THE AMERICAN COLLEGE DICTIONARY

C. L. BARNHART, *Editor in Chief*

JESS STEIN, *Managing Editor*

Assisted and Advised

By 355 Authorities and Specialists

RANDOM HOUSE · NEW YORK

THE L. W. SINGER COMPANY · SYRACUSE

Copyright acknowledgments to the American Institute of Electrical Engineers for the use of certain definitions from *American Standard Definitions of Electrical Terms;* to the American Society of Civil Engineers for the use of certain definitions from *Manual of Engineering Practice No. 15, Definitions of Surveying Terms* (1938); to the Porcelain Enamel Institute for the use of certain definitions from *Porcelain Enamel Terms and Their Definitions;* and to the Viking Press for the use of a quotation from *Grapes of Wrath* by John Steinbeck. Acknowledgment is also made to the United States Department of Defense for the use of certain definitions in *Dictionary of United States Army Terms* (TM 20–205) and *The Weather Observer* (TM 1–235).

Pronunciation Key

The symbol (′), as in **moth·er** (mŭth′ər), is used to mark primary stress; the syllable preceding it is pronounced with greater prominence than the other syllables in the word. The symbol (′), as in **grand·moth·er** (grănd′mŭth′ər), is used to mark secondary stress; a syllable marked for secondary stress is pronounced with less prominence than the one marked (′) but with more prominence than those bearing no stress mark at all.

ă	act, bat	m	my, him	ŭ	up, love
ā	able, cape	n	now, on	ū	use, cute
â	air, dare	ng	sing, England	û	urge, burn
ä	art, calm				
		ŏ	box, hot	v	voice, live
b	back, rub	ō	over, no	w	west, away
ch	chief, beach	ô	order, ball	y	yes, young
d	do, bed	oi	oil, joy	z	zeal, lazy, those
		ŏŏ	book, put	zh	vision, measure
ĕ	ebb, set	ōō	ooze, rule		
ē	equal, bee	ou	out, loud	ə	occurs only in un-accented syllables and indicates the sound of
f	fit, puff				a *in* alone
g	give, beg	p	page, stop		e *in* system
h	hit, hear	r	read, cry		i *in* easily
ĭ	if, big	s	see, miss		o *in* gallop
ī	ice, bite	sh	shoe, push		u *in* circus
j	just, edge	t	ten, bit		
k	kept, make	th	thin, path		
l	low, all	th	that, other		

FOREIGN SOUNDS

à as in French *ami* [a vowel intermediate in quality between the ă of *cat* and the ä of *calm*, but closer to the former]

KH as in German *ach;* Scottish *loch* [a consonant made by bringing the tongue into the position for *k*, as in *key, coo*, while pronouncing a strong *h*]

N [a symbol used to indicate nasalized vowels as in *bon*. There are four such vowels in French, found in *un bon vin blanc* (œN bōN văN bläN)]

œ as in French *feu;* German *schön* [a vowel made with the lips rounded in position for ō as in *over*, while trying to say ā as in *able*]

Y as in French *tu;* German *über* [a vowel made with the lips rounded in position for ōō as in *ooze*, while trying to say ē as in *easy*]

PRESENTED BY

AND

INDIANA
NATIONAL
THE BANK IN INDIANAPOLIS

THE
AMERICAN
COLLEGE
DICTIONARY

CONTENTS

General Introduction: CLARENCE L. BARNHART   vii

Editorial Advisory Committee and Special Editors   ix

Special Consultants   x

Editorial Staff and Special Acknowledgments   xviii

Prefaces

     Selection of Entries and Definitions: IRVING LORGE   xix

     Pronunciation: W. CABELL GREET   xx

     Treatment of Etymologies: KEMP MALONE   xxi

     Synonyms and Antonyms: MILES L. HANLEY   xxiii

     Usage Levels and Dialect Distribution: CHARLES C. FRIES   xxiv

     British and American Usage: ALLEN WALKER READ   xxvi

Table of Common English Spellings   xxvii

Explanatory Notes   xxviii

A DICTIONARY OF THE ENGLISH LANGUAGE   1–1421

Appendices

     Common Signs and Symbols   1422

     A Guide to Usage: HARRISON PLATT, JR.   1425

Colleges and Universities   1433

GENERAL INTRODUCTION

The American College Dictionary is a record of the English language prepared by more than 350 scholars, specialists, and editors to meet the essential needs of the reader, speaker, and writer who want to know the meaning of a word, how to pronounce it, how to spell it, its history, or some important fact of usage. The first abridged dictionary to be prepared by a staff larger than is usually assembled for an unabridged dictionary, the ACD is the latest record of current usage made by any dictionary staff since World War II. This fact alone justifies publishing this new dictionary.

The ACD, however, differs from other similar dictionaries in many important particulars. Linguists have made significant advances in the study of language and psychologists have developed techniques of presenting facts which have been neglected by dictionary-makers who base the dictionaries they prepare today on the same general principles they used one hundred years ago. In order to insure that the ACD would be carefully planned in accordance with the current knowledge of scholars in the various fields of language study, we secured the services of a distinguished editorial board, representing the fields of general linguistics, psychology, phonetics, usage, and etymology. This board laid down certain general principles, formulated in accordance with the findings of modern scholarship, which the sixteen special editors followed.

This dictionary records the usage of the speakers and writers of our language; no dictionary founded on the methods of modern scholarship can prescribe as to usage; it can only inform on the basis of the facts of usage. A good dictionary is a guide to usage much as a good map tells you the nature of the terrain over which you may want to travel. It is not the function of the dictionary-maker to tell you how to speak, any more than it is the function of the mapmaker to move rivers or rearrange mountains or fill in lakes. A dictionary should tell you what is commonly accepted usage and wherein different classes of speakers or regions differ in their use of the language. We have taken special pains to give an accurate record of the distribution of usage (Colloq., Slang, Brit., U.S., etc.) so far as we can determine it; a committee of five special editors who are experts in the study of levels of usage and dialect distribution have recorded their observations in the ACD. This is the first time that a dictionary has attempted such an undertaking, the principles of which are explained by Charles C. Fries on page xxiv and by Allen Walker Read on page xxvi.

New techniques have been worked out for the selection of information to go into the ACD. It is necessary to select from the hundreds of thousands of words in the language and over a million possible definitions the meanings that will be most needed by a person of wide reading. At the same time it is essential that the basic vocabularies of all the special fields of knowledge should be covered. To select the words and meanings needed by the general user we utilized the Lorge-Thorndike Semantic Count which measures the occurrences of various meanings in the general vocabulary. By using this count, which is based upon a reading of modern standard literature, we have been able to select the important meanings needed by the reader of today and to have some statistical assurance of the occurrence of the meanings. This count has also been of considerable importance in the arrangement of meanings, since it has enabled us to determine with some certainty which are the common meanings and to put them first. The uses of this count are explained by Irving Lorge on page xix.

The selection of the basic vocabularies of various special fields has been a more difficult matter; here the usage of today is important. The only satisfactory way to get current usage in special fields is to go directly to the users of the special vocabularies. With the aid of librarians and of the specialists themselves, we divided knowledge systematically into various narrow fields and secured experts in each field. By utilizing the services of experts in this fashion, we have been able to record the usage of today. It is not enough to read and record usage from books and magazines—although this is important—since any reading must be a very inadequate sampling of the current vocabulary. By going directly to the specialists who know and use the words, however, we have been able to speed up by many years the recording of current usage. We have also made certain that relevant and basic facts needed today are included in the definitions. Such a group of specialists has two functions, then: (1) to make sure that we include basic current terms; (2) to check the accuracy of the facts in the definitions themselves.

The pronunciations in the ACD are represented by a system which gives only forty-four symbols for the 251 common spellings of sounds in the language. This system has proved useful in the training of radio speakers, since it focuses attention on the pronunciation instead of on the spelling; it utilizes the traditional textbook key so far as possible, but takes one symbol from the International Phonetic Alphabet—the standard alphabet used by phoneticians everywhere. By the use of this symbol (ə) we have been able to avoid cluttering the key with a dozen additional symbols based on spelling instead of on sound and to give natural pronunciations in cultivated use rather than the artificial pronunciations so common in existing dictionaries. Variant pronunciations common in extensive regions of the country or used by large groups of people are recorded. Any pronunciation in this dictionary is a good pronunciation and may be safely used. If the second or third pronunciation is your natural pronunciation, it is the one to use. In pronunciation, as in vocabulary, we are a record of usage. For a fuller explanation of the principles of pronunciation, see the preface by W. Cabell Greet on page xx.

So far as synonym studies and lists are concerned the ACD differs from similar dictionaries in keying studies and lists to the definitions. Realization of the fact that different words are not synonymous in their entirety but only in certain relatively narrow areas of meaning will lead to a more precise use of words. For example, *unqualified* and *utter* are synonyms of *absolute* in the meaning "free from limitation or restriction"; *complete* and *perfect*, however, are synonyms of *absolute* in the meaning "free from imperfection." For other areas of meaning of *absolute*, other synonyms exist; it is all-important to settle first on the common or core meaning of the synonyms to be distinguished, discriminate carefully among them, and give examples illustrating the use of the synonymous words. Clear examples are almost as important as the discriminations; we have been especially careful to provide illustrative examples for each synonym. We have also placed synonym studies under the well-known word, since it is more likely that the writer will go from the well-known word to the unknown or unfamiliar one. For a further explanation of the principles of handling synonyms and antonyms see the preface by Miles L. Hanley on page xxiii.

The most important fact to learn about the etymology of a word is whether it is a native word or borrowed one. We differ from other dictionaries in immediately indicating this fact. We employ a method of presentation of etymologies which enables the user of the dictionary to read etymologies with a more precise idea of the development of the word. In general, the treatment of the etymologies has been conservative, but a survey of research in this field has been made, and the reader will find many new etymologies recorded here for the first time, particularly of Americanisms, words derived from the American Indian languages, and words from the Romance languages. The preface on etymologies by Kemp Malone, explaining the system carefully and in detail, is on page xxi.

All facts have been arranged in the easiest possible fashion for the user. All entries are in one alphabetical list; the reader will not have to look in a half dozen lists to find an entry. All inflected forms of verbs, nouns, etc., in which the stem is changed in any way by the addition of a suffix have been entered in this dictionary; so have all foreign plurals and all regular plurals likely to be confused with irregular plurals. All definitions are numbered. Central or common meanings are put first. By using different kinds of type for different kinds of information, we have been able to distinguish clearly between main and secondary entries and between definitions and illustrative phrases. The type page has been specially designed so that the user can quickly find the entry for which he is looking.

By putting proper names in the main vocabulary list we have been able to apply the same standards of defining to proper names that we do to the common vocabulary. We have tried to give the most significant facts about each person or place having importance today. Data have been checked against the most recent and reliable sources available and are presented in a clear, readily intelligible manner.

The illustrations have been chosen as aids to the definitions. We have avoided picturing common birds, flowers, and fishes that can be of value only when shown in color or in magnified detail. Captions explaining the illustrations, as under *abacus*, are also designed to supplement the definitions. Actual sizes of animals are given instead of ratios of reduction which the user must figure out and usually doesn't. There are over three hundred spot maps throughout the dictionary giving locations of historically important places (as *Acadia*), places that are hard to find in current atlases (as *Alaska Highway*), and places of literary interest (as *Sherwood Forest*).

The editor, the special editors, the office staff, and the special consultants have had available for their use two outstanding products of American lexicography: *The Century Dictionary* and *The New Century Dictionary*. We were also fortunate in being able to secure the right from the University of Chicago Press to use definitions and sentences from *The Dictionary of American English* (1944).

It is impossible adequately to thank all who have helped in the cooperative project of writing this dictionary, but I am specially grateful to Mr. Jess Stein for his efficient management of the staff and his many editorial suggestions which have materially improved the book. Two editors at Random House, Mr. Robert N. Linscott and Mr. Saxe Commins, have given helpful counsel and support whenever needed. To them I am deeply indebted. Finally, I express my appreciation to Messrs. Bennett A. Cerf, Robert K. Haas, and Donald S. Klopfer for the opportunity to edit a modern dictionary based on present-day scholarship.

Clarence L Barnhart

SPECIAL CONSULTANTS

ANATOMY, PHYSIOLOGY, AND EMBRYOLOGY

Brain and Nervous System, Sensory Organs
THEODORE C. RUCH, Professor of Physiology and Biophysics (Chairman of Department), School of Medicine, University of Washington (Au., *Bibliographia primatologica*).

Circulatory System
R. BURTON-OPITZ, Lecturer in Physiology, Columbia University; Consulting Cardiologist.

Comparative Anatomy
DANIEL P. QUIRING. Associate Professor of Biology, Western Reserve University; Head of the Anatomy Department, Cleveland Clinic Foundation.

Dental Structure and Dentistry
MOSES DIAMOND, Associate Professor, Department of Anatomy, College of Physicians and Surgeons, Columbia University.

Embryology
EMIL WITSCHI, Professor of Zoölogy, Embryology, and Endocrinology, State University of Iowa (Au., *Sex Deviations, Inversions and Parabiosis; Development of Vertebrates*).

Endocrinology
EARL A. DENNIS, Professor of Biology, American University.

Gastro-intestinal System
ALFRED E. WILHELMI, Professor of Biochemistry, Emory University.

General Anatomical Terms
L. F. NIMS, Senior Physiologist, Biology Department, Brookhaven National Laboratory.

Genito-urinary System
EDWARD A. BOYDEN, Professor Emeritus of Anatomy, University of Minnesota; Research Professor of Anatomy, University of Washington.

Histology and Cytology
CHARLES WRIGHT HOOKER, Professor of Anatomy, University of North Carolina.

Major Body Parts
NORMAND L. HOERR, Professor of Anatomy, Western Reserve University.

Physiological Processes
ALBERT TYLER, Professor of Embryology, California Institute of Technology.

Skeletal Structure
G. KASTEN TALLMADGE, Professor and Director of the Department of the History of Medicine, Marquette University (Au., *Basic Biology of Man*).

ANTHROPOLOGY

Archaeology
ALFRED V. KIDDER, Chairman (Retired), Division of Historical Research, Carnegie Institute of Washington (Au., *Introduction to Southwestern Archaeology; Basketmaker Caves in Northeastern Arizona*).

Cultural Anthropology
RALPH LINTON, Professor of Anthropology, Yale University (Au., *The Study of Man; The Material Culture of the Marquesas Islands; Cultural Background of Personality*).

Ethnology: American Indian Tribes
C. F. VOEGELIN. See: ETYMOLOGY.

Ethnology: General
A. L. KROEBER, Professor Emeritus of Anthropology, University of California (Au., *Cultural and Natural Areas; Configurations of Culture Growth; Anthropology; The Nature of Culture; Style and Civilizations*).

Physical Anthropology
WILTON M. KROGMAN, Professor of Physical Anthropology, University of Pennsylvania (Au., *Physical Anthropology of the Seminole Indians of Oklahoma; Growth of Man*)-

APPLIED SCIENCE

Aeronautics
ALEXANDER KLEMIN, Aeronautical Consultant; formerly, Guggenheim Research Professor of Aeronautical Engineering, New York University; Aviation Editor, *Scientific American;* Helicopter Editor, *Aero Digest.*

Agricultural Machinery
R. I. SHAWL, Professor of Farm Machinery, University of Illinois.

Agriculture
W. A. ALBRECHT, Professor of Soils (Chairman of Department), University of Missouri.

Automobiles
RAY F. KUNS, Au., *Automotive Essentials; Automotive Service; Auto-Mechanics;* formerly, Editor of *Automotive Digest* and Principal of Automotive High School of Cincinnati.

Ceramics
R. K. HURSH, Professor of Ceramic Engineering, University of Illinois.

Civil Engineering
CHARLES H. NORRIS, Professor of Structural Engineering and Executive Officer, Department of Civil and Sanitary Engineering, Massachusetts Institute of Technology.

Coke and Petroleum Industries
E. DeGOLYER, Senior Partner, DeGolyer and MacNaughton, Consulting Geologists and Engineers; formerly, Professor of Geology, University of Texas, and Director of American Petroleum Institute; Associate Editor, *Journal of Economic Geology.*

Electrical Devices
NORMAN L. TOWLE, Professor of Electrical Engineering (Head of Department), The Cooper Union School of Engineering.

Electronics
W. L. EVERITT, Dean of Engineering and Professor of Electrical Engineering, University of Illinois; formerly, Director of Operational Research, Office Chief Signal Officer, United States War Department; Past President, Institute of Radio Engineers, and American Society of Engineering Education.

G. H. FETT, Professor of Electrical Engineering, University of Illinois.

Foundry and Ferrous Metallurgy
C. W. MORISETTE, Instructor, Milwaukee Vocational School.

General and Nonferrous Metallurgy
ALFRED BORNEMANN, Professor of Metallurgy (Head of Department), Stevens Institute of Technology.

Glass Industries
S. R. SCHOLES, Professor Emeritus of Glass Technology, New York State College of Ceramics, Alfred University (Au., *Modern Glass Practice;* editor, *Glass Industry Handbook*).

Horse-drawn Vehicles
CARL W. MITMAN, Head Curator, Department of Engineering and Industries, United States National Museum (Au., *An Outline Development of Highway Travel; Beginning of Mechanical Transport Era in America*).

Mining
R. D. PARKS, Associate Professor of Mineral Industry, Massachusetts Institute of Technology (Au., *Examination and Valuation of Mineral Property*).

Photography
C. B. NEBLETTE, Chairman, Division of Photography, Printing and Graphic Arts, Rochester Institute of Technology.

Plumbing
G. W. FARNDALE, Industrial Representative, Milwaukee Vocational and Adult Schools.

Railroads
CARLTON J. CORLISS, Section Manager, Public Relations Office, Association of American Railroads.

Surveying
A. J. BONE, Associate Professor of Transportation Engineering, Massachusetts Institute of Technology.

Telegraphy and Telephony
K. S. JOHNSON, Transmission Standards Engineer, Bell Telephone Laboratories, Inc.

ARCHITECTURE

Construction
FRED N. SEVERUD, Consulting Engineer.

Decorative Treatment
KENNETH J. CONANT, Professor Emeritus of Architecture, Harvard University.

General and Stylistic Terms
RICHARD KRAUTHEIMER, Professor of Art, Institute of Fine Arts, New York University.

x

Miscellaneous Terms
HENRY WRIGHT, Technical Consultant to Building Products Manufacturers. Formerly, Managing Editor, *Architectural Forum*.

Structure
TALBOT F. HAMLIN, Professor of Architecture, Columbia University (Au., *Architecture through the Ages; Greek Revival Architecture in America; Architecture, an Art for All Men*).

ARTS

Dance
ANATOLE CHUJOY, Editor, *Dance News, The Dance Encyclopedia*.

Decorative Arts
EDWIN J. HIPKISS, Curator Emeritus of Department of Decorative Arts of Europe and America, Museum of Fine Arts, Boston.

Engraving Techniques
A. HYATT MAYOR, Curator of Prints, Metropolitan Museum of Art.

General and Stylistic Terms
DIMITRI TSELOS, Professor of Art, University of Minnesota.

Motion Pictures
WILLARD VAN DYKE, Motion-Picture Director and Producer.

Painting and Graphic Arts
HARRY B. WEHLE, Formerly, Curator of Paintings, Metropolitan Museum of Art.

Sculpture
WILLIAM ZORACH, Sculptor; Instructor of Sculpture, Art Students' League (Au., *Zorach Explains Sculpture*).

Theater
EDWARD C. COLE, Associate Professor and Production Manager, Department of Drama, School of the Fine Arts, Yale University.

ASTRONOMY

Astronomical Instruments
CHARLES A. FEDERER, JR., Editor, *Sky and Telescope*.

Astrophysics
OTTO STRUVE, Professor of Astrophysics, University of California (Berkeley).

Celestial Mechanics
DIRK BROUWER, Professor of Astronomy and Director of Observatory, Yale University (Editor, *Astronomical Journal*).

General Terms
NEWTON LACY PIERCE, Associate Professor of Astronomy, Princeton University.

The Solar System
SETH B. NICHOLSON, Astronomer (Retired), Mount Wilson and Palomar Observatories. (Formerly, Editor, *Publications of the Astronomical Society of the Pacific*).

Stellar Astronomy
WILLIAM W. MORGAN, Professor of Astronomy, Yerkes Observatory, University of Chicago.

BOTANY

Algae
GILBERT M. SMITH, Professor of Botany, Stanford University (Au., *Freshwater Algae of United States; Cryptogamic Botany; Marine Algae of the Monterey Peninsula, California*; co-au., *A Textbook of General Botany*).

Angiosperms
LEON CROIZAT, Ministerio de Agricultura y Cría, Caracas, Venezuela; formerly, Staff Member of Arnold Arboretum, Harvard University.

Bacteria
MARIO MOLLARI, Professor of Bacteriology and Immunology (Chairman of Department), Georgetown University.

Bryophytes
HENRY S. CONARD, Research Professor, State University of Iowa; Professor of Botany (Retired), Grinnell College.

Fungi
H. M. FITZPATRICK, Professor of Mycology, Cornell University (Au., *The Lower Fungi; Phycomycetes*).

Grasses
MASON A. HEIN, Research Agronomist, United States Department of Agriculture, Agricultural Research Service, Crops Research Division, Plant Industry Station, Beltsville, Maryland.

Gymnosperms
JOHN T. BUCHHOLZ, Professor of Botany, University of Illinois.

Medicinal Plants
ELMER H. WIRTH, Professor of Pharmacognosy and Pharmacology, College of Pharmacy, University of Illinois; Director, University of Illinois Drug Plant Experiment Station.

North Temperate Edible Vegetables
H. C. THOMPSON, Professor Emeritus, Vegetable Crops, Cornell University (Au., *Vegetable Crops; Sweet Potato Production and Marketing; Asparagus Production*).

North Temperate Fruits, Plant Propagation, and Nursery Practice
H. B. TUKEY, Professor of Horticulture (Head of Department), Michigan State University (Au., *The Pear and Its Culture; Plant Regulators in Agriculture*; Associate Editor, *American Fruitgrower*).

Ornamental Flowering Plants
CHARLES H. CONNORS, Professor Emeritus of Ornamental Horticulture, Rutgers University; Formerly, Head of Department of Ornamental Horticulture, New Jersey State Agricultural Experiment Station.

Ornamental Woody Plants
DONALD WYMAN, Horticulturist, Arnold Arboretum, Harvard University.

Plant Anatomy
H. E. HAYWARD, Director and Plant Anatomist, U.S. Salinity Laboratory, Agricultural Research Service, United States Department of Agriculture, Riverside, California (Au., *The Structure of Economic Plants*).

Plant Ecology
PAUL B. SEARS, Professor of Conservation, Yale University (Au., *Life and Environment*).

Plant Genetics
DONALD FORSHA JONES, Head of Department of Genetics, Connecticut Agricultural Experiment Station.

Plant Physiology
JAMES BONNER, Professor of Biology, California Institute of Technology.

Plants of Economic Use
ALBERT F. HILL, Formerly, Research Fellow, Botanical Museum of Harvard University (Au., *Economic Botany*).

Pteridophytes
C. A. WEATHERBY, Research Associate, Gray Herbarium, Harvard University.

Tropical Edible Plants
ROBERT WILLARD HODGSON, Professor of Subtropical Horticulture, University of California; Dean, College of Agriculture, Los Angeles; Assistant Director, California Agricultural Experiment Station.

BUILDING TRADES

Carpentry
DeWITT T. HUNT, Professor Emeritus of Industrial Arts Education, Oklahoma State University.

Masonry and Bricklaying, Painting and Plastering
HENRY P. ADAMS, Professor and Director of The Technical Institute, Oklahoma State University.

Structural Elements and Materials
VERNON C. GRESHAM, Associate Professor of Industrial Arts and Director of Vocational Training, Tennessee Polytechnic Institute; Educational Specialist, USNR Publications Project, Naval Gun Factory, Washington, D. C.

CHEMISTRY

Biochemistry
RUDOLPH J. ANDERSON, Professor Emeritus of Chemistry, Yale University (Member of Editorial Board, *Journal of Biological Chemistry*).

Chemical Apparatus
W. T. READ, Consultant. Formerly, Dean, Rutgers University; formerly, Chemical Consultant, Department of the Army (Au., *Industrial Chemistry*).

Chemical Industries
DONALD B. BROUGHTON, Research Engineer, Universal Oil Products Co.; formerly, Assistant Professor of Chemical Engineering, Massachusetts Institute of Technology.

The Elements
H. S. BOOTH, Professor of Chemistry (Chairman of Department), Western Reserve University (Editor, *Inorganic Syntheses, Vol. I*).

General Chemical Terms
A. H. BLATT, Professor of Chemistry, Queens College.
LEE F SUPPLE, Professor of Organic Chemistry, Illinois Institute of Technology.

Inorganic Compounds

ROBERT D. FOWLER, Leader, CMF Division, Los Alamos Scientific Laboratory; formerly, Professor of Chemistry (Chairman of Department), Johns Hopkins University.

Inorganic Radicals

HUBERT N. ALYEA, Professor of Chemistry, Princeton University.

Organic Chemistry

L. F. AUDRIETH, Professor of Inorganic Chemistry, University of Illinois.

A. H. BLATT, Professor of Chemistry, Queens College.

CHARLES D. HURD, Clare Hamilton Hall Research Professor of Chemistry, Northwestern University.

R. A. PENNEMAN, Research Fellow, University of Illinois.

Physical Chemistry

FRANK T. GUCKER, JR., Professor of Chemistry (Dean, College of Arts and Sciences), Indiana University.

Selection of Terms

LOUIS SATTLER, Professor of Chemistry, Brooklyn College.

COINS

Current Money and Coinage

F. LELAND HOWARD, Assistant Director, United States Mint.

Numismatics and Older Monetary Units

SYDNEY P NOE, formerly, Secretary, Librarian, and Editor of the Publications of The American Numismatic Society; Chief Curator Emeritus, Museum of The American Numismatic Society.

COMMERCE

Accounting, Bookkeeping, and Business Statistics

MARTIN LEE BLACK, JR., Professor of Accounting, Duke University.

Banking, Credit, and Foreign Exchange

CHARLES R. WHITTLESEY, Professor of Finance and Economics, University of Pennsylvania (Au., *National Interest and International Cartels; International Monetary Issues; Principles and Practices of Money and Banking*).

Bonds and Stocks

HARRY G. GUTHMANN, Morrison Professor of Finance, Northwestern University (Au., *The Analysis of Financial Statements;* co-au., *Corporate Financial Policy; Investment Principles and Practices*).

Corporations

JAMES C. BONBRIGHT, Professor of Finance, Columbia University (Au., *Public Utilities and the National Power Policies; Railroad Capitalization; Valuation of Property;* co-au., *The Holding Company*).

Import and Export

J. S. DAVIS, Professor Emeritus of Economic Research and Director of Food Research Institute, Stanford University

Insurance

S. S. HUEBNER, Professor Emeritus of Insurance and Commerce, University of Pennsylvania; formerly, President, American College of Life Underwriters; Chairman, Board of Trustees of American Institute for Property and Liability Underwriters, Inc. (Au., *Life Insurance; Property Insurance;* co-au., *Life Insurance and Investment*).

Labor

WILLIAM M. LEISERSON, Visiting Professor of Political Economy, Johns Hopkins University; Former Member of National Labor Relations Board; Former Chairman of National Mediation Board (Au., *Right and Wrong in Labor Relations*).

Transportation

C. O. RUGGLES, Professor of Public Utility Management and Regulation, Harvard University (Au., *Terminal Charges at United States Ports; Problems in Public Utility Economics and Management*).

Wholesale and Retail Marketing

PAUL D. CONVERSE, Professor Emeritus of Marketing, University of Illinois (Au., *Marketing Methods and Policies; Selling Policies; Essentials of Distribution; Elements of Marketing;* co-au., *Introduction to Marketing*).

EDUCATION

Administration

DONALD P. COTTRELL, Dean, College of Education, Ohio State University; formerly, Professor of Education and Executive Director of Horace Mann-Lincoln School of Teachers College, Columbia University (Co-au., *Redirecting Teacher Education; Teacher Education for a Free People*).

Comparative and Foreign Education

I. L. KANDEL, Professor Emeritus of Education, Teachers College, Columbia University; Professor Emeritus of American Studies, University of Manchester (Au., *Intellectual Coöperation: National and International; Conflicting Theories of Education; History of Secondary Education; Comparative Education; Essays in Comparative Education; The Classics in Germany, England, and France; The New Era in Education; American Education in the Twentieth Century;* editor, *Educational Yearbook of the International Institute*).

Higher Education

JOHN DALE RUSSELL, Chancellor and Executive Secretary, Board of Educational Finance, State of New Mexico; formerly, Director, Division of Higher Education, United States Office of Education; Professor of Education and Dean of Students, Division of Social Sciences, University of Chicago.

Philosophy of Education

EDGAR W. KNIGHT, Kenan Professor of Education, University of North Carolina (Au., *Twenty Centuries of Education; Education in the United States; Public Education in the South; Reports on European Education; What College Presidents Say; Henry Harrisse on Collegiate Education;* co-au., *Culture in the South; The Graduate School; Research and Publications*).

GEOGRAPHY

Cartography

ARTHUR H. ROBINSON, Professor of Geography, University of Wisconsin (Au., *Elements of Cartography;* co-au., *Elements of Geography*).

ROBERT L. REYNOLDS, Professor of History, University of Wisconsin.

General Geography

RICHARD HARTSHORNE, Professor of Geography, University of Wisconsin (Au., *The Nature of Geography*).

Oceanography

HARRY AARON MARMER, Assistant Chief of Division of Tides and Currents, United States Coast and Geodetic Survey (Au., *Tides and Currents in New York Harbor; Coastal Currents Along the Pacific Coast of the United States; The Sea; The Tide*).

Physical Geography

ROBERT BOWMAN, Professor of Geography, University of Nebraska.

Political Geography and Population Data

G. ETZEL PEARCY, Geographer, United States Department of State.

ROBERT D. HODGSON, Assistant Geographer, United States Department of State.

Statistical Data

HENRY J. DUBESTER, Chief, General Reference and Bibliography Division, Library of Congress.

GEOLOGY

Crystallography

CLIFFORD FRONDEL, Professor of Mineralogy, Harvard University (Co-au., *Dana's System of Mineralogy, 7th ed.*).

Gems and Jewelry

FREDERICK H. POUGH, Consulting Mineralogist; formerly, Curator of Physical Geology and Mineralogy, American Museum of Natural History (Au., *The Jewelers Dictionary; The Field Guide to Rocks and Minerals*).

Mineralogy: General Mineralogical Terms

S. JAMES SHAND, Newberry Professor of Geology, Columbia University.

Mineralogy: Mineral Names

MICHAEL FLEISCHER, Geochemist, United States Geological Survey, Washington, D. C.; Professorial Lecturer, George Washington University (Assistant Editor, *Chemical Abstracts*).

Paleontology

JOHN ERIC HILL, Assistant Curator of Mammals, American Museum of Natural History.

Petrology: General Petrological Terms

KENNETH K. LANDES, Professor of Geology, University of Michigan.

Petrology: Igneous Rocks

CORNELIUS S. HURLBUT, JR., Professor of Mineralogy, Harvard University.

Petrology: Metamorphic and Sedimentary Rocks

See: Mineralogy: General Mineralogical Terms.

Physical Geology

KIRTLEY F. MATHER, Professor Emeritus of Geology, Harvard University; formerly, Geologist, United States Geological Survey (Au., *Old Mother Earth; Sons of the Earth;* co-au., *A Source Book in Geology*).

Stratigraphy

RAYMOND C. MOORE, Professor of Geology, University of Kansas; President, International Commission on Stratigraphy; Member, American Commission of Stratigraphic Nomenclature; formerly, Geologist, United States Geological Survey; State Geologist of Kansas (Au., *Historical Geology*).

GOVERNMENT

Comparative Government: England

R. K. GOOCH, Professor of Political Science, University of Virginia (Au., *The Government of England*; editor, *Source Book on the Government of England*).

Comparative Government: Europe

NORMAN L. HILL, Professor of Political Science, Nebraska University (Au., *Claims to Territory*; co-au., *The Background of European Governments*).

International Law and Diplomacy

PITMAN B. POTTER, Professor of International Relations and Organization, American University School of International Service (Editor, *American Journal of International Law*; au., *Introduction to the Study of International Organization*; *Manual Digest of Common International Law*).

International Relations

W. E. DIEZ, Professor of Government, University of Rochester.

Legislation

ALPHEUS THOMAS MASON, McCormick Professor of Jurisprudence, Princeton University (Au., *Brandeis: A Free Man's Life*; *Free Government in the Making*; *Harlan Fiske Stone: Pillar of the Law*).

Local and State Government

AUSTIN F. MACDONALD, Professor of Political Science, University of California (Au., *American State Government and Administration*; *American City Government and Administration*).

National Government

ARTHUR N. HOLCOMBE, Eaton Professor Emeritus of the Science of Government, Harvard University (Au., *Our More Perfect Union*; *The Middle Classes in American Politics*; *The Foundations of the Modern Commonwealth*).

Political Economy

ALVIN H. HANSEN, Lucius N. Littauer Professor Emeritus of Political Economy, Harvard University (Au., *America's Role in the World Economy*; *Fiscal Policy and Business Cycles*; *Economic Stabilization in an Unbalanced World*; *Economic Policy and Full Employment*; *Monetary Theory and Fiscal Policy*; *A Guide to Keynes*; *The American Economy*).

Political Parties

V. O. KEY, JR., Professor of Government, Harvard University.

Political Theory

R. M. MacIVER, Lieber Professor Emeritus of Political Philosophy and Sociology, Columbia University (Au., *Social Causation*; *Society: A Textbook of Sociology*; *The Web of Government*; *Democracy and the Economic Challenge*; *The Pursuit of Happiness*).

HERALDRY

CHARLES K. BOLTON, Au., *Bolton's American Armory*; formerly, Associate Professor, Simmons College, and Librarian, Boston Athenaeum.

HISTORY

Ancient History

A. E. R. BOAK, Richard Hudson Professor Emeritus of Ancient History (formerly, Chairman of Department), University of Michigan (Au., *History of Rome to 565 A.D.*; *Manpower Shortage and the Fall of Rome*).

The British Empire

PAUL ALEXANDER KNAPLUND, Professor Emeritus of History, University of Wisconsin (Au., *Gladstone and Britain's Imperial Policy*; *Gladstone's Foreign Policy*; *The British Empire, 1815–1939*; *James Stephen and the British Colonial System, 1813–1847*; *Britain, Commonwealth and Empire, 1901–1955*).

China and Japan

OWEN LATTIMORE, Lecturer in History, Johns Hopkins University; formerly, Political Advisor to General Chiang Kai-shek, 1941–42; Deputy Director of Pacific Operations, Office of War Information (Au., *Solution in Asia*; *Ordeal by Slander*).

England to 1689

WILLIAM EDWARD LUNT, Walter D. and Edith M. L. Scull Professor of English Constitutional History, Haverford College (Au., *History of England*; *Financial Relations of the Papacy with England to 1327*; associate editor, *American Historical Review*).

England from 1689

ARTHUR H. BASYE, Professor of History, Dartmouth College.

France

ARTHUR L. DUNHAM, Professor Emeritus of History, University of Michigan.

Italy

MARY LUCILLE SHAY, Assistant Professor of History, University of Illinois.

Medieval History

SIDNEY R. PACKARD, Professor of History, Smith College (Au., *Europe and the Church under Innocent III*)

Middle and Near Eastern History

ALBERT HOWE LYBYER, Professor Emeritus of History, University of Illinois (Au., *The Government of the Ottoman Empire in the Time of Suleiman the Magnificent*).

Modern European History

DWIGHT ERWIN LEE, Professor of Modern European History, Clark University (Au., *Great Britain and the Cyprus Convention Policy of 1878*; *Ten Years: The World on the Way to War, 1930–40*).

Russia

SIR BERNARD PARES, formerly, Professor of Russian History, Language, and Literature, and Director of the School of Slavonic and East European Studies, University of London; Visiting Professor of History, Sarah Lawrence College (Au., *History of Russia*; *The Fall of the Russian Monarchy*; *Russia and the Peace*).

Spain and Latin America

C. H. HARING, Robert Woods Bliss Professor Emeritus of Latin-American History and Economics, Harvard University (Au., *Trade and Navigation Between Spain and the Indies in the Time of the Hapsburgs*; *The Spanish Empire in America*; *Empire in Brazil*).

United States

WILLIAM B. HESSELTINE, Professor of History, University of Wisconsin (Au., *Ulysses S. Grant, Politician*; *The South in American History*; *Lincoln and the War Governors*).

HOME ECONOMICS

Clothing

MARY EVANS, Professor Emeritus of Home Economics, Teachers College, Columbia University (Au., *Costume Silhouettes*; *Costume Throughout the Ages*; *Draping and Dress Design*; *How to Make Historic American Costumes*; *The Story of Textiles*; *A Guide to Textiles*; *Fundamentals of Textiles and Clothing*; *Better Clothes for Your Money*).

Food

MYRNA JOHNSTON, Director, Better Foods and Home Equipment Departments, *Better Homes and Gardens*.

JEAN GUTHRIE DUMONT, Home Economics Consultant and Writer; formerly, Director, Better Foods and Home Equipment Departments, *Better Homes and Gardens*.

Furniture and Furnishings

RUTH A. FOLGER, Associate Professor of Fine Arts (Head of Department), Russell Sage College.

Textiles

GRACE G. DENNY, Professor Emeritus of Home Economics, University of Washington (Au., *Fabrics*).

LAW

Attorney and Client Relationship

ELLIOTT E. CHEATHAM, Charles Evans Hughes Professor Emeritus of Law, Columbia University (Au., *Cases and Materials on the Legal Profession*).

Business and Membership Organizations

HENRY WINTHROP BALLANTINE, Professor of Law, University of California (Au., *Problems in Law*; *Law of Corporations*).

Contracts

LON L. FULLER, Professor of Law, Harvard University (Au., *The Law in Quest of Itself*).

Conveyancing

W. BARTON LEACH, Professor of Law, Harvard University.

Copyright, Patent, and Trademark Law

HORACE G. BALL, Au., *The Law of Copyright and Literary Property*.

Criminal Law

LIVINGSTON HALL, Professor of Law (Vice Dean, Law School) Harvard University (Co-au., *Cases on Criminal Law*).

Decedents' Estates

MAX RHEINSTEIN, Max Pam Professor of Comparative Law, University of Chicago (Au., *Cases and Materials on Decedents' Estates*).

Domestic Relations and Persons

ALBERT CHARLES JACOBS, President, Trinity College; formerly, Professor of Law, Columbia University (Au., *Cases and Materials on Domestic Relations*; *Cases and Materials on Landlord and Tenant*).

English and Scottish Law

JOHN P. DAWSON, Professor of Law, Harvard University.

Evidence

CHARLES T. McCORMICK, Professor of Law, School of Law, University of Texas (Au., *Handbook on Law of Damages; Cases and Materials on the Law of Evidence; Cases and Materials on Law of Damages; co-au., Texas Law of Evidence; Cases and Materials on Federal Courts*).

Fiduciaries and Insolvent Estates

AUSTIN W. SCOTT, Dane Professor of Law, Harvard University (Au., *The Law of Trusts*).

International and Military Law

EARLE H. KETCHAM, Professor of Political Science (Chairman of Department), Syracuse University.

Judges and Courts

EDSON R. SUNDERLAND, Professor of Law and Legal Research, University of Michigan (Au., *Cases on Code Pleading; Cases on Common Law Pleading; Cases on Trial and Appellate Practice; Cases on Judicial Administration*).

Maritime Law

HOBART COFFEY, Professor of Law and Director of the Law Library, University of Michigan.

Penology

EDWIN H. SUTHERLAND, Professor of Sociology (Head of Department), Indiana University; formerly, President, Indiana University Institute of Criminal Law and Criminology (Au., *Principles of Criminology; The Professional Thief*).

Personal Property

HORACE E. WHITESIDE, Professor of Law, Cornell University.

Procedure

GEORGE H. DESSION, Professor of Law, Yale University; formerly, Special Assistant to Attorney General, Anti-Trust Division, United States Department of Justice; Member, Advisory Committee on Rules of Criminal Procedure, United States Supreme Court.

Quasi-judicial Public Offices

KENNETH C. SEARS, Professor Emeritus of Law, University of Chicago (Au., *Cases on Administrative Law; co-au., May on Crimes, 4th ed.*).

Real Property

RICHARD R. POWELL, Dwight Professor of Law, Columbia University (Au., *Law of Property; Future Interests; Trusts*).

Roman and Civil Law

MAX RADIN, John Henry Boalt Professor of Law, University of California (Au., *Handbook of Roman Law; Handbook of Anglo-American Legal History*).

Torts

PHILIP MECHEM, Professor of Law, University of Pennsylvania (Au., *Cases on Agency; Outlines of Agency; co-au., Cases on Wills*).

LINGUISTICS

General

BERNARD BLOCH, Professor of Linguistics, Yale University (Assistant Editor, *Linguistic Atlas of New England;* co-au., *Outline of Linguistic Analysis;* editor, *Language*).

ALBERT H. MARCKWARDT, Professor of English, University of Michigan (Au., *Introduction to the English Language; Scribner Handbook of English; American English*).

Phonetics and Phonemics

W. FREEMAN TWADDELL, Professor of Linguistics, Brown University.

Semitic-Hamitic Languages (Special Review)

ZELLIG S. HARRIS, Professor of Linguistics, University of Pennsylvania (Au., *Development of the Canaanite Dialects; Methods in Structural Linguistics*).

Speech

KARL R. WALLACE, Professor of Speech (Head of Department), University of Illinois.

LITERATURE

Classical Myths and Legends in Literature

DOUGLAS BUSH, Gurney Professor of English, Harvard University (Au., *Mythology and the Renaissance Tradition in English Poetry; Mythology and the Romantic Tradition in English Poetry*).

Drama

ARTHUR H. QUINN, John Welsh Centennial Emeritus Professor of History and English Literature, University of Pennsylvania (Au., *History of American Drama from the Beginning to the Civil War; History of American Drama from the Civil War to the Present Day*).

General Terms in Literature

GEORGE W. SHERBURN, Professor Emeritus of English, Harvard University.

Journalism

FRANK LUTHER MOTT, Dean Emeritus of School of Journalism, University of Missouri (Au., *A History of American Magazines; American Journalism: A History; Jefferson and the Press*).

Library Science

NATHANIEL STEWART, Professorial Lecturer, American University; formerly, Associate, Columbia University and Library of Congress.

Proper Names

JOSEPH WOOD KRUTCH, formerly, Brander Matthews Professor of Dramatic Literature, Columbia University.

Prosody

DONALD A. STAUFFER, Professor of English (Chairman of Department), Princeton University (Au., *The Nature of Poetry;* editor, *The Intent of the Critic*).

MACHINES AND MACHINERY

Air Machines and Refrigeration

H. G. VENEMANN, Professor Emeritus of Refrigeration, Purdue University (Au., *Refrigeration Theory and Applications*).

Boilers and Furnaces

ROBERT P. KOLB, Consulting Engineer; formerly, Professor of Heat-Power Engineering, Worcester Polytechnic Institute.

Horology

WARREN TeRONDE, Instructor, Milwaukee Vocational School.

Internal Combustion Engines

HAROLD C. HERRMANN, Diesel Engineering Department, Milwaukee Institute of Technology.

Machine Shop Tools and Practice

W. N. LATHROP, Supervisor of Trade and Industry, Milwaukee Vocational and Adult School.

MATHEMATICS

Algebra

A. ADRIAN ALBERT, Professor of Mathematics, University of Chicago; Chairman, Section of Mathematics, National Academy of Sciences.

Analytic Geometry

FRANCIS D. MURNAGHAN, Mathematical Consultant, David Taylor Model Basin.

Calculus and Function Theory

M. R. HESTENES, Professor of Mathematics, University of California, Los Angeles.

General Terms in Mathematics

R. G. SANGER, Professor of Mathematics (Chairman of Department), Kansas State College of Agriculture and Applied Science.

Number Theory and Arithmetic

D. H. LEHMER, Professor of Mathematics, University of California.

Statistics

SAMUEL S. WILKS, Professor of Mathematical Statistics, Princeton University.

Synthetic Geometry

S. B. MYERS, Associate Professor of Mathematics, University of Michigan (Associate Editor, *American Journal of Mathematics*).

MILITARY TERMS

Air Warfare, Cutting and Thrusting Weapons, Subsistence

S. L. A. MARSHALL, Military Critic, *Detroit News;* Brigadier General, U.S.A.R.; Chief Historian, European Theater of Operations (Au., *Men Against Fire; River and the Gauntlet; Pork Chop Hill*).

Armor, Obsolete Weapons and Firearms

STEPHEN V. GRANCSAY, Curator of Arms and Armor, Metropolitan Museum of Art.

Artillery and Gunnery

RICHARD ERNEST DUPUY, Colone , Retired, U.S.A.

Equipment, Organization, and Tactics

JOSEPH INGHAM GREENE, Colonel, Infantry, Retired, U.S.A., Editor, *Infantry Journal*.

Explosives and Fortifications

WILLIAM FRANCIS HEAVEY, Brigadier General, Retired, Corps of Engineers, U.S.A.

MUSIC

General Terms in Music
JAMES H. HALL, Professor Emeritus of the History and Criticism of Music, Oberlin College (Au., *The Art Song*).

Harmony
WALTER PISTON, Professor of Music, Harvard University; Composer (Au., *Harmony; Harmonic Analysis; Counterpoint; Orchestration*).

Jazz
WILLIAM RUSSELL, President, American Music Records.

Musical Forms
OTTO LUENING, Professor of Music, Barnard College, Columbia University; Composer; formerly, Chairman of Music Department, Bennington College.

Musical Instruments: Ancient
EMANUEL WINTERNITZ, Curator of Collection of Musical Instruments, Metropolitan Museum of Art; Professor, School of Music, Yale University.

Musical Instruments: Modern
CURT SACHS, Adjunct Professor of Music, Columbia University; Corresponding Member, German Academy of the Arts, Berlin (Au., *The History of Musical Instruments*).

Notation
CARL DEIS, Formerly, Music Editor in Chief, G. Schirmer, Inc.; Composer.

Proper Names
FREDERICK JACOBI, Teacher of Composition, Juilliard School of Music; Composer.

ROSS LEE FINNEY, Professor of Music Composition and Composer in Residence, University of Michigan; Composer.

MYTHS AND LEGENDS

General
STITH THOMPSON, Professor of English and Folklore, Indiana University (Au., *Our Heritage of World Literature; Motif-Index of Folk-Literature; The Folktale*).

Greek Legends
WHITNEY J. OATES, West Professor of Classics, Princeton University.

Greek Myths
GILBERT HIGHET, Anthon Professor of Latin, Columbia University (Au., *The Classical Tradition; Poets in a Landscape*).

Medieval and Arthurian Myths
JOHN WEBSTER SPARGO, Professor of English, Northwestern University (Au., *Chaucer's Shipman's Tale; Juridical Folklore in England*).

Roman Legends and Myths
GEORGE E. DUCKWORTH, Giger Professor of Classics, Princeton University.

NAUTICAL AND NAVAL TERMS

Boats and Inland Vessels
WENDELL P. ROOP, Captain, Retired, U.S.N.

General Seamanship and Gear
HERBERT L. STONE, President, Yachting Publishing Company; Editor, *Yachting*.

Nautical Science
GEORGE S. BRYAN, Rear Admiral, Retired, U.S.N.; Hydrographer of the Navy, 1938–1946; Dean of the Faculty, International Correspondence Schools, 1948–1952.

Ships and Ship Repair
THOMAS B. RICHEY, Rear Admiral, Retired, U.S.N.; attached to Joint Chiefs of Staff, Washington, D. C., 1943–45.

PHILATELY

WINTHROP S. BOGGS, Director, The Philatelic Foundation (Au., *The Postage Stamps and Postal History of Canada; Foundations of Philately*).

PHILOSOPHY

Ethics
T. V. SMITH, Professor Emeritus of Citizenship and Philosophy, Maxwell School, Syracuse University (Au., *Ethics of Compromise and the Art of Containment; Live Without Fear*).

General
RICHARD McKEON, Professor of Greek and Philosophy (formerly, Dean of Division of Humanities), University of Chicago (Au., *The Philosophy of Spinoza; Freedom and History; Thought, Action, and Passion;* co-au., *Studies in the History of Ideas, Vol. III;* editor and translator *Selections from Medieval Philosophers;* editor, *The Basic Works of Aristotle; Introduction to Aristotle*).

Logic
ERNEST NAGEL, Professor of Philosophy, Columbia University (Au., *Principles of the Theory of Probability; Sovereign Reason; Logic Without Metaphysics;* co-au., *Introduction to Logic and Scientific Method*).

Metaphysics
R. W. SELLARS, Professor Emeritus of Philosophy, University of Michigan (Au., *Critical Realism; Principles and Problems of Philosophy; The Philosophy of Physical Realism*).

PHYSICS

Acoustics
LEONARD O. OLSEN, Professor of Physics, Case Institute of Technology.

Color
MATTHEW LUCKIESH, formerly, Director of Lighting Research Laboratory, General Electric Company (Au., *Light; Vision and Seeing; Color and Colors; The Science of Seeing; Torch of Civilization; Reading as a Visual Task*).

Electricity and Magnetism
NORMAN E. GILBERT, Professor Emeritus of Physics, Dartmouth College; Visiting Professor of Physics, Rollins College (Au., *Electricity and Magnetism*).

General Terms in Physics
DUANE ROLLER, Member of Senior Staff, The Ramo-Wooldridge Corporation; Professor of Physics, Harvey Mudd College (Co-au., *Mechanics, Molecular Physics, Heat and Sound; Harvard Case Histories in Experimental Science*).

Geometric Optics
P. G. NUTTING, formerly, Consulting Engineer in Charge of Research, Westinghouse Electric and Manufacturing Company; Geophysicist, United States Geological Survey.

Heat and Thermodynamics
J. M. CORK, Professor of Physics, University of Michigan (Au., *Pyrometry, Heat, Radioactivity and Nuclear Physics*).

Hydraulics and Hydraulic Engineering
HUNTER ROUSE, Professor of Fluid Mechanics, State University of Iowa; Director, Iowa Institute of Hydraulic Research (Au., *Fluid Mechanics for Hydraulic Engineers; Elementary Mechanics of Fluids;* co-au., *Basic Mechanics of Fluids; History of Hydraulics;* editor and co-au., *Engineering Hydraulics; Advanced Mechanics of Fluids*).

Light and Light Measurements
WILLIAM W. WATSON, Professor of Physics (Chairman of Department), Yale University.

Mechanics
GUSTAV G. FREYGANG, Professor of Mechanics, Department of Mechanical Engineering, Stevens Institute of Technology.

Meteorology
MICHAEL FERENCE, Director, Scientific Laboratory, Ford Motor Co.; formerly, Associate Professor of Physics and Meteorology, University of Chicago (Associate Editor, *Journal of Meteorology*).

Pneumatics and Aerodynamics
FREDERICK K. TEICHMANN, Professor of Aeronautical Engineering and Assistant Dean, College of Engineering, New York University (Au., *Airplane Design Manual*).

Radiation and Nuclear Physics
I. I. RABI, Higgins Professor of Physics, Columbia University; Member, President's Science Advisory Committee; Nobel Prize 1944.

HENRY M. FOLEY, Professor of Physics, Columbia University.

PRINTING

Presswork
AUGUSTUS E. GIEGENGACK, formerly, The Public Printer, Government Printing Office, Washington, D. C.

Typography
BRUCE ROGERS, Printer and Book Designer; formerly, Printing Adviser to the Cambridge University Press and the Harvard University Press (Co-au., *Paragraphs on Printing*).

PSYCHOLOGY

Personality Traits and Their Expression
GARDNER MURPHY, Director of Research, Menninger Foundation (Au., *Personality; Historical Introduction to Modern Psychology;* co-au., *Experimental Social Psychology*).

Psychoanalysis
LAWRENCE S. KUBIE, Lecturer in Psychiatry, College of Physicians and Surgeons, Columbia University; Clinical Professor of Psychiatry, School of Medicine, Yale University; Faculty, New York Psychoanalytic Institute (Au., *Practical and Theoretical Aspects of Psychoanalysis*).

Tests and Measurements

LEWIS M. TERMAN, Professor Emeritus of Psychology (Executive Head, Department of Psychology), Stanford University (Au., *The Stanford Revision of the Binet-Simon Intelligence Scale; Genetic Studies of Genius;* co-au., *Measuring Intelligence;* editor, *The Measurement and Adjustment Series*).

RELIGION

Anglicanism

REV. WALTER RUSSELL BOWIE, Professor, Virginia Seminary; formerly, Dean of Students and Professor of Practical Theology, Union Theological Seminary; Member, American Standard Bible Revision Committee (Associate editor, *The Interpreter's Bible;* au., *The Story of the Bible; The Master, the Life of Jesus Christ*).

The Bible: Apocrypha and General Terms

EDGAR J. GOODSPEED, Distinguished Service Professor Emeritus of Biblical and Patristic Greek, University of Chicago; Member, American Standard Bible Revision Committee (Au., *The Apocrypha, An American Translation; The Story of the Apocrypha*).

The Bible: New Testament

FREDERICK C. GRANT, Professor of Biblical Theology, Union Theological Seminary; Member, American Standard Bible Revision Committee (Au., *The Gospels, their Origin and Growth; The Earliest Gospel; The Economic Background of the Gospels; Introduction to New Testament Thought*).

The Bible: Old Testament

JAMES MUILENBURG, Professor of Hebrew and Cognate Languages, Union Theological Seminary; Member, American Standard Bible Revision Committee.

Buddhism, Hinduism, Mohammedanism, and the Persian Religion

ROBERT E. HUME, Professor Emeritus of History of Religions, Union Theological Seminary (Au., *The World's Living Religions; Treasure House of the Living Religions;* translator, *Thirteen Principal Upanishads*).

Christian Theology

ALBERT C. KNUDSON, Dean Emeritus and Professor Emeritus of Systematic Theology, Boston University.

General Theology

A. EUSTACE HAYDON, Professor Emeritus of History of Religions (Chairman, Department of Comparative Religion), University of Chicago (Au., *Biography of the Gods; Man's Search for the Good Life; The Quest of the Ages*).

Greek Orthodox Church

RT. REV. EZEKIEL D. TSOUKALAS, Titular Bishop of Nazianzos, Head of the second District Greek Archdiocese of North and South America; formerly, Assistant Dean, Greek Orthodox Theological School.

Judaism

H. A. WOLFSON, Professor of Hebrew Literature and Philosophy, Harvard University (Au., *The Philosophy of Spinoza; Philo: Foundations of Religious Philosophy in Judaism, Christianity, and Islam; Cresca's Critique of Aristotle; The Philosophy of the Church Fathers, I: Faith, Trinity, Incarnation*).

Mormonism

L. H. CREER, Professor of History (Head of Department), University of Utah (Contributor, "Mormonism," *Encyclopedia of the Social Sciences;* "The Church of Jesus Christ of Latter Day Saints," *Encyclopedia Britannica;* "The Life of George H. Dern," *Dictionary of American Biography;* au., *Utah and the Nation; The Founding of an Empire*).

Protestantism

H. RICHARD NIEBUHR, Sterling Professor of Christian Ethics, Divinity School, Yale University (Au., *The Kingdom of God in America; The Meaning of Revelation; Social Sources of Denominationalism; Christ and Culture*).

Roman Catholicism: Church Calendar, Orders and Ranks, Vestments

REV. VINCENT L. KENNEDY, Professor of Greek, St. Michael's College; Professor of History of Christian Worship, Institute of Medieval Studies, University of Toronto.

Roman Catholicism: Dogma

MOST REV. FULTON J. SHEEN, National Director of the Pontifical Society for the Propagation of the Faith; Auxilary Bishop of New York.

Roman Catholicism: General Terms

MOST REV. JOHN FEARNS, Auxiliary Bishop of New York.

SOCIOLOGY

HERBERT BLUMER, Professor of Sociology, University of California, Berkeley. (Formerly, Editor, *American Journal of Sociology*).

SPORTS AND GAMES

Baseball, Boxing, Football, and General Terms

ARCH WARD, Sports Editor, *Chicago Tribune.*
EDWARD PRELL, Sports Writer, *Chicago Tribune.*

Basketball, Swimming, and Gymnastics

AUGUSTA W. NEIDHARDT, Professor of Physical Education (Chairman of Department), Hunter College.

Card, Dice, and Parlor Games

ALBERT A. OSTROW, Brooklyn College (Au., *The Complete Card Player; Planning Your Home for Play; Pastimes for Two; Time-Fillers*).

Chess and Checkers

FRED REINFELD, Chess Editor, Sterling Publishing Company.

Golf, Tennis, and Track

RICHARD F. VAUGHAN, Athletic Coach, Princeton University; formerly, Staff Writer, *Life* magazine.

Hunting and Fishing

J. P. CUENIN, Outdoor Sports Writer, *San Francisco Examiner.*

Miscellaneous

MARTY BERG, Editor, *Sports-Week.*

THERAPEUTICS

Blood and Heart Pathology

H. ROSS MAGEE, Internist, New York City; formerly, Associate in Medicine, Mayo Clinic and Mayo Foundation.

Brain and Nervous Pathology

GEORGE B. HASSIN, Professor Emeritus of Neurology, College of Medicine, University of Illinois (Chief Editor, *Journal of Neuropathology and Experimental Neurology*).

Curative Processes

J. C. MEAKINS, formerly, Dean of Faculty of Medicine, Professor Emeritus of Medicine, McGill University.

Deformities and Skeletal Pathology

ARTHUR STEINDLER, Professor of Orthopedics, State University of Iowa.

Dermatology

U. J. WILE, Professor Emeritus of Dermatology and Syphilology, University of Michigan; formerly, Chief Medical Consultant, United States Public Health Service.

Digestive Pathology

ALFRED E. WILHELMI, Professor of Biochemistry, Emory University.

Fevers

E. V. COWDRY, Director, Wernse Cancer Research Laboratory, Washington University; formerly, Director of Research, Barnard Free Skin and Cancer Hospital (Au., *Textbook of Histology; Microscopic Technique; Cancer Cells*).

General Pathology

J. FURTH, Associate Director of Research, Children's Cancer Research Foundation; Lecturer in Pathology, Harvard Medical School; formerly, Professor of Pathology, Medical College, Cornell University.

Gynecology

J. NOVAK, Formerly, Clinical Professor of Gynecology, Columbia University.

Medical Instruments

MORRIS I. GERNER, Chester, New York; formerly, Assistant Surgeon, Third Auxiliary Surgical Group. A.U.S.

Medical Substances

CARL F. SCHMIDT, Professor of Pharmacology, University of Pennsylvania.

Miscellaneous Diseases

GEORGE F. DICK, Professor of Medicine (Chairman of Department), University of Chicago.

Ophthalmology

ARTHUR GERARD DeVOE, Professor of Ophthalmology (Chairman of Department), New York University–Bellevue Medical Center.

Pharmacology

M. H. SEEVERS, Professor of Pharmacology (Chairman of Department), University of Michigan.

Psychiatry

NOLAN D. C. LEWIS, Consultant in Research, New Jersey Institutions and Agencies, New Jersey Neuro-Psychiatric Institute (Au., *History of Psychiatric Achievement; Pathological Firesetting; War Psychiatry*).

Surgery

HENRY NELSON HARKINS, Professor of Surgery (Executive Officer of Department), University of Washington; formerly, Associate Professor of Surgery, Johns Hopkins University (Au., *The Treatment of Burns*; editor in chief, *Quarterly Review of Surgery*; co-editor, *Surgery: Principles and Practices*; Member of Editorial Boards of *Annals of Surgery* and *Western Journal of Surgery*).

Trauma

MARK M. RAVITCH, Associate Professor of Surgery, Johns Hopkins University.

Tumors and Pustular Disorders

N. C. FOOT, Professor Emeritus of Surgical Pathology, Cornell University; Consulting Surgical Pathologist, New York Hospital.

Veterinary Science

WILLIAM A. HAGAN, Dean of New York State Veterinary College, Cornell University (Au., *The Infectious Diseases of Domestic Animals*).

WEIGHTS AND MEASURES

LEWIS V. JUDSON, Physicist, National Bureau of Standards.

WINES, SPIRITS, AND BEER

HAROLD J. GROSSMAN, Au., *Grossman's Guide to Wines, Spirits, and Beer*.

ZOOLOGY

Animal Ecology

RALPH BUCHSBAUM, Professor of Zoölogy, University of Pittsburgh.

Animal Embryology

JERRY J. KOLLROS, Professor of Zoölogy (Chairman of Department), State University of Iowa.

Arachnids

A. M. CHICKERING, Professor Emeritus of Biology (Chairman, Division of Science and Mathematics), Albion College.

Beef and Dual-purpose Cattle

W. H. BLACK, Senior Animal Husbandman in Charge of Beef and Dual-purpose Cattle Investigations, Bureau of Animal Industry, Agricultural Research Administration, United States Department of Agriculture.

Classification

WILLIAM C. SCHROEDER, Associate Curator of Fishes, Museum of Comparative Zoölogy, Harvard University; Ichthyologist, Woods Hole Oceanographic Institution, Massachusetts.

Crustaceans

J. H. WELSH, Professor of Zoölogy, Harvard University.

Dairy Cattle and Dairying

O. E. REED, formerly, Director of Livestock Research, Agricultural Research Administration; Chief of Bureau of Dairy Industry, United States Department of Agriculture, 1928–1953.

Dogs

LEONARD WHITTLESEY GOSS, Professor of Veterinary Pathology, Ohio State University.

Entomology: General Entomological Terms

R. E. SNODGRASS, Research Associate, Smithsonian Institution; Collaborator in Entomology, United States Department of Agriculture (Au., *Principles of Insect Morphology*; *Insects, Their Ways and Means of Living*; *A Textbook of Arthropod Anatomy*; *Anatomy of the Honey Bee*).

Entomology: Insect Names

C. H. SEEVERS, Research Associate, Chicago Natural History Museum; Professor of Biology, Roosevelt University.

Evolution

EDWIN G. CONKLIN, Professor Emeritus of Biology, Princeton University (Co-editor, *Biological Bulletin*; *Journal of Experimental Zoology*; *Genetics*; au., *The Mechanism of Evolution*).

General Biological Terms

JAMES A. MULLEN, Associate Professor of Biology, Fordham University.

Genetics

E. W. LINDSTROM, Professor of Genetics (Head of Department), Dean of Graduate College, Iowa State College.

Ichthyology: Fish Names

CARL L. HUBBS, Professor of Biology, The Scripts Institution of Oceanography, University of California, La Jolla; Past Secretary, Editor, and President, American Society of Ichthyologists and Herpetologists (Co-au., *The Improvement of Lakes for Fishing*; *Guide to the Fishes of the Great Lakes and Tributary Waters*).

Ichthyology: General Ichthyological Terms

LOREN P. WOODS, Curator of Fishes, Chicago Natural History Museum.

Ichthyology: Salt-water Food Fish

GEORGE S. MYERS, Professor of Biology, Stanford University; Curator, Zoölogical Collections, Natural History Museum (Editor, *Stanford Ichthyological Bulletin*).

Ichthyology: Tropical Marine Fish

SAMUEL F. HILDEBRAND, Senior Ichthyologist, Fish and Wildlife Service, Division of Fishes, National Museum, Washington, D.C. (Au., *A Descriptive Catalog of the Shore Fishes of Peru*; co-au., *Marine Fishes of Panama*).

Lower Invertebrates

L. H. HYMAN, Research Associate in Invertebrates, American Museum of Natural History.

Mammalogy: African Mammals and Primates

JOHN ERIC HILL, Assistant Curator of Mammals, American Museum of Natural History.

Mammalogy: Anatomy and General Mammalogical Terms

WILLIAM K. GREGORY, Curator Emeritus, Department of Comparative Anatomy and Fishes, American Museum of Natural History; Da Costa Professor Emeritus of Vertebrate Paleontology, Columbia University (Au., *The Orders of the Mammals*).

Mammalogy: Asiatic, European, and South American Mammals

GEORGE H. H. TATE, Curator of Mammals, American Museum of Natural History.

Mammalogy: North American and European Mammals

W. J. HAMILTON, JR., Professor of Zoölogy, Cornell University (Au., *American Mammals*; *Mammals of the Eastern United States*).

Microscopy

RUDOLF T. KEMPTON, Professor of Zoölogy (Chairman of Department), Vassar College; Trustee, Marine Biological Laboratory, Woods Hole, Massachusetts (Au., *Laboratory Manual for Comparative Anatomy*).

Myriapods

R. V. CHAMBERLIN, Professor Emeritus of Zoölogy (Head of Division of Biology), University of Utah (Au., *The Myriapoda of the Australian Region*; *Lithobiida of North America*; *Tropical Pacific Annelida*).

Nomenclature and Sizes in Picture Captions

COLIN C. SANBORN, Curator of Mammalogy, Retired, Chicago Natural History Museum.

Ornithology: African, Asiatic, South American, and Mexican Birds

HERBERT FRIEDMANN, Curator of Birds, United States National Museum (Au., *Birds Collected by the Childs Frick Expedition in Ethiopia and Kenya Colony*; *Birds of North and Middle America*; *Check-list, Birds of Mexico*).

Ornithology: Anatomy and General Ornithological Terms

ALEXANDER WETMORE, Research Associate (formerly, Secretary) Smithsonian Institution; formerly, Director, United States National Museum (Au., *The Migration of Birds*; *Systematic Classification for Birds of the World*; *Fossil Birds of North America*.

Ornithology: North American and European Birds

GEORGE MIKSCH SUTTON, Professor of Zoölogy and Curator of Birds, University of Oklahoma (Contributing Editor, *Audubon Magazine*).

Parasitology

ASA C. CHANDLER, Professor of Biology, Rice Institute; formerly, Special Consultant, United States Public Health Service (Au., *Introduction to Parasitology*).

Poultry

THEODORE C. BYERLY, Deputy Administrator, Agricultural Research Service, United States Department of Agriculture.

Reptiles and Amphibians

KARL PATTERSON SCHMIDT, Chief Curator Emeritus of Zoölogy, Chicago Natural History Museum (Au., *Homes and Habits of Wild Animals*; co-au., *Field Book of Snakes*).

Sheep and Goats

D. A. SPENCER, Senior Animal Husbandman in Charge of Sheep, Goat, and Animal Fiber Investigations, Agricultural Research Administration, United States Department of Agriculture.

Stockbreeding and Horses

RALPH W. PHILLIPS, Director of International Organization Affairs, Foreign Agricultural Service, United States Department of Agriculture; Senior Animal Husbandman in Charge of Genetics Investigations, United States Department of Agriculture.

Swine

JOHN H. ZELLER, Acting Chief, Swine Research Branch, Animal Husbandry Research Division, Agricultural Research Service, United States Department of Agriculture, Beltsville, Maryland.

EDITORIAL STAFF

MANAGING EDITOR: Jess Stein

EDITORS: Rosemary Barnsdall Blackmon, Harriet Cassell, William A. Frankel, Leonore Crary Hauck, Kiyoko Hosoura, Dimmes McDowell, Merle E. Severy, Laurence Urdang

ASSOCIATE EDITORS: Elizabeth J. Denning, Elizabeth Gedney, William J. Gedney, Cecil P. Golann, Martha L. Huot, Babette Keeler, Frederick S. Pease, Jr., Constance Stark, Burton D. Thiel, John S. Wasley, Ralph Weiman

EDITORIAL ASSISTANTS: Noreen E. Barron, Emmy Bloch, Mary Ellis, Mary E. Fallon, Henry Florman, William Franklin, Frances Halsey, Walter Heartsill, Philip Krapp, David A. Lawson, Ellen Nelson, N. Bryce Nelson, Alma Nespital, Nancy Rayfiel, Herbert Rowen, Thomas R. Royston, Phyllis Ruckgaber, Priscilla Smith, Dorothy R. Thelander, Abraham Waisglass, Mabel Wilcox

RESEARCH ASSISTANTS: Doris Alexander, Rodney W. Alexander, John C. Brunner, William Cannastra, Emily Cloud, Elizabeth Diez, Norman Hoss, Joseph Kaplan, Arthur Kohlenberg, Lawrence Krader, Herbert J. Landar, Evelyn Leverah, Leon F. Schwartz, Anne Thomson

OFFICE ASSISTANTS: Grace Bergh, Lorraine Binder, John Brothers, Jean Connors, Natalie Firstenberg, Gerald Gottlieb, Shirley Heckel, Mary Hodge, Sally Horan, Paul Kessler, Eleanor Morse, Ruth Rosoff, Evelyn Smith, Marjorie Waldo, Evelyn Wexler, Luise Wickel, Florence Woolf

ARTISTS: Leon Pray, Thomas Voter, Edward Willms

SPECIAL ACKNOWLEDGMENTS

GEORGE O. CURME, Professor Emeritus of Germanic Philology, Northwestern University

WILLIAM ETKIN, Associate Professor of Biology, College of the City of New York

RICHMOND Y. HATHORN, Assistant Professor of English and Latin, Northwestern State College of Louisiana

CHARLES HOCKETT, Professor of Linguistics, Cornell University

MARTIN JOOS, Professor of German, University of Wisconsin

JOHN KEPKE, New York City

SAMUEL LIEBERMAN, Department of Classical Languages, Queens College

W. ROSS MARVIN, Editor in Chief, World Book Company

BERNARD MATTSON, Department of History, Evanston Township High School

NORMAN McQUOWN, Assistant Professor of Anthropology, University of Chicago

HAROLD RASHKIS, Research Associate, Eastern Pennsylvania Psychiatric Institute

ELIZABETH SCANLAN, Assistant Professor of Speech, Queens College

JOEL SHOR, Clinical Psychologist, Department of Health, Yale University

S. STEPHENSON SMITH, Department of English, New York University

WILLIAM B. S. SMITH, Advisory Editor, Columbia University Press

GEORGE L. TRAGER, Professor of Anthropology and Linguistics, University of Buffalo

CHARLES F. WILKINSON, JR., Professor and Chairman, Department of Medicine, New York University Post-Graduate Medical School

MORRIS WINOKUR, Assistant Professor of Biology, College of the City of New York

SELECTION OF ENTRIES AND DEFINITIONS: IRVING LORGE

The intricate architecture of a dictionary rests on the basic blueprint of the entries that are defined, illustrated, explained, and clarified. The selection of the words, names, places for inclusion in a dictionary must consider how and why a person goes to a dictionary. He goes to find the meaning of words such as *aorist*, or the preferred spelling of words such as *enclose*, or the pronunciation of words such as *stupefacient*. He also goes to find the location of places such as *Pohai* or the significance of names such as *Marie Antoinette*. Such a list of possible uses of the dictionary may, of course, be extended and amplified.

A dictionary, therefore, must include within it those words, names, pronunciations, and other facts that the user is likely to need for meaning, spelling, pronunciation, significant fact, or location.

The primary consideration in the selection of entries therefore, is the specification of words, places, names, and borrowings from other languages that should be included. A reasonable rule would be to include all words that are likely to be read. No one can quarrel with so sagacious a principle. The difficulty is how to put it into practice. If a tabulation were made of every word printed in every book, a master list could be prepared. Then the lexicographer would have a basis for selecting the words to be defined. No such master list exists. There are, however, word counts which have been made of *samples* of printed materials. The most recent word count is based on the tabulation of the frequency of occurrence of each different word in about twenty-five million running words of text. Such a count provides the listing of the words appearing most frequently in printed materials, i.e. in novels, essays, textbooks, monographs, pamphlets, magazines and in business and social letters. In this count[1] are listed the 30,000 words including names of places, people, and characters which were most frequently found.

Words such as *boycott*, *brummagem*, and *macadam* have been incorporated in the stock of English words although they were originally the names of people or places. The reader, however, will find many illustrations of the uses of names or places in factual or metaphoric reference. References to *Paul* or *Moses*, to *Confucius* or *Aristotle*, to *Robin Hood* or *Robinson Crusoe*, to *Galileo* or *Magellan*, to *Bach* or *Kant*, to *Lincoln* or *Roosevelt*, to *Ford* or *Edison*, to *Shaw* or *Wells*, or to *Balzac* or *Zola* need explanation just as much as do references to the words of the language. For names of these persons and characters as well as for the names of places, a dictionary should include significant material about the facts and achievements that will give the reference adequate meaning.

The lexicographer may be reasonably certain that all (or most) of the words in a list of the most frequent 30,000 words will occur in the reading of high school and college students and literate adults. Such a list, however, has defects: first, it cannot include the new words that are added to the stock of the language; second, it does not include the large technical vocabulary that is needed in the specialized study of the humanities, the social studies, and the sciences.

A list of the most frequently occurring words, therefore, must be supplemented by the judgment of specialists in all fields of practice and knowledge. The final list of entries, therefore, is based not only on such facts about word frequency as are available, but, more, on the judgment of hundreds of experts in all fields from astronomy

through zoölogy. All in all, more than 350 experts indicated what words, names, places should be defined or explained. Thus, words like *ant lion*, *Antofagasta*, *Antoinette*, *Antoninus*, *antonomasia*, *antre*, and *antrum* are added to *antlered*, *anvil*, *anxious*, and *any*. The master list for this dictionary included more than 200,000 basic entries.

When the list of entries was established, the next problem was the selection of senses to be defined. Most of the words that occur with great frequency are words used in many different senses. The word *point*, for instance, means a sharp end, an extremity, a period, a size of type, a location, a score, an electrical contact, a kind of lace, and many other things. Trained editors who specialized in recognizing the distinction among the meanings of words found that 1100 separate occurrences of the word *point* were used in 55 different senses. Other words were even more startling in the variety of senses: the editors distinguished 109 different meanings of the word *run*. The available knowledge about word frequency and the expert judgment of specialists is as essential in choosing the senses to be defined as in choosing the basic entry to be included. The variety of different senses of a homograph has been recognized by all who read or write. So far only one count of the frequency of the occurrence of different senses or meanings has been made. Professors Lorge and Thorndike, with the aid of a staff of 270 persons, counted the frequency of the occurrence of different meanings of a sample of about four and a half million words in context.[2]

This dictionary has utilized the semantic count to select the different senses of a homograph for definition. The word *style*, for instance, is given with eighteen different senses. These eighteen senses include those which were found and discriminated as different by the semanticists; to these senses were added those suggested by the experts in botany and zoölogy. Not only is the sense given by definition, it is also explained, elucidated and illustrated to help the reader to make the distinction. Thus, sense 13, **Old Style or New Style** is more than a definition; and sense 14 is pictured for clarity. The word *appeal* is another illustration of the multi-meaning character of common words. The dictionary distinguishes ten different senses which were recognized as different by semantic specialists. These distinctions of *appeal*, further, are clarified by the explanation of the synonyms of the word.

This dictionary, therefore, is based on the accumulated facts about which words are likely to occur in the reading and listening of high school and college students and of literate adults in general. To those words which have been found in the printed materials that people read has been added the scientific and technical vocabulary of business, art, and industry and of the humanities, the social studies, and the sciences. Moreover, the dictionary has combined the facts about the frequency of the occurrence of different meanings that were tabulated by scholars with the judgments of experts in choosing the senses of each word that were to be discriminated and clarified. As such, the dictionary utilizes the last forty years of scholarship in vocabulary selection and discrimination in the choice of senses of words to be defined, and in the selection of names of persons, places, and characters to be described or explained.

[1] Thorndike, Edward L. and Lorge, Irving. *The Teacher's Word Book of 30,000 Words*, New York: Bureau of Publications, Teachers College, Columbia University, 1944, 274 + xii pp.

[2] Lorge, Irving. "The English Semantic Count," *Teachers College Record*, Vol. 39, 65–77: October, 1937.

Lorge, Irving and Thorndike, Edward L. *A Semantic Count of English Words*, New York: The Institute of Educational Research, Teachers College, Columbia University, 1938. [Hectographed; approximately 1200 pages.]

PRONUNCIATION: W. CABELL GREET

Correct pronunciation is one of the many kinds of information that Americans expect to find in their dictionaries. If we may judge from the usual absence of pronunciation in general encyclopedias and technical handbooks, pronunciation may be the distinguishing mark of the American or encyclopedic dictionary. This statement is extravagant and humorous, but whatever else we may find in our dictionaries—and over the years they have approached encyclopedias in breadth of learning—we are certain to find pronunciation; whereas in other reference books and indexes of particular fields of knowledge pronunciation is ordinarily excluded. Their compilers have dedicated themselves to assisting the practitioners, the writers, and the printers of the science or art: meaning and spelling take all their care, as if we were still living in a world where mass communication was entirely a matter of the printing press without radio and phonograph. But the American dictionary! How often have hard-pressed broadcasters blessed the happy result of our "dictionary wars" of the last century. The competing dictionaries have got larger and larger. Everything with a name—and everything known has a name—animal, vegetable, mineral, personal, geographical, supernatural—is more likely than not to appear in an American dictionary, and there it is pronounced. This practice has been justified, for in our time the spoken word, as in the classical past of Greece and Rome and Elizabethan England, has become quite as important as the written word. Rhetoric, which once meant oratory, was used by our fathers and grandfathers to mean the rules of written composition. But the new rhetoric, of the printed page as well as of radio, is based more on the sounds and rhythms of speech than upon visual patterns. Pronunciation is important.

American spelling is phonetic. That is to say, the letters of our alphabet stand for sounds, and when they are arranged in certain patterns they "spell out" words for people who know how to "read English." But the phonetic principles of American spelling must provide for so many exceptions and the position of the accent is so uncertain, that when we are faced with a new word, or when we hear a strange pronunciation, we ask that the dictionary supplement the conventional spelling of English by marking the accents and indicating the sounds by unequivocal and independent letters and symbols.

The uncertainties of English spelling are due to the remarkable conservatism of the spelling tradition that accompanied an equally remarkable disposition to change in pronunciation. Many explanations have been suggested. Without doubt the unbroken length of the tradition is of the greatest importance. More than seven hundred years divide Orm, an orthographer of the twelfth century, and the spelling reformers who were backed by Andrew Carnegie and encouraged by Theodore Roosevelt. It is no wonder that old rules have survived, as is shown by the table of English spellings on page xxvii, where 44 sounds are represented by 251 spellings. There have been no social strains, internal or external, sufficient to break the scribal tradition of English. Sufficient changes were made to keep the spelling from chaos. The machine was tinkered with to keep it running. Good people are always fearful that language may become unintelligible, but that, as a matter of fact, is what never seems to happen so long as there are active speakers and writers. They may occasionally mislead one another, but a minimum degree of intelligibility sufficient to the pressing needs of society the users of a language always provide, no matter how careless they seem as pronouncers and spellers. And so, as there has always been an England—if so many centuries may pass muster for "always"—there will always be an England and the English language and its curious ways of spelling until disaster overtakes us, perhaps bringing in its wake orthographic improvements. The new American scene was able to simplify pounds, shillings, and pence, but even in America the spelling tradition has been cultivated with loving and stubborn care.

In bold black type this dictionary presents the conventional spelling. In most instances this will suggest the pronunciation, but on the chance that the user may wish confirmation of his supposition or additional information, a pronunciation is added in a simple phonetic alphabet, auxiliary to the conventional spelling and subject always to the speech ways that are standard in the major regions. For instance, as in all American dictionaries, r after vowels is included in the phonetic respelling but without the expectation or desire that southern and northeastern Americans should change their pronunciation of words like *farther*. The symbol schwa (ə) is used for vowels, however spelled conventionally, which with lack of stress tend to lose their distinctive values and to merge, more or less, in a common centralized sound like the *a* of *about*

or the *i* of *sensible*. The symbol schwa is not a command to utter this undistinguished vowel where you fancy you pronounce one of more definite character. It is, however, a sign, placed by a sincere and conscientious staff of phoneticians, that the vowel of this syllable, when uttered in connected discourse, has less than the full values indicated by breve (ᵛ) and macron (−). Occasionally one is in doubt whether the reduced vowel is a kind of *uh*-sound or an enfeebled *ih, eh,* or *oh.* Such uncertainty is difficult to resolve because of many varieties of pronunciation and shifting stresses and because of the shortness and the lax quality of the sounds. But the symbol schwa (ə) may be taken as a sign supplementary to the spelling. It signifies that a vowel is reduced in strength, relaxed, and dulled to a degree that may vary with speakers and circumstances. It matters not whether one pronounces the word *added,* ad/ihd or ad/uhd (this transcription and the opinion are my own), but it is essential for intelligibility that the vowel of the last syllable be "reduced, relaxed, and dulled"; otherwise someone may think that Ad is dead. Particularly in these days of radio we must realize that unstressed and therefore reduced vowels are a respectable and essential element in the English language. No broadcaster is so tedious, annoying, and difficult to understand, as he who "overpronounces," stressing syllables and preserving vowels that are neglected in idiomatic and correct English speech.

Inferior teaching in the first grade has sometimes been responsible for a mistaken idea of correct English. The child points out, "Thee boy has ay pen— . . ." and hesitates. The teacher adds, "c i l spells 'sil'—pen/ -sil/." By imitating other speakers the child learns to say "thuh boi/ haz uh pen/səl," but an unfortunate experience of the schoolroom may persist in the erroneous notion that "correct English" is something artificial and apart. And in the past many dictionaries have willy-nilly encouraged the error by giving the pronunciation of a word when isolated, as in a list, instead of the pronunciation when it is joined with other words in discourse. The pronunciation of *a* as a single word is (ā), but as one of a group of words it is "uh." This simple illustration does not illustrate the complexity of the problem for the makers of dictionaries, because the user, having encountered a difficult word in a phrase, nevertheless looks it up in isolation. What pronunciation shall he be given, for instance, of *Roosevelt* or *government?* It is the practice of this dictionary to give a conservative pronunciation of the word per se, and to indicate by the use of schwa and by additional transcriptions, if necessary, some of the striking changes that may take place in speech. This middle course may grieve young radicals and old conservatives, but it is hoped that it will please the judicious.

The use of schwa and attention to actual speech make these pronunciations exceedingly practical as well as correct. But the symbols are not themselves sound nor are they convertible into sound except through the minds and the linguistic habits of individuals. The most efficient indication of pronunciation, in black on white, is the sound track of talking motion pictures. It is really a translation of sound into corresponding values of another medium, because the outlines or the shades of black on white can be reconverted into sound with a predetermined percentage of loss or error. It is possible, though it would be expensive, to construct a machine which would give you, on the pressing of keys in code, the pronunciation of each and every word of this dictionary in, if you wish, the voice of Mickey Mouse or Clark Gable or any other notable who might be willing to record the tens of thousands of words. The advantage would be a lifelike reproduction of sound. A disadvantage might be that the pronunciation would be personal and individual. A dictionary phonetic-transcription is after all general, not individual, abstract, not personal. Perhaps this is as it should be. The American people, like the British, have shown remarkable resistance to every movement towards establishing a dictatorship of speech. Pronunciations and voices may wax and wane in popular acceptance.

In selecting pronunciations, the staff of the American College Dictionary have exercised due care under the circumstances. As I have elsewhere described the procedure, "Without seeking to impair any citizen's right to be his own professor of English, we look for what is national, contemporary, and reputable." This is our standard of correctness, and pronunciations which do not meet it are clearly labeled. The authority of a dictionary is based completely upon the actual speech and writing of the community of effective citizens, with admiration for those skilled in the arts and with respect for those who do but serve the nation.

TREATMENT OF ETYMOLOGIES:
KEMP MALONE

Scientific investigation into the origin and history of words has never been more active than it is at the present time. English etymologists in particular have been busy, and their researches have cleared up many points once enigmatic or wrongly set forth. Our etymological staff have taken due account of the learned publications in this field, and in a number of cases have made contributions of their own. They have provided in this dictionary a presentation of etymologies which is up to date in form and substance. Outmoded and pre-scientific terms like *Anglo-Saxon, Teutonic,* and *Zend* have been avoided, and the reader will find, instead, the terminology now usual in linguistic science. The terms used are duly defined in the dictionary proper.

The treatment of the etymological material is conservative. The use of hypothetical or reconstructed forms has, in general, been avoided, and where such forms appear, they are marked with an asterisk. The origin of many words is put down as "uncertain" or "unknown," and plausible but doubtful etymologies are given (if at all) with a question mark. Rival explanations have been carefully weighed and, if the balance seemed even, both alternatives have been included. In sum, the etymologies here set down present, in succinct form, the fruits of scholarly research, old and new, on the origins of English words.

Extreme brevity of presentation commonly marks the etymologies given in a college dictionary. In this dictionary, too, limitations of space have made brevity needful, but the etymological treatment remains remarkably full, and is combined with an exactness of detail rarely found even in unabridged dictionaries. The method of presentation used is described in the paragraphs which follow.

METHOD OF PRESENTATION

The etymological part of a word entry is normally the final section of the entry proper; it is set off from the rest of the entry by square brackets. In some cases, where the entry word needs two etymologies (thus, one for the noun, one for the verb, if noun and verb have been treated in a single entry), each etymology will be found at the end of the definition group to which it applies.

The etymology begins with some indication of the age of the word in English. This item of information is not etymological, strictly speaking, and might have been given elsewhere in the entry, but it has proved convenient to include it in the etymological part. If the word was current in English in the Middle Ages (before A.D. 1500), it is marked ME (Middle English); if the word was current in the early Middle Ages (before A.D. 1100), it is marked OE (Old English). Thus, the etymological part of the entry **guilt** reads: [ME *gilt,* OE *gylt* offense]. If the modern written form (spelling) of the word was already in use in Middle English, it is not repeated after "ME." Thus, for **name** we have: [ME; OE *nama,* . . .]. Here the semicolon marks the fact that ME and Modern English agree in the spelling of the word. If the Old English spelling likewise agrees with the one now current, the entry word is not repeated at all in the etymology. Thus, for **god** we have: [ME and OE, . . .]. If the word does not occur in English before the 16th century, no indication of its date is set down; this want of indication serves to mark the word as postmedieval.

NATIVE WORDS

Next comes the etymology proper. The fundamental distinction here is that between native words and words of foreign origin. The etymology of a native word like *guilt* or *god* is comparatively simple: after giving the oldest recorded form (if it differs from the current form), one lists the cognates; that is, the words in kindred tongues that correspond both formally and semantically. The etymological part of the word entry **god** reads: [ME and OE, c. D *god,* G *gott,* Icel. *godh,* Goth. *guth*]. This means that *god* occurs in Middle English and Old English, and that it is cognate with Dutch *god,* German *gott,* Icelandic *godh,* and Gothic *guth.* Not all the cognates are listed, of course. Thus, the Danish cognate *gud* is here omitted, and in most cases only one or two cognates can be given, for want of space. The etymology of *guilt* (given above) includes no cognates for the simple reason that none exist; this word occurs in English only, the kindred languages having no words with which *guilt* can be etymologically connected.

Most native words lack the simplicity of *guilt* and *god.* Even so, however, their etymology can usually be presented in a line, or less. Only now and then is more space required, as it is with **godsend:** [earlier *God's send,* var. (under influence of SEND, v.) of *God's sond* or *sand,* OE *sond, sand* message, service]. Here a mere analysis into *god* and *send* would have been insufficient. In many composite words, however, such an analysis meets every etymological need. Often, indeed, the word explains itself, so to speak. Thus, the structure of the adjective *godly* is evident, and the reader in search of etymological explanations need only take the word apart and look up its elements *god* and *-ly* in the dictionary. For this reason the entry **godly,** and many like entries, have no etymological section.

FOREIGN WORDS

The etymology of words of foreign origin takes up more space, on the average, if only because the language of origin must be specified. Moreover, many such words got into English, not directly from the tongues to which they were native, but through other tongues, and the etymology usually gives the intermediate stages as well as the ultimate source, so far as these can be determined. The word **heroine** is one of the simpler examples: [t. L, t. Gk., der. *hḗrōs* hero]. This means that the English word was taken from Latin, and that the Latin word had been taken from Greek, in both cases without change in spelling; further, that the Greek word was derived from the corresponding masculine word. The etymology of **honorary,** too, is simple: [t. L: m.s. *honōrārius* relating to honor]. This means that *honorary* was taken (into English) from Latin; more precisely, that the English form of the word is a modification of the stem of the Latin form. The technical term *stem* (abbreviated s.) is defined in the entry **stem** of this dictionary, and is used accordingly in the etymologies. The stem of Latin *honōrārius* is *honōrāri-* (the *-us* is an inflectional ending that marks the form as nominative, singular, and masculine). The Latin word was not taken into English in its stem form, however, but in a modification (m.) of that form required by a rule of English spelling; the letter *i* is not permitted at the end of a word and in this position is regularly replaced by *y.* In accordance with this rule we write *honorarium* but *honorary,* and the English word-form *honorary* is explained, in our etymology above, as m.s. (that is, a modification of the stem of) L *honōrārius.* The colon in the etymology makes a division between the general statement of origin (namely, that the word was taken from Latin) and the particulars which explain the precise written form of the English word.

The colon is also used in etymologies like that of **biceps:** [t. L: two-headed]. Here the English word and its Latin etymon agree in written form but differ in meaning. In English the word is a noun, used to name a muscle with a double attachment; in Latin, it is an adjective with no particular reference to muscles, though applicable enough to a muscle thought of as two-headed. In such cases the meaning of the etymon is set after the colon. In cases like **inspector,** however, no gloss is needed, and the etymological part of the entry reads simply: [t. L]. This etymology might have been expanded by reference to the entries INSPECT and -OR, where further etymological information is given, but space is precious and the user of the dictionary may be trusted to make for himself this analysis of *inspector.*

CROSS REFERENCES

References to other entries are made by printing the entry word in small capitals. Thus, the etymology of **mischance** reads: [ME *meschance,* t. OF: m. *mescheance.* See MIS-[1], CHANCE]. Here, at the end of the etymology, the reader is referred to two other entries, MIS- and CHANCE, where he will find further etymological information. In this case the reference takes the form "see MIS-, CHANCE." But a mere gloss, if printed in small capitals, serves also as an entry reference. There are two such references in the etymology of **interregnum:** [t. L, f. *inter-* INTER- + *regnum* REIGN]. This etymological statement means that *interregnum* was taken from Latin, and that the Latin word was formed from *inter-* and *regnum,* both the meaning and the etymology of which may be found by consulting the entries INTER- and REIGN in this dictionary. The repetition here may seem needless, but is actually needful, because one must distinguish between Latin and English, even though the word forms are the same. In the sequence "*inter-* INTER-" the first form is Latin; the second, its English gloss.

FORMATIONS

Many English words were not taken, as such, from a foreign tongue but were made by putting together words or word elements of foreign origin, and therefore have a distinctly foreign look. Thus, the learned term **homeomorphism** looks like a Greek word because its parts are Greek in origin. Its etymology reads: [f. m.s. Gk. *homoiómorphos* of like form + -ISM]. This means that the word was formed from a modification of the stem of Greek *homoiómorphos* plus the English word element *-ism*, itself of Greek origin. In this dictionary such words are carefully distinguished from words actually taken from a foreign language. The reader will note that the etymology begins with the abbreviation f. (formed from), not with t. (taken from).

REPLACEMENT

Another important feature of the English vocabulary is brought out in the etymologies by the abbreviation r. (replacing). The etymology of **horizon** serves for illustration: [t. L, t. Gk.: bounding circle, horizon, prop. ppr., bounding; r. ME *orizonte*, t. OF]. The modern form of the word, which agrees with the Latin and Greek etymon, replaced a medieval form taken from Old French. This change marks part of a process of Latinization which the English language underwent during the Renaissance, a process which has continued, in various ways, to the present day. One result of it has been to reduce greatly the number of French words in the English vocabulary, replacing them by the corresponding Latin or Greek words. In this dictionary systematic account has been taken of such replacements.

DESCENT VS. ADOPTION

The etymology of words taken from French and the other Romance languages makes special problems of presentation because of the very fact that these words can usually be traced back to Latin, the language out of which all the Romance languages grew. The Romance vocabulary is made up, in part, of words Latin by descent, having been handed down from generation to generation while spoken Latin was becoming Romance. In this dictionary such words are said to go back to Latin (abbreviated g. L). In the same way a native English word might go back to Germanic, but since such words are rarely traced back, in the etymologies, to Germanic times (for want of records), this parallel is of little practical importance here. Most of the Romance words of Latin origin, however, like the corresponding words in English, German, and other European languages, were simply taken from Latin by learned men at various times and added to the vernacular vocabulary. Such words are of course marked t. L, not g. L, in the etymologies. The two etymologies which follow illustrate the difference between the two kinds of Romance words of Latin origin:

ire [ME, t. OF, t. L: m. *īra*]
isle [ME *isle*, *ile*, t. OF, g. L *insula*]

SCANDINAVIAN WORDS

The English vocabulary includes many words of Scandinavian origin, most of them taken into English in the 10th and 11th centuries, though rarely recorded until Middle English times and often without record even then. It is usually impossible to say which particular Scandinavian language they came from. In such cases the etymology specifies Scandinavian origin and gives a pertinent form from some Scandinavian tongue, usually Icelandic, the classical language of the North. We illustrate with **bulk**: [ME *bolke* heap, t. Scand.; cf. Icel. *bulki* heap, cargo]. A like difficulty arises with many Romance words of Germanic origin, and the etymology of these is given in a like form.

DERIVATIVES

The expression "derived from" (abbreviated der.) is used in the etymologies in its strict or narrow sense only. Thus, it appears in the etymology of **jaundice**: [ME *jaunes*, *jaundis*, t. OF: m. *jaunisse*, der. *jaune* yellow, g. L *galbinus* greenish-yellow]. Here we are told that Old French *jaunisse* was derived from *jaune*. The derivative was made by adding to the basic word *jaune* the noun suffix *-isse* -ICE, but this is left unexplained in the etymology, its obviousness being taken for granted. The reader

will not find "der." used loosely in an etymology, to signify mere origin or the like. Thus, the etymology just given does not say that the English word *jaundice* was derived from French, or from Old French.

COMBINING FORMS

Most English words are composite; that is, they were made by putting together other words or word elements. In composition a word may have a special form, different from the one it has when used alone. In the etymologies of this dictionary such a special form is called a combining form (abbreviated comb. form). A familiar example is *thir-*, the combining form of *three*, as in *thirteen* and *thirty*. The numeral *ten* has two combining forms: *-teen*, as in *thirteen* (3 plus 10), and *-ty*, as in *thirty* (3 times 10). Other native words have combining forms, of course, but by far the greatest number of such forms are of classical (Latin and Greek) origin. These classical combining forms have a special interest for the historical linguist. Thus, the initial combining forms usually end in a vowel, often identical with the stem vowel of prehistoric times. In the classical period the vowel with which most prehistoric stems ended had become, functionally, a part (or the whole) of the inflectional ending, and was no longer treated as belonging to the stem. In an uninflected combining form, however, the old stem vowel may be kept as such. It must be added that these forms, even in classical times, tended to end in *o*, irrespective of etymology, and this tendency is still more marked in modern formations. The vowel *i* was also favored in this position. In this dictionary many combining forms have entries of their own, and the others used in English words are duly identified in the etymologies. The same holds for the prefixes, the suffixes, and even the inflectional endings of English.

BLENDS

Many English words, though a very small proportion of the whole, are compounds of a special kind, technically known as blends (abbreviated b.). They usually have the appearance of simple words because of the way in which they were put together. An example is the word *boost*, a blend of *boom* and *hoist*. Each of the sources of a blend contributes something to the final product, but the contribution may be small. If a whole word as such enters into a compound, that compound is not a blend. In origin, the blend is usually slangy and jocular, but blends often become serious and respectable members of linguistic society. The importance of this method of making words was first brought out by the American scholar Louise Pound in her book on the subject. In this dictionary a number of words are etymologized as blends, and a few of these etymologies are new.

TRANSLITERATIONS

The forms given in the etymologies reproduce the spelling of the originals, with certain conventional changes. Letters not in the modern English alphabet are not used, but ligatures like æ and marks like the tilde are kept. The letter yogh of Middle English is represented by *y* or *gh*, according to its phonetic value. Old and Middle English thorn and eth are replaced by *th*, but for obvious phonetic reasons the treatment of the corresponding Icelandic letters is different, thorn being represented by *th*, eth by *dh*. Old English and Icelandic long vowels are marked with a macron, but Middle English long vowels are left unmarked. In general, long vowels are marked in ancient word forms. In marking Latin quantities, Harper's dictionary has been followed. Greek quantities have been conformed to Liddell and Scott. The transliterations from languages which do not use the Latin alphabet are conventional, and need no further comment here.

ABBREVIATIONS

In the course of the discussion above, some of the abbreviations used in the etymologies have been explained. Many other abbreviations are used, of course, but these are too familiar to need explanation. A key to all the abbreviations will be found on the inside of each cover, and a shorter key, giving only the most frequent abbreviations, appears at the bottom of every other page. By the use of abbreviation it has proved possible to present in limited space a substantial amount of etymological information with clarity and precision. It is hoped that the reader will find the presentation convenient and informative.

SYNONYMS AND ANTONYMS:
MILES L. HANLEY

I. WHAT ARE SYNONYMS?

Early writers referred to synonyms as words of identical meaning. To be sure, there have been groups of words in English which, for a period of time, could be considered synonymous in this oldest and strictest sense. But, like other languages, English has had what is known as *semantic change*, affecting the meanings of words. Many words, while usually keeping earlier meanings, have developed new ones; together with figurative uses, specialized uses, and differences of various other kinds. English has also borrowed freely from the languages with which it has come in contact; and when words have been borrowed, the meaning of any corresponding English terms. or that of the borrowed terms, or both, has commonly been changed. For example, at the time when the word *animal*—already widely known as a Latin word—was adopted into English, there was the native word *deer*, which had the same meaning. But after *animal* had come in as the general term, the word *deer* developed the specialized meaning of "a horned beast." Between words originally identical in meaning, therefore, differences, great and small, have developed, in one of their senses or in several.

That a word may now be truly synonymous with another word or words in some meanings but not in others, needs little proof. *Steal*, *rob*, and *pilfer* are quite clearly synonymous in the sense of "to take away that which belongs to another." They are quite as clearly not synonymous in the sense of "to move quietly or furtively," another of the meanings of *steal*. Thus, the college student who wrote "The sun came pilfering through the leaves," was making the mistake of considering these synonyms as identical in all their meanings.

Important as semantic change is, a discussion of it is not practical here; obviously we must consider words according to their current meanings and uses. We can, however, take some account of it in our definition of synonyms: THOSE WORDS ARE SYNONYMS FOR ONE ANOTHER WHICH HAVE THE SAME, OR A VERY SIMILAR, GENERAL MEANING, THOUGH ONE OR MORE OF THEIR OTHER MEANINGS MAY DIFFER MORE OR LESS WIDELY.

II. WHY STUDY SYNONYMS?

"To consider synonymous words *identical* is fatal to accuracy; to forget that they are *similar*, to some extent *equivalent*, and sometimes *interchangeable* is destructive of freedom and variety." This statement (*Standard Dictionary*, 1894), which remains one of the best on the subject, points to some of the principal values in studying synonyms.

If one becomes aware of distinctions commonly (sometimes even unconsciously) made between similar words, he has added to his understanding of those words. If his attention is also drawn to some of the *ways* of distinguishing between words, and to some of the *kinds of differences* between words in some ways similar, he then has the equipment for gaining an understanding of further words which he may encounter.

One can be said truly to have enlarged his vocabulary only with those words which he can use with precision and with judgment. A corollary of the statements preceding is, then, that by studying synonyms one may learn not to use undiscriminatingly words which he does not understand, lest, in his attempts to be elegant, he succeed only in being ridiculous.

Discriminated studies of synonyms, especially, therefore, can be of assistance if one has such purposes as: (1) gaining freedom and ease in speaking and writing, (2) gaining a sense of appropriateness which will encourage careful discrimination, and (3) acquiring accuracy and precision in the use of words.

III. PRINCIPLES OF SELECTION OF SYNONYMS

A partial treatment of all possible synonyms, or a full treatment of even a part of all possible synonyms, would require volumes devoted exclusively to the subject. A chosen vocabulary of synonyms must necessarily be limited according to some principle or principles of selection.

In this book, lists of synonymous words have been provided where it was thought that these would be useful in throwing further light on the meaning, or meanings, of entry words of high frequency. The lists are in addition to, and exclusive of, words given in definitions and in the studies. Such lists were to serve not only as "finding lists," but to encourage further exploration into the meanings of the head word.

In the discriminated studies, however, the first consideration was frequency of use. In the past, just as the earliest English dictionaries were lists of "hard words," words of a literary tinge or words considered particularly difficult were likely to be selected for such study. Or those might be chosen which would be used in "elegant" conversation (Mrs. Thrale, *British Synonymy*, 1794). But a modern reference book cannot anticipate the infinite variety of needs that individual readers may have; only a word list chosen on the basis of frequency has a chance of being frequently useful to many.

It is, moreover, the frequently used, long-established word, which has developed the great variety of meanings. And it is here that the general reader needs help. For example, in what contexts is "little" more appropriate than "small"? When and why is "small" to be preferred?

It is only fair to say, at this point, that there are still many unsolved problems in determining frequency. The work of Thorndike, Lorge, Buckingham, Dolch, Zipf, and others, as well as the writer's own *Word Index of James Joyce's Ulysses*, has revealed many useful facts. But so far, the choice of material for the study of frequency has necessarily been limited, and to a degree distorted, the findings. Most of the material studied has been either literary or at least written; no account has been taken of the differences between vocabularies in oral and written materials. Much of the material has not been concerned with current usage, and until recently there has been no separation according to levels of formality, informality, etc.; or of parts of speech (when a single form may be used as noun and verb or as noun and adjective) though one part of speech may account for all but a small percentage of the occurrences, leaving the other part of speech as a rare word; or of the different definitions of any word (some uses being out of fashion so that only one or two may account for all or most of a fairly high frequency).

An outstanding advantage of the ACD is the extensive use that has been made of the semantic word count of Drs. Irving Lorge and Edward L. Thorndike. In this, the classifications and subdivisions of the great Oxford English Dictionary have been used in showing the relative frequency of various uses of a word. With this help we have been able to build on the studies and analyses made by some of our most distinguished English scholars over a period of more than seventy years.

Insofar as frequency has been established, we have used it as our first principle. Almost all the words selected for study are from Thorndike's first 10,000, and well up in frequency as indicated in *The Teacher's Word Book of 30,000 Words*, by Thorndike and Lorge.

Other principles were used to a lesser degree. Some of them follow:

1. We have chosen words with which general readers have difficulty; that is, some of the words often inquired about in newspaper columns, radio programs, college classes, and the like.

2. We have attempted to state concisely the distinctions between some words confused with one another and mistakenly thought to be synonyms, in such a way that the preferred usages will be clear.

3. We have taken into account the kinds of difficulty which persons learning English have; such studies as *judicious, judicial* are intended to be useful to this group of readers.

4. We have included a few examples from required readings in literature, which students need to understand.

5. Some of the words traditionally included in any treatment of synonyms have, of course, been considered.

6. A few groups needed to illustrate important principles (see Section V) have been added.

IV. METHOD OF TREATMENT OF SYNONYMS

In the synonym studies, the words discriminated have been limited to groups which have a considerable area of meaning in common. In order that the core meaning might be clear and might be stated in each study, the number of words compared in a study has been kept small—usually three or four, though sometimes only two, and only in a few instances five or more.

A study has practically always been placed under the entry of highest frequency, unless for a special reason (as *ado*, important for occurrence in literature; or *await*, a contrast with the modern form) it has seemed desirable to call greater attention to a word now less frequently used.

To call attention to the fact that the same word may have a number of different meanings; that other words may be its synonyms in one sense but not in another; and that a frequently used sense of one word may be a synonym for a less frequent one of another word, we have keyed each study to a particular sense of a word. With the other definitions of each word easily available, the reader may compare the other senses of the words as he wishes, and discover whatever additional area of synonymy there is. In some cases, different definitions of the same word are closely related in meaning—so closely at times that a number had to be arbitrarily assigned to the study—but in other cases the differences are great (as for example, *brazen*, "of brass," and *brazen*, "bold"). The hope is to lead the reader to consider the *various* definitions of a word and not merely to take the first one or two, if it has several. To examine all the meanings is essential to finding one which fits a context; and the habit is essential in learning to use unfamiliar synonyms discriminatingly—or even to discover which of the meanings are synonymous (the No. 1 definition of one word may be synonymous with the No. 5 of another word, but not with the first four).

In each study we give first a statement of the idea that the words have in common, to show how they are alike. We then go on to show how they differ, by giving the distinctive characteristics of each word. Sometimes it is felt that little more than a comparison of definitions is necessary—a first step in any discrimination. But various methods have been used to illustrate a variety of differences (see Section V).

In most cases, examples in context have been given, not to limit use by a single idiomatic example, but to illustrate an accepted use. It would have been possible to use literary, especially poetic, quotations, for many of the examples; but it has seemed wiser not to do so, since the poet or literary artist frequently finds an original, striking, or suggestive use which, in itself properly memorable, would be usable only rarely in everyday life. Therefore, the examples are expressions that are, or could be, found in ordinary conversation or writing. In a few instances, it has been possible to use all of the discriminated words in a single context, to show how the use of each word produces some difference in the meaning.

V. POINTS ILLUSTRATED IN THE SYNONYM STUDIES

We have tried to illustrate various ways in which words may be discriminated, or ways in which "words that mean the same thing" may differ to the degree that they must be discriminated. A common question is, "What if the difference between this word and that one?" Some of the differences we have illustrated are the following:

1. Between general and specific.
2. Between shades of meaning.
3. In emphasis.
4. In implication.
5. In application.
6. In connotation.
7. In emotional effect.
8. In levels of usage.
9. Between literary and colloquial usage.

10. Effects of prefixes and suffixes.
11. In idiom.
12. In British and American usage.
13. Between borrowed and native words.
14. Between literal and figurative uses.
15. Between concrete and abstract uses.
16. Between technical (or occupational) uses and popular uses.
17. In aspect of action.
18. Between local or provincial usages and general usage.

VI. WHAT ARE ANTONYMS?

When, in 1867, C. J. Smith coined the term *antonym*, he meant it to be used in the sense of "counter-term" (such as "non-x" for "x"), a name already well known. *Antonym*, however, has since his time been variously interpreted.

As with *synonym*, the strictest interpretation has turned out to be too strict. If the strictest sense, "word of (completely) contradictory meaning," were adopted, most English words would not have antonyms. This is true, in any case, of scientific words, most of which are monosemantic. But it is perfectly obvious that, for a very large percentage of the nonscientific words, there are other words which offer a sharp contrast to at least some of the aspects or meanings.

Even such an unpromising word as *man*, for example, may be contrasted with other words which most emphatically do not mean the same thing as *man: woman* (different sex); *boy* (different age); *officer* (different rank), etc. Naturally this process could not be carried to the extreme of saying that all words not *man* are its antonyms because they differ from it in some respect. As with synonyms, there must first be some basis of likeness in classification; that is, for *man* the antonyms must be those referring to human beings, or at least to something living; an antonym for *black* should be the name of a color; for *anger* should be the name of an emotion, and the like. Perhaps, however, this likeness in classification may be taken for granted.

Since there are, as yet, many unsolved problems concerning antonyms, trying to give a definition is very difficult. A narrow definition is unsatisfactory; but a broad one must have limitations. A tentative statement might be made as follows: AN ANTONYM IS A WORD WHICH EXPRESSES THE OPPOSITE OR THE NEGATIVE OF ONE OR MORE OF THE MEANINGS OF ANOTHER WORD.

The number of antonyms which any word can have is not limited to one. Indeed, most words which would have antonyms at all would have several, and some words have great numbers. In this book we have not attempted to give as many antonyms as possible (either for any word or in total). As with synonyms, we have keyed antonyms to specific meanings of entry words, and have usually given only one antonym; but that one a word whose usual meaning is in sharp contrast to the sense of the entry word indicated.

USAGE LEVELS AND DIALECT DISTRIBUTION: CHARLES C. FRIES

Even a very superficial examination of the language practices of native speakers of English will reveal many differences in those practices from person to person. A hasty glance at the materials gathered for the *Linguistic Atlas of New England* will not only confirm the impression one receives from casually listening to the speech of those who talk English but will furnish convincing evidence that the differences of usage among native speakers of English are much greater and much more intricate than is usually believed. These differences of English usage occur not only in matters of vocabulary but also in matters of grammar and especially in matters of pronunciation. It is these differences in the practice of those who speak English that give rise to the many discussions concerning our language and often send students and others to our dictionaries for the information necessary to understand these differences. Ever since the publication of Samuel Johnson's *English Dictionary* in 1755 the "dictionary" has been looked to and consulted as the "authority" concerning the acceptability of words and the proper use of word meanings. "What does the dictionary say?" occurs as the common question in all our disputes concerning our language—as if there were

but one dictionary with ultimate authority and as if the statements recorded in any dictionary were valid for all time. Those who ask "What does the dictionary say?" practically never inquire concerning the publication date of the particular dictionary consulted or the qualifications of those who have produced it. The desire for an easily accessible "authority" on the part of the general public has created an enormous market for many cheap dictionaries, often produced by unscrupulous publishers who have achieved cheapness by reprinting old dictionary materials upon which the copyright has expired—adding, of course, a few of the well-known new words in order to give the appearance of being up-to-date.

ATTITUDES TOWARD USAGE DIFFERENCES

Part of the difficulty lies in the common and traditional view of the differences of English usage. Often it s assumed that there exist in any language only two kinds of words, word meanings, and pronunciations:—those that are correct and proper and those that are incorrect or mistakes. The "mistakes" are thought to be derived by ignorance and carelessness from the correct or proper uses. It is assumed also that the separation and labeling of the mistakes is a simple process and that grammarians and lexicographers have long ago made the proper decisions and the results of their work need only be preserved and made known to succeeding generations. It is assumed that all dictionaries will incorporate these "accepted" decisions and therefore there is no reason to inquire concerning the qualifications of the editors of a new dictionary or even the means employed to make the assignment of usage labels valid.

NECESSITY OF RECORDING USAGE

From the point of view of modern linguistic science these common naïve assumptions concerning the differences of usage in English must be discarded. They belong to a pre-scientific period in the study of language—to an age that still believes the earth to be flat and denies the circulation of the blood. The modern dictionary editor who is aware of the principles and methods of the modern scientific study of language and of the accumulations of knowledge concerning our language built up by the patient study of many scholars, cannot in honesty follow the easy path of copying the usage labels as they are attached to words and word meanings in former dictionaries. He cannot, as Samuel Johnson often did, condemn words and word meanings in accord with his special prejudices. Johnson, in spite of the fact that his quotations show the word *excepting* is used by Dryden and Collier, condemns it with the label "an improper word." In similar fashion he attaches the label "low words" to *budge*, *fun*, and *clever*, although his own quotations give examples of these words from Shakespeare and from Moore, from Addison, Pope, and Arbuthnot.

Constant change—in pronunciation, in grammatical structure, in word meanings, and in the words themselves—is, as far as we know, the normal condition of every language spoken by a living people. The careful study of these changes by the rigorous techniques developed by linguistic science has given us linguistic history. A hundred years of scholarly work has gone into establishing the details of the history of the English language and has forced us to turn away from the methods of "authority" as they are represented in Samuel Johnson's *Dictionary* and its successors. It has demanded the patient recording of the facts of usage as the language is and has been employed by the hosts of speakers of English in this country and in the other countries where English is the language in which the major affairs of the people are conducted. The editor of a modern dictionary is thus confronted with a wide range of constantly changing differences in English usage that cannot be easily separated into correct and proper forms on the one hand and mistakes on the other. These changes in usage render the older dictionaries inaccurate and make necessary continually new examinations of the status of the words and word meanings in English. A dictionary can be an "authority" only in the sense in which a book of chemistry or of physics or of botany can be an "authority"—by the accuracy and the completeness of its record of the observed facts of the field examined, in accord with the latest principles and techniques of the particular science. Older "authorities" in the uses of words are thus superseded by those which incorporate the latest results of the more scientific investigations in the English language.

REGIONAL DIFFERENCES

In the matter of English usage it is not always possible to define precisely the boundaries within which a word or a word meaning is used or recognized. The facilities of travel have so developed in modern times that many speakers of English hear constantly the language of those from other geographical areas. And the radio has brought into even the most secluded communities the speech of all sections of the country. This mixing of speech forms from various geographical areas is not by any means limited to the upper classes.

"I knowed you wasn't Oklahomy folks. You talk queer kinda—That ain't no blame, you understan'."

"Ever'body says words different," said Ivy. "Arkansas folks says 'em different, and Oklahomy folks says 'em different. And we seen a lady from Massachusetts, an' she said 'em differentest of all. Couldn' hardly make out what she was sayin'."

(J. Steinbeck, *The Grapes of Wrath*, p. 168.)

In the great mass of differences of usage that appear in the practice of English speakers, however, some words and word meanings and some pronunciations are in common use in special parts of the English-speaking world and appear much less frequently or never in other areas. For these this dictionary marks the geographical areas of special use. Some of the areas thus indicated within this country are New England, the old South, and the Southwest for such words as the following: *selectman*, *sharpie*, *levee*[1] (def. 1), *granny* (def. 4), *corn pone*, *alamo*, *chaps*, *chuck wagon* (see the definitions of these words).

British usage differs from the usage of the United States in such words as *lift* (def. 21), *navvy*, *lorry* (def. 1), *petrol* (def. 1), *gorse* (see the definitions of these words, and the preface by A. W. Read on "British and American Usage," page xxvi).

And Australia has its particular words and word meanings, as *paddock* (def. 3), *swag*[2] (def. 2), *billabong*, *billy* (def. 3) (see the definitions of these words).

Many words and word meanings are characteristic of certain fields of human activity. Each trade and occupation and sport has its technical vocabulary. Some of this technical vocabulary consists of special words used only in science, art, trade, or sport, such as *Binet test*, *electrode*, *binnacle*, *chiaroscuro*, *silo*, *forward pass* (see the definitions of these words).

Much of these technical vocabularies, however, consists of special meanings and uses of words that are employed generally in the language. The *field* in baseball has a special sense, as does *sacrifice*, *run*, *hit*, *out*, *plate*, *pitcher*. In the preparation and marketing of alcoholic beverages, the words *proof*, *dry*, *mash*, and *smooth* are used with special meanings.

"LEVELS" OF USAGE

Most frequently, however, discussions of language center upon what are often called the "levels" of usage. Some words and word meanings are frequently called "slang." The term "slang" has suffered such a wide extension of its signification and has been applied to so many varieties of words that it is extremely difficult to draw the line between what is slang and what is not. The difference between slang and not-slang does not rest in the meanings of the words themselves. To say that a man is "recalcitrant" is using an acceptable and somewhat learned word; to call him "a kicker" in the same situation is using slang, although the meanings are similar. Some clipped words, as *gent*, are often regarded as slang; others, such as *piano*, *phone*, and *cello*, are not slang. Slang cannot be defined in terms of either the forms or the strict meanings of the words themselves; it can, however, be characterized in terms of the suggested feelings accompanying certain words—their connotations rather than their denotations. Flippant humor marks the expressions we call slang. Some examples are *Java* (def. 3), *ice* (def. 8), *croak* (def. 4), *hangout*, *corking* (see the definitions of these words).

Some expressions appear only in poetry. They suggest then those circumstances in which they usually occur. Others are now found only in the written material of books. To mark them "*Poetic*" and "*Literary*" serves to record the special areas in which they are commonly used. Some examples are: *gloaming*, *e'er*, *lidless* (def. 3), *naught* (def. 2), *scarce* (def. 4) (see the definitions of these words).

Many expressions occur primarily in conversation rather than in formal writing. The occasions for their use are chiefly conversational situations. These are marked "*Colloq.*" Even teachers of English frequently misunderstand the application of the label *Colloquial* in our best dictionaries. Some confuse it with *localism* and think of the words and constructions marked "colloquial" as peculiarities of speaking which are characteristic of a particular locality. Others feel that some stigma attaches to the label "*Colloquial*" and would strive to avoid as incorrect (or as of a low level) all words so marked. The word *colloquial*, however, as used to label words and phrases in a modern scientifically edited dictionary has no such meaning. It is used to mark those words and constructions whose range of use is primarily that of the polite conversation of cultivated people, of their familiar letters and informal speeches, as distinct from those words and constructions which are common also in formal writing. The usage of our better magazines and of public addresses generally has, during the past generation, moved away from the formal and literary toward the colloquial.

Some words and expressions occur primarily in the language of those without much conventional education. These expressions are often called "illiterate" or "vulgar English," and are considered "incorrect." As a matter of fact, many of these expressions are survivals from an older period of the language and are "incorrect" only in the sense that they do not occur in the usage of standard English—the practice of the socially accepted, those who are carrying on the important affairs of English-speaking people. Much of the language spoken by the uneducated is the same as that of the polite conversation of cultivated people and also duplicates the expressions of formal literary discourse. The usage labels in a dictionary attempt to mark only those expressions that are peculiar to a particular type or dialect of English. If one ignores the differences that characterize the various geographical areas and the differences of the separate fields of human activity, of trades and vocations and sports, the situation may be roughly represented by the following diagram:

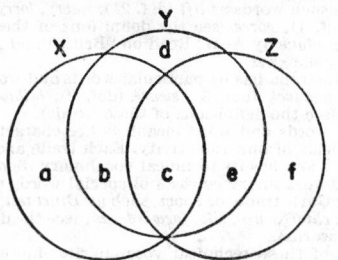

The three circles X, Y, Z, represent the three sets of language habits indicated above.

X—formal literary English, the words, the expressions, and the structures one finds in serious books.

Y—colloquial English, the words, expressions, and the structures of the informal but polite conversation of cultivated people.

Z—illiterate English, the words, the expressions, and the structures of the language of the uneducated.

b, c, and e represent the overlappings of the three types of English.

c—that which is common to all three: formal literary English, colloquial English, and illiterate English.

b—that which is common to both formal literary English and colloquial English.

e—that which is common to both colloquial English and illiterate English.

a, d, and f represent those portions of each type of English that are peculiar to that particular set of language habits.

The following is a list of some of the other usage labels used in this dictionary with typical examples under each of the particular words and expressions to which each label is assigned.

Archaic: impose (def. 8), hugger-mugger (def. 2), glister (def. 1), lief (def. 2), angle² (def. 3).

Colloq.: angel (def. 6), brass tacks, fizzle (def. 2), flimflam, goner.

Humorous: celestial (def. 5), human (def. 4).

Obs.: loblolly boy, lust (def. 5), flittermouse, murther, drugget (def. 2).

Obsolesc.: saloon (def. 6), regimen (def. 5).

Rare: image (def. 17), impassionate, faulty (def. 2), instancy (def. 2), genial¹ (def. 3).

Scot.: chap¹ (def. 5), laird, hag² (def. 1), icker.

Scot. and N. Eng.: unco, kirk (def. 1), ilk (def. 2), braw, bairn.

South African: laager, kraal (def. 3).

U.S.: chain lightning, challenge (def. 14), biscuit (def. 1), boss (def. 2), quilting bee.

BRITISH AND AMERICAN USAGE:

ALLEN WALKER READ

The passengers on the Mayflower, we may assume, were not troubled with problems of British and American usage. These came as a result of natural linguistic developments, on both sides of the ocean, in succeeding centuries. But so much cultural interchange between England and America has regularly taken place that the lines of linguistic division have never been clear-cut nor easily marked. However, most speakers of English recognize that certain expressions have their chief currency in one country or the other; and we have attempted to mark such currency more systematically and thoroughly than has been done in any previous dictionary.

Our criterion has been current usage. Thus the country of origin is not relevant to our marking. Words like *blizzard, jingoism, O. K.,* or *teetotaler* are well known either as Americanisms or Briticisms in origin, but they have now come to be used wherever English is spoken, and a regional label for them belongs only in a historical dictionary.

An unscientific attitude towards language has often in the past interfered with an impartial consideration of regional variation. Many people have regarded the "standard" language as the prime, original form and any deviation from it as a degenerate, deteriorated form. But the contrary is the case: the "standard" form of English developed, by means of social and commercial prestige, out of a multiplicity of dialects. The old, mistaken view has often influenced the attitude toward Americanisms, and most Americans themselves had a "colonial" attitude in language until very recent years. For their part, many Englishmen have assumed that their form of English is the only one with validity, and such a thing as a "Briticism" is impossible—it is simply "English." But in this dictionary, where normal usage is our all-important guide, we have taken an impartial, scientific view: if the frequency or incidence of a word is greater in one region of the English-speaking world than in another, it is a fact that deserves to be recorded. Our symbols *Brit.* and *U. S.* thus have a basis of an informal statistical type. The

Brit. or *U. S.* is not a "stigma" but a record of current usage, as accurate as we can determine it.

Americans have always adopted British expressions with very little reluctance. A few terms, such as *dustman, lift, petrol, tram, treacle,* etc., are conspicuously British, often used to identify the "stage Englishman"; and Americans, except for a few avowed Anglophiles, tend to avoid these. But if a British expression does not get strongly identified as such, Americans adopt it with little hesitation. Englishmen have been somewhat more cautious in adopting American expressions, but even here a constant borrowing has been going on for generations. The symbols *Brit.* and *U. S.* cannot be taken in any "absolute" sense, for exceptions are sure to be found. Sometimes, when usage is much divided, and only a preponderance will be found in one country or the other, the labels *Chiefly Brit* and *Chiefly U. S.* are used. Some matters of currency are taken care of in the definition, and the word or meaning therefore is not specially labeled. If a political or social institution is described as being "in Great Britain" or "in U. S." or if the range of a plant or animal is given in the definition, no further label is needed.

The graphic reflection of words (or spelling) sometimes differs between England and America, and typically British spellings are so labeled in this work. The *-our* and *-re* endings, rather than *-or* and *-er*, often find favor in England, and in the derived forms of a two-syllabled word the final consonant is the redoubled even when the accent is on the first syllable, as in *travel, travelled, travelling,* or *counsel, counselled, counselling.* Other typical British forms are *cheque, connexion, jewellery, gaol, kerb, pyjamas,* etc.

Most British-American differences occur in the language of everyday life rather than on literary levels, and one can sometimes read long passages of solid discussion in books or newspapers in both England and America without coming on distinctive peculiarities of language. But whenever they are found they should be an object of the lexicographer's comment, and we have paid particular attention in this work to such material.

TABLE OF COMMON ENGLISH SPELLINGS

The most frequent spelling or spellings of each sound, shown in boldface italics, are related below to the phonetic symbols of the American College Dictionary (ACD) and the International Phonetic Alphabet (IPA).

ACD Symbol	IPA Symbol	Spellings	Examples
ă	æ	*a, ai*	hat, plaid
ā	eɪ, e	*a, ai, ao, au, ay, ea, eh, ei, ey*	ate, rain, gaol, gauge, ray, steak, eh, veil, obey
âr	ɛː	*a, ai, ay, e, ea, ei*	dare, chair, prayer, there, wear, their
ä	ɑ	*a, e, ea*	father, sergeant, hearth
b	b	*b, bb*	bed, hobby
ch	tʃ	*ch, tch, te, ti, tu*	chief, catch, righteous, question, natural
d	d	*d, dd, ed*	do, ladder, pulled
ĕ	ɛ	*a, ae, ai, ay, e, ea, ei, eo, ie, oe, u*	any, aesthetic, said, says, ebb, leather, heifer, leopard, friend, foetid, bury
ē	i	*ae, ay, e, ea, ee, ei, eo, ey, i, ie, oe*	Caesar, quay, equal, team, see, deceive, people, key, machine, field, amoeba
f	f	*f, ff, gh, ph*	feed, muffin, tough, physics
g	g	*g, gg, gh, gu, gue*	give, egg, ghost, guard, demagogue
h	h	*h, wh*	hit, who
ĭ	ɪ	*e, ee, i, ie, o, u, ui, y*	England, been, if, sieve, women, busy, build, hymn
ī	aɪ	*ai, ay, ei, ey, i, ie, uy, y, ye*	aisle, aye, height, eye, ice, tie, buy, sky, lye
j	dʒ	*ch, d, dg, dge, di, g, gg, j*	Greenwich, graduate, judgment, bridge, soldier, magic, exaggerate, just
k	k	*c, cc, cch, ch, ck, cq, cque, cu, gh, k, qu*	car, account, bacchanal, character, back, acquaint, sacque, biscuit, lough, kill, liquor
l	l	*l, ll*	live, call
m	m	*chm, gm, lm, m, mb, mm, mn*	drachm, paradigm, calm, more, limb, hammer, hymn
n	n	*gn, kn, n, nn, pn*	gnat, knife, not, runner, pneumatic
ng	ŋ	*n, ng, ngue*	pink, ring, tongue
ŏ	ɒ	*a, o*	wander, box
ō	ou, o	*au, eau, eo, ew, o, oa, oe, oh, oo, ou, ow*	hautboy, beau, yeoman, sew, note, road, toe oh, brooch, soul, flow
ô	ɔ	*a, ah, al, au, aw, o, oa, ou*	tall, Utah, talk, fault, raw, order, broad, fought
ōō	u	*eu, ew, o, oe, oo, u, ue, ui*	maneuver, grew, move, canoe, ooze, troupe, rule, flue, fruit
ŏŏ	ʊ	*o, oo, ou, u*	wolf, look, should, pull
oi	ɔɪ	*oi, oy*	oil, toy
ou	aʊ	*ou, ough, ow*	out, bough, brow
p	p	*p, pp*	pen, stopper
r	r	*r, rh, rr*	red, rhythm, carrot
s	s	*c, ce, s, sc, sch, ss*	city, mice, see, scene, schism, loss
sh	ʃ	*ce, ch, ci, psh, s, sch, sci, se, sh, si, ss, ssi, ti, chsi*	ocean, machine, special, pshaw, sugar, schist, conscience, nauseous, ship, mansion, tissue, mission, mention, fuchsia
t	t	*ed, ght, t, th, tt, phth*	talked, bought, toe, thyme, bottom, phthisic
th	θ	*th*	thin
th	ð	*th, the*	then, bathe
ŭ	ʌ	*o, oe, oo, ou, u*	son, does, flood, couple, cup
ū	ju, ɪu	*eau, eu, eue, ew, ieu, iew, u, ue, yu, yew, you*	beauty, feud, queue, few, adieu, view, use, cue, yule, yew, you
ûr	ɜr, ɝ	*er, ear, ir, or, our, ur, yr*	term, learn, thirst, worm, courage, hurt, myrtle
v	v	*f, ph, v, vv*	of, Stephen, visit, flivver
w	w	*o, u, w*	choir, quiet, well
y	j	*g, i, j, y*	lorgnette, union, hallelujah, yet
z	z	*s, sc, ss, x, z, zz*	has, discern, scissors, Xerxes, zone, dazzle
zh	ʒ	*g, s, si, z, zi*	garage, measure, division, azure, brazier
ə	ə	*a, ai, e, ei, eo, i, ia, o, oi, ou, u*	alone, mountain, system, mullein, dungeon, easily, parliament, gallop, porpoise, curious, circus
ər	ər, ɚ	*ar, er, ir, or, our, ur, yr*	liar, father, elixir, labor, labour, augur, martyr

EXPLANATORY NOTES

Material in this dictionary has been arranged in the order considered to be the most convenient for the user. All items in the dictionary are in one alphabetical list: words of the common vocabulary, names of persons, geographical names, abbreviations, foreign words and phrases, etc.

Similarly, all information within a vocabulary entry has been arranged for the convenience of the user. In general, information about spelling and pronunciation comes first, meanings next, etymologies and synonyms last. The sequence of material in the entries is as follows:

   I. the entry word or words.
   II. the pronunciation.
   III. the parts of speech.
   IV. the inflected forms.
   V. the restrictive label.
   VI. the definition or definitions, including subentries and idiomatic phrases.
   VII. variant spellings.
   VIII. etymology.
   IX. run-on (or, undefined derivative) entries.
   X. synonym lists and studies.
   XI. antonym lists.

Abbreviations used in this dictionary have been limited as far as possible to familiar ones. All abbreviations used appear in their individual alphabetical places in the dictionary itself.

I. ENTRY WORD OR WORDS.

(A) The entry word appears in large boldface type at the left, slightly further into the left margin than the usual line of the text. (Example: **guard**)

(B) Syllables are separated by a centered dot, while entries of two or more words have open spaces between the words. (Example: **guarantee**)

(C) Syllabication is not shown in phrases unless the individual words are not separately entered.

(D) Each foreign word and phrase is always followed by a label indicating the language of the word or phrase. (Example: **anno Domini**)

(E) Separate entries are made for all words which, though spelled identically, are of completely unrelated derivation; in such cases, each entry word is followed by a small superscript number. (Example: **gum**[1] and **gum**[2])

II. PRONUNCIATION.

(A) The pronunciation follows the entry word, within parentheses. (Example: **grow**)

(B) The first pronunciation shown is, as a rule, the form in widest general use.

(C) Variations preferred in some sections of the country, in British usage, or by any other substantial group of speakers of the language are shown, usually with only the variant syllable or syllables isolated, to focus the reader's attention on the point or points of difference.

(D) Pronunciations are generally given for run-on entries, unless the pronunciation is easily ascertained from the combination of the main entry and the suffix. (Example: **guardedly**)

A full key to the pronunciation system appears inside both the front and back covers of this dictionary. In addition, for ready reference, an abbreviated pronunciation key appears at the bottom of each right-hand page.

III. PARTS OF SPEECH.

(A) The pronunciation is followed by an abbreviation in italics, indicating the part of speech of the entry word.

(B) If the entry word is used in more than one grammatical form, an italicized abbreviation indicating the part of speech precedes each set of definitions to which it refers.

IV. INFLECTED FORMS.

(A) If an entry word has irregularly inflected forms (any form not formed by the simple addition of the suffix to the main entry), the summary of these forms is given immediately after the pronunciation.

(B) If a word has variant inflected forms, these variants are shown. (Example: **grovel**)

(C) Regularly inflected forms, not generally shown, include:

   (1) Nouns forming a plural merely by the addition of *-s* or *-es*, such as *dog* (*dogs*) or *class* (*classes*).

   (2) Verbs forming the past tense by adding *-ed*, such as *halt* (*halted*).

   (3) Verbs forming the present tense by adding *-s* or *-es*, such as *talk* (*talks*) or *smash* (*smashes*);

   (4) Verbs forming the present participle by adding *-ing*, such as *walk* (*walking*).

Regular forms are given when necessary, however, for clarity, or the avoidance of confusion.

(D) In the case of inflected forms of verbs, if two forms are shown, the first represents the past tense and the past participle, while the second represents the present participle.

(E) If three inflected forms of verbs are shown, the first represents the past tense, the second the past participle, and the third the present participle.

(F) If necessary, variants of inflected forms are labeled as to level of usage or dialect distribution.

V. RESTRICTIVE LABELS.

(A) Entries that are limited in usage as to level, region, time, or subject, are marked with such labels as: *Colloq., Slang, Brit., Western U. S., Obs., Archaic, Electronics, Psychiatry,* etc.

(B) If the restrictive label applies to the entire entry, it appears before the first part of speech label. (Example: **grouch**)

(C) If the restrictive label applies to only one part of speech, it appears after that part of speech label but before the definition numbers.

(D) If the restrictive label applies only to one definition, it appears after the definition number but before the definition itself. (Example: **grub**, def. 3)

VI. DEFINITIONS.

(A) Definitions are individually numbered; numbers appear in a single sequence without regard to part of speech. The central meaning of each part of speech is put first; usually this is also the commonest meaning. The usual order after the central meaning is: figurative or transferred meanings, specialized meanings, general meanings, obsolete, archaic, or rare meanings. This order, however, has been broken whenever it is desirable to group related meanings together and for other reasons.

(B) In some cases in which two definitions are very closely related, usually within the same field of information, they are marked with boldface letters of the alphabet under the same definition number.

(C) If a meaning occurs with both capitalized and lowercase forms, an indication of this is given at the beginning of the definition. (Example: **Guernsey**, def. 2)

(D) Special effort has been made to indicate unique grammatical context wherever possible. Thus, the customary prepositional forms following certain words are often shown. (Example: **gulp**, def. 2)

(E) Idiomatic phrases, etc., are often shown in secondary boldface under main entries. Such subentries are usually placed under the difficult or key word. Noun phrases, in general, have been given separate main entries. (Example: **ground**)

VII. VARIANT SPELLINGS.

Definitions always appear under the commonest spelling of a word.

(A) Less common variants merely cross-refer to the more common ones.

(B) At the end of the definitions of the most common spellings, the variants are usually shown.

(C) Variants are often labeled as to usage, either within specific fields (as *Law*) or within specific levels, regions, or times (as *Colloq., Brit., Archaic,* etc.).

VIII. ETYMOLOGIES.

Etymologies appear in square brackets after the definition or definitions of the entry.

A full key to the etymology appears inside both the front and back of this dictionary, and a short abbreviated key appears at the bottom of every left-hand page.

IX. RUN-ON ENTRIES.

Words which are simple derivatives of the main entry, and which present no meaning problem, are run on after the etymology, or (if there is no etymology) after the last definition in the entry. Such entries appear in secondary boldface type. They are syllabicated and pronounced (or only stressed, if no pronunciation is needed), and followed by an indication of their grammatical form.

X. SYNONYMS.

(A) Studies discriminating between synonyms appear with numbers corresponding to the definitions involved. These studies have been placed under the commonest of the synonyms under discussion, and cross references are placed under the other terms.

(B) At the end of certain entries, lists of synonyms appear, each list being preceded by a number indicating the particular definition to which that list applies. In these lists, semicolons have been used to set off clusters of words with slightly different facets of meaning within the same general definitions.

XI. ANTONYMS.

Lists of antonyms are shown throughout the book, preceded by a number indicating the definition to which the antonym list refers.

A DICTIONARY OF THE
ENGLISH LANGUAGE

A

A, a (ā), *n., pl.* **A's** or **As, a's** or **as.** **1.** the first letter of the English alphabet. **2.** *U.S.* the highest mark for school or college work. **3.** *Music.* **a.** the sixth tone in the scale of C major, or the first in the relative minor scale of A minor. **b.** a written or printed note indicating this tone. **c.** a string, key, or pipe tuned to this note. **d.** (in the fixed system of solmization) the sixth tone of the scale, called **la.** **4. from A to Z,** from beginning to end.

a[1] (ā; *unstressed* ə), *adj. or indef. article.* a doublet of **an** used before words beginning with consonant sounds to mean: **1.** some (indefinite singular referring to one individual of a class): *a man, a house, a star.* **2.** another: *he is a Cicero in eloquence.* **3.** one: *two of a kind, a thousand.* **4.** any (a single): *not a one.* **5.** indefinite plural: *a few, a great many.* [ME, phonetic var. of AN]

a[2] (ā; *unstressed* ə), *adj. or indef. article.* each; every: *three times a day.* [orig. *a*, prep., OE *an, on,* confused with the indefinite article. See A-1]

a[3] (ə), *prep. Colloq. or Dial.* of: *cloth a gold.* [OE *of* of]

a' (ä, ô), *adj. Scot.* all: *for a' that.* Also, **a.**

a-[1], a reduced form of Old English prep. *on,* meaning "on," "in," "into," "to," "towards," preserved before a noun in a prepositional phrase, forming a predicate adjective or an adverbial element, as in *afoot, abed, ashore, apart, aside,* and in archaic and dialectal use before a present participle in *-ing,* as in *to set the bells aringing.* [ME and late OE *a-,* var. of OE *an, on,* on. See ON]

a-[2], a reduced form of Old English *of,* as in *akin, afresh, anew.* [ME *a-,* OE *of* (prep.) off, of]

a-[3], an old point-action prefix, not referring to an act as a whole, but only to the beginning or end: *she awoke* (became awake), *they abided by these conclusions* (remained faithful to the end). [OE ā-; in some cases confused with OF *a-* (g. L *ad-* AD-) and erroneously refashioned after supposed L analogies, as in *a(l)lay*]

a-[4], var. of **ab-** before *m, p,* and *v,* as in *amove, aperient, avert.* [ME *a-,* t. F, g. L *ab-;* or t. L, reduced form of *ab-.* See AB-]

a-[5], var. of **ad-,** used: (1) before *sc, sp, st,* as in *ascend.* (2) in words of French derivation (often with the sense of increase, addition), as in *amass.* [ME *a-,* t. F, g. L *ad-,* or assimilated forms of *ad-,* such as *ab-, ac-, af-,* etc.; or t. L, reduced form of *ad-* AD-]

a-[6], var. of **an-**[1] before consonants, as in *achromatic.* [t. Gk., called alpha privative, before vowels *an-;* akin to L *in-* not, L *un-*[1]]

A, **1.** *Chem.* argon. **2.** *Physics.* angstrom unit.

a., **1.** about. **2.** acre; acres. **3.** adjective. **4.** *Baseball.* assists.

A-1, A one.

AAA, *U.S.* **1.** Agricultural Adjustment Administration. **2.** Anti-aircraft Artillery.

A.A.A.L., American Academy of Arts and Letters.

A.A.A.S., American Association for the Advancement of Science.

Aa·chen (ä′kən; *Ger.* ä′кнən), *n.* a city in W West Germany: taken by U.S. forces, Oct., 1944. 151,148 (1955). French, **Aix-la-Chapelle.**

AAF, *U.S.* Army Air Forces.

Aal·borg (ôl′bôr), *n.* a seaport in N Denmark. 79,806 (1950).

Aalst (älst), *n.* Flemish name of Alost.

aard·vark (ärd′värk′), *n.* a large, nocturnal, burrowing mammal of Africa, subsisting largely on termites, and having a long, extensile tongue, claws, and conspicuously long ears. There is only one genus, *Orycteropus,* constituting a separate order, *Tubulidentata.* [t. S Afr. D, f. m. *aarde* earth + *vark* pig]

Aardvark. *Orycteropus afer*
(Overall length 5 to 6 ft.,
tail 2 to 2½ ft.)

aard·wolf (ärd′wŏŏlf′), *n.* a striped, hyenalike African mammal, *Proteles cristatus,* that feeds largely on insects. [t. S Afr. D, f. m. *aarde* earth + *wolf* wolf]

Aar·hus (ôr′hōōs′), *n.* a seaport in Denmark, in E Jutland. 118,888 (est. 1954).

Aar·on (âr′ən), *n.* the first high priest of the Hebrews and the brother of Moses. Exodus 4:14.

Aa·ron·ic (â rŏn′ĭk), *adj.* **1.** pertaining to Aaron. **2.** pertaining or belonging to the Jewish priestly order. **3.** priestly; ecclesiastical. **4.** of the second or lesser order of priesthood among the Mormons. Also, **Aa·ron′i·cal** (esp. def. 3).

A.A.U.P., American Association of University Professors.

Ab (ăb, äb), *n.* (in the Jewish calendar) the eleventh month of the year.

ab-, a prefix meaning "off," "away," "from," as in *abduct, abjure.* Also, **abs-, a-**[4]. [t. L, repr. *ab,* prep., from, away; akin to Gk. *apó,* Skt. *ápa* from]

Ab, *Chem.* alabamine.

ab., **1.** about. **2.** *Baseball.* (times) at bat.

A.B., **1.** (L *Artium Baccalaureus*) Bachelor of Arts. **2.** able-bodied (seaman).

a·ba (ä′bə), *n.* a sleeveless outer garment, worn by Arabs. [t. Ar.: m. *'abā'a*]

a·ba·cá (ä′bä kä′), *n.* **1.** a Philippine plant, *Musa textilis.* **2.** the fiber of this plant, used in making rope.

a·back (ə băk′), *adv.* **1. taken aback. a.** suddenly disconcerted. **b.** (of a ship) caught by the wind so as to press the sails back against the mast. **c.** (of sails) caught by a wind on the forward surface. **2.** with the wind blowing against the forward side of a sail or sails, instead of the after side. **3.** back against the mast, as when sails are so placed. **4.** toward the back. [ME *abak,* OE *on,* prep., + *bæc* on or to the back]

ab·a·cus (ăb′ə kəs), *n., pl.* **-cuses, -ci** (-sī′). **1.** a contrivance for calculating, consisting of beads or balls strung on wires or rods set in a frame. **2.** *Archit.* a slab forming the top of the capital of a column. See diag. under **column.** [t. L, t. Gk.: m. *ábax*]

Chinese abacus:
(Each vertical column = one integer: each bead in group A = 5 when lowered; each bead in group B = 1 when raised; value of this setting is 203,691,500)

A·ba·dan (ä′bä dän′), *n.* a city in S W Iran, on the Shatt-al-Arab; oil refineries. 100,000 (est. 1949).

A·bad·don (ə băd′ən), *n.* **1.** the place of destruction; the depth of hell. **2.** Apollyon. Rev. 9:11. [Heb.: destruction]

a·baft (ə băft′, ə bäft′), *Naut.* —*prep.* **1.** in the rear of; behind. —*adv.* **2.** at or toward the stern; aft. [ME, f. A-1 + *baft,* OE *bæftan, be æftan.* See BY, AFT]

ab·a·lo·ne (ăb′ə lō′nĭ), *n.* a large snail of the genus *Haliotis* having a bowllike shell bearing a row of respiratory holes. The flesh is used for food and the shell for ornament and mother-of-pearl objects. [t. Sp.]

a·ban·don[1] (ə băn′dən), *v.t.* **1.** to leave completely and finally; forsake utterly: *to abandon one's home.* **2.** to give up all concern in: *to abandon the cares of empire.* **3.** to give up the control of: *to abandon a city to a conqueror.* **4.** to yield (oneself) unrestrainedly: *to abandon oneself to grief.* **5.** *Law.* to cast away or leave (one's property) with no intention to reclaim it, thereby making the property available for appropriation by any person. **6.** to relinqu sh (insured property) to the underwriter in case of partial loss, thus enabling the insured to claim a total loss. **7.** *Obs.* to banish. [ME *abandone(n),* t. OF: m. *abandoner,* der. phrase *a bandon* under one's jurisdiction] —**a·ban′don·er,** *n.* —**a·ban′don·ment,** *n.* —**Syn. 2.** ABANDON, RELINQUISH, RENOUNCE mean to give up all concern in something. ABANDON means to give up (or

---

ăct, āble, dâre, ärt; ĕbb, ēqual; Ĭf, īce; hŏt, ōver, ôrder, oil, bŏŏk, ōoze, out; ŭp, ūse, ûrge; ə = a in alone; ch, chief; g, give; ng, ring; sh, shoe; th, thin; ᵺ, that; zh, vision. See the full key on inside cover.
b., blend of, blended; c., cognate with; d., dialect, dialectal; der., derived from; f., formed from; g., going back to; m., modification of; r., replacing; s., stem of; t., taken from; ?, perhaps. See the full key on inside cover.

discontinue any further) interest in something, because of discouragement, weariness, distaste, or the like: *to abandon one's efforts.* RELINQUISH implies being (or feeling) compelled to give up something one would prefer to keep: *to relinquish a long-cherished desire.* RENOUNCE implies making (and perhaps formally stating) a voluntary decision to give something up: *to renounce worldly pleasures.* See also desert². **3.** give up, yield, surrender, resign, waive, abdicate. —Ant. 3. keep.

a·ban·don² (ə băn′dən; *Fr.* á băN dôN′), *n.* a giving up to natural impulses; freedom from constraint or conventionality: *to do something with abandon.* [t. F]

a·ban·doned (ə băn′dənd), *adj.* **1.** forsaken. **2.** unrestrained. **3.** shamelessly and recklessly wicked. —Syn. **3.** See immoral.

a bas (à bä′), *French.* down with (the person or thing named)!

a·base (ə bās′), *v.t.* abased, abasing. **1.** to reduce or lower, as in rank, office, estimation; humble; degrade. **2.** *Archaic.* to lower; bring down. [b. BASE² and ME *abesse(n)* (t. OF: m. *abaissier*, f. *a-* A-⁵+ *baissier* lower, ult. der. LL *bassus* low] —a·base′ment, *n.* —a·bas′er, *n.*

a·bash (ə băsh′), *v.t.* to destroy the self-possession of; make ashamed or embarrassed; *stand or feel abashed.* [ME *abashe(n),* t. AF: m. *abaïss-,* var. of OF *esbaïss-,* s. *esbaïr* astonish] —a·bash′ment, *n.*

a·bate (ə bāt′), *v.,* abated, abating. —*v.t.* **1.** to reduce in amount, intensity, etc.; lessen; diminish: *to abate a tax, one's enthusiasm, etc.* **2.** *Law.* to put an end to or suppress (a nuisance); suspend or extinguish (an action); annul (a writ). **3.** to deduct or subtract. **4.** to omit. —*v.i.* **5.** to decrease or become less in strength or violence: *the storm has abated.* **6.** *Obs. except Law.* to fail; become void. [ME *abate(n),* t. OF: m. *abatre,* f. *a-* A-⁵ + *batre* beat] —a·bat′a·ble, *adj.* —a·bat′er; *Law* a·ba′tor, *n.* —Ant. **5.** increase, intensify.

a·bate·ment (ə bāt′mənt), *n.* **1.** alleviation; mitigation. **2.** suppression or termination: *abatement of a nuisance.* **3.** *Law.* **a.** a wrongful entry on land made by a stranger, after the owner's death and before the owner's heir or devisee has obtained possession. **b.** a decrease in the legacies of a will when the assets of an estate are insufficient to pay all general legacies in full.

ab·a·tis (ăb′ə tĭs; *Mil.* ăb′ə tē′), *n.* an obstacle of trees with bent or sharpened branches directed toward the enemy, and now often interlaced with barbed wire. [t. F; akin to ABATE]

ab·at·toir (ăb′ə twär′), *n.* a slaughterhouse. [t. F]

ab·ax·i·al (ăb ăk′sĭ əl), *adj.* away from the axis: *the abaxial surface of a leaf.* [f. AB- + L *axi*(s) axle + -AL¹]

ab·ba·cy (ăb′ə sĭ), *n., pl.* **-cies. 1.** an abbot's office, rights, privileges, or jurisdiction. **2.** the period of office of an abbot. [var. of ME *abbatie,* t. LL: m. *abbātia*]

Ab·bas·side (ə băs′ĭd, ăb′ə sĭd′), *n.* a caliph of the dynasty which ruled at Bagdad, A.D. 750 to 1258, claiming descent from Abbas, uncle of Mohammed.

ab·ba·tial (ə bā′shəl), *adj.* of or pertaining to an abbot, abbess, or abbey. [t. LL: s. *abbātiālis*]

ab·bé (ăb′ā; *Fr.* á bā′), *n.* (esp. in France) **1.** an abbot. **2.** any ecclesiastic, esp. one who has no other title. [F]

ab·bess (ăb′ĭs), *n.* the female superior of a convent, regularly in the same religious orders in which monks are governed by an abbot. [ME *abbesse,* t. OF, g. LL *abbātissa*]

ab·bey (ăb′ĭ), *n., pl.* **-beys. 1.** the religious body or establishment under an abbot or abbess; a monastery or convent. **2.** the monastic buildings. **3.** the church of an abbey. **4. the Abbey,** *Brit.* Westminster Abbey. **5.** *Brit.* a country residence that was formerly an abbatial house: *Newstead Abbey.* [ME *abbeye,* t. OF: m. *abaie,* g. LL *abbātia*]

Abbey Theatre, a theater in Dublin associated with the Irish National Theatre Society (founded 1901) and the dramas of Synge, Yeats, and Lady Gregory.

ab·bot (ăb′ət), *n.* the head or superior of a monastery. [ME, var. of ME and OE *abbod,* t. LL: m.s. *abbās,* t. LGk., t. Aram.: m. *abbā* father] —ab′bot·ship, *n.*

Ab·bot (ăb′ət), *n.* **Charles Greeley,** born 1872, U.S. astrophysicist.

Ab·bots·ford (ăb′əts fərd), *n.* Sir Walter Scott's residence from 1812 to 1832, near Melrose, in SE Scotland.

abbr., abbreviation. Also, **abbrev.**

ab·bre·vi·ate (ə brē′vĭ āt′), *v.t.,* -ated, -ating. to make briefer; make shorter by contraction or omission: *to abbreviate "foot" to "ft."* [t. L: s. *abbreviātus,* pp.] —ab·bre′vi·a′tor, *n.* —Syn. See shorten.

ab·bre·vi·a·tion (ə brē′vĭ ā′shən), *n.* **1.** a shortened or contracted form of a word or phrase, used as a symbol for the whole. **2.** reduction in length; abridgment. **3.** *Music.* any of several signs or symbols used to abbreviate musical notation, as those indicating the repetition of a phrase or a note. [t. L: s. *abbreviātio*]

ABC (ā′bē′sē′), *n.* **1.** the main or the basic facts, principles, etc. (of any subject). **2.** ABC's.

ABC's (ā′bē′sēz′), *n.pl.* the alphabet.

Abd-el Krim (äb′děl krēm′), *n.* born, 1881, Riff leader of a native revolt in Morocco, 1921–26.

Ab·di·as (ăb dī′əs), *n.* (in the Douay Bible) Obadiah.

ab·di·cate (ăb′də kāt′), *v.,* -cated, -cating. —*v.i.* **1.** to renounce a throne or some claim; relinquish a right, power, or trust. —*v.t.* **2.** to give up or renounce (office, duties, authority, etc.), esp. in a voluntary, public, or formal manner. [t. L: m.s. *abdicātus,* pp.] —ab·di·ca-

ble (ăb′də kə bəl), *adj.* —ab′di·ca′tive, *adj.*— ab′·di·ca′tor, *n.*

ab·di·ca·tion (ăb′də kā′shən), *n.* act of abdicating; renunciation, esp. of sovereign power.

ab·do·men (ăb′də mən, ăb dō′-), *n.* **1.** that part of the body of a mammal between the thorax and the pelvis; the visceral cavity containing most of the digestive organs; the belly. **2.** (in vertebrates below mammals) a region of the body corresponding to but not coincident with the human abdomen. **3.** *Entomol.* the posterior section of the body of an arthropod, behind the thorax or the cephalothorax. See diag. under **insect.** [t. L]

ab·dom·i·nal (ăb dŏm′ə nəl), *adj.* of, in, or on the abdomen: *abdominal muscles.* —ab·dom′i·nal·ly, *adv.*

ab·dom·i·nous (ăb dŏm′ə nəs), *adj.* potbellied.

ab·duce (ăb dūs′, -dōōs′), *v.t.,* -duced, -ducing. *Physiol.* to draw away or aside, as by the action of a muscle. [t. L: m.s. *abdūcere*]

ab·du·cent (ăb dū′sənt, -dōō′-), *adj. Physiol.* drawing away (applied to muscles, etc.).

ab·duct (ăb dŭkt′), *v.t.* **1.** to carry off surreptitiously or by force, esp. to kidnap. **2.** *Physiol.* to draw away from the original position (opposed to *adduct*). [t. L: s. *abductus,* pp.] —ab·duc′tion, *n.* —ab·duc′tor, *n.*

Ab·dul-Ha·mid II (ăb′dōōl hä mēd′), 1842–1918, sultan of Turkey, 1876–1909.

a·beam (ə bēm′), *adv. Naut.* at right angles to the keel of a ship; directly opposite the middle part of a ship.

a·be·ce·dar·i·an (ā′bĭ sĭ dâr′ĭ ən), *n.* **1.** a pupil who is learning the letters of the alphabet. **2.** a beginner. —*adj.* **3.** alphabetical. **4.** primary; rudimentary. [f. s. ML *abecedārius* ABCD book + -AN]

a·be·ce·da·ry (ā′bĭ sē′də rĭ), *n., pl.* **-ries,** *adj.* abecedarian.

a·bed (ə bĕd′), *adv.* **1.** in bed. **2.** confined to bed.

A·bed·ne·go (ə bĕd′nĭ gō′), *n.* See **Shadrach.**

A·bel (ā′bəl), *n. Bible.* the second son of Adam and Eve, slain by his brother, Cain. Gen. 4.

Ab·e·lard (ăb′ə lärd′; *Fr.* á bě lär′), *n.* **Pierre** (pyĕr′), *(Peter Abelard)* 1079–1142, French scholastic philosopher, teacher, and theologian. His love affair with Héloïse is one of the famous romances of history.

a·bele (ə bēl′, ā′bəl), *n.* the white poplar tree, *Populus alba.* [t. D: m. *abeel,* t. OF: m. *abel,* g. LL *albellus,* dim. of L *albus* white]

a·bel·mosk (ā′bəl mŏsk′), *n.* a malvaceous plant, *Hibiscus Abelmoschus,* of warm countries, cultivated for its musky seed, which is used in perfumery, etc. [t. NL: m. s. *Abelmoschus,* t. Ar.: m. *habb el-mosk* grain of musk]

Ab·er·deen (ăb′ər dēn′), *n.* **1.** Also, **Ab·er·deen·shire** (ăb′ər dēn′shĭr, -shər). a county in NE Scotland. 330,200 pop. (est. 1956); 1974 sq. mi. **2.** its county seat: a seaport. 186,800 (est. 1954). **3.** a seaport in W Washington. 19,653 (1950). **4.** a city in NE South Dakota. 21,051 (1950). —Ab·er·do·ni·an (ăb′ər dō′nĭ ən), *adj., n.*

Aberdeen An·gus (ăng′gəs), one of a breed of hornless beef cattle with smooth black hair, originally bred in Scotland.

A·ber·glau·be (ä′bər glou′bə), *n. German.* belief beyond what is justified by experience and knowledge.

ab·er·rant (ăb ĕr′ənt), *adj.* **1.** straying from the right or usual course. **2.** deviating from the ordinary or normal type. [t. L: s. *aberrans,* ppr.] —ab·er′rance, ab·er′ran·cy, *n.*

ab·er·ra·tion (ăb′ə rā′shən), *n.* **1.** act of wandering from the usual way or normal course. **2.** deviation from truth or moral rectitude. **3.** lapse from a sound mental state. **4.** *Astron.* apparent displacement of a heavenly body, due to the joint effect of the motion of the rays of light proceeding from it and the motion of the earth. **5.** *Optics.* any disturbance of the rays of a pencil of light such that they can no longer be brought to a sharp focus or form a clear image. [t. L: s. *aberrātio*]

a·bet (ə bĕt′), *v.t.,* abetted, abetting. to encourage or countenance by aid or approval (used chiefly in a bad sense): *to abet evildoers, to abet a crime or offense.* [ME *abbette(n),* t. OF: m. *abeter,* f. *a-* A-⁵ + *beter* t. Scand.; cf. Icel. *beita* cause to bite. See BAIT] —a·bet′ment, *n.*

a·bet·tor (ə bĕt′ər), *n.* one who abets. Also, **a·bet′ter.**

ab ex·tra (ăb ĕks′trə), *Latin.* from the outside.

a·bey·ance (ə bā′əns), *n.* **1.** temporary inactivity or suspension. **2.** a state of waiting for the ascertainment of the person entitled to ownership: *an estate in abeyance.* [t. AF: m. *abeiance* expectation, der. OF *abeer* gape after, f. *a-* A-⁵ + *beer, baer* gape, g. LL *badāre*]

a·bey·ant (ə bā′ənt), *adj.* in abeyance.

ab·hor (ăb hôr′), *v.t.,* -horred, -horring. to regard with repugnance; loathe or abominate. [late ME, t. L: m. s. *abhorrēre*] —ab·hor′rer, *n.* —Syn. See hate.

ab·hor·rence (ăb hôr′əns, -hŏr′-), *n.* **1.** a feeling of extreme aversion. **2.** something detested.

ab·hor·rent (ăb hôr′ənt, -hŏr′-), *adj.* **1.** feeling horror (fol. by *of*): *abhorrent of excess.* **2.** utterly opposed (fol. by *to*): *abhorrent to reason.* **3.** exciting horror; detestable. **4.** remote in character (fol. by *from*): *abhorrent from the principles of law.* —ab·hor′rent·ly, *adv.*

a·bid·ance (ə bī′dəns), *n.* **1.** act of abiding. **2.** conformity (fol. by *by*): *abidance by rules.*

a·bide (ə bīd′), *v.,* abode or abided, abiding. —*v.i.* **1.** to remain; continue; stay: *abide with me.* **2.** to dwell; reside. **3.** to continue in a certain condition; remain steadfast or faithful. **4. abide by, a.** to stand by: *to abide by a friend.* **b.** to await or accept the consequences of: *to abide by the event.* —*v.t.* **5.** to wait for. **6.** to stand one's ground against; await or sustain defiantly. **7.** *Colloq.* to put up with; tolerate: *I can't abide such people.* **8.** to pay the price or penalty of; suffer for. [ME *abide(n)*, OE *ābīdan*. See A-³. In def. 8 confused with ABY] —**a·bid′er,** *n.*

a·bid·ing (ə·bī′dǐng), *adj.* continuing; steadfast: *an abiding faith.* —**a·bid′ing·ly,** *adv.* —**a·bid′ing·ness,** *n.*

ab·i·et·ic acid (ǎb′ī·ět′ĭk), a yellow crystalline acid, C₁₉H₂₉COOH, derived from the resin of a species of pine, used in driers, varnishes, and soaps. [f. s. L *abiēs* fir + -IC + ACID]

ab·i·gail (ǎb′ə·gāl′), *n.* a lady's maid. [from *Abigail,* the "waiting gentlewoman," in Beaumont and Fletcher's *The Scornful Lady.* See also I Sam. 25:23–42]

Ab·i·lene (ǎb′ə·lēn′), *n.* a city in central Texas. 90,368 (1960).

a·bil·i·ty (ə·bǐl′ə·tĭ), *n., pl.* **-ties. 1.** power or capacity to do or act in any relation. **2.** competence in any occupation or field of action, from the possession of capacity, skill, means, or other qualification. **3.** (*pl.*) talents; mental gifts or endowments. [ME (*h*)*abilite,* t. F, t. L: m.s. *habilitas;* r. ME *ablete,* t. OF]
—**Syn. 1.** capability; proficiency, expertness, dexterity. **2.** ABILITY, FACULTY, TALENT denote mental qualifications or powers. ABILITY is a general word for mental power, native or acquired, enabling one to do things well: *a person of great ability, ability in mathematics.* FACULTY denotes a natural ability for a particular kind of action: *a faculty of saying what he means.* TALENT is often used to mean a native ability or aptitude in a special field: *a talent for music or art.*

ab in·i·ti·o (ǎb′ ĭ·nǐsh′ĭ·ō), *Latin.* from the beginning.

ab in·tra (ǎb ǐn′trə), *Latin.* from inside; from within.

ab·i·o·gen·e·sis (ǎb′ī·ō·jěn′ə·sǐs), *n. Biol.* the (hypothetical) production of living things from inanimate matter; spontaneous generation. [f. A-⁶ + BIO- + GENESIS] —**ab·i·o·ge·nist** (ǎb′ī·ǒj′ə·nǐst), *n.*

ab·i·o·ge·net·ic (ǎb′ī·ō·jə·nět′ĭk), *adj. Biol.* of or pertaining to abiogenesis. —**ab′i·o·ge·net′i·cal·ly,** *adv.*

ab·ir·ri·tant (ǎb·ǐr′ə·tənt), *Pathol.* —*n.* **1.** a soothing agent. —*adj.* **2.** allaying irritability.

ab·ir·ri·tate (ǎb·ǐr′ə·tāt′), *v.t.,* **-tated, -tating.** *Med.* to make less irritable. —**ab·ir′ri·ta′tion,** *n.*

ab·ject (ǎb′jěkt, ǎb·jěkt′), *adj.* **1.** utterly humiliating or disheartening: *abject poverty.* **2.** contemptible; despicable: *an abject liar.* **3.** *Obs.* cast aside. [ME, t. L: s. *abjectus,* pp., thrown away] —**ab·jec′tion,** *n.* —**ab′ject·ly** (ǎb·jěkt′lǐ, ǎb′jěkt lǐ), *adv.* —**ab′ject′ness,** *n.*

ab·ju·ra·tion (ǎb′jŏŏ·rā′shən), *n.* act of abjuring; renunciation upon oath.

ab·jure (ǎb·jŏŏr′), *v.t.,* **-jured, -juring. 1.** to renounce or repudiate; retract, esp. with solemnity: *to abjure one's errors.* **2.** to renounce upon oath; forswear: *to abjure allegiance.* [t. L: m.s. *abjūrāre*] —**ab′jur′a·to·ry,** *adj.* —**ab·jur′er,** *n.*

Ab·kha·zi·a (ǎb·hä′sǐ·ä′), *n.* an autonomous republic in the SW Soviet Union, on the E coast of the Black Sea. 200,500 pop. (1926); 3360 sq. mi. *Cap.:* Sukhum. Also, **Ab·kha′si·a.**

abl., ablative.

ab·lac·tate (ǎb·lǎk′tāt), *v.t.,* **-tated, -tating.** to wean. [t. L: m. s. *ablactātus,* pp.] —**ab′lac·ta′tion,** *n.*

ab·la·tion (ǎb·lā′shən), *n.* removal, esp. of organs, abnormal growths, or harmful substances, from the body by mechanical means, as by surgery. [t. L: s. *ablātio* a carrying away]

ab·la·tive (ǎb′lə·tǐv), *Gram.* —*adj.* **1.** (in some inflected languages) denoting a case which has among its functions the indication of place from which, place in which, manner, means, instrument, agent, etc. —*n.* **2.** the ablative case. **3.** a word in that case, as *Troiā* in Latin *Ænēas Troiā vēnit,* "Aeneas came from Troy." [t. L: m. s. *ablātivus* of removal; r. late ME *ablatif,* t. F]

ablative absolute, (in Latin grammar) a construction not dependent upon any other part of the sentence, consisting of a noun and a participle. noun and adjective, or two nouns, in which both members are in the ablative case, as Latin *viā factā,* "the road having been made."

ab·laut (ǎb′lout, ǎb′-; *Ger.* äp′lout), *n. Gram.* **1.** regular change in the internal structure of roots, particularly in the vowel, showing alteration in function and meaning. **2.** such change in Indo-European languages, as in English *sing, sang, sung, song;* gradation. [t. G: f. *ab* off + *laut* sound]

a·blaze (ə·blāz′), *adv.* **1.** on fire. —*adj.* **2.** gleaming. **3.** excited; eagerly desirous. **4.** very angry.

a·ble (ā′bəl), *adj.,* **abler, ablest. 1.** having sufficient power, strength, or qualifications; qualified: *a man able to perform military service.* **2.** having unusual intellectual qualifications: *an able minister.* **3.** showing talent or knowledge: *an able speech.* [ME, t. OF, g. L *habilis* easy to handle, fit]
—**Syn. 1.** ABLE, CAPABLE, COMPETENT all mean possessing adequate power for doing something. ABLE implies power equal to effort required: *able to finish in time.* CAPABLE implies power to meet or fulfill ordinary, usual requirements: *a capable workman.* COMPETENT suggests power to meet demands in a completely satisfactory manner: *a competent nurse.* **2.** talented, accomplished, gifted; skilled, clever.

-able, a suffix used to form adjectives, esp. from verbs,

to denote ability, liability, tendency, worthiness, or likelihood, as in *teachable, perishable, obtainable,* but also attached to other parts of speech (esp. nouns) as in *objectionable, peaceable,* and even verb phrases, as in *come-at-able.* Many of these adjectives, such as *durable, tolerable,* have been borrowed directly from Latin or French, in which language they were already compounded. However, **-able** is attached freely (now usually with passive force) to stems of any origin. Also, **-ble, -ible.** [ME, t. OF, g. s. L *-ābilis*]

a·ble-bod·ied (ā′bəl·bŏd′ĭd), *adj.* physically competent.

able-bodied seaman, an experienced seaman who has passed certain tests in the practice of seamanship.

ab·le·gate (ǎb′lǐ·gāt′), *n.* a papal envoy to a newly appointed dignitary.

a·blins (ā′blǐnz), *adv. Scot.* perhaps. Also, **aiblins.**

a·bloom (ə·blōōm′), *adv., adj.* in blossom.

ab·lu·ent (ǎb′lōō·ənt), *adj.* **1.** cleansing. —*n.* **2.** a cleansing agent; a detergent. [t. L: m.s. *abluens,* ppr.]

ab·lu·tion (ǎb·lōō′shən), *n.* **1.** a cleansing with water or other liquid, as in ceremonial purification. **2.** the liquid used. [ME, t. L: s. *ablūtio*] —**ab·lu′tion·ar′y,** *adj.*

a·bly (ā′blǐ), *adv.* in an able manner; competently.

ab·ne·gate (ǎb′nə·gāt′), *v.t.,* **-gated, -gating.** to refuse or deny to oneself; reject; renounce. [t. L: m.s. *abnegātus,* pp.] —**ab′ne·ga′tion,** *n.* —**ab′ne·ga′tor,** *n.*

ab·nor·mal (ǎb·nôr′məl), *adj.* not conforming to rule; deviating from the type or standard. [f. s. L *abnormis* irregular + -AL¹; r. *anormal,* t. F, t. ML: s. *anormalus,* for L *anōmalus,* t. Gk.: m. *anōmalos.* See ANOMALOUS] —**ab·nor′mal·ly,** *adv.* —**Syn.** anomalous, aberrant, peculiar; exceptional, unusual; odd. See **irregular.**

ab·nor·mal·i·ty (ǎb′nôr·mǎl′ə·tǐ), *n., pl.* **-ties. 1.** an abnormal thing, happening, or feature. **2.** deviation from the standard, rule, or type; irregularity.

abnormal psychology, the study of mental phenomena, behavior patterns, etc., of individuals who deviate widely from the average.

ab·nor·mi·ty (ǎb·nôr′mə·tǐ), *n., pl.* **-ties. 1.** abnormality; irregularity. **2.** malformation; monstrosity.

Å·bo (ō′bōō), *n.* Swedish name of **Turku.**

a·board (ə·bôrd′), *adv.* **1.** on board; on or in a ship, railroad car, etc. (in England applied esp. to ships, but in the U.S. also applied to railroad cars, buses, etc.). **2.** alongside. —*prep.* **3.** on board of.

a·bode (ə·bōd′), *n.* **1.** a dwelling place; a habitation. **2.** continuance in a place; sojourn; stay. —*v.* **3.** pt. and pp. of **abide.** [ME *abood,* OE *ābād,* p.t. of *ābīdan* ABIDE]

a·bol·ish (ə·bŏl′ĭsh), *v.t.* to do away with; put an end to; annul or make void; destroy: *to abolish slavery.* [t. F: m. *aboliss-.* s. *abolir* make perish, g. s. L *abolescere* perish] —**a·bol′ish·a·ble,** *adj.* —**a·bol′ish·er,** *n.* —**a·bol′ish·ment,** *n.*
—**Syn.** suppress; annihilate; exterminate. ABOLISH, ERADICATE, STAMP OUT mean to do away completely with something. To ABOLISH is to cause to cease, often by a summary order: *to abolish a requirement.* STAMP OUT, stronger though less formal, implies forcibly making an end to something considered undesirable or harmful: *to stamp out the opium traffic.* ERADICATE (literally, to tear out by the roots), a formal word, suggests extirpation, leaving no vestige or trace: *to eradicate the dandelions in the lawn.*

ab·o·li·tion (ǎb′ə·lǐsh′ən), *n.* **1.** utter destruction; annulment; abrogation: *the abolition of laws, customs, debts, etc.* **2.** the legal extinction of Negro slavery. [t. L: s. *abolitio*] —**ab′o·li′tion·ar′y,** *adj.* —**ab′o·li′tion·ist,** *n.*

ab·o·li·tion·ism (ǎb′ə·lǐsh′ən·ǐz′əm), *n.* the principle or policy of abolition, esp. of Negro slavery.

ab·o·ma·sum (ǎb′ə·mā′səm), *n.* the fourth or true stomach of cud-chewing animals, lying next to the omasum. Also, **ab·o·ma·sus** (ǎb′ə·mā′səs). [t. NL, f. L *ab*-AB- + *omāsum* bullock's tripe]

A-bomb (ā′bŏm′), *n.* atomic bomb.

a·bom·i·na·ble (ə·bŏm′ə·nə·bəl), *adj.* detestable; loathsome. [ME, t. F, t. L: m.s. *abōminābilis*] —**a·bom′i·na·ble·ness,** *n.* —**a·bom′i·na·bly,** *adv.*

a·bom·i·nate (ə·bŏm′ə·nāt′), *v.t.,* **-nated, -nating. 1.** to regard with intense aversion; abhor. **2.** to dislike strongly. [t. L: m.s. *abōminātus,* pp., having deprecated as an ill omen] —**a·bom′i·na′tor,** *n.* —**Syn. 1.** See **hate.**

a·bom·i·na·tion (ə·bŏm′ə·nā′shən), *n.* **1.** an object greatly disliked or abhorred. **2.** intense aversion; detestation. **3.** a detestable action; a shameful vice.

ab·o·rig·i·nal (ǎb′ə·rǐj′ə·nəl), *adj.* **1.** pertaining to aborigines; primitive: *aboriginal customs.* **2.** original; native; indigenous. —*n.* **3.** an aborigine. —**ab′o·rig′i·nal′i·ty,** *n.* —**ab′o·rig′i·nal·ly,** *adv.*

ab o·rig·i·ne (ǎb ō·rǐj′ə·nē′), *Latin.* from the very first; from the source or origin.

ab·o·rig·i·nes (ǎb′ə·rǐj′ə·nēz′), *n., pl.* of **aborigine. 1.** the primitive inhabitants of a country; the people living in a country at the earliest period. **2.** the original fauna or flora of a region. [t. L, der. *ab orīgine* from the beginning]

a·bort (ə·bôrt′), *v.i.* **1.** to miscarry. **2.** to develop incompletely, remaining in a rudimentary state or degenerating. **3.** *Mil. Slang.* to fail to complete a mission. [t. L: s. *abortus,* pp., having miscarried]

a·bor·ti·cide¹ (ə·bôr′tə·sīd′), *n.* destruction of a fetus in the uterus; feticide. [f. s. L *abortus* miscarriage + -(I)CIDE²]

ǎct, āble, dâre, ärt; ěbb, ēqual; ǐf, īce; hŏt, ōver, ôrder, oil, bŏŏk, ōōze, out; ŭp, ūse, ûrge; ə = a in alone; ch, chief; g, give; ng, ring; sh, shoe; th, thin; ᵺ, that; zh, vision. See the full key on inside cover.

a·bor·ti·cide[2] (ə·bôr′tə·sīd′), *n.* an abortifacient. [f. s. L *abortus* miscarriage + -(I)CIDE[1]]

a·bor·ti·fa·cient (ə·bôr′tə·fā′shənt), *adj.* **1.** causing abortion. —*n.* **2.** something used to produce abortion. [f. s. L *abortus* miscarriage + -(I)FACIENT]

a·bor·tion (ə·bôr′shən), *n.* **1.** the expulsion of a human fetus before it is viable (within the first 28 weeks of pregnancy). **2.** an immature and not viable birth product; miscarriage. **3.** *Biol.* the arrested development of an embryo or an organ at its (more or less) early stage. **4.** anything which fails in its progress before it is matured or perfected, as a design or project. [t. L: s. *abortio* miscarriage] —**a·bor′tion·al,** *adj.*

a·bor·tion·ist (ə·bôr′shən·ïst), *n.* one who produces or aims to produce a criminal abortion, esp. one who makes a practice of so doing.

a·bor·tive (ə·bôr′tĭv), *adj.* **1.** failing to succeed; miscarrying: *an abortive scheme.* **2.** born prematurely. **3.** imperfectly developed; rudimentary. **4.** *Med.* a. producing or intended to produce abortion; abortifacient. b. acting to halt progress of a disease. **5.** *Pathol.* (of the course of a disease) short and mild without the commonly pronounced clinical symptoms. —**a·bor′tive·ly,** *adv.* —**a·bor′tive·ness,** *n.*

A·bou·kir (ä′bōō·kēr′), *n.* Abukir.

a·bou·li·a (ə·bōō′lĭ·ə), *n.* abulia. —**a·bou′lic,** *adj.*

a·bound (ə·bound′), *v.i.* **1.** to be in great plenty; be very prevalent: *the discontent which abounds in the world.* **2.** to be rich (fol. by *in*): *some languages abound in figurative expressions.* **3.** to be filled; teem (fol. by *with*): *the ship abounds with rats.* [ME *abounde(n),* t. OF: m. *abunder,* g. L *abundāre*] —**a·bound′ing,** *adj.*

a·bout (ə·bout′), *prep.* **1.** of; concerning; in regard to: *to talk about secrets.* **2.** connected with: *instructions about the work.* **3.** somewhere near or in: *he is about the house.* **4.** near; close to: *about my height.* **5.** on every side of; around: *the railing about the tower.* **6.** on or near (one's person): *they had lost all they had about them.* **7.** on the point of (fol. by an infinitive): *about to leave.* **8.** here and there in or on: *wander about the place.* **9.** *Archaic.* concerned with; engaged in doing. —*adv.* **10.** near in time, number, degree, etc.; approximately: *about a hundred miles.* **11.** *Colloq.* nearly; almost: *about ready.* **12.** nearby: *he is somewhere about.* **13.** on every side; in every direction: *look about.* **14.** half round; in the reverse direction: *to spin about.* **15.** to and fro; here and there: *move furniture about.* **16.** in rotation or succession; alternately: *turn about is fair play.* **17.** on the move: *be up and about.* **18.** *Archaic.* around. [ME; OE *abūtan,* var. of *onbūtan, on būtan* on the outside (of)]

about face, *U.S.* the military command to face to the rear in a prescribed manner while standing. Also, *Brit.,* **about turn.**

a·bout-face (*n.* ə·bout′fās′; *v.* ə·bout′fās′), *n., v.,* **-faced, -facing.** —*n.* **1.** a complete, sudden change in position, principle, attitude, etc. —*v.i.* **2.** to turn in the opposite direction.

a·bout-ship (ə·bout′shĭp′), *v.i. Naut.* to tack a ship.

a·bove (ə·bŭv′), *adv.* **1.** in or to a higher place; overhead: *the blue sky above.* **2.** higher in rank or power: *appeal to the courts above.* **3.** before in order, esp. in a book or writing: *from what has been said above.* **4.** in heaven. —*prep.* **5.** in or to a higher place than: *fly above the earth.* **6.** more in quantity or number than: *the weight is above a ton.* **7.** superior to: *above mean actions.* —*adj.* **8.** said, mentioned, or written above; foregoing: *the above explanation.* —*n.* **9. the above,** that which was said, mentioned, or written above. [ME; OE *abufan,* f. A[1] + *bufan* above]

a·bove-board (ə·bŭv′bôrd′), *adv., adj.* in open sight; without tricks or disguise: *an honest man deals aboveboard, his actions are open and aboveboard.*

ab o·vo (ăb ō′vō), from the beginning. [L: from the egg]

ab·ra·ca·dab·ra (ăb′rə·kə·dăb′rə), *n.* **1.** a mystical word used in incantations, or written in triangular form as a charm on an amulet. **2.** any word charm or empty jingle of words. **3.** gibberish; nonsense. [t. L]

a·bra·dant (ə·brā′dənt), *adj.* **1.** having the property or quality of abrading. —*n.* **2.** an abrasive.

a·brade (ə·brād′), *v.t., v.i.,* **abraded, abrading.** to wear off or down by friction; scrape off. [t. L: m. s. *abrādere* scrape off] —**a·brad′er,** *n.*

A·bra·ham (ā′brə·hăm′, -həm), *n. Bible.* the first of the great patriarchs, father of Isaac, and traditional founder of the Hebrew people. Gen. 11–25. [t. Heb.]

a·bran·chi·ate (ā·brăng′kĭ·ĭt, -āt), *adj. Zool.* without gills. Also, **a·bran·chi·al** (ā·brăng′kĭ·əl). [f. A-[6] + s. Gk. *bránchia* gills + -ATE[1]]

a·bra·sion (ə·brā′zhən), *n.* **1.** the result of rubbing or abrading; an abraded spot or place. **2.** act or process of abrading. [t. L: s. *abrāsio* a scraping off]

a·bra·sive (ə·brā′sĭv, -zĭv), *n.* **1.** any material or substance used for grinding, polishing, lapping, etc., as emery or sand. —*adj.* **2.** tending to produce abrasion.

ab·re·act (ăb′rĭ·ăkt′), *v.t. Psychoanal.* to remove by abreaction.

ab·re·ac·tion (ăb′rĭ·ăk′shən), *n. Psychoanal.* the release of psychic tension through verbalizing or acting out an adequate resolution of a repressed traumatic experience, with the appropriate emotion or affect. [f. AB- + REACTION. Cf. G *abreagieren*]

a·breast (ə·brĕst′), *adv., adj.* **1.** side by side. **2.** along-side in progress or attainment; equally advanced (fol. by *of* or *with*): *to keep abreast of the times in science.*

a·bridge (ə·brĭj′), *v.t.,* **abridged, abridging. 1.** to shorten by condensation or omission, or both; rewrite or reconstruct on a smaller scale. **2.** to lessen; diminish. **3.** to deprive; cut off. [ME *abrege(n),* t. OF: m. *abreger,* g. L *abbreviāre* shorten] —**a·bridg′a·ble,** *adj.* —**a·bridged′,** *adj.* —**a·bridg′er,** *n.* —Syn. **1.** cut down; epitomize; condense. See **shorten. 2.** contract. **3.** curtail. —Ant. **1.** lengthen. **2.** expand.

a·bridg·ment (ə·brĭj′mənt), *n.* **1.** a condensation, as of a book; a reproduction of anything in reduced or condensed form. **2.** act of abridging. **3.** state of being abridged. Also, esp. *Brit.,* **a·bridge′ment.**

a·broach (ə·brōch′), *adv.* **1.** broached. **2. set abroach,** a. to cause (a cask, a barrel, etc.) to flow or to let out liquor. b. to give rise to; spread abroad.

a·broad (ə·brôd′), *adv.* **1.** in a foreign country or countries: *to live abroad.* **2.** out of doors: *the owl ventures abroad at night.* **3.** astir; in circulation: *rumors of disaster are abroad.* **4.** broadly; widely. **5.** wide of the truth. [ME *a brood;* f. A-[1] + FROAD. Cf. E *at large*]

ab·ro·gate (ăb′rə·gāt′), *v.t.,* **-gated, -gating.** to abolish summarily; annul by an authoritative act; repeal: *to abrogate a law.* [t. L: m. s. *abrogātus,* pp.] —**ab·ro·ga·ble** (ăb′rə·gə·bəl), *adj.* —**ab′ro·ga′tion,** *n.* —**ab′ro·ga·tive,** *adj.* —**ab′ro·ga′tor,** *n.*

ab·rupt (ə·brŭpt′), *adj.* **1.** terminating or changing suddenly: *an abrupt turn in a road.* **2.** sudden; unceremonious: *an abrupt entrance.* **3.** lacking in continuity; having sudden transitions from one subject to another: *an abrupt literary style.* **4.** steep; precipitous: *an abrupt descent.* **5.** *Bot.* truncate. [t. L: m. s. *abruptus,* pp., broken off] —**ab·rupt′ly,** *adv.* —**ab·rupt′ness,** *n.* —Syn. **1.** See **sudden.**

ab·rup·tion (ə·brŭp′shən), *n.* a sudden breaking off.

A·bruz·zi (ä·brōōt′sē), *n.* **Duke of the,** (Prince Luigi Amedeo of Savoy-Aosta) 1873–1933, Italian naval officer, mountain climber, and arctic explorer.

abs-, var. of **ab-,** before *c, q, t,* as in *abscond, absterge.*

Ab·sa·lom (ăb′sə·ləm), *n. Bible.* third son of David, who rebelled against his father and was slain. II Sam. 13–19.

ab·scess (ăb′sĕs), *n.* a localized collection of pus in the tissues of the body, often accompanied by swelling and inflammation and often caused by bacteria. [t. L: s. *abscessus* a going away] —**ab′scessed,** *adj.*

ab·scis·sa (ăb·sĭs′ə), *n., pl.* **-scis·sas, -scis·sae** (-sĭs′ē). *Math.* (in plane Cartesian coördinates) the x-coördinate of a point, i.e., its horizontal distance from the y-axis measured parallel to the x-axis. [t. L: short for *linea abscissa* line cut off]

ab·scis·sion (ăb·sĭzh′ən, -sĭsh′-), *n.* act of cutting off; sudden termination. [t. L: s. *abscissio*]

Abscissa: P, any point; AP or OB, axis of P; XX, axis of abscissa; YY, axis of the ordinate

ab·scond (ăb·skŏnd′), *v.i.* to depart in a sudden and secret manner, esp. to avoid legal process. [t. L: s. *abscondere* put away] —**ab·scond′er,** *n.*

ab·sence (ăb′səns), *n.* **1.** state of being away: *speak ill of no one in his absence.* **2.** period of being away: *an absence of several weeks.* **3.** lack: *the absence of proof.* [ME, t. F, t. L: m. s. *absentia*]

absence of mind, absent-mindedness.

ab·sent (*adj.* ăb′sənt; *v.* ăb·sĕnt′), *adj.* **1.** not in a certain place at a given time; away (opposed to *present*). **2.** lacking: *revenge is absent from his mind.* **3.** absent-minded. —*v.t.* **4.** to take or keep (oneself) away: *to absent oneself from home.* [ME, t. L: s. *absens,* ppr.] —**ab·sen·ta·tion** (ăb′sən·tā′shən), *n.* —**ab·sent′er,** *n.* —**ab′sent·ness,** *n.*

ab·sen·tee (ăb′sən·tē′), *n.* **1.** one who is absent. **2.** one who withdraws from his country, office, post, duty, etc. —**ab′sen·tee′ism,** *n.*

absentee landlord, an owner, investor, or incumbent who lives in a place, region, or country other than that from which he draws his income.

ab·sent·ly (ăb′sənt·lĭ), *adv.* inattentively.

ab·sent-mind·ed (ăb′sənt·mĭn′dĭd), *adj.* forgetful of one's immediate surroundings; preoccupied. —**ab′sent-mind′ed·ly,** *adv.* —**ab′sent-mind′ed·ness,** *n.* —Syn. ABSENT-MINDED, ABSTRACTED, OBLIVIOUS all mean inattentive to immediate surroundings. ABSENT-MINDED suggests an unintentional wandering of the mind from the present: *an absent-minded professor.* ABSTRACTED implies that the mind has been drawn away from the immediate present by reflection upon some engrossing subject: *wearing an abstracted air.* OBLIVIOUS implies absorption in some thought which causes one to be completely forgetful of or unaware of his surroundings: *oblivious of danger.*

absent without leave, away from military duties without permission, but without the intention of deserting (usually used in the abbreviation A.W.O.L.).

ab·sinthe (ăb′sĭnth), *n.* **1.** a strong, bitter, green-colored, aromatic liqueur, 68 per cent alcohol, made with wormwood and other herbs, having a pronounced licorice flavor. **2.** wormwood (defs. 1, 3). **3.** *U.S.* sagebrush. Also, **ab′sinth.** [t. F, t. L: m. s. *absinthium,* t. Gk.: m. *apsinthion* wormwood] —**ab·sin′thi·al, ab·sin′thi·an,** *adj.*

---

b., blend of, blended; c., cognate with; d., dialect, dialectal; der., derived from; f., formed from; g., going back to; m., modification of; r., replacing; s., stem of; t., taken from; ?, perhaps. See the full key on inside cover.

ab·sinth·ism (ăb/sĭn thĭz´əm), *n.* a morbid condition due to the excessive use of absinthe.

ab·so·lute (ăb/sə lōōt/), *adj.* 1. free from imperfection; complete; perfect: *absolute liberty.* 2. not mixed; pure. 3. free from restriction or limitation; unqualified: *absolute command.* 4. arbitrary or despotic: *an absolute monarchy.* 5. viewed independently; not comparative or relative: *absolute position.* 6. positive: *absolute in opinion.* 7. *Gram.* **a.** syntactically independent; not grammatically connected with any other element in the sentence, as *It being Sunday* in *It being Sunday, the family went to church.* **b.** (of a transitive verb) used with no object expressed, as *to give* in *the solicitors for the community chest asked him to give.* **c.** (of an adjective) having its noun understood, not expressed, as *poor* in *the poor are always with us.* **d.** characterizing the phonetic or phonemic form of a word or phrase occurring by itself, not influenced by surrounding forms (distinguished from *sandhi form*). Example: "not" in "is not" as opposed to "isn't," or "will" in "they will" as opposed to "they'll." 8. *Physics.* **a.** as nearly independent as possible of arbitrary standards or of properties of special substances or systems: *absolute zero of temperature.* **b.** pertaining to a system of units based on some primary units, esp. units of length, mass, and time: *cgs units are absolute units.* **c.** pertaining to a measurement based on an absolute zero or unit: *absolute pressure.* —*n.* **9. the absolute, a.** that which is free from any restriction, or is unconditioned; the ultimate ground of all things. **b.** that which is independent of some or all relations. **c.** that which is perfect or complete. [ME, t. L: m. s. *absolūtus*, pp., loosened from] —ab/so·lute/ness, *n.*
—Syn. 2. sheer. 3. ABSOLUTE, UNQUALIFIED, UTTER all mean unmodified. ABSOLUTE implies an unquestionable finality: *an absolute coward.* UNQUALIFIED means without reservations or conditions: *an unqualified success.* UTTER expresses totality or entirety: *an utter failure.*

absolute alcohol, ethyl alcohol containing not more than one per cent by weight of water.

ab·so·lute·ly (ăb/sə lōōt/lĭ; *emphatic* ăb/sə lōōt/lĭ), *adv.* 1. completely; wholly. 2. positively. 3. (of a transitive verb) without an object.

absolute majority, (in England) over half, as *majority* alone can mean plurality.

absolute music, music whose patterns in sound are not illustrative of or dependent upon a text or program.

absolute pitch, *Music.* 1. the exact pitch of a tone in terms of vibration per second. 2. the ability to sing or recognize the pitch of a tone by ear.

absolute zero, the lowest possible temperature which the nature of matter admits, or that temperature at which the particles whose motion constitutes heat would be at rest, being a hypothetical point 273 degrees below the zero of the centigrade scale. Cf. **absolute** (def. 8a).

ab·so·lu·tion (ăb/sə lōō/shən), *n.* 1. act of absolving; release from consequences, obligations, or penalties. 2. state of being absolved. 3. *Rom. Cath. Theol.* **a** a remission of sin or of the punishment due to sin, which the priest, on the ground of authority received from Christ, makes in the sacrament of penance. **b.** the formula declaring such remission. 4. *Prot. Theol.* a declaration or assurance of divine forgiveness to penitent believers, upon after confession of sins. [t. L: s. *absolūtio* an acquittal; r. ME *absolucioun*, t. F]

ab·so·lut·ism (ăb/sə lōō tĭz´əm), *n.* 1. the principle or the exercise of absolute power in government. 2. *Philos.* the doctrine of an absolute or nonrelative being. —ab/so·lut/ist, *n.* —ab/so·lu·tis/tic, *adj.*

ab·so·lu·to·ry (ăb sŏl/yə tōr/ĭ), *adj.* giving absolution.

ab·solve (ăb sŏlv/, -zŏlv/), *v.t.*, **-solved, -solving.** 1. to free from the consequences or penalties attaching to actions (fol. by *from*): *to absolve one from moral blame.* 2. to set free or release, as from some duty, obligation, or responsibility (fol. by *from*): *absolved from his oath.* 3. to grant pardon for. 4. *Eccles.* **a.** to grant or pronounce remission of sins to. **b.** to remit (sin). **c.** to declare (censure, as excommunication) removed. [t. L: m. s. *absolvere* loosen from] —ab·solv/a·ble, *adj.* —ab·sol/vent, *adj.* n. —ab·solv/er, *n.*
—Syn. 1. ABSOLVE, ACQUIT, EXONERATE mean to free from blame. ABSOLVE is a general word for this idea. To ACQUIT is to release from a specific and usually formal accusation: *the court must acquit the accused if there is enough evidence of innocence.* To EXONERATE is to consider a person clear of blame or consequences for an act (even when the act is admitted), or to justify him for having done it: *to exonerate one for a crime committed in self-defense.* 2. liberate; exempt. —Ant. 1. blame.

ab·so·nant (ăb/sə nənt), *adj.* discordant (fol. by *from* or *to*). [f. AB- + s. L *sonans*, ppr., sounding]

ab·sorb (ăb sôrb/, -zôrb/), *v.t.* 1. to swallow up the identity or individuality of: *the empire absorbed all the small states.* 2. to engross wholly: *absorbed in a book.* 3. to suck up or drink in (liquids): *a sponge absorbs water.* 4. to take up or receive in by chemical or molecular action: *carbonic acid is formed when water absorbs carbon dioxide.* 5. to take in without echo or recoil: *to absorb sound.* 6. *Obs.* to swallow up. [t. L: s. *absorbēre*] —ab·sorb/a·ble, *adj.* —ab·sorb/a·bil/i·ty, *n.* —ab·sorb/er, *n.* —Syn. 1. imbibe, consume, engulf.

ab·sorbed (ăb sôrbd/, -zôrbd/), *adj.* engrossed; preoccupied. —ab·sorb·ed·ly (ăb sôr/bĭd lĭ, -zôr/-), *adv.* —ab·sorb/ed·ness, *n.*

ab·sor·be·fa·cient (ăb sôr/bə fā/shənt, -zôr/-), *adj.* causing absorption. [f. L *absorbē(re)* absorb + -FACIENT]

ab·sorb·ent (ăb sôr/bənt, -zôr/-), *adj.* 1. capable of absorbing; performing the function of absorption. —*n.* 2. a thing that absorbs. —ab·sorb/en·cy, *n.*

absorbent cotton, raw cotton for surgical dressings and toilet purposes which has had its natural wax chemically removed.

ab·sorb·ing (ăb sôr/bĭng, -zôr/-), *adj.* engrossing: *an absorbing pursuit.* —ab·sorb/ing·ly, *adv.*

ab·sorp·tion (ăb sôrp/shən, -zôrp/-), *n.* 1. assimilation: *the absorption of small farms into one big one.* 2. passage of substances to the blood, lymph, and cells, as from the alimentary canal (e.g., digested foods) or from the tissues. 3. a taking in or reception by molecular or chemical action: *absorption of gases, light, heat, etc.* 4. preoccupation. [t. L: s. *absorptio*] —ab·sorp/tive, *adj.* —ab·sorp/tive·ness, *n.*

absorption coefficient, *Optics.* a constant of any material giving its absorption power for light passing through it.

ab·sorp·tiv·i·ty (ăb/sôrp tĭv/ə tĭ, -zôrp-), *n. Physics.* the ratio between the radiation absorbed by a surface and the total energy striking the surface.

ab·stain (ăb stān/), *v.i.* to refrain voluntarily, esp. from doing or enjoying something (fol. by *from*): *abstain from using intoxicating liquor.* [ME *absteine(n)*, t. F: m. *abstenir*, r. OF *astenir*, g. L *abstinēre*] —ab·stain/er, *n.* —Syn. forbear; desist, cease.

ab·ste·mi·ous (ăb stē/mĭ əs), *adj.* 1. sparing in diet; moderate in the use of food and drink; temperate. 2. characterized by abstinence: *an abstemious life.* 3. sparing: *an abstemious diet.* [t. L: m. *abstēmius*] —ab·ste/mi·ous·ly, *adv.* —ab·ste/mi·ous·ness, *n.*

ab·sten·tion (ăb stĕn/shən), *n.* a holding off or refraining; abstinence from action. [f. s. L *abstentus*, pp., abstained + -ION] —ab·sten/tious, *adj.*

ab·sterge (ăb stûrj/), *v.t.*, **-sterged, -sterging.** 1. *Med.* to purge. 2. to make clean by wiping. [t. L: m. s. *abstergēre* wipe off]

ab·ster·gent (ăb stûr/jənt), *adj.* 1. cleansing; detergent. —*n.* 2. a cleansing agent; a detergent, as soap.

ab·ster·sion (ăb stûr/shən), *n.* act of absterging.

ab·ster·sive (ăb stûr/sĭv), *adj.* abstergent. —ab·ster/sive·ness, *n.*

ab·sti·nence (ăb/stə nəns), *n.* 1. forbearance from any indulgence of appetite, esp. from the use of alcoholic liquors: *total abstinence.* 2. self-restraint; forbearance. 3. *Eccles.* the refraining from certain kinds of food on certain days, as from flesh on Fridays. Also, **ab/sti·nen·cy.** [ME *abstynens*, t. L: m. s. *abstinentia*] —ab/sti·nent, *adj.* —ab/sti·nent·ly, *adv.* —Syn. 1. abstemiousness; moderation, temperance.

ab·stract (*adj.* ăb/străkt, ăb străkt/; *n.* ăb/străkt; *v.* ăb străkt/ *for 10–13,* ăb/străkt *for 14*), *adj.* 1. conceived apart from matter and from special cases: *an abstract number.* 2. theoretical; not applied: *abstract science.* 3. difficult to understand; abstruse: *abstract speculations.* 4. of or pertaining to nonrepresentational art; using only lines, colors, generalized or geometrical forms, etc. —*n.* 5. a summary of a statement, document, speech, etc. 6. that which concentrates in itself the essential qualities of anything more extensive or more general, or of several things; essence. 7. an idea or term considered apart from some material basis or object. 8. **the abstract,** the ideal. 9. **in the abstract,** without reference to special circumstances or particular applications. —*v.t.* 10. to draw or take away; remove. 11. to withdraw or divert (the attention). 12. to steal. 13. to consider as a general object apart from special circumstances: *to abstract the notions of time, of space, or of matter.* 14. to summarize. [t. L: s. *abstractus*, pp., drawn away] —ab·stract/er, *n.* —ab/stract·ly, *adv.* —ab/stract·ness, *n.*

ab·stract·ed (ăb străk/tĭd), *adj.* lost in thought; preoccupied. —ab·stract/ed·ly, *adv.* —ab·stract/ed·ness, *n.* —Syn. See absent-minded.

ab·strac·tion (ăb străk/shən), *n.* 1. an abstract or general idea or term. 2. an idea which cannot lead to any practical result; something visionary. 3. act of considering something as a general object apart from special circumstances. 4. act of taking away or separating; withdrawal: *the sensation of cold is due to the abstraction of heat from our bodies.* 5. absent-mindedness; reverie. 6. *Fine Arts.* **a.** a work of art (**pure abstraction**) using lines, shapes, and colors without reference to natural objects. **b.** a work of art (**near abstraction**) retaining representational characteristics but expressing them through geometrical or generalized forms. [t. L: s. *abstractio*]

ab·strac·tive (ăb străk/tĭv), *adj.* 1. having the power of abstracting. 2. pertaining to an epitome or summary.

abstract noun, *Gram.* 1. a noun having an abstract (as opposed to concrete) meaning, as *dread.* 2. a noun made with an abstract suffix, as *witness.*

abstract of title, *Law.* an outline history of the title to a parcel of real estate, showing the original grant, subsequent conveyances, mortgages, etc.

ab·stric·tion (ăb strĭk/shən), *n. Bot.* a method of spore formation in which successive portions of the sporophore are cut off through the growth of septa. [f. AB- + s. L *strictio* a drawing together]

ăct, āble, dâre, ärt; ĕbb, ēqual; Ĭf, īce; hŏt, ōver, ôrder, oil, bŏŏk, ōōze, out; ŭp, ūse, ûrge; ə = a in alone; ch, chief; g, give; ng, ring; sh, shoe; th, thin; ŧh, that; zh, vision. See the full key on inside cover.

ab·struse (ăb strōōs′), *adj.* **1.** difficult to understand; esoteric: *abstruse questions.* **2.** *Obs.* hidden. [t. L: m. s. *abstrūsus*, pp., concealed] —**ab·struse′ly**, *adv.* —**ab·struse′ness**, *n.*

ab·surd (ăb sûrd′, -zûrd′), *adj.* contrary to reason or common sense; obviously false or foolish; logically contradictory; ridiculous: *an absurd statement.* [t. L: s. *absurdus*] —**ab·surd′ly**, *adv.* —**ab·surd′ness**, *n.*
—**Syn.** ABSURD, RIDICULOUS, PREPOSTEROUS all mean inconsistent with reason or common sense. ABSURD means glaringly opposed to manifest truth or reason: *an absurd claim.* RIDICULOUS implies that something is fit only to be laughed at, perhaps contemptuously or derisively: *a ridiculous suggestion.* PREPOSTEROUS implies an amazing extreme of foolishness: *a preposterous proposal.*

ab·surd·i·ty (ăb sûr′də tǐ, -zûr′-), *n., pl.* **-ties. 1.** state or quality of being absurd. **2.** something absurd.

A·bu-Bek·r (ə bōō′bĕk′ər), *n.* A.D. 573–634, first caliph of Mecca, A.D. 632–634; Mohammed's father-in-law and successor.

A·bu·kir (ä′bōō kēr′), *n.* a bay of the Mediterranean, in N Egypt: "Battle of the Nile," 1798. Also, **Aboukir.**

a·bu·li·a (ə bū′lǐ ə), *n. Psychiatry.* a form of mental derangement in which volition is impaired or lost. Also, **aboulia.** [t. Gk.: m. *aboulía* ill counsel] —**a·bu′lic**, *adj.*

a·bun·dance (ə bŭn′dəns), *n.* **1.** an overflowing quantity or supply: *an abundance of grain.* **2.** overflowing fullness: *abundance of the heart.* **3.** affluence; wealth. [ME, t. OF, g. L *abundantia*] —**Syn. 1.** copiousness, profusion. See **plenty.**

a·bun·dant (ə bŭn′dənt), *adj.* **1.** present in great quantity; fully sufficient: *an abundant supply.* **2.** possessing in great quantity; abounding (fol. by *in*): *a river abundant in salmon.* [ME, t. OF, g. s. L *abundans*, ppr.] —**a·bun′dant·ly**, *adv.* —**Syn. 1.** plentiful, copious, profuse, overflowing.

ab ur·be con·di·ta (ăb ûr′bǐ kŏn′də tə), *Latin.* from the founding of the city (Rome, ab. 753 B.C.). *Abbr.:* A.U.C. The year 360 A.U.C. would be the 360th year after the founding of Rome.

a·buse (*v.* ə būz′), *v.*, **abused, abusing,** *n.* —*v.t.* **1.** to use wrongly or improperly; misuse: *to abuse rights or authority.* **2.** to do wrong to; act injuriously toward: *to abuse one's wife.* **3.** to revile; malign. **4.** *Archaic.* to deceive. [ME *abuse(n)*, t. F: m. *abuser*, ult. der. L *abūsus*, pp., having used up] —*n.* **5.** wrong or improper use; misuse: *the abuse of privileges.* **6.** insulting language. **7.** ill-treatment of a person. **8.** a corrupt practice or custom; an offense: *the abuses of bad government.* **9.** *Archaic.* deception. [t. F: m. *abus*, t. L: s. *abūsus* a wasting, misuse] —**a·bus′er**, *n.* —**Syn. 1.** ill-use, maltreat. **3.** vilify, vituperate, berate, upbraid. **6.** ABUSE, CENSURE, INVECTIVE all mean strongly expressed disapproval. ABUSE implies an outburst of harsh and scathing words against another (often one who is defenseless): *abuse directed against an opponent.* CENSURE implies blame, adverse criticism, or hostile condemnation: *severe censure of acts showing bad judgment.* INVECTIVE applies to strong but formal denunciation in speech or print, often in the public interest: *invective against graft.*

a·bu·sive (ə bū′sǐv), *adj.* **1.** using harsh words or ill treatment: *an abusive author.* **2.** characterized by or containing abuse: *an abusive satire.* **3.** wrongly used; corrupt: *an abusive exercise of power.* [t. L: m. s. *abūsīvus*] —**a·bu′sive·ly**, *adv.* —**a·bu′sive·ness**, *n.*

a·but (ə bŭt′), *v.i.* abutted, abutting. to be adjacent to (often fol. by *on, upon,* or *against*): *this piece of land abuts upon a street.* [ME abutte(n), t. OF: coalescence of *abouter* join end to end (der. a- A⁻⁵ + *bout* end) and *abuter* make contact with end on end (der. a- A⁻⁵ + *but* end)]

a·bu·ti·lon (ə bū′tə lŏn′), *n.* any plant of the malvaceous genus *Abutilon,* esp. the flowering maple. [t. NL, t. Ar.: m. *aubūṭīlūn*]

a·but·ment (ə bŭt′mənt), *n.* **1.** that on which something abuts, as the part of a pier which receives the thrust of an arch; a part for sustaining or resisting pressure, as the part of a bridge pier exposed to the force of the current or of floating ice, or the structure supporting the shore ends of a bridge and restraining the embankment which supports the approaches. **2.** the place where projecting parts meet; junction.

a·but·ter (ə bŭt′ər), *n.* U.S. an owner of adjacent land.

a·by (ə bī′), *v.t.* and pp. **abought.** *Archaic.* to pay the penalty of. Also, **a·bye′.** [ME abye(n), OE ābȳg- s. ābycgan, f. ā- A⁻³ + bycgan buy]

Abutment: A, Arch abutment; B, Current abutment

A·by·dos (ə bī′dŏs), *n.* **1.** an ancient ruined city in central Egypt: temples and tombs. **2.** an ancient town in NW Asia Minor, at the narrowest part of the Hellespont. See **Hero and Leander.**

a·bysm (ə bǐz′əm), *n.* an abyss. [ME abi(s)me, t. OF, g. VL *abyssimus,* superl. of L *abyssus* ABYSS]

a·bys·mal (ə bǐz′məl), *adj.* of or like an abyss; immeasurable: *abysmal ignorance.* —**a·bys′mal·ly**, *adv.*

a·byss (ə bǐs′), *n.* **1.** a bottomless gulf; any deep, immeasurable space. **2.** anything profound and unfathomable: *the abyss of time.* **3.** the bottomless pit; hell. [t. L: s. *abyssus,* t. Gk.: m. *ábyssos* without bottom]

a·byss·al (ə bǐs′əl), *adj.* **1.** abysmal. **2.** of or pertaining to the lowest depths of the ocean.

Ab·ys·sin·i·a (ăb′ə sǐn′ǐ ə), *n.* Ethiopia (def. 1). —**Ab′ys·sin′i·an,** *adj., n.*

ac-, var. of **ad-** (by assimilation) before *c* and *qu,* as in *accede, acquire,* etc.

-ac, an adjective suffix meaning "pertaining to," as in *elegiac, cardiac.* [repr. Gk. adj. suffix *-akos,* whence L *-acus,* F *-aque*]

Ac, *Chem.* actinium.

AC, 1. Air Corps. **2.** *Chem.* hydrocyanic acid.

A.C., *Elect.* alternating current. Also, **a.c.**

a·ca·cia (ə kā′shə), *n.* **1.** any tree or shrub of the mimosaceous genus *Acacia,* native in warm regions. **2.** one of several other plants, as the locust tree. **3.** gum arabic. [t. L, t. Gk.: m. *akakía* a thorny Egyptian tree]

Ac·a·deme (ăk′ə dēm′), *n. Poetic.* **1.** the Academy of Athens. **2.** (*l.c.*) any place of instruction.

ac·a·dem·ic (ăk′ə dĕm′ǐk), *adj.* **1.** pertaining to an advanced institution of learning, as a college, university, or academy; relating to higher education. **2.** *U.S.* pertaining to the classical, mathematical, and general literary departments of a college or university, as distinguished from the professional and scientific departments. **3.** theoretical; not practical. **4.** conforming to set rules and traditions; conventional. —*n.* **5.** a member of a college or university. —**Syn. 4.** See **formal.**

ac·a·dem·i·cal (ăk′ə dĕm′ə kəl), *adj.* **1.** academic. —*n.* **2.** (*pl.*) cap and gown. —**ac′a·dem′i·cal·ly,** *adv.*

academic freedom, freedom of a teacher to discuss social, economic, or political problems without interference from school or public officials.

ac·a·de·mi·cian (ə kăd′ə mǐsh′ən, ăk′ă də-), *n.* a member of a society for promoting literature, art, or science.

ac·a·dem·i·cism (ăk′ə dĕm′ə sǐz′əm), *n.* traditionalism or conventionalism in art, literature, etc.

a·cad·e·mism (ə kăd′ə mǐz′əm), *n.* **1.** academicism. **2.** *Philos.* the doctrines of the school founded by Plato.

a·cad·e·my (ə kăd′ə mǐ), *n., pl.* **-mies. 1.** a secondary school, esp. a private one. **2.** a school for instruction in a particular art or science: *a military academy.* **3.** an association or institution for the promotion of literature, science, or art: *the Academy of Arts and Letters.* **4.** **the Academy, a.** the French Academy. **b.** (in England) the Royal Academy. **c.** the public grove in Athens, in which Plato taught. **d.** the Platonic school of philosophy. [t. L: m.s. *academīa,* t. Gk.: m. *Akadḗmeia* (der. *Akádēmos,* an Attic hero)]

A·ca·di·a (ə kā′dǐ ə), *n.* a former French colony in SE Canada: ceded to Great Britain, 1713. French, **A·ca·die** (à kà dē′).

A·ca·di·an (ə kā′dǐ ən), *adj.* **1.** of or pertaining to Acadia or its inhabitants. —*n.* **2.** Also, *Dial.,* Cajun, Cajian. a native or inhabitant of Acadia, or one of the descendants of these in Louisiana.

Acadia, c1605–1713

ATLANTIC OCEAN

ac·a·leph (ăk′ə lĕf′), *n.* one of the *Acalephae,* a group of coelenterate marine animals including the sea nettles and jellyfishes. Also, **ac·a·lephe** (ăk′ə lĕf′). [t. NL: s. *Acalĕpha,* t. Gk.: m. *akalḗphe* nettle]

ac·an·tha·ceous (ăk′ən thā′shəs), *adj.* **1.** having prickly growths. **2.** belonging to the *Acanthaceae,* or acanthus family of plants.

acan·tho-, *Bot.* a word element meaning "thorn," or "thorny." Also, before vowels, **acanth-.** [t. Gk.: m. *akantho-,* comb. form of *ákantha* thorn]

a·can·tho·ceph·a·lan (ə kăn′thə sĕf′ə lən), *n.* any of the worms belonging to a phylum or class of internal parasitic worms, *Acanthocephala,* having a protrusile proboscis covered with recurved hooks and a hollow body without digestive tract, found in the intestine of vertebrates.

ac·an·tho·di·an (ăk′ən thō′dǐ ən), *n.* a spiny-finned sharklike fish of the late Silurian and Devonian.

a·can·thoid (ə kăn′thoid), *adj.* spiny; spinous.

ac·an·thop·ter·yg·i·an (ăk′ən thŏp′tə rǐj′ǐ ən), *adj.* **1.** belonging or pertaining to the *Acanthopterygii,* the group of fishes with spiny fins, as the bass and perch. —*n.* **2.** an acanthopterygian fish. [f. ACANTHO- + s. Gk. *pterýgion* fin + -AN]

a·can·thous (ə kăn′thəs), *adj.* spinous.

a·can·thus (ə kăn′thəs), *n., pl.* **-thuses, -thi** (-thī). **1.** a plant of the genus *Acanthus,* of the Mediterranean regions, with large spiny or toothed leaves. **2.** an architectural ornament resembling the leaves of this plant, as in the Corinthian capital. [t. L, t. Gk.: m. *ákanthos* a thorny tree]

Acanthus: A, Leaf of plant, *Acanthus mollis;* B, Architectural ornament, front and side view

a cap·pel·la (ä′ kə pĕl′ə; *It.* ä′ käp pĕl′lä), *Music.* **1.** without instrumental accompaniment. **2.** in the style of church or chapel music. [It.]

A·ca·pul·co (ä′kä pōōl′kō), *n.* a seaport in SW Mexico. 27,913 (1950).

ac·a·ri·a·sis (ăk′ə rī′ə sǐs), *n.* **1.** infestation with acarids, esp. mites. **2.** a skin disease caused by such infestation. [f. m. Gk. *ákar(i)* mite + -IASIS]

---

b., blend of, blended; c., cognate with; d., dialect, dialectal; der., derived from; f., formed from; g., going back to; m., modification of; r., replacing; s., stem of; t., taken from; ?, perhaps.   See the full key on inside cover.

ac·a·rid (ăk'ə·rĭd), *n.* any animal belonging to the *Acari* (or *Acarida*), an order of arachnids including the mites, ticks, etc. [f. m. Gk. *ákar(i)* mite + -ID²]

a·car·i·dan (ă·kăr'ə·dən), *adj.* **1.** belonging to the acarids. —*n.* **2.** an acarid.

ac·a·roid (ăk'ə·roid'), *adj.* resembling an acarid.

acaroid gum, a red resin exuded from the trunk of the liliaceous Australian grass tree, *Xanthorrhoea hastilis,* and other species. Also, **acaroid resin.**

a·car·pel·ous (ā·kär'pəl·əs), *adj.* *Bot.* having no carpels. Also, **a·car'pel·lous.**

a·car·pous (ā·kär'pəs), *adj.* *Bot.* not producing fruit; sterile; barren. [t. Gk.: m. *ákarpos* without fruit]

ac·a·rus (ăk'ə·rəs), *n., pl.* **-ri** (-rī'). an animal of the genus *Acarus;* a mite. [t. L, t. Gk.: m. *ákari*]

a·cat·a·lec·tic (ā·kăt'ə·lĕk'tĭk), *Pros.* —*adj.* **1.** not catalectic; complete. —*n.* **2.** a verse having the complete number of syllables in the last foot. See example under **catalectic.**

a·cau·dal (ā·kô'dəl), *adj.* *Zool.* tailless. Also, **a·cau·date** (ā·kô'dāt).

ac·au·les·cent (ăk'ô·lĕs'ənt), *adj.* *Bot.* not caulescent; stemless; without visible stem. Also, **a·cau·line** (ā·kô'lĭn, -līn), **a·cau·lose** (ā·kô'lōs), **a·cau·lous** (ā·kô'ləs). —**ac'au·les'cence,** *n.*

acc., **1.** account. **2.** accusative.

Ac·cad (ăk'ăd, ä'kăd), *n.* Akkad.

ac·cede (ăk·sēd'), *v.i.,* **-ceded, -ceding.** **1.** to give consent; agree; yield: *to accede to terms.* **2.** to attain, as an office or dignity; arrive at (fol. by *to*): *to accede to the throne.* **3.** *Internat. Law.* to become a party (*to*), as a nation signing a treaty. [t. L: m. s. *accēdere* go to] —**ac·ced'ence,** *n.* —**ac·ced'er,** *n.*

accel., accelerando.

ac·cel·er·an·do (ăk·sĕl'ə·răn'dō; *It.* ät·chĕ'lĕ·rän'dō), *adv., adj.* *Music.* gradually increasing in speed. [It.]

ac·cel·er·ant (ăk·sĕl'ər·ənt), *n.* *Chem.* accelerator.

ac·cel·er·ate (ăk·sĕl'ə·rāt'), *v.,* **-ated, -ating.** —*v.t.* **1.** to cause to move or advance faster: *accelerate growth.* **2.** to help to bring about more speedily than would otherwise have been the case: *to accelerate the fall of a government.* **3.** to increase or otherwise change the velocity of (a body) or the rate of (motion); cause to undergo acceleration. —*v.i.* **4.** to become faster; increase in speed. [t. L: m.s. *accelerātus,* pp.]

ac·cel·er·a·tion (ăk·sĕl'ə·rā'shən), *n.* **1.** act of accelerating; increase of speed or velocity. **2.** a change in velocity. **3.** the time rate of change in velocity.

acceleration of gravity, the acceleration of a falling body due to gravity which is a little more than 32 feet per second, per second, at sea level, and which varies with latitude and altitude: represented by the letter *g.*

ac·cel·er·a·tive (ăk·sĕl'ə·rā'tĭv), *adj.* tending to accelerate; increasing the velocity (*of*). Also, **ac·cel·er·a·to·ry** (ăk·sĕl'ər·ə·tôr'ĭ).

ac·cel·er·a·tor (ăk·sĕl'ə·rā'tər), *n.* **1.** one that accelerates. **2.** *Auto.* a device for opening and closing the throttle, esp. when operated by the foot. **3.** *Photog.* any substance, device, or the like, that shortens the time of exposure or development. **4.** *Chem.* **a.** any substance that increases the speed of a chemical change. **b.** any chemical which increases the rate of vulcanization of rubber. **5.** *Anat.* any muscle, nerve, or activating substance that quickens a movement. **6.** *Physics.* a device for producing high-energy particles, as a cyclotron.

ac·cel·er·om·e·ter (ăk·sĕl'ə·rŏm'ə·tər), *n.* an instrument used for measuring acceleration, used in aircraft.

ac·cent (*n.* ăk'sĕnt; *v.* ăk'sĕnt, ăk·sĕnt'), *n.* **1.** the distinctive character of a vowel or syllable determined by its degree or pattern of stress or musical tone. **2.** any one of the degrees or patterns of stress used in a particular language as essential features of vowels, syllables, or words: *primary accent, falling accent, sentence accent.* **3.** a mark indicating stress, musical tone, or vowel quality. In English the accent mark (´) is used to indicate the syllable which is stressed. French has three accent marks, the acute (´), the grave (`), and the circumflex (^), which indicate vowel quality (or sometimes merely distinguish meaning, as *la* "the" and *là* "there"). **4.** *Pros.* **a.** regularly recurring stress. **b.** a mark indicating stress or some other distinction in pronunciation or value. **5.** any one of the musical tones or melodies used in a particular language as essential features of vowels or syllables. **6.** characteristic style of pronunciation: *foreign accent.* **7.** *Music.* **a.** stress or emphasis given to certain notes. **b.** a mark denoting this. **c.** stress or emphasis regularly recurring as a feature of rhythm. **8.** *Math., etc.* a mark, or one of a number of marks, placed after a letter or figure: **a.** to distinguish similar quantities which differ in value, as in b', b'', b''', etc. (called *b prime, b second, b third,* etc., respectively). **b.** to indicate a particular unit or measure, as feet (′) or inches (″): 5'3″, meaning *5 feet, 3 inches;* or as minutes (′) or seconds (″) of time at a degree: 18'25″, meaning *18 minutes, 25 seconds.* **c.** to indicate the operation of differentiation in calculus. **9.** words or tones expressive of some emotion. **10.** (*pl.*) *Poetic.* words; language. **11.** distinctive character or tone. —*v.t.* **12.** to pronounce (a vowel, syllable, or word) with one of the distinctive accents of the language, esp. with a stress accent. **13.** to mark with a written accent or accents: *to accent a word to indicate its pronunciation.*

14. to emphasize; accentuate. [t. L: s. *accentus* tone]

ac·cen·tu·al (ăk·sĕn'chŏŏ·əl), *adj.* **1.** pertaining to accent; rhythmical. **2.** *Pros.* of, pertaining to, or characterized by syllabic accent (distinguished from *quantitative*). —**ac·cen'tu·al·ly,** *adv.*

ac·cen·tu·ate (ăk·sĕn'chŏŏ·āt'), *v.t.,* **-ated, -ating.** **1.** to emphasize. **2.** to mark or pronounce with an accent. [t. ML: m. s. *accentuātus,* pp.] —**ac·cen'tu·a'tion,** *n.*

ac·cept (ăk·sĕpt'), *v.t.* **1.** to take or receive (something offered); receive with approval or favor: *his proposal was accepted.* **2.** to admit and agree to; accede or assent to: *to accept a treaty, an excuse, etc.* **3.** to take with formal acknowledgment of responsibility or consequences: *to accept office.* **4.** to accommodate oneself to: *accept the situation.* **5.** to believe: *to accept a fact.* **6.** to receive as to meaning; understand. **7.** *Com.* to acknowledge, by signature, as calling for payment, and thus to agree to pay, as a draft. **8.** (in a deliberative body) to receive as an adequate performance of the duty with which an officer or a committee has been charged; receive for further action: *the report of the committee was accepted.* —*v.i.* **9.** to accept an invitation, gift, position, etc. (sometimes fol. by *of*). [ME *accept(en),* t. L: m. *acceptāre,* freq. of *accipere* take] —**ac·cept'er;** *esp. in Com.* **ac·cep'tor,** *n.*

ac·cept·a·ble (ăk·sĕp'tə·bəl), *adj.* **1.** capable or worthy of being accepted. **2.** pleasing to the receiver; agreeable; welcome. —**ac·cept'a·bil'i·ty, ac·cept'a·ble·ness,** *n.* —**ac·cept'a·bly,** *adv.*

ac·cept·ance (ăk·sĕp'təns), *n.* **1.** act of taking or receiving something offered. **2.** favorable reception; favor. **3.** act of assenting or believing: *acceptance of a theory.* **4.** fact or state of being accepted or acceptable. **5.** *Com.* **a.** an engagement to pay an order, draft, or bill of exchange when it becomes due, as by the person on whom it is drawn. **b.** an order, draft, etc., which a person has accepted as calling for payment and has thus promised to pay: *a trade acceptance.*

acceptance sampling, a procedure by which a decision is made to accept or reject a lot of articles on the basis of the results of the inspection of one or more samples of articles from the lot.

ac·cept·ant (ăk·sĕp'tənt), *adj.* accepting; receptive.

ac·cep·ta·tion (ăk'sĕp·tā'shən), *n.* **1.** favorable regard. **2.** belief. **3.** usual or received meaning.

ac·cept·ed (ăk·sĕp'tĭd), *adj.* approved.

ac·cess (ăk'sĕs), *n.* **1.** act or privilege of coming to; admittance; approach: *to gain access to a person.* **2.** approachability; accessibility: *the house is difficult of access.* **3.** way or means of approach. **4.** *Theol.* approach to God through Jesus Christ. Eph. 2:18. **5.** an attack, as of disease. **6.** sudden outburst of passion. **7.** accession. [ME, t. L: s. *accessus* approach]

ac·ces·sa·ry (ăk·sĕs'ə·rĭ), *n., pl.* **-ries,** *adj. Chiefly Law.* accessory. —**ac·ces·sa·ri·ly,** *adv.* —**ac·ces·sa·ri·ness,** *n.*

ac·ces·si·ble (ăk·sĕs'ə·bəl), *adj.* **1.** easy of access; approachable. **2.** attainable: *accessible evidence.* **3.** open to the influence of (fol. by *to*): *accessible to bribery.* —**ac·ces'si·bil'i·ty.** —**ac·ces'si·bly,** *adv.*

ac·ces·sion (ăk·sĕsh'ən), *n.* **1.** act of coming into the possession of a right, dignity, office, etc.: *accession to the throne.* **2.** an increase by something added: *an accession of territory.* **3.** something added. **4.** *Law.* addition to property by growth or improvement. **5.** consent: *accession to a demand.* **6.** *Internat. Law.* formal acceptance of a treaty, international convention, or other agreement between states. **7.** act of coming near; approach. [t. L: s. *accessio* increase] —**ac·ces'sion·al,** *adj.*

ac·ces·so·ri·al (ăk'sə·sôr'ĭ·əl), *adj.* accessory.

ac·ces·so·ry (ăk·sĕs'ə·rĭ), *n., pl.* **-ries,** *adj.* —*n.* **1. a.** subordinate part or object; something added or attached for convenience, attractiveness, etc., such as a spotlight, heater, rear-vision mirror, etc., for an automobile. **2.** *Law.* one who, without being present at its commission, is guilty of aiding or abetting another who commits a felony: **an accessory before the fact** is not present when the act is done; **an accessory after the fact** knowingly conceals or assists another who has committed a felony. —*adj.* **3.** contributing to a general effect; subsidiary: *accessory sounds in music.* **4.** *Law.* giving aid as an accessory. **5.** *Petrog.* denoting minerals present in relatively small amounts in a rock, and not mentioned in its definition, as zircon in granite. Also, *esp. Law,* **accessary.** [t. LL: m. s. *accessōrius*] —**ac·ces'so·ri·ly,** *adv.* —**ac·ces'so·ri·ness,** *n.* —**Syn.** **1.** See **addition.**

ac·ciac·ca·tu·ra (ät·chäk'kä·tōō'rä), *n.* *Music.* **1.** a short appoggiatura. **2.** a short grace note one half step below, and struck at the same time with, a principal note. [It.]

Acciaccatura
A. Grace note; B. Principal note

ac·ci·dence (ăk'sə·dəns), *n.* **1.** the rudiments of any subject. **2.** *Gram.* **a.** that part of morphology dealing with inflection. **b.** an inflected form of a word. **c.** a property shown by such inflection. [var of *accidents,* pl. of *accident* (def. 5). or t. L: m. s. *accidentia,* neut. pl. of *accidens,* ppr., striking, happening (as if fem. noun)]

ac·ci·dent (ăk'sə·dənt), *n.* **1.** an undesirable or unfortunate happening; casualty; mishap. **2.** anything that happens unexpectedly, without design, or by chance. **3.** the operation of chance: *I was there by accident.* **4.** a nonessential circumstance; occasional characteristic. **5.** *Gram.* an inflectional variation of a word, as *them* (an inflected form of *they*). **6.** *Geol.* an irregularity, generally on a small scale, on a surface, the explanation for which is not readily apparent. [ME, t. L: s. *accidens*, ppr., happening] —Syn. **1.** mischance, misfortune, disaster, calamity, catastrophe.

ac·ci·den·tal (ăk′sə dĕn′təl), *adj.* **1.** happening by chance or accident, or unexpectedly: *an accidental meeting.* **2.** nonessential; incidental; subsidiary: *accidental benefits.* **3.** *Music.* relating to or indicating sharps, flats, or naturals. —*n.* **4.** a nonessential or subsidiary circumstance or feature. **5.** *Music.* a sign placed before a note indicating a change of its pitch. —ac′ci·den′·tal·ly, *adv.* —ac′ci·den′tal·ness, *n.*

—Syn. **1.** ACCIDENTAL, CASUAL, FORTUITOUS al· describe something outside the usual course of events. ACCIDENTAL implies occurring unexpectedly or by chance: *an accidental blow.* CASUAL describes a passing event of slight importance: *a casual reference.* FORTUITOUS is applied to events occurring without known cause: *a fortuitous shower of meteors.*

ac·cip·i·ter (ăk sĭp′ə tər), *n.*, *pl.* **-tres** (-trēz′). any bird of the subfamily *Accipitrinae* and genus *Accipiter*, which comprises short-winged, long-tailed hawks. [t. L]

ac·cip·i·tral (ăk sĭp′ə trəl), *adj.* accipitrine.

ac·cip·i·trine (ăk sĭp′ə trīn, -trĭn′), *adj.* **1.** belonging to the *Accipitridae*, a hawk family. **2.** raptorial; like or related to the birds of prey.

ac·claim (ə klām′), *v.t.* **1.** to salute with words or sounds of joy or approval; applaud. **2.** to announce or proclaim by acclamation. —*v.i.* **3.** to make acclamation; applaud. —*n.* **4.** acclamation (defs. 1, 2). [t. L: m. s. *acclāmāre*] —ac·claim′er, *n.*

ac·cla·ma·tion (ăk′lə mā′shən), *n.* **1.** a shout or other demonstration of welcome, good will, or applause. **2.** act of acclaiming. **3.** (in parliamentary procedure) an oral vote, often unanimous, usually taken after the sense of a meeting is clear and unmistakable. —ac·clam·a·to·ry (ə klăm′ə tôr′ĭ), *adj.*

ac·cli·mate (ə klī′mĭt, ăk′lə māt′). *v.t.*, *v.i.*, **-mated, -mating.** *Chiefly U.S.* to habituate or become habituated to a new climate or environment. [t. F: m.s. *acclimater*, der. à to + *climat* climate] —ac·cli·mat·a·ble (ə klī′mĭt ə bəl), *adj.* —ac·cli·ma·tion (ăk′lə mā′shən), *n.*

ac·cli·ma·tize (ə klī′mə tīz′), *v.t.*, *v.i.*, **-tized, -tizing.** *Chiefly Brit.* to acclimate. —ac·cli′ma·tiz′a·ble, *adj.* —ac·cli′ma·ti·za′tion, *n.* —ac·cli′ma·tiz′er, *n.*

ac·cliv·i·ty (ə klĭv′ə tĭ), *n.*, *pl.* **-ties.** an upward slope, as of ground; an ascent. [t. L: m. s. *acclīvitas* steepness]

ac·co·lade (ăk′ə lād′, -läd′), *n.* **1.** a ceremony used in conferring knighthood, consisting at one time of an embrace, and afterward of giving the candidate a light blow upon the shoulder with the flat of a sword. **2.** the blow itself. **3.** any award; honor. **4.** *Music.* a brace joining several staves. [t. F, t. It.: m. *accollata*, prop. fem. pp. of *accollare* embrace about the neck; r. ME *acolee*, t. OF]

ac·com·mo·date (ə kŏm′ə dāt′), *v.*, **-dated, -dating.** —*v.t.* **1.** to do a kindness or a favor to; oblige: *to accommodate a friend.* **2.** to provide suitably; supply (fol. by *with*): *to accommodate a friend with money.* **3.** to provide with room and sometimes with food and entertainment. **4.** to make suitable or consistent; adapt: *to accommodate oneself to circumstances.* **5.** to bring into harmony; adjust; reconcile: *to accommodate differences.* **6.** to furnish with accommodations. —*v.i.* **7.** to become or be conformable; act conformably; agree. [t. L: m.s. *accommodātus*, pp., suited] —ac·com′mo·da′tor, *n.* —Syn. **1.** serve, aid, assist. See **oblige. 6.** See **contain.**

ac·com·mo·dat·ing (ə kŏm′ə dā′tĭng), *adj.* easy to deal with; obliging. —ac·com′mo·dat′ing·ly, *adv.*

ac·com·mo·da·tion (ə kŏm′ə dā′shən), *n.* **1.** act of accommodating; state or process of being accommodated; adaptation. **2.** adjustment of differences; reconciliation. **3.** *Sociol.* a process of mutual adaptation between persons or social groups, usually through eliminating or lessening of factors of hostility. **4.** anything which supplies a want; a convenience. **5.** (*chiefly pl.*) lodging, or food and lodging. **6.** readiness to aid others; obligingness. **7.** *U.S.* a loan or pecuniary favor. **8.** *Physiol.* the automatic adjustment by which the eye adapts itself to distinct vision at different distances. **9.** an accommodation bill, draft, note, etc.

accommodation bill, draft, note, etc. *U.S.* a bill, draft, note, etc., drawn, accepted, or endorsed by one person for another without consideration, to enable the second person to obtain credit or raise money.

accommodation ladder, a ladder or stairway hung from a ship's side to connect with boats below.

ac·com·mo·da·tive (ə kŏm′ə dā′tĭv), *adj.* tending to accommodate; adaptive. —ac·com′mo·da·tive·ness, *n.*

ac·com·pa·ni·ment (ə kŭm′pə nĭ mənt, ə kŭmp′nĭ-), *n.* **1.** something incidental or added for ornament, symmetry, etc. **2.** *Music.* any subsidiary part or parts added to a solo or concerted composition to enhance the effect.

ac·com·pa·nist (ə kŭm′pə nĭst, ə kŭmp′nĭst), *n.* *Music.* one who plays an accompaniment. Also, **accompanyist.**

ac·com·pa·ny (ə kŭm′pə nĭ), *v.t.*, **-nied, -nying. 1.** to go along or in company with; join in action: *to accompany a friend on a walk.* **2.** to be or exist in company with: *thunder accompanies lightning.* **3.** to put in company with; cause to be or go along; associate (fol. by *with*): *he accompanied his speech with gestures.* **4.** *Music.*

to play or sing an accompaniment to. [ME *accompanye(n)*, t. F: m. *accompagner*, der. à to + *compagne* COMPANION] —ac·com′pa·ni·er, *n.*

—Syn. **1.** ACCOMPANY, ATTEND, CONVOY, ESCORT mean to go along with someone (or something). To ACCOMPANY is to go along as an associate on equal terms: *to accompany a friend on a shopping trip.* ATTEND implies going along with, usually to render service or perform duties: *to attend one's employer on a business trip.* To CONVOY is to accompany (especially ships) with an armed guard, for protection: *to convoy a fleet of merchant vessels.* To ESCORT is to accompany in order to protect, guard, honor, or show courtesy: *to escort a visiting dignitary.*

ac·com·pa·ny·ist (ə kŭm′pə nĭ ĭst), *n.* accompanist.

ac·com·plice (ə kŏm′plĭs), *n.* an associate in a crime; partner in wrongdoing. [earlier *complice*, t. F, t. ML: m. s. *complex, complicis* close associate, confederate: the phrase *a complice* became *accomplice* by failure to recognize it as made up of two words]

ac·com·plish (ə kŏm′plĭsh), *v.t.* **1.** to bring to pass; carry out; perform; finish: *to accomplish one's mission.* **2.** to complete (a distance or period of time). **3.** to make complete; equip perfectly. [ME *accomplice(n)*, t. OF: m. *acompliss-*, s. *acomplir*, g. LL *accomplēre*] —ac·com′plish·a·ble, *adj.* —ac·com′plish·er, *n.* —Syn. **1.** complete, fulfill; execute. See **do.**

ac·com·plished (ə kŏm′plĭsht), *adj.* **1.** completed; effected: *an accomplished fact.* **2.** perfected; expert: *an accomplished scholar.* **3.** perfected in the graces and attainments of polite society.

ac·com·plish·ment (ə kŏm′plĭsh mənt), *n.* **1.** act of carrying into effect; fulfillment: *the accomplishment of our desires.* **2.** anything accomplished; achievement: *the accomplishments of scientists.* **3.** (*often pl.*) an acquired art or grace; polite attainment. —Syn. **1.** completion.

ac·compt (ə kount′), *n.*, *v.i.*, *v.t.* *Archaic.* account.

ac·cord (ə kôrd′), *v.i.* **1.** to be in correspondence or harmony; agree. —*v.t.* **2.** to make to agree or correspond; adapt. **3.** to grant; concede: *to accord due praise.* **4.** *Archaic.* to settle; reconcile. —*n.* **5.** just correspondence of things; harmony of relation. **6.** a harmonious union of sounds. **7.** consent or concurrence of opinions or wills; agreement. **8.** an international agreement; settlement of questions outstanding between nations. **9.** of one's own accord, voluntarily. [t. LL: s. *accordāre*; r. ME *acorde(n)*, t. OF: m. *acorder*] —ac·cord′a·ble, *adj.* —ac·cord′er, *n.* —Syn. **1.** See **agree.**

ac·cord·ance (ə kôr′dəns), *n.* **1.** agreement; conformity. **2.** act of according.

ac·cord·ant (ə kôr′dənt), *adj.* agreeing; conformable. —ac·cord′ant·ly, *adv.*

ac·cord·ing (ə kôr′dĭng), *adv.* **1. according to,** **a.** in accordance with: *according to his judgment.* **b.** proportionately. **c.** on the authority of; as stated by. **2. according as,** conformably or proportionately as. —*adj.* **3.** agreeing.

ac·cord·ing·ly (ə kôr′dĭng lĭ), *adv.* **1.** in accordance; correspondingly. **2.** in due course; therefore; so. —Syn. **1, 2.** consequently, hence, thus. See **therefore.**

ac·cor·di·on (ə kôr′dĭ ən), *n.* **1.** a portable, keyed, bellowslike wind instrument sounded by means of metallic reeds. —*adj.* **2.** having folds like the bellows of an accordion. [f. ACCORD + -ION] —ac·cor′di·on·ist, *n.*

Boy playing an accordion

ac·cost (ə kŏst′, ə kôst′), *v.t.* **1.** to approach, esp. with a greeting or remark. —*n.* **2.** greeting. [t. F: s. *acoster*, g. LL *accostāre* put side by side]

ac·couche·ment (ə kōosh′mənt; *Fr.* à kōosh män′), *n.* *French.* period of confinement in childbirth.

ac·cou·cheur (ăk′ōō shûr′; *Fr.* à kōō shœr′), *n.* *French.* a man who acts as a midwife.

ac·count (ə kount′), *n.* **1.** a verbal or written recital of particular transactions and events; narrative: *an account of everything as it happened.* **2.** an explanatory statement of conduct, as to a superior. **3.** a statement of reasons, causes, etc., explaining some event. **4.** reason; consideration (prec. by *on*): *on all accounts.* **5.** consequence; importance: *things of no account.* **6.** estimation; judgment: *to take into account.* **7.** profit; advantage: *to turn anything to account.* **8. on account of,** **a.** because of; by reason of. **b.** for the sake of. **9.** a statement of pecuniary transactions. **10.** *Bookkeeping.* **a.** a formal record of the debits and credits relating to the person named (or caption placed) at the head of the ledger account. **b.** a balance of a specified period's receipts and expenditures. [ME *accompt*, t. OF: m. *acont, acunt*, later *acompt*, f. à to + *cont*, g. LL *comptum*, L *computum* calculation] —*v.i.* **11.** to give an explanation (fol. by *for*): *to account for the accident.* **12.** to answer concerning one's conduct, duties, etc. (fol. by *for*): *to account for shortages.* **13.** to render an account, esp. of money. **14.** to cause death, capture, etc. (fol. by *for*). —*v.t.* **15.** to count; consider as: *I account myself well paid.* **16.** to assign or impute (fol. by *to*). [ME *acunte(n)*, t. OF: m. *acunter*, g. LL *accomptāre*] —Syn. **1.** See **narrative.**

ac·count·a·ble (ə koun′tə bəl), *adj.* **1.** liable to be called to account; responsible. **2.** that can be explained. —ac·count′a·bil′i·ty, ac·count′a·ble·ness, *n.* —ac·count′a·bly, *adv.*

ac·count·an·cy (əkoun′tənsĭ), *n.* the art or practice of an accountant.

ac·count·ant (əkoun′tənt), *n.* a person whose profession is inspecting and auditing business accounts. —**ac·count′ant·ship′**, *n.*

ac·count·ing (əkoun′tĭng), *n.* the theory and system of setting up, maintaining, and auditing the books of a firm; the art of analyzing the financial position and operating results of a business house from a study of its sales, purchases, overhead, etc. (distinguished from *bookkeeping* in that a bookkeeper only makes the proper entries in books set up to the accountant's plan).

ac·cou·ple·ment (əkŭp′əlmənt), *n.* 1. act of coupling. 2. that which couples, esp. (in building) a tie or brace. [t. F, der. *accoupler*, der. *à* to + *couple* COUPLE]

ac·cou·ter (əkōō′tər), *v.t.* to equip or array, esp. with military accouterments. Also, *Brit.*, **ac·cou′tre**. [t. F: m. s. *accoutrer*]

ac·cou·ter·ments (əkōō′tər mənts), *n.pl.* 1. equipage, trappings. 2. the equipment of a soldier except arms and clothing. Also, *Brit.*, **ac·cou′tre·ments**.

Ac·cra (ăk′rə; *native* əkrä′), *n.* a seaport in W Africa on Gulf of Guinea: the capital of Ghana. 135,926 (est. 1948). Also, **Akkra**.

ac·cred·it (əkrĕd′ĭt), *v.t.* 1. to ascribe or attribute to (fol. by *with*): *he was accredited with having said it.* 2. to attribute; consider as belonging: *a discovery accredited to Edison.* 3. to send with credentials: *to accredit an envoy.* 4. to certify as meeting official requirements: *to accredit a school.* 5. to bring into credit; invest with credit or authority. 6. to believe. [t. F: s. *accréditer*]

ac·crete (əkrēt′), *v.*, -**creted**, -**creting**, *adj.* —*v.i.* 1. to grow together; adhere (fol. by *to*). —*v.t.* 2. to add as by growth. —*adj.* 3. *Bot.* grown together. [t. L: m. s. *accrētus*, pp., increased]

ac·cre·tion (əkrē′shən), *n.* 1. an increase by natural growth or by gradual external addition; growth in size or extent. 2. the result of this process. 3. an extraneous addition: *the last part of the legend is a later accretion.* 4. the growing together of separate parts into a single whole. 5. *Law.* increase of property by gradual additions caused by acts of nature, as of land by alluvion. 6. *Pathol.* conglomeration; piling up of substance. [t. L: s. *accrētio*] —**ac·cre′tive**, *adj.*

ac·cru·al (əkrōō′əl), *n.* 1. act or process of accruing. 2. something accrued; accretion.

ac·crue (əkrōō′), *v.i.*, -**crued**, -**cruing**. 1. to happen or result as a natural growth; arise in due course; come or fall as an addition or increment. 2. *Law.* to become a present and enforceable right or demand. [der. *accrue*, obs. n., t. F, orig. fem. pp. of *accroître* increase, g. L *accrescere*] —**ac·crue′ment**, *n.*

accrued interest, the amount of interest accumulated at a given time but not yet paid (or received).

acct., account.

ac·cul·tur·a·tion (əkŭl′chərā′shən), *n.* *Sociol.* the process and result of adopting the culture traits of another group.

ac·cum·bent (əkŭm′bənt), *adj.* 1. reclining: *accumbent posture.* 2. *Bot.* lying against something. [t. L: m. s. *accumbens*, ppr.] —**ac·cum′ben·cy**, *n.*

ac·cu·mu·late (əkū′myəlāt′), *v.*, -**lated**, -**lating**. —*v.t.* 1. to heap up; gather as into a mass; collect: *to accumulate wealth.* —*v.i.* 2. to grow into a heap or mass; form an increasing quantity: *public evils accumulate.* [t. L: m. s. *accumulātus*, pp., heaped up]

ac·cu·mu·la·tion (əkū′myəlā′shən), *n.* 1. a collecting together. 2. that which is accumulated. 3. growth by continuous additions, as of interest to principal.

ac·cu·mu·la·tive (əkū′myəlā′tĭv), *adj.* tending to or arising from accumulation; cumulative. —**ac·cu′mu·la′tive·ly**, *adv.* —**ac·cu′mu·la·tive·ness**, *n.*

ac·cu·mu·la·tor (əkū′myəlā′tər), *n.* 1. one that accumulates. 2. *Brit.* a storage battery. [t. L]

ac·cu·ra·cy (ăk′yərəsĭ), *n.* condition or quality of being accurate; precision or exactness; correctness.

ac·cu·rate (ăk′yərĭt), *adj.* in exact conformity to truth, to a standard or rule, or to a model; free from error or defect: *an accurate typist.* [t. L: m. s. *accūrātus*, pp., exact, cared for] —**ac′cu·rate·ly**, *adv.* —**ac′cu·rate·ness**, *n.* —**Syn.** See **correct**.

ac·curs·ed (əkûr′sĭd, əkûrst′), *adj.* 1. subject to a curse; ruined. 2. worthy of curses; detestable. Also, **ac·curst** (əkûrst′). —**ac·curs·ed·ly** (əkûr′sĭd lĭ), *adv.* —**ac·curs′ed·ness**, *n.*

ac·cu·sa·tion (ăk′yŏŏ zā′shən), *n.* 1. a charge of wrongdoing; imputation of guilt or blame. 2. the specific offense charged: *the accusation is murder.* 3. act of accusing or charging. Also, **ac·cus·al** (əkū′zəl). [t. L: s. *accūsātio*]

ac·cu·sa·ti·val (əkū′zətī′vəl), *adj.* pertaining to the accusative case.

ac·cu·sa·tive (əkū′zətĭv), *adj.* 1. (in Greek, Latin, and English grammar) denoting in Latin and Greek by means of its form, in English by means of its form or its position, a case which has as one of its chief functions the indication of the direct object of a finite verb, as in "the boy loves *the girl*." 2. similar to such a case form in function or meaning. —*n.* 3. the accusative case. 4. a word in that case: *Latin "puellam" may be spoken of as an accusative.* 5. a form or construction of similar meaning. [t. L: m.s. *accūsātīvus*, trans. of Gk. (*ptōsis*) *aitiātikē*

pertaining to that which is caused] —**ac·cu′sa·tive·ly**, *adv.*

ac·cu·sa·to·ri·al (əkū′zətōr′ĭəl), *adj.* pertaining to an accuser. —**ac·cu′sa·to′ri·al·ly**, *adv.*

ac·cu·sa·to·ry (əkū′zə tōr′ĭ), *adj.* containing an accusation; accusing: *he looked at the jury with an accusatory expression.*

ac·cuse (əkūz′), *v.t.*, -**cused**, -**cusing**. 1. to bring a charge against; charge with the fault or crime (*of*). 2. to blame. [t. L: m. s. *accūsāre* accuse, blame; r. ME *acuse*, t. OF] —**ac·cus′er**, *n.* —**ac·cus′ing·ly**, *adv.* —**Syn.** 1. arraign, indict; incriminate; impeach.

ac·cus·tom (əkŭs′təm), *v.t.* to familiarize by custom or use; habituate: *to accustom oneself to cold weather.* [late ME *acustume*(*n*), t. OF: m. *acostumer*, der. *a* to + *costume* custom]

ac·cus·tomed (əkŭs′təmd), *adj.* 1. customary; habitual: *in their accustomed manner.* 2. in the habit of: *accustomed to doing good.* —**ac·cus′tomed·ness**, *n.*

ace (ās), *n.* 1. a single spot or mark on a card or die. 2. a card or die marked with a single spot. 3. (in tennis, badminton, etc.) a. a serve which the opponent fails to touch. b. the point thus scored. 4. a very small quantity, amount, or degree; a particle: *within an ace of winning.* 5. a highly skilled person; an adept: *an ace at tap dancing.* 6. a fighter pilot officially credited with shooting down five or more enemy airplanes. —*adj.* 7. excellent; first in quality; outstanding. [ME *as*, t. OF, g. L, supposedly t. d. Gk., var. of Gk. *heîs* one]

-acea, *Zool.* a suffix of (Latin) names of classes and orders of animals, as in *Crustacea*. [t. L, neut. pl. of *-āceus*. See -ACEOUS]

-aceae, *Bot.* a suffix of (Latin) names of families of plants, as in *Rosaceae*. [t. L, fem. pl. of *-āceus*. See -ACEOUS]

A·cel·da·ma (əsĕl′dəmə), *n.* 1. the "field of blood," near Jerusalem, purchased with the bribe Judas took for betraying Jesus. Matt. 27:8; Acts 1:19. 2. any place of slaughter. [t. L, t. Gk.: m. *Akeldamá*, t. Aram.: m. *hagal damā*]

a·cen·tric (āsĕn′trĭk), *adj.* not centered; having no center.

-aceous, a suffix of adjectives used in scientific terminology, as in *cretaceous, herbaceous*, and in adjectives derived from *-acea, -aceae*. [t. L: m. *-āceus* of the nature of]

a·ceph·a·lous (āsĕf′ələs), *adj.* 1. headless; lacking a distinct head. 2. without a leader. [t. LL: m. *acephalus*, t. Gk.: m. *aképhalos*. See A-⁶, CEPHALOUS]

a·ce·quia (əsā′kyə; *Sp.* äsĕ′kyä), *n.* *Southwestern U.S.* an irrigation ditch. [t. Sp.]

ac·er·bate (*v.* ăs′ərbāt′; *adj.* əsûr′bĭt), *v.*, -**bated**, -**bating**, *adj.* —*v.t.* 1. to make sour or bitter. 2. to exasperate. —*adj.* 3. embittered. [t. L: m. s. *acerbātus*, pp.]

a·cer·bi·ty (əsûr′bətĭ), *n.*, *pl.* -**ties**. 1. sourness, with roughness or astringency of taste. 2. harshness or severity, as of temper or expression. [t. F: m. *acerbité*, t. L: m. s. *acerbitas*]

ac·er·ose (ăs′ərōs′), *adj.* *Bot.* needle-shaped, as the leaves of the pine. Also, **ac·er·ate** (ăs′ər ĭt, -ərāt′), **ac·er·ous** (ăs′ər əs). [t. L: m.s. *acerōsus*, der. *acus* chaff, but confused with *acus* needle]

a·cer·vate (əsûr′vĭt, -vāt), *adj.* *Bot.* heaped; growing in heaps, or in closely compacted clusters. [t. L: m. s. *acervātus*, pp., heaped] —**a·cer′vate·ly**, *adv.*

a·ces·cent (əsĕs′ənt), *adj.* turning sour; slightly sour; acidulous. [t. L: m. s. *acescens*, ppr.] —**a·ces′cence**, **a·ces′cen·cy**, *n.*

acet-, var. of *aceto-*, used before vowels, as in *acetal*.

ac·e·tab·u·lum (ăs′ə tăb′yələm), *n.*, *pl.* -**la** (-lə). *Anat.* the socket in the hipbone which receives the head of the thighbone. [t. L: vinegar cup, saucer] —**ac′e·tab′u·lar**, *adj.*

ac·e·tal (ăs′ə tăl′), *n.* 1. a colorless, volatile fluid, $C_6H_{14}O_2$, used as a hypnotic or solvent. 2. (*pl.*) a class of compounds of aldehydes or ketones with alcohols.

ac·et·al·de·hyde (ăs′ə tăl′də hīd′), *n.* a volatile, colorless, aromatic liquid, CH_3CHO, used commercially in the silvering of mirrors and in organic synthesis.

ac·et·am·ide (ăs′ə tăm′ĭd, -ĭd; əsĕt′ə mĭd′, -mĭd), *n.* *Chem.* the amide of acetic acid, a white crystalline solid, CH_3CONH_2, melting at 80°C. Also, **ac·et·am·id** (ăs′ə tăm′ĭd, ə sĕt′ə mĭd′). [f. ACET(YL) + AMIDE]

ac·et·an·i·lide (ăs′ə tăn′ə lĭd′, -lĭd), *n.* an organic compound, C_8H_9ON, derived by the action of glacial acetic acid upon aniline, used as a remedy for fever, headache, rheumatism, etc., and in the lacquer industry. Also, **ac·et·an·i·lid** (ăs′ə tăn′ə lĭd). [f. ACET(YL) + ANIL(INE) + -IDE]

ac·e·tate (ăs′ə tāt′), *n.* *Chem.* a salt or ester of acetic acid. [f. ACET- + -ATE²] —**ac′e·tat′ed**, *adj.*

acetate rayon, a rayon made from the acetic ester of cellulose, differing from viscose rayon in having a greater strength when wet and in being more sensitive to high temperature.

a·ce·tic (əsē′tĭk, əsĕt′ĭk), *adj.* pertaining to, derived from, or producing vinegar or acetic acid.

acetic acid, a colorless liquid, CH_3COOH, the essential constituent of vinegar, used in the manufacture of acetate rayon and the production of numerous esters as solvents and flavoring agents.

ăct, āble, dâre, ärt; ĕbb, ēqual; ĭf, īce; hŏt, ōver, ôrder, oil, bŏŏk, ōōze, out; ŭp, ūse, ûrge; ə = a in alone; ch, chief; g, give; ng, ring; sh, shoe; th, thin; ŧℏ, that; zh, vision.   See the full key on inside cover.

acetic anhydride, a colorless, pungent fluid, $(CH_3.CO)_2O$, the anhydride of acetic acid, used as a reagent and in the production of plastics, film, and fabrics derived from cellulose.

a·cet·i·fy (ə sĕt'ə fī'), v.t., v.i., **-fied, -fying.** to turn into vinegar; make or become acetous. [f. ACET- + -(I)FY] **—a·cet'i·fi·ca'tion,** n. **—a·cet'i·fi'er,** n.

aceto-, a word element indicating the presence of acetic acid or the radical acetyl. Also, **acet-.** [comb. form repr. L acētum vinegar]

ac·e·tone (ăs'ə tōn'), n. a colorless, volatile, inflammable liquid, $(CH_3)_2CO$, formed in the distillation of acetates, etc., used as a solvent and in smokeless powders, varnishes, etc. [f. ACET- + -ONE]

ac·e·tous (ăs'ə təs, ə sē'-). adj. 1. containing or producing acetic acid. 2. sour; vinegary. Also, **ac·e·tose** (ăs'ə tōs'). [t. LL: m. s. acētōsus]

a·ce·tum (ə sē'təm), n. a preparation made with vinegar or dilute acetic acid as the solvent. [t. L: vinegar]

ac·e·tyl (ăs'ə tĭl), n. Chem. a radical, CH_3CO, in acetic acid. [f. ACET- + -YL] **—ac/e·tyl'ic,** adj.

ac·et·y·late (ə sĕt'ə lāt'), v.t., **-lated, -lating.** Chem. to combine (a compound) with one or more acetyl groups. **—a·cet/y·la'tion,** n.

ac·e·tyl·cho·line (ăs'ə tĭl kō'lēn, -kŏl'ēn, -ĭn), n. an alkaline organic compound, $C_7H_{17}O_3N$, prepared from ergot, and used medicinally to decrease the blood pressure or to set up peristalsis.

a·cet·y·lene (ə sĕt'ə lēn'), n. a colorless gas, C_2H_2, prepared by the action of water on calcium carbide, used in metal welding and cutting, as an illuminant, etc.

acetylene series, Chem. a series of unsaturated aliphatic hydrocarbons containing a triple bond and having the general formula C_nH_{2n-2}.

ac·e·tyl·sal·i·cyl·ic acid (ăs'ə tĭl săl'ə sĭl'ĭk, ə sē'təl-), aspirin.

ace·y·deuc·y (ā'sĭ dū'sĭ, -dōō'-), n. a form of backgammon.

A·chae·an (ə kē'ən), adj. 1. of Achaia or the Achaeans. 2. Greek. **—n. 3.** an inhabitant of Achaia. 4. a Greek. Also, **A·cha·ian** (ə kā'ən, ə kī'-). [f. s. L Achaeus (t. Gk.: m. Achaiós) + -AN]

Achaean League, a political confederation of Achaean and other Greek cities, 281–146 B.C.

A·cha·ia (ə kā'ə, ə kī'ə), n. an ancient country in S Greece, on the Gulf of Corinth. Also, **A·chae·a** (ə kē'ə). See map under **Attica.**

A·cha·tes (ə kā'tēz), n. **1.** (in Vergil's Aeneid) the companion and friend of Aeneas. 2. a faithful comrade.

ache (āk), v., **ached, aching.** **—v.i. 1.** to suffer pain; have or be in continued pain: his whole body ached. 2. Colloq. to be eager; yearn; long. [pseudo-Gk. sp. of ake, ME aken, OE acan] **—n. 3.** pain of some duration, in contrast to sudden twinges or spasmodic pain. [ME; OE æce, der. acan] **—ach/ing·ly,** adv. **—Syn. 3.** See **pain.**

Ach·e·lo·us (ăk'ə lō'əs), n. Gk. Myth. a river god, defeated by Hercules in a struggle over Deianira.

a·chene (ə kēn'), n. Bot. a small, dry, hard, oneseeded, indehiscent fruit. Also, **akene.** [t. NL: m. s. achaenium, f. Gk. a- A⁻⁶ + m. s. Gk. chainein gape + -ium -IUM] **—a·che·ni·al** (ā kē'nĭ əl), adj.

Ach·er·on (ăk'ə rŏn), n. 1. Gk. and Rom. Myth. a river in Hades, over which Charon ferried the souls of the dead. 2. the lower world; hell.

Ache·son (ăch'ə sən), n. Dean Gooderham, born 1893, U.S. Secretary of State, 1949–1953.

à che·val (à shə vàl'), French. by horse; on horseback.

a·chieve (ə chēv'), v., **achieved, achieving. —v.t. 1.** to bring to a successful end; carry through; accomplish. 2. to bring about, as by effort; gain or obtain: to achieve victory. **—v.i. 3.** to accomplish some enterprise; bring about a result intended. [ME acheve(n), t. F: m. achever, der. phrase (venir) à chief = LL ad caput venīre bring to a head] **—a·chiev'a·ble,** adj. **—a·chiev'er,** n. **—Syn. 1.** consummate, complete; effect, execute. See **do.** 2. attain, realize, win.

a·chieve·ment (ə chēv'mənt), n. 1. something accomplished, esp. by valor, boldness, or superior ability; a great or heroic deed. 2. act of achieving; accomplishment: the achievement of one's object.
—Syn. 1. ACHIEVEMENT, EXPLOIT, FEAT are terms for a noteworthy act. ACHIEVEMENT connotes final accomplishment of something noteworthy, after much effort and often in spite of obstacles and discouragements: a scientific achievement. EXPLOIT connotes boldness, bravery, and usually ingenuity: the famous exploit of an aviator. FEAT connotes the performance of something difficult, generally demanding skill and strength: a feat of horsemanship.

achievement age, Psychol. the average age at which any given score is made on an achievement test. Cf. **achievement quotient.**

achievement quotient, Psychol. educational age divided by actual age. Thus, a child of 10 years whose educational achievement equals that of the average 12-year-old has an achievement quotient of 1.2 (commonly expressed as 120). Abbr.: A.Q.

achievement test, Psychol. a test designed to measure the results of learning or teaching, as contrasted with tests of native ability or aptitude.

A·chil·les (ə kĭl'ēz), n. Gk. Legend. the hero of Homer's Iliad, the greatest Greek warrior in the Trojan war, who came to be the ideal of Greek manhood. According to legend, he died when Paris wounded him in the heel, where alone he was vulnerable. **—Ach·il·le·an** (ăk'ə lē'ən), adj.

Achilles heel, a vulnerable spot.

Achilles tendon, Anat. the tendon joining the calf muscles to the heelbone.

a·chlam·y·date (ə klăm'ə dāt', -dĭt), adj. Zool. not chlamydate; having no mantle or pallium.

ach·la·myd·e·ous (ăk'lə mĭd'ēəs), adj. Bot. not chlamydeous; having no floral envelope. [f. A- + s. Gk. chlamỹs cloak + -EOUS]

ach·ro·mat·ic (ăk'rə măt'ĭk), adj. **1.** Optics. free from color due to the decomposition of light in chromatic aberration. 2. Biol. a. containing or consisting of achromatin. b. resisting dyes. 3. Music. without accidentals or changes in key. [f. s. Gk. achrōmatos colorless + -IC] **—ach'ro·mat/i·cal·ly,** adv.

a·chro·ma·tin (ā krō'mə tĭn), n. Biol. that portion of the nucleus of a cell which is less highly colored by staining agents than the rest of the cell.

a·chro·ma·tism (ā krō'mə tĭz'əm), n. freedom from chromatic aberration. Also, **a·chro·ma·tic·i·ty** (ā krō'mə tĭs'ə tĭ).

a·chro·ma·tize (ā krō'mə tīz'), v.t., **-tized, -tizing.** to make achromatic; deprive of color.

a·chro·ma·tous (ā krō'mə təs), adj. without color; of a lighter color than normal. [t. Gk.: m. achrōmatos]

a·chro·mic (ā krō'mĭk), adj. colorless; without coloring matter. Also, **a·chro'mous.** [f. A⁻⁶ + m. Gk. chrōma color + -IC]

a·cic·u·la (ə sĭk'yələ), n., pl. **-lae** (-lē'). a needle-shaped part or process; a spine, bristle, or needlelike crystal. [t. L, dim. of acus needle]

a·cic·u·lar (ə sĭk'yə lər), adj. needle-shaped. **—a·cic'u·lar·ly,** adv.

a·cic·u·late (ə sĭk'yə lĭt, -lāt'), adj. **1.** having aciculae. 2. marked as with needle scratches. 3. needle-shaped; acicular. Also, **a·cic'u·lat'ed.**

a·cic·u·lum (ə sĭk'yə ləm), n., pl. **-lums, -la** (-lə). 1. an acicula. 2. Zool. one of the slender sharp stylets embedded in the parapodia of some annelids, as the Polychaeta. [erroneous var. of ACICULA]

ac·id (ăs'ĭd), n. **1.** Chem. a compound (usually having a sour taste and capable of neutralizing alkalis and reddening blue litmus paper) containing hydrogen which can be replaced by a metal or an electropositive radical to form a salt. Acids are proton donors, and yield hydronium ions in water solution. 2. a substance with a sour taste. **—adj. 3.** Chem. **a.** belonging or pertaining to acids or the anhydrides of acids. **b.** having only a part of the hydrogen of an acid replaced by a metal or its equivalent: an acid phosphate, etc. 4. tasting like vinegar: acid fruits. 5. sour; sharp; ill-tempered: an acid remark, wit, etc. 6. Petrog. containing much silica. [t. L: s. acidus sour] **—ac'id·ly,** adv. **—ac'id·ness,** n.
—Syn. 5. ACID, ASTRINGENT are terms used figuratively of wit or humor. ACID suggests a sharp, biting, or ill-natured quality: an acid joke about an opponent. ASTRINGENT connotes severity but usually also a bracing quality, as of something applied with curative intent: much-needed astringent criticism.

ac·id-fast (ăs'ĭd făst', -fäst'), adj. resistant to decoloring by acid after staining.

ac·id-forming (ăs'ĭd fôr'mĭng), adj. **1.** yielding acid in chemical reaction; acidic. 2. (of food) containing a large amount of acid ash after complete oxidation.

a·cid·ic (ə sĭd'ĭk), adj. **1.** Petrog. containing a large amount of silica. 2. acid-forming (def. 1).

a·cid·i·fy (ə sĭd'ə fī'), v.t., v.i., **-fied, -fying.** to make or become acid; convert into an acid. [f. ACID + -(I)FY] **—a·cid/i·fi'a·ble,** adj. **—a·cid/i·fi·ca'tion,** n. **—a·cid/i·fi'er,** n.

a·cid·i·ty (ə sĭd'ə tĭ), n., pl. **-ties. 1.** quality of being acid. 2. sourness; tartness. 3. excessive acid quality, as of the gastric juice.

ac·i·do·phil (ăs'ə dō fĭl', ə sĭd'ə-), n. Biol. a cell or cell constituent with selective affinity for acid dyes.

ac·i·doph·i·lus (ăs'ə dŏf'ə ləs), n. See **lactobacillus.**

acidophilus milk, a fermented milk which alters the bacterial content of the intestines. The fermenting bacteria are Lactobacilli acidophili.

ac·i·do·sis (ăs'ə dō'sĭs), n. Pathol. poisoning by acids forming within the body under morbid conditions. [irreg. f. ACID + -OSIS] **—ac·i·dot·ic** (ăs'ə dŏt'ĭk), adj.

acid soil, a soil of acid reaction, or having predominance of hydrogen ions, tasting sour in solution.

acid test, a critical test; final analysis.

a·cid·u·late (ə sĭj'ə lāt'), v.t., **-lated, -lating. 1.** to make somewhat acid. 2. to sour; embitter. **—a·cid/u·la'tion,** n.

a·cid·u·lous (ə sĭj'ə ləs), adj. **1.** slightly sour. 2. sharp; caustic. 3. subacid. [t. L: m. acidulus, dim. of acidus]

ac·i·er·ate (ăs'ĭ ə rāt'), v.t., **-ated, -ating.** to convert (iron) into steel. [f. F acier steel + -ATE¹] **—ac/i·er·a'tion,** n.

ac·i·form (ăs'ə fôrm'), adj. needle-shaped; acicular. [f. L ac(us) needle + -(I)FORM]

ac·i·nac·i·form (ăs'ə năs'ə fôrm'), adj. Bot. scimitar-shaped, as a leaf. [f. s. L acinacēs short sword (t. Gk.: m. akinákēs) + -(I)FORM]

Acinaciform leaf

a·cin·i·form (ə sĭn'ə fôrm'), adj. **1.** clustered like grapes. 2. acinous. [f. s. L acinus grape + -(I)FORM]

---

b., blend of, blended;   c., cognate with;   d., dialect, dialectal;   der., derived from;   f., formed from;   g., going back to; m., modification of;   r., replacing;   s., stem of;   t., taken from;   ?, perhaps.   See the full key on inside cover.

ac·i·nous (ăs'ə nəs), *adj.* consisting of acini. Also, **ac·i·nose** (ăs'ə nōs'). [t. L: m. s. *acinōsus* like grapes]

ac·i·nus (ăs'ə nəs), *n., pl.* **-ni** (-nī'). **1.** *Bot.* one of the small drupelets or berries of an aggregate baccate fruit, as the blackberry, etc. **2.** a berry, as a grape, currant, etc. **3.** *Anat.* a. a minute rounded lobule. **b.** the smallest secreting portion of a gland. [t. L: berry, grape]

-acious, an adjective suffix made by adding **-ous** to nouns ending in **-acity** (the *-ty* being dropped), as *audacious.*

-acity, a suffix for nouns denoting quality and the like. [t. F: m. *-acité,* t. L: m. s. *-ācitas,* or directly t. L]

ack-ack (ăk'ăk'), *n. Slang.* **1.** anti-aircraft fire. **2.** anti-aircraft arms. [used by Brit. radio operators for A. A. (anti-aircraft)]

ac·knowl·edge (ăk nŏl'ĭj), *v.t.,* **-edged, -edging. 1.** to admit to be real or true; recognize the existence, truth, or fact of: *to acknowledge belief in God.* **2.** to express recognition or realization of: *to acknowledge an acquaintance by bowing.* **3.** to recognize the authority or claims of: *to acknowledge his right to vote.* **4.** to indicate appreciation or gratitude for. **5.** to admit or certify the receipt of: *to acknowledge a letter.* **6.** *Law.* to own as binding or of legal force: *to acknowledge a deed.* [b. obs. *acknow* (OE *oncnāwan* confess) and *knowledge,* v., admit] **—ac·knowl'edge·a·ble,** *adj.* **—ac·knowl'edg·er,** *n.* **—Syn. 1.** ACKNOWLEDGE, ADMIT, CONFESS agree in the idea of declaring something to be true. ACKNOWLEDGE implies making a statement reluctantly, often about something previously denied: *to acknowledge a fault.* ADMIT especially implies acknowledging something under pressure: *to admit a charge.* CONFESS usually means stating somewhat formally an admission of wrongdoing, crime, or shortcoming: *to confess guilt, to an inability to understand.* **—Ant. 1.** deny

ac·knowl·edg·ment (ăk nŏl'ĭj mant), *n.* **1.** act of acknowledging or admitting. **2.** a recognition of the existence or truth of anything: *the acknowledgment of a sovereign power.* **3.** an expression of appreciation. **4.** a thing done or given in appreciation or gratitude. **5.** *Law.* **a.** declaration by a person before an official that he executed a legal document. **b.** an official certificate of a formal acknowledging. Also, *esp. Brit.,* **ac·knowl'edge·ment.**

a·clin·ic (ā klĭn'ĭk), *adj.* free from inclination or dip of the magnetic needle (applied to an imaginary line near the equator). [f. m.s. Gk. *aklinēs* not bending + -IC]

ac·me (ăk'mĭ), *n.* the highest point. [t. Gk.: m. *akmē*]

ac·ne (ăk'nĭ), *n.* an inflammatory disease of the sebaceous glands, characterized by an eruption (often pustular) of the skin, esp. of the face. [orig. uncert.]

ac·node (ăk'nōd), *n. Math.* a double point belonging to a curve, but separated from other real points of the curve. [f. s. L *acus* needle + NODE] **—ac·no'dal,** *adj.*

a·cock (ə kŏk'), *adv., adj.* in a cocked position.

ac·o·lyte (ăk'ə līt'), *n.* **1.** an altar attendant of minor rank; altar boy. **2.** *Rom. Cath. Ch.* a member of the highest of the four minor orders, ranking next below a subdeacon. **3.** an attendant; an assistant. [ME *acolyt,* t. ML: m. s. *acolitus,* t. Gk.: m. *akólouthos* follower]

A·con·ca·gua (ä'kŏn kä'gwä), *n.* a mountain in W Argentina, in the Andes: the highest peak in the Western Hemisphere. 22,834 ft.

ac·o·nite (ăk'ə nīt'), *n.* **1.** any plant of the ranunculaceous genus *Aconitum,* including plants with poisonous and medicinal properties, as monkshood or wolf'sbane. **2.** an extract or tincture made from the root of any of these plants. Also, **ac·o·ni·tum** (ăk'ə nī'təm). [t. L: m.s. *aconitum,* t. Gk.: m. *akóniton*] **—ac·o·nit·ic** (ăk'ə nĭt'ĭk), *adj.*

a·corn (ā'kôrn, ā'kərn), *n.* the fruit of the oak, a nut in a hardened scaly cup. [d. ME *acorne,* r. ME *akern,* OE *æcern,* c. Icel. *akarn*]

a·cot·y·le·don (ā'kŏt'ə lē'dən), *n. Bot.* a plant without cotyledons. [f. A-⁶ + COTYLEDON] **—a·cot·y·le·don·ous** (ā'kŏt'ə lē'dən əs, -lěd'ən əs, ā kŏt'-), *adj.*

a·cous·tic (ə koōs'tĭk *or, esp. Brit.,* ə koūs'-), *adj.* **1.** Also, **a·cous'ti·cal,** pertaining to the sense or organs of hearing, or to the science of sound. **—n. 2.** a remedy for deafness or imperfect hearing. [t. F: m. *acoustique,* t. Gk.: m.s. *akoustikós*] **—a·cous'ti·cal·ly,** *adv.*

ac·ous·ti·cian (ăk'ōō stĭsh'ən *or, esp. Brit.,* ăk'ou-), *n.* an acoustic engineer.

a·cous·tics (ə koōs'tĭks *or, esp. Brit.,* ə koūs'-), *n.* **1.** *Physics.* the science of sound. **2.** (*construed as pl.*) acoustic properties, as of an auditorium. [pl. of ACOUSTIC. See -ICS]

à cou·vert (à koō věr'), *French.* under cover.

ac·quaint (ə kwānt'), *v.t.* **1.** to make more or less familiar or conversant (fol. by *with*): *to acquaint him with our plan.* **2.** to furnish with knowledge; inform: *to acquaint a friend with one's efforts.* [ME *acointe(n),* t. OF: m. *acointer,* g. LL *adcognitāre* make known]

ac·quaint·ance (ə kwān'təns), *n.* **1.** a person (or persons) known to one, esp. a person with whom one is not on terms of great intimacy. **2.** state of being acquainted; personal knowledge. **—ac·quaint'ance·ship',** *n.* **—Syn. 1.** ACQUAINTANCE, ASSOCIATE, COMPANION, FRIEND refer to a person with whom one is in contact. An ACQUAINTANCE is someone recognized by sight or someone known, though not intimately: *a casual acquaintance.* An ASSOCIATE is a person who is often in one's company, usually because of some work, enterprise, or pursuit in common: *a business associate.* A COMPANION is a person who shares one's activities, fate, or condition: *a traveling companion, companion in despair.* A FRIEND is a person with whom one is on intimate

terms and for whom one feels a warm affection: *a trusted friend.* **2.** association, familiarity, intimacy.

ac·quaint·ed (ə kwān'tĭd), *adj.* having personal knowledge; informed (fol. by *with*): *acquainted with law.*

ac·qui·esce (ăk'wĭ ĕs'), *v.i.,* **-esced, -escing.** to assent tacitly; comply quietly; agree; consent (often fol. by *in*): *to acquiesce in an opinion.* [t. L: m.s. *acquiescere*] **—ac'qui·esc'ing·ly,** *adv.*

ac·qui·es·cence (ăk'wĭ ĕs'əns), *n.* **1.** act or condition of acquiescing or giving tacit assent; a silent submission, or submission with apparent consent. **2.** *Law.* such neglect to take legal proceedings in opposition to a matter as implies consent thereto.

ac·qui·es·cent (ăk'wĭ ĕs'ənt), *adj.* disposed to acquiesce or yield; submissive. **—ac'qui·es'cent·ly,** *adv.*

ac·quire (ə kwīr'), *v.t.,* **-quired, -quiring. 1.** to come into possession of; get as one's own: *to acquire property, a title, etc.* **2.** to gain for oneself through one's actions or efforts: *to acquire learning, a reputation, etc.* [t. L: m.s. *acquīrere;* r. ME *acquere(n),* t. OF: m. *acquerre*] **—ac·quir'a·ble,** *adj.* **—ac·quir'er,** *n.* **—Syn. 1.** obtain, procure, secure; win, earn; attain. See get.

acquired characters, *Biol.* characters that are tho results of environment, use, or disuse, rather than of heredity. Also, **acquired characteristics.**

ac·quire·ment (ə kwīr'mənt), *n.* **1.** act of acquiring, esp. the gaining of knowledge or mental attributes. **2.** (*often pl.*) that which is acquired; attainment.

ac·qui·si·tion (ăk'wə zĭsh'ən), *n.* **1.** act of acquiring or gaining possession: *the acquisition of property.* **2.** something acquired: *a valued acquisition.* [t. L: s. *acquīsītio*]

ac·quis·i·tive (ə kwĭz'ə tĭv), *adj.* tending to make acquisitions; fond of acquiring: *an acquisitive society.* **—ac·quis'i·tive·ly,** *adv.* **—ac·quis'i·tive·ness,** *n.*

ac·quit (ə kwĭt'), *v.t.,* **-quitted, -quitting. 1.** to relieve from a charge of fault or crime; pronounce not guilty (fol. by *of*). **2.** to release or discharge (a person) from an obligation. **3.** to settle (a debt, obligation, claim, etc.). **4.** acquit oneself, **a.** to behave; bear or conduct oneself: *he acquitted himself well in battle.* **b.** to clear oneself: *he acquitted himself of suspicion.* [ME *aquite(n),* t. OF: m. *aquiter.* See AD-, QUIT] **—ac·quit'ter,** *n.* **—Syn. 1.** See absolve.

ac·quit·tal (ə kwĭt'əl), *n.* **1.** act of acquitting; discharge. **2.** state of being acquitted; release. **3.** discharge of an obligation or a debt. **4.** *Law.* judicial deliverance from a criminal charge on a verdict or finding of not guilty.

ac·quit·tance (ə kwĭt'əns), *n.* **1.** act of acquitting. **2.** discharge of or from debt or obligation. **3.** a receipt or quittance.

acr-, var. of acro-, used before vowels.

a·cre (ā'kər), *n.* **1.** a common variable unit of land measure, now equal in the U.S. and Great Britain to 43,560 sq. ft. or ¹/₆₄₀ sq. mile. **2.** (*pl.*) fields or land in general. **3.** (*pl.*) *Colloq.* large quantities. **4.** *Obs.* an open plowed or sowed field. [ME *aker,* OE *æcer,* c. G *acker*]

A·cre (ä'kər, ā'kər), *n.* a seaport in NW Israel: captured during the Third Crusade by Richard the Lion-Hearted, 1191. 20,000 (est. 1956).

a·cre·age (ā'kər ĭj), *n.* acres collectively; extent in acres.

a·cred (ā'kərd), *adj.* having acres; landed.

a·cre-foot (ā'kər foŏt'), *n.* a unit of volume of water in irrigation: the amount covering one acre to a depth of one foot (43,560 cubic feet).

a·cre-inch (ā'kər ĭnch'), *n.* one twelfth of an acre-foot.

ac·rid (ăk'rĭd), *adj.* **1.** sharp or biting to the taste; bitterly pungent; irritating. **2.** violent; stinging: *acrid remarks.* [f. s. L *ācer* sharp + -ID⁴] **—a·crid'i·ty,** **ac'rid·ness,** *n.* **—ac'rid·ly,** *adv.*

ac·ri·dine (ăk'rə dēn'. -dĭn), *n.* a crystalline substance, $C_{13}H_9N$, part of the anthracene fraction of coal tar. It occurs as needle-shaped crystals and is a source of synthetic dyes and drugs.

ac·ri·fla·vine (ăk'rə flā'vĭn, -vēn), *n.* a derivative of acridine, $C_{14}H_{14}N_3Cl$, used as an antiseptic; trypaflavine.

ac·ri·mo·ni·ous (ăk'rə mō'nĭ əs), *adj.* caustic; stinging; bitter; virulent: *an acrimonious answer.* **—ac'ri·mo'ni·ous·ly,** *adv.* **—ac'ri·mo'ni·ous·ness,** *n.*

ac·ri·mo·ny (ăk'rə mō'nĭ), *n., pl.* **-nies.** sharpness or severity of temper; bitterness of expression proceeding from anger or ill nature. [t. L: m. s. *ācrimōnia*]

acro-, a word element meaning "tip," "top," "apex," or "edge," as in *acrogen.* Also, before vowels, **acr-.** [t. Gk.: m. *akro-,* comb. form of *ákros* at the top or end]

ac·ro·bat (ăk'rə băt'), *n.* **1.** a skilled performer who can walk on a tightrope, perform on a trapeze, or do other similar feats. **2.** one who makes striking changes of opinion, as in politics, etc. [t. F: m. *acrobate,* t. Gk.: m. s. *akróbatos* walking on tiptoe] **—ac·ro·bat·ic,** *adj.* **—ac'ro·bat'i·cal·ly,** *adv.*

ac·ro·bat·ics (ăk'rə băt'ĭks), *n. pl.* **1.** the feats of an acrobat; gymnastics. **2.** skilled tricks like those of an acrobat. Also, **ac'ro·bat'ism.**

ac·ro·car·pous (ăk'rə kär'pəs), *adj. Bot.* having the fruit at the end of the primary axis.

ac·ro·dont (ăk'rə dŏnt'), *adj. Anat., Zool.* **1.** with rootless teeth fastened to the alveolar ridge of the jaws. **2.** with sharp tips on the crowns of the cheek teeth.

ac·ro·drome (ăk'rə drōm'), *adj. Bot.* running to a point: said of a nervation with the nerves terminating in, or curving inward to, the point of a leaf. Also, **a·crod·ro·mous** (ə krŏd'rə məs).

ăct, āble, dâre, ärt; ĕbb, ēqual; ĭf, īce; hŏt, ōver, ôrder, oil, bŏok, ōoze, out; ŭp, ūse, ûrge; ə = a in alone; ch, chief; g, give; ng, ring; sh, shoe; th, thin; ŧħ, that; zh, vision. See the full key on inside cover.

ac·ro·gen (ăk/rə jən), *n. Bot.* a flowerless plant growing at the apex only, as ferns and mosses. —**ac·ro·gen·ic** (ăk/rə jĕn/ĭk), **a·crog·e·nous** (ə krŏj/ə nəs), *adj.* —**a·crog/e·nous·ly,** *adv.*

a·cro·le·in (ə krō/lĭ ĭn), *n. Chem.* a yellowish, pungent liquid, acrylic aldehyde, C₃H₄O, obtained in the decomposition of glycerol. [f. ACR(ID) + L *olē(re)* smell + -IN²]

ac·ro·lith (ăk/rə lĭth), *n.* a sculptured figure having only the head and extremities made of marble or other stone. [t. L: s. *acrolithus,* t. Gk.: m. *akrólithos*]

ac·ro·me·gal·ic (ăk/rō mə găl/ĭk), *adj.* 1. pertaining to or suffering from acromegaly. —*n.* 2. a person suffering from acromegaly.

ac·ro·meg·a·ly (ăk/rō mĕg/ə lĭ), *n. Pathol.* a chronic nervous disease characterized by enlargement of the head, feet, hands, and sometimes the chest extremities and other structures, due to dysfunction of the pituitary gland. [t. F: m. *acromégalie.* See ACRO-, MEGALO-]

a·cro·mi·on (ə krō/mĭ ən), *n., pl.* **-mia** (-mĭ ə). *Anat.* the outward end of the spine of the scapula or shoulder blade. See diag. under **shoulder.** [t. NL, t. Gk.: m. *akrōmion*] —**a·cro/mi·al,** *adj.*

a·cron·i·cal (ə krŏn/ə kəl), *adj.* occurring at sunset, as the rising or setting of a star. Also, **a·cron/y·cal.** [f. m.s. Gk. *akrónychos* at nightfall + -AL¹]

ac·ro·nym (ăk/rə nĭm), *n.* a word formed from the initial letters of other words, as WAC (from *Women's Army Corps*) or *loran* (from *long range navigation*). [f. ACR(O)- + m. Gk. *ónyma* name (Doric), modeled on HOMONYM]

a·crop·e·tal (ə krŏp/ə təl), *adj. Bot.* (of an inflorescence) developing upwards, toward the apex.

ac·ro·pho·bi·a (ăk/rə fō/bĭ ə), *n. Psychiatry.* a pathological dread of high places.

a·crop·o·lis (ə krŏp/ə lĭs), *n.* 1. the citadel of an ancient Greek city. 2. **the Acropolis,** the citadel of Athens. [t. L, t. Gk.: m. *akrópolis* the upper city]

ac·ro·spire (ăk/rə spīr/), *n. Bot.* the first sprout appearing in the germination of grain; the developed plumule of the seed. [f. ACRO- + SPIRE¹]

a·cross (ə krôs/, ə krŏs/), *prep.* 1. from side to side of: *a bridge across a river.* 2. on the other side of: *across the sea.* 3. so as to meet or fall in with: *we came across our friends.* —*adv.* 4. *U.S.* from one side to another: *I came across in a steamer.* 5. *U.S.* on the other side: *we'll soon be across.* 6. crosswise: *with arms across.* 7. *U.S. Colloq.* so as to pay or own up: *come across.* [f. A-¹ + CROSS]

a·cros·tic (ə krôs/tĭk, ə krŏs/-), *n.* 1. a series of lines or verses in which the first, last, or other particular letters form a word, phrase, the alphabet, etc. —*adj.* 2. of or forming an acrostic. [t. L: m. s. *acrostichis,* t. Gk.: m. *akrostichis.* See ACRO-, STICHIC] —**a·cros/ti·cal·ly,** *adv.*

ac·ro·tism (ăk/rə tĭz/əm), *n. Pathol.* absence or weakness of the pulse. [f. A-⁶ + m.s. Gk. *krótos* a beat + -ISM] —**a·crot·ic** (ə krŏt/ĭk), *adj.*

ac·ryl (ăk/rĭl), *n. Chem.* the hypothetical radical of the allyl series, C₃H₃O. [f. ACR(OLEIN) + -YL]

a·cryl·ic acids (ə krĭl/ĭk), *Chem.* a series of acids derived from the alkenes, with the general formula, CₙH₂ₙ₋₂O₂.

acrylic esters, *Chem.* the series of esters derived from the acrylic acids.

acrylic resins, *Chem.* the group of thermoplastic resins formed by polymerizing the esters or amides of acrylic acid, used chiefly when transparency is desired. Lucite and plexiglass are in this group.

act (ăkt), *n.* 1. anything done or performed; a doing; deed. 2. the process of doing: *caught in the act.* 3. a decree, edict, law, statute, judgment, resolve, or award: *an act of Parliament or of Congress.* 4. a deed or instrument recording a transaction. 5. one of the main divisions of a play or opera. 6. an individual performance forming part of a variety show, radio program, etc. —*v.i.* 7. to do something; exert energy or force; be employed or operative: *his mind acts sluggishly.* 8. to be employed or operate in a particular way; perform specific duties or functions: *to act as chairman.* 9. to produce effect; perform a function: *the medicine failed to act.* 10. to behave: *to act well under pressure.* 11. to pretend. 12. to perform as an actor: *did she ever act on the stage?* 13. to be capable of being acted on the stage: *his plays don't act well.* 14. to serve or substitute (fol. by *for*). 15. **act on** or **upon,** a. to act in accordance with; follow: *he acted upon my suggestion.* b. to affect: *alcohol acts on the brain.* —*v.t.* 16. to represent (a fictitious or historical character) with one's person: *to act Macbeth.* 17. to feign; counterfeit: *to act outraged virtue.* 18. to behave as: *he acted the fool.* 19. *Obs.* to actuate. [ME, t. L: s. *actum* a thing done, and s. *actus* a doing] —**Syn.** 1. feat, exploit; achievement; transaction. See **action.**

act·a·ble (ăk/tə bəl), *adj.* 1. capable of being acted (on the stage). 2. capable of being carried out in practice. —**act/a·bil/i·ty,** *n.*

Ac·tae·on (ăk tē/ən), *n. Class. Legend.* a hunter, who, having seen Artemis (Diana) bathing, was changed by her into a stag.

actg., acting.

ACTH (ā/sē/tē/āch/), *n.* a hormone extracted from the pituitary glands of hogs, which stimulates the activity of the cortical substance of human adrenal glands. It is especially effective against rheumatic fever, rheumatoid arthritis, and various allergic disorders. [initials of *adreno-cortico-tropic hormone*]

ac·tin (ăk/tən), *n. Biochem.* a globulin present in muscle plasma which, in connection with myosin, plays an important role in muscle contraction.

ac·ti·nal (ăk/tə nəl, ăk tī/-), *adj. Zool.* having tentacles or rays. —**ac/ti·nal·ly,** *adv.*

act·ing (ăk/tĭng), *adj.* 1. serving temporarily; substitute: *acting governor.* 2. that acts; functioning. 3. provided with stage directions; designed to be used for performance: *an acting version of a play.*

ac·tin·i·a (ăk tĭn/ĭ ə), *n., pl.* **-tiniae** (-tĭn/ĭ ē/). a sea anemone of the genus *Actinia.*

ac·tin·ic (ăk tĭn/ĭk), *adj.* 1. pertaining to actinism. 2. (of radiation) chemically active. —**ac·tin/i·cal·ly,** *adv.*

actinic rays, light of shorter wave lengths (violet and ultraviolet) which produces photochemical effects.

ac·tin·i·form (ăk tĭn/ə fôrm/), *adj. Zool.* having a radiate form.

ac·tin·ism (ăk/tə nĭz/əm), *n.* the action or the property of radiant energy of producing chemical change.

ac·tin·i·um (ăk tĭn/ĭ əm), *n. Chem.* a radioactive chemical element, an isotope of mesothorium occurring in pitchblende, and resembling the rare earths in chemical behavior and valence. *Symbol:* Ac; *at. no.:* 89; *at. wt.:* 227; radioactive half life 13.5 years. [f. ACTINO- + -IUM]

actino-, 1. *Chem.* a word element used in compounds relating to actinism or actinic activity, as in *actinotherapy.* 2. *Zool.* a word element used in compounds relating to chambered structures, as in *actinoid.* Also, **actin-.** [t. Gk.: m. *aktīno-,* comb. form of *aktīs* ray]

ac·tin·o·gram (ăk tĭn/ə grăm/), *n.* a record made by an actinograph.

ac·tin·o·graph (ăk tĭn/ə grăf/, -gräf/), *n.* a recording actinometer. —**ac·tin/o·graph/ic,** *adj.*

ac·ti·nog·ra·phy (ăk/tə nŏg/rə fĭ), *n.* the recording of actinic power by the actinograph.

ac·ti·noid (ăk/tə noid/), *adj.* raylike; radiate.

ac·tin·o·lite (ăk tĭn/ə līt/), *n.* a variety of amphibole, occurring in greenish bladed crystals or in masses.

ac·ti·nom·e·ter (ăk/tə nŏm/ə tər), *n.* an instrument for measuring the intensity of radiation, whether by the chemical effects or otherwise.

ac·ti·nom·e·try (ăk/tə nŏm/ə trĭ), *n.* measurement of the intensity of radiation. —**ac·ti·no·met·ric** (ăk/tə nō mĕt/rĭk), **ac/ti·no·met/ri·cal,** *adj.*

ac·ti·no·mor·phic (ăk/tə nō môr/fĭk), *adj.* 1. having radial symmetry. 2. *Bot.* (of certain flowers, as the buttercup) divisible vertically into similar halves by each of a number of planes. Also, **ac/ti·no·mor/phous.**

ac·ti·no·my·cete (ăk/tə nō/mĭ sēt/), *n.* any member of the *Actinomycetes,* a group of microörganisms commonly regarded as filamentous bacteria.

ac·ti·no·my·co·sis (ăk/tə nō/mĭ kō/sĭs), *n. Vet. Sci., Med.* an infectious, inflammatory disease of cattle and other animals and of man, due to certain parasites and causing lumpy, often suppurating tumors, esp. about the jaws. —**ac·ti·no·my·cot·ic** (ăk/tə nō/mĭ kŏt/ĭk), *adj.*

ac·ti·non (ăk/tə nŏn/), *n. Chem.* an inert gas, an isotope of radon. It is a member of the actinium series of radioactive elements. *Symbol:* An; *at. no.:* 86; *at. wt.:* 219.

ac·ti·no·zo·an (ăk/tə nə zō/ən), *n., adj. Zool.* anthozoan.

ac·tion (ăk/shən), *n.* 1. process or state of acting or of being active: *the machine is not now in action.* 2. something done; an act; deed. 3. (*pl.*) habitual or usual acts; conduct. 4. energetic activity. 5. an exertion of power or force: *the action of wind upon a ship's sails.* 6. *Physiol.* a change in organs, tissues, or cells leading to performance of a function, as in muscular contraction. 7. way or manner of moving: *the action of a machine,* or (chiefly British) *of a horse.* 8. the mechanism by which something is operated, as that of a breechloading rifle or a piano. 9. a small battle. 10. military and naval combat. 11. *Poetry and Drama.* the main subject or story, as distinguished from an incidental episode. 12. *Drama.* a. one of the three unities. See **unity** (def. 11). b. an event or happening that is part of a dramatic plot: *the action of a scene, a bit of action.* 13. the gestures or deportment of an actor or speaker. 14. *Fine Arts.* the appearance of animation, movement, or passion given to figures by their attitude, position, or expression. 15. *Law.* a. a proceeding instituted by one party against another. b. the right of bringing it. c. **take action,** to commence legal proceedings. [t. L: s. *actio;* r. ME *accioun,* t. OF] —**ac/tion·less,** *adj.* —**Syn.** 2. ACTION, ACT both mean something done. ACTION applies esp. to the doing; ACT to the result of the doing. An ACTION usually lasts through some time and consists of more than one act: *to take action on a petition.* An ACT is single and of slight duration: *an ac. of kindness.* 9. See **battle¹.**

ac·tion·a·ble (ăk/shən ə bəl), *adj.* 1. furnishing ground for a law suit. 2. liable to a law suit. —**ac/tion·a·bly,** *adv.*

Ac·ti·um (ăk/tĭ əm, -shĭ/-), *n.* a promontory in NW ancient Greece: Antony and Cleopatra were defeated by Agrippa in a naval battle near here, 31 B.C.

ac·ti·vate (ăk/tə vāt/), *v.t.,* **-vated, -vating.** 1. to make active. 2. *Physics.* to render radioactive. 3. to aerate (sewage) as a purification measure. 4. *Chem.* a. to make more active: *to activate carbon, a catalyst, molecules.* b. to hasten (reactions) by various means, such as heating. 5. *U.S. Army* to place (a military unit) in an active status by assigning to it officers, enlisted men, and all necessary equipment for war strength and training for war service. —**ac/ti·va/tion,** *n.*

ac·ti·va·tor (ăk/tə vā/tər), *n.* a catalyst.

ac·tive (ăk′tĭv), *adj.* **1.** in a state of action; in actual progress or motion: *active hostilities.* **2.** constantly engaged in action; busy: *an active life.* **3.** having the power of quick motion; nimble: *an active animal.* **4.** moving in considerable volume; brisk; lively: *an active market.* **5.** causing change; capable of exerting influence: *active treason.* **6.** *Gram.* denoting a voice of verb inflection, in which the subject is represented as performing the action expressed by the verb (opposed to *passive*). For example: In English, *he writes the letter* (active); *the letter was written* (passive). **7.** requiring action; practical: *the intellectual and the active mental powers.* **8.** (of a volcano) in eruption. **9.** *Accounting.* profitable; busy: *active accounts* (ones having current transactions). **10.** interest-bearing: *active paper.* **11.** *Med.* acting quickly; producing immediate effects: *active remedies.* —*n.* **12.** *Gram.* **a.** the active voice. **b.** a form or construction in that voice. [t. L: m.s. *activus*; r. ME *actif*, t. F] —**ac′tive·ly**, *adv.* —**ac′tive·ness**, *n.*
—**Syn. 1.** acting; working; operative. ACTIVE, ENERGETIC, STRENUOUS, VIGOROUS imply a liveliness and briskness in accomplishing something. ACTIVE suggests quickness and diligence as opposed to laziness or dilatory methods: *an active and useful person.* ENERGETIC suggests forceful and intense, sometimes nervous, activity: *conducting an energetic campaign.* STRENUOUS implies eager and zealous activity with a sense of urgency: *making a strenuous effort.* VIGOROUS suggests strong, effective activity: *using vigorous measures to accomplish an end.* **3.** agile, sprightly.

active duty, *Mil.* **1.** the status of full duty: *on active duty.* **2.** full duty.

active immunity, immunity achieved by the manufacture of antibodies within the organism.

active service, 1. *U.S. Army.* state of being on full duty with full pay. **2.** the performance of military duty in the field in time of war.

ac·tiv·ist (ăk′tə vĭst′), *n.* an especially zealous worker, as in a political cause. —**ac′tiv·ism**, *n.*

ac·tiv·i·ty (ăk tĭv′ə tĭ), *n., pl.* **-ties. 1.** state of action; doing. **2.** quality of acting promptly; energy. **3.** a specific deed or action; sphere of action: *social activities.* **4.** an exercise of energy or force; an active movement or operation. **5.** liveliness; agility.

act of God, *Law.* a direct, sudden, and irresistible action of natural forces, such as could not humanly have been foreseen or prevented.

act of war, an illegal act of aggression by a country against another with which it is nominally at peace.

ac·tor (ăk′tər), *n.* **1.** one who represents fictitious or historical characters in a play, motion picture, broadcast, etc. **2.** one who acts; doer. [t. L]

ac·tress (ăk′trĭs), *n.* a female actor.

Acts of the Apostles, the fifth book in the New Testament. Also, **Acts.**

ac·tu·al (ăk′chŏŏ əl), *adj.* **1.** existing in act or fact; real. **2.** now existing; present: *the actual position of the moon.* **3.** *Obs.* exhibited in action. [t. LL: s. *actuālis* active, practical; r. ME *actuel*, t. OF] —**ac′tu·al·ness**, *n.* —Syn. **1.** true, genuine. See **real**[1].

actual grace, *Rom. Cath. Ch.* supernatural help given by God to enlighten the mind and strengthen the will to do good and avoid evil.

ac·tu·al·i·ty (ăk′chŏŏ ăl′ə tĭ), *n., pl.* **-ties. 1.** actual existence; reality. **2.** (*pl.*) actual conditions or circumstances; facts: *he had to adjust to the actualities of life.*

ac·tu·al·ize (ăk′chŏŏ ə līz′), *v.t.*, **-ized, -izing.** to make actual; realize in action or fact. —**ac′tu·al·i·za′tion**, *n.*

ac·tu·al·ly (ăk′chŏŏ ə lĭ), *adv.* as an actual or existing fact; really.

actual sin, *Theol.* the sin of an individual, as contrasted with original sin.

ac·tu·ar·y (ăk′chŏŏ ĕr′ĭ), *n., pl.* **-aries. 1.** *Insurance.* an officer who computes risks, rates, and the like according to probabilities indicated by recorded facts. **2.** (formerly) a registrar or clerk. [t. L: m.s. *actuārius*] —**ac·tu·ar·i·al** (ăk′chŏŏ âr′ĭ əl), *adj.* —**ac′tu·ar·i·al·ly**, *adv.*

ac·tu·ate (ăk′chŏŏ āt′), *v.t.*, **-ated, -ating. 1.** to incite to action: *actuated by selfish motives.* **2.** to put into action. [t. ML: m. s. *actuātus*, pp.] —**ac′tu·a′tion**, *n.* —**ac′tu·a′tor**, *n.*

ac·u·ate (ăk′yŏŏ ĭt, -āt′), *adj.* sharpened; pointed. [t. ML: m.s. *acuātus*, pp.]

a·cu·i·ty (ə kū′ə tĭ), *n.* sharpness; acuteness: *acuity of vision.* [t. L: m.s. *acuitas*]

a·cu·le·ate (ə kū′lĭ ĭt, -āt′), *adj.* **1.** *Biol.* having or denoting any sharp-pointed structure. **2.** having a slender ovipositor or sting, as the hymenopterous insects. **3.** pointed; stinging. Also, **a·cu′le·at′ed.** [t. L: m.s. *aculeātus* prickly]

a·cu·men (ə kū′mən), *n.* quickness of perception; mental acuteness; keen insight. [t. L]

a·cu·mi·nate (*adj.* ə kū′mə nĭt, -nāt′; *v.* ə kū′mə nāt′), *adj., v.,* **-nated, -nating.** —*adj.* **1.** *Bot., Zool., etc.* pointed; tapering to a point. —*v.t.* **2.** to make sharp or keen. [t. L: m.s. *acūminātus*, pp.] —**a·cu′mi·na′tion**, *n.*

a·cut·ance (ə kū′təns), *n.* a measure of the sharpness with which a film can reproduce the edge of an object.

a·cute (ə kūt′), *adj.* **1.** sharp at the end; ending in a point (opposed to *blunt* or *obtuse*). **2.** sharp in effect; intense; poignant: *acute sorrow.* **3.** severe; crucial: *an acute shortage.* **4.** brief and

Acuminate leaf

severe, as disease (opposed to *chronic*). **5.** sharp or penetrating in intellect, insight, or perception: *an acute observer.* **6.** having quick sensibility; susceptible to slight impressions: *acute eyesight.* **7.** high in pitch, as sound (opposed to *grave*). **8.** *Geom., etc.* (of an angle) less than 90°. See diag. under **angle**. **9.** *Gram.* designating or having a particular accent (′) indicating: **a.** (orig.) a raised pitch (as in ancient Greek). **b.** (later) stress (as in the Spanish *adiós*), quality of sound (as in the French *résumé*), vowel length (as in Hungarian), etc. —*n.* **10.** the acute accent. [t. L: m.s. *acūtus*, pp., sharpened] —**a·cute′ly**, *adv.* —**a·cute′ness**, *n.*
—**Syn. 5.** keen, astute, discerning, perspicacious; sharp-witted. ACUTE, PENETRATING, SHREWD imply a keenness of understanding, perception, or insight. ACUTE suggests particularly a clearness of perception and a realization of related meanings: *an acute intellect.* PENETRATING adds the idea of depth of perception and a realization of implications: *a wise and penetrating judgment.* SHREWD adds the idea of knowing how to apply practically (or to one's own advantage) what one perceives and understands: *wary and shrewd.*

-acy, a suffix of nouns of quality, state, office, etc., many of which accompany adjectives in *-acious* or nouns or adjectives in *-ate*, as in *efficacy, fallacy, etc., advocacy, primacy, etc., accuracy, delicacy, etc.* [repr. L *-ācia, -ātia,* and Gk. *-āteia*]

a·cy·clic (ā sī′klĭk, ā sĭk′lĭk), *adj. Bot.* not cyclic; not arranged in whorls. [f. A-[6] + CYCLIC]

ad[1] (ăd), *n. Colloq.* advertisement.

ad[2] (ăd), *n. Tennis.* advantage (def. 5).

ad-, a prefix of direction, tendency, and addition, attached chiefly to stems not found as words themselves, as in *advert, advent.* Also, **ac-, af-, ag-, al-, an-, ap-, ar-, as-, at-,** and **a-**[5]. [t. L, repr. *ad*, prep., to, toward, at, about]

-ad, 1. a suffix forming nouns denoting a collection of a certain number, as in *triad.* **2.** a suffix found in words and names proper to Greek myth, as in *dryad, Pleiad.* **3.** a literary suffix used in titles imitating *Iliad,* as in *Dunciad.* [repr. Gk. *-áda,* acc. (nom. *-ás*)]

A.D., (L *anno Domini*) in the year of our Lord; since Christ was born. From 20 B.C. to A.D. 50 is 70 years.

a·dac·ty·lous (ā dăk′tə ləs), *adj. Zool.* without fingers or toes. [f. A-[6] + DACTYL + -OUS]

ad·age (ăd′ĭj), *n.* a proverb. [t. F, t. L: m.s. *adagium*]

a·da·gio (ə dä′jō, -zhĭ ō′; *It.* ä dä′jō), *adv., adj., n., pl.* **-gios.** *Music, etc.* —*adv.* **1.** in a leisurely manner; slowly. —*adj.* **2.** slow. —*n.* **3.** an adagio movement or piece. [It.]

Ad·am (ăd′əm), *n.* **1.** the name of the first man: progenitor of the human race. Genesis 2:7. **2.** the old Adam, the evil inherent in man. —**A·dam·ic** (ə dam′ĭk), *adj.*

Ad·am (ăd′əm), *n.* **1. James,** 1730–94, and his brother, **Robert,** 1728–92, British architects and furniture designers in the classic manner. —*adj.* **2.** (of furniture) pertaining to or in the style of these two brothers.

Ad·am-and-Eve (ăd′əm ənd ēv′), *n. U.S.* the putty-root (plant).

ad·a·mant (ăd′ə mănt′ *or, esp. Brit.,* -mənt), *n.* **1.** (in ancient times) some impenetrably hard substance, variously identified later as the diamond or loadstone. **2.** any impenetrably hard substance. —*adj.* **3.** hard as adamant; adamantine. **4.** hard-hearted. [t. L: s. *adamas,* t. Gk.; r. ME *adamaunt,* t. OF; and OE *athamans* (repr. LL var. of *adamas*)]

ad·a·man·tine (ăd′ə măn′tĭn, -tēn, -tīn), *adj.* **1.** impenetrable. **2.** like a diamond in luster.

Ad·am·ite (ăd′ə mīt′), *n.* **1.** a descendant of Adam; a human being. **2.** a nudist. —**Ad·am·i·tic** (ăd′ə mĭt′ĭk), *adj.*

Ad·ams (ăd′əmz), *n.* **1. Charles Francis,** 1807–86, U.S. statesman: minister to Great Britain, 1861–68 (son of John Quincy Adams). **2. Franklin Pierce,** ("F.P.A.") 1881–1960, U.S. author and columnist. **3. Henry (Brooks),** 1838–1918, U.S. historian, writer, and teacher (son of Charles Francis Adams). **4. James Truslow** (trŭs′lō), 1878–1949, U.S. historian. **5. John,** 1735–1826, second president of the U.S., 1797–1801; leader in the American Revolution. **6. John Quincy** (kwĭn′sĭ), 1767–1848, sixth president of the U.S., 1825–1829; secretary of state, 1817–25 (son of John Adams). **7. Maude,** (*Maude Kiskadden*) 1872–1953, U.S. actress. **8. Samuel,** 1722–1803, leader in the American Revolution. **9. Samuel Hopkins,** 1871–1958, U.S. writer.

Ad·ams (ăd′əmz), *n.* **Mount, 1.** a peak in SW Washington, in the Cascade Range. 12,307 ft. **2.** a peak in N New Hampshire, in the White Mountains. 5798 ft.

Adam's ale, *Colloq.* water.

Adam's apple, a projection of the thyroid cartilage at the front of the (male) throat.

ad·ams·ite (ăd′əmz īt′), *n.* a yellow irritant smoke, containing a form of arsenic that is poisonous, used as a harassing agent. *Symbol:* DM. [named after Major Roger Adams, U.S. soldier (born 1889), who invented it. See -ITE[1]]

Ad·am's-nee·dle (ăd′əmz nē′dəl), *n. U.S.* a species of yucca, *Yucca filamentosa,* much cultivated for ornament.

A·da·na (ä′dä nä′), *n.* a city in S Turkey., 117,642 (1950).

a·dapt (ə dăpt′), *v.t.* to make suitable to requirements; adjust or modify fittingly. [t. L: s. *adaptāre*] —Syn. fit, accommodate, suit, compose, reconcile. See **adjust.**

a·dapt·a·ble (ə dăp′tə bəl), *adj.* **1.** capable of being adapted. **2.** able to adapt oneself easily to new conditions. —**a·dapt′a·bil′i·ty, a·dapt′a·ble·ness**, *n.*

ad·ap·ta·tion (ăd/ǝp tā/shǝn), *n.* **1.** act of adapting. **2.** state of being adapted; adjustment. **3.** something produced by adapting. **4.** *Biol.* **a.** alteration in the structure or function of organisms which fits them to survive and multiply in a changed environment. **b.** a form or structure modified to fit changed environment. **5.** *Physiol.* the response of sensory receptor organs, as those of vision, touch, temperature, olfaction, audition, and pain, to changed, constantly applied, environmental conditions. **6.** Also, **a·dap·tion** (ǝ dăp/shǝn). *Sociol.* a slow, usually unconscious modification of individual and social activity in adjustment to cultural surroundings. —**ad/ap·ta/tion·al**, *adj.*

a·dapt·er (ǝ dăp/tǝr), *n.* **1.** one that adapts. **2.** a device for fitting together parts having different sizes or designs. **3.** an accessory to convert a machine, tool, etc., to a new or modified use. Also, **a·dap/tor.**

a·dap·tive (ǝ dăp/tĭv), *adj.* serving to adapt; showing adaptation: *adaptive coloring of a chameleon.* —**a·dap/tive·ly,** *adv.* —**a·dap/tive·ness,** *n.*

A·dar (ǝdär/), *n.* (in the Jewish calendar) the sixth month of the year. [Heb.]

ad a·stra per a·spe·ra (ăd ăs/trǝ pǝr ăs/pǝ rǝ), *Latin.* to the stars through difficulties (motto of Kansas).

ad·ax·i·al (ăd ăk/sĭ ǝl), *adj. Bot.* situated on the side toward the axis. [f. AD- + L *axi*(s) axle + -AL¹]

A.D.C., aide-de-camp.

ad cap·tan·dum (vul·gus) (ăd kăp tăn/dǝm vŭl/gǝs), *Latin.* in order to please (the mob); emotional.

add (ăd), *v.t.* **1.** to unite or join so as to increase the number, quantity, size, or importance: *to add another stone to the pile.* **2.** to find the sum of (often fol. by *up*). **3.** to say or write further. **4.** to include (fol. by *in*). —*v.i.* **5.** to perform the arithmetical operation of addition. **6.** to be or serve as an addition (fol. by *to*): *to add to one's grief.* **7.** to make the desired or expected total (fol. by *up*): *these figures don't add up.* [ME *adde*(n), t. L: m. *addere*] —**add/a·ble, add/i·ble,** *adj.* —**add/er,** *n.* —**Syn. 1.** append; attach.

Ad·dams (ăd/ǝmz), *n.* **Jane,** 1860–1935, U.S. social worker and writer.

ad·dax (ăd/ăks), *n.* a large, pale-colored antelope, *Addax nasomaculatus,* of North Africa, with loosely spiral horns. [t. L; of African orig.]

added line, *Music.* a leger line. See illus. under **leger line.**

ad·dend (ăd/ĕnd, ǝ dĕnd/), *n. Math.* summand.

Addax (3 ft. high at the shoulder, 6 ft. long, horns 3 or 4 ft. long)

ad·den·dum (ǝ dĕn/dǝm), *n.,* *pl.* **-da** (-dǝ). **1.** a thing to be added; an addition. **2.** an appendix to a book. **3.** *Mach.* **a.** that part of a tooth which projects beyond the pitch circle or pitch line of a toothed wheel or rack. **b.** Also, **addendum circle.** an imaginary circle touching the ends of the teeth of a toothed wheel. [t. L, neut. ger. of *addere* add]

ad·der (ăd/ǝr), *n.* **1.** the common European viper, *Vipera berus,* a small venomous snake, widespread in northern Eurasia. **2.** any of various other snakes, venomous or harmless, resembling the viper. [var. of ME *nadder* (a *nadder* being taken as *an adder*). OE *nædre*]

ad·der's-mouth (ăd/ǝrz mouth/), *n. U.S.* **1.** either of two small terrestrial orchids, *Malaxis monophyllos* and *M. unifolia,* natives of North America, bearing minute white or greenish flowers. **2.** any of the delicate North American orchids of the genus *Pogonia.*

ad·der's-tongue (ăd/ǝrz tŭng/), *n.* **1.** a fern of the genus *Ophioglossum,* with a fruiting spike. **2.** *U.S.* the American species of dogtooth violet.

ad·dict (*n.* ăd/ĭkt; *v.* ǝ dĭkt/), *n.* **1.** one who is addicted to a practice or habit: *a drug addict.* —*v.t.* **2.** to give (oneself) over, as to a habit or pursuit; apply or devote habitually (fol. by *to*): *addict oneself to science.* [t. L: s. *addictus,* pp., adjudged, devoted]

ad·dict·ed (ǝ dĭk/tĭd), *adj.* devoted or given up (to a practice or habit) (fol. by *to*): *addicted to the drug habit.* —**ad·dict/ed·ness,** *n.*

ad·dic·tion (ǝ dĭk/shǝn), *n.* state of being given up to some habit, practice, or pursuit, esp. to narcotics.

Ad·dis A·ba·ba (ăd/ĭs ä/bǝ bä/), the capital of Ethiopia, in the central part. 400,000 (est. 1954).

Ad·di·son (ăd/ǝ sǝn), *n.* **Joseph,** 1672–1719, British essayist and poet. —**Ad·di·so·ni·an** (ăd/ǝ sō/nĭ ǝn), *adj.*

Addison's disease, *Pathol.* a disease characterized by asthenia, low blood pressure, and a brownish coloration of the skin, due to disturbance of the suprarenal glands. [named after T. *Addison,* British physician (1793–1860), who first described it]

ad·dit·a·ment (ǝ dĭt/ǝ mǝnt), *n.* something added; an addition. [t. L: s. *additāmentum.*]

ad·di·tion (ǝ dĭsh/ǝn), *n.* **1.** act or process of adding or uniting. **2.** the process of uniting two or more numbers into one sum, denoted by the symbol +. **3.** the result of adding; anything added. **4.** *U.S.* wings, rooms, etc., added to a building or abutting land added to real estate already owned. **5.** *Obs. except Law.* a particularizing designation added to a person's name, as *Plaintiff*

in *John Doe, Plaintiff.* **6. in addition to,** besides; as well as. [t. L: s. *additio*; r. ME *addicioun,* t. F] —**Syn. 3.** increase, enlargement; increment; accession, supplement; appendix. ADDITION, ACCESSORY, ADJUNCT, ATTACHMENT mean something joined onto or used with something else. ADDITION is the general word, carrying no implication of size, importance, or kind, but merely that of being joined to something previously existing: *an addition to an income, to a building, to one's cares.* An ACCESSORY is a subordinate addition to a more important thing, for the purpose of aiding, completing, ornamenting, etc.: *accessories to a costume.* An ADJUNCT is a subordinate addition that aids or assists a main thing or person but is often separate: *a second machine as an adjunct to the first.* An ATTACHMENT is an accessory part which may be easily connected and removed: *a sewing machine attachment for pleating.*

ad·di·tion·al (ǝ dĭsh/ǝn ǝl), *adj.* added; supplementary: *additional information.* —**ad·di/tion·al·ly,** *adv.*

ad·di·tive (ăd/ǝ tĭv), *adj.* to be added; of the nature of an addition; characterized by addition: *an additive process.* [t. L: m.s. *additīvus*] —**ad/di·tive·ly,** *adv.*

ad·dle (ăd/ǝl), *v.,* **-dled, -dling,** *adj.* —*v.t., v.i.* **1.** to make or become muddled or confused. **2.** to make or become spoiled or rotten, as eggs. —*adj.* **3.** mentally confused; muddled, as in the combinations **ad/dle-brained/, ad/dle-head/ed. 4.** rotten: *addle eggs.* [OE *adela* liquid filth, c. MLG *adele* mud]

ad·dress (*n.* ǝ drĕs/, ăd/rĕs; *v.* ǝ drĕs/), *n., v.,* **-dressed** or **-drest, -dressing.** —*n.* **1.** a formal speech or writing directed to a person or a group of persons: *an address on current problems.* **2.** a direction as to name and residence inscribed on a letter, etc. **3.** a place where a person lives or may be reached. **4.** manner of speaking to persons; personal bearing in conversation. **5.** skillful management; ready skill: *to handle a matter with address.* **6.** *Govt.* a request to the executive by the legislature to remove a judge for unfitness. **7.** (*usually pl.*) attentions paid by a lover; courtship. **8.** (*usually cap.*) the reply to the King's speech in the English parliament. **9.** *Obs.* preparation. —*v.t.* **10.** to direct speech or writing to: *to address an assembly, how does one address the governor?* **11.** to direct to the ear or attention: *to address a warning to someone.* **12.** to apply in speech (used reflexively, fol. by *to*): *he addressed himself to the chairman.* **13.** to direct for delivery; put a direction on: *to address a letter.* **14.** *Com.* to consign or entrust to the care of another, as agent or factor. **15.** to direct the energy or force of (used reflexively, fol. by *to*): *he addressed himself to the work in hand.* **16.** to pay court to; woo; court. **17.** *Golf.* to adjust and apply the club to (the ball) in preparing for a stroke. **18.** *Obs. except in Golf.* to give direction to; aim. **19.** *Obs.* to prepare. —*v.i.* **20.** *Obs.* to make an appeal. **21.** *Obs.* to make preparations. [ME *addresse*(n), t. F: m. *adresser,* earlier *adrecier,* ult. der. L *ad* to + *directus* straight] —**ad·dress/er, ad·dres/sor,** *n.* —**Syn. 1.** discourse, lecture. See **speech. 5.** adroitness, dexterity; cleverness, ingenuity; tact.

ad·dress·ee (ǝ drĕ sē/, ăd/rĕ-), *n. U.S.* one to whom anything is addressed.

ad·dress·so·graph (ǝ drĕs/ǝ grăf/, -gräf/), *n.* **1.** a machine that prints addresses upon envelopes, etc., from stencils. **2.** (*cap.*) a trademark for this machine.

ad·duce (ǝ dūs/, ǝ dōōs/), *v.t.,* **-duced, -ducing.** to bring forward in argument; cite as pertinent or conclusive: *to adduce reasons.* [t. L: m.s. *addūcere* lead to] —**ad·duce/a·ble, ad·duc/i·ble,** *adj.* —**ad·duc/er,** *n.*

ad·du·cent (ǝ dū/sǝnt, ǝ dōō/-), *adj. Physiol.* drawing toward; adducting. [t. L: s. *addūcens,* ppr., leading to]

ad·duct (ǝ dŭkt/), *v.t. Physiol.* to draw toward the main axis (opposed to *abduct*). [t. L: s. *adductus,* pp., led to] —**ad·duc/tive,** *adj.* —**ad·duc/tor,** *n.*

ad·duc·tion (ǝ dŭk/shǝn), *n.* **1.** *Physiol.* the action of the adductor or adducent muscles. **2.** act of adducing.

Ade (ād), *n.* **George,** 1866–1944, U. S. humorist.

-ade¹, 1. a suffix found in nouns denoting action or process, product or result of action, person or persons acting, often irregularly attached, as in *blockade, escapade, masquerade.* **2.** a noun suffix indicating a drink made of a particular fruit, as in *orangeade.* [t. F, t. Pr.: m. *-ada,* g. L *-āta*; in some words -ADE is for Sp. and Pg. *-ado,* It. *-ato,* g. L *-ātus*]

-ade², a collective suffix like **-ad** (def. 1), as in *decade* [t. F, t. Gk.: m. *-áda* (acc.), *-ás* (nom.)]

Ad·e·laide (ăd/ǝ lād/), *n.* a city in S Australia: the capital of the state of South Australia. pop. with suburbs 484,093 (1954).

A·dé·lie Coast (ǝ dē/lē/, ăd/ǝ lē/), a coastal region of Antarctica south of Australia: under French sovereignty.

a·demp·tion (ǝ dĕmp/shǝn), *n. Law.* the failure of a specific legacy because the subject matter no longer belongs to the testator's estate at his death. [t. L: s. *ademptio*]

A·den (ä/dǝn, ā/-), *n.* **1.** a British protectorate in SW Arabia. ab. 800,000 pop.; ab. 112,000 sq. mi. **2.** a British colony adjoining this protectorate. 138,441 pop. (1955); 80 sq. mi. **3.** the capital of this protectorate and colony: a seaport. 99,285 pop. (1955). **4.** Gulf of, an arm of the Arabian Sea between the E tip of Africa and the Arabian peninsula.

Aden (defs. 1, 2)

ad·e·nal·gi·a (ăd′ə năl′jĭ ə), *n. Pathol.* pain in a gland.

A·de·nau·er (ăd′nou ər; *Ger.* ä′də nou′ər), *n.* **Konrad** (kŏn′rad; *Ger.* kōn′rät), born 1876, chancellor of the West German Federal Republic 1949–1963.

ad·e·nine (ăd′ə nĭn, -nēn′, -nĭn′), *n.* an alkaloid, $C_5H_5N_5$, obtained from purine, found as a component of nucleic acid in such organs as the pancreas, spleen, etc.

adeno-, *Anat.* a word element meaning "gland." Also, before vowels, **aden-**. [t. Gk., comb. form of *adēn*]

ad·e·noid (ăd′ə noid′), *n.* **1.** (*usually pl.*) an enlarged mass of lymphoid tissue in the upper pharynx, as in children, often preventing nasal breathing. —*adj.* **2.** Also, **ad′e·noi′dal.** pertaining to the lymphatic glands. [t. Gk.: m.s. *adenoeidēs* glandular]

ad·e·noid·ec·to·my (ăd′ə noi děk′tə mĭ′), *n., pl.* **-mies.** *Surg.* the operation of removing the adenoids.

ad·e·no·ma (ăd′ə nō′mə), *n., pl.* **-mata** (-mə tə), **-mas.** *Pathol.* **1.** a tumor originating in a gland. **2.** a tumor of glandlike structure. —**ad·e·nom·a·tous** (ăd′ə nŏm′ə təs, -nō′mə-), *adj.*

ad·e·no·vi·rus (ăd′ə nō vī′rəs), *n.* a virus which attacks the lymph glands. [f. ADENO- + VIRUS]

ad·ept (*n.* ăd′ĕpt, ə dĕpt′; *adj.* ə dĕpt′), *n.* **1.** one who has attained proficiency; one fully skilled in anything. —*adj.* **2.** well-skilled; proficient. [t. L: s. *adeptus*, pp., having attained] —**a·dept′ly**, *adv.* —**a·dept′ness**, *n.*

ad·e·qua·cy (ăd′ə kwə sĭ′), *n.* state or quality of being adequate; a sufficiency for a particular purpose.

ad·e·quate (ăd′ə kwĭt), *adj.* **1.** equal to the requirement or occasion; commensurate; fully sufficient, suitable, or fit (often fol. by *to*). **2.** *Law.* reasonably sufficient for starting legal action: *adequate grounds.* [t. L: m.s. *adaequātus*, pp., equalized] —**ad′e·quate·ly**, *adv.* —**ad′e·quate·ness**, *n.* —**Syn. 1.** satisfactory; capable.

à deux (ȧ dœ′), *French.* of or for two; two at a time.

ad ex·tre·mum (ăd ĕks trē′məm), *Latin.* to the extreme; at last; finally.

ad fin., (L *ad finem*) to, toward, or at the end.

ad glo·ri·am (ăd glôr′ĭ ăm′) *Latin.* for glory.

ad·here (ăd hǐr′), *v.i.* **-hered, -hering. 1.** to stick fast; cleave; cling (fol. by *to*). **2.** to be devoted; be attached as a follower or upholder (fol. by *to*): *to adhere to a party, a leader, a church, a creed, etc.* **3.** to hold closely or firmly (fol. by *to*): *to adhere to a plan.* **4.** *Obs.* to be consistent. [t. L: m.s. *adhaerēre*] —**ad·her′er,** *n.* —**Syn. 1.** See **stick.**

ad·her·ence (ăd hǐr′əns), *n.* **1.** quality of adhering; fidelity; steady attachment: *adherence to a party, rigid adherence to rules.* **2.** act or state of adhering; adhesion.

ad·her·ent (ăd hǐr′ənt), *n.* **1.** one who follows or upholds a leader, cause, etc.; supporter; follower (fol. by *of*). —*adj.* **2.** sticking; clinging; adhering. **3.** *Bot.* adnate. **4.** *Gram.* standing before a noun. —**ad·her′ent·ly,** *adv.* —**Syn. 1.** See **follower.**

ad·he·sion (ăd hē′zhən), *n.* **1.** act or state of adhering, or of being united: *the adhesion of parts united by growth.* **2.** steady attachment of the mind or feelings; adherence. **3.** assent; concurrence. **4.** *Physics.* the molecular force exerted across the surface of contact between unlike liquids and solids which resists their separation. **5.** *Pathol.* **a.** the abnormal union of adjacent tissues due to inflammation. **b.** the tissue involved. [t. L: m.s. *adhaesio*]

ad·he·sive (ăd hē′sĭv), *adj.* **1.** clinging; tenacious; sticking fast. **2.** gummed: *adhesive tape.* —*n.* **3.** adhesive plaster. —**ad·he′sive·ly,** *adv.* —**ad·he′sive·ness,** *n.*

adhesive plaster, cotton or other fabric coated with an adhesive preparation, used for covering slight cuts, etc., on the skin. Also **adhesive tape.**

ad·hib·it (ăd hĭb′ĭt), *v.t.* **1.** to take or let in; admit. **2.** to use or apply. **3.** *Rare.* to attach. [t. L: s. *adhibitus,* pp., applied] —**ad·hi·bi·tion** (ăd′hə bĭsh′ən), *n.*

ad hoc (ăd hŏk′), *Latin.* for this (special purpose); with respect to this (subject or thing).

ad hom·i·nem (ăd hŏm′ə něm′), *Latin.* to the man; personal. An argument *ad hominem* appeals to a person's prejudices or special interests instead of to his intellect.

ad·i·a·bat·ic (ăd′Ĭ ə băt′Ĭk, ā′dĬ-), *adj. Physics, Chem.* without gain or loss of heat (distinguished from *isothermal*). [f. s. Gk. *adiábatos* impassable + -IC] —**ad′i·a·bat′i·cal·ly,** *adv.*

ad·i·aph·or·ism (ăd′Ĭ ăf′ə rĬz′əm), *n.* tolerance by the Church of actions not specifically prohibited by the Scriptures; indifferentism. [t. Gk.: m. *adiáphoros*]

ad·i·aph·o·rous (ăd′Ĭ ăf′ə rəs), *adj.* doing neither good nor harm, as a medicine.

ad·i·a·ther·man·cy (ăd′Ĭ ə thûr′mən sĬ′), *n. Physics.* inability to transmit heat radiation. —**ad′i·a·ther′ma·nous,** *adj.*

a·dieu (ə dū′, ə doo′; *Fr.* ȧ dyœ′), *interj., n., pl.* **adieus, adieux** (ə dūz′, ə dooz′; *Fr.* ȧ dyœ′). —*interj.* **1.** good-by; farewell. —*n.* **2.** act of taking one's leave; a farewell. [ME, t. F, g. L *ad Deum* (I commend you) to God]

A·di·ge (ä′dē jē), *n.* a river in N Italy, flowing SE to the Adriatic. ab. 220 mi.

ad in·fi·ni·tum (ăd Ĭn′fə nī′təm), *Latin.* to infinity; endlessly; without limit. *Abbr.* **ad inf.**

ad int., *at* interim.

ad in·te·rim (ăd Ĭn′tə rĬm), *Latin.* in the meantime. *Abbr.* **ad int.**

a·dios (ä dyōs′), *interj. Spanish.* good-by; farewell.

ad·i·po·cere (ăd′ə pō sĭr′), *n.* a waxy substance sometimes formed from dead animal bodies in moist burial places or under water. [f. adipo- (comb. form repr.

L *adeps* fat) + m. L *cēra* wax] (ăd′ə pōs′ər əs), *adj.*

ad·i·pose (ăd′ə pōs′), *adj.* **1.** fatty; consisting of, resembling, or having relation to fat: *adipose tissue.* —*n.* **2.** animal fat stored in the fatty tissue of the body. [t. NL: m.s. *adipōsus* fatty, der. L *adeps* fat] —**ad′i·pose·ness, ad·i·pos·i·ty** (ăd′ə pŏs′ə tĬ), *n.*

adipose fin, *Ichthyol.* a finlike projection, fleshy and lacking rays, behind the dorsal fin.

Ad·i·ron·dack Mountains (ăd′ə rŏn′dăk), a mountain range in NE New York: a part of the Appalachian system. Highest peak, Mt. Marcy, 5344 ft. Also, **Adirondacks.**

ad·it (ăd′Ĭt), *n.* **1.** an entrance or a passage. **2.** *Mining.* a nearly horizontal passage leading into a mine. **3.** access. [t. L: s. *aditus* approach]

ADIZ (ā′dĬz′),*U.S.A.F.* Air Defense Identification-Zone.

adj., 1. adjective. **2.** adjourned. **3.** adjunct. **4.** *Banking.* adjustment. **5.** adjutant.

ad·ja·cen·cy (ə jā′sən sĬ′), *n., pl.* **-cies. 1.** state of being adjacent. **2.** (*usually pl.*) that which is adjacent.

ad·ja·cent (ə jā′sənt), *adj.* lying near, close, or contiguous; adjoining; neighboring: *a field adjacent to the highway.* [t. L: s. *adjacens,* ppr.] —**ad·ja′cent·ly,** *adv.* —**Syn.** abutting, bordering. See **adjoining.**

adjacent angles, *Geom.* two angles having the same vertex and having a common side between them.

ad·jec·tive (ăj′Ĭk tĬv), *n.* **1.** *Gram.* **a.** one of the major form classes, or parts of speech, of many languages, comprising words used to qualify or limit a noun. **b.** such a word, as *wise* in *a wise ruler,* or in *he is wise.* **c.** any word or phrase of similar function or meaning. —*adj.* **2.** *Gram.* pertaining to an adjective; functioning as an adjective; adjectival: *the adjective use of a noun.* **3.** not able to stand alone; dependent. **4.** *Law.* concerning methods of enforcement of legal rights, as pleading and practice (opposed to *substantive*). **5.** *Dyeing.* (of colors) requiring a mordant or the like to render them permanent (opposed to *substantive*). [t. L: m.s. *adjectīvus*] —**ad·jec·ti·val** (ăj′Ĭk tĬ′vəl, ăj′Ĭk tĬ′vəl), *adj.* —**ad′jec·ti′val·ly, ad′jec·tive·ly,** *adv.*

ad·join (ə join′), *v.t.* **1.** to be in connection or contact with; abut on: *his house adjoins the lake.* —*v.i.* **2.** to lie or be next, or in contact. [ME *ajoine(n),* t. OF: m. *adjoindre,* g. L *adjungere* join to]

ad·join·ing (ə join′nĬng), *adj.* bordering; contiguous: *the adjoining room.*
—**Syn.** ADJOINING, ADJACENT, BORDERING all mean near or close to something. ADJACENT implies being near by or next to: *adjacent angles.* ADJOINING implies touching, having a common point or line: *an adjoining yard.* BORDERING means having a common boundary with: *Ohio borders on Indiana.*

ad·journ (ə jûrn′), *v.t.* **1.** to suspend the meeting of, as a public or private body, to a future day or to another place: *adjourn the court.* **2.** to defer or postpone to a future meeting of the same body: *the court adjourned consideration of the question.* **3.** to put off; defer; postpone. —*v.i.* **4.** to postpone, suspend, or transfer proceedings. [ME *ajourne(n),* t. OF: m. *ajorner,* g. LL *adjurnāre* fix a day]

ad·journ·ment (ə jûrn′mənt), *n.* **1.** act of adjourning. **2.** state or period of being adjourned.

adjt., adjutant.

ad·judge (ə jŭj′), *v.t.* **-judged, -judging. 1.** to pronounce formally; decree: *the will was adjudged void.* **2.** to award judicially; assign: *the prize was adjudged to him.* **3.** to decide by a judicial opinion or sentence: *to adjudge a case.* **4.** to sentence or condemn: *he was adjudged to die.* **5.** to deem: *it was adjudged wise to avoid war.* [ME *ajuge(n),* t. OF: m. *ajugier,* g. L *adjūdicāre*]

ad·ju·di·cate (ə jōō′də kāt′), *v..* **-cated, -cating.** |—*v.t.* **1.** to pronounce or decree by judicial sentence; settle judicially; pass judgment on; to determine (an issue or dispute) judicially. —*v.i.* **2.** to sit in judgment (fol. by *upon*). [t. L: m. s. *adjūdicātus,* pp.] —**ad·ju′di·ca′tive,** *adj.* —**ad·ju′di·ca′tor,** *n.*

ad·ju·di·ca·tion (ə jōō′də kā′shən), *n.* **1.** act of adjudicating. **2.** *Law.* **a.** act of a court in making an order, judgment, or decree. **b.** a judicial decision or sentence.

ad·junct (ăj′ŭngkt), *n.* **1.** something added to another thing but not essentially a part of it. **2.** a person joined to another in some duty or service; an assistant. **3.** *Gram.* a qualifying form, word, phrase, etc., depending on some other form, word, phrase, etc. —*adj.* **4.** joined to a thing or person, esp. subordinately; associated; auxiliary. [t. L: s. *adjunctus,* pp.] —**Syn. 1.** See **addition.**

ad·junc·tive (ə jŭngk′tĬv), *adj.* forming an adjunct. —**ad·junc′tive·ly,** *adv.*

ad·jure (ə joor′), *v.t.,* **-jured, -juring. 1.** to charge, bind, or command, earnestly and solemnly, often under oath or the threat of a curse. **2.** to entreat or request earnestly. [ME *adjure(n),* t. L: m. *adjūrāre*] —**ad·ju·ra·tion** (ăj′ōō rā′shən), *n.* —**ad·jur·a·to·ry** (ə jōōr′ə tôr′Ĭ), *adj.* —**ad·jur′er,** and/or **ad·ju′ror,** *n.*

ad·just (ə jŭst′), *v.t.* **1.** to fit, as one thing to another; make correspondent or conformable; adapt; accommodate: *to adjust things to a standard.* **2.** to put in working order; regulate; bring to a proper state or position: *to adjust an instrument.* **3.** to settle or bring to a satisfactory state, so that parties are agreed in the result: *to adjust differences.* **4.** *Insurance.* to fix (the sum to be paid on a claim); settle (a claim). **5.** to systematize. **6.** *Mil.* to correct the elevation and deflection of (a gun). —*v.i*

7. to adapt oneself; become adapted. [t. F (obs.): s. *adjuster*, t. ML: m. *adjūstāre*, erroneous Latinization of OF *ajouster*, g. LL *adjūtāre*] —**ad·just/a·ble**, *adj.* —**ad·just/a·bly**, *adv.* —**ad·just/er, ad·jus/tor**, *n.* —**Syn.** 2. ADJUST, ADAPT, ALTER in their literal meanings imply making necessary or desirable changes (as in position, shape, and the like). To ADJUST is to move into proper position for use: *to adjust the eyepiece of a telescope*. To ADAPT is to make a change in character, to make something useful in a new way: *to adapt a paper clip for a hairpin*. To ALTER is to change the appearance but not the use: *to alter the height of a table*. 3. arrange; rectify; reconcile.

adjustable pitch, *Aeron.* (of a propeller) having blades whose pitch can be changed while the propeller is stationary to suit various conditions of flight.

ad·just·ment (ə·jŭst/mənt), *n.* 1. act of adjusting; act of adapting to a given purpose. 2. state of being adjusted; orderly relation of parts or elements. 3. a means of adjusting: *the adjustment of a microscope.* 4. *Sociol.* a process of fitting individual or collective patterns of activity to other such patterns made with some awareness or purposefulness. 5. *Insurance.* act of ascertaining the amount of indemnity which the party insured is entitled to receive under the policy, and of settling the claim. 6. a settlement of a disputed account or claim.

ad·ju·tant (ăj/ə·tənt), *n.* 1. *Mil.* a staff officer who assists the commanding officer in issuing orders. 2. *Brit.* an executive officer. 3. an assistant. 4. the adjutant bird. [t. L: s. *adjūtans*, ppr., aiding] —**ad/ju·tan·cy**, *n.*

adjutant bird, a large East Indian stork, *Leptoptilus dubius*. Also, **adjutant crane, adjutant stork**.

adjutant general, *pl.* **adjutants general**. 1. *U.S. Army.* **a.** the Adjutant General, the chief administrative officer of the Army. **b.** a member of the Adjutant General's Department, from which adjutants for higher command are assigned. 2. a high (often highest) officer of the National Guard of a State or Territory.

ad·ju·vant (ăj/ə·vənt), *adj.* 1. serving to help or assist. —*n.* 2. a person or thing aiding or helping. 3. *Med.* whatever aids in removing or preventing a disease, esp. a substance added to a prescription to aid the operation of the main ingredient. [t. L: s. *adjuvans*, ppr.]

Ad·ler (ăd/lər), *n.* 1. Alfred, 1870–1937, Austrian psychiatrist and psychologist. 2. Felix, 1851–1933, U.S. educator, reformer, and writer.

ad-lib (ăd lĭb/), *v.i., v.t.,* **-libbed, -libbing**. *Colloq.* to improvise, as notes, words, or business, during rehearsal or performance. [v. use of AD LIB.]

ad lib·i·tum (ăd lĭb/ə·təm), *Latin.* at pleasure; to any extent; without restriction: used in music to indicate that the manner of performance of a passage is left to the discretion of the performer. *Abbr.:* **ad lib.**

ad lit·te·ram (ăd lĭt/ə·răm/), *Latin.* to the letter; exactly. One cites an author *verbatim* and *ad litteram*.

ad loc., (L *ad locum*) at or to the place.

Adm., 1. Admiral. 2. Admiralty.

ad ma·jo·rem De·i glo·ri·am (ăd ma·jōr/ĕm dē/ĭ glôr/ĭ ăm/), *Latin.* for the greater glory of God (motto of the Jesuit order).

ad·meas·ure (ăd mĕzh/ər), *v.t.* **-ured, -uring**. to measure off or out; apportion. [f. AD- + MEASURE; r. ME *amesure*, t. OF: m. *amesurer*, g. LL *admēnsūrāre*]

ad·meas·ure·ment (ăd mĕzh/ər mənt), *n.* 1. process of measuring. 2. number, dimensions, or measure of anything. 3. apportionment.

Ad·me·tus (ăd mē/təs), *n. Gk. Legend.* a Thessalian king, one of the Argonauts and husband of Alcestis.

ad·min·i·cle (ăd mĭn/ə·kəl), *n.* an aid; auxiliary. [t. L: m.s. *adminiculum* a prop] —**ad·min·ic·u·lar** (ăd/mə·nĭk/yə·lər), *adj.*

ad·min·is·ter (ăd mĭn/əs·tər), *v.t.* 1. to manage (affairs, a government, etc.); have executive charge of: *to administer laws.* 2. to bring into use or operation; dispense: *to administer justice.* 3. to make application of; give: *to administer medicine.* 4. to tender or impose: *to administer an oath.* 5. *Law.* to manage or dispose of, as a decedent's estate by an executor or administrator, or a trust estate by a trustee. —*v.i.* 6. to contribute assistance; bring aid or supplies (fol. by *to*): *to administer to the needs of the poor.* 7. to perform the duties of an administrator. [t. L: m.s. *administrāre*, t. ME *amynistre*, t. OF: m. *aministrer*] —**ad·min·is·tra·ble** (ăd mĭn/əs·trə·bəl), *adj.* —**ad·min·is·trant** (ăd mĭn/əs·trənt), *adj., n.* —**Syn.** 1. conduct, control. See **rule**. 3. apply.

ad·min·is·trate (ăd mĭn/ə·strāt/), *v.t.,* **-trated, -trating.** *U.S.* to administer.

ad·min·is·tra·tion (ăd mĭn/ə·strā/shən), *n.* 1. the conducting of any office or employment; direction; management. 2. the function of a political state in exercising its governmental duties. 3. the duty or duties of an administrator, specif., the executive functions of government, both general and local, which are neither legislative nor judicial. 4. the executive officers, collectively. 5. *U.S.* their period of service. 6. *U.S.* any body of men entrusted with executive or administrative powers. 7. *Law.* management of a decedent estate by an executor or administrator, or of a trust estate by a trustee. 8. act of dispensing, esp. formally: *administration of the sacraments.* 9. act of tendering: *the administration of an oath.* 10. the applying of a medicine, etc.

ad·min·is·tra·tive (ăd mĭn/ə·strā/tĭv), *adj.* pertaining to administration; executive: *administrative ability, problems, etc.* —**ad·min/is·tra/tive·ly**, *adv.*

ad·min·is·tra·tor (ăd mĭn/ə·strā/tər), *n.* 1. one who directs or manages affairs of any kind. 2. a person with a talent for managing or organizing. 3. *Law.* a person appointed by a court to take charge of the estate of a decedent, but not appointed in the decedent's will. [t. L] —**ad·min·is·tra/tor·ship/**, *n.*

ad·min·is·tra·trix (ăd mĭn/ə strā/trĭks, ăd/mĭn ə-)-), *pl.* **-istratrices** (-ə strā/trə sēz/, -ə strə tri/sēz). *Law.* a female administrator.

ad·mi·ra·ble (ăd/mə rə bəl), *adj.* worthy of admiration; exciting approval, reverence, or affection; excellent. [t. L: m.s. *admīrābilis*] —**ad/mi·ra·ble·ness**, *n.* —**ad/mi·ra·bly**, *adv.* —**Syn.** estimable, praiseworthy.

ad·mi·ral (ăd/mə rəl), *n.* 1. the commander in chief of a fleet. 2. a naval officer of the highest rank. 3. a naval officer of a high rank. The grades in the U. S. Navy are: fleet admiral, admiral, vice-admiral, and rear admiral. 4. the flagship of an admiral. 5. *Brit.* a master who directs a fishing fleet. 6. any of various handsome butterflies, as the **red admiral** (*Vanessa atalanta*). [var. of ME *amiral*, t. OF, t. Ar: m. *amir al* (chief of) in various phrases, e.g. *amir al baḥr* commander of the sea; var. *admiral* arose by assoc. with L *admīrābilis* admirable, etc.] —**ad/mi·ral·ship/**, *n.*

ad·mi·ral·ty (ăd/mə rəl tĭ). *n., pl.* **-ties**, *adj.* —*n.* 1. the office or jurisdiction of an admiral. 2. the officials or the department of state having charge of naval affairs, as in Great Britain. 3. maritime law. 4. a tribunal administering it. 5. the **Admiralty**, the official building, at London, of the British commissioners for naval affairs. —*adj.* 6. pertaining to the sea: *admiralty law.*

Admiralty Islands, a group of islands in the SW Pacific, N of New Guinea: under Australian administration. 14,000 native pop. (est. 1952); ab. 800 sq. mi.

Admiralty Range, a mountain range in Antarctica, NW of the Ross Sea.

ad·mi·ra·tion (ăd/mə rā/shən), *n.* 1. a feeling of wonder, pleasure, and approbation. 2. act of looking on or contemplating with pleasure: *admiration of a pretty girl.* 3. an object of wonder or approbation: *she was the admiration of everyone.* 4. *Archaic.* wonder. —**Syn.** 1. approval; esteem; veneration.

ad·mire (ăd mīr/), *v.,* **-mired, -miring.** —*v.t.* 1. to regard with wonder, pleasure, and approbation. 2. to regard with wonder or surprise (now usually ironical or sarcastic): *I admire your audacity.* —*v.i.* 3. to feel or express admiration. 4. *U.S. or Dial.* to like or desire (to do something). [t. L: m. s *admīrāri* wonder at] —**ad·mir/er**, *n.* —**ad·mir/ing·ly**, *adv.* —**Syn.** 1. esteem; revere, venerate.

ad·mis·si·ble (ăd mĭs/ə bəl), *adj.* 1. that may be allowed or conceded; allowable. 2. capable or worthy of being admitted. —**ad·mis/si·bil/i·ty, ad·mis/si·ble·ness**, *n.* —**ad·mis/si·bly**, *adv.*

ad·mis·sion (ăd mĭsh/ən), *n.* 1. act of allowing to enter; entrance afforded by permission, by provision or existence of means, or by the removal of obstacles: *the admission of aliens into a country.* 2. power or permission to enter: *to grant a person admission.* 3. the price paid for entrance, as to a theater, etc. 4. act or condition of being received or accepted in a position or office; appointment: *admission to the practice of law.* 5. confession of a charge, an error, or a crime; acknowledgment: *his admission of the theft solved the mystery.* 6. an acknowledgment of the truth of something. 7. a point or statement admitted; concession. [t. L: s. *admissio*] —**Syn.** 1. See **entrance**[1].

Admission Day, *U.S.* a legal holiday in some States commemorating the day of their admission into the Union: Feb. 14 in Arizona, Sept. 9 in California, and Oct. 31 in Nevada.

ad·mis·sive (ăd mĭs/ĭv), *adj.* tending to admit.

ad·mit (ăd mĭt/), *v.,* **-mitted, -mitting.** —*v.t.* 1. to allow to enter; grant or afford entrance to: *to admit a student to college.* 2. to give right or means of entrance to. 3. *U.S.* to permit to exercise a certain function or privilege: *admitted to the bar.* 4. to permit; allow. 5. to allow as valid: *to admit the force of an argument.* 6. to have capacity for the admission of at one time: *this passage admits two abreast.* 7. to acknowledge; confess: *he admitted his guilt.* 8. to grant in argument; concede: *the fact is admitted.* —*v.i.* 9. to permit entrance; to give access: *this key admits to the garden.* 10. to grant opportunity or permission (fol. by *of*): *circumstances do not admit of this.* [t. L: m. s. *admittere*; r. late ME *amitte*(n), t. F] —**ad·mit/ter**, *n.* —**Syn.** 7. own; avow. See **acknowledge**.

ad·mit·tance (ăd mĭt/əns), *n.* 1. permission to enter; the power or right of entrance: *admittance into the church.* 2. act of admitting. 3. actual entrance. 4. *Elect.* the reciprocal of impedance. —**Syn.** 1. See **entrance**[1].

ad·mit·ted·ly (ăd mĭt/ĭd lĭ), *adv.* by acknowledgment; confessedly: *he was admittedly the one who had lost the documents.*

ad·mix (ăd mĭks/), *v.t., v.i.* to mingle with or add to something else. [back formation from ME *admixt*, t. L: s. *admixtus*, pp., mingled with]

ad·mix·ture (ăd mĭks/chər), *n.* 1. act of mixing. 2. state of being mixed. 3. anything added; any alien element or ingredient.

---

b., blend of, blended; c., cognate with; d., dialect, dialectal; der., derived from; f., formed from; g., going back to; m., modification of; r., replacing; s., stem of; t., taken from; ?, perhaps. See the full key on inside cover.

ad·mon·ish (ăd mŏn′ĭsh), *v.t.* **1.** to counsel against something; caution or advise. **2.** to notify of or reprove for a fault, esp. mildly: *to admonish someone as a brother.* **3.** to recall or incite to duty; remind: *to admonish someone about his obligations.* [back formation from ADMONITION; r. ME *amonesten*, t. OF] —**ad·mon′ish·er,** *n.* —**ad·mon′ish·ing·ly,** *adv.* —**ad·mon′ish·ment,** *n.* —**Syn. 1.** See warn. **2.** rebuke, censure.

ad·mo·ni·tion (ăd′mə nĭsh′ən), *n.* act of admonishing; counsel or advice; gentle reproof; caution. [t. L: s. *admonitio*; r. ME *amonicioun*, t. OF]

ad·mon·i·tor (ăd mŏn′ə tər), *n.* an admonisher. [t. L]

ad·mon·i·to·ry (ăd mŏn′ə tôr′ĭ), *adj.* tending or serving to admonish: *an admonitory gesture.*

ad·nate (ăd′nāt), *adj.* *Bot., Zool., etc.* grown fast to something; congenitally attached. [t. L: m. s. *adnātus* born to]

ad·na·tion (ăd nā′shən), *n.* adnate condition.

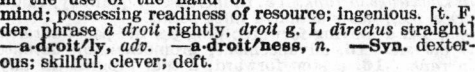
A. Adnate stipule

ad nau·se·am (ăd nô′shĭ ăm′,-sĭ-), *Latin.* to a sickening or disgusting extent.

ad·noun (ăd′noun′), *n.* **1.** *Gram.* an adjective in its substantival use: *the useful.* The more common term is *adjective used as a noun.* —*adj.* **2.** *Rare.* adjective. [f. AD- + NOUN, modeled on ADVERB] —**ad·nom·i·nal** (ăd nŏm′ə nəl), *adj.*

a·do (ə dōō′), *n.* activity; bustle; fuss. [d. ME *ado, at do* to do] —**Syn.** ADO, TO-DO, COMMOTION, STIR, TUMULT suggest a great deal of fuss and noise. ADO implies a confused bustle of activity, a considerable emotional upset, and a great deal of talking: *Much Ado About Nothing.* TO-DO, now more commonly used, may mean merely excitement and noise, and may be pleasant or unpleasant: *a great to-do over a movie star.* COMMOTION suggests a noisy confusion and babble: *commotion at the scene of an accident.* STIR suggests excitement and noise, with a hint of emotional cause: *the report was followed by a tremendous stir in the city.* TUMULT suggests disorder with noise and violence: *a tumult as the mob stormed the Bastille.*

a·do·be (ə dō′bĭ), *n.* **1.** the sun-dried brick in common use in countries having little rainfall. **2.** a yellow silt or clay, deposited by rivers, used to make bricks. **3.** a building constructed of adobe. **4.** a dark, heavy soil, containing clay. [t. Sp.]

adobe flat, a plain consisting of adobe deposited by short-lived rainfall or thaw streams, usually having a smooth or unmarked surface.

ad·o·les·cence (ăd′ə lĕs′əns), *n.* **1.** the transition period between puberty (boyhood or girlhood) and adult stages of development; youth. It extends from about 14 to 25 years of age in man, and from 12 to 21 in woman. **2.** quality or state of being adolescent; youthfulness. Also, **ad·o·les′cen·cy.**

ad·o·les·cent (ăd′ə lĕs′ənt), *adj.* **1.** growing to manhood or womanhood; youthful. **2.** having the characteristics of adolescence or of an adolescent. —*n.* **3.** an adolescent person. [t. L: s. *adolescens*, ppr.]

A·don·ic (ə dŏn′ĭk), *adj.* **1.** *Pros.* noting a verse consisting of a dactyl (– ◡ ◡) followed by a spondee (– –) or trochee (– ◡). **2.** of Adonis. —*n.* **3.** *Pros.* an Adonic verse or line. [t. ML: s. *adōnicus*]

A·do·nis (ə dō′nĭs *or. esp. for 2*, ə dŏn′ĭs), *n.* **1.** *Gk. Myth.* a favorite of Aphrodite, slain by a wild boar, but permitted by Zeus to pass four months every year in the lower world with Persephone, four with Aphrodite, and four wherever else he chose. In another account he spent half the year on earth and thus symbolically represented the vegetation cycle. **2.** a very handsome young man.

a·dopt (ə dŏpt′), *v.t.* **1.** to choose for or take to oneself; make one's own by selection or assent: *to adopt a name or idea.* **2.** to take as one's own child, specif. by a formal legal act. **3.** to vote to accept: *the House adopted the report.* **4.** to take or receive into any kind of new relationship: *to adopt a person as an heir.* **5.** *Brit.* to nominate (a candidate) for political office. [t. L: s. *adoptāre*] —**adopt′a·ble,** *adj.* —**a·dopt′er,** *n.* —**a·dop′tion,** *n.*

a·dop·tive (ə dŏp′tĭv), *adj.* **1.** *Brit.* related by adoption: *an adoptive father or son.* **2.** tending to adopt. —**a·dop′tive·ly,** *adv.*

a·dor·a·ble (ə dôr′ə bəl), *adj.* **1.** worthy of being adored. **2.** *Colloq.* arousing strong liking. —**a·dor′a·ble·ness, a·dor·a·bil′i·ty,** *n.* —**a·dor′a·bly,** *adv.*

ad·o·ra·tion (ăd′ə rā′shən), *n.* **1.** act of paying honor, as to a divine being; worship. **2.** reverent homage. **3.** fervent and devoted love.

a·dore (ə dôr′), *v.t.* **1.** adored, adoring. —*v.t.* **1.** to regard with the utmost esteem, love, and respect; honor. **2.** to pay divine honor to; worship: *to be adored as gods.* **3.** *Colloq.* to like greatly. —*v.i.* **4.** to worship [t. LL: m.s. *adorāre* worship, L address; r. ME *aoure*(*n*), t. OF: m. *ao*(*u*)*rer*] —**a·dor′er,** *n.* —**a·dor′ing,** *adj.* —**a·dor′ing·ly,** *adv.* —**Syn. 1.** reverence, revere, venerate.

a·dorn (ə dôrn′), *v.t.* **1.** to make pleasing or more attractive; embellish; add luster to: *the piety which adorns his character.* **2.** to increase or lend beauty to, as by dress or ornaments; decorate: *garlands of flowers adorning her hair.* [t. L: s. *adornāre*; r. ME *aourne,* t. OF: m. *ao*(*u*)*rner*] —**a·dorn′er,** *n.* —**a·dorn′ing·ly,** *adv.* —**Syn. 2.** beautify; deck, bedeck.

a·dorn·ment (ə dôrn′mənt), *n.* **1.** ornament: *the adornments and furnishings of a room.* **2.** an adorning; ornamentation: *personal adornment.*

a·down (ə doun′), *adv., prep.* *Poetic.* down.

---

ad pa·tres (ăd pä′trēz), *Latin.* to (his) fathers; dead.

ad quem (ăd kwĕm′), *Latin.* at or to which; the goal.

A·dras·tus (ə drăs′təs), *n.* *Gk. Legend.* a king of Argos and leader of the Seven against Thebes (which see).

ad rem (ăd rĕm′), *Latin.* to the matter or thing. To reply *ad rem* is to keep to the subject being considered.

ad·re·nal (ə drē′nəl), *Anat., Zool.* —*adj.* **1.** situated near or on the kidneys; suprarenal. **2.** of or produced by the adrenal glands. —*n.* **3.** one of the adrenal glands. [f. AD- + s. L *rēnēs* kidneys + -AL¹]

ad·re·nal·ec·to·my (ə drē′nə lĕk′tə mĭ), *n., pl.* -**mies.** *Surg.* the removal of one or both adrenal glands.

adrenal glands, *Anat., Zool.* a pair of ductless glands, located above the kidneys, which secrete at least two hormones, adrenalin and cortin.

ad·ren·al·in (ə drĕn′əl ĭn), *n.* **1.** a white crystalline drug, $C_9H_{13}NO_3$, purified from the suprarenal secretion of animals and used to speed heart action, contract blood vessels, etc.; epinephrine. **2.** (*cap.*) a trademark for this drug. Also, **a·dren·al·ine** (ə drĕn′əl ĭn, -ə lēn′).

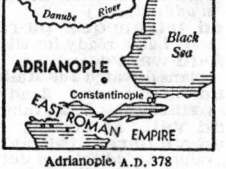
ADRIANOPLE
Danube River
Constantinople
Black Sea
EAST ROMAN EMPIRE
Adrianople, A.D. 378

A·dri·an (ā′drĭ ən), *n.* **1.** name of six popes, esp. **Adrian I,** died A.D. 795, pope from A.D.772-795, and **Adrian IV,** c1100-1159, pope from 1154-1159, the only Englishman ever to become pope. **2.** Hadrian. **3.** Edgar **Douglas,** born 1889, British physiologist.

A·dri·an·o·ple (ā′drĭ ə nō′pəl), *n.* Edirne.

A·dri·at·ic Sea (ā′drĭ ăt′ĭk), an arm of the Mediterranean between Italy and Yugoslavia. ab. 500 mi. long.

a·drift (ə drĭft′), *adv., adj.* **1.** not fastened by any kind of moorings; at the mercy of winds and currents. **2.** swayed by any chance impulse. [f. A-¹ + DRIFT]

a·droit (ə droit′), *adj.* expert in the use of the hand or mind; possessing readiness of resource; ingenious. [t. F, der. phrase *à droit* rightly, *droit* g. L *dīrectus* straight] —**a·droit′ly,** *adv.* —**a·droit′ness,** *n.* —**Syn.** dexterous; skillful, clever; deft.

à droite (á drwät′), *French.* to the right.

ad·sci·ti·tious (ăd′sə tĭsh′əs), *adj.* added or derived from without; supplemental; additional. [f. s. L *adscītus,* pp., derived + -ITIOUS]

ad·script (ăd′skrĭpt), *adj.* written after (distinguished from *subscript*). [t. L: s. *adscriptus,* pp.]

ad·scrip·tion (ăd skrĭp′shən), *n.* ascription.

ad·sorb (ăd sôrb′), *v.t.* to gather (a gas, liquid, or dissolved substance) on a surface in a condensed layer, as when charcoal adsorbs gases. [f. AD- + s. L *sorbēre* suck in] —**ad·sorb′ent,** *adj., n.* —**ad·sorp·tion** (ăd-sôrp′shən), *n.* —**ad·sorp′tive,** *adj., n.*

ad·su·ki bean (ăd sōō′kĭ, -zōō′-), a kind of bean, *Phaseolus angularis,* extensively grown in parts of Asia and to a limited degree in the U. S. Also, **adzuki bean.** [t. Jap.: m. *adzuki*]

ad·u·lar·i·a (ăj′ə lâr′ĭ ə), *n.* *Mineral.* a transparent or translucent variety of orthoclase, often pearly or opalescent, as the moonstone. [named after the *Adula* mountain group in Switzerland. See -ARIA]

ad·u·late (ăj′ə lāt′), *v.t.,* -**lated, -lating.** to show pretended or undiscriminating devotion to; flatter servilely. [t. L: m. s. *adūlātus,* pp.] —**ad′u·la′tion,** *n.* —**ad′u·la′tor,** *n.* —**ad·u·la·to·ry** (ăj′ə lə tôr′ĭ), *adj.*

a·dult (ə dŭlt′, ăd′ŭlt), *adj.* **1.** having attained full size and strength; grown up; mature: *an adult person, animal, or plant.* **2.** pertaining to or designed for adults: *adult education.* —*n.* **3.** a person who is grown up or of age. **4.** a full-grown animal or plant. **5.** *Common Law.* a designation of a person who has attained 21 years of age. **6.** *Civil Law.* a male after attaining 14, or a female after attaining 12, years of age. [t. L: s. *adultus,* pp.] —**a·dult′hood,** *n.* —**a·dult′ness,** *n.*

a·dul·ter·ant (ə dŭl′tər ənt), *n.* **1.** a substance used for adulterating. —*adj.* **2.** adulterating.

a·dul·ter·ate (*v.* ə dŭl′tə rāt′; *adj.* ə dŭl′tər ĭt, -tə rāt′), *v.,* -**ated, -ating,** *adj.* —*v.t.* **1.** to debase by adding inferior materials or elements; make impure by admixture; use cheaper, inferior, or less desirable goods in the production or marketing of (any professedly genuine article): *to adulterate food.* —*adj.* **2.** adulterated. **3.** adulterous. [t. L: m. s. *adulterātus,* pp., defiled] —**a·dul·ter·a′tor,** *n.*

a·dul·ter·a·tion (ə dŭl′tər ā′shən), *n.* **1.** act or process of adulterating. **2.** state of being adulterated. **3.** something adulterated.

a·dul·ter·er (ə dŭl′tər ər), *n.* a person, esp. a man, guilty of adultery. —**a·dul·ter·ess** (ə dŭl′tər ĭs, -trĭs), *n.fem.*

a·dul·ter·ine (ə dŭl′tər ĭn, -tə rīn′), *adj.* **1.** characterized by adulteration; spurious. **2.** born of adultery. **3.** of or involving adultery. [t. L: m.s. *adulterīnus*]

ăct, āble, dâre, ärt; ĕbb, ēqual; ĭf, īce; hŏt, ōver, ôrder, oil, bŏŏk, ōōze, out; ŭp, ūse, ûrge; ə = a in alone; ch, chief; g, give; ng, ring; sh, shoe; th, thin; ŧħ, that; zh, vision.   See the full key on inside cover.

a·dul·ter·ous (ə dŭl′tər əs), *adj.* **1.** characterized by or given to adultery; illicit. **2.** spurious. **—a·dul′ter·ous·ly,** *adv.*

a·dul·ter·y (ə dŭl′tər ĭ), *n.*, *pl.* **-ter·ies.** voluntary sexual intercourse between a married person and any other than the lawful spouse. [t. L: m.s. *adulterium;* r. ME *avoutrie,* t. OF]

ad·um·bral (ăd ŭm′brəl), *adj.* shadowy; shady.

ad·um·brate (ăd ŭm′brāt, ăd′əm brāt′), *v.t.,* **-brated, -brating. 1.** to give a faint shadow or resemblance of; outline or shadow forth. **2.** to foreshadow; prefigure. **3.** to darken or conceal partially; overshadow. [t. L: m. s. *adumbrātus,* pp., shadowed] **—ad·um·bra′tion,** *n.*

ad·um·bra·tive (ăd ŭm′brə tĭv), *adj.* shadowing forth; indicative. **—ad·um′bra·tive·ly,** *adv.*

a·dunc (ə dŭngk′), *adj.* curved inward; hooked. Also, **a·dun·cous** (ə dŭng′kəs). [t. L: s. *aduncus* crooked]

a·dust (ə dŭst′), *adj.* **1.** dried or darkened as by heat; burned; scorched. **2.** atrabilious; sallow; gloomy. [t. L: s. *adūstus,* pp.]

ad u·trum·que pa·ra·tus (ăd ū trŭm′kwĭ pə rā′təs), *Latin.* ready for either alternative.

A·du·wa (ä′dōō wä′), *n.* a town in N Ethiopia: the Ethiopians defeated the Italians here, 1896. 5000 (est. 1948).

adv., 1. adverb. **2.** adverbial. **3.** adverbially. **4.** advertisement. **5.** ad valorem.

ad val., ad valorem.

ad va·lo·rem (ăd və lōr′ĕm), in proportion to the value. An *ad valorem* duty charged on goods entering a country is fixed at a percentage of the customs value as stated on the invoice. [t. L]

ad·vance (ăd văns′, -väns′), *v.,* **-vanced, -vancing,** *n., adj.* **—***v.t.* **1.** to move or bring forward in place: *the troops were advanced to the new position.* **2.** to bring to view or notice; propose: *to advance an argument.* **3.** to improve; further: *to advance one's interests.* **4.** to raise in rank; promote. **5.** to raise in rate: *to advance the price.* **6.** to bring forward in time; accelerate: *to advance growth.* **7.** to supply beforehand; furnish on credit, or before goods are delivered or work is done. **8.** to furnish as part of a stock or fund. **9.** to supply or pay in expectation of reimbursement: *to advance money on loan.* **10.** *Archaic.* to raise, as a banner. **—***v.i.* **11.** to move or go forward; proceed: *the troops advanced.* **12.** to improve or make progress; grow: *to advance in knowledge or rank.* **13.** to increase in quantity, value, price, etc.: *stocks advanced three points.* **—***n.* **14.** a moving forward; progress in space: *advance to the sea.* **15.** advancement; promotion: *an advance in rank.* **16.** a step forward; actual progress in any course of action: *the advance of knowledge.* **17.** (*usually pl.*) an effort to bring about acquaintance, accord, understanding, etc. **18.** addition to price; rise in price: *an advance on cottons.* **19.** Com. **a.** a giving beforehand; a furnishing of something before an equivalent is received. **b.** the money or goods thus furnished. **20.** *U.S.* the leading body of an army. **21.** *Mil.* (formerly) the order or a signal to advance. **22. in advance, a.** before; in front. **b.** beforehand; ahead of time: *he insisted on paying his rent in advance.* **—***adj.* **23.** going before: *the advance section of a train.* **24.** made or given in advance: *an advance payment.* **25. is-sued in advance:** *an advance copy.* **26.** having gone beyond others or beyond the average. [ME *avaunce(n)* t. OF: m. *avancier,* g. LL *abanteāre,* der. *abante* (f. *ab* + *ante*) from before] **—ad·vanc′er,** *n.* **—Syn. 2.** adduce; propound, offer. **5.** increase. **6.** quicken, hasten, speed up. **11.** ADVANCE, MOVE ON, PROCEED all imply movement forward. ADVANCE applies to forward movement, esp. toward an objective: *to advance to a platform.* PROCEED emphasizes movement as from one place to another, and often implies continuing after a halt: *to proceed on one's journey.* MOVE ON, a more informal expression, is similar in meaning to PROCEED; it does not, however, imply a definite goal: *the crowd was told to move on.* **12.** thrive, flourish; prosper. **13.** rise. **17.** overture; proposal.

ad·vanced (ăd vănst′, -vänst′), *adj.* **1.** placed in advance: *with foot advanced.* **2.** far on in progress; beyond the average: *an advanced class in French.* **3.** far on in time: *an advanced age.*

advanced standing, acceptance by a college of credits which a student has earned in another school.

advance guard, a body of troops going before the main force to clear the way, guard against surprise, etc.

ad·vance·ment (ăd văns′mənt, -väns′-), *n.* **1.** act of moving forward. **2.** promotion in rank or standing; preferment: *his hopes of advancement failed.* **3.** *Law.* money or property given during his lifetime by a person subsequently dying intestate and deducted from the intestate share of the recipient.

ad·van·tage (ăd văn′tĭj, -văn′-), *n., v.,* **-taged, -taging. —***n.* **1.** any state, circumstance, opportunity, or means specially favorable to success, interest, or any desired end: *the advantage of a good education.* **2.** benefit; gain; profit: *it is to his advantage.* **3.** superiority or ascendancy (often fol. by *over* or *of*): *to have the advantage of age.* **4.** a position of superiority (often fol. by *over* or *of*): *don't let him get the advantage of us.* **5.** *Tennis.* the first point scored after deuce, or the resulting state of the score; vantage. **6. take advantage of, a.** to make use of: *to take advantage of an opportunity.* **b.** to impose upon: *to take advantage of someone.* **7. to advantage,** with good effect; advantageously. **—***v.t.* **8.** to be of service to; yield profit or gain to; benefit. [ME *avantage,*

t. OF, der. *avant* before, forward, g. LL *abante.* See ADVANCE] **—Syn. 2.** ADVANTAGE, BENEFIT, PROFIT all mean something that is of use or value. ADVANTAGE is anything that places one in an improved position, esp. in coping with competition or difficulties: *it is to one's advantage to have traveled widely.* BENEFIT is anything that promotes the welfare or improves the state of a person or group: *a benefit to society.* PROFIT is any valuable, useful, or helpful gain: *profit from trade or experience.*

ad·van·ta·geous (ăd′vən tā′jəs), *adj.* of advantage; furnishing convenience or opportunity; profitable; useful; beneficial: *an advantageous position.* **—ad′van·ta′geous·ly,** *adv.* **—ad′van·ta′geous·ness,** *n.*

ad·vec·tion (ăd věk′shən), *n.* **1.** the transfer of heat by horizontal movements of air; horizontal convection. **2.** the movement of air horizontally. [t. L: s. *advectio* a carrying]

ad·vent (ăd′věnt), *n.* **1.** a coming into place, view, or being; arrival: *the advent of death.* **2.** (*cap. or l.c.*) the coming of Christ into the world. **3.** (*cap.*) a season (including four Sundays) preceding Christmas, commemorative of Christ's coming. **4. Second Advent,** the second coming of Christ to establish a personal reign upon the earth as its king. [ME, t. L: s. *adventus* arrival]

Ad·vent·ist (ăd′věn tĭst, ăd věn′-), *n.* a member of any of certain Christian denominations which maintain that the second coming of Christ is near at hand; Second Adventist. Cf. **Millerite. —Ad′vent·ism,** *n.*

ad·ven·ti·tious (ăd′vən tĭsh′əs), *adj.* **1.** accidentally or casually acquired; added extrinsically; foreign. **2.** *Bot., Zool.* appearing in an abnormal or unusual position or place, as a root. [t. L: m. *adventicius* coming from abroad] **—ad′ven·ti′tious·ly,** *adv.* **—ad′ven·ti′tious·ness,** *n.*

ad·ven·tive (ăd věn′tĭv), *Bot., Zool.* **—***adj.* **1.** not native and usually not yet well established, as exotic plants or animals. **—***n.* **2.** an adventive plant or animal.

Advent Sunday, the first Sunday in Advent, being the Sunday nearest to St. Andrew's Day (Nov. 30).

ad·ven·ture (ăd věn′chər), *n., v.,* **-tured, -turing. —***n.* **1.** an undertaking of uncertain outcome; a hazardous enterprise. **2.** an exciting experience. **3.** participation in exciting undertakings or enterprises: *the spirit of adventure.* **4.** a commercial or financial speculation of any kind; a venture. **5.** *Obs.* peril; danger. **6.** *Obs.* chance. **—***v.t.* **7.** to risk or hazard. **8.** to take the chance of; dare. **9.** to venture to say or utter: *to adventure an opinion.* **—***v.i.* **10.** to take the risk involved. **11.** to venture. [ME *aventure,* t. OF, g. L *adventūra,* future p., (sc. *rēs*) (a thing) about to happen]

ad·ven·tur·er (ăd věn′chər ər), *n.* **1.** one who adventures. **2.** a seeker of fortune in daring enterprises; a soldier of fortune. **3.** one who undertakes any great commercial risk; a speculator. **4.** a seeker of fortune by underhand or equivocal means.

ad·ven·ture·some (ăd věn′chər səm), *adj.* bold; daring; adventurous.

ad·ven·tur·ess (ăd věn′chər ĭs), *n.* **1.** a female adventurer. **2.** a woman who schemes to win social position, money, etc., by equivocal methods.

ad·ven·tur·ism (ăd věn′chə rĭz′əm), *n.* defiance of accepted standards of behavior.

ad·ven·tur·ous (ăd věn′chər əs), *adj.* **1.** inclined or willing to engage in adventures. **2.** attended with risk; requiring courage: *an adventurous undertaking.* **—ad·ven′tur·ous·ly,** *adv.* **—ad·ven′tur·ous·ness,** *n.* **—Syn. 1.** daring, venturous, venturesome.

ad·verb (ăd′vûrb), *n.* **1.** one of the major form classes or "parts of speech," comprising words used to qualify or limit a verb, a verbal noun (also, in Latin, English, and some other languages, an adjective or another adverb), or an adverbial phrase or clause. An adverbial element expresses some relation of place, time, manner, attendant circumstance, degree, cause, inference, result, condition, exception, concession, purpose, or means. **2.** such a word, as *well* in English *she sings well.* **3.** any word or phrase of similar function or meaning. [earlier *adverbe,* t. L: m. s. *adverbium*] **—ad·ver·bi·al** (ăd vûr′bĭ əl), *adj.* **—ad·ver′bi·al·ly,** *adv.* **—ad′verb·less,** *adj.*

ad ver·bum (ăd vûr′bəm), *Latin.* to the word; exact in wording according to an original.

ad·ver·sar·y (ăd′vər sĕr′ĭ), *n., pl.* **-saries. 1.** an unfriendly opponent. **2.** an opponent in a contest; a contestant. **3. the Adversary,** the Devil; Satan. [ME *adversarie,* t. L: m. *adversārius*] **—Syn. 1.** ADVERSARY, ANTAGONIST mean a person, a group, or a personified force, contending against another. ADVERSARY suggests an enemy who fights determinedly, continuously, and relentlessly: *a formidable adversary.* ANTAGONIST suggests one who, in hostile spirit, opposes another, often in a particular contest or struggle: *a duel with an antagonist.* **—Ant. 1.** ally, supporter.

ad·ver·sa·tive (ăd vûr′sə tĭv), *adj.* **1.** expressing contrariety, opposition, or antithesis: "*but*" *is an adversative conjunction.* **—***n.* **2.** an adversative word or proposition. [t. LL: m. s. *adversātivus*] **—ad·ver′sa·tive·ly,** *adv*

ad·verse (ăd vûrs′, ăd′vûrs), *adj.* **1.** antagonistic in purpose or effect: *adverse criticism, adverse to slavery.* **2.** opposing one's interests or desire: *adverse fate, fortune, influences, or circumstances.* **3.** being or acting in a contrary direction; opposed or opposing: *adverse winds.* **4.** opposite; confronting: *the adverse page.* **5.** *Bot.* turned toward the axis, as a leaf. [ME, t. L: m. *adversus,* pp.,

b., blend of, blended; **c.,** cognate with; **d.,** dialect, dialectal; **der.,** derived from; **f.,** formed from; **g.,** going back to; **m.,** modification of; **r.,** replacing; **s.,** stem of; **t.,** taken from; **?,** perhaps.   See the full key on inside cover.

turned against, turned towards] —**ad·verse·ly**, *adv.* —**ad·verse′ness**, *n.* —**Syn. 1.** hostile, inimical. **2.** unfavorable; unlucky, disastrous. See **contrary.**

ad·ver·si·ty (ăd vûr′sə tĭ), *n.*, *pl.* **-ties.** **1.** adverse fortune or fate; a condition marked by misfortune, calamity, or distress: *his struggles with adversity.* **2.** an unfortunate event or circumstance: *the prosperities and adversities of this life.* [ME *adversite*, t. L: m. *adversitas* opposition] —**Syn. 2.** See **affliction.**

ad·vert¹ (ăd vûrt′), *v.i.* **1.** to make a remark or remarks (about or in relation to); refer (fol. by *to*): *he adverted briefly to the occurrences of the day.* **2.** to turn the attention (fol. by *to*). [t. L: s. *advertere* turn to; r. ME *averte(n)*, t. OF: m. *avertir*]

ad·vert² (ăd′vərt), *n.* *Brit. Colloq.* advertisement.

ad·vert·ent (ăd vûr′tənt), *adj.* attentive; heedful. —**ad·vert′ence, ad·vert′en·cy,** *n.* —**ad·vert′ent·ly,** *adv.*

ad·ver·tise (ăd′vər tīz′, ăd′vər tīz′), *v.*, **-tised, -tising.** —*v.t.* **1.** to give information to the public concerning; make public announcement of, by publication in periodicals, by printed bills, by broadcasting over the radio, etc.: *to advertise a reward.* **2.** to praise the good qualities of, in order to induce the public to buy or invest in. **3.** to give notice, advice, or information to; inform: *I advertised him of my intention.* **4.** *Obs.* to admonish; warn. —*v.i.* **5.** to ask (*for*) by placing an advertisement in a newspaper, magazine, etc., or by broadcasting over the radio: *to advertise for a house to rent.* Also, **ad′ver·tize′.** [ME *advertise(n)*, t. MF: m. *advertiss-*, s. *advertir*, t. L: m. *advertere.* See ADVERT¹, -ISE] —**ad·ver·tis·er, ad′ver·tiz′er,** *n.*

ad·ver·tise·ment (ăd′vər tīz′mənt, ăd vûr′tĭs mənt, -tĭz-), *n.* **1.** a printed announcement, as of goods for sale, in a newspaper, magazine, etc. **2.** a public notice, esp. in print. Also, **ad′ver·tize′ment.** [ME, t. MF: m. *advertissement*]

ad·ver·tis·ing (ăd′vər tī′zĭng), *n.* **1.** act or practice of bringing anything, as one's wants or one's business, into public notice, esp. by paid announcements in periodicals, on billboards, etc., or on the radio: *to secure customers by advertising.* **2.** paid announcements; advertisements. **3.** the profession of designing and writing advertisements. Also, **ad′ver·tiz·ing.**

ad·vice (ăd vīs′), *n.* **1.** an opinion recommended, or offered, as worthy to be followed: *I shall act on your advice.* **2.** a communication, esp. from a distance, containing information: *advice from abroad.* [late ME *advyse*, t. MF: m. *advis* opinion, f. L: ad- AD- + s. *vīsum*, pp. neut., what seems best; r. ME *avis*, t. OF] —**Syn. 1.** admonition. ADVICE, COUNSEL are suggestions given by a (presumably) wiser or more highly trained person to one considered in need of guidance. ADVICE is a practical recommendation as to action or conduct: *advice about purchasing land.* COUNSEL is weighty and serious advice, given after careful deliberation: *counsel about one's career.* **2.** information, news, tidings; report.

ad·vis·a·ble (ăd vī′zə bəl), *adj.* **1.** proper to be advised or to be recommended. **2.** open to or desirous of advice. —**ad·vis′a·bil′i·ty, ad·vis′a·ble·ness,** *n.* —**ad·vis′a·bly,** *adv.* —**Syn. 1.** expedient, politic, proper, prudent, sensible.

ad·vise (ăd vīz′), *v.*, **-vised, -vising.** —*v.t.* **1.** to give counsel to; offer an opinion to, as worthy or expedient to be followed: *I advise you to be cautious.* **2.** to recommend as wise, prudent, etc.: *he advised secrecy.* **3.** to give (a person, etc.) information or notice (fol. by *of*): *the merchants were advised of the risk.* —*v.i.* **4.** to take counsel (fol. by *with*): *I shall advise with my friends.* **5.** to offer counsel; give advice: *I shall act as you advise.* [t. LL: m.s. *advisāre*; r. ME *avise(n)*, t. OF] —**Syn. 1.** admonish, caution. See **warn.** **3.** inform, notify, apprise. **4.** consult, confer.

ad·vised (ăd vīzd′), *adj.* **1.** considered: now chiefly in *ill-advised* or *well-advised.* **2.** informed: *kept thoroughly advised.* —**ad·vis·ed·ness** (ăd vī′zĭd nĭs), *n.*

ad·vis·ed·ly (ăd vī′zĭd lĭ), *adv.* after due consideration; deliberately.

ad·vise·ment (ăd vīz′mənt), *n.* careful deliberation; consultation: *the application was taken under advisement.*

ad·vis·er (ăd vī′zər), *n.* **1.** one who gives advice. **2.** *Educ.* a teacher who helps students select their course of studies, etc. Also, **ad·vi′sor.**

ad·vi·so·ry (ăd vī′zər ĭ), *adj.* of, or giving, advice; having power to advise: *an advisory council.*

ad·vo·ca·cy (ăd′və kə sĭ), *n.* act of pleading for, supporting, or recommending; active espousal.

ad·vo·cate (*v.* ăd′və kāt′; *n.* ăd′və kĭt, -kāt′), *v.*, **-cated, -cating.** —*v.t.* **1.** to plead in favor of; support or urge by argument; recommend publicly: *he advocated isolationism.* —*n.* **2.** one who defends, vindicates, or espouses a cause by argument; an upholder; a defender (fol. by *of*): *an advocate of peace.* **3.** one who pleads for or in behalf of another; intercessor. **4.** *Chiefly Scot., sometimes English, and formerly U.S.* one who pleads the cause of another in a court of law. [t. L: m. s. *advocātus* (prop. pp.) one summoned to help another (in legal case); r. ME *avocat*, t. OF] —**ad′vo·ca′tor,** *n.*

ad·vo·ca·tion (ăd′və kā′shən), *n.* **1.** *Law.* the calling of an action before itself by a superior (papal or Scottish) court. **2.** *Obs.* advocacy. **3.** *Obs.* act of summoning.

ad·vo·ca·to·ry (ăd vŏk′ə tōr′ĭ), *adj.* of an advocate or his functions.

ad·vo·ca·tus di·a·bo·li (ăd′və kā′təs dī ăb′ə lī′), Me-

---

dieval Latin. **1.** the devil's advocate. **2.** an adverse critic, esp. of what is deemed good; a detractor.

ad·vow·son (ăd vou′zən), *n.* *Eng. Law.* the right of presentation to a benefice. [t. AF; r. ME *avoweson*, t. OF: m. *avoeson*, g. L *advocātio*]

advt., advertisement.

ad·y·na·mi·a (ăd′ə nā′mĭ ə), *n.* *Pathol.* weakness; debility; asthenia. [t. Gk.]

ad·y·nam·ic (ăd′ə năm′ĭk, ā′dī-), *adj.* *Pathol.* lacking strength; asthenic.

ad·y·tum (ăd′ə təm), *n.*, *pl.* **-ta** (-tə). **1.** (in ancient worship) a sacred place which the public might not enter; an inner shrine. **2.** the most sacred or reserved part of any place of worship. [t. L, t. Gk.: m. *ádyton* not to be entered]

adz (ădz), *n.* a heavy chisellike steel tool fastened at right angles to a wooden handle, used to remove surplus material, etc. Also, **adze.** [ME *adese*, OE *adesa*]

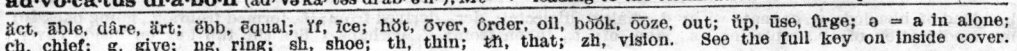

ad·zu·ki bean (ăd zōō′kĭ), adsuki bean.

Adz
A, Cooper's adz; B, Carpenter's adz

ae¹ (ā), *adj.* *Scot.* one.

ae² or **æ, 1.** a digraph or ligature appearing in Latin and Latinized Greek words. In English words of Latin or Greek origin, *ae* is now usually reduced to *e*, except generally in proper names (*Caesar*), in words belonging to Roman or Greek antiquities (*aegis*), and in modern words of scientific or technical use (*aecium*). **2.** an early English ligature representing a vowel sound like the *a* in modern *bad.* The long *æ* continued in use until about 1250, but was finally replaced by *e.* The short *æ* was given up by 1150, being replaced usually by *a* but sometimes by *e.*

ae-. For words with initial ae-, see also e-.

Æ, pen name of George William Russell. Also, **A.E.**

ae., (L *aetatis*) at the age of; aged.

Ae·a·cus (ē′ə kəs), *n.* *Gk. Myth.* a son of Zeus; grandfather of Achilles and a j dge in the lower world. Cf. **Minos, Rhadamanthus.**

ae·ci·al stage (ē′shĭ əl), *Bot.* the part of the life cycle of the rust fungi in which aecia are formed.

ae·cid·i·al stage (ē sĭd′ĭ əl), *Bot.* the part of the life cycle of the rust fungi in which aecidia are formed.

ae·cid·i·um (ē sĭd′ĭ əm), *n.*, *pl.* **-cidia** (-sĭd′ĭ ə). *Bot.* an aecium in which the spores are always formed in chains and enclosed in a cup-shaped peridium, as in the form genus *Aecidium.* [NL dim. of Gk. *aikia* injury]

ae·ci·o·spore (ē′sĭ ə spōr′), *n.* *Bot.* a spore borne by an aecium.

ae·ci·um (ē′shĭ əm, ē′sĭ-), *n.*, *pl.* **-cia** (-shĭ ə, -sĭ ə). *Bot.* the sorus of rust fungi which arises from the haploid mycelium, commonly accompanied by spermogonia and bearing chainlike or stalked spores. [t. NL: f. m.s. Gk. *aikia* an injurious effect + *-ium* -IUM] —**ae·ci·al** (ē′shĭ əl), *adj.*

a·ë·des (ā ē′dēz), *n.* **1.** the mosquito, *Aëdes aegypti,* which transmits yellow fever and dengue. **2.** any mosquito of the genus *Aëdes.* [t. NL, t. Gk: unpleasant]

ae·dile (ē′dīl), *n.* (in ancient Rome) one of a board of magistrates in charge of public buildings, streets, markets, games, etc. Also, **edile.** [t. L: m. s. *aedilis*] —**ae′dile·ship′,** *n.*

Ae·ë·tes (ē ē′tēz), *n.* *Gk. Legend.* a king of Colchis, father of Medea, and custodian of the Golden Fleece.

A.E.F., American Expeditionary Forces.

Ae·ge·an (ē jē′ən), *adj.* denoting or pertaining to the civilization which preceded the historic Hellenic period and which flourished in various islands in, and lands adjacent to, the Aegean Sea, as Crete, Argolis, etc. [f. m. s. L *Aegaeus* (t. Gk.: m. *Aigaios*) + -AN]

Aegean Islands, Greek and Turkish islands of the Aegean Sea, including the Dodecanese, Cyclades, and Sporades groups.

Aegean Sea, an arm of the Mediterranean between Greece and Asia Minor. ab. 350 mi. long; ab. 200 mi. wide.

Ae·geus (ē′jōōs, ē′jĭ əs), *n.* *Gk. Legend.* king of Athens and father of Theseus.

Ae·gi·na (ē jī′nə), *n.* **1.** Gulf of, a gulf in SE Greece. **2.** an island in this gulf. 11,000 pop. (est. 1948); 32 sq. mi. **3.** a seaport on this island. 6000 (est. 1948).

Ae·gir (ā′gĭr, ē′jĭr), *n.* *Scand. Myth.* the sea god, the husband of Ran. Te. Icel.]

ae·gis (ē′jĭs), *n.* **1.** *Gk. Myth.* **a.** the shield of Zeus. **b.** the shield lent by Zeus to other deities, esp. Athene. **2.** protection; sponsorship: *under the imperial aegis.* Also, **egis.** [t. L, t. Gk.: m. *aigis*, lit., a goatskin]

Ae·gis·thus (ē jĭs′thəs), *n.* *Gk. Legend.* the cousin of Agamemnon. He seduced Clytemnestra in the absence of her husband, Agamemnon, and was later slain by her son, Orestes.

Ae·gos·pot·a·mi (ē′gəs pŏt′ə mī′), *n.* a creek in ancient Thrace, flowing into the Hellespont: near its mouth the Athenian fleet was defeated by Lysander, 405 B.C. leading to the termination of the Peloponnesian War.

Ae·gyp·tus (ē jĭp'təs), n. Gk. Legend. a king of Egypt and twin brother of Danaüs.

Æl·fric (ăl'frĭk), n. ("Ælfric Grammaticus") A.D. c955–c1020, English abbot and writer.

-aemia, var. of **-emia**, as in toxaemia.

Ae·ne·as (ĭ nē'əs), n. Class. Myth. the son of Anchises and Aphrodite (Venus): a Trojan hero, who became the founder of Rome. See Aeneid. [t. L, t. Gk.: m. Aineías]

Ae·ne·id (ĭ nē'ĭd), n. a Latin epic poem by Vergil, reciting the adventures of Aeneas after the fall of Troy.

a·ë·ne·ous (ā ē'nĭ əs), adj. bronze-colored. [t. L: m. aēneus brazen]

Ae·o·li·an (ē ō'lĭ ən), adj. **1.** belonging to a branch of the Greek race named from Aeolus, the legendary founder; Aeolic. **—n. 2.** a member of one of the three great divisions of the ancient Greek race, the two other divisions being the Dorian and the Ionian. **3.** Aeolic. Also, **Eolian**. [f. m.s. Gk. Aioleús Aeolus + -AN]

Ae·o·li·an (ē ō'lĭ ən), adj. **1.** pertaining to Aeolus, or to the winds in general. **2.** (l.c.) due to atmospheric action; wind-blown. [f. m.s. Gk. Aíolos Aeolus + -IAN]

aeolian harp, a box over which are stretched a number of strings of equal length, tuned in unison and sounded by the wind. Also, **aeolian lyre**.

Ae·ol·ic (ē ŏl'ĭk), n. **1.** the dialect of Greek spoken by the Aeolians. **—adj. 2.** Aeolian. Also, **Eolic**.

ae·o·li·pile (ē ŏl'ə pīl'), n. an instrument consisting essentially of a round vessel rotated by the force of steam generated within, and escaping through, bent arms. Also, **ae·ol'i·pyle'**. [t. L: m. s. aeolīpila, orig. Aeolī pila ball of Aeolus, or Aeolī pylae doorway of Aeolus]

Ae·o·lis (ē'ə lĭs), n. an ancient coastal region and Greek colony in NW Asia Minor.

ae·o·lo·trop·ic (ē'ə lō trŏp'ĭk), adj. Physics. not isotropic; anisotropic. [f. m. Gk. aiólo(s) changeful + -TROPIC] **ae·o·lot·ro·py** (ē'ə lŏt'rə pĭ), **ae·o·lot·ro·pism** (ē'ə lŏt'rə pĭz'əm), n.

Ae·o·lus (ē'ə ləs), n. Gk. Myth. the ruler of the winds.

ae·on (ē'ən, ē'ŏn), n. **1.** an indefinitely long period of time; an age. **2.** (in the Gnostic doctrine) one of a class of powers or beings conceived as emanating from the Supreme Being and performing various functions in the operations of the universe. **3.** Geol. eon. [t. L, t. Gk.: m. aiṓn lifetime, age]

ae·o·ni·an (ē ō'nĭ ən), adj. eternal. [f. m. s. Gk. aiṓnios agelong + -AN]

aer-, var. of **aero-** before vowels. Also, **aër-**.

aer·ate (âr'āt, ā'ə rāt'), v.t., **-ated**, **-ating**. **1.** to expose to the free action of the air: to aerate milk in order to remove odors. **2.** to charge or treat with air or a gas, esp. with carbon dioxide. **3.** Physiol. to expose (a medium or tissue) to air, as in the oxygenation of the blood in respiration. [f. AER- + -ATE¹] **—aer·a'tion**, n.

aer·a·tor (âr'ā tər, ā'ə rā'tər), n. **1.** an apparatus for aerating water or other fluids. **2.** a contrivance for fumigating wheat and other grain, to bleach it and destroy fungi and insects.

aer·i·al (adj. âr'ĭ əl, ā Yr'ĭ əl; n. âr'ĭ əl), adj. **1.** of, in, or produced by the air: aerial currents. **2.** inhabiting or frequenting the air: aerial creatures. **3.** reaching far into the air; high; lofty: aerial spires. **4.** partaking of the nature of air; airy: aerial beings. **5.** unsubstantial; visionary: aerial fancies. **6.** having a light and graceful beauty; ethereal: aerial music. **7.** Bot. growing in the air, as the adventitious roots of some trees. See illus. under banyan. **8.** pertaining to or used for, against, or in aircraft. **—n. 9.** Radio. an antenna. [f. s. L āerius airy (t. Gk.: m. āérios) + -AL¹] **—aer'i·al·ly**, adv.

aer·i·al·ist (âr'ĭ əl ĭst, ā Yr'ĭ əl-), n. a trapeze artist.

aer·i·al·i·ty (âr'Y̆ ăl'ə tĭ, ā Yr'-), n. unsubstantiality.

aerial perspective, that branch of perspective which considers the variations of light, shade, and color in objects delineated, according to their distances, the quality of light falling on them, and the medium through which they are seen.

aer·ie (âr'Y, Yr'Y), n. **1.** the nest of a bird of prey, as an eagle or a hawk. **2.** a lofty nest of any large bird. **3.** the brood in the nest; the young of a bird of prey. **4.** an elevated habitation or situation. **5.** Archaic. children. Also, **aery**, **eyrie**, **eyry**. [t. ML: m. aeria, t. OF: m. aire, g. L ārea (see AREA) or L ātrium ATRIUM]

aer·if·er·ous (â rĭf'ər əs), adj. conveying air, as the bronchial tubes. [f. AER- + -(I)FEROUS]

aer·i·fi·ca·tion (âr'ə fə kā'shən, ā Yr'-), n. **1.** act of combining with air. **2.** state of being filled with air.

aer·i·form (âr'ə fôrm', ā Yr'-), adj. **1.** having the form or nature of air; gaseous. **2.** unsubstantial; unreal.

aer·i·fy (âr'ə fī', ā Yr'-), v.t., **-fied**, **-fying**. **1.** to aerate. **2.** to make aeriform; convert into vapor.

aer·o (âr'ō), adj. **1.** of or for aircraft. **2.** of aeronautics.

aero-, a word element meaning: **1.** air; atmosphere. **2.** gas. **3.** airplane. Also, **aëro-**. [t. Gk., comb. form of āēr air]

aer·obe (âr'ōb), n. a bacterium or other microörganism whose existence requires, or is not destroyed by, the presence of free oxygen (opposed to anaerobe). [t. NL: m. aerobia, f. Gk.: āero- AERO- + m. bíos life]

aer·o·bee (âr'ə bĭ'), n. a recently developed rocket, capable of attaining an altitude of 100 miles and a speed of 3000 miles an hour, used mainly for carrying scientific recording instruments.

aer·o·bic (â rō'bĭk), adj. **1.** (of organisms or tissues) requiring, or not destroyed by, the presence of free oxygen. **2.** pertaining to or caused by the presence of oxygen: aerobic respiration. **—aer·o'bi·cal·ly**, adv.

aer·o·bi·um (â rō'bĭ əm), n., pl. **-bia** (-bĭ ə). aerobe.

aer·o·do·net·ics (âr'ō də nĕt'ĭks), n. the study of gliding or soaring flight; the science dealing with gliding craft. [f. s. Gk. āerodónētos air-tossed + -ICS]

aer·o·drome (âr'ə drōm'), n. Chiefly Brit. an airdrome.

aer·o·dy·nam·ics (âr'ō dī năm'Yks, -dY-), n. the science that treats of the motion of the air and other gases, or of their properties and mechanical effects when in motion. **—aer'o·dy·nam'ic**, adj.

aer·o·dyne (âr'ə dīn'), n. any heavier-than-air craft.

aer·o·em·bo·lism (âr'ō ĕm'bə lĭz'əm), n. a morbid condition caused by substantial decrease in atmospheric pressure, as in high-altitude flying, and characterized by the formation of nitrogen bubbles in the blood, pains in the lungs, etc. Cf. bends and caisson disease.

aer·o·gram (âr'ə grăm'), n. **1.** a radiogram. **2.** a message carried by aircraft.

aer·og·ra·phy (â rŏg'rə fĭ), n. description of the air or atmosphere. **—aer·og'ra·pher**, n. **—aer·o·graph·ic** (âr'ə grăf'Yk), **aer'o·graph'i·cal**, adj.

aer·o·lite (âr'ə līt'), n. a meteorite consisting mainly of stony matter. Also, **aer·o·lith** (âr'ə lĭth). **—aer·o·lit·ic** (âr'ə lĭt'Yk), adj.

aer·ol·o·gy (â rŏl'ə jĭ), n. the study of the properties of air and of the atmosphere. **—aer·o·log·ic** (âr'ə lŏj'Yk), **aer'o·log'i·cal**, adj. **—aer·ol'o·gist**, n.

aer·o·ma·rine (âr'ō mə rēn'), adj. Aeron. relating to navigation of aircraft above the ocean.

aer·o·me·chan·ic (âr'ō mə kăn'Yk), n. **1.** an aviation mechanic. **—adj. 2.** of or pertaining to aeromechanics.

aer·o·me·chan·ics (âr'ō mə kăn'Yks), n. the mechanics of air or gases. **—aer'o·me·chan'i·cal**, adj.

aer·om·e·ter (â rŏm'ə tər), n. an instrument for determining the weight, density, etc., of air or other gases.

aer·om·e·try (â rŏm'ə trĭ), n. pneumatics. **—aer·o·met·ric** (âr'ə mĕt'rY̆k), adj.

aeron., aeronautics.

aer·o·naut (âr'ə nôt'), n. **1.** the pilot of a balloon or other lighter-than-air craft. **2.** a traveler in an airship. [back formation from AERONAUTICS. Cf. F aéronaute]

aer·o·nau·tic (âr'ə nô'tĭk), adj. of aeronautics or aeronauts. Also, **aer'o·nau'ti·cal**. [t. NL: s. aeronautica, neut. pl. adj. pertaining to sailing in the air] **—aer'o·nau'ti·cal·ly**, adv.

aer·o·nau·tics (âr'ə nô'tY̆ks), n. the science or art of flight. [pl. of AERONAUTIC. See -ICS]

aer·o·pha·gi·a (âr'ə fā'jĭ ə), n. Psychiatry. morbid swallowing of air due to neurotic gastric disturbances.

aer·o·pho·bi·a (âr'ə fō'bĭ ə), n. Psychiatry. morbid fear of drafts of air, gases, and air-borne noxious influences.

aer·o·phore (âr'ə fōr'), n. a portable device filled with compressed air and used in cases of asphyxia, etc.

aer·o·phyte (âr'ə fīt'), n. Bot. epiphyte.

aer·o·plane (âr'ə plăn'), n. Chiefly Brit. airplane.

aer·o·scope (âr'ə skōp'), n. an apparatus for collecting microscopic objects from the air. **—aer·o·scop·ic** (âr'ə skŏp'Yk), adj.

aer·o·sol (âr'ə sŏl', -sŏl'), n. Phys. Chem. a system consisting of colloidal particles dispersed in a gas; a smoke or fog. [f. AERO- + SOL⁵]

aerosol bomb, a small metal container that sprays insecticide in a mist.

aer·o·stat (âr'ə stăt'), n. **1.** a balloon, airship, or any lighter-than-air craft. **2.** an aviator. [f. AERO- + s. Gk. statós placed]

aer·o·stat·ic (âr'ə stăt'Yk), adj. **1.** of aerostatics. **2.** of, or capable of supporting, aerostats. Also, **aer'o·stat'i·cal**.

aer·o·stat·ics (âr'ə stăt'Yks), n. **1.** the science of the equilibrium of air and other gases, and of the equilibrium of bodies sustained in them. **2.** the science of lighter-than-air craft. [pl. of aerostatic. See AEROSTAT, -ICS]

aer·o·sta·tion (âr'ə stā'shən), n. operation of aerostats. [t. F, der. aérostat AEROSTAT]

aer·o·ther·a·peu·tics (âr'ō thĕr'ə pū'tYks), n. that branch of therapeutics which deals with the curative use of air or of artificially prepared atmospheres. Also, **aer·o·ther·a·py** (âr'ō thĕr'ə pĭ).

aer·u·gi·nous (Yrōō'jə nəs), adj. bluish-green; like verdigris. [t. L: m. s. aerūginōsus]

aer·y¹ (âr'Y, ā'ə rĭ), adj. Poetic. ethereal; lofty. [t. L: m. s. āerius airy]

aer·y² (âr'Y, Yr'Y), n., pl. **aeries**. aerie.

aes-. For words with initial aes-, see also **es-**.

Aes·chi·nes (ĕs'kə nēz' or, esp. Brit., ĕs'-), n. 389–314 B.C., Athenian orator: rival of Demosthenes.

Aes·chy·lus (ĕs'kə ləs or, esp. Brit., ĕs'-), n. 525–456 B.C., Greek tragic poet and dramatist. **—Aes·chy·le·an** (ĕs'kə lē'ən or, esp. Brit., ĕs'-), adj.

Aes·cu·la·pi·an (ĕs'kyə lā'pĭ ən or, esp. Brit., ĕs'-), adj. **1.** pertaining to Aesculapius. **2.** medical. **—n. 3.** physician.

Aes·cu·la·pi·us (ĕs'kyə lā'pĭ əs or, esp. Brit., ĕs'-), n. Rom. Myth. the god of medicine and healing.

Ae·sir (ā'sĭr, ĕ'-), n. pl. the gods of the Scandinavian mythology, dwelling in Asgard. [t. Icel., pl. of āss god]

---

b., blend of, blended; c., cognate with; d., dialect, dialectal; der., derived from; f., formed from; g., going back to; m., modification of; r., replacing; s., stem of; t., taken from; ?, perhaps.   See the full key on inside cover.

Ae·sop (ē′səp, ē′sŏp), n. 620?–560? B.C., Greek writer of fables. **—Ae·so·pi·an** (ē sō′pĭ an), adj.

aes·the·sia (ĕs thē′zhə), n. esthesia. Also, **aes·the·sis** (ĕs thē′sĭs). [t. Gk.: m. aisthēsia]

aes·thete (ĕs′thēt or, esp. Brit., ēs′-), n. 1. one who cultivates the sense of the beautiful; one very sensitive to the beauties of art or nature. 2. one who affects great love of art, music, poetry, etc., and indifference to practical matters. Also, **esthete**. [t. Gk.: m.s. aisthētēs one who perceives]

aes·thet·ic (ĕs thĕt′ĭk or, esp. Brit., ēs-), adj. 1. pertaining to the sense of the beautiful or the science of aesthetics. 2. having a sense of the beautiful; characterized by a love of beauty. Also, **esthetic**. [t. Gk.: m.s. aisthētikós perceptive]

aes·thet·i·cal (ĕs thĕt′ə kəl or, esp. Brit., ēs-), adj. of or relating to aesthetics. Also, **esthetical**.

aes·thet·i·cal·ly (ĕs thĕt′ĭk lĭ or, esp. Brit., ēs-), adv. 1. according to aesthetics or its principles. 2. in an aesthetic manner.

aes·the·ti·cian (ĕs′thə tĭsh′ən or, esp. Brit., ēs′-), n. one versed in aesthetics. Also, **esthetician**.

aes·thet·i·cism (ĕs thĕt′ə sĭz′əm or, esp. Brit., ēs-), n. 1. the acceptance of artistic beauty and taste as a fundamental standard, ethical and other standards being secondary. 2. an exaggerated devotion to art, music, or poetry, with indifference to practical matters. Also, **estheticism**.

aes·thet·ics (ĕs thĕt′ĭks or, esp. Brit., ēs-), n. 1. Philos. the science which deduces from nature and taste the rules and principles of art; the theory of the fine arts; the science of the beautiful, or that branch of philosophy which deals with its principles or effects; the doctrines of taste. 2. Psychol. the study of the mind and emotions in relation to the sense of beauty. Also, **esthetics**. [pl. of AESTHETIC. See -ICS]

aes·ti·val (ĕs′tə vəl, ĕs tī′- or, esp. Brit., ĕs′-, ēs-), adj. estival.

aes·ti·vate (ĕs′tə vāt′ or, esp. Brit., ēs′-), v.i., -vated, -vating. estivate. **—aes′ti·va′tion**, n.

aet-. For words with initial aet-, see also et-.

ae·ta·tis su·ae (ē tā′tĭs sōō′ē), Latin. in a certain year of one's age.

ae·ther (ē′thər), n. ether (defs. 2, 3, 4). **—ae·the·re·al** (ĭ thĭr′ĭ əl), adj.

ae·ti·ol·o·gy (ē′tĭ ŏl′ə jĭ), n. etiology. **—ae·ti·o·log·i·cal** (ē′tĭ ə lŏj′ə kəl), adj.

Aet·na (ĕt′nə), n. Mount. See **Etna, Mount**.

Ae·to·li·a (ē tō′lĭə), n. ancient district in W Greece.

af-, var. of ad- (by assimilation) before f, as in affect.

AF, Anglo-French. Also, **A.F.**

A.F., audio frequency. Also, **a.f.**

A.F.A.M., Ancient Free and Accepted Masons.

a·far (ə fär′), adv. 1. from a distance (usually prec. by from): he came from afar. 2. far away; at or to a distance (usually fol. by off): he saw the place afar off. [ME a far. See A-¹, FAR]

a·feard (ə fĭrd′), adj. Archaic or Dial. afraid. Also, **a·feared**. [ME afered, OE āfǣred]

a·fe·brile (ā fē′brəl, ā fĕb′rəl), adj. without fever; feverless. [f. A-⁶ + FEBRILE]

aff (ăf), prep., adv. Scot. off.

af·fa·ble (ăf′ə bəl), adj. 1. easy to talk to or to approach; polite; friendly: an affable and courteous gentleman. 2. expressing affability; mild; benign: an affable countenance. [t. F, t. L: m.s. affābilis able to be spoken to] **—af′fa·bil′i·ty, af′fa·ble·ness,** n. **—af′fa·bly,** adv. **—Syn. 1.** courteous, urbane. See **civil**.

af·fair (ə fâr′), n. 1. anything done or to be done; that which requires action or effort; business; concern: an affair of great moment, the affairs of state. 2. (pl.) matters of interest or concern; particular doings or interests: put your affairs in order. 3. an event or a performance; a particular action, operation, or proceeding: when did this affair happen? 4. thing; matter (applied to anything made or existing, with a descriptive or qualifying term): this machine is a complicated affair. 5. a private or personal concern; a special function, business, or duty: attend to your own affairs. 6. a love affair. [f. m. affaire, g. à faire to do; r. ME afere, t. OF: m. afaire]

af·faire d'a·mour (à fĕr′ dà mōōr′), French. a love affair.

af·faire de cœur (à fĕr′ də kœr′), French. an affair of the heart; a love affair.

af·faire d'hon·neur (à fĕr′ dô nœr′), French. a duel.

af·fect¹ (ə fĕkt′), v.t. 1. to act on; produce an effect or a change in: cold affects the body. 2. to impress; move (in mind or feelings): the poetry affected me deeply. 3. (of pain, disease, etc.) to attack or lay hold of. —n. 4. Psychol. feeling or emotion. 5. Obs. affection; passion; sensation; inclination; inward disposition or feeling. [t. L: s. affectus, pp., influenced, attacked] **—Syn. 1.** AFFECT, EFFECT agree in the idea of exerting influence. To AFFECT is to concern, be of interest or importance to; to produce an effect or in upon something: to affect one's conduct or health. To EFFECT is to accomplish or bring about something: to effect a reconciliation. 2. touch; move, stir.

af·fect² (ə fĕkt′), v.t. 1. to make a show of; put on a pretense of; pretend; feign: to affect ignorance. 2. to make a show of liking or imitating: to affect a Southern accent. 3. to use or adopt by preference; choose; prefer: the peculiar costume which he affected. 4. to assume the character or attitude of: to affect the freethinker. 5. to

tend toward habitually or naturally: a substance which affects colloidal form. 6. (of animals and plants) to inhabit; frequent: moss affects the northern slopes. 7. Archaic. to take pleasure in; fancy; like. 8. Archaic. to aim at; aspire to. —v.i. 9. to profess; pretend: he affected to be wearied. [t. F: s. affecter, t. L: m. affectāre] **—af·fect′-er,** n. **—Syn. 1.** See **pretend**.

af·fec·ta·tion (ăf′ĭk tā′shən, -ĕk-), n. 1. a striving for the appearance of (a quality not really or fully possessed); pretense of the possession or character; effort for the reputation (fol. by of): an affectation of wit, affectation of great wealth. 2. artificiality of manner or conduct; effort to attract notice by pretense, assumption, or any assumed peculiarity: his affectations are insufferable. 3. Obs. strenuous pursuit or desire (fol. by of). [t. L: s. affectātio a pursuit after] **—Syn. 2.** airs, mannerisms.

af·fect·ed¹ (ə fĕk′tĭd), adj. 1. acted upon; influenced. 2. influenced injuriously; impaired; attacked, as by climate or disease. 3. moved; touched: she was deeply affected. [pp. of AFFECT¹]

af·fect·ed² (ə fĕk′tĭd), adj. 1. assumed artificially: affected airs, affected diction. 2. assuming or pretending to possess characteristics which are not natural: an affected lady. 3. inclined or disposed: well affected toward a project. 4. having to some extent: affected with the national interest. [pp. of AFFECT²] **—af·fect′ed·ly,** adv. **—af·fect′ed·ness,** n. **—Syn. 1.** pretended, feigned.

af·fect·ing (ə fĕk′tĭng), adj. having power to excite or move the feelings; tending to move the affections. **—af·fect′ing·ly,** adv. **—Syn.** touching, pathetic.

af·fec·tion¹ (ə fĕk′shən), n. 1. a settled good will, love, or zealous attachment: the affection of a parent for his child. 2. the state of having one's feelings affected; emotion or feeling: over and above our reason and affections. 3. Pathol. a disease, or the condition of being diseased; a morbid or abnormal state of body or mind: a gouty affection. 4. act of affecting; act of influencing or acting upon. 5. state of being affected. 6. Philos. a contingent, alterable, and accidental state or quality of being. 7. Psychol. the affective aspect of a mental process. 8. Archaic. a bodily state due to any influence. 9. Obs. bent or disposition of mind. [t. L: s. affectio influence (active), state of mind, favorable disposition (passive)] **—Syn. 1.** devotion, fondness. See **love**. 3. See **disease**. **—Ant. 1.** dislike.

af·fec·tion² (ə fĕk′shən), n. Obs. affectation. [f. AFFECT², v. + -ION]

af·fec·tion·al (ə fĕk′shən əl), adj. relating to or implying affection. [f. AFFECTION¹ + -AL¹]

af·fec·tion·ate (ə fĕk′shən ĭt), adj. 1. characterized by or manifesting affection; possessing or indicating love; tender: an affectionate embrace. 2. having great love or affection; warmly attached: your affectionate brother. 3. Obs. strongly disposed or inclined. 4. Obs. biased; partisan. **—af·fec′tion·ate·ly,** adv. **—af·fec′tion·ate·ness,** n. **—Syn. 1.** loving, fond. 2. devoted.

af·fec·tive (ə fĕk′tĭv), adj. 1. pertaining to the affections; emotional. 2. exciting emotion; affecting. 3. Psychol. pertaining to feeling or emotion, esp. to pleasurable or unpleasurable aspects of a mental process.

af·fer·ent (ăf′ər ənt), adj. Physiol. bringing to or leading toward a central organ or point (opposed to efferent): afferent nerves or veins. [t. L: s. afferens, ppr., bringing to]

af·fi·ance (ə fī′əns), v., -anced, -ancing, n. —v.t. 1. to bind by promise of marriage; betroth: to affiance a daughter. —n. 2. the pledging of faith; esp. a marriage contract. 3. trust; confidence; reliance. [ME, t. OF: m. afiance, der. afier, g. LL affidāre pledge]

af·fi·anced (ə fī′ənst), adj. betrothed.

af·fi·ant (ə fī′ənt), n. Law. one who makes an affidavit.

af·fiche (à fēsh′), n. French. a posted notice; a poster.

af·fi·da·vit (ăf′ə dā′vĭt), n. Law. a written declaration upon oath, esp. one made before an authorized official. [t. L: he has made oath]

af·fil·i·ate (v. ə fĭl′ĭ āt′; n. ə fĭl′ĭ ĭt, -āt′), v., -ated, -ating, n. —v.t. 1. to bring into association or close connection: the two banks were affiliated by a common ownership of stock. 2. to attach or unite on terms of fellowship; associate (fol. by with in U. S. usage, by to in Brit. usage): affiliated with the church. 3. to connect in the way of descent or derivation (fol. by upon). 4. to adopt. 5. Law. a. to fix the paternity of, as a bastard child: the mother affiliated her child upon John Doe. b. to refer to as being the child of or belonging to. —v.i. 6. to associate oneself; be intimately united in action or interest. —n. 7. U.S. a branch organization. 8. one who is affiliated; associate; auxiliary. [t. LL: m. s. affiliātus, pp., adopted as a son]

af·fil·i·a·tion (ə fĭl′ĭ ā′shən), n. 1. act of affiliating. 2. state of being affiliated; association; relationship.

af·fined (ə fīnd′), adj. 1. related; connected. 2. Obs. bound. [f. s. F affiné related + -ED²]

af·fin·i·tive (ə fĭn′ə tĭv), adj. characterized by affinity; closely related.

af·fin·i·ty (ə fĭn′ə tĭ), n., pl. -ties. 1. a natural liking for, or attraction to, a person or thing. 2. one for whom such a natural liking or attraction is felt. 3. relationship by marriage or by ties other than those of blood (distinguished from consanguinity). 4. inherent likeness or agreement as between things; close resemblance or connection. 5. Biol. the phylogenetic relationship between

---

ăct, āble, dâre, ärt; ĕbb, ēqual; ĭf, īce; hŏt, ōver, ôrder, oil, bŏok, ōōze, out; ŭp, ūse, ûrge; ə = a in alone; ch, chief; g, give; ng, ring; sh, shoe; th, thin; th, that; zh, vision.   See the full key on inside cover.

two organisms or groups of organisms resulting in **a** resemblance in general plan or structure, or in the essential structural parts. **6.** *Chem.* that force by which the atoms or bodies of dissimilar nature unite in certain definite proportions to form a compound. [ME, t. F: m. *af(f)inité,* t. L: m. s. *affīnitas*]

af·firm (ə fûrm′), *v.t.* **1.** to state or assert positively; maintain as true: *to affirm one's loyalty to one's country.* **2.** to establish, confirm, or ratify: *the appellate court affirmed the judgment of the lower court.* —*v.i.* **3.** to declare positively; assert solemnly. **4.** *Law.* to declare solemnly before a court or magistrate, but without oath (a practice allowed where the affirmant has scruples, usually religious, against taking an oath). [t. L: s. *affirmāre;* r. ME *aferme(n),* t. OF: m. *afermer*] —**af·firm′a·ble,** *adj.* —**af·firm′a·bly,** *adv.* —**af·firm′er,** *n.* —Syn. **1.** See **declare.**

af·firm·ant (ə fûr′mənt), *n.* one who affirms.

af·fir·ma·tion (ăf′ər mā′shən), *n.* **1.** the assertion that something is, or is true. **2.** that which is affirmed; a proposition that is declared to be true. **3.** establishment of something of prior origin; confirmation; ratification. **4.** *Law.* a solemn declaration accepted instead of a statement under oath. Also, **af·firm·ance** (ə fûr′məns).

af·firm·a·tive (ə fûr′mə tĭv), *adj.* **1.** giving affirmation or assent; confirmatory; not negative: *an affirmative answer.* **2.** *Logic.* denoting a proposition in which a property is affirmed of a subject, as "all men are happy." —*n.* **3.** that which affirms or asserts; a positive proposition: *two negatives make an affirmative.* **4.** an affirmative word or phrase, as *yes* or *I do.* **5.** the affirmative, the agreeing or concurring side. [t. LL: m. s. *affirmātīvus;* r. ME *affirmatyff,* t. F] —**af·firm′a·tive·ly,** *adj.*

af·firm·a·to·ry (ə fûr′mə tōr′Y), *adj.* affirmative.

af·fix (*v.* ə fĭks′; *n.* ăf′ĭks), *v.t.* **1.** to fix; fasten, join, or attach (fol. by *to*): *to affix stamps to a letter.* **2.** to impress (a seal or stamp). **3.** to attach (blame, reproach, ridicule, etc.). —*n.* **4.** that which is joined or attached. **5.** *Gram.* any meaningful element (prefix, infix, or suffix) added to a stem or base, as *-ed* added to *want* to form *wanted.* [t. ML: s. *affixāre* freq. of L *affīgere* fasten to] —**af·fix′er,** *n.*

af·fix·ture (ə fĭks′chər), *n.* act of affixing; attachment.

af·fla·ted (ə flā′tĭd), *adj.* inspired.

af·fla·tus (ə flā′təs), *n.* **1.** inspiration; an impelling mental force acting from within. **2.** divine communication of knowledge. [t. L: a blast]

af·flict (ə flĭkt′), *v.t.* **1.** to distress with mental or bodily pain; trouble greatly or grievously: *to be afflicted with the gout.* **2.** *Obs.* to overthrow; rout. [t. L: s. *afflictus,* pp., thrown down] —**af·flict′er,** *n.* —Syn. **1.** vex, harass, torment, plague.

af·flic·tion (ə flĭk′shən), *n.* **1.** a state of pain, distress, or grief: *they sympathized with us in our affliction.* **2.** a cause of continued pain of body or mind, as sickness, loss, calamity, persecution, etc. [ME, t. L: s. *afflictio*] —Syn. **1.** AFFLICTION, ADVERSITY, MISFORTUNE, TRIAL refer to an event or circumstance which is hard to bear. A MISFORTUNE is any seriously adverse or unfavorable occurrence: *he had the misfortune to break his leg.* AFFLICTION suggests not only a misfortune but the emotional effect of this: *blindness is one kind of affliction.* ADVERSITY suggests one of a succession of mishaps and afflictions: *Job remained patient under all his adversities.* TRIAL emphasizes the testing of one's character in undergoing misfortunes, trouble, etc.: *his son's conduct was a great trial to him.*

af·flic·tive (ə flĭk′tĭv), *adj.* characterized by or causing pain; distressing. —**af·flic′tive·ly,** *adv.*

af·flu·ence (ăf′lōō əns), *n.* **1.** abundance of material goods; wealth: *to live in great affluence.* **2.** an abundant supply, as of thoughts, words, etc.; a profusion. **3.** a flowing to or onward; afflux. [t. F, t. L: m. s. *affluentia*]

af·flu·ent (ăf′lōō ənt), *adj.* **1.** abounding in means; rich: *an affluent person.* **2.** abounding in anything; abundant. **3.** flowing freely: *an affluent fountain.* —*n.* **4.** a tributary stream. [ME, t. L: s. *affluens,* ppr., flowing to] —**af′flu·ent·ly,** *adv.* —Syn. **1.** See **rich.**

af·flux (ăf′lŭks), *n.* **1.** that which flows to or toward a point: *an afflux of blood to the head.* **2.** act of flowing to; a flow. [t. ML: s. *affluxus,* n., der. L *affluere* flow to]

af·ford (ə fōrd′), *v.t.* **1.** to be able, or have the means (often prec. by *can* or *may* and fol. by an infinitive): *we can afford to sell cheap.* **2.** to be able to meet the expense of; spare the price of (often prec. by *can* or *may*): *he can't afford a car.* **3.** to be able to give or spare (often prec. by *can* or *may*): *I can't afford the loss of a day.* **4.** to supply; furnish: *the transaction afforded him a good profit.* **5.** to be capable of yielding or providing: *the records afford no explanation.* **6.** to give or confer upon: *to afford one great pleasure, etc.* [ME *aforthen,* OE *geforthian* further, accomplish] —**af·ford′a·ble,** *adj.*

af·for·est (ə fōr′Yst, ə fŏr′Yst), *v.t.* to convert (bare or cultivated land) into forest, originally for the purpose of providing hunting grounds. [t. ML: s. *afforestāre.* See AD-, FOREST] —**af·for·est·a′tion,** *n.*

af·fran·chise (ə frăn′chīz), *v.t.,* **-chised, -chising.** to free from a state of dependence, servitude, or obligation. [t. F: m. (by assoc. with FRANCHISE, n.) *affranchiss-,* s. of *affranchir.* See A-⁵, FRANK¹]

af·fray (ə frā′), *n.* **1.** a public fight; a noisy quarrel; a brawl. **2.** *Law.* the fighting of two or more persons in a public place. —*v.t.* **3.** *Archaic.* to frighten. [ME *a(f)fray-(en),* t. AF, var. of *effrayer* of *effreer,* g. LL *exfridāre,* f. ex- EX-¹ + *-fridāre,* der. *fridus* peace (of Gmc. orig.)]

af·fri·cate (ăf′rə kĭt), *n. Phonet.* a composite speech sound beginning with a stop and ending with a fricative, such as *ch* in *church* (which begins like *t* and ends like *sh*). Also, **af·fric·a·tive** (ə frĭk′ə tĭv). [t. L: m.s. *affricātus,* pp., rubbed on or against]

af·fright (ə frīt′), *Archaic.* —*v.t.* **1.** to frighten. —*n.* **2.** sudden fear or terror; fright. **3.** a source of terror. **4.** act of terrifying. [ME *afrighten,* OE *āfyrhtan,* f. ā- (intensive) + *fyrhtan* frighten]

af·front (ə frŭnt′), *n.* **1.** a personally offensive act or word; an intentional slight; an open manifestation of disrespect; an insult to the face: *an affront to the king.* **2.** an offense to one's dignity or self-respect. —*v.t.* **3.** to offend by an open manifestation of disrespect or insolence: *an affronting speech.* **4.** to put out of countenance; make ashamed or confused. **5.** to meet or encounter face to face; confront: *to affront death.* **6.** *Archaic.* to front; face. [ME *afront(en),* t. OF: m. *afronter,* g. LL *affrontāre*] —**af·front′er,** *n.* —**af·front′ing·ly,** *adv.* —Syn. **1.** impertinence, contumely, indignity.

af·fron·tive (ə frŭn′tĭv), *adj. Archaic.* insulting.

af·fu·sion (ə fū′zhən), *n.* the pouring on of water or other liquid. [f. s. L *affūsus,* pp., poured + -ION]

Afgh., Afghanistan.

Af·ghan (ăf′gən, -găn), *n.* **1.** a native of Afghanistan. **2.** Pushtu (language). **3.** *(l.c.)* a kind of woolen blanket, knitted, crocheted, or woven, usually in a geometric pattern. **4.** a breed of hound with a long narrow head and a long silky coat. —*adj.* **5.** of Afghanistan or its people.

Af·ghan·i·stan (ăf găn′ə stăn′), *n.* a kingdom in S Asia, NW of India, E of Iran, and S of the Soviet Union. ab. 12,000,000 (est. 1955); 250,000 sq. mi. *Cap.:* Kabul.

a·fi·cio·na·do (ə fĭsh′yə nä′dō; *Sp.* ä fē′thyô nä′Ŧħô), *n.* an ardent devotee. [Sp.]

a·field (ə fēld′), *adv.* **1.** abroad; away from home. **2.** off the beaten path; far and wide: *to stray far afield in one's reading.* **3.** in or to the field or fields.

a·fire (ə fīr′), *adv., adj.* on fire: *to set something afire.*

A.F.L., American Federation of Labor. Also, **A.F. of L.**

a·flame (ə flām′), *adv., adj.* **1.** on fire; ablaze: *the house was all aflame.* **2.** glowing: *aflame with curiosity.*

a·float (ə flōt′), *adv., adj.* **1.** borne on the water; in a floating condition: *the ship is afloat.* **2.** on board ship; at sea: *cargo afloat and ashore.* **3.** flooded: *the main deck was afloat.* **4.** moving without guide or control: *our affairs are all afloat.* **5.** passing from place to place; in circulation: *a rumor is afloat.*

a·flut·ter (ə flŭt′ər), *adv., adj.* in a flutter.

a·foot (ə fŏŏt′), *adv., adj.* **1.** on foot; walking: *I came afoot.* **2.** astir; in progress: *there is mischief afoot.*

a·fore (ə fōr′), *adv., prep., conj. Archaic* or *Dial.* before. [ME *aforne,* OE *on foran.* See A-¹, FORE¹]

a·fore·men·tioned (ə fōr′měn′shənd), *adj.* mentioned earlier or previously.

a·fore·said (ə fōr′sĕd′), *adj.* said or mentioned previously.

a·fore·thought (ə fōr′thôt′), *adj.* **1.** thought of beforehand; premeditated: *malice aforethought.* —*n.* **2.** premeditation; forethought.

a·fore·time (ə fōr′tīm′), *adv.* **1.** in time past; in a former time; previously. —*adj.* **2.** former; previous.

a for·ti·o·ri (ā fōr′shY ōr′ī), *Latin.* for a still stronger reason; even more certain; all the more.

a·foul (ə foul′), *adv., adj.* **1.** *U.S.* in a state of collision or entanglement: *a ship with its shrouds afoul.* **2. run afoul of,** to become entangled with: *run afoul of the law.*

Afr., **1.** Africa. **2.** African.

a·fraid (ə frād′), *adj.* feeling fear; filled with apprehension: *afraid to go.* [ME *afraied,* orig. pp. of AFFRAY] —Syn. scared, fearful. AFRAID, ALARMED, FRIGHTENED, TERRIFIED all indicate a state of fear. AFRAID implies inner apprehensive disquiet: *afraid of (or in) the dark.* ALARMED implies that the feelings are aroused through realization of some imminent or unexpected danger to oneself or others: *alarmed by (or about) someone's illness.* FRIGHTENED means shocked with sudden, but usually short-lived, fear, esp. that arising from apprehension of physical harm: *frightened by (or about) an accident.* TERRIFIED suggests the emotional reaction when one is struck with a violent, overwhelming fear: *terrified by an earthquake.*

af·reet (ăf′rēt, ə frēt′), *n. Arabian Myth.* a powerful evil demon or monster. Also, **afrit.** [t. Ar.: m. ¹*ifrīt*]

a·fresh (ə frĕsh′), *adv.* anew; again: *to start afresh.*

Af·ric (ăf′rYk), *adj.* African.

Af·ri·ca (ăf′rə kə), *n.* the second largest continent, S of Europe and between the Atlantic and Indian Oceans. 213,386,554 pop. (latest censuses 1946-1954); ab. 11,700,000 sq. mi.; ab. 4970 mi. long; ab. 4700 mi. wide.

Af·ri·can (ăf′rə kən), *adj.* **1.** of or from Africa; belonging to the black race of Africa; Negro. —*n.* **2.** a native of Africa; a member of the black race of Africa; a Negro.

African lily, agapanthus.

African sleeping sickness, *Pathol.* a disease, generally fatal, common in parts of Africa, usually marked by fever, wasting, and progressive lethargy, and caused by a parasitic protozoan, *Trypanosoma gambiense*. It is carried by a tsetse fly, *Glossina palpalis*.

Af·ri·can vi·o·let, a plant, *Saintpaulia ionantha*, with violet, pink, or white flowers, popular in cultivation.

Af·ri·kaans (ăf'rə käns', -känz'), *n.* a language of South Africa, developed out of the speech of 17th century settlers from Holland and still very like Dutch; South African Dutch. [t. S Afr. D, sp. var. of D *Afrikansch*]

Af·ri·kan·der (ăf'rə kăn'dər), *n.* a native of Cape Colony or the neighboring regions of Africa born of white parents, esp. Dutch or Huguenot; a descendant of European settlers in southern Africa. [t. S Afr. D: m. *Afrikaander*, b. *Afrikaans* and *Hollander*]

Af·ri·kan·der·ism (ăf'rə kăn'dər ĭz'əm), *n.* a word, usage, etc., peculiar to or originating among Afrikanders.

af·rit (ăf'rēt, ə frēt'), *n.* afreet.

Afro-, a combining form meaning "African," "Negro." [t. L: m. s. *Afer* African]

Af·ro-A·mer·i·can (ăf'rō ə mĕr'ə kən), *U.S.* —*adj.* 1. pertaining to Negroes of America. —*n.* 2. an American Negro.

aft (ăft, äft), *adv. Naut.* at, in, or toward the stern. [OE *æftan* from behind (f. *æft-* behind + *-an*, suffix marking motion from), c. Goth. *aftana*]

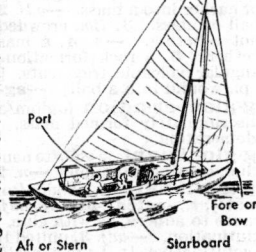

Port
Fore or Bow
Aft or Stern   Starboard

af·ter (ăf'tər, äf'-), *prep.* 1. behind in place; following behind: *men placed in a line one after another.* 2. in pursuit of; in search of; with or in desire for: *run after him.* 3. concerning: *to inquire after a person.* 4. later in time than; in succession to; at the close of: *after supper, time after time I urged him to do it.* 5. subsequent to and in consequence of: *after what has happened, I can never return.* 6. below in rank or excellence; next to: *Milton is usually placed after Shakespeare among English poets.* 7. in imitation of, or in imitation of the style of: *after Raphael, to make something after a model.* 8. with the name of; for: *he was named after his uncle.* 9. in proportion to; in accordance with: *after their intrinsic value.* 10. according to the nature of; in agreement or unison with; in conformity to: *he swore after the manner of his faith, a man after my own heart.* —*adv.* 11. behind; in the rear: *Jill came tumbling after.* 12. later in time; afterward: *it was about three hours after, happy ever after.* —*adj.* 13. later in time; next; subsequent; succeeding: *in after years.* 14. *Naut.* farther aft, or toward the stern of the ship: *the after sail.* —*conj.* 15. subsequent to the time that: *after the boys left.* [ME: OE *æfter* (f. *æf-* away from + *-ter*, comp. suffix)] —**Syn.** 1. See **behind**.

af·ter·birth (ăf'tər bûrth', äf'-), *n.* the placenta and fetal membranes expelled from the uterus after parturition.

af·ter·brain (ăf'tər brān', äf'-), *n.* metencephalon.

af·ter·burn·er (ăf'tər bûr'nər, äf'-), *n.* a ramjet coupled to the exhaust of a jet engine to provide added thrust.

af·ter·damp (ăf'tər dămp', äf'-), *n.* an irrespirable mixture of gases, consisting chiefly of carbon dioxide and nitrogen, left in a mine after an explosion or fire.

af·ter·deck (ăf'tər dĕk', äf'-), *n. Naut.* the weather deck abaft the midship house.

af·ter·din·ner (ăf'tər dĭn'ər, äf'-), *adj.* following dinner: *an after-dinner speech.*

af·ter·ef·fect (ăf'tər ə fĕkt', äf'-), *n.* 1. a delayed effect; effect that follows later. 2. *Med.* a result appearing after the first effect due to an agent, usually a drug, has gone.

af·ter·glow (ăf'tər glō', äf'-), *n.* 1. the glow frequently seen in the sky after sunset. 2. a second or secondary glow, as in heated metal before it ceases to become incandescent.

af·ter·im·age (ăf'tər ĭm'ĭj, Yj, äf'-), *n. Psychol.* a visual image or other sense impression that persists after the withdrawal of the exciting stimulus.

af·ter·math (ăf'tər măth', äf'-), *n.* 1. results, esp. of a catastrophe: *the aftermath of the storm.* 2. a second mowing or crop of grass from land in the same season. [f. AFTER + *math* a mowing (OE *mǣth*)]

af·ter·most (ăf'tər mōst', -məst, äf'-), *adj.* 1. *Naut.* farthest aft. 2. hindmost. [ME *aftermest*, OE *æftemest* last; the *-r-* owing to assoc. with *after*. See AFT, -MOST]

af·ter·noon (ăf'tər nōōn', äf'-), *n.* 1. the time from noon until evening. 2. the latter part: *the afternoon of life.* —*adj.* 3. pertaining to the latter part of the day.

afternoon tea, 1. light refreshments served late in the afternoon. 2. an afternoon social gathering.

af·ter·piece (ăf'tər pēs', äf'-), *n.* a short dramatic piece performed after a play.

af·ter·shaft (ăf'tər shăft', äf'tər shäft'), *n. Ornith.* 1. a supplementary feather, usually small, arising from the under side of the base of the shafts of certain feathers in many birds. 2. the shaft of such a feather.

af·ter·taste (ăf'tər tāst', äf'-), *n.* a taste remaining after the substance causing it is no longer in the mouth.

af·ter·thought (ăf'tər thôt', äf'-), *n.* 1. reflection after an act; some explanation, answer, expedient, or the

like, that occurs to one's mind too late, or afterward. 2. a later or second thought.

af·ter·time (ăf'tər tīm', äf'-), *n.* future time.

af·ter·ward (ăf'tər wərd, äf'-), *adv.* in later or subsequent time; subsequently. Also, **af'ter·wards.** [OE *æfterweard*, var. of OE *æfteweard*. See AFT, -WARD; for *-r-*, see AFTERMOST]

af·ter·world (ăf'tər wûrld', äf'-), *n.* the future world.

ag-, var. of **ad-** (by assimilation) before *g*, as in *agglutinate.*

Ag, *Chem.* (L *argentum*) silver.

Ag., August.

A.G., 1. Adjutant General. 2. Attorney General.

a·ga (ä'gə), *n.* (in Turkey) 1. a title of honor, usually implying respect for age. 2. a general. Also, **agha.**

A·ga·dir (ä'gä dēr'), *n.* a seaport in SW Morocco: a center of international tension, 1911. 30,111 (1952).

a·gain (ə gĕn' or, esp. Brit., ə gān') *adv.* 1. once more; in addition; another time; anew: *he did it all over again.* 2. in an additional case or instance; moreover; besides; furthermore. 3. on the other hand: *it might happen and again it might not.* 4. back; in return; in reply: *to answer again.* 5. in the opposite direction; to the same place or person: *to return again.* 6. again and again, often; with frequent repetition. 7. as much again, twice as much. [ME; OE *ongegn*, adv. and prep., opposite (to); toward, again, f. *on* in + *gegn* straight]

a·gainst (ə gĕnst' or, esp. Brit., ə gānst'), *prep.* 1. in an opposite direction to, so as to meet; toward; upon: *to ride against the wind, the rain beats against the window.* 2. in contact with: *to lean against a wall.* 3. in opposition to; adverse or hostile to: *twenty votes against ten, against reason.* 4. in resistance to or defense from: *protection against burglars.* 5. in preparation for; in provision for: *money saved against a rainy day.* 6. having as background: *the pictures stand out against the dark wall.* 7. in exchange for; in return for; as a balance to: *draw against merchandise shipped.* 8. *Obs.* directly opposite; facing; in front of (now *over against*). —*conj.* 9. Archaic or *Dial.* by the time that. [AGAIN + -(e)s, adv. gen. suff. + -*t* added later; for this -*t* see WHILST, etc.]

A·ga Khan III (ä'gə kän'), (*Aga Sultan Sir Mohammed Shah*) 1872–1957, leader (1885–1957) of the Ismailian sect of Mohammedans in India.

Aga Khan IV, (*Shah Karim al-Husainy*), born 1936, grandson of Aga Khan III, leader (since 1957) of the Ismailian sect of Mohammedans in India.

a·ga·ma (ăg'ə mə), *n.* any lizard of the Old World family *Agamidae*, allied to the iguanas and including large and brilliantly colored species. [t. Carib]

Ag·a·mem·non (ăg'ə mĕm'nŏn, -nən), *n.* 1. *Gk. Legend.* a king of Mycenae, son of Atreus and brother of Menelaus. He led the Greeks against Troy. Upon his return he was treacherously slain by his faithless wife, Clytemnestra. 2. a tragedy by Aeschylus.

a·gam·ic (ə găm'Yk), *adj.* 1. *Biol.* a. asexual. b. occurring without sexual union; germinating without impregnation; not gamic. 2. *Bot.* cryptogamic. Also, **ag·a·mous** (ăg'ə məs). [f. s. Gk. *ágamos* unwed + -IC] —**a·gam'i·cal·ly**, *adv.*

ag·a·mo·gen·e·sis (ăg'ə mō jĕn'ə sĭs), *n. Biol.* asexual reproduction by buds, offshoots, cell division, etc. [f. Gk. *ágamo(s)* unmarried + GENESIS] —**ag·a·mo·ge·net·ic** (ăg'ə mō jənĕt'Yk), *adj.*

A·ga·ña (ä gä'nyä), *n.* capital of Guam. 1,330 (1950).

ag·a·pan·thus (ăg'ə păn'thəs), *n.* any of several African liliaceous plants constituting the genus *Agapanthus* with umbels of blue or white flowers; African lily. [f. Gk.: s. *agápē* love + m. *ánthos* flower]

a·gape (ə găp', ə gāp'), *adv. adj.* with the mouth wide open; in an attitude of wonder or eagerness.

a·gar (ä'gär), *n.* 1. *Biol.* a culture medium with an agar-agar base: *a spore agar.* 2. agar-agar.

a·gar-a·gar (ä'gär ä'gär, ăg'ər äg'ər), *n.* a gelatinlike product of certain seaweeds, used to solidify culture media and, in the Orient, for soups, etc. [t. Malay]

ag·a·ric (ăg'ə rYk, ə gär'Yk), *n.* an agaricaceous fungus. [t. L: s. *agaricum*, t. Gk.: m. *agarikón*; named after Agaria, a place in Sarmatia]

a·gar·i·ca·ceous (ə găr'ə kā'shəs), *adj.* belonging to the *Agaricaceae*, a family of fungi including mushrooms having blade-shaped gills on the underside of the cap.

Ag·as·siz (ăg'ə sĭ; *for 2 also, Fr.* ägäsē'), *n.* 1. Alexander, 1835–1910, U.S. zoölogist and geologist. 2. his father, (Jean) Louis (Rodolphe) (zhän lwē rō dôlf'), 1807–73, Swiss zoölogist and geologist, in the U. S.

ag·ate (ăg'Yt), *n.* 1. a variegated variety of quartz (chalcedony) showing colored bands or other markings (clouded, mosslike, etc.). 2. a child's playing marble made of this substance, or of glass in imitation of it. 3. a printing type (5½ point) of a size between pearl and nonpareil, known in England as *ruby*. [t. F: m. *agathe*, g. L *achatēs*, t. Gk.] —**ag'ate·like'**, *adj.*

agate line, a measure of advertising space, 1/14 of an inch deep and one column wide.

ag·ate·ware (ăg'Yt wâr'), *n.* 1. steel or iron household ware enameled in an agatelike pattern. 2. pottery variegated to resemble agate.

A·gath·o·cles (ə găth'ə klēz'), *n.* 361–289 B.C., tyrant of Syracuse.

ag·a·tize (ăg'ə tīz'), *v.t.*, **-ized, -izing.** to change into, or make like, agate.

a gauche (ȧ gōsh′), *French.* on or to the left-hand side.

a·ga·ve (əgā′vĭ), *n.* any plant of the American (chiefly Mexican) amaryllidaceous genus *Agave*, species of which yield useful fibers, are used in making a fermented beverage, a distilled spirit, or a soap substitute, or are cultivated for ornament, as the century plant. [t. NL, t. Gk.: m. *Agauē*, proper n., fem. of *agauós* noble]

agcy., agency.

age (āj), *n., v.,* **aged, aging** or **ageing.** —*n.* **1.** the length of time during which a being or thing has existed; length of life or existence to the time spoken of or referred to: *his age is 20 years, a tree or building of unknown age.* **2.** the lifetime of an individual, or of the individuals of a class or species on an average: *the age of the horse is from 25 to 30 years.* **3.** a period of human life usually marked by a certain stage of physical or mental development, esp. a degree of development, measured by years from birth, which involves legal responsibility and capacity: *the age of discretion, the age of consent.* **4. of age,** *Law.* **a.** being any of several ages, usually 21 or 18, at which certain legal rights, as voting or marriage, are acquired. **b.** being 21 years old, in possession of full legal rights and responsibilities. **5.** the particular period of life at which one becomes naturally or conventionally qualified or disqualified for anything: *under age or over age for conscription.* **6.** one of the periods or stages of human life: *a person of middle age.* **7.** old age: *his eyes were dim with age.* **8.** a particular period of history, as distinguished from others; a historical epoch: *the age of Pericles, the Stone Age, the Middle Ages.* **9.** the people who live at a particular period. **10.** a generation or a succession of generations: *ages yet unborn.* **11.** *Colloq.* a great length of time: *I haven't seen you for an age or for ages.* **12.** *Cards.* edge (def. 11). **13.** *Psychol.* the comparative mental, emotional, etc., development, of a person, expressed by equating performance in various tests to the average age at which the same result is attained. **14.** *Geol.* a long or short part of earth history distinguished by special features: *the Ice Age.* **15.** any one of the stages in the history of mankind divided, according to Hesiod, into the golden, silver, bronze, heroic, and iron ages. The happiest and best was the first (or golden) age, and the worst the iron age.
—*v.i.* **16.** to grow old: *he is aging rapidly.*
—*v.t.* **17.** to make old; cause to grow or to seem old: *fear aged him overnight.* **18.** to bring to maturity or to a state fit for use: *to age wine.*
[ME, t. OF: m. *aage*, earlier *e(d)age*, ult. f. m. L *aetas* + suffix *-āticum* -AGE]
—**Syn. 8.** AGE, EPOCH, ERA, PERIOD all refer to an extent of time. AGE usually implies a considerable extent of time, esp. one associated with a dominant personality, influence, characteristic, or institution: *the age of chivalry.* EPOCH and ERA are often used interchangeably, but an ERA is an extent of time characterized by changed conditions and new undertakings: *an era of invention.* An EPOCH is properly the beginning of an era: *an epoch of armed aggression.* A PERIOD may be long or short, but usually has a marked condition or feature: *the glacial period, a period of expansion.*

-age, a noun suffix, frequent in words taken from French, as in *baggage, language, savage, voyage*, etc., now a common English formative, forming: **1.** collective nouns from names of things, as in *fruitage, leafage.* **2.** nouns denoting condition, rank, service, fee, etc., from personal terms, as in *bondage, parsonage.* **3.** nouns expressing various relations, from verbs, as in *breakage, cleavage, postage.* [t. OF, g. L *-āticum*, neut. adj. suffix]

a·ged (ā′jĭd *for 1, 2, 4;* ājd *for 3*), *adj.* **1.** having lived or existed long: *an aged man or tree.* **2.** pertaining to or characteristic of old age: *aged wrinkles.* **3.** of the age of: *a man aged 40 years.* **4.** *Phys. Geog.* old; approaching the state of a peneplain. —**a′ged·ly,** *adv.* —**a′ged·ness.** *n.* —**Syn. 1.** See **old.** —**Ant. 1.** young.

a·gee (əjē′), *adv., adj. Dial.* to one side; awry. Also, **ajee.** [f. A-[1] + GEE]

age·less (āj′lĭs), *adj.* never growing old.

age·long (āj′lông′, -lŏng′), *adj.* lasting for an age.

a·gen·cy (ā′jənsĭ), *n., pl.* **-cies.** **1.** a commercial or other bureau furnishing some form of service for the public: *an advertising agency.* **2.** the place of business of an agent. **3.** *U.S.* an Indian agency. **4.** the office of agent; the business of an agent entrusted with the concerns of another. **5.** state of being in action or of exerting power; action; operation: *the agency of Providence.* **6.** a mode of exerting power; a means of producing effects; instrumentality: *by the agency of friends.*

a·gen·da (əjĕn′də), *n.pl., sing.* **-dum** (-dəm). **1.** things to be done. **2.** matters to be brought before a committee, council, board, etc., as things to be done. [t. L, neut. pl. of gerundive of *agere* do]

a·gent (ā′jənt), *n.* **1.** a person acting on behalf of another, called his principal: *my agent has power to sign my name.* **2.** one who or that which acts or has the power to act: *a moral agent.* **3.** a natural force or object producing or used for obtaining specific results; instrumentality: *many insects are agents of fertilization.* **4.** an active cause; an efficient cause. **5.** an official: *an agent of the F.B.I.* **6.** *U.S.* an Indian agent. **7.** *Colloq.* a representative of a business firm, esp. a traveling salesman; a canvasser; solicitor. **8.** *Chem.* a substance which causes a reaction. **9.** *Brit.* a campaign manager; an election agent. —*adj.* **10.** acting (opposed to *patient* in the sense of sustaining action). [t. L: s. *agens*, ppr., driving, doing] —**Syn. 1.** representative, deputy.

a·gen·tial (ā jĕn′shəl), *adj.* **1.** pertaining to an agent or to an agency. **2.** *Gram.* agentive.

a·gen·ti·val (ā′jən tī′vəl), *adj.* agentive.

a·gen·tive (ā′jən tĭv), *Gram.* —*adj.* **1.** pertaining to, or productive of, a form which indicates agent or agency. —*n.* **2.** an agentive element or formation, as English *-er* in *painter.*

a·gent pro·vo·ca·teur (ȧ zhäN′ prô vô kȧ tœr′), *pl.* **agents provocateurs** (ȧ zhäN′ prô vô kȧ tœr′). *French.* a secret agent hired to incite suspected persons to some illegal action, outbreak, etc., that will make them liable to punishment.

ag·er·a·tum (ăj′ərā′təm, əjĕr′ə-), *n.* **1.** any plant of the asteraceous genus *Ageratum*, as *A. Houstonianum*, a garden annual with small, dense, blue or white flower heads. **2.** any of various other composite plants, bearing blue, or sometimes white, flowers. [t. L, t. Gk.: m. *ageraton* kind of plant, prop. neut. adj., not growing old]

Ag·ge·us (əgē′əs), *n.* (in the Douay Bible) Haggai.

ag·glom·er·ate (*v.* əglŏm′ərāt′; *adj., n.* əglŏm′ərĭt, -ərāt′), *v.,* **-ated, -ating,** *adj., n.* —*v.t., v.i.* **1.** to collect or gather into a mass. —*adj.* **2.** gathered together into a ball or mass. **3.** *Bot.* crowded into a dense cluster, but not cohering. —*n.* **4.** a mass of things clustered together. **5.** a rock formation composed of rounded or angular volcanic fragments. [t. L: m. s. *agglomerātus*, pp., wound into a ball] —**ag·glom′er·a′tive,** *adj.*

ag·glom·er·a·tion (əglŏm′ərā′shən), *n.* **1.** an indiscriminately formed mass. **2.** act or process of agglomerating.

ag·glu·ti·nant (əglōō′tənənt), *adj.* **1.** uniting, as glue; causing adhesion. —*n.* **2.** an agglutinating agent.

ag·glu·ti·nate (*v.* əglōō′tənāt′; *adj.* əglōō′tənĭt, -nāt′), *v.,* **-nated, -nating,** *adj.* —*v.t., v.i.* **1.** to unite or cause to adhere, as with glue. **2.** *Gram.* to form by agglutination. —*adj.* **3.** united by or as by glue. **4.** *Gram.* agglutinative. [t. L: m.s. *agglūtinātus*, pp., pasted to]

agglutinating language, a language whose affixes are invariable and are juxtaposed instead of fused. Turkish and Hungarian are agglutinating languages. See **agglutination,** def. 5.

ag·glu·ti·na·tion (əglōō′tənā′shən), *n.* **1.** act or process of uniting by glue or other tenacious substance. **2.** state of being thus united; adhesion of parts. **3.** that which is united; a mass or group cemented together. **4.** *Immunol.* the clumping of bacteria, red blood corpuscles, or other cells, due to introduction of an antibody. **5.** *Gram.* a pattern or process of inflection and word formation in some languages, in which the constituent elements of words are relatively distinct and constant in form and meaning; esp. such a process involving the addition of several suffixes to a single root or stem. In Turkish *ev* means "house," *ev-ler* means "houses," *ev-den* means "from a house," and *ev-ler-den* means "from houses."

ag·glu·ti·na·tive (əglōō′tənā′tĭv), *adj.* **1.** tending or having power to agglutinate or unite: *an agglutinative substance.* **2.** *Gram.* (of a language or construction) characterized by agglutination.

ag·glu·ti·nin (əglōō′tənĭn), *n. Immunol.* an antibody which causes agglutination.

ag·glu·tin·o·gen (ăg′lōō tĭn′əjən), *n. Immunol.* an antigen present in a bacterial body which when injected into an animal causes the production of agglutinins.

ag·grade (əgrād′), *v.t.,* **-graded, -grading.** *Phys. Geog.* to raise the grade or level of (a river valley, a stream bed, etc.), as by depositing detritus. [f. AG- + GRADE, v.] —**ag·gra·da·tion** (ăg′rə dā′shən), *n.*

ag·gran·dize (ăg′rən dīz′, əgrăn′dīz), *v.t.,* **-dized, -dizing.** **1.** to widen in scope; increase in size or intensity; enlarge; extend. **2.** to make great or greater in power, wealth, rank, or honor. **3.** to make (something) appear greater. [t. F: m. *agrandiss-*, s. *agrandir*, g. L *ad-* AD- + *grandīre* make great] —**ag·gran·dize·ment** (əgrăn′dĭz mənt), *n.* —**ag′gran·diz′er,** *n.*

ag·gra·vate (ăg′rəvāt′), *v.t.,* **-vated, -vating.** **1.** to make worse or more severe; intensify, as anything evil, disorderly, or troublesome: *to aggravate guilt; grief aggravated her illness.* **2.** *Colloq.* to provoke; irritate; exasperate: *threats will only aggravate her.* [t. L: m. s. *aggravātus*, pp., added to the weight of] —**ag′gra·vat′ed,** *adj.* —**ag′gra·vat′ing,** *adj.* —**ag′gra·vat′ing·ly,** *adv.* —**ag′gra·va′tive,** *adj.* —**ag′gra·va′tor,** *n.*
—**Syn. 1.** heighten. AGGRAVATE, INTENSIFY both mean to increase in degree. To AGGRAVATE is to make more serious or more grave: *to aggravate a danger, an offense, a wound.* To INTENSIFY is perceptibly to increase intensity, force, energy, vividness, etc.: *to intensify heat, color, rage.*

ag·gra·va·tion (ăg′rəvā′shən), *n.* **1.** increase of the intensity or severity of anything; act of making worse: *an aggravation of pain.* **2.** *Colloq.* something that irritates or exasperates.

ag·gre·gate (*adj., n.* ăg′rəgĭt, -gāt′; *v.* ăg′rəgāt′), *adj., n., v.,* **-gated, -gating.** —*adj.* **1.** formed by the conjunction or collection of particulars into a whole mass or sum; total; combined: *the aggregate amount of indebtedness.* **2.** *Bot.* **a.** (of a flower) formed of florets collected in a dense cluster but not cohering as in composite plants. **b.** (of a fruit) composed of a cluster of carpels belonging to the same flower, as the raspberry. —*n.* **3.** a sum, mass, or assemblage of particulars; a total or gross amount: *the aggregate of all past experience.* **4. in the aggregate,** taken together; considered as a whole; collectively. **5.** *Geol.* a mixture of

b., blend of, blended; c., cognate with; d., dialect, dialectal; der., derived from; f., formed from; g., going back to; m., modification of; r., replacing; s., stem of; t., taken from; ?, perhaps. See the full key on inside cover.

different mineral substances separable by mechanical means, as granite. **6.** any hard material added to cement to make concrete. —*v.t.* **7.** to bring together; collect into one sum, mass, or body. **8.** to amount to (the number of): *the guns captured will aggregate five or six hundred.* —*v.i.* **9.** to combine and form a collection or mass. [t. L: m. s. *aggregātus,* pp., added to] **ag·gre·ga·ly,** *adv.* —**ag·gre·ga·tive** (ăg′rə gā′tĭv), *adj.*

ag·gre·ga·tion (ăg′rə gā′shən), *n.* **1.** a combined whole; an aggregate: *an aggregation of isolated settlements.* **2.** act of collection into an unorganized whole. **3.** state of being so collected. **4.** *Ecol.* a group of organisms of the same or different species living closely together but less integrated than a society.

ag·gress (ə grĕs′), *v.i.* **1.** to commit the first act of hostility or offense; attack first. **2.** to begin a quarrel.

ag·gres·sion (ə grĕsh′ən), *n.* **1.** the action of a state in violating by force the rights of another state, particularly its territorial rights. **2.** any offensive action or procedure; an inroad or encroachment: *an aggression upon one's rights.* **3.** the practice of making assaults or attacks; offensive action in general. [t. L: s. *aggressio*]

ag·gres·sive (ə grĕs′ĭv), *adj.* **1.** characterized by aggression; tending to aggress; making the first attack: *an aggressive foreign policy.* **2.** energetic; vigorous. —**ag·gres·sive·ly,** *adv.* —**ag·gres·sive·ness,** *n.*

ag·gres·sor (ə grĕs′ər), *n.* a person who attacks first; one who begins hostilities; an assailant or invader. [t. L]

ag·grieve (ə grēv′), *v.t.* **-grieved, -grieving.** to oppress or wrong grievously; injure by injustice (used now chiefly in the passive). [ME *agreve(n)*, t. OF: m. *agrever,* g. L *aggravāre* exasperate]

ag·grieved (ə grēvd′), *adj.* **1.** injured; oppressed; wronged: *he felt himself aggrieved.* **2.** *Law.* deprived of legal rights or claims.

a·gha (ä′gə), *n.* aga.

a·ghast (ə găst′, ə gäst′), *adj.* struck with amazement; filled with sudden fright or horror: *they stood aghast at this unforeseen disaster.* [ME *agast,* pp. of *agasten* terrify. Cf. OE *gǣstan* in same sense]

ag·ile (ăj′əl or, esp. Brit., ăj′īl), *adj.* **1.** quick and light in movement: *a robust and agile frame.* **2.** active; lively: *an agile mind.* [t. L: m.s. *agilis*] —**ag′ile·ly,** *adv.* —Syn. **1.** nimble, sprightly.

a·gil·i·ty (ə jĭl′ə tĭ), *n.* the power of moving quickly and easily; nimbleness: *agility of the body or mind.* [late ME *agilitie,* t. F, t. L: m.s. *agilitas*]

Ag·in·court (ăj′ĭn kōrt′; *Fr.* ā zhăn kōōr′), *n.* a village in N France, near Calais: site of a decisive victory of the English under Henry V over the French, 1415.

a·gi·o (ăj′ĭ ō′), *n., pl.* **-os. 1.** a premium on money in exchange. **2.** an allowance for the difference in value of two currencies. **3.** an allowance given or taken on bills of exchange from other countries, as to balance out exchange expenses. **4.** agiotage. [t. It: m. *aggio* exchange, premium = *aggio,* g. L *habeo* I have]

ag·i·o·tage (ăj′ĭ ə tĭj), *n.* **1.** the business of exchange. **2.** speculative dealing in securities. [t. F]

ag·i·tate (ăj′ə tāt′), *v.,* **-tated, -tating.** —*v.t.* **1.** to move or force into violent irregular action; shake or move briskly: *the wind agitates the sea.* **2.** to move to and fro; impart regular motion to: *to agitate a fan, etc.* **3.** to disturb, or excite into tumult; perturb: *the mind of man is agitated by various emotions.* **4.** to call attention to by speech or writing; discuss; debate: *to agitate the question.* **5.** to consider on all sides; revolve in the mind; plan. —*v.i.* **6.** to arouse or attempt to arouse public interest, as in some political or social question: *to agitate for the repeal of a tax.* [t. L: m. s. *agitātus,* pp., aroused, excited] —**ag′i·tat′ed·ly,** *adv.*

ag·i·ta·tion (ăj′ə tā′shən), *n.* **1.** act of agitating. **2.** state of being agitated: *she walked away in great agitation.* **3.** persistent urging of a political or social question before the public.
—Syn. **2.** AGITATION, DISTURBANCE, EXCITEMENT, TURMOIL imply inner unrest and a nervous condition. AGITATION implies a shaken state of emotions, usually perceptible in the face or movements: *with evident agitation she opened the telegram.* DISTURBANCE implies an inner disquiet caused by worry, indecision, apprehension, and the like: *long-continued mental disturbance is a cause of illness.* EXCITEMENT implies a highly emotional state caused by either agreeable or distressing circumstances: *excitement over a proposed trip, unexpected good news, a fire.* TURMOIL suggests such a struggle or conflict of emotions that one is unable to think consecutively: *her thoughts were in a hopeless turmoil.*

a·gi·ta·to (ä′jē tä′tō), *adj. Music.* agitated; restless or hurried in movement or style. [It.]

ag·i·ta·tor (ăj′ə tā′tər), *n.* **1.** one who stirs up others, with the view of strengthening his own cause or that of his party, etc. **2.** a machine for agitating and mixing.

A·glai·a (ə glā′ə), *n. Gk. Myth.* one of the Graces.

a·gleam (ə glēm′), *adv., adj.* gleaming.

ag·let (ăg′lĭt), *n.* **1.** a metal tag at the end of a lace. **2.** the points or ribbons generally used in the 16th and 17th centuries to fasten or tie dresses. **3.** aiguillette. Also, **aiglet.** [ME, t. F: m. *aiguillette* point, ult. der. L *acus* needle]

a·gley (ə glē′, ə glī′), *adv.* Chiefly Scot. and N. Eng. off the right line; awry; wrong. [f. A⁻¹ + Scot. *gley* squint]

a·glim·mer (ə glĭm′ər), *adv., adj.* glimmering.

a·glit·ter (ə glĭt′ər), *adv., adj.* glittering.

a·glow (ə glō′), *adv., adj.* glowing.

ag·mi·nate (ăg′mə nĭt, -nāt′), *adj.* aggregated or clustered together. Also, **ag′mi·nat′ed.** [f. s. L *agmen* troop + -ATE¹]

ag·nail (ăg′nāl′), *n.* **1.** hangnail. **2.** whitlow.

ag·nate (ăg′nāt), *n.* **1.** a kinsman whose connection is traceable exclusively through males. **2.** any male relation by the father's side. —*adj.* **3.** related or akin through males or on the father's side. **4.** allied or akin. [t. L: m. s. *agnātus,* pp., born to] —**ag·nat·ic** (ăg nāt′ĭk), *adj.* —**ag·na·tion** (ăg nā′shən), *n.*

Ag·ni (ŭg′nĭ), *n. Hindu Myth.* the god of fire, one of the three chief divinities of the Vedas. [t. Skt.]

ag·no·men (ăg nō′mən), *n., pl.* **-nomina** (-nŏm′ə nə). **1.** an additional (fourth) name given to a person by the ancient Romans in allusion to some achievement or other circumstance, as *Africanus* in *Publius Cornelius Scipio Africanus.* **2.** any nickname. [t. L: f. ag- AG- + *nōmen* name] —**ag·nom·i·nal** (ăg nŏm′ə nəl), *adj.*

ag·nos·tic (ăg nŏs′tĭk), *n.* **1.** one who holds that the ultimate cause (God) and the essential nature of things are unknown or unknowable or that human knowledge is limited to experience. —*adj.* **2.** pertaining to the agnostics or their doctrines. **3.** asserting the relativity and uncertainty of all knowledge. [f. A⁻³ + Gk. *gnōstos* known, unknowable + -IC] —**ag·nos′ti·cal·ly,** *adv.* —Syn. See **atheist.**

ag·nos·ti·cism (ăg nŏs′tə sĭz′əm), *n.* **1.** the doctrine maintained by agnostics. **2.** an intellectual attitude or doctrine which asserts the relativity and therefore the uncertainty of all knowledge.

Ag·nus De·i (ăg′nəs dē′ĭ), **1.** *Eccles.* **a.** a figure of a lamb as emblematic of Christ. **b.** such a representation with the nimbus inscribed with the cross about its head, and supporting the banner of the cross. **2.** *Rom. Cath. Ch.* **a.** a wax medallion stamped with this figure and blessed by the Pope, or a fragment of such a medallion. **b.** a triple chant preceding the communion in the Mass. **c.** the music accompanying this prayer. **3.** *Anglican Ch.* **a.** an invocation beginning "O Lamb of God," said or sung in the communion service. **b.** a musical setting for this. [LL: Lamb of God. See John 1:29]

a·go (ə gō′), *adj.* **1.** gone; gone by; past (now follows noun): *some time ago.* —*adv.* **2.** in past time: *long ago.* [ME, var. of *agoon,* OE *āgān,* pp. of *āgān* go by, pass]

a·gog (ə gŏg′), *adj.* **1.** highly excited by eagerness or curiosity. —*adv.* **2.** in a state of eager desire; with excitement. [t. F: m. *en gogues* in a merry mood]

-agogue, a word element meaning "leading" or "guiding," found in a few agent nouns (often with pejorative value), as in *demagogue, pedagogue.* [t. Gk.: m.s. *agōgós* leading]

ag·on (ăg′ōn, -ŏn), *n., pl.* **agones** (ə gō′nēz). *Gk. Antiq.* a contest for a prize, whether of athletes in the games or of poets, musicians, painters, and the like. [t. Gk.]

a·gone (ə gŏn′, ə gōn′), *adv., adj. Archaic.* ago.

a·gon·ic (ā gŏn′ĭk), *adj.* not forming an angle. [f. s. Gk. *ágōnos* without angles + -IC]

agonic line, a line on the earth's surface connecting points at which the declination of the earth's magnetic field is zero.

ag·o·nist (ăg′ə nĭst), *n. Physiol.* an actively contracting muscle considered in relation to its opposing muscle.

ag·o·nis·tic (ăg′ə nĭs′tĭk), *adj.* **1.** combative; striving to overcome in argument. **2.** aiming at effect; strained. **3.** pertaining to contests. Also, **ag·o·nis·ti·cal.** [t. Gk.: m.s. *agōnistikós*] —**ag·o·nis′ti·cal·ly,** *adv.*

ag·o·nize (ăg′ə nīz′), *v.,* **-nized, -nizing.** —*v.i.* **1.** to writhe with extreme pain; suffer violent anguish. **2.** to make great effort of any kind. —*v.t.* **3.** to distress with extreme pain; torture. [t. ML: m. s. *agōnizāre,* t. Gk.: m. *agōnizesthai* contend] —**ag·o·niz′ing·ly,** *adv.*

ag·o·ny (ăg′ə nĭ), *n., pl.* **-nies. 1.** extreme, and generally prolonged, pain; intense suffering. **2.** intense mental excitement of any kind. **3.** the struggle preceding natural death: *mortal agony.* **4.** *Rare.* a violent struggle. [ME *agonye,* t. LL: m. *agōnia,* t. Gk.: contest, anguish] —Syn. **1.** throe, paroxysm, pang; ache. See **pain. 2.** anguish, torment, torture.

ag·o·ra (ăg′ə rə), *n., pl.* **-rae** (-rē′). *Anc. Greece.* **1.** a popular political assembly. **2.** the place of such assembly, originally the market place. [t. Gk.]

ag·o·ra·pho·bi·a (ăg′ə rə fō′bĭ ə), *n. Psychiatry.* a morbid fear of being in an open space. [f. AGORA + -PHOBIA]

a·gou·ti (ə gōō′tĭ), *n., pl.* **-tis, -ties. 1.** any of several short-haired, short-eared, rabbitlike rodents of the genus *Dasyprocta,* of South and Central America and the West Indies, destructive to sugar cane. **2.** an irregularly barred pattern of the fur of certain rodents. **3.** an animal having fur of this pattern. [t. F, t. Sp.: m. *aguti,* native Guiana name]

Agouti, *Dasyprocta aguti* (19 to 22 in. long)

a·gou·ty (ə gōō′tĭ), *n., pl.* **-ties.** agouti.

A·gra (ä′grə), *n.* a city in N India, in Uttar Pradesh; site of the Taj Mahal. 333,530 (1951).

a·graffe (ə gräf′), *n.* 1. a small cramp iron. 2. a clasp for hooking together parts of clothing, etc. 3. a device for checking vibration in a piano string. [t. F, var. of *agrafe* hook, f. à A⁻⁵ + *grafe* sharp-pointed tool (g. L *graphium*, t. Gk.: m. *graphion*); F meaning influenced by *agrappe* hook]

A·gram (ä′gräm), *n.* German name of Zagreb.

a·gran·u·lo·cy·to·sis (ə grän′yŏŏ lō sī tō′sĭs), *n.* *Pathol.* a serious, often fatal, blood disease, marked by a great reduction of the leucocytes.

a·graph·i·a (ə gräf′Yə), *n.* *Pathol.* a cerebral disorder marked by total or partial inability to write. [t. NL, f. Gk.: a- A⁻⁵ + -*graphia* writing] —**a·graph′ic,** *adj.*

a·grar·i·an (ə grär′Yən), *adj.* 1. relating to land, land tenure, or the division of landed property: *agrarian laws.* 2. pertaining to the advancement of agricultural groups: *an agrarian experiment.* 3. rural; agricultural. 4. growing in fields; wild: *an agrarian plant.* —*n.* 5. one who favors the equal division of land. [f. s. L *agrārius* pertaining to land + -AN] —**a·grar′i·an·ism,** *n.*

a·gree (ə grē′), *v.,* **agreed, agreeing.** —*v.i.* 1. to yield assent; consent (often fol. by *to,* esp. with reference to things and acts): *he agreed to accompany the ambassador, do you agree to the conditions?* 2. to be of one mind; harmonize in opinion or feeling (often fol. by *with,* esp. with reference to persons): *I don't agree with you.* 3. to live in concord or without contention; harmonize in action. 4. to come to one opinion or mind; come to an arrangement or understanding; arrive at a settlement. 5. to be consistent; harmonize (fol. by *with*): *this story agrees with others.* 6. to be applicable or appropriate; resemble; be similar (fol. by *with*): *the picture does not agree with the original.* 7. to be accommodated or adapted; suit (fol. by *with*): *the same food does not agree with every person.* 8. *Gram.* to correspond in inflectional form, as in number, case, gender, or person (fol. by *with*). —*v.t.* 9. to concede; grant (fol. by noun clause): *I agree that he is the ablest of us.* [MP *agre*(en), t. OF: m. *agreer,* der. phrase *a gre* at pleasure]

—**Syn.** 5. AGREE, ACCORD, CORRESPOND imply comparing persons or things and finding that they harmonize. AGREE implies having or arriving at a condition in which no essential difference of opinion or detail is evident: *all the reports agree.* ACCORD emphasizes agreeing exactly, both in fact and in point of view: *this report accords with the other.* CORRESPOND suggests having an obvious similarity, though not agreeing in every detail: *part of this report corresponds with the facts.*

a·gree·a·ble (ə grē′ə bəl), *adj.* 1. to one's liking; pleasing: *agreeable manners.* 2. *Colloq.* willing or ready to agree or consent: *are you agreeable?* 3. suitable; conformable (fol. by *to*). —**a·gree′a·bil′i·ty, a·gree′a·ble·ness,** *n.* —**a·gree′a·bly,** *adv.*

a·greed (ə grēd′), *adj.* arranged by common consent: *they met at the agreed time.*

a·gree·ment (ə grē′mənt), *n.* 1. act of coming to a mutual arrangement. 2. the arrangement itself. 3. unanimity of opinion; harmony in feeling: *agreement among the members.* 4. state of being in accord; concord; harmony; conformity: *agreement between observation and theory.* 5. *Gram.* correspondence in number, case, gender, person, or some other formal category between syntactically connected words, esp. between one or more subordinate words and the word or words upon which they depend. For example: in *the boy runs,* *boy* is a singular noun and *runs* is a distinctively singular form of the verb. 6. collective agreement. 7. *Law.* a. an expression of assent by two or more parties to the same object. b. the phraseology, written or oral, of an exchange of promises.

—**Syn.** 2. AGREEMENT, BARGAIN, COMPACT, CONTRACT all suggest a binding arrangement between two or more parties. AGREEMENT ranges in meaning from mutual understanding to binding cbligation. BARGAIN applies particularly to agreements about buying and selling. COMPACT applies to treaties or alliances between nations or to solemn personal pledges. CONTRACT is used especially in law and business for such agreements as are legally enforceable.

a·gré·ments (à grē mäN′), *n.pl.* French. agreeable qualities or circumstances. Also, **a·gré·mens′.**

a·gres·tic (ə grĕs′tYk), *adj.* 1. rural; rustic. 2. unpolished. [f. s. L *agrestis* rural + -IC]

agric., 1. agricultural. 2. agriculture. Also, **agr.**

A·gric·o·la (ə grYk′ə lə), *n.* Gnaeus Julius (nē′əs jōōl′yəs), A.D. 37–93, Roman general: governor of Britain.

ag·ri·cul·ture (äg′rə kŭl′chər), *n.* the cultivation of land, as in the raising of crops; husbandry; tillage; farming (in a broad sense, including horticulture, forestry, stock raising, etc.). [t. L: m.s. *agricultūra,* f. *agri,* gen. of *ager* land + *cultūra* cultivation) —**ag′ri·cul′tur·al,** *adj.* —**ag′ri·cul′tur·al·ly,** *adv.*

ag·ri·cul·tur·ist (äg′rə kŭl′chər Ist), *n.* 1. a farmer. 2. an expert in agriculture. Also, *now U.S.,* **ag·ri·cul·tur·al·ist** (äg′rə kŭl′chər əl Ist).

A·gri·gen·to (ä′grē jĕn′tō), *n.* a city in S Sicily. 32,951 (1951). Formerly, **Girgenti.**

ag·ri·mo·ny (äg′rə mō′nĭ), *n., pl.* **-nies.** 1. any plant of the rosaceous genus *Agrimonia,* esp. *A. Eupatoria,* a perennial herb with pinnate leaves and small yellow flowers. 2. any of certain other plants, as hemp agrimony or bur marigold. [t. L: m.s. *agrimōnia,* var. of *argemōnia* a plant, t. Gk.: m. *argemōne;* r. OE *agrimonia,*

t. L, and ME *egrimoigne,* t. OF: m. *aigremoine*]

A·grip·pa (ə grĭp′ə), *n.* **Marcus Vipsanius** (mär′kəs vĭp sä′nĭ əs), 63–12 B.C., Roman statesman, general, engineer: victor over Antony and Cleopatra at Actium.

Ag·rip·pi·na II (äg′rə pī′nə), A.D. 16?–59?, mother of the Roman emperor Nero.

agro-, a word element meaning "soil," "field," as in *agrology.* [t. Gk., comb. form of *agrós*]

ag·ro·bi·ol·o·gy (äg′rō bī ŏl′ə jY), *n.* the quantitative science of plant life and plant nutrition. —**ag·ro·bi·o·log·ic** (äg′rō bī′ə lŏj′Yk), **ag·ro·bi′o·log′i·cal,** *adj.* —**ag′ro·bi′o·log′i·cal·ly,** *adv.* —**ag′ro·bi·ol′o·gist,** *n.*

a·grol·o·gy (ə grŏl′ə jY), *n.* the applied phases of soil science. See **pedology¹.** —**ag·ro·log·ic** (äg′rə lŏj′Yk), **ag′ro·log′i·cal,** *adj.*

agron., agronomy.

ag·ro·nom·ics (äg′rə nŏm′Yks), *n.* the art and science of managing land and crops.

a·gron·o·my (ə grŏn′ə mY), *n.* 1. the applied phases of both soil science and the several plant sciences, often limited to applied plant sciences dealing with crops. 2. agriculture. —**ag·ro·nom·ic** (äg′rə nŏm′Yk), **ag·ro·nom′i·cal,** *adj.* —**a·gron′o·mist,** *n.*

ag·ros·tol·o·gy (äg′rə stŏl′ə jY), *n.* the part of botany that treats of grasses. [f. s. Gk. *ágrōstis* kind of grass + -(o)LOGY]

a·ground (ə ground′), *adv., adj.* on the ground; stranded: *the ship ran aground.*

Agt., agent. Also, **agt.**

A·guas·ca·lien·tes (ä′gwäs kä lyĕn′tĕs), *n.* 1. a state in central Mexico. 188,075 (1950); 2499 sq. mi. 2. the capital of this state. 93,363 (1950).

a·gue (ä′gū), *n.* 1. *Pathol.* a malarial fever characterized by regularly returning paroxysms, marked by successive cold, hot, and sweating fits. 2. a fit of shaking or shivering as if with cold; a chill. [ME, t. OF, t. Pr., t. L: m.s. *acūta* (*febris*) acute (fever)] —**a′gue·like′,** *adj.* —**a′gu·ish,** *adj.* —**a′gu·ish·ly,** *adv.*

a·gue·weed (ä′gū wēd′), *n. U.S.* 1. the common boneset. 2. a species of gentian, *Gentiana quinquefolia.*

A·gui·nal·do (ä′gē näl′dō), *n.* **Emilio** (ĕ mē′lyō), 1869–1964, Filipino leader against Spain during the Spanish-American War and against the U. S. after the war.

A·gul·has (ə gŭl′əs; *Port.* ä gōō′lyäs), *n.* **Cape,** the southernmost point of Africa.

ah (ä), *interj.* an exclamation expressing pain, surprise, pity, complaint, dislike, joy, etc., according to the manner of utterance. [ME]

A.H., (L *anno Hejirae*) in the year of or from the Hejira (A.D. 622).

a.h., *Elect.* ampere-hour.

a·ha (ä hä′), *interj.* an exclamation expressing triumph, contempt, mockery, irony, surprise, etc., according to the manner of utterance. [ME]

A·hab (ä′häb), *n. Bible.* king of Israel of the ninth century B.C., husband of Jezebel. I Kings 16–22.

A·has·u·e·rus (ə häz′yŏŏ Yr′əs, ə häs′-, ə häzh′ŏŏ-), *n. Bible.* king of Persia (known by the Greeks as Xerxes), husband of Esther. Book of Esther; Ezra 4:6.

a·head (ə hĕd′), *adv.* 1. in or to the front; in advance; before. 2. forward; onward. 3. be ahead, *U.S.* to be to the good; be winning: *I was ahead $10 in the deal.* 4. get ahead of, to surpass. [f. A⁻¹ + HEAD]

a·hem (ə hĕm′), *interj.* an utterance designed to attract attention, express doubt, etc.

Ah·med·a·bad (ä′məd ä bäd′), *n.* a city in W India, in Bombay province. 788,333 (1951). Also, **Ah′mad·a·bad′.**

Ah·med·na·gar (ä′məd nŭg′ər), *n.* a city in W India, in Bombay province. 80,873 (1951). Also, **Ah′mad·na′gar.**

a·hoy (ə hoi′), *interj. Naut.* a call used in hailing. [f. *a,* interj. + HOY]

Ah·ri·man (ä′rY mən), *n. Zoroastrianism.* the wicked Devil, supreme spirit of evil, antagonistic to Ormazd.

a·hun·gered (ə hŭng′gərd), *adj. Archaic.* hungry.

A·hu·ra Maz·da (ä′hŏŏ rə mäz′də), Ormazd.

Ah·ve·nan·maa (à KH′vĕ nän mä′), *n.* Finnish name of Aland Islands.

ai (ä′Y), *n., pl.* **ais** (ä′Yz). a large three-toed sloth, *Bradypus tridactylus,* of Central and South America. [t. Brazilian: m. *(h)aí,* imit. of its cry]

ai·blins (ä′blYnz), *adv. Scot.* ablins.

aid (äd), *v.t.* 1. to afford support or relief to; help. 2. to promote the course or accomplishment of; facilitate. —*v.i.* 3. to give help or assistance. —*n.* 4. help; support; assistance. 5. one who or that which aids or yields assistance; a helper; an auxiliary. 6. *U.S.* an aide-decamp. 7. a payment made by feudal vassals to their lord on special occasions. 8. *Eng. Hist.* any of a variety of revenues received by the king in the Middle Ages after 1066 from his feudal vassals and from others of his subjects. [ME *aide*(n), t. OF: m. *aidier,* g. L *adjūtāre*] —**aid′er,** *n.* —**aid′less,** *adj.* —**Syn.** 1. See help. 4. succor; relief; subsidy; subvention. —**Ant.** 2. hinder.

A·ï·da (ä ē′dä), *n.* an opera (1871) by Verdi.

aid-de-camp (äd′də kämp′), *n., pl.* **aids-de-camp.** *Chiefly U.S.* aide-de-camp.

aide (äd), *n.* 1. an aide-de-camp. [t. F]

aide-de-camp (äd′də kämp′), *n., pl.* **aides-de-camp.** a subordinate military or naval officer acting as a confidential assistant to a superior. [t. F: camp assistant]

---

b., blend of, blended; c., cognate with; d., dialect, dialectal; der., derived from; f., formed from; g., going back to; m., modification of; r., replacing; s., stem of; t., taken from; ?, perhaps. See the full key on inside cover.

aide-mé·moire (ĕd mĕ mwâr′), *n. French.* a memorandum of discussion, agreement, or action.

Ai·din (īdēn′). *n.* Aydin.

ai·glet (ā′glĭt). *n.* aglet.

ai·grette (ā′grĕt, ā grĕt′), *n.* 1. a plume or tuft of feathers arranged as a head ornament, esp. the back plumes of various herons. 2. a copy in jewelry of such a plume. [t. F]

ai·guille (ā gwēl′, ā′gwēl), *n.* a needlelike rock mass or mountain peak. [t. F, in OF *aguille* needle, g. LL dim. of L *acus* needle]

ai·guil·lette (ā′gwĭ lĕt′), *n.* an ornamental tagged cord or braid on a uniform; aglet. [t. F, dim. of *aiguille*. See AGLET]

Ai·ken (ā′kən), *n.* Conrad Potter, born 1889, U.S. poet.

ail (āl), *v.t.* 1. to affect with pain or uneasiness; trouble. —*v.i.* 2. to feel pain; be ill (usually in a slight degree); be unwell. [ME *ailen*, OE *eglan*, c. Goth, *agljan*]

ai·lan·thus (ā lăn′thəs), *n.* a simaroubaceous tree, *Ailanthus altissima*, with pinnate leaves and ill-scented greenish flowers, native in eastern Asia and planted in Europe and America as a shade tree. [t. NL, t. Amboinan: m. *aylanto* tree of heaven] —**ai·lan′thic,** *adj.*

ai·ler·on (ā′lə rŏn′), *n. Aeron.* a hinged, movable part of an airplane wing, usually part of the trailing edge, used primarily to maintain lateral balance or to bank, roll, etc. [t. F, dim. of *aile* wing. See AISLE]

ail·ing (ā′lĭng), *adj.* sickly. —**Syn.** See **sick.**

ail·ment (āl′mənt), *n.* a morbid affection of the body or mind; indisposition: *a slight ailment*.

aim (ām), *v.t.* 1. to give a certain direction and elevation to (a gun, etc.), for the purpose of causing the projectile, when the weapon is discharged, to hit the object. 2. to direct or point (something) at something: *to aim a satire at some vice.* —*v.i.* 3. to strive; try (followed in the U.S. by *to* plus the infinitive, in England by *at* plus the gerund): *they aim to save something every month, they aim at saving something every month.* 4. *U.S. and Dial.* to intend: *she aims to go tomorrow.* 5. to direct efforts toward an object: *to aim high, at the highest.* 6. *Obs.* to estimate; guess. —*n.* 7. act of aiming or directing anything at or toward a particular point or object. 8. the direction in which a missile is pointed; the line of sighting: *to take aim.* 9. the point intended to be hit; thing or person aimed at. 10. something intended or desired to be attained by one's efforts; purpose. 11. *Obs.* conjecture; guess. [ME *ayme(n)*, t. OF: m. (*a)esmer*, g. L (*ad)aestimāre* estimate] —**aim′er,** *n.* —**Syn.** 10. AIM, END, OBJECT all imply something which is the goal of one's efforts. AIM implies that toward which one makes a direct line, refusing to be diverted from it: *a nobleness of aim, one's aim in life.* END emphasizes the goal as a cause of efforts: *the end for which one strives.* OBJECT emphasizes the goal as that toward which all efforts are directed: *the object of years of study.*

aim·less (ām′lĭs), *adj.* without aim; purposeless. —**aim′less·ly,** *adv.* —**aim′less·ness,** *n.*

ain (ān), *adj. Scot.* own.

aî·né (ĕ nĕ′), *adj. French.* of the greater age; elder; eldest. —**aî·née′,** *adj. fem.*

ain't (ānt), *Now Illiterate or Dial.* 1. a contraction of *am not*, extended in use as contraction of *are not* and *is not.* 2. a contraction (with loss of *h*) of *have not*.

Ain·tab (īn′täb′). *n.* Gaziantep.

Ai·nu (ī′nōō), *n.* 1. a member of an aboriginal race of the northernmost islands of Japan, having Caucasian features, light skin, and hairy bodies. 2. the language of the Ainus, of uncertain relationship.

air[1] (âr), *n.* 1. a mixture of oxygen, nitrogen, and other gases, which surrounds the earth and forms its atmosphere. 2. a movement of the atmosphere; a light breeze. 3. *Obs.* breath. 4. circulation; publication; publicity. 5. the general character or complexion of anything; appearance. 6. the peculiar look, appearance, and bearing of a person. 7. (*pl.*) affected manner; manifestation of pride or vanity; assumed haughtiness: *to put on airs.* 8. *Music.* **a.** a tune; a melody. **b.** the soprano or treble part. **c.** an aria. **d.** an Elizabethan art song. 9. *Radio.* the atmosphere through which radio waves are sent. 10. **in the air, a.** without foundation or actuality; visionary or uncertain. **b.** in circulation. **c.** undecided or unsettled (often prec. by *up*). **d.** angry; perturbed (often prec. by *up*). 11. **on the air,** in the act of broadcasting; being broadcast. 12. **take the air,** to go out-of-doors; walk or ride a little distance. 13. **walk on air,** to feel very happy or elated. —*v.t.* 14. to expose to the air; give access to the open air; ventilate. 15. to expose ostentatiously; bring into public notice; display: *to air one's opinions or theories.* [ME *ayre, eir,* t. OF: m. *air,* g. L *āer,* t. Gk.: air, mist] —**Syn.** 2. See **wind**[1]. 6. demeanor; attitude. See **manner.**

air[2] (âr), *adv., adj. Scot.* 1. before. 2. early. [see ERE]

A·ïr (ä′ĭr), *n.* a native kingdom in E French West Africa, consisting of a plateau and oasis region in the Sahara. ab. 30,000 sq. mi. *Cap.:* Agadès. Also, **Asben.**

air alert, 1. act of flying while waiting for combat orders or for enemy airplanes to appear. 2. the signal to take stations for such action.

air base, an operations center for units of an air force.

air bladder, 1. a vesicle or sac containing air. 2. *Ichthyol.* a symmetrical sac filled with air whose principal function is the regulation of the hydrostatic equilibrium of the body; a swim bladder. Also, **air cell.**

air-borne (âr′bôrn′), *adj. Mil.* (of ground forces) carried in airplanes or gliders: *air-borne infantry.*

air-bound (âr′bound′), *adj.* stopped up by air.

air brake, *U.S.* a brake, or system of brakes, operated by compressed air.

air brush, *Orig. U.S.* a kind of atomizer for spraying liquid paint upon a surface.

air castle, a daydream; a visionary scheme.

air chamber, 1. a chamber containing air, as in a pump or a lifeboat or in an organic body. 2. a compartment of a hydraulic system containing air which by its elasticity equalizes the pressure and flow of liquid within the system.

air cock, *Mach.* a special type of valve for controlling the flow of air.

air-con·di·tion (âr′kən dĭsh′ən), *v.t. Orig. U.S.* 1. to furnish with an air-conditioning system. 2. to treat (air) with such a system. —**air′-con·di′tioned,** *adj.* —**air′-con·di′tion·er,** *n.*

air conditioning, *Orig. U.S.* a system of treating air in buildings to assure temperature, humidity, dustlessness, and movement at levels most conducive to personal comfort or manufacturing processes.

air-cool (âr′kōōl′), *v.t.* 1. *Mach.* to remove the heat of combustion, friction, etc., from, as by air streams flowing over an engine jacket. 2. to air-condition. —**air′cooled′,** *v.t.*

Air Corps, *U.S. Army.* former name (before May 1, 1942) of the **Army Air Forces.**

air·craft (âr′krăft′, -kräft′). *n., pl.* **-craft.** any machine supported for flight in the air by buoyancy (such as balloons and other lighter-than-air craft) or by dynamic action of air on its surfaces (such as airplanes, helicopters, gliders, and other heavier-than-air craft).

aircraft carrier, a warship, of varying size, equipped with a deck for the taking off and landing of aircraft, and storage space for the aircraft.

air-craft·man (âr′krăft′mən, -kräft′-), *n., pl.* **-men.** *Brit.* a private in the Royal Air Force.

air cushion, 1. an inflatable airtight cushion. 2. air chamber (def. 2).

air cylinder, a cylinder containing air, esp. (with a piston) as a device for checking the recoil of a gun.

air drain, a space below a building to prevent dampness.

air·drome (âr′drōm′), *n.* a landing field for airplanes which has permanent or extensive buildings, equipment, shelters, etc. Also, esp. *Brit.*, **aerodrome.**

air·drop (âr′drŏp′), *n.* delivery of supplies, troops, etc., by parachute.

air-dry (âr′drī′), *v.,* **-dried, -drying,** *adj.* —*v.t.* 1. to remove moisture from by evaporation in free air. —*adj.* 2. dry beyond further evaporation.

Aire·dale (âr′dāl′), *n.* a large, heavy kind of terrier with a rough brown or tan coat which is black or grizzled over the back. [from *Airedale* in Yorkshire, England]

air·field (âr′fēld′), *n.* a level area, usually equipped with hard-surfaced runways, on which airplanes take off and land.

Airedale
(23 in. high at the shoulder)

air·flow (âr′flō′), *n.* air currents caused by a moving aircraft, automobile, etc.

air·foil (âr′foil′), *n. Aeron.* any surface, such as a wing, aileron, or stabilizer, designed to help in lifting or controlling the aircraft by making use of the current of air through which it moves. [f. AIR + FOIL[2]]

Air Force, 1. *U.S.* the department consisting of practically all military aviation forces, established July 26, 1947. 2. (*l.c.*) *U.S.* (formerly) the largest unit in the Army Air Forces. 3. *Brit.* Royal Air Force.

air·graph (âr′grăf′, -gräf′), *Brit.* —*n.* 1. a letter photographed on film, sent by air, and then enlarged, similar to American V-Mail. —*v.t.* 2. to send by airgraph.

air gun, a gun operated by compressed air.

air hole, 1. an opening to admit or discharge air. 2. *U.S.* a natural opening in the frozen surface of a river or pond. 3. *Aeron.* air pocket.

air·i·ly (âr′ə lĭ), *adv.* 1. in a gay manner; jauntily. 2. lightly; delicately. —**air·i·ness** (âr′ĭ nĭs), *n.*

air·ing (âr′ĭng), *n.* 1. an exposure to the air, or to a fire, as for drying. 2. a walk, drive, etc., in the open air.

air jacket, 1. an envelope of enclosed air about part of a machine, as for checking the transmission of heat. 2. *Brit.* a life belt.

air lane, a route regularly used by airplanes; airway.

air·less (âr′lĭs), *adj.* 1. lacking air. 2. without fresh air; stuffy. 3. still.

air lift, 1. a system of transportation by aircraft, esp. that established in 1948 by the Western powers to supply Berlin during the Soviet blockade. 2. the act or process of transporting such a load. Also, **air′lift.**

air line, 1. *Aeron.* **a.** a system furnishing (usually) scheduled air transport between specified points. **b.** the airplanes, airports, navigational aids, etc., of such a system. **c.** a company that owns or operates such a system. **d.** a scheduled route followed by such a system. 2. *Chiefly U.S.* a direct line; a line as direct as a beeline.

air-line (âr′līn′), *adj.* straight as a line in the air.

ăct, āble, dâre, ärt; ĕbb, ēqual; ĭf, īce; hŏt, ōver, ôrder, oil, bŏŏk, ōōze, out; ŭp, ūse, ûrge; ə = a in alone; ch, chief; g, give; ng, ring; sh, shoe; th, thin; ŧh, that; zh, vision. See the full key on inside cover.

air liner, a passenger aircraft operating over an air line.

air lock, *Civ. Eng.* an airtight transition compartment at the entrance of a pressure chamber in which men work, as in a submerged caisson.

air mail, *Orig. U.S.* 1. the system of transmitting mail by aircraft. 2. mail transmitted by aircraft.

air-mail (âr′māl′), *adj.* of or sent by air mail.

air·man (âr′mən), *n., pl.* **-men.** 1. an aviator. 2. *U.S. Air Force.* an enlisted man of one of the four lowest ranks: **basic airman, airman third class, airman second class,** (formerly *corporal*), **airman first class** (formerly *sergeant*). 3. *U.S. Navy.* an enlisted man with duties relating to aircraft. 4. (in other countries) an enlisted man in the Air Force.

air mass, *Meteorol.* a body of air which approximates horizontal uniformity in its properties.

air-mind·ed (âr′mīn′dĭd), *adj.* 1. interested in aviation or in the aviation aspects of problems. 2. favoring increased use of aircraft. **—air′-mind′ed·ness,** *n.*

Air Ministry, (in England) the government department dealing with civil and military aeronautics.

air·plane (âr′plān′), *n.* an aircraft, heavier than air, kept aloft by the upward thrust exerted by the passing air on its fixed wings, and driven by propellers, jet propulsion, etc. Also, *esp. Brit.,* **aeroplane.**

airplane carrier, aircraft carrier.

airplane cloth, 1. a cotton fabric of plain weave constructed to specification for parts of airplanes. 2. a similar fabric used for shirts and pajamas.

air plant, *Bot.* epiphyte.

air pocket, *Aeron.* a downward current of air, usually causing a sudden loss of altitude.

air·port (âr′pōrt′), *n.* a tract of land or water with facilities for aircraft landing, take-off, shelter, supply, and repair, often used regularly for receiving or discharging passengers and cargo.

air post, *Brit.* air mail.

air pressure, the pressure of the atmosphere.

air·proof (âr′prōōf′), *adj.* 1. impervious to air. —*v.t.* 2. to make impervious to air.

air pump, an apparatus for drawing in, compressing, and discharging air.

air raid, a raid or incursion by hostile aircraft, esp. for dropping bombs or other missiles. **—air′-raid′,** *adj.* **—air raider.**

air-raid shelter, a security area or place used as a refuge during an air attack.

air-raid warden, a person who has temporary police duties during an air-raid alert.

air rifle, an air gun with rifled bore.

air sac, *Orig. U.S.* 1. a sac containing air. 2. any of certain cavities in a bird's body connected with the lungs. 3. a saclike dilatation of an insect trachea.

air·screw (âr′skrōō′), *n. Brit.* an airplane propeller.

air shaft, a ventilating shaft.

air·ship (âr′shĭp′), *n.* a self-propelled, lighter-than-air craft with means of controlling the direction of flight, usually classed as rigid, semirigid, or nonrigid.

air-sick (âr′sĭk′), *adj.* ill as the result of traveling in the air. **—air′sick′ness,** *n.*

air-slake (âr′slāk′), *v.t.,* **-slaked, -slaking.** to slake by moist air, as lime.

air speed, the forward speed of an aircraft relative to the air through which it moves.

air-spray (âr′sprā′), *adj.* pertaining to compressed-air spraying devices or to liquids used in them.

air·strip (âr′strĭp′), *n. Aeron.* runway (def. 2).

air switch, *Elect.* a switch in which the interruption of the circuit occurs in air.

airt (ârt; *Scot.* ärt), *Scot.* **—n.** 1. a direction. —*v.t.* 2. to point out the way. Also, **airth** (ârth; *Scot.* ärth). [t. Gaelic: m. *aird* height]

air·tight (âr′tīt′), *adj.* 1. so tight or close as to be impermeable to air. 2. having no weak points or openings of which an opponent may take advantage.

air turbine. See **turbine** (def. 2).

air valve, a device for controlling the flow of air through a pipe.

air vesicle, *Bot.* a large air-filled pocket, present mainly in plants which float on water.

air·way (âr′wā′), *n.* 1. an air route fully equipped with emergency landing fields, beacon lights, radio beams, etc. 2. any passage in a mine used for purposes of ventilation; an air course.

air well, air shaft.

air-wom·an (âr′wŏŏm′ən), *n., pl.* **-women.** a woman aviator.

air-wor·thy (âr′wûr′thǐ), *adj. Aeron.* meeting accepted standards for safe flight; equipped and maintained in condition to fly. **—air′wor′thi·ness,** *n.*

air·y (âr′ĭ), *adj.,* **airier, airiest.** 1. consisting of or having the character of air; immaterial: *airy phantoms.* 2. light in appearance; thin: *airy lace.* 3. light in manner; sprightly; gay; lively: *airy songs.* 4. light in movement; graceful; delicate: *an airy tread.* 5. light as air; unsubstantial; unreal; imaginary: *airy dreams.* 6. visionary; speculative. 7. performed in the air; aerial. 8. lofty; high in the air. 9. open to a free current of air; breezy: *airy rooms.*

A·i·sha (ä′ēshä′), *n.* A.D. 613?–678, favorite wife of Mohammed and daughter of Abu-Bekr. Also, **Ayesha.**

aisle (īl), *n.* 1. a passageway between seats in a church, hall, etc. 2. *Archit.* a. a lateral division of a church or other building separated from the nave by piers or columns. See diag. under **basilica. b.** a similar division at the side of the choir or a transept. c. any of the lateral divisions of a church or hall, as the nave. [var. of *isle,* trans. of late ML *insula* aisle (in L island); r. ME *ele,* t. OF, g. L *āla* shoulder, wing; *ai-* of current sp. from F *aile*] **—aisled** (īld), *adj.*

Aisne (ān; *Fr.* ĕn), *n.* a river in N France, flowing into the Oise river. 175 m. See map under **Compiègne.**

ait (āt), *n. Brit.* a small island. [ME *eyt,* OE *igeoth,* dim. of *ieg* island; history of forms not clear]

aitch (āch), *n.* the letter *H, h.*

aitch·bone (āch′bōn′), *n. Brit.* 1. the rump bone, as of beef. 2. the cut of beef which includes this bone. [ME *nache-bone; a nache-bone* became *an aitch-bone* by false division into words; *nache,* t. OF, ult. der. L *natis* buttock]

Ait·ken (āt′kən), *n.* 1. **Robert Grant,** 1864–1951, U.S. astronomer. 2. See **Beaverbrook.**

Aix-en-Pro·vence (ĕks äN prō väNs′), *n.* a city in SE France, N of Marseilles. 52,217 (1954). Also, **Aix.**

Aix-la-Cha·pelle (ĕks′lä shä pĕl′; *Fr.* ĕks lä shä pĕl′), *n.* French name of **Aachen.**

A·jac·cio (ä yät′chō), *n.* a seaport in and the capital of Corsica: birthplace of Napoleon. 32,997 (1954).

a·jar[1] (ə jär′), *adj., adv.* neither quite open nor shut; partly opened: *leave the door ajar.* [ME *on char* on the turn; *char,* OE *cerr* turn. See **A-[1], CHARWOMAN**]

a·jar[2] (ə jär′), *adv., adj.* out of harmony; jarring: *ajar with the world.* [for *at jar* at discord. See **JAR[3],** n.]

A·jax (ā′jăks), *n. Gk. Legend.* 1. a mighty warrior of the Greeks before Troy. He killed himself in chagrin when Achilles' armor was awarded to Odysseus. 2. **the lesser Ajax,** a Locrian king, a hero in the Trojan War, second in swiftness only to Achilles. [t. L, t. Gk.: m. *Aíās*]

a·jee (ə jē′), *adj. Dial.* agee.

Aj·mer (ŭj mŭr′), *n.* a city in NW India in Rajasthan. 196,633 (1951). Formerly part of Ajmer-Merwara province within, though not part of, Rajputana.

Ak·bar (ăk′bär), *n.* 1542–1605, Mogul emperor of India, 1556–1605.

a·kene (ā kēn′), *n.* achene.

a·kim·bo (ə kĭm′bō), *adj., adv.* with hand on hip and elbow bent outward: *to stand with arms akimbo.* [ME *in kene bowe,* appar., in keen bow, in a sharp bent; but cf. Icel. *kengboginn* bent double, crooked]

a·kin (ə kĭn′), *adj.* 1. of kin; related by blood. 2. allied by nature; partaking of the same properties. [contr. of phrase *of kin*] **—Syn.** 2. cognate; similar, analogous.

A·kins (ā′kǐnz), *n.* **Zoë** (zō′ĭ), 1886–1958, U.S. playwright.

A·ki·ta (ä′kē tä′), *n.* a seaport in N Japan, on Honshu island. 126,074 (1950).

Ak·kad (ăk′ăd, ä′käd), *n.* 1. Also, **Accad.** one of the four cities of Nimrod's kingdom. Gen. 10:10. In the cuneiform inscriptions it evidently includes most of N Babylonia. **—adj.** 2. Akkadian.

Ak·ka·di·an (ə kä′dĭ′ən, əkä′-), *n.* 1. the eastern group of Semitic languages, all extinct, including Babylonian and Assyrian. 2. any member of this group. 3. one of the Akkadian people. —*adj.* 4. of or belonging to Akkad. 5. designating or pertaining to the primitive inhabitants of Babylonia or the non-Semitic language ascribed to them. 6. designating or pertaining to the (later) Semitic language of Babylonia.

Ak·ker·man (ăk′ər män′), *n.* former name for **Belgo-Rod-Dnestrovski.**

Ak·kra (ăk′rə; *native* ə krä′), *n.* Accra.

Ak·ron (ăk′rən), *n.* a city in NE Ohio. 290,351 (1960).

Ak·sum (äk′sōōm), *n.* the capital of an ancient Ethiopian kingdom. Also, **Axum.**

à l′, French. form of **à la** used for either gender before a vowel or *h.*

al-, var. of ad- before *l,* as in *allure.*

-al[1], *adj.* a suffix meaning "of or pertaining to," "connected with," "of the nature of," "like," "befitting," etc., occurring in numerous adjectives and in many nouns of adjectival origin, as *annual, choral, equal, regal.* [t. L: s. *-ālis* (neut. *-āle*) pertaining to; often r. ME *-el,* t. F]

-al[2], a suffix forming nouns of action from verbs, as in *refusal, denial, recital, trial.* [t. L: m. *-āle* (pl. *ālia*), neut. of adj. suffix *-ālis;* often r. ME *-aille,* t. OF]

-al[3], *Chem.* a suffix indicating that a compound includes an alcohol or aldehyde group, as in *chloral.* [short for AL(COHOL) or AL(DEHYDE)]

AL, Anglo-Latin. Also, **AL., A.L.**

Al, *Chem.* aluminum.

a·la (ā′lə), *n., pl.* **alae** (ā′lē). 1. a wing. 2. a winglike part, process, or expansion, as of a bone, a shell, a seed, a stem, etc. 3. one of the two side petals of a papilionaceous flower. [t. L: wing]

à la (ä′lä, ä′lə; *Fr.* ä lä), 1. according to: *à la mode, à la Brooklyn.* 2. *Cookery.* with: **à la jardinière,** with various vegetables. Also, **a la.** [t. F: at, to, in + the; fem. form used before a word beginning with a consonant]

Ala., Alabama.

A.L.A., American Library Association.

A·la·ba·ma (ăl'ə băm'ə), *n.* **1.** a State in the SE United States. 3,266,740 pop. (1960); 51,609 sq. mi. *Cap.:* Montgomery. *Abbr.:* Ala. **2.** a river flowing from central Alabama SW to the Mobile river. 315 mi. —**Al·a·bam·i·an** (ăl'ə băm'Yən), **Al'a·bam'an,** *adj., n.*

al·a·bam·ine (ăl'ə băm'ēn, -Yn), *n. Chem.* former name of astatine. [f. ALABAM (A)+ -INE²]

al·a·bas·ter (ăl'ə băs'tər, -bäs'-), *n.* **1.** a finely granular variety of gypsum, often white and translucent, used for ornamental objects or work, such as lamp bases, figurines, etc. **2.** a variety of calcite, often with a banded structure, used for similar purposes (**Oriental alabaster**). —*adj.* Also, **al·a·bas·trine** (ăl'ə băs'trĭn, -bäs'-). **3.** made of alabaster: *an alabaster column.* **4.** resembling alabaster; smooth and white as alabaster: *her alabaster throat.* [ME, t. L, t. Gk.: m. *alábastros,* var. of *alábastos* an alabaster box]

à la bonne heure (à lȧ bô nœr'), *French.* **1.** at the right moment. **2.** just right; excellent; very well.

à la carte (ä'/ə kärt'; *Fr.* ä lȧ kärt'), by the bill of fare; with a stated price for each dish: *dinner à la carte.* [t. F]

a·lack (ə lăk'), *interj. Archaic.* an exclamation of sorrow, regret, or dismay. Also, **a·lack·a·day** (ə lăk'ə dā').

a·lac·ri·ty (ə lăk'rə tY), *n.* **1.** liveliness; briskness; sprightliness. **2.** cheerful readiness or willingness. [t. L: m. s. *alacritas*] —**a·lac'ri·tous,** *adj.*

A·la Dagh (ä'lä däкн'), **1.** a mountain range in S Turkey. Highest peak, ab. 11,000 ft. **2.** a mountain range in E Turkey. Highest peak, ab. 11,500 ft.

A·lad·din (ə lăd'Yn), *n.* (in *The Arabian Nights' Entertainments*) the son of a poor widow in China. He becomes the possessor of a magic lamp and ring, with which he commands two jinns who gratify all his wishes.

A·la·göz (ä'lä gœz'), *n.* a volcanic mountain in the SE Soviet Union in the Armenian Republic. 13,435 ft.

A·lai Mountains (ä lī'), a mountain range in the SW Soviet Union in Asia, in Kirghiz Republic: a part of the Tien Shan mountain system. Peaks, 16,000 to 19,500 ft.

à la King (ä lä kYng'), (of a dish of diced cooked fowl, fish, etc.) creamed with pimiento or green pepper: *chicken à la King.*

Al·a·me·da (ăl'ə mē'də, -mä'-), *n.* a city in W California, E of San Francisco. 61,316 (1960).

al·a·me·da (ăl'ə mä'də), *n. Chiefly Southwestern U.S.* a public walk shaded with poplar or other trees. [t. Sp., der. *alamo* poplar]

al·a·mo (ăl'ə mō', ä'lə-), *n., pl.* **-mos.** *Southwestern U.S.* a cottonwood.

Al·a·mo (ăl'ə mō'), *n.* a mission building in San Antonio, Texas, which underwent a terrible siege by Mexicans in February, 1836, but was taken on March 6, and its entire garrison of American rebels killed.

al·a·mode (ăl'ə mōd'), *n.* glossy silk for scarfs, etc.

à la mode (ä' lə mōd', ăl'ə; *Fr.* ä lä môd'), **1.** in or according to the fashion. **2.** *Cookery.* **a.** (of pie or other dessert) served with a portion of ice cream. **b.** (of beef) larded and braised or stewed with vegetables, herbs, etc., and served with a rich brown gravy. Also, **a la mode, a'la·mode'.** [t. F]

à la mort (ä lä môr'), *French.* —*adj.* **1.** half dead. **2.** melancholy; dispirited. —*adv.* **3.** mortally.

Å·land Islands (ä'lənd, ô'-; *Swed.* ō'län), a group of Finnish islands in the Baltic between Sweden and Finland. 28,000 pop. (est. 1952); 572 sq. mi. Finnish, **Ahvenanmaa.**

à la Newburg (ä' lə nū'bûrg, noo'-), cooked with a sauce of cream, egg yolk, butter, and usually wine.

al·a·nine (ăl'ə nēn', -nYn), *n.* an amino acid, CH₃·CH(NH₂)COOH, found in many proteins.

a·lar (ä'lər), *adj.* **1.** pertaining to or having wings; alary. **2.** winglike; wing-shaped. **3.** *Anat., Bot.* axillary. [t. L: s. *ālāris,* der. *āla* wing]

A·lar·ic (ăl'ərYk), *n.* A.D. c370–410, king of the Visigoths: captured Rome, A.D. 410.

a·larm (ə lärm'), *n.* **1.** a sudden fear or painful suspense excited by an apprehension of danger; apprehension; fright. **2.** any sound, outcry, or information intended to give notice of approaching danger: *a false alarm.* **3.** a self-acting contrivance of any kind used to call attention, rouse from sleep, warn of danger, etc. **4.** a warning sound; signal for attention. **5.** a call to arms. **6.** *Fencing.* an appeal or a challenge made by a step or stamp on the ground with the advancing foot. —*v.t.* **7.** to surprise with apprehension of danger; disturb with sudden fear. **8.** to give notice of danger to; rouse to vigilance and exertions for safety. [ME *alarme,* t. OF, t. It.: m. *allarme* tumult, fright, der. *all' arme* to arms] —**a·larmed',** *adj.* —**a·larm'ing·ly,** *adv.* —Syn. **1.** consternation; terror; panic. See **fear. 7.** See **afraid.**

a·larm·ist (ə lär'mYst), *n.* one given to raising alarms, esp. without sufficient reason, as by exaggerating dangers, prophesying calamities, etc. —**a·larm'ism,** *n.*

a·lar·um (ə lăr'əm, ə lär'-), *n. Archaic.* alarm.

a·la·ry (ä'lə rY, ăl'ə-), *adj.* **1.** of or pertaining to wings. **2.** *Biol.* wing-shaped. [t. L: m. s. *ālārius,* der. *āla* wing]

a·las (ə läs', ə lăs'), *interj.* an exclamation expressing sorrow, grief, pity, concern, or apprehension of evil. [ME *allas,* t. OF: m. *a las, ha las,* f. *a, ha* ah + *las* miserable, t. L *lassus* weary]

Alas., Alaska.

A·las·ka (ə lăs'kə), *n.* **1.** a State of the United States, in NW North America. 226,167 (1960); 586,400 sq. mi. *Cap.:* Juneau. **2.** Gulf of, a large gulf of the Pacific, on the S coast of Alaska. —**A·las'kan,** *adj., n.*

Alaska Highway, a highway extending from E British Columbia, Canada, to Fairbanks, Alaska: built as a U.S. military supply route, 1942. 1523 mi. Unofficially, **Alcan Highway.**

Alaska Peninsula, a long, narrow peninsula forming the SW extension of the mainland of Alaska. ab. 400 mi. long.

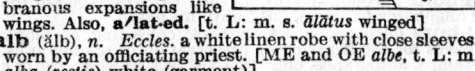

Alaska Range, a mountain range in S Alaska. Highest peak, Mt. McKinley, 20,300 ft.

a·late (ä'lāt), *adj.* **1.** winged. **2.** having membranous expansions like wings. Also, **a'lat·ed.** [t. L: m. s. *ālātus* winged]

alb (ălb), *n. Eccles.* a white linen robe with close sleeves, worn by an officiating priest. [ME and OE *albe,* t. L: m. *alba* (*vestis*) white (garment)]

Alb., 1. Also, **Alba.** Alberta (Canada). **2.** Albania.

Al·ba (ăl'bə, äl'bä), *n.* Duke of. See **Alva.**

Al·ba·ce·te (äl'bä thā'tĕ, -sĕ'tĕ), *n.* a city in SE Spain. 71,882 (1950).

al·ba·core (ăl'bə kōr'), *n., pl.* **-cores,** (*sometimes*) **-core. 1.** the long-finned tunny, *Germo alalunga,* common in all warm or temperate seas, and highly valued for canning. **2.** any of various fishes related to or resembling the tunny. [t. Pg.: m. *albacor*(*a*), t. Ar.: m. *al-bakūra*]

Al·ba Lon·ga (ăl'bə lŏng'gə, lŏng'-), a city of ancient Latium, SE of Rome: fabled birthplace of Romulus and Remus.

Alb worn by a priest

Al·ba·ni·a (ăl bā'nYə, -bān'yə), *n.* **1.** a republic in S Europe, in the Balkan Peninsula between Yugoslavia and Greece. 1,394,000 (est. 1955); 10,632 sq. mi. *Cap.:* Tirana. **2.** *Poetic and Rare.* Scotland.

Al·ba·ni·an (ăl bā'nYən, -bān'yən), *adj.* **1.** pertaining to Albania (def. 1), its inhabitants, or their language. —*n.* **2.** a native or inhabitant of Albania. **3.** the language of Albania (def. 1), an Indo-European language.

Al·ba·ny (ôl'bənY), *n.* **1.** the capital of New York, in the E part, on the Hudson. 129,726 (1960). **2.** a city in SW Georgia. 31,155 (1950). **3.** a river in central Canada, flowing from W Ontario E to James Bay. 610 mi.

al·ba·ta (ăl bā'tə), *n.* German silver. [t. NL, prop. fem. of L *albatus,* pp., made white]

al·ba·tross (ăl'bə trôs', -trŏs'), *n.* any of various large webfooted, tube-nosed sea birds related to the petrels, esp. of the genus *Diomedea,* of the Pacific and southern waters, noted for their powers of flight. [var. of *algatross,* t. Pg.: m. *alcatraz* seafowl, cormorant; change of -g- to -b- ? by association with L *alba* white (the bird's color)]

Wandering albatross, Diomedea exulans (42 in. long, wingspread 11 ft.)

Al·bay (äl bī'), *n.* former name of Legaspi.

al·be·do (ăl bē'dō), *n. Astron.* the ratio of the light reflected by a planet or satellite to that received by it. [t. L: whiteness]

al·be·it (ôl bē'Yt), *conj.* although; notwithstanding that: *to choose a peaceful albeit inglorious retirement.* [ME *al be it* although it be]

Al·be·marle Sound (ăl'bə märl'), a sound in NE North Carolina. ab. 60 mi. long.

Al·bé·niz (äl bĕ'nēth), *n.* Isaac (ē'sä äk'), 1860–1909, Spanish composer and pianist.

Al·ber·ich (ăl'bər Yкн), *n. Medieval Legend.* king of the dwarfs and chief of the Nibelungs.

Al·bert (ăl'bərt), *n.* **1.** Prince, (*Francis Charles Augustus Albert Emanuel, Prince of Saxe-Coburg-Gotha*) 1819–61, German prince, husband of Queen Victoria of Great Britain; known as Prince Consort. **2.** Lake, a lake in central Africa between Uganda and the Belgian Congo: a source of the Nile. ab. 100 mi. long; ab. 2000 sq. mi.; ab. 2200 ft. high.

Albert I, 1875–1934, king of the Belgians, 1909–34.

Al·ber·ta (ăl bûr'tə), *n.* a province in W Canada. 1,002,000 (est. 1953); 255,285 sq. mi. *Cap.:* Edmonton.

Albert Edward, a mountain peak of the Owen Stanley range, in SE New Guinea. 13,030 ft.

Al·ber·tian (ăl bûr'shən), *adj.* pertaining to Prince Albert.

al·bert·ite (ăl'bər tīt'), *n.* an asphalt from the Albert mine in New Brunswick.

Albert Memorial, a monument to Prince Albert in Kensington Gardens, London.

Al·bert Ny·an·za (nī ăn'zə, nyän'zä), Albert (def. 2).

Al·ber·tus Mag·nus (ăl bûr'təs măg'nəs), (*Albert von Böllstadt*) 1193?–1280, German scholastic philosopher; teacher of Thomas Aquinas; canonized in 1932.

al·bes·cent (ăl bĕs'ənt), *adj.* becoming white; whitish. [t. L: s. *albescens,* ppr.] —**al·bes'cence,** *n.*

Al·bi (ăl bē′), *n.* a city in S France: center of the Albigenses. 34,693 (1954).

Al·bi·gen·ses (ăl′bə jĕn′sēz), *n.pl.* the members of several sects in the south of France in the 12th and 13th centuries. [ML. der. *Albi* ALBI] —**Al·bi·gen·si·an** (ăl′bə jĕn′sĭ ən, -shən), *adj.*, *n.*

al·bi·nism (ăl′bə nĭz′əm), *n.* state or condition of being an albino. —**al·bi·nis·tic** (ăl′bə nĭs′tĭk), *adj.*

al·bi·no (ăl bī′nō *or, esp. Brit.*, -bē′-), *n., pl.* -**nos.** **1.** a person with a pale, milky skin, light hair, and pink eyes. **2.** an animal or plant with a marked deficiency in pigmentation. [t. Pg., der. *albo*, g. L *albus* white] —**al·bin·ic** (ăl bĭn′ĭk), *adj.*

Al·bi·on (ăl′bĭ ən), *n. Poetic.* Britain. [t. L, said to be der. *albus* white]

al·bite (ăl′bīt), *n.* a very common mineral of the plagioclase feldspar group, sodium aluminum silicate, NaAlSi₃O₈, usually white, occurring in many igneous rocks. [f. s. L *albus* white + -ITE¹]

Al·boin (ăl′boin, -bō ĭn), *n.* died A.D. 573?, king of the Langobards from A.D. 561? until his death.

al·bum (ăl′bəm), *n.* **1.** a book consisting of blank leaves for the insertion or preservation of photographs, stamps, autographs, etc. **2.** a visitor's register; visitor's book. [t. L: tablet, prop. neut. of *albus* white]

al·bu·men (ăl bū′mən), *n.* **1.** the white of an egg. **2.** *Bot.* the nutritive matter about the embryo in a seed. **3.** *Chem.* albumin. [t. L (def. 1), der. *albus* white]

al·bu·men·ize (ăl bū′mə nīz′), *v.t.*, -**ized**, -**izing.** to treat with an albuminous solution.

al·bu·min (ăl bū′mən), *n. Biochem.* any of a class of water-soluble proteins composed of nitrogen, carbon, hydrogen, oxygen, and sulfur, occurring in animal and vegetable juices and tissues. [t. L: s. *albūmen* ALBUMEN]

al·bu·mi·nate (ăl bū′mə nāt′), *n. Biochem.* a compound resulting from the action of an alkali or an acid upon albumin.

al·bu·mi·noid (ăl bū′mə noid′), *n. Biochem.* **1.** any of a class of simple proteins which are insoluble in all neutral solvents, as keratin, gelatin, collagen, etc. —*adj.* **2.** resembling albumen or albumin. [f. s. L *albūmen* white of egg + -OID] —**al·bu′mi·noi′dal,** *adj.*

al·bu·mi·nous (ăl bū′mə nəs), *adj.* **1.** of albumin. **2.** containing albumin. **3.** resembling albumin. Also, **al·bu·mi·nose** (ăl bū′mə nōs′).

al·bu·mi·nu·ri·a (ăl bū′mə nyŏŏr′Ĭ ə, -nŏŏr′-), *n. Pathol.* the presence of albumin in the urine. [f. ALBUMIN + -URIA] —**al·bu′mi·nu′ric,** *adj.*

al·bu·mose (ăl′byə mōs′), *n. Biochem.* any of a class of compounds derived from albumins, etc., by the action of proteolytic enzymes. [f. ALBUM(IN) + -OSE²]

Al·bu·quer·que (ăl′bə kûr′kĭ), *n.* a city in central New Mexico. 201,189 (1960).

al·bur·num (ăl bûr′nəm), *n. Bot.* the softer part of the wood between the inner bark and the heartwood; sapwood. [t. L, der. *albus* white]

Al·cae·us (ăl sē′əs), *n.* fl. c600 B.C., Greek lyric poet of Mytilene.

al·ca·hest (ăl′kə hĕst′), *n.* alkahest.

Al·ca·ic (ăl kā′ĭk), *adj.* **1.** pertaining to Alcaeus or to certain meters or a form of strophe or stanza used by, or named after, him. —*n.* **2.** (*pl.*) Alcaic verses or strophes.

al·caide (ăl kād′; *Sp.* äl kä′ē dĕ′), *n.* (in Spain, Portugal, Southwestern U.S., etc.) **1.** a commander of a fortress. **2.** a jailer; the warden of a prison. Also, **al·cayde′.** [t. Sp., t. Ar.: m. *al-qā′id* the commander]

al·cal·de (ăl käl′dĭ; *Sp.* älkäl′dĕ), *n.* (in Spain and Southwestern U.S.) a chief municipal officer with judicial powers. Also, *Southwestern U.S.*, **al·cade** (ălkād′). [t. Sp., t. Ar.: m. *al-qāḍī* the judge. See CADI]

Al·can Highway (ăl′kăn), unofficial name of Alaska Highway.

Al·ca·traz (ăl′kə trăz′), *n.* **1.** an island in San Francisco Bay, in W California. **2.** the U.S. federal penitentiary on this island.

Al·ca·zar (ăl′kə zär′, ăl kăz′ər; *Sp.* äl kä′thär), *n.* **1.** the palace of the Moorish kings (later, of Spanish royalty) at Seville. **2.** (*l.c.*) a palace of the Spanish Moors. [t. Sp., t. Ar.: m. *al-qaṣr* the castle (*qaṣr*, t. L: m. s. *castrum* fortress)]

Al·ces·tis (ăl sĕs′tĭs), *n. Gk. Legend.* the wife of the Thessalian king Admetus, whose life she saved by dying in his place. She was brought back from Hades by Hercules.

al·che·mist (ăl′kə mĭst), *n.* one who practices or is versed in alchemy. —**al′che·mis′tic, al′che·mis′ti·cal,** *adj.*

al·che·mize (ăl′kə mīz′), *v.t.*, -**mized**, -**mizing.** to change by alchemy; transmute, as metals.

al·che·my (ăl′kə mĭ), *n.* **1.** *Medieval Chem.* an art which sought in particular to transmute baser metals into gold, and to find a universal solvent and an elixir of life. **2.** any magical power or process of transmuting. [ME *alkamye*, t. OF: m. *alcamie*, t. ML: m. *alchimia*, t. Ar.: m. *al-kīmīya*' (*kīmīyā*' ? t. LGk.: m. *chýma* molten metal)] —**al·chem·ic** (ăl kĕm′Ĭk), **al·chem′i·cal,** *adj.* —**al·chem′i·cal·ly,** *adv.*

Al·ci·bi·a·des (ăl′sə bī′ə dēz′), *n.* 450?–404 B.C., Athenian politician and general.

Al·ci·des (ăl sī′dēz), *n.* Hercules.

al·ci·dine (ăl′sə dīn′, -dĭn), *adj. Ornith.* pertaining to or resembling the *Alcidae*, the auk family.

Al·cin·o·üs (ăl sĭn′ō əs), *n. Homeric Legend.* the father of Nausicaä, a king of the Phaeacians, at whose court Ulysses related the story of his wanderings.

Alc·me·ne (ălk mē′nĭ), *n. Gk. Myth.* mother of Hercules by Zeus, who visited her in the guise of her husband.

al·co·hol (ăl′kə hôl′, -hŏl′), *n.* **1.** a colorless, inflammable liquid (ethyl alcohol, C₂H₅OH), the intoxicating principle of fermented liquors, formed from certain sugars (esp. glucose) by fermentation, now usually prepared by treating grain with malt and adding yeast. **2.** any intoxicating liquor containing this spirit. **3.** *Chem.* any of a class of chemical compounds having the general formula ROH, where R represents an alkyl group; derived from the hydrocarbon by replacement of a hydrogen atom by the hydroxyl radical, OH. [t. ML: orig., fine powder; hence, essence or rectified spirits, t. Ar.: m. *al-kuhl* the powdered antimony, kohl]

al·co·hol·ic (ăl′kə hôl′Ĭk, -hŏl′Ĭk), *adj.* **1.** pertaining to or of the nature of alcohol. **2.** containing or using alcohol. **3.** caused by alcohol. **4.** suffering from alcoholism. **5.** preserved in alcohol. —*n.* **6.** a person suffering from alcoholism. **7.** one addicted to intoxicating drinks.

al·co·hol·ic·i·ty (ăl′kə hō lĬs′ə tĬ, -hŏ-), *n.* alcoholic quality or strength.

al·co·hol·ism (ăl′kə hôl Ĭz′əm, -hŏl-), *n.* a diseased condition due to the excessive use of alcoholic beverages.

al·co·hol·om·e·ter (ăl′kə hō lŏm′ə tər, -hŏ-), *n.* an instrument for finding the percentage of alcohol in a liquid. —**al′co·hol·om′e·try,** *n.*

Al·co·ran (ăl′kō rän′, -rän′), *n.* the Koran. [ME *alkaron*, ult. t Ar.: m. *al-qor'ān*, lit., the reading]

Al·cott (ôl′kət), *n.* **1.** (Amos) **Bronson,** 1799–1888, U.S. transcendentalist philosopher, writer, and reformer. **2.** his daughter, **Louisa May,** 1832–88, U. S. author.

al·cove (ăl′kōv), *n.* **1.** a recess opening out of a room. **2.** a recess in a room for a bed, for books in a library, or for other similar permanent furnishings. **3.** any recessed space, as in a garden. [t. F, t. Sp.: m. *alcoba*, t. Ar.: m. *al-qubba* the vaulted space]

Al·cuin (ăl′kwĭn), *n.* A.D. 735–804, English churchman and scholar: teacher and friend of Charlemagne.

Al·cy·o·ne (ăl sī′ə nē′), *n.* a star of the third magnitude in the constellation Taurus: the brightest star in the group known as the Pleiades. [t. L, t. Gk.: m. *Alkyónē*]

Ald., Alderman. Also, **ald.**

Al·dan (ăl dän′), *n.* a river flowing from the Yabloni Mountains in the SE Soviet Union in Asia NE to the Lena river. ab. 1300 mi.

Al·deb·a·ran (ăl dĕb′ə rən), *n.* one of the brightest stars in the sky, orange in color, in the constellation Taurus. [t. Ar.: the follower (i.e. of the Pleiades)]

al·de·hyde (ăl′də hīd′), *n.* one of a group of organic compounds with the general formula R–CHO, which yield acids when oxidized and alcohols when reduced. [short for L *al*(*cohol*) *dehyd*(*rogenátum*) alcohol deprived of hydrogen] —**al′de·hy′dic,** *adj.*

Al·den (ôl′dən), *n.* **John,** 1599?–1687, Pilgrim settler (1620) in Plymouth, Mass.

al·der (ôl′dər), *n.* **1.** any shrub or tree of the betulaceous genus *Alnus* growing in moist places in northern temperate or colder regions. **2.** any of various trees or shrubs resembling this genus. [ME; OE *alor, aler*]

al·der·man (ôl′dər mən), *n., pl.* -**men.** **1.** *U.S.* one of a body of municipal officers with powers (executive, judicial, or legislative) varying according to locality, often representing a municipal ward. **2.** *Eng.* one of the members, chosen by the elected councilors, in a borough or county council. **3.** *Eng. Hist.* ealdorman. [ME; OE *aldormann, ealdormann*, f. *ealdor* chief, elder + *mann* man] —**al′der·man·cy, al′der·man·ship′,** *n.*

al·der·man·ic (ôl′dər măn′Ĭk), *adj.* **1.** of an alderman. **2.** characteristic of aldermen.

al·der·man·ry (ôl′dər mən rĬ), *n., pl.* -**ries.** a district of a borough represented by an alderman.

Al·der·ney (ôl′dər nĭ), *n.* **1.** one of the Channel Islands in the English Channel. 1350 pop. (1956); 3 sq. mi. **2.** one of a breed of medium-sized dairy cattle, originating in Alderney.

Al·der·shot (ôl′dər shŏt′), *n.* **1.** a city in S England, SW of London. 36,184 (1951) **2.** a large military training center there.

Al·dine (ôl′dĭn, -dēn), *adj.* **1.** of or from the press of Aldus Manutius and his family, of Venice (about 1490–1597), chiefly noted for compactly printed editions of the classics. —*n.* **2.** Aldine and other early editions. **3.** any of certain styles of printing types.

Al·ding·ton (ôl′dĭng tən), *n.* **Richard,** 1892–1962, British poet and novelist.

Aldm., Alderman. Also, **aldm.**

al·dol (ăl′dôl), *n. Chem.* a colorless fluid, C₄H₈O₂, from an acetaldehyde condensation, used medicinally as a sedative and hypnotic. [f. ALD(EHYDE) + (ALCOH)OL]

al·dose (ăl′dōs), *n. Chem.* a sugar containing the aldehyde group or its hemiacetal equivalent.

Al·drich (ôl′drĭch), *n.* **Thomas Bailey,** 1836–1907, U. S. short-story writer, poet, and novelist

Al·dus Ma·nu·ti·us (ôl′dəs mə nū′shĬ əs, -nōō′-, ăl′dəs). See **Manutius.**

ale (āl), *n.* a malt beverage, darker, heavier, and more bitter than beer, containing about 6 percent of alcohol by volume. [ME; OE *ealu*, c. Icel. öl]

b., blend of, blended; c., cognate with; d., dialect, dialectal; der., derived from; f., formed from; g., going back to; m., modification of; r., replacing; s., stem of; t., taken from; ?, perhaps. See the full key on inside cover.

a·le·a·to·ry (ā'lǐ ə tōr'ǐ), *adj.* **1.** *Law.* depending on a contingent event: *an aleatory contract.* **2.** *Sociol.* having or pertaining to accidental causes and hence not predictable; felt as a matter of good or bad luck and thus easily attributed to benevolent or malevolent forces. [t. L: m. s. *āleātōrius*, der. *āleātor* dice player]

A·lec·to (ə lěk'tō), *n. Gk. Myth.* one of the Furies.

a·lee (ə lē'), *adv., adj. Naut.* on or toward the lee side of a ship (opposed to *aweather*).

al·e·gar (ăl'ə gər, ā'lə-), *n.* ale vinegar; sour ale.

ale·house (āl'hous'), *n.* a house where ale is retailed.

A·lek·san·dro·pol (ä lě'ksän drō'pōl), *n.* former name of Leninakan.

A·lek·san·drovsk (ä'lě ksän'drōfsk), *n.* former name of Zaporozhe.

A·le·mán (ä'lě män'), *n.* **1. Mateo** (mä tě'ō), 1547?–1610, Spanish novelist. **2. Miguel** (mē gěl'), born 1902, president of Mexico, 1946–52.

A·le·man·nic (ăl'ə măn'ǐk), *n.* the High German speech of Swabia, Württemberg, Switzerland, and Alsace.

A·lem·bert (dá län běr'), *n.* **Jean le Rond d'** (zhän lə rōn'), 1717?–83, French mathematician, philosopher, and writer: associate of Diderot.

a·lem·bic (ə lěm'bǐk), *n.* **1.** a vessel with a beaked cap or head, formerly used in distilling; an ancient retort. **2.** anything that transforms, purifies, or refines. [ME *alambic*, t. ML: s. *alambicus*, t. Ar.: m. *alanbīq* the still (*anbīq* t. Gk.: m. *ámbix* cup)]

A. Alembic; B, Lamp; C, Receiver

A·len·çon (á län sōn'), *n.* a city in N W France: lace. 21,893 (1954).

A·len·çon lace (ə lěn'sən, -sōn; *Fr.* á län sōn'), **1.** a delicate needle-point lace made in France. **2.** a machine reproduction of this lace, with a cordlike outline.

A·lep·po (ə lěp'ō), *n.* a city in N W Syria. 389,942 (est. 1953). French, **A·lep** (á lěp').

Aleppo nutgall, the gall of *Quercus infectoria*, grown in Aleppo and rich in tannin.

a·lert (ə lûrt'), *adj.* **1.** vigilantly attentive: *an alert mind.* **2.** moving with celerity; nimble. —*n.* **3.** an attitude of vigilance or caution: *on the alert.* **4.** an air-raid alarm. **5.** the period during which an air-raid alarm is in effect. —*v.t.* **6.** to prepare (troops, etc.) for action. **7.** to warn of an impending raid or attack. [t. F: m. *alerte*, t. It.: m. *all' erta* on the lookout] —**a·lert'ed,** *adj.* —**a·lert'ly,** *adv.* —**a·lert'ness,** *n.*
—**Syn. 1.** ALERT, VIGILANT, WATCHFUL imply a wide-awake attitude, as of someone keenly aware of his surroundings. ALERT describes a ready and prompt attentiveness together with a quick intelligence: *the visitor to the city was alert nd eager to see the points of interest.* VIGILANT suggests some immediate necessity for keen, active observation, and for continuing alertness: *knowing the danger, the scout was unceasingly vigilant* WATCHFUL suggests carefulness and preparedness: *watchful waiting.* **2.** brisk, lively, quick, active.

-ales, *Bot.* a suffix of (Latin) names of order. [t. L, pl. of *-ālis*, adj. suffix. See -AL[1]]

A·les·san·dri·a (ä'lěs sän'drē ä'), *n.* a city in N W Italy, in Piedmont. 86,678 (1951).

a·leu·rone (ə lŏŏr'ōn, ä'lyə rōn'), *n.* minute albuminoid granules (protein) found in connection with starch and oily matter, in the endosperm of ripe seeds, and in a special layer of cells in grains of wheat, etc. [t. Gk.: m. *āleuron* flour] —**al·eu·ron·ic** (ăl'yŏŏ rŏn'ǐk), *adj.*

A·le·ut (ăl'ē ōot'), *n.* **1.** a native of the Aleutian Islands. **2.** the language spoken by the Aleutian Indians.

A·leu·tian (ə lōō'shən), *adj.* **1.** of or pertaining to the Aleutian Islands. —*n.* **2.** Aleut (def. 1).

Aleutian Islands, an archipelago extending W from the Alaska Peninsula for ab. 1200 mi.: a part of Alaska. 5600 (1950). Also, **Aleutians.**

ale·wife[1] (āl'wīf'), *n., pl.* **-wives.** a North American fish, *Pomolobus pseudoharengus*, resembling a small shad but inferior as food. [orig. unexplained. Cf. obs. *allize*, t. F: m. *alose* shad]

ale·wife[2] (āl'wīf'), *n., pl.* **-wives.** a woman who keeps an alehouse. [f. ALE + WIFE]

Al·ex·an·der (ăl'ǐg zăn'dər, -zän'-), *n.* **Sir Harold R.L.G.,** born 1891, British field marshal: gov. gen. of Canada, 1946–52; British minister of defense since 1952.

Alexander I, **1.** (Russ.: *Aleksandr Pavlovich*) 1777–1825, czar of Russia, 1801–25. **2.** (Serb.: *Alexander Obrenović*) 1876–1903, king of Serbia. 1889–1903. **3.** (son of Peter I of Serbia). 1888–1934, king of Yugoslavia, 1921–34.

Alexander I Island, an island off the coast of Antarctica, in the Bellingshausen Sea, W of Palmer Peninsula.

Alexander II, (Russ.: *Aleksandr Nikolaevich*) 1818–1881, czar of Russia, 1855–81.

Alexander III, (Russ.: *Aleksandr Aleksandrovich*) 1845–94, czar of Russia, 1881–94 (son of Alexander II).

Alexander VI, (*Roderigo Lanzol y Borgia*) 1431?–1503, pope, 1492–1503.

Alexander Archipelago, numerous coastal islands in SE Alaska.

Alexander Nev·ski (něv'skǐ, něf'-), 1220?–63, Russian prince, warrior, and statesman.

Alexander Se·ve·rus (sə vǐr'əs), A.D. 208?–235, Roman emperor, A.D. 222–235.

Al·ex·an·der·son (ăl'ǐg zăn'dər sən), *n.* **Ernst F. W.,** born 1878, U.S. engineer and inventor.

Alexander the Great, 356–323 B.C., king of Macedonia, 336–323 B.C.; conqueror of Greek city-states and Persian Empire from Asia Minor and Egypt to India.

Empire of Alexander the Great

Al·ex·an·dret·ta (ăl'-ǐg zăn drět'ə,-zän-), *n.* **Is·kenderun.**

Al·ex·an·dri·a (ăl'ǐg zăn'drǐ ə, -zän'-), *n.* **1.** a seaport in N Egypt, on the Nile delta: founded by Alexander the Great, 332 B.C.; ancient center of learning. 1,070,100 (est. 1952). **2.** a city in NE Virginia, opposite the District of Columbia. 91,023 (1960). **3.** a city in central Louisiana, on the Red River. 40,279 (1960).

Al·ex·an·dri·an (ăl'ǐg zăn'drǐ ən, -zän'-), *adj.* **1.** of Alexandria, Egypt. **2.** pertaining to the schools of philosophy, literature, and science in ancient Alexandria. **3.** of Alexander the Great. **4.** Alexandrine.

Al·ex·an·drine (ăl'ǐg zăn'drǐn, -drēn', -zän'-), *n.* **1.** *Pros.* a verse or line of poetry of six iambic feet. —*adj.* **2.** *Pros.* designating such verse or line. **3.** of or pertaining to Alexandria, Egypt. [t. F: m. *alexandrin*, from poems in this meter on *Alexander* the Great]

al·ex·an·drite (ăl'ǐg zăn'drǐt, -zän'-), *n.* a variety of chrysoberyl, green by daylight and red-violet by artificial light, used as a gem. [f. ALEXANDER II of Russia +-ITE[1]]

A·le·xan·drou·po·lis (ä'lěk sän drōō'pô lěs'), *n.* a seaport in NE Greece, in Western Thrace. 18,453 (1950). Formerly, **Dede Agach.**

a·lex·i·a (ə lěk'sǐ ə), *n. Psychiatry.* a cerebral disorder marked by inability to understand written speech. [f. A-[6] + s. Gk. *léxis* a speaking + -IA]

a·lex·in (ə lěk'sǐn), *n. Immunol.* **1.** any of certain substances in normal blood serum which destroy bacteria, etc. **2.** complement (def. 9). [f. s. Gk. *aléxein* ward off + -IN[2]] —**al·ex·in·ic** (ăl'lěk sǐn'ǐk), *adj.*

a·lex·i·phar·mic (ə lěk'sə fär'mǐk), *Med.* —*adj.* **1.** warding off poisoning or infection; antidotal; prophylactic. —*n.* **2.** an alexipharmic agent, esp. an internal antidote. [t. Gk.: m.s. *alexiphármakon* a remedy against poison; final syll., prop. *-ac*, conformed to the suffix -IC]

A·lex·i·us I (ə lěk'sǐ əs), (*Alexius Comnenus*) 1048–1118, emperor of the Byzantine Empire, 1081–1118.

al·fal·fa (ăl făl'fə), *n.* a European fabaceous forage plant, *Medicago sativa*, with bluish-purple flowers, now much cultivated in the U. S.; lucerne. [t. Sp., t. Ar.: m. *al-faṣfaṣa* the best sort of fodder]

Al·fie·ri (äl fyā'rē), *n.* **Count Vittorio** (vět tô'ryô), 1749–1803, Italian dramatist and poet.

al·fil·a·ri·a (ăl fǐl'ə rē'ə), *n.* a low geraniaceous herb, *Erodium cicutarium*, with long-beaked fruit, native in Europe but widely naturalized elsewhere for forage. [t. Mex. Sp., der. Sp. *alfiler* pin, t. Ar.: m. *alkhilāl* a wooden pin; so called from the shape of the carpels]

al fi·ne (äl fē'ně), *Music.* to the end (a direction, as after a *da capo* or *dal segno*, to continue to *fine*, the indicated end). [It.]

Al·fon·so XII (äl fŏn'sō, -zō; *Sp.* äl fôn'sō), 1857–85 king of Spain, 1874–85.

Alfonso XIII, 1886–1941, king of Spain from 1886 until deposed in 1930.

al·for·ja (äl fôr'jə; *Sp.* äl fôr'hä), *n. Southwestern U.S.* **1.** a leather bag; saddlebag. **2.** a cheek pouch. [t. Sp., t. Ar.: m. *al-khorj* the double saddlebag]

Al·fred the Great (ăl'frǐd), A.D. 849–899, king of England, A.D. 871–899: defeated invading Danes and clinched the overlordship of the West Saxon royal house, built the first English fleet, encouraged education, and translated several Latin works into English, becoming the father of English prose literature.

al fres·co (ăl frěs'kō), in the open air; out-of-doors: *to dine al fresco.* [t. It.: in the cool]

al·fres·co (ăl frěs'kō), *adj.* open-air: *an alfresco café.*

alg., algebra.

al·ga (ăl'gə), *n., pl.* **-gae** (-jē). **1.** any chlorophyll-containing plant belonging to the phylum *Thallophyta*, comprising the seaweeds and various fresh-water forms and varying in form and size, from a single microscopic or sometimes large and branching cell, to forms with trunklike stems many feet in length. They constitute a subphylum, the *Algae.* **2.** a seaweed (def. 1). [t. L: sea-weed] —**al'gal,** *adj.*

al·ga·ro·ba (ăl'gə rō'bə), *n.* **1.** any of certain mesquites, esp. *Prosopis juliflora* and its botanical variety *glandulosa.* **2.** its beanlike pod. **3.** the carob (tree). **4.** its beanlike fruit. [t. Sp., t. Ar.: m. *al-kharrūba.* See CAROB]

al·ge·bra (ăl'jə brə), *n.* **1.** the mathematical art of reasoning about (quantitative) relations by means of a systematized notation including letters and other symbols; the analysis of equations, combinatorial analysis, theory of fractions, etc. 2. any special system of notation adapted to the study of a special system of relationship: *algebra of classes.* [t. ML, t. Ar.: m. *al-jebr*, *al-jabr* bone setting, hence algebraic reduction]

al·ge·bra·ic (ăl′ə brā′ĭk), *adj.* of or occurring in algebra. Also, **al·ge·bra′i·cal.** —**al′ge·bra′i·cal·ly,** *adv.*

al·ge·bra·ist (ăl′jə brā′ĭst), *n.* an expert in algebra.

Al·ge·ci·ras (ăl′jə sÿr′əs; *Sp.* äl′hĕ thē′räs, -sē′räs), *n.* seaport in S Spain, on Strait of Gibraltar. 25,671 (1950).

Al·ger (ăl′jər), *n.* **Horatio,** 1834–99, U.S. author of novels, esp. for boys.

Al·ge·ri·a (ăl jÿr′ĭ ə), *n.* a republic in NW Africa: formerly comprising 13 departments of France; became independent, July 3, 1962. 9,925,000 pop. (est. 1960); 113,- 833 sq. mi. *Cap.*: Algiers.—**Al·ge′ri·an, Al·ge·rine** (ăl′jə rēn′), *adj., n.*

-algia, a noun suffix meaning "pain," as in *neuralgia.* [t., NL, t. Gk.]

al·gid (ăl′jĭd), *adj.* cold; chilly. [t. L: s. *algidus*] —**al·gid′i·ty,** *n.*

Al·giers (ăl jÿrz′), *n.* 1. a seaport in and the capital of Algeria, in the N part, 883,879 (1960). 2. one of the former Barbary States in N Africa, notorious for its pirates; modern Algeria.

al·gi·nate (ăl′jə nāt′), *n.* a gelatinous substance extracted from various kelps, esp. *Macrocystis pyrifera,* used in the manufacture of ice cream, in sizing cloth, and for various other industrial purposes. [f. *algin(ic)* (der. *algin,* substance obtained from algae) + -ATE²]

algo-, a word element meaning "pain," as in *algometer.* [comb. form repr. Gk. *álgos*]

al·goid (ăl′goid), *adj.* like algae. [f. ALG(A) + -OID]

Al·gol (ăl′gŏl), *n.* a star of the second magnitude in the constellation Perseus (def. 2). It is remarkable for its variability, which is due to periodic eclipse by a fainter stellar companion. [t. Ar.: the demon]

al·go·lag·ni·a (ăl′gə lăg′nĭ ə), *n. Psychiatry.* morbid enjoyment of sexually related pain, including both sadism and masochism. [f. ALGO- + m. Gk. *lagneia* lust]

al·gol·o·gy (ăl gŏl′ə jĭ), *n.* the branch of botany that deals with algae. —**al·go·log·i·cal** (ăl′gə lŏj′ə kəl), *adj.* —**al·gol′o·gist,** *n.*

al·gom·e·ter (ăl gŏm′ə tər), *n.* a device for determining sensitiveness to pain due to pressure. —**al·go·met·ric** (ăl′gə mĕt′rĭk), **al′go·met′ri·cal,** *adj.* —**al·gom′e·try,** *n.*

Al·gon·ki·an (ăl gŏng′kĭ ən), *adj.* 1. *Stratig.* pertaining to a division of late pre-Cambrian rocks. 2. Algonquian. —*n.* 3. *Stratig.* a division of predominantly sedimentary rocks next older than Cambrian in parts of North America. 4. Algonquian.

Al·gon·kin (ăl gŏng′kĭn), *n.* Algonquin.

Al·gon·qui·an (ăl gŏng′kĭ ən, -kwĭ ən), *n.* 1. one of the principal linguistic stocks of North America, belonging to the Algonquian-Mosan phylum. and including languages spoken or formerly spoken from Labrador southward and westward through Canada and northern U.S. to the Rocky Mountains, including Micmac, Ojibwa, Penobscot, Delaware, Cree, Fox, Blackfoot, Cheyenne, Arapaho, etc., as well as Yurok in California. 2. an Algonquian tribe member. —*adj.* 3. belonging to or constituting this stock.

Algonquian-Mo·san (mō′sən), *n.* a great linguistic phylum of North America including Algonquian, Salishan, and Wakashan.

Al·gon·quin (ăl gŏng′kĭn, -kwĭn), *n.* 1. a member of a group of North American Indian tribes formerly along the Ottawa river and the northern tributaries of the St. Lawrence. 2. their language, of Algonquian stock. 3. any Algonquian Indian. Also, **Algonkin.**

al·go·pho·bi·a (ăl′gə fō′bĭ ə), *n. Psychiatry.* an abnormal dread of pain.

al·gor (ăl′gôr), *n. Pathol.* coldness or chill, esp. at the onset of fever. [t. L: cold]

al·go·rism (ăl′gə rĭz′əm), *n.* 1. the Arabic system of arithmetical notation (with the figures 1, 2, 3, etc.). 2. the art of computation with the Arabic figures, one to nine, plus the zero; arithmetic. [ME *algorisme,* t. OF, t. ML: m.s. *algorismus,* t. Ar.: m. *al-Khwārizmī* the native of *Khwārizm* Khiva (i.e., *Abū Ja'far Mohammed ibn Mūsā,* Arabian mathematician, author of a famous treatise on algebra translated into ML]

al·go·rithm (ăl′gə rĭth′əm), *n.* any peculiar method of computing, as the rule for finding the greatest common divisor. [var. of ALGORISM]

Al·ham·bra (ăl hăm′brə), *n.* 1. the palace of the Moorish kings at Granada, Spain, completed in the 14th century. 2. a city in SW California, near Los Angeles. 54,807 (1960). [t. Sp., t. Ar.: m. *al-hamā'* the red (referring to the color of the soil)]

al·ham·bresque (ăl′hăm brĕsk′), *adj.* resembling the fanciful style of ornamentation of the Spanish Alhambra.

A·li (ä′lē, ä lē′), *n.* 1. (*"the Lion of God"*) A.D. 600?–661, Arabian caliph, cousin and son-in-law of Mohammed. Also **A·li ibn-a·bu-Ta·lib** (ä′lē ĭb′ən ä bōō tä lēb′). 2. See **Mehemet Ali.** 3. See **Mohammed Ali.**

a·li·as (ā′lĭ əs), *adv., n., pl.* **aliases.** —*adv.* 1. at another time; in another place; in other circumstances; otherwise. "Simpson *alias* Smith" means a person calling himself at one time or one place "Smith," at another "Simpson." —*n.* 2. assumed name; another name. [t. L: at another time or place]

A·li Ba·ba (ä′lē bä′bä, ăl′ĭ băb′ə), the poor woodchopper, hero of a tale in *The Arabian Nights Entertainments,* who uses the magic words "open sesame" to open the door to the wealth in the cave of the Forty Thieves.

al·i·bi (ăl′ə bī′), *n., pl.* **-bis.** 1. *Law.* the defense by an accused person that he was elsewhere at the time the offense with which he is charged was committed. 2. *U.S. Colloq.* an excuse. [t. L: elsewhere]

al·i·ble (ăl′ə bəl), *adj.* nutritive. [t. L: m.s. *alibilis*] —**al·i·bil′i·ty,** *n.*

Al·i·can·te (ăl′ə kän′tĭ; *Sp.* ä′lē kän′tĕ), *n.* a seaport in SE Spain, on the Mediterranean. 109,588 (est. 1955).

al·i·cy·clic (ăl′ə sī′klĭk, -sÿk′lĭk), *adj.* denoting organic compounds, essentially aliphatic in chemical behavior but differing structurally in that the essential carbon atoms are connected as in a ring instead of open chain.

al·i·dade (ăl′ə dād′), *n. Survey.* 1. a telescope equipped with vertical circle and stadia cross hairs and mounted on a flat base, used to make measurements from a plane table. 2. a similar instrument consisting of a brass rule with sighting holes at the ends. Also, **al·i·dad** (ăl′ə dăd′). [ME, t. ML: m. s. *alhidada,* t. Ar.: m. *al-'idāda* the revolving radius of a graduated circle]

al·ien (āl′yən, ā′lĭ ən), *n.* 1. one born in or belonging to another country who has not acquired citizenship by naturalization and is not entitled to the privileges of a citizen. 2. a foreigner. 3. one who has been estranged or excluded. —*adj.* 4. residing under another government or in another country than that of one's birth, and not having rights of citizenship in such place of residence. 5. belonging or relating to aliens: *alien property.* 6. foreign; strange; not belonging to one: *alien speech.* 7. adverse; hostile; opposed (fol. by *to* or *from*): *ideas alien to our way of thinking.* [ME, t. L: s. *aliēnus* belonging to another] —**Syn.** 2. See **stranger.**

al·ien·a·ble (āl′yən ə bəl, ā′lĭ ən-), *adj.* capable of being sold or transferred. —**al′ien·a·bil′i·ty,** *n.*

al·ien·age (āl′yən ĭj, ā′lĭ ən-), *n.* state of being an alien; the legal standing of an alien.

al·ien·ate (āl′yə nāt′, ā′lĭ ə-), *v.t.,* **-ated, -ating.** 1. to make indifferent or averse; estrange. 2. to turn away: *to alienate the affections.* 3. *Law.* to transfer or convey, as title, property, or other right, to another: *to alienate lands.* [t. L: m. s. *aliēnātus,* pp., estranged] —**al′ien·a′tor,** *n.*

al·ien·a·tion (āl′yə nā′shən, ā′lĭ ə-), *n.* 1. a withdrawal or estrangement, as of feeling or the affections. 2. *Law.* a transfer of the title to property by one person to another by conveyance (as distinguished from *inheritance*). 3. *Psychiatry.* a. mental or psychiatric illness. b. legal insanity. [ME, t. L: s. *aliēnātio* a transferring, also insanity]

al·ien·ee (āl′yə nē′, ā′lĭ ə-), *n. Law.* one to whom property is alienated.

al·ien·ism (āl′yə nĭz′əm, ā′lĭ ə-), *n.* 1. alienage. 2. the study or treatment of mental diseases.

al·ien·ist (āl′yən ĭst, ā′lĭ ən-), *n.* a psychiatrist who specializes in giving legal evidence. [t. F: m. *aliéniste,* f. s. L *aliēnus* insane + *-iste* -IST]

al·ien·or (āl′yən ər, ā′lĭ ən-, āl′yə nôr′, ā′lĭ ə-), *n. Law.* one who transfers property. Also, **al′ien·er.**

al·i·form (āl′ə fôrm′, ā′lĭ ə-), *adj.* wing-shaped; winglike; alar. [f. s. L *āla* wing + -(I)FORM]

A·li·garh (ä′lē ôgûr′), *n.* a city in N India, in Uttar Pradesh. 141,618 (1951).

a·light¹ (ə līt′), *v.i.,* **alighted** or (*Rare*) **alit, alighting.** 1. to get down from a horse or out of a vehicle; dismount. 2. to settle or stay after descending: *a bird alights on a tree.* 3. to come accidentally, or without design (fol. by *on* or *upon*). [ME *alighte(n),* OE *ālīhtan,* f. A-¹ + *līhtan* LIGHT²,*v.*]

a·light² (ə līt′), *adv., adj.* provided with light; lighted up; burning. [ME; orig. pp. of *alight,* v., light up, but now regarded as f. A-¹ + LIGHT¹, n. Cf. AFIRE]

a·lign (ə līn′), *v.t.* 1. to adjust to a line; lay out or regulate by line; form in line. 2. to bring into line. —*v.i.* 3. to fall or come into line; be in line. 4. to join with others in a cause. Also, **aline.** [t. F: s. *aligner,* f. à A-⁵ + *ligner* (g. L *līneāre* line)] —**a·lign′er,** *n.*

a·lign·ment (ə līn′mənt), *n.* 1. an adjustment to a line; arrangement in a line. 2. the line or lines formed. 3. a ground plan of a railroad or highway. 4. *Archaeol.* a line or an arrangement of parallel or converging lines of upright stones (menhirs). Also, **alinement.**

a·like (ə līk′), *adv.* 1. in the same manner, form, or degree; in common; equally: *known to treat all customers alike.* —*adj.* 2. having resemblance or similarity; having or exhibiting no marked or essential difference (used regularly of a plural substantive or idea, and only in the predicate): *he thinks all politicians are alike.* [ME, t. Scand.; cf. Icel. *ālīka* similar]

---

al·i·ment (ăl′ə mənt; *v.* -měnt′), *n.* **1.** that which nourishes; nutriment; food. **2.** that which sustains; support. —*v.t.* **3.** to sustain; support. [t. L: s. *alimentum* food] —**al′i·men′tal**, *adj.* —**al′i·men′tal·ly**, *adv.*

al·i·men·ta·ry (ăl′ə měn′tə rĭ), *adj.* **1.** concerned with the function of nutrition. **2.** pertaining to food; nutritious. **3.** providing sustenance or maintenance.

alimentary canal, the food passage in any animal from mouth to anus.

al·i·men·ta·tion (ăl′ə měn tā′shən), *n.* **1.** nourishment; nutrition. **2.** maintenance; support.

al·i·men·ta·tive (ăl′ə měn′tə tĭv), *adj.* nutritive.

al·i·mo·ny (ăl′ə mō′nĭ), *n.* *Law.* an allowance paid to a woman by her husband or former husband for her maintenance, granted by a court, upon a legal separation or a divorce, or while action is pending. In exceptional cases, in some States, a husband may receive alimony. **2.** maintenance. [t. L: m. s. *alimōnia* sustenance]

a·line (ə līn′), *v.t.*, *v.i.*, **alined, alining.** align. —**a·line′ment**, *n.* —**a·lin′er**, *n.*

Ali Pa·sha (ä′lĭ pä shä′), (*"the Lion of Janina"*) 1741–822, Turkish governor of Albania and part of Greece.

al·i·ped (ăl′ə pěd′), *adj.* *Zool.* having the toes connected by a winglike membrane, as the bats. [t. L: s. *lipes* having winged feet]

al·i·phat·ic (ăl′ə făt′ĭk), *adj.* *Chem.* pertaining to or concerned with those organic compounds which are open chains, as the paraffins or olefins. [f. m.s. Gk. *leiphar* oil, fat + -IC]

al·i·quant (ăl′ə kwənt), *adj.* *Math.* contained in a number or quantity, but not dividing it evenly: *5 is an aliquant part of 16.* [t. L: s. *aliquantus* some]

Al·i·quip·pa (ăl′ə kwĭp′ə), *n.* a borough in W Pennsylvania. 26,369 (1960).

al·i·quot (ăl′ə kwŏt), *adj.* *Math.* forming an exact proper divisor: *5 is an aliquot part of 15.* [t. L: some, several]

alis vo·lat pro·pri·is (ā′lĭs vō′lăt prō′prĭ′ĭs), *Latin.* she flies with her own wings (motto of Oregon).

a·lit (ə lĭt′), *v.* *Rare.* pt. and pp. of alight[1].

a·li·un·de (ā′lĭ ŭn′dĭ), *adv.*, *adj.* from another place: *evidence aliunde* (evidence outside the record). [L: from another place]

a·live (ə līv′), *adj.* (*rarely used attributively*) **1.** in life or existence; living. **2.** (by way of emphasis) of all living: *the proudest man alive.* **3.** in a state of action; in force or operation; unextinguished: *keep a memory alive.* **4.** full of life; lively: *alive with excitement.* **5.** alive to, attentive to; awake or sensitive to. **6.** filled as with living things; swarming; thronged; teeming [ME; OE *on life* in life] —**a·live′ness**, *n.* —Ant. **1.** dead. **4.** lifeless.

al·i·za·rin (ə lĭz′ə rĭn), *n.* one of the earliest known dyes, orig. obtained from madder but now made from anthraquinone. Also, **a·liz·a·rine** (ə lĭz′ə rĭn, -rēn′). [t. F: m. *alizarine*, der. *alizari*, t. Ar.: m. *al-'uṣāra* the extract]

alk., alkali.

al·ka·hest (ăl′kə hěst′), *n.* the universal solvent sought by the alchemists. Also, **alcahest**. [t. NL, prob. coined by Paracelsus]

al·ka·les·cent (ăl′kə lěs′ənt), *adj.* tending to become alkaline; slightly alkaline. —**al′ka·les′cence, al′ka·les′cen·cy**, *n.*

al·ka·li (ăl′kə lī′), *n.*, *pl.* **-lis, -lies. 1.** *Chem.* **a.** any of various bases, the hydroxides of the alkali metals and of ammonium, which neutralize acids to form salts and turn red litmus paper blue. **b.** any of various other more or less active bases, as calcium hydroxide. **c.** *Obsolesc.* any of various other compounds, as the carbonates of sodium and potassium. **2.** *Agric.* a soluble mineral salt, or a mixture of soluble salts, occurring in soils, etc., usually to the damage of crops. [ME *alkaly*, t. MF: m. *alcali*, t. Ar.: m. *al-qily*, later *al-qalī* the saltwort ashes]

alkali disease, *Vet. Sci.* botulism in wild ducks.

al·ka·li·fy (ăl′kə lə fī′, ăl kăl′ə-), *v.*, **-fied, -fying.** —*v.t.* **1.** to alkalize. —*v.i.* **2.** to become alkaline. —**al·ka·li·fi·a·ble** (ăl′kə lə fī′ə bəl, ăl kăl′ə-), *adj.*

alkali metal, *Chem.* a monovalent metal, one of the group including potassium, sodium, lithium, rubidium, cesium and francium, whose hydroxides are alkalis.

al·ka·lim·e·ter (ăl′kə lĭm′ə tər), *n.* an instrument for determining the quantity of carbon dioxide, usually in baking powder. —**al′ka·lim′e·try**, *n.*

al·ka·line (ăl′kə līn′, -lĭn), *adj.* of or like an alkali; having the properties of an alkali.

alkaline-earth metals, *Chem.* barium, strontium, calcium, and sometimes magnesium.

alkaline earths, *Chem.* the oxides of barium, strontium, calcium, and sometimes magnesium.

al·ka·lin·i·ty (ăl′kə lĭn′ə tĭ), *n.* alkaline condition; the quality which constitutes an alkali.

alkali soil, any of various soils in poorly drained or arid regions, containing a large amount of soluble mineral salts (chiefly of sodium) which in dry weather appear on the surface as a (usually white) crust or powder.

al·ka·lize (ăl′kə līz′), *v.t.*, **-lized, -lizing.** to make alkaline; change into an alkali. [f. ALKAL(I) + -IZE] —**al′ka·li·za′tion**, *n.*

al·ka·loid (ăl′kə loid′), *n.* **1.** one of a class of basic nitrogenous organic compounds occurring in plants, such

as nicotine, atropine, morphine, or quinine. —*adj.* **2.** Also, **al′ka·loi′dal.** resembling an alkali; alkaline.

al·ka·lo·sis (ăl′kə lō′sĭs), *n.* *Physiol.* excessively alkaline state of the body tissue and blood. [f. ALKAL(I) + -OSIS]

al·kanes (ăl′kānz), *n.pl.* *Chem.* methane series.

al·ka·net (ăl′kə nět′), *n.* **1.** a European boraginaceous plant, *Alkanna tinctoria*, whose root yields a red dye. **2.** the root. **3.** the dye. **4.** any of several similar plants, as the bugloss (*Anchusa officinalis*) and the puccoon (*Lithospermum*). [ME, t. Sp.: m. *alcaneta*, dim. of *alcana* henna]

al·kene (ăl′kēn), *n.* *Chem.* any of a group of unsaturated aliphatic hydrocarbons, with the general formula C_nH_{2n}, containing an unsaturated linkage or double bond, as ethylene, C_2H_4. [f. ALK(YL GROUP) + -ENE]

Alk·maar (älk mär′), *n.* a city in W Netherlands. 41,126 (1947).

Al·ko·ran (ăl′kō rän′, -rän′), *n.* the Koran.

al·kyd resins (ăl′kĭd), *Chem.* a group of sticky resins derived from dicarboxylic acids, as phthalic or maleic acids, in reaction with glycols or glycerol, and used as adhesives.

al·kyl·a·tion (ăl′kə lā′shən), *n.* *Chem.* the replacement of a hydrogen atom in an organic compound by an alkyl group.

al·kyl group (ăl′kĭl), *Chem.* a univalent group or radical derived from an aliphatic hydrocarbon, by removal of a hydrogen atom, having the general formula C_nH_{2n+1}. Also, **alkyl radical**. [f. ALK(ALI) + -YL]

alkyl halide, *Chem.* an organic compound with the type formula RX, where R is a radical derived from a hydrocarbon of the methane series and X is a halogen, as methyl chloride, CH_3Cl.

al·kyne (ăl′kīn), *n.* *Chem.* an unsaturated, aliphatic hydrocarbon containing a triple bond; a member of the acetylene series. [f. ALKY(L) + -(I)NE[2]]

all (ôl), *adj.* **1.** the whole of (with reference to quantity, extent, duration, amount, or degree): *all Europe, all year.* **2.** the whole number of (with reference to individuals or particulars, taken collectively): *all men.* **3.** the greatest possible: *with all speed.* **4.** every (chiefly with *kinds, sorts, manner*). **5.** any; any whatever: *beyond all doubt.* —*pron.* **6.** the whole quantity or amount: *to eat all of something.* **7.** the whole number: *all of us.* **8.** everything: *is that all?* —*n.* **9.** a whole; a totality of things or qualities. **10.** one's whole interest, concern, or property: *to give, or lose, one's all.* **11.** Some special noun phrases are:
above all, before everything else.
after all, **1.** after everything has been considered; notwithstanding. **2.** in spite of all that was done, said, etc.: *he lost the fight after all.*
all in all, everything together.
at all, **1.** in any degree: *not bad at all.* **2.** for any reason: *I was surprised at his coming at all.* **3.** in any way: *no offense at all.*
for all (that), notwithstanding; in spite of.
in all, all included: *a hundred people in all.*
once and for all, for the final time.
—*adv.* **12.** wholly; entirely; quite: *all alone.* **13.** only; exclusively: *he spent his income all on pleasure.* **14.** each; apiece: *the score was one all.* **15.** *Poetic.* even; just. [ME; OE *all, eall*, c. G *all*]

all-, var. of all- before vowels, as in *allonym*.

al·la bre·ve (ä′lə brěv′ä; *It.* äl′lä brě′vě), *Music.* **1.** an expression denoting a species of time in which every measure contains a breve, or four minims. **2.** a time value of two minims or four crotchets to a measure, but taken at a rate twice as fast. [It.]

Al·lah (ăl′ə, ä′lə), *n.* the Mohammedan name of the Supreme Being. [t. Ar.: m. *Allāh*, contr. of *al-ilāh* the God]

Al·lah·a·bad (ăl′ə hə băd′, ä′lə hä bäd′), *n.* a city in N India, on the Ganges river. 312,259 (1951).

all-A·mer·i·can (ôl′ə měr′ə kən), *adj.* **1.** representing the entire U. S. **2.** composed exclusively of American members or elements. **3.** representing the best in any field of U.S. sport. —*n.* **4.** an all-American player.

Al·lan-a-Dale (ăl′ən ə dāl′), *n.* (in English balladry) a youth, befriended by Robin Hood, who kept his sweetheart from wedding an aged knight and took her for his own bride.

al·lan·ite (ăl′ə nīt′), *n.* a mineral, a silicate of calcium, cerium, aluminum, and iron, chiefly occurring in brown to black masses or prismatic crystals. [named after Thomas *Allan*, 1777–1833, mineralogist. See -ITE[1]]

al·lan·to·ic (ăl′ən tō′ĭk), *adj.* *Zool.* pertaining to the allantois.

al·lan·toid (ə lăn′toid), *Zool.* —*adj.* **1.** allantoic. —*n.* **2.** the allantois. —**al·lan·toi·dal** (ăl′ən toi′dəl), *adj.*

al·lan·to·is (ə lăn′tō ĭs), *n.* *Zool.* a fetal appendage of mammals, birds, and reptiles, typically developing as an extension of the urinary bladder. [t. NL, earlier *allantoides*, t. Gk.: m. *allantoeídes* sausage-shaped]

al·lar·gan·do (ăl′lär gän′dō), *adj.* *Music.* progressively slower and frequently increasing in power. [It.]

all-a·round (ôl′ə round′), *adj.* *U.S.* all-round.

al·lay (ə lā′), *v.t.*, **-layed, -laying. 1.** to put at rest; quiet (tumult, fear, suspicion, etc.); appease (wrath). **2.** to mitigate; relieve or alleviate: *to allay pain.* [ME *aleyen*, OE *ālecgan* put down, suppress, f. *ā-* away +

lecgan lay; sp. *all-* by false identification of prefix *a-* with L *ad-*] —**al·lay·er,** *n.*

—**Syn. 1.** ALLAY, MODERATE, SOOTHE mean to reduce excitement or emotion. To ALLAY is to lay to rest or lull to a sense of security, possibly by making the emotion seem unjustified: *to allay suspicion, anxiety, fears.* To MODERATE is to tone down any excess and thus to restore calm: *to moderate the expression of one's grief.* To SOOTHE is to exert a pacifying or tranquilizing influence: *to soothe a terrified child.* **2.** lessen, diminish, reduce. —**Ant. 1.** excite.

all clear, a signal, etc., that an air raid is over.

al·le·ga·tion (ăl′ə gā′shən), *n.* **1.** act of alleging; affirmation. **2.** a statement offered as a plea, an excuse, or a justification. **3.** a mere assertion made without any proof. **4.** an assertion made by a party in a legal proceeding, which he undertakes to prove. [ME, t. L: s. *allēgātio*]

al·lege (ə lĕj′), *v.t.,* **-leged, -leging. 1.** to declare with positiveness; affirm; assert: *to allege a fact.* **2.** to declare before a court, or elsewhere as if upon oath. **3.** to assert without proof. **4.** to plead in support of; urge as a reason or excuse. **5.** *Archaic.* to cite or quote in confirmation. [ME *allegg(n)*, t. AF: m. *ategier* (g. L *ex-* EX¹- + *lītigāre* sue), with sense of L *allēgāre* adduce] —**al·lege′a·ble,** *adj.* —**al·leg′er,** *n.* —**Syn. 1.** state, asseverate, aver. —**Ant. 1.** deny.

al·leg·ed·ly (ə lĕj′Yd lY), *adv.* according to allegation.

Al·le·ghe·ny (ăl′ə gā′nY), *n.* a river flowing from SW New York through W Pennsylvania into the Ohio river at Pittsburgh. 325 mi.

Allegheny Mountains, a mountain range in Pennsylvania, Maryland, West Virginia, and Virginia: a part of the Appalachian system. Also, **Alleghenies.**

al·le·giance (ə lē′jəns), *n.* **1.** the obligation of a subject or citizen to his sovereign or government; duty owed to a sovereign or state. **2.** observance of obligation; faithfulness to any person or thing. [ME *alegeaunce* (with *a-* of obscure orig.), t. OF: m. *ligeance.* See LIEGE] —**Syn. 1, 2.** See **loyalty.**

al·le·giant (ə lē′jənt), *adj.* loyal.

al·le·gor·i·cal (ăl′ə gôr′ə kəl, -gōr′-), *adj.* consisting of or pertaining to allegory; of the nature of or containing allegory; figurative: *an allegorical poem, meaning, etc.* Also, **al′le·gor′ic.** —**al′le·gor′i·cal·ly,** *adv.*

al·le·go·rist (ăl′ə gôr′Yst, ăl′ə gə rYst), *n.* one who uses or writes allegory.

al·le·go·ris·tic (ăl′ə gə rYs′tYk), *adj.* relating in the form of allegory; interpreting with allegorical meaning.

al·le·go·rize (ăl′ə gə rīz′), *v.,* **-rized, -rizing.** —*v.t.* **1.** to turn into allegory; narrate in allegory. **2.** to understand in an allegorical sense; interpret allegorically. —*v.i.* **3.** to use allegory. —**al·le·go·ri·za·tion** (ăl′ə gôr′ə zā′shən, -gôr′-), *n.* —**al′le·go·riz′er,** *n.*

al·le·go·ry (ăl′ə gōr′Y), *n., pl.* **-ries. 1.** figurative treatment of one subject under the guise of another; a presentation of an abstract or spiritual meaning under concrete or material forms. **2.** a symbolical narrative: *the political allegory of Piers Plowman.* **3.** an emblem. [ME *allegorie,* t. L *allēgoria,* t. Gk.]

al·le·gret·to (ăl′ə grĕt′ō; *It.* äl′lĕ grĕt′tô), *adj., n., pl.* **-tos.** *Music.* —*adj.* **1.** more rapid than andante, but slower than allegro. —*n.* **2.** an allegretto movement, or a graceful character. [It., dim. of *allegro* ALLEGRO]

al·le·gro (ə lā′grō, ə lĕg′-; *It.* äl lĕ′grō), *adj., n., pl.* **-gros.** *Music.* —*adj.* **1.** brisk; rapid. —*n.* **2.** an allegro movement. [It., g. L *alacer* brisk]

al·lele (ə lēl′), *n. Biol.* shortened form of **allelomorph.** [t. Gk.: m.s. *allēlōn* (gen.) reciprocally] —**al·lel·ic** (ə lē′lYk), *adj.*

al·le·lo·morph (ə lē′lə môrf′, ə lĕl′ə-), *n. Biol.* one of two or more alternative, hereditary units or genes at identical loci of homologous chromosomes, giving rise to contrasting Mendelian characters. [f. *allelo-* (comb. form of ALLELE) + -MORPH] —**al′le·lo·mor′phic,** *adj.* —**al′le·lo·mor′phism,** *n.*

al·le·lu·ia (ăl′ə lōō′yə), *interj.* **1.** praise ye the Lord; hallelujah. —*n.* **2.** a song of praise to God. [t. L, t. Gk.: m. *allēlouia,* t. Heb.: m. *hallēlūyāh* praise ye Jehovah]

al·le·mande (ăl′ə mănd′; *Fr.* âl mänd′), *n.* **1.** either of two German dances. **2.** a piece of music based on their rhythms, often following the prelude in the classical suite. **3.** a figure in a quadrille. **4.** the dance itself. [F: lit., German]

Al·len (ăl′ən), *n.* **1. Ethan** (ē′thən), 1738–89, American soldier in the Revolutionary War: leader of "Green Mountain Boys" of Vermont. **2. Grant,** 1848–99, British novelist and writer on science. **3. (William) Hervey** (hûr′vY), 1889–1949, U.S. author.

Al·len·by (ăl′ən bY), *n.* **Edmund, 1st Viscount,** 1861–1936, British field marshal: commander of British forces in Palestine and Syria in World War I.

Al·len·town (ăl′ən toun′), *n.* a city in E Pennsylvania. 108,347 (1960).

al·ler·gen (ăl′ər jĕn′), *n. Immunol.* any substance which might induce an allergy. [f. ALLER(GY) + -GEN]

al·ler·gen·ic (ăl′ər jĕn′Yk), *adj.* causing allergic sensitization.

al·ler·gic (ə lûr′jYk), *adj.* **1.** of or pertaining to allergy. **2.** affected with allergy.

al·ler·gy (ăl′ər jY), *n., pl.* **-gies. 1.** a state of hypersensitiveness to certain things, as pollens, food, fruits, etc., to which an individual is abnormally sensitive in comparison with the majority of people who remain un-

affected. Hay fever, asthma, and hives are common allergies. **2.** altered susceptibility due to a first inoculation, treatment, or the like, as exhibited in reaction to a subsequent one of the same nature. See **anaphylaxis.** [t. NL: m. s. *allergia,* f. Gk.: s. *állos* other + *-ergia* work]

al·le·vi·ate (ə lē′vY āt′), *v.t.,* **-ated, -ating.** to make easier to be endured; lessen; mitigate: *to alleviate sorrow, pain, punishment, etc.* [t. LL: m. s. *alleviātus,* pp.] —**al·le′vi·a·tor,** *n.*

al·le·vi·a·tion (ə lē′vY ā′shən), *n.* **1.** act of alleviating. **2.** something that alleviates.

al·le·vi·a·tive (ə lē′vY ā′tYv), *adj.* **1.** serving to alleviate. —*n.* **2.** something that alleviates.

al·le·vi·a·to·ry (ə lē′vY ə tōr′Y), *adj.* alleviative.

al·ley¹ (ăl′Y), *n., pl.* **-leys. 1.** a narrow, back street. **2.** a walk, enclosed with hedges or shrubbery, in a garden. **3.** a long narrow enclosure with a smooth wooden floor for bowling, etc. [ME *aley,* t. OF: m. *alee* a going, passage, der. *aler* go] —**Syn. 1.** See **street.**

al·ley² (ăl′Y), *n., pl.* **-leys.** a choice large playing marble. [dim. abbr. of ALABASTER]

al·ley·way (ăl′Y wā′), *n.* **1.** *U.S.* an alley or lane. **2.** a narrow passageway.

All Fools' Day, April Fools' Day.

all fours. 1. all four legs of an animal, or both arms and both legs of man (formerly *all four): to crawl on all fours.* **2. on all fours,** *Brit.* even (*with*); presenting exact comparison (*with*). **3.** *Cards.* seven-up.

all hail, *Archaic.* a salutation of greeting or welcome.

All-hal·low·mas (ôl′hăl′ō məs), *n.* the feast of Allhallows.

All-hal·lows (ôl′hăl′ōz), *n.* All Saints' Day.

All-hal·low·tide (ôl′hăl′ō tīd′), *n.* the time or season of Allhallows.

all-heal (ôl′hēl′), *n.* **1.** valerian (def. 1). **2.** selfheal.

al·li·a·ceous (ăl′Y ā′shəs), *adj.* **1.** *Bot.* belonging to the genus *Allium,* which includes the garlic, onion, leek, etc. **2.** having the odor or taste of garlic, onion, etc.

al·li·ance (ə lī′əns), *n.* **1.** state of being allied or connected; relation between parties allied or connected. **2.** marriage, or the relation or union brought about between families through marriage. **3.** formal agreement by two or more nations to coöperate for specific purposes. **4.** any joining of efforts or interests by persons, families, states, or organizations: *an alliance between church and state.* **5.** the persons or parties allied. **6.** relationship in qualities; affinity: *the alliance between logic and metaphysics.* [ME *aliaunce,* t. OF: m. *aliance,* g. L *alligantia*] —**Syn. 1.** association; coalition, combination; partnership. **3.** ALLIANCE, CONFEDERATION, LEAGUE, UNION all mean the joining of states for mutual benefit or to permit the joint exercise of functions. An ALLIANCE may apply to any connection entered into for mutual benefit. LEAGUE usually suggests closer combination or a more definite object or purpose. CONFEDERATION applies to a permanent combination for the exercise in common of certain governmental functions. UNION implies an alliance so close and permanent that the separate states or parties become essentially one.

Al·li·ance (ə lī′əns), *n.* a city in NE Ohio. 28,362 (1960).

al·lied (ə līd′, ăl′īd), *adj.* **1.** joined by treaty. **2.** related: *allied species.* **3.** (*cap.*) pertaining to the Allies.

Al·lier (â lyĕ′), *n.* a river flowing from S France N to the Loire river. ab. 250 mi.

al·lies (ăl′īz, ə līz′), *n.pl.* **1.** pl. of **ally. 2.** (*cap.*) (in World War I) the powers of the Triple Entente (Great Britain, France, Russia), with the nations allied with them (Belgium, Serbia, Japan, Italy, etc., not including the United States), or, in loose use, with all the nations (including the United States) allied or associated with them as opposed to the Central Powers. **3.** (*cap.*) (in World War II) the United Nations.

al·li·ga·tor (ăl′ə gā′tər), *n.* **1.** the broad-snouted representative of the crocodile group found in the southeastern U. S. **2.** any crocodilian (usually but not always applied to broad-snouted species) in other parts of the world. **3.** *Metall.* a machine for bringing the balls of iron from a puddling furnace into compact form so that they can be handled. [t. Sp.: m. *el lagarto* the lizard, ult. g. L *lacertus* lizard]

alligator pear, avocado (def. 1).

all in, *U.S. Colloq.* exhausted.

all-in (ôl′Yn′), *adj. Brit.* **1.** with extras included; inclusive: *at the all-in rate.* **2.** without restrictions: *all-in wrestling.*

al·lit·er·ate (ə lYt′ə rāt′), *v.,* **-ated, -ating.** —*v.i.* **1.** to show alliteration (with): *the "h" in "harp" does not alliterate with the "h" in "honored."* **2.** to use alliteration: *Swinburne often alliterates.* —*v.t.* **3.** to compose or arrange with alliteration: *he alliterates the "w's" in that line.*

al·lit·er·a·tion (ə lYt′ə rā′shən), *n.* **1.** the commencement of two or more stressed syllables of a word group: **a.** with the same consonant sound or sound group (**consonantal alliteration**), as in *from stem to stern.* **b.** with a vowel sound which may differ from syllable to syllable, (**vocalic alliteration**), as in *each to all.* **2.** the commencement of two or more words of a word group with the same letter, as in *apt alliteration's artful aid.* [f. AL- + s. L *lītera* letter + -ATION]

al·lit·er·a·tive (ə lYt′ə rā′tYv), *adj.* pertaining to or characterized by alliteration: *alliterative verse.* —**al·lit′er·a′tive·ly,** *adv.* —**al·lit′er·a′tive·ness,** *n.*

al·li·um (ăl′Y əm), *n. Bot.* a flower or plant of the liliaceous genus *Allium,* comprising bulbous plants with a

---

b., blend of, blended; c., cognate with; d., dialect, dialectal; der., derived from; f., formed from; g., going back to; m., modification of; r., replacing; s., stem of; t., taken from; ?, perhaps. See the full key on inside cover.

peculiar pungent odor, including the onion, leek, shallot, garlic, and chives. [t. L: garlic]

allo-, a word element indicating difference, alternation, or divergence, as in *allonym, allomerism.* Also, **all-.** [t. Gk., comb. form of *állos* other]

al·lo·cate (ăl′ə kāt′), *v.t.,* **-cated, -cating.** **1.** to set apart for a particular purpose; assign or allot: *to allocate shares.* **2.** to fix the place of; locate. [t. ML: m. s. *allocātus,* pp. of *allocāre,* f. L: *al-* AL- + *locāre* place] —Syn. 1. See assign.

al·lo·ca·tion (ăl′ə kā′shən), *n.* **1.** act of allocating; apportionment. **2.** the share or proportion allocated. **3.** *Accounting.* a system of dividing expenses and incomes among the various branches, etc., of a business.

al·lo·cu·tion (ăl′ə kū′shən), *n.* an address, esp. a formal, authoritative one. [t. L: s. *allocūtio*]

al·lo·di·al (ə lō′dĭ əl), *adj.* free from the tenurial rights of a feudal overlord. Also, **alodial.** [t. ML: s. *allōdiālis*]

al·lo·di·um (ə lō′dĭ əm), *n., pl.* **-dia** (-dĭ ə). land owned absolutely, not subject to any rent, service, or other tenurial right of an overlord. Also, **alodium.** [t. ML, t. OLG: m. *allōd* (f. *all* ALL + *ōd* property). See -IUM.]

al·log·a·my (ə lŏg′ə mĭ), *n.* cross-fertilization in plants. —**al·log′a·mous,** *adj.*

al·lom·er·ism (ə lŏm′ər ĭz′əm), *n.* variability in chemical constitution without change in crystalline form. [f. ALLO- + s. Gk. *méros* part + -ISM] —**al·lom′er·ous,** *adj.*

al·lo·mor·phism (ăl′ə môr′fĭz′əm), *n.* allotropy.

al·lo·nym (ăl′ə nĭm), *n.* the name of someone else assumed by the author of a work. [f. ALL(O)- + m. Gk. *ónyma* name]

al·lo·path (ăl′ə păth′), *n.* one who practices or favors allopathy. Also, **al·lop·a·thist** (ə lŏp′ə thĭst).

al·lop·a·thy (ə lŏp′ə thĭ), *n.* the method of treating disease by the use of agents, producing effects different from those of the disease treated (opposed to *homeopathy*). —**al·lo·path·ic** (ăl′ə păth′ĭk), *adj.* —**al′lo·path′i·cal·ly,** *adv.*

al·lo·phane (ăl′ə fān′), *n.* a mineral, an amorphous hydrous silicate of aluminum, occurring in blue, green, or yellow masses, resinous to earthy. [t. Gk.: m. s. *allophanēs* appearing otherwise (with reference to its change of appearance under the blowpipe)]

al·lo·phone (ăl′ə fōn′), *n. Phonet.* one of several phones belonging to the same phoneme.

al·lo·plasm (ăl′ə plăz′əm), *n. Biol.* that part of protoplasm which is differentiated to perform a special function, as that of the flagellum.

al·lot (ə lŏt′), *v.t.,* **-lotted, -lotting.** **1.** to divide or distribute as by lot; distribute or parcel out; apportion: *to allot money for a new park.* **2.** to appropriate to a special purpose: *to assign as a portion (to);* set apart; appoint. [t. MF: m. s. *aloter,* f. *a* to + *loter* divide by lot, der. *lot* lot, of Gmc. orig.] —**al·lot′ter,** *n.* —Syn. 1. See assign.

al·lot·ment (ə lŏt′mənt), *n.* **1.** distribution as by lot; apportionment, esp. in U.S. military use, the assignment of personnel to an organization for service or use. **2.** a portion or thing allotted; a share granted, esp. in U.S. military use, that portion of the pay of an officer or enlisted person that he authorizes to be paid directly to another person, such as a dependent, or an institution, such as an insurance company. **3.** *Brit.* one of a set of plots of ground separately let out for gardening.

al·lo·trope (ăl′ə trōp′), *n.* one of two or more existing forms of a chemical element: *charcoal, graphite, and diamond are allotropes of carbon.*

al·lo·trop·ic (ăl′ə trŏp′ĭk), *adj.* pertaining to or characterized by allotropy. Also, **al′lo·trop′i·cal.** —**al′lo·trop′i·cal·ly,** *adv.* —**al·lo·tro·pic·i·ty** (ăl′ə trə pĭs′ə tĭ), *n.*

al·lot·ro·py (ə lŏt′rə pĭ), *n.* a property of certain chemical elements, as carbon, sulfur, and phosphorus, of existing in two or more distinct forms; allomorphism. Also, **al·lot′ro·pism.** [t. Gk.: m. s. *allotropía* variety. See ALLO-, -TROPY]

al′ ot·ta·va (ăl′lŏt tä′və), *Music.* a direction (8va), placed above or below the staff, to indicate that the passage covered is to be played one octave higher or lower respectively. [It.]

al·lot·tee (ə lŏt′ē′), *n.* one to whom something is allotted.

all-out (ôl′out′), *adj.* using all one's resources; complete; total: *an all-out effort.*

all-ov·er (adj. ôl′ō′vər; n. ôl′ō′vər), *adj.* **1.** extending or repeated all over, as a decorative pattern on embroidered or lace fabrics. **2.** having a pattern of this kind. —*n.* **3.** fabric with an allover pattern.

al·low (ə lou′), *v.t.* **1.** to grant permission to or for; permit: *to allow a student to be absent, no smoking allowed.* **2.** to let have; grant or give as one's share or suited to one's needs; assign as one's right: *to allow a person 100 for expenses, to allow someone so much a year.* **3.** to permit involuntarily, by neglect or oversight: *to allow a door to stand open.* **4.** to admit; acknowledge; concede: *to allow a claim.* **5.** to take into account; set apart; abate or deduct: *to allow an hour for changing trains.* **6.** *U.S. Dial.* to say; think. **7.** *Archaic.* to approve; sanction. —*v.i.* **8.** allow of, to permit; admit: *to allow of one's authority.* **9. allow for,** to make concession, allowance, or provision for: *to allow for breakage.* [ME *alowe(n),* t. OF: m. *alower* praise (g. L *allaudāre*) confused with OF *alower* assign (g. LL *allocāre*)]

—**Syn. 1.** ALLOW, LET, PERMIT imply granting or conceding the right of someone to do something. ALLOW and PERMIT are often interchangeable, but PERMIT is the more positive. ALLOW implies complete absence of an attempt, or even an intent, to hinder. PERMIT suggests formal or implied assent or authorization. LET is the familiar, conversational term for both ALLOW and PERMIT. —**Ant. 1.** forbid.

al·low·a·ble (ə lou′ə bəl), *adj.* that may be allowed; legitimate; permissible. —**al·low′a·ble·ness,** *n.* —**al·low′a·bly,** *adv.*

al·low·ance (ə lou′əns), *n., v.,* **-anced, -ancing.** —*n.* **1.** a definite amount or share allotted. **2.** a definite sum of money allotted or granted to meet expenses or requirements: *an allowance of pocket money.* **3.** an addition on account of some extenuating or qualifying circumstance. **4.** a deduction: *the allowance for breakages.* **5.** acceptance; admission: *the allowance of a claim.* **6.** sanction; tolerance: *the allowance of slavery.* **7.** *Minting.* tolerance (def. 4). **8.** *Mach.* a prescribed variation in dimensions. Cf. **tolerance** (def. 3). —*v.t.* **9.** to put upon an allowance. **10.** to limit (supplies, etc.) to a fixed or regular amount. —**Syn. 4.** discount, rebate.

Al·lo·way (ăl′ə wā′), *n.* a hamlet in SW Scotland, near Ayr: birthplace of Robert Burns.

al·low·ed·ly (ə lou′ĭd lĭ), *adv.* admittedly; in a manner that is allowed.

al·loy (n. ăl′oi, ə loi′; v. ə loi′), *n.* **1.** a substance composed of two or more metals (or, sometimes, a metal and a nonmetal) which have been intimately mixed by fusion, electrolytic deposition, or the like. **2.** a less costly metal mixed with a more valuable one. **3.** standard; quality; fineness. **4.** admixture, as of good with evil. **5.** a deleterious element. [t. F: m. *aloi,* OF *alei*] —*v.t.* **6.** to mix (metals) so as to form an alloy. **7.** to reduce in value by an admixture of a less costly metal. **8.** to debase, impair, or reduce by admixture. [t. F: m. *aloyer,* in OF *aleier,* g. L *alligāre* combine]

all right, 1. safe and sound: *are you all right?* **2.** yes; okay. **3.** satisfactory (often ironically): *all right! you'll be sorry.* **4.** correctly; satisfactorily. **5.** without fail; certainly.

all-round (ôl′round′), *adj.* **1.** *U.S.* extending all about. **2.** able to do many things; having general use; not too specialized: *all-round education.* Also, *U.S.,* **all-around.**

All Saints′ Day, a church festival celebrated Nov. 1 in honor of all the saints; Allhallows.

all-seed (ôl′sēd′), *n.* any of various many-seeded plants, as a goosefoot, *Chenopodium polyspermum,* and the knotgrass, *Polygonum aviculare.*

All Souls′ Day, *Rom. Cath. Ch.* Nov. 2, a day of solemn prayer for mercy for all the souls in Purgatory.

all-spice (ôl′spīs′), *n.* **1.** the berry of a tropical American myrtaceous tree, *Pimenta officinalis.* **2.** a mildly sharp and fragrant spice made from it; pimento.

All·ston (ôl′stən), *n.* **Washington,** 1779–1843, U.S. artist and author.

All′s Well That Ends Well, a comedy (extant form dated about 1602) by Shakespeare.

al·lude (ə lōōd′), *v.i.,* **-luded, -luding.** **1.** to make an allusion: refer casually or indirectly (foı. by *to*): *he often alluded to his poverty.* **2.** to contain a casual or indirect reference (foı. by *to*): *the letter alludes to something now forgotten.* [t. L: m.s. *allūdere* play with]

al·lure (ə lōōr′), *v.,* **-lured, -luring,** *n.* —*v.t.* **1.** to attract by the offer of some real or apparent good; tempt by something flattering or acceptable. **2.** to fascinate; charm. —*n.* **3.** fascination; charm. [ME *alure(n),* t. OF: m. *alurer,* f. *a* to + *lurer* LURE] —**al·lur′er,** *n.*

al·lure·ment (ə lōōr′mənt), *n.* **1.** fascination; charm. **2.** the means of alluring. **3.** act or process of alluring.

al·lur·ing (ə lōōr′ĭng), *adj.* **1.** tempting; enticing; seductive. **2.** fascinating; charming. —**al·lur′ing·ly,** *adv.* —**al·lur′ing·ness,** *n.*

al·lu·sion (ə lōō′zhən), *n.* **1.** a passing or casual reference; an incidental mention of something, either directly or by implication: *a classical allusion.* **2.** *Obs.* a metaphor. [t. L: s. *allūsio* playing with]

al·lu·sive (ə lōō′sĭv), *adj.* **1.** having reference to something not fully expressed; containing, full of, or characterized by allusions. **2.** *Archaic.* metaphorical. —**al·lu′sive·ly,** *adv.* —**al·lu′sive·ness,** *n.*

al·lu·vi·al (ə lōō′vĭ əl), *adj.* **1.** of or pertaining to alluvium. —*n.* **2.** alluvial soil. **3.** *Australia.* gold-bearing alluvial soil. [f. s. L *alluvium* ALLUVIUM + -AL¹]

alluvial fan, *Phys. Geog.* a fan-shaped alluvial deposit formed by a stream where its velocity is abruptly decreased, as at the mouth of a ravine or at the foot of a mountain. Also, **alluvial cone.**

al·lu·vi·on (ə lōō′vĭ ən), *n.* **1.** alluvium. **2.** *Law.* gradual increase of land on a shore or a river bank by the recent action or recession of water, whether from natural or artificial causes. **3.** overflow; flood. [t. F, t. L: s. *alluvio* inundation]

al·lu·vi·um (ə lōō′vĭ əm), *n., pl.* **-viums,** **-via** (-vĭ ə). **1.** a deposit of sand, mud, etc., formed by flowing water. **2.** the sedimentary matter deposited thus within recent times, esp. in the valleys of large rivers. [t. L, neut. of *alluvius* alluvial, washed to]

al·ly (v. ə lī′; n. ăl′ī, ə lī′), *v.,* **-lied, -lying,** *n., pl.* **-lies.** —*v.t.* **1.** to unite by marriage, treaty, league, or confederacy; connect by formal agreement (fol. by *to* or *with*). **2.** to bind together; connect by some relation, as by resemblance or friendship; associate. —*v.i.* **3.** to enter into an alliance; join or unite. —*n.* **4.** one united or associated with another, esp. by treaty or league; an allied nation, sovereign, etc. **5.** one who helps another or coöperates with him; supporter; associate. [t. F: m. *allier*, g. L *alligāre* bind to; r. ME *alie(n)*, t. OF: m. *alier*]

al·lyl alcohol (ăl'ĭl), a colorless liquid, C₃H₅OH, whose vapor is very irritating to the eyes.

allyl group or **radical,** *Chem.* a univalent aliphatic radical, C₂H₅, with a double bond. [f. L *all(ium)* garlic + -YL] —**al·lyl·ic** (ə lĭl'ĭk), *adj.*

allyl sulfide, *Chem.* a colorless or pale-yellow liquid (C₃H₅)₂S, found in garlic and used medicinally.

Al·ma-A·ta (äl'mä ä'tä), *n.* a city in the S Soviet Union in Asia: the capital of Kazak Republic. 330,000 (est. 1956). Formerly, **Vyernyi.**

Al·ma·dén (äl'mä dĕn'), *n.* a town in S Spain: mercury mines. 12,998 (1950).

Al·ma·gest (ăl'mə jĕst'), *n.* **1.** the famous Greek work on astronomy by Ptolemy. **2.** (*l.c.*) any of various medieval works of a like kind, as on astrology or alchemy. [ME *almageste*, t. OF, ult. t. Ar.: m. *al-majistī*, f. *al* the + m. Gk. *megistē* (*syntaxis*) greatest (composition)]

al·mah (ăl'mə), *n.* (in Egypt) a professional dancing or singing girl. Also, **al'ma, alme, almeh.** [t. Ar.: m. *'ālima* (fem.) learned]

al·ma ma·ter (ăl'mə mä'tər, ăl'-, ăl'mə mā'tər), (*also caps.*) the school, college, or university in which one has been trained or is being trained. [t. L: fostering mother]

al·ma·nac (ôl'mə năk'), *n.* a calendar of the days of the year, in weeks and months, indicating the time of various events or phenomena during the period, as anniversaries, sunrise and sunset, changes of the moon and tides, etc., or giving other pertinent information. [ME *almenak*, t. ML: m. *almanac, almanach*, t. Sp., t. Ar.: m. *al-manākh* orig. the relative position of the sun and the planets throughout a given year, thence calendar]

al·man·dine (ăl'mən dēn', -dĭn), *n.* a mineral, iron aluminum garnet, Fe₃Al₂Si₃O₁₂, used as a gem and abrasive. [f. ML *almand(īna)* (var. of *alabandīna*, der. L. *Alabanda*, name of a city in Asia Minor) + -INE²]

al·man·dite (ăl'mən dīt'), *n.* almandine.

al-Man·sur (ăl'män sōōr'), *n.* (*Abu Djafar Abdallah*) A.D. 712?-775, Eastern calif, A.D. 754-775; founder of Bagdad.

Al·ma-Tad·e·ma (ăl'mə tăd'ə mə), *n.* **Sir Lawrence,** 1836-1912, British painter of Dutch descent.

al·me (ăl'mĕ), *n.* almah. Also, **al'meh.**

Al·me·ri·a (ăl'mĕ rē'ä), *n.* a seaport in S Spain, on the Mediterranean. 82,957 (est. 1955).

al·might·y (ôl mī'tĭ), *adj.* **1.** possessing all power; omnipotent: *God Almighty.* **2.** having unlimited might; overpowering: *the almighty power of the press.* **3.** *U.S. Colloq.* great; extreme: *he's in an almighty fix.* —*n.* **4.** **the Almighty,** God. [ME; OE *ælmihtig, ealmihtig* all mighty] —**al·might'i·ly,** *adv.* —**al·might'i·ness,** *n.*

almighty dollar, *Colloq.* the power of money.

al·mond (ä'mənd, ăm'ənd), *n.* **1.** the stone (nut) or kernel (sweet or bitter) of the fruit of the almond tree, *Amygdalus Prunus*, which grows in warm temperate regions. **2.** the tree itself. **3.** a delicate, pale tan. **4.** anything shaped like an almond. [ME *almonde*, t. OF: m. *almande, alemandle*, g. L *amygdala*, t. Gk.: m. *amygdálē*] —**al'mond·like',** *adj.*

al·mond-eyed (ä'mənd īd', ăm'ənd-), *adj.* having eyes with a long or narrow oval shape, as some Chinese.

al·mon·er (ăl'mən ər, ä'mən-), *n.* a dispenser of alms or charity, esp. for a religious house, a princely household, etc. [ME *aumoner*, t. OF, g. LL *eleēmosynārius* of alms, der. LL *eleēmosyna* ALMS]

al·mon·ry (ăl'mən rĭ, ä'mən-), *n., pl.* **-ries.** the place where an almoner resides, or where alms are distributed.

al·most (ôl'mōst, ôl mōst'), *adv.* very nearly; all but [ME; OE *eal mæst*, var. of *æl mæst* nearly]
—**Syn.** ALMOST (MOST), NEARLY, WELL-NIGH all mean within a small degree of or short space of. ALMOST implies very little short of: *almost exhausted, almost home.* MOST is colloquial for ALMOST. NEARLY implies a slightly greater distance or degree than ALMOST: *nearly well, nearly to the city.* WELL-NIGH, a more literary word, implies a barely appreciable distance or extent: *well-nigh forgotten, well-nigh home.*

alms (ämz), *n. sing. or pl.* that which is given to the poor or needy; anything given as charity. [ME *almes*, OE *ælmysse*, t. LL: m. s. *eleēmosyna*, t. Gk.: m. *eleēmosȳnē* compassion, alms]

alms·house (ämz'hous'), *n.* *Brit.* a poorhouse (in U. S. use, only in historical or sentimental contexts).

alms·wom·an (ämz'wŏm'ən), *n., pl.* **-women.** a woman supported by alms.

al·muce (ăl'mūs), *n.* **1.** (formerly) a headdress shaped like a cowl. **2.** (later) a fur-lined tippet with a hood. [var. of AMICE²]

al·ni·co (ăl'nĭ kō'), *n.* an alloy of iron, nickel, aluminum, and cobalt, used for permanent magnets.

a·lo·di·um (ə lō'dĭ əm), *n., pl.* **-dia** (-dĭ ə). allodium. —**a·lo'di·al,** *adj.*

al·oe (ăl'ō), *n., pl.* **-oes.** **1.** any plant of the liliaceous genus *Aloe*, chiefly African, various species of which yield a drug (aloes) and a fiber. **2.** (*often pl. construed as sing.*) a bitter purgative drug, the inspissated juice of several species of *Aloe*. **3.** *U.S.* the century plant (**American aloe**). **4.** (*pl. construed as sing.*) a fragrant resin of wood

(aloes wood) from an East Indian tree, *Aquilaria Agallocha*. [ME (usually pl.) *aloen*, OE *aluwan*, t. L: m. *aloē*, t. Gk.] —**al·o·et·ic** (ăl'ō ĕt'ĭk), *adj.*

a·loft (ə lôft', ə lŏft'), *adv., adj.* **1.** high up; in or into the air; above the ground. **2.** *Naut.* at or toward the masthead; in the upper rigging. [ME, t. Scand.; cf. Icel. *ā lopti* in the air]

a·lo·ha (ə lō'ə, ä lō'hä), *n., interj.* *Hawaiian.* **1.** greetings. **2.** farewell.

al·o·in (ăl'ō ĭn), *n.* *Chem.* an intensely bitter, crystalline, purgative substance obtained from aloe.

a·lone (ə lōn'), *adj.* (*used in the pred. or following the noun*). **1.** apart from another or others: *to be alone.* **2.** to the exclusion of all others or all else: *man shall not live by bread alone.* **3.** **leave alone, a.** to allow (someone) to be by himself. **b.** *Colloq.* to refrain from bothering or interfering with. **4. let alone, a.** to refrain from bothering or interfering with. **b.** not to mention. **5.** *Obs.* unique. —*adv.* **6.** solitarily. **7.** only. [ME *al one* ALL (wholly) ONE] —**a·lone'ness,** *n.*
—**Syn. 1.** ALONE, LONE, LONELY, LONESOME all imply being without companionship or association. ALONE is colorless unless reinforced by *all*; it then suggests solitariness or desolation: *alone in the house, all alone on an island.* LONE is somewhat poetic or is intended humorous: *a lone sentinel, widow.* LONELY implies a sad or disquieting feeling of isolation. LONESOME connotes emotion, a longing for companionship.

a·long¹ (ə lông', ə lŏng'), *prep.* **1.** implying motion or direction through or by the length of; from one end to the other of: *to walk along a highway.* —*adv.* **2.** by the length; lengthwise; parallel to or in a line with the length: *a row of primroses along by the hedge.* **3.** in a line, or with a progressive motion; onward. **4.** *U.S. Colloq.* (of time) some way on: *along towards evening.* **5.** in company; together (fol. by *with*): *I'll go along with you.* **6.** *U.S.* as a companion; with one: *he took his sister along.* **7. all along, a.** all the time. **b.** throughout; continuously. **c.** from end to end. **d.** at full length. **8. be along,** *Orig. U.S. Colloq.* to come to a place: *he will soon be along.* [ME; OE *andlang*]

a·long² (ə lông', ə lŏng'), *adv.* *Dial.* owing to; on account of (fol. by *of*). [ME; OE *gelang*]

a·long·shore (ə lông'shôr', ə lŏng'-), *adv.* by or along the shore or coast.

a·long·side (ə lông'sīd', ə lŏng'-), *adv.* **1.** along or by the side; at or to the side of anything: *we brought the boat alongside.* —*prep.* **2.** beside; by the side of.

a·loof (ə lōōf'), *adv.* **1.** at a distance, but within view; withdrawn: *to stand aloof.* —*adj.* **2.** reserved; unsympathetic; disinterested. [f. A-¹ + *loof* LUFF, windward] —**a·loof'ly,** *adv.* —**a·loof'ness,** *n.* —**Ant. 1.** near.

al·o·pe·ci·a (ăl'ə pē'shĭ ə), *n.* *Pathol.* loss of hair; baldness. [t. L, t. Gk.: m. *alōpekía* mange of foxes]

A·lost (ä lōst'), *n.* a city in central Belgium, NW of Brussels. 42,939 (1947). Flemish, **Aalst.**

a·loud (ə loud'), *adv.* **1.** with the natural tone of the voice as distinguished from whispering: *to read aloud.* **2.** with a loud voice; loudly: *to cry aloud.*

a·low (ə lō'), *adv.* *Archaic* or *Naut.* low down; below.

alp (ălp), *n.* **1.** a high mountain. **2. the Alps.** See **Alps.** [t. L: s. *Alpēs*, pl., the Alps; ? from Celtic]

al·pac·a (ăl păk'ə), *n.* **1.** a domesticated sheeplike South American ruminant of the genus *Lama* allied to the llama and the guanaco, having long, soft, silky hair or wool. **2.** the hair. **3.** a fabric made of it. **4.** a glossy, wiry, commonly black woolen fabric with cotton warp. **5.** a rayon and alpaca crepe, with a viscose and acetate rayon warp. [t. Sp., from *paco*, Peruv. animal name (to which the Ar. article, *al*, has been prefixed)]

Alpaca, *Lama pacos* (5 ft. high)

al·pen·glow (ăl'pən glō'), *n.* a reddish glow often seen on the summits of mountains before sunrise and after sunset. [trans. of G *alpenglühen*]

al·pen·horn (ăl'pən hôrn'), *n.* a long, powerful horn of wood or bark used in the Alps, as by cowherds. Also **alphorn.** [t. G]

al·pen·stock (ăl'pən stŏk'), *n.* a strong staff pointed with iron, used by mountain climbers. [t. G]

al·pes·trine (ăl pĕs'trĭn), *adj.* **1.** alpine. **2.** *Bot.* subalpine (def. 2). [f. s. ML *alpestris* (der. L *Alpēs* Alps) + -INE¹]

al·pha (ăl'fə), *n.* **1.** the first letter in the Greek alphabet (A, α), corresponding to A. **2.** the first; beginning. **3.** *Astron.* a star, usually the brightest of a constellation. **4.** *Chem.* (of a compound) one of the possible positions or substituted atoms or groups.

alpha and omega, beginning and end. Rev. 1:8

al·pha·bet (ăl'fə bĕt'), *n.* **1.** the letters of a language in their customary order. **2.** any system of characters or signs for representing sounds or ideas. **3.** first elements; simplest rudiments: *the alphabet of radio.* [t. L: s. *alphabētum*, t. Gk.: m. *alphábētos*, f. *álpha* A + m. *bēta* B]

al·pha·bet·i·cal (ăl'fə bĕt'ə kəl), *adj.* **1.** in the order of the alphabet: *alphabetical arrangement.* **2.** pertaining to an alphabet; expressed by an alphabet: *alphabetical writing.* Also, **al'pha·bet'ic.** —**al'pha·bet'i·cal·ly,** *adv.*

b., blend of, blended; c., cognate with; d., dialect, dialectal; der., derived from; f., formed from; g., going back to m., modification of; r., replacing; s., stem of; t., taken from; ?, perhaps. See the full key on inside cover

al·pha·bet·ize (ăl/fə bə tīz/), *v.t.*, **-ized, -izing. 1.** to arrange in the order of the alphabet: *to alphabetize a list of names.* **2.** to express by an alphabet. —**al·pha·bet·i·za·tion** (ăl/fə bĕt/ə zā/shən), *n.* —**al/pha·bet·iz/er,** *n.*

alpha particle, *Physics.* a positively charged particle composed of two protons and two neutrons (and therefore equivalent to the nucleus of a helium atom) and spontaneously emitted by some radioactive material such as radium.

alpha ray, *Physics.* a stream of alpha particles.

alpha test, a psychological test measuring learning ability for those able to read and write, used by the U.S. Army in World War I.

Al·phe·us (ăl fē/əs), *n. Gk. Myth.* a river god, son of Oceanus and Tethys, who fell in love with the nymph Arethusa and, when she became a fountain to escape him, changed into a river and mingled with her.

alp·horn (ălp/hôrn/), *n.* alpenhorn.

al·pho·sis (ăl fō/sĭs), *n. Pathol.* lack of pigment in the skin, as in albinism. [f. s. Gk. *alphós* kind of leprosy + -OSIS]

al·pine (ăl/pīn, -pĭn), *adj.* **1.** of or pertaining to any lofty mountain. **2.** very high; elevated. **3.** (*cap.*) of or pertaining to the Alps. **4.** *Bot.* growing on mountains, above the limit of tree growth. [t. L: m. s. *Alpīnus,* der. *Alpēs* the Alps]

alpine garden, a rock garden.

Al·pin·ism (ăl/pə nĭz/əm), *n.* mountain climbing, esp. in the Alps. —**Al/pin·ist,** *n.*

Alps (ălps), *n.* a mountain system in S Europe, extending from France through Switzerland and Italy into Austria and Yugoslavia. Highest peak, Mont Blanc, 15,781 ft. [see ALP]

al·read·y (ôl rĕd/ĭ), *adv.* by this (or that) time; previously to or at some specified time. [ME *al redy* all ready. See ALL, READY.]

al·right (ôl rīt/), *adv.* all right (not generally regarded as good usage).

Al·sace (ăl săs/, ăl/săs; *Fr.* ăl zàs/), *n.* a region in NE France between the Vosges Mountains and the Rhine: a former province.

Al·sace-Lor·raine (ăl/săs lō-rān/, -săs; *Fr.* ăl zàs lô rĕn/), *n.* a region in NE France, including the former provinces of Alsace and Lorraine: a part of Germany, 1871–1919 and 1940–44. 1,986,-969 (1954); 5607 sq. mi.

Al·sa·tia (ăl sā/shə), *n.* a district in central London, England, once a sanctuary for debtors and lawbreakers: formerly called Whitefriars. [t. ML, Latinization of G *Elsass,* lit., foreign settlement]

Al·sa·tian (ăl sā/shən), *adj.* **1.** of or pertaining to Alsace. **2.** of or pertaining to Alsatia. —*n.* **3.** a native or inhabitant of Alsace. **4.** an inhabitant of Alsatia (Whitefriars).

Al·sib (ăl/sĭb), *n.* the route for air travel between Montana and Moscow, which lies across Alaska and Siberia.

al·sike (ăl/sīk, -sĭk, ôl/-), *n.* a European clover, *Trifolium hybridum,* with whitish or pink flowers, much grown in the U.S. for forage. Also, **alsike clover.** [named after *Alsike,* in Sweden]

al·si·na·ceous (ăl/sə nā/shəs), *adj. Bot.* **1.** caryophyllaceous. **2.** relating to or resembling the chickweed. [f. Gk. *alsīn(ē)* + -ACEOUS]

Al Si·rat (ăl sĭ rät/), *Mohammedanism.* **1.** the correct path of religion. **2.** the bridge, fine as a razor's edge, over which all who enter paradise must pass. [t. Ar.: m. *al-ṣirāṭ* the road, from L (*via*) *strata* paved (road). Cf. STREET.]

al·so (ôl/sō), *adv.* in addition; too; further. [ME; OE *alswā, ealswā* all (wholly or quite) so] —Syn. likewise, besides, moreover.

alt (ălt), *Music.* —*adj.* **1.** high. —*n.* **2. in alt, in** the first octave above the treble staff. [t. It.: s. *alto* high]

alt-, var. of **alto-** before vowels, as in *altazimuth.*

alt., 1. alternate. **2.** altitude. **3.** alto.

Alta., Alberta (Canada).

Al·ta·ic (ăl tā/ĭk), *n.* a group of languages made up of the Turkish, Manchurian, and Mongolian families.

Al·tai Mountains (ăl tī/, -tä/-), a mountain system in central Asia, mostly in the Mongolian People's Republic and the S Soviet Union in Asia. Highest peak, Belukha, 15,157 ft.

Al·ta·ir (ăl tä/ĭr), *n.* a star of the first magnitude in the constellation Aquila. [t. Ar.: m. *al-ṭā'ir* the bird]

Al·ta·mi·ra (ăl/tä mē/rä), *n.* a cave in N Spain, near Santander: Old Stone Age color drawings of animals.

al·tar (ôl/tər), *n.* **1.** an elevated place or structure, on which sacrifices are offered or at which religious rites are performed. **2.** (in most Christian churches) the communion table. **3. lead to the altar,** to marry. [ME *alter,* OE *altar(e)*; t. LL. Cf. L *altāria,* pl., high altar]

altar boy, acolyte (def. 1).

al·tar·piece (ôl/tər pēs/), *n.* a decorative screenlike piece behind and above an altar; a reredos.

al·t·az·i·muth (ăl tăz/ə məth), *n.* a mounting of telescopes or transits which provides two axes, one hori-

zontal and one vertical, so that the instrument may be turned in the plane of the horizon and in any vertical plane. Altazimuths are used to determine altitudes and azimuths of heavenly bodies. [f. ALT- + AZIMUTH]

Alt·dorf (ält/dôrf), *n.* a town in central Switzerland: the legendary home of William Tell. 6576 (1950).

al·ter (ôl/tər), *v.t.* **1.** to make different in some particular; modify. **2.** *Colloq.* to castrate or spay. —*v.i.* **3.** to become different in some respect. [t. F: s. *altérer,* ult. der. L *alter* other] —**Syn. 1.** See **adjust** and **change.**

alter., alteration.

al·ter·a·ble (ôl/tər ə bəl), *adj.* capable of being altered. —**al/ter·a·bil/i·ty, al/ter·a·ble·ness,** *n.* —**al/ter·a·bly,** *adv.*

al·ter·ant (ôl/tər ənt), *adj.* **1.** producing alteration. —*n.* **2.** something that causes alteration.

al·ter·a·tion (ôl/tə rā/shən), *n.* **1.** act of altering. **2.** condition of being altered. **3.** a change; modification.

al·ter·a·tive (ôl/tə rā/tĭv), *adj.* **1.** tending to alter. **2.** *Med.* gradually restoring healthy bodily functions. —*n.* **3.** *Med.* an alterative remedy.

al·ter·cate (ôl/tər kāt/, ăl/-), *v.i.,* **-cated, -cating.** to argue with zeal, heat, or anger; wrangle. [t. L: m. s. *altercātus,* pp., having wrangled]

al·ter·ca·tion (ôl/tər kā/shən, ăl/-), *n.* a heated or angry dispute; a noisy wrangle.

altered chord, *Music.* a chord in which at least one tone has been changed from its normal pitch in the key.

al·ter e·go (ăl/tər ē/gō, ĕg/ō), *Latin.* **1.** a second self. **2.** an inseparable friend. [L: lit., another I]

al·ter i·dem (ăl/tər ī/dĕm), *Latin.* another exactly similar.

al·ter·nant (ôl tûr/nənt, ăl-), *adj.* alternating. [t. L: s. *alternans,* ppr.]

al·ter·nate (*v.* ôl/tər nāt/, ăl/-; *adj., n.* ôl/tər nĭt, ăl/-), *v.,* **-nated, -nating,** *adj., n.* —*v.i.* **1.** to follow one another in time or place reciprocally (usually fol. by *with*): *day and night alternate with each other.* **2.** to change about by turns between points, states, actions, etc.: *he alternates between hope and despair.* **3.** *Elect.* to reverse direction or sign periodically. —*v.t.* **4.** to perform by turns, or one after another. **5.** to interchange successively: *to alternate hot and cold compresses.* —*adj.* **6.** being by turns; following each the other, recurringly, in succession: *alternate winter and summer.* **7.** reciprocal: *alternate acts of kindness.* **8.** every other one of a series: *read only the alternate lines.* **9.** *Bot.* **a.** (of leaves, etc.) placed singly at different heights on the axis, on each side alternately, or at definite angular distances from one another. **b.** opposite to the intervals between other organs: *petals alternate with sepals.* —*n.* **10.** *U.S.* a person authorized to take the place of and act for another in his absence; substitute. [t. L: m.s. *alternātus*] —**al/ter·nate·ness,** *n.* —**Ant. 6.** successive.

Alternate leaves

alternate angles, *Geom.* two nonadjacent angles made by the crossing of two lines by a third line, both angles being either interior or exterior, and being on opposite sides of the third line.

al·ter·nate·ly (ôl/tər nĭt lĭ, ăl/-), *adv.* **1.** in alternate order; by turns. **2.** in alternate position.

alternating current, *Elect.* a current that reverses direction in regular cycles.

al·ter·na·tion (ôl/tər nā/shən, ăl/-), *n.* alternate succession; appearance, occurrence, or change by turns.

alternation of generations, *Biol.* an alternating in a line of reproduction, between generations unlike and generations like a given progenitor, esp. the alternation of asexual with sexual reproduction.

al·ter·na·tive (ôl tûr/nə tĭv, ăl-), *n.* **1.** a possibility of one out of two (or, less strictly, more) things: *the alternative of remaining neutral or attacking.* **2.** one of the things thus possible: *they chose the alternative of attacking.* **3.** a remaining course or choice: *we had no alternative but to move.* —*adj.* **4.** affording a choice between two things, or a possibility of one thing out of two. **5.** (of two things) mutually exclusive, so that if one is chosen the other must be rejected: *alternative results of this or that course.* **6.** *Logic.* (of a proposition) asserting two or more alternatives, at least one of which is true. [t. ML: m. s. *alternātivus*] —**al·ter/na·tive·ly,** *adv.* —**al·ter/na·tive·ness,** *n.* —**Syn. 1.** option, selection. See **choice.**

al·ter·na·tor (ôl/tər nā/tər, ăl/-), *n. Elect.* a generator of alternating current.

Alt·geld (ôlt/gĕld), *n.* **John Peter,** 1847–1902, governor of Illinois, 1892–96.

al·the·a (ăl thē/ə), *n.* **1.** any plant of of the genus *Althaea.* **2.** a malvaceous flowering garden shrub, *Hibiscus syriacus;* the rose of Sharon. **3.** (*cap.*) *Gk. Legend.* the mother of Meleager. Also, **al·the/a.** [t. L, t. Gk.: m. *althata* wild mallow]

alt·horn (ălt/hôrn/), *n.* a valved, brasswind horn, a fourth or fifth below the ordinary cornet; a tenor saxhorn. Also, **alto horn.**

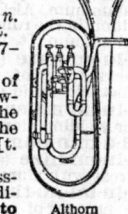

Althorn

al·though (ôl ŧhō/), *conj.* even though (practically equivalent to *though,* and preferred to it only for euphonic or metrical reasons). Also, **al·tho′**. [ME, f. *al* even + THOUGH. See ALL, adv.] —**Syn.** though, notwithstanding (that), even if.

al·tim·e·ter (ăl tǐm′ə tər, ăl′tə mē′tər), *n.* **1.** a sensitive aneroid barometer used to measure altitudes, and graduated and calibrated accordingly, used in aircraft for finding distance above sea level, terrain, or some other reference point, by means of air pressure. **2.** any device used for the same purpose which operates by some other means, as by radio waves, etc. [f. ALTI- + METER]

al·tim·e·try (ăl tǐm′ə trǐ), *n.* the art of measuring altitudes, as with an altimeter.

al·tis·si·mo (ăl tǐs′ə mō′; *It.* äl tēs′sē mō′), *Music.* —*adj.* **1.** very high. —*n.* **2. in altissimo,** in the second octave above the treble staff. [It.]

al·ti·tude (ăl′tə tūd′, -tōōd′), *n.* **1.** the height above sea level of any point on the earth's surface or in the atmosphere. **2.** extent or distance upward. **3.** *Astron.* the angular distance of a star, planet, etc., above the horizon. **4.** *Geom.* **a.** the perpendicular distance from the base of a figure to its highest point. **b.** the line through the highest point of a figure perpendicular to the base. **5.** a high point or region: *mountain altitudes.* **6.** high or exalted position, rank, etc. [ME, t. L: m. *altitūdo* height] —**Syn. 2.** See **height.** —**Ant. 2.** depth.

al·ti·tu·di·nal (ăl′tə tū′də nəl, -tōō′-), *adj.* relating to height.

al·to (ăl′tō), *n., pl.* **-tos,** *adj.* —*n. Music.* **1.** the lowest female voice; contralto. **2.** the highest male voice; countertenor. **3.** a singer with an alto voice. **4.** a musical part for an alto voice. **5.** the viola. **6.** an althorn. —*adj.* **7.** *Music.* of the alto; having the compass of the alto. **8.** high. [t. It., g. L *altus* high]

alto-, a word element meaning "high," as in *alto-stratus.* Also, **alt-, alti-.** [comb. form repr. L *altus*]

alto clef, *Music.* a sign locating middle C on the third line of the staff.

al·to-cu·mu·lus (ăl′tō kū′myə ləs), *n. Meteorol.* a cloud type consisting of globular masses or patches, more or less in a layer, somewhat darker underneath and larger than cirro-cumulus.

al·to·geth·er (ôl′tə gĕth′ər), *adv.* **1.** wholly; entirely; completely; quite: *altogether bad.* **2.** in all: *the debt amounted altogether to twenty dollars.* **3.** on the whole: *altogether, I'm glad it's over.* —*n.* **4.** a whole. [var. of ME *altogeder,* f. *al* ALL, adj. + *togeder* TOGETHER]

alto horn, althorn.

Al·ton (ôl′tən), *n.* a city in SW Illinois. 43,047 (1960).

Al·to·na (äl′tō nä), *n.* a metropolitan district of Hamburg in N West Germany. Formerly an independent city.

Al·too·na (ăl tōō′nə), *n.* a city in central Pennsylvania. 69,407 (1960).

al·to-re·lie·vo (ăl′tō rǐ lē′vō), *n., pl.* **-vos.** sculpture in high relief, in which at least one half the figures project from the background. [t. It.: m. *alto rilievo*]

al·to-ri·lie·vo (äl′tō rē lyě′vō), *n., pl.* **alti-rilievi** (äl′tē rē lyě′vē). *Italian.* alto-relievo.

al·to-stra·tus (ăl′tō strā′təs), *n. Meteorol.* a moderately high, veillike or sheetlike cloud, without definite configurations, more or less gray or bluish.

al·tri·cial (ăl trǐsh′əl), *adj. Ornith.* confined to the nesting place for a period after hatching. [t. NL: s. *altriciālis,* der. L *altrix* nurse]

al·tru·ism (ăl′trŏŏ ǐz′əm), *n.* the principle or practice of seeking the welfare of others (opposed to *egoism*). [t. F: m. *altruisme,* der. It. *altrui* of or to others]

al·tru·ist (ăl′trŏŏ ǐst), *n.* a person devoted to the welfare of others (opposed to *egoist*).

al·tru·is·tic (ăl′trŏŏ ǐs′tǐk), *adj.* regardful of others; having regard to the well-being or best interests of others (opposed to *egoistic*). —**al′tru·is′ti·cal·ly,** *adv.*

al·u·la (ăl′yə lə), *n., pl.* **-lae** (-lē). *Ornith.* the group of 3 to 6 small, rather stiff, feathers growing on the first digit, pollex, or thumb of a bird's wing. [t. NL, dim. of L *āla* wing] —**al′u·lar,** *adj.*

al·um (ăl′əm), *n.* **1.** an astringent crystalline substance, a double sulfate of aluminum and potassium, $K_2SO_4 \cdot Al_2(SO_4)_3 \cdot 24H_2O$, used in medicine, dyeing, and many technical processes. **2.** one of a class of double sulfates analogous to the potassium alum, having the general formula $R_2SO_4 \cdot X_2(SO_4)_3 \cdot 24H_2O$, where R is a monovalent alkali metal or ammonium, and X one of a number of trivalent metals. **3.** *Obsolesc.* aluminum sulfate. $Al_2(SO_4)_3$. [ME, t. OF, g. L *alūmen*]

a·lu·mi·na (ə lōō′mə nə), *n.* **1.** *Mineral.* the oxide of aluminum, Al_2O_3, occurring widely in nature as corundum (in the ruby and sapphire, emery, etc.). **2.** *Obsolesc.* aluminum. [t. NL, der. L *alūmen* alum]

a·lu·mi·nate (ə lōō′mə nāt′), *n.* **1.** *Chem.* a salt of the acid form of aluminum hydroxide. **2.** *Mineral.* a metallic oxide combined with alumina.

a·lu·mi·nif·er·ous (ə lōō′mə nǐf′ər əs), *adj.* containing or yielding aluminum.

a·lu·min·i·um (ăl′yə mǐn′ǐ əm), *n. Brit.* aluminum.

a·lu·mi·nize (ə lōō′mə nīz′), *v.t.* **-nized, -nizing.** to treat with aluminum.

a·lu·mi·no·ther·my (ə lōō′mə nō thûr′mǐ), *n. Metall.* a process of producing high temperatures by causing finely divided aluminum to react with the oxygen from another metallic oxide. Also, **a·lu′mi·no·ther′mics.** [f. *alumino-* (comb. form of ALUMINUM) + -THERMY]

a·lu·mi·nous (ə lōō′mə nəs), *adj.* of the nature of or containing alum or alumina. [t. L: m. s. *alūminōsus*]

a·lu·mi·num (ə lōō′mə nəm), *n.* Also, *Brit.*, **aluminium.** **1.** a silver-white metallic element, light in weight, ductile, malleable, and not readily oxidized or tarnished, occurring combined in nature in igneous rocks, shales, clays, and most soils. It is much used in alloys and for lightweight utensils, castings, airplane parts, etc. *Symbol:* Al; *at. wt.:* 26.97; *at. no.:* 13; *sp. gr.:* 2.70 at 20°C. —*adj.* **2.** belonging to or containing aluminum. [t. NL, der. L *alūmen* alum]

a·lum·na (ə lŭm′nə), *n., pl.* **-nae** (-nē). *Chiefly U.S.* fem. of **alumnus.**

a·lum·nus (ə lŭm′nəs), *n., pl.* **-ni** (-nī). a graduate or former student of a school, college, university, etc. [t. L: foster child, pupil]

al·um·root (ăl′əm rōōt′, -rŏŏt′), *n.* **1.** any of several plants of the saxifragaceous genus *Heuchera,* with astringent roots, esp. *H. americana.* **2.** the root.

al·u·nite (ăl′yə nīt′), *n.* a mineral, a hydrous sulfate of potassium and aluminum, $KAl_3(SO_4)_2(OH)_6$, commonly occurring in fine-grained masses. [f. F *alun* alum + -ITE¹]

Al·va (äl′və; *Sp.* äl′vä), *n.* **Fernando Álvarez de Toledo** (fĕr nän′dō äl′vä rĕth′ dĕ tô lĕ′dō), **Duke of,** 1508–82, Spanish general who ruthlessly suppressed a Protestant rebellion in the Netherlands in 1567. Also, **Alba.**

Al·va·ra·do (äl′vä rä′dō), *n.* **1. Alonso de** (ä lôn′sō dĕ), died 1553?, Spanish soldier in conquests of Mexico and Peru. **2. Pedro de** (pě′drō dĕ), 1495?–1541, Spanish soldier: chief aide of Cortez in conquest of Mexico.

Ál·va·rez Quin·te·ro (äl′vä rĕth′ kēn tĕ′rō), **Joaquín** (hwä kēn′), 1873–1944, and his brother **Serafín** (sĕ′rä fēn′), 1871–1938, Spanish dramatists.

al·ve·o·lar (äl vē′ə lər), *adj.* **1.** *Anat., Zool.* pertaining to an alveolus or to alveoli. **2.** *Phonet.* with the tongue touching or near the alveolar ridge.

alveolar arch, that part of the upper jawbone in which the teeth are set.

alveolar ridge, the ridgelike inward projection of the gums between the hard palate and the upper front teeth.

al·ve·o·late (äl vē′ə lǐt, -lāt′), *adj.* having alveoli; deeply pitted, as a honeycomb. Also, **al·ve′o·lat′ed.** —**al·ve′o·la′tion,** *n.*

al·ve·o·lus (äl vē′ə ləs), *n., pl.* **-li** (-lī′). *Anat., Zool.* **1.** a little cavity, pit, or cell, as a cell of a honeycomb. **2.** an air cell of the lungs, formed by the terminal dilation of tiny air passageways. **3.** one of the terminal secretory units of a racemose gland. **4.** the socket within the jawbone in which the root or roots of a tooth are set. **5.** (*pl.*) alveolar ridge. [t. L, dim. of *alveus* a hollow]

al·vine (äl′vǐn, -vīn), *adj. Med.* pertaining to the belly; intestinal. [t. L: m. s. *alvīnus,* der. *alvus* belly]

al·way (ôl′wā), *adv. Archaic* or *Poetic.* always. [ME; OE *ealneweg,* orig. *ealne weg.* See ALL, WAY]

al·ways (ôl′wāz, -wǐz), *adv.* **1.** all the time; uninterruptedly. **2.** every time; on every occasion (opposed to *sometimes* or *occasionally*): *he always works on Saturday.* [ME, f. ALWAY + adv. gen. suffix -(e)s] —**Syn. 1.** perpetually, everlastingly, forever, continually. Both ALWAYS and EVER refer to uniform or perpetual continuance. ALWAYS often expresses or implies repetition as producing the uniformity or continuance: *the sun always rises in the east.* EVER implies an unchanging sameness throughout: *natural law is ever to be reckoned with.*

a·lys·sum (ə lǐs′əm), *n.* **1.** any of the herbs constituting the brassicaceous genus *Alyssum,* characterized by small yellow or white racemose flowers. **2.** sweet alyssum. [t. NL, t. Gk.: m. *álysson* name of a plant, lit., curing (canine) madness]

am (ăm; *unstressed* əm, m), *v.* 1st pers. sing. pres. indic. of be. [OE *am, eam,* var. of *eom,* c. Icel. *em,* Goth. *im.* Cf. Irish *am,* Gk. *eimí*]

Am, *Chem.* americium.

Am., **1.** America. **2.** American.

A.M., **1.** (L *ante meridiem*) before noon. **2.** the period from 12 midnight to 12 noon. Also, **a.m.**

A.M., amplitude modulation. Also, **AM**

A.M., (L *Artium Magister*) Master of Arts. Also, **M.A.**

A.M.A., American Medical Association.

am·a·da·vat (ăm′ə də văt′), *n.* a small finchlike East Indian bird, *Estrilda amandava,* exported as a cage bird. [East Indian]

am·a·dou (ăm′ə dōō′), *n.* a spongy substance prepared from fungi (*Polyporus* [*Fomes*] *fomentarius* and allied species) growing on trees, used as tinder and in surgery. [t. F]

A·ma·ga·sa·ki (ä′mä gä sä′kē), *n.* a city in S Japan, on Honshu island, near Osaka. 279,264 (1950).

a·mah (ä′mə, ăm′ə), *n.* (used among Europeans in India and the Orient) **1.** a nurse, esp. a wet nurse. **2.** a maidservant. [Anglo-Indian, t. Pg.: m. *ama*]

a·main (ə mān′), *adv. Archaic and Poetic.* **1.** with full force. **2.** at full speed. **3.** suddenly; hastily. **4.** exceedingly; greatly. [f. A-¹ + MAIN¹]

a·mal·gam (ə măl′gəm), *n.* **1.** an alloy of mercury with another metal or metals. **2.** a rare mineral, an alloy of silver and mercury, occurring as silver-white crystals or grains. **3.** a mixture or combination. [ME t. ML: s. *amalgama,* appar. m. L *malagma,* poultice, t. Gk.

mal·gam·ate (ə măl′gə māt′), v., -ated, -ating. —v.t. 1. to mix so as to make a combination; blend; nite; combine: to amalgamate two companies. 2. Metall. o mix or alloy (a metal) with mercury. —v.i. 3. to combine, unite, or coalesce. 4. to blend with another metal, s mercury. —a·mal′gam·a·ble, adj. —a·mal′gam-/tive, adj. —a·mal′gam·a′tor, n.

mal·gam·a·tion (ə măl′gə mā′shən), n. 1. act of amalgamating. 2. the resulting state. 3. Com. a consolidation of two or more corporations. 4. Ethnol. the iological fusion of diverse racial stocks. 5. Metall. the xtraction of the precious metals from their ores by reatment with mercury.

m·al·thae·a (ăm′ăl thē′ə), n. Gk. Myth. 1. a nymph vho nursed Zeus on a goat's milk. 2. the goat itself. Also, Am′al·the·a.

m·a·ni·ta (ăm′ə nī′tə), n. Bot. any fungus of the garicaceous genus Amanita, comprised chiefly of poisonous species. [t. NL, t. Gk.: m. amanītai, pl., kind of ungi]

man·u·en·sis (ə măn′yōō ĕn′sĭs), n., pl. -ses (-sēz). person employed to write what another dictates or to opy what has been written by another; secretary. [t. L: ecretary, orig. adj., f. (servus) ā manū secretary + -ensis elonging to]

m·a·ranth (ăm′ə rănth′), n. 1. Poetic. a flower that ever fades. 2. any plant of the genus Amaranthus, vhich includes species cultivated for their showy flowers, .s the love-lies-bleeding, or their colored foliage (green, urple, etc.). 3. a purplish-red azo dye used to color oods. [var. (by assoc. with Gk. ánthos flower) of amant, t. L: s. amarantus, t. Gk.: m. amárantos unfading]

m·a·ran·tha·ceous (ăm′ə răn thā′shəs), adj. Bot. elonging to the family Amaranthaceae (or Amaranaceae), comprising mostly herbaceous or shrubby plants, .s the cockscomb, the pigweed, the amaranth, etc.

m·a·ran·thine (ăm′ə răn′thĭn, -thĭn), adj. 1. of or ike the amaranth. 2. unfading; everlasting. 3. purplish.

m·a·relle (ăm′ə rĕl′), n. any variety of the sour herry, Prunus Cerasus, with colorless juice.

m·a·ril·lo (ăm′ə rĭl′ō), n. a city in NW Texas. .37,969 (1960).

m·a·ryl·li·da·ceous (ăm′ə rĭl′ə dā′shəs), adj. Bot. elonging to the Amaryllidaceae, or amaryllis family of lants, which includes the amaryllis, arcissus, snowdrop, agave, etc.

m·a·ryl·lis (ăm′ə rĭl′ĭs), n. 1. a ulbous plant, Amaryllis Belladonna, he belladonna lily, with large, lily-ike, normally rose-colored flowers. 2. any of several related plants once eferred to the genus Amaryllis. 3. cap.) a shepherdess or country girl in classical and later pastoral poet-y). [t. L, t. Gk. (def. 3)]

mass (ə măs′), v.t. 1. to gather or oneself; collect as one's own: to mass a fortune. 2. to collect into a nass or pile; bring together. [t. F: s. amasser, der. masse nass, g. L massa lump (of dough, etc.)] —a·mass′a-le, adj. —a·mass′er, n. —a·mass′ment, n.

Amaryllis.
Amaryllis Belladonna

m·a·teur (ăm′ə chŏŏr′, -tyŏŏr′, ăm′ə tûr′), n. 1. one vho cultivates any study or art or other activity for ersonal pleasure instead of professionally or for gain. 2. an athlete who has never competed for money. 3. a superficial or unskillful worker; dabbler. 4. one vho admires. [t. F, t. L: m.s. amātor lover] —am′a-eur·ship′, n. —Syn. 3. dilettante, tyro, novice.

m·a·teur·ish (ăm′ə chŏŏr′ĭsh, -tyŏŏr′-, -tûr′-), adj. haracteristic of an amateur; having the faults or deiciencies of an amateur. —am′a·teur′ish·ly, adv. —am′a·teur′ish·ness, n.

m·a·teur·ism (ăm′ə chŏŏ rĭz′əm, -tyōō-, ăm′ə tûr′-(z əm), n. the practice or character of an amateur.

·ma·ti (ä mä′tē), n. 1. the name of a famous family of violinmakers of Cremona, Italy, who flourished in the 16th and 17th centuries. 2. a violin made by a member of this family. 3. Nicolò (nē′kō lō′), 1596-1684, Italian violinmaker: teacher of Antonio Stradivari.

m·a·tive (ăm′ə tĭv). adj. disposed to loving; amorous. [f. s. L amātus, pp., loved + -IVE] —am′a·tive·ly, adv. —am′a·tive·ness, n.

m·a·tol (ăm′ə tōl′, -tōl′), n. an explosive mixture of ammonium nitrate and TNT.

m·a·to·ry (ăm′ə tōr′ĭ), adj. pertaining to lovers or ovemaking; expressive of love: amatory poems, an amatory look. Also, am′a·to′ri·al. [t. L: m.s. amātōrius] —am′a·to′ri·al·ly, adv.

m·au·ro·sis (ăm′ô rō′sĭs), n. partial or total loss of sight. [NL, t. Gk., der. amaurós dim] —am·au·rot·ic (ăm′ô rŏt′ĭk), adj.

·maze (ə māz′), v., amazed, amazing, n. —v.t. 1. to overwhelm with surprise; astonish greatly. 2. Obs. to bewilder. —n. 3. Archaic. amazement. [OE āmasian. Cf. MAZE] —a·maz·ed·ly (ə māz′ĭd lĭ), adv. —a·maz′ed·ness, n. —Syn. 1. astound, dumfound. See surprise.

·maze·ment (ə māz′mənt), n. 1. overwhelming surprise or astonishment. 2. Obs. stupefaction. 3. Obs. perplexity. 4. Obs. consternation.

·maz·ing (ə māz′ĭng), adj. causing great surprise; wonderful. —a·maz′ing·ly, adv.

m·a·zon (ăm′ə zŏn′, -zən), n. 1. a river in N South America, flowing from the Peruvian Andes E through N Brazil to the Atlantic: the largest river in the world.

ab. 3600 mi. 2. Gk. Legend. one of a race of female warriors said to dwell near the Black Sea. 3. one of a fabled tribe of female warriors in South America. 4. (often l.c.) a tall, powerful, aggressive woman. [ME, t. L, t. Gk.; orig. uncert.; the name of the river refers to female warriors seen in its vicinity]

Amazon ant, a species of red ant, Polyergus rufescens that steals and enslaves the young of other species.

Am·a·zo·ni·an (ăm′ə zō′nĭ ən), adj. 1. characteristic of an Amazon; warlike; masculine. 2. pertaining to the Amazon river or the country adjacent to it.

am·a·zon·ite (ăm′ə zən īt′), n. Mineral. a green feldspar, a variety of microcline, used as an ornamental material. Also, **Amazon stone**. [f. Amazon river + -ITE¹]

am·ba·ges (ăm bā′jēz), n.pl. winding or roundabout ways. [t. L: circuits]

am·ba·gious (ăm bā′jəs), adj. roundabout. —am·ba′gious·ly, adv. —am·ba′gious·ness, n.

Am·ba·la (əm bä′lə), n. a city in N India, in E Punjab. 52,685 (1951).

am·ba·ry (ăm bär′ĭ), n. 1. an East Indian plant, Hibiscus cannabinus, yielding a useful fiber. 2. the fiber itself. Also, **am·ba′ri**. [t. Hind.]

am·bas·sa·dor (ăm băs′ə dər), n. 1. a diplomatic agent of the highest rank, sent by one sovereign or state to another either as resident representative (ambassador extraordinary and plenipotentiary) or on temporary special service. 2. an authorized messenger or representative. Also, **embassador**. [ME ambassadour, t. F: m. ambassadeur, t. It.: m. ambasciatore; prob. of Celtic orig.] —am·bas·sa·do·ri·al (ăm băs′ə dōr′ĭ əl), adj. —am·bas′sa·dor·ship′, n.

am·bas·sa·dress (ăm băs′ə drĭs), n. 1. a female ambassador. 2. the wife of an ambassador.

am·ber (ăm′bər), n. 1. a pale-yellow, sometimes reddish or brownish, fossil resin of vegetable origin, translucent, brittle, and capable of gaining a negative electrical charge by friction. 2. the yellowish-brown color of resin. —adj. 3. of amber. 4. like amber. [ME ambra, t. ML., t. Ar.: m. ·anbar ambergris]

am·ber·gris (ăm′bər grēs′, -grĭs), n. an opaque. ash-colored substance, a morbid secretion of the sperm whale, fragrant when heated, usually found floating on the ocean or cast ashore, used chiefly in perfumery. [late ME imbergres, t. F: m. ambre gris gray amber]

am·ber·oid (ăm′bə roid′), n. synthetic amber made by compressing pieces of various resins, esp. amber, at a high temperature. Also, **ambroid**.

ambi-, a word element meaning "both," "around," "on both sides," as in ambidextrous. [comb. form repr. L ambi- around, or ambo both]

am·bi·dex·ter (ăm′bə dĕk′stər), adj. 1. using both hands with equal facility. 2. double-dealing. —n. 3. a person who uses both hands equally well. 4. a double-dealer. [t. ML, f. ambi- AMBI- + dexter right] —am′bi·dex′tral, adj.

am·bi·dex·ter·i·ty (ăm′bə dĕks tĕr′ə tĭ), n. 1. ambidextrous facility. 2. unusual cleverness. 3. duplicity.

am·bi·dex·trous (ăm′bə dĕks′trəs), adj. 1. able to use both hands equally well. 2. unusually skillful; facile. 3. double-dealing; deceitful. —am′bi·dex′trous·ly, adv. —am′bi·dex′trous·ness, n.

am·bi·ent (ăm′bĭ ənt), adj. 1. completely surrounding: ambient air. 2. circulating. [t. L: s. ambiens, ppr., going around]

am·bi·gu·i·ty (ăm′bə gū′ə tĭ), n., pl. -ties. 1. doubtfulness or uncertainty of meaning: to speak without ambiguity. 2. an equivocal or ambiguous word or expression: the law is free of ambiguities. [ME ambiguite, t. L: m.s. ambiguitas] —Ant. 1. explicitness.

am·big·u·ous (ăm bĭg′yōō əs), adj. 1. open to various interpretations; having a double meaning; equivocal: an ambiguous answer. 2. of doubtful or uncertain nature; difficult to comprehend, distinguish, or classify: a rock of ambiguous character. 3. lacking clearness or definiteness; obscure; indistinct. [t. L: m.s. ambiguus doubtful] —am·big′u·ous·ly, adv. —am·big′u·ous·ness, n. —Syn. 1. AMBIGUOUS, EQUIVOCAL describe that which is not clear in meaning. That which is AMBIGUOUS leaves the intended sense doubtful; it need not be purposely deceptive. That which is EQUIVOCAL is equally capable of two or more interpretations, and is usually intended to be so for the purpose of mystifying. 3. puzzling, enigmatic.

am·bit (ăm′bĭt), n. 1. circumference. 2. boundary; limits. [ME, t. L: s. ambitus compass]

am·bi·tend·en·cy (ăm′bə tĕn′dən sĭ), n. Psychol. the coexistence of opposite tendencies.

am·bi·tion (ăm bĭsh′ən), n. 1. an eager desire for distinction, preferment, power, or fame. 2. the object desired or sought after: the crown was his ambition 3. desire for work or activity; energy. —v.t. 4. to seek after eagerly; aspire to. [ME, t. L: s. ambitio striving for honors] —am·bi′tion·less, adj. —Syn. 1. aspiration.

am·bi·tious (ăm bĭsh′əs), adj. 1. having ambition; eagerly desirous of obtaining power, superiority, or distinction. 2. showing ambition: an ambitious attempt. 3. strongly desirous; eager: ambitious of power. 4. showy; pretentious: an ambitious style. [ME, t. L: m.s. ambitiōsus] —am·bi′tious·ly, adv. —am·bi′tious·ness, n. —Syn. 1. AMBITIOUS, ASPIRING, ENTERPRISING describe one who wishes to rise above his present position or condition. The AMBITIOUS man wishes to attain worldly success, and puts forth effort toward this end: ambitious for social position. The ENTERPRISING man, interested especially in

ct, āble, dâre, ärt; ĕbb, ēqual; ĭf, īce; hŏt, ōver, ôrder, oil, bŏŏk, ōoze, out; ŭp, ūse, ûrge; ə = a in alone; h, chief; g, give; ng, ring; sh, shoe; th, thin; ᵺ, that; zh, vision.   See the full key on inside cover.

wealth, is characterized by energy and daring in undertaking projects. The ASPIRING man wishes to rise (mentally or spiritually) to a higher level or plane, or to attain some end that he feels to be above his ordinary expectations.

am·biv·a·lence (ăm bĭv/ə ləns), n. Psychol. the coexistence of opposite and conflicting feelings about the same person or object. —**am·biv/a·lent**, adj.

am·bi·ver·sion (ăm/bə vûr/zhən, -shən), n. Psychol. state or condition intermediate between extrovert and introvert personality types.

am·bi·vert (ăm/bə vûrt/), n. Psychol. one who is intermediate between an introvert and an extrovert.

am·ble (ăm/bəl), v., -**bled**, -**bling**, n. —v.i. 1. to move with the gait of a horse when it lifts first the two legs on one side and then the two on the other. 2. to go at an easy pace. —n. 3. an ambling gait. 4. an easy or gentle pace. [ME, t. OF: m. ambler, g. L ambulāre walk] —**am/bler**, n. —**am/bling·ly**, adv.

am·blyg·o·nite (ăm blĭg/ə nīt/), n. a mineral, a lithium aluminum fluorophosphate, Li(AlF)PO₄. [t. G: m. amblygonit, f. s. Gk. amblygōnios obtuse-angled + -it -ITE¹]

am·bly·o·pi·a (ăm/blĭ ō/pĭ ə), n. Pathol. dimness of sight, without apparent organic defect. [t. NL, t. Gk.] —**am·bly·op·ic** (ăm/blĭ ŏp/ĭk), adj.

am·bo (ăm/bō), n., pl. -**bos**. (in early Christian churches) one of the two raised desks from which gospels and epistles were read or chanted. [t. ML, t. Gk.: m. ámbōn]

am·bo·cep·tor (ăm/bə sĕp/tər), n. Immunol. a substance which develops during infection in the blood and which according to Ehrlich has affinities for both the bacterial cell or red blood cells and the complement. [f. L ambo both + -CEPTOR]

Am·boi·na (ăm boi/nə), n. 1. an island in Indonesia, in the Moluccas. 64,486 (est. 1954); 314 sq. mi. 2. a seaport on this island. 17,000 (est. 1948).

Amboina wood, Padouk wood. Also, **Am·boy/na wood.**

Am·boise (äⁿbwäz/), n. a historic town in central France, E of Tours: famous castle, long a royal residence. 6736 (1954).

am·broid (ăm/broid), n. amberoid.

Am·brose (ăm/brōz), n. Saint, A.D. 340?–397, bishop of Milan. —**Am·bro·si·an** (ăm brō/zĭ ən, -zhən), adj.

am·bro·sia (ăm brō/zhə), n. 1. the food of the gods of classical mythology, imparting immortality. 2. anything imparting the sense of divinity, as poetic inspiration, music, etc. 3. something especially delicious to taste or smell. 4. (cap.) Bot. the genus comprising the ragweeds. [t. L, t. Gk.: food of the gods, der. ámbrotos immortal]

am·bro·si·a·ceous (ăm brō/zĭ ā/shəs), adj. Bot. belonging to the Ambrosiaceae, or ragweed family of plants, which includes the ragweed, marsh elder, etc.

am·bro·sial (ăm brō/zhəl), adj. 1. exceptionally pleasing to taste or smell: especially delicious, fragrant, or sweet-smelling. 2. worthy of the gods; divine. Also, **am·bro/sian.** —**am·bro/sial·ly**, adv.

Ambrosian chant, a mode of singing or chanting introduced by St. Ambrose in Milan.

am·bro·type (ăm/brə tīp/), n. Photog. a picture or positive made from a glass negative by combining it with a dark background. [named after James Ambrose Cutting (1814–67), the inventor. See -TYPE]

am·bry (ăm/brĭ), n., pl. -**bries**. 1. a storeroom; closet. 2. a pantry. [ME almarie, ult. t. L: m. armārium closet]

ambs·ace (āmz/ās/, ămz/-), n. 1. the double ace, the lowest throw at dice. 2. bad luck; misfortune. 3. the smallest amount or distance. Also, **amesace.** [ME ambes as, t. OF, g. L ambās as double ace]

am·bu·la·cral (ăm/byə lā/krəl), adj. Zool. denoting the radial areas of an echinoderm bearing the tubular protrusions by which locomotion is accomplished. [f. s. L ambulācrum walk, avenue + -AL¹]

am·bu·lance (ăm/byə ləns), n. a vehicle, boat, or aircraft equipped for carrying the sick or wounded. [t. F, der. (hôpital) ambulant walking (hospital)]

ambulance chaser, Slang. a lawyer who incites persons to sue for damages because of accident.

am·bu·lant (ăm/byə lənt), adj. 1. moving from place to place; shifting. 2. Med. ambulatory (def. 4). [t. L: s. ambulans, ppr., walking]

am·bu·late (ăm/byə lāt/), v.i., -**lated**, -**lating**. to walk or move about, or from place to place. [t. L: m. s. ambulātus, pp., walked] —**am/bu·la/tion**, n.

am·bu·la·to·ry (ăm/byə lə tōr/ĭ), adj., n., pl. -**ries**. —adj. 1. pertaining to or capable of walking. 2. adapted for walking, as the limbs of many animals. 3. moving about; not stationary. 4. Med. not confined to bed: ambulatory patient. 5. Law. not fixed; alterable or revocable: ambulatory will. —n. 6. Archit. a place for walking: a. the side aisle surrounding the choir or chancel of a church. b. the arcaded walk around a cloister.

am·bus·cade (ăm/bəs kād/), n., v., -**caded**, -**cading**. —n. 1. an ambush. —v.i. 2. to lie in ambush. —v.t. 3. to attack from a concealed position. [t. F: m. embuscade, der. embusquer, b. It. imboscata and OF embûcher. See AMBUSH] —**am/bus·cad/er**, (U.S.) n.

am·bus·ca·do (ăm/bəs kā/dō), n., pl. -**dos**. Obs. ambuscade.

am·bush (ăm/bŏŏsh), n. Also, **am/bush·ment. 1.** act of lying concealed so as to attack by surprise. **2.** act of

attacking unexpectedly from a concealed position. 3. Mil. a secret or concealed station where troops lie in wait to attack unawares. —v.t. 4. to attack from ambush. [ME enbusshe, t. OF: m. embusche, ult. der. bûche bush, of Gmc. orig.] —**am/bush·er**, n. —**am/-bush·like/**, adj.

A. M. D. G., (L ad majorem Dei gloriam) to the greater glory of God. Also, **AMDG**

a·me·ba (ə mē/bə), n., pl. -**bas**, -**bae** (-bē). amoeba. —**a·me/bic**, adj. —**a·me·boid** (ə mē/boid), adj.

a·meer (ə mĭr/), n. amir.

a·mel·io·rate (ə mēl/yə rāt/), v.t., v.i., -**rated**, -**rating.** to make or become better; improve; meliorate. [f. s. F améliorer + -ATE¹; modeled on earlier MELIORATE] —**a·mel/io·ra·ble**, adj. —**a·mel·io·rant** (ə mēl/yə rənt), n. —**a·mel/io·ra/tive**, adj. —**a·mel/io·ra/tor**, n. —Syn. See **improve.**

a·mel·io·ra·tion (ə mēl/yə rā/shən), n. 1. act of ameliorating. 2. the resulting state. 3. something which is improving; an improvement.

a·men (ā/mĕn/, ä/-), interj. 1. it is so; so be it (used after a prayer, creed, or other formal statement). —adv. 2. verily; truly. —n. 3. an expression of concurrence or assent. [OE, t. LL, t. Gk., t. Heb.: certainty, truth]

A·men (ä/mən), n. a minor Theban god with the head of a ram, symbolizing fertility and life, later identified by the Egyptians with the sun god, Amen-Ra, their principal deity. Also, **Amon.** [t. Egypt., explained as "the one who hides his name"]

a·me·na·ble (ə mē/nə bəl, ə mĕn/ə-), adj. 1. disposed or ready to answer, yield, or submit; submissive; tractable. 2. liable to be called to account; answerable; legally responsible. 3. liable or exposed (to charge, claim, etc.): amenable to criticism. [f. s. F amener bring to (f. à to + mener bring, g. L mināre drive) + -ABLE] —**a·me/na·bil/i·ty, a·me/na·ble·ness**, n. —**a·me/na·bly**, adv.

amen corner, 1. U.S. a place in a church, usually at one side of the pulpit, once occupied by those worshipers who led the responsive amens during the service. 2. any special place in a church occupied by zealous worshipers.

a·mend (ə mĕnd/), v.t. 1. to alter (a motion, bill, constitution, etc.) by due formal procedure. 2. to change for the better; improve: to amend one's ways. 3. to remove or correct faults in; rectify: an amended spelling. —v.i. 4. to grow or become better by reforming oneself. [ME amende(n), t. OF: m. amender, g. L ēmendāre correct] —**a·mend/a·ble**, adj. —**a·mend/er**, n.

a·mend·a·to·ry (ə mĕn/də tōr/ĭ), adj. U.S. serving to amend; corrective.

a·mend·ment (ə mĕnd/mənt), n. 1. act of amending; correction; improvement. 2. alteration of a motion, bill, constitution, etc. 3. a change so made, either by way of correction or addition.

a·mends (ə mĕndz/), n. sing. or pl. 1. reparation or compensation for a loss, damage, or injury of any kind; recompense. 2. Obs. recovery of health. [ME amendes, t. OF, pl. of amende reparation]

A·men·ho·tep III (ä/mən hō/tĕp, ăm/ən-), king of Egypt, 1411? B.C. –1375 B.C. Also, **A·me·no·phis III** (ăm/ə nō/fĭs).

Amenhotep IV, (Ikhnaton) died c1357 B.C., king of Egypt, c1375–c1357 B.C., the first ruler in history to declare his belief in one God. Also, **Amenophis IV.**

a·men·i·ty (ə mĕn/ə tĭ, -mē/nə-), n., pl. -**ties.** 1. (pl.) agreeable features, circumstances, ways, etc.; civilities. 2. the quality of being pleasant or agreeable in situation, prospect, disposition, etc.; pleasantness: the amenity of the climate. [late ME, t. L: m.s. amoenitas]

a·men·or·rhe·a (ā mĕn/ə rē/ə), n. Pathol. absence of the menses. Also, **a·men/or·rhoe/a.** [f. A-⁶ + meno- (comb. form repr. Gk. mēn month) + -(R)RHEA]

A·men·Ra (ä/mən rä/), n. See **Amen** (god).

am·ent (ăm/ənt, ā/mənt), n. Bot. a spike of unisexual apetalous flowers with scaly bracts, usually deciduous; a catkin. [t. L: s. amentum strap, thong]

am·en·ta·ceous (ăm/ən tā/shəs), adj. 1. consisting of an ament. 2. bearing aments.

a·men·tia (ā mĕn/shə), n. Psychiatry. lack of intellectual development; imbecility; idiocy. [t. L: lack of reason]

am·en·tif·er·ous (ăm/ən tĭf/ər əs), adj. Bot. bearing aments or catkins.

a·men·ti·form (ə mĕn/tə fôrm/), adj. ament-shaped.

Amer., 1. America. 2. American.

a·merce (ə mûrs/), v.t., **amerced**, **amercing. 1.** to punish by an arbitrary or discretionary fine, i.e., one not fixed by statute. 2. to punish by inflicting a discretionary penalty of any kind. [ME amercy, ult. der. OF phrase (estre) a merci (to be) at the mercy of] —**a·merce/a·ble**, adj. —**a·merce/ment**, n. —**a·merc/er**, n.

A·mer·i·ca (ə mĕr/ə kə), n. 1. the United States of America. 2. North America. 3. South America. 4. North America and South America. [named after Americus Vespucius. See VESPUCCI]

A·mer·i·can (ə mĕr/ə kən), adj. 1. of or pertaining to the United States of America: an American citizen. 2. of or pertaining to North or South America. 3. Ethnol.

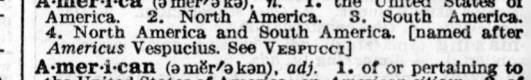

Aments

A. Staminate;
B. Pistillate

..oting or pertaining to the so-called "red" race, characterized by a reddish or brownish skin, dark eyes, black hair, and prominent cheekbones, and embracing the aborigines of North and South America (sometimes excluding the Eskimos), known as American Indians. **–n. 4.** a citizen of the United States of America. **5.** a native or an inhabitant of the western hemisphere. **3.** an aborigine of the western hemisphere.

·mer·i·ca·na (ə měr′ə kā′nə, -kǎn′ə, -kä′nə), *n. pl.* books, papers, etc., relating to America, esp. to its history and geography. [t. NL. See -ANA]

merican aloe, the century plant.

merican Beauty, an American variety of rose, periodically bearing large crimson blossoms.

merican cheese, a smooth white or yellow hard cheese with a slightly acid flavor; cheddar.

merican eagle, the bald eagle, esp. as depicted on the coat of arms of the United States.

merican Expeditionary Forces, troops sent into Europe by the U.S. Army during World War I.

merican Federation of Labor, a federation of trade unions organized in 1886; united with C.I.O., 1955.

merican Indian, Indian (def. 1).

·mer·i·can·ism (ə měr′ə kə nǐz′əm), *n.* **1.** devotion to or preference for the United States and its institutions. **2.** a custom, trait, or thing peculiar to the United States of America or its citizens. **3.** an English usage peculiar to the people of the United States.

·mer·i·can·ize (ə měr′ə kə nīz′), *v.t., v.i.,* **-ized, -izing.** to make or become American in character; assimilate to the customs and institutions of the United States. **—A·mer′i·can·i·za′tion,** *n.*

merican Legion, a society, organized in 1919, now composed of veterans of the armed forces of the United States in World Wars I and II.

merican party. See **know-nothing** (def. 3).

merican plan, (in hotels) a system of paying a single fixed sum that includes both room and meals.

merican Revolution, the war between Great Britain and her American colonies, 1775–83, by which the colonies won their independence. Also, *Brit.,* **War of American Independence.**

merican Samoa, the islands of the Samoa group belonging to the U. S., including mainly Tutuila and the Manua islands. 22,000 (est. 1955); 76 sq. mi. *Cap.;* Pago Pago.

m·er·i·ci·um (ăm′ə rĭsh′Y əm), *n.* a radioactive element, one of the products of the bombardment of uranium and plutonium by very energetic helium ions. *Symbol:* Am; *at. no.:* 95. [f. AMERIC(A) + -IUM]

·me·ri·go Ves·puc·ci (ä′mě rē′gō vě spōot′chē). See **Vespucci.**

m·er·ind (ăm′ər ĭnd), *n.* American Indian. [b. AMER(ICAN) and IND(IAN)] **—Am′er·in′di·an,** *adj., n.* **—Am′er·in′dic,** *adj.*

·mes (āmz), *n.* a city in central Iowa. 27,003 (1960).

mes·ace (āmz′ās′, ämz′-), *n.* ambsace.

m·e·thyst (ăm′ə thĭst), *n.* **1.** *Mineral.* a coarsely crystallized purple or violet quartz used in jewelry. **2.** the violet sapphire (**oriental amethyst**). **3.** a purplish tint. [t. L: s. *amethystus,* t. Gk.: m. *améthystos* lit., remedy for drunkenness; r. ME *ametiste,* t. OF] **—am·e·thys·tine** (ăm′ə thĭs′tĭn, -tīn), *adj.* **—am′e·thyst·like′,** *adj.*

m·e·tro·pi·a (ăm′ə trō′pĭ ə), *n. Pathol.* an abnormal condition of the eye causing faulty refraction of light rays, as in astigmatism, myopia, etc. [t. NL, f. Gk.: s. *ámetros* irregular + *-opia* -OPIA] **—am·e·trop·ic** (ăm′ə trŏp′Yk), *adj.*

m·ha·ra (ämhä′rə), *n.* a former kingdom in NW Ethiopia. *Cap.:* Gondar.

m·har·ic (ăm här′Yk, ämhär′Yk), *n.* **1.** the Semitic language which is official in Ethiopia. **—adj. 2.** of or pertaining to Amhara.

m·herst (ăm′ərst), *n.* **Jeffrey, Baron,** 1717–97, British field marshal.

·mi (ä mē′), *n. masc., pl.* **amis** (ä mē′). *French.* a friend.

·mi·a·ble (ā′mĭ ə bəl), *adj.* **1.** having or showing agreeable personal qualities, as sweetness of temper, kindheartedness, etc. **2.** friendly; kindly: *an amiable mood.* **3.** *Obs.* lovable; lovely. [ME *amyable,* t. OF: m. *amiable,* g. L *amīcābilis* friendly] **—a′mi·a·bil′i·ty, a′mi·a·ble·ness,** *n.* **—a′mi·a·bly,** *adv.* **—Syn. 1.** gracious.

·m·i·an·thus (ăm′Y ăn′thəs), *n. Mineral.* a fine variety of asbestos, with delicate, flexible filaments. [var. (with *-th* from *polyanthus*) of *amiantus,* t. L, t. Gk.: m. *amíantos* (*líthos*) undefiled (stone)]

m·ic (ăm′Yk), *adj. Chem.* of an amide or amine.

m·i·ca·ble (ăm′ə kə bəl), *adj.* characterized by or exhibiting friendliness; friendly; peaceable: *an amicable settlement.* [t. L: m.s. *amīcābilis*] **—am′i·ca·bil′i·ty, am′i·ca·ble·ness,** *n.* **—am′i·ca·bly,** *adv.*

m·ice¹ (ăm′Ys), *n. Eccles.* an oblong piece of linen worn about the neck and shoulders under the alb, or, formerly, on the head. [ME *amyse,* t. OF: m. *amis,* g. L *amictus* cloak]

m·ice² (ăm′Ys), *n.* a furred hood or hooded cape, with long ends hanging down in front, formerly worn by the clergy. [late ME *amisse,* t. F: m. *aumusse,* t. Pr.: m. *almussa,* f. Ar. *al-* the + m. G *mütze* cap]

·mi·cus cu·ri·ae (ə mī′kəs kyŏor′Y ē′), *Law.* a per-

son not a party to the litigation who volunteers or is invited by the court to give advice to the court upon some matter pending before it. [L: a friend of the court]

a·mid (ə mĭd′), *prep.* in the midst of or surrounded by; among; amidst. [ME *amidde,* OE *amiddan,* for *on middan* in the middle. See MID¹] **—Syn.** See **among.**

am·ide (ăm′īd, -Yd), *n. Chem.* **1.** a metallic derivative of ammonia in which the NH₂ grouping is retained, as *potassium amide,* KNH₂. **2.** an organic compound obtained by replacing the OH group in acids by the NH₂ radical. Also, **am·id** (ăm′Yd). [f. AM(MONIA) + -IDE] **—a·mid·ic** (ə mĭd′Yk), *adj.*

am·i·din (ăm′ə dĭn), *n.* the soluble matter of starch. [f. s. ML *amidum,* var. of L *amylum* (t. Gk.: m. *ámylon* fine meal) + -IN²]

amido-, *Chem.* **1.** a prefix denoting the replacement of a hydroxyl group by the NH₂ radical. **2.** (sometimes) amino-. [comb. form of AMIDE] **—a·mi·do** (ə mē′do, ăm′ə dō′), *adj.*

a·mi·do·gen (ə mē′də jən, ə mĭd′ə-), *n. Chem.* the NH₂ radical. If attached to CO in a compound it is called an **amido group;** without CO, an **amino group.**

am·i·dol (ăm′ə dōl′, -dōl′), *n.* a colorless crystalline phenol derivative, $C_6H_8N_2O \cdot 2HCl$, used as a photographic developer.

a·mid·ships (ə mĭd′shĭps), *adv. Naut.* **1.** in or toward the middle of a ship, or the part midway between stem and stern. **2.** lengthwise. Also, **a·mid′ship.**

a·midst (ə mĭdst′), *prep.* amid. [ME *amiddes,* f. *amidde* amid + adv. gen. *-s;* for later *-t,* cf. AGAINST, etc.]

a·mie (ä mē′), *n., pl.* **amies** (ä mē′). *French.* fem. of **ami.**

Am·i·ens (ăm′Y ənz; *Fr.* ä myăN′), *n.* a city in N France, on the Somme river: cathedral; battles, 1914, 1918, 1944. 92,506 (1954).

am·i·gen (ăm′ə jən), *n. Biochem.* **1.** a protein prepared by predigesting hog pancreas and milk with various enzymes, and used in the treatment of malnutrition and widespread burns, and as an aid to surgical convalescence. **2.** (*cap.*) a trademark for this substance.

a·mi·go (ä mē′gō; *Sp.* -gō), *n., pl.* **-gos** (-gōz; *Sp.* -gôs). **1.** a friend. **2.** a Spanish-speaking native friendly toward Americans. [Sp., g. L *amīcus*]

a·mine (ə mēn′, ăm′Yn), *n. Chem.* any of a class of compounds prepared from ammonia by replacing one, two, or all hydrogen atoms with organic radicals. Also, **am·in** (ăm′Yn). [f. AM(MONIA) + -INE²]

amino-, *Chem.* a prefix denoting amino group. [comb. form of AMINE]

a·mi·no acids (ăm′ə nō′, ə mē′nō), *Chem.* a group of organic compounds derived from the acids, RCOOH, by replacement of hydrogen in the (R) group by the (NH₂) radical. They are the basic constituents of proteins.

amino group, the universal basic radical, NH₂. Also, **amino radical.**

a·mir (ə mĭr′), *n.* **1.** a Mohammedan prince, lord, or nobleman. **2.** a title of honor of the descendants of Mohammed. **3.** (*cap.*) the former title of the ruler of Afghanistan. **4.** a title of certain Turkish officials. Also, **ameer.** [t. Ar.: m. *amīr* commander. See EMIR]

Am·ish (ăm′Ysh, ä′mYsh), *U.S.* **—adj. 1.** pertaining to Jakob Ammann, a Swiss Mennonite of the 17th century, or his followers. **—n. 2.** (*pl.*) the Amish Mennonites.

a·miss (ə mĭs′), *adv.* **1.** out of the proper course or order; in a faulty manner; wrongly: *to speak amiss.* **2.** take amiss, to be offended at; resent. **—adj. 3.** improper; wrong; faulty (used only in the predicate). [ME *amis,* f. A-¹ + *mis* wrong. See MISS¹]

am·i·to·sis (ăm′ə tō′sĭs), *n. Biol.* the direct method of cell division characterized by simple cleavage of the nucleus, without the formation of chromosomes. [f. A-⁶ + MITOSIS] **—am·i·tot·ic** (ăm′ə tŏt′Yk), *adj.*

am·i·ty (ăm′ə tY), *n., pl.* **-ties.** friendship; harmony; good understanding, esp. between nations. [ME *amytie,* t. F: m. *amitié,* ult. der. L *amīcus* friend]

Am·man (ăm′măn), *n.* capital of Jordan. 103,304 (1952).

am·me·ter (ăm′mē′tər), *n. Elect.* an instrument for measuring the strength of electric currents in amperes. [f. AM(PERE) + -METER]

am·mi·a·ceous (ăm′Y ā′shəs), *adj. Bot.* apiaceous.

am·mine (ăm′ēn, ə mēn′), *n. Chem.* a compound containing one or more ammonia molecules in coördinate linkage. [f. AMM(ONIA) + -INE²]

am·mo (ăm′ō), *n. Colloq.* ammunition.

am·mo·cete (ăm′ə sēt′), *n.* the larval stage of a lamprey, used as bait. It resembles the theoretical ancestor of the vertebrates. Also, **am′mo·coete′.** [f. AMMO(NIUM) + -CETE]

Am·mon (ăm′ən), *n.* classical name of the Egyptian divinity Amen, whom the Greeks identified with Zeus, the Romans with Jupiter. [t. L, t. Gk., t. Egypt.: m. *Amen*]

Am·mon (ăm′ən), *n.* a Biblical seminomadic Semitic people living east of the Jordan.

am·mo·ni·a (ə mōn′yə, ə mō′nY ə), *n.* **1.** a colorless, pungent, suffocating gas, NH₃, a compound of nitrogen and hydrogen, very soluble in water. **2.** Also, **ammonia water** or **aqueous ammonia.** this gas dissolved in water, the common commercial form. [t. NL; so called as being obtained from sal *ammoniac.* See AMMONIAC]

am·mo·ni·ac (ə mō′nY ăk′), *n.* **1.** gum ammoniac. **—adj. 2.** ammoniacal. [ME, t. L: s. *ammōniacum,* t. Gk.: m. *ammōniakón,* applied to a salt and a gum said to come from near the shrine of *Ammon* in Libya]

ăct, āble, dâre, ärt; ĕbb, ēqual; Yf, īce; hŏt, ōver, ôrder, oil, bŏŏk, ōoze, out; ŭp, ūse, ûrge; ə = a in alone; n, chief; g, give; ng, ring; sh, shoe; th, thin; ŧħ, that; zh, vision. See the full key on inside cover.

am·mo·ni·a·cal (ăm/ə nī/ə kəl), *adj.* 1. consisting of, containing, or using ammonia. 2. like ammonia.

am·mo·ni·ate (ə mō/nĭ āt/), *v.t.* -ated, -ating. to treat or cause to unite with ammonia.

am·mon·ic (ə mŏn/ĭk, ə mō/nĭk), *adj.* of or pertaining to ammonia or ammonium.

am·mon·i·fi·ca·tion (ə mŏn/ə fə kā/shən, ə mō/nə-), *n.* 1. act of impregnating with ammonia, as in fertilizer manufacture. 2. state of being so impregnated. 3. the formation of ammonia or its compounds, as in soil, etc., by soil organisms. [f. AMMONI(A) + -FICATION]

am·mon·i·fy (ə mŏn/ə fī/, ə mō/nə-), *v.*, -fied, -fying. —*v.t.* 1. to combine or impregnate with ammonia. 2. to form into ammonia or ammonium compounds. —*v.i.* 3. to become ammonified; produce ammonification.

am·mo·nite (ăm/ə nīt/), *n.* one of the coiled, chambered fossil shells of the extinct cephalopod mollusks, suborder *Ammonoidea*. [t. NL: m. s. *Ammōnītes*, der. ML *cornū Ammōnis* horn of Ammon]

am·mo·ni·um (ə mō/nĭ əm), *n.* *Chem.* a radical, NH₄, which plays the part of a metal in the compounds (**ammonium salts**) formed when ammonia reacts with acids. [f. AMMON(IA) + -IUM]

ammonium chloride, a white granular powder, NH₄Cl, used medicinally and industrially; sal ammoniac.

ammonium hydroxide, a basic compound, NH₄OH, made by dissolving ammonia in water and used extensively as a weak alkali.

ammonium nitrate, a white, soluble solid, the nitrate of ammonia, NH₄NO₃, used in explosives, freezing mixtures, and the preparation of nitrous oxide.

am·mu·ni·tion (ăm/yə nĭsh/ən), *n.* 1. all the material used in discharging all types of firearms or any weapon that throws projectiles; powder, shot, shrapnel, bullets, cartridges, and the means of igniting and exploding them, as primers and fuzes. Chemicals, bombs, grenades, mines, pyrotechnics are also ammunition. 2. any material or means used in combat. 3. *Obs.* military supplies. [t. F (obs.): m. *amunition* for *munition*, la *munition* being understood as *l'amunition*]

am·ne·sia (ăm nē/zhə), *n.* *Psychiatry.* loss of a large block of interrelated memories. [t. NL, t. Gk.: forgetfulness] —**am·ne·sic** (ăm nē/sĭk, -zĭk), **am·nes·tic** (ăm-nĕs/tĭk), *adj.*

am·nes·ty (ăm/nəs tĭ), *n.*, *pl.* -ties, *v.*, -tied, -tying. —*n.* 1. a general pardon for offenses against a government. 2. the granting of immunity for past offenses against the laws of war. 3. *Law.* protection against punishment granted a witness in order to compel him to testify to incriminating facts. 4. a forgetting or overlooking of any offense. —*v.t.* 5. to grant amnesty to; pardon. [t. L: m.s. *amnēstia*, t. Gk.: forgetfulness]

am·ni·on (ăm/nĭ ən), *n.*, *pl.* -nions, -nia (-nĭ'ə). *Anat.*, *Zool.* the innermost of the embryonic or fetal membranes of insects, reptiles, birds, and mammals; the sac containing the amniotic fluid and the embryo. [t. NL, t. Gk.] —**am·ni·on·ic** (ăm/nĭ ŏn/ĭk), *adj.*

am·ni·ot·ic (ăm/nĭ ŏt/ĭk), *adj.* *Anat.*, *Zool.* of or pertaining to the amnion.

a·moe·ba (ə mē/bə), *n.*, *pl.* -bae (-bē), -bas. *Zool.* 1. a microscopic, one-celled animal consisting of a naked mass of protoplasm constantly changing in shape as it moves and engulfs food. 2. a protozoan of the genus *Amoeba*. Also, **ameba.** [t. NL, t. Gk.: m. *amoibē* change] —**a·moe/ba·like/,** *adj.*

am·oe·bae·an (ăm/ĭ bē/ən), *adj.* *Pros.* alternately responsive, as verses in dialogue. Also, **am/oe·be/an.**

a·moe·bic (ə mē/bĭk), *adj.* 1. of, pertaining to, or resembling an amoeba. 2. characterized by, or due to the presence of, amoebae, as certain diseases. Also, **amebic.**

amoebic dysentery, a variety of dysentery whose causative agent is a protozoan, the *Endamoeba histolytica*, characterized esp. by intestinal ulceration.

a·moe·boid (ə mē/boid), *adj.* *Biol.* resembling or related to amoebae. Also, **ameboid.** [f. AMOEB(A) + -OID]

a·mok (ə mŭk/, ə mŏk/), *n.*, *adj.* 1. (among Malays) a psychic disturbance characterized by depression followed by overwhelming desire to murder. —*adv.* 2. **run amok.** See **amuck.** [t. Malay: m. *amoq*]

a·mo·le (ə mō/lā; *Sp.* ä mō/lĕ), *n.* *Southwestern U.S.* 1. the roots, etc., of various plants, as Mexican species of *Agave*, used as a substitute for soap. 2. any such plant. [t. Mex. Sp., from Nahuatl]

A·mon (ä/mən), *n.* Amen (god).

a·mong (ə mŭng/), *prep.* 1. in or into the midst of; in association or connection with; surrounded by: *he fell among thieves.* 2. to each of; by or for distribution to: *divide these among you.* 3. in the number, class, or group of; of or out of: *that's among the things we must do.* 4. with or by all or the whole of: *popular among the people.* 5. by the joint or reciprocal action of: *settle it among yourselves.* 6. each with the other; mutually: *to quarrel among themselves.* [OE *amang*, for *on* (*ge*)*mang* in the crowd, in the midst of]
—**Syn.** 1. AMONG, AMID, BETWEEN imply a position in the middle of. AMONG suggests a mingling with more than two objects: *he went among the crowd.* AMID, a more literary word implies being in a middle place or surrounded by something: *to stand amid ruins.* BETWEEN refers to only two objects: *between two pillars.* In some special instances, in which each object is individually related to the rest, BETWEEN is used of more than two objects: *dealings between the states.*

a·mongst (ə mŭngst/), *prep.* *Literary* or *Brit.* among.

[ME *amonges*, f. AMONG + adv. gen. -*es*; for later -*t* after the gen. -s, cf. AGAINST, etc.]

a·mon·til·la·do (ə mŏn/tə lä/dō; *Sp.* ä mōn/tē lyä/dō), *n.* a pale-colored, quite dry, Spanish sherry. [t. Sp.]

a·mor·al (ā mŏr/əl, ā mŏr/-, ă-), *adj.* without moral quality; neither moral nor immoral. [f. A-⁶ + MORAL] —**a·mo·ral·i·ty** (ā/mə răl/ə tĭ, ăm/ə-), *n.* —**a·mor/al·ly,** *adv.*

am·o·ret·to (ăm/ə rĕt/ō; *It.* ä/mō rĕt/tō), *n.*, *pl.* -retti (-rĕt/ĭ; *It.* -rĕt/tē). a little cupid. [t. It., dim. of *amore*, g. L *amor* love]

a·mo·ri·no (ä/mō rē/nō), *n.*, *pl.* -ni (-nē). amoretto.

am·o·rist (ăm/ə rĭst), *n.* 1. a lover; a gallant. 2. one who writes about love. [f. L *amor* love + -IST]

am·o·rous (ăm/ə rəs), *adj.* 1. inclined or disposed to love: *an amorous disposition.* 2. in love; enamored. 3. showing love: *amorous sigh.* 4. pertaining to love: *amorous poetry.* [ME, t. OF, g. L *amōrōsus*, der. *amor* love] —**am/o·rous·ly,** *adv.* —**am/o·rous·ness,** *n.* —**Syn.** 1. loving; amatory. 3. fond, tender.

a·mor pa·tri·ae (ā/môr pā/trĭ ē/), *Latin.* love of country; patriotism.

a·mor·phism (ə môr/fĭz əm), *n.* 1. state or quality of being amorphous. 2. nihilism (def. 3).

a·mor·phous (ə môr/fəs), *adj.* 1. lacking definite form; having no specific shape. 2. of no particular kind or character; indeterminate; formless; unorganized: *an amorphous style.* 3. *Geol.* occurring in a mass, as without stratification or crystalline structure. 4. *Chem.* noncrystalline. [t. Gk.: m. *ámorphos*] —**a·mor/phous·ly,** *adv.* —**a·mor/phous·ness,** *n.*

am·or·ti·za·tion (ăm/ər tə zā/shən, ə môr/-), *n.* 1. act of amortizing a debt. 2. the money devoted to this purpose. Also, **a·mor·tize·ment** (ə môr/tĭz mənt).

am·or·tize (ăm/ər tīz/, ə môr/tīz), *v.t.*, -tized, -tizing. 1. to liquidate or extinguish (an indebtedness or charge) usually by periodic payments (or by entries) made to a sinking fund, to a creditor, or to an account. 2. *Old Eng. Law.* to convey to a corporation; alienate in mortmain. Also, *Brit.*, **am/or·tise/.** [ME *amortise(n)*, t. OF: m. *amortiss-*, s. *amortir* deaden, buy out, der. *mort* death. Cf. ML *admortizāre*] —**am/or·tiz/a·ble,** *adj.*

A·mos (ā/məs), *n.* 1. a Hebrew prophet of the eighth century B.C., author of the Old Testament book bearing his name. 2. this book.

a·mount (ə mount/), *n.* 1. the sum total of two or more sums or quantities; the aggregate: *the amount of 7 and 9 is 16.* 2. the sum of the principal and interest of a loan. 3. quantity: *the amount of resistance.* 4. the full effect, value, or import. —*v.i.* 5. to reach, extend, or be equal in number, quantity, effect, etc. (fol. by *to*). [ME *amount(en)*, t. OF: m. *amonter* mount up to, der. *amont* upward, orig. phrase *a mont* to the mountain]

a·mour (ə mŏŏr/), *n.* 1. a love affair. 2. an illicit love affair. [t. F, prob. t. Pr.: m. *amor*, g. L *amor* love]

a·mour-pro·pre (á mŏŏr prô/pr), *n.* *French.* self-esteem; self-respect.

A·moy (ä moi/), *n.* a seaport in SE China, on an island in Formosa Strait. 158,000 (est. 1948).

amp., 1. amperage. 2. ampere.

am·pe·lop·sis (ăm/pə lŏp/sĭs), *n.* any plant of the vitaceous genus *Ampelopsis*, comprising climbing woody vines or shrubs. [t. NL, f. s. Gk. *ámpelos* vine + -*opsis* -OPSIS]

am·per·age (ăm pīr/ĭj, ăm/pər-), *n.* *Elect.* the strength of an electric current measured in amperes.

am·pere (ăm/pĭr, ăm pĭr/), *n.* *Elect.* the usual unit of current strength; the current produced by an electromotive force of one volt acting through a resistance of one ohm; one coulomb per second. Also, **am·père** (ăm pĕr/). [named after A. M. AMPERE]

Am·père (ăm pîr/; *Fr.* äɴ pĕr/), *n.* **André Marie** (äɴ-drĕ/ má rĕ/), 1775–1836, French physicist.

am·pere-hour (ăm/pĭr our/), *n.* *Elect.* a unit equal to 3600 coulombs; the quantity of electricity transferred by a current of one ampere in one hour.

ampere turn, *Elect.* 1. one complete turn or convolution of a conducting coil, through which one ampere of current passes. 2. the magnetomotive force produced by one ampere passing through one complete turn or convolution of a coil.

am·per·sand (ăm/pər sănd/, ăm/pər sănd/), *n.* the name of the character (&) meaning *and.* [contraction of *and per se* – *and*, & by itself (as a mere symbol given after the letters of the alphabet, and called *and*)]

am·phet·a·mine (ăm fĕt/ə mēn/, -mĭn), *n.* *Pharm.* a drug which, diluted with water, is used as a spray or inhaled to relieve nasal congestion and is taken internally to stimulate the central nervous system.

amphi-, a word element meaning "on both sides," "on all sides," "around," "round about," as in *Amphibia.* [t. Gk., repr. *amphi*, prep. and adv.]

am·phi·ar·thro·sis (ăm/fĭ är thrō/sĭs), *n.*, *pl.* -ses (-sēz). *Anat.* a form of articulation which permits slight motion, as that between the bodies of the vertebrae. [t. AMPHI- + Gk. *árthrōsis* articulation]

am·phi·as·ter (ăm/fĭ ăs/tər), *n.* *Biol.* the achromatic spindle with two asters that forms during mitosis.

Am·phib·i·a (ăm fĭb/ĭ ə), *n. pl. Zool.* the class of vertebrates that comprises the frogs, salamanders, and caecilians (with various extinct types), representing the essential, basic characteristics of the ancestral stock of all land vertebrates. Typically they lay eggs that hatch in water, and the young go through a fishlike larval, or tadpole, stage, later metamorphosing into lung-breathing quadrupeds. [t. NL, neut. pl. of *amphibius*, t. Gk.: m. *amphibios* living a double life]

am·phib·i·an (ăm fĭb′Ɏ ən), *n.* **1.** any animal of the class *Amphibia.* **2.** an amphibious plant. **3.** an airplane that can take off from and land on either land or water. —*adj.* **4.** belonging to the class *Amphibia.* **5.** capable of operating on land or water; amphibious.

am·phi·bi·ot·ic (ăm′fə bī ŏt′Ɏk), *adj. Zool.* living on land during an adult stage and in water during a larval stage. [f. AMPHI- + m. s. Gk. *biōtikós* pertaining to life]

am·phib·i·ous (ăm fĭb′Ɏəs), *adj.* **1.** living both on land and in water; belonging to both land and water. **2.** capable of operating on both land and water; *amphibious plane.* **3.** of a twofold nature. [t. Gk.: m. *amphibios* living a double life] —**am·phib′i·ous·ly,** *adv.* —**am·phib′i·ous·ness,** *n.*

am·phi·bole (ăm′fə bōl′), *n. Mineral.* any of a complex group of hydrous silicate minerals, containing chiefly calcium, magnesium, sodium, iron, and aluminum, and including hornblende, tremolite, asbestos, etc., and occurring as important constituents of many rocks. [t. F, t. Gk.: m.s. *amphibolos* ambiguous]

am·phi·bol·ic¹ (ăm′fə bŏl′Ɏk), *adj.* of or pertaining to amphibole. [f. AMPHIBOL(E) + -IC]

am·phi·bol·ic² (ăm′fə bŏl′Ɏk), *adj.* equivocal; uncertain; changing; ambiguous. [f. AMPHIBOL(Y) + -IC]

am·phib·o·lite (ăm fĭb′ə līt′), *n. Petrog.* a metamorphic rock composed basically of amphibole or hornblende. [f. AMPHIBOL(E) + -ITE¹]

am·phi·bol·o·gy (ăm′fə bŏl′ə jɎ), *n., pl.* -gies. ambiguity of speech, esp. from uncertainty of the grammatical construction rather than of the meaning of the words, as in *The Duke yet lives that Henry shall depose.* [t. LL.: m. s. *amphibologia*, r. L *amphibolia* (see AM-PHIBOLY), which was remodeled after *tautologia* and the like] —**am·phib·o·log·i·cal** (ăm′fə lŏj′ə kəl), *adj.*

am·phib·o·lous (ăm fĭb′ə ləs), *adj. Logic.* ambiguous; equivocal; susceptible of two meanings. [t. L: m. *amphibolus*, t. Gk.: m. *amphíbolos* thrown around]

am·phib·o·ly (ăm fĭb′ə lɎ), *n., pl.* -lies. amphibology. [t. L: m. s. *amphibolia* ambiguity, t. Gk.]

am·phi·brach (ăm′fə brăk′), *n. Pros.* a trisyllabic foot in which the syllables come in the following order: short, long, short (quantitative meter), or unstressed, stressed, unstressed (accentual meter). Thus, *together* is an accentual amphibrach. [t. L: s. *amphibrachys*, t. Gk.: short on both sides]

am·phi·chro·ic (ăm′fə krō′Ɏk), *adj. Chem.* giving either of two colors, one with acids and one with alkalis. Also, **am·phi·chro·mat·ic** (ăm′fə krō măt′Ɏk). [f. AMPHI- + s. Gk. *chróa* color + -IC]

am·phi·coe·lous (ăm′fə sē′ləs), *adj. Anat., Zool.* concave on both sides, as the bodies of the vertebrae of fishes. [t. Gk.: m. *amphíkoilos* hollowed all around]

am·phic·ty·on (ăm fĭk′tɎ ən), *n.* a deputy to the council of an amphictyony. [t. Gk.: m. s. *amphiktyones,* pl., dwellers around, neighbors]

am·phic·ty·on·ic (ăm fĭk′tɎ ŏn′Ɏk), *adj.* of or pertaining to an amphictyon or an amphictyony.

am·phic·ty·o·ny (ăm fĭk′tɎ ə nɎ), *n., pl.* -nies. a religious league of ancient Greek states participating in the cult of a common deity. [t. Gk.: m. s. *amphiktyonia*]

am·phi·dip·loid (ăm′fə dɎ′ploid), *n. Genetics.* a plant type possessing the sum of the chromosome numbers of two parental species, ordinarily arising from the doubling of the chromosomes of a hybrid of two species.

am·phi·go·ry (ăm′fə gŏr′Ɏ), *n., pl.* -ries. a meaningless rigmarole, as of nonsense verses or the like; a nonsensical parody. [t. F: m. *amphigouri;* orig. unknown] —**am·phi·gor·ic** (ăm′fə gŏr′Ɏk, -gŏr′-), *adj.*

am·phi·gou·ri (ăm′fə gŏŏr′Ɏ), *n., pl.* -ris. amphigory.

am·phim·a·cer (ăm fĭm′ə sər), *n. Pros.* a trisyllabic foot in which the syllables come in the following order: long, short, long (quantitative meter), or stressed, unstressed, stressed (accentual meter). Thus, *anodyne* is an accentual amphimacer. [t. L: m. s. *amphimacrus,* t. Gk.: m. *amphímakros* long on both sides]

am·phi·mix·is (ăm′fə mĭk′sɎs), *n.* **1.** *Biol.* the merging of the germ plasm of two organisms in sexual reproduction. **2.** *Embryol., Genetics.* the combining of paternal and maternal hereditary substances. [f. AMPHI- + Gk. *mixis* a mingling]

am·phi·on (ăm fī′ən), *n. Gk. Myth.* the son of Antiope by Zeus, twin brother of Zethus, and husband of Niobe, who with his brother fortified Thebes with a wall, charming the stones into place by his lyre.

am·phi·ox·us (ăm′fɎ ŏk′səs), *n. Zool.* a small fishlike animal, the lancelet, showing vertebrate characteristics but lacking a vertebral column, important in discussions of vertebrate ancestry. [t. NL, f. Gk.: *amphi-* AMPHI- + m. *oxýs* sharp]

am·phi·pod (ăm′fə pŏd′), *n.* **1.** any of a type of small crustaceans, *Amphipoda,* including beach fleas, etc. —*adj.* **2.** of or pertaining to the amphipods.

am·phi·ro·style (ăm fĭp′rə stil′, ăm′fə prō′stil), *adj. Archit.* having a prostyle porch in front and rear but no columns along the sides. [t. L: m. s. *amphiprostylos,* t. Gk.]

am·phis·bae·na (ăm′fɎs bē′nə), *n.* **1.** a burrowing, blind, and limbless snakelike lizard of the family *Amphisbaenidae,* with obtuse head and tail, moving

forward or backward with equal ease. **2.** *Classical Myth.* a fabulous venomous serpent having a head at each end and able to move in either direction. [t. L, t. Gk.: m. *amphísbaina*] —**am′phis·bae′nic,** *adj.*

am·phi·the·a·ter (ăm′fə thē′ə tər), *n.* **1.** a level area of oval or circular shape surrounded by rising ground. **2.** any place for public contests or games; an arena. **3.** a building with tiers of seats around an arena or central area, as those used in ancient Rome for gladiatorial contests. **4.** a semicircular sloping gallery in a modern theater. Also, *esp. Brit.,* **am′phi·the′a·tre.** [t. L: m.s. *amphitheātrum,* t. Gk.: m. *amphitheātron*] —**am·phi·the·at·ric** (ăm′fə thɎ ăt′rɎk), **am′phi·the·at′ri·cal,** *adj.* —**am′phi·the·at′ri·cal·ly,** *adv.*

am·phi·the·ci·um (ăm′fə thē′shɎ əm), *n., pl.* -cia (-shɎ ə). *Bot.* the layer or layers of cells in the capsule of a moss surrounding the spores. [t. NL, f. *amphi-* AMPHI- + *thēcium* (s. Gk.: m. *thēkton,* dim. of *thēkē* case)]

am·phit·ri·cha (ăm fĭt′rə kə), *n.pl.* bacteria having the organs of locomotion on both poles. [f. AMPHI- + m. *trich-* (s. Gk. *thríx* hair)] —**am·phit′ri·chous,** *adj.*

Am·phi·tri·te (ăm′fə trī′tɎ), *n. Gk. Myth.* the goddess of the sea, daughter of Nereus and wife of Poseidon.

Am·phit·ry·on (ăm fĭt′rɎ ən), *n.* **1.** *Gk. Legend.* the husband of Alcmene. **2.** a host; an entertainer.

am·pho·ra (ăm′fə rə), *n., pl.* -rae (-rē′). a two-handled, narrow-necked vessel, commonly big-bellied and narrowed at the base, used by the ancient Greeks and Romans for holding wine, oil, etc. [t. L, t. Gk.: m. *amphoreús,* short for *amphi-phoreús*] —**am′pho·ral,** *adj.*

am·pho·ter·ic (ăm′fə tĕr′Ɏk), *adj. Chem.* functioning as an acid or as a base. [f. s. Gk. *amphóteros* (comp. of *amphó* both) + -IC]

Amphorae

am·ple (ăm′pəl), *adj.,* -pler, -plest. **1.** of great extent, size, or amount; large; spacious. **2.** in full or abundant measure; copious; liberal. **3.** fully sufficient for the purpose or for needs; enough and to spare. [late ME, t.L: m.s. *amplus*] —**am′ple·ness,** *n.* —**Syn. 2.** AMPLE, COPIOUS, LIBERAL describe an abundant supply of something. AMPLE describes a plentiful amount: *to give ample praise.* COPIOUS implies an apparently inexhaustible and lavish abundance: *a copious flow of tears.* LIBERAL implies a generous supply (more than AMPLE but less than COPIOUS) together with a free and unrestricted dispensing of it: *liberal amounts of food were distributed to the needy.* —**Ant. 2.** scanty, meager.

am·plex·i·caul (ăm plĕk′sə kôl′), *adj. Bot.* clasping the stem, as some leaves do at their base. [t. NL: s. *amplexicaulis,* f. L: m. s. *amplexus* embracing + *caulis* stem]

am·pli·a·tion (ăm′plɎ ā′shən), *n. Now Rare or Obs.* enlargement; amplification. [t. L: s. *ampliātio*]

am·pli·fi·ca·tion (ăm′plə fə kā′shən), *n.* **1.** act of amplifying. **2.** expansion of a statement, narrative, etc., as for rhetorical purposes. **3.** a statement, narrative, etc., so expanded. **4.** an addition made in expanding. **5.** *Elect.* increase in the strength of current, voltage, or power. [t. L: s. *amplificātio*]

Amplexicaul leaves

am·pli·fi·ca·to·ry (ăm plɎf′ə kə tōr′Ɏ), *adj.* of the nature of enlargement or extension.

am·pli·fi·er (ăm′plə fī′ər), *n.* **1.** one who amplifies or enlarges. **2.** *Elect.* a device for increasing the amplitudes of electric waves or impulses by means of the control exercised by the input over the power supplied to the output from a local source of energy. Commonly it is a vacuum tube or a device employing vacuum tubes, but it may be an electric dynamo.

am·pli·fy (ăm′plə fī′), *v.,* -fied, -fying. —*v.t.* **1.** to make larger or greater; enlarge; extend. **2.** to expand in stating or describing, as by details, illustrations, etc. **3.** to exaggerate. **4.** *Elect.* to increase the amplitude of (impulses or waves). —*v.i.* **5.** to discourse at length; expatiate or dilate (usually fol. by *on*). [ME *amplify(en),* t. F: m. *amplifier,* t. L: m. s. *amplificāre* enlarge. See -FY] —**Ant. 1.** contract. **2.** condense.

am·pli·tude (ăm′plə tūd′, -tōōd′), *n.* **1.** extension in space, esp. breadth or width; largeness; extent. **2.** large or full measure; abundance; copiousness. **3.** *Physics.* the distance or range from one extremity of an oscillation to the middle point or neutral value. **4.** *Elect.* the maximum strength of an alternating current during its cycle, as distinguished from the mean or effective strength. **5.** *Astron.* the arc of the horizon from the east or west point to a heavenly body at its rising or setting. [t. L: m. *amplitūdo*]

amplitude modulation, *Electronics.* a system of radio transmission in which the carrier wave is modulated by changing its amplitude (distinguished from *frequency modulation*).

am·ply (ăm′plɎ), *adv.* in an ample manner; sufficiently.

am·poule (ăm′pool), *n. Med.* a sealed glass bulb used to hold hypodermic solutions. Also, **am·pule** (ăm′pūl). [t. F, g. L *ampulla* bottle]

am·pul·la (ăm pŭl′ə), *n., pl.* -pullae (-pŭl′ē). **1.** *Anat.* a dilated portion of a canal or duct, esp. of the semicircular canals of the ear. **2.** *Eccles.* **a.** a vessel for the wine and water used at the altar. **b.** a vessel for holding consecrated oil. **3.** a two-handled bottle used by the ancient Romans for oil, etc. [t. L]

ct, āble, dāre, ärt; ĕbb, ēqual; Ɏf, īce; hŏt, ōver, ôrder, oil, bŏŏk, ōōze, out; ŭp, ūse, ûrge; ə = a in alone; h, chief; g, give; ng, ring; sh, shoe; th, thin; ᵺ, that; zh, vision. See the full key on inside cover.

am·pul·la·ceous (ăm′pə lā′shəs), *adj.* like an ampulla; bottle-shaped. Also, **am·pul·lar** (ăm pŭl′ər).

am·pu·tate (ăm′pyŏŏ tāt′), *v.t.,* **-tated, -tating. 1.** to cut off (a limb, arm, etc.) by a surgical operation. **2.** *Obs.* to prune, as branches of trees. [t. L: m. s. *amputātus,* pp.] **—am′pu·ta′tion,** *n.* **—am′pu·ta′tor,** *n.*

am·pu·tee (ăm′pyŏŏ tē′), *n.* one who has lost an arm, hand, leg, etc., by amputation.

am·ri·ta (əm rē′tə), *n. Hindu Myth.* **1.** the beverage of immortality. **2.** the immortality conferred by it. Also, **am·ree′ta.** [t. Skt.: m. *amrta* immortal; as n., the drink of immortality. Cf. Gk. *ăm*(*b*)*rotos* immortal]

Am·rit·sar (əm rĭt′sər), *n.* a city in NW India, in Punjab. 325,747 (1951).

Am·ster·dam (ăm′stər dăm′; *Du.* äm′stər däm′), *n.* **1.** a seaport in and the parliamentary capital of the Netherlands, in the W part, on the Ijsselmeer: ship canal. 858,702 (est. 1954). **2.** a city in E New York. 28,772 (1960).

amt., *government.*

a·muck (ə mŭk′), *adv. (orig. adj.)* **1. run amuck, a.** to rush about in a murderous frenzy. **b.** to rush about wildly. **—n. 2.** amok. [var. of AMOK]

A·mu Dar·ya (ä mŏŏ′ där′yä), a river flowing from the Pamirs in central Asia NW to the Aral Sea. ab. 1400 mi. Also, **Oxus.**

am·u·let (ăm′yə lĭt), *n.* an object superstitiously worn to ward off evil; a protecting charm. [t. L: s. *amulētum*]

A·mund·sen (ä′mənd sən; *Nor.* ä′mŏŏn sən), *n.* **Roald** (rō′äl), 1872–1928, Norwegian explorer: discovered the South Pole in December, 1911.

A·mur (ä mŏŏr′), *n.* a river in E Asia, forming most of the boundary between N Manchuria and the SE Soviet Union, flowing into the Sea of Okhotsk. ab. 2700 mi.

a·muse (ə mūz′), *v.t.,* **amused, amusing. 1.** to hold the attention of agreeably; entertain; divert. **2.** to excite mirth in. **3.** to cause (time, leisure, etc.) to pass agreeably. **4.** *Archaic.* to keep in expectation by flattery, pretenses, etc. **5.** *Obs.* to engross. **6.** *Obs.* to puzzle. [late ME, t. MF: m. s. *amuser* occupy with trifles, divert, f. *a* to + *muser* stare. See | MUSE¹] **—a·mus′a·ble,** *adj.* **—a·mus′er,** *n.*
—Syn. 1. AMUSE, DIVERT, ENTERTAIN mean to occupy the attention with something pleasant. That which AMUSES dispels the tedium of idleness or pleases the fancy. DIVERT implies turning the attention from serious thoughts or pursuits to something light, amusing, or lively. That which ENTERTAINS usually does so because of a plan or program which engages and holds the attention by being pleasing and sometimes instructive.

a·mused (ə mūzd′), *adj.* **1.** filled with interest; pleasurably occupied. **2.** displaying amusement: *an amused expression.* **3.** aroused to mirth. **—a·mus·ed·ly** (ə mū′zĭd lĭ), *adv.*

a·muse·ment (ə mūz′mənt), *n.* **1.** state of being amused; enjoyment. **2.** that which amuses; pastime; entertainment. [t. F] **—Syn. 1.** recreation, frolic, p easure, merriment. **2.** diversion, game.

a·mus·ing (ə mū′zĭng), *adj.* **1.** pleasantly entertaining or diverting. **2.** exciting moderate mirth; delighting the fancy. **—a·mus′ing·ly,** *adv.* **—a·mus′ing·ness,** *n.*
—Syn. 2. AMUSING, COMICAL, DROLL describe that which causes mirth. That which is AMUSING is quietly humorous or funny in a gentle, good-humored way: *the baby's attempts to talk were amusing.* That which is COMICAL causes laughter by being incongruous, witty, or ludicrous: *his huge shoes made the clown look comical.* DROLL adds to COMICAL the idea of strange or peculiar, and sometimes that of sly or waggish humor: *droll antics of a kitten, a droll initiation.*

a·mu·sive (ə mū′zĭv), *adj.* affording amusement or entertainment.

a·myg·da·la (ə mĭg′də lə), *n., pl.* **-lae** (-lē′). **1.** an almond. **2.** *Anat.* **a.** an almond-shaped part. **b.** a tonsil. [t. L, t. Gk.: m. *amygdălē* almond. Cf. OE *amygdal*]

a·myg·da·late (ə mĭg′də lĭt, -lāt′), *adj.* pertaining to, resembling, or made of almonds.

a·myg·da·lin (ə mĭg′də lĭn), *n.* a crystalline principle, $C_{20}H_{27}NO_{11} + 3H_2O$, existing in bitter almonds, and in the leaves, etc., of species of the genus *Prunus* and of some of its near allies.

a·myg·da·line (ə mĭg′də lĭn, -lĭn′), *adj.* of or pertaining to the amygdalae.

a·myg·da·loid (ə mĭg′də loid′), *n.* **1.** *Petrog.* an igneous rock in which rounded cavities formed by the expansion of steam have later become filled with various minerals. **—adj.** Also, **a·myg·da·loi′dal. 2.** (of rocks) containing amygdules. **3.** almond-shaped. [f. s. Gk. *amygdălē* almond + -OID]

a·myg·dule (ə mĭg′dŭl, -dŏŏl), *n. Petrog.* one of the mineral nodules in amygdaloid.

am·yl (ăm′ĭl), *n. Chem.* a univalent radical, C_5H_{11}, derived from pentane. Its compounds are found in fusel oil, fruit extracts, etc. [t. L: s. *amylum* starch (t. Gk.: m. *ămylon*); the -*yl* was identified with -YL]

am·y·la·ceous (ăm′ə lā′shəs), *adj.* of the nature of starch; starchy. [f. AMYL(O)- + -ACEOUS]

amyl alcohol, *Chem.* a colorless liquid, $C_5H_{11}OH$, consisting of a mixture of two or more isomeric alcohols, derived from the pentanes and serving as a solvent and intermediate for organic syntheses.

am·y·lase (ăm′ə lās′), *n. Biochem.* **1.** a starch-splitting enzyme in the blood and in certain plants, which hydrolyzes complex sugars to glucose. **2.** any of several

digestive enzymes, as amylopsin or ptyalin, which break down starches.

am·yl·ene (ăm′ə lēn′), *n. Chem.* any of certain unsaturated isomeric hydrocarbons with the formula C_5H_{10}.

amylo-, a combining form of **amyl** and **amylum.** Also, **amyl-.**

am·y·loid (ăm′ə loid′), *n. Pathol.* a hard, homogeneous, glossy substance deposited in tissues in certain kinds of degeneration. **—am′y·loi′dal,** *adj.*

am·y·lol·y·sis (ăm′ə lŏl′ə sĭs), *n. Biochem.* the conversion of starch into sugar. [f. AMYLO- + -LYSIS] **—am·y·lo·lyt·ic** (ăm′ə lō lĭt′ĭk), *adj.*

am·y·lo·pec·tin (ăm′ə lō pĕk′tĭn), *n. Chem.* the gel component of starch. It turns red in iodine.

am·y·lop·sin (ăm′ə lŏp′sĭn), *n. Biochem.* an enzyme of the pancreatic juice, capable of converting starch into sugar. [b. AMYLO(LYSIS) and (PE)PSIN]

am·y·lose (ăm′ə lōs′), *n. Chem.* the sol component of starch. It turns intense blue in iodine.

am·y·lum (ăm′ə ləm), *n.* starch (def. 1). [t. L, t. Gk.: m. *ămylon* fine meal, starch]

am·y·tal (ăm′ə tŏl′, -tăl′), *n. Pharm.* a colorless crystalline substance, $C_{11}H_{18}N_2O_3$, used esp. as a sedative.

an¹ (ăn; *unstressed* ən), *adj. or indefinite article.* the form of *a* before an initial vowel sound. See a¹. [ME; OE *ăn.* See ONE]

an² (ăn; *unstressed* ən), *conj.* **1.** *Dial. and Colloq.* and. **2.** *Archaic and Dial.* if. Also, **an′.** [var. of AND]

an-¹, a prefix meaning "not," "without," "lacking," used before vowels and *h,* as in *anarchy.* Also, a-⁶. [t. Gk.]

an-², var. of ad-, before *n,* as in *announce.*

an-³, var. of ana-, used before vowels, as in *anaerobe.*

-an, a suffix meaning: **1.** "belonging to," "pertaining or relating to," "adhering to," and commonly expressing connection with a place, person, ,eader, class, order, sect, system, doctrine, or the like, serving to form adjectives, many of which are also used as nouns, as *American, Christian, Elizabethan, republican,* and hence serving to form other nouns of the same type, as *historian, theologian.* **2.** *Zool.* "relating to a certain class," as in *Mammalian.* [t. L: s. *-ānus;* r. ME *-ain, -en,* t. OF]

AN, Anglo-Norman. Also, **A.N.**

an., (L *anno*) in the year.

a·na¹ (ā′nə, ä′nə), *n.* **1.** a collection of miscellaneous information about a particular subject. **2.** the information so collected. [independent use of -ANA]

an·a² (ăn′ə), *adv. Pharm.* in equal quantities; of each (used in medical prescriptions, with reference to ingredients, and often written āā). [ML, t. Gk. See ANA-]

ana-, a prefix meaning "up," "throughout," "again," "back," occurring originally in words from the Greek, but used also in modern words (English and other) formed after the Greek type, as in *anabatic.* [t. Gk., repr. *ană,* prep.]

-ana, a noun suffix denoting a collection of material pertaining to a given subject, as in *Shakespeariana, Americana.* [t. L, neut. pl. of *-ānus* -AN]

an·a·bae·na (ăn′ə bē′nə), *n., pl.* **-nas.** *Bot.* any of the fresh-water algae constituting the genus *Anabaena,* commonly occurring in masses, and often contaminating drinking water, giving it a fishy odor and taste. [t. NL, der. Gk. *anabaínein* go up]

An·a·bap·tist (ăn′ə băp′tĭst), *n.* **1.** an adherent of a religious and social movement which arose in Europe shortly after 1520 and was distinguished by its strict requirements for church membership, insistence upon being baptized over again, rejection of infant baptism, and by its demands for social reforms. **2.** a member of a later sect or religious body holding the same doctrines. **3.** *Archaic.* Baptist (def. 1). **—An′a·bap′tism,** *n.*

an·a·bas (ăn′ə băs′), *n.* any fish of the genus *Anabas* of southern Asia, etc., as the climbing fish, *A. testudineus.* [t. NL, t. Gk., aorist participle of *anabaínein* go up]

a·nab·a·sis (ə năb′ə sĭs), *n., pl.* **-ses** (-sēz′). **1.** a march from the coast into the interior, as that of Cyrus the Younger against Artaxerxes II, described by Xenophon in his *Anabasis.* **2.** any military expedition. [t. Gk.]

an·a·bat·ic (ăn′ə băt′ĭk), *adj. Meteorol.* (of winds and air currents) moving upward or up a slope. [t. Gk.: m. s. *anabatikós* pertaining to climbing]

an·a·bi·o·sis (ăn′ə bī ō′sĭs), *n.* a bringing back to consciousness; reanimation (after apparent death). [t. NL, t. Gk.: revival] **—an·a·bi·ot·ic** (ăn′ə bī ŏt′ĭk), *adj.*

a·nab·o·lism (ə năb′ə lĭz′əm), *n. Biol.* constructive metabolism (opposed to *catabolism*). [f. s. Gk. *anabolē* a throwing up + -ISM] **—an·a·bol·ic** (ăn′ə bŏl′ĭk), *adj.*

an·a·branch (ăn′ə brănch′, -bränch′), *n. Phys. Geog.* a branch of a river which leaves the main stream and either enters it again, dries up, or sinks into the ground. [short for *anastomosing branch*]

an·a·car·di·a·ceous (ăn′ə kär′dĭ ā′shəs), *adj.* belonging to the *Anacardiaceae,* a family of trees and shrubs including the cashew, mango, pistachio, sumac, etc. [f. s. NL *Anacardiăceae* (f. *ana-* ANA- + s. Gk. *kardía* heart + -āceae -ACEAE) + -OUS]

a·nach·ro·nism (ə năk′rə nĭz′əm), *n.* **1.** a crediting of a person or thing to a time other, esp. earlier, than the actual period. **2.** something placed or occurring out of its proper time. [t. Gk.: s. *anachronismós*]

a·nach·ro·nis·tic (ə năk′rə nĭs′tĭk), *adj.* containing an anachronism. Also, **a·nach′ro·nis′ti·cal.**

a·nach·ro·nous (ə·năk'rə·nəs), *adj.* anachronistic. —a·nach'ro·nous·ly, *adv.*

an·a·cli·sis (ăn'ə·klī'sĭs), *n. Psychoanal.* the choice of an object of libidinal attachment on the basis of a resemblance to early childhood protective and parental figures. [t. Gk.: m. *anáklisis* a leaning back]

an·a·clit·ic (ăn'ə·klĭt'ĭk), *adj. Psychoanal.* exhibiting or pertaining to anaclisis.

an·a·co·lu·thi·a (ăn'ə·kə·loō'thĭ·ə), *n.* lack of grammatical sequence or coherence, esp. in the same sentence. [t.L, t.Gk.: m. *anakolūthía*] —an'a·co·lu'thic, *adj.*

an·a·co·lu·thon (ăn'ə·kə·loō'thŏn), *n., pl.* -tha (-thə) *Rhet.* a construction involving a break in grammatical sequence; a case of anacoluthia. [t. L, t. Gk.: m. *ana-kólouthon*, neut. adj., inconsequent]

an·a·con·da (ăn'ə·kŏn'də), *n.* 1. a large South American snake, *Eunectes murinus*, of the boa family. 2. any boa constrictor. [orig. unknown; ? t. Singhalese]

An·a·con·da (ăn'ə·kŏn'də), *n.* a city in SW Montana; largest copper smelter in the world. 12,054 (1960).

A·nac·re·on (ə·năk'rĭ'ən), *n.* c563–c478 B.C., Greek lyric poet known for his love poems and drinking songs.

A·nac·re·on·tic (ə·năk'rĭ·ŏn'tĭk), *adj.* Also, **anacreon·tic.** 1. of or in the manner of Anacreon. 2. convivial; amatory. —*n.* 3. (*l.c.*) an Anacreontic poem.

an·a·cru·sis (ăn'ə·kroō'sĭs), *n. Pros.* an unstressed syllable or syllable group which begins a line of verse but is not counted as part of the first foot, which properly begins with a stressed syllable. [t. L, t. Gk.: m. *aná-krousis*, der. *anakroúein* strike up]

an·a·dem (ăn'ə·dĕm'), *n. Poetic.* a garland or wreath for the head. [t. L: m. *anadēma*, t. Gk.: fillet]

an·a·di·plo·sis (ăn'ə·də·plō'sĭs), *n. Rhet.* repetition in the first part of one clause of a prominent word in the latter part of the preceding clause. [t. Gk.: repetition]

a·nad·ro·mous (ə·năd'rə·məs), *adj.* (of fishes) going from the sea up a river to spawn (contrasted with *catadromous*). [t. Gk.: m. *anádromos* running up]

a·nae·mi·a (ə·nē'mĭ'ə), *n.* anemia. —a·nae'mic, *adj.*

an·aer·obe (ăn·âr'ōb), *n.* a bacterium or other micro-organism which does not require free oxygen or is not destroyed by its absence (opposed to *aerobe*). [back formation from *anaerobia*, pl. of ANAEROBIUM]

an·aer·o·bic (ăn'âr·ō'bĭk), *adj.* 1. *Biol., Physiol.* (of organisms or tissues) requiring the absence of free oxygen or not destroyed by its absence. 2. pertaining to or caused by the absence of oxygen.

an·aer·o·bi·um (ăn'âr·ō'bĭ'əm), *n., pl.* -bia (-bĭ'ə). *Biol.* anaerobe. [NL, f. Gk.: *an-* AN-¹ + *áero-* AERO- + m. *bios* life]

an·aes·the·sia (ăn'əs·thē'zhə), *n.* anesthesia. —**an·aes·thet·ic** (ăn'əs·thĕt'ĭk), *adj., n.* —**an·aes·the·tist** (ə·nēs'thə·tĭst), *n.* —**an·aes'the·tize,** *v.t.* —**an·aes'the·ti·za'tion,** *n.*

an·a·glyph (ăn'ə·glĭf), *n.* something executed in low relief, as a cameo or an embossed ornament. [t. Gk.: s. *anáglyphos* wrought in low relief] —**an·a·glyph·ic** (ăn'-ə·glĭf'ĭk), **an·a·glyp·tic** (ăn'ə·glĭp'tĭk), *adj.*

an·a·go·ge (ăn'ə·gō'jĭ), *n.* 1. the spiritual interpretation or application of words, as of Scriptures. 2. *Theol.* the application of the types and allegories of the Old Testament to subjects of the New Testament. [t. LL. t. Gk.: a bringing up, elevation] —**an·a·gog·ic** (ăn'-ə·gŏj'ĭk), **an·a·gog'i·cal,** *adj.* —**an'a·gog'i·cal·ly,** *adv.*

an·a·gram (ăn'ə·grăm'), *n.* 1. a transposition of the letters of a word or sentence to form a new word or sentence, as *Galenus* is an anagram of *angelus.* 2. (*pl.* construed as *sing.*) a game in which the players build words by transposing or adding letters. [t. NL: m. *anagramma*, back formation from Gk. *anagrammatismós* transposition of letters] —**an·a·gram·mat·ic** (ăn'ə·grə·măt'ĭk), **an'-a·gram·mat'i·cal,** *adj.* —**an'a·gram·mat'i·cal·ly,** *adv.*

an·a·gram·ma·tize (ăn'ə·grăm'ə·tīz'), *v.t.,* -tized, -tizing. to transpose into an anagram.

An·a·heim (ā'nə·hīm), *n.* a city in SW California, SE of Los Angeles. 104,184 (1960).

a·nal (ā'nəl), *adj.* of, pertaining to, or near the anus.

anal., 1. analogous. 2. analogy. 3. analysis.

an·al·cite (ăn·ăl'sīt, ăn'əl·sīt'), *n.* a white or slightly colored zeolite mineral, generally found in crystalline form. Also, **an·al·cime** (ăn·ăl'sīm, -sīm). [f. m.s. Gk. *analkēs* weak + -ITE¹]

an·a·lects (ăn'ə·lĕkts'), *n.pl.* selected passages from the writings of an author or of different authors. Also, **an·a·lec·ta** (ăn'ə·lĕk'tə). [t. L: (m.) *analecta*, pl., t. Gk.: m. *análekta* things gathered]

an·a·lep·tic (ăn'ə·lĕp'tĭk), *Med.* —*adj.* 1. restoring; invigorating; giving strength after disease. 2. awakening, esp. from drug stupor. —*n.* 3. an analeptic remedy. [t. Gk.: m.s. *analēptikós* restorative]

anal fin, (in fishes) the median ventral unpaired fin.

an·al·ge·si·a (ăn'əl·jē'zĭ'ə, -sĭ'ə), *n. Med.* absence of sense of pain. [t. NL, t. Gk.]

an·al·ge·sic (ăn'əl·jē'zĭk, -sĭk), *Med.* —*n.* 1. a remedy that relieves or removes pain. —*adj.* 2. pertaining to or causing analgesia.

an·a·log·i·cal (ăn'ə·lŏj'ə·kəl), *adj.* based on, involving, or expressing an analogy. Also, **an'a·log'ic.**

an·a·log·i·cal·ly (ăn'ə·lŏj'ə·kəl·ĭ), *adv.* by analogy.

a·nal·o·gist (ə·năl'ə·jĭst), *n.* 1. one who employs or argues from analogy. 2. one who looks for analogies.

a·nal·o·gize (ə·năl'ə·jīz'), *v.i.,* -gized, -gizing. 1. to make use of analogy in reasoning, argument, etc. 2. to be analogous; exhibit analogy.

a·nal·o·gous (ə·năl'ə·gəs), *adj.* 1. having analogy; corresponding in some particular. 2. *Biol.* corresponding in function, but not evolved from corresponding organs, as the wings of a bee and those of a hummingbird. [t. L: m. *analogus*, t. Gk.: m. *análogos* proportionate] —**a·nal'o·gous·ly,** *adv.* —**a·nal'o·gous·ness,** *n.*

an·a·logue (ăn'ə·lŏg', -lŏg'), *n.* 1. something having analogy to something else. 2. *Biol.* an organ or part analogous to another. Also, **an'a·log'.** [t. F, t. Gk.: m. s. *análogon*]

analogue computer. See **computer.**

a·nal·o·gy (ə·năl'ə·jĭ), *n., pl.* -gies. 1. an agreement, likeness, or correspondence between the relations of things to one another; a partial similarity in particular circumstances on which a comparison may be based: *the analogy between the heart and a pump.* 2. agreement; similarity. 3. *Biol.* an analogous relationship. 4. (in linguistic change) the tendency of inflections and formations to follow existing models and regular patterns: *"adnoun" is formed on the analogy of "adverb."* 5. *Logic.* a form of reasoning in which similarities are inferred from a similarity of two or more things in certain particulars. [t. L: m.s. *analogia*, t. Gk.: orig., equality of ratios, proportion]

a·nal·y·sis (ə·năl'ə·sĭs), *n., pl.* -ses (-sēz'). 1. separation of a whole, whether a material substance or any matter of thought, into its constituent elements (opposed to *synthesis*). 2. this process as a method of studying the nature of a thing or of determining its essential features: *the grammatical analysis of a sentence.* 3. a brief presentation of essential features; an outline or summary, as of a book; a synopsis. 4. *Math.* a. an investigation based on the properties of numbers. b. the discussion of a problem by algebra as opposed to geometry. 5. *Chem.* a. intentionally produced decomposition or separation of a substance into its ingredients or elements, as to find their kind or quantity. b. the ascertainment of the kind or amount of one or more of the constituents of a substance, whether actually obtained in separate form or not. 6. psychoanalysis. [t. ML, t. Gk.: a breaking up]

analysis of variance, *Statistics.* a procedure for resolving the total variance of a set of variates into component variances, which are associated with various factors affecting the variates.

an·a·lyst (ăn'ə·lĭst), *n.* 1. one who analyzes or who is skilled in analysis. 2. a psychoana·yst.

an·a·lyt·ic (ăn'ə·lĭt'ĭk), *adj.* 1. pertaining to or proceeding by analysis (opposed to *synthetic*). 2. (of languages) characterized by the use of separate words (free forms) rather than of inflectional adjuncts (bound forms) to show syntactic relationships (opposed to *synthetic*). 3. *Logic.* (of a proposition) necessarily true because its denial involves a contradiction, as *all spinsters are unmarried.* Also, **an·a·lyt'i·cal.** [t. ML: s. *analyticus*, t. Gk.: m. *analytikós*] —**an'a·lyt'i·cal·ly,** *adv.*

analytic geometry, geometry treated by algebra, the position of any point being determined by numbers which are its coördinates with respect to a system of coördinates.

an·a·lyt·ics (ăn'ə·lĭt'ĭks), *n.* mathematical or algebraic analysis. [n. use of ANALYTIC. See -ICS]

an·a·lyze (ăn'ə·līz'), *v.t.,* -lyzed, -lyzing. 1. to resolve into elements or constituent parts; determine the elements or essential features of: *to analyze an argument.* 2. to examine critically, so as to bring out the essential elements or give the essence of: *to analyze a poem.* 3. to subject to mathematical, chemical, grammatical, etc., analysis. Also, *esp. Brit.,* **an'a·lyse'.** [back formation from ANALYSIS] —**an'a·lyz'a·ble,** *adj.* —**an'a·lyz'er,** *n.*

A·nam (ə·năm'), *n.* Annam.

an·am·ne·sis (ăn'ăm·nē'sĭs), *n.* 1. the recalling of things past; recollection. 2. *Psychiatry.* a case history. [t. NL, t. Gk.: a recalling to mind]

an·a·mor·pho·scope (ăn'ə·môr'fə·skōp'), *n.* a curved mirror or other optical device for giving a correct image of a picture or the like distorted by anamorphosis.

an·a·mor·pho·sis (ăn'ə·môr'fə·sĭs, -môr·fō'sĭs), *n., pl.* -ses (-sēz', -sēz). 1. a kind of drawing presenting a distorted image which appears in natural form under certain conditions, as when viewed at a raking angle or reflected from a curved mirror. 2. the method of producing such drawings. [t. NL, t. Gk.: a forming anew]

an·an·drous (ă·năn'drəs), *adj. Bot.* having no stamens. [t. Gk.: m. *ánandros* without a man]

An·a·ni·as (ăn'ə·nī'əs), *n.* 1. *Bible.* a man who was struck dead for lying. Acts 5:1–5. 2. a liar.

an·an·thous (ă·năn'thəs), *adj. Bot.* without flowers. [f. AN-¹ + s. Gk. *ánthos* flower + -OUS]

an·a·pest (ăn'ə·pĕst'), *n. Pros.* a foot of three syllables, two short followed by one long (quantitative meter), or two unstressed followed by one stressed (accentual meter). Thus, *for the nonce* is an accentual anapest. Also, **an'a·paest'.** [t. L: m.s. *anapaestus*, t. Gk.: m. *anápaistos* struck back, reversed (as compared with a dactyl)] —**an·a·pes'tic,** *adj., n.*

an·a·phase (ăn'ə·fāz'), *n. Biol.* the stage in mitotic cell division after cleavage of the chromosomes, in which the chromosomes move away from each other to opposite ends of the cell.

ăct, āble, dâre, ärt; ĕbb, ēqual; Yf, īce; hŏt, ōver, ôrder, oil, bŏŏk, ōōze, out; ŭp, ūse, ûrge; ə = a in alone; ch, chief; g, give; ng, ring; sh, shoe; th, thin; ᵺ, that; zh, vision. See the full key on inside cover.

a·naph·o·ra (ə năf′ə rə), *n. Rhet.* repetition of the same word or words at the beginning of two or more successive verses, clauses, or sentences. [t. L, t. Gk.: a bringing up]

an·aph·ro·dis·i·ac (ăn ăf′rə dĭz′ĭ ăk′), *Med. —adj.* **1.** capable of diminishing sexual desire. *—n.* **2.** an anaphrodisiac agent. [f. AN-¹ + APHRODISIAC]

an·a·phy·lax·is (ăn′ə fə lăk′sĭs), *n. Pathol.* increased susceptibility to a foreign protein resulting from previous exposure to it, as in serum treatment. [t. NL, f. Gk.: *ana-* ANA- + *phýlaxis* a guarding] **—an′a·phy·lac′tic** *adj.*

an·a·plas·mo·sis (ăn′ə plăz mō′sĭs), *n. Vet. Sci.* a disease of cattle caused by a blood-infecting protozoan parasite, transmitted by bloodsucking flies and ticks.

an·a·plas·tic (ăn′ə plăs′tĭk), *adj.* **1.** *Surg.* replacing lost tissue or parts, or remedying natural defects, as by transplanting. **2.** *Pathol.* **a.** (of cells) having reverted to a more primitive form. **b.** (of tumors) having a high degree of malignancy.

an·a·plas·ty (ăn′ə plăs′tĭ), *n.* anaplastic surgery. [f. s. Gk. *anáplastos* plastic + -Y³]

an·ap·tot·ic (ăn′ăp tŏt′ĭk), *adj.* (of languages) tending to become uninflected, in accordance with a theory that languages evolve from uninflected to inflected and back. [f. AN-³ + s. Gk. *áptōtos* indeclinable + -IC]

an·arch (ăn′ärk), *n.* an anarchist.

an·ar·chic (ăn är′kĭk), *adj.* **1.** of, like, or tending to anarchy. **2.** advocating anarchy. **3.** lawless. Also, **an·ar′chi·cal.** **—an·ar′chi·cal·ly,** *adv.*

an·ar·chism (ăn′ər kĭz′əm), *n.* **1.** the doctrine (advocated under various forms) urging the abolition of government and governmental restraint as the indispensable condition of political and social liberty. **2.** the methods or practices of anarchists. **—an·ar·chis·tic** (ăn′ər kĭs′tĭk), *adj.*

an·ar·chist (ăn′ər kĭst), *n.* **1.** one who advocates anarchy as a political idea; a believer in an anarchic theory of society, esp. an adherent of the social theory of Proudhon, Bakunin, or Kropotkin. **2.** one who seeks to overturn by violence all constituted forms and institutions of society and government, with no purpose of establishing any other system of order in the place of that destroyed. **3.** any person who promotes disorder or excites revolt against an established rule, law, or custom. [f. s. Gk. *ánarchos* without a ruler + -IST]

an·ar·chy (ăn′ər kĭ), *n.* **1.** a state of society without government or law. **2.** political and social disorder due to absence of governmental control. **3.** absence of government or governmental restraint. **4.** a theory which regards the union of order with the absence of all direct or coercive government as the political ideal. **5.** confusion in general; disorder. [t. Gk.: m.s. *anarchía* lack of a ruler]

an·ar·throus (ăn är′thrəs), *adj.* **1.** *Zool.* without joints or articulated limbs. **2.** (esp. in Greek grammar) used without the article. [t. Gk.: m. *ánarthros*]

an·a·sar·ca (ăn′ə sär′kə), *n. Pathol.* a pronounced generalized dropsy. [? m. Gk. phrase *aná sárka* up flesh] **—an/a·sar′cous,** *adj.*

an·as·tig·mat·ic (ăn′ə stĭg măt′ĭk, ă năs′tĭg-), *adj.* (of a lens) not astigmatic; forming point images of a point object located off the lens axis.

a·nas·to·mose (ə năs′tə mōz′), *v.t., v.i.,* **-mosed, -mosing.** *Physiol.* to communicate or connect by anastomosis.

a·nas·to·mo·sis (ə năs′tə mō′sĭs), *n., pl.* **-ses** (-sēz). **1.** *Physiol.* communication between blood vessels by means of collateral channels. **2.** *Biol.* connection between parts of any branching system. [t. NL, t. Gk.: opening] **—a·nas·to·mot·ic** (ə năs′tə mŏt′ĭk), *adj.*

a·nas·tro·phe (ə năs′trə fĭ), *n. Rhet.* inversion of the usual order of words. [t. L, t. Gk.: a turning back]

anat., **1.** anatomical. **2.** anatomy.

an·a·tase (ăn′ə tāz′), *n.* a black to brown mineral, titanium dioxide, TiO₂, occurring in octahedral crystals; octahedrite. [t. F, t. Gk.: m. *anátasis* extension]

a·nath·e·ma (ə năth′ə mə), *n., pl.* **-mas. 1.** a formal ecclesiastical curse involving excommunication. **2.** any imprecation of divine punishment. **3.** a curse; an execration. **4.** a person or thing accursed or consigned to damnation or destruction. **5.** a person or thing detested or loathed. [t. LL, t. Gk.: something devoted (to evil)]

a·nath·e·ma·tize (ə năth′ə mə tīz′), *v.,* **-tized, -tizing.** *—v.t.* **1.** to pronounce an anathema against; denounce; curse. *—v.i.* **2.** to pronounce anathemas; curse. **—a·nath′e·ma·ti·za′tion,** *n.*

an·a·tine (ăn′ə tīn′, -tĭn), *adj.* **1.** of or pertaining to the *Anatidae,* the duck family. **2.** resembling a duck; ducklike. [t. L: m.s. *anatínus*]

An·a·to·li·a (ăn′ə tō′lĭ ə), *n.* a vast plateau between the Black and the Mediterranean seas: in ancient usage, synonymous with the peninsula of Asia Minor; in modern usage, applied to Turkey in Asia.

An·a·to·li·an (ăn′ə tō′lĭ ən), *adj.* **1.** of Anatolia. **2.** of, or belonging to, a group or family of languages that includes cuneiform Hittite and its nearest congeners.

an·a·tom·i·cal (ăn′ə tŏm′ə kəl), *adj.* pertaining to anatomy. Also, **an/a·tom′ic. —an/a·tom′i·cal·ly,** *adv.*

a·nat·o·mist (ə năt′ə mĭst), *n.* an expert in anatomy.

a·nat·o·mize (ə năt′ə mīz′), *v.t.,* **-mized, -mizing. 1.** to dissect, as a plant or an animal, to show the position, structure, and relation of the parts; display the

anatomy of. 2. to analyze or examine very minutely. **—a·nat′o·mi·za′tion,** *n.*

a·nat·o·my (ə năt′ə mĭ), *n., pl.* **-mies. 1.** the structure of an animal or plant, or of any of its parts. **2.** the science of the structure of animals and plants. **3.** dissection of animals or plants, or their parts, for study of structure, position, etc. **4.** an anatomical subject or model. **5.** a skeleton. **6.** any analysis or minute examination. [t. LL: m.s. *anatomia,* t. Gk., var. of *anatomē* dissection; r. ME *anothomia,* t. ML]

a·nat·ro·pous (ə năt′rə pəs), *adj. Bot.* (of an ovule, inverted at an early stage of growth, so that the micropyle is turned toward the funicle, the chalaza being situated at the opposite end. [t. NL: m. *anatropus* inverted. See ANA-, -TROPOUS]

a·nat·to (ə năt′ō, ä nä′tō), *n.* annatto.

An·ax·ag·o·ras (ăn′ăk săg′ə rəs), *n.* 500?–428 B.C., Greek philosopher.

A·nax·i·man·der (ə năk′sə măn′dər), *n.* 611?–547? B.C., Greek philosopher.

anc., ancient.

-ance, a suffix of nouns denoting action, state, or quality, or something exemplifying one of these, often corresponding to adjectives in *-ant,* as *brilliance, distance,* or formed directly from verbs, as in *assistance, defiance.* [ME *-ance,* t. F, g. L *-antia, -entia,* orig. ppr. endings]

an·ces·tor (ăn′sĕs tər), *n.* **1.** one from whom a person is descended, usually distantly; a forefather; a progenitor. **2.** *Biol.* the actual or hypothetical form or stock of an earlier and presumably lower type, from which any organized being is known or inferred to have developed. **3.** *Law.* one from whom an inheritance is derived (correlative of *heir*). [ME *ancestre,* t. OF, g. L *antecessor* predecessor] **—an·ces·tress** (ăn′sĕs trĭs), *n. fem.*

an·ces·tral (ăn sĕs′trəl), *adj.* pertaining to ancestors; descending or claimed from ancestors: *an ancestral home.* **—an·ces′tral·ly,** *adv.* **—Syn.** hereditary, inherited.

an·ces·try (ăn′sĕs trĭ), *n., pl.* **-tries. 1.** ancestral descent. **2.** honorable descent. **3.** a series of ancestors.

An·chi·ses (ăn kī′sēz), *n. Classical Legend.* a prince of Troy, father of Aeneas.

an·chor (ăng′kər), *n.* **1.** a device for holding boats, vessels, floating bridges, etc., in place. **2.** any similar device for holding fast or checking motion. **3.** a metallic strap or belt built into masonry to hold facing or other materials. **4.** a means of stability: *hope is his anchor.* **5.** *Mil.* a key position in defense lines. **6. at anchor,** anchored. **7. cast anchor,** to put down or drop the anchor. **8. weigh anchor,** to take up the anchor. *—v.t.* **9.** to hold fast by an anchor. **10.** to fix or fasten; affix firmly. *—v.i.* **11.** to drop anchor; lie or ride at anchor. **12.** to keep hold or be firmly fixed. [ME *anker, ancre,* OE *ancor,* t. L: s. *ancora,* t. Gk.: m. *ánkȳra*] **—an′chor·less,** *adj.* **—an′chor·like′,** *adj.*

an·chor·age (ăng′kər ĭj), *n.* **1.** a place for anchoring. **2.** a charge for anchoring. **3.** act of anchoring. **4.** state of being anchored. **5.** that to which anything is fastened. **6.** a means of anchoring or making fast.

An·chor·age (ăng′kər ĭj), *n.* a seaport in S Alaska: earthquake 1964. 44,237 (1960).

an·cho·ress (ăng′kə rĭs), *n.* a female anchorite.

an·cho·ret (ăng′kə rĭt, -rĕt′), *n.* anchorite. [t. LL: m.s. *anachōrēta* (t. Gk.: m. *anachōrētēs* a recluse) by assoc. with obs. *anchor* hermit (OE *ancora*)] **—an·cho·ret·ic** (ăng′kə rĕt′ĭk), *adj.*

an·cho·rite (ăng′kə rīt′), *n.* one who has retired to a solitary place for a life of religious seclusion; a hermit. [ME *ancorite,* t. ML: m. s. *anachōrīta,* var. of LL *anachōrēta*] **—an·cho·rit·ic** (ăng′kə rĭt′ĭk), *adj.*

an·cho·vy (ăn′chō vĭ, -chə vĭ, ăn chō′vĭ), *n., pl.* **-vies. 1.** a small herringlike marine fish, *Engraulis encrasicholus,* abundant in South Europe, much used pickled and in the form of a salt paste. **2.** any fish of the same family (*Engraulidae*). **3.** *U.S.* any smelt. [t. Sp. and Pg.: m. *anchova,* prob. t. d. It. (Genoese): m. *anciova,* g. LL *apiuva,* t. Gk.: m. *aphýē*]

anchovy pear, 1. the fruit of a West Indian tree, *Grias cauliflora,* often pickled, and somewhat resembling the mango. **2.** the tree.

An·chu·sa (ăng kū′sə), *n.* a boraginaceous genus of rough hairy plants including the oxtongue. [t. L, t. Gk.: m. *ánchousa* alkanet]

an·chu·sin (ăng kū′sĭn), *n.* a red coloring matter obtained from the root of the alkanet, *Alkanna tinctoria.*

an·chy·lose (ăng′kə lōs′), *v.t., v.i.,* **-losed, -losing.** ankylose. **—an′chy·lo′sis,** *n.* **—an·chy·lot·ic** (ăng′kə lŏt′ĭk), *adj.*

an·cienne no·blesse (ăɴ syĕn′ nô blĕs′), *French.* the ancient nobility, esp. of the ancien régime.

an·cien ré·gime (ăɴ syăɴ′ rĕ zhēm′), *French.* **1.** the political and social system of France before the Revolution of 1789. **2.** the old system of government.

an·cient¹ (ān′shənt), *adj.* **1.** of or in time long past, esp. before the end of the Western Roman Empire, A.D. 476: *ancient history.* **2.** dating from a remote period; of great age. **3.** *Archaic.* very old (applied to persons). **4.** *Archaic.* venerable. **5.** *Law.* of 30 years' standing, or sometimes a lesser period, as 20 years: *in ancient matters the normal requirements of proof are relaxed.* *—n.* **6.** a person who lived in ancient times, esp. one of the ancient Greeks, Romans, Hebrews, etc. **7.** (*usually pl.*) one of the classical writers of antiquity. **8.** *Archaic.* an old man. [ME *auncien,* t. OF: m. *ancien,* g. LL *antiānus*

former, old, der. L *ante* before] —an′cient·ness, *n.*
—Syn. 2. ANCIENT, ANTIQUATED, ANTIQUE, OLD-FASHIONED refer to something dating from the past. ANCIENT implies existence or first occurrence in the past: *an ancient custom.* ANTIQUATED connotes something too old or no longer useful: *an antiquated building.* ANTIQUE suggests a curious or pleasing quality in something old: *antique furniture.* OLD-FASHIONED may disparage something as being out of date or may approve something old as being superior: *an old-fashioned hat, old-fashioned courtesy.* —Ant. 2. new.

an·cient² (ăn′shənt), *n.* *Obs.* 1. the bearer of a flag. 2. a flag, banner, or standard; an ensign. [var. of ENSIGN]

an·cient·ly (ăn′shənt lǐ), *adv.* in ancient times; of old.

Ancient of Days, the eternal Supreme Being.

an·cient·ry (ăn′shən trǐ), *n.* *Archaic.* 1. ancient character or style. 2. ancient times. 3. ancient lineage.

an·cil·lar·y (ăn′sə lĕr′ĭ), *adj.* accessory; auxiliary. [t. L: m. *ancillāris* pertaining to a handmaid]

an·cip·i·tal (ăn sĭp′ə tal), *adj.* *Bot., Zool.* two-edged: *ancipital stems.* [f. s. L *anceps* two-headed + -AL¹]

An·co·hu·ma (äng′kō ōō′mä), *n.* See **Sorata, Mount.**

an·con (ăng′kŏn), *n., pl.* **ancones** (ăng kō′nēz). 1. *Archit.* any projection, as a console, supporting a cornice or the like. 2. *Anat.* the elbow. [t. L, t. Gk.: m. *ankōn* a bend, the elbow] —an·co·ne·al (ăng kō′nĭ al), *adj.*

An·co·na (ăn kō′nä), *n.* a seaport in E Italy, on the Adriatic. 90,000 (est. 1954).

-ancy, an equivalent of **-ance,** used chiefly in nouns denoting state or quality, as in *buoyancy.* [t. L: m.s. *-antia*]

an·cy·los·to·mi·a·sis (ăn′sə lŏs′tə mī′ə sĭs), *n.* hookworm disease. Also, **ankylostomiasis.** [f. NL *Ancylostom(a)* genus of hookworms (f. Gk.: *ankýlo(s)* bent, hooked + *stóma* mouth) + -IASIS]

and (ănd; *unstressed* ənd, ən), *conj.* 1. with; along with; together with; besides; also; moreover (used to connect grammatically coördinate words, phrases, or clauses): *pens and pencils.* 2. as well as: *nice and warm.* 3. *Colloq.* to (used between verbs): *try and do it.* 4. *Archaic or Literary.* also; then (used to introduce a sentence, implying continuation): *And he said unto Moses.* 5. *Archaic or Dial.* if: *and you please.* [OE; akin to G *und*]

and., andante.

An·da·lu·si·a (ăn′də lōō′zhə, -shĭ ə), *n.* a region in S Spain, bordering on the Atlantic and the Mediterranean. 33,712 sq. mi. Spanish, **An·da·lu·cí·a** (än′dä lōō thē′ä). —An′da·lu′sian, *adj.*, *n.*

an·da·lu·site (ăn′də lōō′sīt), *n.* a mineral, aluminum silicate, Al₂SiO₅, found in schistose rocks. [named after ANDALUSIA. See -ITE¹]

An·da·man and Nic·o·bar Islands (ăn′də mən; nĭk′ə bär′), two groups of islands in the Bay of Bengal, SW of Burma, a centrally administered territory of India. 30,963 (1951); 3143 sq. mi. *Cap.*: Port Blair.

Andaman Islands, a group of islands in the E part of the Bay of Bengal, W of the Malay Peninsula. 18,939 pop. (1951); 2508 sq. mi.

an·dan·te (ăn dän′tǐ; *It.* än dän′tĕ), *Music.* —*adj., adv.* 1. moderately slow and even. —*n.* 2. an andante movement or piece. [It.: lit., walking]

an·dan·ti·no (ăn′dän tē′nō; *It.* än′dän tē′nô), *adj., adv., n., pl.* **-nos.** *Music.* —*adj., adv.* 1. slightly faster than andante. —*n.* 2. an andantino movement or piece. [It., dim. of *andante* ANDANTE]

An·de·an (ăn dē′ən, ăn′dĭ-), *adj.* of or like the Andes.

An·der·lecht (ăn′dər lĕкHт′), *n.* a city in central Belgium, near Brussels. 88,326 (est. 1952).

An·der·sen (ăn′dər sən), *n.* **Hans Christian** (hänz krĭs′chən), 1805–75, Danish author. esp. of fairy tales.

An·der·son (ăn′dər sən), *n.* 1. **Marian,** born 1908, U.S. contralto. 2. **Maxwell,** 1888–1959, U.S. dramatist. 3. **Sherwood,** 1876–1941, U.S. short-story writer and novelist. 4. a city in central Indiana. 49,061 (1960).

An·der·son·ville (ăn′dər sən vĭl′), *n.* a village in SW Georgia: site of a Confederate military prison.

An·des (ăn′dēz), *n.pl.* a lofty mountain system in W South America, extending ab. 4500 mi. from N Colombia and Venezuela S to Cape Horn. Highest peak (of the western hemisphere), Aconcagua, 22,834 ft.

an·des·ite (ăn′də zīt′), *n.* a volcanic rock composed essentially of plagioclase feldspar, resembling trachyte in appearance. [f. ANDES + -ITE¹]

An·dhra Pra·desh (än′drä prə dāsh′), a state in SE India, formed from Madras and Hyderabad states. 31,260,000 (est. 1956); 105,963 sq. mi. *Cap.*: Hyderabad.

and·i·ron (ănd′ī′ərn), *n.* one of a pair of metallic stands, usually of iron, used to support wood burned in an open fireplace. [ME *andyre,* t. OF: m. *andier,* ? t. Gallic: m. *andera* young cow (through use of cows' heads as decorations on andirons); *-iron* by assoc. with *iron*]

An·di·zhan (än′dǐ zhän′), *n.* a city in the SW Soviet Union in Asia, in Uzbek Republic. 115,000 (est. 1956).

and/or, and *or* or: *history and/or science* (meaning "history and science" or "history or science").

An·dor·ra (ăn dôr′ə, -dôr′ə; *Sp.* än dôr′rä), *n.* a small republic in the E Pyrenees between France and Spain, under the joint suzerainty of France and the Spanish Bishop of Urgel. 5664 (1954); 191 sq. mi. *Cap.*: Andorra. French, **An·dorre** (än dôr′).

andr-, var. of **andro-,** used before vowels, as in *androecium.*

an·dra·dite (ăn′drə dīt′), *n.* a mineral, calcium-iron garnet, Ca₃Fe₂Si₃O₁₂, occurring in brown, green, or black crystals. [f. D′*Andrada* (Pg. mineralogist) + -ITE¹]

An·drás·sy (än dräs′ĭ; *Hung.* ŏn′drä shǐ), *n.* 1. **Count Julius,** 1823–90, Hungarian statesman. 2. his son, **Count Julius,** (Gyula) 1860–1929, Hungarian statesman.

An·dré (än′drā, än′drĭ), *n.* **Major John,** 1751–80, British officer hanged as spy in American Revolution.

An·dre·a del Sar·to (än drě′ä děl sär′tô). See **Sar·to.**

An·dre·a·nof Islands (än′drě ä′nŏf), a group of islands in the W part of the Aleutian Islands. 1432 sq. mi.

An·dre·ev (än drě′yěf), *n.* **Leonid Nikolaevich** (lĕ ō-nēt′ nǐ kō lä′yə vĭch), 1871–1919, Russian short-story writer, dramatist, and novelist. Also, **An·dre′yev.**

An·drew (ăn′drōō), *n.* *Bible.* one of the twelve apostles of Jesus. Mark 3:18; John 1:40–42.

An·drews (ăn′drōōz), *n.* **Roy Chapman,** 1884–1960, U. S. naturalist, explorer, and author.

andro-, *Biol.* a word element meaning "man," "male," as contrasted with "female," as in *androsphinx.* Also, **andr-.** [t. Gk., comb. form of *anēr* man, male]

An·dro·cles (ăn′drə klēz′), *n.* *Rom. Legend.* a slave spared in the arena by a lion from whose foot he had years before extracted a thorn. Also, **An·dro·clus** (ăn′drə kləs).

an·dro·clin·i·um (ăn′drə klĭn′ĭ əm), *n.* *Bot.* clinandrium.

an·droe·ci·um (ăn drē′shĭ əm), *n., pl.* **-cia** (-shĭ ə). *Bot.* the stamens of a flower collectively. [t. NL, f. Gk.: *andr-* ANDR- + m. *oikion* house] —an·droe′cial, *adj.*

an·dro·gen (ăn′drə jən), *n.* *Biochem.* any substance, natural or synthetic, which promotes masculine characteristics. —an·dro·gen·ic (ăn′drə jĕn′ĭk), *adj.*

an·drog·y·nous (ăn drŏj′ə nəs), *adj.* 1. *Bot.* having staminate and pistillate flowers in the same inflorescence. 2. being both male and female; hermaphroditic. [t. L: m. *androgynus,* t. Gk.: m. *andrógynos* hermaphrodite] —an·drog′y·ny, *n.*

An·drom·a·che (ăn drŏm′ə kē′), *n.* *Gk. Legend.* the wife of Hector and mother of Astyanax.

An·drom·e·da (ăn drŏm′ə də), *n.* 1. *Gk. Myth.* the daughter of Cassiopeia and wife of Perseus, by whom she was rescued from a sea monster. 2. *Astron.* a northern constellation containing within its borders the external stellar system known as the Great Nebula in Andromeda.

An·dros (ăn′drəs), *n.* **Sir Edmund,** 1637–1714, British governor in the American Colonies.

An·dros·cog·gin (ăn′drə skŏg′ĭn), *n.* a river flowing from NE New Hampshire through SW Maine into the Kennebec river. 171 mi.

an·dro·sphinx (ăn′drə sfĭngks′), *n.* a sphinx with the head of a man.

an·dros·ter·one (ăn drŏs′tə rōn′), *n.* *Biochem.* a sex hormone, C₁₉H₃₀O₂, usually present in male urine.

-androus, a word element meaning "male," as in *polyandrous.* [t. NL: m. *-andrus,* t. Gk.: m. *-andros* of a man]

An·dva·ri (än′dwä rē′), *n.* *Scand. Myth.* a dwarf who owned a great treasure (the hoard of the Nibelungs). It was taken from him by Loki.

-ane, 1. a noun suffix used in chemical terms, esp. names of hydrocarbons of the methane or paraffin series, as *decane, pentane, propane.* 2. an adjective suffix used when a similar form (with a different meaning) exists in **-an,** as *human, humane,* etc. [t. L: m. *-ānus,* adj. suffix]

a·near (ə nĭr′), *adv., prep.* *Poetic.* near.

an·ec·dot·age (ăn′ĭk dō′tĭj), *n.* 1. *Rare.* anecdotes collectively. 2. *Colloq. or Humorous.* old age.

an·ec·do·tal (ăn′ĭk dō′təl, ăn′ĭk dō′təl), *adj.* pertaining to, marked by, or consisting of anecdotes.

an·ec·dote (ăn′ĭk dōt′), *n.* a short narrative of a particular incident or occurrence of an interesting nature: *anecdotes of the president's childhood.* [t. ML: m. s. *anecdota,* t. Gk.: m. *anékdota* things unpublished]

an·ec·dot·ic (ăn′ĭk dŏt′ĭk), *adj.* 1. anecdotal. 2. given to relating anecdotes. Also, **an·ec·dot′i·cal.**

an·ec·dot·ist (ăn′ĭk dō′tĭst), *n.* a relater of anecdotes.

a·nele (ə nēl′), *v.t.,* **aneled, aneling.** *Archaic.* to administer extreme unction to. [ME *anelien,* f. *an-* on + *elien* to oil, der. OE *ele* oil, t. L: m. *oleum*]

a·ne·mi·a (ə nē′mĭ ə), *n.* *Pathol.* a quantitative deficiency of the hemoglobin, often accompanied by a reduced number of red blood cells, and causing pallor, weakness, and breathlessness. Also, **anaemia.** [NL, t. Gk.: m. *anaimia* want of blood]

a·ne·mic (ə nē′mĭk), *adj.* suffering from anemia. Also, **anaemic.**

anemo-, a word element meaning "wind," as in *anemometer.* [t. Gk., comb. form of *ánemos* wind]

a·nem·o·graph (ə něm′ə grăf′, -gräf′), *n.* *Meteorol.* an instrument for measuring and recording the velocity, force, or direction of the wind. —a·nem·o·graph·ic, *adj.*

an·e·mog·ra·phy (ăn′ĭ mŏg′rə fĭ), *n.* *Meteorol.* the art of measuring and recording the velocity and direction of the wind.

an·e·mom·e·ter (ăn′ə mŏm′ə tər), *n.* *Meteorol.* an instrument for indicating wind velocity. —an·e·mo·met·ric (ăn′ə mō mĕt′rĭk), an′e·mo·met′ri·cal, *adj.*

an·e·mom·e·try (ăn′ə mŏm′ə trĭ), *n.* *Meteorol.* determination of the velocity of the wind by an anemometer.

ăct, āble, dâre, ärt; ĕbb, ēqual; ĭf, īce; hŏt, ōver, ôrder, oil, bŏŏk, ōōze, out; ŭp, ūse, ûrge; ə = a in alone; ch, chief; g, give; ng, ring; sh, shoe; th, thin; ᵺ, that; zh, vision. See the full key on inside cover.

a·nem·o·ne (ənĕm′ənē′), *n.* **1.** any plant of the ranunculaceous genus *Anemone*, esp. *A. quinquefolia*, a spring wild flower with slender stem and delicate whitish blossoms. **2.** a common marine animal of the phylum *Coelenterata*, of sedentary habits, with one or more circles of tentacles surrounding the mouth. [t. L, t. Gk.: wind flower]

an·e·moph·i·lous (ăn′ə mŏf′ələs), *adj. Bot.* (of seed plants) fertilized by wind-borne pollen. [f. ANEMO- + -PHILOUS; lit., wind-loving] —**an′e·moph′i·ly,** *n.*

a·nem·o·scope (ənĕm′əskōp′), *n. Meteorol.* any device showing the existence and direction of the wind.

a·nenst (ənĕnst′), *prep.* anent. [earlier *anent(i)st*, var. (with excrescent *-t*) of ME *anentes*, gen. of ANENT]

a·nent (ənĕnt′), *prep.* **1.** *Archaic and Scot.* in regard to; concerning. **2.** *Brit. Dial.* in line with; beside. [var. (with excrescent *-t*) of ME *anen*, OE *on emn, on efen* on even (ground) with, beside]

an·er·gy (ăn′ər jǐ), *n.* **1.** *Pathol.* deficiency of energy. **2.** *Immunol.* lack of immunity to an antigen. [t. NL: m. s. *anergia*. f. Gk.: *an-* AN-[1] + *-ergia* work]

an·er·oid (ăn′ə roid′), *adj.* **1.** using no fluid. —*n.* **2.** an aneroid barometer. [f. A-[6] + s. Gk. *nērós* liquid + -OID]

aneroid barometer, an instrument for measuring atmospheric pressure and, indirectly, altitude, by registering the pressure exerted on the elastic top of a box or chamber exhausted of air.

an·es·the·sia (ăn′əs thē′zhə), *n.* **1.** *Med.* general or local insensibility, as to pain and other sensation, induced by certain drugs. **2.** *Pathol.* general loss of the senses of feeling, such as pain, heat, cold, touch, and other less common varieties of sensation. Also, **anaesthesia.** [t. NL, t. Gk.: m. *anaisthēsia* insensibility]

an·es·the·si·ol·o·gy (ăn′ěs thē′zǐ ŏl′ə jǐ), *n.* the science of administering anesthetics. [f. ANESTHESI(A) + -O + -LOGY —**an′es·the′si·ol′o·gist,** *n.*

an·es·thet·ic (ăn′əs thĕt′ĭk), *n.* **1.** a substance such as ether, chloroform, cocaine, etc., that produces anesthesia. —*adj.* **2.** pertaining to or causing physical insensibility. **3.** insensitive. Also, **anaesthetic.**

an·es·the·tist (ənĕs′thə tĭst), *n.* a person who administers anesthetics, usually a specially trained doctor or nurse. Also, **anaesthetist.**

an·es·the·tize (ənĕs′thə tīz′), *v.t.,* **-tized, -tizing.** to render physically insensible, as by an anesthetic. Also, **anaesthetize.** —**a·nes′the·ti·za′tion,** *n.*

an·e·thole (ăn′ə thōl′), *n. Chem.* a compound, $C_{10}H_{12}O$, found in anise and fennel oils, and used in perfumes and as an antiseptic and carminative, etc. [f. s. Gk. *ánēthon* anise (prop., dill) + -OLE]

A·ne·to (ä nĕ′tô), *n.* Spanish name of Néthou, Pic de.

an·eu·rysm (ăn′yərĭz′əm), *n. Pathol.* a permanent cardiac or arterial dilatation usually caused by weakening of the vessel wall by diseases such as syphilis or arteriosclerosis. Also, **an′eu·rism.** [t. Gk.: m. *aneúrysma* dilation] —**an′eu·rys′mal,** an/eu·ris′mal, *adj.*

a·new (ənū′, ənōō′), *adv.* **1.** over again: once more: *to write a story anew.* **2.** in a new form or manner. [ME *onew*, etc., OE *of-niowe, of-niowe*, t. OE *edniwe* once more]

an·frac·tu·os·i·ty (ăn frăk′chŏō′ə tǐ), *n., pl.* **-ties.** **1.** state or quality of being anfractuous. **2.** a channel, crevice, or passage full of windings and turnings.

an·frac·tu·ous (ăn frăk′chŏō əs), *adj.* characterized by windings and turnings; sinuous; circuitous: *an anfractuous path.* Also, **an·frac·tu·ose** (ăn frăk′chŏō ōs′). [t. L.: m. s. *anfractuōsus* winding]

An·ga·ra (än′gär ä′), *n.* a river in the S Soviet Union in Asia, rising NE of Lake Baikal and flowing through it NW to the Yenisei river: called the Upper Tunguska in its lower course. ab. 1300 mi.

an·ga·ry (ăng′gərǐ), *n. Internat. Law.* the right of a belligerent state to seize and use the property of neutrals for purposes of warfare, subject to payment of full compensation. [t. L: m. s. *angaria* forced service (to a lord), t. Gk.: m. *angareía* post service]

an·gel (ān′jəl), *n.* **1.** *Theol.* one of a class of spiritual beings, attendants of God (in medieval angelology divided, according to their rank, into nine orders, ranging from highest to lowest as follows: seraphim, cherubim, thrones, dominations or dominions, virtues, powers, principalities or princedoms, archangels, angels). **2.** a conventional representation of such a being, in human form, with wings. **3.** a messenger, esp. of God. **4.** a person, esp. a woman, who resembles an angel in beauty, kindliness, etc. **5.** an attendant or guardian spirit. **6.** *Colloq.* a financial backer of a play, campaign, actor, candidate, etc. **7.** an English gold coin, struck from 1470 to 1634, in value from 6s. 8d. to 10s., bearing a figure of the archangel Michael overcoming the dragon. [ME and OE, var. of *engel*, pre-E *angil*, t. L: m.s. *angelus*, t. Gk.: m. *ángelos*, orig., messenger]

an·gel·fish (ān′jəl fǐsh′), *n., pl.* **-fishes,** (*esp. collectively*) **-fish.** **1.** any shark of the genus *Squatina*, of Atlantic and Pacific waters, with a depressed flat body and large, winglike pectoral fins. **2.** any of several brightly colored marine fishes, as *Chaetodipterus faber* and *Angelichthys ciliaris.*

angel food cake, a delicate white cake made without shortening. Also, **angel cake.**

an·gel·ic (ănjĕl′ĭk), *adj.* **1.** of or belonging to angels. **2.** like or befitting an angel; saintly. Also, **an·gel′i·cal.** —**an·gel′i·cal·ly,** *adv.*

an·gel·i·ca (ănjĕl′ə kə), *n.* **1.** any plant of the genus

Angelica, tall umbelliferous plants found in both hemispheres, esp. *A. Archangelica* (*Archangelica officinalis*), cultivated in Europe for its aromatic odor and medicinal root and for its stalks, which are candied; archangel. **2.** the candied stalks. **3.** (*cap.*) a sweet white California wine. [t. ML: angelic (herb)]

angelica tree, *U.S.* the Hercules' club (def. 2).

An·ge·li·co (än jĕ′lē kô′), *n.* **Fra** (frä), (*Giovanni da Fiesole*) 1387–1455, Italian painter.

An·gell (ăn′jəl), *n.* **1. James Rowland** (rō′lənd), 1869–1949, U. S. educator. **2. Sir Norman,** (*Ralph Norman Angell Lane*) born 1874, British writer.

angelo-, a combining form of **angel.**

an·gel·ol·o·gy (ăn′jə lŏl′ə jǐ), *n.* doctrine concerning angels.

an·gel·shark (ān′jəl shärk′), *n.* angelfish (def. 1).

An·ge·lus (ăn′jə ləs), *n. Rom. Cath. Ch.* **1.** a devotion in memory of the Annunciation. **2.** the bell (**Angelus bell**) tolled in the morning, at noon, and in the evening, to indicate the time when the Angelus is to be recited. [t. LL (the first word of the recitation). See ANGEL]

an·ger (ăng′gər), *n.* **1.** a revengeful passion or emotion directed against one who inflicts a real or supposed wrong; wrath; ire. **2.** *Obs. or Dial.* pain or smart, as of a sore. **3.** *Obs.* grief; trouble. —*v.t.* **4.** to excite to anger or wrath. **5.** *Obs. or Dial.* to cause to smart; inflame. [ME, t. Scand.; cf. Icel. *angr* grief, sorrow]
—**Syn. 1.** displeasure; resentment, exasperation. ANGER, FURY, INDIGNATION, RAGE imply deep and strong feelings aroused by injury, injustice, wrong, etc. ANGER is a sudden violent displeasure accompanied by an impulse to retaliate: *a burst of anger.* INDIGNATION, a more formal word, implies deep and justified anger, often directed against something unworthy: *indignation at cruelty or against corruption.* RAGE is vehement anger: *rage at being frustrated.* FURY is rage so great that it resembles insanity: *the fury of a woman scorned.*

an·ger·ly (ăng′gər lǐ), *adv.* *Archaic.* angrily.

An·gers (ăn′jərz, äng′gärz; *Fr.* än zhě′), *n.* a city in W France. 102,142 (1954).

An·ge·vin (ăn′jə vǐn), *adj.* **1.** of or from Anjou. **2.** relating to the counts of Anjou or their descendants, esp. those who ruled in England, or to the period when they ruled. —*n.* **3.** an inhabitant of Anjou. **4.** a member of an Angevin royal house, esp. that of the Plantagenets in England. Also, **An·ge·vine** (ăn′jə vǐn, -vīn′). [t. F]

an·gi·na (ăn jī′nə; *in Med. often* ăn′jə-), *n. Pathol.* **1.** any inflammatory affection of the throat or fauces, as quinsy, croup, mumps, etc. **2.** angina pectoris. [t. L: quinsy, lit., strangling. Cf. Gk. *anchónē*]

angina pec·to·ris (pĕk′tərǐs), *Pathol.* a syndrome characterized by paroxysmal, constricting pain below the sternum, most easily precipitated by exertion or excitement and caused by ischemia of the heart muscle, usually due to a coronary artery disease, such as arteriosclerosis. [NL: angina of the chest]

angio-, a word element meaning "vessel," or "container," as in *angiology.* [t. NL, t. Gk.: m. *angeio-*, comb. form of *angeíon* vessel]

an·gi·ol·o·gy (ăn′jǐ ŏl′ə jǐ), *n.* the part of the science of anatomy that deals with blood vessels and lymphatics.

an·gi·o·ma (ăn′jǐ ō′mə), *n., pl.* **-mas, -mata** (-mə tə). a tumor consisting chiefly of dilated or newly formed blood or lymph vessels. [f. ANGIO-+-OMA] —**an·gi·om·a·tous** (ăn′jǐ ŏm′ə təs, -ō′mə-), *adj.*

an·gi·o·sperm (ăn′jǐ ə spûrm′), *n.* a plant having its seeds enclosed in an ovary (opposed to *gymnosperm*). —**an′gi·o·sper′mous,** *adj.*

Ang·kor (ăng′kôr), *n.* a ruined city in NW Cambodia (formerly part of French Indochina); the site of **Angkor Wat** (wät), an ancient Khmer temple.

an·gle[1] (ăng′gəl), *n., v.,* **-gled, -gling.** —*n.* **1.** *Geom.* a. the space within two lines or three planes diverging from a common point, or within two planes diverging from a common line. **b.** the figure so formed. **c.** the amount of rotation needed to bring one line or plane into coincidence with another. **2.** an angular projection; a projecting corner: *the angles of a building.* **3.** a point of view; standpoint: *a new angle on the problem.* **4.** an aspect; side; phase: *to consider all angles of the question.* —*v.t., v.i.* **5.** to move or bend in angles. [ME, t. F, g, L *angulus*]

Right Angle (90°)   Acute Angle (60°)   Acute Angle (30°)

Angles

an·gle[2] (ăng′gəl), *v.,* **-gled, -gling,** *n.* —*v.i.* **1.** to fish with hook and line. **2.** to try by artful means to get: *to angle for a compliment.* [v. use of n.] —*n.* **3.** *Archaic.* a fishhook or fishing tackle. [OE *angel, angul;* akin to ANGLE[1]]

an·gled (ăng′gəld), *adj.* having an angle or angles.

angle iron, **1.** a bar of iron in the form of an angle. **2.** a rolled iron or steel bar with an L-shaped cross section, used mainly in iron constructions.

angle of attack, the acute angle between the chord of an aircraft wing or other airfoil and its direction of motion relative to the air.

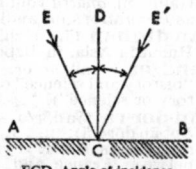

ECD, Angle of incidence on surface AB; CD, Perpendicular; E′CD, Angle of reflection

angle of incidence, 1. the angle that a line, ray of light, etc., meeting a surface, makes with the perpendicular to that surface at the point of meeting. **2.** the fixed angle between the plane of the wing chord and the axis of the fuselage. **3.** *Brit.* angle of attack.

angle of reflection, the angle that a ray of light, or the like, reflected from a surface, makes with a perpendicular to that surface at the point of reflection.

an·gle·pod (ăng/gəl pŏd/), *n.* an asclepiadaceous plant, *Vincetoxicum* (or *Gonolobus*) *gonocarpos*, of the southern and central U.S.

an·gler (ăng/glər), *n.* **1.** one who angles; one who fishes for pleasure. **2.** a fish, *Lophius piscatorius* of the coasts of Europe or *L. americanus* of America, which attracts small fish by the movement of a wormlike filament attached to its head just above the mouth. **3.** any of various related fishes, with a modified free dorsal spine above the mouth, constituting the order *Pediculati*.

An·gles (ăng/gəlz), *n.* a West Germanic people that migrated from Sleswick to Britain in the fifth century A.D. and founded the kingdoms of East Anglia, Mercia, and Northumbria. As early as the 6th century their name was extended to all the Germanic inhabitants of Britain. [OE *Angle,* orig. the inhabitants of *Angel,* a district of Sleswick, named from its hooklike shape]

An·gle·sey (ăng/gəl sĭ), *n.* an island and county in NW Wales. 50,660 pop. (1951); 276 sq. mi. *Co. seat:* Holyhead.

an·gle·site (ăng/gəl sīt/), *n.* a mineral, lead sulfate, PbSO₄, found in massive forms or in colorless or variously tinted crystals: a minor ore of lead. [named after *Anglesey,* Wales. See -ITE¹]

an·gle·smith (ăng/gəl smĭth/), *n.* a blacksmith skilled in forging angle irons, beams, etc., into various forms used in shipbuilding.

an·gle·worm (ăng/glə wûrm/), *n.* an earthworm used for bait in angling.

An·gli·a (ăng/glĭ ə), *n.* Latin name of England.

An·gli·an (ăng/glĭ ən), *adj.* **1.** of or relating to the Angles or to East Anglia. **—n. 2.** an Angle. **3.** the northern and eastern group of Old English dialects.

An·glic (ăng/glĭk), *n.* **1.** a simplified form of English, devised by R. E. Zachrisson (1880–1937) and intended for use as an international auxiliary language. **—adj. 2.** Anglian.

An·gli·can (ăng/glə kən), *adj.* **1.** of or pertaining to the Church of England. **2.** related in origin to and in communion with the Church of England, as various episcopal churches in other parts of the world. **3.** *Chiefly U.S.* English. **—n. 4.** a member of the Church of England or of a church in communion with it. **5.** one who upholds the system or teachings of the Church of England. **6.** one who emphasizes the authority of that church; a High Churchman. [t. ML: s. *Anglicānus*]

Anglican Church, the Church of England and the churches in other countries in full accord with it as to doctrine and church order, as the Church of Ireland, the Episcopal Church of Scotland, the Church of Wales, the Protestant Episcopal Church in the U.S., etc.

An·gli·can·ism (ăng/glə kə nĭz/əm), *n.* Anglican principles; the Anglican Church system.

An·gli·ce (ăng/glə sĭ), *adv.* in English; as the English would say it; according to the English way, as *Córdoba, Anglice Cordova.* [t. ML, der. *Anglicus* English]

An·gli·cism (ăng/glə sĭz/əm), *n.* **1.** an English idiom. **2.** *U.S.* a Briticism. **3.** state or quality of being English.

An·gli·cist (ăng/glə sĭst), *n.* an authority on English language and literature. [L *Anglic*(*us*) *English* + -IST]

An·gli·cize (ăng/glə sīz/), *v.t., v.i.,* -cized, -cizing. to make or become English in form or character: to *Anglicize the pronunciation of a Russian name.* Also, **anglicize.** —An/gli·ci·za/tion, *n.*

An·gli·fy (ăng/glə fī/), *v.t.,* -fied, -fying. to Anglicize.

an·gling (ăng/glĭng), *n.* act or art of fishing with a hook and line, usually attached to a rod.

An·glist (ăng/glĭst), *n.* an authority on England. [t. G]

Anglo-, a word element meaning "pertaining to England or the English," as in *Anglo-American.* [comb. form repr. ML *Anglus* Englishman, *Anglī* (pl.) the English]

An·glo-A·mer·i·can (ăng/glō ə mĕr/ə kən), *adj.* **1.** belonging or relating to, or connected with, England and America, esp. the United States, or with the people of both: *Anglo-American commerce.* **2.** pertaining to the English who have settled in America, esp. in the United States, or have become American citizens. **—n. 3.** a native or descendant of a native of England who has settled in America, esp. in the United States, or has become an American citizen.

An·glo-Cath·o·lic (ăng/glō kăth/ə lĭk), *n.* **1.** one who emphasizes the Catholic character of the Anglican Church. **2.** an Anglican Catholic, as opposed to a Roman or Greek Catholic. **—adj. 3.** of or pertaining to Anglo-Catholicism or Anglo-Catholics. **—An·glo-Ca·thol·i·cism** (ăng/glō kə thŏl/ə sĭz/əm), *n.*

An·glo-E·gyp·tian Sudan (ăng/glō ĭ jĭp/shən), a former condominium of Egypt and Great Britain in NE Africa; now an independent country. See **Sudan.**

An·glo-French (ăng/glō frĕnch/), *adj.* **1.** English and French. **2.** pertaining to Anglo-French (def. 3). **—n. 3.** that dialect of French current in England from the Norman Conquest to the end of the Middle Ages.

An·glo-In·di·an (ăng/glō ĭn/dĭ ən), *n.* **1.** a person of

British birth who has lived long in India. **—adj. 2.** of, pertaining to, or relating to England and India.

An·glo·ma·ni·a (ăng/glō mā/nĭ ə), *n.* an excessive attachment to, respect for, or imitation of English institutions, manners, customs, etc. **—An/glo·ma/ni·ac,** *n.*

An·glo-Nor·man (ăng/glō nôr/mən), *adj.* **1.** pertaining to that period, 1066–1154, when England was ruled by Normans. **2.** pertaining to the Normans who settled in England, or their descendants, or their dialect of French. **—n. 3.** a Norman who settled in England after 1066, or one of his descendants. **4.** Anglo-French.

An·glo·phile (ăng/glə fīl/, -fĭl), *n.* one who is friendly to or likes England or English customs, institutions, etc.

An·glo·phobe (ăng/glə fōb/), *n.* one who hates or fears England or the English.

An·glo·pho·bi·a (ăng/glə fō/bĭ ə), *n.* an intense hatred or fear of England, or of whatever is English.

An·glo-Sax·on (ăng/glō săk/sən), *n.* **1.** one who belongs to the English-speaking world, irrespective of historical periods, political boundaries, geographical areas, or racial origins (the only medieval sense). **2.** an Englishman of the period before the Norman conquest. **3.** a person of English stock and traditions; in the U.S., usually a person of colonial descent and /or British origin. **4.** Old English (def. 1). **5.** the English language. **6.** plain English. **7.** pre-English (def. 1). **—adj. 8.** of, pertaining to, or characteristic of the Anglo-Saxons. **9.** pertaining to Anglo-Saxon. [t. ML: s. *Anglo-Saxonēs* the English people; r. OE *Angulseaxan,* t. ML: m. *Anglī Saxonēs,* Latinizations of the OE *Angle* and *Seaxan*]

An·go·la (ăng gō/lə), *n.* an overseas territory of Portugal in SW Africa. 4,317,000 (est. 1946); 481,226 sq. mi. *Cap.*: Luanda. Also, **Portuguese West Africa.**

An·go·ra (ăng gôr/ə, ăn- *for 1;* ăng gôr/ə, ăng/gə rə *for 2*), *n.* **1.** an Angora cat. **2.** Ankara.

Angora cat, a long-haired variety of the domestic cat, orig. from Angora.

Angora goat, a variety of goat, orig. from Angora, reared for its long, silky hair which is called mohair.

an·gos·tu·ra bark (ăng/gəs tyŏŏr/ə, -tŏŏr/ə), *n.* the bitter aromatic bark of a South American rutaceous tree of the genus *Cusparia* (or *Galipea*), supposed to be valuable as a tonic. Also, **angostura.** [named after *Angostura,* town in Venezuela]

angostura bitters, 1. a bitter aromatic tonic prepared in Trinidad from barks, roots, herbs, etc., under a secret formula. **2.** (*caps.*) a trademark for this tonic.

An·gra do He·ro·is·mo (ăng/grə dŏŏ ĕ/rŏŏ ēzh/mŏŏ), a seaport in the Azores, on Terceira island: former capital of the Azores. 10,296 (1950).

an·gry (ăng/grĭ), *adj.,* -grier, -griest. **1.** feeling or showing anger or resentment (*with* or *at* a person, *at* or *about* a thing). **2.** characterized by anger; wrathful: *angry words.* **3.** *Med.* inflamed, as a sore; exhibiting inflammation. [ME; f. ANGER + -Y¹] **—an/gri·ly,** *adv.* **—an/gri·ness,** *n.* **—Syn. 1.** irate, incensed, enraged.

an/gry young/ man/, 1. (*often cap.*) one of a group of British writers since the late 1950's whose works reflect strong dissatisfaction with, frustration by, and rebellion against tradition and society. **2.** any author writing in this manner. **3.** any frustrated, rebellious person. Also, *referring to a woman,* **an/gry young/ wom/an.**

ang·strom unit (ăng/strəm), one tenth of a millimicron, i.e., a ten millionth of a millimeter: a unit used to express the length of very short waves. Also, **angstrom.** [after A. J. *Angstrom* (1814–74), Swedish physicist]

an·guil·li·form (ăng gwĭl/ə fôrm/), *adj.* having the shape or form of an eel. [f. s. L *anguilla* eel + -(I)FORM]

an·guine (ăng/gwĭn), *adj.* pertaining to or resembling a snake. [t. L: m.s. *anguinus*]

an·guish (ăng/gwĭsh), *n.* **1.** excruciating or agonizing pain of either body or mind; acute suffering or distress: *the anguish of grief.* **—v.t., v.i. 2.** to affect with or suffer anguish. [ME, t. OF: m. *anguisse, angoisse,* g. L *angustia* straitness, pl. straits, distress] **—Syn. 1.** agony, torment, torture. See **pain.** **—Ant. 1.** delight.

an·gu·lar (ăng/gyə lər), *adj.* **1.** having an angle or angles. **2.** consisting of, situated at, or forming an angle. **3.** of, pertaining to, or measured by an angle. **4.** bony; gaunt. **5.** acting or moving awkwardly. **6.** stiff in manner; unbending. [t. L: s. *angulāris*] **—an/gu·lar·ly,** *adv.* **—an/gu·lar·ness,** *n.* **—Ant. 1.** round. **—2.** rotund.

an·gu·lar·i·ty (ăng/gyə lăr/ə tĭ), *n., pl.* -ties. **1.** angular quality. **2.** (*pl.*) sharp corners; angular outlines.

an·gu·late (ăng/gyə lĭt, -lāt/), *adj.* of angular form; angled: *angulate stems.* Also, **an/gu·lat/ed.** [t. L: m. s. *angulātus,* pp., made angular] **—an/gu·late·ly,** *adv.*

an·gu·la·tion (ăng/gyə lā/shən), *n.* angular formation.

An·gus (ăng/gəs), *n.* a county in E Scotland. 274,876 pop. (1951); 873 sq. mi. *Co. seat:* Forfar.

An·halt (än/hält), *n.* a former state in central Germany.

an·hin·ga (ăn hĭng/gə), *n.* snakebird.

An·hwei (än/hwā/), *n.* a province in eastern China. 30,343,637 pop. (1953); 56,371 sq. mi. *Cap.*: Hofei. Also, **Nganhwei.**

an·hy·dride (ăn hī/drīd, -drĭd), *n. Chem.* **1.** a compound formed by abstraction of water, an oxide of a nonmetal (**acid anhydride**) or a metal (**basic anhydride**) which forms an acid or a base, respectively, when united with water. **2.** a compound from which water has been abstracted. Also, **an·hy·drid** (ăn hī′drĭd). [f. s. Gk. *ánydros* without water (with etymological *h* inserted) + -IDE]

an·hy·drite (ăn hī′drīt), *n.* a mineral, calcium sulfate, CaSO₄, usually in whitish or slightly colored masses.

an·hy·drous (ăn hī′drəs), *adj. Chem.* indicating loss of all water, esp. water of crystallization. [t. Gk.: m. *ánydros* without water (with *h* from *hydrous*)]

a·ni (ä′nē), *n., pl.* **anis.** either of two black cuckoolike birds of the genus *Crotophaga*, inhabiting the warmer parts of America. [native name]

an·il (ăn′Ĭl), *n.* **1.** a fabaceous shrub, *Indigofera suffruticosa*, one of the plants which yield indigo, native to the West Indies. **2.** indigo; deep blue. [t. F, t. Pg., t. Ar.: m. *al-nil*, f. *al the* + *nil* (t. Skt.: m. *nīlī* indigo)]

an·ile (ăn′Ĭl, ā′nĭl), *adj.* of or like a weak old woman: *anile ideas*. [t. L: m. s. *anīlis*, der. *anus* old woman]

an·i·line (ăn′ə lĭn, -līn′), *n.* **1.** an oily liquid, C₆H₅NH₂, obtained first from indigo but now prepared from benzene, and serving as the basis of many brilliant dyes, and in the manufacture of plastics, resins, etc. —*adj.* **2.** pertaining to or derived from aniline: *aniline colors.* Also, **an·i·lin** (ăn′ə lĭn). [f. ANIL + -INE²]

aniline dye, any organic dye made from a coal-tar base (because the earliest ones were made from aniline).

a·nil·i·ty (ə nĬl′ə tĬ), *n., pl.* **-ties. 1.** anile state. **2.** an anile notion or procedure.

an·i·mad·ver·sion (ăn′ə măd vûr′zhən, -shən), *n.* **1.** a remark, usually implying censure; a criticism or comment: *to make animadversions on someone's conduct.* **2.** act or fact of criticizing. [t. L: s. *animadversio*]

an·i·mad·vert (ăn′ə măd vûrt′), *v.i.* **1.** to comment critically; make remarks by way of criticism or censure (fol. by *on* or *upon*). **2.** *Obs.* to take cognizance or notice. [t. L: s. *animadvertere* regard, notice]

an·i·mal (ăn′ə məl), *n.* **1.** any living thing that is not a plant, generally capable of voluntary motion, sensation, etc. **2.** any animal other than man. **3.** an inhuman person; brutish or beastlike person. —*adj.* **4.** of, pertaining to, or derived from animals: *animal life, animal fats.* **5.** pertaining to the physical or carnal nature of man, rather than his spiritual or intellectual nature: *animal needs.* [t. L: living being]
—**Syn. 1, 3.** ANIMAL, BEAST, BRUTE refer to sentient creatures as distinct from minerals and plants; fig., they usually connote qualities and characteristics below the human level. ANIMAL is the general word; fig., it applies merely to the body or to animallike characteristics: *an athlete is a magnificent animal.* BEAST refers to four-footed animals; fig., it suggests a base, sensual nature: *a glutton is a beast.* BRUTE implies absence of ability to reason; fig., it connotes savagery as well: *a drunken brute.*

an·i·mal·cule (ăn′ə măl′kūl), *n.* **1.** a minute or microscopic animal, nearly or quite invisible to the naked eye, as an infusorian or rotifer. **2.** *Rare.* a tiny animal, such as a mouse, fly, etc. [t. NL: m. s. *animalculum*, dim. of L *animal* animal] —**an′i·mal′cu·lar,** *adj.*

an·i·mal·cu·lum (ăn′ə măl′kyə ləm), *n., pl.* **-la** (-lə). animalcule.

animal husbandry, the science of breeding, feeding, and care of animals, esp. on a farm.

an·i·mal·ism (ăn′ə məl Ĭz′əm), *n.* **1.** animal state; state of being actuated by sensual appetites, and not by intellectual or moral forces; sensuality. **2.** the doctrine that human beings are without a spiritual nature.

an·i·mal·ist (ăn′ə məl Ĭst), *n.* one who believes in the doctrine of animalism. —**an′i·mal·is′tic,** *adj.*

an·i·mal·i·ty (ăn′ə măl′ə tĬ), *n.* **1.** the animal nature in man. **2.** animal life.

an·i·mal·ize (ăn′ə mə līz′), *v.t.,* **-ized, -izing.** to excite the animal passions of; brutalize; sensualize. —**an′i·mal·i·za′tion,** *n.*

animal kingdom, the animals of the world collectively (distinguished from *vegetable kingdom*).

an·i·mal·ly (ăn′ə məl Ĭ), *adv.* physically.

animal magnetism, hypnotism.

animal spirits, exuberance of health and life; animation and good humor; buoyancy.

an·i·mate (*v.* ăn′ə māt′; *adj.* ăn′ə mĬt), *v.,* **-mated, -mating,** *adj.* —*v.t.* **1.** to give life to; make alive. **2.** to make lively, vivacious, or vigorous. **3.** to encourage: *to animate weary troops.* **4.** to move to action; actuate: *animated by religious zeal.* —*adj.* **5.** alive; possessing life: *animate creatures.* **6.** lively. [t. L: m. s. *animātus*] —**an′i·mat′er,** *n.* —**an′i·mat′ing·ly,** *adv.*
—**Syn. 1.** vivify, quicken, vitalize. **2.** ANIMATE, INVIGORATE, STIMULATE mean to enliven. To ANIMATE is to create a liveliness: *health and energy animated his movements.* To INVIGORATE means to give physical vigor, to refresh, to exhilarate: *mountain air invigorates.* To STIMULATE is to arouse a latent liveliness on a particular occasion: *alcohol stimulates.*

an·i·mat·ed (ăn′ə māt′Ĭd), *adj.* full of life, action, or spirit; lively; vigorous: *an animated debate.* —**an′i·mat′ed·ly,** *adv.*

animated cartoon, a motion picture consisting of a series of drawings, each slightly different from the ones before and after it, run through a projector.

an·i·ma·tion (ăn′ə mā′shən), *n.* **1.** animated quality; liveliness; vivacity; spirit; life. **2.** act of animating; act of enlivening. **3.** the process of preparing animated cartoons. —**Syn. 1.** vigor, energy; enthusiasm, ardor.

an·i·ma·tism (ăn′ə mə tĬz′əm), *n.* the attribution of consciousness to inanimate objects.

a·ni·ma·to (ä′nē mä′tô), *adj. Music.* animated. [It.]

an·i·ma·tor (ăn′ə mā′tər), *n.* **1.** one who or that which animates. **2.** one who draws animated cartoons. [t. L]

an·i·mé (ăn′ə mā′, -mĬ), *n.* any of various resins or copals, esp. that from *Hymenaea Courbaril*, a tree of tropical America, used in making varnish, scenting pastilles, etc. [t. Sp., prob. t. native dialect]

an·i·mism (ăn′ə mĬz′əm), *n.* **1.** the belief that all natural objects and the universe itself possess a soul. **2.** the belief that natural objects have souls which may exist apart from their material bodies. **3.** the doctrine that the soul is the principle of life and health. **4.** belief in spiritual beings or agencies. [f. s. L *anima* soul + -ISM] —**an′i·mist,** *n., adj.* —**an′i·mis′tic,** *adj.*

a·ni·mis o·pi·bus·que pa·ra·ti (ăn′ə mĬs ō′pə bŭs′kwē pə rä′tĬ), *Latin.* prepared in mind and resources (motto of South Carolina).

an·i·mos·i·ty (ăn′ə mŏs′ə tĬ), *n., pl.* **-ties.** a feeling of ill will or enmity animating the conduct, or tending to display itself in action (fol. by *between* or *against*). [late ME *animosite*, t. L: m. s. *animōsitas* courage]

an·i·mus (ăn′ə məs), *n.* **1.** hostile spirit; animosity: *to feel an animus against someone.* **2.** purpose; intention; animating spirit. [t. L: mind, feeling, will]

an·i·on (ăn′ī′ən), *n. Phys. Chem.* **1.** a negatively charged ion which is attracted to the anode in electrolysis. **2.** any negatively charged atom, radical, or molecule. [t. Gk.: going up (ppr. neut.)]

an·ise (ăn′Ĭs), *n.* **1.** an herbaceous plant, *Pimpinella Anisum*, of Mediterranean regions, yielding aniseed. **2.** aniseed. [ME *anys*, t. OF: m. *anis*, t. L: s. *anisum*, t. Gk.: m. *ánīson* dill, anise]

an·i·seed (ăn′ə sēd′, ăn′Ĭs sēd′), *n.* the aromatic seed of the anise, used in medicine, in cookery, etc.

an·i·sette (ăn′ə zĕt′, -sĕt′), *n.* a cordial or liqueur flavored with aniseed. [t. F]

aniso-, a word element meaning "unlike" or "unequal." [comb. form repr. Gk. *ánisos* unequal]

an·i·so·car·pic (ăn Ĭ′sə kär′pĬk, ăn′Ĭ-), *adj. Bot.* (of a flower) having a lower number of carpels than of other floral parts.

an·i·so·dac·ty·lous (ăn Ĭ′sə dăk′tə ləs, ăn′Ĭ-), *adj. Zool.* unequal-toed; having the toes unlike.

an·i·sole (ăn′ə sōl′), *n.* a colorless fluid, C₇H₈O, used in the perfume industry and for killing lice. [f. s. L *anisum* ANISE + -OLE]

an·i·som·er·ous (ăn′Ĭ sŏm′ər əs), *adj. Bot.* unsymmetrical (applied to flowers which do not have the same number of parts in each circle).

an·i·so·met·ric (ăn Ĭ′sə mĕt′rĬk, ăn′Ĭ-), *adj.* **1.** not isometric; of unequal measurement. **2.** (of crystals) having three dimensionally unequal axial directions.

an·i·so·me·tro·pi·a (ăn Ĭ′sə mə trō′pĬ ə, ăn′Ĭ-), *n. Pathol.* inequality in the power of the two eyes to refract light. [t. NL: f. *aniso-* ANISO- + s. Gk. *métron* measure + *-opia* -OPIA]

an·i·so·trop·ic (ăn Ĭ′sə trŏp′Ĭk, ăn′Ĭ-), *adj.* **1.** *Physics.* of different properties in different directions. **2.** *Bot.* of different dimensions along different axes. —**an·i·sot·ro·py** (ăn′Ĭ sŏt′rə pĬ), *n.*

An·jou (ăn′jōō; *Fr.* äN zhōō′), *n.* a region and former province in W France, in the Loire valley.

An·ka·ra (äng′kä rä, -kə rə), *n.* the capital of Turkey, in the central part. 288,536 (1950). Also, **Angora.**

an·ker·ite (ăng′kə rīt′), *n.* a mineral related to dolomite but containing iron in place of part of the magnesium. [named after Prof. M. J. Anker, of Styria. See-ITE¹]

ankh (ăngk), *n. Egyptian Art.* a tau cross with a loop at the top, used as a symbol of generation or enduring life. [t. Egypt.: life, soul]

An·king (än′kĬng′), *n.* a city in E China, on the Yangtze; former capital of Anhwei province.

an·kle (ăng′kəl), *n.* **1.** the aggregate joint connecting the foot with the leg. **2.** the slender part of the leg above the foot. [ME *ankel*, t. Scand. (cf. Dan. *ankel*); r. OE *anclēow(e)*]

an·kle·bone (ăng′kəl bōn′), *n. Anat.* the astragalus.

an·klet (ăng′klĬt), *n.* **1.** a sock which reaches just above the ankle. **2.** an ornament for the ankle, corresponding to a bracelet for the wrist or forearm.

an·ky·lose (ăng′kə lōs′), *v.t., v.i.,* **-losed, -losing.** to grow together and consolidate, as two otherwise freely approximating similar or dissimilar hard tissues, like the bones of a joint or the root of a tooth and its surrounding bone. Also, **anchylose.**

an·ky·lo·sis (ăng′kə lō′sĬs), *n.* **1.** *Pathol.* morbid adhesion of the bones of a joint. **2.** *Anat.* union or consolidation of two similar or dissimilar hard tissues previously freely approximating, as the bones of a joint, or the root of a tooth and its surrounding bone. Also, **anchylosis.** [t. NL, t. Gk.: stiffening of the joints] —**an·ky·lot·ic** (ăng′kə lŏt′Ĭk), *adj.*

an·ky·los·to·mi·a·sis (ăng′kə lŏs′tə mī′ə sĬs), *n.* ancylostomiasis.

an·lace (ăn′lĭs), *n.* a medieval dagger or short sword, worn in front of the person. [ME. t. OF: m. *ale(s)naz*, der. *alesne* awl, t. Gmc.: m. *alisna*]

An·la·ge (än′lä gə), *n.*, *pl.* **-gen** (-gən). *(also l.c.)* Embryol. **1.** primordium. **2.** blastema. [G: setup, layout]

ann., **1.** annual. **2.** annuity. **3.** (L *anni*) years.

an·na (ăn′ə), *n.* **1.** a money of account in India, the sixteenth part of a rupee. **2.** a coin of this value, equivalent to about 2 cents. [t. Hind.: m. *ānā*]

an·na·berg·ite (ăn′ə bûr′gīt), *n.* a mineral, hydrous nickel arsenate, Ni₃As₂O₈·8H₂O, occurring in apple-green masses. [named after *Annaberg*, town in Saxony. See -ITE¹]

an·nal (ăn′əl), *n.* a register or record of the events of a year. See **annals.**

an·nal·ist (ăn′əl ĭst), *n.* a chronicler of yearly events. —**an′nal·is′tic,** *adj.* —**an′nal·is′ti·cal·ly,** *adv.*

an·nals (ăn′əlz), *n.pl.* **1.** history or relation of events recorded year by year. **2.** historical records generally. **3.** a periodical publication containing formal reports of learned societies, etc. [t. L: m. *annālēs* (sc. *libri* books) a yearly record]

An·nam (ə năm′), *n.* a former kingdom and French protectorate along the E coast of French Indochina: now part of Vietnam. Also, **Anam.**

An·na·mese (ăn′ə mēz′, -mēs′), *adj.*, *n.*, *pl.* **-mese.** —*adj.* **1.** of or pertaining to Annam, its people, or their language. —*n.* **2.** a native of Annam. **3.** a literary language of Annam. **4.** the linguistic family to which this belongs, widespread in Tonkin and Annam, and of no certainly known relationships.

An·na·mite (ăn′ə mīt′), *n.*, *adj.* Annamese.

An·nap·o·lis (ə năp′ə lĭs), *n.* the capital of Maryland, in the central part: a seaport on Chesapeake Bay; U. S. Naval Academy. 23,385 (1960).

Annapolis Royal, a town in W Nova Scotia, on an arm of the Bay of Fundy: the first settlement in Canada (1605). Formerly, **Port Royal.**

An·na·pur·na (ə pŏŏr′nə), *n.* a mountain in the Himalayas, in Nepal. 26,503 ft.

Ann Ar·bor (ăn är′bər), a city in SE Michigan. 67,340 (1960).

an·nates (ăn′āts, -ĭts), *n.pl. Eccles.* (formerly) the first year's revenue of a see or benefice, payable to the Pope. Also, **an·nats** (ăn′ăts, -ĭts). [t. ML: m. *annāta* time, work, yield of a year, der. L *annus* year]

an·nat·to (ə năt′ō, ə nä′tō), *n.* **1.** a small tree, *Bixa orellana*, of tropical America. **2.** a yellowish-red dye obtained from the pulp enclosing its seeds, used for coloring fabrics, butter, varnish, etc. Also, **anatto.** [t. Carib]

Anne (ăn), *n.* 1665–1714. queen of England, 1702–14. (daughter of James II of England).

an·neal (ə nēl′), *v.t.* **1.** to heat (glass, earthenware. metals, etc.) to remove or prevent internal stress. **2.** to free from internal stress by heating and gradually cooling. **3.** to toughen or temper: *to anneal the mind.* [ME *anele(n)*, OE *ænælan*, f. *an* on + *ælan* burn]

Anne Bol·eyn (bŏŏl′ən). See **Boleyn.**

an·ne·lid (ăn′ə lĭd), *n. Zool.* a member of the *Annelida.* [t. F: m. *annélide*, f. m. s. L *ānellus* (dim. of *ānulus* ring) + -*ide* -ID²] —**an·nel·i·dan** (ə nĕl′ə dən), *adj.*, *n.*

An·nel·i·da (ə nĕl′ə də), *n.pl. Zool.* a phylum of worms comprising earthworms, leeches, various marine worms, etc., characterized by their ringed or segmented bodies.

Anne of Austria, 1601–66, queen of Louis XIII of France: regent during minority of her son Louis XIV.

Anne of Bohemia, 1366–94, queen of Richard II of England.

Anne of Cleves (klēvz), 1515–57, the fourth wife of Henry VIII of England.

an·nex (*v.* ə nĕks′; *n.* ăn′ĕks), *v.t.* **1.** to attach, join, or add, esp. to something larger or more important; unite; append; subjoin. **2.** to attach as an attribute, concomitant, or consequence. —*n.* Also, *Brit.*, **an·nexe** (ə nĕks′). **3.** something annexed. **4.** a subsidiary building or an addition to a building. **5.** something added to a document; appendix; supplement: *an annex to a treaty.* [ME *a(n)nexe(n)*, t. ML: m. *annexāre*, ult. der. L *annexus*, pp., joined] —**an·nex′a·ble,** *adj.*

an·nex·a·tion (ăn′ĭk sā′shən, -ĕk-), *n.* **1.** act of annexing, esp. new territory. **2.** fact of being annexed. **3.** something annexed. —**an′nex·a′tion·ist,** *n.*

an·nex·ment (ə nĕks′mənt), *n.* that which is annexed.

an·ni·hi·la·ble (ə nī′ə ləbəl), *adj.* susceptible of annihilation. —**an·ni′hi·la·bil′i·ty,** *n.*

an·ni·hi·late (ə nī′ə lāt′), *v.t.*, **-lated, -lating.** **1.** to reduce to nothing; destroy utterly: *the bombing annihilated the city.* **2.** to destroy the form or collective existence of: *to annihilate an army.* **3.** to cancel the effect of; annul: *to annihilate a law.* **4.** *Rare.* to reduce to silence, helplessness, etc. [t. LL: m. s. *annihilātus*, pp.] —**an·ni′hi·la·tive,** *adj.* —**an·ni′hi·la′tor,** *n.*

an·ni·hi·la·tion (ə nī′ə lā′shən), *n.* **1.** act of annihilating. **2.** extinction; destruction. —**an·ni′hi·la′tion·ist,** *n.*

An·nis·ton (ăn′ĭs tən), *n.* a city in E Alabama. 33,657 (1960).

an·ni·ver·sa·ry (ăn′ə vûr′sə rĭ), *n.*, *pl.* **-ries,** *adj.* —*n.* **1.** the yearly recurrence of the date of a past event. **2.** the celebration of such a date. —*adj.* **3.** returning or recurring each year. **4.** pertaining to an anniversary: *an anniversary gift.* [t. L: m. s. *anniversārius*]

an·no Dom·i·ni (ăn′ō dŏm′ə nī′), *Latin.* in the year of our Lord. *Abbr.:* A.D., as A.D. 597.

an·no·tate (ăn′ō tāt′), *v.*, **-tated, -tating.** —*v.t.* **1.** to supply with notes; remark upon in notes: *to annotate the works of Bacon.* —*v.i.* **2.** to make annotations or notes. [t. L: m. s. *annotātus*, pp.] —**an′no·ta′tor,** *n.*

an·no·ta·tion (ăn′ō tā′shən), *n.* **1.** act of annotating. **2.** a note commenting upon, explaining, or criticizing some passage of a book or other writing.

an·nounce (ə nouns′), *v.t.*, **-nounced, -nouncing. 1.** to make known publicly; give notice of. **2.** to state the approach or presence of: *to announce guests or dinner.* **3.** to make known to the mind or senses. [ME *anounce(n)*, t. OF: m. *anoncier*, g. L *annuntiāre*] —**Syn. 1.** ANNOUNCE, PROCLAIM, PUBLISH mean to communicate something in a formal or public way. To ANNOUNCE is to give out news, often of something expected in the future: *to announce a lecture series.* To PROCLAIM is to make a widespread and general announcement of something of public interest: *to proclaim a holiday.* To PUBLISH is to make public in an official way, now esp. by printing: *to publish a book.*

an·nounce·ment (ə nouns′mənt), *n.* **1.** public or formal notice announcing something: *the announcement appeared in the newspapers.* **2.** act of announcing.

an·nounc·er (ə noun′sər), *n.* one who announces, esp. over the radio.

an·no ur·bis con·di·tae (ăn′ō ûr′bĭs kŏn′də tā′), *Latin.* in the year _____ after the founding of the city (Rome, traditionally in 753 B.C.). *Abbr.:* A.U.C.

an·noy (ə noi′), *v.t.* **1.** to disturb (a person) in a way that displeases, troubles, or slightly irritates him. **2.** *Mil.* to molest; harm. —*v.i.* **3.** to be hateful or troublesome. —*n.* **4.** *Archaic or Poetic.* something annoying. [ME *anoye*, t. OF: m. *enui*, der. *en(n)uyer* displease, g. LL *inodiāre*, der. *in odiō* in hatred] —**an·noy′er,** *n.* —**Syn. 1.** harass, pester. See **bother, worry.**

an·noy·ance (ə noi′əns), *n.* **1.** that which annoys; a nuisance: *some visitors are an annoyance.* **2.** act of annoying. **3.** the feeling of being annoyed.

an·noy·ing (ə noi′ĭng), *adj.* causing annoyance: *annoying habits.* —**an·noy′ing·ly,** *adv.* —**an·noy′ing·ness,** *n.*

an·nu·al (ăn′yŏŏ əl), *adj.* **1.** of, for, or pertaining to a year; yearly. **2.** occurring or returning once a year: *an annual celebration.* **3.** *Bot.* living but one growing season, as beans or maize. **4.** performed during a year: *the annual course of the sun.* —*n.* **5.** a plant living but one year or season. **6.** a literary production published annually. [t. LL: s. *annuālis*; r. ME *annuel*, t. OF] —**an′nu·al·ly,** *adv.*

annual parallax. See **parallax** (def. 3).

an·nu·i·tant (ə nū′ə tant,|ə nōō′-), *n.* one who receives an annuity.

an·nu·it coep·tis (ăn′yŏŏ ĭt sĕp′tĭs), *Latin.* He (God) has favored our undertakings (adapted from Vergil, *Aeneid*, IX, 625; motto on reverse of the great seal of the United States).

an·nu·i·ty (ə nū′ə tĭ, ə nōō′-), *n.*, *pl.* **-ties. 1.** a specified income payable at stated intervals for a fixed or a contingent period, often for the recipient's life, in consideration of a stipulated premium paid either in prior installment payments or in a single payment. **2.** the right to receive such an income, or the duty to make such a payment or payments. [ME *annuitee*, t. F: m. *annuité*, ult. der. L *annuus* yearly]

an·nul (ə nŭl′), *v.t.*, **-nulled, -nulling. 1.** to make void or null; abolish (used esp. of laws or other established rules, usages, and the like): *to annul a marriage.* **2.** to reduce to nothing; obliterate. [ME *anulle(n)*, t. LL: m. *annullāre*] —**an·nul′la·ble,** *adj.*

an·nu·lar (ăn′yə lər), *adj.* having the form of a ring. [t. L: s. *annulāris*] —**an·nu·lar·i·ty** (ăn′yə lăr′ə tĭ), *n.* —**an′nu·lar·ly,** *adv.*

annular eclipse, *Astron.* an eclipse of the sun in which a portion of its surface is visible as a ring surrounding the dark moon (opposed to *total eclipse*).

annular ligament, *Anat.* the general ligamentous envelope which surrounds the joints of the wrist or ankle.

An·nu·la·ta (ăn′yə lā′tə), *n.pl. Zool.* Annelida.

an·nu·late (ăn′yə lĭt, -lāt′), *adj.* **1.** formed of ringlike segments, as an annelid worm. **2.** having rings or ring-like bands. Also, **an′nu·lat′ed.**

an·nu·la·tion (ăn′yə lā′shən), *n.* **1.** formation with or into rings. **2.** a ringlike formation or part.

an·nu·let (ăn′yə lĭt), *n.* **1.** a little ring. **2.** *Archit.* an encircling band, molding, or fillet, as on a Doric capital. [f. s. L *annulus* ring + -ET]

an·nul·ment (ə nŭl′mənt), *n.* **1.** an invalidation, as of a marriage. **2.** act of annulling.

an·nu·lose (ăn′yə lōs′), *adj.* furnished with rings; composed of rings: *annulose animals.* [t. NL: m. s. *annulōsus*, der. L *annulus* ring]

an·nu·lus (ăn′yə ləs), *n.*, *pl.* **-li** (-lī′), **-luses.** a ring; a ringlike part, band, or space. [t. L, var. of *ānulus* ring]

an·nun·ci·ate (ə nŭn′shĭ āt′, -sĭ-), *v.t.*, **-ated, -ating.** to announce. [ME *annunciat*, ppl. adj., announced, t. ML: s. *annunciātus*, r. L *annuntiātus*, pp.]

an·nun·ci·a·tion (ə nŭn′sĭ ā′shən, -shĭ-), *n.* **1.** *(often cap.)* the announcement by the angel Gabriel to the Virgin Mary of the incarnation of Christ. **2.** *(cap.)* the festival (March 25) instituted by the church in memory of this. **3.** *Rare.* act of announcing; proclamation.

ăct, āble, dâre, ärt; ĕbb, ēqual; ĭf, īce; hŏt, ōver, ôrder, oil, bŏŏk, ōoze, out; ŭp, ūse, ûrge; ə = a in alone; ch, chief; g, give; ng, ring; sh, shoe; th, thin; t̴h, that; zh, vision. See the full key on inside cover.

an·nun·ci·a·tor (ənŭn/shĭ ā/tər, -sĭ-), n. 1. an announcer. 2. U.S. a signaling apparatus, generally used in conjunction with a buzzer, which displays a visual indication when energized by electric current.

An·nun·zi·o (dän nōōn/tsyō), n. Gabriele d' (gä/brē-ĕ/lĕ), 1863–1938, Italian writer and soldier.

an·nus mi·ra·bi·lis (ăn/əs mə răb/ə lĭs), Latin. year of wonders; wonderful year.

a·no·ci·as·so·ci·a·tion (ə nō/sĭ ə sō/sĭ ā/shən, -shĭ ā/-shən), n. Surg. a method for preventing shock and other harmful effects resulting from an operation, consisting principally in giving general and local anesthesia and in avoiding all unnecessary trauma during the operation. Also, **a·no·ci·a·tion** (ə nō/sĭ ā/shən, -shĭ-), [f. A-⁶ + noci-(comb. form repr. L nocēre harm) + ASSOCIATION]

an·ode (ăn/ōd), n. 1. the electrode which gives off positive ions, or toward which negative ions or electrons move or collect, in a voltaic cell, electronic tube, or other device. 2. the positive pole of a battery or other source of current. 3. the plate of an electron tube. [t. Gk.: m. s. ánodos way up]

an·od·ic (ăn ŏd/ĭk), adj. pertaining to an anode or the phenomena in its vicinity.

an·o·dize (ăn/ə dīz/), v.t., anodized, anodizing. Chem. to coat a metal, esp. magnesium or aluminum, with a protective film by chemical or electrolytic means. [f. ANOD(E) + -IZE]

an·o·dyne (ăn/ə dīn/), n. 1. a medicine that relieves or removes pain. 2. anything relieving distress. —adj. 3. relieving pain. 4. soothing to the feelings. [t. L: m. s. anōdynus, t. Gk.: m. anōdynos freeing from pain]

a·noint (ə noint/), v.t. 1. to put oil on; apply an unguent or oily liquid to. 2. to smear with any liquid. 3. to consecrate by applying oil. [ME anoynte(n), t. OF: m. enoint, pp. of enoindre, g. L inunguere] —a·noint/er, n. —a·noint/ment, n.

an·o·lyte (ăn/ə līt/), n. that part of an electrolyte which surrounds the anode in electrolysis. [b. ANODE and ELECTROLYTE]

a·nom·a·lism (ə nŏm/ə lĭz/əm), n. Rare. 1. anomalous quality. 2. an anomaly.

a·nom·a·lis·tic (ə nŏm/ə lĭs/tĭk), adj. of or pertaining to an anomaly.

anomalistic month, Astron. the average interval between consecutive passages of the moon through the perigee.

anomalistic year, Astron. the average interval between consecutive passages of the earth through the perihelion.

a·nom·a·lous (ə nŏm/ə ləs), adj. deviating from the common rule, type, or form; abnormal; irregular. [t. L: m. anōmalus, t. Gk.: m. anōmalos irregular] —a·nom/a·lous·ly, adv. —a·nom/a·lous·ness, n.

a·nom·a·ly (ə nŏm/ə lĭ), n., pl. -lies. 1. deviation from the common rule or analogy. 2. something anomalous: the anomalies of human nature. 3. Astron. a. an angular quantity used in defining the position of a point in an orbit. b. true anomaly, the angular distance of a planet from the perihelion of its orbit, as observed from the sun. c. mean anomaly, a quantity increasing uniformly with the time and equal to the true anomaly at perihelion and aphelion. [t. L: m. s. anōmalia, t. Gk.]

an·o·mie (ăn ō mē/), n. Sociol. a social vacuum marked by the absence of social norms or values, as in the case of a rooming-house area for single people in a large city. [t. F, t. Gk.: m. anomia lawlessness] —a·nom/ic, adj.

a·non (ə nŏn/), adv. Archaic. 1. in a short time; soon. 2. at another time. 3. at once; immediately. 4. ever and anon, now and then. [ME; OE on ān into one, on āne in one, immediately]

anon., anonymous.

an·o·nym (ăn/ə nĭm), n. 1. an assumed or false name. 2. an anonymous person or publication.

a·non·y·mous (ə nŏn/ə məs), adj. 1. without any name acknowledged, as that of author, contributor, or the like: an anonymous pamphlet. 2. of unknown name; whose name is withheld: an anonymous author. [t. Gk.: m. anōnymos] —an·o·nym·i·ty (ăn/ə nĭm/ə tĭ), a·non/y·mous·ness, n. —a·non/y·mous·ly, adv.

a·noph·e·les (ə nŏf/ə lēz/), n., pl. -les. any mosquito of the genus Anopheles, which, when infested with the organisms causing malaria, may transmit the disease to human beings. [t. NL, t. Gk.: useless, hurtful]

a·no·rak (ä/nə räk/), n. a jacket with a hood, used in the polar regions. [t. Eskimo: m. anoraq]

an·or·thic (ăn ôr/thĭk), adj. Crystall. triclinic.

an·or·thite (ăn ôr/thīt), n. a mineral of the plagioclase feldspar group, calcium aluminum silicate, CaAl₂Si₂O₈, occurring in basic igneous rocks. [f. AN-¹ + s. Gk. orthós straight + -ITE¹] —an·or·thit·ic (ăn/ôr thĭt/ĭk), adj.

an·or·tho·site (ăn ôr/thə sīt/), n. Petrog. a granular igneous rock composed largely of labradorite or a more calcic feldspar. [f. AN-¹ + Gk. orthós straight + -ITE¹. Cf. F anorthose a feldspar]

an·os·mi·a (ăn ŏz/mĭ ə, ăn ŏs/-), n. Pathol. loss of the sense of smell. [t. NL, f. Gk.: an- AN-¹ + s. osmē smell + -ia -IA] —an·os/mic, adj.

an·oth·er (ə nŭth/ər), adj. 1. a second; a further; an additional: another piece of cake. 2. a different; a dis-

tinct; of a different kind: at another time, another man. —pron. 3. one more; an additional one: try another. 4. a different one; something different: going from one house to another. 5. one just like. 6. one another, one the other; each other: love one another. [ME; orig. an other]

ans., answer.

an·sate (ăn/sāt), adj. having a handle or handlelike part: ansate cross (ankh). [t. L: m. s. ansātus]

An·schluss (än/shlŏŏs), n. German. union, esp. the political union of Austria with Germany in 1938.

An·selm (ăn/sĕlm), n. Saint, 1033–1109, archbishop of Canterbury, scholastic theologian and philosopher.

an·ser·ine (ăn/sə rīn/, -sər ĭn), adj. 1. Ornith. of or pertaining to the subfamily Anserinae, the goose family. 2. resembling a goose; gooselike. 3. stupid; foolish; silly. Also, **an/ser·ous**. [t. L: m.s. anserīnus]

an·swer (ăn/sər, än/-), n. 1. a spoken or written reply to a question, request, letter, etc. 2. a reply or response in act: the answer was a volley of fire. 3. a reply to a charge or an accusation. 4. Law. a pleading of facts by a defendant in opposition to those stated in the plaintiff's declaration. 5. a solution to a problem, esp. in mathematics. 6. Music. the entrance of a fugue subject, usually on the dominant, after its first presentation in the main key. —v.i. 7. to make answer; reply. 8. to respond by a word or act: to answer with a nod. 9. to act or suffer in consequence of (fol. by for): to answer for one's sins. 10. to be or declare oneself responsible or accountable (fol. by for): I will answer for his safety. 11. to be satisfactory or serve (fol. by for): to answer for a purpose. 12. to conform; correspond (fol. by to): to answer to a description. 13. answer back, to make a rude or impertinent reply. —v.t. 14. to make answer to; to reply or respond to: to answer a person, or a question. 15. to act in reply or response to: to answer the bell. 16. to serve or suit: this will answer the purpose. 17. to discharge (a responsibility, claim, debt, etc.). 18. to conform or correspond to; be similar or equivalent to: to answer a description. 19. to atone for; make amends for. [ME; OE andswaru, f. and- against + -swaru, akin to swerian swear] —an/swer·er, n. —an/swer·less, adj.

—Syn. 1. ANSWER, REPLY, RESPONSE, RETORT all mean words used to meet a question, remark, charge, etc. An ANSWER is a return remark: an answer giving the desired information. REPLY is somewhat more formal than ANSWER: a reply to a letter. A RESPONSE often suggests an answer to an appeal, exhortation, etc., or an expected or fixed reply: a response to inquiry, a response in a church service. A RETORT implies a keen, prompt answer, esp. one that turns a remark upon the person who made it: a sharp retort.

an·swer·a·ble (ăn/sər ə bəl, än/-), adj. 1. liable to be asked to give account; responsible (to a person, for an act, etc.): he is answerable to me for all his acts. 2. capable of being answered. 3. proportionate; correlative (fol. by to). 4. corresponding; suitable (fol. by to). —an/swer·a·ble·ness, n. —an/swer·a·bly, adv.

ant (ănt), n. 1. any of certain small hymenopterous insects constituting the family Formicidae, very widely distributed in thousands of species, all of which have some degree of social organization. 2. a termite. [ME amte, OE æmete] —ant/like/, adj.

an't (ănt, änt, änt), 1. contraction of are not. 2. Chiefly Brit. contraction of am not. 3. Illiterate or Dial. contraction of is not, has not, or have not.

ant-, var. of anti- esp. before a vowel or h, as in antacid.

-ant, 1. adjective suffix, orig. participial, as in ascendant, pleasant. 2. noun suffix used in words of participial origin, denoting agency or instrumentality, as in servant, irritant. [t. F, g. L -ant-, -ent-, nom. -ans, -ens, ppr. ending]

ant., antonym.

an·ta (ăn/tə), n., pl. -tae (-tē). Archit. a pier or pillar, formed by thickening a wall at its extremity, often having a base and a capital. [t. L (found only in pl.)]

Ant·a·buse (ăn/tə būs), n. Trademark. a drug, tetraethylthiuram disulfide, used in the treatment of alcoholism. It produces highly unpleasant symptoms when alcohol is taken following administration of the drug.

ant·ac·id (ănt ăs/ĭd), adj. 1. neutralizing acids; counteracting acidity, as of the stomach. —n. 2. an antacid agent or remedy. [f. ANT- + ACID]

An·tae·us (ăn tē/əs), n. Gk. Myth. an African giant who was invincible when in contact with the earth but was lifted into the air by Hercules and crushed. —An·tae/an, adj.

an·tag·o·nism (ăn tăg/ə nĭz/əm), n. 1. the activity or the relation of contending parties or conflicting forces; active opposition. 2. an opposing force, principle, or tendency. [t. Gk.: m.s. antagōnisma]

an·tag·o·nist (ăn tăg/ə nĭst), n. 1. one who is opposed to or strives with another in any kind of contest; opponent; adversary. 2. Physiol. a muscle which acts in opposition to another (the agonist). [t. Gk.: s. antagōnistēs] —Syn. 1. See adversary.

an·tag·o·nis·tic (ăn tăg/ə nĭs/tĭk), adj. acting in opposition; mutually opposing. —an·tag/o·nis/ti·cal·ly, adv.

an·tag·o·nize (ăn tăg/ə nīz/), v., -nized, -nizing. —v.t. 1. to make hostile; make an antagonist of: his speech antagonized half the voters. 2. to act in opposition to; oppose. —v.i. 3. Rare. to act antagonistically.

An·ta·ki·ya (än/tä kē/yä), n. Arabic name of Antioch.

ant·al·ka·li (ănt ăl/kə lī/), n., pl. -lis, -lies. something that neutralizes alkalis or counteracts alkalinity. —ant·al·ka·line (ănt ăl/kə lĭn/, -lĭn), adj., n.

---

b., blend of, blended; c., cognate with; d., dialect, dialectal; der., derived from; f., formed from; g., going back to; m., modification of; r., replacing; s., stem of; t., taken from; ?, perhaps. See the full key on inside cover.

An·ta·na·na·ri·vo (än'tə nä/nə rē/vō, än'-), n. Tananarive.

ant·arc·tic (änt ärk/tYk, -är/-), adj. 1. of, at, or near the South Pole. —n. 2. **the Antarctic,** the Antarctic Ocean and Antarctica. [t. L: s. *antarcticus,* t. Gk.: m. *antarktikós* opposite the north; r. ME *antartik,* t. OF: m. *antartique*]

Ant·arc·ti·ca (änt ärk/tə kə, -är/-), n. an uninhabited continent around the South Pole, almost wholly covered by a vast continental ice sheet. ab. 5,000,000 sq. mi. Also, **Antarctic Continent.**

Antarctic Circle, the northern boundary of the South Frigid Zone, 23° 28' from the South Pole.

Antarctic Ocean, the ocean S of the Antarctic Circle.

Antarctic Zone, the South Frigid Zone, between the Antarctic Circle and the South Pole.

An·tar·es (än tär/ēz), n. a red giant star of the first magnitude in Scorpio. [t. Gk., f. *ant*(í) compared with + *Árēs* Mars; so called because its color resembles that of the planet]

ant bear, 1. a large terrestrial tropical American edentate, the great anteater, *Myrmecophaga jubata,* subsisting on termites, ants, and other insects, and having powerful front claws, a long, tapering snout and extensile tongue, and a shaggy gray coat marked with a conspicuous black band. 2. the aardvark.

Ant bear (def. 1),
Myrmecophaga jubata
(23 in. high, overall length 7 ft.,
tail 2½ ft.

an·te (än/tY), n., v., -ted or -teed, -teing. —n. 1. *Poker.* a stake put into the pool by each player after seeing his hand but before drawing new cards, or sometimes, before seeing his hand. —v.i., v.t. 2. *Poker.* to put (one's stake) into the pool. 3. to pay (one's share) (usually fol. by *up*). [cf. L *ante* before]

ante-, a prefix meaning "before in space or time," as in *antedate, antediluvian, anteroom, antecedent.* [t. L]

ant·eat·er (änt/ē/tər), n. 1. any of three related edentates of tropical America, feeding chiefly on termites: **a.** the ant bear or **great anteater. b.** the tamandua or **lesser anteater. c.** silky or **two-toed anteater, a** yellowish, arboreal, prehensile-tailed species, *Cyclopes didactylus,* about the size of a rat. 2. the aardvark. 3. any of the pangolins or scaly anteaters of Africa and tropical Asia. 4. any of the echidnas or spiny anteaters of Australia and New Guinea. 5. banded anteater, an almost extinct insectivorous marsupial, *Myrmecobius fasciatus,* of South and West Australia.

an·te-bel·lum (än/tY bĕl/əm), adj. 1. before the war. 2. *U.S.* before the American Civil War. 3. before World War I. [L: *ante bellum*]

an·te·cede (än/tə sēd/), v.t., -ceded, -ceding. to go before, as in order; precede. [t. L: m. s. *antecēdere*]

an·te·ced·ence (än/tə sē/dəns), n. 1. act of going before; precedence. 2. *Astron.* (of a planet) apparent retrograde motion.

an·te·ced·en·cy (än/tə sē/dən sY), n. quality or condition of being antecedent.

an·te·ced·ent (än/tə sē/dənt), adj. 1. going or being before; preceding; prior (often fol. by *to*): *an antecedent event.* —n. 2. (*pl.*) a. ancestry. b. one's past history. 3. a preceding circumstance, event, etc. 4. *Gram.* the word or phrase, usually a noun or its equivalent, which is replaced by a pronoun or other substitute later (or rarely, earlier) in the sentence or in a subsequent sentence. In *Jack lost a hat and he can't find it, Jack* is the antecedent of *he,* and *hat* is the antecedent of *it.* 5. *Math.* the first term of a ratio; the first or third term of a proportion. 6. *Logic.* the first member of a conditional or hypothetical proposition. [t. L: s. *antecēdens,* ppr.] —**an/te·ced'ent·ly,** adv.

an·te·ces·sor (än/tə sĕs/ər), n. *Rare.* one who goes before; a predecessor.

an·te·cham·ber (än/tY chām/bər), n. a chamber or an apartment through which access is had to a principal apartment. [t. F: m. *antichambre,* t. It.: m. *anticamera,* f. *anti-* ANTE- + *camera* chamber (g. L *camera* vault)]

an·te·choir (än/tY kwīr/), n. an enclosed space in front of the choir of a church.

an·te·date (v. än/tY dāt/, än/tY dāt/; n. än/tY dāt/), v., -dated, -dating, n. —v.t. 1. to be of older date than; precede in time: *the Peruvian empire antedates that of Mexico.* 2. to date before the true time: *to antedate a check.* 3. to assign to an earlier date: *to antedate a historical event.* 4. to cause to return to an earlier time. 5. to cause to happen sooner; accelerate. 6. to take or have in advance; anticipate. —n. 7. a prior date.

an·te·di·lu·vi·an (än/tY dY loo/vY ən), adj. 1. belonging to the period before the Flood. Gen. 7, 8. 2. antiquated; primitive: *antediluvian ideas.* —n. 3. one who lived before the Flood. 4. one who is very old or old-fashioned. [f. ANTE- + s. L *diluvium* deluge + -AN]

an·te·fix (än/tə fYks/), n., pl. -fixes, -fixa. *Archit.* 1. an upright ornament at the eaves of a tiled roof, to conceal the foot of a row of convex tiles which cover the joints of the flat tiles. 2. an ornament above the top molding of a cornice. [t. L: s. *antefixum,* prop. neut. of *antefixus* fixed before] —**an/te·fix/al,** adj.

an·te·flex·ion (än/tə flĕk/shən), n. *Pathol.* a bending forward, esp. of the body of the uterus.

an·te·lope (än/tə lōp/), n., pl. -lope, -lopes. 1. a slenderly built, hollow-horned ruminant allied to cattle, sheep, and goats, found chiefly in Africa and Asia. 2. leather made from its hide. 3. *U.S.* pronghorn. [ME, t. OF: m. *antelop,* t. ML: m.s. *antalopus,* t. LGk.: m. *anthólops*]

an·te me·rid·i·em (än/tY mə rYd/Y ĕm/, -əm), *Latin.* 1. before noon. 2. the time between 12 midnight and 12 noon. *Abbr.:* A.M. or a.m. —**an/te·me·rid/i·an,** adj.

an·te·mor·tem (än/tY môr/təm), adj. *Latin.* before death: *an ante-mortem confession.*

an·te·mun·dane (än/tY mŭn/dān), adj. before the creation of the world.

an·te·na·tal (än/tY nā/təl), adj. prenatal.

an·ten·na (än tĕn/ə), n., pl. -tennas *for* 1; -tennae (-tĕn/ē) *for* 2. 1. *Radio.* the conductor by which the electromagnetic waves are sent out or received, consisting commonly of a wire or set of wires; an aerial. 2. *Zool.* one of the jointed appendages occurring in pairs on the heads of insects, crustaceans, etc., often called feelers. See diag. under **insect.** [t. L: a sailyard]

an·ten·nule (än tĕn/ūl), n. a small antenna, specif. one of the anterior pair in crustacea.

an·te·pen·di·um (än/tə pĕn/dY əm), n., pl. -dia (-dY ə). the decoration of the front of an altar, as a covering of silk, or a painted panel. [t. ML. See ANTE, PEND, -IUM]

an·te·pe·nult (än/tY pē/nŭlt, -pY nŭlt/), n. the last syllable but two in a word, as *syl-* in *monosyllable.* [t. L: short for *antepaenultima* (*syllaba*)] —**an·te·pe·nul·ti·mate** (än/tY pY nŭl/tə mYt), adj., n.

an·te·ri·or (än tîr/Y ər), adj. 1. placed before; situated more to the front (opposed to *posterior*). 2. going before in time; preceding; earlier: *an anterior age.* [t. L, compar. adj. der. *ante* before] —**an·te·ri·or·i·ty** (än tîr/Y-ôr/ə tY, -ŏr/-), n. —**an·te/ri·or·ly,** adv.

an·te·room (än/tY room/, -rŏŏm/), n. 1. a smaller room through which access is had to a chief apartment. 2. a waiting room.

an·te·ver·sion (än/tY vûr/zhən, -shən), n. *Pathol.* a tipping forward of the uterus with its fundus directed toward the pubis. [t. L: s. *anteversio* a putting before]

an·te·vert (än/tY vûrt/), v.t. *Pathol.* to displace (the uterus) by tipping forward. [t. L: s. *antevertere* precede]

An·theil (än/tīl), n. George, 1900–1959, U.S. composer.

ant·he·li·on (änt hē/lY ən, än thē/-), n., pl. -lia (-lY ə). a luminous ring seen around the shadow of the observer's head as thrown by the sun on a cloud, fog bank, or moist surface. [t. Gk., prop. neut. of *anthélios* opposite the sun]

an·thel·min·tic (än/thĕl mYn/tYk), Med. —adj. 1. destroying or expelling intestinal worms. —n. 2. an anthelmintic remedy. [f. ANT- + m. s. Gk. *hélmins* worm + -IC. See HELMINTHIC]

an·them (än/thəm), n. 1. a hymn, as of praise, devotion, or patriotism. 2. a piece of sacred vocal music, usually with words taken from the Scriptures. 3. a hymn sung in alternate parts. —v.t. 4. to celebrate with an anthem. [ME *antem,* OE *antemn*(*e*), *antefn*(*e*), t. VL: m. *antefna,* g. LL *antifona,* var. of *antiphóna,* var. Gk. See ANTIPHON]

an·the·mi·on (än thē/mY ən), n., pl. -mia (-mY ə). an ornament of floral forms in a flat radiating cluster, as in architectural decoration, vase painting, etc. [t. NL, t. Gk.: flower]

an·ther (än/thər), n. *Bot.* the pollen-bearing part of a stamen. See diag. under **flower.** [t. NL: s. *anthéra,* t. Gk., fem. of *anthērós* flowery]

an·ther·id·i·um (än/thə rYd/Y əm), n., pl. -theridia (-thə rYd/Y ə). *Bot.* a male sex organ containing motile male gametes. [t. NL, dim. of Gk. *anthērā* ANTHER] —**an/ther·id/i·al,** adj.

an·ther·o·zo·id (än/thər ə zō/Yd, än/thər ə zoid/), n. *Bot.* the motile male gamete produced in an antheridium.

an·the·sis (än thē/sYs), n. *Bot.* the period or act of expansion in flowers, esp. the maturing of the stamens. [t. NL, t. Gk.: full bloom]

ant hill, a mound of earth, leaves, etc., formed by a colony of ants in constructing their habitation.

antho-, a word element meaning "flower," as in *anthocyanin.* [t. Gk., comb. form of *ánthos*]

an·tho·cy·a·nin (än/thə sī/ə nYn), n. any of a class of water-soluble pigments including most of those that give red and blue flowers these colors. Also, **an·tho·cy·an** (än/thə sī/ən).

an·tho·di·um (än thō/dY əm), n., pl. -dia (-dY ə). *Bot.* a flower head or capitulum, esp. the head (or so-called compound flower) of a composite plant. See illus. under **inflorescence.** [t. NL, f. s. Gk. *anthódes* flowerlike + -ium -IUM]

an·thol·o·gize (än thŏl/ə jīz/), v., -gized, -gizing. —v.i. 1. to make an anthology. —v.t. 2. to include in an anthology.

an·thol·o·gy (än thŏl/ə jY), n., pl. -gies. 1. a collection of short, choice poems, especially epigrams, of varied authorship. 2. any collection of literary pieces of varied authorship. [t. Gk.: m. s. *anthologia,* lit., a flower gathering] —**an·tho·log·i·cal** (än/thə lŏj/ə kəl), adj. —**an·thol/o·gist,** n.

An·tho·ny (än/thə nY, -thə- *for 1;* än/thə nY *for 2*), n. 1. **Saint,** A.D. 251?-356?, Egyptian hermit; founder of Christian monasticism. 2. **Susan Brownell** (brou/nĕl), 1820–1906, U.S. reformer and suffragist.

ăct, āble, dâre, ärt; ĕbb, ēqual; Yf, īce; hŏt, ōver, ôrder, oil, bŏŏk, ōoze, out; ŭp, ūse, ûrge; ə = a in alone; ch, chief; g, give; ng, ring; sh, shoe; th, thin; ŧh, that; zh, vision. See the full key on inside cover.

An·tho·ny of Pad·ua (ăn′tə nĭ′, -thə-), **Saint**, 1195–1231, Franciscan monk and preacher in Italy and France.

an·tho·phore (ăn′thə fōr′), *n.* *Bot.* a form of floral stipe, produced by the elongation of the internode between the calyx and the corolla, and bearing the corolla, stamens, and pistil. [t. Gk.: m.s. *anthophóros* flower-bearing]

an·tho·tax·y (ăn′thə tăk′sĭ), *n.* *Bot.* the arrangement of flowers on the axis of growth; inflorescence.

An·tho·zo·a (ăn′thə zō′ə), *n.pl.* *Zool.* a class of the phylum *Coelenterata*, comprising sessile marine animals of the polyp type, single or colonial, having a columnar body with the interior partitioned by septa and an oral disk with one to many circles of tentacles. It includes anemones, corals, sea pens, etc. **—an′·tho·zo′an**, *adj.*, *n.*

Section of flower of wild pink, *Silene caroliniana*, showing A. anthophore within the calyx

an·thra·cene (ăn′thrə sēn′), *n.* a hydrocarbon, $C_{14}H_{10}$, found in coal tar, important commercially as a source of alizarin. [f. m.s. Gk. *ánthrax* coal + -ENE]

an·thra·cite (ăn′thrə sīt′), *n.* a mineral coal containing little of the volatile hydrocarbons and burning almost without flame; hard coal. [t. L: m. s. *anthracītes*, t. Gk.: m. *anthrakītes* kind of precious stone (prop., coallike)] **—an·thra·cit·ic** (ăn′thrə sĭt′ĭk), *adj.*

an·thrac·nose (ăn′thrăk′nōs), *n.* a necrotic plant disease with restricted lesions, as of bean and cotton plants. [f. Gk.: m.s. *ánthrax* carbuncle, coal + m. s. *nósos* disease]

an·thra·coid (ăn′thrə koid′), *adj.* resembling anthrax.

an·thra·qui·none (ăn′thrə kwə nōn′, -kwĭn′ōn), *n.* *Chem.* a yellow crystalline substance, $C_{14}H_8O_2$, obtained from anthracene or phthalic anhydride, used in the preparation of alizarin. [f. ANTHRA(CENE) + QUINONE]

an·thrax (ăn′thrăks), *n.*, *pl.* **-thrac·es** (-thrə sēz′). **1.** a malignant infectious disease of cattle, sheep, and other animals and of man, caused by *Bacillus anthracis*. **2.** a malignant carbuncle which is the diagnostic lesion of anthrax disease in man. [t. L, t. Gk.: carbuncle, coal]

anthrop., **1.** anthropological. **2.** anthropology.

anthropo-, a word element meaning "man," "human being," as in *anthropocentric*. Also, **anthrop-**. [t. Gk., comb. form of *ánthrōpos*]

an·thro·po·cen·tric (ăn′thrə pō sĕn′trĭk), *adj.* **1.** regarding man as the central fact of the universe. **2.** assuming man to be the final aim and end of the universe. **3.** viewing and interpreting everything in terms of human experience and values.

an·thro·po·gen·e·sis (ăn′thrə pō jĕn′ə sĭs), *n.* the genesis or development of the human race, esp. as a subject of scientific study. Also, **an·thro·pog·e·ny** (ăn′thrə pŏj′ə nĭ).

an·thro·pog·ra·phy (ăn′thrə pŏg′rə fĭ), *n.* the branch of anthropology that describes the varieties of mankind and their geographical distribution.

an·thro·poid (ăn′thrə poid′), *adj.* **1.** resembling man. **—n. 2.** an anthropoid ape. [t. Gk.: m. s. *anthrōpoeidēs*]

anthropoid ape, any ape of the family *Pongidae* comprising the gorilla, chimpanzee, orangutan, and gibbon, without cheek pouches or developed tail.

anthropol., anthropology.

an·thro·pol·o·gist (ăn′thrə pŏl′ə jĭst), *n.* one who studies or is versed in anthropology.

an·thro·pol·o·gy (ăn′thrə pŏl′ə jĭ), *n.* **1.** the science that treats of the origin, development (physical, intellectual, moral, etc.), and varieties, and sometimes esp. the cultural development, customs, beliefs, etc., of mankind. **2.** the study of man's agreement with and divergence from other animals. **3.** the science of man and his works. **—an·thro·po·log·i·cal** (ăn′thrə pə lŏj′ə kəl) **an·thro·po·log′ic**, *adj.* **—an·thro·po·log′i·cal·ly**, *adv.*

an·thro·pom·e·try (ăn′thrə pŏm′ə trĭ), *n.* the measurement of the size and proportions of the human body. **—an·thro·po·met·ric** (ăn′thrə pō mĕt′rĭk), **an·thro·po·met′ri·cal**, *adj.*

an·thro·po·mor·phic (ăn′thrə pō mōr′fĭk), *adj.* ascribing human form or attributes to beings or things not human, esp. to a deity.

an·thro·po·mor·phism (ăn′thrə pō mōr′fĭz əm), *n.* anthropomorphic conception or representation, as of a deity. **—an·thro·po·mor′phist**, *n.*

an·thro·po·mor·phize (ăn′thrə pō mōr′fīz), *v.t.*, *v.i.*, **-phized, -phizing.** to ascribe human form or attributes (to).

an·thro·po·mor·pho·sis (ăn′thrə pō mōr′fə sĭs), *n.* transformation into human form.

an·thro·po·mor·phous (ăn′thrə pō mōr′fəs), *adj.* **1.** having or resembling the human form. **2.** anthropomorphic. [t. Gk.: m. *anthrōpómorphos*]

an·thro·pon·o·my (ăn′thrə pŏn′ə mĭ), *n.* the science that treats of the laws regulating the development of the human organism in relation to other organisms and to environment. Also, **an·thro·po·nom·ics** (ăn′thrə pō nŏm′ĭks). **—an′thro·po·nom′i·cal**, *adj.*

an·thro·pop·a·thy (ăn′thrə pŏp′ə thĭ), *n.* ascription of human passions or feelings to beings not human, esp. to God. Also, **an′thro·pop′a·thism**. [t. Gk.: m. s. *anthrōpopátheia* humanity]

an·thro·poph·a·gi (ăn′thrə pŏf′ə jī′), *n. pl.*, *sing.* **-agus** (-ə gəs). man-eaters; cannibals. [t. L, pl. of *anthrōpophagus*, t. Gk.: m. *anthrōpophágos*]

an·thro·poph·a·gite (ăn′thrə pŏf′ə jīt′), *n.* a man-eater; a cannibal.

an·thro·poph·a·gy (ăn′thrə pŏf′ə jĭ), *n.* the eating of human flesh; cannibalism. **—an·thro·po·phag·ic** (ăn′thrə pō făj′ĭk), **an·thro·po·phag′i·cal**, **an·thro·poph·a·gous** (ăn′thrə pŏf′ə gəs), *adj.*

an·ti (ăn′tĭ, ăn′tī), *n.*, *pl.* **-tis.** *Colloq.* one who is opposed to a particular practice, party, policy, action, etc.

anti-, a prefix meaning "against," "opposed to," with the following particular meanings: **1.** opposed; in opposition: *anti-British*, *antislavery*. **2.** rival or spurious; pseudo-: *antibishop*, *anti-Messiah*. **3.** the opposite or reverse of: *antihero*, *anticlimax*. **4.** not; un-: *antilogical*, *antigrammatical*. **5.** placed opposite: *antipole*, *antichorus*. **6.** moving in a reverse or the opposite direction: *anticyclone*. **7.** *Med.* corrective; preventive; curative: *antifat*, *antipyretic*; *antistimulant*. Also, **ant-**. [t. Gk.]

an·ti·air·craft (ăn′tĭ âr′krăft′, -krăft′), *adj.* designed for or used in defense against enemy aircraft.

an·ti·ar (ăn′tĭ är′), *n.* **1.** the upas tree. **2.** an arrow poison prepared from its sap. [t. Javanese: m. *antjar*]

an·ti·bi·o·sis (ăn′tĭ bī ō′sĭs), *n.* *Biol.* an association between organisms which is injurious to one of them. [f. ANTI- + Gk. *bíōsis* act of living]

an·ti·bi·ot·ic (ăn′tĭ bī ŏt′ĭk), *Biochem.* **—n. 1.** a chemical substance produced by microörganisms that has the capacity, in dilute solutions, to inhibit the growth of and even to destroy bacteria and other microörganisms. Antibiotics (examples: penicillin, streptomycin) are used largely in the treatment of infectious diseases of man, animals, and plants. **—adj. 2.** of or involving antibiotics.

an·ti·bod·y (ăn′tĭ bŏd′ĭ), *n.*, *pl.* **-bodies.** any of various substances existing in the blood or developed in immunization which counteract bacterial poisons or destroy bacteria in the system.

an·tic (ăn′tĭk), *n.*, *adj.*, *v.*, **-ticked, -ticking. —n. 1.** (*often pl.*) a grotesque, fantastic, or ludicrous gesture or posture; fantastic trick. **2.** *Archaic.* a grotesque pageant; ridiculous interlude. **3.** *Archaic.* an actor using a mask. **4.** *Archaic.* a buffoon; clown. **—adj. 5.** *Archaic.* fantastic; odd; grotesque: *an antic disposition.* **—v.i. 6.** to perform antics; to caper. [t. It.: m. *antico* old (but used as if It. *grottesco* grotesque), g. L *antīquus*]

an·ti·cat·a·lyst (ăn′tĭ kăt′ə lĭst), *n.* *Chem.* a substance which prevents or slows a chemical reaction (opposed to *catalyst*).

an·ti·cath·ode (ăn′tĭ kăth′ōd), *n.* the plate, often of platinum, on which cathode rays impinge in an x-ray tube, thus producing x-rays.

an·ti·chlor (ăn′tĭ klôr′), *n.* *Chem.* any of various substances, esp. sodium thiosulfate, used for removing excess chlorine from paper pulp, textile, fiber, etc., after bleaching. [f. ANTI- + CHLOR(INE)] **—an·ti·chlo·ris·tic** (ăn′tĭ klō rĭs′tĭk), *adj.*

An·ti·christ (ăn′tĭ krīst′), *n.* *Theol.* **1.** a particular personage or power (variously identified or explained) conceived as appearing in the world as a mighty antagonist of Christ. **2.** (*sometimes l.c.*) an opponent of Christ; a person or power antagonistic to Christ. [t. Gk.: s. *antíchristos*; r. ME *antecrist*, t.OF] **—an·ti·chris·tian** (ăn′tĭ krĭs′chən), *adj.*, *n.*

an·tic·i·pant (ăn tĭs′ə pənt) *adj.* **1.** anticipative (fol. by *of*). **—n. 2.** one who anticipates.

an·tic·i·pate (ăn tĭs′ə pāt′), *v.t.*, **-pated, -pating. 1.** to realize beforehand; foretaste or foresee: *to anticipate pleasure.* **2.** to expect: *to anticipate an acquittal.* **3.** to perform (an action) before another has had time to act. **4.** to be before (another) in doing something; forestall: *anticipated by his predecessors.* **5.** to consider or mention before the proper time: *to anticipate more difficult questions.* **6.** to cause to happen earlier; accelerate; precipitate: *to anticipate his arrival.* **7.** *Finance.* **a.** to expend (funds) before they are legitimately available for use. **b.** to discharge (an obligation) before it is due. [t. L: m.s. *anticipātus*, pp.] **—an·tic′i·pa′tor**, *n.* **—Syn. 1.** See expect. **3.** preclude, obviate, prevent.

an·tic·i·pa·tion (ăn tĭs′ə pā′shən), *n.* **1.** act of anticipating. **2.** realization in advance; foretaste; expectation; hope. **3.** previous notion; slight previous impression; intuition. **4.** *Law.* a premature drawing from or assignment of money from a trust estate. **5.** *Music.* a tone introduced in advance of its harmony so that it sounds against the preceding chord.

A. Anticipation (def. 5)

an·tic·i·pa·tive (ăn tĭs′ə pā′tĭv), *adj.* anticipating or tending to anticipate; containing anticipation: *an anticipative action or look.* **—an·tic′i·pa·tive·ly**, *adv.*

an·tic·i·pa·to·ry (ăn tĭs′ə pə tōr′ĭ), *adj.* of, showing, or expressing anticipation. **—an·tic′i·pa·to·ri·ly**, *adv.*

an·ti·clas·tic (ăn′tĭ klăs′tĭk), *adj.* *Math.* (of a surface) having principal curvatures of opposite sign at a given point (opposed to *synclastic*).

an·ti·cler·i·cal (ăn′tĭ klĕr′ə kəl), *adj.* opposed to the influence and activities of the clergy in public affairs. **—an′ti·cler′i·cal·ism**, *n.*

an·ti·cli·max (ăn′tĭ klī′măks), *n.* **1.** a noticeable or ludicrous descent in discourse from lofty ideas or expressions to what is much less impressive. **2.** an abrupt descent in dignity; an inglorious conclusion. —**an·ti·cli·mac·tic** (ăn'tĭ klī măk'tĭk), *adj.*

an·ti·cli·nal (ăn'tĭ klī'nəl), *adj.* **1.** inclining in opposite directions from a central axis. **2.** *Geol.* **a.** inclining downward on both sides from a median line or axis, as an upward fold of rock strata. **b.** pertaining to such a fold. [f. ANTI- + CLIN(O)- + AL¹]

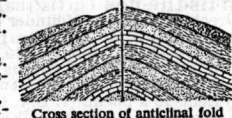

Axis

an·ti·cline (ăn'tĭ klīn'), *n. Geol.* an anticlinal rock structure.

Cross section of anticlinal fold

an·ti·cli·no·ri·um (ăn'tĭ klĭ nōr'ĭ əm), *n., pl.* **-no·ria** (-nōr'ĭ). *Geol.* a compound anticline, consisting of a series o ə subordinate anticlines and synclines, the whole having f he general contour of an arch.

An·ti·co·sti (ăn'tə kôs'tĭ, -kŏs'-), *n.* an island in E Canada,t in the estuary of the St. Lawrence: **a part of** Quebec. ab. 130 mi. long; 3043 sq. mi.

an·ti·cy·clone (ăn'tĭ sī'klōn), *n. Meteorol.* an extensive horizontal movement of the atmosphere spirally around and away from a gradually progressing central region of high barometric pressure, the spiral motion being clockwise in the Northern Hemisphere, counterclockwise in the Southern. —**an·ti·cy·clon·ic** (ăn'tĭ sĭ klŏn'ĭk), *adj.*

an·ti·diph·the·rit·ic (ăn'tĭ dĭf'thə rĭt'ĭk), *Med.* —*adj.* **1.** curing or preventing diphtheria. —*n.* **2.** an antidiphtheritic remedy.

an·ti·dote (ăn'tĭ dōt'), *n.* **1.** a medicine or other remedy for counteracting the effects of poison, disease, etc. **2.** whatever prevents or counteracts injurious effects. [t. L: m. s. *antidotum*, t. Gk.: m. *antidotos* (verbal adj.) given against] —**an'ti·dot'al,** *adj.*

an·ti·drom·ic (ăn'tĭ drŏm'ĭk), *adj. Physiol.* conducting nerve impulses in a direction opposite to the usual one. [ANTI- + s. Gk. *dromos* a running + -IC]

an·ti·en·er·gis·tic (ăn'tĭ ĕn'ər jĭs'tĭk), *adj.* acting in a manner opposite to the energy applied.

An·tie·tam (ăn tē'təm), *n.* a creek flowing from S Pennsylvania through NW Maryland into the Potomac. One of the bloodiest battles of the Civil War was fought here (1862), after which McClellan allowed Lee to retreat across the Potomac.

an·ti·fe·brile (ăn'tĭ fē'brəl, -fĕb'rəl), *Med.* —*adj.* **1.** efficacious against fever; febrifuge; antipyretic. —*n.* **2.** an antifebrile agent.

An·ti·fed·er·al·ist (ăn'tĭ fĕd'ər əl ĭst, -fĕd'rəl-). *n. U.S. Hist.* a member or supporter of the Antifederal Party. —**An'ti·fed'er·al·ism,** *n.*

An·ti·fed·er·al Party (ăn'tĭ fĕd'ər əl, -fĕd'rəl), *U.S. Hist.* the party which, before 1789, opposed the adoption of the proposed Constitution and after that favored its strict construction.

an·ti·freeze (ăn'tĭ frēz'), *n.* a liquid used in the radiator of an internal-combustion engine to lower the freezing point of the cooling medium.

an·ti·fric·tion (ăn'tĭ frĭk'shən), *n.* something that prevents or reduces friction; a lubricant.

an·ti·gen (ăn'tə jən), *n.* any substance which when injected into animal tissues will stimulate the production of antibodies. [f. ANTI(BODY) +-GEN] —**an·ti·gen·ic** (ăn'tə jĕn'ĭk), *adj.*

An·tig·o·ne (ăn tĭg'ə nē'), *n. Gk. Legend.* a daughter of Oedipus by his mother, Jocasta. For performing funeral rites (forbidden by edict of Creon, King of Thebes) over her brother Polynices, she was condemned to be immured alive, and hanged herself.

An·tig·o·nus (ăn tĭg'ə nəs), *n.* ("Cyclops") 382?-301 B.C., Macedonian general under Alexander the Great.

An·ti·gua (ăn tē'gwə, -gə), *n.* one of the Leeward Islands, in the Federation of the West Indies. 52,454 (est. 1955); 108 sq. mi. *Cap.:* St. John's.

an·ti·he·lix (ăn'tĭ hē'lĭks), *n., pl.* **-helices** (-hĕl'ə sēz'), **-helixes.** *Anat.* the inner curved ridge of the pinna of the ear. See diag. under **ear.**

an·ti·his·ta·mine (ăn'tĭ hĭs'tə mēn', -mĭn'), *n. Pharm.* any of certain medicines or drugs which neutralize or inhibit the effect of histamine in the body, used mainly in the treatment of allergic disorders and colds. —**an'ti·his'ta·mine', an'ti·his'ta·min'ic,** *adj.*

an·ti·im·pe·ri·al·ist (ăn'tĭ ĭm pĭr'ĭ əl ĭst), *n.* an opponent of imperialism. —**an'ti·im·pe'ri·al·is'tic,** *adj.*

an·ti·ke·to·gen·e·sis (ăn'tĭ kē'tə jĕn'ə sĭs), *n. Med.* prevention of the excessive formation of acetone bodies in the body, such as occurs in diabetes. [f. ANTI- + KETO(SIS) + -GENESIS] —**an'ti·ke'to·gen'ic,** *adj.*

an·ti·knock (ăn'tĭ nŏk'), *n.* a material, usually a lead compound, added to the fuel to eliminate or minimize detonation in an internal-combustion engine.

An·ti·Leb·a·non (ăn'tĭ lĕb'ə nən), *n.* a mountain range in SW Syria, E of the Lebanon Mountains.

An·til·les (ăn tĭl'ēz), *n.pl.* a chain of islands in the West Indies, divided into the **Greater Antilles** (Cuba, Hispaniola, Jamaica, and Puerto Rico), and the **Lesser**

Antilles (a group of smaller islands to the SE). —**An·til·le·an** (ăn'tə lē'ən, ăn tĭl'ĭ-), *adj.*

an·ti·log·a·rithm (ăn'tĭ lôg'ə rĭth'əm, -lŏg'ə-), *n. Math.* the number corresponding to a logarithm.

an·til·o·gy (ăn tĭl'ə jĭ'), *n., pl.* **-gies.** a contradiction in terms or ideas. [t. Gk.: m. s. *antilogia* contradiction]

an·ti·ma·cas·sar (ăn'tĭ mə kăs'ər), *n.* an ornamental covering for the backs and arms of chairs, sofas, etc., to keep them from being soiled by hair oil; a tidy. [f. ANTI- + *Macassar*, hair oil obtained from MACASSAR]

an·ti·ma·lar·i·al (ăn'tĭ mə lâr'ĭ əl), *Med.* —*adj.* **1.** preventive of or efficacious against malaria. —*n.* **2.** an antimalarial agent.

an·ti·masque (ăn'tə măsk', -mäsk'), *n.* a comic or grotesque interlude between the acts of a masque. Also, **an'ti·mask'.**

an·ti·mat·ter (ăn'tĭ măt'ər), *n. Physics, Chem.* the analogue of matter, possessing charges opposite to those of matter, as negatively-charged nuclei (antiprotons) surrounded by positively-charged electrons (positrons).

an·ti·mere (ăn'tə mĭr'), *n. Zool.* a segment or division of the body in the direction of one of the secondary or transverse axes, as either half of a bilaterally symmetrical animal or a radiating part of a radially symmetrical animal. —**an·ti·mer·ic** (ăn'tə mĕr'ĭk), *adj.* —**an·tim·er·ism** (ăn tĭm'ə rĭz'əm), *n.*

an·ti·mis·sile (ăn'tĭ mĭs'əl), *adj.* designed or used in defense against guided missiles. —*n.* **2.** a ballistic device with a homing instrument, for defense.

an·ti·mon·ic (ăn'tə mō'nĭk, -mŏn'ĭk), *adj.* of or containing antimony, esp. in the pentavalent state (Sb⁺⁵).

an·ti·mo·nous (ăn'tə mō'nəs), *adj. Chem.* containing trivalent antimony (Sb⁺³). Also, **an·ti·mo·ni·ous** (ăn'tə mō'nĭ əs).

an·ti·mon·soon (ăn'tĭ mŏn sōōn'), *n. Meteorol.* a current of air moving in a direction opposite to that of a given monsoon and lying above it.

an·ti·mo·ny (ăn'tə mō'nĭ), *n.* a brittle, lustrous, white metallic element occurring in nature free or combined, used chiefly in alloys and (in compounds) in medicine. *Symbol:* Sb; *at. no.:* 51; *at. wt.:* 121.76. [late ME, t. ML: m.s. *antimōnium*] —**an'ti·mo'ni·al,** *a dj.*, *n.*

antimony glance, stibnite.

an·ti·mo·nyl (ăn'tə mə nĭl, ăn tĭm'ə-), *n. Chem.* a radical containing antimony and oxygen (SbO⁺¹) which forms salts. [f. ANTIMON(Y) + -YL]

an·ti·neu·ral·gic (ăn'tĭ nyōō răl'jĭk, -nŏō-), *Med.* —*adj.* **1.** preventing or relieving neuralgia or neuralgic pain. —*n.* **2.** an antineuralgic substance.

an·ti·node (ăn'tə nōd'), *n. Physics.* a point, line, or region in a vibrating medium at which the amplitude of variation of the disturbance is greatest, situated halfway between two adjacent nodes.

an·ti·no·mi·an (ăn'tə nō'mĭ ən), *n.* one who maintains that Christians are freed from the moral law by the dispensation of grace set forth in the gospel. —**an'ti·no'mi·an,** *adj.* —**an'ti·no'mi·an·ism,** *n.*

an·tin·o·my (ăn tĭn'ə mĭ), *n., pl.* **-mies.** **1.** opposition between laws and principles. **2.** *Philos.* the mutual contradiction of two principles or correctly drawn inferences, each of which is supported by reason. [t. L m. s. *antinomia*, t. Gk.]

An·ti·och (ăn'tĭ ŏk'), *n.* a city in S Turkey: capital of the ancient kingdom of Syria, 300–64 B.C. 30,385 (1950). Arabic, **Antakiya.** —**An·ti·o·chi·an** (ăn'tĭ ō'kĭ ən), *adj.*

An·ti·o·chus III (ăn tī'ə kəs), ("the Great") 241?-187 B.C., king of Syria, 223–187 B.C.; fought against the Romans.

Antiochus IV, (*Antiochus Epiphanes*), died 164? B.C., king of Syria 175–164? B.C.

an·ti·ox·i·dant (ăn'tĭ ŏk'sə dənt), *n.* **1.** any substance which when added to rubber inhibits its deterioration. **2.** any substance inhibiting oxidation.

an·ti·pas·to (ăn'tē päs'tō), *n. Italian.* an appetizer course of relishes, smoked meat, fish, etc.; hors d'oeuvres.

An·tip·a·ter (ăn tĭp'ə tər), *n.* 398?-319 B.C. general, under Alexander the Great; regent of Macedonia.

an·ti·pa·thet·ic (ăn'tĭp'ə thĕt'ĭk, ăn'tĭ pə-), *adj.* having a natural antipathy, contrariety, or constitutional aversion (often fol. by *to*): *he was antipathetic to any change.* Also, **an·tip'a·thet'i·cal.** —**an·tip'a·thet'i·cal·ly,** *adv.*

an·tip·a·thy (ăn tĭp'ə thĭ), *n., pl.* **-thies. 1.** a natural or settled dislike; repugnance; aversion. **2.** an instinctive contrariety or opposition in feeling. **3.** an object of natural aversion or settled dislike. [t. L: m. s. *antipathia*, t. Gk.: m. *antipatheia*, der. *antipathēs* having opposite feelings] —**Syn. 1.** See **aversion.** —**Ant. 1.** attraction.

an·ti·pe·ri·od·ic (ăn'tĭ pĭr'ĭ ŏd'ĭk), *adj.* **1.** efficacious against periodic diseases, as intermittent fever. —*n.* **2.** an antiperiodic agent.

an·ti·per·i·stal·sis (ăn'tĭ pĕr'ə stăl'sĭs), *n. Physiol.* inverted peristaltic action of the intestines, by which their contents are carried upward.

an·ti·per·son·nel (ăn'tĭ pûr'sə nĕl'), *adj. Mil.* used against individuals rather than against mechanized vehicles, materiel, etc.: *antipersonnel bombs.*

an·ti·phlo·gis·tic (ăn'tĭ flō jĭs'tĭk), *adj.* **1.** checking inflammation. —*n.* **2.** an antiphlogistic remedy.

an·ti·phon (ăn'tə fŏn'), n. 1. a verse sung in response. 2. *Eccles.* a. a psalm, hymn, or prayer sung in alternate parts. b. a verse or a series of verses sung as a prelude or conclusion to some part of the service. [t. ML: s. *antiphōna*, t. Gk.: (prop. neut. pl.) sounding in answer]

an·tiph·o·nal (ăn tĭf'ə nəl), adj. 1. pertaining to antiphons or antiphony; responsive. —n. 2. an antiphonary. —**an·tiph'o·nal·ly**, adv.

an·tiph·o·nar·y (ăn tĭf'ə nĕr'ĭ), n., pl. -naries. a book of antiphons.

an·tiph·o·ny (ăn tĭf'ə nĭ), n., pl. -nies. 1. alternate or responsive singing by a choir in two divisions. 2. a psalm, etc., so sung; an antiphon. 3. a responsive musical utterance. —**an·ti·phon·ic** (ăn'tə fŏn'ĭk), adj.

an·tiph·ra·sis (ăn tĭf'rə sĭs), n. *Rhet.* the use of words in a sense opposite to the proper meaning. [t. L, t. Gk.]

an·tip·o·dal (ăn tĭp'ə dəl), adj. 1. *Geog.* on the opposite side of the globe; belonging to the antipodes. 2. diametrically opposite: *antipodal characters.*

an·ti·pode (ăn'tə pōd'), n. a direct or exact opposite.

an·tip·o·des (ăn tĭp'ə dēz'), n.pl. 1. places diametrically opposite to each other on the globe. 2. those who dwell there. [t. L, t. Gk., pl. of *antipous* with feet opposite] —**an·tip·o·de·an** (ăn tĭp'ə dē'ən), adj., n.

An·tip·o·des (ăn tĭp'ə dēz'), n.pl. a group of small uninhabited islands, ab. 460 mi. SE of and belonging to New Zealand. ab. 20 sq. mi.

an·ti·pope (ăn'tĭ pōp'), n. one who is elected pope in opposition to another held to be canonically chosen.

an·ti·pro·ton (ăn'tə prō'tŏn), n. *Physics, Chem.* a subatomic particle of unit negative charge with a mass equal to that of a proton. [f. ANTI- + PROTON]

an·ti·py·ret·ic (ăn'tĭ pī rĕt'ĭk), *Med.* —adj. 1. checking or preventing fever. —n. 2. an antipyretic agent.

an·ti·py·rine (ăn'tĭ pī'rĭn), n. *Pharm.* a white powder, $C_{11}H_{12}N_2O$, used as a sedative, antipyretic, antirheumatic, and antineuralgic.

antiq., antiquity.

an·ti·quar·i·an (ăn'tə kwâr'ĭ ən), adj. 1. pertaining to the study of antiquities or to antiquaries. —n. 2. antiquary. —**an'ti·quar'i·an·ism**, n.

an·ti·quar·y (ăn'tə kwĕr'ĭ), n., pl. -quaries. an expert on ancient things; a student or collector of antiquities. [t. L: m.s. *antiquārius* of antiquity]

an·ti·quate (ăn'tə kwāt'), v.t., -quated, -quating. 1. to make old and useless by substituting something newer and better. 2. to make antique. [t. L: m.s. *antiquātus*, pp., made old] —**an'ti·qua'tion**, n.

an·ti·quat·ed (ăn'tə kwā'tĭd), adj. 1. grown old; obsolete or obsolescent. 2. ill-adapted to present use. 3. aged. —**an'ti·quat'ed·ness**, n. —**Syn.** 2. See **ancient¹.**

an·tique (ăn tēk'), adj., n., v., -tiqued, -tiquing. —adj. 1. belonging to former times as contrasted with modern. 2. dating from an early period: *antique furniture.* 3. oldfashioned; antiquated: *an antique robe.* 4. *Archaic.* aged; ancient. —n. 5. an object of art or a furniture piece of a former period. 6. the antique (usually Greek or Roman) style, esp. in art. 7. *Print.* a style of type. —v.t. 8. to make appear antique. [t. L: m. s. *antiquus* old] —**an·tique'ly**, adv. —**an·tique'ness**, n. —**Syn.** 2. See **ancient¹.**

an·tiq·ui·ty (ăn tĭk'wə tĭ), n., pl. -ties. 1. the quality of being ancient; great age: *a family of great antiquity.* 2. ancient times; former ages: *the errors of dark antiquity.* 3. the time before the Middle Ages. 4. the ancients collectively; the people of ancient times. 5. (*usually pl.*) something belonging to or remaining from ancient times.

an·ti·ra·chit·ic (ăn'tĭ rə kĭt'ĭk), adj. pertaining to the prevention or cure of rickets.

an·ti·re·mon·strant (ăn'tĭ rĭ mŏn'strənt), n. 1. one opposed to remonstrance or to those who remonstrate. 2. (*cap.*) one of that party in the Dutch Calvinistic Church which opposed the Remonstrants or Arminians.

an·ti·rheu·mat·ic (ăn'tĭ rōō măt'ĭk), *Med.* —adj. 1. preventing or relieving rheumatism or rheumatic pain. —n. 2. an antirheumatic substance.

an·tir·rhi·num (ăn'tə rī'nəm), n. any of the genus, *Antirrhinum*, of herbs, family *Scrophulariaceae*, natives of the Old World, introduced into North America; the snapdragon. [t. NL, t. Gk.: m. *antirrhīnon* calf's snout]

an·ti·scor·bu·tic (ăn'tĭ skôr bū'tĭk), *Med.* —adj. 1. efficacious against scurvy. —n. 2. an antiscorbutic agent.

an·ti-Sem·ite (ăn'tĭ sĕm'īt, -sē'mīt), n. one hostile to the Jews. —**an·ti-Se·mit·ic** (ăn'tĭ sə mĭt'ĭk), adj. —**an'ti-Sem'it·i·cal·ly**, adv. —**an·ti-Sem·i·tism** (ăn'tĭ sĕm'ə tĭz'əm), n.

an·ti·sep·sis (ăn'tə sĕp'sĭs), n. destruction of the microörganisms that produce sepsis or septic disease.

an·ti·sep·tic (ăn'tə sĕp'tĭk), adj. 1. pertaining to or affecting antisepsis. —n. 2. an antiseptic agent.

an·ti·sep·ti·cal·ly (ăn'tə sĕp'tĭk lĭ), adv. with the help of antiseptics.

an·ti·sep·ti·cize (ăn'tə sĕp'tə sīz'), v.t., -cized, -cizing. to treat with antiseptics.

an·ti·se·rum (ăn'tĭ sĭr'əm), n., pl. -serums, -sera (-sĭr'ə). a fluid containing antibodies, as antitoxins or agglutinins obtained by inoculation of animals and used for injection into the blood stream of other animals to provide immunity to a specific disease.

an·ti·slav·er·y (ăn'tĭ slā'vər ĭ), adj. opposed to slavery, esp. Negro slavery.

an·ti·so·cial (ăn'tĭ sō'shəl), adj. 1. unwilling or unable to associate normally with one's fellows. 2. opposed to social order, or to the principles on which society is constituted. Also, **an'ti·so·cial·is'tic.**

an·ti·spas·mod·ic (ăn'tĭ spăz mŏd'ĭk), adj. 1. checking spasms. —n. 2. an antispasmodic agent.

An·tis·the·nes (ăn tĭs'thə nēz'), n. 444?–365? B.C., Greek philosopher, founder of the Cynic philosophy.

an·tis·tro·phe (ăn tĭs'trə fĭ), n. 1. the part of an ancient Greek choral ode, answering to a previous strophe, sung by the chorus when returning from left to right. 2. the second of two metrically corresponding systems in a poem. [t. L, t. Gk.: a turning about] —**an·ti·stroph·ic** (ăn'tĭ strŏf'ĭk), adj.

an·ti·tank (ăn'tĭ tăngk'), adj. *Mil.* designed for use against tanks or other armored vehicles: *antitank gun.*

an·tith·e·sis (ăn tĭth'ə sĭs), n., pl. -ses (-sēz'). 1. opposition; contrast: *the antithesis of theory and fact.* 2. the direct opposite (fol. by *of* or *to*). 3. *Rhet.* a. the setting of one clause or other member of a sentence against another to which it is opposed. b. a clause or member thus set in opposition, [t. LL, t. Gk.: opposition]

an·ti·thet·ic (ăn'tə thĕt'ĭk), adj. 1. of the nature of or involving antithesis. 2. directly opposed or contrasted. Also, **an'ti·thet'i·cal.** —**an'ti·thet'i·cal·ly**, adv.

an·ti·tox·ic (ăn'tĭ tŏk'sĭk), adj. 1. counteracting toxic influences. 2. of or serving as an antitoxin.

an·ti·tox·in (ăn'tĭ tŏk'sĭn), n. 1. a substance formed in the body, which counteracts a specific toxin. 2. the antibody formed in immunization with a given toxin, used in treating certain infectious diseases or in immunizing against them. Also, **an·ti·tox·ine** (ăn'tĭ tŏk'sĭn, -sēn).

an·ti·trade (ăn'tĭ trād'), n. 1. any of the upper tropical winds moving counter to and above the trade winds, but descending beyond the trade wind limits, and becoming the westerly winds of middle latitudes. —adj. 2. denoting such a wind.

an·ti·tra·gus (ăn tĭt'rə gəs), n., pl. -gi (-jī'). *Anat.* a process of the external ear. See diag. under **ear.** [t. NL, t. Gk.: m. *antitragos*]

an·ti·trust (ăn'tĭ trŭst'), adj. opposed to or designed to restrain trusts or large combinations of capital.

an·ti·type (ăn'tə tīp'), n. that which is foreshadowed by a type or symbol, as a New Testament event prefigured in the Old Testament. [t. Gk.: m. s. *antitypos* corresponding as a stamp to the die] —**an·ti·typ·ic** (ăn'tə tĭp'ĭk), **an'ti·typ'i·cal**, adj.

an·ti·un·ion (ăn'tĭ ūn'yən), adj. *U.S.* not recognizing or favoring trade unions or unionism.

an·ti·ven·in (ăn'tĭ vĕn'ĭn), n. 1. an antitoxin produced in the blood by repeated injections of venom, as of snakes. 2. the antitoxic serum obtained from such blood.

ant·ler (ănt'lər), n. one of the solid deciduous horns, usually branched, of an animal of the deer family. [ME *auntelere*, t. OF: m. *antoillier* ult. der. L *ant(e)* before + *oculus* eye]

Antler of a stag
A. Brow antler; B. Bay antler; C. Royal antler; D. Crown antler

ant·lered (ănt'lərd), adj. 1. having antlers. 2. decorated with antlers.

ant lion, a larval neuropterous insect of the family *Myrmeleontidae*, the larva of which (doodlebug) digs a pit in sand, where it lies in wait for ants, etc.

An·to·fa·gas·ta (än'tō fä gäs'tä), n. a seaport in N Chile. 100,000 (est. 1954).

An·toi·nette (än'twə nĕt'; *Fr.* än twȧ nĕt'), n. **Marie** (mə rē'; *Fr.* mȧ rē'), 1755–93, wife of Louis XVI: queen of France, 1774–93; executed during French Revolution.

An·to·ni·nus (ăn'tə nī'nəs), n. **Marcus Aurelius** (mär'kəs ô rēl'yəs), A.D. 121–180, emperor of Rome, A.D. 161–180: Stoic philosopher and writer.

Antoninus Pi·us (pī'əs), A.D. 86–161, emperor of Rome, A.D. 138–161.

An·to·ni·us (ăn tō'nĭ əs), n. See **Antony, Mark.**

an·to·no·ma·sia (ăn'tə nō mā'zhə), n. *Rhet.* 1. the identification of a person by an epithet or appellative not his name, as *his lordship.* 2. the use of a personal name to denote a class of similar persons, as a *Shylock.* [t. L, t. Gk., der. *antonomázein* call instead]

An·to·ny (ăn'tə nĭ), n. **Mark,** (*Marcus Antonius*) 83?–30 B.C., Roman general: friend of Caesar; member of second triumvirate and rival of Octavian.

an·to·nym (ăn'tə nĭm), n. a word opposed in meaning to another (opposed to *synonym*): "good" *is the antonym of* "bad." [t. Gk.: m. *antōnymía*]

an·tre (ăn'tər), n. *Chiefly Poetic.* a cavern; a cave. [t. F, t. L: m. s. *antrum*, t. Gk.: m. *ántron*]

An·trim (ăn'trĭm), n. a county in NE Northern Ireland. 231,149 (1951); 1098 sq. mi. *Co. seat:* Belfast.

an·trorse (ăn trôrs'), adj. *Bot., Zool.* bent or directed forward or upward. [t. NL: m.s. *antrorsus*, f. L *anterofront-* + *versus*, pp., turned] —**an·trorse'ly**, adv.

an·trum (ăn'trəm), n., pl. -tra (-trə). *Anat.* a cavity in a bone, esp. that in the maxilla. [t. L, t. Gk.: m. *ántron*]

An·tung (än'tŏŏng'; *Chin.* än'dŏŏng'), n. 1. a former province in NE China, in Manchuria. 3,334,000 pop. (1946); 24,487 sq. mi. *Cap.:* Tunghua. 2. a seaport in this province, at the mouth of the Yalu river. 217,000 (est. 1950).

Ant·werp (ănt′wərp), *n.* a seaport in N Belgium, on the Scheldt river. 261,405 (est. 1952). French, **An·vers** (äⁿ vĕr′). Flemish, **Ant·wer·pen** (änt′vĕr pən).

A·nu·bis (ə nū′bĭs, ə nōō′-), *n. Egyptian Myth.* a son of Osiris, identified by the Greeks with Hermes, and represented as having the head of a dog. [t. L, t. Gk.: m. *Anoubis,* t. Egypt.: m. *Anup* jackal]

A number 1, A one (def. 2).

an·u·ran (ə nyŏŏr′ən, ə nōŏr′-), *adj., n. Zool.* salientian. [f. AN-¹ + m. s. Gk. *ourá* tail + -AN]

a·nus (ā′nəs), *n. Anat.* the opening at the lower end of the alimentary canal, through which the solid refuse of digestion is excreted. [t. L]

an·vil (ăn′vĭl), *n.* 1. a heavy iron block with a smooth face, frequently of steel, on which metals, usually red- or white-hot, are hammered into desired shapes. 2. anything on which blows are struck. 3. the fixed jaw in certain measuring instruments. 4. *Anat.* the incus. [ME *anvilt,* OE *anfilt(e),* c. MD *anvilte]*

Anvil (def. 1)

anx·i·e·ty (ăng zī′ə tĭ), *n., pl.* **-ties.** 1. distress or uneasiness of mind caused by apprehension of danger or misfortune. 2. solicitous desire; eagerness. 3. *Psychiatry.* a state of apprehension and psychic tension found in most forms of mental disorder. [t. L: m.s. *anxietas]*

anx·ious (ăngk′shəs, ăng′-), *adj.* 1. full of anxiety or solicitude; greatly troubled or solicitous: *to be anxious about someone's safety.* 2. earnestly desirous (fol. by infinitive or *for*): *anxious to please.* 3. attended with or showing solicitude or uneasiness: *anxious forebodings.* [t. L: m. *anxius* troubled] —**anx′ious·ly,** *adv.* —**anx′ious·ness,** *n.* —**Syn.** 1. concerned, worried, disturbed.

anxious seat, *U.S.* a seat reserved in a revival meeting for those troubled by conscience and eager for spiritual assistance. Also, **anxious bench.**

an·y (ĕn′ĭ), *adj.* 1. one, a, an, or (as *pl.*) some; whatever or whichever it may be: *if you have any witnesses, produce them.* 2. in whatever quantity or number, great or small: *have you any butter?* 3. every: *any schoolboy would know that.* 4. (with a negative) none at all. 5. any one, any single or individual (person or thing): *any one part of town.* —*pron.* 6. (sing.) any person; anybody, or (as *pl.*) any persons: *he does better than any before him; unknown to any.* 7. any single one or any ones; any thing or things; any quantity or number. —*adv.* 8. in any degree; to any extent; at all: *do you feel any better?* [ME; OE *ænig,* der. *ān* one]

an·y·bod·y (ĕn′ĭ bŏd′ĭ, -bə dĭ), *pron., n., pl.* **-bodies.** 1. any person. 2. a person of some importance.

an·y·how (ĕn′ĭ hou′), *adv.* 1. in any way whatever. 2. in any case; at all events. 3. in a careless manner.

an·y·one (ĕn′ĭ wŭn′, -wən), *pron.* any person; anybody. (Note: for anyone as two words, see **any,** def. 5.)

an·y·thing (ĕn′ĭ thĭng′), *pron.* 1. any thing whatever; something, no matter what. —*n.* 2. a thing of any kind. —*adv.* 3. in any degree; to any extent.

an·y·way (ĕn′ĭ wā′), *adv.* 1. in any way or manner. 2. in any case; anyhow. 3. carelessly; haphazard.

an·y·ways (ĕn′ĭ wāz′), *adv. Colloq.* in any way.

an·y·where (ĕn′ĭ hwâr′), *adv.* in, at, or to any place.

an·y·wise (ĕn′ĭ wīz′), *adv.* in any way or respect.

An·zac (ăn′zăk), *n.* 1. a member of the Australian and New Zealand Army Corps during World War I. 2. a soldier from Australia or New Zealand.

ANZUS (an′zəs), *n.* Australia, New Zealand, and the United States, esp. as associated in the mutual defense treaty (ANZUS Pact or Treaty) of 1952.

A·o·mo·ri (ä′ō mô′rē), *n.* a seaport in N Japan, at the N end of Honshu island. 106,417 (1950).

A one (ā′ wŭn′), 1. (in shipping registers) a symbol indicating a ship of the highest grade, used for insurance, etc. 2. *Colloq.* first-class; excellent. Also, **A-1.**

A·o·ran·gi (ä′ō räng′gĭ), *n.* See **Cook, Mount.**

a·o·rist (ā′ə rĭst), *n. Gram.* 1. a tense of the Greek verb expressing action (in the indicative, past action) without further limitation or implication. —*adj.* 2. of or in the aorist. [t. Gk.: s. *aóristos* indefinite]

a·o·ris·tic (ā′ə rĭs′tĭk), *adj.* 1. *Gram.* pertaining to the aorist. 2. indefinite; indeterminate.

a·or·ta (ā ôr′tə), *n., pl.* **-tas, -tae** (-tē) *Anat.* the main trunk of the arterial system, conveying blood from the left ventricle of the heart to all of the body except the lungs. See diag. under **heart.** [t. NL, t. Gk.: m. *aortē]* —**a·or′tic, a·or′tal,** *adj.*

a·ou·dad (ä′ŏŏ dăd′), *n.* a wild sheep of northern Africa, *Ammotragus lervia.* [t. F, t. Berber: m. *audad]*

ap-, var. of ad-, before *p,* as in *appear.*

Ap., 1. Apostle. 2. April.

A.P., Associated Press.

a·pace (ə pās′), *adv.* with speed; quickly; swiftly.

A·pach·e (ə păch′ĭ), *n., pl.* **Apaches, Apache.** 1. one of a group of Indian tribes of Athabascan speech stock in the southwestern U. S. 2. any of several Athabascan languages of Arizona and the Rio Grande basin.

a·pache (ə päsh′, ə päsh′; Fr. ā·päsh′), *n.* a Parisian gangster or tough. [t. F, special use of APACHE]

Ap·a·lach·ee Bay (ăp′ə lăch′ĭ), a bay in N Florida.

Ap·a·lach·i·co·la (ăp′ə lăch′ĭ kō′lə), *n.* a navigable river flowing through NW Florida into the Gulf of Mexico. 90 mi.

ap·a·nage (ăp′ə nĭj), *n.* appanage.

a·pa·re·jo (ä′pä rā′hō), *n., pl.* **-jos** (-hōs). *Spanish.* a Mexican packsaddle formed of stuffed leather cushions.

A·par·ri (ä pär′rē), *n.* a seaport in the Philippine Islands, on N Luzon. 10,125 (1948).

a·part (ə pärt′), *adv.* 1. in pieces, or to pieces: *to take a watch apart.* 2. separately or aside in motion, place, or position. 3. to or at one side, with respect to purpose or function: *to set something apart.* 4. separately or individually in consideration. 5. aside (used with a gerund or noun): *joking apart, what do you think?* 6. apart from, aside from: *apart from other considerations.* —*adj.* 7. separate; independent: *a class apart.* [ME, t. OF: m. *a part,* g. L *ad partem* to the side]

a·part·heid (ä pärt′hīt′), *n.* (in South Africa) racial segregation. [t. S. Afr. D, f. *apart* + -*heid* -HOOD]

a·part·ment (ə pärt′mənt), *n. U.S.* 1. a set of rooms, among other sets in one building, designed for use as a dwelling. 2. a single room in a building. [t. F: m. *appartement,* t. It.: m. *appartemento,* der. *appartare* separate. See APART]

—**Syn.** 1. APARTMENT, COMPARTMENT agree in denoting a space enclosed by partitions or walls. APARTMENT, however, emphasizes the idea of separateness or privacy: *one's own apartment.* COMPARTMENT suggests a section of a larger space: *compartments in a ship's hold, in an orange crate.*

apartment house, *U.S.* a building divided into apartments (def. 1). Also, **apartment building.**

ap·a·tet·ic (ăp′ə tĕt′ĭk), *adj. Zool.* assuming colors and forms which effect deceptive camouflage. [t. Gk.: m.s. *apatētikós* fallacious]

ap·a·thet·ic (ăp′ə thĕt′ĭk), *adj.* 1. having or exhibiting little or no emotion. 2. indifferent. Also, **ap′a·thet′·i·cal.** —**ap′a·thet′i·cal·ly,** *adv.*

ap·a·thy (ăp′ə thĭ), *n., pl.* **-thies.** 1. lack of feeling; absence or suppression of passion, emotion, or excitement. 2. lack of interest in things which others find moving or exciting. [t. L: m. s. *apathia,* t. Gk.: m. *apátheia* insensibility] —**Ant.** 1. ardor.

ap·a·tite (ăp′ə tīt′), *n.* a common mineral, calcium fluophosphate, Ca₅F₃O₁₂, occurring crystallized and massive, and varying in color, used in the manufacture of phosphate fertilizers. [f. s. Gk. *apátē* deceit + -ITE¹; so called because often mistaken for other minerals]

ape (āp), *n., v.,* **aped, aping.** —*n.* 1. a tailless monkey or a monkey with a very short tail. 2. an anthropoid ape. 3. an imitator; a mimic. 4. any monkey. —*v.t.* 5. to imitate servilely; mimic. [ME; OE *apa;* c. G *affe]* —**ape′like′,** *adj.*

a·peak (ə pēk′), *adv. Naut.* in a vertical position or direction, or nearly so.

A·pel·doorn (ä′pəl dōrn′), *n.* a city in central Netherlands. 93,090 (est. 1954).

Ap·en·nines (ăp′ə nīnz′), *n.pl.* a mountain range traversing Italy from NW to SW. Highest peak, Monte Corno. 9585 ft.

a·per·çu (ä pĕr sy′), *n., pl.* **-çus** (-syz′; *Fr.* -sy′). *French.* 1. a hasty glance; a glimpse. 2. an outline or summary. [F, prop. pp. of *apercevoir* perceive]

a·per·i·ent (ə pĭr′ĭ ənt), *Med.* —*adj.* 1. purgative; laxative. —*n.* 2. a medicine or an article of diet that acts as a mild laxative. [t. L: s. *aperiens,* ppr., opening]

a·pe·ri·od·ic (ā′pĭr ĭ ŏd′ĭk), *adj.* 1. not periodic; irregular. 2. *Physics.* deadbeat. [f. A-⁶ + PERIODIC]

a·pé·ri·tif (ä pĕ′rĭ tēf′), *n. French.* a small drink of alcoholic liquor taken to whet the appetite before a meal.

ap·er·ture (ăp′ər chər), *n.* 1. a hole, slit, crack, gap, or other opening. 2. *Optics.* an opening that limits the size of the bundle of rays that can traverse an optical instrument. [t. L: m. s. *apertūra]*

ap·er·y (ā′pər ĭ), *n., pl.* **-eries.** 1. apish behavior; mimicry. 2. a silly trick. [APE + -RY]

a·pet·al·ous (ā pĕt′əl əs), *adj. Bot.* having no petals.

a·pex (ā′pĕks), *n., pl.* **apexes, apices** (ăp′ə sēz′, ā′pə-). 1. the tip, point, or vertex of anything; the summit. 2. climax; acme. [t. L: point, summit]

aph-, var. of **ap-, apo-** used before an aspirate.

aph., aphetic.

a·phaer·e·sis (ə fĕr′ə sĭs), *n.* apheresis.

aph·a·nite (ăf′ə nīt′), *n. Petrog.* any fine-grained igneous rock having such compact texture that the constituent minerals cannot be detected with the naked eye. [f. s. Gk. *aphanēs* obscure + -ITE¹] —**aph·a·nit·ic** (ăf′ə nĭt′ĭk), *adj.*

a·pha·sia (ə fā′zhə), *n. Pathol.* impairment or loss of the faculty of using or understanding spoken or written language. [t. NL, t. Gk.: speechlessness]

a·pha·si·ac (ə fā′zĭ ăk′), *n. Pathol.* one affected with aphasia.

a·pha·sic (ə fā′zĭk, -sĭk), *Pathol.* —*adj.* 1. pertaining to or affected with aphasia. —*n.* 2. an aphasiac.

a·phe·li·on (ə fē′lĭ ən), *n., pl.* **-lia** (-lĭ ə). *Astron.* the point of a planet's or comet's orbit most distant from the sun (opposed to *perihelion*). [Hellenized form of NL *aphēlium.* See APH-, HELIO-]

a·pher·e·sis (ə fĕr′ə sĭs), *n.* the omission of a letter, phoneme, or unstressed syllable at the beginning of a word, as in *squire* for *esquire.* Also, **aphaeresis.** [t. L, t. Gk.: m. *aphaíresis* removal] —**aph·e·ret·ic** (ăf′ə rĕt′ĭk), *adj.*

ăct, āble, dâre, ärt; ĕbb, ēqual; Ĭf, īce; hŏt, ōver, ôrder, oil, bŏŏk, ōōze, out; ŭp, ūse, ûrge; ə = a in alone; ch, chief; g, give; ng, ring; sh, shoe; th, thin; ŧh, that; zh, vision. See the full key on inside cover.

aph·e·sis (ăf´ə sĭs), *n.* (in historical linguistic process) the disappearance of an unstressed initial vowel or syllable. [t. Gk.: a letting go]

a·phet·ic (ə fĕt´ĭk), *adj.* pertaining to or due to aphesis.

a·phid (ā´fĭd, ăf´ĭd), *n.* any of the plant-sucking insects of the family *Aphididae*; a plant louse. [t. NL: s. *aphis*] **—a·phid·i·an** (ə fĭd´Y ən), *adj.*, *n.*

Apple tree aphid. *Aphis mali* (¼ in. long)

a·phis (ā´fĭs, ăf´ĭs), *n.*, *pl.* **aphides** (ăf´ə dēz´), an aphid.

a·pho·ni·a (ā fō´nĭ ə), *n. Pathol.* loss of voice, due to an organic or functional disturbance of the vocal organs. [t. Gk.: speechlessness]

a·phon·ic (ā fŏn´ĭk), *adj.* **1.** *Phonet.* **a.** unvoiced; without sound. **b.** voiceless (def. 5). **2.** *Pathol.* affected with aphonia. **—n. 3.** *Pathol.* one affected with aphonia.

aph·o·rism (ăf´ə rĭz´əm), *n.* a terse saying embodying a general truth. [ML: s. *aphorismus*, t. Gk.: m. *aphorismós* definition, a short pithy sentence] **—aph´o·ris´mic, aph·o·ris·mat·ic** (ăf´ə rĭz măt´Yk), *adj.*

aph·o·rist (ăf´ə rĭst), *n.* a maker of aphorisms.

aph·o·ris·tic (ăf´ə rĭs´tĭk), *adj.* **1.** of, like, or containing aphorisms: *his sermons were always richly aphoristic.* **2.** given to making or quoting aphorisms. **—aph´o·ris´ti·cal·ly,** *adv.*

aph·o·rize (ăf´ə rīz´), *v.i.*, **-rized, -rizing.** to utter aphorisms; write or speak in aphorisms.

aph·ro·dis·i·ac (ăf´rə dĭz´Y ăk´), *Med.* **—adj. 1.** arousing sexual desire. **—n. 2.** a drug or food that arouses sexual desire. [t. Gk.: m. s. *aphrodisiakós* venereal]

Aph·ro·di·te (ăf´rə dī´tē), *n.* the Greek goddess of love and beauty, identified by the Romans with Venus.

a·phyl·lous (ā fĭl´əs), *adj. Bot.* naturally leafless. [t. Gk.: m. *áphyllos* leafless]

a·phyl·ly (ā fĭl´Y), *n. Bot.* leaflessness.

A·pi·a (ä pē´ä, ä´pēä´), *n.* a seaport in and the capital of Western Samoa, on Upolu island.

a·pi·a·ceous (ā´pĭ ā´shəs), *adj. Bot.* related to the umbelliferous genus *Apium*, including parsley, celery, etc. [t. s. L *apium* parsley + -ACEOUS]

a·pi·an (ā´pĭ ən), *adj.* of or pertaining to bees. [t. L: s. *apiānus*]

a·pi·ar·i·an (ā´pĭ âr´Y ən), *adj.* relating to bees or to the breeding and care of bees.

a·pi·a·rist (ā´pĭ ə rĭst), *n.* one who keeps an apiary.

a·pi·ar·y (ā´pĭ ĕr´Y), *n.*, *pl.* **-aries.** a place in which bees are kept; a stand or shed for bees; a beehouse containing a number of beehives. [t. L: m.s. *apiārium*]

ap·i·cal (ăp´ə kəl, ā´pə-), *adj.* of, at, or forming the apex. [f. s. L *apex* summit + -AL¹] **—ap´i·cal·ly,** *adv.*

ap·i·ces (ăp´ə sēz´, ā´pə-), *n.* pl. of **apex.**

a·pic·u·late (ə pĭk´yəl´ĭt, -lāt´), *adj. Bot.* tipped with a short, abrupt point, as a leaf.

a·pi·cul·ture (ā´pə kŭl´chər), *n.* the rearing of bees. [f. L: *api(s)* bee + CULTURE] **—a´pi·cul´tur·al,** *adj.* **—a´pi·cul´tur·ist,** *n.*

a·piece (ə pēs´), *adv.* for each piece, thing, or person; for each one; each: *an orange apiece, costing a dollar apiece.* [orig. two words, *a* to or for each + PIECE]

à pied (á pyē´), *French.* afoot; walking; on foot.

A·pis (ā´pĭs), *n.* the sacred bull of the ancient Egyptians, to which divine honors were paid. [t. L, t. Gk.: m. *Apis*, t. Egyptian: m. *ḥapi*, prob. the running (bull)]

ap·ish (ā´pĭsh), *adj.* **1.** having the qualities, appearance, or ways of an ape. **2.** slavishly imitative. **3.** foolishly affected. **—ap´ish·ly,** *adv.* **—ap´ish·ness,** *n.*

a·piv·o·rous (ā pĭv´ə rəs), *adj. Zool.* feeding on bees, as certain birds. [f. L *api(s)* bee + -VOROUS]

Apl., April.

a·pla·cen·tal (ā´plə sĕn´təl, ăp´lə-), *adj. Zool.* not placental; having no placenta, as the lowest mammals.

ap·la·nat·ic (ăp´lə năt´Yk), *adj. Optics.* free from spherical aberration and coma. [f. m. s. Gk. *aplánētos* not wandering + -IC]

a·plas·tic anemia (ā plăs´tYk), *Pathol.* a severe anemia due to destruction or depressed function of the bone marrow, with no regenerative hyperplasia.

ap·lite (ăp´līt), *n.* a fine-grained granite composed essentially of feldspar and quartz. [f. m.s. Gk. *haplóos* single, simple + -ITE¹] **—ap·lit·ic** (ăp lĭt´Yk), *adj.*

a·plomb (ə plŏm´; *Fr.* á plôn´), *n.* **1.** imperturbable self-possession, poise, or assurance. **2.** the perpendicular position. [t. F: f. *à* according to + *plomb* plummet]

ap·ne·a (ăp nē´ə), *n. Pathol.* **1.** suspension of respiration. **2.** asphyxia. Also, **ap·noe·a.** [t. NL, t. Gk.: m. *ápnoia* lack of wind] **—ap·ne´al, ap·ne´ic,** *adj.*

A·po (ä´pō), *n.* a volcano in the Philippine Islands, on S Mindanao, near Davao: the highest peak in the Philippine Islands. 9610 ft.

apo-, a prefix meaning "from," "away," "off," "asunder," as in *apomorphine, apophyllite.* Also, **ap-, aph-.** [t. Gk. Cf. AB-]

Apoc., **1.** Apocalypse. **2.** Apocrypha. **3.** Apocryphal.

a·poc·a·lypse (ə pŏk´ə lĭps), *n.* **1.** (*cap.*) the Revelation of St. John the Divine. **2.** any of a class of writings, Jewish and Christian, which appeared from about 200 B.C. to A.D. 350, assuming to make revelation of the ultimate divine purpose. **3.** revelation; discovery; disclosure. [ME *apocalipse,* t. L: m.s. *apocalypsis,* t. Gk.: m. *apokálypsis*]

a·poc·a·lyp·tic (ə pŏk´ə lĭp´tYk), *adj.* **1.** of or like an apocalypse; affording a revelation. **2.** pertaining to the Apocalypse, or book of Revelation. Also, **a·poc´a·lyp´ti·cal. —a·poc´a·lyp´ti·cal·ly,** *adv.*

ap·o·carp (ăp´ə kärp´), *n. Bot.* a gynoecium with acarpous carpels.

ap·o·car·pous (ăp´ə kär´pəs), *adj. Bot.* having the carpels separate. [f. APO- + m. s. Gk. *karpós* fruit + -OUS]

Apocarpous fruit of rue anemone

ap·o·chro·mat·ic (ăp´ə krō măt´Yk), *adj. Optics.* having a high degree of correction for chromatic and spherical aberration and for coma. [modeled on ACHROMATIC. See APO-]

ap·o·co·pate (ə pŏk´ə pāt´), *v.t.,* **-pated, -pating.** to shorten by apocope. **—ap·oc´o·pa´tion,** *n.*

a·poc·o·pe (ə pŏk´ə pY), *n.* the cutting off of the last sound of a word. [t. L, t. Gk.: m. *apokopé* a cutting off]

a·poc·ry·pha (ə pŏk´rə fə), *n.pl.* (*now construed as sing.*) **1.** (*cap.*) fourteen books, not considered canonical, included in the Septuagint and the Vulgate as an appendix to the Old Testament, but usually omitted from Protestant editions of the Bible. **2.** various religious writings of uncertain origin regarded by some as inspired, but rejected by most authorities. **3.** works of doubtful authorship or authenticity. [t. LL, neut. pl. of *apocryphus,* t. Gk.: m. *apókryphos* hidden]

a·poc·ry·phal (ə pŏk´rə fəl), *adj.* **1.** of doubtful authorship or authenticity. **2.** *Eccles.* **a.** (*cap.*) of or pertaining to the Apocrypha. **b.** of doubtful sanction; uncanonical. **3.** false; spurious. **—a·poc´ry·phal·ly,** *adv.* **—a·poc´ry·phal·ness,** *n.*

a·poc·y·na·ceous (ə pŏs´ə nā´shəs), *adj. Bot.* belonging to the Apocynaceae, or dogbane family, which includes the dogbane, periwinkle, oleander, and various other plants, mostly tropical, some having medicinal and industrial uses. [f. s. NL *Apocynum* the dogbane genus (t. Gk.: m. *apókynon* kind of plant) + -ACEOUS]

ap·o·dal (ăp´ə dəl), *adj. Zool.* **1.** having no distinct feet or footlike members. **2.** belonging to the *Apoda* or *Apodes* (various groups of apodal animals). Also, **ap·od** (ăp´ŏd). [f. s. Gk. *ápous* footless + -AL¹]

ap·o·dic·tic (ăp´ə dĭk´tYk), *adj.* **1.** incontestable because demonstrated or demonstrable. **2.** *Logic.* denoting a proposition in which the relation of subject and predicate is asserted to be necessary. Also, **ap·o·deic·tic** (ăp´ə dīk´tYk), **ap´o·dic´ti·cal.** [t. Gk.: m.s. *apodeiktikós* demonstrative] **—ap´o·dic´ti·cal·ly,** *adv.*

a·pod·o·sis (ə pŏd´ə sĭs), *n.*, *pl.* **-ses** (-sēz´). (in a conditional sentence) the clause stating the consequence. [t. L, t. Gk.: return, answering clause]

a·pog·a·my (ə pŏg´ə mY), *n. Bot.* the development of a sporophyte from a cell or cells of the gametophyte other than the egg. [f. APO- + -GAMY] **—ap·o·gam·ic** (ăp´ə găm´Yk), **a·pog´a·mous** *adj.*

ap·o·gee (ăp´ə jē´), *n.* **1.** *Astron.* the point in the orbit of a heavenly body (usually the moon) most distant from the earth (opposed to *perigee*). **2.** the highest or most distant point; climax. [t. F: m. *apogée,* t. L: m. *apogēum,* t. Gk.: m. *apógaion* (*diástēma*) (distance) from the earth] **—ap´o·ge´al, ap´o·ge´an,** *adj.*

Apogee   Earth   Perigee

ap·o·ge·ot·ro·pism (ăp´ə jY´ŏt´rə pYz´əm), *n. Bot.* growth or tendency away from the earth; negative geotropism. **—ap·o·ge·o·trop·ic** (ăp´ə jē´ə trŏp´Yk), *adj.*

A·pol·lo (ə pŏl´ō), *n.*, *pl.* **-los. 1.** a Greek (and Roman) deity, the god of light, healing, music, prophecy, youthful manly beauty, etc. **2.** a very beautiful young man. [t. L, t. Gk.: m.s. *Apóllōn*]

ap·ol·lo·ni·an (ăp´ə lō´nY ən), *adj.* **1.** (*cap.*) pertaining to the cult of Apollo. **2.** serene; majestic; poised; having the properties of classic beauty.

A·pol·lyon (ə pŏl´yən), *n. Bible.* the destroyer; the angel of the bottomless pit. Rev. 9:11. [t. Gk.: prop. adj., destroying]

ap·ol·o·get·ic (ə pŏl´ə jĕt´Yk), *adj.* **1.** making apology or excuse for fault, failure, etc. **2.** defending by speech or writing. Also, **a·pol´o·get´i·cal.** [t. LL: s. *apologēticus,* t. Gk.: m. *apologētikós*] **—a·pol´o·get´i·cal·ly,** *adv.*

ap·ol·o·get·ics (ə pŏl´ə jĕt´Yks), *n.* the branch of theology concerned with the defense of Christianity.

ap·o·lo·gi·a (ăp´ə lō´jY ə), *n.* an apology, as in defense or justification. [t. L, t. Gk.: a speech in defense]

a·pol·o·gist (ə pŏl´ə jYst), *n.* **1.** one who makes an apology or defense in speech or writing. **2.** *Eccles.* **a.** a defender of Christianity. **b.** one of the authors of the early Christian apologies.

a·pol·o·gize (ə pŏl´ə jīz´), *v.i.,* **-gized, -gizing. 1.** to offer excuses or regrets for some fault, insult, failure, or injury. **2.** to make a formal defense in speech or writing. **—a·pol´o·giz´er,** *n.*

ap·o·logue (ăp´ə lôg´, -lŏg´), *n.* **1.** a didactic narrative; a moral fable. **2.** an allegory. [t. F, t. L: m. s. *apologus,* t. Gk.: m. *apólogos* a story, tale]

a·pol·o·gy (ə pŏl´ə jY), *n.*, *pl.* **-gies. 1.** an expression of regret offered for some fault, failure, insult, or injury. **2.** a formal defense in speech or writing, as of a cause or doctrine. **3.** a poor specimen or substitute; a makeshift: *a sad apology for a hat.* [see APOLOGIA] **—Syn. 1.** See **excuse. 2.** justification, vindication.

---

b., blend of, blended; c., cognate with; d., dialect, dialectal; der., derived from; f., formed from; g., going back to; m., modification of; r., replacing; s., stem of; t., taken from; ?, perhaps. See the full key on inside cover.

ap·o·mor·phine (ăp'ə môr'fēn, -fĭn), n. Pharm. an artificial crystalline alkaloid prepared from morphine: used in the form of the hydrochloride as an emetic and expectorant. Also, **ap·o·mor·phin** (ăp'ə môr'fĭn), **ap·o·mor·phi·a** (ăp'ə môr'fĭ ə).

ap·o·neu·ro·sis (ăp'ə nyŏŏ rō'sĭs, -nŏŏ-), n., pl. **-ses** (-sēz). Anat. a whitish fibrous membrane formed by the expansion of a tendon. [t. NL, t. Gk., der. aponeuroústhai become a tendon] **—ap·o·neu·rot·ic** (ăp'ə nyŏŏ rŏt'ĭk, -nŏŏ-), adj.

ap·o·pemp·tic (ăp'ə pĕmp'tĭk), adj. pertaining to sending away; valedictory. [t. Gk.: m.s. apopemptikós]

a·poph·a·sis (ə pŏf'ə sĭs), n. Rhet. denial of an intention to speak of something which is at the same time hinted or insinuated. [t. L, t. Gk.: denial]

ap·o·phthegm (ăp'ə thĕm'), n. apothegm. **—ap·o·phtheg·mat·ic** (ăp'ə thĕg măt'ĭk), **ap·o·phtheg·mat'·i·cal**, adj.

a·poph·y·ge (ə pŏf'ə jē'), n. Archit. 1. the small, hollow outward spread at the bottom of the shaft of a column by which it joins the base. See diag. under **column.** 2. a similar but slighter spread at the top of the shaft. [t. Gk.: lit. an escape]

a·poph·yl·lite (ə pŏf'ə lĭt', ăp'ə fĭl'ĭt), n. a mineral, a hydrous potassium and calcium, occurring in white crystals. [f. APO- + s. Gk. phýllon leaf + -ITE¹; so named because of its tendency to exfoliate]

a·poph·y·sis (ə pŏf'ə sĭs), n., pl. **-ses** (-sēz). Anat., Bot., etc. an outgrowth; a process; a projection or protuberance. [t. NL, t. Gk.: an offshoot]

ap·o·plec·tic (ăp'ə plĕk'tĭk), adj. Also, **ap·o·plec·ti·cal.** 1. of or pertaining to apoplexy. 2. having or inclined to apoplexy. **—n.** 3. a person having or predisposed to apoplexy. **—ap·o·plec·ti·cal·ly,** adv.

ap·o·plex·y (ăp'ə plĕk'sĭ), n. Pathol. 1. a sudden, usually marked, loss of bodily function due to rupture or occlusion of a blood vessel. 2. hemorrhage into the tissue of any organ. [ME apoplexie, t. L: m. apoplēxia, t. Gk., der. apoplēssein disable by a stroke]

a·port (ə pôrt'), adv. Naut. on or toward the port side.

ap·o·si·o·pe·sis (ăp'ə sī'ə pē'sĭs), n. Rhet. a sudden breaking off in the midst of a sentence, as if from unwillingness to proceed. [t. L, t. Gk., der. aposiōpân be silent] **—ap·o·si·o·pet·ic** (ăp'ə sī'ə pĕt'ĭk), adj.

ap·os·ta·sy (ə pŏs'tə sĭ), n., pl. **-sies.** a total desertion of, or departure from, one's principles, party, cause, etc. [ME apostasie, t. L: m. apostasia, t. Gk., var. of apóstasis defection, revolt]

a·pos·tate (ə pŏs'tāt, -tĭt), n. 1. one who forsakes his church, cause, party, etc. **—adj.** 2. guilty of apostasy

a·pos·ta·tize (ə pŏs'tə tīz'), v.i., -tized, -tizing. to commit apostasy.

a pos·te·ri·o·ri (ā pŏs tĭr'ĭ ōr'ī), from effect to cause; based upon actual observation or upon experimental data (opposed to a priori): an a posteriori argument. [t. L: from the subsequent or latter]

a·pos·til (ə pŏs'tĭl), n. a marginal annotation or note. Also, **a·pos·tille.** [t. F: (m.) apostille, der. apostiller, f. à to + postille marginal note, prob. t. ML: m. postilla, f. post after + illa those things]

a·pos·tle (ə pŏs'əl), n. 1. one of the twelve disciples sent forth by Christ to preach the gospel. 2. (among the Jews of the Christian epoch) a title borne by persons sent on foreign missions. 3. Mormon Ch. one of a council of twelve officials presiding over the Church and administering its ordinances. 4. a pioneer of any great moral reform. [ME apostel, OE apostol, t. L: s. apostolus, t. Gk.: m. apóstolos one sent away. Cf. ME apostle, t. OF] **—a·pos'tle·ship',** n.

Apostles' Creed, a creed of virtually universal acceptance in the Christian church, dating back to about A.D. 500 and traditionally ascribed to Christ's apostles. It begins "I believe in God the Father Almighty."

a·pos·to·late (ə pŏs'tə lĭt, -lāt'), n. 1. the dignity or office of an apostle. 2. Rom. Cath. Ch. the dignity or office of the Pope, the holder of the Apostolic See.

ap·os·tol·ic (ăp'ə stŏl'ĭk), adj. 1. pertaining to or characteristic of an apostle, esp. of the twelve apostles. 2. derived from the apostles in regular sequence. 3. of the Pope: papal. Also, **ap·os·tol'i·cal. —ap·os·tol'i·cal·ly,** adv. **—ap·os·tol·i·cism** (ăp'ə stŏl'ə sĭz'əm), n. **—a·pos·to·lic·i·ty** (ə pŏs'tə lĭs'ə tĭ), n.

Apostolic Fathers, 1. the fathers of the church whose lives overlapped those of any of the apostles. 2. works dating back to the second century, reputed to have been written by them.

Apostolic See, 1. the Church of Rome, traditionally founded by St. Peter. 2. (l.c.) any of the churches founded by apostles.

a·pos·tro·phe¹ (ə pŏs'trə fĭ), n. the sign (') used to indicate: **a.** the omission of one or more letters in a word, as in o'er for over. **b.** the possessive case, as in lion's. **c.** certain plurals, as in several M.D.'s. [special use of APOSTROPHE², by confusion with F apostrophe, t. L: m. s. apostrophus, t. Gk.: m. apóstrophos turned away, elided] **—ap·os·troph·ic** (ăp'ə strŏf'ĭk), adj.

a·pos·tro·phe² (ə pŏs'trə fĭ), n. a digression from a discourse, esp. in the form of a personal address to someone not present. [t. L, t. Gk.: a turning away] **—ap·os·troph·ic** (ăp'ə strŏf'ĭk), adj.

a·pos·tro·phize (ə pŏs'trə fīz'), v., -phized, -phizing. Rhet. **—v.t.** 1. to address by apostrophe. **—v.i.** 2. to utter an apostrophe.

apothecaries' measure, a system of units used in compounding and dispensing liquid drugs. In the United States 60 minims (℥) = 1 fluid dram (f ℨ); 8 fluid drams = 1 fluid ounce (f ℨ); 16 fluid ounces = 1 pint (O.); 8 pints = 1 gallon (C.) (231 cubic inches). In Great Britain 20 minims = 1 fluid scruple; 3 fluid scruples = 1 fluid dram; 8 fluid drams = 1 fluid ounce; 20 fluid ounces = 1 pint; 8 pints = 1 imperial gallon (277.274 cubic inches).

apothecaries' weight, a system of weights used in compounding and dispensing drugs: 20 grains = 1 scruple (℈); 3 scruples = 1 dram (℥); 8 drams = 1 ounce (℥); 12 ounces = 1 pound. The grain, ounce, and pound are the same as in troy weight, the grain alone being the same as in avoirdupois weight.

a·poth·e·car·y (ə pŏth'ə kĕr'ĭ), n., pl. **-caries.** 1. a druggist; a pharmacist. 2. (esp. in England and Ireland) a druggist licensed to prescribe medicine. [ME apothecarie, t. LL: m. apothēcārius shopkeeper, der. L apothēca, t. Gk.: m. apothēkē storehouse; r. ME apotecarie, t. OF: m. apotecaire. See -ARY¹]

ap·o·the·ci·um (ăp'ə thē'shĭ əm, -sĭ-), n., pl. **-cia** (-shĭ ə, -sĭ ə). Bot. the fruit of certain lichens, usually an open, saucer- or cup-shaped body, the inner surface of which is covered with a layer which bears asci. [t. NL, f. L: s. apothēca (t. Gk.: m. apothēkē storehouse) + dim. -ium] **—ap·o·the·cial** (ăp'ə thē'shəl), adj.

ap·o·thegm (ăp'ə thĕm'), n. a short, pithy, instructive saying; a terse remark or aphorism. Also, **apophthegm.** [t. Gk.: m. apóphthegma] **—ap·o·theg·mat·ic** (ăp'ə thĕg măt'ĭk), **ap·o·theg·mat·i·cal,** adj.

ap·o·them (ăp'ə thĕm'), n. Geom. a perpendicular from the center of a regular polygon to one of its sides. [f. APO- + m. Gk. thēma, der. tithēnai set]

a·poth·e·o·sis (ə pŏth'ĭ ō'sĭs, ăp'ə thē'ə sĭs), n., pl. **-ses** (-sēz, -sēz'). 1. exaltation to the rank of a god. 2. the glorification of any person. 3. a deified or glorified ideal. [t. L, t. Gk.: deification]

AB, Apothem

a·poth·e·o·size (ə pŏth'ĭ ə sīz', ăp'ə thē'ə sīz'), v.t., -sized, -sizing. to deify; glorify.

app., 1. apparent. 2. appendix. 3. appointed.

ap·pal (ə pôl'), v.t., -palled, -palling. appall.

Ap·pa·lach·i·an Mountains (ăp'ə lăch'ĭ ən, -lā'-chĭ ən, -chən), a mountain system of E North America, extending from Quebec province in Canada to N Alabama. Highest peak, Mt. Mitchell, 6684 ft. Also, **Appalachians.**

Appalachian tea, 1. the leaves of any of certain plants of the genus Ilex of the eastern U.S., as the shrub or small tree, I. vomitoria, sometimes used as a tea. 2. a plant yielding such leaves. 3. a shrub, Viburnum cassinoides, of the eastern U.S.

ap·pall (ə pôl'), v.t. to overcome with fear; fill with consternation and horror. Also, **appal.** [ME apalle(n), t. OF: m. apallir become or make pale] **—Syn.** See **frighten.**

ap·pall·ing (ə pô'lĭng), adj. causing dismay or horror: an appalling accident. **—ap·pall'ing·ly,** adv.

ap·pa·nage (ăp'ə nĭj), n. 1. land or some other source of revenue assigned for the maintenance of a member of the family of a ruling house. 2. whatever belongs or falls to one's rank or station in life. 3. a natural or necessary accompaniment. Also, **apanage.** [t. F, der. OF apaner, t. ML: m. apānāre furnish with bread]

appar., 1. apparent. 2. apparently.

ap·pa·ra·tus (ăp'ə rā'təs, -răt'əs), n., pl. **-tus, -tuses.** 1. an assemblage of instruments, machinery, appliances, materials, etc., for a particular use. 2. any complex appliance for a particular purpose. 3. Physiol. a collection of organs, differing in structure, which all minister to the same function. 4. a subdivison of a political organization: a communist espionage apparatus. [t. L: preparation]

ap·par·el (ə păr'əl), n., v., -eled, -eling or (esp. Brit.) -elled, -elling. **—n.** 1. a person's outer clothing; raiment. 2. aspect; guise. 3. Naut. the furnishings or equipment of a ship, as sails, anchors, guns, etc. **—v.t.** 4. to dress or clothe; adorn; ornament. [ME aparaile(n), t. OF: m. apareiller clothe, ult. der. L ad- AD- + dim. of pār equal] **—Syn.** 1. clothes, dress, attire, garb.

ap·par·ent (ə păr'ənt, ə pâr'-), adj. 1. capable of being clearly perceived or understood; plain or clear. 2. seeming; ostensible (as opposed to actual or real): the apparent motion of the sun. 3. exposed to the sight; open to view. 4. absolutely entitled to an inherited throne, title, or other estate, by right of birth (opposed to presumptive): the heir apparent. [t. L: s. appārens appearing; r. ME aparant, t. OF] **—ap·par'ent·ly,** adv. **—ap·par'ent·ness,** n.

—Syn. 1. APPARENT, EVIDENT, OBVIOUS, PATENT all refer to something easily perceived. APPARENT applies to that which can readily be seen or perceived: an apparent effort. EVIDENT applies to that which facts or circumstances make plain: his innocence was evident. OBVIOUS applies to that which is unquestionable, because completely manifest or noticeable: an obvious change of method. PATENT, a more formal word, applies to that which is open to view or understanding by all: a patent error.

ap·pa·ri·tion (ăp'ə rĭsh'ən), n. 1. a ghostly appearance; a specter or phantom. 2. anything that appears, esp. something remarkable or phenomenal. 3. act of appearing. [t. LL: s. *appāritio*, in L service]. —**ap'pa-ri'tion-al**, *adj.*

—**Syn. 1.** APPARITION, PHANTASM, PHANTOM are terms for a supernatural appearance. An APPARITION of a person or thing is an immaterial appearance which seems real, and is generally sudden or startling in its manifestation: *an apparition of a headless horseman.* Both PHANTOM and PHANTASM denote an illusory appearance, as in a dream; the former is usually pleasant and the latter frightening: *a phantom of a garden*, a *monstrous phantasm.*

ap·par·i·tor (ə pãr'ə tər), *n.* a subordinate official of an ancient Roman magistrate or of a court. [t. L: (public) servant]

ap·pas·sio·na·to (äp päs'syō nä'tō), *adj. Music.* impassioned; with passion or strong feeling. [It.]

ap·peal (ə pēl'), *n.* **1.** a call for aid, support, mercy, etc.; an earnest request or entreaty. **2.** application or reference to some person or authority for corroboration, vindication, decision, etc. **3.** *Law.* **a.** an application or proceeding for review by a higher tribunal. **b.** *Obs.* a formal charge or accusation. **4.** power to attract or to move the feelings: *the game has lost its appeal, sex appeal.* **5.** *Obs.* a summons or challenge. —*v.i.* **6.** to call for aid, mercy, sympathy, or the like; make an earnest entreaty. **7.** *Law.* to apply for review of a case or particular issue to a higher tribunal. **8.** to resort for proof, decision, or settlement: *to appeal to force.* **9.** to offer a peculiar attraction, interest, enjoyment, etc.: *this color appeals to me.* —*v.t.* **10.** *Law.* **a.** to apply for review of (a case) to a higher tribunal. **b.** *Obs.* to charge with a crime before a tribunal. [ME *apele*(n), t. OF: m. *apeler*, g. L *appellāre* approach, address, summon] —**ap·peal'a·ble**, *adj.* —**ap·peal'er**, *n.* —**ap·peal'ing·ly**, *adv.*

—**Syn. 1.** prayer, supplication. **6.** APPEAL, ENTREAT, PETITION, SUPPLICATE mean to ask for something wished for or needed. APPEAL and PETITION may concern groups and formal or public requests. ENTREAT and SUPPLICATE are usually more personal and emotional. To APPEAL is to ask earnestly for help or support, on grounds of reason, justice, common humanity, etc.: *to appeal for contributions to a cause.* To PETITION is to ask by written request, by prayer, or the like, that something be granted: *to petition for more playgrounds.* ENTREAT suggests pleading: *the child entreated his father not to punish him.* To SUPPLICATE is to beg humbly, usually from a superior, powerful, or stern (official) person: *to supplicate that the lives of prisoners be spared.*

ap·pear (ə pĭr'), *v.i.* **1.** to come into sight; become visible: *a cloud appeared on the horizon.* **2.** to have an appearance; seem; look: *to appear wise.* **3.** to be obvious; be clear or made clear by evidence: *it appears to me that you are right.* **4.** to come or be placed before the public: *his biography appeared last year.* **5.** *Law.* to come formally before a tribunal, authority, etc., as defendant, plaintiff, or counsel. [ME *apere*(n), t. OF: m. *aper-*, s. *apareir*, g. L *appārēre*] —**Syn. 2.** see **seem.**

ap·pear·ance (ə pĭr'əns), *n.* **1.** the act or fact of appearing, as to the eye, the mind, or the public. **2.** *Law.* the coming into court of a party to a suit. **3.** outward look or aspect; mien: *a man of noble appearance.* **4.** outward show or seeming; semblance: *to avoid the appearance of coveting an honor.* **5.** (*pl.*) indications or circumstances. **6.** an apparition. **7.** *Philos.* the sensory, or phenomenal, aspect of existence to an observer.

—**Syn. 3.** APPEARANCE, ASPECT, GUISE refer to the way in which something outwardly presents itself to view. APPEARANCE refers to the outward look: *the shabby appearance of his car.* ASPECT refers to the appearance at some particular time or in special circumstances; it often has emotional implications, either ascribed to the object itself or felt by the beholder: *in the dusk the forest had a terrifying aspect.* GUISE suggests a misleading appearance, assumed for an occasion or a purpose: *under the guise of friendship.*

ap·pease (ə pēz'), *v.t.*, **-peased, -peasing. 1.** to bring to a state of peace, quiet, ease, or content: *to appease an angry king.* **2.** to satisfy: *to appease one's hunger.* **3.** to accede to the belligerent demands of (a country, government, etc.) by a sacrifice of justice. [ME *apese*(n), t. OF: m. *apaisier*, der. *a* to + *pais* (g. L *pax*) peace] —**ap·peas'a·ble**, *adj.* —**ap·pease'ment**, *n.* —**appeas'er**, *n.*

—**Syn. 1.** pacify, calm, placate. **2.** allay, assuage. **3.** APPEASE, CONCILIATE, PROPITIATE imply trying to preserve or obtain peace. To APPEASE is to make anxious overtures and often undue concessions to satisfy the demands of someone with a greed for power, territory, etc.: *Chamberlain tried to appease Hitler at Munich.* To CONCILIATE is to win an enemy or opponent over by displaying a willingness to be just and fair: *when mutual grievances are recognized, conciliation is possible.* To PROPITIATE is to admit a fault, and, by trying to make amends, to allay hostile feeling: *to propitiate an offended neighbor.* —**Ant. 1.** enrage. **2.** sharpen. **3.** defy.

ap·pel (á pĕl'), *n. Fencing.* **1.** a tap or stamp of the foot, formerly serving as a warning of one's intent to attack. **2.** a smart stroke with the blade used for the purpose of procuring an opening. [t. F]

ap·pel·lant (ə pĕl'ənt), *n.* **1.** one who appeals. **2.** *Law.* one who appeals to a higher tribunal. —*adj.* **3.** appellate. [t. L: s. *appellans*, ppr., appealing]

ap·pel·late (ə pĕl'ĭt), *adj. Law.* **1.** pertaining to appeals. **2.** having power to review and decide appeals. [t. L: m. s. *appellātus*, pp., appealed]

ap·pel·la·tion (ăp'ə lā'shən), *n.* **1.** a name, title, or designation. **2.** act of naming. [t. L: s. *appellātio* name]

ap·pel·la·tive (ə pĕl'ə tĭv), *n.* **1.** a common noun as opposed to a proper name. **2.** a descriptive name; a designation, as *Odd* in *Odd John.* —*adj.* **3.** pertaining to a common noun. **4.** designative; descriptive.

ap·pel·lee (ăp'ə lē'), *n. Law.* the defendant or respondent in an appellate proceeding. [t. F: m. *appelé*, pp. of *appeler* APPEAL]

ap·pend (ə pĕnd'), *v.t.* **1.** to add, as an accessory; subjoin; annex. **2.** to attach as a pendant. [t. L: s. *appendere* hang (something) on]

ap·pend·age (ə pĕn'dĭj), *n.* **1.** a subordinate attached part of anything. **2.** *Biol.* any member of the body diverging from the axial trunk. **3.** *Bot.* any subsidiary part superadded to another part.

ap·pend·ant (ə pĕn'dənt), *adj.* **1.** hanging to; annexed; attached. **2.** associated as an accompaniment or consequence: *the salary appendant to a position.* **3.** *Law.* pertaining to a legal appendant. —*n.* **4.** a person or thing attached or added. **5.** *Law.* an interest (usually in land) connected with or dependent on some other interest. Also, **ap·pend'ent.** —**ap·pend'ance, ap·pend'ence,** *n.*

ap·pen·dec·to·my (ăp'ən dĕk'tə mĭ), *n., pl.* **-mies.** *Surg.* excision of the vermiform appendix. [f. APPEND(IX) + -ECTOMY]

ap·pen·di·ci·tis (ə pĕn'də sī'tĭs), *n. Pathol.* inflammation of the vermiform appendix. [t. NL, f. s. L *appendix* APPENDIX + -*itis* -ITIS]

ap·pen·di·cle (ə pĕn'də kəl), *n.* a small appendage. [t. L: m. s. *appendicula*, dim. of *appendix* APPENDIX] —**ap·pen·dic·u·lar** (ăp'ən dĭk'yə lər), *adj.*

ap·pen·dix (ə pĕn'dĭks), *n., pl.* **-dixes, -dices** (-də-sēz'). **1.** matter which supplements the main text of a book, generally explanatory, statistical, or bibliographic material. **2.** *Anat.* **a.** a process or projection. **b.** the vermiform appendix. **3.** *Aeron.* the short tube at the bottom of a balloon bag, by which the intake and release of buoyant gas is controlled. [t. L: appendage, addition]

—**Syn. 1.** APPENDIX, SUPPLEMENT both mean material added after the end of a book. An APPENDIX gives useful additional information, without which, however, the rest of the book is complete: *in the appendix are forty detailed charts.* A SUPPLEMENT, bound in the book or published separately, is given for comparison, as an enhancement, to provide corrections, to present later information, and the like: *a yearly supplement is issued.*

ap·per·ceive (ăp'ər sēv'), *v.t.*, **-ceived, -ceiving.** *Psychol.* **1.** to be conscious of perceiving; comprehend. **2.** to comprehend by assimilating (a new idea) with the mass of concepts, etc., already in the mind. [der. APPERCEPTION, modeled on *perceive, perception*]

ap·per·cep·tion (ăp'ər sĕp'shən), *n. Psychol.* **1.** conscious perception. **2.** act of apperceiving. [t. F] —**ap·per·cep'tive**, *adj.*

ap·per·tain (ăp'ər tān'), *v.i.* to belong as a part, member, possession, attribute, etc.; pertain (fol. by *to*). [ME *aperteine*(n), t. OF: m. *apartenir*, g. LL *appertinēre*]

ap·pe·tence (ăp'ə təns), *n.* **1.** strong natural craving; appetite; intense desire. **2.** instinctive inclination or natural tendency. **3.** material or chemical attraction or affinity. [t. L: m. s. *appetentia* seeking after]

ap·pe·ten·cy (ăp'ə tən sĭ), *n., pl.* **-cies.** appetence.

ap·pe·tite (ăp'ə tīt'), *n.* **1.** a desire for food or drink: *to work up an appetite.* **2.** a desire to supply any bodily want or craving: *the natural appetites.* **3.** an innate or acquired demand or propensity to satisfy a want: *an appetite for reading.* [ME *appetit*, t. OF, t. L: s. *appetītus* onset, desire for] —**Syn. 1-3.** longing, hunger.

ap·pe·ti·tive (ăp'ə tī'tĭv), *adj.* pertaining to appetite.

ap·pe·tiz·er (ăp'ə tī'zər), *n.* a food or drink that stimulates the desire for food.

ap·pe·tiz·ing (ăp'ə tī'zĭng), *adj.* exciting or appealing to the appetite. —**ap'pe·tiz'ing·ly**, *adv.*

Ap·pi·an way (ăp'ĭ an), an ancient Roman highway extending from Rome to Brundisium (now Brindisi): begun 312 B.C. by Appius Claudius Caecus. ab. 350 mi.

ap·plaud (ə plôd'), *v.i.* **1.** to express approval by clapping the hands, shouting, etc. **2.** to give praise; express approval. —*v.t.* **3.** to praise or show approval of by clapping the hands, shouting, etc.: *to applaud an actor.* **4.** to praise in any way; commend; approve: *to applaud one's conduct.* [t. L:s. *applaudere*] —**ap·plaud'er**, *n.*

ap·plause (ə plôz'), *n.* **1.** hand clapping, shouting, or other demonstrations of approval. **2.** any expression of approbation or approval. [t. L: m. s. *applausus*, pp.] —**ap·plau·sive** (ə plô'sĭv) *adj.* —**Syn. 2.** acclamation.

ap·ple (ăp'əl), *n.* **1.** the edible fruit, usually round and red, of a rosaceous tree, *Malus pumila (Pyrus Malus).* **2.** the tree, cultivated in most temperate regions. **3.** the fruit of any of certain other species of tree of the same genus. **4.** any of these trees. **5.** any of various other fruits, or fruitlike products or plants, usually specially designated, as the custard apple, love apple (tomato), May apple, oak apple. [ME; OE *æppel*, c. G *apfel*]

apple butter, a kind of thick, spiced applesauce.

apple green, a clear, light green.

ap·ple·jack (ăp'əl jăk'), *n. U.S.* **1.** a brandy distilled from fermented (i.e. hard) cider. **2.** See cider.

apple of discord, *Gk. Myth.* the golden apple inscribed "For the fairest," thrown by the goddess of discord among the Greek gods and awarded by Paris to Aphrodite. His award led to the destruction of Troy.

apple of the eye, **1.** the pupil of the eye. **2.** something very precious or dear.

ap·ple·sauce (ăp'əl sôs'), *n.* **1.** apples stewed to a soft pulp. **2.** *U.S. Slang.* nonsense; bunk.

Ap·ple·ton (ăp'əl tən), *n.* a city in E Wisconsin. 48,411 (1960).

Appleton layers, the upper layers of the ionosphere, beyond the Heaviside layer, important in the reflection of radio waves. [named after E. V. *Appleton*, British scientist (1892–1965)]

ap·pli·ance (ə plī′əns), *n.* **1.** an instrument, apparatus, or device for a particular use. **2.** act of applying; application. **3.** *Obs.* compliance. [f. m. APPLY + -ANCE]

ap·pli·ca·ble (ăp′lə kə bəl, ə plĭk′ə-), *adj.* capable of being applied; fit; suitable; relevant. —**ap′pli·ca·bil′i·ty, ap′pli·ca·ble·ness,** *n.* —**ap′pli·ca·bly,** *adv.*

ap·pli·cant (ăp′lə kənt), *n.* one who applies; a candidate: *an applicant for a position.* [t. L: s. *applicans,* ppr.]

ap·pli·ca·tion (ăp′lə kā′shən), *n.* **1.** act of putting to a special use or purpose: *the application of common sense to a problem.* **2.** quality of being usable for a particular purpose or in a special way; relevance: *this has no application to the case.* **3.** act of applying: *the application of salve to a wound.* **4.** the thing or remedy applied. **5.** act of requesting. **6.** a written or spoken request or appeal. **7.** close attention; persistent effort: *application to one's studies.* [t. L: s. *applicātio* a joining to] —**Syn. 6.** solicitation, petition. **7.** See **effort.**

ap·pli·ca·tive (ăp′lə kā′tĭv), *adj.* applying or capable of being applied; applicatory; practical.

ap·pli·ca·tor (ăp′lə kā′tər), *n. Med.* a rodlike instrument for applying medication.

ap·pli·ca·to·ry (ăp′lə kə tôr′ĭ), *adj.* fitted for application or use; practical.

ap·plied (ə plīd′), *adj.* put to practical use, as a science when its laws are concrete phenomena (distinguished from *abstract, theoretical,* or *pure* science).

ap·pli·qué (ăp′lə kā′; *Fr.* å plē kĕ′), *adj., n., v.,* **-quéd, -quéing.** —*adj.* **1.** formed with ornamentation of one material sewed or otherwise applied to another. —*n.* **2.** the ornamentation used to make an appliqué material. **3.** work so formed. —*v.t.* **4.** to apply or form as in appliqué work. [t. F, pp. of *appliquer* put on]

ap·ply (ə plī′), *v.,* **-plied, -plying.** —*v.t.* **1.** to lay on; bring into physical proximity or contact: *to apply a match to powder.* **2.** to bring to bear; put into practical operation, as a principle, law, rule, etc. **3.** to put to use; employ: *they know how to apply their labor.* **4.** to devote to some specific purpose: *to apply a sum of money to pay a debt.* **5.** to use (a word or statement) with reference to some person or thing as applicable or pertinent: *to apply the testimony to the case.* **6.** to give with earnestness or assiduity; employ with attention; set: *to apply one's mind to one's lessons.* —*v.i.* **7.** to have a bearing or reference; be pertinent: *the argument applies to the case.* **8.** to make application or request; ask: *to apply for a job.* [ME *aplie(n),* t. OF: m. *aplier,* g. L *applicāre* attach] —**ap·pli′er,** *n.* —**Syn. 4.** appropriate, allot, assign. **8.** petition.

ap·pog·gia·tu·ra (ə pŏj′ə tyōōr′ə, -tōōr′ə; *It.* äp-pōd′jä tōō′rä), *n. Music.* a note of embellishment (short or long) preceding another note and taking a portion of its time. [It., der. *ap-poggiare,* prop., lean]

Written   Played

Appoggiatura
A, short; B, long

ap·point (ə point′), *v.t.* **1.** to nominate or assign to a position, or to perform a function; set apart; designate: *to appoint a new secretary.* **2.** to constitute, ordain, or fix by decree, order, or decision; decree: *laws appointed by God.* **3.** to determine by authority or agreement; fix; settle: *a time appointed for the meeting.* **4.** *Law.* to designate (a person) to take the benefit of an estate created by a deed or will. **5.** to provide with what is requisite; equip. **6.** *Obs.* to point at by way of censure. —*v.i.* **7.** *Obs.* to ordain; resolve; determine. [ME *apoint(en),* t. OF: m. *apointer,* g. LL *appunctāre* repair, appoint] —**ap·point′er,** *n.* —**Syn. 2.** prescribe, establish. **5.** supply. See **furnish.**

ap·point·ee (ə poin tē′, ăp′oin tē′), *n.* **1.** a person appointed. **2.** a beneficiary under a legal appointment.

ap·poin·tive (ə poin′tĭv), *adj.* pertaining to or dependent on appointment: *an appointive office.*

ap·point·ment (ə point′mənt), *n.* **1.** act of appointing, designating, or placing in office: *to fill a vacancy by appointment.* **2.** an office held by a person appointed. **3.** act of fixing by mutual agreement; engagement: *an appointment to meet at six o'clock.* **4.** (*usually pl.*) equipment, as for a ship, hotel, etc. **5.** decree; ordinance. —**Syn. 2.** APPOINTMENT, OFFICE, POST, STATION mean a place of duty or employment. APPOINTMENT refers to a position for which special qualifications are required. OFFICE often suggests a position of trust or authority. POST in the U.S. is usually restricted to military or other public positions; in England it may be used of any position. STATION means a sphere of duty or occupation; it emphasizes the location of work to be done. See **position.**

ap·poin·tor (ə poin′tər, ə poin tôr′), *n. Law.* one who exercises a power of appointment of property.

Ap·po·mat·tox (ăp′ə măt′əks), *n.* **1.** a town in central Virginia: Lee surrendered to Grant here, April 9, 1865. **2.** a river flowing from near this town E to the James river. ab. 150 mi.

ap·por·tion (ə pôr′shən), *v.t.* to divide and assign in just proportion or according to some rule; distribute or allocate proportionally: *to apportion expenses.* [t. F: m. s. *apportionner,* f. à to + *portionner* PORTION, v.]

ap·por·tion·ment (ə pôr′shən mənt), *n.* **1.** act of ap-portioning. **2.** *U.S.* the distribution of representation in the federal House of Representatives among the several States (or, in State legislatures, among the counties or other local areas).

ap·pose (ə pōz′), *v.t.,* **-posed, -posing. 1.** to put or apply (one thing) to or near to another. **2.** to place next, as one thing to another; place side by side, as two things. [t. F: m. s. *apposer,* f. à AD- + *poser* POSE[2], assoc. with derivatives of L *apponere.* See APPOSITE]

ap·po·site (ăp′ə zĭt), *adj.* suitable; well-adapted; pertinent: *an apposite answer.* [t. L: m. s. *appositus,* pp., put to] —**ap′po·site·ly,** —**ap′po·site·ness,** *n.*

ap·po·si·tion (ăp′ə zĭsh′ən), *n.* **1.** act of adding to or together; a placing together; juxtaposition. **2.** *Gram.* a syntactic relation between expressions, usually consecutive, which have the same function and the same relation to other elements in the sentence, the second expression identifying or supplementing the first. For example: *Washington, our first President,* has our *first President* in apposition with *Washington.* —**ap′po·si′tion·al,** *adj.* —**ap′po·si′tion·al·ly,** *adv.*

ap·pos·i·tive (ə pŏz′ə tĭv), *Gram.* —*n.* **1.** a word or phrase in apposition. —*adj.* **2.** placed in apposition. —**ap·pos′i·tive·ly,** *adv.*

ap·prais·al (ə prā′zəl), *n.* **1.** act of placing an estimated value on an asset or assets. **2.** valuation; an estimate of value, as for sale, assessment, or taxation. Also, **ap·praise′ment.**

ap·praise (ə prāz′), *v.t.,* **-praised, -praising. 1.** to estimate generally, as to quality, size, weight, etc. **2.** to value in current money; estimate the value of. Also, **ap·prize**[1]. [b. APPRIZE[2] and PRAISE] —**ap·prais′a·ble,** *adj.* —**ap·prais′er,** *n.* —**ap·prais′ing·ly,** *adv.*

ap·pre·ci·a·ble (ə prē′shĭ ə bəl, -shə bəl), *adj.* capable of being perceived or estimated. —**ap·pre′ci·a·bly,** *adv.*

ap·pre·ci·ate (ə prē′shĭ āt′), *v.,* **-ated, -ating.** —*v.t.* **1.** to place a sufficiently high estimate on: *his great ability was not appreciated.* **2.** to be fully conscious of; be aware of; detect: *to appreciate the dangers of a situation.* **3.** to raise in value. —*v.i.* **4.** to increase in value. [t. L: m. s. *appretiātus,* pp., appraised] —**ap·pre′ci·a′tor,** *n.* —**Syn. 1.** APPRECIATE, ESTEEM, PRIZE, VALUE imply holding something in high regard. To APPRECIATE is to exercise wise judgment, delicate perception, and keen insight in realizing the worth of something. To ESTEEM is to feel respect combined with a warm, kindly feeling. To VALUE is to attach importance to a thing because of its worth (material or otherwise). To PRIZE is to value highly and cherish.

ap·pre·ci·a·tion (ə prē′shĭ ā′shən), *n.* **1.** act of estimating the qualities of things and giving them their due value. **2.** clear perception or recognition, esp. of aesthetic quality. **3.** increase in value of property. **4.** critical notice; critique.

ap·pre·ci·a·tive (ə prē′shĭ ə tĭv, -shə tĭv), *adj.* capable of appreciating; feeling or manifesting appreciation. —**ap·pre′ci·a·tive·ly,** *adv.* —**ap·pre′ci·a·tive·ness,** *n.*

ap·pre·ci·a·to·ry (ə prē′shĭ ə tôr′ĭ, -shə-), *adj.* appreciative. —**ap·pre′ci·a·to′ri·ly,** *adv.*

ap·pre·hend (ăp′rĭ hĕnd′), *v.t.* **1.** to take into custody; arrest by legal warrant or authority. **2.** to grasp the meaning of; understand; conceive. **3.** to entertain suspicion or fear of; anticipate: *I apprehend no violence.* —*v.i.* **4.** to understand. **5.** to be apprehensive; fear. [t. L: s. *apprehendere*] —**ap·pre·hend′er,** *n.*

ap·pre·hen·si·ble (ăp′rĭ hĕn′sə bəl), *adj.* capable of being understood. —**ap′pre·hen′si·bil′i·ty,** *n.*

ap·pre·hen·sion (ăp′rĭ hĕn′shən), *n.* **1.** anticipation of adversity; dread or fear of coming evil. **2.** the faculty of apprehending; understanding. **3.** a view, opinion, or idea on any subject. **4.** act of arresting; seizure. [t. L: s. *apprehensio*] —**Syn. 1.** APPREHENSION, ANXIETY, MISGIVING imply an unsettled and uneasy state of mind. APPREHENSION is an active state of fear, usually of some danger or misfortune: *apprehension before opening a telegram.* ANXIETY is a somewhat prolonged state of apprehensive worry: *anxiety because of a reduced income.* MISGIVING implies a dubious uncertainty or suspicion, as well as uneasiness: *to have misgivings about the investment.*

ap·pre·hen·sive (ăp′rĭ hĕn′sĭv), *adj.* **1.** uneasy or fearful about something that may happen: *apprehensive of (or for) one's safety.* **2.** quick to learn or understand. **3.** perceptive (fol. by *of*). —**ap′pre·hen′sive·ly,** *adv.* —**ap′pre·hen′sive·ness,** *n.*

ap·pren·tice (ə prĕn′tĭs), *n., v.,* **-ticed, -ticing.** —*n.* **1.** one who works for another with obligations to learn a trade. **2.** a learner; a novice. **3.** *U.S. Navy,* an enlisted man receiving specialized training. —*v.t.* **4.** to bind to or put under the care of an employer for instruction in a trade. [ME *aprentys,* t. OF: m. *aprentis,* ult. der. L *appre(he)ndre* seize] —**ap·pren′tice·ship′,** *n.*

ap·pressed (ə prĕst′), *adj.* pressed closely against or fitting closely to something.

ap·prise[1] (ə prīz′), *v.t.,* **-prised, -prising.** to give notice to; inform; advise (often fol. by *of*). Also, **apprize.** [t. F: m. *appris,* pp. of *apprendre* learn, teach. See APPRENTICE]

ap·prise[2] (ə prīz′), *v.t.,* **-prised, -prising.** appraise[1].

ap·prize[1] (ə prīz′), *v.t.,* **-prized, -prizing.** appraise. Also, **apprise.** [ME *aprise(n),* t. OF: m. *apriser,* der. phrase *à pris* for sale] —**ap·priz′er,** *n.*

ap·prize[2] (ə prīz′), *v.t.,* **-prized, -prizing.** apprise[1].

ap·proach (ə prōch′), *v.t.* **1.** to come nearer or near to: *to approach the city.* **2.** to come near to in quality, char-

acter, time, or condition: *approaching Homer as a poet.*
3. to bring near to something. **4.** to make advances or a proposal to: *to approach the President with a suggestion.*
5. to begin work on; set about: *to approach a problem.*
—*v.i.* **6.** to come nearer; draw near: *the storm approaches.*
7. to come near in character, time, amount, etc.; approximate. —*n.* **8.** act of drawing near: *the approach of a horseman.* **9.** nearness or close approximation: *a fair approach to accuracy.* **10.** any means of access: *the approaches to a city.* **11.** the method used or steps taken in setting about a task, problem, etc. **12.** (*sing. or pl.*) advances made to a person. **13.** (*pl.*) *Mil.* works for protecting forces in an advance against a fortified position. **14.** *Golf.* a stroke after teeing off, by which a player endeavors to get his ball on the putting green. [ME *aproche(n)*, t. OF: m. *aprochier*, g. LL *appropiāre*]

ap·proach·a·ble (ə·prōch′chə bəl), *adj.* **1.** capable of being approached; accessible. **2.** (of a person) easy to approach. —**ap·proach′a·bil′i·ty, ap·proach′a·ble·ness,** *n.*

ap·pro·bate (ăp′rə bāt′), *v.t.,* -bated, -bating. *U.S.* to approve officially. [t. L: m.s. *approbātus,* pp., favored]

ap·pro·ba·tion (ăp′rə bā′shən), *n.* **1.** approval; commendation. **2.** sanction. **3.** *Obs.* conclusive proof.

ap·pro·ba·tive (ăp′rə bā′tĭv). *adj.* approving; expressing approbation. Also, **ap·pro·ba·to·ry** (ə prō′bə tōr′ĭ). —**ap·pro·ba′tive·ness,** *n.*

ap·pro·pri·a·ble (ə prō′prĭ ə bəl), *adj.* capable of being appropriated.

ap·pro·pri·ate (*adj.* ə prō′prĭ ĭt; *v.* ə prō′prĭ āt′), *adj., v.,* -ated, -ating. —*adj.* **1.** suitable or fitting for a particular purpose, person, occasion, etc.: *an appropriate example.* **2.** belonging or peculiar to one: *each played his appropriate part.* —*v.t.* **3.** to set apart for some specific purpose or use: *the legislature appropriated funds for the university.* **4.** to take to or for oneself; take possession of. [t. L: m.s. *appropriātus,* pp., made one's own] —**ap·pro′pri·ate·ly,** *adv.* —**ap·pro′pri·ate·ness,** *n.* —**ap·pro′pri·a′tive,** *adj.* —**ap·pro′pri·a′tor,** *n.* —**Syn. 1.** befitting, apt, meet, felicitous.

ap·pro·pri·a·tion (ə prō′prĭ ā′shən), *n.* **1.** anything appropriated for a special purpose, as money. **2.** act of appropriating. **3.** an act of a legislature authorizing money to be paid from the treasury for a special use.

ap·prov·al (ə prōō′vəl). *n.* **1.** act of approving; approbation. **2.** sanction; official permission. **3. on approval,** for examination, without obligation to buy.

ap·prove (ə prōōv′), *v.,* -proved, -proving. —*v.t.* **1.** to pronounce or consider good; speak or think favorably of: *to approve the policies of the administration.* **2.** to confirm or sanction officially; ratify. **3.** *Obs.* to demonstrate in practice; show. **4.** *Obs.* to make good; attest. **5.** *Obs.* to prove by trial. **6.** *Obs.* to convict. —*v.i.* **7.** to speak or think favorably (usually fol. by *of*): *to approve of him.* [ME *approve(n),* t. OF: m. *approver,* g. L *approbāre*] —**ap·prov′a·ble,** *adj.* —**ap·prov′er,** *n.* —**ap·prov′ing·ly,** *adv.* —**Syn. 1.** APPROVE, COMMEND, PRAISE mean to have, and usually to express, a favorable opinion. To APPROVE is to have a very good opinion, expressed or not, of someone or something: *he approved the new plan.* To COMMEND is to speak or write approvingly, often formally and publicly, to congratulate or honor for something done: *to commend a fireman for a heroic act.* To PRAISE is to speak or write, often in glowing and emotional terms, to or about one or more persons: *to praise the Boy Scouts.* **2.** authorize, endorse.

approx., approximately.

ap·prox·i·mal (ə prŏk′sə məl), *adj. Anat.* near or adjacent, as surfaces of teeth.

ap·prox·i·mate (*adj.* ə prŏk′sə mĭt; *v.* ə prŏk′sə māt′), *adj., v.,* -mated, -mating. —*adj.* **1.** nearly exact, equal, or perfect. **2.** near; close together. **3.** very similar. —*v.t.* **4.** to come near to; approach closely to: *to approximate a solution to a problem.* **5.** to bring near. —*v.i.* **6.** to come near in position, character, amount, etc. [t. L: m.s. *approximātus,* pp.] —**ap·prox′i·mate·ly,** *adv.*

ap·prox·i·ma·tion (ə prŏk′sə mā′shən), *n.* **1.** a drawing, moving, or advancing near in space, position, degree, or relation. **2.** *Math., Physics.* a result which is not exact, but is sufficiently so for a given purpose.

ap·pur·te·nance (ə pûr′tə nəns), *n.* **1.** something accessory to another and more important thing; an adjunct. **2.** *Law.* a right, privilege, or improvement belonging to and passing with a principal property. **3.** (*pl.*) apparatus; mechanism. [ME *appurtena(u)nce,* t. AF: m. *apurtenance,* ult. der. L *appertinēre* belong to]

ap·pur·te·nant (ə pûr′tə nənt), *adj.* **1.** appertaining or belonging; pertaining. —*n.* **2.** an appurtenance.

Apr., April.

a·près moi le dé·luge (å prě mwå′ lə dě lȳzh′), *French.* after me the deluge (attributed to Louis XV).

a·pri·cot (ā′prə kŏt′, ăp′rə-), *n.* **1.** the downy yellow fruit, somewhat resembling a small peach, of the tree *Prunus armeniaca.* **2.** the tree. **3.** a pinkish yellow or yellowish pink. [var. of *apricock,* appar. b. L *praecoqua* apricots (neut. pl. of *praecoquus* early ripe) and F *abricot* apricot, t. Pg.: m. *albricoque,* t. Sp.: m. *albar*(i)-*coque,* t. Ar.: m. *al-barqūq,* t. Gk.: m. *praikókion,* t. L (as above)]

A·pril (ā′prəl), *n.* the fourth month of the year, containing 30 days. [t. L: s. *Aprīlis*]

April fool, a victim on April Fools' Day.

April Fools' Day, April 1; All Fools' Day; the day observed by playing jokes on unsuspecting people.

a pri·o·ri (ā prī ōr′ī, ä prī ōr′ī), **1.** from cause to

effect; from a general law to a particular instance; valid independently of observation (opposed to *a posteriori*). **2.** claiming to report matters of fact but actually not supported by factual study. [t. L: from something prior] —**a·pri·or·i·ty** (ā′prī ŏr′ə tĭ, -ŏr′-), *n.*

a·pron (ā′prən), *n.* **1.** a piece of apparel made in various ways for covering, and usually also protecting, the front of the person more or less completely. **2.** a flat continuous conveyor belt. **3.** *Mach.* that part of a lathe carriage containing the clutches and gears that transmit feeder or lead screw motion to the carriage. **4.** *Civ. Eng.* **a.** any device for protecting a surface of earth, such as a river bank, from the action of moving water. **b.** a platform to receive the water falling over a dam. **5.** a paved or hard-packed area abutting on airfield buildings and hangars. **6.** the part of the stage in front of the closed curtain. **7.** *Geol.* a deposit of gravel and sand extending forward from a moraine. —*v.t.* **8.** to put an apron on; furnish with an apron. [ME *napron* (*a napron* being later taken as *an apron*), t. OF: m. *naperon.* dim. of *nape,* g. L *nappa* napkin, cloth] —**a′pron-like′,** *adj.*

ap·ro·pos (ăp′rə pō′), *adv.* **1.** to the purpose; opportunely. **2.** with reference or regard; in respect (fol. by *of*): *apropos of nothing.* **3.** by the way. —*adj.* **4.** opportune; pertinent: *apropos remarks.* [t. F: m. *à propos*]

apse (ăps), *n.* **1.** *Archit.* a vaulted semicircular or polygonal recess in a building, esp. at the end of the choir of a church. See diag. under **basilica.** **2.** *Astron.* an apsis. [t. L: m. s. *apsis,* t. Gk.: m. (*h*)*apsis* loop, circle, bow, arch, apse] —**ap·si·dal** (ăp′sə dəl), *adj.*

ap·sis (ăp′sĭs), *n., pl.* -sides (-sə dēz′). **1.** *Astron.* **a.** either of two points in an eccentric orbit, the one (**higher apsis**) furthest from the center of attraction, and the one (**lower apsis**) nearest to it. **b.** line of apsides, the line coinciding with the major axis of an orbit. **2.** *Archit.* an apse. [t. L. See APSE]

apt (ăpt), *adj.* **1.** inclined; disposed; prone: *too apt to slander others.* **2.** likely: *am I apt to find him at home?* **3.** unusually intelligent; quick to learn: *an apt pupil.* **4.** suited to the purpose or occasion: *an apt metaphor.* **5.** *Archaic.* prepared; ready; willing. [ME, t. L: s. *aptus* fastened, joined fitted] —**apt′ly,** *adv.* —**apt′ness,** *n.* —**Syn. 2.** See likely. **3.** clever, bright. **4.** APT, PERTINENT, RELEVANT all refer to something suitable or fitting. APT means to the point and particularly appropriate: *an apt comment.* PERTINENT means pertaining to the matter in hand: *a pertinent remark.* RELEVANT means directly related to and important to the subject: *a relevant opinion.*

apt., *pl.* apts. apartment.

ap·ter·al (ăp′tər əl), *adj. Archit.* without columns or a porch along the sides.

ap·ter·ous (ăp′tər əs), *adj.* **1.** *Zool.* wingless, as some insects. **2.** *Bot.* without membranous expansions, as a stem. [t. Gk.: m. *ápteros* without wings]

ap·ter·yg·i·al (ăp′tərĭj′ĭəl), *adj. Zool.* without wings, fins, or limbs, as snakes and eels. [f. A-⁶ + s. Gk. *pterýgion* little wing + -AL¹]

ap·ter·yx (ăp′tər ĭks), *n., pl.* -teryxes (-tər ĭk sĭz). any of several flightless ratite birds of New Zealand, constituting the genus *Apteryx,* allied to the extinct moas; kiwi. [t. NL, f. Gk.: a-, A-⁶ + *ptéryx* wing]

ap·ti·tude (ăp′tə tūd′, -tōōd′), *n.* **1.** a natural tendency or acquired inclination; both capacity and propensity for a certain course. **2.** readiness in learning; intelligence; talent. **3.** state or quality of being apt; special fitness. [t. ML: m. *aptitūdo,* der. L *aptus* fit]

Apteryx. *Apteryx australis* (27 in. long)

aptitude test, a test for special fitness; a test given to find out what sort of work a person has the ability to learn, such as clerical work, mechanical work, etc.

A·pu·le·ius (ăp′yə lē′əs), *n.* Lucius (lōō′shəs), born A.D. 125?, Roman philosopher and satirist.

A·pu·lia (ə pū′lyə), *n.* a department in SE Italy. 3,220,485 (1951); 7442 sq. mi.

A·pu·re (ä pōō′rě), *n.* a river flowing from W Venezuela E to the Orinoco. ab. 300 mi.

A·pu·ri·mac (ä′pōō rē′mäk), *n.* a river flowing from S Peru NW to the Ucayali river. ab. 500 mi.

a·py·ret·ic (ā′pī rĕt′ĭk), *adj. Pathol.* free from fever. [f. s. Gk. *apýretos* without fever + -IC]

AQ, achievement quotient.

Aq., (L *aqua*) water. Also, **aq.**

A·qa·ba (ä′kä bä′), *n.* a seaport in SW Jordan at the N end of the **Gulf of Aqaba,** an arm of the Red Sea. 2835 (1950).

aqua (ăk′wə, ä′kwə), *n., pl.* aquae (ăk′wē, ä′kwē). *Chiefly Pharm.* water; a liquid; a solution. [t. L: water]

aqua am·mo·ni·ae (ə mō′nĭ ē′), ammonia (def. 2). Also, **aqua ammonia.** [NL]

aqua for·tis (fôr′tĭs), nitric acid. [NL: strong water]

aq·ua·lung (ăk′wə lŭng′), *n.* a cylinder of compressed air, usually strapped onto the back, with a tube leading to a special mouthpiece or watertight mask, which enables a swimmer to move about freely at a considerable depth for an extended length of time.

aq·ua·ma·rine (ăk′wə mə rēn′), *n.* **1.** a transparent light-blue or greenish-blue variety of beryl, used as a gem. **2.** light blue-green or greenish blue. [t. L: m. *aqua marīna* sea water; r. *aigue marine,* t. F]

aq·ua·plane (ăk′wə plān′), *n., v.,* -planed, -planing. —*n.* **1.** a board which skims over water when pulled at

b., blend of, blended; c., cognate with; d., dialect, dialectal; der., derived from; f., formed from; g., going back to; m., modification of; r., replacing; s., stem of; t., taken from; ?, perhaps. See the full key on inside cover.

high speed, used **to carry a rider behind a towing speed-boat.** —*v.i.* 2. to ride an aquaplane. [f. L *aqua* water + -PLANE²; modeled on AIRPLANE]

qua re·gi·a (rē′jĭ̄ə), a mixture of one part of nitric acid and three parts of hydrochloric acid. [t. NL: royal water (with allusion to its power to dissolve gold)]

·qua·relle (ăk′wərĕl′), *n.* a painting in transparent water colors. [t. F, t. It.: m. *acquarello,* dim. of *acqua* water] —aq′ua·rel′list, *n.*

·quar·i·um (əkwâr′Yəm), *n., pl.* **aquariums, aquaria** (əkwâr′Yə). a pond, tank, or establishment in which living aquatic animals or plants are kept, as for exhibition. [t. L, prop. neut. of *aquārius* pertaining to water]

·quar·i·us (əkwâr′Yəs), *n., gen.* **Aquarii** (əkwâr′Yī′). 1. *Astron.* a zodiacal constellation; the water bearer. 2. the eleventh sign of the zodiac. See diag. under zodiac. [t. L: water bearer, prop. adj., pertaining to water]

·quat·ic (əkwăt′Yk, əkwŏt′-), *adj.* 1. of or pertaining to water. 2. living or growing in water. 3. practiced on or in water: *aquatic sports.* —*n.* 4. (*pl.*) sports practiced on or in water. [t. L: s. *aquāticus* watery]

·qua·tint (ăk′wətĭnt′), *n.* 1. a process imitating the broad flat tints of ink or wash drawings by etching a microscopic crackle on the copperplate intended for printing. 2. an etching made by this process. —*v.t., v.i.* 3. to etch in aquatint. [t. F: m. *aquatinte,* t. It.: m. *acqua tinta,* g. L *aqua tincta* tinted water]

qua vi·tae (vī′tē), 1. alcohol. 2. spirituous liquor, as brandy or whiskey. [t. ML: water of life]

q·ue·duct (ăk′wədŭkt′), *n.* 1. *Civ. Eng.* **a.** a conduit or artificial channel for conducting water from a distance, the water usually flowing by gravity. **b.** a structure which carries a conduit or canal across a valley or over a river. 2. *Anat.* a canal or passage through which liquids pass. [t. L: m. *aquae ductus* conveyance of water]

·que·ous (ā′kwYəs, ăk′wY-), *adj.* 1. of, like, or containing water; watery. 2. (of rocks) formed of matter deposited in or by water.

queous ammonia, ammonia (def. 2).

queous humor, *Anat.* the limpid watery fluid which fills the space between the cornea and the crystalline lens in the eye.

·qui·la (ăk′wələ), *n., gen.* **-lae** (-lē′). *Astron.* a northern constellation lying south of Cygnus, and containing the bright star Altair. [t. L: eagle]

·qui·le·gi·a (ăk′wəlē′jĭ̄ə, ā′kwə-), *n. Bot.* any columbine. [t. ML, var. of *aquilēja* columbine]

·qui·le·ia (ā′kwē lē′yə), *n.* an ancient city at the N end of the Adriatic: important Roman center.

q·ui·line (ăk′wəlĭn′, -lĭn), *adj.* 1. of or like the eagle. 2. (of the nose) curved like an eagle's beak; hooked. [t. L: m. s. *aquilīnus*]

·qui·nas (əkwī′nəs), *n.* **Thomas,** (*"the Angelic Doctor"*) 1225?-1274, Italian scholastic philosopher and one of the great theologians of the Roman Catholic Church.

q·ui·taine (ăk′wətān′), *n.* a lowland region in SW France: an ancient Roman province in Gaul; later a duchy. Latin, **Aq·ui·ta·ni·a** (ăk′wətā′nĭ̄ə).

Duchy of Aquitaine, 1360

quo (ā kwō′), *Latin.* from which; a point of departure (for something, an idea, etc.).

·r-, var. of ad- (by assimilation) before *r,* as in *arrear.*

ar¹, 1. an adjective suffix meaning "of or pertaining to," "of the nature of," "like," as in *linear, regular.* 2. a suffix forming adjectives not directly related to nouns, as *similar, singular.* [t. L: s. -*āris*; r. ME -*er,* t. AF]

ar², a noun suffix, as in *vicar, scholar, collar.* [repr. L -*ārius,* -*āris,* etc.]

ar³, a noun suffix denoting an agent (replacing regular -er¹), as in *beggar, liar.* [special use of -AR²]

r., 1. Arabic. 2. Aramaic. 3. argentum.

r., 1. arrival. 2. arrive; arrives.

r·ab (ăr′əb), *n.* 1. a native of Arabia, or a member of the Arabic race (now widely spread in Asia and Africa, and formerly in southern Europe); an Arabian. 2. a horse of a graceful, intelligent breed, native to Arabia and adjacent countries. 3. a street Arab. —*adj.* 4. Arabian. [back formation from ARABY]

rab., 1. Arabia. 2. Arabic.

r·a·besque (ăr′əbĕsk′), *n.* 1. a kind of ornament in which flowers, foliage, fruits, vases, animals, and figures (in strict Mohammedan use, no animate objects) are represented in a fancifully combined pattern. 2. a pose in ballet in which the dancer stands on one leg with one arm extended in front, and the other leg and arm behind. —*adj.* 3. in the Arabian style, esp. of ornamentation. [t. F: Arabian, t. It.: m. *arabesco,* der. *Arabo* Arab]

·ra·bi·a (ərā′bĭ̄ə), *n.* a peninsula in SW Asia, including Saudi Arabia, Yemen, Muscat and Oman, Aden, and other political divisions: divided in ancient time into **Arabia De·ser·ta** (dĭ zûr′tə), the N part, **Arabia Fe·lix** (fē′lĭks), the S part (sometimes restricted to Yemen), and **Arabia Pe·trae·a** (pə trē′ə) the NW part. 2,638,000 sq. mi. (est. 1950-55); ab. 1,000,000 sq. mi.

A·ra·bi·an (ərā′bĭ̄ən), *adj.* 1. pertaining to Arabia or the Arabs. —*n.* 2. an Arab (def. 1).

Arabian camel. See **camel** (def. 1a).

Arabian Desert, a large desert in Egypt between the Nile valley and the Red Sea.

Arabian Nights' Entertainments, The, a collection of Eastern folk tales derived in part from Indian and Persian sources and dating from the 10th century A.D. Also known as **The Thousand and One Nights.**

Arabian Sea, the NW part of the Indian Ocean, between India and Arabia.

Ar·a·bic (ăr′ə bĭk), *adj.* 1. belonging to or derived from Arabia or the Arabians. 2. (*l.c.*) designating certain species of acacia growing in Arabia and other eastern countries. —*n.* 3. any of the languages that developed out of the language of the Arabians of the time of Mohammed, now spoken in North Africa, Egypt, Arabia, Palestine, Syria, and Iraq. 4. the standard literary and classical language as established by the Koran. [t. L: s. *Arabicus*]

Arabic numerals, the characters 0, 1, 2, 3, 4, 5, 6, 7, 8, 9, introduced into general European use since the 12th century. Also, **Arabic figures.**

a·rab·i·nose (ərăb′ənōs′, ăr′əbə-), *n.* the pentose sugar, $C_5H_{10}O_5$, derived from plant gums or made synthetically from glucose. [f. ARAB(IC) + -IN² + -OSE²]

Ar·ab·ist (ăr′əb Yst), *n.* an authority on Arabia and the Arabs or on the Arabic language and literature.

ar·a·ble (ăr′əbəl). *adj.* 1. capable, without much modification, of producing crops by means of tillage. —*n.* 2. arable land. [t. L: m. s. *arābilis* that can be plowed; r. *earable* (f. *ear,* v., plow + -ABLE)] —ar′a·bil′i·ty, *n.*

Arab League, a limited confederation formed in 1945 by Arab Palestine and Trans-Jordan (now Jordan), Egypt, Iraq, Lebanon, Saudi Arabia, Syria, and Yemen; now includes: Algeria, Kuwait, Morocco, Sudan, and Tunisia.

Arab Palestine. See **Palestine** (def. 2).

Ar·a·by (ăr′əbĭ), *n. Poetic.* Arabia. [ME *Arabye,* t. F]

a·ra·ceous (ərā′shəs), *adj. Bot.* belonging to the *Araceae,* or arum family of plants, which includes the arums, skunk cabbage, sweet flag, calla lily, taro, etc. [f. AR(UM) + -ACEOUS]

A·rach·ne (ərăk′nĭ), *n. Gk. Myth.* a Lydian maiden who challenged Athene to a contest in weaving, and was turned into a spider. [t. L, t. Gk.: spider]

a·rach·nid (ərăk′nĭd), *n.* any arthropod of the class *Arachnida,* which includes the spiders, scorpions, mites, etc. [f. s. Gk. *aráchnē* spider, spider's web + -ID²] —a·rach·ni·dan (ərăk′nədən), *adj., n.*

a·rach·noid (ərăk′noid), *adj.* 1. resembling a spider's web. 2. of or belonging to the arachnids. 3. *Anat.* pertaining to the serous membrane (between the dura mater and the pia mater) enveloping the brain and spinal cord. 4. *Bot.* formed of or covered with long, delicate hairs or fibers. —*n.* 5. an arachnid. 6. the arachnoid membrane. [t. Gk.: m. s. *arach-noeidēs* like a cobweb]

A·rad (ärăd′), *n.* a city in W Rumania, on the Mures river. 87,291 (1948).

A·ra·fu·ra Sea (ä-rəfōōr′ə), a sea between N Australia and SW New Guinea.

Ar·a·gon (ăr′əgŏn′; *Sp.* ä′rägŏn′), *n.* a region in NE Spain: formerly a kingdom; later a province. 18,181 sq. mi.

Kingdom of Aragon, 1212-1492

A·ra·gon (ä rä gŏn′), *n.* **Louis** (lwē), born 1891. French novelist and poet.

a·rag·o·nite (ərăg′ənīt′, ăr′əgə-), *n.* a mineral, calcium carbonate, $CaCO_3$, chemically identical with calcite but differing in crystallization, and in having a higher specific gravity, less marked cleavage, etc. [f. ARAGON + -ITE¹]

A·ra·gua·ya (ä′rägwī′yä), *n.* a river in central Brazil, flowing N to the Tocantins river. ab. 1000 mi.

a·ra·li·a·ceous (ərā′lĭ̄ā′shəs), *adj. Bot.* belonging to the *Araliaceae,* a large family of plants incl. the American spikenard, ginseng, etc.

Ar·al Sea (ăr′əl), an inland sea in the SW Soviet Union in Asia, E of the Caspian Sea. 26,166 sq. mi. Also, **Lake Aral.**

A·ram (ā′răm, âr′əm), *n.* Hebrew name of ancient Syria.

Aram., Aramaic.

Ar·a·ma·ic (ăr′ə mā′Yk), *n.* 1. any of a group of Semitic languages which became the speech of Syria, Palestine, and Mesopotamia after circa 300 B.C., including Syriac and the language of Christ. —*adj.* 2. pertaining to Aram, or to the languages spoken there.

Ar·a·me·an (ăr′əmē′ən), *n.* 1. a Semite of the division associated with Aram. 2. the Aramaic language. Also, **Ar·a·mae·an.** [f. s. L *Aramaeus* (t. Gk.: m. *Aramaios*) pertaining to Aram or Syria + -AN]

A·rap·a·ho (ər̆ăp′ə hō′), *n.*, *pl.* **-ho.** **1.** (*pl.*) a tribe of North American Indians, of Algonquian speech stock, once dwelling in the Colorado plains, and now in Oklahoma and Wyoming. **2.** a member of this tribe. Also, **A·rap′a·hoe′.**

ar·a·pai·ma (är′ə pī′mə), *n.* a large fresh-water fish, *Arapaima gigas*, of Brazil and Guiana, said to attain a length of 15 feet and a weight of 400 pounds. [S Amer. native name]

Ar·a·rat (ăr′ə răt′), *n.* a volcanic mountain with two peaks in E Turkey, near the boundary with Iran and the Soviet Union: mentioned in Gen. 8:4. 16,696 ft.

A·ras (ä räs′), *n.* a river flowing from E Turkey along a portion of the border between NW Iran and the SW Soviet Union into the Kura river. Ancient, **A·rax·es** (ə răk′sēz).

Ar·au·ca·ni·a (är′ô kä′nǐ ə; *Sp.* ä′rou kä′nyä), *n.* a former region in central Chile.

Ar·au·ca·ni·an (är′ô kä′nǐ ən), *n.* **1.** one of a tribe of Indians in central Chile. **2.** a linguistic stock of Chile and northern Argentina.

A·ra·wak (ä′rä wäk′), *n.* one of a numerous and widely scattered Indian language stock of northern and northeastern South America and the West Indies. **—A′ra·wa′kan,** *adj.*

ar·ba·lest (är′bə lĭst), *n.* a powerful medieval crossbow. Also, **ar′ba·list.** [OE *arblast*, t. OF: m. *arbaleste* kind of catapult, g. L *arcuballista*. See ARC, BALLISTA] **—ar′ba·lest·er,** *n.*

Ar·be·la (är bē′lə), *n.* an ancient city of Assyria, E of Nineveh: Alexander defeated Darius near here, 331 B.C.

ar·bi·ter (är′bə tər), *n.* **1.** a person empowered to decide points at issue. **2.** one who has the sole or absolute power of judging or determining. [t. L: witness, judge]

ar·bi·tra·ble (är′bə trə bəl), *adj.* capable of arbitration; subject to the decision of an arbiter or arbitrator.

ar·bi·trage (är′bə trĭj, är′bə träzh′ *for 1*; är′bə trĭj *for 2*), *n.* **1.** *Finance.* the simultaneous purchase and sale of the same securities, commodities, or moneys in different markets to profit from unequal prices. **2.** *Rare.* arbitration. [t. F, der. *arbitrer* arbitrate]

ar·bi·tral (är′bə trəl), *adj.* pertaining to an arbiter or to arbitration. [t. LL: s. *arbitrālis*, der. L *arbiter* judge]

ar·bit·ra·ment (är bĭt′rə mənt), *n.* **1.** arbitration. **2.** the decision or sentence pronounced by an arbiter. **3.** the power of absolute and final decision. [t. ML: s. *arbitrāmentum*; r. ME *arbitrement*, t. OF]

ar·bi·trar·y (är′bə trĕr′ĭ), *adj.* **1.** subject to individual will or judgment; discretionary. **2.** capricious; uncertain; unreasonable: *an arbitrary interpretation.* **3.** uncontrolled by law; using or abusing unlimited power; despotic; tyrannical: *an arbitrary government.* [t. L: m. s. *arbitrārius* of arbitration, uncertain] **—ar′bi·trar′i·ly,** *adv.* **—ar′bi·trar′i·ness,** *n.*

ar·bi·trate (är′bə trāt′), *v.*, **-trated, -trating.** **—v.t.** **1.** to decide as arbiter or arbitrator; determine. **2.** to submit to arbitration; settle by arbitration: *to arbitrate a dispute.* **—v.i.** **3.** to act as arbiter; decide between opposing parties or sides. **4.** to submit a matter to arbitration. [t. L: m. s. *arbitrātus*, pp.] **—ar′bi·tra′tive,** *adj.*

ar·bi·tra·tion (är′bə trā′shən), *n.* **1.** *Law.* the hearing and determining of a dispute between parties by a person or persons chosen or agreed to by them. **2.** *Internat. Law.* the application of judicial methods to the settlement of international disputes. **—ar′bi·tra′tion·al,** *adj.*

ar·bi·tra·tor (är′bə trā′tər), *n.* a person chosen to decide a dispute, esp. one empowered to examine the facts and to decide an issue. Also, *Obs.,* **ar·bi·trer** (är′bə trər).

ar·bi·tress (är′bə trĭs), *n.* a female arbiter.

Ar·blay (där′blā; *Fr.* där blĕ′), *n.* **Madame d′,** (*Frances or Fanny Burney*) 1752–1840, British novelist.

ar·bor¹ (är′bər), *n.* **1.** a bower formed by trees, shrubs, or vines, often on a latticework. **2.** *Obs.* a grass plot; lawn; garden; orchard. Also, *esp. Brit.,* **arbour.** [ME (h)erber, t. AF, var. of OF (h)erbier, g. L herbārium, der. herba plant; influenced by L arbor tree]

ar·bor² (är′bər), *n.* **1.** *Mach.* **a.** a beam, shaft, axis, or spindle. **b.** a bar or shaft used to support either the work or the cutting tools during a machining process. **2.** *Foundry.* a reinforcing member of a core or mold. [Latinized var. of earlier *arber*, t. F: m. *arbre*]

ar·bor³ (är′bər), *n.*, *pl.* **arbores** (är′bə rēz′). a tree (used chiefly in botanical names). [t. L]

Arbor Day, a day, varying in date, observed in individual States of the U.S. for the planting of trees.

ar·bo·re·al (är bōr′ĭ əl), *adj.* **1.** pertaining to trees; treelike. **2.** living in or among trees. **3.** *Zool.* adapted for living and moving about in trees, as the limbs and skeleton of opossums, squirrels, monkeys, and apes.

ar·bo·re·ous (är bōr′ĭ əs), *adj.* **1.** abounding in trees; wooded. **2.** arboreal. **3.** arborescent. [t. L: m. *arboreus* pertaining to trees]

ar·bo·res·cent (är′bə rĕs′ənt), *adj.* treelike in size and form. [t. L: s. *arborescens*, ppr., becoming a tree] **—ar′bo·res′cence,** *n.*

ar·bo·re·tum (är′bə rē′təm), *n.*, *pl.* **-tums, -ta** (-tə). a

plot of land where different trees or shrubs are grown for study or popular interest. [t. L: a plantation of trees]

ar·bo·ri·cul·ture (är′bərə kŭl′chər), *n.* the cultivation of trees and shrubs. [f. *arbori-* (comb. form repr. L *arbor* tree) + CULTURE]

ar·bor·i·za·tion (är′bərə zā′shən), *n.* a treelike appearance, as in certain minerals or fossils.

ar·bor·ous (är′bərəs), *adj.* of or pertaining to trees.

ar·bor vi·tae (är′bər vī′tē), **1.** an evergreen tree of the coniferous genus *Thuja*, esp. *T. occidentalis*, planted for hedges, etc. See **red cedar** (def. 2). **2.** *Anat.* a treelike appearance in a vertical section of the cerebellum, due to the arrangement of the white and gray nerve tissues. Also, **ar′bor·vi′tae.** [t. L: tree of life]

ar·bour (är′bər), *n.* *Chiefly Brit.* arbor¹.

Ar·buth·not (är bŭth′nət, är′bəth nŏt′), *n.* **John,** 1667–1735, British satirist and physician: friend of Swift.

ar·bu·tus (är bū′təs), *n.* **1.** any of the evergreen shrubs or trees of the ericaceous genus *Arbutus*, esp. *A. unedo*, of southern Europe, with scarlet berries, cultivated for ornament and food. **2.** a creeping ericaceous plant, *Epigaea repens*, of the U. S., with fragrant white and pink flowers (**trailing arbutus**). [t. L: strawberry tree]

arc (ärk), *n.*, *v.*, **arced** (ärkt), **arcing** (är′kĭng) or **arcked, arcking.** **—n.** **1.** *Geom.* any part of a circle or other curved line. **2.** *Elect.* the luminous bridge formed by the passage of a current across a gap between two conductors or terminals, due to the incandescence of the conducting vapors. **3.** *Astron.* the part of a circle representing the apparent course of a heavenly body. **4.** anything bow-shaped. **—v.i.** **5.** to form an electric arc. [ME *ark*, t. L: m. s. *arcus* bow]

Arc (därk), *n.* **Jeanne d′** (zhän). See Joan of Arc.

ARC, American Red Cross. Also, **A.R.C.**

ar·cade (är kād′), *n.*, *v.*, **-caded, -cading.** **—n.** **1.** *Archit.* **a.** a series of arches supported on piers or columns. **b.** an arched, roofed-in gallery. **2.** an arched or covered passageway, usually with shops on either side. **—v.t.** **3.** to provide with or form as an arcade or arcades. [t. F, t. It.: m. *arcata* arch, der. *arco* bow, arch, g. L *arcus*]

Arcs of circles

Ar·ca·di·a (är kā′dĭ ə), *n.* **1.** a city in SW California, E of Los Angeles. 41,005 (1960). **2.** a mountainous district in ancient Greece, proverbial for the contented pastoral simplicity of its people. [t. L, t. Gk.: m. *Arkadía*]

Ar·ca·di·an (är kā′dĭ ən), *adj.* **1.** of Arcadia. **2.** pastoral; rustic; simple; innocent. **—n.** **3.** a native of Arcadia.

Ar·ca·dy (är′kə dĭ), *n.* *Poetic.* Arcadia.

ar·cane (är kān′), *adj.* mysterious; secret; obscure: *Poor writing can make even the most familiar things seem arcane.* [f. s. L *arcānus* g. *arcēre* shut up, keep + -ānus -ANE]

ar·ca·num (är kā′nəm), *n.*, *pl.* **-na** (-nə). **1.** (*often pl.*) a secret; a mystery. **2.** a supposed great secret of nature which the alchemists sought to discover. **3.** a secret and powerful remedy. [t. L, neut. of *arcānus* secret, hidden]

ar·ca·ture (är′kə chər), *n.* *Archit.* **1.** an arcade of small dimensions. **2.** a blind arcade, used merely to decorate. [f. s. ML *arcāta* arch + -URE]

arc-bou·tant (är bōō tän′), *n.*, *pl.* **arcs-boutants** (är bōō tän′). *French.* a flying buttress.

arch¹ (ärch), *n.* **1.** a curved structure resting on supports at both extremities, used to sustain weight, to bridge or roof an open space, etc. **2.** something bowed or curved; any bowlike part: *the arch of the foot.* **3.** any curvature in the form of an arch: *the arch of the heavens.* **—v.t.** **4.** to cover with a vault, or span with an arch. **5.** to throw or make into the shape of an arch or vault; curve: *a horse arches its neck.* **—v.i.** **6.** to form an arch. [ME, t. OF: m. *arche*, a fem. var. of *arc* (g. L *arcus* bow), due to confusion with *arche* ark (g. L *arca* coffer)]

Arch
A. Abutment; S. Springer; V. Voussoir; In. Intrados; Ex. Extrados; K. Keystone; I. Impost; P. Pier

arch² (ärch), *adj.* **1.** chief; most important; principal: *the arch rebel.* **2.** cunning; sly; roguish: *an arch smile.* **—n.** **3.** *Obs.* a chief. [separate use of ARCH-] **—arch′ly,** *adv.* **—arch′ness,** *n.*

arch-, a prefix meaning "first," "chief," as in *archbishop, archpriest.* [ME *arch-*, OE *arce-, erce-,* t. L: m. *arch-, arche-, archi-,* t. Gk., comb. forms of *archós* chief]

Arch., Archbishop.

arch., **1.** archaic. **2.** archaism. **3.** archery. **4.** archipelago. **5.** architect. **6.** architectural. **7.** architecture.

Ar·chae·an (är kē′ən), *adj., n.* Archean.

archaeo-, a word element meaning "primeval," "primitive," "ancient," as in *archaeology, archaeopteryx.* [t. Gk.: m. *archaio-,* comb. form of *archaios*]

archaeol., **1.** archaeological. **2.** archaeology.

ar·chae·o·log·i·cal (är′kĭ ə lŏj′ə kəl), *adj.* of or pertaining to archaeology. Also, **archeological,** **ar′chae·o·log′ic.** **—ar′chae·o·log′i·cal·ly,** *adv.*

---

b., blend of, blended; **c.,** cognate with; **d.,** dialect, dialectal; **der.,** derived from; **f.,** formed from; **g.,** going back to; **m.,** modification of; **r.,** replacing; **s.,** stem of; **t.,** taken from; **?,** perhaps. See the full key on inside cover.

ar·chae·ol·o·gy (är'kĭ ŏl'ə jĭ), *n.* 1. the scientific study of any prehistoric culture by excavation and description of its remains. 2. *Now Rare.* ancient history; the study of antiquity. Also, **archeology**. [t. Gk.: m. s. *archaiologia* antiquarian lore] —**ar'chae·ol'o·gist,** *n.*

ar·chae·op·ter·yx (är'kĭ ŏp'tər ĭks), *n.* a fossil bird, the oldest known avian type, with teeth and a long, feathered, vertebrate tail, found in the later Jurassic. [t. NL, f. *archǣo-* ARCHAEO- + Gk. *ptéryx* wing, bird]

Ar·chae·o·zo·ic (är'kĭ ə zō'ĭk), *adj., n.* Archeozoic.

ar·cha·ic (är kā'ĭk), *adj.* 1. marked by the characteristics of an earlier period; antiquated. 2. no longer used in ordinary speech or writing; borrowed from older usage. [t. Gk.: m.s. *archaïkós* antique] —**ar·cha'i·cal·ly,** *adv.*

ar·cha·ism (är'kĭ ĭz'əm, -kā-), *n.* 1. something archaic, as a word or expression. 2. the use of what is archaic, as in literature. 3. archaic quality or style. [t. Gk.: s. *archaïsmós*] —**ar'cha·ist,** *n.* —**ar'cha·is'tic,** *adj.*

ar·cha·ize (är'kĭ īz', -kā-), *v.,* -**ized,** -**izing.** —*v.t.* 1. to give an archaic appearance or quality to. —*v.i.* 2. to use archaisms. —**ar'cha·iz'er,** *n.*

arch·an·gel (ärk'ān'jəl), *n.* 1. a chief or principal angel; one of a particular order of angels. 2. *Bot.* angelica (def. 1). [ME, t. L: s. *archangelus,* t. Gk.: m. *archángelos* chief angel] —**arch·an·gel·ic** (ärk'ănjĕl'ĭk), *adj.*

Arch·an·gel (ärk'ān'jəl), *n.* a seaport in the NW Soviet Union, on the **Gulf of Archangel** (Dvina Bay), an arm of the White Sea. 238,000 (est. 1956). Russian, **Arkhangelsk.**

arch·bish·op (ärch'bĭsh'əp), *n.* a bishop of the highest rank. [OE *arcebiscop* (r. *hēahbiscop* high bishop), repr. L *archiepiscopus,* t. Gk.: m. *archiepískopos.* See ARCH-, BISHOP]

arch·bish·op·ric (ärch'bĭsh'əp rĭk), *n.* the see, diocese, or office of an archbishop.

archd., 1. archdeacon. 2. archduke.

arch·dea·con (ärch'dē'kən), *n.* 1. an ecclesiastic who has charge of the temporal and external administration of a diocese, with jurisdiction delegated from the bishop. 2. *Rom. Cath. Ch.* (generally) a title of honor conferred only on a member of a cathedral chapter. [OE *arcediacon,* t. L: m. s. *archidiāconus,* t. Gk.: m. *archidiákonos*] —**arch·dea·con·ate** (ärch'dē'kən ĭt), **arch'dea'con·ship',** *n.*

arch·dea·con·ry (ärch'dē'kən rĭ), *n., pl.* -**ries.** the jurisdiction, residence, or office of an archdeacon.

arch·di·o·cese (ärch'dī'ə sēs', -sĭs), *n.* the diocese of an archbishop.

arch·du·cal (ärch'dū'kəl, -dōō'-), *adj.* pertaining to an archduke or an archduchy.

arch·duch·ess (ärch'dŭch'ĭs), *n.* 1. the wife of an archduke. 2. a princess of the Austrian imperial family.

arch·duch·y (ärch'dŭch'ĭ), *n., pl.* -**duchies.** the territory of an archduke or an archduchess.

arch·duke (ärch'dūk', -dōōk'-), *n.* a title of the sovereign princes of the former ruling house of Austria.

arche-¹, var. of **archi-,** as in *archegonium.*

arche-², var. of **archeo-** before vowels.

Ar·che·an (är kē'ən), *adj.* 1. pertaining to the oldest known rocks. —*n.* 2. a division of early pre-Cambrian rocks, predominantly igneous and metamorphic. Also, **Archaean.** [f. ARCHE(O)- + -AN]

arched (ärcht), *adj.* 1. made, covered, or spanned with an arch. 2. having the form of an arch.

ar·che·go·ni·um (är'kə gō'nĭ əm), *n., pl.* -**nia** (-nĭ ə). *Bot.* the female reproductive organ in ferns, mosses, etc. [t. NL, f. s. Gk. *archégonos* first of a race + -*ium* -IUM] —**ar'che·go'ni·al,** *adj.* —**ar·che·go·ni·ate** (är'kəgō'nĭ ĭt, -āt'), *adj.*

arch·en·e·my (ärch'ĕn'ə mĭ), *n., pl.* -**mies.** 1. a chief enemy. 2. Satan; the Devil.

arch·en·ter·on (är kĕn'tə rŏn'), *n. Embryol.* the primitive enteron or digestive cavity of a gastrula. [f. ARCH- + Gk. *énteron* intestine] —**ar·chen·ter·ic** (är'kən tĕr'ĭk), *adj.*

archeo-, var. of **archaeo-,** as in *Archeozoic.*

ar·che·ol·o·gy (är'kĭ ŏl'ə jĭ), *n.* archaeology. —**ar·che·o·log·i·cal** (är'kĭ ə lŏj'ə kəl), **ar'che·o·log'ic,** *adj.* —**ar'che·o·log'i·cal·ly,** *adv.* —**ar'che·ol'o·gist,** *n.*

Ar·che·o·zo·ic (är'kĭ ə zō'ĭk), *adj.* 1. pertaining to the oldest part of earth history during which earliest forms of life presumably appeared. —*n.* 2. the Archeozoic era or series of rocks. Also, **Archaeozoic.** [f. ARCHEO- + s. Gk. *zōē* life + -IC]

arch·er (är'chər), *n.* 1. one who shoots with a bow and arrow; a bowman. 2. (*cap.*) *Astron.* **a.** the zodiacal constellation Sagittarius. **b.** the sign named from it. [ME, t. AF, var. of OF *archier,* g. L *arcārius,* der. *arcus* bow]

arch·er·y (är'chər ĭ), *n.* 1. the practice, art, or skill of an archer. 2. archers collectively. 3. an archer's bows, arrows, and other weapons.

ar·che·spore (är'kə spōr'), *n. Bot.* the primitive cell, or group of cells, which give rise to the cells from which spores are derived. Also, **ar·che·spo·ri·um** (är'kə spōr'ĭ əm) —**ar'che·spo'ri·al,** *adj.*

ar·che·type (är'kə tĭp'), *n.* a model or first form; the original pattern or model after which a thing is made. [t. L: m. s. *archetypum,* t. Gk.: m. s. *archétypon,* neut. of *archétypos* first-molded, original] —**ar·che·typ·al** (är'kə tī'pəl), **ar·che·typ·i·cal** (är'kə tĭp'ə kəl), *adj.*

arch·fiend (ärch'fēnd'), *n.* 1. a chief fiend. 2. Satan.

archi-, a prefix: 1. var. of **arch-.** 2. *Biol.* "original" or "primitive," as in *archiplasm.* [t. L, t. Gk. See ARCH-]

ar·chi·carp (är'kə kärp'), *n. Bot.* the female sex organ in various ascomycetous fungi, commonly a pluricellular coiled hypha differentiated into a terminal trichogyne and the ascogonium.

ar·chi·di·ac·o·nal (är'kĭ dī ăk'ə nəl), *adj.* of or pertaining to an archdeacon or his office. —**ar·chi·di·ac·o·nate** (är'kĭ dī ăk'ə nĭt), *n.*

ar·chi·e·pis·co·pal (är'kĭ ĭ pĭs'kə pəl), *adj.* of or pertaining to an archbishop or his office. —**ar·chi·e·pis·co·pate** (är'kĭ ĭ pĭs'kə pĭt, -pāt'), *n.*

ar·chi·man·drite (är'kə măn'drīt), *n. Gk. Ch.* 1. the head of a monastery; an abbot. 2. a superior abbot, having charge of several monasteries. 3. a title given to distinguished celibate priests. [t. ML: m. *archimandrīta,* t. LGk.: m. s. *archimandrítēs*]

Archimedean screw, a device consisting essentially of a spiral passage within an inclined cylinder for raising water to a height when rotated.

Ar·chi·me·des (är'kə mē'dēz), *n.* 287?-212 B.C., a Greek mathematician, physicist, and inventor: discovered principles of specific gravity and of the lever. —**Ar·chi·me·de·an** (är'kə mē'dĭ ən, -mə dē'ən), *adj.*

ar·chine (är shēn'), *n.* a Russian unit of length equal to 28 inches.

arch·ing (är'chĭng), *n.* arched work or formation.

ar·chi·pel·a·go (är'kə pĕl'ə gō'), *n., pl.* -**gos,** -**goes.** 1. any large body of water with many islands. 2. the island groups in such a body of water. 3. the **Archipelago,** the Aegean Sea, with its many islands. [t. It.: m. *arcipelago,* lit., chief sea, f. *arci-* ARCHI- + m. Gk. *pélagos* sea] —**ar·chi·pe·lag·ic** (är'kə pə lăj'ĭk), *adj.*

ar·chi·plasm (är'kə plăz'əm), *n.* 1. the most basic or primitive living substance; protoplasm. 2. *Cytology.* (in cell division) the substance surrounding the centrosome. Also, **archoplasm.**

archit., architecture.

ar·chi·tect (är'kə tĕkt'), *n.* 1. one whose profession it is to design buildings and superintend their construction. 2. the deviser, maker, or creator of anything. [t. L: s. *architectus,* t. Gk.: m. *architéktōn* chief builder]

ar·chi·tec·ton·ic (är'kə tĕk tŏn'ĭk), *adj.* 1. pertaining to architecture. 2. pertaining to construction or design of any kind. 3. resembling architecture in manner or technique of structure. 4. (of a science or structure) giving the principle of organization of a system. [t. L: s. *architectonicus,* t. Gk.: m. *architektonikós*]

ar·chi·tec·tur·al (är'kə tĕk'chər əl), *adj.* 1. of or pertaining to architecture. 2. conforming to the basic principles of architecture. 3. having the qualities of architecture. —**ar'chi·tec'tur·al·ly,** *adv.*

ar·chi·tec·ture (är'kə tĕk'chər), *n.* 1. the art or science of building, including plan, design, construction, and decorative treatment. 2. the character or style of building: *the architecture of Paris.* 3. the action or process of building; construction. 4. a building. 5. buildings collectively. [t. L: m. s. *architectūra*]

ar·chi·trave (är'kə trāv'), *n. Archit.* 1. the lowest division of an entablature, resting immediately on the columns. See diag. under **column.** 2. a band of moldings or other ornamentation about a rectangular door or other opening or a panel. 3. a decorative band about openings or panels of any shape. [t. It.: f. *archi-* ARCHI- + *trave* (g. L *trabs* beam)]

ar·chi·val (är kī'vəl), *adj.* pertaining to archives or valuable records; contained in such archives or records.

ar·chives (är'kīvz), *n.pl.* 1. a place where public records or other historical documents are kept. 2. documents or records relating to the activities, rights, claims, treaties, constitutions, etc., of a family, corporation, community, or nation. [t. F, t. L: m. *archīvum,* t. Gk.: m. *archeîon* public building, pl., records]

ar·chi·vist (är'kə vĭst), *n.* a custodian of archives.

ar·chi·volt (är'kə vōlt'), *n. Archit.* a band of moldings or other ornamentation about an arched opening. [t. It.: s. *archivolto,* f. *archi-* arch + *volto* turned]

ar·chon (är'kŏn), *n.* 1. a higher magistrate in ancient Athens. 2. any ruler. [t. Gk.: m. *árchōn* ruler, prop. ppr. of *árchein* be first, rule] —**ar'chon·ship',** *n.*

ar·cho·plasm (är'kə plăz'əm), *n.* archiplasm.

arch·priest (ärch'prēst'), *n.* 1. a priest holding first rank, as among the members of a cathedral chapter or among the clergy of a district outside the episcopal city. 2. *Rom. Cath. Ch.* a priest acting as superior of the Roman Catholic secular clergy in England, first appointed in 1598 and superseded by a vicar apostolic in 1623. —**arch'priest'hood,** *n.*

arch·way (ärch'wā'), *n. Archit.* 1. an entrance or passage under an arch. 2. a covering or enclosing arch.

-archy, a word element meaning "rule," "government," as in *monarchy.* [t. Gk.: m. *-archía*]

arc light, 1. Also, **arc lamp.** a lamp in which the light source of high intensity is an electric arc, usually between carbon rods. 2. the light produced.

arc·o·graph (är'kə grăf', -gräf'), *n. Geom., etc.* an instrument for drawing arcs, having a flexible arc-shaped part adjusted by an extensible straight bar connecting its sides; cyclograph.

arc sine, tangent, etc. *Trig.* the angle, measured in radians, whose sine, tangent, etc., is a given number.

arc·tic (ärk′tĭk or, esp. for 4, är′tĭk), adj. **1.** of, at, or near the North Pole; frigid. **2.** Astron. of, near, or lying under the Great and the Little Bear. —n. **3.** the arctic regions. **4.** (pl.) warm waterproof overshoes. [t. L: s. arcticus, t. Gk.: m. arktikós of the Bear (constellation), northern; r. ME artik, t. OF: m. artique]

Arctic Circle, the southern boundary of the North Frigid Zone, 23°28′ from the North Pole.

Arctic Ocean, an ocean N of North America, Asia, and the Arctic Circle. ab. 5,400,000 sq. mi.

Arctic Zone, the section of the earth's surface lying between the Arctic Circle and the North Pole.

Arc·tu·rus (ärk tyŏŏr′əs, -tŏŏr′-), n. Astron. a bright star of the first magnitude in the constellation Boötes. [t. L, t. Gk.: m. Arktoûros, lit., guard of the Bear, f. árktos a bear, the Great Bear + oûros guardian]

ar·cu·ate (är′kyŏŏĭt, -āt′), adj. bent or curved like a bow. Also, **ar′cu·at·ed.** [t. L: m. s. arcuātus, pp.]

-ard, a noun suffix, orig. intensive but now often depreciative or without special force, as in coward, drunkard, wizard. Also, **-art.** [t. OF: -ard, -art, t. G: m. -hart, -hard hardy, c. HARD]

ar·deb (är′děb), n. a unit of capacity used for dry measure in Egypt and neighboring countries, officially equivalent in Egypt to 5.62 U. S. bushels, but varying greatly in different localities. [t. Ar.: m. ardabb, t. Gk.: m. artábē, t. O Pers.: m. artaba]

Ar·den (är′dən), n. **Forest of,** a forest district formerly in central and E England, now restricted to N Warwickshire: scene of Shakespeare's As You Like It.

ar·den·cy (är′dən sĭ), n. warmth of feeling; ardor.

Ar·dennes (är děn′), n. **Forest of,** a wooded plateau along the Meuse river, in NE France, SE Belgium, and Luxemburg: German counteroffensive, Dec., 1944–Jan., 1945.

ar·dent (är′dənt), adj. **1.** glowing with feeling, earnestness, or zeal; passionate; fervent: ardent vows, an ardent patriot. **2.** glowing; flashing. **3.** burning, fiery, or hot. [t. L: s. ardens, ppr., burning; r. ME ardaunt, t. OF: m. ardant] —ar′dent·ly, adv. —Syn. **1.** fervid, eager, enthusiastic; vehement.

Forest of Ardennes

ardent spirits, strong alcoholic liquors made by distillation, as brandy, whiskey, or gin.

ar·dor (är′dər), n. **1.** warmth of feeling; fervor: eagerness; zeal. **2.** burning heat. Also, esp. Brit., **ar′dour.** [ME, t. OF, g. L] —Syn. **1.** fervency, passion.

ar·du·ous (är′jŏŏ əs), adj. **1.** requiring great exertion; laborious; difficult: an arduous enterprise. **2.** energetic; strenuous: making an arduous effort. **3.** hard to climb; steep: an arduous path. **4.** hard to endure; full of hardships: an arduous winter. [t. L: m. arduus] —ar′du·ous·ly, adv. —ar′du·ous·ness, n. —Syn. **1.** toilsome, onerous, wearisome, exhausting.

are¹ (är; unstressed ər), v. pres. indic. pl. of the verb **be.** [d. OE (Northumbrian) aron]

are² (âr, är), n. Metric System. a surface measure equal to 100 square meters, or 119.6 square yards; a hundredth of a hectare. [t. F, t. L: m. s. ārea AREA]

ar·e·a (âr′Yə), n., pl. **areas,** (in Biol., often) **areae** (âr′-Yē′). **1.** any particular extent of surface; region; tract: the settled area. **2.** extent, range, or scope: the whole area of science. **3.** a piece of unoccupied ground; an open space. **4.** the space or site on which a building stands; the yard attached to or surrounding a house. **5.** Brit. areaway (def. 1). **6.** Math. amount of surface (plane or curved); two-dimensional extent. **7.** Anat., Physiol. a zone of the cerebral cortex with a specific function. [t. L: piece of level ground, open space] —ar′e·al, adj.

ar·e·a·way (âr′Yə wā′), n. **1.** a sunken area leading to a cellar or basement entrance, or in front of basement or cellar windows. **2.** U.S. a passageway.

ar·e·ca (âr′ə kə, ərē′-), n. **1.** any palm of the genus Areca, of tropical Asia and the Malay Archipelago, esp. A. Catechu, the betel palm, which bears a nut (the areca nut). **2.** the nut itself. **3.** any of various palms formerly referred to the genus Areca. Also, **areca palm** for 1, 3. [t. Pg., t. Malayalam: m. ādekka, ult. t. Tamil]

A·re·ci·bo (ä′rě sē′bŏ), n. a seaport in N Puerto Rico. 28,659 (1950).

a·re·na (ə rē′nə), n. **1.** the oval space in a Roman amphitheater for combats or other performances. **2.** the scene of any contest. **3.** a field of conflict or endeavor: the arena of politics. [t. L: sand, sandy place]

ar·e·na·ceous (âr′ə nā′shəs), adj. sandlike; sandy. [t. L: m. arēnāceus sandy]

ar·e·nic·o·lous (âr′ə nĭk′ə ləs), adj. inhabiting sand. [f. s. L arēna sand + -(I)COLOUS]

aren't (ärnt for 1, änt for 2), **1.** contraction of are not. **2.** Chiefly Brit. an't (def. 2).

ar·e·o·cen·tric (âr′Yŏ sĕn′trĭk), adj. Astron. having the planet Mars as center. [f. areo- (comb. form of ARES) + CENTRIC]

a·re·o·la (ə rē′ə lə), n., pl. **-lae** (-lē′), **-las.** Biol. **1.** a ring of color, as around a pustule or the human nipple.

2. a small interstice, as between the fibers of connective tissue. [t. L, dim. of ārea AREA] —a·re′o·lar, adj. —a·re·o·late (ə rē′ə lĭt, -lāt′), adj. —ar·e·o·la·tion (âr′Yə lā′shən), n.

ar·e·ole (âr′Yōl′), n. Biol. an areola. [t. F, t. L: m. areola, dim. of ārea open space]

Ar·e·op·a·gite (âr′Yŏp′ə jĭt′, -gĭt′), n. Gk. Hist. a member of the council of the Areopagus. —Ar·e·op·a·git·ic (âr′Yŏp′ə jĭt′Yk), adj.

Ar·e·op·a·git·i·ca (âr′Yŏp′ə jĭt′ə kə), n. a pamphlet (1644) by Milton, advocating freedom of the press.

Ar·e·op·a·gus (âr′Yŏp′ə gəs), n. **1.** a hill in Athens, Greece, to the west of the Acropolis. **2.** Gk. Hist. the council which met on this hill, originally having wide public functions but later a purely judicial body. **3.** any high tribunal. [t. L, t. Gk.: m. Areiópagos hill of Ares (Mars.) Cf. Acts, 17, 19, 22]

A·re·qui·pa (ä′rě kē′pä), n. a city in S Peru. 79,185 (1940).

Ar·es (âr′ēz), n. the Greek god of war, identified by the Romans with Mars. [t. L, t. Gk.]

a·rête (ə rāt′), n. Phys. Geog. a sharp ridge of a mountain; the divide between two glaciated valleys. [t. F, g. L arista awn, spine]

ar·e·thu·sa (âr′ə thŏŏ′zə), n. **1.** any plant of the North American genus Arethusa, consisting of one species, A. bulbosa, a small bog orchid with a pink, or occasionally white, flower. **2.** (cap.) Gk. Myth. a nymph metamorphosed into a spring on the island of Ortygia (near Syracuse, Sicily) to save her from the pursuing river god, Alpheus.

A·re·ti·no (ä′rě tē′nō), n. **Pietro** (pyě′trŏ), 1492–1556, Italian satirist and dramatist.

A·rez·zo (ä rět′tsŏ), n. a city in central Italy. 69,000 (est. 1954).

Arg., Argentina.

arg., argentum.

ar·gal¹ (är′gəl), n. argol.

ar·gal² (är′gəl), n. argali.

ar·ga·li (är′gə lĭ), n., pl. **-li.** a wild sheep of Asia, Ovis ammon, with long, thick, spirally curved horns. Also, **argal.** [t. Mongolian]

Siberian argali, Ovis ammon (4 ft. high at the shoulder, spread of horns 3 ft.)

ar·gent (är′jənt), n. **1.** Archaic or Poetic. silver. **2.** something resembling it. **3.** Obs. money. —adj. **4.** like silver; silvery-white. [t. F, g. L argentum silver]

ar·gen·tal (är jěn′təl), adj. of, pertaining to, containing, or resembling silver.

ar·gen·te·ous (är jěn′tY əs), adj. silvery. [t. L: m. argenteus]

Ar·gen·teuil (ár zhän tœ′Y), n. a city in N France, on the Seine near Paris. 63,316 (1954).

ar·gen·tic (är jěn′tĭk), adj. Chem. of or containing silver, with a valence greater than the corresponding argentous compound.

ar·gen·tif·er·ous (är′jən tĭf′ər əs), adj. silver-bearing. [f. s. L argentum silver + -(I)FEROUS]

Ar·gen·ti·na (är′jən tē′nə; Sp. är′hěn tē′nä), n. a republic in S South America. 19,470,000 pop. (est. 1956); 1,084,120 sq. mi. Cap.: Buenos Aires.

Ar·gen·tine (är′jən tēn′, -tīn′), n. **1.** a native or inhabitant of Argentina. —adj. **2.** of or pertaining to Argentina. Also, **Ar·gen·tin·e·an** (är′jən tĭn′Yən).

ar·gen·tine (är′jən tĭn, -tīn), adj. **1.** pertaining to or resembling silver. [f. s. L argentum silver + -INE¹] —n. **2.** a silvery substance obtained from fish scales, used in making imitation pearls. [f. s. L argentum silver + -INE²]

ar·gen·tite (är′jən tīt′), n. a mineral, silver sulfide, Ag₂S, a dark lead-gray sectile mineral occurring in crystals and massive: an important ore of silver. [f. s. L argentum silver + -ITE¹]

ar·gen·tous (är jěn′təs), adj. Chem. containing monovalent silver (Ag+1), as argentous chloride, AgCl.

ar·gen·tum (är jěn′təm), n. Chem. silver. [t. L]

ar·gil (är′jĭl), n. clay, esp. potter's clay. [var. of argil(l)e, t. L: m. argilla, t. Gk.: white clay]

ar·gil·la·ceous (är′jə lā′shəs), adj. **1.** of the nature of or resembling clay; clayey. **2.** containing a considerable amount of clayey matter.

ar·gil·lite (är′jə līt′), n. any compact sedimentary rock composed mainly of clay minerals. [f. s. L argilla white clay + -ITE¹]

ar·gi·nine (är′jə nīn′), n. one of the essential amino acids, C₆H₁₄O₂N₄, which make up plant and animal proteins, present in the sperm of salmon and herring.

Ar·give (är′jĭv, -gĭv), adj. **1.** of or pertaining to Argos. **2.** Greek. —n. **3.** a native of Argos. **4.** any Greek.

Ar·go (är′gŏ), n. **1.** Astron. a very large southern constellation, now divided into four, lying largely south of Canis Major. **2.** Gk. Legend. the ship in which Jason sailed in quest of the Golden Fleece.

ar·gol (är′gəl), n. crude tartar. Also, **argal.** [ME argotile, t. AF: m. argoil?]

Ar·go·lis (är′gə lĭs), n. **1.** an ancient district in SE Greece. **2. Gulf of,** a gulf of the Aegean, in SE Greece.

ar·gon (är′gŏn), n. a colorless, odorless, chemically inactive, monatomic, gaseous element. Symbol: Ar; at. no.: 18; at. wt.: 39.94. [t. NL, prop. neut. of argós idle]

---

b., blend of, blended; c., cognate with; d., dialect, dialectal; der., derived from; f., formed from; g., going back to; m., modification of; r., replacing; s., stem of; t., taken from; ?, perhaps. See the full key on inside cover.

Ar·go·naut (är′gə nôt′), *n.* **1.** *Gk. Legend.* a member of the band that sailed to Colchis with Jason in the ship Argo in search of the Golden Fleece. **2.** a person who emigrated to California in 1848 at the time of the discovery of gold there. **3.** (*l.c.*) the paper nautilus. [t. L: s. *Argonauta*, t. Gk.: m. *Argonautēs* (f. *Argō* Argo + *nautēs* sailor)] —**Ar′go·nau′tic**, *adj.*

Ar·gonne Forest (är′gŏn; *Fr.* är gôn′), a wooded region in NE France: battles, 1918, 1944.

Ar·gos (är′gŏs, -gəs), *n.* an ancient city in SE Greece, the center of Argolis: a powerful rival of Sparta, Athens, and Corinth.

ar·go·sy (är′gə sĭ), *n., pl.* **-sies.** **1.** a large merchant ship, esp. one with a rich cargo. **2.** a fleet of such ships. [t. It.: m. *Ragusea* a vessel of Ragusa, Dalmatian port]

ar·got (är′gō, -gət), *n.* the peculiar language or jargon of any class or group; originally, that of thieves and vagabonds, devised for purposes of disguise and concealment. [t. F; orig. unknown] —**ar·got·ic** (är gŏt′ĭk), *adj.*

ar·gue (är′gū), *v.*, **-gued**, **-guing.** —*v.i.* **1.** to present reasons for or against a thing: *to argue for or against a proposed law.* **2.** to contend in argument; dispute: *to argue with someone.* —*v.t.* **3.** to state the reasons for or against: *the counsel argued the cause.* **4.** to maintain in reasoning: *to argue that something must be so.* **5.** to persuade, drive, etc., by reasoning: *to argue one out of a plan.* **6.** to show; prove; imply: *his clothes argue poverty.* [ME *argue(n)*, t. OF: m. *arguer*, g. L *argūtāre*, freq. of *arguere* show] —**ar·gu·a·ble**, *adj.* —**ar′gu·er**, *n.* —**Syn. 1.** Argue, debate, discuss imply using reasons or proofs to support or refute an assertion, proposition, or principle. Argue implies reasoning or trying to understand; it does not necessarily imply opposition: *to argue with oneself.* To discuss is to present varied opinions and views: *to discuss ways and means.* To debate is to interchange formal (usually opposing) arguments, esp. on public questions: *to debate a proposed amendment.*

ar·gu·fy (är′gyə fī′), *v.t.*, *v.i.*, **-fied, -fying.** *Colloq.* or *Dial.* to argue or wrangle. [f. argu(e) + -fy]

ar·gu·ment (är′gyə mənt), *n.* **1.** an argumentation; debate. **2.** a process of reasoning; series of reasons. **3.** a statement or fact tending to improve a point. **4.** an address or composition intended to convince others of the truth of something. **5.** an abstract or summary of the chief points in a book or sections of a book. **6.** *Math.* (of a function) an independent variable. **7.** *Obs.* evidence or proof. **8.** *Obs.* a matter of contention. [ME, t. L: s. *argūmentum* proof] —**Syn. 1.** Argument, controversy, dispute imply the expression of opinions for and against some idea. An argument usually arises from a disagreement between two persons, each of whom advances facts supporting his own point of view. A controversy or a dispute may involve two or more persons. A dispute is an oral contention, usually brief, and often of a heated, angry, or undignified character: *a violent dispute over a purchase.* A controversy is an oral or written expression of contrary opinions, and may be dignified and of some duration: *a political controversy.*

ar·gu·men·ta·tion (är′gyə mĕn tā′shən), *n.* **1.** reasoning; discussion. **2.** a discussion dealing with a controversial point. **3.** the setting forth of reasons together with the conclusion drawn from them. **4.** the premises and conclusion so set forth.

ar·gu·men·ta·tive (är′gyə mĕn′tə tĭv), *adj.* **1.** addicted to argument; disputatious. **2.** controversial. —**ar′gu·men′ta·tive·ly**, *adv.* —**ar′gu·men′ta·tive·ness**, *n.*

ar·gu·men·tum (är′gyə mĕn′təm), *n. Latin.* argument, as **argumentum ad hominem**, argument using the opponent's own words or acts as evidence for one's views.

Ar·gus (är′gəs), *n.* **1.** *Gk. Legend.* a giant with a hundred eyes, set to guard the heifer Io. His eyes were transferred, after his death, to the peacock's tail. **2.** any observant or vigilant person. **3.** (*l.c.*) any pheasant of the Malayan genera *Argusianus* and *Rheinardia*, marked with eyelike spots.

Ar·gus-eyed (är′gəs īd′), *adj.* keen-eyed; vigilant.

Ar·gyle (är′gīl), *n.* **1.** (*also l.c.*) a diamond-shaped pattern of two or more colors, used in knitting socks, sweaters, etc. —*adj.* **2.** (*also l.c.*) having such a pattern. [var. argyll; arbitrary designation]

Ar·gyll (är gīl′), *n.* a county in W Scotland. 63,361 pop. (est. 1951); 3110 sq. mi. Also, **Ar·gyll·shire** (är gīl′shǐr, -shər).

ar·gy·rol (är′jə rōl′, -rŏl′), *n. Pharm.* **1.** a compound of silver and a protein, applied to mucous membranes as a mild antiseptic. **2.** (*cap.*) a trademark for this substance. [f. s. Gk. *árgyros* silver + *-ol* (unexplained)]

a·rhyth·mi·a (ə rĭth′mǐ ə), *n. Pathol.* arrhythmia.

a·ri·a (ä′rǐ ə, âr′ǐ ə), *n.* **1.** an air or melody. **2.** an elaborate melody for a single voice, with accompaniment, in an opera, oratorio, etc., esp. one consisting of a principal and a subordinate section, and a repetition of the first with or without alterations. [t. It., g. L *āēr* air]

-aria, *Bot., Zool.* a suffix used in names of genera and groups. [t. L, neut. pl. n. and adj. termination]

Ar·i·ad·ne (är′ĭ ăd′nǐ), *n. Gk. Legend.* a daughter of Minos and Pasiphaë. She gave Theseus the thread whereby he escaped from the labyrinth.

Ar·i·an (âr′ǐ ən), *adj.* **1.** pertaining to Arius. —*n.* **2.** an adherent of the Arian doctrine. See Arius. [t. L: s. *Ariānus*, der. *Arius*] —**Ar′i·an·ism**, *n.*

Ar·i·an (âr′ǐ ən), *adj.*, *n.* Aryan.

-arian, a compound suffix of adjectives and nouns, often referring to pursuits, doctrines, etc., or to age, as in *antiquarian, humanitarian, octogenarian*. [f. -ary¹ + -an]

A·ri·ca (ä rē′kä), *n.* a seaport in N Chile. 18,947 (1950). **2.** See **Tacna-Arica**.

ar·id (ăr′ĭd), *adj.* **1.** dry; without moisture; parched with heat. **2.** uninteresting; dull; lifeless. [t. L: s. *āridus* dry] —**a·rid·i·ty** (ə rĭd′ə tĭ), **ar′id·ness**, *n.* —**ar′id·ly**, *adv.* —**Syn. 1.** See **dry.** —**Ant. 1.** humid.

A·ri·el (âr′ǐ əl), *n.* **1.** (in Shakespeare's *Tempest*) a spirit of the air who is required to use his magic to help Prospero. **2.** *Astron.* one of the five satellites of Uranus. [t. LL, t. Gk., t. Heb: m. *arī′ēl*]

ar·i·el (âr′ǐ əl), *n.* an Arabian gazelle, *Gazella arabica*. Also, **ariel gazelle**. [t. Ar.: m. *aryal* stag or ibex]

A·ri·es (âr′ēz, -ǐ ēz′), *n., gen.* **Arietis** (ə rī′ə tĭs). **1.** the Ram, a zodiacal constellation between Pisces and Taurus. **2.** the first sign of the zodiac (♈), which the sun enters about March 21. See **zodiac**. [t. L: a ram]

ar·i·et·ta (är′ǐ ĕt′ə; *It.* ä′rēĕt′tä), *n. Music.* a short aria. Also, **ar·i·ette** (är′ǐ ĕt′). [It. dim. of *aria*. See Aria]

a·right (ə rīt′), *adv.* rightly; correctly; properly.

a·ril (ăr′ĭl), *n. Bot.* an accessory covering or appendage of certain seeds, esp. one arising from the placenta, funicle or hilum. [t. NL: m. s. *arillus*, der. ML *arilli* dried grapes, t. Sp.: m. *arillos*]

ar·il·late (ăr′ə lāt′), *adj. Bot.* having an aril.

ar·il·lode (ăr′ə lōd′), *n. Bot.* a false aril; an aril which originates from the micropyle instead of at or below the hilum, as in the nutmeg. [see aril, -ode¹]

Ar·i·ma·thae·a (är′ə mə thē′ə), *n.* a town in ancient Palestine. Matt. 27:57. Also, **Ar′i·ma·the′a**.

ar·i·ose (âr′ǐ ōs′, är′ǐ ōs), *adj.* characterized by melody; songlike. [Anglicization of Arioso]

a·ri·o·so (ä′rǐ ō′sō), *adj., adv. Music.* in the manner of an air or melody. [It., der. *aria* Aria]

A·ri·os·to (ä′rē ôs′tô), *n.* **Ludovico** (lōō′dō vē′kō), 1474–1533, Italian poet, author of *Orlando Furioso*.

-arious, an adjective suffix meaning "connected with," "having to do with," as in *gregarious*. [t. L: m. *-ārius*]

a·rise (ə rīz′), *v.i.*, **arose, arisen, arising. 1.** to come into being or action; originate; appear: *new questions arise.* **2.** to result or proceed (fol. by *from*). **3.** to move upward. **4.** to get up from sitting, lying, or kneeling. [ME *arise(n)*, OE *ārīsan*, f. *ā-* up + *rīsan* rise]

a·ris·ta (ə rĭs′tə), *n., pl.* **-tae** (-tē). **1.** *Bot.* a bristlelike appendage of grain, etc.; an awn. **2.** *Entomol.* a prominent bristle on the antenna of some dipterous insects. [t. L. See arete]

a·ris·tate (ə rĭs′tāt), *adj.* **1.** *Bot.* having aristae; awned. **2.** *Zool.* tipped with a thin spine. [t. LL: m. s. *aristātus*, der. L *arista* awn]

Ar·is·ti·des (är′ə stī′dēz), *n.* ("the Just") 530?–468? b.c., Athenian statesman and general.

Ar·is·tip·pus (är′ə stĭp′əs), *n.* 435?–356? b.c., Greek philosopher who founded a school at Cyrene.

aristo-, a word element meaning "best," "superior," as in *aristocratic*. [t. Gk., comb. form of *áristos* best]

ar·is·toc·ra·cy (är′ə stŏk′rə sĭ), *n., pl.* **-cies. 1.** a government or a state characterized by the rule of a nobility, elite, or privileged upper class. **2.** a body of persons holding exceptional prescriptive rank or privileges; a class of hereditary nobility. **3.** government by the best men in the state. **4.** a governing body composed of the best men in the state. **5.** any class ranking as socially or otherwise superior. [t. L: m.s. *aristocratia*, t. Gk.: m. *aristokratia* rule of the best. See Aristo-, -cracy]

a·ris·to·crat (ə rĭs′tə krăt′, ăr′ĭs tə-), *n.* **1.** one who has the tastes, manners, etc., of the members of a superior group or class. **2.** a member of an aristocracy. **3.** an advocate of an aristocratic form of government.

a·ris·to·crat·ic (ə rĭs′tə krăt′ĭk, ăr′ĭs-), *adj.* **1.** befitting an aristocrat; stylish, grand, or exclusive. **2.** belonging to or favoring the aristocracy. **3.** of or pertaining to government by an aristocracy. Also, **a·ris′to·crat′i·cal.** —**a·ris′to·crat′i·cal·ly**, *adv.*

a·ris·to·lo·chi·a·ceous (ə rĭs′tə lō′kǐ ā′shəs), *adj. Bot.* belonging to the *Aristolochiaceae*, a family of plants including birthwort, Dutchman's-pipe, etc. [f. s. *Aristolochia* birthwort genus (t. Gk.: m. *aristolócheia*) + -aceous]

Ar·is·toph·a·nes (är′ə stŏf′ə nēz′), *n.* 448?–385? b.c., Athenian poet and writer of comedy.

Ar·is·to·te·lian (ăr′ĭs tə tē′lyən, -tēl′yən), *adj.* **1.** of or pertaining to Aristotle or to his doctrines. —*n.* **2.** a follower of Aristotle. **3.** one who thinks in particulars and scientific deductions as distinct from the metaphysical speculation of Platonism. —**Ar′is·to·te′lian·ism**, *n.*

Aristotelian logic, 1. the logic of Aristotle, esp. in the modified form taught in the Middle Ages. **2.** formal logic, dealing with the logical form, rather than the content, of propositions, and based on the four propositional forms: all S is P; no S is P; some S is P; some S is not P.

Ar·is·tot·le (ăr′ə stŏt′əl), *n.* 384–322 b.c., Greek philosopher: pupil of Plato; tutor of Alexander the Great.

a·ris·to·type (ə rĭs′tə tīp′), *n.* **1.** a process of photographic printing in which paper coated with silver chloride in gelatin is used. **2.** a print made by this process.

arith., **1.** arithmetic. **2.** arithmetical.

ăct, āble, dâre, ärt; ĕbb, ēqual; ĭf, īce; hŏt, ōver, ôrder, oil, bŏŏk, ōōze, out; ŭp, ūse, ûrge; ə = a in alone; ch, chief; g, give; ng, ring; sh, shoe; th, thin; ŧħ, that; zh, vision. See the full key on inside cover.

a·rith·me·tic (n. ə rĭth′mə tĭk; adj. ăr′ĭth mĕt′ĭk), n. **1.** the art of computation with figures (the most elementary branch of mathematics). **2.** Also, **theoretical arithmetic.** the theory of numbers; the study of the divisibility of whole numbers, the remainders after division, etc. **3.** a book on this subject. **4.** Also, **ar′ith·met′i·cal.** of or pertaining to arithmetic. [t. L: s. arithmētica, t. Gk.: m. arithmētikē, prop. fem. of arithmētikós of or for reckoning; r. ME arsmetik, t. OF: m. arismetique] —**ar′ith·met′i·cal·ly,** adv.

a·rith·me·ti·cian (ə rĭth′mə tĭsh′ən, ăr′ĭth-), n. an expert in arithmetic.

arithmetic mean, Math. the mean obtained by adding several quantities together and dividing the sum by the number of quantities. For example: the arithmetic mean of 1, 5, 2, 8 is 4.

arithmetic progression, a sequence in which each term is obtained by the addition of a constant number to the preceding term. For example: 1, 4, 7, 10, 13, and 6, 1, —4, —9, —14. Also, **arithmetic series.**

A·ri·us (ə rī′əs, âr′ĭ-), n. died A.D. 336, Christian priest at Alexandria, who held that Christ the Son was not consubstantial with God the Father.

a ri·ve·der·ci (ä′rē vē dĕr′chē), Italian. See **arrivederci.**

Ariz., Arizona.

Ar·i·zo·na (ăr′ə zō′nə), n. a State in the SW United States. 1,302,161 (1960); 113,909 sq. mi. Cap.: Phoenix. Abbr.: Ariz. —**Ar′i·zo′nan, Ar·i·zo·ni·an** (ăr′ə zō′nĭ ən), adj., n.

Ar·ju·na (är′jŏŏ nə), n. Hindu Myth. the chief hero of the great epic of India, the Mahabharata.

ark (ärk), n. **1.** the vessel built by Noah for safety during the Flood. Gen. 6–9. **2.** Also, **ark of the covenant.** a chest or box of great sanctity representing the presence of the Deity, borne by the Israelites in their desert wandering (Num. 10:35), the most sacred object of the tabernacle and of the temple in Jerusalem, where it was kept in the holy of holies. **3.** Now Dial. a chest; box. [ME; OE arc, earc, t. L: m. s. arca a chest, coffer]

Ark., Arkansas.

Ar·kan·sas (är′kən sô′; also for 2 är kän′zəs), n. **1.** a State in the S central United States. 1,786,272 pop. (1960); 53,103 sq. mi. Cap.: Little Rock. Abbr.: Ark. **2.** a river flowing from the Rocky Mountains in central Colorado into the Mississippi in SE Arkansas. 1450 mi. —**Ar·kan·san** (är kän′zən), n.

Ar·khan·gelsk (är hän′gĕlsk), n. Russian name of **Archangel.**

Ark·wright (ärk′rīt), n. **Sir Richard,** 1732–92, British inventor of the spinning jenny.

Arl·berg (ärl′bĕrкн), n. **1.** a mountain pass in W Austria. ab. 5900 ft. high. **2.** a tunnel beneath this pass.

arles (ärlz), n. pl. or sing. Scot. and N. Eng. money paid in advance as a pledge. [ME erles, appar. through OF, der. L arrha earnest money]

Arles (ärlz; Fr. ärl), n. a city in SE France, on the Rhone river: Roman ruins. 37,443 (1954).

Ar·ling·ton (är′lĭng tən), n. **1.** a county in NE Virginia, opposite Washington, D.C.: site of a national cemetery; Tomb of the Unknown Soldier. 163,401 (1960). **2.** a town in E Massachusetts. 49,953 (1960).

arm[1] (ärm), n. **1.** the upper limb of the human body from the shoulder to the hand. **2.** this limb, exclusive of the hand. **3.** the forelimb of any vertebrate. **4.** some part of an organism like or likened to an arm. **5.** any armlike part, as of a lever or of the yard (**yardarm**) of a ship. **6.** a projecting support for the forearm at the side of a chair, sofa, etc. **7.** an inlet or cove: an arm of the sea. **8.** power; might; strength; authority: the arm of the government. **9. at arm's length,** at a distance, yet almost in reach. **10. with open arms,** cordially. [OE arm, earm, c. G arm, L armus shoulder, Gk. harmós joint] —**arm′less,** adj. —**arm′like′,** adj.

arm[2] (ärm), n. **1.** (usually pl.) an offensive or defensive implement for use in war; a weapon. **2.** Mil. a combat branch of the military service, as the infantry, cavalry, field artillery, air corps, etc. [rarely used sing. of ARMS] —v.i. **3.** to enter into a state of hostility or of readiness for war. —v.t. **4.** to equip with arms. **5.** to activate (a fuze) so that it will explode the charge at the time desired. **6.** to cover or provide with whatever will add strength, force, or security. **7.** to fit or prepare (a thing) for any specific purpose or effective use. [ME arme(n), t. F: m. armer, g. L armāre]

Ar·ma·da (är mä′də, -mā′-), n. **1.** Also, the **Spanish** or **Invincible Armada.** a fleet sent by Spain against England in 1588, but shattered and dispersed by storms. **2.** (l.c.) any fleet of warships. [t. Sp., g. L armāta armed forces (prop. pp. neut. pl. of armāre ARM[2], v.). See ARMY]

ar·ma·dil·lo (är′mə dĭl′ō), n., pl. **-los.** any of a great variety of burrowing mammals, having a jointed, protective covering of bony plates. They constitute a suborder, Cingulata, of the edentates, distributed in many species throughout South America and north to Texas, and widely used for food. They are omnivo-

Texas armadillo, Dasypus novemcinctus
(2½ ft. long)

rous and mostly nocturnal. The **Texas armadillo,** Dasypus novemcinctus, is unique for always producing quadruplets of identical sex. [t. Sp., dim. of armado armed, g. L armātus, pp.]

Ar·ma·ged·don (är′mə gĕd′ən), n. **1.** Bible. the place where the final battle will be fought between the forces of good and evil (probably named in reference to Megiddo). Rev. 16:16. **2.** any great crucial armed conflict.

Ar·magh (är mä′), n. a county in Northern Ireland. 114,254 pop. (1951); 489 sq. mi. Co. seat: Armagh.

ar·ma·ment (är′mə mənt), n. **1.** the weapons with which a military unit, esp. a combat airplane, armored vehicle, or warship, is equipped. **2.** a land, sea, or air force equipped for war. **3.** the process of equipping or arming for war. [t. L: s. armāmenta, pl., implements, equipment, ship's tackle]

ar·ma·ture (är′mə chər), n. **1.** armor. **2.** Biol. the protective covering of an animal or plant, or any part serving for defense or offense. **3.** Elect. a. the iron or steel applied across the poles of a permanent magnet to close it, or to the poles of an electromagnet to communicate mechanical force. See illus. under **electromagnet.** b. the part of an electrical machine which includes the main current-carrying winding (distinguished from the field). c. a pivoted part of an electrical device, as a buzzer or relay, activated by a magnetic field. **4.** Sculpture. a framework built as a support for clay figures during construction. [t. L: m.s. armātūra armor]

arm·chair (ärm′châr′), n. a chair with arms to support the forearms or elbows.

armed (ärmd), adj. **1.** bearing arms. **2.** supported or maintained by arms: armed peace.

armed forces, all of the principal naval or military forces, including the army, navy, marines, air forces, coast guard, etc. Also, **armed services.**

Ar·me·ni·a (är mē′nĭ ə, -mēn′yə), n. **1.** an ancient country in W Asia: now a region in the SW Soviet Union, E Turkey, and NW Iran. **2.** Official name, **Armenian Soviet Socialist Republic.** a constituent republic of the Soviet Union, in S Caucasia. 1,600,000 (est. 1956); ab. 11,500 sq. mi. Cap.: Erivan.

Armenia (def 2)

Ar·me·ni·an (är mē′nĭ ən, -mēn′yən), adj. **1.** pertaining to Armenia or to its inhabitants. —n. **2.** a native of Armenia. **3.** the language of the Armenians, an Indo-European language.

Ar·men·tières (är män tyĕr′), n. a city in extreme N France: battles, 1914, 1918. 24,940 (1954).

ar·met (är′mĕt), n. Armor. a helmet with movable front plates to cover the face. [t. F, dim. of arme ARM[2]]

arm·ful (ärm′fŏŏl′), n., pl. **-fuls.** as much as the arm, or both arms, can hold.

arm·hole (ärm′hōl′), n. a hole in a garment for the arm.

ar·mi·ger (är′mə jər), n. **1.** one entitled to armorial bearings. **2.** an armorbearer to a knight; a squire. [ML: squire, L armorbearer]

ar·mil·lar·y (är′mə lĕr′ĭ, är mĭl′ə rĭ), adj. consisting of hoops or rings. [f. s. L armilla armlet, ring + -ARY[1]]

armillary sphere, Astron. an arrangement of rings, all circles of a single sphere, showing the relative positions of the principal circles of the celestial sphere.

arm·ing (är′mĭng), n. Naut. a piece of tallow placed in a cavity at the lower end of a sounding lead to bring up a sample of the sand, mud, etc., of the sea bottom.

Ar·min·i·an (är mĭn′ĭ ən), adj. **1.** of or pertaining to Jacobus Arminius or his doctrines. —n. **2.** an adherent of the Arminian doctrines. —**Ar·min′i·an·ism,** n.

Ar·min·i·us (är mĭn′ĭ əs), n. **1.** (Hermann) 177 B.C.–A.D. 21, Germanic hero: defeated Roman army, A.D. 9. **2.** **Jacobus** (jə kō′bəs), (Jacob Harmensen) 1560–1609, Dutch Protestant theologian who modified certain Calvinistic doctrines, esp. that of predestination.

ar·mip·o·tent (är mĭp′ə tənt), adj. mighty in arms or war. [ME, t. L: s. armipotens powerful in arms]

ar·mi·stice (är′mə stĭs), n. a temporary suspension of hostilities by agreement of the parties, as to discuss peace; a truce. [t. NL: m. s. armistitium, f. L: armi- (comb. form of arma arms) + -stitium (der. sistere stop)]

Armistice Day, November 11, the anniversary of the cessation of hostilities of World War I in 1918: since 1954 called Veterans' Day.

arm·let (ärm′lĭt), n. **1.** Chiefly Brit. an ornamental arm band. **2.** a little arm: an armlet of the sea.

ar·moire (är mwär′), n. a large wardrobe or movable cupboard, with doors and shelves. [t. F. See AMBRY]

ar·mor (är′mər), n. **1.** defensive equipment; any covering worn as a protection against offensive weapons. **2.** a metallic sheathing or protective covering, esp. metal plates.

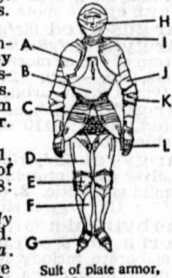

Suit of plate armor,
15th century
A. Palette; B. Breastplate; C. Tasset;
D. Cuisse; E. Kneepiece
F. Jambeau; G. Solleret
H. Helmet; I. Gorset;
J. Brassard; K. Elbow
piece; L. Gauntlet

used on warships, armored vehicles, airplanes, and fortifications. **3.** any protective covering, as the scales of a fish. **4.** that which serves as a protection or safeguard. **5.** the outer wrapping of metal, usually fine, braided steel wires, on a cable, primarily for the purpose of mechanical protection. —*v.t.* **6.** to cover with armor or armor plate. Also, *esp. Brit.*, **armour.** [ME *armure*, t. OF: m. *armeüre*, g. L *armātūra*]

armor., arms and armor.

ar·mor·bear·er (är′mər bâr′ər), *n.* a retainer bearing the armor or arms of a warrior.

ar·mored (är′mərd), *adj.* **1.** protected by armor or armor plate. **2.** consisting of troops using armored vehicles: *armored engineers.* Also, *esp. Brit.*, **ar′moured.**

armored car, a military combat vehicle with wheels, light armor, and, usually, machine guns.

armored forces, military forces composed of tank units and armored infantry, artillery, and other supporting troops. Also, *Brit.*, **armoured troops.**

ar·mor·er (är′mər ər), *n.* **1.** a maker or repairer of armor. **2.** a manufacturer of arms. **3.** an enlisted man in charge of the upkeep of small arms, machine guns, bicycles, etc. Also, *esp. Brit.*, **ar′mour·er.**

ar·mo·ri·al (är mōr′ĭ əl), *adj.* **1.** belonging to heraldry or to heraldic bearing. —*n.* **2.** a book containing heraldic bearings and devices.

armorial bearings, a coat of arms.

Ar·mor·ic (är môr′ĭk, -mŏr′-), *adj.* **1.** pertaining to Armorica. —*n.* **2.** a native of Armorica. **3.** the Breton language. Also, **Ar·mor′i·can.**

Ar·mor·i·ca (är môr′ə kə, -mŏr′-), *n.* an ancient region in NW France, corresponding generally to Brittany.

armor plate, a plate or plating of specially hardened steel used to cover warships, tanks, aircraft, fortifications, etc., to protect them from enemy fire. Also, **armor plating.** —**ar′mor·plat′ed,** *adj.*

ar·mor·y (är′mər ĭ), *n., pl.* **-mories.** **1.** a storage place for weapons and other war equipment. **2.** *U.S. Army.* a building which is the headquarters and drill center of a National Guard unit. **3.** *U.S.* a place where arms and armor are made; an armorer's shop; an arsenal. **4.** (formerly) arms or armor collectively. **5.** *Archaic.* heraldic bearings or arms. **6.** the art of blazoning arms. **7.** heraldry. Also, *esp. Brit.*, **ar′mour·y.** [ME *armurie.* See ARMOR, -Y³]

ar·mour (är′mər), *n., v.t.* *Chiefly Brit.* armor.

arm·pit (ärm′pĭt′), *n.* *Anat.* the hollow under the arm at the shoulder; the axilla.

arms (ärmz), *n.pl.* **1.** arm² (def. 1). **2.** *Mil.* **small arms,** all weapons of small caliber operated or carried by hand, as rifles, pistols, submachine guns, and machine guns. **3.** heraldic bearings. [ME *armes*, t. OF, g. L *arma*]

ar·mure (är′myər), *n.* a woolen or silk fabric woven with ridges in a small pattern. [t. F. See ARMOR]

ar·my (är′mĭ), *n., pl.* **-mies.** **1.** (*cap. or l.c.*) the military forces of a nation, exclusive of the naval and, in some countries, the air forces. **2.** (in large military land forces) the second largest unit, consisting of two or more corps. **3.** a large body of men trained and armed for war. **4.** any body of persons organized for any cause: *the Salvation Army.* **5.** a host; a great multitude. [ME *armee*, t. OF, g. L *armāta* armed forces]

Army Air Forces, *U.S. Army.* a unit comprising almost all aviation, with its personnel, equipment, etc. It became part of the **Air Force** on July 26, 1947.

army ant, any of the driver ants of the American tropics, genus *Eciton.*

army of occupation, an army established in conquered territory to maintain order and to ensure the carrying out of peace or armistice terms.

Army of the United States, the temporary military organization of the U.S. in time of war or emergency, including the Regular Army, the National Guard, selective service personnel, etc. Cf. **United States Army.**

army worm, 1. a kind of caterpillar, the larva of a noctuid moth, *Leucania unipuncta*, which often travels in hosts over a region, destroying grass, grain, etc. **2.** some similarly destructive larva.

Arn·hem (ärn′hĕm), *n.* a city in central Netherlands, on the Rhine: battle, 1944. 114,002 (est. 1954).

ar·ni·ca (är′nə kə), *n.* **1.** any plant of the asteraceous genus *Arnica.* esp. *A. montana*, of Europe. **2.** a tincture of the flowers of *A. montana* and other species of *Arnica* much used as an external application in sprains and bruises. [t. NL; orig. unknown]

Ar·no (är′nō), *n.* a river flowing from the Apennines in central Italy W to the Ligurian Sea near Pisa. ab. 140 mi.

Ar·nold (är′nəld), *n.* **1.** Benedict, 1741–1801, American general in the Revolutionary War who turned traitor. **2.** Sir Edwin, 1832–1904, British poet and journalist. **3.** Henry H., ("Hap") 1886–1950, U. S. general. **4.** Matthew, 1822–88, British essayist, poet, and literary critic. **5.** Thomas, 1795–1842, British clergyman: headmaster of Rugby (father of Matthew). **6.** Thurman Wesley, born 1891, U. S. lawyer and writer.

Ar·nold von Win·kel·ried (är′nōlt fən vĭng′kəl rēt′), died 1386?, Swiss hero in the battle of Sempach (1386), fought against the Austrians.

ar·oid (âr′oid, âr′-), *Bot.* —*adj.* **1.** araceous. —*n.* **2.** any araceous plant. [f. AR(UM) + -OID]

a·roi·de·ous (ə roi′dĭ əs), *adj.* araceous.

a·roint thee! (ə roint′), *Archaic.* avaunt! begone!

a·ro·ma (ə rō′mə), *n.* **1.** an odor arising from spices, plants, etc., esp. an agreeable odor; fragrance. **2.** (of wines and spirits) the odor or bouquet. **3.** a characteristic, subtle quality. [t. L, t. Gk.: spice, sweet herb] —**Syn. 1.** See **perfume.**

ar·o·mat·ic (ăr′ə măt′ĭk), *adj.* **1.** having an aroma; fragrant; sweet-scented; spicy. **2.** *Chem.* of or pertaining to aromatic compounds. —*n.* **3.** a plant, drug, or medicine which yields a fragrant smell, as sage, certain spices and oils, etc. —**ar′o·mat′i·cal·ly,** *adv.*

aromatic compounds, *Chem.* a class of organic compounds including benzene, naphthalene, anthracene, and their derivatives, which contain an unsaturated ring of carbon atoms. Many have an agreeable odor.

a·ro·ma·ti·za·tion (ə rō′mə tə zā′shən), *n. Chem.* the catalytic conversion of aliphatic hydrocarbons to aromatic hydrocarbons.

a·ro·ma·tize (ə rō′mə tīz′), *v.t.*, **-tized, -tizing.** to make aromatic or fragrant.

A·roos·took (ə rōōs′tŏŏk, -tˈk), *n.* a river flowing from N Maine NE to the St. John river. ab. 140 mi.

a·rose (ə rōz′), *v.* pt. of **arise.**

a·round (ə round′), *adv.* **1.** in a circle or sphere; round about; on every side. **2.** *U.S.* here and there; about: *to travel around.* **3.** *U.S. Colloq.* somewhere about or near: *to wait around for a person.* —*prep.* **4.** about; on all sides; encircling; encompassing: *a halo around his head.* **5.** *U.S. Colloq.* here and there in: *to roam around the country.* **6.** *U.S. Colloq.* somewhere in or near: *to stay around the house.* **7.** *U.S. Colloq.* approximately; near in time, amount, etc.: *around ten o'clock, around a million.*

a·rouse (ə rouz′), *v.*, **aroused, arousing.** —*v.t.* **1.** to excite into action; stir or put in motion or exertion; awaken: *arouse attention, arouse one from sleep.* —*v.i.* **2.** to become aroused. [der. ROUSE¹, modeled on ARISE] —**a·rous·al** (ə rou′zəl), *n.* —**a·rous′er,** *n.* —**Syn. 1.** animate, inspirit; incite; stimulate.

ar·peg·gi·o (är pĕj′ĭ ō′, -pĕj′ō), *n., pl.* **-gios.** *Music.* **1.** the sounding of the notes of a chord in rapid succession instead of simultaneously. **2.** a chord thus sounded. [t. It., der. *arpeggiare* play on the harp]

Written   Played

Arpeggio

ar·pent (är′pənt; *Fr.* àr pän′), *n.* an old French unit of area equal to about one acre. It is still used in the province of Quebec and in parts of Louisiana.

ar·que·bus (är′kwə bəs), *n.* harquebus.

arr., 1. arranged. **2.** arrival. **3.** arrive; arrived.

ar·rack (ăr′ək), *n.* any of various spirituous liquors distilled in the East Indies and elsewhere in the East from toddy (def. 2), molasses, or other materials. [ult. t. Ar: m. *'araq* (fermented) juice]

ar·raign (ə rān′), *v.t.* **1.** *Law.* to call or bring before a court to answer to a charge or accusation. **2.** to accuse or charge in general. —*n.* **3.** arraignment. [ME *araine*(n), t. AF: m. *arainer*, ult. g. L *arrationāre* call to account] —**ar·raign′er,** *n.*

ar·raign·ment (ə rān′mənt), *n.* **1.** *Law.* act of arraigning. **2.** a calling in question for faults; accusation.

Ar·ran (ăr′ən), *n.* an island in SW Scotland, in the Firth of Clyde. 4500 pop. (1931); 166 sq. mi.

ar·range (ə rānj′), *v.*, **-ranged, -ranging.** —*v.t.* **1.** to place in proper, desired, or convenient order; adjust properly: *to arrange books on a shelf.* **2.** to come to an agreement or understanding regarding: *to arrange a bargain.* **3.** to prepare or plan: *to arrange the details of a meeting.* **4.** *Music.* to adapt (a composition) for a particular mode of rendering by voices or instruments. —*v.i.* **5.** to make a settlement; come to an agreement. **6.** to make preparations. [ME *arange*(n), t. OF: m.s. *arangier*, f. a- A⁻⁵ + *rangier* RANGE, V.] —**ar·rang′er,** *n.* —**Syn. 1.** array; group, sort. **2.** settle, determine.

ar·range·ment (ə rānj′mənt), *n.* **1.** act of arranging. **2.** state of being arranged. **3.** the manner in which things are arranged. **4.** a final settlement; adjustment by agreement. **5.** (*usually pl.*) preparatory measure; previous plan; preparation. **6.** something arranged in a particular way: *a floral arrangement.* **7.** *Music.* **a.** the adaptation of a composition to voices or instruments, or to a new purpose. **b.** a piece so adapted. [t. F]

ar·rant (ăr′ənt), *adj.* **1.** downright; thorough: *an arrant fool.* **2.** notorious. **3.** *Obs.* wandering. [var. of ERRANT] —**ar′rant·ly,** *adv.*

ar·ras (ăr′əs), *n.* **1.** rich tapestry. **2.** a tapestry weave. **3.** a wall hanging. [named after ARRAS]

Ar·ras (ăr′əs; *Fr.* à räs′), *n.* a city in N France: battles in World War I. 36,242 (1954).

ar·ray (ə rā′), *v.t.* **1.** to place in proper or desired order, as troops for battle. **2.** to clothe with garments, esp. of an ornamental kind; deck. [ME *araye*(n), t. AF: m. *arayer*, var. of OF *areyer*, der. *arei*, n., array] —*n.* **3.** order, as of troops drawn up for battle. **4.** an impressive group of things on exhibition, as a window display. **5.** regular order or arrangement. **6.** attire; dress. [ME, t. AF: m. *arai*, var. of OF *arei*, f. a to + *rei* order, of Gmc. origin] —**Syn. 1.** arrange, range, marshal.

ar·ray·al (ə rā′əl), *n.* **1.** act of arraying; muster; array. **2.** whatever is arrayed.

ar·rear (ə rĭr′), *n.* **1.** state of being behind or behindhand. **2.** (*usually pl.*) that which is behind in payment; a debt which remains unpaid, though due. **3. in arrear** or **in arrears,** behind in payments. **4.** *Archaic.* the rear. [ME *arere*, t. OF, g. L *ad-* AD- + *retrō* backward]

ăct, āble, dâre, ärt; ĕbb, ēqual; ĭf, īce; hŏt, ōver, ôrder, oil, bŏŏk, ōōze, out; ŭp, ūse, ûrge; ə = a in alone; ch, chief; g, give; ng, ring; sh, shoe; th, thin; ŧħ, that; zh, vision. See the full key on inside cover.

ar·rear·age (ə·rĭr′ĭj), *n.* **1.** state or condition of being behind in payments due or in arrears. **2.** arrears; amount or amounts overdue. **3.** a thing or part kept in reserve. [ME *arerage*, t. OF. See ARREAR, -AGE]

ar·rest (ə·rĕst′), *v.t.* **1.** to seize (a person) by legal authority or warrant. **2.** to capture; seize. **3.** to catch and fix: *to arrest the attention.* **4.** to bring to a standstill; stop; check: *to arrest the current of a river.* **5.** *Med.* to stop the active growth of: *arrested cancer.* —*n.* **6.** taking a person into custody in connection with a legal proceeding. **7.** any seizure or taking by force. **8.** act of stopping. **9.** state of being stopped. **10.** *Mach.* any device for arresting motion in a mechanism. [ME *arest*(*e*), t. OF: (m.) *areste* stoppage, der. *arester*, g. LL *adrestāre* (f. L: *ad-* AD- + *restāre* stop)] —**ar·rest′er**, *n.* —**ar·rest′ment**, *n.* —**Syn.** 4. See **stop**. 6. apprehension, imprisonment. 8. stoppage, halt.

ar·rest·ing (ə·rĕs′tĭng), *adj.* catching the attention; striking: *an arresting painting.*

Ar·rhe·ni·us (ä·rā′nē·ŏŏs), *n.* **Svante August** (svän′tĕ ou′gŏŏst), 1859–1927, Swedish physicist and chemist.

ar·rhyth·mi·a (ə·rĭth′mĭ′ə), *n.* *Pathol.* any disturbance in the rhythm of the heart beat. Also, **arhythmia.** [t. Gk.: want of rhythm] —**ar·rhyth·mic** (ə·rĭth′mĭk, ə·rĭth′-), *adj.*

ar·ride (ə·rīd′), *v.t.,* **-rided, -riding.** *Archaic.* to be agreeable or pleasing to. [t. L: m.s. *arrīdēre* smile at]

ar·ri·ère·ban (ăr′ĭ·âr′băn′; *Fr.* à·ryĕr·bän′), *n.* **1.** a group of vassals who owed military service, esp. to French kings. **2.** the message calling on this group for duty. [t. F. f. Gmc.: *hari, heri* army + *ban* proclamation]

ar·rière·pen·sée (à·ryĕr·pän·sĕ′), *n.* *French.* a mental reservation; hidden motive.

ar·ris (ăr′ĭs), *n.* *Archit.* **1.** a sharp ridge, as between adjoining channels of a Doric column. **2.** the line, edge, or hip in which the two straight or curved surfaces of a body, forming an exterior angle, meet. [t. F: m. *areste*, g. L *arista* ear of grain, bone of a fish]

ar·riv·al (ə·rī′vəl), *n.* **1.** act of arriving: *the time of arrival.* **2.** the reaching or attainment of any object or condition: *arrival at a decision.* **3.** the person or thing that arrives, or has arrived. —**Syn.** 1. advent, coming.

ar·rive (ə·rīv′), *v.,* **-rived, -riving.** —*v.i.* **1.** to come to a certain point in the course of travel; reach one's destination. **2.** to reach in any course or process; attain (fol. by *at*): *to arrive at a conclusion.* **3.** to come: *the time has arrived.* **4.** to attain a position of success in the world. **5.** *Obs.* to come to shore. —*v.t.* **6.** *Obs.* to reach; come to. **7.** *Obs.* to happen to. [ME *a*(*r*)*rive*(*n*), t. OF: m. *a*(*r*)*river*, g. LL *arrīpāre* come to shore] —**Syn.** 1. ARRIVE, COME both mean to reach a stopping place. ARRIVE directs the attention to the final point of an activity or state: *the train arrived at noon.* COME rarely refers to the actual moment of arrival but refers instead to the progress toward it. —**Ant.** 1. depart.

ar·ri·ve·der·ci (ä′rē·vĕ·dĕr′chē), *Italian.* until we see each other again; good-by for the present.

ar·ro·ba (är·rō′bä), *n.* **1.** a Spanish and Portuguese unit of weight of varying value, in Mexico, etc., equal to 25.37 pounds avoirdupois, and in Brazil to 32.38 pounds avoirdupois. **2.** a unit of liquid measure of varying value, used in Spain, etc., and commonly equal (when used for wine) to 4.26 U.S. gallons. [t. Sp., t. Ar.: m. *al-rub*′ the quarter]

ar·ro·gance (ăr′ə·gəns), *n.* quality of being arrogant; offensive exhibition of assumed or real superiority; overbearing pride. Also, **ar′ro·gan·cy.** [ME, t. F, t. L: m.s. *arrogantia*] —**Syn.** haughtiness, insolence, disdain.

ar·ro·gant (ăr′ə·gənt), *adj.* **1.** making unwarrantable claims or pretensions to superior importance or rights; overbearingly assuming; insolently proud. **2.** characterized by or proceeding from arrogance: *arrogant claims.* [ME, t. L: s. *arrogans,* ppr., assuming] —**ar′ro·gant·ly,** *adv.* —**Syn.** 1. presumptuous, haughty, imperious, supercilious. See **proud.** —**Ant.** 1. meek. 2. modest.

ar·ro·gate (ăr′ə·gāt′), *v.t.,* **-gated, -gating.** **1.** to claim unwarrantably or presumptuously; assume or appropriate to oneself without just right. **2.** to attribute or assign to another without just reason. [t. L: m. s. *arrogātus,* pp., assumed, asked of] —**ar′ro·ga′tion,** *n.*

ar·ron·disse·ment (à·rôn·dēs·män′), *n., pl.* **-ments** (-män′). *French.* **1.** the largest administrative division of a French department. Each arrondissement is divided into cantons. **2.** a borough of Paris.

ar·row (ăr′ō), *n.* **1.** a slender, straight, generally pointed, missile weapon made to be shot from a bow. The shaft is nearly always made of light wood, fitted with feathers at the nock end to help guide it. **2.** anything resembling an arrow in form. **3.** a figure used in maps, architectural drawings, etc., to indicate direction, as of winds, currents, rivers. **4.** (*cap.*) *Astron.* Sagitta. **5.** See **broad arrow.** [ME and OE *arwe*, c. Icel. ŏr] —**ar′row·less,** *adj.* —**ar′row·like**′, *adj.*

ar·row·head (ăr′ō·hĕd′), *n.* **1.** the head of an arrow, usually wedge-shaped or barbed. **2.** any plant of the genus *Sagittaria,* usually aquatic, species of which have arrowheaded leaves. **3.** *Art.* the dart in an egg-and-dart ornament. See illus. under **egg-and-dart.**

ar·row·root (ăr′ō·rŏŏt′, -rŏŏt′), *n.* **1.** a tropical American plant, *Maranta arundinacea,* or related species, whose rhizomes yield a nutritious starch. **2.** the starch itself. **3.** a similar starch from other plants, used in light puddings, cookies, etc.

ar·row·wood (ăr′ō·wŏŏd′), *n.* any of several shrubs

and small trees, as the wahoo and certain viburnums, with tough, straight shoots, once used for arrows.

ar·row·worm (ăr′ō·wûrm′), *n.* a small transparent pelagic animal of elongate form with fins, comprising the class or phylum *Chaetognatha.*

ar·row·y (ăr′ō·ĭ), *adj.* **1.** like an arrow in shape, peed, effect, etc.; swift or piercing. **2.** consisting of arrows.

ar·roy·o (ə·roi′ō), *n., pl.* **-os** (-ōz). (chiefly in southwest U.S. and parts of Spanish America) a small, steep-sided watercourse or gulch, usually dry except after heavy rains, and with a nearly flat floor and U-shaped cross section. [t. Sp., ult. g. L *arrūgia* shaft, pit]

ar·se·nal (ăr′sə·nəl), *n.* **1.** a repository or magazine of arms and military stores of all kinds for land or naval service. **2.** a building having that incidental purpose but used mainly for the training of troops. **3.** a public establishment where military equipment or munitions are manufactured. [t. : m.: m. *arsenale* dock (d. Venetian *arzaná*), t. Ar.: m. *dar ṣinā′a* workshop]

ar·se·nate (ăr′sə·nāt′, -nĭt), *n.* *Chem.* salt of arsenic acid.

ar·se·nic (*n.* ăr′sə·nĭk, ärs′nĭk; *adj.* är·sĕn′ĭk), *n.* **1.** a grayish-white element having a metallic luster, volatilizing when heated, and forming poisonous compounds. *Symbol:* As; *at. wt.:* 74.91; *at. no.:* 33. **2.** arsenic trioxide, As₂O₃, which is used in medicine and the arts, and in poisons for vermin. **3.** a mineral, the native element, occurring in white or gray masses. —*adj.* **4.** of or containing arsenic, esp. in the pentavalent state (As+5). [ME *arsenik,* t. L: m. s. *arsenicum,* t. Gk.: m. *arsenikón* orpiment]

arsenic acid, *Chem.* a water-soluble crystalline compound, H₃AsO₄, used in the manufacture of arsenates.

ar·sen·i·cal (är·sĕn′ə·kəl), *adj.* **1.** containing or relating to arsenic. —*n.* **2.** (*pl.*) a group of insecticides, drugs, etc., containing arsenic.

ar·se·nide (ăr′sə·nīd′, -nĭd), *n.* *Chem.* a compound containing two elements, of which arsenic is the negative one, as *silver arsenide,* Ag₃As.

ar·se·nite (ăr′sə·nīt′), *n.* *Chem.* **1.** a salt of any of the hypothetical arsenous acids. **2.** arsenic (def. 2).

ar·se·niu·ret (är·sē′nyə·rĕt′, -sĕn′yə-), *n.* *Chem.* arsenide. [f. ARSENI(c) + -URET]

ar·se·niu·ret·ed (är·sē′nyə·rĕt′ĭd, -sĕn′yə-), *adj. Chem.* combined with arsenic so as to form an arsenide.

ar·se·no·py·rite (är′sə·nō·pī′rīt, är′sĕn′ə-), *n.* a common mineral, iron arsenic sulfide, FeAsS, occurring in silver-white to steel-gray crystals or masses, an ore of arsenic. [f. *arseno-* (comb. form of ARSENIC) + PYRITE]

ar·se·nous (ăr′sə·nəs), *adj. Chem.* containing trivalent arsenic (As+3), as *arsenous chloride,* AsCl₃.

ar·sine (är·sēn′, är′sēn, -sĭn), *n.* *Chem.* **1.** arseniuretted hydrogen, AsH₃, a colorless, inflammable, highly poisonous gas, with a fetid garliclike odor, used in chemical warfare. **2.** any derivative of this compound, in which one or more hydrogen atoms are replaced by organic radicals. [f. ARS(ENIC) + -INE²]

ar·sis (ăr′sĭs), *n., pl.* **-ses** (-sēz). **1.** *Pros.* **a.** (originally) the unaccented syllable of a foot in verse. **b.** (in later use) the unstressed part of a rhythmical unit (opposed to *thesis*). **2.** *Music.* the anacrusis, or upbeat (opposed to *thesis*). [t. L, t. Gk.: a raising (appar. of hand or voice)]

ar·son (ăr′sən), *n.* *Law.* the malicious burning of a house or outbuilding belonging to another, or (as fixed by statute) the burning of any building (including one's own). [t. AF, g. LL *arsio* a burning]

ars·phen·a·mine (ärs′fĕn·ə·mēn′, -fĕn·ăm′ĭn), *n.* *Pharm.* a yellow crystalline powder subject to rapid oxidation, C₁₂H₁₂N₂O₂As₂.2HCl + 2H₂O, used to treat diseases caused by spirochete organisms, esp. syphilis and trench mouth; first known as "606." [f. ARS(ENIC) + PHEN(YL) + AMINE]

ars poe·ti·ca (ärz′ pō·ĕt′ə·kə), *Latin.* the art of poetry or poetics.

art¹ (ärt), *n.* **1.** the production or expression of what is beautiful, appealing, or of more than ordinary significance. **2.** *Journ.* any illustration in a newspaper or magazine. **3.** a department of skilled performance: *industrial art.* **4.** (*pl.*) a branch of learning or university study. **5.** (*pl.*) liberal arts. **6.** skilled workmanship, execution, or agency (often opposed to *nature*). **7.** craft; cunning: *glib and oily art.* **8.** studied action; artificiality in behavior. **9.** (*usually pl.*) an artifice or artful device: *the innumerable arts and wiles of politics.* **10.** *Archaic.* learning or science. [ME, t. OF, g. L *ars* skill, art]

art² (ärt), *v. Archaic or Poetic.* 2nd pers. sing. pres. indic. of *be.* [ME; OE *eart*]

-art, var. of **-ard,** as in *braggart.*

art., *pl.* **arts.** **1.** article. **2.** artificial.

ar·tal (är′täl), *n. pl.* of *rotl.*

Ar·ta·xerx·es II (är′tə·zûrk′sēz), died 359? B.C., king of Persia, 404?–359? B.C.

ar·te·fact (är′tə·fäkt′), *n.* artifact.

ar·tel (är·tĕl′; *Russ.* -tĕl′y), *n.* (in the Soviet Union) a peasants' or workers' cooperative enterprise. [Russ.]

Ar·te·mis (är′tə·mĭs), *n. Gk. Myth.* a goddess, sister of Apollo, represented as a virgin huntress and associated with the moon: identified with Diana. [t. L, t. Gk.]

ar·te·mis·i·a (är′tə·mĭz′ĭ·ə, -mĭsh′-), *n.* **1.** any of a very large genus of plants, *Artemisia,* of the family *Compositae,* abundant in dry regions, and mostly of the northern hemisphere. **2.** a North American species, A.

tridentata, the sagebrush of the western plains. [t. L, t. Gk.: herb like wormwood]

ar·te·ri·al (är tĭr′ĭəl), *adj.* **1.** *Physiol.* pertaining to the blood in the arteries which has been charged with oxygen during its passage through the lungs, and, in the higher animals, is usually bright red. **2.** *Anat.* of, pertaining to, or resembling the arteries. **3.** having a main channel and many branches: *arterial drainage.*

ar·te·ri·al·ize (är tĭr′ĭə līz′), *v.t.,* **-ized, -izing.** *Physiol.* to convert (venous blood) into arterial blood by the action of oxygen in lungs. **—ar·te′ri·al·i·za′tion,** *n.*

ar·te·ri·o·scle·ro·sis (är tĭr′ĭ ō skla rō′sĭs), *n. Pathol.* an arterial disease occurring esp. in the elderly, characterized by inelasticity and thickening of the vessel walls, with lessened blood flow. [t. NL, f. Gk.: *arterio-* (comb. form of *artēria* artery) + m. *sklērōsis* hardening] **—ar·te·ri·o·scle·rot·ic** (är tĭr′ĭ ō skla rŏt′ĭk), *adj.*

ar·ter·y (är′tə rĭ), *n., pl.* **-teries. 1.** *Anat.* a blood vessel which conveys blood from the heart to any part of the body. **2.** a main channel in any ramifying system of communication, or transportation, as in drainage or highways. [ME *arterie,* t. L: m. *arteria,* t. Gk.]

ar·te·sian well (är tē′zhən), a well whose shaft penetrates through an impervious layer into a water-bearing stratum from which the water rises under pressure. [t. F: m. *artēsien* pertaining to Artois]

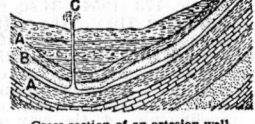

Cross section of an artesian well
A, Impermeable strata;
B, Permeable strata;
C, Artesian boring and well

Ar·te·veld (är′tə vĕlt′), *n.* **1.** Jacob van (yä′kŏp vän), 1290?–1345, statesman of Flanders. **2.** his son, Philip van (fē′lĭp vän), 1340?–82, popular leader of Flanders. Also, **Ar·te·vel·de** (är′tə vĕl′də).

art·ful (ärt′fəl), *adj.* **1.** crafty; cunning; tricky: *artful schemes.* **2.** skillful in adapting means to ends; ingenious. **3.** done with or characterized by art or skill. **4.** *Rare.* artificial. **—art′ful·ly,** *adv.* **—art′ful·ness,** *n.*

ar·thral·gia (är thrăl′jə), *n. Pathol.* pain in a joint. **—ar·thral′gic,** *adj.*

ar·thri·tis (är thrī′tĭs), *n. Pathol.* inflammation of a joint, as in gout or rheumatism. [t. L, t. Gk.: joint disease] **—ar·thrit·ic** (är thrĭt′ĭk), *adj.*

arthro-, *Anat.* a word element meaning "joint," as in *arthropathy.* Also, **arthr-.** [t. Gk., comb. form of *árthron*]

ar·thro·mere (är′thrə mĭr′), *n. Zool.* one of the segments or parts into which the body of articulate animals is divided.

ar·thro·pod (är′thrə pŏd′), *n.* any of the *Arthropoda,* the phylum of segmented invertebrates, having jointed legs, as the insects, arachnids, crustaceans, and myriapods. **—ar·throp·o·dous** (är thrŏp′ə dəs), *adj.*

ar·thro·spore (är′thrə spôr′), *n.* **1.** *Bacteriol.* an isolated vegetative cell which has passed into a resting state, occurring in bacteria, and not regarded as a true spore. **2.** *Bot.* one of a number of spores of various low fungi and algae, united in the form of a string of beads, formed by fission.

Ar·thur (är′thər), *n.* **1.** legendary king in ancient Britain: leader of Knights of the Round Table. **2.** Chester Alan, 1830–86, 21st president of the U.S., 1881–85.

Ar·thu·ri·an (är thŏŏr′ĭ ən), *adj.* of or pertaining to Arthur, who, with his knights, formed the subject of a great body of medieval romantic literature.

ar·ti·choke (är′tə chōk′), *n.* **1.** a herbaceous, thistlelike plant, *Cynara Scolymus,* with an edible flower head. **2.** the edible portion, used as a table vegetable. **3.** Jerusalem artichoke. [t. d. It.: m. *articiocco,* t. Pr.: m. *arquichaut,* t. Ar.: m. *al-kharshūf*]

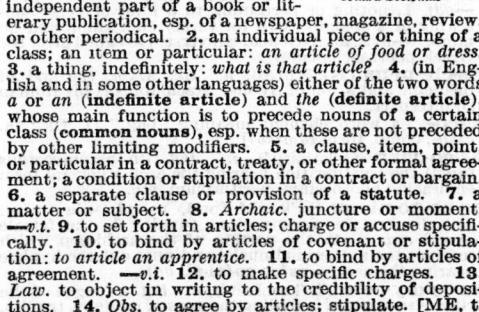

Artichoke.
Cynara Scolymus

ar·ti·cle (är′tə kəl), *n., v.,* **-cled, -cling. —n. 1.** a literary composition on a specific topic, forming an independent part of a book or literary publication, esp. of a newspaper, magazine, review, or other periodical. **2.** an individual piece or thing of a class; an item or particular: *an article of food or dress.* **3.** a thing, indefinitely: *what is that article?* **4.** (in English and in some other languages) either of the two words *a* or *an* (**indefinite article**) and *the* (**definite article**), whose main function is to precede nouns of a certain class (**common nouns**), esp. when these are not preceded by other limiting modifiers. **5.** a clause, item, point, or particular in a contract, treaty, or other formal agreement; a condition or stipulation in a contract or bargain. **6.** a separate clause or provision of a statute. **7.** a matter or subject. **8.** *Archaic.* juncture or moment. **—v.t. 9.** to set forth in articles; charge or accuse specifically. **10.** to bind by articles of covenant or stipulation: *to article an apprentice.* **11.** to bind by articles of agreement. **—v.i. 12.** to make specific charges. **13.** *Law.* to object in writing to the credibility of depositions. **14.** *Obs.* to agree by articles; stipulate. [ME, F, t. L: m. *articulus,* dim. of *artus* joint]

Articles of Confederation, the first constitution of the thirteen American colonies, adopted in 1781 by the Continental Congress and lasting till 1788.

ar·tic·u·lar (är tĭk′yə lər), *adj.* of or pertaining to the joints. [t. L: s. *articulāris*]

ar·tic·u·late (*adj., n.* är tĭk′yə lĭt; *v.* är tĭk′yə lāt′), *adj., v.,* **-lated, -lating,** *n.* **—adj. 1.** clear; distinct. **2.** uttered clearly in distinct syllables. **3.** capable of speech; not speechless. **4.** having joints or articulations; composed of segments. **—v.t. 5.** to utter articulately. **6.** *Phonet.* to make the movements and adjustments of the speech organs necessary to utter (a speech sound). **7.** to unite by a joint or joints. **—v.i. 8.** to utter distinct syllables or words: *to articulate distinctly.* **9.** *Phonet.* to articulate a speech sound. **10.** to form a joint. **11.** *Obs.* to make terms of agreement. **—n. 12.** a segmented invertebrate. [t. L: m. s. *articulātus,* pp.] **—ar·tic′u·late·ly,** *adv.* **—ar·tic′u·late·ness,** *n.* **—ar·tic′u·la·tive,** *adj.* **—ar·tic′u·la·tor,** *n.*

ar·tic·u·la·tion (är tĭk′yə lā′shən), *n.* **1.** *Phonet.* **a.** act or process of articulating speech. **b.** the adjustments and movements of speech organs involved in pronouncing a particular sound, taken as a whole. **c.** any of these adjustments and movements. **d.** any speech sound, esp. a consonant. **2.** act of jointing. **3.** a jointed state or formation; a joint. **4.** *Bot.* **a.** a joint or place between two parts where separation may take place spontaneously, as at the point of attachment of a leaf. **b.** a node in a stem, or the space between two nodes. **5.** *Anat., Zool.* a joint, as the joining or juncture of bones or of the movable segments of an arthropod.

ar·ti·fact (är′tə făkt′), *n.* **1.** any object made by man with a view to subsequent use. **2.** *Biol.* a substance, structure, or the like, not naturally present in tissue but formed by reagents, death, etc. Also, **artefact.** [f. L: *arti-* (comb. form of *ars* art) + s. *factus,* pp., made]

ar·ti·fice (är′tə fĭs), *n.* **1.** a crafty device or expedient; a clever trick or stratagem. **2.** craft; trickery. **3.** skillful or apt contrivance. **4.** *Obs.* workmanship. [t. F, t. L: m. s. *artificium*] **—Syn. 1.** ruse, subterfuge, wile. **2.** guile, deception, deceit. See **cunning.**

ar·tif·i·cer (är tĭf′ə sər), *n.* **1.** a skillful or artistic worker; craftsman. **2.** one who is skillful in devising ways of making things; an inventor. **3.** *Mil.* a soldier mechanic who does repairs.

ar·ti·fi·cial (är′tə fĭsh′əl), *adj.* **1.** made by human skill and labor (opposed to *natural*). **2.** made in imitation of or as a substitute; not genuine. **3.** feigned; fictitious; assumed. **4.** full of affectation; affected. **5.** *Biol.* based on arbitrary rather than organic criteria. **6.** *Obs.* artful; crafty. [ME t. L: s. *artificiālis*] **—ar′ti·fi′cial·ly,** *adv.* **—ar′ti·fi′cial·ness,** *n.*

artificial horizon, 1. a level reflector, as a surface of mercury, used in determining the altitudes of stars, etc. **2.** the bubble in a sextant or octant for aerial use.

ar·ti·fi·ci·al·i·ty (är′tə fĭsh′ĭ ăl′ə tĭ), *n., pl.* **-ties. 1.** artificial quality. **2.** an artificial thing or trait.

artificial selection. See **selection** (def. 3).

ar·til·ler·y (är tĭl′ər ĭ), *n.* **1.** mounted guns, movable or stationary, light or heavy, as distinguished from small arms. **2.** the troops, or the branch of an army, concerned with the service of such guns. **3.** the science which treats of the use of such guns. [ME *artilrie,* t. OF: m. *artillerie* implements of war]

ar·til·ler·y·man (är tĭl′ər ĭ mən), *n., pl.* **-men.** one who serves a piece of artillery. Also, **ar·til′ler·ist.**

ar·ti·o·dac·tyl (är′tĭ ō dăk′tĭl), *adj.* **1.** *Zool.* having an even number of toes or digits on each foot. **—n. 2.** any animal of the mammalian order *Artiodactyla,* which comprises the even-toed quadrupeds, as the swine, the hippopotami, and the ruminants: cattle, sheep, goats, deer, camels, etc., sometimes classified as a suborder of ungulates. [f. Gk.: *ártio(s)* even + m.s. *dáktylos* finger or toe] **—ar′ti·o·dac′ty·lous,** *adj.*

ar·ti·san (är′tə zən), *n.* **1.** one skilled in an industrial art. **2.** *Obs.* an artist. [t. F, t. It.: m. *artigiano,* der. *arte* guild] **—Syn. 1.** See **artist.**

art·ist (är′tĭst), *n.* **1.** a person who practices one of the fine arts, esp. a painter or a sculptor. **2.** a member of one of the histrionic professions, as an actor or singer. **3.** one who exhibits art in his work, or makes an art of his employment. **4.** a trickster. **5.** *Obs.* an artisan. [t. F: m. *artiste,* t. L: m. *artista,* g. L. See ART[1], -IST] **—Syn 1.** ARTIST, ARTISAN are persons having superior skill or ability, or capable of a superior kind of workmanship. An ARTIST is a person engaged in some type of fine art. An ARTISAN is engaged in a commercial or manual enterprise.

ar·tiste (är tēst′; *Fr.* är tēst′), *n. French.* an artist, esp. an actor, singer, dancer, or other public performer.

ar·tis·tic (är tĭs′tĭk), *adj.* **1.** conformable to the standards of art; aesthetically excellent or admirable. **2.** of, like, or befitting an artist. Also, **ar·tis′ti·cal. —ar·tis′ti·cal·ly,** *adv.*

art·ist·ry (är′tĭs trĭ), *n., pl.* **-ries. 1.** artistic workmanship, effect, or quality. **2.** artistic pursuits.

art·less (ärt′lĭs), *adj.* **1.** free from deceit, cunning, or craftiness; ingenuous: *an artless mind.* **2.** natural; simple: *artless beauty.* **3.** lacking art, knowledge, or skill. **—art′less·ly,** *adv.* **—art′less·ness,** *n.*

Ar·tois (är twä′), *n.* a former province in N France: artesian wells. See map under **Agincourt.**

art·y (är′tĭ), *adj.,* **artier, artiest.** *Colloq.* ostentatious in display of artistic interest. **—art′i·ness,** *n.*

A·ru·ba (ä rōō′bä), *n.* an island in the Netherlands Antilles, off the NW coast of Venezuela. 55,483 pop. (1955); 69 sq. mi.

A·ru Islands (ä′rōō), an island group in Indonesia, SW of New Guinea. 3306 sq. mi.

ar·um (âr′əm), n. 1. any plant of the genus *Arum*, having an inflorescence consisting of a spadix enclosed in a large spathe, as the cuckoopint. 2. any of various allied plants in cultivation, as the calla lily. [t. L, t. Gk.: m. *âron* the wake-robin] —**ar′um·like′**, adj.

Ar·un·del (âr′ən dəl; *local* ärn′dəl), n. a town in S England, in Sussex: famous old castle; 2680 (1951).

a·run·di·na·ceous (ərŭn′də nā′shəs), adj. Bot. pertaining to or like a reed or cane; reedlike; reedy. [t. L: m. *arundinăceus*]

A.R.V., American Revised Version (of the Bible).

-ary[1], 1. an adjective suffix meaning "pertaining to," attached chiefly to nouns (*honorary*) and to stems appearing in other words (*voluntary*). 2. a suffix forming nouns from other nouns or adjectives indicating location or repository (*dictionary, granary, apiary*), officers (*functionary, secretary*), or other relations (*adversary*). 3. a suffix forming collective numeral nouns, esp. in time units (*centenary*). [t. L: m. *-ārius*, neut. *-ārium*]

-ary[2], var. of **-ar**[1], as in *exemplary, military.*

Ar·y·an (âr′Ĭən, -yən, ăr′-; är′Ĭən), n. 1. Ethnol. a member or descendant of the prehistoric people who spoke Indo-European. 2. (in Nazi doctrine) a gentile of Indo-European stock. —adj. 3. of or pertaining to an Aryan or the Aryans. Also, **Arian.** [f. Skt. *Arya*, name by which the Sanskrit-speaking immigrants into India called themselves + -AN] —**Ar′y·an,** adj.

Ar·y·an·ize (âr′Ĭə nīz′, -yə-, ăr′-; är′-), v.t., **-ized, -iz·ing.** (in Nazi doctrine) to remove all non-Aryan persons from (office, business, etc.).

ar·yl (ăr′Ĭl), adj. Chem. of or pertaining to any of the organic radicals obtained from the aromatic hydrocarbons by removing a hydrogen atom, as phenyl (C_6H_5) from benzene (C_6H_6). [f. AR(OMATIC) + -YL]

ar·yl·a·mines (ăr′Ĭl ə mēnz′, -ăm′Ĭnz), n. pl. Chem. a group of amines in which one or more of the hydrogen atoms of ammonia are replaced with aromatic radicals.

ar·y·te·noid (ăr′ə tē′noid, ər Ĭt′ə noid′), Anat. —adj. 1. ladle- or cup-shaped (applied to two small cartilages at the top of the larynx, and to some of the muscles connected with them). —n. 2. an arytenoid cartilage. [t. Gk.: m. s. *arytainoeidēs* ladle-shaped] —**ar·y·te·noi·dal** (ăr′ə tə noi′dəl, ə rĬt′ə-), adj.

as[1] (ăz; *unstressed* əz), adv. 1. to such a degree or extent: *as good as gold.* 2. as well as, as much or as truly as; just as; as also: *good as well as beautiful.* 3. as well, equally; also; too: *beautiful, and good as well.* —conj. 4. the consequent in the correlations *as . . . as, same . . . as,* etc., noting degree, extent, manner, etc. (*as good as gold, in the same way as before*), or in the correlations *so as, such as,* noting purpose or result (fol. by infinitive): *to listen so as to hear.* 5. (without antecedent) in the degree, manner, etc., of or that: *to be good as gold, do as we do.* 6. when or while. 7. since; because. 8. for instance. 9. even or just (now chiefly in the phrase, *as yet*). 10. Colloq. (in independent clauses) that: *I don't know as I do.* 11. Eng. Dial. than. 12. as for, as to, with respect to. 13. as if, as though, as it would be if. 14. as it were, in some sort; so to speak. —rel. pron. 15. that; who; which (esp. after *such* and *the same*): *I had the same troubles as you had.* —prep. 16. in the role, function, or status of: *to appear as Othello.* [ME, *as, als, alse, also,* OE *alswā, ealswā* all so, quite so, quite as, as. Cf. ALSO] —Syn. 7. See **because.**

as[2] (ăs), n., pl. **asses** (ăs′Ĭz). 1. a copper coin, the unit of the early monetary system of Rome, first nominally of the weight of a pound (12 ounces). About 80 B.C., having fallen to half an ounce, it ceased to be issued. 2. a unit of weight: 12 ounces; the pound, equal to 327.4 grams, or 5053 grains. [t. L]

as-, var. of **ad-,** before *s,* as in *assert.*

As, Chem. arsenic.

AS., Anglo-Saxon. Also, **A.-S., A.S.**

as·a·fet·i·da (ăs′ə fĕt′ə də), n. a gum resin having an alliaceous odor, obtained from the roots of several species of the umbelliferous genus *Ferula* and used in medicine. Also, **as′a·foet′i·da, assafetida, assafoetida.** [t. ML: f. *asa* (t. Pers.: m. *azā* mastic) + L *fētida, foetida* fetid]

As·ben (äs bĕn′), n. Aïr (French West Africa).

as·bes·tos (ăs bĕs′təs, ăz-), n. 1. Mineral. a. a fibrous amphibole, used for making incombustible or fireproof articles. b. the mineral chrysotile, similarly used. 2. a fabric woven from asbestos fibers, used for theater curtains, firemen's gloves, etc. 3. Theat. a fireproof curtain. Also, **as·bes′tus.** [t. L, t. Gk.: unquenchable; r. ME *asbeston,* t. OF] —**as·bes·tine** (ăs bĕs′tĬn, ăz-), adj.

As·bur·y (ăz′bər Ĭ), n. Francis, 1745–1816, first bishop of the Methodist Episcopal Church in America.

As·bur·y Park (ăz′bĕr′Ĭ, -bər Ĭ), a city in E New Jersey: seacoast resort. 17,366 (1960).

as·ca·rid (ăs′kə rĬd), n. Zool. any of the *Ascaridae,* a family of nematode worms including the roundworm and pinworm. [t. NL: s. *ascaridae,* t. Gk.: m. *askarĭdes* (pl.) threadworms]

as·cend (ə sĕnd′), v.i. 1. to climb or go upward; mount; rise. 2. to rise to a higher point or degree; proceed from an inferior to a superior degree or level. 3. to go toward the source or beginning; go back in time. 4. Music. to rise in pitch; pass from any tone to a higher one. —v.t. 5. to go or move upward upon or along; climb; mount: *to ascend a hill or ladder.* [ME *ascende(n),*

t. L: m. *ascendere* climb up] —**as·cend′a·ble, as·cend′-i·ble,** adj. —Syn. 1. soar. 2. tower. 5. See **climb.**

as·cend·an·cy (ə sĕn′dən sĬ), n. state of being in the ascendant; governing or controlling influence; domination. Also, **as·cend′en·cy, as·cend′ance, as·cend′ence.**

as·cend·ant (ə sĕn′dənt), n. 1. the position of dominance or controlling influence; superiority; predominance. 2. an ancestor (opposed to *descendant*). 3. Astrol. a. the point of the ecliptic or the sign of the zodiac rising above the horizon at the time of a birth, etc. b. the horoscope. —adj. 4. superior; predominant. 5. Bot. directed or curved upward. Also, **as·cend′ent.**

as·cend·er (ə sĕn′dər), n. 1. one who or that which ascends. 2. Print. the part of such letters as *b, h, d,* and *f* that rises above the body of most lower-case letters.

as·cend·ing (ə sĕn′dĬng), adj. Bot. growing or directed upward, esp. obliquely or in a curve from the base.

as·cen·sion (ə sĕn′shən), n. 1. act of ascending; ascent. 2. (*often cap.*) Eccles. the bodily passing of Christ from earth to heaven. Acts 1:9. 3. (*cap.*) Ascension Day. [ME, t. L: s. *ascensio*]

As·cen·sion (ə sĕn′shən), n. a British island in the S Atlantic. 173 (1954); 34 sq. mi.

Ascension Day, the fortieth day after Easter, commemorating the ascension of Christ; Holy Thursday.

as·cen·sive (ə sĕn′sĬv), adj. ascending; rising.

as·cent (ə sĕnt′), n. 1. act of ascending; upward movement; rise. 2. a rising from a lower to a higher state, degree, or grade; advancement. 3. act of climbing or traveling up. 4. the way or means of ascending; upward slope. 5. a procedure toward a source or beginning. 6. gradient. [der. ASCEND, modeled on DESCENT]

as·cer·tain (ăs′ər tān′), v.t. 1. to find out by trial, examination, or experiment, so as to know as certain; determine. 2. Archaic. to make certain, clear, or definitely known. [ME *acertain,* t. OF: s. *acertener* make certain, der. a- A-[5] + *certain* CERTAIN] —**as′cer·tain′a·ble,** adj. —**as′cer·tain′a·ble·ness,** n. —**as′cer·tain′a·bly,** adv. —**as′cer·tain′ment,** n. —Syn. 1. See **learn.**

as·cet·ic (ə sĕt′Ĭk), n. 1. a person who leads an abstemious life. 2. one who practices religious austerities. 3. (in the early Christian Church) a monk; hermit. —adj. 4. pertaining to asceticism or ascetics. 5. rigorously abstinent; austere. 6. unduly strict in religious exercises or mortifications. [t. Gk.: m. s. *askētikós* pertaining to a monk or hermit, der. *askētēs* monk, hermit (orig. athlete)]

as·cet·i·cal (ə sĕt′ə kəl), adj. pertaining to ascetic discipline or practice. —**as·cet′i·cal·ly,** adv.

as·cet·i·cism (ə sĕt′ə sĬz′əm), n. 1. the life or practice of an ascetic; the principles and historic course of the ascetics. 2. Theol. the theory or systemic exposition of the means (whether negative, as self-denial and abstinence, or positive, as the exercise of natural and Christian virtues) by which a complete conformity with the divine will may be attained. 3. rigorous self-discipline.

Asch (äsh), n. Sholom (shō′ləm), 1880–1957, U.S. author, born in Poland.

As·cham (ăs′kəm), n. Roger, 1515–68, English scholar and writer: tutor of Queen Elizabeth.

as·ci (ăs′ī), n. pl. of **ascus.**

As·cid·i·a (ə sĬd′Ĭə), n.pl. Zool. the Tunicata.

as·cid·i·an (ə sĬd′Ĭən), Zool. —n. 1. a tunicate or sea squirt. See **Tunicata.** —adj. 2. of or belonging to the *Ascidia* or *Tunicata.* [f. ASCIDI(UM) + -AN]

as·cid·i·um (ə sĬd′Ĭəm), n., pl. **-cidia** (-sĬd′Ĭə). Bot. a baglike or pitcherlike part. See illus. under **pitcher plant.** [t. NL, t. Gk.: m. *askidion,* dim. of *askós* bag]

as·ci·tes (ə sī′tēz), n. Pathol. dropsy of the belly or peritoneum. [t. L, t. Gk.: m. *askîtēs* (sc. *nósos* disease) a kind of dropsy, der. *askós* bag, belly] —**as·cit·ic** (ə sĬt′Ĭk), adj.

as·cle·pi·a·da·ceous (ăs klē′pĬ ə dā′shəs), adj. Bot. belonging to the *Asclepiadaceae,* or milkweed family of plants. [f. s. NL *Asclēpias* the milkweed genus (t. Gk.: m. *asklēpiás* kind of plant, named after *Asklēpiós* Asclepius) + -ACEOUS]

As·cle·pi·a·de·an (ăs klē′pĬ ə dē′ən), Class. Pros. —adj. 1. noting or pertaining to a kind of verse consisting of a spondee, two (or three) choriambi, and an iamb. —n. 2. an Asclepiadean verse. [so called after the Greek poet Asclepiades]

As·cle·pi·us (ăs klē′pĬ əs), n. Gk. Myth. the god of medicine and the son of Apollo. Aesculapius is his Roman counterpart.

asco-, a word element meaning "bag." [t. Gk.: m. *asko-,* comb. form of *askós*]

as·co·carp (ăs′kə kärp′), n. Bot. (in ascomycetous fungi) the fructification bearing the asci, a general term embracing apothecium, perithecium, etc.

as·co·go·ni·um (ăs′kə gō′nĬ əm), n., pl. **-nia** (-nĬ ə). Bot. (in certain ascomycetous fungi) 1. the female sexual organ. 2. the portion of the archicarp which receives the antheridial nuclei and puts out the hyphae bearing the asci. —**as′co·go′ni·al,** adj.

as·co·my·cete (ăs′kə mī sēt′), n. Bot. a fungus of the class *Ascomycetes,* including the yeasts, mildews, truffles, etc., characterized by bearing the sexual spores in a sac.

as·co·my·ce·tous (ăs′kə mī sē′təs), adj. Bot. belonging or pertaining to the *Ascomycetes.*

---

b., blend of, blended; c., cognate with; d., dialect, dialectal; der., derived from; f., formed from; g., going back to; m., modification of; r., replacing; s., stem of; t., taken from; ?, perhaps. See the full key on inside cover.

a·scor·bic acid (ə·skôr′bĭk), *Biochem.* the antiscorbutic vitamin, or Vitamin C, $C_6H_8O_6$, found in citrus fruits, tomatoes, paprika, and green vegetables, and also made industrially.

as·co·spore (ăs′kə·spôr′), *n. Bot.* a spore formed within an ascus. —**as·cos·po·rous** (ăs kŏs′pə rəs, ăs′kə spôr′əs), **as·co·spor·ic** (ăs′kə spôr′ĭk, -spôr′-), *adj.*

as·cot (ăs′kət), *n.* **1.** a kind of scarf or necktie with broad ends, tied and arranged so that the ends are laid flat, one across the other. —*adj.* **2.** (*cap.*) noting or pertaining to the celebrated race course at Ascot, in Berkshire, England, or the horse races held there.

Ascot

as·cribe (ə·skrīb′), *v.t.*, **-cribed, -crib·ing. 1.** to attribute, impute, or refer, as to a cause or source; assign: *the alphabet is usually ascribed to the Phoenicians.* **2.** to consider or allege to belong. [t. L: m.s. *ascribere* add to a writing; r. ME *ascrive*(n), t. OF: m. *ascriv-*, s. *ascrire*] —**as·crib′a·ble,** *adj.* —**Syn. 1.** See **attribute.**

as·crip·tion (ə·skrĭp′shən), *n.* **1.** act of ascribing. **2.** a statement ascribing something, specif., praise to the Deity. Also, **adscription.**

as·cus (ăs′kəs), *n.*, *pl.* **asci** (ăs′ī). *Bot.* the sac in ascomycetes in which the sexual spores are formed. [t. NL, t. Gk.: m. *askós* bag, wineskin, bladder]

-ase, *Chem.* a noun suffix used in names of enzymes, as in *glucase, lactase, pectase.* [from (DIAST)ASE]

a·sep·sis (ə·sĕp′sĭs, ā-), *n.* **1.** absence of the microörganisms that produce sepsis or septic disease. **2.** *Med.* methods or treatment, as by surgical operation, characterized by the use of instruments, dressings, etc., that are free from such microörganisms. [f. A-⁶ + SEPSIS]

a·sep·tic (ə·sĕp′tĭk, ā-), *adj.* free from the living germs of disease, fermentation, or putrefaction. —**a·sep′ti·cal·ly,** *adv.*

a·sex·u·al (ā sĕk′shŏŏ əl), *adj. Biol.* **1.** not sexual. **2.** having no sex or no sexual organs. **3.** independent of sexual processes. —**a·sex·u·al·i·ty** (ā sĕk′shŏŏ ăl′ə tĭ), *n.* —**a·sex′u·al·ly,** *adv.*

As·gard (ăs′gärd, äs′-), *n. Scand. Myth.* the heavenly abode of the gods, connected with the earth by a rainbow bridge (Bifrost). Also, **As·garth** (ăs′gärth), **as·gar·dhr** (ăs′gär′thər). [t. Icel.: m.s. *āsgardhr,* f. *āss* god + *gardhr* yard]

ash¹ (ăsh), *n.* **1.** the powdery residue of matter that remains after burning: *the ashes are still hot;* (used as sing. chiefly in scientific and commercial language as in *soda ash*). **2.** *Geol.* finely pulverized lava thrown out by a volcano in eruption. See **ashes.** [ME; OE *æsce, æsce*]

ash² (ăsh), *n.* **1.** any tree of the oleaceous genus *Fraxinus,* esp. *F. excelsior* of Europe and Asia or *F. americana* of North America (**white ash**). **2.** the wood, tough, straight-grained, and elastic, and valued as timber. [ME *asch,* OE *æsc,* c. G *esche*]

a·shamed (ə·shāmd′), *adj.* **1.** feeling shame; abashed by guilt. **2.** unwilling or restrained through fear of shame. —**a·sham·ed·ly** (ə shā′mĭd lĭ), *adv.* —**a·sham′ed·ness,** *n.*

—**Syn. 1.** ASHAMED, HUMILIATED, MORTIFIED refer to a condition of discomfort and embarrassment. ASHAMED describes a feeling of guilt combined with regret: *ashamed of a fault.* HUMILIATED describes a feeling of being humbled or disgraced: *humiliated by public ridicule.* MORTIFIED describes a feeling of deep chagrin, embarrassment, and confusion: *mortified by her clumsiness.* —**Ant.** 1. proud.

A·shan·ti (ə shän′tĭ), *n.* **1.** a former British colony in W Africa: now a part of Ghana; a former native kingdom. 818,944 pop. (1948); 24,379 sq. mi. *Cap.:* Kumasi. **2.** a native or an inhabitant of Ashanti.

Ash·bur·ton (ăsh′bûr′tən, -bər tən), *n.* **Alexander Baring, 1st Baron,** 1774–1848, British statesman.

ash can, 1. a can or metal receptacle for ashes. **2.** *Colloq.* a depth bomb.

ash·en¹ (ăsh′ən), *adj.* **1.** ash-colored; gray. **2.** consisting of ashes. [f. ASH¹ + -EN²]

ash·en² (ăsh′ən), *adj.* **1.** pertaining to the ash tree or its timber. **2.** made of wood from the ash tree. [f. ASH² + -EN²]

ash·es (ăsh′ĭz), *n. pl.* **1.** ruins, as from destruction by burning: *the ashes of an ancient empire.* **2.** the remains of the human body after cremation. **3.** a dead body or corpse; mortal remains. See also **ash¹.**

Ashe·ville (ăsh′vĭl), *n.* a city in W North Carolina. 60,192 (1960).

ash gray, pale gray of ashes. Also, **ash color.**

Ash·ke·naz·im (ăsh′kə năz′ĭm), *n.pl.* German, Polish, and Russian Jews (as distinguished from the *Sephardim* or Spanish-Portuguese Jews). [Heb., pl. of *Ashk'naz,* a descendant of Japheth (Gen. 10:3); also, in medieval use, Germany] —**Ash′ke·naz′ic,** *adj.*

Ash·kha·bad (ăsh′kä bäd′), *n.* the capital of the Turkmen republic of the U.S.S.R., in the S central part. 142,000 (est. 1956). Formerly, **Poltoratsk.**

Ash·land (ăsh′lənd), *n.* a city in NE Kentucky, on the Ohio river. 31,283 (1960).

ash·lar (ăsh′lər), *n. Bldg. Trades.* **1.** a squared block of building stone, finished or rough. **2.** such stones collectively. **3.** masonry made of them. Also, **ash′ler.** [ME *asheler,* t. OF: m. *aisselier,* ult. der. L *axis* board]

a·shore (ə shôr′), *adv., adj. Naut.* **1.** to shore; on or to the land. **2.** on land (opposed to *aboard* or *afloat*).

Ash·ta·bu·la (ăsh′tə bū′lə), *n.* a city in NE Ohio: a port on Lake Erie. 24,559 (1960).

Ash·ton-un·der-Lyne (ăsh′tən ŭn′dər līn′), *n.* a city in W England, near Manchester. 46,490 (1951).

Ash·to·reth (ăsh′tə rĕth′), *n.* an ancient Semitic goddess. See **Astarte.** [t. Heb.]

A·shur (ä′shŏŏr), *n.* Assur.

A·shur·ba·ni·pal (ä′shŏŏr bä′nĭ päl′), *n.* died 626? B.C., king of Assyria, 668?–626? B.C.

Ash Wednesday, the first day of Lent.

ash·y (ăsh′ĭ), *adj.*, **ashier, ashiest. 1.** ash-colored; pale. **2.** of ashes. **3.** sprinkled or covered with ashes.

A·sia (ā′zhə, ā′shə), *n.* the largest continent, bounded by Europe and the Pacific, Arctic, and Indian Oceans. 1,480,000,000 pop. (est. 1955); ab. 16,000,000 sq. mi.

Asia Minor, a peninsula in W Asia between the Black and the Mediterranean seas, including most of Asiatic Turkey. See **Anatolia.**

A·si·at·ic (ā′zhĭ ăt′ĭk, ā′shĭ-), *adj.* **1.** of, belonging to, or characteristic of Asia or its inhabitants. —*n.* **2.** a native of Asia. Also, **A·sian** (ā′zhən, ā′shən).

Asiatic beetle, a scarabaeid beetle, *Anomala orientalis,* that destroys crops, introduced into the U.S. from the Orient.

Asiatic cholera, *Pathol.* an infectious epidemic disease, originally from Asia, which is often fatal. See **cholera** (def. 1b).

Asiatic flu, *Pathol.* a form of influenza caused by a microörganism believed to have been carried from Asia. Also, **Asiatic influenza, Asian flu, Asian influenza.**

a·side (ə sīd′), *adv.* **1.** on or to one side; to or at a short distance; apart; away from some position or direction: *to turn aside.* **2.** away from one's thoughts or consideration: *to put one's cares aside.* **3.** aside from, *U.S.* a. apart from; excluding. b. except for. —*n.* **4.** *Theat.* a part of an actor's lines not supposed to be heard by others on the stage and intended only for the audience.

as·i·nine (ăs′ə nīn′), *adj.* stupid; obstinate. [t. L: m.s. *asininus,* der. *asinus* ass] —**as′i·nine′ly,** *adv.* —**as·i·nin·i·ty** (ăs′ə nĭn′ə tĭ), *n.*

A·sir (ä sēr′), *n.* a district in SW Saudi Arabia.

-asis, a word element forming names of diseases. [t. L, t. Gk.]

ask (ăsk, äsk), *v.t.* **1.** to put a question to: *ask him.* **2.** to seek to be informed about: *to ask the way;* (or, with a double object) *to ask him the way.* **3.** to seek by words to obtain; request: *to ask advice or a favor.* **4.** to solicit from; request of (with a personal object, and with or without *for* before the thing desired): *I ask you a great favor, ask him for advice.* **5.** to demand; expect: *to ask a price for something.* **6.** to call for; require: *the job asks time.* **7.** to invite: *to ask guests.* **8.** to publish (banns); publish the banns of (persons). —*v.i.* **9.** to make inquiry; inquire: *she asked after or about him.* **10.** to request or petition (fol. by *for*): *ask for bread.* [ME *asken,* OE *āscian,* also *ācsian,* c. OHG *eiscōn*] —**ask′er,** *n.* —**Syn. 9.** See **inquire.**

a·skance (ə skăns′), *adv.* **1.** with suspicion, mistrust, or disapproval: *he looked askance at my offer.* **2.** with a side glance; sidewise. Also, **a·skant** (ə skănt′). [orig. uncert.]

a·skew (ə skū′), *adv.* **1.** to one side; out of line; obliquely; awry. —*adj.* **2.** oblique. [f. A-¹ + SKEW]

Ask·ja (ăsk′yä), *n.* a volcano in Iceland. 3376 ft.

a·slant (ə slänt′, ə slănt′), *adv.* **1.** at a slant; slantingly; obliquely. —*adj.* **2.** slanting; oblique. —*prep.* **3.** slantingly across; athwart. [ME *on slont, on slent* on slope. Cf. Sw. *slänt* slope]

a·sleep (ə slēp′), *adv.* **1.** in or into a state of sleep. —*adj.* **2.** sleeping. **3.** dormant; inactive. **4.** (of the foot, hand, leg, etc.) numb. **5.** dead.

a·slope (ə slōp′), *adv.* **1.** at a slope. —*adj.* **2.** sloping.

As·ma·ra (äs mä′rə), *n.* the capital of Eritrea, in Ethiopia. 120,000 (est. 1954); ab. 7700 ft. high.

As·mo·de·us (ăz′mə dē′əs, ăs′-), *n.* (in Jewish demonology) an evil spirit. [t. L: m. *Asmodaeus,* t. Gk.: m. *Asmodaîos,* t. Heb.: m. *Ashmadai*]

As·nières (ä nyěr′), *n.* a city near Paris. 77,838 (1954).

a·so·cial (ā sō′shəl), *adj.* **1.** *Psychol., Sociol., etc.* avoiding or withdrawn from the environment; not social. **2.** inconsiderate of others; selfish; not scrupulous.

A·so·ka (ə sō′kə), *n.* died 264?–226? B.C., Buddhist king in India, 264?–226? B.C.

A·so·san (ä′sō sän′), *n.* a volcano in SW Japan, on Kyushu island. 5225 ft. high; crater, 12 mi. across.

asp¹ (ăsp), *n.* **1.** any of several poisonous snakes, esp. the Egyptian cobra, *Naje haje,* said to have caused Cleopatra's death, and much used by snake charmers. **2.** the common European viper or adder. **3.** *Archaeol.* the uraeus. [t. L: m. *aspis,* t. Gk.]

asp² (ăsp), *n., adj.* aspen. [OE *æspe* (see ASPEN)]

as·par·a·gus (ə spăr′ə gəs), *n.* **1.** any plant of the liliaceous genus *Asparagus,* esp. *A. officinalis,* cultivated for its edible shoots. **2.** the shoots, used as a table vegetable. [t. L, t. Gk.: m. *asparagos*]

as·par·tic acid (ə spär′tĭk), *Biochem.* an amino acid, $HOOCCH(NH_2)CH_2COOH$, occurring in proteins.

As·pa·sia (ăs pā′shə -zhə), *n.* fl. c445 B.C., Athenian courtesan, mistress of Pericles.

ăct, āble, dâre, ärt; ĕbb, ēqual; ĭf, īce; hŏt, ōver, ôrder, oil, bŏŏk, ōōze, out; ŭp, ūse, ûrge; ə = a in alone; ch, chief; g, give; ng, ring; sh, shoe; th, thin; ŧħ, that; zh, vision. See the full key on inside cover.

as·pect (ăs′pĕkt), *n.* **1.** appearance to the eye or mind; look: *the physical aspect of the country.* **2.** countenance; facial expression. **3.** a way in which a thing may be viewed or regarded: *both aspects of a question.* **4.** view commanded; exposure: *the house has a southern aspect.* **5.** the side or surface facing a given direction: *the dorsal aspect of a fish.* **6.** *Gram.* **a.** (in some languages) a category of verb inflection denoting various relations of the action or state of the verb to the passage of time, as duration, repetition, or completion. Examples: *he ate* (completed action); *he was eating* (incompleted action); *he ate and ate* (durative action). **b.** (in other languages) one of several contrasting constructions with similar meanings: *the durative aspect.* **c.** a set of such categories or constructions in a particular language. **d.** the meaning of, or typical of, such a category or construction. **e.** such categories or constructions, or their meanings collectively. **7.** *Astrol.* the relative position of planets as determining their influence. **8.** *Archaic.* a look; glance. [ME, t. L: s. *aspectus,* der. *aspicere* look at] —**Syn. 1.** See **appearance. 4.** prospect, outlook.

aspect ratio, *Aeron.* the ratio of the span of an airfoil to its mean chord.

as·pec·tu·al (ăs·pĕk′chŏŏ əl), *adj. Gram.* **1.** of, pertaining to, or producing a particular aspect or aspects. **2.** used as or like a form inflected for a particular aspect.

as·pen (ăs′pən), *n.* **1.** any of various species of poplar, as *Populus tremula* of Europe, and *P. tremuloides* (**quaking aspen**) or *P. alba* (**white aspen**) in America, with leaves that tremble in the slightest breeze. —*adj.* **2.** of or pertaining to the aspen. **3.** trembling or quivering, like the leaves of the aspen. Also, **asp.** [ME *aspen,* adj., f. *asp* white poplar (OE *æspe*) + -EN²]

as·per (ăs′pər), *n.* an old Egyptian and Turkish silver coin, now only a money of account equal to ¹/₁₂₀ of a piaster. [t. F: m. *aspre* (or t. It.: m. *aspero*), t. MGk.: m. *áspron,* t. L: m. *asper* (*nummus*) rough (coin)]

As·per·ges (ə spûr′jĕz), *n. Rom. Cath. Ch.* **1.** the rite of sprinkling the altar, clergy, and people with holy water before High Mass on Sundays. **2.** the anthem beginning "Asperges," sung while the priest performs this rite. [L: thou shalt sprinkle]

as·per·gil·lo·sis (ăs pûr′jə lō′sĭs), *n., pl.* -**ses** (-sēz). *Vet. Sci.* disease in an animal caused by aspergilli.

as·per·gil·lum (ăs′pər jĭl′əm), *n., pl.* -**gilla** (-jĭl′ə), -**gillums.** *Rom. Cath. Ch.* a brush or instrument for sprinkling holy water; aspersorium. [f. L: s. *aspergere* sprinkle + -*illum,* dim. suffix]

as·per·gil·lus (ăs′pər jĭl′əs), *n., pl.* -**gilli** (-jĭl′ī). *Bot.* any fungus of the genus *Aspergillus,* family *Aspergillaceae,* whose sporophores are distinguished by a bristly, knoblike top. [see ASPERGILLUM]

as·per·i·ty (ăs pĕr′ə tĭ), *n., pl.* -**ties. 1.** roughness or sharpness of temper; severity; acrimony. **2.** hardship; difficulty; rigor. **3.** roughness of surface; unevenness. **4.** something rough or harsh. [t. L: m. s. *asperitas* roughness; r. ME *asprete,* t. OF]

as·perse (ə spûrs′), *v.t.,* -**persed,** -**persing. 1.** to assail with damaging charges or insinuations; cast reproach upon; slander. **2.** to sprinkle; bespatter. [t. L: m. s. *aspersus,* pp., sprinkled] —**as·pers′er,** *n.*

as·per·sion (ə spûr′zhən, -shən), *n.* **1.** a damaging imputation; a derogatory criticism: *to cast aspersions on one's character.* **2.** act of aspersing: *to baptize by aspersion.* **3.** a shower or spray.

as·per·so·ri·um (ăs′pər sōr′ĭ əm), *n., pl.* -**soria** (-sōr′ĭ ə), -**soriums.** *Rom. Cath. Ch.* **1.** a vessel for holding holy water. See illus. under **stoup. 2.** aspergillum. [t. ML. See ASPERSE, -ORIUM]

as·phalt (ăs′fôlt, -fält), *n.* **1.** any of various dark-colored, solid bituminous substances, composed mostly of mixtures of hydrocarbons, occurring native in various parts of the earth. **2.** a similar artificial substance, the by-product of petroleum-cracking operations. **3.** a mixture of such a substance with crushed rock, etc., used for pavements, etc. —*v.t.* **4.** to cover or pave with asphalt. [t. LL: s. *asphaltum,* t. Gk.: m. *ásphalton*] —**as·phal′tic,** *adj.* —**as′phalt·like′,** *adj.*

as·phal·tum (ăs fäl′təm), *n.* asphalt.

as·pho·del (ăs′fə dĕl′), *n.* **1.** any of various liliaceous plants of the genera *Asphodelus* and *Asphodeline,* native in southern Europe, with white, pink, or yellow flowers. **2.** any of various other plants, as the daffodil. [t. L: s. *asphodelus,* t. Gk.: m. *asphódelos*]

as·phyx·i·a (ăs fĭk′sĭ ə), *n. Pathol.* the extreme condition caused by lack of oxygen and excess of carbon dioxide in the blood, caused by sufficient interference with respiration, as in choking. [t. Gk.: stopping of the pulse]

as·phyx·i·ant (ăs fĭk′sĭ ənt), *adj.* **1.** asphyxiating or tending to asphyxiate. —*n.* **2.** an asphyxiating agent or substance. **3.** an asphyxiating condition.

as·phyx·i·ate (ăs fĭk′sĭ āt′), *v.,* -**ated,** -**ating.** —*v.t.* **1.** to produce asphyxia in. —*v.i.* **2.** to become asphyxiated. —**as·phyx′i·a′tion,** *n.* —**as·phyx′i·a′tor,** *n.*

as·pic¹ (ăs′pĭk), *n.* an appetizing jelly used as a garnish or as a base for meat, vegetables, etc. [t. F; orig. uncert.]

as·pic² (ăs′pĭk), *n. Poetic.* an asp¹. [t. F, g. L *aspis*]

as·pic³ (ăs′pĭk), *n.* the great lavender, *Lavandula latifolia,* yielding an oil used in perfumery. [t. F, t. ML: m. (*lavendula*) *spica* (lavender) spike]

as·pi·dis·tra (ăs′pə dĭs′trə), *n.* a smooth, stemless Asiatic herb, *Aspidistra elatior,* family *Liliaceae,* bearing large evergreen leaves often striped with white, widely grown as a house plant. [t. NL, der. Gk. *aspis* shield]

as·pir·ant (ə spīr′ənt, ăs′pə rənt), *n.* **1.** a person who aspires; one who seeks advancement, honors, a high position, etc. —*adj.* **2.** aspiring.

as·pi·rate (*v.* ăs′pə rāt′; *n., adj.* ăs′pə rĭt), *v.,* -**rated,** -**rating,** *n., adj.* —*v.t.* **1.** *Phonet.* **a.** to release (a stop) in such a way that the breath escapes with audible friction, as in *title* where the first *t* is aspirated, the second is not. **b.** to begin (a word or syllable) with an *h* sound, as in *when* (pronounced *hwen*), *howl,* opposed to *wen, owl.* **2.** *Med.* to remove (fluids) from body cavities by use of an aspirator. **3.** to draw or remove by suction. —*n.* **4.** *Phonet.* a puff of unvoiced air before or after another sound, represented in many languages by *h,* and in Greek by the "sign of rough breathing" ('). —*adj.* **5.** *Phonet.* aspirated. [t. L: m. s. *aspīrātus,* pp., breathed on]

as·pi·ra·tion (ăs′pə rā′shən), *n.* **1.** act of aspiring; lofty or ambitious desire. **2.** act of aspirating; a breath. **3.** *Phonet.* **a.** the fricative unstopping or release of a stop consonant, as in *too,* where the breath escapes with audible friction as the *t* is brought to an end by the withdrawal of the tongue from contact with the gums **b.** the use of an aspirate in pronunciation. **4.** *Med.* act of removing a fluid, as pus or serum, from a cavity of the body, by a hollow needle or trocar connected with a suction syringe.

as·pi·ra·tor (ăs′pə rā′tər), *n.* **1.** an apparatus or device employing suction. **2.** a jet pump used in laboratories to produce a partial vacuum. **3.** *Med.* an instrument for removing fluids from the body by suction.

as·pi·ra·to·ry (ə spīr′ə tōr′ĭ), *adj.* pertaining to or suited for aspiration.

as·pire (ə spīr′), *v.i.,* -**pired,** -**piring. 1.** to long, aim, or seek ambitiously; be eagerly desirous, esp. for something great or lofty (fol. by *to, after,* or an infinitive): *to aspire after immortality, to aspire to be a leader among men.* **2.** *Archaic* or *Poetic.* to rise up; soar; mount; tower. [ME *aspyre,* t. L: m. s. *aspīrāre* breathe on] —**as·pir′er,** *n.* —**as·pir′ing,** *adj.* —**Syn. 1.** See **ambitious.**

as·pi·rin (ăs′pə rĭn), *n. Pharm.* a white crystalline derivative of salicylic acid, $C_9H_8O_4$, used to relieve the pain of headache, rheumatism, gout, neuralgia, etc. [f. A(CETYL) + SPIR(AEIC) acid (old name for salicylic acid) + -IN²; G coinage, orig. used as trademark]

a·squint (ə skwĭnt′), *adv., adj.* with an oblique glance. [f. A-¹ + *squint* (of obscure orig.; cf. D *schuinte* slope]

As·quith (ăs′kwĭth), *n.* Herbert Henry, (*1st Earl of Oxford and Asquith*) 1852–1928, British statesman: prime minister of Great Britain, 1908–16.

ass (ăs), *n.* **1.** a long-eared, usually ash-colored mammal, *Equus asinus,* related to the horse, serving as a slow, patient, sure-footed beast of burden; the donkey. **2.** any allied wild species, as the **Mongolian wild ass,** *E. hemionus.* See illus. under **onager. 3.** a fool; a blockhead. [ME; OE *assa,* t. OWelsh: m. *asyn* ass, t. L: m. s. *asinus*]

as·sa·fet·i·da (ăs′ə fĕt′ə də), *n.* asafetida. Also, **as′sa·foet′i·da.**

as·sa·gai (ăs′ə gī′), *n., pl.* -**gais,** *v.t.,* -**gaied,** -**gaiing.** assegai.

as·sa·i¹ (ä sä′ē), *adv. Music.* very: *allegro assai* (very quick). [It.]

as·sa·i² (ə sä′ē), *n.* **1.** any of several slender Brazilian palms of the genus *Euterpe,* esp. *E. edulis,* a species bearing a purple fruit from which a beverage is made by infusion. **2.** the beverage itself. [t. Pg.: m. *assahy,* t. Brazilian]

as·sail (ə sāl′), *v.t.* **1.** to set upon with violence; assault. **2.** to set upon vigorously with arguments, entreaties, abuse, etc. **3.** to undertake with the purpose of mastering. [ME *asaile*(*n*), t. OF: m. *asalir,* g. VL *adsalīre,* f. L: *ad-* AD- + *salīre* leap] —**as·sail′a·ble,** *adj.* —**as·sail′er,** *n.* —**as·sail′ment,** *n.* —**Syn. 1.** See **attack.**

as·sail·ant (ə sā′lənt), *n.* **1.** one who assails. —*adj.* **2.** assailing; attacking.

As·sam (ăs säm′), *n.* a state in NE India. 9,043,700 (1951); 85,012 sq. mi. *Cap.:* Shillong. —**As·sa·mese** (ăs′ə mēz′, -mēs′), *adj., n.*

as·sas·sin (ə săs′ĭn), *n.* **1.** one who undertakes to murder, esp. from fanaticism or for a reward. **2.** (*cap.*) one of an order of Mohammedan fanatics, active in Persia and Syria from about 1090 to 1272, whose chief object was to assassinate Crusaders. [t. F, t. ML: s. *assassinus,* t. Ar.: m. *hashshāshīn,* pl., hashish eaters]

as·sas·si·nate (ə săs′ə nāt′), *v.t.,* -**nated,** -**nating. 1.** to kill by sudden or secret, premeditated assault. **2.** to blight or destroy treacherously: *to assassinate a person's character.* [t. ML: m. s. *assassinātus,* pp.] —**as·sas′si·na′tion,** *n.* —**as·sas′si·na′tor,** *n.* —**Syn. 1.** murder.

assassin bug, any insect of the heteropterous family *Reduviidae.* All are predacious and some are bloodsucking parasites of warm-blooded animals.

as·sault (ə sôlt′), *n.* **1.** act of assailing; an attack; onslaught. **2.** *Mil.* the stage of close combat in an attack. **3.** *Law.* an unlawful physical attack upon another; an attempt or offer to do violence to another, with or without a battery, as by holding a stone or club

Ass. *Equus asinus* (Ab. 3 ft. high at the shoulder)

---

b., blend of, blended; c., cognate with; d., dialect, dialectal; der., derived from; f., formed from; g., going back to; m., modification of; r., replacing; s., stem of; t., taken from; ?, perhaps. See the full key on inside cover.

in a threatening manner. **4.** rape[1]. —*v.t.* **5.** to make an assault upon; attack; assail. [ME *assaut*, t. OF, der. *asalir* ASSAIL] —**as·sault'er,** *n.* —**Syn. 1.** onset, charge. **5.** See **attack.**

assault and battery, *Law.* an assault with an actual touching or other violence upon another.

as·say (*v.* ə sā'; *n.* ə sā', ăs'ā), *v.t.* **1.** to examine by trial; put to test or trial: *to assay one's strength.* **2.** *Metall.* to analyze (an ore, alloy, etc.) in order to determine the quantity of gold, silver, or other metal in it. **3.** *Pharm., etc.* to subject (a drug, etc.) to an analysis for the determination of its potency. **4.** to try in combat. **5.** to attempt; endeavor; essay. **6.** to judge the quality of; evaluate. —*v.i.* **7.** *U.S.* to contain, as shown by analysis, a certain proportion of (usually precious) metal. —*n.* **8.** *Metall.* determination of the amount of metal, esp. gold or silver, in an ore, alloy, etc. **9.** *Pharm., etc.* determination of the strength, purity, etc., of a pharmaceutical substance or ingredient. **10.** a substance undergoing analysis or trial. **11.** a listing of the findings in assaying a substance. **12.** *Obs.* examination; trial; attempt; essay. [ME, t. OF, g. LL *exagium* a weighing. Cf. ESSAY, n.] —**as·say'er,** *n.*

as·se·gai (ăs'ə gī'), *n., pl.* -**gais,** *v.,* -**gaied, -gaing.** —*n.* **1.** the slender throwing spear of the Kaffirs. **2.** a South African cornaceous tree, *Curtisia faginea,* from whose wood such spears are made. —*v.t.* **3.** to pierce with an assegai. Also, **assagai.** [t. Sp.: m. *azagaya,* t. Ar.: f. *al* the + (Berber) *zaghāyah* spear]

as·sem·blage (ə sĕm'blĭj), *n.* **1.** a number of persons or things assembled; an assembly. **2.** act of assembling. **3.** state of being assembled. [t. F]

as·sem·ble (ə sĕm'bəl), *v.,* -**bled, -bling.** —*v.t.* **1.** to bring together; gather into one place, company, body, or whole. **2.** to put or fit (parts) together; put together the parts of (a mechanism, etc.). —*v.i.* **3.** to come together; gather; meet. [ME *as(s)emble(n),* t. OF: m. *as(s)embler,* g. L *assimulāre* compare, imitate] —**as·sem'bler,** *n.* —**Syn. 1.** See **gather. 2.** See **manufacture. 3.** congregate.

as·sem·bly (ə sĕm'blĭ), *n., pl.* -**blies. 1.** a company of persons gathered together, usually for the same purpose, whether religious, political, educational, or social. **2.** (*cap.*) *Govt.* a legislative body, sometimes esp. a lower house of a legislature. **3.** *French Hist.* the first of the Revolutionary assemblies, in session 1789–91. **4.** act of assembling. **5.** state of being assembled. **6.** *Mil.* **a.** a signal, as by drum or bugle, for troops to fall into ranks or otherwise assemble. **b.** the movement of forces, tanks, soldiers, etc., scattered by battle or battle drill, toward and into a small area. **7.** the putting together of complex machinery, as airplanes, from interchangeable parts of standard dimensions. **8.** such parts, before or after assembling. [ME *as(s)emblee,* t. OF] —**Syn. 1.** assemblage, gathering. See **convention.**

assembly line, an arrangement of machines, tools, and workers in which each worker performs a special operation on an incomplete unit, which usually passes down a line of workers until it is finished.

as·sem·bly·man (ə sĕm'blĭ mən), *n., pl.* -**men.** *U.S.* a member of a legislative assembly, esp. of a lower house.

as·sent (ə sĕnt'), *v.i.* **1.** to agree by expressing acquiescence or admitting truth; express agreement or concurrence (often fol. by *to*): *to assent to a statement.* —*n.* **2.** agreement, as to a proposal; acquiescence; concurrence. [ME *as(s)ente(n),* t. OF: m. *as(s)enter,* g. L *assentārī,* freq. of *assentīrī*] —**Syn. 1.** acquiesce, accede, concur. See **consent.**

as·sen·ta·tion (ăs'ĕn tā'shən), *n.* the practice of assenting, esp. obsequiously.

as·sen·tor (ə sĕn'tər), *n.* **1.** Also, **as·sent'er.** one who assents. **2.** *Brit. Govt.* one of the eight voters who endorse the nomination, by a proposer and seconder, of a candidate for election to Parliament, as required by law.

as·sert (ə sûrt'), *v.t.* **1.** to state as true; affirm; declare: *to assert that one is innocent.* **2.** to maintain or defend (claims, rights, etc.). **3.** to put (oneself) forward boldly and insistently. [t. L: s. *assertus,* pp., joined to] —**as·sert'er, as·ser'tor,** *n.* —**Syn. 1.** See **declare.** —**Ant. 1.** deny.

as·ser·tion (ə sûr'shən), *n.* **1.** a positive statement; an unsupported declaration. **2.** act of asserting. —**Syn. 1.** allegation.

as·ser·tive (ə sûr'tĭv), *adj.* given to asserting; positive; dogmatic. —**as·ser'tive·ly,** *adv.* —**as·ser'tive·ness,** *n.*

as·ser·to·ry (ə sûr'tər ĭ), *adj.* affirming; assertive.

asses' bridge, *Geom.* pons asinorum (Euclid, I 5).

as·sess (ə sĕs'), *v.t.* **1.** to estimate officially the value of (property, income, etc.) as a basis for taxation. **2.** to fix or determine the amount of (damages, a tax, a fine, etc.). **3.** to impose a tax or other charge on. [ME *assesse(n),* t. OF: m. *assesser,* g. LL *assessāre* fix a tax, freq. of L *assidēre* sit at] —**as·sess'a·ble,** *adj.*

as·sess·ment (ə sĕs'mənt), *n.* **1.** act of assessing. **2.** an amount assessed as payable; an official valuation of taxable property, etc., or the value assigned.

as·ses·sor (ə sĕs'ər), *n.* **1.** one who makes assessments for purposes of taxation. **2.** an advisory associate or assistant. **3.** a judge or magistrate. **4.** one who shares another's position, rank, or dignity. [t. L: assistant judge, ML *assessor* of taxes; r. ME *assessour,* t. OF] —**as·ses·so·ri·al** (ăs'ə sôr'ĭ əl), *adj.*

as·set (ăs'ĕt), *n.* **1.** a useful thing or quality: *neatness is an asset.* **2.** a single item of property.

as·sets (ăs'ĕts), *n.pl.* **1.** *Com.* resources of a person or business consisting of such items as real property, machinery, inventories, notes, securities, cash, etc. **2.** property or effects (opposed to *liabilities*). **3.** *Accounting.* the detailed listing of property owned by a firm and money owing to it. **4.** *Law.* **a.** property in the hands of an executor or administrator sufficient to pay the debts or legacies of the testator or intestate. **b.** any property available for paying debts, etc. [orig. sing., t. OF: what is assigned, der. *asseter* place, ult. der. VL *adsidēre* seat at]

as·sev·er·ate (ə sĕv'ə rāt'), *v.t.,* -**ated, -ating.** to declare earnestly or solemnly; affirm positively. [t. L: m. s. *asseverātus,* pp.,]

as·sev·er·a·tion (ə sĕv'ə rā'shən), *n.* **1.** act of asseverating. **2.** an emphatic assertion.

As·shur (ă'shŏor), *n.* Assur.

as·si·du·i·ty (ăs'ə dū'ə tĭ, -dōō'-), *n., pl.* -**ties. 1.** constant or close application; diligence. **2.** (*pl.*) devoted or solicitous attentions.

as·sid·u·ous (ə sĭj'ōō əs), *adj.* **1.** constant; unremitting: *assiduous reading.* **2.** constant in application; attentive; devoted. [t. L: m. *assiduus* sitting down to] —**as·sid'u·ous·ly,** *adv.* —**as·sid'u·ous·ness,** *n.*

as·sign (ə sīn'), *v.t.* **1.** to make over or give, as in distribution; allot: *to assign rooms at a hotel.* **2.** to appoint, as to a post or duty: *assign to stand guard.* **3.** to designate; specify: *to assign a day.* **4.** to ascribe; attribute; refer: *to assign a reason.* **5.** *Law.* to transfer: *to assign a contract.* **6.** *Mil.* to place permanently on duty with a unit or under a commander. —*v.i.* **7.** *Law.* to transfer property, esp. in trust for the benefit of creditors. —*n.* **8.** (*usually pl.*) *Law.* a person to whom the property or interest of another is or may be transferred: *my heirs and assigns.* [ME *assigne(n),* t. OF: m. *as(s)igner,* g. L *assignāre*] —**as·sign'er,** *Chiefly Law* **as·sign·or** (ə sĭ nôr'), *n.* —**Syn. 1.** ASSIGN, ALLOCATE, ALLOT mean to apportion or measure out. To ASSIGN is to distribute available things, designating them to be given to or reserved for specific persons or purposes: *to assign duties.* To ALLOCATE is to earmark or set aside parts of things available or expected in the future, each for a specific purpose: *to allocate income to various types of expenses.* To ALLOT implies making restrictions as to amount, size, purpose, etc., and then apportioning or assigning: *to allot spaces for parking.*

as·sign·a·ble (ə sī'nə bəl), *adj.* **1.** capable of being specified. **2.** capable of being attributed. **3.** *Law.* capable of being assigned. —**as·sign'a·bil'i·ty,** *n.* —**as·sign'a·bly,** *adv.*

as·sig·nat (ăs'ĭg năt'; *Fr.* ȧ sē nyȧ'), *n.* *French Hist.* one of the notes (paper currency) issued from 1789 to 1796 by the revolutionary government on the security of confiscated lands. [t. F, t. L: s. *assignātus,* pp. See ASSIGN, v.]

as·sig·na·tion (ăs'ĭg nā'shən), *n.* **1.** an appointment for a meeting, now esp. an illicit love meeting. **2.** act of assigning; assignment.

as·sign·ee (ə sī nē', ăs'ə nē'), *n.* *Law.* one to whom some right or interest is transferred, either for his own enjoyment or in trust.

as·sign·ment (ə sīn'mənt), *n.* **1.** something assigned, as a particular task or duty. **2.** act of assigning. **3.** *Law.* **a.** the transference of a right, interest, or title, or the instrument of transfer. **b.** a transference of property to assignees for the benefit of creditors.

as·sim·i·la·ble (ə sĭm'ə lə bəl), *adj.* capable of being assimilated. —**as·sim'i·la·bil'i·ty,** *n.*

as·sim·i·late (ə sĭm'ə lāt'), *v.,* -**lated, -lating.** —*v.t.* **1.** to take in and incorporate as one's own; absorb (fol. by *to* or *with*). **2.** *Physiol.* to convert (food, etc.) into a substance suitable for absorption into the system. **3.** to make like; cause to resemble (fol. by *to* or *with*). **4.** to compare; liken (fol. by *to* or *with*). **5.** *Phonet.* to articulate more like another sound in the same utterance, as *ant* for earlier *amt.* —*v.i.* **6.** to be or become absorbed. **7.** *Physiol.* (of food, etc.) to be converted into the substance of the body; be absorbed into the system. **8.** to become or be like; resemble (fol. by *to* or *with*). [t. L: m. s. *assimilātus,* pp., likened]

as·sim·i·la·tion (ə sĭm'ə lā'shən), *n.* **1.** act or process of assimilating. **2.** state or condition of being assimilated. **3.** *Physiol.* the conversion of absorbed food into the substance of the body. **4.** *Bot.* the total process of plant nutrition, including absorption of external foods and photosynthesis. **5.** *Sociol.* the merging of cultural traits from previously distinct cultural groups, not involving biological amalgamation.

as·sim·i·la·tive (ə sĭm'ə lā'tĭv), *adj.* characterized by assimilation; assimilating. Also, **as·sim·i·la·to·ry** (ə sĭm'ə lə tôr'ĭ).

As·sin·i·boin (ə sĭn'ə boin'), *n.* a Siouan language.

As·sin·i·boine (ə sĭn'ə boin'), *n.* a river in S Canada, flowing from SE Saskatchewan into the Red River in S Manitoba. ab. 450 mi.

As·si·si (äs sē'zē), *n.* a town in central Italy, SE of Perugia: birthplace of St. Francis. 24,164 (1951).

as·sist (ə sĭst'), *v.t.* **1.** to give support, help, or aid to in some undertaking or effort, or in time of distress. **2.** to be associated with as an assistant. —*v.i.* **3.** to give aid or help. **4.** to be present, as at a meeting, ceremony, etc. —*n.* **5.** *Baseball.* a play which helps to put a

---

ăct, āble, dâre, ärt; ĕbb, ēqual; ĭf, īce; hŏt, ōver, ôrder, oil, bŏok, ōoze, out; ŭp, ūse, ûrge; ə = a in alone; ch, chief; g, give; ng, ring; sh, shoe; th, thin; th, that; zh, vision. See the full key on inside cover.

runner out, officially scored and credited as such. **6.** a helpful act. [t. F: s. *assister*, t. L: m. *assistere* stand by] —**as·sist′er**, (*Law.*) **as·sis′tor**, *n.* —Syn. **1.** sustain, befriend; back. See **help.** —Ant. **1.** block, frustrate.

as·sist·ance (ə sĭs′təns), *n.* act of assisting; help; aid. [t. F; r. ME *assystence*, t. ML: m. s. *assistentia*]

as·sist·ant (ə sĭs′tənt), *n.* **1.** one who assists a superior in some office or work; helper. —*adj.* **2.** assisting; helpful. **3.** associated with a superior in some office or work: *assistant manager.* —Syn. **1.** aide, adjutant.

As·siut (ä süt′), *n.* Asyut.

as·size (ə sīz′), *n.* **1.** a sitting or session of a legislative or administrative agency. **2.** an edict, ordinance, or enactment made at such a session or sitting, or issued by such an agency. **3.** (*usually pl.*) a trial session, civil or criminal, held periodically in specific locations in England, usually by a judge of a superior court or circuit. **3.** judgment: *the last or great assize.* [ME, t. OF: m. *as(s)ise* session, der. *aseeir*, g. L *assidēre* sit by]

assn., association. Also, **Assn.**

assoc., **1.** associate. **2.** associated. **3.** association.

as·so·ci·a·ble (ə sō′shĭ ə bəl, -sha bəl), *adj.* capable of being associated. [t. F] —**as·so′ci·a·bil′i·ty,** *n.*

as·so·ci·ate (*v.* ə sō′shĭ āt′; *n., adj.* ə sō′shĭ ĭt, -āt′), *v.,* **-ated, -ating,** *n., adj.* —*v.i.* **1.** to connect by some relation, as in thought. **2.** to join as a companion, partner, or ally. **3.** to unite; combine: *coal associated with shale.* —*v.i.* **4.** to enter into a league or union; unite. **5.** to keep company, as a comrade or intimate: *to associate only with wealthy people.* —*n.* **6.** a partner in interest, as in business or in an enterprise or action. **7.** a companion or comrade: *my most intimate associates.* **8.** a confederate; an accomplice; an ally. **9.** anything usually accompanying or associated with another; an accompaniment or concomitant. **10.** one who is admitted to a subordinate degree of membership in an association or institution: *an associate of the Royal Academy.* —*adj.* **11.** associated, esp. as a companion or colleague: *an associate partner.* **12.** having subordinate membership; without full rights and privileges. **13.** allied; concomitant. [orig. adj., ME *associat*, t. L: s. *associātus*, pp. joined to] —Syn. **6.** See **acquaintance.**

Associated Press, a business organization of newspapers throughout the U.S. together with correspondents abroad for the reporting and distribution of news.

as·so·ci·a·tion (ə sō′sĭ ā′shən, -shĭ′-), *n.* **1.** an organization of people with a common purpose and having a formal structure. **2.** act of associating. **3.** state of being associated. **4.** companionship or intimacy. **5.** connection or combination. **6.** the connection of ideas in thought, or an idea connected with or suggested by a subject of thought. **7.** *Ecol.* a group of plants of one or more species living together under uniform environmental conditions and having a uniform and distinctive aspect. **8.** *Brit.* association football. —**as·so′ci·a′tion·al,** *adj.* —Syn. **1.** alliance, union. **4.** fellowship.

association football, *Chiefly Brit.* soccer.

association of ideas, *Psychol.* the tendency of a sensation, perception, thought, etc., to recall others previously coexisting in consciousness with it or with states similar to it.

as·so·ci·a·tive (ə sō′shĭ ā′tĭv), *adj.* **1.** pertaining to or resulting from association. **2.** tending to associate or unite. —**as·so′ci·a·tive·ly,** *adv.*

as·soil (ə soil′), *v.t. Archaic.* **1.** to absolve; acquit; pardon. **2.** to atone for. [ME, t. OF, pres. indic. of *a(s)soldre*, g. L *absolvere* loosen]

as·so·nance (ăs′ə nəns), *n.* **1.** resemblance of sounds. **2.** *Pros.* a substitute for rhyme, in which the same vowel sounds, though with different consonants, are used in the terminal words of lines, as *penitent* and *reticence.* **3.** partial agreement. [t. F, der. *assonant,* t. L: s. *assonans,* ppr., sounding to] —**as′so·nant,** *adj., n.*

as·sort (ə sôrt′), *v.t.* **1.** to distribute according to sort or kind; classify. **2.** to furnish with a suitable assortment or variety of goods; make up of articles likely to suit a demand. **3.** to group or classify (*with*). —*v.i.* **4.** to agree in sort or kind; be matched or suited. **5.** to associate; consort. [ME t. MF: s. *assorter* distribute, join, der. *a-* A⁻⁵ + *sorte* kind, b. with *sort* lot, fate]

as·sort·ed (ə sôr′tĭd), *adj.* **1.** consisting of selected kinds; arranged in sorts or varieties. **2.** consisting of various kinds; miscellaneous. **3.** matched; suited.

as·sort·ment (ə sôrt′mənt), *n.* **1.** act of assorting; distribution; classification. **2.** an assorted collection.

ASSR, Autonomous Soviet Socialist Republic. Also, **A.S.S.R.**

asst., assistant.

as·suage (ə swāj′), *v.t.,* **-suaged, -suaging. 1.** to make milder or less severe; mitigate; ease: *to assuage grief or wrath.* **2.** to appease; satisfy: *to assuage appetite, thirst, craving, etc.* **3.** to mollify; pacify. [ME *assuage(n),* t. OF: m. *a(s)suagier,* ult. f. L: ad- + deriv. of *suāvis* sweet] —**as·suage′ment,** *n.* —**as·suag′er,** *n.*

As·suan (ăs wän′), *n.* Aswan. Also, **As·souan′.**

as·sua·sive (ə swā′sĭv), *adj.* soothing; alleviative.

as·sume (ə sōōm′), *v.t.,* **-sumed, -suming. 1.** to take for granted or without proof; suppose as a fact: *assume a principle in reasoning.* **2.** to take upon oneself; undertake: *to assume office, an obligation, etc.* **3.** to take on or put on oneself: *to assume new habits of life.* **4.** to pretend to have or be; feign: *to assume a false humility.* **5.** to appropriate or arrogate: *to assume a right to oneself.*

6. *Archaic.* to take into relation or association; adopt. [late ME t. L: m.s. *assūmere* take up] —**as·sum′a·ble,** *adj.* —**as·sum′er,** *n.* —Syn. **1.** presuppose. **4.** See **pretend.**

as·sumed (ə sōōmd′), *adj.* **1.** pretended. **2.** taken for granted. **3.** usurped.

as·sum·ing (ə sōō′mĭng), *adj.* arrogant; presuming.

as·sump·sit (ə sŭmp′sĭt), *n. Law.* **1.** a legal action for breach of a simple contract (a promise not under seal). **2.** an actionable promise. [t. L: he undertook]

as·sump·tion (ə sŭmp′shən), *n.* **1.** act of taking for granted or supposing. **2.** something taken for granted; a supposition. **3.** act of taking to or upon oneself. **4.** arrogance; presumption. **5.** *Eccles.* a. (*often cap.*) the bodily taking up into heaven of the Virgin Mary after her death. b. (*cap.*) a feast commemorating it, celebrated on August 15. —Syn. **2.** conjecture, hypothesis, theory, postulate. **4.** effrontery, forwardness.

as·sump·tive (ə sŭmp′tĭv), *adj.* **1.** taken for granted. **2.** characterized by assumption. **3.** presumptuous.

As·sur (äs′ər), *n.* the supreme national god of Assyria. Also, **Ashur, Asshur, Asur.**

as·sur·ance (ə shŏŏr′əns), *n.* **1.** a positive declaration intended to give confidence. **2.** pledge; guaranty; surety. **3.** full confidence or trust; freedom from doubt; certainty. **4.** freedom from timidity; self-reliance; courage. **5.** presumptuous boldness; impudence. **6.** *Brit.* insurance. —Syn. **3.** See **trust. 4, 5.** See **confidence.**

as·sure (ə shŏŏr′), *v.t.,* **-sured, -suring. 1.** to declare earnestly to; inform or tell positively. **2.** to make (one) sure or certain; convince, as by a promise or declaration. **3.** to make (a future event) sure; ensure: *this assures the success of our work.* **4.** to secure or confirm; render safe or stable: *to assure a person's position.* **5.** to give confidence to; encourage. **6.** to insure, as against loss. [ME *assure(n),* t. OF: m. *aseūrer,* g. LL *assēcūrāre*] —**as·sur·er** (ə shŏŏr′ər), *n.*

as·sured (ə shŏŏrd′), *adj.* **1.** made sure; sure; certain. **2.** bold; confident. **3.** boldly presumptuous. —*n.* **4.** *Insurance.* a. the beneficiary under a policy. b. the person whose life or property is covered by a policy. —**as·sur·ed·ly** (ə shŏŏr′ĭd lĭ), *adv.* —**as·sur′ed·ness,** *n.*

as·sur·gent (ə sûr′jənt), *adj. Bot.* curving upward, as leaves; ascending. [t. L: s. *assurgens,* ppr., rising up] —**as·sur′gen·cy,** *n.*

As·syr·i·a (ə sĭr′ĭ ə), *n.* an ancient empire in SW Asia; greatest extent from ab. 750–612 B.C. *Cap.:* Nineveh.

As·syr·i·an (ə sĭr′ĭ ən), *adj.* **1.** pertaining to Assyria, the Assyrians, or their language. —*n.* **2.** a native or an inhabitant of Assyria. **3.** a Semitic language of the Akkadian group, spoken in northern Mesopotamia.

[map showing *Black Sea, 660 B.C., PHRYGIAN, LYDIAN KINGDOM, Caspian Sea, MEDES, MÉDIT. SEA, EMPIRE OF ASSYRIA, EGYPT, Persian Gulf, ARABS*]

As·syr·i·ol·o·gy (ə sĭr′ĭ ŏl′ə jĭ), *n.* the science of Assyrian antiquities. —**As·syr′i·ol′o·gist,** *n.*

As·tar·te (ăs tär′tĭ), *n.* an ancient Semitic deity, goddess of fertility and reproduction worshiped by the Phoenicians, corresponding to the Hebrew Ashtoreth and the Babylonian and Assyrian Ishtar, and regarded as a moon goddess by the Greeks and Romans. [t. L, t. Gk., t. Phoenician: m. *Ashtareth*]

a·stat·ic (ā stăt′ĭk), *adj.* **1.** unstable; unsteady. **2.** *Physics.* having no tendency to take a definite position. [f. s. Gk. *ástatos* unstable + -ıc] —**a·stat′i·cal·ly,** *adv.* —**a·stat·i·cism** (ā stăt′ə sĭz′əm), *n.*

as·ta·tine (ăs′tə tēn′, -tĭn), *n. Chem.* a rare element of the halogen family. *Symbol:* At; *at. no.:* 85. [f. Gk. *ástatos* unstable + -ıne²]

as·ter (ăs′tər), *n.* **1.** *Bot.* any plant of the large composite genus *Aster,* having rays varying from white or pink to blue around a yellow disk. **2.** a plant of some allied genus, as *Callistephus chinensis* (China aster). **3.** *Biol.* either of two star-shaped structures formed in a cell during mitosis. [t. L, t. Gk.: star]

-aster¹, a suffix used to form nouns denoting something that imperfectly resembles or merely ape. the true thing, or an inferior or petty instance of someth ng, as *criticaster, poetaster, oleaster.* [t. L]

-aster², *Chiefly Biol.* a suffix meaning "star." [repr. Gk. *astēr*]

as·ter·a·ceous (ăs′tə rā′shəs), *adj. Bot.* belonging to the *Asteraceae* or *Carduaceae,* the aster family of plants. usually included in the *Compositae.*

as·te·ri·at·ed (ăs tĭr′ĭ ā′tĭd), *adj. Crystall.* exhibiting asterism. [f. s. Gk. *astérios* starry + -ATE¹ + -ED²]

as·ter·isk (ăs′tər ĭsk), *n.* **1.** the figure of a star (*), used in writing and printing as a reference mark or to indicate omission, doubtful matter, etc. **2.** something in the shape of a star or asterisk. [t. LL: m.s. *asteriscus,* t. Gk.: m. *asterískos,* dim. of *astēr* star]

as·ter·ism (ăs′tə rĭz′əm), *n.* **1.** *Astron.* a. a group of stars. b. a constellation. **2.** *Crystall.* a property of some crystallized minerals of showing a starli ̈ luminous figure in transmitted light or, in a cabochon-cut stone, by reflected light. **3.** three asterisks (*₊* or *₊*₊) placed before a passage to direct attention to it. [t. Gk.: s. *asterismós,* der. *asterízein* mark with stars]

a·stern (ə stûrn′), *adv., adj. Naut.* **1.** to the rear (of); behind; in a backward direction. **2.** in the rear; in a position behind.

---

a·ster·nal (ā·stûr′nəl), *adj. Anat., Zool.* not reaching to or connected with the sternum. [f. A-⁶ + STERNAL]

as·ter·oid (ăs′tə·roid′), *n.* **1.** *Zool.* any of the *Asteroidea*; a starfish. **2.** *Astron.* one of several hundred planetoids with orbits lying mostly between those of Mars and Jupiter. —*adj.* **3.** starlike. [t. Gk.: m. s. *asteroeidḗs* starlike] —**as′ter·oi′dal**, *adj.*

As·ter·oi·de·a (ăs′tə·roi′dĭ′ə), *n.pl. Zool.* a class of echinoderms characterized by a starlike body with radiating arms or rays, as the starfishes. —**as′ter·oi′de·an**, *n., adj.*

as·the·ni·a (ăs·thē′nĭ·ə, ăs′thə·nĭ′ə), *n. Pathol.* lack or loss of strength; debility. [NL, t. Gk.: m. *asthéneia*] —**as·then·ic** (ăs·thĕn′ĭk), *adj.*

asth·ma (ăz′mə, ăs′-), *n.* a paroxysmal disorder of respiration, with labored breathing, a feeling of constriction in the chest, and coughing. [t. Gk.: panting; r. ME *asma*, t. ML]

asth·mat·ic (ăz·măt′ĭk, ăs-), *adj.* **1.** suffering from asthma. **2.** pertaining to asthma. —*n.* **3.** one suffering from asthma. —**asth·mat′i·cal·ly**, *adv.*

As·ti (ăs′tē), *n.* a city in NW Italy, in Piedmont. 54,000 (est. 1954).

as·tig·mat·ic (ăs′tĭg·măt′ĭk), *adj.* pertaining to, exhibiting, or correcting astigmatism.

a·stig·ma·tism (ə·stĭg′mə·tĭz′əm), *n.* a defect of the eye or of a lens whereby rays of light from an external point converge unequally in different meridians, thus causing imperfect vision or images. [f. A-⁶ + s. Gk. *stigma* point + -ISM]

a·stir (ə·stûr′), *adj., adv.* **1.** in a stir; in motion or activity. **2.** up and about; out of bed.

As·to·lat (ăs′tō·lăt′), *n.* a place in the Arthurian romances, possibly in Surrey.

a·stom·a·tous (ā·stŏm′ə·təs, ā·stō′mə-), *adj. Zool., Bot.* having no mouth, stoma, or stomata. [f. A-⁶ + s. Gk. *stóma* mouth + -OUS]

as·ton·ied (ə·stŏn′ĭd), *adj. Archaic.* dazed; bewildered.

as·ton·ish (ə·stŏn′ĭsh), *v.t.* to strike with sudden and overpowering wonder; surprise greatly; amaze. [earlier *astony*, ? OE *āstunian*, intensive of *stunian* resound. Cf. ASTOUND, STUN] —**as·ton′ish·er**, *n.* —**Syn.** astound, startle, shock. See **surprise.**

as·ton·ish·ing (ə·stŏn′ĭsh·ĭng), *adj.* causing astonishment; amazing. —**as·ton′ish·ing·ly**, *adv.*

as·ton·ish·ment (ə·stŏn′ĭsh·mənt), *n.* **1.** overpowering wonder or surprise; amazement. **2.** an object or cause of amazement.

As·tor (ăs′tər), *n.* **John Jacob**, 1763–1848, U.S. capitalist and fur merchant.

As·to·ri·a (ăs·tōr′ĭ·ə), *n.* a seaport in NW Oregon, near the mouth of the Columbia river. 12,331 (1950).

as·tound (ə·stound′), *v.t.* **1.** to overwhelm with amazement; astonish greatly. —*adj.* **2.** *Archaic.* astonished. [pp. of obs. *astone, astun.* See ASTONISH, STUN] —**as·tound′ing·ly**, *adv.* —**Syn.** **1.** See **surprise.**

astr., **1.** astronomer. **2.** astronomical. **3.** astronomy.

as·tra·chan (ăs′trə·kən), *n.* **1.** astrakhan. **2.** (*cap.*) a tart variety of apple, usually red or yellow.

a·strad·dle (ə·străd′əl), *adv., adj.* with one leg on each side; in a straddling position; astride.

As·trae·a (ăs·trē′ə), *n. Gk. Myth.* the goddess of justice, daughter of Zeus and Themis, the last of the immortals to leave mankind.

as·tra·gal (ăs′trə·gəl), *n. Archit.* **1.** a small convex molding cut into the form of a string of beads. **2.** a plain convex molding. See diag. under **column.** [t. L: s. *astragalus.* See ASTRAGALUS]

as·trag·a·lus (ăs·trăg′ə·ləs), *n., pl.* **-li** (-lī′). *Anat.* the uppermost bone of the tarsus; anklebone; talus. [t. L, t. Gk.: m. *astrágalos*] —**as·trag′a·lar**, *adj.*

as·tra·khan (ăs′trə·kən), *n.* **1.** a kind of fur of young lambs, with lustrous closely curled wool, from Astrakhan. **2.** Also, **astrakhan cloth.** a fabric with curled pile resembling it. Also, **astrachan.**

As·tra·khan (ăs′trə·kăn′; *Russ.* ä′strä·hän′y), *n.* a city at the mouth of the Volga, in the SE Soviet Union in Europe. 276,000 (est. 1956).

as·tral (ăs′trəl), *adj.* **1.** pertaining to or proceeding from the stars; consisting of or resembling stars; starry; stellar. **2.** *Biol.* relating to or resembling an aster; starshaped. **3.** *Theosophy.* pertaining to a supersensible substance supposed to pervade all space and form the substance of a second body belonging to each individual. [t. L: s. *astrālis*, der. *astrum* star, t. Gk.: m. *ástron*]

astral lamp, an oil lamp designed to avoid the shadow cast upon the table by ordinary lamps.

a·stray (ə·strā′), *adv., adj.* out of the right way or away from the right; straying; wandering.

as·trict (ə·strĭkt′), *v.t.* **1.** to bind fast; confine; constrain or restrict. **2.** to bind morally or legally. [t. L: s. *astrictus*, pp., drawn close] —**as·tric′tion**, *n.*

a·stride (ə·strīd′), *adv., adj.* **1.** in the posture of striding or straddling. —*prep.* **2.** with a leg on each side of.

as·tringe (ə·strĭnj′), *v.t.* **-tringed, -tringing.** to compress; bind together; constrict. [t. L: m. s. *astringere*]

as·trin·gent (ə·strĭn′jənt), *adj.* **1.** *Med.* contracting; constrictive; styptic. **2.** stern or severe; austere. —*n.* **3.** *Med.* a substance which contracts the tissues or canals of the body, thereby diminishing discharges, as of blood, [t. L: s. *astringens*, ppr.] —**as·trin′gen·cy**, *n.* —**as·trin′gent·ly**, *adv.* —**Syn. 2.** See **acid.**

astro-, a word element meaning ' star," as in *astrology*. [t. Gk., comb. form of *ástron*]

astrol., **1.** astrologer. **2.** astrological. **3.** astrology.

as·tro·labe (ăs′trə·lāb′), *n.* an astronomical instrument for taking the altitude of the sun or stars and for the solution of other problems in astronomy and navigation. [t. ML: m. s. *astrolabium*, t. Gk.: m. *astrolábon* (*órganon*) armillary sphere; r. ME *astrelabe*, t. OF]

as·trol·o·gy (ə·strŏl′ə·jĭ), *n.* **1.** a study or science which assumes, and professes to interpret, the influence of the heavenly bodies on human affairs. **2.** (*formerly*) practical astronomy, the earliest form of the science. [ME, t. L: m. s. *astrologia*, t. Gk. See ASTRO-, -LOGY] —**as·trol′o·ger**, *n.* —**as·tro·log·i·cal** (ăs′trə·lŏj′ə·kəl), **as′tro·log′ic**, *adj.* —**as′tro·log′i·cal·ly**, *adv.*

as·trom·e·try (ə·strŏm′ə·trĭ), *n.* measurement of the positions, motions, and distances of the celestial bodies.

astron., **1.** astronomer. **2.** astronomical. **3.** astronomy.

as·tro·naut (ăs′trə·nôt′), *n.* a traveler outside the atmosphere of the earth. [back formation from ASTRONAU-TICS]

as·tro·nau·tic (ăs′trə·nô′tĭk), *adj.* of astronautics or astronauts. Also, **as′tro·nau′ti·cal.** [f. ASTRO- + NAU-TIC(AL)] —**as′tro·nau′ti·cal·ly**, *adv.*

as·tro·nau·tics (ăs′trə·nô′tĭks), *n.* the science or art of flight outside the atmosphere of the earth. [pl. of ASTRONAUTIC, see -ICS]

as·tron·o·mer (ə·strŏn′ə·mər), *n.* an expert in astronomy; a scientific observer of the celestial bodies.

as·tro·nom·i·cal (ăs′trə·nŏm′ə·kəl), *adj.* **1.** of, pertaining to, or connected with astronomy. **2.** very large, like the numbers used in astronomical calculations. Also, **as′tro·nom′ic.** —**as′tro·nom′i·cal·ly**, *adv.*

astronomical year. See year (def. 5).

as·tron·o·my (ə·strŏn′ə·mĭ), *n.* the science of the celestial bodies, their motions, positions, distances, magnitudes, etc. [ME *astronomie*, t. L: m. *astronomia*, t. Gk. See ASTRO-, -NOMY]

as·tro·pho·tog·ra·phy (ăs′trō·fə·tŏg′rə·fĭ), *n.* the photography of stars and other celestial objects. —**as·tro·pho·to·graph·ic** (ăs′trō·fō′tə·grăf′ĭk), *adj.*

as·tro·phys·ics (ăs′trō·fĭz′ĭks), *n.* astronomical physics, treating of the physical properties and phenomena of the celestial bodies. —**as′tro·phys′i·cal**, *adj.* —**as·tro·phys·i·cist** (ăs′trō·fĭz′ə·sĭst), *n.*

as·tro·sphere (ăs′trə·sfîr′), *n. Biol.* **1.** the central portion of an aster, in which the centrosome lies. **2.** the whole aster exclusive of the centrosome.

as·tu·cious (ăs·tū′shəs, -tōō′-), *adj.* astute. [t. F: m. *astucieux*]

As·tu·ri·as (ăs·tŏŏr′ĭ·əs; *Sp.* ä·stōōr′yäs), *n.* a former kingdom and province in NW Spain.

as·tute (ə·stūt′, ə·stōōt′), *adj.* of keen penetration or discernment; sagacious; shrewd; cunning. [t. L: m. s. *astūtus*, der. *astus* adroitness, cunning] —**as·tute′ly**, *adv.* —**as·tute′ness**, *n.* —**Syn.** artful, crafty, wily, sly.

As·ty·a·nax (ăs·tī′ə·năks′), *n. Gk. Legend.* the young son of Hector and Andromache, thrown from the walls of Troy by the victorious Greeks.

a·sty·lar (ā·stī′lər), *adj. Archit.* without columns. [f. s. Gk. *ástylos* without columns + -AR¹]

A·sun·ción (ä′sōōn·syōn′, -thyōn′), *n.* the capital of Paraguay, on the Paraguay river. 206,634 (1950).

a·sun·der (ə·sŭn′dər), *adv., adj.* **1.** into separate parts; in or into pieces: *to tear asunder.* **2.** apart or widely separated: *as wide asunder as the poles.* [ME *asunder*, o(n)*sunder*, OE *on sundran* apart. See A-¹, SUNDER]

A·sur (ä′sōōr), *n. Assur.*

As·wan (ăs·wän′), *n.* **1.** a city in SE Egypt, on the Nile. 25,397 (1947). **2.** a large dam across the Nile nearby. 6400 ft. long. Also, **As·wân′**, **Assuan, Assouan.**

a·syl·lab·ic (ā′sĭ·lăb′ĭk), *adj.* not syllabic.

a·sy·lum (ə·sī′ləm), *n.* **1.** an institution for the maintenance and care of the blind, the insane, orphans, etc. **2.** an inviolable refuge, as formerly for criminals and debtors; a sanctuary. **3.** *Internat. Law.* a temporary refuge granted political offenders, esp. in a foreign legation. **4.** any secure retreat. [t. L, t. Gk.: m. *ásylon*, neut. of *ásylos* inviolable] —**Syn. 1.** See **hospital.**

a·sym·met·ric (ā′sə·mĕt′rĭk, ăs′ə-), *adj.* **1.** not symmetrical; without symmetry. **2.** *Logic.* denoting relations which, if they hold between one term and a second, do not hold between the second and the first: *the relation "being an ancestor of" is asymmetric.* Also, **a′sym·met′ri·cal.** —**a′sym·met′ri·cal·ly**, *adv.*

a·sym·me·try (ā·sĭm′ə·trĭ), *n.* lack of symmetry or proportion. [t. Gk.: m. s. *asymmetría*]

as·ymp·tote (ăs′ĭm·tōt′), *n. Math.* a straight line that is the limit of a tangent to a curve as the point of contact moves off to infinity. [t. Gk.: m.s. *asýmptōtos* not close] —**as·ymp·tot·ic** (ăs′ĭm·tŏt′ĭk), **as′ymp·tot′i·cal**, *adj.* —**as′ymp·tot′i·cal·ly**, *adv.*

a·syn·chro·nism (ā·sĭng′krə·nĭz′əm, ā·sĭn′-), *n.* want of synchronism, or coincidence in time. —**a·syn′chro·nous**, *adj.*

a·syn·de·ton (ə·sĭn′də·tŏn′, -tən), *n. Rhet.* the omission of conjunctions. [t. L, t. Gk., neut. of *asýndetos* unjoined] —**as·yn·det·ic** (ăs′ən·dĕt′ĭk), *adj.* —**as′yn·det′i·cal·ly**, *adv.*

As·yut (ä·sūt′), *n.* a city in central Egypt, on the Nile. 86,400 (est. 1952). Also, **A·syût′**, **Assiut.**

at (ăt; *unstressed* ət, ĭt), *prep.* a particle specifying a point occupied, attained, sought, or otherwise concerned, as in place, time, order, experience, etc., and hence used in many idiomatic phrases expressing circumstantial or relative position, degree or rate, action, manner: *to stand at the door, to aim at a mark, at home, at hand, at noon, at zero, at work, at ease, at length, at a risk, at cost, at one's best.* [ME; OE æt; c. Icel. *at*, L *ad* AD-]

at-, var. of ad- before *t*, as in *attend.*

at·a·bal (ăt′ə·bäl′), *n.* a kind of drum used by the Moors. Also, **attabal.** [t. Sp., t. Ar.: m. *at-tabl* the drum]

at·a·brine (ăt′ə·brĭn, -brēn′), *n. Pharm.* **1.** Also **atebrin.** an antimalarial substance, $C_{23}H_{30}N_3OCl$, with properties similar to plasmochin. **2.** (*cap.*) a trademark for this substance.

at·a·ghan (ăt′ə·găn′), *n.* yataghan.

A·ta·hual·pa (ä′tä·wäl′pä), *n.* died 1533, last Inca king of Peru.

At·a·lan·ta (ăt′ə·lăn′tə), *n. Gk. Myth.* a virgin huntress who helped to kill the Calydonian boar (see **Meleager**). All suitors whom she could outrun were put to death, but she was vanquished by one who dropped three golden apples given him by Aphrodite, which Atalanta stopped to pick up.

at·a·man (ăt′ə·mən), *n., pl.* **-mans.** a chief of Cossacks, elected by the whole group, serving as a chairman in peace, a leader in war; a hetman. [t. Russ.]

at·a·mas·co (ăt′ə·măs′kō), *n.* **1.** an amaryllidaceous plant, *Zephyranthes atamasco*, of the southeastern U.S., bearing a single white lilylike flower. **2.** any species of this genus. Also, **atamasco lily.** [t. N Amer. Ind.]

At·a·rax (ăt′ə·răks′), *n. Trademark.* a drug employed to induce ataraxia. [back formation from ATARAXIA]

at·a·rax·i·a (ăt′ə·răk′sĭ·ə), *n.* a state of tranquillity, free from emotional disturbance and anxiety. Also, **at·a·rax·y** (ăt′ə·răk′sĭ). [NL, t. Gk.: impassiveness] **—at′a·rac′tic** (-răk′tĭk), **at·a·rax′ic,** *adj., n.*

a·tav·ic (ə·tăv′ĭk), *adj.* **1.** of or pertaining to remote ancestors. **2.** atavistic.

at·a·vism (ăt′ə·vĭz′əm), *n.* **1.** *Biol.* the reappearance in an individual of characteristics of some more or less remote ancestor that have been absent in intervening generations. **2.** reversion to an earlier type. [f. s. L *atavus* ancestor + -ISM] **—at′a·vist,** *n.* **—at′a·vis′·tic,** *adj.*

a·tax·i·a (ə·tăk′sĭ·ə), *n. Pathol.* **1.** loss of coördination of the muscles, esp. of the extremities. **2.** locomotor ataxia. [t. NL, t. Gk.: disorder] **—a·tax′ic,** *adj.*

At·ba·ra (ăt′bä·rä′), *n.* a river flowing from NW Ethiopia NW to the Nile in the Sudan. ab. 500 mi.

Atch·i·son (ăch′ə·sən), *n.* a city in NE Kansas, on the Missouri river. 12,529 (1960).

ate (ăt; *Brit.* ĕt), *v.* pt. of **eat.**

A·te (ā′tĭ), *n. Gk. Myth.* a goddess personifying the fatal blindness or recklessness which produces crime, and the divine punishment which follows it. [t. Gk.]

-ate[1], a suffix forming: **1.** adjectives equivalent to -ed (in participial and other adjectives), as in *accumulate, separate.* **2.** nouns denoting esp. persons charged with some duty or function, or invested with some dignity, right, or special character, as in *advocate, candidate, curate, legate, prelate.* **3.** nouns denoting some product or result of action, as in *mandate* (lit., a thing commanded). **4.** verbs, orig. taken from Latin past participles but now formed from any Latin or other stem, as in *actuate, agitate, calibrate.* [t. NL, t. L: m. -ātus, -āta, -ātum]

-ate[2], *Chem.* a suffix forming nouns denoting a salt formed by action of an acid on a base, added to the stem of the name of the acid, as in *acetate.* [t. L: m. -ātum neut. of -ātus -ATE[1]]

-ate[3], a suffix forming nouns denoting condition, estate, office, officials, or an official, etc., as in *consulate, episcopate, magistrate, senate* [t. L: m. -ātus, suffix making nouns of 4th declension]

at·e·brin (ăt′ə·brĭn), *n. Pharm.* atabrine (def. 1).

at·el·ier (ăt′əl·yā′; *Fr.* ȧ·tə·lyĕ′), *n.* the workshop or studio of an artist. [t. F: workplace, orig. pile of chips, der. OF *astele* chip, t. LL *astella*, r. L *astula*]

a tem·po (ä těm′pō), *Music.* resuming the speed which obtained preceding *rit.* or *accel.* [It.]

A·ten (ä′tən), *n.* sun god introduced into Egyptian religion by Amenhotep IV as the only god. Also, **Aton.**

Ath·a·bas·can (ăth′ə·băs′kən), *n.* an American Indian linguistic stock of the Na-Dene phylum, including languages of northwest Canada and Alaska (e.g., Chippewa), of the Pacific coast, esp. Oregon and California (e.g., Hupa), and of Arizona and the Rio Grande basin (notably Navaho and Apache). Also, **Athapascan.**

Ath·a·bas·ka (ăth′ə·băs′kə), *n.* **1.** Lake, a lake in W Canada, in NW Saskatchewan and NE Alberta. ab. 200 mi. long; ab. 3000 sq. mi. **2.** a river flowing from W Alberta NE to Lake Athabaska. 765 mi.

ath·a·na·sia (ăth′ə·nā′zhə), *n.* deathlessness; immortality. Also, **a·than·a·sy** (ə·thăn′ə·sĭ). [t. Gk.]

Ath·a·na·sian (ăth′ə·nā′zhən), *adj.* **1.** of or pertaining to Athanasius. **—n. 2.** *Theol.* a follower of Athanasius or a believer in his creed.

Athanasian Creed, *Theol.* a (probably) post-Augustinian creed or formulary of Christian faith, of unknown authorship, formerly ascribed to Athanasius.

Ath·a·na·sius (ăth′ə·nā′shəs), *n.* **Saint,** A.D. 296?-373, bishop of Alexandria: opponent of Arianism.

Ath·a·pas·can (ăth′ə·păs′kən), *n.* Athabascan.

A·thar·va-Ve·da (ə·tär′və vā′də, -vē′də), *n.* See **Veda.**

a·the·ism (ā′thĭ·ĭz′əm) *n.* **1.** the doctrine that there is no God. **2.** disbelief in the existence of a God (or gods). **3.** godlessness. [f. s. Gk. *átheos* without a god + -ISM]

a·the·ist (ā′thĭ·ĭst), *n.* one who denies or disbelieves the existence of God or gods.
—Syn. ATHEIST, AGNOSTIC, INFIDEL, SKEPTIC refer to persons not inclined toward religious belief. An ATHEIST is one who denies the existence of a Deity or divine beings. An AGNOSTIC is one who believes it impossible to know anything about God or about the creation of the universe. INFIDEL means an unbeliever, especially a nonbeliever in Mohammedanism or Christianity. A SKEPTIC doubts and is critical of all accepted doctrines and creeds.

a·the·is·tic (ā′thĭ·ĭs′tĭk), *adj.* pertaining to or characteristic of atheists; involving, containing, or tending to atheism. Also, **a′the·is′ti·cal. —a′the·is′ti·cal·ly,** *adv.*

ath·el·ing (ăth′əl·ĭng, ăth′-), *n. Early English Hist.* a man of royal blood; a prince. [ME; OE *ætheling*, f. *æthelu* noble family + -*ing*, suffix of appurtenance]

Ath·el·stan (ăth′əl·stăn′), *n.* A.D. 895?-940, king of England, A.D. 925–940.

A·the·na (ə·thē′nə), *n.* the Greek goddess of wisdom, arts, industries, and prudent warfare, identified by the Romans with Minerva. Also, **A·the·ne** (ə·thē′nĭ). [t. Gk.: m. *Athēnē*]

ath·e·nae·um (ăth′ə·nē′əm), *n.* **1.** an institution for the promotion of literary or scientific learning. **2.** a library or reading room. **3.** (*cap.*) a sanctuary of Athena at Athens, built by the Roman emperor Hadrian, and frequented by poets and men of learning. Also, **ath′e·ne′um.** [t. L, t. Gk.: m. *Athēnaion* temple of Athena]

A·the·ni·an (ə·thē′nĭ·ən), *adj.* **1.** pertaining to Athens, Greece. **—n. 2.** a native or citizen of Athens, Greece.

Ath·ens (ăth′ĭnz), *n.* **1.** the capital of Greece, in the SE part. 565,084 pop. (1951). Greek, **A·the·nai** (ä thē′nē). **2.** a city in N Georgia. 28,180 (1950).

a·ther·man·cy (ə·thûr′mən·sĭ), *n. Physics.* the power of stopping radiant heat.

a·ther·ma·nous (ə·thûr′mə·nəs), *adj. Physics.* impermeable to or able to stop radiant heat. [f. A-[6] + s. Gk. *thermaínein* heat + -OUS]

ath·er·o·scle·ro·sis (ăth′ə·rō′sklə·rō′sĭs, ăth′-), *n. Pathol.* a form of arteriosclerosis in which fatty substances deposit in and beneath the intima. [NL, f. m. Gk. *atherē* groats + SCLEROSIS]

Ath·er·ton (ăth′ər·tən), *n.* **Gertrude Franklin** (*Gertrude Franklin Horn*), 1857–1948, U.S. novelist.

a·thirst (ə·thûrst′), *adj.* **1.** having a keen desire; eager (often fol. by *for*). **2.** *Archaic or Poetic.* thirsty.

ath·lete (ăth′lēt), *n.* **1.** anyone trained to exercises of physical agility and strength. **2.** *Brit.* one trained for track and field events only. [t. L: m.s. *āthlēta*, t. Gk.: m. *athlētēs* contestant in games]

athlete's foot, a contagious disease, a ringworm of the feet, caused by a fungus that thrives on moist surfaces.

ath·let·ic (ăth·lĕt′ĭk), *adj.* **1.** physically active and strong. **2.** of, like, or befitting an athlete. **3.** of or pertaining to athletics. **—ath·let′i·cal·ly,** *adv.* **—ath·let·i·cism** (ăth·lĕt′ə·sĭz′əm), *n.*

ath·let·ics (ăth·lĕt′ĭks), *n.* **1.** (*usually construed as pl.*) athletic sports, as running, rowing, boxing, etc. **2.** *Brit.* track and field events only. **3.** (*usually construed as sing.*) the practice of athletic exercises; the principles of athletic training.

at-home (ət hōm′), *n.* a reception of visitors at certain hours during which a host or hostess has announced he or she will be "at home."

Ath·os (ăth′ŏs, ā′thŏs; *Gk.* ä′thôs), *n.* **Mount, 1.** the easternmost of three prongs of the peninsula of Chalcidice, in NE Greece: site of an independent republic of 20 monasteries. 3086 pop. (1951); 131 sq. mi.; ab. 35 mi. long. **2.** a headland there. 6350 ft.

a·thwart (ə·thwôrt′), *adv.* **1.** from side to side; crosswise. **2.** perversely; awry; wrongly. **3.** *Naut.* at right angles to a ship's keel. **—prep. 4.** from side to side of; across. **5.** in opposition to; contrary to. **6.** *Naut.* across the line or course of. [f. A-[1] + THWART, adv.]

a·tilt (ə·tĭlt′), *adj., adv.* **1.** at a tilt or inclination; tilted. **2.** in a tilting encounter.

-ation, a suffix forming nouns denoting action or process, state or condition, a product or result, or something producing a result, often accompanying verbs or adjectives of Latin origin ending in -ate, as in *agitation, decoration, elation, migration, separation,* but also formed in English from any stem, as in *botheration, flirtation, starvation.* See -ion, -tion. [t. L: s. -*ātio* = -ATE[1] + -ION; identical with G -*ation*, F -*ation*, etc., all from L]

-ative, an adjective suffix expressing tendency, disposition, function, bearing, connection, etc., as in *affirmative, demonstrative, talkative.* See -ive. [t. L: m. s. -*ātivus* = -ATE[1] + -IVE; repr. also F -*atif* (masc.), -*ative* (fem.)]

At·kins (ăt′kĭnz), *n.* **Tommy.** See **Tommy Atkins.**

At·lan·ta (ăt·lăn′tə), *n.* the capital of Georgia, in the N part. 331,314 (1950).

At·lan·te·an (ăt′lăn·tē′ən), *adj.* **1.** pertaining to the demigod Atlas. **2.** having the strength of Atlas. **3.** pertaining to Atlantis. [f. s. L. *Atlantēus* pertaining to Atlas + -AN. See ATLAS]

at·lan·tes (ăt·lăn′tēz), *n.pl., sing.* **atlas.** *Archit.* figures of men used as supporting or decorative columns. [t. L, t. Gk. See ATLAS (def. 4)]

---

b., blend of, blended; c., cognate with; d., dialect, dialectal; der., derived from; f., formed from; g., going back to; m., modification of; r., replacing; s., stem of; t., taken from; ?, perhaps.   See the full key on inside cover.

At·lan·tic (ăt lăn′tĭk), *n.* **1.** the Atlantic Ocean. —*adj.* **2.** of or pertaining to the Atlantic Ocean. **3.** pertaining to the demigod Atlas. [t. L: s. *Atlanticus*, t. Gk.: m. *Atlantikós* pertaining to Atlas]

Atlantic Charter, the joint declaration of Roosevelt and Churchill (August 14, 1941) resulting from a meeting at sea, and setting forth a program of peace purposes and principles to which each power admitted to the United Nations subsequently subscribed.

Atlantic City, a city in SE New Jersey: seashore resort. 59,544 (1960).

Atlantic Ocean, an ocean bordered by North and South America in the Western Hemisphere, and Europe and Africa in the Eastern Hemisphere: divided by the equator into the **North Atlantic** and the **South Atlantic.** ab. 31,530,000 sq. mi.; with connecting seas, ab. 41,-000,000 sq. mi.; greatest known depth, 30,246 ft.

Atlantic Pact, a treaty (1949) providing for collective defense, signed by the U. S., Canada, Great Britain, France, Belgium, The Netherlands, Luxembourg, Norway, Denmark, Iceland, Italy, and Portugal.

At·lan·tis (ăt lăn′tĭs), *n.* a mythical island in the Atlantic Ocean, first mentioned by Plato, supposedly west of Gibraltar, said to have finally sunk into the sea.

at·las (ăt′ləs), *n.* **1.** a bound collection of maps. **2.** a volume of plates or tables illustrating any subject. **3.** *Anat.* the first cervical vertebra, which supports the head. **4.** (*cap.*) a demigod in classical mythology, condemned to support the sky on his shoulders, and identified with the Atlas Mountains. **5.** (*cap.*) one who supports a heavy burden; a mainstay. **6.** sing. of **atlantes**. [t. L, t. Gk.; def. 1–3, 5, 6 are special uses of 4]

atlas folio, *Bibliog.* largest book-size folio, with leaves 16 x 25 inches.

Atlas Mountains, a mountain range in NW Africa, extending for ab. 1500 mi. through Morocco, Algeria, and Tunisia. Highest peak, Mt. Tizi, 14,764 ft.

At·li (ăt′lĭ), *n. Scand. Legend.* the king of the Huns who married Gudrun, widow of Sigurd, for her inheritance, slew her brothers, and was killed by her in turn. [Icel. var. of ATTILA]

at·man (ăt′mən), *n. Hinduism.* **1.** the breath. **2.** the principle of life. **3.** the individual soul. **4.** (*cap.*) the World Soul, from which all individual souls derive, and to which they return as the supreme goal of existence. **5.** (*cap.*) Brahma, the Supreme Being. [Skt.]

at·mos·phere (ăt′məs fĭr′), *n.* **1.** the gaseous fluid surrounding the earth; the air. **2.** this medium at a given place. **3.** *Astron.* the gaseous envelope surrounding any of the heavenly bodies. **4.** *Chem.* any gaseous envelope or medium. **5.** a conventional unit of pressure, the normal pressure of the air at sea level, about 15 pounds per square inch. **6.** environing or pervading influence: *an atmosphere of freedom.* **7.** the quality in a work of art which produces a predominant mood or impression. [t. NL: m. s. *atmosphaera*, f. Gk.: *atmó(s)* vapor + m. *sphaîra* SPHERE]

at·mos·pher·ic (ăt′məs fĕr′ĭk), *adj.* Also, **at·mos·pher·i·cal. 1.** pertaining to, existing in, or consisting of the atmosphere: *atmospheric vapors.* **2.** caused, produced, or operated on by the atmosphere: *atmospheric pressure.* —*n.* **3.** (*pl.*) *Radio.* extraneous noises, crackling, etc., caused by stray electrical currents from storms or other atmospheric disturbance being picked up by the receiver; static. —**at′mos·pher′i·cal·ly,** *adv.*

at. no., atomic number.

at·oll (ăt′ŏl, ə tŏl′), *n.* a ringlike coral island enclosing a lagoon. [? t. Malayalam: m. *adal* uniting]

Atoll

at·om (ăt′əm), *n.* **1.** *Physics, Chem.* the smallest unitary constituent of a chemical element, composed of a more or less complex aggregate of protons, neutrons, and electrons, whose number and arrangement determine the element. **2.** a hypothetical particle of matter so minute as to admit of no division. **3.** anything extremely small; a minute quantity. [t. L: s. *atomus*, t. Gk.: m. *átomos* indivisible] —Syn. **3.** iota.

a·tom·ic (ə tŏm′ĭk), *adj.* **1.** pertaining to atoms. **2.** propelled or driven by atomic energy. **3.** *Chem.* existing as free uncombined atoms. **4.** extremely minute. Also, **a·tom′i·cal.** —**a·tom′i·cal·ly,** *adv.*

atomic age, the period in history initiated by the first use of the atomic bomb and characterized by atomic energy as a military, political, and industrial factor.

atomic bomb, 1. a bomb whose potency is derived from nuclear fission of atoms of fissionable material, with consequent conversion of part of their mass into energy. **2.** a bomb whose explosive force comes from a chain reaction based on nuclear fission in U-235 or in plutonium. It was first used militarily on Hiroshima, Japan (August 6, 1945). The explosion of such a bomb is extremely violent and is attended by great heat, a brilliant light, and strong gamma-ray radiation. Also, **atom bomb, A-bomb.**

atomic energy, energy obtained from changes within the atomic nucleus, chiefly from nuclear fission.

Atomic Energy Commission, *U.S.* a board formed in 1946, consisting of 5 civilian members, for the domestic control of atomic energy.

at·o·mic·i·ty (ăt′ə mĭs′ə tĭ), *n. Chem.* **1.** the number of atoms in the molecule of a gas. **2.** valence.

atomic number, *Chem., Physics.* the number of positive charges on the nucleus of an atom of a given element, and therefore also the number of electrons normally surrounding the nucleus, or the number of protons within the nucleus.

atomic power, energy released in nuclear reactions.

a·tom·ics (ə tŏm′ĭks), *n.* the branch of nuclear physics dealing with atomic energy, nuclear fission, etc.

atomic structure, *Physics.* the theoretically derived concept of an atom composed of a positively charged nucleus surrounded and electrically neutralized by negatively charged electrons, revolving in orbits at varying distances from the nucleus, the constitution of the nucleus and the arrangement of the electrons differing with the different chemical elements.

atomic theory, 1. *Physics, Chem.* the modern theory of the atom as having a complex internal structure and electrical properties. **2.** *Physics.* the mathematical and geometrical description of the motions of the electrons in the atom about the nucleus. **3.** *Philos.* atomism (def. 2). Also, **atomic hypothesis.**

atomic warfare, warfare by atomic bombs, etc.

atomic weight, *Chem.* the average weight of an atom of an element measured in units each of which corresponds to one sixteenth of the average weight of the oxygen atom. *Abbr.:* at. wt.

at·om·ism (ăt′ə mĭz′əm), *n.* **1.** the atomic theory. **2.** *Philos.* the theory that minute discrete, finite, and indivisible elements are the ultimate constituents of all matter. —**at′om·ist,** *n.* —**at·om·is′tic,** *adj.*

at·om·ize (ăt′ə mīz′), *v.t.* -ized, -izing. **1.** to reduce to atoms. **2.** to reduce to fine particles or spray. —**at′-om·i·za′tion,** *n.*

at·om·iz·er (ăt′ə mī′zər), *n.* an apparatus for reducing liquids to a fine spray, as for medicinal application.

at·o·my[1] (ăt′ə mĭ), *n., pl.* -mies. *Archaic.* **1.** an atom; a mote. **2.** a pygmy. [t. L: m. *atomi* atoms]

at·o·my[2] (ăt′ə mĭ), *n., pl.* -mies. *Obs.* a skeleton. [der. ANATOMY, taken as *an atomy*]‘

A·ton (ä′tŏn), *n.* Aten.

a·ton·al (ā tō′nəl), *adj. Music.* having no key. [f. A-⁶ + TONAL] —**a·ton′al·ism,** *n.* —**a·ton′al·is′tic,** *adj.* —**a·ton′al·ly,** *adv.*

a·to·nal·i·ty (ā′tō năl′ə tĭ), *n. Music.* **1.** the absence of key or tonal center. **2.** an atonal principle or style of composition.

a·tone (ə tōn′), *v.,* **atoned, atoning.** —*v.i.* **1.** to make amends or reparation, as for an offense or a crime, or for an offender (fol. by *for*). **2.** to make up, as for errors or deficiencies (fol. by *for*). **3.** *Obs.* to agree. —*v.t.* **4.** to make amends for; expiate. **5.** to harmonize; make harmonious. **6.** *Rare.* to bring into unity. [back formation from ATONEMENT] —**a·ton′er,** *n.*

a·tone·ment (ə tōn′mənt), *n.* **1.** satisfaction or reparation for a wrong or injury; amends. **2.** *Theol.* the reconciliation of God and man by means of the life, sufferings, and death of Christ. **3.** *Archaic.* reconciliation; agreement. [f. phrase *at one* in accord + -MENT]

a·ton·ic (ə tŏn′ĭk), *adj.* **1.** *Phonet.* **a.** unaccented. **b.** *Obs.* voiceless (def. 5). **2.** *Pathol.* characterized by atony. —*n.* **3.** *Gram.* an unaccented word, syllable, or sound.

at·o·ny (ăt′ə nĭ), *n. Pathol.* lack of tone or energy; muscular weakness, esp. in a contractile organ. [t. ML: m. s. *atonia*, t. Gk.: languor]

a·top (ə tŏp′), *adj., adv.* **1.** on or at the top. —*prep.* **2.** on the top of: *atop the house.*

a·tra·bil·ious (ăt′rə bĭl′yəs), *adj.* melancholic or hypochondriac; splenetic. Also, **at′ra·bil′iar.** [f. L *ātra bīli(s)* black bile + -ous] —**at′ra·bil′ious·ness,** *n.*

a·trem·ble (ə trĕm′bəl), *adv.* in a trembling state.

A·treus (ā′trŏŏs, ā′trĭ əs), *n. Gk. Legend.* a king of Mycenae, and a son of Pelops. His evil deeds and those of his house gave many themes to the Greek dramatists.

a·trip (ə trĭp′), *adj. Naut.* (of an anchor) raised just enough to clear the bottom.

a·tri·um (ā′trĭ əm), *n., pl.* atria (ā′trĭ ə). **1.** *Archit.* **a.** the central main room of an ancient Roman private house. **b.** a courtyard, mostly surrounded by colonnades, in front of early Christian or medieval churches. **2.** *Anat.* an auricle of the heart. [(def. 1) t. L; (def. 2) t. NL, special use of L *atrium*]

a·tro·cious (ə trō′shəs), *adj.* **1.** extremely or shockingly wicked or cruel; heinous. **2.** shockingly bad or lacking in taste; execrable. [f. ATROCI(TY) + -OUS] —**a·tro′cious·ly,** *adv.* —**a·tro′cious·ness,** *n.*

a·troc·i·ty (ə trŏs′ə tĭ), *n., pl.* -ties. **1.** quality of being atrocious. **2.** an atrocious deed or thing. [t. L: m.s. *atrōcitas*]

at·ro·phied (ăt′rə fĭd), *adj.* exhibiting or affected with atrophy; wasted.

at·ro·phy (ăt′rə fĭ), *n., v.,* -phied, -phying. —*n.* **1.** *Pathol.* a wasting away of the body or of an organ or part, as from defective nutrition or other cause. **2.** degeneration. —*v.t., v.i.* **3.** to affect with or undergo atrophy. [earlier *atrophie,* t. L: m. *atrophia,* t. Gk.: lack of nourishment] —**a·troph·ic** (ə trŏf′ĭk), *adj.*

at·ro·pine (ăt′rə pēn′, -pĭn), *n.* a poisonous crystalline alkaloid, $C_{17}H_{22}NO_3$, obtained from belladonna and other solanaceous plants, which prevents the response of various body structures to certain types of nerve stimulation. Also, **at·ro·pin** (ăt′rə pĭn). [f. s. NL *Atropa*, the belladonna genus (t. Gk.: m. *átropos*. See ATROPOS) + -INE[2]]

at·ro·pism (ăt′rə pĭz′əm), *n. Pathol.* the morbid state induced by atropine.

At·ro·pos (ăt′rə pŏs′), *n. Gk. Myth.* one of the Fates. She cut off the thread of life. [t. Gk.: lit., inflexible]

att., attorney.

at·ta·bal (ăt′ə băl′), *n.* atabal.

at·tach (ə tăch′), *v.t.* **1.** to fasten to; affix; join; connect: *to attach a cable.* **2.** to join in action or function. **3.** *Mil.* to place on duty with or in assistance to a military unit temporarily. **4.** to connect as an adjunct; associate: *a curse is attached to this treasure.* **5.** to assign or attribute: *to attach significance to a gesture.* **6.** to bind by ties of affection or regard. **7.** *Law.* to take (persons or property) by legal authority. **8.** *Obs.* to lay hold of; seize. —*v.i.* **9.** to adhere; pertain; belong (fol. by *to* or *upon*): *no blame attaches to him.* [ME *attache(n)*, t. OF: m. *atachier*, f. *a-* AD- + word akin to TACK[1]] —**at·tach′a·ble,** *adj.* —**Syn. 1.** subjoin.

at·ta·ché (ăt′ə shā′ or, esp. Brit., ə tăsh′ā; *Fr.* à tà shĕ′), *n.* one attached to an official staff, esp. that of an embassy or legation. [F, prop. pp. of *attacher* ATTACH]

at·tach·ment (ə tăch′mənt), *n.* **1.** act of attaching. **2.** state of being attached. **3.** affection that binds one to another person or to a thing; regard. **4.** that which attaches; a fastening or tie: *the attachments of a pair of skis or of a harness.* **5.** an adjunct or supplementary device: *attachments to a reaping machine.* **6.** *Law.* seizure of property or person by legal authority; esp., seizure of a defendant's property before obtaining judgment against him. —**Syn. 3.** love, devotedness, devotion. **4.** junction, connection. **5.** See **addition**.

at·tack (ə tăk′), *v.t.* **1.** to set upon with force or weapons; begin hostilities against: *attack the enemy.* **2.** to direct unfavorable criticism, argument, etc., against; blame or abuse violently. **3.** to set about (a task) or go to work on (a thing) vigorously. **4.** (of disease, destructive agencies, etc.) to begin to affect. —*v.i.* **5.** to make an attack; begin hostilities. —*n.* **6.** the act of attacking; onslaught; assault. **7.** an offensive military operation with the aim of overcoming the enemy and destroying his armed forces and will to resist. **8.** *Pathol.* seizure by disease. **9.** the initial movement in a performance or contest; onset. [t. F: m. *attaquer*, t. It.: m. *attaccare* attack, ATTACH] —**at·tack′er,** *n.* —**Syn. 1.** ATTACK, ASSAIL, ASSAULT, MOLEST all mean to set upon someone forcibly, with hostile or inimical intent. ATTACK is the most general word and applies to a beginning of hostilities, esp. those definitely planned: *to attack from ambush.* ASSAIL implies vehement, sudden, and sometimes repeated attack: *to assail with weapons, with gossip.* ASSAULT almost always implies bodily violence: *to assault with intent to kill.* MOLEST is to interfere with, to threaten, or to assault: *he was safe, and where no one could molest him.* **2.** criticize, censure; impugn. —**Ant. 1.** defend.

at·tain (ə tān′), *v.t.* **1.** to reach, achieve, or accomplish by continued effort: *to attain one's ends.* **2.** to come to or arrive at in due course: *to attain the opposite shore.* —*v.i.* **3.** attain to, to arrive at; succeed in reaching or obtaining. [ME *attaine(n)*, t. OF: m. *ataindre*, g. L *attingere* touch upon] —**Syn. 1.** secure. See **gain**[1].

at·tain·a·ble (ə tā′nə bəl), *adj.* capable of being attained. —**at·tain′a·bil′i·ty, at·tain′a·ble·ness,** *n.*

at·tain·der (ə tān′dər), *n.* **1.** the legal consequence of judgment of death or outlawry for treason or felony, involving the loss of all civil rights. **2.** *Obs.* dishonor. [ME, t. OF: m. *ataindre* ATTAIN; later assoc. with F *taindre* stain, g. L *tingere.* See ATTAINT]

at·tain·ment (ə tān′mənt), *n.* **1.** act of attaining. **2.** something attained; a personal acquirement.

at·taint (ə tānt′), *v.t.* **1.** *Law.* to condemn by a sentence or a bill or act of attainder. **2.** to disgrace. **3.** *Archaic.* to accuse. **4.** *Obs.* to prove the guilt of. —*n.* **5.** attainder. **6.** a stain, disgrace; taint. **7.** *Obs.* a touch or hit, esp. in tilting. [ME *ataynte(n)*, t. OF: m. *ataint*, pp. of *ataindre* ATTAIN; in part confused with TAINT]

at·tain·ture (ə tān′chər), *n.* **1.** attainder. **2.** imputation.

at·tar (ăt′ər), *n.* a perfume or essential oil obtained from flowers or petals, esp. of damask roses. [t. Pers.: m. *'aṭar*, t. Ar.: m. *'iṭr*]

at·tem·per (ə těm′pər), *v.t.* **1.** to qualify, modify, or moderate by mixing or blending (with something different or opposite). **2.** to regulate or modify the temperature of. **3.** to soothe; mollify; mitigate. **4.** to accommodate; adapt (fol. by *to*). [t. L: s. *attemperāre* fit; r. ME *atempre(n)*, t. OF: m. *atemprer*]

at·tempt (ə těmpt′), *v.t.* **1.** to make an effort at; try; undertake; seek: *to attempt a conversation, to attempt to study.* **2.** to attack; make an effort against: *to attempt a person's life.* **3.** *Archaic.* to tempt. —*n.* **4.** effort put forth to accomplish something; a trial or essay. **5.** an attack or assault: *an attempt upon one's life.* [t. L: s. *attemptāre* try] —**at·tempt′a·bil′i·ty, at·tempt′a·ble,** *adj.* —**at·tempt′er,** *n.* —**Syn. 1.** See **try. 4.** undertaking, endeavor.

at·tend (ə těnd′), *v.t.* **1.** to be present at: *to attend school or a meeting.* **2.** to go with as a concomitant or result; accompany: *a cold attended with fever.* **3.** to minister to; devote one's services to. **4.** to wait upon or accompany as a servant. **5.** to take charge of; tend. **6.** to give heed to; listen to. **7.** *Archaic.* to wait for; expect. —*v.i.* **8.** to be present. **9.** to give attention; pay re-

gard or heed. **10.** to apply oneself: *to attend to one's work.* **11.** to take care or charge of: *to attend to a task.* **12.** to be consequent (*on*). **13.** to wait (*on*) with service. **14.** *Obs.* to wait. [ME *atende(n)*, t. OF: m. *atendre*, g. L *attendere* stretch toward] —**Syn. 4.** See **accompany**.

at·tend·ance (ə těn′dəns), *n.* **1.** act of attending. **2.** the persons present. **3.** *Obs.* attendants collectively.

at·tend·ant (ə těn′dənt), *n.* **1.** one who attends another, as for service or company. **2.** *Chiefly Brit.* an usher or clerk. **3.** one who is present, as at a meeting. **4.** that which goes along with or follows as a natural consequence. —*adj.* **5.** being present or in attendance; accompanying. **6.** concomitant; consequent: *attendant evils.* —**Syn. 1.** escort; retainer, servant.

at·ten·tion (ə těn′shən), *n.* **1.** act or faculty of attending. **2.** *Psychol.* concentration of the mind upon an object; maximal integration of the higher mental processes. **3.** observant care; consideration; notice: *your letter will receive early attention.* **4.** civility or courtesy: *attention to a stranger.* **5.** (*pl.*) acts of courtesy indicating regard, as in courtship. **6.** *Mil.* **a.** a command to take an erect position, with eyes to the front, arms hanging to the sides, heels together, and toes turned outward at an angle of 45 degrees. **b.** state of so standing: *at attention.* [ME *attencioun*, t. L: m. s. *attentiō*] —**Syn. 4.** homage, deference; respect.

at·ten·tive (ə těn′tĭv), *adj.* **1.** characterized by or giving attention; observant. **2.** assiduous in service or courtesy; polite; courteous. —**at·ten′tive·ly,** *adv.* —**at·ten′tive·ness,** *n.* —**Syn. 1.** regardful, mindful.

at·ten·u·ant (ə těn′yŏŏ ənt), *adj.* **1.** diluting, as a liquid. —*n.* **2.** *Med.* a medicine or agent that thins the blood, etc. [t. L: s. *attenuans*, ppr.]

at·ten·u·ate (*v.* ə těn′yŏŏ āt′; *adj.* ə těn′yŏŏ ĭt, -āt′), *v.,* -**ated, -ating,** *adj.* —*v.t.* **1.** to make thin; make slender or fine. **2.** to weaken or reduce in force, intensity, effect, quantity, or value. —*v.i.* **3.** to become thin or fine; lessen. —*adj.* **4.** attenuated; thin. **5.** *Bot.* tapering gradually to a narrow extremity. [t. L: m. s. *attenuātus*, pp., made thin]

at·ten·u·a·tion (ə těn′yŏŏ ā′shən), *n.* **1.** act of attenuating. **2.** the resulting state.

at·test (ə těst′), *v.t.* **1.** to bear witness to; certify; declare to be correct, true, or genuine; declare the truth of, in words or writing; esp., affirm in an official capacity: *to attest the truth of a statement.* **2.** to give proof or evidence of; manifest: *his works attest his industry.* —*v.i.* **3.** to certify to the genuineness of a document by signing as witness. —*n.* **4.** *Archaic.* witness; testimony; attestation. [t. L: s. *attestāri* bear witness] —**at·test′er, at·tes′tor,** *n.*

at·tes·ta·tion (ăt′ĕs tā′shən), *n.* **1.** act of attesting. **2.** an attesting declaration; testimony; evidence.

at·tic (ăt′ĭk), *n.* **1.** (*often pl. in Brit.*) that part of a building, esp. a house, directly under a roof; a garret. **2.** a room or rooms in that part. **3.** a low story or decorative wall above an entablature or the main cornice of a building. [t. F: m. *attique*, t. L: m.s. *Atticus* Attic]

At·tic (ăt′ĭk), *adj.* **1.** pertaining to Attica. **2.** (*often l.c.*) displaying simple elegance, incisive intelligence, and delicate wit. —*n.* **3.** a native or an inhabitant of Attica; an Athenian. **4.** the Ionic dialect of ancient Athens which became the standard of Greek literature (from the 5th century B.C.). [t. L: s. *Atticus*, t. Gk.: m. *Attikós*]

At·ti·ca (ăt′ə kə), *n.* the region about ancient Athens, in SE Greece.

Attic faith, inviolable faith.

Attica, 431 B. C.

At·ti·cism (ăt′ə sĭz′əm), *n.* **1.** peculiarity of style or idiom belonging to Attic Greek. **2.** Attic elegance of diction. **3.** concise and elegant expression. Also, **at′ti·cism.**

At·ti·cize (ăt′ə sīz′), *v.,* -**cized, -cizing.** —*v.i.* **1.** to affect Attic style, usages, etc.; intermingle with Attic elements. **2.** to favor or side with the Athenians. —*v.t.* **3.** to make conformable to Attic usage. Also, **atticize.** [t. Gk.: m.s. *Attikízein* (def. 2)]

Attic salt, dry, delicate wit. Also, **Attic wit.**

At·ti·la (ăt′ə lə), *n.* ("*Scourge of God*") died A.D. 453, king of Huns who invaded Europe: defeated at Châlons-sur-Marne, A.D. 451, by the Romans and Visigoths.

at·tire (ə tīr′), *v.,* -**tired, -tiring,** *n.* —*v.t.* **1.** to dress, array, or adorn, esp. for special occasions, ceremonials, etc. —*n.* **2.** clothes or apparel, esp. rich or splendid garments. **3.** the horns of a deer. [ME *atire(n)*, t. OF: m. *atirer* put in order, der. *a-* AD- + *tire* row]

at·tire·ment (ə tīr′mənt), *n. Obs.* dress; attire.

at·ti·tude (ăt′ə tūd′, -tŏŏd′), *n.* **1.** position, disposition, or manner with regard to a person or thing: *a menacing attitude.* **2.** position of the body appropriate to an action, emotion, etc. **3.** *Aeron.* the inclination of the three principal axes of an aircraft relative to the wind, to the ground, etc. **4.** a pose in ballet in which the dancer stands on one leg, the other bent behind. [t. F, t. It.: m. *attitudine* aptness, t. ML: m.s. *aptitūdō* APTITUDE] —**Syn. 2.** See **position**.

at·ti·tu·di·nize (ăt′ə tū′də nīz′, -tŏŏ′-), *v.i.,* -**nized, -nizing,** to assume attitudes; pose for effect. —**at′ti·tu/di·niz′er,** *n.*

---

t·tle·bor·o (ăt'əl bŭr'ō), *n.* a city in SE Massachusetts. 27,118 (1960).

t·lee (ăt'lĭ), *n.* **Clement Richard,** born 1883, British statesman: prime minister, 1945–1951.

t·torn (ətûrn'), *Law.* —*v.i.* **1.** to acknowledge the relation of tenant to a new landlord. —*v.t.* **2.** to turn over to another; transfer. [t. ML: s. *attornāre,* t. OF: m. *atorner transfer, f.a-* AD- + *torner* turn] —**at·torn'ment,** *n.*

t·tor·ney (ətûr'nĭ), *n., pl.* -**neys. 1.** a lawyer; attorney at law. **2.** one duly appointed or empowered by another to transact any business for him (**attorney in fact**). [ME *atorne,* t. OF, pp. of *atorner* assign] —**at·tor'ney·ship',** *n.*

ttorney at law, *Law.* an officer of the court authorized to appear before it as representative of a party to a legal controversy.

ttorney general, *pl.* **attorneys general, attorney generals.** the chief law officer of the state or nation and head of its legal department.

t·tract (ətrăkt'), *v.t.* **1.** to act upon by a physical force causing or tending to cause approach or union (opposed to *repel*). **2.** to draw by other than physical influence; invite or allure; win: *to attract attention or admirers.* —*v.i.* **3.** to possess or exert the power of attraction. [t. L: s. *attractus,* pp., drawn to] —**at·tract'-a·ble,** *adj.* **at·trac'tor, at·tract'er,** *n.*

t·trac·tion (ətrăk'shən), *n.* **1.** act, power, or property of attracting. **2.** allurement; enticement. **3.** that which allures or entices; a charm. **4.** *Physics.* a situation in which, under the influence of forces, bodies tend to draw together and particles of matter tend to unite or cohere. **5.** an entertainment offered to the public.

t·trac·tive (ətrăk'tĭv), *adj.* **1.** appealing to one's liking or admiration; engaging; alluring; pleasing. **2.** having the quality of attracting. —**at·trac'tive·ly,** *adv.* —**at·trac'tive·ness,** *n.*

t·tra·hent (ăt'rəhənt), *adj.* drawing; attracting. [t· L: s. *attrahens,* ppr., drawing to]

ttrib., **1.** attribute. **2.** attributive. **3.** attributively.

t·trib·ute (*v.* ətrĭb'ūt; *n.* ăt'rəbūt'), *v.,* -**uted,** -**uting,** *n.* —*v.t.* **1.** to consider as belonging; regard as owing, as an effect to a cause (often fol. by *to*). —*n.* **2.** something attributed as belonging; a quality, character, characteristic, or property: *wisdom is one of his attributes.* **3.** *Gram.* **a.** a word or phrase grammatically subordinate to another, serving to limit (identify, particularize, describe, or supplement) the meaning of the form to which it is attached. For example: in *the red house, red* limits the meaning of *house;* it is an attribute of *house.* **b.** an attributive word; adjunct. **4.** *Fine Arts.* a symbol of office, character, or personality. **5.** *Logic.* that which is predicated or affirmed of a subject. **6.** *Obs.* reputation. [ME (as adj.), t. L: m. s. *attribūtus,* pp., assigned] —**at·trib'ut·a·ble,** *adj.* —**at·trib'ut·er, at·trib'u·tor,** *n.*

—**Syn. 1.** ATTRIBUTE, ASCRIBE, IMPUTE imply regarding something as having had a definite origin. ATTRIBUTE and ASCRIBE are often used interchangeably, to imply something's having originated with a definite person or from a definite cause. ASCRIBE is, however, neutral as to implications; whereas, possibly because of an association with *tribute,* ATTRIBUTE is coming to have a complimentary connotation: *to ascribe one's health to outdoor life, an accident to carelessness; to attribute one's success to a friend's encouragement.* IMPUTE has gained uncomplimentary connotations, and usually means to accuse or blame someone or something as a cause or origin: *to impute dishonesty to him.* **2.** See **quality**.

t·tri·bu·tion (ăt'rəbū'shən), *n.* **1.** act of attributing; ascription. **2.** that which is ascribed; an attribute. **3.** authority or function assigned.

t·trib·u·tive (ətrĭb'yətĭv), *adj.* **1.** pertaining to or having the character of attribution or an attribute. **2.** *Gram.* expressing an attribute; in English, applied esp. to adjectives and adverbs preceding the words which they modify (distinguished from *predicate* and *appositive*), as *first* in *the first day.* —*n.* **3.** a word expressing an attribute; attributive word, phrase, or clause. —**at·trib'u·tive·ly,** *adv.* —**at·trib'u·tive·ness,** *n.*

t·trite (ətrīt'), *adj.* worn by rubbing or attrition. Also, **a·trit'ed.** [t. L: m. s. *attrītus,* pp.]

t·tri·tion (ətrĭsh'ən), *n.* **1.** a rubbing against; friction. **2.** a wearing down or away by friction; abrasion.

t·tu (ăt'tōō'), *n.* the westernmost of the Aleutian Islands: taken by U.S. forces, May–June, 1943.

t·tune (ətūn', ətōōn'), *v.t.,* -**tuned,** -**tuning.** to adjust to tune or harmony; bring into accord, or sympathetic relationship. [f. AT- + TUNE]

tty., attorney.

·twain (ətwān'), *adv. Archaic.* in twain; in two; asunder. [ME; f. A-¹ + TWAIN]

·tween (ətwēn'), *prep., adv. Archaic.* between.

t. wt., atomic weight.

·typ·i·cal (ətĭp'əkal), *adj.* not typical; not conforming to the type; irregular; abnormal. Also, **a·typ'ic.** [f. A-⁵ + TYPICAL] —**a·typ'i·cal·ly,** *adv.*

u (ō), *French.* to the; at the; with the. See **à la.**

u, *Chem.* (L *aurum*) gold.

.U., angstrom unit. Also, **a.u., A.U., Au., A.u.**

u·bade (ōbåd'), *n. French.* a piece sung or played outdoors at dawn, usually as a compliment to someone.

u·ber (ōbĕr'), *n.* **Daniel François Esprit** (då nyēl' frän swä' zĕs prē'), 1782–1871, French composer.

---

au·berge (ōbĕrzh'), *n. French.* an inn; tavern.

Au·ber·vil·liers (ōbĕr vēlyē'), *n.* a suburb of Paris in N France. 58,740 (1954).

au·burn (ô'bərn), *n.* **1.** a reddish-brown or golden-brown color. —*adj.* **2.** having auburn color: *auburn hair.* [ME *auburne,* t. OF: m. *auborne,* g. L *alburnus* whitish, der. *albus* white]

Au·burn (ô'bərn), *n.* **1.** a city in central New York: State prison. 35,249 (1960). **2.** a city in SW Maine, on the Androscoggin river. 24,449 (1960).

Au·bus·son rug (ōbысōn'), a fine French rug, hand-made, with a flat tapestry weave.

A.U.C., 1. ab urbe condita. **2.** anno urbis conditae.

Auck·land (ôk'lənd), *n.* the principal seaport of New Zealand, on N North Island. 127,406 (1951).

au con·traire (ō kôn trĕr'), *French.* **1.** on tne contrary. **2.** on the opposite or adverse side.

au cou·rant (ō kōōrän'), *French.* up to date.

auc·tion (ôk'shən), *n.* **1.** a public sale at which property or goods are sold to the highest bidder. **2.** *Cards.* **a.** auction bridge. **b.** (in bridge or certain other games) the competitive bidding to fix a contract that a player or players undertake to fulfill. —*v.t.* **3.** to sell by auction (fol. by *off*): *he auctioned off his furniture.* [t. L: s. *auctio* an increasing]

auction bridge, a variety of bridge in which the players bid to declare the trump or no-trump.

auc·tion·eer (ôk'shə nŕr'), *n.* **1.** one who conducts sales by auction. —*v.t.* **2.** to auction.

auction pitch, *Cards.* a form of seven-up with bidding to determine the trump or "pitch."

au·da·cious (ōdā'shəs), *adj.* **1.** bold or daring; spirited; adventurous: *audacious warrior.* **2.** reckless or bold in wrongdoing; impudent and presumptuous. [f. AUDACI(TY) + -OUS] —**au·da'cious·ly,** *adv.* —**au·da'·cious·ness,** *n.* —**Syn. 2.** unabashed, shameless.

au·dac·i·ty (ōdăs'ətĭ), *n.* **1.** boldness or daring, esp. reckless boldness. **2.** effrontery or insolence. [f. s. L *audācia* daring + -TY²]

Au·den (ô'dən), *n.* **Wystan Hugh** (wĭs'tən), born 1907, British poet in U.S.

au·di·ble (ô'dəbəl), *adj.* capable of being heard; actually heard; loud enough to be heard. [t. ML: m. s. *audibilis,* der. L *audīre* hear] —**au/di·bil'i·ty, au/di·ble·ness,** *n.* —**au'di·bly,** *adv.*

au·di·ence (ô'dĭ əns), *n.* **1.** an assembly of nearers or spectators: *the audience at a movie.* **2.** the persons reached by a book, radio broadcast, etc.; public. **3.** liberty or opportunity of being heard or of speaking with or before a person or group. **4.** *Govt.* admission of a diplomatic representative to a sovereign or high officer of government; formal interview. **5.** act of hearing or attending to words or sounds. [ME, t. OF. g. L *audientia* attention, hearing]

au·di·ent (ô'dĭ ənt), *adj.* hearing; listening. [t. L: s. *audiens,* ppr.]

au·dile (ô'dĭl), *n. Psychol.* one in whose mind auditory images are especially distinct. [f. AUD(IO)- + -ILE]

au·di·o (ô'dĭ ō'), *adj. Electronics.* designating electronic apparatus using audio frequencies: *audio amplifier.*

audio-, a word element meaning "hear," "of or for hearing," as in *audiometer.* [comb. form repr. L *audīre* hear]

audio frequency, *Physics, Electronics.* a frequency of the order of audible frequencies of sound waves; a frequency between 15 and 20,000 cycles per second.

au·di·om·e·ter (ô'dĭ ŏm'ə tər), *n. Med.* an instrument for gauging and recording the power of hearing.

au·di·o·phile (ô'dĭ ə fil), *n.* a person especially interested in high-fidelity sound reproduction, on radios, phonographs, tape recorders, etc. [f. AUDIO- + -PHILE]

au·di·o·vis·u·al aids (ô'dĭ ō vĭzh'ōō əl), films, recordings, photographs, and other nontextual materials, used in classroom instruction and library collections.

au·di·phone (ô'də fōn'), *n. Med.* a kind of diaphragm held against the upper teeth to assist hearing by transmitting sound vibrations to the auditory nerve.

au·dit (ô'dĭt), *n.* **1.** an official examination and verification of accounts and records, esp. of financial accounts. **2.** an account or a statement of account. **3.** *Archaic.* a judicial hearing. **4.** *Rare.* audience. —*v.t.* **5.** to make audit of; examine (accounts, etc.) officially. **6.** *U.S.* to attend (classes, lectures, etc.) as an auditor. —*v.i.* **7.** to examine and verify an account or accounts by reference to vouchers. [late ME *audite,* t. L: m.s. *audītus* a hearing]

au·di·tion (ôdĭsh'ən), *n.* **1.** act, sense, or power of hearing. **2.** a hearing given to a musician, speaker, etc. to test voice capabilities, performance, etc. **3.** what is heard. —*v.t., v.i.* **4.** to give an audition (to). [t. L: s. *audītio* a hearing]

au·di·tive (ô'də tĭv), *adj.* auditory.

au·di·tor (ô'də tər), *n.* **1.** a hearer; listener. **2.** a person appointed and authorized to examine accounts and accounting records, compare the charges with the vouchers, verify balance sheet and income items, and state the result. **3.** *U.S.* a university student who is registered as taking a given course but not for credit and without obligation to do the work of the course. —**au·di·tress** (ô'də trĭs), *n. fem.*

au·di·to·ri·um (ô'də tôr'ĭəm), *n., pl.* -**toriums, -toria** (-tôr'ĭə). **1.** the space for the audience in a church,

---

ăct, āble, dâre, ärt; ĕbb, ēqual; ĭf, īce; hŏt, ōver, ôrder, oil, bŏŏk, ōōze, out; ŭp, ūse, ûrge; ə = a in alone; ʰ, chief; g, give; ng, ring; sh, shoe; th, thin; t̶h̶, that; zh, vision. See the full key on inside cover.

theater, school, or other building. 2. a building for public gatherings; a hall. [t. L]

au·di·to·ry (ô′də tôr′ĭ), *adj., n., pl.* **-ries.** —*adj.* 1. *Anat., Physiol.* pertaining to hearing, to the sense of hearing, or to the organs of hearing: *the auditory nerve.* —*n.* 2. an assembly of hearers; an audience. 3. an auditorium; specif., the nave in a church. [t. L: m.s. *audītōrius* (-*ōrium*, neut.)]

Au·du·bon (ô′də bŏn′), *n.* **John James,** 1785?–1851, U. S. naturalist, who painted and wrote about the birds of North America.

Au·er (ou′ər), *n.* **Leopold** (lā′ô pôlt′), 1845–1930, Hungarian violinist.

au fait (ō fā′; *Fr.* ō fĕ′), *French.* having experience or practical knowledge of a thing; expert; versed.

Auf·klä·rung (ouf′klĕ′ro͝ong), *n. German.* 1. enlightenment. 2. *Europ. Hist.* enlightenment (def. 3). [G.: lit., clearing up]

au fond (ō fôɴ′), *French.* at bottom or to the bottom; thoroughly; in reality; fundamentally.

auf Wie·der·seh·en (ouf vē′dər zā′ən), *German.* until we meet again; good-by for the present.

Aug., August.

aug., augmentative.

Au·ge·an sta·bles (ô jē′ən), *Gk. Legend.* the stables in which a king (**Augeas**) kept 3000 oxen and which had not been cleaned for thirty years. Hercules accomplished the task in a single day by turning the river Alpheus through the stable.

au·ger (ô′gər), *n.* 1. a carpenter's tool larger than a gimlet, with a spiral groove for boring holes in wood. 2. a large tool for boring holes deep in the ground. [ME, var. of *nauger* (*a nauger* being taken as *an auger*), OE *nafogār*]

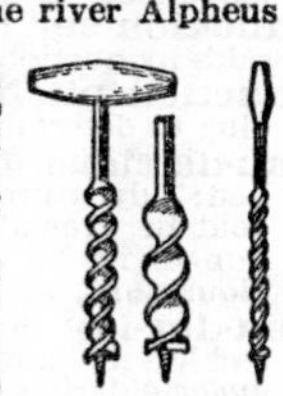

Augers (def. 1)

aught[1] (ôt), *n.* 1. anything whatever; any part: *for aught I know.* —*adv.* 2. in any degree; at all; in any respect. Also, **ought.** [ME *aught, ought,* OE *āwiht, ōwiht* at all, anything, f. *ā, ō* ever + *wiht* thing]

aught[2] (ôt), *n.* a cipher (0). [appar. alter. of NAUGHT; *a naught* being taken as *an aught*]

Au·gier (ō zhyĕ′), *n.* **Guillaume Victor Émile** (gēyōm′ vēk tôr′ ĕ mēl′), 1820–89, French dramatist.

au·gite (ô′jīt), *n.* a mineral, a silicate, chiefly of calcium, magnesium, iron, and aluminum, a dark-green to black variety of pyroxene, characteristic of basic eruptive rocks like basalt. [t. L: m. *augītēs* precious stone, t. Gk.] —**au·git·ic** (ô jĭt′ĭk), *adj.*

aug·ment (*v.* ôg mĕnt′; *n.* ôg′mĕnt), *v.t.* 1. to make larger; enlarge in size or extent; increase. 2. *Gram.* to add an augment to. —*v.i.* 3. to become larger. —*n.* 4. *Gram.* (in Greek, Sanskrit, etc.) a prefixed vowel or a lengthened initial vowel, which characterizes certain forms in the inflection of verbs. [ME *augment(en)*, t. L: m. *augmentāre* increase] —**aug·ment′a·ble,** *adj.* —**aug·ment′er,** *n.* —**Syn.** 1. See **increase.**

aug·men·ta·tion (ôg′mĕn tā′shən), *n.* 1. act of augmenting. 2. augmented state. 3. that by which anything is augmented. 4. *Music.* modification of a theme by increasing the time value of all its notes.

aug·ment·a·tive (ôg mĕn′tə tĭv), *adj.* 1. serving to augment. 2. *Gram.* pertaining to or productive of a form denoting increased size or intensity. In Spanish, *-ón* added to a word indicates increased size, (*silla,* "chair"; *sillón,* "armchair"); hence it is an augmentative suffix. —*n.* 3. *Gram.* an augmentative element or formation.

aug·ment·ed (ôg mĕn′tĭd), *adj. Music.* (of an interval) greater by a half step than the corresponding perfect or major interval.

au gra·tin (ō grä′tən; *Fr.* ō grȧ tăɴ′), *French.* cooked or baked covered with either browned crumbs or cheese, or with both.

Augs·burg (ôgz′bûrg; *Ger.* ouks′bo͝orкн), *n.* a city in S West Germany, in Bavaria. 202,675 (est. 1955).

au·gur (ô′gər), *n.* 1. one of a body of ancient Roman officials charged with observing and interpreting omens, for guidance in public affairs. 2. any soothsayer; prophet. —*v.t.* 3. to divine or predict, as from omens; prognosticate. 4. to afford an omen of. —*v.i.* 5. to conjecture from signs or omens; presage. 6. to be a sign; bode (*well* or *ill*). [t. L]

au·gu·ry (ô′gyə rĭ), *n., pl.* **-ries.** 1. the art or practice of an augur; divination. 2. a rite or observation of an augur. 3. an omen, token, or indication. [ME, t. L: m. s. *augurium*]

Au·gust (ô′gəst), *n.* the eighth month of the year, containing 31 days. [named after AUGUSTUS]

au·gust (ô gŭst′), *adj.* 1. inspiring reverence or admiration; of supreme dignity or grandeur; majestic: *an august spectacle.* 2. venerable: *your august father.* [t. L: s. *augustus*] —**au·gust′ly,** *adv.* —**au·gust′ness,** *n.*

Au·gus·ta (ô gŭs′tə), *n.* 1. a city in E Georgia, on the Savannah river. 71,508 (1950). 2. the capital of Maine, in the SW part, on the Kennebec river. 21,680 (1960).

Au·gus·tan (ô gŭs′tən), *adj.* 1. pertaining to Augustus Caesar, the first Roman emperor, or to his reign (the **Augustan Age**), which marked the golden age of Latin literature. 2. pertaining to the Augustan Age in Roman literature or to the highest point in the literature of any country. 3. having some of the characteristics of Augustan literature, as classicism, correctness, brilliance, nobility. —*n.* 4. an author in an Augustan age.

Au·gus·tine (ô′gə stēn′, ô gŭs′tĭn), *n.* 1. **Saint,** (*Austin*) A.D. 354–430, leader of the early Christian Church: author of *City of God* and *Confessions*; bishop of Hippo in N Africa. 2. **Saint,** died A.D. 604, Roman monk: headed group of missionaries that landed in England A.D. 597 and began the conversion of the English to Christianity; first archbishop of Canterbury.

Au·gus·tin·i·an (ô′gə stĭn′ĭ ən), *adj.* 1. pertaining to St. Augustine (A.D. 354–430), to his doctrines, or to any religious order following his rule. —*n.* 2. a member of any of several religious orders deriving their name and rule from St. Augustine, esp. a member of the order of mendicant friars (**Hermits of St. Augustine** or **Austin Friars**). 3. one who adopts the views or doctrines of St. Augustine. —**Au′gus·tin′i·an·ism, Au·gus·tin·ism** (ô gŭs′tə nĭz′əm), *n.*

Au·gus·tus (ô gŭs′təs), *n.* (*Gaius Julius Caesar Octavianus, Augustus Caesar*) 63 B.C.–A.D. 14, first Roman emperor, 27 B.C. to A.D. 14: reformer, patron of arts and literature; heir and successor to Julius Caesar. Before 27 B.C., called **Octavian.**

au jus (ō zhʏ′), *French.* (meat) served in its own gravy.

auk (ôk), *n.* any of certain short-winged, three-toed diving birds of the family *Alcidae* of northern seas, esp. certain species of this family, as the **razor-billed auk,** *Alca torda,* and the extinct, flightless **great auk,** *Pinguinis impennis.* [t. Scand.; cf. Dan. *alke*]

Razor-billed auk. *Alca torda* (17 in. long)

auk·let (ôk′lĭt), *n.* any of various small members of the auk family found in north Pacific waters, as the **crested auklet,** *Aethia cristatella,* and its allies.

au lait (ō lā′; *Fr.* ō lĕ′), *French.* prepared or served with milk.

auld (ôld), *adj. Scot.* old.

auld lang syne (ôld′ lăng sīn′), *Scot.* 1. old times, esp. times fondly remembered. 2. old or long friendship.

au·lic (ô′lĭk), *adj.* pertaining to a royal court. [t. L: s. *aulicus,* t. Gk.: m. *aulikós* of the court]

Aulic Council, a personal council of the Holy Roman Emperor exercising chiefly judicial powers.

au na·tu·rel (ō nȧ tʏ rĕl′), *French.* 1. in the natural state; naked. 2. cooked plainly. 3. uncooked.

aunt (ănt, änt), *n.* 1. the sister of one's father or mother. 2. the wife of one's uncle. 3. *Chiefly Brit.* a benevolent elderly lady. [ME, t. OF: m. *ante,* g. L *amita*]

aunt·ie (ăn′tĭ, än′-), *n.* a familiar or diminutive form of **aunt.** Also, **aunt′y.**

au·ra (ôr′ə), *n., pl.* **auras, aurae** (ôr′ē). 1. a distinctive air, atmosphere, character, etc.: *an aura of culture.* 2. a subtle emanation proceeding from a body and surrounding it as an atmosphere. 3. *Elect.* the motion of the air at an electrified point. 4. *Pathol.* a sensation, as of a current of cold air, or other sensory experience, preceding an attack of epilepsy, hysteria, etc. [t. L, t. Gk.: air]

au·ral[1] (ôr′əl), *adj.* of or pertaining to an aura. [f. AUR(A) + -AL[1]]

au·ral[2] (ôr′əl), *adj.* of, or perceived by, the organs of hearing. [f. s. L *auris* ear + -AL[1]] —**au′ral·ly,** *adv.*

Au·rang·zeb (ôr′əng zĕb′), *n.* 1618–1707, Mogul emperor of Hindustan, 1658–1707. Also, **Au′rung·zeb′.**

au·re·ate (ôr′ĭ ĭt, -āt′), *adj.* 1. golden. 2. brilliant; splendid. [ME *aureat,* t. L: s. *aureātus* adorned with gold]

Au·re·li·an (ô rē′lĭ ən, -rēl′yən), *n.* (*Lucius Domitius Aurelianus*) A.D. 212?–275, Roman emperor, 270–275.

Au·re·li·us (ô rē′lĭ əs, ô rēl′yəs), *n.* See **Antoninus.**

au·re·ole (ôr′ĭ ōl′), *n.* 1. a radiance surrounding the head or the whole figure in the representation of a sacred personage. 2. any encircling ring of light or color; a halo. 3. *Astron.* corona (defs. 1, 2). Also, **au·re·o·la** (ô rē′ə lə). [t. L: m. *aureola,* fem. of *aureolus* golden]

au·re·o·my·cin (ô′rĭ ō mī′sĭn), *n.* a recently developed antibiotic that is especially effective against certain diseases caused by viruses or Rickettsia, such as Rocky Mountain spotted fever.

au re·voir (ō rə vwȧr′), *French.* until we see each other again; good-by for the present.

au·ric (ôr′ĭk), *adj. Chem.* of or containing gold, esp. in the trivalent state (Au^{+3}). [f. s. L *aurum* gold + -IC]

au·ri·cle (ôr′ə kəl), *n.* 1. *Anat.* **a.** the projecting outer portion of the ear; the pinna. **b.** one of two chambers of the heart through which blood from the veins passes into the ventricles. See diag. under **heart.** 2. *Bot., Zool.* a part like or likened to an ear. [t. L: m.s. *auricula,* dim. of *auris* ear] —**au′ri·cled,** *adj.*

au·ric·u·la (ô rĭk′yə lə), *n., pl.* **-lae** (-lē′), **-las.** a yellow primrose, *Primula Auricula,* native in the Alps; bear's-ear. [t. L: the external ear. See AURICLE]

au·ric·u·lar (ô rĭk′yə lər), *adj.* 1. of or pertaining to the organs of hearing. 2. perceived by or addressed to the ear: *auricular confession.* 3. dependent on hearing; aural. 4. shaped like an ear; auriculate. 5. *Anat.* pertaining to an auricle of the heart. 6. *Ornith.* noting certain feathers, usually of peculiar structure, which overlie and defend the outer opening of a bird's ear. —*n.* 7. (*usually pl.*) *Ornith.* an auricular feather.

au·ric·u·late (ô rĭk′yə lĭt, -lāt′), *adj.* 1. having auricles, or earlike parts. 2. shaped like an ear.

au·rif·er·ous (ô rĭf′ər əs), *adj.* yielding or containing gold. [f. L *aurifer* gold-bearing + -ous]

Au·ri·ga (ô rī′gə), *n.* a northern constellation containing Capella. [t. L: charioteer]

au·rist (ôr′ĭst), *n.* a physician expert in treating diseases of the ear; an otologist. [f. s. L *auris* ear + -ist]

au·rochs (ôr′ŏks), *n., pl.* **-rochs.** a European wild ox, *Bos primigenius*, now extinct. [t. G. var. of *auerochs*, MHG *ūr-ochse*, f. *ūr* (c. OE *ūr* wild ox) + *ochse* ox]

Aurochs, *Bos primigenius*
(Ab.[6 ft. high at the shoulder)

Au·ro·ra (ô rôr′ə), *n.* **1.** *Class. Myth.* dawn, often personified, by the Romans and others, as a goddess (Eos). **2.** (*l.c.*) the rise or dawn of something. **3.** (*l.c.*) *Meteorol.* an electrical atmospheric phenomenon, consisting of streamers, bands, curtains, arcs, etc., of light, ordinarily confined to high altitudes; the polar lights (aurora borealis or aurora australis). **4.** a city in NE Illinois. 65,715 (1960). [t. L]

aurora aus·tra·lis (ô strā′lĭs). *Meteorol.* the aurora of the Southern Hemisphere, a phenomenon similar to the aurora borea'is. [NL]

aurora bo·re·al·is (bôr′ĭ al′ĭs, -ā′lĭs), *Meteorol.* the aurora of the Northern Hemisphere, a luminous meteoric phenomenon appearing at night. [NL]

au·ro·ral (ô rôr′əl), *adj.* **1.** of or like the dawn. **2.** pertaining to a polar aurora. **—au·ro′ral·ly,** *adv.*

au·ro·re·an (ô rôr′ĭ ən), *adj. Poetic.* belonging to the dawn; auroral.

au·rous (ôr′əs), *adj.* **1.** *Chem.* containing monovalent gold (Au+1). **2.** of or containing gold. [f. AUR(UM) + -OUS]

au·rum (ôr′əm), *n. Chem.* gold. *Symbol:* Au. [t. L]

Au·sa·ble (ô sā′bəl), *n.* a river in NE New York, flowing through **Ausable Chasm,** a scenic gorge 2 mi. long, into Lake Champlain.

aus·cul·tate (ô′skəl tāt′), *v.t., v.i.,* **-tated, -tating.** *Med.* to examine by auscultation. **—aus·cul·ta·tive** (ô′skəl tā′tĭv, ô skŭl′tə-), **aus·cul·ta·to·ry** (ô skŭl′tə tôr′ĭ), *adj.* **—aus′cul·ta′tor,** *n.*

aus·cul·ta·tion (ô′skəl tā′shən), *n.* **1.** *Med.* the act of listening, either directly or through a stethoscope or other instrument, to sounds within the body, as a method of diagnosis, etc. **2.** act of listening. [t. L: s. *auscultātiō* a listening]

Aus·gleich (ous′glīкн), *n., pl.* **-gleiche** (-glī′кнə). *German.* **1.** an arrangement or compromise between parties. **2.** the agreement made between Austria and Hungary in 1867, regulating the relations between the countries and setting up the Dual Monarchy.

aus·pex (ô′spĕks), *n., pl.* **auspices** (ô′spə sēz′). an augur (def. 1). [t. L]

aus·pi·cate (ô′spə kāt′), *v.,* **-cated, -cating.** *Obs. or Rare.* **—v.t.** **1.** to initiate with ceremonies calculated to ensure good luck; inaugurate. **—v.i.** **2.** to augur. [t. L: m.s. *auspicātus,* pp.]

aus·pice (ô′spĭs), *n., pl.* **auspices** (ô′spə sĭz′). **1.** (*usually pl.*) favoring influence; patronage: *under the auspices of the State Department.* **2.** a propitious circumstance. **3.** a divination or prognostication, originally from birds. [t. F, t. L: m.s. *auspicium*]

aus·pi·cial (ô spĭsh′əl), *adj.* **1.** of or pertaining to auspices: *auspicial rites.* **2.** auspicious.

aus·pi·cious (ô spĭsh′əs), *adj.* **1.** of good omen; betokening success; favorable: *an auspicious moment.* **2.** favored by fortune; prosperous; fortunate. [f. s. L *auspicium* divination + -ous] **—aus·pi′cious·ly,** *adv.* **—aus·pi′cious·ness,** *n.*

Aus·ten (ô′stən), *n.* **Jane,** 1775–1817, British novelist.

Aus·ter (ô′stər), *n. Poetic.* the south wind personified. [t. L]

aus·tere (ô stĭr′), *adj.* **1.** harsh in manner; stern in appearance; forbidding. **2.** severe in disciplining or restraining oneself; morally strict. **3.** grave; sober; serious. **4.** severely simple; without ornament: *austere writing.* **5.** rough to the taste; sour or harsh in flavor. [ME, t. L: m.s. *austērus,* t. Gk.: m. *austērós*] **—aus·tere′ly,** *adv.* **—aus·tere′ness,** *n.*

aus·ter·i·ty (ô stĕr′ə tĭ), *n., pl.* **-ties.** **1.** austere quality; severity of manner, life, etc. **2.** (*usually pl.*) a severe or ascetic practice. **—Syn. 2.** See **hardship.**

Aus·ter·litz (ô′stər lĭts; *Ger.* ous′tar-), *n.* a town in central Czechoslovakia, in Moravia: Napoleon defeated the combined Russian and Austrian armies here, 1805.

Aus·tin (ô′stən), *n.* **1.** the capital of Texas, in the central part, on the Colorado river. 186,545 (1960). **2.** a city in SE Minnesota. 27,908 (1960). **3. Alfred,** 1835–1913, British poet. **4. John,** 1790–1859, British writer on law. **5. Warren Robinson,** 1877–1962, U.S. diplomat. **6.** Augustine (def. 1).

Austin friar. See **Augustinian** (def. 2).

aus·tral (ô′strəl), *adj.* **1.** southern. **2.** (*cap.*) Australian. [t. L: s. *austrālis* (def. 2)]

Austral, **1.** Australasia. **2.** Australia.

Aus·tral·a·sia (ô′strə lā′zhə, -shə), *n.* Australia, New Zealand, and neighboring islands of the S Pacific Ocean. **—Aus′tral·a′sian,** *adj., n.*

Aus·tral·ia (ô strāl′yə), *n.* **1.** the continent SE of Asia. 9,107,000 (est. 1956); 2,948,366 sq. mi. **2. Commonwealth of,** a member of the British Commonwealth of Nations, consisting of the federated states and territories of Australia and Tasmania. 9,428,000 (est. 1956); 2,974,581 sq. mi. *Cap.:* Canberra.

Aus·tral·ian (ô strāl′yən), *adj.* **1.** of or pertaining to Australia. **—n. 2.** a native or inhabitant of Australia. **3.** an Australian aborigine. **4.** any of the languages of the Australian aborigines.

Australian Alps, a mountain range in SE Australia. Highest peak, Mt. Kosciusko, 7328 ft.

Australian ballot, *Govt.* a ballot which ensures secrecy in voting, originally used in South Australia.

Australian Capital Territory, a federal territory in SE Australia, within New South Wales: Canberra, the capital, is located there. 34,189 (est. 1956); 939 sq. mi. Formerly, **Federal Capital Territory.**

Aus·tra·sia (ô strā′zhə, -shə), *n.* the E part of the kingdom of the Franks comprising parts of what is now NE France, W Germany, and Belgium. *Cap.:* Metz. **—Aus·tra′sian,** *adj., n.*

Austrasia, A.D. 481–814

Aus·tri·a (ô′strĭ ə), *n.* a country in central Europe. 6,974,000 pop. (est. 1955); 32,381 sq. mi. *Cap.:* Vienna. German, *Österreich.* **—Aus′tri·an,** *adj., n.*

Aus·tri·a-Hun·ga·ry (ô′strĭ ə hŭng′gə rĭ), *n.* a former monarchy in central Europe, including the empire of Austria, kingdom of Hungary, and various crownlands: dissolved, 1918. **—Aus·tro-Hun·gar·i·an** (ô′strō hŭng gâr′ĭ ən), *adj.*

Austria-Hungary, 1871–1914

Austro-, a word element meaning "Austria," "Austrian."

Aus·tro·ne·sia (ô′strō nē′zhə, -shə), *n.* islands of the central and south Pacific. [f. *austro-* (repr. AUSTER) + s. Gk. *nêsos* island + -IA]

Aus·tro·ne·sian (ô′strō nē′zhən, -shən), *adj.* **1.** of or pertaining to Austronesia. **—n. 2.** a family of languages spoken in the Pacific, consisting of four divisions, Indonesian, Melanesian, Micronesian, and Polynesian; Malayo-Polynesian.

aut-, var. of auto-1 before most vowels, as in *autacoid.*

au·ta·coid (ô′tə koid′), *n. Physiol.* a substance secreted by one organ into the blood stream or lymph, and controlling organic processes elsewhere in the body; a hormone. [f. AUT- + m.s. Gk. *ākos* remedy + -OID]

au·tar·chy (ô′tär kĭ), *n., pl.* **-chies.** **1.** absolute sovereignty. **2.** self-government. **3.** autarky. [t. Gk.: m.s. *autarchía* self-rule] **—au·tar′chic,** *adj.*

au·tar·ky (ô′tär kĭ), *n., pl.* **-kies.** **1.** the condition of self-sufficiency, esp. economic, as applied to a state. **2.** a national policy of economic independence. Also, **autarchy.** [t. Gk.: m.s. *autárkeia*] **—au·tar′ki·cal,** *adj.* **—au′tar·kist,** *n., adj.*

au·te·cism (ô tē′sĭz əm), *n.* autoecism. **—au·te·cious** (ô tē′shəs), *adj.*

au·te·col·o·gy (ô′tə kŏl′ə jĭ), *n.* that branch of ecology which deals with the individual organism and its environment. Cf. **synecology.**

auth., **1.** author. **2.** authorized.

au·then·tic (ô thĕn′tĭk), *adj.* **1.** entitled to acceptance or belief; reliable; trustworthy: *an authentic story.* **2.** of the authorship or origin reputed; of genuine origin: *authentic documents.* **3.** *Law.* executed with all due formalities: *an authentic deed.* **4.** *Obs.* authoritative. Also, **au·then′ti·cal.** [t. LL: s. *authenticus,* t. Gk.: m. *authentikós* warranted] **—au·then′ti·cal·ly,** *adv.*

au·then·ti·cate (ô thĕn′tə kāt′), *v.t.,* **-cated, -cating.** **1.** to make authoritative or valid. **2.** to establish as genuine. **—au·then′ti·ca′tion,** *n.* **—au·then′ti·ca′tor,** *n.*

au·then·tic·i·ty (ô′thən tĭs′ə tĭ, -thĕn-), *n.* quality of being authentic; reliability; genuineness.

au·thor (ô′thər), *n.* **1.** a person who writes a novel, poem, essay, etc.; the composer of a literary work, as distinguished from a compiler, translator, editor, or copyist. **2.** the originator, beginner, or creator of anything. **3.** the literary production(s) of a writer: *to find a passage in an author.* [ME *autor,* t. OF, t. L: m. *auctor* originator] **—au·thor·ess** (ô′thər ĭs), *n. fem.* **—au·tho·ri·al** (ô thôr′ĭ əl), *adj.* **—au′thor·less,** *adj.*

au·thor·i·tar·i·an (ə thôr′ə târ′ĭ ən, ə thôr′-), *adj.* **1.** favoring the principle of subjection to authority as opposed to that of individual freedom. **—n. 2.** one who favors authoritarian principles. [f. AUTHORIT(Y) + -ARIAN] **—au·thor′i·tar′i·an·ism,** *n.*

ăct, āble, dâre, ärt; ĕbb, ēqual; ĭf, īce; hŏt, ōver, ôrder, oil, bŏŏk, ōōze, out; ŭp, ūse, ûrge; ə = a in alone; ch, chief; g, give; ng, ring; sh, shoe; th, thin; ŧh, that; zh, vision. See the full key on inside cover.

au·thor·i·ta·tive (əthôr′ətā′tĭv, əthŏr′-), *adj.* **1.** having due authority; having the sanction or weight of authority: *an authoritative opinion.* **2.** having an air of authority; positive; peremptory; dictatorial. **—au·thor′·i·ta′tive·ly,** *adv.* **—au·thor′i·ta′tive·ness,** *n.* **—Syn.** 1. conclusive, unquestioned. 2. impressive, dogmatic.

au·thor·i·ty (əthôr′ətĭ, əthŏr′-), *n., pl.* **-ties. 1.** the right to determine, adjudicate, or otherwise settle issues or disputes; the right to control, command, or determine. **2.** a person or body with such rights. **3.** an accepted source of information, advice, etc. **4.** a standard author or his writing; an expert on a subject. **5.** a statute, court rule, or judicial decision which establishes a rule or principle of law; a ruling. **6.** title to respect or acceptance; commanding influence. **7.** a warrant for action; justification. **8.** testimony; witness. [t. F: m. *authorité*; r. ME *auctorite,* t. L: m.s. *auctōritas*]
—Syn. 1. AUTHORITY, CONTROL, INFLUENCE denote a power or right to direct the actions or thoughts of others. AUTHORITY is a power or right, usually because of rank or office, to issue commands and to punish for violations: *to have authority over subordinates.* CONTROL is either authority or influence applied to the complete and successful direction or manipulation of persons or things: *to be in control of a project.* INFLUENCE is a personal and unofficial power derived from deference of others to one's character, ability, or station; it may be exerted unconsciously or may operate through persuasion: *to have influence over one's friends.*

au·thor·i·za·tion (ô′thər ə zā′shən), *n.* act of authorizing; permission from or establishment by an authority.

au·thor·ize (ô′thərīz′), *v.t.* **-ized, -izing. 1.** to give authority or legal power to; empower (to do something): *to authorize a sheriff.* **2.** to give authority for; formally sanction (an act or proceeding). **3.** to establish by authority or usage: *authorized by custom.* **4.** to afford a ground for; warrant; justify. **—au′thor·iz′er,** *n.*

au·thor·ized (ô′thərīzd′), *adj.* **1.** authoritative; endowed with authority. **2.** legally or duly sanctioned.

Authorized Version, 1. an English revision of the Bible prepared in England under James I and published in 1611. **2.** any translation of the Bible endorsed by church authority for use in public worship.

au·thor·ship (ô′thərshĭp′), *n.* **1.** the occupation or career of writing books, articles, etc. **2.** origin as to author, composer, or compiler: *the authorship of a book.*

Auth. Ver., Authorized Version (of the Bible).

au·tism (ô′tĭzəm), *n.* **1.** *Psychol.* fantasy; introverted thought; daydreaming; marked subjectivity of interpretation. **2.** *Psychiatry.* such a state, with introversive behavior, noted in several psychopathological conditions. [f. AUT- + -ISM] **—au·tis·tic** (ôtĭs′tĭk), *adj.*

au·to (ô′tō), *n., pl.* **-tos.** automobile. [shortened form]

auto-[1], a word element meaning "self," "same" as in *autograph.* Also, **aut-.** [t. Gk., comb. form of *autós*]

auto-[2], a combining form of **automobile,** as in *autocade.*

auto., automobile.

Au·to·bahn (ou′tōbän′), *n., pl.* **-bahnen** (-bä′nən). (in Germany) a superhighway having no speed limit.

au·to·bi·o·graph·ic (ô′tōbī′əgrăf′ĭk), *adj.* dealing with one's life history. Also, **au′to·bi′o·graph′i·cal. —au′to·bi′o·graph′i·cal·ly,** *adv.*

au·to·bi·og·ra·phy (ô′təbīŏg′rəfĭ, -bĭ-), *n., pl.* **-phies.** an account of a person's life written by himself. **—au′to·bi·og′ra·pher,** *n.*

au·to·cade (ô′təkād′), *n.* a procession or train of motor vehicles. [f. AUTO-[2] + (CAVAL)CADE]

au·toch·thon (ôtŏk′thən), *n., pl.* **-thons, -thones** (-thə nēz′). **1.** an aboriginal inhabitant. **2.** *Ecol.* one of the indigenous animals or plants of a region. [t. Gk.: lit., sprung from the land itself]

au·toch·tho·nous (ôtŏk′thə nəs), *adj.* pertaining to autochthons; aboriginal; indigenous. Also, **au·toch′·tho·nal, au·toch·thon·ic** (ô′tŏk thŏn′ĭk). **—au·toch′·tho·nism, au·toch′tho·ny,** *n.*

au·to·clave (ô′təklāv′), *n.* **1.** a heavy vessel in which chemical reactions take place under high pressure. **2.** a pressure cooker. **3.** *Med.* a strong closed vessel in which steam under pressure effects sterilization. [t. F: self-regulation, f. *auto-* AUTO-[1] + m.s. L *clāvis* key]

au·toc·ra·cy (ôtŏk′rəsĭ), *n., pl.* **-cies. 1.** uncontrolled or unlimited authority over others, invested in a single person; the government or power of an absolute monarch. **2.** independent or self-derived power. [t. Gk.: m.s. *autokráteia* absolute power]

au·to·crat (ô′təkrăt′), *n.* **1.** an absolute ruler; a monarch who holds and exercises the powers of government as by inherent right, not subject to restrictions. **2.** a person invested with, or claiming to exercise, absolute authority. [t. Gk.: m.s. *autokratēs* ruling by oneself]

au·to·crat·ic (ô′təkrăt′ĭk), *adj.* pertaining to or of the nature of autocracy; absolute; holding independent and unlimited powers of government. Also, **au′to·crat′·i·cal. —au′to·crat′i·cal·ly,** *adv.*

au·to·da·fé (ô′tō də fā′), *n., pl.* **autos-da-fé.** the public declaration of the judgment passed on persons tried in the courts of the Spanish Inquisition, followed by execution of the sentences imposed, including burning (by civil authorities) of heretics at the stake. Also, *Spanish,* **au·to de fé** (ou′tō dĕ fĕ′). [t. Pg.: act of (the) faith]

au·toe·cism (ôtē′sĭzəm), *n. Bot.* the development of the entire life cycle of a parasitic fungus on a single host or group of hosts. Also, **autecism.** [f. AUT- + m.s. Gk. *oîkos* house + ISM] **—au·toe·cious** (ôtē′shəs), *adj.*

au·to·e·rot·ic (ô′tōĭrŏt′ĭk),*adj. Psychoanal.* producing sexual emotion without association with another person.

au·to·er·o·tism (ô′tōĕr′ətĭz′əm), *n. Psychoanal.* the arousal and satisfaction of sexual emotion within or by oneself, usually by masturbation. Also, **au·to·e·rot·i·cism** (ô′tō Ĭ rŏt′ə sĭz′əm).

au·tog·a·my (ôtŏg′əmĭ), *n. Bot.* fecundation of the ovules of a flower by its own pollen; self-fertilization (opposed to *allogamy*). **—au·tog′a·mous,** *adj.*

au·to·gen·e·sis (ô′tō jĕn′əsĭs), *n. Biol.* abiogenesis. Also, **au·tog·e·ny** (ôtŏj′ənĭ).

au·to·ge·net·ic (ô′tō jə nĕt′ĭk), *adj.* **1.** self-generated. **2.** *Biol.* of autogenesis. **—au′to·ge·net′i·cal·ly,** *adv.*

au·tog·e·nous (ôtŏj′ə nəs), *adj.* **1.** self-produced; self-generated. **2.** *Physiol.* pertaining to substances generated in the body. [f. s. Gk. *autogenēs* self-produced + -OUS] **—au·tog′e·nous·ly,** *adv.*

au·to·gi·ro (ô′tə jī′rō), *n., pl.* **-ros. 1.** an aircraft with horizontal revolving wings on a shaft above the fuselage which sustain the machine or allow it to descend slowly and steeply, forward propulsion being secured by a conventional propeller. **2.** (*cap.*) a trademark for this aircraft. Also, **au′to·gy′ro.** [t. Sp. See AUTO-[1], GYRO.]

au·to·graph (ô′təgrăf′, -gräf′), *n.* **1.** a person's own signature. **2.** a person's own handwriting. **3.** a manuscript in the author's handwriting. **—adj. 4.** written by a person's own hand: *an autograph letter.* **5.** containing autographs: *an autograph album.* **—v.t. 6.** to write one's name on or in: *to autograph a book.* **7.** to write with one's own hand. [t. L: s. *autographum,* t. Gk.: m. *autógraphon.* See AUTO-[1], -GRAPH] **—au′to·graph′ic, au′to·graph′i·cal,** *adj.* **—au′to·graph′i·cal·ly,** *adv*

au·tog·ra·phy (ôtŏg′rəfĭ), *n.* autograph writing.

au·to·harp (ô′tōhärp′), *n.* a zither played with the fingers or a plectrum, which is capable of playing chords by arrangements of dampers and is easily learned.

au·to·hyp·no·sis (ô′tō hĭp nō′sĭs), *n.* self-induced hypnosis or hynotic state. **—au·to·hyp·not·ic** (ô′tō-hĭp nŏt′ĭk), *adj.*

au·toi·cous (ôtoi′kəs), *adj. Bot.* having antheridia and archegonia on the same plant: synoicous, paroicous, or otherwise. [f. AUT(o)- + m. s. Gk. *oîkos* house + -OUS]

au·to·in·fec·tion (ô′tō ĭn fĕk′shən), *n. Pathol.* infection from within the body.

au·to·in·oc·u·la·tion (ô′tō Ĭn ŏk′yə lā′shən), *n.* inoculation of a healthy part with an infective agent from a diseased part of the same body.

au·to·in·tox·i·ca·tion (ô′tō Ĭn tŏk′sə kā′shən), *n. Pathol.* poisoning with toxic substances formed within the body, as during intestinal digestion.

au·to·ki·net·ic (ô′tō kĭ nĕt′ĭk, -kī-), *adj.* self-moving; automatic. Also, **au′to·ki·net′i·cal.** [f. s. Gk. *autokĭnētos* self-moved + -IC]

au·to·ly·sin (ô′tə lī′sĭn, ô tŏl′ə-), *n.* an autolytic agent.

au·tol·y·sis (ô tŏl′əsĭs), *n. Biochem.* the breakdown of plant or animal tissue by the action of enzymes contained in the tissue affected; self-digestion. [f. AUTO-[1] + -LYSIS] **—au·to·lyt·ic** (ô′tə lĭt′Ĭk), *adj.*

au·to·mat (ô′tə măt′), *n.* a restaurant using automatic apparatus for serving articles of food to customers upon the dropping of the proper coins or tokens into a slot. [t. Gk.: s. *autómaton.* See AUTOMATON]

au·tom·a·ta (ô tŏm′ə tə), *n.* pl. of automaton.

au·to·mate (ô′tə māt′), *v.t.* **-mated, -mating. 1.** to apply the principles of automation to (a mechanical process). **2.** to operate or control by automation. [back formation from AUTOMATION]

au·to·mat·ic (ô′tə māt′ĭk), *adj.* **1.** having the power of self-motion; self-moving or self-acting; mechanical. **2.** *Physiol.* occurring independently of volition, as certain muscular actions. **3.** (of a firearm, pistol, etc.) utilizing the recoil, or part of the force of the explosive, to eject the spent cartridge shell, introduce a new cartridge, cock the arm, and fire it repeatedly. **4.** done unconsciously or from force of habit; mechanical (opposed to *voluntary*). **—n. 5.** a machine which operates automatically. **6.** automatic rifle. **7.** automatic pistol. [f. s. Gk. *automatos* self-acting + -IC] **—au′to·mat′i·cal·ly,** *adv.* **—Syn. 2.** AUTOMATIC, INVOLUNTARY both mean not under the control of the will. That which is AUTOMATIC, however, is an invariable reaction to a fixed type of stimulus: *the patella reflex is automatic.* That which is INVOLUNTARY is an unexpected response which varies according to the occasion circumstances, mood, etc: *an involuntary cry of pain.*

automatic pilot, *Aeron.* an automatic steering device in an aircraft.

automatic pistol, a pistol that has a mechanism that throws out the empty shell, puts in a new one, and prepares the pistol to be fired again.

automatic rifle, a type of light machine gun which can be fired by single shots or automatically.

au·to·ma·tion (ô′tə mā′shən), *n.* the science of operating or controlling a mechanical process by highly automatic means, such as electronic devices. [b. AUTOM(ATIC) and (OPER)ATION]

au·tom·a·tism (ô tŏm′ə tĭz′əm), *n.* **1.** action or condition of being automatic; mechanical or involuntary action. **2.** *Philos.* the doctrine that all activities of animals, including men, are being controlled only by physiological causes, consciousness being considered a noncausal byproduct; epiphenomenonalism. **3.** *Physiol.* the involuntary functioning of an organic process, esp. muscular, without neural stimulation. **4.** *Psychol.* an act performed by an individual without his awareness or will, as sleepwalking. **5.** *Surrealism.* relaxing on

---

b., blend of, blended; c., cognate with; d., dialect, dialectal; der., derived from; f., formed from; g., going back to; m., modification of; r., replacing; s., stem of; t., taken from; ?, perhaps. See the full key on inside cover.

evading of conscious thought to bring unconscious and repressed ideas and feelings to artistic expression. —au·tom′a·tist, n.

au·tom·a·ton (ô·tŏm′ə·tŏn′, -tən), n., pl. -tons, -ta (-tə). 1. a mechanical figure or contrivance constructed to act as if spontaneously through concealed motive power. 2. a person who acts in a monotonous routine manner, without active intelligence. 3. something capable of acting spontaneously or without external impulse. [t. Gk., prop. neut. of automatos self-acting]

au·to·mo·bile (n. ô′tə·mə·bēl′, ô′tə·mō′bēl, -mə·bēl′; adj. ô′tə·mō′bĭl, -bēl), n. 1. Chiefly U.S. a vehicle, esp. one for passengers, carrying its own power-generating and propelling mechanism, for travel on ordinary roads. —adj. 2. automotive. [f. F. See AUTO-¹, MOBILE] —au·to·mo·bil·ist (ô′tə·mə·bē′lĭst, -mō′bĭl·ĭst), n.

au·to·mo·tive (ô′tə·mō′tĭv), adj. 1. pertaining to the design, operation, manufacture, and sale of automobiles. 2. propelled by a self-contained power plant.

au·to·nom·ic (ô′tə·nŏm′ĭk), adj. 1. autonomous. 2. Physiol. pertaining to or designating a system of nerves and ganglia (the autonomic, involuntary, or vegetative nervous system) leading from the spinal cord and brain to glands, blood vessels, the viscera, and the heart and smooth muscles, constituting their efferent innervation and controlling their involuntary functions (opposed to cerebrospinal). 3. Bot. produced by internal forces or causes; spontaneous. —au′to·nom′i·cal·ly, adv.

au·ton·o·mous (ô·tŏn′ə·məs), adj. 1. Govt. a. self-governing; independent; subject to its own laws only. b. pertaining to an autonomy. 2. Biol. existing as an independent organism and not as a mere form or state of development of an organism. 3. Bot. spontaneous. [t. Gk.: m. autónomos (def. 1)] —au·ton′o·mous·ly, adv.

au·ton·o·my (ô·tŏn′ə·mĭ), n., pl. -mies. Govt. 1. the condition of being autonomous; self-government, or the right of self-government; independence. 2. a self-governing community. [t. Gk.: m. s. autonomía] —au·ton′o·mist, n.

au·to·plas·ty (ô′tə·plăs′tĭ), n. Surg. the repair of defects with tissue from another part of the patient. [f. s. Gk. autóplastos self-formed + -Y³] —au′to·plas′tic, adj.

au·top·sy (ô′tŏp·sĭ, ô′təp-), n., pl. -sies. 1. inspection and dissection of a body after death, as for determination of the cause of death; a post-mortem examination. 2. personal observation. [t. Gk.: m. s. autopsía seeing with one's own eyes]

au·to·some (ô′tə·sōm′), n. Genetics. any chromosome other than the sex chromosome in species having both types of chromosomes.

au·to·sug·ges·tion (ô′tō·səg·jĕs′chən), n. Psychol. suggestion arising from within a person (as opposed to one from an outside source, esp. another person).

au·tot·o·my (ô·tŏt′ə·mĭ), n. Zool. self-crippling by casting off damaged or trapped appendages such as tails by lizards, legs by spiders and crabs, etc.

au·to·tox·e·mi·a (ô′tō·tŏk·sē′mĭ·ə), n. auto-intoxication. Also, au′to·tox·ae·mi·a.

au·to·tox·in (ô′tə·tŏk′sĭn), n. Pathol. a toxin or poisonous principle formed within the body and acting against it. —au′to·tox′ic, adj.

au·to·troph·ic (ô′tə·trŏf′ĭk), adj. Bot. (of plants) building their own nutritive substances, esp. by photosynthesis or chemosynthesis.

au·to·truck (ô′tō·trŭk′), n. an automobile truck.

au·to·type (ô′tə·tīp′), n. 1. facsimile. 2. a photographic process for producing permanent prints in a carbon pigment. 3. a picture so produced. —au·to·typ·ic (ô′tə·tĭp′ĭk), adj. —au·to·typ·y (ô′tə·tī′pĭ), n.

au·tox·i·da·tion (ô tŏk′sə·dā′shən), n. Chem. 1. the oxidation of a compound by its exposure to air. 2. an oxidation reaction in which another substance must be included for the reaction to be completed.

au·tumn (ô′təm), n. 1. the third season of the year, between summer and winter; fall. (In the U.S. autumn is formal or poetic; in England it is the usual word.) 2. a period of maturity passing into decline. [t. L: s. autumnus; r. ME autompne, t. OF]

au·tum·nal (ô·tŭm′nəl), adj. 1. belonging to or suggestive of autumn; produced or gathered in autumn. 2. past maturity or middle life. —au·tum′nal·ly, adv.

autumnal equinox. See equinox (def. 1). Also, autumnal point.

au·tun·ite (ô′tə·nīt′), n. a yellow mineral, a hydrous calcium uranium phosphate, $CaU_2P_2O_{12}.8H_2O$, occurring in crystals as nearly square tablets: a minor ore of uranium. [named after Autun, city in eastern France. See -ITE¹]

Au·vergne (ō vârn′, ō vûrn′; Fr. ō vĕrn′y), n. a former province in central France.

aux (ō), French. to the; at the; with the. See à la.

aux., auxiliary. Also, auxil.

Aux Cayes (ō kā′), former name of Les Cayes.

aux·il·i·a·ry (ôg zĭl′yə·rĭ, -zĭl′ə-), adj., n., pl. -ries. —adj. 1. giving support; helping; aiding; assisting. 2. subsidiary; additional: auxiliary troops. 3. used as a reserve: an auxiliary engine. —n. 4. person or thing that gives aid of any kind; helper. 5. auxiliary verb. 6. (pl.) foreign troops in the service of a nation at war. 7. Naval. a naval vessel designed for other than combat purposes, as a tug, supply ship, transport, etc. 8. a sailing vessel

carrying auxiliary power. [t. L: m.s. auxiliārius, der. auxilium aid] —Syn. 2. subordinate, ancillary. 4. ally.

auxiliary verb, a verb customarily preceding certain forms of other verbs, used to express distinctions of time, aspect, mood, etc., as do, am, etc., in I do think; I am going; we have spoken; may we go?; can they see?; we shall walk.

aux·in (ôk′sĭn), n. Bot., Chem. a class of substances which in minute amounts regulate or modify the growth of plants, esp. root formation, bud growth, fruit and leaf drop, etc. [? var. of auxein, f. Gk. aúxē increase + -IN²]

aux·o·chrome (ôk′sə·krōm′), n. Chem. any group of atoms which make a chromogen acidic or basic, giving it the ability to adhere to wool and silk. [f. auxo- (repr. Gk. auxánein increase) + CHROME]

av., 1. avenue. 2. average. 3. avoirdupois.
A/V, ad valorem. Also, a.v.
A.V., Authorized Version (of the Bible).

a·vail (ə vāl′), v.i. 1. to have force or efficacy; be of use; serve. 2. to be of value or profit. —v.t. 3. to be of use or value to; profit; advantage. 4. avail oneself of, to give oneself the advantage of. —n. 5. efficacy for a purpose; advantage to an object or end: of little or no avail. 6. (pl.) profits or proceeds. [ME. f. OF: a- A-⁵ + vail, 1st person sing. pres. indic. of valoir, g. L valēre be strong, have effect] —a·vail′ing·ly, adv.

a·vail·a·bil·i·ty (ə vā′lə·bĭl′ə·tĭ), n., pl. -ties. 1. state of being available: the availability of a candidate. 2. that which or one who is available.

a·vail·a·ble (ə vā′lə·bəl), adj. 1. suitable or ready for use; at hand; of use or service: available resources. 2. having sufficient power or efficacy; valid. 3. Archaic. profitable; advantageous. —a·vail′a·ble·ness, n. —a·vail′a·bly, adv. —Syn. 1. accessible, usable.

av·a·lanche (ăv′ə·lănch′, -länch′), n., v., -lanched, -lanching. —n. 1. a large mass of snow, ice, etc., detached from a mountain slope and sliding or falling suddenly downward. 2. anything like an avalanche in suddenness and destructiveness: an avalanche of misfortunes. —v.i. 3. to come down in, or like, an avalanche. [b. d. F avalanche (der. OF avaler go down, der. L ad- AD- + vallis valley) and d. F (Swiss) lavenche of pre-Latin orig.]

Av·a·lon (ăv′ə·lŏn′; Fr. à và lôn′), n. Celtic Legend. an island represented as an earthly paradise in the western seas, to which King Arthur and other heroes were carried at death. Also, Av′al·lon′. [t. ML: s. (insula island) Avallōnis (Geoffrey of Monmouth)]

a·vant-garde (à vän gàrd′), n. French. the vanguard.

av·a·rice (ăv′ə·rĭs), n. insatiable greed for riches; inordinate, miserly desire to gain and hoard wealth. [ME, t. OF, t. L: m.s. avāritia greed] —Syn. cupidity.

av·a·ri·cious (ăv′ə·rĭsh′əs), adj. characterized by avarice; greedy of wealth; covetous. —av′a·ri·cious·ly, adv. —av′a·ri·cious·ness, n.

a·vast (ə văst′, ə väst′), interj. Naut. stop! hold! cease! stay! [prob. t. D: m. houd vast hold fast]

av·a·tar (ăv′ə tär′), n. 1. Hindu Myth. the descent of a deity to the earth in an incarnate form or some manifest shape; the incarnation of a god. 2. a concrete manifestation; embodiment. [t. Skt.: m. avatāra descent]

a·vaunt (ə vônt′, ə vänt′), adv. Archaic. away! go! [ME, t. F: m. avant forward, g. L abante from before]

A.V.C., American Veterans' Committee, an organization of veterans of World War II.

avdp., avoirdupois.

a·ve (ä′vĭ, ä′vā), interj. 1. hail! welcome! 2. farewell! good-by! —n. 3. the salutation "ave." 4. (cap.) Ave Maria. 5. (cap.) the time for the recitation of the Angelus, so called because the Ave Maria is thrice repeated in it. [t. L, impv. of avēre be or fare well]

Ave., avenue. Also, ave.

Ave·bur·y (āv′bər·ĭ), n. See Lubbock, Sir John.

a·vec plai·sir (à věk′ plě zēr′), French. with pleasure.

A·vel·la·ne·da (ä vě′yä nĕ′dä), n. a city in E Argentina, near Buenos Aires. 285,000 (est. 1952).

A·ve Ma·ri·a (ä′vĭ mə rē′ə, ä′vā), 1. the "Hail, Mary," a prayer in the Roman Catholic Church, based on the salutation of the angel Gabriel to the Virgin Mary and the words of Elizabeth to her. Luke 1:28, 42. 2. the hour for saying the prayer. 3. a recitation of this prayer. 4. the bead or beads on a rosary used to count off each prayer as spoken. Also, A·ve Mar·y (ä′vĭ mâr′ĭ). [L: hail, Mary]

av·e·na·ceous (ăv′ə nā′shəs), adj. Bot. of or like oats; of the oat kind. [t. L: m. avēnāceus, der. avēna oats]

a·venge (ə věnj′), v., avenged, avenging. —v.t. 1. to take vengeance or exact satisfaction for: to avenge a death. 2. to take vengeance on behalf of: avenge your brother. —v.i. 3. to take vengeance. [ME avenge(n), t. OF: m. avengier, f. a- A-⁵ + vengier revenge, g. L vindicāre punish] —a·veng′er, n. —a·veng′ing·ly, adv.

—Syn. 1, 2. AVENGE, REVENGE both mean to inflict pain or harm in return for pain or harm inflicted on oneself or those persons or causes to which one feels loyalty. The two words were formerly interchangeable, but have been differentiated until they now convey widely diverse ideas. AVENGE is now restricted to inflicting punishment as an act of retributive justice or as a vindication of the right: to avenge a murder by bringing the criminal to trial. REVENGE implies inflicting pain or harm to retaliate for real or fancied wrongs; a reflexive pronoun is now always used with this verb: Iago wished to revenge himself upon Othello.

av·ens (ăv′ĭnz), *n.* any of the perennial rosaceous herbs constituting the genus *Geum*. [ME, t. OF: m. *avence*, t. ML: m.s. *avencia* kind of clover]

Av·en·tine (ăv′ən tīn′, -tĭn), *n.* one of the seven hills on which Rome was built. [t. L: m.s. *Aventīnus*]

a·ven·tu·rine (ə vĕn′chərĭn), *n.* 1. an opaque, brown glass containing fine, gold-colored particles. 2. any of several varieties of minerals, esp. quartz or feldspar, spangled with bright particles of mica, hematite, or other minerals. Also, **a·ven′tu·rin.** [t. F, t. It.: m. *avventurina*, der. *avventura* chance (the mineral being rare and found only by chance)]

av·e·nue (ăv′ə nū′, -nōō′), *n.* 1. a wide street. 2. the main way of approach, usually lined with trees, through grounds to a country house or monumental building (in England, limited to one bordered by trees). 3. a way or an opening for entrance into a place: *the avenue to India.* 4. means of access or attainment: *avenue of escape, avenues of success.* [t. F, orig. pp. fem. of *avenir*, g. L *advenīre* come to] —**Syn.** 1. See **street.**

a·ver (ə vûr′), *v.t.,* **averred, averring.** 1. to affirm with confidence; declare in a positive or peremptory manner. 2. *Law.* to allege as a fact. [ME *aver(en)*, t. OF: s. *averer*, ult. der. L *ad-* AD- + *vērus* true]

av·er·age (ăv′ər ĭj, ăv′rĭj), *n., adj., v.,* **-aged, -aging.** —*n.* 1. an arithmetical mean. 2. *Math.* a quantity intermediate to a set of quantities. 3. the ordinary, normal, or typical amount, rate, quality, kind, etc.; the common run. 4. *Com.* **a.** a small charge paid by the master on account of the ship and cargo, such as pilotage, towage, etc. **b.** an expense, partial loss, or damage to ship or cargo. **c.** the incidence of such an expense or loss on the owners or their insurers. **d.** an equitable apportionment among all the interested parties of such an expense or loss. —*adj.* 5. of or pertaining to an average; estimated by average; forming an average. 6. intermediate, medial, or typical in amount, rate, quality, etc. —*v.t.* 7. to find an average value for; reduce to a mean. 8. to result in, as an arithmetical mean; amount to, as a mean quantity: *wheat averages 56 pounds to a bushel.* —*v.i.* 9. *U.S.* to have or show an average: *to average as expected.* 10. **average down,** to purchase more of a security or commodity at a lower price to reduce the average cost of one's holdings. 11. **average up,** to purchase more of a security or commodity at a higher price to take advantage of a contemplated further rise in prices. [cf. F *avarie* customs duty, etc. c. It. *avaria*, t. Ar.: m. *'awārīya* damages. See -AGE] —**a·ver·age·ly,** *adv.*

a·ver·ment (ə vûr′mənt), *n.* 1. act of averring. 2. a positive statement.

A·ver·nus (ə vûr′nəs), *n.* 1. a lake near Naples, Italy, looked upon by the ancients as an entrance to hell, from whose waters vile-smelling vapors arose, supposedly killing birds over it. 2. hell. [t. L] —**A·ver′nal,** *adj.*

A·ver·ro·ës (ə vĕr′ō ēz′), *n.* 1126?–1198, Arabian philosopher in Spain: influence on Christian and Jewish thought. Arabic, **ibn-Rushd.** Also, **A·ver′rho·ës′.**

Av·er·ro·ism (ăv′ə rō′ĭz əm), *n.* the philosophy of Averroës, consisting chiefly of a pantheistic interpretation of the doctrines of Aristotle. Also, **Av′er·rho′ism.** —**Av′er·ro′ist,** *n.* —**Av′er·ro·is′tic,** *adj.*

a·verse (ə vûrs′), *adj.* 1. disinclined, reluctant, or opposed: *averse to* (formerly *from*) *flattery.* 2. *Bot.* turned away from the central axis (opposed to *adverse*). [t.L: m.s. *āversus*, pp., turned away] —**a·verse′ly,** *adv.* —**a·verse′ness,** *n.* —**Syn.** 1. unwilling, loath. See **reluctant.**

a·ver·sion (ə vûr′zhən, -shən), *n.* 1. an averted state of the mind or feelings; repugnance, antipathy, or rooted dislike (usually fol. by *to*). 2. a cause of dislike; an object of repugnance. 3. *Obs.* a turning away. —**Syn.** 1. distaste, abhorrence. AVERSION, ANTIPATHY, LOATHING connote strong dislike or detestation. AVERSION is an unreasoning desire to avoid that which displeases, annoys, or offends: *an aversion to* (or *toward*) *cats.* ANTIPATHY is a distaste, dislike, or disgust toward something: *an antipathy toward* (or *for*) *braggarts.* LOATHING connotes a combination of hatred and disgust, or detestation: *a loathing for* (or *toward*) *venison, a criminal.*

a·vert (ə vûrt′), *v.t.* 1. to turn away or aside: *to avert one's eyes.* 2. to ward off; prevent: *to avert evil.* [ME, t. OF: s. *avertir,* g. L *āvertere* turn away] —**a·vert′er,** *n.* —**a·vert′i·ble, a·vert′a·ble,** *adj.*

a·ver·tin (ə vûr′tĭn), *n.* 1. tribromoethanol. 2. (*cap.*) a trademark for it.

A·ves (ā′vēz), *n.pl. Zool.* the class of vertebrates comprising the birds, distinguished from all other animals by their feathers, and from their closest relatives, the *Reptilia,* by their warm-bloodedness, the hard shell of their eggs, and significant anatomical features. [t. L, pl. of *avis* bird]

A·ves·ta (ə vĕs′tə), *n.* the Books of Wisdom, or sacred scriptures, of Zoroastrianism.

A·ves·tan (ə vĕs′tən), *n.* 1. the language of the Avesta, closely related to Old Persian. —*adj.* 2. of or pertaining to the Avesta or its language. [f. AVESTA + -AN]

avi-, a word element meaning "bird". [t. L, comb. form of *avis* bird]

a·vi·an (ā′vĭ ən), *adj. Zool.* of or pertaining to birds.

a·vi·ar·y (ā′vĭ ĕr′ĭ), *n., pl.* **-aries.** a large cage or a house or enclosure in which birds are kept. [t. L: m. s. *aviārium,* der. *avis* bird]

a·vi·ate (ā′vĭ āt′, ăv′ĭ-), *v.i.,* **-ated, -ating.** to fly in an aircraft. [back formation from AVIATION]

a·vi·a·tion (ā′vĭ ā′shən, ăv′ĭ-), *n.* 1. act, art, or science of flying by mechanical means, esp. with heavier-than-air craft. 2. the aircraft (with its equipment) of an air force. [t. F. See AVI-, -ATION]

a·vi·a·tor (ā′vĭ ā′tər, ăv′ĭ-), *n.* a pilot of an airplane or other heavier-than-air craft. —**a·vi·a·trix** (ā′vĭ ā′trĭks, ăv′ĭ-), **a·vi·a·tress** (ā′vĭ ā′trĭs, ăv′ĭ-), *n. fem.*

Av·i·cen·na (ăv′ə sĕn′ə), *n.* A.D. 980–1037, Arabian physician and philosopher. Arabic, **ibn-Sina.**

a·vi·cul·ture (ā′vĭ kŭl′chər), *n.* the rearing or keeping of birds. —**a′vi·cul′tur·ist,** *n.*

av·id (ăv′ĭd), *adj.* 1. keenly desirous; eager; greedy (often fol. by *of* or *for*): *avid of pleasure or power.* 2. keen: *avid hunger.* [t. L: s. *avidus* eager] —**av′id·ly,** *adv.*

av·i·din (ăv′ə dĭn, ə vĭd′ĭn), *n. Biochem.* a substance found in the white of egg which prevents the action of biotin and thus injures the egg white.

a·vid·i·ty (ə vĭd′ə tĭ), *n.* eagerness; greediness.

a·vi·fau·na (ā′və fô′nə), *n.* the birds of a given region; avian fauna. —**a′vi·fau′nal,** *adj.*

av·i·ga·tion (ăv′ə gā′shən), *n.* aerial navigation. [b AVIATION and NAVIGATION]

A·vi·gnon (ȧ vē nyôⁿ′), *n.* a city in SE France, on the Rhone river: papal residence, 1309–77. 62,768 (1954).

Á·vi·la Ca·ma·cho (ȧ′vē lȧ′ kȧ mä′chō), **Manuel** (mä nwĕl′), 1897–1955, president of Mexico, 1940–46.

a·vion (ȧ vyôⁿ′), *n. French.* airplane.

a·vi·ru·lent (ā′vĭr′yə lənt, ā vĭr′ə-), *adj.* (of organisms) having no virulence, as a result of age, heat, etc.

a·vi·so (ə vī′zō), *n., pl.* **-sos.** 1. dispatch. 2. a boat used esp. for carrying dispatches. [t. Sp.]

a·vi·ta·min·o·sis (ā vī′tə mə nō′sĭs, ā′və tăm′ə nō′sĭs), *n. Pathol.* a disease caused by a lack of vitamins. [f. A-⁶ + VITAMIN + -OSIS]

A·vlo·na (äv lō′nä), *n.* Valona.

av·o·ca·do (ăv′ə kä′dō, ä′və-), *n., pl.* **-dos.** 1. a tropical American fruit, green to black in color and commonly pear-shaped, borne by the lauraceous tree, *Persea americana,* and its variety *drymifolia,* eaten raw, esp. as a salad fruit; alligator pear. 2. the tree. [t. d. Sp. (prop. lawyer), alter. of *aguacate,* t. Mex.: m. *ahuacatl*]

Avocado,
Persea americana

av·o·ca·tion (ăv′ə kā′shən), *n.* 1. a minor or occasional occupation; a hobby. 2. *Colloq.* one's regular occupation, calling, or vocation. 3. *Archaic.* diversion or distraction. 4. *Obs.* a calling away. [t. L: s. *āvocātio* a calling off]

a·voc·a·to·ry (ə vŏk′ə tōr′ĭ), *adj.* calling away, off, or back.

av·o·cet (ăv′ə sĕt′), *n.* any of several long-legged, web-footed shore birds constituting the genus *Recurvirostra,* of both New World and Old, having a long, slender beak curving upward toward the end. Also, **avoset.** [t. F: m. *avocette.* t. It.: m. *avocetta*]

A·vo·ga·dro (ä′vō gä′drō), *n.* **Count Amadeo** (ä′mä dĕ′ō), 1776–1856, Italian physicist and chemist.

a·void (ə void′), *v.t.* 1. to keep away from; keep clear of; shun; evade: *to avoid a person or a danger.* 2. *Law.* to make void or of no effect; invalidate. 3. *Obs.* to empty; eject or expel. [ME *avoide(n),* t. AF: m. *avoider,* var. of OF *esvuidier* empty out; f. *es-* EX-¹ + *vuidier* (g. L *viduāre*) empty. See VOID, adj.] —**a·void′a·ble,** *adj.* —**a·void′a·bly,** *adv.* —**a·void′er,** *n.* —**Syn.** 1. AVOID, ESCAPE mean to come through peril, actual or potential, without suffering serious consequences. To AVOID is to succeed in keeping away from something harmful or undesirable: *to avoid meeting an enemy.* ESCAPE suggests encountering peril but coming through it safely: *to escape drowning.*

a·void·ance (ə voi′dəns), *n.* 1. act of keeping away from: *avoidance of scandal.* 2. *Law.* a making void.

avoir., avoirdupois.

av·oir·du·pois (ăv′ər də poiz′), *n.* 1. avoirdupois weight. 2. *U.S. Colloq.* weight. [ME *avoir de pois,* t. OF: goods sold by weight, lit., to have weight]

avoirdupois weight, the system of weights in British and U. S. use for goods other than gems, precious metals, and drugs: $27^{11}/_{32}$ grains = 1 dram; 16 drams = 1 ounce; 16 ounces = 1 pound; 112 pounds (Brit.) or 100 pounds (U. S.) = 1 hundredweight; 20 hundredweight = 1 ton. The pound contains 7000 grains.

A·von (ā′vən, ăv′ən), *n.* 1. a river in central England, flowing SE past Stratford (Shakespeare's birthplace) to the Severn. 80 mi. 2. a river in S England, flowing W to the mouth of the Severn. 75 mi. 3. a river in S England, flowing S to the English Channel. ab. 60 mi.

av·o·set (ăv′ə sĕt′), *n.* avocet.

à vo·tre san·té (ȧ vô′tr săn tĕ′), *French.* to your health.

a·vouch (ə vouch′), *v.t.* 1. to make frank acknowledgment or affirmation of; declare or assert with positiveness. 2. to assume responsibility for; guarantee. 3. to admit; confess. [ME *avouche(n),* t. OF: m. *avochier,* t. L: m. *advocāre* summon] —**a·vouch′ment,** *n.*

a·vow (ə vou′), *v.t.* to declare frankly or openly; own; acknowledge; confess: *to avow one's principles.* [ME *avowe(n),* t. OF: m. *avoer,* g. L *advocāre* summon] —**a·vow′a·ble,** *adj.* —**a·vow′er,** *n.*

a·vow·al (ə vou′əl), *n.* an open statement of affirmation; frank acknowledgment or admission.

a·vowed (ə voud′), *adj.* acknowledged; declared: *an avowed enemy.* —**a·vow·ed·ly** (ə vou′ĭd lĭ), *adv.* —**a·vow′ed·ness,** *n.*

a·vul·sed (ə vŭl′sĭd), *adj. Surg.* (of a wound) having the tissue torn away.

a·vul·sion (ə vŭl′shən), *n.* **1.** a tearing away. **2.** *Law.* the sudden removal of soil by change in a river's course or by a flood, from the land of one owner to that of another. **3.** a part torn off. [t. L: s. *āvulsio*]

a·vun·cu·lar (ə vŭng′kyə lər), *adj.* **1.** of or pertaining to an uncle: *avuncular affection.* **2.** *Humorous.* of or pertaining to a pawnbroker. [f. s. L *avunculus* uncle (dim. of *avus* grandfather) + -AR¹]

a·wa (ə wô′, ə wä′), *adv. Scot.* away.

a·wait (ə wāt′), *v.t.* **1.** to wait for; look for or expect. **2.** to be in store for; be ready for. **3.** *Obs.* to lie in wait for. —*v.i.* **4.** to wait as in expectation. [ME *awaite(n),* t. ONF: m. *awaitier,* f. a- A⁻⁵ + *waitier* watch. See WAIT] —**Syn.** 1. See **expect.**

a·wake (ə wāk′), *v.,* **awoke** or **awaked, awaking,** *adj.* —*v.t., v.i.* **1.** to wake up; rouse from sleep. **2.** to come or bring to a realization of the truth; to rouse to action, attention, etc.: *he awoke to the realities of life.* —*adj.* **3.** waking; not sleeping. **4.** vigilant; alert: *awake to a danger.* [ME; OE *weak* v. *awacian* and (for pret. and pp.) OE strong v. *onwæcnan,* later *awæcnan* (pret. *onwōc, awōc,* pp. *onwacen, awacen*)]

a·wak·en (ə wā′kən), *v.t., v.i.* to awake; waken. [ME *awak(e)ne(n),* OE *onwæcnian,* later *awæcnian*] —**a·wak′en·er,** *n.*

a·wak·en·ing (ə wā′kən ĭng), *adj.* **1.** rousing; alarming. —*n.* **2.** act of awaking from sleep. **3.** a revival of interest or attention.

a·ward (ə wôrd′), *v.t.* **1.** to adjudge to be due or merited; assign or bestow: *to award prizes.* **2.** to bestow by judicial decree; assign or appoint by deliberate judgment, as in arbitration. —*n.* **3.** something awarded, as a payment or medal. **4.** *Law.* **a.** a decision after consideration; a judicial sentence. **b.** the decision of arbitrators on points submitted to them. [ME *awarde(n),* t. AF: m. *awarder,* var. of *esguarder* observe, decide, f.: *ex* EX¹- + *guardāre* watch, guard, of Gmc. orig.] —**a·ward′a·ble,** *adj.* —**a·ward′er,** *n.*

a·ware (ə wâr′), *adj.* cognizant or conscious (*of*); informed: *aware of the danger.* [ME; OE *gewær* watchful. See WARE², WARY] —**a·ware′ness,** *n.* —**Syn.** See **conscious.**

a·wash (ə wŏsh′, ə wôsh′), *adv., adj.* **1.** *Naut.* just level with the surface of the water, so that the waves break over. **2.** covered with water. **3.** washing about; tossed about by the waves.

a·way (ə wā′), *adv.* **1.** from this or that place; off: *to go away.* **2.** far; apart: *away back, away from the subject.* **3.** aside: *turn your eyes away.* **4.** out of possession, notice, use, or existence: *to give money away.* **5.** continuously; on: *to blaze away.* **6.** without hesitation: *fire away.* **7.** away with, take away: *away with this man.* **8.** do or make away with, to put out of existence; get rid of; kill. —*adj.* **9.** absent: *away from home.* **10.** distant: *six miles away.* [ME; OE *aweg,* earlier *on weg* on way]

awe (ô), *n., v.,* **awed, awing.** —*n.* **1.** respectful or reverential fear, inspired by what is grand or sublime: *in awe of God.* **2.** *Archaic.* power to inspire fear or reverence. **3.** *Obs.* fear or dread. —*v.t.* **4.** to inspire with awe. **5.** to influence or restrain by awe. [ME, t. Scand.; cf. Icel. *agi* fear]

a·weath·er (ə wĕth′ər), *adv., adj. Naut.* on or to the weather side; toward the wind.

a·weigh (ə wā′), *adj. Naut.* (of an anchor) raised just enough to be clear of the bottom.

awe·less (ô′lĭs), *adj.* awless.

awe·some (ô′səm), *adj.* **1.** inspiring awe. **2.** characterized by awe. —**awe′some·ly,** *adv.* —**awe′some·ness,** *n.*

awe-struck (ô′strŭk′), *adj.* filled with awe. Also, **awe-strick·en** (ô′strĭk′ən).

aw·ful (ô′fəl), *adj.* **1.** inspiring fear; dreadful; terrible. **2.** *Colloq.* extremely bad; unpleasant; ugly. **3.** *Colloq.* very; very great. **4.** full of awe; reverential. **5.** inspiring reverential awe; solemnly impressive. [ME; f. AWE + -FUL, r. OE *egeful* dreadful] —**aw′ful·ly,** *adv.* —**aw′ful·ness,** *n.*

a·while (ə hwīl′), *adv.* for a short time or period.

awk·ward (ôk′wərd), *adj.* **1.** lacking dexterity or skill; clumsy; bungling. **2.** ungraceful; ungainly; uncouth: *awkward gestures.* **3.** ill-adapted for use or handling; unhandy: *an awkward method.* **4.** requiring caution; somewhat hazardous: *there's an awkward step there.* **5.** difficult to handle; dangerous: *an awkward customer.* **6.** embarrassing or trying: *an awkward predicament.* **7.** *Obs.* untoward; perverse. [f. *auk* backhanded (t. Scand.; cf. Icel. *öfugr* turned the wrong way) + -WARD] —**awk′ward·ly,** *adv.* —**awk′ward·ness,** *n.* —**Syn.** 1. unskillful, unhandy, inexpert; inept.

awl (ôl), *n. Carp., etc.* a pointed instrument for piercing small holes in leather, wood, etc. [ME *al,* OE *æl,* c. G *ahle*]

A. Bradawl; B. Sewing awl

aw·less (ô′lĭs), *adj.* without awe; fearless; not to be awed. Also, **awe·less.**

awl·wort (ôl′wûrt′), *n.* a small, stemless, aquatic

cruciferous plant, *Subularia aquatica,* with slender, sharp-pointed leaves.

awn (ôn), *n. Bot.* **1.** a bristlelike appendage of a plant, esp. on the glumes of grasses. **2.** such appendages collectively, as those forming the beard of wheat, barley, etc. **3.** any similar bristle. [ME, t. Scand.; cf. Sw. *agn,* Icel. *ögn* husk] —**awned,** *adj.* —**awn′less,** *adj.*

awn·ing (ô′nĭng), *n.* **1.** a rooflike shelter of canvas, etc., before a window or door, over a deck, etc., as for protection from the sun. **2.** a shelter. [orig. unknown]

a·woke (ə wōk′), *v.* pt. and pp. of **awake.**

A.W.O.L. (*pronounced as initials or,* in *Mil. slang,* ā′wŏl), *Mil.* absent without leave.

a·wry (ə rī′), *adv., adj.* **1.** with a turn or twist to one side; askew: *to glance or look awry.* **2.** away from reason or the truth. **3.** amiss; wrong: *our plans went awry.* [ME *on wry.* See A-¹, WRY]

ax (ăks), *n., pl.* **axes,** *v.,* **axed, axing.** —*n.* **1.** an instrument with a bladed head on a handle or helve, used for hewing, cleaving, chopping, etc. **2.** have an ax to grind, *Orig. U.S.* to have a private purpose or selfish end to attain. —*v.t.* **3.** to shape or trim with an ax. Also, **axe.** [ME; OE *æx,* akin to G *axt,* L *ascia,* Gk. *axīnē*] —**ax′like′,** *adj.*

ax., axiom.

ax·es¹ (ăk′sēz), *n.* pl. of **axis.**

ax·es² (ăk′sĭz), *n.* pl. of **ax.**

ax·i·al (ăk′sĭ əl), *adj.* **1.** of, pertaining to, or forming an axis. **2.** situated in an axis or on the axis. Also, **ax·ile** (ăk′sĭl, -sīl).

ax·i·al·ly (ăk′sĭ əlĭ), *adv.* in the line of the axis.

ax·il (ăk′sĭl), *n. Bot.* the angle between the upper side of a leaf or stem and the supporting stem or branch. [t. L: m.s. *azilla* armpit]

ax·il·la (ăk sĭl′ə), *n., pl.* **axil·lae** (ăk sĭl′ē). **1.** *Anat.* the armpit. **2.** *Ornith.* the corresponding region on a bird. **3.** *Bot.* an axil. [t. L]

ax·il·lar (ăk′sə lər), *n. Ornith.* (*usually pl.*) a feather growing from the axilla (def. 2).

A. Axil

ax·il·lar·y (ăk′sə lĕr′ĭ), *adj., n., pl.* **-laries.** —*adj.* **1.** pertaining to the axilla. **2.** *Bot.* pertaining to or growing from the axil (of plants). —*n.* **3.** *Ornith.* axillar.

ax·i·ol·o·gy (ăk′sĭ ŏl′ə jĭ), *n. Philos.* the science of values in general, including ethics, aesthetics, religion, etc. [f. Gk. *áxio(s)* worthy + -LOGY] —**ax·i·o·log·i·cal** (ăk′sĭ ə lŏj′ə kəl), *adj.*

ax·i·om (ăk′sĭ əm), *n.* **1.** a recognized truth. **2.** an established and universally accepted principle or rule. **3.** *Logic, Math., etc.* a proposition which is assumed without proof for the sake of studying the consequences that follow from it. [t. L: m. *axīoma,* t. Gk.: a requisite]

ax·i·o·mat·ic (ăk′sĭ ə măt′ĭk), *adj.* **1.** pertaining to or of the nature of an axiom; self-evident. **2.** aphoristic. Also, **ax′i·o·mat′i·cal.** —**ax′i·o·mat′i·cal·ly,** *adv.*

ax·is¹ (ăk′sĭs), *n., pl.* **axes** (ăk′sēz). **1.** the line about which a rotating body, such as the earth, turns. **2.** the central line of any symmetrical, or nearly symmetrical, body: *the axis of a cylinder, of the eye, etc.* **3.** *Anat.* **a.** a central or principal structure, about which something turns or is arranged: *the skeletal axis.* **b.** the second cervical vertebra. **4.** *Bot.* the longitudinal support on which organs or parts are arranged; the stem, root; the central line of any body. **5.** *Aeron.* any one of three lines defining the attitude of an airplane, one being generally determined by the direction of forward motion and the other two at right angles to it. **6.** *Fine Arts.* one or more theoretical central lines around which an artistic form is organized or composed. **7.** an alliance of two or more nations to coördinate their foreign and military policies, and to draw in with them a group of dependent or supporting powers. **8.** the Axis, the alliance of Germany, Italy, and Japan prior to and during World War II, beginning with the Rome-Berlin Axis (1936). [t. L: axle, axis, board. Cf. AXLE]

ax·is² (ăk′sĭs), *n.* any of several species of East Asiatic deer, as *Axis axis* and related forms, with white spots. Also, **axis** deer. [t. L]

ax·le (ăk′səl), *n.* **1.** *Mach.* the pin, bar, shaft, or the like, on which or with which a wheel or pair of wheels rotate. **2.** either end (spindle) of an axletree or the like. **3.** the whole (fixed) axletree, or a similar bar connecting and turning with two opposite wheels of a vehicle. [OE *earl(e)* shoulder, crossbeam (in *eazle-gespann* crossbeam attachment place). Cf. Icel. *öxl* shoulder, axle]

ax·le·tree (ăk′səl trē′), *n.* a bar fixed crosswise under an animal-drawn vehicle, with a rounded spindle at each end upon which a wheel rotates. [ME, f. AXLE + TREE]

ax·man (ăks′mən), *n., pl.* **-men.** one who wields an ax.

Ax·min·ster carpet (ăks′mĭn′stər), a kind of carpet having a stiff jute back and a cut pile of wool.

ax·o·lotl (ăk′sə lŏt′əl), *n., pl.* **axolotyles.** **1.** any of several Mexican salamanders that breed in the larval stage, in Mexico prized as food. **2.** the larva of any salamander (esp. of the genus *Ambystoma*

Axolotl, *Ambystoma mexicanus* (6 to 12 in. long)

ăct, āble, dâre, ärt; ĕbb, ēqual; ĭf, īce; hŏt, ōver, ôrder, oil, bŏŏk, ōōze, out; ŭp, ūse, ûrge; ə = a in alone; ch, chief; g, give; ng, ring; sh, shoe; th, thin; ŧħ, that; zh, vision.   See the full key on inside cover.

that matures sexually in the larval stage. [t. Mex.]

ax·on (ăk′sŏn), *n. Anat.* the appendage of the neuron which transmits impulses away from the cell. Also, **ax·one** (ăk′sōn). [t. Gk.: axis]

ax·seed (ăks′sēd′), *n.* an Old World fabaceous plant, *Cornilla varia,* with pink flowers, naturalized in the U. S.

Ax·um (äk′sōom), *n.* Aksum.

ay[1] (ā), *adv. Poetic or Dial.* ever; always. Also, **aye.** [ME *ei, ai,* t. Scand.; cf. Icel. *ei,* c. OE *ā* ever]

ay[2] (ā), *interj. Archaic or Dial.* Ah! Oh! [ME *ey,* m. phrase *ay me,* t. F: m. *ahi, aï.* Cf. It. *ahime,* Sp. *ay de mi*]

ay[3] (ī), *adv., n.* aye[1].

A·ya·cu·cho (ä′yäkōō′chō), *n.* a city in SW Peru: victory of the revolutionists near here ended Spain's domination in the New World, 1824. 23,800 (est. 1952).

a·yah (ä′yə), *n.* (in India) a native maid or nurse. [t. Hind.: m. *āya,* t. Pg.: m. *aia,* fem. of *aio* tutor]

Ay·din (ī dēn′), *n.* a city in W Turkey, SE of Izmir: ancient ruins. 20,421 (1950). Also, **Aidin.**

aye[1] (ī), *adv.* **1.** yes. —*n.* **2.** an affirmative vote or voter, esp. in British Parliament, corresponding to *yea* in Congress. Also, **ay.** [earlier *I,* ? var. of ME *yie,* OE *gī* YEA (with loss of *y* as in if)]

aye[2] (ā), *adv.* ay[1].

aye-aye (ī′ī), *n.* a nocturnal lemur, *Daubentonia madagascariensis,* of Madagascar, about the size of a cat and with rodentline front teeth. [t. F, t. Malagasy: m. *aiay;* prob. imit. of its cry]

A·ye·sha (ä′Ishä′), *n.* Aisha.

Aye-aye
Daubentonia madagascariensis
(Total length 3 ft. 8 in. high)

Ay·ma·ra (I′märä′), *n.* an important Indian nationality and speech group in Bolivia and Peru, still existing about Lake Titicaca. —**Ay′ma·ran′,** *adj.*

Ayr (âr), *n.* **1.** Also, **Ayrshire.** a county in SW Scotland. 329,100 pop. (est. 1956); 1132 sq. mi. **2.** its county seat: a seaport. 43,200 (est. 1956).

Ayr·shire (âr′shĬr, -shər), *n.* **1.** one of a hardy breed of dairy cattle, well-muscled, of medium size, brown and white in color, originating in the shire of Ayr. **2.** Ayr (def. 1).

A·yu·thi·a (ä ū′thēä; *Thai* -tēä), *n.* a city in central Thailand, on the Menam: former capital of country. ab. 50,000. Also, **A·yudh·ya** (ä ūd′yä), **A·yut·tha·ya** (ä ū′tä yä).

az-, var. of azo- used before vowels, as in *azole.*

a·zal·ea (ə zāl′yə), *n.* any plant of a particular group (*Azalea*) of the ericaceous genus *Rhododendron,* comprising species with handsome, variously colored flowers, some of which are familiar in cultivation. *Azalea* was once a botanical genus but is now a nursery or horticultural classification. [t. NL, t. Gk.: (fem. adj.) dry; so named as growing in dry soil]

a·zan (ä zän′), *n.* (in Mohammedan countries) the call to prayer, proclaimed by the crier (muezzin) from the minaret of a mosque five times daily. [t. Ar.: m. *adhān* invitation. See MUEZZIN]

A·za·ña y Dí·ez (ä thä′nyä ē dē′ĕth), **Manuel** (mänwĕl′), 1880–1940, Spanish statesman: prime minister, 1931–33, 1936; president, 1936–39.

A·za·zel (ə zā′zəl, ăz′ə zĕl′), *n.* **1.** the leader of the rebellious sons of God who entered into sexual relations with the daughters of men. Gen. 6:1–4. **2.** (in Arabic writers) one of the jinns taken prisoners by the angels for their transgressions. [t. Heb : m. *‘azā′ zēl*]

a·zed·a·rach (ə zĕd′ərăk′), *n.* the chinaberry tree (def. 1).

a·ze·o·trope (ə zē′ə trōp′), *n. Phys. Chem.* any solution having constant minimum and maximum boiling points. [f. A-⁶ + zeo- (comb. form repr. Gk. *zein* boil) + -TROPE]

Az·er·bai·jan (äz′ərbī jän′; *Russ.* ä′zĕr bĬ jän′), *n.* **1.** Official name, **Azerbaijan Soviet Socialist Republic.** one of the constituent republics of the Soviet Union, in Caucasia. 3,400,000 (est. 1956); ab. 33,000 sq. mi. *Cap.:*

Baku. **2.** a province in NW Iran. 3,266,517 (est. 1953); ab. 35,000 sq. mi. *Cap.:* Tabriz. Also, **Az′er·bai·dzhan′.**

A·zer·bai·ja·ni·an (ä′zər bǐ jä′nĬ ən), *n.* a Turkic language.

az·i·muth (ăz′ə məth), *n.* **1.** *Astron., Navig.* the arc of the horizon from the celestial meridian to the foot of the great circle passing through the zenith, the nadir, and the point of the celestial sphere in question (in astronomy commonly reckoned from the south point of the horizon toward the west point: in navigation reckoned from the north point of the horizon toward the east point). **2.** *Survey., Gunnery, etc.* an angle measured clockwise from the south or north. [ME *azimut,* t. OF, t. Ar.: m. *assumūt,* f. *as* (=*al*) the + *sumūt,* pl. of *samt* way] —**az·i·muth·al** (ăz′ə müth′əl), *adj.* —**az′-i·muth′al·ly,** *adv.*

az·ine (ăz′ēn, -Ĭn), *n. Chem.* any of a group of organic compounds having six atoms, one or more of them nitrogen, arranged in a ring, the number of nitrogen atoms being indicated by a prefix, as in *diazine, triazine, tetrazine.* Also, **az·in** (ăz′Ĭn). [f. AZ- + -INE²]

azo-, *Chem.* a word element meaning nitrogen. [t. Gk.: s. *ázōos* lifeless] —**az·o** (ăz′ō, ā′zō), *adj.*

az·o·ben·zene (ăz′ō bĕn′zēn, -bĕn zēn′, ā′zō-), *n. Chem.* an orange-red crystalline substance, $C_6H_5N = NC_6H_5$, obtained from nitrobenzene in an alkaline solution.

azo dyes, *Chem.* a large group of synthetic coloring substances which contain the azo group, -N=N-.

a·zo·ic (ə zō′Ĭk), *adj. Geol.* pertaining to geologic time before life appeared. [f. s. Gk. *ázōos* lifeless + -IC]

az·ole (ăz′ōl, əzōl′), *n. Chem.* any of a group of organic compounds having five atoms, one or more of them nitrogen, arranged in a ring. The number of nitrogen atoms is indicated by a prefix, as in *diazole.* [f. AZ- + -OLE]

az·on bomb (ăz′ŏn), *n.* a half-ton aerial bomb fitted with radio equipment and a special tail assembly which enables the bombardier to change the direction of its fall (to a certain extent) by remote control.

a·zon·ic (ā zŏn′Ĭk), *adj.* not confined to any particular zone or region; not local.

A·zores (ə zōrz′, ā′zōrz), *n.* a group of islands in the N Atlantic, W of and belonging to Portugal. 318,558 pop. (1950); 890 sq. mi.

az·ote (ăz′ōt, ə zōt′), *n. Obs.* nitrogen. [t. F, t. Gk.: m.s. *ázōtos,* prop., ungirt (mistakenly thought to mean lifeless, the gas being unfit to support life in respiration] —**az·ot·ed** (ăz′ō tĬd, ə zō′tĬd), *adj.*

az·oth (ăz′ŏth), *n. Alchemy.* **1.** mercury, as the assumed first principle of all metals. **2.** the universal remedy of Paracelsus. [t. F, var. of *azoch,* t. Ar.: m. *az-zāwūq* the mercury]

a·zot·ic (ə zŏt′Ĭk), *adj.* of or pertaining to azote; nitric.

az·o·tize (ăz′ə tīz′), *v.t.,* **-tized, -tizing.** to nitrogenize.

A·zov (ä zŏf′), *n.* **Sea of,** a sea NE of the Black Sea and connected with it by Kerch Strait. ab. 14,500 sq. mi. Also, **A·zof′.** See map under **Black Sea.**

Az·ra·el (ăz′rĬ əl), *n.* (in Jewish and Mohammedan angelology) the angel who separates the soul from the body at the moment of death. [t. Heb.]

Az·tec (ăz′tĕk), *n.* **1.** a member of an Indian people dominant in Central Mexico at the time of the Spanish invasion (1519). **2.** a Uto-Aztecan language of the Nahuatl subgroup, still extensively spoken in Mexico; Nahuatl. —**Az′tec·an,** *adj.*

az·ure (ăzh′ər, ā′zhər), *adj.* **1.** of a sky-blue color. —*n.* **2.** blue of unclouded sky. **3.** a blue pigment, now esp. cobalt blue. **4.** the sky. [ME, t. OF: m. *azur,* t. Ar.: m. *lāzward,* t. Pers.: m. *lajward* lapis lazuli]

az·u·rite (ăzh′ə rīt′), *n.* **1.** a blue mineral, a hydrous copper carbonate $[Cu_3(CO_3)_2(OH)_2]$, an ore of copper. **2.** a gem of moderate value, ground from this mineral.

az·y·gous (ăz′ə gəs), *adj. Zool., Bot.* not being one of a pair; single. [t. Gk.: m. *ázygos*]

B

B, b (bē), *n., pl.* **B's** or **Bs, b's** or **bs. 1.** the second letter of the English alphabet. **2.** the second in any series: *schedule B.* **3.** *U.S.* the second highest mark for school or college work. **4.** *Music.* a. the seventh tone in the scale of C major or the second tone in the relative minor scale of A minor. b. a string, key, or pipe tuned

b., blend of, blended; c., cognate with; d., dialect, dialectal; der., derived from; f., formed from; g., going back to; m., modification of; r., replacing; s., stem of; t., taken from; ?, perhaps. See the full key on inside cover.

to this note. **c.** a written or printed note representing this tone. **d.** (in solmization) the seventh tone of the scale of C.

B, *Chem.* boron.

B., 1. bay. **2.** Bible. **3.** British. **4.** Brotherhood.

b., 1. *Baseball.* base; baseman. **2.** bass. **3.** basso. **4.** book. **5.** born. **6.** breadth. **7.** brother. **8.** blend of; blended.

Ba, *Chem.* barium.

B.A., 1. (L *Baccalaureus Artium*) Bachelor of Arts. **2.** British America.

baa (bä, bȧ), *v.,* **baaed, baaing,** *n.* —*v.i.* **1.** to cry as a sheep; bleat. —*n.* **2.** the bleating of a sheep. [imit.]

Ba·al (bā′əl, bäl), *n., pl.* **Baalim** (bā′əl Ym). **1.** any of numerous local deities among the ancient Semitic peoples, typifying the productive forces of nature and worshiped with much sensuality. **2.** a solar deity, the chief god of the Phoenicians. **3.** any false god. [t. Heb.: m. *ba′al* lord] —**Ba′al·ism,** *n.* —**Ba′al·ist, Ba·al·ite** (bā′ə lit′), *n.*

Baal·bek (bäl′bĕk), *n.* a ruined city in E Lebanon: Temple of the Sun. Ancient Greek name, **Heliopolis.**

ba·ba (bä′bə; *Fr.* bȧ bȧ′), *n.* a yeast-raised cake of brioche dough, flavored with rum, etc., and baked.

bab·bitt (băb′Yt), *n. Metall.* **1.** Babbitt metal. **2.** a bearing or lining of Babbitt metal. —*v.t.* **3.** to line, face, or furnish with Babbitt metal.

Bab·bitt (băb′Yt), *n.* **1.** a self-satisfied person who conforms readily to middle-class ideas and ideals, esp. of business success. Cf. **Babbittry. 2.** Irving, 1865–1933, U.S. educator and critic.

Babbitt metal, *Metall.* **1.** an antifriction metal, an alloy of tin, antimony, lead, and copper, used for bearings, etc. **2.** any of various similar alloys. [named after Isaac *Babbitt* (1799–1862), U.S. inventor]

Bab·bitt·ry (băb′Yt rY), *n.* (*often l.c.*) the attitude of the self-satisfied middle class, having social conformity and business success as its ideals, as typified by the title character of Sinclair Lewis' novel *Babbitt* (1922).

bab·ble (băb′əl), *v.,* **-bled, -bling,** *n.* —*v.i.* **1.** to utter words imperfectly or indistinctly. **2.** to talk idly, irrationally, or foolishly; chatter. **3.** to make a continuous murmuring sound: *a babbling stream.* —*v.t.* **4.** to utter incoherently or foolishly. **5.** to reveal foolishly or thoughtlessly: *to babble a secret.* —*n.* **6.** inarticulate speech. **7.** senseless or foolish prattle. **8.** a murmuring sound. [ME *babele*(n); of imit. orig. Cf. Icel. *babla*] —**bab′ble·ment,** *n.* —**bab′bler,** *n.*

babe (bāb), *n.* **1.** baby. **2.** an innocent or inexperienced person. **3.** *Slang.* girl. [ME]

Ba·bel (bā′bəl), *n.* **1.** *Bible.* an ancient city (Babylon) where the building of a tower intended to reach heaven was begun and a confounding of the language of the people took place. Gen. 11:4–9. **2.** (*usually l.c.*) a confused mixture of sounds. **3.** (*usually l.c.*) a scene of noise and confusion. [t. Heb.: m. *Bābel* Babylon]

Bab el Man·deb (băb′ ĕl măn′dĕb), a strait between E Africa and SW Arabia, connecting the Red Sea and the Gulf of Aden. 20 mi. wide.

Ba·ber (bä′bər), *n.* (*Zahir ed-Din Mohammed*) 1483–1530, founder of Mogul Empire. Also, **Ba′bar.**

ba·bies′-breath (bā′bYz brĕth′), *n.* **1.** a tall herb, *Gypsophila paniculata,* of the pink family, bearing numerous small, fragrant, white or pink flowers. **2.** any of certain other plants, as the grape hyacinth, *Muscari.* Also, **baby′s-breath.**

bab·i·ru·sa (băb′ə rōō′sə, bä′bə-) *n.* an East Indian swine, *Babirussa babyrussa.* The male has peculiar curved tusks growing upward, one pair from each jaw. Also, **bab′i·rous′sa, bab′-i·rus′sa.** [t. Malay: m. *bābi rūsa* hog deer]

Bab·ism (bä′bYzəm), *n.* the doctrine of a pantheistic Persian sect, founded about 1844, inculcating a high morality, recognizing the equality of the sexes, and forbidding polygamy. —**Bab′ist,** *n., adj.*

Babirusa. *Babirussa babyrussa* (2 ft. or more high at the shoulder)

ba·boo (bä′bōō), *n., pl.* **-boos. 1.** a Hindu gentleman. **2.** a native clerk who writes English. **3.** any native having a smattering of English culture, esp. with a ludicrous effect. Also, **ba′bu.** [t. Hind.: m. *bābū*] —**ba′boo·ism,** *n.*

ba·boon (bă bōōn′), *n.* any of various large, terrestrial monkeys, with a doglike muzzle, large cheek pouches, and a short tail, which constitute the genus *Papio* of Africa and Arabia. [ME *babewyne,* t. OF: m. *babouin* stupid person] —**ba·boon′ish,** *adj.*

ba·boon·er·y (bă bōō′nər Y), *n.* baboonish condition or behavior.

ba·bul (bä bōōl′, bä′bōōl), *n.* **1.** any of several trees of the mimosaceous genus *Acacia,* which yield a gum, esp. *A. arabica* of India. **2.** the gum, pods, or bark of such a tree. [t. Hind.]

ba·bush·ka (bə bōōsh′kə), *n.* a woman's scarf, often triangular, used as a hood with the ends tied under the chin. [t. Russ.: lit., grandmother]

ba·by (bā′bY), *n., pl.* **-bies,** *adj., v.,* **-bied, -bying.** —*n.* **1.** an infant; young child of either sex. **2.** the youngest member of a family, group, etc. **3.** a childish person.

4. *Slang.* an invention or creation of which one is particularly proud. **5.** *Slang.* girl. —*adj.* **6.** of, like, or suitable for a baby; *baby carriage.·* **7.** infantile; babyish: *baby face.* **8.** *Colloq.* small; comparatively little: *a baby grand* (piano). —*v.t.* **9.** to treat like a young child; pamper. [ME *babi, babee,* dim. of *babe*] —**ba′by·hood′,** *n.* —**ba′by·ish,** *adj.* —**ba′by·ish·ly,** *adv.* —**ba′-by·ish·ness,** *n.* —**ba′by·like′,** *adj.*

ba·by-blue-eyes (bā′bY blōō′Yz′), *n.* **1.** a plant, *Nemophila insignis,* of the Pacific coast of the U.S., with spotted blue blossoms. **2.** a similar plant, *Nemophila phaceloides,* common in Oklahoma. **3.** a plant, *N. menziesi atomaria,* occurring in Northwestern U.S.

Bab·y·lon (băb′ə lən, -lŏn′), *n.* **1.** an ancient city of SW Asia, on the Euphrates river, famed for its magnificence and culture: the capital of Babylonia and later of the Chaldean Empire. **2.** any great, rich, and luxurious or wicked city. [t. L, t. Gk., t. Akkadian: m. *Bāb Ilu* the gate of the god *Il*]

Bab·y·lo·ni·a (băb′ə lō′nY ə), *n.* an ancient empire in SW Asia, in the lower Euphrates valley: period of greatness, 2800 B.C.–1750 B.C.

Bab·y·lo·ni·an (băb′ə lō′nY ən), *adj.* **1.** pertaining to Babylon or Babylonia. **2.** sinful. —*n.* **3.** an inhabitant of ancient Babylonia. **4.** a language of Babylonia, esp. the Semitic language of the Akkadian group.

ba·by's-breath (bā′bYz brĕth′), *n.* babies'-breath.

ba·by-sit (bā′bY sYt′), *v.i.* **-sat, -sitting.** to take charge of a child (usually for an evening) while the parents are away. —**ba′by-sit′ter,** *n.*

bac·ca·lau·re·ate (băk′ə lôr′Yt), *n.* **1.** the bachelor's degree. **2.** a religious service usually associated with commencement ceremonies. **3.** *Chiefly U.S.* a baccalaureate sermon. [t. ML: m.s. *baccalaureātus,* der. *baccalaureus* (as if f. L *bacca* berry + *laureus* of laurel), var. of *baccalarius* BACHELOR]

baccalaureate sermon, (in some U.S. colleges and schools) a farewell sermon to a graduating class.

bac·ca·rat (băk′ə rä′, băk′ə rä′; *Fr.* bä kȧ rä′), *n.* a gambling game at cards played by a banker and two or more punters. Also, **bac′ca·ra′.** [t. F; orig. unknown]

bac·cate (băk′āt), *adj. Bot.* **1.** berrylike. **2.** bearing berries. [t. L: m. s. *baccātus* berried]

Bac·chae (băk′ē), *n.pl. Class. Myth.* **1.** the female attendants of Bacchus. **2.** the priestesses of Bacchus. **3.** the women who took part in the Bacchanalia.

bac·cha·nal (băk′ə nəl), *n.* **1.** a follower of Bacchus. **2.** a drunken reveler. **3.** an occasion of drunken revelry; an orgy. —*adj.* **4.** pertaining to Bacchus; bacchanalian. [t. L: s. *bacchānālis*]

Bac·cha·na·li·a (băk′ə nā′lY ə, -nāl′yə), *n.pl.* **1.** a Roman festival in honor of Bacchus. **2.** (*l.c.*) drunken orgies. [L, neut. pl. of *bacchānālis* BACCHANAL, adj.] —**bac′cha·na·li·an,** *adj.* —**bac′cha·na′li·an·ism,** *n.*

bac·chant (băk′ənt), *n., pl.* **bacchants, bacchantes** (bə kän′tēz). **1.** a priest, priestess, or votary of Bacchus; a bacchanal. **2.** a drunken reveler. [t. L: s. *bacchans,* celebrating the festival of Bacchus] —**bac·chan·tic** (bə kän′tYk), *adj.*

bac·chan·te (bə kän′tY, bə känt′, băk′ənt), *n.* a female bacchant. [t. F, L: m. s. *bacchans* BACCHANT]

Bac·chic (băk′Yk), *adj.* **1.** relating to or in honor of Bacchus; connected with bacchanalian rites or revelries. **2.** (*l.c.*) jovial; riotously or jovially intoxicated; drunken.

Bac·chus (băk′əs), *n. Rom. Myth.* the god of wine. See Dionysus. [t. L, t. Gk.: m. *Bákchos*]

bacci-, *Bot.* a word element meaning "berry," as in *bacciform.* [t. L, comb. form of *bacca*]

bac·cif·er·ous (băk sYf′ər əs), *adj. Bot.* bearing or producing berries. [f. L *baccifer* + -OUS]

bac·ci·form (băk′sə fôrm′), *adj. Bot.* berry-shaped.

bac·civ·o·rous (băk sYv′ə rəs), *adj.* feeding on berries.

bach (băch), *v.i. U.S. Slang.* to keep house alone. [der. BACHELOR]

Bach (bäkH), *n.* **1.** Johann Sebastian (yō′hän sä bäs′tY än′), 1685–1750, German organist and composer. **2.** his son, Karl Philipp Emanuel (kärl fē′lYp ā mä′nŏŏ əl′), 1714–88, German composer.

bach·e·lor (băch′ə lər, băch′lər), *n.* **1.** an unmarried man of any age. **2.** a person who has taken the first or lowest degree at a college or university: *bachelor of arts.* **3.** a young knight who followed the banner of another. **4.** a young male fur seal kept from the breeding grounds by the older males. [ME *bacheler,* t. OF, t. ML: m.s. *baccalāris, baccalārius,* appar. orig. small farmholder; ? akin to L *baculum* staff] —**bach·e·lor·dom** (băch′ə lər dəm, băch′lər-), *n.* —**bach′e·lor·hood′,** *n.* —**bach′e·lor·ship′,** *n.*

bach·e·lor-at-arms (băch′ə lər ət ärmz′, băch′lər-), *n., pl.* **bachelors-at-arms.** bachelor (def. 3).

bach·e·lor′s-but·ton (băch′ə lərz bŭt′ən, băch′lərz-), *n.* any of various plants with round flower heads, esp. the cornflower, or double-flowered varieties of ranunculus.

bac·il·lar·y (băs′ə lĕr′Y), *adj.* **1.** Also, **ba·cil·li·form** (bə sYl′ə fôrm′), of or like a bacillus; rod-shaped. **2.** Bac-

teriol. characterized by bacilli. Also, **ba·cil·lar** (bə·sĭl'ər, băs'ə·lər). [f. s. L *bacillus* little rod + -ARY²]

ba·cil·lus (bə·sĭl'əs), *n.*, *pl.* **-cilli** (-sĭl'ī). *Bacteriol.* 1. any of the group of rod-shaped bacteria which produce spores in the presence of free oxygen. See illus. under **bacteria.** 2. (formerly) any of the rod-shaped or cylindrical bacteria. 3. any bacterium. [t. LL, dim. of *baculus* rod].

back¹ (băk). *n.* 1. the hinder part of the human body, extending from the neck to the end of the spine. 2. the part of the body of animals corresponding to the human back. 3. the rear portion of any part or organ of the body: *the back of the head.* 4. the whole body, with reference to clothing: *the clothes on his back.* 5. the part opposite to or farthest from the face or front; the hinder side; the rear part: *the back of a hall.* 6. the part covering the back, as of clothing. 7. the spine: *to break one's back.* 8. any rear part of an object serving to support, protect, etc.: *the back of a book.* 9. the strength to carry a burden. 10. *Football, etc.* **a.** a player behind the forward line. **b.** the position occupied by this player. 11. **behind one's back,** in secret; when one is absent. 12. **turn one's back on,** to forsake or neglect. —*v.t.* 13. to support, as with authority, influence, or money (often fol. by *up*). 14. to cause to move backward; reverse the action of (often fol. by *up*): *to back a car.* 15. to bet in favor of: *to back a horse in the race.* 16. to get upon the back of; mount. 17. to furnish with a back: *to back a book.* 18. to lie at the back of; form a back or background for: *a beach backed by hills.* 19. to write or print on the back of; endorse. —*v.i.* 20. to go backward (often fol. by *up*). 21. *Naut.* (of wind) to change direction counterclockwise. 22. Some special verb phrases are: **back and fill,** 1. *Naut.* to trim the sails so that the wind strikes them first on the forward and then on the after side (done against the wind in a narrow channel to maneuver a ship from bank to bank without making headway but floating with the current). 2. *U.S. Colloq.* to vacillate. **back down,** to retreat from or abandon an argument, opinion, claim, etc. **back off,** to recede from contact. **back out** or **out of,** to withdraw from or abandon (an engagement, promise, etc.). **back water,** 1. *Naut.* to reverse the direction of a vessel. 2. *U.S. Colloq.* to retreat from an opinion, etc. —*adj.* 23. lying or being behind: *a back door.* 24. (in) **back of,** *U.S. Colloq.* behind. 25. away from the front position or rank; remote: *back settlements.* 26. belonging to the past: *back files.* 27. overdue: *back pay.* 28. coming or going back; backward: *back current.* 29. *Phonet.* pronounced with the tongue drawn back in the mouth, as, in most varieties of English, the vowels of *bought*, *boat*, and *boot*. [ME *bak*, OE *bæc*, c. Icel. *bak*] —Syn. 23. BACK, HIND, POSTERIOR, REAR refer to something situated behind something else. BACK means the opposite of front: *back window.* HIND, and the more formal word POSTERIOR, suggest the rearmost of two or more, often similar, objects: *hind legs, posterior lobe.* REAR is used of buildings, conveyances, etc., and in military language it is the opposite of fore: *rear end of a truck, rear echelon.*

back² (băk). *adv.* 1. at, to, or toward the rear; backward: *to step back.* 2. toward the past: *to look back on one's youth.* 3. toward the original starting point, place, or condition: *to go back to the old home.* 4. in reply; in return: *to pay back a loan.* 5. in reversal of the usual course: *to take back a gift.* [aphetic var. of ABACK]

back³ (băk). *n.* a tub or vat. [t. D: m. *bak*, t. F: m. *bac* tub, trough, ferryboat]

back·ache (băk'āk'). *n.* an ache in one's back.

Back Bay, a fashionable residential section of Boston.

back·bite (băk'bīt'). *v.*, **-bit, -bitten** or (*Colloq.*) **-bit, ·biting.** —*v.t.* 1. to attack the character or reputation of secretly. —*v.i.* 2. to speak evil of the absent. —**back'bit'er,** *n.* —**back'bit'ing,** *n.*

back·board (băk'bōrd'). *n.* 1. a board placed at or forming the back of anything. 2. *Med.* a board worn to support or straighten the back. 3. *Basketball.* the vertical surface to which the basket is attached. —*v.t.* 4. *Med.* to subject to the wearing of a backboard.

back·bone (băk'bōn'). *n.* 1. *Anat.* the spinal or vertebral column; the spine. 2. something resembling a backbone in appearance, position, or function. 3. strength of character; resolution. 4. *Bibliog.* the back or bound edge of a book; spine. —**back'boned',** *adj.*

back·break·ing (băk'brā'kĭng). *adj.* physically exhausting.

back·cross (băk'krôs', -krŏs'), *Genetics.* —*v.t.* 1. to cross a hybrid (of the first generation) with either of its parents. —*n.* 2. an instance of such crossing.

back·door (băk'dôr'). *adj.* secret; clandestine.

back·drop (băk'drŏp'). *n.* *Theat.* the rear curtain of a stage setting.

backed (băkt). *adj.* having a back: *a high-backed chair.*

back·er (băk'ər). *n.* anything, esp. a person, that supports or gives aid in an enterprise.

back·fall (băk'fôl'). *n.* 1. that which falls back. 2. a fall in which a wrestler is thrown upon his back.

back·field (băk'fēld'). *n.* *Football.* those players who are in back of the front line, consisting of the quarterback, the two halfbacks, and the fullback.

back·fire (băk'fīr'). *v.*, **-fired, -firing,** *n.* —*v.i.* 1. (of

an internal-combustion engine) to have a premature explosion in the cylinder or in the admission or exhaust passages. 2. to check a forest or prairie fire by burning off an area in advance of it. 3. to bring results opposite to those planned: *the plot backfired.* —*n.* 4. (in an internal-combustion engine) premature ignition of the fuel, resulting in loss of power and loud explosive sound in the manifold. 5. an explosion coming out of the breech of a firearm. 6. a fire purposely started in advance of a fire in order to fight it.

back formation, *Gram.* 1. the formation of a word from one that looks like its derivative, as *typewrite* from *typewriter, donate* from *donation.* 2. a word so formed.

back·gam·mon (băk'găm'ən, băk'găm'ən), *n.* 1. a game played by two persons on a board having two tables or parts, with pieces or men moved in accordance with throws of dice. 2. a victory at this game, esp. one resulting in a tripled score. —*v.t.* 3. to defeat at backgammon; esp. to win a triple score over. [f. BACK¹, adj. + GAMMON; game so called because the pieces often must go back and reënter]

back·ground (băk'ground'). *n.* 1. the ground or parts situated in the rear. 2. the surface or ground against which the parts of a picture are relieved, or the portions of a picture represented as more distant (opposed to *foreground*). 3. the social, historical, and other antecedents which explain an event or condition: *the background of the war.* 4. a person's origin, education, etc. in relation to present character, status, etc. 5. **in the background,** out of sight or notice; in obscurity.

back·hand (băk'hănd'). *n.* 1. the hand turned backward in making a stroke, as in tennis. 2. a stroke, as in tennis, by a right-handed player from the left of the body (or the reverse for a left-handed player). 3. writing which slopes backward or to the left. —*adj.* 4. backhanded. —Ant. 1. forehand.

back·hand·ed (băk'hăn'dĭd). *adj.* 1. performed with the hand turned backward, crosswise, or in any oblique direction, or with the back of the hand in the direction of the stroke. 2. sloping to the left: *backhanded writing.* 3. oblique or opposite in meaning; insincere; indirect: *a backhanded compliment.* 4. (of a rope) twisted in the opposite way from the usual or right-handed method. —**back'hand'ed·ly,** *adv.* —**back'hand'ed·ness,** *n.*

back·house (băk'hous'). *n.* 1. an outhouse at the back of a main building. 2. a privy.

back·ing (băk'ĭng). *n.* 1. aid or support of any kind. 2. supporters or backers collectively. 3. that which forms the back or is placed at or attached to the back of anything to support or strengthen it.

back·lash (băk'lăsh'). *n.* 1. *Mach.* the jarring reaction, or the play, between loosely fitting or worn parts of a machine or mechanical device. 2. *Angling.* a tangled line on a reel, caused by a faulty cast.

back·log (băk'lôg', -lŏg'), *n.* *U.S.* 1. a large log at the back of the hearth to keep up the fire. 2. something serving as a reserve, or support.

back number, *Orig. U.S.* 1. an out-of-date issue of a serial publication. 2. anything out-of-date.

back·set (băk'sĕt'). *n.* 1. a setback; a reverse. 2. an eddy or countercurrent.

back·sheesh (băk'shēsh), *n.*, *v.t.*, *v.i.* baksheesh. Also, **back·shish.**

back·side (băk'sīd'). *n.* 1. the back part. 2. the rump.

back·sight (băk'sīt'). *n.* *Survey.* 1. a sight on a previously occupied instrument station. 2. (in leveling) the reading on a rod that is held on a point of known elevation, and which is to be used in computing the height of the instrument.

back·slide (băk'slīd'). *v.i.*, **-slid, -slidden** or **-slid, -sliding.** to relapse into error or sin. —**back'slid'er,** *n.*

back·spin (băk'spĭn'). *n.* reverse spinning of a ball causing it to bounce backwards, as in tennis.

back·stage (băk'stāj'). *adv.* 1. behind the curtain in a theater; on the stage, or in the wings or dressing rooms. 2. toward the rear of the stage; upstage. —*adj.* 3. located, occurring, etc., backstage.

back·stairs (băk'stârz'). *adj.* indirect; underhand. Also, **back·stair'.**

back·stay (băk'stā'). *n.* 1. *Mach.* a supporting or checking piece in a mechanism. 2. *Naut.* a stay or supporting rope leading from a masthead backward to the ship's side or stern.

back·stitch (băk'stĭch'). *n.* 1. stitching or a stitch in which the thread doubles back each time on the preceding stitch. —*v.t.*, *v.i.* 2. to sew by backstitch.

back·stop (băk'stŏp'). *n.* *U.S. Sports.* a wall, wire screen, player, etc., to prevent a ball from going too far.

back·stroke (băk'strōk'). *n.* 1. a backhanded stroke. 2. a blow or stroke in return; recoil. 3. *Swimming.* a stroke made while on one's back.

back·sword (băk'sōrd'). *n.* 1. a sword with only one sharp edge; a broadsword. 2. a cudgel with a basket hilt, used like a foil in fencing. 3. a backswordsman.

back·sword·man (băk'sōrd'mən), *n.*, *pl.* **-men.** one who uses a backsword. Also, **back'swords'man.**

back talk, impertinent talk; answering back.

back·track (băk'trăk'), *v.i.* *U.S.* 1. to return over the same course or route. 2. to withdraw from an undertaking, position, etc.; pursue a reverse policy.

back·ward (băk'wərd). *adv.* Also, **back'wards.** 1. toward the back or rear. 2. with the back foremost.

3. in the reverse of the usual or right way; retrogressively: *to read or spell backward.* **4.** toward the past. **5.** in time past. —*adj.* **6.** directed toward the back or past. **7.** reversed; returning: *a backward movement or journey.* **8.** behind in time or progress; late; slow: *a backward learner or country.* **9.** reluctant; hesitating; bashful: *a backward child.* [ME *bakward*, f. *bak* BACK- + -WARD] —back'ward·ly, *adv.* —back'ward·ness, *n.* —Syn. **9.** disinclined; timid, retiring. —Ant. **1.** forward.

back·wash (băk'wŏsh', -wŏsh'), *n.* **1.** *Naut.* the water thrown back by oars, paddle wheels, or the like. **2.** a condition lasting after the event which caused it.

back·wa·ter (băk'wŏ'tər, -wôt'ər), *n.* **1.** water held or forced back, as by a dam, flood, tide, etc. **2.** a place or state of stagnant backwardness.

back·woods (băk'wŏŏdz'), *n.pl. Orig. U.S.* **1.** wooded or partially uncleared and unsettled districts. —*adj.* Also, back'wood'. **2.** of or pertaining to the backwoods. **3.** unsophisticated; uncouth.

back·woods·man (băk'wŏŏdz'mən), *n., pl.* -men. **1.** one living in the backwoods. **2.** an uncouth person.

ba·con (bā'kən), *n.* the back and sides of the hog, salted and dried or smoked. [ME, t. OF, t. Gmc.; cf. OHG *bahho*, MHG *bache* buttock, ham]

Ba·con (bā'kən), *n.* **1. Francis**, (*Baron Verulam, Viscount St. Albans*) 1561–1626, British essayist, philosopher, and statesman. **2. Nathaniel**, 1642?–76, American colonist, born in England: leader of a rebellion in 1676, demanding greater suffrage and lower taxes. **3. Roger**, (*Friar Bacon or "the Admirable Doctor"*) 1214?–1294?, British philosopher and scientist.

Ba·co·ni·an (bākō'nĭən), *adj.* **1.** of or pertaining to Francis Bacon or his doctrines. —*n.* **2.** an adherent of the Baconian philosophy.

Baconian theory, the theory attributing the authorship of Shakespeare's plays to Francis Bacon.

bac·te·re·mi·a (băk'tə rē'mĭ ə), *n. Pathol.* the presence (for transient periods) of bacteria in the blood.

bacteri-, a word element meaning "bacteria" or "bacterial." Also, **bacter-, bacterio-, bactero-**. [comb. form of BACTERIUM]

bac·te·ri·a (băk tĭr'ĭ ə), *n., pl.* of **bacterium.** the morphologically simplest group of nongreen vegetable organisms, various species of which are concerned in fermentation and putrefaction, the production of disease, the fixing of atmospheric nitrogen, etc.; a schizomycete. [t. NL. See BACTERIUM] —bac·te'ri·al, *adj.* —bac·te'ri·al·ly, *adv.*

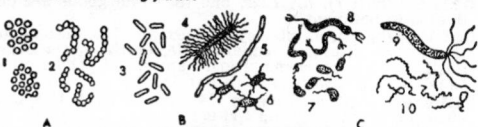

Bacteria (greatly magnified)

A. Cocci (spherical): **1.** *Staphylococcus pyogenes aureus,* **2.** *Streptococcus pyogenes.* B. Bacilli (rod): **3.** *Bacillus sporogenes,* **4.** *Bacillus proteus,* **5.** *Bacillus subtilis,* **6.** *Bacillus typhosus.* C. Spirilla (spiral): **7.** *Vibrio cholerae asiaticae,* **8.** *Spirillum undulum,* **9.** *Theospirillum,* **10.** *Spirochaeta*

bac·te·ri·cide (băk tĭr'ə sīd'), *n.* an agent capable of destroying bacteria. —bac·te'ri·cid'al, *adj.*

bac·te·rin (băk'tə rĭn), *n. Immunol.* a vaccine prepared from bacteria. [f. BACTER- + -IN²]

bacteriol., bacteriology.

bac·te·ri·ol·o·gy (băk tĭr'ĭ ŏl'ə jĭ), *n.* the science that deals with bacteria. —bac·te·ri·o·log·i·cal (băk tĭr'ĭ ə lŏj'ə kəl), *adj.* —bac·te·ri·o·log'i·cal·ly, *adv.* —bac·te·ri·ol'o·gist, *n.*

bac·te·ri·ol·y·sis (băk tĭr'ĭ ŏl'ə sĭs), *n.* disintegration or dissolution of bacteria. —bac·te·ri·o·lyt·ic (băk tĭr'ĭ ə lĭt'ĭk), *n., adj.*

bac·te·ri·o·phage (băk tĭr'ĭ ə fāj'), *n. Bacteriol.* an ultramicroscopic agent which causes the dissolution of certain bacteria (regarded by some as a living agent, by others as an enzyme).

bac·te·ri·o·sta·sis (băk tĭr'ĭ ə stā'sĭs), *n. Bacteriol.* the prevention of the development of bacteria. —bac·te·ri·o·stat·ic (băk tĭr'ĭ ə stăt'ĭk), *adj.*

bac·te·ri·um (băk tĭr'ĭ əm), *n. Bacteriol.* **1.** sing. of **bacteria. 2.** a group of nonsporeforming bacteria (in distinction to the bacillus and clostridium groups). [t. NL, t. Gk.: m. *baktērion,* dim. of *baktron* stick]

bac·ter·ize (băk'tə rīz'), *v.t.,* -ized, -izing. to change in composition by means of bacteria. —bac'ter·i·za'tion, *n.*

bactero-, var. of bacteri-.

bac·ter·oid (băk'tə roid'), *n. Bacteriol.* one of the minute rodlike or branched organisms (regarded as forms of bacteria) in the root nodules of nitrogen-fixing plants, as the legumes. —bac'te·roi'dal, *adj.*

Bac·tri·a (băk'trĭ ə), *n.* an ancient country in W Asia between the Oxus river and the Hindu Kush Mountains. —Bac'tri·an, *adj., n.*

Bactrian camel, *Camelus bactrianus* (Ab. 9 ft. long, ab. 7½ ft. high at the humps)

Bactrian camel, the two-humped camel, *Camelus bactrianus.* See illus. in preceding column.

ba·cu·li·form (bə kū'lə fôrm', băk'yə-), *adj. Biol.* rod-shaped. [f. s. L *baculum* rod + -(I)FORM]

bac·u·line (băk'yə lĭn, -līn), *adj.* pertaining to the rod or to its use in punishing. [f. s. L *baculum* rod + -INE¹]

bad¹ (băd), *adj.* worse, worst, *n., adv.* —*adj.* **1.** not good: *bad conduct, a bad life* **2.** defective; worthless: *a bad coin, a bad debt.* **3.** not sufficient for use; inadequate: *bad heating.* **4.** incorrect; faulty: *a bad shot.* **5.** not valid; not sound: *a bad claim.* **6.** having an injurious or unfavorable tendency or effect: *bad air or food.* **7.** in ill health; sick: *to feel bad.* **8.** regretful; contrite; sorry; upset: *to feel bad about an error.* **9.** unfavorable; unfortunate: *bad news.* **10.** offensive; disagreeable; painful: *a bad temper.* **11.** severe: *a bad sprain.* **12.** rotten; decayed. —*n.* **13.** that which is bad. **14.** a bad condition, character, or quality. —*adv.* **15.** badly. [ME *badde;* ? back formation from OE *bæddel* effeminate person] —bad'ness, *n.*

—Syn. **1.** depraved, corrupt, base, sinful, criminal, villainous, atrocious. BAD, EVIL, ILL, WICKED are closest in meaning, in reference to that which is lacking in moral qualities or is actually vicious and reprehensible. BAD is the broadest and simplest term: *a bad man, bad habits.* EVIL applies to that which violates or leads to the violation of moral law: *evil practices.* ILL now appears mainly in certain fixed expressions, with a milder implication than that in evil: *ill will, ill-natured.* WICKED implies willful and determined doing of what is very wrong: *a wicked plan.* **3.** inferior, poor, deficient. **6.** disadvantageous. **9.** adverse.

bad² (băd), *v.* pt. of bid.

Ba·da·joz (bä'dä hôth'), *n.* a city in SW Spain. 90,398 (est. 1955).

bad blood, hate; long-standing enmity; dislike.

bade (băd), *v.* pt. of bid.

Ba·den (bä'dən), *n.* **1.** a former state in SW West Germany. **2.** Also, **Ba/den-Ba/den.** a city in Baden-Württemberg. 40,000 (1951).

Ba·den-Pow·ell (bä'dən pō'əl), *n.* **Robert Stephenson Smyth, 1st Baron,** 1857–1941, British general who founded the Boy Scouts in 1908.

Ba·den-Würt·tem·berg (bä'dən vyrt'əm bĕrKH), *n.* a state in SW West Germany; formerly Baden. 7,232,-100 pop. (est. 1956); 13,803 sq. mi. *Cap.:* Stuttgart.

bad form, *Chiefly Brit.* a breach of good manners.

badge (băj), *n., v.,* **badged, badging.** —*n.* **1.** a mark, token, or device worn as a sign of allegiance, membership, authority, achievement, etc. **2.** any emblem, token, or distinctive mark. —*v.t.* **3.** to furnish or mark with a badge. [ME *bage, bagge;* orig. unknown]

badg·er (băj'ər), *n.* **1.** any of the various burrowing carnivorous mammals of the *Mustelidae,* as *Meles meles,* a European species about two feet long, and *Taxidea taxus,* a similar American species. **2.** the fur of this mammal. **3.** (in Australia) **a.** a wombat.

American badger, *Taxidea taxus* (28 in. long, tail ab. 5¼ in.)

b. a bandicoot (def. 2). —*v.t.* **4.** to harass; torment. [earlier *bageard.* ? f. BADGE (with allusion to white mark on head) + -ARD]

bad·i·nage (băd'ə näzh', băd'ə nĭj), *n., v.,* -naged, -naging. —*n.* **1.** light playful banter or raillery. —*v.t.* **2.** to drive or force by badinage. [t. F, der. *badiner* jest, der. *badin* fool, t. Pr., der. *badar* gape, g. LL *badāre*]

bad·lands (băd'lăndz'), *n.pl.* a barren area in which soft rock strata are eroded into varied, fantastic forms.

Bad Lands, a barren, badly eroded region in SW South Dakota and NW Nebraska.

bad·ly (băd'lĭ), *adv.* **1.** in a bad manner; ill. **2.** very much: *to need or want badly.*

bad·min·ton (băd'mĭn tən), *n.* a game, similar to lawn tennis, but played with a high net and shuttlecock. [named after *Badminton,* in Gloucestershire, England]

Ba·do·glio (bä dô'lyô), *n.* **Pietro** (pyĕ'trô), 1871–1956, Italian general.

bad-tem·pered (băd'tĕm'pərd), *adj.* cross; cranky.

Bae·da (bē'də), *n.* Bede.

Bae·de·ker (bā'də kər), *n.* any of the series of guidebooks for travelers issued by the German publisher Karl Baedeker, 1801–59, and his successors.

Baeke·land (bä'kländ'; *Flem.* bä'kə länt'), *n.* **Leo Hendrik** (lē'ō hĕn'drĭk; *Flem.* lā'ō), 1863–1944, Belgian-American chemist. Cf. **Bakelite.**

baff (băf), *Golf.* —*v.i.* **1.** to strike the ground with the club in making a stroke. —*n.* **2.** a baffling stroke, unduly lofting the ball. [? imit.]

Baf·fin (băf'ĭn), *n.* **William,** 1584?–1622, British navigator who explored arctic North America.

Baffin Bay, a part of the Arctic Ocean between Greenland and the Canadian arctic islands.

Baffin Island, a large Canadian island between Greenland and Hudson Bay. ab. 1000 mi. long.

baf·fle (băf/əl), v., **-fled, -fling,** n. —v.t. **1.** to thwart or frustrate disconcertingly; balk; confuse. **2.** Naut. (of the wind, current, etc.) to beat about; force to take a variable course. **3.** Obs. to hoodwink; cheat. —v.i. **4.** to struggle ineffectually, as a ship in a gale. —n. **5.** a balk or check; perplexity. **6.** an artificial obstruction for checking or deflecting the flow of gases (as in a boiler), sounds (as in a radio), etc. [orig. uncert.] —**baf/fle·ment,** n. —**baf/fler,** n. —**baf/fling,** adj. —**baf/fling·ly,** adv.

baff·y (băf/ĭ), n., pl. **baffies.** Golf. a short wooden club with a deeply pitched face, for lofting the ball.

bag (băg), n., v., **bagged, bagging.** —n. **1.** a receptacle of leather, cloth, paper, etc., capable of being closed at the mouth; a pouch. **2.** Chiefly Brit. a suitcase or other portable receptacle for carrying articles as in traveling. **3.** a purse or moneybag. **4.** the contents of a bag. **5.** Hunting. a sportsman's take of game, etc. **6.** any of various measures of capacity. **7.** something resembling or suggesting a bag. **8.** a sac, as in an animal body. **9.** an udder. **10.** a baggy part. **11.** Baseball. **a.** a base (def. 7). **b.** a bag of sand used to mark a base. **12. hold the bag,** U.S. Colloq. to be left with the blame, responsibility, etc. —v.i. **13.** to swell or bulge. **14.** to hang loosely like an empty bag. —v.t. **15.** to cause to swell or bulge; distend. **16.** to put into a bag. **17.** to kill or catch, as in hunting. [ME bagge, t. Scand.; cf. Icel. baggi pack, bundle] —**Syn. 1.** BAG, SACK, referring to a pouchlike object, are often used interchangeably, esp. in the Middle West. A BAG, though it may be of any size, is usually small, and made of such materials as paper, leather, etc. A SACK is usually large, oblong, and made of coarse material.

B. Ag. (L Baccalaureus Agriculturae) Bachelor of Agriculture. Also, **B. Agr.**

ba·gasse (bagás/), n. crushed sugar cane or beet refuse from sugar making. [t. F, t. Pr.: m., bagasso]

bag·a·telle (băg/ətĕl/), n. **1.** a trifle. **2.** a game played on a board having at one end holes into which balls are to be struck with a cue. **3.** pinball. **4.** a short and light musical composition, usually for the piano. [t. F, t. It.: m. bagatella, dim. of baga, baca berry]

Bage·hot (băj/ət), n. **Walter,** 1826–77, British economist, political journalist, and critic.

ba·gel (bā/gəl), n. a small doughnut-shaped roll, often eaten with cream cheese, etc.

bag·gage (băg/ĭj), n. **1.** trunks, suitcases, etc., used in traveling; luggage. **2.** Brit. the portable equipment of an army. [ME, t. OF: m. bagage, der. bagues, pl., bundles, or der. baguer tie up]

bag·ging (băg/ĭng), n. woven material, as of hemp or jute, for bags.

bag·gy (băg/ĭ), adj., **-gier, -giest.** baglike; hanging loosely. —**bag/gi·ly,** adv. —**bag/gi·ness,** n.

Bagh·dad (băg dăd/, băg/dăd), n. the capital of Iraq, in the central part, on the Tigris river. 352,137; with suburbs, 558,820 (1947). Also, **Bag·dad** (băg/dăd, băg dăd/).

bag·man (băg/mən), n., pl. **-men.** Brit., Now Rare or Obs. a traveling salesman.

bagn·io (băn/yō, băn/-), n., pl. **bagnios. 1.** a prison for slaves, as in the Orient. **2.** a brothel. **3.** a bath or bathing house. [t. It.: m. bagno, g. L balneum bath]

bag·pipe (băg/pīp/), n. (often pl.) a reed instrument consisting of a melody pipe and one or more accompanying drone pipes protruding from a windbag into which the air is blown by the mouth or a bellows. —**bag/pip/er,** n.

ba·guette (bă gĕt/), n. **1.** a gem cut in a long, rectangular shape. **2.** this shape. **3.** Archit. a small, convex, semicircular molding. Also, **ba·guet/.** [t. F: wand, rod, t. It.: m. bacchetta, dim. of bacchio, g. L baculum]

Scottish bagpipe

Ba·gui·o (băg/ĭō/; Sp. bä/gyō), n. a city in the Philippine Islands, on Luzon: summer capital. 29,262 (1948); 4961 ft. high.

bag·worm (băg/wûrm/), n. the caterpillar of any moth of the family Psychidae. It constructs a bag of silk, leaves, etc., in which it lives.

bah (bä, bă), interj. an exclamation of contempt.

ba·ha·dur (bə hō/dŏŏr, -hä/-), n. a title of respect commonly affixed to the names of European officers in Indian documents, or used in ceremonious mention by natives: Jonas Sahib Bahadur. [t. Hind.: brave, hero]

Ba·hai (bə hä/ē), n., pl. **-hais,** adj. —n. **1.** an adherent of Bahaism. —adj. **2.** of or pertaining to Bahaism or a Bahai. [t. Pers.: m. Bahā (u'llāh) splendor (of God), title of the leader]

Ba·ha·ism (bə hä/ĭz əm), n. Relig. Babism as accepted by the followers of Mirza Husayn Ali, who in 1863 proclaimed himself leader of the Babists under the name Baha-ullah. —**Ba·ha/ist** n., adj.

Ba·ha·ma Islands (bə hä/mə; esp. Brit. and locally bə hä/mə), a group of islands in the British West Indies, SE of Florida: a British colony. 98,489 pop. (est. 1955); 4404 sq. mi. Cap. Nassau. Also, **Bahamas.**

Ba·ha·wal·pur (bə hä/wəl pŏŏr/, bä/wäl-), n. **1.** a state in Pakistan, in the Punjab. 1,823,000 pop. (1951); 17,471 sq. mi. **2.** capital of the state. 41,646 (1951).

Ba·hi·a (bäē/ə, bəē/ə), n. São Salvador.

Ba·hi·a Blan·ca (bäē/ä bläng/kä), a seaport in E Argentina. 112,597 (1947).

Bah·rein Islands (bärān/), a group of islands in the W Persian Gulf: a British protectorate. 120,000 pop. (est. 1954); 232 sq. mi. Cap.: Manama.

baht (bät), n., pl. **bahts, baht.** the Siamese monetary unit in silver, with a U.S. gold equivalent of $.4424. [t. Siamese]

Ba·iae (bā/yē), n. an ancient resort city in SW Italy: villas of Julius Caesar, Nero, and Pompey.

Bai·kal (bī käl/), n. **Lake,** a lake in the S Soviet Union in Asia: the deepest lake in the world. ab. 13,000 sq. mi.; ab. 5000 ft. deep.

bail¹ (bāl), Law. —n. **1.** property given as surety that a person released from custody will return at an appointed time. **2.** the person or persons giving it. **3.** the position or the privilege of being bailed. **4.** release from prison on bond. **5.** the court granting such a release. —v.t. **6.** to grant or to obtain the liberty of (a person under arrest) on security given for his appearance when required, as in court for trial. **7.** to deliver possession of (goods, etc.) for storage, hire, or other special purpose, without transfer of ownership. [ME bayle, t. OF: m. bail control, baillier deliver, g. L bājulāre carry]

bail² (bāl), n. **1.** the semicircular handle of a kettle or pail. **2.** a hooplike support, as for a wagon cover. [ME beyl, prob. t. Scand.; cf. Icel. beyglast become bent]

bail³ (bāl), v.t. **1.** to dip out of a boat, as with a bucket: to bail water out of a boat. **2.** to clear of water by dipping (usually fol. by out): to bail out a boat. —v.i. **3.** to bail water. **4.** to make a parachute jump (fol. by out). —n. **5.** a bucket or other vessel for bailing. [ME bayle, t. OF: m. baille bucket, g. VL bajula vessel] —**bail/er,** n.

bail⁴ (bāl), n. **1.** Cricket. either of the two small bars or sticks laid across the tops of the stumps which form the wicket. **2.** a bar for separating horses in a stable. **3.** (pl.) Obs. the wall of an outer court of a feudal castle. [ME baile, t. OF: barrier; of obscure origin]

bail·a·ble (bā/lə bəl), adj. Law. **1.** capable of being set free on bail. **2.** admitting of bail: a bailable offense.

bail·ee (bā/lē/), n. Law. one to whom goods are delivered in bailment.

bai·ley (bā/lĭ), n., pl. **-leys.** the wall of defense about the outer court of a feudal castle, or the outer court itself (still used in some proper names, as in Old Bailey, London). [ME baily; var. of BAIL⁴]

Bai·ley (bā/lĭ), n. **Liberty Hyde,** 1858–1954, U.S. botanist, horticulturist, and writer.

bail·ie (bā/lĭ), n. (in Scotland) a municipal officer or magistrate, corresponding to an English alderman. [ME bailli, t. OF, var. of baillif BAILIFF]

bail·iff (bā/lĭf), n. **1.** an officer similar to a sheriff or his deputy, employed to execute writs and processes, make arrests, keep order in the court, etc. **2.** (in England) a person charged with local administrative authority, or the chief magistrate in certain towns. **3.** (esp. in England) an overseer of a landed estate. [ME baillif, t. OF, der. baillir govern. See BAIL⁴]

bail·i·wick (bā/lə wĭk), n. **1.** the district within which a bailie or bailiff has jurisdiction. **2.** a person's area of skill, work, etc. [f. BAILIE + wick office (ME wike, OE wíce)]

bail·ment (bāl/mənt), n. Law. **1.** act of bailing a prisoner or accused person. **2.** act of bailing goods, etc.

bail·or (bā/lər, bā/lôr/), n. Law. one who delivers goods, etc., in bailment.

bails·man (bālz/mən), n., pl. **-men.** Law. one who gives bail or security.

bain-ma·rie (băN mä rē/), n., pl. **bains-marie** (băN mä rē/) Chiefly Brit. a vessel containing hot water, in which another vessel is placed to heat its contents. [F: bath of Miriam (sister of Moses), in the Middle Ages considered an alchemist]

Bai·ram (bī räm/, bĭ/räm), n. either of two Mohammedan festivals, one (lesser Bairam) immediately after Ramadan, the other (greater Bairam) 70 days after it. [t. Turk.: m. bai ram]

Baird Mountains (bârd), a mountain range in NW Alaska, forming the W end of the Brooks Range.

bairn (bârn; Scot. bärn), n. Scot. and N. Eng. a child; a son or daughter. [Scot. var. of obs. E barn(e) child, OE bearn]

bait (bāt), n. **1.** food, or some substitute, used as a lure in angling, trapping, etc. **2.** an allurement; enticement. **3.** a halt for refreshment or rest during a journey. —v.t. **4.** to prepare (a hook or trap) with bait. **5.** to lure as with bait; captivate. **6.** to set dogs upon (an animal) for sport. **7.** to worry; torment. **8.** to give food and drink to (horses, etc.), esp. during a journey. —v.i. **9.** Now Chiefly Brit. to stop for food or refreshment during a journey. **10.** to take food; feed. [ME, t. Scand.; cf. Icel. beita] —**bait/er,** n.

baize (bāz), n. **1.** a soft, usually green, woolen fabric resembling felt, used chiefly for the tops of billiard tables. **2.** an article of this fabric. [earlier bays, t. F: m. baies, pl., der. bai bay-colored, g. L badius]

Ba·ja Ca·li·for·nia (bä/hä kä/lē fôr/nyä), Spanish name of Lower California.

bake (bāk), v., **baked, baking,** n. —v.t. 1. to cook by dry heat in an oven, under coals, or on heated metals or stones. 2. to harden by heat. —v.i. 3. to bake bread etc. 4. to become baked. —n. 5. U.S. a social occasion, at which the chief food is baked. 6. Scot. a cracker. [ME bake(n), OE bacan, c. G backen]

bake·house (bāk/hous/), n. a building or room to bake in; a bakery.

Ba·ke·lite (bā/kə līt/), n. a trademark for a thermosetting plastic derived by heating phenol or cresol with formaldehyde and ammonia under pressure, used for radio cabinets, telephone receivers, electric insulators, and molded plastic ware. [named after L. H. Baekeland]

bak·er (bā/kər), n. 1. one who bakes; one who makes and sells bread, cake, etc. 2. a small portable oven.

Bak·er (bā/kər), n. 1. **Mount,** a mountain in NW Washington, in the Cascade Range. 10,750 ft. 2. **George Pierce,** 1866–1935, U.S. critic, author, and professor of drama. 3. **Newton Diehl** (dēl), 1871–1937, U.S. lawyer: Secretary of War, 1916–21. 4. **Ray Stannard,** ("David Grayson") 1870–1946, U.S. author.

Baker Island, a small island in the Pacific, near the equator, belonging to the U.S. 1 sq. mi.

baker's dozen, thirteen, reckoned as a dozen.

Bak·ers·field (bā/kərz fēld/), n. a city in S California, N of Los Angeles. 56,848 (1960).

bak·er·y (bā/kər ĭ), n., pl. **-eries.** a baker's shop; place where baked goods are made or sold.

bak·ing (bā/kĭng), n. 1. act of one who or that which bakes. 2. the quantity baked at one time; a batch.

baking powder, any of various powders used as a substitute for yeast in baking, composed of sodium bicarbonate mixed with an acid substance capable of setting carbon dioxide free when the mixture is moistened.

baking soda, sodium bicarbonate, $NaHCO_3$.

bak·sheesh (bāk/shēsh), (used in India, Turkey, etc.) —n. 1. a tip, present, or gratuity. —v.t., v.i. 2. to give a tip (to). Also, **bak/shish, backsheesh, backshish.** [t. Pers.: m. bakhshish, der. bakhshidan give]

Bakst (bäkst), n. **Léon Nikolaevich** (lĕ ôN' nĭ kō lä/yə vĭch), 1866–1924, Russian painter and designer.

Ba·ku (bä kōō/), n. a seaport in the Soviet Union on the Caspian Sea: capital of Azerbaijan. 901,000 with suburbs (est. 1956).

Ba·ku·nin (bä kōō/nĭn), n. **Mikhail Aleksandrovich** (mĭ hä ēl/ ä/lĕ ksän/drō vĭch), 1814–76, Russian anarchist and writer.

bal., balance.

Ba·laam (bā/ləm), n. a Mesopotamian diviner, who, when commanded to curse the Israelites, blessed them and uttered favorable prophecies, after having been rebuked by the ass he rode. Num. 22–23.

Bal·a·kla·va (bäl/ə klä/və; Russ. bä/lä klä/vä), n. a seaport in the SW Soviet Union, on the Black Sea: scene of the "Charge of the Light Brigade" in the Crimean War, 1854.

bal·a·lai·ka (bäl/ə lī/kə), n. a Russian musical instrument with a triangular body and a guitar neck. [t. Russ.]

bal·ance (bäl/əns), n., v., **-anced, -ancing.** —n. 1. an instrument for weighing, typically a bar poised or swaying on a central support according to the weights borne in scales (pans) suspended at the ends. 2. power to decide as by a balance; authoritative control: his fate hung in the balance. 3. state of equilibrium or equipoise; equal distribution of weight, amount, etc. 4. mental steadiness; habit of calm behavior, judgment, etc. 5. harmonious arrangement or adjustment, esp. in the arts of design. 6. something used to produce equilibrium; a counterpoise. 7. act of balancing; comparison as to weight, amount, importance, etc.; estimate. 8. U.S. the remainder or rest. 9. Com. a. equality between the totals of the two sides of an account. b. difference between the debit total and the credit total of an account. c. unpaid difference represented by the excess of debits over credits. 10. an adjustment of accounts. 11. Dancing. a balancing movement. 12. Horol. a wheel which oscillates against the tension of a hairspring for regulating the beats of a watch or clock. 13. (cap.) Astron. the zodiacal constellation Libra or the sign named for it. —v.t. 14. to weigh in a balance. 15. to estimate the relative weight or importance of; compare: balance probabilities. 16. to serve as a counterpoise to; counterbalance; offset. 17. to bring to or hold in equilibrium; poise: to balance a book on one's head. 18. to arrange, adjust, or proportion the parts of symmetrically. 19. to be equal or proportionate to. 20. Com. a. to add up the two sides of (an account) and determine the difference. b. to make the necessary entries in (an account) so that the sums of the two sides will be equal. c. to settle by paying what remains due on an account; equalize or adjust. 21. Dancing. to move in rhythm to and from: to balance one's partner. —v.i. 22. to have an equality or equivalence in weight, parts, etc.; be in equilibrium: the account doesn't balance, do these scales balance? 23. Com. to reckon or adjust accounts. 24. to waver, hesitate. 25. Dancing. to move forward and backward, or in opposite directions. [ME, t. OF, g. LL bilanx having two scales] —Syn. 4. poise, composure. 8. See remainder.

balance of power, a distribution and an opposition of forces among nations such that no single nation will be strong enough to dominate all the others.

balance of trade, the difference between the exports and imports of a country, said to be favorable or unfavorable as exports are greater or less than imports.

bal·anc·er (bäl/ən sər), n. 1. one who or that which balances. 2. Entomol. halter². 3. an acrobat.

balance sheet, Com. 1. a tabular statement of both sides of a set of accounts, in which the debit and credit balances add up as equal. 2. a statement of the financial position of a business on a specified date.

balance wheel, Horol. balance (def. 12).

Ba·la·ra·ma (bül/ərä/mə), n. Hindu Myth. the elder brother of Krishna and an incarnation of Vishnu.

bal·as (bäl/əs, bä/ləs), n. Mineral. a rose-red variety of spinel. Also, **balas ruby.** [ME, t. OF: m. balais, t. Ar.: m. balakksh kind of ruby, t. Pers.: m. Badakhshān, a province where found]

bal·a·ta (bäl/ə tə), n. 1. the dried juice or gum (balata gum) obtained from the bully tree, Manikara bidentata, used as a substitute for gutta-percha and in making chewing gum. 2. the bully tree. [t. Amer. Sp.]

Ba·la·ton (bô/lō tôn/), n. a lake in W Hungary: the largest lake in central and western Europe. ab. 50 mi. long. German, **Platten See.**

Bal·bo (bäl/bō), n. Italo (ē/tä lō/), 1896–1940, Italian aviator, general, and statesman.

Bal·bo·a (bäl bō/ə; Sp. bäl bō/ä), n. 1. **Vasco Núñez de** (väs/kō nōō/nyĕth dĕ), 1475?–1517, Spanish adventurer and explorer who discovered the Pacific Ocean in 1513. 2. a seaport in the Canal Zone at the Pacific terminus of the Panama Canal. 4162 (1950). 3. (l.c.) a silver coin of Panama, valued at one U.S. dollar.

bal·brig·gan (bäl brĭg/ən), n. a kind of unbleached cotton, originally made at Balbriggan, in Ireland, used esp. in hosiery and underwear.

bal·co·ny (bäl/kə nĭ), n., pl. **-nies.** 1. a balustrade or raised and railed platform projecting from the wall of a building. 2. a gallery in a theater. [t. It.: m. balcone, der. balco scaffold, t. OHG. See BALK] —**bal/co·nied,** adj.

bald (bôld), adj. 1. lacking hair on some part of the scalp: a bald head or person. 2. destitute of some natural growth or covering: a bald mountain. 3. bare; plain; unadorned: a bald prose style. 4. open; undisguised: a bald lie. 5. Zool. having white on the head: bald eagle. [ME balled, f. obs. ball white spot (cf. Welsh bali whiteness) + -ED³] —**bald/ly,** adv. —**bald/ness,** n.

bal·da·chin (bäl/də kĭn, bôl/-), n. 1. Archit. a fixed canopy, of metal, wood, or stone, above the isolated high altar of a church or above a tomb. 2. a portable canopy carried in religious processions. Also, **bal/da·quin.** [t. F: m. baldaquin, t. It.: m. baldacchino, orig., silk from Bagdad, der. Baldacco Bagdad]

bald cypress, a tree, Taxodium distichum, of the Southern swamplands of the U.S.

bald eagle, a large eagle, Haliaeetus leucocephalus, of the U. S. and Canada, having a fully feathered head and, when adult, a white head and tail.

Bal·der (bôl/dər), n. Scand. Myth. son of Odin, and one of the chief deities, god of the summer sun, and called "the Good." Also, **Bal·dr** (bäl/dər).

Bald eagle.
Haliaeetus leucocephalus
(Ab. 3 ft. high, wingspread 7 ft.)

bal·der·dash (bôl/dər däsh/), n. 1. a senseless jumble of words; nonsense. 2. Obs. mixture of liquors.

bald·head (bôld/hĕd/), n. 1. one who has a bald head. 2. a breed of domestic pigeons. —**bald/head/ed,** adj.

bald·pate (bôld/pāt/), n. 1. one who has a bald head. 2. the American widgeon. —**bald/pat/ed,** adj.

bal·dric (bôl/drĭk), n. a belt, sometimes richly ornamented, worn diagonally from shoulder to hip, supporting a sword, horn, etc. [ME bawdrik, orig. and history obscure; akin to MHG balderich girdle; r. ME baudry, t. OF, t. MHG (as above)]

Bald·win (bôld/wĭn), n. 1. **James Mark,** 1861–1934, U.S. psychologist. 2. **Stanley** (Earl Baldwin of Bewdley), 1867–1947, British statesman: prime minister, 1923–1924, 1924–29, 1935–37. 3. a variety of red, or red-and-yellow, winter apple, grown esp. in the northeast U.S.

Baldwin I, 1058–1118, crusader and first king of Jerusalem, 1100–18.

bale¹ (bāl), n., v., **baled, baling.** —n. 1. a large bundle or package prepared for storage or transportation, esp. one closely compressed and secured by cords, wires, hoops, or the like, sometimes with a wrapping: a bale of hay. —v.t. 2. to make into bales. [ME, t. Flem., t. OF: m. balle, t. OHG: m. balla BALL¹] —**bal/er,** n.

bale² (bāl), n. Archaic. 1. evil; harm; misfortune. 2. woe; misery; sorrow. [ME; OE balu, bealo]

Bâle (bäl), n. French name of Basel.

Bal·e·ar·ic Islands (bäl/ĭ är/ĭk), a group of islands in the W Mediterranean: a province of Spain. 428,821 (est. 1955); 1936 sq. mi. Cap.: Palma. Spanish, **Ba·le·a·res** (bä/lĕ ä/rĕs).

ba·leen (bə lēn/), n. Zool. whalebone (def. 1). [ME balene, t. OF: m. baleine, g. L bālaena whale]

bale·fire (bāl′fīr′), n. **1.** a large fire in the open air; bonfire. **2.** a beacon or signal fire. **3.** the fire of a funeral pile. [ME *balefyre*, OE *bǣlfȳr*]

bale·ful (bāl′fəl), adj. **1.** full of menacing or malign influences; pernicious. **2.** Obs. wretched; miserable. [ME; OE *bealofull*] —**bale′ful·ly**, adv. —**bale′ful·ness**, n.

Bal·four (băl′fŏŏr), n. **Arthur James** (*1st Earl of Balfour*), 1848–1930, British statesman and writer: prime minister, 1902–05.

Balfour Declaration, a statement (Nov. 2, 1917) that the British government "view with favour the establishment in Palestine of a National Home for the Jewish people," but that "nothing shall be done which may prejudice the civil and religious rights of existing non-Jewish communities in Palestine."

Ba·li (bä′lē), n. an island in Indonesia, E of Java. 1,101,393 pop. (1930): 2147 sq. mi. Cap.: Singaraja.

Ba·li·nese (bä′lə nēz′, -nēs′), adj., n., pl. **-nese.** —adj. **1.** of or pertaining to Bali, its people, or their language. —n. **2.** a native or inhabitant of Bali. **3.** the language of Bali, an Indonesian language.

Bal·iol (bāl′yəl, bā′lY əl), n. **John de**, 1249–1315, king of Scotland, 1292–96.

balk (bôk), v.i. **1.** to stop, as at an obstacle: *he balked at making the speech.* **2.** (of horses) to stop short and stubbornly refuse to go on. —v.t. **3.** to place a balk in the way of; hinder; thwart: *balked in one's hopes.* **4.** to let slip; fail to use: *to balk an opportunity.* —n. **5.** a check or hindrance; a defeat or disappointment. **6.** a miss, slip, or failure: *to make a balk.* **7.** a strip of land left unplowed. **8.** a crossbeam in the roof of a house which unites and supports the rafters; tie beam. **9.** Civ. Eng. one of the stringers of a military bridge. **10.** Baseball. an illegal deceptive motion of a pitcher as if to pitch when a runner or runners are on base. **11.** Billiards. **a.** any of the eight panels or compartments lying between the cushions of the table and the balk lines. **b.** in balk, inside any of these spaces. Also, **baulk.** [ME; OE *balca* ridge, c. OHG *balco* beam] —**balk′er**, n.

Bal·kan (bôl′kən), adj. **1.** pertaining to the Balkan States or their inhabitants. **2.** pertaining to the Balkan Peninsula. **3.** pertaining to the Balkan Mountains. —n. **4. the Balkans**, the Balkan States.

Bal·kan·ize (bôl′kə nīz′), v.t., **-ized, -izing.** to divide into small states hostile to one another. —**Bal′kan·i·za′tion**, n.

Balkan Mountains, a mountain range extending from W Bulgaria to the Black Sea. Highest peak, ab. 7800 ft.

Balkan Peninsula, a peninsula in S Europe, lying S of the Danube and bordered by the Adriatic, Ionian, Aegean, and Black Seas.

Balkan States, the countries in the Balkan Peninsula: Yugoslavia, Rumania, Bulgaria, Albania, Greece, and the European part of Turkey.

Bal·khash (băl häsh′), n. a salt lake in the SW Soviet Union in Asia, in Kazak Republic. 7115 sq. mi.

balk line (bôk), **1.** Sports. in track events) the starting line. **2.** Billiards. **a.** a straight line drawn across the table, behind which the cue balls are placed in beginning a game. **b.** any of four lines, each near to and parallel with one side of the cushion, which divide the table into a large central panel or compartment and eight smaller compartments (**balks**) lying between this. **c.** balk (def. 11a).

balk·y (bô′kY), adj., **balkier, balkiest.** U.S. given to balking: *a balky horse.*

ball¹ (bôl), n. **1.** a spherical or approximately spherical body; a sphere. **2.** a round or roundish body, of different materials and sizes, hollow or solid, for use in various games, as baseball, football, tennis, or golf. **3.** a game played with a ball, esp. baseball. **4.** Baseball. **a.** a ball in play or action, as tossed, thrown, struck, etc.: *a low or high ball, a curved ball.* **b.** a ball pitched too high or low or not over the plate, and not struck at by the batter. **5.** Mil. **a.** a solid projectile for a cannon, rifle, pistol, etc. (as distinguished from a shell), usually spherical. **b.** projectiles, esp. bullets, collectively. **6.** any part of a thing, esp. of the human body, that is rounded or protuberant: *the ball of the thumb.* **7.** Astron. a planetary or celestial body, esp. the earth. **8. play ball, a.** (in games) to put the ball in motion. **b.** to start any action. **c.** U.S. Colloq. to work together; coöperate. —v.t. **9.** to make into a ball. **10.** to wind into balls: *to ball cotton.* **11.** U.S. Slang. to bring to a state of hopeless confusion or difficulty (fol. by *up*). —v.i. **12.** to form or gather into a ball. [ME *bal*, t. Scand.; cf. Icel. *böllr*] —**Syn. 1.** BALL, GLOBE, SPHERE, ORB agree in referring to a round or rounded object. BALL may be applied to any round or roundish object or part: *a rubber ball.* GLOBE and SPHERE denote something thought of as either exactly or approximately round: *in the form of a globe, a perfect sphere.* ORB is now found only in elevated or scientific use; it is applied esp. to the eye and to the heavenly bodies: *the orb of the full moon.*

ball² (bôl), n. a social assembly for dancing. [t. F: m. *bal*, der. OF *baler* dance, g. LL *ballāre*]

Ball (bôl), n. **John**, died 1381, English priest: one of the leaders of Wat Tyler's peasants' revolt in 1381.

bal·lad (băl′əd), n. **1.** a simple, often crude, narrative poem, of popular origin, composed in short stanzas, esp. one of romantic character and adapted for singing. **2.** any poem written in similar style. **3.** any light, simple song, esp. one of sentimental or romantic character, having two or more stanzas, all sung to the same melody. **4.** the musical setting for a folk or literary ballad. [ME *balade*, t. OF, t. Pr.: m. *balada* dancing song, dance, der. *balar* dance, g. LL *ballāre*]

bal·lade (bə läd′, bă-; Fr. bá läd′), n. **1.** a poem consisting commonly of 3 stanzas having an identical rhyme scheme, followed by an envoy. The same last line is used for each of the stanzas and the envoy. **2.** Music. a composition in free style and romantic mood, often for solo piano or for orchestra. [t. F. See BALLAD]

bal·lad·mon·ger (băl′əd mŭng′gər), n. **1.** a seller of ballads. **2.** a bad poet.

bal·lad·ry (băl′ə drY), n. ballad poetry.

ballad stanza, the metrical form for ballad verse, ordinarily consisting of four lines.

ball and chain, **1.** a heavy iron ball fastened by a chain to a prisoner's leg. **2.** any restraint.

ball-and-sock·et joint (bôl′ən sŏk′Yt), a joint formed by a ball or knob in a socket, admitting a degree of rotary movement in every direction.

Bal·la·rat (băl′ə răt′, băl′ə răt′), n. a city in SE Australia, in Victoria. 39,964 (1954).

bal·last (băl′əst), n. **1.** any heavy material carried by a ship or boat for insuring proper stability, so as to avoid capsizing and to secure the greatest effectiveness of the propelling power. **2.** something heavy, as bags of sand, placed in the car of a balloon for control of altitude or, less frequently, of attitude. **3.** anything that gives mental, moral, or political stability or steadiness. **4.** gravel, broken stone, slag, etc., placed between and under the ties of a railroad to give stability, provide drainage, and distribute the load. —v.t. **5.** to furnish with ballast: *to ballast a ship.* **6.** to give steadiness to; keep steady. [t. ODan.: m. *barlast* (f. *bar* mere + *last* load), or t. MLG: f. *bal* bad + *last* load]

ball bearing, Mach. **1.** a bearing in which the shaft or journal turns upon a number of steel balls running in an annular track. **2.** any of the steel balls so used. —**ball′-bear′ing**, adj.

ball cock, a device for regulating the supply of water in a tank, cistern, or the like, consisting essentially of a valve connected with a hollow floating ball which by its rise or fall shuts or opens the valve.

bal·le·ri·na (băl′ə rē′nə; It. bäl′ lĕ rē′nä), n., pl. **-nas,** (It.) **-ne** (-nĕ). **1.** the principal female dancer in a ballet company. **2.** any female ballet dancer. [t. It.]

bal·let (băl′ā, bă lā′; Fr. bá lĕ′), n. **1.** a spectacular entertainment, often designed to tell a story, and rendered by a company of professional dancers. **2.** a dance interlude in an operatic performance. **3.** the style of dancing used in such a performance, using intricate steps and expressive gestures. **4.** the company of dancers. [F, t. It.: m. *balletto*, dim. of *ballo* dance]

bal·let·o·mane (bă lĕt′ə mān′), n. a ballet enthusiast.

ball·flow·er (bôl′flou′ər), n. Archit. a medieval ornament resembling a ball placed in a circular flower, the three (or four) petals of which form a cup around it.

Bal·liol (băl′yəl, bā′lY əl), n. a college of Oxford University founded before 1268.

bal·lis·ta (bə lYs′tə), n., pl. **-tae** (-tē). an ancient military engine for throwing stones or other missiles. [t. L, der. Gk. *bállein* throw]

bal·lis·tics (bə lYs′tYks), n. the science or study of the motion of projectiles, such as bullets, shells, bombs, etc. **Interior ballistics** is the study of the motion of projectiles within the bore of a gun; **exterior ballistics** is the study of the motion of projectiles after they leave the muzzle of a gun. —**bal·lis′tic**, adj. —**bal·lis·ti·cian** (băl′Ys tYsh′ən), n

Ballista

bal·lo·net (băl′ə nĕt′), n. an air or gasbag compartment in a balloon or airship, used to control buoyancy and maintain shape. [t. F: m. *ballonnet*, dim. of *ballon* balloon]

bal·loon (bə lōōn′), n. **1.** a bag made of some material impermeable to gas and filled with some gas lighter than ordinary air, designed to rise and float in the atmosphere, and in the large forms having a car or compartment attached for passengers. **2.** an inflatable rubber bag, usually brightly colored, used as a children's toy. **3.** Chem. a round-bottomed flask. **4.** (in drawings, etc.) a balloon-shaped figure enclosing words represented as issuing from the mouth of the speaker. —v.i. **5.** to go up or ride in a balloon. **6.** to swell or puff out like a balloon. —v.t. **7.** to fill with air; inflate or distend (something) like a balloon. —adj. **8.** puffed out like a balloon: *balloon sleeves.* [t. It.: m. *ballone*, aug. of *balla* ball] —**bal·loon′ist**, n.

balloon jib, Naut. a large triangular sail of light canvas used by yachts in light winds, instead of the jib.

balloon tire, Auto., etc. a low-pressure pneumatic tire with a broad tread for reducing the shock of bumps.

---

b., blend of, blended; c., cognate with; d., dialect, dialectal; der., derived from; f., formed from; g., going back to; m., modification of; r., replacing; s., stem of; t., taken from; ?, perhaps. See the full key on inside cover.

balloon vine, a sapindaceous tropical climbing plant, *Cardiospermum Halicacabum*, with big bladderlike pods.

bal·lot (băl′ət), *n., v.,* **-loted, -loting.** —*n.* **1.** a ticket, paper, etc., used in voting. **2.** the whole number of votes cast or recorded: *there was a large ballot.* **3.** the method of secret voting by means of printed or written ballots, or by means of voting machines. **4.** voting in general, or a round of voting. **5.** (formerly) a little ball used in voting. —*v.i.* **6.** to vote by ballot. **7.** to draw lots: *to ballot for places.* —*v.t.* **8.** to vote on by ballot. [t. It.: m. *ballotta*, bullet, tot, dim. of *balla* ball] —**bal′·lot·er,** *n.*

bal·lotte·ment (bə lŏt′mənt), *n. Med.* **1.** an unreliable method of diagnosing pregnancy by the rebound of a fetal part displaced from its position by a sudden push with the examining finger. **2.** a similar method employed in testing for floating kidney, movable abdominal tumors, etc. [t. F.: a tossing, der. *ballotter* toss as a ball]

ball·play·er (bôl′plā′ər), *n.* **1.** a baseball player. **2.** one who plays ball.

ball point pen, a fountain pen in which the point is a fine ball bearing, depositing an extremely thin film of ink. It will write for a longer period with a single reservoir of ink than a conventional pen.

ball·room (bôl′rōōm′, -rŏŏm′), *n.* a large room with a polished floor for balls or dancing.

ball valve, *Mach.* a valve controlled by a ball which is lifted by the upward pressure of the fluid and descends by gravity.

bal·ly (băl′ĭ), *Eng. Slang.* —*adj.* **1.** confounded (used humorously or for emphasis). —*adv.* **2.** very.

bal·ly·hoo (n. băl′ĭ hōō′; v. băl′ĭ hōō′, băl′ĭ hōō′), *n., pl.* **-hoos,** *v.,* **-hooed, -hooing.** *U.S. Slang.* —*n.* **1.** a clamorous attempt to win customers or advance any cause; blatant advertising or publicity. **2.** clamor or outcry. —*v.t., v.i.* **3.** to advertise or push by ballyhoo. [orig. obscure]

bal·ly·rag (băl′ĭ răg′), *v.t.* bullyrag.

balm (bäm), *n.* **1.** any of various oily, fragrant, resinous substances, often of medicinal value, exuding from certain plants, esp. tropical trees of the burseraceous genus *Commiphora*. **2.** a plant or tree yielding such a substance. **3.** any aromatic or fragrant ointment. **4.** aromatic fragrance; sweet odor. **5.** any of various aromatic menthaceous plants, esp. of the genus *Melissa*, as *M. officinalis*, a lemon-scented perennial herb. **6.** anything which heals, soothes, or mitigates pain. [ME *basme*, t. OF, g. L *balsam* BALSAM]

bal·ma·caan (băl′mə kän′), *n.* a man's short, full-skirted overcoat of rough woolen cloth, with raglan shoulders. [named after *Balmacaan*, in Scotland]

balm of Gilead, **1.** any of several species of the genus *Commiphora* (esp. *C. opobalsamum* and *C. mecanensis*), which yield a fragrant oleoresin. **2.** the resin itself. **3.** a North American poplar, *Populus candicans*.

Bal·mor·al (băl môr′əl, -mŏr′əl), *n.* **1.** a colored woolen petticoat formerly worn under a looped-up skirt. **2.** (*also l.c.*) a kind of laced shoe. **3.** a kind of brimless Scotch cap with a flat top projecting all around the head. [named after *Balmoral* Castle in Scotland]

Bal·mung (băl′mŏŏng), *n.* (in the *Nibelungenlied*) the sword of Siegfried.

balm·y (bä′mĭ), *adj.,* **balmier, balmiest. 1.** mild and refreshing; soft; soothing: *balmy weather.* **2.** having the qualities of balm; aromatic; fragrant: *balmy leaves.* **3.** producing balm. **4.** *Eng. Slang.* weak-minded; silly. —**balm′i·ly,** *adv.* —**balm′i·ness,** *n.* —**Syn. 1.** fair, gentle, temperate, clement.

bal·ne·al (băl′nĭ əl), *adj.* of or pertaining to baths or bathing. [f. s. L *balneum* bath + -AL¹]

bal·ne·ol·o·gy (băl′nĭ ŏl′ə jĭ), *n. Med.* the science of using baths and bathing in therapeutics. [f. s. L *balneum* bath + -(o)LOGY]

ba·lo·ney (bə lō′nĭ), *n.* **1.** *Slang.* nonsense; foolishness. **2.** *Colloq.* bologna sausage. Also, **boloney.**

bal·sa (bôl′sə, bäl′-), *n.* **1.** a bombacaceous tree, *Ochroma lagopus*, of tropical America, with an exceedingly light wood used for life preservers, rafts, etc. **2.** a raft made of balsa wood. **3.** any life raft. [t. Sp.]

bal·sam (bôl′səm), *n.* **1.** any of various fragrant exudations from certain trees, esp. of the burseraceous genus *Commiphora* (see **balm** def. 1), as the balm of Gilead (**balsam of Mecca**). **2.** the similar products (**balsam of Peru** and **balsam of Tolu**) yielded by the leguminous trees, *Myroxylon Pereirae* and *M. Balsamum* of Central and South America. **3.** oleoresin (def. 1). **4.** any of certain transparent turpentines, as Canada balsam. **5.** a plant or tree yielding a balsam. **6.** the balsam fir. **7.** any of various plants of the balsaminaceous genus *Impatiens*, as *I. Balsamina*, a common garden annual. **8.** any aromatic ointment, whether for ceremonial or medicinal use. **9.** any healing or soothing agent or agency. [OE, t. L: s. *balsamum*, t. Gk.: m. *bálsamon*] —**bal·sa·ma·ceous** (bôl′sə mā′shəs, băl′-), *adj.*

balsam fir, **1.** a North American species of fir, *Abies balsamea*, which yields Canada balsam. **2.** the wood of this tree. **3.** any of certain other firs.

bal·sam·ic (bôl săm′ĭk, băl′-), *adj.* of, like, or containing balsam. —**bal·sam′i·cal·ly,** *adv.*

bal·sam·if·er·ous (bôl′səm ĭf′ər əs, băl′-), *adj.* yielding balsam. [f. BALSAM + -(I)FEROUS]

bal·sa·mi·na·ceous (bôl′sə mĭ nā′shəs, băl′-), *adj. Bot.* belonging to the Balsaminaceae, a family of plants

with odd-shaped flowers, including many tropical species and also the balsams of the genus *Impatiens.* [f. s. Gk. *balsaminē* balsam plant + -ACEOUS]

balsam poplar, a poplar, *Populus Tacamahaca*, with broad heart-shaped leaves, cultivated as a shade tree.

balsam spruce, an evergreen conifer of genus *Abies.*

Balt., Baltic.

Bal·tic (bôl′tĭk), *adj.* **1.** of, near, or on the Baltic Sea. **2.** of or pertaining to the Baltic States. —*n.* **3.** a group of Indo-European languages, including Lettish, Lithuanian, and the extinct Old Prussian. [t. ML: s. *Balticum*, ? der. L *balteus* belt]

Baltic Sea, a sea in N Europe, bounded by Sweden, Finland, the Soviet Union, Poland, Germany, and Denmark. ab. 160,000 sq. mi.

Baltic States, the formerly independent republics of Estonia, Latvia, and Lithuania, sometimes including Finland.

Bal·ti·more (bôl′tə môr′), *n.* **1.** a seaport in N Maryland, on an estuary near Chesapeake Bay. 939,024 (1960). **2. Lord.** See **Calvert,** Sir George.

Baltic Sea

Baltimore oriole, an American oriole, *Icterus galbula.* [so named because the black and orange of the male were the colors of Lord Baltimore's livery]

Bal·to-Sla·vic (bôl′tō slä′vĭk, -slăv′ĭk), *n.* a grouping of Indo-European languages comprising the Baltic and Slavic groups.

Ba·lu·chi·stan (bə lōō′chə stän′, -stăn′), *n.* **1.** a province in W Pakistan, bordering the Arabian Sea; formerly subdivided into British territory and three native states. 1,374,000 pop. (1951); 134,002 sq. mi. *Cap.:* Quetta. **2.** a region in SE Iran.

bal·us·ter (băl′ə stər), *n. Archit.* **1.** one of a series of short, pillarlike supports for a railing, as of a staircase. **2.** (*pl.*) balustrade. [t. F: m. *balustre*, t. It.: m. *balaust(r)o*, t. L: m. *balaustium*, t. Gk.: m. *balaustion* pomegranate flower]

bal·us·trade (băl′ə strād′), *n. Archit.* a series of balusters supporting a railing. [t. F, t. It.: m. *balaustrata*]

Bal·zac (băl′zăk, bôl′-; *Fr.* bál-zák′), *n.* **Honoré de** (ō nô rě′ də), 1799–1850, French novelist.

Baluster and balustrade

Bam·berg (băm′bûrg; *Ger.* bäm′běrкн), *n.* a city in West Germany, in N Bavaria. 76,800 (1951).

bam·bi·no (băm bē′nō; *It.* bäm bē′nō), *n., pl.* **-ni** (-nē). **1.** a child or baby. **2.** an image of the infant Jesus. [t. It., dim. of *bambo* simple]

bam·boo (băm bōō′), *n., pl.* **-boos. 1.** any of the woody or treelike tropical and semitropical grasses of the genus *Bambura* (or *Bambos*) and allied genera. **2.** the hollow woody stem of such a plant, used for building purposes and for making furniture, poles, etc. [earlier *bambus*, t. D: m. *bamboes.* Cf. Malay *bambu*]

bamboo curtain, the state of rigid censorship and secrecy in Communist Asia, esp. China.

bam·boo·zle (băm bōō′zəl), *v.,* **-zled, -zling.** —*v.t.* **1.** to deceive by trickery; impose upon. **2.** to perplex; mystify. —*v.i.* **3.** to practice imposition or trickery. —**bam·boo′zle·ment,** *n.* —**bam·boo′zler,** *n.*

ban¹ (băn), *v.,* **banned, banning,** *n.* —*v.t.* **1.** to prohibit; interdict: *to ban a meeting or book.* **2.** *Archaic.* to pronounce an ecclesiastical curse upon. **3.** *Archaic.* to curse; execrate. —*n.* **4.** an authoritative interdiction. **5.** informal denunciation or prohibition, as by public opinion. **6.** *Law.* a sentence of outlawry. **7.** *Eccles.* a formal ecclesiastical denunciation; excommunication. **8.** a malediction; curse. [ME, t. Scand.; cf. Icel. *banna* forbid, curse, c. OE *bannan* summon] —**Syn. 1.** forbid, taboo. **4.** prohibition, proscription.

ban² (băn), *n.* **1.** a public proclamation or edict. **2.** (*pl.*) banns. **3.** (in feudal times) the summons of the sovereign's vassals for military service, or the whole body liable to the summons. [OE *gebann*]

ban³ (băn), *n.* **1.** the governor of Croatia and Slavonia. **2.** *Hist.* one of the wardens of the southern marches of Hungary. [t. Hung., t. Pers.: lord]

ban⁴ (băn), *n., pl.* **bani** (bä′nĭ). a Rumanian coin worth one-hundredth part of a leu. [Rum.]

ba·nal (bā′nəl, bə näl′, -näl′, băn′əl), *adj.* hackneyed; trite. [t. F, der. OF *ban*, t. Gmc.: proclamation, c. BAN²] —**ba·nal·i·ty** (bə näl′ə tĭ, bā-), *n.* —**ba′nal·ly,** *adv.* —**Syn.** See **commonplace.**

ba·nan·a (bə năn′ə), *n.* **1.** a plant of the tropical genus *Musa*, of which various species are cultivated for their nutritious fruit. **2.** the fruit, esp. that of *M. sapientum*, with yellow or red rind. [t. Pg., Sp., from native name]

banana oil, *Chem.* amyl acetate, $CH_3CO_2C_5H_{11}$, a sweet-smelling, colorless, liquid ester, used as a solvent and in artificial fruit flavors.

Ban·bur·y (băn′běr′ĭ, -bə rĭ, băm′-), *n.* a historic town in Oxfordshire, S England, esp. important in 16th and 17th centuries. 18,917 (1951).

ăct, āble, dâre, ärt; ĕbb, ēqual; ĭf, īce; hŏt, ōver, ôrder, oil, bŏŏk, ōōze, out; ŭp, ūse, ûrge; ə = a in alone; ch, chief; g, give; ng, ring; sh, shoe; th, thin; ŧħ, that; zh, vision. See the full key on inside cover.

Ban·croft (băn′krôft, -krŏft), *n.* **George**, 1800–91, U. S. historian and statesman.

band¹ (bănd), *n.* **1.** a company of persons (rarely animals) joined or acting together; a company, party, or troop. **2.** a company of musicians playing instruments usually for marching or open-air performance, namely, brass wind, wood wind, and percussion. **3.** an orchestra playing popular music, esp. for dancing. **4.** a division of a nomadic tribe; a group of individuals who move and camp together. —*v.t.* **5.** to unite in a troop, company, or confederacy. —*v.i.* **6.** to unite; confederate. [t. F: m. *bande*, ult. from Gmc., but sense devel. purely Rom.] —**Syn. 1.** See **company**.

band² (bănd), *n.* **1.** a thin, flat strip of some material for binding, confining, trimming, or some other purpose: *hat band, rubber band.* **2.** a fillet, belt, or strap. **3.** a stripe, as of color or decorative work. **4.** the form of falling or flat collar commonly worn by men and women in the seventeenth century in western Europe. **5.** a linen or cambric collar with two pendent strips in front, sometimes worn by clergymen (Geneva bands). **6.** one of the pendent strips. **7.** *Radio.* a group of frequencies which can be tuned in closely together, as by means of a particular set of condensers. —*v.t.* **8.** to mark with bands; stripe. [ME *bande*, t. F, ult. c. BAND³]

band³ (bănd), *n.* **1.** (*usually pl.*) anything which binds the person or the limbs; a shackle, manacle, or fetter. **2.** an obligation; bond: *the nuptial bands.* [ME, t. Scand.; cf. Icel. *band*]

band·age (băn′dĭj), *n., v.,* **-aged, -aging.** —*n.* **1.** a strip of cloth or other material used to bind up a wound, etc. **2.** anything used as a band or ligature. —*v.t.* **3.** to bind or cover with a bandage. [t. F, der. *bande* band] —**band′ag·er,** *n.*

ban·dan·na (băn dăn′ə), *n.* **1.** a large colored handkerchief with spots or figures, usually white on a red or blue background. **2.** any large handkerchief. Also, **ban·dan′a.** [appar. der. Hind. *bandhnu*, mode of dyeing in which the cloth is tied so as to prevent parts from receiving the dye]

Ban·da Sea (băn′dä), a sea between Celebes and New Guinea, S of the Moluccas and N of Timor.

band·box (bănd′bŏks′), *n.* a light box of pasteboard, thin wood, etc., for holding a hat, collars, etc.

ban·deau (băn dō′, băn′dō), *n., pl.* **-deaux** (-dōz′, -dōz). a band worn about or on the head; a headband; a fillet. [t. F, dim. of *bande* BAND²]

ban·de·role (băn′də rōl′), *n.* **1.** a small flag or streamer borne on a lance, at a masthead, etc. **2.** a narrow scroll usually bearing an inscription. **3.** a sculptured band adapted to receive an inscription. **4.** a square banner borne at the funeral of a great man and placed over the tomb. Also, **ban′de·rol′, bannerol.** [t. F, t. It.: m. *banderola* small banner, der. *bandiera* banner]

ban·di·coot (băn′də kōōt′), *n.* **1.** any of the very large East Indian rats constituting the genus *Nesokia*, as *N. bandicota*. **2.** any of various long-clawed, insectivorous marsupials of the family *Peramelidae* of Australia, etc. [t. Telugu: m. *pandikokku* pig rat]

ban·dit (băn′dĭt), *n., pl.* **-dits, ban·ditti** (băn dĭt′ĭ). **1.** a robber, esp. one who robs by violence. **2.** an outlaw. [t. It.: m. *bandito*, prop. pp. of *bandire* proscribe]

ban·dit·ry (băn′dĭt rĭ), *n.* **1.** the work or practice of bandits. **2.** bandits collectively; banditti.

Ban·djer·ma·sin (băn′jər mä′sĭn), *n.* Dutch name of Banjermasin.

band·mas·ter (bănd′măs′tər, -mäs′tər), *n.* the conductor of a band.

Ban·doeng (băn′dōōng), *n.* Dutch name of Bandung.

ban·dog (băn′dôg′, -dŏg′), *n.* **1.** any dog kept tied or chained. **2.** a mastiff or bloodhound. [ME *band-dogge;* f. BAND³ + DOG]

ban·do·leer (băn′də lĭr′), *n.* a broad belt worn over the shoulder by soldiers, and having a number of small loops or pockets each containing a cartridge or cartridges. Also, **ban·do·lier′.** [t. F: m. *bandoulière*, t. Sp.: m. *bandolera*, der. *banda* band, sash, t. It., of Gmc. orig.]

ban·do·line (băn′də lēn′, -lĭn), *n.* a mucilaginous preparation used for keeping the hair smooth or in curls, waves, etc. [t. F, b. *bandeau* band and L *linere* smear]

ban·dore (băn dōr′, băn′dōr), *n.* an old musical string instrument resembling the lute or the guitar. Also, **pandora, pandore.** [t. Sp.: m. *bandurria*, var. of *pandora*, t. LL: m. *pandūra*, t. Gk.: m. *pandoûra* musical instrument with three strings]

band saw, *Mach.* a saw consisting of an endless toothed steel band passing over two wheels.

band shell, an open, elliptical or spherical, acoustically resonant structure in which music is played.

bands·man (băndz′mən), *n., pl.* **-men.** a musician who plays in a band.

band·stand (bănd′stănd′), *n.* a platform, often roofed, for outdoor band performances.

Ban·dung (băn′dōōng), *n.* a city in Indonesia, in W Java. 800,000 (est. 1951). Dutch, **Bandoeng.**

band wagon, **1.** a wagon carrying a band of music, as at the head of a procession or parade. **2.** **climb aboard the band wagon,** *U.S. Colloq.* to shift one's vote or aid to an apparently successful candidate or cause.

ban·dy (băn′dĭ), *v.,* **-died, -dying,** *adj., n., pl.* **-dies.** —*v.t.* **1.** to throw or strike to and fro, or from side to side, as a ball in tennis. **2.** to pass from one to another, or back and forth; give and take: *to bandy blows or words.* —*adj.* **3.** (of legs) having a bend or crook outward. —*n. Obs.* **4.** an old method of playing tennis. **5.** *Chiefly Brit.* hockey or shinny. **6.** a hockey or shinny club. [orig. obscure. Cf. F *bander* bandy, *se bander* band together, ? der. *bande* side]

ban·dy-leg·ged (băn′dĭ lĕg′ĭd, -lĕg′d′), *adj.* having crooked legs; bowlegged.

bane (băn), *n.* **1.** that which causes death or destroys life. **2.** a deadly poison. **3.** a thing that ruins or spoils. **4.** ruin; destruction; death. [ME; OE *bana* slayer]

bane·ber·ry (băn′bĕr′ĭ), *n., pl.* **-ries.** **1.** any plant of the ranunculaceous genus *Actaea*, comprising herbs which bear nauseous poisonous berries. **2.** the berry.

bane·ful (băn′fəl), *adj.* destructive; pernicious; poisonous: *a baneful superstition, baneful herbs.* —**bane′ful·ly,** *adv.* —**bane′ful·ness,** *n.*

Banff (bămf), *n.* **1.** Also, **Banff·shire** (bămf′shĭr, -shər). a county in NE Scotland. 51,100 pop. (est. 1956); 630 sq. mi. **2.** its county seat: a seaport. 3359 (1951). **3.** a resort town in Banff National Park, a scenic park (2585 sq. mi.) in the Rocky Mountains in SW Alberta, Canada. 2357 pop. (1951).

bang¹ (băng), *n.* **1.** a loud, sudden, explosive noise, as the discharge of a gun. **2.** a resounding stroke or blow. **3.** *Colloq.* a sudden, impetuous movement: *he started off with a bang.* **4.** energy; spirit. **5.** *U.S. Slang.* thrill, excitement. —*v.t.* **6.** to strike or beat resoundingly; slam: *to bang a door.* —*v.i.* **7.** to strike violently or noisily: *to bang on the door.* **8.** to make a loud noise as of violent blows: *the guns banged away.* —*adv.* **9.** with a bang; suddenly and loudly; abruptly. [cf. Icel. *banga* to hammer, *bang* hammering, bungling]

bang² (băng), *n.* **1.** (*often pl.*) a fringe of banged hair. —*v.t.* **2.** to cut (the hair) so as to form a fringe over the forehead. **3.** to dock (the tail of a horse, etc.). [short for *bangtail* docked (horse's) tail, f. *bang* (nasal var. of *bag* cut) + TAIL¹]

bang³ (băng), *n.* bhang.

Ban·ga·lore (băng′gə lôr′), *n.* a city in S India: the capital of Mysore state. 778,977 (1951).

Bang·ka (băng′kə; *Du.* bäng′kä), *n.* an island in Indonesia, E of Sumatra: tin mines. 205,363 (1930); 4611 sq. mi. *Cap.:* Muntok. Also, **Banka.**

Bang·kok (băng′kŏk), *n.* **1.** the capital of Thailand, on the Menam river: the principal port of Thailand. with suburbs, 1,052,924 (1947). **2.** (*l.c.*) a kind of Siamese straw. **3.** (*l.c.*) a hat woven of strands of this straw.

ban·gle (băng′gəl), *n.* **1.** a bracelet in the form of a ring, without a clasp. **2.** an ornamental anklet. [t. Hind.: m. *bangrī* bracelet of glass]

Ban·gor (băng′gôr, -gər), *n.* a city in S Maine: a port on the Penobscot river. 38,912 (1960).

Bang's disease (băngz), *Vet. Sci.* an infectious disease of cattle caused by a bacterium, *Brucella abortus*, which infects the genital organs and frequently causes abortions. This organism is one of several which causes undulant fever or brucellosis in man.

bang-up (băng′ŭp′), *adj. Slang.* first-rate.

Bang·we·u·lu (băng′wĭ ōō′lōō), *n.* a shallow lake and swamp in NE Northern Rhodesia. ab. 50 mi. long.

ba·ni (bä′nĭ), *n.* pl. of ban⁴.

ban·ian (băn′yən), *n.* **1.** a loose shirt, jacket, or gown worn in India. **2.** a Hindu trader or merchant of a particular caste which abstains from eating flesh. **3.** banyan. [t. Pg., prob. t. Ar.: m. *banyān*, t. Gujarati: m. *vāniyo* merchant, t. Skt.: m. *vanij*]

ban·ish (băn′ĭsh), *v.t.* **1.** to condemn to exile; expel from or relegate to a country or place by authoritative decree. **2.** to compel to depart; send, drive, or put away: *to banish sorrow.* [ME *banysshe(n)*, t. OF: m. *baniss-, s. banir*, g. LL *bannīre* ban; of Gmc. orig. and akin to BAN¹, v.] —**ban′ish·er,** *n.* —**ban′ish·ment,** *n.* —**Syn. 1.** exile, expatriate, outlaw.

ban·is·ter (băn′ĭs tər), *n.* **1.** baluster. **2.** (*pl.*) the balustrade of a staircase. Also, **bannister.** [var. of BALUSTER]

Ban·jer·ma·sin (băn′jər mä′sĭn), *n.* a seaport on the S coast of Borneo. 100,000 (est. 1951). Dutch, **Bandjermasin.**

ban·jo (băn′jō), *n., pl.* **-jos.** a musical instrument of the guitar family, having a circular body covered in front with tightly stretched parchment, and played with the fingers or a plectrum. [var. of BANDORE] —**ban′jo·ist,** *n.*

bank¹ (băngk), *n.* **1.** a long pile or heap: *a bank of earth, snow, or clouds.* **2.** a slope or acclivity. **3.** *Phys. Geol.* the slope immediately bordering a stream course along which the water normally runs. **4.** *Oceanog.* a broad submarine elevation on the continental shelf lying some distance off the coast, over which the water is relatively shallow. **5.** *Coal Mining.* the surface around the mouth of a shaft. **6.** *Aeron.* the lateral inclination of an airplane, esp. during a curve. **7.** *Billiards, Pool.* the cushion of the table. —*v.t.* **8.** to border with or like a bank; embank. **9.** to form into a bank or heap (fol. by *up*): *to bank up the snow.* **10.** *Aeron.* to tip or incline (an airplane) laterally. **11.** *Billiards, Pool.* **a.** to drive (a ball) to the cushion.

Bandicoot.
Macrotis lagotis
(Total length 2 ft., tail 8 in.)

Banjo

b. to pocket (the object ball) by driving it against the bank. **12.** to cover up (a fire) with ashes or fuel and close the dampers, to make it burn long and slowly. —*v.i.* **13.** to rise in or form banks, as clouds or snow. **14.** *Aeron.* to tip or incline an airplane laterally. [ME *banke*, prob. t. Scand.] —**Syn. 1.** embankment, mound, ridge. **3.** See shore¹.

bank² (băngk), *n.* **1.** an institution for receiving and lending money (in some cases, issuing notes or holding demand deposits that serve as money) or transacting other financial business. **2.** the office or quarters of such an institution. **3.** (in games) **a.** the stock or fund of pieces from which the players draw. **b.** the fund of the manager or the dealer. **4.** any storage place. **5.** any store or reserve: *a blood bank.* **6.** *Obs.* a sum of money, esp. as a fund for use in business. **7.** *Obs.* a money changer's table, counter, or shop. —*v.i.* **8.** to exercise the functions of a bank or banker. **9.** to keep money in, or have an account with, a bank. **10.** (in games) to hold the bank. **11.** *Colloq.* to rely or count (fol. by *on* or *upon*). —*v.t.* **12.** to deposit in a bank. [ME *banke*, t. F: m. *banque*, t. It.: m. *banca*, orig. bench, table; of Gmc. orig. See BANK¹, BENCH]

bank³ (băngk), *n.* **1.** an arrangement of objects in line. **2.** *Music.* a row of keys in an organ. **3.** a bench for rowers in a galley. **4.** a row or tier of oars. **5.** the rowers on one bench or to one oar. —*v.t.* **6.** to arrange in a bank. [ME *banck*, t. OF: m. *banc* bench, t. LL: s. *bancus;* from the Gmc. source of BENCH]

Ban·ka (băng′kə), *n.* Bangka.

bank·a·ble (băngk′ə bəl), *adj.* receivable by a bank.

bank acceptance, a draft endorsed or otherwise formally acknowledged by a bank on which it is drawn.

bank account, 1. an account with a bank. **2.** balance standing to the credit of a depositor at a bank.

bank bill, a draft drawn by one bank on another, payable on demand or at a specified future date.

bank·book (băngk′bŏŏk′), *n.* a book held by a depositor in which a bank enters a record of his account.

bank clerk, *Brit.* a teller (def. 2).

bank discount, interest on a loan, deducted in advance from the face value of the note.

bank·er¹ (băngk′ər), *n.* **1.** one who manages or works for a bank, usually a bank officer. **2.** (in games) the keeper or holder of the bank. [f. BANK² + -ER²]

bank·er² (băngk′ər), *n.* a vessel employed in the cod fishery on the banks off Newfoundland. [f. BANK¹ + -ER²]

bank·er³ (băngk′ər), *n.* *Bldg. Trades.* the bench or table upon which bricklayers and stone masons prepare and shape their material. [f. BANK³ + -ER². Cf. It. *banco*]

banker's acceptance, bank acceptance.

banker's bill, bank bill.

bank holiday, 1. a weekday on which banks are closed by law; legal holiday. **2.** *Brit.* a secular day on which banks are closed and the law therefore exempts the parties to negotiable paper from their obligations.

bank·ing (băngk′ĭng), *n.* the business of a bank or banker.

banking account, *Brit.* bank account.

bank note, a promissory note, payable on demand, issued by a bank and intended to circulate as money.

bank paper, 1. drafts, bills, and acceptances payable by banks. **2.** commercial paper which may be discounted in a bank.

bank rate, 1. the rate of discount fixed by a bank or banks. **2.** the discount charge set by a central bank, as by the Federal Reserve Bank.

bank·rupt (băngk′rŭpt, -rəpt), *n.* **1.** *Law.* a person who upon his own petition or that of his creditors is adjudged insolvent by a court, and whose property is distributed among his creditors, under a bankruptcy law. **2.** any insolvent debtor; one unable to satisfy any just claims made upon him. —*adj.* **3.** *Law.* subject to, or under, legal process because of insolvency; insolvent. **4.** at the end of one's resources; lacking (fol. by *in*): *to be bankrupt in thanks.* **5.** pertaining to bankrupts. —*v.t.* **6.** to make bankrupt. [t. F. (after L *ruptus* broken) *banqueroute*, t. It.: m. *bancarotta* bankruptcy, f. *banca* bank + *rotta*, pp. fem. of *rompere* break, g. L *rumpere*]

bank·rupt·cy (băngk′rŭpt sĭ, -rəp sĭ), *n., pl.* **-cies. 1.** state of being or becoming bankrupt. **2.** utter ruin.

Banks (băngks), *n.* Sir Joseph, 1743–1820, British naturalist.

bank·si·a (băngk′sĭ ə), *n.* any plant of the Australian genus *Banksia* comprising shrubs and trees with leathery leaves and dense cylindrical heads of flowers. [t. NL, named after Sir Joseph BANKS]

Bank·side (băngk′sīd′), *n.* a former theatrical district in London, England, along the south bank of the Thames, the site of Shakespeare's Globe Theater.

ban·ner (băn′ər), *n.* **1.** the flag of a country, army, troop, etc. **2.** an ensign or the like bearing some device or motto, as one borne in processions. **3.** a piece of cloth, attached by one side to a pole or staff, formerly used as the standard of a sovereign, lord, or knight. **4.** anything displayed as a profession of principles: *the banner of freedom.* **5.** *Her.* a square flag bearing heraldic devices. **6.** *Journalism.* the headline which extends across the width of the newspaper, usually at the top of the first page. —*adj.* **7.** leading or foremost: *a banner year for crops.* [ME *banere*, t. OF, der. LL *bandum* standard; of Gmc. orig. (cf. Goth. *bandwo* sign)]

ban·ner·et¹ (băn′ər ĭt, -ə rĕt′), *n.* **1.** *Hist.* a knight who could bring a company of followers into the field under his own banner. **2.** a rank of knighthood; knight banneret. [ME *baneret*, t. OF, der. *baniere* BANNER]

ban·ner·et² (băn′ə rĕt′), *n.* a small banner. Also, **ban′ner·ette′.** [t. OF, dim. of *baniere* BANNER]

ban·ner·ol (băn′ə rōl′), *n.* banderole.

ban·nis·ter (băn′ĭs tər), *n.* banister.

ban·nock (băn′ək), *n.* *Scot. and Brit. Dial.* a flat cake made of oatmeal, barley meal, etc., commonly baked on a griddle. [OE *bannuc* bit, small piece, t. OBrit. Cf. OCornish *banna* drop]

Ban·nock·burn (băn′ək bûrn′, băn′ək bûrn′), *n.* a village in central Scotland, in Stirling county: site of the victory of the Scots (1314) under Robert Bruce over the English, which assured the independence of Scotland.

banns (bănz), *n.pl.* *Eccles.* notice of an intended marriage, given three times in the parish church of each of the espoused. Also, **bans.** [var. of *bans*, pl. of BAN², n.]

ban·quet (băng′kwĭt), *n., v.,* **-queted, -queting.** —*n.* **1.** a feast. **2.** a ceremonious public dinner. —*v.t., v.i.* **3.** to entertain (another) or regale (oneself) at a banquet. [t. F, t. It.: m. *banchetto*, dim. of *banco* bench] —**ban′·quet·er,** *n.* —**Syn. 1.** See feast.

ban·quette (băng kĕt′), *n.* **1.** *Fort.* a platform or step along the inside of a parapet, for soldiers to stand on when firing. **2.** a bench for passengers on top of a stagecoach. **3.** *Southern U.S.* a sidewalk. **4.** a ledge running across the back of a buffet. [t. F]

Ban·quo (băng′kwō, -kō), *n.* (in Shakespeare's *Macbeth*) a murdered thane whose ghost appears to Macbeth.

ban·shee (băn′shē, băn shē′), *n.* *Irish and Scot.* a supernatural being supposed to give warning by its wails of an approaching death in the family. Also, **ban′shie.** [t. Irish: m. *bean sidhe* woman of the fairies]

ban·tam (băn′təm), *n.* **1.** (*often cap.*) a domestic fowl of any of certain varieties or breeds characterized by very small size. **2.** a small, quarrelsome person. —*adj.* **3.** diminutive; tiny. [prob. named after BANTAM]

Ban·tam (băn′təm; *Du.* băn tăm′), *n.* a village in W Java: first Dutch settlement in the East Indies.

ban·tam·weight (băn′təm wāt′), *n.* a boxer of very light weight (not more than 118 pounds).

ban·ter (băn′tər), *n.* **1.** playfully teasing language; good-humored raillery. —*v.t.* **2.** to address with banter; chaff. —*v.i.* **3.** to use banter. [orig. unknown] —**ban′·ter·er,** *n.* —**ban′ter·ing·ly,** *adv.* —**Syn. 1.** badinage, joking, jesting. **2.** tease.

Ban·ting (băn′tĭng), *n.* Sir Frederick Grant, 1891–1941, Canadian physician: discoverer of insulin treatment of diabetes.

Ban·ting·ism (băn′tĭng ĭz′əm), *n.* *Med.* a method of reducing one's weight, based upon a high protein and low fat and carbohydrate diet. [named after William *Banting*, 1797–1878, British dietitian]

bant·ling (bănt′lĭng), *n.* *Contemptuous.* a young child; brat. [f. var. of obs. *bandle* swaddling band + -ING⁴]

Ban·tu (băn′tōō), *n., pl.* **-tu, -tus,** *adj.* —*n.* **1.** (*pl.*) a large family of Negro tribes inhabiting central and southern Africa. **2.** a member of any of these tribes. **3.** a principal linguistic family of Africa, its languages being prevalent from the Equator to South Africa, including Swahili, Kaffir, and Zulu. —*adj.* **4.** of or pertaining to the Bantu tribes or languages.

Ban·ville (băn vēl′), *n.* Théodore Faullain de (tě ō-dôr′ fō lăn′ də), 1823–91, French poet and dramatist.

ban·yan (băn′yən), *n.* an East Indian fig tree, *Ficus benghalensis*, whose branches send out adventitious roots to the ground, sometimes causing the tree to spread over a wide area. Also, **banian.** [orig. a particular tree under which Banian traders had built a pagoda]

Banyan, *Ficus benghalensis*
(70 to 100 ft. high)

ban·zai (băn′zä ē′, -zī′), *interj.* **1.** a Japanese complimentary salutation or patriotic shout, as in honor of the emperor, meaning: **a.** long life. **b.** forward; attack. —*adj.* **2.** reckless; suicidal. [t. Jap.: ten thousand years]

ba·o·bab (bā′ō băb′, bä′-), *n.* a large, exceedingly thick-trunked bombacaceous tree of the genus *Adansonia*, esp. *A. digitata*, native to tropical Africa, bearing a gourdlike fruit. [t. native African]

Bap., Baptist. Also, **Bapt.**

bap·tism (băp′tĭz əm), *n.* **1.** *Eccles.* a ceremonial immersion in water, or application of water, as an initiatory rite or sacrament of the Christian church. **2.** any similar ceremony or action of initiation, dedication, etc. —**bap·tis·mal** (băp tĭz′məl), *adj.* —**bap·tis′mal·ly,** *adv.*

baptism of fire, 1. the first battle a soldier experiences. **2.** any severe ordeal; crucial test.

Bap·tist (băp′tĭst), *n.* **1.** *Relig.* a member of a Christian denomination which maintains that baptism (usually implying immersion) should follow only upon a personal profession of Christian faith. **2.** one who baptizes. **3.** the Baptist, John, the forerunner of Christ.

bap·tis·ter·y (băp′tĭs tər ĭ, -tĭs′trĭ), *n., pl.* **-teries. 1.** a building, or a part of a church, in which baptism is administered. **2.** (in Baptist churches) a tank containing water for baptism by immersion. [t. L: m.s. *baptistérium*, t. Gk.: m. *baptistérion*]

bap·tist·ry (băp′tĬstrĭ), *n.*, *pl.* **-ries.** baptistery.

bap·tize (băp tīz′, băp′tīz), *v.*, **-tized, -tizing.** —*v.t.* **1.** to immerse in water, or sprinkle or pour water on, in the Christian rite of baptism. **2.** to cleanse spiritually; initiate or dedicate by purifying. **3.** to christen. —*v.i.* **4.** to administer baptism. [ME *baptise(n)*, t. OF: m. *baptiser*, t. LL: m. *baptizāre*, t. Gk.: m. *baptizein* immerse] —**bap·tiz′er,** *n.*

bar[1] (bär), *n.*, *v.*, **barred, barring,** *prep.* —*n.* **1.** a relatively long and evenly shaped piece of some solid substance, esp. of wood or metal used as a guard or obstruction, or for some mechanical purpose: *the bars of a fence or gate.* **2.** crowbar. **3.** an oblong piece of any solid material: *a bar of soap or candy.* **4.** the amount of material in a bar. **5.** *Com.* an ingot, lump, or wedge of gold or silver. **6.** a band or stripe: *a bar of light.* **7.** *Oceanog.* a long ridge of sand or gravel in coastal waters, near or slightly above the surface, and extending across the mouth of a bay or parallel to the shore. **8.** anything which obstructs, hinders, or impedes; an obstacle; a barrier: *a bar to vice.* **9.** *Music.* **a.** the line marking the division between two measures of music. **b.** See **double bar. c.** the unit of music contained between two bar lines; measure. **10.** a counter or a place where liquors, etc., are served to customers. **11.** the legal profession. **12.** the practicing members of the legal profession in a given community. **13.** a railing in a courtroom separating the general public from the part of the room occupied by the judges, jury, attorneys, etc. **14.** the place in court where prisoners are stationed: *a prisoner at the bar.* **15.** *Law.* **a.** an objection which nullifies an action or claim. **b.** a stoppage or defeat of an alleged right of action. **16.** any tribunal: *the bar of public opinion.* **17.** *Physics.* a unit of pressure equal to 1,000,000 dynes per square centimeter. **18.** a space, between the molar and canine teeth of a horse, in which the bit is fitted. **19.** *U.S.* (in a bridle) the mouthpiece connecting the checks. **20.** (in lace) bride[2] (def. 1). **21.** *Her.* a band, properly horizontal, crossing the field. —*v.t.* **22.** to provide or fasten with a bar or bars: *to bar the door.* **23.** to shut in or out by or as by bars. **24.** to block (a way, etc.) as with a barrier; prevent or hinder; as access. **25.** to exclude; except. **26.** to mark with bars, stripes, or bands. —*prep.* **27.** except; omitting; but: *bar none.* [ME *barre*, t. OF, g. LL *barra*, of disputed origin] —**Syn. 8.** BAR, BARRIER, BARRICADE mean something put in the way of advance. BAR has the general meaning of hindrance or obstruction: *a bar across the doorway.* BARRIER suggests an impediment to progress, literal or figurative, or a defensive obstruction against attack: *a river barrier.* A BARRICADE is esp. a pile of articles hastily gathered or a rude earthwork for protection in street fighting: *a barricade of wooden boxes.*

Bar (def. 9)
A, single; B, double

bar[2] (bär), *n.* *U.S.* a mosquito net.

bar., **1.** barometer. **2.** barrel. **3.** barrister.

B. Ar., Bachelor of Architecture.

Bar·ab·bas (bə răb′əs), *n.* *Bible.* a condemned robber or insurrectionist whose release was demanded of Pilate by the mob when they had an opportunity to free Jesus. Mark 15:6–11; John 18:40.

barb[1] (bärb), *n.* **1.** a point or pointed part projecting backward from a main point, as of a fishhook, an arrowhead, or a fence wire. **2.** *Bot., Zool.* a beardlike growth or part. **3.** *Ornith.* one of the processes attached to the rachis of a feather. **4.** a breed of domestic pigeons similar to the carriers or homers, having a short, broad bill. **5.** any of a large number of small, Old World cyprinid fishes of the genera *Barbus* or *Puntius*, widely cultivated for use in home aquariums. **6.** (*usually pl.*) *Vet. Sci.* a small protuberance under the tongue in horses and cattle, esp. when inflamed and swollen. **7.** a linen covering for the throat and breast, formerly worn by women mourners, and now by nuns. **8.** a band or small scarf of lace, worn by women. **9.** *Obs.* a beard. —*v.t.* **10.** to furnish with a barb or barbs: *to barb a hook.* [ME *barbe*, t. OF, g. L *barba* beard] —**barbed,** *adj.*

barb[2] (bärb), *n.* a horse of a breed brought from Barbary to Spain by the Moors. [t. F: m. *barbe*]

Bar·ba·dos (bär bā′dōz, bär bə dōz′), *n.* an island in the West Indies: a British colony. 228,897 pop. (est. 1955); 166 sq. mi. *Cap.:* Bridgetown.

bar·bar·i·an (bär bâr′Ĭ ən), *n.* **1.** a man in a rude, savage state; an uncivilized person **2.** an uncultured person; a philistine. **3.** a foreigner (orig. a non-Greek). —*adj.* **4.** uncivilized. **5.** foreign. [t. F: m. *barbarien*, der. L *barbaria* barbarous country] —**bar·bar′i·an·ism,** *n.* —**Syn. 4.** rude, savage, primitive, wild. BARBARIAN, BARBARIC, BARBAROUS pertain to uncivilized people. BARBARIAN is the general word for anything uncivilized: *a barbarian tribe.* BARBARIC has both unfavorable and mildly favorable connotations, implying crudeness of taste or practice, or conveying an idea of rude magnificence and splendor: *barbaric noise.* BARBAROUS emphasizes the inhumanity and cruelty of barbarian life: *barbarous customs.*

bar·bar·ic (bär bâr′Ĭk), *adj.* **1.** uncivilized: *barbaric invaders.* **2.** of, like, or befitting barbarians: *a barbaric empire.* **3.** crudely rich or splendid: *barbaric decorations.* [ME *barbarik*, t. L: m. s. *barbaricus* t. Gk.: m.: *barbarikós*

foreign, barbaric] —**bar·bar′i·cal·ly,** *adv.* —**Syn. 1.** See **barbarian.**

bar·ba·rism (bär′bə rĬz′əm), *n.* **1.** barbarous or uncivilized condition. **2.** something belonging or proper to a barbarous condition; a barbarous act. **3.** the use in a language of forms or constructions felt by some to be undesirably alien to the established mode or custom of the language. **4.** such a form or construction, as completed, all the farther.

bar·bar·i·ty (bär bâr′ə tĬ), *n.*, *pl.* **-ties.** **1.** brutal or inhuman conduct; cruelty. **2.** act of cruelty or inhumanity. **3.** crudity of style, taste, etc.

bar·ba·rize (bär′bə rīz′), *v.i.*, *v.t.*, **-rized, -rizing.** to make or become barbarous. —**bar′ba·ri·za′tion,** *n.*

Bar·ba·ros·sa (bär′bə rŏs′ə), *n.* surname of Emperor Frederick I of Germany, meaning "red beard."

bar·ba·rous (bär′bə rəs), *adj.* **1.** uncivilized: *barbarous countries.* **2.** excessively harsh: *barbarous treatment.* **3.** harsh-sounding: *wild and barbarous music.* **4.** not conforming or conformed to classical standards or accepted usage, as language. **5.** foreign (orig. non-Greek). [t. L: m. *barbarus*, t. Gk.: m. *bárbaros*, orig., babbling] —**bar′ba·rous·ly,** *adv.* —**bar′ba·rous·ness,** *n.* —**Syn. 1.** See **barbarian. 2.** cruel, ferocious, inhuman, brutal.

Bar·ba·ry (bär′bə rĬ), *n.* a region in N Africa, extending from W of Egypt to the Atlantic, and including the former Barbary States.

Barbary ape, an ape, *Macaca sylvana*, of northern Africa and Gibraltar.

Barbary Coast, the Mediterranean coastline of the former Barbary States: once infested with pirates who harassed Mediterranean trade.

Barbary States, Morocco, Algiers, Tunis, and Tripoli.

Barbary Coast (Ca. 1800)

bar·bate (bär′bāt), *adj. Zool., Bot.* bearded; tufted or furnished with hairs. [t. L: m. s. *barbātus* bearded]

bar·be·cue (bär′bə kū′), *n.*, *v.*, **-cued, -cuing.** —*n.* **1.** *U.S.* a large social or political entertainment, usually in the open air, at which animals are roasted whole. **2.** a dressed ox or other animal roasted whole. **3.** a framework on which animals are broiled or roasted whole or in large pieces. —*v.t.* **4.** to broil or roast whole or in large pieces before an open fire, on a spit or gridiron, often seasoning with vinegar, spices, salt, and pepper. **5.** to cook (sliced or diced meat or fish) in a highly seasoned sauce. [t. Sp.: m. *barbacoa*, t. Haitian: m. *barboka*]

barbed wire, iron wire to which barbs are attached at short intervals, used largely for fencing in livestock, protecting a defensive military position, etc.

bar·bel (bär′bəl), *n.* **1.** a slender cylindrical tactile process appended to the mouth of certain fishes. **2.** any of various cyprinoid fishes of the genus *Barbus*, esp. *B. barbus*, of Europe. [ME *barbelle*, t. OF: m. *barbel*, g. LL *barbellus*, dim. of *barbus*]

bar·bel·late (bär′bə lāt′, bär bĕl′Ĭt, -āt), *adj. Bot., Zool.* having short, stiff hairs. [f. s. NL *barbella* (dim. of L *barbula* little beard) + -ATE[1]]

bar·ber (bär′bər), *n.* **1.** one whose occupation it is to shave or trim the beard and to cut and dress the hair of customers. —*v.t.* **2.** to trim or dress the beard and hair of. [ME *barbour*, t. AF, ult. der. L *barba* beard]

Bar·ber (bär′bər), *n.* **Samuel,** born 1910, American composer.

bar·ber·ry (bär′bĕr′Ĭ), *n.*, *pl.* **-ries. 1.** a shrub of the genus *Berberis*, esp. *B. vulgaris*. **2.** its red, elongated, acid fruit. [ME *barbere*, t. ML: m.s. *barbaris*, *berberis*]

Bar·ber·ton (bär′bər tən), *n.* a city in NE Ohio, near Akron. 33,805 (1960).

bar·bet (bär′bĬt), *n.* **1.** a dog with long curly hair; poodle. **2.** any of numerous tropical nonpasserine birds of the family *Capitonidae*, most of which are brightly colored and large-headed, and have bristles at the base of the bill. [t. F, masc. dim. of *barbe* beard]

bar·bette (bär bĕt′), *n.* **1.** a platform or mound of earth within a fortification, from which guns may be fired over the parapet instead of through embrasures. **2.** *Naval.* an armored cylinder to protect a turret on a warship. [t. F, fem. dim. of *barbe* beard]

bar·bi·can (bär′bə kən), *n.* **1.** an outwork of a castle or fortified place. **2.** an outpost of any nature, as a bridge tower, or a defense outside of the moat protecting the approach to the drawbridge. [ME, t. OF: m. *barbacane*, t. ML: m. *barbicana*; ult. orig. obscure, ? t. Ar.-Pers.: m. *bāb khāne* gate house, or Pers. *bālā khāne* high house]

bar·bi·cel (bär′bə sĕl′), *n. Ornith.* one of the minute processes fringing the barbules of certain feathers. [t. NL: m. s. *barbicella*, dim. of L *barbula*]

Bar·bi·rol·li (bär′bə rŏl′Ĭ, -rŏl′lĬ), *n.* **John,** born 1899, British conductor, formerly in the U.S.

bar·bi·tal (bär′bə tăl′, -tŏl), *n. Pharm.* a drug, diethyl-barbituric acid, sold as sleeping pills; Veronal. [f. BARBIT(URIC) + -AL[3]]

barbital sodium, *Pharm.* a sleeping powder, $C_8H_{11}N_2O_3Na$, the sodium salt of barbital.

bar·bi·tu·rate (bär bĭch/ə rāt/, -rĭt; bär/bə tyŏŏr/āt, -ĭt), n. Chem. a derivative of barbituric acid.

bar·bi·tu·ric acid (bär/bə tyŏŏr/ĭk, -tŏŏr/-), Chem. an acid, C₄H₄N₂O₃, a crystalline powder from which several hypnotic and sedative drugs are derived. [*barbituric*, f. s. Gk. *bárbiton* lyre + URIC]

Bar·bi·zon School (bär/bə zŏn/, Fr. bár bē zôn/), a group of French landscape painters of the third quarter of the 19th century, including Théodore Rousseau and Daubigny, who worked chiefly at Barbizon, a village in N France.

Bar·bu·da (bär bōō/də), n. a British colony in the Leeward Islands, in the Federation of the West Indies: a dependency of Antigua. 902 pop. (1946); 62 sq. mi.

bar·bule (bär/būl), n. 1. a little barb. 2. one of the small processes fringing the barbs of a feather. [t. L: m. s. *barbula*, dim. of *barba* beard]

Bar·busse (bár bys/), n. Henri (äⁿ rē/), 1873?-1935, French journalist and author.

Bar·ca (bär/kə), n. 1. a politically influential family of ancient Carthage. Hamilcar, Hasdrubal, and Hannibal belonged to it. 2. Cyrenaica.

bar·ca·role (bär/kə rōl/), n. 1. a boating song of the Venetian gondoliers. 2. a piece of music composed in the style of such songs. Also, **bar/ca·rolle/**. [t. F: m. *barcarolle*, t. It.: m. *barcar(u)ola* boatman's song, der. *barcar(u)olo* a boatman, der. *barca* BARK³]

Bar·ce·lo·na (bär/sə lō/nə; Sp. bär/thē lō/nä), n. a seaport in NE Spain, on the Mediterranean. 1,361,379 (est. 1955).

B. Arch., Bachelor of Architecture.

Bar·clay de Tol·ly (bär kli/ də tô/lĭ), Prince Mikhail (mĭ hä ēl/), 1761-1818, Russian field marshal: commander in chief against Napoleon in 1812.

bard¹ (bärd), n. 1. one of an ancient Celtic order of poets. 2. a poet. [ME, t. Celtic (cf. Irish *bard*, Welsh *bardd*), whence also L *bardus*, Gk. *bárdos*] —**bard/ic**, adj.

bard² (bärd), Armor. —n. 1. any of various pieces of defensive armor for a horse. —v.t. 2. to caparison with bards. Also, **barde**. [t. F, t. Ar.: m. *bardha'ah* packsaddle]

bare¹ (bâr), adj., **barer**, **barest**, v., **bared**, **baring**. —adj. 1. without covering or clothing; naked or nude: *bare knees*. 2. with the head uncovered. 3. without the usual furnishings, contents, etc.: *bare walls*. 4. open to view; unconcealed; undisguised. 5. unadorned; bald; plain: *the bare facts*. 6. napless or threadbare. 7. scarcely or just sufficient; mere: *bare necessaries*. —v.t. 8. to make bare. [ME; OE *bær*, c. G *bar*] —**bare/ness**, n. —Syn. 7. See mere¹. 8. uncover, strip; unmask.

bare² (bâr), v. Archaic. pt. of bear.

bare·back (bâr/băk/), adv., adj. with the back (of a horse, etc.) bare; without saddle. —**bare/backed/**, adj.

bare·faced (bâr/fāst/), adj. 1. with the face uncovered. 2. undisguised; boldly open. 3. shameless; impudent; audacious: *a barefaced lie*. —**bare·fac·ed·ly** (bâr/fā/sĭd lĭ, -fāst/lĭ), adv. —**bare/fac/ed·ness**, n.

bare·foot (bâr/fŏŏt/), adj., adv. with the feet bare.

bare·foot·ed (bâr/fŏŏt/ĭd), adj. having the feet bare.

bare·hand·ed (bâr/hăn/dĭd), adj. 1. with hands uncovered. 2. with empty hands; without means.

bare·head·ed (bâr/hĕd/ĭd), adj., adv. with the head uncovered.

Ba·reil·ly (bə rā/lĭ),n. a city in N India, in Uttar Pradesh. 194,679 (1951). Also, **Ba·re/li**.

bare·leg·ged (bâr/lĕg/ĭd, -lĕgd/), adj. with bare legs.

bare·ly (bâr/lĭ), adv. 1. only; just; no more than: *she is barely sixteen*. 2. without disguise or concealment; openly: *a question barely put*. 3. nakedly. 4. Archaic. merely; only. —Syn. 1. See hardly.

Bar·ents Sea (bâr/ĕnts; Russ. bä rĕnts/), a part of the Arctic Ocean between NE Europe and the islands of Spitzbergen, Franz Josef Land, and Novaya Zemlya.

bare·sark (bâr/särk), n. 1. Scand. Legend. a berserker. —adv. 2. without armor. [translation var. of *berserk*, taken as *bare* + *serk* sark, shirt]

bar·gain (bär/gĭn), n. 1. an agreement between parties settling what each shall give and take, or perform and receive, in a transaction. 2. such an agreement as affecting one of the parties: *a losing bargain*. 3. that which is acquired by bargaining. 4. an advantageous purchase. 5. **into the bargain**, over and above what is stipulated; moreover; besides. 6. **strike a bargain**, to make a bargain; come to terms. —v.i. 7. Colloq. to discuss the terms of a bargain; haggle over terms. 8. to come to an agreement; make a bargain. —v.t. 9. to arrange by bargain; stipulate. [ME, t. OF: m. *bargaigne*] —**bar/gain·er**, n. —Syn. 1. See agreement. 7. See trade.

barge (bärj), n., v., **barged**, **barging**. —n. 1. an unpowered vessel used for transporting freight; a lighter. 2. a vessel of state used in pageants. 3. a ship's boat used in visits of courtesy. 4. Naval. a boat reserved for a flag officer. 5. (in New England) a large two-seated, four-wheel coach. —v.t. 6. to carry or transport by barge. —v.i. 7. to move in the slow, heavy manner of a barge. 8. Colloq. to force oneself rudely (fol. by *into*). 9. Colloq. to bump; collide. [ME, t. OF, g. der. of L *bāris*, t. Gk.: (Egyptian) boat, barge]

barge·board (bärj/bōrd/), n. an overhanging board along the projecting sloping edge of a gable roof.

barge couple, one of the pair of rafters in a gable carrying the overhanging portion of the roof.

barge course, the part of a gable roof that projects beyond the end wall.

barge·man (bärj/mən), n., pl. -men. 1. one of the crew of a barge. 2. one who has charge of a barge. Also, esp. Brit., **bar·gee** (bär jē/).

Bar Harbor, a town on Mount Desert island, in S Maine: summer resort. 2444 (1960).

Ba·ri (bä/rĭ), n. a seaport in SE Italy, on the Adriatic. 288,000 (est. 1954). Italian, **Ba·ri del·le Pu·glie** (bä/rē dĕl/lĕ pŏō/lyĕ).

bar·ic¹ (bâr/ĭk), adj. Chem. of or containing barium. [f. BAR(IUM) + -IC]

bar·ic² (bâr/ĭk), adj. of or pertaining to weight, esp. that of the atmosphere. [f. s. Gk. *báros* weight + -IC]

ba·ril·la (bə rĭl/ə), n. 1. either of two European saltworts, *Salsola Kali* and esp. *S. Soda*, whose ashes yield an impure carbonate of soda. 2. the alkali obtained from the ashes of these and certain other maritime plants. [t. Sp.: m. *barrilla*]

Bar·ing (bâr/ĭng), n. Alexander. See Ashburton.

barit., Music. baritone.

bar·ite (bâr/īt, bâr/-), n. a common mineral, barium sulfate, BaSO₄, occurring in tabular crystals: the principal ore of barium. Also, **barytes**. [f. BAR(IUM) + -ITE¹]

bar·i·tone (bâr/ə tōn/), Music. —n. 1. a male voice or voice part intermediate between tenor and bass. 2. a singer with such a voice. 3. a large, valved brass instrument, slightly smaller in bore than a euphonium, used chiefly in military bands. —adj. 4. of or pertaining to the baritone; having the compass of the baritone. Also, **barytone**. [t. Gk.: m. s. *barýtonos* deep-sounding]

bar·i·um (bâr/ĭəm, bâr/-), n. Chem. a whitish malleable, active, divalent, metallic element occurring in combination chiefly as barite or as witherite. Symbol: Ba; at. wt.: 137.36; at. no.: 56; sp. gr.: 3.5 at 20°C. [t. NL; f. BAR(YTES) + -IUM]

bark¹ (bärk), n. 1. the abrupt, explosive cry of a dog. 2. a similar sound made by another animal or by a person. 3. Colloq. a cough. —v.i. 4. to utter an abrupt, explosive cry or a series of such cries, as a dog. 5. to make a similar sound: *the big guns barked*. 6. to speak or cry out sharply or gruffly. 7. Slang. to advertise a cheap show at its entrance. 8. U.S. Colloq. to cough. 9. **bark up the wrong tree**, U.S. to mistake one's object; assail or pursue the wrong person or purpose. —v.t. 10. to utter or give forth with a bark: *to bark out an order*. [ME *berke(n)*, OE *beorcan*]

bark² (bärk), n. 1. Bot. the external covering of the woody stems, branches, and roots of plants, as distinct and separable from the wood itself. 2. Tanning. a mixture of oak and hemlock barks. —v.t. 3. to strip off the bark of; peel. 4. to remove a circle of bark from. 5. to cover or enclose with bark. 6. to treat with a bark infusion; tan. 7. to rub off the skin of: *to bark one's shins*. [ME, t. Scand.; cf. Dan. *bark*] —**bark/er**, n.

bark³ (bärk), n. 1. Naut. a. a three-masted vessel, fore-and-aft-rigged on the mizzenmast, and square-rigged on the two other masts. b. a sailing vessel of small size. 2. Poetic. a boat or sailing vessel. Also, **barque**. [t. F: m. *barque*, t. It.: m. *barca*, g. LL]

bark beetle, any beetle of the family Scolytidae, the adults and larvae of which do great damage to living trees, esp. to conifers.

bar·keep·er (bär/kē/pər), n. 1. one who owns or manages a bar where liquors are served to customers. 2. a bartender. Also, **bar/keep/**.

bark·en·tine (bär/kən tēn/), n. Naut. a three-masted vessel with the foremast square-rigged and the mainmast and mizzenmast fore-and-aft-rigged. Also, **bark/an·tine/**, barquentine. [extension of BARK³ after *brigantine*]

bark·er (bär/kər), n. 1. an animal or person that barks. 2. Colloq. one who stands before a store, theater, etc., calling passers-by to enter. [f. BARK¹ + -ER¹]

Bark·ley (bärk/lĭ), n. Alben William, 1877-1956, vice-president of the U.S., 1949-1953.

bark·y (bär/kĭ), adj., **barkier**, **barkiest**. consisting of or containing bark; covered with or resembling bark.

bar·ley (bär/lĭ), n. a widely distributed cereal plant of the genus *Hordeum*, whose awned flowers grow in tightly bunched spikes, with three small additional spikes at each node. It is used as food, and in the making of beer, ale, and whiskey. [ME *barly*, OE *bærlīc*; cf. BARN]

bar·ley·corn (bär/lĭ kôrn/), n. 1. barley, or a grain of barley. 2. a measure equal to one third of an inch.

Bar·ley·corn (bär/lĭ kôrn/), n. John, a humorous personification of barley as used in malt liquor, or malt liquor itself.

barley sugar, sugar boiled, formerly in a decoction of barley, until it has become brittle and transparent.

Bar·low (bär/lō), n. Joel, 1754-1812, U.S. poet and diplomat.

barm (bärm), n. yeast formed on malt liquors while fermenting. [ME *beorma*, OE *beorma*, c. G *bärme*]

bar·maid (bär/mād/), n. Brit. a woman or girl who serves customers in a bar.

Bar·me·cide (bär/mə sīd/), n. a member of a noble Persian family of Bagdad who, according to a tale in *The Arabian Nights' Entertainments*, gave a beggar a pretended feast with empty dishes.

Bar·men (bär/mən), n. See Wuppertal.

äct, āble, dâre, ärt; ĕbb, ēqual; ĭf, īce; hŏt, ōver, ôrder, oil, bŏŏk, ōōze, out; ŭp, ūse, ûrge; ə = a in alone; ch, chief; g, give; ng, ring; sh, shoe; th, thin; ᵺ, that; zh, vision. See the full key on inside cover.

bar miz·vah (bär mĭts′və), *Jewish Relig.* 1. a boy of thirteen, the age at which he acquires religious obligations. 2. *U.S. Colloq.* the ceremony and feast marking this. Also, **bar mitz′vah.** [t. Heb.]

barm·y (bär′mĭ), *adj.* **barmier, barmiest.** 1. containing or resembling barm; frothy. 2. *Brit. Slang.* flighty; silly; weak-minded.

barn (bärn), *n.* a building for storing hay, grain, etc., and often for stabling live stock. [ME *bern*, OE *berern*, f. *bere* barley + *ærn* place, house]

Bar·na·bas (bär′nə bəs), *n.* the surname of the Cyprian Levite Joseph, an apostle and companion of Paul. Acts 4:36, 37.

bar·na·cle[1] (bär′nə kəl), *n.* 1. any of certain crustaceans of the group *Cirripedia*, as the **goose barnacle**, the stalked species which cling to ship bottoms and floating timber, and the **rock barnacles**, the species which attach themselves to marine rocks. 2. a thing or person that clings tenaciously. [late ME *bernacle*, of obscure orig. (cf. ML *bernacula*, F *bernicle*, *barnacle*); r. ME *bernekke*, *bernake* (cf. ML *bernaca*, OF *bernaque*)]   **—bar′na·cled**, *adj.*

Goose barnacle.
Lepas fasicularis

bar·na·cle[2] (bär′nə kəl), *n.* 1. (*usually pl.*) an instrument with two hinged branches for pinching the nose of an unruly horse. 2. (*pl.*) *Colloq.* spectacles. [ME *bernacle*, t. OF: m. *bernac*]

Bar·nard (bär′nərd), *n.* **George Gray,** 1863–1938, U.S. sculptor.

Bar·na·ul (bär′nä ōōl′), *n.* a city in the S Soviet Union in Asia, on the Ob river. 255,000 (est. 1956).

Bar·ne·veldt (bär′nə vĕlt′), *n.* **Jan van Olden** (yän vän ōl′dən), 1547–1619, Dutch statesman and patriot.

barn owl, a widely distributed owl, *Tyto alba*, commonly frequenting barns, where it destroys mice.

Barns·ley (bärnz′lĭ), *n.* a city in central England, N of Sheffield. 75,625 (1951).

barn·storm (bärn′stôrm′), *v.i.* *U.S. Colloq.* 1. to conduct a campaign or speaking tour in rural areas. 2. *Theat.* to act in plays in small country towns where there are no theaters. [back formation from *barnstormer*, lit., one who storms the barn]   **—barn′storm′er,** *n.*   **—barn′storm′ing,** *n.*, *adj.*

barn swallow. See **swallow**[2] (def. 1).

Bar·num (bär′nəm), *n.* **Phineas Taylor** (fĭn′ĭ əs), 1810–91, U.S. showman; established circus (1871).

barn·yard (bärn′yärd′), *n.* a yard next to a barn.

baro-, a word element meaning "weight," "pressure," as in *barogram*. [comb. form repr. Gk. *báros* weight]

Ba·roc·chio (bä rōk′kyō), *n.* See **Vignola.**

Ba·ro·da (bə rō′də), *n.* 1. a former native state in W India, now part of Bombay State. 2. a city north of Bombay, formerly capital of Baroda State. 211,407 (1951).

bar·o·gram (bär′ə grăm′), *n.* *Meteorol.* a record traced by a barograph or similar instrument.

bar·o·graph (bär′ə grăf′, -gräf′), *n.* *Meteorol.* an automatic recording barometer. **—bar′o·graph′ic,** *adj.*

Ba·ro·ja (bä rō′hä), *n.* **Pío** (pē′ō), 1872–1956, Spanish novelist.

ba·rom·e·ter (bə rŏm′ə tər), *n.* 1. an instrument for measuring atmospheric pressure, thus determining height, weather changes, etc. 2. anything that indicates changes.   **—bar·o·met·ric** (bär′ə mĕt′rĭk), **bar′o·met′ri·cal,** *adj.* **—bar′o·met′ri·cal·ly,** *adv.*

bar·on (bär′ən), *n.* 1. a member of the lowest grade of nobility. 2. *Brit.* **a.** a feudal vassal holding his lands directly from the king; a member of the House of Lords. **b.** a member of a borough holding directly from the crown. 3. *U.S.* a powerful industrialist or financier. [ME, t. OF, g. L *báro* hulking fellow]

bar·on·age (bär′ən ĭj), *n.* 1. the whole body of British barons. 2. the dignity or rank of a baron.

bar·on·ess (bär′ən ĭs), *n.* 1. the wife of a baron. 2. a lady holding a baronial title in her own right.

bar·on·et (bär′ən ĭt, -ə nĕt′), *n.* a member of a British hereditary order of honor, ranking below the barons and made up of commoners, designated by *Sir* before the name, and *Baronet*, usually abbrev.ated *Bart.*, after: *Sir John Smith, Bart.*

bar·on·et·age (bär′ən ĭt ĭj, -ə nĕt′-), *n.* 1. the dignity or rank of a baronet. 2. the order of baronets; baronets collectively.

bar·on·et·cy (bär′ən ĭt sĭ, -ə nĕt′-), *n.*, *pl.* **-cies.** the rank or patent of a baronet.

ba·rong (bä rông′, -rŏng′), *n.* a large, broad-bladed knife or cleaver used by the Moros. [native name]

ba·ro·ni·al (bə rō′nĭ əl), *adj.* 1. pertaining to a baron, a barony, or to the order of barons. 2. befitting a baron.

bar·o·ny (bär′ə nĭ), *n.*, *pl.* **-nies.** 1. the rank or dignity of a baron. 2. the domain of a baron. [ME *baronie*, t. OF, der. *baron* BARON]

ba·roque (bə rōk′; Fr. bå rōk′), *n.* 1. *Art.* **a.** a style developed in Italy in the 16th century characterized by heavy and contorted forms and exaggeration of ornamental and pictorial effects. **b.** work of this style and period. 2. anything so extravagantly ornamented as to be in bad taste. **—adj.** 3. pertaining to the baroque. 4. irregular in shape. [t. F, t. Pg.: m. *barroco* irregular]

bar·o·scope (bär′ə skōp′), *n.* an instrument showing roughly the variations in atmospheric pressure. **—bar·o·scop·ic** (bär′ə skŏp′ĭk), **bar′o·scop′i·cal,** *adj.*

ba·rouche (bə rōōsh′), *n.* a four-wheeled carriage with a seat outside for the driver, and seats inside for two couples facing each other, and with a calash top over the back seat. [t. d. G: m. *barutsche*, t. It.: m. *biroccio*, g. L *birotus* two-wheeled]

Barouche

bar pin, a long, slender, decorative pin or brooch.

barque (bärk), *n.* **bark**[3].

bar·quen·tine (bär′kən tēn′), *n.* barkentine.

bar·rack[1] (bär′ək), *n.* (*usually pl.*) 1. a building or range of buildings for lodging soldiers, esp. in garrison. 2. any large, plain building in which many people are lodged.   **—v.t., v.i.** 3. to lodge in barracks. [t. F: m. *baraque*, t. It.: m. *baracca*; orig. uncert.]

bar·rack[2] (bär′ək), *Austral. and Brit.* **—v.i.** 1. to shout boisterously for or against a player or team; to root.   **—v.t.** 2. to shout for or against. [back formation from *barracking* banter, var. of *barrakin*, *barrikin* gibberish (Cockney slang)] **—bar′rack·er,** *n.*

bar·ra·cu·da (bär′ə kōō′də), *n.*, *pl.* **-da, -das.** any of several species of elongate, predaceous, tropical and subtropical marine fishes of the genus *Sphyraena*, some of which are extensively used for food. [t. Sp., t. W. Ind.]

bar·rage (bə räzh′; *esp. Brit.* băr′äzh for 1, 2, 4; băr′ĭj for 3), *n.*, *v.*, **-raged, -raging.** **—n.** 1. *Mil.* a barrier of artillery fire used to prevent the enemy from advancing, to enable troops behind it to operate with a minimum of casualties, or to cut off the enemy's retreat in one or more directions. 2. any overwhelming quantity: *a barrage of questions.* 3. *Civ. Eng.* an artificial obstruction in a watercourse to increase the depth of the water, facilitate irrigation, etc.   **—v.t.** 4. to cut off by or subject to a barrage. [t. F, der. *barrer* BAR[1], v. Cf. F phrase *tir de barrage* barrage fire]

bar·ra·mun·da (bär′ə mŭn′də), *n.*, *pl.* **-da, -das.** a lungfish, *Neoceratodus forsteri*, of the rivers of Australia. Also, **bar·ra·mun·di** (bär′ə mŭn′dĭ). [native Australian]

bar·ran·ca (bə räng′kə; *Sp.* bär räng′kä), *n.* a steepwalled ravine or gorge. [t. Sp.]

Bar·ran·quil·la (bär′än kē′yä), *n.* a port in N Colombia, on the Magdalena river. 279,627 (1951).

bar·ra·tor (băr′ə tər), *n.* *Law.* one who commits barratry. Also, **bar′ra·ter.** [ME *baratour*, t. OF: m. *barateor* fraudulent dealer, der. *barater* exchange, cheat]

bar·ra·try (băr′ə trĭ), *n.* *Law.* 1. fraud by a master or crew at the expense of the owners of the ship or its cargo. 2. the offense of frequently exciting and stirring up suits and quarrels. 3. the purchase or sale of ecclesiastical preferments or of offices of state. [ME *barratrie*, t. OF: m. *baraterie*. See BARRATOR] **—bar′ra·trous,** *adj.* **—bar′ra·trous·ly,** *adv.*

barred (bärd), *adj.* 1. provided with one or more bars: *a barred gate.* 2. striped; streaked: *barred fabrics.*

barred owl, a large owl, *Strix varia*, of eastern North America, with dark brown eyes and with no feather "horns" on the head.

bar·rel (băr′əl), *n.*, *v.*, **-reled, -reling** or (*esp. Brit.*) **-relled, -relling.** **—n.** 1. a wooden cylindrical vessel, with slightly bulging sides made of staves hooped together and with flat, parallel ends. 2. the quantity which such a vessel of some standard size can hold (as 31½ U.S. gallons of liquid, 105 U.S. dry quarts of fruits and vegetables). 3. any vessel, case, or part similar in form. 4. *Ordn.* the tube of a gun. 5. *Mach.* the chamber of a pump, in which the piston works. 6. *Horol.* the cylindrical case in a watch or clock within which the mainspring is coiled. 7. *Ornith.* the hard, horny, hollow part of the stem at the base of a feather; the calamus or quill. 8. *Naut.* the main portion of a capstan, about which the rope winds, between the drumhead at the top and the pawl rim at the bottom. See illus. under *capstan*.   **—v.t.** 9. to put or pack in a barrel or barrels. [ME *barel*, t. OF: m. *baril*, prob. der. *barre* bar, stave]

bar·rel-house (băr′əl hous′), *adj.* *Jazz.* in a rough and crude style, as in low-class night clubs where (usually) only blues are played and sung. [orig. a cheap drinking establishment with a row of barrels in evidence]

barrel organ, a musical instrument in which air from a bellows is admitted to a set of pipes by means of pins inserted into a revolving barrel; hand organ.

barrel roll, *Aeron.* a complete rotation of an airplane on its main or longitudinal axis.

bar·ren (băr′ən), *adj.* 1. incapable of producing, or not producing, offspring; sterile: *a barren woman.* 2. unproductive; unfruitful: *barren land.* 3. destitute of interest or attraction. 4. mentally unproductive; dull; stupid. 5. not producing results; fruitless: *a barren pen.*   **—n.** 6. (*usually pl.*) level or slightly rolling land, usually with a sandy soil and few trees, relatively infertile. [ME *barein*, t. OF: m. *baraine*, of pre-L orig.] **—bar′ren·ly,** *adv.* **—bar′ren·ness,** *n.*

Barren Grounds, a region of windswept, almost uninhabited tundras in N Canada, esp. around Hudson Bay. Also, **Barren Lands.**

Bar·rès (bá·rĕs′), n. **Maurice** (mō·rĕs′), 1862–1923, French novelist, writer on politics, and politician.

bar·ret (băr′ĭt), n. a kind of small cap, esp. a biretta. [t. F: m. *barrette* cap, t. It.: m. *berretta*. See BIRETTA.]

bar·rette (bə·rĕt′), n. a clasp for holding a woman's hair. [t. F, dim. of *barre* bar]

bar·ri·cade (băr′ə·kād′, băr′ə·kād′), n., v., **-caded,** **-cading.** —n. **1.** a defensive barrier hastily constructed, as in a street, to stop an enemy. **2.** any barrier or obstruction to passage: *a barricade of rubbish.* —v.t. **3.** to obstruct or block with a barricade. **4.** to shut in and defend with or as with a barricade. [t. F, prob. t. Pr.: m. *barricada* a barricade, orig. made of casks filled with earth, der. *barrica* cask] —**bar′ri·cad′er,** n. —Syn. **1.** See **bar**[1].

Bar·rie (băr′ĭ), n. **Sir James Matthew,** 1860–1937, Scottish novelist, short-story writer, and playwright.

bar·ri·er (băr′ĭ·ər), n. **1.** anything built or serving to bar passage, as a stockade or fortress, or a railing. **2.** any natural bar or obstacle: *a mountain barrier.* **3.** anything that restrains or obstructs progress, access, etc.: *a trade barrier.* **4.** a limit or boundary of any kind: *the barriers of caste.* **5.** (*often cap.*) *Phys. Geog.* the portion of the polar icecap of Antarctica extending miles out beyond land, and resting in places on the ocean bottom. **6.** *Oceanog.* a bar built off shore by waves and currents, separated from the mainland by lagoons or marshes. **7.** (*pl.*) the palisades or railing surrounding the ground where tourneys and jousts were carried on. [ME *barrere,* t. AF, der. *barre* bar] —Syn. **1.** See **bar**[1].

barrier reef, *Oceanog.* a long narrow ridge of coral close to or above the surface of the sea off the coast of a continent or island: *the Great Barrier Reef.*

bar·ring (bär′ĭng), prep. excepting; except for: *barring accidents, I'll be there.*

bar·ri·o (bär′rē·ô), n., pl. -os. (in Spain and countries colonized by Spain) one of the divisions into which a town or city, together with the contiguous rural territory, is divided. [t. Sp.]

bar·ris·ter (băr′ĭs·tər), n. **1.** *Eng.* a counselor admitted to plead at the bar in any court. **2.** *Colloq.* a lawyer. [f. *barri-* (comb. form of BAR[1]) + -STER]

bar·room (bär′rōōm′, -rŏŏm′), n. *U.S.* a room containing a bar for the sale of liquors.

Bar·ros (bär′rŏŏsh), n. **Joao de** (zhwoUN də), ("the Portuguese Livy") 1496–1570, Portuguese historian.

bar·row[1] (băr′ō), n. **1.** a flat rectangular frame used for carrying a load, esp. such a frame with projecting shafts at each end for handles. **2.** a wheelbarrow. **3.** *Brit.* a pushcart used by costermongers. [ME *barewe,* OE *bearwe;* prob. akin to OE *beran* BEAR[1], v.]

bar·row[2] (băr′ō), n. **1.** *Anthropol.* a burial mound of the prehistoric inhabitants of Great Britain. **2.** a hill (now chiefly in place names). [ME *berwe,* OE *beorg* hill, mound, c. G *berg* hill, mountain]

bar·row[3] (băr′ō), n. a castrated male swine. [ME *barow,* OE *bearg*]

Bar·row (băr′ō), n. **1.** Also, **Barrow-in-Furness** (băr′ō·in·fur′nes). a seaport in NW England, in Lancashire. 67,473 (1951). **2. Point,** the N tip of Alaska.

Bar·ry (băr′ĭ; *Fr.* bä·rē′), n. Du. See **Du Barry.**

Bar·ry·more (băr′ə·mōr′), n. *U.S.* family of actors: **Maurice,** (*Herbert Blythe*) 1847–1905, father of **Ethel,** 1879–1959, **John,** 1882–1942, and **Lionel,** 1878–1954.

bar sinister, 1. *Her.* (erroneously) a baton or a bend sinister. See illus. under **bend sinister. 2.** the implication or proof of bastard birth.

Bart., Baronet.

bar·tend·er (bär′tĕn′dər), n. *U.S.* a man who mixes and serves drinks in a bar.

bar·ter (bär′tər), v.i. **1.** to trade by exchange of commodities rather than by the use of money. —v.t. **2.** to exchange in trade, as one commodity for another; trade. **3.** to bargain away unwisely or dishonorably (fol. by *away*). —n. **4.** act of bartering. **5.** the thing bartered. [ME *bartre,* freq. of obs. *barrat.* v., t. OF: m. *barater* exchange, cheat. Cf. BARRATOR.] —**bar′-ter·er,** n. —Syn. **1, 2.** See **trade.**

Bar·thol·di (bär·thŏl′dĭ; *Fr.* bár·tōl·dē′), n. **Frédéric Auguste** (frĕ·dĕ·rĕk′ ō·gyst′), 1834–1904, French sculptor who executed the Statue of Liberty.

Bar·thol·o·mew (bär·thŏl′ə·mū′), n. *Bible.* one of the twelve apostles. Mark 3:18.

bar·ti·zan (bär′tə·zən, bär′tə·zăn′), n. *Archit.* a small overhanging turret on a wall or tower. [alter. of BRATTICING] —**bar·ti·zaned** (bär′tə·zənd, bär′tə·zănd′), adj.

Baruzan
A, Merlon; B, Embrasure; C, Loophole; D, Machicolation

Bart·lett (bärt′lĭt), n. **1.** Also, **Bartlett pear.** *Hort.* a large, yellow, juicy variety of pear. **2. John,** 1820–1905, U. S. publisher and compiler.

Bar·tók (bŏr′tōk), n. **Béla** (bā′lŏ), 1881–1945, Hungarian composer.

Bar·to·lom·me·o (bär′tô·lôm·mĕ′ō), **Fra** (frä), (*Baccio della Porta*) 1475–1517, Italian painter.

Bar·ton (bär′tən), n. **Clara,** 1821–1912, U.S. woman who organized the American Red Cross in 1881.

Bar·uch (bär′ək), n. *Bible.* the amanuensis and friend of Jeremiah and nominal author of the Book of Baruch in the Apocrypha. Jer. 32:13.

Ba·ruch (bə·rōōk′), n. **Bernard Mannes** (măn′əs), 1870–1965, U. S. statesman and financier.

ba·ry·ta (bə·rī′tə), n. *Chem.* **1.** barium oxide, BaO. **2.** barium (in phrases): *carbonate of baryta.* [see BARYTES] —**ba·ryt·ic** (bə·rĭt′ĭk), adj.

ba·ry·tes (bə·rī′tēz), n. barite. [t. Gk.: weight]

bar·y·tone[1] (băr′ə·tōn′), adj., n. *Music.* baritone.

bar·y·tone[2] (băr′ə·tōn′), adj. **1.** (in Greek) pronounced with the (theoretical) grave accent on the last syllable. —n. **2.** a barytone word. [t. Gk.: m. s. *barȳtonos* with grave accent]

bas·al (bā′səl), adj. **1.** of, at, or forming the base. **2.** fundamental: *basal characteristics.* **3.** *Physiol.* **a.** indicating a standard low level of activity of an organism as present during total rest. **b.** of an amount required to maintain this level. —**bas′al·ly,** adv.

basal metabolic rate, *Physiol.* the rate of oxygen intake and heat discharge in an organism in a basal state.

basal metabolism, *Physiol.* the energy turnover of the body at a standard low level of activity.

ba·salt (bə·sŏlt′, băs′ŏlt, bā′sŏlt′), n. the dark, dense igneous rock of a lava flow or minor intrusion, composed essentially of labradorite and pyroxene, and often displaying a columnar structure. [t. L: s. *basaltes* a dark, hard marble in Ethiopia] —**ba·sal′tic,** adj.

ba·salt·ware (bə·sŏlt′wâr′, băs′ŏlt–, bā′sŏlt–), n. unglazed stoneware developed by Josiah Wedgwood, usually black, with a dull gloss.

bas bleu (bä blœ′), bluestocking. [E word trans. into F]

bas·cule (băs′kūl), n. *Civ. Eng.* a device operating like a balance or seesaw, esp. an arrangement of a movable bridge (**bascule bridge**) by which the rising floor or section is counterbalanced by a weight. [t. F: a seesaw, r. *bacule,* appar. f. *ba(ttre)* strike and *cul* the posteriors]

base[1] (bās), n., adj., v., **based, basing.** —n. **1.** the bottom of anything, considered as its support; that on which a thing stands or rests. **2.** a fundamental principle or groundwork; foundation; basis: *the base of needed reforms.* **3.** *Archit.* **a.** that part of a column on which the shaft rests. See diag. under **column.** **b.** the lowest member of a wall, monument, or the like. **c.** the lower elements of a complete structure. **4.** *Bot., Zool.* **a.** the part of an organ nearest its point of attachment. **b.** the point of attachment. **5.** the principal element or ingredient of anything, considered as its fundamental part. **6.** that from which a commencement, as of action or reckoning, is made. **7.** *Baseball.* one of the four corners of the diamond. **8.** a starting point for racers, etc. **9.** the goal in hockey and in certain other games. **10.** *Mil.* **a.** a fortified or more or less protected area or place from which the operations of an army or an air force proceed. **b.** a supply installation for a large military force. **11.** *Geom.* the line or surface forming that part of a figure on which it is supposed to stand. **12.** *Math.* the number which serves as a starting point for a logarithmic or other numerical system. **13.** *Survey.* an accurately measured line forming one side of a triangle or system of triangles from which all other sides are computed. **14.** *Chem.* **a.** a compound which reacts with an acid to form a salt, as ammonia, calcium hydroxide, certain nitrogen-containing organic compounds (as the amines and alkaloids) etc. **b.** the hydroxide of a metal or of an electropositive element or radical. **c.** a radical or molecule which takes up or accepts protons. **15.** *Gram.* the form to which affixes are added in the construction of a complex word, sometimes equivalent to *stem* or *theme.* For example: *want* is the base in *unwanted.* **16.** *Her.* the lower part of a shield. —adj. **17.** serving as a base. —v.t. **18.** to make or form a base or foundation for. **19.** to establish, as a fact or conclusion (fol. by *on* or *upon*). **20.** to place or establish on a base or basis; ground; found; establish. [ME, t. OF, t. L: m.s. *basis,* t. Gk.: a stepping, a step, pedestal, base] —Syn. **1.** BASE, BASIS, FOUNDATION refer to anything upon which a structure is built and upon which it rests. BASE usually refers to a literal supporting structure: *the base of a statue.* BASIS more often refers to a figurative support: *the basis of a report.* FOUNDATION implies a solid, secure understructure: *the foundation of a skyscraper or a rumor.*

base[2] (bās), adj., **baser, basest,** n. —adj. **1.** morally low; without dignity of sentiment; mean-spirited; selfish; cowardly. **2.** characteristic of an inferior person or thing. **3.** of little value: *the base metals.* **4.** debased or counterfeit: *base coin.* **5.** of illegitimate birth. **6.** *Old Eng. Law.* **a.** not held or holding by honorable tenure. **b. base estate,** an estate held by services not honorable, or by villeinage. **c. base tenant,** the tenant of such an estate. **7.** deep or grave in sound; bass: *the base tones of a piano.* **8.** not classical or refined: *base language.* **9.** *Archaic.* of humble origin or station. **10.** *Archaic.* of small height. **11.** *Archaic.* low in place, position, or degree. —n. **12.** *Music. Obs.* bass[1]. [ME, t. OF: m. *bas,* g. LL *bassus* low] —**base′ly,** adv. —**base′ness,** n. —Syn. **1.** despicable, contemptible. See **mean**[2]. **2.** servile, ignoble.

base·ball (bās′bôl′), n. **1.** a game of ball played by two sides of nine players each, on a diamond enclosed by

---

ăct, āble, dâre, ärt; ĕbb, ēqual; ĭf, īce; hŏt, ōver, ôrder, oil, bŏŏk, ōōze, out; ŭp, ūse, ûrge; ə = a in alone; ch, chief; g, give; ng, ring; sh, shoe; th, thin; ŧh, that; zh, vision. See the full key on inside cover.

lines connecting four bases, a complete circuit of which must be made by a player after batting, in order to score a run. 2. the ball used in playing this game.

base·board (bās′bôrd′), *n.* 1. a line of boarding around the interior walls of a room, next to the floor. 2. a board forming the base of anything.

base·born (bās′bôrn′), *adj.* 1. of humble birth. 2. born out of wedlock. 3. base-natured; mean.

base·burn·er (bās′bûr′nər), *n. U.S.* a stove or furnace with a self-acting fuel hopper over the fire chamber.

base hit, *Baseball.* a hit on which a batter runs to first base or beyond unless a fielder has made an error or another runner is forced out by the batter's advance.

Ba·sel (bä′zəl), *n.* a city in NW Switzerland, on the Rhine. 183,543 (1950). British **Basle,** French **Bâle.**

base·less (bās′lĭs), *adj.* having no base; without foundation; groundless: *a baseless claim.*

base level, *Phys. Geog.* the lowest level to which running water can theoretically erode the land.

base·man (bās′mən), *n., pl.* **-men.** *Baseball.* a player stationed at first, second, or third base.

base·ment (bās′mənt), *n.* 1. a story of a building partly or wholly underground. 2. the portion of a structure which supports those portions which come above it. 3. the substructure of a columnar or arched construction.

ba·ses[1] (bā′sēz), *n.* pl. of **basis.**

bas·es[2] (bā′sĭz), *n.* pl. of **base**[1].

bash (băsh), *Dial. or Slang.* —*v.t.* 1. to strike with a crushing or smashing blow. —*n.* 2. a crushing blow. [b. BAT[1] and MASH]

Ba·shan (bā′shən), *n.* a fertile region E of the Jordan in ancient Palestine: famous for its cattle and sheep.

ba·shaw (bə shô′), *n.* 1. pasha. 2. *Colloq.* an important personage; a bigwig. [t. Turk.: m. *bâsha,* var. of *pâsha* PASHA]

bash·ful (băsh′fəl), *adj.* 1. uncomfortably diffident or shy; timid and easily embarrassed. 2. indicative of bashfulness, accompanied with, or proceeding from bashfulness. [f. obs. *bash,* v. (aphetic var. of ABASH) + -FUL] —**bash′ful·ly,** *adv.* —**bash′ful·ness,** *n.* —Syn. 1. See **shy**[1].

bash·i-ba·zouk (băsh′ĭ bə zōōk′), *n.* one of a class of irregular mounted troops in the Turkish military service. [t. Turk.: m. *bashi-bozuq* irregular soldier]

Bash·kir (băsh kĭr′) *n.* an autonomous republic in the E Soviet Union in Europe. 3,144,713 pop. (1939); ab. 54,200 sq. mi. *Cap.:* Ufa. Official name, **Bashkir Autonomous Soviet Socialist Republic.**

bas·ic (bā′sĭk), *adj.* 1. of, pertaining to, or forming a base; fundamental: *a basic principle, ingredient, etc.* 2. *Chem.* **a.** pertaining to, of the nature of, or containing a base. **b.** not having all of the hydroxyls of the base replaced by the acid radical, or having the metal or its equivalent united partly to the acid radical and partly to oxygen. **c.** alkaline. 3. *Metall.* noting, pertaining to, or made by a steelmaking process in which the furnace is lined with a basic or nonsiliceous material, principally burned magnesite and a small amount of ground basic slag, to aid in sintering. 4. *Geol.* (of rocks) having relatively little silica. 5. *Mil.* **a.** primary: *basic training.* **b.** of lowest rank: *basic soldier; basic airman.* —*n.* 6. *Mil.* a soldier or airman receiving basic training.

bas·i·cal·ly (bā′sĭk lĭ), *adv.* fundamentally.

Basic English, a simplified English with a restricted vocabulary, intended as an international auxiliary language and for use in teaching English.

ba·sic·i·ty (bā sĭs′ə tĭ), *n. Chem.* 1. state of being a base. 2. the power of an acid to react with bases, dependent on the number of replaceable hydrogen atoms of the acid.

basic slag, the slag in a basic lined furnace used to remove impurities from metal, as in steelmaking, and as a fertilizer.

ba·sid·i·o·my·cete (bə sĭd′ĭ ō mī sēt′), *n. Bot.* a basidiomycetous organism. [t. NL: m. *Basidiomycētes.* See BASIDIUM, -MYCETES]

ba·sid·i·o·my·ce·tous (bə sĭd′ĭ ō mī sē′təs), *adj. Bot.* belonging or pertaining to the *Basidiomycetes,* a large group of fungi which bear the spores on a basidium, including the smuts, rusts, mushrooms, puffballs, etc.

ba·sid·i·um (bə sĭd′ĭ əm), *n., pl.* **-sidia** (-sĭd′ĭ ə). *Bot.* a special form of sporophore, characteristic of basidiomycetous fungi, on which the sexual spores are borne, usually at the tips of slender projections. [f. BAS(IS) + -IDIUM] —**ba·sid′i·al,** *adj.*

bas·il (băz′əl), *n.* a plant of the mint family *Labiatae,* genus *Ocimum,* as *O. Basilicum* (sweet basil). [ME *basile,* t. OF, t. L: short for *basilicum,* t. Gk.: m. *basilikón* (neut.), lit., royal]

Basidia

Bas·il (băz′əl), *n.* **Saint,** ("*the Great*") A.D. 329?–379. bishop of Caesarea, in Asia Minor. Also, **Basilius.**

bas·i·lar (băs′ə lər), *adj.* 1. pertaining to or situated at the base, esp. the base of the skull. 2. basal. Also, **bas·i·lar·y** (băs′ə lĕr′ĭ).

ba·sil·ic (bə sĭl′ĭk), *adj.* 1. kingly; royal. 2. of a basilica. Also, **ba·sil·i·can** (bə sĭl′ə kən). [t. F: m. *basilique,* t. L: m. s. *basilicus,* t. Gk.: m. *basilikós* kingly]

ba·sil·i·ca (bə sĭl′ə kə), *n.* 1. (*cap.*) (in ancient Rome) a large oblong building near the forum, used as a hall of justice and public meeting place. 2. *Archit.* an oblong building, esp. a church with a nave higher than its aisles. 3. one of the seven main churches of Rome or another Roman Catholic church accorded the same religious privileges. See illus. in preceding column. [t. L, t. Gk.: m. *basilikē,* fem. of *basilikós* royal]

basilic vein, *Anat.* a large vein on the inner side of the arm.

bas·i·lisk (băs′ə lĭsk, băz′-), *n.* 1. *Class. Legend.* a fabulous creature (serpent, lizard, or dragon) said by the ancients to kill by its breath or look. 2. a tropical American lizard of the genus *Basiliscus,* of the family *Iguanidae,* with a crest on the back of the head and along the back and tail. [t. L: m.s. *basiliscus,* t. Gk.: m. *basiliskos,* prop. dim. of *basileús* king]

Ba·sil·i·us (bə sĭl′ĭ əs, -zĭl′-), *n.* Basil. (saint).

ba·sin (bā′sən), *n.* 1. a circular container of greater width than depth, contracting toward the bottom, used chiefly to hold water or other liquid, esp. for washing. 2. any container of similar shape, as the pan of a balance. 3. the quantity held by such a container. 4. a natural or artificial hollow place containing water. 5. *Geol.* an area in which the strata dip from the margins toward a common center. 6. *Phys. Geog.* **a.** a hollow or depression in the earth's surface, wholly or partly surrounded by higher land: *ocean basin, lake basin, river basin.* **b.** the tract of country drained by a river and its tributaries. [ME, t. OF: m. *bacin,* g. LL *bachīnus,* der. *bacca* water vessel] —**ba′sined,** *adj.* —**ba′sin-like′,** *adj.*

Hooded basilisk, *Basiliscus mitratus* (2½ to 3 ft. long)

bas·i·net (băs′ə nĭt, -nĕt′), *n. Armor.* a steel globe-shaped cap. [ME, t. OF: m. *bacinet,* dim. of *bacin* BASIN]

ba·si·on (bā′sĭ ŏn′), *n. Craniom.* a point on the anterior margin of the foramen magnum, in the mid-sagittal plane of the skull. [t. NL, der. Gk. *bāsis* base]

ba·sip·e·tal (bā sĭp′ə təl), *adj. Bot.* (of a plant structure) developing toward the base during growth.

ba·sis (bā′sĭs), *n., pl.* **-ses** (-sēz). 1. the bottom or base of anything, or that on which it stands or rests. 2. a groundwork or fundamental principle. 3. the principal constituent; a fundamental ingredient. [t. L, t. Gk. See BASE[1]] —Syn. 1, 2. See **base**[1].

bask (băsk, bäsk), *v.i.* 1. to lie in or be exposed to a pleasant warmth: *to bask in the sunshine.* 2. to enjoy a pleasant situation: *he basked in royal favor.* —*v.t.* 3. to expose to warmth, heat, etc. [ME *baske(n),* t. Scand.; cf. Icel. *badhask,* refl. of *badha* bathe]

Bas·ker·ville (băs′kər vĭl), *n.* a style of type.

bas·ket (băs′kĭt, bäs′-), *n.* 1. a receptacle made of twigs, rushes, thin strips of wood, or other flexible material, woven together. 2. a container made of pieces of thin veneer, used for packing berries, vegetables, etc. 3. the contents of a basket. 4. anything like a basket in shape or use. 5. *Basketball.* **a.** a short open net suspended before the backboard through which the ball must pass to score points. **b.** a score, counting one point on a free throw and two for a field goal. [ME; orig. unknown] —**bas′ket·less,** *adj.* —**bas′ket·like′,** *adj.*

bas·ket·ball (băs′kĭt bôl′, bäs′-), *n.* 1. a game played, usually indoors, by two teams of five (six, if women) players each. Points are scored by throwing the ball through the baskets placed at either end of the oblong court. 2. the round leather ball used in this game.

basket hilt, a basketlike hilt of a sword, etc., designed to cover and protect the hand. —**bas′ket·hilt′ed,** *adj.*

bas·ket·ry (băs′kĭt rĭ, bäs′-), *n.* 1. basketwork; baskets. 2. the art or process of making baskets.

basket weave, a plain weave with two or more yarns woven together, resembling that of a basket.

bas·ket·work (băs′kĭt wûrk′, bäs′-), *n.* work of the basket kind or weave; wickerwork; interwoven work.

bask·ing shark (băs′kĭng, bäs′-), a very large shark, *Cetorhinus maximus,* which frequently comes to the surface to bask in the sun.

Basle (bäl), *n.* British name of **Basel.**

ba·so·phile (bā′sə fīl′, -fĭl), *n. Biol.* a cell or cell constituent with an affinity for basic dyes. [f. *baso-* (repr. BASIC) + -PHILE] —**ba·so·phil·ic** (bā′sə fĭl′ĭk), *adj.*

Basque (băsk), *n.* 1. one of a people of unknown origin inhabiting the western Pyrenees regions in France and Spain. 2. their language, historically connected only with Iberian. 3. (*l.c.*) a woman's bodice extending over the hips. 4. (*l.c.*) a short skirt or piece hanging from the waistline of a woman's (formerly a man's) garment. —*adj.* 5. of or pertaining to the Basques or their language. [t. F, g. L *Vasco* inhabitant of *Vasconia*]

Christian basilica (def. 2)
A. Apse; B. Secondary apse; C. High altar; D. Transept; E. Nave; F. Aisle

---

b., blend of, blended; c., cognate with; d., dialect, dialectal; der., derived from; f., formed from; g., going back to; m., modification of; r., replacing; s., stem of; t., taken from; ?, perhaps. See the full key on inside cover.

Basque Provinces, a region in N Spain, bordering on the Bay of Biscay, populated mostly by Basques.

Bas·ra (bŭs′rə, bäs′rä), *n.* a port in SE Iraq, N of the Persian Gulf. 101,535 (1947). Also, **Busra, Busrah.**

bas·re·lief (bä′rĭ lēf′, bäs′-; bä′rĭ lēf′, bäs′-), *n.* sculpture in low relief, in which the figures project only slightly from the background. [t. F, t. It.: m. *basso-rilievo* low relief]

bass¹ (bās), *Music.* —*adj.* **1.** low in pitch; of the lowest pitch or range: *a bass voice, part, singer, or instrument.* **2.** of or pertaining to the lowest part in the harmonized music. —*n.* **3.** the bass part. **4.** a bass voice, singer, or instrument. [var. of BASE² (see def. 12)]

bass² (bās), *n., pl.,* **basses,** (*esp. collectively*) **bass. 1.** any of various spiny-finned fishes, as: **a.** any fish of the family *Serranidae.* **b.** any of certain fishes of the family *Centrarchidae.* **c.** any of several similar fishes of other families. **2.** (orig.) the European perch, *Perca fluviatilis.* [var. of d. E *barse,* OE *bærs*]

bass³ (bās), *n.* **1.** the basswood or linden. **2.** *Bot.* bast. [alter. of BAST]

bass clef (bās), *Music.* the symbol placed on the fourth line of a staff to indicate that the notes are pitched below middle C; F clef. See illus. under **clef.**

bass drum (bās), *Music.* a musical instrument, the largest of the drum family, having a cylindrical body and two membranes.

bas·set¹ (bās′ĭt), *n.* a long-bodied, short-legged dog resembling a dachshund but larger and heavier. Also, **basset hound.** [t. F, orig. dim. of *bas* low]

bas·set² (bās′ĭt), *n., v.,* **-seted, -seting.** *Geol., Mining.* —*n.* **1.** an outcrop, as of the edges of strata. —*v.i.* **2.** to crop out. [? t. F: something low. See BASSET¹]

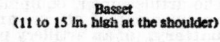

Basset
(11 to 15 in. high at the shoulder)

Basse·terre (bäs târ′), *n.* a seaport in the Federation of the West Indies: the capital of St. Kitts. 12,000 (est. 1952).

Basse-Terre (bäs târ′; *Fr.* bås tĕr′), *n.* a seaport in and the capital of Guadeloupe, in the French West Indies. 11,837 (1954).

basset horn, *Music.* an alto clarinet with a soft tone. [t. G: m. *bassett-horn,* f. *bassett* voice (or instrument) pitched between tenor and bass (t. It.: m. *bassetto,* dim. of *basso* low) + *horn,* pun on name of inventor]

bass horn (bās), *Music.* **1.** a tuba. **2.** *Obsolesc.* a wind instrument related to the serpent.

bas·si·net (bās′ə nĕt′, bās′ə nĕt′), *n.* **1.** a basket with a hood over one end, for use as a baby's cradle. **2.** a form of perambulator. [t. F, dim. of *bassin* BASIN]

bas·so (bās′ō, bäs′ō; *It.* bäs′sō), *n., pl.* **-sos, -si** (-sē). *Music.* one who sings bass; a bass. [t. It., g. LL *bassus* low]

bas·soon (bä sōōn′, bə-), *n. Music.* a wood-wind instrument of the oboe class in baritone range, having a doubled wooden tube or body and a long, curved metallic crook to receive the reed. [t. F: m. *basson,* t. It.: m. *bassone,* aug. of *basso* low]

basso pro·fun·do (prō fŭn′dō; *It.* prō fōōn′dō), *Music.* the lowest bass singer. [t. It.: deep bass]

Bassoon

bas·so-re·lie·vo (bäs′ō rĭ lē′vō), *n., pl.* **-vos.** bas-relief. [t. It.]

bas·so-ri·lie·vo (bäs′ō rē lye′vō), *n., pl.* **bassi-rilievi** (bäs′sē rē lye′vē). basso-relievo. [It.]

Bass Strait (bās), a strait between Australia and Tasmania. 80–150 mi. wide.

bass viol (bās), *Music.* viola da gamba (def. 1).

bass·wood (bās′wōōd′), *n.* **1.** a linden, esp. *Tilia americana.* **2.** its wood.

bast (bāst), *n.* **1.** *Bot.* phloem. **2.** the inner bark of the linden and other trees, used in making matting, etc. [ME; OE *bæst,* c. G *bast*]

bas·tard (bās′tərd), *n.* **1.** an illegitimate child. **2.** something irregular, inferior, spurious, or unusual. —*adj.* **3.** illegitimate in birth. **4.** spurious; not genuine; false. **5.** of abnormal or irregular shape or size; of unusual make or proportions. **6.** having the appearance of; resembling in some degree. [ME, t. OF: prob. f. *bast* packsaddle + *-ard* -ARD, through meaning of mule; for semantic development, cf. MULATTO]

bas·tard·ize (bās′tər dīz′), *v.,* **-ized, -izing.** —*v.t.* **1.** to declare or prove to be a bastard. **2.** to debase. —*v.i.* **3.** to become debased. —**bas′tard·i·za′tion,** *n.*

bas·tard·ly (bās′tərd lĭ), *adj.* **1.** bastard; baseborn. **2.** spurious; counterfeit.

bastard wing, *Ornith.* alula.

bas·tar·dy (bās′tər dĭ), *n., pl.* **-dies. 1.** condition of a bastard; illegitimacy. **2.** act of begetting a bastard.

baste¹ (bāst), *v.t.,* **basted, basting.** to sew slightly; sew with temporary stitches, as a garment in the first stages of making; tack. [ME, t. OF: m. *bastir,* t. OG; cf. OHG *bestan* sew with bast, der. *bast* BAST]

baste² (bāst), *v.t.,* **basted, basting.** to moisten (meat, etc.) while cooking, as with drippings, butter, etc. [? t. F; cf. OF *basser* soak, moisten]

baste³ (bāst), *v.t.,* **basted, basting. 1.** to beat with a stick; thrash; cudgel. **2.** to denounce or scold vigorously. [t. Scand.; cf. Icel. *beysta* beat, thresh]

Bas·ti·a (bäs tē′ä), *n.* a seaport on the NE coast of Corsica: the former capital of Corsica. 47,729 (1954).

bas·tille (bäs tēl′; *Fr.* bås tē′y), *n.* **1. the Bastille,** a famous fortress in Paris, used as a prison, built in the 14th century and destroyed July 14, 1789. **2.** any prison, esp. one conducted in a tyrannical way. **3.** a tower, as of a castle; a small fortress. Also, **bas·tile′.** [ME, t. F, g. LL *bastilia* (pl.), der. *bastire* build]

Bastille Day, July 14, a national holiday of the French republic, commemorating the fall of the Bastille.

bas·ti·na·do (bäs′tə nā′dō), *n., pl.* **-does,** *v.,* **-doed, -doing.** —*n.* **1.** a blow or a beating with a stick, etc. **2.** an Oriental mode of punishment consisting in blows with a stick on the soles of the feet, or on the buttocks. **3.** a stick or cudgel. —*v.t.* **4.** to beat with a stick, etc., esp. on the soles of the feet or on the buttocks. Also, *Archaic,* **bas·ti·nade** (bäs′tə nād′). [t. Sp.: m. *basto-nada,* der. *baston* stick]

bast·ing (bās′tĭng), *n.* **1.** sewing with slight or temporary stitches. **2.** (*pl.*) the stitches taken, or the threads used. [f. BASTE¹ + -ING¹]

bas·tion (bās′chən, -tĭ′ən), *n.* **1.** *Fort.* a projecting portion of a rampart or fortification, forming an irregular pentagon attached at the base to the main work. **2.** a fortified place. [t. F, t. It.: m. *bastione,* der *bastire* build] —**bas′tioned,** *adj.*

Bas·togne (bäs tōn′; *Fr.* bås tōn′y), *n.* a town in SE Belgium: U. S. forces were besieged here during the German counteroffensive, Dec., 1944. 5602 (1947).

Ba·su·to·land (bə sōō′tō-länd′), *n.* a British protectorate in, but not an administrative part of, the Union of South Africa. 563,854 pop. (1946); 11,716 sq. mi. *Cap.:* Maseru.

Bastion: A. Salient angle; B. Flank; C. Ramp; D. Gorge; E. Parapet; F. Face; G. Moat; H. Curtain

bat¹ (bāt), *n., v.,* **batted, batting.** —*n.* **1.** *Sports* **a.** the club used in certain games, as baseball and cricket, to strike the ball. **b.** a racket, esp. one used in ping-pong and tennis. **c.** act of batting in a game. **d.** the right or turn to bat. **e. at bat,** in the position of the batter. **2.** a heavy stick, club, or cudgel. **3.** *Colloq.* a blow as with a bat. **4.** any fragment of brick or hardened clay. **5.** *Brit. Dial.* or *Colloq.* rate of motion, or speed. **6.** *Slang.* a spree; binge: *to go on a bat.* **7.** batt. —*v.t.* **8.** to strike or hit with or as with a bat or club. —*v.i.* **9.** *Baseball, etc.* **a.** to strike at the ball with the bat. **b.** to take one's turn as a batter. **10.** *Slang.* to rush. [ME *batte,* OE *batt* cudgel]

bat² (bāt), *n.* **1.** any of the nocturnal or crepuscular flying mammals constituting the order *Chiroptera,* characterized by modified forelimbs which serve as wings and are covered with a membranous skin extending to the hind limbs. **2.** blind as a bat, blind. [var. of ME *bakke,* t. Scand.; cf. Dan. *-bakke*] —**bat′like,** *adj.*

Silver-haired bat,
Lasionycteris noctivagans
(4 in. long)

bat³ (bāt), *v.t.,* **batted, batting.** *Colloq.* to wink. [var. of *bate* flutter, t. OF: m. *batre,* g. LL *batere* beat]

Ba·taán (bə tän′; *local* bä′tä-än′), *n.* a peninsula on W Luzon, in the Philippine Islands: U. S. troops surrendered to the Japanese, April 9, 1942.

Ba·tan·gas (bä täng′gäs), *n.* a seaport in the Philippines, on SW Luzon. 59,582 (1948).

Ba·ta·vi·a (bə tä′vĭ ə), *n.* a former Dutch name for Djakarta.

batch (bāch), *n.* **1.** the quantity of bread made at one baking. **2.** a quantity or number coming at one time or taken together: *a batch of prisoners.* **3.** the quantity of material prepared or required for one operation. [ME *batche,* OE *gebæc* baking, der. *bacan* bake]

bate (bāt), *v.t.,* **bated, bating. 1.** to moderate or restrain (the breath): *to wait with bated breath.* **2.** to lessen; abate. [aphetic var. of ABATE]

ba·teau (bä tō′; *Fr.* bå tō′), *n., pl.* **-teaux** (-tōz′; *Fr.* -tō′). **1.** a light boat, esp. one having a flat bottom and tapering ends. **2.** a pontoon of a floating bridge. [t. F, in OF *batel.* Cf. ML *batellus,* dim. of *bat(t)us* boat, prob. t. OE: m. *bāt*]

bat·fish (bāt′fĭsh′), *n.* **1.** any of the flat-bodied marine fishes of the family *Ogcocephalidae,* as *Ogcocephalus vespertilio,* common along the southern Atlantic coast of the U.S. **2.** a California sting ray, *Aetobatis californicus.* [f. BAT² + FISH, n.]

bat·fowl (bāt′foul′), *v.i.* to catch birds at night by dazzling them with a light, then taking them in a net. [prob. f. BAT¹ + FOWL, v.] —**bat′fowl′er,** *n.*

ăct, āble, dâre, ärt; ĕbb, ēqual; ĭf, īce; hŏt, ōver, ôrder, oil, bŏŏk, ōōze, out; ŭp, ūse, ûrge; ə = a in alone; ch, chief; g, give; ng, ring; sh, shoe; th, thin; ŧh, that; zh, vision. See the full key on inside cover.

bath[1] (băth, bäth), n., pl. **baths** (băthz, bäthz), v. —n.
1. a washing of the body in, or an exposure of it to the action of, water or other liquid, or vapor, etc., as for cleansing, refreshment, medical treatment, etc. 2. water or other agent used for this purpose. 3. a vessel for containing this, as a bathtub. 4. a room equipped for bathing; bathroom. 5. a building containing apartments for bathing, or fitted up for bathing. 6. (often pl.) one of the elaborate bathing establishments of the ancients. 7. (usually pl.) a town or place resorted to for medical treatment by bathing, etc. 8. a preparation, as an acid solution, in which something is immersed. 9. the vessel containing such a preparation. 10. a device for heating or cooling apparatus by means of a surrounding medium such as sand, water, or oil. 11. state of being covered by a liquid. —v.t. 12. to put or wash in a bath. [ME; OE bæth, c. G bad] —**bath′less**, adj.

bath[2] (băth), n. either of two Hebrew units of liquid measure, about 10 and 10¾ U.S. gallons respectively.

Bath (băth, bäth), n. 1. a city in SW England: mineral springs. 79,800 (est. 1956). 2. a seaport in SW Maine. 10,717 (1960).

Bath brick, a compacted mass of fine siliceous sand, used for scouring metal. [named after Bath, England]

Bath chair, an invalid's wheeled chair. Also, **bath chair**.

bathe (băth), v., **bathed**, **bathing**, n. —v.t. 1. to immerse in water or other liquid for cleansing, refreshment, etc. 2. to wet; wash. 3. to moisten or suffuse with any liquid. 4. to apply water or other liquid to, with a sponge, cloth, etc. 5. to cover or surround with anything like water. —v.i. 6. to take a bath. 7. to swim for pleasure. 8. to be covered or surrounded as if with water. —n. 9. Brit. act of bathing, as in the sea. [ME bathien, OE bathian, der. bæth bath] —**bath′er**, n.

bath·house (băth′hous′, bäth′-), n. 1. a house or building for bathing. 2. a structure, as at the seaside, containing dressing rooms for bathers.

batho-, a word element meaning "deep," as in batholith. [comb. form repr. Gk. bathos depth]

bath·o·lith (băth′ə lĭth), n. Geol. a large body of igneous rock, bounded by irregular, cross-cutting surfaces or fault planes, and believed to have crystallized at a considerable depth below the earth's surface. Also, **bath·o·lite** (băth′ə līt′). —**bath′o·lith′ic**, **bath·o·lit·ic** (băth′ə lĭt′ĭk), adj.

ba·thom·e·ter (bə thŏm′ə tər), n. Oceanog. a device for ascertaining the depth of water.

ba·thos (bā′thŏs), n. 1. a ludicrous descent from the elevated to the commonplace; anticlimax. 2. triteness or triviality in style. 3. insincere pathos; sentimentality. [t. Gk.: depth] —**ba·thet·ic** (bə thĕt′ĭk), adj.

bath·robe (băth′rōb′, bäth′-), n. a long, loose garment for wear in going to and from a bath.

bath·room (băth′rōōm′, -rŏŏm′, bäth′-), n. 1. a room fitted up for taking a bath. 2. toilet.

Bath·she·ba (băth shē′bə, băth′shĭ-), n. Bible. wife of Uriah the Hittite, loved by David; later, David's wife and mother of Solomon. II Sam. 11, 12.

bath·tub (băth′tŭb′, bäth′-), n. a tub to bathe in, esp. one forming a permanent fixture in a bathroom.

Bath·urst (băth′ərst), n. 1. a seaport in and the capital of Gambia. 21,000 (est. 1957). 2. a town in SE Australia, in New South Wales. 16,090 (1954).

bath·y·sphere (băth′ə sfîr′), n. Oceanog. a spherical diving apparatus from which to study deep-sea life. [f. Gk. bathy(s) deep + -SPHERE]

ba·tik (bə tēk′, băt′ĭk), n. 1. a method of printing cloth using a wax deposit in the desired pattern. 2. the fabric so decorated. Also, **battik**. [t. Malay (Javanese)]

Ba·tis·ta y Zal·dí·var (bä tēs′tä ē säl dē′vär), n. Fulgencio (fōōl hĕn′syō), born 1901, Cuban military leader: president of Cuba, 1940–44, 1952–59.

ba·tiste (bə tēst′), n. a fine, delicate cotton fabric of plain weave. [t. F: m. Baptiste, name of the alleged first maker]

bat·man (băt′mən), n., pl. **-men**. a British army officer's assigned soldier-servant.

ba·ton (bə tŏn′, băt′ən; Fr. bä tôn′), n. 1. a staff, club, or truncheon, esp. as a mark of office or authority. 2. Music. the wand used by a conductor. 3. Her. a sinisterwise ordinary cut off at each end, borne in England as a mark of bastardy. [t. F, r. obs. baston, t. OF, der. LL bastum; orig. uncert.]

Bat·on Rouge (băt′ən rōōzh′), the capital of Louisiana, in SE part: a port on the Mississippi. 152,419 (1960).

ba·tra·chi·an (bə trā′kĭ ən), Zool. —adj. 1. of or pertaining to the Batrachia, a term formerly applied to the Amphibia, though sometimes restricted to the salientians. —n. 2. an amphibian, sometimes more esp. a salientian. [f. s. Gk. bátrachos frog + -IAN]

bats·man (băts′mən), n., pl. **-men**. Brit. a batter[3].

batt (băt), n. a sheet of matted cotton wool. Also, **bat**.

batt., 1. battalion. 2. battery.

bat·tal·ion (bə tăl′yən), n. 1. Mil. a ground force unit composed of three or more companies or similar units. 2. an army in battle array. 3. (often pl.) a large number; force. [t. F: m. bataillon, t. It.: m. battaglione]

bat·ten[1] (băt′ən), v.i. 1. to thrive as by feeding; grow fat. 2. to feed gluttonously; live in luxury at the expense of others. —v.t. 3. to cause to thrive as by feeding; fatten. [t. Scand.; cf. Icel. batna improve, der. bati change for the better. Cf. OE bet better]

bat·ten[2] (băt′ən), n. 1. a light strip of wood usually having an oblong cross section and used to fasten main members of a structure together. 2. Naut. a. a thin strip of wood inserted in a sail to keep it flat. b. a strip of wood, as one used to secure the edges of a tarpaulin over a hatchway. —v.t. 3. to furnish with battens. 4. Naut. to fasten (as hatches) with battens and tarpaulins (usually fol. by down). [var. of BATON]

bat·ter[1] (băt′ər), v.t. 1. to beat persistently or hard; pound. 2. to damage by beating or hard usage. —v.i. 3. to deal heavy, repeated blows; pound. —n. 4. Print. a. a damaged spot on the face of type or a plate. b. the resulting defect in print. [ME batere(n); freq. of BAT[1]]

bat·ter[2] (băt′ər), n. a mixture of flour, milk or water, eggs, etc., beaten together for use in cookery. [late ME bater, n. use of batter[1], but cf. OF bature beating]

bat·ter[3] (băt′ər), n. U.S. one who wields a bat or whose turn it is to bat, as in baseball, cricket, etc. [f. BAT[1] + -ER[1]]

bat·ter[4] (băt′ər), Archit. —v.i. 1. (of walls, etc.) to slope backward from the base. —n. 2. the receding slope, usually decreasing in thickness. [orig. uncert.]

battering ram, an ancient military engine with a heavy horizontal beam for battering down walls, etc.

Bat·ter·sea (băt′ər sĭ), n. a SW borough of London, England, on the Thames. 117,130 (1951).

bat·ter·y (băt′ə rĭ), n., pl. **-teries**. 1. Elect. a combination of two or more galvanic cells electrically connected to work together to produce electric energy. 2. a set or series of similar machines, parts, or the like, as a group of boilers. 3. Mil. a. a parapet or fortification equipped with artillery. b. two or more pieces of artillery used for combined action. c. a tactical unit of artillery, usually consisting of four guns together with the artillerymen, equipment, etc. d. the personnel or complement of officers and men attached to it. e. in battery, (of an artillery piece) in firing position, having recuperated from recoil. 4. Naval. a group of guns on, or the whole armament of, a vessel of war. 5. Baseball. the pitcher and catcher together. 6. act of beating or battering. 7. Law. an unlawful attack upon another by beating or wounding, or even by touching in an offensive manner. 8. the instrument used in battering. [t. F: m. batterie, der. battre beat]

Bat·ter·y (băt′ə rĭ), n. a park in New York City at the S tip of Manhattan, on upper New York Bay.

bat·tik (băt′ĭk), n. batik.

bat·ting (băt′ĭng), n. 1. act or manner of using a bat in a game of ball. 2. cotton or wool in batts or sheets, used as filling for quilts or bedcovers.

bat·tle[1] (băt′əl), n., v., **-tled**, **-tling**. —n. 1. a hostile encounter or engagement between opposing forces. 2. participation in such hostile engagements: wounds received in battle. 3. a fight between two persons or animals. 4. Archaic. a battalion. —v.i. 5. to engage in battle. 6. to struggle; strive: to battle for freedom. —v.t. 7. to fight. [ME batayle, t. OF: m. bataille, g. LL battālia, der. L battuere beat] —**bat′tler**, n.

—Syn. 1. BATTLE, ACTION, SKIRMISH mean a conflict between organized armed forces. A BATTLE is a prolonged and general conflict pursued to a definite decision: the Battle of the Bulge in World War II. An ACTION is part of a spirited military operation, offensive or defensive: the army was involved in a number of brilliant actions during the battle. A SKIRMISH is a slight engagement, often preparatory to larger movements: several minor skirmishes. 2. warfare, combat.

bat·tle[2] (băt′əl), v.t. Archaic. to furnish with battlements. [see BATTLEMENT]

bat·tle-ax (băt′əl ăks′), n. 1. an ax for use as a weapon of war. 2. Slang. a cantankerous old woman. Also, **bat′tle-axe′**.

Battle Creek, a city in S Michigan. 44,169 (1960).

battle cruiser, a warship of maximum speed and firepower, but with lighter armor than a battleship.

battle cry, 1. a cry or shout of troops in battle. 2. the phrase or slogan in any contest or campaign.

bat·tle·dore (băt′əl dōr′), n., v., **-dored**, **-doring**. —n. 1. an instrument shaped like a tennis racket, but smaller, used in striking a shuttlecock in play. 2. Also, **battledore and shuttlecock**. the game played with this racket and a shuttlecock. —v.t., v.i. 3. to toss to and fro. [ME batyldore, ? f. bater BATTER[1] + dore beetle, with dissimilation]

battle fatigue, Psychiatry. a type of psychoneurosis occurring among soldiers engaged in active warfare, and often making continued service in danger zones impossible; combat fatigue.

bat·tle·field (băt′əl fēld′), n. the field or ground on which a battle is fought. Also, **bat·tle·ground** (băt′əl-ground′).

bat·tle·ment (băt′əl mənt), n. (often pl.) Archit. an indented parapet, having a series of openings, orig. for shooting through; a crenelated upper wall. [ME batelment, ? ult. der. OF bastiller fortify] —**bat·tle·ment·ed** (băt′əl mĕn′tĭd), adj.

bat·tle·plane (băt′əl plān′), n. an airplane designed for combat use.

battle royal, 1. a fight in which more than two combatants are engaged. 2. a hard fight or a heated argument; a fight to the finish.

Battlement: A. Merlon;
B. Crenel; C. Loophole;
D. Machicolation

bat·tle-scarred (băt/əl skärd/), *adj.* bearing scars or damages received in battle.

bat·tle·ship (băt/əl shĭp/), *n.* one of a class of warships which are the most heavily armored and equipped with the most powerful batteries.

battle wagon, *Slang.* a battleship.

bat·tue (bă tōō/, -tū/; Fr. bà tỹ/), *n. Chiefly Brit.* **1.** *Hunting.* **a.** the beating or driving of game from cover, to be killed by sportsmen. **b.** a hunt of this kind. **2.** undiscriminating slaughter of defenseless or unresisting crowds. [t. F, prop. fem. pp. of *battre* beat]

bat·ty (băt/ĭ), *adj.* **-tier, -tiest. 1.** *U.S. Slang.* crazy; silly. **2.** of or like a bat.

Ba·tum (bä tōōm/), *n.* a seaport in the SW Soviet Union, on the SE coast of the Black Sea. 70,000 (est. 1956).

bau·ble (bô/bəl), *n.* **1.** a cheap piece of ornament; trinket; gewgaw. **2.** a jester's staff. [ME *babel*, t. OF: toy, prob. der. *bel*, g. L *bellus* pretty]

Bau·cis and Phi·le·mon (bô/sĭs; fə lē/mən), a poor and aged Phrygian couple who offered hospitality to Zeus and Hermes in disguise, and were rewarded.

Bau·de·laire (bōd lĕr/), *n.* **Pierre Charles** (pyĕr shärl), 1821–67, French poet and critic.

Bau·douin I (bō dwăn/), *n.* born 1930, king of Belgium since 1951.

bau·drons (bô/drənz), *n. Scot.* a cat.

Bau·haus (bou/hous/), *n. German.* a school established in Weimar in 1918 by Walter Gropius (born 1883) to create a functional experimental architecture, utilizing all the resources of art, science, and technology.

baulk (bôk), *v.i., v.t., n.* balk.

Baut·zen (bout/sən), *n.* a city in E East Germany, on the Spree river: Napoleon's victory over the Prussians and Russians, 1813. 42,008 (1955).

baux·ite (bôk/sīt, bō/zīt), *n.* a rock, consisting chiefly of aluminum oxide or hydroxide with various impurities: the principal ore of aluminum. [f. *Les Baux*, in southern France + -ITE¹]

Ba·var·i·a (bə vâr/ĭə), *n.* a state in S West Germany: formerly a kingdom. 9,191,800 (est. 1956); 27,239 sq. mi. *Cap.*: Munich. German, **Bayern.**

Ba·var·i·an (bə vâr/ĭən), *adj.* **1.** of or pertaining to Bavaria, its inhabitants, or their dialect. —*n.* **2.** a native or an inhabitant of Bavaria. **3.** the High German speech of most of Bavaria and Austria, and of the Sudeten Germans.

baw·bee (bô/bē/, bô/bē), *n. Scot.* **1.** an old Scotch bullion coin, originally worth about 3 halfpence of English coin, later 6d. **2.** *Colloq.* a halfpenny. [named after a mint master, the laird of Sillebawby]

baw·cock (bô/kŏk/), *n. Archaic or Dial.* (used familiarly) a fine fellow. [t. F: m. *beau coq* fine cock]

bawd (bôd), *n.* a procuress or procurer. [ME *bawde*, ? t. F: m. *baud* gay, t. WGmc.; cf. OE *bald* bold]

bawd·y (bô/dĭ), *adj.* **bawdier, bawdiest.** obscene; indecent. —**bawd/i·ly,** *adv.* —**bawd/i·ness,** *n.*

bawl (bôl), *v.t.* **1.** to utter or proclaim by outcry; shout out. **2.** to cry for sale, as a hawker. **3.** *U.S. Colloq.* to scold (fol. by *out*). **4.** to cry or wail lustily. —*n.* **5.** a loud shout; an outcry. [ME *bawl*(en), prob. t. ML: m. *baulāre* bark as a dog; but cf. Icel. *baula* low as a cow] —**bawl/er,** *n.*

Bax·ter (băk/stər), *n.* **Richard,** 1615–91, British Puritan preacher, scholar, and writer.

bay¹ (bā), *n. Phys. Geog.* **1.** a recess or inlet in the shore of a sea or lake between two capes or headlands, not as large as a gulf but larger than a cove. **2.** a recess of land, partly surrounded by hills. **3.** *U.S.* an arm of a prairie, extending into woods and partly surrounded by them. [ME *baye*, t. OF: m. *baie*, g. LL *baia*, of doubtful orig.]

bay² (bā), *n.* **1.** *Archit.* **a.** the part of a window included between two mullions. **b.** a recessed space projecting outward from the line of a wall, as to contain a window. **c.** a bay window. **d.** *Chiefly Brit.* a space or division of a wall, building, etc., between two vertical architectural features or members. **2.** *Aeron.* **a.** any portion of an airplane set off by two successive bulkheads or other bracing members. **b.** a compartment in an aircraft: *a bomb bay, an engine bay.* **3.** a compartment, as in a barn for storing hay. **4.** *Naut.* the forward part of a ship between decks on either side, formerly often used as a hospital. [ME, t. OF: m. *baee* an opening, ult. der. LL *badāre* gape]

bay³ (bā), *n.* **1.** a deep, prolonged bark, as of a hound in hunting. **2.** a stand made by a hunted animal to face or repel pursuers, or of a person forced to face a foe or difficulty: *to stand at bay, be brought to bay.* **3.** the position of the pursuers or foe thus kept off. —*v.i.* **4.** to bark, esp. with a deep prolonged sound, as a hound in hunting. —*v.t.* **5.** to beset with deep prolonged barking. **6.** to express by barking. **7.** to bring to or hold at bay. [ME *baye*(n), t. OF: m. *baier*, ? g. LL *badāre* gape]

Architectural bays
F. Window bay;
C. Triforium bay; A. Arch of aisle

bay⁴ (bā), *n.* **1.** the European laurel, *Laurus nobilis* sweet bay. **2.** a West Indian tree, *Pimenta acris,* whose leaves are used in making bay rum. **3.** any of various laurellike trees. **4.** *U.S.* any of several magnolias. **5.** an honorary garland or crown bestowed for victory or excellence. **6.** (*pl.*) fame; renown. [ME, t. OF: m. *baie,* g. L *bāca, bacca* berry]

bay⁵ (bā), *n.* **1.** reddish-brown. **2.** a bay horse or animal. —*adj.* **3.** (of horses, etc.) of the color bay. [ME, t. OF: m. *bai,* g. L *badius*]

Ba·yard (bā yär/), *n.* **1.** **Pierre Terrail, Seigneur de** (pyĕr tĕ rä/y, sĕn yœr/ də), c1473–1524, the heroic French knight "without fear and without reproach." **2.** any man of heroic courage and unstained honor.

bay·ard (bā/ərd), *n.* **1.** a magical legendary horse in medieval chivalric romances. **2.** a mock-heroic name for any horse. **3.** (*l.c.*) *Archaic.* a bay horse. [ME, t. OF: f. *bai* BAY⁵ + -*ard* -ARD]

bay·ber·ry (bā/bĕr/ĭ), *n., pl.* **-ries. 1.** any of certain shrubs or trees of the genus *Myrica,* as *M. carolinensis,* a shrub common on seacoasts, and *M. cerifera* (wax myrtle). **2.** the berry of such a plant. **3.** a West Indian tree, *Pimenta acris,* whose leaves are used in making bay rum. [f. BAY⁴ + BERRY]

Bay City, a city in E Michigan: a port near the mouth of the Saginaw river. 53,604 (1960).

Bay·ern (bī/ərn), *n.* German name of **Bavaria.**

Ba·yeux tapestry (bā yōō/, bä-; *Fr.* bä yœ/), a strip of linen 231 feet long and 20 inches wide, preserved in Bayeux, a town in NW France. Its colored embroidery pictures events leading to the Norman conquest of England, and it probably dates from the 12th century.

Bayle (bĕl), *n.* **Pierre** (pyĕr), 1647–1706, French philosopher and critic.

bay·o·net (bā/ə nĭt), *n., v.,* **-neted, -neting.** —*n.* **1.** a stabbing or slashing instrument of steel, made to be attached to or at the muzzle of a rifle. —*v.t.* **2.** to kill or wound with the bayonet. [t. F: m. *baïonette,* der. *Bayonne,* in France, where first made]

Ba·yonne (bā yŏn/ for 1; bä yŏn/ for 2), *n.* **1.** a city in NE New Jersey. 74,215 (1960). **2.** a seaport in SW France, near the Bay of Biscay. 32,575 (1954).

bay·ou (bī/ōō), *n., pl.* **-ous.** *Southern U.S.* an arm or outlet of a lake, river, etc. [t. Louisiana F, t. Choctaw (Muskhogean): m. *bayuk* small stream]

Bay·reuth (bī/roit/), *n.* a city in West Germany, in N Bavaria: music festivals founded by Richard Wagner. 60,500 (1950).

bay rum, a fragrant liquid used as a cosmetic, etc., esp. after shaving, prepared by distilling the leaves of the bayberry, *Pimenta acris,* with rum, or by mixing oil from them with alcohol, water, and other oils.

Bay State, Massachusetts.

bay tree, the European laurel, *Laurus nobilis.*

bay window, 1. a window forming an extension in a room and projecting outward from the wall of the building, esp. one rising from the ground or basement. **2.** *Humorous.* a fat man's protuberance in front.

bay·wood (bā/wood/), *n.* a kind of mahogany, esp. found near the Gulf of Campeche, in Mexico.

ba·zaar (bə zär/), *n.* **1.** a market place or quarter containing shops. **2.** any place or establishment for the sale of miscellaneous goods. **3.** a sale of miscellaneous articles for some charitable or other special object. Also, **ba·zar/.** [t. F: m. *bazar,* t. Ar., t. Pers.]

Ba·zaine (bä zĕn/), *n.* **François Achille** (frän swä/ ä shēl/), 1811–88, French general and marshal.

Ba·zin (bä zăn/), *n.* **René François Nicolas Marie** (rə nĕ/ frän swä/ nē kō lä/ mà rē/), 1853–1932, French novelist.

ba·zoo·ka (bə zōō/kə), *n. Mil.* a cylindrical rocket launcher, an individual infantry weapon penetrating several inches of armor plate, used to destroy tanks and other armored military vehicles.

B.B.A., Bachelor of Business Administration.

bbl., *pl.* **bbls.** barrel.

B.C., 1. before Christ. From 20 B.C. to A.D. 50 is 70 years. **2.** Bachelor of Chemistry. **3.** British Columbia.

B.C.E., Bachelor of Civil Engineering.

B.Ch.E., Bachelor of Chemical Engineering.

bd., *pl.* **bds. 1.** board. **2.** bond. **3.** bound. **4.** bundle.

B.D., Bachelor of Divinity.

B/D, bank draft.

bdel·li·um (dĕl/ĭəm, -yəm), *n.* **1.** a fragrant gum resin obtained from certain burseraceous plants, as *Commiphora.* **2.** a plant yielding it. **3.** a substance mentioned in the Bible (Gen. 2:12 and Num. 11:7), variously interpreted to mean gum resin, carbuncle, crystal, or pearl. [ME *bdelyum* (Wyclif), t. L (Vulgate): m. *bdellium* (Gen. 2:12 and Num. 11:7), t. Gk.: m. *bdéllion,* translating Heb. *b'dōlakh*]

bd. ft., **1.** board feet. **2.** board foot.

bdl., *pl.* **bdls.** bundle.

B.D.S., Bachelor of Dental Surgery.

be (bē; *unstressed* bĭ), *v., pres. indic. sing.* 1 **am;** 2 **are** or (*Archaic*) **art;** 3 **is;** *pl.* **are;** *pt. indic.* 1 **was;** 2 **were** or (*Archaic*) **wast** or **wert;** 3 **was;** *pl.* **were;** *pres. subj.* **be;** *pt. subj.* 1 **were;** 2 **were** or (*Archaic*) **wert;** 3 **were;** *pl.* **were;** *pp.* **been;** *ppr.* **being.** —*substantive.* **1.** to exist; have reality; live; take place; remain as before: *he is no more, it was not to be, think what might have been, the wedding was last week.* —*copula.* **2.** a link con-

ct, āble, dâre, ärt; ĕbb, ēqual; ĭf, īce; hŏt, ōver, ôrder, oil, bŏŏk, ōoze, out; ŭp, ūse, ûrge; ə = a in alone; ħ, chief; g, give; ng, ring; sh, shoe; th, thin; ŧħ, that; zh, vision. See the full key on inside cover.

necting a subject with predicate or qualifying words in assertive, interrogative, and imperative sentences, or serving to form infinitive and participial phrases: *you are late, he is much to blame, is he here? try to be just, the art of being agreeable.* —*auxiliary.* 3. used with the present participle of a principal verb to form the progressive tense (*I am waiting*), or with a past participle in passive forms, regularly of transitive verbs (*the date was fixed, it must be done*) and formerly, as still to some extent, of intransitives (*I am done, he is come*). [ME been, OE beon, g. IE base *bheu-* become; now used to make inf., pres. and past participles, and pres. subj.; for pres. ind., see AM, IS, ARE (g. IE base *es-* exist); for pret., see WAS, WERE (g. IE base *wes-* remain)]

be-, a prefix of W Germanic origin, meaning "about," "around," "all over," and hence having an intensivae nd often disparaging force, much used as an English formative of verbs (and their derivatives), as in *besiege, becloud, bedaub, beplaster, bepraise,* and often serving to form transitive verbs from intransitives or from nouns or adjectives, as in *begrudge, belabor, befriend, belittle.* [OE, unstressed form of *bī* by]

Be, *Chem.* beryllium.

B.E., 1. Bachelor of Education. 2. Bachelor of Engineering. 3. bill of exchange.

B/E, bill of exchange. Also, **b.e.**

beach (bēch), *n.* 1. the sand or loose waterworn pebbles of the seashore. 2. that part of the shore of the sea, or of a large river or lake, washed by the tide or waves. —*v.t., v.i.* 3. *Naut.* to run or haul up (a ship or boat) on the beach. [cf. OE *bece* brook] —**beach′less,** *adj.* —Syn. 2. coast, seashore, strand. See **shore**[1].

beach·comb·er (bēch′kō′mər), *n.* 1. one who lives by gathering articles along the beaches, as from wreckage; a vagrant of the beach or coast, esp. a white man in South Pacific regions. 2. a long wave rolling in from the ocean.

beach flea, any of various small hopping amphipods (family *Orchestidae*) found on beaches; a sand hopper.

Beach flea, *Orchestia ag ills.* (enlarged)

beach·head (bēch′hed′), *n.* the area of lodgment which is the first objective of a military force landing on an enemy shore.

beach-la-Mar (bēch′lə mär′), *n.* a pidgin language based on English, spoken in the Southwest Pacific.

beach wagon, *U.S.* station wagon.

beach·y (bē′chǐ), *adj. Obs.* or *Rare.* covered with pebbles or sand.

bea·con (bē′kən), *n.* 1. a guiding or warning signal, such as a fire, esp. one on a pole, tower, hill, etc. 2. a tower or hill used for such purposes. 3. a lighthouse, signal buoy, etc., on a coast or over dangerous spots at sea to warn and guide vessels. 4. a radio beacon. 5. any person, thing, or act that warns or guides. —*v.t.* 6. to serve as a beacon to; guide. 7. to furnish or mark with beacons. —*v.i.* 8. to serve or shine as a beacon. [ME *beken,* OE *bēac(e)n*] —**bea′con·less,** *adj.*

Bea·cons·field (bē′kənz fēld′), *n.* See **Disraeli.**

bead (bēd), *n.* 1. a small ball of glass, pearl, wood, etc., with a hole through it, strung with others like it, and used as an ornament or in a rosary. 2. (*pl.*) a necklace. 3. (*pl.*) a rosary. 4. **say, tell, or count one's beads,** to say prayers and count them off by means of the beads on the rosary. 5. any small globular or cylindrical body. 6. a bubble rising through effervescent liquid. 7. a mass of such bubbles on the surface of a liquid. 8. a drop of liquid: *beads of sweat, etc.* 9. the front sight of a gun. 10. aim. 11. *Archit., etc.* **a.** a narrow convex molding, usually more or less semicircular in section. **b.** any of various pieces similar in some sections to this type of molding. 12. *Chem.* a globule of borax or some other flux, supported on a platinum wire, in which a small amount of some substance is heated in a flame as a test for its constituents, etc. 13. *Metall.* the rounded mass of refined metal obtained by cupellation. —*v.t.* 14. to ornament with beads. —*v.i.* 15. to form beads; form in beads or drops. [ME *bede* prayer, rosary bead, aphetic var. of *ibed,* OE *gebed* prayer] —**bead′ed,** *adj.* —**bead′-like′,** *adj.*

bead·house (bēd′hous′), *n.* an almshouse whose beneficiaries were required to pray for the founder. Also, **bedehouse.**

bead·ing (bē′dǐng), *n.* 1. material composed of or adorned with beads. 2. narrow lacelike trimming. 3. narrow openwork trimming through which ribbon may be run. 4. *Archit.* **a.** a bead. **b.** beads collectively.

bea·dle (bē′dəl), *n.* 1. an official in British universities who, bearing a mace, supervises and leads processions. 2. *Eccles.* a parish officer having various subordinate duties, as keeping order during services, waiting on the clergyman, etc. Also, *Archaic,* **bedel, bedell.** [southeastern ME *bedel,* OE *bydel* apparitor, herald]

bea·dle·dom (bē′dəl dəm), *n.* a stupid show or exercise of authority, as by subordinate officials.

bead·roll (bēd′rōl′), *n.* 1. *Rom. Cath. Ch.* a list of persons to be prayed for. 2. any list or catalogue.

bead-ru·by (bēd′rōō′bǐ), *n., pl.* **-bies.** the false lily of the valley, *Maianthemum canadense,* a low herb with small white flowers and red bead-shaped berries.

beads·man (bēdz′mən), *n., pl.* **-men.** 1. one who prays for another, as a duty, and esp. when paid for it. 2. an inmate of a poorhouse. Also, **bedesman.** —**beads·wom·an** (bēdz′wŏŏm′ən), *n., fem.*

bead·work (bēd′wûrk′), *n.* 1. ornamental work made of or with beads. 2. beading.

bead·y (bēd′ĭ), *adj.,* **beadier, beadiest.** 1. beadlike; small, globular, and glittering: *beady eyes.* 2. covered with or full of beads.

bea·gle (bē′gəl), *n.* one of a breed of small hounds with short legs and drooping ears, used esp. in hunting. [ME *begle;* orig. uncert.]

Beagle. (15 in. high at the shoulder

beak[1] (bēk), *n.* 1. the horny bill of a bird; the neb. 2. a horny head part in animals, as in turtle, duckbill, etc., similar to a bird's beak. 3. *Slang.* a person's nose. 4. anything beaklike or ending in a point, as the lip of a pitcher or a beaker. 5. *Bot.* a narrowed or prolonged tip. 6. *Naut.* a powerful construction of metal, or of timber sheathed with metal, forming a part of the bow of many older type warships for ramming an enemy's ship. 7. *Archit.* a little pendent fillet with a channel behind it forming a drip and preventing water from trickling down the faces of lower architectural members. [ME *beke,* t. OF: m. *bec,* g. LL *beccus,* of Celtic orig.] —**beaked** (bēkt, bē′kǐd), *adj.* —**beak′less,** *adj.* —**beak′like′,** *adj.*

beak[2] (bēk), *n.* **Brit. Collog.** 1. magistrate; judge. 2. *Brit. Slang.* schoolmaster. [orig. unknown]

beak·er (bē′kər), *n.* 1. a large drinking vessel with a wide mouth. 2. contents of a beaker. 3. a flat-bottomed cylindrical vessel, usually with a pouring lip. [var. (influenced by *beak*[1]) of d. E *bicker,* ME *biker,* t. Scand.; cf. Icel. *bikarr* (? ult. t. L: m. *bicārium*)]

beam (bēm), *n.* 1. a thick and relatively long piece of timber, shaped for use. 2. a similar piece of metal, stone, etc. 3. *Bldg. Trades.* one of the principal horizontal supporting members in a building or the like, as for supporting a roof or floor. 4. *Shipbuilding.* one of the strong transverse pieces of timber or metal stretching across a ship to support the deck or hold the sides in place, etc. 5. *Naut.* **a.** the side of a vessel, or the direction at right angles to the keel, with reference to the wind, sea, etc. **b.** the greatest breadth of a ship. 6. the widest part. 7. *Mach.* **a.** an oscillating lever of a steam engine, transferring the motion from piston root to crankshaft. **b.** a roller or cylinder in a loom, on which the warp is wound before weaving **c.** a similar cylinder on which cloth is wound as it is woven. 8. the transverse bar of a balance from the ends of which the scales or pans are suspended. 9. a ray, or bundle of parallel rays, of light or other radiation. 10. the angle at which a microphone or loud-speaker functions best. 11. the cone-shaped range of effective use of a microphone or loud-speaker. 12. a gleam; suggestion: *a beam of hope.* 13. *Radio, Aeron.* a signal transmitted along a narrow course, used to guide planes through darkness, bad weather, etc. 14. **on the beam** **a.** on the course indicated by a radio beam. **b.** *Naut.* at right angles with the keel. **c.** *Slang.* just right; exactly correct. 15. **off the beam, a.** not on the course indicated by a radio beam. **b.** *Slang.* wrong; incorrect. 16. **fly the beam,** *Radio, Aeron.* to be guided by a beam. —*v.t.* 17. to emit in or as in beams or rays. 18. *Radio* to transmit (a signal) on a narrow beam. —*v.i.* 19. to emit beams, as of light. 20. to look or smile radiantly [ME *beem,* OE *bēam* tree, piece of wood, ray of light, c G *baum* tree] —**beamed,** *adj.* —**beam′less,** *adj.* —**beam′like′,** *adj.* —Syn. 19. See **shine.**

beam-ends (bēm′endz′), *n.pl. Naut.* 1. the ends of a ship's beams. 2. **on her beam-ends,** so far inclined on one side that the deck beams are practically vertical.

beam·ing (bē′mǐng), *adj.* radiant; bright; cheerful —**beam′ing·ly,** *adv.*

beam-pow·er tube (bēm′pou′ər), *Radio.* a vacuum tube in which the stream of electrons flowing to the plate is focused by the action of a set of auxiliary, charged elements, giving an increase in output power.

beam·y (bē′mǐ), *adj.,* **beamier, beamiest.** 1. emitting beams, as of light; radiant. 2. broad in the beam, as a ship. 3. *Zool.* having antlers, as a stag.

bean (bēn), *n.* 1. the edible nutritious seed of various species of leguminous plants, esp. of the genus *Phaseolus.* 2. a plant producing such seeds, used as a snap bean as a shell bean, or as dry beans. 3. any of various other beanlike seeds or plants, as the coffee bean. 4. *Slang.* head. —*v.t.* 5. *Slang.* to hit on the head, esp. with a base ball. [ME *bene,* OE *bēan,* c G *bohne*] —**bean′like′,** *adj.*

bean·bag (bēn′băg′), *n.* a small cloth bag filled with beans, used as a toy.

bean caper, a small tree, *Zygophyllum Fabago,* of the eastern Mediterranean regions, whose flower buds are used as a substitute for capers.

bean·ie (bē′nǐ), *n.* a small brimless hat.

bean·o (bē′nō), *n.* bingo.

bean-pole (bēn′pōl′), *n.* 1. a tall pole for a bean plant to climb on. 2. *Slang.* a tall, lanky person.

bean·stalk (bēn′stôk′), *n.* the stem of a bean plant.

bean tree, any of several trees bearing pods resembling those of a bean, as the catalpa and the carob tree

---

b., blend of, blended; c., cognate with; d., dialect, dialectal; der., derived from; f., formed from; g., going back to; m., modification of; r., replacing; s., stem of; t., taken from; ?, perhaps. See the full key on inside cover

bear[1] (bâr), v., **bore** or (*Archaic*) **bare, borne** or **born, bearing.** —v.t. **1.** to hold up; support: *to bear the weight of the roof.* **2.** to carry: *to bear gifts.* **3.** to conduct; guide; take: *they bore him to his quarters.* **4.** to press or push against: *the crowd was borne back by the police.* **5.** to render; afford; give: *to bear testimony.* **6.** to transmit or spread (gossip, tales, etc.). **7.** to sustain without yielding or suffering injury (usually negative unless qualified): *I can't bear your scoldin.* **8.** to undergo: *to bear the blame.* **9.** to accept or have as an obligation: *to bear responsibility, cost, etc.* **10.** to hold up under; be capable of: *his claim doesn't bear close examination.* **11.** to be fit for or worthy of: *the story doesn't bear repeating.* **12.** to have and be entitled to: *to bear title.* **13.** to possess as a quality, characteristic, etc.; have in or on: *bear traces, an inscription, etc.* **14.** to stand in (a relation or ratio): *the relation that price bears to profit.* **15.** to carry in the mind: *to bear love, a grudge, etc.* **16.** to exhibit; show. **17.** to have and use; exercise: *to bear sway.* **18.** to manage (oneself, one's body, head, etc.): *to bear oneself erectly.* **19.** to conduct (oneself). **20.** to give birth to: *to bear quintuplets.* **21.** to produce by natural growth: *plants bear leaves.* **22.** to confirm; prove (fol. by *out*): *the facts bear me out.* —v.i. **23.** to hold, or remain firm, as under pressure (often fol. by *up*). **24.** to be patient (fol. by *with*). **25.** to press (fol. by *on, against, down,* etc.). **26.** to have an effect, reference, or bearing (fol. by *on*): *time bears heavily on him.* **27.** to tend in course or direction; move; go. **28.** to be situated: *the ship bears due west.* **29.** to bring forth young, fruit, etc. [ME *bere(n),* OE *bæran;* akin to G *gebären* bring forth, L *ferre* bear, Gk. *phérein,* Skt. *bhar-*] —Syn. **4.** thrust, drive, force. **7.** tolerate, brook, abide. **8.** BEAR, STAND, ENDURE refer to supporting the burden of something distressing, irksome, or painful. BEAR is the general word and STAND its colloquial equivalent, but with an implication of stout spirit: *to bear a disappointment well, to stand a loss.* ENDURE implies continued resistance and patience in bearing through a long time: *to endure torture.*

bear[2] (bâr), n., v., **beared, bearing.** —n. **1.** any of the plantigrade, carnivorous or omnivorous mammals of the family *Ursidae,* having massive bodies, coarse heavy fur, relatively short limbs, and almost rudimentary tails. **2.** any of various animals resembling the bear, as the ant bear. **3.** a gruff, clumsy, or rude person. **4.** (in general business) one who believes that conditions are or will be unfavorable. **5.** *Stock Exchange.* one who sells short with the expectation of covering at a lower price (opposed to a *bull*). **6.** *Astron.* either of two constellations in the northern hemisphere, the **Great Bear** (Ursa Major) and the **Little Bear** (Ursa Minor). **7. the Bear,** Russia. —adj. **8.** of, having to do with, or caused by declining prices in stocks, etc.: *bear market.* —v.t. **9.** *Stock Exchange, etc.* to attempt to lower the price of; operate in for a decline in price. [ME *bere,* OE *bera,* c. G *bär*] —**bear'a·ble,** adj. —**bear'a·ble·ness,** n. —**bear'a·bly,** adv.

American black bear,
Euarctos americanus (5 ft. long)

bear-bait·ing (bâr'bā'tǐng), n. the sport of setting dogs to fight a captive bear.

bear·ber·ry (bâr'běr'ǐ), n., pl. **-ries. 1.** a trailing evergreen ericaceous shrub, *Arctostaphylos Uva-ursi,* bearing small bright-red berries and tonic, astringent leaves. **2.** a related species, *A. alpina,* bearing black berries (**alpine bearberry** or **black bearberry**). **3.** any of certain other plants, as *Ilex decidua,* a holly of the southern U.S. **4.** the cranberry, *Oxycoccus macrocarpus.*

beard (bǐrd), n. **1.** the growth of hair on the face of an adult man, sometimes exclusive of the mustache. **2.** *Zool.* a tuft, growth, or part resembling or suggesting a human beard, as the tuft of long hairs on the lower jaw of a goat, or a cluster of fine, hairlike feathers at the base of the beak of certain birds. **3.** *Bot.* a tuft or growth of awns or the like, as in wheat, barley, etc. **4.** a barb or catch on an arrow, fishhook, knitting needle, crochet needle, etc. **5.** *Print.* the part of a type which connects the face with the shoulder of the body; the neck. See diag. under **type.** —v.t. **6.** to seize, pluck, or pull the beard of. **7.** to oppose boldly; defy. **8.** to supply with a beard. [ME *berd,* OE *beard,* c. G *bart*] —**beard'ed,** adj. —**beard'less,** adj. —**beard'less·ness,** n. —**beard'like',** adj.

Beard (bǐrd), n. **1. Charles Austin,** 1874–1948, and his wife, **Mary,** 1876–1958, U.S. historians. **2. Daniel Carter,** 1850–1941, founder of Boy Scouts of America.

Beards·ley (bǐrdz'lǐ), n. **Aubrey Vincent** (ô'brǐ), 1872–98, British illustrator.

beard·tongue (bǐrd'tǔng'), n. any plant of the scrophulariaceous genus *Penstemon.*

bear·er (bâr'ər), n. **1.** a person or thing that carries, upholds, or brings. **2.** one who presents an order for money or goods. **3.** a tree or plant that yields fruit or flowers. **4.** the holder of rank or office. **5.** pallbearer.

bear garden, 1. a place for keeping or exhibiting bears, as for bearbaiting. **2.** any place of tumult.

bear grass, 1. any of several American plants of the liliaceous genus *Yucca,* having grasslike foliage. **2.** any of certain similar liliaceous plants, such as the camass.

bear·ing (bâr'ǐng), n. **1.** the manner in which a person bears or carries himself, including posture, gestures, etc.: *a man of dignified bearing.* **2.** act, capability, or period of producing or bringing forth: *a tree past bearing.* **3.** that which is produced; a crop. **4.** act of enduring or capacity to endure. **5.** reference or relation (fol. by *on*): *some bearing on the problem.* **6.** *Archit.* **a.** a supporting part, as in a structure. **b.** the contact area between a load-carrying member and its support. **7.** *Mach.* a part in which a journal, pivot, or the like, turns or moves. **8.** (*often pl.*) direction or relative position: *the pilot lost his bearings.* **9.** *Geog.* a horizontal angle measured from 0 to 90° fixing the direction of a line with respect to either the north or south direction. **True bearings** are referred to the true north direction, **magnetic bearings** to magnetic north (or south). **10.** *Her.* any single device on a coat of arms; a charge. —Syn. **1.** See **manner.**

bearing rein, a checkrein (def. 1).

bear·ish (bâr'ǐsh), adj. **1.** like a bear; rough; burly; morose; rude. **2.** *Stock Exchange, etc.* unfavorable and tending to cause a decline in price. —**bear'ish·ly,** adv. —**bear'ish·ness,** n.

Bear River, a river in Utah, Wyoming, and Idaho flowing into Great Salt Lake. ab. 450 mi.

bear's-ear (bârz'ǐr'), n. a primrose, the auricula.

bear's-foot (bârz'fòòt'), n. any of various species of hellebore, esp. *Helleborus foetidus.*

bear·skin (bâr'skǐn'), n. **1.** the skin or pelt of a bear. **2.** a tall black fur cap worn esp. by soldiers. **3.** a coarse, shaggy woolen cloth for overcoats.

bear·wood (bâr'wòòd'), n. a buckthorn, *Rhamnus purshiana.*

beast (bēst), n. **1.** any animal except man, but esp. a large four-footed one. **2.** the animal nature common to man and nonhumans. **3.** a coarse, filthy, or otherwise beastlike human. [ME *beste,* t. OF. g. LL *besta,* var. of L *bestia*] —**beast'like',** adj. —Syn. **1.** See **animal.**

beast·ly (bēst'lǐ), adj., **-lier, -liest. 1.** of or like a beast; bestial. **2.** *Brit. Colloq.* nasty; disagreeable. —adv. **3.** *Brit. Colloq.* exceedingly. —**beast'li·ness,** n.

beast of burden, an animal used to carrying loads.

beat (bēt), v., **beat, beaten** or **beat, beating,** n. —v.t. **1.** to strike repeatedly, as in chastising, threshing, metalworking, making a batter, etc. **2.** to dash against: *rain beating the trees.* **3.** to flutter, flap, or rotate in. **4.** to sound as on a drum. **5.** to break, forge, or make by blows. **6.** to produce or destroy (an idea, habit, etc.) by repeated efforts. **7.** to make (a path) by repeated treading. **8.** *Music.* to mark (time) by strokes, as with the hand or a metronome. **9.** *Hunting.* to scour (the forest, grass, or brush) for game. **10.** to overcome in a contest; defeat. **11.** to be superior to. **12.** to be too difficult for; baffle. **13.** *U.S. Slang.* to swindle; get ahead of: *he beat him.* **14. beat a retreat,** to withdraw hurriedly. —v.i. **15.** to strike repeated blows; pound. **16.** to throb or pulsate. **17.** to dash (*against, on,* etc.). **18.** to resound under blows, as a drum. **19.** to win in a contest. **20.** to play, as on a drum. **21.** to scour cover for game. **22.** *Physics.* to make a beat or beats. **23.** to permit beating. **24.** *Naut.* to make progress to windward by sailing full and by, first on one tack and then on the other. **25. beat about the bush,** to approach a matter in a roundabout way; avoid coming to the point. —n. **26.** a stroke or blow. **27.** the sound made by it. **28.** a throb or pulsation. **29.** *Horol.* the stroke made by the action of the escapement of a watch or clock. **30.** one's beaten path or habitual round. **31.** *Music.* **a.** the audible, visual, or mental marking of the metrical divisions of music. **b.** a stroke of the hand, baton, etc., marking time division or accent for music during performance. **32.** *Pros.* the accent stress, or ictus, in a foot or rhythmical unit of poetry. **33.** *Physics.* a periodic pulsation caused by simultaneous occurrence of two waves, currents, or sounds of slightly different frequency. **34.** *U.S. Journalism.* the publishing of some piece of news in advance of, or to the exclusion of, its rivals. **35.** a subdivision of a county, as in Mississippi. —adj. **36.** *U.S. Colloq.* exhausted; worn out. [ME *bete(n),* OE *béatan,* c. Icel. *bauta*] —Syn. **1.** BEAT, HIT, POUND, STRIKE, THRASH refer to the giving of a blow or blows. BEAT implies the giving of repeated blows: *to beat a rug.* To HIT is usually to give a single blow, definitely directed: *to hit a ball.* To POUND is to give heavy and repeated blows, often with the fist: *to pound a nail, the table.* To STRIKE is to give one or more forceful blows suddenly or swiftly: *to strike a gong.* To THRASH implies inflicting repeated blows as punishment, to show superior strength, and the like: *to thrash a child.* **16.** See **pulsate.**

beat·en (bē'tən), adj. **1.** having undergone blows; hammered. **2.** much trodden; commonly used: *the beaten path.* **3.** defeated. **4.** exhausted.

beat·er (bē'tər), n. **1.** a person or thing that beats. **2.** an implement or device for beating something: *an egg beater.* **3.** *Hunting.* one who rouses or beats up game.

beat generation, members of the generation that came of age after World War II who espouse mystical detachment and relaxation of social and sexual tensions, supposedly as a result of disillusionment stemming from the cold war. [coined by John Kerouac, born 1920, American author]

be·a·tif·ic (bē'ə tǐf'ǐk), adj. **1.** rendering blessed. **2.** blissful: *a beatific vision or smile.* [t. LL: s. *beātificus*] —**be'a·tif'i·cal·ly,** adv.

be·at·i·fi·ca·tion (bǐ ăt/ə fə kā/shən), n. **1.** act of beatifying. **2.** state of being beatified. **3.** *Rom. Cath. Ch.* the official act of the Pope whereby a deceased person is declared to be enjoying the happiness of heaven, and therefore a proper subject of religious honor and public cult in certain places.

be·at·i·fy (bǐ ăt/ə fī/), v.t., **-fied, -fying. 1.** to make blissfully happy. **2.** *Rom. Cath. Ch.* to declare (a deceased person) to be among the blessed, and thus entitled to specific religious honor. [t. F: m.s. *beatifier*, t. L: m. *beātificāre* make happy]

beat·ing (bē/tǐng), n. **1.** act of a person or thing that beats. **2.** the same act administered as punishment; whipping. **3.** a defeat. **4.** a pulsation or throb.

be·at·i·tude (bǐ ăt/ə tūd/, -tōōd/), n. **1.** supreme blessedness; exalted happiness. **2.** (*often cap.*) *Theol.* any one of the declarations of blessedness pronounced by Christ in the Sermon on the Mount, as "Blessed are the poor," etc. Matt. 5:3–11. [t. L: m. *beātitūdo*]

beat·nik (bēt/nǐk), n. *Colloq.* **1.** a member of the beat generation. **2.** one who avoids the conventions of behavior, dress, etc.

Be·a·trice (bē/ə trǐs; *It.* bě/ä trē/chě), n. (in Dante's *Vita Nuova* and *Commedia Divina*) a symbolic figure developed from the lady of Dante's love on earth.

Beat·ty (bē/tǐ), n. **David,** (1st Earl of the North Sea and of Brooksby) 1871–1936, British admiral.

beau (bō), n., pl. **beaus, beaux** (bōz; *Fr.* bō). **1.** a lover; swain. **2.** an escort. **3.** a dandy; fop. [ME, t. OF, n. use of *beau* (earlier *bel*) handsome, g. L *bellus.* See BELLE] —**beau/ish,** adj.

Beau Brum·mell (brǔm/əl), **1.** (*George Bryan Brummell*) 1778–1840, a man who set the fashion in men's clothes in England. **2.** a fop; dandy.

Beau·fort scale (bō/fərt), *Meteorol.* a numerical scale for indicating the force or velocity of the wind, ranging from 0 for calm to 12 for hurricane, or velocities above 75 miles per hour. [named after Sir Francis *Beaufort,* 1774–1857, British admiral who devised it]

beau geste (bō zhěst/), pl. **beaux gestes** (bō zhěst/). *French.* a fine gesture, often only for effect.

Beau·har·nais (bō är ně/), n. **1. Eugénie Hortense de,** (œ zhě ně/ ôr täns/ də), 1783–1837, queen of Holland: wife of Louis Bonaparte. **2. Joséphine de,** (jō/zə fēn/; *Fr.* zhō zě fēn/), 1763–1814, first wife of Napoleon: empress of France, 1804–09.

beau i·de·al (ĭ dē/əl, ĭ dēl/), **1.** a conception of perfect beauty. **2.** a model of excellence. [t. F]

Beau·mar·chais (bō mär shě/), n. **Pierre Augustin Caron de** (pyěr ō gys tăn/ kà rón/ də), 1732–99, French dramatist.

beau monde (bō/ mŏnd/; *Fr.* bō mônd/), *French.* the fashionable world.

Beau·mont (bō/mŏnt), n. **1.** a city in SE Texas. 119,175 (1960). **2. Francis,** 1584–1616, English dramatist: collaborated with John Fletcher.

Beau·re·gard (bō/rə gärd/; *Fr.* bōr gàr/), n. **Pierre Gustave Toutant de** (pyěr gys tàv/ tōō tän/ də), 1818–93, Confederate general in the U.S. Civil War.

beau·te·ous (bū/tǐ əs), adj. *Chiefly Poetic.* beautiful. —**beau/te·ous·ly,** adv. —**beau/te·ous·ness,** n.

beau·ti·cian (bū tǐsh/ən), n. a person who operates or works in a beauty parlor.

beau·ti·ful (bū/tə fəl), adj. having beauty; delighting the eye; admirable to the taste or the mind. —**beau/ti·ful·ly,** adv. —**beau/ti·ful·ness,** n.
—Syn. BEAUTIFUL, HANDSOME, LOVELY, PRETTY refer to a pleasing appearance. That is BEAUTIFUL which has perfection of form, color, etc., or noble and spiritual qualities: *a beautiful landscape, girl* (not *man*). HANDSOME often implies stateliness or pleasing proportion and symmetry: *a handsome man.* That which is LOVELY is beautiful but in a warm and endearing way: *a lovely smile.* PRETTY implies a moderate but noticeable beauty, esp. in that which is small or of minor importance: *a pretty child.* —Ant. ugly.

beau·ti·fy (bū/tə fī/), v.t., v.i., **-fied, -fying.** to make or become beautiful. [f. BEAUTY + -FY] —**beau·ti·fi·ca·tion** (bū/tə fə kā/shən), n. —**beau/ti·fi/er,** n.

beau·ty (bū/tǐ), n., pl. **-ties. 1.** that quality of any object of sense or thought whereby it excites an admiring pleasure; qualification of a high order for delighting the eye or the aesthetic, intellectual, or moral sense. **2.** something beautiful, esp. a woman. **3.** a grace, charm, or pleasing excellence. [ME *beute,* t. OF: m. *beaute,* der. *beau.* See BEAU] —Syn. **1.** loveliness, pulchritude.

beauty parlor, *U.S.* an establishment for the hairdressing, manicuring, etc., of women. Also, **beauty shop.**

beauty spot, 1. a patch worn on the face or elsewhere to set off the fairness of the skin. **2.** a mole or other trifling mark on the skin. **3.** any spot, place, or feature of especial beauty.

beaux (bōz; *Fr.* bō), n. a pl. of beau.

beaux-arts (bō zàr/), n.pl. *French.* the fine arts, as painting, sculpture, etc.

beaux-es·prits (bō zěs prē/), n. *French.* pl. of **bel-esprit.**

bea·ver[1] (bē/vər), n. **1.** an amphibious rodent of the genus *Castor,* valued for its fur and formerly for castor, and noted for its ingenuity in damming

Beaver, *Castor canadensis* (43 in. long, including tail)

streams with trees, branches, stones, mud, etc. **2.** its fur. **3.** a flat, round hat made of beaver fur or a similar fabric. **4.** a man's high silk hat. **5.** a heavy woolen cloth. [ME *bever,* OE *beofor,* akin to G *biber*] —**bea/ver·like/,** adj.

bea·ver[2] (bē/vər), n. *Armor.* **1.** a piece of armor protecting the lower part of the face. **2.** a visor (def. 1). [late ME. *baviere,* t. MF: orig., bib, der. *bave* saliva]

B, Beaver[2] (def. 1)

bea·ver·board (bē/vər bôrd/), n. **1.** a light, stiff sheeting made of wood fiber and used in building, esp. for partitions, temporary structures, etc. **2.** (*cap.*) a trademark for this substance.

Bea·ver·brook (bē/vər brŏŏk/), n. **William Maxwell Aitken** (āt/kǐn), **1st Baron,** 1879–1964, British newspaper publisher, born in Canada.

be·be·rine (bə bǐr/ēn, -ǐn), n. *Pharm.* an alkaloid resembling quinine, obtained from the bark of the greenheart and other plants.

be·bee·ru (bə bǐr/ōō), n. greenheart (def. 1). [native name in Guiana]

Be·bel (bā/bəl), n. **Ferdinand August** (fěr/dǐ nänt/ ou/gōōst), 1840–1913, German socialist and writer.

be·bop (bē/bŏp), n. *Jazz.* a style of composition and performance characterized by dissonant harmony, complex rhythmic devices, and experimental, often bizarre instrumental effects. [fanciful coinage] —**be/bop·per,** n.

be·calm (bǐ käm/), v.t. **1.** (*usually in pp.*) to halt (a ship, etc.) by a lack of wind. **2.** to calm.

be·came (bǐ kām/), v. pt. of become.

be·cause (bǐ kôz/, -kŏz/, -kŭz/) ,conj. **1.** for the reason that; due to the fact that: *the game was called because it rained.* —adv. **2.** by reason; on account (fol. by *of*): *the game was called because of rain.* [ME *bi cause* by cause]
—Syn. **1.** BECAUSE, AS, SINCE, FOR, INASMUCH AS agree in implying a reason for an occurrence or action. BECAUSE introduces a direct reason: *I was sleeping because I was tired.* As and SINCE are so casual as to imply merely circumstances attendant on the main statement: *as (or since) I was tired, I was sleeping.* The reason, proof, or justification introduced by FOR is like an afterthought or a parenthetical statement: *I was sleeping, for I was tired.* INASMUCH AS implies concession; the main statement is true in view of the circumstances introduced by this conjunction: *inasmuch as I was tired, it had seemed best to sleep.*

bec·ca·fi·co (běk/ə fē/kō), n., pl. **-cos.** any of several small European birds, esp. the garden warbler, *Sylvia hortensis,* esteemed as a delicacy in Italy. [t. It.: f. *becca(re)* peck + *fico* fig]

bé·cha·mel sauce (bě shä měl/), a white sauce flavored with carrots, onions, seasoning, etc. [t. F, named after the inventor, Louis de *Béchamel*]

be·chance (bǐ chăns/, -chäns/), v.i., v.t., **-chanced, -chancing.** to befall.

be·charm (bǐ chärm/), v.t. to charm; captivate.

bêche-de-mer (běsh də měr/), n. **1.** a trepang. **2.** Beach-la-Mar. [F: sea spade]

Bech·u·a·na (běch/ōō ä/nə, běk/yōō-), n., pl. **-anas, -ana.** a Bantu living in the region of S Africa between the Orange and Zambesi rivers.

Bech·u·a·na·land (běch/ōō ä/nə länd/, běk/yōō-), n. a British protectorate in S Africa. 293,000 (est. 1953); ab. 275,000 sq. mi. *Cap.:* Mafeking.

beck[1] (běk), n. **1.** a beckoning gesture. **2.** *Scot.* a bow or curtsy of greeting. **3. at one's beck and call,** ready to obey one immediately; subject to one's slightest wish. —v.t., v.i. **4.** to beckon. [short for BECKON]

beck[2] (běk), n. *Chiefly Brit. Dial.* a brook. [ME, t. Scand.; cf. Icel. *bekkr,* akin to OE *bece*]

beck·et (běk/ĭt), n. *Naut.* **1.** any of various contrivances for holding spars, etc., in position, as a short rope with a knot at one end which can be secured in a loop at the other end. **2.** a loop or ring of rope forming a handle, or the like. [orig. unknown]

Beck·et (běk/ĭt), n. **Saint Thomas à,** 1118?–70, archbishop of Canterbury: murdered because of his opposition to Henry II's policies toward the church.

becket bend, *Naut.* sheet bend.

Beck·ford (běk/fərd), n. **William,** 1759–1844, British writer.

beck·on (běk/ən), v.t., v.i. **1.** to signal, summon, or direct by a gesture of the head or hand. **2.** to lure; entice. —n. **3.** a beckoning. [ME *beknen,* OE *bēcnan,* der. *bēacen* sign. Cf. BEACON] —**beck/on·er,** n.

be·cloud (bǐ kloud/), v.t. **1.** to darken or obscure with clouds. **2.** to make confused: *becloud the argument.*

be·come (bǐ kŭm/), v., **became, become, becoming.** —v.i. **1.** to come into being; come or grow to be (as stated): *he became tired.* **2.** to be the fate (*of*): *what will become of him?* —v.t. **3.** to befit in appearance; suit: *that dress becomes you.* [ME *becume(n),* OE *becuman* come about, happen]

be·com·ing (bǐ kŭm/ĭng), adj. **1.** attractive: *a becoming dress.* **2.** suitable; proper: *a becoming sentiment.* —n. **3.** any process of change. **4.** *Aristotelian Metaphys.* change involving realization of potentialities, as a movement from the lower level of potentiality to the higher level of actuality. —Syn. **2.** fitting, meet, appropriate. —**be·com/ing·ly,** adv. —**be·com/ing·ness,** n.

Bec·que·rel (běk rěl/), n. **1. Alexandre Edmond** (à lěk sän/dr ěd môn/), 1820–91, French physicist (son of Antoine César and father of Antoine Henri). **2. Antoine

b., blend of, blended; c., cognate with; d., dialect, dialectal; der., derived from; f., formed from; g., going back to; m., modification of; r., replacing; s., stem of; t., taken from; ?, perhaps. See the full key on inside cover

César (än twän′ sĕ zàr′), 1788–1878, French physicist. 3. **Antoine Henri** (än twän′ än rē′), 1852–1908, French physicist.

Becquerel rays, *Obsolesc.* rays emitted by radio-active substances. [named after A. H. *Becquerel*]

bed (bĕd), *n., v.* **bedded, bedding.** —*n.* 1. a piece of furniture upon which or within which a person sleeps. 2. the mattress and bedclothes together with the bed-stead. 3. the bedstead alone. 4. the use of a bed for the night; lodging. 5. matrimonial rights and duties. 6. any resting place. 7. something resembling a bed in form or position. 8. a piece of ground (in a garden) in which plants are grown. 9. the bottom of a body of water. 10. a piece or part forming a foundation or base. 11. a rock layer or stratum. 12. a foundation surface of earth or rock supporting a track or pavement: *a road bed.* 13. the under surface of a brick, shingle, slate, or tile in position. 14. either of the horizontal surfaces of a stone in position. 15. the flat surface in a printing press on which the form of type is laid. 16. *Zool.* flesh enveloping the base of a claw. —*v.t.* 17. to provide with a bed. 18. to put to bed. 19. to make a bed for (a horse, cattle, etc.) (fol. by *down*). 20. *Hort.* to plant in or as in a bed. 21. to lay flat, or in a bed or layer. 22. to embed, as in a substance. 23. *Archaic.* to go to bed with. —*v.i.* 24. to go to bed. 25. *Geol.* to form a compact layer or stratum. [ME; OE *bedd,* c. D *bed,* G *bett*] —**bed′less,** *adj.* —**bed′like′,** *adj.*

be·daub (bĭ dôb′), *v.t.* 1. to daub all over; besmear; soil. 2. to ornament gaudily or excessively.

be·daz·zle (bĭ dăz′əl), *v.t.,* **-zled, -zling.** to blind or confuse by dazzling.

bed·bug (bĕd′bŭg′), *n.* a small flat, wingless, hemipterous, bloodsucking insect, *Cimex lectularius,* that infests houses and esp. beds; cimex.

Bedbug. *Cimex lectularius* (⅓ in. long)

bed·cham·ber (bĕd′chăm′bər), *n.* bedroom.

bed·clothes (bĕd′klōz′, -klōⁿz′), *n.pl.* coverings for a bed; sheets, blankets, etc.

bed·ding (bĕd′ĭng), *n.* 1. blankets, sheets, for a bed; bedclothes. 2. litter; straw, etc., as a bed for animals. 3. *Bldg. Trades.* foundation or bottom layer of any kind. 4. *Geol.* arrangement of rocks in strata.

Bed·does (bĕd′ōz), *n.* **Thomas Lovell** (lŭv′əl), 1803–1849, British dramatist and poet.

Bede (bĕd), *n.* **Saint,** (*"the Venerable Bede"*) A.D. 673?–735, English monk, historian, and theologian: wrote earliest history of England. Also, **Baeda.**

be·deck (bĭ dĕk′), *v.t.* to deck out; showily adorn.

bede·house (bĕd′hous′), *n.* beadhouse.

be·del (bĕ′dəl), *n. Archaic.* beadle. Also, **be′dell.**

bedes·man (bĕdz′mən), *n., pl.* **-men.** beadsman. —**bedes·wom·an** (bĕdz′woŏm′ən). *n. fem.*

be·dev·il (bĭ dĕv′əl), *v.t.,* **-iled, -iling** or (*Brit.*) **-illed, -illing.** 1. to treat diabolically; torment maliciously. 2. to possess as with a devil; bewitch. 3. to confound; muddle; spoil. —**be·dev′il·ment,** *n.*

be·dew (bĭ dū′, -dōō′), *v.t.* to wet with or as with dew.

bed·fast (bĕd′făst′, -fäst′), *adj.* confined to bed.

bed·fel·low (bĕd′fĕl′ō), *n.* 1. a sharer of one's bed. 2. close companion: *politics makes strange bedfellows.*

Bed·ford (bĕd′fərd), *n.* 1. **John Plantagenet, Duke of,** 1389–1435, English regent of France. 2. a city in central England. 56,450 (est. 1956). 3. Bedfordshire.

Bedford cord, cotton, worsted, rayon, or silk, distinctively woven with a lengthwise, corded effect.

·**Bed·ford·shire** (bĕd′fərd shĭr′, -shər), *n.* a county in central England. 311,920 pop. (1951); 473 sq. mi. *Co. seat:* Bedford. Also, **Bedford, Beds.**

be·dight (bĭ dīt′), *v.t.,* **-dight, -dight** or **-dighted, -dighting.** *Archaic.* to deck out; array.

be·dim (bĭ dĭm′), *v.t.,* **-dimmed, -dimming.** to make dim. —Ant. illumine, illumine.

Bed·i·vere (bĕd′ə vĭr′), *n.* **Sir,** *Arthurian Legend.* the knight who brought the dying King Arthur to the barge in which the three queens bore him to the Isle of Avalon.

be·di·zen (bĭ dī′zən, -dĭz′ən), *v.t.* to dress or adorn gaudily. [f. BE- + DIZEN] —**be·di′zen·ment,** *n.*

bed·lam (bĕd′ləm), *n.* 1. a scene of wild uproar and confusion. 2. (*cap.*) an insane asylum in SE London, Hospital of St. Mary of Bethlehem. 3. any lunatic asylum; a madhouse. [ME *bedlem,* alter. of *Bethlehem*]

bed·lam·ite (bĕd′lə mīt′), *n.* a lunatic.

bed linen, sheets and pillowcases.

Bed·loe Island (bĕd′lō), a small island in upper New York Bay: site of the Statue of Liberty.

bed molding, *Archit.* 1. the molding, or series of moldings, between the corona and the frieze of an entablature. 2. any molding under a projection.

Bed·ou·in (bĕd′oŏ ĭn), *n.* 1. an Arab of the desert, in Asia or Africa; nomadic Arab. 2. a nomad; wanderer. [t. F, t. Ar.: m. *badawīyin,* pl. of *badawī* desert dweller]

bed·pan (bĕd′păn′), *n.* 1. a shallow toilet pan for use by persons confined to bed. 2. a warming pan.

bed·plate (bĕd′plāt′), *n.* a plate, platform, or frame supporting the lighter parts of a machine.

bed·post (bĕd′pōst′), *n.* one of the upright supports of a bedstead.

be·drag·gle (bĭ drăg′əl), *v.t.,* **-gled, -gling.** to make limp and soiled as with wet or dirt.

bed·rail (bĕd′rāl′), *n.* the board between the head- and footboards at the side of a bed.

bed·rid (bĕd′rĭd′), *adj.* 1. bedridden. 2. worn out. [ME *bedrede,* OE *bedreda, -rida,* lit., bed rider]

bed·rid·den (bĕd′rĭd′ən), *adj.* confined to bed. [var. (by confusion with pp.) of BEDRID]

bed·rock (bĕd′rŏk′), *n.* 1. *Geol.* unbroken solid rock, overlaid in most places by soil or rock fragments. 2. bottom layer; lowest stratum. 3. any firm foundation.

bed·room (bĕd′rōōm′, -rōōm′), *n.* a sleeping room.

Beds (bĕdz), *n.* Bedfordshire.

bed·side (bĕd′sīd′), *n.* 1. the side of a bed, esp. as the place of one in attendance on the sick. —*adj.* 2. attending a sick person: *a good bedside manner.* 3. at or for a bedside: *a bedside table.*

bed·sore (bĕd′sōr′), *n.* a sore due to prolonged contact with a bed, as in a long illness.

bed·spread (bĕd′sprĕd′), *n.* an outer covering, usually decorative, for a bed.

bed·spring (bĕd′sprĭng′), *n.* a set of springs for the support of a mattress.

bed·stead (bĕd′stĕd′, -stŷd′), *n.* the framework of a bed supporting the springs and a mattress.

bed·straw (bĕd′strô′), *n.* a rubiaceous plant, *Galium verum* (our Lady's bedstraw) or some allied species: formerly used as straw for beds.

bed·time (bĕd′tīm′), *n.* time to go to bed.

bed·ward (bĕd′wərd), *adv.* to bed. Also, **bed′wards.**

bee[1] (bē), *n.* 1. any of various hymenopterous insects of the superfamily *Apoidea,* which includes many social and solitary bees of several families, as the bumblebees, honeybees, etc. 2. the common honeybee, *Apis mellifera.* 3. **bee in one's bonnet** or **head, a.** an obsession. **b.** a slightly crazy idea, attitude, fad, etc. 4. *U.S.* a local gathering for work, entertainment, contests, etc.: *husking bee, spelling bee.* [ME; OE *bēo,* c. D *bij,* Icel. *bȳ*] —**bee′like′,** *adj.*

Common honeybee. *Apis mellifera* A. Queen; B. Worker; C. Drone

bee[2] (bē), *n. Naut.* a piece of hard wood, bolted to the side of the bowsprit, through which to reeve stays. [ME *beh* ring, OE *bēag, bēah* ring]

bee balm, a perennial garden flower of the genus *Monarda,* esp. the Oswego tea, *Monarda didyma.*

Bee·be (bē′bĭ), *n.* **Charles William,** 1877–1962, U.S. naturalist, explorer, and writer.

bee beetle, a European beetle, *Trichodes apiarius,* which sometimes infests beehives.

bee·bread (bē′brĕd′), *n.* a protein food mixture, containing pollen, manufactured and stored up by bees for their young.

beech (bēch), *n.* 1. any tree of the genus *Fagus,* of temperate regions, having a smooth gray bark, and bearing small edible triangular nuts. 2. the wood of such a tree. [ME *beche,* OE *bēce*] —**beech′en,** *adj.*

Bee·cham (bē′chəm), *n.* **Sir Thomas,** 1879–1961, British orchestral conductor and impresario.

beech·drops (bēch′drŏps′), *n.* 1. a low annual plant, *Leptamnium virginianum,* without green foliage, parasitic upon the roots of the beech. 2. the squawroot.

Bee·cher (bē′chər), *n.* 1. **Henry Ward,** 1813–87, U.S. preacher and writer. 2. his father, **Lyman** (lī′mən), 1775–1863, U.S. preacher and theologian.

beech mast, the edible nuts of the beech, esp. when lying on the ground.

beech·nut (bēch′nŭt′), *n.* the small, triangular, edible nut of the beech.

bee eater, any of the family *Meropidae,* comprising Old World insectivorous birds with long, slender bills and brilliant plumage.

beef (bēf). *n., pl.* **beeves** (bēvz) for 1; **beefs** for 5, *v.* —*n.* 1. a bull, cow, or steer of the genus *Bos,* esp. if intended for meat. 2. the flesh of such an animal, used for food. 3. *Colloq.* brawn; muscular strength. 4. *Colloq.* weight, as of human flesh. 5. *U.S. Slang.* a complaint. —*v.i.* 6. *U.S. Slang.* to complain; grumble. [ME, t. OF: m. *boef,* g. L *bōs* ox] —**beef′less,** *adj.*

beef cattle, cattle raised for beef, such as Hereford.

beef·eat·er (bēf′ē′tər), *n.* 1. one who eats beef. 2. a well-fed person. 3. a yeoman of the English royal guard or a warder of the Tower of London.

bee fly, any fly of the dipterous family *Bombyliidae,* members of which more or less resemble bees.

beef·steak (bēf′stāk′), *n.* a slice of beef for broiling, etc.

beef tea, an extract of beef made by heating chopped beef in water and straining it.

beef·wit·ted (bēf′wĭt′ĭd), *adj.* thick-witted; stupid.

beef·y (bē′fĭ), *adj.,* **beefier, beefiest.** fleshy; brawny; solid; heavy. —**beef′i·ness,** *n.*

bee gum, *South and West U.S.* 1. a gum tree, hollowed up by decay, in which bees live or from which hives are made. 2. a beehive.

bee·hive (bē′hīv′), *n.* 1. a hive or receptacle, conventionally dome-shaped, serving as a habitation for bees. 2. a crowded, busy place.

bee·keep·er (bē′kē′pər), *n.* one who raises bees.

bee killer, a robber fly (family *Asilidae*).

bee·line (bē′līn′), *n.* a direct line, like the course of bees returning to a hive.

Be·el·ze·bub (bȳ·ĕl′zə·bŭb′), *n.* **1.** *Bible.* "the prince of the devils" (Matt. 12:24); the devil. **2.** a devil. **3.** (in Milton's *Paradise Lost*) one of the fallen angels, second only to Satan himself. [ult. t. Heb.: m. *Ba'al-zebub* Philistine god, II Kings 1:2 (? meaning "lord of flies")]

bee martin, the kingbird, *Tyrannus tyrannus*.

been (bĭn), *v.* pp. of be.

bee plant, any plant much used by bees for food materials, esp. the cleome (*Cleome surrelata*) or figwort.

beer (bĭr), *n.* **1.** an alcoholic beverage made by brewing and fermentation from cereals, usually malted barley, and flavored with hops, etc., to give a bitter taste. **2.** any of various beverages, whether alcoholic or not. made from roots, molasses or sugar, yeast, etc.: *root beer, ginger beer.* [ME *bere*, OE *bēor*, c. G *bier*]

Beer (bĭr), *n.* Thomas, 1889–1940, U.S. author.

beer and skittles, *Brit.* drinks and pleasure.

Beer·bohm (bĭr′bōm), *n.* Sir Max, 1872–1956, British author and caricaturist.

Beer·she·ba (bĭr·shē′bə, bĭr′shĭ-), *n.* *Bible.* a town near the southern extremity of Biblical Palestine. See Dan (def. 2).

beer·y (bĭr′ĭ), *adj.,* **beerier, beeriest. 1.** of, like, or abounding in beer. **2.** affected by or suggestive of beer. **—beer′i·ness,** *n.*

beest·ings (bēs′tĭngz), *n.pl.* colostrum, the first milk of a mammal, esp. a cow, after giving birth. Also, **biestings.** [OE var. of *bysting*, der. *bēost* beestings, c. G *biest*]

bees·wax (bēz′wăks′), *n.* **1.** the wax secreted by bees, of which they construct their honeycomb; wax (def. 1). *—v.t.* **2.** to rub, polish, or treat with beeswax.

bees·wing (bēz′wĭng′), *n.* a thin film formed in port and some other wines after long keeping.

beet (bēt), *n.* **1.** any of various biennial plants of the chenopodiaceous genus *Beta*, whose varieties include the red beet, which has a fleshy edible root, and the **sugar beet,** which yields sugar. **2.** the root of such a plant. **3.** the leaves served as a salad or cooked vegetable. [OE *bēte*, t. L: m. *bēta*] **—beet′like′,** *adj.*

Bee·tho·ven (bā′tō·vən; *Ger.* bāt′hō·fən), *n.* Ludwig **van** (lōōd′vĭκн fän), 1770–1827, German composer.

bee·tle[1] (bē′tal), *n.* **1.** any insect of the order Coleoptera, characterized by having forewings modified as hard, horny structures, useless in flight. **2.** any of various insects resembling beetles, as the common cockroach. [ME *bētylle, bityl,* OE *bitula,* lit., biter]

Ground beetle,
Calosoma scrutator
(1¼ in. long)

bee·tle[2] (bē′tal), *n., v.,* **-tled, -tling.** *—n.* **1.** a heavy hammering or ramming instrument, usually of wood, used to drive wedges, force down paving stones, consolidate earth, etc. **2.** any of various wooden instruments for beating linen, mashing potatoes, etc. *—v.t.* **3.** to use a beetle on; drive, ram, beat, or crush with a beetle. **4.** to finish (cloth) by means of a beetling machine. [ME and d. OE *bētel,* r. OE *bietl,* der. *bēatan* beat]

bee·tle[3] (bē′tal), *adj., v.,* **-tled, -tling.** *—adj.* **1.** projecting, overhanging; *beetle brows.* *—v.i.* **2.** to project; jut out; overhang. [back formation from BEETLE-BROWED] **—bee′tling,** *adj.*

bee·tle-browed (bē′tal·broud′), *adj.* **1.** having heavy projecting eyebrows. **2.** scowling; sullen. [ME *bitel-browed,* f. *bitel* biting + BROW + -ED³. See BEETLE¹]

bee·tle-head (bē′tal·hĕd′), *n.* a stupid person; blockhead. [see BEETLE²] **—bee′tle·head′ed,** *adj.*

bee tree, a hollow tree used by wild bees as a hive, esp. the basswood or American linden.

beet sugar, sugar from the roots of the sugar beet.

beeves (bēvz), *n.* pl. of beef (def. 1).

bef., before.

B.E.F., British Expeditionary Forces.

be·fall (bĭ·fôl′), *v.,* **-fell, -fallen, -falling.** *—v.i.* **1.** to happen or occur. **2.** *Archaic.* to come (*to*) as by right. *—v.t.* **3.** to happen to. [ME *befallen,* OE *befeallan*]

be·fit (bĭ·fĭt′), *v.t.,* **-fitted, -fitting.** to be fitting or appropriate for; be suited to: *his clothes befit the occasion.*

be·fit·ting (bĭ·fĭt′ĭng), *adj.* fitting; proper. **—be·fit′ting·ly,** *adv.* **—Syn.** appropriate, suitable, seemly.

be·fog (bĭ·fôg′, -fŏg′), *v.t.,* **-fogged, -fogging.** to involve in fog or obscurity; confuse.

be·fool (bĭ·fōōl′), *v.t.* **1.** to fool; deceive; dupe. **2.** to treat as a fool.

be·fore (bĭ·fōr′), *adv.* **1.** in front; in advance; ahead. **2.** in time preceding; previously. **3.** earlier or sooner: *begin at noon, not before.* *—prep.* **4.** in front of; ahead of; in advance of: *before the house.* **5.** previously to; earlier than: *before the war.* **6.** ahead of; in the future of; awaiting: *the golden age is before us.* **7.** in preference to; rather than: *they would die before yielding.* **8.** in precedence of, as in order or rank: *we put freedom before fame.* **9.** in the presence or sight of: *before an audience.* **10.** under the jurisdiction or consideration of: *before a magistrate.* *—conj.* **11.** previously to the time when: *before we go.* **12.** sooner than; rather than: *I will die before I submit.* [ME *before(n),* OE *beforan,* f. *be* by + *foran* before] **—Ant. 1.** behind. **2.** afterward. **3.** later.

---

be·fore·hand (bĭ·fōr′hănd′), *adv., adj.* in anticipation; in advance; ahead of time.

be·fore·time (bĭ·fōr′tĭm′), *adv.* *Archaic.* formerly.

be·foul (bĭ·foul′), *v.t.* to make foul; defile; sully.

be·friend (bĭ·frĕnd′), *v.t.* to act as a friend to; aid.

be·fud·dle (bĭ·fŭd′əl), *v.t.,* **-dled, -dling. 1.** to make stupidly drunk. **2.** to confuse, as with glib argument.

beg (bĕg), *v.,* **begged, begging.** *—v.t.* **1.** to ask for in charity; ask as alms. **2.** to ask for, or of, with humility or earnestness, or as a favor: *to beg forgiveness, to beg him to forgive me.* **3.** to take for granted without warrant: *to beg the point.* **4.** beg the question, to assume the very point raised in a question. *—v.i.* **5.** to ask alms or charity; live by asking alms. **6.** to ask humbly or earnestly: *begging for help.* [ME *beggen,* OE *bedecian*] **—Syn. 2.** entreat, pray, crave, implore, beseech, petition. BEG and REQUEST are used in certain conventional formulas, in the sense of *ask.* BEG, once a part of many formal expressions used in letter writing, debate, etc., is now used chiefly in courteous formulas like *I beg your pardon, the Committee begs to report,* etc. REQUEST, more impersonal and now more formal, is used in giving courteous orders (*you are requested to report*) and in commercial formulas like *to request payment.*

be·gan (bĭ·găn′), *v.* pt. of begin.

be·gat (bĭ·găt′), *v.* *Archaic.* pt. of beget.

be·get (bĭ·gĕt′), *v.t.,* **begot, begotten** or **begot, begetting. 1.** to procreate or generate (used chiefly of the male parent). **2.** to cause; produce as an effect. [ME *begeten,* f. BE- + GET, r. OE *begitan*] **—be·get′ter,** *n.*

beg·gar (bĕg′ər), *n.* **1.** one who begs alms, or lives by begging. **2.** a penniless person. **3.** (in playful use) a wretch or rogue: *a cute little beggar.* *—v.t.* **4.** to reduce to beggary; impoverish. **5.** to exhaust the resources of: *to beggar description.* [ME *begger,* f. BEG + -ER¹. See -AR³] **—beg·gar·dom** (bĕg′ərdəm), **beg′gar·hood′,** *n.*

beg·gar·ly (bĕg′ərlĭ), *adj.* like or befitting a beggar; wretchedly poor; mean. **—beg′gar·li·ness,** *n.*

beg·gar's-lice (bĕg′ərz·līs′), *n.* **1.** (construed as pl.) seeds or fruits which stick to clothing. **2.** (*sing.* or *pl.*) any plant producing them. Also, **beg′gar·lice′.**

beg·gar's-tick (bĕg′ərs·tĭk′), *n.* **1.** one of the prickly awns of *Bidens frondosa* or similar plants. **2.** (*pl.*) the plant itself.

beg·gar-tick (bĕg′ər·tĭk′), *n.* **1.** beggar's-tick. **2.** beggar's-lice.

beg·gar·y (bĕg′ərĭ), *n.* **1.** the condition of utter poverty. **2.** beggar's collectively.

Beg·hard (bĕg′ərd, bĭ·gärd′), *n.* a member of one of certain former religious communities of men which arose in Flanders in the 13th century, living after the manner of the Beguines. [t. ML: s. *Beghardus*]

be·gin (bĭ·gĭn′), *v.,* **began, begun, beginning.** *—v.i.* **1.** to enter upon an action; take the first step; commence; start. **2.** to come into existence; arise; originate. *—v.t.* **3.** to take the first step in; set about; start; commence. **4.** to originate; be the originator of. [ME *beginne(n),* OE *beginnan*] **—be·gin′ner,** *n.* **—Syn. 3.** BEGIN, COMMENCE, INITIATE, START (when followed by noun or gerund) refer to setting into motion or progress something which continues for some time. BEGIN is the common term: *to begin knitting a sweater.* COMMENCE is a more formal word, often suggesting a more prolonged or elaborate beginning: *to commence proceedings in court.* INITIATE implies an active and often ingenious first act in a new field: *to initiate a new procedure.* START means to make a first move or to set out on a course of action: *to start paving a street.* **4.** institute, inaugurate, initiate. **—Ant. 1.** end.

be·gin·ning (bĭ·gĭn′ĭng), *n.* **1.** act or fact of entering upon an action or state. **2.** the point of time or space at which anything begins: *the beginning of the Christian era.* **3.** the first part or initial stage of anything: *the beginnings of science.* **4.** origin; source; first cause: *humility is the beginning of wisdom.* **—Syn. 1.** initiation, inauguration, inception. **2.** start. **—Ant. 1.** ending. **2.** end.

be·gird (bĭ·gûrd′), *v.t.,* **-girt** or **-girded, -girding.** to gird about; encompass; surround. [ME *begirden,* OE *begyrdan.* See BE-, GIRD¹]

be·gone (bĭ·gôn′, -gŏn′), *v.i.* to go away; depart (usually as an imperative).

be·gon·ia (bĭ·gōn′yə, -gō′nĭ·ə), *n.* any plant of the tropical genus *Begonia,* including species much cultivated for their handsome, succulent, often varicolored leaves and waxy flowers. [named after Michel *Bégon* (1638–1710), French patron of science]

be·got (bĭ·gŏt′), *v.* pt. and pp. of beget.

be·got·ten (bĭ·gŏt′ən), *v.* pp. of beget.

be·grime (bĭ·grīm′), *v.t.,* **-grimed, -griming.** to make grimy.

be·grudge (bĭ·grŭj′), *v.t.,* **-grudged, -grudging. 1.** to be discontented at seeing (a person) have (something): *to begrudge a man his good fortune.* **2.** to be reluctant to give, grant, or allow: *to begrudge him the money he earned.* **—Syn. 1.** See envy.

be·guile (bĭ·gīl′), *v.t.,* **-guiled, -guiling. 1.** to influence by guile; mislead; delude. **2.** to take away from by artful tactics (fol. by *of*). **3.** to charm or divert. **4.** to while away (time) pleasantly. **—be·guile′ment,** *n.* **—be·guil′er,** *n.* **—Syn. 1.** deceive, cheat.

Be·guin (bĕg′ĭn; *Fr.* bĕ·găN′), *n.* a Beghard.

be·guine (bĭ·gēn′), *n.* **1.** a South American dance in bolero rhythm. **2.** a modern social dance based on the beguine. **3.** music for either of these dances.

---

b., blend of, blended; c., cognate with; d., dialect, dialectal; der., derived from; f., formed from; g., going back to; m., modification of; r., replacing; s., stem of; t., taken from; ?, perhaps.   See the full key on inside front cover.

Beg·uine (bĕg'ēn; *Fr.* bĕ gēn'), *n.* a member of one of certain communities of Roman Catholic women who devote themselves to a religious life but retain private property and may leave at any time. The first of these communities was founded at Liège in the 12th century. [ME *begyne*, t. MFlem., t. OF: m. *beguine*, der. *beg-* in *begarde*, t. MD: m. *begaert* mendicant (friar)]

be·gum (bē'gəm), *n. India.* 1. a Mohammedan woman ruler. 2. a high-ranking Mohammedan lady, often a widow. [t. Hind.: m. *begam*]

be·gun (bĭ gŭn'), *v.* pp. of **begin**.

be·half (bĭ hăf', -häf'), *n.* 1. side or part (prec. by *on*): *on behalf of his country.* 2. interest, favor, or aid (prec. by *in*): *to plead in behalf of a cause.* [ME *behalve* beside, in OE a phrase, *be healfe* (*him*) by (his) side; later used as n. by confusion with ME *on his halve* on his side. See HALF]

be·have (bĭ hāv'), *v.*, **-haved**, **-having.** —*v.i.* 1. to conduct oneself or itself; act: *the ship behaves well.* 2. to act properly: *did the child behave?* —*v.t.* 3. behave oneself, a. to conduct oneself in a specified way. b. to conduct oneself properly. [late ME, appar. f. BE- + HAVE hold oneself a certain way]

be·hav·ior (bĭ hāv'yər), *n.* 1. manner of behaving or acting. 2. *Psychol.* the actions or activities of the individual as matters of psychological study. 3. the action of any material: *the behavior of tin under heat.* Also, *Brit.,* **be·hav·iour.** —**be·hav·ior·al,** *adj.*
—**Syn.** 1. demeanor, manners. BEHAVIOR, CONDUCT, DEPORTMENT refer to one's mode of acting. BEHAVIOR refers to one's actions before or toward others, esp. on a particular occasion: *his behavior at the party was childish.* CONDUCT refers to actions viewed collectively, esp. as measured by an ideal standard of behavior: *conduct is judged according to principles of ethics.* DEPORTMENT is behavior as related to a code or to an arbitrary standard: *deportment is guided by rules of etiquette.*

be·hav·ior·ism (bĭ hāv'yə rĭz'əm), *n.* *Psychol.* a theory or method that regards objective and accessible facts of behavior or activity of man and animals as the only proper subject for psychological study. —**be·hav'·ior·ist,** *n.,* *adj.* —**be·hav'ior·is'tic,** *adj.*

behavior pattern, *Sociol.* a recurrent way of acting by an individual or group toward a given object or in a given situation.

be·head (bĭ hĕd'), *v.t.* to cut off the head of; kill or execute by decapitation.

be·held (bĭ hĕld'), *v.* pt. and pp. of **behold.**

be·he·moth (bĭ hē'məth, bē'ə-), *n.* 1. *Bible.* an animal, perhaps the hippopotamus, mentioned in Job 40:15. 2. *U.S. Colloq.* a huge and powerful man, beast, etc. [t. Heb.: m. *behēmōth,* pl. of *behēmah* beast]

be·hest (bĭ hĕst'), *n.* bidding or injunction; mandate or command. [ME; OE *behǣs* promise]

be·hind (bĭ hīnd'), *prep.* 1. at the back of; in the rear of: *behind the house.* 2. after; later than: *behind schedule.* 3. less advanced than; inferior to: *behind his class in mathematics.* 4. on the farther side of; beyond: *behind the mountain.* 5. supporting; promoting: *he is behind the play.* 6. hidden or unrevealed by: *malice lay behind her smile.* —*adv.* 7. at or toward the back; in the rear. 8. in a place, state, or stage already passed. 9. remaining; in reserve: *greater support is behind.* 10. in arrears; behindhand: *behind in his rent* 11. slow, as a watch or clock. [ME *behinden,* OE *behindan.* See BE-, HIND¹]
—**Syn.** 1, 2. BEHIND, AFTER both refer to a position following something else. BEHIND applies primarily to position in space, and suggests that one person or thing is at the back of another: *it may also refer to (a fixed) time: he stood behind the chair, the train is behind schedule.* AFTER applies primarily to time; when it denotes position in space, it is not used with precision, and refers usually to bodies in motion: *rest after a hard day's work; they entered the room, one after another.*

be·hind·hand (bĭ hīnd'hănd'), *adv.* 1. late. 2. behind in progress; backward. 3. in debt.

be·his·tun (bā'hĭs tōon'), *n.* a ruined town in W Iran: site of a cliff containing an account carved in Persian, Elamite, and Babylonian cuneiform, which provided the key to cuneiform. Also, **Bisutun.**

be·hold (bĭ hōld'), *v.,* **beheld, beholding,** *interj.* —*v.t.* 1. to observe; look at; see. —*interj.* 2. look! see! [ME *beholde(n),* OE *behaldan* keep] —**be·hold'er,** *n.*

be·hold·en (bĭ hōl'dən), *adj.* obligated; indebted.

be·hoof (bĭ hōōf'), *n.* use; advantage; benefit. (ME *behove,* OE *behōf* profit, need, c. G *behuf*]

be·hoove (bĭ hōōv'), *v.,* **-hooved, -hooving.** —*v.t.* 1. to be needful or proper for or incumbent on (chiefly in impersonal use): *it behooves me to see him.* —*v.i.* 2. *Archaic.* to be needful, proper, or due (chiefly in impersonal use). Also, *esp. Brit.,* **be·hove** (bĭ hōv'). [ME *behove(n),* OE *behōfian* need. See BEHOOF]

beh·ring (bā'rĭng), *n.* 1. Emil von (ā'mēl fən), 1854–1917, German physician and bacteriologist. 2. Vitus (vē'tōōs). See **Bering, Vitus.**

behr·man (bâr'mən), *n.* S(amuel) N(athaniel), born 1893, U.S. dramatist.

beige (bāzh), *n.* very light brown, as of undyed wool; light gray with brownish tinge. [t. F]

bei·lan Pass (bā'län'), a mountain pass NW of Aleppo: the ancient gateway from Asia Minor to Syria.

be·ing (bē'ĭng), *n.* 1. existence, as opposed to nonexistence. 2. conscious existence; life: *the aim of our being.* 3. mortal existence; lifetime. 4. substance or nature: *of such a being as to arouse fear.* 5. something that exists: *inanimate beings.* 6. a living thing. 7. a

human being; person. 8. (*cap.*) God. 9. *Philos.* a. that which has actuality either materially or in idea. b. absolute existence in a complete or perfect state, lacking no essential characteristic; essence.

Bei·ra (bā'rə), *n.* a seaport in Mozambique. 42,539 (1950).

Bei·rut (bā'rōot, bā rōot'), *n.* a seaport in and the capital of Lebanon. 400,000 (est. 1953). Also, **Beyrouth.**

be·jew·el (bĭ jōō'əl), *v.t.,* **-eled, -eling** or (*esp. Brit.*) **-elled, -elling.** to adorn with or as with jewels.

bel (bĕl), *n.* *Physics.* the unit which measures power ratios equal to the logarithm to the base 10 of the ratio of any two powers. [named after A. G. BELL]

Bel (bāl), *n.* a deity of the Babylonians and Assyrians, god of the earth. [t. L: s. *Bēlus,* t. Gk.: m. *Bēlos* BAAL]

be·la·bor (bĭ lā'bər), *v.t.* 1. to beat vigorously; ply with heavy blows. 2. to assail persistently, as with ridicule. 3. *Obs.* to labor at. Also, *Brit.,* **be·la'bour.**

Be·las·co (bĭ lăs'kō), *n.* David, 1854–1931, U.S. playwright and theatrical manager.

be·lat·ed (bĭ lā'tĭd), *adj.* coming or being late or too late. —**be·lat'ed·ly,** *adv.* —**be·lat'ed·ness,** *n.*

be·lay (bĭ lā'), *v.t.,* *v.i.,* **-layed, -laying.** 1. *Naut.* to fasten (a rope) by winding around a pin or short rod inserted in a holder so that both ends of the rod are clear. 2. to stop (used chiefly in the imperative). [ME *belegge(n),* OE *belecgan* cover. See BE-, LAY¹]

belaying pin, *Naut.* a pin for use in securing the ends of ropes.

bel can·to (bĕl kän'tō), *Music.* a smooth, cantabile style of singing. [It.]

belch (bĕlch), *v.i.* 1. to eject wind spasmodically and noisily from the stomach through the mouth; eructate. 2. to emit contents violently, as a gun, geyser, or volcano. 3. to issue spasmodically; gush forth. —*v.t.* 4. to eject spasmodically or violently; give forth. —*n.* 5. a belching; eructation. 6. a burst of flame, smoke, gas, etc. [ME *belche(n).* Cf. OE *belcettan*] —**belch'er,** *n.*

Belaying pins, with ropes belayed on them

bel·dam (bĕl'dəm), *n.* 1. an old woman, esp. an ugly one; hag. 2. *Obs.* grandmother. Also, **bel·dame** (bĕl'dəm, -dām'). [ME, grandmother, f. *bel-* (t. OF: *bel-, belle* fair) used like GRAND (def. 12) + *dam* DAME]

be·lea·guer (bĭ lē'gər), *v.t.* 1. to surround with an army. 2. to surround; *beleaguered with annoyances.* [t. D: m.s. *belegeren,* der. *be-* about + *leger* camp] —**be·lea'guered,** *adj.* —**be·lea'guer·er,** *n.*

Be·lém (bĕ lĕn'), *n.* a seaport in N Brazil, on the Pará river. 225,218 (1950). Also, **Pará.**

bel·em·nite (bĕl'əm nīt'), *n.* *Paleontol.* a conical fossil, several inches long, consisting of the internal calcareous rod of an extinct animal allied to the cuttlefish; a thunderstone. [f. s. Gk. *bélemnon* dart + -ITE¹]

bel·es·prit (bĕl ĕs prē'), *n.,* *pl.* **beaux-esprits** (bō zĕs prē'). *French.* a person of great wit or intellect.

Bel·fast (bĕl'făst, -fäst; bŭl făst', -fäst'), *n.* a seaport in and the capital of Northern Ireland. 443,671 (1951).

Bel·fort (bĕl fôr'), *n.* a fortress city in E France, strategically located on a pass between the Vosges and Jura Mountains: siege 1870–71; battle, 1944. 43,434 (1954).

bel·fry (bĕl'frĭ), *n.,* *pl.* **-fries.** 1. a bell tower, either attached to a church or other building or standing apart. 2. that part of a steeple or other structure in which a bell is hung. 3. a frame of timberwork which sustains a bell. [ME *belfray,* dissimilated var. of *berfrey,* t. OF: m. *berfrei,* t. Gmc.; cf. MHG *bercfrit* defense shelter]

Belg., 1. Belgian. 2. Belgium.

bel·ga (bĕl'gə), *n.* the Belgian currency unit in foreign exchange, introduced 1926, worth five Belgian francs.

Bel·gian (bĕl'jən, -jÝən), *n.* 1. a native or an inhabitant of Belgium. —*adj.* 2. of or pertaining to Belgium.

Belgian Congo, a former Belgian colony in central Africa: now an independent republic. See **Congo** (def. 2a).

Belgian hare, one of a breed of domestic rabbits notable for large size.

Bel·gic (bĕl'jĭk), *adj.* 1. of the Belgae, an ancient people of N Gaul. 2. Belgian. [t. L: s. *Belgicus,* der. *Belgae*]

Bel·gium (bĕl'jəm, -jÝəm), *n.* a kingdom in W Europe, on the North Sea, N of France. 8,868,000 pop. (est. 1955); 11,779 sq. mi. *Cap.:* Brussels. French, **Bel·gique** (bĕl zhēk').

Bel·go·rod-Dnes·trov·ski (byĕl'gə rət dnyĕs trôf'skĭ), *n.* a seaport in the SW Soviet Union, on the Black Sea at the mouth of the Dniester river. 30,000 (est. 1948). Formerly, **Akkerman.**

Bel·grade (bĕl grād', bĕl'grād), *n.* the capital of Yugoslavia, in the E part, on the Danube. 469,988 (1953). Serbian, **Beograd.**

Bel·gra·vi·a (bĕl grā'vÝə), *n.* a fashionable district in London, England, adjoining Hyde Park.

Bel·gra·vi·an (bĕl grā'vÝən), *adj.* 1. of Belgravia. 2. aristocratic; fashionable.

Be·li·al (bē'lÝəl, bēl'yəl), *n.* 1. *Theol.* the spirit of evil personified; the devil; Satan. 2. (in Milton's *Paradise Lost*) one of the fallen angels. 3. (in the Bible and rabbinical commentary) worthlessness, wickedness, or destruction. [t. Heb.: m. *belī-ya'al* worthlessness]

be·lie (bǐ lī′), v.t., **-lied, -lying. 1.** to misrepresent: *his face belied his thoughts.* **2.** to show to be false: *his trembling belied his words.* **3.** to prove false to; fail to justify: *to belie one's faith.* **4.** to lie about; slander. [ME *belye(n)*, OE *belēogan*, f. *be-* BE- + *lēogan* LIE[1]] —be·li′er, n.

be·lief (bǐ lēf′), n. **1.** that which is believed; an accepted opinion. **2.** conviction of the truth or reality of a thing, based upon grounds insufficient to afford positive knowledge: *statements unworthy of belief.* **3.** confidence; faith; trust: *a child's belief in his parents.* **4.** a religious tenet or tenets: *the Christian belief.* [ME *bilēve* (with -ē- from v.), r. early ME *bilēafe*, r. OE *gelēafa*, c. G *glaube*] —**Syn. 2.** BELIEF, CERTAINTY, CONVICTION refer to acceptance of, or confidence in, an alleged fact or body of facts as true or right without positive knowledge or proof. BELIEF is such acceptance in general: *belief in astrology.* CERTAINTY indicates unquestioning belief and positiveness in one's own mind that something is true: *I know this for a certainty.* CONVICTION is settled, profound, or earnest belief that something is right: *a conviction that a decision is just.*

be·lieve (bǐ lēv′), v., **-lieved, -lieving. —v.i. 1.** to have confidence (*in*); trust; rely through faith (*on*). **2.** to be persuaded of the truth of anything; accept a doctrine, principle, system, etc. (fol. by *in*): *to believe in public schools.* —v.t. **3.** to have belief in; credit; accept as true: *to believe a person or a story.* **4.** to think: *I believe he has left the city.* [ME *bileve(n)*, f. *bi-* + *lēven*, d. OE *lēfan*; r. OE (ge)*liefan*, c. G *glauben*] —**believ′a·ble,** adj. —**be·liev′er,** n. —**be·liev′ing·ly,** adv.

be·like (bǐ līk′), adv. Archaic, or Dial. very likely; perhaps; probably. [f. BE- + LIKE[1]]

Bel·i·sar·i·us (běl′ə sâr′ĭəs), n. A.D. 505?–565, general of the Eastern Roman Empire.

Be·li·tong (bě lē′tŏng), n. Billiton.

be·lit·tle (bǐ lǐt′əl), v.t. **-littled, -littling.** to make little or less important; depreciate; disparage.

be·live (bǐ līv′), adv. Scot. before long; soon.

Be·lize (bě lēz′), n. a seaport in and the capital of British Honduras. 21,886 (1946).

bell[1] (běl), n. **1.** a metallic sounding instrument, typically cup-shaped with flaring mouth, rung by the strokes of a tongue or clapper or a hammer. **2.** the stroke or sound of such an instrument (used on shipboard to indicate time): *rise at the bell.* **3.** anything of the form of a bell. **4.** the large end of a funnel, or the end of a pipe, tube, or any musical wind instrument, when its edge is turned out and enlarged. **5.** Zool. umbrella (def. 2). —v.t. **6.** to put a bell on. **7.** to cause to swell (*out*) like a bell. —v.i. **8.** to take or have the form of a bell. **9.** to produce bells; be in bell (said of hops when the seed vessels are forming). [ME and OE *belle*. See BELL[2], BELLOW] —**bell′-like′,** adj.

bell[2] (běl), v.i., v.t. **1.** to bellow like a deer in rutting time. **2.** Obs. to bellow; roar. —n. **3.** the cry of a rutting deer. [ME *belle(n)*, OE *bellan* roar, c. G *bellen* bark]

Bell (běl), n. **Alexander Graham,** 1847–1922, U.S. scientist, born in Scotland: invented the telephone.

bel·la·don·na (běl′ə dŏn′ə), n. **1.** a poisonous solanaceous plant, *Atropa Belladonna*; deadly nightshade. **2.** a poisonous drug from this plant. [t. It.: lit., fair lady]

belladonna lily, the amaryllis (def. 1).

Bel·la·my (běl′ə mǐ), n. **Edward,** 1850–98, U.S. author.

bell·bird (běl′bûrd′), n. any of various birds of the southern hemisphere whose notes resemble the sound of a bell, as the honey eater.

bell·boy (běl′boi′), n. U.S. an employee in a hotel who attends to the wants of guests in their rooms.

bell buoy, Naut. a buoy having a bell hung on it to ring from the action of the waves. See illus. under **buoy.**

belle (běl), n. a woman or girl admired for her beauty; a reigning beauty. [t. F, fem. of *beau* BEAU]

Bel·leau Wood (běl′ō; Fr. bě lō′), a forest in N France, NW of Château-Thierry: now a memorial to the U. S. Marines who won a battle there, 1918.

Bel·leek (bə lēk′), n. a fragile, ornamental porcelain with a bright luster. Also, **Belleek ware.** [named after *Belleek*, Northern Ireland]

Belle Isle, Strait of, the strait between Labrador and Newfoundland. 10–15 mi. wide.

Bel·ler·o·phon (bə lěr′ə fŏn′), n. Gk. Legend. a hero of Corinth who, on the winged horse Pegasus, slew the monster Chimera.

belles-let·tres (běl lět′r), n.pl. the finer or higher forms of literature; literature regarded as a fine art. [F] —**bel·let·rist** (běl lět′rǐst), n. —**bel·le·tris·tic** (běl′lě trǐs′tǐk), adj. —**Syn.** See literature.

Belle·ville (běl′vǐl), n. **1.** a city in SW Illinois. 37,264 (1960). **2.** a city in NE New Jersey. 35,005 (1960).

bell·flow·er (běl′flou′ər), n. a campanula.

bell glass, bell jar.

bell·hop (běl′hŏp′), n. U.S. Colloq. bellboy.

bel·li·cose (běl′ə kōs′), adj. inclined to war; warlike; pugnacious. [t. L: m. s. *bellicōsus*, der. *bellum* war] —**bel·li·cose′ly,** adv. —**bel·li·cos·i·ty** (běl′ə kŏs′ə tǐ), n.

bel·lig·er·ence (bə lǐj′ərəns), n. **1.** warlike nature. **2.** act of carrying on war; warfare.

bel·lig·er·en·cy (bə lǐj′ərənsǐ), n. position or status as a belligerent; state of being actually engaged in war.

bel·lig·er·ent (bə lǐj′ərənt), adj. **1.** warlike; given to waging war. **2.** of warlike character: *a belligerent tone.* **3.** waging war; engaged in war: *the belligerent powers.* **4.** pertaining to war, or to those engaged in war: *belligerent rights, etc.* —n. **5.** a state or nation at war, or a member of the military forces of such a state. [t. L: m. s. *belligerans,* ppr.] —**bel·lig′er·ent·ly,** adv.

Bel·ling·ham (běl′ǐng hǎm′), n. a seaport in NW Washington. 34,688 (1960).

Bel·li·ni (běl lē′nē), n. **1. Gentile** (jěn tē′lě), 1427?–1507, Venetian painter (son of Jacopo). **2. Giovanni** (jō vän′nē), 1430?–1516, Venetian painter (son of Jacopo). **3. Jacopo** (yä′kō pō′), 1400?–70, Venetian painter. **4. Vincenzo** (věn chěn′tsō), 1801?–35, Italian composer of opera.

bell jar, a bell-shaped glass vessel or cover, as for protecting delicate instruments, bric-a-brac, etc., or for holding gases in chemical operations. Also, **bell glass.**

bell·man (běl′mən), n., pl. **-men,** a man who carries or rings a bell, esp. a town crier or watchman.

bell metal, a hard alloy of copper and tin of low damping capacity, used for bells.

bell-mouthed (běl′mouthd′, -moutht′), adj. having a flaring mouth like that of a bell.

Bel·loc (běl′ək, -ŏk), n. **Hilaire** (hǐlâr′), 1870–1953, British essayist, poet, and satirist, born in France.

Bel·lo Ho·ri·zon·te (bě′lō rē zōn′tə), Belo Horizonte.

Bel·lo·na (bə lō′nə), n. Rom. Myth. goddess of war (sister or wife of Mars). [t. L]

bel·low (běl′ō), v.i. **1.** to make a hollow, loud, animal cry, as a bull or cow. **2.** to roar; bawl: *bellowing with rage.* —v.t. **3.** to utter in a loud deep voice: *to bellow forth an answer.* —n. **4.** act or sound of bellowing. [ME *belwe(n)*, appar. b. OE *bellan* BELL[2] and *bylgan* bellow] —**bel′low·er,** n. —**Syn. 2.** See cry.

bel·lows (běl′ōz, -əs), n. sing. and pl. **1.** an instrument or machine for producing a strong current of air, as for a draft for a fire or sounding a musical instrument, consisting essentially of an air chamber which can be expanded to draw in air through a valve and contracted to expel the air through a tube or tubes. **2.** anything resembling or suggesting a bellows, as the collapsible part of a camera or enlarger. **3.** the lungs. [ME *belwes,* pl., OE *belg* short for *blǣst-belg* blast-bag. See BELLY]

Bel·lows (běl′ōz), n. **George,** 1882–1925, U.S. artist.

bell·weth·er (běl′wěth′ər), n. **1.** a wether or other male sheep which leads the flock, usually bearing a bell. **2.** a person whom others follow blindly.

bell·wort (běl′wûrt′), n. **1.** any campanulaceous plant. **2.** a plant of the liliaceous genus *Uvularia,* bearing a delicate, slenderly bell-shaped, yellow flower.

bel·ly (běl′ǐ), n., pl. **-lies,** v., **-lied, -lying.** —n. **1.** the front or under part of a vertebrate body from the breastbone to the pelvis, containing the abdominal viscera; the abdomen. **2.** the stomach with its adjuncts. **3.** appetite for food; gluttony. **4.** the womb. **5.** the inside or interior of anything: *the belly of a ship.* **6.** a protuberant or bulging surface of anything: *the belly of a flask.* **7.** Anat. the fleshy part of a muscle. **8.** the front, inner, or under surface or part (opposed to *back*). **9.** Music. the front surface of a violin or similar instrument. —v.t., v.i. **10.** to swell out. [ME *bely,* OE *belig* bag, skin, var. of *belg* (whence *bellow(s)*)]

bel·ly·band (běl′ǐ bǎnd′), n. a band worn about the belly, as of a harnessed horse. See illus. under **harness.**

Bel·mont (běl′mŏnt), n. a town in E Massachusetts, near Boston. 28,715 (1960).

Be·lo Ho·ri·zon·te (bě′lō rē zōn′tə), a city in SE Brazil. 338,585 (1950). Also, **Bello Horizonte.**

Be·loit (bə loit′), n. a city in S Wisconsin. 32,846 (1960).

be·long (bǐ lông′, -lŏng′), v.i. **1.** to have one's rightful place; to bear relation as a member, adherent, inhabitant, etc. (fol. by *to*): *he belongs to the Grange.* **2. belong to, a.** to be the property of: *the book belongs to him.* **b.** to be an appurtenance, adjunct, or part of: *that cover belongs to this jar.* **c.** to be a property, function, or concern of: *attributes which belong to nature.* **3.** to have the proper social qualifications: *he doesn't belong.* **4.** to be proper or due. [ME *belonge(n)*, f. BE- + *longen* belong, der. adj., aphetic var. of d. *along,* OE *gelang* belonging to]

be·long·ing (bǐ lông′ǐng, -lŏng′-), n. **1.** something that belongs. **2.** (pl.) possessions; goods; personal effects.

be·lov·ed (bǐ lŭv′ǐd, -lŭvd′), adj. **1.** greatly loved; dear to the heart. —n. **2.** one who is greatly loved.

be·low (bǐ lō′), adv. **1.** in or to a lower place; lower down; beneath. **2.** on or to a lower floor; downstairs. **3.** on earth. **4.** in hell or the infernal regions. **5.** at a later point on a page or in writing: *see the statistics below.* **6.** in a lower rank or grade: *he was demoted to the class below.* —prep. **7.** lower down than: *below the knee.* **8.** lower in rank, degree, amount, rate, etc., than: *below cost, below freezing.* **9.** too low or base to be worthy of: [ME *bilooghe* by low. See BE-, LOW[1]] —**Syn. 7.** BELOW, UNDER, BENEATH indicate position in some way lower than something else. BELOW implies being in a lower plane: *below the horizon, the water line.* UNDER implies being lower in a perpendicular line: *the plaything is under a chair.* BENEATH may have a meaning similar to BELOW, but more usually denotes being under so as to be covered, overhung, or overtopped: *the pool beneath the falls.*

Bel·shaz·zar (běl shǎz′ər), n. son of Nebuchadnezzar, and king of Babylonia. Dan. 5. [t. Heb.]

belt (bĕlt), *n.* **1.** a band of flexible material for encircling the waist. **2.** any encircling or transverse band, strip, or stripe. **3.** *Ecol.* a region having distinctive properties or characteristics: *the cotton belt.* **4.** *Mach.* **a.** a flexible band or cord connecting and passing about each of two or more wheels, pulleys, or the like, to transmit or change the direction of motion. See illus. under **shafting. b. belt conveyor,** a similar belt used to transport objects from one place to another in an industrial plant. **5.** *Naval.* a series of armor plates around a ship. **6.** *Mil.* **a.** a cloth strip with loops, or a series of metal links with grips, for holding cartridges which are fed into an automatic gun. **b.** a band of leather or webbing, worn around the waist and used as a support for weapons, ammunition, etc. —*v.t.* **7.** to gird or furnish with a belt. **8.** to surround or mark as if with a belt. **9.** to fasten on (a sword, etc.) by means of a belt. **10.** to beat with a belt, strap, etc. **11.** *Colloq.* to give a thwack or blow to. [ME and OE, prob. ult. t. L: m.s. *balteus*] —**belt′less,** *adj.* —**Syn. 3.** BELT and ZONE agree in their original meaning of a girdle or band. BELT is more used in popular or journalistic writing: *the corn or wheat belt.* ZONE tends to be used in technical language: *the Torrid Zone, a parcel-post zone.*

Bel·tane (bĕl′tān), *n.* an ancient Celtic festival observed on May Day in Scotland and Ireland. [ME (Scot.), t. Gaelic: m. *bealltainn*; of obscure orig.]

belt·ing (bĕl′tĭng), *n.* **1.** material for belts. **2.** belts collectively. **3.** a belt.

belt line, a transportation system partially or wholly surrounding a city, terminal, district, or port.

be·lu·ga (bəlōō′gə), *n.* a cetacean, *Delphinapterus leucas,* chiefly Arctic, having a rounded head, and white in color. [t. Russ.: m. *bielukha,* der. *bielo-* white]

bel·ve·dere (bĕl′vədĭr′; *It.* bĕl′vĕdĕ′rĕ), *n.* **1.** an upper story or any structure or building designed to afford a fine view. **2.** (*cap.*) the Vatican art gallery in Rome. [t. It.: beautiful view]

be·ma (bē′mə), *n., pl.* **-mata** (-mətə). *Gk. Orth. Ch.* the enclosed space surrounding the altar; the sanctuary or chancel. [t. Gk.: step, platform]

be·maul (bĭmôl′), *v.t.* to maul severely.

be·mean (bĭmēn′), *v.t.* to make mean; debase (oneself).

be·mire (bĭmīr′), *v.t.,* **-mired, -miring. 1.** to soil with mire. **2.** to sink in mire.

be·moan (bĭmōn′), *v.t.* **1.** to moan over; bewail; lament. **2.** to express pity for. —*v.i.* **3.** to lament; mourn. [f. BE- + moan; r. ME *bemene(n),* OE *bemǣnan*]

be·mused (bĭmūzd′), *adj.* **1.** confused; muddled; stupefied. **2.** lost in thought; preoccupied.

ben[1] (bĕn), *n. Scot.* the inner room (parlor) of a cottage. [ME, var. of *binne,* OE *binnan* within, c. G *binnen*]

ben[2] (bĕn), *n.* **1.** a tree, *Moringa oleifera,* of Arabia, India, and elsewhere, bearing a winged seed (nut) which yields an oil (**oil of ben**), used in extracting flower perfumes, lubricating delicate machinery, etc. **2.** the seed of such a tree. [t. Ar.: m. *bān*]

ben·a·dryl (bĕn′ədrĭl), *n. Pharm.* **1.** a synthetic drug used esp. to relieve hay fever and hives. **2.** (*cap.*) a trademark for this drug.

be·name (bĭnām′), *v.t.,* **-named; -named, -nempt,** or **-nempted; -naming.** *Archaic.* to name; denominate.

Be·na·res (bənä′rĭz), *n.* a city in N India, on the Ganges: holy city of Hinduism. 341,811 (1951).

Ben·bow (bĕn′bō), *n.* **John,** 1653-1702, English admiral.

bench (bĕnch), *n.* **1.** a long seat for several people. **2.** the seat on which judges sit in court. **3.** the position or office of a judge: *elected to the bench.* **4.** the body of persons sitting as judges. **5.** a seat occupied by persons in their official capacity. **6.** the office or dignity of those occupying it. **7.** the persons themselves. **8.** the strong work table of a carpenter or other mechanic. **9.** a platform on which animals are placed for exhibition, esp. at a dog show. **10.** a dog show. **11.** *Phys. Geog.* a flat, terracelike tract of land on a valley slope, above the stream bed, or along a coast, above the level of sea or lake. **12.** *Mining.* a step or working elevation in a mine. **13. on the bench,** *Sports.* not participating. —*v.t.* **14.** to furnish with benches. **15.** to seat on a bench. **16.** to place in exhibition: *to bench a dog.* **17.** *Sports.* to remove from a game: *the player was benched for too many fouls.* [ME; OE *benc.* See BANK[2], BANK[3]] —**bench′less,** *adj.*

bench dog, a dog on exhibition, as at a dog show.

bench·er (bĕn′chər), *n.* **1.** (in England) a senior member of an Inn of Court. **2.** one who handles an oar.

bench mark, *Survey.* a point of known elevation, usually a mark cut into some durable material, as stone or a concrete post with a bronze plate to serve as a reference point in running a line of levels for the determination of elevations.

bench warrant, *Law.* a warrant issued or ordered by a judge or court for the apprehension of an offender.

bend[1] (bĕnd), *v.,* **bent** or (*Archaic*) **bended, bending,** *n.* —*v.t.* **1.** to bring (a bow, etc.) into a state of tension by curving it. **2.** to force into a different or particular, esp. curved, shape, as by pressure. **3.** to cause to submit: *to bend someone to one's will.* **4.** to turn in a particular direction. **5.** to incline mentally (fol. by *to* or *towards*). **6.** *Naut.* to fasten. **7.** *Archaic.* to strain or brace tensely (fol. by *up*). —*v.i.* **8.** to become curved, crooked, or bent. **9.** to assume a bent posture; stoop. **10.** to bow in submission or reverence; yield; submit. **11.** to turn

or incline in a particular direction; be directed. **12.** to direct one's energies. —*n.* **13.** act of bending. **14.** state of being bent. **15.** a bent thing or part; curve; crook. **16. the bends,** *U.S. Colloq.* **a.** caisson disease. **b.** aeroembolism. **17.** *Naut.* **a.** (*pl.*) the wales of a ship. **b.** a knot by which a rope is fastened to another rope or to something else. [ME *bende(n),* OE *bendan* bind, bend (a bow)] —**bend′a·ble,** *adj.* —**Syn. 2.** curve, crook, flex. **9.** BEND, BOW, STOOP imply taking a bent posture. BEND and BOW are used of the head and upper body; STOOP is used of the body only.

bend[2] (bĕnd), *n. Her.* a diagonal band extending from the dexter chief to the sinister base. [OE *bend* band; in ME identified with OF *bende* band]

Ben Da·vis (bĕn dā′vĭs), a variety of red winter apple.

bend·ed (bĕn′dĭd), *adj.* **1.** *Archaic.* bent. —*v.* **2.** *Archaic.* pt. and pp. of **bend**[1].

bend·er (bĕn′dər), *n.* **1.** one who or that which bends, as a pair of pliers. **2.** *U.S. Slang.* a drinking spree. **3.** *Baseball.* a curve (def. 5). **4.** *Brit. Slang.* a sixpence.

Ben·di·go (bĕn′dəgō′), *n.* a city in SE Australia, in Victoria: gold mining. 28,726 (1951).

bend sinister, *Her.* a diagonal band extending from the sinister chief to the dexter base (a supposed mark of bastardy).

bene-, a word element meaning "well," as in *benediction.* [t. L, comb. form of *bene,* adv.]

Bend sinister

be·neath (bĭnēth′, -nēth′), *adv.* **1.** below; in a lower place, position, state, etc. **2.** underneath: *the heaven above and the earth beneath.* —*prep.* **3.** below; under: *beneath the same roof.* **4.** further down than; underneath; lower in place than. **5.** lower down on a slope than: *beneath the crest of a hill.* **6.** inferior in position, power, etc. to: *a captain is beneath a major.* **7.** unworthy of; below the level or dignity of: *beneath contempt.* [ME *benethe,* OE *beneothan,* f. *be* by + *neothan* below] —**Syn. 3.** See below. —**Ant. 1.** above.

Ben·e·dic·i·te (bĕn′ə dĭs′ə tĭ), *n.* **1.** *Eccles.* the canticle beginning in Latin "Benedicite, omnia opera Domini," and in English "O all ye works of the Lord." **2.** a musical setting for it. **3.** (*l.c.*) an invocation for a blessing. —*interj.* **4.** (*l.c.*) bless you! [t. L, 2d pers. pl. impv. of *benedicere* bless]

Ben·e·dick (bĕn′ə dĭk), *n.* **1.** (in Shakespeare's *Much Ado About Nothing*) the confident bachelor who courts and finally marries Beatrice. **2.** (*l.c.*) benedict.

ben·e·dict (bĕn′ə dĭkt), *n.* **1.** a newly married man, esp. one who has been long a bachelor. **2.** a married man. [var. of BENEDICK]

Ben·e·dict (bĕn′ə dĭkt), *n.* **Saint,** A.D. 480?-543?, Italian monk: founded Benedictine order.

Benedict, *n.* the name adopted by 15 popes, esp.: **1. XIV,** 1675-1758, Italian pope, 1704-58: patron of art, archaeology, and learning. **2. XV,** 1854-1922, Italian pope, 1914-22.

Ben·e·dic·tine (bĕn′ə dĭk′tĭn, -tēn, -tĭn *for 1;* bĕn′ə dĭk′tēn *for 2*), *n.* **1.** *Rom. Cath. Ch.* a member of an order of monks founded at Monte Cassino, between Rome and Naples, by St. Benedict about A.D. 530 or of various congregations of nuns following his rule. The rules of the order (**Benedictine rule**) enjoined silence and useful employment when not in divine service. **2.** (*usually l.c.*) a French liqueur orig. made by Benedictine monks. —*adj.* **3.** pertaining to St. Benedict or to an order following his rule. [t. F: m. *bénédictin*]

ben·e·dic·tion (bĕn′ə dĭk′shən), *n. Eccles.* **1.** act of uttering a blessing. **2.** the form of blessing pronounced by an officiating minister, as at the close of divine service, etc. **3.** a ceremony by which things are set aside for sacred uses, as a church, vestments, bells, etc. **4.** the advantage conferred by blessing; a mercy or benefit. [ME, t. L: s. *benedictio*] —**ben′e·dic′tion·al,** *adj.* —**ben·e·dic·to·ry** (bĕn′ə dĭk′tə rĭ), *adj.*

Ben·e·dic·tus (bĕn′ə dĭk′təs), *n. Eccles.* **1.** the short canticle or hymn beginning in Latin "Benedictus qui venit in nomine Domini," and in English "Blessed is He that cometh in the name of the Lord." **2.** the canticle or hymn beginning in Latin "Benedictus Dominus Deus Israel," and in English "Blessed be the Lord God of Israel." **3.** a musical setting of either of these canticles. [t. L: pp., blessed]

ben·e·fac·tion (bĕn′ə făk′shən), *n.* **1.** act of conferring a benefit; doing of good. **2.** the benefit conferred; charitable donation. [t. LL: s. *benefactio*]

ben·e·fac·tor (bĕn′ə făk′tər, bĕn′ə făk′-), *n.* **1.** one who confers a benefit; kindly helper. **2.** one who makes a bequest or endowment. [t. L] —**ben·e·fac·tress** (bĕn′ə făk′trĭs, bĕn′ə făk′-), *n. fem.*

be·nef·ic (bə nĕf′ĭk), *adj.* beneficent. [t. L: s. *beneficus*]

ben·e·fice (bĕn′ə fĭs), *n., v.,* **-ficed, -ficing.** —*n.* **1.** an ecclesiastical living. **2.** the revenue itself. —*v.t.* **3.** to invest with a benefice or ecclesiastical living. [ME, t. OF, t. L: m.s. *beneficium* benefit, favor]

be·nef·i·cence (bə nĕf′ə səns), *n.* **1.** the doing of good; active goodness or kindness; charity. **2.** beneficent act or gift; benefaction. [t. L: m. s. *beneficentia*]

be·nef·i·cent (bə nĕf′ə sənt), *adj.* doing good or causing good to be done; conferring benefits; kindly in action or purpose. —**be·nef′i·cent·ly,** *adv.*

ben·e·fi·cial (bĕn′ə fĭsh′əl), *adj.* **1.** conferring benefit; advantageous; helpful. **2.** *Law.* **a.** helpful in the meeting of needs: *a beneficial association.* **b.** involving the personal enjoyment of proceeds: *a beneficial owner.* —ben′e·fi′cial·ly, *adv.* —ben′e·fi′cial·ness, *n.* —Syn. **1.** salutary, wholesome, serviceable. —Ant. **1.** harmful.

ben·e·fi·ci·ar·y (bĕn′ə fĭsh′ĭ ĕr′ĭ, -fĭsh′ər ĭ), *n., pl.* -aries. **1.** one who receives benefits, profits, or advantages. **2.** *Law.* a person designated as the recipient of funds or other property under a trust, insurance policy, etc. **3.** *Eccles.* the holder of a benefice.

ben·e·fit (bĕn′ə fĭt), *n., v.,* -fited, -fiting. —*n.* **1.** act of kindness. **2.** anything that is for the good of a person or thing. **3.** a theatrical performance or other public entertainment to raise money for a worthy purpose. **4.** a payment or other assistance given by an insurance company, mutual benefit society, or public agency. —*v.t.* **5.** to do good to; be of service to. —*v.i.* **6.** to gain advantage; make improvement. [partial Latinization of ME *benfet,* t. AF, g. L *benefactum,* f. *bene-* BENE- + *factum* thing done. See FACT and cf. FEAT] —ben′e·fit·er, *n.* —Syn. **1.** favor, service. **2.** See **advantage.**

benefit of clergy, 1. church rites, as of marriage. **2.** an early right of church authorities to try, in an ecclesiastical court, any clergyman accused of serious crime (abolished in U.S. in 1790 and in England in 1827).

benefit society, *Insurance.* an association of persons to create a fund (as by dues or assessments) for the assistance of members and their families in sickness, death, etc. Also, **benefit association.**

Ben·e·lux (bĕn′ə lŭks), *n.* a customs union (since Jan. 1, 1948) of Belgium, the Netherlands, and Luxembourg.

be·nempt (bĭ nĕmpt′), *v. Archaic.* a pp. of **bename.**

Be·neš (bĕn′ĕsh), *n.* **Eduard** (ĕ′dŏŏ ärt′), 1884–1948, Czechoslovakian patriot and statesman: president of Czechoslovakia, 1935–1938 and 1945–1948.

Be·nét (bĭ nā′), *n.* **1. Stephen Vincent,** 1898–1943, U.S. poet. **2.** his brother, **William Rose,** 1886–1950, U.S. writer.

Be·ne·ven·to (bĕ′nĕ vĕn′tō), *n.* a city in S Italy: location of the Arch of Trajan. 51,000 (est. 1954).

be·nev·o·lence (bə nĕv′ə ləns), *n.* **1.** desire to do good for others; good will; charitableness. **2.** an act of kindness; charitable gift. **3.** *Eng. Hist.* a forced contribution to the sovereign. —Ant. **1.** malevolence.

be·nev·o·lent (bə nĕv′ə lənt), *adj.* **1.** desiring to do good for others. **2.** intended for benefits rather than profit: *a benevolent institution.* [t. L: s. *benevolens* well-wishing; r. ME *benyvolent,* t. OF: m. *benivolent*] —be·nev′o·lent·ly, *adv.*

Ben·gal (bĕn gôl′, bĕng-), *n.* **1.** a former province in NE India: now divided into **East Bengal** (in Pakistan) and **West Bengal** (in India). **2. Bay of,** a part of the Indian Ocean between India and Burma.

Ben·ga·lese (bĕn′gə lēz′, -lēs′, bĕng′-), *adj., n., pl.* -lese. —*adj.* **1.** of or pertaining to Bengal. —*n.* **2.** a native or inhabitant of Bengal.

Ben·ga·li (bĕn gô′lĭ, bĕng-), *n.* **1.** a native or an inhabitant of Bengal. **2.** the language of Bengal, an Indic language. —*adj.* **3.** of or pertaining to Bengal, its inhabitants, or their language; Bengalese.

ben·ga·line (bĕng′gə lēn′, bĕng′gə lēn′), *n.* a corded fabric resembling poplin but with heavier cords. It may be silk or rayon with worsted cord. [t. F]

Bengal light (bĕn′gôl, bĕng′-), a vivid, sustained, blue light used in signaling, fireworks, etc.

Ben·gha·zi (bĕn gä′zĭ), *n.* a seaport in N Libya. 62,300 (est. 1954). Also **Ben·ga′si.**

Ben-Gu·rion (bĕn′gŏŏ ryōn′), *m.* **David,** born 1886, Israeli statesman: prime minister of Israel, 1948–53, 1955–63.

Be·ni (bĕ′nē), *n.* a river flowing from W Bolivia NE to the Madeira river. ab. 600 mi.

be·night·ed (bĭ nī′tĭd), *adj.* **1.** intellectually or morally ignorant; unenlightened. **2.** overtaken by darkness or night. [pp. of *benight,* v., der. BE- + NIGHT]

be·nign (bĭ nīn′), *adj.* **1.** of a kind disposition; kind. **2.** showing or caused by gentleness or kindness: *a benign smile.* **3.** favorable; propitious: *benign planets.* **4.** (of weather) salubrious. **5.** *Pathol.* not malignant: *a benign tumor.* [ME *benigne,* t. OF, t. L: s. *benignus* kind] —be·nign′ly, *adv.* —Ant. **2.** sinister. **3.** malign.

be·nig·nant (bĭ nĭg′nənt), *adj.* **1.** kind, esp. to inferiors; gracious: *benignant sovereign.* **2.** exerting a good influence; beneficial. **3.** *Pathol.* benign. [b. BEN(IGN) and (MAL)IGNANT] —be·nig·nan·cy (bĭ nĭg′nən sĭ), *n.* —be·nig′nant·ly, *adv.*

be·nig·ni·ty (bĭ nĭg′nə tĭ), *n., pl.* -ties. **1.** quality of being benign; kindness. **2.** a good deed; favor.

Be·ni Ha·san (bĕ′nĭ hä′sän), a village in central Egypt, on the Nile, N of Asyut: ancient cliff tombs.

Be·nin (bĕ nēn′), *n.* **1.** a former native kingdom in W Africa: now a district in Nigeria. 901,000 pop. (1953); 8482 sq. mi. **2.** a river in S Nigeria flowing into the Bight of Benin, a wide bay in the Gulf of Guinea.

ben·i·son (bĕn′ə zən, -sən), *n. Archaic.* benediction. [ME *benisoun,* t. OF: m. *beneison,* g. L *benedictio*]

ben·ja·min (bĕn′jə mən), *n.* benzoin (def. 1). [var. (by assimilation to *Benjamin*) of *benjoin* BENZOIN]

Ben·ja·min (bĕn′jə mən), *n.* **1.** *Bible.* **a.** the youngest son of Jacob by Rachel, and brother of Joseph. **b.** a tribe of Israel said to have Benjamin as its ancestor. **2. Judah Philip,** 1811–84, Confederate statesman.

Ben·ja·min-Con·stant (băN zhà măN′ kôN stäN′), *n.* See **Constant, Jean Joseph Benjamin.**

Ben Lo·mond (bĕn lō′mənd), *n.* a mountain in W Scotland, E of Loch Lomond. 3192 ft.

ben·ne (bĕn′ĭ), *n.* the sesame, *Sesamum indicum,* from the seeds of which a fixed oil (oil of benne or benne oil) is expressed. [t. Malay]

ben·net (bĕn′ĭt), *n. Bot.* **1.** the American avens, esp. the species *Geum virginianum* and *G. canadense.* **2.** herb bennet. [ME *beneit* in *herbe beneit,* prob. t. OF: m. *herbe beneite,* trans. of ML *herba benedicta* blessed herb]

Ben·nett (bĕn′ĭt), *n.* **1.** (**Enoch**) **Arnold,** 1867–1931, British novelist. **2. James Gordon,** 1795–1872, U.S. journalist. **3. Richard Bedford,** 1870–1947, Canadian statesman.

Ben Ne·vis (bĕn nĕ′vĭs, nĕv′ĭs), a peak in W Scotland in Inverness county: the highest point in the British Isles. 4406 ft.

Ben·ning·ton (bĕn′ĭng tən), *n.* a village in SW Vermont: the British were defeated near here by the "Green Mountain Boys," 1777. 8002 (1950).

Be·no·ni (bĕ nō′nĭ), *n.* a city in the Republic of South Africa, near Johannesburg: gold mines. 94,029 (1951).

bent[1] (bĕnt), *adj.* **1.** curved; crooked: *a bent stick, bow, etc.* **2.** determined; set; resolved (fol. by *on*). —*n.* **3.** bent state or form. **4.** direction taken (usually figurative); inclination; leaning; bias: *a bent for painting.* **5.** capacity of endurance. **6.** *Civ. Eng.* a transverse frame of a bridge or a building, designed to support either vertical or horizontal loads. [pp. of BEND[1]] —Syn. **4.** tendency, propensity, proclivity, predilection

bent[2] (bĕnt), *n.* **1.** bent grass. **2.** a stalk of such grass. **3.** (formerly) any stiff grass or sedge. **4.** *Scot. and N Eng.* a grassy tract, a moor, or a hillside. [ME; OE *beonet,* c. G *binse* rush]

bent grass, any of the species of the gramineous genus *Agrostis,* esp. the redtop.

Ben·tham (bĕn′thəm, -təm), *n.* **Jeremy** (jĕr′ə mĭ) 1748–1832, British jurist and utilitarian philosopher.

Ben·tham·ism (bĕn′thə mĭz′əm, bĕn′tə-), *n.* the variety of utilitarianism put forth by Jeremy Bentham characterized esp. by moral and ethical evaluation of actions in terms of their power to produce pleasure (the only good) or pain (the only evil). —Ben·tham·ite (bĕn′thə mīt′, bĕn′tə-), *n.*

ben·thos (bĕn′thŏs), *n. Ecol.* the animals and plants that are fixed to or crawl upon the sea bottom. [t. Gk. *depth* (of the sea)] —ben′thic, ben·thon·ic (bĕn thŏn′ĭk), *adj.*

Bent·ley (bĕnt′lĭ), *n.* **Richard,** 1662–1742, British scholar and critic.

Ben·ton (bĕn′tən), *n.* **Thomas Hart,** born 1889, U.S. painter.

Be·nu·e (bā′nŏŏ ā′), *n.* a river in W Africa, flowing from the Cameroons W to the Niger river in Nigeria. ab. 800 mi.

be·numb (bĭ nŭm′), *v.t.* **1.** to make numb; deprive of sensation: *benumbed by cold.* **2.** to render inactive; stupefy. [ME *benome(n),* OE *benumen,* pp. of *beniman* deprive]

benz-, var. of **benzo-,** used before vowels.

benz·al·de·hyde (bĕn zăl′də hīd′), *n. Chem.* an aldehyde, C_6H_5CHO, obtained from natural oil of bitter almonds or other oils, or produced artificially, used in dyes, as a flavoring agent, etc.

Ben·ze·drine (bĕn′zə drēn′, -drĭn), *n. Pharm.* a trademark for amphetamine.

ben·zene (bĕn′zēn, bĕn zēn′), *n. Chem.* a colorless, volatile, inflammable, liquid, aromatic hydrocarbon, C_6H_6, obtained chiefly from coal tar, and used as a solvent for resins, fats, etc., and in the manufacture of dyes, etc.

benzene ring, *Chem.* the graphic representation of the structure of benzene as a hexagon with a carbon atom at each of its points. Each carbon atom is united with an atom of hydrogen, one or more of which may be replaced to form benzene derivatives. Also, **benzene nucleus.**

ben·zi·dine (bĕn′zə dēn′, -dĭn), *n. Chem.* a basic compound, $H_2C_6H_4C_6H_4NH_2$, occurring as grayish scales or a crystalline powder, used in the manufacture of certain dyes, as Congo red. [f. BENZ- + -ID[3] + -INE[2]]

ben·zine (bĕn′zēn, bĕn zēn′), *n.* a colorless, volatile, inflammable liquid, a mixture of various hydrocarbons obtained in the distillation of petroleum, and used in cleaning, dyeing, etc.

benzo-, *Chem.* a combining form meaning "pertaining to or derived from benzoin" or designating the presence of benzoic acid. Also, **benz-.**

ben·zo·ate (bĕn′zō āt′, -ĭt), *n. Chem.* a salt or ester of benzoic acid.

ben·zo·ic acid (bĕn zō′ĭk), *Chem., Pharm., etc.* a white, crystalline acid, C_6H_5COOH, obtained from benzoin and other balsams or from toluene, used in medicine, aniline dye manufacture, as a food preservative, etc.

---

b., blend of, blended; c., cognate with; d., dialect, dialectal; der., derived from; f., formed from; g., going back to; m., modification of; r., replacing; s., stem of; t., taken from; ?, perhaps. See the full key on inside cover

ben·zoin (běn'zoin, -zō'ĭn, běn zō'ĭn), *n.* **1.** a balsamic resin obtained from species of *Styrax*, esp. *S. Benzoin*, a tree of Java, Sumatra, etc., and used in perfumery, medicine, etc. **2.** any plant of the lauraceous genus *Lindera* (also known as *Benzoin*) which includes the spicebush and other aromatic plants. [earlier *benzoin*, t. F. through Sp. or Pg., t. Ar.: m. *lubān jāwi* incense of Java (*lu-* appar. taken as "the")]

ben·zol (běn'zōl, -zŏl), *n.* crude industrial benzene.

ben·zo·phe·none (běn'zō fĭ nōn'), *n.* *Chem.* a water-insoluble crystalline ketone, $C_6H_5COC_6H_5$, used in organic synthesis. [f. BENZO- + PHEN- + -ONE]

ben·zo·yl (běn'zō ĭl, -ĭl), *n.* *Chem.* a univalent radical, C_6H_5CO, present in benzoic acid and allied compounds.

ben·zyl (běn'zĭl, -zēl), *n.* *Chem.* a univalent organic radical, $C_6H_5CH_2$, from toluene.

Be·o·grad (bĕ ō'gräd), *n.* Serbian name of **Belgrade**.

Be·o·wulf (bā'ō woolf'), *n.* **1.** an English alliterative epic poem of the early 8th century. **2.** its hero.

be·queath (bĭ kwēth', -kwēth'), *v.t.* **1.** *Law.* to dispose by last will of (personal property, esp. money). **2.** to hand down; pass on. **3.** *Obs.* to commit; entrust. [ME *bequethe(n)*, OE *becwethan*, f. BE- + *cwethan* say] —**be·queath·al** (bĭ kwē'thal), *n.*

be·quest (bĭ kwěst'), *n.* **1.** *Law.* a disposition in a will concerning personal property, esp. money. **2.** a legacy. [ME *biqueste*, OE *gequis*, c. Goth. *gakwiss* consent]

Bé·ran·ger (bĕ rän zhĕ'), *n.* Pierre Jean de (pyĕr zhän də), 1780–1857, French poet.

Be·rar (bā rär'), *n.* a former division of the Central Provinces in central India; now part of Bombay state.

be·rate (bĭ rāt'), *v.t.*, **-rated, -rating.** to scold.

Ber·ber (bûr'bər), *n.* **1.** a member of a group of North African tribes living in Barbary and the Sahara. **2.** the Hamitic languages of the Berbers, spoken from Tunisia, west to the Atlantic and in the Sahara, including Kabyle, Tuareg, and other languages. —*adj.* **3.** of or pertaining to the Berbers or their language.

Ber·ber·a (bûr'bər ə), *n.* a seaport in Somalia, on the Gulf of Aden; formerly, capital of British Somaliland. 9080 (1951).

ber·be·ri·da·ceous (bûr'bərĭ dā'shəs), *adj.* belonging to the *Berberidaceae*, a family of plants including the barberry, May apple, blue cohosh, etc.

ber·ber·ine (bûr'bə rēn'), *n.* *Chem.* a widely distributed alkaloid, $C_{20}H_{19}NO_5$, found in the barberry and a considerable number of other plants whose extracts have a yellow color and a bitter taste.

ber·ceuse (běr sœz'), *n.*, *pl.* **-ceuses** (-sœz'). *Music.* a cradlesong; lullaby. [F]

Berch·tes·ga·den (běrκΗ'təs gä'dən), *n.* a town in West Germany, in S Bavaria: site of the fortified mountain chalet of Adolf Hitler. 5736 (1950).

Ber·di·chev (běr dē'chěf), *n.* a city in the SW Soviet Union, in the Ukrainian Republic. 70,000 (est. 1956).

be·reave (bĭ rēv'), *v.t.*, **-reaved** or **-reft, -reaving. 1.** to deprive (*of*) ruthlessly, esp. of hope, joy, etc.: *bereft of all their lands.* **2.** to make desolate through loss (*of*), esp. by death: *bereaved of their mother.* **3.** *Obs.* to take away by violence. [ME *bereve(n)*, OE *berēaflan*, f. BE- + *rēaflan* rob] —**be·reave'ment,** *n.*

Ber·e·ni·ce's Hair (běr'ə nī'sēz), *Astron.* the constellation Coma Berenices.

be·ret (bə rā', běr'ā; *Fr.* bĕ rĕ'), *n.* a soft, round, visorless cap that fits closely. [t. F., t. Bearnese: m. *berreto*, g. Gallo-Rom. *birretum* cap, der. LL *birrum* cloak]

Be·re·zi·na (*Pol.* bĕ'rĕ zē'nä; *Russ.* -zĭ nä'), *n.* a river in the W Soviet Union, flowing SE to the Dnieper river: crossed with heavy losses by Napoleon's army during the retreat of 1812. ab. 350 mi.

berg (bûrg), *n.* *Oceanog.* iceberg. [short for ICEBERG]

Ber·ga·mo (běr'gä mō'), *n.* a city in N Italy, in Lombardy. 108,000 (est. 1954).

ber·ga·mot (bûr'gə mŏt'), *n.* **1.** a small tree of the citrus family, *Citrus Bergamia*, the rind of whose fruit yields a fragrant essential oil (**essence of bergamot**). **2.** the oil or essence itself. **3.** any of various plants of the mint family, as *Monarda fistulosa*, yielding an oil resembling essence of bergamot. **4.** *Hort.* one of a group of globular oblate, evenly and regularly shaped pears. [t. F: m. *bergamote*, t. It.: m. *bergamotta*, appar. t. Turk.: m. *begarmüdi* prince's pear]

Ber·gen (bûr'gən; *Nor.* běr'gən), *n.* a seaport in SW Norway, on the Atlantic. 112,845 (1950).

Ber·ge·rac (běr zhe räk'), *n.* **Savinien Cyrano de** (sá vē nyän' sĕ rä nō' də), 1619–55, French soldier, duelist, and romantic writer: hero of play by Rostand.

Berg·son (bûrg'sən, běrg'-; *Fr.* běrg sôn'), *n.* **Henri** (än rē'), 1859–1941, French philosopher and writer. —**Berg·so·ni·an** (bûrg sō'nĭ ən, běrg-), *adj.*, *n.*

Berg·son·ism (bûrg'sə nĭz'əm, běrg'-), *n.* *Philos.* Henri Bergson's doctrine of creative evolution, emphasizing duration as the central fact of experience and an *élan vital* (vital drive) as an original life force essentially governing all organic processes.

be·rhyme (bĭ rīm'), *v.t.*, **-rhymed, -rhyming.** to celebrate in verse. Also, **be·rime.**

Be·ri·a (bě'rĭ ə), *n.* **Lavrenti** (lə vrěn'tĭ) **Pavlovitch,** 1899–1953, Soviet leader; executed for treason in 1953.

be·rib·boned (bĭ rĭb'ənd), *adj.* adorned with ribbons.

ber·i·ber·i (běr'ĭ běr'ĭ), *n.* *Pathol.* a disease of the peripheral nerves caused by deficiency in vitamin B_1, and marked by pain in and paralysis of the extremities, and severe emaciation or swelling of the body. It is common in China, Japan, and the Philippines. [t. Singhalese, redupl. of *beri* weakness]

Ber·ing (bĭr'ĭng, bâr'-; *Dan.* bā'rĭng), *n.* **Vi·tus** (vē'tōōs), 1680–1741, Danish navigator and explorer of the N Pacific for Russia. Also, **Behring.**

Ber·ing Sea (bĭr'ĭng, bâr'-), a part of the N Pacific N of the Aleutian Islands. ab 878,000 sq. mi.

Bering Strait, the strait between Alaska and the Soviet Union in Asia, connecting the Bering Sea and the Arctic Ocean. 36 mi. wide.

Berke·le·ian (bûrk lē'ən; *Brit.* bärk-), *adj.* **1.** pertaining or relating to George Berkeley, or his philosophy. —*n.* **2.** one who holds George Berkeley's system of idealism; one who denies the existence of a material world. —**Berke·le'ian·ism,** *n.*

Berke·ley (bûrk'lĭ; *Brit.* bärk'lĭ), *n.* **1. George,** 1685–1753, Irish bishop and philosopher. **2. Sir William,** 1610?–77, British royal governor of Virginia.

Berke·ley (bûrk'lĭ), *n.* a city in W California, on San Francisco Bay. 111,268 (1960).

ber·ke·li·um (bər kē'lĭ əm), *n.* *Chem.* a synthetic, radioactive, metallic element. *Symbol:* Bk; *at. no.:* 97. [f. BERKEL(EY), Calif., where first identified + -IUM]

Berk·shire (bûrk'shĭr, -shər; *Brit.* bärk'-), *n.* **1.** Also, **Berks** (bûrks; *Brit.* bärks). a county in S England. 403,141 pop. (1951); 725 sq. mi. *Co. seat:* Reading. **2.** one of a breed of black hogs originating in Berkshire, England, with white markings on feet, face, and tail.

Berk·shire Hills (bûrk'shĭr, -shər), a range of low mountains in N Massachusetts: resort region. Highest peak, Mt. Greylock, 3505 ft. Also, **Berkshires.**

Ber·lin (bər lĭn' *or Ger.* běr lēn' *for 1;* bûr'lĭn *for 2*), *n.* **1.** a city in E Germany. 3,345,000 (est. 1955). Former capital of Germany: now divided into a **western zone** (part of West Germany), 2,204,000 (est. 1956); and an **eastern zone**, (*Soviet Zone, Russian Zone;* part of East Germany), 1,150,000 (est. 1955): capital of East Germany. **2.** a city in N New Hampshire. 16,615 (1951).

Ber·lin (bər lĭn'), *n.* **Ir·ving,** born 1888, U.S. song writer.

ber·lin (bər lĭn', bûr'-lĭn), *n.* **1.** large four-wheeled closed carriage hung between two perches, having two interior seats. **2.** *Auto.* berline. **3.** Berlin wool. [named after *Berlin*, capital of Prussia]

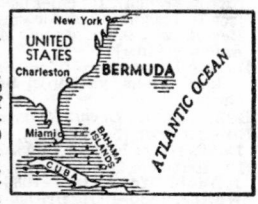
Berlin

ber·line (bər lĭn'; *Fr.* běr'l ēn'), *n.* *Auto.* a limousine with a movable glass partition behind the driver's seat.

Berlin wool, a soft woolen yarn for knitting, etc.

Ber·li·oz (běr'lĭ ōz'; *Fr.* běr lyôz'), *n.* **Louis Hector** (lwē ěk tôr'), 1803–69, French composer.

berm (bûrm), *n.* **1.** *U.S.* the dirt shoulder alongside a road. **2.** *Fort.* Also, **berme.** a narrow terrace between the rampart and moat. [t. F: (m.) *berme*, t. MD]

Ber·me·jo (běr mě'hō), *n.* a river in N Argentina, flowing SE to the Paraguay river. ab. 1000 mi.

Ber·mu·da (bər mū'də), *n.* a group of islands in the Atlantic, 580 miles E of North Carolina: a British colony; resort. 42,000 pop. (est. 1956); 19 sq. mi. *Cap.:* Hamilton. Also, **Bermudas.** —**Ber·mu·di·an** (bər mū'dĭ ən), *adj.*, *n.*

Bermuda onion, *Hort.* any of several mild flat varieties of onion grown on a large scale in Texas and, to some extent, in other parts of the U.S. and in Bermuda.

Bermuda shorts, shorts reaching almost to the knee, worn by men and women for informal dress.

Bern (bûrn; *Fr.* běrn), *n.* **1.** the capital of Switzerland, in the W part. 146,499 pop. (1950). **2.** a canton in W Switzerland. 817,000 pop. (est. 1952); 2658 sq. mi. *Cap.:* Bern. Also, **Berne.** —**Ber·nese** (bûr nēz', -nēs'), *n.*, *adj.*

Ber·na·dotte (bûr'nə dŏt'; *Fr.* běr nà dôt'), *n.* **Jean Baptiste Jules** (zhän bâ tēst' zhyl), 1764–1844, French marshal under Napoleon: king of Sweden and Norway, 1818–44, as Charles XIV.

Ber·nard (bûr'närd), **1. Saint,** A.D. 923–1008 (*Bernard of Menthon*), French monk. **2. Saint,** (*Bernard of Cluny*) fl. 1140, French monk. **3. Saint,** (*Bernard of Clairvaux*, "*the Mellifluous Doctor*") 1090?–1153, French monk, preacher, and mystical writer.

Ber·nard·ine (bûr'nər dĭn, -dēn'), *adj.* **1.** of or pertaining to St. Bernard of Clairvaux. **2.** of or pertaining to the Cistercians. —*n.* **3.** a Cistercian.

Ber·nese Alps (bûr nēz', -nēs'), a range of the Alps in SW Switzerland. Highest peak, 14,026 ft.

Bern·har·di (běrn här'dĭ), *n.* **Friedrich A. J. von** (frē'drĭκΗ fən), 1849–1930, German general.

Bern·hardt (bûrn'härt; *Fr.* běr när'), *n.* **Sarah,** (*Rosine Bernard*) 1845–1923, French actress.

Ber·ni·na (běr nē'nä), *n.* a mountain peak (13,295 ft.) in SE Switzerland, in the Rhaetian Alps, traversed by Bernina Pass (7640 ft. high), leading into N Italy.

ber·ret·ta (bə rět'ə), *n.* *Eccles.* biretta.

ber·ried (bĕr′ĭd), *adj.* **1.** covered with berries. **2.** of or like a berry; baccate. **3.** (of lobsters, etc.) having eggs.

ber·ry (bĕr′ĭ), *n., pl.* **-ries,** *v.* **-ried, -rying.** —*n.* **1.** any small, (usually) stoneless, juicy fruit, irrespective of botanical structure, as the gooseberry, strawberry, hackberry, etc. **2.** the hip of the rose. **3.** a dry seed or kernel, as of wheat. **4.** *Bot.* a simple fruit having a pulpy pericarp in which the seeds are embedded, as the grape, gooseberry, currant, tomato, etc. **5.** one of the eggs of the lobster. —*v.i.* **6.** to bear or produce berries. **7.** to gather berries. [ME and OE *berie,* c. G *beere*] —**ber′ry·less,** *adj.* —**ber′ry·like′,** *adj.*

Ber·ry (bĕr′ĭ; *Fr.* bĕ·rē′), *n.* a former province in central France. Also, **Ber·ri′.**

ber·sa·glie·re (bĕr′sä·lyĕ′rĕ), *n.* one of a class of riflemen or sharpshooters in the Italian army.

ber·serk (bûr′sûrk), *adj.* **1.** violently and destructively frenzied. —*n.* **2.** berserker.

ber·serk·er (bûr′sûr·kər), *n. Scand. Legend.* one of the ancient Norse warriors of great strength and courage, reputed to have fought with frenzied fury in battle; baresark. [t. Icel.: m. *berserkr* wild warrior; orig. uncert.]

berth (bûrth), *n.* **1.** *Railroads.* a shelflike space allotted to a passenger in a vessel or in a railroad sleeping car as a sleeping space. **2.** *Naut.* **a.** an apartment in a ship where a number of officers or men mess and reside. **b.** a sailor's bunk on board ship. **c.** a place for a hammock, or a repository for chests. **d.** a space allowed for safety or convenience between a vessel and other vessels, rocks, etc. **e.** room for a vessel to moor at a dock or to ride at anchor. **3.** *Brit.* job; position. —*v.t.* **4.** *Naut.* to assign or allot anchoring ground to; give space to lie in, as a ship in a dock. —*v.i.* **5.** *Naut.* to come to a dock, anchorage, or moorage. [orig. uncert.; prob. der. BEAR¹]

ber·tha (bûr′thə), *n.* a kind of collar or trimming, as of lace, worn about the shoulders by women, as on a low-necked waist. [t. F: m. *berthe,* der. *Berthe* Bertha, Charlemagne's mother, noted for her modesty]

Ber·til·lon system (bûr′tə·lŏn′; *Fr.* bĕr·tē·yôN′), a system of identifying persons, esp. criminals, by a record of individual physical measurements and peculiarities. [named after the inventor, A. *Bertillon*]

Ber·wick (bĕr′ĭk), *n.* a county in SE Scotland. 24,500 pop. (est. 1956); 457 sq. mi. *Co. seat:* Duns. Also, **Berwick·shire** (bĕr′ĭk·shĭr′, -shər).

Ber·wyn (bûr′wĭn), *n.* a city in NE Illinois, near Chicago. 54,224 (1960).

ber·yl (bĕr′əl), *n.* a mineral, beryllium aluminum silicate, Be₃Al₂Si₆O₁₈, usually green (but also blue, rose, white, and golden) and both opaque and transparent, the latter variety including the gems emerald and aquamarine: the principal ore of beryllium. **2.** pale bluish green; sea green. [ME, f. L: m.s. *bēryllus,* t. Gk.: m. *bēryllos*] —**ber·yl·ine** (bĕr′ə·lĭn, -lĭn′), *adj.*

be·ryl·li·um (bĕ·rĭl′ĭ·əm), *n. Chem.* a steel-gray, divalent, hard, light, metallic element, the salts of which are said to have a sweetish taste (hence it is called glucinum by the French). Its chief use is in copper alloys not subject to fatigue, used for springs and contacts. *Symbol:* Be; *at. wt.:* 9.02; *at. no.:* 4; *sp. gr.:* 1.8 at 20°C. [t. BERYL + -IUM]

Ber·ze·li·us (bər·zē′lĭ·əs; *Swed.* bĕr·sā′lĭ·ŏŏs), *n.* **Jöns Jakob** (yœns yä′kôp), **Baron,** 1779–1848, Swedish chemist.

Bes (bĕs), *n. Egypt. Relig.* a beneficent god of pleasure.

Be·san·çon (bə·zän·sôN′), *n.* a city in E France, on the Doubs river: Roman ruins. 73,445 (1954).

Bes·ant (bĕz′ənt *for 1;* bə·zănt′, *older* bĕz′ənt *for 2*), *n.* **1.** Annie (Wood), 1847–1933, British theosophist. **2.** Sir Walter, 1836–1901, British novelist.

be·seech (bĭ·sēch′), *v.t.,* **-sought, -seeching. 1.** to implore urgently. **2.** to beg eagerly for; solicit. [ME *bisēche(n),* f. BE- + *sechen,* OE *sēcan* seek] —**beseech′er,** *n.* —**be·seech′ing,** *adj.* —**be·seech′ing·ly,** *adv.* —**be·seech′ing·ness,** *n.* —Syn. **1.** entreat, pray.

be·seem (bĭ·sēm′), *v.t.* **1.** to be fit for or worthy of. —*v.i.* **2.** to be seemly or fitting.

be·set (bĭ·sĕt′), *v.t.,* **-set, -setting. 1.** to attack on all sides; assail; harass: *beset by enemies, difficulties, etc.* **2.** to surround; hem in. **3.** to set or place upon; bestud: *beset with jewels.* [ME *besete(n),* OE *besettan,* f. BE- + *settan* SET] —**be·set′ment,** *n.*

be·set·ting (bĭ·sĕt′ĭng), *adj.* constantly attacking, tempting, etc.: *our besetting sins.*

be·shrew (bĭ·shrōō′), *v.t. Archaic.* to curse; invoke evil upon: *beshrew me.* [ME *beshrewen,* f. BE- + SHREW¹]

be·side (bĭ·sīd′), *prep.* **1.** by or at the side of; near: *sit down beside me.* **2.** compared with. **3.** over and above; in addition to. **4.** apart from; not connected with: *beside the point or question.* **5.** beside oneself, out of one's senses through strong emotion. —*adv.* **6.** in addition; besides. [ME; OE *be sīdan* by side] —Syn. **1.** BESIDE, BESIDES may both be used as prepositions, though with different meanings. BESIDE is almost exclusively used as a preposition meaning "by the side of": *beside the house, the stream.* BESIDES is used as a preposition meaning "in addition to" or "over and above": *besides these honors he received a sum of money.*

be·sides (bĭ·sīdz′), *adv.* **1.** moreover. **2.** in addition. **3.** otherwise; else. —*prep.* **4.** over and above; in addition to. **5.** other than; except. [f. BESIDE + adv. *-s*] —Syn. **1.** BESIDES, MOREOVER both indicate something additional to what has already been stated. BESIDES often suggests that the addition is in the nature of an afterthought: *the bill cannot be paid as yet; besides the work is not completed.* MOREOVER is more formal and implies that the addition is something particular, emphatic, or important: *I did not like the house; moreover, it was too high-priced.* **4.** See **beside.**

be·siege (bĭ·sēj′), *v.t.,* **-sieged, -sieging. 1.** to lay siege to. **2.** to crowd around. **3.** to assail or ply, as with requests, etc. —**be·siege′ment,** *n.* —**be·sieg′er,** *n.*

be·smear (bĭ·smĭr′), *v.t.* **1.** to smear over. **2.** to sully; soil. [ME *bismeren,* OE *besmerian.* See BE-, SMEAR]

be·smirch (bĭ·smûrch′), *v.t.* **1.** to soil; discolor. **2.** to detract from the honor of: *to besmirch one's name.*

be·som (bē′zəm), *n.* **1.** brush or twigs bound together as a broom. **2.** a broom of any kind. [ME *besum* broom, rod, OE *besema,* c. G *besen*]

be·sot (bĭ·sŏt′), *v.t.,* **-sotted, -sotting. 1.** to stupefy with drink; make a drunkard of. **2.** to make stupid or foolish. **3.** to infatuate.

be·sought (bĭ·sôt′), *v.* pt. and pp. of **beseech.**

be·spake (bĭ·spāk′), *v. Archaic.* pt. of **bespeak.**

be·span·gle (bĭ·spăng′gəl), *v.t.,* **-gled, -gling.** to adorn with, or as with, spangles.

be·spat·ter (bĭ·spăt′ər), *v.t.* **1.** to soil by spattering; sprinkle with dirt, water, etc. **2.** to slander.

be·speak (bĭ·spēk′), *v.t.,* **-spoke** or (*Archaic*) **-spake, -spoken** or **-spoke, -speaking. 1.** to ask for in advance: *to bespeak a calm hearing or the reader's patience.* **2.** *Brit.* to reserve beforehand; engage in advance; make arrangements for: *to bespeak a seat in a theater.* **3.** *Poetic.* to speak to; address. **4.** to show; indicate: *this bespeaks a kindly heart.* **5.** *Obs.* to foretell; forebode. [ME *bespeken,* OE *besprecan* speak against, speak of, f. *be-* BE- + *sprecan* (for loss of *-r-* see SPEAK)]

be·spec·ta·cled (bĭ·spĕk′tə·kəld), *adj.* wearing eyeglasses.

be·spread (bĭ·sprĕd′), *v.t.,* **-spread, -spreading.** to spread over; cover with.

be·sprent (bĭ·sprĕnt′), *adj. Poetic.* besprinkled; bestrewed. [pp. of *bespreng* (obs.), OE *besprengan*]

be·sprin·kle (bĭ·spring′kəl), *v.t.,* **-kled, -kling.** to sprinkle over with something; bespatter.

Bes·sa·ra·bi·a (bĕs′ə·rā′bĭ·ə), *n.* a territory in the SW Soviet Union: formerly a province of Rumania. 17,151 sq. mi. —**Bes′sa·ra′bi·an,** *adj., n.*

Bes·se·mer (bĕs′ə·mər), *n.* **1.** Sir Henry, 1813–98, British engineer: inventor of Bessemer process. **2.** a city in central Alabama. 28,445 (1950).

Bessemer converter, *Metall.* a huge pear-shaped metal container used in the Bessemer process.

Bessemer process, *Metall.* a process of producing steel, in which impurities are removed by forcing a blast of air through molten iron.

best (bĕst), *adj.* (*superlative of* **good**). **1.** of the highest quality, excellence, or standing: *the best judgment.* **2.** most advantageous, suitable, or desirable: *the best way.* **3.** largest; most: *the best part of a day.* —*adv.* (*superlative of* **well**). **4.** most excellently or suitably; with most advantage or success. **5.** in or to the highest degree; most fully. **6. had best,** would be wiser, safer, etc., to. —*n.* **7.** the best thing, state, or part. **8.** one's finest clothing. **9.** utmost or best quality: *at one's best.* **10. at best,** under the best circumstances. **11. get or have the best of,** to defeat. **12. make the best of,** to manage as well as one can (under unfavorable or adverse circumstances). —*v.t.* **13.** to defeat; beat. **14.** to outdo; surpass. [ME *beste,* OE *betst,* c. Goth. *batist-*]

be·stead (bĭ·stĕd′), *v.,* **-steaded, -steaded** or **-stead, -steading.** —*v.t.* **1.** to help; assist; serve; avail. —*adj.* **2.** *Archaic.* placed; situated. [ME, f. BE- + *stead,* v., help, be of use to, der. *stead,* n., profit, support]

bes·tial (bĕs′chəl, bĕs′yəl), *adj.* **1.** of or belonging to a beast. **2.** brutal; inhuman; irrational. **3.** depravedly sensual; carnal. [ME, t. L: s. *bestiālis*] —**bes′tial·ly,** *adv.*

bes·ti·al·i·ty (bĕs′chĭ·ăl′ə·tĭ, -tĭ·ăl′-), *n.* **1.** bestial character or conduct; beastliness. **2.** excessive appetites or indulgence. **3.** unnatural sexual relations with an animal; sodomy.

bes·tial·ize (bĕs′chə·līz′, bĕst′yə-), *v.t.,* **-ized, -izing.** to make bestial.

bes·ti·ar·y (bĕs′tĭ·ĕr′ĭ), *n., pl.* **-aries.** a collection of moralized fables about natural history objects, mostly animals, attributed to an Alexandrian Greek of the 4th century after Christ. It was universally known in the Middle Ages. [t. ML: m. s. *bestiārium,* prop. neut. of L *bestiārius* pertaining to beasts]

be·stir (bĭ·stûr′), *v.t.,* **-stirred, -stirring.** to stir up; rouse to action. [ME *bestyrie(n),* OE *bestyrian* heap up]

best man, the chief attendant of the bridegroom at a wedding.

be·stow (bĭ·stō′), *v.t.* **1.** to present as a gift; give; confer. **2.** to dispose of; apply to some use. **3.** *Colloq.* to provide quarters for. **4.** to put; stow; deposit; store. —**be·stow′al,** *n.* —**be·stow′ment,** *n.*

be·strad·dle (bĭ·străd′əl), *v.t.,* **-dled, -dling.** to bestride.

---

be·strew (bǐ'strōō'), *v.t.*, **-strewed, -strewed** or **-strewn, -strewing. 1.** to strew or cover (a surface). **2.** to strew or scatter about. **3.** to lie scattered over. [ME *bistrewe(n)*, OE *bestrēowian*]

be·stride (bǐ'strīd'), *v.t.*, **-strode** or **-strid, -stridden** or **-strid, -striding. 1.** to get or be astride of; spread the legs on both sides of. **2.** to step over or across. [ME *bestride(n)*, OE *bestrīdan*, f. BE- + *strīdan* stride]

best seller, 1. a book that has a very large sale during a given period. **2.** the author of such a book.

be·stud (bǐ'stŭd'), *v.t.*, **-studded, -studding.** to set with studs distributed over a surface; dot.

bet (bĕt), *v.*, **bet** or **betted, betting,** *n.* —*v.t.* **1.** to pledge as a forfeit to another who makes a similar pledge in return, in support of an opinion; stake; wager. —*v.i.* **2.** to lay a wager. —*n.* **3.** a pledge of something to be forfeited, in case one is wrong, to another who has the opposite opinion. **4.** that which is pledged. [orig. uncert.] —**bet'ter, bet'tor,** *n.*

bet., better.

be·ta (bā'tə, bē'-), *n.* the 2nd letter of the Greek alphabet (B, β), often used to designate the second in a series, esp. in scientific classification, as: **a.** *Astron.* (of a constellation) the second brightest star: *Rigel is β (or Beta) Orionis.* **b.** *Chem.* (of a compound) one of the possible positions of substituted atoms or groups: *β eucaine* or *betaeucaine.*

be·ta·eu·caine (bā'tə ū'kān, bē'tə-), *n.* eucaine (def. 2).

be·ta·ine (bē'tə ēn', -ǐn; bǐ tā'ēn, -ǐn), *n. Chem.* a nonpoisonous crystalline substance, $C_5H_{11}O_2N(H_2O)$, a sweetish-tasting alkaloid, found in sugar beets, cottonseed, the sprouts of wheat and barley; related chemically to glycine. Also, **be·ta·in** (bē'tə ǐn, bǐ tā'-). [f. L *bēta* beet + -INE²]

be·take (bǐ tāk'), *v.t.*, **-took, -taken, -taking.** (Fol. by *oneself*, etc.) **1.** to go: *she betook herself to the market.* **2.** to resort to; undertake: *he betook himself to flight.*

be·ta·naph·thol (bā'tə năf'thōl, -thôl, -năp'-, bē'tə-), *n. Chem.* a crystalline antiseptic, $C_{10}H_7OH.$

beta particle, *Physics.* an electron in a beta ray.

beta ray, *Physics.* a ray emitted by radium and other radioactive substances, resembling the cathode ray and consisting of electrons.

beta test, *Psychol.* an intelligence test requiring no use of written or spoken language, used by the U. S. Army in World War I.

be·ta·tron (bā'tə trŏn', bē'-), *n. Physics.* a device based on the principle of the transformer, which accelerates electrons to high energy by a magnetic field varying with time.

be·tel (bē'təl), *n.* an East Indian pepper plant, *Piper Betle.* Cf. betel nut. [t. Pg.: m. *betele*, earlier *vitele*, t. Malay: m. *vettila*, Tamil *vettilei*]

Be·tel·geuse (bē'təl jōōz', bĕt'əl jœz'), *n. Astron.* a giant reddish star of the first magnitude in the constellation Orion. Also, **Be'tel·geux'.** [t. F, ? t. Ar.: m. *bīt-al-jāuza* the giant's shoulder]

betel nut, the areca nut, chewed extensively with lime by East Indian natives.

betel palm, a tall, graceful, Asiatic palm, *Areca Catechu,* that bears the areca nut or betel nut, so named from its association in native usage with the betel plant.

bête noire (bāt' nwär'; *Fr.* bĕt nwär'), *French.* something that one especially dislikes or dreads, either a person, task, or object; bugbear. [F: black beast]

Beth·a·ny (bĕth'ə nĭ), *n.* a village in Arab Palestine, near Jerusalem, at the foot of the Mount of Olives.

beth·el (bĕth'əl), *n.* **1.** a hallowed spot. Gen. 28:19. **2.** a church or chapel for seamen, often afloat in a harbor. **3.** *Brit.* a dissenters' chapel or meeting house. [t. Heb.: m. *bēth-ēl* house of God]

Beth·el (bĕth'əl), *n.* ancient town in Arab Palestine.

Be·thes·da (bə thĕz'də), *n.* **1.** *Bible.* a pool in Jerusalem, having healing powers. John 5:2–4. **2.** a city in central Maryland; residential suburb of Washington, D.C. 56,527 (1960). **3.** a chapel.

be·think (bǐ thǐngk'), *v.*, **-thought, -thinking.** —*v.t.* (generally reflexive) **1.** to think; consider. **2.** to remember; recall. **3.** to determine; resolve. **4.** *Obs.* to bear in mind; remember. —*v.i.* **5.** *Archaic.* to consider; meditate. [ME *bethenken*, OE *bethencan*, f. BE- + *thencan* consider]

Beth·le·hem (bĕth'lĭ əm, -hĕm'), *n.* **1.** a town in central Arab Palestine, near Jerusalem; birthplace of Jesus and of David. 19,155 pop. (1952). **2.** a city in E Pennsylvania. 75,408 (1960).

Beth·mann-Holl·weg (bāt'män höl'vākH), *n.* **Theobald von** (tā'ō bält' fən), 1856–1921, German statesman: chancellor 1909–17.

Beth·nal Green (bĕth'nəl), a NE industrial borough of London, England. 53,374 (1951).

be·thought (bǐ thôt'), *v.* pt. and pp. of **bethink.**

Beth·sa·i·da (bĕth sā'ə də), *n.* an ancient town in N Israel, near the N shore of the Sea of Galilee.

MEDITERRANEAN SEA / SYRIA / Sea of Galilee / ISRAEL / JORDAN / Jerusalem / BETHLEHEM° / Dead Sea

be·tide (bǐ tīd'), *v.*, **-tided, -tiding. 1.** to happen; befall; come to: *woe betide the villain!* —*v.i.* **2.** to come to pass. [ME *betide(n)*, f. BE-, OE *tīdan* betide]

be·times (bǐ tīmz'), *adv.* **1.** before it is too late; early. **2.** soon. [ME *betymes*, f. *betime* by time + adv. -s]

bê·tise (bĕ tēz'), *n.* **1.** stupidity. **2.** a stupid or foolish act or remark. **3.** an absurdity; trifle. [F, der. *bête* beast]

be·to·ken (bǐ tō'kən), *v.t.* **1.** to give evidence of; indicate. **2.** to be or give a token of; portend.

bé·ton (bĕ tôn'), *n.* a kind of concrete composed of a mixture of cement, sand, and gravel.

bet·o·ny (bĕt'ə nĭ), *n.* **1.** a plant, *Stachys* (formerly *Betonica*) *officinalis,* of the mint family, formerly used in medicine and dyeing. **2.** any of various similar plants. [t. LL: m. *betoni(ca)*; r. ME *beteine*, t. OF; r. OE *betonice*, t. LL (as above)]

be·took (bǐ tŏŏk'), *v.* pt. of betake.

be·tray (bǐ trā'), *v.t.* **1.** to deliver or expose to an enemy by treachery or disloyalty. **2.** to be unfaithful in keeping or upholding: *to betray a trust.* **3.** to be disloyal to; disappoint the hopes or expectations of. **4.** to reveal or disclose in violation of confidence: *to betray a secret.* **5.** to reveal unconsciously (something one would preferably conceal). **6.** to show; exhibit. **7.** betray oneself, to reveal one's real character, plans, etc. **8.** to deceive; mislead. **9.** to seduce and desert. [ME *bitraien*, f. *bi-* + *traien*, t. OF: m. *traïr*, ult. g. L *trādere* give over] —**be·tray'al,** —**be·tray'er,** *n.*

be·troth (bǐ trōth', -trôth'), *v.t.* **1.** to promise to marry. **2.** to arrange for the marriage of; affiance. [ME *betrouthen*, var. of *betreuthien*, der. BE- + *treuthe*, OE *trēowth* pledge. See TROTH, TRUTH]

be·troth·al (bǐ trō'thəl, -trô'thəl), *n.* act or ceremony of betrothing; engagement. Also, **be·troth'ment.**

be·trothed (bǐ trōthd', -trôtht'), *adj.* **1.** engaged to be married. —*n.* **2.** an engaged person.

bet·ter (bĕt'ər), *adj.* (comparative of good). **1.** of superior quality or excellence: *a better position.* **2.** of superior value, use, fitness, desirability, acceptableness, etc.: *a better time for action.* **3.** larger; greater: *the better part of a lifetime.* **4.** improved in health; healthier. —*adv.* (comparative of *well*). **5.** in a more excellent way or manner: *to behave better.* **6.** in a superior degree: *to know a man better.* **7.** more: *better than a mile to town.* **8.** had better, would be wiser, safer, etc., to. **9.** better off, in better circumstances. **10.** think better of, to reconsider and decide more favorably or wisely. —*v.t.* **11.** to make better; improve; increase the good qualities of. **12.** better oneself, to improve one's social standing, education, etc. **13.** to improve upon; surpass; exceed: *they bettered working conditions.* —*n.* **14.** that which has superior excellence, etc.: *the better of two choices.* **15.** (usually pl.) one's superior in wisdom, wealth, etc. **16.** superiority: *to get the better of someone.* [ME *bettre,* OE *betera,* c. Goth. *batiza*] —**Syn. 11.** See improve.

bet·ter·ment (bĕt'ər mənt), *n.* **1.** improvement. **2.** (*usually pl.*) *Law.* an improvement of real property, other than mere repairs.

Bet·ter·ton (bĕt'ər tən), *n.* **Thomas,** 1635?–1710, British actor.

bet·u·la·ceous (bĕch'ŏŏ lā'shəs), *adj. Bot.* belonging to the *Betulaceae,* a family of trees and shrubs including the birch, alder, etc. [f. s. L *betula* birch + -ACEOUS]

be·tween (bǐ twēn'), *prep.* **1.** in the space separating (two points, objects, etc.). **2.** intermediate to, in time, quantity, or degree: *between 12 and 1 o'clock, between pink and red.* **3.** connecting: *a link between parts.* **4.** involving; concerning: *war between nations, choice between things.* **5.** by joint action or possession of: *to own land between them.* —*adv.* **6.** in the intervening space or time; in an intermediate position or relation: *visits far between.* [ME *betwene,* OE *betwēonan, betwēonum,* f. be by + -twēonan, twēonum,* der. *twā* two] —**Syn. 1.** See among.

be·twixt (bǐ twǐkst'), *prep., adv.* **1.** *Archaic and Poetic* between. **2.** betwixt and between, neither the one nor the other; in a middle position. [ME *betwix,* OE *betweox, betweon;* for final *-t,* cf. *against,* etc.]

Beu·lah (bū'lə), *n. Bible.* the land of Israel. Isa. 62:4. [t. Heb.: m. *be'ulāh* married]

Beu·then (boi'tən), *n.* German name of Bytom.

BEV (bĕv), billion electron volts.

bev·a·tron (bĕv'ə trŏn'), *n. Physics.* a type of electro-nuclear machine.

bev·el (bĕv'əl), *n., v.,* **-eled, -eling** or (*esp. Brit.*) **-elled, -elling,** *adj.* —*n.* **1.** the inclination that one line or surface makes with another when not at right angles. **2.** an adjustable instrument for drawing angles or adjusting the surface of work to a particular inclination. —*v.t., v.i.* **3.** to cut or slant at a bevel. —*adj.* **4.** oblique; sloping; slanted. [orig. obscure]

bevel gear, *Mach.* a gear in which the axis or shaft of the driver forms an angle with the axis or shaft of the wheel driven. See illus. under gear.

bevel square, an adjustable tool used by woodworkers for laying out angles and for testing the accuracy of surfaces worked to a slope.

Bevel square

bev·er·age (bĕv'ər ĭj, bĕv'rĭj), *n.* a drink of any kind: *intoxicating beverages.* [ME, t. OF: m. *bevrage,* der. *bevre,* g. L *bibere* drink]

Bev·er·idge (bĕv'ər ĭj, bĕv'rĭj), *n.* **Sir William Henry,** 1879–1963, British economist.

Bev·er·ly (bĕv′ərlĭ), n. a city in NE Massachusetts. 36,108 (1960).

Beverly Hills, a city in SW California, near Los Angeles. 30,817 (1960).

Bev·in (bĕv′ĭn), n. Ernest, 1881–1951, British labor leader: foreign minister, 1945–1951.

bev·y (bĕv′ĭ), n., pl. bevies. 1. a flock of birds, esp. larks or quails. 2. a group, esp. of girls or women. [ME bevey; orig. uncert.]

be·wail (bĭ wāl′), v.t. 1. to express deep sorrow for; lament. —v.i. 2. to express grief.

be·ware (bĭ wâr′), v.i., v.t., -wared, -waring. to be wary, cautious, or careful (of). [prop. two words, BE + WARE², adj.]

be·wil·der (bĭ wĭl′dər), v.t. to confuse or puzzle completely; perplex. [f. BE- + WILDER] —be·wil′dered, adj. —be·wil′dered·ly, adv. —be·wil′der·ing, adj. —be·wil′der·ing·ly, adv. —Syn. mystify, nonplus, confound, daze. See puzzle.

be·wil·der·ment (bĭ wĭl′dər mənt), n. 1. bewildered state. 2. a confusing maze or tangle.

be·witch (bĭ wĭch′), v.t. 1. to affect by witchcraft or magic; throw a spell over. 2. to enchant. —be·witch′er, n. —be·witch′er·y, n. —be·witch′ing, adj. —be·witch′ing·ly, adv. —be·witch′ment, n. —Syn. 2. fascinate, captivate.

be·wray (bĭ rā′), v.t. Obs. 1. to reveal. 2. to betray. [ME bewreien, f. BE- + wreien, OE wrēgan accuse]

bey (bā), n., pl. beys. 1. the governor of a minor Turkish province. 2. a Turkish title of respect for important persons (placed after the proper name). 3. the title of the native head of Tunis. [t. Turk.: m. beg]

Beyle (bĕl), n. Marie Henri (må rē′ än rē′), real name of Stendhal.

be·yond (bĭ yŏnd′), prep. 1. on or to the farther side of: beyond the house. 2. farther on than; more distant than: beyond the horizon. 3. later than: they stayed beyond the time limit. 4. outside the understanding, limits, or reach of; past: beyond human comprehension. 5. superior to; surpassing; above: wise beyond all others. 6. more than; in excess of; over and above. —adv. 7. farther on or away: as far as the house and beyond. —n. 8. the life after the present one. [ME beyonde, OE begeondan, f. be by + geondan beyond]

Bey·routh (bā′rōōt, bā rōōt′), n. Beirut.

bez·ant (bĕz′ənt, bə zănt′), n. 1. the solidus, a gold coin of the Byzantine emperors, widely circulated in Europe during the Middle Ages. 2. Archit. an ornament in the form of a flat disk. [ME, t. OF: m. besant, g. L Byzantius Byzantine]

bez·el (bĕz′əl), n. 1. a sloping face or edge of a chisel or other cutting tool. 2. the upper oblique faces of a brilliant-cut gem. 3. the grooved ring or rim holding a gem or watch crystal in its setting. [prob. t. F, der. biais slant. See BIAS]

Bé·ziers (bĕ zyĕ′), n. a city in S France. 64,929 (1954).

be·zique (bə zēk′), n. Cards. a game, resembling pinochle, played with 64 cards. [t. F: m. bésigue]

be·zoar (bē′zōr), n. 1. a calculus or concretion found in the stomach or intestines of certain animals, esp. ruminants, formerly reputed to be efficacious against poison. 2. Obs. a counterpoison or antidote. [t. Ar.: m. bāzahr, t. Pers.: m. pādzahr counterpoison]

be·zo·ni·an (bĭ zō′nĭ ən), n. Archaic. an indigent rascal; scoundrel. [der. obs. besonio, t. It.: m. bisogno need, needy fellow]

b.f., Printing. boldface. Also, bf.

B.F.A., Bachelor of Fine Arts.

Bha·ga·vad-Gi·ta (bŭg′ə vəd gē′tä), n. Hinduism. a famous episode of eighteen chapters, in the Mahabharata, wherein the divine incarnation Krishna expounds the duties of the caste system along with devotion to Deity. [t. Skt.: the Song of the Blessed One]

bhang (băng), n. 1. the Indian hemp plant. 2. a preparation of its leaves and tops used in India as an intoxicant and narcotic. Also, bang. [t. Hind.: m. bhāng, g. Skt. bhangā hemp]

Bhau·na·gar (bou nŭg′ər), n. a seaport in W India. 137,951 (1951). Also, Bhav·na·gar (băv nŭg′ər).

bhees·ty (bēs′tĭ), n. India. water carrier. Also, bhees′tie. [t. Hind.: m. bhīstī, t. Pers.: m. bihishtī water carrier, deriv. (presumably jocular) of bihisht paradise]

Bho·pal (bō päl′), n. 1. a former state in the central part of the peninsula of India. 836,474 pop. (1951); 6878 sq. mi. Now part of Madhya Pradesh. 2. Capital of Madhya Pradesh. 102,333 (1951).

Bhu·tan (bōō tän′), n. a principality in the Himalayas NE of India: partly controlled by India. 300,000 pop. (est. 1950); ab. 19,300 sq. mi. Cap.: Punaka.

bi-, a prefix meaning: 1. twice, doubly, two, as in bilateral, binocular, biweekly. 2. (in science) denoting (in general) two, as in bicarbonate. Also, bin-. [t. L, comb. form of bis twice, doubly, der. L duo two]

Bi, Chem. bismuth.

B.I., British India.

Bi·a·fra (bē ä′frə), n. Bight of, a wide bay in the E part of the Gulf of Guinea, off the W coast of Africa.

Bia·ly·stok (byä lĭ′stŏk), n. a city in E Poland. 95,000 (est. 1954). Russian, Byelostok.

bi·an·gu·lar (bī ăng′gyə lər), adj. having two angles or corners.

bi·an·nu·al (bī ăn′yōō əl), adj. occurring twice a year. —bi·an′nu·al·ly, adv.

bi·an·nu·late (bī ăn′yōō lĭt, -lāt′), adj. Zool. having two rings or ringlike bands, as of color.

Bi·ar·ritz (bē′ə rĭtz′; Fr. byà rēts′), n. a city in SW France, on the Bay of Biscay: resort. 22,922 (1954).

bi·as (bī′əs), n., adj., adv., v., biased, biasing or (esp. Brit.) biassed, biassing. —n. 1. an oblique or diagonal line of direction, esp. across a woven fabric: to cut cloth on the bias. 2. a particular tendency or inclination, esp. one which prevents unprejudiced consideration of a question. 3. Bowling. a. a bulge or a greater weight on one side of the bowl, causing it to swerve. b. the swerved course of a bowl, due to shape or weighting. 4. Radio. the direct voltage placed on the grid of an electronic tube. —adj. 5. cut, set, folded, etc., diagonally. —adv. 6. slantingly; obliquely. —v.t. 7. to influence, usually unfairly; prejudice; warp. [t. F: m. biais slant, prob. g. L *biazius having two axes]

—Syn. 2. BIAS, PREJUDICE mean a strong inclination of the mind or a preconceived opinion about something or someone. A BIAS may be favorable or unfavorable: bias in favor of or against an idea. PREJUDICE implies a preformed judgment even more unreasoning than BIAS, and usually implies an unfavorable opinion: prejudice against a race. —Ant. 2. impartiality. 5. straight.

bi·au·ric·u·lar (bī′ô rĭk′yə lər), adj. Anat. 1. having two auricles. 2. pertaining to the two ears.

bi·au·ric·u·late (bī′ô rĭk′yə lĭt, -lāt′), adj. Biol. having two auricles or earlike parts.

bi·ax·i·al (bī ăk′sĭ əl), adj. 1. having two axes. 2. (of a crystal) having two directions in which no double refraction occurs. —bi·ax′i·al·ly, adv.

bib (bĭb), n., v., bibbed, bibbing. —n. 1. an article of clothing worn under the chin by a child, esp. while eating, to protect the dress. 2. the upper part of an apron. —v.t. 3. Obs. to tipple. [ME bibben; orig. uncert., ? t. L: m. bibere drink] —bib′like′, adj.

Bib., 1. Bible. 2. Biblical.

bib and tucker, Colloq. clothes.

bi·bas·ic (bī bā′sĭk), adj. Chem. dibasic.

bib·ber (bĭb′ər), n. a steady drinker; tippler.

bib·cock (bĭb′kŏk′), n. Plumbing. a faucet having a nozzle bent downward.

bi·be·lot (bĭb′lō; Fr. bē blō′), n. small object of curiosity, beauty, or rarity. [t. F]

bi·bi·va·lent (bī′bī vā′lənt, bī bĭv′ə-), adj. Chem. denoting an electrolytic compound which splits into two ions, each with a valence of two.

Bibl., 1. Biblical. 2. Also, bibl. bibliographical.

Bi·ble (bī′bəl), n. 1. the collection of sacred writings of the Christian religion, comprising the Old and the New Testament. 2. the Old Testament only. 3. (often l.c.) the sacred writings of any religion. 4. (l.c.) any book accepted as authoritative. [ME bibul, t. ML: m. s. biblia, t. Gk., pl. of biblíon, dim. of bíblos book]

Bib·li·cal (bĭb′lə kəl), adj. 1. of or in the Bible. 2. in accord with the Bible. —Bib′li·cal·ly, adv.

Biblical Latin, the form of Latin used in the translation of the Bible, which became current in Western Europe at the beginning of the Middle Ages.

Bib·li·cist (bĭb′lə sĭst), n. 1. an adherent of the letter of the Bible; a fundamentalist. 2. a Biblical scholar. Also, Biblicist.

biblio-, a word element meaning: 1. book, as in bibliophile. 2. Bible, as in bibliolatry. [t. Gk., comb. form of biblíon book]

bib·li·o·film (bĭb′lĭ ə fĭlm′), n. a microfilm used esp. in libraries for reproducing valuable or much-used books.

bibliog., 1. bibliographer. 2. bibliography.

bib·li·og·ra·pher (bĭb′lĭ ŏg′rə fər), n. an expert in bibliography. Also, bib·li·o·graph (bĭb′lĭ ə grăf′, -gräf′). [f. s. Gk. bibliográphos bookwriter + -ER¹]

bib·li·og·ra·phy (bĭb′lĭ ŏg′rə fĭ), n., pl. -phies. 1. a compilation of a complete or a selective literature on a particular subject; a list of works by a given author. 2. the art of describing books authoritatively with respect to authorship, format, imprint, etc.; the study of variations in editions, issues, etc. —bib·li·o·graph·ic (bĭb′lĭ ə grăf′ĭk), bib·li·o·graph′i·cal, adj.

bib·li·ol·a·try (bĭb′lĭ ŏl′ə trĭ), n. excessive reverence for the Bible. —bib·li·ol′a·ter, n. —bib·li·ol′a·trous, adj.

bib·li·o·man·cy (bĭb′lĭ ō măn′sĭ), n. divination by means of a book, as the Bible, opened at random to some verse taken as significant.

bib·li·o·ma·ni·a (bĭb′lĭ ō mā′nĭ ə), n. an enthusiasm for collecting books. —bib·li·o·ma·ni·ac (bĭb′lĭ ō mā′nĭ ăk′), adj., n. —bib·li·o·ma·ni·a·cal (bĭb′lĭ ō mə nī′ə kəl), adj.

bib·li·o·peg·y (bĭb′lĭ ŏp′ə jĭ), n. art of binding books. [f. BIBLIO- + m.s. Gk. -pēgia, der. pēgnýnai fasten]

bib·li·o·phile (bĭb′lĭ ə fīl′, -fĭl), n. a lover of books. Also, bib·li·o·phil (bĭb′lĭ ə fĭl), bib·li·oph·i·list (bĭb′lĭ ŏf′ə lĭst). [t. F. See BIBLIO-, -PHILE] —bib·li·oph′i·lism, n. —bib·li·oph′i·lis′tic, adj.

bib·li·o·pole (bĭb′lĭ ə pōl′), n. a bookseller, esp. a dealer in books unique for their rarity, artistic format, etc. Also, bib·li·o·po·list (bĭb′lĭ ŏp′ə lĭst). [t. L: m. bibliopōla, t. Gk.: m. bibliopōlēs] —bib·li·o·pol·ic (bĭb′lĭ ə pŏl′ĭk), bib·li·o·pol′i·cal, adj. —bib·li·op·o·lism (bĭb′lĭ ŏp′ə lĭz′əm), bib·li·op′o·list, n.

Bib·list (bĭb′lĭst, bĭ′blĭst), n. 1. one who regards the Bible as the only rule of faith. 2. a Biblicist.

---

b., blend of, blended; c., cognate with; d., dialect, dialectal; der., derived from; f., formed from; g., going back to; m., modification of; r., replacing; s., stem of; t., taken from; ?, perhaps. See the full key on inside cover.

bib·u·lous (bĭb′yə ləs), *adj.* **1.** addicted to alcoholic drinking. **2.** absorbent; spongy. [t. L: m. *bibulus* freely drinking] —**bib′u·lous·ly**, *adv.* —**bib′u·lous·ness**, *n.*

bi·cam·er·al (bī kăm′ər əl), *adj. Govt.* having two branches, chambers, or houses, as a legislative body.

bicarb., sodium bicarbonate.

bi·car·bo·nate (bī kär′bə nĭt, -nāt′), *n. Chem.* a salt of carbonic acid, containing the HCO₃⁻¹ radical; an acid carbonate, as *sodium bicarbonate*, NaHCO₃.

bice (bīs), *n.* blue or green as of carbonates of copper. [ME *bis*, t. OF: dark-colored, brownish-gray]

bi·cen·te·nar·y (bī sĕn′tə nĕr′Y, bī′sĕn tĕn′ə rY), *adj., n., pl.* -**naries.** *Chiefly Brit.* bicentennial.

bi·cen·ten·ni·al (bī′sĕn tĕn′Y əl), *adj.* **1.** consisting of or lasting 200 years: *a bicentennial period.* **2.** occurring every 200 years. —*n.* **3.** a 200th anniversary. **4.** its celebration. Also, *esp. Brit.*, bicentenary.

bi·ceph·a·lous (bī sĕf′ə ləs), *adj. Bot., Zool.* having two heads. [f. BI- + m. s. Gk. *kephalē* head + -ous]

bi·ceps (bī′sĕps), *n. Anat., Zool.* a muscle having two heads of origin, esp. in *Anat.* **a.** biceps brachii, the muscle on the front of the upper arm, which bends the forearm. **b.** biceps femoris, the hamstring muscle on the back of the thigh. [t. L: two-headed]

bi·chlo·ride (bī klōr′īd, -Yd), *n. Chem.* **1.** a compound in which two atoms of chlorine are combined with another element or radical. **2.** bichloride of mercury.

bichloride of mercury, *Chem.* corrosive sublimate.

bi·chro·mate (bī krō′māt), *n. Chem.* **1.** dichromate. **2.** chromate of potassium, K₂Cr₂O₃.

bi·cip·i·tal (bī sĭp′ə təl), *adj.* **1.** having two heads. **2.** *Anat.* pertaining to the biceps. [f. s. L *biceps* two-headed + -AL¹]

bick·er (bĭk′ər), *v.i.* **1.** to engage in petulant argument; wrangle. **2.** to run rapidly; move quickly; rush; hurry. **3.** to quiver; flicker; glitter. —*n.* **4.** an angry dispute; squabble. [ME *biker(en)*. Cf. MLG *bicken* prick, thrust] —**bick′er·er**, *n.*

Bi·col (bē kōl′), *n.* Bikol.

bi·col·lat·er·al (bī′ka lăt′ər əl), *adj. Bot.* (of a bundle) having the xylem lined with phloem on both its inner and outer faces.

bi·col·or (bī′kŭl′ər), *adj.* of two colors: *a bicolor flower.* Also, **bi′col′ored.**

bi·con·cave (bī kŏn′kāv, bī′kŏn kāv′), *adj.* concave on both sides, as a lens. See illus. under **lens.**

bi·con·vex (bī kŏn′vĕks, bī′kŏn vĕks′), *adj.* convex on both sides, as a lens. See illus. under **lens.**

bi·corn (bī′kôrn), *adj. Bot., Zool.* having two horns or hornlike parts. Also, **bi·cor·nu·ate** (bī kôr′nyŏŏ Yt, -āt′). [t. L: s. *bicornis* two-horned]

bi·cor·po·ral (bī kôr′pə rəl), *adj.* having two bodies. Also, **bi·cor·po·re·al** (bī′kôr pōr′Y əl).

bi·cron (bī′krŏn, bĭk′rŏn), *n. Physics.* one billionth (.000,000,001) of a meter.

bi·cus·pid (bī kŭs′pĭd), *adj.* Also, **bi·cus·pi·date** (bī-kŭs′pĭ dāt′). **1.** having two cusps or points, as certain teeth. —*n.* **2.** *Anat.* one of eight such teeth in man, four on each jaw between the cuspid and the first molar teeth. [f. BI- + s. L *cuspis* point]

bi·cy·cle (bī′sə kəl, -sĭk′əl), *n., v.,* -**cled,** -**cling.** —*n.* **1.** a vehicle with two wheels, one in front of the other, and having a saddlelike seat for the rider. It is steered by turning a handlebar and driven by pedals or a motor. —*v.i.* **2.** to ride a bicycle. [t. F: f. *bi-* BI- + m.s. Gk. *kýklos* circle, wheel] —**bi′cy·cler, bi′cy·clist,** *n.*

bi·cy·clic (bī sī′klĭk, -sĭk′lĭk), *adj.* **1.** consisting of or having two circles. **2.** *Bot.* in two whorls, as the stamens of a flower. Also, **bi·cy·cli·cal.**

bid (bĭd), *v.,* **bade** or **bad** (for 1, 2) or **bid** (for 3-8), **bidden** or **bid, bidding,** *n.* —*v.t.* **1.** to command; order; direct: *bid them depart.* **2.** to say as a greeting or benediction: *to bid farewell.* **3.** *Com.* to offer, as a price at an auction or as terms in a competition to secure a contract. **4.** *Com.* **a.** to overbid all offers for (property) at an auction in order to retain ownership (fol. by *in*). **b.** to increase (the market price) by increasing bids (fol. by *up*). **5.** *Cards.* to enter a bid of a given quantity or suit: *to bid two no-trump, bid spades.* —*v.i.* **6.** to make an offer to purchase at a price. **7.** **bid fair,** to seem likely. —*n.* **8.** act of one who bids. **9.** *Cards.* **a.** the number of points or tricks a player offers to make. **b.** the turn of a person to bid. **10.** *Colloq.* an invitation. **11.** an attempt to attain some goal or purpose: *a bid for election.* [ME *bidde(n)*, OE *(ge)biddan* beg, ask, pray; sense devel. influenced by ME *bede(n)*, OE *bēodan* offer, proclaim, command] —**bid′der**, *n.* —**Syn. 1.** charge.

bi·dar·ka (bī där′kə), *n.* the sealskin boat of the Alaskan Eskimo. Also, **bi·dar·kee** (bī där′kē). [t. Russ., dim. of *baidara* coracle]

bid·da·ble (bĭd′ə bəl), *adj.* **1.** willing to do what is asked; obedient; docile. **2.** *Cards.* adequate to bid upon: *a biddable hand at bridge.*

Bid·de·ford (bĭd′ə fərd), *n.* a city in SW Maine. 19,255 (1960).

bid·den (bĭd′ən), *v.* pp. of bid.

bid·ding (bĭd′Yng), *n.* **1.** invitation; command; order. **2.** a bid. **3.** bids collectively.

Bid·dle (bĭd′əl), *n.* **1.** John, 1615–62, British theologian: founder of Unitarianism in England. **2.** Nicholas, 1786–1844, U.S. financier.

bid·dy (bĭd′Y), *n., pl.* -**dies.** chicken. [orig. uncert.]

bide (bīd), *v.,* **bided** (for 1, 2) or **bode** (for 3), **biding.** —*v.t.* **1.** bide one's time, to wait for a favorable opportunity. **2.** *Archaic.* to encounter. **3.** *Archaic.* to endure; bear. —*v.i.* **4.** *Archaic.* to dwell; abide; wait; remain; continue. [ME *biden*, OE *bīdan*]

bield (bēld), *n. Scot.* shelter.

Bie·le·feld (bē′lə fĕlt′), *n.* a city in N West Germany. 172,732 (est. 1955).

bien en·ten·du (byăN näN täN dY′). *French.* naturally; of course.

Bienne (byĕn), *n.* **Lake of,** a lake in NW Switzerland: traces of prehistoric lake dwellings. 16 sq. mi. Also, **Bie·ler·see** (bē′lər zā′).

bi·en·ni·al (bī ĕn′Y əl), *adj.* **1.** happening every two years: *biennial games.* **2.** *Bot.* completing its normal term of life in two years, flowering and fruiting the second year, as beet, winter wheat. —*n.* **3.** any event occurring once in two years. **4.** *Bot.* a biennial plant. [f. s. L *biennium* two-year period + -AL¹] —**bi·en′ni·al·ly**, *adv.*

bien·ve·nu (byăN və nY′), *adj. French.* welcome. —**bien·ve·nue′**, *adj., fem.*

Bien·ville (byăN vēl′), *n.* **Jean Baptiste Le Moyne, Sieur de** (zhäN bå tēst′ lə mwäN′, syœr də), 1680–1768, French governor of Louisiana: founder of New Orleans.

bier (bYr), *n.* a frame or stand on which a corpse, or the coffin containing it, is laid before burial. [ME *bere*, OE *bēr, bær*, c. G *bahre*]

Bierce (bYrs), *n.* **Ambrose Gwinett** (gwĭ nĕt′), 1842–1914?, U.S. journalist and short-story writer.

biest·ings (bēs′tYngz), *n. pl.* beestings.

bi·fa·cial (bī fā′shəl), *adj.* **1.** having two faces or fronts. **2.** having the opposite surfaces alike. **3.** *Bot.* having the opposite surfaces unlike, as a leaf.

bi·far·i·ous (bī fâr′Y əs), *adj. Bot.* in two vertical rows. [t. L: m. *bifārius* twofold] —**bi·far′i·ous·ly**, *adv.*

biff (bĭf), *U.S. Slang.* —*n.* **1.** a blow; punch. —*v.t.* **2.** to hit; punch.

bif·fin (bĭf′Yn), *n. Brit.* a red variety of winter cooking apple. [var. of *beefing*, f. BEEF (from the color) + -ING¹]

bi·fid (bī′fYd), *adj.* cleft into two parts or lobes. [t. L: s. *bifidus*] —**bi·fid′i·ty**, *n.* —**bi′fid·ly**, *adv.*

bi·fi·lar (bī fī′lər), *adj.* furnished or fitted with two filaments or threads. —**bi·fi′lar·ly**, *adv.*

bi·flag·el·late (bī flăj′ə lāt′, -lYt), *adj. Zool.* having two whiplike appendages or flagella.

bi·flex (bī′flĕks), *adj.* bent at two places.

bi·fo·cal (bī fō′kəl), *adj.* **1.** (esp. in *Optics*) having two foci. **2.** (of spectacle or eyeglass lenses) having two portions, one for near and one for far vision. —*n.* **3.** (*pl.*) eyeglasses with bifocal lenses.

bi·fo·li·ate (bī fō′lY Yt, -āt), *adj.* having two leaves.

bi·forked (bī′fôrkt′), *adj.* bifurcate.

bi·form (bī′fôrm′), *adj.* having or combining two forms, as a centaur, mermaid, etc. Also, **bi′formed′.** [t. L: s. *biformis*]

Bif·rost (bĭv′rŏst), *n. Scand. Myth.* the rainbow bridge of the gods from heaven to earth. [t. Icel.: m. *Bifröst*]

bi·fur·cate (*v.,* *adj.* bī′fər kāt′, bĭ fûr′kāt; *adj.* also -kYt), *v.,* -**cated, cating,** *adj.* —*v.t., v.i.* **1.** to divide or fork into two branches. —*adj.* **2.** divided into two branches. [t. ML: m.s. *bifurcātus*, der. L *bi-* BI- + *furca* fork] —**bi·fur·ca′tion**, *n.*

big (bĭg), *adj.,* **bigger, biggest,** *adv.* —*adj.* **1.** large in size, height, width, amount, etc. **2.** pregnant: *big with child.* **3.** filled; teeming: *eyes big with tears.* **4.** important in influence, standing, wealth, etc.: *the big man of his town.* **5.** haughty; pompous; boastful: *a big talker.* **6.** generous; kindly: *a big person forgives others.* **7.** loud: *a big voice.* **8.** *Obs.* very strong; powerful. —*adv.* **9.** *Colloq.* boastfully: *to talk big.* [ME; orig. uncert.] —**big′gish**, *adj.* —**big′ly**, *adv.* —**big′ness**, *n.* —**Syn. 1.** large, huge, immense; bulky, massive; capacious, voluminous; extensive. See **great.** **4.** important, consequential. **5.** inflated, arrogant. —**Ant. 1.** little, small.

big·a·mist (bĭg′ə mYst), *n.* a person guilty of bigamy.

big·a·mous (bĭg′ə məs), *adj.* **1.** having two wives or husbands at the same time; guilty of bigamy. **2.** involving bigamy. [t. ML: m. *bigamus*, f. *bi-* BI- + *-gamus* (t. Gk.: m. *-gamos* married)] —**big′a·mous·ly**, *adv.*

big·a·my (bĭg′ə mY), *n. Law.* the crime of marrying while one has a wife or husband still living, from whom no valid divorce has been effected. [ME *bigamie*, t. OF, der. *bigame* BIGAMOUS]

big·ar·reau (bĭg′ə rō′, bĭg′ə rō′), *n. Hort.* a kind of large, sweet, heart-shaped cherry with firm flesh. [t. F]

Big Ben, the bell in the clock tower of the Houses of Parliament in London, England.

Big Bertha, *Colloq.* a German gun or cannon, esp. one of large size, as used during World War I.

Big Dipper, *Astron.* the Dipper (def. 3a).

Big Five, **1.** the United States, Great Britain, France, Italy, and Japan in World War I and at the Paris Peace Conference, 1919. **2.** the United States, Great Britain, Russia, China, and France, in the United Nations.

big game, **1.** large animals, esp. when hunted for sport. **2.** an important prize or objective.

big·gin (bĭg′Yn), *n.* **1.** a cap, esp. a child's. **2.** *Brit. Dial.* a nightcap. [t. F: m. *béguin* cap worn by Beguines]

big·ging (bĭg′Yn), *n. Scot. and N. Eng.* a building; home. [der. *big* build (ME *biggen*, t. Scand.)]

ăct, āble, dâre, ärt; ĕbb, ēqual; Yf, īce; hŏt, ōver, ôrder, oil, bŏŏk, ōōze, out; ŭp, ūse, ûrge; ə = a in alone; ch, chief; g, give; ng, ring; sh, shoe; th, thin; t͟h, that; zh, vision. See the full key on inside cover.

big·head (bĭg′hĕd′), *n.* **1.** *Vet. Sci.* an inflammatory swelling of the tissues of the head of sheep. **2.** *Colloq.* conceit. —**big′-head′ed,** *adj.*

big-heart·ed (bĭg′här′tĭd), *adj.* generous; kind.

big·horn (bĭg′hôrn′), *n.*, *pl.* **-horn, -horns.** a wild sheep, *Ovis canadensis*, of the Rocky Mountains, with large, curving horns.

Big Horn, a river flowing from central Wyoming to the Yellowstone river in S Montana. 336 mi.

Big Horn Mountains, a mountain range in N Wyoming, in the Rocky Mountains. Highest peak, Cloud Peak, 13,165 ft. Also, **Big Horns.**

Bighorn. *Ovis canadensis*
(3¼ ft. high at the shoulder.
5 ft. 10 in. long)

bight (bīt), *n.* **1.** the part of a rope between the ends. **2.** the loop or bent part of a rope, as distinguished from the ends. **3.** a bend or curve in the shore of a sea or a river. **4.** a body of water bounded by such a bend; a bay. —*v.t.* **5.** to fasten with a bight of rope. [ME *byght*, OE *byht* a bend]

big·no·ni·a (bĭg nō′nĬ ə), *n.* any plant of the genus *Bignonia*, which comprises climbing shrubs, American and mostly tropical, much cultivated for their showy trumpet-shaped flowers. [t. NL; named after Bignon, librarian to Louis XV]

big·no·ni·a·ceous (bĭg nō′nĬ ā′shəs), *adj. Bot.* belonging or pertaining to the *Bignoniaceae*, a family of plants including trumpet creeper, catalpa, etc.

big·ot (bĭg′ət), *n.* a person who is intolerantly convinced of a particular creed, opinion, practice, etc. [t. F; orig. uncert.]

big·ot·ed (bĭg′ə tĭd), *adj.* intolerantly convinced of a particular creed, practice, etc. —**big′ot·ed·ly,** *adv.*

big·ot·ry (bĭg′ə trĬ), *n.*, *pl.* **-ries.** **1.** intolerant attachment to a particular creed, opinion, practice, etc. **2.** actions or beliefs of a bigot.

big tree, an extremely large coniferous tree of California, *Sequoiadendron giganteum* (formerly *Sequoia gigantea*). Cf. **sequoia.**

big·wig (bĭg′wĭg′), *n. Colloq.* a very important person.

Bi·har (bē här′), *n.* **1.** a state in NE India. 38,779,562 pop. (est. 1956); 67,164 sq. mi. *Cap.*: Patna. **2.** a city in this state. 63,124 (1951).

Bihar and O·ris·sa (ōrĬs′ə). a former province in NE India: now divided into **Bihar** and **Orissa.**

bi·hour·ly (bī our′lĬ), *adj.* occurring every two hours.

bi·jou (bē′zhoo, bē zhoo′), *n.*, *pl.* **-joux** (-zhooz, -zhooz′). **1.** a jewel. **2.** something small and choice. [t. F]

bi·jou·te·rie (bē zhoo′tə rĬ), *n.* jewelry. [t. F]

bi·ju·gate (bī′joo gāt′, bĬ joo′gāt), *adj. Bot.* (of leaves) having two pairs of leaflets or pinnae. Also, **bi·ju·gous** (bĬ′joo gəs). [f. BI- + JUGATE]

Bi·ka·ner (bē′kə nĬr′), *n.* **1.** formerly a native state in NW India, in Rajputana. Now in Rajasthan. **2.** former capital of native state. 117,113 (1951).

bike (bīk), *n.*, *v.*, **biked, biking.** *Colloq.* bicycle. [alter. of BICYCLE]

Bi·ki·ni (bē kē′nē), *n.* an atoll in the N Pacific, in the Marshall Islands: atomic bomb tests, 1946. 3 sq. mi.

bi·ki·ni (bĬ kē′nĬ), *n.* a very brief swimsuit.

Bi·kol (bē kōl′), *n.* a member of a Malayan tribe in SE Luzon and nearby Philippine islands, converted to Christianity early in the Spanish conquest. Also, **Bicol.**

bi·la·bi·al (bī lā′bĬ əl), *Phonet.* —*adj.* **1.** pronounced with the two lips brought close together or touching. In the English bilabial consonants *p, b,* and *m,* the lips touch; in the bilabial *w,* they do not. —*n.* **2.** a bilabial speech sound.

bi·la·bi·ate (bī lā′bĬ āt′, -Ĭt), *adj. Bot.* two-lipped, as a corolla.

bi·lan·der (bĬl′ən dər, bī′lən-), *n. Naut.* a small merchant vessel with two masts, used on canals and along the coast in Holland, etc. [t. D: m. *bijlander*, f. *bij* by + *land* land + *-er* -ER[1]]

bi·lat·er·al (bī lăt′ər əl), *adj.* **1.** *Bot., Zool.* pertaining to both sides. **1.** *bilateral symmetry.* **2.** pertaining to or affecting two or both sides. **3.** disposed on opposite sides of an axis; two-sided; often, symmetrical. **4.** *Law, etc.* (of a contract) binding the parties to reciprocal obligations. —**bi·lat′er·al·ism, bi·lat′-er·al·ness,** *n.* —**bi·lat′er·al·ly,** *adv.*

Bilabiate calyx and corolla of sage, *Salvia*

Bil·ba·o (bĕl bä′ō), *n.* a seaport in N Spain, near the Bay of Biscay. 252,460 (est. 1955).

bil·ber·ry (bĬl′bĕr′Ĭ), *n.*, *pl.* **-ries.** the fruit of the shrub of several species of *Vaccinium*. [f. *bil* (t. Scand.; cf. Dan. *bölle* bilberry) + BERRY]

bil·bo[1] (bĬl′bō), *n.*, *pl.* **-boes.** (usually *pl.*) a long iron bar or bolt with sliding shackles and a lock, formerly used to confine the feet of prisoners. [orig. uncert.]

Bilbo

bil·bo[2] (bĬl′bō), *n.*, *pl.* **-boes.** *Archaic.* a sword. [short for *Bilbo sword* sword of Bilbao (Spain)]

bile (bīl), *n.* **1.** *Physiol.* a bitter yellow or greenish liquid secreted by the liver and aiding in digestion, principally by emulsifying fats. **2.** ill nature; peevishness. [t. F, t. L: m. s. *bilis*]

bi·lec·tion (bĬ lĕk′shən), *n. Archit.* bolection.

bile-stone (bīl′stōn′), *n. Pathol.* a gallstone.

bilge (bĬlj), *n.*, *v.*, **bilged, bilging.** —*n.* **1.** *Naut.* **a.** the approximately flat under portion of a ship's hull. **b.** the lowest portion of a ship's interior. **c.** Also, **bilge water.** foul water that collects in a ship's bilge. **2.** *Slang.* foolishness. **3.** the wider part or belly of a cask. —*v.i.* **4.** *Naut.* to spring a leak in the bilge. **5.** to bulge or swell out. —*v.t.* **6.** to break in the bilge of. [orig. unknown]

bilge keel, *Naut.* either of two keellike projections extending lengthwise along a ship's bilge, one on each side, to retard rolling. Also, **bilge piece.**

bilg·y (bĬl′jĬ), *adj. Naut.* smelling like bilge water.

bil·i·ar·y (bĬl′Ĭ ĕr′Ĭ), *adj.* **1.** *Physiol.* **a.** of bile. **b.** conveying bile: *a biliary duct.* **2.** *Pathol.* bilious: *biliary colic.* [t. NL: m. *biliaris*, der. L *bilis* bile]

bi·lin·e·ar (bī lĬn′Ĭ ər), *adj. Math.* of, pertaining to, or having reference to two lines: *bilinear coördinates.*

bi·lin·gual (bī lĬng′gwəl), *adj.* **1.** able to speak one's native language and another with approximately equal facility. **2.** expressed or contained in two different languages. —*n.* **3.** a bilingual person. [f. s. L *bilinguis* speaking two languages + -AL[1]] —**bi·lin′gual·ly,** *adv.*

bi·lin·gual·ism (bī lĬng′gwə lĬz′əm), *n.* **1.** habitual use of two languages. **2.** ability in being bilingual.

bil·ious (bĬl′yəs), *adj.* **1.** *Physiol., Pathol.* pertaining to bile or to an excess secretion of bile. **2.** *Pathol.* suffering from, caused by, or attended by trouble with the bile or liver. **3.** peevish; testy; cross. [t. L: m. s. *biliosus* full of bile] —**bil′ious·ly,** *adv.* —**bil′ious·ness,** *n.*

-bility, a suffix forming nouns from adjectives in *-ble,* as in *nobility.* [ME *-bilite,* t. F, t. L: m. s. *-bilitas*]

bilk (bĬlk), *v.t.* **1.** to evade payment of (a debt). **2.** to defraud; cheat. **3.** to frustrate. **4.** to escape from; elude. —*n.* **5.** a trick; a fraud. **6.** a cheater; a swindler. [orig. unknown] —**bilk′er,** *n.*

bill[1] (bĬl), *n.* **1.** an account of money owed for goods or services supplied. **2.** a bill of exchange. **3.** *U.S.* a piece of paper money (usually with its amount): *a dollar bill.* **4.** *Govt.* a form or draft of a proposed statute presented to a legislature, but not yet enacted or passed and made law. **5.** a written or printed public notice or advertisement. *post no bills.* **6.** any written paper containing a statement of particulars: *a bill of charges or expenditures.* **7.** *Law.* a written statement, usually of complaint, presented to a court. **8.** a printed theater program or the like. **9.** program; entertainment: *good bill at the theater.* **10.** *Obs.* an acknowledgment of debt; a promissory note. —*v.t.* **11.** to enter in a bill; make a bill or list of: *to bill goods.* **12.** to charge for by bill; send a bill to: *the store will bill me.* **13.** to announce by bill or public notice: *a new actor was billed for this week.* **14.** to schedule on a program. [ME *bille,* t. Anglo-L: m. *billa,* var. of ML *bulla* seal (see BULLA)] —**Syn. 5.** bulletin.

bill[2] (bĬl), *n.* **1.** that part of the jaws of a bird covered with a horny sheath; a beak. —*v.i.* **2.** to join bills or beaks, as doves. [ME; OE *bile* beak]

bill[3] (bĬl), *n.* **1.** a medieval shafted weapon with a broad hook-shaped blade and a spike at the back. **2.** a sharp, hooked instrument used for pruning, etc.; billhook. **3.** *Naut.* the point or extremity of the fluke of an anchor. [OE *bill* sword, c. G *bille* pickax]

bill[4] (bĬl), *n.* the cry of the bittern. [cf. OE *bylgan* bellow, c. Icel. *bylga* roar]

bil·la·bong (bĬl′ə bŏng′), *n. Australia.* **1.** a branch of a river flowing away from the main stream, in some cases returning to it lower down. **2.** a stagnant backwater. [native Australian]

bill·board[1] (bĬl′bôrd′), *n. U.S.* a board on which notices or advertisements are posted. [f. BILL[1] (def. 5) + BOARD]

bill·board[2] (bĬl′bôrd′), *n. Naut.* a projection placed abaft the cathead, for the bill or fluke of an anchor to rest on. [f. BILL[3] (def. 3) + BOARD]

bil·let[1] (bĬl′Ĭt), *n.*, *v.*, **-leted, -leting.** —*n.* **1.** lodging for a soldier, esp. lodging in private or nonmilitary public buildings. **2.** *Mil.* an official order, written or verbal, directing the person to whom it is addressed to provide such lodging. **3.** a place assigned, as to each of the crew of a man-of-war for slinging his hammock. **4.** job; appointment. **5.** a small paper or note in writing. —*v.t.* **6.** *Mil.* to direct (a soldier) by ticket, note, or verbal order, where to lodge. **7.** to provide lodging for; quarter. [ME *billette,* t. OF, b. *bille* a writing and *bullette* certificate, der. *bulle* BULL[2]]

bil·let[2] (bĬl′Ĭt), *n.* **1.** a small thick stick of wood, esp. one cut for fuel. **2.** *Metall.* a bar or slab of iron or steel, esp. when obtained from an ingot by forging, etc. **3.** *Archit.* one of a series of short rods forming part of a molding. **4.** a short strap used for connecting various straps and portions of a harness. **5.** a pocket or loop into which the end of a strap is inserted after passing through a buckle. [ME *billette,* t. OF: m. *billete,* dim. of *bille* log]

Architectural billets

bil·let-doux (bĭl′ĭ dōō′, bĭl′ā-; Fr. bē yĕ dōō′), n., pl. **billets-doux** (bĭl′ĭ dōōz′, bĭl′ā-; Fr. bē yĕ dōō′). a love letter. [t. F: lit., sweet note]

bill·fish (bĭl′fĭsh′), n., pl. **-fishes,** (esp. collectively) **-fish.** one of various fishes with a long beak or snout, as the gar, needlefish, or spearfish.

bill·fold (bĭl′fōld′), n. U.S. a folding leather case for carrying banknotes, personal cards, etc.

bill·head (bĭl′hĕd′), n. **1.** a printed heading on paper for making out bills. **2.** a sheet of paper with such a heading. **3.** a printed form for itemized statements.

bill·hook (bĭl′hŏŏk′), n. bill³ (def. 2).

bil·liard (bĭl′yərd), adj. **1.** of or used in billiards. —n. **2.** U.S. Colloq. carom (def. 1).

bil·liards (bĭl′yərdz), n. a game played by two or more persons on a rectangular table enclosed by an elastic ledge or cushion, with balls (**billiard balls**) of ivory or other hard material, driven by means of cues. [t. F: m. billard, der. bille log. Cf. BILLET²] —**bil′liard·ist,** n.

bill·ing (bĭl′ĭng), n. the relative position in which a performer or act is listed on handbills, posters, etc.

Bil·lings (bĭl′ĭngz), n. **1.** a city in S Montana. 52,851 (1960). **2.** Josh, pen name of H. W. Shaw.

bil·lings·gate (bĭl′ĭngz gāt′; esp. Brit. -gĭt), n. coarse language or abuse. [orig., the kind of language heard at Billingsgate, a gate and fish market in London]

bil·lion (bĭl′yən), n. **1.** U.S. a thousand millions. **2.** Brit. a million millions. [t. F: f. bi- + (mi)llion, i.e., the second power of one million (def. 2 agrees with earlier, def. 1 with later F usage)] —**bil′lionth,** adj., n.

bil·lion·aire (bĭl′yə nâr′), n. the owner of a billion dollars, francs, pounds, etc.

Bil·li·ton (bĕl′lē tŏn′, bĭ′lē′tŏn), n. an island in Indonesia, SW of Borneo. 73,429 pop. (1930); 1866 sq. mi. Also, **Belitong.**

bill of attainder, a legal act depriving a person of his property if found guilty of treason or felony.

bill of exchange, a written authorization or order to pay a specified sum of money to a specified person.

bill of fare, a list of foods that are served; menu.

bill of health, a certificate as to the health of a ship's company at the time of her clearing any port.

bill of lading, a written receipt given by a carrier for goods accepted for transportation.

bill of rights, 1. a formal statement of the fundamental rights of the people of a nation. **2.** (cap.) such a statement incorporated in the Constitution of the United States as Amendments 1–10, and in all State constitutions. **3.** (caps.) an English statute of 1689 confirming, with minor changes, the Declaration of Rights, declaring the rights and liberties of the subjects and settling the succession in William III and Mary II.

bill of sale, a document transferring title in personal property from seller to buyer.

bil·lon (bĭl′ən), n. **1.** an alloy used in coinage, consisting of gold or silver with a preponderating admixture of some base metal. **2.** an alloy of silver with copper or the like, used for coins of small denomination. **3.** any coin struck from such an alloy. [t. F, der. bille log]

bil·low (bĭl′ō), n. **1.** a great wave or surge of the sea. **2.** any surging mass: billows of smoke. —v.i. **3.** to rise or roll in or like billows; surge. [t. Scand.; cf. Icel. bylgja]

bil·low·y (bĭl′ō ĭ), adj., **-lower, -lowiest.** full of billows; surging: billowy flames. —**bil′low·i·ness,** n.

bill-post·er (bĭl′pōs′tər), n. one who posts bills and advertisements. Also, **bill-stick·er** (bĭl′stĭk′ər).

bil·ly (bĭl′ĭ), n., pl. **-lies. 1.** Colloq. a policeman's club. **2.** a small cudgel. **3.** Also, **bil·ly·can** (bĭl′ĭ kăn′). Australia. tin kettle or pot, used by bushmen in making tea. [special use of Billy, pet var. of William, man's name]

bil·ly·cock (bĭl′ĭ kŏk′), n. **1.** Brit. a round, low-crowned, soft felt hat. **2.** a derby hat. [var. of bully-cocked (hat), i.e. hat cocked in the style of a bully]

billy goat, a male goat.

bi·lo·bate (bī lō′bāt), adj. having or divided into two lobes. Also, **bi·lo·bat·ed, bi·lobed** (bī′lōbd′).

bi·loc·u·lar (bī lŏk′yə lər), adj. divided into two chambers or cells, or containing two cells internally. Also, **bi·loc·u·late** (bī lŏk′yə lĭt, -lāt′).

Bi·lox·i (bĭ lŏk′sĭ), n. a city in SE Mississippi, on the Gulf of Mexico. 44,053 (1960).

bil·sted (bĭl′stĕd), n. the liquidambar tree.

bil·tong (bĭl′tŏng′), n. (in South Africa) strips of lean meat dried in the open air. [t. S Afr. D]

bim·a·nous (bĭm′ə nəs, bī mā′-), adj. Zool. two-handed. [f. s. NL bimana (animālia) two-handed (animals) + -ous]

bi·man·u·al (bī măn′yŏŏ əl), adj. involving the use of both hands. —**bi·man′u·al·ly,** adv.

bi·men·sal (bī mĕn′səl), adj. occurring once in two months; bimonthly.

bi·mes·tri·al (bī mĕs′trĭ əl), adj. **1.** occurring every two months; bimonthly. **2.** lasting two months. [f. L bimestri(s) of two months' duration + -AL¹]

bi·me·tal·lic (bī′mə tăl′ĭk), adj. **1.** of two metals. **2.** pertaining to bimetallism. [t. F: m. bimétallique]

bi·met·al·ism (bī mĕt′ə lĭz′əm), n. the use of two metals, ordinarily gold and silver, at a fixed relative value, as the monetary standard. **2.** the doctrine or policies supporting such a standard. —**bi·met′al·list,** n.

bi·month·ly (bī mŭnth′lĭ), adj., n., pl. **-lies,** adv. —adj. **1.** occurring every two months. **2.** occurring twice a

month; semimonthly. —n. **3.** a bimonthly publication. —adv. **4.** every two months. **5.** twice a month; semimonthly.

bi·mo·tored (bī mō′tərd), adj. Aeron. having two separate engines.

bin (bĭn), n., v., **binned, binning.** —n. **1.** a box or enclosed place used for storing grain, coal, and the like. —v.t. **2.** to store in a bin. [ME binne, OE binn(e) crib]

bin-, a form of bi-, sometimes used before a vowel, as in binoxide. [prob. t. L: m. bīnī two apiece]

bi·nal (bī′nəl), adj. **1.** double; twofold. **2.** Phonet. (of a syllable) having two pitch peaks. [t. NL: s. bīnālis, der. L bīnī two apiece. Cf. G zweigipfelig]

bi·na·ry (bī′nə rĭ), adj., n., pl. **-ries.** —adj. **1.** consisting of, indicating, or involving two. —n. **2.** a whole composed of two. **3.** Astron. a binary star. [t. L: m. s. bīnārius consisting of two things]

binary compound, Chem. a compound containing only two elements or radicals.

binary star, Astron. a system of two stars which revolve round their common center of gravity.

binary system, any system of counting or measurement whose units are powers of two.

bi·nate (bī′nāt), adj. Bot. double; produced or borne in pairs. [t. NL: m. s. bīnātus, der. L bīnī two at a time] —**bi′nate·ly,** adv.

bin·au·ral (bĭn ôr′əl), adj. **1.** of, with, or for both ears: binaural hearing, a binaural stethoscope. **2.** having two ears.

binaural broadcasting, a system of radio broadcasting in which a microphone in one part of a studio broadcasts via FM and one in another part via AM. FM and AM receivers similarly placed provide a stereophonic effect.

Binate leaf

bind (bīnd), v., **bound, binding,** n. —v.t. **1.** to make fast with a band or bond. **2.** to encircle with a band or ligature: bind one's hair up. **3.** to swathe or bandage (often fol. by up). **4.** to fasten around; fix in place by girding. **5.** to cause to cohere. **6.** to unite by any legal or moral tie: bound by duty, debt, etc. **7.** to hold to a particular state, place, employment, etc. **8.** to place under obligation or compulsion (usually passive): all are bound to obey the laws. **9.** Law. to put under legal obligation (often with over): to bind a man over to keep the peace. **10.** to make compulsory or obligatory: to bind the order with a deposit. **11.** to indenture as an apprentice (often fol. by out). **12.** Pathol. to hinder or restrain (the bowels) from their natural operations; constipate. **13.** to fasten or secure within a cover, as a book. **14.** to cover the edge of, as for protection or ornament. —v.i. **15.** to become compact or solid; cohere. **16.** to be obligatory: an obligation that binds. **17.** to tie up anything, esp. sheaves of grain. —n. **18.** something that binds. **19.** Music. a tie, slur or brace. [ME binden, OE bindan, c. G binden] —Syn. **1.** gird, fasten, attach, tie. —Ant. **1.** free.

bind·er (bīn′dər), n. **1.** person or thing that binds. **2.** a detachable cover for loose papers. **3.** one who binds books; a bookbinder. **4.** Agric. a. an attachment to a harvester or reaper for binding the cut grain. b. a machine that both cuts and binds grain. **5.** Law. an informal contract, operative pending the execution of a more formal document. **6.** Metall. a substance used: a. to hold crushed ore dust together before and during sintering or refining. b. to hold metallic powders (mixed sometimes with nonmetals) together after compacting and before sintering in powder metallurgy.

bind·er·y (bīn′də rĭ), n., pl. **-eries.** an establishment for binding books.

bind·ing (bīn′dĭng), n. **1.** act of fastening or uniting. **2.** anything that binds. **3.** the covering within which the leaves of a book are bound. **4.** a strip that protects or adorns the edge of cloth, etc. —adj. **5.** having power to bind or oblige; obligatory: a binding engagement. —**bind′ing·ly,** adv. —**bind′ing·ness,** n.

bind·weed (bīnd′wēd′), n. any of various twining or vinelike plants, esp. certain species of Convolvulus.

bine (bīn), n. **1.** a twining plant stem, as of the hop. **2.** any bindweed. **3.** woodbine (defs. 1, 2). [var. of BIND]

Bi·net (bǐ nā′; Fr. bē nĕ′), n. Alfred (ȧl frĕd′), 1857–1911, French psychologist: deviser of Binet test.

Bi·net test (bĭ nā′; Fr. bē nĕ′), Psychol. a test for determining the relative development of the intelligence of children and others, consisting of a series of questions and tasks graded with reference to the ability of the normal child to deal with them at successive age levels. Also, **Binet-Si·mon test** (-sī′mən; Fr. -sē mōn′).

binge (bĭnj), n. Slang. a spree; a period of excessive indulgence, as in eating or drinking.

Bing·en (bĭng′ən), n. a town in W West Germany, on the Rhine: whirlpool; tourist center. 17,900 (1950).

Bing·ham·ton (bĭng′əm tən), n. a city in S New York, on the Susquehanna river. 75,941 (1960).

bin·go (bĭng′gō), n. a game similar to lotto; beano.

Binh Dinh (bĭn′y dĭn′y, bĭn′ dĭn′), n. a city in E Indochina, in Vietnam. ab. 147,000.

bin·na·cle (bĭn′ə kəl), n. Naut. a special stand of nonmagnetic material built in the hull for housing the compass and fitted with lights by which the compass can be read at night. [earlier bittacle, t. Pg.: m. bitácola, or t. Sp.: m. bitácula, ult. t. L: m. habitāculum dwelling place]

bin·o·cle (bĭn′ə kəl), n. binocular. [t. F, t. NL: m. s. bīn(ī) two at a time + m. oculus eye]

bin·oc·u·lar (bə nŏk′yə lər, bī-), *adj.* 1. involving two eyes: *binocular vision.* —*n.* 2. (*often pl.*) a double telescope, microscope, or field glass used by both eyes at once. —**bin·oc′u·lar/i·ty,** *n.* —**bin·oc′u·lar·ly,** *adv.*

bi·no·mi·al (bī nō′mǐ əl), *n.* 1. *Alg.* an expression which is a sum or difference of two terms, as $3x+2y$ and x^2-4x. 2. *Zool., Bot.* a name of two terms, denoting respectively genus and species, as *Felis leo,* the lion. —*adj.* 3. *Alg.* consisting of or pertaining to two terms or a binomial. 4. *Zool., Bot.* consisting of or characterized by binomials. [f. s. LL *binōmius* having two names + -AL¹] —**bi·no′mi·al·ly,** *adv.*

binomial distribution, *Statistics.* a distribution giving the probability of obtaining a specified number of successes in a set of trials where each trial can end in either a success or a failure.

bi·nu·cle·ate (bī nū′klǐ āt′, -nōō′-), *adj.* having two nuclei, as some cells. Also, **bi·nu′cle·ar, bi·nu′cle·at′ed.**

Bin·yon (bĭn′yən), *n.* Lawrence, 1869–1943, British poet, translator, and art historian.

bio-, a word element meaning "life," "living things," as in *biology.* [t. Gk., comb. form of *bios* life]

bi·o·as·tro·nau·tics (bī′ō ăs′trə nô′tĭks), *n.* (construed as sing.) the science dealing with the effects of space travel on animals and plants.

Bí·o-Bí·o (bē′ō bē′ō), *n.* a river in central Chile from the Andes NW to the Pacific at Concepción. ab. 250 mi.

bi·o·cat·a·lyst (bī′ō kăt′ə lĭst), *n. Biochem.* a substance, as an enzyme, vitamin, or hormone, which acts as a biochemical catalyst.

bi·o·cel·late (bī ŏs′ə lāt′, bī′ō sĕl′ĭt), *adj. Zool., Bot.* marked with two ocelli or eyelike parts.

bi·o·chem·is·try (bī′ō kĕm′ĭs trĭ), *n.* the chemistry of living matter. *Abbrev.:* **biochem.** —**bi·o·chem′i·cal** (bī′ō kĕm′ə kəl), **bi·o·chem′ic,** *adj.* —**bi·o·chem′i·cal·ly,** *adv.* —**bi′o·chem′ist,** *n.*

bi·o·dy·nam·ics (bī′ō dī năm′ĭks, -dĭ′-), *n.* the branch of biology that treats of energy, or of the activity of living organisms (opposed to *biostatics*). —**bi′o·dy·nam′ic, bi′o·dy·nam′i·cal,** *adj.*

biog., 1. biographical. 2. biography.

bi·o·gen (bī′ə jən), *n. Biol., Biochem.* a hypothetical protein molecule, large and unstable, assumed to be basic to fundamental biological processes, as assimilation and dissimilation.

bi·o·gen·e·sis (bī′ō jĕn′ə sĭs), *n. Biol.* the doctrine that living organisms come from other living organisms. Also, **bi·og·e·ny** (bī ŏj′ə nĭ). —**bi·o·ge·net·ic** (bī′ō jə nĕt′ĭk), *adj.* —**bi·o·ge·net′i·cal·ly,** *adv.*

bi·o·ge·og·ra·phy (bī′ō jĭ ŏg′rə fĭ), *n. Ecol.* the study of the geographical distribution of living things.

bi·og·ra·pher (bī ŏg′rə fər, bĭ-), *n.* a writer of biography.

bi·o·graph·i·cal (bī′ə grăf′ə kəl), *adj.* 1. of or pertaining to a person's life. 2. pertaining to biography. Also, **bi′o·graph′ic.** —**bi′o·graph′i·cal·ly,** *adv.*

bi·og·ra·phy (bī ŏg′rə fĭ, bĭ-), *n., pl.* **-phies.** 1. a written account of a person's life. 2. such writings collectively. [t. Gk.: m. s. *biographia*]

biol., 1. biological. 2. biography.

bi·o·log·i·cal (bī′ə lŏj′ə kəl), *adj.* Also, **bi′o·log′ic.** 1. pertaining to biology. 2. of or pertaining to the products and operations of applied biology: *a biological preparation or test.* —*n.* 3. *Biol., Pharm.* any biochemical product, esp. serums, vaccines, etc., produced from microörganisms. —**bi′o·log′i·cal·ly,** *adv.*

biological warfare, warfare which makes use of biologically-produced poisons that affect man, domestic animals or food crops, esp. bacteria or viruses. Also, **B.W.**

bi·ol·o·gy (bī ŏl′ə jĭ), *n.* the science of life or living matter in all its forms and phenomena, often esp. with reference to origin, growth, reproduction, structure, etc. —**bi·ol′o·gist,** *n.*

bi·o·lu·mi·nes·cence (bī′ō lōō′mə nĕs′əns), *n.* the production of light by living organisms. —**bi′o·lu′mi·nes′cent,** *adj.*

bi·ol·y·sis (bī ŏl′ə sĭs), *n. Biol.* dissolution of a living being; death; the destruction of the phenomena of life. —**bi·o·lyt·ic** (bī′ə lĭt′ĭk), *adj.*

bi·o·met·rics (bī′ō mĕt′rĭks), *n.* 1. *Biol.* the application of mathematical-statistical theory to biology. 2. biometry. —**bi′o·met′ric, bi′o·met′ri·cal,** *adj.* —**bi′o·met′ri·cal·ly,** *adv.*

bi·om·e·try (bī ŏm′ə trĭ), *n.* the calculation of the probable duration of human life.

Bi·on (bī′ŏn), *n.* fl. c100 B.C., Greek pastoral poet.

bi·o·nom·ics (bī′ō nŏm′ĭks), *n.* ecology (def. 1). [f. BIO- + -*nomics,* as in ECONOMICS] —**bi′o·nom′ic, bi′o·nom′i·cal,** *adj.* —**bi′o·nom′i·cal·ly,** *adv.* —**bi·on·o·mist** (bī ŏn′ə mĭst), *n.*

bi·o·phys·ics (bī′ō fĭz′ĭks), *n.* that branch of biology which deals with biological structures and processes in terms of physics. —**bi′o·phys′i·cal,** *adj.*

bi·op·sy (bī′ŏp sĭ), *n. Med.* the excision and diagnostic study of a piece of tissue from a living body.

bi·o·scope (bī′ō skōp′), *n.* an early form of motion-picture projector (about 1900).

bi·os·co·py (bī ŏs′kə pĭ), *n. Med.* examination of the body to discover whether or not it is alive.

-biosis, a word element meaning "way of life," as in *symbiosis.* [comb. form repr. Gk. *bíōsis*]

bi·o·stat·ics (bī′ō stăt′ĭks), *n.* the branch of biology

that treats of the structure of organisms in relation to their functions (opposed to *biodynamics*). —**bi′o·stat′ic, bi′o·stat′i·cal,** *adj.*

bi·o·ta (bī ō′tə), *n. Ecol.* the animal and plant life of a region or period. [t. NL, t. Gk.: m. *biotē* life]

bi·ot·ic (bī ŏt′ĭk), *adj.* concerning life. Also, **bi·ot′i·cal.**

bi·o·tin (bī′ə tĭn), *n. Biochem,* a crystalline acid, $C_{10}H_{16}N_2O_3S$, one of the vitamin B complex factors; vitamin H. It will prevent the death of animals that have been fed large quantities of raw white of eggs.

bi·o·tite (bī′ə tīt′), *n.* a very common mineral of the mica group, occurring in dark-black, brown, or green sheets and scales, an important constituent of igneous rocks. [named after J. B. *Biot* (1774–1862), French physicist. See -ITE¹] —**bi·o·tit·ic** (bī′ə tĭt′ĭk), *adj.*

bi·o·type (bī′ə tīp′), *n. Biol.* a group of organisms with the same hereditary characteristics; genotype. —**bi′o·typ·ic** (bī′ə tĭp′ĭk), *adj.*

bi·pa·ri·e·tal (bī′pə rī′ə təl), *adj. Anat.* pertaining to both parietal bones.

bip·a·rous (bĭp′ə rəs), *adj.* 1. *Zool.* bringing forth offspring in pairs. 2. *Bot.* bearing two branches or axes.

bi·par·ti·san (bī pär′tə zən), *adj.* representing or characterized by two parties. —**bi·par′ti·san·ship′,** *n.*

bi·par·tite (bī pär′tīt), *adj.* 1. *Law.* being in two corresponding parts: *a bipartite contract.* 2. *Bot.* divided into two parts nearly to the base, as a leaf. [t. L: m. s. *bipartītus,* pp., divided into two parts] —**bi·par′tite·ly,** *adv.* —**bi·par·ti·tion** (bī′pär tĭsh′ən), *n.*

bi·ped (bī′pĕd), *Zool.* —*n.* 1. a two-footed animal. —*adj.* 2. having two feet. [t. L: s. *bipēs* two-footed]

bi·pe·dal (bī′pə dəl, bĭp′ə-), *adj.* biped.

bi·pet·al·ous (bī pĕt′əl əs), *adj. Bot.* having two petals.

bi·phen·yl (bī fĕn′əl, -fē′nəl), *n. Chem.* a colorless crystalline compound, $C_6H_5C_6H_5$, composed of two phenyl groups. The benzidine dyes are derivatives of biphenyl.

bi·pin·nate (bī pĭn′āt), *adj. Bot.* pinnate, as a leaf, with the divisions also pinnate.

bi·plane (bī′plān′), *n.* an airplane with two wings, one above and usually slightly forward of the other.

bi·pod (bī′pŏd), *n.* a two-legged support, as for an automatic rifle. [f. BI- + -POD. Cf. TRIPOD.]

Bipinnate leaf

bi·po·lar (bī pō′lər), *adj.* 1. having two poles. 2. pertaining to or found at both poles. —**bi·po·lar·i·ty** (bī′pō lăr′ə tĭ), *n.*

bi·quad·rate (bī kwŏd′rāt, -rĭt), *n. Math.* the fourth power.

bi·quad·rat·ic (bī′kwŏd răt′ĭk), *adj. Math.* involving the fourth power of the unknown or variable.

bi·ra·di·al symmetry (bī rā′dǐ əl), *Biol.* symmetry manifested both bilaterally and radially in the same creature, as in ctenophores.

birch (bûrch), *n.* 1. any tree or shrub of the genus *Betula,* comprising species with a smooth, laminated outer bark and close-grained wood. 2. the wood itself. 3. a birch rod, or a bundle of birch twigs, used as a whip. —*adj.* 4. birchen. —*v.t.* 5. to beat or punish with a birch. [ME *birche,* OE *bierce,* c. G *birke*]

birch·en (bûr′chən), *adj.* 1. of or pertaining to birch. 2. consisting or made of birch.

bird (bûrd), *n.* 1. any of the *Aves,* a class of warm-blooded vertebrates having a body more or less completely covered with feathers, and the forelimbs so modified as to form wings by means of which most species fly. 2. *Sports.* a. a game bird. b. a clay pigeon. 3. *Slang.* a person, esp. one having some peculiarity. 4. *Slang.* a sound of derision: *to get the bird.* 5. *Archaic.* the young of any fowl. —*v.i.* 6. to catch or shoot birds. [ME *byrd, bryd,* OE *brid(d)* young bird, chick]

bird call, 1. a sound made by a bird. 2. a sound imitating that of a bird. 3. a device used to imitate the sound of a bird.

bird dog, a dog trained to help hunt birds, usually a pointer or setter, sometimes a spaniel.

bird-foot (bûrd′fōōt′), *n.* bird's-foot.

bird grass, 1. a grass, *Poa trivialis,* grown in temperate climates of North America largely for lawns and turf. 2. knotgrass, *Polygonum aviculare.*

bird·ie (bûr′dĭ), *n.* 1. bird; small bird. 2. *Golf.* a score of one stroke under par on a hole.

bird·lime (bûrd′līm′), *n., v.,* **-limed, -liming.** —*n.* 1. a sticky material, prepared from holly, mistletoe or other plants and smeared on twigs to catch small birds that light on it. —*v.t.* 2. to smear or catch with or as with birdlime.

bird·man (bûrd′măn′, -mən), *n., pl.* **-men** (-mĕn′, -mən). 1. fowler. 2. ornithologist. 3. *Colloq.* aviator.

bird of paradise, any bird of the family *Paradiseidae,* of New Guinea, etc., noted for magnificent plumage, as *Paradisea apoda.*

bird of passage, a bird that migrates seasonally.

bird of peace, dove.

bird of prey, *Ornith.* any of numerous predacious, flesh-eating birds such as the eagles, hawks, kites, vultures, owls, etc., most of which have strong beaks and claws for catching, killing and tearing to pieces the animals on which they feed.

---

bird pepper, a variety of extremely strong pepper, *Capsicum frutescens,* with small, elongated berries.

bird-seed (bûrd'sēd'), *n.* small seed, esp. that of a grass, *Phalaris canariensis,* used as food for birds.

bird's-eye (bûrdz'ī'), *adj.* 1. seen from above: *a bird's-eye view of a city.* 2. general; not detailed: *a bird's-eye view of history.* 3. having spots or markings resembling birds' eyes: *bird's-eye maple.* —*n.* 4. any of various plants with small, round, bright-colored flowers, as a primrose, *Primula farinosa,* or the germander speedwell, *Veronica chamaedrys.* 5. a type of weave with small, eyelike figures. 6. a fabric, either cotton or linen, with this weave, used for diapers or toweling.

bird's-foot (bûrdz'fŏŏt'), *n.* 1. any of various plants whose leaves, flowers, or pods resemble or suggest the foot or claw of a bird, esp. plants of the leguminous genus *Ornithopus,* which have clawlike pods. 2. any similar plant, esp. bird's-foot trefoil or fenugreek. Also, **birdfoot.**

bird's-foot fern, 1. a fern, *Adiantopsis radiata,* of tropical America. 2. a fern, *Pellea mucronata,* growing in hilly parts of the U. S. Pacific seaboard.

bird's-foot trefoil, 1. a fabaceous plant, *Lotus corniculatus,* the legumes of which spread like a crow's foot. 2. any similar plant of the same genus.

bird's-foot violet, *Bot.* a handsome violet, *Viola pedata,* cultivated for its large light-blue or whitish flowers with yellow eyes (the State flower of Wisconsin).

bird-wom·an (bûrd'wŏŏm'ən), *n., pl.* **-women.** *Colloq.* a female aviator.

bi·reme (bī'rēm), *n.* a galley having two banks or tiers of oars. [t. L: m.s. *birēmis,* lit., two-oared]

bi·ret·ta (bə rĕt'ə), *n.* a stiff, square cap with three (or four) upright projecting pieces extending from the center of the top to the edge, worn by Roman Catholic ecclesiastics. Also, **berretta.** [t. It.: m. *berretta,* der. L *birrus* cap]

Biretta

Bir·ken·head (bûr'kən hĕd', bûr'kən hĕd'), *n.* 1. a seaport in W England, on the Mersey opposite Liverpool. 141,600 (est. 1956). 2. Frederick Edwin Smith, 1st Earl of, 1872–1930, British lawyer, statesman, and writer.

birl (bûrl), *v.t., v.i.* *Lumbering.* to cause (a floating log) to rotate rapidly by treading upon it. [orig. Scot.]

Bir·ming·ham (bûr'mĭng əm *for 1;* -hăm' *for 2*), *n.* 1. a city in central England, 1,110,800 (est. 1956). 2. a city in central Alabama. 340,887 (1960).

birth (bûrth), *n.* 1. fact of being born: *the day of his birth.* 2. act of bearing or bringing forth; parturition. 3. lineage; extraction; descent: *of Grecian birth.* 4. high or noble lineage. 5. supposedly natural heritage: *a musician by birth.* 6. that which is born. 7. any coming into existence; origin: *the birth of Protestantism.* [ME *byrth(e),* t. Scand.; cf. Icel. *byrdh*] —**Syn.** 3. parentage, race, family.

birth control, the regulation of birth through the deliberate control or prevention of conception.

birth·day (bûrth'dā'), *n.* 1. (of persons) the day of one's birth. 2. (of things) origin or beginning. 3. the anniversary of one's birth or the origin of something.

birth·mark (bûrth'märk'), *n.* a congenital mark on the body.

birth·night (bûrth'nīt'), *n.* the night of one's birth.

birth·place (bûrth'plās'), *n.* place of birth or origin.

birth rate, the proportion of the number of births in a place in a given time to the total population.

birth·right (bûrth'rīt'), *n.* any right or privilege to which a person is entitled by birth.

birth·root (bûrth'rōōt', -rŏŏt'), *n.* 1. a species of trillium, *Trillium erectum,* the roots of which are used in medicine. 2. any of certain other species of trillium.

birth·stone (bûrth'stōn'), *n.* a stone which has been selected as appropriate for wear by persons born within a designated period, superstitiously endowed with mystic powers for good or ill fortune.

birth·wort (bûrth'wûrt'), *n.* 1. a plant, *Aristolochia Clematitis,* a native of Europe, reputed to facilitate childbirth. 2. any of certain other species of the same genus. 3. the birthroot.

bis (bĭs), *adv.* 1. twice. 2. a second time: used (esp. in music) to direct a repetition. [t. L. See BI-]

Bi·sa·yan (bē sä'yən), *n.* Visayan.

Bi·sa·yas (bē sä'yäs), *n.* Spanish name of the **Visayan Islands.**

Bis·cay (bĭs'kā, -kī), *n.* **Bay of,** a large bay of the Atlantic between W France and N Spain.

bis·cuit (bĭs'kĭt), *n.* 1. *U.S.* a kind of bread in small, soft cakes, raised with baking powder or soda, sometimes with yeast. 2. *Brit.* a dry and crisp or hard bread in thin, flat cakes, made without yeast or other raising agent; a cracker. 3. a pale-brown color. 4. pottery after the first baking and before glazing. [ME *besquite,* t. OF: m. *bescuit,* f. *bes* (g. L *bis*) twice + *cuit,* pp. of *cuire* cook (g. L *coquere*)] —**bis'cuit·like'**, *adj.*

bise (bēz), *n.* a dry, cold north or northeast wind in southeastern France, Switzerland, and adjoining regions. [t. F, t. Gmc.; cf. OHG *bîsa*]

bi·sect (bī sĕkt'), *v.t.* 1. to cut or divide into two parts. 2. *Geom.* to cut or divide into two equal parts. —*v.i.* 3. to split into two, as a road; fork. —**bi·sec'tion,** *n.* —**bi·sec'tion·al,** *adj.* —**bi·sec'tion·al·ly,** *adv.*

bi·sec·tor (bī sĕk'tər), *n.* *Geom.* a line or plane bisecting an angle or line segment.

bi·sec·trix (bī sĕk'trĭks), *n., pl.* **bisectrices** (bī'sĕk trī'sēz). 1. *Crystal.* either of the two directions which bisect the acute (**acute bisectrix**) or obtuse (**obtuse bisectrix**) angles of the optic axes in a biaxial crystal. 2. *Geom.* a bisector.

bi·ser·rate (bī sĕr'āt, -ĭt), *adj.* *Bot.* doubly serrate; notched like a saw, with the teeth also notched.

bi·sex·u·al (bī sĕk'shŏŏ əl), *adj.* *Biol.* 1. of both sexes. 2. combining male and female organs in one individual; hermaphroditic. —*n.* 3. *Biol.* one who has the reproductive organs of both sexes. 4. *Psychiatry.* a person sexually attracted by either sex. —**bi·sex'u·al·ism,** *n.* —**bi·sex'u·al·ly,** *adv.*

bish·op (bĭsh'əp), *n., v.,* -oped, -oping. —*n.* 1. an overseer over a number of local churches or a diocese, being in the Greek, Roman Catholic, Anglican, and other churches a member of the highest order in the ministry. 2. a spiritual overseer. 3. *Chess.* a piece which moves obliquely on squares of the same color. 4. a hot drink made of port wine, oranges, cloves, etc. —*v.t.* 5. to appoint to the office of bishop. —*v.i.* 6. to function as bishop. [ME; OE *bisc(e)op,* t. VL: (m.) s. *(e)biscopus,* var. of L *episcopus,* t. Gk.: m. *epískopos* overseer] —**bish'op·less,** *adj.*

bish·op·ric (bĭsh'əp rĭk), *n.* the see, diocese, or office of a bishop. [ME *bisshoprike,* OE *bisceoprīce,* f. *bisceop* bishop + *rīce* dominion]

bish·op's-cap (bĭsh'əpskăp'), *n.* miterwort (def. 1).

Bis·kra (bĭs'krä), *n.* a town and oasis in NE Algeria, in the Sahara. 52,511 (1954).

Bis·marck (bĭz'märk; *Ger.* bĭs'-), *n.* 1. **Otto von** (ô'tō fən), (*Prince Otto Eduard Leopold von Bismarck Schönhausen*) 1815–98, German statesman: first chancellor of modern German Empire, 1871–1890. 2. the capital of North Dakota, in the central part. 27,670 (1960).

Bismarck Archipelago, a group of islands in the SW Pacific NE of New Guinea, including the Admiralty Islands, New Britain, New Ireland, and adjacent islands: under Australian administration. ab. 23,000 sq. mi.

bis·muth (bĭz'məth), *n.* *Chem.* a brittle, metallic element, having compounds used in medicine. *Symbol:* Bi; *at. no.:* 83; *at. wt.:* 209.00; *sp. gr.:* 9.8 at 20° C. [t. G, var. of *wismut;* orig. uncert.] —**bis'muth·al,** *adj.*

bis·mu·thic (bĭz mū'thĭk, -mŭth'ĭk), *adj.* *Chem.* of or containing bismuth, esp. in the pentavalent state, Bi⁺⁵.

bis·muth·in·ite (bĭz mŭth'ə nīt'), *n.* a mineral, bismuth sulfide, Bi₂S₃, occurring in lead-gray masses, an ore of bismuth.

bis·muth·ous (bĭz'məth əs), *adj.* *Chem.* containing trivalent bismuth, Bi⁺³.

bi·son (bī'sən, -zən), *n., pl.* **-son.** *Zool.* a large North American bovine ruminant, *Bison bison* (**American bison,** or **buffalo**), with high, well-haired shoulders. [t. L, t. Gmc.; g. G *wisent*]

American Bison, *Bison bison* (10 to 12 ft. long. ab. 6 ft. high at the shoulder)

bisque¹ (bĭsk), *n.* 1. any smooth, creamy soup. 2. a thick soup made of shellfish or game stewed long and slowly. 3. ice cream made with powdered macaroons or nuts. [t. F]

bisque² (bĭsk), *n.* a point, extra turn, or the like, allowed to a player as odds in tennis and other games. [t. F; orig. unknown]

bis·sex·tile (bĭ sĕks'tĭl), *adj.* 1. containing or noting the extra day of leap year. —*n.* 2. leap year. [t. LL: m. s. *bissextīlis* (*annus*) leap year]

bis·ter (bĭs'tər), *n.* 1. a brown pigment extracted from the soot of wood, much used in pen and wash drawings. 2. a dark-brown color. Also, **bis'tre.** [t. F: m. *bistre;* orig. unknown, ? akin to F *bis* dark gray]

bis·tort (bĭs'tôrt), *n.* 1. a European perennial herb, *Polygonum Bistorta,* with a twisted root, which is sometimes used as an astringent; snakeweed. 2. a plant of other allied species, as **Virginia bistort,** *P. virginianum,* and **Alpine bistort,** *P. viviparum.* [f. L: *bis* twice + s. *torta,* pp. fem., twisted]

bis·tou·ry (bĭs'tə rĭ), *n., pl.* **-ries.** a small, narrow surgical knife. [t. F: m. *bistouri,* der. *bistourner* turn out of shape, castrate, t. Pr.: m. *bistornar* (r. OF *bestorner*)]

bis·tro (bĭs'trō; *Fr.* bē strō'), *n.* *Colloq.* 1. a small, unpretentious tavern or café. 2. a bartender.

bi·sul·fate (bī sŭl'fāt), *n.* *Chem.* a salt of sulfuric acid, containing the radical HSO₄⁻¹. Also, **bi·sul'phate.**

bi·sul·fide (bī sŭl'fīd, -fĭd), *n.* *Chem.* a disulfide. Also, **bi·sul'phide.**

bi·sul·fite (bī sŭl'fīt), *n.* *Chem.* a salt of sulfurous acid, containing the radical HSO₃⁻¹. Also, **bi·sul'phite.**

Bi·su·tun (bē soo tōōn'), *n.* Behistun.

bi·sym·met·ri·cal (bī'sĭ mĕt'rə kəl), *adj.* *Bot.* having two planes of symmetry at right angles to each other. Also, **bi·sym'met·ric.** —**bi·sym·met·ri·cal·ly,** *adv* —**bi·sym·me·try** (bī sĭm'ə trĭ), *n.*

---

bit[1] (bĭt), n., v., **bitted, bitting.** —n. **1.** the metallic mouthpiece of a bridle, with the adjacent parts to which the reins are fastened. See illus. under **harness. 2.** anything that curbs or restrains. **3.** Mach. the cutting or penetrating part of various tools: **a.** the cutting portion of an ax or hatchet or the removable cutter in the plane, bitstock, etc. **b.** the movable boring or drilling part (in many forms) used in a carpenter's brace, a drilling machine, or the like. **4.** the part of a key which enters the lock and acts on the bolt and tumblers. —v.t. **5.** to put a bit in the mouth of. **6.** to curb; restrain. **7.** to grind a bit on. [ME byt, OE bite action of biting] —**bit'less,** adj.

Spiral bits (def. 3b)

bit[2] (bĭt), n. **1.** a small piece or quantity of anything: a bit of string, a bit of one's mind. **2.** a short time: wait a bit. **3.** U.S. Colloq. twelve and a half cents: two bits (25 cents). **4.** any small coin: a threepenny bit. **5.** a Spanish or Mexican silver real worth twelve and a half cents, formerly current in parts of the U. S. [ME bite, OE bita bit, morsel] —**Syn. 1.** particle, speck, grain, mite; whit, iota, jot; scrap, fragment.

bit[3] (bĭt), n. a single, basic unit of information, used in connection with computers and communication theory. [short for B(INARY DIG)IT]

bi·tar·trate (bī tär'trāt), n. Chem. a tartrate in which only one of the acid hydrogens of tartaric acid is replaced by a metal or a positive radical; an acid tartrate.

bitch (bĭch), n. **1.** a female dog. **2.** a female of canines generally. **3.** Vulgar. a woman, esp. a disagreeable or lewd one. **4.** Slang. a complaint. —v.i. **5.** Slang. to complain. —v.t. **6.** Slang. to spoil; bungle. [ME biche, OE bicce, c. Icel. bikkja]

bite (bīt), v., **bit, bitten or bit, biting,** n. —v.t. **1.** to cut into or wound, or cut (off, out, etc.) with the teeth. **2.** to grip with the teeth. **3.** to cut or pierce. **4.** to sting, as an insect. **5.** to cause to smart or sting. **6.** to eat into or corrode, as an acid does. **7.** Etching. to use acid for eating into such parts of a copper or other surface as are left bare of a protective coating. **8.** to make a great impression on. **9.** to close the teeth tightly on. **10.** to take firm hold or act effectively on. **11.** to cheat; deceive. —v.i. **12.** to press the teeth (into, on, etc.); snap. **13.** Angling. (of fish) to take the bait. **14.** to accept a deceptive offer or suggestion. **15.** to act effectively; grip; hold. —n. **16.** act of biting. **17.** a wound made by biting. **18.** a cutting, stinging, or nipping effect. **19.** a piece bitten off. **20.** food: not a bite to eat. **21.** a small meal. **22.** Mach. **a.** the catch or hold that one object or one part of a mechanical apparatus has on another. **b.** a surface brought into contact to obtain a hold or grip, as in a lathe, chuck, or similar device. **23.** (in a file) the roughness or power of abrasion. [ME biten, OE bītan, c. G beissen] —**bit'er,** n.

Bi·thyn·i·a (bĭ thĭn'ĭ ə), n. an ancient country in NW Asia Minor.

bit·ing (bī'tĭng), adj. **1.** nipping; keen: biting cold. **2.** cutting; sarcastic: a biting remark. —**bit'ing·ly,** adv.

Bi·tolj (bē'tōl'y), n. a city in S Yugoslavia. 37,732 (1953). Turkish, **Monastir.**

bit·stock (bĭt'stŏk'), n. Mach. the stock or handle by which a boring bit is held and rotated; a brace.

bitt (bĭt), Naut. —n. **1.** a strong post of wood or iron projecting (usually in pairs) above the deck of a ship, and used for securing cables, lines for towing, etc. —v.t. **2.** to put (a cable, etc.) round the bitts. [var. of BIT[1]]

bit·ten (bĭt'ən), v. pp. of **bite.**

bit·ter (bĭt'ər), adj. **1.** having a harsh, disagreeable taste, like that of quinine. **2.** hard to admit or receive: a bitter lesson. **3.** hard to bear; grievous; distressful: a bitter sorrow. **4.** causing pain; piercing; stinging: bitter cold. **5.** characterized by intense animosity: bitter hatred. **6.** harsh; sarcastic; cutting: bitter words. —n. **7.** that which is bitter; bitterness. —v.t. **8.** to make bitter. [OE biter; akin to BITE] —**bit'ter·ish,** adj. —**bit'ter·ly,** adv. —**bit'ter·ness,** n. —Syn. **6.** acrimonious, caustic. —Ant. **1.** sweet. **2.** pleasant.

bitter end, Naut. the extreme tail end of a cable or rope. The bitter end of an anchor cable is secured to the ship inside the chain locker. [f. bitter (f. BITT + -ER[1]) + END[1]]

Bitter Lakes, two lakes that form part of the Suez Canal, in NE Egypt.

bit·tern[1] (bĭt'ərn), n. any of several herons, as Botaurus lentiginosus of North America, and the common bittern, Botaurus stellaris, of Europe. [ME bitter, botor, t. OF: m. butor; orig. uncert. Cf. L būtio bittern]

bit·tern[2] (bĭt'ərn), n. a bitter, oily liquid remaining in saltmaking after the salt has crystallized out of sea water or brine, used as a source of bromine, etc. [d. var. of bittering, f. BITTER + -ING[1]]

American bittern.
Botaurus lentiginosus
(27 in. long)

bitter principle, Chem. any of several hundred natural compounds, usually of vegetable origin, having a bitter taste, and not admitting of any chemical classification.

bit·ter·root (bĭt'ər rōōt', -rŏŏt'), n. a portulacaceous plant, Lewisia rediviva, having fleshy roots and hand-

some pink flowers, growing in the mountains of Idaho, Montana, etc. (the State flower of Montana).

Bitterroot Range, a range of the Rocky Mountains, on the boundary between Idaho and Montana. Highest peak, ab. 10,000 ft. Also, **Bitter Root Range.**

bit·ters (bĭt'ərz), n.pl. **1.** a liquor (generally a spirituous liquor) in which bitter herbs or roots are steeped. **2.** Pharm. **a.** a liquid, usually alcoholic, impregnated with a bitter medicine, as gentian, quassia, etc., used as a stomachic, tonic, or the like. **b.** bitter medicinal substances in general, as quinine, gentian, etc.

bit·ter·sweet (n. bĭt'ər swēt'; adj. bĭt'ər swēt'), n. **1.** the woody nightshade, Solanum Dulcamara, a climbing or trailing solanaceous plant with scarlet berries. **2.** any climbing plant of the genus Celastrus, with orange capsules opening to expose red-coated seeds, esp. Celastrus scandens. —adj. **3.** both bitter and sweet to the taste. **4.** both pleasant and painful.

bit·ter·weed (bĭt'ər wēd'), n. **1.** any of various plants containing a bitter principle, as the ragweed. **2.** any sneezeweed of genus Helenium, esp. H. tenuifolium.

bi·tu·men (bĭ tū'mən, -tōō'-, bĭch'ŏŏ-), n. **1.** any of various natural substances, as asphalt, maltha, gilsonite, etc., consisting mainly of hydrocarbons. **2.** a brown tar or asphaltlike substance used in painting. [t. L] —**bi·tu·mi·noid** (bĭ tū'mə noid', -tōō'-), adj.

bi·tu·mi·nize (bĭ tū'mə nīz', -tōō'-), v.t., **-nized, -nizing.** to convert into or treat with bitumen. —**bi·tu·mi·ni·za'tion,** n.

bi·tu·mi·nous (bĭ tū'mə nəs, -tōō'-), adj. of, like, or containing bitumen: bituminous shale.

bituminous coal, soft coal; a mineral coal which contains volatile hydrocarbons and tarry matter, and burns with a yellow, smoky flame.

bi·va·lent (bī vā'lənt, bĭv'ə-), adj. **1.** Chem. **a.** having a valence of two. **b.** having two valences, as mercury, with valences 1 and 2. **2.** Biol. pertaining to composites of two similar or identical chromosomes, or chromosome sets. —n. **3.** Biol. a bivalent pair or set of chromosomes. —**bi·va·lence** (bī vā'ləns, bĭv'ə ləns), **bi·va·len·cy,** n.

bi·valve (bī'vălv'), n. Zool. **1.** a mollusk having two shells hinged together, as the oyster, clam, mussel; a lamellibranch. —adj. **2.** Bot. having two valves, as a seedcase. **3.** Zool. having two shells, usually united by a hinge. —**bi·val·vu·lar** (bī văl'vyə lər), adj.

biv·ou·ac (bĭv'ŏŏ ăk', bĭv'wăk), n., v., **-acked, -acking.** —n. **1.** an area in the field where troops rest or assemble, usually having no shelter or protection from enemy fire, or only tents, or shelter made from anything available. —v.i. **2.** to rest or assemble in such an area. [t. F, prob. t. d. G: m. biwache. Cf. G beiwacht patrol]

bi·week·ly (bī wēk'lĭ), adj., n., pl. **-lies,** adv. —adj. **1.** occurring every two weeks. **2.** occurring twice a week; semiweekly. —n. **3.** a periodical issued every other week. —adv. **4.** every two weeks. **5.** twice a week.

bi·year·ly (bī yĭr'lĭ), adj., adv. **1.** biennial. **2.** twice yearly.

bi·zarre (bĭ zär'), adj. singular in appearance, style, or general character; whimsically strange; odd. [t. F: odd, prob. t. Sp.: m. bizarro brave, ? t. Basque: m. bizar beard] —**bi·zarre'ly,** adv. —**bi·zarre'ness,** n.

Bi·zer·te (bĭ zûr'tə; Fr. bē zĕrt'). n. a seaport in N Tunisia. 44,681 (1956). Also, **Bi·zer·ta** (bē zĕr'tä). Ancient, **Hippo Zarytus.**

Bi·zet (bē zā'; Fr. bē zĕ'), n. **Georges** (zhôrzh), (Alexandre César Léopold Bizet) 1838–75, French composer.

Bi·zo·ni·a (bī zō'nĭ ə, bī'-), n. the combined U.S. and British zones of occupation in Germany after World War II.

Bjoerling (byœr'lĭng), n. **Jussi** (yŏŏ'sĭ), 1911–1960, Swedish operatic tenor.

Björn·son (byœrn'sŏn), n. **Björnstjerne** (byœrn'styĕr'nə), 1832–1910, Norwegian poet, novelist, and dramatist.

bk., 1. bank. **2.** book.

bkg., banking.

bl., 1. bale; bales. **2.** barrel; barrels.

B.L., Bachelor of Laws.

b.l., 1. Com. bill of lading. **2.** Ordn. breech loading.

blab (blăb), v., **blabbed, blabbing,** n. —v.t. **1.** to reveal indiscreetly and thoughtlessly. —v.i. **2.** to talk or chatter indiscreetly and thoughtlessly. —n. **3.** idle, indiscreet chattering. **4.** a person who blabs. —**blab'ber,** n.

black (blăk), adj. **1.** without brightness or color. **2.** wearing black or dark clothing, armor, etc.: the black prince. **3.** Anthropol. **a.** pertaining or belonging to an ethnic group characterized by dark skin pigmentation. **b.** pertaining specif. to the "black races" of Africa, Oceania, and Australia: the Negroes, Negritos, Papuans, Melanesians, and Australian aborigines. **4.** soiled or stained with dirt. **5.** characterized by absence of light; involved or enveloped in darkness: a black night. **6.** gloomy; dismal: a black outlook. **7.** boding ill; sullen; forbidding: black words, black looks. **8.** without any moral light or goodness; evil; wicked. **9.** caused or marked by ruin or desolation. **10.** indicating censure, disgrace, or liability to punishment: a black mark on one's record. **11.** (of coffee) without milk or cream. —n. **12.** a member of a dark-skinned people; a Negro. **13.** a black speck, flake, or spot, as of soot. **14.** black clothing, esp. as a sign of mourning: to be in black. **15.** Chess, Checkers. the dark-colored men or pieces. **16.** black pigment: lamp black. **17. in the black,** financially solvent. —v.t. **18.** to make black; put black on. **19.** to clean and polish (shoes) with blacking. **20.** *Mil.* to obscure by concealing all light in defense against air raids (fol. by *out*). —*v.i.* **21.** to become black; take on a black color. **22.** to lose consciousness (fol. by *out*). [ME *blak*, OE *blæc*, c. OHG *blah-*, *blach-*] —**black′ish,** *adj.* —**black′ish·ly,** *adv.* —**black′ness,** *n.* —**Syn. 1.** sable, ebon; swart, swarthy; dark, dusky; sooty, inky. —**Ant. 1.** colorful. **4.** clean. **6.** hopeful.

Black (blăk), *n.* Hugo Lafayette, born 1886, U.S. political official: associate justice of U.S. Supreme Court since 1937.

black·a·moor (blăk′ə moŏr′), *n.* **1.** a Negro. **2.** any dark-skinned person. [var. of *black Moor*]

black-and-blue (blăk′ən blōō′), *adj.* discolored, as by bruising.

Black and Tan, 1. an armed force of about 6,000 men sent by the British government to Ireland in June, 1920, to suppress revolutionary activity; so called from the color of their uniforms. **2.** a member of this force.

black and white, 1. print or writing. **2.** a drawing or picture done in black and white only.

black art, witchcraft; magic.

black·ball (blăk′bôl′), *n.* **1.** an adverse vote. **2.** a black ball placed in a ballot box signifying a negative vote. —*v.t.* **3.** to vote against. **4.** to ostracize. **5.** to reject (a candidate) by placing a black ball in the ballot box. —**black′ball′er,** *n.*

black bass, an American fresh-water fish of the genus *Micropterus*, which comprises five species of which the best-known are the **large-mouthed bass,** *M. salmoides*, the **small-mouthed bass,** *M. dolomieu*, and the **spotted bass,** *M. punctulatus*.

black bear, a species of American bear, *Euarctos americanus*, with a pale face and dense black fur.

black belt, *U.S.* **1.** a preponderantly Negro area in a city or State. **2.** a narrow belt of dark-colored, calcareous soils in central Alabama and Mississippi highly adapted to agriculture, esp. cotton growing.

black·ber·ry (blăk′bĕr′ĭ), *n., pl.* **-ries. 1.** the fruit, black or very dark purple when ripe, of certain species of the genus *Rubus*. **2.** the plant. [ME *blakeberie*, OE *blace berian* (pl.)] —**black′ber′ry·like′,** *adj.*

blackberry lily, a perennial iridaceous plant, *Belamcanda chinensis*, with red-spotted, orange, lilylike flowers and globose seeds resembling blackberries.

black bindweed, **1.** a twining Old World vine, *Tamus communis*, with red berries. **2.** a climbing European herb, *Polygonum Convolvulus*, found widely in America as a tenacious weed.

black·bird (blăk′bûrd′), *n.* **1.** one of various birds of the American family *Icteridae*, as the **crow blackbird,** *Quiscalus quiscula*, the **rusty blackbird,** *Euphagus carolinus*, and the **red-winged blackbird,** *Agelaius phoeniceus*. **2.** any of various unrelated birds having black plumage in the male.

black·board (blăk′bôrd′), *n.* a smooth dark board, used in schools, etc., for writing or drawing with chalk.

black book, 1. a book of names of people liable to censure or punishment. **2.** be in **one's black books,** to be in disfavor.

black·boy (blăk′boi′), *n.* the grass tree.

black buck, a common Indian antelope, *Antilope cervicapra*, of medium size and blackish-brown color.

Black·burn (blăk′bərn), *n.* **1.** a city in NW England, in Lancashire. 107,900 (est. 1956). **2. Mount,** a peak in SE Alaska, in the Wrangell Mountains. 16,140 ft.

Black Canyon, a canyon of the Colorado river between Arizona and Nevada: site of Boulder Dam.

black·cap (blăk′kăp′), *n.* **1.** any of several birds having the top of the head black, as the chickadee and certain warblers, esp. the Old World blackcap, *Sylvia atricapilla*. **2.** *U.S.* a popular name of the plant and fruit of the black raspberry, *Rubus occidentalis*.

black·cock (blăk′kŏk′), *n.* the male of the European black grouse, *Lyrurus tetrix*.

Black Country, a midlands district around Birmingham, England, begrimed by numerous factories, etc.

black·damp (blăk′dămp′), *n.* *Mining.* chokedamp.

Black Death, bubonic plague, which spread over Europe in the 14th century.

black diamond, 1. a carbonado (def. 2). **2.** (*pl.*) coal.

black disease, *Vet. Sci.* an acute, highly fatal disease of sheep caused by general intoxication from *Clostridium novyi*, an anaerobic organism which multiplies in the liver in areas damaged by the common liver fluke.

black dog, *Colloq.* melancholy; the blues.

black·en (blăk′ən), *v.* **-ened, -ening.** —*v.t.* **1.** to make black; darken. **2.** to speak evil of; defame. —*v.i.* **3.** to grow or become black. —**black′en·er,** *n.*

black eye, 1. discoloration of the skin around the eye, resulting from a blow, etc. **2.** *Colloq.* a cause of shame, dishonor, etc.

black-eyed Su·san (blăk′īd′ sōō′zən), any of a number of plants having flowers with a dark center against a lighter, usually yellow, background, such as the composite herb, *Rudbeckia hirta*, and the acanthaceous vine, *Thunbergia alata* (the State flower of Maryland).

black·face (blăk′fās′), *n.* **1.** *Theat.* **a.** an entertainer playing a Negro. **b.** the make-up for the role of a Negro. **2.** *Print.* a heavy-faced type.

black·fel·low (blăk′fĕl′ō), *n.* an aboriginal of Australia.

black·fish (blăk′fĭsh′), *n., pl.* **-fishes,** (*esp. collectively*) **-fish. 1.** the black whale. **2.** any of various dark-colored fishes, as the tautog, *Tautoga onitis*, or the sea bass, *Centropristes striatus*, or a small fresh-water food fish, *Dallia pectoralis*, of Alaska and Siberia, notable for its ability to revive after having been long frozen.

black flag, the pirate flag, usually of black cloth with the white skull and crossbones on it.

black fly, any of the minute, black-bodied gnats of the dipterous family *Simuliidae*; the larvae are aquatic.

Black·foot (blăk′foŏt′), *n., pl.* **-feet** (-fēt′), **-foot. 1.** a member of a North American tribe of Indians (the Blackfeet) of Algonquian stock. **2.** an Algonquian language of Saskatchewan, Alberta, and Montana. —*adj.* **3.** of or pertaining to the Blackfeet.

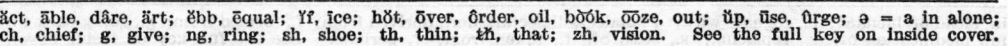

Black Forest, a forest-covered mountainous region in SW West Germany. Highest peak, Feldberg, ab. 4700 ft. German, Schwarzwald.

Black Friar, 1. a Dominican friar (from the distinctive black mantle). **2.** a Benedictine monk.

black grouse, a large grouse, *Lyrurus tetrix*, found in the northern parts of Europe and western Asia. The male is black, the female mottled gray and brown.

black·guard (blăg′ärd, -ərd), *n.* **1.** a coarse, despicable person; a scoundrel. —*v.t.* **2.** to revile in scurrilous language. —*v.i.* **3.** to behave like a blackguard. [f. BLACK + GUARD] —**black′guard·ism,** *n.*

black·guard·ly (blăg′ərd lĭ′), *adj.* **1.** of, like, or befitting a blackguard. —*adv.* **2.** in the manner of a blackguard.

black gum, a tree of the family *Nyssaceae*, as *Nyssa sylvatica* and *N. biflora*. See tupelo.

Black Hand, 1. an anarchistic society in Spain, repressed in 1883. **2.** *U.S.* a criminal secret society, esp. of Italians, organized for blackmail and deeds of violence about the last decade of the 19th century. **3.** *U.S.* any similar group. [trans. of Sp. *mano negra*]

black haw, 1. a North American shrub or small tree of the honeysuckle family, *Viburnum prunifolium*, bearing white flowers and black drupes. **2.** the sheepberry.

Black Hawk, 1767–1838, American Indian chief of the Sac and Fox tribes.

black·head (blăk′hĕd′), *n.* **1.** a small wormlike, black-tipped, fatty mass in a follicle of the face. **2.** any of several birds having a black head, as the scaup duck, *Aythya marila*. **3.** *Vet. Sci.* a malignant, infectious, protozoan disease of turkeys, chickens, and many wild birds, attacking esp. the intestines and liver.

black·heart (blăk′härt′), *n.* **1.** a plant disease, as of potatoes and various trees, in which internal plant tissues blacken. **2.** a kind of cherry bearing a large, sweet, somewhat heart-shaped fruit with a nearly black skin.

black·heart·ed (blăk′här′tĭd), *adj.* evil.

Black Hills, a group of mountains in W South Dakota and NE Wyoming. Highest peak, Harney Peak, 7242 ft.

Black Hole, 1. a small prison cell in Fort William, Calcutta, into which, in 1756, 146 Europeans were thrust for a night, only 23 of whom were alive in the morning. **2.** (*l.c.*) a military cell or lockup.

black horehound, a fetid European weed, *Ballota nigra*, with purple flowers, prevalent in waste land.

black·ing (blăk′ĭng), *n.* any preparation for producing a black coating or finish, as on shoes, stoves, etc.

black·jack (blăk′jăk′), *n.* **1.** a short club, usually leather-covered, consisting of a heavy head on an elastic shaft. **2.** a large drinking cup or jug for beer, ale, etc., orig. one made of leather coated externally with tar. **3.** the black flag of a pirate. **4.** a small oak, *Quercus marilandica*, of the eastern U. S., with a nearly black bark and a wood of little value except for fuel. **5.** *Mineral.* a dark, iron-rich variety of sphalerite. **6.** caramel or burnt sugar for coloring spirits, vinegar, coffee, etc. **7.** *Cards.* twenty-one. —*v.t.* **8.** to strike or beat with a blackjack. **9.** to compel by threat.

Leather blackjacks

black knot, a fungus plant disease appearing as black knotlike masses on the branches, esp. on plums and cherries.

black lead (lĕd), graphite; plumbago.

black·leg (blăk′lĕg′), *n.* **1.** *Vet. Sci.* an infectious, generally fatal disease of cattle and sheep characterized by painful, gaseous swellings in the muscles, usually of the upper parts of the legs. **2.** a plant disease, as of cabbage and potato, in which the lower stems turn black and decay. **3.** a swindler, esp. in racing or gambling. **4.** *Brit. Colloq.* a strikebreaker; scab.

black letter, *Print.* a heavy-faced type in gothic style like that in early English printed books. —**black′let′ter,** *adj.*

black-letter day, an unlucky day.

black list, a list of persons under suspicion, disfavor, censure, etc.

ăct, āble, dâre, ärt; ĕbb, ēqual; ĭf, īce; hŏt, ōver, ôrder, oil, boŏk, ōōze, out; ŭp, ūse, ûrge; ə = a in alone; ch, chief; g, give; ng, ring; sh, shoe; th, thin; ŧℎ, that; zh, vision. See the full key on inside cover.

black-list (blăk′lĭst′), v.t. to put on a black list.
black·ly (blăk′lĭ), adv. darkly; gloomily; wickedly.
black magic, magic used for evil purposes.
black·mail (blăk′māl′), n. 1. Law. a. any payment extorted by intimidation, as by threats of injurious revelations or accusations. b. the extortion of such payment. 2. a tribute formerly exacted in the north of England and in Scotland by freebooting chiefs for protection from pillage. —v.t. 3. to extort blackmail from. [f. BLACK + mail coin, rent (ME maille, t. OF)] —black′mail′er, n.
Black Ma·ri·a (mə rī′ə), Colloq. a closed vehicle used for conveying prisoners to and from jail.
black mark, a mark of failure or censure.
black market, an illegal market violating price controls, rationing, etc.
black measles, Pathol. a malignant form of measles.
Black·more (blăk′mōr), n. Richard Doddridge (dŏd′rĭj), 1825–1900, British novelist.
Black Mountains, a mountain range in W North Carolina, a part of the Appalachian system. Highest peak, Mt. Mitchell, 6684 ft.
black nightshade, a common weed, Solanum nigrum, with white flowers and black edible berries.
black·out (blăk′out′), n. 1. Mil. the extinguishing of all visible lights in a city, etc., as a war protection. 2. Theat. the extinguishing of all stage lights. 3. unconsciousness, esp. in aviation. 4. loss of memory.
black pepper, a hot, sharp condiment prepared from the dried berries of a tropical vine, Piper nigrum.
black·poll (blăk′pōl′), n. a North American warbler, Dendroica striata, the adult male of which has the top of the head black.
Black·pool (blăk′pōōl′), n. a seaport in NW England, in Lancashire: resort. 146,500 (est. 1956).
Black Prince, 1330–76. Edward, Prince of Wales (the son of Edward III of England).
Black Rod, 1. (in England) an usher (**gentleman usher of the black rod**) of the King's chamber, the Order of the Garter, and the House of Lords (so called from the rod he carries). 2. a similar official in British colonial legislatures.
Black Sea, a sea S of E Europe, bounded by the Soviet Union, Turkey, Rumania, and Bulgaria. ab. 168,000 sq. mi.; greatest depth, ab. 7200 ft. Also, Euxine Sea. Ancient, Pontus Euxinus.
black sheep, a person worthless despite good background.
Black Shirt, Europ. Hist. a member of a fascist organization in Europe, such as the Italian fascist militia, or Hitler's Schutzstaffel.
black·smith (blăk′smĭth′), n. 1. a person who makes horseshoes and shoes horses. 2. an artisan who works in iron. [f. BLACK (in ref. to iron or black metal) + SMITH¹. Cf. WHITESMITH]
black·snake (blăk′snāk′), n. 1. a nonvenomous snake, Coluber constrictor, of the U. S., attaining a length of 5 to 6 ft., and notably agile and strong. 2. any of various other snakes of a black or very dark color. 3. U.S. a heavy, tapering, flexible whip of braided cowhide or the like. Also, **snake**, **black snake**.
black spruce, 1. a conifer of North America, Picea mariana, noted for its extremely dark green needles. 2. an easily worked light wood from this tree.
Black·stone (blăk′stōn, -stən), n. Sir William, 1723–80, British judge and writer on law.
black·tail (blăk′tāl′), n. the mule deer.
black tea, a tea which has been allowed to wither and ferment in the air for some time, before being subjected to a heating process.
black·thorn (blăk′thôrn′), n. 1. a much-branched, thorny shrub of the Old World, Prunus spinosa, bearing white flowers and small plumlike fruits; sloe. 2. a species of the genus Crataegus, as C. tomentosa.
black·top (blăk′tŏp′), n. 1. a bituminous substance, usually asphalt, for paving roads, etc. 2. a road covered with blacktop. —adj. 3. of or covered by blacktop.
Black Volta. See Volta (def. 2).
black vomit, Pathol. 1. a dark-colored substance, consisting chiefly of altered blood, vomited in some cases of yellow fever, usually presaging a fatal issue of the disease. 2. act of throwing up this matter. 3. the disease itself.
Black·wall hitch (blăk′wôl′), a hitch made with a rope over a hook so that it holds fast when pulled but is loose otherwise. See illus. under knot.
black walnut, 1. a tree, Juglans nigra, of North America, which yields a valuable timber. 2. the nut thereof. 3. the wood of this tree.
black·wa·ter fever (blăk′wô′tər, -wŏt′ər), Pathol. a severe form of malaria found chiefly in the tropics but occasionally in the southern U. S.
black·weed (blăk′wēd′), n. the common ragweed.
Black·wells Island (blăk′wĕlz, -wəlz), former name of Welfare Island.
black whale, a dolphinlike cetacean of the genus Globicephalus; a blackfish.

black widow, a poisonous female spider, Latrodectus mactans, common in the U. S., that eats its mate.
blad·der (blăd′ər), n. 1. Anat., Zool. a. a distensible pelvic sac with membranous and muscular walls, for storage and expulsion of urine secreted by the kidneys. b. any similar sac or receptacle. 2. Pathol. a vesicle, blister, cyst, etc., filled with fluid or air. 3. Bot. a sac or the like containing air, as in certain seaweeds. 4. anything inflated, empty, or unsound. [ME; OE blædre bladder, blister, akin to BLOW², v., BLAST] —blad′der·less, adj. —blad′der·like′, adj. —blad′der·y, adj.
bladder campion, a plant, Silene latifolia (Silene inflata), so called from its inflated calyx.
bladder ket·mi·a (kĕt′mĭ ə), a cultivated annual plant, Hibiscus Trionum, with a bladdery calyx.
blad·der·nose (blăd′ər nōz′), n. a large seal, Cystophora cristata, of the northern Atlantic, the male of which has a large, distensible, hoodlike sac upon the head; the hooded seal.
blad·der·nut (blăd′ər nŭt′), n. 1. the bladderlike fruit capsule of any shrub or small tree of the genus Staphylea, as S. trifolia of the eastern U. S. 2. the shrub itself.
bladder worm, Zool. the bladderlike encysted larva of a tapeworm; a cysticercus, coenurus, or hydatid.
blad·der·wort (blăd′ər wûrt′), n. any of various herbs of the large genus Utricularia, including aquatic, terrestrial, and epiphytic forms throughout the world.
blade (blād), n. 1. the flat cutting part of sword, knife, etc. 2. a sword. 3. the leaf of a plant, esp. of a grass or cereal. 4. Bot. the broad part of a leaf, as distinguished from the stalk or petiole. See illus. under leaf. 5. a thin, flat part of something, as of an oar or a bone. 6. a dashing, swaggering, or rakish young fellow. 7. Anat. the scapula or shoulder blade. 8. Phonet. the upper surface and edges of the tongue for a short distance back from the tip. [ME; OE blæd, c. G blatt] —blad′ed, adj. —blade′less, adj. —blade′like′, adj.
Bla·go·vesh·chensk (blä′gŏ vĕsh′chĕnsk), n. a city in the SE Soviet Union in Asia. 60,000 (est. 1956).
blah (blä), n. U.S. Slang. nonsense; rubbish.
blain (blān), n. Pathol. an inflammatory swelling or sore. [ME bleine, OE blegen]
Blaine (blān), n. James Gillespie (gĭ lĕs′pĭ), 1830–1893, U. S. statesman.
Blake (blāk), n. 1. Robert, 1599–1657, British admiral. 2. William, 1757–1827, British poet and artist.
blam·a·ble (blā′mə bəl), adj. deserving blame; censurable. —blam′a·ble·ness, n. —blam′a·bly, adv.
blame (blām), v., blamed, blaming, n. —v.t. 1. to lay the responsibility of (a fault, error, etc.) on a person: I blame the accident on him. 2. to find fault with; censure: I don't blame you for doing that. 3. U.S. Slang and Dial. to blast (as a humorous imperative or optative): Blame my hide if I go. —n. 4. imputation of fault; censure. 5. responsibility for censure. [ME blamen, t. OF: m. blasmer, g. LL blasphēmāre BLASPHEME]
—Syn. 1, 2. reproach, reprove, reprehend. BLAME, CENSURE, CONDEMN imply finding fault with someone (or something). To BLAME is to hold accountable for, and disapprove because of, some error, mistake, omission, neglect, or the like: who is to blame for the disaster? The verb CENSURE differs from the noun in connoting scolding or rebuking even more than adverse criticism: to censure for extravagance. To CONDEMN is to express an adverse (esp. legal) judgment, without recourse: to condemn conduct, a building, a man to death. 4. reprehension, condemnation, stricture. 5. guilt, culpability, fault. —Ant. 2. praise.
blamed (blāmd), U.S. Slang and Dial. —adj. 1. confounded. 2. confoundedly; excessively. —adv.
blame·ful (blām′fəl), adj. deserving blame. —blame′ful·ly, adv. —blame′ful·ness, n.
blame·less (blām′lĭs), adj. free from blame; guiltless. —blame′less·ly, adv. —blame′less·ness, n. —Syn. irreproachable. See innocent. —Ant. guilty.
blame·wor·thy (blām′wûr′thĭ), adj. deserving blame. —blame′wor′thi·ness, n.
Blanc (blän), n. 1. Jean Joseph Charles Louis (zhän zhô zĕf′ shàrl lwē), 1811–82, French socialist and historian. 2. Mont (môn), a mountain on the French-Italian border: the highest peak of the Alps. 15,781 ft.
Blan·ca Peak (blăng′kə), a mountain in S Colorado; the highest peak in the Sangre de Cristo range. 14,390 ft.
blanch (blănch, blänch), v.t. 1. to whiten by removing color. 2. Hort. to whiten or prevent from becoming green by excluding the light (a process applied to the stems or leaves of plants, such as celery, lettuce, etc.). 3. to remove the skin from (nuts, fruits, etc.) by immersion in boiling water, then in cold. 4. to separate (the grains or strands of rice, macaroni, etc.) by immersing in boiling water, then in cold. 5. to scald (meat, etc.). 6. Metall. to give a white luster to (metals), as by means of acids. 7. to make pale, as with sickness or fear. —v.i. 8. to become white; turn pale. [ME blaunche(n), t. OF: m. blanchir, der. blanc white. See BLANK] —blanch′er, n. —Syn. 1. See whiten.
blanc·mange (blə mänzh′, -mänzh′), n. a jellylike preparation of milk thickened with cornstarch, gelatin, or the like, and flavored. [ME blancmanger, t. OF: lit. white food]
bland (blănd), adj. 1. gentle or agreeable, as of persons. 2. soothing or balmy, as air. 3. nonirritating, as food or medicines. 4. nonstimulating, as medicines. [t. L: s. blandus] —bland′ly, adv. —bland′ness, n. —Syn. 1. suave, urbane. 3. soft, mild.

blan·dish (blăn′dĭsh), *v.t.* to treat flatteringly; coax; cajole. [ME *blaundysh*(*en*), t. OF: m. *blandiss-*, s. *blandir*, g. L *blandīre* flatter] —**blan′dish·er**, *n.*

blan·dish·ment (blăn′dĭsh mənt), *n.* 1. flattering action or speech. 2. something that pleases or allures.

blank (blăngk), *adj.* 1. (of paper, etc.) free from marks; not written or printed on. 2. not filled out: *a blank check.* 3. unrelieved or unbroken by ornament or opening: *a blank wall.* 4. lacking some usual or completing feature. 5. void of interest, results, etc. 6. showing no attention, interest, or emotion: *a blank face.* 7. disconcerted; nonplussed: *a blank look.* 8. complete, utter, or unmitigated: *blank stupidity.* 9. white or pale. —*n.* 10. a place where something is lacking: *a blank in one's memory.* 11. a space in a printed form to be filled in. 12. a printed form containing such spaces. 13. a dash put in place of an omitted letter or word, esp. profanity or obscenity. 14. *Mach.* a piece of metal prepared to be stamped or cut into a finished object, such as a coin or key. 15. *Archery.* the white mark in the center of a butt or target at which an arrow is aimed. 16. the object toward which anything is directed; aim; target. —*v.t.* 17. to make blank or void: *to blank out an entry.* 18. *Colloq.* to keep (an opponent) from scoring in a game. 19. *Mach.* to stamp or punch out of flat stock as with a die. [ME, t. OF: m. *blanc* white, t. Gmc.; cf. G *blank* bright, shining] —**blank′ness**, *n.* —Syn. 1-4. See **empty.**

blank cartridge, *Ordn.* a cartridge containing powder only, without a bullet.

blank check, 1. a check bearing a signature but no stated amount. 2. a free hand; carte blanche.

blank endorsement, *Com.* an endorsement on a check or note naming no payee, and payable to bearer.

blan·ket (blăng′kĭt), *n.* 1. a large rectangular piece of soft, loosely woven fabric, usually wool, used esp. as a bedcovering. 2. a covering for a horse, etc. 3. *U.S. and Canada.* the chief garment worn by some Indians. 4. any thin, extended covering: *a blanket of snow.* —*v.t.* 5. to cover with or as with a blanket. 6. to obscure by increasing prominence of the background (often fol. by *out*). 7. to toss in a blanket, as for punishment. 8. *Naut.* to take the wind out of the sails of (a vessel) by passing to windward of it. —*adj.* 9. covering or intended to cover a group or class of things conditions, etc.: *a blanket indictment.* [ME, t. OF: m. *blankete*, dim. of *blanc* white] —**blan′ket·less**, *adj.*

blan·ket·ing (blăng′kĭt ĭng), *n.* *Radio.* the effect of a signal from a powerful transmitter which interferes with or prevents the reception of other signals.

blank·ly (blăngk′lĭ), *adv.* 1. without expression or understanding. 2. totally; fully; in every respect.

blank verse, 1. unrhymed verse. 2. the unrhymed iambic pentameter verse most frequently used in English dramatic, epic, and reflective poems.

blare (blâr), *v.*, **blared**, **blaring**, *n.*—*v.i.* 1. to emit a loud raucous sound. —*v.t.* 2. to sound loudly; proclaim noisily. —*n.* 3. a loud raucous noise. 4. glaring intensity of color. [ME *blaren*, t. MD]

blar·ney (blär′nĭ), *n.*, *v.*, **-neyed**, **-neying**. —*n.* 1. flattering or wheedling talk; cajolery. —*v.t.*, *v.i.* 2. to ply or beguile with blarney; use blarney; wheedle. [see **Blarney stone**]

Blarney stone, a stone in Blarney Castle near Cork, Ireland, said to confer skill in flattery to anyone who kisses it.

Blas·co I·bá·ñez (blăs′kō ē bä′nyĕth), **Vicente** (vĕ-thĕn′tĕ), 1867–1928, Spanish novelist.

bla·sé (blä zā′, blä′zā; *Fr.* blå zĕ′), *adj.* indifferent to and bored by pleasures of life. [t. F, pp. of *blaser* exhaust, satiate, ? t. D: m. *blasen* blow]

blas·pheme (blăs fēm′), *v.*, **-phemed**, **-pheming.**—*v.t.* 1. to speak impiously or irreverently of (God or sacred things). 2. to speak evil of; abuse. —*v.i.* 3. to utter impious words. [t. LL: m. s. *blasphēmāre*, t. Gk.: m. *blasphēmein* speak ill; r. ME *blasfeme*(*n*), t. OF: m. *blasfemer*, t. Gk.] —**blas·phem′er**, *n.* —Syn. 1. See **curse.**

blas·phe·mous (blăs′fə məs), *adj.* uttering, containing, or exhibiting blasphemy. —**blas′phe·mous·ly**, *adv.* —**blas′phe·mous·ness**, *n.*

blas·phe·my (blăs′fə mĭ), *n.*, *pl.* **-mies.** 1. impious utterance or action concerning God or sacred things. 2. *Jewish Relig.* a. (in Talmudic law) cursing and reviling the "ineffable name" of the Lord. b. (in later Hebrew history) the violation of religious law by pronouncing one of the four-letter symbols for God rather than using one of the substitute words. 3. *Theol.* the crime of assuming to oneself the rights or qualities of God. 4. irreverent behavior toward anything held sacred. [t. LL: m. s. *blasphēmia*, t. Gk.: slander; r. ME *blasfemie*, t. OF] —Syn. 1. profanity, cursing, swearing.

blast (blăst, bläst), *n.* 1. a sudden blowing or gust of wind. 2. the blowing of a trumpet, whistle, etc. 3. the sound produced by this. 4. a forcible stream of air from the mouth, from bellows, or the like. 5. *Metall.* air under pressure directed into a blast furnace, cupola, etc. to support combustion. 6. a jet of exhaust steam directed into a smokestack to augment the draft, as in a locomotive. 7. a draft thus increased. 8. *Mining, Civ. Eng.*, *etc.* the charge of dynamite or other explosive used at one firing in blasting operations. 9. the act of exploding; explosion. 10. any pernicious or destructive influence, esp. on animals or plants; a blight. —*v.t.*

11. to blow (a trumpet, etc.). 12. to cause to shrivel or wither; blight. 13. to affect with any pernicious influence; ruin; destroy: *to blast one's hope.* 14. to tear (rock, etc.) to pieces with an explosive. —*v.i.* 15. to wither; be blighted. [ME; OE *blǣst*] —**blast′er**, *n.* —Syn. 1. See **wind**[1].

-blast, *Biol.* a combining form meaning "embryo," "sprout," "germ," as in *ectoblast.* [t. Gk.: s. *blastós*]

blast·ed (blăs′tĭd, bläs′tĭd), *adj.* 1. withered; shriveled; blighted. 2. damned (a euphemism).

blas·te·ma (blăs tē′mə), *n.*, *pl.* **-mata** (-mə tə). *Embryol.* an aggregation of embryonic cells, capable of differentiation into primordia and organs. [t. NL, t. Gk.: sprout] —**blas·tem·ic** (blăs tĕm′ĭk, -tē′mĭk), *adj.*

blast furnace, *Metall.* a vertical, steel, cylindrical furnace using a forced blast to produce molten iron which may be converted into steel or formed into pig iron.

blas·tie (blăs′tĭ, bläs′-), *n.* *Scot.* a dwarf.

blast·ment (blăst′mənt, bläst′-), *n.* a blasting; a blast or blight.

blasto-, *Biol.* a word element meaning "embryo" or "germ," as in *blastocyte.* Also, before vowels, **blast-**. [t. Gk., comb. form of *blastós*]

blas·to·coele (blăs′tə sēl′), *n.* *Embryol.* the cavity of a blastula, arising in the course of cleavage. Also, **blas′to·coel′.**

blas·to·cyst (blăs′tə sĭst), *n.* *Embryol.* 1. the germinal vesicle. 2. the vesicular stage in early mammalian development, following cleavage.

blas·to·derm (blăs′tə dûrm′), *n.* *Embryol.* 1. the primitive membrane or layer of cells which results from the segmentation of the ovum. 2. the membrane forming the wall of the blastula, and in most vertebrates enclosing a cavity or a yolk mass. —**blas′to·der′mic**, *adj.*

blas·to·disc (blăs′tə dĭsk), *n.* *Embryol.* the small disk of protoplasm, containing the egg nucleus, which appears on the surface of the yolk mass in the very heavily yolked eggs, as in birds and reptiles. Also, **blas′to·disk.**

blas·to·gen·e·sis (blăs′tə jĕn′ə sĭs), *n.* *Biol.* 1. reproduction by gemmation or budding. 2. the theory of the transmission of hereditary characters by germ plasm.

blas·to·mere (blăs′tə mĭr′), *n.* *Embryol.* any cell produced during cleavage. —**blas·to·mer·ic** (blăs′tə-mĕr′ĭk), *adj.*

blas·to·pore (blăs′tə pōr′), *n.* *Embryol.* the orifice of an archenteron. —**blas·to·por·ic** (blăs′tə pōr′ĭk, -pŏr′-) *adj.*

blas·to·sphere (blăs′tə sfĭr′), *n.* *Embryol.* 1. a blastula. 2. a blastocyst (def. 2).

blas·tu·la (blăs′təchoō lə), *n.*, *pl.* **-lae** (-lē′). *Embryol.* an early developmental stage of a metazoan, consisting in typical cases of a hollow sphere formed by a single layer of cells. [t. NL, dim. of Gk. *blastós* sprout, germ] —**blas′tu·lar**, *adj.*

blat (blăt), *v.*, **blatted**, **blatting.** —*v.i.* 1. to cry out, as a calf or sheep. —*v.t.* 2. *Colloq.* to utter loudly and indiscreetly; blurt. [imit. Cf. **bleat**]

Blastula
After numerous cleavages: A, Exterior view; B, Cross section

bla·tant (blā′tənt), *adj.* 1. loud-mouthed; offensively noisy; in coarse taste. 2. obtrusive: *a blatant error.* 3. bleating: *blatant herds.* [coined by Spenser. Cf. L *blatīre* babble] —**bla′tan·cy**, *n.* —**bla′tant·ly**, *adv.*

blath·er (blăth′ər), *n.* 1. foolish talk. —*v.i.*, *v.t.* 2. to talk or utter foolishly. Also, **blether.** [ME, t. Scand.; cf. Icel. *bladhra* talk nonsense]

blath·er·skite (blăth′ər skĭt′), *n.* one given to voluble, empty talk. [f. **blather** + *skite* **skate**[3]]

blau·bok (blou′bŏk′), *n.*, *pl.* **-bok**, **-boks.** a bluish South African antelope, *Hippotragus leucophaeus*, extinct since 1800, with backward-curving horns. [t. S Afr. D: m. *blauwbok* blue buck]

Bla·vat·sky (blə văt′skĭ), *n.* **Madame**, (*Elena Petrovna Blavatskaya, nee Hahn*) 1831–91, Russian theosophist.

blaw (blô), *v.t.*, *v.i.* *Scot. and Brit. Dial.* to blow.

blaze[1] (blāz), *n.*, *v.*, **blazed**, **blazing.** —*n.* 1. a bright flame or fire. 2. a bright, hot gleam or glow: *the blaze of day.* 3. a sparkling brightness: *a blaze of jewels.* 4. a sudden, intense outburst, as of fire, passion, fury. 5. (*pl.*) *Slang.* hell. —*v.i.* 6. to burn brightly. 7. to shine like flame. 8. *Poetic.* to be meritoriously conspicuous. —*v.t.* 9. to exhibit vividly. [ME and OE *blase* torch, flame] —Syn. 1. See **flame.**

blaze[2] (blāz), *n.*, *v.*, **blazed**, **blazing.** —*n.* 1. a spot or mark made on a tree, as by removing a piece of the bark, to indicate a boundary or a path in a forest. 2. a white spot on the face of a horse, cow, etc. —*v.t.* 3. to mark with blazes: *to blaze a trail.* [t. LG: m. *blåse* white mark on head of horse or steer, c. Icel. *blesa*]

blaze[3] (blāz), *v.t.*, **blazed**, **blazing.** 1. to make known; proclaim; publish. 2. *Obs.* to blow, as from a trumpet. [ME *blase*(*n*), t. MD, c. Icel. *blåsa* blow]

blaz·er (blā′zər), *n.* 1. *Colloq.* anything intensely bright or hot. 2. a bright-colored jacket worn by tennis players and others. 3. a dish under which there is a receptacle for coals to keep it hot.

blazing star, 1. a person whose rare qualities attract universal attention. 2. any of certain plants with showy flower clusters, as the liliaceous herb *Aletris farinosa* or the composite perennial *Liatris squarrosa*.

bla·zon (blā′zən), *v.t.* 1. to describe in heraldic terminology. 2. to depict (heraldic arms, etc.) in proper form and color. 3. to set forth conspicuously or publicly; display; proclaim. —*n.* 4. a heraldic shield; armorial bearings. 5. the heraldic description of armorial bearings. 6. pompous display. [ME *blason,* t. OF: shield, later armorial bearings] —**bla′zon·er,** *n.* —**bla′zon·ment,** *n.*

bla·zon·ry (blā′zən rĭ), *n.* 1. brilliant decoration or display. 2. *Her.* a. armorial bearings. b. a description of heraldic devices.

bldg., building.

-ble, var. of **-able,** as in *noble;* occurring first in words of Latin origin which came into English through French, later in words taken directly from Latin. Also, after consonant stems, **-ible.** [t. OF, g. L *-bilis,* suffix forming verbal adjectives]

bleach (blēch), *v.t., v.i.* 1. to make or become white, pale, or colorless. —*n.* 2. a bleaching agent. 3. degree of paleness achieved in bleaching. 4. act of bleaching. [ME *blechen,* OE *blǣcean*] —**Syn.** 1. See **whiten.**

bleach·er (blē′chər), *n.* 1. one who or that which bleaches. 2. a vessel used in bleaching. 3. (*usually pl.*) an uncovered seat or stand for spectators at games.

bleach·er·y (blē′chər ĭ), *n., pl.* **-er·ies.** a place or establishment where bleaching is carried on.

bleaching powder, a powder used for bleaching, esp. chloride of lime.

bleak (blēk), *adj.* 1. bare, desolate, and windswept: *a bleak plain.* 2. cold and piercing: *a bleak wind.* 3. dreary: *a bleak prospect.* [ME *bleke* pale, b. *bleche* (OE *blǣc*) and *blake* (OE *blāc*), c. G *bleich*] —**bleak′ly,** *adv.* —**bleak′ness,** *n.*

blear (blĭr), *v.t.* 1. to make (the eyes or sight) dim, as with tears or inflammation. —*adj.* 2. (of the eyes) dim from a watery discharge. 3. *Rare.* dim; indistinct. —*n.* 4. a blur; a bleared state. [ME *blere(n);* orig. uncert.]

blear-eyed (blĭr′īd′), *adj.* 1. having blear eyes. 2. dull of perception.

blear·y (blĭr′ĭ), *adj.,* **blearier, bleariest.** bleared. —**blear′i·ness,** *n.*

bleat (blēt), *v.i.* 1. to cry as a sheep, goat, or calf. —*v.t.* 2. to give forth with a bleat. 3. to babble; prate. —*n.* 4. the cry of a sheep, goat, or calf. 5. any similar sound. [ME *blete(n),* OE *blǣtan*] —**bleat′er,** *n.*

bleb (blĕb), *n. Rare.* 1. a blister or pustule. 2. a bubble. —**bleb′by,** *adj.*

bleed (blēd), *v.,* **bled** (blĕd), **bleeding,** *adj.* —*v.i.* 1. to lose blood, from the body or internally from the vascular system. 2. to be severely wounded or die, as in battle: *bled for the cause.* 3. to cause blood to flow, esp. surgically. 4. (of blood, etc.) to flow out. 5. to exude sap, juice, etc. 6. (of color in dyeing) to run. 7. to feel pity, sorrow, or anguish: *a nation bleeds for its dead heroes.* 8. *Slang.* to pay money as when overcharged or threatened with extortion. 9. *Print.* to run off the edges of a printed page, either by design or through mutilation caused by too close trimming. —*v.t.* 10. to cause to lose blood, esp. surgically. 11. to lose or emit (blood or sap). 12. to drain, draw sap, liquid, etc., from. 13. *Colloq.* to obtain, as in excessive amount, or extort money from. 14. *Print.* a. to permit (printed illustrations or ornamentation) to run off the page or sheet. b. to trim the margin of (a book or sheet) so closely as to mutilate the text or illustration. —*n.* 15. *Print.* a sheet or page margin trimmed in this way. 16. a part thus trimmed off. —*adj.* 17. characterized by bleeding: *a bleed page.* [ME *blede(n),* OE *blēdan,* der. *blōd* blood]

bleed·er (blē′dər), *n.* a person predisposed to bleeding; hemophiliac.

bleeding heart, any of various plants of the genus *Dicentra,* esp. *D. spectabilis,* a common garden plant with racemes of red heart-shaped flowers.

blem·ish (blĕm′ĭsh), *v.t.* 1. to destroy the perfection of. —*n.* 2. a defect; a disfigurement; stain. [ME *blemissh(en),* t. OF: m. *blemiss-,* s. *ble(s)mir* make livid] —**blem′ish·er,** *n.* —**Syn.** 1. injure, mar, damage, impair, deface. 2. See **defect.**

blench¹ (blĕnch), *v.i.* to shrink; flinch; quail. [ME *blenchen,* OE *blencan* deceive] —**blench′er,** *n.*

blench² (blĕnch), *v.i., v.t.* to make or become pale or white; blanch. [var. of BLANCH]

blend (blĕnd), *v.,* **blended** or **blent, blending,** *n.* —*v.t.* 1. to mix smoothly and inseparably together. 2. to mix (various sorts or grades) in order to obtain a particular kind or quality. 3. to prepare by such mixture. —*v.i.* 4. to mix or intermingle smoothly and inseparably. 5. to have no perceptible separation: *sea and sky seemed to blend.* —*n.* 6. act or manner of blending: *tea of our own blend.* 7. a mixture or kind produced by blending. 8. *Linguistics.* a word made by putting together parts of other words, as *dandle,* a blend of *dance* and *handle.* [ME *blenden,* OE *blendan, blandan,* c. Icel. *blanda*] —**Syn.** 1. mingle, combine, coalesce. See **mix.**

blende (blĕnd), *n.* 1. sphalerite; zinc sulfide. 2. any of certain other sulfides. [t. G, der. *blenden* blind, deceive]

blend·ed (blĕn′dĭd), *adj.* (of a whiskey) consisting of either two or more straight whiskeys, or of whiskey or whiskeys and neutral spirits.

Blen·heim (blĕn′əm), *n.* village in S West Germany, on the Danube: famous victory of the Duke of Marlborough over the French, 1704. German, **Blindheim.**

Blenheim spaniel, one of a breed of small spaniels with short heads and very long ears, kept as pets. [from *Blenheim* Palace, in Oxfordshire, England]

blen·ni·oid (blĕn′ĭ oid′), *adj. Ichthyol.* 1. resembling a blenny. 2. pertaining to the blennies.

blen·ny (blĕn′ĭ), *n., pl.* **-nies.** any of various fishes of the genus *Blennius* and allied genera, with an elongated tapering body and small pelvic fins inserted farther forward than the pectoral fins. [t. L: m. s. *blennius,* t. Gk.: m. *blénnos* blenny, orig. slime]

blent (blĕnt), *v.* pt. and pp. of **blend.**

bleph·a·ri·tis (blĕf′ə rī′tĭs), *n. Pathol.* inflammation of the eyelids. [f. s. Gk. *blépharon* eyelid + -ITIS]

Blé·riot (blē′ryō′), *n.* **Louis** (lwē), 1872–1936, French airplane inventor and aviator.

bles·bok (blĕs′bŏk′), *n.* a large South African antelope, *Damaliscus albifrons,* having a blaze on the face. Also, **bles·buck** (blĕs′bŭk′). [t. S Afr. D: blaze buck]

bless (blĕs), *v.t.,* **blessed** or **blest, blessing.** 1. to consecrate by a religious rite; make or pronounce holy. 2. to request of God the bestowal of divine favor on. 3. to bestow good of any kind upon: *a nation blessed with peace.* 4. to extol as holy; glorify. 5. to protect or guard from evil. 6. *Eccles.* to make the sign of the cross over. [ME *blessen,* OE *blētsian, blēdsian* consecrate, orig. with blood, der. *blōd* blood]

bless·ed (blĕs′ĭd, blĕst), *adj.* 1. consecrated; sacred; holy. 2. divinely or supremely favored; fortunate; happy. 3. beatified. 4. bringing happiness; pleasurable. 5. damned (euphemism). 6. (used for emphasis): *every blessed cent.* —**bless′ed·ly,** *adv.* —**bless′ed·ness,** *n.*

Blessed Sacrament. See **sacrament** (def. 3).

Blessed Trinity, trinity (def. 1).

Blessed Virgin, the Virgin Mary.

bless·ing (blĕs′ĭng), *n.* 1. act or words of one who blesses. 2. a special favor, mercy, or benefit. 3. a favor or gift bestowed by God, thereby bringing happiness. 4. the invoking of God's favor upon a person. 5. praise; devotion; worship. 6. a cursing (euphemism).

blest (blĕst), *v.* 1. pt. and pp. of **bless.** —*adj.* 2. blessed.

bleth·er (blĕth′ər), *v.i., v.t., n.* blather.

blew (bloo), *v.* pt. of **blow.**

Bli·da (blē′dä), *n.* a city in N Algeria. 61,808 (1954).

blight (blīt), *n.* 1. a widespread and destructive plant disease, such as chestnut blight, potato late blight, and apple fire blight. 2. any cause of destruction, ruin, or frustration. —*v.t.* 3. to cause to wither or decay; blast. 4. to destroy; ruin; frustrate. —*v.i.* 5. to suffer blight. [orig. unknown]

blimp (blĭmp), *n.* 1. a small, nonrigid airship or dirigible, used chiefly for observation. 2. *Colloq.* any dirigible. [orig. uncert.]

blind (blīnd), *adj.* 1. lacking the sense of sight. 2. unwilling, or unable to try, to understand: *blind to all arguments.* 3. not controlled by reason: *blind tenacity.* 4. not possessing or proceeding from intelligence. 5. lacking all awareness: *a blind stupor.* 6. drunk. 7. hard to see or understand: *blind reasoning.* 8. hidden from view: *a blind corner.* 9. having no outlets. 10. closed at one end: *a blind street.* 11. done without seeing: *blind flying.* 12. made without knowledge in advance: *a blind bargain.* 13. of or pertaining to blind persons. —*v.t.* 14. to make blind, as by injuring, dazzling, or bandaging the eyes. 15. to make obscure or dark. 16. to deprive of discernment or judgment. 17. to outshine; eclipse. —*n.* 18. something that obstructs vision or keeps out light, as a window shade or a blinker for a horse. See illus. under **harness.** 19. a lightly built structure of brush or other growths, esp. one in which hunters conceal themselves while hunting. 20. a cover for masking action or purpose; decoy. 21. **the blind,** sightless people. [OE, c. G *blind*] —**blind′ing,** *adj.* —**blind′ing·ly,** *adv.* —**blind′ly,** *adv.* —**blind′ness,** *n.*

—**Syn.** 1. BLIND, STONE-BLIND, PURBLIND mean lacking in vision. BLIND means unable to see with the physical eyes. STONE-BLIND emphasizes complete blindness. PURBLIND refers to weakened vision, literally or figuratively. 3. irrational, uncritical. 18. See **curtain.** 19. hiding place, ambush.

blind·age (blīn′dĭj), *n. Mil.* a screen or other structure as for protecting men in a trench. [t. F, der. *blinder* to armor, t. G: m. *blinden* blind]

blind alley, 1. a road, street, etc., closed at one end. 2. a position or situation offering no hope of progress or improvement.

blind·er (blīn′dər), *n.* 1. person or thing that blinds. 2. *U.S.* a blinker for a horse.

blind·fish (blīnd′fĭsh′), *n.* any of several small fishes with rudimentary, functionless eyes, found in subterranean streams, as *Amblyopsis spelaeus,* best known from the Mammoth Cave, in Kentucky.

blind·fold (blīnd′fōld′), *v.t.* 1. to prevent sight by covering (the eyes); cover the eyes of. 2. to impair the clear thinking of. —*n.* 3. a bandage cover the eyes. —*adj.* 4. with eyes covered: *a blindfold test.* 5. rash; unthinking. [f. BLIND + FOLD¹ wrap up, r. *blindfell,* lit., a blind-fall. Cf. OE *(ge)blindfellian* make blind]

Blind·heim (blĭnt′hīm), *n.* German name of **Blenheim.**

blind·man's buff (blīnd′mănz bŭf′), a game in which a blindfolded player tries to catch and identify one of the others. [see BUFF²]

blind spot, 1. *Anat.* a small area on the retina, insensitive to light, at which the optic nerve leaves the eye. See diag. under **eye. 2.** a matter about which one is ignorant or unintelligent, despite knowledge of related things. **3.** *Radio.* an area in which signals are weak and their reception poor.

blind staggers, *Vet. Sci.* stagger (def. 13).

blind·sto·ry (blīnd′stōr′ĭ), n., pl. -ries. *Archit.* a story without windows or windowlike openings. See illus. under **clerestory.**

blind tiger, *Obs. U.S. Slang.* an illegal liquor saloon. Also, **blind pig.**

blind·worm (blīnd′wûrm′), n. a European species of limbless lizard, *Anguis fragilis*, related to the glass snakes, *Ophisaurus*.

blink (blĭngk), v.i. **1.** to wink, esp. rapidly and repeatedly. **2.** to look with winking or half-shut eyes. **3.** to cast a glance; take a peep. **4.** to look evasively or with indifference; ignore (often fol. by *at*). **5.** to shine unsteadily or dimly; twinkle. —v.t. **6.** to cause to blink. **7.** to see dimly. **8.** to shut the eyes to; evade; shirk. —n. **9.** a blinking. **10.** a glance or glimpse. **11.** a gleam; glimmer. **12.** *Meteorol.* iceblink. [ME *blinken*, var. of *blenken* blench. Cf. G *blinken*] —Syn. **1.** See **wink.**

blink·ard (blĭngk′ərd), n. **1.** one who blinks habitually or who sees imperfectly. **2.** one who lacks intellectual perception.

blink·er (blĭngk′ər), n. **1.** a device for flashing light signals. **2.** either of two flaps on a bridle, to prevent a horse from seeing sidewise or backward; a blinder. **3.** (*pl.*) goggles.

blip (blĭp), n. a spot of light on a radar screen indicating the position of a plane, submarine, or other object.

bliss (blĭs), n. **1.** lightness of heart; blitheness; gladness. **2.** supreme happiness or delight. **3.** *Theol.* the joy of heaven. **4.** a cause of great joy or happiness. [ME *blisse*, OE *bliss*, *blīths*, der. *blīthe* BLITHE] —Syn. **2.** See **happiness.** —Ant. **2.** despair.

bliss·ful (blĭs′fəl), adj. full of, abounding in, enjoying, or conferring bliss; supremely joyful. —**bliss′ful·ly,** adv. —**bliss′ful·ness,** n.

blis·ter (blĭs′tər), n. **1.** a thin vesicle on the skin, containing watery matter or serum, as from a burn or other injury. **2.** any similar swelling, as an air bubble in a casting or a paint blister. **3.** *Mil.* a transparent bulge on the fuselage of an airplane, usually for mounting a gun. —v.t. **4.** to raise a blister or blisters on. **5.** to subject to burning shame or disgrace. —v.i. **6.** to rise in blisters; become blistered. [ME *blister, blester,* ? t. OF: m. *blestre* clod, lump (prob. of Gmc. orig.)] —**blis′ter·y,** adj.

blister beetle, any of various beetles of the family *Meloidae*, many of which produce a secretion capable of blistering the skin, as the Spanish fly.

blister gas, *Chem. Warfare.* a poison gas that burns or blisters the tissues of the body.

blister rust, *Bot.* a disease, esp. of white pine trees, manifested by cankers and in the spring by blisters, raised by fungi of the genus *Cronartium*.

B. Lit., Bachelor of Literature.

blithe (blīth, blĭth), adj. joyous, merry, or gay in disposition; glad; cheerful. [ME; OE *blīthe* kind, pleasant, joyous] —**blithe′ly,** adv. —**Syn.** mirthful, sprightly, lighthearted, buoyant. —**Ant.** solemn.

blithe·some (blīth′səm, blĭth′-), adj. light-hearted; merry; cheerful: *a blithesome nature.* —**blithe′some·ly,** adv. —**blithe′some·ness,** n.

B. Litt., Bachelor of Letters.

blitz (blĭts), n. **1.** *Mil.* war waged by surprise, swiftly and violently, as by the use of aircraft, tanks, etc. **2.** any swift, vigorous attack. —v.t. **3.** to attack with a blitz. Also, **blitz·krieg** (blĭts′krēg′). [t. G: lightning war]

bliz·zard (blĭz′ərd), n. **1.** a violent windstorm with dry, driving snow and intense cold. **2.** a widespread and heavy snowstorm. [var. of d. *blizzer* blaze, flash, blinding flash of lightning; sense widened from lightning to storm. Cf. OE *blysa, blyse* torch, and *blysian* burn. Appar. first used in present sense in Iowa in 1870.]

B. LL., Bachelor of Laws.

bloat (blōt), v.t. **1.** to make distended, as with air, water, etc.; cause to swell. **2.** to puff up; make vain or conceited. **3.** to cure (fishes) as bloaters. —v.i. **4.** to become swollen; be puffed out or dilated. —n. **5.** *Vet. Sci.* (in cattle, sheep, and horses) a distention of the rumen or paunch or of the large colon by gases of fermentation, caused by eating ravenously of green forage, esp. legumes. [der. *bloat,* adj., ME *blout* puffy, t. Scand.; cf. Icel. *blautr* soft]

bloat·er (blō′tər), n. **1.** a herring cured by being salted and briefly smoked and dried. **2.** a mackerel similarly cured. **3.** a deep-water cisco, of the whitefish family, *Leucichthys* species, of the Great Lakes.

blob (blŏb), n. **1.** a small globe of liquid; a bubble. **2.** a small lump, drop, splotch, or daub. [? imit.]

bloc (blŏk), n. **1.** *Europ. Pol.* a coalition of factions or parties for a particular measure or purpose. **2.** *U.S. Pol.* a group of legislators, usually of both parties, who vote together for some particular interest: *the Farm bloc in Congress.* [t. F. See BLOCK]

block (blŏk), n. **1.** a solid mass of wood, stone, etc., usually with one or more plane or approximately plane faces. **2.** a blockhead. **3.** a mold or piece on which something is shaped or kept in shape, as a hat block. **4.** a piece of wood prepared for cutting, or as cut, for wood engraving. **5.** *Print.* the base on which a plate is mounted to make it type-high. **6.** a platform on which a person is beheaded. **7.** a platform from which an auctioneer sells. **8.** *Mach.* a device consisting of one or more grooved pulleys mounted in a casing or shell, to which a hook or the like is attached, used for transmitting power, changing the direction of motion, etc.

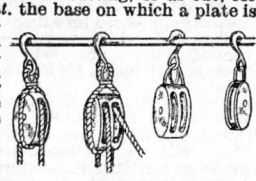
Single and double blocks (def. 8)

9. an obstacle or hindrance. **10.** a blocking or obstructing, or blocked or obstructed state or condition. **11.** *Pathol.* an obstruction, as of a nerve. **12.** *Sports.* a hindering of an opponent's actions. **13.** a quantity, portion, or section taken as a unit or dealt with at one time: *block of tickets.* **14.** *U.S.* a portion of a city, town, etc. enclosed by (usually four) neighboring and intersecting streets. **15.** *U.S.* the length of one side of this. **16.** *Chiefly Brit.* a large building divided into separate houses, shops, etc. **17.** a large number of shares taken together, as on the stock exchange. **18.** one of the short divisions into which a railroad is divided for signaling purposes. **19.** *Philately.* a group of four or more unseparated stamps, not in a strip. —v.t. **20.** to fit with blocks; mount on a block. **21.** to shape or prepare on or with a block. **22.** to sketch or outline roughly or in a general plan, without details (often fol. by *out*). **23.** to obstruct (a space, progress); check (a person) by placing obstacles in the way; stop up. **24.** *Pathol., Physiol.* to stop the passage of impulses in (a nerve, etc.). **25.** *Football.* to bump (an opponent) out of the play. —v.i. **26.** to act so as to obstruct an opponent, as in football, boxing, and baseball. [ME *blok,* appar. t. OF: m. *bloc* block, mass, t. Gmc. (cf. G *block*)] —**block′er,** n.

block·ade (blŏ kād′), n., v., -aded, -ading. —n. **1.** *Naval, Mil.* the shutting up of a place, esp. a port, harbor, or part of a coast by hostile ships or troops to prevent entrance or exit. **2.** any obstruction of passage or progress. —v.t. **3.** to subject to a blockade. —**block·ad′er,** n.

block·age (blŏk′ĭj), n. an obstruction.

block and tackle, the pulley blocks and ropes used for hoisting.

block·bust·er (blŏk′bŭs′tər), n. *Colloq.* an aerial bomb containing high explosives and weighing from 4 to 8 tons, used as a large scale demolition bomb.

block·head (blŏk′hĕd′), n. a stupid fellow; a dolt.

block·house (blŏk′hous′), n. **1.** *Mil.* a fortified structure with ports or loopholes for gunfire, used against bombs, artillery, and small arms fire. **2.** (formerly) a building, usually of hewn timber and with a projecting upper story, having loopholes for musketry. **3.** a house built of squared logs.

block·ish (blŏk′ĭsh), adj. like a block; dull; stupid. —**block′ish·ly,** adv. —**block′ish·ness,** n.

Block Island, an island in the Atlantic, S of Rhode Island: a part of that State.

block lava, *Geol.* lava flows composed of rough angular blocks.

block letter, *Print.* a type face or letter designed without serifs.

block line, *Mach.* a rope, wire, chain, etc., running through a series of pulleys.

block plane, a small plane used for cutting across the grain of the wood.

block print, *Fine Arts.* a design printed by means of blocks of wood or metal.

block signal, a fixed railway signal governing the movements of trains entering and using a block.

block system, 1. a series of consecutive railroad blocks. **2.** a method of controlling train movements by means of blocks and block signals.

block·y (blŏk′ĭ), adj., blockier, blockiest. **1.** heavily built; stocky. **2.** marked by blocks or patches of unequally distributed light and shade, as in a photograph.

Bloem·fon·tein (blōōm′fŏn tān′), n. a city in the central part of the Republic of South Africa: capital of Orange Free State. 80,606; with suburbs, 109,180 (1951).

Blois (blwä), n. a city in central France, on the Loire river: historic castle. 28,190 (1954).

bloke (blōk), n. *Chiefly Brit. Slang.* man; fellow; guy.

blond (blŏnd), adj. **1.** (of hair, skin, etc.) light-colored. **2.** (of a person) having light-colored hair and skin. —n. **3.** a blond person. **4.** lace or net of silk, orig. unbleached, manufactured in France, now, esp., black silk lace. [t. F, t. ML: s. *blondus* yellow. Cf. OE *blondenfeax* gray-haired] —**blonde,** adj. n. fem. —**blond′ness,** n.

blood (blŭd), n. **1.** the fluid that circulates in the arteries and veins or principal vascular system of animals, in man being of a red color and consisting of a pale-yellow plasma containing semisolid corpuscles. **2.** body fluids spilling or spilled out; gore. **3.** the vital principle; life. **4.** bloodshed; slaughter; murder. **5.** the juice or

ăct, āble, dâre, ärt; ĕbb, ēqual; ĭf, īce; hŏt, ōver, ôrder, oil, bŏŏk, ōōze, out; ŭp, ūse, ûrge; ə = a in alone; ch, chief; g, give; ng, ring; sh, shoe; th, thin; th, that; zh, vision. See the full key on inside cover.

sap of plants. **6.** temper or state of mind: *a person of hot blood.* **7.** man's fleshly nature: *the frailty of men's blood.* **8.** *Chiefly Brit.* a man of fire or spirit. **9.** a rake. **10.** physical and cultural extraction. **11.** royal extraction. **12.** descent from a common ancestor: *related by blood.* **13.** *Stock Breeding.* recorded and respected ancestry; purebred breeding. **14. in cold blood,** calmly, coolly, and deliberately. —*v.t.* **15.** *Hunting.* to give (hounds, etc.) a first taste or sight of blood. **16.** *Obs.* to stain with blood. [ME; OE *blōd*, c. G *blut*] —**blood**-**like′,** *adj.*

blood bank, 1. a place where blood plasma is stored. **2.** such a supply of blood.

blood count, the count of the number of red or white blood cells in a specific volume of blood.

blood·cur·dling (blŭd′kûrd′lĭng), *adj.* frightening; terrifyingly horrible.

blood·ed (blŭd′ĭd), *adj.* **1.** having blood: *warm-blooded animals.* **2.** (of horses, etc.) derived from ancestors of good blood; having a good pedigree. **3.** having been through battle: *blooded troops.*

blood group, blood type.

blood·guilt·y (blŭd′gĭl′tĭ), *adj.* guilty of murder or bloodshed. —**blood′guilt′i·ness,** *n.*

blood heat, the normal temperature (about 98.6°F.) of human blood.

blood·hound (blŭd′hound′), *n.* one of a breed of large, powerful dogs with a very acute sense of smell, used for tracking game, human fugitives, etc.

Bloodhound
(25 to 27 in. high at the shoulder)

blood·less (blŭd′lĭs), *adj.* **1.** without blood; pale. **2.** free from bloodshed: *a bloodless victory.* **3.** spiritless; without energy. **4.** cold-hearted: *bloodless charity.* —**blood′-less·ly,** *adv.* —**blood′less·ness,** *n.*

blood·let·ting (blŭd′lĕt′ĭng), *n.* act of letting blood by opening a vein.

blood·mo·bile (blŭd′mə bēl′), *n.* a small truck with medical equipment for receiving blood donations.

blood money, 1. a fee paid to a hired murderer. **2.** compensation paid to the survivors of a slain man.

blood plasma, the liquid part of human blood, often stored in hospitals, etc., for transfusions.

blood poisoning, *Pathol.* a morbid condition of the blood due to the presence of toxic matter or microörganisms; toxemia; septicemia; pyemia.

blood pressure, *Physiol.* the pressure of the blood against the inner walls of the blood vessels, varying in different parts of the body, during different phases of contraction of the heart, and under different conditions of health, exertion, etc.

blood-red (blŭd′rĕd′), *adj.* **1.** of the deep-red color of blood. **2.** red with blood.

blood relation, one related by birth. Also, **blood relative.**

blood·root (blŭd′rōōt′, -rŏŏt′), *n.* **1.** a North American papaveraceous plant, *Sanguinaria canadensis,* with red root and root sap. **2.** an Old World rosaceous plant, *Potentilla tormentilla,* with a reddish root.

blood serum, serum (def. 1).

blood·shed (blŭd′shĕd′), *n.* destruction of life; slaughter. Also, **blood′shed′ding.**

blood·shot (blŭd′shŏt′), *adj.* (of the eyes) red from dilated blood vessels. [var. of *blood-shotten,* f. BLOOD + *shot(ten),* pp. of SHOOT]

blood·stain (blŭd′stān′), *n.* a spot or trace of blood.

blood·stained (blŭd′stānd′), *adj.* **1.** stained with blood. **2.** guilty of bloodshed.

blood·stone (blŭd′stōn′), *n.* *Jewelry.* a greenish variety of chalcedony with small bloodlike spots of red jasper scattered through it; heliotrope.

blood stream, the blood flowing through a circulatory system.

blood·suck·er (blŭd′sŭk′ər), *n.* **1.** any animal that sucks blood, esp. a leech. **2.** an extortioner. **3.** sponger (def. 2).

blood test, a test of a sample of blood to determine blood type, presence of infection, parentage, etc.

blood·thirst·y (blŭd′thûrs′tĭ), *adj.* eager to shed blood; murderous. —**blood′thirst′i·ly,** *adv.* —**blood′-thirst′i·ness,** *n.*

blood transfusion, the injection of blood from one person or animal into the blood stream of another.

blood type, one of several classifications into which the blood may be grouped with reference to its agglutinogens. Also, **blood group.**

blood vessel, any of the vessels (arteries, veins, capillaries) through which the blood circulates.

blood·wort (blŭd′wûrt′), *n.* **1.** any of the plants, with red roots, constituting the family *Haemodoraceae,* esp. the redroot, *Gyrotheca tinctoria,* of North America. **2.** any of various other plants with red roots, leaves, etc., as the dock or the rattlesnake weed. **3.** bloodroot.

blood·y (blŭd′ĭ), *adj.*, **blood·i·er, blood·i·est,** *v.,* **blood·ied, blood·y·ing,** *adv.* —*adj.* **1.** stained with blood. **2.** attended with bloodshed: *a bloody battle.* **3.** inclined to bloodshed. **4.** of, of the nature of, or pertaining to blood; containing or composed of blood. **5.** *Brit. Slang.* damned. —*v.t.* **6.** to stain with blood. —*adv.* **7.** *Brit.*

Slang. very. [ME *blody,* OE *blōdig*] —**blood′i·ly,** *adv.* —**blood′i·ness,** *n.* —**Syn. 3.** bloodthirsty, murderous.

bloom[1] (blōōm), *n.* **1.** the flower of a plant. **2.** flowers collectively. **3.** state of having the buds opened. **4.** a flourishing, healthy condition: *the bloom of youth.* **5.** a glow or flush on the cheek indicative of youth and health. **6.** *Bot.* a whitish powdery deposit or coating, as on the surface of certain fruits and leaves. **7.** any similar surface coating or appearance. **8.** any of certain minerals occurring as a pulverulent incrustation. —*v.i.* **9.** to produce or yield blossoms. **10.** to flourish. **11.** to be in a state of healthful beauty and vigor. **12.** to glow with a warm color. —*v.t.* **13.** to cause to yield blossoms. **14.** to cause to flourish. **15.** to invest with luster or beauty. **16.** to cause a cloudy area on (something shiny). [ME *blom(e),* t. Scand.; cf. Icel. *blōm* flower, *blōmi* prosperity] —**bloom′less,** *adj.* —**Syn. 4.** freshness, glow, flush.

bloom[2] (blōōm), *n.* a semifinished steel ingot rolled to reduced size. [OE *blōma* lump of metal]

bloom·er (blōō′mər), *n.* **1.** (*pl.*) loose trousers gathered at the knee, worn by women as part of gymnasium, riding, or other like dress. **2.** (*pl.*) a woman's undergarment so designed. **3.** a costume for women, advocated about 1850 by Mrs. Amelia Bloomer of New York, consisting of a short skirt and loose trousers buttoned around the ankle. [named after Mrs. *Bloomer.* See def. 3]

Bloom·field (blōōm′fēld′), *n.* a city in NE New Jersey. 51,867 (1960).

bloom·ing (blōō′mĭng), *adj.* **1.** in bloom; blossoming; in flower. **2.** glowing as with youthful freshness and vigor. **3.** flourishing; prospering. **4.** *Slang.* (as a euphemism) damned. —**bloom′ing·ly,** *adv.*

Bloom·ing·ton (blōō′mĭng tən), *n.* **1.** a city in central Illinois. 36,271 (1960). **2.** a city in S Indiana. 31,357 (1960). **3.** a city in SE Minnesota. 50,498 (1960).

bloom·y (blōō′mĭ), *adj.* **1.** covered with blossoms; in full flower. **2.** having a bloom (def. 6), as fruit.

blos·som (blŏs′əm), *n. Bot.* **1.** the flower of a plant, esp. of one producing an edible fruit. **2.** the state of flowering: *the apple tree is in blossom.* —*v.i.* **3.** *Bot.* to produce or yield blossoms. **4.** to flourish; develop (often fol. by *out*). [ME *blosme, blossem,* OE *blōs(t)m(a)* flower] —**blos′som·less,** *adj.* —**blos′som·y,** *adj.*

blot[1] (blŏt), *n., v.,* **blotted, blotting.** —*n.* **1.** a spot or stain, esp. of ink on paper. **2.** a blemish or reproach on character or reputation. **3.** an erasure or obliteration, as in a writing. —*v.t.* **4.** to spot, stain, or bespatter. **5.** to darken; make dim; obscure or eclipse. **6.** to make indistinguishable (fol. by *out*): *blot out a memory.* **7.** to dry with absorbent paper or the like. **8.** to destroy; wipe out completely (fol. by *out*). **9.** to paint coarsely; daub. —*v.i.* **10.** (of ink, etc.) to spread in a stain. **11.** to become blotted or stained: *this paper blots easily.* [ME; orig. uncert.] —**blot′less,** *adj.* —**Syn. 1.** blotch.

blot[2] (blŏt), *n.* **1.** *Backgammon.* an exposed piece liable to be taken or forfeited. **2.** an exposed or weak point, as in an argument or course of action. [cf. Dan. *blot* bare]

blotch (blŏch), *n.* **1.** a large irregular spot or blot. —*v.t.* **2.** to mark with blotches; blot, spot, or blur. [b. BLOT[1] and BOTCH[2]] —**blotch′y,** *adj.*

blot·ter (blŏt′ər), *n.* **1.** a piece of blotting paper used to absorb excess ink, to protect a desk, etc. **2.** a book in which transactions or occurrences, as sales, arrests, etc., are recorded as they take place.

blotting paper, a soft, absorbent, unsized paper.

blouse (blous, blouz), *n.* **1.** a loosely fitting waist worn by women or children, sometimes worn outside the skirt and belted. **2.** a single-breasted, semifitting jacket worn with the service uniform of the U. S. Army. **3.** a loose upper garment, reaching about to the knees, worn esp. by peasants in France, Russia, etc. [t. F, ? t. Pr.: m. (*lano) blouso* short (wool)] —**blouse′like′,** *adj.*

blow[1] (blō), *n.* **1.** a sudden stroke with hand, fist, or weapon. **2.** a sudden shock, or a calamity or reverse. **3.** a sudden attack or drastic action. **4.** at one blow, with a single act. **5.** come to blows, to start to fight. [northern ME *blaw;* orig. uncert.] —**Syn. 1.** buffet, thump, thwack, rap, slap, cuff, box. BLOW, STROKE both refer to a sudden and forceful impact, but differ both literally and figuratively, in that the first emphasizes the violence of the impact: *a blow from a hammer, a blow to one's hopes.* STROKE indicates precision and finality, often together with the idea of unexpectedness: *the stroke of a piston, a forehand stroke, a stroke of lightning.*

blow[2] (blō), *v.,* **blew, blown, blowing,** —*v.i.* **1.** (of the wind or air) to be in motion. **2.** to move along, carried by or as by the wind: *the dust was blowing.* **3.** to produce or emit a current of air, as with the mouth, a bellows, etc.: *blow on your hands.* **4.** *Music.* (of horn, trumpet, etc.) to give out sound. **5.** to make a blowing sound; whistle. **6.** to breathe hard or quickly; pant. **7.** *Colloq.* to boast; brag. **8.** *Zool.* (of a whale) to spout. **9.** (of a fuse, light bulb, vacuum tube, tire, etc.) to go bad; become unusable (often fol. by *out*). **10. blow over, a.** to cease; subside. **b.** to be forgotten. **11. blow up, a.** to come into being: *a storm blew up.* **b.** to explode: *the ship blew up.* **c.** *Colloq.* to lose one's temper. **d.** *Colloq.* to scold; abuse. —*v.t.* **12.** to drive by means of a current of air. **13.** to spread by report. **14.** to drive a current of air upon. **15.** to clear or empty by forcing air through. **16.** to shape (glass, etc.) with a current of air. **17.** to cause to sound, emp. by a current of air. **18.** to cause to explode (fol. by *up, to bits,* etc.). **19.** *Photog.* to reproduce by enlargement (fol. by *up*). **20.** to expel

b., blend of, blended; c., cognate with; d., dialect, dialectal; der., derived from; f., formed from; g., going back to; m., modification of; r., replacing; s., stem of; t., taken from; ?, perhaps. See the full key on inside cover.

noisily (fol. by *off*). **21.** to put (a horse) out of breath by fatigue. **22.** (*pp.* **blowed**) *Slang.* to damn (a euphemism). **23.** *U.S. Slang.* to spend money on. **24.** *U.S. Slang.* to squander; spend quickly. —*n.* **25.** a blast of air or wind. **26.** act of producing a blast of air, as in playing a wind instrument. **27.** *Colloq.* boasting or brag. **28.** *Metall.* **a.** the blast of air used in making steel in a converter. **b.** the time during which, or that part of a process in which, it is used. [ME *blowe(n)*, OE *blāwan*]

low³ (blō), *v.,* **blew, blown, blowing,** *n.* —*v.i., v.t.* **1.** to blossom; bloom; flower. —*n.* **2.** a yield or display of blossoms. **3.** state of blossoming. [ME *blowen*, OE *blōwan*]

low·er (blō′ər), *n.* **1.** a person or thing that blows. **2.** a machine for forcing air through a furnace, building, mine, etc. **3.** *Colloq.* a boaster.

low·fish (blō′fĭsh′), *n.* puffer (def. 2).

low·fly (blō′flī′), *n., pl.* **-flies.** any of various true flies, *Diptera,* which deposit their eggs or larvae on carcasses or meat, or in sores, wounds, etc.

low·gun (blō′gŭn′), *n.* a pipe or tube through which missiles are blown by the breath.

low·hole (blō′hōl′), *n.* **1.** an air or gas vent. **2.** either of two nostrils or spiracles, or a single one, at the top of the head in whales and other cetaceans, through which they breathe. **3.** a hole in the ice to which whales or seals come to breathe. **4.** *Metall.* a defect in a casting caused by trapped steam or gas.

low·ing (blō′ĭng), *n.* **1.** the sound of any vapor or gas issuing from a vent under pressure. **2.** *Metall.* a disturbance caused by gas or steam blowing through molten metal.

lown¹ (blōn), *adj.* **1.** inflated; distended. **2.** out of breath; fatigued; exhausted. **3.** flyblown. **4.** formed by blowing: *blown glass.* [see BLOW²]

lown² (blōn), *adj.* *Hort.* fully expanded or opened, as a flower. [see BLOW³]

low·off (blō′ôf′, -ŏf′), *n.* **1.** a current of escaping surplus steam, water, etc. **2.** a device which permits and channels such a current. **3.** *Slang.* one who brags.

low·out (blō′out′), *n.* **1.** a rupture of an automobile tire. **2.** a sudden or violent escape of air, steam, or the like. **3.** *Colloq.* a big entertainment or spree.

low·pipe (blō′pīp′), *n.* **1.** a tube through which a stream of air or gas is forced into a flame to concentrate and increase its heating action. **2.** *Glass Blowing.* a long iron pipe used to gather and blow the viscous glass into hollow ware. **3.** blowgun. **4.** *Med.* an instrument used to observe or clean a cavity.

low·torch (blō′tôrch′), *n.* a small portable apparatus which gives an extremely hot gasoline flame intensified by a blast, used in plumbing, etc.

low·tube (blō′tūb′, -tōōb′), *n.* **1.** blowgun. **2.** blowpipe (def. 2).

low·up (blō′ŭp′), *n.* **1.** an explosion or other drastic trouble. **2.** a violent outburst of temper or scolding. **3.** *Photog.* an enlargement.

low·y (blō′ĭ), *adj.* windy.

lowz·y (blou′zĭ), *adj.,* **blowzier, blowziest. 1.** disheveled; unkempt: *blowzy hair.* **2.** red-faced. Also, **blowzed** (blouzd). [der. *blowze* wench, of unknown origin]

.L.S., Bachelor of Library Science.

lub·ber (blŭb′ər), *n.* **1.** *Zool.* the fat found between the skin and muscle of whales and other cetaceans, from which oil is made. **2.** act of blubbering. —*v.i.* **3.** to weep, usually noisily and with contorted face. —*v.t.* **4.** to say while weeping. **5.** to disfigure with weeping. —*adj.* **6.** disfigured with blubbering. [ME *bluber,* n., *blubren,* v.; appar. imit.] —**blub′ber·er,** *n.* —**blub′-ber·ing·ly,** *adv.*

lub·ber·y (blŭb′ə rĭ), *adj.* **1.** abounding in or resembling blubber. **2.** (of a cetacean) fat. **3.** blubbered; disfigured; swollen.

lu·cher (blōō′kər, -chər), *n.* **1.** a kind of strong leather half boot. **2.** a shoe with the vamp continued up beneath the top, which laps over it from the sides. [named after Field Marshal von *Blücher*]

Blü·cher (blōō′kər, -chər; *Ger.* blý′кнәr), *n.* **Gebhart Leberecht von** (gĕp′härt lā′bə rĕкнt′ fən), 1742-1819, Prussian field marshal.

ludg·eon (blŭj′ən), *n.* **1.** a short, heavy club with one end loaded, or thicker and heavier than the other. —*v.t.* **2.** to strike or fell with a bludgeon. **3.** to force (someone) into something; bully. [orig. unknown] —**bludg′eon·er, bludg·eon·eer** (blŭj′ə nîr′), *n.*

lue (blōō), *n., adj.,* **bluer, bluest,** *v.,* **blued, bluing** or **blueing.** —*n.* **1.** the pure hue of clear sky; deep azure (between green and violet in the spectrum). **2.** the blue, *Poetic.* **a.** the sky. **b.** the sea. **3.** bluing. **4.** a blue thing. **5.** a person who wears blue, or is a member of a group characterized by some blue symbol. **6.** bluestocking. **7.** (*pl.*) See **blues. 8.** out of the blue, unexpectedly; from an unforeseen or unknown source. —*adj.* **9.** of the color of blue. **10.** (of the skin) discolored by cold, contusion, fear, or vascular collapse. **11.** depressed in spirits. **12.** dismal: *a blue outlook.* **13.** characterized by or stemming from rigid morals or religion; *blue laws.* **14.** marked by blasphemy: *the air was blue with oaths.* **15.** once in a blue moon, rarely and exceptionally. —*v.t.* **16.** to make blue; dye a blue color. **17.** to tinge with bluing. [ME *blewe,* t. OF: m. *bleu,* t. Gmc. (cf. G *blau*)] —**blue′ly,** *adv.* —**blue′ness,** *n.* —**Syn. 11.** despondent, dejected.

blue baby, an infant with congenital cyanosis.

Blue·beard (blōō′bîrd′), *n.* **1.** (in folklore) a nickname of the Chevalier Raoul, whose seventh wife found in a forbidden room the bodies of the other six. **2.** any person alleged to have murdered a number of his wives or other women.

blue·bell (blōō′bĕl′), *n.* **1.** any of various plants with blue bell-shaped flowers, as the harebell (**bluebell of Scotland**), or a liliaceous plant, *Scilla nonscripta,* of the Old World. **2.** (*usually pl.*) the lungwort, *Mertensia virginica,* of the U.S.

blue·ber·ry (blōō′bĕr′ĭ), *n., pl.* **-ries. 1.** the edible berry, usually bluish, of any of various shrubs of the ericaceous genus *Vaccinium.* **2.** any of these shrubs.

blue·bill (blōō′bĭl′), *n.* scaup duck.

blue·bird (blōō′bûrd′), *n.* **1.** any bird of the genus *Sialia,* comprising small North American passerine songbirds whose prevailing color is blue; esp. the well-known eastern bluebird, *S. sialis,* which appears early in the spring. **2.** any of various other birds of which the predominant color is blue.

blue blood, 1. the alleged hereditary exclusiveness or trait of aristocratic families. **2.** *Colloq.* an aristocrat. —**blue′-blood′ed,** *adj.*

blue·bon·net (blōō′bŏn′ĭt), *n.* **1.** the cornflower, *Centaurea Cyanus.* **2.** *Bot.* a blue-flowering lupine, esp. one, *Lupinus subcarnosus,* adopted as the State flower of Texas. **3.** a broad, flat bonnet of blue wool, formerly much worn in Scotland. **4.** a Scottish soldier who wore such a bonnet. **5.** any Scot. Also, **blue bonnet, blue·cap** (blōō′kăp′).

blue book, 1. *U.S. Colloq.* a directory of socially prominent persons. **2.** *U.S.* a blank book used in taking college examinations, usually with a blue cover. **3.** a British parliamentary or other official publication, bound in a blue cover. Also, **blue/book/.**

blue·bot·tle (blōō′bŏt′əl), *n.* **1.** the cornflower (def. 1). **2.** any of various other plants with blue flowers, esp. of the genera *Campanula* and *Scilla.* **3.** bluebottle fly.

bluebottle fly, any of several large, metallic blue-and-green flies of the dipterous family *Calliphoridae.* The larvae of some are parasites of domestic animals.

blue cheese, an American type of Roquefort cheese.

blue·coat (blōō′kōt′), *n.* **1.** a person who wears a blue coat or uniform. **2.** a policeman. **3.** a soldier in the U.S. Army in earlier times. —**blue′-coat′ed,** *adj.*

blue-curls (blōō′kûrlz′), *n.* **1.** any plant of the labiate genus *Trichostema,* comprising herbs with blue to pink or (rarely) white flowers and long, curved filaments. **2.** the selfheal (def. 1). Also, **blue curls.**

blue devils, 1. low spirits. **2.** delirium tremens.

blue-eyed grass (blōō′īd′), any of numerous plants of the iridaceous genus *Sisyrinchium,* having grasslike leaves and small, usually blue, flowers.

Blue·fields (blōō′fēldz′), *n.* a seaport in E Nicaragua. 8016 (1950).

blue·fish (blōō′fĭsh′), *n., pl.* **-fishes,** (*esp. collectively*) **-fish. 1.** a predacious marine food fish, *Pomatomus saltatrix,* bluish or greenish in color, of the Atlantic coast of the Americas. **2.** any of many diverse kinds of fishes, usually of a bluish color.

blue flag, any North American plant of the genus *Iris,* esp. *I. versicolor* (**larger blue flag**), and *I. prismatica* (**slender blue flag**), the former being the State flower of Tennessee.

blue fox, 1. a variety of the small Arctic fox, *Alopex lagopus,* having a year-round bluish pelt. **2.** any fox of this species while having a bluish fur in the summer season. **3.** the blue fur. **4.** any white fox fur dyed blue.

blue-gill (blōō′gĭl′), *n.* a fresh-water sunfish, *Lepomis macrochirus,* of the Mississippi valley, much used for food and important among the smaller game fishes.

blue grama. See **grama grass.**

blue-grass (blōō′grăs′, -gräs′), *n.* **1.** any of the grasses in the genus *Poa,* as the Kentucky bluegrass, *P. pratensis,* etc. **2.** the **Bluegrass,** the Bluegrass Region.

Bluegrass Region, a region in central Kentucky, famous for its luxuriant crops of bluegrass.

blue-green (blōō′grēn′), *n.* a color about midway between blue and green in the spectrum.

blue-green algae, *Bot.* unicellular or filamentous, asexual algae belonging to the class *Myxophyceae* (*Cyanophyceae*), usually bluish-green as the result of blue pigments added to their chlorophyll.

blue grouse, a local name for any grouse of the North American genus *Dendragapus,* as the dusky grouse (*D. obscurus*) of the Rocky Mountain region.

blue gum, eucalyptus.

blue-hearts (blōō′härts′), *n.* a perennial North American scrophulariaceous herb, *Buchnera americana,* with deep-purple flowers.

blue·ing (blōō′ĭng), *n.* bluing.

blue·ish (blōō′ĭsh), *adj.* bluish.

blue·jack (blōō′jăk′), *n.* a small oak, *Quercus cinerea* (or *brevifolia*), of the southern U.S.

blue·jack·et (blōō′jăk′ĭt), *n.* a sailor.

blue·jay (blōō′jā′), *n.* a well-known crested jay, *Cyanocitta cristata,* of the Eastern U.S. and Canada.

blue jeans, trousers or overalls of dark blue denim.

blue laws, *U.S.* severe or puritanical laws (from an alleged code said to have been adopted in the colonies of Connecticut and New Haven).

ăct, āble, dâre, ärt; ĕbb, ēqual; Yf, īce; hŏt, ōver, ôrder, oil, bŏŏk, ōōze, out; ŭp, ūse, ûrge; ə = a in alone; ch, chief; g, give; ng, ring; sh, shoe; th, thin; t̄h, that; zh, vision. See the full key on inside cover.

blue mass, *Pharm.* a preparation of metallic mercury with other ingredients, used for making blue pills.

Blue Mountains, a low range of mountains in NE Oregon and SE Washington.

Blue Nile. See Nile, Blue.

blue-pen·cil (bloo´pĕn´sal), *v.t.,* **-ciled, -ciling** or (*esp. Brit.*) **-cilled, -cilling.** to alter, abridge, or cancel with, or as with, a pencil that makes a blue mark, as in editing a manuscript.

blue peter, *Naut.* a blue flag with a white square in the center, hoisted as a signal for immediate sailing, to recall boats, etc. [f. BLUE + *peter,* orig. REPEATER]

blue pill, *Pharm.* a pill of blue mass, used as an alterative, cathartic, etc.

blue·point (bloo´point´), *n.* a small oyster suitable for serving raw.

Blue peter

blue·print (bloo´print´), *n.* **1.** a process of photographic printing, based on ferric salts, in which the prints are white on a blue ground: used chiefly in making copies of tracings. **2.** a detailed outline or plan. —*v.t.* **3.** to make a blueprint of.

blue racer, a variety of black snake, occurring in central U.S.

blue ribbon, 1. first prize; highest award. **2.** a badge indicating a pledge of abstinence from alcohol. **3.** a blue ribbon worn as a badge of honor, esp. by members of the Order of the Garter of the British knighthood.

Blue Ridge, a mountain range extending from N Virginia SW to N Georgia: a part of the Appalachians.

blues (blooz), *n. pl.* **1.** despondency; melancholy. **2.** *Jazz.* a type of song, of American Negro origin, predominantly melancholy in character and usually performed in slow tempo. [short for BLUE DEVILS]

blue-sky law (bloo´ski´), a law designed to prevent the sale of fraudulent securities.

blue·stock·ing (bloo´stŏk´Yng), *n.* **1.** a woman who affects literary or intellectual tastes. **2.** a member of a mid-eighteenth century London literary circle. [so called because members of this group (def. 2) did not wear formal dress] —**blue´stock´ing·ism,** *n.*

blue·stone (bloo´stōn´), *n.* a bluish argillaceous sandstone used for building purposes, flagging, etc.

blue streak, *Colloq.* something moving very fast.

blu·et (bloo´Yt), *n.* **1.** any of various plants with blue flowers, as the cornflower. **2.** (*often pl.*) any of various species of *Houstonia,* esp. *Houstonia caerulea.* [ME *blewet,* t. F: m. *bluet,* dim. of *bleu* blue]

blue vitriol, sulfate of copper, $CuSO_4 \cdot 5H_2O$, a compound occurring in large, transparent, deep-blue triclinic crystals, used in calico printing, medicine, etc.

blue·weed (bloo´wēd´), *n.* a bristly, boraginaceous weed, *Echium vulgare,* with showy blue flowers, a native of Europe naturalized in the U.S.

blue whale, the sulphur-bottom.

blue-winged teal (bloo´wYngd´), a small pond and river duck, *Anas discors,* of North America, with grayish-blue patches on the wings.

blue·wood (bloo´wood´), *n.* a rhamnaceous shrub or small tree, *Condalia obovata,* of western Texas and northern Mexico, often forming dense chaparral.

bluff¹ (blŭf), *adj.* **1.** somewhat abrupt and unconventional in manner; hearty; frank. **2.** presenting a bold and nearly perpendicular front, as a coastline. **3.** *Naut.* (of a ship) presenting a broad, flattened front. —*n.* **4.** a cliff, headland, or hill with a broad, steep face. [prob. t. LG: m. *blaf* flat] —**bluff´ly,** *adv.* —**bluff´ness,** *n.* —Syn. **1.** See **blunt. 2.** steep, precipitous.

bluff² (blŭf), *v.t.* **1.** to mislead by presenting a bold front. **2.** to gain by bluffing: *he bluffed his way.* **3.** *Poker.* to deceive by a show of confidence in the strength of one's cards. —*v.i.* **4.** to mislead someone by presenting a bold front. —*n.* **5.** act of bluffing. **6.** one who bluffs; a bluffer. [orig. uncert.] —**bluff´er,** *n.*

blu·ing (bloo´Yng), *n.* a substance, as indigo, used to whiten clothes or give them a bluish tinge. Also, **blueing.**

blu·ish (bloo´Ysh), *adj.* somewhat blue. Also, **blueish.** —**blu´ish·ness,** *n.*

Blum (bloom), *n.* **Léon** (lĕ ôN´), 1872–1950, French statesman.

blun·der (blŭn´dər), *n.* **1.** a gross or stupid mistake. —*v.i.* **2.** to move or act blindly, stupidly, or without direction or steady guidance. **3.** to make a gross or stupid mistake, esp. through mental confusion. —*v.t.* **4.** to bungle; botch. **5.** to utter thoughtlessly; blurt out. [ME *blondren,* orig. uncert.] —**blun´der·er,** *n.* —**blun´der·ing·ly,** *adv.* —Syn. **1.** error. See **mistake.**

blun·der·buss (blŭn´dər bŭs´), *n.* **1.** a short musket of wide bore with expanded muzzle to scatter shot, bullets, or slugs at close range. **2.** a stupid, blundering person. [alter. of D *donderbus,* f. *donder* thunder + *buss* gun, orig. box]

Blunderbuss

blunge (blŭnj), *v.t.,* **blunged, blunging.** to mix (clay or the like) with water, forming a liquid suspension. [b. BLEND and PLUNGE]

blung·er (blŭn´jər), *n.* a large vessel containing rotating arms for mechanical mixing.

blunt (blŭnt), *adj.* **1.** having an obtuse, thick, or dull edge or point; rounded; not sharp. **2.** abrupt in address or manner. **3.** slow in perception or understanding; dull. —*v.t.* **4.** to make blunt. **5.** to weaken or impair the force, keenness, or susceptibility of. [ME; orig. unknown] —**blunt´ly,** *adv.* —**blunt´ness,** *n.* —Syn. **1.** See **dull. 2.** BLUNT, BLUFF, BRUSQUE, CURT characterize manners and speech. BLUNT suggests lack of polish and of regard for the feelings of others: *blunt and tactless.* BLUFF implies an unintentional roughness together with so much good-natured heartiness that others rarely take offense: *a bluff sea captain.* BRUSQUE connotes sharpness and abruptness of speech or manner: *a brusque denial.* CURT applies esp. to disconcertingly concise language: *a curt reply.*

blur (blûr), *v.,* **blurred, blurring,** *n.* —*v.t.* **1.** to obscure or sully as by smearing with ink, etc.; stain. **2.** to obscure by making confused in form or outline; make indistinct. **3.** to dim the perception or susceptibility of; make dull or insensible. —*v.i.* **4.** to become indistinct: *the vision blurred.* **5.** to make blurs. —*n.* **6.** a smudge or smear which obscures. **7.** a blurred condition; indistinctness. [? akin to BLEAR] —**blur´ry,** *adj.*

blurb (blûrb), *n.* an announcement or advertisement, esp. an effusively laudatory one. [a word coined by Gelett BURGESS]

blurt (blûrt), *v.t.* **1.** to utter suddenly or inadvertently; divulge unadvisedly (usually fol. by *out*). —*n.* **2.** an abrupt utterance. [appar. imit.]

blush (blŭsh), *v.i.* **1.** to redden as from embarrassment or shame. **2.** to feel shame (*at, for,* etc.). **3.** (of the sky, flowers, etc.) to become rosy. —*v.t.* **4.** to make red; flush. **5.** to make known by a blush. —*n.* **6.** a reddening, as of the face. **7.** rosy or pinkish tinge. [ME *blusche*(n), OE *blyscan* redden] —**blush´er,** *n.* —**blush´ful,** *adj.* —**blush´ing·ly,** *adv.*

blus·ter (blŭs´tər), *v.i.* **1.** to roar and be tumultuous, as wind. **2.** to be loud, noisy, or swaggering; utter loud empty menaces or protests. —*v.t.* **3.** to force or accomplish by blustering. —*n.* **4.** boisterous noise and violence. **5.** noisy, empty menaces or protests; inflated talk. [cf. Icel. *blāstr* blowing] —**blus´ter·er,** *n.* —**blus´ter·ing·ly,** *adv.* —**blus´ter·y, blus´ter·ous,** *adj.*

blvd., boulevard.

B.M., 1. Bachelor of Medicine. **2.** British Museum.

B.M.E., 1. Bachelor of Mechanical Engineering. **2.** Bachelor of Mining Engineering.

B. Met., Bachelor of Metallurgy.

B. Mus., Bachelor of Music.

bn., battalion.

B'nai B'rith (bə nā´ bə rēth´, brYth´), a fraternal organization of Jewish men. [t. Heb.: m. *bĕnē bĕrīth* sons of the covenant]

bo·a (bō´ə), *n., pl.* **boas. 1.** any of various nonvenomous snakes of the family *Boidae,* notable for their vestiges of hind limbs, as the boa constrictor of the American tropics. **2.** a long, snake-shaped wrap of silk, feather, or other material, worn about the neck by women. [t. L]

Bo·ab·dil (bō´ăb dēl´; *Sp.* bō´äb dēl´), *n.* (*abu-Abdallah,* "*El Chico*") died 1492?, last Moorish king of Granada, 1482–92.

boa constrictor, 1. a boa, *Constrictor constrictor,* of Central and South America, noted for its size and crushing power. **2.** any large python or other snake of the boa family.

Bo·a·di·ce·a (bō´ăd ə sē´ə), *n.* Boudicca.

Bo·a·ner·ges (bō´ə nûr´jēz), *n.* **1.** (*construed as pl.*) *Bible.* surname given by Christ to James and John, explained as meaning "sons of thunder." Mark, 3:17. **2.** (*construed as sing.*) a vociferous preacher or orator. [t. LL, t. Gk., t. Aram.: surname equiv. to Heb. *bĕnē regesh* "sons of thunder"]

boar (bōr), *n.* **1.** the uncastrated male of swine. **2.** the wild boar. [ME *boor,* OE *bār*]

board (bōrd), *n.* **1.** a piece of timber sawed thin, and of considerable length and breadth compared with the thickness. **2.** (*pl.*) *Theat.* the stage. **3.** a flat slab of wood for some specific purpose: *an ironing board.* **4.** a sheet of wood, paper, etc., with or without markings, for some special use: *a chessboard.* **5.** stiff cardboard covered with paper, cloth, or the like, to form the binding for a book. **6.** a table, esp. to serve food on. **7.** daily meals, esp. as provided for pay. **8.** an official body of persons who direct or supervise some activity: *a board of directors, of trade, of health.* **9.** the border or edge of anything, as in *seaboard.* **10.** *Naut.* **a.** the side of a ship. **b.** one leg, or tack, of the course of a ship beating to windward. **11. by the board,** over the ship's side. **12. go by the board,** to be destroyed, neglected, or forgotten. **13. on board,** on or in a ship, plane, or vehicle. —*v.t.* **14.** to cover or close with boards. **15.** to furnish with food, or with food and lodging, esp. for pay. **16.** to arrange for the furnishing of meals to. **17.** to go on board of or enter (a ship, train, etc.). **18.** to come up alongside of (a ship), as to attack or to go on board. **19.** *Obs.* to approach; accost. —*v.i.* **20.** to take one's meals, or be supplied with food and lodging at a fixed price: *several of us board at the same rooming house.* [OE *bord* board, table, shield]

board·er (bōr´dər), *n.* **1.** one who is supplied with meals. **2.** a person chosen to board an enemy ship.

board foot, a unit of measure equal to the cubic contents of a piece of lumber one foot square and one inch thick, used in measuring logs and lumber.

board·ing (bôr′dĭng), *n.* **1.** wooden boards collectively. **2.** a structure of boards, as in a fence or a floor.

boarding house, a place, usually a home, at which board is furnished, often with lodging.

boarding school, a school at which board and lodging are furnished for the pupils.

board measure, *Bldg. Trades.* a system of cubic measure in which the unit is the board foot.

board of health, a government department concerned with public health.

board of trade, **1.** a businessmen's association. **2.** (*cap.*) (in England) the national ministry that supervises and encourages commerce and industry.

board rule, a measuring device having scales for finding the cubic contents of a board without calculation.

board·walk (bôrd′wôk′), *n.* **1.** *U.S.* a promenade made of wooden boards, usually along a beach. **2.** any walk made of boards or planks.

boar·fish (bôr′fĭsh′), *n.* any of various fishes of different genera which have a projecting snout, esp. a small spiny-rayed European fish, *Capros aper.*

boar·hound (bôr′hound′), *n.* any of various large dogs used orig. for hunting wild boars, esp. a dog of a German breed (**German boarhound**) or a Great Dane.

boar·ish (bôr′ĭsh), *adj.* swinish; sensual; cruel.

Bo·as (bō′ăz), *n.* **Franz** (fränts), 1858–1942, U. S. anthropologist, born in Germany.

boast[1] (bōst), *v.i.* **1.** to speak exaggeratedly and objectionably, esp. about oneself. **2.** to speak with pride (fol. by *of*). —*v.t.* **3.** to speak of with excessive pride, vanity, or exultation. **4.** to be proud in the possession of: *the town boasts a new school.* —*n.* **5.** a thing boasted of. **6.** exaggerated or objectionable speech; bragging. [ME *bosten*; orig. unknown] —**boast′er,** *n.* —**boast′ing·ly,** *adv.*
—Syn. **1, 2.** BOAST, BRAG imply vocal self-praise or claims to superiority over others. BOAST usually refers to a particular ability, possession, etc., which may be one of such kind as to justify a good deal of pride: *he boasts of his ability as a singer.* BRAG, a more colloquial term, usually suggests a more ostentatious and exaggerated boasting but less well-founded: *he loudly brags of his marksmanship.*

boast[2] (bōst), *v.t.* to dress or shape (stone, etc.) roughly. [orig. uncert.]

boast·ful (bōst′fəl), *adj.* given to or characterized by boasting. —**boast′ful·ly,** *adv.* —**boast′ful·ness,** *n.*

boat (bōt), *n.* **1.** a vessel for transport by water, constructed to provide buoyancy by excluding water and shaped to give stability and permit propulsion. **2.** a small ship, generally for specialized use. **3.** a small vessel carried for use by a large one. **4.** *Colloq.* a ship. **5.** an open dish resembling a boat: *a gravy boat.* **6.** **in the same boat,** faced with the same, esp. unfortunate, circumstances. —*v.i.* **7.** to go in a boat. —*v.t.* **8.** to transport in a boat. [ME *boot*, OE *bāt*, c. Icel. *beit*]

boat·bill (bōt′bĭl′), *n.* a bird of the genus *Cochlearius*, of the heron family, containing the single species *C. cochlearius*, of tropical America.

boat hook, a metal hook fixed to a pole, for pulling or pushing a boat.

boat·house (bōt′hous′), *n.* a house or shed for sheltering boats.

boat·ing (bō′tĭng), *n.* the use of boats, esp. for pleasure.

boat·load (bōt′lōd′), *n.* **1.** the cargo that a vessel carries. **2.** the cargo that a vessel is capable of carrying.

boat·man (bōt′mən), *n., pl.* **-men.** a person skilled in the use of small craft. —**boat′man·ship′,** *n.*

boat·swain (bō′sən; *rarely* bōt′swān′), *n.* a warrant officer on a warship, or a petty officer on a merchant vessel, in charge of rigging, anchors, cables, etc. Also, **bo's′n, bosun.**

Bo·az (bō′ăz), *n. Bible.* husband of Ruth. Ruth 2–4. [t. Heb.: m. *Bo'az*]

bob[1] (bŏb), *n., v.,* **bobbed, bobbing.** —*n.* **1.** a short jerky motion: *a bob of the head.* —*v.t.* **2.** to move quickly down and up: *to bob the head.* **3.** to indicate with such a motion: *to bob a greeting.* —*v.i.* **4.** to make a jerky motion with head or body. **5.** to move about with jerky motions. [ME; orig. uncert.]

bob[2] (bŏb), *n., v.,* **bobbed, bobbing.** —*n.* **1.** a style of short haircut for women and children. **2.** a horse's tail cut short. **3.** a small dangling or terminal object, as the weight on a pendulum or a plumb line. **4.** *Angling.* **a.** a knot of worms, rags, etc., on a string. **b.** a float for a fishing line. **5.** *Colloq.* a bunch; a cluster. **6.** a bobsled or bob skate. —*v.t.* **7.** to cut short; dock. —*v.i.* **8.** *Angling.* to fish with a bob. [ME *bobbe* bunch, cluster, knob; orig. obscure]

bob[3] (bŏb), *n., v.,* **bobbed, bobbing.** —*n.* **1.** a tap; light blow. —*v.t.* **2.** to tap; strike lightly. [ME *bobben*? imit.]

bob[4] (bŏb), *n. Brit. Colloq.* a shilling. [orig. uncert.]

Bo·ba·dil·la (frän thĕs′kō dē, -yä), *n.* **Francisco de** (frän thēs′kō dē), died 1502, Spanish colonial governor in the West Indies: sent Columbus back to Spain in chains.

bob·ber (bŏb′ər), *n.* **1.** one who or that which bobs. **2.** a fishing bob.

bob·ber·y (bŏb′ər·ĭ), *n., pl.* **-beries.** *Colloq.* a disturbance. [Anglo-Ind.: t. Hindu: m. *bāp re* O father!]

bob·bin (bŏb′ĭn), *n.* a reel, cylinder, or spool upon which yarn or thread is wound, as used in spinning, machine sewing, etc. [t. F: m. *bobine*, der. *bobiner* to wind up, der. OF *baube* stammering, g. L *balbus*]

Bobbin and Joan (jōn), the European arum, *Arum maculatum.*

bob·bi·net (bŏb′ə·nĕt′), *n.* lacelike fabric of hexagonal mesh, made on a lace machine. [var. of *bobbin-net*, f. BOBBIN + NET[1]]

bobbin lace, lace made by hand with bobbins of thread, the threads being twisted around pins stuck into a pattern placed on a pillow.

bob·by (bŏb′ĭ), *n., pl.* **-bies.** *Brit. Colloq.* a policeman. [special use of *Bobby*, for Sir *Robert Peel* (1788–1850), who improved the police system of London]

bobby pin, a metal hairpin with close prongs.

bob·by·socks (bŏb′ĭ·sŏks′), *n.pl. Colloq.* anklets (def. 1), esp. as worn by young girls.

bob·by·sox·er (bŏb′ĭ·sŏk′sər), *n. Colloq.* a girl or young woman who enthusiastically follows adolescent fashions and fads. Also, **bob·by sox′er.**

bob·cat (bŏb′kăt′), *n.* an American wildcat, esp. the species *Lynx rufus*, which is widespread in the U.S.

Bobolink.
Dolichonyx oryzivorus
(7 to 7¼ in. long)

bob·o·link (bŏb′ə·lĭngk′), *n.* a common North American passerine songbird, *Dolichonyx oryzivorus*, which winters in South America. [short for *Bob o' Lincoln*, supposed to be the bird's call]

bob skate, a type of skate with two parallel runners.

bob·sled (bŏb′slĕd′), *n., v.,* **-sledded, -sledding.** *U.S.* —*n.* **1.** (formerly) a sled formed of two short sleds coupled one behind the other. The modern bobsled couples the runners only, the seat portion being continuous. **2.** either of the short sleds. —*v.i.* **3.** to ride on a bobsled. Also, **bob·sleigh** (bŏb′slā′). [f. BOB[2] + SLED]

bob·stay (bŏb′stā′), *n. Naut.* a rope, chain, or rod from the outer end of the bowsprit to the cutwater, holding the bowsprit in. See illus. under **bowsprit.**

bob·tail (bŏb′tāl′), *n.* **1.** a short or docked tail. **2.** a bobtailed animal. —*adj.* **3.** bobtailed; cut short. —*v.t.* **4.** to cut short the tail of; dock.

bob·white (bŏb′hwīt′), *n.* a common North American quail, *Colinus virginianus*, known locally as the partridge. [imit. of its call]

bo·cac·cio (bō·kä′chō), *n.* a brown or reddish species of rock cod of the California coast. [t. It.: m. *boccaccio* one having a large mouth]

Boc·cac·ci·o (bō·kä′chĭ·ō; *It.* bōk·kät′chō), *n.* **Giovanni** (jō·vän′nē), 1313–75, Italian writer and poet.

Boche (bôsh, bŏsh), *n. Slang.* (in World War I) a German. Also, **boche.** [t. F, ? alter. of F *caboche* head, pate, noodle, der. d. stem *cab-*, g. L *caput* head]

Bo·chum (bō′kʜōōm), *n.* a city in W West Germany, in the Ruhr. 342,436 (est. 1955).

bock beer (bŏk), a strong, dark beer, commonly brewed in the spring. Also, **bock.** [t. G: m. *bockbier*, for *Eimbocker bier* beer of Eimbock, or Einbeck, in Prussia]

bode[1] (bōd), *v.,* **boded, boding.** —*v.t.* **1.** to be an omen of; portend. **2.** *Archaic.* to announce beforehand; predict. —*v.i.* **3.** to portend. [ME *boden*, OE *bodian* announce, foretell, der. *boda* messenger] —**bode′ment,** *n.*

bode[2] (bōd), *v.* pt. and pp. of **bide** (def. 3).

bo·de·ga (bō·dē′gä), *n.* a wineshop. [Sp., g. L *apothēca*, t. Gk.: m. *apothēkē* storehouse]

Bo·den See (bō′dən zā′), German name of the **Lake of Constance.**

bod·ice (bŏd′ĭs), *n.* **1.** a woman's laced outer garment covering the waist and bust, common in peasant dress. **2.** *Chiefly Brit.* a woman's fitted waist or dress body. **3.** *Obs.* stays or a corset. [var. of *bodies*, pl. of BODY]

Bodice

bod·i·less (bŏd′ĭ·lĭs), *adj.* having no body or material form; incorporeal.

bod·i·ly (bŏd′ĭ·lĭ), *adj.* **1.** of or pertaining to the body. **2.** corporeal or material, in contrast with spiritual or mental. —*adv.* **3.** as a whole; without taking apart. —Syn. **2.** See **physical.**

bod·ing (bō′dĭng), *n.* **1.** a foreboding; omen. —*adj.* **2.** foreboding; ominous. —**bod′ing·ly,** *adv.*

bod·kin (bŏd′kĭn), *n.* **1.** a small pointed instrument for making holes in cloth, etc. **2.** a long pin-shaped instrument used by women to fasten up the hair. **3.** a blunt needlelike instrument for drawing tape, cord, etc., through a loop, hem, or the like. **4.** *Obs.* a small dagger; a stiletto. [ME *boydekin* dagger; orig. unknown]

Bod·lei·an (bŏd′lē·ən, bŏd′lĭ-), *n.* the library of Oxford University reëstablished by Sir Thomas Bodley, 1545–1613, English diplomat and scholar.

Bo·do·ni (bə·dō′nĭ *for 1;* bō·dô′nē *for 2*), *n.* **1.** *Print.* a style of type. **2. Giambattista** (jäm′bät·tēs′tä), 1740–1813, Italian printer.

bod·y (bŏd′ĭ), *n., pl.* **bodies,** *v.,* **bodied, bodying,** *adj.* —*n.* **1.** the physical structure of an animal (and sometimes, in *Biol.*, of a plant) living or dead. **2.** a corpse; carcass. **3.** the trunk or main mass of a thing. **4.** *Zool.* the physical structure of an animal minus limbs and head. **5.** *Archit.* the central structure of a building, esp. the nave of a church; the major mass of a building. **6.** a vehicle minus wheels and other appendages. **7.** *Naut.* the hull of a ship. **8.** *Aeron.* the fuselage of a plane. **9.**

Print. the shank of a type, supporting the face. **10.** *Geom.* a figure having the three dimensions, length, breadth, and thickness; a solid. **11.** *Physics.* anything having inertia; a mass. **12.** the major portion of an army, population, etc. **13.** the central part of a speech or document, minus introduction, conclusion, indexes, etc. **14.** *Colloq. and Dial.* a person. **15.** *Law.* the physical person of an individual. **16.** a collective group, or an artificial person: *body politic, body corporate.* **17.** a number of things or people taken together. **18.** consistency or density; substance; strength as opposed to thinness: *wine of a good body.* **19.** that part of a dress which covers the trunk, or the trunk above the waist. —*v.t.* **20.** to invest with or as with a body. **21.** to represent in bodily form (usually fol. by *forth*). —*adj.* **22.** *Print.* (of type) used mainly for the text, generally less than 14 pts. (as distinguished from *display type*). —**bod/ied,** *adj.* [ME; OE *bodig,* c. MHG *potih*]
—Syn. **1, 2.** BODY, CARCASS, CORPSE agree in referring to a physical organism. BODY refers to the material organism of an individual man or animal, either living or dead: *the muscles in a horse's body, the body of a victim (man or animal).* CARCASS refers only to the dead body of an animal, unless applied humorously or contemptuously to the human body: *a sheep's carcass, save your carcass.* CORPSE refers only to the dead body of man: *preparing a corpse for burial.*

body cavity, *Zool., Anat., etc.* the general or common cavity of the body, as distinguished from special cavities or those of particular organs.

body corporate, *Law.* a person, association, or group of persons legally incorporated; a corporation.

bod·y·guard (bŏd/ĭ gärd/), *n.* **1.** a personal or private guard, as for a high official. **2.** a retinue; escort.

body politic, *Pol. Sci.* a people as forming a political body under an organized government.

body snatching, act of robbing a grave to obtain a subject for dissection. —**body snatcher.**

Boe·o·tia (bē ō/shə), *n.* a district and republic in ancient Greece, NW of Athens. *Cap.*: Thebes.

Boe·o·tian (bē ō/shən), *adj.* **1.** of or pertaining to Boeotia or the Boeotians. **2.** dull; stupid. —*n.* **3.** a native or inhabitant of Boeotia. **4.** a dull, stupid person.

Boer (bōr; *Du.* bōōr), *n.* **1.** a South African of Dutch extraction. —*adj.* **2.** of or pertaining to the Boers. [t. D: peasant, countryman. See BOOR]

Boer War, 1. a war in which Great Britain fought against the Transvaal and Orange Free State, 1899–1902. **2.** a war between Great Britain and the Transvaal, 1880–81.

Bo·e·thi·us (bō ē/thĭ əs), *n.* **Anicius Manlius Severinus** (ə nĭsh/ĭ əs măn/lĭ əs sĕv/ə rī/nəs), A.D. 475?–525?, Roman philosopher and statesman. Also, **Bo·ece** (bō ēs/), **Bo·e·tius** (bō ē/shəs).

bog (bŏg, bôg), *n., v.,* **bogged, bogging.** —*n.* **1.** wet, spongy ground, with soil composed mainly of decayed vegetable matter. **2.** an area or stretch of such ground. —*v.i., v.i.* **3.** to sink in or as in a bog. [t. Irish or Gaelic: soft] —**bog/gish,** *adj.* —**bog/gy,** *adj.*

bog asphodel, either of two liliaceous plants, *Nathecium ossifragum* of Europe, and *N. americanum* of the U.S., growing in boggy places.

bo·gey (bō/gĭ), *n., pl.* **-geys. 1.** a bogy. **2.** *Golf.* **a.** par (def. 4). **b.** one stroke above par on a hole. [var. of BOGY]

bog·gle¹ (bŏg/əl), *v.,* **-gled, -gling,** *n.* —*v.i.* **1.** to take alarm; start with fright. **2.** to hesitate, as if afraid to proceed; waver; shrink. **3.** to dissemble; equivocate. **4.** to be awkward; bungle. —*n.* **5.** act of shying or taking alarm. **6.** *Colloq.* bungle; botch. [? special use of BOGGLE²] —**bog/gler,** *n.*

bog·gle² (bŏg/əl), *n.* bogle.

bo·gie (bō/gĭ), *n.* bogy.

bo·gle (bō/gəl, bŏg/əl), *n.* a bogy; a specter. Also, **boggle.** [der. obs. *bog,* var. of BUG bugbear]

bog oak, oak (or other wood) preserved in peat bogs.

Bo·gor (bō/gôr), *n.* a city in Indonesia, in W Java. 124,000 (est. 1951).

Bo·go·tá (bō/gə tä/), *n.* the capital of Colombia, in the central part. 765,360 (est. 1954).

bog·trot·ter (bŏg/trŏt/ər, bôg/-), *n.* **1.** one who lives among bogs. **2.** *Contemptuous.* a rural Irishman.

bo·gus (bō/gəs), *adj.* U.S. counterfeit; spurious; sham.

bo·gy (bō/gĭ), *n., pl.* **-gies. 1.** a hobgoblin; evil spirit. **2.** anything that haunts and annoys one. **3.** *Mil. Slang.* an unidentified or unrecognized aircraft. Also, **bogey, bogie.** [der. obs. *bog.* See BOGLE]

Bo·he·mi·a (bō hē/mĭ ə, -hēm/yə), *n.* **1.** Czech, **Čechy.** a region in W Czechoslovakia: formerly in Austria; a part of Bohemia-Moravia, 1939–45. 5,988,000 pop. (est. 1954); 20,101 sq. mi. **2.** a district inhabited by Bohemians (def. 3). **3.** the social circles in which a Bohemian atmosphere is prevalent.

Bo·he·mi·a-Mo·ra·vi·a (bō hē/mĭ ə mō rä/vĭ ə, bō-hēm/yə-), *n.* a former German protectorate including Bohemia and Moravia (1939–1945).

Bo·he·mi·an (bō hē/mĭ ən, -hēm/yən), *n.* **1.** a native or inhabitant of Bohemia. **2.** the Czech language.

3. (*often l.c.*) a person with artistic or intellectual tendencies who lives and acts with disregard for conventional rules of behavior. **4.** a Gypsy. —*adj.* **5.** pertaining to Bohemia, its people, or their language. **6.** pertaining to or characteristic of Bohemians (def. 3) —**Bo·he/mi·an·ism,** *n.*

Bohemian Forest, a low forest-covered mountain range on the boundary between SW Czechoslovakia and SE West Germany. Highest peak, Arber, 4780 ft. German, **Böh·mer Wald** (bœ/mər vält/).

Bo·hol (bō hōl/), *n.* one of the Philippine Islands, in the central part. 553,407 (1948); 1492 sq. mi.

Bohr (bōr), *n.* **Niels** (nēls), 1885–1962, Danish physicist.

Bohr theory, *Physics.* a theory of atomic structure in which the electrons are described as revolving in individual orbits about a central part.

bo·hunk (bō/hŭngk/), *n.* U.S. Slang. (in contemptuous use) an unskilled or semiskilled foreign-born laborer specif., a Bohemian, Magyar, Slovak, or Croatian. Cf. hunky².

Bo·iar·do (bō yär/dō), *n.* **Matteo Maria** (mät tĕ/ō mä-rē/ä), 1434–94, Italian poet.

boil¹ (boil), *v.i.* **1.** to change from liquid to gaseous state, producing bubbles of gas that rise to the surface of the liquid, agitating it as they rise. **2.** to be in a similarly agitated state: *the sea was boiling.* **3.** to be agitated by angry feeling. **4.** to contain, or be contained in, a liquid that boils: *the pot is boiling, the meat is boiling.* **5.** *boil over,* **a.** to overflow while boiling. **b.** to be unable to repress excitement, anger, etc. —*v.t.* **6.** to cause to boil. **7.** to separate (sugar, salt, etc.) from something containing it by heat. **8.** *boil down,* **a.** to reduce by boiling. **b.** to shorten; abridge. —*n.* **9.** act of boiling. **10.** state or condition of boiling. [ME *boile(n),* t. OF: *m. boillir,* g. L *bullīre*]
—Syn. **3.** BOIL, SEETHE, SIMMER, STEW are used figuratively to refer to agitated states of emotion. To BOIL suggests the state of being very hot with anger or rage: *rage made his blood boil.* To SEETHE is to be deeply stirred, violently agitated, or greatly excited: *a mind seethes with conflicting ideas.* To SIMMER means to be on the point of bursting out or boiling over: *to simmer with curiosity, with anger.* To STEW is colloquial for to worry, to be in a restless state of anxiety and excitement: *to stew about (or over) one's troubles.*

boil² (boil), *n.* *Pathol.* a painful suppurating inflammatory sore forming a central core, caused by microbic infection; a furuncle. [ME *bule,* OE *byl,* c. G *beule*]

Boi·leau-Des·pré·aux (bwá lō/ dĕ prē ō/), *n.* **Nicolas** (nē kō lä/), 1636–1711, French critic and poet.

boiled shirt, U.S. a white or dress shirt.

boil·er (boi/lər), *n.* **1.** a closed vessel together with its furnace, in which steam or other vapor is generated for heating or for driving engines. **2.** a vessel for boiling or heating. **3.** *Brit.* a stove for heating water. **4.** a tank for storing hot water.

boiling point, the temperature at which the vapor pressure of a liquid is equal to the pressure of the atmosphere on the liquid, equal for water to 212°F or 100°C at sea level.

Boi·se (boi/zĭ, -sĭ), *n.* the capital of Idaho, in the SW part, built on the site of Fort Boise, a post on the Oregon trail. 34,481 (1960).

Bois-le-Duc (bwá lə dŷk/), *n.* French name of 's Hertogenbosch.

bois·ter·ous (boi/stər əs), *adj.* **1.** rough and noisy; clamorous; unrestrained. **2.** (of waves, weather, wind, etc.) rough and stormy. **3.** *Obs.* rough and massive. [ME *boistrous,* earlier *boistous;* orig. unknown] —**bois/ter·ous·ly,** *adv.* —**bois/ter·ous·ness,** *n.* —Syn. **1.** uproarious, obstreperous, roistering. —Ant. **1.** sedate.

Bo·jar·do (bō yär/dō), *n.* See Boiardo.

Bo·jer (boi/ər), *n.* **Johan** (yō hän/), 1872–1959, Norwegian novelist and playwright.

Bok (bŏk), *n.* **Edward William,** 1863–1930, U.S. editor and writer, born in the Netherlands.

Bo·kha·ra (bō kä/rə; *Russ.* bŏŏ hä/rä), *n.* Bukhara.

Bol., Bolivia.

bo·la (bō/lä; *Sp.* bō/lä), *n.* a weapon used by the Indians and Gauchos of southern South America, consisting of two or more heavy balls secured to the ends of one or more strong cords, which entangle the victim at which it is thrown. Also, **bo·las** (bō/ləs; *Sp.* bō/läs). [t. Sp.: a ball, g. L *bulla* bubble, round object]

Bo·lan Pass (bō län/), a pass in NE Baluchistan. ab. 54 mi. long.

bo·lar (bō/lər), *adj.* of or pertaining to bole or clay.

bold (bōld), *adj.* **1.** not hesitating in the face of actual or possible danger or rebuff. **2.** not hesitating to breach the rules of propriety; forward. **3.** calling for daring, unhesitating action. **4.** overstepping usual bounds or conventions. **5.** conspicuous to the eye: *bold handwriting.* **6.** steep; abrupt: *a bold promontory.* **7.** *Obs.* trusting; assured. **8.** *make bold to,* to venture to. [ME; OE *b(e)ald,* c. G *bald*] —**bold/ly,** *adv.* —**bold/ness,** *n.*
—Syn. **1.** fearless, courageous, brave, intrepid, daring. **2.** BOLD, BRAZEN, FORWARD, PRESUMPTUOUS may refer to manners in a derogatory sense. BOLD suggests impudence, shamelessness, and immodesty (esp. in women): *a bold stare.* BRAZEN suggests the same, together with a defiant manner: *a brazen hussy.* FORWARD implies making oneself unduly prominent or bringing oneself to notice with too much assurance. PRESUMPTUOUS implies overconfidence, effrontery, taking too much for granted. —Ant. **2.** modest.

b., blend of, blended; c., cognate with; d., dialect, dialectal; der., derived from; f., formed from; g., going back to; m., modification of; r., replacing; s., stem of; t., taken from; ?, perhaps. See the full key on inside cover.

bold·face (bōld′fās′), *n.* *Print.* type that has thick, heavy lines, used for emphasis, etc.

bold-faced (bōld′fāst′), *adj.* **1.** impudent; brazen. **2.** *Print.* (of type) having thick lines.

bole¹ (bōl), *n.* *Bot.* the stem or trunk of a tree. [ME, t. Scand.; cf. Icel. *bolr*]

bole² (bōl), *n.* any one of a class of soft, brittle, unctuous clays varying in color and affording pigments. [t. LL: m.s. *bolus*, t. Gk.: m. *bōlos* clod, lump]

bo·lec·tion (bō lĕk′shən), *n.* *Archit.* a molding which projects beyond the surface of the work it decorates. Also, **bilection**. [orig. uncert.]

bo·le·ro (bō lâr′ō; *Sp.* bō lē′rō), *n.*, *pl.* **-ros. 1.** a lively Spanish dance in three-four time. **2.** the music for it. **3.** a short jacket ending above or at the waistline. [t. Sp.]

bo·le·tus (bō lē′təs), *n.* any species of the genus *Boletus*, a group of umbrella-shaped mushrooms in which the stratum of tubes on the underside of the cap is easily separable. [t. L, t. Gk.: m. *bōlĭtēs* kind of mushroom]

Bol·eyn (bŏŏl′ĭn), *n.* **Anne,** 1507–36, second wife of Henry VIII of England: mother of Queen Elizabeth I.

bo·lide (bō′līd, -lĭd), *n.* *Astron.* a large, brilliant meteor, esp. one that explodes. [t. F, t. L: m. s. *bolis* large meteor, t. Gk.: missile]

Bol·ing·broke (bŏl′ĭng brŏŏk′; *older* bŏŏl′-), *n.* **Henry St. John** (sĭn′jən), **1st Viscount,** 1678–1751, British statesman and writer.

Bol·i·var (bō′lə vär′; *Sp.* bō lē′vär), *n.* **Simón** (sī′mən; *Sp.* sē mōn′), 1783–1830, Venezuelan statesman: leader of revolt of South American colonies from Spanish rule.

bol·i·var (bō′lə vär′; *Sp.* bō lē′vär), *n.*, *pl.* **bolivars;** *Sp.***bolivares** (bō lē′väres). the silver coin of Venezuela and its monetary unit, equal to 30 cents. [named after Simon Bolívar]

Bo·liv·i·a (bō lĭv′ĭ ə, bə-; *Sp.* bō lē′vyä), *n.* a republic in W South America. 3,235,000 pop. (est. 1956); 404,388 sq. mi. *Capitals:* La Paz and Sucre. —**Bo·liv′i·an,** *adj.*, *n.*

bo·li·via·no (bō lē′vyä′nō), *n.*, *pl.* **-nos** (-nōs). the monetary unit of Bolivia; equal to 2.3 cents. [t. Bolivian Sp.]

boll (bōl), *n.* *Bot.* a rounded seed vessel or pod of a plant, as of flax or cotton. [var. of BOWL¹]

bol·lard (bŏl′ərd), *n.* *Naut.* a vertical post on which hawsers are made fast. [? f. BOLE¹ + -ARD]

boll weevil (bōl), a snout beetle, *Anthonomus grandis,* that attacks the bolls of cotton.

boll·worm (bōl′wûrm′), *n.* **1.** the larva, **pink bollworm,** of the moth *Platyeara gossypiella,* one of the worst pests of cotton. **2.** corn earworm.

Cotton boll weevil, *Anthonomus grandis* A. Larva; B. Adult; C. Pupa (line = actual total length of adult; lower section of line = length of body)

bo·lo (bō′lō), *n.*, *pl.* **-los** (-lōz). large, heavy single-edged knife for hacking used in the Philippine Islands and in the U.S. Army. [t. Sp., t. native d.]

Bo·lo·gna (bə lōn′yə; *It.* bō lō′nyä), *n.* a city in N Italy. 364,000 (est. 1954). —**Bo·lo·gnese** (bō′lə nēz′, -nēs′), *adj.*, *n. sing. and pl.*

bologna sausage, a large-sized variety of sausage containing a mixture of meats. Also, **bo·lo·gna** (bə lō′nə, -lōn′yə, -lō′nĭ).

bo·lo·graph (bō′lə grăf′, -gräf′), *n.* *Physics.* a record made by a bolometer. [f. s. Gk. *bolē* ray + -(o)GRAPH] —**bo′lo·graph′ic,** *adj.*

bo·lom·e·ter (bō lŏm′ə tər), *n.* *Physics.* an electrical resistance element for measuring minute amounts of radiant energy. [f. s. Gk. *bolē* ray + -(o)METER] —**bo·lo·met·ric** (bō′lə mĕt′rĭk), *adj.*

bo·lo·ney (bə lō′nĭ), *n.* *U.S.* baloney.

Bol·she·vik (bŏl′shə vĭk, bōl′-), *n.*, *pl.* **Bolsheviki** (-vē′kē; *Russ.* bŏl′shĕ vĭ kē′), **-viks. 1.** (in Russia), **a.** (1903–1917) a member of the more radical majority of the Social Democratic Party, advocating abrupt and forceful seizure of power by the proletariat. **b.** (since 1918) a member of the Russian Communist Party. **2.** (in any country) a member of the Communist Party. **3.** (in derisive use) any radical or progressive. Also, **bolshevik.** [t. Russ., der. *bolshe* greater, more, with allusion to the majority (Russ. *bolshinstvo*) of the party]

Bol·she·vism (bŏl′shə vĭz′əm, bōl′-), *n.* **1.** the doctrines, methods, or procedure of the Bolsheviki. **2.** (*sometimes l.c.*) the principles or practices of ultraradical socialists or political ultraradicals generally.

Bol·she·vist (bŏl′shə vĭst, bōl′-), *n.* **1.** a follower or advocate of the doctrines or methods of the Bolsheviki. **2.** (*sometimes l.c.*) an ultraradical socialist; any political ultraradical. —*adj.* **3.** Bolshevistic.

Bol·she·vis·tic (bŏl′shə vĭs′tĭk, bōl′-), *adj.* pertaining to or characteristic or suggestive of Bolshevists or Bolshevism. Also, **bolshevistic.**

Bol·she·vize (bŏl′shə vīz′, bōl′-), *v.*, **-vized, -vizing.** —*v.t.* **1.** to bring under the influence or domination of Bolshevists; render Bolshevik or Bolshevistic. —*v.i.* **2.** to become Bolshevik or Bolshevistic; act like a Bolshevik. Also, **bolshevize.** —**Bol′she·vi·za′tion,** *n.*

bol·són (bŏl sōn′; *Sp.* bōl sōn′), *n.* *Phys. Geog.* a broad and nearly flat mountain-rimmed desert basin with interior drainage. [t. Sp.: large purse. See BURSE]

bol·ster (bōl′stər), *n.* **1.** a long ornamental pillow for a bed, sofa, etc. **2.** something resembling this in form or use. **3.** a pillow, cushion, or pad. —*v.t.* **4.** to support with or as with a pillow. **5.** to prop, support, or uphold (something weak, unworthy, etc.) (often fol. by *up*). [ME *bolstre*, OE *bolster*, c. G *polster*] —**bol′ster·er,** *n.*

bolt¹ (bōlt), *n.* **1.** a movable bar which when slid into a socket fastens a door, gate, etc. **2.** the part of a lock which is protruded from and drawn back into the case, as by the action of the key. **3.** a strong metal pin, often with a head at one end and with a screw thread at the other to receive a nut. See illus. under nut. **4.** a sudden swift motion or escape. **5.** sudden desertion of a meeting, political party, program, etc. **6.** a woven length of cloth. **7.** a roll of wall paper. **8.** a sudden dash, run, flight, etc. **9.** a jet of water, molten glass, etc. **10.** an arrow, esp. one for a crossbow. **11.** a shaft of lightning; a thunderbolt. —*v.t.* **12.** to fasten with or as with bolts. **13.** *U.S. Pol.* to break away from; refuse to support. **14.** to shoot; discharge (a missile). **15.** to blurt; utter hastily. **16.** to swallow (one's food) hurriedly or without chewing. **17.** to make (cloth, wall paper, etc.) into bolts. —*v.i.* **18.** to make a sudden, swift movement; spring away suddenly. **19.** *U.S. Pol.* to break away, as from a party; refuse to support one's party. **20.** to eat hurriedly or without chewing. —*adv.* **21.** suddenly; with sudden meeting or collision. **22. bolt upright,** stiffly upright. [ME and OE, c. G *bolz*] —**bolt′er,** *n.* —**bolt′less,** *adj.* —**bolt′like′,** *adj.*

bolt² (bōlt), *v.t.* **1.** to sift through a cloth or sieve. **2.** to examine or search into, as if by sifting. [ME *bult*(*en*), t. OF: m. *bulter* sift, t. MD: m. *buitelen*] —**bolt′er,** *n.*

bolt·head (bōlt′hĕd′), *n.* **1.** the head of a bolt. **2.** *Chem.* (formerly) a matrass.

Bol·ton (bōl′tən), *n.* a city in W England, in Lancashire. 163,380 (est. 1956).

bol·to·ni·a (bōl tō′nĭ ə), *n.* a tall asteraceous perennial, genus *Boltonia,* of the U.S., sometimes cultivated. [t. NL; after James Bolton (d. 1795), Brit. botanist]

bolt·rope (bōlt′rōp′), *n.* **1.** *Naut.* a rope or the cordage sewed on the edges of a sail or the like to strengthen it. **2.** a superior grade of rope.

bo·lus (bō′ləs), *n.* a round mass of medicine, larger than an ordinary pill, forming a dose. [t. LL, t. Gk.: m. *bōlos* lump]

bomb (bŏm), *n.* **1.** *Mil.* a hollow (usually spherical) projectile filled with a bursting charge, and exploded by means of a fuse, by impact, or otherwise. **2.** any similar missile or device: *a dynamite bomb, an aerial bomb.* **3.** *Geol.* a rough spherical or ellipsoidal mass of lava ejected from a volcano. —*v.t.* **4.** to hurl bombs at; drop bombs upon, as from an airplane; bombard. —*v.i.* **5.** to hurl or drop bombs. **6.** to explode a bomb or bombs. [t. F: m. *bombe,* t. It.: m. *bomba,* g. L *bombus* a booming sound, t. Gk.: m. *bómbos*]

bom·ba·ca·ceous (bŏm′bə kā′shəs), *adj.* *Bot.* belonging to the *Bombacaceae,* a family of woody plants including the silk-cotton trees and the baobab. [f. s. LL *bombax* (for L *bombyx,* t. Gk.: silkworm, silk) + -ACEOUS]

bom·bard (*v.* bŏm bärd′; *n.* bŏm′bärd), —*v.t.* **1.** to attack or batter with artillery. **2.** to attack with bombs. **3.** to assail vigorously: *bombard someone with questions.* —*n.* **4.** the earliest kind of cannon, orig. throwing stone balls. [ME *bombarde,* t. OF: cannon, der. L *bombus* loud noise. See BOMB] —**bom·bard′er,** *n.* —**bom·bard′ment,** *n.*

bom·bar·dier (bŏm′bər dĭr′), *n.* **1.** *Mil.* member of bombing plane crew who operates the bomb release mechanism. **2.** *Hist.* artilleryman. [t. F]

bom·bar·don (bŏm′bər dən, bŏm bär′dən), *n.* *Music.* **1.** a bass reed stop of the organ. **2.** a large, deep-toned, valved brass-wind instrument not unlike a tuba. [t. It.: m. *bombardone;* akin to BOMBARD]

bom·bast (bŏm′băst), *n.* **1.** high-sounding words; speech too high-flown for the occasion. **2.** *Obs.* cotton or other material used to stuff garments; padding. —*adj.* **3.** *Obs.* bombastic. [earlier *bombace,* t. F, g. LL *bombax* cotton, for L *bombyx* silkworm, silk, t. Gk.]

bom·bas·tic (bŏm băs′tĭk), *adj.* (of speech, etc.) high-sounding; high-flown; inflated; turgid. Also, **bom·bas′ti·cal.** —**bom·bas′ti·cal·ly,** *adv.*

Bom·bay (bŏm bā′), *n.* **1.** a state in W India: formerly a province in British India; enlarged in 1956 by Reorganization Act, adding 12,000,000 pop. and ab. 73,000 sq. mi. 48,000,000 (est. 1956); 190,919 sq. mi. **2.** the capital of this state: a port on the Arabian Sea. 2,839,270 (1951).

bom·ba·zine (bŏm′bə zēn′, bŏm′bə zēn′), *n.* a fine-twilled fabric with a silk warp and worsted weft, formerly much used (in black) for mourning. Also, **bom′ba·sine′.** [t. F: m. *bombasin,* t. LL: s. *bombbasinum,* der. *bombax.* See BOMBAST]

bomb bay, *Aeron., Mil.* the compartment from which bombs are dropped.

bombe (bôNb), *n.* *French.* a melon or circular mold containing one or more flavors of ice cream or ice.

bomb·er (bŏm′ər), *n.* *Mil.* an airplane employed to drop bombs.

bomb·proof (bŏm′prŏŏf′), *adj.* **1.** strong enough to resist the impact and explosive force of bombs or shells striking on the outside. —*n.* **2.** a structure of such design and strength as to resist the penetration and the shattering force of shells, usually, at least in part, beneath the level of the ground.

ăct, āble, dâre, ärt; ĕbb, ēqual; ĭf, īce; hŏv, ōver, ôrder, oil, bŏŏk, ōōze, out; ŭp, ūse, ûrge; ə = a in alone; ch, chief; g, give; ng, ring; sh, shoe; th, thin; ŧħ, that; zh, vision. See the full key on inside cover.

bomb rack, a device for carrying bombs in an air craft.

bomb·shell (bŏm′shĕl′), *n.* **1.** a bomb. **2.** like a bombshell, with sudden or devastating effect: *his resignation came like a bombshell.*

bomb·sight (bŏm′sīt′), *n.* *Mil.* an aiming instrument used to tell when to drop a bomb from an aircraft so that it will hit a specified target.

bom·by·cid (bŏm′bə sĭd), *n.* any of the *Bombycidae,* the family of moths that includes the silkworm moths. [f. s. L *bombyx* silkworm (t. Gk.) + -ID²]

Bon (bŏn), *n.* **Cape,** a cape on the NE coast of Tunisia: surrender of the German Afrika Korps, May 12, 1943.

bo·na fi·de (bō′nə fī′dĭ), in good faith; without fraud. [t. L] **—bo·na-fide** (bō′nə fĭd′, bŏn′ə-), *adj.*

Bon·aire (bō′nâr′), *n.* an island in the Netherlands Antilles. 5661 pop. (1955); 95 sq. mi.

bon a·mi (bôn nà mē′), *French.* **1.** a good friend. **2.** a lover.

bo·nan·za (bō năn′zə), *n.* *U.S.* **1.** a rich mass of ore, as found in mining. **2.** a mine of wealth; good luck. [t. Sp.: fair weather, prosperity, der. L *bonus* good]

Bo·na·parte (bō′nə pärt′; *Fr.* bô nà pàrt′), *n.* **1.** **Jérôme** (jə rōm′; *Fr.* zhě rōm′), 1784–1860, king of Westphalia (brother of Napoleon I). **2.** **Joseph** (jō′zəf; *Fr.* zhô zěf′), 1768–1844, king of Naples and Spain (brother of Napoleon I). **3.** **Louis** (*Fr.* lwē; *Du.* lōō ē′), 1778–1846, king of Holland (brother of Napoleon I). **4.** **Louis Napoléon,** 1808–73, president of France, 1848–52; as Napoleon III, emperor of France, 1852–70 (son of Louis Bonaparte). **5.** **Lucien** (lōō′shən; *Fr.* ly syăn′), 1775–1840, Prince of Cannino (brother of Napoleon I). **6.** **Napoléon** (nə pō′lĭ ən; *Fr.*. nà pô lě ôN′), 1769–1821, Corsican-born French general: emperor of France as Napoleon I, 1804–1815. **7.** **Napoléon,** (*Duke of Reichstadt*) 1811–32, called Napoleon II, but never ruled France (son of Napoleon I). Also, *Italian,* **Buonaparte.**

Bo·na·part·ist (bō′nə pär′tĭst), *n.* an adherent of the Bonapartes or their policies. **—Bo′na·part′ism,** *n.*

Bo·na·ven·ture (bō′nə věn′chər), *n.* **Saint,** ("*the Seraphic Doctor*") 1221–74, Italian scholastic theologian. Also, *Italian,* **Bo·na·ven·tu·ra** (bō′nä věn tōō′rä).

bon·bon (bŏn′bŏn′; *Fr.* bôN bôN′), *n.* **1.** a fondant, fruit, or nut center dipped in fondant or chocolate. **2.** a piece of confectionery. [t. F, der. *bon* good]

bon·bon·nière (bŏN bôN nyěr′), *n.* *French.* a box for candies.

bond (bŏnd), *n.* **1.** something that binds, fastens, confines, or holds together. **2.** a cord; rope; band; ligament. **3.** something that unites individual people into a group. **4.** something that constrains a person to a certain line of behavior. **5.** a bondsman or security. **6.** a sealed instrument under which a person or corporation guarantees to pay a stated sum of money on or before a specified day. **7.** any written obligation under seal. **8.** *Law.* the written promise of a surety, originally expressed as a promise to pay a sum of money to be void in case no default occurs by the person whose conduct or performance is guaranteed. **9.** *Govt.* the state of dutiable goods on which the duties are unpaid, when stored, under a bond, in charge of the government (esp. in phrase *in bond*). **10.** *Finance.* a certificate of ownership of a specified portion of a debt due by government, a railroad, or other corporation to individual holders, and usually bearing a fixed rate of interest. **11.** *Insurance.* **a.** a surety agreement. **b.** the money deposited, or the promissory arrangement entered into, under any such agreement. **12.** a substance that causes particles to adhere; a binder. **13.** *Chem.* a unit of combining power equivalent to that of one hydrogen atom. **14.** bond paper. **15.** *Masonry.* the connection of the stones or bricks in a wall, etc., made by overlapping them in order to bind the whole into a compact mass. **—***v.t.* **16.** to put (goods, an employee, official, etc.) on or under bond. **17.** *Finance.* to place a bonded debt on; mortgage. **18.** *Masonry.* to cause (bricks or other building materials) to hold together firmly by laying them in some overlapping pattern. **—***v.i.* **19.** to hold together from being bonded, as bricks in a wall. [ME, var. of BAND³] **—bond′er,** *n.*

—Syn. 3. BOND, LINK, TIE agree in referring to a force or influence which unites people. BOND and TIE are sometimes used interchangeably. BOND, however, usually emphasizes the strong and enduring quality of affection; whereas TIE may refer more especially to duty, obligation, or responsibility: *bonds of memory, blessed be the tie that binds, family ties.* A LINK is a definite connection, though a slighter one; it may indicate affection or merely some traceable influence or desultory communication: *a close link between friends.*

bond·age (bŏn′dĭj), *n.* **1.** slavery or involuntary servitude; serfdom. **2.** state of being bound by or subjected to external control. **3.** *Early Eng. Law.* tenure of land by villeinage. **—Syn. 1.** See **slavery.**

bond·ed (bŏn′dĭd), *adj.* **1.** secured by or consisting of bonds: *bonded debt.* **2.** placed in bond: *bonded goods.*

bonded warehouse, a warehouse for holding goods in bond. See **bond,** def. 9.

bond·hold·er (bŏnd′hōl′dər), *n.* a holder of a bond or bonds issued by a government or corporation. **—bond′hold′ing,** *adj., n.*

bond·maid (bŏnd′mād′), *n.* **1.** a female slave. **2.** a female bound to service without wages.

bond·man (bŏnd′mən), *n., pl.* **-men.** **1.** a male slave. **2.** a man bound to service without wages. **3.** *Old Eng. Law.* a villein or other unfree tenant.

bond paper, a superior variety of white paper.

bond servant, one who serves in bondage; a slave.

bonds·man (bŏndz′mən), *n., pl.* **-men.** *Law.* one who is bound or who by bond becomes surety for another.

bond·wom·an (bŏnd′wŏōm′ən), *n., pl.* **-women.** a female slave.

bone (bōn), *n., v.,* **boned, boning.** **—***n.* **1.** *Anat., Zool.* **a.** any of the discrete pieces of which the skeleton of a vertebrate is composed. **b.** the hard tissue which composes the skeleton. **2.** a bone or piece of a bone with the meat adhering to it, as an article of food. **3.** (*pl.*) the skeleton. **4.** (*pl.*) a body. **5.** any of various similar substances, such as ivory, whalebone, etc. **6.** something made of bone, or of a substance resembling bone. **7.** (*pl.*) *U.S. Slang.* the dice in the game of craps. **8.** (*pl.*) *Theat.* **a.** noisemakers of bone or wood used by a minstrel end man. **b.** an end man in a minstrel troupe. **9.** a strip of whalebone used to stiffen corsets, etc. **10.** feel in one's bones, *U.S.* to feel intuitively. **11. make no bones of or about,** to be quite direct in dealing with. **—***v.t.* **12.** to take out the bones of: *to bone a turkey.* **13.** to put whalebone into (clothing). **14.** *Agric.* to put ground bone into, as fertilizer. **—***v.i.* **15.** *Slang.* to study hard and fast; cram (often fol. by *up*). [ME *boon,* OE *bān,* c. G *bein* leg] **—bone′less,** *adj.* **—bone′like′,** *adj.*

Bône (bōn), *n.* a seaport in NE Algeria. 112,010 (1954). Also, **Bo·na** (bō′nä). See **Hippo Regius.**

bone ash, the remains of bones calcined in the air.

bone·black (bōn′blăk′), *n.* a black carbonaceous substance obtained by calcining bones in closed vessels. Also, **bone black.**

bone china, a kind of china in which bone ash is used.

bone-dry (bōn′drī′), *adj.* *Colloq.* dry as a bone (applied esp. to the effect of rigidly enforced prohibition laws).

bone·head (bōn′hěd′), *n.* a stupid, obstinate person; a blockhead. **—bone′head′ed,** *adj.*

bone meal, *Agric.* bones ground to a coarse powder, used as a fertilizer or animal feed.

bone oil, a fetid, tarry liquid obtained in the dry distillation of bone.

bon·er (bō′nər), *n.* *Colloq.* a foolish blunder.

bone·set (bōn′sĕt′), *n.* the plant, *Eupatorium perfoliatum;* thoroughwort.

bon·fire (bŏn′fīr′), *n.* **1.** a large fire in an open place, for entertainment, celebration, or as a signal. **2.** any fire built in the open. [earlier *bonefire;* heaps of wood and bones were burned at certain old festivals]

bon·go (bŏng′gō), *n., pl.* **-gos.** a large forest-dwelling antelope, *Taurotragus eurycerus,* of tropical Africa, of a chestnut color striped with white, with spiraling horns.

Bon·heur (bô nœr′), *n.* **Rosa** (rô zä′), (*Marie Rosalie Bonheur*) 1822–99, French painter of animals.

bon·ho·mie (bŏn′ə mē′; *Fr.* bô nô mē′), *n.* frank and simple good-heartedness; a good-natured manner. Also, **bon′hom·mie′.** [t. F, der. *bonhomme* good man]

Bon·i·face (bŏn′ə fās′), *n.* **1.** name given to 9 popes, esp. **Boniface VIII** (*Benedetto Gaetani*), c.1235–1303, Italian ecclesiastic: pope 1294–1303. **2. Saint,** (*Wynfrith*) A.D. 680?–755?, English monk who became a missionary in Germany. **3.** a jovial innkeeper in *The Beaux' Stratagem* (1707) by George Farquhar. **4.** (*l.c.*) any landlord or innkeeper.

Bo·nin Islands (bō′nĭn), a group of islands in the N Pacific, SE of Japan; under U.S. administration. Uninhabited since WW II. 40 sq. mi. Japanese, **Ogasawara Jima.**

bo·ni·to (bə nē′tō), *n., pl.* **-tos, -toes.** **1.** any of the mackerellike fishes of the genus *Sarda,* as *S. sarda* of the Atlantic. **2.** any of several related species, as the oceanic bonito or skipjack, *Katsuwonus pelamis.* [t. Sp]

bon jour (bôN zhōōr′), *French.* good day; hello.

bon mot (bôN mō′), *pl.* **bons mots** (bôN mōz′; *Fr.* mō′), an especially fitting word or expression; a clever saying; witticism. [F: lit., good word]

Bonn (bŏn; *Ger.* bôn), *n.* a city in W West Germany, on the Rhine: capital of Federal Republic of Germany; Beethoven's birthplace. 140,761 (est. 1955).

Bon·nard (bô när′), *n.* **Pierre** (pyâr), 1867–1947, French impressionist painter.

bonne (bŏn, bûn), *n. French.* **1.** a maidservant. **2.** a child's nurse. [F, fem. of *bon* good. See BOON²]

bonne a·mie (bŏn à mē′), *French.* fem. of **bon ami.**

bonne bouche (bŏn bōōsh′), *French.* a tidbit.

bonne foi (bŏn fwà′), *French.* good faith; sincerity.

bon·net (bŏn′ĭt), *n.* **1.** a woman's or child's outdoor head covering, commonly fitting down over the hair, and often tied on with strings. **2.** *Chiefly Scot.* a man's or boy's cap. **3.** a bonnetlike headdress. **4.** any of various hoods, covers, or protective devices. **5.** a cowl or wind cap for a chimney to stabilize the draft. **6.** *Brit.* an automobile hood. **7.** *Naut.* an additional piece of canvas laced to the foot (formerly the top) of a jib or other sail. **—***v.t.* **8.** to put a bonnet on. [ME *bonet,* t. OF: cap (orig. its material); ? of Gmc. orig.] **—bon′net·like′,** *adj.*

bon·net rouge (bô ně rōōzh′), *pl.* **bonnets rouges** (bô ně rōōzh′), *French.* **1.** a red liberty cap, worn by extremists at the time of the French Revolution. **2.** an extremist or radical. [F: red cap]

bon·ny (bŏn′ĭ), *adj.,* **-nier, -niest. 1.** pleasing to the eye; handsome; pretty. **2.** *Brit. Dial.* plump and healthy. **3.** *Scot. and N. Eng.* fine (often used ironically). Also, **bon′nie.** [ME *bonie*. See BOON²] —**bon′ni·ly,** *adv.* —**bon′ni·ness,** *n.*

bon·ny·clab·ber (bŏn′Ĭ klăb′ər), *n.* sour, thick milk. [t. Irish: m. *bainne clabair,* lit., milk of the clabber (i.e.? the churn dasher)]

bon soir (bôn swȧr′), *French.* good evening; good night.

bon·spiel (bŏn′spēl, -spəl), *n.* *Scot.* a curling match between two clubs, parishes, etc. [orig. obscure]

bon·te·bok (bŏn′tĭ bŏk′), *n.* a large, red, South African antelope, *Damaliscus pygargus,* with a blaze on the face, now almost extinct. [t. S Afr. D: pied buck]

bon ton (bôn tôn′), good or elegant form or style; good breeding; fashionable society. [F: good tone]

bo·nus (bō′nəs), *n.* **1.** something given or paid over and above what is due. **2.** a sum of money paid to an employee, an agent of a company, a returned soldier, etc., over and above his regular pay. **3.** something free added in a corporate sale of securities. **4.** *Insurance.* dividend. **5.** a premium paid for a loan, contract, etc. **6.** something extra. [t. L: (adj.) good]
—**Syn. 2.** BONUS, BOUNTY, PREMIUM refer to something extra beyond a stipulated payment. A BONUS is a gift to reward performance, paid either by a private employer or by a government: *a bonus based on salary, the soldiers' bonus.* A BOUNTY is a public aid or reward offered to stimulate interest in a specific purpose or undertaking and to encourage performance: *a bounty for killing wolves.* A PREMIUM is usually something additional given as an inducement to buy, produce, or the like: *a premium with a magazine subscription.*

bon vi·vant (bŏn vē văn′), *pl.* **bons vivants** (bŏn vē văn′). *French.* **1.** a person who lives luxuriously, self-indulgently, etc. **2.** a jovial companion.

bon vo·yage (bôn vwȧ yȧzh′), *French.* pleasant trip.

bon·y (bō′nĬ), *adj.,* **bonier, boniest. 1.** of or like bone. **2.** full of bones. **3.** having prominent bones; big-boned. —**bon′i·ness,** *n.*

bonze (bŏnz), *n.* a Buddhist monk, esp. of Japan or China. [t. F, t. Pg.: m. *bonzo,* t. Jap.: m. *bonzō,* t. Chinese: m. *fan sung* ordinary (member) of the assembly]

boo (boo), *interj., n., pl.* **boos,** *v.,* **booed, booing.** —*interj.* **1.** an exclamation used to express contempt, disapprobation, etc., or to frighten. —*n.* **2.** this exclamation. —*v.i.* **3.** to cry "boo." —*v.t.* **4.** to cry "boo" at; show disapproval of by booing.

boob (boob), *n.* *U.S. Slang.* a fool; a dunce. [see BOOBY]

boo·by (boo′bĬ), *n., pl.* **-bies. 1.** a stupid person; a dunce. **2.** the worst student, player, etc., of a group. **3.** Also, **booby gannet,** any of various gannets, as the white-bellied booby (*Sula leucogaster*) of the Bahama Islands, etc. [prob. t. Sp.: m. *bobo* fool, also the bird booby, g. L *balbus* stammering] —**boo′by·ish,** *adj.*

booby hatch, 1. *Naut.* a wooden hood over a hatch. **2.** *U.S. Colloq.* insane asylum. **3.** *U.S. Slang.* jail.

booby prize, a prize given in good-natured ridicule to the worst player in a game or contest.

booby trap, a hidden bomb or mine so placed that it will be set off by an unsuspecting person through such means as moving an apparently harmless object.

boo·dle (boo′dəl), *n., v.,* **-dled, -dling.** *U.S. Slang.* —*n.* **1.** (often in contemptuous use) the lot, pack, or crowd: *the whole boodle.* **2.** a bribe or other illicit gain in politics. —*v.i.* **3.** to obtain money dishonestly, as by corrupt bargains. [t. D: m. *boedel, boel* stock, lot] —**boo′dler,** *n.*

boog·ie-woog·ie (boog′Ĭ woog′Ĭ), *Jazz.* a form of instrumental blues using melodic variations over a constantly repeated bass figure.

boo·hoo (boo′hoo′), *v.,* **-hooed, -hooing,** *n., pl.* **-hoos.** —*v.i.* **1.** to weep noisily; blubber. —*n.* **2.** the sound of noisy weeping. [imit.]

book (book), *n.* **1.** a written or printed work of some length, as a treatise or other literary composition, esp. on consecutive sheets fastened or bound together. **2.** a number of sheets of writing paper bound together and used for making entries, as of commercial transactions. **3.** a division of a literary work, esp. one of the larger divisions. **4. the Book,** the Bible. **5.** *Music.* the text of an opera, operetta, etc. **6.** *Theat.* a play script. **7.** a record of bets, as on a horserace. **8.** *Cards.* the number of tricks or cards which must be taken before any trick counts in the score. In bridge it is six tricks. **9.** a set of tickets, checks, stamps, etc., bound together like a book. **10.** a pile or package of leaves, as of tobacco. **11.** anything that serves for the recording of facts or events: *the book of Nature.* **12. bring to book,** to bring to account. **13. by (the) book, a.** formally. **b.** authoritatively; correctly. **14. in one's books,** in one's favor. **15. on the books,** entered on the list of members. **16. without book, a.** by memory. **b.** without authority. —*v.t.* **17.** to enter in a book or list; record; register. **18.** to engage (a place, passage, etc.) beforehand. **19.** to put down for a place, passage, etc. **20.** to engage (a person or company) for a performance or performances. —*v.i.* **21.** to register one's name. **22.** to engage a place, services, etc. [ME; OE *bōc,* c. G *buch*] —**book′less,** *adj.*

book·bind·er (book′bīn′dər), *n.* one whose business or work is the binding of books.

book·bind·er·y (book′bīn′dərĬ), *n., pl.* **-eries.** an establishment for binding books.

book·bind·ing (book′bīn′dĬng), *n.* the process or art of binding books.

book·case (book′kās′), *n.* a set of shelves for books.

book club, 1. a club which lends or sells (usually at a discount) books to its members. **2.** a club organized for the discussion and reviewing of books.

book end, a support placed at the end of a row of books to hold them upright.

book·ie (book′Ĭ), *n.* *Colloq.* bookmaker (def. 2).

book·ing (book′Ĭng), *n.* an engagement to perform.

book·ish (book′Ĭsh), *adj.* **1.** given to reading or study. **2.** more acquainted with books than with real life. **3.** of or pertaining to books; literary. **4.** stilted; pedantic. —**book′ish·ly,** *adv.* —**book′ish·ness,** *n.*

book jacket, a detachable paper cover, usually attractively illustrated, protecting the binding of a book.

book·keep·er (book′kē′pər), *n.* one who keeps account books, as for a business house.

book·keep·ing (book′kē′pĬng), *n.* the work or art of keeping account books or systematic records of money transactions.

book learning, knowledge gained by reading books, in distinction to that obtained through observation and experience. Also, **book knowledge, book·lore** (book′lōr′). —**book-learn·ed** (book′lûr′nĬd), *adj.*

book·let (book′lĬt), *n.* a little book, esp. one with paper covers; pamphlet.

book louse, any insect of the order *Corrodentia,* which damages books by eating away the glue, and is injurious to other products in houses, granaries, etc.

book·mak·er (book′mā′kər), *n.* **1.** a maker of books. **2.** a professional betting man who accepts the bets of others, as on horses in racing.

book·man (book′mən), *n., pl.* **-men. 1.** a studious or learned man; a scholar. **2.** *Colloq.* a person whose occupation is selling or publishing books.

book·mark (book′märk′), *n.* **1.** a ribbon or the like placed between the pages of a book to mark a place. **2.** a bookplate.

book·mo·bile (book′mə bēl′), *n.* *U.S.* an automobile or small truck constructed to carry books, serving as a traveling library as for small communities in which libraries are not accessible.

book of account, *Com.* **1.** (*pl.*) the original records and books used in recording business transactions. **2.** an original entry or other account book.

Book of Common Prayer, the service book of the Church of England, essentially adopted but changed in details by other churches of the Anglican communion.

Book of Mormon. See Mormon (def. 2).

book·plate (book′plāt′), *n.* a label, bearing the owner's name, a design, etc., for pasting in a book.

book·rack (book′răk′), *n.* **1.** a rack for supporting an open book. **2.** a rack for holding books.

book review, critical discussion of a book, esp. of a newly published book. —**book reviewer.** —**book reviewing.**

book scorpion, any of the minute arachnids, superficially resembling a tailless scorpion, which constitute the order *Chelonethi* (*Pseudoscorpionida*), as *Chelifer cancroides,* found in old books, etc.

book·sell·er (book′sĕl′ər), *n.* a person whose occupation or business is selling books.

book·stack (book′stăk′), *n.* a set of bookshelves one above another, as in a library; a stack.

book·stall (book′stôl′), *n.* **1.** a stall at which books (usually secondhand) are sold. **2.** *Brit.* a newsstand.

book·stand (book′stănd′), *n.* **1.** bookrack. **2.** bookstall.

book·store (book′stōr′), *n.* *U.S.* a store where books are sold. Also, *orig. Brit.,* **book·shop** (book′shŏp′).

book·worm (book′wûrm′), *n.* **1.** any of various insects that feed on books. **2.** a person closely addicted to reading or study.

boom¹ (boom), *v.i.* **1.** to make a deep, prolonged, resonant sound; make a rumbling, humming, or droning noise. **2.** to move with a resounding rush or great impetus. **3.** to progress or flourish vigorously, as a business, a city, etc. —*v.t.* **4.** to give forth with a booming sound (usually fol. by *out*): *the clock boomed out twelve.* **5.** to push (a cause, a new product, etc.) vigorously. —*n.* **6.** a deep, hollow, continued sound. **7.** a roaring, rumbling, or reverberation, as of waves or distant guns. **8.** the cry of the bittern. **9.** a buzzing, humming, or droning, as of a bee or beetle. **10.** a rapid increase in price, development, numbers, etc. **11.** a rise in popularity, as of a political candidate, or efforts to bring it about. —*adj.* **12.** *U.S.* caused by a boom: *boom prices.* [imit. Cf. ZOOM]

boom² (boom), *n.* **1.** *Naut.* a long pole or spar used to extend the foot of certain sails. **2.** a chain or cable or a series of connected floating timbers, etc., serving to obstruct navigation, to confine floating timber, etc. **3.** the area thus shut off. **4.** *Mach.* a spar or beam projecting from the mast of a derrick, supporting or guiding the weights to be lifted. [t. D: tree, beam. See BEAM]

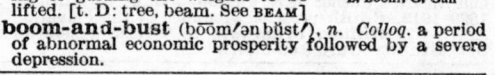

B, Boom; G, Gaff

boom-and-bust (boom′ən bŭst′), *n.* *Colloq.* a period of abnormal economic prosperity followed by a severe depression.

boom·er·ang (bōō'mə răng'), n. 1. a bent or curved piece of hard wood used as a missile by the native Australians, one form of which can be so thrown as to return to the thrower. 2. a scheme, plan, argument, etc., which recoils upon the user. —v.i. 3. (of a scheme, etc.) to cause unexpected harm to the originator. [t. natived.]

Boomerangs

Boom·er State (bōō'mər), Oklahoma.

boon[1] (bōōn), n. 1. a benefit enjoyed; a thing to be thankful for; a blessing. 2. Archaic. that which is asked; a favor sought. [ME, t. Scand.; cf. Icel. bōn request, petition]

boon[2] (bōōn), adj. 1. jolly; jovial; convivial: boon companion. 2. Poetic. kindly; gracious; bounteous. [ME, t. OF: m. bon, g. L bonus good]

boon·docks (bōōn'dŏks'), n. U.S. Slang. an uninhabited and densely overgrown area, as a backwoods, marsh, etc.

boon·dog·gle (bōōn'dŏg'əl), n., v., -gled, -gling. U.S. —n. 1. a belt, knife sheath, ax handle, or other product of simple manual skill. 2. a cord of plaited leather worn round the neck by Boy Scouts. 3. Slang. work of little or no practical value. —v.i. 4. Slang. to do work of little or no practical value. —boon'dog'gler, n.

Boone (bōōn), n. **Daniel**, 1735–1820, American pioneer, esp. in Kentucky.

boor (bōōr), n. 1. a clownish, rude, or unmannerly person. 2. a peasant; a rustic. 3. an illiterate or clownish peasant. 4. a Dutch or German peasant. 5. any foreign peasant. 6. (cap.) a Dutch colonist. [t. D: m. boer peasant, or t. LG: m. būr peasant]

boor·ish (bōōr'ish), adj. of or like a boor; rustic; rude. —boor'ish·ly, adv. —boor'ish·ness, n.

boost (bōōst), U.S. —v.t. 1. to lift or raise by pushing from behind or below. 2. to advance or aid by speaking well of. 3. to increase; push up: to boost prices. —n. 4. an upward shove or push. 5. an aid that helps one to rise in the world. [b. BOOM and HOIST]

boost·er (bōō'stər), n. U.S. 1. one that boosts. 2. Elect. a device connected in series with a current for increasing or decreasing the nominal circuit voltage. 3. a. a rocket engine used as the main supply of thrust in a missile flight. b. the stage of a missile containing this engine, often detached at burnout. 4. Pharm. a substance, usually injected, for prolonging a person's immunity to a specific infection.

boot[1] (bōōt), n. 1. a covering, usually of leather, for the foot and leg, reaching at least to the middle of the calf, and often to the knee or higher. 2. Brit. any shoe or outer foot covering reaching above the ankle. 3. an instrument of torture for the leg. 4. any sheathlike protective covering: a boot for a weak automobile tire. 5. a protective covering for the foot and part of the leg of a horse. 6. a protecting apron or cover for the driver's seat of a vehicle. 7. U.S. Navy or Marines. a recruit. 8. Chiefly Brit. a receptacle or place for baggage at either end of a vehicle. 9. Music. the box in the reed pipe of an organ which holds the reed. 10. a kick. 11. Slang. a dismissal; discharge. 12. lick the boots of, to be subservient to; flatter. —v.t. 13. to put boots on. 14. to torture with the boot. 15. Slang. to kick; drive by kicking. 16. Football. to kick; punt. 17. Slang. to dismiss; discharge. 18. Sports. to fumble. —adj. 19. U.S. Navy or Marines. for primary training: boot camp. [ME bote, t. OF; orig. uncert. See SABOT.]

boot[2] (bōōt), n. 1. to boot, into the bargain; in addition. 2. Archaic or Dial. something given into the bargain. 3. Obs. advantage. 4. Obs. remedy. —v.i. 5. Obs. or Poetic. to be of profit, advantage, or avail: it boots not to complain. [ME bote, OE bōt advantage]

boot[3] (bōōt), n. Archaic. booty; spoil; plunder. [special use of BOOT[2] by assoc. with BOOTY]

boot·black (bōōt'blăk'), n. a person whose occupation it is to shine shoes, boots, etc.

boot·ed (bōō'tĭd), adj. 1. equipped with boots. 2. Ornith. (of the tarsus of certain birds) covered with a continuous horny, bootlike sheath.

boot·ee (bōō tē'; or esp. for 1 bōō'tĭ), n. 1. a baby's knitted shoe. 2. a kind of half boot for women.

Bo·ö·tes (bō ō'tēz), n. a northern constellation containing the first magnitude star Arcturus. [t. L, t. Gk.: ox driver]

booth (bōōth, bōōth), n., pl. booths (bōōthz). 1. a temporary structure of boughs, canvas, boards, etc., as for shelter. 2. a stall or light structure for the sale of goods or for display purposes, as at a market or fair. 3. a small compartment for a telephone, motion picture projector, etc. 4. a small temporary structure used by voters at elections. [ME bōthe, t. Scand.; cf. Dan. bod]

Booth (bōōth; Brit. bōōth), n. 1. Ballington, 1859–1940, founder of the Volunteers of America (son of William). 2. Edwin Thomas, 1833–93, U. S. actor (brother of John Wilkes). 3. Evangeline Cory, 1865?–1950, general of the Salvation Army, 1934–39 (daughter of William). 4. John Wilkes, 1838–65, U.S. actor: assassin of Abraham Lincoln (brother of Edwin T.). 5. Junius Brutus, 1796–1852, British actor in England and America (father of Edwin and John). 6. William, 1829–1912, British preacher: founder of the Salvation Army. 7. William Bramwell, 1856–1929, general of the Salvation Army (son of William).

Boo·thi·a (bōō'thĭ ə), n. 1. an arctic peninsula in N Canada: northernmost part of the mainland of North America; former location of the north magnetic pole. 2. Gulf of, a gulf between this peninsula and Baffin Island.

boot·jack (bōōt'jăk'), n. a device used to hold a boot while the foot is drawn out of it.

Boo·tle (bōō'təl), n. a seaport in W England, on the Mersey estuary near Liverpool. 74,302 (1951).

boot·leg (bōōt'lĕg'), n., v. -legged, -legging, adj. U.S. —n. 1. alcoholic liquor secretly and unlawfully made, sold, or transported. 2. that part of a boot which covers the leg. —v.t. 3. to deal in (liquor or other goods) illicitly. —v.i. 4. to carry goods, as liquor, about secretly for illicit sale. —adj. 5. made, sold, or transported unlawfully. 6. unlawful; clandestine. 7. of or pertaining to bootlegging. [def. 2 orig. meaning; others arose from the practice of concealing illegal liquor in the bootleg] —boot'leg'ger, n.

boot·less (bōōt'lĭs), adj. without advantage; unavailing; useless. [OE bōtlēas unpardonable, f. bōt BOOT[2] + -lēas -LESS] —boot'less·ly, adv. —boot'less·ness, n.

boot·lick (bōōt'lĭk'), U.S. Slang. —v.t. 1. to curry favor with; toady to (a person). —v.i. 2. to be a toady. —boot'lick'er, n. —boot'lick'ing, n., adj.

boots and saddles, U.S. Army. a cavalry bugle call for mounted formation.

boot tree, an instrument inserted into a boot or shoe to stretch it or preserve its shape.

boo·ty (bōō'tĭ), n., pl. -ties. 1. spoil taken from an enemy in war; plunder; pillage. 2. that which is seized by violence and robbery. 3. a prize or gain, without reference to use of force. [late ME boyte; cf. G beute]

booze (bōōz), n., v. boozed, boozing. Colloq. —n. 1. alcoholic liquor. 2. a drinking bout; spree. —v.i., v.t. 3. to drink immoderately. [var. of BOUSE[2]] —booz'er, n.

booz·y (bōō'zĭ), adj., boozier, booziest. Colloq. 1. drunken. 2. addicted to liquor. —booz'i·ness, n.

bop (bŏp), n. bebop.

bor., 1. borough. 2. boron.

bo·ra (bôr'ə), n. Meteorol. a violent, dry, cold wind on the coasts of the Adriatic, blowing from the north or northeast. [t. d. It., g. L boreas north wind]

bo·rac·ic (bə răs'ĭk, bō-), adj. Chem. boric.

bo·ra·cite (bôr'ə sīt'), n. a mineral, a borate and chloride of magnesium, $Mg_6Cl_2B_{14}O_{26}$, occurring in white or colorless crystals or fine-grained masses, strongly pyroelectric.

bor·age (bûr'ĭj, bôr'-, bŏr'-), n. 1. a plant, Borago officinalis, native of southern Europe, with hairy leaves and stems, used in salads and medicinally. 2. any of various allied or similar plants. [ME, t. AF: m. burage, var. of OF bourrace, der. bourrer stuff, ult. der. ML burra wool]

bo·rag·i·na·ceous (bə răj'ə nā'shəs, bō-), adj. belonging to the Boraginaceae, or borage family of plants, including borage, bugloss, heliotrope, forget-me-not, etc.

Bo·rah (bôr'ə), n. William Edgar, 1865–1940, U. S. senator from Idaho, 1906–40.

bo·rate (n. bôr'āt, -ĭt; v. bôr'āt), n., v., -rated, -rating. Chem. —n. 1. a salt of orthoboric acid. 2. (loosely) a salt of any boric acid. —v.t. 3. to treat with borate, boric acid, or borax.

bo·rax (bôr'ăks, -ăks), n. a white, crystalline sodium borate, $Na_2B_4O_7.10H_2O$, occurring native or prepared artificially and used as a flux, cleansing agent, in the manufacture of glass, etc. [t. ML, t. Ar.: m. buwraq, t. Pers.: m. bōrah (OPers. bōrak); r. ME boras, t. OF]

Bor·deaux (bôr dō'), n. 1. a seaport in SW France, on the Garonne river. 257,946 (1954). 2. wine produced in the region surrounding Bordeaux. Red Bordeaux wines are called clarets. White Bordeaux wines include sauternes (sweet) and graves (dry). 3. Bordeaux mixture.

Bordeaux mixture, Hort. a fungicide consisting of a mixture of copper sulfate, lime, and water.

bor·del·lo (bôr dĕl'ō), n. a house of prostitution.

bor·der (bôr'dər), n. 1. a side, edge, or margin. 2. the line that separates one country, state, or province from another; frontier line. 3. the district or region that lies along the boundary line of a country. 4. U.S. the frontier of civilization. 5. the Border, the region along the boundary between England and Scotland. 6. brink; verge. 7. an ornamental strip or design around the edge of a printed page, a drawing, etc. 8. a piece of ornamental trimming around the edge of a garment, cap, etc. 9. Hort. a narrow strip of ground in a garden, enclosing a portion of it. —v.t. 10. to make a border about; adorn with a border. 11. to form a border or boundary to. 12. to lie on the border of; adjoin. —v.i. 13. border on or upon, a. to touch or abut at the border. b. to approach closely in character; verge. [ME bordure, t. OF, der. bord side, edge; of Gmc. orig. See BOARD] —bor'dered, adj. —bor'der·er, n.

bor·der·er (bôr'dər ər), n. one who dwells on or near the border of a country, region, etc.

bor·der·land (bôr'dər lănd'), n. 1. land forming a border or frontier. 2. an uncertain intermediate district, space, or condition.

bor·der·line (bôr'dər līn'), adj. 1. on or near a border or boundary. 2. uncertain; indeterminate; debatable.

Border States, 1. U.S. Hist. the slave States inclined to compromise instead of seceding: Delaware, Maryland, Virginia, Kentucky, Missouri; sometimes extended to include North Carolina, Tennessee, and Arkansas. **2.** *U.S.* the States touching the Canadian border. **3.** certain of the countries of central and northern Europe, bordering on the Soviet Union and formerly belonging to the Russian Empire: Finland, Poland (prior to 1940), Estonia, Latvia and Lithuania.

bor·dure (bôr′jər), *n.* *Her.* the outer fifth of the shield. [ME, t. OF. See BORDER]

bore[1] (bôr), *v.*, **bored, boring,** *n.* —*v.t.* **1.** *Mach.* to pierce (a solid substance) or make (a round hole, etc.) with an auger, drill, or other rotated instrument. **2.** to force by persistent forward thrusting. —*v.i.* **3.** *Mach.* to make a hole, as with an auger or drill. **4.** to admit of being pierced with an auger or the like, as a substance. —*n.* *Mach.* **5.** a hole made by boring, or as if by boring. **6.** the inside diameter of a hollow cylindrical object or device, such as a bushing or bearing, or the barrel of a gun. [ME *boren*, OE *borian*, c. G *bohren*; akin to L *forāre* pierce] —Syn. **1.** perforate.

bore[2] (bôr), *v.*, **bored, boring,** *n.* —*v.t.* to weary by tedious repetition, dullness, unwelcome attentions, etc. —*n.* **2.** a dull, tiresome, or uncongenial person. **3.** a cause of ennui or annoyance. [orig. unknown]

bore[3] (bôr), *n.* *Oceanog.* an abrupt rise of the tide which breaks in an estuary, rushing violently up the channel. [ME, t. Scand.; cf. Icel. *bāra* wave]

bore[4] (bôr), *v.* pt. of **bear**[1].

bo·re·al (bôr′ĭ əl), *adj.* **1.** pertaining to the north wind. **2.** northern. **3.** pertaining to Boreas. [t. L: s. *boreālis*, der. *Boreas* north wind]

Bo·re·as (bôr′ĭ əs), *n.* the north wind, as personified or deified by the Greeks.

bore·dom (bôr′dəm), *n.* bored state; tedium; ennui.

bor·er (bôr′ər), *n.* **1.** one that bores or pierces. **2.** *Mach.* a tool used for boring; an auger. **3.** *Entomol.* any insect that burrows in trees, fruits. etc., esp. any beetle of certain groups. **4.** *Zool.* any of various mollusks, etc., that bore into wood, etc. **5.** a marsipobranch fish, as a hagfish, that bores into other fish to feed on their flesh.

bore·some (bôr′səm), *adj.* tedious; dull; boring.

Bor·ger·hout (bôr′кнәr hout′), *n.* a city in N Belgium, near Antwerp. 50,694 (est. 1952).

Bor·ghe·se (bôr gĕ′sĕ), *n.* a noble Italian family, orig. from the republic of Siena, important in Italian society and politics from the 16th to the early 19th century.

Bor·gia (bôr′jä), *n.* **1. Cesare** (chĕ′zä rĕ), 1476–1507, Italian cardinal, military leader, and politician. **2. Lucrezia** (lōō krĕ′tsyä), 1480–1519, sister and the political tool of Cesare; patroness of culture; Duchess of Ferrara. **3. Rodrigo Lanzol** (rô drē′gô län zôl′), 1431–1503, Italian cardinal: became Pope Alexander VI (father of Cesare and Lucrezia Borgia).

Bor·glum (bôr′gləm), *n.* **(John)** Gutzon (gŭt′sən), 1867–1941, U. S. sculptor and painter.

bo·ric (bôr′ĭk), *adj.* *Chem.* of or containing boron; boracic.

boric acid, 1. *Chem., Pharm.* a white crystalline acid, H_3BO_3, occurring in nature or prepared from borax, used in aqueous solution as a mild antiseptic. **2.** *Chem.* any of a group of acids containing boron.

bo·ride (bôr′ĭd), *n.* *Chem.* a compound usually containing two elements only, of which boron is the more electropositive one.

bor·ing (bôr′ĭng), *n.* *Mach.* **1.** act or process of piercing or perforating. **2.** the hole so made. **3.** (*pl.*) the chips, fragments, or dust produced in boring.

Bo·ris III (bôr′ĭs), 1894–1943, king of Bulgaria, 1918–1943.

born (bôrn), *adj.* **1.** brought forth by birth. **2.** possessing from birth the quality or character stated: *a born fool.* [prop. pp. of BEAR[1]; ME and OE *boren*]

borne (bôrn), *v.* **1.** pp. of **bear** in all meanings except in the sense "brought forth" where *born* is now used, except after *have* or when followed by *by: the child was born, she had borne a child.* **2.** p.a. of **bear.**

Bor·ne·o (bôr′nĭ ō′), *n.* an island in the Malay Archipelago, including Sabah and Sarawak (formerly British), the British controlled territory of Brunei, and Indonesian Borneo (formerly Dutch). ab. 1,115,000 pop.; ab. 290,000 sq. mi.

bor·ne·ol (bôr′nĭ ōl′, -ŏl′), *n.* *Chem. Bot.* terpene alcohol, $C_{10}H_{17}OH$, closely resembling common camphor, found in concrete masses in the trunk of *Dryobalanops aromatica,* a large tree of Borneo, Sumatra, etc. [f. BORNEO + -OL[1]]

Born·holm (bôrn′hōlm), *n.* a Danish island in the Baltic, S of Sweden. 48,392 pop. (est. 1954); 227 sq. mi.

born·ite (bôr′nīt), *n.* a common mineral, copper iron sulfide, Cu_5FeS_4, occurring in masses of brownish color on fresh surfaces: an important ore of copper. [after I. von *Born* (1742–91), Austrian mineralogist. See -ITE[1]]

Bor·nu (bôr′nōō′), *n.* a former sultanate in W Africa, S and W of Lake Chad: now largely a province in Nigeria. ab. 50,000 sq. mi.

Bo·ro·din (bŏ rŏ dēn′), *n.* **Aleksandr Porfirevich** (ä′lĕ ksän′dər pŏr fîr yĕ′vĭch), 1834–87, Russian composer.

Bo·ro·di·no (bŏ rŏ dĭ′nô′), *n.* a village in the W Soviet Union, 70 mi. W of Moscow: Napoleon's victory here made possible the capture of Moscow, 1812.

bo·ron (bôr′ŏn), *n.* *Chem.* a nonmetallic element present in borax, etc., and obtained in either an amorphous or a crystalline form when reduced from its compound. *Symbol:* B; *at. wt.:* 10.82; *at. no.:* 5. [b. BORAX and CARBON]

bo·ro·sil·i·cate (bôr′ō sĭl′ə kĭt, -kāt′), *n.* *Chem.* a salt of boric and silicic acids.

bo·ro·sil·ic·ic acids (bôr′ō sə lĭs′ĭk), *Chem.* hypothetical acids yielding borosilicate.

bor·ough (bûr′ō), *n.* **1.** (in certain States of the U.S.) an incorporated municipality smaller than a city. **2.** one of the five administrative divisions of New York City. **3.** *Brit.* **a.** an urban community incorporated by royal charter, equivalent in general to *city* in U. S. **b.** an urban election constituency, usually subdivided. **c.** (formerly) a fortified town, or a town possessing municipal organization. [ME *burgh* town, OE *burg* stronghold, c. G *burg*]

bor·ough-Eng·lish (bûr′ō ĭng′glĭsh), *n.* *Law.* a customary system of inheritance in parts of England which gave the entire estate to the youngest son.

bor·row (bŏr′ō, bôr′ō), *v.t.* **1.** to take or obtain (a thing) on the promise to return it or its equivalent; obtain the temporary use of. **2.** to get from another or from a foreign source; appropriate or adopt: *borrowed words.* **3.** *Arith.* (in subtraction) to take from one denomination to add to the next lower. —*v.i.* **4.** to borrow something. [ME *borowe(n)*, OE *borgian*, der. *borg* a pledge] —**bor′row·er,** *n.*

Bor·row (bŏr′ō, bôr′ō), *n.* **George,** 1803–81, British traveler, writer, and student of languages, esp. Romany.

Bors (bôrs), *n.* *Arthurian Legend.* **1.** Also, **Sir Bors de Ganis.** a knight of the Round Table, nephew of Lancelot. **2.** a natural son of King Arthur.

borsch (bôrsh), *n.* a Russian stock soup containing beets, served hot or chilled. Also, **borscht** (bôrsht).

bort (bôrt), *n.* flawed, low quality diamonds, and diamond fragments, valuable only for crushing to diamond dust. [cf. OF *bort* bastard] —**bort′y,** *adj.*

bor·zoi (bôr′zoi), *n., pl.* **-zois.** a Russian wolfhound.

Bo·san·quet (bō′zan kĕt′, -kĭt), *n.* **Bernard,** 1848–1923, British philosopher and writer.

bos·cage (bŏs′kĭj), *n.* a mass of growing trees or shrubs; woods, groves, or thickets. Also, **bos′kage.** [ME, t. OF, der. *bosc,* t. Gmc. See BOSK]

Bosch (bŏs), *n.* **Hieronymus** (hĕ′ə rŏ′nĭ məs), 1450?–1516, Dutch painter.

bosch·bok (bŏsh′bŏk′), *n.* bushbuck. [t. S Afr. D: f. *bosch* wood + *bok* buck]

bosch·vark (bŏsh′värk′), *n.* bush pig. [t. S Afr. D: wood pig]

Bose (bōs), *n.* **Sir Jagadis Chandra** (jə gə dēs′ chŭn′drə), 1858–1937, Indian physicist and plant physiologist.

bosh[1] (bŏsh), *n.* *Colloq.* complete nonsense; absurd or foolish talk or opinions. [t. Turk.: empty, vain]

bosh[2] (bŏsh), *n.* the lower portion of a blast furnace, extending from the widest part to the hearth. [cf. G *böschung* slope]

bosk (bŏsk), *n.* *Archaic or Poetic.* a thicket; a small wood, esp. of bushes. [ME, var. of *busk,* var. of BUSH[1]]

bos·ket (bŏs′kĭt), *n.* a grove; a thicket. Also, **bosquet.** [t. F: m. *bosquet,* t. It.: m. *boschetto,* dim. of *bosco* wood. See BUSH[1]]

bosk·y (bŏs′kĭ), *adj.* **1.** woody; covered with bushes. **2.** shady. —**bosk′i·ness,** *n.*

bo's'n (bō′sən), *n.* *Naut.* boatswain.

Bos·ni·a (bŏz′nĭ ə), *n.* a former Turkish province in S Europe: a part of Austria, 1878–1918; now a part of Bosnia and Herzegovina. See map under **Austria-Hungary.** —**Bos′ni·an,** *adj., n.*

Bosnia and Her·ze·go·vi·na (hĕr′tsə gō vē′nə), a constituent republic of Yugoslavia, in the W part. 4,043,000 (est. 1956); 19,909 sq. mi. *Cap.*: Sarajevo.

bos·om (bŏŏz′əm, bŏō′zəm), *n.* **1.** the breast of a human being. **2.** that part of a garment which covers the breast. **3.** the breast, conceived of as the seat of thought or emotion. **4.** the enclosure formed by the breast and the arms; affectionate embrace. **5.** something likened to the human bosom: *the bosom of the earth.* —*adj.* **6.** of or pertaining to the bosom. **7.** intimate or confidential: *a bosom friend.* —*v.t.* **8.** to take to the bosom; embrace; cherish. **9.** to hide from view; conceal. [ME *bōsm,* c. G *busen*]

Bos·po·rus (bŏs′pə rəs), *n.* a strait connecting the Black Sea and the Sea of Marmara. 18 mi. long.

bos·quet (bŏs′kĭt), *n.* bosket.

boss[1] (bôs, bŏs), *n.* **1.** *Chiefly U.S. Colloq.* one who employs or superintends workmen; a foreman or manager. **2.** *U.S.* a politician who controls his party organization, as in a particular district. —*v.t.* **3.** to be master of or over; manage; direct; control. —*v.i.* **4.** to be boss. **5.** to be too domineering and authoritative. —*adj.* **6.** chief; master. **7.** *Slang.* first-rate. [t. D: m. *baas* master]

boss[2] (bôs, bŏs), *n.* **1.** *Bot., Zool.* a protuberance or roundish excrescence on the body or some organ of an animal or plant. **2.** *Geol.* a knoblike mass of rock, esp. such an outcrop of eruptive rock. **3.** an ornamental protuberance of metal, ivory, etc. **4.** *Archit.* a knoblike projection of ornamental character, as at the intersection of ribs or groins. **5.** *Mach.* the enlarged part of a shaft. *—v.t.* **6.** to ornament with bosses. **7.** to emboss. [ME *bos*, t. OF: m. *boce*. See BOTCH²]

boss³ (bôs, bŏs), *n.* *U.S.* a name for a cow. [cf. L *bōs* ox]

bos·sa no·va (bŏs′ə nō′və), **1.** jazz-influenced music of Brazilian origin, rhythmically related to the samba. **2.** a dance performed to this music.

boss·ism (bôs′ĭz əm, bŏs′ĭz-), *n.* *U.S.* control by bosses, esp. political bosses.

Bos·suet (bō swĕ′), *n.* **Jacques Bénigne** (zhàk bĕ-nēn′y), 1627-1704, French bishop and writer.

boss·y¹ (bôs′ĭ, bŏs′ĭ), *adj.*, **bossier, bossiest.** *Colloq.* given to acting like a boss; domineering. [f. BOSS¹ + -Y¹]

boss·y² (bôs′ĭ, bŏs′ĭ), *adj.* studded with bosses; projecting as decorative work. [f. BOSS² + -Y¹]

bos·sy³ (bôs′ĭ, bŏs′ĭ), *n.*, *pl.* **-sies.** *U.S.* a familiar name for a cow or calf. [f. BOSS³ + -Y²]

Bos·ton (bôs′tən, bŏs′tən), *n.* **1.** the capital of Massachusetts, in the E part: the largest city and seaport in New England. 697,197 (1960). **2.** (*l.c.*) a game of cards, played by four persons with two packs of cards. **3.** (*l.c.*) a social dance, a modification of the waltz.—**Bos·to·ni·an** (bôs tō′nĭ ən, bŏs tō′-), *adj.*, *n.*

Boston brown bread, a dark-brown steamed bread made of corn meal and rye meal (or graham or wheat flour), sweetened with molasses.

Boston ivy, *Hort.* Japanese ivy.

Boston Massacre, *U.S. Hist.* a riot on March 5 1770, arising from the resentment of Boston citizens against British troops quartered in the city.

Boston rocker, a wooden American rocking chair having curved seat, spindle back, and headpiece usually stenciled with gilt design.

Boston Tea Party, *U.S. Hist.* a raid on British ships in Boston Harbor on Dec. 16, 1773, in which colonists of Boston, disguised as Indians, threw tea into the harbor as a protest against British taxes on the commodity.

Boston terrier, any of a breed of small, smooth-coated dogs with short hair and brindle or dark-brown coat with white markings, originated in the U. S. by crossing the English bulldog and the bull terrier. Also, **Boston bull.**

Boston terrier
(12 to 16 in. high)

bo·sun (bō′sən), *n.* *Naut.* boatswain.

Bos·well (bŏz′wĕl, -wəl), *n.* **1. James,** 1740-95, Scottish author: biographer of Samuel Johnson. **2.** any devoted biographer.

Bos·worth Field (bŏz′wûrth, -wərth), a battlefield in central England, near Leicester, where Richard III was defeated and slain by the future Henry VII (the first Tudor ruler of England) in 1485.

bot (bŏt), *n.* an insect larva infesting the skin, sinuses, nose, eye, stomach, or other parts of animals or man. Also, **bott.** See botfly. [orig. uncert.]

bot., 1. botanical. **2.** botanist. **3.** botany.

bo·tan·i·cal (bə tăn′ə kəl), *adj.* Also, **bo·tan′ic. 1.** pertaining to plants: *botanical survey, botanical drugs.* *—n.* **2.** *Pharm.* a drug made from part of a plant, as from roots, leaves, bark, etc. [f. ML *botanicus* (t. Gk.: m. *botanikós*) + -AL¹] —**bo·tan′i·cal·ly,** *adv.*

bot·a·nist (bŏt′ə nĭst), *n.* one who is skilled in botany.

bot·a·nize (bŏt′ə nīz′), *v.*, **-nized, -nizing.** *—v.i.* **1.** to study plants botanically. **2.** to collect plants for botanical study. *—v.t.* **3.** to explore botanically.

bot·a·ny (bŏt′ə nĭ), *n.*, *pl.* **-nies. 1.** the science of plants; branch of biology that deals with plant life. **2.** the plant life of a region: *the botany of Cuba.* **3.** the biology of a plant or plant group: *the botany of deciduous trees.* [f. *botan*(ic) (see BOTANICAL) + -Y³]

Botany Bay, 1. a bay on the SE coast of Australia, near Sydney: former British penal colony. **2.** any place of detention or punishment.

botch¹ (bŏch), *v.t.* **1.** to spoil by poor work; bungle. **2.** to do or say in a bungling manner. **3.** to mend or patch in a clumsy manner. *—n.* **4.** a clumsy or poor piece of work; a bungle: *his baking was a complete botch.* **5.** a clumsily added part or patch. [ME *bocchen*; orig. uncert.] —**botch′er,** *n.* —**botch′er·y,** *n.*

botch² (bŏch), *n.* *Archaic* or *Dial.* a swelling on the skin; a boil; an eruptive disease. [ME *boche*, t. ONF, var. of *boce* ulcer]

botch·y (bŏch′ĭ), *adj.*, **botchier, botchiest.** poorly made or done; bungled.

bot·fly (bŏt′flī′), *n.*, *pl.* **-flies.** *Parasitol.* any of various dipterous insects of the families *Oestridae* and *Gastrophilidae*, the larvae of which are parasitic in the skin or other parts of animals or man. [see BOT]

both (bōth), *adj.*, *pron.* **1.** the one and the other; the two together: *give both dates, both had been there. —conj.* **2.** alike; equally: *both men and women, he is both ready and willing.* [ME *bothe, bathe,* t. Scand.; cf. Icel. *bādhir,* c. G *beide*]

Bo·tha (bō′tə), *n.* **Louis** (lōŏ ē′), 1863-1919, South African general and statesman.

both·er (bŏth′ər), *v.t.* **1.** to give trouble to; annoy; pester; worry. **2.** to bewilder; confuse. *—v.i.* **3.** to trouble oneself. **4.** to cause annoyance or trouble. *—n.* **5.** something bothersome. **6.** an annoying disturbance. **7.** worried or perplexed state. **8.** someone who

bothers. *—interj.* **9.** *Chiefly Brit.* a mild exclamation. [orig. unknown]

—Syn. 1. BOTHER, ANNOY, PLAGUE, TEASE imply persistent interference with one's comfort or peace of mind. BOTHER suggests causing trouble or weariness or repeatedly interrupting in the midst of pressing duties. To ANNOY is to vex or irritate by bothering. PLAGUE is a strong word, connoting unremitting annoyance and harassment. To TEASE is to pester, as by long-continued whining and begging.

both·er·a·tion (bŏth′ə rā′shən), *interj.* **1.** an exclamation indicating vexation or annoyance. *—n.* **2.** act of bothering. **3.** state of being bothered.

both·er·some (bŏth′ər səm), *adj.* troublesome.

Both·ni·a (bŏth′nĭ ə), *n.* Gulf of, an arm of the Baltic, extending N between Sweden and Finland. ab. 400 mi.

Both·well (bŏth′wĕl, -wəl, bŏth′-), *n.* **James Hepburn, Earl of,** 1536?-78, third husband of Mary, Queen of Scots.

both·y (bŏth′ĭ, bŏth′ĭ), *n.*, *pl.* **bothies.** *Scot.* a hut or small cottage, esp. for lodging farm hands or workmen. [? der. BOOTH]

bo tree (bō), the pipal or sacred fig tree, *Ficus religiosa,* of India, under which the founder of Buddhism is reputed to have attained the enlightenment which constituted him the Buddha. [*bo,* t. Sinhalese, t. Pali: m. *bodhi-(taru)* perfect knowledge (tree)]

bot·ry·oi·dal (bŏt′rĭ oi′dal), *adj.* having the form of a bunch of grapes. Also, **bot′ry·oid′.** [f. m. s. Gk. *botryoeidḗs* + -AL¹] —**bot′ry·oi′dal·ly,** *adv.*

bot·ry·o·my·co·sis (bŏt′rĭ ō mī kō′sĭs), *n.* a disease of horses, usually following castration, in which there is tumefaction of the stump of the spermatic cord.

bot·ry·ose (bŏt′rĭ ōs′), *adj.* **1.** botryoidal. **2.** racemose.

bots (bŏts), *n.* a disease caused by the attachment of the larvae of botflies to the stomach of a horse.

Bot·sa·res (bŏt′sä rĕs′), *n.* **Markos** (mär′kŏs). See Bozzaris, Marco.

bott (bŏt), *n.* *Parasitol.* bot.

Bot·ti·cel·li (bŏt′ə chĕl′ĭ; *It.* bôt′tē chĕl′lē), *n.* **Sandro** (sän′drō), (*Alessandro di Mariano dei Filipepi*) 1447-1510, Italian painter.

bot·tle¹ (bŏt′əl), *n.*, *v.*, **-tled, -tling.** *—n.* **1.** a portable vessel with a neck or mouth, now commonly made of glass, used for holding liquids. **2.** the contents of a bottle; as much as a bottle contains: *a bottle of wine.* **3.** the bottle, intoxicating liquor. **4.** bottled milk for babies: *raised on the bottle. —v.t.* **5.** to put into or seal in a bottle; esp. in England, to can or put up fruit or vegetables. **6.** bottle up, to shut in or restrain closely: *to bottle up one's feelings.* [ME *botel,* t. OF: m. *botele,* g. LL *butticula,* dim. of *buttis* BUTT⁴] —**bot′tler,** *n.*

bot·tle² (bŏt′əl), *n.* *Brit. Dial.* a bundle, esp. of hay. [ME *botel,* t. OF, dim. of *botte* bundle]

bottle green, a deep green.

bot·tle·neck (bŏt′əl nĕk′), *n.* **1.** a narrow entrance or passageway. **2.** a place, or stage in a process, where progress is retarded.

bot·tle·nose (bŏt′əl nōz′), *n.* *Zool.* any of various cetaceans, as *Hyperoodon ampullatus.*

bottle tree, any of several trees, species of the genus *Sterculia* (*Firmiana*), native to warmer regions, as *S. rupestris* (**narrow-leaved bottle tree**) and *S. trichosiphon* (**broad-leaved bottle tree**).

bot·tom (bŏt′əm), *n.* **1.** the lowest or deepest part of anything, as distinguished from the top: *the bottom of a hill, of a page, etc.* **2.** the under side: *the bottom of a flatiron.* **3.** the ground under any body of water: *the bottom of the sea.* **4.** (*usually pl.*) *Phys. Geog.* low-lying alluvial land adjacent to a river. **5.** *Naut.* the part of a ship below the wales. **6.** a ship. **7.** the seat of a chair. **8.** the buttocks. **9.** the fundamental part; basic aspect: *from the bottom of my heart.* **10.** *Brit.* the inmost part or inner end of a recess, bay, lane, etc. **11.** at bottom, in reality; fundamentally. *—v.t.* **12.** to furnish with a bottom. **13.** to base or found (fol. by *on* or *upon*). **14.** to get to the bottom of; fathom. *—v.i.* **15.** to be based; rest. **16.** to strike against the bottom or end; reach the bottom. *—adj.* **17.** lowest; undermost: *bottom prices.* **18.** fundamental: *the bottom cause.* [ME; *botm,* c. G *boden*] —**Syn. 1.** base, foot.

bottom land, *Phys. Geog.* bottom (def. 4).

bot·tom·less (bŏt′əm lĭs), *adj.* **1.** without a bottom. **2.** immeasurably deep. **3.** the bottomless pit, hell.

bot·tom·ry (bŏt′əm rĭ), *n.*, *pl.* **-ries.** *Marine Law.* a contract, of the nature of a mortgage, by which the owner of a ship borrows money to make a voyage, pledging the ship as security. [modeled on D *bodemerij*]

bot·u·lin (bŏch′ə lĭn), *n.* the toxin causing botulism.

bot·u·li·nus (bŏch′ə lī′nəs), *n.* the bacterium *Clostridium botulinum,* which forms botulin.

bot·u·lism (bŏch′ə lĭz′əm), *n.* a disease of the nervous system caused by botulin developed in spoiled foods eaten by animals and man. [f. s. L *botulus* sausage + -ISM]

Bou·cher (bōō shā′), *n.* **François** (frän swä′), 1703-70, French painter.

Bou·ci·cault (bōō′sĭ kôlt′, -kō′), *n.* **Dion** (dī′ŏn, -ən), 1822-90, Irish dramatist and actor.

bou·clé (bōō klā′; *Fr.* bōō klĕ′), *n.* yarn with loops, which produces a woven or knitted fabric with rough appearance. [t. F]

Bou·dic·ca (bōō dĭk′ə), *n.* died A.D. 62, queen who led an unsuccessful revolt against the Roman government of Britain. Also, **Boadicea.**

bou·doir (bōō′dwär, -dwôr), *n.* a lady's bedroom or private sitting room. [t. F, der. *bouder* pout, sulk]

bouf·fant (bōō fän′), *adj. French.* puffed out; full, as sleeves or draperies. —**bouf·fante** (bōō fänt′), *adj. fem.*

bou·gain·vil·lae·a (bōō′gən vǐl′ǐ ə), *n.* any plant of the nyctaginaceous South American genus *Bougainvillaea*, comprising shrubs with small flowers, species of which are cultivated for ornament.

Bou·gain·ville (bōō gǎn vēl′ *for 1;* bōō′gən vǐl′, *Fr.* bōō gǎn vēl′ *for 2*), *n.* **1. Louis Antoine de** (lwē än twän′ də) 1729–1811, French navigator. **2.** the largest of the Solomon Islands, in the S Pacific. 48,990 (1954); 4080 sq. mi.

bough (bou), *n.* **1.** a branch of a tree, esp. one of the larger of main branches. **2.** *Archaic.* the gallows. [ME; OE *bōg, bōh* shoulder, bough, c. D *boeg,* LG *bug,* Icel. *bōgr* shoulder, bow of a ship] —**bough′less,** *adj.* —Syn. 1. See branch.

bought (bôt), *v.* pt. and pp. of **buy.**

bought·en (bôt′ən), *adj. Dial.* bought or purchased, esp. as opposed to homemade.

bou·gie (bōō′jǐ, bōō′zhǐ; *Fr.* bōō zhē′), *n.* **1.** *Med.* **a.** a slender flexible instrument for introduction into passages of the body for dilating or opening, etc. **b.** a suppository. **2.** a wax candle. [t. F, prop., name of an Algerian town, center of wax trade]

Bou·gue·reau (bōō grō′), *n.* **Adolphe William** (ȧ dôlf′ wĕl yȧm′), 1825–1905, French painter.

bouil·la·baisse (bōōl′yə bās′; *Fr.* bōō yȧ bĕs′), *n.* a kind of stew or chowder made of fish and vegetables. [t. F, t. Pr.: m. *bouiabaisso,* f. *boui* boil + *abaisso* (go) down]

bouil·lon (bōōl′yŏn, -yən; *Fr.* bōō yôn′), *n.* a clear, thin soup made by boiling meat, etc. [t. F, der. *bouillir* boil]

Bou·lan·ger (bōō län zhě′), *n.* **Georges Ernest Jean Marie** (zhôrzh ĕr nĕst′ zhän mȧ rē′), 1837–91, French general and politician.

boul·der (bōl′dər), *n.* a detached and rounded or worn rock, esp. one of some size. Also, **bowlder.** [short for *boulder stone,* ME *bulder-,* t. Scand.; cf. d. Sw. *buldersten* big stone (in a stream)]

Boul·der (bōl′dər), *n.* a city in N Colorado. 37,718 (1960).

Boulder Canyon, the canyon of the Colorado river above Boulder Dam, between Arizona and Nevada.

Boulder Dam, a large dam on the Colorado river, in SE Nevada and NW Arizona: the highest dam in the world. 727 ft. high; 1180 ft. long. Official name, **Hoover Dam.**

Bou·le (bōō′lē), *n.* **1.** the legislative assembly of modern Greece. **2.** (*sometimes l.c.*) a legislative, advisory, or administrative council in ancient Greek states. [t. Gk.]

boul·e·vard (bōōl′ə värd′, bōō′lə-), *n.* a broad avenue of a city, often having trees and used as a promenade. [t. F, t. MLG: m. *boleverk.* See BULWARK] —Syn. See **street.**

bou·le·ver·se·ment (bōōl vĕrs män′), *n. French.* an overturning; upsetting; confusion; turmoil.

Bou·logne (bōō lōn′, -loin′, bə-; *Fr.* bōō lôn′y), *n.* a seaport in N France. 41,870 (1954). Also, **Bou·logne-sur-Mer** (bōō lôn′y sʏr mĕr′).

Bou·logne Bil·lan·court (bōō lôn′y bē yän kōōr′), a suburb of Paris in N France. 93,998 (1954). Also, **Bou·logne-sur-Seine** (bōō lôn′y sʏr sĕn′).

boul·ter (bōl′tər), *n.* a long, stout fishing line with several hooks attached.

bounce (bouns), *v.,* **bounced, bounc·ing,** *n., adv.* —*v.i.* **1.** to move with a bound, and rebound, as a ball: *a ball bounces back from the wall.* **2.** to burst noisily or angrily (*into* or *out of*): *to bounce into and out of a room.* —*v.t.* **3.** to cause to bound or rebound: *to bounce a ball,* to *bounce a child up and down.* **4.** *Slang.* to eject or discharge summarily. **5.** *Brit.* to persuade (someone) by bluff. —*n.* **6.** a rebound or bound: *catch the ball on the first bounce.* **7.** a sudden spring or leap. **8.** *Brit.* impudence; bluster; swagger. **9.** ability to bounce; resilience. **10.** *Slang.* expulsion; discharge; dismissal. —*adv.* **11.** with a bounce; suddenly. [ME *bunsen* thump, t. LG, der. *bums!* thump! Cf. D *bonzen* thwack, etc.]

bounc·er (boun′sər), *n.* **1.** one who or that which bounces. **2.** *U.S. Slang.* one employed in a place of public resort to eject disorderly persons. **3.** something large of its kind. **4.** *Brit.* an impudent, pert person.

bounc·ing (boun′sǐng), *adj.* **1.** stout, strong, or vigorous: *a bouncing baby.* **2.** exaggerated; big; hearty; noisy: *a bouncing lie.*

bouncing Bet (bĕt), the common soapwort. Also, **bouncing Bess** (bĕs).

bound[1] (bound), *adj.* **1.** tied; in bonds: *a bound prisoner.* **2.** made fast as by a band or bond: *bound by one's word.* **3.** secured within a cover, as a book. **4.** under obligation, legally or morally: *in duty bound to help.* **5.** destined or sure: *it is bound to happen.* **6.** determined or resolved: *he is bound to go.* **7.** *Pathol.* constipated; costive. **8.** *bound up in* or *with,* a. inseparably connected with. b. having the affections centered in: *his life is bound up in his children.* [pp. of BIND]

bound[2] (bound), *v.i.* **1.** to move by leaps; leap; jump; spring. **2.** to rebound, as a ball. —*v.t.* **3.** to cause to bound. —*n.* **4.** a leap onward or upward; a jump. **5.** a rebound. [t. F: m. s. *bondir* leap, orig., resound, ? g. L *bombitäre* hum] —Syn. 1. See skip[1].

bound[3] (bound), *n.* **1.** (*usually n.*) a limiting line, or boundary: *the bounds of space and time.* **2.** that which limits, confines, or restrains. **3.** (*pl.*) territory on or near a boundary. **4.** (*pl.*) an area included within boundary lines: *within the bounds of his estate, within the bounds of reason.* —*v.t.* **5.** to limit as by bounds. **6.** to form the boundary or limit of. **7.** to name the boundaries of. —*v.i.* **8.** to have its boundaries (*on*); abut. [ME *bounde, boune,* t. OF: m. *bodne,* g. LL *butina*] —Syn. 1. border, frontier. 5. demarcate, circumscribe.

bound[4] (bound), *adj.* **1.** going or intending to go; on the way (*to*); destined (*for*): *the train is bound for Denver.* **2.** *Archaic.* prepared; ready. [ME *boun,* t. Scand.; cf. Icel. *büinn,* pp. of *büa* get ready]

bound·a·ry (boun′dər ǐ, -drǐ), *n., pl.* **-ries.** something that indicates bounds or limits; a limiting or bounding line. [f. BOUND[3], n. + -ARY[1]]

bound·en (boun′dən), *adj.* **1.** obliged; under obligation. **2.** obligatory: *one's bounden duty.* [var. of BOUND[1]]

bound·er (boun′dər), *n. Chiefly Brit. Colloq.* an obtrusive, ill-bred person; a vulgar upstart.

bound form, a linguistic form which never occurs by itself but always as part of some larger construction, as *-ed* in *seated.*

bound·less (bound′lǐs), *adj.* without bounds; unlimited: *his boundless energy amazed them.* —**bound′less·ly,** *adv.* —**bound′less·ness,** *n.*

boun·te·ous (boun′tǐ əs), *adj.* **1.** giving or disposed to give freely; generously liberal. **2.** freely bestowed; plentiful; abundant. [f. *bounte* (earlier var. of BOUNTY) + -ous; r. ME *bontyvous,* der. OF *bontif* benevolent] —**boun′te·ous·ly,** *adv.* —**boun′te·ous·ness,** *n.*

boun·ti·ful (boun′tə fəl), *adj.* **1.** liberal in bestowing gifts, favors, or bounties; munificent; generous. **2.** abundant; ample: *a bountiful supply.* —**boun′ti·ful·ly,** *adv.* —**boun′ti·ful·ness,** *n.*

boun·ty (boun′tǐ), *n., pl.* **-ties. 1.** generosity in giving. **2.** whatever is given bounteously; a benevolent, generous gift. **3.** a premium or reward, esp. one offered by a government. [ME *bounte,* t. OF: m. *bonte(t),* g. L *bonitas* goodness] —Syn. 1. munificence, liberality, charity. 3. See **bonus.**

bou·quet (bō kā′, bōō-, *for 1;* bōō kā′ *for 2; Fr.* bōō kĕ′), *n.* **1.** a bunch of flowers; a nosegay. **2.** the characteristic aroma of wines, liquors, etc. [t. F: bunch, clump of trees, d. var. of OF *bosquet* little wood, dim. of *bosc* wood. See BUSH[1]]

Bour·bon (bōōr′bən, *Fr.* bōōr bôn′ *for 1–3;* bûr′bən *for 4, occas. for 3*), *n.* **1.** a member of the last house of the royal family of France, or of any of its branches, as the former royal family of Spain. **2. Charles** (shärl), 1490–1527, French general. **3.** (in derogatory use) an extreme conservative, or one devoted to ideas suited only to past conditions. **4.** (*l.c.*) Also, **bourbon** whiskey, a straight whiskey distilled from a mash containing 51% or more corn, orig. the corn whiskey produced in Bourbon county, Ky.

Bour·bon·ism (bōōr′bə nǐz′əm; *occas.* bûr′-), *n.* **1.** adherence to the system of government and the ideas for which the Bourbons stood. **2.** extreme conservatism, as in politics. —**Bour′bon·ist,** *n.*

bour·don (bōōr′dən, bûr′-), *n. Music.* **1.** the drone of a bagpipe, or of a monotonous and repetitious ground melody. **2.** a low-pitched tone; a bass. [t. F]

bourg (bōōrg; *Fr.* bōōr), *n.* **1.** a town. **2.** a French market town. [t. F, g. LL *burgus,* t. Gmc. See BOROUGH]

bour·geois[1] (bōōr zhwä′, bōōr′zhwä; *Fr.* bōōr zhwä′), *n., pl.* **-geois,** *adj.* —*n.* **1.** a member of the middle class. **2.** any person owning property. —*adj.* **3.** belonging to or consisting of the middle class. **4.** lacking in refinement or elegance. [t. F] —**bour·geoise** (bōōr zhwäz′; *Fr.* bōōr zhwäz′), *n., adj. fem.*

bour·geois[2] (bər jois′), *n.* a printing type (9 point) of a size between brevier and long primer. [? proper name]

bour·geoi·sie (bōōr′zhwä zē′; *Fr.* bōōr zhwä zē′), *n.* **1.** the bourgeois class. **2.** (in Marxist ideology) the antithesis of the proletariat or wage-earning class. [t. F]

bour·geon (bûr′jən), *n., v.* burgeon.

Bourges (bōōrzh), *n.* a city in central France. 53,879 (1954).

Bour·get (bōōr zhě′), *n.* **Paul** (pōl), 1852–1935, French novelist and critic.

Bour·gogne (bōōr gôn′y), *n.* French name of **Burgundy.**

bourn[1] (bōrn), *n.* burn[2]. Also, **bourne.**

bourn[2] (bōrn, bōōrn), *n.* **1.** a bound; limit. **2.** destination; goal. **3.** realm; domain. Also, **bourne.** [t. F: m. *borne*]

Bourne·mouth (bōōrn′məth, bōrn′-), *n.* a city in S England; seaside resort. 142,600 (est. 1956).

bour·rée (bōō rě′), *n.* **1.** an old French and Spanish dance, somewhat like a gavotte. **2.** the music for it.

Bourse (bōōrs), *n.* a stock exchange, esp. that of Paris. [t. F: orig. purse, g. LL *bursa,* t. Gk.: m. *býrsa* hide]

bouse[1] (bous, bouz), *v.t.* **boused, bousing.** *Naut.* to haul with tackle. Also, **bowse.** [orig. unknown]

bouse[2] (boōz, bouz), *n., v.,* **boused, bousing.** *—n.*
1. liquor or drink. **2.** a drinking bout; a carouse. *—v.t.,*
v.i. **3.** to drink, esp. to excess. [ME *bous* drinking vessel,
t. MD: m. *buse*]

bou·stro·phe·don (boō/strəfē/dən, bou/-), *n.* an ancient method of writing in which the lines run alternately from right to left and from left to right. [t. Gk.:
adv., with turning like that of oxen in plowing]

bous·y (boō/zY, bou/-), *adj.* intoxicated; boozy.

bout (bout), *n.* **1.** a contest; a trial of strength. **2.** a
turn at work or any action. **3.** period; spell: *a bout of
illness.* [var. of obs. *bought* bend, turn, der. BOW[1]]

bou·ton·niere (boō/tənyâr/), *n.* a buttonhole bouquet or flower. Also, *French,* **bou·ton·nière** (boō tô-
nyĕr/). [t. F: buttonhole]

bo·vid (bō/vYd), *adj. Zool.* of or pertaining to the *Bovidae,* or ox family, comprising the hollow-horned ruminants, as oxen, sheep, and goats.

bo·vine (bō/vīn, -vYn), *adj.* **1.** of the ox family
(*Bovidae*). **2.** oxlike. **3.** stolid; dull. *—n.* **4.** a bovine
animal. [t. LL: m. s. *bovīnus,* der. L *bōs* ox]

bow[1] (bou), *v.i.* **1.** to bend or curve downward; stoop:
the pines bowed low. **2.** to yield; submit: *to bow to the
inevitable.* **3.** to bend the body or head in worship,
reverence, respect, or submission. **4.** to incline the head
or body, or both, in salutation. *—v.t.* **5.** to bend or
incline in worship, submission, respect, civility, or agreement: *to bow one's head.* **6.** to cause to submit; subdue;
crush. **7.** to cause to stoop: *age had bowed his head.* **8.** to
express by a bow, or by bowing: *to bow one's thanks.*
9. to usher (*in, out,* etc.) with a bow. **10.** *Archaic and
Dial.* to cause to bend; make curved or crooked. *—n.*
11. an inclination of the head or body in salutation,
assent, thanks, reverence, respect, or submission. [ME
bouce(n), OE *būgan,* c. G *biegen* bend] **—Syn. 1.** See *bend*[1].

bow[2] (bō), *n.* **1.** a strip of elastic wood or other material
bent by a string stretched between its ends, used for
shooting arrows. **2.** a bend or curve. **3.** a looped knot,
as of ribbon, composed of one or two loops and two ends;
a bowknot. **4.** *Music.* **a.** an implement, orig. curved but
now almost always straight, with horsehairs stretched
upon it, for playing any member of the violin family of
instruments. **b.** a single stroke of such an implement.
5. something curved or arc-shaped. **6.** *U. S.* one of the
supports for a pair of spectacles, reaching to the ears.
7. a U-shaped piece under an animal's neck to hold a
yoke. **8.** a rainbow. *—adj.* **9.** curved; bent like a bow:
bow legs. *—v.t., v.i.* **10.** to bend into the form of a bow;
curve. **11.** *Music.* to perform by means of a bow upon a
stringed instrument. [ME *bowe,* OE *boga,* c. G *bogen*]
—bow/less, *adj.* **—bow/like/,** *adj.*

bow[3] (bou), *n.* **1.** the front or forward end of a ship,
boat, airship, etc. See illus. under **aft.** **2.** the foremost
oar used in rowing a boat. **3.** the person who pulls that
oar; the bow oar; bowman. [? t. Dan.: m. *bov,* c. BOUGH]

bow compass (bō), *Geom.* any of various compasses,
as one having the legs joined by a bow-shaped piece.

bowd·ler·ize (boud/ləriz/), *v.t.,* **-ized, -izing.** to expurgate prudishly. [from Thomas *Bowdler,* who in 1818
published an expurgated edition of Shakespeare]
—bowd/ler·ism, *n.* **—bowd/ler·i·za/tion,** *n.*

bow·el (bou/əl, boul), *n., v.,* **-eled, -eling** or (esp. *Brit.*)
-elled, -elling. *—n.* **1.** *Anat.* a, an intestine. **b.** (*usually
pl.*) the parts of the alimentary canal below the stomach;
the intestines or entrails. **2.** the inward or interior parts.
3. (*pl.*) *Archaic.* feelings of pity or compassion. *—v.t.*
4. to disembowel. [ME *bouel,* t. OF: m. *boel,* g. L
botellus, dim. of *botulus* sausage]

bow·er[1] (bou/ər), *n.* **1.** a leafy shelter or recess; an
arbor. **2.** *Now Only Poetic.* a rustic dwelling; a cottage.
3. *Poetic.* a chamber; a boudoir. *—v.t.* **4.** to enclose in
or as in a bower; embower. [ME *bour,* OE *būr* a dwelling,
cottage, akin to *būan* dwell] **—bow/er·like/,** *adj.*

bow·er[2] (bou/ər), *n.* an anchor carried at a ship's bow.
Also, **bower anchor.** [f. BOW[3] + -ER[2]]

bow·er[3] (bou/ər), *n.* (in euchre and other card games)
the knave of trumps (**right bower**) or the other knave
of the same color (**left bower**); the highest cards in the
game, unless the joker (often called the **best bower**) is
used. [t. G: m. *bauer* peasant, jack (in cards)]

bow·er[4] (bou/ər), *n.* one who or that which bows or
bends. [f. BOWER[1] + -ER[1]]

bow·er[5] (bō/ər), *n. Music.* a player with the bow on a
violin or other stringed instrument. [f. BOW[2] + -ER[1]]

bow·er·bird (bou/ər bûrd/), *n.* any of various Australian and Papuan oscine birds, related to birds of
paradise, as *Ptilonorhynchus violaceus,* which build
bowerlike structures, used, not as nests, but as places of
resort to attract the females.

Bow·ers (bou/ərz), *n.* **Claude Gernade** (zhər nād/),
1878-1958, U.S. diplomat and historian.

bow·er·y[1] (bou/ər Y), *adj.* bowerlike; containing bow-
ers; shady: *a bowery maze.* [f. BOWER[1] + -Y[1]]

bow·er·y[2] (bou/ər Y, bou/rY), *n., pl.* **-eries.** **1.** (among
the Dutch settlers of New York) a farm or country seat.
2. the Bowery, a long, wide street in New York City,
notorious for its saloons, run-down hotels, etc. [t. D:
m. *bouwerij* (farm); l. der. *bouwer* farmer]

bow·fin (bō/fYn/), *n.* a North American fresh-water
ganoid fish, *Amia calva,* not highly regarded as food.

bow hand (bō), **1.** *Archery.* the hand that holds the
bow, usually the left hand. **2.** *Music.* the hand that
draws the bow, usually the right hand.

bow·head (bō/hĕd/), *n.* the whale, *Balaena mysticetus,*
of arctic seas.

bow·ie knife (bō/Y, boō/Y),
a heavy sheath-knife having a
long, single-edged blade.
[named after James *Bowie*
(1796-1836), U.S. pioneer]

Bowie State, Arkansas.

bow·knot (bō/nŏt/), *n.* bow[2]
(def. 3).

Bowie knife and sheath

bowl[1] (bōl), *n.* **1.** a rather deep, round dish or basin,
used chiefly for holding liquids, food, etc. **2.** the contents of a bowl. **3.** a rounded, hollow part: *the bowl of a
pipe.* **4.** a large drinking cup; a goblet. **5.** festive
drinking; conviviality. **6.** any bowl-shaped depression
or formation. **7.** an edifice with a bowllike interior,
as for athletic contests, etc. [ME *bolle,* OE *bolla,* c.
Icel. *bolli.* See BOLL] **—bowl/like/,** *adj.*

bowl[2] (bōl), *n.* **1.** one of the balls, having little or no
bias, used in playing ninepins or tenpins. **2.** one of the
biased or weighted balls used in the game of bowls. **3.** a
cast or delivery of the ball in bowling. **4.** *Mach.* a
rotating cylindrical part in a machine, as one to reduce
friction. *—v.i.* **5.** to play with bowls, or at bowling.
6. to roll a bowl, as in the game of bowls. **7.** to move
along smoothly and rapidly. **8.** *Cricket.* to deliver the
ball to be played by the batsman. *—v.t.* **9.** to roll or
trundle, as a ball, hoop, etc. **10.** to knock or strike, as
by the ball in bowling (fol. by *over* or *down*). **11.** to disconcert; upset (fol. by *over*). **12.** to carry or convey as
in a wheeled vehicle. **13.** *Cricket.* to eliminate (a batsman) by bowling (fol. by *out*). [ME *boule,* t. OF: ball, g.
L *bulla* bubble] **—bowl/er,** *n.*

bowl·der (bōl/dər), *n.* boulder.

bow·leg (bō/lĕg/), *n. Pathol.* **1.** outward curvature of
the legs causing a separation of the knees when the
ankles are close or in contact. **2.** a leg so curved. **—bow-
leg·ged** (bō/lĕg/Yd, bō/lĕgd/), *adj.*

bowl·er (bō/lər), *n. Brit.* derby (def. 4). [f. BOWL[1] + -ER[1]]

Bowles (bōlz), *n.* **Samuel,** 1826-78, U.S. journalist.

bow·line (bō/lYn, -līn/), *n.* **1.** Also, **bowline knot.** a
knot which forms a nonslipping loop. **2.**
Naut. **a.** a rope leading forward and
fastened to the leech of a square sail, used
to steady the weather leech of the sail and
keep it forward. **b. on a bowline,** sailing
close to the wind.   Bowline (def. 1)

bowl·ing (bō/lYng), *n.* **1.** act of playing with or at
bowls. **2.** the game of bowls. **3.** *U.S., Canada.* tenpins.

bowling alley, 1. a long enclosure for playing at
bowls, etc. **2.** a covered place with a long, narrow
planked enclosure, for playing at tenpins.

bowling green, *Chiefly Brit.* a level plot of turf for
bowling.

Bowling Green, 1. a city in S Kentucky. 28,338 (1960).
2. a small open space in New York City, at the foot of
Broadway.

bowls (bōlz), *n.* **1.** a game, common in Great Britain
and parts of the U. S. and Canada, in which the players
roll biased or weighted balls along the sward in an effort
to bring them as near as possible to a stationary ball
called the *jack.* **2.** skittles, ninepins or (*U.S.*) tenpins.

bow·man[1] (bō/mən), *n., pl.* **-men.** **1.** an archer. **2.** (in
medieval warfare) a soldier armed with a bow. [f. BOW[2]
+ MAN]

bow·man[2] (bou/mən), *n.,*
pl. **-men.** *Naut.* bow[3] (def.
3). [f. BOW[3] + MAN]

bow oar (bou), bow[3] (def.
3).

bow pen (bō), *Geom.* a
bow compass with a pen at
the end of one leg.

bowse (bous, bouz), *v.t.,*
bowsed, bowsing. bouse[1].

bow·shot (bō/shŏt/), *n.*
the distance a bow sends an
arrow.

bow·sprit (bou/sprYt,
bō/-), *n. Naut.* a large spar   A. Bowsprit; B. Jib boom; C. Bobstay
projecting forward from the
stem of a ship or other vessel. [ME *bouspret,* f. *bou* bow
of a ship + *spret* (OE *sprēot* pole)]

Bow Street (bō), a street in London, England, on
which is the principal metropolitan police court.

bow·string (bō/strYng), *n., v.,* **-stringed** or **-strung,
-stringing.** *—n.* **1.** the string of a bow. **2.** a string
used, as by the Turks, for strangling offenders. *—v.t.*
3. to strangle with a bowstring or any string or band.

bowstring hemp, any of various fibrous plants
(genus *Sansevieria*) of Asia and Africa, cultivated in
the U.S. for ornament.

bow tie (bō), a small bow-shaped necktie.

bow window (bō), a rounded bay window.

bow-wow (bou/wou/), *n.* **1.** the bark of a dog. **2.** an
imitation of this. **3.** (in childish use) a dog.

bow·yer (bō/yər), *n.* a maker or seller of bows.

box[1] (bŏks), *n.* **1.** a case or receptacle, usually rectangular, of wood, metal, cardboard, etc., with a lid or
removable cover. **2.** the quantity contained in a box.
3. a package or case containing presents. **4.** the present

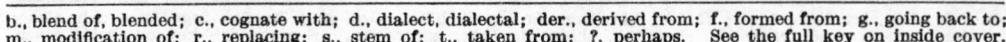
b., blend of, blended; c., cognate with; d., dialect, dialectal; der., derived from; f., formed from; g., going back to;
m., modification of; r., replacing; s., stem of; t., taken from; ?, perhaps.   See the full key on inside cover.

box 143 Brachiopoda

or gift itself. **5.** a compartment or place shut or railed off for the accommodation of a small number of people in a public place, esp. in theaters, opera houses, ballrooms, etc. **6.** a small shelter: *a sentry's box.* **7.** *Brit.* a small house, as for use while following some sport: *a shooting box.* **8.** a box stall. **9.** the driver's seat on a coach. **10.** the section of a wagon in which passengers or parcels are carried. **11.** part of a page of a periodical set off by lines, border, or white space. **12.** *Mach.* an enclosing, protecting, or hollow part; a casing; a chamber; a bush; a socket. **13.** *Baseball.* the space where the batter stands (or, less often, the pitcher or coaches). **14.** *Agric.* a bowl or pit cut in the side of a tree for collecting sap. —*v.t.* **15.** to put into a box. **16.** to enclose or confine as in a box (often fol. by *up*). **17.** to furnish with a box. **18.** to form into a box or the shape of a box. **19.** *Naut.* to boxhaul (often fol. by *off*). **20.** to make a hole or cut in (a tree) for the sap to collect. **21.** box the compass, *Naut.* to name the points of the compass in their order. [special use of BOX³] —**box/like′**, *adj.*

box² (bŏks), *n.* **1.** a blow as with the hand or fist. —*v.t.* **2.** to strike with the hand or fist, esp. on the ear. **3.** to fight in a boxing match. —*v.i.* **4.** to fight with the fists; spar. [ME; orig. unknown]

box³ (bŏks), *n.* **1.** an evergreen shrub or small tree of the genus *Buxus*, esp. *B. sempervirens*, much used for ornamental borders, hedges, etc., and yielding a hard, durable wood. **2.** the wood itself. See **boxwood**. **3.** any of various other shrubs or trees, esp. species of eucalyptus. [ME and OE, t. L: m.s. *buxus*, t. Gk.: m. *pyxos*]

box bed, 1. a bed completely enclosed so as to resemble a box. **2.** a bed that folds up in the form of a box.

box·ber·ry (bŏks/bĕr′ĭ), *n., pl.* **-ries. 1.** the checkerberry. **2.** the partridgeberry.

box calf, a chrome-tanned calfskin with square markings produced by graining.

box camera, a boxlike camera, without bellows.

box·car (bŏks/kär′), *n.* **1.** *Railroads.* an enclosed and covered freight car. **2.** (*pl.*) a pair of sixes on the first throw in the game of craps.

box coat, 1. an outer coat with a straight, unfitted back. **2.** a heavy overcoat worn by coachmen.

box elder, a fast-growing North American maple, *Acer negundo*, cultivated for shade.

box·er (bŏk/sər), *n.* **1.** one who boxes; a pugilist. **2.** a handsome, smooth-coated, brown dog of medium size, related to the bulldog and terrier.

Box·er (bŏk/sər), *n.* a member of a Chinese secret society, which practiced ritualistically the traditional Chinese posture boxing, supposed to make them immune to bullets and swords. In 1900 they attacked foreigners and native Christians and besieged the legations at Peking until an international expeditionary force raised the siege.

box·haul (bŏks/hôl′), *v.t. Naut.* to veer (a ship) round on her heel by bracing the head yards aback, etc.

box·ing¹ (bŏk/sĭng), *n.* **1.** the material used to make boxes or casings. **2.** a boxlike enclosure; a casing. **3.** act of putting into or furnishing with a box. [f. BOX¹ + -ING¹]

box·ing² (bŏk/sĭng), *n.* act or art of fighting with the fists, with or without boxing gloves. [f. BOX² + -ING¹]

Boxing Day, *Brit.* the first weekday after Christmas, when Christmas gifts are given to employees, etc.

boxing glove, a padded glove worn in boxing.

box iron, a smoothing iron which is heated by placing a hot iron in its boxlike holder.

box kite, a kite consisting of a light box-shaped frame, covered except on the ends and a space along the middle.

box office, *Theat.* **1.** the office in which tickets are sold. **2.** receipts from a play or other entertainment. **3.** the ability of an entertainment or performer to draw an audience: *this show will be good box office.*

box pleat, a double pleat, with the material folded under at each side. Also, **box plait.**

box seat, a seat in a theater box, etc.

box stall, a stall for a horse or other large animal.

box·thorn (bŏks/thôrn′), *n.* matrimony vine.

box·wood (bŏks/wŏŏd′), *n.* **1.** the hard, fine-grained, compact wood of the box (genus *Buxus*), much used for wood engravers' blocks, musical and mathematical instruments, etc. **2.** the tree or shrub itself. Cf. **box³** (def. 1).

boy (boi), *n.* **1.** a male child, from birth to full growth, but esp. to the beginning of youth. **2.** a young man who lacks maturity, vigor, judgment, etc. **3.** a grown man. **4.** a young servant; a page. **5.** (in India, China, Japan, etc.) a native male servant, working as a butler, waiter, house boy, etc. [ME *boy, boi*; orig. uncert.]

bo·yar (bō yär′, boi′ər), *n.* **1.** *Russian Hist.* a member of the old nobility of Russia, before Peter the Great made rank depend on state service. **2.** one of a privileged class in Rumania. Also, **bo·yard** (bō yärd′, boi′ərd). [t. Russ.: m. *boyarin* lord]

boy·cott (boi/kŏt), *v.t.* **1.** to combine in abstaining from, or preventing dealings with, as a means of intimidation or coercion: *to boycott a person, business house, etc.* **2.** to abstain from buying or using: *to boycott a commercial product.* —*n.* **3.** the practice of boycotting. **4.** an instance of boycotting. [from Captain *Boycott*, the first victim (1880), agent of an Irish landlord]

boy·hood (boi/hŏŏd), *n.* **1.** state or period of being a boy. **2.** boys collectively.

boy·ish (boi/ĭsh), *adj.* of, like, or befitting a boy. —**boy/ish·ly**, *adv.* —**boy/ish·ness**, *n.*

Boyle (boil), *n.* **Robert**, 1627–91, British chemist and physicist.

Boyne (boin), *n.* a river in E Ireland, near which William III defeated James II (1690). 70 mi.

boy scout, 1. a member of an organization of boys (the **Boy Scouts**), founded in England in 1908 by Lieut. Gen. Sir Robert S. S. Baden-Powell, to develop in its members manly character, self-reliance, and usefulness to others. **2.** a member of any similar society elsewhere.

boy·sen·ber·ry (boi/zən bĕr′ĭ), *n., pl.* **-ries.** a blackberrylike fruit with a flavor similar to that of raspberries, developed by crossing various species of *Rubus*.

Boz·ca·da (bŏz/jä ä dä′), *n.* Tenedos.

Boz·zar·is (bō zăr/ĭs, -zär′-; *Gk.* bôt/sä rēs′), *n.* **Marco** (mär′kō), 1788?–1823, Greek patriot.

bp., **1.** baptized. **2.** birthplace. **3.** bishop.

b.p., 1. Also, **B/P**. *Com.* bills payable. **2.** *Physics, Chem.* boiling point.

B.P.E., Bachelor of Physical Education.

B.P.H., Bachelor of Public Health.

B.Ph., Bachelor of Philosophy. Also, **B.Phil.**

B.P.O.E., Benevolent and Protective Order of Elks.

Br, *Chem.* bromine.

Br., 1. Britain. **2.** British.

br., 1. branch. **2.** brig. **3.** bronze. **4.** brother.

b.r., *Com.* bills receivable. Also, **B/R.**

bra (brä), *n. Colloq.* brassière.

Bra·bant (bra bănt′, brä/bănt; *Du.* brä/bänt; *Fr.* brä bän′), *n.* **1.** a former duchy in W Europe: now divided into two provinces, one in Belgium (Brabant) and one in the Netherlands (North Brabant). See map under **Agincourt. 2.** a province in central Belgium. 1,849,087 pop. (est. 1952); 1268 sq. mi. *Cap.*: Brussels. **3.** a province in S Netherlands. 1,332,033 pop. (est. 1954); 1894 sq. mi. *Cap.*: s'Hertogenbosch.

brace (brās), *n., v.*, **braced, bracing.** —*n.* **1.** something that holds parts together or in place, as a clasp or clamp. **2.** anything that imparts rigidity or steadiness. **3.** *Mach.* a device for holding and turning tools for boring or drilling; a bitstock. See illus. under **brace and bit. 4.** *Bldg. Trades.* a piece of timber, metal, etc., used to support or position another piece or portion of a framework. **5.** *Naut.* (on a square-rigged ship) a rope by which a yard is swung about and secured horizontally. **6.** *Music.* leather loops sliding upon the tightening cords of a drum to change their tension and therewith the pitch. **7.** (*often pl.*) *Dentistry.* a round or flat metal wire placed against surfaces of the teeth, and used to straighten irregularly arranged teeth. **8.** *Med.* an appliance for supporting a weak joint or joints. **9.** (*pl.*) *Chiefly Brit.* suspenders. **10.** a pair; a couple. **11.** one of two characters { or } for connecting written or printed lines. **12.** *Music.* connected staves. **13.** a defense or protection for the arm, specif. one used in archery. [ME *brase*, t. OF (see BRACE, V.)] —*v.t.* **14.** to furnish, fasten, or strengthen with or as with a brace. **15.** to fix firmly; make steady. **16.** to make tight; increase the tension of. **17.** to act as a stimulant to. **18.** *Naut.* to swing or turn around (the yards of a ship) by means of the braces. —*v.i.* **19.** brace up, *Colloq.* to rouse one's strength or vigor. [ME *brase*(n), t. OF: m. *bracier* embrace, der. *brace* the two arms (cf. def. 10), g. L *brāchia*] —**Syn. 10.** See **pair.**

brace and bit, *Mach.* a boring tool consisting of a bit and a handle for rotating it.

brace·let (brās/lĭt), *n.* **1.** an ornamental band or circlet for the wrist or arm. **2.** *Humorous.* a handcuff. [ME, t. OF, dim. of *bracel*, ult. der. L *brāc*(c)*hium* arm]

brac·er¹ (brā/sər), *n.* **1.** one who or that which braces, binds, or makes firm. **2.** *U.S. Colloq.* a stimulating drink; tonic. [f. BRACE + -ER¹]

brac·er² (brā/sər), *n. Archery.* a guard for the left wrist and lower arm worn as a protection against the friction or the catching of the bowstring. [ME *bracer*, t. OF: m. *brasseüre*, der. *bras* arm, g. L *brāchium*]

brach (brăch, brăk), *n. Obs.* a bitch of the hound kind. Also, **brach·et** (brăch/ĭt). [ME *braches*, pl., t. OF, pl. of *brachet*, dim of *brac*, t. OHG: m. *bracco* a hound hunting by scent]

bra·chi·al (brā/kĭ·al, brăk/ĭ-), *adj. Zool.* **1.** belonging to the arm, foreleg, wing, pectoral fin, or other forelimb of a vertebrate. **2.** belonging to the upper part of such member, from the shoulder to the elbow. **3.** armlike, as an appendage. [t. L: adj. *brāchiālis*]

bra·chi·al·gi·a (brā/kĭ ăl/jĭ a, brăk/ĭ-), *n. Pathol.* pain in the nerves of the upper arm.

bra·chi·ate (brā/kĭ ĭt, -āt′, brăk/ĭ-), *adj. Bot.* having widely spreading branches in alternate pairs.

brachio-, a word element meaning "arm," as in *brachiopod.* Also, before vowels, **brachi-**. [t. NL, comb. form repr. L *brāchium*, or its source, Gk. *brachīon*]

bra·chi·o·pod (brā/kĭ ə pŏd′, brăk/ĭ-), *n. Zool.* any of the Brachiopoda.

Bra·chi·op·o·da (brā/kĭ ŏp′ə də, brăk/ĭ-), *n.pl. Zool.* a phylum of mollusklike animals, the lamp shells, having dorsal and ventral shells. Most members are now extinct.

Brace and bit

bra·chi·um (brā′kĭ əm, brăk′Y-), n., pl. **brachia** (brā′-kĭ ə, brăk′Y ə). *Anat.*, *Zool.* **1.** the upper arm, from the shoulder to the elbow. **2.** the part of any limb, as in the wing of a bird, corresponding to it. **3.** an armlike part or process. [t. L: arm]

brachy-, a word element meaning "short," as in *brachycephalic.* [t. Gk., comb. form of *brachýs*]

brach·y·ce·phal·ic (brăk′Y sə făl′Yk), adj. *Cephalom.* short-headed; having a breadth of head at least four fifths the length front to back. Also, **brach·y·ceph·a·lous** (ĭsĕf′ə ləs). —**brach′y·ceph′a·ly,** n.

brach·y·cra·nic (brăk′Y krā′nYk), adj. *Craniom.* short-headed; having a breadth of skull at least four fifths as great as the length from front to back.

bra·chyl·o·gy (brə kYl′ə jY), n., pl. **-gies.** brevity of diction; a concise or abridged form of expression. [t. Gk.: m.s. *brachylogia.* See BRACHY-, -LOGY]

bra·chyp·ter·ous (brə kYp′tər əs), adj. *Ornith.* short-winged. [f. BRACHY- + -PTEROUS]

brach·y·u·ran (brăk′Y yŏŏr′ən), adj. **1.** belonging or pertaining to the *Brachyura,* a group of stalk-eyed decapod crustaceans with short tails, the common crabs. —n. **2.** a brachyuran crustacean.

brach·y·u·rous (brăk′Y yŏŏr′əs), adj. *Zool.* short-tailed, as the crabs (opposed to *macrurous*).

brac·ing (brā′sYng), adj. **1.** strengthening; invigorating. —n. **2.** a brace. **3.** braces collectively.

brack·en (brăk′ən), n. *Brit.* **1.** a large fern or brake, esp. *Pteridium aquilinum.* **2.** a clump of brakes. [ME *braken,* t. Scand.; cf. Sw. *bräken* fern]

brack·et (brăk′Yt), n. **1.** a wooden, metal, etc., support of triangular outline placed under a shelf or the like. **2.** a shelf or shelves supported by a bracket. **3.** *Archit.* an ornamental projection from the face of a wall, intended to support a statue, pier, etc.; a corbel. See illus. under **corbel. 4.** a projecting fixture for gas or electricity. **5.** one of two marks, [or] used in writing or printing to enclose parenthetical matter, interpolations, etc. **6.** *Math.* **a.** (pl.) parentheses of various forms indicating that the enclosed quantity is to be treated as a unit. **b.** (loosely) vinculum (def. 2). **7.** a grouping of taxpayers based on the amount of their income: *low income bracket.* **8.** *Gunnery.* range or elevation producing both shorts and overs on a target. —v.t. **9.** to furnish with or support by a bracket or brackets. **10.** to place within brackets; couple with a brace. **11.** to associate or mention together. **12.** *Gunnery.* to place (shots) both over and short of a target. [earlier *bragget,* t. F: m. *braguette,* t. Pr., or Sp., dim. of *braga,* g. L *brācae,* pl., breeches of Celtic orig.]

brack·et·ing (brăk′Yt Yng), n. *Archit.* the series of wooden supports, often of fanciful jigsaw form, nailed to the ceiling, joists, and battening to support cornices.

brack·ish (brăk′Ysh), adj. **1.** slightly salt; having a saltish or briny flavor. **2.** distasteful. [f. *brack* brackish (t. D: m. *brak*) + -ISH¹] —**brack′ish·ness,** n.

bract (brăkt), n. *Bot.* a specialized leaf or leaflike part, usually situated at the base of a flower or inflorescence. [t. L: m. s. *bractea* thin plate of metal] —**brac·te·al** (brăk′tY əl), adj. —**bract′less,** adj.

brac·te·ate (brăk′tY Yt, -āt′), adj. *Bot.* having bracts.

brac·te·o·late (brăk′tY ə lYt, -lāt′), adj. having bracteoles.

brac·te·ole (brăk′tY ōl′), n. *Bot.* a small or secondary bract, as on a pedicel. Also, **bract·let** (brăkt′lYt).

Bracts of marigold A. of pedicel; B. of flower

brad (brăd), n. **1.** a small wire nail with a head like a finishing nail. —v.t. **2.** to turn down (the end of a nail which projects a short way through the work). [ME *brad,* var. of *brod,* t. Scand.; cf. Icel. *broddr* spike]

brad·awl (brăd′ôl′), n. *Carp.* an awl for making small holes in wood for brads, etc. See illus. under **awl.**

Brad·dock (brăd′ək), n. **1.** Edward, 1695–1755, British general in America. **2.** a city in SW Pennsylvania, near Pittsburgh: the site of General Braddock's defeat by the French and Indians, 1755. 16,488 (1950).

Brad·ford (brăd′fərd), n. **1.** Gamaliel (gə mā′lY əl) 1863–1932, U. S. writer. **2.** William, 1590–1657, second governor of English colony, Plymouth, Massachusetts. **3.** a city in N England, in Yorkshire, 286,400 (est. 1956). **4.** a city in N Pennsylvania. 17,354, (1950).

Brad·ley (brăd′lY), n. Omar Nelson, born 1893, U.S. general: Chief of Staff 1948–49; chairman, Joint Chiefs of Staff, 1949–1953.

Brad·street (brăd′strēt′), n. **1.** Anne, 1612?–72, American poet. **2.** her husband, Simon, 1603–97, governor of the Massachusetts colony.

Bra·dy (brā′dY), n. Mathew B., 1823?–1896, U.S. photographer, esp. of the Civil War.

brae (brā, brē), n. *Scot. and N. Eng.* a slope; a declivity; a hillside. [ME *bra,* t. Scand.; cf. Icel. *brā* eyelash, c. OE *brēaw* eyebrow, eyelid, G *braue* eyebrow]

brag (brăg), v., **bragged, bragging,** n., adj. —v.i. **1.** to use boastful language; boast: *he likes to brag.* —v.t. **2.** to boast of. —n. **3.** a boast or vaunt; bragging. **4.** a thing to boast of. **5.** a boaster. —adj. **6.** unusually fine; first rate. [t. Scand.; cf. Icel. *bragga sig* take heart, *braggast* thrive] —**brag′ger,** n. —**Syn. 1.** See **boast¹.**

Bragg (brăg), n. **1.** Braxton, 1817–76, Confederate

general in the U.S. Civil War. **2.** Sir William Henry, 1862–1942, British physicist who with his son William Lawrence, born 1890, won the Nobel Prize in 1915.

brag·ga·do·ci·o (brăg′ə dō′shY ō′), n., pl. **-os. 1.** empty boasting; brag. **2.** a boasting person; a braggart. [from *Braggadochio,* name of a boastful character in Spenser's "Faerie Queen"]

brag·gart (brăg′ərt), n. **1.** one given to bragging. —adj. **2.** bragging; boastful. [t. F (obs.): m. *bragard* boastful] —**brag′gart·ism,** n.

Bra·gi (brä′gY), n. *Scand. Myth.* son of Odin, and god of poetry; Odin's principal skald in Valhalla. His wife is Ithunn. Also, **Bra·ge** (brä′gə).

Brahe (brä; *Dan.* brä′ĕ), n. Tycho (tY′kō), 1546–1601, Danish astronomer.

Brah·ma (brä′mə), n. **1.** (in philosophic Hinduism) the impersonal Supreme Being, the primal Source and the ultimate Goal of all being; Atman, the World Soul. **2.** (in later Hinduism) a trinity of the personal Creator along with Vishnu the Preserver and Siva the Destroyer. [t. Skt.: m. *brăhma,* neut., worship, prayer, the impersonal divinity (see def. 1); m. *brahmă,* masc., worshiper, priest, the divinity as personified (see def. 2)]

brah·ma (brä′mə, brä′-), n. a breed of large domestic fowls, of Asiatic origin, with feathered legs and small wings and tail. [named after and short for BRAHMAPUTRA]

Brah·man (brä′mən), n., pl. **-mans.** a member of the highest, or priestly, caste among the Hindus. Also, **Brahmin.** [t. Skt.: m. *brāhmana*] —**Brah·man·ic** (brä măn′-Yk), **Brah·man′i·cal,** adj.

Brah·man (brä′mən), n. U.S. an animal of a breed of cattle of the species *Bos indicus,* originating in India.

Brah·man·ism (brä′mə nYz′əm), n. the religious and social system of the Brahmans and orthodox Hindus, characterized by the caste system and diversified pantheism. —**Brah′man·ist,** n.

Brah·ma·pu·tra (brä′mə pŏŏ′trə), n. a river flowing from SW Tibet through NE India, joining the Ganges in E Pakistan to flow into the Bay of Bengal. ab. 1800 mi.

Brah·min (brä′mYn), n., pl. **Brahmin. 1.** Brahman. **2.** a person of great culture and intellect. **3.** a snobbish or aloof intellectual.

Brahms (brämz; *Ger.* bräms), n. Johannes (yō hän′-əs), 1833–97, German composer.

braid (brād), v.t. **1.** to weave together strips or strands of; plait. **2.** to form by such weaving. **3.** to bind or confine (the hair) with a band, ribbon, etc. **4.** to trim (garments) with braid. —n. **5.** a braided length, or plait, of hair, etc. **6.** a narrow band or tape, formed by plaiting or weaving together several strands of silk, cotton wool, or other material, used as trimming for garments, etc. **7.** a band, ribbon, etc., for binding or confining the hair. [ME *braide(n),* OE *bregdan* move quickly, move to and fro, weave, c. Icel. *bregdha*] —**braid′er,** n.

braid·ing (brā′dYng), n. **1.** braids collectively. **2.** braided work.

brail (brāl), n. **1.** *Naut.* one of certain ropes made fast to the after leech of a sail, to assist in taking in the sail. —v.t. **2.** to gather or haul in (a sail) by means of brails (usually fol. by *up*). [ME *brayle,* t. OF: m. *braiel* cincture, g. L *brācāle* belt, der. *brācae* breeches]

Bră·i·la (brə ē′lä), n. a city in E Rumania: a port on the Danube. 95,514 (1948).

Braille (brāl), n. a system of writing or printing for the blind, in which combinations of tangible dots or points are raised to represent letters, etc. Also, **braille.** [after Louis *Braille* (1809–52)]

Brails on sail A. Peak brail; B. Throat brail; C. Lower brail

brain (brān), n. **1.** (*sometimes pl.*) the soft convoluted mass of grayish and whitish nerve substance which fills the cranium of man and other vertebrates. **2.** *Zool.* (in many invertebrates) a part of the nervous system more or less corresponding to the brain of vertebrates. **3.** (usually *pl.*) understanding; intellectual power; intelligence. —v.t. **4.** to dash out the brains of. [ME; OE *brægen,* c. MLG *bregen*] —**Syn. 3.** See **mind¹.**

brain cell, *Anat.* a neuron in the brain.

brain·child (brān′chYld′), n., pl. **-children.** a product of one's creative work or thought.

brain fever, *Pathol.* cerebrospinal meningitis.

brain·less (brān′lYs), adj. mentally weak; witless; stupid. —**brain′less·ness,** n.

brain·pan (brān′păn′), n. the skull or cranium.

brain·sick (brān′sYk′), adj. crazy; mad. —**brain′-sick′ly,** adv. —**brain′sick′ness,** n.

brain storm, 1. a sudden, violent attack of mental disturbance. **2.** *Colloq.* sudden inspiration, idea, etc.

brain·storm·ing (brān′stôrm′Yng), n. a technique in which a group meets in order to stimulate creative thinking, develop new ideas, etc.

brain trust, a group of experts who give counsel, help shape policy, etc. —**brain truster.**

brain washing, systematic indoctrination that changes or undermines one's political convictions. —**brain-wash,** v.

brain wave, 1. (*pl.*) *Med.* electroencephalogram **2.** *Colloq.* a sudden idea or inspiration.

b., blend of, blended; c., cognate with; d., dialect, dialectal; der., derived from; f., formed from; g., going back to; m., modification of; r., replacing; s., stem of; t., taken from; ?, perhaps. See the full key on inside cover.

brain·y (brā'nĭ), *adj.*, **brainier, brainiest.** having brains; intelligent; clever. —**brain'i·ness,** *n.*

braise (brāz), *v.t.*, **braised, braising.** to cook (meat or vegetables) by sautéing in fat and then cooking slowly in very little moisture. [t. F: m. *braiser,* der. *braise* hot charcoal, live coals; of Gmc. orig.]

brake¹ (brāk), *n., v.,* **braked, braking.** —*n.* **1.** any mechanical device for arresting the motion of a wheel or a vehicle by means of friction. **2.** (*pl.*) the drums, shoes, tubes, levers, etc., making up the brake system. **3.** a tool or machine for breaking up flax or hemp, to separate the fiber. **4.** Also, **break.** *Brit.* a large, high-set, four-wheeled vehicle, with crosswise seats, a seat in front for the driver, and another behind for footmen, now little used. **5.** *Obs.* an old instrument of torture. —*v.t.* **6.** to slow or stop the motion of (a wheel, automobile, etc.) as by a brake. **7.** to furnish with brakes. **8.** to process (flax or hemp) by crushing it in a brake. —*v.i.* **9.** to use or run a brake. **10.** to run a hoisting machine. [ME, t. MLG and /or MD] —**brake'less,** *adj.*

brake² (brāk), *n.* a place overgrown with bushes, shrubs, brambles, or cane; a thicket. [cf. MLG *brake*]

brake³ (brāk), *n.* any large or coarse fern, esp. *Pteridium aquilina* or some allied species. [ME, var. of BRACKEN]

brake⁴ (brāk), *v. Obs.* or *Archaic.* pt. of **break.**

brake·age (brā'kĭj), *n.* **1.** the action of a brake or set of brakes, as in stopping a vehicle. **2.** brakes collectively.

brake band, a part of brake mechanism consisting of a flexible band which grips a drum when tightened.

brake drum, the steel or cast-iron part attached to the wheel hub or transmission shaft to which a brake lining is applied.

brake horsepower, the amount of horsepower delivered to the transmission by the engine.

brake lining, the material, usually asbestos combined with other materials, used as the friction-producing element of a brake.

brake·man (brāk'mən), *n., pl.* **-men.** *Railroads.* a member of a train crew, assisting the conductor in the operation of a train; trainman. Also, *Brit.,* **brakes'man.**

Bra·man·te (brä män'tě), *n.* **Donato d'Agnolo** (dō-nä'tō dä'nyō lō), 1444?–1514, Italian architect and painter.

bram·ble (brăm'bəl), *n., v.,* **-bled, -bling.** —*n.* **1.** any plant of the rosaceous genus *Rubus.* **2.** *Scot.* the common blackberry, *R. fruticosus.* **3.** any rough prickly shrub, as the dog rose. —*v.i.* **4.** *Brit.* to gather blackberries. [OE *bræmbel, brembel,* var. of *bræmel, brēmel,* der. *brōm* broom] —**bram'bly,** *adj.*

bram·bling (brăm'blĭng), *n.* an Old World finch, *Fringilla montifringilla,* closely related to the chaffinch.

bran (brăn), *n.* **1.** the ground husk of wheat or other grain, separated from flour or meal by bolting. **2.** by-products of grain processing used as feed. [ME, t. OF]

Bran (brăn), *n.* a Brython deity, and early mythical king of Britain.

branch (brănch, bränch), *n.* **1.** *Bot.* a division or subdivision of the stem or axis of a tree, shrub, or other plant (the ultimate or smaller ramifications being called branchlets, twigs, or shoots). **2.** a limb, offshoot, or ramification: *the branches of a deer's horns.* **3.** any member or part of a body or system; a section or subdivision: *the various branches of learning.* **4.** a local operating division of a business house, a library, or the like. **5.** a line of family descent, in distinction from some other line or lines from the same stock. **6.** (in the classification of languages) a subdivision of a family; a group. **7.** *Geog.* **a.** a tributary stream. **b.** any stream that is not a large river or a bayou. —*v.i.* **8.** to put forth branches; spread in branches. **9.** to divide into separate parts or subdivisions; diverge. —*v.t.* **10.** to divide as into branches. **11.** to adorn with needlework; decorate with embroidery, as in textile fabrics. [ME, t. OF: m. *branche,* g. LL *branca* paw, claw] —**branch'less,** *adj.* —**branch'like',** *adj.*

—**Syn. 1.** BRANCH, BOUGH, LIMB refer to divisions of a tree. BRANCH is general, meaning either a large or a small division. BOUGH refers only to the larger branches: *a bough loaded with apples.* A LIMB is a large primary division of a tree trunk or of a bough: *to climb out on a limb.*

bran·chi·a (brăng'kĭ ə), *n. pl.* *Ichthyol.* branchiae. [t. L (sing.), t. Gk.: m. *bránchia* (neut. pl.) gills] —**bran'-chi·al,** *adj.*

bran·chi·ae (brăng'kĭ ē'), *n. pl. Ichthyol.* the respiratory organs or gills of fishes, etc.

bran·chi·ate (brăng'kĭ ĭt, -āt'), *adj. Ichthyol.* having branchiae.

bran·chi·o·pod (brăng'kĭ ə pŏd'), *n. Zool.* any of the *Branchiopoda,* a group of crustaceans having branchiae or gills on the feet. [f. s. Gk. *bránchia* gills + -(o)POD]

brand (brănd), *n.* **1.** a trademark or trade name to identify a product, as that of a distributor, or a manufacturer or other producer. **2.** kind, grade, or make, as indicated by a brand, stamp, trademark, or the like. **3.** a mark made by burning or otherwise, to indicate kind, grade, make, ownership, etc. **4.** a mark formerly put upon criminals with a hot iron. **5.** any mark of infamy; a stigma. **6.** an iron for branding. **7.** a burning or partly burned piece of wood. **8.** *Archaic* or *Poetic.* a sword. —*v.t.* **9.** to mark with a brand. **10.** to mark with infamy; stigmatize. [ME and OE; akin to BURN¹] —**brand'er,** *n.*

Bran·deis (brăn'dīs), *n.* **Louis Dembitz,** 1856–1941, U.S. lawyer and writer: associate justice of the U.S. Supreme Court, 1916–39.

Bran·den·burg (brăn'dən bûrg'; *Ger.* brän'dən-bōōrkн'), *n.* **1.** a former province in East Germany. 10,412 sq. mi. (1946). **2.** the former capital of this province. 87,143 (1955).

Bran·des (brăn'dĕs), *n.* **Georg Morris Cohen** (gĭ'org mō'rĭs kō'ən), 1842–1927, Danish critic and scholar.

bran·died (brăn'dĭd), *adj.* flavored or treated with brandy.

bran·dish (brăn'dĭsh), *v.t.* **1.** to shake or wave, as a weapon; flourish. —*n.* **2.** a wave or flourish, as of a weapon. [ME *braundish(en),* t. OF: m. *brandiss-,* s. *brandir,* der. *brand* sword; of Gmc. orig. See BRAND] —**bran'dish·er,** *n.*

brand·ling (brănd'lĭng), *n.* a small, reddish-brown earthworm, *Helodrilus foetidus,* with yellow markings, found chiefly in manure piles.

brand-new (brănd'nū', -nōō'), *adj.* quite new. Also, **bran-new** (brăn'nū', -nōō'). [f. BRAND + NEW]

bran·dy (brăn'dĭ), *n., pl.* **-dies,** *v.,* **-died, -dying.** —*n.* **1.** the spirit distilled from the fermented juice of grapes or, sometimes, of apples, peaches, plums, etc. —*v.t.* **2.** to mix, flavor, or preserve with brandy. [short for *brandy-wine,* t. D: m. *brandewijn* burnt (i.e. distilled) wine]

Bran·dy·wine (brăn'dĭ wīn'), *n.* a creek in SE Pennsylvania and N Delaware: American defeat by the British, 1777.

branks (brăngks), *n.* a bridle formerly used to punish a scold. [orig. uncert.]

bran·ny (brăn'ĭ), *adj.* of, containing, or like bran.

brant (brănt), *n., pl.* **brants,** (*esp. collectively*) **brant.** any of several species of small, dark-colored geese of the genus *Branta. B. bernicla,* breeding in high northern latitudes and migrating south in the autumn. Also, **brent.** [cf. Icel. *brandgås*]

Brant (brănt), *n.* **Joseph** (native name, *Thayenda-negea*), 1742–1807, Mohawk Indian chief who fought with the British in the American Revolution.

Brant·ford (brănt'fərd), *n.* a city in SE Canada, in Ontario, near Hamilton. 52,231 with suburbs (1951).

Braque (bräk), *n.* **Georges,** 1881–1963, French painter.

brash (brăsh), *adj.* **1.** headlong; hasty; rash. **2.** impertinent; impudent. **3.** *U.S. Local.* (used esp. of timber) brittle. —*n.* **4.** loose fragments of rock. **5.** *Naut.* small fragments of crushed ice collected by winds or currents near the shore. **6.** *Dial.* an attack of illness. **7.** *Dial.* a shower. [orig. obscure] —**brash'y,** *adj.*

bra·sier (brā'zhər), *n.* brazier.

Bra·sil (brə sēl'), *n.* Portuguese and Spanish for **Brazil.**

Bra·si·li·a (brə zĭl'Y ə), *n.* a city in and the capital of Brazil, on the central plateau. 130,968 (est. 1960).

bras·i·lin (brăz'ə lĭn), *n. Chem.* brazilin.

Bra·șov (brä shôv'), *n.* a city in central Rumania. 82,984 (1948). Renamed Stalin. German, **Kronstadt.** Hungarian, **Brassó.**

brass (brăs, bräs), *n.* **1.** a durable, malleable, and ductile yellow alloy, consisting essentially of copper and zinc. **2.** a utensil, ornament, or other article made of brass. **3.** *Mach.* a bearing, bush, or the like. **4.** *Music.* **a.** a musical instrument of the trumpet or horn families. **b.** such instruments collectively in a band or orchestra. **5.** *Brit.* a memorial tablet incised with an effigy, coat of arms or the like. **6.** metallic yellow; lemon, amber, or reddish yellow. **7.** *U.S. Slang.* **a.** high-ranking military officers. **b.** any important officials. **8.** *Colloq.* excessive assurance; impudence; effrontery. **9.** *Brit. Slang.* money. —*adj.* **10.** of brass. **11.** using musical instruments made of brass. [ME *bras,* OE *bræs*] —**brass'-like',** *adj.*

brass·age (brăs'ĭj, bräs'ĭj), *n.* a charge to cover costs of coining money. [t. F, der. *brasser* stir (welded metal), ult. der. L *brace* white corn, of Celtic orig.]

bras·sard (brăs'ärd), *n.* **1.** a badge worn around the upper arm. **2.** Also, **bras·sart** (brăs'ərt), a piece of armor for the arm. See under **armor.** [t. F, der. *bras* arm]

brass hat, *Slang.* a high-ranking army or navy officer.

bras·si·ca·ceous (brăs'ĭ kā'shəs), *adj. Bot.* belonging to the family *Brassicaceae* (often called *Cruciferae*) of herbaceous plants, including the common cabbage, watercress, etc. [f. s. L *brassica* cabbage + -ACEOUS]

brass·ie (brăs'Y, bräs'Y), *n.* a long-shafted golf club with a wooden head soled with a brass plate. Also, **brassy.**

bras·sière (brə zĭr'), *n.* a woman's undergarment which supports the breasts. Also, **bras·siere'.** [t. F: little camisole, der. *bras* arm]

brass knuckles, piece of metal fitted across the knuckles, used in fighting.

Bras·só (brŏsh'shō), *n.* Hungarian name of **Brasov.**

brass tacks, *Colloq.* basic facts; realities.

brass·ware (brăs'wâr', bräs'-), *n.* articles of brass.

brass winds, *Music.* brass (def. 4b).

brass·y¹ (brăs'Y, bräs'Y), *adj.,* **brassier, brassiest. 1.** made of or covered with brass. **2.** resembling brass. **3.** harsh and metallic: *brassy tones.* **4.** *Colloq.* brazen. [f. BRASS + -Y¹] —**brass'i·ly,** *adv.* —**brass'i·ness,** *n.*

brass·y² (brăs'Y, bräs'Y), *n., pl.* **-ies.** *Golf.* brassie.

brat (brăt), *n.* **1.** a child (used usually in contempt or irritation). [cf. d. *brat* rag, trash, OE *bratt* cloak]

Bra·ti·sla·va (brä/tĭ slä/və), *n.* a city in S Czechoslovakia, on the Danube: a former capital of Hungary. 172,664 (1947). German, **Pressburg.** Hungarian, **Pozsony.**

brat·tice (brăt/ĭs), *n., v.,* **-ticed, -ticing.** —*n.* 1. a partition or lining, as of planks or cloth, forming an air passage in a mine. —*v.t.* 2. to provide with a brattice; line with planks or cloth. [ME *bretage,* t. OF: m. *bretesche* parapet, ? t. OE: m. *brittisc* British, i.e., foreign (fortification)]

brat·tle (brăt/əl), *n., v.,* **-tled, -tling.** —*n.* 1. a clattering noise. —*v.i.* 2. to scamper noisily.

braun·ite (brou/nīt), *n.* a mineral, manganese oxide and silicate, Mn₇SiO₁₂, an ore of manganese.

Braun·schweig (broun/shvīкн), *n.* German name of **Brunswick.**

bra·va·do (brə vä/dō), *n., pl.* **-does, -dos.** boasting; swaggering; pretense. [t. Sp.: m. *bravada.* See BRAVE] —**Syn.** See **courage.**

brave (brāv), *adj.,* **braver, bravest,** *n., v.,* **braved, braving.** —*adj.* 1. possessing or exhibiting courage or courageous endurance. 2. making a fine appearance. 3. *Archaic.* excellent; fine; admirable. —*n.* 4. a brave person. 5. a North American Indian or other savage warrior. 6. *Obs.* a bully. 7. *Obs.* a boast; a challenge; a defiance. —*v.t.* 8. to meet or face courageously: *to brave misfortunes.* 9. to defy; challenge; dare. 10. *Obs.* to make splendid. —*v.i.* 11. *Obs.* to boast; brag. [t. F, t. It.: m. *bravo* brave, bold, fine, t. Sp.: vicious (first applied to bulls), g. L *prāvus*] —**brave/ly,** *adv.* —**brave/ness,** *n.*

—**Syn.** 1. BRAVE, COURAGEOUS, FEARLESS, GALLANT refer to confident bearing in the face of difficulties or dangers. BRAVE is the most comprehensive; it is especially used of that confident fortitude or daring that actively faces and endures anything threatening. COURAGEOUS implies a higher or nobler kind of bravery, esp. as resulting from an inborn quality of mind or spirit which faces or endures perils or difficulties without fear and even with enthusiasm. FEARLESS implies unflinching spirit and coolness in the face of danger. GALLANT implies chivalrous, impetuous, dashing, or showy bravery.

brav·er·y (brā/vər ĭ), *n., pl.* **-eries.** 1. brave spirit or conduct; courage; valor. 2. showiness; splendor; magnificence. —**Syn.** 1. intrepidity, fearlessness, boldness, daring, prowess, heroism, pluck. See **courage.**

bra·vo¹ (brä/vō), *interj., n., pl.* **-vos.** —*interj.* 1. well done! good! —*n.* 2. a shout of "bravo!" [t. It., prop. adj. See BRAVE]

bra·vo² (brä/vō, brä/-), *n., pl.* **-voes, -vos.** a daring bandit or assassin or murderer. [t. It. See BRAVE]

bra·vu·ra (brə vyŏŏr/ə; *It.* brä/vōō/rä), *n.* 1. *Music.* a florid passage or piece, requiring great skill and spirit in the performer. 2. a display of daring; brilliant performance. —*adj.* 3. *Music.* spirited; florid; brilliant (chiefly applied to vocal compositions, but occasionally to instrumental). [t. It.: bravery, spirit]

braw (brô, brä), *adj. Scot. and N. Eng.* fine or finelooking; excellent. [var. of BRAVE]

brawl¹ (brôl), *n.* 1. a noisy quarrel; a squabble. 2. a bubbling or roaring noise; a clamor. —*v.i.* 3. to quarrel angrily, noisily; wrangle. 4. to make a bubbling or roaring noise, as water flowing over a rocky bed. [ME *brall(en),* der. *brawl* brawler, var. of *broll* brat, contr. of *brothel* good-for-nothing, der. OE *brēothan* go to ruin] —**brawl/er,** *n.* —**Syn.** 1. See **disorder.**

brawl² (brôl), *n.* an old folk dance of French origin. [orig. unknown]

brawn (brôn), *n.* 1. well-developed muscles. 2. muscular strength. 3. a boar's or swine's flesh, esp. when boiled and pickled. [ME *brawne,* t. OF: m. *braon,* t. Gmc.; cf. G *braten* roast]

brawn·y (brô/nĭ), *adj.,* **brawnier, brawniest.** muscular; strong. —**brawn/i·ness,** *n.*

brax·y (brăk/sĭ), *Vet. Sci.* —*n.* 1. an acute bacterial disease of sheep involving inflammation of the bowels, usually fatal. —*adj.* 2. affected with braxy. [prob. n. use of adj., OE *bræcsēoc* ill with falling sickness, f. *bræc* rheum + *sēoc* sick]

bray¹ (brā), *n.* 1. a harsh, breathy cry, as of the donkey. 2. any similar loud, harsh sound. —*v.i.* 3. to utter a loud and harsh cry as the donkey. 4. to make a loud, harsh, disagreeable sound, as a trumpet. —*v.t.* 5. to utter with a loud, harsh sound, like the donkey. [ME *braye(n),* t. OF: m. *braire*] —**bray/er,** *n.*

bray² (brā), *v.t.* to pound or crush fine, as in a mortar. [ME *braye(n),* t. OF: m. *breier*]

bray·er (brā/ər), *n. Print.* a small roller for inking type or plates by hand (usually for making a proof). [f. BRAY² + -ER¹]

Braz., 1. Brazil. 2. Brazilian.

bra·za (brä/thä, -sä), *n.* a unit of length in Spanish-speaking countries, representing the reach of outspread arms, officially 5.48 U.S. ft. in Spain, and 5.68 U.S. ft. in Argentina. [t. Sp., der. *brazo* arm, g. L *brāchium*]

braze¹ (brāz), *v.t.,* **brazed, brazing.** 1. to make of brass. 2. to cover or ornament with brass, or as if with brass. 3. to make brasslike. [OE *brasian,* der. *bræs* brass]

braze² (brāz), *v.t.,* **brazed, brazing.** *Metall.* to unite (pieces of brass, steel, etc.) by intensely heating the parts to be joined and applying any one of a number of high melting solders which range in melting point from alloys rich in silver to pure copper. [? t. F: m. *braser,* der. *braise* live coals. See BRAISE]

bra·zen (brā/zən), *adj.* 1. made of brass. 2. like brass, as in sound, color, strength, etc. 3. shameless or impudent: *brazen effrontery.* —*v.t.* 4. to face with boldness and effrontery (fol. by *out*). 5. to make brazen or bold. [ME *brasen,* OE *bræsen,* der. *bræs* brass] —**bra/zen·ly,** *adv.* —**bra/zen·ness,** *n.* —**Syn.** 3. See **bold.**

bra·zen-faced (brā/zən fāst/), *adj.* openly shameless; impudent.

bra·zier¹ (brā/zhər), *n.* a person who works in brass. Also, **brasier.** [ME *brasiere;* f. BRAZE², v. + -IER]

bra·zier² (brā/zhər), *n.* a metal receptacle for holding burning charcoal or other fuel, as for heating a room. Also, **brasier.** [t. F: m. *brasier,* der. *braise* live coals.]

Bra·zil (brə zĭl/), *n.* a republic in South America. 65,743,303 (est. 1960); 3,286,170 sq. mi. *Cap.:* Brasília. Official name, **United States of Brazil,** Portuguese and Spanish, **Brasil.** —**Bra·zil·ian** (brə zĭl/yən), *adj., n.*

bra·zil (brə zĭl/), *n.* 1. a dyewood from various tropical American trees of the genus *Caesalpinia* (esp. *C. echinata*) and allied genera, yielding reds and purples. 2. the red dyestuff extracted from it. 3. (*orig.*) a hard East Indian dyewood yielding a red color, from the tree *Caesalpinia sappan.* [ME *brasile,* t. Sp. or Pg.: m. *brasil,* t. OF: m. *brésil* reddish-tinted wood, der. *brēze, braise* glowing coals; Brazil was named after the tree]

braz·i·lin (brăz/ə lĭn), *n. Chem.* a yellow substance, $C_{16}H_{14}O_5$, from brazil, used as a dye and indicator. Also, **brasilin.**

Brazil nut, the triangular edible seed (nut) of the tree *Bertholletia excelsa* and related species, of Brazil, etc.

bra·zil·wood (brə zĭl/wŏŏd/), *n.* brazil.

Bra·zos (brā/zōs; *locally* brăz/əs, brä/zəs), *n.* a river flowing from N Texas SE to the Gulf of Mexico. 870 mi.

Braz·za·ville (brä zä vēl/), *n.* the capital of the Republic of Congo and former capital of French Equatorial Africa: a port on the Congo river. 99,144 (1959).

breach (brēch), *n.* 1. act or result of breaking; a break or rupture. 2. a gap made in a wall, dike, fortification, etc.; rift; fissure. 3. an infraction or violation, as of law, trust, faith, promise, etc. 4. a severance of friendly relations. 5. the springing of a whale from the water. 6. *Archaic.* the breaking of waves; the dashing of surf. 7. *Obs.* wound. —*v.t.* 8. to make a breach or opening in. [ME *breche,* OE *bræce*] —**Syn.** 4. alienation, quarrel.

breach of promise, *Law.* a violation of one's promise, esp. of a promise to marry.

breach of the peace, *Law.* a violation of the public peace, by a riot, disturbance, etc.

breach of trust, 1. *Law.* a violation of duty by a trustee. 2. *Colloq.* a violation of duty by any fiduciary.

bread (brĕd), *n.* 1. a kind of food made of flour or meal, milk or water, etc., made into a dough or batter, with or without yeast or the like, and baked. 2. food or sustenance; livelihood: *to earn one's bread.* 3. *Eccles.* the wafer or bread used in the Eucharist. 4. **break bread, a.** to partake of or share food. **b.** *Eccles.* to administer or join in Communion. —*v.t.* 5. *Cookery.* to cover or dress with bread crumbs or meal. [ME *breed,* OE *brēad,* c. G *brot*] —**bread/less,** *adj.*

bread and butter, 1. bread spread with butter. 2. *Colloq.* means of living; livelihood.

bread-and-but·ter (brĕd/ən bŭt/ər), *adj.* 1. seeking the means of living; mercenary. 2. *Colloq.* belonging to or in the stage of adolescence. 3. *Colloq.* matter-of-fact. 4. expressing thanks for hospitality, as a letter.

bread·fruit (brĕd/frŏŏt/), *n.* 1. a large, round, starchy fruit yielded by a moraceous tree, *Artocarpus communis* (*A. altilis*), of the Pacific islands, etc., much used, baked or roasted, for food. 2. the tree bearing this fruit.

bread line, a line of needy persons assembled to receive food given as charity.

bread mold, a black fungus, *Rhizopus nigricans,* often seen on bread.

bread·root (brĕd/rŏŏt/, -rŏŏt/), *n.* the edible farinaceous root of *Psoralea esculenta,* a fabaceous plant of central North America.

bread·stuff (brĕd/stŭf/), *n.* 1. grain, flour, or meal for making bread. 2. bread.

breadth (brĕdth, brĕtth), *n.* 1. *Math.* the measure of the second principal diameter of a surface or solid, the first being length, and the third (in the case of a solid) thickness; width. 2. an extent or piece of something as measured by its width, or of definite or full width: *a breadth of cloth.* 3. freedom from narrowness or restraint; liberality: *breadth of view.* 4. size in general; extent. 5. *Art.* broad or general effect due to subordination of details or nonessentials. [f. earlier *breade* (OE *brǣdu*) + -TH¹; modeled on LENGTH]

breadth·ways (brĕdth/wāz/, brĕtth/-), *adv.* in the direction of the breadth. Also, **breadth·wise** (brĕdth/wīz/, brĕtth/-).

bread·win·ner (brĕd/wĭn/ər), *n.* one who earns a livelihood for himself and those dependent upon him.

break (brāk), *v.,* **broke** or (*Archaic*) **brake; broken,** or (*Archaic*) **broke; breaking.** —*v.t.* 1. to divide into parts violently; reduce to pieces or fragments. 2. to violate: *to break a law or promise.* 3. to dissolve or annul (often fol. by *off*). 4. to fracture a bone of. 5. to lacerate; wound: *break the skin.* 6. to discontinue abruptly; interrupt; suspend: *to break the silence.* 7. to destroy the regularity of. 8. to put an end to; overcome.

---

b., blend of, blended; c., cognate with; d., dialect, dialectal; der., derived from; f., formed from; g., going back to; m., modification of; r., replacing; s., stem of; t., taken from; ?, perhaps. See the full key on inside cover.

9. to interrupt the uniformity or sameness of: *to break the monotony.* 10. to destroy the unity, continuity, or arrangement of. 11. to exchange for a smaller amount or smaller units. 12. to make one's way through; penetrate. 13. *Law.* a. to open or force one's way into (a dwelling, store, etc.). b. to contest (a will) successfully by judicial action. 14. to make one's way out of: *to break jail.* 15. to exceed; outdo: *to break a record.* 16. to disclose or divulge, with caution or delicacy. 17. to disable or destroy by or as by shattering or crushing. 18. (pp. **broke**) to ruin financially, or make bankrupt. 19. to reduce in rank. 20. to impair or weaken in strength, spirit, force, or effect. 21. to train to obedience; tame (often fol. by *in*). 22. to train away from a habit or practice (fol. by *of*). 23. *Elect.* to render (a circuit) incomplete; stop the flow of (a current). —*v.i.* 24. to become broken; separate into parts or fragments, esp. suddenly and violently. 25. to become suddenly discontinuous or interrupted; leave off abruptly. 26. to become detached (fol. by *off*, etc.). 27. to dissolve and separate (fol. by *up*). 28. to sever relations (fol. by *with*). 29. to change suddenly, as in sound, movement, or direction. 30. to free oneself or escape suddenly, as from restraint (often fol. by *away*). 31. to force a way (fol. by *in, through*, etc.). 32. to burst (fol. by *in, forth, from*, etc.). 33. to come suddenly, as into notice. 34. to dawn, as the day. 35. (of a fish) to come to the surface. 36. to give way or fail as under strain (often fol. by *down*). 37. (of the heart) to be crushed or overwhelmed. 38. (of stock exchange prices) to drop quickly and considerably. 39. *Music.* a. to change or go from one register to another, as a musical instrument or the voice. b. to change or be interrupted unmusically, as a voice or tone. 40. *Ling.* to undergo breaking. 41. *Pool.* to make a break (def. 59). 42. Some special verb phrases are:
break away, (in racing) to start prematurely.
break camp, to pack up tents and equipment and resume a march.
break down, 1. to take down or destroy by breaking. **2.** to overcome. **3.** to analyze.
break off, 1. to sever by breaking. **2.** to put a sudden stop to; discontinue.
break out, 1. to issue forth; arise. **2.** *Pathol.* (of certain diseases) to appear in eruptions. **3.** to have a sudden appearance of various eruptions on the skin.
break step, *Mil.* to cease marching in cadence.
break up, 1. to separate; disband. **2.** to put an end to; discontinue. **3.** to cut up (fowl, etc.).
—*n.* 43. a forcible disruption or separation of parts; a breaking; a fracture, rupture, or shattering. 44. an opening made by breaking; a gap. 45. a rush away from a place; an attempt to escape: *a break for freedom.* 46. an interruption of continuity; suspension; stoppage. 47. an abrupt or marked change, as in sound or direction. 48. *Colloq.* an opportunity; chance. 49. *Colloq.* a social error or slip; an unfortunate remark. 50. a small amount; portion. 51. a brief rest, as from work. 52. *Pros.* a pause or caesura. 53. *Jazz.* a solo passage, usually of about two bars, during which the band accompaniment breaks off, or rests. 54. *Music.* the point in the scale where the quality of voice of one register changes to that of another, as from chest to head. 55. (on the stock exchange) a sudden drop in prices. 56. *Elect.* an opening or discontinuity in a circuit. 57. *Print.* a. one or more blank lines between two paragraphs. b. (*pl.*) dots (. . .) to show where something has been omitted in printed material. 58. *Billiards.* run (def. 99). 59. *Pool.* a. the shot that breaks or scatters the balls as piled together at the beginning of the game. b. the right to the first play. 60. *Baseball, Cricket, etc.* change in direction of a ball, usually caused by spinning it when thrown. 61. *Bowling.* a failure to knock down all ten pins after bowling twice. 62. brake (def. 4). [ME *breke(n)*, OE *brecan*, c. G *brechen*, Goth. *brikan*] —**break'a·ble,** *adj.*
—**Syn.** 1. BREAK, CRUSH, SHATTER, SMASH mean to reduce to parts, violently or by force. BREAK means to divide by means of a blow, a collision, a pull, or the like: *to break a chair, a leg, a strap.* To CRUSH is to subject to (usually heavy or violent) pressure so as to press out of shape or reduce to shapelessness or to small particles: *to crush a beetle.* SHATTER is to break in a way to cause the pieces to fly in many directions: *to shatter a light globe.* To SMASH is to smash noisily and suddenly into many pieces: *to smash a glass.* 2. transgress, disobey, contravene.

break·age (brā'kĭj), *n.* 1. act of breaking; a break. 2. the amount or quantity of things broken. 3. *Com.* an allowance or compensation for loss or damage of articles broken in transit or in use.
break·bone fever (brāk'bōn'), *Pathol.* dengue.
break·down (brāk'doun'), *n.* 1. a breaking down, as of a machine, of physical or mental health, etc.; a collapse. 2. *Chem.* a. decomposition. b. analysis. 3. *U.S.* a noisy, lively folk dance.
break·er¹ (brā'kər), *n.* 1. one who or that which breaks. 2. a wave that breaks or dashes into foam. [f. BREAK + -ER¹] —**Syn.** 2. See **wave.**
break·er² (brā'kər) *n.* *Naut.* a small water cask for use in a boat. [t. Sp.: alter. of *barrica* cask]
break·fast (brĕk'fəst), *n.* 1. the first meal of the day; a morning meal. 2. the food eaten at the first meal. 3. a meal or food in general. —*v.i.* 4. to take breakfast. —*v.t.* 5. to supply with breakfast. [ME *brekfast*, f. *brek* break + *fast* FAST²] —**break'fast·er,** *n.*

breakfast food, a cold or hot cereal generally eaten for breakfast.
break·ing (brā'kĭng), *n.* (in the history of English and of some other languages) the change of a vowel to diphthong under the influence of a following consonant or combination of consonants; e.g., in Old English, the change of *-a-* to *-ea-* and of *-e-* to *-eo-* before preconsonantal *-r-* or *-l-* and before *-h-*, as in *earm* (arm) developed from *arm* and *eorthe* (earth) from *erthe.*
break·neck (brāk'nĕk'), *adj.* dangerous; hazardous.
break of day, dawn; daybreak.
break·through (brāk'thrōō'), *n.* 1. *Mil.* a movement or advance all the way through and beyond a defensive system into the unorganized areas in the rear. 2. any development, as in science, technology, or diplomacy, which removes a barrier to progress.
break·up (brāk'ŭp'), *n.* disintegration; disruption; dispersal.
break·wa·ter (brāk'wô'tər, -wŏt'ər), *n.* a barrier which breaks the force of waves, as before a harbor.
bream¹ (brēm), *n., pl.* **breams,** (*esp. collectively*) **bream** 1. any of various fresh-water cyprinoid fishes of the genus *Abramis,* as *A. brama* of Europe, with a compressed, deep body. 2. any of various related and similar species, as the **white bream,** *Blicca bjoerkna.* 3. a sea bream. 4. Also, *Southern U.S.,* **brim.** any of various fresh-water sunfishes of the genus *Lepomis.* [ME *breme*, t. F; in OF *bresme*, t. OG; cf. OS *bressemo*]
bream² (brēm), *v.t.* *Naut.* to clean (a ship's bottom) by applying burning furze, reeds, etc., to soften the pitch and loosen adherent matter. [cf. MD *brem(e)* furze]
breast (brĕst), *n.* 1. *Anat., Zool.* the outer front part of the thorax, or the front part of the body from neck to belly; the chest. 2. *Zool.* the corresponding part in lower animals. 3. *Anat., Zool.* a mammary or milk gland, esp. of a woman, or of female animals whose milk glands are similarly formed. 4. that part of a garment which covers the chest. 5. the bosom regarded as the seat of thoughts and feelings. 6. thoughts; feelings; mind. 7. any surface or part resembling or likened to the human breast. 8. *Mining.* the face or heading at which the working is going on. —*v.t.* 9. to meet or oppose with the breast. 10. to meet boldly or advance against; face. [ME *brest*, OE *brēost*, akin to G *brust*]
breast·bone (brĕst'bōn'), *n.* *Anat., Zool.* sternum.
Breas·ted (brĕs'tĭd), *n.* **James Henry,** 1865–1935, U. S. archaeologist, and historian o. ancient Egypt.
breast·pin (brĕst'pĭn'), *n.* a pin worn on the breast or at the throat; a brooch.
breast·plate (brĕst'plāt'), *n.* 1. armor for the front of the torso. 2. part of the harness that runs across a saddle horse's breast. 3. a square ornament worn on the breast by the Jewish high priest.

Breastplate. (def. 1)
16th century

breast stroke, *Swimming.* a stroke made in the prone position in which both hands move simultaneously forward, outward and rearward from in front of the chest.
breast·work (brĕst'wûrk'), *n.* *Fort.* a defensive work usually breast high, hastily thrown up.
breath (brĕth), *n.* 1. *Physiol.* the air inhaled and exhaled in respiration. 2. respiration, esp. as necessary to life. 3. ability to breathe, esp. freely: *out of breath.* 4. time to breathe; pause or respite. 5. a single respiration. 6. the brief time required for it; an instant. 7. an utterance; whisper. 8. a light current of air. 9. *Phonet.* voiceless expiration of air, used in the production of many speech sounds, such as *p* or *f.* 10. moisture emitted in respiration, esp. when condensed and visible. 11. a trivial circumstance; a trifle. 12. an odorous exhalation, or the air impregnated by it. 13. *Obs.* odor; vapor. 14. **below** or **under one's breath,** in a low voice or whisper. [ME *breeth*, OE *brǣth* odor, exhalation; akin to G *brodem* exhalation, vapor]
breathe (brēth), *v.,* **breathed** (brēthd), **breathing.** —*v.i.* 1. to inhale and exhale air; respire. 2. (in speech) to control the outgoing breath in producing voice and speech sounds. 3. to pause, as for breath; take rest (only in infinitive): *give me a chance to breathe.* 4. to blow lightly, as air. 5. to live; exist. 6. to exhale an odor. 7. to be redolent (*of*). —*v.t.* 8. to inhale and exhale in respiration. 9. to allow to rest or recover breath. 10. to put out of breath; tire or exhaust. 11. to give utterance to; whisper. 12. to express; manifest. 13. to exhale: *dragons breathing fire.* 14. to inject by breathing; infuse. 15. to exercise briskly. —**breath'a·ble,** *adj.*
breathed (brĕtht, brēthd *for* 1; brĕtht *for* 2), *adj.* 1. *Phonet.* without use of the vocal chords; voiceless. 2. having a breath, as in *sweet-breathed.*
breath·er (brē'thər), *n.* 1. a pause, as for breath. 2. *Colloq.* something, as exercise, that stimulates or exhausts the breath. 3. one who breathes.
breath·ing (brē'thĭng), *n.* 1. act of one that breathes; respiration. 2. a single breath. 3. the short time required for it. 4. a pause, as for breath. 5. utterance or words. 6. aspiration or longing. 7. gentle blowing, as of wind. 8. *Gram.* a. aspiration; pronunciation with reference to the use or omission of an *h*-sound. b. a sign to indicate this, as in Greek.

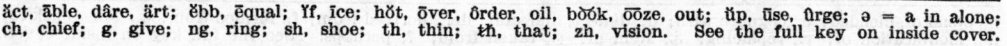

breathing space, opportunity to breathe easily; time to rest.

breath·less (brĕth′lĭs), *adj.* **1.** out of breath: *the blow left him breathless.* **2.** with the breath held, as in suspense: *breathless listeners.* **3.** that takes away the breath: *a breathless ride.* **4.** dead. **5.** motionless, as the air. —breath′less·ly, *adv.* —breath′less·ness, *n.*

breath-tak·ing (brĕth′tā/kĭng), *adj.* causing extreme excitement: *a breath-taking performance.*

breath·y (brĕth′Y), *adj.* (of the voice) characterized by excessive emission of breath.

brec·ci·a (brĕch′Y ə, brĕsh′-), *n.* rock composed of angular fragments of older rocks cemented together. [t. It.]

Breck·in·ridge (brĕk′ĭn rĭj), *n.* **John Cabell** (kăb′əl), 1821–75, vice-president of the U. S., 1857–61: Confederate general in the U.S. Civil War.

Breck·noch·shire (brĕk′nək shĭr/), *n.* a county in S Wales. 56,508 pop. (1951); 733 sq. mi. *Co. seat:* Brecon. Also, **Brech′noch, Brec·on** (brĕk′ən).

bred (brĕd), *v.* pt. and pp. of **breed.**

Bre·da (brā dä′), *n.* a city in S Netherlands. 96,317 (est. 1954).

brede (brĕd), *n. Archaic.* a braid. [var. of BRAID]

bree (brē), *n. Scot.* broth; juice. [cf. OE *briw* pottage]

breech (*n.* brĕch; *v.* brĕch, brĭch), *n.* **1.** the lower part of the trunk of the body behind; the posteriors or buttocks. **2.** the hinder or lower part of anything. **3.** *Ordn.* the mass of metal behind the bore of a cannon, or the part of a small arm back of the barrel. **4.** *Mach.* the lowest part of a pulley. —*v.t.* **5.** *Ordn.* to fit or furnish (a gun) with a breech. **6.** to clothe with breeches. [ME *breeche,* OE *brēc,* pl., c. Icel. *brœkr,* pl. of *brōk.* Cf. L *brācae,* pl., breeches, of Celtic orig.]

breech·block (brĕch′blŏk/), *n.* a piece of metal which closes the breech of the barrel in certain firearms.

breech·cloth (brĕch′klôth/, -klŏth/), *n.* a cloth worn about the breech. Also, **breech·clout** (brĕch′klout/).

breech·es (brĭch′Yz), *n.pl.* **1.** a garment worn by men (and by women for riding, etc.), covering the hips and thighs. **2.** trousers. [f. BREECH + *-es* (pl. ending)]

breeches buoy, *Naut.* a lifesaving apparatus, like a short pair of breeches, moving on a rope stretched from a wreck to the shore or another ship.

breech·ing (brĭch′ĭng, brē′chĭng), *n.* **1.** the part of a harness which passes around a horse's breech. See illus. under **harness. 2.** a smoke pipe connecting one or more boilers with a chimney. **3.** *Naval.* a strong rope fastened to a ship's side, to check the recoil of a gun or to secure it.

breech·load·er (brĕch′lō/dər), *n. Ordn.* a firearm, as a rifle, loaded at the breech.

breech·load·ing (brĕch′lō/dĭng), *adj. Ordn.* loaded at the breech.

Breeches buoy

breed (brēd), *v.,* bred, breeding, *n.* —*v.t.* **1.** to produce (offspring). **2.** to procure by the mating of parents; propagate. **3.** *Hort.* **a.** to cause to reproduce by controlled pollination. **b.** to improve by controlled pollination and selection. **4.** to raise (livestock, etc.). **5.** to procreate; engender. **6.** to cause; occasion; produce: *dirt breeds disease.* **7.** to be the native place or the source of: *stagnant water breeds mosquitoes.* **8.** to produce by training. —*v.i.* **9.** to produce offspring. **10.** to be engendered or produced; grow; develop. **11.** to procure the birth of young, as in raising stock. —*n.* **12.** *Genetics.* a relatively homogenous group of animals within a species, developed and maintained by man. **13.** race; lineage; strain. **14.** sort; kind. [ME *brede(n),* OE *brēdan* nourish, der. *brōd* brood] —breed′er, *n.*

breed·er (brē′dər) *n. Physics.* a nuclear reactor in which fissionable material is used as a source of neutrons to produce more nuclei than are consumed.

breed·ing (brē′dĭng), *n.* **1.** act of one who or that which breeds. **2.** the rearing of livestock to improve their quality or merit. **3.** *Hort.* the production of new forms by selection, crossing, and hybridizing. **4.** nurture; training. **5.** the results of training as shown in behavior and manners; manners; esp. good manners.

Breed's Hill (brēdz). See **Bunker Hill.**

breeze[1] (brēz), *n.* **1.** a wind or current of air, esp. a light or moderate one. **2.** *Meteorol.* any wind of Beaufort scale numbers 2 to 6 inclusive, comprising velocities from 4 to 31 miles per hour. **3.** *Chiefly Brit. Colloq.* a disturbance or quarrel. [t. Sp. (and Pg.): m. *briza*] —Syn. **1.** See **wind**[1].

breeze[2] (brēz), *n.* a gadfly. [ME *brese,* OE *breosa*]

breeze[3] (brēz), *n. Brit.* cinders; dust of charcoal, coke, or coal. [prob. t. F: m. *braise* live coals, cinders]

breeze·way (brēz′wā/), *n.* a roofed passageway, open at the sides, usually connecting the garage and house.

breez·y (brē′zĭ), *adj.,* breezier, breeziest. **1.** abounding in breezes; windy. **2.** fresh; sprightly. —breez′i·ly, *adv.* —breez′i·ness, *n.*

Bre·genz (brā′gĕnts), *n.* a city in W Austria: a port on the Lake of Constance. 20,277 (1951).

breg·ma (brĕg′mə), *n., pl.* -mata (-mə tə) *Craniom.* the point of junction of the sagittal and coronal sutures of the skull. [t. Gk.: front of the head] —breg·mat·ic (brĕg măt′Yk), *adj.*

Brem·en (brĕm′ən; *Ger.* brā′mən), *n.* **1.** a small state in N West Germany. 648,800 pop. (est. 1956); 156 sq. mi.

2. the capital of this state: a port on the Weser river; a member of the Hanseatic League. 508,637 (est. 1955).

Brem·er·ha·ven (brĕm′ər hä′vən; *Ger.* brā′mər hä′fən), *n.* a seaport in N West Germany at the mouth of the Weser river. 131,012 (est. 1955). Formerly, **Wesermünde.**

Brem·er·ton (brĕm′ər tən), *n.* a city in W Washington, on Puget Sound: navy yard; largest drydocks in the U.S. 28,922 (1960).

Bren gun (brĕn), *Brit.* a kind of machine gun. [f. *Br(no),* in Czechoslovakia, where they were first manufactured + *En(field),* where construction was perfected]

Bren·ner Pass (brĕn′ər), a pass in the Alps, on the Italian-Austrian border. 4494 ft. high-

[map: WEST GERMANY / SWITZ-ERLAND / AUSTRIA / BRENNER PASS / ITALY]

brent (brĕnt), *n.* brant.

br′er (brûr, brĕr), *n. Southern U.S. Dial.* brother.

Bre·scia (brĕ′shä), *n.* a city in N Italy, in Lombardy. 147,000 (est. 1954).

Bres·lau (brĕz′lou; *Ger.* brĕs′-), *n.* a city in SW Poland, on the Oder river: formerly in Germany. 374,000 (est. 1955). Polish, **Wroclaw.**

Brest (brĕst), *n.* a seaport in NW France: surrendered by German forces, Sept., 1944. 110,713 (1954).

Brest Li·tovsk (brĕst′ lĭ tôfsk′), a city in the W Soviet Union, on the Bug river: formerly in Poland; German-Russian peace treaty, 1918. 60,000 (est. 1948). Polish, **Brzesc nad Bugiem.**

Bre·tagne (brə tän′y), *n.* French name of **Brittany.**

breth·ren (brĕth′rĭn), *n.* **1.** pl. of **brother. 2.** fellow members. —Syn. **1, 2.** See **brother.**

Bret·on (brĕt′ən; *Fr.* brə tôn′), *n.* **1.** a native of Brittany. **2.** the Celtic language of Brittany. —*adj.* **3.** pertaining to Brittany, the Bretons, or their language. [t. F. See BRITON]

Bre·ton (brə tôn′), *n.* **André** (än drĕ′), born 1896, French poet, essayist, and critic.

Bret·ton Woods Conference (brĕt′ən), an international conference called at Bretton Woods, N.H., in July, 1944, to deal with international monetary and financial problems.

Breu·ghel (brœ′gəl); *n.* **Brueghel.**

breve (brēv), *n.* **1.** a mark (˘) placed over a vowel to show that it is short, as in ŭ. **2.** *Law.* **a.** an initial writ. **b.** a writ, as one issued by a court of law. **3.** *Music.* the longest modern note, equivalent to two semibreves or whole notes. See illus. under **note.** [t. It., g. L *brevis* short]

bre·vet (brə vĕt′ *or,* esp. *Brit.,* brĕv′Yt), *n., v.,* -vetted, -vetting *or* -veted, -veting. —*n.* **1.** a commission promoting a military officer to a higher rank without increase of pay and with limited exercise of the higher rank. —*v.t.* **2.** to appoint or promote by brevet. [ME, t. F, dim. of *bref* letter. See BRIEF]

brevi-, a word element meaning "short," as in *brevirostrate.* [t. L, comb. form of *brevis*]

bre·vi·ar·y (brē′vĭ ĕr/Y, brĕv′Y-), *n., pl.* -aries. **1.** *Rom. Cath. Ch.* a book of daily prayers and readings to be read by those in major orders. **2.** *Eccles.* a similar book in some other churches. [t. L: m.s. *breviārium* abridgment, prop. neut. of *breviārius* abridged]

bre·vier (brə vĭr′), *n.* a printing type (8 point) of a size between minion and bourgeois. [so called from use in printing breviaries; said to be t. G: breviary, t. F: m. *brēviaire,* g. L *brevis* short]

brev·i·ros·trate (brĕv′ə rŏs′trāt), *adj. Ornith.* having a short beak or bill.

brev·i·ty (brĕv′ə tĭ), *n., pl.* -ties. **1.** shortness of time or duration; briefness: *the brevity of human life.* **2.** condensation in speech; conciseness. [t. L: m. s. *brevitas,* der. *brevis* short]

—Syn. **2.** BREVITY, CONCISENESS refer to the use of few words in speaking. BREVITY emphasizes the short duration of speech: *reduced to extreme brevity.* CONCISENESS emphasizes compactness of expression: *clear despite conciseness.*

brew (brōō), *v.t.* **1.** to make (beer, ale, etc.) from malt, etc., by steeping, boiling, and fermentation. **2.** to prepare (a beverage) by or as by brewing. **3.** to concoct or contrive; bring about: *to brew mischief.* —*v.i.* **4.** to brew beer, ale, etc. **5. be brewing,** to be in preparation; be forming or gathering: *trouble was brewing.* —*n.* **6.** a quantity brewed in a single process. **7.** a particular brewing or variety of malt liquor. [ME *brewen,* OE *brēowan.* Cf. BROTH] —brew′er, *n.*

brew·age (brōō′Yj), *n.* a fermented liquor brewed from malt.

brew·er·y (brōō′ə rĭ, brŏŏr′Y), *n., pl.* -eries. an establishment for brewing malt liquors.

brew·ing (brōō′Yng), *n.* **1.** act of one who brews. **2.** a quantity brewed at once.

brew·is (brōō′Ys), *n. Now Dial.* **1.** broth. **2.** bread soaked in broth, gravy, etc. [ME *browes,* t. OF: m. *broez,* ult. t. OHG: m. *brod* BROTH]

Brew·ster (brōō′stər), *n.* **William,** 1560?–1644, English colonist: leader of the Pilgrims at Plymouth.

Brezh·nev (brĕzh nĕf′), *n.* **Le·o·nid Il·yich** (lĕ ô nēt′ il yēch′), born 1906, Russian politician: First Secretary of the Soviet Communist Party since 1964.

Bri·and (brē än′), *n.* **Aristide** (à rēs tēd′), 1862–1932, French statesman: minister of France 11 times.

bri·ar (brī′ər), *n.* brier. —bri′ar·y, *adj.*

b., blend of, blended; **c.,** cognate with; **d.,** dialect, dialectal; der., derived from; **f.,** formed from; **g.,** going back to; **m.,** modification of; **r.,** replacing; **s.,** stem of; **t.,** taken from; **?,** perhaps.   See the full key on inside cover.

Bri·ar·e·us (brī âr′y əs), *n.* *Gk. Myth.* a hundred-armed, fifty-headed giant who helped Zeus against the Titans. —**Bri·ar′e·an,** *adj.*

bri·ar·root (brī′ər rōōt′, -rŏŏt′), *n.* brierroot.

bri·ar·wood (brī′ər wŏŏd′), *n.* brierwood.

bribe (brīb), *n., v.,* **bribed, bribing. —***n.* 1. any valuable consideration given or promised for corrupt behavior in the performance of official or public duty. 2. anything given or serving to persuade or induce. —*v.t.* 3. to give or promise a bribe to. 4. to influence or corrupt by a bribe. —*v.i.* 5. to give bribes; practice bribery. [ME; cf. OF *bribe* piece of bread given to a beggar, *briber* beg, c. Sp. *bribar*] —**brib′a·ble,** *adj.* —**brib′a·bil′i·ty,** *n.* —**brib′er,** *n.*

brib·er·y (brī′bər), *n., pl.* **-eries.** act or practice of giving or accepting bribes.

bric-a-brac (brĭk′ə brăk′), *n.* miscellaneous ornamental articles of antiquarian, decorative, or other interest. [t. F]

brick (brĭk), *n.* 1. a block of clay, usually rectangular, hardened by drying in the sun or burning in a kiln, and used for building, paving, etc. 2. such blocks collectively. 3. the material. 4. any similar block. 5. *Colloq.* a good fellow. —*v.t.* 6. to lay, line, wall, or build with brick. [ME *bryke,* t. F: m. *brique,* t. MD: m. *bricke,* akin to BREAK] —**brick′like′,** *adj.*

brick·bat (brĭk′băt′), *n.* 1. a piece of broken brick, esp. one used as a missile. 2. any rocklike missile. 3. *Colloq.* an unkind remark; caustic criticism.

brick·kiln (brĭk′kĭl′, -kĭln′), *n.* a kiln or furnace in which bricks are baked or burned.

brick·lay·ing (brĭk′lā′ĭng), *n.* the art or occupation of laying bricks in construction. —**brick′lay′er,** *n.*

brick red, yellowish or brownish red.

brick·work (brĭk′wûrk′), *n.* brick construction (as contrasted with that of other materials).

brick·y (brĭk′ĭ), *adj.* consisting or made of bricks.

brick·yard (brĭk′yärd′), *n.* a place where bricks are made.

bri·cole (brĭ kōl′, brĭk′əl), *n.* 1. *Billiards.* a shot in which the cue ball strikes the cushion first. 2. an indirect action or unexpected stroke. [t. F, t. Pr.: m. *bricola* catapult]

brid·al (brī′dəl), *adj.* 1. of or pertaining to a bride or a wedding. —*n.* 2. a wedding. 3. *Archaic.* a wedding feast. [ME *bridale,* OE *brȳdealo* bride ale, f. *brȳd* bride + *ealo* ale, feast, assoc. with adj. suffix -AL¹]

Bridal Veil, a waterfall in Yosemite National Park, California. 620 ft. high.

bridal wreath, any of several shrubs of the rosaceous genus *Spiraea,* bearing sprays of small white flowers, esp. *S. prunifolia.*

bride¹ (brīd), *n.* a woman newly married, or about to be married. [ME; OE *brȳd,* c. G *braut*]

bride² (brīd), *n.* 1. (in needlework, lacemaking, etc.) a bar, link, or tie. 2. an ornamental bonnet string. [t. F: bridle, string, tie, t. Gmc. See BRIDLE]

Bride (brīd), *n.* Saint. See Brigid, Saint.

bride·groom (brīd′grōōm′, -grŏŏm′),*n.* a man newly married, or about to be married. [var. of ME *bridegome,* OE *brȳdguma,* f. *brȳd* bride + *guma* man (c. L *homo*)]

brides·maid (brīdz′mād′), *n.* a young unmarried woman who attends the bride at a wedding.

bride·well (brīd′wěl, -wəl), *n.* 1. *Brit.* a house of correction for the confinement of vagrants and disorderly persons (so called from a former prison in London at St. Bride's well). 2. *Colloq.* any prison or house of correction.

bridge¹ (brĭj), *n., v.,* **bridged, bridging. —***n.* 1. a structure spanning a river, chasm, road, or the like, and affording passage. 2. *Naut.* a raised platform from side to side of a ship above the rail, for the officer in charge. 3. *Anat.* the ridge or upper line of the nose. 4. *Dentistry.* an artificial replacement of a missing tooth or teeth, supported by natural teeth adjacent to the space. A bridge may be fixed or removable. 5. *Music.* a piece raising the strings of a musical instrument above the sounding board. 6. (on eyeglasses) the part which joins the two lenses and rests on the bridge or side of the nose. 7. *Elect.* an instrument for measuring electrical impedance. 8. *Railroads.* an overhead structure above railroad tracks on which signals are placed. 9. *Metall.* a ridge or wall-like projection of fire brick or the like, at either end of the hearth in a metallurgical furnace. 10. *Billiards.* a notched piece of wood with a long handle, sometimes used to support a cue when the distance is otherwise too great to reach; rest. —*v.t.* 11. to make a bridge over; span. 12. to make (a way) by a bridge. [ME *brigge,* OE *brycg,* c. G *brücke*] —**bridge′a·ble,** *adj.*

bridge² (brĭj), *n.* *Cards.* a game derived from whist in which one partnership plays to fulfill a certain declaration against opponents acting as defenders. See contract (def. 6) and **auction bridge.** [orig. uncert.]

bridge-board (brĭj′bōrd′), *n.* a notched board at the side of a wooden stair, supporting the treads and risers.

bridge-head (brĭj′hĕd′), *n.* 1. a position held on the enemy side of a river or defile, to cover the crossing of friendly troops. 2. a defensive work covering or protecting the end of a bridge toward the enemy.

Bridge of Sighs, a bridge in Venice through which prisoners were led for trial in the ducal palace.

Bridge·port (brĭj′pōrt′), *n.* a seaport in SW Connecticut, on Long Island Sound. 156,748 (1960).

Bridg·es (brĭj′ĭz), *n.* **Robert,** 1844–1930, British poet laureate, 1913–30.

Bridges Creek, an estate in E Virginia, on the Potomac: birthplace of George Washington; restored as a national monument, 1932. Now called **Wakefield.**

Bridg·et (brĭj′ĭt), *n.* **Saint.** See Brigid, Saint.

Bridge·town (brĭj′toun′), *n.* a seaport in and the capital of Barbados, in the Federation of the West Indies. 18,500 (est. 1955).

bridge·work (brĭj′wûrk′), *n.* 1. *Dentistry.* **a.** dental bridges collectively. **b.** any of several different types of dental bridges. 2. the building of bridges.

bridg·ing (brĭj′ĭng), *n.* *Bldg. Trades.* a piece or an arrangement of pieces fixed between floor or roof joists to keep them in place.

bri·dle (brī′dəl), *n., v.,* **-dled, -dling. —***n.* 1. the part of the harness of a horse, etc., about the head, consisting usually of headstall, bit, and reins, and used to restrain and guide the animal. 2. anything that restrains or curbs. 3. *Mach.* a link, flange, or other attachment for limiting the movement of any part of a machine. 4. *Naut.* a short chain or rope span both ends of which are made fast. 5. a bridling, or drawing up the head, as in disdain. —*v.t.* 6. to put a bridle on. 7. to control as with a bridle; restrain; curb. —*v.i.* 8. to draw up the head and draw in the chin, as in disdain or resentment. [ME; OE *brīdel,* earlier *brigdils*] —**bri′dler,** *n.*

bridle path, a path used by horseback riders.

bri·doon (brĭ dōōn′), *n.* a light snaffle or bit without crossbars, and on a rein, used in certain military bridles in addition to the principal bit and its rein. [t. F: m. *bridon,* der. *bride* bridle]

Brie cheese (brē), a kind of salted, white, soft cheese, ripened with bacterial action, waxy to semiliquid, originating in Brie, a district in northern France.

brief (brēf), *adj.* 1. of little duration. 2. using few words; concise; succinct. 3. abrupt or curt. —*n.* 4. a short and concise writing or statement. 5. an outline, the form of which is determined by set rules, of all the possible arguments and information on one side of a controversy: *a debater's brief.* 6. *Law.* **a.** a writ summoning one to answer to any action. **b.** a memorandum of points of fact or of law for use in conducting a case. 7. briefing. 8. *Rom. Cath. Ch.* a papal letter less formal than a bull, sealed with the Pope's signet ring or stamped with the device borne on this ring. 9. *Obs.* a letter. 10. **in brief,** in few words; in short. —*v.t.* 11. to make an abstract or summary of. 12. to instruct by a brief or briefing. 13. *Law.* to retain as advocate in a suit. [t. F, g. L *brevis*] —**brief′ly,** *adv.* —**brief′ness,** *n.* —**Syn.** 1. short-lived, fleeting, transitory, ephemeral. See **short.** 2. terse, compact. 4. See **summary.**

brief case, a flat, rectangular leather case used for carrying documents, books, manuscripts, etc.

brief·ing (brē′fĭng), *n.* a short, accurate summary of the details of a flight mission, given to the crew of a combat plane just before it takes off on a mission.

brief·less (brēf′lĭs), *adj.* having no brief, as a lawyer without clients.

brief of title, an abstract of the legal documents concerning the conferring and transferring of ownership of a given piece of property.

bri·er¹ (brī′ər), *n.* 1. a prickly plant or shrub, esp. the sweetbrier, or the greenbriers. 2. a tangled mass of prickly plants. 3. a thorny stem or twig. Also, **briar.** [ME *brere,* OE *brēr*] —**bri′er·y,** *adj.*

bri·er² (brī′ər), *n.* 1. the white heath, *Erica arborea,* of France and Corsica, whose woody root is used for making tobacco pipes. 2. a pipe made of this woody root. Also, **briar.** [t. F: m. *bruyère* heath, g. a LL deriv. of Gallic *brūcus* heather]

bri·er·root (brī′ər rōōt′, -rŏŏt′), *n.* 1. the root wood of the brier. 2. certain other woods from which tobacco pipes are made. 3. a pipe made of brierroot. Also, **briarroot.**

bri·er·wood (brī′ər wŏŏd′), *n.* brierroot. Also, **briarwood.**

Bri·eux (brē œ′), *n.* **Eugène** (œ zhĕn′), 1858–1932, French dramatist.

brig¹ (brĭg), *n.* *Naut.* 1. a two-masted vessel square-rigged on both masts. 2. the compartment of a ship where prisoners are confined. [short for BRIGANTINE]

brig² (brĭg), *n., v.* *Scot. and N. Eng.* bridge.

Brig., *Mil.* 1. Brigade. 2. Brigadier.

bri·gade (brĭ gād′), *n., v.,* **-gaded, -gading. —***n.* 1. a unit consisting of several regiments, squadrons, groups, or battalions. 2. a large body of troops. 3. a body of individuals organized for a special purpose: *a fire brigade.* —*v.t.* 4. to form into a brigade. 5. to group together. [t. F, t. It.: m. *brigata* troop, der. *brigare* strive, contend]

brig·a·dier (brĭg′ə dîr′), *n.* 1. *Brit. Army.* a rank between colonel and major general. 2. *Colloq. U.S. Army.* a brigadier general. 3. (formerly) a noncommissioned rank in the Napoleonic armies. [t. F, der. *brigade* BRIGADE]

brigadier general, *pl.* **brigadier generals.** *U.S. Army.* an officer between colonel and major general.

ăct, āble, dâre, ärt; ĕbb, ēqual; ĭf, īce; hŏt, ōver, ôrder, oil, bŏŏk, ōōze, out; ŭp, ūse, ûrge; ə = a in alone; ch, chief; g, give; ng, ring; sh, shoe; th, thin; ŧh, that; zh, vision. See the full key on inside cover.

brig·and (brĭg'ənd), n. a bandit; one of a gang of robbers in mountain or forest regions. [ME *brigant*, t. OF. t. It.: m. *brigante*, der. *brigare*. See BRIGADE] —**brig'and·ish,** adj.

brig·and·age (brĭg'ən dĭj), n. the practice of brigands; plundering. Also, **brig'and·ism.**

brig·an·dine (brĭg'ən dēn', -dĭn'), n. Armor. a flexible body armor of overlapping steel plates riveted to the exterior covering of linen, velvet, leather, etc. [late ME *brigandyne,* t. OF: m. *brigandine*]

brig·an·tine (brĭg'ən tēn', -tĭn'), n. Naut. a two-masted vessel in which the foremast is square-rigged and the mainmast bears a fore-and-aft mainsail and square topsails. [t. F: m. *brigantin,* t. It.: m. *brigantino,* der. *brigante* BRIGAND]

bright (brīt), adj. 1. radiating or reflecting light; luminous; shining. 2. filled with light. 3. vivid or brilliant, as color. 4. clear or translucent, as liquids. 5. radiant or splendid. 6. illustrious or glorious, as a period. 7. quick-witted or intelligent. 8. clever or witty, as a remark. 9. animated; lively; cheerful, as a person. 10. characterized by happiness or gladness. 11. favorable or auspicious: *bright prospects.* —n. 12. Archaic. brightness; splendor. —adv. 13. in a bright manner; brightly. [ME; OE *bryht, beorht,* c. OHG *beraht,* Icel. *bjartr,* Goth. *bairhts*] —**bright'ly,** adv. —**Syn.** 1. refulgent, effulgent, lustrous, lucent, beaming, lambent. BRIGHT, BRILLIANT, RADIANT, SHINING refer to that which gives forth, is filled with, or reflects light. BRIGHT suggests the general idea: *bright flare, stars, mirror.* BRILLIANT implies a strong, unusual, or sparkling brightness, often changeful or varied and too strong to be agreeable: *brilliant sunlight.* RADIANT implies the pouring forth of steady rays of light, esp. such as is agreeable to the eyes: *a radiant face.* SHINING implies giving forth or reflecting a strong or steady light: *shining eyes.* —**Ant.** 1. dull, dim.

Bright (brīt), n. **John,** 1811–89, British orator and statesman.

bright·en (brī'tən), v.i., v.t. to become or make bright or brighter.

bright·ness (brīt'nĭs), n. 1. bright quality. 2. luminosity apart from hue; value. Pure white is of maximum brightness and pure black is of zero brightness.

Brigh·ton (brī'tən), n. 1. a city in SE England, on the English channel: seaside resort. 158,700 (est. 1956). 2. a city in SE Australia, near Melbourne. 39,769 (1947).

Bright's disease, Pathol. a disease characterized by albuminuria and heightened blood pressure. [named after R. *Bright,* British physician, who described it]

Brig·id (brĭj'ĭd, brē'ĭd), n. **Saint,** A.D. 453–523, Irish abbess: a patron saint of Ireland. Also, **Bride, Bridget, Brig·it** (brĭj'ĭt, brē'ĭt).

brill (brĭl), n., pl. **brill** or **brills,** a European flatfish, *Scophthalmus rhombus,* closely allied to the turbot.

Brill (brĭl), n. **Abraham Arden,** 1874–1948, U.S. psychoanalyst and author, born in Austria.

bril·liance (brĭl'yəns), n. 1. great brightness; splendor; luster. 2. remarkable excellence or distinction; conspicuous mental ability. 3. Color. brightness (def. 2). Also, **bril'lian·cy.** —**Syn.** 1. radiance, effulgence.

bril·liant (brĭl'yənt), adj. 1. shining brightly; sparkling; glittering; lustrous. 2. distinguished; illustrious: *a brilliant achievement.* 3. having or showing great intelligence or keenness. —n. 4. a diamond (or other gem) of a particular cut, typically round in outline and shaped like two pyramids united at their bases, the top one cut off near the base and the bottom one close to the apex, with many facets on the slopes. 5. this form. 6. a printing type (about 3½ point). [t. F: m. *brillant,* ppr. of *briller,* corresponding to It. *brillare* shine, sparkle, ? g. LL *brillāre,* der. L *bēryllus* BERYL] —**bril'liant·ly,** adv. —**bril'liant·ness,** n. —**Syn.** 1. See bright.

bril·lian·tine (brĭl'yən tēn'), n. 1. a toilet preparation for the hair. 2. a dress fabric resembling alpaca. [t. F]

brim[1] (brĭm), n., v., **brimmed, brimming.** —n. 1. the upper edge of anything hollow; rim: *the brim of a cup.* 2. a projecting edge: *the brim of a hat.* 3. Archaic. edge or margin. —v.i. 4. to be full to the brim: *a brimming glass.* —v.t. 5. to fill to the brim. [ME *brimme* shore, OE *brim* sea. Cf. Icel. *brim* surf] —**Syn.** 1. See rim.

brim[2] (brĭm), n. Southern U.S. bream (def. 4). [var. of BREAM[1]]

brim·ful (brĭm'fŏŏl'), adj. full to the brim; all full.

brim·mer (brĭm'ər), n. a cup or bowl full to the brim.

brim·stone (brĭm'stōn'), n. 1. sulfur. 2. virago. [ME *brinston,* etc., f. *brinn(en)* burn + *ston* stone] —**brim'ston·y,** adj.

Brin·di·si (brēn'dē zē), n. a seaport in SE Italy: an important Roman city and naval station. 63,000 (est. 1954). Ancient, **Brundisium.**

brin·dle (brĭn'dəl), n. 1. a brindled coloring. 2. brindled animal. [back formation from BRINDLED]

brin·dled (brĭn'dəld), adj. gray or tawny with darker streaks or spots. Also, **brin·ded** (brĭn'dĭd). [cf. Icel. *brönddöttr;* ? akin to BRAND]

brine (brīn), n., v., **brined, brining.** —n. 1. water saturated or strongly impregnated with salt. 2. water strongly salted for pickling. 3. the sea or ocean. 4. the water of the sea. —v.t. 5. to treat with or steep in brine. [ME; OE *brȳne,* c. D *brijn*] —**brin'ish,** adj.

Bri·nell machine (brĭ nĕl'), Metall. an instrument for calculating the hardness (**Brinell hardness**) of metal, esp. heat-treated steels, by forcing a hard steel or tungsten carbide ball of standard dimensions into the material being tested, under a fixed pressure. [named after J. A. *Brinell* (1849–1925), Swedish engineer]

Brinell number, Metall. a numerical expression of Brinell hardness, found by determining the diameter of a dent made by the Brinell machine.

bring (brĭng), v.t., **brought, bringing.** 1. to cause to come with oneself; take along to the place or person sought; conduct or convey. 2. to cause to come, as to a recipient or possessor to the mind or knowledge, into a particular position or state, to a particular opinion or decision, or into existence, view, action, or effect. 3. to lead or induce: *he couldn't bring himself to do it.* 4. Law. to put forward before a tribunal; declare in or as if in court. 5. Some special verb phrases are:

bring about, to cause; accomplish.

bring around or **round,** 1. to convince of an opinion. 2. to restore to consciousness, as after a faint.

bring forth, 1. to produce. 2. to give rise to; cause.

bring forward, 1. to produce to view. 2. to adduce.

bring out, 1. to expose; show; reveal. 2. to publish.

bring to, 1. to bring back to consciousness. 2. Naut. to head a ship close to or into the wind and kill her headway by manipulating helm and sails.

bring up, 1. to care for during childhood; rear. 2. to introduce to notice or consideration. 3. to cause to advance, as troops. [ME *bringen,* OE *bringan,* c. G *bringen*] —**bring'er,** n. —**Syn.** 1. transport. BRING, FETCH imply conveying or conducting to or towards the place where the speaker is. To BRING is simply so to convey or conduct: *bring it to me, I'm permitted to bring my dog here with me.* (It is the opposite of TAKE, which means to convey or conduct away from the place where the speaker is: *bring it back here, take it back there.*) FETCH is chiefly British and means to go, get, and bring back: *fetch it here tomorrow.* —**Ant.** 1. take.

bring·ing-up (brĭng'ĭng ŭp'), n. childhood training or care.

brink (brĭngk), n. 1. the edge or margin of a steep place or of land bordering water. 2. any extreme edge; verge. [ME, t. Scand.; cf. Dan. *brink*]

brin·y (brī'nĭ), adj., **brinier, briniest.** of or like brine; salty: *a briny taste.* —**brin'i·ness,** n.

bri·oche (brē ōsh', -ŏsh; Fr. brē ōsh'), n. a kind of light, sweet bun or roll, raised with eggs and yeast. [t. F, der. *brier,* d. form of *broyer* knead]

bri·o·lette (brē'ə lĕt'; Fr. brē ô-), n. a pear-shaped gem having its entire surface cut with triangular facets. [t. F]

bri·quette (brĭ kĕt'), n. a molded block of compacted coal dust for fuel. Also, **bri·quet'.** [t. F]

bri·sance (brē zäns'), n. the shattering power of high explosives.

Bris·bane (brĭz'bān, -bən), n. a seaport in E Australia: capital of Queensland. 501,871 with suburbs (1954).

Bri·se·is (brī sē'ĭs), n. (in the *Iliad*) a beautiful maiden captured by Achilles: the cause of his quarrel with Agamemnon.

brisk (brĭsk), adj. 1. quick and active; lively: *a brisk breeze, a brisk walk.* 2. sharp and stimulating: *brisk weather.* 3. (of liquors) effervescing vigorously: *brisk cider.* —v.t., v.i. 4. to make or become brisk; liven (up). [? akin to BRUSQUE] —**brisk'ly,** adv. —**brisk'ness,** n. —**Syn.** 1. spry, energetic. —**Ant.** 1. languid.

bris·ket (brĭs'kĭt), n. the breast of an animal, or the part of the breast lying next to the ribs. [ME *brusket,* appar. t. OF: m. *bruschet,* t. Gmc.; cf. LG *bröske,* Icel. *brjōsk* cartilage]

bris·ling (brĭs'lĭng), n. the sprat.

bris·tle (brĭs'əl), n., v., **-tled, -tling.** —n. 1. one of the short, stiff, coarse hairs of certain animals, esp. hogs, used extensively in making brushes, etc. 2. any short, stiff hair or hairlike appendage (often used facetiously of human hair). —v.i. 3. to stand or rise stiffly, like bristles. 4. to erect the bristles, as an irritated animal (often fol. by up): *the hog bristled up.* 5. to be thickly set with something suggestive of bristles: *the plain bristled with bayonets, the enterprise bristled with difficulties.* 6. to be visibly roused or stirred (usually fol. by up). —v.t. 7. to erect like bristles: *the rooster bristled up his crest.* 8. to furnish with a bristle or bristles. 9. to make bristly. [ME *bristel,* f. *brist* (OE *byrst*) + *-el,* dim. suffix] —**bris'tly,** adj.

bris·tle·tail (brĭs'əl tāl'), n. any of various wingless insects of the order *Thysanura,* having long bristlelike caudal appendages.

Bris·tol (brĭs'təl), n. 1. a seaport in SW England, on the Avon river near its confluence with the Severn estuary. 440,500 (est. 1956). 2. a city in central Connecticut. 45,499 (1960).

Bristol board, a fine, smooth kind of pasteboard, sometimes glazed.

Bristol Channel, an arm of the Atlantic between Wales and SW England.

brit (brĭt), n. 1. small animals forming the food of whalebone whales. 2. the young of herring and sprat.

Brit., 1. Britain. 2. British.

Brit·ain (brĭt'ən), n. 1. Great Britain. 2. Britannia (def. 1a).

Bri·tan·ni·a (brĭ tăn'ĭ ə, -tăn'yə), n. 1. Roman name for: **a.** the largest island of the British Isles. **b.** the Roman province in that island. 2. British Empire. 3. Great Britain. 4. *Chiefly Poetic.* England, Scotland,

and Ireland. **5.** the feminine personification of Great Britain or the British Empire. **6.** Britannia metal. [t. L]

Britannia metal, a white alloy of tin, copper, and antimony, usually with small amounts of zinc, etc.

Bri·tan·nic (brǐ tăn′ǐk), *adj.* **1.** British: *His Britannic Majesty.* **2.** Brythonic. [t. L: s. *Britannicus*]

Brit·i·cism (brǐt′ə sǐz′əm), *n.* an English usage peculiar to British people. The use of *lift* (cf. U.S. *elevator*) is a typical Briticism.

Brit·ish (brǐt′ǐsh), *adj.* **1.** of or pertaining to Great Britain, the British Empire, or its inhabitants. **2.** of or pertaining to the ancient Britons. —*n.* **3.** the British people, taken collectively. **4.** the language spoken in southern England (now regarded as the English standard). **5.** the language of the ancient Britons and the languages which have developed from it, namely Welsh, Cornish (no longer spoken), and Breton. [ME *Brytysshe,* OE *Bryttisc,* der. *Bryttas, Brettas* Britons, from Celtic]

British America, British North America.

British Columbia, a province in W Canada, on the Pacific coast. 1,230,000 (est. 1953); 366,255 sq. mi. *Cap.:* Victoria.

British Commonwealth of Nations, a group of nations linked by a common allegiance to the British crown: the United Kingdom of Great Britain and Northern Ireland, Canada, Australia, New Zealand, India, Pakistan, Ceylon, Ghana, Nigeria, Rhodesia, Sierra Leone, Cyprus, Jamaica, Trinidad and Tobago, Uganda, Malaysia, Kenya, Malawi, Gambia, Tanzania, Zambia, and the Colonies and Protectorates.

British East Africa, a former comprehensive term for Kenya, Tanganyika Territory, Uganda, and Zanzibar.

British Empire, formerly the territories under the leadership or control of the British crown, including those in the British Commonwealth of Nations together with their colonies, protectorates, dependencies, and trusteeships.

Brit·ish·er (brǐt′ǐsh ər), *n.* a native or inhabitant o Britain.

British Guiana, former name of **Guyana.**

British Honduras, a British crown colony in N Central America. 79,000 pop. (est. 1955); 8867 sq. mi. *Cap.:* Belize.

British India, that part of India (17 provinces) which prior to 1947 was subject to British law; now divided between India and Pakistan.

British Isles, a group of islands in W Europe: Great Britain, Ireland, the Isle of Man, and adjacent islands. 54,261,000 pop. (est. 1956); 120,592 sq. mi.

British Malaya, a comprehensive term for that part of the Malay peninsula formerly under British influence which now is part of the federation of Malaysia.

British North America, 1. Canada. **2.** all parts of the British Empire in or near North America.

British North Borneo. See **Sabah.**

British Somaliland, a former British protectorate in E Africa, on the Gulf of Aden: now part of the republic of Somalia.

British thermal unit, the amount of heat required to raise the temperature of one pound of water one degree Fahrenheit.

British West Africa, a former comprehensive term for Nigeria, Sierra Leone, Gambia, and the Gold Coast.

British West Indies, formerly, the British islands in the West Indies, including the Bahama Islands, Jamaica, Barbados, Trinidad, Tobago, and islands of the Leeward and Windward groups.

Brit·on (brǐt′ən), *n.* **1.** a native or inhabitant of Great Britain, or (sometimes) of the British Empire. **2.** one of the Celtic people who in early times occupied the southern part of the island of Britain. [t. ML: s. *Brito;* r. ME *Breton,* t. OF, g. L *Bretto*]

brits·ka (brǐts′kə), *n.* an open carriage with a calash top. Also, **britzka, britzska.** [t. Pol.: m. *bryczka,* dim. of *bryka* freight wagon]

Brit·ta·ny (brǐt′ə nǐ), *n.* a peninsula in NW France between the English Channel and the Bay of Biscay: a former duchy and province. French, **Bretagne.**

Brit·ten (brǐt′ən), *n.* Benjamin, born 1913, British composer, pianist and conductor.

brit·tle (brǐt′əl), *adj.* **1.** breaking readily with a comparatively smooth fracture, as glass. —*n.* **2.** a confection of melted sugar, usually with nuts, brittle when cooled: *peanut brittle.* [ME *britel,* der. OE *brēotan* break] —**brit′tle·ness,** *n.* —Syn. 1. fragile See frail¹.

Brit·ton (brǐt′ən), *n.* Nathaniel Lord (nə thăn′yəl), 1859–1934, U. S. botanist.

britz·ka (brǐts′kə), *n.* britska. Also, **britz′ska.**

Br·no (bûr′nô), *n.* a city in central Czechoslovakia: the capital of Moravia. 273,127 (1947). German, **Brunn.**

bro., *pl.* **bros.** brother. Also, **Bro.**

broach (brōch), *n.* **1.** *Mach.* an elongated and tapered tool with serrations which enlarges a given hole as the tool is pulled through the hole, which may be round, square, etc. See illus. under **reamer.** **2.** a spit for roasting meat. **3.** a gimlet for tapping casks. —*v.t.* **4.** to enlarge and finish with a broach. **5.** to tap or pierce. **6.** to draw as by tapping: *to broach liquor.* **7.** to mention or suggest for the first time: *to broach a subject.* —*v.i.* **8.** *Naut.* (of a ship) to veer to windward, esp. so as to be broadside to the wind (fol. by *to*). [ME *broche,* t. OF, g. L *brocc(h)us* projecting] —**broach′er,** *n.*

broad (brôd), *adj.* **1.** of great breadth: *a broad river or street.* **2.** of great extent; large: *the broad expanse of ocean.* **3.** widely diffused; open; full: *broad daylight.* **4.** not limited or narrow; liberal: *broad experience.* **5.** of extensive range or scope: *broad sympathies.* **6.** main or general: *the broad outlines of a subject.* **7.** plain or clear: *a broad hint.* **8.** bold; plain-spoken. **9.** indelicate; indecent: *a broad joke.* **10.** (of conversation) rough; coarse; countrified. **11.** unconfined; free; unrestrained: *broad mirth.* **12.** (of pronunciation) strongly dialectal: *broad Scots.* **13.** broad a, the *a* (ä) sound in *father,* esp. in a word customarily pronounced, in standard American usage, with the *a* (ă) of *glad,* as in *half* or *can't* or *laughable.* —*adv.* **14.** fully: *broad awake.* —*n.* **15.** the broad part of anything. [ME *brood,* OE *brād,* c. G *breit*] —**broad′ish,** *adj.* —**broad′ly,** *adv.* —Syn. 1. See **wide.** **2.** extensive, ample, vast. —Ant. 1. narrow.

broad arrow, 1. a mark of the shape of a broad arrowhead, placed upon British governmental stores. **2.** *Archery.* an arrow having an expanded head.

broad·ax (brôd′ăks′), *n.* **1.** an ax for hewing timber. **2.** a battle-ax. Also, **broad′axe′.**

broad bean, a variety of edible bean, *Vicia faba.*

broad·bill (brôd′bǐl′), *n.* **1.** any of various birds with a broad bill, as the scaup duck, shoveler, and spoonbill. **2.** a swordfish.

broad·brim (brôd′brǐm′), *n.* **1.** a hat with a broad brim, as that worn by Quakers. **2.** (*cap.*) *U.S. Colloq.* a Friend or Quaker.

broad·cast (brôd′kăst′, -käst′), *v.,* **-cast** or **-casted, -casting,** *n., adj., adv.* —*v.t.* **1.** to send (messages, speeches, music, etc.) by radio. **2.** to cast or scatter abroad over an area, as seed in sowing. **3.** to spread or disseminate widely: *to broadcast gossip.* —*v.i.* **4.** to send radio messages, speeches, etc. **5.** to scatter or disseminate something widely. —*n.* **6.** that which is broadcast. **7.** *Radio.* **a.** the broadcasting of radio messages, speeches, etc. **b.** a radio program. **c.** a single period of broadcasting. **8.** a method of sowing by scattering seed. —*adj.* **9.** sent out by broadcasting, as radio messages, speeches, music, etc. **10.** of or pertaining to broadcasting. **11.** cast abroad or all over an area, as seed sown thus. **12.** widely spread or disseminated: *broadcast discontent.* —*adv.* **13.** so as to reach an indefinite number of radio receiving stations or instruments in various directions. **14.** so as to be cast abroad over an area: *seed sown broadcast.* —**broad′cast′er,** *n.*

Broad Church, *Eccles.* those members of the Anglican communion who favor a liberal interpretation of doctrine and ritual, and such conditions of membership as will promote wide Christian inclusiveness. —**Broad′-Church′,** *adj.* —**Broad′-Church′man,** *n.*

broad·cloth (brôd′klôth′, -klŏth′), *n.* **1.** cotton broadcloth, cotton shirting or dress material, usually mercerized, resembling fine poplin. **2.** rayon broadcloth, spun rayon fabric similar to cotton broadcloth. **3.** woolen broadcloth, woolen dress goods with nap laid parallel with selvage.

broad·en (brôd′ən), *v.i., v.t.* to become or make broad; widen.

broad gauge. See **gauge** (def. 10). Also, **broad′gage′.** —**broad′-gauged′, broad′-gaged′,** *adj.*

broad jump, *Sports.* **1.** a jump horizontally, either from rest (**standing broad jump**) or with a running start (**running broad jump**). **2.** an athletic contest for the longest such jump.

broad·leaf (brôd′lēf′), *n.* any of several cigar tobaccos which have broad leaves.

broad·loom carpet (brôd′lōōm′), any kind of carpet, from 54 inches to 18 feet wide, woven on a broad loom to avoid the need for seams.

broad·mind·ed (brôd′mīn′dǐd), *adj.* free from prejudice or bigotry; liberal; tolerant. —**broad′-mind′ed·ly,** *adv.* —**broad′-mind′ed·ness,** *n.*

broad seal, the official seal of a country or state.

broad·side (brôd′sīd′), *n.* **1.** *Naut.* the whole side of a ship above the water line, from the bow to the quarter. **2.** *Naval.* **a.** all the guns that can be fired to one side of a ship. **b.** a simultaneous discharge of all the guns on one side of a vessel of war. **3.** any comprehensive attack, as of criticism. **4.** Also, **broad·sheet** (brôd′shēt′). a sheet of paper, esp. of large size, printed on one side only, as for distribution or posting. **5.** any broad surface or side, as of a house.

broad·sword (brôd′sōrd′), *n.* a straight, broad, flat, sword, usually with a basket hilt.

Broad·way (brôd′wā′). *n.* a street in New York City, famous for its theaters.

Brob·ding·nag (bröb′dĭng năg′), n. the region in Swift's *Gulliver's Travels* where everything was of enormous size. —**Brob′ding·nag′i·an**, adj., n.

bro·cade (brō kād′), n., v., **-caded, -cading.** —n. 1. fabric woven with an elaborate design from any yarn. The right side has a raised effect. —v.t. 2. to weave with a design or figure. [t. Sp.: m. *brocado*, c. It. *broccato* der. *broccare* interweave with gold or silver, der. L *brocc(h)us*. See BROACH] —**bro·cad′ed**, adj.

broc·a·tel (brŏk′ə tĕl′), n. 1. a kind of brocade, in which the design is in high relief. 2. an ornamental marble with variegated coloring esp. from Italy and Spain. Also, **broc′a·telle′.** [t. F.: m. *brocatelle*, t. It.: m. *broccatello*]

broc·co·li (brŏk′ə lĭ), n. 1. a plant of the mustard family, *Brassica oleracea* var. *botrytis*, resembling the cauliflower. 2. a form of this plant which does not produce a head, the green saps and the stalk of which are a common vegetable. Also, **broccoli sprouts.** [t. It., pl. of *broccolo* sprout, der. L *broccus* projecting]

bro·ché (brō shā′; *Fr.* brō shě′), adj. woven with a pattern; brocaded. [t. F, pp. of *brocher* BROCADE, v.]

bro·chette (brō shĕt′; *Fr.* brō-), n. 1. a skewer, for use in cookery. 2. **en brochette** (ĕn; *Fr.* än), on a small spit. [t. F, dim. of *broché* spit. See BROACH]

bro·chure (brō shoõr′; *Fr.* brō shyr′), n. a pamphlet. [t. F, der. *brocher* stitch]

Brock·en (brŏk′ən), n. a mountain in E West Germany and W East Germany: the highest peak in the Harz Mountains; prominent in German folklore. 3745 ft.

brock·et (brŏk′ĭt), n. 1. a small swamp deer, genus *Mazama*, of tropical America. 2. the male red deer in the second year, with the first growth of straight horns.

Brock·ton (brŏk′tən), n. a city in E Massachusetts. 72,813 (1960).

bro·gan (brō′gən), n. a coarse, stout shoe. [t. Irish]

Bro·glie (brō glē′), n. **Achille Charles Léonce Victor de** (å shĕl′ shärl lĕ ôns′ vĕk tôr′ də), 1785–1870, French statesman.

brogue¹ (brōg), n. an Irish accent in the pronunciation of English. [appar. special use of BROGUE²]

brogue² (brōg), n. a strongly made, comfortable type of ordinary shoe, often with decorative perforations on the vamp and upper. [t. Irish, Gaelic: m. *brōg* shoe]

broi·der (broi′dər), v.t. Archaic. to embroider. [ME *broudre(n)*, t. OF: m. *bro(u)der*, *brosder*, of Gmc. orig.] —**broi′der·y**, n.

broil¹ (broil), v.t. 1. to cook by direct heat, as on a gridiron or in an oven broiler; grill. 2. to scorch; make very hot. —v.i. 3. to be subjected to great heat. 4. to burn with impatience, etc. —n. 5. a broiling. 6. something broiled. [ME *brule(n)*, ? t. OF: m. *bruiller* burn, g. LL verb, prob. b. Gmc. *brand* a burning and L *ustulāre* burn a little (der. *ūrere* burn)]

broil² (broil), n. 1. an angry quarrel or struggle; a disturbance; a tumult. —v.i. 2. to quarrel; brawl. [ME, t. OF: m. *brouiller* disorder, prob. der. *bro(u)* broth, t. OHG: m. *brod*. Cf. BREWIS]

broil·er (broil′ər), n. 1. any device for broiling meats or fish; a grate or pan for broiling. 2. a young chicken suitable for broiling.

bro·kage (brō′kĭj), n. brokerage.

broke (brōk), v. 1. pt. of **break.** 2. Archaic and still often Colloq. pp. of **break.** —adj. 3. Slang. out of money; bankrupt.

bro·ken (brō′kən), v. 1. pp. of **break.** —adj. 2. reduced to fragments. 3. ruptured; torn; fractured. 4. changing direction abruptly: *a broken line.* 5. fragmentary or incomplete: *a broken set.* 6. infringed or violated. 7. interrupted or disconnected: *broken sleep.* 8. weakened in strength, spirit, etc. 9. reduced to submission; tamed: *the horse was not yet broken to the saddle.* 10. imperfectly spoken, as language. 11. ruined; bankrupt: *the broken fortunes of his family.* —**bro′ken·ly**, adv. —**bro′ken·ness**, n.

bro·ken-down (brō′kən doun′), adj. shattered or collapsed; having given way.

bro·ken-heart·ed (brō′kən här′tĭd), adj. crushed by grief.

Broken Hill, a city in SE Australia, in New South Wales: the center of a rich mining district. 31,351 (1954).

broken wind, heaves. —**bro′ken-wind′ed**, adj.

bro·ker (brō′kər), n. 1. an agent who buys or sells for a principal on a commission basis without having title to the property. 2. a middleman or agent. [ME *brocor*, t. AF: m. *brocour*, orig., broacher (of casks), tapster (hence retailer); akin to BROACH]

bro·ker·age (brō′kər ĭj), n. 1. the business of a broker. 2. the commission of a broker.

bro·mal (brō′măl), n. Chem., Pharm. a colorless, oily liquid, CBr₃CHO, used in medicine as an anodyne and hypnotic. [f. BROM(INE) + AL(COHOL)]

bro·mate (brō′māt), n., v., **-mated, -mating.** —n. 1. Chem. a salt of bromic acid. —v.t. 2. to combine with bromine.

Brom·berg (brŏm′bûrg; *Ger.* brŏm′bĕrҡ), n. German name of Bydgoszcz.

brome grass (brōm), any grass of the genus *Bromus*, widely distributed in about 40 species, esp. *B. inermis*, a perennial used for hay and pasture. Also, **brome.** [*brome*, t. L: m. s. *bromus*, t. Gk.: m. *brōmos* kind of oats]

bro·me·li·a·ceous (brō mē′lĭ ā′shəs), adj. Bot. belonging to the *Bromeliaceae*, a large family of herbaceous plants, mostly of tropical Americas, and including the pineapple, the Spanish moss, and many ornamentals. [f. s. NL *Bromelia* (named after Olaf *Bromel* (1639–1705), Swedish botanist) + -ACEOUS]

Brom·field (brŏm′fēld′), n. **Louis,** 1896–1956, U.S. novelist.

bro·mic (brō′mĭk), adj. Chem. containing pentavalent bromine (Br+5).

bromic acid, Chem. an acid, HBrO₃, containing bromine and oxygen, used as an oxidizing agent.

bro·mide (brō′mīd, -mĭd), n. 1. Also, **bro·mid** (brō′mĭd). Chem. a compound usually containing two elements only, one of which is bromine. 2. Slang. a person who is platitudinous and boring. 3. Slang. a tiresome platitude. [def. 2 and 3 from the use of certain bromides as sedatives]

bro·mid·ic (brō mĭd′ĭk), adj. Colloq. pertaining or proper to a bromide; being a bromide; trite.

bro·mi·nate (brō′mə nāt′), v.t., **-nated, -nating.** Chem. to treat or combine with bromine. —**bro′mi·na′tion**, n.

bro·mine (brō′mēn, -mĭn), n. Chem. an element, a dark-reddish fuming liquid, resembling chlorine and iodine in chemical properties. Symbol: Br; at. wt.: 79.92; at. no.: 35; sp. gr. (liquid): 3.119 at 20°C. Also, **bro·min** (brō′mĭn). [f. s. Gk. *brōmos* stench + -INE²]

bro·mism (brō′mĭz əm), n. Pathol. a morbid skin condition due to excessive use of bromides.

bron·chi (brŏng′kī), n. Anat. pl. of **bronchus.**

bron·chi·a (brŏng′kĭ ə), n. pl. Anat. the ramifications of the bronchi or tubes. [t. LL, t. Gk., der. *brónchos* windpipe]

bron·chi·al (brŏng′kĭ əl), adj. Anat. pertaining to the bronchia or bronchi.

bronchial tube, Anat. the bronchi, or the bronchi and their ramifications. See diag. under **lung.**

bron·chi·tis (brŏng kī′tĭs), n. Pathol. inflammation of the membrane lining of the windpipe and bronchial tubes. [NL; f. BRONCH(O)- + -ITIS] —**bron·chit·ic** (brŏng kĭt′ĭk), adj.

bron·cho (brŏng′kō), n., pl. **-chos.** bronco.

broncho-, a word element meaning "bronchial." Also, **bronch-.** [t. Gk., comb. form of *brónchos* windpipe]

bron·cho·bust·er (brŏng′kō bŭs′tər), n. broncobuster.

bron·cho·pneu·mo·nia (brŏng′kō nyoõ mō′nyə, -noõ-), n. Pathol. inflammation of the bronchia and lungs; a form of pneumonia.

bron·chor·rha·gi·a (brŏng′kə rā′jĭ ə), n. Obs. Pathol. hemorrhage from the bronchial tubes.

bron·cho·scope (brŏng′kə skōp′), n. Med. a tubular instrument for examining bronchi and for the removal of foreign bodies therefrom.

bron·chus (brŏng′kəs), n., pl. **-chi** (-kī). Anat. either of the two main branches of the trachea. See diag. under **lung.** [t. NL, t. Gk.: m. *brónchos* windpipe]

bron·co (brŏng′kō), n., pl. **-cos.** a pony or mustang of the western U.S., esp. one that is not broken, or is only imperfectly broken. Also, **broncho.** [t. Sp.: rough, rude]

bron·co·bust·er (brŏng′kō bŭs′tər), n. Western U.S. one who breaks broncos to the saddle. Also, **bronchobuster.**

Bron·të (brŏn′tĭ), n. 1. **Anne,** (Acton Bell) 1820–49, British novelist. 2. her sister, **Charlotte,** (Currer Bell) 1816–55, British novelist. 3. her sister, **Emily Jane,** (Ellis Bell) 1818–48, British novelist.

bron·to·sau·rus (brŏn′tə sôr′əs), n. Paleontol. a large amphibious herbivorous dinosaur of the American Jurassic, 60 feet or more in length. [f. *bronto-*, comb. form of Gk. *brontē* thunder + -SAURUS]

Bronx (brŏngks), n. **The, a** N borough of New York City. 1,424,815 (1960); 43.4 sq. mi.

bronze (brŏnz), n., v., bronzed, bronzing. —n. 1. Metall. a. a durable brown alloy, consisting essentially of copper and tin. b. any of various other copper base alloys, such as aluminum bronze, manganese bronze, silicon bronze, etc. The term implies a product superior in some way to brass. 2. a metallic brownish color. 3. a work of art, as a statue, statuette, bust, or medal, composed of bronze, whether cast or wrought. —v.t. 4. to give the appearance or color of bronze to. 5. to make brown, as by exposure to the sun. [t. F, t. It.: m. *bronzo*] —**bronz′y**, adj.

Brontosaurus, *Apatasaurus excelsus* (66 ft. long. 12 ft. high)

Bronze Age, 1. Archaeol. the age in the history of Old World mankind (between the Stone and Iron Ages) marked by the use of bronze implements. 2. (l.c.) Gk. Myth. the third period of the history of man, marked by war and violence, following the gold and silver ages.

brooch (brōch, broõch), n. a clasp or ornament for the dress, having a pin at the back for passing through the clothing and a catch for securing the point of the pin. [var. of BROACH, n.]

brood (broõd), n. 1. a number of young creatures produced or hatched at one time; a family of offspring or

young. **2.** breed or kind. —*v.t.* **3.** to sit as a bird over (eggs or young); incubate. **4.** to dwell persistently or moodily in thought on; ponder. —*v.i.* **5.** to sit as a bird over eggs to be hatched. **6.** to rest fixedly. **7.** to meditate with morbid persistence. —*adj.* **8.** kept for breeding purposes: *a brood mare.* [ME; OE *brōd*, c. G *brut.* Cf. BREED]
—**Syn. 1.** BROOD, LITTER refer to young creatures. BROOD is esp. applied to the young of fowls and birds hatched from eggs at one time and raised under their mother's care: *a brood of young turkeys.* LITTER is applied to a group of young animals brought forth at a birth: *a litter of kittens or pups.*
brood·er (brōō′dər), *n.* **1.** a device or structure for the artificial rearing of young chickens or other birds. **2.** one who or that which broods.
brood·y (brōō′dĭ), *adj.*, **broodier, broodiest. 1.** moody. **2.** inclined to brood or sit on eggs: *a broody hen.*
brook[1] (brŏŏk), *n.* a small, natural stream of fresh water, flowing through a glen or through woods, meadows, etc. [ME; OE *brōc* stream, c. G *bruch* marsh; akin to BREAK] —**Syn.** rivulet, run, burn, branch.
brook[2] (brŏŏk), *v.t.* to bear; suffer; tolerate (usually in a negative sentence). [ME *brouke*(n), OE *brūcan*, c. G *brauchen* use; akin to L *fruī* enjoy]
Brooke (brŏŏk), *n.* **1. Sir James,** (1803–68), British soldier and adventurer: rajah of Sarawak. **2. Rupert,** 1887–1915, British poet.
Brook Farm, the scene of a famous, but unsuccessful, communistic experiment at West Roxbury, Mass., 1841–47, participated in by George Ripley, C. A. Dana, Nathaniel Hawthorne, and others.
brook·let (brŏŏk′lĭt), *n.* a little brook.
Brook·line (brŏŏk′lĭn), *n.* a town in E Massachusetts, near Boston. 54,044 (1960).
Brook·lyn (brŏŏk′lĭn), *n.* a borough of New York City, on W Long Island. 2,627,319 (1960); 76.4 sq. mi.
Brooklyn Bridge, a large suspension bridge over the East River, in New York City, uniting the boroughs of Manhattan and Brooklyn: built 1867–84. 5989 ft. long.
Brooks (brŏŏks), *n.* **1. Phillips,** 1835–93, U.S. Protestant Episcopal bishop and pulpit orator. **2. Van Wyck,** born 1886, U.S. author and critic.
Brooks Range, a mountain range in N Alaska, forming a watershed between the Yukon river and the Arctic Ocean. Highest peak, ab. 10,000 ft.
brook trout, 1. the common speckled trout of eastern North America, *Salvelinus fontinalis.* **2.** the common stream trout of northern Europe, *Salmo trutta fario;* brown trout.
brook·weed (brŏŏk′wēd′), *n.* either of two primulaceous plants, *Samolus valerandi,* of the Old World, and *S. floribundus,* of North America, both bearing small white flowers.
broom (brōōm, brŏŏm), *n.* **1.** a sweeping implement consisting of a brush of twigs or plant stems on a handle. **2.** any of the shrubby fabaceous plants of the genus *Cytisus,* esp. *C. scoparius,* common in western Europe, which grows on uncultivated ground and has long, slender branches bearing yellow flowers. —*v.t.* **3.** to sweep. [ME *brōme,* OE *brōm,* c. OHG *brāmo.* Cf. BRAMBLE] —**broom′y,** *adj.*
broom·corn (brōōm′kôrn′, brŏŏm′-), *n.* a variety of sorghum with long, stiff panicles, used in brooms.
broom·rape (brōōm′rāp′, brŏŏm′-), *n.* any of various parasitic plants, esp. of the genus *Orobanche,* living on the roots of broom and other plants.
broom·stick (brōōm′stĭk′, brŏŏm′-), *n.* the long stick forming the handle of a broom.
bros., brothers. Also, **Bros.**
brose (brōz), *n.* *Scot.* a dish made by stirring boiling liquid into oatmeal or other meal. [Scot. var. of BREWIS]
broth (brôth, brŏth), *n.* **1.** thin soup of concentrated meat or fish stock. **2.** water in which meat or fish has been boiled, sometimes with vegetables or barley. [ME and OE, c. OHG *brod.* Cf. BREW, BREWIS]
broth·el (brŏth′əl, brŏ*th*′-, brôth′əl), *n.* a house of prostitution. [ME; orig. worthless person, later whore, der. OE *brothen* ruined, degenerate, pp. of *brēothan* decay; in mod. use, short for *brothel house* whore house]
broth·er (brŭth′ər), *n.,* *pl.* **brothers, brethren,** *v.*
—*n.* **1.** a male child of the same parents (**whole brother**). **2.** a male child of only one of one's parents (**half brother**). **3.** a male member of the same kinship group, nationality, profession, etc.; an associate; a fellow countryman, fellow man, etc. **4.** *Eccles.* **a.** a male lay member of a religious organization which has a priesthood. **b.** a man who devotes himself to the duties of a religious order without taking holy orders, or while preparing for holy orders. **5.** (*pl.*) all members of a particular race, or of the human race in general. —*v.t.* **6.** to treat or address as a brother. [ME; OE *brōthor,* c. G *bruder*]
—**Syn. 1.** BROTHERS, BRETHREN are plurals of *brother.* BROTHERS are kinsmen, sons of the same parents: *my mother lives with my brothers.* BRETHREN, now archaic in the foregoing sense, is used of male members of a congregation or of a fraternal organization: *the brethren will meet at the church.*
broth·er·hood (brŭth′ər hŏŏd′), *n.* **1.** condition or quality of being a brother or brothers. **2.** quality of being brotherly. **3.** a fraternal or trade organization. **4.** all those engaged in a particular trade or profession.
broth·er-in-law (brŭth′ər ĭn lô′), *n.,* *pl.* **brothers-in-law. 1.** one's husband's or wife's brother. **2.** one's sister's husband. **3.** the husband of one's wife's or husband's sister.

Brother Jon·a·than (jŏn′ə thən), **1.** the government of the United States of America. **2.** a typical American.
broth·er·ly (brŭth′ər lĭ), *adj.* **1.** of, like, or befitting a brother; fraternal. —*adv.* **2.** as a brother; fraternally. —**broth′er·li·ness,** *n.*
brough·am (brōō′əm, brōōm, brō′əm), *n.* **1.** a four-wheeled, boxlike, closed carriage for two or four persons, with the driver's perch outside. **2.** *Auto.* **a.** a limousine having an open driver's compartment. **b.** an early type of automobile resembling a coupé, often with electric power. [named after Lord *Brougham* (1778–1868), British statesman]
brought (brôt), *v.* pt. and pp. of **bring.**
Broun (brōōn), *n.* (**Matthew**) **Heywood Campbell** 1888–1939, U. S. journalist.
brow (brou), *n.* **1.** *Anat.* the ridge over the eye. **2.** the hair growing on that ridge; eyebrow. **3.** (*sing. or pl.*) the forehead: *to knit one's brows.* **4.** the countenance. **5.** the edge of a steep place. [ME *browe,* OE *brū*]
brow·beat (brou′bēt′), *v.t.,* **-beat, -beaten, -beating.** to intimidate by overbearing looks or words; bully.
brown (broun), *n.* **1.** a dark shade with yellowish or reddish hue. —*adj.* **2.** of the color brown. **3.** having skin of that color. **4.** sunburned or tanned. **5.** pertaining to the Malay race. —*v.t., v.i.* **6.** to make or become brown. [ME; OE *brūn,* c. G *braun*] —**brown′ish,** *adj.* —**brown′ness,** *n.*
Brown (broun), *n.* **1. Charles Brockden,** 1771–1810, U.S. novelist. **2. John** ("*of Osawatomie*"), 1800–1859, U.S. abolitionist who incited the slaves to a rebellion but was captured at Harpers Ferry, tried, and hanged. **3. Robert,** 1773–1858, Scottish botanist.
brown algae, *Bot.* algae belonging to the class *Phaeophyceae,* usually brown as a result of brown pigments added to their chlorophyll.
brown bear, 1. a variety of the common black bear, *Ursus americanus,* having a brownish coat. **2.** a variety of the black bear of Europe and America, *Ursus arctos,* inhabiting northern regions.
brown betty, a baked pudding made of apples, or other fruit, bread crumbs, sugar, butter, spice, etc.
brown bread, 1. any bread made of flour darker in color than the bolted wheat flour, esp. graham or whole wheat bread. **2.** Boston brown bread.
brown coal, lignite.
Browne (broun), *n.* **1. Charles Farrar** (făr′ər). ("*Artemus Ward*") 1834–67, U.S. humorist. **2. Sir Thomas,** 1605–82, British physician and author.
Brown·i·an movement (brou′nĭ ən), *Physics.* a rapid oscillatory motion often observed in very minute particles suspended in water or other liquid: first noticed (in 1827) by Robert Brown. Also, **Brownian motion.**
brown·ie (brou′nĭ), *n.* **1.** (in folklore) a little brown goblin, esp. one who helps secretly in household work. **2.** *U.S.* a small, highly shortened chocolate cake, often containing nuts. **3.** (*cap.*) a trademark for a type of inexpensive camera. **4.** any inexpensive camera. **5.** (*cap.*) a member of the junior division (ages 8–11) of the Girl Scouts or (*Brit.*) the Girl Guides. —**Syn. 1.** See **fairy.**
Brown·ing (brou′nĭng), *n.* **1. Elizabeth Barrett** (băr′ĭt), 1806–61, British poetess. **2.** her husband, **Robert,** 1812–89, British poet.
brown rice, rice from which the bran layers and germs have not been removed by polishing.
brown rot, *Plant Pathol.* a disease, esp. of apples, peaches, plums, and cherries, caused by fungi of the genus *Sclerotinia.*
Brown Shirt, 1. a member of Hitler's storm troopers (Sturmabteilungen). **2.** (loosely) any Nazi.
brown·stone (broun′stōn′), *n.* **1.** a reddish-brown sandstone, extensively used as a building material. —*adj.* **2.** belonging or pertaining to the well-to-do class.
brown study, deep, serious absorption in thought.
brown sugar, unrefined or partially refined sugar.
Browns·ville (brounz′vĭl), *n.* a seaport in S Texas, near the mouth of the Rio Grande. 48,040 (1960).
Brown Swiss, one of a breed of large-boned and well-muscled dairy cattle, giving large quantities of milk.
brown-tail moth (broun′tāl′), a tussock moth, *Euproctis chrysorrhoea,* having white wings, in the larval stage very destructive to trees.
brown thrasher, a well-known songbird, *Toxostoma rufum,* of the eastern U.S. Also, **brown thrush.**
brown trout, brook trout (def. 2).
browse (brouz), *v.,* **browsed, browsing,** *n.* —*v.t.* **1.** (of cattle, deer, etc.) to nibble at; eat from. **2.** (of cattle, deer, etc.) to feed on; pasture on; graze. —*v.i.* **3.** (of cattle, etc.) to graze. **4.** to glance at random through a book or books. —*n.* **5.** tender shoots or twigs of shrubs and trees as food for cattle, deer, etc. [appar. t. MF: m. *broust* young sprout; t. Gmc.; cf. OS *brustian* to sprout] —**brows′er,** *n.*
Bruce (brōōs), *n.* **1. Robert the,** (*Robert I, Robert Bruce*) 1274–1329, king of Scotland, 1306–29: preserved the independence of Scotland by victory over the English at Bannockburn in 1314. **2. Stanley Melbourne,** born 1883, prime minister of Australia, 1923–29.
bru·cel·lo·sis (brōō′sə lō′sĭs), *n.* *Vet. Sci., Pathol.* infection with bacteria of the *Brucella* group, frequently causing abortions in animals and undulant fever in man.

bruc·ine (broo′sēn, -sĭn), *n. Pharm., Chem.* a bitter, poisonous alkaloid, $C_{23}H_{26}N_2O_4$, obtained from the nux vomica tree, *Strychnos nux vomica*, and from other species of the same genus, resembling strychnine in action but less powerful. Also, **bruc·in** (broo′sĭn). [f. James *Bruce* (1730–94), Scottish explorer of Africa + -INE²]

Brue·ghel (broe′gəl), *n.* a Flemish family of genre and landscape painters: **Pieter**, 1525?–1569, and his sons **Pieter**, 1564–1637, and **Jan**, 1568–1625. Also, **Brue/gel, Breu/ghel.**

Bru·ges (broo′jĭz, broozh; *Fr.* bryzh), *n.* a city in NW Belgium: connected by canal with its seaport, Zeebrugge. 51,924 (est. 1952). Flemish, **Brug·ge** (broekн′ə).

bru·in (broo′ĭn), *n.* a bear. [t. MD: lit., brown, the name of the bear in *Reynard the Fox*]

bruise (brooz), *v.*, **bruised, bruising,** *n.* —*v.t.* **1.** to injure by striking or pressing, without breaking the skin or drawing blood. **2.** to injure or hurt superficially: *to bruise a person's feelings.* **3.** to crush (drugs or food) by beating or pounding. —*v.i.* **4.** to develop a discolored spot on the skin as the result of a blow, fall, etc. **5.** to be injured superficially: *his feelings bruise easily.* —*n.* **6.** an injury due to bruising; a contusion. [ME *bruse*(*n*), *brise*(*n*), coalescence of OE *brўsan* crush, bruise and OF *br*(*u*)*isier* break, ult. der. Gallic *bris-, brus-* beat]

bruis·er (broo′zər), *n.* **1.** a boxer. **2.** *Colloq.* a tough fellow; bully.

bruit (broot), *v.t.* **1.** to noise abroad; rumor (mainly in the passive): *the report was bruited about.* —*n.* **2.** *Archaic.* rumor. **3.** *Archaic.* a din. [ME, t. OF, der. *bruire* make a noise]

Bru·maire (brȳ mĕr′), *n.* the second month, October 22 to November 20, in the calendar adopted (1793) by the first French republic. [t. F, der. *brume* BRUME]

bru·mal (broo′məl), *adj.* wintry. [t. L: s. *brūmālis*]

brume (broom), *n.* mist; fog. [t. F: fog, t. Pr.: m. *bruma*, g. L *brūma* winter, winter solstice, lit., shortest day] —**bru·mous** (broo′məs), *adj.*

brum·ma·gem (brŭm′ə jəm), *adj.* **1.** showy but inferior and worthless. —*n.* **2.** a showy but inferior and worthless thing. [alter. of *Birmingham*, in England]

Brum·mell (brŭm′əl), *n.* See **Beau Brummell.**

brunch (brŭnch), *n.* a mid-morning meal that serves both as breakfast and lunch. [b. BREAKFAST and LUNCH]

Brun·dis·i·um (brŭn dĭz′Ȳəm), *n.* ancient name of **Brindisi.**

Bru·nei (broo nī′), *n.* **1.** a British sultanate in NW Borneo. 65,000 (est. 1955); ab. 2220 sq. mi. **2.** the capital of this sultanate: a seaport. 11,000 (est. 1955).

Bru·nel·les·chi (broo′nĕl lĕs′kē), *n.* **Filippo** (fē lēp′ pô), 1377?–1446, Florentine architect.

bru·net (broo nĕt′), *adj.* **1.** (of skin, eyes, or hair) dark; brown. **2.** (of a person) having dark or brown hair, eyes, or skin. —*n.* **3.** a man or boy with dark hair, skin, and eyes. [t. F, dim. of *brun*, fem. *brune* brown; of Gmc. orig. Cf. BROWN]

bru·nette (broo nĕt′), *adj.* **1.** brunet. —*n.* **2.** a woman or girl with dark hair, skin, and eyes.

Brün·hild (brŭn′hĭld; *Ger.* broon′hĭlt), *n.* **1.** (in the *Nibelungenlied*) a legendary queen of Iceland, wife of King Gunther, for whom she is won by Siegfried. **2.** (in the corresponding Scandinavian legend) a Valkyrie, won by Sigurd for Gunnar. Also, **Brynhild.** [t. G. Cf. Icel. *Brynhildr*]

Brünn (bryn), *n.* German name of **Brno.**

Brün·ne·hil·de (bryn′ə hĭl′də), *n.* the heroine of Wagner's *Ring of the Nibelungs.* Cf. Siegfried.

Bru·no (broo′nô), *n.* **1. Giordano** (jôr dä′nô), 1548?–1600, Italian philosopher. **2. Saint,** c1030–1101, monk, born at Cologne: founder of Carthusian order.

Bruns·wick (brŭnz′wĭk), *n.* **1.** a former state in central Germany. 1418 sq. mi. Now part of Lower Saxony. **2.** Former capital of this state. 244,479 (est. 1955). German, **Braunschweig.**

brunt (brŭnt), *n.* **1.** the shock or force of an attack, etc.; the main stress, force, or violence: *to bear the brunt of their criticism.* **2.** *Rare or Archaic.* a violent attack.

Bru·sa (broo′sä), *n.* Bursa.

brush¹ (brŭsh), *n.* **1.** an instrument consisting of bristles, hair, or the like, set in or attached to a handle, used for painting, cleaning, polishing, rubbing, etc. **2.** act of brushing; an application of a brush. **3.** the bushy tail of an animal, esp. that of a fox. **4.** the art or skill of a painter of pictures. **5.** a brief encounter. **6.** a quick ride across country. **7.** *Elect.* **a.** a conductor serving to maintain electric contact between stationary and moving parts of a machine or other apparatus. **b.** corona (def. 6). —*v.t.* **8.** to sweep, rub, clean, polish, etc., with a brush. **9.** to touch lightly in passing; pass lightly over. **10.** to remove by brushing or by lightly passing over. —*v.i.* **11.** to move or skim with a slight contact. **12.** to move quickly or in haste; rush. [ME *brusshe*, t. OF: m. *broisse*, t. Gmc.; cf. MHG *bürste* brush] —**brush/y,** *adj.* —Syn. 5. See **struggle.**

brush² (brŭsh), *n.* **1.** a dense growth of bushes, shrubs, etc.; scrub; a thicket. **2.** *U.S.* lopped or broken branches; brushwood. **3.** *U.S.* backwoods; a sparsely settled wooded region. [ME *brusche*, t. OF: m. *broche*, ? of Gallic orig.] —**brush/y,** *adj.*

brush discharge, *Elect.* corona (def. 6).

brush-off (brŭsh′ôf′, -ŏf′), *n. U.S. Slang.* an abrupt or final dismissal or refusal.

brush·wood (brŭsh′wŏŏd′), *n.* **1.** branches of trees cut or broken off. **2.** densely growing small trees and shrubs. [f. BRUSH² + WOOD¹]

brusque (brŭsk; *esp. Brit.* brŏŏsk; *Fr.* brysk), *adj.* abrupt in manner; blunt; rough: *a brusque welcome.* Also, **brusk.** [t. F, t. It.: m. *brusco* rude, sharp, g. L *bruscum*, b. L *ruscum* butcher's-broom and *brūcum* broom] —**brusque/ly,** *adv.* —**brusque/ness,** *n.* —Syn. See **blunt.**

brus·que·rie (bryskə rē′), *n.* brusqueness. [F]

Brus·sels (brŭs′əlz), *n.* the capital of Belgium, in the central part. 955,929 with suburbs (1947). French, **Bruxelles.**

Brussels carpet, a kind of worsted carpet woven on a Jacquard loom, in which uncut loops form a heavy pile.

Brussels lace, handmade lace from Brussels.

Brussels sprouts, 1. plants of *Brassica oleracea,* var. *gemmifera,* having small edible heads or sprouts along the stalk, which resemble miniature cabbage heads. **2.** the heads or sprouts themselves.

Brussels sprouts

brut (bryt), *adj.* (of wines, usually champagne) very dry. [t. F: raw]

bru·tal (broo′təl), *adj.* **1.** savage; cruel; inhuman. **2.** crude; coarse; harsh. **3.** irrational; unreasoning. **4.** of or pertaining to lower animals. —**bru/tal·ly,** *adv.* —Syn. 1. See **cruel.**

bru·tal·i·ty (broo tăl′ə tĬ), *n., pl.* **-ties. 1.** quality of being brutal. **2.** a brutal act.

bru·tal·ize (broo′tə līz′), *v.t., v.i.* **-ized, -izing.** to make or become brutal. —**bru/tal·i·za/tion,** *n.*

brute (broot), *n.* **1.** a nonhuman animal; beast. **2.** a brutal person. **3.** the animal qualities, desires, etc., of man. —*adj.* **4.** wanting reason; animal; not human. **5.** not characterized by intelligence; irrational. **6.** characteristic of animals; of brutal character or quality. **7.** savage; cruel. **8.** sensual; carnal. [t. F: m. *brut,* t. L: s. *brūtus* dull] —Syn. 1. See **animal.**

bru·ti·fy (broo′tə fĬ′), *v.t., v.i.* **-fied, -fying.** to brutalize.

brut·ish (broo′tĬsh), *adj.* **1.** brutal. **2.** gross; carnal; bestial. **3.** uncivilized; like an animal. —**brut/ish·ly,** *adv.* —**brut/ish·ness,** *n.* —Syn. 2. See **beastly.**

Bru·tus (broo′təs), *n.* **Marcus Junius** (mär′kəs jŏŏn′yəs), 85?–42 B.C., Roman provincial administrator; one of the assassins of Julius Caesar.

Brux·elles (bry sĕl′; *local* bryk sĕl′), *n.* French name of **Brussels.**

Bry·an (brī′ən), *n.* **William Jennings,** 1860–1925, U.S. political leader.

Bry·ansk (brĬ yänsk′; *Russ.* bryänsk), *n.* a city in the W Soviet Union. 111,000 (est. 1956).

Bry·ant (brī′ənt), *n.* **William Cullen,** 1794–1878, U.S. poet.

Bryce (brīs), *n.* **James, Viscount,** 1838–1922, British historical and political writer, and diplomat.

Bryce Canyon National Park, a national park in SW Utah: fantastically eroded pinnacles. 55 sq. mi.

Bryn·hild (brĬn′hĬld; *Icelandic* bryn′-), *n.* Brünhild.

bry·ol·o·gy (brī ŏl′ə jĬ), *n.* the part of botany that treats of bryophytes. [f. Gk. *brўo*(*n*) moss + -LOGY] —**bry·o·log·i·cal** (brī′ə lŏj′ə kəl), *adj.* —**bry·ol′o·gist,** *n.*

bry·o·ny (brī′ə nĬ), *n., pl.* **-nies.** any plant of the Old World cucurbitaceous genus *Bryonia,* comprising vines or climbers with acrid juice and emetic and purgative properties. [t. L: m.s. *brўōnia,* t. Gk.]

bry·o·phyte (brī′ə fĬt′), *n. Bot.* any of the *Bryophyta,* a primary division or group of plants comprising the true mosses and liverworts. [t. NL: m. *Bryophyta,* pl., f. Gk. *brўo*(*n*) moss + -*phyta* (see -PHYTE)] —**bry·o·phyt·ic** (brī′ə fĬt′Ĭk), *adj.*

Bry·o·zo·a (brī′ə zō′ə), *n. pl. Zool.* a phylum of marine and fresh-water animals, of sessile habits, forming branching, encrusting, or gelatinous colonies of many small polyps, each having a circular or horseshoe-shaped ridge bearing ciliated tentacles. Branching marine types are termed sea moss and are used as ornaments.

bry·o·zo·an (brī′ə zō′ən), *Zool.* —*adj.* **1.** of or pertaining to the *Bryozoa.* —*n.* **2.** any of the *Bryozoa.* [f. Gk. *brўo*(*n*) moss + zo- + -AN]

Bryth·on (brĬth′ən), *n.* **1.** a Celt in Britain using the Brythonic form of the Celtic language, which was confined mainly to the western part of southern Britain after the English conquest. **2.** a Briton. [t. Welsh]

Bry·thon·ic (brĬ thŏn′Ĭk), *adj.* **1.** pertaining to the Celtic dialects used in northwestern and southwestern England, Wales, and Brittany. —*n.* **2.** the British subgroup of Celtic.

Brześć nad Bu·giem (bzhĕshch′ näd bŏŏ′gyĕm), *n.* Polish name of **Brest Litovsk.**

B.S., 1. Bachelor of Science. **2.** Bachelor of Surgery.

b.s., *Com.* **1.** balance sheet. **2.** bill of sale.

B.S.A., 1. Bachelor of Scientific Agriculture. **2.** Boy Scouts of America.

B.Sc., (L *Baccalaureus Scientiae*) Bachelor of Science.

Bt., Baronet.

B.T., (L *Baccalaureus Theologia*) Bachelor of Theology. Also, **B.Th.**

---

b., blend of, blended; c., cognate with; d., dialect, dialectal; der., derived from; f., formed from; g., going back to; m., modification of; r., replacing; s., stem of; t., taken from; ?, perhaps. See the full key on inside cover.

B.T.U., *Physics.* British thermal unit, or units. Also, **B.t.u., B.th.u., Btu.**

bu., bushel; bushels.

bu·bal (bū′bəl), *n.* a large antelope, one of the hartebeests, *Alcelaphus boselaphus,* of northern Africa. Also, **bu·ba·lis** (bū′bə lĭs). [t. L: s. *būbalus* an oxlike antelope, t. Gk.: m. *boúbalos*]

bu·ba·line (bū′bə lĭn′, -lῑn), *adj.* **1.** (of antelopes) resembling or like the bubal, as the hartebeests, blesbok, etc. **2.** pertaining to or resembling the true buffaloes.

bub·ble (bŭb′əl), *n., v.,* **-bled, -bling.** —*n.* **1.** a small globule of gas in or rising through a liquid. **2.** a small globule of gas in a thin liquid envelope. **3.** a globule of air or gas, or a globular vacuum, in a solid substance. **4.** anything that lacks firmness, substance, or permanence; a delusion; a worthless, deceptive matter. **5.** an inflated speculation; fraud. **6.** act or sound of bubbling. —*v.i.* **7.** to send up bubbles; effervesce. **8.** to flow or run with a gurgling noise; gurgle. —*v.t.* **9.** to cause to bubble; make (bubbles) in. **10.** *Archaic.* to cheat; deceive; swindle. [ME *bobel,* c. D *bobbelen,* Sw. *bubla.* Cf. BURBLE] —**bub′bly,** *adj.*

bubble chamber, an apparatus for determining the movements of charged particles by producing visible tracks of bubbles in their paths as they traverse a transparent medium.

bub·bler (bŭb′lər), *n.* a drinking fountain from which one drinks without a cup.

bu·bo (bū′bō), *n., pl.* **-boes.** *Pathol.* an inflammatory swelling of a lymphatic gland, esp. in the groin or armpit. [t. LL, t. Gk.: m. *boubōn,* lit., groin]

bu·bon·ic (bū bŏn′ῐk), *adj. Pathol.* **1.** of or pertaining to a bubo. **2.** accompanied by or affected with buboes.

bubonic plague, *Pathol.* a contagious epidemic disease in which the victims suffer chills, fevers, and buboes and are prostrate, and which often has rat fleas as its carrier.

bu·bon·o·cele (bū bŏn′ə sēl′), *n. Pathol.* an inguinal hernia, esp. one in which the protrusion of the intestine is limited to the region of the groin.

Bu·ca·ra·man·ga (bōō kä′rä mäng′gä), *n.* a city in N Colombia. 136,170 (est. 1954).

buc·cal (bŭk′əl), *adj. Anat.* **1.** of or pertaining to the cheek. **2.** pertaining to the sides of the mouth or to the mouth; oral. **3.** pertaining to the mouth as a whole. [f. s. L *bucca* cheek, mouth + -AL¹]

buc·ca·neer (bŭk′ə nῑr′), *n.* **1.** a pirate. **2.** one of the piratical adventurers who raided Spanish colonies and shipping in America. [t. F: m. *boucanier,* der. *boucan* frame for curing meat, of Carib orig.]

buc·ci·na·tor (bŭk′sə nā′tər), *n. Anat.* a thin, flat muscle lining the cheek, assisting in mastication, blowing wind instruments, etc. [t. L: trumpeter, der. *buccināre* blow a trumpet]

bu·cen·taur¹ (bū sĕn′tôr), *n.* the state barge of Venice, from which the doge and other officials on Ascension Day performed the ceremonial marriage of the state with the Adriatic, by dropping a ring into the sea. [t. It.: m. *bucentoro,* orig. unknown]

bu·cen·taur² (bū sĕn′tôr), *n.* a mythical monster, half man and half bull; a centaur with the body of a bull instead of a horse. [f. Gk.: m. *boûs* ox + m.s. *kéntauros* centaur]

Bu·ceph·a·lus (bū sĕf′ə ləs), *n.* the war horse of Alexander the Great.

Buch·an (bŭk′ən; *Scot.* bŭкʜ′ən), *n.* **John,** (*Baron Tweedsmuir*) 1875–1940, Scottish novelist and historian; governor general of Canada, 1935–40.

Bu·chan·an (bū kăn′ən, bə-), *n.* **James,** 1791–1868, 15th president of the U.S., 1857–61.

Bu·cha·rest (bōō′kə rĕst′, bŏŏ′-), *n.* the capital of Rumania. 1,042,000 (est. 1952). Rumanian, **Bucuresti.**

Buch·en·wald (bōōk′ən wôld′; *Ger.* bōō кʜ′ən vält′), *n.* a Nazi concentration camp in central Germany, near Weimar, infamous for atrocities perpetrated there.

Buch·man·ism (bōōk′mə nῑz′əm), *n.* a religious movement emphasizing Christian fellowship or "sharing" in small groups, public confession of sins, divine guidance, absolute honesty, purity, love, and unselfishness; the Oxford Group. [named after Frank *Buchman* (1878–1961) who founded it] —**Buch·man·ite** (bōōk′mə nῑt), *n.*

buck¹ (bŭk), *n.* **1.** the male of the deer, antelope, rabbit, hare, sheep, or goat. **2.** male of certain other animals: *buck shad.* **3.** a fop; a dandy. **4.** *U.S. Colloq.* a male Indian or Negro. **5.** *U.S. Slang.* a dollar. —*adj.* **6.** *Mil. Slang.* of the lowest of several ranks involving the same principal designation: *buck private, buck sergeant.* [ME *bukke,* coalescence of OE *bucca* he-goat and *bucc* male deer, c. G *bock*]

buck² (bŭk), *v.i.* **1.** (of a saddle or pack animal) to leap with arched back and come down with head low and forelegs stiff, in order to dislodge rider or pack. **2.** *U.S. Colloq.* to resist obstinately; object strongly: *to buck at improvements.* **3.** *U.S. Colloq.* (of a vehicle) to jerk and bounce. **4.** *Colloq.* to become more cheerful, vigorous, etc. (fol. by *up*). **5.** *Brit.* to boast. —*v.t.* **6.** to throw or attempt to throw (a rider) by bucking. **7.** *U.S.* to strike with the head; butt. **8.** *U.S. Colloq.* to resist obstinately; object strongly to. **9.** *Colloq.* to make more cheerful, vigorous, etc. (fol. by *up*). **10.** *Football.* to charge into (the line of opponents) with the ball. —*n.* **11.** act of bucking. [special use of BUCK¹; in def. 7, alter. of BUTT³]

buck³ (bŭk), *n.* **1.** a sawhorse. **2.** *Gymnastics.* a leather-covered cylindrical block, adjustable in height, used for leaping or diving over, etc. [t. D: m. *zaagbok*]

buck⁴ (bŭk), *n.* **1.** *Poker.* any object in the pot which reminds the winner that he has some privilege or duty when his turn to deal next comes. **2. pass the buck,** *U.S. Colloq.* to shift the responsibility or blame to another person. [orig. uncert.]

Buck (bŭk), *n.* **Pearl,** born 1892, U.S. novelist.

buck·a·roo (bŭk′ə rōō′, bŭk′ə rōō′), *n., pl.* **-roos.** *Western U.S.* a cowboy. Also, **buck·ay·ro** (bə kär′ō). [alter. of Sp. *vaquero,* der. *vaca* cow, g. L *vacca*]

buck bean, a plant, *Menyanthes trifoliata,* with white or pink flowers, growing in bogs.

buck·board (bŭk′bôrd′), *n.* a light four-wheeled carriage in which a long elastic board or lattice frame is used in place of body and springs.

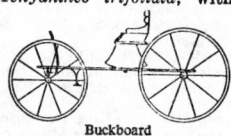

Buckboard

buck·een (bŭk ēn′), *n. Ireland.* a young man of the middle class or lower aristocracy who copies the habits of wealthier people.

buck·er (bŭk′ər), *n.* a horse that bucks.

buck·et (bŭk′ῑt), *n., v.,* **-eted, -eting.** —*n.* **1.** a vessel, usually round with flat bottom and a semicircular handle, for carrying water, sand, etc. **2.** anything resembling or suggesting this. **3.** one of the scoops attached to or forming the endless chain in certain types of conveyers or elevators. **4.** a cupped vane of a water wheel, turbine, etc. **5.** a bucketful. —*v.t.* **6.** to lift, carry, or handle in a bucket (often fol. by *up* or *out*). **7.** to ride (a horse) fast and without care about its fatigue. **8.** to handle (orders, etc.) as in a bucket shop. —*v.i.* **9.** *Colloq.* to move or ride fast. [ME *buket,* appar. t. OF: m. *buket* pail, tub, prob. der. some cognate of OE *būc* pitcher] —**buck·et·ful** (bŭk′ῑt fŏŏl′), *n.*

bucket seat, a folding seat for one person in racing cars, and in some airplanes.

bucket shop, *Finance.* a fraudulent establishment operating ostensibly for the transaction of a legitimate stock exchange or similar business, but actually speculating on its own account against its customers' purchases and sales by failing to execute some so that customers' gains are the establishment's loss and vice versa. [orig. a place where liquor was obtained and carried away in buckets brought by the customers]

buck·eye (bŭk′ῑ′), *n.* **1.** any of various trees or shrubs, genus *Aesculus,* allied to the true horse chestnut, as *A. glabra* (**Ohio buckeye**), a large tree with an ill-smelling bark. **2.** (*cap.*) *Colloq.* an inhabitant of Ohio, the **Buckeye State.** [f. BUCK¹ stag + EYE, in allusion to the appearance of the seed]

buck fever, *U.S. Colloq.* nervous excitement of an inexperienced hunter upon the approach of game.

buck·hound (bŭk′hound′), *n.* a hound for hunting bucks, etc., similar to the staghound, but smaller.

Buck·ing·ham (bŭk′ῑng əm), *n.* **1. George Villiers** (vῑl′ōrz, -yərz), **1st Duke of,** 1592–1628, British courtier, politician, and military leader: lord high admiral, 1617. **2.** his son, **George Villiers, 2nd Duke of,** 1628–1687, British courtier and writer. **3.** Buckinghamshire.

Buckingham Palace, the London residence of the British sovereign, at the west end of St. James's Park.

Buck·ing·ham·shire (bŭk′ῑng əm shῑr′, -shər), *n.* a county in S England. 386,291 pop. (1951); 749 sq. mi. *Co. seat:* Aylesbury. Also, **Buckingham, Bucks.**

buck·ish (bŭk′ῑsh), *adj.* dapperish; foppish. —**buck′ish·ly,** *adv.* —**buck′ish·ness,** *n.*

buck·le (bŭk′əl), *n., v.,* **-led, -ling.** —*n.* **1.** a clasp consisting of a rectangular or curved rim with one or more movable tongues, used for fastening together two loose ends, as of a belt or strap. **2.** any similar contrivance used for such a purpose. **3.** an ornament of metal, beads, etc., of similar appearance. **4.** a bend, bulge, or kink, as in a saw blade. —*v.t.* **5.** to fasten with a buckle or buckles. **6.** to shrivel, by applying heat or pressure; bend; curl. **7.** to prepare (oneself) for action; apply (oneself) vigorously to something. —*v.i.* **8.** to set to work with vigor (fol. by *down to*). **9.** to bend, warp, or give way suddenly, as with heat or pressure. **10.** to grapple; contend. [ME *bocle,* t. OF: m. *boucle* buckle, boss of a shield, g. L *buccula,* dim. of *bucca* cheek, mouth]

buck·ler (bŭk′lər), *n.* **1.** a round shield, with grip for holding, and sometimes with straps through which the arm is passed. **2.** any means of defense; a protection. —*v.t.* **3.** to be a buckler or shield to; support; defend. [ME *bokeler,* t. OF: m. *boucler* shield, orig., one with a boss, der. *boucle* boss. See BUCKLE, n.]

buck·o (bŭk′ō), *n., pl.* **-oes.** a bully.

buck·ra (bŭk′rə), *n.* a white man (used among the Negroes of the African coast, the West Indies, and the southern U.S.). [? t. West African (Calabar): m. *mbākara* demon, powerful being, white man]

buck·ram (bŭk′rəm), *n., v.,* **-ramed, -raming.** —*n.* **1.** stiff cotton fabric for interlining, binding books, etc. **2.** stiffness of manner; extreme preciseness or formality. —*v.t.* **3.** to strengthen with buckram. **4.** to give (a person, etc.) a false appearance of importance or strength. [ME *bokeram.* Cf. OF *boquerant,* It. *bucherame,* ? ult. der. *Bukhāra,* town and region in C Asia whence cloth was exported]

Bucks (bŭks), *n.* Buckinghamshire.

buck·saw (bŭk′sô′), *n.* a saw consisting of a blade set across an upright frame or bow, used with both hands in cutting wood on a sawbuck or saw-horse.

buck·shot (bŭk′shŏt′), *n.* a large size of lead shot used on big game.

buck·skin (bŭk′skĭn′), *n.* **1.** the skin of a buck or deer. **2.** a strong, soft, yellowish or grayish leather, orig. prepared from deerskins, now usually from sheepskins. **3.** (*pl.*) breeches made of buckskin. **4.** (*cap.*) a buckskin-clad American soldier of the Revolutionary War. **5.** *U.S.* a horse of the color of buckskin.

Bucksaw

buck·thorn (bŭk′thôrn′), *n.* **1.** any of several trees or shrubs (sometimes thorny) belonging to the genus *Rhamnus*, as *R. cathartica*, a shrub whose berries were formerly much used in medicine as a purgative, and *R. frangula*, yielding the **buckthorn bark** used in medicine. **2.** a tree or shrub of the sapotaceous genus *Bumelia*, esp. *B. lycioides*, a tree common in the southern and part of the central U.S.

buck·tooth (bŭk′tooth′), *n.*, *pl.* **-teeth** (-tēth′). a projecting tooth.

buck·wheat (bŭk′hwēt′), *n.* **1.** a herbaceous plant, *Fagopyrum sagittatum*, cultivated for its triangular seeds, which are used as a food for animals, and made into a flour for pancakes, etc. **2.** the seeds. **3.** the flour. [f. *buck* (OE *bōc* beech) + WHEAT. Cf. obs. *buckmast* beech mast, D *boekweit*, G *buchweizen* buckwheat, lit., beech wheat, from its beechnut-shaped seed]

bu·col·ic (bū·kŏl′ĭk), *adj.* Also, **bu·col′i·cal. 1.** of or pertaining to shepherds; pastoral. **2.** rustic; rural; agricultural: *bucolic isolation.* —*n.* **3.** *Humorous.* a farmer; a shepherd; a rustic. **4.** a pastoral poem. [t. L: s. *bucólicus*, t. Gk.: m. *boukolikós* rustic] —**bu·col′i·cal·ly**, *adv.*

Bu·co·vi·na (boo′kə vē′nə; *Rum.* bŏō kô vē′nä), *n.* **1.** a province in N Rumania. 300,751 pop. (1948); 1912 sq. mi. **2.** *Northern*, a region in the SW Soviet Union, in the Ukrainian Republic: formerly a part of Rumania. Also, **Bukovina**.

Bu·cu·reş·ti (boo kŏō rĕsht′), *n.* Rumanian name of Bucharest.

bud[1] (bŭd), *n.*, *v.*, **budded**, **budding.** —*n.* **1.** *Bot.* **a.** a small axillary or terminal protuberance on a plant, containing rudimentary foliage (**leaf bud**), the rudimentary inflorescence (**flower bud**), or both (**mixed bud**). **b.** an undeveloped or rudimentary stem or branch of a plant. **2.** *Zool.* (in certain animals of low organization) a prominence which develops into a new individual, sometimes permanently attached to the parent and sometimes becoming detached; a gemma. **3.** *Anat.* any small rounded part, as a tactile bud or a gustatory bud. **4.** an immature or undeveloped person or thing. **5.** nip in the bud, to stop (something) before it really gets started. —*v.i.* **6.** to put forth or produce buds, as a plant. **7.** to begin to grow and develop. **8.** to be in an early stage of development. —*v.t.* **9.** to cause to bud. **10.** *Hort.* to graft by inserting a single bud into the stock. [ME *budde*; orig. uncert.]

Leaf buds of the elm (def. 1a)

bud[2] (bŭd), *n.* *Familiar.* **1.** brother. **2.** man or boy (as a term of address). [alter. of BROTHER]

Bu·da·pest (boo′də pĕst′, boo′də pĕst′; *Hung.* bŏō′dŏ-pĕsht′), *n.* the capital of Hungary, on the Danube: formed by the union of the cities of Buda and Pest (1872). 1,781,085 (est. 1954).

Bud·dha (bŏōd′ə), *n.* "The Enlightened One," a title applied esp. to the great religious teacher, variously known as Siddhartha and Gautama (or Gotama), or Sakyamuni, who flourished in India about the 6th century B.C., regarded by his followers as the latest of a series of teachers (Buddhas) possessing perfect enlightenment and wisdom. [t. Skt.: wise, enlightened]

Bud·dhism (bŏōd′ĭz əm), *n.* the cult, founded by Buddha, which teaches that life is intrinsically full of suffering and that the supreme felicity (Nirvana) is to be striven for by psychological and ethical self-culture. —**Bud′dhist**, *n.*, *adj.* —**Bud·dhis′tic**, *adj.*

bud·dle·ia (bŭd lē′ə, bŭd′lĭ ə), *n.* any of the genus *Budleja*, mainly tropical ornamental perennials of the family Loganiaceae, having a two-celled many-seeded fruit. [NL; after Adam *Buddle* (d. 1715), botanist]

bud·dy (bŭd′ĭ), *n.*, *pl.* **-dies.** *U.S. Colloq.* a comrade or mate. [see BUD[2]]

Bu·dën·ny (boo dĕn′ĭ; *Russ.* bŏō dyŏn′nĭ), *n.* **Semën Mikhailovich** (sĕ myŏn′ mī′ hī′lŏ vĭch), born 1883, Russian general in 1917 Revolution and World War II.

budge (bŭj), *v.*, **budged**, **budging.** —*v.i.* **1.** to move slightly; give way (usually with negative). —*v.t.* **2.** to cause to budge (usually with negative). [t. F: m. s. *bouger*, ult. der. L *bullīre* BOIL[1]]

budg·et (bŭj′ĭt), *n.*, *v.*, **-eted**, **-eting.** —*n.* **1.** an estimate, often itemized, of expected income and expense, or operating results, for a given period in the future. **2.** a plan of operations based on such an estimate. **3.** an itemized allotment of funds for a given period. **4.** a stock; a collection. **5.** *Obs.* a small bag; a pouch. —*v.t.* **6.** to plan allotment of (funds, time, etc.). **7.** to

deal with (specific funds) in a budget. [late ME *bougette*, t. F, dim. of *bouge* bag, g. L *bulga*] —**budg·et·ar·y** (bŭj′ə tĕr′ĭ), *adj.*

Bud·weis (bŏōt′vīs), *n.* a city in W Czechoslovakia, on the Moldau river. 38,194 (1947). Czech, **Česke Budějovice**.

Bu·ell (bū′əl), *n.* **Don Carlos** (dŏn kär′lŏs), 1818–98, Union general in the U.S. Civil War.

Bue·na Park (bwā′nə pärk), a city in SW California. 46,401 (1960).

Bue·na Vis·ta (bwĕ′nä vēs′tä), a battlefield in N Mexico, near Saltillo: the American forces withstood a severe attack here in the Mexican War, 1847.

Bue·nos Ai·res (bwā′nəs ī′rĭz, bŏ′nəs âr′ĕz; *Sp.* bwĕ′nōs ī′rĕs), a seaport in and the capital of Argentina, in the E part, on the Río de la Plata. 3,403,600 (est. 1952).

buff[1] (bŭf), *n.* **1.** a kind of thick leather, orig. and properly made of buffalo skin but later also of other skins, light-yellow with napped surface, used for making belts, pouches, etc. **2.** a thick coat of buff leather, worn esp. by soldiers. **3.** yellowish-brown; medium or dark tan. **4.** *Colloq.* the bare skin. —*adj.* **5.** made of buff (leather). **6.** having the color of buff. —*v.t.* **7.** to polish (metal) or to give a grainless finish of high luster to (plated surfaces). **8.** to dye or stain in a buff color. [appar. for earlier *buffle*, t. F: buffalo, t. It.: m. *buffalo*. See BUFFALO]

buff[2] (bŭf), *v.t.* **1.** to reduce or deaden the force of, as a buffer. —*n.* **2.** *Obs.* a blow; a slap; a buffet (surviving in *blindman's buff*). [late ME *buffe*, ? t. OF; or back formation from BUFFET[1]. But cf. LG *buff* blow]

buf·fa·lo (bŭf′ə lŏ′), *n.*, *pl.* **-loes**, **-los**, (*esp. collectively*) **-lo**, *v.*, **-loed**, **-loing.** —*n.* **1.** any of several mammals of the ox kind, as **a.** *Bos bubalus* or *Bubalus buffelus*, an Old World species, orig. from India, valued as a draft animal **b.** *Bos caffer* or *Bulbalus caffer* (**Cape buffalo**), a South African species **c.** *Bison bison* (the **American buffalo** or bison). **2.** buffalo robe. **3.** buffalo fish. —*v.t.* *U.S. Slang.* **4.** to baffle; confound; mystify. **5.** to impress or intimidate by a display of power, importance, etc. [t. It.: m. *bufalo*, g. d. L *būfalus*, var. of *būbalus* BUBAL]

Buf·fa·lo (bŭf′ə lŏ′), *n.* a city in W New York: a port on Lake Erie. 532,759 (1960).

buffalo berry, **1.** the edible scarlet berry of *Shepherdia argentea* of the oleaster family of the U.S. and Canada. **2.** the shrub itself.

Buffalo Bill, sobriquet of **William Frederick Cody**.

buffalo bug, carpet beetle. Also, **buffalo moth**.

buffalo fish, any of several large carplike North American fresh-water fishes of the subfamily *Ictiobinae* of the sucker family (*Catostomidae*), comprising the genera *Ictiobus* and *Megastomatobus*.

buffalo grass, **1.** a short grass, *Buchloë dactyloides*, very prevalent on the dry plains east of the Rocky Mountains. **2.** any of many species of short grasses.

Buffalo Indian, Plains Indian.

buffalo robe, the skin of an American bison, prepared with the hair on, used as a lap robe.

buff·er[1] (bŭf′ər), *n.* **1.** an apparatus, such as the one at the end of a railroad car, for deadening the concussion between a moving body and something against which it strikes. **2.** anything serving to neutralize the shock of opposing forces. [f. BUFF[2], v. + -ER[1]]

buff·er[2] (bŭf′ər), *n.* **1.** a device for polishing; buffing wheel; buff stick. **2.** a worker who uses such a device. [f. BUFF[1] + -ER[1]]

buffer state, a smaller state lying between potentially hostile larger states.

buf·fet[1] (bŭf′ĭt), *n.*, *v.*, **-feted**, **-feting.** —*n.* **1.** a blow, as with the hand or fist. **2.** a violent shock or concussion. —*v.t.* **3.** to strike, as with the hand or fist. **4.** to contend against; battle. —*v.i.* **5.** to struggle with blows of hand or fist. **6.** to force one's way by a fight, struggle, etc. [ME, t. OF, dim. of *buffe* a blow] —*buff′fet·er*, *n.*

buf·fet[2] (bə fā′, bŏō-; *Brit.* bŭf′ĭt; *Fr.* bỹ fĕ′), *n.* **1.** a sideboard or cabinet for holding china, plate, etc. **2.** a counter, bar, or the like, for lunch or refreshments. **3.** a restaurant containing such a counter or bar. —*adj.* **4.** (of a meal) spread on tables or buffets from which the guests serve themselves. [t. F: orig., chair, table]

buffing wheel (bŭf′ĭng), buff wheel.

buf·fle·head (bŭf′əl hĕd′), *n.* a small North American duck, *Glaucionetta albeola*, the male of which has fluffy head plumage; butterball. [f. *buffle* buffalo + HEAD]

buf·fo (boo′fŏ; *It.* bŏōf′fô), *n.*, *pl.* **-fi** (-fē). *Music.* (in opera) a comedy part, usually bass. [t. It.: ridiculous, der. *buffare* blow with puffed cheeks]

Buf·fon (bỹ fôn′), *n.* **Georges Louis Leclerc** (zhôrzh lwē lə klĕr′), **Comte de**, 1707–88, French naturalist.

buf·foon (bə foon′), *n.* **1.** one who amuses others by tricks, odd gestures and postures, jokes, etc. **2.** one given to coarse or undignified joking. [t. F: m. *bouffon*, t. It.: m. *buffone* jester, der. *buffa* a jest] —**buf·foon′er·y**, *n.* —**buf·foon′ish**, *adj.*

buff stick, a small stick covered with leather or the like, used in polishing.

buff wheel, a wheel for polishing metal, etc., commonly covered with leather bearing a polishing powder.

bug (bŭg), *n.*, *v.t.*, **bugged**, **bugging.** —*n.* **1.** any insect of the suborder *Heteroptera* (order *Hemiptera*), characterized by having the forewings thickened at base and membranous at tip, and the hindwings membranous. Sucking mouth parts enable the majority to suck plant juices and others to feed on animals, including man. 2. (in popular usage) almost any insect. 3. *Chiefly Brit.* a bedbug. 4. (*often pl.*) *U.S. Colloq.* defect or difficulty: *eliminating the bugs in television.* 5. *Lit. or dial.* a bogy; hobgoblin. 6. *U.S. Slang.* a microphone hidden in a room to tap conversation there. —*v.t.* 7. *U.S. Slang.* to install a bug in (a room, etc.). [ME *bugge.* Cf. Welsh *bug* bogy, ghost]

Bug (*Pol.* bŏŏg, bŏŏk; *Russ.* bōōg), *n.* **1.** a river forming part of the boundary between E Poland and the W Soviet Union, flowing NW to the Vistula. 450 mi. **2.** a river in the SW Soviet Union, flowing SE to the estuary of the Dnieper. 470 mi.

bug·a·boo (bŭg′ə bōō′), *n., pl.* **-boos.** some imaginary thing that causes fear or worry; a bugbear; a bogy. [f. BUG bogy + BOO (def. 1); for the *-a-*, cf. BLACKAMOOR]

bug·bane (bŭg′bān′), *n.* any of various tall erect herbs of the ranunculaceous genus *Cimicifuga,* as *C. americana* of the eastern U.S., bearing clusters of white flowers supposed to repel insects.

bug·bear (bŭg′bâr′), *n.* **1.** any source, real or imaginary, of needless fright or fear. **2.** *Obs.* a goblin that eats up naughty children. [f. BUG (def. 5) + BEAR²]

bug·ger (bŭg′ər), *n.* **1.** one guilty of bestiality or sodomy. **2.** *Low Slang.* a foul, contemptible person. **3.** *Dial.* person; child. [t. F: m. *bougre,* t. ML: m. s. *Bulgarus* a Bulgarian, a heretic; certain Bulgarian heretics being charged with this crime] —**bug′ger·y,** *n.*

bug·gy¹ (bŭg′ĭ), *n., pl.* **-gies.** *U.S.* a light four-wheeled carriage with a single seat and a transverse spring. [orig. uncert.]

bug·gy² (bŭg′ĭ), *adj.,* **-gier,** **-giest.** infested with bugs. [f. BUG + -Y¹]

Buggy

bu·gle¹ (bū′gəl), *n., v.,* **-gled, -gling.** —*n.* **1.** a cornet-like military wind instrument, usually metal, used for sounding signals, and sometimes furnished with keys or valves. —*v.i.* **2.** to sound a bugle. —*v.t.* **3.** to call by bugle. [ME, t. OF. g. L *būculus,* dim. of *bōs* ox]

Bugle

bu·gle² (bū′gəl), *n.* any plant of the menthaceous genus *Ajuga,* esp. *A. reptans,* a low, blue-flowered herb. [t. F. g. LL *bugula* kind of plant]

bu·gle³ (bū′gəl), *n.* a tubular glass bead, usually black, used for ornamenting dresses. [orig. uncert.]

bu·gle·weed (bū′gəl wēd′), *n.* **1.** a plant of the menthaceous genus *Lycopus,* esp. *L. virginicus,* an herb with reputedly medicinal properties. **2.** the wild indigo. **3.** the bugle².

bu·gloss (bū′glŏs, -glôs), *n.* any of various boraginaceous plants, as *Anchusa officinalis,* an Old World medicinal herb with rough leaves, and *Lycopsis arvensis,* a bristly, blue-flowered herb. [t. F: m. *buglosse,* t. L: m. *būglossa,* t. Gk.: m. *boúglōssos* oxtongue]

bug·seed (bŭg′sēd′), *n.* an annual chenopodiaceous herb, *Corispermum hyssopifolium,* of northern temperate regions (so called from the flat, oval shape of its seeds).

buhl (bōōl), *n.* elaborate inlaid work of woods, metals, tortoise shell, ivory, etc. Also, **buhl·work** (bōōl′wŭrk′). [appar. Germanized sp. of F *boulle* or *boule,* named after A.C. *Boulle* or *Boule* (1642–1732), French cabinetmaker]

buhr (bûr), *n.* **1.** burr¹ (def. 2). **2.** burr⁴.

buhr·stone (bûr′stŏn′), *n.* burstone.

build (bĭld), *v.,* **built** or (*Archaic*) **builded, building,** *n.* —*v.t.* **1.** to construct (something relatively complex) by assembling and combining parts: *build a house or an empire.* **2.** to establish, increase, and strengthen (often fol. by *up*): *build up a business.* **3.** to base; form; construct: *to build one's hopes on promises.* **4.** to fill in with houses (fol. by *up*). **5.** *Games.* a. to make (words) from letters. **b.** to add (cards) to each other according to number, suit, etc. —*v.i.* **6.** to engage in the art or business of building. **7.** to form or construct a plan, system of thought, etc. (fol. by *on* or *upon*). —*n.* **8.** manner or form of construction: *a person's build.* [ME *bilden, bulde(n),* OE *byldan,* der. *bold* dwelling, house]

build·er (bĭl′dər), *n.* **1.** a person who builds. **2.** a person who contracts for the construction of buildings and supervises the workmen who build them. **3.** a substance, as an abrasive or filler, used with soap or another cleaning compound.

build·ing (bĭl′dĭng), *n.* **1.** anything built or constructed. **2.** the act, business, or art of constructing houses, etc.

—**Syn. 1.** BUILDING, EDIFICE, STRUCTURE refer to something built. BUILDING and STRUCTURE may apply to either a finished or an unfinished product of construction, and carry no implications as to size or condition. EDIFICE is not only a more formal word, but narrower in application, referring to a completed structure, and usually a large and imposing one. BUILDING generally connotes a useful purpose (houses, schools, business offices, etc.); STRUCTURE suggests the planning and constructive process.

building and loan association, *Finance.* an organization featuring a savings plan for members who intend to purchase or build a home.

built (bĭlt), *v.* pt. and pp. of **build.**

built-in (bĭlt′ĭn′), *adj.* built so as to be an integral, permanent part of a larger unit, as a bookcase.

Bui·ten·zorg (boi′tən zôrkH′, boĕ′-), *n.* the former Dutch name for **Bogor.**

Bu·kha·ra (bŏŏ hä′rä), *n.* **1.** a former state in W Asia: now a region in the Uzbek Republic of the Soviet Union. **2.** the chief city of this region. 60,000 (est. 1948). Also, **Bokhara.**

Bu·kha·rin (bŏŏ hä′rĭn), *n.* **Nikolai Ivanovich** (nĭ kō lī′ Ĭ vä′nō vĭch), 1888–1938, Russian editor, writer, and communist leader.

Bu·ko·vi·na (bōō′kə vē′nə; *Rum.* bŏŏ kō vē′nä), *n.* Bucovina.

Bu·la·wa·yo (bōō′lə wä′yō), *n.* a city in SW Southern Rhodesia: mining center. 82,395 with suburbs (est. 1953).

bulb (bŭlb), *n.* **1.** *Bot.* **a.** a bud, having fleshy leaves and usually subterranean, in which the stem is reduced to a flat disk, rooting from the under side, as in the onion, lily, etc. **b.** a plant growing from a bulb. **2.** any round, enlarged part, esp. one at the end of a long, slender body: *the bulb of a thermometer.* **3.** *Elect.* **a.** the glass housing, in which partial vacuum has been established, which contains the filament of an incandescent electric lamp. **b.** an incandescent electric lamp. **4.** an electron tube. **5.** *Anat.* **a. bulb of the spinal cord** or **brain,** the medulla oblongata. **b. bulb of the urethra,** the rounded mass of erectile tissue that surrounds the urethra at the posterior end of the penis, just in front of the anus. [t. L: s. *bulbus,* t. Gk.: m. *bolbós*] —**bulb·ar** (bŭl′bər), *adj.*

bulb·if·er·ous (bŭl bĭf′ər əs), *adj.* producing bulbs.

bul·bil (bŭl′bĭl), *n. Bot.* **1.** a little bulb. **2.** a small aerial bulb growing in the axils of leaves, as in the tiger lily, or replacing flower buds, as in the common onion. [t. NL: m.s. *bulbillus,* dim. of L *bulbus* BULB]

bulb·ous (bŭl′bəs), *adj.* **1.** bulb-shaped; bulging. **2.** having, or growing from, bulbs. Also, **bul·ba·ceous** (bŭl bā′shəs).

bul·bul (bŏŏl′bŏŏl), *n.* any bird of the tropical Old World family *Pycnonotidae,* much referred to in Persian poetry, and famed as songsters. [t. Pers.]

Bul·finch (bŏŏl′fĭnch), *n.* **1. Charles,** 1763–1844, U.S. architect. **2.** his son, **Thomas,** 1796–1867, author and compiler of myths.

Bulg., **1.** Bulgaria. **2.** Bulgarian.

Bul·ga·nin (bŏŏl gä′nĭn), *n.* **Nikolai A.,** born 1895, Soviet official: premier from 1955 to 1958.

Bul·gar (bŭl′gər, bŏŏl′gär), *n.* Bulgarian.

Bul·gar·i·a (bŭl gâr′Ĭ ə, bŏŏl-), *n.* a republic in SE Europe. 7,629,000 pop. (est. 1956); 42,800 sq. mi. (1946). *Cap.:* Sofia.

Bul·gar·i·an (bŭl gâr′Ĭ ən, bŏŏl-), *n.* **1.** a native or inhabitant of Bulgaria. **2.** a Slavic language, the language of Bulgaria. —*adj.* **3.** of or pertaining to Bulgaria, its people, or their language.

bulge (bŭlj), *n., v.,* **bulged, bulging.** —*n.* **1.** a rounded projecting or protruding part; protuberance; hump. **2.** *Naut.* the bilge, or bottom of a ship's hull. —*v.i.* **3.** to swell out; be protuberant. —*v.t.* **4.** to make protuberant. [ME, t. OF: m. *boulge,* g. L *bulga* bag, of Celtic orig.] —**bulg′y,** *adj.*

Bulge (bŭlj), *n.* **Battle of the,** the final German counter-offensive of World War II, begun Dec. 16, 1944, and thrusting deep into Allied territory in N and E Belgium: repulsed, Jan., 1945.

bulg·er (bŭl′jər), *n. Golf.* a club with a convex face.

bu·lim·i·a (bū lĭm′Ĭ ə), *n. Pathol.* morbidly voracious appetite; a disease marked by constant hunger. [t. NL, t. Gk.: m. *boulīmía* great hunger] —**bu·lim′ic,** *adj.*

bulk¹ (bŭlk), *n.* **1.** magnitude in three dimensions: *a ship of great bulk.* **2.** the greater part; the main mass or body: *the bulk of a debt.* **3.** goods or cargo not in packages, boxes, bags, etc. **4. in bulk,** unpackaged. **b.** in large quantites. **5** *Rare.* the body of a living creature. —*v.i.* **6.** to be of bulk, size, weight, or importance. **7.** to increase in size; grow large; swell. —*v.t.* **8.** to cause to swell or grow large. [ME *bolke* heap, t. Scand.; cf. Icel. *būlki* heap, cargo] —**Syn. 1.** See size.

bulk² (bŭlk), *n.* a structure, as a stall, projecting from the front of a building. [orig. uncert. Cf. BALK (def. 8)]

bulk·head (bŭlk′hĕd′), *n.* **1.** *Naut.* one of the upright partitions dividing a ship into compartments. **2.** *Civ. Eng.* a partition built in a subterranean passage to prevent the passage of air, water, or mud. **3.** *Bldg. Trades.* **a.** a horizontal or inclined outside door over a stairway leading to the cellar. **b.** a boxlike structure on a roof, etc., covering the head of a staircase or other opening.

bulk·y (bŭl′kĭ), *adj.,* **bulkier, bulkiest.** of great and cumbersome bulk or size. —**bulk′i·ly,** *adv.* —**bulk′i·ness,** *n.* —**Syn.** massive, ponderous, unwieldy.

bull¹ (bŏŏl), *n.* **1.** the male of a bovine animal, esp. of the genus *Bos,* with sexual organs intact and capable of reproduction. **2.** the male of certain other animals: *a bull elephant.* **3.** a bull-like person. **4.** (in general business) one who believes that conditions are or will be favorable. **5.** (in stock exchange slang) one who buys in the hope of profit from a rise in prices (opposed to *bear*). **6.** (*cap.*) *Astron.* **a.** the zodiacal constellation Taurus. **b.** the sign named for it. **7.** bulldog. —*adj.* **8.** male. **9.** bull-like; large. **10.** (in the stock exchange, etc.) pertaining to the bulls; marked by a rise in price. —*v.t.* **11.** (in the stock exchange, etc.) to endeavor to raise the price of (stocks, etc.). **12.** to operate in, for a rise in price. [ME *bule*, OE *bula; also ME *bulle*, OE *bull-* in *bulluc* bull calf. Cf. Icel. *boli*]

bull² (bŏŏl), *n.* 1. a bulla or seal. 2. *Rom. Cath. Ch.* a formal papal document having a bulla attached. [ME *bulle*, t. L: m. *bulla*, ML seal, document, L *bubble*, knob]

Bull (bŏŏl), *n.* **Ole Bornemann** (ō'lə bôr'nə män'), 1810–80, Norwegian violinist and composer.

bul·la (bŏŏl'ə, bŭl'ə), *n., pl.* **bullae** (bŏŏl'ē, bŭl'ē). 1. a seal attached to an official document, as a papal bull. 2. *Pathol.* a. a large vesicle. b. a blisterlike or bubble-like part of a bone. [t. ML. See BULL²]

bul·late (bŏŏl'āt, -ĭt, bŭl'-), *adj.* 1. *Bot., Zool.* having the surface covered with irregular and slight elevations, giving a blistered appearance. 2. *Anat.* inflated; vaulted. [t. L: m. s. *bullātus* having bubbles.]

bull·bat (bŏŏl'băt'), *n.* the nighthawk (def. 1).

bull brier, a smilacaceous North American plant, *Smilax Pseudochina*, with tuberous rootstocks.

bull·dog (bŏŏl'dôg', -dŏg'), *n.* 1. a large-headed, short-haired, heavily built variety of dog, of comparatively small size but very muscular and courageous. 2. a short-barreled revolver of large caliber. 3. the servant or assistant who accompanies the proctor at Oxford and Cambridge Universities when on duty. —*adj.* 4. like or characteristic of a bulldog: *bulldog tenacity.* —*v.t.* 5. to attack in the manner of a bulldog. 6. *Western U.S.* to throw (a calf, etc.) by seizing it by the horns.

English bulldog (13 in. or more high at the shoulder)

bull·doze (bŏŏl'dōz'), *v.t.,* **-dozed, -dozing.** 1. *U.S. Slang.* to coerce or intimidate by violence or threats. 2. to use a bulldozer on.

bull·doz·er (bŏŏl'dō'zər), *n.* *U.S. Slang.* 1. a person who intimidates. 2. a powerful caterpillar tractor having a vertical blade at the front end for moving earth, tree stumps, rocks, etc.

Bul·ler (bŏŏl'ər), *n.* **Sir Redvers Henry** (rĕd'vərz), 1839–1908, British general.

bul·let (bŏŏl'ĭt), *n.* 1. a small metal projectile, part of a cartridge, for firing from small arms. See diag. under **cartridge.** 2. a small ball. [t. F: m. *boulet(te)*, dim. of *boule* ball]

bul·let·head (bŏŏl'ĭt hĕd'), *n.* 1. a round head. 2. a person having such a head. 3. an obstinate or stupid person. —**bul'let·head'ed,** *adj.*

bul·le·tin (bŏŏl'ə tən, -tĭn), *n.* 1. a brief account or statement, as of news or events, issued for the information of the public. 2. a periodical publication, as of a learned society. —*v.t.* 3. to make known by a bulletin. [t. F, t. It.: m. *bullettino*, dim. of *bulletta*, dim. of *bulla* edict. See BULL², BULLA]

bulletin board, a board for the posting of bulletins, notices, announcements, etc.

bul·let·proof (bŏŏl'ĭt prōōf'), *adj.* capable of resisting the impact of a bullet.

bull·fight (bŏŏl'fīt'), *n.* a combat between men and a bull or bulls in an enclosed arena. —**bull'fight'er,** *n.* —**bull'fight'ing,** *n.*

bull·finch¹ (bŏŏl'fĭnch'), *n.* 1. a rosy-breasted European fringilline bird, *Pyrrhula pyrrhula*, with a short, stout bill, valued as a cage bird. 2. any of various allied or similar birds. [f. BULL¹ + FINCH]

bull·finch² (bŏŏl'fĭnch'), *n.* a hedge high enough to impede hunters. [orig. uncert.]

bull·frog (bŏŏl'frŏg', -frôg'), *n.* a large frog, as the American *Rana catesbeiana*, which has an exceptionally deep bass voice.

bull·head (bŏŏl'hĕd'), *n.* 1. (in America) any species of *Ameiurus*; horned pout. See catfish (def. 1). 2. any of various edible fishes with a large or broad head, esp. those with a spine on each side of the head. 3. an obstinate or stupid person.

bull·head·ed (bŏŏl'hĕd'ĭd), *adj.* obstinate; blunderingly stubborn; stupid. —**bull'head'ed·ness,** *n.*

bul·lion (bŏŏl'yən), *n.* 1. gold or silver in the mass. 2. gold or silver in the form of bars or ingots. 3. a cordlike trimming made of twisted gold or silver wire, or a trimming of cord covered with gold or silver thread (bullion fringe), used to ornament uniforms, etc. [ME *bullioun*, t. AF: m. *bouillir* boil, g. L *bullīre*; in part confused with OF *billon* debased metal]

bull·ish (bŏŏl'ĭsh), *adj.* 1. like a bull. 2. obstinate or stupid. 3. (in the stock exchange, etc.) tending to cause a rise in price. 4. optimistic.

Bull Moose, member of the Progressive Party (def. 1).

bull-necked (bŏŏl'nĕkt'), *adj.* thick-necked.

bull nose, *Vet. Sci.* a disease of swine caused by bacterial infection of the tissues of the snout causing gross malformation of the part and frequently serious blocking of the nasal passages.

bull·ock (bŏŏl'ək), *n.* a castrated male of a bovine animal, not having been used for reproduction; ox; steer. [ME *bullok*, OE *bulluc*. See BULL¹, -OCK]

bull pen, *U.S.* 1. a pen for a bull or bulls. 2. *Colloq.* a place for the temporary confinement of prisoners or suspects. 3. *Colloq.* any other place of temporary or crowded

stay, as sleeping quarters in a lumber camp. 4. *Baseball.* a place where relief pitchers warm up during a game.

bull·pout (bŏŏl'pout'), *n.* horned pout.

bull ring, an arena for a bullfight.

bull·roar·er (bŏŏl'rōr'ər), *n.* a long, thin, narrow piece of wood attached to a string, by which it is whirled in the air, making a roaring sound: used for religious rites by certain primitive tribes, as of Australian aborigines, American Indians, etc., and as a children's toy; thunder stick.

Bull Run, a small river in NE Virginia: two important battles of the Civil War were fought near here, both resulting in defeat for the Union forces, 1861, 1862. See map under **Antietam.**

bull's-eye (bŏŏlz'ī'), *n.* 1. the central spot, usually black, of a target. 2. a shot that strikes the bull's-eye. 3. a small circular opening or window. 4. a thick disk or lenslike piece of glass inserted in a deck or the like to admit light. 5. *Naut.* an oval or circular wooden block having a groove around it and a hole in the center through which to reeve a rope. 6. *Chiefly Brit.* a round, hard lump of candy.

bull snake, the gopher snake. See **gopher** (def. 4).

bull terrier, one of a breed of dogs produced by crossing the bulldog and the terrier.

bull tongue, a simple form of plow, so called from its shape.

bull-tongue (bŏŏl'tŭng'), *v.t., v.i.* to plow with a bull tongue.

Bull terrier, white variety (18 in. high at the shoulder)

bul·ly¹ (bŏŏl'ĭ), *n., pl.* **-lies,** *v.,* **-lied, -lying,** *adj., interj.* —*n.* 1. a blustering, quarrelsome, overbearing person who browbeats smaller or weaker people. 2. *Archaic.* a man hired to do violence. 3. *Obs.* a pimp; procurer. 4. *Obs.* good friend; good fellow. 5. *Obs.* sweetheart; darling. —*v.t.* 6. to act the bully toward. —*v.i.* 7. to be loudly arrogant and overbearing. —*adj.* 8. *Colloq.* fine; excellent; very good. 9. dashing; jovial; high-spirited. —*interj.* 10. *Colloq.* good! well done! [orig. uncert.]

bul·ly² (bŏŏl'ĭ), *n.* bully beef. [? t. F: m. *bouilli* boiled beef, prop. pp. of *bouillir* boil]

bully beef, canned or pickled beef.

bul·ly·rag (bŏŏl'ĭ răg'), *v.t.,* **-ragged, -ragging.** to bully; badger; abuse; tease. Also, **ballyrag.**

bully tree, any of various sapotaceous trees of tropical America, as *Manilkara bidentata* of Guiana, which yields the gum balata. [said to be f. m. *balata* + TREE]

Bü·low (by'lō), *n.* **Prince Bernhard von** (bĕrn'härt fən), 1849–1929, chancellor of Germany, 1900–09.

bul·rush (bŏŏl'rŭsh'), *n.* 1. (in Biblical use) the papyrus, *Cyperus papyrus*. 2. any of various large rushes or rushlike plants, as *Scirpus lacustris*, a tall perennial from which mats, bottoms of chairs, etc., are made. 3. any of various rushes of the genus *Scirpus*. [f. *bull* large (cf. *bull trout*) + RUSH²]

bul·wark (bŏŏl'wərk), *n.* 1. *Fort.* a defensive mound of earth or other material situated round a place; a rampart. 2. any protection against annoyance or injury from outside. 3. (*usually pl.*) *Naut.* a solid part of a ship's side extending like a fence above the level of the deck. —*v.t.* 4. to fortify with a bulwark or rampart; secure by a fortification; protect. [ME *bulwerk*. Cf. G *bollwerk*, appar. orig. bole (tree trunk) work. Cf. BOULEVARD]

Bul·wer (bŏŏl'wər), *n.* **William Henry Lytton Earle** (lĭt'ən), (*Baron Dalling and Bulwer*) 1801–72, British diplomat and author, known as Sir Henry Bulwer.

Bul·wer-Lyt·ton (bŏŏl'wər lĭt'ən), *n.* See **Lytton.**

bum (bŭm), *n., v.,* **bummed, bumming.** *U.S. Colloq.* —*n.* 1. a shiftless or dissolute person. 2. a habitual loafer and tramp. 3. a drunken orgy; a debauch. —*v.t.* 4. to get for nothing; borrow without expectation of returning. —*v.i.* 5. to sponge on others for a living; lead an idle or dissolute life. —*adj.* 6. of poor, wretched, or miserable quality; bad. [orig. meaning "rump"; akin to BUMP] —**bum'mer,** *n.*

bum-bail·iff (bŭm'bā'lĭf), *n. Brit. Contemptuous.* a bailiff or under-bailiff employed in serving writs, making arrests, etc.

bum·ble·bee (bŭm'bəl bē'), *n.* any of various large, hairy social bees of the family *Bombidae*. [f. *bumble* buzz + BEE¹]

Bumblebee (queen), *Bombus americanorum* (Ab. ¾ in. long)

bum·boat (bŭm'bōt'), *n. Naut.* a boat used in peddling provisions and small wares among vessels lying in port or off shore. —**bum·boat·man** (bŭm'bōt'mən), *n.*

bum·kin (bŭm'kĭn), *n. Naut.* a bumpkin².

bump (bŭmp), *v.t.* 1. to come more or less violently in contact with; strike; collide with. 2. to cause to strike or collide: *to bump one's head against the wall.* —*v.i.* 3. to come in contact with; collide (often fol. by *against, into*). —*n.* 4. act of bumping; a blow. 5. the shock of a blow or collision. 6. a swelling or contusion from a blow. 7. a small area raised above the level of the surrounding surface, as on the skull or on a road. 8. *Aeron.* a rapidly rising current of air which gives an airplane a dangerous jolt or upward thrust. [imit.]

---

b., blend of, blended; c., cognate with; d., dialect, dialectal; der., derived from; f., formed from; g., going back to; m., modification of; r., replacing; s., stem of; t., taken from; ?, perhaps. See the full key on inside cover.

bump·er (bŭm′pər), *n.* **1.** a person or thing that bumps. **2.** *Auto.* a horizontal bar affixed to the front or rear of a car to give protection in collisions. **3.** a cup or glass filled to the brim, esp. when drunk as a toast. **4.** *Colloq.* something unusually large. —*adj.* **5.** unusually abundant: *bumper crops.* —*v.t.* **6.** to fill to the brim. **7.** to drink a bumper as a toast to. —*v.i.* **8.** to drink toasts.

bump·kin[1] (bŭmp′kĭn), *n.* an awkward, clumsy yokel. [t. MD: m. *bommekyn* little barrel]

bump·kin[2] (bŭmp′kĭn), *n. Naut.* a beam or spar projecting outward from the bow, side, or stern of a ship to extend a sail, secure blocks, or the like. Also, **bumkin.** [t. MD: m. *boomken* little tree]

bump·tious (bŭmp′shəs), *adj.* offensively self-assertive: *he's a bumptious young upstart.* [f. BUMP + -tious, modeled on FRACTIOUS, etc.] —**bump′tious·ly,** *adv.* —**bump′tious·ness,** *n.*

bump·y (bŭm′pĭ), *adj.*, **bumpier, bumpiest. 1.** of uneven surface: *a bumpy road.* **2.** full of jolts: *a bumpy ride.* **3.** giving rise to jolts: *bumpy air.* —**bump′i·ly,** *adv.* —**bump′i·ness,** *n.*

bun (bŭn), *n.* **1.** a kind of bread roll, variously shaped, usually only slightly sweetened, and sometimes containing spice, dried currants, citron, etc. **2.** hair arranged in a bun shape. [ME *bunne;* orig. uncert.]

bu·na (bōō′nə, bū′-), *n. Chem.* **1.** any synthetic rubber made by copolymerizing butadiene with other material. **2.** (*orig.*) a synthetic rubber made by polymerizing butadiene by means of styrene. [f. BU(TADIENE) + NA (the symbol for sodium)]

bunch (bŭnch), *n.* **1.** a connected group; cluster: *a bunch of bananas.* **2.** a group of things; lot: *a bunch of papers.* **3.** *Colloq.* a group of human beings: *a fine bunch of boys.* **4.** a knob; lump; protuberance. **5.** to group together; make a bunch of. —*v.i.* **6.** to gather into a cluster or protuberance; gather together. [ME *bunche;* orig. uncert.] —**Syn. 1, 2.** See **bundle.**

bunch·ber·ry (bŭnch′bĕr′ĭ), *n.*, *pl.* **-ries.** a dwarf species of cornel, *Cornus canadensis* bearing dense clusters of bright-red berries.

Bunche (bŭnch), *n.* **Ralph,** born 1904, U. S. diplomat.

buncher resonator. See **klystron.**

bunch·flow·er (bŭnch′flou′ər), *n.* **1.** a liliaceous plant, *Melanthium virginicum,* of the U.S., bearing grasslike leaves and a panicle of small greenish flowers. **2.** any other plant of the same genus.

bunch grass, any of various grasses in different regions of the U.S. growing in distinct clumps.

bunch·y (bŭn′chĭ), *adj.*, **bunchier, bunchiest. 1.** having bunches. **2.** bulging or protuberant.

bun·co (bŭng′kō), *n.*, *pl.* **-cos,** *v.*, **-coed, -coing.** *U.S. Colloq.* —*n.* **1.** a swindle in which a person is lured to some place and there fleeced at a game or otherwise victimized; a confidence game. **2.** any swindle or misrepresentation. —*v.t.* **3.** to victimize by a bunco. Also, **bunko.** [short for BUNCOMBE]

bun·combe (bŭng′kəm), *n.* **1.** insincere speechmaking intended merely to please political constituents. **2.** insincere talk; claptrap; humbug. Also, **bunkum.** [from a Congressional representative's phrase, "talking for *Buncombe*" (county of North Carolina)]

bunco steerer, *U.S. Colloq.* a swindler.

Bund (bŏŏnd; *Ger.* bŏŏnt), *n.*, *pl.* **Bünde** (byn′də). **1.** a short form of "German-American Volksbund," a Nazi-inspired and directed organization in the U.S. **2.** an alliance or league. [t. G]

bund (bŭnd), *n.* (in India, China, Japan, etc.) an embankment; an embanked quay. [t. Hind.: m. *band*]

Bun·del·khand (bŭn′dəl kŭnd′, -кнŭnd′), *n.* formerly a group of native states in central India: now a part of Vindhya Pradesh.

Bun·des·rat (bŏŏn′dəs rät′), *n.* **1.** (formerly) a federal legislative council of representatives from the 26 states of the German Empire. Now upper house of German Federal Parliament. **2.** the federal council of Switzerland. Also, **Bun·des·rath** (bŏŏn′dəs rät′). [G]

bun·dle (bŭn′dəl), *n.*, *v.*, **-dled, -dling.** —*n.* **1.** a group bound together: *a bundle of hay.* **2.** something wrapped for carrying; package. **3.** a number of things considered together. **4.** *Bot.* an aggregation of strands of specialized conductive and mechanical tissue. —*v.t.* **5.** to tie or wrap in a bundle. **6.** to dress snugly (fol. by *up*). **7.** to send away hurriedly or unceremoniously (fol. by *off, out,* etc.). —*v.i.* **8.** to leave hurriedly or unceremoniously (fol. by *off, out,* etc.). **9.** to dress warmly (fol. by *up*). **10.** to sleep or lie in the same bed without undressing, esp. of sweethearts, as in early New England. [ME *bundel,* t. MD, c. G *bündel;* akin to OE *byndele* binding together] —**bun′dler,** *n.*
—**Syn. 1.** BUNDLE, BUNCH refer to a number of things or an amount of something fastened or bound together BUNDLE implies a close binding or grouping together, and often refers to a wrapped package: *a bundle of laundry, of dry goods.* A BUNCH is a number of things, usually all of the same kind, fastened together: *a bunch of roses or of keys.*

bung (bŭng), *n.* **1.** a stopper for the hole of a cask. **2.** a bunghole. —*v.t.* **3.** to close with or as a bung (often fol. by *up*). **4.** to beat; bruise; maul (often fol. by *up*). [ME *bunge,* t. MD: m. *bonghe*]

bun·ga·low (bŭng′gə lō′), *n.* **1.** a cottage, commonly of one story or a story and a half, esp. for country or seaside residence. **2.** (in India) a one-storied thatched or tiled house, usually surrounded by a veranda. [t. Hind.: m. *banglā,* lit., of Bengal]

bung·hole (bŭng′hōl′), *n.* a hole or orifice in a cask through which it is filled.

bun·gle (bŭng′gəl), *v.*, **-gled, -gling,** *n.* —*v.i.* **1.** to do something awkwardly and clumsily. **2.** to do clumsily and awkwardly; botch. —*n.* **3.** a bungling performance. **4.** a bungled job. [? imit.] —**bun′gler,** *n.* —**bun′gling·ly,** *adv.*

Bu·nin (bōō′nĭn), *n.* **Ivan Alekseevich** (ĭ vän′ ä′lĕk-sĕ′yə vĭch), 1870–1953, Russian poet and novelist.

bun·ion (bŭn′yən), *n. Pathol.* a swelling on the foot caused by the inflammation of a synovial bursa, esp. of the great toe. [orig. obscure]

bunk[1] (bŭngk), *n.* **1.** a built-in platform bed, as on a ship. **2.** *Colloq.* any bed. —*v.i.* **3.** *Colloq.* to occupy a bunk; sleep, esp. in rough quarters. [orig. unknown]

bunk[2] (bŭngk), *n.* *U.S. Slang.* humbug; nonsense. [short for BUNCOMBE]

bunk·er (bŭng′kər), *n.* **1.** a fixed chest or box; a large bin or receptacle: *a coal bunker.* **2.** *Golf.* **a.** an obstruction or obstacle on a course. **b.** a sandy hollow or other rough place on the course. **c.** an obstacle, usually a small ridge, generally preceded by a sand trap. —*v.t.* **3.** *Golf.* to drive (a ball) into a bunker. [orig. uncert.]

Bunker Hill, a hill in Charlestown, Massachusetts: the first major battle of the American Revolution was fought on adjoining Breed's Hill, June 17, 1775.

bun·ko (bŭng′kō), *n.*, *pl.* **-kos,** *v.*, **-koed, -koing.** **bunco.**

bun·kum (bŭng′kəm), *n.* **buncombe.**

bun·ny (bŭn′ĭ), *n.*, *pl.* **-nies.** *Colloq.* **1.** a rabbit. **2.** *U.S.* a squirrel.

Bun·sen (bŭn′sən; *Ger.* bŏŏn′zən), *n.* **Robert Wilhelm** (rō′bĕrt vĭl′hĕlm), 1811–99, German chemist.

Bunsen burner, a type of gas burner with which a very hot, practically nonluminous flame is obtained by allowing air to enter at the base and mix with the gas.

bunt[1] (bŭnt), *v.t.* **1.** (of a goat or calf) to push with the horns or head. **2.** *Baseball.* to bounce (the ball) from the loosely held bat so that it goes only a short distance. —*v.i.* **3.** to push (something) with the horns or head. **4.** *Baseball.* to bunt a ball. —*n.* **5.** a push with the head or horns; butt. **6.** *Baseball.* **a.** act of bunting. **b.** a bunted ball. [nasalized var. of BUTT²]

bunt[2] (bŭnt), *n.* **1.** *Naut.* the middle part of a square sail. **2.** the bagging part of a fishing net or the like. [orig. unknown]

bunt[3] (bŭnt), *n.* a disease of wheat in which the kernels are replaced by black fungus spores. [orig. unknown]

bunt·ing[1] (bŭn′tĭng), *n.* **1.** a coarse open fabric of worsted or cotton used for flags, signals, etc. **2.** flags, esp. a vessel's flags, collectively. [cf. G *bunt* parti-colored]

bunt·ing[2] (bŭn′tĭng), *n.* any of numerous small fringilline birds of the genera *Emberiza, Passerina,* and *Plectrophenax* as, respectively, the reed bunting (*E. schoeniclus*) of Europe, the indigo bunting (*P. cyanea*) of U.S. and Canada, and the snow bunting (*P. nivalis*) of arctic regions. [ME *bountyng;* orig. uncert.]

bunt·line (bŭnt′lĭn, -lĭn′), *n. Naut.* one of the ropes attached to the foot of a square sail to haul it up to the yard for furling. [f. BUNT² + LINE¹]

Bun·yan (bŭn′yən), *n.* **1. John,** 1628–88, British preacher: author of *Pilgrim's Progress.* **2. Paul,** hero of American lumberjack tall tales.

Buo·na·par·te (bwô′nä pär′tĕ), *n.* Italian spelling of **Bonaparte.**

Buo·nar·ro·ti (bwô′när rô′tĕ), *n.* See **Michelangelo.**

buoy (boi, bōō′ĭ), *n. Naut.* **1.** a distinctively marked and shaped anchored float, sometimes carrying a light, whistle, or bell, marking a channel or obstruction. **2.** a life buoy. —*v.t.* **3.** to support by or as by a buoy; keep afloat in a fluid. **4.** *Naut.* to furnish or mark with a buoy or buoys: *to buoy or buoy off a channel.* **5.** to bear up or sustain, as hope or courage does. —*v.i.* **6.** to float; rise by reason of lightness. [ME *boye,* t. MD: m. *boeie* buoy, ult. t. L: m. *boia* fetter]

Buoys (def. 1)
A. Bell buoy; B. Spar buoy;
C. Light buoy; D. Whistle buoy

buoy·age (boi′ĭj, bōō′ĭj), *n. Naut.* **1.** a system of buoys. **2.** buoys collectively. **3.** the providing of buoys.

buoy·an·cy (boi′ən sĭ, bōō′yən sĭ), *n.* **1.** the power to float or rise in a fluid; relative lightness. **2.** the power of supporting a body so that it floats; upward pressure exerted by the fluid in which a body is immersed. **3.** elasticity of spirit; cheerfulness.

buoy·ant (boi′ənt, bōō′yənt), *adj.* **1.** tending to float or rise in a fluid. **2.** capable of keeping a body afloat, as a liquid. **3.** not easily depressed; cheerful. **4.** cheering or invigorating. —**buoy′ant·ly,** *adv.*

bu·pres·tid (bū prĕs′tĭd), *n.* any beetle of the family *Buprestidae,* comprising the metallic wood borers, noted for their brilliant coloration. [f. s. L *būprestis,* t. Gk.: m. *boúprēstis,* lit., ox-burner + -ID²]

bur (bûr), *n.*, *v.*, **burred, burring.** —*n.* **1.** *Bot.* the rough, prickly case around the seeds of certain plants, as of the chestnut and burdock. **2.** any bur-bearing plant. **3.** something that adheres like a bur. **4.** *Mach.* burr¹ (defs. 1, 2, 3). —*v.t.* **5.** to extract or remove burs from. Also, **burr.** [ME *burre,* t. Scand.; cf. Dan. *borre*]

bu·ran (bōōrän′), *n.* a violent storm of wind on the steppes of Russia and Siberia, esp. one accompanied by driving snow and intense cold. [t. Turk.]

Bur·bage (bûr′bĭj), *n.* **Richard,** 1567?–1619, English actor: associate of Shakespeare.

Bur·bank (bûr′băngk), *n.* **1. Luther,** 1849–1926, U.S. horticulturist who produced a number of new varieties. **2.** a city in SW California. 90,155 (1960)

bur·ble (bûr′bəl), *v.,* **-bled, -bling,** *n.* —*v.i.* **1.** to make a bubbling sound; bubble. **2.** to speak with a burble. —*n.* **3.** a bubbling or gentle gush. **4.** a bubbling flow of speech. **5.** *Aeron.* the breakdown of smooth airflow around a wing at a high angle of attack. [prob. imit.]

bur·bot (bûr′bət), *n., pl.* **-bots,** (*esp. collectively*) **-bot.** a fresh-water fish of the cod family, *Lota lota,* of Europe, Asia, and North America, with an elongated body and a barbel on the chin. [ME *borbot,* t. F: m. *borbote* (appar. der. L *barba* beard, b. with *borbe* slime)]

burd (bûrd), *n. Obs. except Poetic.* a lady; a maiden.

bur·den[1] (bûr′dən), *n.* **1.** that which is carried; a load. **2.** that which is borne with difficulty: *burden of responsibilities.* **3.** *Naut.* **a.** the weight of a ship's cargo. **b.** the carrying capacity of a ship: *a ship of a hundred tons burden.* —*v.t.* **4.** to load heavily. **5.** to load oppressively; oppress. Also, *Archaic,* **burthen.** [var. of *burthen,* OE *byrthen;* akin to BEAR[1]] —**Syn. 1.** See **load.**

bur·den[2] (bûr′dən), *n.* **1.** something often repeated or much dwelt upon; the principal idea. **2.** *Music.* the refrain or recurring chorus of a song. [ME *burdoun,* t. OF: m. *bourdon* a humming, the drone of a bagpipe, der. L *burda* pipe; later assoc. with BURDEN[1]]

burden of proof, *Chiefly Law.* **1.** the obligation to offer evidence which the court or jury could reasonably believe, in support of a contention, failing which the party will lose its case. **2.** the obligation to establish an alleged fact by convincing the tribunal of its probable truth (**the burden of persuasion**).

bur·den·some (bûr′dən səm), *adj.* oppressively heavy. Also, *Archaic,* **burthensome.** —**bur′den·some·ly,** *adv.* —**bur′den·some·ness,** *n.*

bur·dock (bûr′dŏk), *n.* a plant of the composite genus *Arctium,* esp. *A. lappa,* a coarse, broad-leaved weed with prickly heads or burs which stick to the clothing. [f. BUR + DOCK[1]]

bu·reau (byŏŏr′ō), *n., pl.* **-eaus, -eaux** (-ōz). **1.** a chest of drawers for holding clothing, etc., often provided with a mirror. **2.** *Brit.* a desk or writing table with drawers for papers. **3.** a division of a government department or independent administrative unit. **4.** an office for giving out information, etc.: *travel bureau.* [t. F: desk, office, OF *burel* cloth-covered table, kind of woolen cloth, ult. der. L *būra,* var. of *burra* long-haired woolen cloth]

bu·reauc·ra·cy (byŏŏrŏk′rə sĭ), *n., pl.* **-cies.** *Govt.* **1.** government by bureaus. **2.** the body of officials administering bureaus. **3.** excessive multiplication of, and concentration of power in, administrative bureaus. **4.** excessive governmental red tape and routine. [t. F: m. *bureaucratie.* See BUREAU, -CRACY]

bu·reau·crat (byŏŏr′ə krăt′), *n. Govt.* **1.** an official of a bureaucracy. **2.** an official who works by fixed routine without exercising intelligent judgment. —**bu′reau·crat′ic,** *adj.* —**bu′reau·crat′i·cal·ly,** *adv.*

bu·rette (byŏŏ rĕt′), *n. Chem.* a graduated glass tube, commonly having a stopcock at the bottom, used for accurately measuring, or measuring out, small quantities of liquid. Also, **bu·ret′.** [t. F: cruet, dim. of *buire* vessel for wine, etc. Cf. BUCKET]

burg (bûrg), *n.* **1.** *Colloq.* a city or town. **2.** *Hist.* a fortified town. [var. of BURGH]

-burg, (in compound names) "city" or "town," as in *Parkersburg.* [var. of BOROUGH]

burg·age (bûr′gĭj), *n. Law.* **1.** (in England) a tenure whereby burgesses or townsmen hold their lands or tenements of the king or other lord, usually for a fixed money rent. **2.** (in Scotland) that tenure by which the property in royal burghs is held under the crown, proprietors being liable to the (nominal) service of watching and warding. [t. ML: m. *burgāgium,* der. *burgus,* Latinized form of BURG(H), BOROUGH]

Bur·gas (bŏŏr gäs′), *n.* a seaport in E Bulgaria, on the **Gulf of Burgas** (inlet of Black Sea). 43,684 (1948).

bur·gee (bûr′jē), *n. Naut.* a swallow-tailed flag or pennant, in the merchant service generally bearing the ship's name. [orig. uncert.; ? der. *burge* burgeon?]

bur·geon (bûr′jən), *n.* **1.** a bud; a sprout. —*v.i.* **2.** to begin to grow, as a bud; to put forth buds, shoots, as a plant (often fol. by *out, forth*). —*v.t.* **3.** to put forth as buds. Also, **bourgeon.** [ME *burjon,* t. OF, ? t. Gmc.]

bur·gess (bûr′jĭs), *n.* **1.** an inhabitant, esp. a citizen or freeman, of an English borough. **2.** *Hist.* a representative of a borough, corporate town, or university in the British Parliament. **3.** *U.S. Hist.* a representative in the popular branch of the colonial legislature of Virginia or Maryland. [ME *burgeis,* t. OF, g. LL *burgēnsis* a citizen. Cf. BOURGEOIS]

Bur·gess (bûr′jĭs), *n.* **(Frank) Gelett** (jə lĕt′), 1866–1951, U.S. illustrator and humorist.

burgh (bûrg; *Scot.* bŭr′ō, -ə), *n.* a borough (applied to chartered towns in Scotland). [var. of BOROUGH] —**burgh′al** (bûr′gəl), *adj.*

burgh·er (bûr′gər), *n.* an inhabitant of a borough; a citizen.

Burgh·ley (bûr′lĭ), *n.* **William Cecil,** 1520–98, British statesman: adviser to Elizabeth. Also, **Burleigh.**

bur·glar (bûr′glər), *n.* one who commits burglary. [cf. Anglo-L *burglātor,* var. of *burgātor,* Latinization of AF *burgur* burglar, der. *burgier* pillage]

bur·glar·i·ous (bər glâr′ĭ əs), *adj.* pertaining to or involving burglary. —**bur·glar′i·ous·ly,** *adv.*

bur·glar·ize (bûr′glə rīz′), *v.t.,* **-ized, -izing.** *Colloq.* to commit burglary upon.

bur·gla·ry (bûr′glə rĭ), *n., pl.* **-ries.** *Criminal Law.* the felony of breaking into and entering the house of another at night with intent to commit a felony therein, extended by statute to cover the breaking and entering of any of various buildings, by night or day.

bur·gle (bûr′gəl), *v.t., v.i.,* **-gled, -gling.** *Colloq.* to commit burglary; burglarize.

bur·go·mas·ter (bûr′gə măs′tər, -mäs′tər), *n.* the chief magistrate of a municipal town of Holland, Flanders, Germany, or Austria. [t. D: m. *burgemeester,* lit., town master]

bur·go·net (bûr′gə nĕt′), *n. Armor.* an open helmet usually with pivoted peak and hinged cheek pieces. [t. F: m. *bourguignotte,* der. *Bourgogne* Burgundy]

bur·goo (bûr′gōō, bûr gōō′), *n., pl.* **-goos. 1.** a thick oatmeal gruel, as used by seamen. **2.** *U.S. Dial.* a kind of thick, highly seasoned soup. **3.** *U.S. Dial.* a picnic at which such soup is served. [orig. uncert.]

Bur·gos (bŏŏr′gōs), *n.* a city in N Spain: famous cathedral. 74,063 (1950).

Bur·goyne (bər goin′), *n.* **John,** 1722–92, British general in American Revolutionary War.

bur·grave (bûr′grāv), *n. Ger. Hist.* **1.** the appointed head of a fortress. **2.** hereditary governor of a castle or town. [t. G: m. *burggraf,* f. *burg* castle +*graf* count]

Bur·gun·di·an (bər gŭn′dĭ ən), *adj.* **1.** of or pertaining to Burgundy or its people. —*n.* **2.** a native or an inhabitant of Burgundy.

Bur·gun·dy (bûr′gən dĭ), *n., pl.* **-dies. 1.** French, **Bourgogne.** a region in SE France: a former kingdom, duchy, and province. See map under **Brittany. 2.** (*often l.c.*) wine, of many varieties, red and white, mostly still, full, and dry, produced in the Burgundy region. **3.** (*often l.c.*) some similar wine made elsewhere. **4.** (*l.c.*) dull reddish-blue (color).

bur·i·al (bĕr′ĭ əl), *n.* act of burying. [f. BURY + -AL[2] (cf. *funeral*); r. ME *buriel,* OE *byrgels* burying place, g. pre-E **burgh-* + -*ils* (var. of -*isl*) suffix; for dropping of -*s* (mistaken for plural sign), cf. RIDDLE, CHERRY]

burial ground, a tract of land for burial of the dead.

bur·i·er (bĕr′ĭ ər), *n.* one who or that which buries.

bu·rin (byŏŏr′ĭn), *n.* **1.** a tempered steel rod, with a lozenge-shaped point and a rounded handle, used for engraving furrows in metal. **2.** a similar tool used by marble workers. [t. F, prob. of Gmc. orig.; cf. OHG *bora* gimlet. See BORE[1]]

burke (bûrk), *v.t.,* **burked, burking. 1.** to murder, as by suffocation, so as to leave no or few marks of violence. **2.** to get rid of by some indirect maneuver. [from W. *Burke,* hanged at Edinburgh in 1829 for murders of this kind]

Burke (bûrk), *n.* **Edmund,** 1729–97, British statesman, orator, and writer.

burl (bûrl), *n.* **1.** a small knot or lump in wool, thread, or cloth. **2.** a dome-shaped growth on the trunk of a tree; a wartlike structure sometimes two feet across and a foot or more in height, sliced to make a veneer known as **burlwood veneer.** —*v.t.* **3.** to remove burls from (cloth) in finishing. [ME *burle,* t. OF: m. *bourle,* ult. der. LL *burra* flock of wool] —**burled,** *adj.*

bur·lap (bûr′lăp), *n.* a coarse fabric made of jute, hemp, or the like; gunny.

Bur·leigh (bûr′lĭ), *n.* **Burghley.**

bur·lesque (bər lĕsk′), *n., adj., v.,* **-lesqued, -lesquing.** —*n.* **1.** an artistic composition, esp. literary or dramatic, which, for the sake of laughter, vulgarizes lofty material or treats ordinary material with mock dignity. **2.** any ludicrous take-off or debasing caricature. **3.** *U.S.* a theatrical entertainment featuring coarse, crude, often vulgar comedy and dancing. —*adj.* **4.** involving ludicrous or debasing treatment of a solemn subject. **5.** of or pertaining to risqué burlesque. —*v.t.* **6.** to make ridiculous by mocking representation. —*v.i.* **7.** to use caricature. [t. F, t. It.: m. *burlesco,* der. *burla* jest, mockery] —**bur·les′quer,** *n.*

bur·ley (bûr′lĭ), *n., pl.* **-leys.** (*often cap.*) an American tobacco grown esp. in Kentucky and southern Ohio.

Bur·lin·game (bûr′lĭn gām′, -lĭng gām′), *n.* **Anson** (ăn′sən), 1820–70, U.S. diplomat.

Bur·ling·ton (bûr′lĭng tən), *n.* **1.** a city in NW Vermont, on Lake Champlain. 35,531 (1960). **2.** a city in SE Iowa, on the Mississippi. 32,430 (1960). **3.** a city in N North Carolina. 33,199 (1960).

bur·ly (bûr′lĭ), *adj.,* **-lier, -liest. 1.** great in bodily size; stout; sturdy. **2.** bluff; brusque. [ME *borli, burlich, burli;* orig. uncert.] —**bur′li·ly,** *adv.* —**bur′li·ness,** *n.*

Bur·ma (bûr′mə), *n.* an independent republic in SE Asia, until 1948 a British dependency: historically subdivided into **Lower Burma** (coastal region W of Siam), **Upper Burma** (inland districts), and the Shan States. 19,846,000 (est. 1956); 261,789 sq. mi. *Cap.:* Rangoon.

Bur·man (bûr′mən), *adj., n.* Burmese.

---

b., blend of, blended; c., cognate with; d., dialect, dialectal; der., derived from; f., formed from; g., going back to; m., modification of; r., replacing; s., stem of; t., taken from; ?, perhaps. See the full key on inside cover.

ur marigold, any of various herbs of the composite genus *Bidens*, esp. those with conspicuous yellow flowers.

urma Road, a strategic highway extending from Lashio, Burma, through mountainous regions to Kunming, China, (in 1938) and later to Chungking: used during World War II for supplying Allied military forces in China.

ur·mese (bər mēz′, -mēs′), *n., pl.* **-mese,** *adj.* —*n.* 1. a native or inhabitant of Burma. 2. the principal language of Burma, a Sino-Tibetan language. —*adj.* 3. of or pertaining to Burma, its people, or their language.

urn¹ (bûrn), *v.,* **burned** *or* **burnt, burning,** *n.* —*v.i.* 1. to be on fire: *the fuel burns.* 2. (of a furnace, etc.) to contain fire. 3. to feel heat or a physiologically identical sensation: *his face burned in the wind.* 4. to give light: *the lights in the house burned all night.* 5. to glow like fire. 6. (in games) to be extremely close to finding a concealed object or guessing an answer. 7. to feel strong passion: *he was burning with anger.* 8. *Chem.* to undergo combustion; oxidize. 9. to become discolored, tanned, or charred through heat. —*v.t.* 10. to consume, partly or wholly, with fire. 11. to cause to feel the sensation of heat. 12. to injure, discolor, char, or treat with heat. 13. to produce with fire: *to burn charcoal.* 14. *Chem.* to cause to undergo combustion; oxidize. —*n.* 15. a burned place. 16. *Pathol.* an injury produced by heat or by abnormal cold, chemicals, poison gas, electricity, or lightning. A **first-degree burn** is characterized by reddening; a **second-degree burn** by blistering; a **third-degree burn** by charring. 17. the operation of burning or baking, as in brickmaking. [coalescence in later ME of OE *beornan,* v.i. (c. Goth. *brinnan*) and OE *bærnan,* v.t. (c. Goth. *brannjan*) with (weak) inflexion of *bærnan* and phonetic form of *beornan*]
—**Syn.** 10. BURN, SCORCH, SEAR, SINGE refer to the effect of fire or heat. To BURN is to consume, wholly or in part, by contact with fire or excessive heat: *to burn leaves.* SCORCH implies superficial or slight burning on the surface, resulting in a change of color or in injury to the texture because of shriveling or curling: *to scorch a dress while ironing.* SEAR refers esp. to the drying or hardening caused by heat: *to sear a roast of meat.* SINGE applies esp. to a superficial burning that takes off ends or projections: *to singe hair.*

urn² (bûrn), *n. Scot. and N. Eng.* a brook or rivulet. Also, **bourn, bourne.** [ME *burne, bourne,* OE *burna, burne,* akin to G *born, brunnen* spring]

Burne-Jones (bûrn′ jōnz′), *n.* **Sir Edward,** 1833–1898, British painter and designer.

urn·er (bûr′nər), *n.* 1. one who or that which burns. 2. that part of a gas fixture, lamp, etc., from which flame issues or in which it is produced.

bur·net (bûr′nĭt), *n.* a plant of the rosaceous genus *Sanguisorba,* esp. *S. minor,* an erect herb whose leaves are used for salad. [ME, t. OF: m. *brunette,* dim. of *brun* brown]

Bur·ney (bûr′nĭ), *n.* **Frances** (or **Fanny**), (*Madame D'Arblay*) 1752–1840. British novelist and diarist.

burn·ing (bûr′nĭng), *adj.* 1. intense; serious; much-discussed: *a burning question.* —*n.* 2. the final heat treatment used to develop hardness and other properties in ceramic products. —**burn′ing·ly,** *adv.*

burn·ing-bush, *n.* any of various plants, esp. the wahoo, *Euonymus atropurpureus.*

burning glass, a lens used to produce heat or ignite substances by focusing the sun's rays.

bur·nish (bûr′nĭsh), *v.t.* 1. to polish (a surface) by friction. 2. to make smooth and bright. —*n.* 3. gloss; brightness; luster. [ME *burnissh(en),* t. OF: m. *burniss-,* s. *burnir* make brown, polish, der. *brun* brown, t. Gmc.; see BROWN]

bur·nish·er (bûr′nĭsh ər), *n.* a tool, usually with a smooth, slightly convex head, used for polishing, as in dentistry, etc.

Burn·ley (bûrn′lĭ), *n.* a city in NW England, in Lancashire. 82,350 (est. 1956).

bur·noose (bər noos′, bûr′noos), *n.* a hooded mantle or cloak, such as that worn by Arabs, etc. See illus. just above. Also, **bur·nous** (bər noos′, bûr′noos). [t. F: (m.) *burnous,* t. Ar.: m. *burnus*]

Burnoose

burn-out (bûrn′out′), *n.* the end of combustion in a rocket engine after the propellant has been exhausted.

Burns (bûrnz), *n.* **Robert,** 1759–96, Scottish poet.

Burn·side (bûrn′sīd′), *n.* **Ambrose Everett,** 1824–81, Union general in the U.S. Civil War.

burn·sides (bûrn′sīdz′), *n.pl.* a style of beard consisting of side whiskers and a mustache, the chin being clean-shaven. [named after Gen. A. E. BURNSIDE]

Burnsides

burnt (bûrnt), *v.* a pt. and pp. of **burn.**

burnt offering, *Relig.* an offering burnt upon an altar in sacrifice to a deity.

burnt umber, 1. reddish brown. 2. See **umber** (def. 1).

bur oak, an oak tree of eastern North America, *Quercus macrocarpa,* having a hard, tough, and durable wood.

burp (bûrp), *n. Colloq.* 1. a belch (def. 5). —*v.i.* 2. to belch (def. 1). —*v.t.* to cause (a baby) to belch, esp. to relieve flatulence after feeding. [imit.]

burr¹ (bûr), *n.* 1. any of various tools and appliances for cutting or drilling. 2. Also, **buhr.** a rough protuberance, ridge, or area left on metal after cutting, drilling, or ploughing with an engraver's tool, etc. 3. a rough or irregular protuberance on any object, as on a tree. 4. bur. —*v.t.* 5. to form a rough point or edge on. [var. of BUR]

burr² (bûr), *n.* 1. a washer placed at the head of a rivet. 2. the blank punched out of a piece of sheet metal. [ME *burwhe* circle, t. Scand.; cf. Icel. *borg* wall]

burr³ (bûr), *n.* 1. a guttural pronunciation of the letter *r* (as in certain Northern English dialects). 2. any rough or dialectal pronunciation. 3. a whirring noise or sound. —*v.i.* 4. to speak with a burr. 5. to speak roughly, indistinctly, or inarticulately. 6. to make a whirring noise or sound. —*v.t.* 7. to pronounce with a burr. [appar. imit.; ? assoc. with idea of roughness in BUR]

burr⁴ (bûr), *n.* 1. burstone. 2. a mass of harder siliceous rock in soft rock. Also, **buhr.** [orig. uncert.; ? akin to BUR]

Burr (bûr), *n.* **Aaron,** 1756–1836, vice-president of the U.S., 1801–05.

bur reed, any plant of the genus *Sparganium,* whose species have ribbonlike leaves and burlike heads of fruit.

bur·ro (bûr′ō, boor′ō), *n., pl.* **-ros.** *Southwestern U.S.* 1. a pack donkey. 2. any donkey. [t. Sp., der. *burrico* small horse, g. L *burricus*]

Bur·roughs (bûr′ōz), *n.* **John,** 1837–1921, U. S. naturalist and writer.

bur·row (bûr′ō), *n.* 1. a hole in the ground made by a rabbit, fox, or similar small animal, for refuge and habitation. 2. a similar place of retreat, shelter, or refuge. —*v.i.* 3. to make a hole or passage (in, into, or under something). 4. to lodge in a burrow. 5. to hide. —*v.t.* 6. to put a burrow or burrows into (a hill, etc.). 7. to hide (oneself), as in a burrow. [ME *borow.* Cf. OE *beorg* burial place, *gebeorg* refuge, *burgen* grave] —**bur′row·er,** *n.*

burrowing owl, a long-legged, terrestrial owl, *Speotyto cunicularia,* of North and South America, which digs its nesting burrow in open prairie land; ground owl.

burr·stone (bûr′stōn′), *n.* burstone.

bur·ry (bûr′ĭ), *adj.* full of burs; burlike; prickly.

bur·sa (bûr′sə), *n., pl.* **-sae** (-sē), **-sas.** *Anat., Zool.* a pouch, sac, or vesicle, esp. a sac containing synovia, to facilitate motion, as between a tendon and a bone. [t. ML: bag, purse, t. Gk.: m. *býrsa* hide] —**bur′sal,** *adj.*

Bur·sa (boor′sä), *n.* a city in NW Turkey: one-time capital of the Ottoman Empire. 103,812 (1950). Also, **Brusa.**

bur·sar (bûr′sər), *n.* a treasurer or business officer, esp. of a college. [t. ML: m. *bursārius,* der. *bursa* purse]

bur·sar·i·al (bər sâr′ĭ əl), *adj.* of, pertaining to, or paid to or by a bursar, or a bursary.

bur·sa·ry (bûr′sə rĭ), *n., pl.* **-ries.** 1. *Eccles.* the treasury of a monastery. 2. (in Scotland) a scholarship granted by a college. [t. ML: m.s. *bursāria*]

Bur·schen·schaft (boor′shən shäft′), *n., pl.* **-schaften** (-shäf′tən). *German.* any of certain associations of students at German universities, formed to promote patriotism, Christian conduct, and liberal ideas, but now purely social fraternities. [G, der. *bursch* student]

burse (bûrs), *n.* 1. a pouch or case for some special purpose. 2. (in Scotland) **a.** a fund to provide allowances for students. **b.** an allowance so provided. 3. *Eccles.* a case or receptacle for the corporal. [t. F: m *bourse* wallet, g. L *bursa,* t. Gk.: m. *býrsa* hide]

bur·seed (bûr′sēd′), *n.* a species of stickseed, *Lappula echinata,* introduced into the U. S. from Europe.

bur·ser·a·ceous (bûr′sə rā′shəs), *adj.* *Bot.* belonging to the family Burseraceae, of shrubs or trees of warm, often arid, countries, with compound leaves.

bur·si·form (bûr′sə fôrm′), *adj.* *Anat., Zool.* pouch-shaped; saccate. [t. ML *bursa* bag, purse + -(I)FORM]

bur·si·tis (bər sī′tĭs), *n.* *Pathol.* inflammation of a bursa. [t. NL BURSA, -ITIS]

burst (bûrst), *v.,* **burst, bursting,** *n.* —*v.i.* 1. to fly apart or break open with sudden violence. 2. to issue forth suddenly and forcibly from or as from confinement. 3. to break or give way from violent pain or emotion: *to burst into speech or tears.* 4. to be extremely full, as if ready to break open. 5. to become visible, audible, evident, etc., suddenly and clearly. —*v.t.* 6. to cause to burst; break suddenly and violently. 7. to cause or suffer the rupture of. —*n.* 8. act of bursting. 9. a sudden display of activity or energy: *a burst of applause or speed.* 10. a sudden expression or manifestation of emotion, etc. 11. a sudden and violent issuing forth. 12. *Mil.* **a.** the explosion of a projectile, esp. in a specified place: *an air burst.* **b.** a series of shots fired by one pressure on the trigger of an automatic weapon. 13. the result of bursting: *a burst in the dike.* 14. a sudden opening to sight or view. [ME *berst(en), burst(en),* etc., OE *berstan;* form *burst* orig. past only; c. G *bersten, Dan. bresta*] —**burst′er,** *n.* —**Syn.** 1. crack, explode. 6. rend, tear.

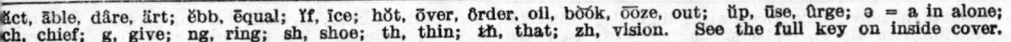

bur·stone (bûr'stōn'), n. 1. Geol. any of various siliceous rocks used for millstones. 2. a millstone of such material. Also, **buhr, buhrstone, burrstone.** [f. BURR⁴ + STONE]

bur·then (bûr'ᵺən), n., v.t. Archaic. burden¹. —**bur'then·some,** adj.

bur·ton (bûr'tən), n. Naut. 1. any of various kinds of tackle used for setting up rigging, raising sails, etc. 2. any of various small tackles, esp. one having a two-sheave and a one-sheave block.

Bur·ton (bûr'tən), n. 1. **Harold Hitz,** 1888–1964, associate justice of U.S. Supreme Court 1945–58. 2. **Sir Richard Francis,** 1821–90, British traveler and author. 3. **Robert,** 1577–1640, British clergyman, scholar, and author.

Bur·ton-on-Trent (bûr'tən ŏn trĕnt'), n. a city in central England, in Staffordshire. 48,910 (est. 1956).

Bu·run·di (bŏŏ rŏŏn'dĭ), n. a kingdom in central Africa, E of the Republic of the Congo: formerly comprising the southern part of the Belgian trust territory of Ruanda-Urundi; became independent on July 1, 1962. 2,213,480 pop. (1962); 10,747 sq. mi. Cap.: Usumbura.

bur·weed (bûr'wēd'), n. any of various plants having a burlike fruit, as the cocklebur, burdock, etc.

bur·y (bĕr'ĭ), v.t., **buried, burying.** 1. to put in the ground and cover with earth. 2. to put (a corpse) in the ground or a vault, or into the sea, often with ceremony. 3. to cause to sink in: to bury a dagger in one's heart. 4. to cover in order to conceal from sight. 5. to withdraw (oneself): he buried himself in his work. 6. to put out of one's mind: to bury an injury. [ME berien, buryen, OE byrgan, akin to OE beorg burial place, burgen, byrgen grave] —**bur'i·er,** n. —Syn. 2. inter, entomb, inhume.

burying ground, a burial ground.

Bur·y St. Ed·munds (bĕr'ĭ sânt ĕd'məndz), a city in E England: famous medieval shrine. 20,045 (1951).

bus (bŭs), n., pl. **buses, busses.** 1. a motor vehicle with a long body equipped with seats or benches for passengers, usually operating as part of a scheduled service line; an omnibus. 2. a similar horse-drawn vehicle. 3. Colloq. a passenger automobile or airplane. [short for OMNIBUS]

bus., 1. business. 2. bushel; bushels.

bus boy, a waiter's helper in a restaurant or other public dining room, doing the more menial tasks.

bus·by (bŭz'bĭ), n., pl. **-bies.** a tall fur hat with a bag hanging from the top over the right side, worn by hussars, etc., in the British Army.

bush¹ (bŏŏsh), n. 1. a plant, esp. a low one with many branches, which usually arise from or near the ground. 2. Bot. a small cluster of shrubs appearing as a single plant. 3. something resembling or suggesting this, as a thick, shaggy head of hair. 4. a fox's tail. 5. Geog. a stretch of land covered with bushy vegetation or trees. 6. a tree branch hung as a sign before a tavern or vintner's shop. 7. any tavern sign. 8. a wineshop. —v.i. 9. to be or become 'bushy; branch or spread as or like a bush. —v.t. 10. to cover with bushes; protect with bushes set round about; support with bushes. [ME; unexplained var. of busk, t. Scand.; cf. Dan. busk]

Busby

bush² (bŏŏsh), Mach. —n. 1. a lining of metal or the like let into an orifice to guard against wearing by friction, erosion, etc. 2. a metal lining, usually detachable, used as a bearing. —v.t. 3. to furnish with a bush; line with metal. [t. MD: m. busse, n.]

bush., bushel; bushels.

bush·buck (bŏŏsh'bŭk'), n. a rather small African antelope, Tragelaphus scriptus, frequenting forests and bushy regions. Also, **boschbok.**

bush cranberry, cranberry tree.

bush·el¹ (bŏŏsh'əl), n. 1. a unit of dry measure containing 4 pecks, equivalent in the U. S. (and formerly in England) to 2,150.42 cubic inches (**Winchester bushel**), and in Great Britain to 2,219.36 cubic inches (**Imperial bushel**). 2. a container of this capacity. 3. a unit of weight equal to the weight of a bushel of a given commodity. [ME boyschel, t. OF: m. boissiel, dim. of boisse, ult. der. Gallic word meaning hollow of the hand]

bush·el² (bŏŏsh'əl), v.t., **-eled, -eling** or (esp. Brit.) **-elled, -elling.** U.S. to alter or repair (a garment). [orig. uncert.] —**bush'el·er;** esp. Brit., **bush'el·ler,** n. —**bush·el·man** (bŏŏsh'əl mən), n.

bush·ham·mer (bŏŏsh'hăm'ər), n. a hammer studded with pyramidal points or the like for dressing stone.

Bu·shi·do (bŏŏ'shē dō'), n. 1. a code of behavior attributed to the warriors of feudal Japan, actually a growth of the end of the feudal period, tinged with Confucian influences. 2. (in modern usage) fanatical disregard of life in the service of the Japanese emperor. Also, **bushido.** [Jap.: lit. the way of the warrior]

bush·i·ness (bŏŏsh'ĭ nĭs), n. bushy state or form.

bush·ing (bŏŏsh'ĭng), n. Elect. a lining for a hole, intended to insulate and/or protect from abrasion conductors which pass through it. [f. BUSH² + -ING¹]

Bu·shire (bŏŏ shēr'), n. a seaport in SW Iran, on the Persian Gulf. 27,317 (est. 1949).

bush league, Baseball, Colloq. a minor league.

bush·man (bŏŏsh'mən), n., pl. **-men.** 1. a woodsman. 2. Australia. a pioneer; dweller in the bush. 3. (cap.) a member of a South African Negroid race. 4. (cap.) the language of the Bushmen.

bush·mas·ter (bŏŏsh'măs'tər, -mäs'tər), n. a large venomous serpent, Lachesis mutus, of tropical America.

bush pig, a wild swine, Potamochaerus porcus, of S and E Africa, with white face markings; boschvark.

bush·rang·er (bŏŏsh'rān'jər), n. 1. a person who ranges or dwells in bush or woods. 2. Australia. a criminal who hides in the bush and leads a predatory life.

bush tit, any of several small chickadeelike birds of the genus Psalliparus, known for their pendent nests.

bush·whack·er (bŏŏsh'hwăk'ər), n. U.S. 1. one accustomed to range in the woods. 2. U.S. Hist. a Confederate guerrilla. 3. any guerrilla.

bush·whack·ing (bŏŏsh'hwăk'ĭng), n. U.S. 1. travel through bushy country, on foot or in a boat. 2. guerrilla tactics.

bush·y (bŏŏsh'ĭ), adj., **bushier, bushiest.** 1. resembling a bush. 2. full of or overgrown with bushes.

bus·i·ly (bĭz'ə lĭ), adv. in a busy manner; actively.

busi·ness (bĭz'nĭs), n. 1. one's occupation, profession, or trade. 2. Econ. the purchase and sale of goods in an attempt to make a profit. 3. Com. a person, partnership, or corporation engaged in this; an established or going enterprise or concern. 4. volume of trade; patronage. 5. one's place of work. 6. that with which one is principally and seriously concerned. 7. that with which one is rightfully concerned. 8. affair; matter. 9. Theat. any movement or gesture by an actor used for dramatic expression (generally not applied to actions like exits, etc.). [ME busines, OE (North) bisignes. See BUSY, -NESS] —Syn. 1. See occupation.

business college, U.S. a school that gives training in the clerical side of business and commerce.

busi·ness·like (bĭz'nĭs lĭk'), adj. conforming to the methods of business or trade; methodical; systematic.

busi·ness·man (bĭz'nĭs măn'), n., pl. **-men** (-mĕn'). a man who engages in business or commerce. —**busi·ness·wom·an** (bĭz'nĭs wŏŏm'ən), n. fem.

busk¹ (bŭsk), v.t. Scot. and Dial. to prepare. [ME buske(n), t. Scand.; cf. Icel. būask, refl. of būa make ready]

busk² (bŭsk), n. 1. a strip of wood, steel, whalebone, or other stiffening material placed in the front of a corset to keep it in form. 2. Dial. the whole corset. [t. F: m. busc, t. It.: m. busco stick]

bus·kin (bŭs'kĭn), n. 1. a half boot, or outer covering for the foot and leg reaching to the calf or higher. 2. the high shoe or cothurnus of ancient Greek and Roman tragic actors. 3. tragedy; tragic drama. [orig. uncert. Cf. F brousequin, D broosken, Sp. borcegui, It. borzacchino]

Ancient buskins

bus·kined (bŭs'kĭnd), adj. 1. wearing buskins. 2. pertaining to tragedy.

bus·man's holiday (bŭs'mənz), a holiday on which, by choice, one does one's regular work.

Bus·ra (bŭs'rə), n. Basra. Also, **Bus'rah.**

buss (bŭs), n., v.t., v.i. Colloq. kiss. [cf. d. G buss]

bus·ses (bŭs'ĭz), n. pl. of **bus.**

bust¹ (bŭst), n. 1. the head and shoulders of a person done in sculpture, either in the round or in relief. 2. the chest or breast; the bosom. [t. F: m. buste, t. It.: m. busto, g. L bustum bust, funeral monument, funeral]

bust² (bŭst) Colloq. or Slang. —v.i. 1. to burst. 2. to go bankrupt (often fol. by up). —v.t. 3. to burst. 4. to bankrupt; ruin (often fol. by up). 5. (in the Army) to reduce in rank or grade, usually to the rank of private. 6. to subdue (a bronco, etc.). 7. to hit. —n. 8. a complete failure; bankruptcy. 9. a drunken party; brawl. [d. or vulgar var. of BURST]

bus·tard (bŭs'tərd), n. any of several large Old World birds of the family Otididae allied to both the cranes and the plovers, inhabiting some country of Europe and Africa. [ME, t. OF, b. bistarde (t. It.: m. bistarda) and oustarde, both g. L avis tarda slow bird]

bust·er (bŭs'tər), n. 1. a person or thing that busts; trustbuster. 2. Slang. something very big or unusual for its kind. 3. Slang. a roisterer. 4. Slang. a frolic; a spree. 5. U.S. Colloq. a small boy. 6. Australia. a violent, cold, southerly wind.

bus·tle¹ (bŭs'əl), v., **-tled, -tling,** n. —v.i. 1. to move or act with a great show of energy (often fol. by about). —v.t. 2. to cause to bustle. —n. 3. activity with great show of energy; stir; commotion. [? var. of obs. buskle, freq. of BUSK¹] —**bus'tling·ly,** adv.

bus·tle² (bŭs'əl), n. 1. fullness outside the skirt, as exaggerated fullness at the back of a peplum, large bows, etc. 2. (formerly) a pad, cushion, or wire framework worn by women on the back part of the body below the waist, to expand and support the skirt. [? der. BUSTLE¹]

bus·y (bĭz'ĭ), adj., **busier, busiest,** v., **busied, busying.** —adj. 1. actively and attentively engaged: busy with his work. 2. not at leisure; otherwise engaged. 3. full of or characterized by activity: a busy life. 4. officious; meddlesome; prying. [ME busi, bisi, OE bysig, c. D bezig, LG besig] —v.t. 5. to keep occupied; make or keep busy: to busy oneself keeping the lawn in order. [ME bisien, OE bysgian, der. bysig BUSY, adj.] —**bus'y·ness,** n.

—Syn. 1. BUSY, DILIGENT, INDUSTRIOUS imply active or earnest effort to accomplish something, or a habitual attitude of such earnestness. **Busy** means actively employed, temporarily or habitually: *a busy official.* **Diligent** suggests earnest and constant effort or application, and usually connotes fondness for, or enjoyment of, what one is doing: *a diligent student.* **Industrious** often implies a habitual characteristic of steady and zealous application, often with a definite goal: *an industrious clerk working for promotion.*

bus·y·bod·y (bĭz'ĭ bŏd'ĭ), *n., pl.* **-bodies.** a person who pries into and meddles in the affairs of others.

but[1] (bŭt; *unstressed* bət), *conj.* **1.** on the contrary; yet: *they all went but I didn't.* **2.** excepting, except, or save: *anywhere but here.* **3.** except that (followed by a clause, often with *that* expressed): *nothing would do but, or but that, I should come in.* **4.** without the circumstance that, or that not: *it never rains but it pours.* **5.** otherwise than: *I can do nothing but go.* **6.** that (esp. after *doubt, deny,* etc., with a negative): *I don't doubt but he will do it.* **7.** that not (after a negative or question): *the children never played but that a quarrel followed.* **8.** who or which not: *no leader worthy of the name ever existed but he was an optimist* (who was not an optimist). —*prep.* **9.** with the exception of; except; save: *no one replied but me.* —*adv.* **10.** only; just: *there is but one God.* **11.** all but, almost: *all but dead.* —*n.* **12.** a restriction or objection: *no buts about it.* [ME; OE *b(e)ūta(n)* on the outside, without, f. *be-* by + *ūt* out + *-an* adv. suffix]
—**Syn. 1.** But, however, nevertheless, still, yet are words implying opposition (with a possible concession). **But** marks an opposition or contrast, though in a casual way: *we are going, but we shall return.* **However** indicates a less marked opposition, but displays a second consideration to be compared with the first: *we are going; however* (notice this also) *we shall return.* **Nevertheless** implies a concession, something which should not be forgotten in making a summing up: *we are going; nevertheless* (do not forget that) *we shall return.* **Still** implies that in spite of a preceding concession, something must be considered as possible or even inevitable: *we have to go on foot; still* (it is probable and possible that) *we'll get there.* **Yet** implies that in spite of a preceding concession, there is still a chance for a different outcome: *we are going; yet* (in spite of all, some day) *we shall return.* **2.** See **except**[1].

but[2] (bŭt), *n. Scot.* the outer room of a house consisting of two rooms; the kitchen, the other room being the ben. [n. use of **but**[1], adv. (etymological sense)]

bu·ta·di·ene (bū'tə dī'ēn, -dī ēn'), *n. Chem.* an inflammable, colorless, hydrocarbon gas, C₄H₆, used in making synthetic rubber. [f. **buta**(ne) + **di-** + **-ene**]

bu·tane (bū'tān, bū tān'), *n. Chem.* a saturated aliphatic hydrocarbon, C₄H₁₀, existing in two isomeric forms and used as a fuel and a chemical intermediate. [f. **but**(yl) + **-ane**]

bu·ta·none (bū'tə nōn'), *n. Chem.* an inflammable ketone, C₄H₈O, used as a solvent and in making plastics.

butch·er (bŏŏch'ər), *n.* **1.** a retail dealer in meat. **2.** one who slaughters certain domesticated animals, or dresses their flesh, for food or for market. **3.** a person guilty of cruel or indiscriminate slaughter. **4.** *U.S.* a person who sells candy, etc., on a train. —*v.t.* **5.** to kill or slaughter for food or for market. **6.** to murder indiscriminately or brutally. **7.** to bungle; botch: *to butcher a job.* [ME *bocher,* t. OF, der. *boc* he-goat, t. Gmc. See **buck**[1]] —**butch·er·er,** *n.* —**Syn. 5.** See **slaughter.**

butch·er·bird (bŏŏch'ər bûrd'), *n.* any of various shrikes of the genus *Lanius,* which impale their prey upon thorns.

butch·er·ly (bŏŏch'ər lĭ), *adj.* like, or characteristic of, a butcher.

butch·er's-broom (bŏŏch'ərz brōōm', -brŏŏm'), *n.* a shrubby liliaceous evergreen, *Ruscus aculeatus,* of England, used for making brooms.

butch·er·y (bŏŏch'ər ĭ), *n., pl.* **-eries. 1.** a slaughterhouse. **2.** the trade or business of a butcher. **3.** brutal slaughter of human beings; carnage.

Bute (būt), *n.* **1.** Also, **Bute·shire** (būt'shĭr, -shər). a county in SW Scotland, composed of islands. 17,600 pop. (est. 1956); 218 sq. mi. *Co. seat:* Rothesay. **2.** an island in the Firth of Clyde: a part of this county. 12,112 pop. (1931); ab. 50 sq. mi.

bu·tene (bū'tēn), *n. Chem.* one of three isomeric butylenes, C₄H₈.

but·ler (bŭt'lər), *n.* **1.** the head male servant of a household. **2.** the male servant having charge of the wines and liquors, etc. [ME *buteler,* t. AF: m. *butuiller,* der. *bouteille* bottle] —**but·ler·ship**[1], *n.*

But·ler (bŭt'lər), *n.* **1. Benjamin Franklin,** 1818–93, U. S. politician and Union general in the Civil War. **2. Joseph,** 1692–1752, British bishop, theologian, and author. **3. Nicholas Murray,** 1862–1947, U. S. educator: president, Columbia University, 1902–45. **4. Samuel,** 1612–80, British poet. **5. Samuel,** 1835–1902, British writer. **6.** a city in W Pennsylvania. 20,975 (1960).

butler's pantry, a room between the kitchen and the dining room arranged for the storage of china and silverware and containing a sink.

but·ler·y (bŭt'lə rĭ), *n., pl.* **-leries.** a butler's room or pantry; a buttery. [f. **butler** + **-y**[3]; r. ME *botelerye,* t. OF: m. *bouteillerie* storeroom for wine]

butt[1] (bŭt), *n.* **1.** the end or extremity of anything. esp. the thicker, larger, or blunt end, as of a musket, fishing rod, whip handle, arrow, log, etc. **2.** an end which is not used up: *a cigarette butt.* **3.** buttock. [ME *bott* buttock; appar. short for **buttock**]

butt[2] (bŭt), *n.* **1.** a person or thing that is an object

of wit, ridicule, sarcasm, etc., or contempt. **2.** (in rifle practice) **a.** a wall of earth behind the targets of a target range, which prevents bullets from scattering over a large area. **b.** (*pl.*) a wall in front of the targets of a target range, behind which men can safely lower, score, and raise targets during firing. **3.** a hinge for a door or the like, secured to the butting surfaces or ends instead of the adjacent sides. **4.** *Obs.* a goal; limit. —*v.i.* **5.** to have an end or projection (*on*); be adjacent (*to*). —*v.t.* **6.** to join an end of (something); join the ends of (two things) together. [late ME, t. OF: m. *bout* end, extremity, of Gmc. orig.]

butt[3] (bŭt), *v.t.* **1.** to strike with the head or horns. —*v.i.* **2.** to strike something or at something with the head or horns. **3.** to project. **4.** *Colloq.* to interrupt; interfere; intrude (fol. by *in*). —*n.* **5.** a push with head or horns. [ME *butt*(en), t. OF: m. *bouter* strike, thrust, abut, touch, der. *bout* end, of Gmc. orig.]

butt[4] (bŭt), *n.* **1.** a large cask for wine, beer, or ale. **2.** any cask or barrel. **3.** a unit of capacity, equal to two hogsheads. [late ME; cf. OF *botte, bote,* c. It. *botte,* g. LL *butta, buttis* vessel, cask]

butte (būt), *n. Western U. S. and Canada.* an isolated hill or mountain rising abruptly above the surrounding land. [t. F: hill, prop., mound for target]

Butte (būt), *n.* a city in SW Montana: important mining center. 27,877 (1960).

but·ter (bŭt'ər), *n.* **1.** the fatty portion of milk, separating as a soft whitish or yellowish solid when milk or cream is agitated or churned. **2.** this substance, processed for cooking and table use. **3.** any of various other soft spreads for breads: *apple butter, peanut butter.* **4.** any of various substances of butterlike consistency, as various metallic chlorides, and certain vegetable oils solid at ordinary temperatures. —*v.t.* **5.** to put butter on or in. **6.** *Colloq.* to flatter grossly (often fol. by *up*). [ME; OE *butere,* t. L: m. s. *būtyrum,* t. Gk.: m. *boútyron*] —**but·ter·like**[1], *adj.*

but·ter-and-eggs (bŭt'ər ən ĕgz'), *n.* any of certain plants whose flowers are of two shades of yellow, as the toadflax.

but·ter·ball (bŭt'ər bôl'), *n.* **1.** the bufflehead. **2.** *Colloq.* a fat, round person.

butter bean, a variety of small-seeded lima beans, *Phaseolus lunatus,* grown in the South.

but·ter·bur (bŭt'ər bûr'), *n.* an Old World perennial herb composite, *Petasites vulgaris,* bearing large woolly leaves said to have been used to wrap butter.

but·ter·cup (bŭt'ər kŭp'), *n.* a plant of the genus *Ranunculus,* esp. *R. acris* or *R. bulbosus,* with yellow cup-shaped flowers.

but·ter·fat (bŭt'ər făt'), *n.* butter; milk fat; a mixture of glycerides, mainly butyrin, olein, and palmitin.

but·ter·fin·gers (bŭt'ər fĭng'gərz), *n.* a person who drops things easily.

but·ter·fish (bŭt'ər fĭsh'), *n., pl.* **-fishes,** (*esp. collectively*) **-fish. 1.** a small, flattened, marine food fish, *Poronotus triacanthus,* of the Atlantic coast of the U. S., having very small scales and smooth skin. **2.** an elongated blenny, *Pholis gunnellus,* of both coasts of the North Atlantic.

but·ter·fly (bŭt'ər flī'), *n., pl.* **-flies. 1.** any of a group of lepidopterous insects characterized by clubbed antennae, large, broad wings, often conspicuously colored and marked, and diurnal habits. **2.** a person who flits aimlessly from one thing to another. [OE *buttorflēoge,* f. *buttor-* (comb. form of *butere*) + *flēoge* fly, c. G *butterfliege;* ? orig. used of a butter-colored (yellow) species]

butterfly fish, any of the tropical marine fishes of the family *Chaetodontidae,* as *Chaetodon copistratus,* which are suggestive of the butterfly.

butterfly table, a small, occasional table with drop leaves having butterfly-shaped supports.

butterfly weed, 1. either of two closely related North American milkweeds, *Asclepias tuberosa* and *A. decumbens,* bearing orange-colored flowers. **2.** an erect North American herb, *Gaura coccinea,* related to the evening primrose, with wandlike spikes of red flowers.

but·ter·ine (bŭt'ə rēn', -ər ĭn), *n.* an artificial butter; oleomargarine.

but·ter·milk (bŭt'ər mĭlk'), *n.* the more or less acidulous liquid remaining after the butter has been separated from milk or cream.

but·ter·nut (bŭt'ər nŭt'), *n.* **1.** the edible oily nut of an American tree, *Juglans cinerea,* of the walnut family. **2.** the tree itself. **3.** the souari nut. **4.** dark brown. **5.** *U.S. Civil War.* **a.** a member of the copperhead branch of the Democratic Party in the North. **b.** a Confederate soldier.

but·ter·scotch (bŭt'ər skŏch'), *n.* **1.** a kind of taffy made with butter. **2.** a flavor produced in puddings, frostings, ice cream, etc., by a combination of brown sugar, vanilla extract, and butter, with other ingredients.

but·ter·weed (bŭt'ər wēd'), *n.* **1.** any wild plant having conspicuously yellow flowers or leaves. **2.** the horseweed. **3.** a ragwort or groundsel, *Senecio glabellus.*

but·ter·wort (bŭt'ər wûrt'), *n.* any plant of the genus *Pinguicula,* small herbs whose leaves secrete a viscid substance in which small insects are caught.

but·ter·y[1] (bŭt'ə rĭ), *adj.* **1.** like, containing, or spread with, butter. **2.** *Colloq.* grossly flattering. [f. **butter** + **-y**[1]]

but·ter·y² (bŭt′ər ĭ, bŭt′rĭ), *n.*, *pl.* **-teries. 1.** a room or apartment in which the wines, liquors, and provisions of a household are kept; a pantry. **2.** a room in colleges at Oxford and Cambridge Universities from which certain articles of food and drink are supplied to the students. [ME *boterie*, t. OF, der. *bot(t)e* cask]

butt joint, *Bldg. Trades.* a joint formed by two pieces of wood or metal united end to end without overlapping.

but·tock (bŭt′ək), *n.* **1.** *Anat.* **a.** either of the two protuberances which form the rump. **b.** (*pl.*) the rump. **2.** (*sing. or pl.*) *Naut.* the convex aftermost portion of a ship's body above the water line. [ME *buttok*, OE *buttuc*]

but·ton (bŭt′ən), *n.* **1.** a disk or knob on a piece of cloth which, when passed through a slit or loop in the same piece or another, serves as a fastening. **2.** anything resembling a button. **3.** *Bot.* a bud or other protuberant part of a plant. **4.** a young or undeveloped mushroom. **5.** a disk pressed to close an electric circuit, as in ringing a bell. **6.** (*pl.*) *Brit. Colloq.* a bellboy or page. **7.** *Assaying, etc.* a globule or mass of metal lying at the bottom of a crucible after fusion. **8.** *Fencing.* the protective knob fixed to the point of a foil. **9.** *Western U.S.* the hard bonelike structure at the end of the rattles of a rattlesnake. **10.** *U.S.* a guessing game. —*v.t.* **11.** to fasten with a button or buttons. **12.** to provide with a button or buttons. **13.** *Fencing.* to touch with the button of the foil. —*v.i.* **14.** to be capable of being buttoned. [ME *boton*, t. OF, der. *bouter* thrust. See BUTT²] —**but′-ton·er,** *n.* —**but′ton·like′,** *adj.*

but·ton·ball (bŭt′ən bôl′), *n.* the buttonwood (def. 1).

but·ton·bush (bŭt′ən bŏŏsh′), *n.* a name given to *Cephalanthus occidentalis,* a North American shrub, on account of its globular flower heads.

but·ton·hole (bŭt′ən hōl′), *n., v.,* **-holed, -holing.** —*n.* **1.** the hole, slit, or loop through which a button is passed. —*v.t.* **2.** to sew with buttonhole stitch. **3.** to make buttonholes in. **4.** to seize by or as by the buttonhole and detain in conversation. —**but′ton·hol′er,** *n.*

buttonhole stitch, *Sewing.* a looped stitch used to strengthen the edge of material, as in a buttonhole.

but·ton·hook (bŭt′ən hŏŏk′), *n.* a small metal or other stiff hook used for buttoning shoes, gloves, etc.

but·ton·mold (bŭt′ən mōld′), *n.* a disk of bone, wood, or metal, to be covered with fabric to form a button.

button snakeroot, any of a composite genus, *Liatris,* of perennial herbs with racemose or spicate heads of handsome rose-purple flowers.

button tree, 1. a tropical tree or shrub, *Conocarpus erecta,* with heavy, hard, compact wood and buttonlike fruits. **2.** the buttonwood.

but·ton·wood (bŭt′ən wŏŏd′), *n.* **1.** a tall, North American plane tree, *Platanus occidentalis,* yielding a useful timber (so called from its small pendulous fruit). **2.** the button tree.

but·ton·y (bŭt′ən ĭ), *adj.* **1.** like a button. **2.** having many buttons.

but·tress (bŭt′rĭs), *n.* **1.** *Archit.* a structure built against a wall or building for the purpose of giving it stability. **2.** any prop or support. **3.** a thing shaped like a buttress. —*v.t.* **4.** *Archit.* to support by a buttress. **5.** to prop up; support. [ME *boterace,* t. OF: m. *bouterez,* pl., der. *bouter* thrust, abut]

A. Buttress;
B. Flying buttress

butt shaft, a blunt or barbless arrow.

butt weld, *Bldg. Trades.* a weld formed by joining the flattened ends of two pieces of iron at a white heat.

bu·tyl (bū′tĭl), *n. Chem.* a univalent radical, C₄H₉, from butane. [f. BUT(YRIC) + -YL]

butyl alcohols, *Chem.* a group of three isomeric alcohols of the formula C₄H₉OH.

bu·tyl·ene (bū′tə lēn′), *n. Chem.* any of three isomeric gaseous hydrocarbons of the formula C₄H₈, belonging to the ethylene series. [f. BUTYL + -ENE]

butyl rubber, *Chem.* **1.** a synthetic rubber, prepared by polymerization of butylene containing a little butadiene, particularly useful for inner tubes of automobile tires because of its leakproof qualities. **2.** (*cap.*) a trademark for this substance.

bu·tyn (bū′tĭn), *n. Chem.* **1.** a colorless para-aminobenzoic ester, H₂NC₆H₄COO(CH₂)₃N(C₄H₉)₂.H₂SO₄, used in dentistry as a local anesthetic. **2.** (*cap.*) a trademark for this substance.

bu·tyr·a·ceous (bū′tə rā′shəs), *adj.* of the nature of, resembling, or containing butter. [f. s. L *būtyrum* butter + -ACEOUS]

bu·tyr·ate (bū′tə rāt′), *n. Chem.* a salt or ester of butyric acid.

bu·tyr·ic (bū tĭr′ĭk), *adj. Chem.* pertaining to or derived from butyric acid. [f. s. L *būtyrum* butter + -IC]

butyric acid, *Chem.* either of two isomeric acids, C₃H₇COOH, esp. the one, a rancid liquid, present in spoiled butter, etc., as an ester and sometimes free.

bu·tyr·in (bū′tər ĭn), *n. Chem.* a colorless liquid fat or ester present in butter, and formed from glycerin and butyric acid. [f. s. L *būtyrum* butter + -IN²]

bux·om (bŭk′səm), *adj.* **1.** (of a woman) full-bosomed, plump, and attractive because of radiant health. **2.** (usually of a woman) healthy, attractive, cheerful, and lively. [ME; early ME *buhsum* pliant, der. OE *būgan* bend, bow. See -SOME¹] —**bux′om·ly,** *adv.* —**bux′om·ness,** *n.*

buy (bī), *v.,* **bought, buying,** *n.* —*v.t.* **1.** to acquire the possession of, or the right to, by paying an equivalent, esp. in money. **2.** to acquire by giving any kind of recompense: *to buy favor with flattery.* **3.** to hire; bribe. **4.** *Chiefly Theol.* to redeem; ransom. **5.** to get rid of (a claim, opposition, etc.) by payment; purchase the nonintervention of; bribe (fol. by *off*). **6.** to secure all of (an owner or partner's) share or interest in an enterprise (fol. by *out*). **7.** to buy as much as one can of (fol. by *up*). —*v.i.* **8.** to be or become a purchaser. —*n.* **9.** act of buying. **10.** *U.S.* something bought or to be bought; a purchase. **11.** *U.S. Colloq.* a bargain. [ME *b(u)yen* etc., OE *byg-,* s. *bycgan,* c. OS *buggian,* Goth. *bugjan*]

—**Syn. 1.** BUY, PURCHASE imply obtaining or acquiring property or goods for a price. BUY is the common and informal word, applying to any such transaction: *to buy a house, vegetables at the market.* PURCHASE is more formal and may connote buying on a larger scale, in a finer store, and the like: *to purchase a year's supplies.* —**Ant. 1.** sell.

buy·er (bī′ər), *n.* **1.** one who buys; a purchaser. **2.** a purchasing agent, as for a department or chain store.

buyers' strike, an attempt on the part of consumers to lower price levels by boycotting retailers or certain types of goods.

buzz (bŭz), *n.* **1.** a low, vibrating, humming sound, as of bees. **2.** a rumor or report. **3.** *Colloq.* a phone call. —*v.i.* **4.** to make a low, vibrating, humming sound. **5.** to speak or whisper with such a sound. **6.** to move busily from place to place. **7.** *Brit. Colloq.* to go; leave (usually fol. by *off* or *along*). —*v.t.* **8.** to make a buzzing sound with: *the fly buzzed its wings.* **9.** to spread (a rumor) secretively. **10.** to communicate with buzzes, as in signaling. **11.** *Colloq.* to make a phone call to. **12.** *Aeron.* **a.** to fly a plane very low over: *to buzz a field.* **b.** to signal or greet (someone) by flying a plane low and slowing the motor spasmodically. [imit.]

buz·zard (bŭz′ərd), *n.* **1.** any of various more or less heavily built hawks of the genus *Buteo* and allied genera, as *B. vulgaris,* a rather sluggish European species. **2.** any of various carrion-eating birds, as the turkey buzzard or turkey vulture, *Cathartes aura.* —*adj.* **3.** *Obs.* senseless; stupid. [ME *busard,* t. OF, der. *buse* buzzard, g. L *būteo* kind of hawk]

Turkey buzzard, *Cathartes aura* (Ab. 2½ ft. long)

Buzzards Bay, an inlet of the Atlantic, in SE Massachusetts. ab. 30 mi. long.

buzz bomb, *Mil.* a type of self-steering aerial bomb, launched from large land-based rocket platforms, and used by the Germans in World War II, esp. over England.

buzz·er (bŭz′ər), *n.* **1.** one who or that which buzzes. **2.** a signaling apparatus similar to an electric bell, but without hammer or gong, and serving to produce sound by the vibration of an armature.

buzz saw, a small circular saw, so named because of the noise it makes.

buzz·wig (bŭz′wĭg′), *n.* **1.** a large, bushy wig. **2.** a person wearing such a wig. **3.** a person of consequence.

B.V., 1. (L *Beata Virgo*) Blessed Virgin. **2.** (L *bene vale*) farewell.

B.V.M., (L *Beata Virgo Maria*) Blessed Virgin Mary.

bvt., 1. brevet. **2.** brevetted.

B.W.I., British West Indies.

bx., *pl.* **bxs.** box.

by (bī), *prep.* **1.** near to: *a house by the river.* **2.** using as a route: *he came by the highway.* **3.** through or on as a means of conveyance: *he journeyed by water.* **4.** to and past a point near: *he went by the church.* **5.** within the compass or period of: *by day, by night.* **6.** not later than: *by two o'clock.* **7.** to the extent of: *larger by a half.* **8.** by evidence or authority of: *by his own account.* **9.** with the participation of: *regretted by all.* **10.** before; in the presence of: *to swear by all that is sacred.* **11.** through the agency or efficacy of: *founded by Napoleon, done by force.* **12.** after; in serial order: *piece by piece.* **13.** combined with in multiplication or relative dimension: *five feet by six feet.* **14.** involving as unit of measure: *beef by the pound.* —*adv.* **15.** near to something: *it's near by.* **16.** to and past a point near something: *the car drove by.* **17.** aside: *put it by for the moment.* **18.** over; past: *in times gone by.* **19.** by and by, at some time in the future; before long; presently. **20.** by and large, in general; on the whole. —*adj.* **21.** situated to one side. **22.** secondary; incidental. —*n.* **23.** bye. [ME; OE *bī,* stressed form answering to unstressed *be-,* c. G *bei* by, near]

—**Syn. 11.** BY, THROUGH, WITH indicate agency or means of getting something done or accomplished. BY is regularly used to denote the agent (person or force) in passive constructions: *it is done by many, destroyed by fire.* It also indicates means: *send it by airmail.* WITH denotes the instrument (usually consciously) employed by an agent: *he cut it with the scissors.* THROUGH designates particularly immediate agency or instrumentality for reason or motive: *through outside aid, to yield through fear, wounded through carelessness.*

---

b., blend of, blended;   **c.,** cognate with;   **d.,** dialect, dialectal;   der., derived from;   **f.,** formed from;   **g.,** going back to;   **m.,** modification of;   **r.,** replacing;   **s.,** stem of;   **t.,** taken from;   **?,** perhaps.   See the full key on inside cover.

by-, a prefix meaning: 1. secondary; incidental, as in *by-product.* 2. out of the way; removed, as in *byway.* 3. near, as in *bystander.* Also, **bye-**.

by-and-by (bī′ən bī′), *n.* the (near) future.

by-bid·der (bī′bĭd′ər), *n.* a person employed to bid at an auction in order to raise the prices.

Byd·goszcz (bĭd′gôshch), *n.* a city in NW Poland. 200,000 (est. 1955). German, **Bromberg.**

bye (bī), *n.* Also, **by.** 1. *Sports.* state of having no competitor in a contest where several competitors are engaged in pairs. 2. *Golf.* the holes of a stipulated course still unplayed after the match is finished. 3. *Cricket.* a run made on a ball not struck by the batsman. 4. something subsidiary, secondary, or out of the way. 5. **by the bye,** incidentally; by the way. —*adj.* 6. by. [var. spelling of BY, prep., in noun use]

bye-, var. of by-, as in *bye-election.*

bye-bye (bī′bī′), *interj. Childish or Colloq.* good-by.

by-e·lec·tion (bī′ĭ lĕk′shən), *n. Brit.* a special election not held at the time of a general election, to fill a vacancy in Parliament. Also, **bye′-e·lec′tion.**

Byel·o·rus·sian Soviet Socialist Republic (bĕl′ō rŭsh′ən), White Russian Soviet Socialist Republic.

Bye·lo·stok (bĕ′lō stôk′), *n.* Russian name of **Bialystok.**

by·gone (bī′gôn′, -gŏn′), *adj.* 1. past; gone by; out of date: *bygone days.* —*n.* 2. that which is past.

by·law (bī′lô′), *n.* 1. a standing rule, as of a corporation or society, not in its constitution. 2. a subsidiary law. 3. *Brit.* an ordinance of a municipality or community. [f. BY- + LAW; r. ME *bilawe,* f. *by* town (t. Scand; cf. Dan. *by*) + *lawe* law]

by-line (bī′līn′), *n. U.S.* a line under the heading of a newspaper or magazine article giving the writer's name.

by-name (bī′nām′), *n.* 1. a secondary name; cognomen; surname. 2. a nickname.

Byng (bĭng), *n.* **Julian Hedworth George,** (*Viscount Byng of Vimy*) 1862–1935, British general: governor general of Canada, 1921–26.

by-pass (bī′păs′, -päs′), *n.* 1. a road enabling motorists to avoid towns and other heavy traffic points or any obstruction to easy travel on a main highway. 2. a secondary pipe or other channel connected with a main passage for conducting a liquid or gas around a fixture, pipe, or appliance. 3. *Elect.* a shunt (def. 8). —*v.t.* 4. to avoid (obstructions, etc.) by following a by-pass. 5. to cause (fluid, etc.) to follow such a channel. 6. to go over the head of (one's immediate supervisor, etc.).

by-past (bī′păst′, -päst′), *adj.* bygone; past.

by-path (bī′păth′, -päth′), *n.* a private path; an indirect course or means; byway.

by-play (bī′plā′), *n.* action or speech carried on aside while the main action proceeds, esp. on the stage.

by-prod·uct (bī′prŏd′əkt), *n.* a secondary or incidental product, as in a process of manufacture.

Byrd (bûrd), *n.* **Richard Evelyn,** 1888–1957, rear admiral in U. S. Navy: polar explorer.

byre (bīr), *n. Brit.* a cow barn or shed. [OE *bÿre,* der. OE *būr* hut. Cf. BOWER¹]

Byrne (bûrn), *n.* **Donn** (dŏn), 1889–1928, U.S. author. *Real name:* Brian Oswald Donn-Byrne.

Byrnes (bûrnz), *n.* **James Francis,** born 1879, U.S. statesman and jurist: secretary of state, 1945–47.

byr·nie (bûr′nĭ), *n.* a shirt of mail; a hauberk. [var. of ME *brynie,* t. Scand.; cf. Icel. *brynja,* c. OE *byrne* coat of mail]

by-road (bī′rōd′), *n.* a side road.

By·ron (bī′rən), *n.* **George Gordon, Lord,** (*6th Baron Byron*) 1788–1824, British poet.

By·ron·ic (bī rŏn′ĭk), *adj.* 1. of or pertaining to Lord Byron. 2. possessing the characteristics of Byron or his poetry, esp. melancholy, melodramatic energy, etc. —**By·ron′i·cal·ly,** *adv.*

bys·sus (bĭs′əs), *n., pl.* **byssuses, byssi** (bĭs′ī). 1. *Zool.* a collection of silky filaments by which certain mollusks attach themselves to rocks. 2. (among the ancients) **a.** (orig.) a fine yellowish flax, or the linen made from it, as the Egyptian mummy cloth. **b.** (later) cotton or silk. [t. L, t. Gk.: m. *býssos,* of Oriental orig.]

by·stand·er (bī′stăn′dər), *n.* a person present but not involved; a chance looker-on.

by-street (bī′strēt′), *n.* a separate, private, or obscure street; a side street; a byway.

By·tom (bĭ′tôm), *n.* a city in S Poland: formerly in Germany. 181,000 (est. 1953). German, **Beuthen.**

by·way (bī′wā′), *n.* 1. a secluded, private, or obscure road. 2. a subsidiary or obscure field of research, endeavor, etc.

by·word (bī′wûrd′), *n.* 1. a word or phrase the frequent use of which characterizes some person or group. 2. a word or phrase used proverbially; a common saying; a proverb. 3. an object of general reproach, derision, scorn, etc. 4. an epithet, often of scorn. [OE *bīword*]

by-work (bī′wûrk′), *n.* work done in addition to one's regular work, as in intervals of leisure.

Byz·an·tine (bĭz′ən tēn′, -tin′, bĭ zăn′tĭn), *adj.* 1. of or pertaining to Byzantium. 2. of or pertaining to the Byzantine Empire. 3. of, pertaining to, or resembling Byzantine architecture. —*n.* 4. a native or inhabitant of Byzantium. [t. L: m. s. *Byzantīnus*]

Byzantine architecture, a style of architecture developed in Byzantium and its provinces during the 5th and 6th centuries A.D., characterized by centralized plans, vaulting, and rich use of light, shade, colorful mosaics, paintings, and decoration.

Byzantine Empire, the Eastern Roman Empire after the fall of the Western Empire in A.D. 476, having Constantinople as its capital. See map just below.

Byzantine Empire. A. D. 814

By·zan·ti·um (bĭ zăn′shĭ əm, -tĭ əm), *n.* an ancient Greek city on the Bosporus, commanding the entrance to the Black Sea: Constantine I built the city of Constantinople on this site, A.D. 330.

Bz., benzene.

C

C, c (sē), *n., pl.* **C's** or **Cs, c's** or **cs.** 1. the third letter of the English alphabet. 2. *Music.* **a.** the first, or keynote, of the C major scale, the third note of the scale of the A minor. **b.** a written or printed note representing this tone. **c.** a string, key, or pipe tuned to this note. **d.** (in solmization) the first tone of the scale of C, called *do.* 3. (as a mark at school or college) fair; satisfactory.

C, 1. *Chem.* carbon. 2. *U.S. Slang.* a hundred-dollar bill. 3. (L *centum*) 100. See **Roman numerals.**

C., 1. Cape. 2. Catholic. 3. Celsius (=Centigrade). 4. Celtic. 5. Centigrade. 6. Conservative.

c., 1. Also, **ç** (L *circa, circiter, circum*) about. 2. *Elect.* capacity. 3. *Baseball.* catcher. 4. cent; cents. 5. *Football.* center. 6. centigrade. 7. centime. 8. centimeter. 9. century. 10. chapter. 11. cognate with. 12. copyright. 13. cubic.

ca′ (kä, kô), *v.t., v.i. Scot.* to call, esp. in the sense "to drive." [var. of CALL]

Ca, *Chem.* calcium.

ca., 1. (L *circa*) about: *ca.* A.D. 476. 2. centiare.

C.A., 1. Central America. 2. Chartered Accountant. 3. Coast Artillery.

CAA, Civil Aeronautics Administration.

Caa·ba (kä′bə), *n.* Kaaba.

cab¹ (kăb), *n.* 1. taxicab. 2. any of various one-horse vehicles for public hire, as the hansom or the brougham. 3. the covered part of a locomotive or truck, where the engineer or driver sits. [short for CABRIOLET]

cab² (kăb), *n.* a Hebrew measure equal to about two quarts. Also, **kab.** [t. Heb.: m. *qab* vessel]

CAB, Civil Aeronautics Board.

ca·bal (kə băl′), *n., v., -balled, -balling.* —*n.* 1. the secret schemes of a small group of plotters; an intrigue. 2. a small group of secret plotters. —*v.i.* 3. to form a cabal; intrigue; conspire; plot. [var. of *cabbal,* t. ML: s. *cabbāla.* See CABALA]

cab·a·la (kăb′ə lə, kə bä′-), *n.* 1. (among certain Jewish rabbis and medieval Christians) a system of esoteric theosophy, based on a mystical interpretation of the Scriptures. 2. any occult or secret doctrine or science. Also, **cabbala, kabala, kabbala.** [t. ML: m. *cabbāla,* t. Heb.: m. *qabbālāh* tradition] —**cab′a·lism,** *n.* —**cab′a·list,** *n.*

cab·a·lis·tic (kăb/ə lĭs/tĭk), *adj.* **1.** pertaining to the cabala. **2.** mystic; occult. Also, **cab/a·lis/ti·cal.**

ca·bal·le·ro (kăb/əl yâr/ō; *Sp.* kä/bä lyĕ/rō), *n., pl.* **-ros. 1.** a Spanish gentleman. **2.** *Southwestern U.S.* **a.** a horseman. **b.** an escort; admirer. [t. Sp., g. L *caballārius* horseman. See CAVALIER]

ca·ba·ña (kä bä/nyä), *n.* **1.** a cabin; cottage; hut. **2.** a bathhouse near water's edge. [t. Sp.]

ca·bane (kə băn/), *n. Aeron.* a mastlike structure on some early airplanes, for anchoring bracing wires. [t. F. See CABIN]

cab·a·ret (kăb/ə rā/ *for 1, 2;* kăb/ə rĕt/ *for 3*), *n.* **1.** a restaurant that provides musical or other entertainment and space for dancing by patrons. **2.** *Brit.* the entertainment; floor show. **3.** a small table, stand, or tray with a set of dishes and utensils for serving tea, coffee, etc. [t. F (prob. Gascon): cellar, der. L *cavus* hollow]

cab·bage¹ (kăb/ĭj), *n., v.,* **-baged, -baging.** —*n.* **1.** any of various cultivated varieties of the cruciferous plant *Brassica oleracea,* var. *capitata,* with short stem and leaves formed into a compact, edible head. **2.** the head of the ordinary cabbage. —*v.i.* **3.** to form a head like a cabbage. [ME *caboche,* t. F, prob. t. Pr.: m. *caboso,* der. *cap* head, g. L *caput*]

cab·bage² (kăb/ĭj), *n., v.,* **-baged, -baging.** —*n.* **1.** something stolen, esp. pieces of cloth by a tailor when making garments. —*v.t., v.i.* **2.** to steal; pilfer: *cabbaging whole yards of cloth.* [orig. uncert.]

cabbage palm, any of several palm trees with large terminal leaf buds which are eaten like cabbage, as *Sabal palmetto* of the southeastern U.S., and *Roystonea oleracea* of the West Indies. Also, **cabbage tree.**

cabbage palmetto, a cabbage palm, *Sabal palmetto.*

cab·ba·la (kăb/ələ, kəbäl/-), *n.* cabala. Also, **kabbala.** —**cab/ba·lism,** *n.* —**cab/ba·list,** *n.*

cab·by (kăb/ĭ), *n., pl.* **-bies.** *Colloq.* a cab driver.

Cab·ell (kăb/əl), *n.* **James Branch,** 1879–1958, U.S. novelist, essayist, and critic.

ca·ber (kā/bər), *n. Scot.* a pole or beam, esp. one thrown as a trial of strength in the Highland game of **tossing the caber.** [t. Gaelic: m. *cabar* pole]

Ca·be·za de Va·ca (kä bĕ/thä dĕ vä/kä), **Álvar Núñez** (äl/vär nōō/nyĕth), c1490–c1557, Spanish explorer in North and South America.

cab·e·zon (kăb/ə zŏn/; *Sp.* kä/bĕ sôn/), *n.* a large Pacific fish, *Scorpaenichthys marmoratus,* of the sculpin family.

cab·in (kăb/ĭn), *n.* **1.** a small house; hut. **2.** an apartment or room in a ship, as for passengers. **3.** (in a passenger ship) a section comprising staterooms, etc., allotted to the use of the higher fare passengers. **4.** (in a warship) the apartment used by the commanding officer or flag officer. **5.** *Aeron.* the enclosed place for the pilot, passengers, or cargo. —*v.i.* **6.** to live in a cabin. —*v.t.* **7.** to confine; enclose tightly; cramp. [ME *cabane,* t. F, t. Pr.: m. *cabana,* g. LL *capanna,* of uncert. orig.] —**Syn. 1.** cot, shanty, shack. See **cottage.**

cabin boy, a boy employed to wait on the officers and passengers of a ship.

cab·i·net (kăb/ə nĭt), *n.* **1.** (*also cap.*) a council advising a sovereign or executive; the group of ministers who help to manage the government of a nation. **2.** a piece of furniture with shelves, drawers, etc., for holding or displaying valuable objects, dishes, etc. **3.** a case with compartments for precious objects, etc. **4.** a private room. **5.** *Archaic.* a small room. **6.** *Obs.* a small cabin. —*adj.* **7.** pertaining to a political cabinet: *a cabinet meeting.* **8.** pertaining to a private room. **9.** private; confidential; secret. **10.** of suitable value, beauty, or size for a private room, small case, etc.: *a cabinet edition of Milton.* [t. F, t. It.: m. *gabinetto,* ? der. *gabbia* cage, g. L *cavea;* in some senses, dim. of CABIN]

cab·i·net·mak·er (kăb/ə nĭt mā/kər), *n.* a workman who uses tools, woodworking machines, and lumber to build items for storage and household equipment.

cab·i·net·work (kăb/ə nĭt wûrk/), *n.* **1.** the making of fine furniture, etc. **2.** the product made.

ca·ble (kā/bəl), *n., v.,* **-bled, -bling.** —*n.* **1.** a thick, strong rope, often one of several wires twisted together. **2.** *Naut.* **a.** the rope or chain used to hold a vessel at anchor. **b.** cable's length. **3.** *Elect.* a stranded conductor, or a combination of conductors insulated from one another. **4.** cablegram. —*v.t.* **5.** to send (a message) by submarine cable. **6.** to send a cablegram to. **7.** to fasten with a cable. **8.** to furnish with a cable or cables. —*v.i.* **9.** to send a message by submarine cable. [ME *cable, cabel,* c. D, MLG, MHG, G *kabel,* all t. Rom.; cf. F *cable* t. Pr.), Sp. *cable,* all g. LL *capulum* halter]

Ca·ble (kā/bəl), *n.* **George Washington,** 1844–1925, U. S. novelist and writer about Southern life.

ca·ble·gram (kā/bəl grăm/), *n.* a telegram sent by a submarine cable.

ca·ble-laid (kā/bəl lād/), *adj.* (of a rope) made by laying three plain-laid ropes together with a left-handed twist.

cable railway, a railway on which the cars (**cable cars**) are pulled by a moving cable under the roadway.

cable's length, *Naut.* a unit of length (720 ft. in the U. S. Navy; 608 ft. in the British Navy).

ca·blet (kā/blĭt), *n.* a small cable, esp. a cable-laid rope under 10 inches in circumference. [f. CABLE + -ET]

cab·man (kăb/mən), *n., pl.* **-men.** a cab driver.

ca·bob (kə bŏb/), *n.* kabob.

ca·bo·chon (kăb/ə shŏn/; *Fr.* kȧ bô shôN/), *n.* a precious stone of convex hemispherical form, which has been polished but not cut into facets. [t. F, der. *caboche* head]

ca·boo·dle (kə bōō/dəl), *n. Colloq.* the (whole) lot, pack, or crowd. [unexplained var. of BOODLE (def. 1)]

ca·boose (kə bōōs/), *n.* **1.** *U.S.* a car (usually the last) on a freight train, used by the train crew. **2.** *Brit.* a kitchen on the deck of a ship; galley. [t. LG: m. *kabuus*]

Cab·ot (kăb/ət), *n.* **1.** **John,** c1450–1498?, Italian navigator who explored for England: discovered continent of North America in 1497. **2.** his son, **Sebastian,** 1474?–1557, English navigator and explorer.

ca·bril·la (kə brĭl/ə), *n.* any of various serranoid fishes, as the grouper, *Epinephelus guttatus,* of the West Indies, etc. [t. Sp.: a prawn, dim. of *cabra* goat]

cab·ri·ole (kăb/rĭ ōl/), *n. Furnit.* a curved, tapering leg, often ending in the form of an animal's paw, used esp. by Chippendale. [t. F. See CAPRIOLE]

A B

Cabrioles
A. 17th century
B. 18th century

cab·ri·o·let (kăb/rĭ ə lā/), *n.* **1.** a type of automobile resembling a coupé, with a folding top; a convertible coupé. **2.** a light, hooded one-horse carriage with two seats. [t. F, der. *cabriole* a leap. See CAPRIOLE]

Cabriolet, 19th century

cac-, var. of **caco-.**

ca′can·ny (kä kän/ĭ, kô-), *Orig. Scot. Slang, now Brit.* deliberate slowdown of production on the part of workers. [lit., drive gently. See CA′ (CALL), V., CANNY]

ca·ca·o (kə kā/ō, -kä/ō), *n., pl.* **-caos. 1.** a small evergreen sterculiaceous tree, *Theobroma cacao,* a native of tropical America, cultivated for its seeds, the source of cocoa, chocolate, etc. **2.** the fruit and seeds of this tree. [t. Sp., t. Mex. (Aztec): m. *caca-uatl*]

cacao bean, the seed of the cacao tree.

cacao butter, a fatty substance obtained from the seeds of the cacao, used in making soaps, cosmetics, etc. Also, **cocoa butter.**

cach·a·lot (kăsh/ə lŏt/, -lō/), *n.* the sperm whale. [t. F, t. Pg.: m. *cacholote,* ult. der. L *caccabus* pot]

cache (kăsh), *n., v.,* **cached, caching.** —*n.* **1.** a hiding place, esp. one in the ground, for provisions, treasure, etc. **2.** the store of provisions, etc., so hidden. —*v.t.* **3.** to put in a cache; conceal; hide. [t. F, der. *cacher* hide]

ca·chet (kä shā/, kăsh/ā; *Fr.* kȧ shĕ/), *n.* **1.** a seal as on a letter. **2.** a distinguishing mark or character. **3.** *Pharm.* a hollow wafer for enclosing an ill-tasting medicine. **4.** *Philately.* a slogan, design, etc., stamped or printed on mail. [t. F, der. *cacher* hide]

ca·chex·i·a (kə kĕk/sĭ ə), *n. Pathol.* general ill health, with emaciation, due to a chronic disease, as cancer. Also, **ca·chex·y** (kə kĕk/sĭ). [t. NL, t. Gk.: bad condition] —**ca·chec·tic** (kə kĕk/tĭk), *adj.*

cach·in·nate (kăk/ə nāt/), *v.i.* **-nated, -nating.** to laugh loudly or immoderately. [t. L: m. s. *cachinnātus,* pp.] —**cach/in·na/tion,** *n.*

ca·chou (kə shōō/, kä-), *n.* **1.** catechu. **2.** a pill or pastille for sweetening the breath. [t. F, t. Pg.: m. *cachu,* t. Malay: m. *kāchu* CATECHU]

ca·chu·cha (kä chōō/chä), *n. Spanish.* **1.** a lively dance. **2.** the music for it.

ca·cique (kə sēk/), *n.* **1.** a chief of an Indian clan or tribe in Mexico and the West Indies. **2.** any of a genus of American oscine passerine birds of the family *Icteridae,* including numerous species of Mexico and Central and South America, typical forms having a large bill somewhat swollen at the base. [t. Sp., t. Arawak]

cack·le (kăk/əl), *v., -led, -ling, n.* —*v.i.* **1.** to utter a shrill, broken sound or cry, as a hen after laying an egg. **2.** to laugh brokenly. **3.** to chatter noisily. —*v.t.* **4.** to utter with cackles; express by cackling. —*n.* **5.** act or sound of cackling. **6.** idle talk. [ME *cakelen;* imit. Cf. D *kakelen,* LG *kākeln,* Swed. *kackla*] —**cack/ler,** *n.*

caco-, a word element meaning "bad," "deformed," or "unpleasant," often used in forming medical terms. Also, **cac-.** [t. Gk.: m. *kako-,* comb. form of *kakós* bad]

cac·o·de·mon (kăk/ə dē/mən), *n.* an evil spirit; a devil. Also, **cac/o·dae/mon.** [t. Gk.: m. *kakodaímōn*]

cac·o·dyl (kăk/ə dĭl), *n. Chem.* **1.** any compound containing the (CH₃)₂As radical. **2.** a poisonous, oily, ill-smelling liquid, As₂(CH₃)₄. [f. m.s. Gk. *kakṓdēs* ill-smelling + -YL] —**cac/o·dyl/ic,** *adj.*

cac·o·ë·thes (kăk/ō ē/thēz), *n.* an irresistible urge; mania. [t. L, t. Gk.: m. *kakóēthes* bad habit (prop. neut. of *kakoēthēs* malignant)]

cac·o·gen·ics (kăk/ə jĕn/ĭks), *n. Sociol.* dysgenics. [f. CACO- + (EU)GENICS] —**cac/o·gen/ic,** *adj.*

ca·cog·ra·phy (kə kŏg/rə fĭ), *n.* **1.** bad handwriting (opposed to *calligraphy*). **2.** incorrect spelling (opposed to *orthography*). —**cac·o·graph·ic** (kăk/ə grăf/ĭk), **cac/o·graph/i·cal,** *adj.*

cac·o·mis·tle (kăk/ə mĭs/əl), n. a carnivorous animal, *Bassariscus astutus*, of Mexico and the southwestern U.S., related to the raccoon but smaller, with a sharper snout and longer tail. Also, **cac·o·mix·le** (kăk/ə mĭks/əl, -mĭk/səl). [t. Sp.: m. *cacomiztle*, t. Aztec, f. *claco* middle-sized + *miztli* lion]

Cacomistle.
Bassariscus astutus
(Total length 32 in., tail 17 in.)

ca·coph·o·nous (kə kŏf/ə nəs), *adj.* having a harsh sound; discordant.

ca·coph·o·ny (kə kŏf/ə nĭ), n., pl. **-nies.** 1. the quality of having a harsh sound; dissonance. 2. *Music.* frequent use of discords of a harshness and relationship difficult to understand. [t. NL: m.s. *cacophonia*, t. Gk.: m. *kakophōnía*]

cac·ta·ceous (kăk tā/shəs), *adj. Bot.* belonging to the *Cactaceae*, or cactus family.

cac·tus (kăk/təs), n., pl. **-tuses, -ti** (-tī). any of various fleshy-stemmed plants of the family *Cactaceae*, usually leafless and spiny, often producing showy flowers, chiefly natives of the hot, dry regions of America. [t. L, t. Gk.: m. *káktos* kind of prickly plant]

ca·cu·mi·nal (kə kū/mə nəl), *Phonet.* —*adj.* 1. pronounced with the tip of the tongue curled back so as to touch the roof of the mouth above the gums; cerebral. —*n.* 2. a cacuminal consonant. [f. s. L *cacūmen* top + -AL¹]

cad (kăd), n. 1. a contemptible, ill-bred person: one who does not behave like a gentleman. 2. *Brit.* (*Oxford Univ. Slang*) townsman (defs. 1, 2). [short for CADDIE (def. 2)]

ca·das·tral map (kə dăs/trəl), *Survey.* a map showing boundaries and ownership of land. [*cadastral* t. F, der. *cadastre* register of property, g. LL *capitāstrum*, der. L *caput* head]

cadastral survey, *Survey.* a survey relating to boundaries and subdivision of land.

ca·dav·er (kə dăv/ər, -dā/vər), n. a dead body, esp. of a human being; a corpse. [t. L] —**ca·dav/er·ic,** *adj.*

ca·dav·er·ine (kə dăv/ə rēn/), n. *Biochem.* a colorless ptomaine, C₅H₁₄N₂, produced by protein hydrolysis and by the putrefaction of animal tissues.

ca·dav·er·ous (kə dăv/ər əs), *adj.* 1. of or like a corpse. 2. pale; wan; ghastly. 3. haggard and thin. —**ca·dav/er·ous·ly,** *adv.* —**ca·dav/er·ous·ness,** *n.*

cad·die (kăd/ĭ), n., v., **-died, -dying.** —n. 1. *Golf.* an attendant, hired to carry the player's clubs, find the ball, etc. 2. a person who runs errands, does odd jobs, etc. —*v.i.* 3. to work as a caddie. Also, **caddy.** [t. F: m. *cadet* CADET]

cad·dis (kăd/ĭs), n. a kind of woolen yarn or braid.

cad·dis fly (kăd/ĭs), any of various adult insects of the order *Trichoptera*, characterized by four membranous, more or less hairy wings. Also, **cad/dice fly.** [orig. uncert.]

cad·dish (kăd/ĭsh), *adj. Chiefly Brit.* ill-bred; ungentlemanly: *caddish behavior.* —**cad/dish·ly,** *adv.* —**cad/dish·ness,** *n.*

caddis worm, the larva of the caddis fly, used as fish bait. Also, **caddis, cad·dice** (kăd/ĭs).

Cad·do·an (kăd/ō ən) n. a family of North American Indian languages spoken in the upper Missouri valley in N Dakota, in the Platte valley in Nebraska (Pawnee), and in SW Arkansas and neighboring parts of Oklahoma, Texas, and Louisiana.

Caddis fly and worms
A. Caddis fly; B. Larva in case formed of small stones; C. Larva in case formed of grass roots

cad·dy¹ (kăd/ĭ), n., pl. **-dies.** *Eng.* a small box, can, or chest, esp. one for holding tea. [var. of CATTY²]

cad·dy² (kăd/ĭ), n., pl. **-dies,** *v.i.,* **-died, -dying.** caddie.

cade¹ (kād), n. a species of juniper, *Juniperus oxycedrus,* of the Mediterranean area, whose wood on destructive distillation yields an oily liquid (**oil of cade**) used in treating skin affections. [t. F, t. Pr.]

cade² (kād), *adj.* (of the young of animals) left by the mother and raised by hand: *a cade lamb.* [orig. uncert.]

ca·delle (kə děl/), n. a small blackish beetle, *Tenebrioides mauritanicus,* all stages of which are commonly destructive to cereals. [t. F, t. Pr.: m. *cadello,* g. L *catellus,* fem. *catella* little animal]

ca·dence (kā/dəns), n. 1. rhythmic flow, as of verses; rhythm. 2. the beat of any rhythmical movement. 3. a fall of the voice, as in speaking. 4. the general modulation of the voice. 5. *Music.* a sequence of notes or chords which indicates the momentary or complete end of a composition, section, phrase, etc. 6. *Mil.* the rate of stepping in marching: *a cadence of 120 steps per minute.* Also, **ca/den·cy.** [ME, t. F, t. It.: m. *cadenza,* g. LL *cadentia,* der. s. L *cadens,* ppr., falling] —**ca/denced,** *adj.*

ca·dent (kā/dənt), *adj.* 1. having cadence. 2. *Archaic.* falling. [t. L: s. *cadens,* ppr., falling]

ca·den·za (kə děn/zə), n. *Music.* an elaborate flourish or showy passage introduced near the end of an aria or in a movement of a concerto. [t. It. See CADENCE]

ca·det (kə dět/), n. 1. a student training for service as an officer in the U.S. Army. (Students in the Naval Academy training for service as officers in the U.S. Navy are called **midshipmen**). 2. a gentleman, usually a younger son, who entered the army to prepare for a subsequent commission. 3. a younger son or brother. 4. the youngest son. 5. *Colloq.* a pander. [t. F, t. Gascon: m. *capdet* chief, ult. der. L *caput* head] —**ca·det/-ship, ca·det·cy** (kə dět/sĭ), n.

cadge (kăj), v., **cadged, cadging.** *Brit.* —*v.i.* 1. to sponge. 2. to peddle or beg. —*v.t.* 3. to get by peddling or begging. —**cadg/er,** n.

cadg·y (kăj/ĭ), *adj. Scot.* 1. cheerful. 2. wanton.

ca·di (kä/dĭ, kā/-), n., pl. **-dis.** a judge in a Moslem community, whose decisions are based on Mohammedan religious law. Also, **kadi.** [t. Ar.: m. *qāḍī* judge]

Cad·il·lac (kăd/ə lăk/; Fr. kȧ dē yȧk/), n. **Antoine de la Mothe** (ȧN twän/ də lȧ môt/), 1657?–1730, French colonial governor in North America: founder of Detroit.

Cá·diz (kā/dĭz, kə dĭz/; Sp. kä/dēth, -dēs), n. a seaport in SW Spain, on the **Gulf of Cadiz,** a bay of the Atlantic, 106,976 (est. 1955).

Cad·me·an (kăd mē/ən), *adj.* pertaining to Cadmus.

Cadmean victory, a victory in which the victor suffers as much as the vanquished. See **Cadmus.**

cad·mi·um (kăd/mĭ əm), n. *Chem.* a white, ductile divalent metallic element like tin in appearance: used in plating and in making certain alloys. *Symbol:* Cd; *at. wt.:* 112.41; *at. no.:* 48; *sp. gr.:* 8.6 at 20°C. [t. NL, der. L *cadmia,* t. Gk.: m. *kadmeia* (gē) Cadmean (earth), i.e. calamine (with which cadmium is usually associated)] —**cad/mic,** *adj.*

cadmium orange, a yellow color approaching orange.

cadmium yellow, a bright, or lemon, yellow color.

Cad·mus (kăd/məs), n. *Gk. Legend.* a Phoenician prince who planted the teeth of a dragon he had slain, from which many warriors suddenly sprang up who fought each other until only five survived. These five, led by Cadmus, founded Thebes. He is said by several accounts to have brought an alphabet from Phoenicia (or Egypt) to Greece.

Ca·dor·na (kä dôr/nä), n. **Count Luigi** (lōō ē/jē), 1850–1928, Italian general: chief of staff, 1914–17.

ca·dre (kä/dər; *Mil. usually* kăd/rĭ), n. 1. *Mil.* the key group of officers and enlisted men necessary to establish and train a new military unit. 2. a framework. [t. F: frame, t. It.: m. *quadro,* g. L *quadrum* a square]

ca·du·ce·us (kə dū/sĭ əs, -dōō/-), n., pl. **-cei** (-sĭ ī/). 1. the staff carried by Hermes, or Mercury, as herald or messenger of the gods. 2. a similar staff used as an emblem of the medical profession and as the insignia of the U. S. Army Medical Corps. [t. L, t. d. Gk.: m. *kārȳkeion* herald's staff] —**ca·du/ce·an,** *adj.*

ca·du·ci·ty (kə dū/sə tĭ, -dōō/-), n. 1. the infirmity of old age; senility. 2. frailty; transitoriness. [t. F: m. *caducité.* See CADUCOUS]

ca·du·cous (kə dū/kəs, -dōō/-), *adj.* 1. *Bot.* a. tending to fall. b. deciduous; dropping off very early, as leaves. 2. *Zool.* subject to shedding. 3. transitory. [t. L: m. *cadūcus* falling]

cae·cil·i·an (sē sĭl/ĭ ən), n. any of the limbless and elongate burrowing amphibians of the order *Apoda.* [f. s. L *caecilia* lizard + -AN]

caeco-, a word element meaning "the caecum." Also, before vowels, **caec-.**

Caduceus
(def. 2)

cae·cum (sē/kəm), n., pl. **-ca** (-kə). *Anat., Zool.* a cul-de-sac, esp. the one at the beginning of the human large intestine, bearing the vermiform appendix. See diag. under **intestine.** [t. L, neut. of *caecus* blind] —**cae/cal,** *adj.*

Cæd·mon (kăd/mən), n. fl. A.D. 670, English poet, the first to compose religious verse in the vernacular.

Cae·li·an (sē/lĭ ən), n. the southeastern hill of the seven hills of ancient Rome.

Caen (kän; *Fr.* käN), n. a seaport in N France, near the English channel. 67,851 (1954).

caeno-, var. of ceno-¹.

cae·o·ma (sē ō/mə), n. *Bot.* (in fungi) an aecium in which the spores are formed in chains and not enclosed in a peridium. [f. m.s. Gk. *kaíein* smelt + -OMA]

Caer·le·on (kär lē/ən), n. a town in SW England, in Monmouthshire: site of an ancient Roman fortress; supposed seat of King Arthur's court. 4709 (1951).

Caer·nar·von·shire (kär när/vən shĭr/, -shər), n. a county in NW Wales. 124,000 pop. (est. 1956); 569 sq. mi. *Co. seat:* Caernarvon. Also, **Caer·nar/von, Car·narvon.**

caes·al·pin·i·a·ceous (sěz/ăl pĭn/ĭ ā/shəs, sěs/-), *adj. Bot.* belonging to the *Caesalpiniaceae,* a family of leguminous plants including the honey locust, royal poinciana, Kentucky coffee tree, and numerous tropical genera. [f. s. NL *Caesalpinia,* the typical genus (named after Andrea *Caesalpino* (1519–1603), Italian botanist) + -ACEOUS]

Cae·sar (sē/zər), n. 1. **Gaius Julius** (gā/əs jōōl/yəs), 102 or 100–44 B.C., Roman general, statesman, and historian: conqueror of Gaul, Britain, etc. 2. a title of the Roman emperors from Augustus to Hadrian, and later of the heir presumptive. 3. any emperor. 4. a tyrant; dictator. [cf. CZAR, KAISER]

ăct, āble, dâre, ärt; ĕbb, ēqual; ĭf, īce; hŏt, ōver, ôrder, oil, bŏŏk, ōōze, out; ŭp, ūse, ûrge; ə = a in alone; ch, chief; g, give; ng, ring; sh, shoe; th, thin; ŧh, that; zh, vision. See the full key on inside cover.

Caes·a·re·a (sĕs/ə rē/ə, sĕz/-), *n.* **1.** an ancient seaport in NW Israel: the Roman capital of Palestine. **2.** ancient name of **Kayseri.**

Cae·sar·e·an (sĭ zâr/ĭ ən), *n.* **1.** a Caesarean operation or section. —*adj.* **2.** pertaining to Caesar or the Caesars: *a Caesarean conquest.* Also, **Cae·sar/i·an, Cesarean, Cesarian.**

Caesarean operation, *Surg.* the operation by which a fetus is taken from the uterus by cutting through the walls of the abdomen and uterus (supposedly performed at the birth of Caesar). Also, **Caesarean section.**

Cae·sar·ism (sē/zə rĭz/əm), *n.* absolute government; imperialism. —**Cae/sar·ist,** *n.*

cae·si·um (sē/zĭ əm), *n. Chem.* cesium.

caes·pi·tose (sĕs/pə tōs/), *adj.* cespitose.

cae·su·ra (sĭ zhŏor/ə, -zyŏor/ə), *n., pl.* **-suras, -surae** (-zhŏor/ē, -zyŏor/ē). **1.** *Eng. Pros.* a break, esp. a sense pause, usually near the middle of a verse, and marked in scansion by a double vertical line, as in *know then thyself* ‖ *presume not God to scan.* **2.** *Greek and Latin Pros.* a division made by the ending of a word within a foot (or sometimes at the end of a foot), esp. in certain recognized places near the middle of a verse. Also, **cesura.** [t. L: a cutting] —**cae·su/ral,** *adj.*

ca·fé (kȧ fā/, kə-; *Fr.* kȧ fĕ/), *n.* **1.** a restaurant. **2.** a barroom. **3.** coffee. [t. F. See COFFEE]

ca·fé au lait (kȧ fā/ ō lā/, kȧf/Y-; *Fr.* kȧ fĕ/ ō lĕ/), *French.* **1.** hot coffee with scalded milk. **2.** a light brown.

ca·fé noir (kȧ fā/ nwär/; *Fr.* kȧ fĕ/ nwär/), *French.* black coffee.

caf·e·te·ri·a (kăf/ə tŷr/ĭ ə), *n.* a restaurant in which the patrons wait on themselves, carrying the food, as served out to them, to tables where it is eaten. [t. Mex. Sp.: coffee shop]

caf·feine (kăf/ēn, kăf/ĭ ĭn), *n.* a bitter crystalline alkaloid, $C_8H_{10}N_4O_2$, obtained from coffee, tea, etc., used in medicine as a stimulant, diuretic, etc. Also, **caf/fein.** [t. F: m. *caféine,* der. *café* coffee. See -INE[2] (def. 3)]

caf·tan (kăf/tən, kăf tän/), *n.* a long garment having long sleeves and tied at the waist by a girdle, worn under a coat in the Near East. Also, **kaftan.** [t. Turk., Pers.: m. *qaftān*] —**caf/taned,** *adj.*

cage (kāj), *n., v.,* **caged, caging.** —*n.* **1.** a boxlike receptacle or enclosure for confining birds or other animals, made with openwork of wires, bars, etc. **2.** anything that confines or imprisons; prison. **3.** something like a cage in structure or purpose. **4.** the car or enclosed platform of an elevator. **5.** any skeleton framework. **6.** *Ordn.* a steel framework upon which guns are supported. **7.** *Baseball.* **a.** a metal backstop used mainly in batting practice. **b.** a catcher's mask. **8.** *Hockey.* the structure forming the goal. —*v.t.* **9.** to put or confine in or as in a cage. [ME, t. OF, g. L *cavea* enclosure]

cage·ling (kāj/lĭng), *n.* a caged bird.

cage·y (kā/jĭ), *adj.,* **cagier, cagiest.** *Colloq.* cautious; shrewd. Also, **cag/y.** —**cag/i·ly,** *adv.* —**cag/i·ness,** *n.*

Ca·glia·ri (kä/lyä rē/), *n.* **1.** a seaport in S Sardinia. 149,000 (est. 1954). **2. Paolo** (pä/ō lō/), 1528-88, *(real name of Paul Veronese)* Venetian painter.

Ca·glios·tro (kä lyôs/trô), *n.* **Count Alessandro di** (ä/lĕs sän/drō dē), *(Giuseppe Balsamo)* 1743-95, unscrupulous Italian adventurer and supposed magician.

ca·hier (kä yā/; *Fr.* kȧ yĕ/), *n.* **1.** a number of sheets of paper or leaves of a book placed together, as for binding. **2.** a report of the proceedings of any body. [t. F, g. LL word meaning fourth, group of four sheets. See QUIRE[1]]

ca·hoot (kə hoot/), *n. U.S. Slang.* **1. in cahoot** or **cahoots,** in partnership; in league. **2. go cahoots,** to become partners. [? t. F: m. *cahute* hut, cabin]

Ca·i·a·phas (kā/ə fəs, kī/-), *n.* a high priest of the Jews from sometime before A.D. 37: presided at the Council of Sadducees which condemned Jesus to death.

Cai·cos Islands (kī/kōs). See **Turks and Caicos Islands.**

cai·man (kā/mən), *n.* cayman.

Cain (kān), *n.* **1.** the first son of Adam and Eve, who murdered his brother Abel. Gen. 4. **2.** a murderer.

Caine (kān), *n.* **(Sir Thomas Henry) Hall,** 1853-1931, British novelist.

caino-, var. of ceno-[1].

Cai·no·zo·ic (kī/nə zō/ĭk. kā/-), *adj., n.* Cenozoic.

ca·ique (kä ēk/), *n.* a long, narrow skiff or rowboat used on the Bosporus. [t. F, t. It.: m. *caicco,* t. Turk.]

ça i·ra (sȧ/ ē rȧ/), *French.* it will go on (refrain of a song of the French Revolution).

caird (kârd), *n. Scot.* a traveling tinker; a tramp or vagrant. [t. Gaelic: m. *ceard* tinker]

Caird (kârd), *n.* **Edward,** 1835-1908, British philosopher and theologian.

cairn (kârn), *n.* a heap of stones set up as a landmark, monument, tombstone, etc. [Scot., t. Gaelic: m. *carn* pile of stones] —**cairned** (kârnd), *adj.*

Cai·ro (kī/rō *for 1;* kâr/ō *for 2*), *n.* **1.** the capital of Egypt, in the N part, on the E bank of the Nile: wartime conference of Roosevelt, Churchill, and Chiang Kaishek, Nov., 1943. 2,367,000 (est. 1952). **2.** a city in S Illinois at the confluence of the Mississippi and Ohio rivers. 12,123 (1950).

cais·son (kā/sən, -sŏn), *n.* **1.** a structure in which men can work on river bottoms, etc., consisting essentially of an airtight box or chamber with an open bottom, the water being kept out by the high air pressure maintained within. **2.** a boatlike structure used as a gate for a dock or the like. **3.** pontoon (def. 3). **4.** a wooden chest containing bombs or explosives, used as a mine; an ammunition chest. **5.** an ammunition wagon. [t. F: b. *caisse* chest and earlier *casson* (t. It.: m. *cassone,* aug. of *cassa,* g. L *capsa* box). See CASE[2]]

caisson disease, *Pathol.* a disease marked by paralysis and other nervous symptoms, developed in coming from an atmosphere of high pressure, as in a caisson, to air of ordinary pressure; bends.

Caith·ness (kāth/nĕs, kāth nĕs/), *n.* a county in NE Scotland. 23,900 (est. 1956); 686 sq. mi. *Co. seat:* Wick.

cai·tiff (kā/tĭf), *Archaic and Poetic.* —*n.* **1.** a base, despicable person. —*adj.* **2.** base; despicable. [ME *caitif,* t. ONF, g. LL*cactīvus,* assimilatory var. of L *captīvus* (see CAPTIVE)]

ca·jole (kə jōl/), *v.t., v.i.,* **-joled, -joling.** to persuade by flattery or promises; wheedle; coax. [t. F: m.s. *cajoler,* ? b. *caresser* caress and *enjôler* capture] —**ca·jole/ment,** *n.* —**ca·jol/er,** *n.*

ca·jol·er·y (kə jō/lə rĭ), *n., pl.* **-eries.** persuasion by flattery or promises; wheedling; coaxing.

Ca·jun (kā/jən), *n. Louisiana.* a descendant of the exiles from Acadia; Acadian. Also, **Ca/jian.** [var. of ACADIAN. Cf. *Injun* for *Indian*]

caj·u·put (kăj/ə pət), *n.* **1.** a small myrtaceous tree or shrub of the Moluccas and neighboring islands, *Melaleuca cajuputi* or *minor,* a variety of *M. leucadendron.* **2.** a green, odorous oil distilled from the leaves of this tree, used as a stimulant, antispasmodic, and diaphoretic. **3.** a lauraceous tree, *Umbellularia californica,* whose aromatic leaves are used medicinally. Also, **caj/e·put.** [t. Malay, f. *kāyu* wood + *pūtih* white]

cake (kāk), *n., v.,* **caked, caking.** —*n.* **1.** a sweet baked food in loaf or layer form, made with or without shortening, usually with flour, sugar, eggs, flavoring, usually with baking powder or soda, and a liquid. **2.** a flat, thin mass of bread, esp. unleavened bread. **3.** pancake; griddlecake. **4.** a shaped or molded mass of other food: *a fish cake.* **5.** a shaped or compressed mass: *a cake of soap, ice, etc.* **6. take the cake, a.** to win the prize. **b.** to surpass all others; excel. —*v.t.* **7.** to form into a cake or compact mass. —*v.i.* **8.** to become formed into a cake or compact mass: *mud caked on his shoes.* [ME, t. Scand.; cf. Icel. *kaka;* akin to D *koek,* G *kuchen*]

cakes and ale, good things and enjoyments of life.

cake·walk (kāk/wôk/), *n.* **1.** a promenade or march, of American Negro origin, in which the couples with the most intricate or eccentric steps receive cakes as prizes. **2.** a dance based on this promenade. **3.** music for this dance. —*v.i.* **4.** to walk or dance in or as in a cakewalk. —**cake/walk/er,** *n.*

Cal., 1. California. **2.** *Physics.* large calorie.

cal., 1. *Physics.* small calorie. **2.** caliber.

Cal·a·bar (kăl/ə bär/, kăl/ə bär/), *n.* **1.** a river and estuary in SE Nigeria. **2.** a seaport near the mouth of this river. 46,000 (est. 1950).

Calabar bean, the violently poisonous seed of a fabaceous African climbing plant, *Physostigma venenosum,* the active principle of which is physostigmine.

cal·a·bash (kăl/ə băsh/), *n.* **1.** any of various gourds, esp. the fruit of the bottle gourd, *Lagenaria siceraria.* **2.** any of the plants bearing them. **3.** the fruit of a bignoniaceous tree, *Crescentia cujete,* of tropical America. **4.** Also, **calabash tree.** the tree itself. **5.** the dried hollow shell of the calabash (either def. 1 or 3) used as a vessel or otherwise. **6.** a bottle, kettle, tobacco-pipe bowl, etc., made from it. **7.** *U.S.* a gourd used as a rattle, drum, etc., esp. by Indians. [t. F: m. *calebasse,* t. Sp.: m. *calabaza* gourd, ? t. Pers.: m. *kharbuz* melon]

cal·a·boose (kăl/ə bōōs, kăl/ə bōōs/), *n. U.S. Colloq.* lockup; jail. [t. Sp.: m. *calabozo* dungeon, orig. uncert.]

Ca·la·bri·a (kə lā/brĭ ə; *It.* kä lä/bryä), *n.* **1.** a department in SW Italy. 2,104,000 pop. (est. 1954); 5828 sq. mi. **2.** an ancient district at the SE extremity of Italy.

ca·la·di·um (kə lā/dĭ əm), *n.* a plant of the araceous genus *Caladium,* mostly herbs of the American tropics, cultivated for their variegated, colorful leaves. [NL, t. Malay: m. *kelády*]

Cal·ais (kăl/ā, -ĭs; *Fr.* kȧ lĕ/), *n.* a seaport in N France, on the Strait of Dover: the nearest French port to England; taken by Canadian forces, Sept., 1944. 60,340 (1954).

cal·a·man·co (kăl/ə măng/kō), *n., pl.* **-cos.** a glossy woolen fabric checkered or brocaded in the warp so that the pattern shows on one side only, much used in the 18th century.

cal·a·man·der (kăl/ə măn/dər), *n.* the hard wood of a tree, *Diospyros quaesita,* of Ceylon and India, used for cabinetwork. [orig. uncert.]

cal·a·mine (kăl/ə mĭn/, -mĭn), *n.* **1.** a mineral, hydrous zinc silicate, $ZnSiO_3(OH_2)$, an ore of zinc; hemimorphite. **2.** *Chiefly Brit.* smithsonite (def. 1). [t. F, t. ML: m. *calamina,* appar. alter. of L *cadmia.* See CADMIUM]

cal·a·mint (kăl/ə mĭnt), *n.* any plant of the labiate genus *Satureja,* esp. *S. calamintha* and *S. nepeta.* [t. L: m. s. *calaminthē,* t. Gk.: m. *kalaminthē;* r. ME *calament,* t. F, t. ML: s. *calamentum*]

cal·a·mite (kăl/ə mīt/), *n.* a Paleozoic fossil plant. [t. NL: m. *Calamītes,* t. Gk.: m. *kalamītēs* reedlike]

b., blend of, blended; c., cognate with; d., dialect, dialectal; der., derived from; f., formed from; g., going back to; m., modification of; r., replacing; s., stem of; t., taken from; ?, perhaps. See the full key on inside cover.

ca·lam·i·tous (kə lăm'ə təs), *adj.* causing or involving calamity; disastrous: *a calamitous defeat.* [t. L: m. s. *calamitōsus*] **—ca·lam'i·tous·ly,** *adv.* **—ca·lam'i·tous-ness,** *n.*

ca·lam·i·ty (kə lăm'ə tĭ), *n., pl.* **-ties. 1.** grievous affliction; adversity; misery. **2.** a great misfortune; a disaster. [late ME *calamyte,* t. L: m.s. *calamitas*] **—Syn. 2.** reverse, blow, catastrophe, cataclysm. See **disaster.**

cal·a·mus (kăl'ə məs), *n., pl.* **-mi** (-mī'). **1.** the sweet flag, *Acorus calamus.* **2.** its aromatic root. **3.** any palm of the genus *Calamus,* yielding rattan, canes, etc. **4.** the hollow base of a feather; a quill. [t. L, t. Gk.: m. *kálamos* reed]

ca·lash (kə lăsh'), *n.* **1.** a light, low-wheeled carriage, either with or without a folding top. **2.** the folding top (**calash top**) of such a vehicle. **3.** a kind of hood formerly worn by women. [t. F: m. *calèche,* t. G: m. *kalesche,* t. Slavic; cf. Bohemian *kolésa*]

Calash

cal·a·ver·ite (kăl'ə vâr'īt), *n.* a silver-white mineral, gold telluride, AuTe₂, containing a little silver: an ore of gold. [f. *Calaver(as)* (county in California where first found) + -ITE[1]]

cal·ca·ne·um (kăl kā'nĭ əm), *n., pl.* **-nea** (-nĭ ə). cal-caneus.

cal·ca·ne·us (kăl kā'nĭ əs), *n., pl.* **-nei** (-nĭ ī'). **1.** (in man) the largest tarsal bone, forming the prominence of the heel. **2.** the corresponding bone in other vertebrates. Also, **calcaneum.** [t. L: heel]

cal·car (kăl'kär), *n., pl.* **calcaria** (kăl kâr'ĭ ə). *Biol* a spur, or spurlike process. [t. L: a spur]

cal·ca·rate (kăl'kə rāt), *adj. Biol.* furnished with a calcar or calcaria; spurred. Also, **cal'ca·rat'ed.**

cal·car·e·ous (kăl kâr'ĭ əs), *adj.* of, containing, or like calcium carbonate; chalky: *calcareous earth.* [var. of *calcarious,* t. L: m. *calcārius* pertaining to lime]

cal·ca·rif·er·ous (kăl'kə rĭf'ər əs), *adj. Biol.* bearing a spur or spurs. [f. CALCAR + -(I)-FEROUS]

cal·ce·i·form (kăl'sĭ ə fôrm', kăl sē'-), *adj. Bot.* calceolate. [f. s. L *calceus* a shoe + -(I)-FORM]

cal·ce·o·lar·i·a (kăl'sĭ ə lâr'ĭ ə), *n.* any plant of the genus *Calceolaria,* often cultivated for its slipperlike flowers. [NL, f. s. L *calceolus* slipper (dim. of *calceus* shoe) + -āria -ARIA]

Calcarate foot of pheasant

cal·ce·o·late (kăl'sĭ ə lāt'), *adj. Bot.* having the form of a shoe or slipper, as the labellum of certain orchids.

cal·ces (kăl'sēz), *n.* pl. of **calx.**

Cal·chas (kăl'kəs), *n.* Gk. Legend. a priest of Apollo who aided the Greeks in the Trojan war.

cal·cic (kăl'sĭk), *adj.* pertaining to or containing lime or calcium. [f. s. L *calx* lime + -IC]

cal·cif·er·ol (kăl sĭf'ə rōl', -rŏl'), *n. Biochem.* vitamin D₂, a fat-soluble, crystalline alcohol, C₂₈H₄₃OH, found in milk and fish-liver oils and produced by the activation of ergosterol by ultraviolet irradiation.

cal·cif·er·ous (kăl sĭf'ər əs), *adj.* **1.** *Chem.* forming salts of calcium, esp. calcium carbonate. **2.** containing calcium carbonate. [f. s. L *calx* lime + -(I)FEROUS]

cal·cif·ic (kăl sĭf'ĭk), *adj. Zool., Anat.* making or converting into salt of lime or chalk.

cal·ci·fi·ca·tion (kăl'sə fə kā'shən), *n.* **1.** a changing into lime. **2.** *Physiol.* the deposition of lime or insoluble salts of calcium and magnesium, as in a tissue. **3.** *Anat., Geol.* a calcified formation. **4.** a soil process in which the surface soil is supplied with calcium in such a way that the soil colloids are always close to saturation.

cal·ci·fy (kăl'sə fī'), *v.t., v.i.,* **-fied, -fying.** *Physiol.* to make or become calcareous or bony; harden by the deposit of calcium salts. [f. s. L *calx* lime + -(I)FY]

cal·ci·mine (kăl'sə mīn', -mĭn), *n., v.,* **-mined, -mining. —n. 1.** a white or tinted wash for walls, ceilings, etc. **—v.t.** to wash or cover with calcimine. Also, **kalsomine.** [m. KALSOMINE by assoc. with CALCIUM]

cal·cine (kăl'sĭn, -sĭn), *v.t., v.i.,* **-cined, -cining. 1.** to convert or be converted into calx by heat. **2.** to burn to a friable substance; roast. **3.** to oxidize by heating. **4.** to frit. [t. F: m.s. *calciner,* ult. der. L *calx* lime] **—cal-cin·a·tion** (kăl'sə nā'shən), *n.* **—cal·cin·a·to·ry** (kăl'sĭn'ə tŏr'ĭ, kăl'sĭn-), *adj., n.*

cal·cite (kăl'sĭt), *n.* one of the commonest minerals, calcium carbonate, CaCO₃, occurring in a great variety of crystalline forms. Limestone, marble, and chalk consist largely of calcite. [f. s. L *calx* lime + -ITE[1]]

cal·ci·um (kăl'sĭ əm), *n. Chem.* a silver-white divalent metal, occurring combined in limestone, chalk, gypsum, etc. Symbol: Ca; at. wt.: 40.08; at. no.: 20; sp. gr.: 1.52 at 20°C. [t. NL, f. s. L *calx* lime + -IUM]

calcium carbide, *Chem.* a crystalline compound of calcium and carbon, CaC₂, which reacts with water to form acetylene.

calcium carbonate, *Chem.* a crystalline compound, CaCO₃, occurring in nature as calcite, etc.

calcium chloride, *Chem.* a white, deliquescent powder, CaCl₂, used as a drying agent, preservative, dust preventer, etc.

calcium hydroxide, *Chem.* slaked lime, Ca(OH)₂.

calcium light, a brilliant white light produced by heating lime to incandescence in an oxyhydrogen or other hot flame.

calcium phosphate, *Chem.* any of several phosphates of calcium occurring naturally in some rocks and in animal bones, and used in medicine, industry, etc.

calc·sin·ter (kălk'sĭn'tər), *n. Mineral.* travertine. [t. G: m. *kalksinter* lime slag]

calc·tu·fa (kălk'tōō'fə), *n. Geol.* calcareous tufa. See tufa (def. 1). Also, **calc-tuff** (kălk'tŭf').

cal·cu·la·ble (kăl'kyə lə bəl), *adj.* **1.** that can be calculated. **2.** that can be counted on; reliable; dependable.

cal·cu·late (kăl'kyə lāt'), *v.,* **-lated, -lating. —v.t. 1.** to ascertain by mathematical methods; compute: *to calculate the velocity of light.* **2.** to make suitable, adapt, or fit for a purpose: *calculated to inspire confidence.* **3.** *U.S. Colloq. or Dial.* to intend; plan. **4.** *U.S. Colloq. or Dial.* to think; guess. **—v.i. 5.** to make a computation; form an estimate. **6.** to count or rely (fol. by *on* or *upon).* [t. L: m.s. *calculātus,* pp., counted. See CALCULUS] **—Syn. 1.** count, figure, cast, estimate, weigh.

cal·cu·lat·ing (kăl'kyə lā'tĭng), *adj.* **1.** that performs calculations: *a calculating machine.* **2.** shrewd; cautious. **3.** selfishly scheming.

cal·cu·la·tion (kăl'kyə lā'shən), *n.* **1.** act or process of calculating; computation. **2.** result or product of calculating. **3.** an estimate based on the various facts in a case; a forecast. **4.** forethought; prior or careful planning. **—cal'cu·la'tive,** *adj.* **—Syn. 4.** circumspection, caution, wariness. See **prudence.**

cal·cu·la·tor (kăl'kyə lā'tər), *n.* **1.** one who calculates or computes. **2.** a machine that performs mathematical operations mechanically. **3.** a set of tables that facilitates calculation. [t. L]

cal·cu·lous (kăl'kyə ləs), *adj. Pathol.* characterized by the presence of calculus or stone.

cal·cu·lus (kăl'kyə ləs), *n., pl.* **-li** (-lī'), **-luses. 1.** *Math.* a method of calculation, esp. a highly systematic method of treating problems by a special system of algebraic notation. See **differential, infinitesimal,** and **integral calculus. 2.** *Pathol.* a stone or concretion found in the gall bladder, kidneys, or other parts of the body. [t. L: stone used in counting, dim. of *calx* small stone, lime]

Cal·cut·ta (kăl kŭt'ə), *n.* a seaport in NE India, in W Bengal, on the Hooghly river: former capital of British India, 1772–1912. 2,548,627 (1951).

cal·dar·i·um (kăl dâr'ĭ əm), *n., pl.* **-daria** (-dâr'ĭ ə). (in Roman baths) a room with hot water. [t. L]

Cal·de·cott award (kôl'də kət), an annual award for an outstanding illustrated juvenile book. [named after Randolph *Caldecott,* 1846–86, British illustrator]

Cal·de·rón de la Bar·ca (kŏl'də rən dĕl'ə bär'kə; Sp. kăl'dĕ'rōn' dĕ lä bär'kä), **Pedro** (pĕ'drō), 1600–81, Spanish dramatist and poet.

cal·dron (kôl'drən), *n.* a large kettle or boiler. Also, **cauldron.** [ME *cauderon,* t. ONF: m. *caudron,* g. deriv. of L *caldāria,* der. *cal(i)dus* hot]

Cald·well (kôld'wĕl, -wəl), *n.* **Erskine** (ûr'skĭn), born 1903, U.S. author.

Ca·leb (kā'ləb), *n.* a Hebrew leader, sent as a spy into the land of Canaan. Num. 13:6, etc.

Cal·e·do·ni·a (kăl'ə dō'nĭ ə), *n. Chiefly Poetic.* Scotland. **—Cal'e·do'ni·an,** *adj., n.*

Caledonian Canal, a ship canal traversing N Scotland, extending from the Atlantic NE to the North sea. 60½ mi.

cal·e·fa·cient (kăl'ə fā'shənt), *n.* **1.** *Med.* a substance which produces a sensation of heat when applied to the body, as mustard. **—adj. 2.** heating; warming. [t. L: s. *calefaciens,* ppr., making hot]

cal·e·fac·tion (kăl'ə făk'shən), *n.* **1.** act of heating. **2.** a heated state. [t. L: s. *calefactio*] **—cal'e·fac'tive,** *adj.*

cal·e·fac·to·ry (kăl'ə făk'tər ĭ), *adj., n., pl.* **-ries. —adj. 1.** serving to heat. **2.** a heated sitting room in a monastery. [t. L: m.s. *calefactōrius* having heating power]

cal·en·dar (kăl'ən dər), *n.* **1.** any of various systems of reckoning time, esp. with reference to the beginning, length, and divisions of the year: *the Gregorian calendar.* **2.** a tabular arrangement of the days of each month and week in a year. **3.** a list or register, esp. one arranged chronologically, as a list of the cases to be tried in a court. **4.** *Obs.* a guide or example. **—v.t. 5.** to enter in a calendar; register. [t. L: m. s. *calendārium* account book, der. *calendae* calends; r. ME *calender,* t. AF]

calendar day, the period from one midnight to the following one.

calendar month. See **month** (def. 1).

calendar year. See **year** (def. 1).

cal·en·der (kăl'ən dər), *n.* **1.** a machine in which cloth, paper, or the like is smoothed, glazed, etc., by pressing between revolving cylinders. **—v.t. 2.** to press in a calender. [t. F: m. *calandre,* prob. t. Pr.: m. *calandra,* ult. g. L *cylindrus* CYLINDER] **—cal'en·der·er,** *n.*

Cal·en·der (kăl'ən dər), *n. (often l.c.)* (in Mohammedan countries) one of an order of mendicant dervishes founded in the 14th century. [t. Pers.: m. *qalandar*]

ăct, āble, dâre, ärt; ĕbb, ēqual; ĭf, īce; hŏt, ōver, ôrder, oil, bŏok, ōoze, out; ŭp, ūse, ûrge; ə = a in alone; ch, chief; g, give; ng, ring; sh, shoe; th, thin; t͟h, that; zh, vision. See the full key on inside cover.

cal·ends (kăl′əndz), *n.pl.* (in the Roman calendar) the first day of the month. Also, **kalends**. [ME *kalendes* (rarely sing.), OE *cālend* (beginning of) a month, t. L: s. *calendae* (usually *kalendae*)]

ca·len·du·la (kə·lĕn′jə·lə), *n.* **1.** any plant of the asteraceous genus *Calendula*, esp. *C. officinalis*, a common marigold. **2.** the dried florets of this plant, used in medicine as a vulnerary, etc. [NL, dim. of L *calendae* CALENDS; so called as flowering almost every month of the year.]

cal·en·ture (kăl′ən·chər, -chŏŏr′), *n.* a violent fever with delirium, affecting persons in the tropics. [t. F, t. Sp.: m. *calentura* heat, der. L *calēre* be hot]

ca·le·sa (kä·lĕ′sä), *n.* (in the Philippines) a calash.

ca·les·cent (kə·lĕs′ənt), *adj.* growing warm; increasing in heat. [t. L: s. *calescens*, ppr., growing hot] —**ca·les′-cence,** *n.*

calf¹ (kăf, käf), *n.*, *pl.* **calves. 1.** the young of the cow or of other bovine mammals (in cattle usually under one year of age). **2.** the young of certain other animals, as the elephant, seal, and whale. **3.** calfskin leather. **4.** *Colloq.* an awkward, silly boy or man. **5.** a mass of ice detached from a glacier, iceberg, or floe. **6. kill the fatted calf,** to prepare an elaborate welcome. [ME and d. OE, r. OE *cealf*, c. G *kalb*]

calf² (kăf, käf), *n.*, *pl.* **calves.** the fleshy part of the back of the human leg below the knee. [ME, t. Scand.; cf. Icel. *kālfi*]

calf love, temporary infatuation of a boy or girl for a person of the opposite sex.

calf·skin (kăf′skĭn′, käf′-), *n.* **1.** the skin or hide of a calf. **2.** leather made from it.

Cal·ga·ry (kăl′gə·rĭ), *n.* a city in SW Canada, in Alberta. 129,060 (1951).

Cal·houn (kăl·hōōn′, kə-), *n.* **John Caldwell,** 1782–1850, vice-president of the U.S., 1825–32.

Ca·li (kä′lē), *n.* a city in SW Colombia. 284,186 (1952).

Cal·i·ban (kăl′ə·băn′), *n.* **1.** the ugly, beastlike slave of Prospero in Shakespeare's *The Tempest*. **2.** a man who has a degraded, bestial nature.

cal·i·ber (kăl′ə·bər), *n.* **1.** the diameter of something of circular section, as a bullet, or esp. that of the inside of a tube, as the bore of a gun. **2.** *Ordn.* the diameter of the bore of a gun taken as a unit in stating its length: *a fifty caliber 1¼-inch gun.* **3.** degree of capacity or ability; personal character. **4.** degree of merit, or importance; quality. Also, esp. *Brit.*, **cal′i·bre.** [t. F: m. *calibre*, t. It.: m. *calibro*, t. Ar.: m. *qālib* mold]

cal·i·brate (kăl′ə·brāt′), *v.t.*, **-brated, -brating.** to determine, check, or rectify the graduation of (any instrument giving quantitative measurements). —**cal′-i·bra′tion,** *n.* —**cal′i·bra′tor,** *n.*

cal·i·ces (kăl′ə·sēz′), *n.* pl. of **calix.**

ca·li·che (kä·lē′chě), *n. Geol.* **1.** a surface deposit consisting of sand or clay impregnated with crystalline salts, such as sodium nitrate or sodium chloride. **2.** a horizon of calcium or mixed carbonates in soils of semiarid regions. [Amer. Sp., der. *cal* lime, g. L *calx*]

cal·i·cle (kăl′ə·kəl), *n.* a cuplike depression or formation, as in corals. [t. L: m. s. *caliculus*, dim. of *calix* cup]

cal·i·co (kăl′ə·kō′), *n.*, *pl.* **-coes, -cos,** *adj.* —*n.* **1.** *U.S.* a printed cotton cloth, superior to percale. **2.** *Brit.* white cotton cloth. **3.** (orig.) cotton cloth imported from India. —*adj.* **4.** made of calico. **5.** resembling printed calico; spotted; piebald. [named after CALICUT]

cal·i·co·back (kăl′ə·kō·băk′), *n.* a brilliantly marked red-and-black bug, *Murgantia histrionica*, destructive to cabbages; the harlequin cabbage bug.

calico bass, a fresh-water food fish, *Pomoxys sparoides*, of the eastern and central U.S.

calico bush, the mountain laurel, *Kalmia latifolia*. Also, **calico flower, calico tree.**

Cal·i·cut (kăl′ə·kŭt′), *n.* a seaport in SW India, in Madras province. 158,724 (1951). Indian **Kozhikode.**

ca·lif (kā′lĭf, kăl′ĭf), *n.* caliph.

Calif., official abbreviation for California.

cal·if·ate (kăl′ə·fāt′, -fĭt), *n.* caliphate.

Cal·i·for·nia (kăl′ə·fôr′nyə, -fôr′nĭ·ə), *n.* **1.** a State in the W United States, on the Pacific coast. 15,717,204 pop. (1960); 158,693 sq. mi. *Cap.:* Sacramento. *Abbr.:* Calif. **2.** Gulf of, an arm of the Pacific, extending N W between the W coast of Mexico and the peninsula of Lower California. ab. 750 mi. long. —**Cal′i·for′nian,** *adj., n.*

California condor, a very rare bird of prey, *Gymnogyps californianus*, inhabiting a restricted part of California. It is the largest land bird of North America.

California fuchsia. See fuchsia (def. 2).

California poppy, a papaveraceous pale-green herb with showy yellow flowers, *Eschscholtzia californica*: the State flower of California.

cal·i·for·ni·um (kăl′ə·fôr′nĭ·əm), *n. Chem.* a synthetic, radioactive, metallic element. *Symbol:* Cf; *at. no.:* 98. [f. (University of) CALIFORN(IA), where first identified, + -IUM]

ca·lig·i·nous (kə·lĭj′ə·nəs), *adj. Rare.* misty; dim; dark. [t. L: m.s. *cālīginōsus* misty] —**ca·lig·i·nos·i·ty** (kə·lĭj′ə·nŏs′ə·tĭ), *n.*

Ca·lig·u·la (kə·lĭg′yə·lə), *n.* **Gaius Caesar** (gā′əs sē′zər), A.D. 12–41, Roman emperor, A.D. 37–41.

cal·i·pash (kăl′ə·păsh′, kăl′ə·păsh′), *n.* that part of a turtle next to the upper shield, a greenish gelatinous substance. Also, **callipash.** [orig. uncert.]

cal·i·pee (kăl′ə·pē′, kăl′ə·pē′), *n.* that part of a turtle next to the lower shield, consisting of a yellowish gelatinous substance. [cf. CALIPASH]

cal·i·per (kăl′ə·pər), *n.* **1.** (*usually pl.*) a tool, in its simplest form having two legs and resembling a draftsman's compass, used for obtaining inside and outside measurements. —*v.t.* **2.** to measure with calipers. Also, **calliper.** [var. of CALIBER]

caliper rule, a caliper with one jaw fixed to, or integral with, a graduated straight bar on which the other jaw slides.

A   B   C
Calipers
A. Outside calipers; B. Inside calipers; C. Spring adjusting calipers

ca·liph (kā′lĭf, kăl′ĭf), *n.* successor (usually of Mohammed): a title for the head of the Moslem state. Also, **calif, kaliph, khalif, khalifa.** [ME *califfe*, t. OF: m. *calife*, t. ML: m. *calipha*, t. Ar.: m. *khalīfa* successor, vicar]

cal·iph·ate (kăl′ə·fāt′, -fĭt), *n.* the rank, jurisdiction or government of a caliph. Also, **califate.**

cal·i·sa·ya (kăl′ə·sä′yə), *n.* the medicinal bark of the tree *Cinchona calisaya*. [t. S. Amer. Sp., prob. t. Kechua]

cal·is·then·ics (kăl′əs·thĕn′ĭks), *n.* **1.** (*construed as sing.*) the practice or art of calisthenic exercises; exercising the muscles for the purpose of gaining health, strength, and grace of form and movement. **2.** (*construed as pl.*) light gymnastic exercises designed to develop grace as well as organic vigor and health. Also, **cal·is·then′ic,** *adj.* —**cal·is·then·ics.** [f. *cali-* (var. of CALLI-) + s. Gk. *sthénos* strength + -ICS]

ca·lix (kā′lĭks, kăl′ĭks), *n.*, *pl.* **calices** (kăl′ə·sēz′). *Rom. Cath. Ch.* a chalice (def. 2). [t. L: cup]

calk¹ (kôk), *v.t.* **1.** to fill or close (a seam, joint, etc.), as in a boat. **2.** to make (a vessel) watertight by filling the seams between its planks with oakum or other material driven snug. **3.** to drive the edges of (plating) together to prevent leakage. **4.** to fill or close seams or crevices of (a tank, window, etc.) in order to make watertight, airtight, etc. Also, **caulk.** [ME *caulke(n)*, t. ONF: m. *cauquer*, g. L. *calcāre* tread, press]

calk² (kôk), *n.* **1.** a projection on a horseshoe to prevent slipping. **2.** *U.S.* a similar device on the heel or sole of a shoe. —*v.t.* **3.** to provide with calks. **4.** to injure with a calk. [ult. L: m. s. *calx* heel, or m. *calcāneum* heel, or m. *calcar* spur]

calk·er (kô′kər), *n.* **1.** one who calks ships, etc. **2.** a calking tool or device. Also, **caulker.** [f. CALK¹ + -ER¹]

call (kôl), *v.t.* **1.** to cry out in a loud voice. **2.** (of a bird or animal) to utter its characteristic cry. **3.** to announce; proclaim: *call a halt.* **4.** to read over (a roll or list) in a loud tone. **5.** to attract the attention of by loudly uttering something. **6.** to rouse from sleep as by a call: *call me at 8 o'clock.* **7.** to command or request to come; summon: *the boy was called by his mother, call a cab, call a witness.* **8.** to summon to an office, duty, etc.: *call someone to the ministry.* **9.** to convoke or convene, as a meeting or assembly: *call Congress into session.* **10.** to bring under consideration or discussion: *call a case.* **11.** to telephone to. **12.** to attract or lure (wild birds, etc.) by a particular cry or sound. **13.** *Baseball.* **a.** to terminate (a game) because of darkness, rain, etc. **b.** to indicate (a pitched ball) as a strike. **14.** to demand payment or fulfillment of (a loan, etc.). **15.** to demand (bonds, etc.) for payment. **16.** to give a name to; name: *his parents named him James but the boys call him Jim.* **17.** to designate as something specified: *he called me a liar.* **18.** to reckon; consider; estimate: *to call a thing a success, I call that mean.* **19.** *Billiards.* to request (the player) to state his intended shot. **20.** *Poker.* to require (a player) to show his hand, after equaling his bet. —*v.i.* **21.** to speak loudly, as to attract attention; shout; cry: *who calls so loudly?* **22.** to make a short visit; stop at a place on some errand or business: *to call at a house or place for a person or thing, or upon a person.* **23.** to telephone a person. **24.** *Poker.* to demand a showing of hands. **25.** Special verb phrases are: **call away,** to order off; divert: *necessity called him.* **call back, 1.** to recall; summon or bring back. **2.** to revoke; retract: *call back an oath.* **call down, 1.** to invoke from above; cause to descend. **2.** to reprimand; scold. **call for, 1.** to go and get. **2.** to require; demand; need: *the occasion calls for a cool head.* **call forth,** to bring or summon into action. **call in, 1.** to collect: *call in debts.* **2.** to withdraw from circulation: *call in gold notes.* **3.** to invite. **call into being,** to create. **call on, 1.** to appeal to: *call on a person for a song.* **2.** to make a short visit to: *to call on friends.* **call out, 1.** to utter in a loud voice. **2.** to summon into service: *call out the militia.* **3.** to bring into play; elicit: *call out new abilities.* **call up, 1.** to bring into action, discussion, etc. **2.** to require payment of. **3.** to communicate (with) by telephone. **4.** to recollect: *call up my sorrows afresh.* —*n.* **26.** a cry or shout. **27.** the cry of a bird or other animal. **28.** an instrument for imitating this cry and attracting or luring the animal. **29.** a summons or

---

b., blend of, blended; c., cognate with; d., dialect, dialectal; der., derived from; f., formed from; g., going back to; m., modification of; r., replacing; s., stem of; t., taken from; ?, perhaps. See the full key on inside cover.

signal sounded by a bugle, bell, etc.   **30.** a note blown on a horn to encourage the hounds.   **31.** a short visit: *to make a call on someone.*   **32.** a summons; invitation; bidding.   **33.** *Theat.* a notice of rehearsal posted by the stage manager.   **34.** a mystic experience of divine appointment to a vocation or service.   **35.** a request or invitation to become pastor of a church, a professor in a university, etc.   **36.** a need or occasion: *he had no call to say such things.*   **37.** a demand or claim: *to make a call on a person's time.*   **38.** a roll call.   **39.** *Poker.* a demand for the showing of hands.   **40.** a contract which permits its purchaser to buy a certain amount of stock, etc., at a specified price for a limited period of time.   **41.** a demand for payment of an obligation, esp. where payment is at the option of the creditor.   **42. call for margin,** a demand for payment upon the balance owed a stock or commodity broker because of the shrinking value of the security.   **43. on call,** payable or subject to return without advance notice. [ME *calle(n)*, (cf. OE *calla* herald), r. OE *ceallian*, c. Icel. *kalla*]   —**Syn. 7.** CALL, INVITE, SUMMON imply requesting the presence or attendance of someone at a particular place. CALL is the general word: *to call a meeting.* To INVITE is to ask someone courteously to come as a guest, a participant, etc., leaving him free to refuse: *to invite guests to a concert, invite them to contribute to a fund.* SUMMON implies sending for someone, using authority or formality in requesting his presence, and (theoretically) not leaving him free to refuse: *to summon a witness, members of a committee.*

cal·la (kăl′ə), *n.*   **1.** a plant of the genus *Zantedeschia* (or *Richardia*), native in Africa, esp. *Z. aethiopicum* (**calla lily**), which has a large white spathe enclosing a yellow spadix, and is familiar in cultivation.   **2.** an araceous plant, *Calla palustris*, of cold marshes of Europe and North America, with heart-shaped leaves. [t. NL, ? special use of L *calla* plant name]

call·a·ble (kô′lə bəl), *adj.*   **1.** that may be called.   **2.** subject to redemption upon notice, as a bond.   **3.** subject to payment on demand, as money loaned.

cal·lant (kă′lənt), *n.*   *Scot. and N. Eng.* a lad; a boy. Also, **cal·lan** (kă′lən). [t. D or LG: m. *kalant*, t. F: m. *chaland* customer]

Cal·la·o (kä yä′ō), *n.*   a seaport in W Peru, near Lima. 104,500 (est. 1952).

call·board (kôl′bôrd′), *n.*   a bulletin board, as in a theater for notices of rehearsal periods, etc.

call·boy (kôl′boi′), *n.*   **1.** a boy who summons actors just before they go on the stage.   **2.** a bellboy.

call·er[1] (kô′lər), *n.*   **1.** one that calls.   **2.** one who makes a short visit. [f. CALL + -ER[1]]   —**Syn. 2.** See **visitor.**

cal·ler[2] (kăl′ər, kä′lər), *adj.*   *Scot. and N. Eng.*   **1.** fresh, as fish, vegetables, etc.   **2.** fresh and cool. [? d. var. of *calver* fresh]

Cal·les (kä′yĕs), *n.*   **Plutarco Elías** (plōō tär′kō ĕ lē′äs), 1877–1945, Mexican general and statesman: president of Mexico, 1924–28.

calli-, a word element meaning "beauty." [t. Gk.: m. *kalli-*, comb form. of *kállos*]

cal·lig·ra·phy (kə lĭg′rə fĭ), *n.*   **1.** beautiful handwriting.   **2.** handwriting; penmanship. [t. Gk.: m. s. *kalligraphía*]   —**cal·lig′ra·pher, cal·lig′ra·phist,** *n.*   —**cal·li·graph·ic** (kăl′ə grăf′ĭk), *adj.*

call·ing (kô′lĭng), *n.*   **1.** act of one that calls.   **2.** vocation, profession, or trade.   **3.** summons.   **4.** invitation.   **5.** convocation.

calling card, a small card bearing one's name, used on various social or business occasions.

cal·li·o·pe (kə lī′ə pē′; *for 1, also* kăl′Ĭ ōp′), *n.*   **1.** a harsh musical instrument consisting of a set of steam whistles, played from a keyboard.   **2.** (*cap.*) *Gk. Myth.* the Muse of heroic poetry. [t. L, t. Gk.: m. *Kalliópē,* lit. beautiful-voiced]

cal·li·op·sis (kăl′Ĭ ŏp′sĬs), *n.*   a coreopsis.

cal·li·pash (kăl′ə păsh′, kăl′ə päsh′), *n.*   calipash.

cal·li·per (kăl′ə pər), *n., v.t.*   caliper.

cal·li·pyg·i·an (kăl′ə pĬj′Ĭ ən), *adj.*   having well-shaped buttocks. Also, **cal·li·py·gous** (kăl′ə pī′gəs). [t. Gk.: m.s. *kallípygos*]

cal·lis·then·ics (kăl′əs thĕn′Ĭks), *n.*   calisthenics.   —**cal′lis·then′ic,** *adj.*

Cal·lis·to (kə lĬs′tō), *n.*   *Gk. Myth.* a nymph attendant on Artemis, punished for an amour with Zeus by being changed into a bear and slain by Artemis.

call loan, a loan repayable on demand.

call market, the market for lending call money.

call money, funds available or loaned on call.

cal·los·i·ty (kə lŏs′ə tĬ), *n., pl.* **-ties.**   **1.** a callous condition.   **2.** *Bot.* a hardened or thickened part of a plant.   **3.** callus (def. 1a).

cal·lous (kăl′əs), *adj.*   **1.** hardened.   **2.** hardened in mind, feelings, etc.   **3.** having a callus; indurated, as parts of the skin exposed to friction.   —*v.i., v.t.*   **4.** to become or make hard or callous. [t. L: m. s. *callōsus* hard-skinned]   —**cal′lous·ly,** *adv.*   —**cal′lous·ness,** *n.*   —**Syn. 1.** See **hard.**

cal·low (kăl′ō), *adj.*   **1.** immature or inexperienced: *a callow youth.*   **2.** (of a young bird) featherless; unfledged. [ME and OE *calu, calw-,* c. G *kahl*]   —**cal′low·ness,** *n.*

call rate, interest charge on call loans.

call slip, a printed form used by a library patron to request the use of a particular book.

call to quarters, *U.S. Army.* a bugle call fifteen minutes before taps warning soldiers to go to quarters.

cal·lus (kăl′əs), *n., pl.* **-luses,** *v.*   —*n.*   **1.** *Pathol., Physiol.* **a.** a hardened or thickened part of the skin; a callosity.   **b.** a new growth of osseous matter at the ends of a fractured bone, serving to unite them.   **2.** *Bot.* **a.** the tissue which forms over the wounds of plants, protecting the inner tissues and causing healing.   **b.** a deposit on the perforated area of a sieve tube.   —*v.i.*   **3.** to make a callus. [t. L: hardened skin]

calm (käm), *adj.*   **1.** without motion; still: *a calm sea.*   **2.** not windy.   **3.** free from excitement or passion; tranquil: *a calm face, voice, manner, etc.*   —*n.*   **4.** freedom from motion or disturbance; stillness.   **5.** absence of wind.   **6.** freedom from agitation, excitement, or passion; tranquillity; serenity.   —*v.t.*   **7.** to make calm: *calm fears, calm an excited dog, etc.*   —*v.i.*   **8.** to become calm (usually fol. by *down*). [ME *calme,* t. OF, t. It.: m. *calma* (as if orig., heat of the day, hence, time for resting, quiet), g. LL b. Gk. *kaûma* burning heat and L *calēre* be hot]   —**calm′ly,** *adv.*   —**calm′ness,** *n.*   —**Syn. 1.** quiet, motionless.   **3.** placid, peaceful, serene, self-possessed. CALM, COLLECTED, COMPOSED, COOL imply the absence of agitation. CALM implies an unruffled state, esp. under disturbing conditions: *calm in a crisis.* COLLECTED implies complete command of oneself, usually as the result of an effort: *he remained collected in spite of the excitement.* One who is COMPOSED has or has gained dignified self-possession: *pale but composed.* COOL implies the apparent absence of strong feeling or excitement, esp. in circumstances of danger or strain: *so cool that he seemed calm.*   **7.** still, quiet, tranquilize.   —**Ant. 3.** agitated, excited.

cal·ma·tive (käl′mə tĬv, kä′mə-), *adj., n.*   *Med.* sedative.

calm·y (kä′mĬ), *adj.*   *Poetic.* calm. [f. CALM, n. + -Y[1]]

cal·o·mel (kăl′ə mĕl′, -məl), *n.*   *Pharm.* mercurous chloride, Hg_2Cl_2, a white, tasteless solid, used in medicine as a mercurial, a purgative, etc. [t. F, short for *calomélas,* f. Gk.: m. s. *kalós* beautiful + *mélās* black]

ca·lor·ic (kə lôr′Ĭk, -lŏr′-), *n.*   **1.** heat.   **2.** *Old Physics.* a hypothetical imponderable fluid whose presence in matter determined its thermal state.   —*adj.*   **3.** pertaining or relating to heat.   **4.** (of engines) driven by heated air. [t. F: m. *calorique,* der. L *calor* heat. Cf. CALORIE]   —**cal·o·ric·i·ty** (kăl′ə rĬs′ə tĬ), *n.*

cal·o·rie (kăl′ərĬ), *n.*   **1.** *Physics.* **a.** gram calorie or small calorie, the quantity of heat required to raise the temperature of one gram of water one degree centigrade, usually specified as determined at, or close to, 16°C.   **b.** kilogram calorie or large calorie, a quantity of heat, equal to 1000 gram calories.   **2.** *Physiol.* **a.** a unit equal to the large calorie, used to express the heat output of an organism and the fuel or energy value of food.   **b.** a quantity of food capable of producing such a unit of energy. Also, **calory.** [t. F, der. L *calor* heat]

cal·o·rif·ic (kăl′ə rĬf′Ĭk), *adj.*   pertaining to conversion into heat. [t. L: s. *calōrificus* heat-producing]

cal·o·rim·e·ter (kăl′ə rĬm′ə tər), *n.*   *Physics, etc.* an apparatus for measuring quantities of heat. [f. L *calor* heat + -(I)METER]

cal·o·rim·e·try (kăl′ə rĬm′ə trĬ), *n.*   *Physics.* the measurement of heat.   —**cal·o·ri·met·ric** (kăl′ə rə mĕt′rĬk, kə lôr′-, -lŏr′-), **cal′o·ri·met′ri·cal,** *adj.*   —**cal′o·ri·met′ri·cal·ly,** *adv.*

cal·o·ry (kăl′ərĬ), *n., pl.* **-ries.**   calorie.

ca·lotte (kə lŏt′), *n.*   a plain skullcap, as that worn by Catholic ecclesiastics. [t. F, dim. of *cale* cap. Cf. CAUL]

cal·o·yer (kăl′ə yər, kə lol′ər), *n.*   a monk of the Greek Orthodox Church. [t. F, t. It.: m. *caloiero,* t. LGk.: m. *kalógeros* venerable, monk]

cal·pac (kăl′păk), *n.*   a large black cap of sheepskin or other heavy material, worn by Armenians, Turks, etc. Also, **cal′pack.** [t. Turk.: m. *qâlpâq*]

cal·trop (kăl′trəp), *n.*   **1.** *Bot.* **a.** any of various plants having spiny heads or fruit, esp. of the genera *Tribulus* and *Kallstroemia.*   **b.** the star thistle.   **c.** an Old World plant, *Tribulus terrestris.*   **d.** the water chestnut.   **2.** *Mil.* an iron ball with four projecting spikes so disposed that when the ball is on the ground one of them always points upward, used to obstruct the passage of cavalry, etc. Also, **cal′trap.** [ME *calketrappe,* OE *col(te)træppe, calcatrippe* spiny plant, appar. f. m. s. L *calx* heel + m. ML *trappa* trap]

Caltrop (def. 2)

cal·u·met (kăl′yə mĕt′, kăl′yə mĕt′), *n.*   a long, ornamented tobacco pipe used by North American Indians on ceremonial occasions, esp. in token of peace. [t. d. F, g. dim. of L *calamus* reed]

ca·lum·ni·ate (kə lŭm′nĬ āt′), *v.t.,* **-ated, -ating.**   to make false and malicious statements about; slander. [t. L: m.s. *calumniātus,* pp.]   —**ca·lum′ni·a′tor,** *n.*

ca·lum·ni·a·tion (kə lŭm′nĬ ā′shən), *n.*   **1.** act of calumniating; slander.   **2.** a calumny.

ca·lum·ni·ous (kə lŭm′nĬ əs), *adj.*   of, involving, or using calumny; slanderous; defamatory. Also, **ca·lum·ni·a·to·ry** (kə lŭm′nĬ ə tôr′Ĭ).   —**ca·lum′ni·ous·ly,** *adv.*

cal·um·ny (kăl′əm nĬ), *n., pl.* **-nies.**   **1.** a false and malicious statement designed to injure someone's reputation.   **2.** slander. [t. L: m.s. *calumnia*]

cal·var·i·a (kăl vâr′Ĭə), *n.*   the dome of the skull. [t. L. See CALVARY]

Cal·va·ry (kăl′vərĬ), *n., pl. for 2* **-ries.**   **1.** Golgotha, the place where Jesus was crucified. Luke 23:33.   **2.** (*l.c.*) a sculptured representation of the Crucifixion, usually erected in the open air. [t. L: m. s. *calvāria* skull, used to render the Aramaic name. See Golgotha]

calve (kăv, käv), *v.*, **calved, calving.** —*v.i.* **1.** to give birth to a calf. **2.** (of a glacier, iceberg, etc.) to give off a detached piece. —*v.t.* **3.** to give birth to (a calf). **4.** to give off (a detached piece). [ME *calve(n)*, der. *calf* calf; r. OE *cealfian*, der. *cealf* calf]

Cal·vé (kȧl vě′), *n.* **Emma** (ěm′ə; *Fr.* ěm mȧ′), *(Emma de Roquer Gaspari)* 1863?–1942, French operatic soprano.

Cal·vert (kăl′vərt), *n.* **1. Sir George,** *(1st Baron Baltimore)* c1580–1632, English statesman: projector of colony of Maryland. **2.** his son, **Leonard,** 1606–47, first governor of the English colony of Maryland.

calves (kăvz, kävz), *n.* pl. of calf.

Cal·vin (kăl′vĭn), *n.* **John,** 1509–64, religious reformer and theologian, born in France: leader of the Protestant Reformation in Geneva, Switzerland.

Cal·vin·ism (kăl′və nĭz′əm), *n.* **1.** *Theol.* **a.** the doctrines and church practices taught by John Calvin, who emphasized the sovereignty of God, predestination, the authority of Scriptures, presbyterian polity, and strict church discipline. **b.** the doctrines of later theologians who accepted Calvin's teachings with various modifications. **2.** adherence to these doctrines. —**Cal′vin·ist,** *n., adj.* —**Cal′vin·is′tic, Cal′vin·is′ti·cal,** *adj.*

cal·vi·ti·es (kăl vĭsh′ĭ ēz′), *n.* baldness. [t. L]

calx (kălks), *n., pl.* **calxes, calces** (kăl′sēz). **1.** the oxide or ashy substance which remains after metals, minerals, etc., have been thoroughly roasted or burned. **2.** lime. [t. L: small stone, lime]

cal·y·ces (kăl′ə sēz′, kā′lə-), *n.* a pl. of calyx.

cal·y·cine (kăl′ə sīn, -sĭn′), *adj.* pertaining to or resembling a calyx. Also, **ca·lyc·i·nal** (kə lĭs′ə nəl).

cal·y·cle (kăl′ə kəl), *n.* *Bot.* a set of bracts resembling an outer calyx. [t. L: m. s. *calyculus,* dim. of *calyx* calyx]

Cal·y·don (kăl′ə dŏn′), *n.* an ancient city in W Greece, in Aetolia. —**Cal·y·do·ni·an** (kăl′ə dō′nĭ ən), *adj.*

Calydonian hunt, *Gk. Legend.* the pursuit, by Meleager and a band of heroes, of a savage boar (**Calydonian boar**) sent by Artemis to ravage Calydon.

Ca·lyp·so (kə lĭp′sō), *n., pl.* **-sos. 1.** *Gk. Legend.* a sea nymph who for seven years detained Odysseus on the island of Ogygia. **2.** (*l.c.*) a terrestrial orchid of the genus *Calypso (Cytherea),* widespread in the Northern Hemisphere, having a single variegated purple, yellow, and white flower. —*adj.* **3.** (*l.c.*) pertaining to a musical style of West Indian Negro origin, influenced by jazz, usually having a flexible accent in its topical, often improvised, lyrics.

ca·lyp·tra (kə lĭp′trə), *n.* *Bot.* **1.** the hood which covers the lid of the capsule in mosses. **2.** a hoodlike part connected with the organs of fructification in flowering plants. **3.** a root cap. [t. NL, t. Gk.: m. *kalýptra* veil]

ca·lyp·tro·gen (kə lĭp′trə jən), *n.* *Bot.* the histogen layer which develops into the root cap.

ca·lyx (kā′lĭks, kăl′ĭks), *n., pl.* **calyxes, calyces** (kăl′ə sēz′, kā′lə-). **1.** *Bot.* the outermost group of floral parts, usually green; the sepals. **2.** *Anat., Zool.* a cuplike part. [t. L, t. Gk.: m. *kályx* covering, husk, calyx]

Floral calyxes
A. Trisepalous calyx; B. Gamosepalous (united) calyx; C. Bilabiate calyx

cam (kăm), *n.* *Mach.* a device for converting regular rotary motion into irregular rotary or reciprocating motion, etc., commonly consisting of an oval-, needle-, or heart-shaped, or other specially shaped flat piece, an eccentric wheel, or the like, fastened on and revolving with a shaft, and engaging with other mechanism [t. D or LG: m. *kam, kamm* cog. See COMB]

Ca·ma·cho (kä mä′chô), *n.* Manuel Ávila. See Ávila Camacho.

Ca·ma·güey (kä′mä gwā′), *n.* a city in central Cuba. 132,059 (1953).

Cams
A. Elliptical cam;
B. Cam wheel;
C. Heart cam

ca·ma·ra·de·rie (kä′mə rä′də rĭ), *n.* comradeship; close friendship. [t. F]

cam·a·ril·la (kăm′ə rĭl′ə; *Sp.* kä′mä rē′lyä), *n.* a group of private advisers; a cabal; a clique. [t. Sp., dim. of *cámara* CHAMBER]

cam·ass (kăm′əs), *n.* **1.** any of various plants of the lily family (genus *Camassia*), esp. *C. quamash,* a species in western North America, with sweet, edible bulbs. **2.** death camass. Also, **cam′as.** [t. N Amer. Ind., from Chinook jargon, der. *chamas* sweet (Nootka)]

cam·ber (kăm′bər), *v.t., v.i.* **1.** to arch slightly; bend or curve upward in the middle. —*n.* **2.** a slight arching or convexity above, as of a ship's deck. **3.** a slightly arching piece of timber. **4.** *Aeron.* the rise of the curve of an airfoil, usually expressed as the ratio of the rise to the length of the chord of the airfoil. [t. d. F: m. *cambre,* adj., bent, g. L *camur*]

Cam·ber·well (kăm′bər wěl′, -wəl), *n.* a residential borough of S London, England. 172,729 (1951).

cam·bist (kăm′bĭst), *n.* **1.** a dealer in bills of exchange. **2.** an expert in the science of monetary exchange. **3.** a manual giving the moneys, weights, and measures of different countries, with their equivalents. [t. F: m. *cambiste,* t. It.: m. *cambista,* der. *cambiare* CHANGE]

cam·bi·um (kăm′bĭ əm), *n.* *Bot.* a layer of soft cellular tissue (or meristem) between the bark and wood (or phloem and xylem) in plants, from which new bark and new wood originate. [t. LL: exchange]

Cam·bo·di·a (kăm bō′dĭ ə), *n.* a kingdom in SE Asia, formerly a part of French Indochina. 3,860,000 (est. 1953); 69,866 sq. mi. *Cap.:* Pnom-Penh. French, **Cambodge** (kän bôj′).

cam·bo·gi·a (kăm bō′jĭ ə), *n.* *Pharm.* gamboge (def. 1).

Cam·bon (kän bôn′), *n.* **1. Jules Martin** (zhyl mär tăn′), 1845–1935, French diplomat and administrator. **2. Pierre Paul** (pyěr pôl), 1843–1924, French diplomat.

Cam·brai (kän brě′), *n.* a city in N France: battles, 1917, 1918. 29,567 (1954).

Cam·bri·a (kăm′brĭ ə), *n.* medieval name of Wales.

Cam·bri·an (kăm′brĭ ən), *adj.* **1.** *Stratig.* pertaining to the oldest geological period or a system of rocks characterized by presence of numerous well-preserved fossils. **2.** pertaining to Cambria (Wales). —*n.* **3.** *Stratig.* the period or system comprising the first main division of the Paleozoic era or rocks. **4.** a Welshman.

cam·bric (kăm′brĭk), *n.* a cotton or linen fabric of fine close weave, usually white. [t. Flem.: m. *Kameryk* CAMBRAI]

cambric tea, a mixture of hot water and milk, with sugar and, sometimes, a little tea.

Cam·bridge (kām′brĭj), *n.* **1.** a city in E England. 91,780 (est. 1956). **2.** the university located there. **3.** a city in E Massachusetts, near Boston. 107,716 (1960). **4.** Cambridgeshire.

Cam·bridge·shire (kām′brĭj shĭr′, -shər), *n.* a county in E England. 166,887 pop. (1951); 492 sq. mi. *Co. seat:* Cambridge. Also, **Cambridge.**

Cam·by·ses (kăm bī′sēz), *n.* died 522 B.C., son of Cyrus the Great and king of Persia, 529–522 B.C.

Cam·den (kăm′dən), *n.* a city in SW New Jersey: a port on the Delaware. 117,159 (1960).

came[1] (kām), *v.* pt. of come.

came[2] (kām), *n.* a slender grooved bar of lead for holding together the pieces of glass in windows of latticework or stained glass. [appar. var. of *calm* mold for casting metallic objects]

cam·el (kăm′əl), *n.* **1.** either of two large Old World ruminant quadrupeds of the genus *Camelus,* used as beasts of burden: **a.** the **Arabian camel,** or dromedary, with one hump (*C. dromedarius*). **b.** the **Bactrian camel,** with two humps (*C. bactrianus*). **2.** *Civ. Eng. Naut.* a pontoon (def. 2). [ME and OE, t. L: s. *camēlus,* t. Gk.: m. *kámēlos* of Semitic orig.]

cam·el·eer (kăm′ə lĭr′), *n.* **1.** a camel driver. **2.** a soldier on a camel.

cam·el·hair (kăm′əl hâr′), *n.* **1.** camel's hair. —*adj.* **2.** camel's-hair.

ca·mel·lia (kə měl′yə, -mē′lĭ ə), *n.* a plant, *Camellia (or Thea) japonica,* native in Asia, with glossy evergreen leaves and white, pink, red, or variegated waxy roselike flowers, familiar in cultivation. [named after G. J. Kamel, Moravian Jesuit missionary]

Ca·mel·o·pard (kə měl′ə pärd′), *n.* **1.** Also, **Ca·mel·o·par·da·lis** (kə měl′ə pär′də lĭs). *Astron.* a northern constellation. **2.** (*l.c.*) *Obsolesc.* a giraffe. [t. LL: s. *camēlopardus,* L *camēlopardālis,* t. Gk.: m. *kamēlopárdalis* giraffe]

Cam·e·lot (kăm′ə lŏt′), *n.* the legendary site of King Arthur's palace and court, probably near Exeter, England.

camel's hair, 1. the hair of the camel, used for cloth, painters' brushes, certain Oriental rugs, etc. **2.** cloth made of this hair, or of a substitute, usually tan in color.

cam·el's-hair (kăm′əlz hâr′), *adj.* **1.** made of camel's hair. **2.** (of a painter's brush) made from the tail hairs of squirrels.

Cam·em·bert (kăm′əm bâr′; *Fr.* kȧ män běr′), *n.* a rich, yellowish variety of soft cheese.

Ca·me·nae (kə mē′nē), *n.pl.* (in early Roman religion) prophetic nymphs of the springs and fountains, later identified with the Greek Muses.

cam·e·o (kăm′ĭ ō′), *n., pl.* **cameos. 1.** an engraving in relief upon a gem, stone, etc., with differently colored layers of the stone often utilized to produce a background of one hue and a design of another. **2.** a gem, stone, etc., so engraved. [t. It.: m. *cammeo;* prob. of Oriental orig.]

cam·er·a (kăm′ərə, kăm′rə), *n., pl.* **-eras** *for 1–2,* **-erae** (-ə rē′) *for 3.* **1.** a photographic apparatus in which sensitive plates or film are exposed, the image being formed by means of a lens. **2.** (in a television transmitting apparatus) the device in which the picture to be televised is formed before it is changed into electrical impulses. **3.** a judge's private room. **4. in camera,** **a.** *Law.* in the privacy of a judge's chambers. **b.** privately. [t. L: arch, vault, ML chamber, treasury. Cf. CHAMBER]

---

b., blend of, blended; **c.,** cognate with; **d.,** dialect, dialectal; **der.,** derived from; **f.,** formed from; **g.,** going back to; **m.,** modification of; **r.,** replacing; **s.,** stem of; **t.,** taken from; **?,** perhaps. See the full key on inside cover.

cam·er·al (kăm′ər əl), *adj.* pertaining to a camera (esp. defs. 3, 4).

camera lu·ci·da (lōō′sə də), *Optics.* an optical instrument by which the image of an external object is projected on a sheet of paper, etc., upon which it may be traced. [t. LL: light chamber]

cam·er·a·man (kăm′ər ə măn′, kăm′rə-), *n.*, *pl.* **-men.** a man who operates a camera, esp. a motion picture camera.

camera ob·scu·ra (ŏb skyŏŏr′ə), a darkened boxlike device in which images of external objects, received through an aperture, as with a convex lens, are exhibited in their natural colors on a surface arranged to receive them: used for sketching, exhibition purposes, etc. [t. LL: dark chamber]

Cam·e·roon (kăm′ə rōōn′), *n.* 1. an active volcano in S Cameroons: the highest peak on the W coast of Africa. 13,370 ft. 2. Cameroun.

Cam·e·roons (kăm′ə rōōnz′), *n.* 1. German. **Kame·run.** a region in W Africa: a former German protectorate; divided into two mandates of Cameroons (to Gt. Britain) and Cameroun (to France), 1919. 2. former name, **British Cameroons.** the N W part of this region, comprising the **Northern Cameroons** (now part of Nigeria) and the **Southern Cameroons** (now part of Cameroun).

Came·roun (kăm rōōn′), *n.* an independent republic in W Africa, comprising the former French trusteeship of Cameroun and the former British trusteeship of Southern Cameroons. ab. 4,700,000 pop. (est. 1961); 183,350 sq. mi. *Cap.:* Yaoundé. Also, **Cameroon.**

cam·i·on (kăm′Yən; *Fr.* kå myôN′), *n.* 1. a strongly built cart or wagon for transporting heavy loads. 2. a truck, as for military supplies. [t. F; orig. uncert.]

cam·i·sole (kăm′ə sōl′), *n.* 1. *Chiefly Brit.* an ornamental underbodice, worn under a thin outer bodice. 2. a woman's dressing jacket. 3. a sleeved jacket or jersey once worn by men. 4. a type of strait jacket. [t. F, f. Sp.: m. camisola, dim. of camisa shirt]

cam·let (kăm′lĭt), *n.* 1. a durable waterproof cloth used for cloaks, etc. 2. apparel made of this material. 3. a rich fabric, apparently orig. made of camel's or goat's hair, formerly in use. [var. of camelot, t. F; r. late ME chamelot, t. OF, prob. t. Ar.: m. khamla, der. khaml nap]

Cam·maerts (kä′märts), *n.* **Émile** (ĕ mēl′), 1878–1953, Belgian poet.

Cam·o·ëns (kăm′ō ĕns′), *n.* **Luis Vaz de** (lōō ēsh′ väzh də), 1524?–80, Portuguese poet. Portuguese, **Ca·mões** (kə môYNsh′).

cam·o·mile (kăm′ə mīl′), *n.* 1. any plant of the asteraceous genus *Anthemis,* esp. *A. nobilis* (the common camomile of Europe and of gardens elsewhere), an herb with strongly scented foliage and flowers which are used medicinally. 2. any of various allied plants, as *Matricaria Chamomilla* (German camomile). Also, **chamomile.** [ME camemille, t. L: m. chamomilla, var. of chamaemēlon, t. Gk.: m. chamaimēlon earth apple]

Ca·mor·ra (kə môr′ə, -môr′ə; *It.* kä môr′rä), *n.* 1. a Neapolitan secret society, first publicly known about 1820, which developed into a powerful political organization and has been associated with blackmail, robbery, etc. 2. (*l.c.*) some similar society or group. [t. It., t. Sp.: dispute, quarrel] —**Ca·mor′rism,** *n.* —**Ca·mor′rist,** *n.*

cam·ou·flage (kăm′ə fläzh′), *n.*, *v.*, **-flaged, -flaging.** —*n.* 1. *Mil.* act, art, means, or result of disguising things to deceive the enemy, as by painting or screening objects so that they are lost to view in the background, or by making up objects which, from a distance, have the appearance of fortifications, guns, roads, etc. 2. disguise; deception; false pretense. —*v.t.* 3. to disguise, hide, or deceive by means of camouflage: *camouflaged ships.* [t. F, der. camoufler disguise]

cam·ou·fleur (kăm′ə flûr′; *Fr.* kå mōō flœr′), *n.* *Mil.* one who conceals military objects by camouflage.

camp (kămp), *n.* 1. a place where an army or other body of persons is lodged in tents or other temporary means of shelter. 2. the tents, etc., collectively. 3. the persons sheltered. 4. an encamping, or camping out. 5. a body of troops, etc., camping and moving together. 6. army life. 7. a group of people favoring the same ideals, doctrines, etc. 8. any position in which ideals, doctrines, etc., are strongly entrenched. —*v.i.* 9. to establish or pitch a camp. 10. to live temporarily in a tent (often fol. by *out*). 11. to take a position stubbornly: *camped in front of the office of the president.* —*v.t.* 12. to put or station (troops, etc.) in a camp; shelter. [t. F, t. It.: m. campo field, g. L *campus*] —**camp′er,** *n.*

Cam·pa·gna (käm pän′yə; *It.* käm pä′nyä), *n.* 1. a low plain surrounding the city of Rome, Italy. 2. (*l.c.*) any flat open plain; champaign. [t. It., g. L *campānia* level plain]

cam·paign (kăm pān′), *n.* 1. the military operations of an army in the field during one season or enterprise. 2. any course of aggressive activities for some special purpose: *a sales campaign.* 3. the competition by rival political candidates and organizations for public office. —*v.i.* 4. to serve in, or go on, a campaign. [t. F: m. campagne, ult. der. L *campus* plain] —**cam·paign′er,** *n.*

Cam·pa·ni·a (käm pä′nĭ yə), *n.* a region and department in SW Italy. 4,509,000 (est. 1954); 5214 sq. mi.

cam·pa·ni·le (kăm′pə nē′lĭ; *It.* käm′pä nē′lĕ), *n.*, *pl.* **-niles, -nili** (-nē′lē). a bell tower (often a detached structure). [t. It., der. *campana* bell, g. L]

cam·pa·nol·o·gy (kăm′pə nŏl′ə jĭ), *n.* 1. the study of bells. 2. the principles of bell founding, bell ringing, etc. [t. NL: m.s. campanologia, f. s. LL *campāna* bell + -(o)*logia* -(o)LOGY] —**cam′pa·nol′o·gist, cam/pa·nol′o·ger,** *n.*

cam·pan·u·la (kăm păn′yə lə), *n.* any plant of the genus *Campanula,* as the harebell or the Canterbury bell; a bellflower. [t. NL, dim. of LL *campāna* bell]

cam·pan·u·la·ceous (kăm păn′yə lā′shəs), *adj.* *Bot.* belonging to the *Campanulaceae,* or campanula family of plants.

cam·pan·u·late (kăm păn′yə lĭt, -lāt′), *adj.* bell-shaped, as a corolla.

Camp·bell (kăm′bəl, kăm′əl), *n.* 1. **Colin** (kŏl′Yn), (*Baron Clyde*) 1792–1863, British general. 2. **Thomas,** 1777–1844, British poet and editor.

Camp·bell-Ban·ner·man (kăm′bəl băn′ər mən, kăm′əl-), *n.* **Sir Henry,** 1836–1908, prime minister of Great Britain, 1905–08.

Camp·bell·ite (kăm′bə līt′, kăm′ə-), *n.* a member of the body of Christians known as Disciples of Christ. [f. *Campbell* + -ITE¹; named after the Rev. Alexander Campbell, founder]

camp chair, a light folding chair.

camp·craft (kămp′kräft′, -kräft′), *n.* the art of outdoor camping.

Cam·pe·che (käm pĕ′chĕ), *n.* 1. a state in SE Mexico, on the peninsula of Yucatán. 125,964 (est. 1952); 19,672 sq. mi. 2. the capital of this state: seaport. 31,279 (1951). 3. **Gulf of,** the SW part of the Gulf of Mexico.

camp·fire (kămp′fīr′), *n.* 1. a fire in a camp for warmth or cooking. 2. a reunion of soldiers, scouts, etc.

campfire girl, a member of an organization for girls from 7 to 18 (**Camp Fire Girls, Inc.**), helping build good character, citizenship, and health.

camp follower, a person who follows a camp or an army without official connection, as a washerwoman, prostitute, etc.

camp·ground (kămp′ground′), *n.* a place for a camp or a camp meeting.

cam·phene (kăm′fēn, kăm fēn′), *n.* *Chem.* a hydrocarbon, $C_{10}H_{16}$, present in certain essential oils.

cam·phol (kăm′fəl, -fōl), *n.* *Chem.* borneol.

cam·phor (kăm′fər), *n.* 1. a whitish, translucent, crystalline, pleasant-odored terpene ketone, $C_{10}H_{16}O$, obtained chiefly from the camphor tree and used in medicine, the manufacture of celluloid, etc. 2. any of various similar substances. [t. ML: s. camphora, t. Ar.: m. kāfūr, t. Malay: m. kāpūr; r. ME caumfre, t. AF] —**cam·phor·ic** (kăm fôr′Yk, -fŏr′-), *adj.*

cam·phor·ate (kăm′fə rāt′), *v.t.*, **-ated, -ating.** to impregnate with camphor.

camphor ball, a moth ball, usually consisting of naphthalene, and sometimes of camphor, etc.

camphor tree, 1. a lauraceous tree, *Cinnamomum camphora,* of Japan, Formosa, China, etc., yielding camphor. 2. any of various similar trees, as *Dryobalanops aromatica* of Borneo, etc., which yields borneol.

Cam·pi·nas (kəm pē′nəs, käm-), *n.* a city in S Brazil. 101,746 (est. 1952).

cam·pi·on (kăm′pĭ ən), *n.* any of certain plants of the pink family, genera *Silene* or *Lychnis,* as the **rose campion,** *L. coronaria.* [prob. ult. der. L *campion* field]

Cam·pi·on (kăm′pĭ ən), *n.* **Thomas,** 1567–1620, English song writer and poet.

camp meeting, a religious gathering, usually lasting for some days, held in a tent or in the open air.

cam·po (kăm′pō, käm′-), *n.*, *pl.* **-pos.** (in South America) an extensive, nearly level, grassy plain. [t. Pg., Sp., g. L *campus* field, plain]

Cam·po·bel·lo (kăm′pō bĕl′ō), *n.* a Canadian island in the Bay of Fundy: a part of New Brunswick.

Cam·po For·mio (käm′pō fôr′myō), a village in NE Italy: treaty between France and Austria, 1797. Modern, **Cam·po·for·mi·do** (käm′pō fôr′mē dō).

cam·po san·to (käm′pō sän′tō), *Italian.* a cemetery. [It.: sacred field]

camp·stool (kămp′stōōl′), *n.* a light folding seat.

cam·pus (kăm′pəs), *n.* *U.S.* the grounds of a college or other school. [L: field]

cam·shaft (kăm′shăft′, -shäft′), *n.* *Mach.* a shaft with cams.

Ca·mus (kå my′), *n.* **Albert** (ål bâr′), 1913–60, French author; Nobel prize for literature, 1957.

can¹ (kăn; *unstressed* kən), *v.*, *pres. sing.* 1 **can;** 2 **can** or (*Archaic*) **canst;** 3 **can;** *pt.* **could.** —*aux.* 1. to know how to; to be able to; have the ability, power, right, qualifications, or means to: *you can lift the box.* 2. *Colloq.* may; have permission: *Can I speak to you a moment?* —*v.t.*, *v.i.* 3. *Obs.* to know. [ME and OE cann, can, 1st and 3d pers. sing. pres. ind. (pret. cūthe) of cunnan, c. G können. Cf. KEN and KNOW]

—**Syn.** 1. CAN denotes power or ability to do something: *the child can talk.* MAY refers to probability, possibility, or permission: *our son may* (possibility or probability) *play football Saturday if the doctor says he may* (permission). The two words are often confused in asking or granting permission; MAY is the better usage, though CANNOT is used informally in denying permission: *May I go? Yes, you may go* (or, *you may not or cannot go*). CANNOT may also be used to express either extreme negation of ability or negation of

---

ăct, āble, dâre, ärt; ĕbb, ēqual; Yf, īce; hŏt, ōver, ôrder, oil, bŏŏk, ōōze, out; ŭp, ūse, ûrge; ə = a in alone; ch, chief; g, give; ng, ring; sh, shoe; th, thin; ŧℏ, that; zh, vision. See the full key on inside cover.

probability: *I cannot work such long hours, I cannot* (possibly) *be mistaken.* **2.** CAN BUT, CANNOT BUT are formal expressions suggesting that there is no possible alternative to doing a certain thing. CAN BUT is equivalent to informal CAN ONLY: *we can but do our best* (1. and *must* make the attempt; or 2. and no more than that should be expected of us). CANNOT BUT (do) is equivalent to informal CAN'T HELP (doing): *we cannot but protest against injustice* (we are under moral obligation to do so). CANNOT HELP BUT is common in familiar use, but is not otherwise considered good usage.

can² (kăn), *n., v.,* **canned, canning.** —*n.* **1.** a container for food, milk, etc., usually of sheet iron coated with tin or other metal. **2.** a receptacle for garbage, ashes, etc. **3.** *Chiefly Brit.* a container for holding or carrying liquids. **4.** a drinking cup; tankard. **5.** *U.S. Colloq.* a depth bomb. —*v.t.* **6.** to put in a can or jar, esp. a sealed one. **7.** *U.S. Slang.* to dismiss; fire. [ME and OE *canne*, c. G *kanne* can, pot, mug]

Can., **1.** Canada. **2.** Canadian.

Ca·na (kā′nə), *n.* an ancient town in N Israel, in Galilee: the scene of Christ's first miracle. John 2:1, 11.

Ca·naan (kā′nən), *n.* **1.** the ancient region, included in modern Palestine (now Israel and Jordan), lying between the Jordan, the Dead Sea, and the Mediterranean: the land promised by God to Abraham. Gen. 12. **2.** Palestine. **3.** any land of promise. **4.** *Bible.* the descendant of Ham, the son of Noah. Gen. 10. [t. Heb.: m. *kana'an*]

Ca·naan·ite (kā′nə nīt′), *n.* **1.** a member of the Semitic people inhabiting Palestine at the time of the Hebrew conquest. **2.** a group of Semitic languages, including Hebrew and Phoenician, spoken chiefly in ancient Palestine and Syria. —**Ca′naan·it′ish, Ca·naan·it·ic** (kā′nə nĭt′ĭk), *adj.*

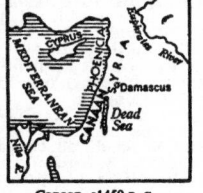

Canaan. c1450 B. C.

Can·a·da (kăn′ə də), *n.* a member of the British Commonwealth of Nations, in N North America. 15,970,000 (est. 1956); 3,690,410 sq. mi. *Cap.:* Ottawa.

Canada balsam, a transparent turpentine obtained from the balsam fir, *Abies balsamea,* used for mounting objects for the microscope.

Canada goose, the common wild goose, *Branta canadensis,* of North America.

Canada jay, a plain gray bird, *Perisoreus canadensis.*

Canada lily, a lily, *Lilium canadense,* with several nodding flowers and recurved sepals, common in NE U.S.

Canada thistle, an Old World herb, *Cirsium arvense,* with small purple or white flower heads, now a troublesome weed in North America.

Ca·na·di·an (kə nā′dʸən), *adj.* **1.** of Canada or its people. —*n.* **2.** a native or inhabitant of Canada.

Canadian River, a river flowing from the Rocky Mountains in NE New Mexico E to the Arkansas river in E Oklahoma. 906 mi.

ca·naille (kə nāl′; *Fr.* kả nä′y), *n.* riffraff; the rabble [t. F, t. It.: m. *canaglia,* der. *cane* dog, g. L *canis*]

ca·nal (kə năl′), *n., v.,* **-nalled, -nalling** or **-naled, -naling.** —*n.* **1.** an artificial waterway for navigation, irrigation, etc. **2.** a long, narrow arm of the sea penetrating far inland. **3.** a tubular passage or cavity for food, air, etc. esp. in an animal or plant; a duct. **4.** *Astron.* one of the long, narrow, dark lines on the surface of the planet Mars. **5.** *Obs.* a channel or watercourse. —*v.t.* **6.** to make a canal through. **7.** to furnish with canals. [late ME, t. L: s. *canālis* pipe, groove, channel]

canal boat, a craft built to fit canal locks.

can·a·lic·u·lus (kăn′ə lĭk′yə ləs), *n., pl.* **-li** (-lī′). *Anat″ Zool.* a small canal or tubular passage, as in bone. [t. L, dim. of *canālis* channel. See CANAL] —**can·a·lic·u·lar,** **can·a·lic·u·late** (kăn′ə lĭk′yə lĭt, -yə lāt′), **can·a·lic′u·lat′ed,** *adj.*

ca·nal·ize (kə năl′īz, kăn′ə līz′), *v.t.,* **-ized, -izing. 1.** to make a canal or canals through. **2.** to convert into a canal. **3.** to divert into certain channels; give a certain direction to or provide a certain outlet for. —**ca·nal·i·za·tion** (kə năl′ə zā′shən, kăn′ə lə-), *n.*

canal rays, *Physics.* the rays (consisting of positively charged ions) which pass through a hole in the cathode, in a direction away from the anode, when an electric discharge takes place in a vacuum tube.

Canal Zone, a strip of territory 10 mi. wide across the Isthmus of Panama, on both sides of the Panama Canal, excl. cities of Panama and Colón: perpetually leased to and governed by U.S. 52,822 pop. (1950); 553 sq. mi.

can·a·pé (kăn′ə pĭ, -pā′; *Fr.* kả nả pĕ′), *n.* a thin piece of bread, toast, etc., spread or topped with cheese, caviar, anchovies, or other appetizing foods. [t. F. See CANOPY]

ca·nard (kə närd′; *Fr.* kả năr′), *n.* **1.** a false story, report, or rumor; a hoax. **2.** *Aeron.* a very early kind of airplane, having a pusher engine with the rudder and elevator assembly in front of the wings. [t. F: lit., duck]

Ca·na·rese (kă′nə rēz′, -rēs′), *n., adj.* Kanarese.

ca·nar·y (kə năr′ĭ), *n., pl.* **-naries. 1.** Also, **canary bird,** a well-known cage bird, a kind of finch, *Serinus canarius,* native of the Canary Islands, and orig. of a brownish or greenish color, but through modification in the domesticated state now usually a light, clear yellow. **2.** Also, **canary yellow,** a light, clear yellow color. **3.** a sweet white wine of the Canary Islands,

resembling sherry. **4.** *Obs.* a lively French and English dance, similar to the jig. [named after the islands]

canary grass, any of various grasses of the genus *Phalaris,* as *P. canariensis,* native in the Canary Islands, which yields a seed used as food for cage birds, or *P. arundinacea* (**reed canary grass**), a species widely used throughout the Northern Hemisphere as fodder.

Canary Islands, a group of mountainous islands in the Atlantic, near the NW coast of Africa, forming two provinces of Spain. 850,157 (est. 1955); 2894 sq. mi. Also, **Canaries.** [t. F: m. *Canarie* (the principal island), t. Sp.: m. *Canaria,* in L *canāria insula* isle of dogs]

canary seed, birdseed.

ca·nas·ta (kə năs′tə), *n.* a card game of the rummy family in which the main object is to meld sets of seven or more cards. [t. Sp.: ? m. *canasta* kind of basket. Cf. CANISTER]

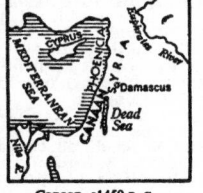

Ca·nav·er·al (kə năv′ər əl), *n.* Cape, former name of Cape Kennedy.

Can·ber·ra (kăn′bĕr ə -bĕr ə) *n.* the capital of Australia, in the SE part, in the Australian Capital Territory. With suburbs, 28,277 (1954).

Can·by (kăn′bĭ), *n.* **Henry Seidel** (sī′dəl), 1878–1961, U.S. author and critic.

can·can (kăn′kăn; *Fr.* kän kän′), *n.* a form of quadrille marked by extravagant leaping and kicking, which came into vogue about 1830 in Paris. [t. F]

can·cel (kăn′səl), *v.,* **-celed, -celing** or (*esp. Brit.*) **-celled, -celling,** *n.* —*v.t.* **1.** to cross out (writing, etc.) by drawing a line or lines over. **2.** to make void; annul. **3.** to mark or perforate (a postage stamp, streetcar transfer, etc.) to render it invalid for re-use. **4.** to neutralize; counterbalance; compensate for. **5.** *Math.* to eliminate by striking out (a factor common to both terms of a fraction, equivalent quantities on opposite sides of an equation, etc.). **6.** *Print.* to omit. —*n.* **7.** act of canceling. **8.** *Print.* omission. **9.** *Print., Bookbinding.* an omitted part, or the replacement for it. [late ME, t. L: m.s. *cancellāre* to make like a lattice, to strike out a writing] —**can′cel·er;** *esp. Brit.,* **can′cel·ler,** *n.* —**Syn. 1, 3.** CANCEL, DELETE, ERASE, OBLITERATE refer to indicating that something is no longer to be considered usable or in force. To CANCEL is to cross something out by stamping a mark over it, drawing lines through it, and the like: *to cancel a stamp, a word.* To DELETE is to omit something from written matter or from matter to be printed, often in accordance with a printer's symbol indicating this is to be done: *to delete part of a line.* To ERASE is to remove by scraping or rubbing: *to erase a capital letter.* To OBLITERATE is to blot out entirely, so as to remove all sign or trace of: *to obliterate a record, an inscription.* **2.** countermand, revoke, rescind.

can·cel·late (kăn′sə lāt′), *adj. Anat.* of spongy or porous structure, as bone. Also, **can′cel·lous.** [t. L: m.s. *cancellātus,* pp., latticed. See CANCEL]

can·cel·la·tion (kăn′sə lā′shən), *n.* **1.** act of canceling. **2.** the marks or perforations made in canceling. **3.** something canceled.

can·cer (kăn′sər), *n.* **1.** *Pathol.* a malignant and invasive growth or tumor, esp. one originating in epithelium, tending to recur after excision and to metastasize to other sites. **2.** any evil condition or thing that spreads destructively. **3.** (*cap.*) *Astron.* a constellation and sign of the zodiac, represented by a crab. See illus. under **zodiac.** [t. L: crab, tumor] —**can′cer·ous,** *adj.*

Cancellate bone structure

Can·cer (kăn′sər), *n.* Tropic of. See **tropic** (1a, 2a).

can·croid (kăng′kroid), *adj.* **1.** *Pathol.* resembling a cancer, as certain tumors. **2.** *Zool.* resembling a crab. —*n.* **3.** *Pathol.* a form of cancer of the skin.

can·de·la·bra (kăn′də lä′brə, -lä′-), *n.* **1.** a pl. of **candelabrum. 2.** (*properly pl. but taken as sing. with pl. -bras*) candelabrum.

can·de·la·brum (kăn′də lä′brəm, -lä′-), *n., pl.* **-bra** (-brə), **-brums.** an ornamental branched candlestick. [t. L, der. *candēla* candle]

can·dent (kăn′dənt), *adj.* glowing with heat; at a white heat. [t. L: s. *candens,* ppr., shining]

can·des·cent (kăn dĕs′ənt), *adj.* glowing; incandescent. [t. L: s. *candescens,* ppr., beginning to glow] —**can·des′cence,** *n.* —**can·des′cent·ly,** *adv.*

Can·di·a (kăn′dʸə), *n.* **1.** Greek, **Herakleion.** a seaport in N Crete. 51,144 (1951). **2.** Crete.

can·did (kăn′dĭd), *adj.* **1.** frank; outspoken; open and sincere: *candid account.* **2.** honest; impartial: *candid mind.* **3.** white. **4.** clear; pure. [t. L: s. *candidus* white, sincere] —**can′did·ly,** *adv.* —**can′did·ness,** *n.* —**Syn. 1.** See **frank.**

can·di·date (kăn′də dāt′, -dĭt), *n.* **1.** one who seeks an office, an honor, etc. **2.** one who is selected by others as a contestant for an office, etc. [t. L: m.s. *candidātus* clad in white, as a Roman candidate for office] —**can·di·da·cy** (kăn′də də sĭ); *Brit.,* **can·di·da·ture** (kăn′də də chər), **can′di·date·ship′,** *n.*

candid camera, a small handy camera, esp. one having a fast lens for unposed or informal pictures.

can·died (kăn′dĭd), *adj.* **1.** impregnated or incrusted with or as with sugar. **2.** crystallized, as sugar. **3.** honeyed or sweet; flattering.

Can·di·ot (kăn′dĭ ŏt′), *adj.* **1.** Cretan. —*n.* **2.** a native or inhabitant of Crete. Also, **Can·di·ote** (kăn′dĭ ōt′).

can·dle (kăn′dəl), *n.*, *v.*, **-dled, -dling.** —*n.* **1.** a long, usually slender, piece of tallow, wax, etc., with an embedded wick, burned to give light. **2.** something like this in appearance or use. **3.** *Photom.* **a.** the luminous intensity of a standard candle. **b. standard candle,** a candle of specified size, composition, character of wick, and rate of burning, whose flame is taken as a unit of luminous intensity. **c. international candle,** a unit of luminous intensity established by international agreement, based on the standard candle but defined in terms of specially constructed electric lamps. —*v.t.* **4.** to examine (esp. eggs for freshness) by holding between the eye and a light. [OE *candel*, t. L: s. *candēla*] —**can′dler**, *n.*

can·dle·ber·ry (kăn′dəl bĕr′ĭ), *n.*, *pl.* **-ries. 1.** the wax myrtle (genus *Myrica*). **2.** its berry. **3.** the candlenut.

can·dle·fish (kăn′dəl fĭsh′), *n.* a small edible fish, *Thaleichthys pacificus*, of the northwestern coast of America, of the smelt family, with flesh so oily that when the fish is dried it may be used as a candle.

can·dle·foot (kăn′dəl fŏŏt′), *n.* a foot-candle.

can·dle·hold·er (kăn′dəl hōl′dər), *n.* candlestick.

can·dle·light (kăn′dəl līt′), *n.* **1.** the light of a candle. **2.** artificial light. **3.** twilight; dusk.

Can·dle·mas (kăn′dəl məs), *n.* an ecclesiastical festival, Feb. 2, in honor of the presentation of the infant Jesus in the Temple and the purification of the Virgin Mary. Candles are blessed on this day. [ME *candelmasse*, OE *candelmæsse*. See CANDLE, -MAS]

can·dle·nut (kăn′dəl nŭt′), *n.* **1.** the oily fruit or nut of a euphorbiaceous tree, *Aleurites moluccana*, of the South Sea Islands, etc., the kernels of which, when strung together, are used as candles by the natives. **2.** the tree itself.

can·dle·pin (kăn′dəl pĭn′), *n.* Tenpins. **1.** a slender, candle-shaped pin. **2.** (*pl.*) a game using such pins.

candle power, *Photom.* **1.** the illuminating capacity or luminous intensity of a standard candle. **2.** luminous intensity (of a light) or illuminating capacity (of a lamp or other device), measured in candles.

can·dle·stick (kăn′dəl stĭk′), *n.* a holder for a candle.

can·dle·wick (kăn′dəl wĭk′), *n.* **1.** the wick of a candle. —*adj.* **2.** of a fabric, usually unbleached muslin, into which small, short bunches of wicking have been hooked to form a design, used for bedspreads, etc.

can·dle·wood (kăn′dəl wŏŏd′), *n.* **1.** any resinous wood used for torches or as a substitute for candles. **2.** any of various trees or shrubs yielding such wood.

can·dor (kăn′dər), *n.* **1.** frankness, as of speech; sincerity; honesty. **2.** freedom from bias; fairness; impartiality. **3.** *Obs.* kindliness. **4.** *Obs.* purity. Also, *Brit.*, **can′dour.** [t. L: radiance, purity, candor]

can·dy (kăn′dĭ), *n.*, *pl.* **-dies,** *v.*, **-died, -dying.** —*n.* **1.** any of a variety of confections made with sugar, syrup, etc., combined with other ingredients. **2.** a single piece of such a confection. —*v.t.* **3.** to cook in sugar or syrup, as sweet potatoes or carrots. **4.** to cook in heavy syrup until transparent, as fruit, fruit peel, or ginger. **5.** to reduce (sugar, etc.) to a crystalline form, usually by boiling down. **6.** to cover with sugarlike crystals, as of ice. **7.** to make sweet, palatable, or agreeable. —*v.i.* **8.** to become covered with sugar. **9.** to crystallize. [short for *sugar candy*, t. F: m. *sucre candi* candied sugar (*candi* der. Ar. *qand* sugar, t. Pers., appar. c. Skt. *khanda* piece)]

candy pull, a social gathering of young people, for the purpose of making taffy or molasses candy.

can·dy·tuft (kăn′dĭ tŭft′), *n.* a plant of the brassicaceous genus *Iberis*, esp. *I. umbellata*, a cultivated annual with tufted flowers, orig. from the island of Candia, and *I. amara*. [f. *Candy* (for CANDIA) + TUFT]

cane (kān), *n.*, *v.*, **caned, caning.** —*n.* **1.** a walking stick. **2.** a long, hollow or pithy, jointed woody stem, as that of bamboo, rattan, sugar cane, certain palms, etc. **3.** a plant having such a stem. **4.** such stems as a material. **5.** any of various tall, woody, bamboolike grasses, esp. of the genus *Arundinaria*, as *A. macrosperma* (**large cane**) and *A. tecta* (**small cane**), of the southern U.S. **6.** the stem of the raspberry or blackberry. **7.** sugar cane. **8.** the stem of a bamboo, etc., used as a rod for flogging. **9.** a slender piece of sealing wax, etc. —*v.t.* **10.** to beat with a cane. **11.** to furnish or make with cane: *to cane chairs*. [ME, t. OF, t. Pr. or It., g. L *canna*, t. Gk.: m. *kánna* reed. Cf. Heb. *qāneh*] —**can′er**, *n.*

Ca·ne·a (kä nē′ä; *Gk.* hän yä′), *n.* a seaport in and the capital of Crete. 33,211 (1951). Greek, **Khania.**

cane·brake (kān′brāk′), *n.* a thicket of canes.

ca·nel·la (kə nĕl′ə), *n.* the cinnamonlike bark of a West Indian tree, *Canella winterana*, used as a condiment and in medicine. [ML: cinnamon, dim. of L *canna* CANE]

ca·neph·o·ra (kə nĕf′ər ə), *n.*, *pl.* **-rae** (-rē′). **1.** (in ancient Greece) one of the maidens who bore upon their heads baskets containing the materials for sacrifice in certain religious festivals. **2.** a caryatid having a basketlike cushion upon the head. [t. L, t. Gk.: m. *kanēphóros* basket bearer]

cane sugar, sugar obtained from sugar cane, identical with that obtained from the sugar beet; sucrose.

can·field (kăn′fēld), *n.* Cards. a game of solitaire often adapted to gambling purposes.

cangue (kăng), *n.* (in China) a kind of portable pillory worn about the neck by criminals. [t. F, prob. t. Pg.: m. *canga* yoke, t. Annamite: m. *gong*]

Ca·nic·u·la (kə nĭk′yə lə), *n.* Astron. Sirius; the Dog Star. [t. L, dim. of *canis* dog]

ca·nic·u·lar (kə nĭk′yə lər), *adj.* Astron., etc. pertaining to the Dog Star or its rising.

ca·nine (kā′nīn, kə nīn′). *adj.* **1.** of or like a dog; pertaining to or characteristic of dogs. **2.** *Anat., Zool.* of or pertaining to the four pointed teeth, esp. prominent in dogs, situated one on each side of each jaw, next to the incisors. —*n.* **3.** *Zool.* any animal of the dog family, the *Canidae*, including the wolves, jackals, hyenas, coyotes, and foxes. **4.** a dog. **5.** a canine tooth. [t. L: m.s. *canīnus* pertaining to a dog]

Ca·nis (kā′nĭs), *n.* Zool. the canine genus that includes the domestic dog, *Canis familiaris*, the wild dogs, the wolves, and the jackals, all having 42 teeth. [t. L: dog]

Ca·nis Ma·jor (kā′nĭs mā′jər), gen. Canis Majoris (mə jôr′ĭs). Astron. the Great Dog, a southern constellation containing Sirius, the Dog Star, the brightest of the stars. [t. L: greater dog]

Ca·nis Mi·nor (kā′nĭs mī′nər), gen. Canis Minoris (mĭ nôr′ĭs). Astron. the Little, or Lesser, Dog, a small ancient constellation following Orion and south of Gemini. It contains the star Procyon. [t. L: lesser dog]

can·is·ter (kăn′ĭs tər), *n.* **1.** a small box, usually of metal, for holding tea, coffee, etc. **2.** case shot (**canister shot**). [t. L: m.s. *canistrum*, t. Gk.: m. *kánastron* wicker basket]

can·ker (kăng′kər), *n.* **1.** *Pathol.* a gangrenous or ulcerous sore, esp. in the mouth. **2.** *Vet. Sci.* a disease affecting horses' feet, usually the soles, characterized by a foul-smelling exudate. **3.** *Plant Pathol* a stem disease in which a dead area is surrounded by living tissue. **4.** anything that corrodes, corrupts, destroys, or irritates. **5.** *Obs.* or *Dial.* dog rose. —*v.t.* **6.** to infect with canker. **7.** to corrupt; destroy slowly. —*v.i.* **8.** to become infected with or as with canker. [ME; OE *cancer*, t. L: m. *cancr-*, s. *cancer* gangrene]

can·ker·ous (kăng′kər əs), *adj.* **1.** of the nature of or resembling canker. **2.** causing canker.

can·ker·worm (kăng′kər wûrm′), *n.* a striped green caterpillar injurious to fruit trees and other plants. It is the larva of any of several geometrid moths.

can·na (kăn′ə), *n.* any plant of the tropical genus *Canna* (family *Cannaceae*), various species of which are cultivated for their large, handsome leaves and showy flowers. [t. L: reed. See CANE]

can·na·bin (kăn′ə bĭn), *n.* a poisonous resin extracted from Indian hemp. [f. CANNAB(IS) + -IN²]

can·na·bis (kăn′ə bĭs), *n.* hashish; the dried pistillate parts of Indian hemp. [t. L: hemp]

Can·nae (kăn′ē), *n.* an ancient town in SE Italy: Romans defeated by Hannibal, 216 B.C.

canned (kănd), *adj.* **1.** preserved in a can or jar. **2.** *Slang.* recorded: *canned music.* **3.** *Slang.* prepared in advance.

can·nel coal (kăn′əl), a compact coal burning readily and brightly. Also, **cannel.** [appar. for *candle coal*]

can·ner (kăn′ər), *n.* one who cans meat, fruit, etc., for preservation.

can·ner·y (kăn′ər ĭ), *n.*, *pl.* **-neries.** a place where meat, fish, fruit, etc., are canned.

Cannes (kăn, kănz; *Fr.* kän), *n.* a city in SE France, on the Mediterranean: coastal resort. 50,192 (1954).

can·ni·bal (kăn′ə bəl), *n.* **1.** a human being, esp. a savage, that eats human flesh. **2.** any animal that eats its own kind. —*adj.* **3.** pertaining to or characteristic of cannibals. **4.** given to cannibalism. [t. Sp.: m. *Caníbal*, for *Caríbal*, der. *Caribe* Carib]

can·ni·bal·ism (kăn′ə bə līz′əm), *n.* **1.** the practice of eating one's own kind. **2.** savage cruelty; barbarism. —**can′ni·bal·is′tic,** *adj.* —**can′ni·bal·is′ti·cal·ly,** *adv.*

can·ni·bal·ize (kăn′ə bə līz′), *v.t.*, **-ized, -izing.** *U.S. Army.* to repair (damaged motor vehicles, airplanes, tanks, etc.) by the use of parts of other assembled vehicles, etc., instead of using spare parts. —**can′ni·bal·i·za′tion,** *n.*

can·ni·kin (kăn′ə kĭn), *n.* a little can; a cup. [t. M Flem. or D: m. *cannekin* little can]

can·ning (kăn′ĭng), *n.* act, process, or business of preserving meat, fruits, etc., in sealed cans or jars.

Can·ning (kăn′ĭng), *n.* **1.** Charles John, (*Earl Canning*) 1812–62, governor general and 1st viceroy of India. **2.** his father, **George,** 1770–1827, British prime minister, 1827.

can·non (kăn′ən), *n.*, *pl.* **-nons,** (esp. collectively) **-non,** *v.* —*n.* **1.** a mounted gun for firing heavy projectiles; a gun, howitzer, or mortar. **2.** *Mach.* a hollow cylinder fitted over a shaft and capable of revolving independently. **3.** a smooth round bit. **4.** the part of a bit that is in the horse's mouth. **5.** the metal loop of a bell by which it is hung. **6.** *Zool.* **a.** the cannon bone. **b.** the part of the leg in which it is situated; instep. **7.** *Brit.* a carom in billiards. —*v.i.* **8.** to discharge cannon. **9.** *Brit.* to make a carom in billiards. [t. F: m. *canon*, t. It.: m. *cannone*, aug. of *canna* tube, g. L *canna*. See CANE]

Can·non (kăn′ən), *n.* **Joseph Gurney** (gûr′nĭ), ("*Uncle Joe*"), 1836–1926, U.S. politician and legislator.

can·non·ade (kăn′ə nād′), *n., v.,* -aded, -ading. —*n.* **1.** a continued discharge of cannon, esp. during an attack. —*v.t., v.i.* **2.** to attack with or discharge cannon. [t. F: m. *cannonnade*]

cannon ball, a missile, usually round and made of iron or steel, designed to be fired from a cannon.

cannon bone, *Zool.* the greatly developed middle metacarpal or metatarsal bone of hoofed quadrupeds, extending from wrist or ankle to the first joint of the digit. See illus. under **horse.** [f. CANNON (as being tube-shaped) + BONE]

can·non·eer (kăn′ə nĭr′), *n.* an artilleryman. [t. F: m. *canonnier*]

cannon fodder, soldiers (as the material used up in war).

can·non·ry (kăn′ən rĭ), *n., pl.* -ries. **1.** a discharge of artillery. **2.** artillery (def. 1).

cannon shot, 1. a ball or shot for a cannon. **2.** the shooting of a cannon. **3.** the range of a cannon.

can·not (kăn′ŏt, kă nŏt′, kə-), *v.* a form of can not. —Syn. See **can¹.**

can·nu·la (kăn′yə lə), *n. Surg.* a metal tube for insertion into the body, used to draw off fluid or to introduce medication. [t. L, dim. of *canna.* See CANE]

can·nu·lar (kăn′yə lər), *adj.* tubular. Also, **can·nu·late** (kăn′yə lāt′, -lĭt).

can·ny (kăn′ĭ), *adj.,* -nier, -niest, *adv. Scot.* —*adj.* **1.** careful; cautious; wary. **2.** knowing; sagacious; shrewd; astute. **3.** frugal; thrifty. **4.** skilled; expert. **5.** (chiefly with a negative) safe to deal or meddle with. **6.** quiet; gentle. **7.** snug; cozy. **8.** pretty; attractive. **9.** *Archaic.* having supernatural powers. —*adv.* **10.** in a canny manner. [appar. der. CAN¹] —**can′ni·ly,** *adv.* —**can′ni·ness,** *n.*

ca·noe (kə nōō′), *n., v.,* -noed, -noeing. —*n.* **1.** any light and narrow boat, often canvas-covered, that is propelled by paddles in place of oars. **2.** any native boat of very light construction, as the Algonquian birch bark canoe. —*v.i.* **3.** to paddle a canoe. **4.** to go in a canoe. —*v.t.* **5.** to transport by canoe. [earlier *canow,* var. of *canoa,* t. Sp., t. Carib: m. *kanoa*] —**ca·noe′ing,** *n.* —**ca·noe′ist,** *n.*

ca·noe·wood (kə nōō′wŏŏd′), *n.* the tulip tree.

can·on¹ (kăn′ən), *n.* **1.** *Chiefly Brit.* an ecclesiastical rule or law enacted by a council or other competent authority, and (in the Rom. Cath. Ch.) approved by the Pope. **2.** the body of ecclesiastical law. **3.** any rule or law. **4.** a fundamental principle. **5.** a standard; criterion. **6.** the books of the Bible recognized by the Christian Church as genuine and inspired. **7.** any officially recognized set of sacred books. **8.** a catalogue or list, as of the saints acknowledged by the church. **9.** *Liturgy.* that part of the Mass between the Sanctus and the Communion. **10.** *Music.* a kind of composition in which the same melody is played or sung through by two or more voice parts at the same or at a different pitch. **11.** a large size of printing type (48 point). [ME and OE, t. L: rule, canon, t. Gk.: m. *kanōn* straight rod, rule, standard] —Syn. **4.** See **principle.**

can·on² (kăn′ən), *n.* **1.** *Chiefly Brit.* one of a body of dignitaries or prebendaries attached to a cathedral or a collegiate church; a member of the chapter of a cathedral or a collegiate church. **2.** *Rom. Cath. Ch.* one of the members (**canons regular**) of certain religious orders. [ME *canoun,* t. ONF: m. *canon,* t. ML. See CANNON]

ca·ñon (kăn′yən; *Sp.* kä nyôn′), *n.* canyon.

canon bit, cannon (def. 4).

can·on·ess (kăn′ən ĭs), *n.* one of a community of women living under a rule, but not under a vow.

ca·non·i·cal (kə nŏn′ə kəl), *adj.* **1.** pertaining to, established by, or conforming to a canon or canons. **2.** included in the canon of the Bible. **3.** authorized; recognized; accepted: *canonical criticism.* —*n.* **4.** (*pl.*) the dress prescribed by canon for the clergy when officiating. [t. ML: s. *canonicālis,* der. L *canonicus,* t. Gk.: m. *kanonikós.* See CANON¹] —**ca·non′i·cal·ly,** *adv.*

canonical hour, 1. *Eccles.* any of certain periods of the day set apart for prayer and devotion, namely, matins (with lauds), prime, tierce, sext, nones, vespers, and complin. **2.** *Brit.* any hour between 8 A.M. and 3 P.M. during which marriage may be legally performed in parish churches.

ca·non·i·cate (kə nŏn′ə kāt′, -kĭt), *n.* the office or dignity of a canon; a canonry.

can·on·ic·i·ty (kăn′ə nĭs′ə tĭ), *n.* canonical character.

can·on·ist (kăn′ən ĭst), *n.* one versed in canon law.

can·on·ize (kăn′ə nīz′), *v.t.,* -ized, -izing. **1.** *Eccles.* to place in the canon of saints. **2.** to glorify. **3.** to make canonical: *canonized books.* —**can′on·i·za′tion,** *n.*

canon law, the body of ecclesiastical law.

can·on·ry (kăn′ən rĭ), *n., pl.* -ries. **1.** the office or benefice of a canon. **2.** the body or group of canons.

can·on·ship (kăn′ən shĭp′), *n.* the position or office of canon; canonry.

can opener, a device for opening cans.

Ca·no·pic (kə nō′pĭk), *adj.* **1.** *Archaeol.* of or from Canopus, as a kind of vase used to hold the entrails of embalmed bodies. **2.** denoting a vase used elsewhere to hold the ashes of the dead. [t. L: s. *Canōpicus,* der. *Canōpus* CANOPUS (def. 2)]

Ca·no·pus (kə nō′pəs), *n.* **1.** *Astron.* a star of the first magnitude in the constellation Carina: the second in order of brightness of the stars; Alpha Carinae. **2.** an ancient seacoast city in Lower Egypt, 15 miles east of Alexandria.

can·o·py (kăn′ə pĭ), *n., pl.* -pies, *v.,* -pied, -pying. —*n.* **1.** a covering suspended or supported over a throne, bed, etc., or held over a person, sacred object, etc. **2.** an overhanging protection or shelter. **3.** *Archit.* an ornamental rooflike projection or covering. **4.** the sky. —*v.t.* **5.** to cover with or as with a canopy: *clouds canopy the sky.* [ME *canape,* t. ML: s. *canapēum,* alter. of L *cōnōpēum* net curtains, t. Gk.: m. *kōnōpeton* mosquito net]

ca·no·rous (kə nōr′əs), *adj.* melodious; musical. [t. L: m. *canōrus*] —**ca·no′rous·ly,** *adv.*

Ca·nos·sa (kə nŏs′ə; *It.* kä nôs′sä), *n.* a ruined castle in N Italy: scene of the penance of Emperor Henry IV of the Holy Roman Empire before Pope Gregory VII in 1077.

Ca·no·va (kä nō′vä), *n.* **Antonio** (än tō′nyō), 1757–1822, Italian sculptor.

Can·ro·bert (kän rō bĕr′), *n.* **François Certain** (frän-swä′ sĕr tăn′), 1809–95, marshal of France.

Can·so (kăn′sō), *n.* **Cape,** the NE extremity of the mainland of Nova Scotia.

canst (kănst), *v. Archaic or Poetic.* 2nd pers. sing. pres. of **can.**

cant¹ (kănt), *n.* **1.** insincere statements, esp. conventional pretense of enthusiasm for high ideals; insincere expressions of goodness or piety. **2.** the special language or jargon spoken by thieves, gypsies, etc. **3.** the words, phrases, etc., peculiar to a particular class, party, profession, etc. **4.** whining or singsong speech, esp. of beggars. —*v.i.* **5.** to make religious remarks insincerely or hypocritically; pretend goodness or piety. **6.** to speak in the whining or singsong tone of a beggar; beg. [cf. OE *cantere* singer, t. L: m. *cantor*] —**can′ter,** *n.*

cant² (kănt), *n.* **1.** a salient angle. **2.** a sudden movement that tilts or overturns a thing. **3.** a slanting or tilted position. **4.** an oblique line or surface, as one formed by cutting off the corner of a square or cube. **5.** an oblique or slanting face of anything. **6.** a sudden pitch or toss. —*v.t.* **7.** *Mech.* to bevel. **8.** to put in an oblique position; tilt; tip. **9.** to throw with a sudden jerk. —*v.i.* **10.** to take or have an inclined position; tilt; turn. [t. MD, or MLG: m. *kant,* both prob. t. ONF: m. *cant,* g. L *canthus* corner, side]

cant³ (kănt), *adj. Brit. Dial.* hearty; merry. [t. LG]

can't (kănt, känt), contraction of *cannot.*

Cant., 1. Canterbury. **2.** Canticles.

Cantab., (L *Cantabrigiensis*) of Cambridge.

can·ta·bi·le (kän tä′bē lē′), *Music.* —*adj.* **1.** songlike and flowing in style. —*n.* **2.** a cantabile style, passage, or piece. [It., t. LL: m.s. *cantābilis* that may be sung]

Can·ta·brig·i·an (kăn′tə brĭj′ĭ ən), *adj.* **1.** of Cambridge (England) or Cambridge University. —*n.* **2.** a native or inhabitant of Cambridge. **3.** a student or graduate of Cambridge University. [f. *Cantabrigia* Latin form of the name Cambridge + -(A)N]

can·ta·lev·er (kăn′tə lĕv′ər, -lē′vər), *n.* cantilever. Also, **can·ta·li·ver** (kăn′tə lē′vər).

can·ta·loupe (kăn′tə lōp′), *n.* a variety of melons, *Cucumis melo,* var. *cantalupensis,* with hard, scaly, or warty rinds, esp. a small, ribbed, delicately flavored muskmelon. Also, **can′ta·loup′.** [t. F: m. *cantaloup,* t. It.: m. *Cantalupo,* a former estate of the Pope near Rome, where it was first grown in Europe]

can·tan·ker·ous (kăn tăng′kər əs), *adj.* ill-natured; quarrelsome; perverse or contrary, as in disposition: *a cantankerous old maid.* [? der. ME *contek* contention] —**can·tan′ker·ous·ly,** *adv.* —**can·tan′ker·ous·ness,** *n.*

can·ta·ta (kən tä′tə), *n. Music.* **1.** a choral composition, either sacred and resembling a short oratorio, or secular, as a lyric drama set to music but not to be acted. **2.** (*orig.*) a metrical narrative set to recitative, or alternate recitative and air, usually for a single voice, accompanied by one or more instruments. [t. It., der. *cantare* sing, g. L]

can·ta·tri·ce (*It.* kän′tä trē′chĕ; *Fr.* kän tä trēs′), *n., pl. It.* -trici (-trē′chē), *Fr.* -trices (-trēs′). a female singer. [F and It., t. L: m.s. *cantātrix*]

can·teen (kăn tēn′), *n.* **1.** U.S. a small container used by soldiers and others for carrying water or other liquids. **2.** a place in a military camp, reservation, etc., for the sale of personal necessities and supplies to members of the army. **3.** U.S. Army (formerly) Post Exchange. **4.** a place where free entertainment is provided for enlisted men, usually in a town or city near an army camp or post or naval shore station. **5.** a box or chest containing table utensils, etc., used by army officers and others. [t. F: m. *cantine,* t. It.: m. *cantina* cellar, wine cellar, der. *canto* side, g. L *canthus*]

can·ter (kăn′tər), *n.* **1.** an easy gallop. —*v.i., v.t.* **2.** to go or ride at a canter. [abbr. of *Canterbury gallop* (as of pilgrims to Canterbury, England)]

Can·ter·bur·y (kăn′tər bĕr′ĭ; *Brit.* -brĭ), *n.* **1.** a city in SE England, in Kent: famous cathedral; medieval pilgrimages to the tomb of Saint Thomas à Becket. 30,000 (est. 1956). **2.** a city in SE Australia, a part of Sydney.

Canterbury bell, a plant, *Campanula medium,* cultivated for its showy violet-blue, pink, or white flowers.

---

b., blend of, blended; c., cognate with; d., dialect, dialectal; der., derived from; f., formed from; g., going back to; m., modification of; r., replacing; s., stem of; t., taken from; ?, perhaps. See the full key on inside cover.

Canterbury Tales, The, an uncompleted sequence of tales by Chaucer, for the most part written after 1387.

can·thar·i·des (kăn thăr′ə dēz′), *n.pl., sing.* **cantharis** (kăn′thə rĭs). **1.** a preparation of powdered blister beetles, esp. the Spanish fly, *Lytta vesicatoria,* used medicinally as a skin irritant, diuretic, and aphrodisiac. **2.** *(sing.)* the beetle itself. [t. L, t. Gk.: pl., blister flies]

cant hook, a wooden lever with a movable iron hook near the lower end, used for grasping and canting or turning over logs, etc.

Cant hook

can·thus (kăn′thəs), *n., pl.* **-thi** (-thī). *Anat.* the angle or corner on each side of the eye, formed by the junction of the upper and lower lids. [t. NL, t. Gk.: m. *kanthós* corner of the eye]

can·ti·cle (kăn′tə kəl), *n.* **1.** one of the nonmetrical hymns or chants, chiefly from the Bible, used in church services. **2.** a little song; a song. **3.** *(cap., pl.)* a book of the Old Testament, also known as the *Song of Solomon.* [ME, t. L: m.s. *canticulum,* dim. of *canticum* song]

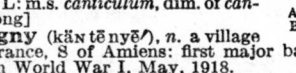
A. Inner canthus;
B. Outer canthus

Can·ti·gny (kän tē nyē′), *n.* a village in N France, S of Amiens: first major battle of U. S. forces in World War I, May, 1918.

can·ti·lev·er (kăn′tə lĕv′ər, -lē′vər), *n.* **1.** *Mach.* a free part of any horizontal member projecting beyond a support. **2.** *Civ. Eng.* either of two bracketlike arms projecting toward each other from opposite banks or piers, serving to form the span of a bridge **(cantilever bridge)** when united. **3.** *Aeron.* a form of wing construction in which no external bracing is employed **(cantilever wing). 4.** *Archit.* an extended bracket for supporting a balcony, cornice, or the like. Also, **cantalever, cantaliver.** [orig. uncert.]

can·ti·na (kän tē′nə; *Sp.* kän tē′nä), *n. Southwestern U.S.* a saloon. [t. Sp.]

can·tle (kăn′təl), *n.* **1.** the hind part of a saddle, usually curved upward. See illus. under **saddle. 2.** a corner; piece; portion. [ME *cantel,* t. ONF, dim. of *cant* corner, CANT²]

can·to (kăn′tō), *n., pl.* **-tos.** one of the main or larger divisions of a long poem, as in Scott's *Marmion.* [t. It., g. L *cantus* song]

can·ton (kăn′tən, -tŏn, kăn tŏn′ *for 1–6;* kăn tŏn′, -tōn′, *esp. Brit.* -tōōn′ *for 7*), *n.* **1.** a small territorial district, esp. one of the states of the Swiss confederation. **2.** a subdivision of a French arrondissement. **3.** *Her.* a square division in the upper dexter corner of an escutcheon, etc. **4.** a division, part, or portion of anything. **—v.t. 5.** to divide into parts or portions. **6.** to divide into cantons or territorial districts. **7.** to allot quarters to (soldiers, etc.). [t. F: corner, ult. der. L *canthus* corner, CANT²] **—can·ton·al** (kăn′tən əl), *adj.*

Can·ton (kăn tŏn′ *for 1;* kăn′tən *for 2*), *n.* **1.** Chinese, **Kwangchow.** a seaport in SE China, on the Chu-Kiang: the capital of Kwangtung province. 1,210,000 (est. 1952). **2.** a city in NE Ohio. 113,631 (1960).

Can·ton crepe (kăn′tən), a thin, light silk or rayon crepe with a finely wrinkled surface, heavier in texture than crepe de chine. [named after *Canton,* China]

Can·ton·ese (kăn′tə nēz′, -nēs′), *n., pl.* **-ese,** *adj.* **—n. 1.** a Chinese language of southern China. **2.** a native or inhabitant of Canton. **—adj. 3.** pertaining to Canton, its inhabitants, or their language.

Can·ton flannel (kăn′tən), a cotton twill fabric, napped on one side.

can·ton·ment (kăn tŏn′mənt, -tōn′-; *esp. Brit.* -tōōn′-), *n.* **1.** a camp (usually of large size) where men are trained for military service. **2.** military quarters. **3.** the winter quarters of an army. [t. F: m. *cantonnement*]

Can·ton River (kăn tŏn′), Chu-Kiang.

can·tor (kăn′tər, -tôr), *n. Eccles.* **1.** an officer whose duty is to lead the singing in a cathedral or in a collegiate or parish church; a precentor. **2.** the Jewish religious official singing the liturgy. [t. L: singer]

can·trip (kăn′trĭp), *n. Orig. and Chiefly Scot.* **1.** a charm; a spell. **2.** a trick. [orig. unknown]

can·tus (kăn′təs), *n., pl.* **-tus.** **1.** a song; melody. **2.** an ecclesiastical piece of music. [t. L. See CHANT]

can·tus fir·mus (kăn′təs fûr′məs), **1.** *Eccles.* the ancient traditional vocal music of the Christian Church, having its form settled and its use prescribed by ecclesiastical authority. **2.** *Music.* a fixed melody to which other melodic parts are added. [ML]

cant·y (kăn′tĭ, kän′-), *adj. Scot. and N. Eng.* **1.** cheerful. **2.** lively; brisk. [t. LG: m. *kantig* cheerful]

Ca·nuck (kə nŭk′), *n. Colloq. or Slang.* a Canadian, esp. a French Canadian.

Ca·nute (kə nōōt′, -nūt′), *n.* A.D. 994?–1035, Danish king of England, 1017–35; of Denmark, 1018–35; and of Norway, 1028–35. Also, **Cnut, Knut.**

can·vas (kăn′vəs), *n.* **1.** a closely woven, heavy cloth of hemp, flax, or cotton, used for tents, sails, etc. **2.** a piece of this material on which an oil painting is made. **3.** an oil painting on canvas. **4.** a tent, or tents collectively. **5.** sailcloth. **6.** sails collectively. **7.** any fabric, of linen, cotton, etc., of a coarse loose weave,

used as a foundation for embroidery stitches, for interlining, etc. [ME *canevas,* t. ONF, ult. der. L *cannabis* hemp]

can·vas·back (kăn′vəs băk′), *n.* a North American wild duck, *Aythya valisineria,* with a whitish back, prized for the delicacy of its flesh.

can·vass (kăn′vəs), *v.t.* **1.** to examine carefully; investigate by inquiry; discuss; debate. **2.** to solicit votes, subscriptions, opinions, etc., from (a district, group of people, etc.). **3.** *Brit.* to engage in a political campaign. **4.** *Obs.* to criticize severely. **—v.i. 5.** to solicit votes, opinions, etc. **6.** to review election returns. **7.** to engage in discussion or debate. **—n. 8.** examination; close inspection; scrutiny. **9.** a soliciting of votes, orders, etc. **10.** a campaign for election to government office. [var. of CANVAS, *n.;* orig. meaning to toss (someone) in a canvas sheet (cf. def. 4)] **—can′vass·er,** *n.*

can·yon (kăn′yən), *n. U.S.* a deep valley with steep sides, often with a stream flowing through it. Also, **cañon.** [t. Sp.: m. *cañón* tube, der. *caña,* g. L *canna* reed]

can·zo·ne (kän tsō′nĕ), *n., pl.* **-zoni** (-tsō′nē). **1.** a variety of lyric poetry in the Italian style, of Provençal origin, which closely resembles the madrigal. **2.** any ballad or song. [It., g. L *cantio* song.]

can·zo·net (kăn′zə nĕt′), *n.* a short song, esp. a light and gay one.

caou·tchouc (kōō′chŏŏk, kou chōŏk′; *esp. Brit.* kou′-chōŏk), *n.* **1.** the gummy coagulated juice of certain tropical plants; India rubber. **2.** pure rubber. [t. F, t. Sp.: m. *cauchú,* of S Amer. orig.]

cap (kăp), *n., v.,* **capped, capping. —n. 1.** a covering for the head, esp. one fitting closely and made of softer material than a hat, and having little or no brim. **2.** a covering of lace, etc., for a woman's head, usually worn indoors. **3.** a special headdress denoting rank, occupation, etc.: *a cardinal's cap, nurse's cap.* **4.** a mortarboard. **5.** anything resembling or suggestive of a covering for the head in shape, use, or position. **6.** the acme. **7.** *Bot.* the pileus of a mushroom. **8.** a percussion cap. **9.** a noise-making device for toy pistols, made of a small quantity of explosive wrapped in paper or other thin material. **10.** capital; capital letter. **11.** a name given (with distinctive qualifications, as in *foolscap*) to several large sizes of writing paper. **—v.t. 12.** to provide or cover with or as with a cap. **13.** to complete. **14.** to surpass; follow up with something as good or better. **15.** to serve as a cap, covering, or top to; overlie. [ME *cappe,* OE *cæppe,* t. LL: m. *cappa, cāpa* cap, hooded cloak, cape, appar. der. *caput* head]

cap., **1.** capital. **2.** capitalize. **3.** capitalized. **4.** *(pl.* **caps.)** capital letter. **5.** (L *capitulum, caput*) chapter.

ca·pa·bil·i·ty (kā′pə bĭl′ə tĭ), *n., pl.* **-ties. 1.** quality of being capable; capacity; ability. **2.** quality of admitting of certain treatment. **3.** *(usually pl.)* a quality, ability, etc., that can be developed or used.

ca·pa·ble (kā′pə bəl), *adj.* **1.** having much intelligence or ability; competent; efficient; able: *a capable instructor.* **2.** capable of, **a.** having the ability, strength, etc., to; qualified or fitted for: *a man capable of judging art.* **b.** susceptible to; open to the influence or effect of: *a situation capable of improvement.* **c.** wicked enough for: *capable of murder.* [t. LL: m. *capabilis*] **—ca′pa·ble·ness,** *n.* **—ca′pa·bly,** *adv.* **—Syn. 1.** See able.

ca·pa·cious (kə pā′shəs), *adj.* capable of holding much. [f. CAPACI(TY) + -OUS] **—ca·pa′cious·ly,** *adv.* **—ca·pa′cious·ness,** *n.* **—Syn.** spacious, roomy.

ca·pac·i·tance (kə păs′ə təns), *n. Elect.* **1.** the ratio of a change in quantity of electricity (in a conductor) to the corresponding change in potential. **2.** the property of being able to collect a charge of electricity. **3.** a condenser. [f. CAPACIT(Y) + -ANCE]

ca·pac·i·tate (kə păs′ə tāt′), *v.t.,* **-tated, -tating. 1.** to make capable; enable. **2.** to furnish with legal powers. **—ca·pac′i·ta′tion,** *n.*

ca·pac·i·tive (kə păs′ə tĭv), *adj. Elect.* pertaining to capacity.

ca·pac·i·tor (kə păs′ə tər), *n. Elect.* a condenser.

ca·pac·i·ty (kə păs′ə tĭ), *n., pl.* **-ties. 1.** the power of receiving or containing. **2.** cubic contents; volume. **3.** power of receiving impressions, knowledge, etc.; mental ability: *the capacity of a scholar.* **4.** power, ability, or possibility of doing something (fol. by *of, for,* or infinitive): *capacity for self-protection.* **5.** quality of being susceptible to certain treatment. **6.** position; function; relation: *in the capacity of legal adviser.* **7.** legal qualification. **8.** *Elect.* **a.** capacitance. **b.** a measure of output performance. [late ME *capacyte,* t. L: m.s. *capācitas*] **Syn.** competence.

Ca·pa·neus (kăp′ə nūs′, -nōōs′, kə pā′nĭ əs), *n. Gk. Legend.* one of the Seven against Thebes, destroyed by Zeus for blasphemy. See **Seven against Thebes.**

cap-a-pie (kăp′ə pē′), *adv.* from head to foot. Also, **cap′-à-pie′.** [t. F (obs.)]

ca·par·i·son (kə păr′ə sən), *n.* **1.** a covering, usually ornamented, laid over the saddle or harness of a horse, etc. **2.** dress; equipment; outfit. **—v.t. 3.** to cover with a caparison. **4.** to dress finely; deck. [t. F: m. *caparasson,* t. Sp.: m. *caparazón,* t. Pr.: m. *caparaso,* der. *capa* CAPE¹]

cape¹ (kāp), *n.* a sleeveless garment fastened round the neck and falling loosely over the shoulders, worn separately or attached to a coat, etc. [t. F, t. Sp.: m. *capa,* g. LL *cāpa.* See CAP]

ăct, āble, dâre, ärt; ĕbb, ēqual; ĭf, īce; hŏt, ōver, ôrder, oil, bŏŏk, ōōze, out; ŭp, ūse, ûrge; ə = a in alone; ch, chief; give; g, ng, ring; sh, shoe; th, thin; ŧħ, that; zh, vision. See the full key on inside cover.

cape² (kāp), *n.* **1.** a piece of land jutting into the sea or some other body of water. **2. the Cape,** the Cape of Good Hope. [ME, t. F: m. *cap,* t. Pr., g. L *caput* head]

Cape Bret·on (brĭt'ən, brĕt'ən), an island forming the NE part of Nova Scotia. 150,157 (1951); 3970 sq. mi.

Cape buffalo. See buffalo (def. 1).

Cape Colony, See Cape of Good Hope (def. 2).

Cape Dutch, South African Dutch.

Cape Gi·rar·deau (jē'rärdō'), a city in SE Missouri, on the Mississippi. 24,947 (1960).

Cape Horn (hôrn), *n.* a headland on a small island at the S extremity of South America.

Ča·pek (chä'pĕk), *n.* Karel (kä'rĕl), 1890–1938, Czech dramatist, novelist, and producer.

cap·e·lin (kăp'əlĭn), *n.* either of two small fishes of the smelt family, of the coasts of the North Atlantic (*Mallotus villosus*) and North Pacific (*M. catervarius*). [t. F: m. *caplan, capelan,* prob. t. Pr. See CHAPLAIN]

Ca·pel·la (kəpĕl'ə), *n.* *Astron.* a brilliant star of the first magnitude in the constellation Auriga. [t. L: lit., she-goat]

Cape of Good Hope, 1. a cape near the S extremity of Africa. **2.** Also, **Cape Province.** Formerly, **Cape Colony.** a province in the Union of South Africa. 4,727,-000 (est. 1955); 277,169 sq. mi. *Cap.:* Cape Town.

ca·per¹ (kā'pər), *v.i.* **1.** to leap or skip about in a sprightly manner; prance. **—n. 2.** a playful leap or skip. **3.** a prank; capricious action; hare-brained escapade. [fig. use of L *caper* he-goat] **—ca'per·er,** *n.*

ca·per² (kā'pər), *n.* **1.** a shrub, *Capparis spinosa,* of Mediterranean regions. **2.** its flower bud, which is pickled and used for garnish or seasoning. [ME *caperis,* t. L: m. *capparis,* t. Gk.: m. *kápparis*]

cap·er·cail·lie (kăp'ərkāl'yĭ), *n.* the wood grouse, *Tetrao urogallus,* a very large gallinaceous bird of northern Europe. Also, **cap·er·cail·zie** (kăp'ər kāl'yĭ, -kāl'zĭ). [t. Gaelic: m. *capullcoille,* lit., horse-wood, with *r* for *l* by dissimilation]

Ca·per·na·um (kəpûr'nāəm, -nĭ-), *n.* an ancient town in N Israel, on the Sea of Galilee: the center of Jesus' ministry in Galilee.

Ca·pet (kā'pĭt, kăp'ĭt; *Fr.* kȧpě'), *n.* Hugh or *Fr.* Hugues (yg), A.D. 938?–996, king of France, 987–996.

Ca·pe·tian (kəpē'shən), *adj.* **1.** pertaining or relating to the French dynasty (987–1328) founded by Hugh Capet. **—n. 2.** a member of this dynasty.

Cape Town, a seaport in the Republic of South Africa, near the Cape of Good Hope: seat of the legislature. With suburbs, 441,203 (1951). Also, **Cape'town'.**

Cape Verde Islands (vûrd), a group of islands in the Atlantic, W of French West Africa, an overseas territory of Portugal. 165,000 pop. (est. 1954); 1557 sq. mi. *Cap.:* Praia.

Cape York Peninsula, a large peninsula in NE Australia between the Gulf of Carpentaria and the Coral Sea.

cap·ful (kăp'fŏŏl), *n., pl.* **-fuls.** as much as a cap will hold.

Cap-Ha·ï·tien (kȧpǡē̇syăN', -tyäN'), *n.* a seaport in N Haiti. 24,423 (1950).

ca·pi·as (kā'pĭəs, kăp'ĭ-), *n.* *Law.* a writ commanding an officer to take a specified person into custody. [t. L: take thou]

cap·i·ba·ra (kăp'əbä'rə), *n.* capybara.

cap·il·la·ceous (kăp'əlā'shəs), *adj.* hairlike; capillary. [t. L: m. *capillāceus* hairy]

cap·il·lar·i·ty (kăp'əlăr'ətĭ), *n.* **1.** state of being capillary. **2.** *Physics.* capillary action.

cap·il·lar·y (kăp'əlĕr'ĭ), *adj., n., pl.* **-laries. —adj. 1.** pertaining to or occurring in or as in a tube of fine bore. **2.** *Physics.* **a.** pertaining to the property of surface tension. **b. capillary action,** the elevation or depression of the surface of liquids in fine tubes, etc., due to surface tension and the forces of cohesion and adhesion. **c. capillary attraction** or **repulsion,** the apparent attraction or repulsion between a liquid and a tube, etc., observed in such phenomena. **3.** *Bot.* resembling hair in the manner of growth or in shape. **4.** *Anat.* pertaining to a capillary or capillaries. **—n. 5.** *Anat.* one of the minute blood vessels between the terminations of the arteries and the beginnings of the veins. **6.** Also, **capillary tube,** a tube with a small bore. [t. L: m. *capillāris* pertaining to the hair]

ca·pi·ta (kăp'ətə), *n.* pl. of **caput.**

cap·i·tal¹ (kăp'ətəl), *n.* **1.** the city or town which is the official seat of government in a county, state, etc. **2.** a capital letter. **3.** the wealth, whether in money or property, owned or employed in business by an individual, firm, corporation, etc. **4.** an accumulated stock of such wealth. **5.** any form of wealth employed or capable of being employed in the production of more wealth. **6.** *Accounting.* **a.** assets remaining after deduction of liabilities; the net worth of a business. **b.** the ownership interest in a business. **7.** any source of profit, advantage, power, etc. **8.** capitalists as a group or class. **9.** resources. **—adj. 10.** pertaining to capital: *capital stock.* **11.** principal; highly important. **12.** chief,

esp. as being the official seat of government of a country, state, etc. **13.** excellent or first-rate. **14.** (of letters) of the large size used at the beginning of a sentence or as the first letter of a proper name. **15.** involving the loss of the head or life, usually as punishment; punishable by death. **16.** fatal; serious: *a capital error.* **17.** of the largest, most heavily armed, etc., type: *a capital ship.* [ME, t. L: s. *capitālis* pertaining to the head or to life, chief (ML *capitāle,* n., wealth)]

—Syn. 11. The adjectives CAPITAL, CHIEF, MAJOR, PRINCIPAL apply to a main or leading representative of a kind. CAPITAL may mean larger or more prominent, or it may suggest preëminence and excellence of quality: *capital letter, city, investment.* CHIEF means leading, highest in office or power: *the chief clerk.* MAJOR may refer to greatness of importance, number, or quantity: *a major operation, the major part of a population.* PRINCIPAL refers to most distinguished, influential, or foremost: *principal officer, export.* **—Ant. 11.** minor, lesser.

cap·i·tal³ (kăp'ətəl), *n.* *Archit.* the head, or uppermost part, of a column, pillar, etc. [ME *capital(e),* t. L: m.s. *capitellum,* dim. of *caput* head; influenced by CAPITAL¹, adj.]

Capitals
A. Doric; B. Ionic; C. Corinthian

capital account, 1. a business account stating the owner's or shareholder's interest in the assets. **2.** (*pl.*) *Accounting.* accounts showing the net worth, as in a business enterprise, as assets minus liabilities.

capital expenditure, *Accounting.* an addition to the value of a fixed asset, as by the purchase of a new building.

capital gain, profit from the sale of assets, such as bonds, real estate, etc.

capital goods, *Econ.* goods used in the production of other goods.

cap·i·tal·ism (kăp'ətəlĭz'əm; *Brit. also* kəpĭt'ə-), *n.* **1.** a system under which the means of production, distribution, and exchange are in large measure privately owned and directed. **2.** the concentration of capital in the hands of a few, or the resulting power or influence. **3.** a system favoring such concentration of wealth.

cap·i·tal·ist (kăp'ətəlĭst; *Brit. also* kəpĭt'əl-), *n.* one who has capital, esp. extensive capital employed in business enterprises.

cap·i·tal·is·tic (kăp'ətəlĭs'tĭk; *Brit. also* kəpĭt'ə-), *adj.* pertaining to capital or capitalists; founded on or believing in capitalism: *capitalistic production.* **—cap'i·tal·is'ti·cal·ly,** *adv.*

cap·i·tal·i·za·tion (kăp'ətələzā'shən; *Brit. also* kəpĭt'əl-), *n.* **1.** act of capitalizing. **2.** the authorized or outstanding stocks and bonds of a corporation. **3.** *Accounting.* **a.** the total investment of the owner or owners in a business enterprise. **b.** the total corporate liability. **c.** the total arrived at after addition of liabilities. **4.** conversion into stocks or bonds. **5.** act of computing the present value of future periodical payments.

cap·i·tal·ize (kăp'ətəlīz'; *Brit. also* kəpĭt'əlīz'), *v.t.* **-ized, -izing. 1.** to write or print in capital letters, or with an initial capital. **2.** to authorize a certain amount of stocks and bonds in the corporate charter: *to capitalize a corporation.* **3.** to convert (floating debt) into stock or shares. **4.** *Accounting.* to set up (expenditures) as business assets in the books of account instead of treating as expense. **5.** to supply with capital. **6.** to estimate the value of (a stock or an enterprise). **7.** to take advantage of; turn to one's advantage (often fol. by *on*): *capitalize on one's opportunities.*

capital levy, a tax based on total assets.

cap·i·tal·ly (kăp'ətəlĭ), *adv.* in a capital manner; excellently; very well.

capital ship, one of a class of the largest warships; a battleship, battle cruiser, or aircraft carrier.

capital stock, 1. the total shares issued by a corporation. **2.** the book value of all the shares of a corporation, including unissued shares and those not completely paid in.

capital surplus, the surplus of a business, exclusive of its earned surplus.

cap·i·tate (kăp'ətāt'), *adj.* *Bot.* having a globular head; collected in a head. [t. L: m. s. *capitātus* having a head]

cap·i·ta·tion (kăp'ətā'shən), *n.* **1.** a numbering or assessing by the head. **2.** a poll tax. **3.** a fee or payment of a uniform amount for each person. [t. LL: s. *capitātio* poll tax]

Cap·i·tol (kăp'ətəl), *n.* **1.** the building at Washington, D.C., used by the Congress of the U. S. for its sessions. **2.** (*often l.c.*) a building occupied by a State legislature; Statehouse. **3.** the ancient temple of Jupiter at Rome, on the Capitoline. **4.** the ancient temple of Jupiter at Rome, t. L: m.s. *Capitōlium* (cf. def. 3, 4), der. *caput* head]

Cap·i·to·line (kăp'ətəlīn'), *adj.* **1.** of or pertaining to the Capitol at Rome, the hill on which it stood, or the god Jupiter (who was worshiped there). **—n. 2.** one of the seven hills of ancient Rome.

ca·pit·u·lar (kəpĭch'ələr), *n.* **1.** a member of an ecclesiastical chapter. **2.** (*pl.*) the laws or statutes of a chapter or of an ecclesiastical council. **—adj. 3.** *Bot.* capitate. **4.** pertaining to an ecclesiastical or other chapter: *a capitular cathedral.* [t. ML: s. *capitulāris,* der. L *capitulum* CAPITULUM]

ca·pit·u·lar·y (kə·pĭch′ə·lĕr′ĭ), *adj.*, *n.*, *pl.* **-laries.** —*adj.* **1.** pertaining to a chapter, esp. an ecclesiastic one. —*n.* **2.** a member of a chapter, esp. an ecclesiastic one. **3.** (*pl.*) the ordinances or laws of a Frankish sovereign.

ca·pit·u·late (kə·pĭch′ə·lāt′), *v.i.*, **-lated, -lating.** to surrender unconditionally or on stipulated terms. [t. ML: m. s. *capitulātus*, pp. of *capitulāre* arrange in chapters, der. L *capitulum* CAPITULUM]

ca·pit·u·la·tion (kə·pĭch′ə·lā′shən), *n.* **1.** a surrender unconditionally or upon certain terms. **2.** the instrument containing a surrender. **3.** a statement of the heads of a subject; a summary or enumeration. **4.** (*pl.*) any of the treaties of the sultans of Turkey which granted to foreigners residing there rights of personality of law, extraterritoriality, etc. **5.** a treaty by which Christian states obtained the right to establish courts for their nationals in non-Christian states.

ca·pit·u·lum (kə·pĭch′ə·ləm), *n.*, *pl.* **-la** (-lə). **1.** *Bot.* a close head of sessile flowers; a flower head. **2.** *Anat.* the head of a bone. [t. L: small head, capital of column, chapter, dim. of *caput* head]

Cap′n (kăp′ən), *n.* Captain.

ca·pon (kā′pŏn, -pən), *n.* a rooster castrated to improve the flesh for use as food. [OE *capun*, t. L: m. s. *cāpo*]

ca·po·ral (kăp′ə·răl′), *n.* a kind of tobacco. [t. F, t. It.: m. *caporale* superior]

Ca·po·ret·to (kăp′ə·rĕt′ō; *It.* kä′pô·rĕt′tô), *n.* a village in NE Italy: scene of a disastrous Italian defeat by the Austrians and Germans, 1917.

ca·pote (kə·pōt′; *Fr.* kȧ·pôt′), *n.* **1.** a long cloak with a hood. **2.** a close, caplike bonnet worn by women and children. **3.** the hood or top of a vehicle. [t. F, dim. of *cape* hood]

Cap·pa·do·cia (kăp′ə·dō′shə), *n.* an ancient country in E Asia Minor: later a Roman province.

cap·pa·ri·da·ceous (kăp′ə·rĭ′dā′shəs), *adj.* *Bot.* belonging to the *Capparidaceae*, or caper family of plants. [f. *capparid* (f. s. L *capparis* + -ID²) the caper plant + -ACEOUS]

capped hock, *Vet. Sci.* any swelling, inflammatory or otherwise, on the point of the hock of horses.

cap·per (kăp′ər), *n.* **1.** one who or that which caps. **2.** *U.S. Slang.* an informer, esp. for gamblers. **3.** *U.S. Slang.* a by-bidder at an auction.

cap·re·o·late (kăp′rĭ′ə·lāt′, kə·prē′-), *adj.* **1.** *Bot.* having tendrils. **2.** *Anat.* resembling tendrils. [f. s. L *capreolus* tendril + -ATE¹]

Ca·pri (kä′prē), *n.* a rocky island in the Bay of Naples, in W Italy: famous for its scenery and grottoes. 6209 pop. (1951); 5½ sq. mi.

ca·pric·ci·o (kə·prē′chʸō′; *It.* kä·prēt′chō), *n.*, *pl.* **-cios,** *It.* **-ci** (-chē). **1.** a caper; a prank. **2.** a caprice. **3.** *Music.* a composition in a free, irregular style. [t. It., der. *capro* goat, g. L *caper*]

ca·pric·ci·o·so (kə·prē′chʸō′sō; *It.* kä·prēt′chō·sô), *adj. Music.* capricious; fantastic in style.

ca·price (kə·prēs′), *n.* **1.** a sudden change of mind without apparent or adequate motive; whim. **2.** a tendency to change one's mind without apparent or adequate motive; whimsicality; capriciousness. **3.** *Music.* capriccio (def. 3). [t. F, t. It.: m. *capriccio* CAPRICCIO]

ca·pri·cious (kə·prĭsh′əs), *adj.* **1.** subject to, led by, or indicative of caprice or whim. **2.** *Obs.* fanciful or witty. —**ca·pri′cious·ly,** *adv.* —**ca·pri′cious·ness,** *n.*

Cap·ri·corn (kăp′rə·kôrn′), *n.* **1.** *Astron.* a zodiacal constellation between Sagittarius and Aquarius. **2.** the tenth sign of the zodiac. See diag. under zodiac. Also, **Cap·ri·cor·nus** (kăp′rə·kôr′nəs). **3.** See **tropic** (1a, 2a) [t. L: *Capricornus*, lit., goat-horned]

cap·ri·fo·li·a·ceous (kăp′rə·fō′lĭ′ā′shəs), *adj.* *Bot.* belonging to the *Caprifoliaceae*, a family of plants including the honeysuckle, elder, viburnum, snowberry, etc. [f. s. ML *caprifolium* honeysuckle + -ACEOUS]

cap·ri·ole (kăp′rĭ·ōl′), *n.*, *v.*, **-oled, -oling.** —*n.* **1.** a caper or leap. **2.** an upward spring made by a horse with all four feet and without advancing. —*v.i.* **3.** to execute a capriole. [t. F, t. It.: m. *capriola* caper, der. *capro* goat, g. L *caper*]

ca·pro·ic (kə·prō′ĭk), *n.* an organic acid, CH₃(CH₂)₄COOH, found in fatty animal tissue and in coconut oil, used to make artificial flavoring agents. [f. *capro-* (comb. form repr. L *caper* goat) + -IC; so called from its smell]

caps. capital letters.

cap·sa·i·cin (kăp·sā′ə·sĭn), *n.* *Chem.* a bitter irritant principle from paprika; colorless crystalline amide, C₁₈H₂₇NO₃, related to guaiacol. [f. L *capsa* box + -IC + -IN²]

cap screw, a screw bolt with a long thread and a square or hexagonal head, used to secure covers of steam cylinders, etc. See illus. under **screw.**

cap·si·cum (kăp′sĭ·kəm), *n.* **1.** any plant of the solanaceous genus *Capsicum,* as *C. frutescens,* the common pepper of the garden, in many varieties, with mild to hot, pungent seeds enclosed in a podded or bell-shaped pericarp which also ranges from mild to extremely hot. **2.** the fruit of these plants, or some preparation of it, used as a condiment and once widely used internally and externally as a local irritant. [t. NL: f. s. L *capsa* box + -icum, neut. of -icus -IC]

cap·size (kăp′sīz′), *v.*, **-sized, -sizing.** —*v.i.* **1.** to overturn: *the boat capsized.* —*v.t.* **2.** to upset: *they capsized the boat.* [orig. unknown] —Syn. See **upset.**

cap·stan (kăp′stən), *n.* a device resembling a windlass but with a vertical axis, commonly turned by a bar or lever, and winding a cable, for raising weights (as an anchor). [ME, t. Pr.: m. *cabestan,* earlier *cabestran,* der. *cabestre,* g. L *capistrum* halter]

Capstan
A, Capstan head; B, Barrel;
C, Toothed rim and pawls;
D, Capstan bar

capstan bar, one of the levers, generally of wood, by which a capstan is turned.

cap·stone (kăp′stōn′), *n.* a finishing stone of a structure.

cap·su·lar (kăp′sə·lər), *adj.* of, in, or like a capsule.

cap·su·late (kăp′sə·lāt′), *adj.* enclosed in or formed into a capsule. Also, **cap′su·lat′ed.**

cap·sule (kăp′səl), *n.* **1.** a gelatinous case enclosing a dose of medicine. **2.** *Bot.* **a.** a dry dehiscent fruit, composed of two or more carpels. **b.** the spore case of various cryptogamic plants. **3.** *Anat., Zool.* **a.** a membranous sac or integument. **b.** either of two strata of white matter in the cerebrum. **4.** a small case, envelope, or covering. **5.** a thin metal covering for the mouth of a corked bottle. [earlier *capsul,* t. L: s. *capsula,* dim. of *capsa* box]

Capsules (def. 2a), after dehiscence
A, Asphodel; B, Prickly poppy; C, Violet

Capt., Captain.

cap·tain (kăp′tən, -tĭn), *n.* **1.** one who is at the head of or in authority over others; a chief; leader. **2.** an officer in most armies, ranking above a first lieutenant and below a major. **3.** a military leader. **4.** the commander or master of a merchant ship or other vessel. **5.** an officer in the navy ranking above a commander and below a rear admiral, usually in command of a warship. **6.** the leader of a baseball team, racing crew, etc. —*v.t.* **7.** to lead or command as a captain. [ME *capitain,* t. OF, t. LL: m.s. *capitāneus* chief, der. L *caput* head] —**cap′tain·cy,** *n.* —**cap′tain·ship,** *n.*

cap·tion (kăp′shən), *n.* **1.** a heading or title, as of a chapter, article, or page. **2.** *Print.* a legend for a picture or illustration. **3.** *Motion Pictures.* the title of a scene, the text of a speech, etc., shown on the screen. **4.** *Law.* that part of a legal document which states time, place, etc., of execution or performance. [t. L: s. *captio*]

cap·tious (kăp′shəs), *adj.* **1.** apt to notice and make much of trivial faults or defects; faultfinding; difficult to please. **2.** proceeding from a faultfinding or caviling disposition: *captious remarks.* **3.** apt or designed to ensnare or perplex, esp. in argument: *captious questions.* [t. L: m. s. *captiōsus* fallacious, sophistical] —**cap′tious·ly,** *adv.* —**cap′tious·ness,** *n.*

cap·ti·vate (kăp′tə·vāt′), *v.t.*, **-vated, -vating.** **1.** to enthrall by beauty or excellence; enchant; charm. **2.** *Obs.* to capture; subjugate. [t. LL: m.s. *captivātus,* pp., taken captive] —**cap′ti·va′tion,** *n.* —**cap′ti·va′tor,** *n.* —Syn. **1.** See **charm.**

cap·tive (kăp′tĭv), *n.* **1.** a prisoner. **2.** one who is enslaved by love, beauty, etc. —*adj.* **3.** made or held prisoner, esp. in war. **4.** kept in confinement or restraint. **5.** enslaved by love, beauty, etc.; captivated. **6.** of or pertaining to a captive. [t. L: m.s. *captivus*]

captive audience, an audience with little or no choice about listening to a broadcast.

captive balloon, a balloon held in a particular place by means of a rope or cable, as for observation purposes.

cap·tiv·i·ty (kăp·tĭv′ə·tĭ), *n.*, *pl.* **-ties.** state or period of being captive. —Syn. bondage, servitude, slavery.

cap·tor (kăp′tər), *n.* a person who captures.

cap·ture (kăp′chər), *v.*, **-tured, -turing,** *n.* —*v.t.* **1.** to take by force or stratagem; take prisoner; seize: *the chief was captured.* [v. use of n.] —*n.* **2.** act of capturing. **3.** the thing or person captured. [t. F, t. L: m. *captūra*] —**cap′tur·er,** *n.* —Syn. **1.** catch, arrest, snare, grab, nab. **2.** seizure, arrest.

Cap·u·a (kăp′yŏŏ·ə; *It.* kä′pwä), *n.* a town in SW Italy, near Naples. 15,427 (1951).

ca·puche (kə·pōōsh′, -pōōch′), *n.* a hood or cowl; esp. the long, pointed cowl of the Capuchins.

cap·u·chin (kăp′yŏŏ·chĭn, -shĭn), *n.* **1.** a prehensile-tailed, Central and South American monkey, *Cebus capucinus,* whose head hair presents a cowllike appearance. **2.** any monkey of the genus *Cebus.* **3.** a hooded cloak for women. **4.** (*cap.*) *Rom. Cath. Ch.* one of an order of Franciscan friars, a reformed branch of the Observants, wearing a long cowl. [t. F, t. It.: m. *cappuccino,* der. *cappuccio* hood]

Capuchin monkey,
Cebus capucinus
(Total length 3 ft.,
tail 15 in.)

Cap·u·let (kăp'yə lĕt', -lĭt), *n.* the family name of Juliet in Shakespeare's *Romeo and Juliet.*

ca·put (kā'pət, kăp'ət), *n.*, *pl.* **capita** (kăp'ə tə). *Anat.* any head or headlike expansion on a structure, as on a bone. [L: the head]

cap·y·ba·ra (kăp'Ĭ bä'rə), *n.* the largest living rodent, *Hydrochaerus hydrochaeris,* 3 or 4 feet long, living along the banks of South American rivers, sand-colored and virtually tailless. Also, **capibara.** [t. Pg.: m. *capibara,* t. Tupi: m. *kapigwara* grass eater]

Capybara.
Hydrochaerus hydrochaeris
(3 to 4 ft. long,
ab. 2 ft. high)

car (kär), *n.* **1.** an automobile. **2.** a vehicle running on rails, as a streetcar. **3.** *Brit.* a wheeled vehicle in many varieties often one with two wheels. **4.** the part of a balloon, elevator, etc., for carrying the passengers, etc. **5.** *Poetic.* a chariot, as of war or triumph. **6.** a perforated box floated in water, used to preserve live fish, etc. [ME *carre,* t. ONF, g. LL *carrus,* of Celtic orig.]

ca·ra·ba·o (kär'ə bä'ō), *n.*, *pl.* **-baos.** (in the Philippine Islands) the water buffalo. [t. Philippine Sp., t. Malay: m. *karbau*]

car·a·bin (kär'ə bĭn), *n.* carbine. Also, **car·a·bine** (kär'ə bin').

car·a·bi·neer (kär'ə bə nĭr'), *n.* a carbineer. Also, **car·a·bi·nier'.**

Car·a·cal·la (kär'ə kăl'ə), *n.* (*Marcus Aurelius Antoninus Bassianus*), A.D. 188–217, Roman emperor, A.D. 211–217.

ca·ra·ca·ra (kär'ə kär'ə), *n.* any of certain vulturelike birds of the subfamily *Polyborinae* of the warmer parts of America, as **Audubon's caracara** (*Polyborus cheriway*). [t. Sp., Pg., t. Tupi; imit. of its cry]

Ca·ra·cas (kə rä'kəs; *Sp.* kä rä'käs), *n.* the capital of Venezuela, in the N part. 611,048 (est. 1953).

car·a·col (kär'ə kŏl'), *n.*, *v.i.* **-colled, -colling.** caracole.

car·a·cole (kär'ə kōl'), *n.*, *v.* **-coled, -coling.** —*n.* **1.** a half turn executed by a horseman in riding. —*v.i.* **2.** to execute caracoles; wheel. [t. F, t. Sp.: m. *caracol* snail, wheeling movement, ult. der. L *scarabaeus* scarab]

Ca·rac·ta·cus (kə răk'tə kəs), *n.* fl. A.D. c50, English chieftain who opposed the Romans. Also, **Ca·rad·oc** (kə răd'ək).

car·a·cul (kär'ə kəl), *n.* **1.** the skin of the very young of certain Asiatic or Russian sheep, karakul, dressed as a fur, resembling astrakhan, but with flatter, looser curl. **2.** karakul (sheep). Also, **karakul.**

ca·rafe (kə răf', -räf'), *n.* a glass water bottle. [t. F, t. It.: m. *caraffa,* prob. t. Sp.: m. *garrafa,* t. Ar.: m. *gharrâf* drinking vessel]

car·a·mel (kär'ə məl, -mĕl'; *Midwest often* kär'məl), *n.* **1.** burnt sugar, used for coloring and flavoring food, etc. **2.** a kind of candy, commonly in small blocks, made from sugar, butter, milk, etc. [t. F, t. Sp.]

car·a·mel·ize (kär'ə mə līz'), *v.t., v.i.,* **-ized, -izing.** to convert or be converted into caramel.

ca·ran·goid (kə răng'goid), *adj.* **1.** belonging to or resembling the *Carangidae,* a family of spiny-rayed fishes including the cavally, pompano, pilot fish, etc. —*n.* **2.** a carangoid fish. [f. s. NL *Caranx,* the typical genus (cf. Sp. *carangue* a West Indian flatfish) + -OID]

car·a·pace (kär'ə pās'), *n.* a shield, test, or shell covering some or all of the dorsal part of an animal. [t. F, t. Sp.: m. *carapacho*]

car·at (kär'ət), *n.* **1.** a unit of weight in gem stones, 200 mg. (about 3 grains of troy or avoirdupois weight). **2.** karat. [t. F, t. It.: m. *carato,* t. Ar.: m. *qīrāt* light weight, t. Gk.: m. *kerátion* carob bean, carat, dim. of *kéras* horn]

car·a·van (kär'ə văn'), *n.* **1.** a group of merchants or others traveling together, as for safety, esp. over deserts, etc., in Asia or Africa. **2.** a large covered vehicle for passengers or goods. **3.** a van. **4.** *Brit.* a house on wheels; a trailer. [t. F: m. *caravane,* t. Pers.: m. *kārwān*]

car·a·van·sa·ry (kär'ə văn'sə rĭ), *n.*, *pl.* **-ries.** **1.** (in the Near East) a kind of inn for the accommodation of caravans. **2.** any large inn or hotel. Also, **car·a·van·se·rai** (kär'ə văn'sə rī', -rā'). [ult. t. Pers.: m. *kārwān-sarāī,* f. *kārwān* caravan + *sarāī* inn]

car·a·vel (kär'ə vĕl'), *n.* a kind of small ship formerly used esp. by the Spaniards and Portuguese. Also, **carvel.** [t. F: m. *caravelle,* t. It.: m. *caravella.* Cf. LL *carabus,* Gk. *kárabos* kind of light ship]

car·a·way (kär'ə wā'), *n.* **1.** an umbelliferous condimental herb, *Carum Carvi,* bearing aromatic seedlike fruit (**caraway seeds**) used in cookery and medicine. **2.** the fruit or seeds. [late ME, t. ML: m. *carui,* t. Ar.: m. *karawyā.* Cf. L *careum,* Gk. *káron*]

carb-, var. of **carbo-** before vowels, as in *carbazole.*

car·bam·ic acid (kär băm'ĭk), a hypothetical compound, NH₂COOH, known only in the form of its salts and esters. [f. CARB- + AM(IDE) + -IC]

car·ba·zole (kär'bə zōl'), *n.* a weakly acidic, crystalline compound, C₁₂H₉N, found with anthracene in coal tar. Many dyes are derived from it. [f. CARB- + AZ- + -OLE]

car·bide (kär'bīd, -bĭd), *n.* *Chem.* a compound of carbon with a more electropositive element or radical. [f. CARB- + -IDE]

car·bine (kär'bīn, -bēn), *n.* a short rifle (or, formerly, musket) carried by combat soldiers and noncommissioned soldiers who are not equipped with rifles. Also, **carabin, carabine.** [t. F: m. *carabine,* orig. a small harquebus, der. *carabin* a mounted soldier armed with this weapon, prob. alter. of ONF *escarrabin* corpsebearer, ult. der. L *scarabaeus* SCARAB]

car·bi·neer (kär'bə nĭr'), *n.* (formerly) a soldier armed with a carbine. Also, **carabineer, carabinier.**

car·bi·nol (kär'bə nōl'), *n.* **1.** methyl alcohol. **2.** an alcohol derived from it. [f. m. CARBON + -OL¹]

carbo-, a word element meaning "carbon," as in *carborundum.* Also, **carb-.** [comb. form of CARBON]

car·bo·cy·clic compounds (kär'bō sī'klĭk, -sĭk'lĭk), *Chem.* a group of organic compounds in which all the atoms composing the ring are carbon atoms, as naphthalene.

car·bo·hy·drate (kär'bō hī'drāt), *n.* any of a class of organic compounds which are polyhydroxy aldehydes or polyhydroxy ketones, or change to such substances on simple chemical transformations, such as hydrolysis, oxidation, or reduction. They form the supporting tissues of plants and are important food for animals.

car·bo·lat·ed (kär'bə lā'tĭd), *adj.* containing carbolic acid.

car·bol·ic acid (kär bŏl'ĭk), phenol (def. 1). [f. CARB- + -OL² + -IC]

car·bo·lize (kär'bə līz'), *v.t.,* **-lized, -lizing.** to treat with carbolic acid.

car·bon (kär'bən), *n.* **1.** *Chem.* a widely distributed element which forms organic compounds in combination with hydrogen, oxygen, etc., and which occurs in a pure state as the diamond and as graphite, and in an impure state as charcoal. Symbol: C; *at. wt.:* 12.010; *at. no.:* 6; *sp. gr.:* (of diamond) 3.51 at 20°C.; (cf graphite) 2.26 at 20° C. **2.** *Elect.* **a.** the carbon rod through which current is conducted between the electrode holder and the arc in carbon arc lighting or welding. **b.** the rod or plate, composed in part of carbon, used in batteries. **3.** a sheet of carbon paper. **4.** a duplicate copy made by using carbon paper: *a carbon of a letter.* [t. F: m. *carbone,* t. L: m.s. *carbo* coal, charcoal]

carbon 14, *Chem.* radiocarbon. Also, **carbon-14.**

car·bo·na·ceous (kär'bə nā'shəs), *adj.* of, like, or containing carbon.

car·bo·na·do (kär'bə nā'dō), *n., pl.* **-does, -dos,** *v.,* **-doed, -doing.** —*n.* **1.** a piece of meat, fish, etc., scored and broiled. **2.** an opaque, dark-colored, massive form of diamond, found chiefly in Brazil, and used for drills; black diamond. —*v.t.* **3.** to score and broil. **4.** to slash; hack. [t. Sp.: m. *carbonada,* der. *carbón,* g. L *carbo* coal]

Car·bo·na·ri (kär'bō nä'rē), *n.pl., sing.* **-ro** (-rō) the members of a 19th century secret political society, of revolutionary aims, in Italy, France, and Spain. [It., pl. of *carbonaro* charcoal burner] —**Car'bo·na'rism,** *n.*

car·bon·a·ta·tion (kär'bən ə tā'shən), *n.* *Chem.* saturation or reaction with carbon dioxide.

car·bon·ate (*n.* kär'bə nāt', -nĭt; *v.* kär'bə nāt'), *n., v.,* **-ated, -ating.** —*n.* **1.** *Chem.* a salt of carbonic acid, as *calcium carbonate,* CaCO₃. —*v.t.* **2.** to form into a carbonate. **3.** to charge or impregnate with carbon dioxide. [t. NL: m. *carbonātum* (something) carbonated]

car·bon·a·tion (kär'bə nā'shən), *n.* **1.** saturation with carbon dioxide, as in making soda water. **2.** reaction with carbon dioxide to remove lime, as in sugar refining. **3.** carbonization.

carbon cycle, *Astrophysics.* a cycle of nuclear transformations, with the release of atomic energy, in the interiors of the stars, by means of which hydrogen is gradually converted into helium.

carbon dioxide, a colorless, odorless, incombustible gas, CO₂, used extensively in industry as dry ice, in carbonated beverages, fire extinguishers, etc. It is present in the atmosphere and formed during respiration.

carbon dioxide snow, *Chem.* carbon dioxide, CO₂, solidified under great pressure; dry ice. It is used as a refrigerant because it passes directly from a solid to a gas, absorbing a great amount of heat.

car·bon·ic (kär bŏn'ĭk), *adj.* *Chem.* containing tetravalent carbon, as *carbonic acid,* H₂CO₃.

carbonic acid, the acid, H₂CO₃, formed when carbon dioxide dissolves in water, known in the form of its salts and esters, the carbonates.

carbonic acid gas, carbon dioxide.

Car·bon·if·er·ous (kär'bə nĭf'ər əs), *Stratig.* —*adj.* **1.** pertaining to a geological period or a system of rocks preceding the Permian and corresponding to combined Mississippian and Pennsylvanian of North American usage. **2.** (*l.c.*) producing coal. —*n.* **3.** a late Paleozoic period or system next following the Devonian. [f. CARBON + -(I)FEROUS]

car·bon·i·za·tion (kär'bən ə zā'shən), *n.* **1.** formation of carbon from organic matter. **2.** coal distillation, as in coke ovens.

car·bon·ize (kär'bə nīz'), *v.t.,* **-ized, -izing.** **1.** to char, forming carbon. **2.** to coat or enrich with carbon.

carbon monoxide, a colorless, odorless, poisonous gas, CO, burning with a pale-blue flame, formed when carbon burns with an insufficient supply of air.

carbon paper, 1. paper faced with a preparation of carbon or other material, used between two sheets of plain paper in order to reproduce upon the lower sheet that which is written or typed on the upper. **2.** a paper for making photographs by the carbon process.

carbon process, a method of making photographic prints by the use of a pigment, such as carbon, contained in sensitized gelatin.

carbon tetrachloride, a noninflammable, colorless liquid, CCl₄, used in medicine, and as a fire extinguisher, cleaning fluid, solvent, etc.

car·bon·yl (kär′bən Yl), *n.* *Chem.* **1.** the divalent radical >CO occurring in acids, ketones, aldehydes, and their derivatives. **2.** a compound containing metal combined with carbon monoxide, as *nickel carbonyl*, Ni(CO)₄. [f. CARBON + -YL] —**car′bon·yl′ic**, *adj.*

car·bo·run·dum (kär′bə rŭn′dəm), *n.* **1.** silicon carbide, SiC, an important abrasive produced in the electric furnace. **2.** (*cap.*) a trademark for this substance. [f. CARBO-+ (CO)RUNDUM]

car·box·yl group (kär bŏk′sYl), *Chem.* a univalent radical, COOH, present in and characteristic of the formulas of all organic acids. Also, **carboxyl radical.** [f. CARB- + OX(YGEN) + -YL]

car·boy (kär′boi), *n.* a large glass bottle, esp. one protected by basketwork or a wooden box, as for containing acids. [t. Pers.: m. *qarābah* large flagon]

car·bun·cle (kär′bŭng kəl), *n.* **1.** a painful circumscribed inflammation of the subcutaneous tissue, resulting in suppuration and sloughing, and having a tendency to spread (somewhat like a boil, but more serious in its effects). **2.** a garnet cut in a convex rounded form without facets. **3.** (formerly) a rounded red gem, as a ruby or garnet. **4.** deep red. **5.** brownish red. [ME, t. ONF, g. L *carbunculus*, dim. of *carbo* (live) coal] —**car′bun·cled**, *adj.* —**car·bun·cu·lar** (kär bŭng′kyə lər), *adj.*

car·bu·ret (kär′bə rāt′, -byə rĕt′), *v.t.*, -reted, -reting or (*esp. Brit.*) -retted, -retting. to combine or mix with carbon or hydrocarbons. [f. CARB- + -URET]

car·bu·re·tion (kär′bə rā′shən, kär′byə rĕsh′ən), *n.* (of internal-combustion engines) the process of metering air and fuel to an engine intake system in the proper proportions for combustion.

car·bu·re·tor (kär′bə rā′tər, -byə rĕt′ər), *n.* an apparatus for adding hydrocarbons to nonluminous or poor gases, or to air for the purpose of producing an illuminating or explosive gas. Also, *esp. Brit.*, **car·bu·ret·tor** (kär′byə rĕt′ər).

car·bu·rize (kär′bə rīz′, -byə-), *v.t.*, -rized, -rizing. **1.** to cause to unite with carbon. **2.** to carburet. —**car′bu·ri·za′tion**, *n.* —**car′bu·riz′er**, *n.*

car·byl·a·mine (kär′bYl ə mēn′, -ăm′Yn), *n.* an organic compound containing the group -NC.

car·ca·jou (kär′kə jōō′, -zhōō′), *n.* the American glutton, *Gulo luscus*; wolverine. [t. Canadian F, t. Amer. Ind. (Algonquian); cf. Montagnais *karkaju*, Ojibwa *gwingwaage*, Cree *kikkwahakes*]

car·ca·net (kär′kə nĕt′, -nYt), *n.* **1.** *Archaic.* an ornamental collar or necklace. **2.** *Obs.* or *Hist.* an ornamental band for the head. [F *carcan* (of Gmc. orig.) + -ET]

car·cass (kär′kəs), *n.* **1.** the dead body of an animal or (now only in contempt) of a human being. **2.** (now chiefly in contempt or humor) a living body. **3.** the body of a slaughtered animal after removal of the offal, etc. **4.** anything from which life and power are gone. **5.** an unfinished framework or skeleton, as of a house or ship. Also, **car′case**, [t. F: m. *carcasse*, t. It.: m. *carcassa*; r. ME *carkeis*, t. AF] —**Syn. 1.** See **body.**

Car·cas·sonne (kár kä sôn′), *n.* a city in S France. 37,035 (1954).

car·cin·o·gen (kär′sYn′ə jən), *n.* *Pathol.* any substance which tends to produce a cancer in a body.

car·ci·no·ma (kär′sə nō′mə), *n.*, *pl.* **-mata** (-mə tə), **-mas.** *Pathol.* a malignant and invasive epithelial tumor that spreads by metastasis and often recurs after excision; a cancer. [t. L, t. Gk.: m. *karkínōma* a cancer]

car·ci·no·ma·to·sis (kär′sə nō mə tō′sYs), *n.* *Pathol.* a condition marked by the production of an overwhelming number of carcinomata throughout the body. —**car·ci·nom·a·tous** (kär′sə nŏm′ə təs, -nō′mə-), *adj.*

card¹ (kärd), *n.* **1.** a piece of stiff paper or thin pasteboard, usually rectangular, for various uses: *a postal card, a union card* (showing membership in a trade union). **2.** one of a set of small cardboards with spots, figures, etc., used in playing various games. **3.** (*pl.*) a game or games played with such a set. **4.** a piece of cardboard with more or less elaborate ornamentation, bearing complimentary greeting: *a Christmas card*. **5.** a program of the events at races, etc. **6.** the circular piece of paper, etc., on which the 32 points indicating direction are marked in a compass. **7.** *Colloq.* a person of some indicated characteristic: *a queer card*. **8.** *Colloq.* an amusing or facetious person. —*v.t.* **9.** to provide with a card. **10.** to fasten on a card. **11.** to write, list, etc., on cards. [ME, t. F: m. *carte*, t. L: m. *charta* (see CHART)]

card² (kärd), *n.* **1.** an implement used in disentangling and combing out fibers of wool, flax, etc., preparatory to spinning. **2.** a similar implement for raising the nap on cloth. —*v.t.* **3.** to dress (wool, etc.) with a card. [late ME *carde*, t. MD: m. *caerde*, ult. t. LL: m. *cardus*, L. *carduus* thistle] —**card′er**, *n.*

Card., Cardinal.

car·da·mom (kär′də məm), *n.* **1.** the aromatic seed capsule of various zingiberaceous plants of the genera *Amomum* and *Elettaria*, native in tropical Asia, used as a spice or condiment and in medicine. **2.** any of the plants. Also, **car·da·mon** (kär′də mən), **car′da·mum.** [t. L: s. *cardamōmum*, t. Gk.: m. *kardámōmon*]

card·board (kärd′bôrd′), *n.* a thin, stiff pasteboard, used for signs, boxes, etc.

card case, a small pocket case for visiting cards, etc.

card catalogue, a definite arrangement of cards of uniform size (**catalogue cards**) in drawers, each card usually identifying a single publication in a library.

Cár·de·nas (kär′də näs′), *n.* **1.** **Lázaro** (lä′sä rô′), born 1895, president of Mexico, 1934–40. **2.** a seaport in N W Cuba. 37,059 (1953).

cardi-, var. of cardio- before vowels, as in *cardialgia*.

car·di·ac (kär′dY ăk′), *adj.* **1.** pertaining to the heart. **2.** pertaining to the esophageal portion of the stomach. —*n.* **3.** *Med.* a cardiac remedy. [t. L: s. *cardiacus* of the heart, t. Gk.: m. *kardiakós*]

cardiac glucoside, *Pharm.* one of a group of drugs used to stimulate the heart in cases of heart failure, obtained from a number of plants, as the foxglove, squill, or yellow oleander.

car·di·al·gi·a (kär′dY ăl′jY ə), *n.* *Pathol.* heartburn (def. 1). [f. CARDI- + -ALGIA]

Car·diff (kär′dYf), *n.* a seaport in SE Wales. 249,800 (est. 1956).

car·di·gan (kär′də gən), *n.* a close-fitting knitted woolen jacket. Also, **cardigan jacket, cardigan sweater.** [named after seventh Earl of Cardigan (1797–1868)]

Car·di·gan (kär′də gən), *n.* **1.** a variety of the Welsh Corgi breed of dogs. See **Welsh Corgi. 2.** Cardiganshire.

Car·di·gan·shire (kär′dY gan shYr′, -shər), *n.* a county in W Wales. 53,278 pop. (1951); 692 sq. mi. *Co. seat:* Cardigan. Also, **Cardigan.**

car·di·nal (kär′də nəl), *adj.* **1.** of prime importance; chief; principal; fundamental: *of cardinal significance*. **2.** deep rich red. —*n.* **3.** one of the seventy members of the Sacred College of the Roman Catholic Church, ranking next to the Pope. **4.** Also, **cardinal bird, cardinal grosbeak.** a crested North American finch, *Richmondina cardinalis*. The male is brilliant red, the female brown, and both sexes sing. **5.** any of various similar birds. **6.** a deep rich red color. **7.** a cardinal number. [ME, t. L: s. *cardinālis* pertaining to a hinge, chief] —**car′di·nal·ly**, *adv.* —**car′di·nal·ship′**, *n.*

car·di·nal·ate (kär′də nə lāt′), *n.* *Rom. Cath. Ch.* **1.** the body of cardinals. **2.** the office, rank, dignity, or incumbency of a cardinal.

cardinal flower, a North American plant, *Lobelia cardinalis*, with showy red flowers.

cardinal number, any of the numbers *one, two, three*, etc. (in distinction from *first, second, third*, etc. which are *ordinal numbers*). Also, **cardinal numeral.**

cardinal points, the four chief directions of the compass; the north, south, east, and west points.

cardinal sins. See **deadly sins.**

cardinal virtues, 1. the most important elements of good character. **2.** *Ancient Philos.* justice, prudence, temperance, and fortitude.

card·ing (kär′dYng), *n.* the process of preparing fibers as wool, cotton, etc. for spinning.

cardio-, a word element meaning "heart." Also, **cardi-.** [t. Gk.: m. *kardio-*, comb. form of *kardía*]

car·di·o·gram (kär′dY ə grăm′), *n.* an electrocardiogram.

car·di·o·graph (kär′dY ə grăf′, -gräf′), *n.* an electrocardiograph. [f. CARDIO- + GRAPH] —**car′di·o·graph′ic**, *adj.* —**car·di·og·ra·phy** (kär′dY ŏg′rə fY), *n.*

car·di·oid (kär′dY oid′), *n.* *Math.* a somewhat heart-shaped curve, being the path of a point on a circle which rolls externally, without slipping on another equal circle. [t. Gk.: m.s. *kardioeidḗs* heart-shaped. See CARDIO-,-OID]

car·di·ol·o·gy (kär′dY ŏl′ə jY), *n.* the study of the heart and its functions.

Cardioid

car·di·tis (kär dī′tYs), *n.* *Pathol.* inflammation of the pericardium, myocardium, or endocardium, separately or in combination. [f. CARD(IO)- + -ITIS]

car·doon (kär dōōn′), *n.* a perennial edible plant, *Cynara Cardunculus*, native in Mediterranean regions, related to the artichoke. [t. F: m. *cardon*, t. Pr., der. L *carduus* thistle]

Car·do·zo (kär dō′zə), *n.* **Benjamin Nathan,** 1870–1938, associate justice, U. S. Supreme Court, 1932–38.

card·sharp (kärd′shärp′), *n.* a person, esp. a professional gambler, who cheats at card games. Also, **card′sharp′er.** —**card′sharp′ing**, *n.*

car·du·a·ceous (kär′jōō ā′shəs), *adj.* *Bot.* belonging to the family Carduaceae, regarded as part of the *Compositae* by most botanists, and including goldenrods, asters, boltonias, fleabanes, and many other genera throughout the world. [f. s. NL *Carduāceae* (der. L *carduus* thistle)+ -OUS]

Car·duc·ci (kär dōōt′chē), *n.* **Giosuè** (jô swě′), 1835–1907, Italian poet.

care (kâr), *n.*, *v.*, **cared, caring.** —*n.* **1.** worry; anxiety; concern: *care had aged him.* **2.** a cause of worry, anxiety, distress, etc.: *to be free from care.* **3.** serious attention; solicitude; heed; caution: *devote great care to work.* **4.** protection; charge: *under the care of a doctor.* **5.** an object of concern or attention. **6.** *Obs.* grief;

mental distress. —*v.i.* **7.** to be concerned or solicitous: have thought or regard. **8.** to be unconcerned or to have no special preference (with a negative): *I don't care if I do.* **9.** to make provision or look out (fol. by *for*): *I'll care for his education.* **10.** to have an inclination, liking, fondness, or affection (fol. by *for*). **11.** to be inclined (fol. by *to*): *I don't care to do it today.* [ME; OE *caru* (*cearu*), c. Goth. *kara*]
—Syn. **1.** See **concern. 3.** To take CARE, PAINS, TROUBLE (to do something) implies watchful, conscientious effort to do something exactly right. To take CARE implies the performance of one particular detail: *she took care to close the cover before striking the match.* To take PAINS suggests a sustained carefulness, an effort to see that nothing is overlooked but that every small detail receives attention: *to take pains with fine embroidery.* To take TROUBLE implies an effort which requires a considerable amount of activity and exertion: *to take the trouble to prepare suitable arrangements.*

ca·reen (kərēn′), *v.t.* **1.** to cause (a ship) to lie wholly or partly on its side, as for repairing or the like. **2.** to clean or repair (a ship in such a position). **3.** to cause (a ship) to heel over. —*v.i.* **4.** to lean, sway, or tip to one side, as a ship. **5.** to careen a ship. —*n.* **6.** a careening. **7.** the position of a careened ship. [t. F: m. *carine*, t. L: m. *carīna* keel] —**ca·reen′er,** *n.*

ca·reer (kərĭr′), *n.* **1.** general course of action or progress of a person through life, as in some profession, in some moral or intellectual action, etc. **2.** an occupation, profession, etc. followed as one's lifework: *a career in law.* **3.** success in a profession, occupation, etc. **4.** a course, esp. a swift one. **5.** speed; full speed. **6.** *Obs.* a charge at full speed. —*v.i.* **7.** to run or move rapidly along. [t. F: m. *carrière,* t. It.: m. *carriera,* der. *carro,* g. L *carrus.* See CAR] —**ca·reer′ist,** *n.*

care·free (kâr′frē′), *adj.* without anxiety or worry.
care·ful (kâr′fəl), *adj.* **1.** cautious in one's actions. **2.** taking pains in one's work; exact; thorough. **3.** (of things) done or performed with accuracy or caution. **4.** solicitously mindful (fol. by *of, about, in*): *careful of the rights of others, about your person, in speech.* **5.** *Archaic.* troubled. **6.** *Archaic.* attended with anxiety. —**care′ful·ly,** *adv.* —**care′ful·ness,** *n.*
—Syn. **1.** watchful, guarded, chary, circumspect. CAREFUL, CAUTIOUS, DISCREET, WARY imply a watchful guarding against something CAREFUL implies guarding against mistakes, by paying strict and close attention to details, and, often, trying to use good judgment: *he was careful to distinguish between them* CAUTIOUS implies a fear of some unfavorable situation, and investigation before coming to conclusions: *cautious about investments.* DISCREET implies being prudent in speech and action, and being trustworthy as a confidant: *discreet in manner, in keeping secrets.* WARY implies a vigilant lookout for a danger suspected or feared: *wary of polite strangers.* **2.** painstaking, meticulous. **4.** solicitous, attentive, heedful, regardful.

care·less (kâr′lĭs), *adj.* **1.** not paying enough attention to what one does. **2.** not exact or thorough: *careless work.* **3.** done or said heedlessly or negligently; unconsidered: *a careless remark.* **4.** not caring or troubling; having no care or concern; unconcerned (fol. by *of, about, in*): *careless of his health, about his person, in speech.* **5.** artless. **6.** *Archaic.* free from anxiety. —**care′less·ly,** *adv.* —**care′less·ness,** *n.* —Syn. **1.** incautious, unwary, indiscreet, reckless. **2.** inaccurate, negligent.

ca·ress (kərĕs′), *n.* **1.** an act or gesture expressing affection, as an embrace, pat, kiss, etc. —*v.t.* **2.** to touch or pat gently to show affection. **3.** to touch, etc., as if in affection. **4.** to treat with favor, kindness, etc. [t. F: m. *caresse,* t. It.: m. *carezza,* der. L *cārus* dear] —**ca·ress′er,** *n.* —**ca·ress′ing·ly,** *adv.*

car·et (kăr′ət), *n.* a mark (∧) made in written or printed matter to show the place where something is to be inserted. [t. L: there is lacking]

care·tak·er (kâr′tā′kər), *n.* a person who takes care of a thing, place, or person.

Ca·rew (kərōō′; *sometimes* kâr′ōō), *n.* **Thomas,** c1595–c1645, British poet.

care·worn (kâr′wôrn′), *adj.* showing signs of care; tired and troubled with worries: *a careworn mother.*

car·fare (kär′fâr′), *n.* the amount charged for a ride on a streetcar, bus, etc.

car·go (kär′gō), *n., pl.* **-goes, -gos. 1.** the lading or freight of a ship. **2.** load. [t. Sp., der. *cargar* load] —Syn. **1.** See **freight.**

Car·ib (kăr′ĭb), *n.* **1.** a member of an Indian people of NE South America, formerly dominant through the Lesser Antilles. **2.** an extensive linguistic stock of the West Indies and of NE South America. [t. Sp.: m. *Caribe.* See CANNIBAL] —**Car′ib·an,** *adj.*

Car·ib·be·an (kăr′ə bē′ən, kə rĭb′ē-), *adj.* **1.** pertaining to the Caribs, the Lesser Antilles, or the Caribbean Sea. —*n.* **2.** a Carib. **3.** Also, **Caribbe·an Sea.** a sea between Central America, the West Indies, and South America. ab. 750,000 sq. mi.; greatest known depth, 22,788 ft.

car·i·bou (kăr′əbōō′), *n., pl.* **-bous** (*esp. collectively*) **bou.** any of several North American species or varieties of reindeer, esp. *Rangifer caribou* (and *R. tarandus*). See illus. in next col. [t. Canadian F, t. Algonquian (Micmac): m. *xalibu* pawer, scratcher]

car·i·ca·ture (kăr′Ykə chər, -chōōr′), *n., v.,* **-tured, -turing.** —*n.* **1.** a picture, description, etc., ludicrously exaggerating the peculiarities or defects of persons or things. **2.** the art or process of making such pictures, etc. **3.** any imitation or copy so inferior as to be ludicrous. —*v.t.* **4.** to make a caricature of; represent in caricature. [t. F, t. It.: m. *caricatura,* der. *caricare* (over)load, exaggerate. See CHARGE, v.] —**car′i·ca·tur·ist,** *n.*

car·ies (kâr′ēz, -Yēz′), *n.* decay, as of bone or teeth, or of plant tissue. [t. L]

car·il·lon (kăr′əlŏn′, -lən, kərĭl′yən), *n., v.,* **-lonned, -lonning.** —*n.* **1.** a set of stationary bells hung in a tower and sounded by manual or pedal action, or by machinery. **2.** a melody played on such bells. **3.** an organ stop which imitates the peal of bells. **4.** a set of horizontal metal plates, struck by hammers, used in the modern orchestra. —*v.i.* **5.** to play a carillon. [t. F: chime of (orig. four) bells, alter. of OF *carignon,* ult. der. L *quattuor* four]

Caribou.
Rangifer caribou
(Total length 6 ft., ab. 4 ft. high at the shoulder)

car·il·lon·neur (kăr′ələnûr′; *Fr.* kȧrēyô nœr′), *n.* one who plays a carillon. [F]

ca·ri·na (kərī′nə), *n., pl.* **-nae** (-nē). *Bot., Zool.* a keel-like part or ridge. [t. L: keel] —**ca·ri′nal,** *adj.*

Ca·ri·na (kərī′nə), *n., gen.* **-nae** (-nē). *Astron.* a southern constellation, containing the bright star, Canopus: one of the subordinate constellations into which Argo is divided.

car·i·nate (kăr′ə nāt′), *adj. Bot., Zool.* formed with a carina; keellike. Also, **car′i·nat′ed.** [t. L: m. s. *carīnātus,* pp., keel-shaped]

Ca·rin·thi·a (kərĭn′thЎə), *n.* a province in S Austria. 479,353 pop. (est. 1953); 3681 sq. mi. *Cap.:* Klagenfurt.

Car·i·o·ca (kăr′Yō′kə; *Port.* kä′rēô′kə), *n.* a native of Rio de Janeiro.

car·i·ole (kăr′Yōl′), *n.* **1.** a small, open, two-wheeled vehicle. **2.** a covered cart. Also, **carriole.** [t. F: m. *carriole,* t. It.: m. *carriuola,* ult. der. L *carrus.* Cf. CARRYALL]

car·i·ous (kâr′Yəs), *adj.* having caries, as teeth; decayed. [t. L: m. s. *cariōsus*] —**car·i·os·i·ty** (kăr′Yŏs′ətY), **car·i·ous·ness,** *n.*

cark·ing (kär′kYng), *adj.* anxious; troubled.

carl (kärl), *n.* **1.** *Scot.* a robust fellow. **2.** *Archaic.* a churl. **3.** *Archaic.* a farmer. **4.** *Obs.* a bondman. Also, **carle.** [ME and OE, t. Scand.; cf. Icel. *karl* man, c. *Charles* proper name. Cf. CHURL]

car·line (kär′lYn, kér′-), *n.* *Chiefly Scot.* **1.** an old woman. **2.** a hag; witch. [northern ME *kerling,* t. Scand.; cf. Icel. *kerling* old woman. See CARL]

car·ling (kär′lYng), *n.* one of the fore-and-aft timbers in a ship which form part of the deck framework.

Car·lisle (kär līl′), *n.* a city in NW England, in Cumberland county. 68,450 (est. 1956).

Car·list (kär′lYst), *n.* **1.** a supporter of the claims of Don Carlos of Spain, or of his successors, to the Spanish throne. **2.** a partizan of Charles X of France, and of the elder branch of the Bourbons. —**Car′lism,** *n.*

car·load (kär′lōd′), *n.* *Chiefly U.S.* **1.** the amount carried by a car, esp. a freight car. **2.** the legal minimum weight entitling a shipper to a rate (**carload rate**) lower than that charged for less than this weight.

carload lot, *U.S.* a standard carload shipment of freight which measures up to the legal minimum amount.

Car·los (kär′ləs; *Sp.* -lôs), *n.* **Don** (dŏn, *Sp.* dôn), (*Count of Molina*) 1788–1855, a Spanish prince and pretender (second son of Charles IV).

Car·lo·ta (kär lō′tä), 1840–1927, wife of Maximilian, Archduke of Austria: Empress of Mexico, 1864–67.

Car·lo·vin·gi·an (kär′lə vYn′jĭ′ən), *adj.* Carolingian.

Carls·bad (kärlz′băd; *Ger.* kärls′bät), *n.* a city in W Czechoslovakia: mineral springs; Carlsbad decrees, 1819. 30,915 (1947). German, **Karlsbad.** Czech, **Karlovy Vary.**

Carlsbad Caverns, a series of enormous limestone caverns in SE New Mexico.

Carl·son (kärl′sən), *n.* **1. Anton Julius** (ăn′tŏn), 1875–1956, U.S. physiologist, born in Sweden. **2. Evans Fordyce** (fôr′dīs), 1896–1947, U.S. Marine Corps general in World War II.

Car·lyle (kär līl′), *n.* **Thomas,** 1795–1881, Scottish essayist and historian.

car·ma·gnole (kär′mən yōl′; *Fr.* kȧr mȧ nyôl′), *n.* a dance and song popular during the French Revolution. [t. F, ? from *Carmagnola,* town in NW Italy]

car·man (kär′mən), *n., pl.* **-men. 1.** one of the crew of a streetcar or the like. **2.** one who drives a car or cart.

Car·man (kär′mən), *n.* **(William) Bliss,** 1861–1929, Canadian poet who spent most of his life in the U.S.

Car·ma·ni·a (kär mā′nĭ ə), *n.* a province of the ancient Persian Empire, on the Gulf of Oman.

Car·mar·then·shire (kär mär′ŦЎen shĭr′, -shər), *n.* a county in S Wales. 172,034 pop. (1951); 919 sq. mi. *Co. seat.:* Carmarthen. Also, **Car′mar′then.**

Car·mel (kär′məl), *n.* **Mount,** a ridge in NW Israel, near the Mediterranean coast. ab. 14 mi. long; highest point, ab. 1800 ft.

---
b., blend of, blended; c., cognate with; d., dialect, dialectal; der., derived from; f., formed from; g., going back to; m., modification of; r., replacing; s., stem of; t., taken from; ?, perhaps. See the full key on inside cover.

Car·mel·ite (kär'məlīt'), n. 1. a mendicant friar belonging to a religious order founded at Mt. Carmel, Palestine, in the 12th century; a white friar. 2. a nun belonging to this order. [t. LL: m. *Carmelītes*, t. Gk.: m. *Karmelítēs* inhabitant of Mt. Carmel]

car·min·a·tive (kär'mĭn'ə tĭv, kär'mə nā'tĭv), n. 1. a drug causing expulsion of gas from the stomach or bowel. —adj. 2. expelling gas from the body; relieving flatulence. [f. s. L *carminātus*, pp., carded + -IVE]

car·mine (kär'mĭn, -mīn), n. 1. a crimson or purplish-red color. 2. a crimson pigment obtained from cochineal. —adj. 3. crimson or purplish-red. [t. ML: m.s. *carmīnus*, contr. of *carmesīnus*, der. Sp. *carmesí* CRIMSON]

car·nage (kär'nĭj), n. 1. the slaughter of a great number, as in battle; butchery; massacre. 2. *Archaic*. dead bodies, as of men slain in battle. [t. F, t. It: m. *carnaggio*, der. *carne* meat, g. s. L *caro* flesh]

car·nal (kär'nəl), adj. 1. not spiritual; merely human; temporal; worldly. 2. pertaining to the flesh or the body, its passions and appetites; sensual. 3. sexual. [ME, t. L: s. *carnālis*, der. L *caro* flesh] —**car·nal'i·ty**, n. —**car'nal·ly**, adv. —Syn. 2. fleshly, bodily, animal. 3. lustful, impure, gross, worldly.

car·nall·ite (kär'nəlīt'), n. a mineral, a hydrous potassium magnesium chloride, KMgCl₃.6H₂O: a valuable source of potassium. [named after R. von *Carnall* (1804–1874), Prussian mining official. See -ITE¹]

Car·nar·von (kär när'vən), n. Caernarvonshire.

car·nas·si·al (kär näs'ī əl), *Zool.* —adj. 1. (of teeth) adapted for shearing flesh, as certain of the upper and lower cheek teeth of cats, civets, dogs, etc. —n. 2. a carnassial tooth, esp. the last upper premolar or the first lower molar tooth of certain carnivores. [f. m. F *carnassier* flesh-eating (t. Pr.: m. *carnasier*, der. L *caro* flesh) + -AL¹]

Car·nat·ic (kär năt'ĭk), n. a historically important region on the SE coast of India: now in Madras province.

car·na·tion (kär nā'shən), n. 1. any of numerous cultivated varieties of clove pink, *Dianthus Caryophyllus*, with fragrant flowers of various colors: the State flower of Ohio. 2. pink; light red. 3. the colors of flesh as represented in painting. [t. L: s. *carnatio* fleshiness, NL representation of flesh in painting]

car·nau·ba (kär nou'bə), n. 1. the Brazilian wax palm, *Copernicia cerifera*. 2. a yellowish or greenish wax derived from the young leaves of this tree, used as a polish, and in phonograph records. [t. Brazilian Pg.]

Car·ne·gie (kär nā'gĭ), n. Andrew, 1835–1919, U. S. steel manufacturer and philanthropist, born in Scotland.

car·nel·ian (kär nĕl'yən), n. a red or reddish variety of chalcedony, used in jewelry, etc. Also, **cornelian**. [alter. (due to assoc. with L *caro* flesh) of ME *corneline*, t. OF, of uncert. orig. Cf. ML *cornelius*]

car·ni·fy (kär'nə fī'), v.i., v.t., -fied, -fying. to turn into or form flesh; make or become fleshlike. [t. L: m. *carnificāre*. See -FY]

Car·ni·o·la (kär'nĭ ō'lä), n. a former duchy and crown land of Austria: now in NW Yugoslavia.

car·ni·val (kär'nə vəl), n. 1. an amusement show, usually traveling from place to place, having side shows, a Ferris wheel, merry-go-rounds, etc. 2. any merrymaking, usually noisy and riotous; revelry. 3. the season immediately preceding Lent, often observed with merrymaking. [t. It.: m. *carnevale*, alter. of *carnesciale*, der. *carnesciolare, carnelasciare* leave off (eating) meat]

Car·niv·o·ra (kär nĭv'ə rə), n.pl. *Zool.* See **carnivore** (def. 1).

car·ni·vore (kär'nə vōr'), n. 1. *Zool.* one of the *Carnivora*, the order of mammals, chiefly flesh-eating, that includes the cats, dogs, bears, seals, etc. 2. *Bot.* a flesh-eating plant. [see CARNIVOROUS]

car·niv·o·rous (kär nĭv'ə rəs), adj. flesh-eating. [t. L: m. *carnivorus*] —**car·niv'o·rous·ly**, adv. —**car·niv'o·rous·ness**, n.

Car·not cycle (kär nō'), a cycle of engine operations giving the maximum thermal efficiency obtainable by an engine working between any two temperatures.

car·no·tite (kär'nə tīt'), n. a mineral, a yellow, earthy, hydrous potassium uranium vanadate: an ore of uranium. [named after A. *Carnot*, French inspector general of mines. See -ITE¹]

car·ob (kär'əb), n. 1. the fruit of a caesalpinaceous tree, *Ceratonia Siliqua*, of the Mediterranean regions, a long, dry pod containing hard seeds in a sweet pulp, used for feeding animals and sometimes eaten by man. 2. the tree. [t. F: m. *carobe*, t. Ar.: m. *kharrūba*]

ca·roche (kə rōch', -rōsh'), n. an old form of stately coach or carriage. [t. F (obs.): m. *caroche*, t. It.: m. *carroccio*, aug. of *carro* chariot, g. L *carrus*; akin to CAR]

car·ol (kär'əl), n., v., -oled, -oling or (esp. *Brit.*) -olled, -olling. 1. a song, esp. of joy. 2. a Christmas song or hymn. 3. *Obs.* a kind of circular dance. —v.i. 4. to sing, esp. in a lively, joyous manner; warble. —v.t. 5. to sing joyously. 6. to praise or celebrate in song. [ME, t. OF: m. *carole*; prob. from Celtic root *cor-* circle, b. with L *choraula* minstrel, chorus leader, t. Gk.: m. *choraúlēs*] —**car'ol·er**; *esp. Brit.*, **car'ol·ler**, n.

Car·ol II (kär'əl; *Rum.* kä'rōl), 1893–1953, king of Rumania, 1930–40.

Car·o·le·an (kär'ə lē'ən), adj. *Brit.* characteristic of the time of Charles I and II: a *Carolean* costume.

Car·o·li·na (kär'ə lī'nə), n. a former English colony on the Atlantic coast of North America: officially divided into North Carolina and South Carolina, 1729. 2. the **Carolinas**, North Carolina and South Carolina.

Car·o·line (kär'ə lĭn', -lĭn), adj. of or pertaining to some person named Charles, as Charles I or Charles II of England, or the period in which he flourished.

Caroline Islands, a group of over 500 islands in the Pacific, E of the Philippine Islands: formerly a Japanese mandate; now under U.S. administration. 42,627 pop. (1955); 525 sq. mi.

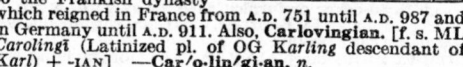

Car·o·lin·gi·an (kär'ə lĭn'jĭ ən), adj. belonging to the Frankish dynasty which reigned in France from A.D. 751 until A.D. 987 and in Germany until A.D. 911. Also, **Carlovingian**. [f. s. ML *Caroling* (Latinized pl. of OG *Karling* descendant of *Karl*) + -IAN] —**Car·o·lin'gi·an**, n.

Car·o·lin·i·an (kär'ə lĭn'ĭ ən), adj. 1. of or pertaining to North and South Carolina or to either one of them. 2. Carolingian. 3. Caroline. —n. 4. a native or inhabitant of North or South Carolina.

car·o·lus (kär'ə ləs), n., pl. -luses, -li (-lī'). any of various coins issued under monarchs named Charles, esp. an English gold coin struck in the reign of Charles I, orig. worth 20 and later 23 shillings. [t. ML: Charles]

car·om (kär'əm), n. 1. *Billiards*. a shot in which the ball struck with the cue is made to hit two balls in succession. 2. any strike and rebound, as a ball striking a wall and glancing off. —v.i. 3. to make a carom. 4. to strike and rebound. Also, **carrom**. [earlier *carambole*, t. F, t. Sp.: m. *carambola*; ? identical with *carambola*, name of fruit, t. Malay: m. *carambil*]

car·o·tene (kär'ə tēn'), n. *Chem.* any of three isomeric red hydrocarbons, C₄₀H₅₆, found in many plants, esp. carrots, and transformed to vitamin A in the liver. Also, **car·o·tin** (kär'ə tĭn). [f. s. L *carota* CARROT + -ENE]

ca·rot·e·noid (kə rŏt'ə noid'), *Chem.* —n. 1. any of a group of red and yellow pigments, chemically similar to carotene, contained in animal fat and some plants. —adj. 2. similar to carotene. 3. pertaining to carotenoids. Also, **ca·rot'i·noid'**. [f. CAROTENE + -OID]

ca·rot·id (kə rŏt'ĭd), *Anat.* —n. 1. either of the two great arteries, one on each side of the neck, which carry blood to the head. —adj. 2. pertaining to the carotids. [t. Gk.: s. *karōtides*, pl., der. *kāros* stupor (thought to be caused by compression of these arteries)] —**ca·rot'id·al**, adj.

ca·rous·al (kə rou'zəl), n. 1. a noisy or drunken feast or other social gathering; jovial revelry. 2. carrousel (def. 2). [f. CAROUSE, v. + -AL²]

ca·rouse (kə rouz'), n., v., -roused, -rousing. —n. 1. a noisy or drunken feast; jovial revelry. —v.i. 2. to engage in a carouse; drink deeply. [n. and v. uses of obs. adv., t. G: m. *gar aus* wholly out]

car·ou·sel (kär'ə zĕl', -sĕl'), n. carrousel.

carp¹ (kärp), v.i. to find fault; cavil; complain unreasonably: *to carp at minor errors*. [ME *carpe(n)*, t. Scand.; cf. Icel. *karpa* wrangle, dispute] —**carp'er**, n. —**carp'ing·ly**, adv.

carp² (kärp), n., pl. **carps**, (*esp. collectively*) **carp**. 1. a large, coarse fresh-water food fish, *Cyprinus carpio* (family *Cyprinidae*), commonly bred in ponds. 2. any of various other fishes of the same family, also known as minnows. [ME *carpe*, t. OF, t. Pr.: m. *carpa*, g. LL *carpa*; of Gmc. orig.]

-carp, a noun termination meaning "fruit," used in botanical terms, as *endocarp*. [comb. form repr. Gk. *karpós*]

carp., carpentry.

car·pal (kär'pəl), *Anat.* —adj. 1. pertaining to the carpus: *the carpal joint*. —n. 2. a carpale. [t. NL: s. *carpālis*, der. L *carpus* wrist]

car·pa·le (kär pā'lī), n., pl. -lia (-lī'ə). *Anat.* any of the bones of the wrist. Also, **carpal**. [t. NL, neut. of *carpālis* CARPAL]

Car·pa·thi·an Mountains (kär pā'thĭ ən), a mountain system in central Europe, extending ab. 800 mi. from N Czechoslovakia to central Rumania. Highest peak, Gerlachovka, 8737 ft. Also, **Carpathians**.

Car·pa·tho-U·kraine (kär pā'thō ū krān'), n. a region in the SW Soviet Union, in the Ukrainian Republic: ceded by Czechoslovakia, 1945. 4871 sq. mi. Formerly, **Ruthenia** or **Carpathian Ruthenia**.

car·pe di·em (kär'pĭ dī'ĕm), *Latin*. enjoy the present day, trusting as little as possible to the future.

car·pel (kär'pəl), n. *Bot.* a simple pistil, or a single member of a compound pistil: regarded as a modified leaf. [t. NL: m. s. *carpellum*, der. Gk. *karpós* fruit] —**car·pel·lar·y** (kär'pə lĕr'ī), adj.

car·pel·late (kär'pə lāt'), adj. *Bot.* having carpels.

Car·pen·tar·i·a (kär'pən târ'ĭ ə), n. Gulf of, a large gulf on the N coast of Australia. ab. 420 mi. wide; ab. 480 mi. long.

Carpels
A. Flower with simple pistils;
B. Tricarpellary fruit

car·pen·ter (kär'pən tər), *n.* **1.** a workman who uses tools and lumber in the building of houses and other wooden structures. —*v.i.* **2.** to do carpenter's work. —*v.t.* **3.** to make by carpentry. [ME, t. ONF: m. *carpentier*, g. LL *carpentārius* wagon maker, der. L *carpentum* wagon] —**car'pen·ter·ing, car'pen·try,** *n.*

Car·pen·ter (kär'pən tər), *n.* **John Alden,** 1876–1951 U.S. composer.

carpenter bee, any of various solitary bees of the family *Xylocopidae* that make their nests in wood, boring tunnels in which to deposit their eggs.

car·pet (kär'pĭt), *n.* **1.** a heavy fabric, commonly of wool, for covering floors. **2.** a covering of this material. **3.** any covering like a carpet: *they walked on the grassy carpet.* **4. on the carpet,** **a.** under consideration or discussion. **b.** before an authority for a reprimand. —*v.t.* **5.** to cover or furnish with, or as with, a carpet. **6.** to reprimand. [ME *carpete*, t. ML: m. *carpeta*, ult. der. L *carpere* card (wool)]

car·pet·bag (kär'pĭt băg'), *n.* a bag for traveling, esp. one made of carpeting.

car·pet·bag·ger (kär'pĭt băg'ər), *n.* **1.** a person who takes up residence in a place, with no more property than he brings in a carpetbag, to seek special advantages for himself. **2.** (in U. S. history) **a.** *Contemptuous.* a Northerner who went to the South after the Civil War to seek political or other advantages made possible by the disorganized condition of political affairs. **b.** a wildcat banker in the western U. S. who had no office and could not be found when wanted.

carpet beetle, a small beetle, *Anthrenus scrophulariae,* whose larvae are destructive to carpets and other woolen fabrics; buffalo bug. Also, **carpet bug.**

car·pet·ing (kär'pĭt ĭng), *n.* **1.** material for carpets. **2.** carpets in general.

car·pet·weed (kär'pĭt wēd'), *n.* a North American prostrate weed, *Mollugo verticillata.*

car·pi (kär'pī), *n.* pl. of **carpus.**

-carpic, a word element related to **-carp,** as in *endocarpic.* [f. -CARP + -IC]

carpo-, a word element meaning "fruit" as in *carpology.* [t. Gk.: m. *karpo-,* comb. form of *karpós*]

car·po·go·ni·um (kär'pə gō'nĭ əm), *n., pl.* **-nia** (-nĭ ə). *Bot.* the one-celled female sex organ of the red algae (*Rhodophyceae*) which, when fertilized, gives rise to the carpospores. [NL; see CARPO-, -GONIUM] —**car'po·go'ni·al,** *adj.*

car·pol·o·gy (kär pŏl'ə jĭ), *n.* the branch of botany that relates to fruits. —**car·po·log·i·cal** (kär'pə lŏj'ə kəl), *adj.* —**car·pol'o·gist,** *n.*

car·poph·a·gous (kär pŏf'ə gəs), *adj.* fruit-eating.

car·po·phore (kär'pə fōr'), *n. Bot.* **1.** a slender prolongation of the floral axis, bearing the carpels in the geranium and in many umbelliferous plants. **2.** the fruit body of the higher fungi.

car·port (kär'pōrt), *n.* a roofed, wall-less shed projecting from the side of a building, used as a shelter for a motor vehicle.

car·po·spore (kär'pə spōr'), *n. Bot.* a nonmotile spore of the red algae.

-carpous, a combining form related to **-carp,** as in *apocarpous.* [f. -CARP + -OUS]

car·pus (kär'pəs), *n., pl.* **-pi** (-pī). *Anat.* **1.** the part of the upper extremity between the hand and the forearm; the wrist. **2.** the wrist bones collectively; the group of bones between the bones of the hand and the radius. See diag. under **shoulder.** [t. NL, t. Gk.: m. *karpós* wrist]

Carpophore (def. 1), with carpels

car·rack (kär'ək), *n. Archaic.* a galleon. [ME *caracke,* t. OF: m. *carraque,* t. Sp., Pg.: m. *carraca,* t. Ar.: m. *qarāqīr,* pl. of *qurqūr* merchant vessel; or m. *ḥarraqa* boat]

car·ra·geen (kär'ə gēn'), *n.* Irish moss (def. 1). Also, **car'ra·gheen'.** [named after *Carragheen,* in S Ireland]

Car·ran·za (kərän'zə; *Sp.* kärrän'sä), *n.* **Venustiano** (vĕ'nōō styä'nō), 1859–1920, president of Mexico, 1915–20.

Car·ra·ra (kärrä'rä), *n.* a city in NW Italy: famous for its marble. 61,903 (1951).

car·rel (kär'əl), *n.* (in a library) a small area or cubicle near the stacks used by faculty members and certain students for individual study.

Car·rel (kərĕl'; *Fr.* kärĕl'), *n.* **Alexis** (əlĕk'sĭs; *Fr.* àlĕk sē'), 1873–1944, U.S. surgeon and biologist, born in France.

car·riage (kär'ĭj; *also for 7* kär'ĭj), *n.* **1.** a wheeled vehicle for conveying persons, usually drawn by horses, esp. one designed for comfort and elegance. **2.** *Brit.* a railway car. **3.** a wheeled support, as for a cannon. **4.** a part, as of a machine, designed for carrying something. **5.** manner of carrying the head and body; bearing: *the carriage of a soldier.* **6.** act of transporting; conveyance: *the expenses of carriage.* **7.** the price or cost of transportation. **8.** management. [ME *cariage,* t. ONF, der. *carier.* See CARRY] —**Syn. 5.** deportment.

car·rick bend (kär'ĭk), *Naut.* a kind of knot for joining cables or hawsers. See illus. under **knot.**

carrick bitt, *Naut.* one of the bitts which support the windlass.

car·ri·er (kär'ĭ ər), *n.* **1.** a person or thing that carries. **2.** a person, company, etc. that undertakes to convey goods or persons for hire. **3.** *Mach.* a mechanism

by which something is carried or moved. **4.** *Immunol.* an individual harboring specific organisms, who, though often immune to the agent harbored, may transmit the disease to others. **5.** *Chem.* a catalytic agent which brings about a transfer of an element or group of atoms from one compound to another. **6.** Also, **carrier wave.** *Radio.* the wave whose amplitude, frequency or phase is to be varied or modulated to transmit a signal. **7.** carrier pigeon.

carrier pigeon, 1. a pigeon trained to fly home from great distances and thus transport written messages; a homing pigeon. **2.** one of a breed of domestic pigeons characterized by a huge wattle at the base of the beak.

car·ri·ole (kär'ĭ ōl'), *n.* cariole.

car·ri·on (kär'ĭ ən), *n.* **1.** dead and putrefying flesh. **2.** rottenness; anything vile. —*adj.* **3.** feeding on carrion. **4.** of or like carrion. [ME *carion, caroine,* t. ONF, var. of central OF *charoigne,* ult. der. L *caro* flesh]

carrion crow, 1. any of various crows, as the common European crow, *Corvus corone.* **2.** a black vulture, *Coragypo atratus,* of the southern U. S., etc.

Car·roll (kär'əl), *n.* **1. Charles,** 1737–1832, American patriot and legislator. **2. Lewis,** (*Charles Lutwidge Dodgson*) 1832–98, British mathematician and writer.

car·rom (kär'əm), *n., v.i.* carom.

car·ro·ma·ta (kär'rō mä'tä), *n.* (in the Philippines) a light, two-wheeled covered vehicle, usually drawn by one horse. [t. Sp.: m. *carromato,* der. *carro* cart, g. L *carrus*]

car·ron·ade (kär'ə nād'), *n.* a short piece of muzzle-loading ordnance, formerly in use, esp. in ships. [der. *Carron* (Scotland), site of a cannon foundry]

car·ron oil (kär'ən), *Pharm.* a liniment containing limewater and oil, used esp. for burns.

car·rot (kär'ət), *n.* **1.** a plant of the umbelliferous genus *Daucus,* esp. *D. Carota,* in its wild form a widespread, familiar weed, and in cultivation valued for its yellowish edible root. **2.** the root. [t. F: m. *carotte,* t. L: m. s. *carōta,* t. Gk.: m. *karōtón*]

car·rot·y (kär'ət ĭ), *adj.* **1.** like a carrot root in color; yellowish-red. **2.** having red hair.

car·rou·sel (kär'ə zĕl', -sĕl'), *n.* **1.** a merry-go-round (def. 1). **2.** a tournament in which horsemen executed various formations. Also, **carousel.** [t. F, t. It.: m. *carosello,* der. *carro,* g. L *carrus* cart]

car·ry (kär'ĭ), *v.,* **-ried, -rying,** *n., pl.* **-ries.** —*v.t.* **1.** to convey from one place to another in a car, ship, pocket, hand, etc. **2.** to transmit or transfer in any manner; take or bring: *the wind carries sounds, he carries his audience with him.* **3.** to bear the weight, burden, etc., of; sustain. **4.** *U.S.* to take a (leading or guiding part) in singing; bear or sustain (a part or melody). **5.** to hold (the body, head, etc.) in a certain manner. **6.** to behave or comport (oneself). **7.** to take, esp. by force; capture; win. **8.** to secure the election of (a candidate) or the adoption of (a motion or bill). **9.** to extend or continue in a given direction or to a certain point: *to carry the war into enemy territory.* **10.** to impel or drive. **11.** *Southern U.S.* to lead, escort, or conduct: *to carry a girl to a dance, a mule to the barn.* **12.** to lead or impel; conduct. **13.** to have as an attribute, property, consequence, etc.: *his opinion carries great weight.* **14.** to support or give validity to (a related claim, etc.): *one decision carries another.* **15.** *Com.* **a.** to keep on hand or in stock. **b.** to keep on one's account books, etc. **16.** to bear as a crop. **17.** to support (cattle): *our grain supply will carry the cattle through the winter.* **18.** *Golf.* to advance beyond or go by (an object or expanse) with one stroke. **19.** *Hunting.* to retain and pursue (a scent). —*v.i.* **20.** to act as a bearer or conductor. **21.** to have or exert propelling force: *the rifle carries almost a mile.* **22.** to be transmitted, propelled, or sustained: *my voice carries farther than his.* **23.** to bear the head in a particular manner, as a horse. **24.** Some special verb phrases: **carry away,** to influence greatly or beyond reason.

carry forward, 1. to make progress with. **2.** *Bookkeeping.* to transfer (an amount, etc.) to the next column, page, etc.

carry off, 1. to win (the prize, honor, etc.) **2.** to face consequences boldly: *he carried it off well.* **3.** to cause the death of.

carry on, 1. to manage; conduct. **2.** *U.S.* to behave in an excited, foolish, or improper manner. **3.** *Chiefly Brit.* to continue; keep up without stopping.

carry out, to accomplish or complete (a plan, scheme, etc.): *to carry out the details of his plan.*

carry over, to postpone; hold off until later.

carry through, 1. to accomplish; complete. **2.** to support or help (in a difficult situation, etc.).

—*n.* **25.** range, as of a gun. **26.** *Golf.* the distance traversed by a ball before it alights. **27.** *U.S.* land separating navigable waters, over which a canoe or boat must be carried; a portage. **28.** a carrying. [ME *carie(n),* t. ONF: m. *carier,* g. LL *carricāre* convey by wagon, der. L *carrus.* See CAR]

—**Syn. 1.** CARRY, CONVEY, TRANSPORT, TRANSMIT, imply taking or sending something from one place to another CARRY means to take by means of the hands, a vehicle, etc.: *to carry a book.* CONVEY is a more formal word, suggesting a means of taking, but not any particular method of taking; it is also used figuratively: *to convey wheat to market, a message of sympathy.* TRANSPORT means to carry or convey goods, now usually by vehicle or vessel: *to transport milk to customers.* TRANSMIT implies chiefly sending or transferring messages, hereditary tendencies, etc.: *to transmit a telegram.*

---

ar·ry·all (kăr′Yôl′), *n.* **1.** a light, covered, one-horse family carriage, with two seats. **2.** a closed motorcar having two passenger benches extending the length of the body. [f. CARRY + ALL; r. CARRIOLE by pop. etym.]

ar·ry-o·ver (kăr′Yō′vər), *n.* **1.** the part left over to a later period, account, etc. **2.** *Bookkeeping.* the total of one page of an account carried forward to the next.

ar·sick (kăr′sĭk′), *adj.* nauseated by the motion of a train, automobile, etc.

Jar·son (kăr′sən), *n.* **1.** Christopher, ("*Kit*") 1809–68, U.S. frontiersman and scout. **2.** Sir **Edward Henry**, (*Baron Carson*) 1854–1935, British public official.

Carson City, the capital of Nevada, in the W part. 5163 (1960).

art (kärt), *n.* **1.** a heavy two-wheeled vehicle, commonly without springs, for the conveyance of heavy goods. **2.** a light two-wheeled vehicle with springs, used for business or pleasure. **3.** any small vehicle moved by hand. **4.** *Obs.* a chariot. —*v.t.* **5.** to convey in or as in a cart. —*v.i.* **6.** to drive a cart. [metathetic var. of OE *crœt*, c. Icel. *kartr*] —**cart′er,** *n.*

art·age (kär′tĭj), *n.* the act or cost of carting.

ar·ta·ge·na (kär′tə jē′nə; *Sp.* kär′tä hĕ′nä), *n.* **1.** a seaport in SE Spain. 118,049 (est. 1955). **2.** a seaport in N Colombia. 142,880 (est. 1954).

arte¹ (kärt; *Fr.* kårt), *n.* *Fencing.* quarte. [t. F: m. *quarte*, t. It.: m. *quarta* fourth]

arte² (kärt; *Fr.* kårt), *n.* **1.** menu. *Cf.* à la carte. **2.** *Now Rare or Obs.* a playing card. **3.** *Obs.* a map or chart. [t. F. See CARD¹]

Carte (kärt), *n.* **Richard D'Oyly** (doi′lY), 1844–1901, British theatrical producer.

arte blanche (kärt′ blänsh′; *Fr.* kårt blänsh′), *pl.* **cartes blanches** (kärts′ blänsh′; *Fr.* kårt blänsh′). *French.* **1.** a signed paper left blank for the person to whom it is given to fill in his own conditions. **2.** unconditional authority; full power.

ar·tel (kär tĕl′, kär′təl), *n.* **1.** an international syndicate, combine or trust generally formed to regulate prices and output in some field of business. **2.** a written agreement between belligerents, esp. for the exchange of prisoners. **3.** (*often cap.*) (in French or Belgian politics) a group acting as a unit toward a common goal. **4.** a challenge to single combat. [t. F, t. It.: m. *cartello*, dim. of *carta*, g. L *charta* paper. See CHART]

ar·te·lize (kär′tə līz), *v.t.*, **-lized, -lizing.** to organize into a cartel (def. 1). —**car′te·li·za′tion,** *n.*

Car·ter (kär′tər), *n.* **Howard,** 1873–1939, British archaeologist in Egypt.

Car·ter·et (kär′tər Yt), *n.* **John** (*Earl Granville*), 1690–1763, British statesman.

Car·te·sian (kär tē′zhən), *adj.* **1.** pertaining to Descartes, to his mathematical methods, or to his dualistic philosophy which began with the famous phrase *Cogito, ergo sum* (I think, therefore I am), saw physical nature mechanistically, and in science emphasized rationalism and logic. —*n.* **2.** a believer in the philosophy of Descartes. [t. NL: s. *Cartesiānus*, der. *Cartesius*, Latinized form of the name of René *Descartes*] —**Car·te′sian·ism,** *n.*

Car·thage (kär′thĭj), *n.* an ancient city-state in N Africa, near modern Tunis: destroyed by the Romans, 146 B.C. —**Car·tha·gin·i·an** (kär′thə jYn′Y ən), *adj.*, *n.*

Carthage, c133 B.C.

Car·thu·sian (kär thoō′zhən), *Rom. Cath. Ch.* —*n.* **1.** a member of an austere monastic order founded by St. Bruno in 1086 near Grenoble, France. —*adj.* **2.** belonging to this order. [t. ML: m.s. *Cartusiānus*, der. *Chatrousse*, name of a village in Dauphiné near which the first monastery of the order was built]

Car·tier (kär tyĕ′), *n.* **Jacques** (zhäk), 1491?–c1557, French navigator: discoverer of the St. Lawrence river.

car·ti·lage (kär′tə lĭj, kärt′lYj), *n.* *Anat., Zool.* **1.** a firm, elastic, flexible substance of a translucent whitish or yellowish color, consisting of connective tissue; gristle. **2.** a part or structure composed of cartilage. [t. F, t. L: m. *cartilāgo* gristle]

cartilage bone, a bone that is developed from cartilage (distinguished from *membrane bone*).

car·ti·lag·i·nous (kär′tə lăj′ə nəs), *adj.* **1.** of or resembling cartilage. **2.** *Zool.* having the skeleton composed mostly of cartilage, as sharks and rays.

cart·load (kärt′lōd′), *n.* the amount a cart can hold.

car·to·gram (kär′tə grăm′), *n.* a diagrammatic presentation in highly abstracted or simplified form, commonly of statistical data, on a map base or distorted map base. [t. F: m. *cartogramme.* See CARD¹, -GRAM]

car·tog·ra·phy (kär tŏg′rə fĭ), *n.* the production of maps, including construction of projections, design, compilation, drafting, and reproduction. Also, **chartography.** [f. *carto-* (comb. form of ML *carta* chart, map) + -GRAPHY] —**car·tog′ra·pher,** *n.* —**car·to·graph·ic** (kär′tə grăf′Yk), **car′to·graph′i·cal,** *adj.* —**car′to·graph′i·cal·ly,** *adv.*

car·ton (kär′tən), *n.* a cardboard box. [t. F. See CARTOON]

car·toon (kär toōn′), *n.* **1.** a sketch or drawing as in a newspaper or periodical, symbolizing or caricaturing some subject or person of current interest, in an exag-

gerated way. **2.** *Fine Arts.* a drawing, of the same size as a proposed decoration or pattern in fresco, mosaic, tapestry, etc., for which it serves as a model to be transferred or copied. **3.** a comic strip. **4.** an animated cartoon. —*v.t.* **5.** to represent by a cartoon. [t. F: m. *carton,* t. It.: m. *cartone* pasteboard, cartoon, aug. of *carta,* g. L *charta* paper. See CHART] —**car·toon′ist,** *n.*

car·touche (kär toōsh′), *n.* **1.** *Archit.* a French Renaissance motif, usually an oval tablet with ornamental scrollwork. **2.** an oval or oblong figure, as on ancient Egyptian monuments, enclosing characters which express royal names. **3.** the case containing the inflammable materials in certain fireworks. **4.** cartridge (def. 1). **5.** a box for cartridges. Also, **car·touch′.** [t. F, t. It.: m. *cartoccio,* aug. of *carta,* g. L *charta* paper. See CHART]

car·tridge (kär′trĭj), *n.* **1.** a cylindrical case of pasteboard, metal, or the like, for holding a complete charge of powder, and often also the bullet or the shot, for a rifle, machine gun, or other small arm. **2.** a case containing any explosive charge, as for blasting. **3.** *Photog.* **a.** a case or holder for a roll of camera film, used in daylight loading. **b.** such a case loaded with film. **4.** a pickup (def. 8). [m. CARTOUCHE]

Cartridge: A. Metallic case of copper or brass; B. Bullet; R. Primer; F. Fulminate; P. Powder

cartridge belt, a belt (def. 6b) for ammunition with loops for cartridges or pockets for clips of cartridges.

cartridge clip, a metal frame or container holding cartridges for a magazine rifle or automatic pistol; clip.

car·tu·lar·y (kär′chŏŏ lĕr′Y), *n., pl.* **-laries.** chartulary.

cart·wheel (kärt′hwēl′), *n.* **1.** a somersault performed sidewise. **2.** *Slang.* any large coin, esp. the silver dollar.

Cart·wright (kärt′rīt′), *n.* **Edmund,** 1743–1823, British clergyman: inventor of the power-driven loom.

car·un·cle (kär′ŭng kəl, kə rŭng′-), *n.* **1.** *Bot.* a protuberance at or surrounding the hilum of a seed. **2.** *Zool.* a fleshy excrescence, as on the head of a bird; a fowl's comb. [t. L: m. s. *caruncula,* dim. of *caro* flesh] —**ca·run·cu·lar** (kə rŭng′kyə lər), **ca·run′cu·lous,** *adj.*

ca·run·cu·late (kə rŭng′kyə lYt, -lāt′), *adj.* having a caruncle. Also, **ca·run′cu·lat′ed.**

Ca·ru·so (kə rōō′sō; *It.* kä rōō′zō), *n.* **Enrico** (ĕn rē′kō), 1873–1921, Italian operatic tenor.

carve (kärv), *v.,* **carved, carving.** —*v.t.* **1.** to fashion by cutting: *to carve a block of stone into a statue.* **2.** to produce by cutting: *to carve a design in wood.* **3.** to cut into slices or pieces, as meat. —*v.i.* **4.** to decorate by cutting figures, designs, etc. **5.** to cut meat. [ME *kerve(n),* OE *ceorfan* cut, c. G *kerben* notch; akin to Gk. *gráphein* mark, write] —**carv′er,** *n.*

car·vel (kär′vəl), *n.* caravel.

car·vel-built (kär′vəl bYlt′), *adj.* (of a ship) built with the planks flush, not overlapping. Cf. **clinker-built.**

carv·en (kär′vən), *adj. Poetic.* carved.

Car·ver (kär′vər), *n.* **1.** **George Washington,** c1864–1943, U.S. botanist and chemist. **2.** **John,** 1575?–1621, Pilgrim leader: first governor of Plymouth Colony.

carv·ing (kär′vYng), *n.* **1.** act of fashioning or producing by cutting. **2.** carved work; a carved design.

Car·y (kâr′Y), *n.* **1.** **Alice,** 1820–71, U.S. poet (sister of Phoebe Cary). **2.** **Henry Francis,** 1772–1844, British writer and translator. **3.** **Phoebe,** 1824–71, U.S. poet (sister of Alice Cary).

car·y·at·id (kär′Y ăt′Yd), *n., pl.* **-ids, -ides** (-ə dēz′). *Archit.* a figure of a woman used like a supporting column. [t. L: s. *Caryātides,* pl., t. Gk.: m. *Karyátides,* lit., women of Caryae] —**car′y·at′i·dal,** *adj.*

car·y·o·phyl·la·ceous (kär′Y ō fə lā′shəs), *adj. Bot.* **1.** belonging to the *Caryophyllaceae* (sometimes called *Silenaceae*) or pink family of plants. **2.** resembling the pink. [f. m.s. Gk. *karyóphyllon* clove tree + -ACEOUS]

car·y·op·sis (kär′Y ŏp′sYs), *n., pl.* **-opses** (-ŏp′sēz), **-opsides** (-ŏp′sə dēz′). *Bot.* a small, one-celled, one-seeded, dry indehiscent fruit with the pericarp adherent to the seed coat, as in wheat. [f. m.s. Gk. *káryon* nut + -OPSIS]

Caryatids

ca·sa·ba (kə sä′bə), *n.* a kind of winter muskmelon, having a yellow rind and sweet, juicy flesh. Also, **casaba melon, cassaba.** [named after *Kassaba,* town near Smyrna, Asia Minor]

Ca·sa·bian·ca (kä zä byän kä′), *n.* **Louis de** (lwē də), c1752–98, French naval officer whose son died trying to save him from his burning ship.

Ca·sa·blan·ca (kä′sä bläng′kä, kăs′ə bläng′kə), *n.* a seaport in NW Morocco: wartime conference of Roosevelt and Churchill, Jan., 1943. 682,288 (1952).

Ca·sa Gran·de (kä′sä grän′dā, -dǐ), a national monument in S Arizona, near the Gila river: remarkable ruins of a prehistoric culture.

Ca·sals (kä sälz′, *Sp.* kä säls′), *n.* **Pablo** (pä′blō), born 1876, Spanish cellist.

Cas·a·no·va (käz′ə nō′və, käs′-; *It.* kä′sä nō′vä). Giovanni Jacopo (jō vän′nē yä′kō pō), 1725–98, Italian adventurer and writer.

Ca·sau·bon (kə sô′bən; *Fr.* kà zō bôN′), *n.* **Isaac** (ē′zăk′), 1559–1614, French classical scholar.

Cas·bah (käz′bä), *n.* Kasbah.

cas·cade (kăs kād′), *n. v.*, **-caded, -cading.** —*n.* **1.** a waterfall over steep rocks, or a series of small waterfalls. **2.** an arrangement of lace, etc., in folds falling one over another in a zigzag fashion. **3.** a type of firework resembling a waterfall in effect. **4.** *Chem.* a series of vessels, from each of which a liquid successively overflows to the next, thus presenting a large absorbing surface, as to a gas. **5.** *Elect.* an arrangement of component devices, each of which feeds into the next in succession. —*v.i.* **6.** to fall in or like a cascade. [t. F, t. It.: m. *cascata,* der. *cascare,* der. L *cadere* fall]

Cascade Range, a mountain range extending from N California to British Columbia: a part of the Coast Range. Highest peak, Mt. Rainier, 14,408 ft.

cas·car·a (kăs kâr′ə), *n.* a species of buckthorn, *Rhamnus Purshiana,* of the Pacific coast of the U.S., yielding cascara sagrada. Also, **cascara buckthorn.** [t. Sp.: bark, der. *casca* bark, skin]

cascara sa·gra·da (sə grä′də), the bark of the cascara, used as a cathartic or laxative. [t. Sp.: sacred bark]

cas·ca·ril·la (kăs′kə rǐl′ə), *n.* **1.** Also, **cascarilla bark.** the bitter aromatic bark of a West Indian euphorbiaceous shrub, *Croton Eluteria,* used as a tonic. **2.** the shrub itself. [t. Sp., dim. of *cáscara* bark]

Cas·co Bay (kăs′kō), a bay in SW Maine.

case¹ (kās), *n.* **1.** an instance of the occurrence, existence, etc. of something. **2.** the actual state of things: *that is not the case.* **3.** a question or problem of moral conduct: *a case of conscience.* **4.** situation; condition; plight. **5.** a state of things involving a question for discussion or decision. **6.** a statement of facts, reasons, etc.: *a strong case for the proposed law.* **7.** an instance of disease, etc., requiring medical or surgical treatment or attention. **8.** a medical or surgical patient. **9.** *Law.* **a.** a suit or action at law; a cause. **b.** a set of facts giving rise to a legal claim, or to a defense to a legal claim. **10.** *Gram.* **a.** a category in the inflection of nouns, pronouns, and adjectives, denoting the syntactic relation of these words to other words in the sentence, indicated by the form or the position of the words. **b.** a set of such categories in a particular language. **c.** the meaning of, or typical of, such a category. **d.** such categories or their meanings collectively. **11.** *Colloq.* a peculiar or unusual person: *he's a case.* **12.** in any case, under any circumstances; anyhow. **13.** in case, if; if it should happen that. **14.** in case of, in the event of. [ME, t. OF: m. *cas,* g. L *cāsus* a falling, occurrence]
—Syn. 1. CASE, INSTANCE, EXAMPLE, ILLUSTRATION suggest the existence or occurrence of a particular thing representative of its type. CASE and INSTANCE are closely allied in meaning, as are EXAMPLE and ILLUSTRATION. CASE is a general word, meaning a fact, occurrence, or situation typical of a class: *a case of assault and battery.* An INSTANCE is a concrete factual case which is adduced to explain a general idea: *an instance of a brawl in which an assault occurred.* An EXAMPLE is one typical case, from many similar ones, used to make clear or explain the working of a principle (what may be expected of any others of the group): *this boy is an example of the effect of strict discipline.* An ILLUSTRATION exemplifies a theory or principle similarly, except that the choice may be purely hypothetical: *the work of Seeing Eye dogs is an illustration of what is thought to be intelligence in animals.*

case² (kās), *n. v.,* **cased, casing.** —*n.* **1.** a thing for containing or enclosing something; a receptacle. **2.** a sheath or outer covering: *a knife case.* **3.** a box with its contents. **4.** the amount contained in a box or other container. **5.** a frame or framework, as of a door. **6.** *Bookbinding.* a completed book cover ready to be fitted to form the binding of a book. **7.** *Print.* a tray, of wood or metal, divided into compartments for holding types for the use of a compositor and usually arranged in a set of two, the **upper case** for capitals, etc., and the **lower case** for small letters, etc. —*v.t.* **8.** to put or enclose in a case; cover with a case. **9.** *U.S. Slang.* to examine or survey (a house, bank, etc.) in planning a crime. [ME *casse,* t. ONF, g. L *capsa* box, receptacle.]

ca·se·ase (kā′sǐ ās′), *n. Biochem.* a bacterial enzyme which dissolves casein. [f. CASE(IN) + -ASE]

ca·se·ate (kā′sǐ āt′), *v.i.,* **-ated, -ating.** *Pathol.* to undergo caseous degeneration; become like cheese in consistency and appearance. [f. s. L *cāseus* cheese + -ATE¹]

ca·se·a·tion (kā′sǐ ā′shən), *n. Pathol.* transformation into a soft cheeselike mass, as of tissue in tuberculosis.

case·hard·en (kās′här′dən), *v.t.* **1.** *Metall.* to make the outside surface of (alloys having an iron base) hard, leaving the interior tough and ductile by carburizing and heat treatment. **2.** to harden in spirit so as to render insensible to external impressions or influences.

case history, all the relevant information or material gathered about an individual, family, group, etc., and ordered so as to give it significance (usually genetic) to the student or the like: used esp. in social work, sociology, psychiatry, and medicine. Also, **case record.**

ca·se·in (kā′sǐ ǐn, -sēn), *n. Biochem.* a protein precipitated from milk, as by rennet, and forming the basis of cheese and certain plastics. [f. s. L *cāseus* cheese + -IN²]

ca·se·in·o·gen (kā′sǐ ǐn′ə jən, -sē′nə-), *n. Biochem.* the principal protein of milk, which in the presence of rennet is converted into casein.

case knife, **1.** a knife carried or kept in a case. **2.** a table knife.

case law, law established by judicial decisions in particular cases, instead of by legislative action.

case·mate (kās′māt′), *n.* **1.** an armored enclosure for guns in a warship. **2.** a vault or chamber, esp. in a rampart, with embrasures for artillery. [t. F, t. It.: m. *casamatta,* ult. t. Gk.: m. *chásmata* opening (as military term)] —**case′mat′ed,** *adj.*

case·ment (kās′mənt), *n.* **1.** a window sash opening on hinges, which are generally attached to the upright side of its frame. **2.** a window with such sashes. **3.** *Poetic.* any window. **4.** a casing or covering. [f. CASE² + -MENT] —**case′ment·ed,** *adj.*

Case·ment (kās′mənt), *n.* **(Sir) Roger (David),** 1864–1916, Irish patriot: hanged by the British for treason.

ca·se·ose (kā′sǐ ōs′), *n. Biochem.* any of various soluble products formed in the gastric and pancreatic digestion of casein and caseinogen. [f. CASE(IN) + -OSE²]

ca·se·ous (kā′sǐ əs), *adj.* of or like cheese. [f. s. L *cāseus* cheese + -OUS]

ca·sern (kə zûrn′), *n.* (formerly) a lodging for soldiers in a garrison town; a barrack. Also, **ca·serne′.** [t. F: m. *caserne,* orig., small room for soldiers, t. Pr.: m. *cazerna,* g. LL var. of *quaterna* group of four]

case shot, a collection of small projectiles in a case, to be fired from a cannon.

case·worm (kās′wûrm′), *n.* a caddis worm or other caterpillar that constructs a case around its body.

cash¹ (kăsh), *n.* **1.** money, esp. money on hand. **2.** money, or an equivalent (as a check), paid at the time of making a purchase. —*v.t.* **3.** to give or obtain cash for (a check, etc.). **4.** *U.S. Colloq.* in poker, etc.) **cash in one's chips,** to hand in and get cash for. **5. cash in on,** *U.S. Colloq.* **a.** to gain a return from. **b.** to turn to one's advantage. —*v.i.* **6.** *U.S. Colloq.* to die (fol by in). [t. F: m. *caisse,* t. Pr.: m. *caissa,* g. L *capsa* box]

cash² (kăsh), *n., pl.* **cash.** any of several low-denomination coins of China, India, and East Indies, esp. a Chinese copper coin. [t. Pg.: m. *caixa,* t. Tamil: m. *kāsu*]

ca·shaw (kə shô′), *n.* cushaw.

cash·book (kăsh′bŏŏk′), *n.* a book in which to record money received and paid out.

cash discount, 1. a term of sale by which the purchaser deducts a percentage from the bill if he pays within a stipulated period. **2.** the amount deducted.

cash·ew (kăsh′ōō, kə shōō′), *n.* **1.** an anacardiaceous tree, *Anacardium occidentale,* native in tropical America, whose bark yields a medicinal gum. **2.** its fruit, a small, edible, kidney-shaped nut (**cashew nut**). [t. F: alter. of *acajou,* t. Brazilian Pg.: m. *acajú,* t. Tupi]

cash·ier¹ (kă shǐr′), *n.* one who has charge of cash or money, esp. one who superintends monetary transactions, as in a bank; in England, a teller. [t. F: m. *caissier,* der. *caisse* cash box. See CASH¹]]

cash·ier² (kă shǐr′), *v.t.* **1.** to dismiss from a position of command or trust, esp. with disgrace. **2.** to discard; reject. [t. D: m. *casseren,* t. F: m. *casser* break, discharge, annul, g. L *quassāre* shake, break, and LL *cassāre* annul]

cashier's check, a check drawn by a bank upon its own funds and signed by its cashier.

cash·mere (kăsh′mǐr), *n.* **1.** the fine downy wool at the roots of the hair of Kashmir goats of India. **2.** a shawl made of this hair. **3.** a wool fabric of twill weave. Also, **kashmir.**

Cash·mere (kăsh mǐr′), *n.* Kashmir.

ca·shoo (kə shōō′), *n.* catechu.

cash register, a cash box with a mechanism for indicating amounts of sales, etc.

cas·i·mire (kăs′ə mǐr′), *n.* cassimere.

cas·ing (kā′sǐng), *n.* **1.** a case or covering. **2.** material for a case or covering. **3.** the framework around a door or window. **4.** *U.S.* the outermost covering of an automobile tire. **5.** any frame or framework. **6.** an iron pipe or tubing, esp. as used in oil and gas wells.

ca·si·no (kə sē′nō), *n., pl.* **-nos. 1.** a building or large room for meetings, amusements, etc.; a clubhouse, in England and Europe, usually understood to be devoted to gambling. **2.** a small country house or lodge. **3.** cassino. [t. It., dim. of *casa* house, g. L *casa* cottage]

cask (kăsk, käsk), *n.* **1.** a barrellike container made of staves, and of varying size, for holding liquids, etc., often one larger and stronger than an ordinary barrel. **2.** the quantity such a container holds. [appar. t. Sp.: m. *casco* skull, helmet, cask (for wine, etc.), der. *cascar* break, g. LL *quassicāre,* der. *quassāre* break, shake]

cas·ket (kăs′kǐt, käs′-), *n.* **1.** *Chiefly U.S.* a coffin. **2.** a small chest or box, as for jewels. —*v.t.* **3.** to put or enclose in a casket. [orig. uncert.]

Cas·lon (kăz′lən), *n.* **1. William,** 1692–1766, British type founder. **2.** *Print.* an old-style type modeled after the types designed by William Caslon.

Cas·par·i·an strip (kăs pâr′ǐ ən), *Bot.* a thickened strip in the radial walls of some endodermal cells.

b., blend of, blended; c., cognate with; d., dialect, dialectal; der., derived from; f., formed from; g., going back to; m., modification of; r., replacing; s., stem of; t., taken from; ?, perhaps. See the full key on inside cover.

Cas·per (kăs'pər), *n.* a city in central Wyoming. 38,930 (1960).

Cas·pi·an Sea (kăs'pǐ ən), a salt lake between SE Europe and Asia: the largest inland body of water in the world. ab. 169,000 sq. mi.; 85 ft. below sea level.

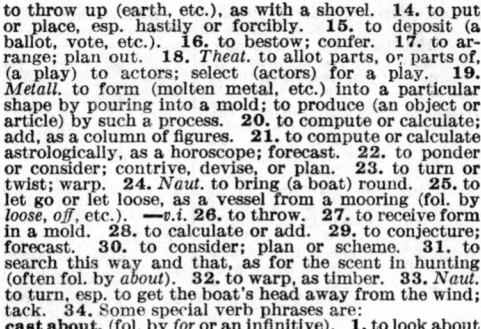
Caspian Sea

casque (kăsk), *n.* *Chiefly Poetic.* a helmet (def. 1, esp. 1b). [t. F, t. Sp.: m. *casco* helmet. See CASK] **—casqued** (kăskt), *adj.*

Cass (kăs), *n.* Lewis, 1782–1866, U. S. statesman.

cas·sa·ba (kə sä'bə), *n.* casaba.

Cas·san·dra (kə săn'drə), *n.* **1.** *Class. Legend.* a prophetess daughter of Priam and Hecuba of ancient Troy, who was fated never to be believed. **2.** any woman who warns in vain of coming evil.

cas·sa·reep (kăs'ə rēp), *n.* the inspissated juice of the root of the bitter cassava, used in cookery.

cas·sa·tion (kă sā'shən), *n.* annulment; cancellation; reversal. [t. LL: s. *cassātio*, der. *cassāre* annul]

Cas·satt (kə săt'), *n.* Mary, 1845?–1926, U. S. painter.

cas·sa·va (kə sä'və), *n.* **1.** any of several tropical euphorbiaceous plants of the genus *Manihot*, as *M. esculenta* (**bitter cassava**) and *M. dulcus* (**sweet cassava**), cultivated for their tuberous roots, which yield important food products. **2.** a nutritious starch from the roots, the source of tapioca. [earlier *casavi*, t. Sp.: m. *cazabe*, t. Haitian (Taino): m. *cacábi*, *cazábbi*]

Cas·se·grain·i·an telescope (kăs'ə grā'nǐ ən), a reflecting telescope in which the primary mirror is perforated so that the light may pass through it to the eyepiece or photographic plate.

Cas·sel (kăs'əl; *Ger.* käs'əl), *n.* Kassel.

cas·se·role (kăs'ə rōl'), *n.* **1.** a baking dish of glass, pottery, etc., usually with a cover. **2.** any food, usually a mixture, cooked in such a dish. **3.** a small dish with a handle, used in chemical laboratories. **4.** *Chiefly Brit.* a stewpan. **5. en casserole** (äṅ käs rōl'), *French.* served or cooked in a casserole. [t. F, ult. der. *casse* pan, g. L *cattia*, t. Gk.: m. *kyáthion* little cup, dim. of *kyáthos*]

cas·sia (kăsh'ə, kăs'ĭ ə), *n.* **1.** a variety of cinnamon from the tree *Cinnamomum Cassia*, of southern China (**cassia bark**). **2.** the tree itself. **3.** any of the caesalpiniaceous herbs, shrubs, and trees constituting the genus *Cassia*, as *C. Fistula*, an ornamental tropical tree with long pods (**cassia pods**) whose pulp (**cassia pulp**) is a mild laxative, and *C. acutifolia* and *C. angustifolia*, which yield senna. **4.** cassia pods. **5.** cassia pulp. [OE, t. L, t. Gk.: m. *kasia*, t. Heb.: m. *qətsī'āh*]

cas·si·mere (kăs'ə mǐr'), *n.* a plain or twilled woolen cloth. Also, **casimire.** [var. of CASHMERE]

cas·si·no (kə sē'nō), *n.* a game in which faced cards on the table are taken with eligible cards in the hand. Also, **casino.** [var. of CASINO]

Cas·si·no (kə sē'nō; *It.* käs sē'nô), *n.* a city in central Italy, ab. 45 mi. NW of Naples: site of **Monte Cassino**, a famous Benedictine abbey; scene of bitter fighting between the Allied and German armies, Jan.-May, 1944.

Cas·si·o·pe·ia (kăs'ĭ ə pē'ə), *n.* **1.** a northern circumpolar constellation east of Cepheus, on the opposite side of Polaris from the Dipper. **2.** *Gk. Myth.* the wife of Cepheus and mother of Andromeda.

Cassiopeia's Chair, the most conspicuous group of stars in the constellation Cassiopeia, supposed to resemble a chair in outline.

cas·sit·er·ite (kə sǐt'ə rīt'), *n.* a common mineral, tin dioxide, SnO$_2$: the principal ore of tin. [f. m.s. Gk. *kassíteros* tin + -ITE[1]]

Cas·sius Lon·gi·nus (kăsh'əs lŏn jī'nəs), **Gaius** (gā'əs), d. 42 B.C., Roman politician and general, who led a conspiracy against Julius Caesar.

cas·sock (kăs'ək), *n.* **1.** a long, close-fitting garment worn by ecclesiastics and others engaged in church functions. **2.** a shorter, light, double-breasted coat or jacket, usually of black silk, worn under the Geneva gown. **3.** a clergyman. [t. F: m. *casaque*, t. It.: m. *casacca*, root *cas-* (cf. F *chasuble*), ? identical with L *casa* house, hut]

cas·so·war·y (kăs'ə wěr'ĭ), *n.*, *pl.* **-war·ies.** any of several large, three-toed, flightless, ratite birds constituting the genus *Casuarius*, of Australasian regions, superficially resembling the ostrich but smaller. [t. Malay: m. *kasuāri*]

cast (kăst, käst), *v.*, **cast, cast·ing,** *n.* —*v.t.* **1.** to throw; fling; hurl (often fol. by *away*, *off*, *out*, etc.). **2.** to throw off or away. **3.** to direct (the eye, a glance, etc.). **4.** to cause (light, etc.) to fall upon something or in a certain direction. **5.** to throw out (a fishline, anchor, etc.). **6.** to throw down; throw (an animal) on its back or side; throw to the ground, as in wrestling. **7.** to part with; lose. **8.** to shed or drop (hair, fruit, etc.), esp. prematurely. **9.** to bring forth (young), esp. abortively. **10.** to send off (a swarm), as bees do. **11.** to throw or set aside; discard or reject; dismiss or disband. **12.** to throw forth, as from within; emit or eject; vomit. **13.**

Cassowary,
Casuarius casuarius
(Total length 5 ft.)

to throw up (earth, etc.), as with a shovel. **14.** to put or place, esp. hastily or forcibly. **15.** to deposit (a ballot, vote, etc.). **16.** to bestow; confer. **17.** to arrange; plan out. **18.** *Theat.* to allot parts, or parts of, (a play) to actors; select (actors) for a play. **19.** *Metall.* to form (molten metal, etc.) into a particular shape by pouring into a mold; to produce (an object or article) by such a process. **20.** to compute or calculate; add, as a column of figures. **21.** to compute or calculate astrologically, as a horoscope; forecast. **22.** to ponder or consider; contrive, devise, or plan. **23.** to turn or twist; warp. **24.** *Naut.* to bring (a boat) round. **25.** to let go or let loose, as a vessel from a mooring (fol. by *loose, off,* etc.). —*v.i.* **26.** to throw. **27.** to receive form in a mold. **28.** to calculate or add. **29.** to conjecture; forecast. **30.** to consider; plan or scheme. **31.** to search this way and that, as for the scent in hunting (often fol. by *about*). **32.** to warp, as timber. **33.** *Naut.* to turn, esp. to get the boat's head away from the wind; tack. **34.** Some special verb phrases are:

cast about, (fol. by *for* or an infinitive). **1.** to look about one mentally, as for an excuse. **2.** scheme.

cast away, 1. to reject. **2.** to shipwreck.

cast back, 1. to refer to something past. **2.** to show resemblance to a remote ancestor.

cast down, to depress; discourage.

cast off, 1. to discard or reject. **2.** to let go.

cast up, 1. to compute; calculate. **2.** to eject; vomit. **3.** to turn up.

—*n.* **35.** act of casting or throwing. **36.** that which is cast. **37.** the distance to which a thing may be cast or thrown. **38.** *Games.* **a.** a throw of dice. **b.** the number rolled. **39.** *Angling.* **a.** act of throwing the line or net on the water. **b.** *Brit.* a line so thrown. **c.** the leader with flies attached, used in angling. **40.** *Hunting.* a dispersal of the dogs in all directions to recapture a scent. **41.** a stroke of fortune; fortune or lot. **42.** a ride offered on one's way. **43.** the form in which something is made or written; arrangement. **44.** *Theat.* the actors to whom the parts in a play are assigned. **45.** *Metall.* **a.** act of casting or founding. **b.** the quantity of metal cast at one time. **46.** something shaped in a mold while in a fluid or plastic state; a casting. **47.** any impression or mold made from a thing. **48.** *Med.* rigid surgical dressing usually made of plaster of paris bandage. **49.** a reproduction or copy, as a plaster model, made in a mold. **50.** outward form; appearance. **51.** sort; kind; style. **52.** tendency; inclination. **53.** a permanent twist or turn: *to have a cast in one's eye.* **54.** a warp. **55.** a slight tinge of some color; hue; shade. **56.** a dash or trace; a small amount. **57.** computation; calculation; addition. **58.** a conjecture; forecast. **59.** *Zool.* one of the wormlike coils of sand passed by the lugworm or other worms. **60.** *Ornith.* a mass of feathers, fur, bones, or other indigestible matters ejected from the stomach by a hawk or other bird. **61.** *Pathol.* effused plastic matter produced in the hollow parts of various diseased organs. —*adj.* **62.** *Theat.* (of a production) having all actors selected. [ME *casten*, t. Scand.; cf. Icel. *kasta* throw] **—Syn.** **1.** See **throw.** **52.** See **turn.**

Cas·ta·li·a (kăs tā'lĭ ə), *n.* **1.** a spring on Mount Parnassus in Greece, sacred to Apollo and the Muses and regarded as a source of inspiration. **2.** any source of inspiration. —**Cas·ta'li·an,** *adj.*

cas·ta·net (kăs'tə nĕt'), *n.* a pair or one of a pair, of shells of ivory or hard wood held in the palm of the hand and struck together as an accompaniment to music and dancing. [t. Sp.: m. *castañeta*, dim. of *castaña*, g. L *castanea* chestnut]

cast·a·way (kăst'ə wā', käst'-), *n.* **1.** a shipwrecked person. **2.** an outcast. —*adj.* **3.** cast adrift. **4.** thrown away.

caste (kăst, käst), *n.* **1.** *Sociol.* an endogamous and hereditary social group limited to persons in a given occupation or trade, having mores distinguishing it from other such groups. **2.** *Hinduism.* **a.** one of the artificial divisions or social classes into which the Hindus are rigidly separated and of which the privileges or disabilities are transmitted by inheritance. **b.** the system or basis of this division. **3.** any rigid system of social distinctions. **4.** the position or rank conferred by the Hindu social system or any similar system: *to lose caste.* [t. Sp., Pg.: m. *casta* breed, race, t. L: m. *castus* pure, CHASTE]

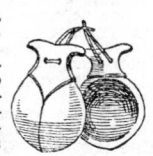
Castanets

cas·tel·lan (kăs'tə lən), *n.* the governor of a castle. [t. L: s. *castellānus* (der. *castellum*; see CASTLE); r. ME *castelain*, t. ONF]

cas·tel·la·ny (kăs'tə lā'nĭ), *n.*, *pl.* **-nies. 1.** the office of a castellan. **2.** the land belonging to a castle.

cas·tel·lat·ed (kăs'tə lā'tĭd), *adj.* **1.** *Archit.* built like a castle, esp. with turrets and battlements. **2.** having very many castles. —**cas·tel·la'tion,** *n.*

cast·er (kăs'tər, käs'-), *n.* **1.** one who or that which casts. **2.** a small wheel on a swivel, set under a piece of furniture, etc., to facilitate moving it. **3.** a bottle or cruet for holding a condiment. **4.** a stand containing a set of such bottles. Also, **castor** for 2, 3, and 4.

cas·ti·gate (kăs'tə gāt'), *v.t.* **-gated, -gating.** to punish in order to correct; criticize severely. [t. L: m.s. *castigātus*, pp.] —**cas·ti·ga'tion,** *n.* —**cas'ti·ga'tor,** *n.*

Ca·sti·glio·ne (käs/tēlyō'nĕ), *n.* **Baldassare** (bäl'-däs sä'rĕ), 1478–1529, Italian diplomat and author.

Cas·tile (käs tēl'), *n.* a former kingdom comprising most of Spain. Spanish, **Cas·til·la** (käs-tē'lyä).

Cas·tile (käs/tēl), *adj.* (of soap, etc.) **1.** (*often l.c.*) made with olive oil and soda. **2.** (*often l.c.*) made with similar ingredients. —*n.* **3.** Castile soap.

Cas·til·ian (käs tĭl'yən), *n.* **1.** the accepted standard form of the Spanish language as spoken in Spain. **2.** the dialect of Castile. **3.** a native or inhabitant of Castile. **4.** of or pertaining to Castile.

cast·ing (käs'tĭng, käs'-), *n.* **1.** act or process of one that casts. **2.** that which is cast; any article which has been cast in a mold.

casting vote, the deciding vote of the presiding officer when the votes are equally divided.

cast iron, an alloy of iron, carbon, and other elements, cast as a soft and strong, or as a hard and brittle iron, depending on the mixture and methods of molding.

cast-i·ron (käst/ī'ərn, käst'-), *adj.* **1.** made of cast iron. **2.** inflexible; rigid; unyielding. **3.** strong; hardy.

cas·tle (käs/əl, käs/əl), *n., v.,* **-tled, -tling.** —*n.* **1.** a fortified residence, as of a prince or noble in feudal times. **2.** the chief and strongest part of the fortifications of a medieval city. **3.** a strongly fortified, permanently garrisoned stronghold. **4.** a large and stately residence, esp. one which imitates the forms of a medieval castle. **5.** *Chess.* the rook. —*v.t.* **6.** to place or enclose in or as in a castle. **7.** *Chess.* to move (the king) in castling. —*v.i.* **8.** *Chess.* **a.** to move the king two squares and bring the castle to the first square the king has passed over. **b.** (of the king) to be moved in this manner. [ME *castel,* t. ONF, g. L *castellum* fortress, dim. of *castrum* fortified place; r. OE *castel* village, t. L (Vulgate): m.s. *castellum*] —**cas'tled,** *adj.* —**Syn. 4.** palace, mansion.

castle in the air, a visionary project; a daydream. Also, **castle in Spain.**

Cas·tle·reagh (käs/əl rā', käs/əl-), *n.* **Robert Stewart, Viscount,** (*2nd Marquess of Londonderry*) 1769–1822, British statesman.

cast·off (käst/ôf', -ŏf', käst'-), *adj.* **1.** thrown away; rejected; discarded: *castoff clothing.* —*n.* **2.** a person or thing that has been cast off.

cas·tor[1] (käs/tər, käs'-), *n.* **1.** a brownish unctuous substance with a strong, penetrating odor, secreted by certain glands in the groin of the beaver, used in medicine and perfumery. **2.** a beaver (hat). **3.** some similar hat. **4.** a beaver. [t. L, t. Gk.: m. *kástōr* beaver]

cas·tor[2] (käs/tər, käs'-), *n.* caster (defs. 2, 3, and 4).

Cas·tor (käs/tər, käs'-), *n. Astron.* Alpha Geminorum; the more northerly of the two bright stars in Gemini.

Castor and Pollux, *Gk. Myth.* twin sons of Leda and brothers of Helen (called the Dioscuri or sons of Zeus), famous for protection of sailors, and for brotherly affection. Pollux, who was immortal, spent alternate days with the gods and with his mortal brother in Hades.

castor bean, *U.S.* **1.** the seed of the castor-oil plant. **2.** the castor-oil plant.

castor oil, a viscid oil obtained from the castor bean, used as a cathartic, lubricant, etc.

cas·tor-oil plant (käs/tər oil', käs'-), a tall euphorbiaceous plant, *Ricinus communis,* native to India but widely naturalized, yielding the castor bean.

cas·tra·me·ta·tion (käs/trə mə tā'shən), *n.* the laying out of camps. [t. F, f. L: *castra* camp + s. *mētātio* measurement]

cas·trate (käs/trāt), *v.t.,* **-trated, -trating. 1.** to deprive of the testicles; emasculate. **2.** to deprive of the ovaries. **3.** to mutilate (a book, etc.) by removing parts; expurgate. [t. L: m.s. *castrātus,* pp.] —**cas·tra'tion,** *n.*

Cas·tro (käs/trō; *Sp.* käs/-)*n.* **Fidel** (fĭ dĕl'; *Sp.* fē-), born 1927, premier of Cuba since 1959.

cast steel, *Metall.* steel rendered homogeneous by being melted in crucibles or pots.

cas·u·al (käzh/ŏŏ əl), *adj.* **1.** happening by chance: *a casual meeting.* **2.** unpremeditated; offhand; without any definite intention: *a casual remark, etc.* **3.** careless; tending to leave things to chance; negligent; unconcerned: *a casual air.* **4.** irregular; occasional: *a casual observer.* **5.** accidental: *a casual fire.* **6.** *Brit.* pertaining to persons receiving charity or work from a district in which they do not permanently live. **7.** *Obs.* uncertain. —*n.* **8.** a worker employed only irregularly. **9.** *Brit.* one who receives occasional relief at a workhouse, etc. **10.** a soldier temporarily at a station or other place of duty, and usually en route to another station. [t. LL: s. *cāsuālis* by chance; r. ME *casuel,* t. OF] —**cas/u·al·ly,** *adv.* —**cas/u·al·ness,** *n.* —**Syn. 1.** fortuitous, unforeseen. See **accidental.** —**Ant. 1.** planned. **2.** deliberate.

cas·u·al·ty (käzh/ŏŏ əl tĭ), *n., pl.* **-ties. 1.** an unfortunate accident, esp. one involving bodily injury or death; a mishap. **2.** *Mil.* **a.** a soldier who is missing in action, or who has been killed, wounded, or captured as a result of enemy action. **b.** (*pl.*) loss in numerical strength through any cause, as death, wounds, sickness,

capture, or desertion. **3.** one who is injured or killed in an accident. **4.** any person injured accidentally.

cas·u·ist (käzh/ŏŏ ĭst), *n.* **1.** one who studies and resolves cases of conscience or conduct. **2.** an oversubtle or disingenuous reasoner upon such matters. [t. F: m. *casuiste,* der. L *cāsus* CASE[1]]

cas·u·is·tic (käzh/ŏŏ ĭs/tĭk), *adj.* **1.** pertaining to casuists or casuistry. **2.** oversubtle; intellectually dishonest; sophistical: *casuistic distinctions.* Also, **cas/-u·is/ti·cal.** —**cas/u·is/ti·cal·ly,** *adv.*

cas·u·ist·ry (käzh/ŏŏ ĭs trĭ), *n., pl.* **-ries.** the application, or, from an outside point of view, misapplication, of general ethical principles to particular cases of conscience or conduct.

ca·sus bel·li (kā/səs bĕl/ī), *Latin.* an event or political occurrence which brings about a declaration of war.

cat (kät), *n., v.,* **catted, catting.** —*n.* **1.** a domesticated carnivore, *Felis domestica* (or *F. catus*), widely distributed in a number of breeds. **2.** any digitate carnivore of the family *Felidae,* as the lion, tiger, leopard, jaguar, etc., of the genus *Felis,* and the short-tailed species that constitute the genus *Lynx,* and esp. any of the smaller species of either genus. **3.** a spiteful and gossipy woman. **4.** cat-o'-nine-tails. **5.** *Games.* **a.** *Chiefly Brit.* the tapering piece of wood used in the game of tipcat. **b.** *Chiefly Brit.* the game itself. **c.** *Chiefly Brit.* the bat used in this game. **d.** a boy's game of ball. **6.** a catboat. **7.** a catfish. **8.** *Naut.* a tackle used in hoisting an anchor to the cathead. —*v.t.* **9.** to flog with a cat-o'-nine-tails. **10.** to hoist (an anchor) to the cathead. [ME; OE *catt, catte,* c. G *katze,* F *chat;* ult. orig. unknown] —**cat/like/,** *adj.*

cat., **1.** catalogue. **2.** catechism.

cata-, a prefix meaning "down," "against," "back," occurring orig. in words from the Greek, but used also in modern words (English and other) formed after the Greek type, as in *catabolism, catalogue, catalysis, catastrophe.* Also, before a vowel, **cat-;** before an aspirate, **cath-.** [t. Gk.: m. *kata-,* also (before a vowel) *kat-,* (before an aspirate) *kath-,* repr. *katá,* prep., down, through, against, according to]

ca·tab·o·lism (kə tăb/ə lĭz'əm), *n. Physiol., Biol.* a breaking down process; destructive metabolism (opposed to *anabolism*). Also, **katabolism.** [f. m.s. Gk. *katabolē* a throwing down + -ISM] —**cat·a·bol·ic** (kăt/ə-bŏl/ĭk), *adj.* —**cat/a·bol/i·cal·ly,** *adv.*

ca·tab·o·lite (kə tăb/ə līt/), *n. Physiol., Biol.* a product of catabolic action.

cat·a·caus·tic (kăt/ə kôs/tĭk), *adj. Math., Optics.* denoting a caustic surface or curve formed by a reflection of light. See **diacaustic.**

cat·a·chre·sis (kăt/ə krē/sĭs), *n., pl.* **-ses** (-sēz). **1.** misuse or strained use of words. **2.** *Philol.* the employment of a word under a false form through misapprehension in regard to its origin: *causeway* and *crawfish* or *crayfish* have their forms by catachresis. [t. L, t. Gk.: m. *katáchrēsis* misuse] —**cat·a·chres·tic** (kăt/ə kres/tĭk), **cat/a·chres/ti·cal,** *adj.* —**cat/a·chres/ti·cal·ly,** *adv.*

cat·a·cli·nal (kăt/ə klī/nəl), *adj. Phys. Geog.* descending with the dip, as a valley. [f. CATA- + CLIN- + -AL]

cat·a·clysm (kăt/ə klĭz'əm), *n.* **1.** any violent upheaval, esp. one of a social or political nature. **2.** *Phys. Geog.* a sudden and violent physical action producing changes in the earth's surface. **3.** an extensive flood. [t. L: s. *cataclysmos,* t. Gk.: m. *kataklysmós* deluge]

cat·a·clys·mic (kăt/ə klĭz/mĭk), *adj.* **1.** of, pertaining to, or resulting from a cataclysm. **2.** of the nature of, or having the effect of, a cataclysm: *cataclysmic changes.* Also, **cat/a·clys/mal.**

cat·a·comb (kăt/ə kōm/), *n.* (*usually pl.*) an underground cemetery, esp. one consisting of tunnels and rooms with recesses dug out for coffins and tombs. [ME *catacombe,* OE *catacumbe,* t. LL: m. *catacumbas*]

cat·a·dro·mous (kə tăd/rə məs), *adj.* (of fishes) going down a river to the sea to spawn.

cat·a·falque (kăt/ə fălk/), *n.* a raised structure on which the body of a deceased personage lies or is carried in state. [t. F, t. It.: m. *catafalco,* g. LL word f. *cata-*CATA- + s. *fala* tower + -*icum* -IC); akin to SCAFFOLD]

Cat·a·lan (kăt/ə lăn/, -lən), *adj.* **1.** pertaining to Catalonia, its inhabitants, or their language. —*n.* **2.** a native or inhabitant of Catalonia. **3.** a Romance language spoken in Catalonia, closely related to Provençal. [t. Sp.]

cat·a·lase (kăt/ə lās/), *n. Chem.* an oxidizing enzyme which decomposes peroxides into water and oxygen. [f. CATAL(YSIS) + -ASE]

cat·a·lec·tic (kăt/ə lĕk/tĭk), *adj.* (of a line of poetry) lacking part of the last foot. Thus the italicized second line is catalectic:

> One more unfortunate,
> Weary of breath.

[t. LL: s. *catalēcticus,* t. Gk.: m. *katalēktikós* incomplete]

cat·a·lep·sy (kăt/ə lĕp/sĭ), *n. Pathol., Psychiatry.* a morbid bodily condition marked by suspension of sensation, muscular rigidity, fixity of posture, and often by loss of contact with environment. [t. LL: m. *catalepsis,* t. Gk.: m. *katálēpsis* seizure] —**cat/a·lep/tic,** *adj.,n.*

cat·a·lin (kăt/ə lĭn), *n.* **1.** a synthetic resin used in costume jewelry, etc. **2.** (*cap.*) a trademark for it.

Cat·a·li·na Island (kăt/ə lē/nə), Santa Catalina.

cat·a·lo (kăt/ə lō'), *n., pl.* **-loes, -los.** a hybrid resulting from crossing the American bison (buffalo) with cattle of the domestic breeds. Also, **cattalo**. [b. CAT(TLE) and (BUFF)ALO]

cat·a·log (kăt′ə lŏg′, -lŏg′), *n., v.t.* catalogue. —**cat′-a·log′er, cat′a·log′ist,** *n.*

cat·a·logue (kăt′ə lŏg′, -lŏg′), *n., v.,* **-logued, -loguing.** —*n.* 1. a list, usually in alphabetical order, with brief notes on the names, articles, etc., listed. 2. a record of the books and other resources of a library or a collection, indicated on cards, or, occasionally, in book form. 3. any list or register. —*v.t.* 4. to make a catalogue of; enter in a catalogue. 5. *Library Science.* to describe the bibliographical and technical features of (a publication and the subject matter it treats). [t. F, t. LL: m.s. *catalogus,* t. Gk.: m. *katálogos* a list] —**cat′a·logu′er, cat′a·logu′ist,** *n.* —**Syn. 1. See list¹.**

Cat·a·lo·ni·a (kăt′ə lō′nĭ ə), *n.* a region in NE Spain, formerly a province. Regional center: Barcelona. Spanish, **Ca·ta·lu·ña** (kä′tä lōō′nyä).

ca·tal·pa (kə tăl′pə), *n.* any tree of the bignoniaceous genus *Catalpa,* of America and Asia, as *C. speciosa,* of the U. S., having large cordate leaves and bell-shaped white flowers. [t. NL, t. N Amer. Ind. (prob. Creek): m. *kutuhlpa* winged head]

ca·tal·y·sis (kə tăl′ə sĭs), *n., pl.* **-ses** (-sēz′). *Chem.* the causing or accelerating of a chemical change by the addition of a substance (**catalyst**) which is not permanently affected by the reaction. [t. NL, t. Gk.: m. *katálysis* dissolution] —**cat·a·lyt·ic** (kăt′ə lĭt′ĭk), *adj., n.* —**cat·a·lyt′i·cal·ly,** *adv.*

cat·a·lyst (kăt′ə lĭst), *n. Chem.* a substance that causes catalysis.

cat·a·lyze (kăt′ə līz′), *v.t.,* **-lyzed, -lyzing.** *Chem.* to act upon by catalysis. —**cat′a·lyz′er,** *n.*

cat·a·ma·ran (kăt′ə mə răn′), *n.* 1. *Naut.* **a.** a float or raft, usually of several logs or pieces of wood lashed together. **b.** any craft with twin parallel hulls. 2. *Colloq.* a quarrelsome person, esp. a woman. [t. Tamil: m. *kaṭṭa-maram* tied tree or wood]

Catamaran

cat·a·me·ni·a (kăt′ə mē′nĭ ə), *n.pl. Physiol.* menses. [t. NL, t. Gk.: m. *kataménia,* neut. pl. of *kataménios* monthly] —**cat′a·me′ni·al,** *adj.*

cat·a·mount (kăt′ə mount′), *n.* 1. a wild animal of the cat family. 2. (in America) **a.** the cougar. **b.** the lynx. 3. catamountain. [var. of CATAMOUNTAIN cat of mountain]

cat·a·moun·tain (kăt′ə moun′tən, -tĭn), *n.* a wild animal of the cat family, as the European wild cat, or the leopard or panther. Also, **cat-o′-mountain.**

Ca·ta·nia (kä tä′nyä), *n.* a seaport in E Sicily. 321,000 (est. 1954).

cat·a·pho·re·sis (kăt′ə fə rē′sĭs), *n.* 1. *Med.* the causing of medicinal substances to pass through or into living tissues in the direction of flow of a positive electric current. 2. *Phys. Chem.* electrophoresis. [t. NL, f. Gk.: m. *kata-* CATA- + *phórēsis* a carrying] —**cat·a·pho·ret·ic** (kăt′ə fə rĕt′ĭk), *adj.*

cat·a·phyll (kăt′ə fĭl), *n. Bot.* a simplified leaf form, as a bud scale or a scale on a cotyledon or rhizome.

cat·a·pult (kăt′ə pŭlt′), *n.* 1. an ancient military engine for throwing darts, stones, etc. 2. a device for launching an airplane from the deck of a ship, esp. a ship not equipped with a flight deck. 3. *Brit.* a slingshot. —*v.t.* 4. to hurl as from a catapult. 5. *Brit.* to hit (an object) by means of a slingshot. [t. L: s. *catapulta,* t. Gk.: m. *katapéltēs*]

Catapult (def. 1)

cat·a·ract (kăt′ə răkt′), *n.* 1. a descent of water over a steep surface; a waterfall, esp. one of considerable size. 2. any furious rush or downpour of water; deluge. 3. an abnormality of the eye, characterized by opacity of the lens. [ME *cataracte,* t. L: m. *cataracta* waterfall, t. Gk.: m. *kataráktēs* down rushing]

ca·tarrh (kə tär′), *n.* inflammation of a mucous membrane, esp. of the respiratory tract, accompanied by excessive secretions. [t. L: m. *catarrhus,* t. Gk.: m. *katárrhous* running down] —**ca·tarrh′al,** *adj.*

ca·tas·ta·sis (kə tăs′tə sĭs), *n., pl.* **-ses** (-sēz′). the part of a drama, preceding the catastrophe, in which the action is at its height. [t. NL, t. Gk.: m. *katástasis* appointment, settlement, condition]

ca·tas·tro·phe (kə tăs′trə fĭ), *n.* 1. a sudden and widespread disaster. 2. a final event or conclusion, usually an unfortunate one; a disastrous end. 3. (in a drama) the point at which the circumstances overcome the central motive, introducing the close or conclusion; the dénouement. 4. a sudden, violent disturbance, esp. of the earth's surface; a cataclysm. [t. Gk.: m. *katastrophḗ* overturning] —**cat·a·stroph·ic** (kăt′ə strŏf′ĭk), *adj.* —**Syn. 2. See disaster.**

ca·tas·tro·phism (kə tăs′trə fĭz′əm), *n. Geol.* the doctrine that certain vast geological changes in the earth's history were caused by catastrophes rather than gradual evolutionary processes. —**ca·tas′tro·phist,** *n.*

cat·a·to·ni·a (kăt′ə tō′nĭ ə), *n. Psychiatry.* a syndrome seen most frequently in schizophrenia, with muscular rigidity and mental stupor, sometimes alternating with great excitement and confusion. [f. CATA- + Gk. *-tonía,* der. *tónos* tension] —**cat·a·ton·ic** (kăt′ə tŏn′ĭk), *adj., n.*

Ca·taw·ba (kə tô′bə), *n.* 1. *Hort.* a reddish grape of the eastern U. S. 2. a light, dry, white wine made from this grape. 3. a Siouan language of Virginia and the Carolinas. 4. name of that part of the Wateree river which is in North Carolina.

cat·bird (kăt′bûrd′), *n.* 1. a slate-colored North American songbird, *Dumetella carolinensis,* allied to the mockingbird, having a call resembling the mewing of a cat. 2. *Australia.* any of several common birds which produce catlike cries.

cat·boat (kăt′bōt′), *n.* a boat with one mast, which is set well forward, and a single sail extended by gaff and boom.

cat brier, any of various species of *Smilax,* as the greenbrier, *Smilax rotundifolia.*

cat·call (kăt′kôl′), *n.* 1. a cry like that of a cat, or an instrument for producing a similar sound, used to express disapproval, at a theater, meeting, etc. —*v.i.* 2. to sound catcalls. —*v.t.* 3. to express disapproval of by catcalls.

catch (kăch), *v.,* **caught, catching,** *n., adj.* —*v.t.* 1. to capture, esp. after pursuit; take captive. 2. to ensnare, entrap, or deceive. 3. to be in time to reach (a train, boat, etc.). 4. to come upon suddenly; surprise or detect, as in some action: *I caught him doing it.* 5. to strike; hit: *the blow caught him on the head.* 6. to intercept and seize (a ball, etc.). 7. to check (one's breath, etc.). 8. to get, receive, incur, or contract (often used figuratively): *to catch a cold, I caught the spirit of the occasion.* 9. to lay hold of; grasp, seize, or snatch; grip or entangle: *a nail caught his sleeve.* 10. to allow to be caught; be entangled with: *to catch one's finger in a door, catch one's coat on a nail.* 11. to fasten with or as with a catch. 12. to get by attraction or impression: *to catch the eye, the attention, etc.* 13. to captivate; charm. 14. to understand by the senses or intellect: *to catch a speaker's words.* 15. **catch it,** to get a scolding or beating. —*v.i.* 16. to become fastened or entangled: *the kite caught in the trees.* 17. to take hold: *the door lock catches.* 18. **catch at, a.** to grasp or snatch. **b.** to be glad to get: *he caught at the chance.* 19. to overtake something moving (fol. by *up, up with,* or *up to*). 20. to play as catcher in a baseball game. 21. to become lighted, take fire, ignite: *the kindling caught instantly.* 22. to spread or be communicated, as a disease. 23. **catch on,** *Colloq.* **a.** to become popular. **b.** to grasp mentally; understand. —*n.* 24. act of catching. 25. anything that catches, esp. a device for checking motion. 26. that which is caught, as a quantity of fish. 27. anything worth getting. 28. *Colloq.* a person of either sex regarded as a desirable matrimonial prospect. 29. a fragment: *catches of a song.* 30. *Music.* a round, esp. one in which the words are so arranged as to produce ludicrous effects. 31. *Baseball, etc.* the catching and holding of a batted or thrown ball before it touches the ground. —*adj.* 32. catchy (defs. 1, 2). [ME *cache(n), cacche(n),* t. ONF: m. *cachier,* g. LL. *captiāre,* der. L *capere* take] —**Syn. 9.** CATCH, CLUTCH, GRASP, SEIZE imply taking hold suddenly of something. To CATCH may be to reach after and get: *he caught my hand.* To CLUTCH is to take firm hold of (often out of fear or nervousness), and retain: *the child clutched his mother's hand.* To GRASP also suggests both getting and keeping hold of, with a connotation of eagerness and alertness, rather than fear (lit. or fig.): *to grasp one's hand in welcome, to grasp an idea.* To SEIZE implies the use of force or energy in taking hold of suddenly (lit. or fig.): *to seize a criminal, seize an opportunity.*

catch·all (kăch′ôl′), *n.* a bag, basket, or other receptacle for odds and ends.

catch basin, a receptacle at an opening into a sewer to retain matter that would not pass readily through the sewer.

catch·er (kăch′ər), *n.* 1. one who or that which catches. 2. *Baseball.* the player who stands behind the bat or home base to catch the pitched ball.

catcher resonator. See **klystron.**

catch·fly (kăch′flī′), *n.* any of various plants, esp. of the genus *Silene,* having a viscid secretion on stem and calyx in which small insects are sometimes caught.

catch·ing (kăch′ĭng), *adj.* 1. infectious. 2. attractive; fascinating; captivating; alluring.

catch·ment basin (kăch′mənt), *Phys. Geog.* a drainage area, esp. of a reservoir or river. Also, **catchment area.**

catch·pen·ny (kăch′pĕn′ĭ), *adj., n., pl.* **-nies.** —*adj.* 1. made to sell readily at a low price, regardless of value or use. —*n.* 2. anything of little value or use, made merely for quick sale.

catch phrase, a phrase that attracts attention.

catch·pole (kăch′pōl′), *n. Archaic or Hist.* a petty officer of justice, esp. one who makes arrests for debt. Also, **catch′poll′.** [ME *cachepol,* OE *kæcepol,* t. ML: m.s *cacepollus* chase-fowl. See CATCH, PULLET]

catch·up (kăch′əp, kĕch′-), *n. Now U.S.* any of several sauces or condiments for meat, fish, as *tomato* or *mushroom catchup.* Also, **catsup, ketchup.** [var. of KETCHUP]

catch·weight (kăch'wāt'), *n.* *Sports.* the chance or optional weight of a contestant, as contrasted with a weight fixed by agreement, etc.

catch·word (kăch'wûrd'), *n.* **1.** a word or phrase caught up and repeated for effect as by a political party. **2.** a word printed at the top of a page in a dictionary or other reference book to indicate the first or last article on that page. **3.** a device, used esp. in old books, to assist the reader by inserting at the foot of the page the first word of the following page. **4.** an actor's cue.

catch·y (kăch'ĭ), *adj.*, **catchier, catchiest. 1.** pleasing and easily remembered: *a catchy tune.* **2.** tricky; deceptive: *a catchy question.* **3.** occurring in snatches; fitful: *a catchy wind.*

cate (kāt), *n.* *(usually pl.)* *Archaic.* a choice food; a delicacy; a dainty. [aphetic var. of ME *acate*, t. ONF: m. *acat*, der. *acater* buy, g. LL *accaptāre* acquire]

cat·e·che·sis (kăt'ə kē'sĭs), *n.*, *pl.* **-ses** (-sēz). oral religious instruction, formerly esp. before baptism or confirmation. [t. L, t. Gk.: m. *katēchēsis* oral instruction]

cat·e·chet·i·cal (kăt'ə kĕt'ĭ kəl), *adj.* pertaining to teaching by question and answer. Also, **cat'e·chet'ic.**

cat·e·chin (kăt'ə chĭn, -kĭn), *n.* an amorphous, yellow compound, $C_{15}H_{14}O_6$, used in tanning and dyeing.

cat·e·chism (kăt'ə kĭz'əm), *n.* **1.** *Eccles.* **a.** an elementary book containing a summary of the principles of the Christian religion, esp. as maintained by a particular church, in the form of questions and answers. **b.** the contents of such a book. **2.** a similar book of instruction in other subjects. **3.** *Pol.* a series of formal questions put to political candidates, etc., to bring out their views. **4.** *Obs.* catechetical instruction. [t. LL: s. *catēchismus*, der. Gk. *katēchizein*. See CATECHIZE]

cat·e·chist (kăt'ə kĭst), *n.* **1.** one who catechizes. **2.** *Eccles.* one appointed to instruct catechumens in the principles of religion as a preparation for baptism. —**cat'e·chis'tic, cat'e·chis'ti·cal,** *adj.*

cat·e·chize (kăt'ə kīz'), *v.t.*, **-chized, -chizing. 1.** to instruct orally by means of questions and answers, esp. in Christian doctrine. **2.** to question with reference to belief. **3.** to question closely or excessively. Also, **cat'e·chise'.** [t. LL: m. s. *catēchizāre*, t. Gk.: m. *katēchizein*, teach orally] —**cat'e·chi·za'tion,** *n.* —**cat'e·chiz'er,** *n.*

cat·e·chol (kăt'ə chôl', -kōl'), *n.* *Chem., etc.* a white crystalline benzene derivative, $C_6H_6O_2$, used in photography; pyrocatechol. [f. CATECH(U) + -OL²]

cat·e·chu (kăt'ə chōō', -kū'), *n.* any of several astringent substances obtained from various tropical plants, esp. from the wood of two East Indian species of acacia, *Acacia Catechu* and *A. Suma*, used in medicine, dyeing, tanning, etc.; cutch. Also, **cashoo.** [t. NL, t. Malay: m. (unexplained) *kachu*]

cat·e·chu·men (kăt'ə kū'mən), *n.* **1.** *Eccles.* one under instruction in the rudiments of Christianity, as in the early church; a neophyte. **2.** a person being taught the elementary facts, principles, etc. of any subject. [t. LL: s. *catēchūmenus*, t. Gk.: m. *katēchoúmenos*, ppr. pass. of *katēchein*. See CATECHIZE] —**cat'e·chu'me·nal,** *adj.*

cat·e·gor·i·cal (kăt'ə gôr'ə kəl, -gŏr'-), *adj.* **1.** not involving a condition, qualification, etc.; explicit; direct: *a categorical answer.* **2.** *Logic.* (of a proposition) analyzable into a subject and an attribute related by a copula, as in *all men are mortal.* **3.** of, pertaining to, or in a category. —**cat'e·gor'i·cal·ly,** *adv.* —**cat'e·gor'i·cal·ness,** *n.*

categorical imperative, 1. *Ethics.* the rule of Immanuel Kant that one must do only what he can will that all others should do under similar circumstances. **2.** the unconditional command of conscience.

cat·e·go·ry (kăt'ə gôr'ĭ), *n.*, *pl.* **-ries. 1.** a classificatory division in any field of knowledge, as a phylum or any of its subdivisions in biology. **2.** any general or comprehensive division; a class. **3.** *Logic, Metaphys.* **a.** a basic mode or phase of existence, as space, quantity, quality. **b.** a basic form or organizing principle of reason as the principle of causality. [t. L: m. s. *catēgoria*, t. Gk.: m. *katēgoria* assertion]

ca·te·na (kə tē'nə), *n.*, *pl.* **-nae** (-nē). a chain or connected series, esp. of extracts from the writings of the fathers of the church. [t. L: chain]

cat·e·nar·y (kăt'ə nĕr'ĭ; *esp. Brit.* kə tē'nə rĭ), *n.*, *pl.* **-naries,** *adj.* *Math.* —*n.* **1.** the curve assumed approximately by a heavy uniform cord or chain hanging freely from two points not in the same vertical line. —*adj.* **2.** Also, **cat·e·nar·i·an** (kăt'ə nâr'ĭ ən). pertaining to a catenary. [t. L; m.s. *catēnārius* relating to a chain]

cat·e·nate (kăt'ə nāt'), *v.t.*, **-nated, -nating.** to link together; form into a connected series: *catenated cells.* —**cat'e·na'tion,** *n.*

ca·ter (kā'tər), *v.i.* **1.** to provide food, service, etc.: *to cater for a banquet.* **2.** to provide means of amusement, pleasure, etc.: *to cater to popular taste.* [v. use of obs. *cater*, ME *catour*, aphetic var. of *acatour* buyer of provisions, t. OF: m. *acateor* buyer. See CATE]

cat·er·an (kăt'ər ən), *n.* a freebooter or marauder of the Scottish Highlands. [t. ML: s. *caterānus*, Latinization of ME (Scot.) *catherein*, etc., t. Gaelic: m. *ceathairne* peasantry. See KERN¹]

cat·er·cor·nered (kăt'ə kôr'nərd, kăt'ər-), *adj.* **1.** diagonal. —*adv.* **2.** diagonally. [f. *cater,* adv., diagonally (t. F: m. *quatre* four) + *cornered*]

ca·ter·cous·in (kā'tər kŭz'ən), *n.* **1.** one related by or as by cousinship. **2.** an intimate friend.

ca·ter·er (kā'tərər), *n.* **1.** a purveyor of food or provisions, as for entertainments, etc. **2.** one who caters. —**ca·ter·ess** (kā'tər ĭs), *n. fem.*

cat·er·pil·lar (kăt'ə pĭl'ər, kăt'ər-), *n.* **1.** the wormlike larva of a butterfly or a moth. **2.** Also, **caterpillar tractor.** a tractor having the driving wheels moving inside endless tracks on either side, thus being capable of hauling heavy loads over rough or soft ground. **3.** *(cap.)* a trademark for this tractor. **4.** any device, as a tank or steam shovel, moving on endless belt (caterpillar) treads. **5.** one who preys on others; extortioner. [late ME *catyrpel*(er), of uncert. orig. Cf. OF *chatepelose,* lit., hairy cat]

cat·er·waul (kăt'ər wôl'), *v.i.* **1.** to cry as cats in rutting time. **2.** to utter a similar sound; howl or screech. **3.** to quarrel like cats. —*n.* Also, **cat'er·waul'ing. 4.** the cry of a cat in rutting time. **5.** any similar sound. [ME *caterw*(r)*awen,* f. *cater* (cf. G *kater* tomcat) + *wrawen* howl]

cat·fall (kăt'fôl'), *n.* *Naut.* the rope or tackle for hoisting an anchor to the cathead.

cat·fish (kăt'fĭsh'), *n.*, *pl.* **-fishes,** *(esp. collectively)* **-fish. 1.** any of numerous fishes having some fancied resemblance to a cat, such as one of the fishes characterized by long barbels, of the North American fresh-water family *Ameiuridae*, many of which are used for food. **2.** any fish of the order *Nematognathi*, as a bullhead.

cat·gut (kăt'gŭt'), *n.* **1.** the intestines of sheep or other animals, dried and twisted, used as strings for musical instruments, etc. **2.** a violin. **3.** stringed instruments collectively.

cath-, var. of cata-, before an aspirate, as in *cathode.*

Cath., Catholic.

ca·thar·sis (kə thär'sĭs), *n.* **1.** *Aesthetics.* the effect of art in purifying the emotions (applied by Aristotle to the relief or purgation of the emotions of the audience or performers effected through pity and terror by tragedy and certain kinds of music). **2.** *Pyschoanal.* an effective discharge with symptomatic relief but not necessarily a cure of the underlying pathology. **3.** *Psychiatry.* psychotherapy which encourages and permits discharge of pent-up and socially unacceptable effects. **4.** *Med.* purgation. [t. NL, t. Gk.: m. *kátharsis* a cleansing]

ca·thar·tic (kə thär'tĭk), *adj.* **1.** Also, **ca·thar'ti·cal.** evacuating the bowels; purgative. —*n.* **2.** a purgative. [t. L: s. *catharticus*, t. Gk.: m. *kathartikós* fit for cleansing, purgative]

Ca·thay (kă thā'), *n.* *Archaic or Poetic.* China. [t. ML: s. *Cat*(h)*aya;* cf. Russ. *Kitai,* said to be of Tatar orig.]

cat·head (kăt'hĕd'), *n.* *Naut.* a projecting timber or beam near the bow, to which the anchor is hoisted.

ca·the·dra (kə thē'drə, kăth'ə-), *n.*, *pl.* **-drae** (-drē, -drē'). **1.** the seat or throne of a bishop in the principal church of his diocese. **2.** an official chair, as of a professor in a university. [t. L, t. Gk.: m. *kathēdra* chair]

ca·the·dral (kə thē'drəl), *n.* **1.** the principal church of a diocese, containing the bishop's throne. **2.** (in nonepiscopal denominations) any of various important churches. —*adj.* **3.** pertaining to or containing a bishop's throne. **4.** pertaining to or emanating from a chair of office or authority.

Cath·er (kăth'ər), *n.* **Willa Sibert** (wĭl'ə sē'bərt), 1876–1947, U. S. novelist.

Cath·er·ine (kăth'rĭn, -ər ĭn), *n.* **Saint,** died A.D. 307, Christian martyr of Alexandria who was beheaded.

Catherine I, c 1683–1727, consort of Peter the Great, and empress of Russia, 1725–27.

Catherine II, *("the Great")* 1729–96, consort of Czar Peter, and empress of Russia, 1762–96.

Catherine of Ar·a·gon (ăr'ə gən, -gŏn'), 1485–1536, first wife of Henry VIII of England and mother of Mary I of England.

Catherine of Sie·na (syĕ'nä), **Saint,** 1347–80, Italian ascetic and mystic (Dominican tertiary).

cath·e·ter (kăth'ə tər), *n.* *Med.* a flexible or rigid hollow tube employed to drain fluids from body cavities or to distend body passages, esp. one for passing into the bladder through the urethra to draw off urine. [t. LL, t. Gk.: m. *kathetēr,* der. *kathiénai* let down]

cath·e·ter·ize (kăth'ə tə rīz'), *v.t.*, **-ized, -izing.** to introduce a catheter into.

ca·thex·is (kə thĕk'sĭs), *n.* *Psychoanal.* **1.** the investment of emotional significance in an activity, object, or idea. **2.** the charge of psychic energy so invested. [t. Gk.: m. *káthexis* holding, retention; rendering G *besetzung* (Freud)]

cath·ode (kăth'ōd), *n.* **1.** the electrode which emits electrons or gives off negative ions and toward which positive ions move or collect, in a voltaic cell, electronic or x-ray tube, or other device. **2.** the negative pole of a battery or other source of electric current (opposed to *anode*). Also, **kathode.** [t. Gk.: m. s. *káthodos* way down] —**ca·thod·ic** (kə thŏd'ĭk), *adj.*

cathode ray, a stream of electrons generated at the cathode during an electric discharge in a vacuum tube; used to generate x-rays.

cathode ray tube, *Electronics.* a vacuum tube that generates a focused beam of electrons which can be deflected by electric and/or magnetic fields. The terminus of the beam is visible as a spot or line of luminescence caused by its impinging on a sensitized screen at one end

---

b., blend of, blended; **c.,** cognate with; **d.,** dialect, dialectal; **der.,** derived from; **f.,** formed from; **g.,** going back to; **m.,** modification of; **r.,** replacing; **s.,** stem of; **t.,** taken from; **?,** perhaps. See the full key on inside cover.

of the tube. Cathode ray tubes are used to study the shapes of electric waves, to reproduce pictures in television receivers, as an indicator in radar sets, etc.

cath·o·lic (kăth′əlÿk, kăth′lÿk), *adj.* **1.** pertaining to the whole Christian body or church. **2.** universal in extent; involving all; of interest to all. **3.** having sympathies with all; broad-minded; liberal: *to be catholic in one's tastes, interests, etc.* [t. L: s. *catholicus*, t. Gk.: m. *katholikós* (def. 2)] —**ca·thol·i·cal·ly** (kəthŏl′ĭklĭ), *adv.*

Cath·o·lic (kăth′əlÿk, kăth′lÿk), *adj.* **1.** *Theol.* **a.** (among Roman Catholics) claiming to possess exclusively the notes or characteristics of the one, only, true, and universal church—unity, visibility, indefectibility, apostolic succession, universality, and sanctity (used in this sense, with these qualifications, only by the Church of Rome, as applicable only to itself and its adherents, and to their faith and organization; often qualified, especially by those not acknowledging these claims, by prefixing the word *Roman*). **b.** (among Anglicans) noting or pertaining to the conception of the Church as the body representing the ancient undivided Christian witness, comprising all the orthodox churches which have kept the apostolic succession of bishops, and including the Anglican Church, the Roman Catholic Church, the Eastern Orthodox Church, Church of Sweden, the Old Catholic Church (in the Netherlands and elsewhere), etc. **2.** pertaining to the Western Church. —*n.* **3.** a member of a Catholic church, esp. of the Church of Rome.

Catholic Church, *Rom. Cath. Ch.* a visible society of baptized, professing the same faith under the authority of the invisible Head (Christ) and the authority of the visible head (the pope and the bishops in communion with him).

Ca·thol·i·cism (kəthŏl′əsĭz′əm), *n.* **1.** the faith, system, and practice of the Catholic Church, esp. the Roman Catholic Church. **2.** (*l.c.*) catholicity (def. 1).

cath·o·lic·i·ty (kăth′əlĭs′ətĭ), *n.* **1.** the quality of being catholic; universality; broad-mindedness. **2.** (*cap.*) the Roman Catholic Church, or its doctrines and usages.

ca·thol·i·cize (kəthŏl′əsīz′), *v.t., v.i.,* -**cized,** -**cizing.** to make or become catholic or (*cap.*) Catholic.

ca·thol·i·con (kəthŏl′əkən), *n.* a universal remedy; a panacea. [t. Gk.: m. *katholikón*]

Cat·i·line (kăt′əlīn′), *n.* **1.** (*Lucius Sergius Catilina*) 108?–62 B.C. Roman politician and conspirator. **2.** any base political conspirator.

cat·i·on (kăt′ī′ən), *n. Phys. Chem.* **1.** a positively charged ion which is attracted to the cathode in electrolysis. **2.** any positively charged ion, radical, or molecule. Also, **kation.** [t. Gk.: m. *katíon*, ppr. neut., going down]

cat·kin (kăt′kĭn), *n. Bot.* an ament, as of the willow or birch. [t. D: m. *katteken* little cat]

cat·ling (kăt′lĭng), *n. Now Rare.* **1.** a little cat; a kitten. **2.** catgut; a catgut string. **3.** a surgical knife. [f. CAT + -LING¹]

cat nap, *U.S.* a short, light nap or doze.

cat·nip (kăt′nĭp), *n.* a plant, *Nepeta Cataria*, of the mint family, with strongly scented leaves of which cats are fond. Also, *Brit.,* **cat·mint** (kăt′mĭnt′). [f. CAT + *nip,* var. of *nep* catnip, var. of *nept,* t. ML: s. *nepta,* L *nepeta*]

Ca·to (kā′tō), *n.* **1. Marcus Porcius** (mär′kəs pôr′shĭəs), ("the Elder" or "the Censor") 234–149 B.C., Roman statesman, soldier, and writer. **2.** his greatgrandson **Marcus Porcius,** ("the Younger") 95–46 B.C., Roman statesman, soldier, and Stoic philosopher.

cat-o′-moun·tain (kăt′əmoun′tən, -tĭn), *n.* catamountain.

cat-o′-nine-tails (kăt′ənīn′tālz′), *n., pl.* **-tails.** a whip, usually having nine knotted lines or cords fastened to a handle, used to flog offenders.

ca·top·trics (kətŏp′trĭks), *n.* that branch of optics dealing with the formation of images by mirrors. [t. Gk.: m.s. *katoptrikós* of or in a mirror. See -ICS] —**ca·top′tric, ca·top′tri·cal,** *adj.*

cat·rigged (kăt′rĭgd′), *adj.* rigged like a catboat.

cat's cradle, a child's game in which two players alternately stretch a looped string over their fingers in such a way as to produce different designs.

cat's-eye (kăts′ī′), *n.* any of certain gems exhibiting a chatoyant luster, but esp. a variety of chrysoberyl (the oriental or precious cat's-eye).

Cats·kill Mountains (kăts′kĭl). a range of low mountains in E New York. Highest peak, Slide Mountain, 4204 ft. Also, **Catskills.**

cat's-paw (kăts′pô′), *n.* **1.** a person used by another to serve his purposes; a tool. **2.** *Naut.* **a.** a kind of hitch in the bight of a rope, made to hook a tackle on. **b.** a light breeze which ruffles the surface of the water over a comparatively small area. Also, **cats′paw′.**

cat·stick (kăt′stĭk′), *n.* a stick used in certain games.

cat·sup (kăt′səp, kĕch′əp), *n.* catchup.

Catt (kăt), *n.* **Carrie Chapman** (kăr′ĭ chăp′mən), 1859–1947, U.S. leader in women's suffrage movements.

cat·tail (kăt′tāl′), *n.* **1.** a tall reedlike marsh plant, *Typha latifolia,* with flowers in long, dense cylindrical

spikes; reed mace. **2.** any of several other plants of the same genus. **3.** *Bot.* an ament or catkin.

cat·ta·lo (kăt′əlō′), *n., pl.* **-loes, -los.** catalo.

Cat·te·gat (kăt′əgăt′), *n.* Kattegat.

cat·tish (kăt′ĭsh), *adj.* **1.** catlike; feline; **2.** spiteful. —**cat′tish·ly,** *adv.* —**cat′tish·ness,** *n.*

cat·tle (kăt′əl), *n.* **1.** *U.S.* ruminants of the bovine kind, of any age, breed, or sex. **2.** (formerly, and still in England) such animals together with horses and other domesticated animals. **3.** insects, vermin, or other animals considered contemptuously or in a mass. **4.** *Contemptuous.* human beings. [ME *catel,* t. ONF, g. L *capitāle* wealth, stock. See CAPITAL¹, n.]

cat·tle·man (kăt′əlmən), *n., pl.* **-men.** **1.** a person employed in tending or rearing cattle. **2.** *U.S.* one who rears cattle on a large scale; the owner of a cattle ranch.

cat·ty¹ (kăt′ĭ), *adj.,* **-tier, -tiest. 1.** catlike. **2.** quietly or slyly malicious; spiteful: *a catty gossip.* [f. CAT + -Y¹] —**cat′ti·ly,** *adv.* —**cat′ti·ness,** *n.*

cat·ty² (kăt′ĭ), *n., pl.* **-ties.** (in China and elsewhere in the East) a weight equal to about 1⅓ pounds avoirdupois. [t. Malay: m. *kati*]

Ca·tul·lus (kətŭl′əs), *n.* **Gaius Valerius** (gā′əs vəlĭr′ĭ əs), 84?–54? B.C., Roman lyric poet.

cat·walk (kăt′wôk′), *n.* any narrow walking space on a bridge, or in an aircraft.

cat whisker, *Radio.* the wire forming one contact of the crystal in a crystal detector.

Cau·ca·sia (kôkā′zhə, -shə), *n.* a region in the Soviet Union between the Black and Caspian seas: divided by the Caucasus Mountains into Ciscaucasia (in Europe) and Transcaucasia (in Asia). Also, **Caucasus.**

Cau·ca·sian (kôkā′zhən, -shən, -kăzh′ən, -kăsh′ən), *adj.* **1.** pertaining to the so-called "white race," embracing the principal peoples of Europe, southwestern Asia, and northern Africa, so named because the native peoples of the Caucasus were considered typical. **2.** of or pertaining to the Caucasus mountain range. Also, **Cau·cas·ic** (kôkăs′ĭk). —*n.* **3.** a member of the Caucasian race. **4.** a native of the Caucasus.

Cau·ca·sus (kô′kəsəs), *n.* **1.** a mountain range in the S Soviet Union in Europe, in Caucasia. Highest peak, Mt. Elbrus (highest in Europe), 18,481 ft. **2.** Caucasia.

cau·cus (kô′kəs), *n.* **1.** *U.S.* a meeting of the local members of a political party to nominate candidates, elect delegates to a convention, etc., or of the members of a legislative body who belong to the same party to determine upon action in that body. **2.** (in England) a local committee of a political party exercising a certain control over its affairs or actions. —*v.i.* **3.** to hold or meet in a caucus. [orig. unknown; ? alter. of *caulkers'* (*meeting*), from the fact that such meetings were orig. held where ship business was carried on, or ? of Amer. Ind. orig.]

cau·dad (kô′dăd), *adv. Anat., Zool.* toward the tail or posterior end of the body (opposed to *cephalad*). [f. L: s. *cauda* tail + *ad* to]

cau·dal (kô′dəl), *adj. Zool.* **1.** of, at, or near the tail. **2.** taillike: *caudal appendages.* [t. NL: s. *caudālis,* der. L *cauda* tail] —**cau′dal·ly,** *adv.*

cau·date (kô′dāt), *adj. Zool.* having a tail or taillike appendage. Also, **cau′dat·ed.** [t. NL: m. s. *caudātus,* der. L *cauda* tail]

cau·dex (kô′dĕks), *n., pl.* **-dices** (-dəsēz′), **-dexes.** *Bot.* **1.** the axis of a plant, including both stem and root. **2.** a stem bearing the remains or scars of petioles. **3.** the woody or thickened persistent base of a herbaceous perennial. [t. L: tree trunk. See CODEX]

cau·dil·lo (kôdēl′yō, -dē′yō; *Sp.* koudē′lyō, -yō), *n., pl.* **-los** (-yōz; *Sp.* -lyōs, -yōs). (in Spanish-speaking countries) the head of the state; leader.

Cau·dine Forks (kô′dĭn), two narrow mountain passes in S Italy, near Benevento: site of a Roman defeat by the Samnites, 321 B.C.

cau·dle (kô′dəl), *n.* a warm drink for the sick, as of wine or ale mixed with eggs, bread, sugar, spices, etc. [ME *caudel,* t. ONF, dim. of *caud,* g. L *calidus* warm]

caught (kôt), *v.* pt. and pp. of **catch.**

caul (kôl), *n.* a part of the amnion sometimes covering the head of a child at birth, superstitiously supposed to bring good luck and to be an infallible preservative against drowning. [ME *calle,* t. F: m. *cale* kind of cap]

cauld (kôld, kăld, kōd), *adj., n. Scot.* cold.

caul·dron (kôl′drən), *n.* caldron.

cau·les·cent (kôlĕs′ənt), *adj. Bot.* having an obvious stem rising above the ground. [f. s. L *caulis* stalk + -ESCENT]

cau·li·cle (kô′ləkəl), *n. Bot.* a small or rudimentary stem. [t. L: m. s. *cauliculus,* dim. of *caulis* stalk]

cau·li·flow·er (kô′lə flou′ər; *Colloq. often* kŏl′ĭ-), *n.* **1.** a cultivated cruciferous plant, *Brassica oleracea* var., *botrytis,* whose inflorescence forms a compact, fleshy head. **2.** the head, used as a vegetable. [half adoption, half trans. of NL *cauliflora,* lit., cabbage-flower]

cauliflower ear, an ear that has been misshaped by battering blows.

cau·line (kô′lĭn, -līn), *adj. Bot.* of or pertaining to a stem, esp. pertaining to or arising from the upper part of a stem. [f. s. L *caulis* stalk + -INE¹]

cau·lis (kô′lĭs), *n., pl.* **-les** (-lēz). *Bot.* the main stalk or stem of a plant or of a herbaceous plant. [t. L]

caulk (kôk), *v.t.* calk¹. —**caulk′er,** *n.*

caus·al (kô/zəl), *adj.* **1.** of, constituting, or implying a cause. **2.** *Gram.* expressing a cause, as a conjunction. —**caus/al·ly,** *adv.*

cau·sal·gi·a (kô zăl/jĭ ə), *n.* a neuralgia distinguished by a burning pain along certain nerves, usually of the upper extremities. [f. m.s. Gk. *kaûsos* burning heat + -ALGIA]

cau·sal·i·ty (kô zăl/ə tĭ), *n., pl.* **-ties. 1.** the relation of cause and effect. **2.** causal quality or agency.

cau·sa si·ne qua non (kô/zə sī/nĭ kwä nŏn/), *Latin.* a requisite or indispensable condition.

cau·sa·tion (kô zā/shən). *n.* **1.** the action of causing or producing. **2.** the relation of cause to effect. **3.** anything that produces an effect; a cause.

caus·a·tive (kô/zə tĭv), *n.* **1.** *Gram.* a word (usually a verb) denoting causation, as *made* in *he made me eat the apple.* —*adj.* **2.** *Gram.* **a.** pertaining to an affix or other form by which causatives are derived from an underlying word. For example: Gothic *jan* is a causative affix in *fulljan* (cause to be full, fill). **b.** pertaining to a word or words so derived, esp. one formed from an underlying word that lacks this meaning: *"to fell" is the causative of "to fall."* **3.** acting as a cause; productive (fol. by *of*). —**caus/a·tive·ly,** *adv.* —**caus/a·tive·ness,** *n.*

cause (kôz), *n., v.,* **caused, causing.** —*n.* **1.** that which produces an effect; the thing, person, etc. from which something results. **2.** the ground of any action or result; reason; motive. **3.** good or sufficient reason: *to complain without cause.* **4.** *Law.* **a.** a ground of legal action; the matter over which a person goes to law. **b.** a case for judicial decision. **5.** any subject of discussion or debate. **6.** that side of a question which a person or party supports; the aim, purpose, etc. of a group. **7.** *Philos.* the end or purpose for which a thing is done or produced (now only in *final causes*). —*v.t.* **8.** to be the cause of; bring about. [ME, t. L: m. *causa*] —**caus/a·ble,** *adj.* —**cause/less,** *adj.* —**caus/er,** *n.*
—**Syn. 1.** CAUSE, OCCASION refer to the starting of effects into motion. A CAUSE is an agency, perhaps acting through a long time, or a long-standing situation, which produces an effect: *the cause of the quarrel between the two men was jealousy.* An OCCASION is an event which provides an opportunity for the effect to become evident, or perhaps promotes its becoming evident: *the occasion was the fact that one man's wages were increased.* **3.** See **reason. 8.** effect, make, create, produce.

cause cé·lè·bre (kôz sĕ lĕb/r), *French.* a celebrated legal case.

cau·se·rie (kō/zə rē/; *Fr.* kōz rē/), *n.* **1.** a talk or chat. **2.** a short, informal essay, article, etc. [t. F, der. *causer* talk, t. L: m. *causārī* plead]

cause·way (kôz/wā/), *n.* **1.** a raised road or path, as across low or wet ground. **2.** a highway or paved way. —*v.t.* **3.** to pave, as a road or street, with cobbles or pebbles. **4.** to provide with a causeway. [var. of *causey way.* See CAUSEY]

cau·sey (kō/zĭ), *n., pl.* **-seys.** *Brit. Dial.* causeway. [ME *cauce,* t. ONF: m. *caucie,* earlier *cauciee* (cf. F *chaussée*), g. LL *calciāta* paved road]

caus·tic (kôs/tĭk), *adj.* **1.** capable of burning, corroding, or destroying living tissue: *caustic soda.* **2.** severely critical or sarcastic: *a caustic remark.* **3.** *Math., Optics.* **a.** denoting a surface to which all the light rays emanating from a single point and reflected by a curved surface (as a concave mirror) are tangent. **b.** denoting a curve formed by a plane section of such a surface. **c.** denoting an analogous surface or curve resulting from refraction. —*n.* **4.** a caustic substance: *lunar caustic.* **5.** *Math., Optics.* a caustic surface or curve. [t. L: s. *causticus,* t. Gk.: m. *kaustikós* capable of burning] —**caus/ti·cal·ly,** *adv.* —**caus·tic·i·ty** (kôs tĭs/ə tĭ), *n.*

caustic potash, potassium hydroxide, KOH, used in the manufacture of soap, and glass.

caustic soda, sodium hydroxide, NaOH, used in metallurgy and photography.

cau·ter·ize (kô/tə rīz/), *v.t.,* **-ized, -izing.** to burn with a hot iron, or with fire or a caustic, esp. for curative purposes; treat with a cautery. —**cau/ter·i·za/tion,** *n.*

cau·ter·y (kô/tər ĭ), *n., pl.* **-teries. 1.** an escharotic substance or a hot iron used to destroy tissue. **2.** the process of destroying tissue with a cautery. [t. L: m.s. *cautērium,* t. Gk.: m. *kautērion,* dim. of *kautḗr* branding iron]

cau·tion (kô/shən), *n.* **1.** prudence in regard to danger or evil; carefulness; wariness: *proceed with caution.* **2.** a warning against danger or evil; anything serving as a warning. **3.** *Colloq.* a person or thing that is unusual, odd, amazing, etc. —*v.t.* **4.** to give warning to; advise or urge to take heed. [t. L: s. *cautio;* r. ME *caucion* security, t. OF] —**Syn. 1.** circumspectness, watchfulness, heed, care. **2.** admonition, advice. **4.** See **warn.** —**Ant. 1.** recklessness.

cau·tion·ar·y (kô/shə nĕr/ĭ), *adj.* of the nature of or containing a warning: *cautionary advice.*

cau·tious (kô/shəs), *adj.* having or showing caution or prudence to avoid danger or evil; very careful. —**cau/tious·ly,** *adv.* —**cau/tious·ness,** *n.* —**Syn.** prudent, discreet, guarded, wary, circumspect. See **careful.** —**Ant.** rash, heedless.

Cau·ver·y (kô/və rĭ), *n.* a river in S India, flowing from the Western Ghats SE to the Bay of Bengal: sacred to the Hindus. ab. 500 mi. Also, **Kaveri.**

Cav., Cavalry.

cav·al·cade. (kăv/əl kād/, kăv/əl kād/), *n.* **1.** a procession of persons on horseback or in horse-drawn carriages. **2.** any procession. [t. F, t. It.: m. *cavalcata,* der. *cavalcare,* g. LL *caballicāre* ride on horseback]

cav·a·lier (kăv/ə lĭr/), *n.* **1.** a horseman, esp. a mounted soldier; a knight. **2.** one having the spirit or bearing of a knight; a courtly gentleman; a gallant. **3.** a man escorting a woman or acting as her partner in dancing. **4.** (*cap.*) an adherent of Charles I of England in his contest with Parliament. —*adj.* **5.** haughty, disdainful, or supercilious. **6.** offhand or unceremonious. **7.** (*cap.*) of or pertaining to the Cavaliers. —*v.i.* **8.** to play the cavalier. **9.** to be haughty or domineering. [t. F, t. It.: m. *cavalliere,* der. *cavallo* horse, g. L *caballus*]

cav·a·lier·ly (kăv/ə lĭr/lĭ), *adv.* **1.** in a cavalier manner. —*adj.* **2.** characteristic of a cavalier; arrogant.

Cavalier poets, a group of English poets (Herrick, Carew, Lovelace, Suckling, etc.), mainly at the court of Charles I, who produced a body of graceful lyrical poetry.

ca·val·la (kə văl/ə), *n., pl.* **-la, -las.** cavally.

ca·val·ly (kə văl/ĭ), *n., pl.* **-lies. 1.** any of various carangoid fishes of the genus *Caranx,* esp. *C. hippos,* a food fish of both coasts of tropical America. **2.** the cero. [t. Pg.: m. *cavalla,* or t. Sp.: m. *caballa* horse mackerel, g. L *caballa* mare]

cav·al·ry (kăv/əl rĭ), *n., pl.* **-ries. 1.** *Mil.* **a.** that part of a military force composed of troops that serve on horseback. **b.** mounted soldiers collectively. **c.** (in armored forces) an element having reconnaissance in force as its principal mission. **2.** horsemen, horses, etc., collectively. **3.** *Obs.* horsemanship, esp. of a knight. [t. F: m. *cavalerie,* t. It.: m. *cavalleria* knighthood, der. *cavalliere.* See CAVALIER[1]] —**cav·al·ry·man** (kăv/əl rĭ man/), *n.*

cav·a·ti·na (kăv/ə tē/nə; *It.* kä/vä tē/nä), *n., pl.* **-ne** (-nĕ). *Music.* a simple song or melody, properly one without a second part and a repeat; an air. [t. It.]

cave (kāv), *n., v.,* **caved, caving.** —*n.* **1.** a hollow in the earth, esp. one opening more or less horizontally into a hill, mountain, etc. **2.** *Eng. Pol.* a secession, or a group of seceders, from a political party on some special question. —*v.t.* **3.** to hollow out. **4.** to cause to fall (fol. by *in*). —*v.i.* **5.** to fall or sink, as ground (fol. by *in*). **6.** *Colloq.* to give, yield, or submit (fol. by *in*). [ME, t. OF, t. L: m. *cava* hollow (places), neut. pl.]

ca·ve·at (kā/vĭ ăt/), *n.* **1.** *Law.* a legal notice to a court or public officer to suspend a certain proceeding until the notifier is given a hearing: *a caveat filed against the probate of a will.* **2.** any warning or caution. [t. L: let him beware]

ca·ve·at emp·tor (kā/vē ăt/ ĕmp/tôr), *Latin.* let the buyer beware (since he buys without recourse).

ca·ve·a·tor (kā/vĭ ā/tər), *n.* one who enters a caveat.

cave-in (kāv/ĭn/), *n.* a collapse, as of a mine, etc.

Cav·ell (kăv/əl), *n.* **Edith Louisa,** 1865–1915, British nurse, executed by the Germans in World War I.

cave man, 1. a cave dweller; a man of the Old Stone Age. **2.** *Colloq.* a man who behaves in a rough, primitive manner, esp. toward women.

cav·en·dish (kăv/ən dĭsh), *n.* tobacco softened, sweetened, and pressed into cakes. [named after the maker]

Cav·en·dish (kăv/ən dĭsh), *n.* **Henry,** 1731?–1810, British physicist and chemist.

cav·ern (kăv/ərn), *n.* a cave, esp. a large cave. [ME *caverne,* t. F, t. L: m. *caverna* cave]

cav·ern·ous (kăv/ər nəs), *adj.* **1.** containing caverns. **2.** deep-set: *cavernous eyes.* **3.** hollow and deep-sounding: *a cavernous voice.* **4.** full of small cavities; porous. **5.** of a cavern: *cavernous darkness.* —**cav/ern·ous·ly,** *adj.*

ca·vet·to (kə vĕt/ō; *It.* kä vĕt/tō), *n., pl.* **-ti** (-tĭ; *It.* -tē), **-tos.** *Archit.* a concave molding, as in a cornice, with the curve usually a quarter circle. See diag. under **column.** [t. It., dim. of *cavo,* g. L *cavum* hollow (place)]

cav·i·ar (kăv/ĭ är/, kä/vĭ-, kăv/ĭ är/), *n.* **1.** the roe of sturgeon and other large fish, pressed and salted as a relish. **2. caviar to the general,** something beyond appeal to the popular taste. Also, **cav/i·are/.** [t. F, t. It.: m. *caviaro,* t. Turk.: m. *khāviār;* r. *cavialy,* t. It.: m. *caviale,* var. of *caviaro;* ult. orig. unknown]

cav·i·corn (kăv/ə kôrn/), *adj. Zool.* hollow-horned, as the ruminants with true horns, as distinguished from bony antlers. [f. L: *cavi-* (comb. form of *cavus* hollow) + s. *-cornis* horned]

cav·il (kăv/əl), *v.,* **-iled, -iling** or (*esp. Brit.*) **-illed, -illing,** *n.* —*v.i.* **1.** to raise irritating and trivial objections; find fault unnecessarily. —*n.* **2.** a trivial and annoying objection. **3.** the raising of such objections. [t. F: m. s. *caviller,* t. L: m. *cavillārī,* der. *cav.lla* a jeering] —**cav/il·er,** *esp. Brit.,* **cav/il·ler,** *n.*

cav·i·ta·tion (kăv/ə tā/shən), *n.* the rapid formation and collapse of vapor pockets in a flowing liquid in regions of very low pressure, a frequent cause of serious structural damage to propellers, pumps, etc.

Ca·vi·te (kä vē/tĕ, kə-), *n.* a seaport in the Philippine Islands, on Manila Bay: naval base. 35,052 (1948).

cav·i·ty (kăv/ə tĭ), *n., pl.* **-ties. 1.** any hollow place; a hollow: *a cavity in the earth.* **2.** *Anat.* a hollow space within the body, an organ, a bone, etc. **3.** *Dentistry.* the loss of tooth structure, most commonly produced by caries. A cavity may be artificially made to support dental restorations. [t. F: m. *cavité,* t. LL: m.s. *cavitas* hollowness] —**Syn. 1.** See **hole.**

ca·vort (kə vôrt′), *v.i.* *U.S. Colloq.* to prance or caper about. [orig. unknown]

Ca·vour (kä vōōr′), *n.* **Camillo Benso di** (kä mēl′lô bĕn′sô dē), 1810–61, Italian statesman who was a leader in the unification of Italy.

ca·vy (kā′vĭ), *n.*, *pl.* **-vies.** any of various short-tailed South American rodents, esp. those of the genus *Cavia* (including the domesticated guinea pig) or the family *Caviidae.* [t. NL: m.s. *Cavia*, t. Galibi: m. *cabiai*]

caw (kô), *n.* **1.** the cry of the crow, raven, etc. —*v.i.* **2.** to utter this cry or a similar sound. [imit.]

Cawn·pore (kôn′pōr′), *n.* a city in N India, on the Ganges. 487,324 (1941). Also, **Cawn·pur** (kôn′pŏŏr′). Indian, **Kanpur.**

Cax·ton (kăk′stən), *n.* **1.** William, 1422?–91, first English printer: translator and author. **2.** *Bibliog.* any book printed by Caxton, all of which are in black letter. **3.** *Print.* a kind of type imitating Caxton's black letter.

cay (kā, kē), *n.* a small island; key.

cay·enne (kī ĕn′, kā-), *n.* a hot, biting condiment composed of the ground pods and seeds of *Capsicum frutescens* var. *longum*; red pepper. Also, **cayenne pepper.** [named after *Cayenne*, in French Guiana]

Cay·enne (kī ĕn′, kā-), *n.* a seaport in and the capital of French Guiana. 11,458 (1954).

cay·man (kā′mən), *n.*, *pl.* **-mans.** any of several tropical American crocodilians having overlapping scutes, constituting the genus *Caiman* and related types. Also, **caiman.** [t. Sp., Pg.: m. *caiman*, t. Carib]

Cay·man Islands (kā′mən), three islands NW of and belonging to Jamaica, in the British West Indies. 8000 pop. (est. 1954); 104 sq. mi.

Ca·yu·ga (kā ū′gə, kī-), *n.*, *pl.* **-ga, -gas.** a member of a tribe of North American Indians, the smallest tribe of the Iroquois Confederacy. [t. d. Amer. Ind.: m. *kweñio/gwen* the place where locusts were taken out]

Cayuga Lake, a lake in central New York: one of the Finger Lakes. ab. 40 mi. long.

cay·use (kī ūs′), *n.* *Western U.S.* an Indian pony. [named after the *Cayuse* Indians, now living in Oregon]

Cb, *Chem.* columbium.

C.B., **1.** (L *Chirurgiae Baccalaureus*) Bachelor of Surgery. **2.** *Brit.* Companion of the Bath.

C.B.E., Commander of the Order of the British Empire.

cc., **1.** cubic centimeter or centimeters. **2.** Also, **cc** carbon copy. Also, **c.c.**

C clef, *Music.* a sign locating the position of middle C on the staff.

Cd, *Chem.* cadmium.

cd., cord; cords.

Ce, *Chem.* cerium.

C.E., Civil Engineer.

Ce·a·rá (sĕ′ä rä′), *n.* Fortaleza.

cease (sēs), *v.*, **ceased, ceasing,** *n.* —*v.i.* **1.** to stop (moving, speaking, etc.): *she ceased to cry.* **2.** to come to an end. **3.** *Obs.* to pass away. —*v.t.* **4.** to put a stop or end to; discontinue: *to cease work.* —*n.* **5.** cessation, obs. except in **without cease,** endlessly. [ME *cess(en)*, t. OF: m. *cesser*, g. L *cessāre*, freq. of *cēdere* go, yield] —Syn. 1. See **stop.** —Ant. 1. begin.

cease-fire (sēs′fīr′), *n.* truce.

cease·less (sēs′lĭs), *adj.* without stop or pause; unending; incessant. —**cease′less·ly,** *adv.*

Ce·bú (sĕ bōō′), *n.* **1.** one of the Philippine Islands, in the central part of the group. 1,123,107 pop. (1948); 1703 sq. mi. **2.** a seaport on this island. 182,000 (est. 1954).

Cech·y (chĕ′hĭ), *n.* Czech name of Bohemia.

Ce·cil (sēs′əl), *n.* **1.** Edgar Algernon Robert (ăl′jər nən), (*1st Viscount Cecil of Chelwood*) born 1864, British statesman. **2.** William. See **Burghley.**

Ce·cil·ia (sĭ sēl′yə), *n.* Saint, died A.D. 230?, Roman martyr: patron saint of music.

Ce·cro·pi·a moth (sĭ krō′pĭ ə), a large North American silk-producing moth, *Samia cecropia.*

Ce·crops (sē′krŏps), *n.* *Gk. Legend.* the founder and first king of Attica: represented as half dragon.

ce·dant ar·ma to·gae (sē′dănt är′mə tō′jē), *Latin.* let military power be subject to civil authority (motto of Wyoming). Cicero, *De Officiis* 1:22,41.

ce·dar (sē′dər), *n.* **1.** any of the Old World coniferous trees constituting the genus *Cedrus*, as *C. libani* (**cedar of Lebanon**), a stately tree native in Asia Minor, etc. **2.** any of various junipers, as *Juniperus virginiana* (**red cedar**), an American tree with a fragrant reddish wood used for making lead pencils, etc. **3.** any of various other coniferous trees, as *Chamaecyparis thyoides*, a species of the swamps of the eastern U. S., *Thuja occidentalis*, the arbor vitae (both called **white cedar**), and *Libocedrus decurrens*, the **incense cedar** of California. **4.** any of various nonpinaceous tropical trees, as *Cedrela odorata* (**Spanish cedar**), a timber tree whose wood is used for cigar boxes. **5.** the wood of any of these trees. [ME *cedir*, etc., OE *ceder*, t. L: m.s. *cedrus*, t. Gk.: m. *kédros*; r. ME *cedre*, t. OF]

cedar bird, *Ornith.* a waxwing, *Bombycilla cedrorum*, of North America. Also, **cedar waxwing.**

ce·darn (sē′dərn), *adj.* *Poetic.* **1.** of cedar trees. **2.** made of cedar wood.

Cedar Rapids, a city in E Iowa. 92,035 (1960).

cede (sēd), *v.t.*, **ceded, ceding.** to yield or formally resign and surrender to another; make over, as by treaty:

to cede territory. [t. L: m.s. *cēdere* go, withdraw, yield, grant] —Syn. grant, transfer. —Ant. retain.

ce·dil·la (sĭ dĭl′ə), *n.* a mark placed under *c* before *a, o*, or *u*, as in *façade*, to show that it has the sound of *s.* [t. Sp.: *cedilla*, now *zedilla*, the mark (orig. a *z* written after *c*) g. dim. of L *zēta*, t. Gk.: name of letter *z*]

ced·u·la (sĕj′ə lə; *Sp.* thĕ′dōō lä′), *n.* **1.** (in Spanish-speaking countries) any of various orders, certificates, or the like. **2.** any of certain securities issued by South and Central American governments. **3.** (in the Philippine Islands) **a.** a personal registration tax certificate. **b.** the tax itself. [t. Sp. See SCHEDULE]

cei·ba (sē′ē bä, thē′-; *also for 2* sī′bä), *n.* **1.** the silk-cotton tree. **2.** silk-cotton; kapok. [t. Sp., t. Carib]

ceil (sēl), *v.t.* **1.** to overlay (the interior upper surface of a building or room) with wood, plaster, etc. **2.** to provide with a ceiling. [late ME. Cf. F *ciel* sky, heaven, canopy, g. L *caelum* sky, heaven]

ceil·ing (sē′lĭng), *n.* **1.** the overhead interior lining of a room; the surface of a room opposite the floor. **2.** a lining applied for structural reasons to a structural framework, esp. in the interior surfaces of a ship. **3.** top limit: *price ceilings on rent.* **4.** *Aeron.* **a.** the maximum altitude from which the earth can be seen on a particular day, usually equal to the distance between the earth and the base of the lowest cloud bank. **b.** the maximum altitude to which a particular aircraft can rise under specified conditions. **5.** act of one who ceils. [der. CEIL]

cel·an·dine (sĕl′ən dīn′), *n.* **1.** a papaveraceous plant, *Chelidonium majus* (**greater celandine**), with yellow flowers. **2.** a ranunculaceous plant, *Ranunculus Ficaria* (**lesser celandine**), with yellow flowers. [ME *celidoine*, t. OF, g. L *chelidonia*, t. Gk.: m. *chelidónion*, der. *chelidōn* swallow]

cel·a·nese (sĕl′ə nēz′), *n.* **1.** an acetate rayon yarn or fabric. **2.** (*cap.*) a trademark for this yarn or fabric.

-cele[1], a word element meaning "tumor," as in *varicocele.* [comb. form repr. Gk. *kēlē*]

-cele[2], var. of **-coele.**

Cel·e·bes (sĕl′ə bēz′; *Du.* sĕ lä′bĕs), *n.* an island in Indonesia, separated from the Philippine Islands by the **Celebes Sea.** With adjacent islands, 6,065,145 pop. (est. 1955); 72,986 sq. mi.

cel·e·brant (sĕl′ə brənt), *n.* **1.** the officiating priest in the celebration of the Eucharist. **2.** a participant in a public religious rite. **3.** a participant in any celebration.

cel·e·brate (sĕl′ə brāt′), *v.*, **-brated, -brating.** —*v.t.* **1.** to observe (a day) or commemorate (an event) with ceremonies or festivities. **2.** to make known publicly; proclaim. **3.** to sound the praises of; extol. **4.** to perform with appropriate rites and ceremonies; solemnize. —*v.i.* **5.** to observe a day or commemorate an event with ceremonies or festivities. **6.** to perform a religious ceremony, esp. Mass. [t. L: m.s. *celebrātus*, pp.] —**cel′e·bra′tor,** *n.* —Syn. 3. laud, glorify, honor.

cel·e·brat·ed (sĕl′ə brā′tĭd), *adj.* famous; renowned; well-known. —Syn. See **famous.**

cel·e·bra·tion (sĕl′ə brā′shən), *n.* **1.** act of celebrating. **2.** that which is done to celebrate anything.

ce·leb·ri·ty (sə lĕb′rə tĭ), *n.*, *pl.* **-ties.** **1.** a famous or well-known person. **2.** fame; renown.

ce·ler·i·ty (sə lĕr′ə tĭ), *n.* swiftness; speed. [ME *celerite*, t. L: m.s. *celeritas*]

cel·er·y (sĕl′ə rĭ), *n.* a plant, *Apium graveolens*, of the parsley family, whose blanched leafstalks are used raw for salad, and cooked as a vegetable. [t. F: m. *céleri*, t. d. It.: m. *sellari* (pl.), g. LL *selinon*, t. Gk.: parsley]

ce·les·ta (sə lĕs′tə), *n.* a musical instrument consisting essentially of steel plates struck by hammers, and having a keyboard. [t. F: m. *céleste*, lit., heavenly]

ce·les·tial (sə lĕs′chəl), *adj.* **1.** pertaining to the spiritual or invisible heaven; heavenly; divine: *celestial bliss.* **2.** pertaining to the sky or visible heaven. **3.** (*cap.*) of the former Chinese Empire or the Chinese people. —*n.* **4.** an inhabitant of heaven. **5.** (*cap.*) *Humorous.* a native of China; a Chinese. [ME, t. OF, f. *celesti-* (m.s. L *caelestis* heavenly) + *-al* -AL] —**ce·les′tial·ly,** *adv.*

Celestial City, the goal of the journey in Bunyan's *Pilgrim's Progress*; the heavenly Jerusalem. Rev. 21.

Celestial Empire, the Chinese Empire.

celestial equator, *Astron., Navig.* a great circle of the celestial sphere, the plane of which is perpendicular to the axis of the earth.

celestial globe, a model of the celestial sphere, on which the relative positions of the stars may be indicated without distortion.

celestial latitude. See **latitude** (def. 3).

celestial longitude. See **longitude** (def. 2).

celestial sphere, the imaginary spherical shell formed by the sky, usually represented as an infinite sphere of which the observer's position is the center.

Cel·es·tine V (sĕl′əs tēn, sə lĕs′tĭn, -tĭn), Saint, c1215–96, Italian hermit: pope in 1294.

cel·es·tite (sĕl′əs tīt′), *n.* a white to delicate-blue mineral, strontium sulfate, $SrSO_4$, occurring in tabular crystals: the principal ore of strontium. Also, **cel·es·tine** (sĕl′əs tĭn, -ə tēn′). [f. m.s. L *caelestis* heavenly (in allusion to the delicate blue of some specimens) + -ITE[1]]

ăct, āble, dâre, ärt; ĕbb, ēqual; Ĭf, īce; hŏt, ōver, ôrder, oil, bŏŏk, ōōze, out; ŭp, ūse, ûrge; ə = a in alone; ch, chief; g, give; ng, ring; sh, shoe; th, thin; ŧħ, that; zh, vision. See the full key on inside cover.

ce·li·ac (sē'lĭ·ăk'), *adj. Anat.* pertaining to the cavity of the abdomen. Also, **coeliac**. [t. L: (m.) s. *coeliacus*, t. Gk.: m. *koiliakós* of the belly]

cel·i·ba·cy (sĕl'ə·bə·sĭ; *esp. Brit.* sə·lĭb'ə·sĭ), *n., pl.* **-cies.** 1. the unmarried state. 2. abstention by vow from marriage: *the celibacy of priests.*

cel·i·bate (sĕl'ə·bĭt, -bāt'), *n.* 1. one who remains unmarried, esp. for religious reasons. —*adj.* 2. unmarried. [t. L: m. s. *caelibātus*, der. *caelebs* unmarried]

cell (sĕl), *n.* 1. a small room in a convent, prison, etc. 2. any small compartment, bounded area, receptacle, case, etc. 3. a small group acting as a unit within a larger organization. 4. *Biol.* a. a plant or animal structure, usually microscopic, containing nuclear and cytoplasmic material, enclosed by a semipermeable membrane (animal) or cell wall (plant); the structural unit of plant and animal life. b. a minute cavity or interstice, as in animal or plant tissue. 5. *Entomol.* one of the areas into which an insect's wing is divided by the veins. 6. *Embryol.* an internal cavity of an ovary.

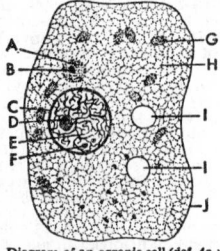

Diagram of an organic cell (def. 4a.)
A. Centrosphere; B. Centrosome; C. Nucleus; D. Nucleolus; E. Chromatin network; F. Karyosome; G. Plastid; H. Cytoplasm; I. Vacuole; J. Cell wall

7. *Bot.* the pollen sac of an anther. 8. *Elect.* a device which generates electricity and which forms the whole, or a part of, a voltaic battery, consisting in one of its simplest forms of two plates, each of a different metal, placed in a jar containing a dilute acid or other electrolyte (**voltaic cell**). 9. *Phys. Chem.* a device for producing electrolysis, consisting essentially of the electrolyte, its container, and the electrodes (**electrolytic cell**). 10. *Aeron.* a. the part of the wing structure of a biplane on either side of the fuselage. b. the gas container of a balloon. 11. *Eccles.* a monastery or nunnery, usually small, dependent on a larger religious house. [ME *celle*, OE *cell*, t. L: s. *cella* room]

cel·la (sĕl'ə), *n., pl.* **cellae** (sĕl'ē). *Archit.* (in ancient Greek or Roman temples) an enclosed inner room, the sanctuary containing the statue of the divinity. [t. L]

cel·lar (sĕl'ər), *n.* 1. a room or set of rooms for the storage of foodstuffs, etc., now always either wholly or partly underground, and usually beneath a building. 2. an underground room or story. 3. a wine cellar. 4. a supply or stock of wines. 5. the cellar, *Sports.* the lowest position in a ranked series: *my team is in the cellar this week.* —*v.t.* 6. to place or store in a cellar. [t. L: m. s. *cellārium* pantry; r. ME *celer*, t. AF, var. of OF *celier*, g. L *cellārium*]

cel·lar·age (sĕl'ər·ĭj), *n.* 1. cellar space. 2. charges for storage in a cellar.

cel·lar·er (sĕl'ər·ər), *n.* the steward of a monastery.

cel·lar·et (sĕl'ə·rĕt'), *n.* a cabinet for wine bottles, etc.

cell division, *Biol.* the division of a cell in reproduction or growth.

Cel·li·ni (chə·lē'nĭ; *It.* chĕl·lē'nē), *n.* **Benvenuto** (bĕn'vĕ·nōō'tō), 1500–71, Italian sculptor, artist in metal, and autobiographer.

cel·list (chĕl'ĭst), *n.* a player on the cello. Also, **'cel/list, violoncellist.**

cel·lo (chĕl'ō), *n., pl.* **-los.** the baritone of the violin family, which is rested vertically on the floor between the player's knees. Also, **'cel/lo, violoncello.** [short form of VIOLONCELLO]

cel·loi·din (sə·loi'dĭn), *n. Microscopy.* a concentrated form of pyroxylin used to embed tissues for cutting and microscopic examination.

cel·lo·phane (sĕl'ə·fān'), *n.* 1. a transparent, paperlike product of viscose, impervious to moisture, germs, etc., used to wrap candy, tobacco, etc. 2. (*cap.*) a trademark for this product. [f. CELL(UL)O(SE) + -PHANE]

Man playing a cello

cel·lu·lar (sĕl'yə·lər), *adj.* pertaining to or characterized by cellules or cells, esp. minute compartments or cavities. [t. NL: s. *cellulāris*, der. L *cellula* little room]

cel·lule (sĕl'ūl), *n.* a little cell. [t. L: m. *cellula*]

cel·lu·li·tis (sĕl'yə·lī'tĭs), *n. Pathol.* inflammation of cellular tissue. [t. NL, f. s. L *cellula* little cell + -ITIS]

cel·lu·loid (sĕl'yə·loid'), *n.* 1. a substance consisting essentially of soluble guncotton and camphor, usually highly inflammable, variously used as a substitute for ivory, vulcanite, etc. 2. (*cap.*) a trademark for this substance. [f. CELLUL(OSE) + -OID]

cel·lu·lose (sĕl'yə·lōs'), *n. Chem.* an inert substance, a carbohydrate, the chief constituent of the cell walls of plants, and forming an essential part of wood, cotton, hemp, paper, etc. [f. s. L *cellula* little cell + -OSE²]

cellulose acetate, *Chem.* an acetic ester of cellulose used to make textiles, artificial leathers, yarns, etc.

cellulose nitrate, *Chem.* a nitric ester of cellulose used in the manufacture of lacquers and explosives.

cel·lu·lous (sĕl'yə·ləs), *adj.* full or consisting of cells.

cell wall, *Biol.* the definite boundary or wall which is usually part of the structure of a biological cell, esp. a plant cell. See **cell** (def. 4a).

ce·lom (sē'ləm), *n. Zool.* coelom.

Cels., Celsius.

Cel·si·us thermometer (sĕl'sĭ·əs), 1. centigrade thermometer. 2. Also, **Celsius scale.** a centigrade scale or thermometer, from which the modern thermometer was developed (1743) by inverting the freezing point (orig. 100°) and boiling point (orig. 0°) of water.

Celt (sĕlt; *esp. Brit.* kĕlt), *n.* a member of an Indo-European people now represented chiefly by the Irish, Gaels, Welsh, and Bretons. Also, **Kelt.** [t. L: s. *Celtae*, pl., t. Gk.: m. *Keltoi*]

celt (sĕlt), *n. Archaeol.* an ax of stone or metal without perforation or groove for hafting. [t. LL: s. *celtis* chisel]

Celt., Celtic.

Celt·ic (sĕl'tĭk; *esp. Brit.* kĕl'tĭk), *n.* 1. a group of Indo-European languages including Irish, Scotch, Gaelic, Welsh, Breton, etc., surviving now in Ireland, the Scottish Highlands, Wales, and Brittany. —*adj.* 2. of the Celts or their language. Also, **Keltic.**

Celto-, a word element meaning "Celtic."

ce·ment (sĭ·mĕnt'), *n.* 1. any of various substances which are soft when first prepared but later become hard or stonelike, used for joining stones, making floors, etc. 2. a material of this kind (the ordinary variety, often called **hydraulic cement**) commonly made by burning a mixture of clay and limestone, used for making concrete for foundations or the like, covering floors, etc. 3. *Petrog.* the compact groundmass surrounding and binding together the fragments of clastic rocks. 4. anything that binds or unites. 5. *Dentistry.* an adhesive plastic substance used to fill teeth or to pack fillings or inlays into teeth. 6. *Metall.* the powder utilized during cementation. —*v.t.* 7. to unite by, or as by, cement: *a friendship cemented by time.* 8. to coat or cover with cement. —*v.i.* 9. to become cemented; join together or unite; cohere. [t. L: m.s. *caementum* rough stone; r. ME *siment*, t. OF] —**ce·ment'er,** *n.*

ce·men·ta·tion (sē'mən·tā'shən, sĕm'ən-), *n.* 1. act, process, or result of cementing. 2. *Metall.* the heating of two substances in contact in order to effect some change in one of them; esp., the formation of steel by heating iron in powdered charcoal.

ce·ment·ite (sĭ·mĕn'tīt), *n. Metall.* a carbide of iron, Fe₃C, used in steel to add strength and hardness.

ce·men·tum (sĭ·mĕn'təm), *n. Dentistry.* a hard tissue which forms the outer surfaces of the root of a tooth. See diag. under **tooth.**

cem·e·ter·y (sĕm'ə·tĕr'ĭ), *n., pl.* **-teries.** a burial ground, esp. one not attached to a church; graveyard. [late ME *cymytery*, t. LL: m.s. *coemētērium*, t. Gk.: m. *koimētērion*]

-cene, a word element meaning "recent," "new," as in *pleistocene*. [comb. form repr. Gk. *kainós*]

ce·nes·the·sia (sē'nəs·thē'zhə), *n.* coenesthesia. Also, **ce·nes·the·sis** (sē'nəs·thē'sĭs).

Ce·nis (sə·nē'), *n.* **Mont** (môN), 1. a pass in the Alps between France and Italy. 6835 ft. high. 2. a railway tunnel to the W of this pass. ab. 8 mi. long.

ceno-¹, a word element meaning "new," "recent," as in *Cenozoic*. Also, **caeno-, caino-.** [see -CENE]

ceno-², a word element meaning "common." Also, **coeno-.** [t. Gk.: m. *koino-*, comb. form of *koinós*]

ce·no·bite (sē'nə·bīt', sĕn'ə-), *n.* one of a religious order living in a convent or community. Also, **coenobite.** [t. LL: m. s. *coenobīta*, der. *coenobium*, t. Gk.: m. *koinóbion* convent, neut. of *koinóbios* living in community] —**ce·no·bit·ic** (sē'nə·bĭt'ĭk, sĕn'ə-), **ce·no·bit·i·cal,** *adj.* —**ce·no·bit·ism** (sē'nə·bī'tĭz·əm, sĕn'ə-), *n.*

ce·no·gen·e·sis (sē'nə·jĕn'ə·sĭs, sĕn'ə-), *n. Biol.* development of an individual which does not repeat the phylogeny of its race, stock, or group (opposed to *palingenesis*). Also, **kenogenesis.** [f. CENO-¹ + GENESIS] —**ce·no·ge·net·ic** (sē'nə·jə·nĕt'ĭk, sĕn'ə-), *adj.*

cen·o·taph (sĕn'ə·tăf', -täf'), *n.* a sepulchral monument erected in memory of a deceased person whose body is elsewhere. [t. L: m. s. *cenotaphium*, t. Gk.: m. *kenotáphion* an empty tomb] —**cen/o·taph'ic,** *adj.*

Ce·no·zo·ic (sē'nə·zō'ĭk, sĕn'ə-), *Stratig.* —*adj.* 1. pertaining to the geological era or rocks of most recent age, extending to the present. —*n.* 2. the era or rocks representing the most recent major division of earth history. Also, **Cainozoic.** [f. CENO-¹ + ZO(O)- + -IC]

cense (sĕns), *v.t.* **censed, censing.** to burn incense near or in front of; perfume with incense. [aphetic var. of INCENSE¹]

cen·ser (sĕn'sər), *n.* a container in which incense is burned. [ME *censere*, t. OF: m. *encensier*. See INCENSE¹]

cen·sor (sĕn'sər), *n.* 1. an official who examines books, plays, news reports, motion pictures, radio programs, etc., for the purpose of suppressing parts deemed objectionable on moral, political, military, or other grounds. 2. any person who supervises the manners or morality of others. 3. an adverse critic; a faultfinder. 4. a member of the board of two officials of republican Rome who kept the register or census of the citizens, let public contracts, and supervised manners and morals. 5. *Psychoanal.* censorship. —*v.t.* 6. to examine and act upon as a censor does. [t. L] —**cen·so·ri·al** (sĕn·sôr'ĭ·əl), *adj.*

Acolyte with censer

cen·so·ri·ous (sĕn sōr′Ĭ əs), *adj.* severely critical; faultfinding; carping. **—cen·so′ri·ous·ly,** *adv.* **—cen·so′ri·ous·ness,** *n.*

cen·sor·ship (sĕn′sər shĬp′), *n.* **1.** act of censoring. **2.** the office or power of a censor. **3.** the time during which a censor holds office. **4.** *Psychoanal.* (in dream theory) Freud's first term for the psychological force which represses ideas, impulses, and feelings, and prevents them from entering consciousness in their original form.

cen·sur·a·ble (sĕn′shэr ə bəl), *adj.* deserving censure. **—cen′sur·a·ble·ness, cen′sur·a·bil′i·ty,** *n.* **—cen′sur·a·bly,** *adv.*

cen·sure (sĕn′shər), *n., v.,* **-sured, -suring.** **—n. 1.** an expression of disapproval; adverse or hostile criticism; blaming. **—v.t. 2.** to criticize adversely; disapprove; find fault with; condemn. **—v.i. 3.** to give censure, adverse criticism, or blame. [ME, t. L: m. *censūra* censorship, judgment. Cf. CENSOR.] **—cen′sur·er,** *n.* **—Syn. 1.** condemnation, reproof. See **abuse. 3.** reprove, rebuke, reprimand. See **blame. —Ant.** praise.

cen·sus (sĕn′səs), *n.* **1.** an official enumeration of inhabitants, with details as to age, sex, pursuits, etc. **2.** (in ancient Rome) the registration of citizens and their property, for purposes of taxation. [t. L]

census tract, a standard area in certain large American cities used by the U. S. Census Bureau for purposes of population enumeration.

cent (sĕnt), *n.* **1.** the hundredth part of the U.S. dollar. **2.** a bronze coin of this value. **3.** the hundredth part of monetary units elsewhere. [? t. L: short for *centēsimus* hundredth]

cent-, var. of centi-, as in *centare.*

cent., 1. centigrade. **2.** central. **3.** centum (in *per-cent.*) **4.** century.

cen·tal (sĕn′təl), *n.* *Rare.* a hundredweight. [f. s. L *centum* hundred + -AL¹]

cen·tare (sĕn′târ; *Fr.* säN tàr′), *n.* centiare.

cen·taur (sĕn′tôr), *n.* **1.** *Gk. Legend.* one of a race of monsters having the head, trunk, and arms of a man, and the body and legs of a horse. **2.** (*cap.*) *Astron.* Centaurus. [ME, t. L: s. *Centaurus,* t. Gk.: m. *Kéntauros*]

Cen·tau·rus (sĕn tôr′əs). *n., gen.* **Centauri** (sĕn tôr′Ī). *Astron.* a southern constellation containing the first magnitude stars Alpha Centauri (the star nearest to the solar system) and Beta Centauri. [see CENTAUR]

cen·tau·ry (sĕn′tôrĬ), *n., pl.* **-ries. 1.** either of two gentianaceous Old World herbs, *Chlora perfoliata* and *Centaurium umbellatum* (*Erythraea centaurium*), with medicinal properties. **2.** any plant of the genus *Centaurium* (*Erythraea*). **3.** any of certain other plants, as those of the gentianaceous genus *Sabatia* (**American centaury**). [ME *centaurie,* t. ML: m. *centauria,* r. L *centaurēum,* t. Gk.: m. *kentaúreion,* der. *Kéntauros* centaur (here the centaur Chiron, reputed discoverer of the plant's medicinal virtues)]

cen·ta·vo (sĕn tä′vō; *Sp.* -vō), *n., pl.* **-vos** (-vōz; *Sp.* -vōs). a small coin or minor monetary unit equal to the hundredth part of a particular monetary unit, esp. **a.** one hundredth of a peso, as in Mexico, the Philippine Islands, Cuba, etc. **b.** one hundredth of an escudo, in Portugal. [t. Amer. Sp. See CENT]

cen·te·nar·i·an (sĕn′tə nâr′Ĭ ən), *adj.* **1.** pertaining to or having lived 100 years. **—n. 2.** one who has reached the age of a hundred.

cen·te·nar·y (sĕn′tə nĕr′Ĭ; *esp. Brit.* sĕn tĕn′ər Ĭ, -tē′-nər Ĭ), *adj., n., pl.* **-naries.** **—adj. 1.** pertaining to a period of 100 years. **2.** recurring once in every 100 years. **—n. 3.** a 100th anniversary. **4.** a period of 100 years; a century. [t. L: m.s. *centēnārius* of or containing 100]

cen·ten·ni·al (sĕn tĕn′Ĭ əl), *adj.* **1.** pertaining to, or marking the completion of, 100 years. **2.** pertaining to a 100th anniversary. **3.** lasting 100 years. **4.** 100 years old. **—n. 5.** a 100th anniversary. **6.** its celebration. [f. s. L *centennium* 100 years + -AL¹; modeled on BIENNIAL] **—cen·ten′ni·al·ly,** *adv.*

cen·ter (sĕn′tər), *n.* **1.** *Geom.* the middle point, as the point within a circle or sphere equally distant from all points of the circumference or surface, or the point within a regular polygon equally distant from the vertices. **2.** a point, pivot, axis, etc., round which anything rotates or revolves. **3.** a principal point, place, or object: *a shipping center.* **4.** a person, thing, group, etc., occupying the middle position, esp. troops. **5.** (*usually cap.*) (in continental Europe). **a.** that part of a legislative assembly which sits in the center of the chamber, a position customarily assigned to representatives holding views intermediate between those of the conservatives or Right and the liberals or Left. **b.** a party holding such views. **6.** *Football, etc.* the middle player in the forward line. **7.** *Basketball.* **a.** the place in the center of the court from which a game is started. **b.** a player, usually very tall, who attempts to tap the ball to a teammate when a jump ball is thrown by a referee at the beginning of play. **8.** *Physiol.* a cluster of nerve cells governing a specific organic process: *the vasomotor center.* **9.** *Math.* the mean position of a figure or system. **10.** *Mach.* **a.** a tapered rod mounted in the headstock spindle (**live center**) or the tailstock spindle (**dead center**) of a lathe, upon which the work to be turned is placed. **b.** one of two similar points on some other machine, as a planing machine, enabling an object to be turned on its axis. **c.** a tapered indentation in a piece to be turned on a lathe into which the center is fitted.

—v.t. 11. to place in or on a center. **12.** to collect at a center. **13.** to determine or mark the center of. **14.** to adjust, shape, or modify (an object, part, etc.) so that its axis or the like is in a central or normal position. **—v.i. 15.** to be at or come to a center. Also, *esp. Brit.,* **centre.** [ME *centre,* t. OF, t. L: m. *centrum,* t. Gk.: m. *kéntron* sharp point, center] **—Syn. 1.** See **middle.**

center bit, a carpenter's bit with a sharp, projecting center point, used for boring holes.

cen·ter·board (sĕn′tər bôrd′), *n.* *Naut.* a movable fin keel that can be drawn up in shoal water into a housing or well. Also, *Brit.,* **centreboard.**

cen·ter·ing (sĕn′tər Ĭng), *n.* a temporary framing, for supporting permanent framework during construction. Also, *Brit.,* **centring.**

center of gravity, *Mech.* that point of a body (or system of bodies) from which it could be suspended or on which it could be supported and be in equilibrium in any position in a uniform gravitational field.

center of mass, *Mech.* that point of a body (or system of bodies) at which its entire mass could be concentrated without changing its linear inertia in any direction. For ordinary bodies near the earth, this point is identical with the center of gravity.

cen·ter·piece (sĕn′tər pēs′), *n.* an ornamental piece of silver, glass, or the like, or of embroidery, lace, or like material, for the center of a table, etc. Also, *Brit.,* **centrepiece.**

cen·tes·i·mal (sĕn tĕs′ə məl), *adj.* hundredth; pertaining to division into 100ths. [f. s. L *centēsimus* hundredth + -AL¹] **—cen·tes′i·mal·ly,** *adv.*

cen·tes·i·mo (sĕn tĕs′ə mō′; *It., Sp.* -tē′sē mō′). *n., pl. It.* **-mi** (-mē′), **-mos** (-mōz′; *Sp.* -mōs′). **1.** an Italian copper coin and monetary unit, the hundredth part of a lira. **2.** the hundredth part of a peso in Uruguay and of a balboa in Panama. [t. It., g. L *centēsimus* hundredth]

centi-, a word element meaning "hundred," applied in the metric system to the division of the unit by 100, as in *centigram.* Also, **cent-.** [t. L, comb. form of *centum*]

cen·ti·are (sĕn′tĬ âr′; *Fr.* säN tyàr′), *n.* a square meter. Also, **centare.** [t. F. See CENTI-, ARE²]

cen·ti·grade (sĕn′tə grād′), *adj.* **1.** divided into 100 degrees, as a scale. **2.** pertaining to the centigrade thermometer. [t. F. See CENTI-, -GRADE]

centigrade thermometer, a thermometer based on a scale of equal degrees between zero (fixed at the melting point of ice) and 100° (fixed at the boiling point of water) at a pressure of 760 mm. of mercury; Celsius thermometer. See illus. under **thermometer.**

cen·ti·gram (sĕn′tə grăm′), *n.* 1/100 of a gram, equivalent to 0.1543 grain. Also, *esp. Brit.,* **cen′ti·gramme′.** [t. F: m. *centigramme.* See CENTIGRAM, *n.*]

cen·ti·li·ter (sĕn′tə lē′tər), *n.* one hundredth of a liter, equivalent to 0.6102 cubic inch, or 0.338 U.S. fluid ounce. Also, *esp. Brit.,* **cen′ti·li′tre.** [t. F: m. *centilitre.* See CENTI-, LITER]

cen·time (sän′tēm; *Fr.* säN tēm′), *n.* the hundredth part of a franc. [t. F: *f. cent* hundred + suffix -*ime*]

cen·ti·me·ter (sĕn′tə mē′tər), *n.* one hundredth of a meter, equivalent to .3937 in. Also, *esp. Brit.,* **cen′ti·me′tre.** [t. F: m. *centimètre.* See CENTI-, -METER]

cen·ti·me·ter-gram-sec·ond (sĕn′tə mē′tər grăm′-sĕk′ənd), *adj.* a system of units employed in science, based on the centimeter, gram, and second as the primary units of length, mass, and time. Also, *Brit.,* **centimetre-gramme-second.**

cen·ti·mo (sĕn′tə mō′; *Sp.* -tē mō′), *n., pl.* **-mos** (-mōz′; *Sp.* -mōs′). the hundredth part of a bolivar, colon, or peseta. [t. Sp., t. F: m. *centime*]

cen·ti·pede (sĕn′tə pēd′), *n.* any member of the class *Chilopoda,* active, predacious, and mostly nocturnal arthropods having an elongated flattened body of numerous segments each with a single pair of legs, the first pair of which is modified into poison fangs. Few are dangerous to man. [t. L: m. s. *centipeda* hundred-footed insect]

cent·ner (sĕnt′nər), *n.* **1.** (in several European countries) a unit of weight of 50 kilograms, equivalent to 110.23 pounds avdp. **2.** *Rare.* a unit of 100 kilograms. [t. Flem.: m. *centener,* t. L: m. s. *centēnārius* of a hundred]

centr-, var. of centro- before vowels.

cen·tra (sĕn′trə), *n.* pl. of **centrum.**

cen·tral (sĕn′trəl), *adj.* **1.** of or forming the center. **2.** in, at, or near the center. **3.** constituting that from which other related things proceed or upon which they depend. **4.** principal; chief; dominant: *the central idea, the central character in a novel.* **5.** *Anat., Physiol.* **a.** pertaining to the brain and spinal cord of the nervous system (as distinguished from *peripheral*). **b.** of or relating to the centrum or body of a vertebra. **6.** *Phonet.* pronounced with the tongue in a neutral position, as for example, the final vowel in *sofa* or *idea.* **—n. 7.** the office of a telephone system, in which connections are made between different lines. **8.** an operator at such an office. [t. L: s. *centrālis.* See CENTER] **—cen′tral·ly,** *adv.*

Central African Republic, an independent member of the French Community in central Africa. 1,177,166 pop. (est. 1960); 238,000 sq. mi. *Cap.:* Bangui. Formerly, **Ubangi-Shari.**

Central America, continental North America S of Mexico, comprising the six republics of Guatemala, Honduras, El Salvador, Nicaragua, Costa Rica, Panama, and the colony British Honduras. 9,800,000 pop. (est. 1953); 227,933 sq. mi. **—Central American.**

ăct, āble, dâre, ärt; ĕbb, ēqual; Ĭf, īce; hŏt, ōver, ôrder, oil, bŏŏk, ōōze, out; ŭp, ūse, ûrge; ə = a in alone; ch, chief; g, give; ng, ring; sh, shoe; th, thin; ŧħ, that; zh, vision.   See the full key on inside cover.

central cylinder, *Bot.* stele (def. 4).

Central Falls, a city in NE Rhode Island. 19,858 (1960).

Central India, a former group of states in central India, which constituted the **Central India Agency.**

cen·tral·ism (sĕn'trə līz'əm), *n.* **1.** centralization, or a centralizing system. **2.** the principle of centralization, esp. in government. —**cen'tral·ist,** *n., adj.*

cen·tral·i·ty (sĕn trăl'ə tǐ), *n.* central position or state.

cen·tral·i·za·tion (sĕn'trəl ə zā'shən), *n.* **1.** act of centralizing. **2.** fact of being centralized. **3.** the concentration of administrative power in a central government. **4.** *Sociol.* a process whereby social groups and institutions become increasingly dependent on a central group or institution.

cen·tral·ize (sĕn'trə līz'), *v.t.,* **-ized, -izing. 1.** to draw to or toward a center. **2.** to bring under one control, esp. in government. —*v.i.* **3.** to come together at a center. —**cen'tral·iz'er,** *n.*

Central Powers, (in World War I) Germany and Austria-Hungary, often with their allies Turkey and Bulgaria, as opposed to the Allies.

Central Provinces and Be·rar (bā rär'), a former province in central India, now a part of Madhyra Pradesh.

Central time. See **standard time.**

cen·tre (sĕn'tər), *n., v.,* **-tred, -tring.** *Chiefly Brit.* center.

centri-, var. of **centro-,** as in *centrifugal.*

cen·tric (sĕn'trĭk), *adj.* **1.** pertaining to or situated at the center; central. **2.** *Physiol.* pertaining to or originating at a nerve center. Also, **cen'tri·cal.** —**cen'tri·cal·ly,** *adv.* —**cen·tric·i·ty** (sĕn trĭs'ə tǐ), *n.*

cen·trif·u·gal (sĕn trĭf'yə gəl), *adj.* **1.** moving or directed outward from the center. **2.** pertaining to or operated by centrifugal force: *a centrifugal pump.* **3.** *Physiol.* efferent. —*n.* **4.** a solid or perforated cylinder rotated rapidly to separate solids from liquids. [f. CENTRI- + s. L *fugere* flee + -AL¹] —**cen·trif'u·gal·ly,** *adv.* —**Ant.** 1. centripetal.

centrifugal force, the force outward exerted by a body moving in a curved path; the reaction of centripetal force. Also, **centrifugal action.**

cen·tri·fuge (sĕn'trə fūj'), *n.* a machine consisting of a rotating container in which substances of different densities may be separated by the centrifugal force. [t. F: centrifugal]

cen·tring (sĕn'trĭng), *n.* *Brit.* centering.

cen·trip·e·tal (sĕn trĭp'ə təl), *adj.* **1.** proceeding or directed toward the center. **2.** operating by centripetal force. **3.** *Physiol.* afferent. [f. s. NL *centripetus* center-seeking + -AL¹] —**cen·trip'e·tal·ly,** *adv.*

centripetal force, a force acting on a body, which is directed toward the center of a circle or curve, which causes it to move in the circle or curve. Also, **centripetal action.**

cen·trist (sĕn'trĭst), *n.* (in continental Europe) a member of a political party of the Center. See **center** (def. 5a). [t. F: m. *centriste,* der. *centre* center]

centro-, a word element meaning "center." Also, **centr-, centri-.** [comb. form repr. L *centrum* and Gk. *kéntron*]

cen·tro·bar·ic (sĕn'trə băr'ĭk), *adj.* pertaining to the center of gravity. [f. CENTRO- + s. Gk. *báros* weight + -IC]

cen·troid (sĕn'troid), *n.* *Mech.* the point in an area common to all lines whose moment of area is zero.

cen·tro·some (sĕn'trə sōm'), *n.* *Biol.* a minute protoplasmic body regarded by some as the active center of cell division in mitosis. See diag. under **cell.** [f. CENTRO- + -SOME³] —**cen·tro·som·ic** (sĕn'trə sŏm'ĭk), *adj.*

cen·tro·sphere (sĕn'trə sfǐr'), *n.* **1.** *Biol.* the protoplasm around a centrosome; the central portion of an aster, containing the centrosome. See diag. under **cell. 2.** *Geol.* the central or interior portion of the earth.

cen·trum (sĕn'trəm), *n., pl.* **-trums, -tra** (-trə). **1.** a center. **2.** *Zool.* the body of a vertebra. [t. L. See CENTER]

cen·tu·ple (sĕn'tyə pəl, -tə-), *adj., v.,* **-pled, -pling.** —*adj.* **1.** a hundred times as great; hundredfold. —*v.t.* **2.** to increase 100 times. [t. F, t. LL: m.s. *centuplus* hundredfold]

cen·tu·pli·cate (*v.* sĕn tū'plə kāt', -tŏŏ'-; *adj., n.* sĕn tū'plə kĭt, -kāt', -tŏŏ'-), *v.,* **-cated, -cating,** *adj., n.* —*v.t.* **1.** to increase 100 times; centuple. —*adj.* **2.** hundredfold. —*n.* **3.** a number or quantity increased a hundredfold. [t. L *centuplicātus*, pp.]

cen·tu·ri·al (sĕn tyŏŏr'ǐ əl, -tŏŏr'-), *adj.* pertaining to a century. [t. L: s. *centuriālis*]

cen·tu·ri·on (sĕn tyŏŏr'ǐ ən, -tŏŏr'-), *n.* (in the ancient Roman Army) the commander of a century. [ME, t. L: s. *centurio,* der. *centuria.* See CENTURY]

cen·tu·ry (sĕn'chə rǐ), *n., pl.* **-ries. 1.** a period of one hundred years. **2.** one of the successive periods of 100 years reckoned forward or backward from a recognized chronological epoch, esp. from the assumed date of the birth of Jesus. **3.** any group or collection of 100. **4.** (in the ancient Roman army) a company, consisting of approximately one hundred men. **5.** one of the voting divisions of the ancient Roman people, each division having one vote. **6.** (*cap.*) *Print.* a style of type. [t. L: m. s. *centuria* a division of a hundred things]

century plant, a Mexican species of agave, *Agave americana,* cultivated for ornament: popularly supposed not to blossom until a century old.

ceorl (chĕôrl), *n.* *Early Eng. Hist.* a freeman of the lowest rank, neither a noble nor a slave. [OE. See CHURL] —**ceorl'ish,** *adj.*

cephal-, var. of **cephalo-,** before vowels, as in *cephalad.*

ceph·al·ad (sĕf'ə lăd'). *adv. Anat., Zool.* toward the head (opposed to *caudad*). [f. CEPHAL- + L *ad* to]

ce·phal·ic (sə făl'ĭk), *adj.* **1.** of or pertaining to the head. **2.** situated or directed toward the head. **3.** of the nature of a head. [t. L: s. *cephalicus,* t. Gk.: m. *kephalikós* of the head]

-cephalic, a word element meaning "head," as in *brachycephalic* (related to **cephalo-**).

cephalic index, *Cephalom.* the ratio of the greatest breadth of head to its greatest length from front to back, multiplied by 100.

ceph·a·li·za·tion (sĕf'ə lə zā'shən), *n. Zool.* a tendency in the development of animals to localization of important organs or parts in or near the head.

cephalo-, a word element denoting the "head," as in *cephalopod.* Also, **cephal-.** [t. Gk.: m. *kephalo-,* comb. form of *kephalē*]

Ceph·a·lo·chor·da·ta (sĕf'ə lō kôr dā'tə), *n. pl.* a chordate subphylum including the lancelets, having fishlike characters but lacking a vertebral column.

ceph·a·lo·chor·date (sĕf'ə lō kôr'dāt), *adj.* **1.** denoting or pertaining to the *Cephalochordata.* —*n.* **2.** a member of the *Cephalochordata.* [f. CEPHALO- + CHORD + -ATE¹]

cephalom., cephalometry.

ceph·a·lom·e·ter (sĕf'ə lŏm'ə tər), *n.* an instrument for measuring the head or skull; a craniometer.

ceph·a·lom·e·try (sĕf'ə lŏm'ə trĭ), *n.* the science of the measurement of heads. [f. CEPHALO- + -METRY]

Ceph·a·lo·ni·a (sĕf'ə lō'nǐ ə, -lōn'yə), *n.* the largest of the Ionian Islands, off the W coast of Greece. 47,369 pop. (1951); 287 sq. mi. Greek, **Kephallenia.**

ceph·a·lo·pod (sĕf'ə lə pŏd'), *n.* a member of the class *Cephalopoda.* [f. CEPHALO- + -POD]

Ceph·a·lop·o·da (sĕf'ə lŏp'ə də), *n.pl.* the most highly organized class of mollusks, including the cuttlefish, squid, octopus, etc., the members of which have tentacles attached to the head. —**ceph'a·lop/o·dan,** *adj., n.*

ceph·a·lo·tho·rax (sĕf'ə lō thôr'ăks), *n. Zool.* the anterior part of the body in certain arachnids and crustaceans, consisting of the coalesced head and thorax.

ceph·a·lous (sĕf'ə ləs), *adj.* having a head. [f. CEPHAL- + -OUS]

-cephalous, a word element related to **cephalo-.** [f. CEPHAL- + -OUS]

Ceph·e·id variable (sĕf'ǐ ĭd), *Astron.* a variable star in which changes in brightness are due to bodily pulsations.

Ce·pheus (sē'fūs, -fǐ əs), *n.* **1.** *Astron.* a northern circumpolar constellation between Cassiopeia and Draco. **2.** *Gk. Legend.* the Ethiopian king who was the husband of Cassiopeia and the father of Andromeda.

-ceptor, a word element meaning "taker," "receiver." [t. L]

cer-, var. of **cero-,** used before vowels, as in *ceraceous.*

ce·ra·ceous (sə rā'shəs), *adj.* waxy.

Ce·ram (sē răm'; *Port.* sē rän'; *Du.* sä'räm), *n.* an island of the Moluccas in Indonesia, W of New Guinea. 100,000 pop. (1930); 7191 sq. mi.

ce·ram·ic (sə răm'ĭk), *adj.* pertaining to products made from clay and similar materials, such as pottery, brick, etc., or to their manufacture: *ceramic art.* Also, **keramic.** [t. Gk.: m. s. *keramikós* of or for potters' clay, pottery]

ce·ram·ics (sə răm'ĭks), *n.* **1.** (*construed as sing.*) the art and technology of making clay products and similar ware. **2.** (*construed as pl.*) articles of earthenware, porcelain, etc. [pl. of CERAMIC. See -ICS] —**cer·a·mist** (sĕr'ə mĭst), *n.*

ce·rar·gy·rite (sə rär'jə rīt'), *n.* a mineral, silver chloride: an important silver ore in some places. [f. m. Gk. *kēr(as)* horn + s. Gk. *árgyros* silver + -ITE¹]

ce·rate (sǐr'āt), *n. Pharm.* an unctuous (often medicated) preparation for external application, consisting of lard or oil mixed with wax, rosin, or the like, esp. one which has a firmer consistency than a typical ointment and does not melt when in contact with the skin. [t. L: m. s. *cērātum,* neut. pp., covered with wax]

cer·a·tin (sĕr'ə tǐn), *n. Zool.* keratin. [f. CERAT- + -IN²]

cerato-, a word element meaning: **1.** *Zool.* horn, horny, or hornlike. **2.** *Anat.* the cornea. Also, before vowels, **cerat-.** [t. Gk.: m. *kerāto-,* comb. form of *kéras* horn]

ce·rat·o·dus (sə răt'ə dəs, sĕr'ə tō'dəs), *n.* a fish of the extinct lungfish genus *Ceratodus,* or of the closely related existent genus *Neoceratodus,* as *N. forsteri,* the barramunda of Australia, so called from the horn like ridges of the teeth. [NL, f. *cerat-* CERAT- + m. Gk. *odoús* tooth]

cer·a·toid (sĕr'ə toid'), *adj.* hornlike; horny. [t. Gk.: m. s. *kerātoeidḗs* hornlike]

Cer·ber·us (sûr'bər əs), *n.* **1.** *Class. Myth.* a dog, usually represented as having three heads, which guarded the entrance of the infernal regions. **2.** a watchful and formidable or surly keeper or guard. —**Cer·be·re·an** (sər bǐr'ǐ ən), *adj.*

cer·car·i·a (sər·kâr′ĭ·ə), *n., pl.* **-cariae** (-kâr′ĭ·ē′). *Zool.* a larval stage of flukes, *Trematoda,* characterized by a body usually bearing a taillike appendage, but sometimes enclosed in the tail. [NL, f. *cerc-* (comb. form repr. Gk. *kérkos* tail) + *-āria* -ARIA] —**cer·car′i·al,** *adj.* —**cer·car′i·an,** *adj., n.*

cere[1] (sĭr), *n. Ornith.* a membrane of waxy appearance at the base of the upper mandible of certain birds, esp. birds of prey and parrots, in which the nostrils open. [late ME *sere,* t. ML: m. *cēra,* in L wax, c. Gk. *kērós*]

cere[2] (sĭr), *v.t.* **cered, cering.** 1. *Poetic.* to wrap in or as in a cerecloth, esp. a corpse. 2. *Obs.* to wax. [ME, t. L: m.s. *cērāre,* to wax]

ce·re·al (sĭr′ē·əl), *n.* 1. any gramineous plant yielding an edible farinaceous grain, as wheat, rye, oats, rice, maize, etc. 2. the grain itself. 3. some edible preparation of it, esp. (*U.S.*) a breakfast food made from some grain. —*adj.* 4. of or pertaining to grain or the plants producing it. [t. L: s. *Cereālis* pertaining to Ceres.]

cer·e·bel·lum (sĕr′ə·bĕl′əm), *n., pl.* **-bellums, -bella** (-bĕl′ə). *Anat., Zool.* a large expansion of the hindbrain, concerned with the coördination of voluntary movements, posture, and equilibrium. In man it lies at the back of and below the cerebrum and consists of two lateral lobes and a central lobe. [t. L, dim. of *cerebrum* brain] —**cer·e·bel′lar,** *adj.*

cer·e·bral (sĕr′ə·brəl; *for 1, 2, also* sə·rē′brəl), *adj.* 1. *Anat., Zool.* of or pertaining to the cerebrum or the brain. 2. thoughtful; intellectual. 3. *Phonetics.* cacuminal. —*n.* 4. *Phonetics.* a cerebral consonant. [t. NL: s. *cerebrālis,* der. L *cerebrum* brain]

cerebral palsy, a form of paralysis caused by injury to the brain, most marked in certain motor areas. It is characterized by involuntary motions and difficulty in control of the voluntary muscles.

cer·e·brate (sĕr′ə·brāt′), *v.,* **-brated, -brating.** —*v.i.* 1. to use the cerebrum or brain; experience brain action. 2. to think. —*v.t.* 3. to perform by brain action.

cer·e·bra·tion (sĕr′ə·brā′shən), *n.* 1. the action of the cerebrum or brain. 2. thinking; thought.

cer·e·bric (sĕr′ə·brĭk, sə·rēb′rĭk, -rē′brĭk), *adj.* pertaining to or derived from the brain.

cerebro-, a word element meaning "cerebrum." Also, before vowels, **cerebr-.**

cer·e·bro·spi·nal (sĕr′ə·brō·spī′nəl), *adj. Anat., Physiol.* 1. pertaining to or affecting both the brain and the spinal cord. 2. pertaining to the brain and the spinal cord together with their cranial and spinal nerves (distinguished from *autonomic*).

cerebrospinal meningitis, *Pathol.* an acute inflammation of the meninges of the brain and spinal cord caused by a specific organism, and accompanied by fever and occasionally red spots on the skin; brain fever.

cer·e·brum (sĕr′ə·brəm), *n., pl.* **-brums, -bra** (-brə). *Anat., Zool.* 1. the anterior and upper part of the brain, consisting of two hemispheres, partially separated by a deep fissure but connected by a broad band of fibers, and concerned with voluntary and conscious processes. 2. these two hemispheres together with other adjacent parts; the prosencephalon, thalamencephalon, and mesencephalon together. [t. L: brain]

cere·cloth (sĭr′klôth′, -klŏth′), *n.* 1. waxed cloth, used esp. for wrapping the dead. 2. a piece of such cloth. [earlier *cered cloth.* See CERE, v.]

cere·ment (sĭr′mənt), *n.* (*usually pl.*) 1. cerecloth. 2. any graveclothes. [f. CERE, v. + -MENT. Cf. F *cirement*]

cer·e·mo·ni·al (sĕr′ə·mō′nĭ·əl), *adj.* 1. pertaining to, marked by, or of the nature of ceremonies or ceremony; ritual; formal. —*n.* 2. a system of ceremonies, rites, or formalities prescribed for or observed on any particular occasion; a rite or ceremony. 3. *Rom. Cath. Ch.* **a.** the order for rites and ceremonies. **b.** a book containing it. 4. a formality, esp. of etiquette; the observance of ceremony. —**cer′e·mo′ni·al·ism,** *n.* —**cer′e·mo′ni·al·ist,** *n.,* —**cer′e·mo′ni·al·ly,** *adv.*

cer·e·mo·ni·ous (sĕr′ə·mō′nĭ·əs), *adj.* 1. carefully observant of ceremony; formally or elaborately polite. 2. pertaining to, marked by, or consisting of ceremony; formal: *a ceremonious reception.* —**cer′e·mo′ni·ous·ly,** *adv.* —**cer′e·mo′ni·ous·ness,** *n.*

cer·e·mo·ny (sĕr′ə·mō′nĭ), *n., pl.* **-nies.** 1. the formalities observed on some solemn or important public or state occasion. 2. a formal religious or sacred observance; a solemn rite. 3. any formal act or observance, esp. a meaningless one. 4. a gesture or act of politeness or civility. 5. formal observances or gestures collectively; ceremonial observances. 6. strict adherence to conventional forms; formality: *to leave a room without ceremony.* 7. **stand on ceremony,** to be excessively formal or polite. [t. ML: m.s. *cēremōnia,* L *caerimōnia* sacred rite; r. ME *serimonie,* t. OF]
—Syn. 1, 2. CEREMONY, RITE, RITUAL refer to set observances and acts traditional in religious services or on public occasions. CEREMONY applies to more or less formal dignified acts on religious or public occasions: *a marriage ceremony, an inaugural ceremony.* A RITE is an established, prescribed, or customary form of religious or other solemn practice: *the rite of baptism.* RITUAL refers to the form of conducting worship or to a code of ceremonies in general: *Masonic rituals.*

Ce·res (sĭr′ēz), *n.* an ancient Italian goddess of agriculture, under whose name the Romans adopted the worship of the Greek goddess Demeter. [t. L]

ce·re·us (sĭr′ĭ·əs), *n.* any plant of the cactaceous genus *Cereus,* of tropical America, as *C. Jamacaru,* of northern Brazil, which grows to about 40 feet. [t. L: wax candle]

ce·ri·a (sĭr′ĭ·ə), *n. Chem.* cerium oxide, CeO_2, used in small percentages in incandescent mantles for gas.

ce·ric (sĭr′ĭk, sĕr′-), *adj. Chem.* containing cerium, esp. in the tetravalent state, Ce^{+4}.

Ce·ri·go (chĕ′rē·gô′), *n.* one of the Ionian Islands, off the S coast of Greece. 6297 pop. (1951); 108 sq. mi. Greek, **Kythera.** See **Cythera.**

ce·rise (sə·rēz′, -rēs′), *n., adj.* bright red; cherry. [t. F]

ce·ri·um (sĭr′ĭ·əm), *n. Chem.* a steel-gray, ductile metallic element of the rare-earth group found only in combination. *Symbol:* Ce; *at. wt.:* 140.13; *at no.:* 58. [t. NL, named after the asteroid *Ceres*]

cerium metals, *Chem.* See **rare-earth elements.**

Cer·nă·u·ţi (chĕr′nə·ōōts′), *n.* a city in the SW Soviet Union: formerly in Rumania. 142,000 (est. 1956). Polish, **Czernowitz.** Russian, **Chernovitsy.**

cer·nu·ous (sŭr′nyŏŏ·əs, -nōō-), *adj. Bot.* drooping or bowing down, as a flower. [t. L: m. *cernuus* stooping]

ce·ro (sĭr′ō), *n., pl.* **ceros.** 1. a large tropical Atlantic mackerellike fish, *Scomberomorus regalis,* of importance for food and game. 2. any related species. [t. Sp.: m. *sierra* saw, sawfish]

cero-, a word element meaning "wax," as in *cerotype.* Also, **cer-.** [t. Gk.: m. *kēro-,* comb. form of *kērós*]

ce·ro·plas·tic (sĭr′ə·plăs′tĭk, sĕr′ə-), *adj.* 1. pertaining to modeling in wax. 2. modeled in wax.

ce·rot·ic acid (sĭ·rŏt′ĭk), *Chem.* the monobasic fatty acid, $C_{26}H_{53}COOH$, of beeswax. [f. m.s. Gk. *kērotón* waxed + -IC]

ce·ro·type (sĭr′ə·tīp′, sĕr′-), *n.* a process of engraving in which the design or the like is cut on a wax-coated metal plate, from which a printing surface is subsequently produced by stereotyping or by electrotyping.

ce·rous (sĭr′əs), *adj. Chem.* containing trivalent cerium (Ce^{+3}). [f. CER(IUM) + -OUS]

Cer·ro de Pas·co (sĕr′rô dĕ păs′kô), a town in central Peru: famous silver mining district. 24,533 (est. 1954); 14,280 ft. high.

Cer·ro Gor·do (sĕr′rô gôr′dô), a mountain pass in E Mexico between Veracruz and Jalapa: battle, 1847.

cert., 1. certificate. 2. certify. 3. certified.

cer·tain (sûr′tən), *adj.* 1. having no doubt; confident; assured (often fol. by *of* before a noun, gerund, or pronoun): *I am certain of being able to finish it by tomorrow.* 2. sure; inevitable; bound to come (fol. by an infinitive): *it is certain to happen.* 3. established as true or sure; unquestionable; indisputable: *it is certain that he tried.* 4. fixed; agreed upon: *on a certain day.* 5. definite or particular, but not named or specified: *certain persons.* 6. that may be depended on; trustworthy; unfailing; reliable: *his aim was certain.* 7. some though not much: *a certain reluctance.* 8. *Obs.* steadfast. —*n.* 9. **for certain,** without any doubt; surely. [ME, t. OF, der. L *certus* fixed, certain, orig. pp.] —Syn. 1. positive, convinced, satisfied. 2. See **sure.** 3. incontrovertible, irrefutable, incontestable. 4. prescribed, specified.

cer·tain·ly (sûr′tən·lĭ), *adv.* 1. with certainty; without doubt; assuredly. —*interj.* 2. yes! of course!

cer·tain·ty (sûr′tən·tĭ), *n., pl.* **-ties.** 1. state of being certain. 2. something certain; an assured fact. [ME *certeinte,* t. AF] —Syn. 2. See **belief.**

cer·tes (sûr′tēz), *adv. Archaic.* certainly; verily. [ME, t. OF, g. LL *certas,* adv., der. L *certus* CERTAIN]

certif., 1. certificate. 2. certificated.

cer·ti·fi·a·ble (sûr′tə·fī′ə·bəl), *adj.* 1. capable of being certified. 2. *Brit.* committable to a mental institution.

cer·tif·i·cate (*n.* sər·tĭf′ə·kĭt; *v.* sər·tĭf′ə·kāt′), *n., v.,* **-cated, -cating.** —*n.* 1. a writing on paper certifying to the truth of something, or to status, qualifications, privileges, etc. 2. a document issued to a person completing an educational course, issued either by an institution not authorized to grant diplomas, or to a student not qualifying for a diploma. 3. *Law.* a statement, written and signed, which is by law made evidence of the truth of the facts stated, for all or for certain purposes. 4. a certificate issued by the U.S. government and circulating as money, bearing a statement that gold (**gold certificate**) or silver (**silver certificate**) to a specified amount has been deposited in the Treasury for its redemption. —*v.t.* 5. to attest by a certificate. 6. to furnish with or authorize by a certificate. [late ME, t. ML: m.s. *certificātum,* neut. pp. of *certificāre.* See CERTIFY]

certificate of deposit, a written acknowledgment of a bank that it has received from the person named a specified sum of money as a deposit.

certificate of incorporation, a statement filed with a state official in forming a corporation, stating its name, purposes, the nature and distribution of the stock to be issued, and other matters required by law.

certificate of indebtedness, a short-term, negotiable, interest-bearing note representing indebtedness.

certificate of origin, a shipping document having consular certification that names a boat's origin and type of goods aboard, often required before importation.

cer·ti·fi·ca·tion (sûr′tə·fə·kā′shən, sər·tĭf′ə-), *n.* 1. act of certifying. 2. state of being certified. 3. a certified statement. 4. the writing on the face of a check by which it is certified. 5. *Law.* a certificate attesting the truth of some statement or event.

ăct, āble, dâre, ärt; ĕbb, ēqual; ĭf, īce; hŏt, ōver, ôrder, oil, bŏŏk, ōōze, out; ŭp, ūse, ûrge; ə = a in alone; ch, chief; g, give; ng, ring; sh, shoe; th, thin; ŧħ, that; zh, vision. See the full key on inside cover.

cer·ti·fied (sûr′tə fīd′), *adj.* **1.** having, or proved by, a certificate. **2.** guaranteed; reliably endorsed. **3.** *Brit.* committed to a mental institution.

certified milk, *U.S.* milk from dairies conforming to official standards of sanitation, etc., and therefore requiring no pasteurization.

certified public accountant, *U.S.* one having an official accountant certificate after fulfilling all legal requisites. *Abbr.:* C.P.A.

cer·ti·fy (sûr′tə fī′), *v.t.,* **-fied, -fy·ing. 1.** to guarantee as certain; give reliable information of. **2.** to testify to or vouch for in writing. **3.** to assure or inform with certainty. **4.** to guarantee; endorse reliably. **5.** (of a bank, or one of its officials) to acknowledge in writing upon (a check) that the bank on which it is drawn has funds of the drawer sufficient to pay it. —*v.i.* **6.** to give assurance; testify (fol. by *to*); vouch (fol. by *for*). [ME *certifie*(*n*), t. F: m. *certifier,* t. ML: m. *certificāre*] —**cer′·ti·fi′er,** *n.*

cer·ti·o·ra·ri (sûr′shī ə rär′ī), *n. Law.* a writ issuing from a superior court calling up the record of a proceeding in an inferior court for review. [t. L: to be informed (lit., made more certain)]

cer·ti·tude (sûr′tə tūd′, -tōōd′), *n.* certainty. [late ME, t. LL: m. *certitūdo*]

ce·ru·le·an (sə rōō′lĭ ən), *adj., n.* deep blue; sky blue; azure. [f. m.s. L *caeruleus* dark blue + -AN]

ce·ru·men (sə rōō′mən), *n. Anat.* a yellowish waxlike secretion from certain glands in the external auditory canal, acting as a lubricant and arresting the entrance of dust, insects, etc.; earwax. [t. NL, der. L *cēra* wax]

ce·ruse (sĭr′ōōs, sĭ rōōs′), *n.* white lead; a mixture or compound of hydrate and carbonate of lead, much used in painting. [ME, t. L: m. *cērussa*]

ce·rus·site (sĭr′ə sīt′), *n.* a mineral, lead carbonate, PbCO₃, in white crystals or massive: an important ore of lead. [f. s. L *cērussa* white lead + -ITE¹]

Cer·van·tes Sa·a·ve·dra (sər văn′tĕz; *Sp*.ther văn′tĕs sä′ä vĕ′drä), **Miguel de** (mē gĕl′ dĕ), 1547–1616, Spanish novelist.

Cer·ve·ra y To·pe·te (ther vĕ′rä ē tô pĕ′tĕ), **Pas·cual** (päs kwäl′), 1839–1909, Spanish admiral.

cervic-, a combining form of cervical. Also, **cervico-.**

cer·vi·cal (sûr′və kəl), *adj. Anat.* pertaining to the cervix or neck. [f. s. L *cervix* neck + -AL¹]

cer·vi·ci·tis (sûr′və sī′təs), *n.* inflammation of the cervix (of the uterus).

cervico-, var. of cervic-, used before consonants.

Cer·vin (sĕr văn′), *n.* **Mont** (môN), French name of the **Matterhorn.**

cer·vine (sûr′vīn, -vĭn), *adj.* **1.** deerlike. **2.** of deer or the deer family, the *Cervidae.* **3.** of a deep tawny color. [t. L: m. s. *cervīnus* pertaining to deer]

cer·vix (sûr′vĭks), *n., pl.* **cervixes, cervices** (sər vī′sēz). **1.** the neck. **2.** the neck of the uterus, which dilates just before parturition. **3.** any necklike part. [t. L]

Ce·sar·e·an (sĭ zâr′ī ən), *adj., n.* Caesarean. Also, **Ce·sar′i·an.**

ce·si·um (sē′zĭ əm), *n. Chem.* a rare, extremely active, soft, monovalent metallic element showing blue lines in the spectrum. *Symbol:* Cs; *at. wt.:* 132.91; *at. no.:* 55; *sp. gr.:* 1.9 at 20° C.; melts at 28.5° C. Also, **caesium.** [NL, special use of L *caesium* (neut.) bluish-gray]

Čes·ké Bu·de·jo·vi·ce (chĕs′kĕ bōō′dyĕ yō′vĭ tsĕ), Czech name of Budweis.

ces·pi·tose (sĕs′pə tōs′), *adj. Bot.* matted together; growing in dense tufts. Also, **caespitose.** [f. m.s. L *caespes* turf + -OSE¹] —**ces′pi·tose′ly,** *adv.*

ces·sa·tion (sĕ sā′shən), *n.* a ceasing; discontinuance; pause: *a cessation of hostilities.* [t. L: s. *cessātio*]

ces·sion (sĕsh′ən), *n.* **1.** act of ceding, as by treaty. **2.** something, as territory, ceded. [t. L: s. *cessio*]

ces·sion·ar·y (sĕsh′ə nĕr′ī), *n., pl.* **-aries. 1.** a transferee. **2.** assignee. **3.** grantee.

cess·pool (sĕs′pōōl′), *n.* **1.** a cistern, well, or pit for retaining the sediment of a drain or for receiving the filth of a water closet, etc. **2.** any filthy receptacle or place: *a cesspool of iniquity.* [orig. uncert.]

c'est-à-dire (sĕ tà dēr′), *French.* that is to say.

c'est la guerre (sĕ là gĕr′), *French.* it is war.

Ces·to·da (sĕs tō′də), *n.pl. Zool.* tapeworms, a class of internally parasitic platyhelminths or flatworms, characterized by the long tapelike body divided into joints.

ces·tode (sĕs′tōd), *n.* a tapeworm. [f. m.s. Gk. *kestós* girdle + -ODE¹]

ces·toid (sĕs′toid), *adj. Zool.* (of worms) ribbonlike.

ces·tus¹ (sĕs′təs), *n.* **1.** a belt or girdle. **2.** *Class. Myth.* the girdle of Aphrodite or Venus, which was said to be decorated with everything that could awaken love. [t. L, t. Gk.: m. *kestós* girdle, lit., stitched]

ces·tus² (sĕs′təs), *n. Rom. Antiq.* a hand covering made of leather strips often loaded with metal, worn by boxers. [t. L: m. *caestus,* prob. var. sp. of *cestus* CESTUS¹]

ce·su·ra (sə zhŏŏr′ə, -zyŏŏr′ə), *n.* caesura. —**ce·su′·ral,** *adj.*

cet-, a word element meaning "whale." [comb. form repr. L *cētus* and Gk. *kētos* whale]

ce·ta·cean (sə tā′shən), *adj.* **1.** belonging to the *Cetacea,* an order of aquatic, chiefly marine, mammals, including the whales, dolphins, porpoises, etc. —*n.* **2.** a cetacean mammal. [f. s. NL *Cetacea,* pl. (see CET-, -ACEA) + -AN] —**ce·ta′ceous,** *adj.*

ce·tane number (sē′tān), *Chem., etc.* a measure of the ignition quality of Diesel engine fuels. The fuel is compared with mixtures of the alpha form of methylnaphthalene (value = 0) and a hydrocarbon, C₁₆H₃₄ of the methane series (**cetane**) (value = 100).

Ce·ta·tea Al·bă (chĕ tä′tyä äl′bə), Rumanian name of Akkerman.

ce·te·ra de·sunt (sĕt′ərə dē′sənt), *Latin.* the remaining (parts) are missing.

ce·te·ris pa·ri·bus (sĕt′ərĭs păr′ə bəs), *Latin.* the others (other things) being equal. *Abbr.:* **cet. par.**

Ce·tin·je (tsĕ′tĭ nyĕ), *n.* a city in SW Yugoslavia: the capital of Montenegro. 9109 (1953).

Ce·tus (sē′təs), *n., gen.* **Ceti** (sē′tī). *Astron.* a constellation lying across the equator and containing an important variable star. [t. L, t. Gk. See CET-]

Ceu·ta (sū′tə; *Sp.* thĕ′ŏŏ tä, sĕ-), *n.* a Spanish seaport in Morocco, on the Strait of Gibraltar. 59,936 (1950).

Cé·vennes (sĕ vĕn′), *n.* a mountain range in S France. Highest peak, Mt. Mézenc, 5753 ft.

Cey·lon (sĭ lŏn′), *n.* an island in the Indian Ocean, S of India: member of Brit. commonwealth. 8,589,000 pop. (est. 1955); 25,232 sq. mi. *Cap.:* Colombo. —**Cey·lo·nese** (sē′lə nēz′, -nēs′), *adj., n.*

Ceylon moss, a seaweed, *Gracilaria lichenoides,* of Ceylon and the East Indies, and one of the algae from which agar-agar is obtained.

Cé·zanne (sĭ zăn′; *Fr.* sĕ zàn′), **Paul** (pōl), 1839–1906, French painter.

cf., 1. *Bookbinding.* calf. **2.** *Baseball.* center fielder. **3.** (L *confer*) compare.

C.F.I., cost, freight, and insurance. Also, **c.f.i.**

· **g.,** centigram; centigrams.

C.G., 1. Coast Guard. **2.** Commanding General.

cgs, centimeter-gram-second (system). Also, **c.g.s.**

Ch., 1. chapter. **2.** *Chess.* check. **3.** church. Also, **ch.**

chab·a·zite (kăb′ə zīt′), *n.* a zeolite mineral, essentially a hydrated sodium calcium aluminum silicate, occurring commonly in red to colorless crystals that are nearly cubes. [earlier *chabazie,* t. F, misspelling of Gk. *chalázie* (voc.), der. *chálaza* hailstone. See -ITE¹]

Cha·blis (shăb′lĭ; *Fr.* shäblē′), *n.* a very dry white table wine from the Burgundy wine region in France. [named after *Chablis,* town in N central France]

cha·bouk (chä′bŏŏk), *n.* a horsewhip, often used in the Orient for inflicting corporal punishment. Also, **cha·buk.** [t. Pers. and Hind.: m. *chābuk*]

cha·cha·la·ca (chä′chä lä′kä), *n.* a loud-voiced guan, *Ortalis vetula,* inhabiting brushlands of southern Texas, Mexico, and Central America. The name is onomatopoeic.

chac·ma (chăk′mə), *n.* a large South African baboon, *Papio comatus,* about the size of a mastiff. [t. Hottentot]

Cha·co (chä′kō), *n.* **1.** a part of the Gran Chaco region in central South America, formerly in dispute between Bolivia and Paraguay: boundary fixed by arbitration, 1938. ab. 100,000 sq. mi. **2.** See **Gran Chaco.**

Chacma.
Papio comatus
(Total length 4½ ft.
tail 21 in.)

cha·conne (shä kôn′), *n.* **1.** an old-time dance, probably of Spanish origin. **2.** music for it. [t. F, t. Sp.: m. *chacona,* t. Basque: m. *chacun* pretty]

cha·cun à son goût (shà kœn nä sôn gōō′). *French.* everyone to his own taste.

Chad (chăd), *n.* **1.** Lake, a lake in N Africa at the junction of Chad, Niger, and Nigeria. 10,000 to 20,000 sq. mi. (seasonal variation). **2.** an independent member of the French community E of this lake; formerly part of French Equatorial Africa. 2,730,000 pop. (est. 1959); 501,000 sq. mi. *Cap.:* Fort-Lamy. Official name, **Republic of Chad.**

FRENCH WEST AFRICA / LAKE CHAD / GHANA / NIGERIA / IVORY COAST / Gulf of Guinea

Chad·wick (chăd′wĭk), *n.* **James,** born 1891, British physicist.

Chaer·o·ne·a (kĕr′ə nē′ə), *n* an ancient city in E Greece, in Boeotia: victory of Philip of Macedon over the Athenians, 338 B.C.

chae·ta (kē′tə), *n., pl.* **-tae** (-tē). *Zool.* a bristle or seta, esp. of a chaetopod. [NL, t. Gk.: m. *chaitē* hair]

chaeto-, a word element meaning "hair," as in *chaetopod.* Also, before vowels, **chaet-.** [comb. form repr. Gk. *chaitē*]

chae·toph·o·rous (kĭ tŏf′ə rəs), *adj. Zool.* bearing bristles; setigerous or setiferous.

chae·to·pod (kē′tə pŏd′), *n. Zool.* any of the *Chaetopoda,* a class or group of annelids having the body made up of more or less similar segments provided with muscular processes bearing setae.

chafe (chāf), *v.,* **chafed, chafing,** *n.* —*v.t.* **1.** to warm by rubbing. **2.** to wear or abrade by rubbing. **3.** to make sore by rubbing. **4.** to irritate; annoy. **5.** to heat; make warm. —*v.i.* **6.** to rub; press with friction. **7.** to become worn or sore by rubbing. **8.** to be irritated

r annoyed. —*n.* **9.** irritation; annoyance. **10.** heat,
wear, or soreness caused by rubbing. [ME *chaufe(n)*, t.
OF: m. *chaufer*, g. LL contr. of L *calefacere* make hot]

chaf·er (chā′fər), *n.* *Chiefly Brit.* any scarabaeid bee-
le. [ME *cheaffer*, *chaver*, OE *ceafor*. Cf. G *käfer*]

chaff[1] (chǎf, chäf), *n.* **1.** the husks of grains and grasses
separated from the seed. **2.** straw cut small for fodder.
3. worthless matter; refuse; rubbish. [ME *chaf*, OE *ceaf*.
t. D *kaf*] —**chaff′y,** *adj.*

chaff[2] (chǎf, chäf), *v.t.*, *v.i.* **1.** to ridicule or tease good-
naturedly; banter. —*n.* **2.** good-natured ridicule or
teasing; raillery. [? special use of CHAFF[1]] —**chaff′er,** *n.*

chaf·fer (chǎf′ər), *n.* **1.** bargaining; haggling. —*v.i.*
2. to bargain; haggle. **3.** to bandy words. —*v.t.* **4.** to
trade or deal in; barter. **5.** to bandy (words). [ME
chaffare, earlier *chapfare* trading journey, f. OE *cēap*
trade + *faru* a going] —**chaf′fer·er,** *n.*

chaf·finch (chǎf′inch), *n.* a common European finch,
Fringilla coelebs, with a pleasant short song, often kept
as a cage bird. [OE *ceaffinc*. See CHAFF[1], FINCH]

chaf·ing dish (chā′fing), **1.** an apparatus consisting
of a metal dish with a lamp or heating appliance beneath it, for cooking food or keeping it hot. **2.** a vessel
to hold charcoal, etc., for heating anything set over it.

ha·gall (shä gäll′), *n.* **Marc,** born 1887, Russian
painter in U.S.

ha·gres (chä′grĕs), *n.* a river in Panama, flowing
through Gatun Lake to the Caribbean.

ha·grin (shə grǐn′), *n.* **1.** a feeling of vexation and
disappointment or humiliation. —*v.t.* **2.** to vex by disappointment or humiliation. [t. F. See SHAGREEN]

ha·har (chä′här), *n.* a former province of Inner
Mongolia in NE China. 3,881,000 (est. 1950); 107,-
398 sq. mi. Divided among adjacent provinces in 1952.

hain (chān), *n.* **1.** a connected series of metal or other
links for connecting, drawing, confining, restraining,
etc., or for ornament. **2.** something that binds or restrains. **3.** (*pl.*) bonds or fetters. **4.** (*pl.*) bondage.
5. a series of things connected or following in succession.
6. a range of mountains. **7.** a number of similar establishments, as banks, theaters, hotels, etc. under one
ownership and management. **8.** *Chem.* a linkage of
atoms of the same element, as carbon to carbon.
9. *Survey.* **a.** a measuring instrument consisting of 100
wire rods or links, each 7.92 inches long (**surveyor's** or
Gunter's chain), or one foot long (**engineer's chain**).
b. the length of a surveyor's chain (66 feet) or engineer's
chain (100 feet). —*v.t.* **10.** to fasten or secure with a
chain. **11.** to fetter; confine: *chained to his desk.* [ME
chayne, t. OF: m. *chaeine*, g. L *catēna*] —**chain′less,** *adj.*

hain gang, *Chiefly U.S.* a group of prisoners usually
chained together when in camp, in transit, etc.

hain lightning, *U.S.* lightning visible in wavy, zigzag, or broken lines.

hain mail, flexible body armor made of metal links.

hain·man (chān′mən), *n.*, *pl.* **-men.** a man who holds
the chain in making surveying measurements.

hain-re·act·ing (chān′rī ǎk′tǐng), *adj.* *Physics.* (of
a substance) undergoing or capable of undergoing a chain
reaction.

hain reaction, **1.** *Physics.* a nuclear reaction which
produces enough neutrons to sustain itself. **2.** *Chem.* a
reaction which results in a product necessary for the
continuance of the reaction.

hain shot, *Ordn.* a shot consisting of two balls or half
balls connected by a short chain.

hain stitch, a kind of ornamental stitching in which
each stitch forms a loop through the forward end of
which the next stitch is taken.

hain store, **1.** a group of retail stores under the
same ownership and management and merchandised
from a common point or points. **2.** one such store.

hain·work (chān′wûrk′), *n.* decorative work esp.
when looped or woven together as in the links of a chain.

hair (châr), *n.* **1.** a seat with a back and legs or other
support, often with arms, usually for one person. **2.** a
seat of office or authority. **3.** the position of a judge,
chairman, presiding officer, etc. **4.** the person occupying
the seat or office, esp. the chairman of a meeting.
5. take the chair, a. to assume the chairmanship of a
meeting; begin or open a meeting. **b.** to preside at a
meeting. **6.** electric chair. **7.** sedan chair. **8.** *Railroads.* a metal block to support and secure a rail. —*v.t.*
9. to place or seat in a chair. **10.** to install in office or
authority. **11.** *Brit.* to place in a chair and carry aloft,
esp. in triumph. [ME *chaiere*, t. OF, g. L *cathedra* seat,
t. Gk.: m. *kathédra*]

hair car, *U.S. Railroads.* **1.** a parlor car. **2.** a car
with two adjustable seats on each side of the aisle.

hair·man (châr′mən), *n.*, *pl.* **-men.** **1.** the presiding
officer of a meeting, committee, board, etc. **2.** someone
employed to carry or wheel a person in a chair.

hair·wom·an (châr′-
wŏŏm′ən), *n.*, *pl.* **-women.**
a female chairman (def. 1).

haise (shāz), *n.* **1.** Also,
Colloq., **shay.** a light, open
carriage, usually with a hood,
esp. a one-horse, two-wheeled
carriage for two persons. **2.** a
post chaise. [t. F: chair,
chaise, var. of *chaire*. See
CHAIR]

Chaise, 18th and 19th centuries

chaise longue (shāz′ lông′; *Fr.* shĕz lông′), a kind
of couch or reclining chair with seat prolonged to form a
full-length leg rest. [t. F: long chair]

cha·la·za (kə lā′zə), *n.*, *pl.* **-zas,** **-zae** (-zē). **1.** *Zool.*
one of the two albuminous twisted cords which fasten
an egg yolk to the shell membrane. **2.** *Bot.* the point of
an ovule or seed where the integuments are united to
the nucellus. [t. NL, t. Gk.: hail, lump] —**cha·la′zal,**
adj.

chal·can·thite (kǎl kǎn′thĭt), *n.* blue vitriol.

Chal·ce·don (kǎl′sĭ dŏn′, kǎl sē′dən), *n.* an ancient city
in NW Asia Minor, on the Bosporus, opposite Byzantium.

chal·ced·o·ny (kǎl sĕd′ə nĭ, kǎl′sə dō′nĭ), *n.*, *pl.* **-nies.**
a microcrystalline translucent variety of quartz, often
milky or grayish. [ME, t. L (Vulgate): m. s. *chalcēdonius*,
t. Gk.: m. *chalkēdōn* in Rev. 21: 19]

chal·cid fly (kǎl′sĭd), any of the *Chalcididae*, a family of small hymenopterous insects, often of bright metallic colors, whose larvae are mostly parasitic on various
stages of other insects. Also, **chalcid.** [*chalcid*, f. s. Gk.
chalkós copper (with allusion to the metallic coloration)
+ -ID[2]]

Chal·cid·i·ce (kǎl sĭd′ə sĭ), *n.* a peninsula in NE
Greece. Greek, **Khalkidike.**

chalco-, a word element meaning "copper" or "brass."
Also, before vowels, **chalc-.** [t. Gk.: m. *chalko-,* comb.
form of *chalkós*]

chal·co·cite (kǎl′kə sīt′), *n.* a common mineral, cuprous sulfide, Cu₂S, an important ore of copper.

chal·cog·ra·phy (kǎl kŏg′rə fĭ), *n.* the art of engraving on copper or brass. —**chal·cog′ra·pher,** *n.* —**chal-
co·graph·ic** (kǎl′kə grăf′ĭk), **chal′co·graph′i·cal,** *adj.*

chal·co·py·rite (kǎl′kə pī′rīt, -pĭr′ĭt), *n.* a very common mineral, copper iron sulfide, CuFeS₂, occurring in
brass-yellow crystals or masses: the most important ore
of copper; copper pyrites.

Chal·de·a (kǎl dē′ə), *n.* ancient region in S Babylonia.

Chal·de·an (kǎl dē′ən), *n.*
1. one of an ancient Semitic
people that formed the dominant element in Babylonia.
2. an astrologer, soothsayer,
or enchanter. Dan. 1:4; 2:2.
3. Biblical Aramaic. —*adj.*
4. of or belonging to ancient
Chaldea. **5.** pertaining to
astrology, occult learning, etc.
Also, **Chal·dee** (kǎl dē′, kǎl′-
dē), *Obsolesc.*, **Chal·da·ic** (kǎl dā′ĭk). [f. m.s. L *Chal-
daeus* (t. Gk.: m. *Chaldaîos*) + -AN]

Chaldea, c1450 B.C.

chal·dron (chôl′drən), *n.* an English dry measure
for coal, coke, lime, etc., equal to 32 or 36 or more
bushels in different commodities and localities. [t. F:
m. *chaudron* kettle; var. of CALDRON]

cha·let (shă lā′, shăl′ā; *Fr.* shă lĕ′), *n.* **1.** a herdsman's
hut in the Swiss mountains. **2.** a kind of cottage, low
and with wide eaves, common in Alpine regions. **3.** any
cottage or villa built in this style. [t. F (Swiss)]

Cha·lia·pin (shä lyä′pĭn), *n.* **Fëdor Ivanovich** (fyô′-
dôr ĭ vä′nô vĭch), 1873–1938, Russian operatic bass
singer.

chal·ice (chăl′ĭs), *n.* **1.** *Poet.* a drinking cup. **2.** *Eccles.*
a. a cup for the wine of the Eucharist or Mass. **b.** the
wine contained in it. **3.** a cuplike blossom. [ME, t.
OF, g. L *calix* cup; r. ME *caliz*, *calc*, OE *calic*, t. L: m.
calix] —**chal′iced** (chăl′ĭst), *adj.*

chalk (chôk), *n.* **1.** a soft powdery limestone consisting
chiefly of fossil shells of foraminifers. **2.** a prepared
piece of chalk or chalklike substance for marking; a
blackboard crayon. **3.** a mark made with chalk. **4.** a
score, or record of credit given, as at a tavern, etc. —*v.t.*
5. to mark or write with chalk. **6.** to rub over or whiten
with chalk. **7.** to treat or mix with chalk. **8.** to make
pale; blanch. **9. chalk up,** to score or earn: *they chalked
up two runs in the first inning.* [ME *chalke*, OE *cealc*, t.
L: m. s. *calx* lime] —**chalk′like′,** *adj.* —**chalk′y,** *adj.*
—**chalk′i·ness,** *n.*

chalk·stone (chôk′stōn′), *n.* *Pathol.* a chalklike concretion in the tissues or small joints of one with gout.

chal·lenge (chăl′inj), *n.*, *v.*, **-lenged,** **-lenging.** —*n.*
1. a call to engage in a contest of skill, strength, etc.
2. a call to fight, as a battle, a duel, etc. **3.** a demand to
explain. **4.** *Mil.* the demand of a sentry for identification or the countersign. **5.** *Law.* a formal objection to
the qualifications of a juror or to the legality of an entire jury. **6.** *U.S.* the assertion that a vote is invalid or
that a voter is not legally qualified. —*v.t.* **7.** to summon
to a contest of skill, strength, etc. **8.** to demand defiantly. **9.** to take exception to; call in question: *to
challenge the wisdom of a procedure.* **10.** *Mil.* to halt and
demand identification or countersign from. **11.** *Law.*
to take formal exception to (a juror or jury). **12.** to
have a claim to because of qualities or character: *a matter which challenges attention.* **13.** *Archaic.* to lay claim
to. **14.** *U.S.* to assert that (a vote) is invalid or (a voter)
is not qualified to vote. —*v.i.* **15.** to make or issue a challenge. **16.** *Hunting.* (of hounds) to cry or give tongue
on picking up the scent. [ME *chalange*, t. OF: m. *chal-
enge*, g. L *calumnia* CALUMNY] —**chal′lenge·a·ble,** *adj.*
—**chal′leng·er,** *n.*

chal·lis (shăl′ĭ), *n.* a printed fabric of plain weave in
wool, cotton, or rayon. Also, **chal′lie.** [orig. uncert.]

ct, āble, dâre, ärt; ĕbb, ēqual; ĭf, īce; hŏt, ōver, ôrder, oil, bŏŏk, ōōze, out; ŭp, ūse, ûrge; ə = a in alone;
h, chief; g, give; ng, ring; sh, shoe; th, thin; ŧh, that; zh, vision. See the full key on inside cover.

chal·one (kăl′ōn), n. *Physiol.* an endocrine secretion which reduces physiological activity. [t. Gk.: m. *chaloûn*, ppr., slackening]

Châ·lons (shä lôn′), n. **1.** Also, **Châ·lons-sur-Marne** (shä lôn′syr märn′). a city in NE France: defeat of Attila, A.D. 451. 36,834 (1954). **2.** Also, **Cha·lon-sur-Saône** (shä lôn′syr sōn′). a city in E France. 37,399 (1954).

Chalons (def. 1)

chal·u·meau (shăl′yə mō′; *Fr.* shȧ ly mō′), n. *Music.* the low register of the clarinet. [t. F, in OF *chalemel* a musical instrument, g. L *calamellus*, dim. of *calamus* reed]

chal·yb·e·ate (kə lĭb′ĭ ĭt, -āt′), adj. **1.** containing or impregnated with salts of iron, as a mineral spring, medicine, etc. —n. **2.** a chalybeate water, medicine, or the like. [appar. t. NL: m. s. *chalybēātus*, der. L *chalybēius* of steel, der. *chalybs*, t. Gk.: m. *chályps* iron]

cham (kăm), n. *Archaic.* khan[1].

cham·ber (chām′bər), n. **1.** a room or apartment, usually a private room, and esp. a bedroom. **2.** (pl.) *Brit.* rooms for residence in the house or building of another; apartments. **3.** a room in a palace or official residence. **4.** the meeting hall of a legislative or other assembly. **5.** (pl.) a place where a judge hears matters not requiring action in court. **6.** (pl.) (in England) quarters of lawyers and others, esp. in the Inns of Court. **7.** the place where the moneys due a government, etc., are received and kept; a treasury or chamberlain's office. **8.** a legislative, judicial, or other like body: *the upper or the lower chamber of a legislature.* **9.** a compartment or enclosed space; a cavity. **10.** a receptacle for one or more cartridges in a firearm, or for a shell in a gun or other cannon. **11.** that part of the barrel of a gun which receives the charge. —v.t. **12.** to put or enclose in, or as in, a chamber. **13.** to provide with a chamber. [ME, t. OF: m. *chambre*, g. L *camera*] —**cham′bered**, adj.

chamber concert, a concert of chamber music.

cham·ber·lain (chām′bər lĭn), n. **1.** an official charged with the management of a sovereign's or nobleman's living quarters. **2.** an official who receives rents and revenues, as of a municipal corporation; a treasurer. **3.** the high steward or factor of a nobleman. **4.** a high official of a royal court. [ME *chamberleyn*, t. OF: m. *chamberlenc*, t. OG; cf. OHG *chamarlinc*]

Cham·ber·lain (chām′bər lĭn), n. **1.** (Arthur) Neville (nĕv′Yl), 1869–1940, British prime minister, 1937–40. **2.** Joseph, 1836–1914, British statesman (father of Sir Austen and Neville Chamberlain). **3.** Sir (Joseph) Austen, 1863–1937, British statesman.

cham·ber·maid (chām′bər mād′), n. a female servant who takes care of bedrooms.

chamber music, music suited for performance in a room or a small concert hall, esp. for two or more (but usually less than ten) solo instruments.

chamber of commerce, an association, primarily of businessmen, to protect and promote the business activities of a city, etc.

cham·bray (shăm′brā), n. a fine variety of gingham, commonly plain, but with the warp and weft of different colors. [var. of CAMBRIC]

cha·me·le·on (kə mē′lĭ ən, -mēl′yən), n. **1.** any of a group of lizards, *Chamaeleontidae,* esp. of the genus *Chamaeleon,* characterized by the greatly developed power of changing the color of the skin, very slow locomotion, and a projectile tongue. **2.** an inconstant person. [ME *camelion,* t. L: m. *chamaeleon,* t. Gk.: m. *chamailéōn,* lit., ground lion] —**cha·me·le·on·ic** (kə mē′lĭ ŏn′ĭk). adj.

African chameleon, *Chamaeleon chamaeleon* (8 in. long)

cham·fer (chăm′fər), n. **1.** an oblique surface cut on the edge or corner of a solid, usually a board, made by removing the arris and usually sloping at 45°. [appar. t. F: m. *chamfrain,* der. *chanfraindre,* f. *chant* side + *fraindre* g. L *frangere* break]

cham·fron (chăm′frən), n. *Armor.* chanfron. Also, **cham·frain** (chăm′frĭn).

cham·ois (shăm ĭ; *Fr.* shȧ mwä′), n., pl. -ois. **1.** an agile goatlike antelope, *Rupicapra rupicapra,* of high mountains of Europe and southwestern Russia. **2.** Also, **cham′my.** a soft, pliable leather made from various skins dressed with oil (esp. fish oil), orig. prepared from the skin of the chamois; shammy. [t. F, g. LL *camox*]

Chamois, *Rupicapra rupicapra* (Total length 3½ ft., 2 ft. 4 in. high at the shoulder)

cham·o·mile (kăm′ə mĭl′), n. camomile.

Cha·mo·nix (shȧ mô nē′; *Fr.* shȧ mô nē′), n. a mountain valley in E France, N of Mont Blanc.

Cha·mor·ro (chä môr′rō), n. an inhabitant of Guam, the Marianas, etc.

champ[1] (chămp), v.t. **1.** to bite upon, esp. impatiently: *horses champing the bit.* **2.** to crush with the teeth and chew

vigorously or noisily; munch. **3.** *Scot.* to mash; crush —v.i. **4.** to make vigorous chewing or biting movement with the jaws and teeth. —n. **5.** act of champing. [nasalized var. (cf. BUNT) of *chop* bite at, der. *chap, cho[* jaw]

champ[2] (chămp), n. *Slang.* a champion.

cham·pac (chăm′păk, chŭm′pŭk), n. an East India tree, *Michelia Champaca,* of the magnolia family, wit[fragrant golden flowers and a handsome wood used fo[making images, furniture, etc. Also, **cham′pak.** [t Hind.]

cham·pagne (shăm pān′), n. **1.** a sparkling whit[wine produced in the wine region of Champagne, France or elsewhere. **2.** the nonsparkling (still) dry white tabl[wine produced in the region of Champagne. **3.** a ver[pale yellow or greenish-yellow color. —adj. **4.** havin[the color of champagne.

Cham·pagne (shăm pān′; *Fr.* shän pän′y), n. a re gion, formerly a province, in E France: famous wine

cham·paign (shăm pān′), n. **1.** level, open country plain. —adj. **2.** level and open. [ME *champaigne,* t OF, g. L *campānia.* See CAMPAIGN]

Cham·paign (shăm pān′), n. a city in E Illinoi[49,583 (1960).

cham·per·ty (chăm′pər tĭ), n. *Law.* a sharing in th[proceeds of litigation by one who promotes it. [MI *champartie,* t. OF: m. *champart* share of the produce o land, g. L *campī pars* part of the field] —**cham′per tous,** adj.

cham·pi·gnon (shăm pĭn′yən; *esp. Brit.* chăm-; *Fr* shän pē nyôn′), n. a mushroom (defs. 2, 3). [t. F, ult der. L *campānia* flat land, der. *campus* field]

cham·pi·on (chăm′pĭ ən), n. **1.** one who holds firs[place in any sport, etc., having defeated all opponents **2.** anything that takes first place in competition. **3.** on[who fights for or defends any person or cause: *a champio[of the oppressed.* **4.** a fighter or warrior. —v.t. **5.** to ac[as champion of; defend; support. **6.** *Obs.* to defy. —ad[**7.** first among all contestants or competitors. **8.** *Collo[* first-rate. [ME, t. OF, g. LL *campio,* der. L *campus* fiel[(of battle)] —**cham·pi·on·ess** (chăm′pĭ ən Ĭs), n fem. —**cham′pi·on·less,** adj. —**Syn. 3.** defender protector, vindicator. **5.** maintain, fight for, advocate

cham·pi·on·ship (chăm′pĭ ən shĭp′), n. **1.** the posi tion of being a champion. **2.** the honor of being a cham pion in competition. **3.** advocacy or defense.

Cham·plain (shăm plān′; *also for 2, Fr.* shän plăn′), n **1.** Lake, a lake between New York and Vermont 125 mi. long; ab. 600 sq. mi. **2.** Samuel de (sȧ my ĕl′ də), 1567–1635, French explorer who founded Quebec the first French governor of Canada.

Cham·pol·lion (shän pô lyôn′). n. Jean François (zhän frän swä′), 1790–1832, French Egyptologist.

Champs É·ly·sées (shän zĕ lē zē′), n. French. a fa mous boulevard in Paris, France; cafés, shops, an[theaters; a tourist center. [F: lit., Elysian Fields]

chance (chăns, chäns), n., v., **chanced, chancing,** adj —n. **1.** the absence of any known reason why an even[should turn out one way rather than another, spoken o[as if it were a real agency: *chance governs all.* **2.** fortune fate; luck. **3.** a possibility or probability of anythin[happening: *the chances are two to one against us.* **4.** a[opportunity: *now is your chance.* **5.** *Baseball.* an op portunity, in fielding, for a put-out or an assist. **6.** [risk or hazard: *take a chance.* **7.** *Archaic.* an unfortunat[event; a mishap. **8.** *U.S. Colloq.* a quantity or numbe[(usually followed by *of*). **9. by chance,** accidentally —v.i. **10.** to happen or occur by chance. **11.** to come by chance (fol. by *on* or *upon*). —v.t. **12.** *Colloq.* to take th[chances or risks of; risk (usually fol. by impersonal *it*) —adj. **13.** due to chance: *a chance occurrence.* [ME *chea(u)nce,* t. OF: m. *cheance,* g. LL *cadentia* a fallin[out, der. *cadens* ppr., falling] —**Syn. 10.** See **happen.** **13.** casual, accidental, fortuitous.

chan·cel (chăn′səl, chän′-), n. the space about th[altar of a church, usually enclosed, for the clergy and other officials. [ME, t. OF, g. LL *cancellus,* L *cancelli* bars, lattice (which enclosed the chancel)]

chan·cel·ler·y (chăn′sə lər Ĭ, -slər Ĭ, chän′-), n., pl -leries. **1.** the position of a chancellor. **2.** the office or department of a chancellor. **3.** the office attached to an embassy, etc. **4.** the building or room occupied by an chancellor's department. [ME *chancelerie,* t. OF, der *chancelier* CHANCELLOR]

chan·cel·lor (chăn′sə lər, -slər, chän′-), n. **1.** the title of various important judges and other high officials. **2.** *U.S.* the presiding judge of a court of equity or chancery. **3.** (formerly) the chief minister of state in Germany or Austria. **4.** a secretary, as of a king, nobleman, or embassy. **5.** the chief administrative officer in certain American universities. **6.** an honorary official in British universities. [ME *chanceler,* t. AF, var. of OF *chancelier,* g. L *cancellārius,* orig. officer stationed at a tribunal. See CHANCEL] —**chan′cel·lor·ship′,** n.

Chancellor of the Exchequer, the minister of finance in the British Government.

Chan·cel·lors·ville (chăn′sə lərz vĭl′, chän′-), n. a village in NE Virginia: site of a Confederate victory, 1863.

chance-med·ley (chăns′mĕd′lĭ, chäns′-), n. *Law.* a sudden quarrel with violence, in the course of which one party kills or wounds another in self-defense or in the heat of passion. [t. AF: m. *chance medlée* mixed chance]

chan·cer·y (chăn′sə rĭ, chăn′-), *n., pl.* **-ceries. 1.** the office or department of a chancellor. **2.** a chancellery. **3.** an office of public records, esp., in England, of the Lord Chancellor. **4.** *Eng.* the Lord Chancellor's court, now a division of the High Court of Justice. **5.** *Law.* **a.** Also, **court of chancery.** court having jurisdiction in equity; court of equity. **b.** equity (defs. 3a, 3b). **6. in chancery, a.** *Law.* in litigation in a court of chancery. **b.** *Boxing.* (of a contestant's head) held under his opponent's arm. **c.** in a helpless or embarrassing position. [ME, var. of CHANCELLERY]

chan·cre (shăng′kər), *n.* the initial lesion of syphilis, commonly a more or less distinct ulcer or sore with a hard base. [t. F, g. L *cancer* crab, cancer]

chanc·y (chăn′sĭ, chăn′-), *adj.,* **chancier, chanciest.** *Colloq. or Dial.* uncertain.

chan·de·lier (shăn′də lĭr′), *n.* a branched support for a number of lights, esp. one suspended from a ceiling. [t. F: f. *chandel* candle + suffix *-ier*]

chan·delle (shăn dĕl′; *Fr.* shän-), *n.* *Aeron.* an abrupt climbing turn approximately to a stall, in which momentum is used to obtain a higher rate of climb. [t. F]

Chan·der·na·gor (chŭn′dər nə gōr′), *n.* a city in NE India, near Calcutta: a port on the Hooghly river. Formerly a French dependency; part of French India. 49,909 (1954). Also, **Chan·dar·na·gar** (chŭn′dər nŭg′ər).

Chan·di·garh (chŭn′dĭ gŭr′), *n.* the capital of the state of Punjab, N W India. Established 1953.

chan·dler (chăn′dlər, chăn′-), *n.* **1.** a dealer or trader: *a ship chandler.* **2.** one who makes or sells candles. **3.** a retailer of groceries, etc. [ME *cha(u)ndeler,* t. AF, var. of OF *chandelier* candle-seller, der. OF *chandeile* CANDLE]

chan·dler·y (chăn′dlə rĭ, chăn′-), *n., pl.* **-dleries. 1.** a storeroom for candles. **2.** the warehouse, wares, or business of a chandler.

Chan·dra·gup·ta (chŭn′drə gŏŏp′tə), *n.* fl. c300 B.C., king of northern India, c315–c296 or c291 B.C. Greek, **Sandrocottus.**

chan·fron (chăn′frən), *n.* armor for a horse's head. Also, **chamfron, chamfrain.** [ME *shamfron,* t. OF: m. *chanfrain;* orig. uncert.]

Chang·chow·fu (chăng′chou′fōō′; *Chin.* chäng′jō′-fōō′), *n.* a city in SE China, in Fukien province. ab. 62,000. Also, **Lungki.**

Chang·chun (chăng′chŏŏn′), *n.* a city in NE China: the former capital of Manchuria. 750,000 (est. 1950). Also, **Hsinking.**

change (chānj), *v.,* **changed, changing,** *n.* —*v.t.* **1.** to make different; alter in condition, appearance, etc.; turn (often fol. by *into*): *change one's habits.* **2.** to substitute another or others for; exchange for something else: *to change trains.* **3.** to give or get smaller money in exchange for: *to change a five-dollar bill.* **4.** to give or get different money in exchange for: *to change dollars into francs.* **5.** to give and take reciprocally; interchange: *to change places with someone.* **6.** to remove and replace the covering or coverings of: *to change a bed.* **7. change front,** *Mil.* to shift a military force in another direction. **8. change hands,** to pass from one hand or possessor to another. —*v.i.* **9.** to become different; alter (fol. by *to* or *into*). **10.** to make a change or an exchange. **11.** to change trains or other conveyances. **12.** to change one's clothes. —*n.* **13.** variation; alteration; modification; deviation; transformation. **14.** the substitution of one thing for another. **15.** variety or novelty. **16.** the passing from one place, state, form, or phase to another: *change of the moon.* **17.** the supplanting of one thing by another. **18.** that which is or may be substituted for another. **19.** a fresh set of clothing. **20.** money given in exchange for an equivalent of higher denomination. **21.** a balance of money that is returned when the sum tendered in payment is larger than the sum due. **22.** coins of low denomination. **23.** Also, **'change.** *Com.* an exchange (def. 10). **24.** any of the various sequences in which a peal of bells may be rung. **25.** *Obs.* changefulness; caprice. [ME *change(n),* t. OF: m. *changier,* g. LL *cambiāre,* L *cambīre*] —**chang′er,** *n.*
—**Syn. 1.** transmute, transform. CHANGE, ALTER both mean to make a difference in the state or condition of a thing or to substitute another state or condition. To CHANGE is to make a material difference so that the thing is distinctly other than it was: *to change one's opinion, one's shoes.* To ALTER is to make some partial change, as in appearance, but usually to preserve the identity: *to alter a dress (to change a dress* would mean to put on a different one).

change·a·ble (chān′jə bəl), *adj.* **1.** liable to change or to be changed; variable. **2.** of changing color or appearance: *changeable silk.* —**change′a·bil′i·ty, change′a·ble·ness,** *n.* —**change′a·bly,** *adv.*

change·ful (chānj′fəl), *adj.* changing; variable; inconstant. —**change′ful·ly,** *adv.* —**change′ful·ness,** *n.*

change·less (chānj′lĭs), *adj.* unchanging. —**change′less·ly,** *adv.* —**change′less·ness,** *n.*

change·ling (chānj′lĭng), *n.* **1.** a child supposedly substituted secretly for another, esp. by fairies. **2.** *Archaic.* an inconstant person. **3.** *Archaic or Dial.* an idiot.

change of life, menopause.

change of venue, *Law.* the removal of trial to another jurisdiction.

change ringing, act of ringing the changes on a peal of bells.

Chang·sha (chăng′shä′), *n.* a city in SE China: the capital of Hunan province. 500,000 (est. 1950).

Chang·teh (chăng′dŭ′), *n.* a city in S China, in Hunan province. ab. 300,000.

Chang Tso-lin (jäng′ tsō′lĭn′), 1873–1928, Chinese general: military ruler of Manchuria, 1918–28.

chan·nel¹ (chăn′əl), *n., v.,* **-neled, -neling** or (esp. Brit.) **-nelled, -nelling.** —*n.* **1.** the bed of a stream or waterway. **2.** the deeper part of a waterway. **3.** a wide strait, as between a continent and an island. **4.** *Naut.* a navigable route between two bodies of water. **5.** a means of access. **6.** a course into which something may be directed. **7.** a route through which anything passes or progresses: *channels of trade.* **8.** a frequency band wide enough for one-way communication, the exact width of a channel depending upon the type of transmission involved (as telegraph, telephone, radio, television, etc.). **9.** a tubular passage for liquids or fluids. **10.** a groove or furrow. —*v.t.* **11.** to convey through a channel. **12.** to direct toward or into some particular course: *to channel one's interests.* **13.** to excavate as a channel. **14.** to form a channel in; groove. [ME *chanel,* t. OF. g. L *canālis* CANAL]

chan·nel² (chăn′əl), *n.* one of the horizontal planks or ledges attached outside of a ship to give more spread to the lower shrouds. [var. of *chain-wale* (see WALE¹)]

channel iron, a rolled iron bar whose section is shaped like three sides of a rectangle.

Channel Islands, a British island group in the English Channel, near the coast of France, consisting of Alderney, Guernsey, Jersey, and smaller islands. 98,224 pop. (est. 1956); 75 sq. mi.

Chan·ning (chăn′ĭng), *n.* **William Ellery** (ĕl′ər ĭ), 1780–1842, U.S. Unitarian clergyman and writer.

chan·son (shăn′sən; *Fr.* shän sôN′), *n.* a song. [t. F, g. L *cantio*]

chan·son de geste (shän sôN′ də zhĕst′), *French.* one of a class of old French epic poems.

chant (chănt, chänt), *n.* **1.** a song; singing. **2.** a short, simple melody, specif. one characterized by single notes to which an indefinite number of syllables are intoned, used in singing the psalms, canticles, etc., in the church service. **3.** a psalm, canticle, or the like, chanted or for chanting. **4.** the singing or intoning of all or portions of a liturgical service. **5.** any monotonous song. **6.** a monotonous intonation of the voice in speaking —*v.t.* **7.** to sing. **8.** to celebrate in song. **9.** to sing to a chant, or in the manner of a chant, esp. in the church service. —*v.i.* **10.** to sing. **11.** to sing a chant. [ME *chaunte(n),* t. OF: m. *chanter,* g. L *cantāre,* freq. of *canere* sing]

chan·tage (chän′tĭj, chän′-; *Fr.* shän täzh′), *n. French.* blackmailing. [cf. F *faire chanter* to make (one) sing, to extort something]

chant·er (chăn′tər, chän′-), *n.* **1.** one who chants; a singer. **2.** a chorister; a precentor. **3.** the chief singer or priest of a chantry. **4.** the pipe of a bagpipe, provided with finger holes for playing the melody.

chan·te·relle (shăn′tə rĕl′, chän′-), *n.* the mushroom *Cantharellus cibarius,* a favorite edible species in France. [t. F, t. NL: m. *cantharella,* dim. of L *cantharus* drinking vessel, t. Gk.: m. *kántharos*]

chan·teuse (shän tœz′), *n. French.* a woman singer.

chant·ey (shăn′tĭ, chăn′-), *n., pl.* **-eys.** a sailors' song, esp. one sung in rhythm to work. Also, **chanty, shanty.** [alter. of F *chanter* sing. See CHANT]

chan·ti·cleer (chăn′tə klĭr′), *n.* a name for the rooster, orig. in the medieval epic *Reynard the Fox.* [ME *chauntecler,* t. OF: m. *Chantecler,* lit., clear singer, f. *chante* (impv. of *chanter* sing) + *cler* clear]

Chan·til·ly (shän tĭl′ĭ; *Fr.* shän tē yē′), *n.* a town in N France, N of Paris: noted for its lace. 7065 (1954).

chant·ress (chăn′trĭs, chän′-), *n.* a female chanter or singer. [ME *chauntresse,* t. OF: m. *chanteresse*]

chan·try (chăn′trĭ, chän′-), *n., pl.* **-tries.** *Eccles.* **1.** an endowment for the singing or saying of mass for the souls of the founders or of persons named by them. **2.** a chapel or the like so endowed. **3.** the priests of a chantry endowment. **4.** a chapel attached to a church, used for minor services. [ME *chanterie,* t. F: singing]

chant·y (shăn′tĭ, chăn′tĭ), *n., pl.* **chanties.** chantey.

Cha·nu·kah (khä′nŏŏ kä′), *n.* Hanukkah.

Chao-an (chou′än′), *n.* a city in SE China. ab. 23,000. Also, **Chao-chow-fu** (chou′jō′fōō′).

Chao Phra·ya (chou′ prä yä′), Menam.

cha·os (kā′ŏs), *n.* **1.** utter confusion or disorder wholly without organization or order. **2.** any assemblage. **3.** the infinity of space or formless matter supposed to have preceded the existence of the ordered universe. **4.** *Obs.* a chasm or abyss. [t. L, t. Gk.]

cha·ot·ic (kā ŏt′ĭk), *adj.* in utter confusion or disorder. —**cha·ot′i·cal·ly,** *adv.* —**Ant.** orderly, systematic. .

chap¹ (chăp), *v.,* **chapped, chapping,** *n.* —*v.t.* **1.** (of cold or exposure) to crack, roughen, and redden (the skin). **2.** to cause (the earth, wood, etc.) to split, crack, open in clefts. —*v.i.* **3.** to become chapped. —*n.* **4.** a fissure or crack, esp. in the skin. **5.** *Scot.* a blow; a knock. [ME *chapp(en);* orig. uncert.]

chap² (chăp), *n.* **1.** *Colloq.* a fellow; man or boy. **2.** *Obs. or Dial.* a customer. [short for CHAPMAN]

chap³ (chŏp, chäp), *n.* chop³. [? special use of CHAP¹]

chap., **1.** Chaplain. **2.** chapter. Also, **Chap.**

cha·pa·ra·jos (chä′pä rä′hōs), *n.pl.* chaps. Also, **cha·pa·re·jos** (chä′pä rā′hōs). [Mex. Sp. var. of *chaparreras,* der. *chaparro* bramble bush]

chap·ar·ral (chăp′ə răl′), n. *Southwestern U.S.* **1.** a close growth of low evergreen oaks. **2.** any dense thicket. [t. Sp., der. *chaparra* evergreen oak, ? t. Basque]

chaparral cock, a terrestrial cuckoo of the SW United States, *Geococcyx californianus;* the road runner.

chaparral pea, a spiny leguminous bush, *Pickeringia montana,* sometimes forming dense thickets in the Pacific coast regions of the U. S.

chap·book (chăp′bŏŏk′), n. one of a type of small books or pamphlets of popular tales, ballads, etc., such as were formerly hawked about by chapmen.

chape (chāp), n. the metal mounting or trimming of a scabbard, esp. at the point. [ME, t. F. See CAP]

cha·peau (shȧ pō′; *Fr.* shä-), n., pl. **-peaux, -peaus** (-pōz′; *Fr.* -pō′). a hat. [t. F, g. L *capellus,* dim. of *capa, cappa.* See CAP]

chapeau bras (brä′), *French.* a small three-cornered hat, formerly in use, which could be folded flat and carried under the arm. [F, f. *chapeau* hat + *bras* arm]

chap·el (chăp′əl), n. **1.** a private or subordinate place of prayer or worship; an oratory. **2.** a separately dedicated part of a church, **or** a small independent churchlike edifice, devoted to special services. **3.** a room or building for worship in a college, royal court, etc. **4.** (in England) a place of worship of a religious body outside of the Established Church. **5.** a separate place of public worship dependent on the church of a parish. **6.** a religious service in a chapel. **7.** a choir or orchestra of a chapel, court, etc. **8.** a print shop or printing house. **9.** the body of printers belonging to a printing house. [ME *chapele,* t. OF, g. LL *cappella* sanctuary for relics (such as the cape of St. Martin), dim. of *capa, cappa.* See CAP]

chap·er·on (shăp′ə rōn′), n. **1.** an older person, usually a matron, who, for propriety, attends a young unmarried woman in public or accompanies a party of young unmarried men and women. —v.t. **2.** to attend or accompany as chaperon. Also, **chaperone.** [t. F: hood, der. *chape* CAPE[1]] —**chap·er·on·age** (shăp′ə rō′nĭj), n.

chap·fall·en (chŏp′fô′lən, chăp′-), adj. dispirited; chagrined; dejected. Also, **chopfallen.**

chap·i·ter (chăp′ə tər), n. *Archit.* a capital[2]. [t. F. See CHAPTER]

chap·lain (chăp′lĭn), n. **1.** an ecclesiastic attached to the chapel of a royal court, college, etc., or to a military unit. **2.** one who says the prayer, invocation, etc., for an organization or at an assembly or gathering. [ME *chapelayn,* t. OF: m. *chapelain,* g. LL *capellānus,* der. *capella* CHAPEL; r. OE *capellān,* t. LL (as above)] —**chap′lain·cy, chap′lain·ship**, n.

chap·let (chăp′lĭt), n. **1.** a wreath or garland for the head. **2.** a string of beads. **3.** *Rom. Cath. Ch.* **a.** a string of beads for counting prayers, one third of the length of a rosary. **b.** the prayers so counted thereon. **4.** *Archit.* a small molding carved in the shape of beads or the like. [ME *chapelet,* t. OF, dim. of *chapel* headdress. See CHAPEAU] —**chap′let·ed**, adj.

Chap·lin (chăp′lĭn), n. **Charles Spencer,** born 1889, U.S. screen actor, born in England.

chap·man (chăp′mən), n., pl. **-men. 1.** *Brit.* a hawker or peddler. **2.** *Archaic.* a merchant. [ME; OE *cēapman,* f. *cēap* trade + *man* man]

Chap·man (chăp′mən), n. **George,** 1559?–1634, British poet, dramatist, and translator.

chaps (chăps, shăps), n.pl. *Western U.S.* strong leather riding breeches or overalls, having no seat, worn esp. by cowboys. Also, **chaparajos, chaparejos.** [short for CHAPARAJOS]

chap·ter (chăp′tər), n. **1.** a main division, usually numbered, of a book, treatise, or the like. **2.** a branch, usually localized, of a society or fraternity. **3.** *Eccles.* **a.** an assembly of the monks in a monastery, or of those in a province, or of the entire order. **b.** a general assembly of the canons of a church. **c.** a meeting of the elected representatives of the provinces or houses of a religious community. **d.** the body of such canons or representatives collectively. **4.** any general assembly. **5.** *Liturgy.* a short Scriptural quotation read at various parts of the office, as after the last psalm in the service of lauds, prime, tierce, etc. —v.t. **6.** to divide into or arrange in chapters. [ME *chapitre,* t. OF, var. of *chapitle,* g. L *capitulum* small head, capital of column, chapter, dim. of *caput* head]

chapter house, 1. *Eccles.* a building, attached to a cathedral or monastery, in which the chapter meets. **2.** the building of a chapter of a society, etc.

Cha·pul·te·pec (chə pŭl′tə pěk′; *Sp.* chä pōōl′tě pěk′), n. a fortress near Mexico City: famous for resistance to the U.S. forces in the Mexican War, 1847.

cha·que·ta (chä kě′tä), n. *Spanish.* a heavy jacket, esp. a leather one worn by cowboys. [Sp., t. F: m. *jaquette* jacket, der. *jaque* short garment, of obscure orig.]

char[1] (chär), v., **charred, charring.** —v.t. **1.** to burn or reduce to charcoal. **2.** to burn slightly; scorch. —v.i. **3.** to become charred. —n. **4.** a charred substance. **5.** charcoal. [? short for CHARCOAL] —**char′ry**, adj.

char[2] (chär), n., pl. **chars,** (*esp. collectively*) **char.** any trout or the genus *Salvelinus,* esp. *S. alpinus* (the common char of Europe). Also, **charr.** [cf. Gaelic *ceara* red]

char[3] (chär), n., v., **charred, charring.** *Chiefly Brit.* —n. **1.** a charwoman. **2.** a turn or single piece of work, esp. household work; an odd job; a chore. —v.i. **3.** to do

small jobs. **4.** to do housework by the day. —v.t. **5.** to do (odd jobs). Also, **chare.** [ME *cherre,* OE *cerr, cyrr* turn, time, occasion, affair]

char-à-banc (shär′ə băng′, -băngk′; *Fr.* shȧ rȧ bän′), n., pl. **-bancs** (-băngz′, -băngks′; *Fr.* -bän′). *Brit.* a long motor bus with transverse seats, much used in sightseeing. Also, **char′a·banc′.** [t. F: m. *char à bancs* car with benches]

char·a·cin (kăr′ə sĭn). n. a fish of the family *Characinidae,* native to Africa or South America.

char·ac·ter (kăr′ĭk tər), n. **1.** the aggregate of qualities that distinguishes one person or thing from others. **2.** one such quality or feature; a characteristic. **3.** moral constitution, as of a person or people. **4.** good moral constitution or status. **5.** reputation. **6.** good repute. **7.** an account of the qualities or peculiarities of a person or thing. **8.** a formal statement from an employer concerning the qualities and habits of a former servant or employee. **9.** status or capacity. **10.** a person: *a good or strange character.* **11.** *Colloq.* an odd person. **12.** a person represented in a drama, story, etc. **13.** *Theat.* a part or role. **14.** *Genetics.* any trait, function, structure, or substance of an organism resulting from the development of a gene interacting with the environment and the remainder of the gene complex; a hereditary characteristic. **15.** a significant visual mark or symbol. **16.** a symbol as used in a writing system, as a letter of the alphabet. **17.** the symbols of a writing system collectively. **18.** a style of writing or printing. **19.** *Obs.* a cipher or cipher message. —v.t. **20.** to portray; describe. **21.** *Archaic.* to engrave or inscribe. [t. L, t. Gk.: m. *charaktēr* instrument for marking, mark; r. ME *caractere,* t. F] —**char′ac·ter·less**, adj.

—**Syn. 1.** CHARACTER, INDIVIDUALITY, PERSONALITY refer to the sum of the characteristics possessed by a person. CHARACTER refers esp. to moral qualities, ethical standards, principles, and the like: *a man of sterling character.* INDIVIDUALITY refers to the distinctive qualities which make one recognizable as a person differentiated from others: *a man of strong individuality.* PERSONALITY refers particularly to the combination of outer and inner characteristics that determine the impression which one makes upon others: *a man of vivid or pleasing personality.* **5.** See **reputation.**

char·ac·ter·is·tic (kăr′ĭk tə rĭs′tĭk), adj. **1.** pertaining to, constituting, or indicating the character or peculiar quality; typical; distinctive. —n. **2.** a distinguishing feature or quality. **3.** *Math.* the integral part of a logarithm. —**Syn. 2.** attribute, property, trait, peculiarity. See **feature.**

char·ac·ter·is·ti·cal·ly (kăr′ĭk tə rĭs′tĭk lĭ), adv. in a characteristic manner; typically.

char·ac·ter·i·za·tion (kăr′ĭk tər ə zā′shən, -trə zā′-), n. **1.** portrayal; description. **2.** act of characterizing. **3.** the creation of fictitious characters.

char·ac·ter·ize (kăr′ĭk tə rīz′), v.t., **-ized, -izing. 1.** to mark or distinguish as a characteristic; be a characteristic of. **2.** to describe the character or peculiar quality of. **3.** to give character to. —**char′ac·ter·iz′er**, n.

char·ac·ter·y (kăr′ĭk tə rĭ, -trĭ), n., pl. **-teries. 1.** the use of characters or symbols for the expression of meaning. **2.** characters or symbols collectively.

cha·rade (shə rād′; *esp. Brit.* shə räd′), n. a parlor game in which a player or players act out in pantomime a word or phrase which the others try to guess. [t. F, t. Pr.: m. *charrado* entertainment, der. *charra* chat]

char·coal (chär′kōl′), n. **1.** the carbonaceous material obtained by the imperfect combustion of wood or other organic substances. **2.** a drawing pencil of charcoal. **3.** a drawing made with charcoal. —v.t. **4.** to blacken, write, or draw with charcoal. [ME *charcole;* orig. uncert.]

charcoal burner, a stove, etc., burning charcoal.

Char·cot (shär kō′), n. **Jean Martin** (zhän mȧr tăn′), 1825–93, French specialist in nervous diseases.

chard (chärd), n. a variety of beet, *Beta vulgaris,* var. *Cicla,* having large leafstalks and midribs which are used as a vegetable (**Swiss chard**). [t. F: m. *charde,* g. L *carduus* thistle, artichoke]

chare (châr), n., v., **chared, charing.** *Chiefly Brit.* **char**[3].

charge (chärj), v., **charged, charging,** n. —v.t. **1.** to put a load or burden on or in. **2.** to fill or furnish (a thing) with the quantity, as of powder or fuel, that it is fitted to receive. **3.** to supply with a quantity of electricity or electrical energy: *to charge a storage battery.* **4.** to fill (air, water, etc.) with other matter in a state of diffusion or solution. **5.** to load or burden (the mind, heart, etc.). **6.** to lay a command or injunction upon. **7.** to instruct authoritatively, as a judge does a jury. **8.** to impute as a fault: *charge him with carelessness.* **9.** to lay blame upon; blame; accuse (usually fol. by *with*): *to charge someone with negligence.* **10.** to hold liable for payment; enter a debit against. **11.** to list or record as a debt or obligation; enter as a debit. **12.** to impose or ask as a price. **13.** to attack by rushing violently against. **14.** *Her.* to place a bearing on (a shield, etc.). —v.i. **15.** to make an onset; rush, as to an attack. **16.** to place the price of a thing to one's debit. **17.** to ask payment. **18.** to make a debit, as in an account. **19.** (of dogs) to lie down at command.

—n. **20.** a load or burden. **21.** the quantity of anything which an apparatus is fitted to hold, or holds, at one time. **22.** a quantity of explosive to be set off at one time. **23.** a duty or responsibility laid upon or entrusted to one. **24.** care, custody, or superintendence: *to have charge of a thing.* **25.** anything or anybody committed to one's

care or management. **26.** *Eccles.* a parish or congregation committed to the spiritual care of a pastor. **27.** a command or injunction; exhortation. **28.** an accusation. **29.** *Law.* an address by a judge to a jury at the close of a trial, instructing them as to the legal points, the weight of evidence, etc., affecting their verdict in the case. **30.** expense or cost: *improvements made at a tenant's own charge.* **31.** a sum or price charged: *a charge of 50 cents for admission.* **32.** a pecuniary burden, encumbrance, tax, or lien; cost; expense; liability to pay. **33.** an entry in an account of something due. **34.** an impetuous onset or attack, as of soldiers. **35.** a signal by bugle, drum, etc., for a military charge. **36.** the accumulation of electricity or electrical energy in or upon a piece of equipment. **37.** *Her.* bearing (def. 10). **38. in charge, a.** in command; having supervision. **b.** *Brit.* under arrest by the police. **39. in charge of, a.** having the care or supervision of: *in charge of the class.* **b.** under the care or supervision of: *in charge of the teacher.* [ME *charge*(n), t. OF: m. *charg*(i)*er*, g. LL *carricāre* load. See CAR]
—**Syn. 6.** enjoin, exhort. **9.** indict, arraign. **28.** indictment, imputation, allegation. **31.** See **price**. **34.** onslaught, assault. —**Ant. 9.** acquit, absolve.

charge·a·ble (chär′jə bəl), *adj.* **1.** that may or should be charged. **2.** liable to be accused or held responsible; indictable. **3.** liable to become a charge on the public.

char·gé d'af·faires (shär zhā′ də fâr′; *Fr.* shär zhā′ dä fêr′), *pl.* **chargés d'affaires** (shär zhāz′ də fâr′; *Fr.* shär zhā′ dä fêr′). *Govt.* **1.** (in full: **chargé d'affaires ad interim**) an official placed in charge of diplomatic business during the temporary absence of the ambassador or minister. **2.** an envoy to a state to which a diplomat of higher grade is not sent. Also, **char·gé′.** [t. F: lit., entrusted with affairs.]

charg·er[1] (chär′jər), *n.* **1.** one who or that which charges. **2.** a horse intended, or suitable, to be ridden in battle. **3.** *Elect.* an apparatus which charges storage batteries. [f. CHARGE, v. + -ER[1]]

charg·er[2] (chär′jər), *n.* **1.** a platter. **2.** a large, shallow dish for liquids. [ME *chargeour*; akin to CHARGE]

char·i·ly (chār′ə lY), *adv.* **1.** carefully; warily. **2.** sparingly. —**Ant. 1.** boldly. **2.** liberally.

char·i·ness (chār′Y nYs), *n.* **1.** chary quality; caution; sparingness. **2.** *Obs.* scrupulous integrity.

Char·ing Cross (chār′Yng), a district in central London, England.

char·i·ot (chār′Y ət), *n.* **1.** a two-wheeled vehicle used by the ancients in war, racing, processions, etc. **2.** a light four-wheeled pleasure carriage. **3.** any more or less stately carriage. —*v.t.* **4.** to convey in a chariot. —*v.i.* **5.** to drive a chariot; ride in a chariot. [ME, t. OF, aug. of *char*. See CAR]

char·i·ot·eer (chār′Y ə tYr′), *n.* **1.** a chariot driver. **2.** (*cap.*) *Astron.* the northern constellation Auriga.

cha·ris·ma (kə rYz′mə), *n., pl.* **-ma·ta** (-mə tə). **1.** *Theol.* a divinely conferred gift or power. **2.** those special spiritual powers or personal qualities that give an individual influence or authority over large numbers of people. Also, **char·ism** (kār′Yzəm). [t. Gk.: *chárisma* gift] —**char·is·mat·ic**, *adj.*

char·i·ta·ble (chār′Y tə bəl), *adj.* **1.** generous in gifts to relieve the needs of others. **2.** kindly or lenient in judging others. **3.** pertaining to or concerned with charity: *a charitable institution.* [ME, t. OF, der. *charite* CHARITY] —**char′i·ta·ble·ness**, *n.* —**char′i·ta·bly**, *adv.* —**Syn. 1.** beneficent, liberal, bountiful. **2.** broadminded. —**Ant. 1.** selfish. **2.** severe, intolerant.

char·i·ty (chār′ə tY), *n., pl.* **-ties. 1.** almsgiving; the private or public relief of unfortunate or needy persons; benevolence. **2.** something given to a person or persons in need; alms. **3.** a charitable act or work. **4.** a charitable fund, foundation, or institution. **5.** benevolent feeling, esp. toward those in need. **6.** Christian love. I Cor. 13. [ME *charite*, t. OF, g. s. L *cāritas* dearness]

cha·riv·a·ri (shə rYv′ə rē′, shYv′ə rē′, shä′rY vä′rY), *n., pl.* **-ris.** a mock serenade of discordant noises made with pans, horns, etc., after a wedding. [t. F]

chark (chärk), *n.* **1.** charcoal (def. 1). —*v.t.* **2.** to char; convert into coke. [back formation from CHARCOAL]

char·kha (chär′kə), *n.* (in India and the East Indies) a cotton gin or spinning wheel. Also, **char′ka**. [t. Hind.]

char·la·dy (chär′lā′dY), *n., pl.* **-dies.** *Brit.* a charwoman.

char·la·tan (shär′lə tən), *n.* one who pretends to more knowledge or skill than he possesses; a quack. [t. F, t. It.: m. *ciarlatano* der. *ciarlare* chatter] —**char·la·tan·ic** (shär′lə tan′Yk), *adj.*

char·la·tan·ism (shär′lə tə nYz′əm), *n.* the practices of a charlatan. Also, **char·la·tan·ry** (shär′lə tən rY).

Char·le·magne (shär′lə mān′; *Fr.* shär lə màn′y), *n.* ("*Charles the Great*") A.D. 742–814, king of the Franks, A.D. 768–814: as Charles I, emperor of the Holy Roman Empire, A.D. 800–814.

Char·le·roi (shär lə rwä′), *n.* a city in S Belgium. 25,982 pop. (1947). Also, **Char′le·roy**.

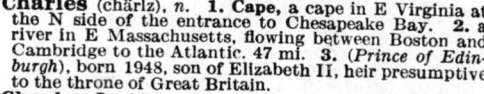

Empire of Charlemagne, A.D. 814

Charles (chärlz), *n.* **1. Cape,** a cape in E Virginia at the N side of the entrance to Chesapeake Bay. **2.** a river in E Massachusetts, flowing between Boston and Cambridge to the Atlantic. 47 mi. **3.** (*Prince of Edinburgh*), born 1948, son of Elizabeth II, heir presumptive to the throne of Great Britain.

Charles I (chärlz; *Fr.* shàrl), **1.** Charlemagne. **2.** ("*the Bald*") A.D. 823–877, king of France, A.D. 840–877: as Charles II, emperor of the Holy Roman Empire, A.D. 875–877. **3.** 1600–49, king of England and Ireland from 1625 until executed in 1649 (son of James I). **4.** 1500–58, king of Spain, 1516–66: as Charles V, emperor of the Holy Roman Empire, 1519–1556. **5.** 1887–1922, emperor of Austria, 1916–18; as Charles IV, king of Hungary, 1916–18.

Charles II, 1. See **Charles I** (def. 2). **2.** 1630–85, king of England and Ireland, 1660–85 (son of Charles I, 1600–49).

Charles IV, 1. ("*Charles the Fair*") 1294–1328, king of France, 1322–28. **2.** See **Charles I** (def. 5).

Charles V, 1. ("*Charles the Wise*") 1337–80, king of France, 1364–80. **2.** See **Charles I** (def. 4).

Charles VI, ("*the Mad*" or "*the Well-Beloved*") 1368–1422, king of France, 1380–1422.

Charles VII, ("*Charles the Victorious*") 1403–61, king of France, 1422–61 (son of Charles VI of France).

Charles IX, 1550–74, king of France, 1560–74.

Charles X, 1757–1836, king of France, 1824–30.

Charles XII, 1682–1718, king of Sweden, 1697–1718.

Charles XIV, John, 1763–1844, king of Sweden and Norway, 1818–44. See **Bernadotte.**

Charles Edward Stuart, ("*the Young Pretender*" or "*Bonnie Prince Charlie*") 1720–88, grandson of James II of Great Britain and Ireland.

Charles Louis, (Ger. *Karl Ludwig Johann*) 1771–1847, archduke of Austria.

Charles Mar·tel (mär tĕl′; *Fr.* mär-), A.D. 690?–741 ruler of the Franks, A.D. 714–741: grandfather of Charlemagne; checked Moorish invasion, A.D. 732.

Charles's Wain (chärl′zYz wān′), *Brit.* the Big Dipper. See **dipper** (def. 3a). [OE *Carles wægn* Carl's wagon (Carl = Charlemagne)]

Charles the Great, Charlemagne.

Charles·ton (chärlz′tən), *n.* **1.** the capital of West Virginia, in the W part. 85,796 (1960). **2.** a seaport in SE South Carolina.65,925 (1960). **3.** a kind of fox trot, of Southern Negro origin, popular in the 1920's.

Charles·town (chärlz′toun′), *n.* a former city in E Massachusetts: since 1874 a part of Boston; navy yard; battle of Bunker Hill, June 17, 1775.

char·ley horse (chär′lY), *U.S. Colloq.* stiffness of the leg or arm due to injury or excessive muscular use.

char·lock (chär′lək), *n.* the wild mustard, *Brassica arvensis*, often troublesome as a weed in grainfields. [ME *carlok*, OE *cerlic*]

char·lotte (shär′lət), *n.* a sweet dish (hot or cold) of many varieties, commonly made by lining a mold with cake or bread and filling with fruit or a cream, custard, or gelatin. [t. F, orig., woman's name]

Char·lotte (shär′lət), *n.* a city in S North Carolina. 134,042 (1950).

Char·lot·te A·ma·li·e (shär lŏt′ə ä mä′lY ə), a seaport in and the capital of the Virgin Islands (U.S.), on St. Thomas. 11,469 (1950). Formerly, **St. Thomas.**

Char·lot·ten·burg (shär lŏt′ən bûrg′; *Ger.* shär lŏt′ən bōōrKH′), *n.* a part of Berlin, Germany. 221,012 (1950).

char·lotte russe (shär′lət rōōs′), a mold of sponge cake filled with whipped cream or a similar preparation. [t. F: Russian charlotte]

Char·lottes·ville (shär′ləts vYl′), *n.* a city in central Virginia. 29,427 (1960).

Char·lotte·town (shär′lət toun′), *n.* the capital of Prince Edward Island, Canada: a seaport. 15,887 (1951).

charm[1] (chärm), *n.* **1.** an irresistible power to please and attract; fascination. **2.** some quality or feature exerting a fascinating influence: *feminine charms.* **3.** something which possesses this power. **4.** a trinket to be worn on a chain, bracelet, etc. **5.** something worn for its supposed magical effect; an amulet. **6.** any action supposed to have magical power. **7.** the chanting or recitation of a magic verse or formula. **8.** a verse or formula credited with magical power. —*v.t.* **9.** to attract powerfully by beauty, etc.; please greatly. **10.** to act upon with or as with a charm; enchant. **11.** to endow with or protect by supernatural powers. —*v.i.* **12.** to be fascinating or pleasing. **13.** to use charms. **14.** to act as a charm. [ME *charme*, t. OF, g. L *carmen* song, incantation] —**charm′er**, *n.* —**Syn. 1.** attractiveness, allurement. **10.** fascinate, captivate, entrance; enrapture, transport, ravish, delight; allure.

charm[2] (chärm), *n.* *Obs.* or *Dial.* blended singing of birds, children, etc. [ME *cherm*(e), OE *cerm, ceorm,* var. of *cierm* outcry. Cf. CHIRM]

char·meuse (shär mœz′), *n.* a soft, flexible variety of satin. [t. F: lit., charmer (fem.)]

charm·ing (chär′mYng), *adj.* **1.** pleasing; delightful. **2.** exercising magic power. —**charm′ing·ly**, *adv.*

char·nel (chär′nəl), *n.* a repository for dead bodies. [ME, t. OF, g. LL *carnāle*, prop. neut. adj. See CARNAL]

charnel house, a house or place in which the bodies or bones of the dead are deposited.

Char·on (kâr'ən, kǎr'-), n. 1. Class. Myth. the ferryman who conveyed souls of the dead across the Styx. 2. (in humorous use) any ferryman.

Char·pen·tier (shär pän tyě'), n. Gustave (gɥs tǎv'), 1860-1956, French composer.

char·poy (chär'poi'), n. the common light bedstead of India. [t. Hind.: m. chärpāī, lit., four-footed, t. Pers.: m. chahār-pāī]

char·qui (chär'kǐ), n. jerked meat, esp. beef. [t. Sp., t. Kechua (Peruvian): m. echarqui]

charr (chär), n., pl. **charrs**, (esp. collectively) **charr**. char².

chart (chärt), n. 1. a sheet exhibiting information in tabulated or methodical form. 2. a graphic representation, as by curves, of a dependent variable such as temperature, price, etc. 3. a map, esp. a hydrographic or marine map. 4. an outline map showing special conditions or facts: a weather chart. —v.t. 5. to make a chart of. 6. to plan: to chart a course of action. [t. F: m. charte, g. L c(h)arta paper, t. Gk.: m. chártēs leaf of paper] —chart'less, adj. —Syn. 3. See map.

char·ter (chär'tər), n. 1. the articles or certificate of incorporation taken in connection with the law under which a corporation is organized. 2. authorization from a central or parent organization to establish a new branch, chapter, etc. 3. a grant by a sovereign power creating a corporation, as the royal charters granted to British colonies in America. 4. Also, **charter party**. a contract by which part or all of a ship is leased for a voyage or a stated time. 5. special privilege or immunity. —v.t. 6. to establish by charter: to charter a bank. 7. to lease or hire by charter. 8. to hire (a car, etc.). —adj. 9. done or held in accordance with a charter. [ME chartre, t. OF, g. L chartula, dim. of charta. See CHART] —char'ter·er, n. —Syn. 8. See hire.

char·tered accountant (chär'tərd), (in the British Empire) a member of the institute of accountants granted a royal charter. Abbr.: C.A.

charter member, one of the original members.

Chart·ism (chär'tǐz əm), n. the principles or movement of a party of political reformers, chiefly workingmen, active in England from 1838 to 1848 (so called from the People's Charter, the document which contained their principles and demands. [f. s. L charta charter + -ISM]; pronunciation influenced by charter] —Chart'ist, n., adj.

char·tog·ra·phy (kär tŏg'rə fǐ), n. cartography.

Char·tres (shär'trə; Fr. shär'tr), n. a city in N France: famous cathedral. 28,750 (1954).

char·treuse (shär trœz'), n. 1. an aromatic liqueur made by the Carthusian monks, at Grenoble, France, and Tarragona, Spain. 2. (cap.) a trademark for this liqueur. 3. a clear, light green with a yellowish tinge. 4. a Carthusian monastery. —adj. 5. of the color chartreuse. [t. F]

char·tu·lar·y (kär'chŏŏ lěr'ǐ), n., pl. -laries. a register of charters, title deeds, etc. Also, **cartulary**. [t. ML: m. s. c(h)artulārium, der. L c(h)artula. See CHARTER]

char·wom·an (chär'wŏŏm'ən), n., pl. -women. a woman hired to do chars, or odd jobs of household work, or to do such work by the day. [f. CHAR³ + WOMAN]

char·y (châr'ǐ), adj., charier, chariest. 1. careful; wary. 2. shy. 3. fastidious; choosy. 4. sparing (often fol. by of): chary of his praise. [ME chari, OE cearig sorrowful, der. caru CARE] —Ant. 1. trustful. 2. confident. 3. uncritical. 4. lavish.

Cha·ryb·dis (kə rǐb'dǐs), n. Gk. Legend. See **Scylla**. —Cha·ryb'di·an, adj.

chase¹ (chās), v., chased, chasing, n. —v.t. 1. to pursue in order to seize, overtake, etc. 2. to pursue with intent to capture or kill, as game; hunt. 3. to drive by pursuing. 4. to put to flight. —v.i. 5. to follow in pursuit: to chase after someone. 6. Colloq. to run or hasten. —n. 7. act of chasing; pursuit. 8. an object of pursuit; a thing chased. 9. the occupation or sport of hunting. 10. Brit. an unenclosed tract of privately owned land reserved for animals to be hunted. 11. Brit. the right of keeping game or of hunting on the land of others. 12. a steeplechase. [ME chace(n), t. OF: m. chacier, g. L captiāre seize. See CATCH]

chase² (chās), n., v., chased, chasing. —n. 1. a rectangular iron frame in which composed type, etc., is secured or locked, for printing or plate-making. 2. a groove, furrow, or trench; a lengthened hollow. 3. Ordn. a. the part of a gun in front of the trunnions. b. the part containing the bore. —v.t. 4. to groove or indent, so as to make into a screw. 5. to cut in making a screw head. [t. F: m. châsse, g. L capsa box]

chase³ (chās), v.t., chased, chasing. to ornament (metal) by engraving or embossing. [aphetic var. of ENCHASE]

Chase (chās), n. 1. **Salmon Portland** (sǎl'mən), 1808-1873, chief justice of the U.S. Supreme Court, 1864-73. 2. **Stuart**, born 1888, U.S. economist and writer.

chas·er¹ (chā'sər), n. 1. one who or that which chases or pursues. 2. U.S. Colloq. a drink of water, beer, or other mild beverage taken after a drink of liquor. 3. Also, **chase gun**. a gun on a vessel esp. for use when in chase or being chased. 4. a hunter. [f. CHASE¹ + -ER¹]

chas·er² (chā'sər), n. a multiple-toothed tool used in cutting screw threads. [f. CHASE² + -ER¹]

chas·er³ (chā'sər), n. a person who engraves metal. [f. CHASE³ + -ER¹]

chasm (kǎz'əm), n. 1. a yawning fissure or deep cleft in the earth's surface; a gorge. 2. a breach or wide fissure in a wall or other structure. 3. a marked interruption of continuity; gap. 4. a sundering breach in relations: the chasm of death. [t. L: m. chasma, t. Gk.] —chas·mal (kǎz'məl), adj.

chas·sé (shǎ sā'; Colloq. sǎ shā'), n..v., chasséd, chasséing. Dancing. —n. 1. a kind of gliding step in which one foot is kept in advance of the other. —v.i. 2. to execute a chassé. [t. F: lit., chased]

chasse·pot (shǎs pō'), n. a breechloading rifle, closed with a sliding bolt, introduced into the French army after the war between Austria and Prussia in 1866. [named after A. A. Chassepot (1833-1905), the (French) inventor]

chas·seur (shǎ sûr'; Fr. shá sœr'), n. 1. (in the French army) one of a body of troops (cavalry or infantry) equipped and trained for rapid movement. 2. a uniformed footman or attendant; a liveried servant. 3. a huntsman. [t. F: lit., chaser]

chas·sis (shǎs'ǐ, -ǐs, chǎs'ǐ), n., pl. chassis (shǎs'ǐz, chǎs'-). 1. Auto. the frame, wheels, and machinery of a motor vehicle, on which the body is supported. 2. Ordn. the frame or railway on which a gun carriage moves backward and forward. 3. the main landing gear of an aircraft; that portion of the landing gear that supports an aircraft. 4. Radio. a. the foundation on which the sections of a radio set are mounted. b. the collection of various sections of a receiving set mounted on a foundation. [t. F. See CHASE²]

chaste (chāst), adj. 1. pure with respect to unlawful sexual intercourse; virtuous. 2. free from obscenity; decent. 3. undefiled or stainless. 4. pure in style; subdued; simple. 5. Obs. unmarried [ME, t. OF, g. L castus pure] —chaste'ly, adv. —chaste'ness, n. —Ant. 1. immoral. 2. coarse. 3. debased. 4. ornate.

chas·ten (chā'sən), v.t. 1. to inflict suffering upon for purposes of moral improvement; chastise. 2. to restrain; subdue. 3. to make chaste in style. [f. obs. chaste, v., chasten (t. OF: m. chastier, g. L castigāre) + -EN¹] —chas'ten·er, n.

chas·tise (chǎs tīz'), v.t., -tised, -tising. 1. to inflict corporal punishment upon. 2. Archaic. to restrain; chasten. 3. Archaic. to refine; purify. [ME; f. obs. chaste CHASTEN + -ISE] —chas·tise·ment (chǎs'tǐz mənt, chǎs tīz'-), n. —chas·tis'er, n.

chas·ti·ty (chǎs'tə tǐ), n. quality of being chaste. [ME chastete, t. OF, f. chaste CHASTE + -te -TY²]

chas·u·ble (chǎz'yə bəl, chǎs'-), n. Eccles. a sleeveless outer vestment worn by the celebrant at Mass. [t. F (r. ME chesible, t. OF). g. LL casubula, for L casula cloak, dim. of casa house]

chat (chǎt), v., chatted, chatting, n. —v.i. 1. to converse in a familiar or informal manner. —n. 2. informal conversation. 3. any of several passerine birds, as the yellowbreasted chat (Icteria virens) of the U. S., known for their chattering cries. [short for CHATTER]

cha·teau (shǎ tō'; Fr. shá-), n., pl. -teaux (-tōz'; Fr. -tō'). 1. a French castle. 2. a stately residence imitating a French castle. 3. a country estate, esp. a fine one. [t. F, g. L castellum]

Cha·teau·bri·and (shǎ tō brē ān'), n. François René (frän swá' rə ně'), **Vicomte de**, 1768-1848, French author and statesman.

Châ·teau-Thier·ry (shǎ tō' tē'ə rǐ; Fr. shá tō tyě rē'), a town in N France, on the Marne river: the scene of heavy fighting, 1918. 8841 (1954).

Château wine, the wine produced from grapes grown at a given vineyard or chateau in the Bordeaux wine region of France.

chat·e·laine (shǎt'ə lān'; Fr. shät lěn'), n. 1. the mistress of a castle. 2. the mistress of an elegant or fashionable household. 3. a device for suspending keys, trinkets, etc., worn at the waist by women. 4. a woman's lapel ornament. [t. F. See CASTELLAN]

Chat·ham (chǎt'əm), n. 1. **1st Earl of**. See **Pitt, William**. 2. a city in SE England. 49,900 (est. 1956).

Chatham Islands, an island group in the S Pacific, ab. 500 mi. E of and belonging to New Zealand. 372 sq. mi.

cha·toy·ant (shə toi'ənt), adj. 1. changing in luster or color. 2. Jewelry. reflecting a single streak of light when cut in a cabochon. [t. F. ppr. of chatoyer change luster like a cat's eye, der. chat cat]

Chat·ta·hoo·chee (chǎt'ə hōō'chǐ), n. a river flowing from N Georgia S along a part of the boundary between Alabama and Georgia into the Apalachicola river. ab. 500 mi.

Chat·ta·noo·ga (chǎt'ə nōō'gə), n. a city in SE Tennessee, on the Tennessee river: two battles of the Civil War were fought near here. 1863. 130,009 (1960).

chat·tel (chǎt'əl), n. 1. a movable article of property. 2. any article of tangible property other than land, buildings, and other things annexed to land. 3. a slave. [ME chatel, t. OF. See CATTLE] —Syn. 1. See property.

chattel mortgage, U.S. a mortgage on household, movable, or other personal property.

chat·ter (chǎt'ər), v.i. 1. to utter a succession of quick, inarticulate, speechlike sounds: a chattering monkey. 2.

to talk rapidly and to little purpose; jabber. **3.** to make a rapid clicking noise by striking together, as the teeth from cold. **4.** *Mach.* to vibrate in cutting, so as to form a series of nicks or notches. —*v.t.* **5.** to utter rapidly or idly. **6.** to cause to chatter. —*n.* **7.** idle or foolish talk. **8.** act or sound of chattering. [ME; imit.]

chat·ter·box (chăt′ər bŏks′), *n.* a very talkative person.

chat·ter·er (chăt′ər ər), *n.* **1.** one who chatters. **2.** any member of the tropical American bird family *Cotingidae*, fruit-eating birds of diverse coloration.

chatter mark, **1.** a mark left by a tool that has been chattering. **2.** one of a series of irregular gouges made on rock surfaces by the slipping of rock fragments held in the lower portion of a glacier.

Chat·ter·ton (chăt′ər tən), *n.* **Thomas**, 1752–70, British poet.

chat·ty (chăt′ĭ), *adj.*, **-tier, -tiest.** given to or full of chat or familiar talk; conversational: *a chatty letter or person.* —**chat′ti·ly,** *adv.* —**chat′ti·ness,** *n.*

Chau·cer (chô′sər), *n.* **Geoffrey** (jĕf′rĭ), 1340?–1400, English poet.

Chau·ce·ri·an (chô sîr′ĭ ən), *adj.* **1.** of, pertaining to, or characteristic of Chaucer's writings. —*n.* **2.** a scholar devoted to Chaucer.

chauf·fer (chô′fər), *n.* a small, portable stove. [t. F: m. *chauffoir* heater]

chauf·feur (shō′fər, shō fûr′), *n.* the paid and licensed driver of a private motor car. [t. F: stoker, der. *chauffer* heat. See CHAFE]

chaul·moo·gra (chôl mōō′grə), *n.* an East Indian tree of the genus *Taraktogenos* (or *Hydnocarpus*), the seeds of which yield a fixed oil used in the treatment of leprosy and skin diseases. [t. E Ind. (Bengali)]

chaunt (chônt, chänt), *n., v.t., v.i.* *Obs.* chant.

chausses (shōs), *n.pl.* medieval armor of mail for the legs and feet. [t. F, der. L *calceus* shoe]

chaus·sure (shō syr′), *n.* French. a foot covering. [F, der. *chausser* to shoe, g. L *calceāre*]

Chau·tau·qua (shə tô′kwə), *n.* **1.** a village in SW New York, on **Chautauqua Lake**: a summer educational center. **2.** the annual Chautauqua assembly. **3.** (*often l.c.*) any similar assembly esp. one of a number meeting in a circuit of communities. —*adj.* **4.** pertaining to an institution, or a system of popular education, employing summer schools assembling annually at Chautauqua, N.Y., with courses of home reading and study. **5.** (*often l.c.*) pertaining to a chautauqua: *a chautauqua program.*

chau·vin·ism (shō′və nĭz′əm), *n.* blind enthusiasm for military glory; zealous and belligerent patriotism or devotion to any cause. [t. F: m. *chauvinisme*; from Nicholas *Chauvin*, an old soldier and overenthusiastic admirer of Napoleon I] —**chau′vin·ist,** *n., adj.* —**chau′vin·is′tic,** *adj.* —**chau′vin·is′ti·cal·ly,** *adv.*

Cha·vannes (shȧ vȧn′), *n.* **Puvis de** (pʏ vē′ də). See **Puvis de Chavannes.**

chaw (chô), *v.t., v.i., n.* *Dial.* chew.

chaz·zan (кнȧ zän′, кнȧ′zən), *n.* a Jewish cantor. Also, **hazzan.** [t. Heb.: lit., governor, prefect]

Ch.B., (L *Chirurgiae Baccalaureus*) Bachelor of Surgery.

Ch.E., Chemical Engineer. Also, **Che.E.**

cheap (chēp), *adj.* **1.** of a relatively low price; at a bargain. **2.** costing little labor or trouble. **3.** charging low prices: *a very cheap store.* **4.** of little account; of small value; mean: *cheap conduct.* **5.** embarrassed; sheepish: *feeling cheap about his mistake.* **6.** obtainable at a low rate of interest: *when money is cheap.* **7.** of decreased value or purchasing power, as currency depreciated due to inflation. —*adv.* **8.** at a low price; at small cost. [ME *cheep* (in phrases, as *greet cheep* cheap, lit., great bargain) OE *cēap,* c. G *kauf* bargain] —**cheap′·ly,** *adv.* —**cheap′ness,** *n.*

—**Syn. 1.** CHEAP, INEXPENSIVE agree in their suggestion of low cost. CHEAP now usually suggests shoddiness, inferiority, showy imitation, complete unworthiness, and the like: *a cheap kind of fur.* INEXPENSIVE emphasizes lowness of price and suggests that the value is fully equal to the cost: *an inexpensive dress.* —**Ant. 1.** expensive, dear.

cheap·en (chē′pən), *v.t.* **1.** to make cheap or cheaper. **2.** to belittle; bring into contempt. **3.** *Archaic.* to bargain for. —*v.i.* **4.** to become cheap or cheaper. —**cheap′en·er,** *n.*

Cheap·side (chēp′sīd′), *n.* the central east-and-west thoroughfare of London, England.

cheat (chēt), *n.* **1.** a fraud; swindle; deception. **2.** a person who cheats or defrauds. **3.** *Law.* the fraudulent obtaining of another's property by a false pretense or trick. **4.** an impostor. **5.** an annual, weedy grass, *Bromus secalinus*; chess. —*v.t.* **6.** to defraud; swindle. **7.** to deceive; impose upon. **8.** to beguile; elude. —*v.i.* **9.** to practice fraud. [ME *chet(e),* aphetic form of *achet,* var. of ESCHEAT] —**cheat′er,** *n.* —**cheat′ing·ly,** *adv.*

—**Syn. 1.** imposture, artifice, trick, hoax. **2.** swindler, trickster, sharper. **6.** CHEAT, DECEIVE, TRICK, VICTIMIZE refer to the use of fraud or artifice deliberately to hoodwink someone or to obtain an unfair advantage over him. CHEAT implies conducting matters fraudulently esp. for profit to oneself: *cheat him at cards.* DECEIVE suggests deliberately misleading or deluding, to produce misunderstanding or to prevent someone from knowing the truth: *to deceive one's parents.* To TRICK is to deceive by a stratagem, often of a petty, crafty, or dishonorable kind: *to trick someone into signing a note.* To VICTIMIZE is to make a victim of; the

emotional connotation makes the cheating, deception, or trickery seem particularly dastardly: *to victimize a blind man.*

che·bec (chĭ′bĕk′), *n.* the least flycatcher.

check (chĕk), *v.t.* **1.** to stop or arrest the motion of suddenly or forcibly. **2.** to restrain; hold in restraint or control. **3.** to investigate or verify as to correctness. **4.** to note (an item, etc.) with a mark, to indicate examination or correctness (often fol. by *off*). **5.** to leave in temporary custody: *check your umbrellas at the door.* **6.** to accept for temporary custody: *small parcels checked here.* **7.** *U.S.* to send to a destination under the privilege of a passage ticket: *we checked two trunks through to Portland.* **8.** *U.S.* to accept for conveyance, and to convey, under the privilege of a passage ticket: *check this trunk to Portland.* **9.** to mark in a pattern of checks or squares: *a checked dress.* **10.** *Agric.* to plant in checkrows. **11.** *Chess.* to place (an opponent's king) under direct attack. **12.** to draw out (money) by checks (fol. by *out*).

—*v.i.* **13.** to prove to be right; to correspond accurately: *the reprint checks with the original item for item.* **14.** *U.S.* to make an inquiry or investigation for verification, etc. (usually fol. by *up* or *on*): *I'll check up on the matter.* **15.** to make a stop; pause. **16.** *Chess.* to make a move that puts the opponent's king in check. **17.** to crack or split, usually in small checks. **18.** *Hunting.* (of dogs) to stop on losing the scent or to verify it. **19.** *Falconry.* (of a hawk) to forsake the proper prey and follow baser game (fol. by *at*). **20.** *U.S.* to leave and pay for one's quarters at a hotel (fol. by *out*).

—*n.* **21.** a person or thing that checks or restrains. **22.** **in check,** under restraint. **23.** a sudden arrest or stoppage; repulse; rebuff. **24.** control with a view to ascertaining performance or preventing error. **25.** a controlled and carefully observed operation or test procedure to determine actual or potential performance. **26.** a means or standard to insure against error, fraud, etc. **27.** a mark put against an item or the like to indicate that it has been examined or verified. **28.** Also, *Brit.,* **cheque.** *Banking.* a written order, usually on a standard printed form, directing a bank to pay money. **29.** a slip or ticket showing amount owed for food or beverages consumed, or goods purchased. **30.** a token given as a means of identification: *a hat check.* **31.** a pattern formed of squares, as on a checkerboard. **32.** one of the squares. **33.** a fabric having a check pattern. **34.** *Chess.* the exposure of the king to direct attack. **35.** a counter used in card games; the chip in poker. **36.** a small crack. **37.** *Masonry.* a rabbet-shaped cutting on the edge of a stone, by which it is fitted to another stone. —*adj.* **38.** serving to check, control, verify, etc. **39.** ornamented with a checkered pattern; checkered. —*interj.* **40.** *Chess.* an optional call to warn one's opponent that his king is exposed to direct attack. [ME *chek,* t. OF: m. *eschec,* b. OF *eschac* check (ult. t. Pers.; see CHECKMATE) and OF *eschiec* booty (t. Gmc.; cf. OHG *scāh*)] —**check′a·ble,** *adj.* —**check′er,** *n.*

—**Syn. 1.** See **stop. 2.** CHECK, CURB, REPRESS, RESTRAIN refer to putting a control on movement, progress, action, etc. CHECK implies arresting suddenly, halting or causing to halt: *to check a movement toward reform.* CURB implies the use of a means such as a chain, strap, frame, wall, etc., to guide or control or to force to stay within definite limits: *to curb a horse.* REPRESS, formerly meaning to suppress, now implies preventing the action or development which might naturally be expected: *to repress evidences of excitement.* RESTRAIN implies the use of force to put under control, or chiefly, to hold back: *to restrain a person from violent acts.* **21.** obstacle, obstruction, hindrance, restriction, restraint, curb, damper. **30.** ticket, coupon, tag.

check·book (chĕk′bo͝ok′), *n.* a book containing blank checks or orders on a bank.

checked (chĕkt), *adj.* **1.** having a pattern of squares checkered. **2.** *Phonet.* situated in a closed syllable.

check·er (chĕk′ər), *n.* **1.** one of the pieces used in checkers. **2.** a checkered pattern. **3.** one of the squares of a checkered pattern. **4.** the checker tree. **5.** its fruit. —*v.t.* **6.** to mark like a checkerboard. **7.** to diversify in color; variegate. **8.** to diversify in character; subject to alternations. Also, *Brit.,* **chequer.** [ME *cheker,* t. AF: m. *escheker* chessboard, der. *eschec* CHECK]

check·er·ber·ry (chĕk′ər bĕr′ĭ), *n., pl.* **-ries. 1.** the red fruit of the American wintergreen, *Gaultheria procumbens.* **2.** the plant itself. **3.** the partridgeberry.

check·er·board (chĕk′ər bôrd′), *n.* a board marked off into sixty-four squares of two alternating colors, on which checkers and chess are played. Also, *Brit.,* **chequerboard.**

check·ered (chĕk′ərd), *adj.* **1.** marked by wide or frequent alternations; diversified: *a checkered career.* **2.** marked with squares. **3.** diversified in color. Also, *Brit.,* **chequered.**

check·ers (chĕk′ərz), *n.* a game played by two persons, each with twelve pieces, on a checkerboard; draughts. Also, *Brit.,* **chequers.**

checker tree, either of the European service trees, *Sorbus domestica* and *S. torminalis.*

check·hook (chĕk′ho͝ok′), *n.* (in a harness) a hook on the saddle for holding the end of the checkrein.

checking account, a bank deposit which is subject to withdrawal by check at any time by the depositor.

check line, a checkrein.

check list, *U.S.* items listed together for convenience of comparison or other checking purposes.

check·mate (chĕk/māt/), *n.*, *v.*, -mated, -mating, *interj.* —*n.* **1.** *Chess.* **a.** act of putting the opponent's king into an inextricable check, thus bringing the game to a close. **b.** the position of the pieces when a king is checkmated. **2.** defeat; overthrow. —*v.t.* **3.** *Chess.* to put (an opponent's king) into inextricable check. **4.** to check completely; defeat. —*interj.* **5.** *Chess.* the announcing by a player that he has put his opponent's king into inextricable check. [ME *chek mat*, ult. t. Ar.: m. *shāh māt* the king is dead]

check·off (chĕk/ôf/, -ŏf/), *n.* collection of union dues by deduction from each worker's wages, as indicated on the employer's payroll.

check·rein (chĕk/rān/), *n.* **1.** a short rein attached to the saddle of a harness to prevent a horse from lowering its head. See illus. under **harness**. **2.** a short rein joining the bit of one of a span of horses to the driving rein of the other.

check·room (chĕk/rōom/, -rŏom/), *n.* a place where hats, coats, parcels, etc., can be left in temporary custody.

check·row (chĕk/rō/), *Agric.* —*n.* **1.** one of a number of rows of trees or plants, esp. corn, in which the distance between adjacent trees or plants is equal to that between adjacent rows. —*v.t.* **2.** to plant in checkrows.

check·up (chĕk/ŭp/), *n.* **1.** an examination or close scrutiny for purposes of verification as to accuracy, comparison, etc. **2.** a comprehensive physical examination.

Ched·dar cheese (chĕd/ər), American cheese. Also, **ched/dar.**

chedd·ite (chĕd/īt, shĕd/īt), *n.* an explosive used for blasting made up of a chlorate or perchlorate mixture with a fatty substance, such as castor oil. [t. F: f. *Chedde* place name (of Savoy) + -*ite* -ITE¹]

cheek (chēk), *n.* **1.** either side of the face below eye level. **2.** the side wall of the mouth between the upper and lower jaws. **3.** something resembling the human cheek in form or position, as either of two parts forming corresponding sides of a thing. **4.** *Colloq.* impudence or effrontery. [ME *cheke*, OE *cēce*, c. D *kaak*]

cheek·bone (chēk/bōn/), *n.* the bone or bony prominence below the outer angle of the eye.

cheek by jowl, side by side; in close intimacy.

cheek pouch, a bag in the cheek of certain animals, as squirrels, for carrying food.

cheek·y (chē/kĭ), *adj.*, **cheekier, cheekiest.** *Colloq.* impudent; insolent: *a cheeky face, cheeky behavior.* —**cheek/i·ly,** *adv.* —**cheek/i·ness,** *n.*

cheep (chēp), *v.i.* **1.** to chirp; peep. —*v.t.* **2.** to express by cheeps. —*n.* **3.** a chirp. [imit.] —**cheep/er,** *n.*

cheer (chĭr), *n.* **1.** a shout of encouragement, approval, congratulation, etc. **2.** that which gives joy or gladness; encouragement; comfort. **3.** state of feeling or spirits: *what cheer?* **4.** gladness, gaiety, or animation: *to make cheer.* **5.** food; provisions. **6.** *Archaic.* expression of countenance. —*v.t.* **7.** to salute with shouts of approval, congratulation, etc. **8.** to inspire with cheer; gladden (often fol. by *up*). **9.** to encourage or incite. —*v.i.* **10.** to utter cheers of approval, etc. **11.** to become cheerful (often fol. by *up*). **12.** *Obs.* to be in a particular state of spirits. [ME *chere*, t. OF: face, g.LL *cara*] —**cheer/er,** *n.* —**cheer/ing·ly,** *adv.* —**Syn. 8.** CHEER, GLADDEN, ENLIVEN mean to make happy or lively. To CHEER is to comfort, to restore hope and cheerfulness to (now often CHEER UP, when thoroughness, a definite time, or a particular point in the action is referred to). (Cf. *eat up, drink up, hurry up*): *to cheer a sick person; soon cheered him up.* To GLADDEN does not imply a state of sadness to begin with, but suggests bringing pleasure or happiness to someone: *to gladden some one's heart with good news.* ENLIVEN suggests bringing vivacity and liveliness: *to enliven a dull evening, a party.* **9.** exhilarate, animate. **10.** shout, applaud, acclaim. —**Ant. 8.** depress. **9.** discourage.

cheer·ful (chĭr/fəl), *adj.* **1.** full of cheer; in good spirits: *a cheerful person.* **2.** promoting cheer; pleasant; bright: *cheerful surroundings.* **3.** arising from good spirits or cheerfulness: *cheerful song.* **4.** hearty or ungrudging: *cheerful giving.* —**cheer/ful·ly,** *adv.* —**cheer/ful·ness,** *n.* —**Syn. 1.** cheery, gay, blithe.

cheer·i·o (chĭr/ĭ·ō/), *interj.*, *n.*, *pl.* -os. *Chiefly Brit. Colloq.* **1.** hello. **2.** good-by.

cheer·less (chĭr/lĭs), *adj.* without cheer; joyless; gloomy. —**cheer/less·ly,** *adv.* —**cheer/less·ness,** *n.*

cheer·ly (chĭr/lĭ), *adv.* cheerfully.

cheer·y (chĭr/ĭ), *adj.*, **cheerier, cheeriest. 1.** in good spirits; blithe; gay. **2.** promoting cheer; enlivening. —**cheer/i·ly,** *adv.* —**cheer/i·ness,** *n.*

cheese¹ (chēz), *n.* **1.** the curd of milk separated from the whey and prepared in many ways as a food. **2.** a cake or definite mass of this substance. **3.** something of similar shape or consistence, as a mass of pomace in cider-making. **4.** a low curtsy. [ME *chese* OE *cēse*, c. G *käse*, ult. t. L: m. *cāseus*]

cheese² (chēz), *v.t.*, **cheesed, cheesing.** *Slang.* to stop. **Cheese it!**, look out! run away! [alter. of CEASE]

cheese³ (chēz), *n.* *Slang.* the correct or proper thing. [prob. t. Pers., Hind.: m. *chīz* thing]

cheese·cake (chēz/kāk/), *n.* *Slang.* photographs of pretty girls in newspapers, magazines, etc., posed to display their legs.

cheese cake, a kind of cake or open pie filled with a custardlike preparation containing cheese.

cheese·cloth (chēz/klôth/, -klŏth/), *n.* a coarse cotton fabric of open texture, orig. used for wrapping cheese.

---

cheese·par·ing (chēz/pâr/ĭng), *adj.* **1.** meanly economical; parsimonious. —*n.* **2.** something of little or no value. **3.** niggardly economy.

chees·y (chē/zĭ), *adj.*, **cheesier, cheesiest. 1.** like cheese: *cheesy taste or consistency.* **2.** *U.S. Slang.* of poor quality. —**chees/i·ness,** *n.*

chee·tah (chē/tə), *n.* an animal of the cat family, *Acinonyx jubatus*, of southwestern Asia and Africa, resembling the leopard but having certain doglike characteristics, often trained for hunting deer, etc. Also, **cheetah.** [t. Hind.: m. *chītā*]

Cheetah, *Acinonyx jubatus*
(Total length ab. 7 ft.; tall 2½ ft., 2½ ft. high at the shoulder)

chef (shĕf), *n.* a cook, esp. a head cook. [t. F. See CHIEF]

chef-d'oeu·vre (shě dœ/vr), *n.*, *pl.* **chefs-d'oeuvre** (shě dœ/vr). *French.* a masterpiece, esp. of an author, painter, etc.

Che·foo (chē/fōō/), *n.* a seaport in NE China, in Shantung province. 227,000 (est. 1950).

cheiro-, var. of chiro-.

Che·ju (chě/jōō/), *n.* an island S of, and belonging to, South Korea. ab. 200,000 (est. 1948); 718 sq. mi. Also, **Quelpart;** Japanese, **Saishuto;** Korean, **Saishu.**

Che·ka (chě/kä), *n.* (formerly) the special commission in the Soviet Union for protection against counterrevolution; a secret police. The name later was changed to Ogpu. [t. Russ.: f. *che* + *ka*, names of the initials of the *chrezvychainaya komissiya* extraordinary commission]

Che·khov (chĕk/ôf, -ŏf/; *Russ.* chĕ/hôf), *n.* **Anton Pavlovich** (än tôn/ pä vlô/vĭch), 1860–1904, Russian short-story writer and dramatist. Also, **Tchekhoff.**

Che·kiang (chě/kyăng/; *Chin.* jü/jyäng/), *n.* a province in E China. 22,865,477 pop. (1953); 39,768 sq. mi.

che·la¹ (kē/lə), *n.*, *pl.* -lae (-lē). the nipperlike organ or claw terminating certain limbs of crustaceans and arachnids. [t. NL, t. Gk.: m. *chēlē* claw]

Chela of lobster

che·la² (chā/lä), *n.* (in India) a disciple of a religious teacher. [t. Hind.: slave, disciple]

che·late (kē/lāt), *adj.* *Zool.* having a chela.

che·lif·er·ous (kĭ lĭf/ər əs), *adj.* bearing chelae.

che·li·form (kē/lə fôrm/), *adj.* nipperlike.

che·loid (kē/loid), *n.* *Pathol.* keloid.

che·lo·ni·an (kĭ lō/nĭ ən), *adj.* **1.** of or belonging to the *Chelonia*, an order or group of reptiles comprising the turtles. —*n.* **2.** a turtle. [f. s. NL *Chelōnia*, pl. (cf. Gk. *chelōnē* tortoise) + -AN]

Chel·sea (chĕl/sĭ), *n.* **1.** a borough in SW London, England: artists' and writers' section. 50,912 pop. (1951). **2.** a city in E Massachusetts, near Boston. 33,749 (1960).

Chel·ten·ham (chĕlt/nəm), *n.* **1.** a city in W England. 68,010 (est. 1956). **2.** *Print.* a style of type.

Chel·ya·binsk (chĕl yä/bĭnsk), *n.* a city in the W Soviet Union in Asia, in the Ural area. 612,000 (est. 1956).

Chel·yus·kin (chĕl yōōs/kĭn), *n.* **Cape,** a cape in the N Soviet Union in Asia: northernmost point of Asia.

chem-, var. of **chemo-**, used before vowels, as in *chemism.*

chem., **1.** chemical. **2.** chemist. **3.** chemistry.

chem·ic (kĕm/ĭk), *adj.* **1.** alchemic. **2.** chemical. [short for ALCHEMIC]

chem·i·cal (kĕm/ə kəl), *adj.* **1.** of or concerned with the science or the operations or processes of chemistry. —*n.* **2.** a substance produced by or used in a chemical process. —**chem/i·cal·ly,** *adv.*

chemical engineering, the science or profession of chemistry applied to industrial processes.

chemical warfare, warfare with asphyxiating, poisonous, and corrosive gases, oil flames, etc.

chem·i·lum·i·nes·cence (kĕm/ə lōō/mə nĕs/əns), *n.* (in chemical reactions) the production of light at low temperatures.

che·min de fer (shə măn/ də fĕr/), *French.* **1.** a railroad. **2.** a variation of baccarat.

che·mise (shə mēz/), *n.* **1.** a woman's loose-fitting shirt-like undergarment. **2.** (in women's fashions) a dress, suit, etc., designed to fit loosely at the waist and more tightly at the hips. [t. F, g. LL *camisia* shirt (prob. t. Celtic); r. ME *kemes*, OE *cemes*, t. LL: m. *camisia*]

chem·i·sette (shĕm/ə zĕt/), *n.* a woman's garment of linen, lace, etc., worn with a low-cut or open bodice to cover the neck and breast. [t. F, dim. of *chemise*]

chem·ism (kĕm/ĭz əm), *n.* chemical action.

chem·ist (kĕm/ĭst), *n.* **1.** one versed in chemistry or professionally engaged in chemical operations. **2.** *Brit.* druggist. **3.** *Obs.* alchemist. [var. of ALCHEMIST]

chem·is·try (kĕm/ĭs trĭ), *n.*, *pl.* -tries. **1.** the science that treats of or investigates the composition of substances and various elementary forms of matter (**chemical elements**). **2.** chemical properties, reactions, etc.: *the chemistry of carbon.* [f. CHEMIST + -RY]

Chem·nitz (kĕm/nĭts), *n.* former name of **Karl-Marx-Stadt.**

chemo-, a word element representing chemic or chemical. Also, **chem-.**

---

b., blend of, blended; c., cognate with; d., dialect, dialectal; der., derived from; f., formed from; g., going back to; m., modification of; r., replacing; s., stem of; t., taken from; ?, perhaps.   See the full key on inside cover.

chem·o·syn·the·sis (kĕm′ō sĭn′thə sĭs), *n. Bot.* production by plants of nutritive substances from carbon dioxide and water with energy derived from other chemical reactions.

chem·o·tax·is (kĕm′ō tăk′sĭs), *n. Biol.* the property in a cell or organism of exhibiting attraction or repulsion to chemical substances.

chem·o·ther·a·peu·tics (kĕm′ō thĕr′ə pū′tĭks), *n. Med.* chemotherapy. —**chem′o·ther′a·peu′tic,** *adj.*

chem·o·ther·a·py (kĕm′ō thĕr′ə pĭ), *n. Med.* the treatment of disease by means of chemicals which have a specific toxic effect upon the disease-producing microörganisms. —**chem′o·ther′a·pist,** *n.*

che·mot·ro·pism (kĭ mŏt′rə pĭz′əm), *n. Bot., Zool.* the property in plants and other organisms of turning or bending (toward or away), as by unequal growth, in response to the presence of chemical substances.

Che·mul·po (chĕ′mŏŏl pō′), *n.* Inchon.

chem·ur·gy (kĕm′ûr jĭ), *n.* a division of applied chemistry concerned with the industrial use of organic substances, esp. from farm produce, as soybeans, peanuts, etc. —**chem·ur′gic, chem·ur′gi·cal,** *adj.*

Che·nab (chĭ năb′), *n.* a river through S Kashmir and SW through Pakistan to the Sutlej in W Punjab.

Cheng·teh (chŭng′dŭ′), *n.* a city in NE China: the capital of Jehol province; the former summer residence of the Manchu emperors. 60,000 (1947). Also, **Jehol.**

Cheng·tu (chŭng′dōō′), *n.* a walled city in central China, the capital of Szechwan. 648,000 (est. 1948).

che·nille (shə nēl′), *n.* **1.** a velvety cord of silk or worsted, used in embroidery, fringe, etc. **2.** fabric made with a fringed silken thread used as the weft in combination with wool or cotton. [t. F: caterpillar, g. L *canicula* little dog]

che·no·pod (kē′nə pŏd′, kĕn′ə-), *n.* any plant of the genus *Chenopodium* or the family *Chenopodiaceae.* [f. *cheno-* (comb. form repr. Gk. *chēn* goose) + -POD]

che·no·po·di·a·ceous (kē′nə pō′dĭ ā′shəs, kĕn′ə-), *adj. Bot.* belonging to the *Chenopodiaceae,* or goosefoot family of plants, which includes the beet and mangelwurzel, spinach, and orach, also many species peculiar to saline, alkaline, or desert regions. [f. s. NL *Chenopodium* (see CHENOPOD) + -ACEOUS]

Che·ops (kē′ŏps), *n.* fl. c3900 or c3700 or c2700 B.C., king of Egypt, of 4th dynasty: builder of great pyramid at El Giza. Also, **Khufu.**

cheque (chĕk), *n. Brit.* check (def. 28).

chequ·er (chĕk′ər), *n. Brit.* checker.

chequ·er·board (chĕk′ər bôrd′), *n. Brit.* checkerboard.

chequ·uered (chĕk′ərd), *adj. Brit.* checkered.

chequ·uers (chĕk′ərz), *n. Brit.* checkers.

Cher (shĕr), *n.* a river in central France, flowing NW to the Loire river. ab. 220 mi.

Cher·bourg (shâr′bŏŏrg; *Fr.* shĕr bōōr′), *n.* a fortified seaport in N W France: taken by U.S. forces, June, 1944. 38,262 (1954).

cher·chez la femme (shĕr shě′ là fàm′), *French-* search for the woman.

cher·ish (chĕr′ĭsh), *v.t.* **1.** to hold or treat as dear. **2.** to care for tenderly; nurture. **3.** to cling fondly to (ideas, etc.): *cherishing no resentment.* [ME *cherische(n),* t. F: m. *cheriss-,* s. *cherir,* der. *cher* dear, g. L *cārus*] —**cher′ish·er,** *n.* —**cher′ish·ing·ly,** *adv.*

—**Syn. 1.** CHERISH, FOSTER, HARBOR imply giving affection, care, or shelter to something. CHERISH suggests regarding or treating something as an object of affection or as valuable: *to cherish a memory or a friendship.* FOSTER implies sustaining and nourishing something with care, esp in order to promote, increase, or strengthen it: *to foster a hope, enmity, crime.* HARBOR suggests giving shelter to or entertaining something undesirable, esp. evil thoughts or intentions: *to harbor malice or a grudge.* —**Ant. 2.** neglect. **3.** relinquish.

Cher·no·vi·tsy (chĕr′nŏ vĭ tsĭ), *n.* Russian name of Cernăuti.

cher·no·zem (chĕr′nŏ zĕm′), *n.* the normal soil of subhumid grasslands, having a deep, rich, black topsoil and a lower layer of lime accumulation. [t. Russ.]

Cher·o·kee (chĕr′ə kē′, chĕr′ə kē′), *n., pl.* -**kee, -kees.** **1.** a member of an important tribe of North American Indians of Iroquoian family whose first known center was in the southern Alleghenies and whose present center is Oklahoma. **2.** an Iroquoian language.

Cherokee rose, a smooth-stemmed white rose, *Rosa laevigata,* of Chinese origin, cultivated in southern U. S.

che·root (shə rōōt′), *n.* a cigar having open, unpointed ends. [t. F: m. *chéroute,* t. Tamil: m. *shuruttu* a roll]

cher·ry (chĕr′ĭ), *n., pl.* -**ries,** *adj.* —**1.** the fruit of any of various trees of the genus *Prunus,* consisting of a pulpy, globular drupe enclosing a one-seeded smooth stone. **2.** the tree itself. **3.** its wood. **4.** any of various fruits or plants resembling the cherry. **5.** bright red; cerise. —**adj. 6.** bright-red; cerise. **7.** made of the wood of the cherry tree. [ME *chery, chiri,* back formation from OE *ciris* (the -s being taken for plural sign), t. VL: m. *ceresia,* der. L *cerasus* cherry tree, t. Gk.: m. *kerasós.* Cf. F *cerise,* ONF *cherise,* etc., g. VL (in place)]

cherry stone, the clam, *Venus mercenaria,* when larger than a littleneck.

cher·so·nese (kûr′sə nēz′, -nēs′), *n.* **1.** a peninsula. **2.** the Chersonese, Gallipoli Peninsula. [t. L: m.s. *chersonēsus,* t. Gk.: m. *chersónēsos*]

chert (chûrt), *n.* a compact rock consisting essentially of cryptocrystalline quartz. —**chert′y,** *adj.*

cher·ub (chĕr′əb), *n., pl.* **cherubs** for 3, 4; **cherubim** (chĕr′ə bĭm, -yŏŏ bĭm) for 1, 2. **1.** *Bible.* a kind of celestial being. Gen. 3:24; Ezek. 1 and 10. **2.** *Theol.* a member of the second order of angels, distinguished by knowledge, often represented as a beautiful winged child or as a winged head of a child. **3.** a beautiful or innocent person, esp. a child. **4.** a person with a chubby, innocent face. [ME and OE *cherubin,* pl., ult. t. Heb.: m. *kerūb* sing., *karubīm,* pl.] —**che·ru·bic** (chə rōō′bĭk), *adj.* —**che·ru′bi·cal·ly,** *adv.*

Che·ru·bi·ni (kě′rōō bē′nē), *n.* **Maria Luigi Carlo Zenobio Salvatore** (mä rē′ä lōō ē′jē kär′lō dzē nō′byō säl′vä tô′rě), 1760–1842, Italian composer in France.

cher·vil (chûr′vĭl), *n.* **1.** a herbaceous plant, *Anthriscus Cerefolium,* of the parsley family, with aromatic leaves used to flavor soups, salads, etc. **2.** any of various plants of the same genus or allied genera. [ME *chervelle,* OE *cerfille,* t. L: m. s. *caerephylla,* pl. of *caerephyllum,* t. Gk.: m. *chairéphyllon*]

cher·vo·nets (chĕr vô′nĭts, -nĕts), *n., pl.* -**vontsi** (-vônt′sĭ). the gold unit of the U.S.S.R. monetary system, equal to ten rubles, or about $8.72. [t. Russ.]

Ches·a·peake Bay (chĕs′pēk′, chĕs′ə pēk′), a large inlet of the Atlantic, in Maryland and Virginia. ab. 200 mi. long; 4–40 mi. wide.

Chesh·ire (chĕsh′ər, -ĭr), *n.* a county in W England. 1,258,507 pop. (1951). 1015 sq. mi. *Co. seat:* Chester. Also, **Chester.**

Cheshire cat, a constantly grinning cat, in *Alice in Wonderland,* named from the old simile "to grin like a Cheshire cat."

chess[1] (chĕs), *n.* a game played by two persons, each with sixteen pieces, on a checkerboard. [ME, t. OF: aphetic m. *esches, eschecs,* pl. See CHECK]

chess[2] (chĕs), *n., pl.* **chess, chesses.** one of the planks forming the roadway of a floating bridge. [orig. uncert.]

chess[3] (chĕs), *n.* cheat (def. 5). [orig. uncert.]

chess·board (chĕs′bôrd′), *n.* the board, identical with a checkerboard, used for playing chess.

chess·man (chĕs′măn′, -mən), *n., pl.* -**men** (-mĕn′, -mən). one of the pieces used in the game of chess.

chest (chĕst), *n.* **1.** the trunk of the body from the neck to the belly; the thorax. **2.** a box, usually a large, strong one, for the safekeeping of valuables. **3.** the place where the funds of a public institution, etc., are kept. **4.** the funds themselves. **5.** a box in which certain goods, as tea, are packed for transit. **6.** the quantity contained in such a box. **7.** chest of drawers. [ME; OE *cest, cist,* t. L: s. *cista,* t. Gk.: m. *kistē* box]

Ches·ter (chĕs′tər), *n.* **1.** a city in SE Pennsylvania. 63,658 (1960). **2.** a walled city in W England. 58,800 (est. 1956). **3.** Cheshire.

Ches·ter·field (chĕs′tər fēld′), *n.* **1. Philip Dormer Stanhope** (dôr′mər stăn′ōp), **4th Earl of,** 1694–1773, British statesman and author. **2.** (*l.c.*) an overcoat, usually single-breasted, with concealed buttons. **3.** (*l.c.*) a sofa or divan with a back and arms.

Ches·ter·field·i·an (chĕs′tər fēl′dĭ ən), *adj.* like the Earl of Chesterfield; lordly; elegant; cold; suave.

Ches·ter·ton (chĕs′tər tən), *n.* **Gilbert Keith,** 1874–1936, British essayist, critic, and novelist.

Chester White, one of an early-maturing white breed of hog which originated in Chester county, Penn.

chest·nut (chĕs′nŭt′, -nət), *n.* **1.** the edible nut of trees of the genus *Castanea,* of the beech family. **2.** any of the trees, as *C. sativa* (**European chestnut**), *C. dentata* (**American chestnut**), or *C. crenata* (**Japanese chestnut**). **3.** the wood. **4.** any of various fruits or trees resembling the chestnut, as the horse chestnut. **5.** reddish brown. **6.** *Colloq.* an old or stale joke, anecdote, etc. **7.** the callosity on the inner side of a horse's leg. —*adj.* **8.** reddish-brown. **9.** (esp. in England, of horses) sorrel. [t. obs. *chesten* chestnut (ME; OE *cisten-,* var. of **cesten,* g. WGmc. **kastinia,* t. L: m. *castanea,* t. Gk.: m. *kastanēa*) + NUT; r. ME *chasteine,* t. OF]

chest of drawers, *Chiefly Brit.* a piece of furniture consisting of a set of drawers fitted into a frame, used for clothing, linen, etc. Cf. *U.S.* **bureau** or **dresser.**

chest-on-chest (chĕst′ŏn chĕst′), *n.* a chest of drawers placed upon a slightly wider chest of drawers.

chest·y (chĕs′tĭ), *adj.,* **chestier, chestiest.** *Slang.* proud; conceited.

che·tah (chē′tə), *n.* cheetah.

che·val-de-frise (shə văl′ də frēz′), *n., pl.* **chevaux-de-frise** (shə vō′ də frēz′). (*usually pl.*) an obstacle of projecting spikes or barbed wire used to close a gap to the enemy. [t. F: lit., horse of Friesland]

cheval glass (shə văl′), a full-length mirror mounted so as to swing in a frame. [*cheval,* t. F: support, horse]

chev·a·lier (shĕv′ə lĭr′), *n.* **1.** a member of certain orders of honor or merit: *a chevalier of the Legion of Honor.* **2.** a knight. **3.** *French Hist.* **a.** the lowest title of rank in the old nobility. **b.** a cadet of the old nobility. **4.** a chivalrous man. [ME *chevalere,* t. OF: m. *chevalier,* der. *cheval* horse, g. L *caballus.* See CAVALIER]

Chev·i·ot (chĕv′ĭ ət, chē′vĭ-; *commonly* shĕv′ĭ ət for 2), *n.* **1.** a breed of sheep valued for their thick wool (so called from the Cheviot Hills). **2.** (*l.c.*) a worsted fabric in a coarse twill weave, used for coats, suits, etc.

Cheviot Hills, a range of hills on the boundary between England and Scotland. Highest point, 2676 ft.

ăct, āble, dâre, ärt; ĕbb, ēqual; ĭf, īce; hŏt, ōver, ôrder, oil, bŏŏk, ōōze, out; ŭp, ūse, ûrge; ə = a in alone; ch, chief; g, give; ng, ring; sh, shoe; th, thin; ŧh, that; zh, vision. See the full key on inside cover.

chev·ron (shĕv′rən), *n.* **1.** a badge consisting of stripes meeting at an angle, worn on the sleeve (by non-commissioned officers, policemen, etc.) as an indication of rank, of service, wounds in war, etc. **2.** *Her.* the lower half of a bend and a bend sinister meeting at the center of the shield, like an inverted V. **3.** a similar decoration, as in an architectural molding. [t. F: rafter, chevron, der. F *chèvre* goat, g. L *caper*]

Chevrons, U.S. Army A. Sergeant; B. Master Sergeant; C. Private, first class

chev·ro·tain (shĕv′rətăn′, -tĭn), *n.* any of the very small deerlike ruminants, family *Tragulidae*, of the genera *Tragulus* of Asia, and *Hyemoschus* of Africa. [t. F, dim. of OF *chevrot* kid, dim. of *chèvre* she-goat]

chev·y (chĕv′ĭ), *v.t.*, *v.i.*, **chevied, chevying,** *n.*, *pl.* **chevies.** *Brit.* chivvy.

Chevy Chase. See Otterburn.

chew (choō), *v.t.* **1.** to crush or grind with the teeth; masticate. **2.** to meditate on; consider deliberately. —*v.i.* **3.** to perform the act of crushing or grinding with the teeth. **4.** *Colloq.* to use tobacco for chewing. **5.** to meditate. —*n.* **6.** act of chewing. **7.** that which is chewed; a portion, as of tobacco, for chewing. [ME *chewen*, OE *cēowan*, akin to G *kauen*] —**chew′er,** *n.*

chew·ing gum (choō′ĭng), a preparation for chewing, usually made of sweetened and flavored chicle.

che·wink (chĭ wĭngk′), *n.* a bird, *Pipilo erythrophthalmus*, of the finch family, common in eastern North America; towhee. [imit. of its note]

Chey·enne (shĭ ĕn′), *n.* the capital of Wyoming, in the SE part. 43,505 (1960).

Chey·enne (shĭ ĕn′), *n.*, *pl.* **-enne, -ennes. 1.** (*pl.*) a Plains tribe of the Algonquian linguistic family, formerly in central Minnesota, later in North and South Dakota; now divided between Montana (**Northern Cheyenne**) and Oklahoma (**Southern Cheyenne**). **2.** a member of this tribe. [t. Dakota Sioux: m. *shahi′yena, shai-ena,* or t. Teton Sioux: m. *shai-ela* people of alien speech, der. *sha′ia* speak a strange tongue]

Cheyenne River, a river flowing from E Wyoming NE to the Missouri in central South Dakota. ab. 300 mi.

Chey·ne (chā′nĭ, chān), *n.* Thomas Kelly, 1841–1915, British clergyman and Biblical scholar.

chg., *pl.* **chgs.** charge.

chi (kī), *n.* the twenty-second letter (X, χ, = English ch or kh) of the Greek alphabet.

Chi·an (kī′ən), *adj.* **1.** of or pertaining to Chios. —*n.* **2.** a native or inhabitant of Chios.

Chiang Kai-shek (chyäng′ kī′shĕk′), born 1886, commander in chief of the Chinese forces; president of China, 1943–49; of Nationalist China since 1950.

Chi·an·ti (kĭ än′tĭ; *It.* kē än′tē), *n.* a dry, red, full-bodied Italian table wine, usually bottled in a colorful straw-covered bottle. [named after the *Chianti* Mountains in Tuscany]

Chi·a·pas (chē ä′päs), *n.* a state in S Mexico. 961,237 (est. 1952); 28,732 sq. mi. *Cap.:* Tuxtla Gutiérrez.

chi·a·ro·scu·ro (kĭ är′ə skyoŏr′ō), *n.*, *pl.* **-ros. 1.** the treatment or general distribution of light and shade in a picture. **2.** pictorial art employing only light and shade. **3.** a sketch in light and shade. Also, **chi·a·ro·o·scu·ro** (kĭ är′ə ō skyoŏr′ō). [t. It.: clear-dark] —**chi·a·ro·scu′rist,** *n.*

chi·asm (kī′ăz əm), *n.* *Anat.* a crossing or decussation, esp. that of the optic nerves at the base of the brain.

chi·as·ma (kĭ äz′mə), *n.*, *pl.* **-mata** (-mə tə). *Biol.* a crossing point in conjugating chromosomes. [t. NL, t. Gk.: arrangement in the form of the Greek letter chi (X)] —**chi·as′mal, chi·as′mic,** *adj.*

chi·as·ma·typ·y (kĭ äz′mə tī′pĭ), *n.* *Biol., Genetics.* the crossing over of segments of allelomorphic chromosomes during synapsis, with possible interchange of factors. —**chi·as′ma·type′,** *adj.*, *n.*

Chi·ba (chē′bä′), *n.* a city in central Japan, on Honshu island, near Tokyo. 138,844 (1950).

Chib·cha (chĭb′chə), *n.* **1.** (*pl.*) an extinct tribe of civilized South American Indians, formerly living in a high plateau of Bogotá, Colombia. **2.** a member of this tribe.

Chib·chan (chĭb′chən), *n.* a South American Indian speech family including the Chibcha and other tribes of Colombia.

chi·bouk (chĭ boōk′, -boŏk′), *n.* a Turkish tobacco pipe with a long, stiff stem (sometimes 4 or 5 feet long). Also, **chi·bouque′.** [t. Turk.: m. *chibūq*]

chic (shēk, shĭk), *adj.* **1.** cleverly attractive in style; stylish. —*n.* **2.** style; cleverly attractive style, esp. in dress. [t. F, ? der. *chicane* CHICANE]

Chi·ca·go (shĭ kô′gō, -kä′-), *n.* a city in NE Illinois; a port on Lake Michigan; the second largest city in the U.S. 3,550,404 (1960). —**Chi·ca′go·an,** *n.*

Chicago Heights, a city in NE Illinois, S of Chicago. 34,331 (1960).

chi·ca·lo·te (chē′kä lô′tě), *n.* any of several prickly papaveraceous plants of arid tropical and subtropical America, as *Argemone mexicana* and *A. platyceras*. [Mex. Sp., t. Nahuatl: m. *chicalotl*]

chi·cane (shĭ kān′), *n.*, *v.*, **-caned, -caning.** —*n.* **1.** chicanery. **2.** *Bridge.* a hand without trumps. —*v.t.*

3. to use chicanery. —*v.t.* **4.** to trick by chicanery. **5.** to quibble over; cavil at. [t. F, der. *chicaner* quibble, ? t. MLG: m. *schikken* arrange] —**chi·can′er,** *n.*

chi·can·er·y (shĭ kā′nə rĭ), *n.*, *pl.* **-eries. 1.** trickery, quibbling, or sophistry. **2.** a quibble or subterfuge.

chic·co·ry (chĭk′ə rĭ), *n.*, *pl.* **-ries.** chicory.

Chi·chen It·zá (chē chĕn′ ēt sä′). the ruins of an ancient Mayan city, in central Yucatán state, Mexico.

chi·chi (shē′shē′), *adj.* pretentiously elegant, sophisticated, or stylish.

chick (chĭk), *n.* **1.** a young chicken or other bird. **2.** a child. **3.** *U.S. Slang.* a young girl.

chick·a·dee (chĭk′ə dē′), *n.* any of several North American birds of the family *Paridae*, esp. the black-capped titmouse, *Parus atricapillus*. [imit. of cry]

Chick·a·mau·ga (chĭk′ə mô′gə), *n.* a creek in NW Georgia: scene of a Confederate victory, 1863.

chick·a·ree (chĭk′ə rē′), *n.* the red squirrel, *Sciurus hudsonius*, of North America. [imit. of cry]

Chick·a·saw (chĭk′ə sô′), *n.*, *pl.* **-saw, -saws. 1.** (*pl.*) a warlike Muskhogean tribe of North American Indians, formerly in northern Mississippi, now in Oklahoma. **2.** a member of this tribe.

chick·en (chĭk′ən, -ĭn), *n.* **1.** the young of the domestic fowl (or of certain other birds). **2.** a domestic fowl of any age, or its flesh. **3.** any of certain other birds as **Mother Carey's chicken** (the stormy petrel) or the **prairie chicken** (the prairie hen). **4.** *Colloq.* a young person, esp. a young girl. —*adj.* **5.** *Slang.* cowardly. [ME *chiken*, OE *cicen, ciken.* Cf. D *kieken*]

chicken breast, *Pathol.* a malformation of the chest in which there is abnormal projection of the sternum and the sternal region, often associated with rickets.

chicken feed, *U.S. Slang.* **1.** small change (pennies, nickels, etc.). **2.** meager wages or other recompense.

chicken hawk, any of various hawks that prey on poultry, esp. *Buteo borealis*, the red-tailed hawk common in the U. S.

chick·en-heart·ed (chĭk′ən här′tĭd, chĭk′ĭn-), *adj.* timid; cowardly.

chicken pox, a mild, contagious eruptive disease, commonly of children; varicella.

chick·pea (chĭk′pē′), *n.* **1.** a leguminous plant. *Cicer arietinum*, bearing edible pealike seeds, much used for food in southern Europe. **2.** its seed. [earlier *chich* (pease), t. F: m. (*pois*) *chiche*, g. L *cicer* vetch]

chick·weed (chĭk′wēd′), *n.* **1.** any of various plants of the caryophyllaceous genus *Stellaria*, as *S. media*, a common Old World weed whose leaves and seeds are relished by birds. **2.** any of various allied plants.

chi·cle (chĭk′əl), *n.* a gumlike substance obtained from certain tropical American trees, as the sapodilla, used in the manufacture of chewing gum, etc. Also, **chicle gum.** [t. Amer. Sp., t. Mex.: m. *tziktli*]

chi·co (chē′kō), *n.*, *pl.* **-cos.** greasewood (def. 1). [t. S. Amer.]

Chic·o·pee (chĭk′ə pē′), *n.* a city in S Massachusetts, oh the Connecticut river. 61,553 (1960).

chic·o·ry (chĭk′ə rĭ), *n.*, *pl.* **-ries. 1.** a perennial plant, *Cichorium intybus*, with bright-blue flowers, cultivated as a salad plant and for its root, which is used roasted and ground as a substitute for or adulterant for coffee. **2.** the root. **3.** *Brit.* endive. Also, **chiccory.** [t. F: m. *chicorée*, t. L: m. s. *cichorēum*, t. Gk.: m. *kichórion*]

chide (chīd), *v.*, **chided or chid; chided, chid or chidden; chiding.** —*v.t.* **1.** to scold; find fault. —*v.t.* **2.** to drive, impel, etc., by chiding. **3.** to express disapproval of. [ME *chiden*, OE *cīdan*] —**chid′er,** *n.* —**chid′ing·ly,** *adv.* —**Syn. 3.** reprove, rebuke, censure.

chief (chēf), *n.* **1.** the head or leader of a body of men; the person highest in authority. **2.** the head or ruler of a clan or tribe. **3.** (*cap.*) *U.S. Army.* a title of some advisors to the Chief of Staff who do not, in most instances, command the troop units of their arms or services: *Chief of Engineers, Chief Signal Officer*, etc. **4.** *Slang.* boss. **5.** *Her.* the upper third of an escutcheon. —*adj.* **6.** highest in rank or authority. **7.** most important: *his chief merit, the chief difficulty.* **8.** standing at the head. —*adv.* **9.** *Archaic.* chiefly; principally. [ME, t. OF, g. L *caput* head] —**Syn. 7.** foremost, essential, leading, principal. See **capital.** —**Ant.** 6. subordinate.

chief constable, *Brit.* chief of police.

chief justice, 1. *Law.* the presiding judge of a court having several members. **2.** (*caps.*) the presiding judge of the U. S. Supreme Court (in full, **Chief Justice of the United States**).

chief·ly (chēf′lĭ), *adv.* **1.** principally; above all. **2.** mainly; mostly. —**Syn. 1, 2.** See especially.

Chief of Staff, *U.S.* **1.** the senior officer of the Army, Navy, or Air Force, responsible to the Secretary of his particular service branch and to the President. **2.** (*l.c.*) *U.S. Army.* the senior staff officer in a division or higher unit.

chief·tain (chēf′tən, -tĭn), *n.* **1.** a leader of a group, band, etc. **2.** the chief of a clan or a tribe. [ME *chieftayne*, var. of *chevetaine*, t. OF, g. LL *capitānus*. See **CAPTAIN**] —**chief′tain·cy, chief′tain·ship′,** *n.*

chield (chēld), *n.* *Scot.* a young man; a fellow. Also, **chiel** (chēl). [var. of **CHILD**]

---

b., blend of, blended; c., cognate with; d., dialect, dialectal; der., derived from; f., formed from; g., going back to; m. modification of; r., replacing; s., stem of t., taken from; ?, perhaps. See the full key on inside cover.

chiff·chaff (chĭf′chăf′, -chăf′), *n.* a common, plain-colored Old World warbler, *Phylloscopus collybita.*

chif·fon (shĭ fŏn′, shĭf′ŏn), *n.* 1. sheer fabric of silk or rayon in plain weave. 2. any bit of feminine finery, as of ribbon or lace. [t. F, der. *chiffe* rag]

chif·fo·nier (shĭf′ə nĭr′), *n.* a high chest of drawers or bureau, often having a mirror. Also, **chif·fon·nier′.** [t. F: m. *chiffonnier*, der. *chiffon* rag]

hig·ger (hĭg′ər), *n.* 1. the parasitic larva of certain kinds of mites, which causes severe itching when attached to the skin; redbug. 2. chigoe. [alter. of CHIGOE]

hi·gnon (shēn′yŏn; *Fr.* shē nyôN′), *n.* a large rolled arrangement of the hair, worn at the back of the head by women. [t. F, ult. der. L *catēna* chain]

hig·oe (chĭg′ō), *n.* a flea, *Tunga Penetrans*, of the West Indies, South America, Africa, etc., the female of which buries itself in the skin of men and animals. [t. W Ind. Cf. F *chique*]

hih·li (chē′lē′; *Chin.* jū′lē′), *n.* 1. former name of **Hopeh.** 2. Gulf of, former name of Pohai.

hi·hua·hua (chĭ wä′wä), *n.* 1. a state in N Mexico. 900,024 (est. 1952); 94,831 sq. mi. 2. the capital of this state. 86,796 (est. 1951). 3. the smallest type of dog, originating in Mexico.

hil-, var. of chilo-, used before vowels.

hil·blain (chĭl′blān′), *n.* (*usually pl.*) *Pathol.* an inflammation on the hands and feet caused by exposure to cold and moisture. [f. CHIL(L) + BLAIN] **—chil′-blained′,** *adj.*

hild (chīld), *n., pl.* **children.** 1. a baby or infant. 2. a boy or girl. 3. a childish person. 4. a son or daughter. 5. any descendant. 6. any person or thing regarded as the product or result of particular agencies, influences, etc.: *children of light.* 7. *Brit. Dial.* a female infant. 8. *Archaic.* childe. 9. **with child,** pregnant. [ME *child*, pl. *childre*(n), OE *cild*, pl. *cild*(*ru*)] **—child′less,** *adj.* **—child′less·ness,** *n.*

hild·bear·ing (chīld′bâr′ĭng), *n.* producing or bringing forth children.

hild·bed (chīld′bĕd′), *n.* the condition of a woman giving birth to a child; parturition.
 hildbed fever, puerperal fever.

hild·birth (chīld′bûrth′), *n.* parturition.

hilde (chīld), *n.* *Archaic.* a youth of noble birth. Also, **child.**

hil·der·mas (chĭl′dər mas), *n.* Obs. Holy Innocents' Day.

hild·hood (chīld′hŏŏd), *n.* state or time of being a child.

hild·ing (chīl′dĭng), *adj.* bearing children; pregnant.

hild·ish (chīl′dĭsh), *adj.* 1. of, like, or befitting a child. 2. puerile; weak; silly. [ME *childisch*, OE *cildisc*] **—child′ish·ly,** *adv.* **—child′ish·ness,** *n.*
 —Syn. 1, 2. CHILDISH, INFANTILE, CHILDLIKE refer to characteristics or qualities of childhood. The ending *-ish* has unfavorable connotations: CHILDISH therefore refers to characteristics which are undesirable and unpleasant: *childish selfishness, outbursts of temper.* INFANTILE, originally a general word, now often carries an even stronger idea of disapproval or scorn than does CHILDISH: *infantile reasoning, behavior.* The ending *-like* has pleasing connotations; CHILDLIKE therefore refers to the characteristics which are desirable and admirable: *childlike innocence, trust.*

hild labor, the employment in gainful occupations of children below a minimum age determined by law or custom. The minimum legal age for full-time employment is 16 years in the U.S., according to federal law; standards regulating intrastate employment vary in different states.

hild·like (chīld′līk′), *adj.* like or befitting a child, as in innocence, frankness, etc. **—child′like′ness,** *n.* **—Syn.** See childish.

hild·ly (chīld′lĭ), *adj.* childlike; childish.

hil·dren (chĭl′drən, -drĭn), *n.* pl. of child.

hildren of Israel, the Hebrews; Jews.

hild's play, something very easy or simple.

hil·e (chĭl′ĭ; *Sp.* chē′lĕ), *n.* a republic in SW South America, on the Pacific coast. 6,944,000 pop. (est. 1956). 286,396 sq. mi. *Cap.:* Santiago. **—Chil′e·an,** *adj., n.*

hil·e con car·ne (chĭl′ĭ kŏn kär′nĭ; *Sp.* chē′lĕ kôn kär′nĕ), a popular Mexican dish made from meat and finely chopped red pepper, served with beans. Also, **chil′i con car′ne.** [t. Sp.: chili with meat]

Chile saltpeter, sodium nitrate, NaNO₃, a crystalline compound used as a fertilizer.

hil·i (chĭl′ĭ), *n., pl.* **chilies.** the pod of species of capsicum, esp. *Capsicum frutescens.* Also, **chil′e, chilli, chili pepper.** [t. Sp.: m. *chile*, t. Mex. (Nahuatl): m. *chilli*]

hil·i·ad (kĭl′ĭ ăd′), *n.* 1. a thousand. 2. a thousand years. [t. Gk.: s. *chīliás,* der. *chīlioi* thousand]

hil·i·arch (kĭl′ĭ ärk′), *n.* the commander of a thousand men. [t. Gk.: s. *chīliárchēs*]

hil·i·asm (kĭl′ĭ ăz′əm), *n.* *Theol.* the doctrine of the reign of Christ on earth for a thousand years. [t. Gk.: s. *chīliasmós,* der. *chīliás.* See CHILIAD] **—chil·i·ast** (kĭl′ĭ ăst′), *n.* **—chil′i·as′tic,** *adj.*

hili sauce, a highly flavored sauce made of tomatoes cooked with chili, spices, and other seasonings.

Chil·koot Pass (chĭl′kōōt), a mountain pass through the Coast Range in SE Alaska, ab. 20 mi. north of Skagway, leading to the upper Yukon valley. ab. 3500 ft. high.

hill (chĭl), *n.* 1. coldness, esp. a moderate but penetrating coldness. 2. a sensation of cold, usually with shivering. 3. the cold stage of ague, etc. 4. a depressing influence or sensation. 5. a metal mold for making chilled castings. **—***adj.* 6. cold; tending to cause shivering. 7. shivering with cold. 8. depressing or discouraging. 9. not warm or hearty: *a chill reception.* **—***v.i.* 10. to become cold. 11. to be seized with a chill. 12. *Metall.* to become hard, esp. on the surface, by sudden cooling, as a metal mold. **—***v.t.* 13. to affect with cold; make chilly. 14. to make cool or freeze: *to chill wines.* 15. to depress; discourage: *chill his hopes.* 16. *Metall.* to harden (cast iron or steel) on the surface by casting in a metal mold. [ME *chile*, OE *ciele, cile* coolness; akin to COOL, COLD] **—chill′er,** *n.* **—chill′ing·ly,** *adv.* **—chill′ness,** *n.* **—Syn.** 6, 13. See cold.

chil·li (chĭl′ĭ), *n., pl.* **-lies.** chili.

Chil·li·coth·e (chĭl′ə kŏth′ĭ), *n.* a city in S Ohio. 24,957 (1960).

Chil·lon (shə lŏn′, shĭl′ən; *Fr.* shē yôN′), *n.* an ancient castle in W Switzerland, at the E end of Lake Geneva.

chil·ly (chĭl′ĭ), *adj.* **-lier, -liest,** *adv.* **—***adj.* 1. producing a sensation of cold; causing shivering. 2. feeling cold; sensitive to cold. 3. without warmth of feeling: *a chilly reception.* **—***adv.* 4. in a chill manner. **—chil′li·ly,** *adv.* **—chil′li·ness,** *n.* **—Syn.** 1. See cold.

chilo-, a word element meaning "lip," "labial." [t. Gk.: m. *cheilo-,* comb. form of *cheilos* lip]

chi·lo·plas·ty (kī′lə plăs′tĭ), *n.* plastic surgery of the lip.

chi·lo·pod (kī′lə pŏd′), *n.* a centipede.

Chil·tern hundreds (chĭl′tərn), *Brit.* an office held under the crown, for which members of Parliament apply, by a legal fiction, when they wish to resign.

chi·mae·ra (kī mĭr′ə, kĭ-), *n.* 1. any of the fishes of the family *Chimaeridae.* The male has a spiny clasping organ over the mouth. 2. any similar fish of the group *Holocephali,* which includes this family. 3. chimera. [t. L. See CHIMERA]

chim·ar (chĭm′ər), *n.* chimere.

chimb (chĭm), *n.* chime².

Chim·bo·ra·zo (chĭm′bə rä′zō, -rä′-; *Sp.* chĕm′bô rä′sô), *n.* a volcanic mountain in central Ecuador, in the Andes. 20,702 ft.

chime¹ (chīm), *n., v.,* **chimed, chiming. —***n.* 1. an arrangement for striking a bell or bells so as to produce a musical sound: *a door chime.* 2. a set of vertical metal tubes struck with a hammer, as used in the modern orchestra. 3. carillon (def. 1, 3). 4. (*often pl.*) carillon (def. 2). 5. harmonious sound in general; music; melody. 6. harmonious relation; accord. **—***v.i.* 7. to sound harmoniously or in chimes, as a set of bells. 8. to produce a musical sound by striking a bell, etc.; ring chimes. 9. to speak in cadence or singsong. 10. to harmonize; agree. 11. **chime in, a.** to break suddenly into a conversation, esp. to express agreement. **b.** to join in harmoniously (in music). **—***v.t.* 12. to give forth (music, etc.), as a bell or bells. 13. to strike a(bell, etc.) so as to produce musical sound. 14. to put, bring, indicate, etc., by chiming. 15. to utter or repeat in cadence or singsong. [ME *chimbe,* appar. back formation from OE *cimbal,* t. L: m.s. *cymbalum* cymbal] **—chim′er,** *n.*

chime² (chīm), *n.* the edge or brim of a cask or the like, formed by the ends of the staves beyond the head or bottom. Also, **chimb, chine.** [ME *chimb*(*e*), OE *cimb* (in compounds and derivatives), c. G *kimme* edge]

chi·me·ra (kī mĭr′ə, kĭ-), *n., pl.* **-ras.** 1. (*often cap.*) a mythological fire-breathing monster, commonly represented with a lion's head, a goat's body, and a serpent's tail. 2. a grotesque monster, as in decorative art. 3. a horrible or unreal creature of the imagination; a vain or idle fancy. 4. *Genetics.* an organism composed of two or more genetically distinct tissues, as **a.** an organism which is partly male and partly female. **b.** an artificially produced individual having tissues of several species. Also, **chimaera.** [t. L: m. *Chimaera,* t. Gk.: m. *Chīmaira* lit., she-goat; r. ME *chimere,* t. F]

chi·mere (chĭ mĭr′, shĭ′-), *n.* a loose upper robe, esp. of a bishop, to which the lawn sleeves are usually attached. Also, **chim·ar, chim·er** (chĭm′ər, shĭm′-). [ME *chemer*, ? t. Anglo-L: m.s. *chimēra.* See SIMAR]

chi·mer·i·cal (kī mĕr′ə kəl, -mĭr′-, kĭ-), *adj.* 1. unreal; imaginary; visionary. 2. wildly fanciful. Also, **chi·mer′ic. —chi·mer′i·cal·ly,** *adv.*

chim·ney (chĭm′nĭ), *n., pl.* **-neys.** 1. a structure, usually vertical, containing a passage or flue by which the smoke, gases, etc., of a fire or furnace are carried off and by means of which a draft is created. 2. that part of such a structure which rises above a roof. 3. *Chiefly Brit.* the smokestack or funnel of a locomotive, steamship, etc. 4. a tube, commonly of glass, surrounding the flame of a lamp to promote combustion and keep the flame steady. 5. anything resembling a chimney, such as the vent of a volcano. 6. *Now Dial.* fireplace. [ME *chimenee,* t. OF, g. LL *camīnāta,* der. L *camīnus* furnace, t. Gk.: m. *kámīnos*] **—chim′ney·less,** *adj.*

chimney corner, 1. the corner or side of a fireplace. 2. a place near the fire. 3. fireside.

chimney piece, 1. *Chiefly Brit.* mantelpiece. 2. *Obs.* a decoration over a fireplace.

chimney pot, *Brit.* a cylindrical or other pipe, as of earthenware or sheet metal, fitted on the top of a chimney to increase the draft and prevent smoking.

chimney swallow, 1. *Brit.* barn swallow. 2. *U.S.* See **swallow** (def. 2).

ct, āble, dâre, ärt; ĕbb, ēqual; ĭf, īce; hŏt, ōver, ôrder, oil, bŏŏk, ōoze, out; ŭp, ūse, ûrge; ə = a in alone; h, chief; g, give; ng, ring; sh, shoe; th, thin; ŧh, that; zh, vision. See the full key on inside cover.

chimney sweep, one whose business it is to clean out chimneys. Also, **chimney sweeper.**

chimney swift, an American swift, *Chaetura pelagica*, which often builds its nest in a disused chimney.

chim·pan·zee (chĭm/păn zē′, chĭm păn/zĭ), *n.* a highly intelligent anthropoid ape, *Pan troglodytes*, of equatorial Africa, smaller, with larger ears, and more arboreal than the gorilla. [t. native language in Angola, W. Afr.]

Chimpanzee. *Pan troglodytes* (4 ft. long)

chin (chĭn), *n.*, *v.*, **chinned, chinning.** —*n.* **1.** the lower extremity of the face, below the mouth. **2.** the point of the under jaw. —*v.t.* **3.** to bring one's chin up to (a horizontal bar, from which one is hanging), by bending the elbows; bring (oneself) to this position. **4.** *Colloq.* to talk to. **5.** *Colloq.* to bring up to the chin, as a violin. —*v.i.* **6.** to chin oneself. **7.** *Colloq.* to talk. [ME; OE *cin*, c. G *kinn*]

Chin., Chinese.

chi·na (chī/nə), *n.* **1.** a vitreous, translucent ceramic ware, orig. produced in China. **2.** any porcelain ware. —*adj.* **3.** indicating the 20th event of a series, as a wedding anniversary.

Chi·na (chī/nə), *n.* **1.** a country in E Asia; under communist control since 1949. Official name: People's Republic of China. 567,000,000 pop. including 6,000,000 in Inner Mongolia and 1,275,000 in Tibet (est. 1953); ab. 4,475,000 sq. mi. *Cap.*: Peking. **2. Republic of,** official name of Nationalist China.

China aster, any variety of a species of asterlike plant, *Callistephus chinensis*.

chi·na bark (kĭ′nə, kē′nə), cinchona (def. 2). [t. Peruvian, var. of *kina*, *quina* bark. See QUININE]

chi·na·ber·ry (chī/nə bĕr′ĭ), *n.*, *pl.* **-ries. 1.** a tree, *Melia Azedarach*, native to Asia but widely planted elsewhere for its ornamental yellow fruits. **2.** a soapberry, *Sapindus marginatus*, of Mexico, the West Indies, and the southern U.S. Also, *U.S.*, **chi·na tree** (chī/nə); **chinaberry tree.**

Chi·na·man (chī/nə mən), *n.*, *pl.* **-men.** *Offensive.* a native or inhabitant of China; a Chinese.

China Sea, a W part of the Pacific, divided by Formosa Strait into the South and East China seas.

Chi·na·town (chī/nə toun′), *n.* the Chinese quarter of a city.

chi·na·ware (chī/nə wâr′), *n.* dishes, etc., of china.

chin·ca·pin (chĭng/kə pĭn), *n.* chinquapin.

chinch (chĭnch), *n.* **1.** the bedbug. **2.** chinch bug. [t. Sp.: m. *chinche*, g. L *cimex* bug]

chinch bug, a small American hemipterous insect of the genus *Blissus*, destructive to wheat, etc., esp. *B. leucopterus*.

chin·chil·la (chĭn chĭl/ə), *n.* **1.** a small South American rodent of the genus *Chinchilla*, whose valuable skin is dressed as a fur. **2.** a thick, napped, woolen fabric for coats, esp. children's coats. [t. Sp., dim. of *chinche* bug]

Chinchilla. *Chinchilla chinchilla* (Total length 17 in. tail 6 in.)

chin·cough (chĭn/kôf′, -kŏf′), *n.* whooping cough.

Chin·dwin (chĭn/dwĭn′), *n.* river in Burma. ab. 550 mi.

chine[1] (chīn), *n.* *Local, Eng.* a ravine formed in rock by the action of running water. [ME, n. use of *chine*, v., crack, OE *cīnan*, akin to OE *cinu*, *cine* chink, fissure]

chine[2] (chīn), *n.* **1.** the backbone or spine. **2.** the whole or a piece of the backbone of an animal with adjoining parts, cut for cooking. **3.** a ridge or crest, as of land. [ME *chyne*, t. OF: m. *eschine*, t. Gmc. See SHIN]

chine[3] (chīn), *n.* chimb[2].

Chi·nese (chī nēz′, -nēs′), *n.*, *pl.* **-nese,** *adj.* —*n.* **1.** the standard language of China, based on the speech of Peking; Mandarin. **2.** a group of languages of the Sino-Tibetan family including standard Chinese and most of the other languages of China. **3.** any of the Chinese languages, which vary among themselves to the point of mutual unintelligibility. **4.** a native of China. —*adj.* **5.** of China, its inhabitants, or their language.

Chinese Empire, China under the rule of various imperial dynasties, usually including China proper, Manchuria, Mongolia, Sinkiang, and Tibet: replaced by a republic, Jan., 1912.

Chinese lantern, a collapsible lantern of thin, colored paper, often used for decorative lighting.

Chinese puzzle, 1. a very complicated puzzle. **2.** anything very complicated.

Chinese red, scarlet; orange red; red chrome.

Chinese Wall. See Great Wall of China.

Chinese white, a pigment made from barium sulfate, largely used in water colors alone and for giving opacity to other colors.

Chinese windlass, *Mach.* a differential windlass.

Chinese wood oil, tung oil.

Ch'ing (chĭng), *n.* the last imperial dynasty in China, 1644–1911, founded by the Manchus.

Ching·hai (chĭng/hī′), *n.* a province in W China. ab. 1,676,534 pop. (1953); 269,187 sq. mi. *Cap.*: Sining. Also, **Tsinghai, Koko Nor.**

chink[1] (chĭngk), *n.* **1.** a crack, cleft, or fissure. **2.** a narrow opening. —*v.t.* **3.** to fill up chinks in. [appar. f. OE *cinu*, *cine* crack, fissure + -*k*, suffix. See -OCK]

chink[2] (chĭngk), *v.t.*, *v.i.* **1.** to make, or cause to make, a short, sharp, ringing sound, as of coins or glasses striking together. —*n.* **2.** a chinking sound. **3.** *Slang.* coin or ready cash. [imit.]

Chink (chĭngk), *n.* *U.S.* (contemptuous) a Chinese.

chin·ka·pin (chĭng/kə pĭn), *n.* chinquapin.

Chin·kiang (chĭn/kyăng′), *n.* a city in E China: a port on the Yangtze. 179,000 (est. 1950).

chi·no (chē/nō), *n.* a tough, twilled cotton cloth used for uniforms, sports clothes, etc.

Chino-, a combining form meaning "Chinese."

Chi·nook (chĭ nook′, -nook′), *n.*, *pl.* **-nook, -nooks. 1. Lower Chinook,** (*pl.*) a North American Indian tribe living on the north side of the Columbia river 15 miles upstream from its mouth. **2. Upper Chinook,** (*pl.*) several extinct tribes (Cascades, Multnomah, Wasco, Wishram, Clackamas) speaking mutually intelligible dialects on the lower Columbia river, east of Lower Chinook. **3.** a member of any of these groups. **4.** a North American Indian linguistic family comprising two languages, **Lower Chinook** and **Upper Chinook,** and assigned by some linguists to the Penutian linguistic family. **5.** (*l.c.*) a warm, dry wind which blows at intervals down the eastern slopes of the Rocky Mountains. **6.** (*l.c.*) a warm, moist southwest wind on the coast of Washington and Oregon (**wet chinook**). **7.** chinook salmon. [m. *Tsinúk* (Chehalis name)]

Chi·nook·an (chĭ nook/kən, -nook/ən), *n.* a family of American Indian languages, of the Penutian linguistic phylum, including Chinook.

Chinook jargon, a lingua franca composed of words from Chinook and other Indian languages and from English and French. It was formerly widely used among traders and Indians in the Columbia river country.

chinook salmon, a variety of salmon, *Oncorhynchus tshawytscha*, largest of the Pacific salmon, and valued as a food fish; king salmon; quinnat salmon.

chin·qua·pin (chĭng/kə pĭn), *n.* **1.** the dwarf chestnut, *Castanea pumila*, a shrub or small tree of the U. S., bearing a small, edible nut, solitary in the bur. **2.** a fagaceous tree of the Pacific coast, *Castanopsis chrysophylla*. **3.** the nut of either of these trees. Also, **chincapin, chinkapin.** [t. N Amer. Ind. (Algonquian); cf. Delaware *chinkwa* large, *min* fruit, seed]

chintz (chĭnts), *n.* **1.** a printed cotton fabric, glazed or unglazed, used esp. for draperies. **2.** (*orig.*) painted or stained calico from India. [var. of *chints*, pl. of *chint*, t. Hind.: m. *chīnt*]

Chi·os (kī/ŏs; *Gk.* hē/ŏs), *n.* **1.** a Greek island in the Aegean, near the W coast of Turkey. 66,823 pop. (1951); 322 sq. mi. **2.** the capital of this island: a seaport. 24,216 (1951). Greek, **Khíos.**

chip[1] (chĭp), *n.*, *v.*, **chipped, chipping.** —*n.* **1.** a small piece, as of wood, separated by chopping, cutting, or breaking. **2.** a very thin slice or piece of food, candy, etc.: *potato chips, chocolate chips.* **3.** (*pl.*) *Brit.* French fried potatoes. **4.** a mark made by chipping. **5.** *Games.* a counter, as of ivory or bone, used in certain card games, etc. **6.** *Colloq.* a small (cut) piece of diamond, etc. **7.** anything trivial or worthless, or dried up or without flavor. **8.** a piece of dried dung. **9.** wood, straw, etc., in thin strips for weaving into hats, baskets, etc. **10.** *Golf.* chip shot. [cf. OE *cipp* log] —*v.t.* **11.** to hew or cut with an ax, chisel, etc. **12.** to cut or break off (bits or fragments). **13.** to disfigure by breaking off fragments. **14.** to shape or produce by cutting away pieces. **15.** *Colloq.* to contribute, as to a fund (often fol. by *in*). **16.** *Games.* to bet by means of chips, as in poker. —*v.i.* **17.** to break off in small pieces. **18. chip in, a.** to contribute money, help, etc. **b.** to interrupt. **19.** *Games.* to bet a chip or chips, as in poker. **20.** *Golf.* to make a chip shot. [ME *chippen*, OE *cippian.* Cf. MLG, MD *kippen* chip eggs, hatch]

chip[2] (chĭp), *v.*, **chipped, chipping,** *n.* —*v.i.* **1.** to utter a short chirping or squeaking sound. —*n.* **2.** a short chirping or squeaking cry. [imit.]

chip[3] (chĭp), *n.* *Wrestling.* a tricky or special method by which an opponent can be thrown. [der. *chip*, v., trip. Cf. Icel. *kippa* scratch, pull]

chip log, See log (def. 2b).

chip·munk (chĭp/mŭngk), *n.* any of various small striped terrestrial squirrels of the American genus *Tamias*, and the Asiatic and American genus *Eutamias*, esp. *T. striatus* of eastern North America. [t. N Amer. Ind. (Ojibwa); m. *acitamo* squirrel]

Chipmunk. *Tamias striatus* (Total length 9 to 10 in.)

chipped beef, *U.S.* very thin slices of smoked beef.

Chip·pen·dale (chĭp/ən dāl′), *n.* **1. Thomas,** 1718?–1779, British cabinetmaker and furniture designer. —*adj.* **2.** of, or in the style of, Thomas Chippendale.

chip·per[1] (chĭp/ər), *adj.* *U.S. Colloq.* lively; cheerful. [cf. Northern E *kipper* frisky]

---

hip·per² (chĭp'ər), *v.i.* **1.** to chirp or twitter. **2.** to chatter or babble. [f. CHIP² + -ER⁶]

hip·per³ (chĭp'ər), *n.* one who or that which chips or cuts. [f. CHIP¹ + -ER¹]

Chip·pe·wa (chĭp'ə wä', -wȧ', -wə), *n.* **1.** an Ojibwa Indian. **2.** the Ojibwa language.

Chip·pe·way (chĭp'ə wā'), *n.* Chippewa. —**Chip'pe·way'an,** *n.*

hip·ping sparrow (chĭp'ĭng), any of several small North American sparrows of the genus *Spizella,* as *S. passerina,* commonly found about houses.

hip·py (chĭp'ĭ), *n., pl.* **-pies.** the chipping sparrow.

hip shot, *Golf.* a short shot using a wrist motion, made in approaching the green.

hi·ri·co (kē'rē kō), *n.* Giorgio de (jôr'jō dā), born 1888, Italian painter.

hirk (chûrk), *U.S. Colloq.* —*v.i.* **1.** to cheer (fol. by *up*). —*adj.* **2.** cheerful. [ME *chirken,* OE *circian* roar]

hirm (chûrm), *v.i.* **1.** to chirp, as a bird; sing; warble. —*n.* **2.** the chirping of birds. [ME; OE *cierm*]

hiro-, a word element meaning "hand," as in *chiropractic.* [t. Gk.: m. *cheiro-,* comb. form of *cheir*]

hi·rog·ra·phy (kī rŏg'rə fĭ), *n.* handwriting. —**chirog'ra·pher,** *n.* —**chi·ro·graph·ic** (kī'rə grăf'ĭk), **chi'·ro·graph'i·cal,** *adj.*

hi·ro·man·cy (kī'rə măn'sĭ), *n.* the art of telling one's fortune by the appearance of the hand; palmistry. —**chi'ro·man'cer,** *n.*

Chi·ron (kī'rŏn), *n. Gk. Myth.* a wise and beneficent centaur, teacher of Achilles, Asclepius, and others.

hi·rop·o·dy (kī rŏp'ə dĭ, kī-), *n.* the treatment of minor foot ailments, such as corns, bunions, etc. [f. CHIRO- + m.s. Gk. *-podia,* der. *poús* foot] —**chirop'o·dist,** *n.*

hi·ro·prac·tic (kī'rə prăk'tĭk), *n.* **1.** a therapeutic system based upon the premise that disease is caused by interference with nerve function, the method being to restore normal condition by adjusting the segments of the spinal column. **2.** a chiropractor. [f. CHIRO- + m.s. Gk. *praktik.s* practical]

hi·ro·prac·tor (kī'rə prăk'tər), *n.* one who practices chiropractic.

hi·rop·ter (kī rŏp'tər), *n.* any of the *Chiroptera,* the order of mammals that comprises the bats. [t. NL: s. *chiroptera,* pl., f. *chiro-* CHIRO- + Gk. *pterá* wings]

hi·rop·ter·an (kī rŏp'tər ən), *n.* **1.** chiropter. —*adj.* **2.** of or pertaining to a chiropter.

hirp (chûrp), *v.i.* **1.** to make a short, sharp sound, as small birds and certain insects. **2.** to make any similar sound. —*v.t.* **3.** to sound or utter in a chirping manner. —*n.* **4.** a chirping sound. [? var. of CHIRK] —**chirp'er,** *n.*

hirp·y (chûr'pĭ), *adj. Colloq.* cheerful; lively; gay.

hirr (chûr), *v.i.* **1.** to make a shrill trilling sound, as a grasshopper. **2.** to make a similar sound. —*n.* **3.** the sound of chirring. Also, **chirre, churr.** [appar. back formation from CHIRRUP]

hir·rup (chĭr'əp, chûr'-), *v.,* **-ruped, -ruping,** *n.* —*v.i.* **1.** to chirp. **2.** to make a chirping sound, as to a cage bird or a horse. —*v.t.* **3.** to utter with chirps. **4.** to make a chirping sound to. —*n.* **5.** act or sound of chirruping. [var. of CHIRP] —**chir'rup·er,** *n.*

hir·rup·y (chĭr'əp ĭ, chûr'-), *adj.* chirpy.

hi·rur·geon (kī rûr'jən), *n. Archaic.* a surgeon. [b. L *chīrūrgus* surgeon (t. Gk.: m. *cheirourgós*) and SURGEON; r. ME *cirurgien,* t. OF]

hi·rur·ger·y (kī rûr'jə rĭ), *n. Archaic.* surgery. —**chi·rur'gic,** **chi·rur'gi·cal,** *adj.*

his·el (chĭz'əl), *v.,* **-eled, -eling** or (*esp. Brit.*) **-elled, -elling.** —*n.* **1.** a tool, as of steel, with a cutting edge at the extremity, usually transverse to the axis, for cutting or shaping wood, stone, etc. —*v.t.* **2.** to cut, shape, etc., with a chisel. **3.** *Now U.S. Slang.* **a.** to cheat; swindle. **b.** to get by cheating or trickery. —*v.i.* **4.** to work with a chisel. **5.** *U.S. Slang.* to use trickery; cheat. [ME, t. ONF, ult. der. L *caesus,* pp., cut] —**chis'el·er;** *esp. Brit.,* **chis'el·ler,** *n.*

chis·eled (chĭz'əld), *adj.* **1.** cut, shaped, etc., with a chisel. **2.** clear-cut. Also, *esp. Brit.,* **chis'elled.**

Chi·shi·ma (chē'shē mä'), *n.* Japanese name for the Kurile Islands.

Chi·și·nă·u (kē'shē nŭ'ŏŏ), *n.* Rumanian name of Kishinev.

chi-square test (kī'skwâr'), *Statistics.* a test devised by Karl Pearson for testing the mathematical goodness of fit of a frequency curve to an observed frequency distribution. The test has a wide variety of applications.

chit¹ (chĭt), *n.* **1.** a voucher of money owed for food, drink, etc. **2.** *Chiefly Brit.* a note; a short memorandum. [short for *chitty,* t. Hind.: m. *chitthī*]

chit² (chĭt), *n.* a young child, esp. a pert girl. [? akin to KITTEN; assoc. with obs. *chit* sprout]

Chi·ta (chĭ tä'), *n.* a city in the SE Soviet Union in Asia, E of Lake Baikal. 162,000 (est. 1956).

chit·chat (chĭt'chăt'), *n.* **1.** light conversation; small talk. **2.** gossip. [varied redupl. of CHAT]

chi·tin (kī'tĭn), *n.* a characteristic horny organic component of the cuticula of arthropods. [t. F: m. *chitine,* der. Gk. *chitōn* tunic] —**chi'tin·ous,** *adj.*

chi·ton (kī'tən, -tŏn), *n.* **1.** *Gk. Antiq.* a garment for both sexes, usually worn next to the skin. **2.** any of a group of sluggish, limpetlike mollusks which adhere to rocks. [t. Gk.]

Chit·ta·gong (chĭt'ə gŏng'), *n.* a seaport in East Pakistan, near the Bay of Bengal. 145,777 (1951).

chit·ter·ling (chĭt'ər lĭng), *n.* **1.** (*usually pl.*) a part of the small intestine of swine, etc., esp. as cooked for food. **2.** *Obs.* a frill or ruff. [cf. G *kutteln* entrails]

chiv·al·ric (shĭv'əl rĭk, shĭ văl'rĭk), *adj.* **1.** pertaining to chivalry. **2.** chivalrous.

chiv·al·rous (shĭv'əl rəs), *adj.* **1.** having the high qualities characteristic of chivalry, such as courage, courtesy, generosity, loyalty, etc. **2.** chivalric. [ME, t. OF: m. *chevalereus,* der. *chevalier* CHEVALIER] —**chiv'al·rous·ly,** *adv.* —**chiv'al·rous·ness,** *n.*

chiv·al·ry (shĭv'əl rĭ), *n.* **1.** the ideal qualifications of a knight, such as courtesy, generosity, valor, dexterity in arms, etc. **2.** the rules and customs of medieval knighthood. **3.** the medieval system or institution of knighthood. **4.** a group of knights. **5.** gallant warriors or gentlemen. **6.** *Obs.* the position or rank of a knight. [ME, t. OF: m. *chevalerie,* der. *chevalier* CHEVALIER]

chive (chīv), *n.* a small bulbous plant, *Allium Schoenoprasum,* related to the leek and onion, with long, slender leaves which are used as a seasoning in cookery. Also, **chive garlic.** [ME, t. ONF, g. L *caepa* onion]

chiv·vy (chĭv'ĭ), *v.,* **-vied, -vying,** *n., pl.* **-vies.** *Brit.* —*v.t.* **1.** to chase; run after. **2.** to harass; nag; torment. —*v.i.* **3.** to race; scamper. —*n.* **4.** a hunting cry. **5.** a hunt, chase, or pursuit. **6.** the game of prisoners' base. Also, **chevy, chiv'y.** [? short for *chevy chase*]

Ch.J., Chief Justice.

Chka·lov (chkä'lŏf), *n.* a city in the E Soviet Union in Europe. 226,000 (est. 1956). Also, **Orenburg.**

chlam·y·date (klăm'ə dāt'), *adj. Zool.* having a mantle or pallium, as a mollusk. [f. s. Gk. *chlamýs* mantle + -ATE¹]

chla·myd·e·ous (klə mĭd'ĭ əs), *adj. Bot.* pertaining to or having a floral envelope. [f. s. NL *chlamydeae,* pl., (der. Gk. *chlamýs* mantle) + -OUS]

chla·mys (klā'mĭs, klăm'ĭs), *n., pl.* **chlamyses** (klā'mĭs ĭz, klăm'ĭs-), **chlamydes** (klăm'ə dēz'). *Gk. Antiq.* a short mantle or cloak worn by men. [t. L, t. Gk.]

Chlod·wig (klŏt'vĭкн), *n.* German name for **Clovis I.**

Chlo·e (klō'ĭ), *n.* (in pastoral and other literature) a name for a maiden, esp. one beloved. Also, **Chlo'ë.**

chlor-¹, a word element meaning "green," as in *chlorine.* Also, **chloro-¹.** [t. Gk., comb. form of *chlōrós*]

chlor-², a combining form denoting "chlorine," as in *chloral.* Also, **chloro-².**

chlo·ral (klōr'əl), *n. Chem., Pharm.* **1.** a colorless, mobile liquid, CCl_3CHO, first prepared from chlorine and alcohol and used as a hypnotic. **2.** a white, crystalline substance, $CCl_3CH(OH)_2$ (**chloral hydrate**), formed by combining liquid chloral with water, and used as a hypnotic. [f. CHLOR-² + AL(COHOL)]

chlo·ra·mine (klōr'ə mēn'), *n. Chem.* an unstable, colorless liquid, NH_2Cl, with a pungent odor, derived from ammonia.

chlo·rate (klōr'āt, -ĭt), *n. Chem.* a salt of chloric acid.

chlo·ren·chy·ma (klə rĕng'kə mə), *n. Bot.* parenchyma tissue containing chlorophyll.

chlo·ric (klōr'ĭk), *adj. Chem.* of or containing chlorine in the pentavalent state.

chloric acid, *Chem.* an acid, $HClO_3$, which exists only in solution and as salts. [f. CHLOR-² + -IC]

chlo·ride (klōr'īd, -ĭd), *n.* **1.** a compound usually of two elements only, one of which is chlorine. **2.** a salt of hydrochloric acid.

chloride of lime, *Chem., etc.* a white powder used in bleaching and disinfecting, made by treating slaked lime with chlorine, and regarded (when dry) as calcium oxychloride, $CaOCl_2$.

chlo·rin·ate (klōr'ə nāt'), *v.t.,* **-ated, -ating. 1.** *Chem.* to combine or treat with chlorine. **2.** to disinfect (water) by means of chlorine. **3.** *Metall.* to treat (a gold ore) with chlorine gas in order that the gold may be removed as a soluble chloride. —**chlo'rin·a'tion,** —**chlo'rin·a'tor,** *n.*

chlo·rine (klōr'ēn, -ĭn), *n. Chem.* a greenish-yellow gaseous element (occurring combined in common salt, etc.), incombustible, and highly irritating to the organs of respiration. It is used as a powerful bleaching agent and in various industrial processes. Symbol: Cl; at. wt.: 35.46; at. no.: 17. Also, **chlo·rin** (klōr'ĭn). [f. CHLOR-² + -INE²]

chlo·rite¹ (klōr'īt), *n.* a group of minerals, hydrous silicates of aluminum, ferrous iron, and magnesium, occurring in green platelike crystals or scales. [t. Gk.: m.s. *chlōrítis* kind of green stone]

chlo·rite² (klōr'īt), *n. Chem.* a salt of chlorous acid, as *potassium chlorite,* $KClO$. [f. CHLOR-² + -ITE¹]

chloro-¹, var. of chlor-¹, used before consonants, as in *chlorophyll.*

chloro-², var. of chlor-², used before consonants, as in *chloroform.*

chlo·ro·a·ce·tic acid (klōr'ō ə sē'tĭk, -ə sĕt'ĭk), *Chem., Pharm., etc.* a colorless, crystalline, deliquescent compound, $CH_2ClCOOH$, used as a corn and wart remover and in the manufacture of dyes.

chlo·ro·form (klōr'ə fôrm'), *n.* **1.** *Chem., Pharm., etc.* a colorless volatile liquid, $CHCl_3$, used as an anesthetic and solvent. —*v.t.* **2.** to administer chloroform to. **3.** to put chloroform on (a cloth, etc.). [f. CHLORO-² + FORM(YL)]

ĭct, ā́ble, dâre, ärt; ĕbb, ḗqual; ĭf, īce; hŏt, ṓver, ôrder, oil, bŏŏk, ōōze, out; ŭp, ūse, ûrge; ə = a in alone; ch, chief; g, give; ng, ring; sh, shoe; th, thin; tͪh, that; zh, vision. See the full key on inside cover.

chlo·ro·hy·drin (klôr′ə·hī′drĭn), *n. Chem.* any of a class of organic compounds containing a chlorine atom and a hydroxyl group, usually on adjacent carbon atoms.

chlo·ro·my·ce·tin (klôr′ə·mī·sē′tən), *n.* a recently developed antibiotic, the first to be synthesized, similar to penicillin, especially effective in the treatment of virus and rickettsial diseases such as Rocky Mountain spotted fever, undulant fever, typhoid fever, and typhus.

chlo·ro·phyll (klôr′ə·fĭl), *n. Bot., Biochem.* the green coloring substance of leaves and plants, having two forms: bluish-black **chlorophyll a,** $C_{55}H_{72}MgN_4O_5$, and yellowish-green **chlorophyll b,** $C_{55}H_{70}MgN_4O_6$. It is associated with the production of carbohydrates by photosynthesis in plants and is used as a dye for cosmetics and oils. Also, **chlo′ro·phyl.** [f. CHLORO-[1] + -PHYLL]

chlo·ro·phyl·lous (klôr′ə·fĭl′əs), *adj.* of or containing chlorophyll. Also, **chlo·ro·phyl·lose** (klôr′ə·fĭl′ōs).

chlo·ro·pic·rin (klôr′ō·pĭk′rĭn, -pĭ/krĭn), *n. Chem., etc.* a colorless liquid, CCl_3NO_2, used as an insecticide and as a chemical agent in warfare. Also, **chlorpicrin.** [f. CHLORO-[1] + PICR(IC) + -IN[2]]

chlo·ro·plast (klôr′ə·plăst), *n. Bot.* a plastid containing chlorophyll. [f. CHLORO-[1] + -PLAST]

chlo·ro·prene (klôr′ə·prēn), *n.* a colorless fluid, $CH_2=CClCH=CH_2$, produced from acetylene and hydrogen chloride, which polymerizes readily to neoprene.

chlo·ro·sis (klō·rō′sĭs), *n.* 1. abnormal yellow color of a plant, as from lack of iron in the soil. 2. a benign type of iron-deficiency anemia in adolescent girls, marked by a pale yellow-green complexion. [t. NL; see CHLOR-[1], -OSIS]

chlo·rous (klôr′əs), *adj.* containing trivalent chlorine, as *chlorous acid,* $HClO_2$, which occurs only in solution or as its salts, the chlorites. [f. CHLOR-[2] + -OUS]

chlor·pic·rin (klôr pĭk′rĭn, -pĭ′krĭn), *n.* chloropicrin.

chm., chairman. Also, **chmn.**

Choate (chōt), *n.* 1. **Joseph Hodges,** 1832–1917, U.S. lawyer and diplomat. 2. **Rufus,** 1799–1859, U.S. lawyer, orator, and statesman.

chock (chŏk), *n.* 1. a block or wedge of wood, etc., for filling in a space, esp. for preventing movement, as of a wheel or a cask. 2. *Naut.* **a.** a metal or wooden fitting through which a mooring line, anchor cable, towline, or similar rope passes, usually on or in the rail. **b.** a shaped standard on which a boat, barrel, or other object rests. —*v.t.* 3. to furnish with or secure by a chock or chocks. 4. *Naut.* to place (a boat) upon chocks. —*adv.* 5. as close or tight as possible; quite: *chock against the edge.* [prob. t. ONF: m. *choque* log or block of wood. Cf. It. *ciocco* burning log]

chock-a-block (chŏk′ə·blŏk′), *adv.* 1. *Naut.* with the blocks drawn close together, as when a tackle is hauled to the utmost. 2. in a jammed or crowded condition.

chock-full (chŏk′fŏŏl′), *adj.* full to the utmost; crammed. Also, **chuck-full, choke-full.**

choc·o·late (chŏk′ə·lĭt, chŏk′-, chôk′lĭt, chôk′-), *n.* 1. a preparation of the seeds of cacao, roasted, husked, and ground (without removing any of the fat), often sweetened and flavored, as with vanilla. 2. a beverage or a candy made from this. 3. dark brown. —*adj.* 4. made or flavored with chocolate. 5. having the color of chocolate. [t. Sp., t. Mex.: m. *chocolatl* bitter water]

Choc·taw (chŏk′tô), *n., pl.* **-taw, -taws.** 1. (*pl.*) a large Muskhogean tribe of North American Indians, formerly living chiefly in southern Mississippi, now in Oklahoma. 2. a member of this tribe.

choice (chois), *n., adj.,* **choicer, choicest.** —*n.* 1. act of choosing; selection. 2. power of choosing; option. 3. the person or thing chosen: *this book is my choice.* 4. an abundance and variety from which to choose: *a wide choice of candidates.* 5. that which is preferred or preferable to others; the best part of anything. 6. an alternative. 7. a well-chosen supply. —*adj.* 8. worthy of being chosen; excellent; superior. 9. carefully selected: *delivered in choice words.* [ME *chois,* t. OF, der. *choisir* choose, of Gmc. orig. and akin to CHOOSE] —**choice′ly,** *adv.* —**choice′ness,** *n.*

—**Syn.** 2. CHOICE, ALTERNATIVE, OPTION, PREFERENCE all suggest the power of choosing between (two) things. CHOICE implies the opportunity to choose: *a choice of evils.* ALTERNATIVE suggests that one has a choice between only two possibilities. It is often used with a negative to mean that there is no second possibility: *to have no alternative.* OPTION emphasizes free right or privilege of choosing: *to exercise one's option.* PREFERENCE applies to a choice based on liking or partiality: *to state a preference.* 8. See **fine**[1].

choir (kwīr), *n.* 1. a company of singers, esp. an organized group employed in church service. 2. any company or band, or a division of one: *string choir.* 3. *Archit.* **a.** that part of a church used by the singers. **b.** (in a medieval cruciform church) the body of the church which extends from the crossing to the east, or altar, end. **c.** (in cathedrals, etc.) the area between the nave and the main altar. 4. *Theol.* any of the nine orders of the celestial hierarchy. —*v.i., v.t.* 5. to sing in chorus. [ME *quer,* t. OF: m. *cuer,* g. L *chorus.* See CHORUS]

choir·boy (kwīr′boi′), *n.* a boy who sings in a choir.

choir loft, a gallery in which the choir is stationed.

choir·mas·ter (kwīr′măs′tər, -mäs′tər), *n.* the leader or director of a choir.

Choi·seul (shwä·zœl′), *n.* one of the British Solomon Islands, E of New Guinea. 4500 (est. 1951); 1500 sq. mi.

choke (chōk), *v.,* **choked, choking,** *n.* —*v.t.* 1. to stop the breath of, by squeezing or obstructing the windpipe;

strangle; stifle; suffocate. 2. to stop, as the breath or utterance, by or as by strangling or stifling. 3. to check the growth, progress, or action of: *to choke off discussion.* 4. to stop by filling; obstruct; clog; congest. 5. to suppress, as a feeling or emotion. 6. to fill chock-full. 7. (in internal-combustion engines) to enrich the fuel mixture by diminishing the air supply to the carburetor, as when starting a motor. —*v.i.* 8. to suffer strangling or suffocation. 9. to be obstructed or clogged. —*n.* 10. act or sound of choking. 11. (in internal-combustion engines) the mechanism by which the air supply to a carburetor is diminished or stopped. 12. *Mach.* any such mechanism which, by blocking a passage, regulates the flow of air, etc. 13. *Elect.* a choke coil. 14. a narrowed part, as in a chokebore. [ME *chok(n), cheke(n),* aphetic variants of ME *achoke(n), acheke(n),* OE *acēocian*]

choke·ber·ry (chōk′bĕr′Y), *n., pl.* **-ries.** 1. the berrylike fruit of shrubs of the North American rosaceous genus *Aronia,* esp. *A. arbutifolia.* 2. the plant bearing it.

choke·bore (chōk′bōr′), *n.* 1. (in a shotgun) a bore which narrows toward the muzzle to prevent shot from scattering too widely. 2. a shotgun with such a bore.

choke·cher·ry (chōk′chĕr′Y), *n., pl.* **-ries.** 1. any of several species of cherry, esp. *Prunus virginiana* of North America, which bears an astringent fruit. 2. the fruit.

choke coil, *Elect.* a coil of large inductance which allows steady currents to pass freely but chokes off or greatly weakens all rapid fluctuations, esp. such a coil as is used in electronic apparatus.

choke·damp (chōk′dămp′), *n. Mining.* mine atmosphere so low in oxygen and high in carbon dioxide as to cause choking; blackdamp.

choke-full (chōk′fŏŏl′), *adj.* chock-full.

chok·er (chō′kər), *n.* 1. one who or that which chokes. 2. *Colloq.* a necklace worn tightly around the neck. 3. *Colloq.* a neckcloth or a high collar.

chok·ing (chō′kĭng), *adj.* 1. so full of emotion one almost chokes: *to speak in a choking voice.* 2. that makes one feel as if he is being choked. —**chok′ing·ly,** *adv.*

chok·y (chō′kY), *adj.,* **chokier, chokiest.** tending to choke or suffocate one. Also, **chok′ey.**

chol-, a word element meaning "gall" or "bile." Also, **chole-, cholo-.** [t. Gk., comb. form of *cholē* bile]

chol·e·cys·tec·to·my (kŏl′ə·sĭs·tĕk′tə·mY), *n., pl.* **-mies.** *Surg.* removal of the gall bladder.

chol·e·cys·tos·to·my (kŏl′ə·sĭs·tŏs′tə·mY), *n., pl.* **-mies.** *Surg.* a draining of the gall bladder with the organ left in place, usually done to remove stones.

chol·er (kŏl′ər), *n.* 1. irascibility; anger; wrath; irritability. 2. *Old Physiol.* bile (that one of the four humors supposed when predominant to cause irascibility and anger). 3. *Obs.* biliousness. [t. LL: s. *cholera* bile, t. Gk.: name of the disease; r. ME *colere,* t. OF]

chol·er·a (kŏl′ər·ə), *n.* 1. *Pathol.* **a.** an acute disorder of the digestive tract, marked by diarrhea, vomiting, cramps, etc. (**sporadic cholera, bilious cholera, or cholera morbus**). **b.** an acute, infectious disease, due to a specific microörganism, endemic in India, etc., and epidemic generally, marked by profuse diarrhea, vomiting, cramps, etc., and often fatal (**Asiatic cholera**). 2. *Vet. Sci.* any disease characterized by violent diarrhea. See **hog cholera** and **fowl cholera.** [t. L, t. Gk.] —**chol·e·ra·ic** (kŏl′ə·rā′Yk), *adj.*

cholera in·fan·tum (Yn·făn′təm), *Pathol.* sporadic cholera in infants. [L: cholera of infants]

cholera mor·bus (môr′bəs), *Pathol.* sporadic cholera. Also, **cholera nos·tras** (nŏs′trăs). [L: cholera disease]

chol·er·ic (kŏl′ər·Yk), *adj.* 1. irascible; angry. 2. *Obs.* bilious. 3. *Obs.* causing biliousness.

cho·les·ter·ol (kə·lĕs′tə·rōl′, -rŏl′), *n. Biochem.* a fat-like substance, $C_{27}H_{45}OH$, found in bile and gallstones, and in the blood and brain, the yolk of eggs, etc. Also, **cho·les·ter·in** (kə·lĕs′tər·Yn). [f. CHOLE- + Gk. *ster(eòs)* solid + -OL[2]]

cho·lic acid (kō′lYk, kŏl′Yk), *Biochem.* a white crystalline hydroxy acid, $C_{24}H_{40}O_5$, derived from bile acids and related to the sex hormones and cholesterol. [*cholic* s. Gk.: m.s. *cholikós* of bile]

cho·line (kō′lēn, kŏl′Yn, -Yn), *n. Biochem.* a viscous ptomaine, $C_5H_{15}NO_2$, found in the lecithin of many plants and animals.

chol·la (chŏl′yä; Sp. chô′yä), *n.* any of several spiny treelike cacti of the genus *Opuntia,* esp. *O. fulgida* of the southwestern U.S. and Mexico.

cholo-, var. of chol- before consonants.

Cho·lon (shô·lôn′; Indo. chə·lōn′), *n.* part of the Saigon-Cholon urban area in Vietnam. 481,000 (est. 1953).

Cho·lu·la (chô·lōō′lä), *n.* a town in S central Mexico, near Puebla: ancient Aztec ruins.

chon·dri·o·somes (kŏn′drY·ə·sōmz′), *n. Biol.* minute structures occurring in the cytoplasm of cells. [f. Gk. *chondrío(n),* dim. of *chóndros* cartilage + -SOME(S)[3]]

chon·dro·ma (kŏn·drō′mə), *n., pl.* **-mas, -mata** (-mə·tə). *Pathol.* a cartilaginous tumor or growth. [f. s. Gk. *chóndros* cartilage + -OMA]

choose (chōōz), *v.,* **chose, chosen** or (*Obs.*) **chose, choosing.** —*v.t.* 1. to select from a number, or in preference to another or other things or persons. 2. to prefer and decide (to do something): *he chose to run for election.* 3. to want; desire. —*v.i.* 4. to make a choice. 5. **cannot choose but,** cannot do otherwise than: *he cannot choose but hear.* [ME *chose(n),* OE *cēosan;* var. of

ME *chēse(n)*, OE *cēosan*, c. G *kiesan*, Goth. *kiusan;* akin to L *gustāre* taste] **—choos′er**, *n.*
—Syn. 1. CHOOSE, SELECT, PICK, ELECT, PREFER indicate a decision that one or more possibilities are to be regarded more highly than others. CHOOSE suggests a decision on one of a number of possibilities because of its apparent superiority: *to choose a course of action.* SELECT suggests a choice made for fitness: *to select the proper golf club.* PICK, an informal word, suggests a selection on personal grounds: *to pick a winner.* The formal word ELECT suggests a kind of official action: *to elect a chairman.* PREFER, also formal, emphasizes the desire or liking for one thing more than for another or others: *to prefer coffee to tea.* **—Ant. 1.** reject.

choos·y (choo′zǐ), *adj. Colloq.* hard to please, particular, fastidious, esp. in making a choice: *choosy about food.* Also, **choos′ey.**

chop[1] (chǒp), *v.,* **chopped, chopping,** *n.* **—v.t. 1.** to cut with a quick, heavy blow or series of blows, using an ax, etc. **2.** to make by so cutting. **3.** to cut in pieces; mince. **4.** *Tennis, Cricket, etc.* to hit (a ball) with a chop stroke. **—v.i. 5.** to make a quick, heavy stroke or a series of strokes, as with an ax. **6.** to go, come, or move suddenly or violently. **—n. 7.** act of chopping. **8.** a cutting blow. **9.** *Boxing.* a short, downward cutting blow. **10.** a piece chopped off. **11.** a slice of mutton, lamb, veal, pork, etc., usually one containing a rib. **12.** a short, irregular, broken motion of waves. **13.** *Obs.* a chap; crack; cleft. [var. of CHAP[1]] **—Syn. 1.** See cut.

chop[2] (chǒp), *v.,* **chopped, chopping.** **—v.i. 1.** to turn, shift, or change suddenly, as the wind. **2.** *Obs.* to barter. **3.** *Obs.* to bandy words; argue. **—v.t. 4. chop logic,** to reason or dispute argumentatively; argue. **5.** *Now Brit. Dial.* to barter; exchange. [var. of obs. *chap* barter, ME *chapien*, OE *cēapian.* Cf. CHEAP]

chop[3] (chǒp), *n.* **1.** (*usually pl.*) a jaw. **2.** (*pl.*) the oral cavity. Also, **chap.** [? special use of CHOP[1]]

chop[4] (chǒp), *n.* **1.** (in India, China, etc.) **a.** an official stamp or seal, or a permit or clearance. **b.** a design, corresponding to a brand or trademark, stamped on goods to indicate their special identity. **2.** *Anglo-Indian Colloq.* quality. [t. Hind.: m. *chhāp* impression, stamp]

chop chop! (chǒp′ chǒp′), "bring it quickly" (common in fiction about China). [Pidgin English *chop* quick]

chop·fall·en (chǒp′fô′lən), *adj.* chapfallen.

chop·house[1] (chǒp′hous′), *n.* an eating house making a specialty of chops, steaks, etc. [f. CHOP[1] + HOUSE]

chop·house[2] (chǒp′hous′), *n.* (in China) a custom house. [f. CHOP[4] + HOUSE]

Cho·pin (shō′pǎn; *Fr.* shô′pǎn′), *n.* Frédéric François (frě dě rěk′ frän swä′), 1810?–49, Polish-French pianist and composer.

cho·pine (chō pēn′, chǒp′ǐn), *n.* a kind of shoe with a very thick sole of cork or the like, sometimes suggesting a short stilt, formerly worn esp. by women. Also, **chop·in** (chǒp′ǐn). [t. Sp., der. *chapa* bit of leather, t. F: m. *chape* CHAPE]

chop·per (chǒp′ər), *n.* **1.** one who or that which chops. **2.** a short ax with a large blade used for cutting up meat, etc.; a butcher's cleaver.

chop·ping[1] (chǒp′ǐng), *adj.* choppy (def. 1).

chop·ping[2] (chǒp′ǐng), *adj. Brit. Colloq.* large and strong; bouncing: *a chopping baby boy.*

chop·py (chǒp′ǐ), *adj.,* **-pier, -piest. 1.** (of the sea, etc.) forming short, irregular, broken waves. **2.** (of the wind) shifting or changing suddenly or irregularly; variable. [f. CHOP[2] + -Y[1]]

chop·stick (chǒp′stǐk′), *n.* one of a pair of thin sticks, as of wood or ivory, used by Chinese, etc., to raise food to the mouth. [f. Pidgin English *chop* quick + STICK[1]]

chop stroke, *Tennis, Cricket, etc.* a downward stroke made with the racket at an angle.

chop su·ey (chǒp′ soo′ǐ), *U.S.* a mixed dish served in Chinese restaurants, consisting of small pieces of meat, chicken, etc., cooked together with onions, bean sprouts, green peppers, mushrooms, or other vegetables and seasoning, in a gravy, eaten commonly with soy sauce and rice. Also, **chop′ soo′y.** [t. Chinese: mixed bits]

cho·ra·gus (kə rā′gəs, kō-), *n., pl.* **-gi** (-jī). **1.** the leader and sponsor of an ancient Greek chorus. **2.** any conductor of an entertainment or festival. [t. L, t. Gk.: m. *chorāgós, chorēgós* leader of the chorus] **—cho·rag·ic** (kə rǎj′ǐk, -rā′jǐk), *adj.*

cho·ral (*adj.* kōr′əl; *n.* kərǎl′, kō-, kōr′əl), *adj.* **1.** of a chorus or a choir. **2.** sung by or adapted for a chorus or a choir. **—n. 3.** a choral composition. **4.** a hymn tune. **5.** a simple sacred tune, having a plain melody, a strong harmony, and a stately rhythm. [t. ML: s. *chorālis*, der. L. *chorus.* See CHORUS] **—cho′ral·ly,** *adv.*

cho·rale (kərǎl′, -räl′, kō-, kōr′əl), *n.* choral.

chord[1] (kôrd), *n.* **1.** a string of a musical instrument. **2.** a feeling or emotion. **3.** *Geom.* that part of a straight line between two of its intersections with a curve. **4.** *Civ. Eng.* one of the main members which lie along the top or bottom edge of a truss framework. **5.** *Aeron.* a straight line joining the trailing and leading edges of an airfoil section. **6.** *Anat.* a cord (def. 4). [t. L: s. *chorda* cord, string, t. Gk.: m. *chordē* gut, string of a musical instrument. Cf. CORD] **—chord′al,** *adj.*

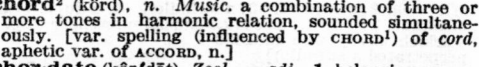

Geometrical chords: AB, AC chords subtending arcs ACB, AC

chord[2] (kôrd), *n. Music.* a combination of three or more tones in harmonic relation, sounded simultaneously. [var. spelling (influenced by CHORD[1]) of *cord*, aphetic var. of ACCORD, n.]

chor·date (kôr′dāt), *Zool.* **—adj. 1.** belonging or pertaining to the *Chordata*, the phylum that includes the true vertebrates and those animals (*protochordates*) that have a notochord, such as the lancelets and the tunicates. **—n. 2.** a chordate animal. [t. NL: m. s. *chordātus* having a chord. See CHORD[1]]

chore (chōr), *n. U.S.* **1.** a small or odd job; a piece of minor domestic work. **2.** (*pl.*) routine work around a house or farm. **3.** a hard or unpleasant task. [ME *churre*, OE *cyrr*, var. of *cierr, cerr.* See CHARE]

cho·re·a (kə rē′ə, kō-), *n.* **1.** *Pathol.* an acute disease of children characterized by irregular, involuntary, and uncontrollable movements in the face or extremities; St. Vitus's dance. **2.** *Vet. Sci.* a disease of the nervous system characterized by degenerations which cause irregular, jerky, involuntary muscular movements. It is frequent in dogs, usually as an aftereffect of canine distemper. [t. NL, t. Gk.: m. *choreia* dance]

cho·re·og·ra·pher (kōr′ǐ ǒg′rə fər), *n.* a person who creates dance compositions; a dance director.

cho·re·og·ra·phy (kōr′ǐ ǒg′rə fǐ), *n.* **1.** the art of composing ballets, etc., and arranging separate dances. **2.** the art of representing the various movements in dancing by a system of notation. **3.** the art of dancing. Also, *esp. Brit.,* **cho·reg·ra·phy** (kə rěg′rə fǐ, kō-). [f. *choreo-* (comb. form repr. Gk. *choreia* dance) + -GRAPHY] **—cho·re·o·graph·ic** (kōr′ǐ ə grǎf′ǐk), *adj.*

cho·ri·amb (kōr′ǐ ǎmb′, kôr′-), *n. Pros.* a foot of four syllables, two short between two long.

cho·ri·am·bus (kōr′ǐ ǎm′bəs, kôr′-), *n., pl.* **-bi** (-bī), **-buses.** choriamb. [t. L, t. Gk.: m. *choriambos*]

cho·ric (kōr′ǐk, kôr′-), *adj.* of or for a chorus.

cho·ri·oid (kōr′ǐ oid′), *adj., n. Anat.* choroid.

cho·ri·on (kōr′ǐ ǒn′), *n. Embryol.* the outermost of the extra embryonic membranes of land vertebrates, contributing to the placenta in the placental mammals and next to the shell (or the shell membrane) in egg-laying types. [t. NL, t. Gk.] **—cho′ri·on′ic,** *adj.*

cho·ris·ter (kōr′ǐs tər, kôr′-), *n.* **1.** a singer in a choir. **2.** a male singer in a church choir; a choirboy. **3.** a choir leader. [f. s. ML *chorista* chorister + -ER[1]; r. ME *queristre*, t. AF, der. *quer* CHOIR]

cho·rog·ra·phy (kə rǒg′rə fǐ, kō-), *n. Geog.* the systematic description and analysis of regions or of a region. [t. L: m.s. *chorographia*, t. Gk.] **—cho·rog′ra·pher,** *n.* **—cho·ro·graph·ic** (kōr′ə grǎf′ǐk), **cho·ro·graph′i·cal,** *adj.* **—cho′ro·graph′i·cal·ly,** *adv.*

cho·roid (kōr′oid), *Anat.* **—adj. 1.** like the chorion; membranous (applied esp. to a delicate, highly vascular membrane or coat of the eyeball between the sclerotic coat and the retina). **—n. 2.** the choroid coat of the eye. Also, **chorioid.** See diag. under eye. [t. Gk.: m.s. *choroeidēs*, prop. *chorioeidēs* like a membrane]

chor·tle (chôr′tal), *v.,* **-tled, -tling,** *n.* **—v.t., v.i. 1.** to chuckle or utter with glee. **—n. 2.** a gleeful chuckle. [b. CHUCKLE and SNORT; coined by Lewis Carroll in *Through the Looking-Glass* (1871)] **—chor′tler,** *n.*

cho·rus (kōr′əs), *n., pl.* **-ruses,** *v.,* **-rused, -rusing. —n. 1.** *Music.* **a.** a group of persons singing in concert. **b.** (in an opera, oratorio, etc.) such a company singing in connection with soloists or individual singers. **c.** a piece of music for singing in concert. **d.** a part of a song in which others join the principal singer or singers. **e.** any recurring refrain. **2.** simultaneous utterance in singing, speaking, etc. **3.** the sounds uttered. **4.** (in musical shows) **a.** the company of dancers and singers. **b.** the singing or song of such a company. **5.** (in ancient Greek use) **a.** a dance performed by a company of persons and accompanied with song or narration, orig. as a religious rite. **b.** a company of singers, dancers, or narrators supplementing the performance of the main actors. **6.** (in later use) **a.** a company of persons, or a single person, having a similar function in a play, esp. in the Elizabethan drama. **b.** a part of a drama rendered by such a company or person. **—v.t., v.i. 7.** to sing or speak in chorus. [t. L, t. Gk.: m. *chorós* dance, band of dancers, chorus]

chorus girl, *Theat.* a female member of the chorus (of a musical comedy or the like). **—chorus boy.**

Cho·rzów (hō′zhōōf), *n.* a city in S Poland. 150,000 (est. 1954). German, **Königshütte.**

chose[1] (chōz), *v.* pt. and obs. pp. of **choose.**

chose[2] (shōz), *n. Law.* a thing; an article of personal property. [t. F: thing, g. L *causa* CAUSE]

cho·sen (chō′zən), *v.* **1.** pp. of **choose.** **—adj. 2.** selected from a number; preferred. **3.** *Theol.* elect.

Cho·sen (chō′sěn′), *n.* Japanese name of Korea.

cho·sen people (chō′zən), the Israelites. Ex. 19, etc.

Chou (jō), *n.* a Chinese dynasty, beginning in legendary times and continuing into historical times. The traditional date for its foundation, 1122 B.C., cannot be verified; it ended c249 B.C.

Chou En-lai (jō′ ěn′lī′), born 1898, Chinese communist leader.

chough (chŭf), *n.* a European crow, *Pyrrhocorax pyrrhocorax*, of a glossy black color, with red feet and head. [ME *choghe.* Cf. OE *cēo*]

chouse (chous), *v.,* **choused, chousing,** *n. Archaic.* **—v.t. 1.** to swindle; cheat; dupe (often fol. by *of* or *out* *of*). **—n.** 2. a swindle. 3. a swindler. 4. a dupe. [var. of *chiaus*, ? t. Turk.: m. *châush* official messenger (esp. a Turkish envoy who in 1609 perpetrated a swindle)]

chow (chou), *n.* 1. one of a Chinese breed of dogs of medium size, with a thick, even coat of brown or black hair and a black tongue. 2. *U.S. Slang.* food. [short for CHOW-CHOW]

Chow
(20 in. high at the shoulder)

chow-chow (chou/chou/), *n.* 1. a Chinese mixed fruit preserve. 2. *China, India, etc.* any mixed food, or food in general, or a meal. 3. a mixed pickle in mustard (orig. East Indian). 4. chow (def. 2). [Pidgin English]

chow·der (chou/dər), *n.* *U.S.* a kind of soup or stew made of clams, fish, or vegetables, with potatoes, onions, other ingredients and seasoning. [prob. t. F: m. *chaudière* caldron, g. LL *caldãria*, der. *caldus*, *calidus* hot]

chow mein (chou/ mān/), a stew of mushrooms, celery, onions, and various Chinese vegetables, topped with shredded chicken, shrimp, etc., and served with fried noodles. [t. Chinese: fried flour]

Chr., Christian.

Chres·tien de Troyes (krĕ·tyăn/ də trwä/), c1140-c1191, French poet. Also, **Chré·tien/ de Troyes.**

chres·tom·a·thy (krĕs·tŏm/ə·thĭ), *n., pl.* **-thies.** a collection of selected passages, esp. from a foreign language. [t. Gk.: m. s. *chrēstomátheia*, lit., useful learning]

chrism (krĭz/əm), *n.* *Eccles.* 1. a consecrated oil used by certain churches in the rites of baptism, confirmation, etc. 2. consecrated oil generally. 3. a sacramental anointing; the rite of confirmation, esp. in the Greek Church. Also, **chrisom.** [learned respelling of ME *crisme*, OE *crisma*, t. L: m. *chrisma*, t. Gk.: unguent, unction] **—chris/mal,** *adj.*

chris·ma·to·ry (krĭz/mə·tōr/ĭ), *n., pl.* **-ries.** *Eccles.* a receptacle for the chrism. [t. ML: m. s. *chrismatōrium*]

chris·om (krĭz/əm), *n.* *Eccles.* 1. chrism. 2. *Obs.* a white cloth or robe formerly put on a child at baptism, and also at burial if the child died soon after baptism. [var. of CHRISM]

Christ (krīst), *n.* *Bible.* 1. the Anointed; the Messiah expected by the Jews. 2. Jesus of Nazareth, as fulfilling this expectation. [learned respelling of ME and OE *Crist*, t. L: m. s. *Christus*, t. Gk.: m. *Christós* anointed, trans. of Heb. *mãshiaḥ* anointed, messiah]

Christ·church (krīst/chûrch/), *n.* a city in New Zealand, near the E coast of South Island. 126,600 (est. 1953).

christ-cross (krīs/krŏs/, -krôs/), *n.* the figure or mark of a cross. [lit., Christ s cross]

christ-cross-row (krĭs/krŏs·rō/, -krôs/-), *n.* *Archaic* or *Dial.* the alphabet. Also, **crisscross-row.**

chris·ten (krĭs/ən), *v.t.* 1. to receive into the Christian church by baptism; baptize. 2. to give a name to at baptism. 3. to name and dedicate; give a name to; name. 4. *Colloq.* to make use of for the first time. [ME *cristene(n)*, OE *cristnian* make Christian (by baptism), der. *cristen* Christian, t. L: m. s. *Christiãnus*]

Chris·ten·dom (krĭs/ən·dəm), *n.* 1. Christians collectively. 2. the Christian world. 3. *Obs.* Christianity. [ME and OE *cristendōm*, f. *cristen* Christian + -DOM]

chris·ten·ing (krĭs/ən·ĭng, krĭs/nĭng), *n.* the ceremony of baptism, esp. as accompanied by the giving of the name to the infant baptized.

Christ·hood (krīst/hŏŏd), *n.* the condition of being the Christ.

Chris·tian (krĭs/chən), *adj.* 1. pertaining to or derived from Jesus Christ or his teachings. 2. believing in or belonging to the religion of Jesus Christ. 3. pertaining to Christianity or Christians. 4. exhibiting a spirit proper to a follower of Jesus Christ; Christlike. 5. *Colloq.* decent or respectable. 6. *Colloq.* human, or not brutal. **—n.** 7. one who believes in Jesus Christ; an adherent of Christianity. 8. one who exemplifies in his life the teachings of Christ. 9. *Colloq.* a decent or presentable person. 10. *Colloq., Dial.* a human being as distinguished from an animal. 11. the hero of Bunyan's *Pilgrim's Progress.* [t. L: s. *Christiãnus*]

Christian X, 1870–1947, king of Denmark, 1912–47.

Christian Brothers, a Roman Catholic religious order of laymen, founded in 1684 for the education of the poor (in full, **Brothers of the Christian Schools**).

Christian Era, the period since the assumed date of the birth of Jesus, adopted in Christian countries.

Chris·tia·ni·a (krĭs·tyă/nĭ·ä; *also for 2* krĭs/chĭ·ăn/yə, -tĭ-), *n.* 1. former name of Oslo. 2. Also, **Christiania turn** or **Christy.** *Skiing.* a type of turn originating in Norway in which the body is swung around from a crouching position, in order to turn the skis into a new direction or to stop quickly.

Chris·ti·an·i·ty (krĭs/chĭ·ăn/ə·tĭ), *n., pl.* **-ties.** 1. the Christian religion. 2. Christian beliefs or practices; Christian quality or character. 3. a particular Christian religious system. 4. state of being a Christian.

Chris·tian·ize (krĭs/chə·nīz/), *v., -ized, -izing.* **—v.t.** 1. to make Christian. 2. to imbue with Christian principles. **—v.i.** 3. to become Christian. **—Chris/tian·i·za/tion,** *n.* **—Chris/tian·iz/er,** *n.*

Chris·tian·like (krĭs/chən·līk/), *adj.* like or befitting a Christian.

Chris·tian·ly (krĭs/chən·lĭ), *adj.* 1. Christianlike. **—adv.** 2. in a Christian manner.

Christian name, the name given one at baptism, as distinguished from the family name; the given name.

Christian Science, a system of religious teaching, based on the Scriptures, the most notable application of which is the treatment of disease by mental and spiritual means, founded about 1866 by Mrs. Mary Baker Glover Eddy of Concord, N. H. **—Christian Scientist.**

Chris·ti·na (krĭs·tē/nə), *n.* 1626–89, queen of Sweden, 1632–54 (daughter of Gustavus Adolphus).

Christ·less (krīst/lĭs), *adj.* 1. without Christ or the spirit of Christ. 2. unchristian. **—Christ/less·ness,** *n.*

Christ·like (krīst/līk/), *adj.* like Christ; showing the spirit of Christ. **—Christ/like/ness,** *n.*

Christ·ly (krīst/lĭ), *adj.* 1. of or like Christ. 2. Christlike. **—Christ/li·ness,** *n.*

Christ·mas (krĭs/məs), *n.* 1. the annual festival of the Christian church commemorating the birth of Jesus; celebrated on December 25. 2. Dec. 25 (**Christmas Day**), now generally observed as an occasion for gifts, greetings, etc. [ME *cristmasse*, OE *Cristes mæsse* mass of Christ. See -MAS]

Christmas Carol, a story (1843) by Dickens.

Christmas Eve, the evening preceding Christmas.

Christmas Island, 1. a British island in the Indian ocean, ab. 190 mi. S of Java. 2050 pop. (est. 1955); 62 sq. mi. 2. one of the Gilbert and Ellice Islands, in the central Pacific: largest atoll in Pacific. 30 mi. across.

Christmas pudding, *Brit.* plum pudding.

Christ·mas·tide (krĭs/məs·tīd/), *n.* the season of Christmas. [f. CHRISTMAS + TIDE[1] time]

Christmas tree, an evergreen, white, or artificial tree hung with decorations at Christmas.

Chris·to et ec·cle·si·ae (krĭs/tō ĕt ĕklē/zĭ·ē/), *Latin.* for Christ and the church, or the Christian congregation.

Chris·tophe (krēs·tôf/), *n.* **Henri** (än·rē/), 1767–1820, Negro general and king of Haiti, 1811–20.

Chris·to·pher (krĭs/tə·fər), *n.* **Saint,** died A.D. 250? Christian martyr: protector of travelers.

Christ's-thorn (krīsts/thôrn/), *n.* any of certain Old World thorny shrubs or small trees supposed to have been used for Christ's crown of thorns, as the rhamnaceous plants *Zizyphus Spina-Christi* and *Paliurus.*

Chris·ty (krĭs/tĭ), *n.* Christiania (def. 2).

Chris·ty (krĭs/tĭ), *n.* **Howard Chandler,** 1873–1952, U.S. illustrator and painter.

-chroic, adjectival word element indicating color (of skin, plants, etc.). Cf. **-chroous.** [t. Gk.: m.s. *chrõikos* colored]

chrom-, 1. a word element referring to color, as in *chromic*, *chromite.* 2. *Chem.* a. a word element referring to chromium, as in *chromic, bichromate.* b. a combining form in chemistry used to distinguish a colored compound from its colorless form. Also, **chromo-.** [def. 1, see -CHROME; def. 2, see CHROMIUM]

-chrom-, a word element synonymous with **chrom-,** as in *polychromatic.*

chro·ma (krō/mə), *n.* 1. purity of a color, or its freedom from white or gray. 2. intensity of distinctive hue; saturation of a color. [t. Gk.: color]

chromat-, var. of **chromato-** before vowels.

chro·mate (krō/māt), *n.* *Chem.* a salt of chromic acid which contains the radical CrO₄⁻².

chro·mat·ic (krō·măt/ĭk), *adj.* 1. pertaining to color or colors. 2. *Music.* a. involving a modification of the normal scale by the use of accidentals. b. progressing by semitone to a tone having the same letter name, as in C to C-sharp. [t. L: s. *chrōmaticus*, t. Gk.: m. *chrōmatikós* relating to color (chiefly in musical sense)] **—chro·mat/i·cal·ly,** *adv.*

chromatic aberration, *Optics.* (of a lens system) the variation of either the focal length or the magnification, with different wave lengths of light, characterized by prismatic coloring at the edges of, and color distortion within, the optical image.

chro·mat·ics (krō·măt/ĭks), *n.* the science of colors. Also, **chro·ma·tol·o·gy** (krō/mə·tŏl/ə·jĭ). **—chro·ma·tist** (krō/mə·tĭst), *n.*

chromatic scale, *Music.* a scale progressing entirely by semitones. See illus. under **scale.**

chro·ma·tid (krō/mə·tĭd), *n.* *Biol.* one of two identical chromosomal strands into which a chromosome splits longitudinally preparatory to cell division.

chro·ma·tin (krō/mə·tĭn), *n.* *Biol.* that portion of the animal or plant cell nucleus which readily takes on stains. See diag. under **cell.** [f. CHROMAT- + -IN²]

chromato-, 1. a word element referring to color. 2. a word element meaning "chromatin." [t. Gk., comb. form of *chrõma* color]

chro·ma·to·gram (krō/mə·tə·grăm/, krō·măt/ə-), *n.* *Chem.* the column or paper strip on which some or all the constituents of a mixture have been adsorbed in chromatographic analysis. [f. CHROMATO- + -GRAM¹]

chro·ma·to·graph (krō/mə·tə·grăf/, -gräf/, krō·măt/ə-), *v.t. Chem.* to separate mixtures by chromatography. [f. CHROMATO- + -GRAPH]

chro·ma·tog·ra·phy (krō/mə·tŏg/rə·fĭ), *n.* *Chem.* the separation of mixtures into their constituents by preferential adsorption by a solid such as a column of silica (column chromatography), or a strip of filter paper (paper chromatography). [f. CHROMATO- + -GRAPHY] —chro·ma·to·graph·ic (krō/mə tə grăf/Ĭk), adj.

chro·ma·tol·y·sis (krō/mə tŏl/ə sĬs), n. Biol., Pathol. the dissolution and disintegration of chromatin.

chro·ma·to·phore (krō/mə tə fōr/), n. 1. Zool. a. a pigmented body or cell, as one of those which through contraction and expansion produce a temporary color in cuttlefishes, etc. b. a colored mass of protoplasm. 2. Bot. one of the plastids in plant cells. —chro·ma·to·phor·ic (krō/mə tə fōr/Ĭk, -fōr/Ĭk), adj.

chrome (krōm), n., v., chromed, chrom·ing. —n. 1. chromium, esp. as a source of various pigments, as chrome yellow and chrome green. 2. the dichromate of potassium or sodium. —v.t. 3. Dyeing. to subject to a bath of dichromate of potassium or sodium. [t. F, t. Gk.: m. chrōma color]

-chrome, a word element meaning "color," as in polychrome. [t. Gk.: m. chrōma]

chrome alum, Chem. 1. ammonium chromic sulfate, $Cr_2(SO_4)_3(NH_4)_2SO_4\cdot24H_2O$, a water-soluble, green, crystalline compound. 2. a dark-violet double sulfate of chromium and potassium, $KCr(SO_4)_2\cdot12H_2O$, crystallizing like common alum, and used in dyeing.

chrome green, the permanent green color made from chromic oxide, or any similar pigment made largely from chromic oxide, employed in printing textiles, etc.

chrome red, a bright-red pigment consisting of the basic chromate of lead.

chrome steel, steel of great hardness and strength, containing chromium, carbon, and other elements. Also, **chromium steel.**

chrome yellow, any of several yellow pigments in shades from lemon to deep orange, composed of chromates of lead, barium, or zinc, esp. the first.

chro·mic (krō/mĬk), adj. Chem. of or containing chromium, esp. in the trivalent state (Cr^{+3}).

chromic acid, Chem. a hypothetical acid, H_2CrO_4, which exists only in solution and forms chromates.

chro·mite (krō/mīt), n. 1. Chem. a salt of chromous acid. 2. a common mineral, iron magnesium chromite, $(Fe, Mg)Cr_2O_4$: the principal ore of chromium.

chro·mi·um (krō/mĬ əm), n. Chem. a lustrous, hard, brittle metallic element occurring in compounds, which are used for making pigments in photography to harden gelatin, as a mordant, etc. Symbol: Cr; at. wt.: 52.01; at. no.: 24; sp. gr.: 7.1. [f. Gk. chrōm(a) color + -IUM]

chromium steel, chrome steel.

chro·mo (krō/mō), n., pl. -mos. chromolithograph.

chromo-, var. of chrom-, used before consonants, as in chromogen.

chro·mo·gen (krō/mə jən), n. 1. Chem. any substance found in organic fluids which forms colored compounds when oxidized. 2. Dyeing. a colored compound which, though not a dye itself, can be converted into a dye.

chro·mo·gen·ic (krō/mə jěn/Ĭk), adj. 1. producing color. 2. pertaining to chromogen or a chromogen. 3. (of bacteria) forming some characteristic color or pigment, usually valuable in identification.

chro·mo·lith·o·graph (krō/mō lĬth/ə grăf/, -grăf/), n. a picture produced by chromolithography.

chro·mo·li·thog·ra·phy (krō/mō lĬ thŏg/rə fĬ), n. the process of lithographing in colors. —chro·mo·li·thog·ra·pher (krō/mō lĬ thŏg/rə fər), n. —chro·mo·lith·o·graph·ic, adj.

chro·mo·mere (krō/mə mĬr/), n. Biol. one of the chromatin granules of a chromosome.

chro·mo·phore (krō/mə fōr/), n. Chem. 1. any chemical group which produces color in a compound, as the azo group -N=N-. 2. the structural layout of atoms which is found in many colored organic compounds.

chro·mo·pho·to·graph (krō/mō fō/tə grăf/, -grăf/), n. a picture produced by chromophotography.

chro·mo·pho·tog·ra·phy (krō/mō fə tŏg/rə fĬ), n. color photography. —chro/mo·pho/to·graph/ic, adj.

chro·mo·plast (krō/mə plăz/əm), n. Biol. chromoplast.

chro·mo·plast (krō/mə plăst/), n. Bot. a plastid, or specialized mass of protoplasm, containing coloring matter other than chlorophyll.

chro·mo·some (krō/mə sōm/), n. Biol. each of several threadlike, rodlike, or beadlike bodies which contain the chromatin during the meiotic and the mitotic processes. [f. CHROMO- + -SOME[3]] —chro/mo·so/mal, adj.

chromosome number, Biol. the characteristic number of chromosomes for each biological species. In sex cells this number is haploid (1n); in fertilized eggs it is diploid (2n), one half coming from the egg, one half from the sperm; more numerous numbers may be triploid (3n), tetraploid (4n), polyploid (5+n).

chro·mo·sphere (krō/mə sfĬr/), n. Astron. 1. a scarlet, gaseous envelope surrounding the sun outside the photosphere, from which enormous masses of hydrogen, and other gases are erupted. 2. a gaseous envelope surrounding a star. —chro·mo·spher·ic (krō/mə sfĬr/Ĭk), adj.

chro·mous (krō/məs), adj. Chem. containing divalent chromium (Cr^{+2}).

chro·myl (krō/məl, -mĕl), adj. Chem. containing the radical CrO_2^{-2}.

chron-, a word element meaning "time," as in chronazie. Also, **chrono-.** [t. Gk., comb. form of chrónos]

Chron., Bible. Chronicles.

chron., 1. chronological. 2. chronology.

chro·nax·ie (krō/năk sĬ), n. Physiol. the minimum time that a current of twice the threshold strength (that value below which no excitation occurs) must flow in order to excite a tissue. Also, **chro/nax·y.** [f. CHRON- + m. Gk. axía value]

chron·ic (krŏn/Ĭk), adj. 1. inveterate; constant: a chronic smoker. 2. continuing a long time: chronic civil war. 3. having long had a disease, habit, or the like: a chronic invalid. 4. (of disease) long continued (opposed to acute). Also, **chron/i·cal.** [t. L: s. chronicus, t. Gk.: m. chronikós concerning time] —chron/i·cal·ly, adv. —Syn. 1. habitual, confirmed, hardened.

chron·i·cle (krŏn/ə kəl), n., v., -icled, -icling. —n. 1. a record of events in the order of time; a history. —v.t. 2. to record in or as in a chronicle. [ME, t. AF, var. of OF cronique, t. ML: m. chronica, t. Gk.: m. chronikā annals, neut. pl.] —chron/i·cler, n.

Chron·i·cles (krŏn/ə kəlz), n. two historical books of the Old Testament, following Kings.

chrono-, var. of chron-, used before consonants, as in chronogram.

chron·o·gram (krŏn/ə grăm/), n. 1. an inscription or the like in which certain letters, usually distinguished from the others, express by their values as Roman numerals a date or epoch. 2. a record made by a chronograph. —chron·o·gram·mat·ic (krŏn/ō grə măt/Ĭk), adj.

chron·o·graph (krŏn/ə grăf/, -grăf/), n. a clock-driven instrument for recording the exact instant of occurrences, or for measuring small intervals of time. —chron/o·graph/ic, adj.

chron·o·log·i·cal (krŏn/ə lŏj/ə kəl), adj. 1. arranged in the order of time: chronological tables. 2. pertaining to or in accordance with chronology: chronological character. Also, **chron·o·log/ic.** —chron·o·log/i·cal·ly, adv.

chro·nol·o·gist (krə nŏl/ə jĬst), n. one versed in chronology. Also, **chro·nol/o·ger.**

chro·nol·o·gy (krə nŏl/ə jĬ), n., pl. -gies. 1. a particular statement of the supposed or accepted order of past events. 2. the science of arranging time in periods and ascertaining the dates and historical order of past events.

chro·nom·e·ter (krə nŏm/ə tər), n. a timekeeper with special mechanism for ensuring accuracy, for use in determining longitude at sea or for any purpose where very exact measurement of time is required. —chron·o·met·ric (krŏn/ə mĕt/rĬk), chron·o·met/ri·cal, adj. —chron/o·met/ri·cal·ly, adv.

chro·nom·e·try (krə nŏm/ə trĬ), n. 1. the art of measuring time accurately. 2. the measuring of time by periods or divisions.

chron·o·scope (krŏn/ə skōp/), n. an instrument for measuring accurately very small intervals of time, as in determining the velocity of projectiles.

-chroous, -chroic. [suffix f. s. Gk. chróa surface, color + -ous]

chrys·a·lid (krĬs/ə lĬd), Entomol. —n. 1. a chrysalis. —adj. 2. of a chrysalis.

chrys·a·lis (krĬs/ə lĬs), n., pl. **chrysa·lises, chrysalides** (krĬ săl/ə dēz/), the hard-shelled pupa of a moth or butterfly; an obtected pupa. [t. L: m. chrýsallis, t. Gk.: gold-colored sheath of butterflies]

Chrysalis of swallowtail butterfly

chry·san·the·mum (krĬ săn/thə məm), n. 1. any of the perennial asteraceous plants constituting the genus Chrysanthemum, as C. Leucanthemum, the oxeye daisy. 2. any of many cultivated varieties of C. mortifolium, a native of China, and of other species of Chrysanthemum, notable for the diversity of color and size of their autumnal flowers. 3. the flower of any such plant. [t. L, t. Gk. m. chrȳsánthemon, lit., golden flower]

Chry·se·is (krĬ sē/Ĭs), n. Gk. Legend. (in the Iliad) the beautiful daughter of Chryses, a priest of Apollo. She was captured and given to Agamemnon.

chrys·el·e·phan·tine (krĬs/ĕl ə făn/tĬn, -tĬn), adj. overlaid with gold and ivory (used in describing objects of ancient Greece). [t. Gk.: m. s. chrȳselephántinos]

chrys·o·ber·yl (krĬs/ə bĕr/əl), n. a mineral, beryllium aluminate, $BeAl_2O_4$, occurring in green or yellow crystals, sometimes used as a gem. [t. L: m.s. chrȳsobēryllus, t. Gk.: m. s. chrȳsobēryllos]

chrys·o·lite (krĬs/ə lĬt/), n. olivine. [ME crisolite, t. ML: m. crisolitus, for L chrȳsolithos, t. Gk.: a bright yellow stone (prob. topaz)]

chrys·o·prase (krĬs/ə prāz/), n. a nickel-stained, apple-green chalcedony, much used in jewelry. [t. L: m. s. chrȳsoprasus, t. Gk.: m. chrȳsóprasos, lit., gold leek; r. ME crisopace, t. OF]

Chrys·os·tom (krĬs/əs təm, krĬ sŏs/təm), n. Saint John, A.D. 347?–407, archbishop of Constantinople.

chrys·o·tile (krĬs/ə tĬl), n. Mineral. a fibrous variety of serpentine.

chtho·ni·an (thō/nĬ ən), adj. Chiefly Gk. Myth. dwelling in the earth; pertaining to the deities or spirits of the underworld. [f. s. Gk. chthónios in the earth + -AN]

chub (chŭb), n., pl. **chubs,** (esp. collectively) **chub.** 1. a common fresh-water fish, Leuciscus cephalus, of Europe, with a thick fusiform body. 2. any of several allied fishes, as the Semotilus atromaculatus of America. 3. any of several unrelated American fishes, esp. the tautog of the Atlantic and the deep-water whitefishes (Coregonidae) of the Great Lakes. [ME chubbe]

chub·by (chŭb′ĭ), *adj.*, **-bier, -biest.** round and plump: *a chubby face, chubby cheeks.*

chuck[1] (chŭk), *v.t.* **1.** to pat or tap lightly, as under the chin. **2.** *Brit.* to throw with a quick motion, usually a short distance. **3.** *Brit. Slang.* to eject (fol. by *out*): *they chucked him out of the cabaret.* **4.** *Brit. Slang.* to resign from: *he's chucked his job.* **5. chuck it,** *Brit. Slang.* stop it. **—n. 6.** a light pat or tap, as under the chin. **7.** *Brit.* a toss; a short throw. [prob. imit., but cf. F *choquer* knock]

chuck[2] (chŭk), *n.* **1.** the cut of beef between the neck and the shoulder blade. **2.** a block or log used as a chock. **3.** *Mach.* a mechanical device for holding tools or work in a machine: *lathe chuck.* [var. of CHOCK]

Simple chuck[2] (def 3)

chuck[3] (chŭk), *v.i., v.t.* **1.** to cluck. **—n. 2.** a clucking sound. **3.** *Archaic.* a term of endearment. [imit.]

chuck-full (chŭk′fŏŏl′), *adj.* chock-full.

chuck·le (chŭk′əl), *v.*, **chuckled, chuckling,** *n.* **—v.i. 1.** to laugh in a soft, amused manner, usually with satisfaction. **2.** to laugh to oneself. **3.** to cluck, as a fowl. **—n. 4.** a soft, amused laugh, usually with satisfaction. **5.** *Obs.* the call of a hen to her young; a cluck. [freq. of CHUCK[3]] **—chuck′ler,** *n.* **—Syn. 4.** See **laugh.**

chuck·le·head (chŭk′əl hĕd′),*n.* *Colloq.* a blockhead. **—chuck′le·head′ed,** *adj.* **—chuck′le·head′ed·ness,** *n.*

chuck-luck (chŭk′lŭk′), *n.* *U.S.* a dice game in which the players bet on the possible combinations formed by three dice thrown from an hourglass-shaped metal container. Also, **chuck′-a-luck′.**

chuck wagon, *Western U.S.* a wagon carrying provisions, stoves, etc., for cowboys, harvest hands, etc.

chuck-will's-wid·ow (chŭk′wĭlz wĭd′ō), *n.* a goat-sucker, *Caprimulgus carolinensis,* of the southern U.S., resembling the whippoorwill but larger.

chud·dar (chŭd′ər), *n.* a kind of fine, plain-colored woolen shawl made in India. Also, **chud·dah** (chŭd′ə), **chud′der.** [t. Hind.: m. *chadar* square piece of cloth]

Chud·sko·e (chŏŏd skô′yĕ), *n.* a lake in the W Soviet Union, on the E boundary of the Estonian Republic. 93 mi. long; 356 sq. mi. Estonian, **Peipsi.** Formerly, **Peipus.**

chuff[1] (chŭf), *n.* **1.** a rustic. **2.** a boor; a churl. **3.** a miserly fellow. [orig. unknown] **—chuff′y,** *adj.* **—chuff′i·ly,** *adv.* **—chuff′i·ness,** *n.*

chuff[2] (chŭf, chŏŏf), *adj.* *Eng. Dial.* fat-cheeked; chubby. [adj. use of obs. *chuff,* n., muzzle]

chug (chŭg), *n., v.,* **chugged, chugging.** **—n. 1.** a short, dull explosive sound: *the steady chug of an engine.* **—v.i. 2.** to make this sound. **3.** to move while making this sound: *the train chugged along.* [imit.]

Chu-Kiang (chōō′jyäng′), *n.* a river in SE China, forming a large estuary below Canton. ab. 100 mi. Also, **Canton River** or **Pearl River.**

chuk·ker (chŭk′ər), *n.* *Polo.* one of the periods of play. Also, **chuk′kar.** [t. Hind.: m. *chakar*]

Chu·la Vis·ta (chōō′lə vĭs′tə), a city in SW California, near San Diego. 42,034 (1960).

chum (chŭm), *n., v.,* **chummed, chumming.** **—n. 1.** an intimate friend or companion: *boyhood chums.* **2.** a roommate, as at college. **—v.i. 3.** to associate intimately. **4.** to share the same room or rooms with another. [orig. uncert.]

chum·my (chŭm′ĭ), *adj.,* **-mier, -miest.** intimate; sociable. **—chum′mi·ly,** *adv.*

chump (chŭmp), *n.* **1.** *Colloq.* a blockhead or dolt. **2.** a short, thick piece of wood. **3.** the thick, blunt end of anything. **4.** *Slang.* the head. **—chump′ish,** *adj.*

Chung·king (chŏŏng′kĭng′; *Chin.* jōŏng′chĭng′), *n.* a city in central China, on the Yangtze: provisional capital of China, 1937–46. 1,620,000 (est. 1953).

chunk (chŭngk), *n.* **1.** a thick mass or lump of anything: *a chunk of bread.* **2.** *Colloq.* a thick-set and strong person. **3.** a strong and stoutly built horse or other animal. **4.** a substantial amount (of something). [nasalized var of CHUCK[2], n.]

chunk·y (chŭng′kĭ), *adj.,* **chunkier, chunkiest.** **1.** thick or stout; thick-set; stocky. **2.** in a chunk or chunks. **—chunk′i·ness,** *n.*

church (chûrch), *n.* **1.** an edifice for public Christian worship. **2.** public worship of God in a church; church service. **3.** the whole body of Christian believers. **4.** any division of this body professing the same creed and acknowledging the same ecclesiastical authority; a Christian denomination: *the Methodist Church.* **5.** that part of the whole Christian body, or of a particular denomination, belonging to the same city, country, nation, etc. **6.** a body of Christians worshiping in a particular building or constituting one congregation. **7.** the ecclesiastical organization or power as distinguished from the state. **8.** the clerical profession. **9.** a place of public worship of a non-Christian religion. **10.** any non-Christian religious society, organization, or congregation: *the Jewish church.* **—v.t. 11.** to conduct or bring to church, esp. for special services. **12.** to subject to church discipline. **13.** to perform a church service of thanksgiving for (a woman after childbirth). [ME *churche, chirche,* OE *cir(i)ce, cyrice* (c. G *kirche*), ult. t. Gk.: m. *kȳriakón (dōma)* Lord's (house)]

church·go·er (chûrch′gō′ər), *n.* **1.** one who goes to church, esp. habitually. **2.** *Chiefly Brit.* a member of the Established Church, in contrast to a Nonconformist. **—church′go′ing,** *n., adj.*

Church·ill (chûrch′ĭl, -əl), *n.* **1. John.** See **Marlborough,** Duke of. **2. Lord Randolph,** 1849–95, British statesman (father of Winston L. S. Churchill). **3. Winston,** 1871–1947, U. S. novelist. **4. Winston Leonard Spencer,** 1874–1965. British statesman and writer: prime minister, 1940–45 and 1951–55. **5.** a river in Canada, flowing from E Saskatchewan NE through Manitoba to Hudson Bay. ab. 1000 mi. **6.** a seaport and railway terminus on Hudson Bay at the mouth of this river.

church·less (chûrch′lĭs), *adj.* **1.** without a church. **2.** not belonging to or attending any church.

church·like (chûrch′līk′), *adj.* resembling, or appropriate to, a church: *churchlike silence.*

church·ly (chûrch′lĭ), *adj.* of or appropriate for the church or a church; ecclesiastical. [OE *ciriclíc;* f. CHURCH + -LY] **—church′li·ness,** *n.*

church·man (chûrch′mən), *n., pl.* **-men. 1.** an ecclesiastic; a clergyman. **2.** an adherent or active supporter of a church. **3.** *Brit.* a member of the Established Church. **—church′man·ly,** *adj.* **—church′man·ship′,** *n.*

Church of Christ, Scientist, (official name) Christian Science.

Church of England, the national Church continuous with English history, Catholic in faith and order, but incorporating many emphases of the Protestant Reformation and establishing independence from the papacy.

Church of Jesus Christ of Latter-day Saints, (official name) the Mormon Church.

Church of Rome, Roman Catholic Church.

church text, *Print.* Old English (def. 2).

church·ward (chûrch′wərd), *adv.* **1.** Also, **church′wards.** toward the church. **—adj. 2.** directed toward the church: *churchward summons.*

church·ward·en (chûrch′wôr′dən), *n.* **1.** *Anglican Ch.* a lay officer who looks after the secular affairs of the church, and who, in England, is the legal representative of the parish. **2.** *Prot. Episc. Ch.* a lay church officer who, with other members of the vestry, is in charge of the temporal management of the parish. **3.** *Colloq.* a clay tobacco pipe with a very long stem.

church·wom·an (chûrch′wŏŏm′ən), *n., pl.* **-women.** a female member of a church, esp. of an Anglican church.

church·yard (chûrch′yärd′), *n.* the yard or ground adjoining a church, often used as a graveyard.

churl (chûrl), *n.* **1.** a peasant; a rustic. **2.** a rude, boorish, or surly person. **3.** a niggard; miser. **4.** *Eng. Hist.* a freeman of the lowest rank. [ME; OE *ceorl* freeman of the lowest rank, c. G *kerl.* Cf. CARL]

churl·ish (chûr′lĭsh), *adj.* **1.** of a churl or churls. **2.** like a churl; boorish; rude; surly. **3.** niggardly; sordid. **4.** difficult to work or deal with, as soil. **—churl′ish·ly,** *adv.* **—churl′ish·ness,** *n.*

churn (chûrn), *n.* **1.** a vessel or machine in which cream or milk is agitated to make butter. **2.** any of various similar vessels or machines. **3.** *Brit.* a milk can. **—v.t. 4.** to stir or agitate in order to make into butter: *to churn cream.* **5.** to make by the agitation of cream: *to churn butter.* **6.** to shake or agitate with violence or continued motion. **—v.i. 7.** to operate a churn. **8.** to move in agitation, as a liquid or any loose matter: *leaves churning.* [ME *chyrne,* OE *cyrin,* c. Icel. *kirna* tub, pail] **—churn′er,** *n.*

churn·ing (chûr′nĭng), *n.* **1.** act of one that churns. **2.** the butter made at one time.

churr (chûr), *v.i., v.t.* chirr. [? var. of CHIRR]

chute[1] (shōōt), *n.* **1.** a channel, trough, tube, shaft, etc., for conveying water, grain, coal, etc., to a lower level; a shoot. **2.** a waterfall; a steep descent, as in a river; a rapid. **3.** parachute. [b. F *chute* a fall (b. OF *cheue* and OF *cheoite,* both der. OF *cheoir* fall, g. L *cadere*) and E SHOOT]

chute[2] (shōōt), *n.* a steep slope, as for tobogganing. [Frenchified spelling of d. E. *shoot, shute,* ME *shote* steep slope, akin to SHOOT *v.*]

Chu Teh (jōō′ dŭ′), born 1886, leader of Chinese communist army.

chut·ney (chŭt′nĭ), *n., pl.* **-neys.** a sauce or relish of East Indian origin compounded of both sweet and sour ingredients (fruits, herbs, etc.) with spices and other seasoning. Also, **chut′nee.** [t. Hind.: m. *chatnī*]

chy·la·ceous (kī lā′shəs), *adj.* of or resembling chyle.

chyle (kīl), *n.* a milky fluid containing emulsified fat and other products of digestion, formed from the chyme in the small intestine and conveyed by the lacteals and the thoracic duct to the veins. [t. NL: m.s. *chýlus,* t. Gk.: m.s. *chȳlós* juice, chyle] **—chy′lous,** *adj.*

chyme (kīm), *n.* the pulpy matter into which food is converted by gastric digestion. [t. L: m.s. *chȳmus,* t. Gk.: m. *chȳmós* juice] **—chy′mous,** *adj.*

chym·is·try (kĭm′ĭs trĭ), *n.* *Archaic.* chemistry. **—chym′ic,** *adj.* **—chym′ist,** *n.*

Cia., (Sp. *Compañía*) Company.

Cib·ber (sĭb′ər), *n.* **Colley** (kŏl′ĭ), 1671–1757, British actor and dramatist.

ci·bo·ri·um (sĭ bôr′ĭ əm), *n., pl.* **-boria** (-bôr′ĭ ə). **1.** a permanent canopy placed over an altar. **2.** any vessel designed to contain the consecrated bread or sacred wafers for the Eucharist. [t. ML: canopy, in L drinking cup, t. Gk.: m. *kibórion* cup, seed vessel of the Egyptian bean]

Ciborium (def. 2)

ci·ca·da (sĭ kā'də, -kä'-), *n.*, *pl.* **-das, -dae** (-dē). any insect of the family *Cicadidae*, which comprises large homopterous insects noted for the shrill sound produced by the male by means of vibrating membranes or drums on the underside of the abdomen. [t. L]

Imago of cicada.
Cicada septendecim

ci·ca·la (sĭ kä'lə; *It.* chē kä'lä), *n.*, *pl.* **-las,** *It.* **-le** (-lě). cicada. [t. It. or L]

cic·a·tri·cle (sĭk'ə trĭk'əl), *n.* *Embryol.* the small blastodisc on the yolk of an unincubated bird's egg. [t. L: m.s. *cicātrīcula* a small scar]

cic·a·trix (sĭk'ə trĭks, sĭ kā'trĭks), *n.*, *pl.* **cicatrices** (sĭk'ə trī'sēz). 1. the new tissue which forms over a wound or the like, and later contracts into the scar. 2. *Bot.* the scar left by a fallen leaf, seed, etc. Also, **cic·a·trice** (sĭk'ə trĭs). [t. L] **—cic·a·tri·cial** (sĭk'ə trĭsh'əl), *adj.* **—ci·cat·ri·cose** (sĭ kăt'rə kōs', sĭk'ə trī'-), *adj.*

cic·a·trize (sĭk'ə trīz'), *v.*, **-trized, -trizing.** **—v.t.** 1. to heal by inducing the formation of a cicatrix. **—v.i.** 2. to become healed by the formation of a cicatrix. **—cic'a·tri·za'tion,** *n.* **—cic'a·triz'er,** *n.*

cic·e·ly (sĭs'ə lĭ), *n.*, *pl.* **-lies.** a plant of the parsley family, *Myrrhis odorata* (the sweet cicely of England), grown for its pleasing odor and sometimes used as a potherb. [? t. L: m.s. *seselis*, t. Gk.: kind of plant]

Cic·e·ro (sĭs'ə rō'), *n.* 1. **Marcus Tullius,** 106–43 B.C., Roman statesman, orator, and writer. Also, **Tully.** 2. a city in NE Illinois, near Chicago. 69,130 (1960). **—Cic·e·ro·ni·an** (sĭs'ə rō'nĭ ən), *adj.*

cic·e·ro·ne (sĭs'ə rō'nĭ, chĭch'ə-; *It.* chē'chĕ rō'ně), *n.*, *pl.* **-nes** (-nĭz), *It.* **-ni** (-nē). a guide who shows and explains the antiquities, curiosities, etc., of a place. [t. It., t. L: abl. sing. of *Cicero* Cicero (def. 1)]

cich·lid (sĭk'lĭd), *n.* any of the *Cichlidae*, a family of spiny-rayed, fresh-water fishes of South America, Africa, and southern Asia, superficially resembling the American sunfishes: often kept in home aquariums. [t. NL: s. *Cichlidae*, pl., der. Gk. *kíchlē* kind of sea fish] **—cich·loid** (sĭk'loid), *n.*, *adj.*

ci·cho·ri·a·ceous (sĭ kōr'ĭ ā'shəs), *adj.* belonging to the *Cichoriaceae*, or chicory family (a composite family) of plants, as the dandelion, endive, lettuce, salsify, etc. [f. s. L *cichorium* chicory + -ACEOUS]

ci·cis·be·o (sĭ sĭs'bĭ ō'; *It.* chē'chēz bě'ō'), *n.*, *pl.* **-bei** (-bĭ ē'; *It.* -bě'ē). a professed gallant of a married woman. [t. It.]

Cid (sĭd; *Sp.* thēd), *n.* ("El Cid Campeador"; *Ruy Díaz de Bivar*) 1040?–99, Spanish soldier and hero of the wars against the Moors. [t. Sp., t. Ar.: m. *sayyid* lord]

-cidal, adjective form of -cide². [f. -CIDE² + -AL¹]

-cide¹, a word element meaning "killer," as in **matricide¹.** [t. L: m. *-cida*, der. *caedere* kill]

-cide², a word element meaning "act of killing," as in **matricide².** [t. L: m. *-cīdium*, der. *caedere* kill]

ci·der (sī'dər), *n.* the expressed juice of apples (or formerly of some other fruit), used for drinking, either before fermentation (**sweet cider**) or after fermentation (**hard cider**), or for making applejack, vinegar, etc. Also, *Brit.*, **cyder.** [ME *sidre*, t. OF, g. L *sīcera*, t. Gk.: m. *sīkera*, repr. Heb. *shēkār* strong drink]

cider press, a press for crushing apples for cider.

ci·de·vant (sē'də vän'), *adj.* French. former; late: *a ci-devant official.* [F: heretofore]

Cie., (*F Compagnie*) Company. Also, **cie.**

Cien·fue·gos (syěn fwĕ'gōs), *n.* a seaport in S Cuba. 70,833 (1953).

C.I.F., cost, insurance, and freight (included in the price quoted). Also, **c.i.f.**

ci·gar (sĭ gär'), *n.* a small, shaped roll of tobacco leaves prepared for smoking. [t. Sp.: m. *cigarro,* ? der. *cigarra* grasshopper, g. L *cicāla,* var. of *cicāda* CICADA]

cig·a·rette (sĭg'ə rĕt', sĭg'ə rĕt'), *n.* a roll of finely-cut tobacco for smoking, usually enclosed in thin paper. Also, **cig'a·ret'.** [t. F, dim. of *cigare* CIGAR]

cil·i·a (sĭl'ĭ ə), *n.pl.,* *sing.* **cilium** (sĭl'ĭ əm). 1. the eyelashes. 2. *Zool.* short hairs on the surface of protozoans or of metazoan cells accomplishing locomotion or producing a current. 3. *Bot.* minute, hairlike processes. [t. L, pl. of *cilium* eyelid, eyelash]

cil·i·ar·y (sĭl'ĭ ĕr'ĭ), *adj.* 1. not-ing or pertaining to a delicate ring of tissue in the eye from which the lens is suspended by means of fine ligaments. See diag. under **eye.** 2. pertaining to cilia.

Flower with cilia

Cil·i·a·ta (sĭl'ĭ ā'tə), *n. pl. Zool.* a class of protozoans distinguished by the cilia on part or all of the body, among the most common of microscopic animals.

cil·i·ate (sĭl'ĭ ĭt, -āt'), *n.* one of the *Ciliata.* **—cil'i·at'ed,** *adj.*

cil·ice (sĭl'ĭs), *n.* 1. a garment of haircloth; a hair shirt. 2. haircloth. [t. F, t. L: m.s. *cilicium,* t. Gk.: m. *kilíkion* coarse cloth made of (orig. Cilician) goat's hair; r. OE *cilic,* t. L (as above)]

Ci·li·cia (sĭ lĭsh'ə), *n.* an ancient country and Roman province in SE Asia Minor.

Ci·li·cian Gates (sĭ lĭsh'ən), a narrow mountain pass in SE Asia Minor, leading from Cappadocia into Cilicia. Turkish, **Gülek Bogaz.**

cil·i·o·late (sĭl'ĭ ə lĭt, -lāt'), *adj.* furnished with minute cilia.

Ci·ma·bu·e (chē'mä boo'ě), *n.* **Giovanni** (jô vän'nē), 1240?–1302?, Florentine painter: teacher of Giotto.

Cim·ar·ron (sĭm'ə rŏn', sĭm'ə rōn', -rŏn'), *n.* a river flowing from NE New Mexico E to the Arkansas river in Oklahoma. ab. 600 mi.

ci·mex (sī'mĕks), *n., pl.* **cimices** (sĭm'ə sēz'). the bedbug (of the genus *Cimex*). [t. L: bug]

Cim·me·ri·an (sĭ mĭr'ĭ ən), *adj.* 1. pertaining to or suggestive of a mythical western people said by Homer to dwell in perpetual darkness. 2. very dark; gloomy.

Ci·mon (sī'mən), *n.* 507?–449 B.C., Athenian military and naval commander, and statesman: son of Miltiades.

cinch¹ (sĭnch), *U.S.* **—n.** 1. a strong girth for a saddle or pack. 2. *Colloq.* a firm hold or tight grip. 3. *Slang.* something sure or easy. **—v.t.** 4. to gird with a cinch; gird or bind firmly. 5. *Slang.* to seize on or make sure of. [t. Sp.: m. *cincha,* g. L *cincta* girdle, der. L *cingere* gird]

cinch² (sĭnch), *n.* *Cards.* a variety of seven-up. [? t. Sp.: m. *cinco* five]

cin·cho·na (sĭn kō'nə), *n.* 1. any of the rubiaceous trees or shrubs constituting the genus *Cinchona,* as *C. calisaya,* native in the Andes, cultivated there and in Java and India for their bark, which yields quinine and other alkaloids. 2. the medicinal bark of such trees or shrubs; Peruvian bark. [t. NL, named after the Countess of *Chinchón* (1576–1639), wife of a Spanish viceroy of Peru] **—cin·chon·ic** (sĭn kŏn'ĭk), *adj.*

cin·cho·nine (sĭn'kə nēn', -nĭn), *n.* a colorless, crystalline alkaloid, $C_{19}H_{22}ON_2,$ obtained from various species of the cinchona bark, used as an antiperiodic and quinine substitute.

cin·cho·nize (sĭn'kə nīz'), *v.t.,* **-nized, -nizing.** to treat with cinchona or quinine.

Cin·cin·nat·i (sĭn'sə năt'ĭ, -năt'ə), *n.* a city in SW Ohio, on the Ohio river. 502,550 (1960).

Cin·cin·na·tus (sĭn'sə nā'təs), *n.* **Lucius Quinctius** (lōō'shəs kwĭngk'tĭ əs), 519?–439? B.C., Roman patriot. He was called from his farm to be dictator in 458 and 439 B.C. Each time he resigned his dictatorship and returned to his farm when the enemy was defeated.

cinc·ture (sĭngk'chər), *n., v.,* **-tured, -turing. —n.** 1. a belt or girdle. 2. something surrounding or encompassing like a girdle; a surrounding border. 3. act of girding or encompassing. **—v.t.** 4. to gird with or as with a cincture; encircle; encompass. [t. L: m.s. *cinctūra* girdle]

cin·der (sĭn'dər), *n.* 1. a burned-out or partially burned piece of coal, wood, etc. 2. *(pl.)* any residue of combustion; ashes. 3. *(pl.) Geol.* coarse scoriae thrown out of volcanoes. **—v.t.** 4. to reduce to cinders: *cindering flame.* [ME *cyndir, sindir,* OE *sinder* cinder, slag, c. G *sinter*] **—cin'der·y,** *adj.*

Cin·der·el·la (sĭn'də rĕl'ə), *n.* 1. heroine of a well-known fairy tale. 2. any girl, esp. one of unrecognized beauty, who is forced to be a household drudge, or who, for the time being, is despised and oppressed.

cinder track, a path covered with small cinders, used in running races.

cin·e·ma (sĭn'ə mə), *n.* 1. a motion picture. 2. the cinema, motion pictures collectively. 3. a motion-picture theater. [short for CINEMATOGRAPH] **—cin·e·mat·ic** (sĭn'ə măt'ĭk), *adj.* **—cin'e·mat'i·cal·ly,** *adv.*

Cin·e·ma·scope (sĭn'ə mə skōp'), *n.* *Trademark.* a process of motion-picture reproduction that achieves a realistic three-dimensional effect by using a single-lens camera or projector, an extra-wide curved screen, and a stereophonic arrangement of speakers.

cin·e·ma·tize (sĭn'ə mə tīz'), *v.t., v.i.,* **-tized, -tizing.** *Brit.* cinematograph (def. 3).

cin·e·mat·o·graph (sĭn'ə măt'ə grăf', -gräf'), *Brit.* **—n.** 1. a motion-picture projector. 2. a motion-picture camera. **—v.t., v.i.** 3. to take motion pictures (of). Also, **kinematograph.** [f. *cinemato-* (comb. form repr. Gk. *kínēma* motion) + -GRAPH] **—cin·e·ma·tog·ra·pher** (sĭn'ə mə tŏg'rə fər), *n.* **—cin·e·mat'o·graph'ic,** *adj.* **—cin'e·ma·tog'ra·phy,** *n.*

cin·e·ole (sĭn'ĭ ōl'), *n.* *Chem.* a colorless liquid, $C_{10}H_{18}O,$ a terpene ether found in eucalyptus and other essential oils and used in medicine; eucalyptol. Also, **cin·e·ol** (sĭn'ĭ ōl, -ŏl'). [t. NL: m. *oleum cinae* (reversed), oil of wormwood]

cin·e·rar·i·a (sĭn'ə râr'ĭ ə), *n.* any of various horticultural varieties of the asteraceous plant *Senecio cruentus* (or *Cineraria cruenta*), a native of the Canary Islands, with heart-shaped leaves and clusters of flowers with white, blue, purple, red, or variegated rays. [t. NL, prop. fem. of L *cinerārius* pertaining to ashes (with reference to the soft white down on the leaves)]

cin·e·rar·i·um (sĭn'ə râr'ĭ əm), *n., pl.* **-raria** (-râr'ĭ ə). a place for depositing the ashes of the dead after cremation. [t. L] **—cin·er·ar·y** (sĭn'ə râr'ĭ), *adj.*

cin·e·ra·tor (sĭn'ə rā'tər), *n.* an incinerator.

cin·e·re·ous (sə nĭr'ĭ əs), *adj.* 1. in the state of ashes: *cinereous bodies.* 2. resembling ashes. 3. ashen; ash-colored; grayish: *cinereous crow.* Also, **cin·er·i·tious** (sĭn'ə rĭsh'əs), *adj.* [t. L: m. *cinereus* ash-colored]

cin·gu·lum (sĭng'gyə ləm), *n., pl.* **-la** (-lə). *Anat., Zool.* a belt, zone, or girdlelike part. [t. L: girdle] **—cin·gu·late** (sĭng'gyə lĭt, -lāt'), **cin'gu·lat'ed,** *adj.*

cin·na·bar (sĭn′ə bär′), *n.* **1.** a mineral, mercuric sulfide, occurring in red crystals or masses: the principal ore of mercury. It is very heavy (*sp. gr.*: 8.1). **2.** red mercuric sulfide, used as a pigment. **3.** bright red; vermilion. [t. L: m. *cinnabaris*, t. Gk.: m. *kinnábari*; of Oriental orig.; r. ME *cynoper*, t. ML]

cin·nam·ic (sĭ năm′ĭk, sĭn′ə mĭk), *adj.* of or obtained from cinnamon.

cinnamic acid, an unsaturated acid, $C_6H_5CH\text{-}CH\text{-}CO_2H$, derived from cinnamon, balsams, etc.

cin·na·mon (sĭn′ə mən), *n.* **1.** the aromatic inner bark of any of several lauraceous trees of the genus *Cinnamomum* of the East Indies, etc., esp. Ceylon Cinnamon, *C. zeylanicum*, much used as a spice, and Saigon cinnamon, *C. loureirii*, used in medicine as a cordial and carminative. **2.** a tree yielding cinnamon. **3.** any of various allied or similar trees. **4.** cassia bark. **5.** yellowish or reddish brown. [t. LL, t. Gk.: m. *kinnamon*; r. ME *cynamome*, t. F: m. *cinnamome*. Ult. of Semitic orig.; cf. Heb. *qinnāmōn*]

cinnamon bear, the cinnamon-colored variety of the black bear of North America, *Euarctos americanus*.

cinnamon stone, a light, brown grossularite garnet.

cinque (sĭngk), *n.* the five at dice, cards, etc. [t. F; r. ME *cink*, t. OF, g. L *quinque* five]

cin·que·cen·tist (chĭng′kwə chĕn′tĭst), *n.* an Italian writer or an artist of the 16th century.

cin·que·cen·to (chĭng′kwə chĕn′tō), *n.* the 16th century, with reference to Italy, esp. to the Italian art or literature of that period. [t. It.: five hundred, short for *mille cinquecento* one thousand five hundred]

cinque·foil (sĭngk′foil′), *n.* **1.** any species of the rosaceous genus *Potentilla*, as the creeping cinquefoil (*P. reptans*) of the Old World and the silvery cinquefoil (*P. argentea*) of North America. **2.** a decorative design or feature resembling the leaf of cinquefoil, as an architectural ornament or opening of a generally circular or rounded form divided into five lobes by cusps. **3.** *Her.* a five-leafed clover, used as a bearing. [ME *synkefoile*, through OF (unrecorded), g. L *quinquefolium*, f. *quinque* five + *folium* leaf]

Cinquefoil (def. 2)

Cinque Ports (sĭngk), an association of maritime towns in SE England, in Sussex and Kent: originally (1278) numbering five (Hastings, Romney, Hythe, Dover, and Sandwich) and receiving special privileges in return for aiding in the naval defense of England.

C I O, Congress of Industrial Organizations. Also, **C.I.O.**

ci·on (sī′ən), *n.* scion (def. 2). (Cion is the usual spelling of scion in U. S. horticulture and nursery practice).

-cion, a suffix having the same function as -tion, as in *suspicion*. [t. L: s. *-cio*, f. *-c*, final vowel in verb stem, + *-io*, n. suffix. Cf. -SION, -TION]

Ci·pan·go (sĭ păng′gō), *n. Poetic.* Japan.

ci·pher (sī′fər), *n.* **1.** an arithmetical symbol (0) which denotes naught, or no quantity or magnitude. **2.** any of the Arabic numerals or figures. **3.** Arabic numerical notation collectively. **4.** something of no value or importance. **5.** a person of no influence; a nonentity. **6.** a secret method of writing, as by a specially formed code of symbols. **7.** writing done by such a method. **8.** the key to a secret method of writing. **9.** a combination of letters, as the initials of a name, in one design; a monogram. —*v.i.* **10.** to use figures or numerals arithmetically. —*v.t.* **11.** to calculate numerically; figure. **12.** to write in, or as in, cipher. Also, *cypher*. [ME *siphre*, t. ML: m. *ciphra*, t. Ar.: m. *ṣifr*, lit., empty. Cf. ZERO]

cip·o·lin (sĭp′ə lĭn), *n.* a variety of marble with alternate white and greenish zones and a laminated structure. [t. F, t. It.: m. *cipollino* (so called from its layered structure), dim. of *cipolla* onion, g. L *cēpa*]

cir., (L *circa, circiter, circum*) about. Also, **circ.**

cir·ca (sûr′kə) *prep., adv.* about (used esp. in approximate dates). *Abbr.*: ca., c. or c: *born ca. 1550*. [t. L]

Cir·cas·sia (sər kăsh′ə, -Ῐə), *n.* a region NW of the Caucasus Mountains in the S Soviet Union in Europe, bordering on the Black Sea.

Cir·cas·sian (sər kăsh′ən, -Ῐən), *n.* **1.** a native or inhabitant of Circassia. **2.** a North Caucasic language.

Cir·ce (sûr′sĭ), *n.* **1.** *Gk. Legend.* the enchantress represented by Homer as turning the companions of Odysseus into swine by a magic drink. **2.** a dangerously or irresistibly fascinating woman. —**Cir·ce·an** (sər sē′ən), *adj.*

cir·ci·nate (sûr′sə nāt′), *adj.* **1** made round; ring-shaped. **2.** *Bot.* rolled up on the axis at the apex, as a leaf, etc. [t. L: m. s. *circinātus*, pp.] —**cir′ci·nate·ly**, *adv.*

cir·cle (sûr′kəl), *n., v.,* -cled, -cling. —*n.* **1.** a closed plane curve consisting of all points equally distant from a point within it, called the center. **2.** the portion of a plane bounded by such a curve. **3.** any circular object, formation, or arrangement. **4.** a ring; a circlet; crown. **5.** the ring of a circus. **6.** a section of seats in a theater: *dress circle*. **7.** the area within

Circinate fronds of a young fern

which something acts, exerts influence, etc. **8.** a series ending where it began, and perpetually repeated: *the circle of the year*. **9.** *Logic.* an inconclusive form of reasoning in which unproved statements, or their equivalents, are used to prove each other; vicious circle. **10.** a complete series forming a connected whole; cycle: *the circle of the sciences*. **11.** a number of persons bound by a common tie; a coterie. **12.** an administrative division, esp. of a province. **13.** *Geog.* a parallel of latitude. **14.** *Astron.* **a.** the orbit of a heavenly body. **b.** its period of revolution. **c.** an instrument for observing the transit of stars across the meridian of the observer. **15.** a sphere or orb. **16.** a ring of light in the sky; halo. —*v.t.* **17.** to enclose in a circle; surround: *the enemy circled the hill*. **18.** to move in a circle or circuit round: *he circled the house cautiously*. —*v.i.* **19.** to move in a circle. [t. L: m.s. *circulus*, dim. of *circus* circle, ring; r. ME *cercle*, t. OF] —**cir′cler**, *n.*

—**Syn. 11.** CIRCLE, CLUB, COTERIE, SET, SOCIETY are terms applied to more or less restricted social groups. A CIRCLE may be a pleasant little group meeting chiefly for conversation; in the plural it often suggests a whole section of society interested in one mode of life, occupation, etc.: *a sewing circle, a language circle,* in theatrical circles. CLUB implies an association with definite requirements for membership, fixed dues, and often a stated time of meeting: *an athletic club*. COTERIE suggests a little group closely and intimately associated because of great congeniality: *a literary coterie*. SET refers to a number of persons of similar background, upbringing, interests, etc., somewhat like a CLIQUE (see RING) but without disapproving connotations; it often implies wealth or interest in social activities: *the country club set*. A SOCIETY is a group associated to further common interests of a cultural or practical kind: *a Humane Society*.

cir·clet (sûr′klĭt), *n.* **1.** a small circle. **2.** a ring. **3.** a ring-shaped ornament, esp. for the head.

circling disease, a fatal infectious bacterial disease of cattle and sheep which damages the nervous system and often causes the afflicted animal to walk in circles.

cir·cuit (sûr′kĭt), *n.* **1.** act of going or moving around. **2.** a circular journey; a round. **3.** a roundabout journey or course. **4.** a periodical journey from place to place, to perform certain duties, as of judges to hold court or ministers to preach. **5.** the persons making such a journey. **6.** the route followed, places visited, or district covered by such a journey. **7.** the line going around or bounding any area or object; the distance about an area or object. **8.** the space within a bounding line. **9.** a number of theaters controlled by one manager or visited in turn by the same actors, etc. **10.** *Elect.* **a.** the complete path of an electric current, including the generating apparatus or other source, or a distinct segment of the complete path. **b.** a more or less elaborately contrived arrangement of conductors, wave guides, electronic tubes, and other devices, for the investigation or utilization of electrical phenomena. **c.** the diagram of the connections of such apparatus. —*v.i.* **11.** to go or move around; make the circuit of. —*v.i.* **12.** to go or move in a circuit. [ME, t. L: s. *circuitus*]

circuit breaker, a device for interrupting an electric circuit between separable contacts under normal or abnormal conditions.

circuit court, 1. a court holding sessions at various intervals in different sections of a judicial district. **2.** the court of general jurisdiction found in a number of the states.

circuit court of appeal, the federal intermediate court which sits in each of the federal circuits and reviews judgments of the federal district courts and whose judgments are in turn reviewed by the Supreme Court of the U. S.

cir·cu·i·tous (sər kū′ə təs), *adj.* roundabout; not direct. —**cir·cu′i·tous·ly**, *adv.* —**cir·cu′i·tous·ness**, *n.*

circuit rider, a Methodist minister who rides from place to place to preach along a circuit.

cir·cu·i·ty (sər kū′ə tĭ), *n.* circuitous quality; roundabout character: *circuity of language or of a path*.

cir·cu·lar (sûr′kyə lər), *adj.* **1.** of or pertaining to a circle. **2.** having the form of a circle; round. **3.** moving in or forming a circle or a circuit. **4.** moving or occurring in a cycle or round. **5.** circuitous; roundabout; indirect. **6.** pertaining to a circle or set of persons. **7.** (of a letter, etc.) addressed to a number of persons or intended for general circulation. —*n.* **8.** a circular letter, notice, or statement for circulation among the general public for business or other purposes. [t. L: s. *circulāris*, der. L *circulus* circle; r. ME *circuler*, t. AF] —**cir·cu·lar·i·ty** (sûr′kyə lăr′ə tĭ), *n.* —**cir′cu·lar·ly**, *adv.*

cir·cu·lar·ize (sûr′kyə lə rīz′), *v.t.,* -ized, -izing. **1.** to send circulars to. **2.** to make into a circular letter, etc. **3.** to make circular. —**cir′cu·lar·i·za′tion**, *n.* —**cir′cu·lar·iz′er**, *n.*

circular measure, a measurement system for circles.

1 circle = 360 degrees (4 quadrants)	
1 quadrant = 90 degrees	
1 degree = 60 minutes	
1 minute = 60 seconds	

circular mil, a unit used principally for measuring the cross-sectional area of wires, being the area of a circle having the diameter of one mil.

circular saw, a saw consisting of a circular plate or disk with a toothed edge, which is rotated at high speed in machines for sawing logs, cutting lumber.

circular triangle, a triangle in which the sides are arcs of circles.

cir·cu·late (sûr′kyə lāt′), v., -lated, -lating. —v.i. 1. to move in a circle or circuit; move or pass through a circuit back to the starting point, as the blood in the body. 2. to pass from place to place, from person to person, etc.; be disseminated or distributed. —v.t. 3. to cause to pass from place to place, person to person, etc.: to circulate a rumor. [t. L: m.s. circulātus, pp., made circular, gathered into a circle] —**cir′cu·la′tive**, adj. —**cir′cu·la′tor**, n. —**cir·cu·la·to·ry** (sûr′kyə lə tôr′ī), adj.

circulating decimal, a decimal in which a series of digits is repeated ad infinitum, as 0.147232323 . . .

circulating library, a library whose books circulate among the members or subscribers.

circulating medium, 1. any coin or note passing, without endorsement, as a medium of exchange. 2. such coins or notes collectively.

cir·cu·la·tion (sûr′kyə lā′shən), n. 1. act of circulating, or moving in a circle or circuit. 2. the recurrent movement of the blood through the various vessels of the body. 3. any similar circuit or passage, as of the sap in plants. 4. the transmission or passage of anything from place to place, person to person, etc. 5. the distribution of copies of a publication among readers. 6. the number of copies of each issue of a newspaper, magazine, etc., distributed. 7. coin, notes, bills, etc., in use as currency; currency.

circum-, a prefix referring to movement around, motion on all sides, as in circumvent, circumnavigate, circumference. [t. L, prefix use of circum, adv. and prep., orig. acc. of circus circle, ring. See CIRCUS]

cir·cum·am·bi·ent (sûr′kəm ăm′bī ənt), adj. surrounding; encompassing: circumambient gloom. —**cir′cum·am′bi·ence, cir·cum·am′bi·en·cy,** n.

cir·cum·am·bu·late (sûr′kəm ăm′byə lāt′), v.t., v.i., -lated, -lating. to walk or go about. —**cir′cum·am′bu·la′tion,** n.

cir·cum·bend·i·bus (sûr′kəm bĕn′də bəs), n. (in humorous use) a roundabout way; a circumlocution.

cir·cum·cise (sûr′kəm sīz′), v.t., -cised, -cising. 1. to remove the foreskin of (males), esp. as a religious rite. 2. to perform an analogous operation on (females). 3. to purify spiritually. [ME circumcise(n), t. L: m. s. circumcīsus, pp., cut around] —**cir′cum·cis′er,** n.

cir·cum·ci·sion (sûr′kəm sĭzh′ən), n. 1. act or rite of circumcising. 2. spiritual purification. 3. the circumcision, a. the Jews, as the circumcised people of the Bible. b. those spiritually purified. 4. (cap.) a church festival in honor of the circumcision of Jesus, observed on Jan. 1. [ME circumcisi(o)un, t. L: m.s. circumcisio]

cir·cum·fer·ence (sər kŭm′fər əns), n. 1. the outer boundary, esp. of a circular area. 2. the length of such a boundary. 3. the space within a bounding line. [t. L: m.s. circumferentia] —**cir·cum·fer·en·tial** (sər kŭm′fə rĕn′shəl), adj.

cir·cum·flex (sûr′kəm flĕks′), adj. 1. noting, or having a particular accent (∧, ⌒, ∼), indicating orig. a combination of rising and falling pitch (as in ancient Greek), later a long vowel (as in the French bête, earlier beste), quality of sound (as in phonetic notation), etc. 2. bending or winding around. —n. 3. the circumflex accent. —v.t. 4. to bend around. [t. L: s. circumflexus, pp., bent round] —**cir·cum·flex·ion** (sûr′kəm flĕk′shən), n.

cir·cum·flu·ent (sər kŭm′flōō ənt), adj. flowing around; encompassing: two circumfluent rivers.

cir·cum·flu·ous (sər kŭm′flōō əs), adj. 1. flowing around; encompassing: circumfluous tides. 2. surrounded by water. [t. L: m. circumfluus flowing around]

cir·cum·fuse (sûr′kəm fūz′), v.t., -fused, -fusing. 1. to pour around; diffuse. 2. to surround as with a fluid; suffuse. [t. L: m.s. circumfūsus, pp., poured around] —**cir′cum·fu·sion** (sûr′kəm fū′zhən), n.

cir·cum·ja·cent (sûr′kəm jā′sənt), adj. lying around; surrounding: the circumjacent parishes.

cir·cum·lo·cu·tion (sûr′kəm lō kū′shən), n. 1. a roundabout way of speaking; the use of too many words. 2. a roundabout expression. [t. L: s. circumlocūtio] —**cir·cum·loc·u·to·ry** (sûr′kəm lŏk′yə tôr′ī), adj.

cir·cum·nav·i·gate (sûr′kəm năv′ə gāt′), v.t., -gated, -gating. to sail around; make the circuit of by navigation. —**cir′cum·nav′i·ga′tion,** n. —**cir′cum·nav′i·ga′tor,** n.

cir·cum·nu·tate (sûr′kəm nū′tāt, -nōō′-), v.i., -tated, -tating. (of the apex of a stem or other growing part of a plant) to bend or move around in an irregular circular or elliptical path. —**cir′cum·nu·ta′tion,** n.

cir·cum·po·lar (sûr′kəm pō′lər), adj. around one of the poles of the earth or of the heavens.

cir·cum·ro·tate (sûr′kəm rō′tāt), v.i., -tated, -tating. to rotate like a wheel.

cir·cum·scis·sile (sûr′kəm sĭs′ĭl), adj. Bot. opening along a transverse circular line, as a seed vessel.

Circumscissile pod of pimpernel

cir·cum·scribe (sûr′kəm skrīb′), v.t., -scribed, -scribing. 1. to draw a line around; encircle; surround. 2. to enclose within bounds; limit or confine, esp. narrowly. 3. to mark off; define. 4. Geom. a. to draw (a figure) around another figure so as to touch as many

points as possible. b. (of a figure) to enclose (another figure) in this manner. [t. L: m.s. circumscrībere draw a line around, limit] —**cir′cum·scrib′er,** n.

cir·cum·scrip·tion (sûr′kəm skrĭp′shən), n. 1. act of circumscribing. 2. circumscribed state; limitation. 3. anything that circumscribes, surrounds, or encloses. 4. periphery; outline. 5. a circumscribed space. 6. a circular inscription on a coin, seal, etc. 7. Archaic. limitation of a meaning; definition. —**cir′cum·scrip′tive,** adj.

cir·cum·so·lar (sûr′kəm sō′lər), adj. around the sun: circumsolar course.

cir·cum·spect (sûr′kəm spĕkt′), adj. 1. watchful on all sides; cautious; prudent: circumspect in behavior. 2. well-considered: circumspect ambition. [late ME, t. L: s. circumspectus, pp., considerate, wary] —**cir′cum·spect′ly,** adv. —**cir′cum·spect′ness,** n.

cir·cum·spec·tion (sûr′kəm spĕk′shən), n. circumspect observation or action; caution; prudence.

cir·cum·spec·tive (sûr′kəm spĕk′tĭv), adj. given to or marked by circumspection; watchful; cautious: a circumspective approach.

cir·cum·stance (sûr′kəm stăns′), n., v., -stanced, -stancing. —n. 1. a condition, with respect to time, place, manner, agent, etc., which accompanies, determines, or modifies a fact or event. 2. (usually pl.) the existing condition or state of affairs surrounding and affecting an agent: forced by circumstances to do a thing. 3. an unessential accompaniment of any fact or event; a secondary or accessory matter; a minor detail. 4. (pl.) the condition or state of a person with respect to material welfare: a family in reduced circumstances. 5. an incident or occurrence: his arrival was a fortunate circumstance. 6. detailed or circuitous narration; specification of particulars. 7. Archaic. ceremonious accompaniment or display: pomp and circumstance. 8. under no circumstances, never; regardless of events. 9. under the circumstances, because of the conditions; such being the case. —v.t. 10. to place in particular circumstances or relations. 11. Obs. to furnish with details. 12. Obs. to control or guide by circumstances. [ME, t. L: m.s. circumstantia surrounding condition] —**cir′cum·stanced′,** adj.

cir·cum·stan·tial (sûr′kəm stăn′shəl), adj. 1. of, pertaining to, or derived from circumstances: circumstantial evidence. 2. of the nature of a circumstance or unessential accompaniment; secondary; incidental. 3. dealing with or giving circumstances or details; detailed; particular. 4. pertaining to conditions of material welfare: circumstantial prosperity. —**cir′cum·stan′tial·ly,** adv.

circumstantial evidence, proof of facts offered as evidence from which other facts are to be inferred (contrasted with direct evidence).

cir·cum·stan·ti·al·i·ty (sûr′kəm stăn′shī ăl′ə tī), n., pl. -ties. 1. the quality of being circumstantial; minuteness; fullness of detail. 2. a circumstance; a particular detail.

cir·cum·stan·ti·ate (sûr′kəm stăn′shī āt′), v.t., -ated -ating. 1. to set forth or support with circumstances or particulars. 2. to describe fully or minutely. —**cir′cum·stan′ti·a′tion,** n.

cir·cum·val·late (sûr′kəm văl′āt), adj., v., -lated, -lating. —adj. 1. surrounded by, or as by, a rampart, etc. —v.t. 2. to surround with, or as with, a rampart, etc. [t. L: m.s. circumvallātus, pp., surrounded with a rampart] —**cir′cum·val·la′tion,** n.

cir·cum·vent (sûr′kəm vĕnt′), v.t. 1. to surround or encompass as by stratagem; entrap. 2. to gain advantage over by artfulness or deception; outwit; overreach. 3. to go around: circumvent the bridge. [t. L: s. circumventus, pp., surrounded] —**cir′cum·vent′er, cir′cum·ven′tor,** n. —**cir′cum·ven′tion,** n. —**cir′cum·ven′tive,** adj.

cir·cum·vo·lu·tion (sûr′kəm və lōō′shən), n. 1. the act of rolling or turning around. 2. a single complete turn. 3. a winding or folding about something. 4. a fold so wound. 5. a winding in a sinuous course; a sinuosity. 6. roundabout course or procedure.

cir·cum·volve (sûr′kəm vŏlv′), v.t., v.i., -volved, -volving. to revolve. [t. L: m.s. circumvolvere roll around]

cir·cus (sûr′kəs), n. 1. a company of performers, animals, etc., esp. a traveling company. 2. the performance itself. 3. a circular arena surrounded by tiers of seats, for the exhibition of wild animals, acrobatic feats, etc. 4. (in ancient Rome) a large, usually oblong, or oval, roofless enclosure, surrounded by tiers of seats rising one above another, for chariot races, public games, etc. 5. anything like the Roman circus, as a natural amphitheater, a circular range of houses, etc. 6. flying circus. 7. Brit. a place, originally circular, where several streets come together: Piccadilly Circus. 8. uproar; a display of rowdy sport. 9. an exhibition. 10. Obs. a circlet or ring. [t. L, t. Gk.: m. kírkos ring]

Circus Max·i·mus (măk′sə məs), the great Roman circus in the hollow between the Palatine and the Aventine.

cirque (sûrk), n. 1. a circular space, esp. a natural amphitheater, as in mountains. 2. Poetic. a circle or ring of any kind. 3. a circus. [t. F, t. L: m. s. circus]

cir·rate (sĭr′āt), adj. having cirri. [t. L: m. s. cirrātus curled, der. cirrus curl]

cir·rho·sis (sĭ rō'sĭs), *n. Pathol.* a disease of the liver characterized by increase of connective tissue and alteration in gross and microscopic make-up. [t. NL, f. m.s. Gk. *kirrhós* tawny + *-osis* -OSIS] —**cir·rhot·ic** (sĭ-rŏt'ĭk), *adj.*

cir·ri·ped (sĭr'ə pĕd'), *n.* **1.** any of the *Cirripedia*, an order or group of crustaceans, typically having slender legs bearing bristles used in gathering food. —*adj.* **2.** having legs like cirri. **3.** pertaining to the *Cirripedia*. [t. NL: m. s. *Cirripedia*, pl.; f. *cirri-* CIRRO- + *-pedia* footed]

cirro-, a combining form of **cirrus**.

cir·ro·cu·mu·lus (sĭr'ō kū'myə ləs), *n. Meteorol.* a cloud of high altitude, consisting of small fleecy balls or flakes, often in rows or ripples.

cir·rose (sĭr'ōs, sĭ rōs'), *adj.* **1.** having a cirrus or cirri. **2.** resembling cirri. **3.** *Meteorol.* of the nature of cirrus clouds. Also, **cir·rous** (sĭr'əs).

cir·ro·stra·tus (sĭr'ō strā'təs), *n. Meteorol.* a high veillike cloud or sheet of haze, often giving rise to halos around the sun and moon, sometimes very thin and only slightly whitening the blue of the sky. —**cir'ro·stra'tive**, *adj.*

cir·rus (sĭr'əs), *n.*, *pl.* **cirri** (sĭr'ī). **1.** *Bot.* a tendril. **2.** *Zool.* a filament or slender appendage serving as a barbel, tentacle, foot, arm, etc. **3.** *Meteorol.* a variety of cloud having a thin, fleecy or filamentous appearance, normally occurring at great altitudes and consisting of minute ice crystals. [t. L: curl, tuft, fringe]

cir·soid (sûr'soid), *adj.* varixlike; varicose. [t. Gk.: m.s. *kirsoeidḗs*]

cis-, a prefix denoting relative nearness (this side of) applied to time as well as space, as in *cisalpine.* Cf. **citra-**. [t. L, prefix use of *cis*, prep.]

cis·al·pine (sĭs ăl'pīn, -pĭn), *adj.* on this (the Roman or south) side of the Alps.

cis·at·lan·tic (sĭs'ət lăn'tĭk), *adj.* on this (the speaker's or writer's) side of the Atlantic.

Cis·cau·ca·sia (sĭs'kô kā'zhə, -shə), *n.* that part of Caucasia north of the Caucasus Mountains.

cis·co (sĭs'kō), *n.*, *pl.* **-coes, -cos.** *U.S.* any of several species of whitefish of the genus *Leucichthys*, esp. *L. artedi*, the lake herring of the Great Lakes. [t. N Amer. Ind.]

cis·mon·tane (sĭs mŏn'tān), *adj.* on this (esp. the north) side of the mountains.

cis·pa·dane (sĭs'pə dān', sĭs pā'dān), *adj.* on this (the Roman or south) side of the river Po. [f. CIS- + m.s. L *Padānus* of the Po river]

cis·soid (sĭs'oid), *Geom.* —*n.* **1.** a curve having a cusp at the origin and a point of inflection at infinity. —*adj.* **2.** included between the concave sides of two intersecting curves (opposed to *sistroid*): *a cissoid angle.* [t. Gk.: m.s. *kissoeidḗs* ivy-like]

cist[1] (sĭst), *n. Class. Antiq.* a box or chest, esp. for sacred utensils. [t. L: s. *cista*, t. Gk.: m. *kístē* CHEST]

cist[2] (sĭst, kĭst), *n.* a prehistoric sepulchral tomb or casket. [t. Welsh, t. L: s. *cista.* See CIST[1]]

cis·ta·ceous (sĭs tā'shəs), *adj.* belonging to the *Cistaceae*, or rockrose family of plants. [f. s. Gk. *kístos* rockrose + -ACEOUS]

Cis·ter·cian (sĭs tûr'shən), *n.* **1.** a member of an order of monks and nuns founded in 1098 at Cîteaux, near Dijon, France, under the rule of St. Benedict. —*adj.* **2.** belonging to this order.

Cistercian Rule, an adaptation of the Benedictine Rule stressing contemplation and extreme asceticism.

cis·tern (sĭs'tərn), *n.* **1.** a reservoir, tank, or vessel for holding water or other liquid. **2.** *Anat.* a reservoir or receptacle of some natural fluid of the body. [ME, t. L: s. *cisterna*, der. *cista* box]

cit., **1.** citation. **2.** cited. **3.** citizen.

cit·a·del (sĭt'ə dəl, -dĕl'), *n.* **1.** a fortress in or near a city, intended to keep the inhabitants in subjection, or, in a siege, to form a final point of defense. **2.** any strongly fortified place; a stronghold. **3.** a heavily armored structure on a warship. [t. F: m. *citadelle*, t. It.: m. *cittadella*, der. *città* CITY]

ci·ta·tion (sī tā'shən), *n.* **1.** act of citing or quoting. **2.** the quoting of a passage, book, author, etc.; a reference to an authority or a precedent. **3.** a passage cited; a quotation. **4.** mention or enumeration. **5.** call or summons, esp. to appear in court. **6.** a document containing such a summons. **7.** *Mil.* mention of a soldier or unit, in orders, usually for gallantry: *Presidential citation.* [ME *citacion*, t. L: m.s. *citātio*] —**ci·ta·to·ry** (sī'tə tōr'ī), *adj.*

cite (sīt), *v.t.*, **cited, citing. 1.** to quote (a passage, book, author, etc.), esp. as an authority. **2.** to mention in support, proof, or confirmation; refer to as an example. **3.** to summon officially or authoritatively to appear in court. **4.** to summon or call; rouse to action: *cited to the field of battle.* **5.** to call to mind; mention: *citing my own praise.* **6.** *Mil.* to mention (a soldier, unit, etc.) in orders, as for gallantry. [late ME, t. L: m. *citāre*, freq. of *ciēre*, *cīre*, move, excite, call] —**cit'a·ble**, **cite'a·ble**, *adj.*

cith·a·ra (sĭth'ə rə), *n.* kithara. [L form of KITHARA]

cith·er (sĭth'ər), *n.* cittern. Also, **cith·ern** (sĭth'ərn). [t. L: m.s. *cithara* CITHARA]

cit·ied (sĭt'īd), *adj.* **1.** occupied by a city or cities. **2.** formed into or like a city.

cit·i·fied (sĭt'ĭ fīd'), *adj.* having city habits, fashions, etc.

cit·i·zen (sĭt'ə zən, -sən), *n.* **1.** a member, native or naturalized, of a state or nation (as distinguished from *alien*). **2.** a person owing allegiance to a government and entitled to its protection. **3.** an inhabitant of a city or town, esp. one entitled to its privileges or franchises. **4.** an inhabitant or denizen. **5.** a civilian (as distinguished from a soldier, police officer, etc.). [ME *citisein*, t. AF, var. of OF *citeain*, der. *cite* CITY] —**cit·i·zen·ess** (sĭt'ə zən ĭs, -sən ĭs), *n. fem.*

citizen of the world, a person who is concerned about all nations, not just his own.

cit·i·zen·ry (sĭt'ə zən rī, -sən-), *n.*, *pl.* **-ries.** citizens collectively.

cit·i·zen·ship (sĭt'ə zən shĭp', -sən-), *n.* the status of a citizen, with its rights and duties.

cit·ole (sĭt'ōl, sĭ tōl'), *n.* cittern.

citra-, a prefix synonymous with **cis-**. [t. L, repr. *citrā*, adv. and prep., akin to *cis.* See CIS-]

cit·ral (sĭt'rəl), *n.* a liquid aldehyde, $C_9H_{15}CHO$, with a strong lemonlike odor, obtained from the oils of lemon, orange, etc., used in perfumery. [f. CITR(US) + AL(DEHYDE)]

cit·rate (sĭt'rāt, sī'trāt), *n. Chem.* a salt or ester of citric acid.

cit·re·ous (sĭt'rĭ əs), *adj.* lemon-yellow; greenish-yellow. [t. L: m. *citreus* of the citron tree]

cit·ric acid (sĭt'rĭk), *Chem.* an acid, $C_6H_8O_7 \cdot H_2O$, contained in many fruits, especially in limes and lemons. [f. s. L *citrus* citron tree + -IC]

cit·rin (sĭt'rĭn), *n. Biochem.* vitamin P.

cit·rine (sĭt'rĭn), *adj.* **1.** pale-yellow; lemon-colored. —*n.* **2.** a pellucid yellow variety of quartz. [ME, t. F: m. *citrin*, der. L *citrus* citron tree]

cit·ron (sĭt'rən), *n.* **1.** a pale-yellow fruit resembling the lemon but larger and with thicker rind, borne by a small tree or large bush, *Citrus medica*, allied to the lemon and lime. **2.** the tree itself. **3.** the rind of the fruit, candied or preserved. [t. F, t. It.: m. *citrone*, der. L *citrus* citron tree]

cit·ron·el·la (sĭt'rə nĕl'ə), *n.* a fragrant grass, *Andropogon nardus*, of southern Asia, cultivated as the source of an oil (**citronella oil**) used in making liniment, perfume, and soap. [t. NL; named from its citronlike odor]

cit·ron·el·lal (sĭt'rə nĕl'ăl), *n.* a colorless, liquid aldehyde, $C_9H_{17}CHO$, found in essential oils, and used as a flavoring agent and in the perfume industry.

citron melon, *U.S.* a round, hard-fleshed watermelon, *Citrullus vulgaris*, var. *citroides*, used for preserving.

citron wood, **1.** the wood of the citron. **2.** the wood of the sandarac.

cit·rus (sĭt'rəs), *n.* **1.** any tree or shrub of the rutaceous genus *Citrus*, which includes the citron, lemon, lime, orange, grapefruit, etc. —*adj.* **2.** Also, **cit'rous.** of or pertaining to such trees or shrubs: *citrus fruit.* [t. L]

cit·tern (sĭt'ərn), *n.* an old musical instrument, related to the guitar, having a flat pear-shaped soundbox and wire strings. Also, either, **cithern, gittern, zittern.** [b. L *cithara* CITHARA and GITTERN]

cit·y (sĭt'ī), *n.*, *pl.* **cities. 1.** a large or important town. **2.** *U.S.* an incorporated municipality, usually governed by a mayor and a board of aldermen or councilmen. **3.** *Canada.* a municipality of high rank, usually based on population. **4.** *Brit.* a borough, usually the seat of a bishop, upon which the dignity of the title has been conferred by the Crown. **5. the City**, the part of London, England, in which the commercial and financial interests are chiefly centered. **6.** city-state. **7.** the inhabitants of a city collectively. [ME *cite*, t. OF, g. L *civitas* citizenship, the state, a city] —**Syn. 1.** See **community**.

Woman playing a cittern

city editor, **1.** *U.S.* the editor in charge of local news. **2.** *Brit.* the editor in charge of the financial and commercial news.

city father, one of the officials and prominent citizens of a city.

city hall, the administration building of a city government.

city man, *Brit.* a financier; a person employed in the banking establishments of the City (def. 5). Also, **City man.**

city manager, a person not publicly elected but appointed by a city council to manage a city.

City of God, heaven.

City of Seven Hills, Rome.

city planning, public control of the physical development of a city, by means of a plan regulating street layout, locations of buildings, etc.

cit·y-state (sĭt'ī stāt'), *n.* a sovereign state consisting of an autonomous city with its dependencies.

Ciu·dad Bo·lí·var (sū däd' bô lē'vär), a city in E Venezuela: a port on the Orinoco. 31,009 (1950).

Ciu·dad Juá·rez (sū dăd' hwä'rĕs), a city in N Mexico, across the Rio Grande from El Paso, Texas. 121,912 (est. 1951).

---

b., blend of, blended; c., cognate with; d., dialect, dialectal; der., derived from; f., formed from; g., going back to; m., modification of; r., replacing; s., stem of; t., taken from; ?, perhaps. See the full key on inside cover.

Ciu·dad Tru·jil·lo (sū dȧd′ trōō hē′yô), the former name of the capital of the Dominican Republic; used from 1936 until 1961 when the original name Santo Domingo was restored.

civ., 1. civil. 2. civilian.

civ·et (sĭv′ĭt), *n.* 1. a yellowish unctuous substance with a strong musklike odor, obtained from a pouch in the genital region of civets and used in perfumery. 2. any of the catlike carnivorous mammals of southern Asia and Africa (subfamily *Viverrinae*) having glands in the genital region that secrete civet. 3. any of certain allied or similar animals, as the **palm civet.** Also, **civet cat** (for defs. 2, 3). [t. F: m. *civette,* t. It.: m. *zibetto,* t. Ar.: m. *zabād*]

African civet. *Civettictis civetta*
(Total length 4 to 4½ ft.;
ab. 1 ft. high)

civ·ic (sĭv′ĭk), *adj.* 1. of or pertaining to a city; municipal: *civic problems.* 2. of or pertaining to citizenship; civil: *civic duties.* 3. of citizens: *civic pride.* [t. L: s. *civicus,* der. *civis* citizen]

civ·ics (sĭv′ĭks), *n.* the science of civic affairs.

civ·ies (sĭv′ĭz), *n.pl. U.S. Colloq.* civilian clothes (as disting. from military). Also, *Brit. Colloq.,* **civvies.**

civ·il (sĭv′əl), *adj.* 1. of or consisting of citizens: *civil life, civil society.* 2. of the commonwealth or state: *civil affairs.* 3. of citizens in their ordinary capacity, or the ordinary life and affairs of citizens (distinguished from *military, ecclesiastical, etc.*). 4. of the citizen as an individual: *civil liberty.* 5. befitting a citizen: *a civil duty.* 6. of, or in a condition of, social order or organized government; civilized. 7. polite; courteous. 8. not rude or discourteous. 9. (of divisions of time) legally recognized in the ordinary affairs of life: *the civil year.* 10. *Law.* a. of or in agreement with Roman civil law. b. of the civil law, as the medieval and modern law derived from the Roman system. c. pertaining to the private rights of individuals and to legal proceedings connected with these (distinguished from *criminal, military, or political*). [ME *civile,* t. L: m.s. *cīvīlis* pertaining to citizens] —**Syn.** 7, 8. respectful, deferential, gracious, complaisant, suave, affable, urbane, courtly. CIVIL, AFFABLE, COURTEOUS, POLITE all imply avoidance of rudeness toward others. CIVIL suggests a minimum observance of social requirements. AFFABLE suggests ease of approach, often with a touch of condescension. COURTEOUS implies positive dignified, sincere, and thoughtful consideration for others. POLITE implies habitual courtesy, arising from a consciousness of one's training and the demands of "good manners." —**Ant.** 7, 8. boorish, churlish.

civil engineer, one versed in the design, construction, and maintenance of public works, such as roads, bridges, dams, canals, aqueducts, harbors, etc.

civil engineering, action, work, or profession of a civil engineer.

ci·vil·ian (sĭ vĭl′yən), *n.* 1. one engaged in civil pursuits (distinguished from a soldier, etc.). 2. one versed in or studying the Roman or civil law.

ci·vil·i·ty (sĭ vĭl′ə tĭ), *n., pl.* **-ties.** 1. courtesy; politeness. 2. a polite attention or expression. 3. *Archaic.* civilization; culture; good breeding.

civ·i·li·za·tion (sĭv′ələ zā′shən), *n.* 1. an advanced state of human society, in which a high level of art, science, religion, and government has been reached. 2. those people or nations that have reached such a state. 3. the type of culture, society, etc. of a specific group: *Irish civilization.* 4. act or process of civilizing.

civ·i·lize (sĭv′ə līz′), *v.t.,* **-lized, -lizing.** to make civil; bring out of a savage state; elevate in social and individual life; enlighten; refine. [t. ML: m.s. *cīvīlizāre.* See CIVIL, -IZE] —**civ′i·liz′a·ble,** *adj.* —**civ′i·liz′er,** *n.*

civ·i·lized (sĭv′ə līzd′), *adj.* 1. having an advanced culture, society, etc. 2. polite; well-bred; refined. 3. of or pertaining to civilized people.

civil law, 1. the laws of a state or nation regulating ordinary private matters (distinguished from criminal, military, or political matters). 2. the body of law proper to the city or state of Rome, as distinct from that common to all nations. 3. the systems of law derived from Roman law (distinguished from *common law, canon law*).

civil liberty, complete liberty of opinion, etc., restrained only as much as necessary for the public good.

civil list, *Brit.* the provision of money by Parliament for the king and his household.

civ·il·ly (sĭv′ə lĭ), *adv.* 1. in accordance with civil law. 2. politely; considerately; gently.

civil marriage, a marriage performed by a government official rather than a clergyman.

civil rights, *U.S.* rights to personal liberty established by the 13th and 14th Amendments to the Constitution and other Congressional Acts.

civil servant, *Chiefly Brit.* a civil-service employee.

civil service, the public service concerned with all affairs not military, naval, legislative, or judicial.

civil war, 1. a war between parties, regions, etc., within their own country. 2. *(caps.)* a. the American war between the North and South (1861–65). b. the war in England between the Parliamentarians and Royalists (1642–52).

civ·ism (sĭv′ĭz əm), *n.* good citizenship.

civ·vies (sĭv′ĭz), *n.pl. Brit. Colloq.* civies.

Cl, *Chem.* chlorine.

cl., 1. carload. 2. centiliter. 3. class. 4. classification. 5. clause.

clab·ber (klăb′ər), *n.* 1. bonnyclabber. —*v.i.* 2. (of milk) to become thick in souring. [t. Irish: m. *clabar,* short for *bainne clabair* bonnyclabber, curds]

clach·an (klăкʜ′ən), *n. Gaelic.* a small village or hamlet. [t. Gaelic, der. *clach* stone]

clack (klăk), *v.i.* 1. to make a quick, sharp sound, or a succession of such sounds, as by striking or cracking. 2. to talk rapidly and continually, or with sharpness and abruptness; chatter. 3. to cluck or cackle. —*v.t.* 4. to utter by clacking. 5. to cause to clack. —*n.* 6. a clacking sound. 7. something that clacks, as a rattle. 8. rapid, continual talk; chatter. 9. *Slang.* the tongue. [ME *clacke;* imit.] —**clack′er,** *n.*

Clack·man·nan (klăk măn′ən), *n.* a county in central Scotland. 39,300 pop. (est. 1956). 55 sq. mi. *Co. seat:* Clackmannan. Also, **Clack·man·nan·shire** (klăk măn′nən shĭr′, -shər)

clad (klăd), *v.* a pt. and pp. of **clothe.**

clado-, a word element meaning "sprout," "branch." Also, before vowels, **clad-.** [comb. form repr. Gk. *kládos* sprout]

clad·o·phyll (klăd′ə fĭl), *n. Bot.* a leaflike flattened branch. Also, **clad·ode** (klăd′ōd).

claim (klām), *v.t.* 1. to demand by or as by virtue of a right; demand as a right or as due. 2. to assert, and demand the recognition of (a right, title, possession, etc.); assert one's right to. 3. to assert or maintain as a fact. 4. to require as due or fitting. —*n.* 5. a demand for something as due; an assertion of a right or alleged right. 6. an assertion of something as a fact. 7. a right to claim or demand; a just title to something. 8. that which is claimed; a piece of public land to which formal claim is made for mining or other purposes. 9. a payment demanded in accordance with an insurance policy, a workmen's compensation law, etc. [ME *claime(n),* t. OF: m. *claimer, clamer,* g. L *clāmāre* call] —**claim′a·ble,** *adj.* —**claim′er,** *n.* —**Syn.** 1. See **demand.** —**Ant.** 3. deny.

Cladophyll

claim·ant (klā′mənt), *n.* one who makes a claim.

claiming race, a race in which horses are "claimed" for a fixed amount prior to the running of the race.

clair·voy·ance (klâr voi′əns), *n.* 1. power of seeing objects or actions beyond the natural range of vision. 2. quick intuitive knowledge of things; sagacity. [t. F]

clair·voy·ant (klâr voi′ənt), *adj.* 1. having the power of seeing objects or actions beyond the natural range of vision. —*n.* 2. a clairvoyant person. [t. F, f. *clair* clear + *voyant,* ppr. of *voir* see, g. L *vidēre*]

clam (klăm), *n., v.,* **clammed, clamming.** —*n.* 1. any of various bivalve mollusks, esp. certain edible species, as *Venus mercenaria* (the **hard clam** or **round clam**) or *Mya arenara* (the **soft clam** or **long clam**) of the Atlantic coast of North America. 2. *U.S. Colloq.* a secretive or silent person. —*v.i.* 3. to gather or dig clams. [special use of CLAM[2], with reference to the shell]

clam[2] (klăm), *n.* 1. a clamp[1] (def. 1). 2. *(pl.)* pincers (def. 1). [ME; OE *clamm* band, bond]

cla·mant (klā′mənt), *adj.* 1. clamorous. 2. urgent. [t. L: s. *clāmans,* ppr., crying out]

clam·a·to·ri·al (klăm′ə tôr′ĭ əl), *adj.* of or pertaining to the *Clamatores,* a large group of passerine birds with relatively simple vocal organs and little power of song, as the flycatchers. [f. s. NL *Clāmātōres* (pl. of L *clāmātor* one who cries out) + -IAL]

clam·bake (klăm′bāk′), *n. U.S.* 1. a picnic at the seashore at which the baking of clams (usually on hot stones under seaweed) is a main feature. 2. *Humorous.* any social gathering, esp. a very gay one. 3. *Slang.* a bungled rehearsal, esp. of a radio program.

clam·ber (klăm′bər), *v.i., v.t.* 1. to climb, using both feet and hands; climb with effort or difficulty. —*n.* 2. a clambering. [ME *clambren, clameren,* ? freq. of OE *clæmman* press; semantic devel. infl. by assoc. with CLIMB] —**clam′ber·er,** *n.*

clam·my (klăm′ĭ), *adj.,* **-mier, -miest.** covered with a cold, sticky moisture; cold and damp. [? t. Flem.: m. *klammig* sticky, etc.] —**clam′mi·ness,** *n.*

clam·or (klăm′ər), *n.* 1. a loud outcry. 2. a vehement expression of desire or dissatisfaction. 3. popular outcry. 4. any loud and continued noise. —*v.i.* 5. to make a clamor; raise an outcry. —*v.t.* 6. to drive, force, put, etc., by clamoring. 7. to utter noisily. 8. *Obs.* to disturb with clamor. Also, *Brit.,* **clam′our.** [ME, t. OF, g. L *clāmor* a cry, shout] —**clam′or·er,** *n.* —**Syn.** 1. shouting, uproar. 2. vociferation. 4. See **noise.**

clam·or·ous (klăm′ər əs), *adj.* 1. full of, marked by, or of the nature of clamor; vociferous; noisy. 2. vigorous in demands or complaints. —**clam′or·ous·ly,** *adv.*

clamp[1] (klămp), *n.* 1. a device, usually of some rigid material, for strengthening or supporting objects or fastening them together. 2. an appliance with opposite sides or parts that may be screwed or otherwise brought together to hold or compress something. 3. one of a pair of movable pieces, made of lead or other soft material, for covering the jaws of a vise and enabling it to grasp without

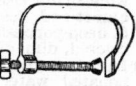
Clamp (def. 2)

bruising. —v.t. 4. to fasten with or fix in a clamp. —v.i. 5. **clamp down**, *Colloq.* a. to press down. b. to become more strict. [t. MD: m. *klampe* clamp, cleat]

clamp² (klămp), v.i. to tread heavily; clump. [imit.]

clamp·er (klăm/pər, klăm/-), n. 1. a clamp; pincer. 2. an iron frame with sharp prongs, fastened to the sole of the shoe to prevent slipping on ice.

clam·shell (klăm/shĕl/), n. 1. the shell of a clam. 2. a dredging bucket made of two similar pieces hinged together at one end.

clan (klăn), n. 1. a group of families or households, as among the Scottish Highlanders, the heads of which claim descent from a common ancestor. 2. a group of people of common descent. 3. a clique, set, society, or party. 4. a social unit in a tribe in which descent is reckoned in the maternal line; a group of people supposed to be descended from a common ancestor, descent being reckoned in the female line. [t. Gaelic: m. *clann* family, stock]

clan·des·tine (klăn·dĕs/tǐn), adj. secret; private; concealed (generally implying craft or deception): *a clandestine marriage.* [t. L: m. s. *clandestīnus*] —**clan·des/tine·ly**, adv. —**clan·des/tine·ness**, n.

clang (klăng), v.i. 1. to give out a loud, resonant sound, as metal when struck; ring loudly or harshly. —v.t. 2. to cause to resound or ring loudly. —n. 3. a clanging sound. [imit. Cf. L *clangere*]

clan·gor (klăng/gər, klăng/ər), n. 1. a loud, resonant sound, as of pieces of metal struck together or of a trumpet; a clang. 2. clamorous noise. —v.i. 3. to make a clangor; clang. Also, *Brit.*, **clan/gour.** [t. L] —**clan/gor·ous**, adj. —**clan/gor·ous·ly**, adv.

clank (klăngk), n. 1. a sharp, hard, metallic sound: *the clank of chains.* —v.i. 2. to make such a sound. 3. to move with such sounds. —v.t. 4. to cause to resound sharply, as metal in collision. [t. D: m. *klank*]

clan·nish (klăn/ǐsh), adj. 1. of, pertaining to, or characteristic of a clan. 2. disposed to adhere closely, as the members of a clan. 3. imbued with or influenced by the sentiments, prejudices, etc., peculiar to clans. —**clan/nish·ly**, adv. —**clan/nish·ness**, n.

clans·man (klănz/mən), n., pl. **-men.** a member of a clan. —**clans·wom·an** (klănz/wŏŏm/ən), n. fem.

clap (klăp), v., **clapped, clapping**, n. —v.t. 1. to strike with a quick, smart blow, producing an abrupt, sharp sound; slap; pat. 2. to strike together resoundingly, as the hands to express applause. 3. to applaud in this manner. 4. to flap (the wings). 5. to put, place, apply, etc., promptly and effectively. 6. *Colloq.* to make or arrange hastily (often fol. by *up* or *together*). —v.i. 7. to make an abrupt, sharp sound, as of bodies in collision. 8. to move or strike with such a sound. 9. to clap the hands, as in applause. —n. 10. act or sound of clapping. 11. a resounding blow; a slap. 12. a loud and abrupt or explosive noise, as of thunder. 13. a sudden stroke, blow, or act. 14. an applauding; applause. 15. a clapper. 16. *Obs.* a sudden mishap. [ME *clappen*, OE *clæppan*, c. D and LG *klappen*]

clap·board (klăb/ərd, klăp/bôrd/), n. 1. *U.S.* a long, thin board, thicker along one edge than along the other, used in covering the outer walls of buildings being laid horizontally, the thick edge of each board overlapping the thin edge of the board below it. 2. *Brit.* a size of oak board used for making barrel staves and for wainscoting. —adj. 3. of or pertaining to clapboard: *a clapboard roof.* —v.t. 4. to cover with clapboards. [t. MD: m. *klapholt*, with BOARD for *-holt* wood]

clap·per (klăp/ər), n. 1. one who or that which claps. 2. the tongue of a bell. 3. *Slang.* the tongue. 4. any clapping contrivance, as either of a pair of bones.

clap·per·claw (klăp/ər·klô/), v.t. *Archaic* or *Dial.* 1. to claw or scratch with the hand and nails. 2. to revile.

clap·trap (klăp/trăp/), n. 1. any artifice or expedient for winning applause or impressing the public. 2. pretentious but insincere or empty language.

claque (klăk), n. 1. a set of hired applauders in a theater. 2. any group of persons ready to applaud from interested motives. [t. F, der. *claquer* clap]

clar·a·bel·la (klăr/ə·bĕl/ə), n. an organ stop which gives soft, sweet tones. [f. L *clāra* (fem. of *clārus* clear) + *bella* (fem. of *bellus* beautiful)]

Clare (klâr), n. a county in W Ireland, in Munster province. 77,107 (prelim. 1956); 1231 sq. mi. *Co. seat:* Ennis.

clar·ence (klăr/əns), n. a closed four-wheeled carriage with a curved glass front and inside seats for four persons. [named after the Duke of *Clarence*, 1765–1837, (afterwards William IV of England)]

Clar·en·don (klăr/ən·dən), n. 1. Edward Hyde, 1st Earl of, 1609–74, British statesman and historian. 2. The Council of, a council (1164) occasioned by the opposition of Thomas à Becket to Henry II. 3. (*l.c.*) a condensed form of printing type, like roman in outline but with thicker lines.

clar·et (klăr/ət), n. 1. the red (orig. the light-red or yellowish) table wine of Bordeaux, France. 2. a similar wine made elsewhere, as California claret. 3. Also, **claret red.** deep purplish red. 4. *Slang.* blood. —adj. 5. deep purplish red. [ME, t. OF: somewhat clear, light-colored, dim. of *cler*, g. L *clārus* clear]

claret cup, an iced beverage made of claret and carbonated water with lemon juice, brandy (or other spirits), fruits, sugar, etc.

clar·i·fy (klăr/ə·fī/), v.t., v.i., **-fied, -fying**. to make or become clear, pure, or intelligible. [ME *clarifie(n)*, t. OF: m. *clarifier*, t. LL: m. *clārificāre*] —**clar/i·fi·ca/tion**, n. —**clar/i·fi/er**, n.

clar·i·net (klăr/ə·nĕt/), n. a wind instrument in the form of a cylindrical tube with a single reed attached to its mouthpiece. Also, **clar·i·o·net** (klăr/Y·ə·nĕt/). [t. F: m. *clarinette*, dim. of *clarine* clarion] —**clar/i·net/ist, clar/i·net/tist**, n.

clar·i·on (klăr/Y·ən), adj. 1. clear and shrill. —n. 2. an old kind of trumpet, having a curved shape. 3. *Poetic.* the sound of this instrument. 4. any similar sound. [ME, t. ML: s. *clārio*, der. L *clārus* clear]

clar·i·ty (klăr/ə·tY), n. clearness: *clarity of thinking.* [t. L: m. s. *clāritas*; r. ME *clarte*, t. OF]

Clark (klärk), n. 1. George Rogers, 1752–1818, U. S. soldier and frontiersman. 2. his brother, William, 1770–1838, U. S. soldier and explorer: joint commander of Lewis and Clark expedition, 1804–06, to Oregon.

Clarks·burg (klärks/bûrg), n. a city in N West Virginia, on the Monongahela river. 28,112 (1960).

cla·ro (klä/rō), adj., n., pl. **-ros.** —adj. 1. (of cigars) light-colored and, usually, mild. —n. 2. such a cigar. [t. Sp., g. L *clārus* clear]

clart (klärt), v.t. *Scot.* and N. *Eng.* to smear or spot with something sticky or dirty.

clar·y (klâr/Y), n., pl. **claries.** any of several ornamental garden plants of the *Salvia* family, esp. *S. sclarea.* [late ME; ? aphetic var. of **esclary*, r. OE *slarie.* Cf. OF *sclaree*, ML *sclarea*]

clash (klăsh), v.i. 1. to make a loud, harsh noise. 2. to collide, esp. noisily. 3. to conflict; disagree. —v.t. 4. to strike with a resounding or violent collision. 5. to produce (sound, etc.) by, or as by, collision. —n. 6. the noise of, or as of, a collision. 7. a collision, esp. a noisy one. 8. a conflict; opposition, esp. of views or interests. [b. CLAP and DASH] —**Syn.** 8. See struggle.

clasp (klăsp, kläsp), n. 1. a device, usually of metal, for fastening things or parts together; any fastening or connection; anything that clasps. 2. a grasp; an embrace. 3. a military decoration consisting of a small design of metal fixed on the ribbon which represents a medal that the bearer has been awarded, the clasp usually indicating an additional award. —v.t. 4. to fasten with, or as with, a clasp. 5. to furnish with a clasp. 6. to take hold of with an enfolding grasp: *clasping hands.* [ME *claspe(n), clapse(n)*; orig. uncert.] —**clasp/er**, n. —**Syn.** 6. grasp, clutch, hug.

clasp knife, a knife with a blade (or blades) folding into the handle.

class (klăs, kläs), n. 1. a number of persons or things, regarded as forming one group through the possession of similar qualities; a kind; sort. 2. any division of persons or things according to rank or grade. 3. *Brit. Univ.* a division of candidates for honors degrees into groups, according to merit. 4. *Sociol.* a social stratum sharing essential economic, political, or cultural characteristics, and having the same social position. 5. the system of dividing society; caste. 6. social rank, esp. high rank. 7. the assembly of such a group. 8. the **classes**, the higher ranks of society, as distinguished from the masses. 9. *Chiefly U.S. Slang.* excellence; merit. 10. *U.S.* a number of pupils in a school, or of students in a college, pursuing the same studies, ranked together, or graduated in the same year. 11. a type of accommodation in railroad carriages and on steamers: *shall we get a ticket for first class?* 12. drafted or conscripted soldiers, or men available for draft or conscription, all of whom were born in the same year. 13. *Zool., Bot.* the usual major subdivision of a phylum or subphylum, commonly comprising a plurality of orders, as the gastropods, the mammals, the angiosperms. 14. *Gram.* a form class. 15. *Eccles.* classis. 16. (in early Methodism) one of several small companies, each composed of about twelve members under a leader, into which each society or congregation was divided. —v.t. 17. to arrange, place, or rate as to class: *to class justice with wisdom.* —v.i. 18. to take or have a place in a particular class: *those who class as believers.* [earlier *classe*, t. F, t. L: m. s. *classis* class (of people, etc.), army, fleet] —**class/a·ble**, adj. —**class/er**, n.

class., 1. classic. 2. classical. 3. classification. 4. classified.

class·book (klăs/bŏŏk/, kläs/-), n. *U.S.* 1. a book in which a record of student attendance, grades, etc., is kept. 2. a souvenir book issued by a graduating class, containing pictures, reports, etc.

class consciousness, awareness of one's social or economic rank in society. —**class-con·scious** (klăs/kŏn/shəs, kläs/-), adj.

class day, (in American colleges and schools) a day during the commencement season on which the members of the graduating class celebrate the completion of their course with special ceremonies.

clas·sic (klăs/Yk), adj. 1. of the first or highest class or rank. 2. serving as a standard, model, or guide. 3. of or characteristic of Greek and Roman antiquity, esp. with reference to literature and art. 4. in the style of the ancient Greek and Roman literature or art;

classical. 5. of, or adhering to, an established set of artistic or scientific standards and methods. 6. of literary or historical renown. —*n.* 7. an author or a literary production of the first rank, esp. in Greek or Latin. 8. (*pl.*) the literature of ancient Greece and Rome. 9. an artist or an artistic production of the highest class. 10. one versed in the classics. 11. one who adheres to classical rules and models. [t. L: s. *classicus* pertaining to a class, of the first or highest class]

clas·si·cal (klăs′ə·kəl), *adj.* 1. classic. 2. in accordance with ancient Greek and Roman models in literature or art, or with later systems of principles modeled upon them. 3. pertaining to or versed in the ancient classics. 4. marked by classicism. 5. conforming to established taste or critical standards; adhering to traditional forms. 6. teaching, or relating to, academic branches of knowledge (the humanities, general sciences, etc.), distinguished from technical subjects. 7. accepted as being standard in a given field of knowledge, as distinguished from novel or unusual theories: *classical physics.* 8. *Eccles.* pertaining to a classis. —**clas′si·cal′i·ty,** *n.* —**clas′si·cal·ly,** *adv.*

classical architecture, 1. any architectural style distinguished by clarity and balance of design and plan, expressive of poise and dignity, and as a rule by the use of a Greek or Roman vocabulary. 2. the architecture of Greek and Roman antiquity. 3. the architectural style popular from 1770–1840, esp. in the Anglo-Saxon countries, France, and central Europe, which intended to revive Greek and Roman architecture.

classical economics, a system of thought developed by Adam Smith and Ricardo, according to whom the wealth of nations is promoted by free competition with a minimum of government intervention and by division of labor (labor being the source of wealth).

clas·si·cism (klăs′ə·sĭz′əm), *n.* 1. the principles of classic literature or art, or adherence to them. 2. the classical style in literature or art, characterized esp. by attention to form with the general effect of regularity, simplicity, balance, proportion, and controlled emotion (contrasted with *romanticism*). 3. a classical idiom or form. 4. classical scholarship or learning. Also, **clas·si·cal·ism** (klăs′ə·kə·lĭz′əm).

clas·si·cist (klăs′ə·sĭst), *n.* 1. one who advocates the study of the ancient classics. 2. an adherent of classicism in literature or art. 3. an authority on Greek and Roman studies. Also, **clas·si·cal·ist** (klăs′ə·kəl·ĭst).

clas·si·cize (klăs′ə·sīz′), *v.*, **-cized, -cizing.** —*v.t.* 1. to make classic. —*v.i.* 2. to conform to the classic style.

clas·si·fi·ca·tion (klăs′ə·fə·kā′shən), *n.* 1. act or the result of classifying. 2. *Zool., Bot.* the assignment of plants and animals to groups within a system of categories distinguished by structure, origin, etc. The usual series of categories is phylum (in zoölogy) or division (in botany), class, order, family, genus, species, and variety. 3. one of the several degrees (restricted, confidential, secret, top secret, etc.) of security protection for government documents, papers, etc. 4. *Library Science.* a system for arranging publications according to broad fields of knowledge and specific subjects within each field. —**clas·si·fi·ca·to·ry** (klăs′ə·fə·kā′tə·rĭ, klə·sĭf′ə·kə·tôr′ĭ), *adj.*

classified ad, want ad.

clas·si·fi·er (klăs′ə·fī′ər), *n.* 1. one who or that which classifies. 2. *Chem.* a device for separating solids of different characteristics by controlled rates of settling.

clas·si·fy (klăs′ə·fī′), *v.t.*, **-fied, -fying.** 1. to arrange or distribute in classes; place according to class. 2. *Mil.* to mark or otherwise declare (a document, paper, etc.) of value to the enemy and limit and safeguard its handling and use. [f. L *classi*(s) CLASS + -FY] —**clas′si·fi′a·ble,** *adj.*

class inclusion, *Logic.* the relation between one class and a second when every object that belongs to the first class also belongs to the second. For example: the class of *men* is included in the class of *animals.*

clas·sis (klăs′ĭs), *n., pl.* **classes** (klăs′ēz). *Eccles.* (in certain Reformed churches) 1. the organization of pastors and elders which governs a group of local churches; a presbytery. 2. the group of churches governed by such an organization. [t. L. See CLASS]

class·mate (klăs′māt′, klás′-), *n.* a member of the same class, as at school or college.

class meaning, *Gram.* 1. the meaning of a grammatical category or a form class, common to all forms showing the category or to all members of the form class, as in the meaning of possession common to all English nouns in the possessive case. 2. that part of the meaning of a linguistic form which it has by virtue of membership in a particular form class, as the past tense meaning of *ate* (opposed to *lexical meaning*).

class number, *Library Science.* the classification number of a book in a library to indicate its subject class and location on the library shelves, usually a Dewey decimal or a Library of Congress classification symbol.

class·room (klăs′rōōm′, -rŏŏm′, klás′-), *n.* a room in a school or college in which classes meet.

class struggle, 1. conflict between different classes in the community. 2. (in Marxist thought) the struggle for political and economic power carried on between capitalists and workers.

class·y (klăs′ĭ), *adj. Slang.* of high class, rank, or grade; stylish; fine.

clas·tic (klăs′tĭk), *adj.* 1. *Biol.* breaking up into fragments or separate portions; dividing into parts; causing or undergoing disruption or dissolution: *clastic action, the clastic pole of an ovum, a clastic cell.* 2. pertaining to an anatomical model made up of detachable pieces. 3. *Geol.* noting or pertaining to rock or rocks composed of fragments or particles of older rocks or previously existing solid matter; fragmental [f. m.s. Gk. *klastós* broken + -IC]

clath·rate (klăth′rāt), *adj.* resembling a lattice; divided or marked like latticework.

clat·ter (klăt′ər), *v.i.* 1. to make a rattling sound, as of hard bodies striking rapidly together. 2. to move rapidly with such a sound. 3. to talk fast and noisily; chatter. —*v.t.* 4. to cause to clatter. —*n.* 5. a clattering noise; disturbance. 6. noisy talk; din of voices. 7. idle talk; gossip. [ME *clatren*, OE *clatrian*; of imit. orig. Cf. D *klateren* rattle] —**clat′ter·er,** *n.*

Clau·del (klō·děl′), *n.* **Paul Louis Charles** (pōl lwē shärl), 1868–1955, French diplomat, poet, and dramatist.

clau·di·ca·tion (klō·dĭ·kā′shən), *n.* a limp.

Clau·di·us I (klō′dĭ·əs), 10 B.C.–A.D. 54, Roman emperor, A.D. 41–54.

Claudius II, (*"Gothicus"*) A.D. 214–70, Roman emperor, A.D. 268–70.

clause (klôz), *n.* 1. *Gram.* a group of words containing a subject and a predicate, forming part of a compound or complex sentence, or coextensive with a simple sentence. 2. part of a written composition containing complete sense in itself, as a sentence or paragraph (in modern use commonly limited to such parts of legal documents, as of statutes, contracts, wills, etc.). [ME *claus,* t. ML: s. *clausa* in sense of L *clausula* clause] —**claus′al,** *adj.*

Clau·se·witz (klou′zə·vĭts), *n.* **Karl von** (kärl fən), 1780–1831, German military officer and author of books on military science.

claus·tral (klôs′trəl), *adj.* cloistral; cloisterlike. [t. LL: s. *claustrālis,* der. *claustrum* enclosure, CLOISTER]

claus·tro·pho·bi·a (klôs′trə·fō′bĭ·ə), *n. Psychiatry.* a morbid dread of closed or narrow places. [t. NL, f. *claustro-* (comb. form repr. L *claustrum* enclosure) + *-phobia* -PHOBIA]

cla·vate (klā′vāt), *adj.* club-shaped. [t. L: m. s. *clāvātus,* pp., studded with nails; sense influenced by assoc. with L *clāva* club]

clave (klāv), *v. Archaic.* pt. of cleave.

cla·ver (klā′vər, klä′-), *Scot.* —*n.* 1. idle talk. —*v.i.* 2. to talk idly; gossip.

clav·i·chord (klăv′ə·kôrd′), *n.* an ancient keyboard instrument, in which the strings were softly struck with metal blades vertically projecting from the rear ends of the keys. [t. ML: m. s. *clāvicordium,* f. L: *clāvi*(s) key + m.s. *chorda* string (see CHORD¹) + *-ium -IUM*]

clav·i·cle (klăv′ə·kəl), *n. Anat. Zool.* 1. a bone of the pectoral arch. 2. (in man) either of two slender bones each articulating with the sternum and a scapula and forming the anterior part of a shoulder; the collarbone. See diag. under **shoulder.** [t. L: m.s. *clāvicula,* dim. of *clāvis* key] —**cla·vic·u·lar** (klə·vĭk′yə·lər), *adj.*

clav·i·corn (klăv′ə·kôrn′), *adj.* 1. having club-shaped antennae, as many beetles of the group *Clavicornia.* 2. belonging to this group. —*n.* 3. a clavicorn beetle. [t. NL: s. *clāvicornis,* f. *clavi-* (comb. form repr. L *clāva* club) + *-cornis* horned] —**clav·i·cor·nate** (klăv′ə·kôr′nāt), *adj.*

clav·i·er¹ (klăv′ĭ·ər, klə·vîr′), *n.* the keyboard of a musical instrument. [t. F, der. L *clāvis* key]

cla·vier² (klə·vîr′), *n.* any musical instrument with a keyboard, as a harpsichord, clavichord, piano, or organ. [t. G, t. F: keyboard]

clav·i·form (klăv′ə·fôrm′), *adj.* club-shaped; clavate.

claw (klô), *n.* 1. a sharp, usually curved, nail on the foot of an animal. 2. *Obs.* the foot of an animal armed with such nails. 3. any part or thing resembling a claw, as the cleft end of the head of a hammer. —*v.t.* 4. to tear, scratch, seize, pull, etc., with or as with claws. 5. to scratch gently, as to relieve itching. 6. to make, bring, etc., by clawing: *claw a hole.* [ME *clawen,* OE *clawian,* der. *clawu,* n., c. G *klaue*]

claw hammer, 1. a hammer having a head with one end curved and cleft for drawing nails. 2. *U.S. Colloq.* a dress coat.

clay (klā), *n.* 1. a natural earthy material which is plastic when wet, consisting essentially of hydrated silicates of aluminum, and used for making bricks, pottery, etc. 2. earth; mud. 3. earth as the material from which the human body was originally formed. 4. the human body. [ME; OE *clæg,* c. D and G *klei*] —**clay·ey** (klā′ĭ), *adj.* —**clay·ish,** *adj.*

Clay (klā), *n.* **Henry,** 1777–1852, U.S. statesman and orator.

clay·bank (klā′băngk′), *n.* a yellow shade; dun; brownish yellow.

clay·more (klā′mōr′), *n.* 1. a heavy two-edged sword formerly used by the Scottish Highlanders. 2. a baskethilted broadsword, often single-edged, used by Highlanders. [t. Gaelic: m. *claidheamh mor* great sword]

clay pigeon, *Trapshooting.* a disc of baked clay or other material hurled into the air as a target.

clay stone, 1. a deeply decomposed igneous rock. 2. argillite.

clay·to·ni·a (klā tō′nĭ ə), *n.* any of the low, succulent portulacaceous herbs constituting the genus *Claytonia.* [named after Dr. J. *Clayton* (1685?–1773), American botanist]

-cle, var. of **-cule.** [t. L: m. *-culus, -cula, -culum;* in some words, t. F]

clean (klēn), *adj.* 1. free from dirt or filth; unsoiled; unstained. 2. **a.** free from foreign or extraneous matter. **b.** *Physics, Chem.* free of radioactivity. 3. free from defect or blemish. 4. unadulterated; pure. 5. entirely (or almost so) without corrections; easily readable: *clean printer's proofs.* 6. free from encumbrances or obstructions: *a clean harbor.* 7. (of a ship) **a.** having its bottom free of marine growth, etc. **b.** empty; having nothing in its cargo spaces. 8. free from any form of defilement; morally pure; innocent; upright; honorable. 9. free from dirty habits, as an animal. 10. (among the Jews) **a.** (of persons) free from ceremonial defilement. **b.** (of animals, fowl, and fish) permissible to eat. 11. neatly or evenly made or proportioned; shapely; trim. 12. free from awkwardness; not bungling; dextrous; adroit: *a clean boxer, a clean leap.* 13. complete; perfect: *a clean sweep.* —*adv.* 14. in a clean manner; cleanly. 15. wholly; completely; quite. —*v.t.* 16. to make clean. 17. **clean out, a.** to rid of dirt, etc. **b.** to use up; exhaust. **c.** *U.S. Slang.* to drive out by force. **d.** *U.S. Colloq.* to empty or rid (a place) of occupants, contents, etc.: *clean out the larder.* 18. **clean up, a.** to rid of dirt, etc. **b.** to put in order; tidy up. **c.** to finish up; reach the end of. **d.** *U.S. Colloq.* to make a large profit. —*v.i.* 19. to perform or to undergo a process of cleaning. 20. to get rid of dirt, etc. (fol. by *up*): *to clean up for dinner.* [ME *clene,* OE *clǣne* pure, clear, c. D and G *klein* small] —**clean′a·ble,** *adj.* —**clean′ness,** *n.* —**Syn.** 1. CLEAN, CLEAR, PURE refer to freedom from soiling, flaw, stain, or mixture. CLEAN refers esp. to freedom from soiling: *a clean dress.* CLEAR refers particularly to freedom from flaw or blemish: *a clear pane of glass.* PURE refers esp. to freedom from mixture or stain: *a pure metal, not diluted but pure and full strength.* 8. unsullied, chaste, virtuous. 16. scour, scrub, sweep, brush, wipe, mop, dust, wash, rinse, lave. CLEAN, CLEANSE refer to removing dirt or impurities. To CLEAN is the general word with no implication of method or means: *to clean windows, a kitchen, streets.* CLEANSE is esp. used of thorough cleaning by chemical or other technical process; figuratively it applies to moral or spiritual purification: *to cleanse parts of machinery, one's soul of guilt.* —**Ant.** 1. unclean. 8. impure. 16. soil.

clean-cut (klēn′kŭt′), *adj.* 1. distinctly outlined. 2. well-shaped. 3. definite. 4. neat and wholesome.

clean·er (klē′nər), *n.* 1. one who or that which cleans. 2. an apparatus or preparation for cleaning.

clean·ly (*adj.* klĕn′lĭ; *adv.* klēn′lĭ), *adj.,* **-lier, -liest,** *adv.* —*adj.* 1. personally neat; careful to keep or make clean. 2. habitually clean. 3. *Obs.* cleansing; making clean. —*adv.* 4. in a clean manner. —**clean·li·ly** (klĕn′la lĭ), *adv.* —**clean·li·ness** (klĕn′lĭ nĭs), *n.*

cleanse (klĕnz), *v.t.,* **cleansed, cleansing.** 1. to make clean. 2. to remove by, or as by, cleaning: *his leprosy was cleansed.* [ME *clense(n),* OE *clǣnsian,* der. *clǣne* clean] —**cleans′er,** *n.* —**Syn.** 1. See **clean.**

clean-shav·en (klēn′shā′vən), *adj.* having all the hairs shaved off.

Cle·an·thes (klĭ ăn′thēz), *n.* c300–c232 B.C., Greek Stoic philosopher.

clean-up (klēn′ŭp′), *n.* 1. act or process of cleaning up, esp. of gambling, vice, graft, etc. 2. *Slang.* a very large profit.

clear (klĭr), *adj.* 1. free from darkness, obscurity, or cloudiness; light. 2. bright; shining. 3. transparent; pellucid: *good, clear wine.* 4. of a pure, even color: *a clear complexion.* 5. distinctly perceptible to the eye, ear, or mind; easily seen, heard, or understood. 6. distinct; evident; plain. 7. free from confusion, uncertainty, or doubt. 8. perceiving or discerning distinctly: *a clear head.* 9. convinced; certain. 10. free from guilt or blame; innocent. 11. serene; calm; untroubled. 12. free from obstructions or obstacles; open: *a clear space.* 13. unentangled or disengaged; free; quit or rid (fol. by *of*). 14. having no parts that protrude, are rough, etc. 15. freed or emptied of contents, cargo, etc. 16. without limitation or qualification: *the clear contrary.* 17. without obligation or liability; free from debt. 18. without deduction or diminution: *a clear $1000.* 19. *Phonet.* (of e sounds) light, palatal, ē-like. 20. *Obs.* illustrious. —*adv.* 21. in a clear manner; clearly; distinctly; entirely. —*v.t.* 22. to make clear; free from darkness, cloudiness, muddiness, indistinctness, confusion, uncertainty, obstruction, contents, entanglement, obligation, liability, etc. 23. to free from imputation, esp. of guilt; prove or declare to be innocent. 24. to pass or get over without entanglement or collision. 25. to pay (a debt) in full. 26. to pass (checks, etc.) through a clearing house. 27. to obtain the money required for. 28. to gain as clear profit: *to clear $1000 in a transaction.* 29. to free (a ship, cargo, etc.) from legal detention at a port by satisfying the customs and other required conditions. 30. *U.S.* to try or otherwise dispose of (the cases awaiting court action): *to clear the docket.* —*v.i.* 31. to become clear. 32. to exchange checks and bills, and settle balances, as in a clearing house. 33. (of a ship) **a.** to comply with the customs and other

conditions legally imposed upon leaving or entering a port. **b.** to leave port after having complied with such conditions. 34. Some special verb phrases are: **clear away, off,** etc., 1. to remove so as to leave something clear. 2. to disappear; vanish. **clear out,** *Colloq.* to go away. **clear up,** 1. to make clear. 2. to solve; explain. 3. to put in order; tidy up. 4. to become brighter, lighter, etc. —*n.* 35. a clear or unobstructed space. 36. **in the clear, a.** between the bounding parts. **b.** free. [ME *cler,* t. OF, g. L *clārus*] —**clear′a·ble,** *adj.* —**clear′er,** *n.* —**Syn.** 1. See **clean.** 3. translucent, limpid, crystalline, diaphanous. 5. intelligible, comprehensible. 6. obvious, manifest, apparent. 7. unmistakable, unambiguous.

clear·ance (klĭr′əns), *n.* 1. act of clearing. 2. a clear space; a clearing. 3. an intervening space, as between machine parts for free play. 4. *Banking.* an exchange of checks and other commercial paper drawn on members of a clearing house, usually effected at a daily meeting of the members. 5. the clearing of a ship at a port. 6. the official certificate or papers (**clearance papers**) indicating this.

Cle·ar·chus (klĭ är′kəs), *n.* died 401 B.C., Spartan general.

clear-cut (klĭr′kŭt′), *adj.* cut or formed with clearly defined outlines; distinctly defined.

clear-eyed (klĭr′īd′), *adj.* 1. having clear, bright eyes; clear-sighted. 2. mentally acute or discerning.

clear-head·ed (klĭr′hĕd′ĭd), *adj.* having or showing a clear head or understanding. —**clear′-head′ed·ness,** *n.*

clear·ing (klĭr′ĭng), *n.* 1. act of one who or that which clears. 2. a tract of cleared land, as in a forest. 3. the mutual exchange between banks of checks and drafts, and the settlement of the differences. 4. (*pl.*) the total of claims settled at a clearing house.

clearing house, a place or institution where mutual claims and accounts are settled, as between banks.

clear·ly (klĭr′lĭ), *adv.* in a clear manner. —**Syn.** CLEARLY, DEFINITELY, DISTINCTLY, EVIDENTLY imply the way in which something is plainly understood or understandable. CLEARLY suggests without doubt or obscurity: *expressed clearly.* DEFINITELY means explicitly, with precision: *definitely phrased.* DISTINCTLY means without blurring or confusion: *distinctly enunciated.* EVIDENTLY means patently, unquestionably: *evidently an error.*

clear·ness (klĭr′nĭs), *n.* state or quality of being clear; distinctness; plainness.

clear-sight·ed (klĭr′sī′tĭd), *adj.* having clear sight; having keen mental perception; discerning; perspicacious: *clear-sighted businessman, reason, etc.* —**clear′-sight′ed·ly,** *adv.* —**clear′-sight′ed·ness,** *n.*

clear-starch (klĭr′stärch′), *v.t., v.i.* to stiffen and dress (linen, etc.) with clear or transparent (boiled) starch. —**clear′starch′er,** *n.*

clear-sto·ry (klĭr′stōr′ĭ), *n., pl.* **-ries.** clerestory.

clear·wing (klĭr′wĭng′), *n.* a moth with wings for the most part destitute of scales and transparent, esp. any of the family *Aegeriidae,* many species of which are injurious to plants.

cleat (klēt), *n.* 1. a small wedge-shaped block, as one fastened to a spar or the like as a support, check, etc. 2. *Naut.* **a.** a piece of wood nailed down to secure something from slipping. **b.** a piece of wood or iron consisting of a bar with arms, to which ropes are belayed. 3. a piece of wood or iron fastened across anything for support, security, etc. 4. a piece of iron fastened under a shoe to preserve the sole. 5. *Coal Mining.* the cleavage (plane) in coal to which it breaks, as **face cleat** (prominent), **butt cleat** (poor). —*v.t.* 6. to supply or strengthen with cleats; fasten to or with a cleat. [ME *clete* wedge, c. D *kloot* ball. Cf. CLOT]

Cleats (def. 2b), one of which is lashed to a stay

cleav·a·ble (klē′və bəl), *adj.* that may be cleft or split.

cleav·age (klē′vĭj), *n.* 1. act of cleaving. 2. state of being cleft or split; division. 3. *Biol.* the total or partial division of the egg into smaller cells or blastomeres. 4. *Crystall.* the tendency to break in certain definite directions, yielding more or less smooth surfaces. 5. *Chem.* the breaking down of a molecule or compound into simpler molecules or compounds.

cleave[1] (klēv), *v.i.,* **cleaved** or (*Archaic*) **clave, cleaved, cleaving.** 1. to stick or adhere; cling or hold fast (fol. by *to*). 2. to be attached or faithful (fol. by *to*). [ME *cleve(n),* OE *cleofian,* c. G *kleben*]

cleave[2] (klēv), *v.,* **cleft** or **cleaved** or **clove, cleft** or **cleaved** or **cloven, cleaving.** —*v.t.* 1. to part by, or as by, a cutting blow, esp. along the grain or any other natural line of division. 2. to split; rend apart; rive. 3. to penetrate or pass through (air, water, etc.). 4. to make by or as by cutting: *to cleave a path through the wilderness.* 5. to separate or sever by, or as by, splitting. —*v.i.* 6. to part or split, esp. along a natural line of division. 7. to penetrate or pass (fol. by *through*). [ME *cleven,* OE *cleofan,* c. D *klieven.* Cf. Gk. *glyphein* carve]

cleav·er (klē′vər), *n.* 1. one who or that which cleaves. 2. a heavy knife or long-bladed hatchet used by butchers for cutting up carcasses.

cleav·ers (klē′vərz), *n. sing.* and *pl.* 1. a rubiaceous plant, *Galium aparine,* with short hooked bristles by means of which it adheres to clothing, etc. **2.** any of certain related species. [ME *clivre* (der. CLEAVE¹), r. OE *clife*]

cleek (klēk), *n. Golf.* a club having an iron head with a long, narrow face. [akin to CLUTCH¹]

clef (klĕf), *n. Music.* a symbol placed upon a staff to indicate the name and pitch of the notes corresponding to its lines and spaces. The **G clef** (or **treble clef**) indicates that the second line of the staff corresponds to the G next above middle C. The **F clef** (or **bass clef**) indicates that the fourth line of the staff corresponds to the F next below middle C. [t. F, g. L *clāvis* key]

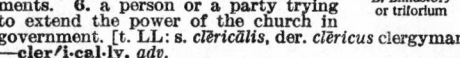
G Clef   F Clef

cleft¹ (klĕft), *n.* **1.** a space or opening made by cleavage; a split. **2.** a division formed by cleaving. **3.** (in horses) a crack on the bend of the pastern. [ME *clift*, OE *geclyft* split, crack, fissure] —**Syn. 1.** fissure, crevice, crack.

cleft² (klĕft), *v.* a pt. and pp. of **cleave².** —*adj.* **2.** cloven; split; divided. **3.** (of a leaf) having divisions formed by incisions or narrow sinuses which extend halfway, or more than halfway, to the midrib or the base.

cleft palate, a congenital defect of the palate in which a longitudinal fissure exists in the roof of the mouth.

clei·do·ic (klī′dō·ĭk), *adj. Embryol.* closed-up. Cleidoic eggs, as those of birds and insects, have little more than gaseous exchange with the environment. [f. m. Gk. *kleidó(ein)* lock up + -ic]

Cleis·the·nes (klīs′thə·nēz′), *n.* fl. 508 B.C., Athenian statesman.

cleis·tog·a·my (klī·stŏg′ə·mĭ), *n. Bot.* the condition of having (usually in addition to the ordinary, fully developed flowers) small, inconspicuous flowers which do not open, but are pollinated from their own anthers, as in the case of the pansy. [f. m. Gk. *kleistó(s)* closed + -GAMY] —**cleis·tog′a·mous, cleis·to·gam·ic** (klī′stə·găm′ĭk), *adj.*

clem·a·tis (klĕm′ə·tĭs), *n.* **1.** any of the flowering vines or erect shrubs constituting the ranunculaceous genus *Clematis*, as *C. virginiana*, the virgin's-bower of the U. S. **2.** any plant of the allied genus *Atragene*. [t. L, t. Gk.: m. *klēmatis*, dim. of *klēma* vine branch]

Cle·men·ceau (klĕm′ən·sō′; *Fr.* klĕ·män·sō′), *n.* Georges Eugène Benjamin (zhôrzh œ·zhĕn′ băn·zhä·män′), 1841–1929, French statesman, journalist, editor, author, and physician: premier of France, 1906–09 and 1917–20.

clem·en·cy (klĕm′ən·sĭ), *n., pl.* -cies. **1.** the quality of being clement; mildness of temper, as shown by a superior to an inferior, or by an aggrieved person to the offender; disposition to spare or forgive; mercy; leniency; forbearance. **2.** an act or deed showing mercy or leniency. **3.** mildness: *the clemency of the weather.* [t. L: m. s. *clēmentia*] —**Ant. 1.** harshness. **3.** severity.

Clem·ens (klĕm′ənz), *n.* **Samuel Langhorne** (lăng′hôrn, -ərn), ("Mark Twain") 1835–1910, U. S. author and humorist.

clem·ent (klĕm′ənt), *adj.* **1.** mild or merciful in disposition; lenient; compassionate. **2.** (of the weather, etc.) mild or pleasant. [late ME, t. L: s. *clēmens*] —**clem′ent·ly,** *adv.*

Clement VII (klĕm′ənt), (Giulio de'Medici) 1478?–1534, Italian ecclesiastic: pope, 1523–34 (nephew of Lorenzo de' Medici).

Clement of Alexandria, A.D. c150–c215, Greek Christian theologian and writer.

clench (klĕnch), *v.t.* **1.** to close (the hands, teeth, etc.) tightly. **2.** to grasp firmly; grip. **3.** to settle decisively; clinch. **4.** *Naut.* to clinch. —*n.* **5.** act of clenching. **6.** a tight hold; grip. **7.** that which holds fast or clenches. **8.** *Naut.* a clinch. [ME *clench(en)*, OE *-clencan* (in *beclencan* hold fast)]

cle·o·me (klĭ·ō′mĭ), *n.* any of the numerous herbaceous or shrubby plants constituting the genus *Cleome*, mostly natives of tropical regions, and often bearing showy flowers.

Cle·om·e·nes III (klĭ·ŏm′ə·nēz′), died 220? B.C., king of Sparta, 235?–220? B.C.

Cle·on (klē′ŏn), *n.* died 422 B.C., Athenian general and political opponent of Pericles.

Cle·o·pa·tra (klē′ō·pă′trə, -păt′rə, -pā′trə), *n.* 69?–30 B.C., queen of Egypt, 47–30 B.C. She saved her kingdom by winning the love of Julius Caesar and Marcus Antonius, but was defeated by Octavian. After her death by suicide, Egypt became a Roman province.

clepe (klēp), *v.t.,* cleped or clept (also ycleped or yclept), cleping. *Archaic.* to call; name (now chiefly in the pp. as ycleped or yclept). [ME *clepien*, OE *cleopian*]

clep·sy·dra (klĕp′sə·drə), *n., pl.* -dras, -drae (-drē′). a device for measuring time by the regulated flow of water or mercury through a small aperture. [t. L, t. Gk.: m. *klepsydra*]

clep·to·ma·ni·a (klĕp′tə·mā′nĭ·ə), *n.* kleptomania. —**clep′to·ma′ni·ac′,** *n.*

clere·sto·ry (klĭr′stōr′ĭ), *n., pl.* -ries. **1.** the upper part of the nave, transepts, and choir of a building, esp. a church, perforated with a series of windows above the aisle roofs, and forming the chief source of light for the building. See illus. in next col. **2.** any similar raised construction, as that for ventilating a railroad car. Also, **clearstory.** [f. *cler-* CLEAR (def. 1) + m. F *estoré* built]

cler·gy (klûr′jĭ), *n., pl.* -gies. the body of men ordained for ministration in the Christian church, in distinction from the laity. [ME *clergie*, t. OF, ult. der. LL *clēricus* CLERIC]

cler·gy·man (klûr′jĭ·mən), *n., pl.* -men. **1.** a member of the clergy. **2.** an ordained Christian minister.

cler·ic (klĕr′ĭk), *n.* **1.** a member of the clergy. **2.** a member of a clerical party. —*adj.* **3.** pertaining to the clergy; clerical. [t. LL: s. *clēricus*, t. Gk.: m. *klērikós*, der. *klēros* clergy, orig., lot, allotment]

cler·i·cal (klĕr′ə·kəl), *adj.* **1.** pertaining to a clerk or copyist, or to clerks: *a clerical error.* **2.** of, pertaining to, or characteristic of the clergy or a clergyman. **3.** upholding the power or influence of the clergy in politics. —*n.* **4.** a cleric. **5.** (*pl.*) *Colloq.* clerical garments. **6.** a person or a party trying to extend the power of the church in government. [t. LL: s. *clēricālis*, der. *clēricus* clergyman] —**cler′i·cal·ly,** *adv.*

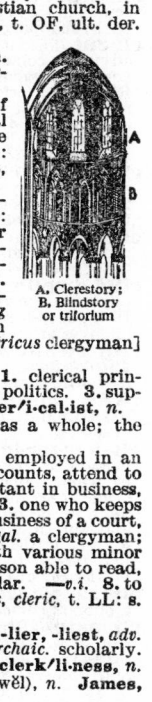
A. Clerestory; B. Blindstory or triforium

cler·i·cal·ism (klĕr′ə·kə·lĭz′əm), *n.* **1.** clerical principles. **2.** clerical power or influence in politics. **3.** support of such power or influence. —**cler′i·cal·ist,** *n.*

cler·i·sy (klĕr′ə·sĭ), *n.* learned men as a whole; the literati. [t. ML: m.s. *clēricia*]

clerk (klûrk; *Brit.* klärk), *n.* **1.** one employed in an office, shop, etc., to keep records or accounts, attend to correspondence, etc. **2.** *U.S.* an assistant in business, esp. a retail salesman or saleswoman. **3.** one who keeps the records and performs the routine business of a court, legislature, board, etc. **4.** *Chiefly Legal.* a clergyman; ecclesiastic. **5.** a layman charged with various minor ecclesiastical duties. **6.** *Archaic.* a person able to read, or to read and write. **7.** *Archaic.* a scholar. —*v.i.* **8.** to act or serve as a clerk. [ME; OE *clerc, cleric,* t. LL: s. *clēricus* CLERIC] —**clerk′ship′,** *n.*

clerk·ly (klûrk′lĭ; *Brit.* klärk′-), *adj.,* -lier, -liest, *adv.* —*adj.* **1.** of a clerk or clerks. **2.** *Archaic.* scholarly. —*adv.* **3.** in the manner of a clerk. —**clerk′li·ness,** *n.*

Clerk-Max·well (klärk′măks′wəl, -wĕl), *n.* **James,** 1831–79, British physicist.

Cler·mont-Fer·rand (klĕr·môN′fĕ·rän′), *n.* a city in central France. 113,391 (1954).

cleve·ite (klēv′īt), *n.* a crystallized variety of uraninite. [named after P. T. *Cleve* (1840–1905), Swedish chemist]

Cleve·land (klēv′lənd), *n.* **1.** (Stephen) Grover (grō′vər), 1837–1908, 22nd and 24th president of the U.S., 1885–89, 1893–97. **2.** a city in NE Ohio: a port on Lake Erie. 876,050 (1960).

Cleveland Heights, a city in NE Ohio, near Cleveland. 61,813 (1960).

clev·er (klĕv′ər), *adj.* **1.** bright mentally; having quick intelligence; able. **2.** dexterous or nimble with the hands or body. **3.** showing adroitness or ingenuity: *a clever remark, a clever device.* **4.** *Colloq. or Dial.* suitable; convenient; satisfactory. **5.** *U.S. Colloq.* good-natured. **6.** *Dial.* handsome. **7.** *Dial.* in good health. [ME *cliver*; orig. uncert.] —**clev′er·ish,** *adj.* —**clev′er·ly,** *adv.* —**clev′er·ness,** *n.* —**Syn. 1.** ingenious, talented, quick-witted. **2.** skillful, adroit. —**Ant. 1.** stupid. **2.** clumsy.

clev·is (klĕv′ĭs), *n.* a piece of metal, usually U-shaped, with a pin or bolt passing through holes at the two ends, as for attaching an implement to a drawbar for pulling. [akin to CLEAVE²]

C. Clevis

clew (klōō), *n.* **1.** a ball or skein of thread, yarn, etc. **2.** *Legend.* a ball of thread unwound to serve as a guide through a labyrinth. **3.** (*often spelled* clue) anything that serves to guide or direct in the solution of a problem, mystery, etc. **4.** (*pl. or sing.*) the rigging for a hammock. **5.** *Naut.* either lower corner of a square sail or the after lower corner of a fore-and-aft sail. —*v.t.* **6.** to coil into a ball. **7.** to direct or point out by a clew. **8.** *Naut.* to haul (the lower corners of a sail) up to the yard by means of the clew lines (fol. by *up*). [ME *clewe*, OE *cleowen, c.* D *kluwen*]

clew iron, a ring in the corner of a sail bearing thimbles to which the clew lines are secured.

clew line, a rope by which a clew of a square sail is hauled to the yard.

cli·ché (klē·shā′; *Fr.* -shĕ′), *n., pl.* -chés (-shäz′; *Fr.* -shĕ′). **1.** a trite, stereotyped expression, idea, practice, etc., as *sadder but wiser,* or *strong as an ox.* **2.** *Print.* **a.** a stereotype or electrotype plate. **b.** a reproduction made in a like manner. [t. F, pp. of *clicher* to stereotype. Cf. G *klitsch* doughy mass]

Cli·chy (klē·shē′), *n.* suburb of Paris, France, on the Seine. 55,591 (1954).

click (klĭk), *n.* **1.** a slight, sharp sound: *the click of a latch.* **2.** some clicking mechanism, as a detent or a pawl. **3.** *Phonet.* a speech sound produced by allowing air to flow suddenly into a partial vacuum in the mouth or in part of the mouth. —*v.i.* **4.** to emit or make a slight, sharp sound, or series of such sounds, as by the cocking of a pistol. **5.** *Slang.* to make a success; make a hit. —*v.t.* **6.** to cause to click; strike with a click. [imit. Cf. D *klikken*] —**click′er,** *n.*

---

click beetle, an elaterid beetle that makes a clicking sound in springing up, as after having been laid on its back; snapping beetle.

cli·ent (klī'ənt), *n.* **1.** one who applies to a lawyer for advice or commits his cause or legal interests to a lawyer's management. **2.** a customer. **3.** (in ancient Rome) **a.** (orig.) a hereditary dependent of one of the nobility. **b.** a plebeian who lived under the patronage of a patrician. **4.** anyone under the patronage of another; a dependent. [ME, t. L: s. *cliens* retainer] —**cli·en·tal** (klī ĕn'təl, klī'ən təl), *adj.*

cli·en·tele (klī'ən těl'), *n.* **1.** the customers, patients, etc. (of a lawyer, doctor, businessman, etc.) as a whole. **2.** dependents or followers. Also, **cli·ent·age** (klī'ən tǐj). [t. L: m. *clientēla* a body of retainers]

cliff (klǐf), *n.* the high, steep face of a rocky mass; precipice. Also, *Archaic or Dial.*, **clift** (klǐft). [ME and OE *clif*, c. Icel. *klif*]

cliff dweller, 1. one who dwells on a cliff. **2.** (*usually cap.*) one of a prehistoric people of the southwestern U. S., ancestors of the Pueblo Indians, who built houses in caves or on ledges of the cliffs. —**cliff dwelling.**

cliff swallow, a colonial North American bird, *Petrochelidon pyrrhonota*, so called because it attaches its bottle-shaped nests of mud to cliffs and walls.

cliff·y (klǐf'ĭ), *adj.* having, or formed by, cliffs; craggy.

Clif·ton (klǐf'tən), *n.* a city in NE New Jersey. 82,084 (1960).

cli·mac·ter·ic (klī măk'tər ĭk, klī'măk těr'ĭk), *adj.* **1.** pertaining to a critical period; crucial. —*n.* **2.** a year in which important changes in health, fortune, etc. occur: *the grand climacteric (the sixty-third year).* **3.** *Physiol.* a period of decrease of reproductive activity in men and women, culminating, in women, in the menopause. **4.** any critical period. Also, **cli·mac·ter·i·cal** (klī'măk těr'ə kəl). [t. L: s. *clīmactēricus*, t. Gk.: m. *klīmaktērikós* of the nature of a critical period]

cli·mac·tic (klī măk'tĭk), *adj.* pertaining to or forming a climax: *climactic arrangement.* Also, **cli·mac'ti·cal.**

cli·mate (klī'mǐt), *n.* **1.** the composite or generalization of weather conditions of a region, as temperature, pressure, humidity, precipitation, sunshine, cloudiness, and winds, throughout the year, averaged over a series of years. **2.** an area of a particular kind of climate. [ME *climat*, t. LL: s. *clima*, t. Gk.: m. *klīma* clime, zone, lit., slope (of the earth from equator to pole)] —**cli·mat·ic** (klī măt'ĭk), *adj.* —**cli·mat'i·cal·ly,** *adv.*

cli·ma·tol·o·gy (klī'mə tŏl'ə jĭ), *n.* the science that deals with climates or climatic conditions. —**cli·ma·to·logic** (klī'mə tə lŏj'ĭk), **cli·ma·to·log'i·cal,** *adj.* —**cli·ma·tol'o·gist,** *n.*

cli·max (klī'măks), *n.* **1.** the highest point of anything; the culmination. **2.** that point in the drama in which it is clear that the central motive will or will not be successful. **3.** *Rhet.* **a.** a figure consisting in a series of related ideas so arranged that each surpasses the preceding in force or intensity. **b.** (popularly) the last term or member of this figure. **4.** *Ecol.* that stage in the ecological succession or evolution of a plant-animal community, which is stable and self-perpetuating. —*v.i., v.t.* **5.** to reach, or bring to, the climax. [t. L, t. Gk.: m. *klīmax* ladder, staircase, climax]

climb (klīm), *v.,* **climbed** or (*Archaic*) **clomb, climbed** or (*Archaic*) **clomb, climbing,** *n.* —*v.i.* **1.** to mount or ascend, esp. by using both hands and feet. **2.** to rise slowly by, or as by, continued effort. **3.** to slope upward. **4.** to ascend by twining or by means of tendrils, adhesive tissues, etc., as a plant. **5.** climb down, **a.** to descend, esp. by using both hands and feet. **b.** *Colloq.* to withdraw from an untenable position. —*v.t.* **6.** to ascend, go up, or get to the top of, esp. by the use of hands and feet. **7.** to descend (a ladder, pole, etc.), esp. by using both hands and feet (fol. by *down*). —*n.* **8.** a climbing; an ascent by climbing. **9.** a place to be climbed. [ME *climben*, OE *climban*, c. D and G *klimmen*] —**climb'a·ble,** *adj.*
—**Syn. 1.** CLIMB, ASCEND, MOUNT, SCALE imply a moving upward. To CLIMB is to make one's way upward with effort: *to climb a mountain.* ASCEND, in its literal meaning (to go up), is general; but it now usually suggests a gradual or stately movement, with or without effort, often to a considerable degree of altitude: *to ascend stairs, to ascend the Hudson River.* MOUNT may be interchangeable with ascend, but also suggests climbing on top of or astride of: *to mount a platform, a horse.* SCALE, a more literary word, implies difficult or hazardous climbing up or over something: *to scale a summit.* —**Ant. 1, 6.** descend.

climb·er (klī'mər), *n.* **1.** one who or that which climbs. **2.** a person who strives to associate with social superiors. **3.** a climbing plant. **4.** a spike attached to a shoe to assist in climbing poles, etc.

climb indicator, *Aeron.* an instrument to show the rate of ascent or descent, operating on a differential pressure principle.

climbing fish, a small East Indian fish, *Anabas testudineus,* which is reputed to climb trees.

climbing irons, iron frames with spikes attached, worn on the feet or legs to help in climbing trees, etc.

clime (klīm), *n.* *Poetic.* **1.** a tract or region of the earth. **2.** climate. [t. L: m. *clima* CLIMATE]

cli·nan·dri·um (klī năn'drĭ əm), *n., pl.* **-dria** (-drĭ ə). a cavity in the apex of the column in orchids, in which the anthers rest; the androclinium. [t. NL, f. s. Gk. *klīnē* bed + s. Gk. *anér* man + *-ium* -IUM]

clinch (klǐnch), *v.t.* **1.** to secure (a driven nail, etc.) by beating down the point. **2.** to fasten (work) together thus. **3.** to settle (a matter) decisively. **4.** *Naut.* to fasten by a clinch. —*v.i.* **5.** *Boxing, etc.* to grasp tightly; grapple. **6.** to beat down the point of a nail, etc. in order to fasten something. —*n.* **7.** act of clinching **8.** *Boxing, etc.* a grasp; grapple. **9.** a clinched nail o fastening. **10.** the clinched part of a nail, etc. **11.** *Naut.* a kind of hitch in which the end of the rope is fastened back by seizing. **12.** *Obs.* a pun. [later var. of CLENCH]

clinch·er (klǐnch'ər), *n.* **1.** one who or that which clinches. **2.** a nail, etc. for clinching. **3.** something decisive.

cling (klǐng), *v.,* **clung, clinging,** *n.* —*v.i.* **1.** to adher closely; stick. **2.** to hold fast, as by grasping or em bracing; cleave. **3.** to be or remain close. **4.** to remain attached (to an idea, hope, memory, etc.). **5.** *Obs.* to cohere. —*n.* **6.** the act of clinging; adherence; attach ment. [ME *clingen*, OE *clingan* stick or draw together shrivel] —**cling'er,** *n.* —**cling'ing·ly,** *adv.*

cling·fish (klǐng'fǐsh'), *n., pl.* **-fishes,** (*esp. collectively fish.* any fish of the family *Gobiesocidae,* all of which have a ventral sucking disc constructed from the pectoral a well as the pelvic fins. They use this disc to adher tightly to rocks.

Cling·mans Dome (klǐng'mənz), a mountain on th border between North Carolina and Tennessee: the highest peak in the Great Smoky Mountains. 6642 ft.

cling·stone (klǐng'stōn'), *adj.* **1.** having a stone t which the pulp adheres closely, as certain peaches —*n.* **2.** a clingstone peach.

cling·y (klǐng'ĭ), *adj.* apt to cling; adhesive or tena cious: *dirt of a wet and clingy nature.*

clin·ic (klǐn'ĭk), *n.* **1.** a place, as in connection with medical school or a hospital, for the treatment of non resident patients. **2.** the instruction of medical student by examining or treating patients in their presence. **3.** class of students assembled for such instruction. **4.** th place for such instruction. —*adj.* **5.** clinical. [t. LL s. *clīnicus* pertaining to a bed, t. Gk.: m. *klīnikós*]

clin·i·cal (klǐn'ə kəl), *adj.* **1.** pertaining to a clinic **2.** pertaining to or used in a sickroom. **3.** concerne with observation and treatment of disease in the patien (as distinguished from an artificial experiment). **4.** ad ministered on a sickbed or deathbed: *clinical conversio or baptism.* —**clin'i·cal·ly,** *adv.*

clinical thermometer, an instrument used to de termine the body temperature.

cli·ni·cian (klǐ nǐsh'ən), *n.* a physician who studie diseases at the bedside, or is skilled in clinical methods

clink[1] (klǐngk), *n., v., v.t.* **1.** to make, or cause to make a light, sharp, ringing sound. **2.** to rhyme or jingle —*n.* **3.** a clinking sound. **4.** a rhyme; jingle. **5.** th rather piercing cry of some birds, as the stonechat. [MF *clynk(e)*. Cf. D *klinken*]

clink[2] (klǐngk), *n.* *Colloq.* a prison; jail; lockup. [appar from *Clink* prison on Clink Street, London]

clink·er[1] (klǐng'kər), *n.* **1.** a hard brick, used for pav ing, etc. **2.** a partially vitrified mass of brick. **3.** th scale of oxide formed on iron during forging. **4.** a mas of incombustible matter fused together, as in the burn ing of coal. —*v.i.* **5.** to form clinkers in burning, a coal. [t. D: m. *klinker* kind of brick]

clink·er[2] (klǐng'kər), *n.* one who or that which clinks [f. CLINK[1] + -ER[1]]

clink·er-built (klǐng'kər bǐlt'), *adj.* made of pieces as boards or plates of metal, which overlap one another

clink·stone (klǐngk'stōn'), *n.* *Petrog.* any of severa varieties of phonolite which give out a ringing sound when struck.

cli·nom·e·ter (klī nŏm'ə tər, klĭ-), *n.* an instrumen used to determine inclination or slope. [f. *clino-* (comb form repr. L *-clīnāre* incline) + -METER]

cli·no·met·ric (klī'nə mĕt'rĭk), *adj.* **1.** (of crystals having oblique angles between one or all axes. **2.** per taining to or determined by a clinometer. Also, **cli'no met'ri·cal.**

clin·quant (klǐng'kənt), *adj.* **1.** glittering, esp. with tinsel; decked with garish finery. —*n.* **2.** imitation gol leaf; tinsel. **3.** *Obs.* tinsel; false glitter. [t. F, ppr. o obs. *clinquer* clink, tinkle, glitter, t. D: m. *klinken*]

Clin·ton (klǐn'tən), *n.* **1.** De Witt (də wǐt'), 1769-1828, U.S. political leader: governor of New York State sponsor of the Erie Canal. **2.** George, 1739-1812, gov ernor of New York State: vice-president of the U.S. 1805-12. **3.** James, 1733-1812, American general in Revolutionary War. **4.** Sir Henry, 1738?-95, com mander in chief of the British forces in the American Revolutionary War. **5.** a city in E Iowa, on the Mis sissippi. 33,589 (1960).

clin·to·ni·a (klǐn tō'nĭ ə), *n.* any plant of the liliaceou genus *Clintonia,* comprising stemless perennial herb with a few broad, ribbed, basal leaves, and white o greenish-yellow flowers on a short peduncle. [t. NL named after De Witt *Clinton*]

Cli·o (klī'ō), *n. Class. Myth.* the Muse of history.

clip[1] (klǐp), *v.,* **clipped, clipping,** *n.* —*v.t.* **1.** to cut, o cut off or out, as with shears; trim by cutting. **2.** t cut or trim the hair or fleece of; shear. **3.** to pare th edge of (a coin). **4.** to cut short; curtail. **5.** to omi sounds of (a word) in pronouncing. **6.** *Colloq.* to hit with a quick, sharp blow. —*v.i.* **7.** to clip or cut something **8.** to cut articles or pictures from a newspaper, magazine etc. **9.** to move swiftly. **10.** *Archaic.* to fly rapidly. —*n.* **11.** act of clipping. **12.** anything clipped off, esp. the wool shorn at a single shearing of sheep. **13.** the amount of wool shorn in one season. **14.** (*pl.*) shears. **15.** *Colloq.* a quick, sharp blow or punch. **16.** *Colloq.* rate; pace: *at a rapid clip.* [ME *clippen*, t. Scand.; cf. Icel. *klippa*]

clip² (klĭp), *n.*, *v.*, **clipped, clipping.** —*n.* **1.** a device for gripping and holding tightly; a metal clasp, esp. one for papers, letters, etc. **2.** a flange on the upper surface of a horseshoe. **3.** cartridge clip. **4.** *Archaic or Dial.* an embrace. —*v.t.*, *v.i.* **5.** to grip tightly; hold together by pressure. **6.** to encircle; encompass. **7.** *Football.* to stop (a player who does not have the ball) by illegally hurling the body across his legs from behind. **8.** *Archaic or Dial.* to embrace or hug. [ME *clippe*(n), OE *clyppan* embrace]

clip-fed (klĭp′fĕd′), *adj.* (of a rifle) loading from a cartridge clip into the magazine.

clip-per (klĭp′ər), *n.* **1.** one who or that which clips or cuts. **2.** (*often pl.*) a cutting tool, esp. shears. **3.** (*often pl.*) a tool with rotating or reciprocating knives for cutting hair. **4.** one that clips, or moves swiftly, as a horse. **5.** a sailing vessel built and rigged for speed. **6.** an airliner, esp. a flying boat, designed for long flights over a sea or ocean. **7.** *Slang.* a first-rate person or thing.

clip-per-built (klĭp′ər·bĭlt′), *adj.* *Naut.* built on sharp, rakish lines conducive to fast sailing.

clip-ping (klĭp′ĭng), *n.* **1.** act of one who or that which clips. **2.** a piece clipped off or out, as from a newspaper. —*adj.* **3.** that clips. **4.** *Colloq.* swift: *a clipping pace.* **5.** *Slang.* first-rate or excellent.

clique (klēk, klĭk), *n.*, *v.*, **cliqued, cliquing.** —*n.* **1.** a small set or coterie, esp. one that is snobbishly exclusive. —*v.i.* **2.** *Colloq.* to form, or associate in, a clique. [t. F, der. OF *cliquer* make a sharp sound. Cf. CLAQUE] —**Syn. 1.** See *ring¹.*

cli-quish (klē′kĭsh, klĭk′ĭsh), *adj.* of, pertaining to, or savoring of a clique: *a cliquish fashion.* —**cli′quish·ly,** *adv.* —**cli′quish·ness,** *n.*

cli-to-ris (klĭ′tə·rĭs, klĭt′ər·ĭs), *n.* *Anat.* the erectile organ of the vulva, homologous to the penis of the male. [t. NL, t. Gk.: m. *kleitoris*, der. *kleiein* shut]

Clive (klīv), *n.* **Robert,** (*Baron Clive of Plassey*) 1725–1774, British general and statesman in India. His victory in the Battle of Plassey in 1757 was important in giving Great Britain control of India.

clk., clerk.

clo-a-ca (klō·ā′kə), *n.*, *pl.* **-cae** (-sē). **1.** a sewer. **2.** a privy. **3.** a place or receptacle of moral filth. **4.** *Zool.* **a.** the common cavity into which the intestinal, urinary, and generative canals open in birds, reptiles, amphibians, many fishes, and certain mammals (*monotremes*). **b.** a similar cavity in invertebrates. [t. L, prob. der. *cluere* cleanse] —**clo-a/cal,** *adj.*

cloak (klōk), *n.* **1.** a loose outer garment. **2.** that which covers or conceals; disguise; pretext.—*v.t.* **3.** to cover with, or as with, a cloak. **4.** to hide; conceal. [ME *cloke*, t. OF, g. LL *cloca* cloak, orig. bell; ? of Celtic orig. See CLOCK¹]

cloak-room (klōk′rōōm′, -rŏŏm′), *n.* **1.** a room where cloaks, overcoats, etc., may be left temporarily. **2.** *Brit.* a toilet or rest room.

clob-ber (klŏb′ər), *v.t.* *Slang.* **1.** to batter severely; maul. **2.** to wound.

cloche (klōsh), *n.* **1.** a bell-shaped cover used in cooking or in greenhouses. **2.** a bell-shaped, close-fitting woman's hat. [t. F: lit., bell. See CLOCK¹]

clock¹ (klŏk), *n.* **1.** an instrument for measuring and indicating time, having pointers which move round on a dial to mark the hour, etc. **2.** such a timepiece not carried on the person (distinguished from a *watch*). —*v.t.* **3.** to time, test, or ascertain by the clock. [ME *clokke*, t. MD: m. *clocke* instrument for measuring time; cf. OE *clugge* bell, ONF *cloke* bell]

clock² (klŏk), *n.* **1.** an embroidered or woven ornament on each side of a stocking, extending from the ankle upward. —*v.t.* **2.** to embroider with such an ornament. [orig. uncert.] —**clocked,** *adj.*

clock-mak-er (klŏk′mā′kər), *n.* a person who makes or repairs clocks.

clock-wise (klŏk′wīz′), *adv.*, *adj.* in the direction of rotation of the hands of a clock.

clock-work (klŏk′wûrk′), *n.* **1.** the mechanism of a clock. **2.** any mechanism similar to that of a clock. **3.** **like clockwork,** with perfect regularity or precision.

clod (klŏd), *n.* **1.** a lump or mass, esp. of earth or clay. **2.** earth; soil. **3.** anything earthy or base, as the body in comparison with the soul: *this corporeal clod.* **4.** a stupid person; blockhead; dolt. **5.** a part of the shoulder of beef. [ME *clodde*, OE *clodd* (in *clodhamer* fieldfare). Cf. CLOUD] —**clod′dish,** *adj.* —**clod′dish·ness,** *n.* —**clod′dy,** *adj.*

clod-hop-per (klŏd′hŏp′ər), *n.* **1.** a clumsy boor; rustic; bumpkin. **2.** (*pl.*) strong, heavy shoes.

clod-hop-ping (klŏd′hŏp′ĭng), *adj.* loutish; boorish.

clod-poll (klŏd′pōl′), *n.* a blockhead; a stupid person. Also, **clod′pole′, clod-pate** (klŏd′pāt′).

clog (klŏg, klôg), *v.*, **clogged, clogging,** *n.* —*v.t.* **1.** to encumber; hamper; hinder. **2.** to hinder or obstruct, esp. by sticky matter; choke up. —*v.i.* **3.** to become clogged, encumbered, or choked up. **4.** to stick; stick together. **5.** to do a clog dance. —*n.* **6.** anything that impedes motion or action; an encumbrance; a hindrance.

7. a heavy block, as of wood, fastened to a man or beast to impede movement. **8.** a kind of shoe with a thick sole usually of wood. **9.** a similar but lighter shoe worn in the clog dance. **10.** a clog dance. **11.** *Now Chiefly Eng.* a thick piece of wood. [ME *clog, clogge*; orig. uncert.] —**clog′gy,** *adj.*

clog dance, a dance performed with clogs to beat time to the music. —**clog dancer.** —**clog dancing.**

cloi-son-né (kloi′zə·nā′; *Fr.* klwȧ·zô·nĕ′), *n.* enamelwork in which color areas are separated by thin, metal bands fixed edgewise to the ground. [t. F, der. *cloison* partition] —**cloi′son·né′,** *adj.*

clois-ter (klois′tər), *n.* **1.** a covered walk, esp. one adjoining a building, as a church, commonly running round an open court (garth) and opening onto it with an open arcade or colonnade. **2.** a place of religious seclusion; a monastery or nunnery; a convent. **3.** any quiet, secluded place. **4.** life in a monastery or nunnery. —*v.t.* **5.** to confine in a cloister or convent. **6.** to confine in retirement; seclude. **7.** to furnish with a cloister or covered walk. **8.** to convert into a cloister or convent. [ME *cloistre*, t. OF, b. *cloison* partition (cf. CLOISONNE) and L *claustrum* enclosed place] —**clois′ter·like′,** *adj.* —**Syn. 2.** See **convent.**

clois-tered (klois′tərd), *adj.* solitary; retired from the world: *cloistered seclusion, cloistered virtue.*

cloister garth. See **garth** (def. 1).

clois-tral (klois′trəl), *adj.* **1.** of, pertaining to, or living in a cloister. **2.** cloisterlike: *a cloistral house.*

cloke (klōk), *n.*, *v.* *Obs.* cloak.

clomb (klōm), *v.* *Archaic and Dial.* pt. and pp. of **climb.**

clone (klōn), *n.* *Hort.* a group of plants originating as parts of the same individual, as from buds or cuttings. Also, **clon** (klōn, klŏn). [t. Gk.: m. *klōn* slip, twig]

clo-nus (klō′nəs), *n.* *Pathol.* a rapid succession of flexion and extension of a group of muscles, usually signifying an affection of the brain or spinal cord. [t. NL, t. Gk.: m. *klōnos* commotion, turmoil] —**clon-ic** (klŏn′ĭk), *adj.* —**clo-nic-i-ty** (klō·nĭs′ə·tĭ), *n.*

Cloots (klōts), *n.* **Jean Baptiste du Val-de-Grâce** (zhäɴ bȧ·tēst′ dü vȧl·də·gräs′), **Baron de,** ("*Anacharsis Clootz*") 1755–94, Prussian leader in French Revolution.

close (*v.* klōz; *adj., adv.* klōs; *n.* klōz for 44–47, klōs for 48–50), *v.*, **closed, closing,** *adj.*, **closer, closest,** *adv.*, *n.* —*v.t.* **1.** to stop or obstruct (a gap, entrance, aperture, etc.). **2.** to stop or obstruct the entrances, apertures, or gaps in. **3.** to shut in or surround on all sides; enclose; cover in. **4.** to bring together the parts of; join; unite: *to close the ranks of troops.* **5.** to bring to an end: *to close a debate, bargain, etc.* **6.** *Naut.* to come close to. **7.** *U.S.* to get rid of, usually at a reduced price (fol. by *out*): *close out a stock of shoes.* —*v.i.* **8.** to become closed; shut. **9.** to come together; unite. **10.** to come close. **11.** to grapple; engage in close encounter (fol. by *with*). **12.** to come to terms (fol. by *with*). **13.** to agree (fol. by *on, upon*). **14.** to come to an end; terminate. **15.** *Stock Exch.* to be worth at the end of a trading period. [ME *close*(n), t. OF: m. *clos-*, s. *clore*, g. L *claudere* shut; r. OE *clȳsan*] —*adj.* **16.** shut; shut tight; not open. **17.** shut in; enclosed. **18.** completely enclosing. **19.** without opening; with all openings covered or closed. **20.** confined; narrow: *close quarters.* **21.** lacking fresh or freely circulating air: *a close room.* **22.** heavy; oppressive: *a spell of close weather.* **23.** narrowly confined, as a prisoner. **24.** practicing secrecy; secretive; reticent. **25.** parsimonious; stingy. **26.** scarce, as money. **27.** not open to public or general admission, competition, etc. **28.** under prohibition as to hunting or fishing: *a close season.* **29.** having the parts near together: *a close texture.* **30.** compact; condensed. **31.** near, or near together, in space, time, or relation: *in close contact.* **32.** intimate; confidential: *close friendship.* **33.** based upon a strong uniting feeling of love, honor, etc.: *a close union of nations.* **34.** fitting tightly, as a cap. **35.** short; near the surface. **36.** not deviating from the subject under consideration: *close attention.* **37.** strict; searching; minute: *close investigation.* **38.** not deviating from a model or original: *a close translation.* **39.** nearly even or equal: *a close contest.* **40.** strictly logical: *close reasoning.* **41.** *Phonet.* pronounced with a relatively small opening above the tongue. *Beet* and *boot* have the closest English vowels. **42.** *Rare.* viscous; not volatile. —*adv.* **43.** in a close manner; closely. [ME *clos*, t. F, g. L *clausus*, pp., shut] —*n.* **44.** act of closing. **45.** the end or conclusion. **46.** a junction; union. **47.** a close encounter; a grapple. **48.** an enclosed place; an enclosure; any piece of land held as private property. **49.** an enclosure about or beside a building, cathedral, etc. **50.** *Scot. and Brit. Dial.* a narrow entry or alley, or a court to which it leads. [(defs. 44–47) n. use of v.; (defs. 48–50) ME *clos*, t. F, g. L *clausum* enclosed place] —**close·ly** (klōs′lĭ), *adv.* —**close·ness** (klōs′nĭs), *n.* —**clos·er** (klō′zər), *n.* —**Syn. 1.** CLOSE, SHUT mean to cause something not to be open. CLOSE suggests blocking an opening or vacant place: *to close a breach in a wall.* It also connotes force and more refinement than SHUT. The informal word SHUT refers esp. to blocking or barring openings intended for literal or figurative ingress and egress: *to shut a door, mouth, gate, etc.* **5.** end, conclude, terminate, finish, complete. **21.** unventilated, muggy. **25.** penurious, miserly. **45.** See *end¹.*

close call (klōs), *U.S. Colloq.* a narrow escape.

closed (klōzd), *adj. Phonet.* (of syllables) ending with a consonant.

closed chain, *Chem.* a linking of atoms in an organic molecule which may be represented by a structural formula which forms a ring or cycle.

closed-circuit television, a system of televising by wire to designated viewing sets, as within a factory for monitoring production operations, in a theater for viewing a special event taking place elsewhere, etc.

closed corporation, an incorporated business the stock of which is owned by a small group.

closed gentian, a gentian, *Gentian* (or *Dasytephana*) *Andrewsii*, of the eastern and central U.S.

closed primary, a direct primary in which only persons meeting tests of party membership may vote.

closed shop, a shop in which union membership is a condition of hiring as well as employment, or one in which the employer must call on the union to furnish employees.

close-fist·ed (klōs'fĭs'tĭd), *adj.* stingy; miserly.

close-grained (klōs'grānd'), *adj.* (of wood) having the grain close or fine in texture.

close-hauled (klōs'hôld'), *adj. Naut.* sailing as close to the wind as a vessel will sail, with sails trimmed as flat as possible.

close-lipped (klōs'lĭpt'), *adj.* not talking or telling much.

close-mouthed (klōs'mouthd', -moutht'), *adj.* reticent; uncommunicative.

close-or·der drill (klōs'ôr'dər), *U.S. Army.* practice in formation marching and other movements, the carrying of arms during formal marching, and the formal handling of arms for ceremonies and guard.

close position (klōs), *Music.* arrangement of a chord so that the parts are as close together as possible.

close quarters, 1. a small, cramped place or position. 2. direct and close contact in a fight.

close shave, *Colloq.* a narrow escape.

clos·et (klŏz'ĭt), *n.* 1. a small room, enclosed recess, or cabinet for clothing, food, utensils, etc. 2. a small private room, esp. one for prayer, thought, etc. 3. a water closet; toilet. —*adj.* 4. pertaining to a closet; private; secluded. 5. suited for use or enjoyment in privacy: *a closet drama* (one to be read rather than acted). 6. engaged in private study or speculation; speculative; unpractical. —*v.t.* 7. to shut up in a private room for a conference, interview. etc. [ME, t. OF, dim. of *clos*, g. L *clausum* enclosed place]

close-up (klōs'ŭp), *n.* 1. a picture taken at close range or with a long focal length lens, on a relatively large scale. 2. an intimate view or presentation of anything.

clos·trid·i·um (klŏs trĭd'ĭ əm), *n.* any of the group of spore-forming, anaerobic bacteria.

clo·sure (klō'zhər), *n., v.,* -sured, -suring. —*n.* 1. act of closing or shutting. 2. state of being closed. 3. a bringing to an end; conclusion. 4. that which closes or shuts. 5. *Obs.* that which encloses or shuts in; enclosure. 6. *Phonet.* an articulation which keeps the breath from moving outward by closing the passage at some point. 7. *Parl. Proc.* a method of closing a debate and causing an immediate vote to be taken on the question under discussion, as by moving the previous question, corresponding to U.S. *cloture.* —*v.t., v.i.* 8. *Parl. Proc.* to end (a debate, etc.) by closure. [ME, t. OF, g. LL *clausūra,* der. L *clausus,* pp., shut]

clot (klŏt), *n., v.,* **clotted, clotting.** —*n.* 1. a mass or lump. 2. a semisolid mass, as of coagulated blood. —*v.i.* 3. to form into clots; coagulate. —*v.t.* 4. to cause to clot; cover with clots. [ME; OE *clott* lump, c. G *klotz* block, log]

cloth (klôth, klŏth), *n., pl.* **cloths** (klôthz, klŏthz; klôths, klŏths). 1. a fabric formed by weaving, felting, etc., from wool, hair, silk, flax, cotton, or other fiber, used for garments, upholstery, and many other purposes. 2. a piece of such a fabric for a particular purpose: *a table-cloth.* 3. a particular profession, esp. that of a clergyman. 4. **the cloth,** the clergy. 5. sails collectively. 6. a sail. 7. *Obs.* a garment; clothing. 8. *Obs.* a livery or customary garb, as of a trade or profession. [ME; OE *clāth,* c. G *kleid* garment]

clothe (klōth), *v.t.,* **clothed** or **clad, clothing.** 1. to dress; attire. 2. to provide with clothing. 3. to cover with, or as with, clothing. [ME *clothen,* OE *clāthian*]

clothes (klōz, klōthz), *n. pl.* 1. garments for the body; articles of dress; wearing apparel. 2. bedclothes. [orig., pl. of CLOTH] —**Syn.** 1. clothing, attire, raiment, vesture, costume, garb; vestments, habiliments.

clothes·horse (klōz'hôrs', klōthz'-), *n.* a frame on which to hang clothes, etc., esp. for drying.

clothes·line (klōz'līn', klōthz'-), *n.* a rope on which to hang clothes, etc., to dry after being washed.

clothes moth, any of certain small moths whose larvae feed on wool, fur, etc.

clothes·pin (klōz'pĭn', klōthz'-), *n.* a forked piece of wood or other device for hanging clothes on a line.

clothes pole, a pole that holds up a clothesline.

clothes·press (klōz'prĕs', klōthz'-), *n.* a receptacle for clothes, as a chest, wardrobe, or closet.

clothes tree, an upright pole with hooks near the top for hanging coats, hats, etc.

cloth·ier (klōth'yər, -ĭ ər), *n.* a maker or seller of woolen cloth or of clothes.

cloth·ing (klō'thĭng), *n.* 1. garments collectively; clothes; raiment; apparel. 2. a covering.

Clo·tho (klō'thō), *n. Gk. Myth.* one of the three Fates [t. L, t. Gk.: m. *Klōthō,* lit., the spinner]

cloth yard, 36 inches; 3 feet.

clot·ty (klŏt'ĭ), *adj.* 1. full of clots. 2. tending to clot

clo·ture (klō'chər), *n. U.S. Parl. Proc.* closure of a de bate. [t. F, g. L *claustūra,* var. of *clausūra* CLOSURE]

cloud (kloud), *n.* 1. a visible collection of particles of water or ice suspended in the air, usually at an elevation above the earth's surface. 2. any similar mass, esp. of smoke or dust. 3. a dim or obscure area in something otherwise clear or transparent. 4. a patch or spot differing in color from the surrounding surface. 5. anything that obscures, darkens, or causes gloom, trouble, suspicion, disgrace, etc. 6. a great number of insects, birds etc., flying together: *a cloud of locusts.* 7. in the clouds a. imaginary; unreal. b. impractical. —*v.t.* 8. to over spread or cover with, or as with, a cloud or clouds. 9. to overshadow; obscure; darken. 10. to make gloomy 11. to place under suspicion, disgrace, etc. 12. to varie gate with patches of another color. —*v.i.* 13. to grow cloudy; become clouded. [ME *cloud(e)* rock, clod, cloud OE *clūd* rock, hill; akin to CLOD] —**Syn.** 7. CLOUD, FOG, HAZE, MIST differ somewhat in thei figurative uses. CLOUD connotes esp. daydreaming: *his min. is in the clouds.* FOG and HAZE connote esp. bewildermen or confusion: *to go around in a fog (haze).* MIST has a emotional connotation and suggests tears: *a mist in one's eyes*

cloud·ber·ry (kloud'bĕr'ĭ), *n., pl.* -ries. 1. the or ange-yellow edible fruit of *Rubus chamaemorus,* a smal raspberry of the northern hemisphere. 2. the plant.

cloud·burst (kloud'bûrst'), *n.* a sudden and ver heavy rainfall.

cloud chamber, *Physics.* a closed chamber contain ing saturated water vapor which indicates the presenc of moving particles by the trails of water condensatio which they produce.

cloud·land (kloud'lănd'), *n.* a region of unreality imagination, etc.; dreamland.

cloud·less (kloud'lĭs), *adj.* without clouds; clear —**cloud'less·ly,** *adv.* —**cloud'less·ness,** *n.*

cloud·let (kloud'lĭt), *n.* a little cloud.

cloud rack, a group of drifting clouds.

cloud·y (klou'dĭ), *adj.,* **cloudier, cloudiest.** 1. full o or overcast with clouds: *a cloudy sky.* 2. of or like a cloud or clouds; pertaining to clouds. 3. having cloud like markings: *cloudy marble.* 4. not clear or trans parent: *a cloudy liquid.* 5. obscure; indistinct: *cloudy notions.* 6. darkened by gloom, trouble, etc.: *cloudy looks.* 7. under suspicion, disgrace, etc.: *a cloudy repu tation.* —**cloud'i·ly,** *adv.* —**cloud'i·ness,** *n.* —**Syn** 1. overclouded, lowering.

clough (klŭf, klou), *n. Prov. Eng.* a narrow valley; ravine; a glen. [ME, c. OHG *klāh*]

Clough (klŭf), *n.* **Arthur Hugh,** 1819–61, British poet

clout (klout), *n.* 1. *Colloq.* or *Dial.* a blow, esp. with th hand; a cuff. 2. *Baseball Slang.* a powerful blow with the bat. 3. the mark shot at in archery. 4. a shot tha hits the mark. 5. *Archaic* or *Dial.* a patch, or piec of cloth or other material used to mend something 6. *Archaic* or *Dial.* any worthless piece of cloth; a rag —*v.t.* 7. *Colloq.* or *Dial.* to strike, esp. with the hand cuff. 8. *Archaic* or *Dial.* to bandage. 9. *Archaic* or *Dial.* to patch; mend. [ME; OE *clūt* piece of cloth or metal. Cf. CLOT]

clove[1] (klōv), *n.* 1. the dried flower bud of a tropica myrtaceous tree, *Eugenia aromatica,* used whole o ground as a spice. 2. the tree. [ME *clowe,* t. OF: m *clou* (g. L *clāvus* nail), in *clou de girofle* nail of clove (se GILLYFLOWER), so called from the shape]

clove[2] (klōv), *n. Bot.* one of the small bulbs formed i the axils of the scales of a mother bulb, as in garlic. [ME OE *clufu* clove, bulb, tuber, c. D *kloof* cleft]

clove[3] (klōv), *v.* pt. of **cleave**[2].

clove hitch, *Naut.* a form of hitch for fastening a rop about a spar, etc., in which two rounds of rope ar crossed about the spar, with the ends of the rope issuin in opposite directions between the crossed parts. Se illus. under **knot.**

clo·ven (klō'vən), *v.* 1. pp. of **cleave**[2]. —*adj.* 2. cleft split; divided: *cloven feet or hoofs.* 3. cleaved.

clo·ven-foot·ed (klō'vən fŏŏt'ĭd), *adj.* 1. havin cloven feet. 2. devilish; Satanic.

cloven hoof, the figurative indication of Satan o evil temptation. Also, **cloven foot.**

clo·ven-hoofed (klō'vən hŏŏft', -hōōft'), *adj.* 1. hav ing split hoofs, once assumed to represent the halves of single undivided hoof, as in cattle. 2. devilish; Satanic

clove pink, a pink, *Dianthus caryophyllus,* with spicy scent like that of cloves; a carnation.

clo·ver (klō'vər), *n.* 1. any of various herbs of th fabaceous genus *Trifolium,* with trifoliolate leaves an dense flower heads, many species of which, as *T. pratens (*the common **red clover**), are cultivated as forage plants 2. any of various plants of allied genera, as melilo (**sweet clover**). 3. **in clover,** in comfort or luxury [ME *clovere,* OE *clāfre,* c. D *klaver*]

clo·ver·leaf (klō'vər lĕf'), *n., pl.* -leaves. *U.S.* system of routing traffic between two intersecting super highways, wherein one highway passes over the othe and the feeder roads connecting them are usually ar ranged in the pattern of a four-leaf clover.

---

b., blend of, blended; c., cognate with; d., dialect, dialectal; der., derived from; f., formed from; g., going back to m., modification of; r., replacing; s., stem of; t., taken from; ?, perhaps. See the full key on inside cover

Clo·vis I (klō′vĭs; *Fr.* klô vēs′), (Ger. *Chlodwig*) A.D. 465?–511, king of the Franks, A.D. 481–511: first of the Merovingian dynasty of Frankish kings.

lown (kloun), *n.* **1.** a jester or buffoon in a circus, pantomime, etc. **2.** a peasant; a rustic. **3.** a coarse, ill-bred person; a boor. —*v.i.* **4.** to act like a clown. [orig. uncert. Cf. Icel. *klunni* clumsy fellow] —**clown′-ish,** *adj.* —**clown′ish·ly,** *adv.* —**clown′ish·ness,** *n.*

lown·er·y (kloun′ər ĭ), *n., pl.* -**eries.** clownish behavior.

loy (kloi), *v.t.* **1.** to weary by an excess of food, sweetness, pleasure, etc.; surfeit; satiate. —*v.i.* **2.** to cause to feel satiated or surfeited: *cloyed palate of the epicure, cloying with particulars.* [aphetic var. of obs. *accloy* to stop up, drive in a nail, ? t. MF: m. *encloyer,* der. *clou,* g. L *clāvus* nail] —**cloy′ing·ly,** *adv.* —**cloy′ing·ness,** *n.*

lub (klŭb), *n., v.,* **clubbed, clubbing.** —*n.* **1.** a heavy stick, usually thicker at one end than at the other, suitable for a weapon; a cudgel. **2.** a stick or bat used to drive a ball, etc., in various games. **3.** a stick with a crooked head used in golf, hockey, etc. **4.** Indian club. **5.** a group of persons organized for a social, literary, athletic, political, or other purpose. **6.** the building or rooms occupied by such a group. **7.** a black trefoil-shaped figure on a playing card. **8.** a card bearing such figures. **9.** (*pl.*) the suit so marked. —*v.t.* **10.** to beat with, or as with, a club. **11.** to gather or form into a clublike mass. **12.** to unite; combine; join together. **13.** to contribute as one's share toward a joint expense; make up by joint contribution (often fol. by *up* or *together*). **14.** to defray by proportional shares: *to club the expense.* **15.** to invert (a rifle, etc.) so as to use as a club. —*v.i.* **16.** to combine or join together as for a common purpose. **17.** to gather into a mass. **18.** to contribute to a common fund. [ME *clubbe,* t. Scand.; cf. Icel. *klubba;* akin to CLUMP] —**Syn. 5.** society, association. See **circle.**

lub·ba·ble (klŭb′ə bəl), *adj.* fit to be a member of a social club; sociable. Also, **club′a·ble.**

lub car, a railroad passenger car equipped with easy chairs, card tables, buffet, etc.

lub·foot (klŭb′fŏŏt′), *n.* **1.** a deformed or distorted foot. **2.** the condition of such a foot; talipes. —**club′-foot′ed,** *adj.*

lub·hand (klŭb′hănd′), *n.* **1.** a deformed or distorted hand, similar in nature and causation to a clubfoot. **2.** the condition of such a hand.

lub·haul (klŭb′hôl′), *v.t. Naut.* to cause (a ship), in an emergency, to go on the other tack by letting go the lee anchor, and pulling on a hawser leading from the anchor to the lee quarter, the hawser being cut when the ship gathers way on the new tack.

lub·house (klŭb′hous′), *n.* a building occupied by a club.

lub·man (klŭb′mən), *n., pl.* -**men.** a member of a fashionable club. —**club′wom′an,** *n. fem.*

lub moss, any plant of the genus *Lycopodium.*

lub·room (klŭb′rŏŏm′), *n.* a room used by a club.

lub sandwich, a sandwich of toast (usually three slices) with a filling of cold chicken, turkey, bacon, or ham, lettuce with tomato, mayonnaise dressing, etc.

lub steak, a loin steak.

luck (klŭk), *v.i.* **1.** to utter the cry of a hen brooding or calling her chicks. **2.** to make a similar sound. —*v.t.* **3.** to call or utter by clucking: *clucking her sympathy.* —*n.* **4.** the sound uttered by a hen when brooding, or in calling her chicks. **5.** any clucking sound. [var. of *clock* (now Scot. and d.), OE *cloccian*]

lue (klŏŏ), *n., v.,* **clued, cluing.** —*n.* **1.** anything that serves to guide or direct in the solution of a problem, mystery, etc. **2.** clew. —*v.t.* **3.** to clew. [var. of CLEW]

luj (klŏŏzh), *n.* a city in N W Rumania. 117,915 (1948). German, **Klausenburg.** Hungarian, **Kolozsvár.**

lum·ber (klŭm′bər), *n.* one of a breed of spaniels with short legs and long, heavy body, valued as retrievers. Also, **clumber spaniel.** [named after *Clumber,* estate of the Duke of Newcastle, in Nottinghamshire, England]

lump (klŭmp), *n.* **1.** a cluster, esp. of trees, or other plants. **2.** *Bacteriol.* a cluster of agglutinated bacteria. **3.** a lump or mass. **4.** a clumping tread, sound, etc. **5.** a thick extra sole on a shoe. —*v.i.* **6.** to walk heavily and clumsily. **7.** *Bacteriol.* to gather or be gathered into clumps. —*v.t.* **8.** to gather into or form a clump; mass. **9.** *Bacteriol.* to gather or form in clumps. [back formation from *clumper* lump, OE *clympre*] —**clump′y, clump′ish,** *adj.*

Clumber
(1½ ft. high)

lum·sy (klŭm′zĭ), *adj.,* -**sier,** -**siest.** **1.** awkward in movement or action; without skill or grace: *a clumsy workman.* **2.** awkwardly done or made; unwieldy; ill-contrived: *a clumsy apology.* [der. obs. v. *clumse* be benumbed with cold, t. Scand.; cf. Swed. *klummsen* benumbed] —**clum′si·ly,** *adv.* —**clum′si·ness,** *n.* —**Syn. 1.** ungraceful, ungainly, lumbering, lubberly. **2.** unhandy, unskillful, maladroit, inexpert, bungling.

lung (klŭng), *v.* pt. and pp. of **cling.**

Clu·ny (klȳ nē′), *n.* a town in E France: ruins of a famous Benedictine abbey. 4032 (1954).

Clu·ny lace (klŏŏ′nĭ), **1.** a lace made by hand with bobbins, originally in France. **2.** a machine lace copied from it.

clu·pe·id (klŏŏ′pĭ ĭd), *n.* **1.** any of the *Clupeidae,* a family of (chiefly) marine, teleostean fishes, including the herrings, sardines, menhaden, and shad. —*adj.* **2.** relating to the family *Clupeidae.* [t. NL: s. *Clupeidae,* pl., f. s. *Clupea* the herring genus (L′clupea kind of small river fish) + -idae (see -ID²)]

clu·pe·oid (klŏŏ′pĭ oid′), *adj.* **1.** herringlike. —*n.* **2.** any member of the *Isospondyli,* an order of fishes including the clupeids, salmon, smelts, etc.

clus·ter (klŭs′tər), *n.* **1.** a number of things of the same kind, growing or held together; a bunch: *a cluster of grapes.* **2.** a group of things or persons near together. **3.** *U.S. Army.* a small metal design placed on the ribbon representing an awarded medal, which indicates that the same medal has been awarded again: *oak-leaf cluster.* —*v.t.* **4.** to gather into a cluster. **5.** to furnish or cover with clusters. —*v.i.* **6.** to form a cluster or clusters. [ME and OE, var. of *clyster* bunch] —**clus′ter·y,** *adj.*

clutch¹ (klŭch), *v.t.* **1.** to seize with, or as with, the hands or claws; snatch. **2.** to grip or hold tightly or firmly. —*v.i.* **3.** to try to seize or grasp (fol. by *at*). —*n.* **4.** the hand, claw, paw, etc., when grasping. **5.** (*chiefly pl.*) power of disposal or control; mastery: *in the clutches of an enemy.* **6.** act of clutching; a snatch; a grasp. **7.** a tight grip or hold. **8.** a device for gripping something. **9.** a coupling or appliance by which working parts of machinery (as a pulley and a shaft) may be made to engage or disengage at will. [ME *clucche(n),* var. of *clycche(n),* OE *clyccan* crook or bend, close (the hand), clench] —**Syn. 1.** See **catch.**

clutch² (klŭch), *n.* **1.** a hatch of eggs; the number of eggs produced or incubated at one time. **2.** a brood of chickens. —*v.t.* **3.** to hatch (chickens). [var. of d. *cletch,* akin to *cleck* hatch, t. Scand.; cf. Sw. *kläcka*]

clut·ter (klŭt′ər), *v.t.* **1.** to heap, litter, or strew in a disorderly manner. —*v.i.* **2.** to run in disorder; move with bustle and confusion. **3.** to make a clatter. **4.** to speak so rapidly and inexactly that distortions of sound and phrasing result. —*n.* **5.** a disorderly heap or assemblage; litter. **6.** confusion; disorder. **7.** confused noise; clatter. [var. of *clotter,* der. CLOT; associated with CLUSTER]

Clyde (klīd), *n.* **1.** a river in S Scotland, flowing into the Firth of Clyde: shipbuilding. 106 mi. **2. Firth of,** an inlet of the Atlantic, in SW Scotland. 64 mi. long.

Clyde·bank (klīd′băngk′), *n.* a city in SW Scotland, on the Clyde. 48,100 (est. 1956).

Clydes·dale (klīdz′dāl′), *n.* one of a breed of active, strong, and hardy draft horses originally raised in Clydesdale, Scotland.

Clydesdale terrier, a variety of Skye terrier bred for smallness.

clyp·e·ate (klĭp′ĭ āt′), *adj.* shaped like a round shield or buckler. [t. L: m. s. *clypeātus,* pp., furnished with a shield]

clyp·e·us (klĭp′ĭ əs), *n., pl.* **clypei** (klĭp′ĭ ē′). the area of the facial wall of an insect's head between the labrum and the front, usually separated from the latter by a groove. [t. L: prop., *clipeus* round shield] —**clyp′e·al,** *adj.*

clys·ter (klĭs′tər), *n. Med.* an enema. [ME *clister,* t. L: m. *clyster,* t. Gk.: m. *klystēr* syringe]

Cly·tem·nes·tra (klī′təm nĕs′trə), *n. Gk. Legend.* the daughter of Tyndareus and Leda, wife of Agamemnon. See **Agamemnon, Aegisthus, Orestes.** Also, **Cly′taem·nes′tra.**

cm., centimeter; centimeters.

cml., commercial.

Cni·dus (nī′dəs), *n.* ancient city of Caria, in SW Asia Minor: Athenian naval victory over the Spartans, 394 B.C.

Cnos·sus (nŏs′əs), *n.* Knossos.

Cnut (kə nŏŏt′, kə nūt′), *n.* Canute.

co-, **1.** a prefix signifying association and accompanying action, occurring mainly before vowels and *h* and *gn,* as in *coadjutor, cohabit, cognate.* Also used in variants of words of Latin origin in place of the regular *com-, con-,* etc. as in *co-centric,* for *concentric, co-mingle,* for *commingle,* etc. Cf. **com-.** **2.** *Math., Astron.* a prefix meaning "complement of," as in *cosine, codeclination.* [t. L, var. of *com-* COM-.]

Co, *Chem.* cobalt.

Co., **1.** Company. **2.** County. Also, **co.**

C.O., **1.** Commanding Officer. **2.** conscientious objector.

c.o., **1.** care of. **2.** carried over. Also, **c/o**

coach (kōch), *n.* **1.** a large, enclosed, four-wheeled carriage. **2.** an enclosed automobile, usually having two doors. **3.** a public passenger bus. **4.** a railroad passenger car, esp. as distinguished from a parlor car, etc. **5.** a person who trains athletes for a contest, etc. **6.** *Baseball.* a person stationed near first or third base to advise the players of his team while they run the bases. **7.** a private tutor who prepares a student for an examination. —*v.t.* **8.** to give instruction or advice to in the capacity of a coach. —*v.i.* **9.** to act as a coach. **10.** to study with or be instructed by a coach. [earlier *cochee,* t. Hung.: m. *kocsi*]

coach-and-four (kōch′ən fôr′), *n.* a coach drawn by four horses.

ăct, āble, dâre, ärt; ĕbb, ēqual; Ĭf, Ice; hŏt, ōver, ôrder, oil, bŏŏk, ōōze, out; ŭp, ūse, ûrge; ə = a in alone; ch, chief; g, give; ng, ring; sh, shoe; th, thin; th, that; zh, vision. See the full key on inside cover.

coach dog, Dalmatian (def. 3).

coach·er (kō′chər), *n.* **1.** one who coaches; a coach. **2.** coach horse.

coach horse, a horse used or fitted to draw a coach.

coach·man (kōch′mən), *n., pl.* **-men.** **1.** a man employed to drive a coach or carriage. **2.** a certain kind of artificial fly for angling. —**coach′man·ship′,** *n.*

co·ac·tion (kō ăk′shən), *n.* force or compulsion, either in restraining or in impelling. [t. F, t. L: s. *coactio*]

co·ac·tive (kō ăk′tĭv), *adj.* compulsory; coercive. —**co·ac′tive·ly,** *adv.*

co·ad·ju·tor (kō ăj′ə tər, kō′ə jōō′tər), *n.* **1.** an assistant. **2.** an assistant to a bishop or other ecclesiastic. **3.** a bishop who assists another bishop, with the right of succession. [t. LL: f. *co-* co- + *adjutor* helper; r. ME *coadiutoure,* t. OF]

co·ad·ju·tress (kō ăj′ə trĭs), *n.* a female coadjutor or assistant.

co·ad·ju·trix (kō ăj′ə trĭks), *n., pl.* **coadjutrices** (kō-ăj′ə tri′sēz). coadjutress.

co·ad·u·nate (kō ăj′ə nĭt, -nāt′), *adj. Zool., Bot.* united by growth. [t. L: m.s. *coadūnātus,* pp., joined together] —**co·ad′u·na′tion,** *n.*

co·ad·ven·ture (kō′əd vĕn′chər), *v.,* **-tured, -turing,** *n.* —*v.i.* **1.** to share in an adventure. —*n.* **2.** adventure in which two or more share. —**co′ad·ven′tur·er,** *n.*

co·ag·u·la·ble (kō ăg′yə lə bəl), *adj.* capable of being coagulated: *this substance is highly coagulable.* —**co·ag′u·la·bil′i·ty,** *n.*

co·ag·u·lant (kō ăg′yə lənt), *n.* a substance that produces coagulation. [t. L: s. *coāgulans,* ppr., curdling]

co·ag·u·late (*v.* kō ăg′yə lāt′; *adj.* kō ăg′yə lĭt, -lāt′), *v.,* **-lated, -lating,** *adj.* —*v.i., v.i.* **1.** to change from a fluid into a thickened mass; curdle; congeal. —*adj.* **2.** *Obs.* coagulated. [t. L: m. s. *coāgulātus,* pp., curdled] —**co·ag′u·la′tion,** *n.* —**co·ag′u·la′tive,** *adj.* —**co·ag′u·la′tor,** *n.*

co·ag·u·lum (kō ăg′yə ləm), *n., pl.* **-la** (-lə). *Physiol., etc.* a clump, clot, curd, precipitate, or gel. [t. L: *rennet*]

Co·a·hui·la (kō′ä wē′lä), *n.* a state in N Mexico. 760,748 pop. (est. 1952); 58,067 sq. mi. *Cap.:* Saltillo.

coal (kōl), *n.* **1.** a black or dark-brown combustible mineral substance consisting of carbonized vegetable matter, used as a fuel: **hard coal** (anthracite), **soft coal** (bituminous coal), **brown coal** (lignite). **2.** a piece of wood or other combustible substance either glowing, charred, or burned out. **3.** charcoal. **4.** **take, call, rake,** etc., **over the coals,** to scold; to reprimand. —*v.t.* **5.** to burn to coal or charcoal. **6.** to provide with coal. —*v.i.* **7.** to take in coal for fuel. [ME *cole,* OE *col* live coal, c. G *kohle*]

coal car, *U.S.* **1.** a railway car designed to carry coal. **2.** a car used in hauling coal in or from a mine.

coal·er (kōl′ər), *n.* a railroad, ship, etc., used mainly to haul or supply coal.

co·a·lesce (kō′ə lĕs′), *v.i.,* **-lesced, -lescing.** **1.** to grow together or into one body. **2.** to unite so as to form one mass, community, etc. [t. L: m. s. *coalescere*] —**co′a·les′cence,** *n.* —**co′a·les′cent,** *adj.*

coal field, an area containing coal deposits.

coal·fish (kōl′fĭsh′), *n.* **1.** the sablefish. **2.** a North Atlantic gadoid food fish, *Pollachius virens,* a species of pollack. [named from the color of its back]

coal gas, 1. the gas formed by burning coal. **2.** a gas used for illuminating and heating, produced by distilling bituminous coal, consisting chiefly of hydrogen, methane and carbon monoxide.

coal heaver, one who carries or shovels coal.

coal hod, *U.S. and Dial.* a small pail for carrying coal.

coal·ing station (kō′lĭng), a place at which coal is supplied to ships, locomotives, etc.

co·a·li·tion (kō′ə lĭsh′ən), *n.* **1.** union into one body or mass; fusion. **2.** a combination or alliance, esp., a temporary one between persons, factions, states, etc. [t. ML: s. *coalitio,* der. L *coalescere* coalesce] —**co′a·li′tion·ist,** *n.*

coal measures, *Geol.* **1.** coal-bearing strata. **2.** (*caps.*) a portion of the Carboniferous system, characterized by coal deposits.

coal mine, a mine or pit from which coal is obtained. —**coal miner.** —**coal mining.**

coal oil, kerosene.

coal pit, 1. a pit where coal is dug. **2.** *U.S.* a place where charcoal is made.

coal·sack (kōl′săk′), *n.* **1.** **southern coalsack,** a large dark space near the southern constellation Crux. **2.** **northern coalsack,** a dark space in the Milky Way in the northern constellation Cygnus. Also, **Coalsack.**

coal tar, a thick, black, viscid liquid formed during the distillation of coal (as in the manufacture of illuminating gas), and which upon further distillation yields benzene, anthracene, phenol, etc. (from which are derived a large number of dyes and synthetic compounds), and a final residuum (**coal-tar pitch**) which is used in making pavements, etc.

coal-tar creosote, impure phenol or carbolic acid, distinct from the creosote of wood tar.

coal·y (kō′lĭ), *adj.* of, like, or containing coal.

coam·ing (kō′mĭng), *n.* **1.** a raised border around an opening in a deck, roof, or floor, designed to prevent water from running below. **2.** *Naut.* one of the pieces, esp. of the fore-and-aft pieces, of such a border.

co·arc·tate (kō ärk′tāt), *adj. Entomol.* denoting a insect pupa enclosed in the hardened cuticula (puparium) of a preceding larval instar. [t. L: m. s. *coarctātus,* pp., pressed together; r. ME *coartate,* t. L: m. s. *coartātus,* var. of *coarctātus*]

coarse (kōrs), *adj.,* **coarser, coarsest.** **1.** of inferior or faulty quality; not pure or choice; common; base: *coarse manners, coarse lad.* **2.** composed of relatively large parts or particles: *coarse sand.* **3.** lacking in fineness or delicacy of texture, structure, etc. **4.** harsh. **5.** lacking delicacy of feeling, manner, etc.; not refined. **6.** (of metals) unrefined. [adjectival var. of **course,** n., with the sense of ordinary] —**coarse′ly,** *adv.* —**coarse′ness,** *n.* —Syn. **5.** vulgar, gross, crass, indelicate, ribald.

coarse-grained (kōrs′grānd′), *adj.* **1.** having coarse texture or grain. **2.** indelicate; crude; gross.

coars·en (kōr′sən), *v.t., v.i.* to make or become coarse.

coast (kōst), *n.* **1.** the land next to the sea; the sea shore. **2.** the region adjoining it. **3.** **the Coast,** (the U. S.) the region bordering on the Pacific Ocean. **4.** *Archaic.* the boundary or border of a country. **5.** hill or slope down which one may slide on a sled. **6.** slide or ride down a hill, etc. **7.** the coast is clear the danger is gone. —*v.i.* **8.** *U.S.* to slide on a sled down a snowy or icy hillside or incline. **9.** *U.S.* to descend hill, etc., as on a bicycle, without using pedals. **10.** proceed or sail along, or sail from port to port of, a coast **11.** to move along after effort has ceased; to keep going on acquired momentum. **12.** *Obs.* to proceed in a roundabout way. **13.** *Obs.* to go or pass (along, etc.). —*v* **14.** to proceed along the coast of. **15.** to go along near to (a coast). **16.** to keep alongside of (a person moving). **17.** *Obs.* to go by the side or border of. [ME *coste,* t. OF, g. L *costa* rib, side] —Syn. **1.** See **shore.**

coast·al (kōs′təl), *adj.* of or at a coast: *coastal defense*

Coast Artillery Corps, a branch and combat arm of the U. S. Army, troops of which man the coast defenses and form the anti-aircraft units of the army.

coast·er (kōs′tər), *n.* **1.** one who or that which coast **2.** a vessel engaged in coastwise trade. **3.** a sled f coasting. **4.** an amusement railway with deep dips a sharp curves. **5.** a tray, sometimes on wheels, for holding a decanter to be passed around a dining table. a small dish or tray placed under glasses, etc., to prote a table from moisture or heat.

coaster brake, a brake on freewheel bicycle operated by back pressure on the pedals.

coast guard, 1. (*caps.*) *U.S.* a military service, und the Treasury Department in peacetime, which enforc maritime laws, saves lives and property at sea, a operates aids to navigation. **2.** any organization for t prevention of smuggling, etc. **3.** a member of any su organization.

coast·ing trade (kōs′tĭng), trade between por along the same coast.

coast·line (kōst′līn′), *n.* outline or contour of a coas

Coast Range, a series of mountain ranges along t Pacific coast of North America, extending from Low California to SE Alaska. Highest peak in U.S., S. Gorgonio in the San Bernardino range, 11,485 ft. Als **Coast Mountains** in British Columbia.

coast·ward (kōst′wərd), *adv.* **1.** Also, **coast′ward** toward the coast. —*adj.* **2.** directed toward the coas *coastward movement.*

coast·wise (kōst′wīz′), *adv.* **1.** Also, **coast′wa** (kōst′wāz′). along the coast. —*adj.* **2.** following th coast: *coastwise drift.*

coat (kōt), *n.* **1.** an outer garment with sleeves, cove ing the upper part of the body. **2.** a natural integume. or covering, as the hair, fur, or wool of an animal, th bark of a tree, or the skin of a fruit. **3.** anything th covers or conceals: *a coat of paint.* **4.** *Obs.* a garme indicating profession, class, etc. **5.** *Obs.* professiona class, etc., so indicated. **6.** *Obs. or Dial.* a petticoat skirt. —*v.t.* **7.** to cover or provide with a coat. **8.** cover with a layer or coating; cover as a layer or coatin does. [ME *cote,* t. OF, t. Gmc.; cf. OS *cott* woolen coa ML *cotta* kind of tunic] —**coat′less,** *adj.*

coat card, *Cards.* face card.

coat·ed (kō′tĭd), *adj.* **1.** (of paper) having a high polished coating applied to provide a smooth surfa for printing. **2.** (of a fabric) having a plastic, paint, pyroxylin coating, making it impervious to moistur **3.** having a coat.

coat·ee (kō tē′), *n.* a short coat.

Coates (kōts), *n.* **Eric,** 1886–1957, British composer.

co·a·ti (kō ä′tĭ), *n., pl.* **-tis.** any of the tropical American plantigrade carnivores constituting the genus *Nasua,* closely related to the raccoon, and having an elongated body, a long, ringed tail, and an attenuated, flexible snout. Also, **co·a·ti·mon·di, co·a·ti·mun·di** (kō-ä′tĭ mŭn′dĭ). [t. Brazilian]

Coati, *Nasua narica* (3½ ft. long, tail 18 in.)

coat·ing (kō′tĭng), *n.* **1.** a layer of any substance spread over a surface. **2.** material f coats.

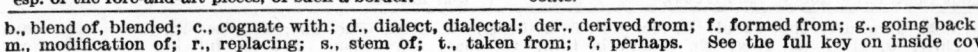

coat of arms, 1. a surcoat or tabard embroidered with heraldic devices, worn by medieval knights over their armor. **2.** the heraldic bearings of a person; a hatchment; an escutcheon. [trans. of F *cotte d'armes*]

coat of mail, *pl.* **coats of mail.** a hauberk; a defensive garment made of interlinked metal rings, overlapping metal plates, etc.

co·au·thor (kō ō′thər), *n.* a joint author.

coax (kōks), *v.t.* **1.** to influence by gentle persuasion, flattery, etc. **2.** to get or win by coaxing. **3.** *Obs.* to fondle. **4.** *Obs.* to befool. —*v.i.* **5.** to use gentle persuasion, etc. [der. obs. *cokes*, n., fool; of doubtful orig. Cf. COCKNEY] —**coax′er,** *n.* —**coax′ing·ly,** *adv.* —Syn. **1.** wheedle, cajole, beguile, inveigle, persuade.

Coat of arms (def. 2)

co·ax·i·al (kō ăk′sĭ əl), *adj.* **1.** having a common axis or coincident axes. **2.** (of a cable) composed of an insulated central conductor with tubular stranded conductors laid over it concentrically and separated by layers of insulation. Also, **co·ax·al** (kō ăk′səl).

cob[1] (kŏb), *n.* **1.** *U.S.* a corncob. **2.** a male swan. **3.** a short-legged, thick-set horse. **4.** *U.S.* a horse with an unnaturally high gait. **5.** *Brit. Dial.* a man of importance; leader. **6.** *Brit. Dial.* a roundish mass, lump, or heap. **7.** *Brit.* a mixture of clay and straw, used as a building material. [ME; orig. obscure]

cob[2] (kŏb), *n.* a gull, esp. the great black-backed gull, *Larus marinus.* Also, **cobb.** [orig. unknown. Cf. D *kob*]

co·balt (kō′bôlt), *n.* **1.** *Chem.* a silver-white metallic element with a faint pinkish tinge, occurring in compounds the silicates of which afford important blue coloring substances for ceramics. *Symbol:* Co; *at. wt.:* 58.94; *at. no.:* 27; *sp. gr.:* 8.9 at 20°C. **2.** a blue pigment containing cobalt. [t: G: m. *kobalt,* var. of *kobold* goblin]

cobalt bloom, the mineral erythrite, hydrous cobalt arsenate, $Co_3As_2O_8\cdot8H_2O$, usually of a peach-red color, and often occurring as a pulverulent incrustation.

cobalt blue, any of a number of pigments containing an oxide of cobalt.

co·bal·tic (kō bôl′tĭk), *adj. Chem.* of or containing cobalt, esp. in the trivalent state (Co+3).

co·bal·tite (kō bôl′tīt, kō′bôl tīt′), *n.* a mineral, cobalt arsenic sulfide, CoAsS, silver-white with a reddish tinge: an ore of cobalt. Also, **co·balt·ine** (kō′bôl tēn′, -tĭn).

co·bal·tous (kō bôl′təs), *adj. Chem.* containing divalent cobalt (Co+2).

Cobb (kŏb), *n.* **Irvin Shrewsbury,** 1876–1944, U.S. humorist and writer.

Cob·bett (kŏb′ĭt), *n.* **William,** 1763–1835, British journalist and politician, in America and England.

cob·bing (kŏb′ĭng), *n. Metall.* old refractory material removed from furnaces.

cob·ble (kŏb′əl), *n., v.,* **-bled, -bling.** —*n.* **1.** a cobble stone. **2.** (*pl.*) cob coal. —*v.t.* **3.** to pave with cobblestones. **4.** to mend (shoes, etc.); patch. **5.** to put together roughly or clumsily. [? der. COB[1], def. 6]

cob·bler (kŏb′lər), *n.* **1.** one who mends shoes. **2.** a clumsy workman. **3.** an iced drink made of wine, fruits, sugar, etc. **4.** *U.S.* a deep-dish fruit pie with a rich biscuit crust, usually only on top.

cob·ble·stone (kŏb′əl stōn′), *n.* a natural rounded stone, large enough for use in paving.

cob coal, a large round lump of coal.

Cob·den (kŏb′dən), *n.* **Richard,** 1804–65, British manufacturer, merchant, economist, and statesman.

co·bel·lig·er·ent (kō′bə lĭj′ər ənt), *n.* a nation, state, or individual that coöperates with, but is not bound by a formal alliance to, another in carrying on war.

Cóbh (kōv), *n.* a seaport in S Ireland; the port for Cork. 5711 (1951). Formerly, **Queenstown.**

Cob·ham (kŏb′əm), *n.* **John Oldcastle** (ōld′käs′əl -käs′əl), **Lord,** died 1417, English martyr: leader of a Lollard conspiracy.

co·ble (kō′bəl, kŏb′əl), *n. Scot. and Eng.* a kind of flat-bottomed rowboat or fishing boat. [ME; cf. OE *cuopl,* Welsh *ceubal,* ML *caupulus*]

Co·blenz (kō′blĕnts), *n.* a city in W West Germany at the junction of the Rhine and Moselle rivers. 80,000 (est. 1953). German, **Koblenz.**

cob·nut (kŏb′nŭt′), *n.* **1.** the nut of certain cultivated varieties of hazel, *Corylus Avellana grandis.* **2.** a tree bearing such nuts.

co·bra (kō′brə), *n.* any snake of the genus *Naja,* exceedingly venomous and characterized by the ability to dilate its neck so that it assumes a hoodlike form. [short for Pg. *cobra* (L *colubra* serpent) *de capello* hood snake]

co·bra de ca·pel·lo (kō′brə dē kə pĕl′ō), *pl.* **cobras** de capello. a cobra, *Naja tripudians,* common in India.

Co·burg (kō′bûrg; *Ger.* kō′bŏŏrk), *n.* a city in West Germany, in N Bavaria. 45,700 (est. 1952).

cob·web (kŏb′wĕb′), *n.* **1.** a web or net spun by a spider to catch its prey. **2.** a single thread spun by a spider. **3.** anything finespun, flimsy, or unsubstantial. **4.** a network of plot or intrigue; an insidious snare. [ME *coppeweb,* f. *coppe* spider (OE *-coppe* in *ātorcoppe* spider) + WEB] —**cob′webbed′,** *adj.* —**cob′web·by,** *adj.*

---

co·ca (kō′kə), *n.* **1.** either of two shrubs, *Erythroxylon coca* and *Erythroxylon truxillense,* native in the Andes and cultivated in Java and elsewhere. **2.** their dried leaves, which are chewed for their stimulant properties and which yield cocaine and other alkaloids. [t. Peruvian: m. *cuca*]

co·caine (kō kān′, kō′kān; *tech. often* kō′kə ēn′), *n.* a bitter crystalline alkaloid, $C_{17}H_{21}NO_4$, obtained from coca leaves, used as a local anesthetic. Also, **co·cain′.** [f. COCA + -INE[2]]

co·cain·ism (kō kā′nĭz əm, kō′kə nĭz′əm), *n.* a morbid condition due to excessive or habitual use of cocaine.

co·cain·ize (kō kā′nīz, kō′kə nīz′), *v.t.,* **-ized, -izing.** to treat with or affect by cocaine. —**co·cain′i·za′tion,** *n.*

coc·cid (kŏk′sĭd), *n.* any insect of the homopterous superfamily *Coccoidea,* including the scale insects, etc.

coc·cid·i·oi·dal gran·u·lo·ma (kŏk sĭd′ĭ oi′dəl grăn′yōō lō′mə), a fungus disease of the lymph nodes of sheep, cattle, dogs, and man, somewhat like tuberculosis.

coc·cid·i·o·sis (kŏk sĭd′ĭ ō′sĭs), *n.* any one of a series of specific infectious diseases caused by epithelial protozoan parasites, which usually affect the intestines. The disease is known in birds, cattle, swine, sheep, and dogs; it rarely occurs in man.

coc·cus (kŏk′əs), *n., pl.* **-ci** (-sī). **1.** *Bacteriol.* a spherical organism when free, slightly flattened when two or more form in apposition, as in the *Neisseria gonorrhoeae* or *N. meningitidis.* **2.** *Bot.* one of the carpels of a schizocarp. **3.** *Pharm.* cochineal. [t. NL, t. Gk.: m. *kókkos* grain, seed] —**coc·coid** (kŏk′oid), *adj.*

Cocci (def. 2)
A, Fruit composed of ten cocci; B, Fruit composed of four cocci

coc·cyx (kŏk′sĭks), *n., pl.* **coccyges** (kŏk sī′jēz). **1.** a small triangular bone forming the lower extremity of the spinal column in man, consisting of four ankylosed rudimentary vertebrae. See diag. under **spinal column. 2.** a corresponding part in certain other animals. [t. L, t. Gk.: m. *kókkyx* coccyx, orig., cuckoo] —**coc·cyg·e·al** (kŏk-sĭj′ĭ əl), *adj.*

Co·cha·bam·ba (kō′chä bäm′bä), *n.* a city in central Bolivia. 74,949 (1950); 8394 ft. high.

co·chin (kō′chĭn, kŏch′ĭn), *n.* a breed of large domestic fowls, of Asiatic origin, resembling the brahma but slightly smaller. Also, **Cochin.** [named after COCHIN-CHINA]

Co·chin (kō′chĭn), *n.* a seaport near the SW extremity of India: the first European fort in India was built here by the Portuguese, 1503. 29,881 (1951).

Co·chin-Chi·na (kō′chĭn chī′nə, kŏch′ĭn), *n.* a former state in S French Indochina: now part of Vietnam. French, **Co·chin·chine** (kō shăn shēn′).

coch·i·neal (kŏch′ə nēl′, kŏch′ə nēl′), *n.* a red dye prepared from the dried bodies of the females of a scale insect, *Dactylopius coccus,* which lives on cactuses of Mexico, Central America, and other warm regions. [t, F: m. *cochenille,* t. Sp.: m. *cochinilla,* orig. wood louse, der. *cochino* pig]

coch·le·a (kŏk′lĭ ə), *n., pl.* **-leae** (-lĭ ē′). a division, spiral in form, of the internal ear, in man and most other mammals. See diag. under **ear.** [t. L, t. Gk.: m. *kochlĭas* snail, something spiral] —**coch′le·ar,** *adj.*

coch·le·ate (kŏk′lĭ āt′), *adj.* shaped like a snail shell; spiral. Also, **coch′le·at′ed.** [t. L: m.s. *cochleātus*]

cock[1] (kŏk), *n.* **1.** a rooster. **2.** the male of any bird, esp. of the gallinaceous kind. **3.** the crowing of the cock. **4.** *Archaic.* the time of its crowing, in the early morning. **5.** a weathercock. **6.** a leader; chief person; ruling spirit. **7.** a device for permitting or arresting the flow of a liquid or gas from a receptacle or through a pipe; a faucet, tap, or stop valve. **8.** (in a firearm) **a.** that part of the lock which by its fall or action causes the discharge; the hammer. **b.** the position into which the cock or hammer is brought by being drawn partly or completely back, preparatory to firing. **9.** *Curling.* the mark aimed at. —*v.t.* **10.** to pull back and set the cock or hammer of (a firearm) preparatory to firing. —*v.i.* **11.** to cock the firing mechanism of a gun. [ME *cok,* OE *cocc,* c. Icel. *kokkr*]

cock[2] (kŏk), *v.t.* **1.** to set or turn up or to one side, often in an assertive, jaunty, or significant manner. —*v.i.* **2.** to stand or stick up conspicuously. **3.** *Dial.* to strut; swagger; put on airs of importance. —*n.* **4.** act of turning the head, a hat, etc. up or to one side in a jaunty or significant way. **5.** the position of anything thus placed. [prob. special use of COCK[1]]

cock[3] (kŏk), *n.* **1.** a conical pile of hay, etc. —*v.t.* **2.** to pile (hay, etc.) in such piles. [ME. Cf. Norw. *kok* heap]

cock·ade (kŏ kād′), *n.* a knot of ribbon, rosette, etc., worn on the hat as a badge or a part of a uniform. [alter. of *cockard,* t. F: m. *cocarde,* der. *coq* cock] —**cock·ad′ed,** *adj.*

cock-a-hoop (kŏk′ə hōōp′, -hŏŏp′), *adj.* in a state of unrestrained joy or exultation.

Cock·aigne (kŏ kān′), *n.* a fabulous land of luxury and idleness. [ME *cokaigne,* t. OF, ? t. MLG: m. *kokenje* sugar cakes given children at fairs]

cock·a·lo·rum (kŏk′ə lōr′əm), *n. Colloq.* a self-important little man.

---

cock-and-bull story (kŏk'ən bŏŏl'), an absurd improbable story told as true.

cock·a·teel (kŏk'ə tēl'), n. a small, crested, long-tailed Australian parrot, *Leptolopus hollandicus*, common as a cage bird. Also, **cock'a·tiel'**. [t. D: m. *kaketielje*. Cf. COCKATOO]

cock·a·too (kŏk'ə tōō'), n. any of the crested parrots constituting the genera *Kakatoë, Callocephalon*, or *Calyptorhynchus*, forming the subfamily *Kakatuinae*, of the East Indies, Australia, etc., often white, or white and yellow, pink, or red. [t. D: m. *kaketoe*. t. Malay: m. *kakatūa*]

cock·a·trice (kŏk'ə trĭs), n. 1. a fabulous serpent with deadly glance, reputed to be hatched by a serpent from a cock's egg, and commonly represented with the head, legs, and wings of a cock and the body and tail of a serpent. 2. *Bible.* an unidentified species of venomous serpent. [ME *cocatris*, t. OF, der. L *calcāre* tread; used to render Gk. *ichneúmōn* ICHNEUMON; assoc. with COCK¹]

Crested cockatoo, *Kakatoe sulphurea* (13 in. long)

cock bead, *Joinery.* a bead which is not flush with the general surface, but raised above it.

cock·boat (kŏk'bōt'), n. a small boat, esp. one used as a tender.

cock·chaf·er (kŏk'chā'fər), n. any of certain scarabaeid beetles, esp. the European species, *Melolontha melolontha*, which is very destructive to forest trees. [f. COCK¹ (def. 6, with reference to size) + CHAFER]

cock·crow (kŏk'krō'), n. the time at which cocks crow; dawn. Also, **cock'crow'ing.**

cocked hat (kŏkt), 1. a hat having the brim turned up on two or three sides. 2. **knock into a cocked hat,** to damage or destroy completely.

cock·er¹ (kŏk'ər), n. 1. a cocker spaniel. 2. one who promotes or patronizes cockfighting. [f. COCK¹, v. + -ER¹]

cock·er² (kŏk'ər), v.t. to pamper. [? freq. of obs. *cock*, v., ? orig. meaning make a cock of]

cock·er·el (kŏk'ər əl, kŏk'rəl), n. a young domestic cock. [dim. of COCK¹. See -REL]

cocker spaniel, one of a breed of small spaniels trained for use in hunting or kept as pets.

cock·eye (kŏk'ī'), n. an eye that squints, or is affected with strabismus. [f. COCK² v. + EYE]

Cocker spaniel (11 in. high)

cock·eyed (kŏk'īd'), adj. 1. having a squinting eye; cross-eyed. 2. *Slang.* twisted or slanted to one side. 3. *Slang.* foolish; absurd.

cock·fight (kŏk'fīt'), n. a fight between gamecocks usually armed with spurs. —**cock'fight'ing,** n., adj.

cock·horse (kŏk'hôrs'), n. a child's rocking horse or hobbyhorse.

cock·ish (kŏk'ĭsh), adj. *Colloq.* cocklike; cocky. —**cock'ish·ly,** adv. —**cock'ish·ness,** n.

cock·le¹ (kŏk'əl), n., v., -led, -ling. —n. 1. any of the bivalve mollusks with somewhat heart-shaped, radially ribbed valves which constitute the genus *Cardium*, esp. *C. edule*, the common edible species of Europe. 2. any of various allied or similar mollusks. 3. cockleshell. 4. a wrinkle; pucker. 5. cockles of the heart, the inmost parts or depths of the heart. 6. a small shallow or light boat. 7. *U.S.* a small crisp candy of sugar and flour, bearing a motto. —v.i. 8. to contract into wrinkles; pucker. 9. to rise into short, irregular waves. —v.t. 10. to cause to wrinkle or pucker: *a book cockled by water*. [ME *cockille*, t. F: m. *coquille*, b. F *coque* shell and L *conchÿlium*, t. Gk.: m. *konchÿlion*, dim. of *kónché* mussel or cockle, CONCH]

cock·le² (kŏk'əl), n. a weed generally, as the darnel *Lolium temulentum*, or rye grass, *L. perenne*. [ME; OE *coccel*]

cock·le·boat (kŏk'əl bōt'), n. a cockboat.

cock·le·bur (kŏk'əl bûr'), n. 1. any plant of the composite genus *Xanthium*, comprising coarse weeds with spiny burs. 2. the burdock, *Arctium Lappa*.

cock·le·shell (kŏk'əl shĕl'), n. 1. a shell of the cockle. 2. a shell of some other mollusk, as the scallop. 3. a small, light boat.

cock·loft (kŏk'lôft', -lŏft'), n. a small upper loft; a small garret.

cock·ney (kŏk'nĭ), n., pl. -neys, adj. —n. (often cap.) 1. a native or resident of London, especially of the East End (often with reference to those who have marked peculiarities of pronunciation and dialect). 2. their pronunciation or dialect. 3. *Obs.* a pampered child. 4. *Obs.* a squeamish, affected, or effeminate person. —adj. 5. of cockneys or their dialect. [ME *cokeney* cock's egg (i.e., malformed egg), f. *coken*, gen. pl. of *cok* cock + *ey*, OE *ǣg* egg] —**cock'ney·ish,** adj.

cock·ney·dom (kŏk'nĭ dəm), n. 1. the region of cockneys. 2. cockneys collectively.

cock·ney·ese (kŏk'nĭ ēz', -ēs'), n. cockney dialect.

cock·ney·fy (kŏk'nĭ fī'), v.t., -fied, -fying. to give a cockney character to.

cock·ney·ism (kŏk'nĭ ĭz'əm), n. 1. cockney quality or usage. 2. a cockney peculiarity, as of speech.

cock-of-the-rock (kŏk'əv thə rŏk'), n. a brilliant orange-red bird of the genus *Rupicola* with the bill hidden by the frontal plumes, found in northern South America.

cock of the woods, the pileated woodpecker *Ceophloeus pileatus*, of North America.

cock·pit (kŏk'pĭt'), n. 1. (in some airplanes) an enclosed space containing seats for the pilot and copilot. 2. a recess aft, in the deck of a yacht or other boat, which provides a small amount of deck space at a lower level. 3. (in old type of warship) an apartment below the water line, used as quarters for certain officers and as a dressing station for the wounded. 4. a pit or enclosed place for cockfights. 5. a place where a contest is fought, or which has been the scene of many contests or battles: *Belgium, the cockpit of Europe.*

cock·roach (kŏk'rōch'), n. any of various orthopterous insects of the family *Blattidae*, usually nocturnal, and having a flattened body, as the following important cosmopolitan species: the pale, yellowish-brown common cockroach (Croton bug, *Blatella germanica*) introduced from Europe, and the dark-brown or black oriental roach (black beetle, *Blatta orientalis*) spread by commerce. These and other species are important household pests. [f. COCK¹ + ROACH, popular analysis of Sp. *cucaracha*. Cf. popular *sparrow grass* for *asparagus*, etc.]

cocks·comb (kŏks'kōm'), n. 1. the comb or caruncle of a cock. 2. the cap of a professional fool, resembling a cock's comb. 3. an amaranthaceous garden plant *Celosia cristata*, with flowers, commonly crimson or purple, in a broad spike somewhat resembling the comb of a cock. 4. some other species of *Celosia*. 5. a coxcomb.

cocks·head (kŏks'hĕd'), n. an herb of the genus *Onobrychis*, esp. *O. Caputgalli* and *O. sativa.*

cock·shut (kŏk'shŭt'), n. *Obs.* or *Brit. Dial.* the close of the day; evening; twilight.

cock·shy (kŏk'shī'), n., pl. -shies. *Brit.* 1. act or sport of throwing missiles at a target. 2. an object of attack.

cock·spur (kŏk'spûr'), n. a North American species of thorn, *Crataegus Crusgalli*, frequently cultivated as a small ornamental tree.

cock·sure (kŏk'shŏŏr'), adj. 1. perfectly sure or certain; completely confident in one's own mind. 2. too certain; overconfident. 3. *Obs.* perfectly secure or safe. —**cock'sure'ness,** n. —Ant. 1. doubtful. 2. cautious.

cock·swain (kŏk'sən, -swān'), n. coxswain.

cock·tail (kŏk'tāl'), n. 1. any of various short mixed drinks, consisting typically of gin, whiskey, or brandy, with different admixtures, such as vermouth, fruit juices, etc., usually chilled and frequently sweetened. 2. a portion of oysters, clams, crabmeat, etc., served in a small glass with a sauce. 3. a mixture of fruits served in a glass. 4. a horse with a docked tail. 5. a horse which is not thoroughbred. 6. an ill-bred person passing as a gentleman. [orig. unknown]

cock·y (kŏk'ĭ), adj., cockier, cockiest. *Colloq.* arrogantly smart; pertly self-assertive; conceited: *a cocky fellow, air, answer.* —**cock'i·ly,** adv. —**cock'i·ness,** n.

cock·y-ol·ly bird (kŏk'ĭ ŏl'ĭ), a pet name for any small bird. Also, **cock'y·ol'y.**

co·co (kō'kō), n., pl. -cos. 1. a tall, slender tropical palm, *Cocos nucifera*, which produces the coconut; coconut palm. 2. the coconut fruit or seed. Also, **cocoa.** [t. Sp., Pg.: grinning face]

co·coa¹ (kō'kō), n. 1. the roasted, husked, and ground seeds of the cacao, *Theobroma cacao*, from which much of the fat has been removed. 2. a beverage made from cocoa powder. 3. brown; yellowish brown; reddish brown. —adj. 4. of or pertaining to cocoa. 5. of the color of cocoa. [var. of CACAO]

co·coa² (kō'kō), n. misspelling of coco.

cocoa butter, cacao butter.

co·con·scious·ness (kō kŏn'shəs nĭs), n. *Psychol.* mental processes dissociated from the main stream of thought or from the dominant personality integration. —**co·con'scious,** adj. —**co·con'scious·ly,** adv.

co·co·nut (kō'kə nŭt', -nət), n. the seed of the coconut palm, large, hard-shelled, lined with a white edible meat, and containing a milky liquid. Also, **co'coa·nut'.**

coconut palm, coco (def. 1). Also, **coconut tree.**

co·coon (kə kōōn'), n. 1. the silky envelope spun by the larvae of many insects, as silkworms, serving as a covering while they are in the chrysalis or pupal state. 2. any of various similar protective coverings, as the silky case in which certain spiders enclose their eggs. [t. F: m. *cocon*, der. *coque* shell]

Co·cos Islands (kō'kōs), a British group of 20 coral islands in the Indian Ocean. SW of Java. 605 pop. (est. 1955); 1½ sq. mi. Also, **Keeling Islands.**

co·cotte (kō kŏt', ka-; *Fr.* kô kôt'), n. a courtesan; immoral woman. [t. F: hen, der. *coq* rooster]

Coc·teau (kôk tō'), n. **Jean** (zhäN), 1889–1963, French poet, novelist, dramatist, critic, and artist.

Co·cy·tus (kō sī'təs), n. *Class. Myth.* a river of Hades connected with the Acheron.

cod¹ (kŏd), n., pl. **cods**, (esp. collectively) **cod.** 1. one of the most important North Atlantic food fishes, *Gadus callarias*. 2. any of several other gadoid fishes, as the Pacific cod, *Gadus macrocephalus.* 3. any of various unrelated fishes, as the rockfish (def. 3). [ME; orig. uncert.]

cod² (kŏd), *n.* **1.** a bag or sack. **2.** *Dial.* a pod. [ME; OE *codd*]

Cod (kŏd), *n.* **Cape,** a sandy peninsula in SE Massachusetts between **Cape Cod Bay** and the Atlantic: traversed near its base by the **Cape Cod Canal** (8 mi. long).

C.O.D., l. *U.S.* collect on delivery. **2.** *Brit.* cash on delivery. Also, **c.o.d.**

co·da (kō′də), *n.* *Music.* a more or less independent passage, at the end of a composition, introduced to bring it to a satisfactory close. [t. It., g. L *cauda* tail]

cod·dle (kŏd′al), *v.t.,* **-dled, -dling. 1.** to boil gently; stew (fruit etc.). **2.** to treat tenderly; nurse or tend indulgently; pamper. [var. of and v. use of *caudle* kind of gruel, t. ONF: m. *caudel*, g. ML *caldellum*, dim. of *cal(i)dum* hot drink, neut. of L *calidus* hot]

code (kōd), *n., v.,* **coded, coding.** —*n.* **1.** any systematic collection or digest of the existing laws of a country, or of those relating to a particular subject: *the Civil Code of France.* **2.** any system or collection of rules and regulations. **3.** a system of signals for communication by telegraph, heliograph, etc. **4.** a system of arbitrarily chosen words, etc., used for brevity or secrecy. —*v.t.* **5.** to arrange in a code; enter in a code. **6.** to translate into a code. [ME, t. F, L: m. s. *cōdex.* See CODEX]

co·dec·li·na·tion (kō′dĕk la nā′shən), *n.* *Astron.* the complement of the declination.

co·de·fend·ant (kō′dĭ fĕn′dənt), *n.* a joint defendant.

co·deine (kō′dēn), *n.* a white, crystalline, slightly bitter alkaloid, $C_{18}H_{21}NO_3H_2O$, obtained from opium, used in medicine as an analgesic, sedative, and hypnotic. Also, **co·de·in** (kō′dĭ ĭn), **co·de·ia** (kō dē′ə). [f. m.s. Gk. *kōdeia* head, poppy head + -INE²]

Code Na·po·lé·on (kōd nà põ lē ôN′), the body of French private law, the Civil Code, promulgated between 1804–07.

co·det·ta (kō dĕt′tä), *n.* *Italian.* a short coda.

co·dex (kō′dĕks), *n., pl.* **codices** (kō də sēz′ kōd′ə-). a manuscript volume of an ancient classic, the Scriptures, etc. [t. L, earlier *caudex* tree trunk, book]

Co·dex Ju·ris Ca·no·ni·ci (kō′dĕks jŏor′ĭs kə nŏn′ə sī′), *Rom. Cath. Ch.* an official collection of general church law made effective in 1918. [L]

cod·fish (kŏd′fĭsh′), *n., pl.* **-fishes,** (*esp. collectively*) **-fish.** cod¹.

codg·er (kŏj′ər), *n.* **1.** *Colloq.* an odd or peculiar (old) person: *a lovable old codger.* **2.** *Brit. Dial.* a mean, miserly person. [? var. of CADGER.]

co·di·ces (kō′də sēz′ kōd′ə-), *n.* pl. of codex.

cod·i·cil (kŏd′ə səl), *n.* **1.** a supplement to a will, containing an addition, explanation, modification, etc., of something in the will. **2.** some similar supplement. [t. L: m. s. *cōdicillus,* dim. of *cōdex.* See CODEX]

cod·i·cil·la·ry (kŏd′ə sĭl′ə rĭ), *adj.* of the nature of a codicil.

cod·i·fi·ca·tion (kŏd′ə fə kā′shən, kō′də-), *n.* **1.** the act, process, or result of arranging in a code. **2.** *Law.* the reducing of unwritten customs or case law to statutory form.

cod·i·fy (kŏd′ə fī′, kō′də-), *v.t.,* **-fied, -fying. 1.** to reduce (laws, etc.) to a code. **2.** to digest; arrange in a systematic collection. [f. COD(E) + -(I)FY. Cf. F *codifier*] —**cod′i·fi′er,** *n.*

cod·ling¹ (kŏd′lĭng), *n.* **1.** *Brit.* any of several varieties of elongated apples, used for cooking purposes. **2.** an unripe, half-grown apple. Also, **cod·lin** (kŏd′lĭn). [ME *querdling,* f. *querd* (orig. unknown) + -LING¹]

cod·ling² (kŏd′lĭng), *n.* the young of the cod. [ME; f. COD¹ + -LING¹]

codling moth, a small moth, *Carpocapsa pomonella,* whose caterpillar (larva) feeds on the pulp around the core of apples and other fruits. Also, **codlin moth.**

cod-liv·er oil (kŏd′lĭv′ər), a fixed oil, extracted from the liver of the common cod or of allied species, extensively used in medicine as a source of vitamins A and D.

cod·piece (kŏd′pēs′), *n.* (in 15th and 16th century male costume) a bagged appendage to the front of tight-fitting hose or breeches. [f. COD² + PIECE]

Co·dy (kō′dĭ), *n.* **William Frederick,** ("*Buffalo Bill*") 1846–1917, U. S. Army scout and showman.

co·ed (kō′ĕd′), *n.* *U.S. Colloq.* a female student in a coeducational institution, esp. in a college or university. Also, **co′-ed′.** [short for COEDUCATIONAL (student)]

co·ed·u·ca·tion (kō′ĕj ə kā′shən), *n.* joint education, esp. of both sexes in the same institution and classes. —**co′ed·u·ca′tion·al,** *adj.*

co·ef·fi·cient (kō′ə fĭsh′ənt), *n.* **1.** *Math.* a number or quantity placed (generally) before and multiplying another quantity: *3 is the coefficient of x in 3x.* **2.** *Physics.* a quantity, constant for a given substance, body, or process under certain specified conditions, that serves as a measure of some one of its properties: *coefficient of friction.* —*adj.* **3.** coöperating.

coe·horn (kō′hôrn), *n.* a small mortar for throwing grenades, used in the 18th century.

coele, a word element referring to some small cavity of the body. Also, **-cele.** [comb. form repr. Gk. *koilía* belly and *koîlos* hollow]

coe·len·ter·a·ta (sĭ lĕn′tə rā′tə), *n. pl.* *Zool.* a phylum of invertebrate animals that includes the hydras, jellyfishes, sea anemones, corals, etc., and is characterized by a single internal cavity serving for digestion, excretion, and other functions, and the tentacles on the oral end.

coe·len·ter·ate (sĭ lĕn′tə rāt′, -tə rĭt), *Zool.* —*n.* **1.** a member of the phylum *Coelenterata.* —*adj.* **2.** belonging to the *Coelenterata.* [f. COELENTER(ON) + -ATE¹]

coe·len·ter·on (sĭ lĕn′tə rŏn′), *n., pl.* **-tera** (-tərə). *Zool.* the body cavity of a coelenterate. [f. *coel-* (comb. form repr. Gk. *koîlos* hollow) + Gk. *énteron* intestine]

coe·li·ac (sē′lĭ ăk′), *adj.* *Anat.* celiac.

coe·lom (sē′ləm), *n.* *Zool.* the body cavity of a metazoan, as distinguished from the intestinal cavity. Also, **coe·lome** (sē′lōm), **celom.** [t. Gk.: m. *koílōma* a hollow]

coe·nes·the·sia (sē′nəs thē′zhə, -zhĭ′ə, sĕn′əs-), *n.* *Psychol.* the general sense of life, the bodily consciousness, or the total impression from all contemporaneous organic sensations, as distinct from special and well-defined sensations, such as those of touch or sight. Also, **cenesthesia, coe·nes·the·sis** (sē′nəs thē′sĭs, sĕn′əs-), **cenesthesis.** [cf. ANESTHESIA]

coeno-, var. of ceno-². Also, before vowels, **coen-.**

coe·no·bite (sē′nə bīt′, sĕn′ə-), *n.* cenobite.

coe·no·cyte (sē′nə sīt′, sĕn′ə-), *n.* *Biol.* an organism made up of many protoplasmic units enclosed by one cell wall, as in some algae and fungi.

coe·nu·rus (sĭ nyŏŏr′əs, -nŏŏr′-), *n.* the larva of a tapeworm of the genus *Multiceps,* in which a number of heads (scolices) form in the bladder. One species causes gid in sheep. [t. NL, f. *coen-* COEN- + m. Gk. *ourá* tail]

co·en·zyme (kō ĕn′zīm), *n.* *Biochem.* a biocatalyst required by certain enzymes to produce their reactions.

co·e·qual (kō ē′kwəl), *adj.* **1.** equal in rank, ability, etc. —*n.* **2.** a person or thing coequal with another. —**co·e·qual·i·ty** (kō′ĭ kwŏl′ə tĭ), *n.* —**co·e′qual·ly,** *adv.*

co·erce (kō ûrs′), *v.t.,* **-erced, -ercing. 1.** to restrain or constrain by force, law, or authority; force or compel, as to do something. **2.** to compel by forcible action: *coerce obedience.* [t. L: m.s. *coercēre* hold together] —**co·er′cer,** *n.* —**co·er′ci·ble,** *adj.*

co·er·cion (kō ûr′shən), *n.* **1.** act or power of coercing; forcible constraint. **2.** government by force.

co·er·cive (kō ûr′sĭv), *adj.* serving or tending to coerce. —**co·er′cive·ly,** *adv.* —**co·er′cive·ness,** *n.*

co·es·sen·tial (kō′ĭ sĕn′shəl), *adj.* united in essence; having the same essence or nature. —**co·es·sen·ti·al·i·ty** (kō′ĭ sĕn′shĭ ăl′ə tĭ), **co′es·sen′tial·ness,** *n.* —**co′es·sen′tial·ly,** *adv.*

co·e·ta·ne·ous (kō′ĭ tā′nĭ əs), *adj.* of the same age or duration. [t. LL: m. *coaetāneus* of the same age]

co·e·ter·nal (kō′ĭ tûr′nəl), *adj.* equally eternal; existing with another eternally. —**co′e·ter′nal·ly,** *adv.*

co·e·ter·ni·ty (kō′ĭ tûr′nə tĭ), *n.* coexistence from eternity with another eternal being.

Coeur-d'A·lène (kûr′də lān′), *n.* a Salishan language.

co·e·val (kō ē′vəl), *adj.* **1.** of the same age, date, or duration; equally old. **2.** contemporary; coincident. —*n.* **3.** a contemporary. **4.** one of the same age. [f. m.s. L *coaevus* of the same age + -AL¹] —**co·e′val·ly,** *adv.*

co·ex·e·cu·tor (kō′ĭg zĕk′yə tər), *n.* a joint executor.

co·ex·e·cu·trix (kō′ĭg zĕk′yə trĭks), *n., pl.* **-executrices** (-ĭg zĕk′yə trī′sēz). a female coexecutor.

co·ex·ist (kō′ĭg zĭst′), *v.i.* to exist together or at the same time. —**co′ex·ist′ence,** *n.* —**co′ex·ist′ent,** *adj.*

co·ex·tend (kō′ĭk stĕnd′), *v.t., v.i.* to extend equally through the same space or duration. —**co·ex·ten·sion** (kō′ĭk stĕn′shən), *n.*

co·ex·ten·sive (kō′ĭk stĕn′sĭv), *adj.* having equal or coincident extension. —**co′ex·ten′sive·ly,** *adv.*

cof·fee (kôf′ĭ, kŏf′ĭ), *n.* **1.** a beverage, consisting of a decoction or infusion of the roasted and ground or crushed seeds (**coffee beans**) of the two-seeded fruit (**coffee berry**) of *Coffea arabica* and other species of *Coffea,* rubiaceous trees and shrubs of tropical regions. **2.** the berry or seed of such plants. **3.** the tree or shrub itself. **4.** dark brown. [t. Turk.: m. *qahveh,* t. Ar.: m. *qahwa*]

coffee break, *U.S.* an intermission from work, usually in the middle of the morning or afternoon, for coffee, cake, etc.

coffee house, a public room where coffee and other refreshments are supplied. British coffee houses formerly held a position similar to modern club houses.

coffee nut, **1.** the fruit of the Kentucky coffee tree. **2.** the tree.

coffee shop, a public room, as in a hotel, where coffee and food are served. Also, **coffee room.**

coffee tree, **1.** any tree, as *Coffea arabica,* yielding coffee beans. **2.** the Kentucky coffee tree.

cof·fer (kôf′ər, kŏf′ər), *n.* **1.** a box or chest, esp. one for valuables. **2.** (*pl.*) a treasury; funds. **3.** any of various boxlike enclosures, as a cofferdam. **4.** an ornamental sunken panel in a ceiling or soffit. —*v.t.* **5.** to deposit or lay up in or as in a coffer or chest. **6.** to ornament with coffers or sunken panels: *a coffered ceiling.* [ME *cofre,* t. OF: chest, g. L *cophinus* basket. See COFFIN]

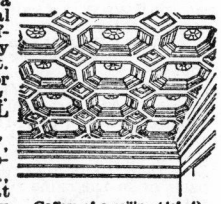

Coffers of a ceiling (def. 4)

cof·fer·dam (kôf′ər dăm′, kŏf′ər-), *n.* a watertight enclosure constructed in rivers, etc., and then pumped dry so that bridge foundations, etc., may be constructed in the open.

cof·fin (kôf'ĭn, kŏf'ĭn), *n.* **1.** the box or case in which a corpse is placed for burial. **2.** the part of a horse's foot containing the coffin bone. —*v.t.* **3.** to put or enclose in or as in a coffin. [ME *cofin*, t. OF: small basket, coffin, t. L: m. s. *cophinus*, t. Gk.: m. *kóphinos* basket]

Cof·fin (kôf'ĭn, kŏf'ĭn), *n.* **Robert P(eter) Tristram** (tris'trəm), 1892–1955, U.S. author.

coffin bone, the terminal phalanx in the foot of the horse and allied animals, enclosed in the hoof.

cof·fle (kôf'əl), *n.* a train of men or beasts, esp. of slaves, fastened together. [t. Ar.: m. *qāfila* caravan]

C. of S., Chief of Staff.

cog[1] (kŏg), *n.* **1.** a tooth or projection (usually one of a series) on a wheel, etc., for transmitting motion to, or receiving motion from, a corresponding tooth or part with which it engages. **2.** a cogwheel. [ME *cogge*, akin to CUDGEL]

cog[2] (kŏg), *v.,* **cogged, cogging.** —*v.t.* **1.** to manipulate or load (dice) unfairly. —*v.i.* **2.** to cheat, esp. at dice. [orig. obscure]

cog., cognate.

co·gen·cy (kō'jən sĭ), *n.* power of proving or producing belief; convincing force.

co·gent (kō'jənt), *adj.* compelling assent or belief; convincing; forcible: *a cogent reason.* [t. L: s. *cōgens,* ppr., forcing, collecting] —**co'gent·ly,** *adv.*

cog·i·tate (kŏj'ə tāt'), *v.,* **-tated, -tating.** —*v.i.* **1.** to think hard; ponder; meditate. —*v.t.* **2.** to think about; devise. [t. L: m.s. *cōgitātus,* pp.] —**cog'i·ta'tor,** *n.*

cog·i·ta·tion (kŏj'ə tā'shən), *n.* **1.** meditation. **2.** the faculty of thinking. **3.** a thought; a design or plan.

cog·i·ta·tive (kŏj'ə tā'tĭv), *adj.* **1.** meditating. **2.** given to meditation; thoughtful: *cogitative pause.* —**cog'i·ta'tive·ly,** *adv.*

co·gi·to, er·go sum (kŏj'ə tō', ûr'gō sŭm'), *Latin.* I think, therefore I exist (the philosophical principle of Descartes).

co·gnac (kōn'yăk, kŏn'-; *Fr.* kô nyák'), *n.* **1.** (*often cap.*) the brandy distilled in and shipped from the legally delimited area surrounding the town of Cognac, France. **2.** French brandy in general. **3.** any good brandy.

cog·nate (kŏg'nāt), *adj.* **1.** related by birth; of the same parentage, descent, etc. **2.** related in origin: *cognate languages, words, etc.* **3.** allied in nature or quality. —*n.* **4.** a person or thing cognate with another. [t. L: m. s. *cognātus*]

cog·na·tion (kŏg nā'shən), *n.* cognate relationship.

cog·ni·tion (kŏg nĭsh'ən), *n.* **1.** act or process of knowing; perception. **2.** the product of such a process; thing thus known, perceived, etc. **3.** *Obs.* knowledge. [ME, t. L: s. *cognitio* a getting to know] —**cog·ni·tive** (kŏg'nə tĭv), *adj.*

cog·ni·za·ble (kŏg'nə zə bəl, kŏn'ə-; kŏg nī'-), *adj.* **1.** capable of being perceived or known. **2.** within the jurisdiction of a court. —**cog'ni·za·bly,** *adv.*

cog·ni·zance (kŏg'nə zəns, kŏn'ə-), *n.* **1.** knowledge; notice; perception: *to have or take cognizance of a fact, remark, etc.* **2.** *Law.* **a.** judicial notice as taken by a court in dealing with a cause. **b.** the right of taking judicial notice, as possessed by a court. **c.** acknowledgment; admission, as a plea admitting the fact alleged in the declaration. **3.** the range or scope of knowledge, observation, etc. [ME *conisance,* t. OF: m. *conoissance,* der. *conoistre,* g. L *cognoscere* come to know]

cog·ni·zant (kŏg'nə zənt, kŏn'ə-), *adj.* **1.** having cognizance; aware (fol. by *of*). **2.** competent to take judicial notice, as of causes.

cog·nize (kŏg'nīz), *v.t.,* **-nized, -nizing.** to perceive; become conscious of; know.

cog·no·men (kŏg nō'mən), *n., pl.* **-nomens, -nomina** (-nŏm'ə nə). **1.** a surname. **2.** any name, esp. a nickname. **3.** the third and commonly the last name (in order) of a Roman citizen, indicating his house or family, as in "Caius Julius *Caesar.*" [t. L] —**cog·nom·i·nal** (kŏg nŏm'ə nəl, -nō'mə-), *adj.*

co·gno·scen·te (kô'nyō shĕn'tĕ), *n., pl.* **-ti** (-tē). a connoisseur. Also, **conoscente.** [It., var. of *conoscente,* ppr. of *conoscere,* g. L *cognoscere* know]

cog·nos·ci·ble (kŏg nŏs'ə bəl), *adj.* capable of being known. —**cog·nos'ci·bil'i·ty,** *n.*

cog·no·vit (kŏg nō'vĭt), *n. Law.* an acknowledgment or confession by a defendant that the plaintiff's cause, or a part of it, is just, wherefore the defendant, to save expense, suffers judgment to be entered without trial. [t. L: he acknowledged]

co·gon (kō gōn'), *n.* a tall, coarse grass, *Imperata cylindrica,* of the tropics and subtropics, furnishing an excellent material for thatching. [t. Sp., t. Tagalog]

cog railway, a railway having locomotives with a cogged center driving wheel engaging with a cogged rail, to provide sufficient traction for climbing steeper grades than is possible with ordinary wheels.

cog·wheel (kŏg'hwēl'), *n.* a wheel with cogs, for transmitting or receiving motion. [late ME]

Cogwheels

co·hab·it (kō hăb'ĭt), *v.i.* **1.** to live together as husband and wife. **2.** *Archaic.* to dwell or reside in company or in the same place. [t. LL: s. *cohabitāre* dwell with] —**co·hab'it·ant, co·hab'it·er,** *n.* —**co·hab'i·ta'tion,** *n.*

Co·han (kō hăn'), *n.* **George Michael,** 1878–1942, U.S. actor, playwright, and producer.

co·heir (kō âr'), *n.* a joint heir. —**co·heir'ess,** *n. fem.*

Co·hen (kō'ən), *n.* **Octavus Roy,** 1891–1959, U.S. shortstory writer and novelist.

co·here (kō hĭr'), *v.i.,* **-hered, -hering. 1.** to stick together; be united; hold fast, as parts of the same mass. **2.** to be naturally or logically connected. **3.** to agree; be congruous. [t. L: m. s. *cohaerēre* stick together] —**Syn. 1.** See **stick**[2].

co·her·ence (kō hĭr'əns), *n.* **1.** act or state of cohering; cohesion. **2.** natural or logical connection. **3.** congruity; consistency. Also, **co·her'en·cy.** —**Syn. 1, 2.** COHERENCE, COHESION imply a sticking together. COHERENCE is more often applied figuratively, relating to the order and consistency of thought or of statements: *the coherence of an argument, of a report.* COHESION usually applies to the literal sticking together of material things: *the cohesion of wood and glue in plywood.*

co·her·ent (kō hĭr'ənt), *adj.* **1.** cohering; sticking together. **2.** having a natural or due agreement of parts; connected. **3.** consistent; logical. —**co·her'ent·ly,** *adv.*

co·her·er (kō hĭr'ər), *n. Radio.* a device, usually a tube filled with a conducting substance in granular form, whose electrical resistance decreases when struck by radio waves: used in detecting radio waves.

co·he·sion (kō hē'zhən), *n.* **1.** act or state of cohering, uniting, or sticking together. **2.** *Physics.* the state or process by which the particles of a body or substance are bound together. **3.** *Bot.* the congenital union of one part with another. —**Syn. 1.** See **coherence.**

co·he·sive (kō hē'sĭv), *adj.* **1.** characterized by or causing cohesion. **2.** cohering; tending to cohere. —**co·he'sive·ly,** *adv.* —**co·he'sive·ness,** *n.*

co·ho·bate (kō'hō bāt'), *v.t.,* **-bated, -bating.** *Pharm.* to distill again from the same or a similar substance, as a distilled liquid poured back upon the matter remaining in the vessel, or upon another mass of similar matter. [t. ML: m.s. *cohobātus,* pp. of *cohobāre;* der. obs. med. term *cohob* of uncert. orig.]

Co·hoes (kō hōz'), *n.* a city in E New York, on the Hudson. 20,129 (1960).

co·hort (kō'hôrt), *n.* **1.** one of the ten divisions in an ancient Roman legion, numbering from 300 to 600 men. **2.** any group of warriors. **3.** any group or company. [t. L: s. *cohors* (orig. enclosure; see COURT)]

co·hosh (kō'hŏsh, kō hŏsh'), *n.* either of two perennial herbs of the Eastern U. S., the ranunculaceous *Cimicifuga racemosa* (**black cohosh**), or the berberidaceous *Caulophyllum thalictroides* (**blue cohosh**), both used medicinally. [t. N Amer. Ind. (Mass.): m. *kuskⁿ* rough]

co·hune (kō hōōn'), *n.* a pinnate-leaved palm, *Orbignya Cohune,* native of Central America, bearing large nuts whose meat yields an oil resembling that of the coconut. Also, **cohune palm.**

coif (koif), *n.* **1.** a hood-shaped cap worn under a veil, as by nuns. **2.** a close-fitting cap of various kinds, as one worn by European peasant women. **3.** a cap like the skullcap, retained until the common introduction of the wig, esp. as the headdress of barristers. **4.** the rank or position of a sergeant at law. —*v.t.* **5.** to cover or dress with, or as with, a coif. [ME, t. OF: m. *coife,* g. LL *cofea* cap; appar. of Gmc. orig. (cf. MHG *kupfe* cap)]

coif·feur (kwä fœr'), *n.* a hairdresser. [t. F, der *coiffer.* See COIFFURE]

coif·fure (kwä fyōōr', *Fr.* kwä fÿr'), *n.* **1.** a style of arranging or combing the hair. **2.** a head covering; headdress. [t. F, der. *coiffer,* lit., furnish with a coif]

coign (koin), *n.* **1.** a projecting corner. **2.** a wedge. Also, **coigne.** [var. of COIN (def. 4)]

coign of vantage, a good position or place for observation or action.

coil[1] (koil), *v.t.* **1.** to wind into rings one above another; twist or wind spirally: *to coil a rope.* —*v.i.* **2.** to form rings, spirals, etc.; wind. **3.** to move in winding course. —*n.* **4.** a connected series of spirals or rings into which a rope or the like is wound. **5.** a single such ring. **6.** an arrangement of pipes, coiled or in a series, as in a radiator. **7.** a continuous pipe having inlet and outlet, or flow and return ends. **8.** *Elect.* **a.** a conductor, as a copper wire, wound up in a spiral or other form. **b.** a device composed essentially of such a conductor. **9.** *Philately.* **a.** a stamp issued in a roll, usually of 500 stamps, and usually perforated vertically or horizontally only. **b.** a roll of such stamps. [cf. F *cueillir* gather, g. a LL form r. L *colligere.* See COLLECT]

coil[2] (koil), *n.* **1.** disturbance; tumult; bustle. **2.** trouble. [orig. unknown]

Co·im·ba·tore (kō'ĭm'bä tōr'), *n.* a city in SW India, in Madras province. 197,755 (1951).

coin (koin), *n.* **1.** a piece of metal stamped and issued by the authority of the government for use as money. **2.** such pieces collectively. **3.** pay (someone) in his own coin, to treat (someone) as he has treated others. **4.** *Archit.* **a.** a corner or an angle. **b.** a cornerstone. **c.** a wedge-shaped stone of an arch. —*v.t.* **5.** to make (money) by stamping metal. **6.** to convert (metal) into money. **7.** *Colloq.* to make or gain (money) rapidly. **8.** to make; invent; fabricate: *to coin words.* —*v.i.* **9.** *Brit. Colloq.* to counterfeit money, etc. [ME, t. F: wedge, corner, die, g. L *cuneus* wedge] —**coin'a·ble,** *adj.* —**coin'er,** *n.*

---

b., blend of, blended; **c.,** cognate with; **d.,** dialect, dialectal; **der.,** derived from; **f.,** formed from; **g.,** going back to; **m.,** modification of; **r.,** replacing; **s.,** stem of; **t.,** taken from; **?,** perhaps. See the full key on inside cover.

coin·age (koi′nĭj), *n.* **1.** act, process, or right of making coins. **2.** that which is coined. **3.** coins collectively; the currency. **4.** anything made, invented, or fabricated.

co·in·cide (kō′ĭn sīd′), *v.i.*, **-cided, -ciding. 1.** to occupy the same place in space, the same point or period in time, or the same relative position. **2.** to correspond exactly (in nature, character, etc.). **3.** to agree or concur (in opinion, etc.). [t. ML: m.s. *coincidere*, f. L: *co- + incidere* fall on]

co·in·ci·dence (kō ĭn′sə dəns), *n.* **1.** condition or fact of coinciding. **2.** a striking occurrence of two or more events at one time apparently by mere chance.

co·in·ci·dent (kō ĭn′sə dənt), *adj.* **1.** coinciding; occupying the same place or position. **2.** happening at the same time. **3.** exactly corresponding. **4.** in exact agreement (fol. by *with*). **—co·in′ci·dent·ly,** *adv.*

co·in·ci·den·tal (kō ĭn′sə děn′təl), *adj.* showing or involving coincidence. **—co·in·ci·den′tal·ly,** *adv.*

co·in·her·it·ance (kō′ĭn hĕr′ə təns), *n.* joint inheritance. **—co′in·her′i·tor,** *n.*

co·in·sur·ance (kō′ĭn shŏŏr′əns), *n.* **1.** insurance jointly with another or others. **2.** a form of fire and various other forms of property insurance in which a person taking out insurance on property for less than its full value is regarded as a joint insurer and becomes jointly and proportionately responsible for losses.

co·in·sure (kō′ĭn shŏŏr′), *v.t.*, *v.i.*, **-sured, -suring.** to insure jointly with another or others; insure on the basis of coinsurance.

coir (koir), *n.* the prepared fiber of the husk of the coconut fruit, used in making rope, matting, etc. [t. Malayalam: m. *kāyar* cord]

co·i·tal ex·an·the·ma (kō′ə təl ĕk′sən thē′mə), a virus disease affecting horses and cattle characterized by the appearance of vesicles which later become pustules on the mucous membranes of the genital organs and neighboring skin. It is transmitted by copulation.

co·i·tion (kō ĭsh′ən), *n.* sexual intercourse. Also, **co·i·tus** (kō′ĭ təs). [t. L: s. *coitio,* der. *coīre* go together]

coke[1] (kōk), *n., v.*, **coked, coking. —***n.* **1.** the solid product resulting from the distillation of coal in an oven or closed chamber, or by imperfect combustion: used as a fuel in metallurgy, etc. It consists almost wholly of carbon. **—***v.t., v.i.* **2.** to convert into or become coke. [? var. of *colk* core]

coke[2] (kōk), *n. Slang.* cocaine. [short for COCAINE]

cok·er (kō′kər), *n.* (*usually pl.*) *U.S.* an inhabitant of the mountains of West Virginia and Pennsylvania.

col (kŏl; *Fr.* kôl), *n.* **1.** *Phys. Geog.* a saddle or pass between two higher-standing parts of a mountain range or ridge. **2.** *Meteorol.* the region of relatively low pressure between two anticyclones. [t. F, g. L *collum* neck]

col-[1], variant of **com-,** by assimilation before *l,* as in *collateral.*

col-[2], variant of **colo-** before vowels, as in *colectomy.*

Col., 1. Colorado. **2.** Colossians. **3.** Colonel.

col., column.

co·la[1] (kō′lə), *n.* kola. [Latinization of *Kola, Kolla, Goora,* in Negro languages of W Africa]

co·la[2] (kō′lə), *n.* pl. of **colon.**

co·lan·der (kŭl′ən dər, kŏl′-), *n.* a strainer for draining off liquids, esp. in cookery. Also, **cullender.** [cf. ML *cōlātōrium,* der. *cōlāre* strain]

cola nut, kola nut.

co·lat·i·tude (kō lăt′ə tūd′, -tōōd′), *n. Astron., Navig.* the complement of the latitude; the difference between a given latitude and 90°.

Col·bert (kôl bĕr′), *n.* **Jean Baptiste** (zhäN bȧ tĕst′), 1619–83, French statesman and financier.

col·can·non (kəl kăn′ən, kôl′kăn-), *n.* an Irish dish made of cabbage (or greens) and potatoes boiled and mashed together. [f. COLE + *-cannon* (of uncert. orig. and meaning)]

Col·ches·ter (kōl′chĕs′tər; *Brit.* kōl′chĭs tər), *n.* a city in E England, in Essex. 61,880 (est. 1956).

col·chi·cine (kŏl′chə sēn′, -sĭn, kŏl′kə-), *n. Pharm.* the active principle of colchicum (def. 3).

col·chi·cum (kŏl′chə kəm, kŏl′kĭ-), *n.* **1.** any plant of the Old World liliaceous genus *Colchicum,* esp. *C. autumnale,* a crocuslike plant. **2.** the dried seeds or corms of this plant. **3.** a medicine or drug prepared from them, used esp. for gout. [t. L, t. Gk.: m. *kolchikón;* appar. named after COLCHIS]

Col·chis (kŏl′kĭs), *n.* the legendary land of Medea and the Golden Fleece.

col·co·thar (kŏl′kə thər), *n.* the brownish-red oxide of iron which remains after the heating of ferrous sulfate: used as a polishing agent, etc. [t. ML, t. Ar.: m. *qolqotār*]

cold (kōld), *adj.* **1.** having a temperature lower than the normal temperature of the body: *cold hands.* **2.** having a relatively low temperature; having little or no warmth: *cold water, a cold day.* **3.** producing or feeling, esp. in a high degree, a lack of warmth: *I am cold.* **4.** dead. **5.** *U.S.* unconscious because of a severe blow, shock, etc. **6.** deficient in passion, emotion, enthusiasm, ardor, etc.: *cold reason.* **7.** not affectionate, cordial, or friendly; unresponsive: *a cold reply.* **8.** lacking sensual desire; frigid. **9.** failing to excite feeling or interest. **10.** imperturbable. **11.** depressing; dispiriting: *cold news.* **12.** faint; weak: *a cold scent.* **13.** distant from the object of search. **14.** *Art.* blue in effect, or inclined toward blue in tone: *a picture cold in tone.* **15.** slow to

absorb heat, as a soil containing a large amount of clay and hence retentive of moisture. **16. cold feet,** *Slang.* loss of courage or confidence for carrying out some undertaking. **17. in cold blood,** calmly; coolly and deliberately. **—***n.* **18.** the relative absence of heat. **19.** the sensation produced by loss of heat from the body, as by contact with anything having a lower temperature than that of the body. **20.** an indisposition caused by exposure to cold, characterized by catarrh, hoarseness, coughing, etc. **21. catch** or **take cold,** to suffer from such a cold. **22.** cold weather. **23. in the cold,** neglected; ignored. [ME; d. OE *cald,* r. OE *ceald,* c. G *kalt.* Cf. L *gelidus* icy] **—cold′ish,** *adj.* **—cold′ly,** *adv.* **—cold′ness,** *n.*

—Syn. 2. COLD, CHILL, CHILLING, CHILLY, COOL refer to various degrees of absence of heat. COLD refers to temperature possibly so low as to cause suffering: *cold water.* CHILL, now chiefly poetical, suggests a raw cold which causes shivering and numbness: *how bitter chill it was.* CHILLING carries a connotation of (killing) frost: *a chilling wind.* CHILLY is a weaker word, though it also connotes shivering and discomfort: *a chilly room.* COOL means merely somewhat cold, not warm: *cool and comfortable.* All have figurative uses. **6.** indifferent **—Ant. 2.** hot. **6.** emotional.

cold-blood·ed (kōld′blŭd′ĭd), *adj.* **1.** without feeling; unsympathetic; cruel: *a cold-blooded murder.* **2.** sensitive to cold. **3.** designating or pertaining to animals, as fishes and reptiles, whose blood temperature ranges from the freezing point upward, in accordance with the temperature of the surrounding medium. **—cold′-blood′ed·ly,** *adv.* **—cold′-blood′ed·ness,** *n.*

cold chisel, a strong steel chisel used on cold metal.

cold cream, a cooling unguent for the skin.

cold frame, a small glass-covered structure, and the bed of earth which it covers, used to protect plants.

cold front, *Meteorol.* **1.** the contact surface between two air masses where the cooler mass is advancing against and under the warmer mass. **2.** the line of intersection of this surface with the surface of the earth.

Cold Harbor, a locality NE of Richmond, Virginia: the scene of Civil War battles, 1862, 1864.

cold-heart·ed (kōld′här′tĭd), *adj.* lacking sympathy or feeling; indifferent; unkind.

cold pack, a cold towel, ice bag, etc., applied to the body to reduce swelling, relieve pain, etc.

cold shoulder, an open show of indifference or disregard: *to give one the cold shoulder.*

cold-shut (kōld′shŭt′), *n. Metall.* an imperfectly fused junction of two streams of metal in a mold.

cold snap, a sudden period of cold weather.

cold sore, a vesicular eruption on the face often accompanying a cold or a febrile condition; herpes simplex.

cold steel, a sword, bayonet, etc.

cold storage, the storage of food, furs, etc. in an artificially cooled place.

cold sweat, perspiration and coldness caused by fear, nervousness, etc.

cold war, intense economic and political rivalry just short of military conflict.

cold wave, *Meteorol.* a rapid and considerable fall in temperature, usually affecting a large area.

cole (kōl), *n.* any of various plants of the genus *Brassica,* esp. rape, *Brassica napus.* [ME *col(e),* OE *cāl,* var. of *cāw(e)l,* t. L: m.s. *caulis* stalk, cabbage]

co·lec·to·my (kə lĕk′tə mĭ), *n., pl.* **-mies.** *Surg.* the removal of all or part of the colon or large intestine.

cole·man·ite (kōl′mə nīt′), *n.* a mineral, hydrous calcium borate, $Ca_2B_6O_{11} \cdot 5H_2O$, occurring in colorless or milky-white crystals. [named after W. T. *Coleman,* to San Francisco]

co·le·op·ter·on (kō′lĭ ŏp′tə rŏn′, kŏl′ĭ-), *n.* a coleopterous insect; a beetle. Also, **co′le·op′ter·an.** [t. NL, t. Gk.: m. *koleópteron,* adj. (neut.), sheath-winged]

co·le·op·ter·ous (kō′lĭ ŏp′tər əs, kŏl′ĭ-), *adj.* belonging or pertaining to the order *Coleoptera,* the beetles. [t. Gk.: m. *koleópteros* sheath-winged]

Coleopteron, *Cicindela campestris*
A. Head; B. Prothorax; C. Abdomen;
D. Elytra; E. Wings; F. Antennae

co·le·op·tile (kō′lĭ ŏp′tĭl, kŏl′ĭ-), *n. Bot.* (in grasses) the first leaf above the ground, forming a sheath around the stem tip.

co·le·o·rhi·za (kō′lĭ ə rī′zə, kŏl′ĭ-), *n., pl.* **-zae** (-zē). *Bot.* the sheath which envelops the radicle in certain plants, and which is penetrated by the root in germination. [t. NL, f. Gk.: m. *koleó(s)* sheath + *rhiza* root]

Cole·ridge (kōl′rĭj), *n.* **Samuel Taylor,** 1772–1834, British poet, critic, and philosopher.

cole·slaw (kōl′slô′), *n. U.S.* a salad of finely sliced cabbage. [t. D: m. *koolsla,* f. *kool* cabbage + *sla,* m. *salade* salad]

Col·et (kŏl′ĭt), *n.* **John,** 1467?–1519, English educator and clergyman: a leader of humanism in England.

Co·lette (kô lĕt′), *n.* (*Sidonie Gabrielle Claudine Colette*), 1873–1954, French novelist.

co·le·us (kō′lĭ əs), *n.* any plant of the menthaceous genus *Coleus,* of tropical Asia and Africa, species of which are cultivated for their showy, colored foliage. [NL, t. Gk.: m. *koleós* sheath (so called from the union of the filaments about the style)]

ăct, āble, dâre, ärt; ĕbb, ēqual; ĭf, īce; hŏt, ōver, ôrder, oil, bŏŏk, ōōze, out; ŭp, ūse, ûrge; ə = a in alone; ch, chief; g, give; ng, ring; sh, shoe; th, thin; th, that; zh, vision.   See the full key on inside cover.

cole·wort (kōl′wûrt′), *n.* any plant of the genus *Brassica*, esp. kale and rape.

Col·fax (kōl′făks), *n.* **Schuyler** (skī′lər), 1823–85, U.S. political leader: vice-president of the U.S., 1869–73.

col·ic (kŏl′ĭk), *Pathol., Vet. Sci.* —*n.* **1.** paroxysmal pain in the abdomen or bowels. —*adj.* **2.** pertaining to or affecting the colon or the bowels. [ME *colyke*, t. L: m.s. *cōlicus*, t. Gk.: m. *kōlikós* pertaining to the colon] —**col·ick·y** (kŏl′ĭk ĭ), *adj.*

col·ic·root (kŏl′ĭk rōōt′, -rŏŏt′), *n.* **1.** either of two North American liliaceous herbs, *Aletris farinosa* and *A. aurea*, having small yellow or white flowers in a spikelike raceme, and a root reputed to relieve colic. **2.** any of certain other plants reputed to cure colic.

col·ic·weed (kŏl′ĭk wēd′), *n.* *U.S.* **1.** the squirrel corn. **2.** the Dutchman's-breeches. **3.** any of a species of *Corydalis* (*Capnoides*), esp. the pale corydalis, *C. flavula* of the eastern U.S.

Co·li·gny (kô lē nyē′), *n.* **Gaspard de** (gȧs pȧr′ də), 1519–72, French admiral and Huguenot leader. Also, **Co·li·gni′**.

Co·li·ma (kô lē′mä), *n.* **1.** a state in SW Mexico, on the Pacific coast. 120,618 pop. (est. 1952); 2010 sq. mi. **2.** the capital of this state. 28,658 (1950). **3.** a volcano NW of this city, in Jalisco state. 12,792 ft.

-coline, -colous. [f. s. L *colere* inhabit + -INE¹]

col·i·se·um (kŏl′ə sē′əm), *n.* **1.** an amphitheater, stadium, large theater, etc., for public meeting and entertainment. **2.** (*cap.*) Colosseum. [t. ML: COLOSSEUM]

co·li·tis (kō lī′tĭs, kə-), *n.* *Pathol.* inflammation of the mucous membrane of the colon. [t. NL; see COL(ON), -ITIS]

coll., **1.** college. **2.** collegiate. **3.** collective. **4.** colloquial.

col·lab·o·rate (kə lăb′ə rāt′), *v.i.*, **-rated, -rating. 1.** to work, one with another; coöperate, as in literary work. **2.** to coöperate treacherously: *collaborating with the Nazis.* [t. LL: m.s. *collabōrātus*, pp.] —**col·lab′o·ra′tion**, *n.* —**col·lab′o·ra′tor**, **col·lab′o·ra′tion·ist**, *n.*

col·lage (kə läzh′, kô-; *Fr.* kô lȧzh′), *n.* *Surrealism.* an abstract composition employing various materials, such as newspaper clippings, fragments of advertisements, etc., with lines and colors supplied by the artist. [F]

col·la·gen (kŏl′ə jən), *n.* *Biochem.* the protein contained in connective tissue and bones which yields gelatin on boiling. [t. F: m. *collagène*, f. m. Gk. *kólla* glue + -gène -GEN]

col·lapse (kə lăps′), *v.*, **-lapsed, -lapsing,** *n.* —*v.i.* **1.** to fall or cave in; crumble suddenly: *the roof collapsed.* **2.** to be made so that parts can be folded, placed, etc., together: *this bridge table collapses.* **3.** to break down; come to nothing; fail: *the project collapsed.* **4.** to lose strength, courage, etc., suddenly. **5.** *Pathol.* **a.** to sink into extreme weakness. **b.** (of lungs) to come into an airless state. —*v.t.* **6.** to cause to collapse. —*n.* **7.** a falling in or together. **8.** a sudden, complete failure; a breakdown. [t. L: m.s. *collapsus*, pp., fallen together] —**col·laps′i·ble, col·laps′a·ble,** *adj.* —**col·laps′i·bil′i·ty,** *n.*

col·lar (kŏl′ər), *n.* **1.** anything worn or placed around the neck. **2.** the part of a shirt, blouse, coat, etc., around the neck, usually folded over. **3.** a leather or metal band put around an animal's neck to restrain or identify it. **4.** part of a harness around the horse's neck that bears some of the weight of the load drawn. See illus. under **harness. 5.** an ornamental necklace worn as insignia of an order of knighthood. **6.** *Zool.* any of various markings, or structures, about the neck, suggesting a collar; a torques. **7.** *Mach.* an enlargement encircling a rod or shaft, and serving usually as a holding or bearing piece. —*v.t.* **8.** to put a collar on; furnish with a collar. **9.** to seize by the collar or neck. **10.** *Slang.* to lay hold of, seize, or take. **11.** to roll up and bind (meat, fish, etc.) for cooking. [t. L: m. *collāre*, der. *collum* neck; r. ME *coler*, t. AF] —**col′lar·less,** *adj.*

col·lar·bone (kŏl′ər bōn′), *n.* clavicle.

col·lard (kŏl′ərd), *n.* a kind of edible kale, *Brassica oleracea*, var. *acephala*, grown in southern U.S. [var. of COLEWORT, with second element assimilated to -ARD]

col·lar·et (kŏl′ə rĕt′), *n.* a woman's small collar or neckpiece of lace, embroidery, chiffon, fur, or other material. Also, **col′lar·ette′.** [f. COLLAR + -ET, r. *colleret*, t. F: m. *collerette*, dim. of *collier* collar]

col·late (kŏ lāt′, kə-, kŏl′āt), *v.t.*, **-lated, -lating. 1.** to compare (texts, statements, etc.) in order to note points of agreement or disagreement. **2.** *Bookbinding.* to verify the arrangement of, as the sheets of a book after they have been gathered, usually by inspecting the signature at the foot of the first page of each sheet. **3.** *Bibliog.* to verify the number and order of the sheets of (a volume) as a means of determining its completeness. **4.** *Eccles.* to present by collation, as to a benefice. [t. L: m.s. *collātus*, pp., brought together] —**col·la·tor** (kŏ lā′tər, kə-, kŏl′ā tər), *n.*

col·lat·er·al (kə lăt′ər əl), *adj.* **1.** situated at the side. **2.** running side by side. **3.** *Bot.* standing side by side. **4.** accompanying; attendant; auxiliary. **5.** additional; confirming: *collateral security.* **6.** secured by collateral: *a collateral loan.* **7.** aside from the main subject, course, etc.; secondary; indirect. **8.** descended from the same stock, but in a different line; not lineal. **9.** pertaining to those so descended. —*n.* **10.** security pledged for the payment of a loan. **11.** a collateral kinsman. [ME, t.

ML: s. *collaterālis*. See COL-, LATERAL] —**col·lat′er·al·ly**, *adv.*

col·la·tion (kŏ lā′shən, kə-), *n.* **1.** act of collating. **2.** description of the technical features of a book; volumes, size, pages, illustrations, etc. **3.** the presentation of a clergyman to a benefice, esp. by a bishop who is himself the patron or has acquired the patron's rights. **4.** a light meal which may be permitted on days of general fast. **5.** a light meal. **6.** act of reading and conversing on the lives of the saints, or the Scriptures (a practice instituted in monasteries by St. Benedict). [ME *collacion*, t. L: m.s. *collātio* a bringing together]

col·la·tive (kŏ lā′tĭv, kŏl′ā-), *adj.* **1.** collating. **2.** *Eccles.* presented by collation: *collative benefices.*

col·league (kŏl′ēg), *n.* an associate in office, professional work, etc. [t. F: m. *collègue* t. L: m. *collēga* one chosen with another] —**col′league·ship′,** *n.*

col·lect¹ (kə lĕkt′), *v.t.* **1.** to gather together; assemble. **2.** to accumulate; make a collection of. **3.** to receive or compel payment of: *to collect a bill.* **4.** to regain control of (one's thoughts, faculties, etc., or oneself). **5.** to infer. —*v.i.* **6.** to gather together; assemble. **7.** to accumulate: *rain water collecting in the drainpipe.* **8.** to gather or bring together books, stamps, coins, etc., usually as a hobby. —*adj.*, *adv.* **9.** to be paid for on delivery: *to send a telegram collect.* [t. L: s. *collectus*, pp., gathered together] —**col·lect′a·ble, col·lect′i·ble,** *adj.* —**Syn. 1.** See **gather.**

col·lect² (kŏl′ĕkt), *n.* any of certain brief prayers used in Western churches as before the epistle in the communion service, and, in Anglican churches, also in morning and evening prayers. [ME *collecte*, t. ML: m. *collecta* short prayer, orig., a gathering together. See COLLECT¹]

col·lec·ta·ne·a (kŏl′ĕk tā′nĭ ə), *n. pl.* collected passages; a miscellany; anthology. [t. L, neut. pl. of *collectāneus* collected]

col·lect·ed (kə lĕk′tĭd), *adj.* having control of one's faculties; self-possessed. —**col·lect′ed·ly,** *adv.* —**col·lect′ed·ness,** *n.* —**Syn.** See **calm.**

col·lec·tion (kə lĕk′shən), *n.* **1.** act of collecting. **2.** that which is collected; a set of objects, specimens, writings, etc., gathered together. **3.** a sum of money collected, esp. for charity or church use. —**Syn. 2.** accumulation, aggregation. [ME, t. L: s. *collectio*]

col·lec·tive (kə lĕk′tĭv), *adj.* **1.** formed by collection. **2.** forming a collection or aggregate; aggregate; combined. **3.** pertaining to a group of individuals taken together. **4.** (of a fruit) formed by the coalescence of the pistils of several flowers, as the mulberry or the pineapple. —*n.* **5.** a collective noun. **6.** a collective body, aggregate. **7.** *Govt.* a unit of organization or the organization in a collectivist system. —**col·lec′tive·ly,** *adv.*

collective agreement, 1. the contract, written or oral, made between an employer or employers and a union in behalf of all the employees represented by the union. **2.** the schedule of wages, rules, and working conditions agreed upon.

collective bargaining, the process by which wages, hours, rules, and working conditions are negotiated and agreed upon by a union with an employer for all the employees collectively whom it represents.

collective behavior, *Sociol.* the concerted behavior of individuals acting under the influence of each other.

collective noun, *Gram.* a noun that under the singular form expresses a grouping of individual objects or persons, as *herd*, *jury*, and *clergy*. The singular verb is used when the noun is thought of as naming a single unit, acting as one, as *family* in *my family is related to Washington.* The plural verb is used when the noun is thought of as composed of individuals who retain their separateness, as *My family are all at home.*

collective security, a policy or principle in international relations, designed to preserve world peace, according to which all countries collectively guarantee the security of individual countries, as by sanctions or multilateral alliances against an aggressor.

col·lec·tiv·ism (kə lĕk′tə vĭz′əm), *n.* the socialistic principle of control by the people collectively, or the state, of all means of production or economic activities —**col·lec′tiv·ist,** *n.*, *adj.* —**col·lec′tiv·is′tic,** *adj.*

col·lec·tiv·i·ty (kŏl′ĕk tĭv′ə tĭ), *n.*, *pl.* **-ties. 1.** collective character. **2.** a collective whole. **3.** the people collectively.

col·lec·ti·vize (kə lĕk′tə vīz′), *v.t.*, **-vized, -vizing.** to organize (a people, industry, economy, etc.) according to the principles of collectivism. —**col·lec′ti·vi·za′tion,** *n.*

col·lec·tor (kə lĕk′tər), *n.* **1.** one who or that which collects. **2.** a person employed to collect debts, duties taxes, etc. **3.** one who collects books, paintings, stamps shells, etc., esp. as a hobby. **4.** *Elect.* any device for collecting current from contact conductors. [ME, t. LL] —**col·lec′tor·ship′,** *n.*

collector electrode. See **klystron.**

col·leen (kŏl′ēn, kə lēn′), *n.* *Irish.* girl. [t. Irish: m. *cailín*]

col·lege (kŏl′ĭj), *n.* **1.** an institution of higher learning, esp. one not divided (like a university) into distinct schools and faculties, and affording a general or liberal education rather than technical or professional training **2.** a constituent unit of a university, furnishing courses of instruction in the liberal arts and sciences, usually leading to the degree of bachelor. **3.** an institution for special or professional instruction, as in medicine, pharmacy, agriculture, or music, often set up as a part of a university. **4.** an endowed, self-governing association of scholars incorporated within a university as at the universities of Oxford and Cambridge in England. **5.** a similar corporation outside a university. **6.** the building or buildings occupied by an institution of higher education. **7.** (in French use) an institution for secondary education. **8.** an organized association of persons having certain powers and rights, and performing certain duties or engaged in a particular pursuit: *an electoral college.* **9.** a company; assemblage. **10.** a body of clergy living together on a foundation for religious service, etc. **11.** *Brit. Slang.* a prison. [ME, t. OF, t. L: m.s. *collēgium* association, a society]

College of Cardinals, *Rom. Cath. Ch.* the Sacred College which comprises all the cardinals and which elects and advises the Pope. Official name, **Sacred College of Cardinals.**

College of Propaganda. See **propaganda** (def. 3).

col·leg·er (kŏl′ĭj ər), *n.* (at Eton College, England) a student supported by funds provided by the college.

college widow, *U.S. Colloq.* an unmarried woman living in a college town who has received the attentions of students of several successive classes.

col·le·gian (kə lē′jən, -jĭ ən), *n.* **1.** a student in, or a graduate of, a college. **2.** a member of a college.

col·le·giate (kə lē′jĭt, -jĭ ĭt), *adj.* **1.** of or pertaining to a college. **2.** of, for, or like college students: *collegiate life, collegiate dictionaries.* **3.** of the nature of or constituted as a college. Also, **col·le·gi·al** (kə lē′jĭ əl).

collegiate church, **1.** a church which is endowed for a chapter of canons (usually with a dean), but which has no bishop's see. **2.** (loosely) a chapel connected with a college. **3.** *U.S.* a church or group of churches under the general management of one consistory or session. **4.** a consolidation of formerly distinct churches under one or more pastors. **5.** (in Scotland) a church or congregation the active pastor of which is the colleague and successor of the emeritus pastor.

col·len·chy·ma (kə lĕng′kə mə), *n. Bot.* a layer of modified parenchyma consisting of cells which are thickened at the angles and commonly elongated. [NL, f. Gk.: m.s. *kólla* glue + *énchyma* infusion]

col·let (kŏl′ĭt), *n., v.,* **-leted, -leting.** —*n.* **1.** a collar or enclosing band. **2.** the enclosing rim within which a jewel is set. **3.** *Horol.* the tiny collar which supports the inner terminal of the hairspring. —*v.t.* **4.** to set in a collet: *colleted in gold.* [t. F, dim. of *col* neck, g. L *collum*]

col·lide (kə līd′), *v.i.,* **-lided, -liding. 1.** to come together with force; come into violent contact; crash: *the two cars collided.* **2.** to clash; conflict. [t. L: m.s. *collīdere*]

col·lie (kŏl′ĭ), *n.* a dog of any of certain intelligent varieties much used for tending sheep, esp. one of Scotch breed, usually with a heavy coat of long hair and a bushy tail.

col·lier (kŏl′yər), *n. Chiefly Brit.* **1.** a ship for carrying coal. **2.** a coal miner. **3.** *Obs.* one who carries or sells coal.

Col·lier (kŏl′yər), *n.* **Jeremy,** 1650–1726, British clergyman and author.

Collie
(2 ft. high at the shoulder)

col·lier·y (kŏl′yər ĭ), *n., pl.* **-lieries.** a coal mine, incl. all buildings and equipment.

col·li·gate (kŏl′ə gāt′), *v.t.,* **-gated, -gating. 1.** to bind or fasten together. **2.** *Logic.* to bind (facts) together by a general description or by a hypothesis which applies to them all. [t. L: m.s. *colligātus,* pp., bound together] —**col′li·ga′tion,** *n.*

col·li·mate (kŏl′ə māt′), *v.t.,* **-mated, -mating. 1.** to bring into line; make parallel. **2.** to adjust accurately the line of sight of (a telescope). [t. L: m.s. *collimātus,* pp., var. (by false reading) of *collineātus,* pp., brought into line with] —**col′li·ma′tion,** *n.*

col·li·ma·tor (kŏl′ə mā′tər), *n. Optics.* **1.** a fixed telescope for use in collimating other instruments. **2.** the receiving lens or telescope of a spectroscope.

col·lin·e·ar (kə lĭn′ē ər), *adj.* lying in the same straight line. [f. COL-¹ + LINEAR] —**col·lin′e·ar·ly,** *adv.*

Col·ling·wood (kŏl′ĭng wŏŏd′), *n.* a city in SE Australia, near Melbourne. 29,758 (1947).

Col·lins (kŏl′ĭnz), *n.* **1. Michael,** 1890–1922, Irish revolutionist and patriot. **2. William,** 1721–59, British poet. **3. (William) Wilkie,** 1824–89, British novelist.

col·lin·si·a (kə lĭn′sĭ ə, -zĭ ə), *n.* any of the scrophulariaceous herbs constituting the genus *Collinsia,* bearing whorled, (usually) parti-colored flowers. [t. NL, named after Z. *Collins* (1764–1831), American botanist]

col·li·sion (kə lĭzh′ən), *n.* **1.** act of colliding; a coming violently into contact; crash. **2.** a clash; conflict. [late ME, t. LL: s. *collīsio,* acc. L *collīdere* COLLIDE]

col·lo·cate (kŏl′ō kāt′), *v.t.,* **-cated, -cating. 1.** to set or place together. **2.** to arrange in proper order: *collocated events.* [t. L: m.s. *collocātus,* pp., set in a place]

col·lo·ca·tion (kŏl′ō kā′shən), *n.* **1.** act of collocating. **2.** state or manner of being collocated. **3.** arrangement, esp. of words in a sentence.

col·lo·di·on (kə lō′dĭ ən), *n.* soluble guncotton dissolved in a mixture of ether and alcohol, used to form a

---

coating or film on wounds, photographic plates, etc. [f. Gk.: m.s. *kollṓdēs* gluelike + *-ion,* suffix]

col·logue (kə lōg′), *v.i.,* **-logued, -loguing.** *Dial.* to confer secretly; plot mischief; conspire.

col·loid (kŏl′oid), *n.* **1.** *Phys. Chem.* a gelatinous or other substance which when dissolved in a liquid will not diffuse readily through vegetable or animal membranes (contrasted with *crystalloid*). Colloidal particles are about 10^{-7} to 5×10^{-5} cm. in diameter, larger than most inorganic molecules, and remain suspended indefinitely. They are large molecules, as proteins, or groups of molecules, with many properties depending upon their large specific surface. **2.** *Med.* a homogeneous gelatinous substance occurring in some diseased states. [f. m.s. Gk. *kólla* glue + -OID]

col·loi·dal (kə loi′dəl), *adj. Phys. Chem.* pertaining to, or of the nature of, a colloid: *colloidal gold, silver, etc.*

col·lop (kŏl′əp), *n. Brit. Dial.* **1.** a small slice of bacon or other meat. **2.** a small slice or piece of anything. **3.** a fold or roll of flesh on the body. [ME *colope, colloppe.* Cf. Sw. *kollops,* now *kalops*]

colloq., **1.** colloquial. **2.** colloquialism. **3.** colloquially.

col·lo·qui·al (kə lō′kwĭ əl), *adj.* **1.** characteristic of or appropriate to ordinary or familiar conversation rather than formal speech or writing. In standard American English, *he hasn't got any* is colloquial, while *he has none* is formal. **2.** conversational. —**col·lo′qui·al·ly,** *adv.*

—**Syn.** 1, 2. COLLOQUIAL, CONVERSATIONAL, INFORMAL refer to types of speech or to usages not on a formal level. COLLOQUIAL is often mistakenly used with a connotation of disapproval, as if it meant vulgar or "bad" or "incorrect" usage, whereas it is merely a familiar style used in speaking rather than in writing. CONVERSATIONAL refers to a style used in the oral exchange of ideas, opinions, etc.: *an easy conversational style.* INFORMAL means without formality, without strict attention to set forms, unceremonious: *an informal manner of speaking.* —**Ant.** 1, 2. formal.

col·lo·qui·al·ism (kə lō′kwĭ ə līz′əm), *n.* **1.** a colloquial expression. **2.** colloquial style or usage.

col·lo·qui·um (kə lō′kwĭ əm), *n.* an informal conference or group discussion.

col·lo·quy (kŏl′ə kwĭ), *n., pl.* **-quies. 1.** a speaking together; a conversation. **2.** a conference. **3.** (in certain Reformed churches) a governing body corresponding to a presbytery. [t. L: m.s. *colloquium* conversation] —**col′lo·quist,** *n.*

col·lo·type (kŏl′ə tīp′), *n.* **1.** a photomechanical process of printing in ink from a gelatin plate. **2.** the plate. **3.** a print made from it. [f. *collo-* (comb. form repr. Gk. *kólla* glue) + -TYPE]

col·lude (kə lōōd′), *v.i.,* **-luded, -luding. 1.** to act together through a secret understanding. **2.** to conspire in a fraud. [t. L: m.s. *collūdere* play with] —**col·lud′er,** *n.*

col·lu·nar·i·um (kŏl′yə när′ĭ əm), *n. Med.* a solution for application to the nose; nose drops.

col·lu·sion (kə lōō′zhən), *n.* **1.** secret agreement for a fraudulent purpose; conspiracy. **2.** *Law.* a secret understanding between two or more persons prejudicial to another, or a secret understanding to appear as adversaries though in agreement: *collusion of husband and wife to obtain a divorce.* [ME, t. L: s. *collūsio* a playing together]

col·lu·sive (kə lōō′sĭv), *adj.* involving collusion; fraudulently concerted: *a collusive treaty.* —**col·lu′sive·ly,** *adv.* —**col·lu′sive·ness,** *n.*

col·ly (kŏl′ĭ), *v.,* **-lied,** *-lying, n. Archaic or Dial.* —*v.t.* **1.** to blacken as with coal dust; begrime. —*n.* **2.** grime; soot. [var. of *collow,* ME *colwen,* der. *col* COAL]

col·lyr·i·um (kə lĭr′ĭ əm), *n., pl.* **-lyria** (-lĭr′ĭ ə), **-lyriums.** *Med.* a solution for application to the eye; an eyewash. [t. L, t. Gk.: m. *kollýrion* poultice, eye salve]

Col·mar (Fr. kôl mär′; Ger. kôl′mär), *n.* a city in NE France. 47,305 (1954).

Cöln (kœln), *n.* German name of **Cologne.**

colo-, a combining form of **colon**².

Colo., Colorado.

col·o·cynth (kŏl′ə sĭnth), *n.* **1.** a cucurbitaceous plant, *Citrullus colocynthis,* of the warmer parts of Asia, the Mediterranean region, etc., bearing a fruit with a bitter pulp which yields a purgative drug. **2.** the fruit. **3.** the drug. [t. L: m. *colocynthis,* t. Gk.: m. *kolokynthís*]

co·logne (kə lōn′), *n.* a perfumed toilet water; eau de Cologne. Also, **Cologne water.** [for *Cologne water* (made at Cologne, Germany, since 1709)]

Co·logne (kə lōn′; Pr. kô lôn′y), *n.* a city in West Germany. 715,914 (est. 1955). German, **Köln, Cöln.**

Co·lombes (kô lôNb′), *n.* city in N France. 67,909 (1954).

Co·lom·bi·a (kə lŭm′bĭ ə; Sp. kô lôm′byä), *n.* a republic in NW South America. 12,939,000 pop. (est. 1956); 439,828 sq. mi. *Cap.:* Bogotá. —**Co·lom′bi·an,** *adj., n.*

Co·lom·bo (kə lŭm′bō), *n.* a seaport in and the capital of Ceylon, on the W coast. 423,481 (1953).

co·lon¹ (kō′lən), *n., pl.* **-lons** *for 1,* **-la** (-lə) *for 2.* **1.** a point of punctuation (:) marking off a main portion of a sentence (intermediate in force between the semicolon and the period). **2.** *Anc. Pros.* one of the members or sections of a rhythmical period, consisting of a sequence of from two to six feet united under a principal ictus or beat. [t. L, t. Gk.: m. *kôlon* limb, member, clause]

co·lon² (kō′lən), *n., pl.* **-lons, -la** (-lə). *Anat.* that portion of the large intestine which extends from the caecum to the rectum. See diag. under **intestine.** [ME, t. L, t. Gk.: m. *kólon* food, colon]

ăct, āble, dâre, ärt; ĕbb, ēqual; ĭf, īce; hŏt, ōver, ôrder, oil, bŏŏk, ōōze, out; ŭp, ūse, ûrge; ə = a in alone; ch, chief; g, give; ng, ring; sh, shoe; th, thin; t͡h, that; zh, vision.   See the full key on inside cover.

co·lon³ (kō′lŏn′; *Sp.* kô·lôn′), *n., pl.* **colons,** *Sp.* **colo·nes** (kô·lô′nĕs). the unit in the Costa Rican monetary system (= 25c in U.S.) and the El Salvador monetary system (= 50c in U.S.). [t. Amer. Sp.: lit., Columbus]

Co·lón (kō·lōn′; *Sp.* kô·lôn′), *n.* a seaport in Panama at the Atlantic end of the Panama Canal. 52,204 (1950).

colo·nel (kûr′nəl), *n.* an officer ranking in most armies between lieutenant colonel and brigadier general. In England it is an honorary rank. [earlier *coronel* (whence the pronunc.), t. F: m. *coronnel,* var. of *colonnel,* t. It.: m. *colonnello,* dim. of *colonna* COLUMN] —**colo′nel·cy, colo′nel·ship′,** *n.*

co·lo·ni·al (kə·lō′nĭ·əl), *adj.* **1.** of or pertaining to a colony or colonies. **2.** pertaining to the thirteen British colonies which became the United States of America, or to their period. **3.** *Ecol.* forming a colony. **4.** (*cap.*) *Archit.* of the American colonies; largely derived from contemporaneous English styles, as Queen Anne, often translated into new building materials (brick, wood) and simpler forms. —*n.* **5.** an inhabitant of a colony. —**co·lo′ni·al·ly,** *adv.*

co·lo·ni·al·ism (kə·lō′nĭ·ə·lĭz′əm), *n.* the policy of a nation seeking to extend or retain its authority over other peoples or territories.

co·lon·ic (kə·lŏn′ĭk), *adj.* of or affecting the colon.

col·o·nist (kŏl′ə·nĭst), *n.* **1.** an inhabitant of a colony. **2.** a member of a colonizing expedition.

col·o·nize (kŏl′ə·nīz′), *v.,* **-nized, -nizing.** —*v.t.* **1.** to plant or establish a colony in; settle: *England colonized Australia.* **2.** to form a colony of: *to colonize laborers in a mining region.* —*v.i.* **3.** to form a colony. **4.** to settle in a colony. —**col′o·ni·za′tion,** *n.* —**col′o·niz′er,** *n.*

col·on·nade (kŏl′ə·nād′), *n.* **1.** *Archit.* a series of columns set at regular intervals, and usually supporting an entablature, a roof, or a series of arches. **2.** a long row of trees. [t. F. t. It.: m. *colonnato,* der. *colonna,* g. L *columna* COLUMN] —**col′on·nad′ed,** *adj.*

col·o·ny (kŏl′ə·nĭ), *n., pl.* **-nies. 1.** a group of people who leave their native country to form in a new land a settlement subject to, or connected with, the parent state. **2.** the country or district settled or colonized. **3.** any people or territory separated from but subject to a ruling power. **4. the Colonies,** those British colonies that formed the original thirteen States of America: New Hampshire, Massachusetts, Rhode Island, Connecticut, New York, New Jersey, Pennsylvania, Delaware, Maryland, Virginia, North Carolina, South Carolina, and Georgia. **5.** a number of foreigners from a particular country living in a city or country, esp. in one locality: *the American colony in Paris.* **6.** any group of individuals of similar occupation, etc., usually living in a community of their own: *a colony of artists.* **7.** the district or quarter inhabited by any such number or group. **8.** an aggregation of bacteria growing together as the descendants of a single cell. **9.** *Ecol.* a group of animals or plants of the same kind living or growing together in close association. [ME *colonie,* t. L: m. *colōnia*]

col·o·phon (kŏl′ə·fŏn′, -fən), *n.* **1.** an inscription at the close of a book, used esp. in the 15th and 16th centuries, giving the title, author, and other publication facts. **2.** a publisher's distinctive emblem. [t. LL, t. Gk.: m. *kolophōn,* finishing touch]

col·o·pho·ny (kŏl′ə·fō′nĭ, kə·lŏf′ə·nĭ), *n.* common rosin, the hard amorphous substance derived from the oleoresin of the pine. [t. L: m. s. *Colophōnia* (*rēsīna*) (resin) of Colophon (Ionian city in Asia Minor)]

col·or (kŭl′ər), *n.* **1.** the evaluation by the visual sense of that quality of light (reflected or transmitted by a substance) which is basically determined by its spectral composition; that quality of a visual sensation distinct from form. Any color may be expressed in terms of three factors: hue, chroma (purity or saturation), and brightness (or value). Generally the most obvious or striking feature of a color is its hue, which gives it its name. The color is qualified if necessary as pale, dark, dull, light, etc. **2.** complexion. **3.** a ruddy complexion. **4.** racial complexion other than white, esp. Negro. **5.** a blush. **6.** vivid or distinctive quality, as of literary work. **7.** details in description, customs, speech, habits, etc., of a place or period, included for the sake of realism: *a novel about the Pilgrims with much local color.* **8.** that which is used for coloring; pigment; paint; dye. **9.** *Painting.* the general effect of all the hues entering into the composition of a picture. **10.** *Print.* the amount and quality of ink used. **11.** any distinctive color, symbol, badge, etc., of identification: *the colors of a school, jockey, etc.* **12.** (*pl.*) **a.** a flag, ensign, etc., as of a military body or a ship. **b.** *U.S. Navy.* the ceremony of hoisting the national flag at 8 A.M. and of lowering it at sunset. **13.** outward appearance or aspect; guise or show. **14.** a pretext. **15.** kind; sort; variety; general character. **16.** timbre of sound. **17.** an apparent or prima-facie right or ground (esp. in legal use): *to hold possession under color of title.* **18.** *U.S.* a trace or particle of valuable mineral, esp. gold, as shown by washing auriferous gravel, etc. **19.** *Her.* heraldic tincture. **20. change color,** to turn pale or red. **21. give or lend color,** to make probable or realistic. **22. lose color,** to turn pale. **23. show one's colors,** to show one's true nature, opinions, etc. [ME, t. OF, g. L] —*v.t.* **24.** to give or apply color to; tinge; paint; dye. **25.** to cause to appear different from the reality. **26.** to give a special character or distinguishing quality to: *an account colored by personal feelings.* —*v.i.* **27.** to take on or change color. **28.** to flush; blush. Also, *Brit.,* **colour.**

[ME *coloure*(*n*), t. OF: m. *colo*(*u*)*rer,* g. L *cōlōrāre*] —**col′or·er,** *n.*

col·or·a·ble (kŭl′ər·ə·bəl), *adj.* **1.** capable of being colored. **2.** specious; plausible. **3.** pretended; deceptive. Also, *Brit.,* **colourable.** —**col′or·a·bil′i·ty, col′or·a·ble·ness,** *n.* —**col′or·a·bly,** *adv.*

Col·o·rad·o (kŏl′ə·răd′ō, -rä′dō), *n.* **1.** a State in the W United States. 1,753,947 pop. (1960); 104,247 sq. mi. *Cap.*: Denver. *Abbr.*: Colo. **2.** a river flowing from N Colorado through Utah and Arizona into the Gulf of California: Grand Canyon; Boulder Dam. 1450 mi. **3.** a river flowing from W Texas SE to the Gulf of Mexico. 840 mi. —**Col′o·rad′an,** *adj., n.*

col·o·rad·o (kŏl′ə·răd′ō, -rä′dō), *adj.* (of cigars) of medium color and strength. [t. Sp.: colored, red]

Colorado Desert, an arid region in SE California, including the Salton Sink. ab. 2000 sq. mi.

Colorado Springs, a city in central Colorado: resort. 70,194 (1960).

col·or·a·tion (kŭl′ə·rā′shən), *n.* coloring; appearance as to color. Also, *Brit.,* **colouration.**

col·o·ra·tu·ra (kŭl′ə·rə·tyŏŏr′ə, -tŏŏr′ə), *n.* **1.** runs, trills, and other florid decorations in vocal music. **2.** music marked by this. **3.** a lyric soprano of high range who specializes in such music. Also, **col·o·ra·ture** (kŭl′ə·rə·chŏŏr′). [t. It., der. *colorare* to color, g. L *colōrāre*]

col·or·bear·er (kŭl′ər·bâr′ər), *n.* one who carries the colors or standard, esp. of a military body.

color blindness, defective color perception, independent of the capacity for distinguishing light and shade, and form. —**col′or-blind′,** *adj.*

col·or·cast (kŭl′ər·kăst′), *n., v.,* **-cast, -casting.** —*n.* **1.** a television program broadcast in color. —*v.t.* **2.** to broadcast a television program in color.

col·ored (kŭl′ərd), *adj.* **1.** having color. **2.** belonging wholly or in part to some other race than the white, esp. to the Negro race. **3.** pertaining to the Negro race. **4.** specious; deceptive: *a colored statement.* **5.** influenced or biased. **6.** *Bot.* of some hue other than green. Also, *Brit.,* **coloured.**

col·or·ful (kŭl′ər·fəl), *adj.* **1.** abounding in color. **2.** richly picturesque: *a colorful historical period.* **3.** presenting or suggesting vivid or striking scenes: *a colorful narrative.* Also, *Brit.,* **col′our·ful.** —**col′or·ful·ly,** *adv.* —**col′or·ful·ness,** *n.*

color guard, *n.* a guard having charge of the colors, as of a regiment.

col·or·if·ic (kŭl′ə·rĭf′ĭk), *adj.* **1.** producing or imparting color. **2.** pertaining to color. [f. COLOR + -(I)FIC]

col·or·im·e·ter (kŭl′ə·rĭm′ə·tər), *n.* an instrument for analyzing colors into their components, as by measuring a given color in terms of a standard color, of a scale of colors, or of certain primary colors. [f. COLOR + -(I)-METER] —**col·or·i·met·ric** (kŭl′ər·ə·mĕt′rĭk), **col·or·i·met′ri·cal,** *adj.* —**col′or·im′e·try,** *n.*

col·or·ing (kŭl′ər·ĭng), *n.* **1.** act or method of applying color. **2.** appearance as to color. **3.** characteristic aspect or tone. **4.** specious appearance; show. **5.** a substance used to color something. Also, *Brit.,* **colouring.**

col·or·ist (kŭl′ər·ĭst), *n.* **1.** a user of color, as in painting. **2.** a painter who devotes himself specially to effects of color. Also, *Brit.,* **colourist.** —**col′or·is′tic,** *adj.*

col·or·less (kŭl′ər·lĭs), *adj.* **1.** without color. **2.** pallid; dull in color. **3.** without vividness or distinctive character: *a colorless description of the parade.* **4.** unbiased; neutral. Also, *Brit.,* **colourless.** —**col′or·less·ly,** *adv.* —**col′or·less·ness,** *n.*

color line, the line of social or political distinction between the white and colored races.

color sergeant, a sergeant who has charge of battalion or regimental colors.

co·los·sal (kə·lŏs′əl), *adj.* **1.** gigantic; huge; vast. **2.** like a colossus. —**co·los′sal·ly,** *adv.* —**Syn. 1.** See **gigantic.**

Col·os·se·um (kŏl′ə·sē′əm), *n.* **1.** an amphitheater in Rome, the greatest in antiquity, begun by Vespasian and inaugurated (A.D. 80) by Titus. **2.** (*l.c.*) coliseum. [t. L, prop. neut. of *colossēus* colossal. Cf. COLOSSUS]

Co·los·sian (kə·lŏsh′ən), *n.* **1.** a native or an inhabitant of Colossae, an ancient city of Phrygia, in Asia Minor. **2.** one of the Christians of Colossae, to whom Paul addressed one of his epistles. **3.** (*pl.*) the book of the New Testament called *The Epistle of Paul the Apostle to the Colossians.* —**Co·los′sian,** *adj.*

co·los·sus (kə·lŏs′əs), *n., pl.* **-lossi** (-lŏs′ī), **-lossuses. 1.** (*cap.*) the legendary bronze statue of Apollo at Rhodes. See **Seven Wonders of the World. 2.** any statue of gigantic size. **3.** anything colossal or gigantic. [ME, t. L, t. Gk.: m. *kolossós*]

co·los·to·my (kə·lŏs′tə·mĭ), *n., pl.* **-mies.** *Surg.* incision of an artificial opening into the colon for drainage.

co·los·trum (kə·lŏs′trəm), *n.* the milk secreted before and for a few days after parturition. [t. L]

col·our (kŭl′ər), *n., v.t., v.i.* *Brit.* color. —**col′our·a′tion,** *n.* —**col′oured,** *adj.* —**col′our·er,** *n.* —**col′our·ful,** *adj.* —**col′our·ing,** *n.* —**col′our·ist,** *n.* —**col′our·less,** *adj.*

col·our·a·ble (kŭl′ər·ə·bəl), *adj. Brit.* colorable. —**col′our·a·bil′i·ty, col′our·a·ble·ness,** *n.*

-colous, a word element indicating habitat. [f. s. L *colere* inhabit + -OUS]

col·pi·tis (kŏl pī′tĭs), n. *Pathol.* vaginitis. [f. m. s. Gk. *kólpos* bosom, womb + -ITIS]

col·por·tage (kŏl′pōr′tĭj; *Fr.* kôl pôr tàzh′), n. the work of a colporteur. [t. F. der. *colporter* hawk, lit., carry on the neck, f. *col* neck + *porter* carry]

col·por·teur (kŏl′pōr′tər; *Fr.* kôl pôr tœr′), n. 1. a hawker of books, etc. 2. one employed to travel about distributing Bibles, religious tracts, etc., gratuitously or at a low price. [t. F. See COLPORTAGE]

colt (kōlt), n. 1. a young horse or animal of the horse kind, esp. a young male. 2. a young or inexperienced person. 3. *Naut.* a rope's end used in chastising. [ME and OE; cf. d. Sw. *kult* pig] —**colt′ish**, adj. —**colt′-ish·ly**, adv. —**colt′ish·ness**, n.

Colt (kōlt), n. *Trademark.* a type of revolver. [named after Samuel Colt, the inventor]

col·ter (kōl′tər), n. a sharp blade or wheel attached to the beam of a plow, used to cut the ground in advance of the plowshare. Also, **coulter**. [ME and OE *culter*, t. L: knife]

colts·foot (kōlts′fŏŏt′), n., pl. -**foots**. a composite perennial, *Tussilago Farfara*, native to the Old World but widespread as a weed, formerly used in medicine.

col·u·brine (kŏl′yə brīn′, -brĭn), adj. 1. of or resembling a snake; snakelike. 2. of or pertaining to the snake family *Colubridae* (or the subfamily *Colubrinae*). In older definitions, this family included various venomous snakes as well as the great majority of nonvenomous snakes of the world. [t. L: m. s. *colubrīnus* like a serpent] **co·lu·go** (kə lōō′gō), n., pl. -**gos**. the flying lemur.

Col·um (kŏl′əm), n. Padraic (pô′drĭk), born 1881, Irish poet.

Co·lum·ba (kə lŭm′bə), n. Saint, A.D. 521–97, Irish missionary to Scotland.

col·um·bar·i·um (kŏl′əm bâr′Ĭ əm), n., pl. -**baria** (-bâr′Ĭ ə). 1. a sepulchral vault or other structure with recesses in the walls to receive the ashes of the dead. 2. one of the recesses. [t. L, orig., dovecote, der. *columba* dove]

Co·lum·bi·a (kə lŭm′bĬ ə), n. 1. the capital of South Carolina, in the central part. 97,433 (1960). 2. a city in central Missouri. 36,650 (1960). 3. a river flowing from SE British Columbia through Washington and along the boundary between Washington and Oregon into the Pacific. 1214 mi. 4. America, or the United States, esp. as a feminine personification: *Columbia, the Gem of the Ocean*. 5. a white-faced breed of sheep developed from a foundation of crossbred sheep. It is noted for its rapid growing lambs, heavy fleeces of medium wool, good size, and vigor.

Co·lum·bi·an (kə lŭm′bĬ ən), adj. 1. pertaining to America or the United States. 2. pertaining to Columbus. —**n.** 3. a printing type (16 point) of a size between English and great primer. [f. s. NL *Columbia* poetic name for America + -AN]

co·lum·bic (kə lŭm′bĬk), adj. *Chem.* niobic.

Col·um·bine[1] (kŏl′əm bīn′), n. any plant of the ranunculaceous genus *Aquilegia*, comprising erect branching herbs with handsome flowers, as *A. canadensis* (the common wild columbine of North America), and various other species, with blue, purple, white, pink, or yellow flowers. [ME, t. LL: m. *columbīna*, prop. fem. of L *columbīnus* dovelike; from the resemblance of the inverted flower to a group of doves]

col·um·bine[2] (kŏl′əm bīn′, -bĭn), adj. 1. of a dove. 2. dovelike; dove-colored. [ME *columbyn*, t. L: m.s. *columbīnus*]

Col·um·bine (kŏl′əm bīn′), n. a female character in comedy (orig. the early Italian) and pantomime, the sweetheart of Harlequin. [t. It.: m. *Colombina*, der. *colomba* dove, g. L *columba*]

co·lum·bite (kə lŭm′bīt), n. a black, crystalline mineral, $FeNb_2O_6$, often containing manganese and tantalum. It is the principal ore of niobium. [f. COLUMB(IUM) + -ITE[1]]

co·lum·bi·um (kə lŭm′bĬ əm), n. *Chem.* former name for niobium. [t. NL, named after *Columbia* the United States.]

co·lum·bous (kə lŭm′bəs), adj. *Chem.* niobous.

Co·lum·bus (kə lŭm′bəs), n. 1. Christopher, (Sp. *Cristóbal Colón*; It. *Cristoforo Colombo*) 1446?–1506, Italian navigator in Spanish service: discoverer of America, 1492. 2. the capital of Ohio, in the central part. 471,316 (1960). 3. a city in W Georgia. 116,779 (1960).

Columbus Day, a day, Oct. 12, publicly appointed or observed as a holiday in various individual States of the U.S. in honor of the discovery of America by Columbus on Oct. 12, 1492.

col·u·mel·la (kŏl′yə mĕl′ə), n., pl. -**mellae** (-mĕl′ē). *Anat., Zool., Bot.* a small columnlike part; an axis. [t. L, dim. of *columna* COLUMN] —**col′u·mel′lar**, adj.

col·u·mel·li·form (kŏl′yə mĕl′ə fôrm′), adj. like a columella.

col·umn (kŏl′əm), n. 1. *Archit.* **a.** an upright shaft or body of greater length than thickness, usually serving as a support; a pillar. **b.** a vertical architectural member consisting typically of an approximately cylindrical shaft with a base and a capital. See the diagram in the next column. 2. any columnlike object, mass, or formation: *a column of smoke*. 3. one of the two or more vertical rows of lines of type or printed matter of a page: *There are two columns on this page*. 4. a regular contri-

bution to a newspaper, usually signed, and consisting of comment, news, or feature material. 5. a journalistic department devoted to short articles, poems, etc., of a humorous, entertaining, or esp. readable kind, furnished by a particular editor or writer without or with the aid of contributors. 6. a line of ships following one after another. 7. a formation of troops, narrow laterally and extended from front to rear. [t. L: s. *columna* pillar, post; r. ME *colompne*, t. OF] —**columned** (kŏl′əmd), adj. —**Syn.** 1. COLUMN, PILLAR refer to upright supports in architectural structures. PILLAR is the general word: *the pillars supporting the roof.* A COLUMN is a particular kind of pillar, esp. one with three identifiable parts: shaft, base, and capital: *columns of the Corinthian style.*

co·lum·nar (kə lŭm′nər), adj. 1. shaped like a column. 2. printed, arranged, etc., in columns.

co·lum·ni·a·tion (kə lŭm′nĬ ā′shən), n. 1. the use of columns in a structure. 2. the columns used.

col·umn·ist (kŏl′əm Ĭst, -əm nĬst), n. the editor or conductor of a special column in a newspaper.

Architectural column, Tuscan order

co·lure (kō lyŏŏr′, kō′lyŏŏr), n. *Astron.* either of two great circles of the celestial sphere intersecting each other at the poles, one passing through the equinoctial and the other through the solstitial points of the ecliptic. [t. L: m.s. *colūrus*, t. Gk.: m. *kólouros* dock-tailed (the colures being cut off by the horizon))]

Col·vin (kŏl′vĬn), n. Sir Sidney, 1845–1927, British literary and art critic.

col·za (kŏl′zə), n. rapeseed. [t. F, t. D: m. *koolzaad* coleseed]

colza oil, rape oil.

com-, a prefix meaning "with," "jointly," "in combination" and (with intensive force) "completely," occurring in this form before *p* and *b*, as in *compare*, and (by assimilation) before *m*, as in *commingle*. Cf. co- (def. 1). Also, **con-, col-, cor-**. [t. L: comb. form of *cum* with]

Com., 1. Commander. 2. Commission. 3. Commissioner. 4. Committee. 5. Commodore.

com., 1. comedy. 2. commerce. 3. common. 4. commonly.

co·ma[1] (kō′mə), n., pl. -**mas**. a state of prolonged unconsciousness from which it is difficult or impossible to rouse a person, caused by disease, injury, poison, etc.; stupor. [t. Gk.: m. *kōma* deep sleep]

co·ma[2] (kō′mə), n., pl. -**mae** (-mē). 1. *Astron.* the nebulous envelope around the nucleus of a comet. 2. *Optics.* that aberration of optical systems by which rays of an oblique pencil cannot be brought to a sharp focus. 3. *Bot.* a tuft of silky hairs at the end of a seed. [t. L, t. Gk.: m. *kómē* hair]

Co·ma Ber·e·ni·ces (kō′mə bĕr′ə nī′sēz), a northern constellation situated north of Virgo and between Boötes and Leo. [t. L]

Co·man·che (kō măn′chĬ), n., pl. -**ches**. 1. (pl.) a Shoshonean tribe, the only one of the group living entirely on the plains, formerly ranging from Wyoming to Texas, now in Oklahoma. 2. a member of this tribe. 3. their language, of the Uto-Aztecan stock.

Coma[2] (def. 3) on seed of willow herb, *Chamaenerion angustifolium*

Co·man·che·an (kō măn′chĬ ən), *Stratig.* —adj. 1. pertaining to an epoch or series of rocks in parts of North America comprising the early portion of the Cretaceous period or system. —n. 2. an epoch or series of early Cretaceous rocks typically represented in the Gulf of Mexico region. [der. *Comanche*, town and county in central Texas]

co·mate[1] (kō′māt′), n. a mate or companion. [f. co- + MATE[1]]

co·mate[2] (kō′māt), adj. 1. *Bot.* having a coma. 2. hairy; tufted. [t. L: m. s. *comātus* having long hair]

com·a·tose (kŏm′ə tōs′, kō′mə-), adj. affected with coma; lethargic; unconscious. [f. *comat-* (comb. form repr. Gk. *kóma* coma) + -OSE[1]] —**com′a·tose′ly**, adv.

Co·mat·u·la (kə măch′ə lə), n., pl. -**lae** (-lē′). *Zool.* a genus of crinoids or feather stars, characterized by lack of a stalk, hence able to move about freely. [t. NL, prop. fem. of L *comātulus*, dim. of *comātus* COMATE[2]]

co·mat·u·lid (kə măch′ə lĭd), *n.* an extant free-swimming crinoid, as *Comatula* and related forms. [t. NL: *s. Comatulidae*, the family containing the *Comatula*]

comb¹ (kōm), *n.* 1. a toothed piece of bone, metal, etc., for arranging or cleaning the hair, or for keeping it in place. 2. a currycomb. 3. any comblike instrument, object, or formation. 4. a card for dressing wool, etc. 5. the fleshy, more or less serrated excrescence or growth on the head of the domestic fowl. 6. something resembling or suggesting this, as the crest of a wave. 7. a honeycomb, or any similar group of cells. —*v.t.* 8. to dress (the hair, etc.) with, or as with, a comb. 9. to card (wool). 10. to scrape as with a comb. 11. to search everywhere in: *she combed the files for the missing letter.* —*v.i.* 12. to roll over or break at the crest, as a wave. [OE *comb*, var. of *camb*, c. G *kamm*]

comb² (kōōm, kōm), *n.* combe.

comb., combining.

com·bat (*v.*, *n.* kŏm′băt, kŭm′-; *v. also* kəm băt′), *v.*, **-bated, -bating** *or* (*esp. Brit.*) **-batted, -batting**, *n.* —*v.t.* 1. to fight or contend against; oppose vigorously. —*v.i.* 2. to fight; battle; contend (fol. by *with* or *against*). —*n.* 3. a fight between two men, armies, etc. [t. F, der. *combattre*, v., g. L *com-* + *batt(u)ere* beat] —**com·bat·a·ble** (kŏm′băt ə bəl, kŭm′-, kəm băt′-), *adj.* —**com′bat·er**, *n.* —Syn. 3. struggle, conflict. See **fight**.

com·bat·ant (kŏm′bə tənt, kŭm′-, kəm băt′ənt), *n.* 1. a person or group that fights. —*adj.* 2. combating; fighting. 3. disposed to combat.

combat fatigue, *Psychiatry.* battle fatigue.

combat infantryman's badge, *U.S.* the badge awarded to every infantryman of World War II who proved himself in battle.

com·ba·tive (kŏm′bə tĭv, kŭm′-, kəm băt′ĭv), *adj.* ready or inclined to fight; pugnacious. —**com′ba·tive·ly**, *adv.* —**com′ba·tive·ness**, *n.*

combe (kōōm, kōm), *n. Eng.* a narrow valley or deep hollow, esp. one enclosed on all sides but one. Also, **comb, coomb.** [OE *cumb*]

combed yarn (kōmd), cotton or worsted yarn made of fibers laid parallel.

comb·er (kō′mər), *n.* 1. one who or that which combs. 2. a long, curling wave.

com·bi·na·tion (kŏm′bə nā′shən), *n.* 1. act of combining. 2. state of being combined. 3. a number of things combined. 4. something formed by combining. 5. an alliance of persons or parties. 6. the set or series of numbers or letters used in setting the mechanism of a certain type of lock (**combination lock**) used on safes, etc. 7. the parts of the mechanism operated by this. 8. a suit of underwear in one piece. 9. *Math.* **a.** the arrangement of a number of individuals into various groups, as *a*, *b*, and *c* into *ab*, *ac*, and *bc*. **b.** a group thus formed. [t. LL: *s. combīnātio*] —**com′bi·na′tion·al**, *adj.* —Syn. 3. COMBINATION, COMPOSITE, COMPOUND all mean a union of individual parts. COMBINATION implies a grouping which is close but which may be easily dissolved. A COMPOSITE is a stronger union, in which the parts have become subordinate to a unity. COMPOUND implies a more or less complete merging of individual parts into an organic whole.

com·bi·na·tive (kŏm′bə nā′tĭv, kəm bī′nə-), *adj.* 1. tending or serving to combine. 2. pertaining to combination.

com·bin·a·to·ri·al analysis (kəm bī′nə tōr′Ÿ əl), *Math.* the branch of mathematics which studies permutations, and combinations, etc., esp. used in statistics and probability.

com·bine (*v.* kəm bīn′; *n.* kŏm′bīn, kəm bīn′ *for 6, 7,* kŏm′bīn *for 8*), *v.*, **-bined, -bining**, *n.* —*v.t.* 1. to bring or join into a close union or whole; unite; associate; coalesce. 2. to possess or exhibit in union: *a plan which combines the best features of several other plans.* —*v.i.* 3. to unite; coalesce. 4. to unite for a common purpose; join forces. 5. to enter into chemical union. —*n.* 6. a combination. 7. *U.S. Colloq.* a combination of persons or groups for the furtherance of their political, commercial or other interests. 8. *U.S.* a machine for cutting and threshing ripe standing grain and seed such as wheat, soybeans, and clover. [late ME *combyne(n)*, t. LL: *m. combīnāre* together] —**com·bin′a·ble**, *adj.* —**com·bin′er**, *n.* —Syn. 1. See **mix**.

combined operations, war operations carried out by coöperation of land, sea, and air forces.

comb·ings (kō′mĭngz), *n.pl.* hairs removed with a comb.

combining form, *Gram.* a special form of a word used in compounds: *England* and *English*, but *Anglo-* in *Anglophile* and *Anglo-French*.

comb jelly, ctenophore.

com·bust (kəm bŭst′), *adj. Astrol.* so near the sun as to be obscured by it. [ME, t. L: *s. combustus*, pp., burned up]

com·bus·ti·ble (kəm bŭs′tə bəl), *adj.* 1. capable of catching fire and burning; inflammable. 2. easily excited. —*n.* 3. a combustible substance. [t. LL: m. s. *combūstibilis*, der. L *combūstus*, pp. See COMBUST] —**com·bus′ti·bil′i·ty, com·bus′ti·ble·ness,** *n.* —**com·bus′ti·bly,** *adv.*

com·bus·tion (kəm bŭs′chən), *n.* 1. act or process of burning. 2. *Chem.* **a.** rapid oxidation accompanied by heat and usually light. **b.** chemical combination attended by heat and light. **c.** slow oxidation not accompanied by high temperature and light. 3. violent excitement; tumult. —**com·bus′tive,** *adj.*

combustion tube, a tube of hard glass in which a substance may be burned in a current of air or oxygen (usually used in a furnace).

comdg., commanding.

Comdr., commander. Also, **comdr.**

Comdt., commandant. Also, **comdt.**

come (kŭm), *v.*, **came, come, coming.** —*v.i.* 1. to move toward the speaker or toward a particular place; approach. 2. to arrive by movement or in course of progress; approach or arrive in time, succession, etc.: *when Christmas comes.* 3. to move into view; appear: *the light comes and goes.* 4. to extend; reach: *the dress comes to her knees.* 5. to take place; occur; happen. 6. to occur at a certain point, position, etc. 7. to be available, produced, offered, etc.: *toothpaste comes in a tube.* 8. to occur to the mind. 9. to befall a person. 10. to issue; emanate; be derived. 11. to arrive or appear as a result: *this comes of carelessness.* 12. to enter or be brought into a specified state or condition: *to come into use.* 13. to enter into being or existence; be born. 14. to become: *to come untied.* 15. to turn out to be: *his dream came true.* 16. (in the imperative, used to call attention, express remonstrance, etc.): *Come, that will do!* 17. to germinate, as grain. 18. Some special verb phrases are:
  come about, 1. to arrive in due course; come to pass. 2. *Naut.* to tack.
  come across, 1. to meet with, esp. by chance. 2. *Colloq.* to pay or give.
  come at, 1. to reach. 2. to get. 3. to rush at; attack.
  come back, 1. to return, esp. in memory. 2. *Colloq.* to return to a former position or state.
  come by, to obtain; acquire.
  come down, 1. to lose wealth, rank, etc. 2. to be handed down by tradition or inheritance.
  come forward, to offer one's services, etc.; volunteer.
  come in, 1. to enter. 2. to arrive. 3. to become useful, fashionable, etc.
  come into, 1. to get. 2. to inherit.
  come off, 1. to happen; occur. 2. to end. 3. to reach the end; acquit oneself: *to come off with honors.*
  come on, 1. to meet unexpectedly. 2. to make progress; develop. 3. to appear on stage.
  come out, 1. to appear; be published. 2. to be revealed; show itself. 3. to make a debut in society, on the stage, etc. 4. to emerge; reach the end.
  come out with, 1. to tell; say. 2. to bring out; publish.
  come over, to happen to: *what's come over him?*
  come round, 1. to relent. 2. to recover; revive. 3. to change (an opinion, direction, etc.).
  come through, *U.S.* 1. to succeed; reach an end. 2. to experience religious conversion. 3. to do as expected or hoped.
  come to, 1. to recover consciousness. 2. to amount to; equal. 3. *Naut.* to take the way off a vessel, as by bringing her head into the wind, anchoring, etc.
  come up, 1. to arise; present itself. 2. *Brit.* to come into residence at a school or university.
—*v.t.* 19. *Slang.* to do; perform. 20. *Colloq. or Slang.* to play the part of. [ME *comen*, OE *cuman*, c. G *kommen*] —Syn. 2. See **arrive**. —Ant. 2. leave, depart.

come-at-a·ble (kŭm ăt′ə bəl), *adj. Colloq.* accessible.

come·back (kŭm′băk′), *n.* 1. *Colloq.* a return to a former position, prosperity, etc. 2. *Slang.* a retort; repartee. 3. *U.S. Slang.* a ground for complaint.

co·me·di·an (kə mē′dʸ ən), *n.* 1. an actor in comedy. 2. a writer of comedy. 3. a very amusing person. [f. m. COMEDY + -AN. Cf. F *comédien*]

co·me·di·enne (kə mē′dʸ ĕn′; *Fr.* kô mē dyĕn′), *n.* an actress in comedy. [t. F, fem. of *comédien* comedian]

com·e·do (kŏm′ə dō′), *n.*, *pl.* **comedos, comedones** (kŏm′ə dō′nēz). a blackhead (def. 1). [t. L: glutton]

come·down (kŭm′doun′), *n. Colloq.* an unexpected or humiliating descent from dignity, importance, or prosperity.

com·e·dy (kŏm′ə dĭ), *n.*, *pl.* **-dies.** 1. a play, movie, etc., of light and humorous character, typically with a happy or cheerful ending; a drama in which the central motive of the play triumphs over circumstances and is therefore successful. 2. that branch of the drama which concerns itself with this form of composition. 3. the comic element of drama, of literature generally, or of life. 4. any literary composition dealing with a theme suitable for comedy, or employing the methods of comedy. 5. any comic or humorous incident or series of incidents. [ME *comedye*, t. ML: m. *comēdia*, L *cōmoedia*, Gk.: m. *kōmōidía*, der. *kōmōidós* comedian, f. *s. kōmos* mirth + *ōidós* singer]

Comedy of Errors, an early comedy (first acted, 1594) by Shakespeare.

come·ly (kŭm′lĭ), *adj.*, **-lier, -liest.** 1. pleasing in appearance; fair. 2. proper; seemly; becoming. [ME; OE *cȳmlic*, f. *cȳme* comely + *līc*. See -LY, LIKE] —**come′li·ness**, *n.* —Syn. 1. pretty, handsome, beautiful, good-looking, personable. —Ant. 1. unattractive.

Co·me·ni·us (kə mē′nʸ əs), *n.* **John Amos,** (*Jan Amos Komensky*) 1592–1670, Moravian educational reformer and bishop.

come-on (kŭm′ŏn′, -ôn′), *n. U.S. Slang.* inducement; lure.

com·er (kŭm′ər), *n.* 1. one who or that which comes, or has lately come. 2. *Colloq.* one who or something that is coming on or promising well.

co·mes·ti·ble (kə mĕs/tə bəl), *adj.* **1.** edible; eatable. —*n.* **2.** something edible; an article of food. [late ME, t. LL: m.s. *comestibilis*, der. L *comestus*, var. of *comēsus*, pp., eaten up]

com·et (kŏm/ĭt), *n.* a celestial body moving about the sun in an elongated orbit, usually consisting of a central mass (the *nucleus*) surrounded by a misty envelope (the *coma*) which extends into a stream (the *tail*) in the direction away from the sun. [ME, t. L: s. *comēta*, t. Gk.: m. *komētēs*, lit., long-haired] —**com·et·ar·y** (kŏm/ə tĕr/ĭ), *adj.* —**co·met·ic** (kə mĕt/ĭk), *adj.*

comet seeker, a telescope of low power but with a wide field, used to search for comets. Also, **comet finder.**

com·fit (kŭm/fĭt, kŏm/-), *n.* a dry sweetmeat; a bonbon. [ME, t. OF, g. L *confectus*, pp., prepared]

com·fort (kŭm/fərt), *v.t.* **1.** to soothe when in grief; console; cheer. **2.** to make physically comfortable. **3.** *Obs.* to aid; encourage. —*n.* **4.** relief in affliction; consolation; solace. **5.** the feeling of relief or consolation. **6.** a person or thing that affords consolation. **7.** a cause or matter of relief or satisfaction. **8.** a state of ease, with freedom from pain and anxiety, and satisfaction of bodily wants. **9.** that which promotes such a state. **10.** *U.S.* a comforter; bedcover. **11.** *Obs.* strengthening aid; assistance. [ME *conforte*(n), t. OF: m. *conforter*, g. L *confortāre* strengthen] —**com/fort·ing·ly,** *adv.* —**com/fort·less,** *adj.* —**com/fort·less·ly,** *adv.* —**com/fort·less·ness,** *n.*

—**Syn. 1.** COMFORT, CONSOLE, RELIEVE, SOOTHE imply assuaging sorrow, worry, discomfort, or pain. To COMFORT is to lessen the sadness or sorrow of someone, and to strengthen by inspiring with hope and restoring a cheerful outlook: *to comfort a despairing person.* CONSOLE, a more formal word, means to make grief or distress seem lighter, by means of kindness and thoughtful attentions: *to console a bereaved parent.* RELIEVE means to lighten, lessen, or remove pain, trouble, discomfort, or hardship: *to relieve a needy person.* SOOTHE means to pacify or calm: *to soothe a child.* **8. See ease.**

com·fort·a·ble (kŭmf/tə bəl, kŭm/fər tə bəl), *adj.* **1.** giving comfort, support, or consolation. **2.** producing or attended with comfort or ease of mind or body. **3.** being in a state of comfort or ease; easy and undisturbed. **4.** adequate. **5.** *Obs.* cheerful. —*n.* **6.** *U.S.* a quilted bedcover. —**com/fort·a·ble·ness,** *n.* —**com/fort·a·bly,** *adv.*

com·fort·er (kŭm/fər tər), *n.* **1.** one who or that which comforts. **2.** (*cap.*) the Holy Spirit. **3.** *Chiefly Brit.* a woolen scarf for wrapping round the neck in cold weather. **4.** *U.S.* a quilted bedcover.

com·frey (kŭm/frĭ), *n.*, *pl.* **-freys.** any plant of the boraginaceous genus *Symphytum,* of Europe and Asia, as *S. officinale,* formerly used as a vulnerary. [ME *cumfirie,* t. ML: m. *cumfiria,* appar. var. of L *conferva*]

com·ic (kŏm/ĭk), *adj.* **1.** of, pertaining to, or of the nature of comedy, as distinct from tragedy. **2.** acting in or composing comedy. **3.** provoking laughter; humorous; funny; laughable. —*n.* **4.** a comic actor. **5.** *Colloq.* a comic periodical. **6.** (*pl.*) *Colloq.* the comic strips. **7.** the amusing element in art, life, etc. [t. L: s. *comicus,* t. Gk.: m. *komikós*]

com·i·cal (kŏm/ə kəl), *adj.* **1.** provoking laughter, or amusing; funny. **2.** *Obs.* pertaining to or of the nature of comedy. —**com/i·cal·i·ty,** *n.* —**com/i·cal·ly,** *adv.* —**com/i·cal·ness,** *n.* —**Syn. 1.** See **amusing.**

comic opera, a diverting opera with spoken dialogue and a happy ending.

comic strip, a series of several drawings, either in color or black and white, relating a comic incident, an adventure or mystery story, etc.

Com. in Chf., Commander in Chief.

Co·mines (kô mēn/), *n.* Philippe de (fē lēp/ də), 1445?–1511?, French historian and diplomat. Also, **Commines.**

Com·in·form (kŏm/ĭn fôrm/), *n.* an organization established in late 1947 by the Communist parties of nine European countries for mutual advice and coördinated activity.

com·ing (kŭm/ĭng), *n.* **1.** approach; arrival; advent. —*adj.* **2.** that comes; approaching. **3.** on the way to fame or success.

Com·in·tern (kŏm/ĭn tûrn/, kŏm/ĭn tûrn/), *n.* the Third Communist International, dissolved, 1943, the organization of the Russian Communist Party, headed by its Politburo, for extending world revolution. Also, **Komintern.** [t. Russ.; short for *Communist International*]

co·mi·ti·a (kə mĭsh/ĭ ə), *n. Rom. Antiq.* an assembly of the people convened to pass on laws, nominate magistrates, etc. [t. L, pl. of *comitium* place of assembly] —**co·mi·tial** (kə mĭsh/əl), *adj.*

com·i·ty (kŏm/ə tĭ), *n.*, *pl.* **-ties. 1.** courtesy; civility. **2.** *Internat. Law.* courtesy between nations, as in respect shown by one country for the laws, judicial decisions, and institutions of another. [t. L: m.s. *cōmitas* courtesy]

Comm., **1.** commander. **2.** commerce. **3.** commission. **4.** committee. **5.** commonwealth. Also, **comm.**

com·ma (kŏm/ə), *n.* **1.** a mark of punctuation (,) used to indicate the smallest interruptions in continuity of thought or grammatical construction. **2.** *Anc. Pros.* **a.** a fragment or smaller section of a colon. **b.** the part of dactylic hexameter ending with, or that beginning with, the caesura. **c.** the caesura itself. [t. L, t. Gk.: m. *kŏmma* short clause]

comma bacillus, a slightly curved bacterium, *Vibrio Cholerae,* which causes Asiatic cholera. It is contracted by eating or drinking contaminated food, and causes a violent form of dysentery.

com·mand (kə mănd/, -mänd/), *v.t.* **1.** to order or direct with authority. **2.** to require with authority; demand: *he commanded silence.* **3.** to have or exercise authority over; be in control over; be master of; have at one's bidding or disposal. **4.** to dominate by reason of location; overlook: *a hill commanding the sea.* **5.** to deserve and get (respect, sympathy, etc.). **6.** to have charge of and authority over (a military or naval unit or station). —*v.i.* **7.** to issue commands. **8.** to occupy a dominating position; look down upon or over a region, etc. —*n.* **9.** act of commanding or ordering. **10.** an order given by a commander. **11.** *Mil.* **a.** an order in prescribed words, usually given in a loud voice to troops at close-order drill. **b.** the second part of any two-part, close-order drill command. **c.** an administrative and tactical unit of the Army Air Forces, usually made up of three or more wings. **d.** a body of troops, etc. or an area, station, etc., under a commander. **12.** the possession or exercise of controlling authority. **13.** control; mastery; disposal. **14.** *Brit.* a royal invitation. **15.** power of dominating a region by reason of location; extent of view or outlook. [ME *comande*(n), t. OF: m. *comander,* g. LL *commandāre,* f. L *com-* COM- + *mandāre* enjoin] —**com·mand/ing·ly,** *adv.* —**Syn. 1.** bid, enjoin, charge, instruct. See **direct. 3.** govern, control, manage. See **rule. 5.** exact, compel, secure. **10.** direction, bidding, injunction, charge.

com·man·dant (kŏm/ən dănt/, -dänt/), *n.* **1.** the commanding officer of a place, group, etc.: *the commandant of a navy yard.* **2.** the title of the senior officer and head of the U.S. Marine Corps. **3.** *U.S. Army.* a title generally given to the heads of military schools. **4.** a commander. [t. F, orig. ppr. of *commander* COMMAND]

com·man·deer (kŏm/ən dĭr/), *v.t.* **1.** to order or force into active military service. **2.** to seize (private property) for military or other public use. **3.** *Colloq.* to seize arbitrarily. [t. S. Afr. D: s. *commandeeren,* t. F: m. *commander* command]

com·mand·er (kə măn/dər, -män/-), *n.* **1.** one who commands. **2.** one who exercises authority; a leader; a chief officer. **3.** the chief commissioned officer (irrespective of rank) of a military unit. **4.** *U.S. Navy.* an officer ranking below a captain and above a lieutenant commander. **5.** the chief officer of a commandery in the medieval orders of Knights Hospitalers, Templars, etc. **6.** a member of a higher class in a modern fraternal order of knighthood. —**com·mand/er·ship/,** *n.*

commander in chief, *pl.* **commanders in chief. 1.** (*sometimes caps.*) the supreme commander of the armed forces of the nation: *the President is the Commander in Chief of the army and the navy.* **2.** an officer in command of a particular portion of an army or navy.

com·mand·er·y (kə măn/də rĭ, -män/-), *n.*, *pl.* **-eries. 1.** the office or district of a commander. **2.** (among certain medieval orders of knights) a district controlled by a commander. **3.** a local branch or lodge in certain secret orders.

commanding officer, *U.S. Army.* a commander of any rank from second lieutenant to colonel.

com·mand·ment (kə mănd/mənt, -mänd/-), *n.* **1.** a command or mandate. **2.** any one of the precepts (the Ten Commandments) spoken by God to Israel (Exodus 20: Deut. 10) or delivered to Moses (Exodus 24:12 and 34) on Mount Sinai. **3.** act, fact, or power of commanding.

com·man·do (kə măn/dō, -män/-), *n.*, *pl.* **-dos, -does. 1.** (in World War II) **a.** a special type of allied military unit used for organized raids against Axis forces. **b.** *Chiefly U.S.* a member of this unit. **2.** *South Africa.* an armed force raised for service against marauders. [t. S Afr. D, t. Pg.]

command performance, a performance of a play, etc., before a ruler, etc., usually at his request.

command post, *U.S. Army.* the field headquarters of the commander of a military unit.

com·meas·ur·a·ble (kə mĕzh/ər ə bəl), *adj.* having the same measure; commensurate.

com·meas·ure (kə mĕzh/ər), *v.t.,* **-ured, -uring.** to equal in measure; be coextensive with.

comme il faut (kô mĕl fō/), *French.* as it should be; proper; properly.

com·mem·o·rate (kə mĕm/ə rāt/), *v.t.,* **-rated, -rating. 1.** to serve as a memento of. **2.** to honor the memory of by some solemnity or celebration. **3.** to make honorable mention of. [t. L: m.s. *commemorātus,* pp., brought to remembrance] —**com·mem/o·ra/tor,** *n.*

com·mem·o·ra·tion (kə mĕm/ə rā/shən), *n.* **1.** act of commemorating. **2.** a service, celebration, etc., in memory of some person or event. **3.** a memorial. —**com·mem/o·ra/tion·al,** *adj.*

com·mem·o·ra·tive (kə mĕm/ə rā/tĭv, -rə tĭv), *adj.* **1.** serving to commemorate. **2.** (of stamps) issued to celebrate a particular historical event, in honor of a famous personage, etc. —*n.* **3.** anything that commemorates. —**com·mem/o·ra/tive·ly,** *adv.*

com·mem·o·ra·to·ry (kə mĕm/ə rə tō/rĭ), *adj.* commemorative (def. 1).

com·mence (kə mĕns/), *v.i., v.t.,* **-menced, -mencing.** to begin; start. [ME *comence*(n), t. OF: m. *comencer,* g. LL *cominitiāre,* f. *com-* COM- + *initiāre* begin] —**com·menc/er,** *n.* —**Syn. See begin. —Ant.** finish, end.

com·mence·ment (kə mĕns′mənt), *n.* **1.** act or fact of commencing; beginning. **2.** (in universities, colleges, etc.) the ceremony of conferring degrees or granting diplomas at the end of the academic year. **3.** the day on which this takes place.

com·mend (kə mĕnd′), *v.t.* **1.** to present or mention as worthy of confidence, notice, kindness, etc.; recommend. **2.** to entrust; give in charge; deliver with confidence: *into Thy hands I commend my spirit.* **3.** *Archaic.* to recommend (a person) to the kind remembrance of another. [ME *commend*(*en*), t. L: m. *commendāre* commit. Cf. COMMAND] —**com·mend′a·ble,** *adj.* —**com·mend′a·ble·ness,** *n.* —**com·mend′a·bly,** *adv.* —**Syn. 1.** praise, laud, extol. See **approve.**

com·men·dam (kə mĕn′dăm), *n. Eccles.* **1.** the tenure of a benefice to be held until the appointment of a regular incumbent, the benefice being said to be held *in commendam.* **2.** a benefice so held. [t. ML, acc. sing. of *commenda,* as in *dare in commendam* give in trust]

com·men·da·tion (kŏm′ən dā′shən), *n.* **1.** act of commending; recommendation; praise. **2.** something that commends. **3.** (*pl.*) *Archaic* or *Obs.* complimentary greeting. —**Syn. 2.** eulogy, encomium.

com·mend·a·to·ry (kə mĕn′də tôr′ĭ), *adj.* **1.** serving to commend; approving; praising. **2.** holding a benefice in commendam. **3.** held in commendam.

com·men·sal (kə mĕn′səl), *adj.* **1.** eating together at the same table. **2.** (of an animal or plant) living with, on, or in another, but neither one at the expense of the other (distinguished from *parasite*). —*n.* **3.** a companion at table. **4.** a commensal animal or plant. [t. ML: s. *commensālis,* f. L: *com-* COM- + *mensālis* belonging to the table] —**com·men′sal·ism,** *n.* —**com·men·sal·i·ty** (kŏm′ĕn săl′ə tĭ), *n.* —**com·men′sal·ly,** *adv.*

com·men·su·ra·ble (kə mĕn′shə rə bəl, -sə rə-), *adj.* **1.** having a common measure or divisor. **2.** suitable in measure; proportionate. [t. LL: m.s. *commensūrābilis* having a common measure] —**com·men′su·ra·bil′i·ty,** *n.* —**com·men′su·ra·bly,** *adv.*

com·men·su·rate (kə mĕn′shə rĭt, -sə-), *adj.* **1.** having the same measure; of equal extent or duration. **2.** corresponding in amount, magnitude, or degree. **3.** proportionate; adequate. **4.** having a common measure; commensurable. [t. LL: m.s. *commensūrātus,* f. L: *com-* COM- + *mensūrātus,* pp., measured] —**com·men′su·rate·ly,** *adv.* —**com·men·su·ra·tion** (kə mĕn′shə rā′shən, -sə-), *n.*

com·ment (kŏm′ĕnt), *n.* **1.** a note in explanation, expansion, or criticism of a passage in a writing, book, etc.; an annotation. **2.** explanatory or critical matter added to a text. **3.** a remark, observation, or criticism. —*v.i.* **4.** to write explanatory or critical notes upon a text. **5.** to make remarks. —*v.t.* **6.** to make comments or remarks on; furnish with comments. [ME, t. LL: s. *commentum* exposition, L contrivance, invention, prop. pp. neut.] —**com′ment·er,** *n.* —**Syn. 3.** See **remark.**

com·men·tar·y (kŏm′ən tĕr′ĭ), *n., pl.* **-taries. 1.** a series of comments or annotations. **2.** an explanatory essay or treatise: *a commentary on the Bible.* **3.** anything serving to illustrate a point; comment. **4.** (*usually pl.*) a record of facts or events: *the Commentaries of Caesar.* —**com·men·tar·i·al** (kŏm′ən târ′ĭ əl), *adj.*

com·men·ta·tor (kŏm′ən tā′tər), *n.* a person who makes critical or explanatory remarks about news events, etc. [t. L]

com·merce (kŏm′ərs), *n.* **1.** interchange of goods or commodities, esp. on a large scale between different countries (**foreign commerce**) or between different parts of the same country (**domestic** or **internal commerce**); trade; business. **2.** social relations. **3.** sexual intercourse. **4.** intellectual interchange. [t. F, t. L: m.s. *commercium* trade] —**Syn. 1.** See **trade.**

com·mer·cial (kə mûr′shəl), *adj.* **1.** of, or of the nature of, commerce. **2.** engaged in commerce. **3.** prepared merely for sale. **4.** not entirely or chemically pure: *commercial soda, etc.* —*n.* **5.** *Radio.* a commercial announcement or program. **6.** *Brit. Colloq.* a traveling salesman. —**com·mer·ci·al·i·ty** (kə mûr′shĭ ăl′ə tĭ), *n.* —**com·mer′cial·ly,** *adv.*

—**Syn. 1.** COMMERCIAL, MERCANTILE refer to the activities of business, industry, and trade. COMMERCIAL is the broader term, covering all the activities and relationships of industry and trade. In a derogatory sense it may mean such a preoccupation with the affairs of commerce as results in indifference to considerations other than wealth: *commercial treaties, relations, law, a merely commercial viewpoint.* MERCANTILE applies to the actual purchase and sale of goods, or to the transactions of business: *a mercantile house or class.*

commercial agency, a concern which investigates for the benefit of its subscribers the financial standing, reputation, and credit rating of individuals, firms, corporations, and others engaged in business.

commercial college, *U.S.* a school that trains people for careers in business.

com·mer·cial·ism (kə mûr′shə lĭz′əm), *n.* **1.** the principles, methods, and practices of commerce. **2.** commercial spirit. **3.** a commercial custom or expression. —**com·mer′cial·ist,** *n.* —**com·mer′cial·is′tic,** *adj.*

com·mer·cial·ize (kə mûr′shə līz′), *v.t.,* **-ized, -izing.** to make commercial in character, methods, or spirit; make a matter of profit. —**com·mer′cial·i·za′tion,** *n.*

commercial paper, negotiable paper, as drafts, bills of exchange, etc., given in the course of business.

commercial traveler, a traveling agent, esp. for a wholesale business house, who solicits orders for goods.

Com·mie (kŏm′ĭ), *n.* (*also l.c.*) *Colloq.* Communist.

com·mi·na·tion (kŏm′ə nā′shən), *n.* **1.** a threat of punishment or vengeance. **2.** a denunciation. **3.** (in the liturgy of the Church of England) a penitential office proclaiming God's anger and judgments against sinners. [late ME, t. L: s. *comminātio* a threatening] —**com·min·a·to·ry** (kə mĭn′ə tôr′ĭ, kŏm′ĭn-), *adj.*

Com·mines (kô mēn′), *n.* Comines.

com·min·gle (kə mĭng′gəl), *v.t., v.i.,* **-gled, -gling.** to mingle together; blend.

com·mi·nute (kŏm′ə nūt′, -nōot′), *v.t.,* **-nuted, -nuting.** to pulverize; triturate. [t. L: m. s. *comminūtus,* pp., made smaller] —**com′mi·nu′tion,** *n.*

com·mis·er·ate (kə mĭz′ə rāt′), *v.t.,* **-ated, -ating.** to feel or express sorrow or sympathy for; pity. [t. L: m.s. *commiserātus,* pp.] —**com·mis′er·a′tion,** *n.* —**com·mis′er·a′tive,** *adj.* —**com·mis′er·a′tive·ly,** *adv.*

com·mis·sar (kŏm′ə sär′), *n.* head of a government department (commissariat) in any republic of the U.S.S.R. [t. Russ: m. *kommisar,* t. F: m. *commissaire*]

com·mis·sar·i·at (kŏm′ə sâr′ĭ ət), *n.* **1.** the department of an army charged with supplying provisions, etc. **2.** the organized method or manner by which food, equipment, transport, etc., is delivered to the armies. **3.** any of the governmental divisions of the U.S.S.R. [t. F, der. *commissaire.* See COMMISSARY]

com·mis·sar·y (kŏm′ə sĕr′ĭ), *n., pl.* **-saries. 1.** a store that supplies food and equipment, esp. in an army, mining camp, or lumber camp. **2.** *Mil.* an officer of the commissariat. **3.** one to whom some charge is committed by a superior power; a deputy. **4.** *Eccles.* an officer who, by delegation from the bishop, exercises spiritual jurisdiction in remote parts of a diocese, or is entrusted with the performance of duties of the bishop in his absence. **5.** (in the Soviet Union) a commissar. **6.** (in France) a police official, usually just below the police chief and mayor. [ME, t. ML: m.s. *commissārius,* der. L *commissus,* pp., committed] —**com·mis·sar·i·al** (kŏm′ə sâr′ĭ əl), *adj.* —**com′mis·sar′y·ship′,** *n.*

com·mis·sion (kə mĭsh′ən), *n.* **1.** act of committing or giving in charge. **2.** an authoritative order, charge, or direction. **3.** authority granted for a particular action or function. **4.** a document or warrant granting authority to act in a given capacity or conferring a particular rank. **5.** a body of persons authoritatively charged with particular functions. **6.** the condition of being placed under special authoritative charge. **7.** the condition of anything in active service or use: *to be in or out of commission.* **8.** a task or matter committed to one's charge. **9.** authority to act as agent for another or others in commercial transactions. **10.** the committing or perpetrating of a crime, error, etc. **11.** that which is committed. **12.** a sum or percentage allowed to an agent for his services. **13.** the position or rank of an officer in the army or navy: *to hold or resign a commission.* **14.** the document conferring authority issued by the President to officers in the army and navy, and others, and by state governments to justices of the peace and others. **15.** the power thus granted. **16.** *Naval.* **a.** the condition of a ship ordered to active service, and supplied with a captain and crew. **b.** put in or into commission, to transfer (a ship) to active service. —*v.t.* **17.** to give a commission to. **18.** to authorize; send on a mission. **19.** to put (a ship, etc.) in commission. **20.** to give a commission or order for. [ME, t. L: s. *commissio* a committing]

com·mis·sion·aire (kə mĭsh′ə nâr′), *n. Brit.* a person who does miscellaneous small errands for the public; messenger; porter. [t. F: m. *commissionaire*]

commissioned officer, an army or naval officer holding rank by commission, including in the U.S. second lieutenants, ensigns, and all above them.

com·mis·sion·er (kə mĭsh′ən ər), *n.* **1.** one commissioned to act officially; a member of a commission. **2.** a government official in charge of a department: *police commissioner.* **3.** *Slang.* a betting broker. —**com·mis′sion·er·ship′,** *n.*

commission merchant, an agent who receives goods for sale on a commission basis, or who buys on this basis and has the goods delivered to a principal.

commission plan, a system of municipal government in which all the powers of the city are concentrated in the hands of a commission.

com·mis·sure (kŏm′ə shŏŏr′), *n.* **1.** a joint; seam; suture. **2.** *Bot.* the joint or face by which one carpel coheres with another. **3.** *Anat., Zool.* a connecting band of nerve tissue, etc. [late ME, t. L: m.s. *commissūra* joining] —**com·mis·su·ral** (kə mĭsh′ə rəl, kŏm′ə sŏŏr′əl), *adj.*

Botanical commissure
AB, line of the commissural faces of the two carpels

com·mit (kə mĭt′), *v.t.,* **-mitted, -mitting. 1.** to give in trust or charge; entrust; consign. **2.** to consign for preservation: *to commit to writing, memory, etc.* **3.** to consign to custody: *to commit a person to jail.* **4.** to consign, esp. for safekeeping; commend: *to commit one's soul to God.* **5.** to hand over for treatment, disposal, etc.: *to commit a manuscript to the flames.* **6.** *Parl.*

Proc. to refer (a bill, etc.) to a committee for consideration. **7.** to do; perform; perpetrate: *to commit murder, an error, etc.* **8.** to bind by pledge or assurance; pledge. [ME *committe(n)*, t. L: m. *committere* bring together, join, entrust] **—com·mit/ta·ble,** *adj.*

com·mit·ment (kə mĭt/mənt), *n.* **1.** act of committing. **2.** state of being committed. **3.** *Parl. Proc.* the act of referring or entrusting to a committee for consideration. **4.** consignment, as to prison. **5.** *Law.* a written order of a court directing that someone be confined in prison (formerly more often termed a *mittimus*). **6.** perpetration or commission, as of a crime. **7.** act of committing, pledging, or engaging oneself. **8.** *Stock Exchange.* an agreement to sell or purchase; a sale or purchase. Also, **com·mit/tal** for defs. 1, 3, 4, 6, 7.

com·mit·tee (kə mĭt/ĭ), *n.* **1.** a person or a group of persons elected or appointed to investigate, report, or act in special cases. **2. standing committee,** a permanent committee, as of a legislature, society, etc., intended to consider all matters pertaining to a designated subject. **3.** *Law.* one to whom the care of a person (as a lunatic) or an estate is committed. [t. AF, orig. pp., committed]

com·mit·tee·man (kə mĭt/ĭ mən, -măn/), *n., pl.* **-men** (-mən, -měn/). a member of a committee. **—com·mit·tee·wom·an** (kə mĭt/ĭ wŏŏm/ən), *n. fem.*

committee of correspondence, (during the American Revolutionary period) a committee appointed by a town or colony to communicate or coördinate the measures variously taken toward redress of grievances.

committee of the whole, a legislative body consisting of all the members present, sitting in a deliberative rather than a legislative capacity, for informal debate and preliminary consideration of matters awaiting legislative action.

Committee of Ways and Means, a committee (usually in a legislative body) to whom financial matters are referred.

com·mix (kə mĭks/), *v.t., v.i.* to mix together; blend.

com·mix·ture (kə mĭks/chər), *n.* a mixing together; the product of mixing; mixture. [t. L: m.s. *commixtūra*]

com·mode (kə mōd/), *n.* **1.** a piece of furniture containing drawers or shelves. **2.** a stand or cupboard containing a chamber pot or washbasin. **3.** a large, high headdress worn by women about 1700. [t. F, t. L: m.s. *commodus* fit, convenient, useful]

com·mo·di·ous (kə mō/dĭ əs), *adj.* **1.** convenient and roomy; spacious: *a commodious harbor.* **2.** convenient or satisfactory for the purpose. [late ME, t. ML: m.s. *commodiōsus.* See COMMODE] **—com·mo/di·ous·ly,** *adv.* **—com·mo/di·ous·ness,** *n.*

com·mod·i·ty (kə mŏd/ə tĭ), *n., pl.* **-ties.** **1.** a thing that is of use or advantage. **2.** an article of trade or commerce. **3.** *Obs.* a quantity of goods.

commodity dollar, *U.S.* a proposed currency unit whose gold content would vary with fluctuations in an official index of commodity prices.

commodity money, *U.S.* a proposed form of currency using commodity dollars as units.

com·mo·dore (kŏm/ə dôr/), *n.* **1.** *U.S. Navy.* an officer of a rank next below that of rear admiral. **2.** *British Navy.* an officer in temporary command of a squadron, sometimes having a captain under him on the same ship. **3.** *Naval.* the senior captain when three or more ships of war are cruising in company. **4.** (in the U. S. Navy or Merchant Marine) the officer in command of a convoy. **5.** the senior captain of a line of merchant vessels. **6.** the president or head of a yacht club or boat club. [earlier *commandore,* possibly t. D: m. *kommandeur,* t. F: m. *commandeur,* der. *commander* command]

Com·mo·dus (kŏm/ə dəs), *n. Lucius Aelius Aurelius* (lōō/shəs ē/lĭ əs ô rē/lĭ əs), A.D. 161–192, Roman emperor, A.D. 180–192 (son and successor of Marcus Aurelius).

com·mon (kŏm/ən), *adj.* **1.** belonging equally to, or shared alike by, two or more or all in question: *common property.* **2.** joint; united: *to make common cause against the enemy.* **3.** pertaining or belonging to the whole community; public: *common council.* **4.** generally or publicly known; notorious: *a common scold.* **5.** widespread; general; ordinary: *common knowledge.* **6.** of frequent occurrence; familiar; usual: *a common event, common salt.* **7.** hackneyed; trite. **8.** of mediocre or inferior quality; mean; low. **9.** coarse; vulgar: *common manners.* **10.** ordinary; having no rank, etc.: *common soldier, the common people.* **11.** *Anat.* denoting a trunk from which two or more arteries, veins, or nerves are given off: *the common carotid arteries.* **12.** *Pros.* (of a syllable) either long or short. **—***n.* **13.** a tract of land owned or used in common, esp. by all of the members of a community, now usually a park in the midst of the town. **14. in common,** in joint possession, use, etc.; jointly. **15.** *Law.* the power, shared with other persons to enter on the land or waters of another, and to remove something therefrom, as by pasturing cattle, catching fish, etc. **16.** (*sometimes cap.*) *Eccles.* an office or form of service used on a festival of a particular kind. **17.** *Obs.* the community or public. **18.** *Obs.* the common people. [ME, *comun,* t. OF, g. L *commūnis* common, general] **—com/mon·ness,** *n.*

—Syn. 5. universal, prevalent, popular See **general. 10.** COMMON, VULGAR, ORDINARY refer to the usual or most often experienced; often with derogatory connotations of cheapness or inferiority. COMMON means the accustomed or

usually experienced; or the inferior, and the opposite of exclusive or aristocratic: *she is a common person.* VULGAR properly means belonging to the peop'e, or characteristic of common peop'e; it connotes low taste, coarseness. or ill breeding: *the vulgar view of things, vulgar in manners and speech.* ORDINARY means what is to be expected in the usual order of things; or only average, or below average: *the quality is just ordinary.*—**Ant. 1.** individual. **6.** unusual.

com·mon·a·ble (kŏm/ən ə bəl), *adj.* **1.** held in common, or subject to general use, as lands. **2.** that may be pastured on common land.

com·mon·age (kŏm/ən ĭj), *n.* **1.** the use of anything in common, esp. of a pasture. **2.** the right to such use. **3.** state of being held in common. **4.** that which is so held, as land. **5.** the commonalty.

com·mon·al·ty (kŏm/ən əl tĭ), *n., pl.* **-ties.** **1.** the common people as distinguished from the nobility, etc. **2.** the members of an incorporated body.

common carrier, an individual or company, such as a railroad or steamship line, which transports the public or goods for hire.

common council, *New Rare.* **1.** the local legislative body of a city. **2.** its lower branch.

common denominator, *Math.* a number, usually the least, divisible by the denominators of a set of fractions.

common divisor, *Math.* a number which is an exact divisor of two or more given numbers. Also, **common factor.**

com·mon·er (kŏm/ən ər), *n.* **1.** one of the common people; a member of the commonalty. **2.** (at Oxford University, etc.) a student who pays for his commons, etc., and is not supported by any foundation. **3.** one who has a joint right in common land.

common fraction, *Math.* a fraction having the numerator above and the denominator below a horizontal or diagonal line (as opposed to a *decimal fraction*).

common gender, *Gram.* (in a language having masculine and feminine gender classes) a class of nouns which change gender according to meaning.

common law, **1.** the system of law originating in England, as distinct from the civil or Roman law and the canon or ecclesiastical law. **2.** the unwritten law, esp. of England, based on custom or court decision, as distinct from statute law. **3.** the law administered through the system of writs, as distinct from equity, admiralty, etc. **—com/mon-law/,** *adj.*

common-law marriage, a marriage without a marriage ceremony, civil or ecclesiastical, generally resulting from living together as man and wife.

common logarithm, *Math.* a logarithm using 10 as the base.

com·mon·ly (kŏm/ən lĭ), *adv.* **1.** in a common manner. **2.** usually; generally; ordinarily. **—Ant. 2.** rarely.

common measure, *Music.* duple and quadruple rhythm. Also, **common time.**

common multiple, *Math.* a number divisible by two or more given numbers. The **least** (or **lowest**) **common multiple** is the smallest common multiple of a set of numbers.

common name. See **name** (def. 9).

common noun, *Gram.* (in English and some other languages) a noun that can be preceded by an article or other limiting modifier, in meaning applicable to any one or all of the members of a class, as *man, men, city, cities,* in contrast to *Lincoln, New York.* Cf. **proper noun.**

com·mon·place (kŏm/ən plās/), *adj.* **1.** ordinary; uninteresting; without individuality: *a commonplace person.* **2.** trite; hackneyed: *a commonplace remark.* **—***n.* **3.** a well-known, customary, or obvious remark; a trite or uninteresting saying. **4.** anything common, ordinary, or uninteresting. **5.** a place or passage in a book or writing noted as important for reference or quotation. [trans. of L *locus commūnis,* Gk. (*koinós*) *topós* a stereotyped topic, argument, or passage in literature] **—com/mon-place/ness,** *n.*

—Syn. 2. COMMONPLACE, BANAL, HACKNEYED. STEREOTYPED, TRITE describe words, remarks, and styles of expression which are lifeless and uninteresting. COMMONPLACE characterizes thought which is dull, ordinary, and platitudinous: *commonplace and boring.* That is BANAL which seems inane, insipid, and pointless: *a heavy and banal affirmation of the obvious.* HACKNEYED characterizes that which seems stale and worn out through overuse: *a hackneyed comparison.* STEREOTYPED emphasizes the fact that situations felt to be similar invariably call for the same thought in exactly the same form and the same words: *so stereotyped as to seem automatic.* TRITE describes that which was originally striking and apt, but which has become so well known and been so commonly used that all interest has been worn out of it: *true but trite.*

commonplace book, a book in which noteworthy passages, poems, comments, etc. are written.

common pleas, **1.** *U.S.* any of various courts of civil jurisdiction in several States. **2.** *England.* (historically) the chief common-law court of civil jurisdiction, now merged in the King's Bench Division of the High Court.

common prayer, **1.** the liturgy or public form of prayer prescribed by the Church of England to be used in all churches and chapels in public worship. **2.** (*cap.*) the Book of Common Prayer.

common room, (in schools and colleges) a cloakroom, latterly extended to factories, sanitariums, etc.

com·mons (kŏm/ənz), *n. pl.* **1.** the common people as distinguished from their rulers or a ruling class; the

commonalty. 2. the body of people not of noble birth or ennobled, as represented in England by the House of Commons. 3. (*cap.*) the representatives of this body. 4. (*cap.*) the elective house of the Parliament of Great Britain and Northern Ireland, Canada, and some of the other Dominions. 5. *Brit.* food provided at a common table, as in colleges. 6. food or provisions in general. 7. a large dining room, esp. at a university.

common school, *U.S.* a public school below the grade of a high school.

common sense, sound practical sense; normal intelligence. —**com′mon-sense′,** *adj.*

Common Sense, an influential pamphlet (1776) by Thomas Paine, advocating American independence.

common stock, stock which ordinarily has no preference in the matter of dividends or assets and represents the residual ownership of a corporate business.

common time, common measure.

com·mon·weal (kŏm′ən wēl′), *n.* 1. the common welfare; the public good. 2. *Archaic.* the body politic; a commonwealth. Also, **common weal.**

com·mon·wealth (kŏm′ən wĕlth′), *n.* 1. the whole body of people of a nation or state; the body politic: *British Commonwealth of Nations.* 2. a state in which the supreme power is held by the people; a republican or democratic state. 3. (*cap.*) the English government from the abolition of the monarchy in 1649 until the establishment of the Protectorate in 1653. 4. any body of persons united by some common interest. 5. *Obs.* the public welfare. [i. COMMON + WEALTH]

com·mo·tion (kə mō′shən), *n.* 1. violent or tumultuous motion; agitation. 2. political or social disturbance; sedition; insurrection. —**Syn.** 1. disturbance, disorder, turmoil, tumult, riot, turbulence. See **ado.**

com·move (kə mōōv′). *v.t.,* **-moved, -moving.** to move violently; agitate; excite. [t. L: m.s. *commovēre;* r. ME *commoeve*(*n*), t. F: m. *commouvoir*]

com·mu·nal (kŏm′yə nəl, kə mū′nəl), *adj.* 1. pertaining to a commune or a community. 2. of or belonging to the people of a community: *communal land.* —**com′mu·nal·ly** (kŏm′yə nə lĭ, kə mū′-), *adv.*

com·mu·nal·ism (kŏm′yə nə lĭz′əm, kə mū′-). *n.* a theory or system of government according to which each commune is virtually an independent state, and the nation merely a federation of such states. —**com′mu·nal·ist,** *n.* —**com′mu·nal·is′tic,** *adj.*

com·mu·nal·ize (kŏm′yə nə līz′, kə mū′-), *v.t.,* **-ized, -izing.** to make communal; convert into municipal property. —**com′mu·nal·i·za′tion,** *n.* —**com′mu·nal·iz′er,** *n.*

Com·mu·nard (kŏm′yə närd′), *n.* (*often l.c.*) a member or supporter of the Paris Commune of 1871. [t. F]

com·mune[1] (*v.* kə mūn′; *n.* kŏm′ūn), *v.,* **-muned, -muning,** —*v.i.* 1. to converse; talk together; interchange thoughts or feelings. —*n.* 2. interchange of ideas or sentiments; friendly conversation. [ME *com*(*m*)*une*(*n*). t. OF: m. *comuner* hare, der. *comun* common]

com·mune[2] (kə mūn′), *v.i.,* **-muned, -muning.** to partake of the Eucharist. [ME *comunen,* t. OF: m. *communier,* g. L *commūnicāre* COMMUNICATE]

com·mune[3] (kŏm′ūn), *n.* 1. the smallest administrative division in France, Italy, Switzerland, etc., governed by a mayor assisted by a municipal council. 2. a similar division in some other country. 3. any community organized for the protection and promotion of local interests, and subordinate to the state. 4. the government or citizens of a commune. 5. *Ethnol.* a representative group in primitive society. 6. **the Commune, a.** a revolutionary committee which took the place of the municipality of Paris in the French Revolution of 1789, and soon usurped the supreme authority in the state. It was suppressed by the Convention in 1794. **b.** a socialistic government of Paris from March 18 to May 27, 1871. [t. F, fem. of *commun* common]

com·mu·ni·ca·ble (kə mū′nə kə bəl), *adj.* 1. capable of being communicated. 2. communicative. [t. ML: m.s. *commūnicābilis*] —**com·mu′ni·ca·bil′i·ty, com·mu′ni·ca·ble·ness,** *n.* —**com·mu′ni·ca·bly,** *adv.*

com·mu·ni·cant (kə mū′nə kənt), *n.* 1. one who partakes, or is entitled to partake, of the Eucharist; a member of a church. 2. one who communicates. —*adj.* 3. communicating; imparting.

com·mu·ni·cate (kə mū′nə kāt′), *v.,* **-cated, -cating.** —*v.t.* 1. to give to another as a partaker; impart; transmit. 2. to impart knowledge of; make known. 3. to administer the Eucharist to. 4. *Archaic.* to share in or partake of. —*v.i.* 5. to have interchange of thoughts. 6. to have or form a connecting passage. 7. to partake of the Eucharist. 8. *Obs.* to take part or participate. [t. L: m.s. *commūni ātus,* pp., shared] —**com·mu′ni·ca′tor,** *n.*
—**Syn.** 1. COMMUNICATE, IMPART denote giving to a person or thing a part or share of something, now usually something immaterial, as knowledge, thoughts, hopes, qualities, or properties. COMMUNICATE the more common word, implies often an indirect or gradual transmission: *to communicate by means of letters, telegrams, etc., to communicate one's wishes to someone else.* IMPART usually implies directness of action: *to impart information.* —**Ant.** 1. withhold. 2. conceal.

com·mu·ni·ca·tion (kə mū′nə kā′shən), *n.* 1. act or fact of communicating; transmission. 2. the imparting or interchange of thoughts, opinions, or information by speech, writing, or signs. 3. that which is communicated

or imparted. 4. a document or message imparting views, information, etc. 5. passage, opportunity of passage, or a means of passage between places. 6. (*pl.*) **a.** the means of sending military messages, orders, etc., as by telephone, telegraph, radio, couriers. **b.** routes and transportation for moving troops and supplies overseas, or in a theater of operations.

com·mu·ni·ca·tive (kə mū′nə kā′tĭv), *adj.* 1. inclined to communicate or impart. 2. talkative; not reserved. 3. of or pertaining to communication. —**com·mu′ni·ca′tive·ly,** *adv.* —**com·mu′ni·ca′tive·ness,** *n.*

com·mu·ni·ca·to·ry (kə mū′nĭ kə tō′rĭ), *adj.* of or pertaining to communication.

com·mun·ion (kə mūn′yən), *n.* 1. act of sharing, or holding in common; participation. 2. state of things so held. 3. association; fellowship. 4. interchange of thoughts or interests; communication; intimate talk. 5. *Eccles.* **a.** a body of persons having one common religious faith; a religious denomination. **b.** reception of the Eucharist. **c.** the celebration of the Lord's Supper; the Eucharist. [ME, t. L: s. *commūnio* fellowship]

com·mun·ion·ist (kə mūn′yən ĭst). *n. Eccles.* 1. a person with a particular view or interpretation of communion. 2. a communicant.

com·mu·ni·qué (kə mū′nə kā′, kə mū′nə kā′), *n.* an official bulletin or communication, usually to the press or public. [t. F]

com·mu·nism (kŏm′yə nĭz′əm), *n.* 1. a theory or system of social organization based on the holding of all property in common, actual ownership being ascribed to the community as a whole or to the state. 2. a system of social organization in which all economic activity is conducted by a totalitarian state dominated by a single and self-perpetuating political party. 3. communalism. [t. F: m. *communisme,* der. *commun.* See COMMON]

com·mu·nist (kŏm′yə nĭst), *n.* 1. an advocate of communism. 2. (*often cap.*) a person who belongs to the Communist Party, esp. the party in the Soviet Union. 3. (*usually cap.*) a Communard. —*adj.* 4. pertaining to communists or communism. —**com′mu·nis′tic, com′mu·nis′ti·cal,** *adj.* —**com′mu·nis′ti·cal·ly,** *adv.*

Communist Manifesto, a pamphlet (1848) by Karl Marx and Friedrich Engels: first statement of the principles of modern communism.

Communist Party, a political party professing the principles of communism.

com·mu·ni·tar·i·an (kə mū′nə târ′ĭ ən), *n.* 1. a member of a communistic community. 2. an advocate of such a community.

com·mu·ni·ty (kə mū′nə tĭ), *n., pl.* **-ties.** 1. a social group of any size whose members reside in a specific locality, share government, and have a cultural and historical heritage. 2. the community, the public. 3. *Eccles.* a group of men or women leading a common life according to a rule. 4. *Ecol.* a group of organisms, both plant and animal, living together in a definite region: *an oak forest community.* 5. joint possession, enjoyment, liability, etc.: *community of property.* 6. similar character; agreement; identity: *community of interests.* [t. L: m.s. *commūnitas;* r. ME *comunete,* t. OF]
—**Syn.** 1. COMMUNITY, HAMLET, VILLAGE, TOWN, CITY are terms for groups of people living in somewhat close association, and usually under common rules. COMMUNITY is a general term, and TOWN is often loosely applied. A commonly accepted set of connotations envisages HAMLET as a small group, VILLAGE as a somewhat larger one, TOWN still larger, and CITY as very large. Size is, however, not the true basis of differentiation, but properly sets off only HAMLET. Incorporation, or the absence of it, and the type of government determine the classification of the others.

community center, *U.S.* a building in which members of a community meet for social or other purposes.

community chest, *U.S. and Canada.* a fund for local welfare activities, built by voluntary contributions.

com·mu·nize (kŏm′yə nīz′), *v.t.,* **-nized, -nizing.** 1. to make the property of the community. 2. to make communistic. —**com′mu·ni·za′tion,** *n.*

com·mut·a·ble (kə mū′tə bəl), *adj.* that may be commuted; exchangeable. —**com·mut′a·bil′i·ty,** *n.*

com·mu·tate (kŏm′yə tāt′), *v.t.,* **-tated, -tating.** *Elect.* 1. to reverse the direction of (a current or currents), as by a commutator. 2. to convert (alternating current) into direct current by use of a commutator.

com·mu·ta·tion (kŏm′yə tā′shən), *n.* 1. act of substituting one thing for another; substitution; exchange. 2. the substitution of one kind of payment for another. 3. *U.S.* regular travel between home (usually distant) and work, generally using a commutation ticket. 4. the changing of a penalty, etc. for another less severe.

commutation ticket, *U.S.* a ticket issued at a reduced rate, as by a railroad company, entitling the holder to be carried over a given route a certain number of times or during a certain period.

com·mu·ta·tive (kə mū′tə tĭv, kŏm′yə tā′tĭv), *adj.* of or pertaining to commutation, exchange, substitution, or interchange.

commutative law, *Logic.* a law asserting that the order in which certain logical operations are performed is indifferent. For example: *Smith is ill or out of town* is equipollent with *Smith is out of town or ill.*

com·mu·ta·tor (kŏm′yə tā′tər), *n. Elect.* 1. a device for reversing the direction of a current. 2. (in a dynamo) a cylindrical ring or disk assembly of conducting members, individually insulated in a supporting structure with an exposed surface for contact with current-collecting brushes, and mounted on the armature shaft.

com·mute (kə mūt'), v., -muted, -muting. —v.t. 1. to exchange for another or something else; give and take reciprocally; interchange. 2. to change (one kind of payment) into or for another, as by substitution. 3. to change (a penalty, etc.) for one less burdensome or severe. —v.i. 4. to make substitution. 5. to serve as a substitute. 6. to make a collective payment, esp. of a reduced amount, as an equivalent for a number of payments. 7. U.S. to travel regularly between home (usually distant) and work, generally using a commutation ticket. [t. L: m.s. *commutāre* change wholly] —**com·mut'er**, n.

Com·ne·nus (kŏm nē'nəs), n. a dynasty of Byzantine emperors that ruled at Constantinople, 1057?–1185, and at Trebizond in Asia Minor, 1204–1461?

Co·mo (kô'mō), n. 1. Lake, a lake in N Italy, in Lombardy. 35 mi. long; 56 sq. mi. 2. a city on this lake. 72,000 (est. 1954).

Com·o·rin (kŏm'ə rĭn), n. Cape, a cape at the S tip of India extending into Indian Ocean.

Com·o·ro Islands (kŏm'ə rō'), a group of French islands in Mozambique Channel between N Madagascar and E Africa. 180,000 pop. (est. 1953); ab. 800 sq. mi.

co·mose (kō'mōs), adj. hairy; comate. [t. L: m.s. *comōsus* covered with hair]

comp., 1. comparative. 2. compare. 3. compilation. 4. compiled. 5. composition. 6. compound.

com·pact[1] (adj., v. kəm pakt'; n. kŏm'pakt), adj. 1. joined or packed together; closely and firmly united; dense; solid. 2. arranged within a relatively small space. 3. expressed concisely; pithy; terse; not diffuse. 4. composed or made (fol. by *of*). —v.t. 5. to join or pack closely together; consolidate; condense. 6. to make firm or stable. 7. to form or make by close union or conjunction; make up or compose. 8. *Metall.* to press (metallic and other powders) in a die. —n. 9. a small case containing a mirror, face powder, a puff, and (sometimes) rouge. 10. *Metall.* the molded shape obtained after pressing metallic and other powders in a die. 11. a comparatively small automobile, somewhat larger than a sports car. [t. L: s. *compactus*, pp., joined together] —**com·pact'ly**, adv. —**com·pact'ness**, n.

com·pact[2] (kŏm'pakt), n. an agreement between parties; a covenant; a contract. [t. L: s. *compactum*, prop. pp. neut., having agreed with] —**Syn.** treaty, pact. See **agreement**.

com·pan·ion[1] (kəm pan'yən), n. 1. one who accompanies or associates with another. 2. a person, usually a woman, employed to accompany or assist another. 3. a mate or match for a thing. 4. a handbook; guide: *Woman's Home Companion.* 5. a member of the lowest rank in an order of knighthood, or of a grade in an order. 6. *Obs.* a fellow (used in contempt). —v.t. 7. to be a companion to; accompany. [t. LL: s. *compānio* messmate, der. L *pānis* bread; r. ME *compainoun*, t. OF: m. *compaignon*] —**com·pan'ion·less**, adj. —**Syn.** 1. mate, comrade, associate, partner. See **acquaintance**.

com·pan·ion[2] (kəm pan'yən), n. 1. a covering or hood over the top of a companionway. 2. a companionway. [t. D: m. *kampanje* quarterdeck. Cf. It. *camera della campagna* storeroom]

com·pan·ion·a·ble (kəm pan'yən ə bəl). adj. fitted to be a companion; sociable. —**com·pan'ion·a·ble·ness**, n. —**com·pan'ion·a·bly**, adv.

com·pan·ion·ate (kəm pan'yən ĭt), adj. of, by, or like companions.

companionate marriage, a suggested form of marriage without the traditional rights and obligations of the spouses and with a simplified divorce completely terminating the relationship of childless couples.

companion cell, *Bot.* a cell associated with a sieve tube and, collectively, forming one of the elements of phloem.

com·pan·ion·ship (kəm pan'yən shĭp'), n. association as companions; fellowship.

com·pan·ion·way (kəm pan'yən wā'), n. *Naut.* 1. the space or shaft occupied by the steps leading down from the deck to a cabin. 2. the steps themselves.

com·pa·ny (kŭm'pə nĭ), n., pl. -nies, v., -nied, -nying. —n. 1. a number of individuals assembled or associated together; group of people. 2. an assemblage of persons for social purposes. 3. companionship; fellowship; association. 4. a guest or guests. 5. society collectively. 6. a number of persons united or incorporated for joint action, esp. for business: *a publishing company.* 7. the member or members of a firm not specifically named in the firm's title: *John Jones and Company.* 8. a medieval trade guild. 9. *Mil.* a. a subdivision of a regiment or battalion. b. any relatively small group of soldiers. 10. *Naut.* a ship's crew, including the officers. 11. bear or keep company, to associate or go with. 12. part company, to cease association or friendship with. —v.i. 13. to associate. —v.t. 14. *Archaic.* to accompany. [ME *compaignie*, t. OF. See **companion**[1]]
—**Syn.** 1. COMPANY, BAND, PARTY, TROOP refer to a group of people, friendly or informally associated. COMPANY is the general word and means any group of people: *a company of travelers.* BAND, used esp. of a band of musicians, suggests a relatively small group pursuing the same purpose or sharing

a common fate: *concert by a band, a band of survivors.* PARTY, except when used of a political group, usually implies an indefinite and temporary assemblage as for some common pursuit: *an exploring party.* TROOP, used specifically of a body of cavalry, usually implies a number of individuals organized as a unit: *a troop of cavalry.* 2. assembly, gathering, concourse, crowd. 5. firm, house, corporation, syndicate.

company union, *U.S.* 1. a union dominated by the employer of its members. 2. a union confined to employees of one business or corporation.

compar., comparative.

com·pa·ra·ble (kŏm'pə rə bəl), adj. 1. capable of being compared. 2. worthy of comparison. —**com'pa·ra·ble·ness**, n. —**com'pa·ra·bly**, adv.

com·par·a·tive (kəm par'ə tĭv), adj. 1. of or pertaining to comparison. 2. proceeding by or founded on comparison: *comparative anatomy.* 3. estimated by comparison; not positive or absolute; relative. 4. *Gram.* a. denoting the intermediate degree of the comparison of adjectives and adverbs. b. denoting the form of an adjective or adverb inflected to show this degree. c. having or pertaining to the function or meaning of this degree of comparison. —n. 5. *Gram.* a. the comparative degree. b. a form in it, as English *lower* in contrast to *low* and *lowest, more gracious* in contrast to *gracious* and *most gracious.* —**com·par'a·tive·ly**, adv.

com·pa·ra·tor (kŏm'pə rā'tər), n. any of various instruments for making comparisons, as of lengths or distances, tints of colors, etc.

com·pare (kəm pâr'), v., -pared, -paring, n. —v.t. 1. to represent as similar or analogous; liken (fol. by *to*). 2. to note the similarities and differences of (fol. by *with*). 3. to bring together for the purpose of noting points of likeness and difference: *to compare two pieces of cloth.* 4. **compare notes**, to exchange views, ideas, impressions, etc. 5. *Gram.* to form or display the degrees of comparison of (an adjective or adverb). —v.i. 6. to bear comparison; be held equal. 7. to vie. —n. 8. comparison: *joy beyond compare.* [ME, t. F: m.s. *comparer*, g. L *comparāre*, lit., bring together] —**com·par'er**, n. —**Syn.** 1, 2. COMPARE, CONTRAST agree in placing together two or more things and examining them to discover characteristics, qualities, etc. To COMPARE means to examine in order to discover like or unlike characteristics. We compare things of the same class *with* each other; one of unlike classes *to* the other: *to compare one story with another, a man to a mountain.* To CONTRAST is to examine with an eye to differences; or to place together so that the differences are striking. We contrast one thing *with* another: *to contrast living conditions in peace and in war.*

com·par·i·son (kəm par'ə sən), n. 1. act of comparing. 2. state of being compared. 3. a likening; an illustration by similitude; a comparative estimate or statement. 4. *Rhet.* the considering of two things with regard to some characteristic which is common to both, as the likening of a hero to a lion in courage. 5. capability of being compared or likened. 6. *Gram.* a. that function of an adverb or adjective used to indicate degrees of superiority or inferiority in quality, quantity, or intensity. b. the patterns of formation involved therein. c. the degrees of a particular word, displayed in a fixed order, as *mild, milder, mildest, less mild, least mild.* [ME, t. OF: m. *comparaison*, g. L *comparātio,* der. *comparāre.* See **COMPARE**]

com·part·ment (kəm pärt'mənt), n. 1. a part or space marked or partitioned off. 2. a separate room, section, etc.: *a compartment on a train, a watertight compartment in a ship.* 3. *Archit., Art.* an ornamental division of a larger design. —v.t. 4. to divide into compartments. [t. F: m. *compartiment,* t. It.: m. *compartimento,* der. LL *compartīrī* divide]

com·pass (kŭm'pəs), n. 1. an instrument for determining directions, consisting essentially of a freely moving needle indicating magnetic north and south. 2. the enclosing line or limits of any area; measurement round. 3. space within limits; area; extent; range; scope. 4. the total range of tones of a voice or of a musical instrument. 5. due or proper limits; moderate bounds. 6. a passing round; a circuit; a detour. 7. (*usually pl.*) an instrument for describing circles, measuring distances, etc., consisting generally of two movable legs hinged at one end. 8. *Obs.* a circle. —v.t. 9. to go or move round; make the circuit of. 10. to extend or stretch around; hem in; encircle. 11. to attain or achieve; accomplish; obtain. 12. to contrive; scheme. 13. to make curved or circular. 14. to grasp with the mind. [ME *compas,* t. OF, der. *compasser* divide exactly, ult. der. L *compassus* equal step] —**com'pass·a·ble**, adj. —**Syn.** 3. See **range**.

compass card, a circular card attached to the needle of a mariner's compass, on which the degrees or points indicating direction are marked.

com·pas·sion (kəm pash'ən), n. 1. a feeling of sorrow or pity for the sufferings or misfortunes of another; sympathy. —v.t. 2. to compassionate.

Compass card

[ME, t. LL: s. *compassio* sympathy] —**Syn. 1.** ruth, commiseration, mercy.

com·pas·sion·ate (*adj.* kəm păsh′ən ĭt; *v.* kəm păsh′-ə nāt′), *adj.*, *v.*, **-ated, -ating.** —*adj.* **1.** having or showing compassion. **2.** *Obs.* pitiable. —*v.t.* **3.** to have compassion for; pity. —**com·pas′sion·ate·ly,** *adv.* —**com·pas′sion·ate·ness,** *n.* —**Syn. 1.** pitying, sympathizing, sympathetic, tender, kind, merciful.

compass plant, any of various plants whose leaves tend to lie in a plane at right angles to the strongest light, hence usually north and south, esp. *Silphium laciniatum,* or *Lactuca* (wild lettuce).

com·pat·i·ble (kəm păt′ə bəl), *adj.* **1.** capable of existing together in harmony; such as to agree; consistent; congruous (usually fol. by *with*). **2.** denoting a system of television in which color broadcasts can be received on ordinary sets in black and white. [t. ML: m.s. *compatibilis,* der. LL *compatī* suffer with] —**com·pat′i·bil′i·ty, com·pat′i·ble·ness,** *n.* —**com·pat′i·bly,** *adv.*

com·pa·tri·ot (kəm pā′trĭ ət *or, esp. Brit.,* -păt′rĭ ət), *n.* **1.** a fellow countryman or fellow countrywoman. —*adj.* **2.** of the same country. [t. L: s. *compatriōta*] —**com·pa′tri·ot·ism,** *n.*

com·peer (kəm pĭr′, kŏm′pĭr), *n.* **1.** an equal or peer; a comrade; an associate. —*v.t.* **2.** *Archaic.* to be the equal of; match. [ME *comper,* t. OF. See COM-, PEER]

com·pel (kəm pĕl′), *v.t.*, **-pelled, -pelling. 1.** to force or drive, esp. to a course of action. **2.** to secure or bring about by force. **3.** to force to submit; subdue. **4.** to overpower. **5.** to drive together; unite by force; herd. [ME *compelle(n),* t. L: m. *compellere*] —**com·pel′la·ble,** *adj.* —**com·pel′ler,** *n.*
—**Syn. 1.** constrain, oblige, coerce. COMPEL, IMPEL agree in the idea of using (physical or other) force to cause something to be done. COMPEL means to constrain someone, in some way, to yield or to do what one wishes: *to compel a recalcitrant debtor to pay, fate compels men to face danger and trouble.* IMPEL may mean literally to push forward; but is usually applied figuratively, meaning to provide a strong motive or incentive toward a certain end: *wind impels a ship, curiosity impels me to speak.*

com·pel·la·tion (kŏm′pə lā′shən), *n.* **1.** act or manner of addressing a person. **2.** form of address or designation; appellation. [t. L: s. *compellātio*]

com·pen·di·ous (kəm pĕn′dĭ əs), *adj.* containing the substance of a subject in a brief form; concise. [t. L: m.s. *compendiōsus* abridged] —**com·pen′di·ous·ly,** *adv.* —**com·pen′di·ous·ness,** *n.*

com·pen·di·um (kəm pĕn′dĭ əm), *n., pl.* **-diums, -dia** (-dĭ ə), a comprehensive summary of a subject; a concise treatise; an epitome. Also, **com·pend** (kŏm′pĕnd). [t. L: a saving, a short way]

com·pen·sate (kŏm′pən sāt′), *v.*, **-sated, -sating.** —*v.t.* **1.** to counterbalance; offset; make up for. **2.** to make up for something to; recompense. **3.** *Mech.* to counterbalance (a force or the like); adjust or construct so as to offset or counterbalance variations or produce equilibrium. **4.** to change the gold content (of the monetary unit) to counterbalance price fluctuations and thereby stabilize its purchasing power. —*v.i.* **5.** to provide or be an equivalent; make up; make amends (fol. by *for*). [t. L: m. s. *compensātus,* pp., counterbalanced] —**com′pen·sa′tor,** *n.* —**Syn. 2.** remunerate, reward, pay.

compensating gear, *Mach.* differential gear.

com·pen·sa·tion (kŏm′pən sā′shən), *n.* **1.** act of compensating. **2.** something given or received as an equivalent for services, debt, loss, suffering, etc.; indemnity. **3.** *Biol.* the improvement of any defect by the excessive development or action of another structure or organ of the same structure. **4.** *Psychol.* behavior which compensates for some personal trait, as a weakness or inferiority. —**com′pen·sa′tion·al,** *adj.* —**Syn. 2.** recompense, remuneration, payment, amends, reparation.

com·pen·sa·to·ry (kŏm pĕn′sə tōr′ĭ), *adj.* serving to compensate. Also, **com·pen·sa·tive** (kŏm′pən sā′tĭv, kəm pĕn′sə tĭv).

com·pete (kəm pēt′), *v.i.*, **-peted, -peting.** to contend with another for a prize, profit, etc.; engage in a contest; vie: *to compete in a race, in business, etc.* [t. L: m. s. *competere* contend for, (earlier) come together]
—**Syn.** COMPETE, CONTEND, CONTEST mean to strive to outdo or excel: they may apply to individuals or groups. COMPETE implies having a sense of rivalry and of striving to do one's best as well as to outdo another: *to compete for a prize.* CONTEND suggests opposition or disputing as well as rivalry: *to contend with an opponent, against obstacles.* CONTEST suggests struggling to gain or hold something, as well as contending or disputing: *to contest a position or ground (in battle), to contest a decision.*

com·pe·tence (kŏm′pə təns), *n.* **1.** quality of being competent; adequacy; due qualification or capacity. **2.** sufficiency; a sufficient quantity. **3.** an income sufficient to furnish the necessities of life, without great luxuries. **4.** *Law.* quality or position of being legally competent; legal capacity or qualification (which presupposes the meeting of certain minimum requirements of age, soundness of mind, citizenship, or the like). **5.** *Embryol.* the sum total of possible reactions of any group of blastemic cells under varied external conditions.

com·pe·ten·cy (kŏm′pə tən sĭ), *n.* **1.** competence (defs. 1–4). **2.** *Law.* (of a witness) eligibility to be sworn and testify (presupposing the meeting of requirements of ability to observe, remember, and recount).

com·pe·tent (kŏm′pə tənt), *adj.* **1.** fitting, suitable, or sufficient for the purpose; adequate; properly qualified. **2.** rightfully belonging; permissible (fol. by *to*). **3.** *Law.* (of a witness, a party to a contract, etc.) having legal capacity or qualification. [t. L: s. *competens,* ppr., being fit] —**com′pe·tent·ly,** *adv.* —**Syn. 1.** fit, qualified, capable, proficient. See **able.**

com·pe·ti·tion (kŏm′pə tĭsh′ən), *n.* **1.** act of competing; rivalry. **2.** a contest for some prize or advantage. **3.** the rivalry between two or more business enterprises to secure the patronage of prospective buyers. **4.** *Sociol.* rivalry for the purpose of obtaining some advantage over some other person or group, but not involving the destruction of such person or group. **5.** *Ecol.* the struggle among organisms, both of the same and of different species, for food, space, and other factors of existence. [t. L: s. *competītio*]

com·pet·i·tive (kəm pĕt′ə tĭv), *adj.* of, pertaining to, involving, or decided by competition: *a competitive examination.* Also, **com·pet·i·to·ry** (kəm pĕt′ə tōr′ĭ). —**com·pet′i·tive·ly,** *adv.* —**com·pet′i·tive·ness,** *n.*

com·pet·i·tor (kəm pĕt′ə tər), *n.* one who competes; a rival. —**com·pet·i·tress** (kəm pĕt′ə trĭs), *n. fem.* —**Syn.** See **opponent.**

Com·piègne (kôN pyĕn′y), *n.* a city in N France, on the Oise river: nearby were signed the armistices between the Allies and Germany, 1918, and between Germany and France, 1940. 22,325 (1954).

com·pi·la·tion (kŏm′pə lā′shən), *n.* **1.** act of compiling: *the compilation of an index to a book.* **2.** something compiled, as a book.

com·pile (kəm pīl′), *v.t.*, **-piled, -piling. 1.** to put together (literary materials) in one book or work. **2.** to make (a book, etc.) of materials from various sources. [ME *compile(n),* t. OF: m. *compiler,* g. L *compīlāre* snatch together and carry off] —**com·pil′er,** *n.*

com·pla·cen·cy (kəm plā′sən sĭ), *n., pl.* **-cies. 1.** a feeling of quiet pleasure; satisfaction; gratification; self-satisfaction. **2.** that which gives satisfaction; a cause of pleasure or joy; a comfort. **3.** friendly civility. **4.** a civil act. Also, **com·pla′cence.**

com·pla·cent (kəm plā′sənt), *adj.* **1.** pleased, esp. with oneself or one's own merits, advantages, etc.; self-satisfied. **2.** pleasant; complaisant. [t. L: s. *complacens,* ppr., pleasing] —**com·pla′cent·ly,** *adv.*

com·plain (kəm plān′), *v.i.* **1.** to express grief, pain, uneasiness, censure, resentment, or dissatisfaction; find fault. **2.** to tell of one's ailments, etc. **3.** to state a grievance; make a formal accusation. [ME *com-playn(en),* t. OF: m. *complaindre,* g. LL *complangere* lament] —**com·plain′er,** *n.* —**com·plain′ing·ly,** *adv.*
—**Syn. 1.** COMPLAIN, GRUMBLE, GROWL, MURMUR, WHINE are terms for expressing dissatisfaction or discomfort. To COMPLAIN is to protest against or lament a condition or cause of wrong, etc.: *to complain about high prices.* To GRUMBLE is to utter surly, ill-natured complaints half to oneself: *to grumble about the service.* To GROWL may express more anger than GRUMBLE: *to growl ungraciously in reply to a question.* To MURMUR is to complain in low or suppressed tones, and may indicate greater dissatisfaction than GRUMBLE: *to murmur against a government.* To WHINE is to complain or beg in a mean-spirited, objectionable way, using a nasal tone; whining often connotes persistence in begging or complaining: *to whine like a coward, like a spoiled child.* —**Ant. 1.** rejoice.

com·plain·ant (kəm plā′nənt), *n.* one who makes a complaint, as in a legal action.

com·plaint (kəm plānt′), *n.* **1.** an expression of grief, regret, pain, censure, resentment, or lament; lament; faultfinding. **2.** a cause of grief, discontent, lamentation, etc. **3.** a cause of bodily pain or ailment; a malady. **4.** *U.S. Law.* the first pleading of the plaintiff in a civil action, stating his cause of action. [ME, t. OF: m. *complainte,* der. *complaindre.* See COMPLAIN]

com·plai·sance (kəm plā′zəns, kŏm′plə zăns′), *n.* **1.** quality of being complaisant. **2.** a complaisant act. [t. F]

com·plai·sant (kəm plā′zənt, kŏm′plə zănt′), *adj.* disposed to please; obliging; agreeable; gracious; compliant. [t. F, ppr. of *complaire* please, g. L *complacēre*] —**com·plai′sant·ly,** *adv.*

com·plect·ed (kəm plĕk′tĭd), *adj. U.S. Dial.* or *Colloq.* complexioned, as in *dark-complected.*

com·ple·ment (*n.* kŏm′plə mənt; *v.* kŏm′plə mĕnt′), *n.* **1.** that which completes or makes perfect. **2.** the quantity or amount that completes anything. **3.** either of two parts or things needed to complete the whole. **4.** full quantity or amount; complete allowance. **5.** the full number of officers and crew required to man a ship. **6.** a word or words used to complete a grammatical construction, esp. in the predicate, as an object (*man in he saw the man*), predicate adjective (*tall in the tree is tall*), or predicate noun (*John in his name is John*). **7.** *Geom.* the angular amount needed to bring a given angle to a right angle. **8.** *Music.* the interval which added to a given interval completes an octave. **9.** *Immunol.* a thermolabile substance which is normally present in all sera. —*v.t.* **10.** to complete; form a complement to. [ME, t. L: s. *complēmentum* that which fills up, (later) fulfillment]
—**Syn. 10.** COMPLEMENT, SUPPLEMENT both mean to make an addition or additions to something. To COMPLEMENT is to

provide something felt to be lacking or needed; it is often applied to putting together two things, each of which supplies what is lacking in the other, to make a complete whole: *two discussions from different points of view may complement each other*. To SUPPLEMENT is merely to add to; no lack or deficiency is implied nor is there an idea of a definite relationship between parts: *some additional remarks may supplement either discussion or both*.

com·ple·men·tal (kŏm′plə mĕn′təl), *adj.* complementary. —**com·ple·men′tal·ly**, *adv.*

com·ple·men·ta·ry (kŏm′plə mĕn′tə rĭ, -trĭ), *adj.* 1. forming a complement; completing. 2. complementing each other.

complementary angle, the complement of the given angle.

complementary cells, *Bot.* cells fitting closely together in the lenticel.

complementary colors, pairs of colors which when mixed in equal proportions produce white or gray, as yellow and blue.

Complementary angles
Angle BCD, complement of angle ACB;
Arc BD, complement of arc AB

com·plete (kəm plēt′), *adj., v.,* -pleted, -pleting. —*adj.* 1. having all its parts or elements; whole; entire; full. 2. finished; ended; concluded. 3. thorough; consummate; perfect in kind or quality. 4. *Archaic.* (of persons) accomplished; skilled; expert. —*v.t.* 5. to make complete; make whole or entire. 6. to make perfect. 7. to bring to an end; finish; fulfill. [ME *compleet,* t. L.: m.s. *complētus,* pp., filled up, completed] —**com·plete′ly**, *adv.* —**com·plete′ness**, *n.* —**com·plet′er**, *n.* —**com·ple′tive**, *adj.*

—**Syn.** 1–3. COMPLETE, ENTIRE, INTACT, PERFECT imply that there is no lack or defect, nor has any part been removed. COMPLETE implies that a certain unit has all its parts, fully developed or perfected; and may apply to a process or purpose carried to fulfillment: *a complete explanation.* ENTIRE means whole, having unbroken unity: *an entire book.* INTACT implies retaining completeness and original condition: *a package delivered intact.* PERFECT emphasizes not only completeness but also high quality and absence of defects or blemishes: *a perfect diamond.* 7. consummate, accomplish, flower. —**Ant.** 1. partial. 3. defective

com·ple·tion (kəm plē′shən), *n.* 1. act of completing. 2. state of being completed. 3. conclusion; fulfillment.

com·plex (*adj.* kəm plĕks′, kŏm′plĕks; *n.* kŏm′plĕks), *adj.* 1. composed of interconnected parts; compound; composite. 2. characterized by an involved combination of parts. 3. complicated; intricate. 4. *Gram.* (of a word) consisting of two parts, at least one of which is a bound form, as *boyish* (consisting of the word *boy* and the bound form *-ish*). —*n.* 5. a complex whole or system; a complicated assemblage of particulars. 6. *Psychol.* a group of related ideas, feelings, memories, and impulses which operate together and may be repressed or inhibited together. 7. *Colloq.* a fixed idea; an obsessing notion. [t. L.: s. *complexus,* pp., having embraced] —**com·plex′ly**, *adv.* —**com·plex′ness**, *n.* —**Syn.** 2, 3. involved, perplexing. —**Ant.** 2, 3. simple.

complex fraction, *Math.* a fraction expressing a ratio between fractions or mixed numbers, or between a fraction or mixed number and a whole number.

com·plex·ion (kəm plĕk′shən), *n.* 1. the natural color and appearance of the skin, esp. of the face. 2. appearance; aspect; character. 3. *Old Physiol.* constitution or nature of body and mind, regarded as the result of certain combined qualities. 4. *Obs.* nature; disposition; temperament. [ME, t. LL.: s. *complexio* constitution, in L combination] —**com·plex′ion·al**, *adj.*

com·plex·i·ty (kəm plĕk′sə tĭ), *n., pl.* -ties. 1. state or quality of being complex; intricacy. 2. something complex: *the automobile was a complexity far beyond her mechanical skill.*

complex sentence, a sentence containing one or more dependent clauses in addition to the main clause. For example: *When the clock strikes* (dependent clause), *it will be three o'clock* (main clause).

com·pli·a·ble (kəm plī′ə bəl), *adj.* compliant. —**com·pli·a·ble·ness**, *n.* —**com·pli′a·bly**, *adv.*

com·pli·ance (kəm plī′əns), *n.* 1. act of complying; an acquiescing or yielding. 2. a disposition to yield to others. 3. base subservience. 4. **in compliance with,** in keeping or accordance with. Also, **com·pli′an·cy** for 1–3.

com·pli·ant (kəm plī′ənt), *adj.* complying; yielding; obliging: *they were uncomfortably compliant.* [f. m. COM-PLY + -ANT] —**com·pli′ant·ly**, *adv.*

com·pli·ca·cy (kŏm′plə kə sĭ), *n., pl.* -cies. 1. complicated state. 2. a complication.

com·pli·cate (*v.* kŏm′plə kāt′; *adj.* kŏm′plə kĭt), *v.,* -cated, -cating, *adj.* —*v.t.* 1. to make complex, intricate, or involved. 2. to fold or twine together; combine intricately (fol. by *with*). —*adj.* 3. complex; involved. 4. *Bot.* folded upon itself: *a complicate embryo.* 5. *Zool.* (of insects' wings) folded longitudinally one or more times. [t. L: m. s. *complicātus,* pp., folded together]

com·pli·cat·ed (kŏm′plə kā′tĭd), *adj.* 1. composed of interconnected parts; not simple; complex. 2. consisting of many parts not easily separable; difficult to analyze, understand, explain, etc. —**com·pli·cat′ed·ly**, *adv.* —**com·pli·cat′ed·ness**, *n.*

com·pli·ca·tion (kŏm′plə kā′shən), *n.* 1. act of complicating. 2. a complicated or involved state or condition. 3. a complex combination of elements or things.

4. a complicating element. 5. *Pathol.* a concurrent disease or a fortuitous condition which aggravates the original disease.

com·plic·i·ty (kəm plĭs′ə tĭ), *n., pl.* -ties. 1. state of being an accomplice; partnership in wrongdoing. 2. complexity.

com·pli·er (kəm plī′ər), *n.* one who complies.

com·pli·ment (*n.* kŏm′plə mənt; *v.* kŏm′plə mĕnt′), *n.* 1. an expression of praise, commendation, or admiration: *he paid you a high compliment.* 2. a formal act or expression of civility, respect, or regard: *the compliments of the season.* 3. polite, esp. insincere, praise or commendation; flattery. 4. a present; gift. —*v.t.* 5. to pay a compliment to: *to compliment a woman on her new hat.* 6. to show kindness or regard for by a gift or other favor: *he complimented us with tickets for the exhibition.* 7. to congratulate; felicitate: *to compliment a prince on the birth of a son.* [t. F, t. It.: m. *complimento,* t. Sp.: m. *cumplimiento,* der. *cumplir* fulfill, ult. g. L *complēre*] —**Syn.** 1. praise, tribute. —**Ant.** 1. disparagement.

com·pli·men·ta·ry (kŏm′plə mĕn′tə rĭ, -trĭ), *adj.* 1. of the nature of, conveying, or addressing a compliment. 2. politely flattering. 3. *U.S.* free: *a complimentary ticket.* —**com′pli·men′ta·ri·ly**, *adv.*

com·plin (kŏm′plĭn), *n. Eccles.* the last of the seven canonical hours, or the service for it, orig. occurring after the evening meal, but now usually following immediately upon vespers. Also, **com·pline** (kŏm′plĭn, -plīn). [ME *compelin,* var. of *cumplie,* t. OF, g. L *complēta* (*hōra*) completed (hour)]

com·plot (*n.* kŏm′plŏt; *v.* kəm plŏt′), *n., v.,* -plotted, -plotting. —*n.* 1. a joint plot; a conspiracy. —*v.t., v.i.* 2. to plot together. [t. F: plot, OF concerted plan, also crowd, struggle; orig. uncert.] —**com·plot′ter**, *n.*

com·ply (kəm plī′), *v.i.,* -plied, -plying. 1. to act in accordance with wishes, requests, commands, requirements, conditions, etc. (fol. by *with*). 2. *Obs.* to be courteous or conciliatory. [appar. t. It.: m. *complire* fulfill, complete, t. Sp.: m. *cumplir,* ult. g. L *complēre* COM-PLETE; in part appar. affected by PLY] —**Syn.** 1. acquiesce, yield, conform, obey. —**Ant.** 1. refuse, resist.

com·po (kŏm′pō), *n., pl.* -pos. shortened form of *composition,* esp. as the name of various composite substances in industrial use.

com·po·nent (kəm pō′nənt), *adj.* 1. composing; constituent. —*n.* 2. a constituent part. 3. *Mech.* one of the parts of a force, velocity, or the like, out of which the whole may be compounded or into which it may be resolved. [t. L: s. *compōnens,* ppr., composing] —**Syn.** 2. See **element.**

com·po·ny (kəm pō′nĭ), *adj. Her.* composed of a single row of squares, metal and color alternating. Also, **com·po·né** (kəm pō′nā; *Fr.* kôn pô nĕ′).

com·port (kəm pōrt′), *v.t.* 1. to bear or conduct (oneself); behave. —*v.i.* 2. to agree or accord; suit (fol. by *with*). [t. F: s. *comporter* bear, behave, g. L *comportāre* carry together]

com·port·ment (kəm pōrt′mənt), *n.* bearing; demeanor; behavior.

com·pose (kəm pōz′), *v.,* -posed, -posing. —*v.t.* 1. to make or form by uniting parts or elements. 2. to be the parts or elements of. 3. to make up; constitute: *currency composed of silver.* 4. to put or dispose in proper form or order. 5. to arrange the parts or elements of (a picture, etc.). 6. to devise and make (a literary or musical production). 7. to arrange or settle, as a quarrel, etc. 8. to bring (the body or mind) to a condition of repose, calmness, etc.; calm; quiet. 9. *Print.* a. to set (type). b. to set the types for (an article, etc.). —*v.i.* 10. to practice composition. 11. to enter into composition. [late ME *compose*(n), t. OF: m. *composer* (see COM-POSE²), but assoc. with derivatives of L *compōnere.* See COMPOSITE]

com·posed (kəm pōzd′), *adj.* calm; tranquil; serene. —**com·pos·ed·ly** (kəm pō′zĭd lĭ), *adv.* —**com·pos·ed·ness**, *n.* —**Syn.** See **calm.** —**Ant.** agitated, perturbed.

com·pos·er (kəm pō′zər), *n.* 1. one who or that which composes. 2. a writer of music. 3. an author.

composing room, the room in which compositors work in a printing establishment.

composing stick, *Print.* a small (usually) metal tray of adjustable width, in which type is set.

com·pos·ite (kəm pŏz′ĭt), *adj.* 1. made up of various parts or elements; compound. 2. *Bot.* belonging to the *Compositae,* a family of plants, including the daisy, dandelion, aster, etc., in which the florets are borne in a close head surrounded by a common involucre of bracts. The *Compositae* are sometimes divided into several families: *Ambrosiaceae, Carduaceae* or *Asteraceae,* and *Cichoriaceae.* 3. (*cap.*) *Archit.* noting or pertaining to a classical order in which capital and entablature combine features of the Corinthian and Ionic orders. —*n.* 4. something composite; a compound. 5. *Bot.* a composite plant. [t. L: m.s. *compositus,* pp. of *compōnere* put together, compound, compose] —**com·pos′ite·ly**, *adv.* —**com·pos′ite·ness**, *n.* —**Syn.** 4. See **combination.**

composite number, *Math.* a number exactly divisible by some number other than itself and unity.

composite photograph, a photograph obtained by combining two or more separate photographs.

com·po·si·tion (kŏm′pə zĭsh′ən), *n.* 1. act of combining parts or elements to form a whole. 2. manner in which such parts are combined. 3. resulting state or product. **4.** make-up; constitution. **5.** a compound or composite substance. **6.** *Fine Arts.* organization or grouping of the different parts of a work of art so as to achieve a unified whole. **7.** the art of putting words and sentences together in accordance with the rules of grammar and rhetoric: *Greek prose composition.* **8.** act of producing a literary work. **9.** the art of composing music. **10.** the resulting production or work. **11.** a short essay written as a school exercise. **12.** *Gram.* the formation of compounds: *the composition of "bootblack" from "boot" and "black."* **13.** a settlement by mutual agreement. **14.** an agreement or compromise, esp. one by which a creditor (or group of creditors) accepts partial payment from a debtor. **15.** a sum of money so paid. **16.** the setting up of type for printing.

com·po·si·tion of forc·es, *Mech.* the union or combination of two or more forces, velocities, or the like (called *components*) acting in the same or in different directions, into a single equivalent force, velocity, or the like (called the *resultant*).

com·pos·i·tor (kəm pŏz′ə tər), *n. Print.* typesetter.

com·pos men·tis (kŏm′pŏs měn′tĭs), *Latin.* sane.

com·post (kŏm′pōst), *n.* **1.** a composition; compound. **2.** a mixture of various substances, as dung, dead leaves, etc., undergoing decay, used for fertilizing land. [ME, t. OF, g. L *compositus,* pp., compounded]

com·po·sure (kəm pō′zhər), *n.* serene state of mind; calmness; tranquillity. **—Syn.** equability, calmness.

com·po·ta·tion (kŏm′pə tā′shən), *n.* a drinking or tippling together. [t. L: s. *compōtātio* drinking together]

com·po·ta·tor (kŏm′pə tā′tər), *n.* one who drinks or tipples with another. [t. LL]

com·pote (kŏm′pōt; *Fr.* kôn pôt′), *n.* a preparation or dish of fruit stewed in a syrup. [t. F, in OF *composte,* g. L *compos(i)ta,* fem. of *compositus.* See COMPOSITE]

com·po·tier (kŏm′pə tîr′; *Fr.* kôn pô tyĕ′), *n.* a dish, usually of glass, china, or silver and having a supporting stem, used for holding compotes, fruit, etc. [t. F]

com·pound[1] (*adj.* kŏm′pound, kŏm pound′; *n.* kŏm′pound; *v.* kəm pound′), *adj.* **1.** composed of two or more parts, elements, or ingredients, or involving two or more actions, functions, etc.; composite. **2.** *Gram.* (of a word) consisting of two or more parts which are also words, but distinguished from a phrase by special phonetic features, in English often consisting of reduction of stress on one constituent, as in *housetop, blackberry,* historically also *cupboard, breakfast.* **3.** *Zool.* (of an animal) composed of a number of distinct individuals which are connected to form a united whole or colony. **—n. 4.** something formed by compounding or combining parts, elements, etc. **5.** *Chem.* a pure substance composed of two or more elements whose composition is constant. **6.** *Gram.* a compound word. **—v.t. 7.** to put together into a whole; combine. **8.** to make or form by combining parts, elements, etc.; construct. **9.** to make up or constitute. **10.** to settle or adjust by agreement, esp. for a reduced amount, as a debt. **11.** *Law.* to agree, for a consideration, not to prosecute or punish a wrongdoer for: *to compound a crime or felony.* **12.** to pay (interest) on the accrued interest as well as the principal. **13.** *Elect.* to connect a portion of the field turns of (a direct-current dynamo) in series with the armature circuit. **—v.i. 14.** to make a bargain; come to terms; compromise. **15.** to settle a debt, etc., by compromise. [ME *compoune(n),* t. OF: m. *compondre,* g. L *compōnere* put together] **—com·pound′a·ble,** *adj.* **—com·pound′-er,** *n.* **—Syn. 4.** See **combination.**

com·pound[2] (kŏm′pound), *n.* (in the Far East) an enclosure containing a residence or other establishment of Europeans. [cf. Malay *kampong* enclosure]

Compound E, cortisone.

compound eye, an arthropod eye subdivided into many individual light-receptive elements, each including a lens, a transmitting apparatus, and retinal cells.

compound flower, the flower head of a composite plant.

compound fraction, *Math.* a complex fraction or a fraction of a fraction.

compound fracture, a break in a bone such that the fracture line communicates with an open wound.

compound interest, interest paid, not only on the principal, but on the interest after it has periodically come due and, remaining unpaid, been added to the principal.

compound leaf, a leaf composed of a number of leaflets on a common stalk. It may be either digitately or pinnately compound, and the leaflets may be themselves compound.

compound number, a quantity expressed in more than one denomination or unit, as the length 1 foot 6 inches.

Pinnately compound leaf

compound sentence, a sentence having two or more coördinate independent clauses, usually joined by one or more conjunctions. For example: *the lightning flashed* (independent clause) *and* (conjunction) *the rain fell* (independent clause).

com·pra·dor (kŏm′prə dôr′), *n.* (in China, etc.) a native agent or factotum, as of a foreign business house. Also, **com/pra·dore′.** [t. Pg.: a buyer, purveyor]

com·pre·hend (kŏm′prĭ hĕnd′), *v.t.* **1.** to understand the meaning or nature of; conceive; know. **2.** to take in or embrace; include; comprise. [ME, t. L: s. *comprehendere* seize] **—com/pre·hend′i·ble,** *adj.* **—com/pre·hend′ing·ly,** *adv.* **—Syn. 1.** See **know. 2.** See **include.**

com·pre·hen·si·ble (kŏm′prĭ hĕn′sə bəl), *adj.* capable of being comprehended; intelligible. **—com/pre·hen/si·bil/i·ty, com/pre·hen/si·ble·ness,** *n.* **—com/pre·hen/si·bly,** *adv.*

com·pre·hen·sion (kŏm′prĭ hĕn′shən), *n.* **1.** act or fact of comprehending. **2.** inclusion; comprehensiveness; perception or understanding. **3.** capacity of the mind to understand; power to grasp ideas; ability to know. **4.** *Logic.* the sum of all those attributes which make up the content of a given conception (distinguished from *extension* or *extent*). For example: *rational, sensible, moral, etc.,* form the comprehension of the conception *man.* [t. L: s. *comprehensio* a comprising]

com·pre·hen·sive (kŏm′prĭ hĕn′sĭv), *adj.* **1.** comprehending; inclusive; comprehending much; of large scope. **2.** comprehending mentally; having a wide mental grasp. **—com/pre·hen/sive·ly,** *adv.* **—com/pre·hen/sive·ness,** *n.* **—Syn. 1.** broad, wide, extensive, full.

com·press (*v.* kəm prĕs′; *n.* kŏm′prĕs), *v.t.* **1.** to press together; force into less space. [ME *compresse(n),* t. L: m. *compressāre*] **—n. 2.** *Med.* a soft pad of lint, linen, or the like, held in place by a bandage, used as a means of pressure or to supply moisture, cold, heat, or medication. **3.** an apparatus or establishment for compressing cotton bales, etc. [t. L: s. *compressa,* prop. fem. pp., pressed together] **—com·press′i·ble,** *adj.* **—com·press/i·bil/i·ty,** *n.* **—Syn. 1.** condense, squeeze, constrict. See **contract.**

com·pressed (kəm prĕst′), *adj.* **1.** pressed into less space; condensed. **2.** pressed together. **3.** flattened. **4.** *Bot.* flattened laterally or along the length. **5.** *Zool.* narrow from side to side, and therefore of greater height than width. **—Ant. 1.** expanded.

compressed air, mechanically compressed air the expansive force of which is used to operate drills, brakes, etc.

com·pres·sion (kəm prĕsh′ən), *n.* **1.** act of compressing. **2.** compressed state. **3.** (in internal-combustion engines) the reduction in volume and increase of pressure of the air or combustible mixture in the cylinder prior to ignition, produced by the motion of the piston toward the cylinder head after intake. Also, **com·pres·sure** (kəm prĕsh′ər) for 1, 2.

com·pres·sive (kəm prĕs′ĭv), *adj.* compressing; tending to compress. **—com·pres/sive·ly,** *adv.*

com·pres·sor (kəm prĕs′ər), *n.* **1.** one who or that which compresses. **2.** *Anat.* a muscle that compresses some part of the body. **3.** *Surg.* an instrument for compressing a part of the body. **4.** a machine, usually driven by electric or steam power, by which a gas is compressed so that its expansion may be utilized as a source of power. In refrigeration the compressor is used to compress the gas so that it can be condensed with water or air at prevailing temperatures. [t. L]

com·prise (kəm prīz′), *v.t.* **-prised, -prising. 1.** to comprehend; include; contain. **2.** to consist of; be composed of. Also, **com·prize′.** [ME *comprise(n),* t. F: s. *compris,* pp. of *comprendre,* g. L *compre(he)ndere* seize] **—com·pris′a·ble,** *adj.* **—com·pris/al,** *n.* **—Syn. 1.** See **include.**

com·pro·mise (kŏm′prə mīz′), *n., v.,* **-mised, -mising. —n. 1.** a settlement of differences by mutual concessions; an adjustment of conflicting claims, principles, etc., by yielding a part of each; arbitration. **2.** anything resulting from compromise. **3.** something intermediate between different things. **4.** an endangering, esp. of reputation; exposure to danger, suspicion, etc. **—v.t. 5.** to settle by a compromise. **6.** to make liable to danger, suspicion, scandal, etc.; endanger the reputation of. **7.** to involve unfavorably; commit. **8.** *Obs.* to bind by bargain or agreement. **9.** *Obs.* to bring to terms. **—v.i. 10.** to make a compromise. [ME, t. F: m. *compromis,* g. L *comprōmissum* a mutual promise to abide by a decision, prop. pp. neut.] **—com/pro·mis/er,** *n.*

comp·tom·e·ter (kŏmp tŏm′ə tər), *n.* **1.** a high-speed adding and calculating machine. **2.** (*cap.*) a trademark for this machine.

Comp·ton (kŏmp′tən), *n.* **1. Arthur Holly,** 1892–1962, U.S. physicist. **2. Karl Taylor,** 1887–1954, U.S. physicist. **3.** a city in SW California. 71,812 (1960).

comp·trol·ler (kən trō′lər), *n.* controller (def. 1). [var. sp. of CONTROLLER] **—comp·trol/ler·ship′,** *n.*

com·pul·sion (kəm pŭl′shən), *n.* **1.** act of compelling; constraint; coercion. **2.** state of being compelled. **3.** *Psychol.* **a.** a strong irrational impulse to carry out a given act. **b.** the act. [late ME, t. LL: s. *compulsio*]

com·pul·sive (kəm pŭl′sĭv), *adj.* **1.** compulsory. **2.** (esp. in *Psychol.*) pertaining to compulsion. **—com·pul/sive·ly,** *adv.*

com·pul·so·ry (kəm pŭl′sə rĭ), *adj.* **1.** using compulsion; compelling; constraining: *compulsory measures.* **2.** compelled; forced; obligatory. **—com·pul/so·ri·ly,** *adv.* **—com·pul/so·ri·ness,** *n.* **—Ant. 1, 2.** voluntary.

com·punc·tion (kəm pŭngk/shən), *n.* uneasiness of conscience or feelings; regret for wrongdoing or giving pain to another; contrition; remorse. [ME, t. LL: s. *compunctio* remorse]

---

b., blend of, blended; **c.,** cognate with; **d.,** dialect, dialectal; **der.,** derived from; **f.,** formed from; **g.,** going back to; **m.,** modification of; **r.,** replacing; **s.,** stem of; **t.,** taken from; **?,** perhaps. See the full key on inside cover.

com·punc·tious (kəm pŭngk/shəs), *adj.* causing compunction; causing misgiving, regret, or remorse.

com·pur·ga·tion (kŏm/pər gā/shən), *n.* an early common-law method of trial in which the defendant is acquitted if a specified number of friends or neighbors would swear to his innocence or veracity. [t. LL: s. *compurgātio,* der. L *compurgāre* purify completely]

com·pur·ga·tor (kŏm/pər gā/tər), *n.* one who testifies to another's innocence or veracity.

com·pu·ta·tion (kŏm/pyə tā/shən), *n.* 1. act, process, or method of computing; calculation. 2. a result of computing; the amount computed.

com·pute (kəm pūt/), *v.,* -puted, -puting, *n.* —*v.t.* 1. to determine by calculation; reckon; calculate: *to compute the distance of the moon from the earth.* —*v.i.* 2. to reckon; calculate. —*n.* 3. computation; reckoning. [t. L: m.s. *computāre* reckon. Cf. COUNT[1]] —**com·put/a·bil/i·ty,** *n.* —**Syn.** 1. estimate, count, figure.

com·put·er (kəm pū/tər), *n.* 1. one who computes. 2. an apparatus for carrying out mathematical operations by mechanical or electrical means or both: an **analogue computer** performs mathematical operations by transforming data received into electrical impulses; a **digital computer** operates directly with information received and can perform only simpler, linear operations.

com·rade (kŏm/răd *or, esp. Brit.,* -rĭd, kŭm/rĭd), *n.* 1. an associate in occupation or friendship; a close companion; a fellow; a mate. 2. fellow member of a political party, fraternal group, etc. [t. F: m. *comrade,* t. Sp.: m. *camarada,* lit., group living in one room, der. *cámara* room, g. L *camera* CHAMBER] —**com/rade·ship/,** *n.*

Com·stock (kŭm/stŏk, kŏm/-), *n.* **Anthony,** 1844–1915, U.S. crusader against vice.

com·stock·er·y (kŭm/stŏk ə rĭ, kŏm/-), *n.* overzealous censorship of the fine arts and literature, often mistaking outspokenly honest works for salacious ones.

Comte (kônt; *Fr.* kônt), *n.* **Auguste** (ō gyst/), 1798–1857, French philosopher, founder of positivism. —**Com·ti·an** (kŏn/tĭ ən, kŏn/-), *adj.* —**Comt·ism** (kŏm/tĭz əm, kŏn/-), *n.* —**Comt/ist,** *n., adj.*

Co·mus (kō/məs), *n. Later Class. Myth.* a young god of revelry, represented by Milton as the son of Bacchus and Circe. [t. L, t. Gk.: m. *kōmos* revel]

con[1] (kŏn), *adv.* 1. against a proposition, opinion, etc.; not pro (for). —*n.* 2. the argument, arguer, or voter against (something). [short for L *contrā,* adv., in opposition, as prep., against]

con[2] (kŏn), *v.t.,* **conned, conning.** to learn; study; commit to memory; peruse or examine carefully. [var. of CAN, OE *can, con,* a finite form of *cunnan* know]

con[3] (kŏn), *v.,* **conned, conning,** *n. Naut.* —*v.t.* 1. to direct the steering of (a ship). —*n.* 2. the station of the person who cons. 3. act of conning. [var. of obs. *cond,* short for *condue,* t. OF: m. *conduire* CONDUCT]

con[4] (kŏn), *adj., v.,* **conned, conning.** *U.S. Slang.* —*adj.* 1. confidence: *con game, con man.* —*v.t.* 2. to swindle; defraud. [short for CONFIDENCE (GAME OR MAN)]

con-, var. of **com-,** before consonants except *b, h, l, p, r, w,* as in *convene, condone,* and, by assimilation, before *n,* as in *connection.* Cf. **co-** (def. 1).

con., 1. conclusion. 2. consolidated. 3. (L *contra*) against.

Co·na·kry (kŏ nà krē/), *n.* a seaport in and the capital of Guinea. 49,200 (1951). Also, **Konakri.**

con a·mo·re (kŏn ä mô/rĕ), *Italian.* 1. with love, tender enthusiasm, or zeal. 2. *Music.* (as a direction) tenderly and lovingly.

Co·nant (kō/nənt), *n.* **James Bryant,** born 1893, U.S. chemist and educator: president of Harvard, 1933–1953.

co·na·tion (kō nā/shən), *n. Psychol.* that portion of mental life having to do with striving, embracing desire and volition. [t. L: s. *cōnātiō* an endeavoring, effort]

con·a·tive (kŏn/ə tĭv, kō/nə-), *adj.* 1. *Psychol.* pertaining to or of the nature of conation. 2. *Gram.* expressing endeavor or effort: *a conative verb.*

co·na·tus (kō nā/təs), *n., pl.* -tus. 1. an effort or striving. 2. a force or tendency simulating a human effort. [t. L: effort, endeavor].

con bri·o (kŏn brē/ō), *Music.* with vigor; vivaciously. [It.]

con·cat·e·nate (kŏn kăt/ə nāt/), *v.,* -nated, -nating, *adj.* —*v.t.* 1. to link together; unite in a series or chain. —*adj.* 2. linked together as in a chain. [t. L: m.s. *concatēnātus,* pp.]

con·cat·e·na·tion (kŏn kăt/ə nā/shən), *n.* 1. act of concatenating. 2. state of being concatenated; connection, as in a chain. 3. a series of interconnected or interdependent things or events.

con·cave (*adj., v.* kŏn kāv/, kŏn/kāv; *n.* kŏn/kāv), *adj., v.,* -caved, -caving. —*adj.* 1. curved like the interior of a circle or hollow sphere; hollow and curved. 2. *Obs.* hollow. —*n.* 3. a concave surface, part, line, etc. —*v.t.* 4. to make concave. [t. L: m.s. *concavus*] —**con·cave/ly,** *adv.* —**con·cave/ness,** *n.* —**Ant.** 1. convex.

A. Concave or plano-concave lens; B. Concavo-concave lens; C. Concavo-convex lens

con·cav·i·ty (kŏn kăv/ə tĭ), *n., pl.* -ties. 1. state of being concave. 2. a concave surface or thing; a hollow; cavity.

con·ca·vo-con·cave (kŏn kā/vō kŏn kāv/), *adj.* concave on both sides.

con·ca·vo-con·vex (kŏn kā/vō kŏn vĕks/), *adj.* 1. concave on one side and convex on the other. 2. denoting or pertaining to a lens in which the concave face has a greater degree of curvature than the convex face, the lens being thinnest in the middle.

con·ceal (kən sēl/), *v.t.* 1. to hide; withdraw or remove from observation; cover or keep from sight. 2. to keep secret; forbear to disclose or divulge. [ME *concele(n),* t. OF: m. *conceler,* g. L *concēlāre* hide] —**con·ceal/a·ble,** *adj.* —**con·ceal/er,** *n.* —**Syn.** 1. See hide.

con·ceal·ment (kən sēl/mənt), *n.* 1. act of concealing. 2. concealed state. 3. a means or place of hiding.

con·cede (kən sēd/), *v.,* -ceded, -ceding. —*v.t.* 1. to admit as true, just, or proper; admit. 2. to grant as a right or privilege; yield. —*v.i.* 3. to make concession; yield; admit. [t. L: m.s. *concēdere*] —**con·ced/ed·ly,** *adv.* —**con·ced/er,** *n.* —**Ant.** 1. deny. 2. refuse.

con·ceit (kən sēt/), *n.* 1. an exaggerated estimate of one's own ability, importance, wit, etc. 2. favorable opinion; esteem. 3. personal opinion or estimation. 4. the faculty of conceiving; apprehension. 5. that which is conceived in the mind; a thought; an idea. 6. imagination; fancy. 7. a fancy; whim; a fanciful notion. 8. a fanciful thought, idea, or expression, esp. of strained or far-fetched nature. 9. the use of such thoughts, ideas, etc., as a literary characteristic. 10. *Obs.* a fancy article. —*v.t.* 11. to flatter (esp. oneself). 12. to conceive mentally; apprehend. 13. to imagine. 14. *Archaic or Dial.* to take a fancy to; have a good opinion of. [ME *conceyte;* der. CONCEIVE, modeled on DECEIT] —**Syn.** 1. self-esteem, vanity, egotism, complacency. See **pride.** —**Ant.** 1. humility.

con·ceit·ed (kən sē/tĭd), *adj.* 1. having an exaggerated opinion of one's abilities, importance, etc. 2. *Dial.* having an opinion. 3. *Obs.* intelligent; clever. 4. *Dial.* fanciful; whimsical. —**con·ceit/ed·ly,** *adv.* —**con·ceit/ed·ness,** *n.* —**Syn.** 1. vain, proud, egotistical.

con·ceiv·a·ble (kən sē/və bəl), *adj.* capable of being conceived; imaginable. —**con·ceiv/a·bil/i·ty, con·ceiv/a·ble·ness,** *n.* —**con·ceiv/a·bly,** *adv.*

con·ceive (kən sēv/), *v.,* -ceived, -ceiving. —*v.t.* 1. to form (a notion, opinion, purpose, etc.). 2. to form a notion or idea of; imagine. 3. to apprehend in the mind; understand. 4. to hold as an opinion; think; believe. 5. to experience or entertain (a feeling). 6. to express, as in words. 7. to become pregnant with. —*v.i.* 8. to form an idea; think (fol. by *of*). 9. to become pregnant. [ME *conceive(n),* t. OF: m. *conceveir,* g. L *concipere* take in] —**con·ceiv/er,** *n.* —**Syn.** 2, 8. See **imagine.**

con·cent (kən sĕnt/), *n.* concord of sounds, voices, etc. [t. L: s. *concentus* a singing together]

con·cen·ter (kŏn sĕn/tər), *v.t., v.i.* to bring or converge to a common center; concentrate. Also, *esp. Brit.,* **concentre.**

con·cen·trate (kŏn/sən trāt/), *v.,* -trated, -trating, *n.* —*v.t.* 1. to bring or draw to a common center or point of union; cause to come close together; bring to bear on one point; direct toward one object; focus. 2. to intensify the action of; make more intense, stronger, or purer by removing or reducing the proportion of what is foreign or inessential. 3. *Mining.* to separate (metal or ore) from rock, sand, etc., so as to improve the quality of the valuable portion. —*v.i.* 4. to converge to a center. 5. to become more intense, stronger, or purer. —*n.* 6. a concentrated form of something; a product of concentration. [f. con- + s. L *centrum* center + -ATE[1]] —**con·cen·tra·tive** (kŏn/sən trā/tĭv, kən sĕn/trə-), *adj.* —**con/cen·tra/tive·ness,** *n.* —**con/cen·tra/tor,** *n.* —**Syn.** 1. See **contract.** —**Ant.** 1. radiate. 4. diverge.

con·cen·tra·tion (kŏn/sən trā/shən), *n.* 1. act of concentrating. 2. concentrated state. 3. exclusive attention to one object; close mental application. 4. *Mil.* a. the assembling of military or naval forces in a particular area in preparation for further operations. b. a specified intensity and duration of artillery fire placed on a small area. 5. something concentrated. 6. *Chem.* (of a solution) a measure of the amount of dissolved substance contained per unit of volume.

concentration camp, 1. a guarded enclosure for the detention or imprisonment of political prisoners, prisoners of war, aliens, refugees, etc. 2. an area for the assembly of military or naval personnel.

con·cen·tre (kŏn sĕn/tər), *v.t., v.i. Chiefly Brit.* concenter.

con·cen·tric (kən sĕn/trĭk), *adj.* having a common center, as circles or spheres. Also, **con·cen/tri·cal.** —**con·cen/tri·cal·ly,** *adv.* —**con·cen·tric·i·ty** (kŏn/sən trĭs/ə tĭ), *n.*

Con·cep·ción (kŏn/sĕp syôn/), *n.* a city in central Chile, near the mouth of the Bío-Bío. 133,580 (est. 1954).

con·cept (kŏn/sĕpt), *n.* 1. a general notion; the predicate of a (possible) judgment. 2. a complex of characters. 3. the immediate object of thought in simple apprehension. [t. L: s. *conceptus* a conceiving]

con·cep·ta·cle (kən sĕp/tə kəl), *n. Biol.* an organ or cavity enclosing reproductive bodies. [t. L: m.s. *conceptāculum* receptacle]

con·cep·tion (kən sĕp/shən), *n.* 1. act of conceiving. 2. state of being conceived. 3. fertilization; inception of pregnancy. 4. that which is conceived. 5. beginning. 6. act or power of forming notions, ideas, or concepts. 7. a notion; idea; concept. 8. a design; plan. —**con·cep/tion·al,** *adj.* —**con·cep/tive,** *adj.*

con·cep·tu·al (kən sĕp′chŏŏ əl), *adj.* pertaining to the forming of concepts or to concepts. [t. ML: s. *conceptuālis*] —**con·cep′tu·al·ly**, *adv.*

con·cep·tu·al·ism (kən sĕp′chŏŏ ə lĭz′əm), *n.* the philosophical doctrine, midway between nominalism and realism, that concepts enable the mind to grasp objective reality. It is often ambiguous as to the existence and status of universals. —**con·cep′tu·al·ist**, *n.* —**con·cep′tu·al·is′tic**, *adj.*

con·cern (kən sûrn′), *v.t.* 1. to relate to; be connected with; be of interest or importance to; affect: *the problem concerns us all.* 2. to interest, engage, or involve (used reflexively or in the passive, often fol. by *with* or *in*): *to concern oneself with a matter, to be concerned in a plot.* 3. to disquiet or trouble (used in the passive): *to be concerned about a person's health.* —*n.* 4. that which relates or pertains to one; business; affair. 5. a matter that engages one's attention, interest, or care, or that affects one s welfare or happiness: *it's no concern of mine.* 6. solicitude or anxiety. 7. important relation or bearing. 8. a commercial or manufacturing firm or establishment. 9. *Colloq.* any material object or contrivance. [t. ML: s. *concernere* relate to, in LL mix, f. L: con- CON- + *cernere* separate, have respect to]
—**Syn.** 6. CONCERN, CARE, WORRY connote an uneasy and burdened state of mind. CONCERN implies an anxious sense of interest in, or responsibility for, something: *concern over a friend's misfortune.* CARE suggests a heaviness of spirit caused by dread, or by the constant pressure of burdensome demands: *poverty weighs one down with care.* WORRY is an active state of agitated uneasiness and restless apprehension: *he was disturbed by worry over the stock market.* —**Ant.** 6. indifference.

con·cerned (kən sûrnd′), *adj.* 1. interested. 2. troubled or anxious: *a concerned look.*

con·cern·ing (kən sûr′nĭng), *prep.* relating to; regarding; about.

con·cern·ment (kən sûrn′mənt), *n.* 1. importance or moment. 2. interest or participation. 3. relation or bearing. 4. anxiety or solicitude. 5. a concern or affair. 6. *Archaic.* a thing in which one is concerned.

con·cert (*n.* kŏn′sûrt, -sərt; *v.* kən sûrt′), *n.* 1. a public musical performance in which several singers or players, or both, participate. 2. agreement of two or more in a design or plan; combined action; accord or harmony. [t. F, t. It.: m. *concerto,* der. *concertare* be in accord] —*v.t.* 3. to contrive or arrange by agreement. 4. to plan; devise. —*v.i.* 5. to plan or act together. [t. F: s. *concerter,* t. It.: m. *concertare* be in accord, g. L *concertāre* contend; influenced in meaning by *consertus,* pp., joined]

con·cert·ed (kən sûr′tĭd), *adj.* 1. contrived or arranged by agreement; prearranged; planned or devised: *concerted action.* 2. *Music.* arranged in parts for several voices or instruments. —**con·cert′ed·ly**, *adv.*

concert grand piano. See **pi·ano** (def. 2).

con·cer·ti·na (kŏn′sər tē′nə), *n.* a small hexagonal accordion. [f. CONCERT + -INA]

con·cer·ti·no (kŏn′chĕr tē′nō), *n., pl.* -ni (-nē). a short concerto. [It.]

con·cert·mas·ter (kŏn′sərt-mäs′tər, -mäs′tər), *n.* the leader, usually the first violinist, of an orchestra, ranking next to the conductor. Also, *Ger.,* **con·cert·meis·ter** (kŏn tsĕrt′mīs′tər).

Man playing a concertina

con·cer·to (kən chĕr′tō; *It.* kôn chĕr′tô), *n., pl.* -tos, *It.* -ti (-tē). *Music.* a composition for one or more principal instruments, with orchestral accompaniment, now usually in symphonic form. [t. It.]

concert pitch, *Music.* a pitch slightly higher than the ordinary pitch, used in tuning instruments for concert use.

con·ces·sion (kən sĕsh′ən), *n.* 1. act of conceding or yielding, as a right or privilege, or as a point or fact in an argument. 2. the thing or point yielded. 3. something conceded by a government or a controlling authority, as a grant of land, a privilege, or a franchise. 4. *U.S.* a space or privilege within certain premises for a business: *the popcorn concession at the theater.* [t. L: s. *concessio,* der. *concēdere.* See CONCEDE]

con·ces·sion·aire (kən sĕsh′ə nâr′), *n.* one to whom a concession has been granted, as by a government. Also, **con·ces′sion·er.** [t. F: s. *concessionnaire*]

con·ces·sion·ar·y (kən sĕsh′ə nĕr′Y), *adj., n., pl.* -aries. —*adj.* 1. pertaining to concession; of the nature of a concession. —*n.* 2. a concessionaire.

con·ces·sive (kən sĕs′Yv), *adj.* 1. tending or serving to concede. 2. *Gram.* expressing concession, as the English conjunction *though.* [t. L: m.s. *concessīvus*]

conch (kŏngk, kŏnch), *n., pl.* **conchs** (kŏngks), **conches** (kŏn′chYz). 1. the spiral shell of a gastropod, often used as a trumpet. 2. any of several marine gastropods, esp. *Strombus gigas.* 3. the fabled shell trumpet of the Tritons. 4. *Archit.* **a.** the concave surface of a dome or half dome. **b.** apse. [t. L: s. *concha,* t. Gk.: m. *kónchē* mussel or cockle, shell-like part or thing. external ear]

con·cha (kŏng′kə), *n., pl.* -chae (-kē). 1. *Anat.* a shell-like structure, esp. the external ear. See diag. under **ear.** 2. *Archit.* a conch. [see CONCH]

con·chif·er·ous (kŏng kĭf′ərəs), *adj.* shell-bearing.
Con·cho·bar (kŏng′kō wər, kŏn′ōŏr), *n.* See **Deirdre.**

con·choid (kŏng′koid), *n.* *Geom.* a plane curve such that if a straight line be drawn from a certain fixed point, called the pole of the curve, to the curve, the part of the line intersected between the curve and its asymptote is always equal to a fixed distance. [see CONCHOIDAL]

con·choi·dal (kŏng koi′dəl), *adj.* *Mineral.* having convex elevations and concave depressions like shells. [f. m. s. Gk. *konchoeidēs* shell-like + -AL[1]]

con·chol·o·gy (kŏng kŏl′ə jĭ), *n.* the branch of zoology dealing with mollusks. [f. *concho-* (t. Gk.: m. *koncho-,* comb. form of *kónchē* mussel) + -LOGY] —**con·cho·log·i·cal** (kŏng′kə lŏj′ə kəl), *adj.* —**con·chol′o·gist,** *n.*

con·chy (kŏn′chǐ), *n., pl.* **-chies.** *Slang.* conscientious objector. [short for CONSCIENTIOUS]

con·ci·erge (kŏn′sĭ ûrzh′; *Fr.* kôN syĕrzh′), *n.* 1. (in France, etc.) one who has charge of the entrance of a building; a janitor or doorkeeper. 2. *Obs.* a custodian or warden. [t. F]

con·cil·i·ate (kən sĭl′Y āt′), *v.t.* -ated, -ating. 1. to overcome the distrust or hostility of, by soothing or pacifying means; placate; win over. 2. to win or gain (regard or favor). 3. to render compatible; reconcile. [t. L: m. s. *conciliātus,* pp., brought together] —**con·cil′i·a′tion,** *n.* —**con·cil′i·a′tor,** *n.* —**Syn.** 1. propitiate. See **appease.**

con·cil·i·a·to·ry (kən sĭl′Y ə tôr′Y), *adj.* tending to conciliate: *a conciliatory manner.* Also, **con·cil·i·a·tive** (kŏn sĭl′Y ā′tĭv). —**con·cil′i·a·to′ri·ly,** *adv.* —**con·cil′i·a·to′ri·ness,** *n.*

con·cin·ni·ty (kən sĭn′ə tY), *n., pl.* **-ties.** 1. *Rhet.* **a.** a close harmony of tone as well as logic among the elements of a discourse. **b.** an instance of this effect. 2. any harmonious adaptation of parts. [t. L: m.s. *concinnitas,* der. *concinnus* put together]

con·cise (kən sīs′), *adj.* expressing much in few words; brief and comprehensive; succinct; terse: *a concise account.* [t. L: m.s. *concīsus,* pp., cut up or off] —**con·cise′ly,** *adv.*

con·cise·ness (kən sīs′nĭs), *n.* quality of being concise. —**Syn.** See **brevity.**

con·ci·sion (kən sĭzh′ən), *n.* 1. concise quality; brevity; terseness. 2. a cutting up or off; mutilation.

con·clave (kŏn′klāv, kŏng′-), *n.* 1. any private meeting. 2. the place in which the cardinals of the Roman Catholic Church meet in private for the election of a pope. 3. the assembly or meeting of the cardinals for the election of a pope. 4. the body of cardinals; the Sacred College. [ME, t. L: lockable place]

con·clav·ist (kŏn′klā vĭst, kŏng′-), *n.* either of two persons who attend upon a cardinal in conclave.

con·clude (kən klood′), *v.* -cluded, -cluding. —*v.t.* 1. to bring to an end; finish; terminate: *to conclude a speech.* 2. to say in conclusion. 3. to bring to a decision or settlement; settle or arrange finally: *to conclude a treaty.* 4. to determine by reasoning; deduce; infer. 5. to decide, determine, or resolve. 6. *Obs.* to shut up or enclose. 7. *Obs.* to restrict or confine. —*v.i.* 8. to come to an end; finish. 9. to arrive at an opinion or judgment; come to a decision; decide. [ME *conclude*(n), t. L: m.s. *conclūdere* shut up] —**con·clud′er,** *n.*

con·clu·sion (kən kloo′zhən), *n.* 1. the end or close; the final part. 2. the last main division of a discourse, containing a summing up of the points. 3. a result, issue, or outcome: *a foregone conclusion.* 4. final settlement or arrangement. 5. try conclusions with, to engage (a person) in a contest or struggle for victory or mastery. 6. final decision. 7. a deduction or inference: *to jump to a conclusion.* 8. *Logic.* a proposition concluded or inferred from the premises of an argument. 9. *Law.* **a.** the effect of an act by which he who did it is bound not to do anything inconsistent therewith; an estoppel. **b.** the end of a pleading or conveyance. 10. *Gram.* apodosis. [ME, t. L: s. *conclūsio*] —**Syn.** 1. ending, termination, completion, finale. See **end.**

con·clu·sive (kən kloo′sĭv), *adj.* serving to settle or decide a question; decisive; convincing: *conclusive evidence.* —**con·clu′sive·ly,** *adv.* —**con·clu′sive·ness,** *n.*

con·coct (kŏn kŏkt′, kən-), *v.t.* 1. to make by combining ingredients, as in cookery: *to concoct a soup or a dinner.* 2. to prepare; make up; contrive: *to concoct a story.* [t. L: s. *concoctus,* pp., cooked together, digested] —**con·coct′er, con·coc′tor,** *n.* —**con·coc′tive,** *adj.*

con·coc·tion (kŏn kŏk′shən, kən-), *n.* 1. act or process of concocting. 2. something concocted. [t. L: s. *concoctio*]

con·com·i·tant (kŏn kŏm′ə tənt, kən-), *adj.* 1. accompanying; concurrent; attending. —*n.* 2. a concomitant quality, circumstance, or thing. [t. LL: s. *concomitans,* ppr., accompanying] —**con·com′i·tance, con·com′i·tan·cy,** *n.* —**con·com′i·tant·ly,** *adv.*

con·cord (kŏn′kôrd, kŏng′-), *n.* 1. agreement between persons; concurrence in opinions, sentiments, etc.; unanimity; accord. 2. peace. 3. a compact or treaty. 4. agreement between things; mutual fitness; harmony. 5. *Gram.* agreement. 6. *Music.* consonance. [ME *concorde,* t. F, t. L: m. *concordia* agreement]

Con·cord (kŏng′kərd for 1-3; *also for 3* kŏn′kôrd), *n.* 1. a town in E Massachusetts, NW of Boston: the second battle of the Revolution was fought here, April 19, 1775. 3,188 (1960). 2. the capital of New Hampshire, in the S part. 28,991 (1960). 3. Concord grape.

---

b., blend of, blended; c., cognate with; d., dialect, dialectal; der., derived from; f., formed from; g., going back to; m., modification of; r., replacing; s., stem of; t., taken from; ?, perhaps. See the full key on inside cover.

con·cord·ance (kŏn kôr′dəns, kən-), *n.* **1.** state of being concordant; agreement; harmony. **2.** an alphabetical index of the principal words of a book, as of the Bible, with a reference to the passage in which each occurs and usually some part of the context. **3.** an alphabetical index of subjects or topics.

con·cord·ant (kŏn kôr′dənt, kən-), *adj.* agreeing; harmonious. **—con·cord′ant·ly,** *adv.*

con·cor·dat (kŏn kôr′dăt), *n.* **1.** an agreement; a compact. **2.** an agreement between the Pope and a secular government regarding the regulation of ecclesiastical matters. [t. F, t. ML: s. *concordātum,* prop. pp. neut. of L *concordāre* agree]

Concord coach, *U.S.* a type of stagecoach.

Con·cord grape (kŏng′kərd, kŏn′kôrd), a large, dark-blue, eastern U.S. grape, grown largely for unfermented juice.

con·course (kŏn′kôrs, kŏng′-), *n.* **1.** an assemblage; a throng: *a mighty concourse of people.* **2.** a driveway or promenade in a park. **3.** an open space in a railroad station. **4.** grounds for racing, athletic sports, etc. **5.** a running or coming together; confluence. [ME *concours,* t. OF, g. L *concursus* running together]

con·cres·cence (kŏn krĕs′əns), *n.* **1.** a growing together, as of parts, cells, etc.; coalescence. **2.** *Embryol.* the moving together and growing together of embryonic parts which give origin to the left and right halves of an embryo or of an organ. [t. L: m. s. *concrescentia* a condensing]

con·crete (kŏn′krēt, kŏn krēt′ for 1–11, 14; kŏn krēt′ for 12, 13), *adj., n., v.,* **-creted, -creting.** *—adj.* **1.** constituting an actual thing or instance; real: *a concrete example.* **2.** pertaining to or concerned with realities or actual instances rather than abstractions; particular as opposed to general: *concrete ideas.* **3.** representing or applied to an actual substance or thing as opposed to an abstract quality: *a concrete noun.* **4.** made of concrete: *a concrete pavement.* **5.** formed by coalescence of separate particles into a mass; united in a coagulated, condensed, or solid state. *—n.* **6.** a concrete idea or term; a concrete object or thing. **7.** a mass formed by coalescence or concretion of particles of matter. **8.** an artificial stonelike material used for foundations, etc., made by mixing cement, sand, and broken stones, etc., with water, and allowing the mixture to harden. **9.** this material strengthened by a system of embedded iron or steel bars, netting, or the like, used for building: *reinforced concrete.* **10.** any of various other artificial building or paving materials, as those containing tar. *—v.t.* **11.** to treat or lay with concrete. **12.** to form into a mass by coalescence of particles; render solid. *—v.i.* **13.** to coalesce into a mass; become solid; harden. **14.** to use or apply concrete. [t. L: m.s. *concrētus,* pp., grown together, hardened] **—con·crete′ly,** *adv.* **—con·crete′ness,** *n.* **—con·cre′tive,** *adj.* **—con·cre′tive·ly,** *adv.* **—Ant.** 1, 2. abstract.

concrete number, *Arith.* a number which relates to a particular object or thing.

con·cre·tion (kŏn krē′shən), *n.* **1.** act or process of concreting. **2.** state of being concreted. **3.** a solid mass formed by or as by coalescence or cohesion. **4.** *Pathol.* a solid or calcified mass in the body formed by a disease process. **5.** *Geol.* a rounded mass of mineral matter occurring in sandstone, clay, etc., often in concentric layers about a nucleus.

con·cre·tion·ar·y (kŏn krē′shə nĕr′Y), *adj.* formed by concretion; consisting of concreted matter or masses.

con·cu·bi·nage (kŏn kū′bə nĬj), *n.* **1.** cohabitation without legal marriage. **2.** the condition of a concubine.

con·cu·bi·nar·y (kŏn kū′bə nĕr′Y), *adj.* **1.** of a concubine. **2.** living in concubinage.

con·cu·bine (kŏng′kyə bĬn′, kŏn′-), *n.* **1.** a woman who cohabits with a man without being married to him. **2.** (among polygamous peoples) a secondary wife. [ME, t. L: m. *concubīna*]

con·cu·pis·cence (kŏn kū′pĬ səns), *n.* **1.** sensual appetite; lust. **2.** eager or illicit desire.

con·cu·pis·cent (kŏn kū′pə sənt), *adj.* **1.** eagerly desirous. **2.** lustful; sensual. [t. L: s. *concupiscens,* ppr.]

con·cur (kən kûr′), *v.i.,* **-curred, -curring. 1.** to accord in opinion; agree. **2.** to coöperate; combine; be associated. **3.** to coincide. **4.** to come together, as lines; unite. **5.** *Obs.* to run together. [late ME, t. L: m.s. *concurrere* run together] **—Syn.** 1. See **consent.**

con·cur·rence (kən kûr′əns, -kûr′-), *n.* **1.** act of concurring. **2.** accordance in opinion; agreement. **3.** coöperation, as of agents or causes. **4.** simultaneous occurrence; coincidence. **5.** *Geom.* a point which is in three or more lines simultaneously. **6.** competition. **7.** *Law.* a power equally held or a claim shared equally. Also, **con·cur′ren·cy** for 1–4, 6.

con·cur·rent (kən kûr′ənt, -kûr′-), *adj.* **1.** occurring or existing together or side by side. **2.** acting in conjunction; coöperating. **3.** having equal authority or jurisdiction. **4.** accordant or agreeing. **5.** tending to or intersecting in the same point: *four concurrent lines.* *—n.* **6.** something joint or contributory. **7.** a rival or competitor. **—con·cur′rent·ly,** *adv.*

concurrent resolution, a resolution adopted by both branches of a legislative assembly which, unlike a joint resolution, does not require the signature of the chief executive.

con·cus·sion (kən kŭsh′ən), *n.* **1.** act of shaking or shocking, as by a blow. **2.** shock occasioned by a blow or collision. **3.** *Pathol.* jarring of the brain, spinal cord, etc., from a blow, fall, etc. [t. L: s. *concussio* shock] **—con·cus·sive** (kən kŭs′Ĭv), *adj.*

Con·dé (kŏn dā′), *n.* **Louis II de Bourbon** (lwē, də bōōr bôn′), **Prince of,** (*Duc d'Enghien, "the Great Condé"*) 1621–86, French general.

con·demn (kən dĕm′), *v.t.* **1.** to pronounce adverse judgment on; express strong disapproval of; censure. **2.** to afford occasion for convicting: *his very looks condemn him.* **3.** to pronounce to be guilty; sentence to punishment; doom. **4.** to judge or pronounce to be unfit for use or service: *the old ship was condemned.* **5.** to declare incurable. **6.** *U.S. Law.* to acquire ownership of for a public purpose, under the right of eminent domain. [ME *condem(p)ne,* t. OF: m. *condem(p)ner,* g. L *condem(p)nāre*] **—con·dem·na·ble** (kən dĕm′nə bəl), *adj.* **—con·demn·er** (kən dĕm′ər), *n.* **—con·demn′ing·ly,** *adv.* **—Syn.** 1. See **blame.**

con·dem·na·tion (kŏn′dĕm nā′shən, -dəm-), *n.* **1.** act of condemning. **2.** strong censure; disapprobation; reproof. **3.** state of being condemned. **4.** cause or reason for condemning. **5.** *U.S.* the seizure (of property) for public use.

con·dem·na·to·ry (kən dĕm′nə tōr′Y), *adj.* serving to condemn.

con·den·sa·ble (kən dĕn′sə bəl), *adj.* capable of being condensed. Also, **condensible.** **—con·den′sa·bil′i·ty,** *n.*

con·den·sate (kən dĕn′sāt), *n.* something formed by condensation.

con·den·sa·tion (kŏn′dĕn sā′shən), *n.* **1.** act of condensing. **2.** condensed state or form. **3.** a condensed mass. **4.** *Chem.* a reaction between two or more like or unlike organic molecules, leading to the formation of a larger molecule and the splitting out of a simple molecule such as water or alcohol. **5.** act of reducing a gas or vapor to a liquid or solid form. **6.** *Psychoanal.* the representation of two or more ideas, memories, feelings, or impulses by one word or image, as in wit, slips, allegories, and dreams.

con·dense (kən dĕns′), *v.,* **-densed, -densing.** *—v.t.* **1.** to make more dense or compact; reduce the volume or compass of. **2.** to reduce to another and denser form, as a gas or vapor to a liquid or solid state. *—v.i.* **3.** to become denser or more compact. **4.** to become liquid or solid, as a gas or vapor. [late ME, t. L: m.s. *condensāre* make thick] **—Syn.** 1. compress, concentrate. See **contract.** **—Ant.** 1, 3. expand.

condensed milk, whole milk reduced by evaporation to a thick consistency with sugar added.

condensed type, a kind of type narrow in proportion to its height.

con·dens·er (kən dĕn′sər), *n.* **1.** one who or that which condenses. **2.** an apparatus for condensing. **3.** any device for reducing gases or vapors to liquid or solid form. **4.** a lens or combination of lenses, used to gather and concentrate the rays of light and direct them upon the object. **5.** *Elect.* a device for accumulating and holding a charge of electricity, consisting of two conducting surfaces separated by a nonconductor or dielectric and used esp. in radio apparatus, as for modifying the electrical capacity in a circuit, for blocking the flow of a direct current, etc.; a capacitor.

con·den·si·ble (kən dĕn′sə bəl), *adj.* condensable.

con·de·scend (kŏn′dĬ sĕnd′), *v.i.* **1.** to waive ceremony voluntarily and assume equality with an inferior. **2.** to stoop or deign (to do something). **3.** to behave as if one is conscious of descending from a superior position, rank, or dignity. **4.** *Obs.* to yield. **5.** *Obs.* to assent. [ME *condescende(n),* t. F: m. *condescendre,* t. LL: m. *condēscendere* stoop] **—con′de·scend′ence,** *n.*

con·de·scend·ing (kŏn′dĬ sĕn′dĬng), *adj.* showing or implying a gracious descent from dignity; patronizing. **—con′de·scend′ing·ly,** *adv.*

con·de·scen·sion (kŏn′dĬ sĕn′shən), *n.* act of condescending; gracious or patronizing complaisance.

con·dign (kən dĬn′), *adj.* (chiefly of punishment, etc.) well-deserved; fitting; adequate. [ME *condigne,* t. F, t. L: m. *condignus* wholly worthy] **—con·dign′ly,** *adv.*

Con·dil·lac (kŏn dē yàk′), *n.* **Étienne Bonnot de** (ē tyĕn′ bō nō′ də), 1715–80, French philosopher.

con·di·ment (kŏn′də mənt), *n.* something used to give flavor and relish to food, as a sauce or seasoning. [t. L: s. *condīmentum* spice] **—con′di·men′tal,** *adj.*

con·di·tion (kən dĬsh′ən), *n.* **1.** particular mode of being of a person or thing; situation with respect to circumstances; existing state or case. **2.** state of health. **3.** fit or requisite state. **4.** social position. **5.** a restricting, limiting, or modifying circumstance. **6.** a circumstance indispensable to some result; a prerequisite; that on which something else is contingent. **7.** something demanded as an essential part of an agreement. **8.** *Law.* **a.** a stipulation in a contract making some liability contingent on the happening of a future uncertain event. **b.** the event. **9. on condition that,** if; provided that. **10.** *U.S.* **a.** a requirement imposed on a college student who fails to reach the prescribed standard in a study at the end of the regular period of instruction, permitting credit to be established by later performance. **b.** the study or subject to which the requirement is attached. **11.** *Gram.* protasis. **12.** *Logic.* antecedent. *—v.t.* **13.** to put in fit or proper state. **14.** to form or be a condition of; determine, limit, or restrict as a condition. **15.** to subject to something as a condition; make conditional (fol. by *on* or *upon*). **16.** to subject to particular conditions or circumstances. **17.** *U.S.* to impose a condition on (a student). **18.** to test (a commodity) to ascertain its condition. **19.** to make it a condition; stipulate. **20.** *Psychol.* to cause a conditioned response in. —*v.i.* **21.** to make conditions. [ME *condicion*, t. L: s. *condicio* (erroneously *conditio*) agreement, stipulation, circumstances] —**con·di′tion·er,** *n.* —**Syn. 1.** See **state. 6.** prerequisite. **7.** requirement, proviso.

con·di·tion·al (kən·dĭsh′ən əl), *adj.* **1.** imposing, containing, or depending on a condition or conditions; not absolute; made or granted on certain terms: *a conditional agreement, sale, etc.* **2.** *Gram.* (of a sentence, clause, or mood) involving or expressing a condition. For example: *If the suit is expensive* (conditional clause), *don't buy it.* **3.** *Logic.* **a.** (of a proposition) asserting that one state of affairs is or will be realized if some other state of affairs is realized, as in *if Smith is 21 years old, he is eligible to vote.* **b.** (of a syllogism) containing a conditional proposition as a premise. —*n.* **4.** (in certain languages) a mood, tense, or other category used in expressing conditions, often corresponding to an English verb preceded by *if: Spanish "comería" (he would eat) is in the conditional.* —**con·di/tion·al′i·ty,** *n.* —**con·di/tion·al·ly,** *adv.*

conditional probability, *Statistics.* the probability of the occurrence of an event under the condition that only a portion of the cases or alternatives are to be considered.

con·di·tioned (kən·dĭsh′ənd), *adj.* existing under or subject to conditions. —**Ant.** free, absolute.

conditioned response, *Psychol.* a learned response resulting from the fact that whenever a stimulus has a motor outlet, another stimulus occurring at the same time will tend to acquire the same outlet. Also, **conditioned reflex.**

con·dole (kən dōl′), *v.,* **-doled, -doling.** —*v.i.* **1.** to express sympathy with one in affliction; grieve (fol. by *with*). —*v.t.* **2.** *Obs.* to grieve with. [t. LL: m.s. *condolēre* suffer greatly] —**con·do·la·to·ry** (kən dō′lə tôr′ĭ), *adj.* —**con·dol′er,** *n.* —**con·dol′ing·ly,** *adv.*

con·do·lence (kən dō′ləns), *n.* expression of sympathy with a person in affliction. Also, **con·dole′ment.**

con do·lo·re (kôn dō lô′rĕ), *Music.* sorrowfully. [It.]

con·do·min·i·um (kŏn′də mĭn′ĭ əm), *n.* **1.** joint or concurrent dominion. **2.** *Internat. Law.* joint sovereignty over a territory by several foreign states. [t. NL, f. L: *con-* CON- + *dominium* lordship]

con·do·na·tion (kŏn′dō nā′shən), *n.* act of condoning; the overlooking or implied forgiving of an offense.

con·done (kən dōn′), *v.t.,* **-doned, -doning. 1.** to pardon or overlook (an offense). **2.** to cause the condonation of. **3.** *Law.* to forgive, or act so as to imply forgiveness of (a violation of the marriage vow). [t. L: m.s. *condōnāre* give up] —**con·don′er,** *n.*

con·dor (kŏn′dər), *n.* **1.** a large vulture of the New World, as the Andean condor (*Sarcorhamphus gryphus*) and California condor (*Gymnogyps californianus*). **2.** a gold coin of South American countries, bearing the figure of a condor, that of Chile being worth about $2.05 and that of Ecuador about $8.49. [t. Sp., t. Kechua: m. *cuntur*]

Con·dor·cet (kôn dôr sĕ′), *n.* **Marie Jean Antoine Nicolas Caritat** (ma rē′ zhän ăn twän′ nē kō lä′ kå rē tä′), **Marquis de,** 1743–94, French mathematician and philosopher.

con·dot·tie·re (kôn′dôt tyĕ′rĕ), *n., pl.* **-ri** (-rĕ). (in Europe, esp. in the 14th and 15th centuries) a professional military captain or leader of mercenaries, in the service of princes or states at war. [It.: leader, der. *condotto* mercenary (soldier), g. L *conductus,* pp., led together, hired]

con·duce (kən dūs′, -dōōs′), *v.i.,* **-duced, -ducing.** to lead or contribute to a result (fol. by *to*). [late ME, t. L: m. s. *condūcere* lead together, hire] —**Ant.** hinder.

con·du·cive (kən dū′sĭv, -dōō′-), *adj.* conducing; contributive; helpful (fol. by *to*). —**con·du/cive·ness,** *n.*

con·duct (*n.* kŏn′dŭkt; *v.* kən dŭkt′), *n.* **1.** personal behavior; way of acting; deportment: *good conduct.* **2.** direction or management; execution: *the conduct of a business.* **3.** act of conducting; guidance; escort. **4.** *Obs.* a guide; an escort. —*v.t.* **5.** to behave (oneself). **6.** to direct in action or course; manage; carry on: *to conduct a campaign.* **7.** to direct as leader: *to conduct an orchestra.* **8.** to lead or guide; escort. **9.** to serve as a channel or medium for (heat, electricity, sound, etc.). —*v.i.* **10.** to behave. **11.** to act as conductor. **12.** *U.S. Obs.* to behave. [t. LL: *conductus,* n., escort, der. L *condūcere* bring together; r. ME *conduyt,* t. OF: m. *conduit*] —**con·duct/i·ble,** *adj.* —**con·duct/i·bil/i·ty,** *n.* —**Syn. 1.** See **behavior. 6.** supervise, regulate. **8.** See **guide.**

con·duct·ance (kən dŭk′təns), *n. Elect.* the conducting power of a conductor (the reciprocal of *resistance*).

con·duc·tion (kən dŭk′shən), *n.* **1.** a conducting, as of water through a pipe. **2.** *Physics.* **a.** transmission through a conductor. **b.** conductivity. **3.** *Physiol.* the carrying of an impulse by a nerve or other tissue.

con·duc·tive (kən dŭk′tĭv), *adj.* having the property of conducting.

con·duc·tiv·i·ty (kŏn′dŭk tĭv′ə tĭ), *n., pl.* **-ties. 1.** *Physics.* the property or power of conducting heat, electricity, or sound. **2.** *Elect.* the conductance between opposite faces of a one centimeter cube of a given material (the reciprocal of *resistivity*).

con·duc·tor (kən dŭk′tər), *n.* **1.** one who conducts; a leader, guide, director, or manager. **2.** the official in charge of a railroad train, bus, or streetcar (in England, only of a bus or streetcar). **3.** the director of an orchestra or chorus, who communicates to the performers by motions of a baton, etc., his interpretation of the music. **4.** that which conducts. **5.** a substance, body, or device that readily conducts heat, electricity, sound, etc. **6.** a lightning rod. —**con·duc/tor·ship′,** *n.* —**con·duc·tress** (kən dŭk′trĭs), *n., esp. Brit., n.fem.*

con·duit (kŏn′dĭt, -dōō ĭt), *n.* **1.** a pipe, tube, or the like, for conveying water or other fluid. **2.** some similar natural passage. **3.** *Elect.* a structure containing one or more ducts. **4.** *Archaic.* a fountain. [ME *condit,* t. OF: m. *conduit,* g. LL *conductus.* See CONDUCT]

con·du·pli·cate (kŏn dū′plə kĭt, -dōō′-), *adj. Bot.* (of a leaf in the bud) folded lengthwise with the upper face of the blade within.

con·dyle (kŏn′dĭl), *n. Anat.* a rounded protuberance on a bone, serving to form an articulation with another bone. [t. F, t. L: m.s. *condylus,* t. Gk.: m. *kóndylos* knuckle, bony knob] —**con/dy·lar,** *adj.*

con·dy·loid (kŏn′də loid′), *adj.* of or like a condyle.

con·dy·lo·ma (kŏn′də lō′mə), *n., pl.* **-mata** (-mə tə). *Pathol.* a wartlike excrescence on the skin, usually in the region of the anus or genitals. [t. L, t. Gk.: m. *kondŷlōma,* der. *kóndylos* CONDYLE] —**con·dy·lom·a·tous** (kŏn′də lŏm′ə təs, -lō′mə-), *adj.*

cone (kōn), *n., v.,* **coned, coning.** —*n.* **1.** *Geom.* a solid whose surface is generated by the straight lines joining a fixed point to the points of a plane curve whose plane does not contain the fixed point. When the plane curve is a circle and the fixed point lies on the perpendicular to the plane of the circle through its center, the cone is a **right circular cone.** When the plane curve is a circle and the fixed point is not so situated, the cone is an **oblique circular cone. 2.** *Mach.* a mechanical part having the shape of a cone or conoid. **3.** *Bot.* **a.** the more or less conical multiple fruit of the pine, fir, etc., consisting of imbricated or valvate scales bearing naked ovules or seeds; a strobile. **b.** a similar fruit, as in cycads, club mosses, etc. **4.** anything cone-shaped: *an ice-cream cone.* —*v.t.* **5.** to shape like a cone or the segment of a cone. [t. L: m.s. *cōnus,* t. Gk.: m. *kōnos*]

Cone

cone·flow·er (kōn′flou′ər), *n.* **1.** a rudbeckia. **2.** any of various allied plants.

Con·el·rad (kŏn′əl răd′), *n. U.S.* a part of the civil defense system in which FM and TV broadcasts cease and AM stations broadcast for brief periods at 640 or 1240 kilocycles: designed to prevent enemy airplanes or guided missiles from homing on radio frequencies. [short for CON(TROL OF) EL(ECTROMAGNETIC) RAD(IATION)]

cone·nose (kōn′nōz′), *n.* assassin bug.

Con·es·to·ga wagon (kŏn′ə stō′gə), a large, heavy, broad-wheeled covered wagon, used esp. for transporting goods, the principal freighting medium westward prior to railroads in North America.

co·ney (kō′nĭ, kŭn′ĭ), *n., pl.* **-neys.** cony.

Co·ney Island (kō′nĭ), an island in New York City, off the S shore of Long Island: seaside resort and amusement center. 5 mi. long.

conf., (L *confer*) compare.

con·fab (kŏn′făb), *n., v.,* **-fabbed, -fabbing.** *Colloq.* —*n.* **1.** a confabulation. —*v.i.* **2.** to confabulate.

con·fab·u·late (kən făb′yə lāt′), *v.i.,* **-lated, -lating.** to talk together; converse. [t. L: m.s. *confābulātus,* pp.] —**con·fab/u·la/tion,** *n.*

con·far·re·a·tion (kŏn făr′ĭ ā′shən), *n.* (among the ancient Romans) the highest form of marriage, marked by the offering of a cake made of spelt. [t. L: s. *confarreātio*]

con·fect (*v.* kən fĕkt′; *n.* kŏn′fĕkt), *v.t.* **1.** to make up, compound, or prepare from ingredients or materials. **2.** to make into a preserve or confection. **3.** to construct, form, or make. —*n.* **4.** a preserved, candied, or other sweet confection. [t. L: s. *confectus,* pp., put together]

con·fec·tion (kən fĕk′shən), *n.* **1.** the process of compounding, preparing, or making. **2.** a sweet preparation (liquid or dry) of fruit or the like, as a preserve or candy. **3.** a candy or bonbon. **4.** a medicinal preparation, now one made with the aid of sugar, honey, or syrup. **5.** a ready-made garment, esp. a woman's frilly garment. —*v.t.* **6.** to prepare as a confection. [ME, t. L: s. *confectio* a making ready]

con·fec·tion·ar·y (kən fĕk′shə nĕr′ĭ), *n., pl.* **-aries,** *adj.* —*n.* **1.** a place where confections are kept or made. **2.** a confection or sweetmeat. **3.** *Obs.* a confectioner. —*adj.* **4.** pertaining to or of the nature of confections or their making.

con·fec·tion·er (kən fĕk′shən ər), *n.* one who makes or sells candies, and sometimes ice cream, cakes, etc.

confectioners' sugar, a finely ground powdered sugar. See **powdered sugar.**

con·fec·tion·er·y (kənfĕk/shə nĕr/ĭ), *n., pl.* **-er·ies.**
1. confections or sweetmeats collectively. 2. the work or business of a confectioner. 3. a confectioner's shop, sometimes used in England for a bakery.

con·fed·er·a·cy (kən fĕd/ər ə sĭ, -fĕd/rə sĭ), *n., pl.* **-cies.** 1. a body of confederated persons, parties, or states. 2. a union of confederated persons, parties, etc. 3. a combination for unlawful purposes; a conspiracy. 4. **the Confederacy,** the Confederate States of America.

con·fed·er·ate (*adj., n.* kən fĕd/ər ĭt, -fĕd/rĭt; *v.* kən-fĕd/ə rāt/), *adj., n., v.,* **-at·ed, -at·ing.** *—adj.* 1. confederated; united in a league or alliance, or a conspiracy. 2. (*cap.*) denoting or pertaining to the Confederate States of America: *the Confederate army.* *—n.* 3. one united with others in a confederacy; an ally. 4. an accomplice. 5. (*cap.*) an adherent of the Confederate States of America. *—v.t., v.i.* 6. to unite in a league or alliance, or a conspiracy. [ME, t. LL: m. s. *confoederātus,* pp., united in a league]

Confederate States of America, the name assumed by the eleven Southern States which seceded from the American Union in 1860–61.

con·fed·er·a·tion (kən fĕd/ə rā/shən), *n.* 1. act of confederating. 2. state of being confederated. 3. a league or alliance. 4. a body of confederates, esp. of states more or less permanently united for common purposes. 5. **the Confederation,** the union of the American colonies from 1781 to 1789 under the Articles of Confederation. **—Syn.** 3. See **alliance.**

con·fed·er·a·tive (kən fĕd/ə rā/tĭv), *adj.* pertaining to a confederation.

con·fer (kən fûr/), *v.t.,* **-ferred, -fer·ring.** *—v.t.* 1. to bestow as a gift, favor, honor, etc. (fol. by *on* or *upon*). 2. to compare. *—v.i.* 3. consult together; compare opinions; carry on a discussion or deliberation. [t. L: s. *conferre* bring together] **—con·fer/ment,** *n.* **—con·fer/ra·ble,** *adj.* **—con·fer/rer,** *n.* **—Syn.** 1. See **give.** 3. See **consult.**

con·fer·ee (kŏn/fə rē/), *n.* 1. *U.S.* one who is conferred with or takes part in a conference. 2. one on whom something is conferred. Also, **con/fer·ree/.**

con·fer·ence (kŏn/fər əns), *n.* 1. a meeting for consultation or discussion. 2. act of conferring or consulting together; consultation, esp. on an important or serious matter. 3. *Govt.* a meeting (usually of committees) to settle disagreements between the two legislative groups. 4. *Eccles.* **a.** an official assembly of clergy, or of clergy and laymen, customary in many Christian denominations. **b.** a group of churches the representatives of which regularly meet in such an assembly. 5. *U.S. Sports.* an organization of teams. **—con·fer·en·tial** (kŏn/fə rĕn/shəl), *adj.* **—Syn.** 1. See **convention.**

con·fer·va (kən fûr/və), *n., pl.* **-vae** (-vē), **-vas.** any simple filamentous green alga. [t. L: kind of water plant] **—con·fer·void** (kən fûr/void), *adj., n.*

con·fess (kən fĕs/), *v.t.* 1. to acknowledge or avow: *to confess a secret, fault, crime, debt, etc.* 2. to own or admit; admit the truth or validity of: *I must confess that I haven't read it.* 3. to acknowledge one's belief in; declare adherence to. 4. to declare (one's sins) or declare the sins of (oneself), esp. to a priest, for the obtaining of absolution. 5. (of a priest) to hear the confession of. 6. *Archaic.* to reveal by circumstances. *—v.i.* 7. to make confession; plead guilty; own (fol. by *to*). 8. to make confession of sins, esp. to a priest. [ME *confesse*(n), t. LL: m. *confessāre,* der. L *confessus,* pp.] **—Syn.** 1. See **acknowledge.** **—Ant.** 1. conceal. 2. deny.

con·fess·ed·ly (kən fĕs/ĭd lĭ), *adv.* by confession or acknowledgment; admittedly.

con·fes·sion (kən fĕsh/ən), *n.* 1. acknowledgment or avowal; admission or concession: *a confession of guilt.* 2. acknowledgment of sin or sinfulness. 3. a disclosing of sins to a priest to obtain forgiveness. 4. that which is confessed. 5. Also, **confession of faith.** a formal profession of belief and acceptance of church doctrines, as before being admitted to church membership. 6. the tomb of a martyr or confessor, or the altar or shrine connected with it. [ME, t. L: s. *confessio*]

con·fes·sion·al (kən fĕsh/ən əl), *adj.* 1. of, or of the nature of, confession. *—n.* 2. the place set apart for the hearing of confessions by a priest.

con·fes·sion·ar·y (kən fĕsh/ə nĕr/ĭ), *adj.* of or pertaining to confession, esp. auricular confession of sins.

con·fes·sor (kən fĕs/ər), *n.* 1. one who confesses. 2. a priest authorized to hear confessions. 3. one who confesses and adheres to the Christian religion, esp. in spite of persecution and torture: *Edward the Confessor.* Also, **con·fess/er.**

con·fet·ti (kən fĕt/ĭ; *It.* kōn fĕt/tē), *n. pl., sing.* **-fetto** (-fĕt/tō). 1. small bits of colored paper, thrown at carnivals, weddings, etc. 2. confections; bonbons. [t. It., pl. of *confetto* comfit]

con·fi·dant (kŏn/fə dănt/, kŏn/fə dănt/), *n.* one to whom secrets are confided. [t. F, t. It.: m. *confidente,* t. L: m. s. *confīdens,* ppr., trusting] **—con/fi·dante/,** *n. fem.*

con·fide (kən fīd/), *v.,* **-fid·ed, -fid·ing.** *—v.i.* 1. to show trust by imparting secrets (fol. by *in*). 2. to have full trust: *confiding in that parting promise.* *—v.t.* 3. to tell in assurance of secrecy. 4. to entrust; commit to the charge, knowledge, or good faith of another. [late ME, t. L: m.s. *confīdere* trust altogether] **—con·fid/er,** *n.*

con·fi·dence (kŏn/fə dəns), *n.* 1. full trust; belief in the trustworthiness or reliability of a person or thing. 2. **in confidence,** as a secret or private matter, not to be divulged or communicated to others: *I told him in confidence.* 3. *Brit. Pol.* the wish to retain the incumbent government in office, as shown by a vote on a particular issue: *this issue is a question of confidence.* 4. self-reliance, assurance, or boldness. 5. presumption. 6. certitude or assured expectation. 7. a confidential communication. 8. a ground of trust. **—Syn.** 1. See **trust.** 4. CONFIDENCE, ASSURANCE both imply a faith in oneself. CONFIDENCE may imply trust in oneself or arrogant self-conceit. ASSURANCE implies even more sureness of oneself; this may be shown as undisturbed calm or as offensive boastfulness or headstrong conduct.

confidence game, the crime of obtaining money or property by fraud, after obtaining the victim's confidence. Also, *Brit.,* **confidence trick.**

confidence limits, *Statistics.* a pair of numbers used to estimate a characteristic of a population from a sample, which are such that it can be stated with a specified probability that the pair of numbers calculated from a sample will include the value of the population characteristic between them.

confidence man, one who swindles by a confidence game.

con·fi·dent (kŏn/fə dənt), *adj.* 1. having strong belief or full assurance; sure: *confident of victory.* 2. sure of oneself; bold: *a confident bearing.* 3. overbold. 4. *Obs.* trustful or confiding. *—n.* 5. a confidant. **—con/fi·dent·ly,** *adv.* **—Syn.** 1. certain, positive. See **sure.**

con·fi·den·tial (kŏn/fə dĕn/shəl), *adj.* 1. spoken or written in confidence; secret: *a confidential communication.* 2. betokening confidence or intimacy; imparting private matters: *a confidential tone.* 3. enjoying another's confidence; entrusted with secrets or private affairs: *a confidential secretary.* **—con/fi·den/ti·al/i·ty, con/fi·den/tial·ness,** *n.* **—con/fi·den/tial·ly,** *adv.* **—Syn.** 3. See **familiar.**

confidential communication, *Law.* a confidential statement made to a lawyer, doctor, or priest, or to one's husband or wife, privileged against disclosure in court if the privilege is claimed by the client, patient, penitent, or spouse.

con·fid·ing (kən fī/dĭng), *adj.* trustful; credulous or unsuspicious. **—con·fid/ing·ly,** *adv.*

con·fig·u·ra·tion (kən fĭg/yə rā/shən), *n.* 1. the relative disposition of the parts or elements of a thing. 2. external form, as resulting from this; conformation. 3. *Astron.* **a.** the relative position or aspect of heavenly bodies. **b.** a group of stars. 4. *Physics, Chem.* the relative position in space of the atoms in a molecule. [t. LL: s. *configūrātio,* der. L *configūrāre* shape after some pattern] **—con·fig/u·ra/tion·al, con·fig·u·ra·tive** (kən-fĭg/yə rə tĭv, -rā/-), *adj.*

con·fig·u·ra·tion·ism (kən fĭg/yə rə/shə nĭz/əm), *n.* Gestalt psychology.

con·fine (kən fīn/ for *1–3, 5, 6b;* kŏn/fīn for *4, 6a*), *v.,* **-fined, -fin·ing.** *—v.t.* 1. to enclose within bounds; limit or restrict. 2. to shut or keep in; imprison. 3. to be in childbed, or be delivered of a child (used in the passive). [t. F: m. s. *confiner,* t. It.: m. *confinare,* der. *confīno* bordering, g. L *confīnis*] *—n.* 4. (*usually pl.*) a boundary or bound; a border or frontier. 5. *Poetic.* confinement. 6. *Obs.* **a.** (*usually pl.*) a region. **b.** a place of confinement. [t. F: m. *confīns* (pl.), g. L *confīnia,* pl. of *confīnium* a border] **—con·fin/er,** *n.* **—Syn.** 1. circumscribe. **—Ant.** 1, 2. free.

con·fine·ment (kən fīn/mənt), *n.* 1. act of confining. 2. state of being confined. 3. the lying-in of a woman in childbed. 4. *Mil.* state of being held in a guard house or prison, while awaiting trial or as punishment (as distinguished from *arrest*). [t. F, der. *confiner* CONFINE, v.]

con·firm (kən fûrm/), *v.t.* 1. to make certain or sure; corroborate; verify: *this confirmed my suspicions.* 2. to make valid or binding by some formal or legal act; sanction; ratify: *to confirm an agreement, appointment, etc.* 3. to make firm or more firm; add strength to; settle or establish firmly: *the news confirmed my resolution.* 4. to strengthen (a person) in habit, resolution, opinion, etc. 5. *Eccles.* to administer the rite of confirmation to. [t. L: s. *confirmāre* make firm; r. ME *conferme*(n), t. OF: m. *confermer*] **—con·firm/a·ble,** *adj.* **—con·firm/-er;** *Law,* **con·firm·or** (kŏn/fər môr/, kən fûr/mər), *n.* **—Syn.** 1. substantiate, authenticate. **—Ant.** 1. disprove. 2. invalidate. 3. shake.

con·fir·ma·tion (kŏn/fər mā/shən), *n.* 1. act of confirming. 2. that which confirms, as a corroborative statement. 3. *Eccles.* **a.** a rite administered to baptized persons, in some churches as a sacrament for confirming and strengthening the recipient in the Christian faith, in others as a rite without sacramental character by which the recipient is admitted to full communion with the church. **b.** (among American Jews) a solemn form of initiation of the Jewish youth into their ancestral faith. In the case of boys, it is used as a substitute for the bar mizvah ceremony, or as supplementary to it, or as the equivalent of it.

con·firm·a·to·ry (kən fûr/mə tôr/ĭ), *adj.* serving to confirm; corroborative. Also, **con·firm/a·tive.**

con·firmed (kən fûrmd/), *adj.* 1. made firm; settled; ratified. 2. firmly established in a habit or condition; inveterate: *a confirmed drunk.* 3. (of a disease) chronic.

con·fis·ca·ble (kənfĭs′kə bəl), *adj.* liable to be confiscated.

con·fis·cate (kŏn′fĭskāt′, kənfĭs′kāt), *v.*, **-cated, -cating,** *adj.* **-v.t. 1.** to seize as forfeited to the public treasury; appropriate, by way of penalty, to public use. **2.** to seize as if by authority; appropriate summarily. **—adj. 3.** confiscated. [t. L: m.s. *confiscātus,* pp., put away in a chest] **—con′fis·ca′tion,** *n.* **—con′fis·ca′tor,** *n.*

con·fis·ca·to·ry (kənfĭs′kə tôr′ĭ), *adj.* characterized by or effecting confiscation.

Con·fit·e·or (kənfĭt′ĭ ôr′), *n. Rom. Cath. Ch.* a form of prayer beginning with "Confiteor," in which a general confession of sinfulness is made, used at the beginning of the mass and on other occasions. [t. L: I confess]

con·fi·ture (kŏn′fĭ chŏŏr′), *n.* a confection; a preserve, as of fruit. [ME, t. F, der. *confit* comfit, pp. of *confire* preserve, prepare, g. L *conficere*]

con·fla·gra·tion (kŏn′flə grā′shən), *n.* a large and destructive fire. [t. L: s. *conflagrātio*] **—Syn.** See **flame.**

con·fla·tion (kənflā′shən), *n. Bibliog.* **1.** the combination of two variant texts into a new one. **2.** the result. [t. LL: s. *conflātio,* der. L *conflāre* blow together]

con·flict (*v.* kənflĭkt′; *n.* kŏn′flĭkt), *v.i.* **1.** to come into collision; clash, or be in opposition or at variance. **2.** to contend; do battle. **—n. 3.** a battle or struggle, esp. a prolonged struggle; strife. **4.** controversy; a quarrel: *conflicts between church and state.* **5.** discord of action, feeling, or effect; antagonism, as of interests or principles: *a conflict of ideas.* **6.** a striking together; collision. [t. L: s. *conflictus,* pp., struck together] **—con·flic′tion,** *n.* **—con·flic′tive,** *adj.* **—Syn. 3.** See **fight. 5.** contention, opposition, variance. **—Ant. 4.** accord.

con·flu·ence (kŏn′flŏŏ əns), *n.* **1.** a flowing together of two or more streams. **2.** the place of junction. **3.** the body of water so formed. **4.** a coming together of people or things. **5.** a throng; an assemblage. Also, **con·flux** (kŏn′flŭks).

con·flu·ent (kŏn′flŏŏ ənt), *adj.* **1.** flowing or running together; blending into one. **2.** *Pathol.* **a.** running together: *confluent efflorescences.* **b.** characterized by confluent efflorescences: *confluent smallpox.* **—n. 3.** one of two or more confluent streams. **4.** a tributary stream. [t. L: s. *confluens,* ppr., flowing together]

con·fo·cal (kŏn fō′kəl), *adj. Math.* having the same focus or foci.

con·form (kənfôrm′), *v.i.* **1.** to act in accord or harmony; comply (fol. by *to*). **2.** to become similar in form or character. **3.** to comply with the usages of the Established Church of England. **—v.t. 4.** to make similar in form or character. **5.** to bring into correspondence or harmony. [ME *conforme(n),* t. F: m. *conformer,* t. L: m. *conformāre* fashion] **—con·form′er,** *n.* **—Syn. 5.** adapt, adjust, accommodate. **—Ant. 1, 3.** dissent. **4.** differ.

con·form·a·ble (kənfôr′mə bəl), *adj.* **1.** corresponding in form or character; similar. **2.** exhibiting agreement in form or harmony (usually fol. by *to*). **3.** compliant, acquiescent, or submissive. **4.** *Geol.* (of strata or beds) having the same dip and strike as a result of successive depositions uninterrupted by crustal movement. **—con·form′a·bil′i·ty,** **con·form′a·ble·ness,** *n.* **—con·form′a·bly,** *adv.*

Conformable and unconformable strata

A and B, two sets of unconformable strata; CD, line of junction of A and B

con·form·ance (kənfôr′məns), *n.* act of conforming; conformity.

con·for·ma·tion (kŏn′fôr mā′shən), *n.* **1.** manner of formation; structure; form. **2.** symmetrical disposition or arrangement of parts. **3.** act of conforming; adaptation; adjustment. **4.** state of being conformed.

con·form·ist (kənfôr′mĭst), *n.* **1.** one who conforms to a usage or practice. **2.** one who conforms to the usages of the Established Church of England.

con·form·i·ty (kənfôr′mə tĭ), *n., pl.* **-ties. 1.** correspondence in form or character; agreement, congruity, or accordance. **2.** compliance or acquiescence. **3.** compliance with the usages of the Church of England.

con·found (kŏn found′, kən-; *for 7 usually* kŏn′found′), *v.t.* **1.** to mingle so that the elements cannot be distinguished or separated. **2.** to treat or regard erroneously as identical; mix or associate by mistake. **3.** to throw into confusion or disorder: *confusion worse confounded.* **4.** to perplex, as with sudden disturbance or surprise. **5.** *Archaic.* to put to shame; abash. **6.** *Archaic.* to defeat or overthrow; bring to ruin or naught. **7.** (in mild imprecations) to damn: *confound it!* **8.** *Obs.* to spend uselessly, or waste. [ME *confounde(n),* t. OF: m. *confondre,* g. L *confundere* pour together, mix, confuse] **—con·found′er,** *n.*

con·found·ed (kŏn foun′dĭd, kən-), *adj.* **1.** damned (a euphemism): *a confounded lie.* **2.** *Colloq.* execrable; odious; detestable. **—con·found′ed·ly,** *adv.*

con·fra·ter·ni·ty (kŏn′frə tûr′nə tĭ), *n., pl.* **-ties. 1.** a lay brotherhood devoted to some particular religious or charitable service. **2.** a society or body of men united for some purpose or in some profession. [late ME *confraternite,* t. ML: m.s. *confrāternitas* brotherhood, der. *confrāter.* See CONFRERE]

con·frere (kŏn′frâr), *n.* a fellow member of a fraternity, profession, etc.; a colleague. [ME, t. F, trans. of ML *confrāter* colleague]

con·front (kənfrŭnt′), *v.t.* **1.** to stand or come in front of; stand or meet facing. **2.** to face in hostility or defiance; oppose. **3.** to set face to face. **4.** to bring together for examination or comparison. [t. F: s. *confronter,* t. ML: m. s. *confrontārī,* f. L: *con-* CON- + s. *frons* forehead + *-ārī,* inf. ending] **—con·fron·ta·tion** (kŏn′frən tā′shən), **con·front′ment,** *n.* **—con·front′er,** *n.*

Con·fu·cius (kənfū′shəs), *n.* (Chin. *Kung-fu-tse*) 551–478 B.C., Chinese philosopher and teacher of principles of conduct. His highest standards of conduct were treating others as you wish to be treated, loyalty, intelligence, and the fullest development of the individual in the five chief relationships of life: ruler and subject, father and son, elder and younger brother, husband and wife, friend and friend. **—Con·fu′cian,** *adj., n.* **—Con·fu′cian·ism,** *n.* **—Con·fu′cian·ist,** *n., adj.*

con·fuse (kənfūz′), *v.t.,* **-fused, -fusing. 1.** to combine without order or clearness; jumble; render indistinct. **2.** to throw into disorder. **3.** to fail to distinguish between; associate by mistake; confound: *to confuse dates.* **4.** to perplex or bewilder. **5.** to disconcert or abash. **6.** *Obs.* to bring to ruin or naught. [back formation from *confused,* f. ME *confus* (t. F, t. L: s. *confūsus,* pp., confounded) + -ED²] **—con·fus·ed·ly** (kənfū′zĭd lĭ, -fūzd′-lĭ), *adv.* **—con·fus′ed·ness,** *n.* **—con·fus′ing·ly,** *adv.* **—Syn. 4.** CONFUSE, DISCONCERT, EMBARRASS imply temporary interference with the clear working of one's mind. To CONFUSE is to produce a general bewilderment: *to confuse by giving complicated directions.* To DISCONCERT is quickly or violently to disturb one's mind by irritation, perplexities, etc., making it difficult for him to collect his thoughts: *to disconcert by asking irrelevant questions.* To EMBARRASS is to cause one to be ill at ease or uncomfortable, so that his usual judgment and presence of mind desert him: *to embarrass by treating with unexpected rudeness.* **—Ant. 5.** compose.

con·fu·sion (kənfū′zhən), *n.* **1.** act of confusing. **2.** state of being confused. **3.** disorder. **4.** lack of clearness or distinctness. **5.** embarrassment or abashment. **6.** perplexity; bewilderment. **7.** *Psychiatry.* a disturbed mental state; a clouding of consciousness; disorientation. [ME, t. L: s. *confūsio*] **—Syn. 3.** turmoil.

con·fu·ta·tion (kŏn′fyŏŏ tā′shən), *n.* **1.** act of confuting. **2.** that which confutes. **3.** (in the classically arranged speech) the fourth section, given over to direct refutation. **—con·fut·a·tive** (kənfū′tə tĭv), *adj.*

con·fute (kənfūt′), *v.t.,* **-futed, -futing. 1.** to prove to be false or defective; disprove: *to confute an argument.* **2.** to prove to be wrong; convict of error by argument or proof: *to confute one's opponent.* **3.** to confound or bring to naught. [t. L: m. s. *confūtāre*] **—con·fut′er,** *n.*

Cong., **1.** Congress. **2.** Congressional.

cong., (L *congius*) gallon.

con·gé (kŏn′zhā; Fr. kôn zhē′), *n.* **1.** leave to depart, or dismissal; leave or permission; leave-taking. **2.** a bow or obeisance. **3.** *Archit.* a type of concave molding. [F. See CONGEE]

con·geal (kən jēl′), *v.t., v.i.* **1.** to change from a fluid or soft to a solid or rigid state, as by freezing or cooling. **2.** to stiffen or coagulate, as blood. **3.** to make or become fixed, as sentiments, principles, etc. [ME *congeal(n),* t. L: m. *congelāre* cause to freeze together] **—con·geal′a·ble,** *adj.* **—con·geal′er,** *n.* **—con·geal′ment,** *n.*

con·gee (kŏn′jē), *n., v.,* **-geed, -geeing.** *Obsolesc.* **—n. 1.** congé. **—v.i. 2.** to take one's leave. **3.** to bow. [ME *congye,* t. OF: m. *congie* (F *congé*), g. L *commeātus* a going to and fro, leave of absence]

con·ge·la·tion (kŏn′jə lā′shən), *n.* **1.** act or process of congealing. **2.** state of being congealed. **3.** the product of congealing; a concretion; a coagulation.

con·ge·ner (kŏn′jə nər), *n.* **1.** one of the same kind or class. **2.** a fellow member of a genus, as of plants or animals. [t. L: of the same kind]

con·ge·ner·ic (kŏn′jə nĕr′ĭk), *adj.* of the same kind or genus. Also, **con·gen·er·ous** (kən jĕn′ər əs).

con·gen·ial (kən jēn′yəl), *adj.* **1.** suited or adapted in spirit, feeling, temper, etc.: *congenial companions.* **2.** agreeable or pleasing; agreeing or suited in nature or character: *a congenial task.* [f. CON- + s. L *genius* spirit + -AL¹] **—con·ge·ni·al·i·ty** (kən jē′nĭ ăl′ə tĭ), *n.* **—con·gen′ial·ly,** *adv.* **—Syn. 1.** kindred, sympathetic.

con·gen·i·tal (kən jĕn′ə təl), *adj.* existing at or from one's birth: *a congenital defect.* [f. s. L *congenitus* born together with + -AL¹] **—con·gen′i·tal·ly,** *adv.*

con·ger (kŏng′gər), *n.* **1.** a large marine eel, *Conger conger,* sometimes growing to a length of 10 feet, which is caught for food along the coast of Europe. **2.** any other species of the family Congridae. Also, **conger eel.** [ME *congre,* t. OF, g. L *conger, congrus,* t. Gk.: m. *góngros*]

con·ge·ries (kŏn jĭr′ēz), *n. sing. and pl.* a collection of several particles or bodies in one mass; an assemblage; aggregation; heap. [t. L: heap, pile]

con·gest (kən jĕst′), *v.t.* **1.** to fill to excess; overcrowd. **2.** *Pathol.* to cause an unnatural accumulation of blood in the vessels of (an organ or part). **3.** *Obs.* to heap together. **—v.i. 4.** to become congested. [t. L: s. *congestus,* pp., brought together] **—con·ges′tion,** *n.* **—con·ges′tive,** *adj.*

con·gi·us (kŏn′jĭ əs), *n., pl.* **congii** (kŏn′jĭ ī′). **1.** *Pharm.* a gallon. **2.** an ancient Roman unit of liquid measure, equal to about 0.8 U.S. gallon. [t. L]

---

b., blend of, blended; c., cognate with; d., dialect, dialectal; der., derived from; f., formed from; g., going back to; m., modification of; r., replacing; s., stem of; t., taken from; ?, perhaps. See the full key on inside cover.

con·glo·bate (kŏn·glō′băt, kŏng′glō·bāt′), *adj., v.,* **-bated, -bating.** —*adj.* 1. formed into a ball. —*v.t., v.i.* 2. to collect or form into a ball or rounded mass. [t. L: m.s. *conglobātus*, pp.] —**con·glo·ba′tion**, *n.*

con·globe (kŏn·glōb′), *v.t., v.i.,* **-globed, -globing.** to conglobate.

con·glom·er·ate (*adj., n.* kən·glŏm′ər·Ĭt; *v.* -ə·rāt′), *n., adj., v.,* **-ated, -ating.** —*n.* 1. anything composed of heterogeneous materials or elements. 2. *Geol.* a rock consisting of rounded and waterworn pebbles, etc., embedded in a finer cementing material; consolidated gravel. —*adj.* 3. gathered into a rounded mass; consisting of parts so gathered; clustered. 4. *Geol.* of the nature of a conglomerate. —*v.t.* 5. to bring together into a cohering mass. 6. to gather into a ball or rounded mass. —*v.i.* 7. to collect or cluster together. [t. L: m.'s. *conglomerātus*, pp., rolled together] —**con·glom·er·at·ic** (kən·glŏm′ə·krăt′Ĭk), **con·glom·er·it·ic** (-rĭt′Ĭk), *adj.*

con·glom·er·a·tion (kən·glŏm′ə·rā′shən), *n.* 1. act of conglomerating. 2. state of being conglomerated. 3. a cohering mass; a cluster. 4. a heterogeneous combination.

con·glu·ti·nate (kən·glōō′tə·nāt′), *v.,* **-nated, -nating,** *adj.* —*v.t., v.i.* 1. to join or become joined as with glue. —*adj.* 2. conglutinated. [t. L: m.s. *conglūtinātus*, pp., glued together] —**con·glu′ti·na′tion**, *n.* —**con·glu′ti·na′tive**, *adj.*

Con·go (kŏng′gō), *n.* 1. a river in central Africa, rising in the SE part of the Republic of the Congo, flowing in a large arc through the Congo and into the Atlantic. ab. 3000 mi. 2. **a. Republic of the,** an independent republic in central Africa. 13,540,082 pop.; 905,063 sq. mi. *Cap.:* Kinshasa. Formerly, **Belgian Congo. b. Republic of,** a republic in Africa. W of this country: member of the French Community. 760,000 pop.; 139,000 sq. mi. *Cap.:* Brazzaville. Formerly, **Middle Congo.** —**Con′go·lese′** (kŏng′gə·lēz′,-lēs′), *adj., n.*

Congo colors, a group of azo dyes derived from benzidine which will dye cotton and other vegetable fibers without the aid of a mordant. Also, **Congo dyes.**

Congo Free State, former name of Congo (def. 2a).

Congo red, one of the Congo colors, used esp. to dye cotton, etc., red. Since it is not acid-fast or light-fast, it is often used as a chemical indicator.

congo snake, either of two eel-shaped salamanders: **a.** *Siren,* of the southern U.S., with small forelimbs but no hind ones. **b.** *Amphiuma,* of the southeastern U.S., having four minute limbs, and sometimes attaining a length of 3 feet. Also, **congo eel.**

con·gou (kŏng′gōō), *n.* a kind of black tea from China. Also, **con·go** (kŏn′gō). [t. Chinese: m. *kung-fu* labor]

con·grat·u·lant (kən·grăch′ə·lənt), *adj.* 1. congratulating. —*n.* 2. one who congratulates.

con·grat·u·late (kən·grăch′ə·lāt′), *v.t.,* **-lated, -lating.** 1. to express sympathetic joy to (a person), as on a happy occasion; compliment with expressions of sympathetic pleasure; felicitate. 2. *Obs.* **a.** to express sympathetic joy or satisfaction at (an event, etc.). **b.** to salute. [t. L: m.s. *congrātulātus*, pp.] —**con·grat′u·la′tor**, *n.*

con·grat·u·la·tion (kən·grăch′ə·lā′shən), *n.* 1. act o congratulating. 2. (*usually pl.*) a congratulatory expression; felicitation.

con·grat·u·la·to·ry (kən·grăch′ə·lə·tôr′Y), *adj.* 1. conveying congratulations. 2. inclined to congratulate.

con·gre·gate (kŏng′grə·gāt′), *v.,* **-gated, -gating,** *adj.* —*v.i.* 1. to come together; assemble, esp. in large numbers. —*v.t.* 2. to bring together in a crowd, body, or mass; assemble; collect. —*adj.* 3. congregated; assembled. 4. collective. [ME, t. L: m.s. *congregātus*, pp., collected into a flock] —**con′gre·ga′tive,** *adj.* —**con′gre·ga′tive·ness,** *n.* —**con′gre·ga′tor,** *n.*

con·gre·ga·tion (kŏng′grə·gā′shən), *n.* 1. act of congregating. 2. a congregated body; an assemblage. 3. an assembly of persons met for common religious worship. 4. an organization formed for the purpose of providing for worship of God, religious education, and other church activities; a local church society. 5. (in the Old Testament) the whole body of the Hebrews. 6. (in the New Testament) the Christian church in general. 7. *Rom. Cath. Ch.* **a.** a committee of cardinals or other ecclesiastics. **b.** a community of men or women who observe the simple vows of poverty, chastity, and obedience: *Congregation of the Holy Cross.* 8. (at English universities) the general assembly of the doctors, fellows, etc. 9. (in colonial North America) a parish, hundred, town, plantation, or other settlement.

con·gre·ga·tion·al (kŏng′grə·gā′shən·əl), *adj.* 1. of or pertaining to a congregation: *congregational singing.* 2. (*cap.*) pertaining or adhering to a form of church government in which each congregation or local church acts as an independent, self-governing body, while maintaining fellowship with other like congregations.

con·gre·ga·tion·al·ism (kŏng′grə·gā′shən·ə lĭz′əm), *n.* 1. the type of church government in which each local religious society is independent and self-governing. 2. (*cap.*) the system of government and doctrine of Congregational churches. —**con′gre·ga′tion·al·ist,** *n., adj.*

con·gress (kŏng′grĬs), *n.* 1. (*cap.*) **a.** the national legislative body of the U.S., consisting of the Senate (upper house) and the House of Representatives (lower house), as a continuous institution. **b.** this body as it exists for the two years during which the representatives hold their seats: *the 69th Congress.* **c.** the session of this body.

2. the national legislative body of a nation, esp. of a republic. 3. a formal meeting or assembly of representatives, as envoys of independent states, for the discussion, arrangement, or promotion of some matter of common interest. 4. act of coming together; an encounter. 5. social relations; converse. —*v.i.* 6. to meet in congress. [t. L: s. *congressus* a meeting]

congress boot, *U.S.* a high shoe with elastic sides, by the stretching of which it is drawn onto the foot.

con·gres·sion·al (kən·grĕsh′ən əl), *adj.* of a congress, esp. (*cap.*) the Congress of the U.S.

con·gress·man (kŏng′grĬs·mən), *n., pl.* **-men.** (*often cap.*) a member of the U.S. Congress, esp. of the House of Representatives. —**con·gress·wom·an** (kŏng′grĬs·wŏom′ən), *n. fem.*

Congress of Industrial Organizations, a federation of affiliated industrial labor unions, originally (1935) within the American Federation of Labor, independent from it (1938–55), and reunited with it in 1955. *Abbr.:* CIO or C.I.O.

Congress of Vienna, an international conference (1814–15) held at Vienna after Napoleon I's banishment to Elba, with Metternich as the dominant figure, aimed at territorial resettlement and restoration to power of the crowned heads of Europe.

Con·greve (kŏn′grēv, kŏng′-), *n.* **William,** 1670–1729, English dramatist.

Con·greve (kŏn′grēv, kŏng′-), *n.* 1. a kind of friction match (**Congreve match**). 2. a kind of rocket formerly used in warfare (**Congreve rocket**). [named after Sir W. *Congreve* (1772–1828), British inventor]

con·gru·ent (kŏng′grōō ənt), *adj.* 1. agreeing; accordant; congruous. 2. *Geom.* coinciding exactly when superposed. [t. L: s. *congruens,* ppr. agreeing] —**con′gru·ence, con′gru·en·cy,** *n.* —**con′gru·ent·ly,** *adv.*

con·gru·i·ty (kən·grōō′ə tY), *n., pl.* **-ties.** 1. state or quality of being congruous; agreement; harmony; appropriateness. 2. *Geom.* equality; capacity of figures of being exactly superposed. 3. a point of agreement.

con·gru·ous (kŏng′grōō əs), *adj.* 1. agreeing or harmonious in character; accordant; consonant; consistent (fol. by *with* or *to*). 2. exhibiting harmony of parts. 3. appropriate or fitting. [t. L: m. *congruus* fit] —**con′gru·ous·ly,** *adv.* —**con′gru·ous·ness,** *n.*

con·ic (kŏn′Yk), *adj.* 1. Also, **con′i·cal.** having the form of, resembling, or pertaining to a cone. —*n.* 2. *Math.* a conic section. [t. Gk.: m.s. *kōnikós* cone-shaped] —**con′i·cal·ly,** *adv.*

conic projection, *Cartog.* a map projection based on the concept of projecting the earth's surface on a conical surface, which is then unrolled to a plane surface.

con·ics (kŏn′Yks), *n.* the branch of mathematics dealing with conic sections.

conic section, *Math.* a curve formed by the intersection of a plane with a right circular cone; an ellipse, a parabola, or a hyperbola.

conic sections, the branch of mathematics dealing with the ellipse, the parabola, and the hyperbola.

Conic sections

The two principal forms are fig. H, hyperbola, and fig. E, ellipse. Fig. P, parabola, is the intermediate case. The degenerate form of the hyperbola is a pair of straight lines, fig. S. Fig. C, circle, is a special case of the ellipse in which the plane becomes perpendicular to the axis of the cone.

co·nid·i·o·phore (kō·nYd′Y·ə·fôr′), *n. Bot.* (in fungi) a special stalk or branch of the mycelium, bearing conidia. [f. *conidio-* (combining form of CONIDIUM) + -PHORE]

co·nid·i·um (kō·nYd′Y·əm), *n., pl.* **-nidia** (-nYd′Yə). *Bot.* (in fungi) an asexual spore formed by abstriction at the top of a hyphal branch, usually thin-walled and windborne. [NL, f. m.s. Gk. *kónis* dust + dim. *-ium*] —**co·nid′i·al, co·nid′i·an,** *adj.*

co·ni·fer (kō′nə·fər, kŏn′ə-), *n.* 1. any of the (mostly evergreen) trees and shrubs constituting the gymnospermous order or group *Coniferales* or *Coniferae,* including the pine, fir, spruce, and other cone-bearing trees and shrubs, and also the yews and their allies which bear drupelike seeds. 2. a plant producing naked seeds in cones, or single naked seeds as in yews, but with pollen always borne in cones. [t. L: cone-bearing]

co·nif·er·ous (kō·nYf′ər·əs), *adj. Bot.* belonging or pertaining to the conifers. See **conifer** (def. 1).

co·ni·ine (kō′nY ēn′, -Yn, -nēn), *n.* a highly poisonous volatile alkaloid, $C_3H_7·C_5H_9NH$, constituting the active principle of the poison hemlock. Also, **co·nin** (kō′nYn). **co·nine** (kō′nēn, -nYn). [f. CONI(UM) + -INE²]

co·ni·um (kō′nY əm), *n.* the poison hemlock, *Conium maculatum.* [t. L, t. Gk.: m. *kóneion* hemlock]

conj. 1. conjugation. 2. conjunction. 3. conjunctive.

con·jec·tur·al (kən·jĕk′chər əl), *adj.* 1. of, or the nature of, or involving conjecture; problematical. 2. given to making conjectures. —**con·jec′tur·al·ly,** *adv.*

con·jec·ture (kən·jĕk′chər), *n., v.,* **-tured, -turing.** —*n.* 1. the formation or expression of an opinion without sufficient evidence for proof. 2. an opinion so formed or expressed. 3. *Obs.* the interpretation of signs or omens. —*v.t.* 4. to conclude or suppose from grounds or evidence insufficient to ensure reliability. —*v.i.* 5. to form conjectures. [ME, t. L: m. *conjectūra* a throwing together, inference] —**con·jec'tur·a·ble,** *adj.* —**con·jec'-tur·a·bly,** *adv.* —**con·jec'tur·er,** *n.* —**Syn.** 2. surmise, inference, supposition, theory, hypothesis. 4. surmise, suppose, presume. See **guess.**

con·join (kən join'), *v.t., v.i.* to join together; unite; combine; associate. [ME *conjoigne*(n), t. F: m. *conjoign-,* s. *conjoindre,* g. L *conjungere* join together] —**con·join'er,** *n.* —**Ant.** disjoin.

con·joint (kən joint'), *adj.* 1. joined together; united; combined; associated. 2. pertaining to or formed by two or more in combination; joint. [t. F, pp. of *conjoindre,* g. L *conjungere* join together] —**con·joint'ly,** *adv.*

con·ju·gal (kŏn'jə gəl), *adj.* 1. of, or of the nature of, marriage. 2. pertaining to the relation of husband and wife. [t. L: s. *conjugālis,* der. *conjux, conjunx* husband or wife] —**con'ju·gal'i·ty,** *n.* —**con'ju·gal·ly,** *adv.*

con·ju·gate (*v.* kŏn'jə gāt'; *adj., n.* kŏn'jə gĭt, -gāt'), *v.,* -**gated, -gating,** *adj., n.* —*v.t.* 1. *Gram.* **a.** to inflect (a verb). **b.** to recite or display all, or some subset of, the inflected forms of (a verb), in a fixed order: *conjugate the present tense verb "be" as I am, you are, he is, we are, you are, they are.* 2. *Obs.* to join together, esp. in marriage. —*v.i.* 3. *Biol.* to unite temporarily. 4. *Gram.* to be characterized by conjugation: *the Latin verb "esse" does not conjugate in the passive voice.* —*adj.* 5. joined together, esp. in a pair or pairs; coupled. 6. *Bot.* (of a pinnate leaf) having only one pair of leaflets. 7. (of words) having a common derivation. 8. *Bibliog.* (of two leaves in a book) forming one sheet. 9. *Math.* (of two points, lines, etc.) so related as to be interchangeable in the enunciation of certain properties. —*n.* 10. one of a group of conjugate words. 11. a conjugate number or axis. [t. L: m.s. *conjugātus,* pp., joined together, yoked] —**con'ju·ga'tive,** *adj.*

con·ju·ga·tion (kŏn'jə gā'shən), *n.* 1. *Gram.* **a.** the inflection of verbs. **b.** the whole set of inflected forms of a verb, or the recital or display thereof in a fixed order: *the conjugation of Latin "amo" begins amō, amas, amat.* **c.** a class of verbs having similar sets of inflected forms, as the Latin *second conjugation.* 2. act of joining. 3. state of being joined together; union; conjunction. 4. *Biol.* **a.** the sexual process in ciliate protozoans in which two animals adhere and exchange nuclear material through a temporary area of fusion. **b.** the temporary union or fusion of two cells or individuals, as in certain plants. —**con'ju·ga'tion·al,** *adj.* —**con'ju·ga'tion·al·ly,** *adv.*

con·junct (kən jŭngkt', kŏn'jŭngkt), *adj.* 1. conjoined; associate. 2. formed by conjunction. 3. *Gram.* **a.** occurring only in combination with an immediately preceding or following form of a particular class, and constituting with this form a single phonetic unit, as *'ll* in English *he'll,* and *n't* in *isn't.* **b.** (of a pronoun) having enclitic or proclitic form and occurring with a verb, as French *me, le, se.* **c.** pertaining to a word so characterized. [late ME, t. L: s. *conjunctus,* pp., joined together] —**con·junct'ly,** *adv.*

con·junc·tion (kən jŭngk'shən), *n.* 1. act of conjoining; combination. 2. state of being conjoined; union; association. 3. a combination of events or circumstances. 4. *Gram.* **a.** (in some languages) one of the major form classes, or "parts of speech," comprising words used to link together words, phrases, clauses, or sentences. **b.** such a word, as English *and* or *but.* **c.** any form of similar function or meaning. 5. *Astron.* **a.** the meeting of heavenly bodies in the same longitude or right ascension. **b.** the situation of two or more heavenly bodies when their longitudes are the same. —**con·junc'-tion·al,** *adj.* —**con·junc'tion·al·ly,** *adv.*

con·junc·ti·va (kŏn'jŭngk tī'və), *n., pl.* -**vas, -vae** (-vē). *Anat.* the mucous membrane which lines the inner surface of the eyelids and is reflected over the forepart of the sclera and the cornea. See diag. under **eye.** [t. NL, short for *membrāna conjunctīva* membrane serving to connect] —**con'junc·ti'val,** *adj.*

con·junc·tive (kən jŭngk'tĭv), *adj.* 1. connective. 2. conjoined; joint. 3. *Gram.* **a.** (of a mode) subjunctive. **b.** (of a pronoun) conjunct. **c.** of the nature of a conjunction. —*n.* 4. *Gram.* a conjunctive word; a conjunction. —**con·junc'tive·ly,** *adv.*

con·junc·ti·vi·tis (kən jŭngk'tə vī'tĭs), *n. Pathol.* inflammation of the conjunctiva. [t. NL. See CONJUNC-TIVA, -ITIS]

con·junc·ture (kən jŭngk'chər), *n.* 1. a combination of circumstances or affairs; a particular state of affairs. 2. a critical state of affairs; a crisis. 3. *Obs.* conjunction; meeting. [f. CON- + JUNCTURE]

con·ju·ra·tion (kŏn'jŏŏ rā'shən), *n.* 1. act of calling on or invoking by a sacred name. 2. an incantation; a spell or charm. 3. supernatural accomplishment by invocation or spell. 4. the practice of legerdemain. 5. *Archaic.* supplication; solemn entreaty.

con·jure (kŭn'jər, kŏn'- for 1-4, 7-9; kən jŏŏr' for 5, 6, 10), *v.,* -**jured, -juring.** —*v.t.* 1. to call upon or command (a devil or spirit) by invocation or spell. 2. to affect or influence by, or as by, invocation or spell. 3. to effect, produce, bring, etc., by, or as by, magic. 4. **conjure up, a.** to call, raise up, or bring into existence by magic. **b.** to bring to mind or recall. 5. to appeal to solemnly or earnestly. 6. to charge solemnly. —*v.i.* 7. to call upon or command a devil or spirit by invocation or spell. 8. to practice magic. 9. to practice legerdemain. 10. *Obs.* to conspire. [ME *conjure*(n), t. OF: m. *conjurer,* t. L: m.s. *conjūrāre* swear together]

con·jur·er (kŭn'jər ər, kŏn'- for 1, 2; kən jŏŏr'ər for 3), *n.* 1. one who conjures spirits or practices magic; magician. 2. one who practices legerdemain; juggler. 3. one who solemnly charges or entreats. Also, **con'jur·or.**

conn (kŏn), *v.t.* to direct the steering of (a ship).

Conn., Connecticut.

con·nate (kŏn'āt), *adj.* 1. existing in a person or thing from birth or origin; inborn; congenital. 2. associated in birth or origin. 3. allied or agreeing in nature; cognate. 4. *Biol.* congenitally or firmly united into one body. [t. LL: m.s. *connātus,* pp., born at the same time] —**con'nate·ly,** *adv.* —**con·na'tion** (kə nā'shən), *n.*

con·nat·u·ral (kə năch'ər əl), *adj.* 1. belonging to a person or thing by nature or from birth or origin. 2. of the same or like nature. [t. ML: s. *connātūrālis*] —**con·nat'u·ral·ly,** *adv.*

Con·naught (kŏn'ôt), *n.* a province in NW Ireland. 446,008 (prelim. 1956); 6611 sq. mi. Irish, **Connacht** (kŏn'ŭKHt, -ŭt).

con·nect (kə nĕkt'), *v.t.* 1. to bind or fasten together; join or unite; link. 2. to establish communication between; put in communication (fol. by *with*). 3. to associate or attach: *the pleasures connected with music.* 4. to associate mentally. —*v.i.* 5. to become connected; join or unite. 6. (of trains, buses, etc.) to run so as to make connections (*with*). [t. L: s. *connectere,* var. of *cōnectere* join, tie] —**con·nect'ed·ly,** *adv.* —**con-nect'er, con·nec'tor,** *n.* —**Syn.** 1. See join. —**Ant.** 1. divide. 3. dissociate.

Con·nect·i·cut (kə nĕt'ə kət), *n.* 1. a State in the NE United States. 2,535,234 pop. (1960); 5009 sq. mi. *Cap.:* Hartford. *Abbr.:* Conn. 2. a river forming the boundary between Vermont and New Hampshire, flowing S through Massachusetts and Connecticut into Long Island Sound. 407 mi.

connecting rod, a rod or bar connecting movable parts, as in an engine.

con·nec·tion (kə nĕk'shən), *n.* 1. act of connecting. 2. state of being connected. 3. anything that connects; a connecting part. 4. association; relationship. 5. a circle of friends or associates, or a member of such a circle. 6. union in due order or sequence of words or ideas. 7. contextual relation. 8. the meeting of means of conveyance for transfer of passengers without delay. 9. a person related to another or others, esp. by marriage or distant consanguinity. 10. a body of persons connected as by political or religious ties. 11. a religious denomination. 12. communication. 13. sexual relation. Also, *Brit.,* **con·nex'ion.** [t. L: m.s. *connexio*] —**con·nec'tion·al,** *adj.* —**Syn.** 1. junction, conjunction, union. 3. bond, tie, link, coupling. 4. affiliation, alliance, combination. 9. relation, relative, kinsman.

con·nec·tive (kə nĕk'tĭv), *adj.* 1. serving or tending to connect. —*n.* 2. that which connects. 3. *Gram.* a word used to connect words, phrases, clauses, and sentences, as a conjunction. 4. *Bot.* the tissue joining the two cells of the anther. —**con·nec'tive·ly,** *adv.* —**con-nec·tiv·i·ty** (kŏn'ĕk tĭv'ə tĭ), *n.*

connective tissue, *Anat.* a tissue, usually of mesoblastic origin, which connects, supports or surrounds other tissues, organs, etc., and occurs in various forms throughout the body.

Con·nel·ly (kŏn'əlĭ), *n.* **Marc,** born 1890, U.S. dramatist.

conn·ing tower (kŏn'ĭng), the low, dome-shaped, armored pilothouse of a warship, used esp. during battle.

con·nip·tion (kə nĭp'shən), *n. U.S. Colloq.* a fit of hysterics or hysterical excitement.

con·niv·ance (kə nī'vəns), *n.* 1. act of conniving. 2. *Law.* **a.** tacit encouragement or assent (without participation) to wrongdoing by another. **b.** the consent by a person to a spouse's conduct, esp. adultery, which is later made the basis of a divorce proceeding or other complaint. Also, **con·niv'ence.**

con·nive (kə nīv'), *v.i.,* -**nived, -niving.** 1. to avoid noticing that which one should oppose or condemn but secretly approves; give aid to wrongdoing, etc., by forbearing to act or speak; be secretly accessory (fol. by *at*): *conniving at their escape.* 2. to coöperate secretly (fol. by *with*). [t. L: s. *connīvēre,* var. of *cōnīvēre* shut the eyes] —**con·niv'er,** *n.*

con·niv·ent (kə nī'vənt), *adj. Bot., Zool.* converging, as petals. [t. L: s. *connīvens,* ppr., winking at]

con·nois·seur (kŏn'ə sûr'), *n.* one competent to pass critical judgments in an art, esp. one of the fine arts, or in matters of taste. [t. F (now *connaisseur*), der. *connaître,* older *connoître,* g. L *cognoscere* come to know]

Con·nor (kŏn'ər), *n.* **Ralph,** (*Charles William Gordon*) 1860-1937, Canadian novelist and clergyman.

con·no·ta·tion (kŏn'ə tā'shən), *n.* 1. act or fact of connoting. 2. that which is connoted; secondary implied or associated meanings (as distinguished from *denotation*): "*It takes a heap o' living to make a house a home.*" 3. *Logic.* the set of attributes constituting the meaning of a term, and thus determining the range of objects to which that term may be applied; comprehension; intension. —**con·no·ta·tive** (kŏn'ə tā'tĭv, kə nō'tə-), *adj.* —**con'no·ta'tive·ly,** *adv.*

con·note (kə nōt'), *v.t.,* -**noted, -noting.** 1. to denote secondarily; signify in addition to the primary meaning; imply. 2. to involve as a condition or accompaniment. [t. ML: m.s. *connotāre* mark with, f. L: *con-* CON- + *notāre* mark. See NOTE, v.]

---

b., blend of, blended; **c.,** cognate with; **d.,** dialect, dialectal; **der.,** derived from; **f.,** formed from; **g.,** going back to; **m.,** modification of; **r.,** replacing; **s.,** stem of; **t.,** taken from; **?,** perhaps. See the full key on inside cover.

con·nu·bi·al (kə nū′bĭ əl, -nōō′-), *adj.* of marriage or wedlock; matrimonial; conjugal. [t. L: s. *connūbiālis,* der. *connūbium* marriage] **—con·nu·bi·al′i·ty,** *n.* **—con·nu′bi·al·ly,** *adv.*

co·noid (kō′noid), *adj.* **1.** Also, **co·noi′dal.** resembling or approaching a cone in shape. **—n. 2.** a geometrical solid formed by the revolution of a conic section about one of its axes. [t. Gk.: m.s. *kōnoeidēs* cone-shaped]

·o·no·scen·te (kô′nō shĕn′tĕ), *n., pl.* **-ti** (-tē). cognoscente.

con·quer (kŏng′kər), *v.t.* **1.** to acquire by force of arms; win in war: *to conquer territories.* **2.** to overcome by force; subdue: *to conquer an enemy.* **3.** to gain or obtain by effort. **4.** to gain the victory over; surmount. **—v.i. 5.** to make conquests; gain the victory. [ME *conquere(n),* t. OF: m. *conquerre,* g. L *conquaerere, conquīrere* seek for] **—con′quer·a·ble,** *adj.* **—con′quer·ing·ly,** *adv.* **—Syn. 2.** vanquish, overpower, overthrow, subjugate. See **defeat.**

·on·quer·or (kŏng′kər ər), *n.* **1.** one who conquers. **2. the Conqueror,** William I of England.

·on·quest (kŏn′kwĕst, kŏng′-), *n.* **1.** act of conquering. **2.** captivation, as of favor or affections. **3.** vanquishment. **4.** territory acquired by conquering. **5.** a person whose favor or affections have been captivated. **6. the Conquest,** the conquering of England by William, Duke of Normandy, in 1066. [ME, t. OF: m. *conqueste,* fem. collective of *conquest,* pp. of *conquerre* conquer] **—Syn. 3.** See **victory.**

con·qui·an (kŏng′kĭ ən), *n.* a card game of the rummy family for two players. [orig. uncert.]

·on·quis·ta·dor (kŏn kwĭs′tə dôr′; *Sp.* kông kēs′tä-dôr′), *n., pl.* **-dors,** *Sp.* **-dores** (-dō′rĕs). one of the Spanish conquerors of Mexico and Peru in the 16th century. [t. Sp.]

Con·rad (kŏn′răd), *n.* **Joseph** (*Teodor Jozef Konrad Korzeniowski*), 1857–1924, Polish-born British novelist.

con·san·guin·e·ous (kŏn′săng gwĭn′Yəs), *adj.* related by birth; akin. Also, **con·san·guine** (kŏn-săng′gwĭn). [t. L: m. *consanguineus*] **—con′san·guin′e·ous·ly,** *adv.*

con·san·guin·i·ty (kŏn′săng gwĭn′ə tY), *n.* **1.** relationship by blood; kinship. **2.** relationship or affinity.

con·science (kŏn′shəns), *n.* **1.** the internal recognition of right and wrong as regards one's actions and motives; the faculty which decides upon the moral quality of one's actions and motives, enjoining one to conformity with the moral law. **2.** conscientiousness. **3.** *Obs.* consciousness. **4.** *Obs.* inmost thought. **5. in** (all) **conscience, a.** in (all) reason and fairness; in truth. **b.** most certainly; assuredly. [ME, t. OF, t. L: m.s. *conscientia* joint knowledge] **—con′science·less,** *adj.*

conscience clause, a clause or article in an act or law which relieves persons whose conscientious or religious scruples forbid their compliance with it.

conscience money, money paid to relieve the conscience, as for obligations previously evaded.

con·sci·en·tious (kŏn′shY ĕn′shəs, kŏn′sY-), *adj.* controlled by or done according to conscience; scrupulous: *a conscientious judge, conscientious conduct.* **—con′sci·en′tious·ly,** *adv.* **—con′sci·en′tious·ness,** *n.* **—Syn.** just, upright, honest, faithful, careful, particular, painstaking.

conscientious objector, one who, when called upon in time of war to fight for his country, refuses to do so because of conscientious scruples, as of religion, morality, etc.

con·scion·a·ble (kŏn′shən ə bəl), *adj.* conformable to conscience; just. **—con′scion·a·bly,** *adv.*

con·scious (kŏn′shəs), *adj.* **1.** awake to one's own existence, sensations, cognitions, etc.; endowed with consciousness. **2.** inwardly sensible or awake to something: *conscious of one's own faults.* **3.** having the mental faculties awake. **4.** present to consciousness; known to oneself; felt: *conscious guilt.* **5.** aware of what one is doing: *a conscious liar.* **6.** aware of oneself; self-conscious. **7.** deliberate or intentional. **8.** *Obs.* inwardly sensible of wrongdoing. [t. L: m. *conscius* knowing] **—con′scious·ly,** *adv.* **—Syn. 2.** Conscious, Aware refer to an individual sense of recognition of something. Conscious implies to be awake or awakened to an inner realization of fact, a truth, a condition, etc.: *he was conscious of an extreme weariness.* Aware lays the emphasis on sense perceptions which lead to consciousness: *he was aware of the odor of tobacco.*

con·scious·ness (kŏn′shəs nYs), *n.* **1.** state of being conscious. **2.** inward sensibility of something; knowledge of one's own existence, sensations, cognitions, etc. **3.** the thoughts and feelings, collectively, of an individual, or of an aggregate of people: *the moral consciousness of a nation.* **4.** activity of mental faculties: *to regain consciousness after a swoon.*

con·script (*adj., n.* kŏn′skrYpt; *v.* kən skrYpt′), *adj.* **1.** enrolled or formed by conscription; drafted: *a conscript soldier or army.* **—n. 2.** a recruit obtained by conscription. **—v.t. 3.** to draft for military or naval service. [t. L: s. *conscriptus,* pp., enrolled]

conscript fathers, 1. the senators of ancient Rome. **2.** any legislators.

con·scrip·tion (kən skrYp′shən), *n.* **1.** compulsory enrollment of men for military or naval service; a draft. **2.** a compulsory monetary payment exacted by a government during war.

con·se·crate (kŏn′sə krāt′), *v.,* **-crated, -crating,** *adj.* **—v.t. 1.** to make or declare sacred; set apart or dedicate to the service of the Deity. **2.** to devote or dedicate to some purpose: *a life consecrated to science.* **3.** to make an object of veneration: *a custom consecrated by time.* **—adj. 4.** *Archaic.* consecrated; sacred. [ME, t. L: m.s. *consēcrātus,* pp., dedicated] **—con′se·cra′tor,** *n.* **—con·se·cra·to·ry** (kŏn′sə krə tōr′Y), *adj.* **—Syn. 2.** devote. **3.** sanctify. **4.** See **holy.**

con·se·cra·tion (kŏn′sə krā′shən), *n.* **1.** act of consecrating; dedication to the service and worship of God. **2.** act of giving the sacramental character to the Eucharistic elements of bread and wine. **3.** ordination to a sacred office, esp. to the episcopate.

con·se·cu·tion (kŏn′sə kū′shən), *n.* **1.** succession; sequence. **2.** logical sequence; inference. [t. L: s. *consecūtio,* der. *consequī* follow after]

con·sec·u·tive (kən sĕk′yə tYv), *adj.* **1.** following one another in uninterrupted succession; uninterrupted in course or succession; successive. **2.** marked by logical sequence. **3.** *Gram.* expressing consequence or result: *a consecutive clause.* [t. F: m. *consécutif,* der. L *consecūtus,* pp., having followed after] **—con·sec′u·tive·ly,** *adv.* **—con·sec′u·tive·ness,** *n.* **—Syn. 1.** See **successive.**

con·sen·su·al (kən sĕn′shŏŏ əl), *adj.* **1.** formed or existing by mere consent: *a consensual marriage.* **2.** *Physiol.* (of an action) involuntarily correlative with a voluntary action, as the contraction of the iris when the eye is opened. [f. L *consensu(s)* agreement + -AL¹] **—con·sen′su·al·ly,** *adv.*

con·sen·sus (kən sĕn′səs), *n.* general agreement or concord: *the consensus is against revision.* [t. L: agreement]

con·sent (kən sĕnt′), *v.i.* **1.** to give assent; agree; comply or yield (fol. by *to* or infinitive). **2.** *Obs.* to agree in sentiment, opinion, etc.; be in harmony. **—n. 3.** assent; acquiescence; permission; compliance. **4.** agreement in sentiment, opinion, a course of action, etc.: *by common consent.* **5.** *Archaic.* accord; concord; harmony. [ME *consente(n),* t. OF: m. *consentir,* g. L *consentīre* feel together] **—con·sent′er,** *n.* **—Syn. 1.** Consent, Assent, Concur imply agreeing with someone. Consent, applying to somewhat important matters, conveys an active and positive idea; it implies making a definite decision to comply with someone's expressed wish: *to consent to become engaged.* Assent conveys a more passive idea; it suggests agreeing intellectually or merely verbally with someone's assertion, request, etc.: *to assent to a speaker's theory, to a proposed arrangement.* To Concur is to show accord in matters of opinion, as of minds independently running along the same channels: *to concur in a judgment about an art exhibit.*

con·sen·ta·ne·ous (kŏn′sĕn tā′nY əs), *adj.* **1.** agreeing or accordant. **2.** done by common consent; unanimous. [t. L: m. *consentāneus* agreeing, fit] **—con′sen·ta′ne·ous·ly,** *adv.* **—con·sen·ta·ne·i·ty** (kən sĕn′tə nē′ə tY), con′sen·ta′ne·ous·ness, *n.*

con·sen·tient (kən sĕn′shənt), *adj.* **1.** agreeing; accordant. **2.** acting in agreement or harmony. **3.** unanimous, as an opinion. **—con·sen′tience,** *n.*

con·se·quence (kŏn′sə kwĕns′), *n.* **1.** act or fact of following as an effect or result upon something antecedent. **2.** that which so follows; an effect or result. **3. in consequence,** as a result. **4.** the conclusion of an argument or inference. **5.** importance or significance: *a matter of no consequence.* **6.** importance in rank or position; distinction. **—Syn. 2.** outcome, issue, upshot, sequel. See **effect. 5.** moment, weight. See **importance. —Ant. 2.** cause.

con·se·quent (kŏn′sə kwĕnt′), *adj.* **1.** following as an effect or result; resulting. **2.** following as a logical conclusion. **3.** logically consistent. **—n. 4.** anything that follows upon something else, with or without implication of causal relation. **5.** *Logic.* the second member of a conditional or hypothetical proposition, as the proposition expressed by the second clause in *If Jones is ill, he will remain indoors.* **6.** *Arith.* the second term of a ratio. [t. L: s. *consequens,* ppr.]

con·se·quen·tial (kŏn′sə kwĕn′shəl), *adj.* **1.** of the nature of a consequence; following as an effect or result, or as a logical conclusion or inference; consequent; resultant. **2.** self-important; pompous. **3.** logically consistent. **4.** of consequence or importance. **—con′se·quen′ti·al′i·ty,** con′se·quen′tial·ness, *n.* **—con′se·quen′tial·ly,** *adv.*

con·se·quent·ly (kŏn′sə kwĕnt′lY), *adv.* by way of consequence; in consequence of something; therefore. **—Syn.** See **therefore.**

con·serv·a·ble (kən sûr′və bəl), *adj.* capable of being conserved; preservable.

con·serv·an·cy (kən sûr′vən sY), *n., pl.* **-cies. 1.** (in England) a commission regulating navigation, fisheries, etc. **2.** conservation of natural resources.

con·ser·va·tion (kŏn′sər vā′shən), *n.* **1.** act of conserving; preservation. **2.** official supervision of rivers, forests, etc. **3.** a district under such supervision. [t. L: s. *conservātio*] **—con′ser·va′tion·al,** *adj.*

con·ser·va·tion·ist (kŏn′sər vā′shən Yst), *n.* one who advocates or promotes conservation, esp. of the natural resources of a country.

conservation of energy, *Physics.* the principle that the total energy of the universe is constant, no energy being created or destroyed in any of the processes of nature.

ăct, āble, dâre, ärt; ĕbb, ēqual; Yf, īce; hŏt, ōver, ôrder, oil, bŏŏk, ōōze, out; ŭp, ūse, ûrge; ə = a in alone; ch, chief; g, give; ng, ring; sh, shoe; th, thin; ŧħ, that; zh, vision. See the full key on inside cover.

con·serv·a·tism (kən sûr′və tĭz′əm), *n.* **1.** the disposition to preserve what is established; opposition to innovation or change. **2.** the principles and practices of political conservatives as (*cap.*) those of the English Conservative Party.

con·serv·a·tive (kən sûr′və tĭv), *adj.* **1.** disposed to preserve existing conditions, institutions, etc. **2.** cautious or moderate: *a conservative estimate.* **3.** having the power or tendency to conserve; preservative. **4.** (*often cap.*) noting or pertaining to a political party whose characteristic principle is opposition to change in the institutions of a country. **—n. 5.** a person of conservative principles. **6.** a member of a conservative party in politics, esp. (*cap.*) in England. **7.** a preservative. **—con·serv′a·tive·ly,** *adv.* **—con·serv′a·tive·ness,** *n.*

Conservative Party, (in Brit. politics) a party now characterized by a tendency to oppose change in prevailing institutions, esp. those associated with capitalism.

con·ser·va·toire (kən sûr′və twär′, -sûr′və twär′; *Fr.* kôn sĕr′vȧ twȧr′), *n.* a conservatory (of music, etc.). [t. F]

con·ser·va·tor (kŏn′sər vā′tər, kən sûr′və tər), *n.* **1.** one who conserves or preserves; a preserver. **2.** *Law.* a guardian; a custodian. **3.** *Brit.* one who has duties in conservancy (def. 1).

con·serv·a·to·ry (kən sûr′və tōr′ĭ), *n., pl.* **-ries,** *adj.* **—n. 1.** *Chiefly Brit.* a greenhouse, usually a glass-covered house or room for growing and displaying plants. **2.** *U.S.* a place for instruction in music and theatrical arts; a school of music. **3.** *Obs.* a place where things are preserved. **—adj. 4.** serving or adapted to conserve; preservative.

con·serve (*v.* kən sûrv′; *n.* kŏn′sûrv, kən sûrv′), *v.,* **-served, -serving,** *n.* **—v.t. 1.** to keep in a safe or sound state; preserve from loss, decay, waste, or injury; keep unimpaired. **2.** to preserve, as fruit, with sugar, etc. [ME, t. L: m.s. *conservāre* preserve] **—n. 3.** (*often pl.*) a mixture of several fruits, cooked to jamlike consistency with sugar, often with nuts and raisins. [t. F, der. *conserver* CONSERVE, v.] **—con·serv′er,** *n.*

con·sid·er (kən sĭd′ər), *v.t.* **1.** to contemplate mentally; meditate or reflect on. **2.** to regard as or deem to be: *I consider him a rascal.* **3.** to think; suppose. **4.** to make allowance for. **5.** to pay attention to; regard: *he never considers others.* **6.** to regard with consideration or respect; hold in honor; respect. **7.** to think about (a position, purchase, etc.) with a view to accepting or buying. **8.** *Archaic.* to view attentively, or scrutinize. **9.** *Obs.* to recompense or remunerate. **—v.i. 10.** to think deliberately or carefully; reflect. **11.** *Obs.* or *Archaic.* to look attentively. [ME *considere(n),* t. L: s. *considerāre* examine closely] **—Syn. 1.** ponder, deliberate, weigh, revolve. See **study.**

con·sid·er·a·ble (kən sĭd′ər ə bəl), *adj.* **1.** worthy of consideration; important; of distinction. **2.** (of an amount, extent, etc.) worthy of consideration; fairly large or great. **—n. 3.** *U.S. Colloq.* much; not a little: *he has done considerable for the community, I found considerable to detain me.* **—con·sid′er·a·bly,** *adv.*

con·sid·er·ate (kən sĭd′ər ĭt), *adj.* **1.** showing consideration or regard for another's circumstances, feelings, etc. **2.** marked by consideration or reflection; deliberate. **3.** *Archaic.* given to consideration or reflection; prudent. **—con·sid′er·ate·ly,** *adv.* **—con·sid′er·ate·ness,** *n.* **—Syn. 1.** See **thoughtful.**

con·sid·er·a·tion (kən sĭd′ər ā′shən), *n.* **1.** act of considering; meditation or deliberation. **2.** regard or account; something taken, or to be taken, into account. **3.** a thought or reflection. **4.** a recompense for service rendered, etc.; a compensation. **5.** *Law.* something which suffices to make an informal promise legally binding, usually some value given in exchange for the promise. **6.** thoughtful or sympathetic regard or respect; thoughtfulness for others. **7.** importance or consequence. **8.** estimation; esteem. **9. in consideration of,** **a.** in view of. **b.** in return for. **10. take into consideration,** to consider; take into account. **11. under consideration,** being considered. **—Syn. 1.** contemplation, advisement, attention. **8.** See **honor.**

con·sid·er·ing (kən sĭd′ər ĭng), *prep.* taking into account; in view of.

con·sign (kən sīn′), *v.t.* **1.** to hand over or deliver formally; commit (fol. by *to*). **2.** to transfer to another's custody or charge; entrust. **3.** to set apart, as to a purpose or use. **4.** *Commerce.* **a.** to transmit, as by public carrier, esp. for sale or custody. **b.** to address for such transmission. **5.** *Obs.* to mark with a sign or seal. **—v.i. Obs. 6.** to yield or submit. **7.** to agree or assent. [t. F: m. *consigner,* t. L: m. *consignāre* furnish or mark with a seal] **—con·sign′a·ble,** *adj.* **—con·sig·na·tion** (kŏn′sĭg nā′shən), *n.*

con·sign·ee (kŏn′sī nē′, -sī nē′), *n.* the person or party to whom merchandise is consigned.

con·sign·ment (kən sīn′mənt), *n.* **1.** act of consigning. **2.** that which is consigned. **3.** *Com.* **a.** property sent to an agent for sale, storage, or shipment. **b. on consignment,** (of goods) sent to an agent for sale, title being held by the consignor until they are sold.

con·sign·or (kən sī′nər, kŏn′sī nôr′), *n.* one who consigns goods, etc. Also, **con·sign·er** (kən sī′nər).

con·sist (kən sĭst′), *v.i.* **1.** to be made up or composed (fol. by *of*). **2.** to be comprised or contained (fol. by *in*). **3.** to be compatible, consistent, or harmonious (fol. by *with*). **4.** *Obs.* to exist together or be capable of existing together. **5.** *Obs.* to stand together; be supported and maintained. [t. L: s. *consistere* place oneself] **—Syn. 1, 2.** CONSIST OF, CONSIST IN are often confused. With CONSIST OF, parts, materials, or ingredients are spoken of: *bread consists of flour, yeast, etc.* With CONSIST IN, something resembling a definition is given: *coöperation consists in helping one another and in sharing losses or gains.*

con·sist·en·cy (kən sĭs′tən sĭ), *n., pl.* **-cies. 1.** material coherence with retention of form; solidity or firmness. **2.** degree of density or viscosity: *the consistency of cream.* **3.** constant adherence to the same principles, course, etc. **4.** agreement, harmony, or compatibility; agreement among themselves of the parts of a complex thing. Also, **con·sist′ence.**

con·sist·ent (kən sĭs′tənt), *adj.* **1.** agreeing or accordant; compatible; not self-opposed or self-contradictory. **2.** constantly adhering to the same principles, course, etc. **3.** holding firmly together; cohering. **4.** *Obs.* fixed; firm; solid. **—con·sist′ent·ly,** *adv.* **—Syn. 1.** congruous, consonant, harmonious. **—Ant. 2.** contradictory.

con·sis·to·ry (kən sĭs′tər ĭ), *n., pl.* **-ries. 1.** any of various ecclesiastical councils or tribunals. **2.** the place where it meets. **3.** the meeting of any such body. **4.** *Rom. Cath. Ch.* an ecclesiastical senate, consisting of the whole body of cardinals, which deliberates upon the affairs of the church. **5.** *Ch. of Eng.* a diocesan court held before the bishop or the bishop's chancellor or commissary in the cathedral church for the trial of ecclesiastical questions. **6.** (in certain Reformed churches) the governing board of a local church or congregation. **7.** an assembly or council. **8.** *Obs.* a council chamber. [ME *consistorie,* t. ONF, t. L: m. *consistōrium* place of assembly] **—con·sis·to·ri·al** (kŏn′sĭs tōr′ĭəl), con·sis·to′ri·an, *adj.*

con·so·ci·ate (*adj., n.* kən sō′shĭ ĭt, -āt′; *v.* kən sō′shĭ āt′), *adj., n., v.i.,* **-ated, -ating.** associate. [t. L: m. s. *consociātus,* pp.] **—con·so·ci·a·tion** (kən sō′sĭ ā′shən, -shĭ-), *n.*

con·so·la·tion (kŏn′sə lā′shən), *n.* **1.** act of consoling. **2.** state of being consoled. **3.** one who or that which consoles. [ME, t. L: s. *consōlātio*] **—Syn. 3.** comfort, solace.

con·sol·a·to·ry (kən sŏl′ə tōr′ĭ), *adj.* affording consolation; consoling.

con·sole¹ (kən sōl′), *v.t.,* **-soled, -soling.** to alleviate the grief or sorrow of; comfort; solace; cheer. [t. L: m. *consōlārī* comfort] **—con·sol′a·ble,** *adj.* **—con·sol′er,** *n.* **—con·sol′ing·ly,** *adv.* **—Syn.** See **comfort.**

con·sole² (kŏn′sōl), *n.* **1.** a desklike structure containing the keyboards, pedals, etc., of an organ, from which the organ is played. **2.** a floor-model radio cabinet. **3.** a console table. **4.** *Archit.* an ornamental bracketlike member, as for supporting a cornice, bust, etc. **5.** a bracket or bracketlike support. [t. F; orig. uncert.]

console table, 1. a table supported by consoles or brackets fixed to a wall. **2.** a table, often with bracketlike legs, designed to fit against a wall.

con·sol·i·date (kən sŏl′ə dāt′), *v.,* **-dated, -dating.** *adj.* **—v.t. 1.** to make solid or firm; solidify; strengthen: *to consolidate gains.* **2.** *Mil.* to strengthen by rearranging the position of ground combat troops after a successful attack. **3.** to bring together compactly in one mass or connected whole; unite; combine: *to consolidate two companies.* **—v.i. 4.** to unite or combine. **5.** to become solid or firm. **—adj. 6.** *Archaic.* consolidated. [t. L: m. s. *consolidātus,* pp., made solid] **—con·sol′i·da′tor,** *n.*

con·sol·i·da·tion (kən sŏl′ə dā′shən), *n.* **1.** act of consolidating; unification. **2.** state of being consolidated; combination. **3.** a consolidated whole. **4.** *Law.* a statutory combination of two or more corporations.

con·sols (kŏn′sŏlz, kən sŏlz′), *n.pl.* the funded government securities of Great Britain, which originated in the consolidation in 1751 of various public securities, chiefly in the form of annuities, into a single debt issue without maturity. [short for *consolidated annuities*]

con·som·mé (kŏn′sə mā′; *Fr.* kôn sô mĕ′), *n.* a strong, clear soup made by boiling meat long and slowly until most of the nutritive properties are extracted. [t. F, prop. pp. of *consommer,* t. L: m. *consummāre* finish]

con·so·nance (kŏn′sə nəns), *n.* **1.** accord or agreement. **2.** correspondence of sounds; harmony of sounds. **3.** *Music.* a simultaneous combination of tones conventionally accepted as being in a state of repose (opposite of *dissonance*). Also, **con′so·nan·cy.**

con·so·nant (kŏn′sə nənt), *n.* **1.** *Phonet.* **a.** (as a member of a syllable) a sound subordinated to another sound that has greater sonority; *w* and *g* in *wig* are subordinate to *i,* the sound of greatest sonority in the syllable, and by virtue of this subordination they are called consonants. **b.** (as a member of an articulation class) a sound made with more or less obstruction of the breath stream in its passage outward, as the *l, s,* and *t* of *list,* each an example of a consonantal subclass: *l* is a *sonorant* (relatively slight obstruction), *s* a *fricative* (relatively great obstruction), and *t* a *stop* (complete obstruction). **2.** a letter which usually represents a consonant sound. **—adj. 3.** in agreement; agreeable or accordant; consistent (fol. by *to* or *with*). **4.** corresponding in sound, as words. **5.** harmonious, as sounds. **6.** *Music.* constituting a consonance. **7.** consonantal. [ME, t. L: s. *consonans* sounding together] **—con′so·nant·ly,** *adv.* **—Ant. 6.** dissonant.

con·so·nan·tal (kŏn'sə nǎn'təl), *adj.* **1.** of, or of the nature of, a consonant. **2.** marked by consonant sounds.

con·sort (*n.* kŏn'sôrt, *v.* kən sôrt'), *n.* **1.** a husband or wife; a spouse. **2.** one vessel or ship accompanying another. **3.** *Obs.* **a.** a companion or partner. **b.** company or association. **c.** accord or agreement. **d.** harmony of sounds. —*v.i.* **4.** to associate; keep company. **5.** to agree or harmonize. —*v.t.* **6.** to associate. **7.** *Obs.* **a.** to accompany; espouse. **b.** to sound in harmony. [late ME, t. F: mate, t. L: s. *consors* partner, sharer, orig. adj., sharing]

con·sor·ti·um (kən sôr'shĭ əm), *n.*, *pl.* **-tia** (-shĭ ə). **1.** a combination of financial institutions, capitalists, etc., for carrying into effect some financial operation requiring large resources of capital. **2.** an association or union. [t. L: partnership]

con·spec·tus (kən spĕk'təs), *n.* **1.** a general or comprehensive view. **2.** a digest; a résumé. [t. L: survey]

con·spic·u·ous (kən spĭk'yŏŏ əs), *adj.* **1.** easy to be seen. **2.** readily attracting the attention. [t. L: m. *conspicuus* visible, striking] —**con·spic'u·ous·ly**, *adv.* —**con·spic'u·ous·ness**, *n.* —**Syn. 1.** visible, manifest, noticeable, clear, marked, salient. **2.** prominent, striking, noteworthy.

con·spir·a·cy (kən spĭr'ə sĭ), *n.*, *pl.* **-cies.** **1.** act of conspiring. **2.** a combination of persons for an evil or unlawful purpose; a plot. **3.** *Law.* an agreement by two or more persons to commit a crime, fraud, or other wrongful act. **4.** *Archaic.* any concurrence in action; combination in bringing about a given result. [f. CONSPIR(E) + -ACY] —**con·spir'a·tor**, *n.* —**con·spir·a·tress** (kən spĭr'ə trĭs), *n. fem.*

con·spire (kən spīr'), *v.*, **-spired, -spiring.** —*v.i.* **1.** to agree together, esp. secretly, to do something reprehensible or illegal; combine for an evil or unlawful purpose. **2.** to act in combination; contribute jointly to a result. —*v.t.* **3.** to plot (something evil or unlawful). [ME *conspire(n)*, t. L: m. *conspīrāre*, lit., breathe together] —**con·spir'er**, *n.* —**con·spir'ing·ly**, *adv.* —**Syn. 1.** complot, intrigue. See **plot**[1]. **2.** combine, concur, coöperate.

con·sta·ble (kŭn'stə bəl, kŏn'-), *n.* **1.** any of various officers of the peace, as one who executes the processes of a justice of the peace. **2.** *Eng.* a policeman. **3.** an officer of high rank in medieval monarchies, usually the commander of all armed forces, particularly in the absence of the ruler. **4.** the keeper or governor of a royal fortress or castle. [ME *conestable*, t. OF, g. LL *comes stabulī* count of the stable, master of the horse] —**con'sta·ble·ship'**, *n.*

Con·sta·ble (kŭn'stə bəl), *n.* **John**, 1776–1837, British painter of landscapes.

con·stab·u·lar·y (kən stăb'yə lĕr'ĭ), *n.*, *pl.* **-laries**, *adj.* —*n.* **1.** the body of constables of a district or locality. **2.** a body of officers of the peace organized on a military basis. **3.** a district under a constable. —*adj.* **4.** pertaining to constables or their duties. [t. ML: m.s. *constabulāria*]

Con·stance (kŏn'stəns), *n.* **1. Lake of,** German, **Boden See.** a lake bounded by Germany, Austria, and Switzerland. 46 mi. long; 207 sq. mi. **2.** German, **Konstanz.** a city in SW Germany, on this lake: important church council, 1414–18. 47,700 (1950).

con·stan·cy (kŏn'stən sĭ), *n.* **1.** quality of being constant; firmness or fortitude; faithfulness to a person or cause. **2.** invariableness, uniformity, or regularity. [t. L: m. s. *constantia* firmness] —**Syn. 1.** steadfastness, fidelity, fealty, loyalty.

con·stant (kŏn'stənt), *adj.* **1.** invariable; uniform; always present. **2.** continuing without intermission. **3.** regularly recurrent; continual; persistent. **4.** steadfast, as in attachment; faithful. **5.** standing firm in mind or purpose; resolute. **6.** *Obs.* certain or confident. —*n.* **7.** something constant, invariable, or unchanging. **8.** *Physics.* a numerical quantity expressing a relation or value that remains unchanged under certain conditions. **9.** *Math.* a quantity assumed to be unchanged throughout a given discussion. [ME, t. L: s. *constans*, ppr., standing firm] —**con'stant·ly**, *adv.* —**Syn. 2.** perpetual, unremitting, uninterrupted. **3.** incessant, ceaseless. See **continual**. **4.** loyal, stanch, true. See **faithful**. **5.** steady, unwavering, unswerving, unshaken. —**Ant. 1.** changeable. **2.** fitful. **3.** sporadic. **4.** unreliable. **5.** wavering.

Con·stant (kôn stän'), *n.* **Jean Joseph Benjamin** (zhän zhō zĕf' bǎn zhà mǎn'), 1845–1902, French portrait painter.

Con·stan·ṭa (kôn stän'tsä), *n.* a seaport in SE Rumania, on the Black Sea. 78,580 (1948).

con·stan·tan (kŏn'stən tǎn'), *n.* an alloy containing 60% copper and 40% nickel, used for electrical resistance heating and thermocouples.

Con·stant de Re·becque (kôn stän' də rə bĕk'), **Henri Benjamin** (än rē' bǎn zhà mǎn'), (*Benjamin Constant*) 1767–1830, French statesman and author.

Con·stan·tine (kŏn'stən tēn'; *Fr.* kôn stän tēn'), *n.* a city in NE Algeria. 143,334 (1954).

Con·stan·tine I (kŏn'stən tīn', -tēn'), **1.** ("*the Great*") A.D. 288?–337, Roman emperor, A.D. 324–337: built Constantinople as new capital; made Christian worship lawful. **2.** 1868–1923, king of Greece, 1913–1917 and 1920–22.

Con·stan·ti·no·ple (kŏn'stǎn tə nō'pəl), *n.* a city built on the site of ancient Byzantium by Constantine the Great, A.D. 330: capital of the Eastern Roman Empire and later of the Ottoman Empire. See **Istanbul.**

con·stel·late (kŏn'stə lāt'), *v.i.*, *v.t.*, **-lated, -lating.** to cluster together, as stars in a constellation.

con·stel·la·tion (kŏn'stə lā'shən), *n.* **1.** *Astron.* **a.** any of various groups of stars to which definite names have been given, as Ursa Major, Ursa Minor, Boötes, Cancer, Orion. **b.** a division of the heavens occupied by such a group. **2.** *Astrol.* **a.** the grouping or relative position of the stars as supposed to influence events, esp. at a person's birth. **b.** *Obs.* character as supposed to be determined by the stars. **3.** any brilliant assemblage. [ME, t. LL: s. *constellātio* group of stars]

con·ster (kŏn'stər), *v.t.*, *v.i.* *Obs.* construe.

con·ster·nate (kŏn'stər nāt'), *v.t.*, **-nated, -nating.** to dismay; terrify (usually used in the passive).

con·ster·na·tion (kŏn'stər nā'shən), *n.* amazement and dread tending to confound the faculties; paralyzing dismay. [t. L: s. *consternātio*] —**Syn.** bewilderment, alarm, terror, fear, panic. —**Ant.** equanimity.

con·sti·pate (kŏn'stə pāt'), *v.t.*, **-pated, -pating. 1.** to cause constipation in; make costive. **2.** *Obs.* to crowd or pack closely together. [t. L: m. s. *constīpātus*, pp., pressed together] —**con'sti·pat'ed**, *adj.*

con·sti·pa·tion (kŏn'stə pā'shən), *n.* **1.** a condition of the bowels marked by defective or difficult evacuation. **2.** *Obs.* act of crowding anything into a smaller compass; condensation.

con·stit·u·en·cy (kən stĭch'ŏŏ ən sĭ), *n.*, *pl.* **-cies. 1.** a body of constituents; the body of voters, or, loosely, of residents, in a district represented by an elective officer. **2.** the district itself. **3.** any body of supporters, customers, etc.; a clientele.

con·stit·u·ent (kən stĭch'ŏŏ ənt), *adj.* **1.** serving to make up a thing; component; elementary: *constituent parts.* **2.** having power to frame or alter a political constitution or fundamental law (as distinguished from lawmaking power): *a constituent assembly.* —*n.* **3.** a constituent element, material, etc.; a component. **4.** a voter, or (loosely) a resident, in a district represented by an elective officer. **5.** *Gram.* an element that forms part of a construction. The **immediate constituents** are the largest parts (usually two) into which a construction is divisible, any or all of them sometimes further divisible into constituents of their own; the **ultimate constituents** are all the parts of a construction which are not further divisible. The sentence *John's hat looked slightly stained* has the immediate constituents *John's hat* (subject) and *looked slightly stained* (predicate), and the ultimate constituents *John, -'s, hat, look, -ed, slight, -ly, stain,* and *-ed.* [t. L: s. *constituens,* ppr., setting up] —**Syn. 3.** See **element.**

con·sti·tute (kŏn'stə tūt', -tōōt'), *v.t.*, **-tuted, -tuting. 1.** (of elements, etc.) to compose; form. **2.** to appoint to an office or function; make or create. **3.** to set up or establish (laws, etc.); found (an institution, etc.). **4.** to give legal form to (an assembly, court, etc.). **5.** to make up or form of elements, material, etc.; frame. **6.** *Obs.* to set or place. [t. L: m. s. *constitūtus,* pp., set up, established] —**con'sti·tut'er, con'sti·tu'tor,** *n.*

con·sti·tu·tion (kŏn'stə tū'shən, -tōō'-), *n.* **1.** the way in which anything is constituted; make-up or composition: *the physical constitution of the sun.* **2.** the physical character of the body as to strength, health, etc.: *a strong constitution.* **3.** character or condition of mind; disposition; temperament. **4.** act of constituting; establishment. **5.** state of being constituted; formation. **6.** any established arrangement or custom. **7.** the system of fundamental principles according to which a nation, state, corporation, etc., is governed: *the British constitution.* **8.** the document embodying these principles. [ME, t. L: s. *constitūtio*]

Con·sti·tu·tion (kŏn'stə tū'shən, -tōō'-), *n.* **The,** an American 44-gun frigate, famous for its exploits in the War of 1812, and popularly called "Old Ironsides."

con·sti·tu·tion·al (kŏn'stə tū'shən əl, -tōō'-), *adj.* **1.** belonging to or inherent in a person's constitution of body or mind: *a constitutional weakness.* **2.** beneficial to, or designed to benefit, the bodily constitution: *a constitutional walk.* **3.** pertaining to the constitution or composition of a thing; essential. **4.** pertaining to, in accordance with, or subject to the constitution of a state, etc.: *a constitutional monarchy.* **5.** having the power of, or existing by virtue of and subject to, a constitution or fundamental organic law: *a constitutional government.* **6.** forming a part of, or authorized by, the constitution or fundamental organic law of a nation or state. —*n.* **7.** a walk or other exercise taken for the benefit of the health. —**con'sti·tu·tion·al·ly,** *adv.*

con·sti·tu·tion·al·ism (kŏn'stə tū'shən əlĭz'əm, -tōō'-), *n.* **1.** the principles of constitutional government, or adherence to them. **2.** constitutional rule or authority.

con·sti·tu·tion·al·ist (kŏn'stə tū'shən əl ĭst, -tōō'-), *n.* **1.** an adherent or advocate of constitutionalism, or of an existing constitution. **2.** a student of or writer on a political constitution.

con·sti·tu·tion·al·i·ty (kŏn'stə tū'shə nǎl'ə tĭ, -tōō'-), *n.* **1.** quality of being constitutional. **2.** accordance with the constitution of a state, etc. (as a measure or norm of lawmaking power).

Constitution of the United States, The, the fundamental or organic law of the U. S., framed in 1787 by the Constitutional Convention. It went into effect March 4, 1789.

con·sti·tu·tive (kŏn′stə tū′tĭv, -tōō′-), *adj.* **1.** constituent; making a thing what it is; essential. **2.** having power to establish or enact. —**con′sti·tu′tive·ly,** *adv.*

con·strain (kən strān′), *v.t.* **1.** to force, compel, or oblige; bring about by compulsion: *to constrain obedience.* **2.** to confine forcibly, as by bonds. **3.** to repress or restrain. [ME *constreign(en),* t. OF: m. *constreindre,* g. L *constringere* draw together] —**con·strain′a·ble,** *adj.* —**con·strain′er,** *n.* —**Syn. 3.** check, bind, confine.

con·strained (kən strānd′), *adj.* forced; cramped; restrained; stiff or unnatural: *a constrained smile or manner.* —**con·strain·ed·ly** (kən strā′nĭd lĭ), *adv.*

con·straint (kən strānt′), *n.* **1.** confinement or restriction. **2.** repression of natural feelings and impulses. **3.** unnatural restraint in manner, etc.; embarrassment. **4.** something that constrains. **5.** act of constraining. **6.** condition of being constrained. [ME *constreinte,* t. OF, prop. pp. fem. of *constreindre* CONSTRAIN]

con·strict (kən strĭkt′), *v.t.* to draw together; compress; cause to contract or shrink. [t. L: s. *constrictus,* pp., drawn together] —**Syn.** cramp, squeeze, bind, tighten. —**Ant.** expand.

con·stric·tion (kən strĭk′shən), *n.* **1.** act of constricting. **2.** state of being constricted. **3.** a constricted part. **4.** something that constricts.

con·stric·tive (kən strĭk′tĭv), *adj.* **1.** constricting, or tending to constrict. **2.** pertaining to constriction.

con·stric·tor (kən strĭk′tər), *n.* **1.** a snake that crushes its prey in its coils. **2.** *Anat.* a muscle that constricts a hollow part of the body, as the pharynx. **3.** one who or that which constricts. [t. NL]

con·stringe (kən strĭnj′), *v.t.,* **-stringed, -stringing.** to constrict; compress; cause to contract. [t. L: m.s. *constringere.* Cf. CONSTRAIN]

con·strin·gent (kən strĭn′jənt), *adj.* **1.** constringing. **2.** causing constriction. —**con·strin′gen·cy,** *n.*

con·struct (*v.* kən strŭkt′, *n.* kŏn′strŭkt), *v.t.* **1.** to form by putting together parts; build; frame; devise. **2.** *Geom., etc.* to draw, as a figure, so as to fulfill given conditions. —*n.* **3.** something constructed. **4.** a complex image or idea resulting from a synthesis by the mind. [t. L: s. *constructus,* pp., constructed, piled or put together] —**con·struc′tor, con·struct′er,** *n.* —**Syn. 1.** erect, form. See **make.**

con·struc·tion (kən strŭk′shən), *n.* **1.** act or art of constructing. **2.** the way in which a thing is constructed; structure: *objects of similar construction.* **3.** that which is constructed; a structure. **4.** *Gram.* **a.** the arrangement of two or more forms in a grammatical unit. Constructions involving bound forms are called morphological, as the bound forms *fif-* and *-teen* in *fifteen.* Those involving only free forms are called syntactic, as *the good man,* *in the house.* Cf. **bound form, free form. b.** a word or phrase consisting of two or more forms arranged in a particular way. **5.** explanation or interpretation, as of a law or a text, or of conduct or the like. —**con·struc′tion·al,** *adj.*

con·struc·tion·ist (kən strŭk′shən ĭst), *n.* one who construes or interprets, esp. laws or the like.

con·struc·tive (kən strŭk′tĭv), *adj.* **1.** constructing, or tending to construct: *constructive (as opposed to destructive) criticism.* **2.** of, pertaining to, or of the nature of construction; structural. **3.** deduced by construction or interpretation; inferential: *constructive permission.* **4.** *Law.* not actually existing, but having the same legal effects as one that does: *a constructive contract.* —**con·struc′tive·ly,** *adv.* —**con·struc′tive·ness,** *n.*

con·strue (kən strōō′ *or,* esp. *Brit.* kŏn′strōō), *v.,* **-strued, -struing.** —*v.t.* **1.** to show the meaning or intention of; explain; interpret; put a particular interpretation on. **2.** to deduce by construction or interpretation; infer. **3.** to translate, esp. orally. **4.** to explain the syntax of: *in construing the sentence "He caught a fish" one says "he" is the subject, "caught a fish" is the predicate, "(a) fish" is the direct object of the verb "caught," etc.* **5.** to arrange or combine (words, etc.) syntactically. —*v.i.* **6.** to admit of grammatical analysis or interpretation. [ME *construe(n),* t. L: m. *construere* build up, pile together] —**con·stru′a·ble,** *adj.* —**con·stru·a·bil′i·ty,** *n.* —**con·stru′er,** *n.*

con·sub·stan·tial (kŏn′səb stăn′shəl), *adj.* of one and the same substance, essence, or nature. [t. LL: s. *consubstantiālis,* f. L: *con-* CON- + *s. substantia* substance + *-ālis* -AL¹] —**con′sub·stan′ti·al·i·ty,** *n.* —**con′sub·stan′tial·ly,** *adv.*

con·sub·stan·ti·ate (kŏn′səb stăn′shĭ āt′), *v.,* **-ated, -ating.** —*v.i.* **1.** to profess the doctrine of consubstantiation. **2.** to become united in one common substance or nature. —*v.t.* **3.** to unite in one common substance or nature. **4.** to regard as so united. [t. ML: m.s. *consubstantiātus,* pp., identified in substance]

con·sub·stan·ti·a·tion (kŏn′səb stăn′shĭ ā′shən), *n.* *Theol.* the doctrine that the substance of the body and blood of Christ coexist in and with the substance of bread and wine of the Eucharist.

con·sue·tude (kŏn′swĭ tūd′, -tōōd′), *n.* custom, esp. as having legal force. [ME, t. L: m. *consuētūdo* custom]

con·sue·tu·di·nar·y (kŏn′swĭ tū′də nĕr′ĭ, -tōō′-), *adj.* customary.

con·sul (kŏn′səl), *n.* **1.** an agent appointed by an independent state to reside in a foreign state and discharge certain administrative duties. **2.** either of the two chief magistrates of the ancient Roman republic. **3.** one of the three supreme magistrates of the French republic from 1799 to 1804. [t. L] —**con′su·lar,** *adj.* —**con′sul·ship,** *n.*

consular agent, an officer performing the duties of a consul at a place of small commercial importance.

con·su·late (kŏn′sə lĭt), *n.* **1.** the premises officially occupied by a consul. **2.** consulship. **3.** (*often cap.*) a government by consuls, as in France from 1799 to 1804. [t. L: m.s. *consulātus*]

consul general, a consular officer of the highest rank, as one stationed at a place of considerable commercial importance.

con·sult (*v.* kən sŭlt′; *n.* kŏn′sŭlt, kən sŭlt′), *v.t.* **1.** to seek counsel from; ask advice of. **2.** to refer to for information. **3.** to have regard for (a person's interest, convenience, etc.) in making plans. **4.** *Obs.* to meditate, plan, or contrive. —*v.i.* **5.** to consider or deliberate; take counsel; confer (fol. by *with*). —*n.* **6.** *Rare.* **a.** consultation. **b.** a council. [t. L: s. *consultāre,* freq. of *consulere* deliberate, take counsel. Cf. COUNSEL, *n.,* CONSUL] —**con·sult′a·ble,** *adj.* —**con·sult′er,** *n.* —**Syn. 1.** CONSULT, CONFER imply talking over a situation or a subject with someone to decide points in doubt. To CONSULT is to seek from a presumably qualified personal or an impersonal source advice, opinion, etc.: *to consult an authority.* To CONFER is to interchange views in order to throw light on a subject under consideration: *the partners conferred concerning their business policy.*

con·sult·ant (kən sŭl′tənt), *n.* **1.** one who consults. **2.** one who gives professional or expert advice.

con·sul·ta·tion (kŏn′səl tā′shən), *n.* **1.** act of consulting; conference. **2.** a meeting for deliberation.

con·sult·a·tive (kən sŭl′tə tĭv), *adj.* of consultation; advisory. Also, **con·sul·ta·to·ry** (kən sŭl′tə tôr′ĭ).

con·sult·ing (kən sŭl′tĭng), *adj.* employed in giving professional advice, either to the public or to those practicing the profession: *a consulting physician.*

con·sume (kən sōōm′), *v.,* **-sumed, -suming.** —*v.t.* **1.** to destroy or expend by use; use up. **2.** to eat or drink up; devour. **3.** to destroy, as by decomposition or burning. **4.** to spend (money, time, etc.) wastefully. **5.** to absorb; engross. —*v.i.* **6.** to be consumed; suffer destruction; waste away. [ME *consume(n),* t. L: m. *consūmere* take up completely] —**con·sum′a·ble,** *adj., n.* —**Syn. 1.** exhaust, expend. **4.** squander, dissipate.

con·sum·ed·ly (kən sōō′mĭd lĭ), *adv.* excessively; extremely.

con·sum·er (kən sōō′mər), *n.* **1.** one who or that which consumes. **2.** *Econ.* one who uses up a commodity or service (opposed to *producer*).

consumers' goods, *Econ.* goods ready for consumption in satisfaction of human wants, as clothing, food, etc., and which are not utilized in any further production.

con·sum·mate (*v.* kŏn′sə māt′, *adj.* kən sŭm′ĭt), *v.,* **-mated, -mating,** *adj.* —*v.t.* **1.** to bring to completion or perfection. **2.** to complete (a marriage) by sexual intercourse. —*adj.* **3.** complete or perfect; supremely qualified; of the highest quality. [late ME, t. L: m. s. *consummātus,* pp., brought to the highest degree] —**con·sum′mate·ly,** *adv.* —**con′sum·ma′tive, con′sum·ma′tor,** *n.* —**Syn. 1.** complete, perfect, fulfill, accomplish, achieve. **3.** excellent, finished, supreme.

con·sum·ma·tion (kŏn′sə mā′shən), *n.* the act of consummating, or the state of being consummated; completion; perfection; fulfillment.

con·sump·tion (kən sŭmp′shən), *n.* **1.** act of consuming; destruction or decay. **2.** destruction by use. **3.** the amount consumed. **4.** *Econ.* the using up of goods and services having an exchangeable value. **5.** *Pathol.* **a.** a wasting disease, esp. tuberculosis of the lungs. **b.** progressive wasting of the body. [ME, t. L: s. *consumptio* a wasting]

con·sump·tive (kən sŭmp′tĭv), *adj.* **1.** tending to consume; destructive; wasteful. **2.** pertaining to consumption by use. **3.** *Pathol.* **a.** pertaining to or of the nature of consumption. **b.** disposed to or affected with consumption. —*n.* **4.** one who suffers from consumption.—**con·sump′tive·ly,** *adv.* —**con·sump′tive·ness,** *n.*

cont., **1.** containing. **2.** contents. **3.** continent. **4.** continental. **5.** continued.

con·tact (kŏn′tăkt), *n.* **1.** state or fact of touching; a touching or meeting of bodies. **2.** immediate proximity or association. **3.** *Elect.* **a.** a junction, usually surface, between electric conductors, usually solids, which may be presumed to permit current flow. **b.** a conducting part which acts together with another part to complete or to interrupt a circuit. **4.** *Med.* **a.** one who has lately been exposed to an infected person. **b.** inflammation of the skin due to contact with an irritating agent. **5.** *Sociol.* **a.** a condition in which two or more individuals or groups are placed in communication with one another. **b. categoric contact,** acting toward one on the basis of the type or group of people he represents rather than on the basis of his personal make-up. **c. primary contact,** a contact characterized by intimacy and personal familiarity. **d. secondary contact,** a contact characterized by impersonal and detached interest on the part of the participants, such as between strangers. **e. sympathetic contact,** acting toward an individual on the basis of his personal or individual make-up instead of on the basis of his group membership. **—*v.t.* 6.** to put or bring into contact. **7.** *Colloq.* to get in touch with (a person). **—*v.i.* 8.** to enter into or be in contact. [t. L: s. *contactus* a touching]

contact flight, *Aeron.* a flight in which the pilot always sees land or water over which he passes.

contact lenses, devices to aid defective vision inconspicuously, consisting of small plastic lenses which cover the irises and are held in place by eye fluid.

con·tac·tor (kŏn′tăk tər), *n. Elect.* a device, operated other than by hand, for repeatedly establishing and interrupting an electric power circuit.

con·ta·gion (kən tā′jən), *n.* **1.** the communication of disease by direct or indirect contact. **2.** a disease so communicated. **3.** the medium by which a contagious disease is transmitted. **4.** pestilential influence; hurtful contact or influence. **5.** the communication of any influence, as enthusiasm, from one to another. [ME, t. L: s. *contāgio* a contact]

con·ta·gious (kən tā′jəs), *adj.* **1.** communicable to other individuals, as a disease. **2.** causing or involving contagion; noxious. **3.** tending to spread from one to another: *panic is contagious.* [ME, t. LL: m. s. *contāgiōsus*] **—con·ta′gious·ly,** *adv.* **—con·ta′gious·ness,** *n.*
—Syn. 3. CONTAGIOUS, INFECTIOUS have scientific uses in which they are precisely defined; but in popular use in referring to disease, the words are often confused. In popular figurative use, in which both have favorable connotations, they are differentiated to some extent. CONTAGIOUS emphasizes the rapidity with which the "contagion" spreads: *contagious laughter ran through the hall.* INFECTIOUS suggests the pleasantly irresistible quality of the source of "contagion": *his infectious enthusiasm stimulated applause.*

con·tain (kən tān′), *v.t.* **1.** to have within itself; hold within fixed limits. **2.** to be capable of holding; have capacity for. **3.** to have as contents or constituent parts; comprise; include. **4.** to keep within proper bounds; restrain: *to contain oneself or one's feelings.* **5.** *Math.* to be divisible by, without a remainder. **6.** to be equal to: *a quart contains two pints.* [ME *conteine(n),* t. OF: m. *contenir,* g. L *continēre* hold together, hold back] **—con·tain′a·ble,** *adj.*
—Syn. 1. CONTAIN, ACCOMMODATE, HOLD express the idea that something is so designed that something else can exist or be placed within it. CONTAIN refers to what is actually within a given container. HOLD emphasizes the idea of causing to remain in position, or keeping within bounds; it refers also to the greatest amount or number that can be kept within a given container. ACCOMMODATE means to contain comfortably or conveniently, or to meet the needs of a certain number. A passenger plane which ACCOMMODATES fifty passengers may be able to HOLD sixty, but at a given time may CONTAIN only thirty.

con·tain·er (kən tā′nər), *n.* anything that contains or can contain, as a carton, box, crate, can, etc.

contam., contamination.

con·tam·i·nate (*v.* kən tăm′ə nāt′; *adj.* -nĭt, -nāt′), *v.,* **-nated, -nating,** *adj.* **—*v.t.* 1.** to render impure by contact or mixture. **—*adj.* 2.** *Archaic.* contaminated. [t. L: m. s. *contāminātus,* pp.] **—con·tam′i·na′tive,** *adj.* **—con·tam′i·na′tor,** *n.* **—Syn. 1.** defile, pollute, befoul, sully, taint, infect, poison, corrupt.

con·tam·i·na·tion (kən tăm′ə nā′shən), *n.* **1.** act of contaminating. **2.** state of being contaminated. **3.** something that contaminates.

contd., continued.

conte (kônt), *n., pl.* **contes** (kônts; *Fr.* kônt). a tale or short story, esp. of extraordinary and usually imaginary events. [t. F]

con·temn (kən těm′), *v.t.* to treat disdainfully or scornfully; view with contempt. [t. L: s. *contemnere* despise] **—con·temn′er, con·tem·nor** (kən těm′nər), *n.*

con·tem·plate (kŏn′təm plāt′, kən těm′plāt), *v.,* **-plated, -plating. —*v.t.* 1.** to look at or view with continued attention; observe thoughtfully. **2.** to consider attentively; reflect upon. **3.** to have as a purpose; intend. **4.** to have in view as a future event. **—*v.i.* 5.** to think studiously; meditate; consider deliberately. [t. L: m. s. *contemplātus,* pp., having surveyed] **—con′tem·pla′tor,** *n.* **—Syn. 1.** observe, regard. **2.** design, plan.

con·tem·pla·tion (kŏn′təm plā′shən), *n.* **1.** act of contemplating; thoughtful observation or consideration; reflection. **2.** religious meditation. **3.** purpose or intention. **4.** prospect or expectation.

con·tem·pla·tive (kŏn′təm plā′tĭv, kən těm′plə-), *adj.* given to or characterized by contemplation. **—con′tem·pla′tive·ly,** *adv.* **—con′tem·pla′tive·ness,** *n.* **—Syn.** thoughtful, reflective, meditative. **—Ant.** active.

con·tem·po·ra·ne·ous (kən těm′pə rā′nĭ əs), *adj.* contemporary. [t. L: m. *contemporāneus*] **—con·tem′po·ra′ne·ous·ly,** *adv.* **—con·tem′po·ra′ne·ous·ness,** *n.*

con·tem·po·rar·y (kən těm′pə rěr′ĭ), *adj., n., pl.* **-raries. —*adj.* 1.** belonging to the same time; existing or occurring at the same time. **2.** of the same age or date. **—*n.* 3.** one belonging to the same time or period with another or others. **4.** a person of the same age as another [f. CON- + TEMPORARY] **—Syn. 1.** coeval, coexistent.

con·tem·po·rize (kən těm′pə rīz′), *v.,* **-rized, -rizing. —*v.t.* 1.** to place in, or regard as belonging to, the same age or time. **—*v.i.* 2.** to be contemporary.

con·tempt (kən těmpt′), *n.* **1.** act of contemning or despising. **2.** the feeling with which one regards anything considered mean, vile, or worthless; disdain; scorn. **3.** state of being despised; dishonor; disgrace. **4.** *Law.* **a.** disobedience to, or open disrespect of, the rules or orders of a court or legislature. **b.** an act showing this disrespect. [ME, t. L: s. *contemptus* scorn]
—Syn. 2. CONTEMPT, DISDAIN, SCORN imply strong feelings of disapproval combined with disgust or derision. CONTEMPT is disapproval tinged with disgust for what seems mean, base, or worthless: *to feel contempt for a weakling.* DISDAIN is a feeling that something is beneath the level of one's own dignity or is unworthy of one's notice or acceptance: *disdain for crooked dealing.* SCORN denotes derisive, open, or undisguised contempt, as for a thing thought unworthy of considerate treatment: *scorn for attempted evasion of punishment by blaming others.* **—Ant. 2.** respect.

con·tempt·i·ble (kən těmp′tə bəl), *adj.* **1.** deserving of or held in contempt; despicable. **2.** *Obs.* contemptuous. **—con·tempt′i·bil′i·ty, con·tempt′i·ble·ness,** *n.* **—con·tempt′i·bly,** *adv.* **—Syn. 1.** mean, abject, low, base. **—Ant. 1.** admirable.

con·temp·tu·ous (kən těmp′chŏŏ əs), *adj.* manifesting or expressing contempt or disdain; scornful. [f. L *contemptu(s)* scorn + -OUS] **—con·temp′tu·ous·ly,** *adv.* **—con·temp′tu·ous·ness,** *n.* **—Syn.** disdainful, sneering, insolent, arrogant, supercilious, haughty.

con·tend (kən těnd′), *v.i.* **1.** to struggle in opposition. **2.** to strive in rivalry; compete; vie. **3.** to strive in debate; dispute earnestly. **—*v.t.* 4.** to assert or maintain earnestly. [t. L: s. *contendere* stretch out] **—con·tend′er,** *n.* **—Syn. 1.** wrestle, grapple, battle, fight. **2.** See **compete. 3.** argue, wrangle. **—Ant. 3.** agree.

con·tent[1] (kŏn′těnt; *rarely* kən těnt′), *n., pl.* **contents** (kŏn′těnts *or, esp. Brit.* kən těnts′). **1.** (*usually pl.*) that which is contained: *the contents of a cask, room, or book.* **2.** substance or purport, as of a document. **3.** the sum of the attributes or notions composing a given conception; the substance or matter of cognition, etc. **4.** power of containing; capacity; volume. **5.** area; extent; size. **6.** the amount contained. [t. L: s. *contentum* that which is contained, prop. pp. neut.]

con·tent[2] (kən těnt′), *adj.* **1.** having the desires limited to what one has; satisfied. **2.** easy in mind. **3.** willing or resigned; assenting. **—*v.t.* 4.** to make content. **—*n.* 5.** state or feeling of being contented; contentment. **6.** (in the British House of Lords) an affirmative vote or voter. [ME, t. L: s. *contentus* satisfied, prop. pp.] **—Syn. 4.** appease, gratify. See **satisfy.**

con·tent·ed (kən těn′tĭd), *adj.* satisfied, as with what one has or with something mentioned; content; resigned. **—con·tent′ed·ly,** *adv.* **—con·tent′ed·ness,** *n.*

con·ten·tion (kən těn′shən), *n.* **1.** a struggling together in opposition; strife. **2.** a striving in rivalry; competition; a contest. **3.** strife in debate; a dispute; a controversy. **4.** a point contended for or affirmed in controversy. [ME, t. L: s. *contentio* strife] **—Syn. 1.** struggle, conflict, combat. **3.** disagreement, dissension, debate, wrangle, altercation.

con·ten·tious (kən těn′shəs), *adj.* **1.** given to contention: *a contentious crew.* **2.** characterized by contention: *contentious issues.* **3.** *Law.* pertaining to causes between contending parties. [t. L: m.s. *contentiōsus*] **—con·ten′tious·ly,** *adv.* **—con·ten′tious·ness,** *n.*

con·tent·ment (kən těnt′mənt), *n.* **1.** state of being contented; satisfaction; ease of mind. **2.** *Archaic.* act of contenting. **—Syn. 1.** See **happiness.**

con·ter·mi·nous (kən tûr′mə nəs), *adj.* **1.** having a common boundary; bordering; contiguous. **2.** meeting at their ends. **3.** having the same boundaries or limits; coextensive. Also, **con·ter′mi·nal.** [t. L: m. *conterminus*] **—con·ter′mi·nous·ly,** *adv.*

con·test (*n.* kŏn′těst; *v.* kən těst′), *n.* **1.** struggle for victory or superiority. **2.** conflict between competitors; a competition. **3.** strife in argument; dispute; controversy. **—*v.t.* 4.** to struggle or fight for, as in battle. **5.** to argue against; dispute. **6.** to call in question. **7.** to contend for in rivalry. **—*v.i.* 8.** to dispute; contend; compete. [t. F: s. *contester,* t. L: m. *contestārī* call to witness, bring a legal action] **—con·test′a·ble,** *adj.* **—con·test′er,** *n.* **—Syn. 1.** See **fight. 2.** rivalry, match, tournament, game. **4.** See **compete. 5.** controvert, oppose. **6.** challenge. **7.** strive, compete, vie.

con·test·ant (kən těs′tənt), *n.* **1.** one who takes part in a contest or competition. **2.** one who contests the result of an election. **3.** *Law.* the party who, in proceedings in the probate court, contests the validity of a will. [t. F, ppr. of *contester* contest, used as n.]

con·tes·ta·tion (kŏn′těs tā′shən), *n.* **1.** act of contesting. **2.** an assertion contended for.

con·text (kŏn′těkst), *n.* the parts of a discourse or writing which precede or follow, and are directly connected with, a given passage or word. [late ME, t. L: s. *contextus* connection]

con·tex·tu·al (kən těks′chŏŏ əl), *adj.* of or pertaining to the context; depending on the context. [f. L *contextu(s)* connection + -AL[1]] **—con·tex′tu·al·ly,** *adv.*

con·tex·ture (kən těks′chər), *n.* **1.** the disposition and union of the constituent parts of anything; constitution; structure. **2.** an interwoven structure; a fabric. **3.** act of weaving together. **4.** fact or manner of being woven together. [t. F, der. L *contexere* weave together. See CON-, TEXTURE]

con·ti·gu·i·ty (kŏn′tə gū′ə tĭ), *n., pl.* **-ties. 1.** state of being contiguous. **2.** a series of things in continuous connection; a continuous mass or extent.

ăct, āble, dâre, ärt; ěbb, ēqual; ĭf, īce; hŏt, ōver, ôrder, oil, bŏŏk, ōōze, out; ŭp, ūse, ûrge; ə = a in alone; ch, chief; g, give; ng, ring; sh, shoe; th, thin; ᵺ, that; zh, vision. See the full key on inside cover.

con·tig·u·ous (kən tǐg′yŏŏ əs), *adj.* **1.** touching; in contact. **2.** in close proximity without actually touching; near. [t. L: m. *contiguus* touching] —**con·tig′u·ous·ly**, *adv.* —**con·tig′u·ous·ness**, *n.*

con·ti·nence (kŏn′tə nəns), *n.* self-restraint, esp. in regard to sexual passion. Also, **con′ti·nen·cy.** [ME, t. L: m. s. *continentia*]

con·ti·nent (kŏn′tə nənt), *n.* **1.** one of the main land masses of the globe, usually reckoned as seven in number (Europe, Asia, Africa, North America, South America, Australia and Antarctica). **2.** the mainland (as distinguished from islands or peninsulas). **3. the Continent,** the mainland of Europe (as distinguished from the British Isles). **4.** a continuous tract or extent, as of land. **5.** *Archaic.* that which contains, holds, or comprises. —*adj.* **6.** exercising restraint in relation to the desires or passions; temperate. **7.** characterized by self-restraint in regard to sexual passion; chaste. **8.** *Rare.* containing; being a container; capacious. **9.** *Obs.* restraining or restrictive. **10.** *Obs.* continuous; forming a continuous tract, as land. [ME, t. L: s. *continens*, pp., lit., holding together]

con·ti·nen·tal (kŏn′tə nĕn′təl), *adj.* **1.** of, or of the nature of, a continent. **2.** (*usually cap.*) of or pertaining to the mainland of Europe. **3.** (*cap.*) of the colonies during and immediately after the Revolutionary War: *the Continental Congress.* —*n.* **4.** (*cap.*) a soldier of the Continental army in the Revolutionary War. **5.** a piece of paper money issued by the Continental Congress during the war: *not worth a continental.* **6.** an inhabitant of a continent, esp. (*usually cap.*) of the mainland of Europe.

Continental Congress, one of the two American legislative congresses during and after the Revolutionary War, responsible for the Declaration of Independence and The Articles of Confederation.

continental divide, 1. a water parting between river systems that flow into different oceans. **2.** (*caps.*) (in North America) the line of summits of the Rocky Mountains, separating streams flowing toward the Gulf of California and the Pacific from those flowing toward the Gulf of Mexico, Hudson Bay, and the Arctic Ocean.

continental shelf, *Phys. Geog.* that portion of a continent submerged under relatively shallow sea, in contrast with the deep ocean basins from which it is separated by the relatively steep **continental slope.**

con·ti·nent·ly (kŏn′tə nənt lǐ), *adv.* in a continent manner; temperately.

con·tin·gence (kən tǐn′jəns), *n.* contact or tangency.

con·tin·gen·cy (kən tǐn′jən sǐ), *n.*, *pl.* **-cies. 1.** fortuitousness; uncertainty; dependence on chance or on the fulfillment of a condition. **2.** a contingent event; a chance, accident, or possibility, conditional on something uncertain. **3.** something incidental to a thing.

contingency table, *Statist.* the frequency distribution for a two-way statistical classification.

con·tin·gent (kən tǐn′jənt), *adj.* **1.** dependent for existence, occurrence, character, etc., on something not yet certain; conditional (often fol. by *on* or *upon*). **2.** liable to happen or not; uncertain; possible. **3.** happening by chance or without known cause; fortuitous; accidental. **4.** *Logic.* (of a proposition) not involving any self-contradiction if denied, so that its truth or falsity can be established only by sensory observation (as opposed to *analytic* or *necessary* propositions). —*n.* **5.** the proportion that falls to one as a share to be contributed or furnished. **6.** a quota of troops furnished. **7.** any one of the representative groups composing an assemblage: *the New York contingent at a national convention.* **8.** something contingent; a contingency. [ME, t. L: s. *contigens*, ppr., touching, bordering on, reaching, befalling] —**con·tin′gent·ly**, *adv.*

con·tin·u·al (kən tǐn′yŏŏ əl), *adj.* **1.** proceeding without interruption or cessation; continuous in time. **2.** of regular or frequent recurrence; often repeated; very frequent. —**Syn. 1.** unceasing, ceaseless, incessant, uninterrupted, unremitting, constant.

—**Syn. 1, 2.** CONTINUAL, CONSTANT, CONTINUOUS, all refer to a succession of occurrences. CONTINUAL implies that successive recurrences are very close together, with only small breaks between them, or none at all: *continual misunderstanding between nations.* CONSTANT implies always recurring in the same way, under uniform conditions, with similar results, and the like: *constant repetition of the same mistakes.* CONTINUOUS emphasizes the idea that the succession is unbroken: *the continuous life of the universe.*

con·tin·u·al·ly (kən tǐn′yŏŏ ə lǐ), *adv.* **1.** without cessation or intermission; unceasingly. **2.** very often; at regular or frequent intervals; habitually.

con·tin·u·ance (kən tǐn′yŏŏ əns), *n.* **1.** act or fact of continuing; continuation. **2.** a continuation or sequel. **3.** *Law.* adjournment of a step in a proceeding to a future day. [ME, t. OF, der. *continuer* CONTINUE]

con·tin·u·ant (kən tǐn′yŏŏ ənt), *n. Phonet.* a consonant, such as *f* or *m*, which may be prolonged without change of quality. [t. L: s. *continuans*, ppr., continuing]

con·tin·u·a·tion (kən tǐn′yŏŏ ā′shən), *n.* **1.** act or fact of continuing or prolonging. **2.** state of being continued. **3.** extension or carrying on to a further point: *the continuation of a story.* **4.** that by which anything is continued; a sequel, as to a story.

continuation school, a school in which instruction (special or general) is given in continuation or extension of that given in the lower schools, for the benefit of those who have left school while in the lower grades to work.

con·tin·u·a·tive (kən tǐn′yŏŏ ā′tǐv), *adj.* **1.** tending or serving to continue, or to cause continuation or prolongation. **2.** expressing continuance of thought. **3.** expressing a following event. In the sentence "They arrested a suspect, who gave his name as John Doe," the second clause is a continuative clause. —*n.* **4.** something continuative. **5.** a continuative word or expression. —**con·tin′u·a·tive·ly**, *adv.* —**con·tin′u·a′tive·ness**, *n.*

con·tin·u·a·tor (kən tǐn′yŏŏ ā′tər), *n.* one who or that which continues: *the continuator of a story.*

con·tin·ue (kən tǐn′ū), *v.*, **-tinued, -tinuing.** —*v.i.* **1.** to go forward or onward in any course or action; keep on. **2.** to go on after suspension or interruption. **3.** to last or endure. **4.** to remain in a place; abide; stay. **5.** to remain in a particular state or capacity. —*v.t.* **6.** to go on with or persist in: *to continue an action.* **7.** to extend from one point to another in space; prolong. **8.** to carry on from the point of suspension or interruption: *to continue a narrative.* **9.** to say in continuation. **10.** to cause to last or endure; maintain or retain, as in a position. **11.** to carry over, postpone, or adjourn; keep pending, as a legal proceeding. [ME *continue(n)*, t. L: m. *continuāre* make continuous] —**con·tin′u·a·ble**, *adj.* —**con·tin′u·er**, *n.*

—**Syn. 3.** CONTINUE, ENDURE, LAST, REMAIN imply existing uninterruptedly for an appreciable length of time. CONTINUE implies duration or existence without break or interruption: *the rain continued two days.* ENDURE implies persistent continuance against influences that tend to weaken, undermine, or destroy: *brass endures through many years.* LAST often applies to that which holds out to a desired end, fresh, unimpaired, or unexhausted, sometimes under conditions that tend to produce the opposite effect: *they had provisions enough to last all winter.* REMAIN is esp. applied to what continues without change in its essential state: *he remained a bachelor.*

continued fraction, a fraction whose denominator contains a fraction whose denominator contains a fraction, and so on, as $2 \cfrac{7+1}{9+3}{\ } \cfrac{}{4+\ldots}$

con·ti·nu·i·ty (kŏn′tə nū′ə tǐ, -nōō′-), *n.*, *pl.* **-ties. 1.** state or quality of being continuous. **2.** a continuous or connected whole. **3.** a motion-picture scenario giving the complete action, scenes, etc., in detail and in the order in which they are to be shown on the screen. **4.** a radio script for the spoken parts.

con·tin·u·ous (kən tǐn′yŏŏ əs), *adj.* **1.** having the parts in immediate connection. **2.** uninterrupted in time; without cessation. [t. L: m. *continuus* hanging together] —**con·tin′u·ous·ly**, *adv.* —**con·tin′u·ous·ness**, *n.* —**Syn. 2.** See **continual.**

continuous waves, *Radio.* electric waves which are not intermittent or broken up into damped wave trains, but (unless intentionally interrupted) follow one another without any interval of time between.

con·tin·u·um (kən tǐn′yŏŏ əm), *n.*, *pl.* **-tinua** (-tǐn′yŏŏə). **1.** a continuous extent, series, or whole. **2.** *Math.* an infinite set of objects such that between any two of them there is a third object: *the continuum of rational numbers.* [t. L, neut. of *continuus* CONTINUOUS]

con·to (kŏn′tō; *Port.* kôn′tŏō), *n.*, *pl.* **-tos** (-tōz; *Port.* -tŏōsh; *Brazil.* -tŏōs). **1.** a Portuguese or Brazilian money of account, in which large sums are calculated, equal to 1,000,000 reis. The sign for the conto is (:) and the thousand conto is (.). One thousand milreis is written Rs. 1:000$000. **2.** *Portugal.* 1000 escudos. **3.** *Brazil.* 1000 milreis. [t. Pg., & L *computus* calculated]

con·tort (kən tôrt′), *v.t.* to twist; bend or draw out of shape; distort. [t. L: s. *contortus*, pp., twisted] —**con·tor′tion**, *n.*

con·tor·tion·ist (kən tôr′shən ǐst), *n.* **1.** one who performs gymnastic feats involving contorted postures. **2.** one who practices contortion: *a verbal contortionist.*

con·tour (kŏn′tŏŏr), *n.* **1.** the outline of a figure or body; the line that defines or bounds anything. **2.** a contour line. —*v.t.* **3.** to mark with contour lines. **4.** to make or form the contour or outline of. **5.** to build (a road, etc.) in conformity to a contour. —*adj.* **6.** *Agric.* of or used in a system of plowing and sowing along the contour lines of the terrain, thereby preventing rain water from washing away the topsoil. [t. F, t. It.: m. *contorno*, der. *contornare*, f. L: con- con + *tornāre* turn]

contour feathers, any of the feathers which form the surface plumage of a bird, apart from wings, tail, and specialized types, as filoplumes.

contour interval, the difference in elevation represented by each contour line on a map.

contour line, 1. a line joining points of equal elevation on a surface. **2.** the representation of such a line on a map.

contour map, a map on which irregularities of land surface are shown by contour lines, the relative spacing of the lines indicating the relative slope of the surface.

contr. 1. contracted. **2.** contraction.

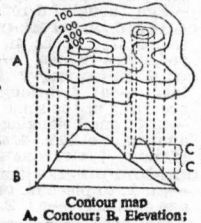

Contour map
A. Contour; B. Elevation; C. Contour interval

contra-, a prefix meaning "against," "opposite," or "opposing." [t. L, prefix use of *contrā*, adv. and prep.]

con·tra·band (kŏn′trə bănd′), *n.* 1. anything prohibited by law from being imported or exported. 2. goods imported or exported illegally. 3. illegal or prohibited traffic; smuggling. 4. *Internal. Law.* goods which neutrals cannot supply to one belligerent except at the risk of seizure and confiscation by the other (**contraband of war**). 5. *U.S.* (during the Civil War) a Negro slave who escaped to or was brought within the Union lines. —*adj.* 6. prohibited from export or import. [t. Sp.: m. *contrabando*; r. *counterband* t. F: m. *contrebande*, t. It.: m. *contrabando*, f. *contra* against (g. L *contrā*) + *bando* proclamation (g. LL *bandum* BAN², n.)]

con·tra·band·ist (kŏn′trə bănd′ist), *n.* a smuggler.

con·tra·bass (kŏn′trə bās′), *Music.* —*n.* 1. (in any family of instruments) the member below the bass. 2. (in the violin family) the double bass. —*adj.* 3. denoting such instruments: *a contrabass trombone.* —**con·tra·bass·ist** (kŏn′trə bā′sĭst, -bās′ĭst), *n.*

con·tra bassoon (kŏn′trə), a bassoon larger in size and an octave lower in pitch than the ordinary bassoon; a double bassoon.

con·tra·cep·tion (kŏn′trə sĕp′shən), *n.* the prevention of conception by deliberate measures, in order to prevent childbirth. [f. CONTRA- + (CON)CEPTION]

con·tra·cep·tive (kŏn′trə sĕp′tĭv), *adj.* 1. tending or serving to prevent conception or impregnation. 2. pertaining to contraception. —*n.* 3. a contraceptive agent or device.

con·tra·clock·wise (kŏn′trə klŏk′wīz′), *adj., adv.* counterclockwise.

con·tract (*n. and usually for v.* 12 kŏn′trăkt; *otherwise v.* kən trăkt′), *n.* 1. an agreement between two or more parties for the doing or not doing of some definite thing. 2. an agreement enforceable by law. 3. the writing containing such an agreement. 4. the division of law dealing with contracts. 5. the formal agreement of marriage; betrothal. 6. Also, **contract bridge.** a modification of auction bridge in which the side which wins the bid can earn towards game only that number of tricks bid, all additional points being credited above the score line. 7. (in auction or contract bridge) a. the highest bid. b. the number of tricks so bid. [ME, t. LL: s. *contractus* agreement] —*v.t.* 8. to draw together or into smaller compass; draw the parts of together: *to contract a muscle.* 9. to wrinkle: *to contract the brows.* 10. to shorten (a word, etc.) by combining or omitting some of its elements. 11. to acquire, as by habit or contagion; incur, as a liability or obligation: *to contract a disease or debts.* 12. to settle or establish by agreement: *to contract an alliance.* 13. to enter into (friendship, acquaintance, etc.). 14. to betroth. —*v.i.* 15. to be drawn together or reduced in compass; become smaller; shrink. 16. to enter into an agreement. [t. L: s. *contractus*, pp., drawn together] —**con·tract′i·ble,** *adj.* —**con·tract′i·bil′i·ty, con·tract′i·ble·ness,** *n.* —**Syn.** 1. See **agreement.** 8. reduce, shorten, lessen, narrow, shrivel, shrink. CONTRACT, COMPRESS, CONCENTRATE, CONDENSE imply retaining original content but reducing the amount of space occupied. CONTRACT means to cause to draw more closely together: *to contract a muscle.* COMPRESS suggests causing to become smaller by means of fairly uniform external pressure: *to compress gases into liquid form, clay into bricks.* CONCENTRATE implies causing to gather around a point, or eliminating nonessentials: *to concentrate troops near an objective, attention, strength.* CONDENSE implies increasing the compactness, or thickening the consistency of a homogeneous mass: *to condense milk.*—**Ant.** 8. expand.

con·tract·ed (kən trăk′tĭd), *adj.* 1. drawn together; shrunken. 2. condensed; abridged. 3. narrow or illiberal; restricted: *contracted circumstances.* —**con·tract′ed·ly,** *adv.* —**con·tract′ed·ness,** *n.*

con·trac·tile (kən trăk′təl, -tĭl), *adj.* capable of undergoing or of producing contraction. —**con·trac·til·i·ty** (kŏn′trăk tĭl′ə tĭ), *n.*

con·trac·tion (kən trăk′shən), *n.* 1. act of contracting. 2. state of being contracted. 3. a shortened form of a word, etc., as *e′er* for *ever, can′t* for *cannot.* 4. *Physiol.* the change in a muscle by which it becomes thickened and shortened. 5. a restriction or withdrawal, as of currency or of funds available as call money. [t. L: s. *contractio* a drawing together]

con·trac·tive (kən trăk′tĭv), *adj.* serving or tending to contract. —**con·trac′tive·ly,** *adv.* —**con·trac′tive·ness,** *n.*

con·trac·tor (kŏn′trăk tər, kən trăk′tər), *n.* 1. one who contracts to furnish supplies or perform work at a certain price or rate. 2. one who or that which contracts. [t. LL]

con·trac·tu·al (kən trăk′chŏŏ əl), *adj.* of, or of the nature of, a contract. [L *contractu(s)* contract + -AL¹]

con·tra·dance (kŏn′trə däns′, -dăns′), *n.* contredanse.

con·tra·dict (kŏn′trə dĭkt′), *v.t.* 1. to assert the contrary or opposite of; deny directly and categorically. 2. to deny the words or assertion of (a person). 3. (of a statement, action, etc.) to be directly contrary to. 4. *Obs.* to speak or declare against; oppose. —*v.i.* 5. to utter a contrary statement. [t. L: s. *contrādictus*, pp., said against] —**con′tra·dict′a·ble,** *adj.* —**con′tra·dict′er,** **con′tra·dic′tor,** *n.* —**Syn.** 1, 2. gainsay, impugn, controvert, dispute. See **deny.**

con·tra·dic·tion (kŏn′trə dĭk′shən), *n.* 1. act of contradicting; gainsaying or opposition. 2. assertion of the contrary or opposite; denial. 3. a statement or proposition that contradicts or denies another or itself. 4. direct opposition between things compared; inconsistency. 5. a contradictory act, fact, etc. 6. See **law of contradictions.**

con·tra·dic·tious (kŏn′trə dĭk′shəs), *adj.* 1. inclined to contradict; disputatious. 2. *Archaic.* self-contradictory. [f. CONTRADICTI(ON) + -OUS]

con·tra·dic·tive (kŏn′trə dĭk′tĭv), *adj.* tending to contradict; involving contradiction.

con·tra·dic·to·ry (kŏn′trə dĭk′tə rĭ), *adj., n., pl.* **-ries.** —*adj.* 1. of the nature of a contradiction; asserting the contrary or opposite; contradicting each other; inconsistent. 2. given to contradiction. —*n.* 3. *Logic.* a proposition so related to a second that it is impossible for both to be true or both to be false. —**con′tra·dic′to·ri·ly,** *adv.* —**con′tra·dic′to·ri·ness,** *n.* —**Syn.** 1. opposing, antagonistic, irreconcilable, paradoxical.

con·tra·dis·tinc·tion (kŏn′trə dĭs tĭngk′shən), *n.* distinction by opposition or contrast: *plants and animals in contradistinction to man.* —**con′tra·dis·tinc′tive,** *adj.* —**con′tra·dis·tinc′tive·ly,** *adv.*

con·tra·dis·tin·guish (kŏn′trə dĭs tĭng′gwĭsh), *v.t.* to distinguish by contrasting opposite qualities.

con·tra·in·di·cate (kŏn′trə ĭn′də kāt′), *v.t.,* **-cated, -cating.** *Med.* (of a symptom or condition) to give indication against the advisability of (a particular or usual remedy or treatment). —**con·tra·in·di·cant** (kŏn′trə ĭn′də kənt), *n.* —**con′tra·in′di·ca′tion,** *n.*

con·tral·to (kən trăl′tō), *n., pl.* **-tos,** *adj.* *Music.* —*n.* 1. the lowest female voice or voice part, intermediate between soprano and tenor. 2. the alto, or highest male voice or voice part. 3. a singer with a contralto voice. —*adj.* 4. pertaining to the contralto or its compass. [t. It., f. *contra* against, counter to + *alto* high]

con·trap·tion (kən trăp′shən), *n.* *Colloq.* a contrivance; a device.

con·tra·pun·tal (kŏn′trə pŭn′təl), *adj.* *Music.* 1. of or pertaining to counterpoint. 2. composed of two or more relatively independent melodies sounded together. [f. m. It. *contrappunto* counterpoint + -AL¹] —**con′tra·pun′tal·ly,** *adv.*

con·tra·pun·tist (kŏn′trə pŭn′tĭst), *n.* one skilled in the practice of counterpoint.

con·tra·ri·e·ty (kŏn′trə rī′ə tĭ), *n., pl.* **-ties.** 1. state or quality of being contrary. 2. something contrary or of opposite character; a contrary fact or statement. [t. LL: m.s. *contrārietas*]

con·trar·i·ous (kən trâr′ĭ əs), *adj.* *Now Rare.* 1. perverse. 2. adverse. [ME, t. ML: m. s. *contrāriōsus*]

con·tra·ri·wise (kŏn′trĕr′ĭ wīz′), *adv.* 1. in the opposite way. 2. on the contrary. 3. perversely.

con·tra·ry (kŏn′trĕr′ĭ; *for* 5 *also* kən trâr′ĭ), *adj., n., pl.* **-ries,** *adv.* —*adj.* 1. opposite in nature or character; diametrically opposed; mutually opposed: *contrary to fact, contrary propositions.* 2. opposite in direction or position. 3. being the opposite one of two. 4. untoward or unfavorable: *contrary winds.* 5. perverse; self-willed. 6. *Bot.* at right angles. —*n.* 7. that which is contrary or opposite: *to prove the contrary of a statement.* 8. either of two contrary things. 9. *Logic.* a proposition so related to a second that it is impossible for both to be true though both may be false. For example: *all judges are male* is the contrary of *no judges are male.* 10. **by contraries,** a. by way of opposition. b. contrary to expectation. 11. **on the contrary,** in extreme opposition to what has been stated. 12. **to the contrary,** to the opposite or a different effect. —*adv.* 13. contrarily; contrariwise. [ME *contrarie* t. AF, t. L: m. *contrārius* opposite, hostile] —**con′tra·ri·ly,** *adv.* —**con′tra·ri·ness,** *n.* —**Syn.** 1. contradictory, conflicting, discordant, counter. See **opposite.** 4. CONTRARY, ADVERSE both describe that which unfavorably opposes. CONTRARY conveys an idea of something impersonal and objective whose opposition happens to be unfavorable: *contrary winds.* ADVERSE suggests something more personally unfriendly or even hostile; it emphasizes the idea of the resulting misfortune to that which is opposed: *the judge rendered a decision adverse to the defendant.* 5. intractable, refractory, obstinate, headstrong.

contrary motion, *Music.* one part rising in pitch while the other descends, and vice versa.

con·trast (*v.* kən trăst′; *n.* kŏn′trăst), *v.t.* 1. to set in opposition in order to show unlikeness; compare by observing differences. 2. to afford or form a contrast to; set off. —*v.i.* 3. to exhibit unlikeness on comparison; form a contrast. —*n.* 4. act of contrasting. 5. state of being contrasted. 6. a striking exhibition of unlikeness. 7. something strikingly unlike. 8. opposition or juxtaposition of different forms, lines, or colors in a work of art to intensify each other's properties and produce a more dynamic expression. [t. F: s. *contraster,* t. It.: m. *contrastare,* g. LL: withstand, oppose] —**con·trast′a·ble,** *adj.* —**Syn.** 1. differentiate, discriminate, distinguish, oppose. See **compare.**

con·trast·y (kən trăs′tĭ), *adj.* *Photog.* having coarse or sharp gradations of tone, esp. between dark and light areas (opposed to *soft*).

con·tra·val·la·tion (kŏn′trə və lā′shən), *n.* *Fort.* a chain of redoubts and breastworks raised by besiegers about the place invested. [t. F: m. *contrevallation,* f. *contre-* CONTRA- + s. LL *vallātio* entrenchment]

con·tra·vene (kŏn′trə vēn′), *v.t.*, **-vened, -vening.**
1. to come or be in conflict with; go or act counter to;.
oppose. **2.** to violate, infringe, or transgress: *to contra*
vene the law. [t. L: m. s. *contrāvenīre* oppose] **—con′tra-**
ven′er, *n.*

con·tra·ven·tion (kŏn′trə vĕn′shən), *n.* act of con-
travening; action counter to something; violation.

con·tra·yer·va (kŏn′trə yûr′və), *n.* the root of certain plants of the tropical American moraceous genus
Dorstenia, esp. *D. contrayerva,* used as a stimulant, tonic,
and diaphoretic. [t. Sp.: counter herb, antidote, f. L
contra- CONTRA- + Sp. *yerva* herb]

con·tre·danse (kŏn′trə däns′), *n.* **1.** a variation of
the quadrille, in which the dancers face each other. **2.** a
piece of music suitable for such a dance. Also, **contra-**
dance. [F, mistranslation of COUNTRY-DANCE]

con·tre·temps (kŏn′trə tän′), *n., pl.* **-temps** (-tänz′;
Fr. -tän′). an inopportune occurrence; an embarrassing
mischance. [t. F, respelling of *contretant,* g. OF *contretant*
opposing, ppr. of *contrester* oppose, g. L *contrāstāre*]

con·trib·ute (kən trĭb′ūt), *v.,* **-uted, -uting.** *—v.t.*
1. to give in common with others; give to a common
stock or for a common purpose: *to contribute money,*
time, help. **2.** to furnish to a magazine or journal. *—v.i.*
3. to make contribution; furnish a contribution. [t. L:
m. s. *contribūtus,* pp., brought together] **—con·trib′-**
ut·a·ble, *adj.* **—con·trib′u·tive,** **—con·trib′u-**
tive·ly, *adv.* **—con·trib′u·tive·ness,** *n.*

con·tri·bu·tion (kŏn′trə bū′shən), *n.* **1.** act of contributing. **2.** something contributed. **3.** an article
contributed to a magazine or the like. **4.** an impost or
levy. **5.** the method of distributing liability, in case of
loss, among several insurers whose policies attach to the
same risk. [ME, t. L: s. *contribūtio*]

con·trib·u·tor (kən trĭb′yə tər), *n.* **1.** one that contributes. **2.** one who contributes articles to a newspaper,
magazine, or other joint literary work.

con·trib·u·to·ry (kən trĭb′yə tōr′Y), *adj., n., pl.* **-ries.**
—adj. **1.** pertaining to or of the nature of contribution;
contributing. **2.** furnishing something toward a result:
contributory negligence. **3.** subject to contribution or
levy. *—n.* **4.** one who or that which contributes.

con·trite (kən trīt′, kŏn′trīt), *adj.* **1.** broken in spirit
by a sense of guilt; penitent: *a contrite sinner.* **2.** proceeding from contrition: *contrite tears.* [ME *contrit,* t.
L: s. *contrītus,* pp., ground, worn down] **—con·trite′ly,**
adv. **—con·trite′ness,** *n.*

con·tri·tion (kən trĭsh′ən), *n.* **1.** sincere penitence.
2. *Theol.* sorrow for and detestation of sin with a true
purpose of amendment, arising from a love of God for his
own perfections (**perfect contrition**), or from some inferior motive, as fear of divine punishment (**imperfect**
contrition). [ME, t. L: s. *contrītio*]

con·triv·ance (kən trī′vəns), *n.* **1.** something contrived; a device, esp. a mechanical one. **2.** act or manner of contriving; the faculty or power of contriving.
3. a plan or scheme; an expedient.

con·trive (kən trīv′), *v.,* **-trived, -triving.** *—v.t.* **1.** to
plan with ingenuity; devise; invent. **2.** to plot (evil,
etc.). **3.** to bring about or effect by a device, stratagem,
plan, or scheme; manage (to do something). *—v.i.* **4.** to
form schemes or designs; plan. **5.** to plot. [ME *con-*
treve(n), controve(n), t. OF: m. *controver,* f. *con-* CON- +
trover find. See TROVER] **—con·triv′a·ble,** *adj.* **—con-**
triv′er, *n.* **—Syn. 1.** See **prepare.**

con·trol (kən trōl′), *v.,* **-trolled, -trolling,** *n.* *—v.t.*
1. to exercise restraint or direction over; dominate; command. **2.** to hold in check; curb. **3.** to test or verify (a
scientific experiment) by a parallel experiment or other
standard of comparison. **4.** to check or regulate (payments, etc.), orig. by means of a duplicate register. *—n.*
5. act or power of controlling; regulation; domination
or command. **6.** check or restraint. **7.** something that
serves to control; a check; a standard of comparison
in scientific experimentation. **8.** a person who acts as a
check; a controller. **9.** a device for regulating and guiding a machine, as a motor, airplane, etc. **10.** (*pl.*) a co-
ordinated arrangement of such devices. **11.** *Auto Rac-*
ing, etc. that portion of the track which is not included in
the timing. [t. F: s. *contrôler,* in OF *contreroller,* der. *con-*
trerolle register. See COUNTER-, ROLL] **—con·trol′la-**
ble, *adj.* **—con·trol′la·bil′i·ty,** *n.* **—con·trol′ment,** *n.*
—Syn. 1. manage, govern, rule. **5.** See **authority.**

control chart, *Statistics.* a chart on which observations are plotted as ordinates in the order in which they
are obtained, and on which **control lines** are constructed
to indicate whether the population from which the observations are being drawn is remaining the same (used
particularly in industrial quality control work).

control experiment, an experiment in which the
variables are controlled so that the effects of varying one
factor at a time may be observed.

con·trol·ler (kən trō′lər), *n.* **1.** one employed to check
expenditures, etc.; a comptroller. **2.** one who regulates,
directs, or restrains. **3.** *Brit. Aeron.* the dispatcher.
4. a regulating mechanism. **—con·trol′ler·ship′,** *n.*

control stick, a lever which, by tubes or cables, controls the ailerons and elevator of an airplane.

con·tro·ver·sial (kŏn′trə vûr′shəl), *adj.* **1.** of, or of
the nature of, controversy; polemical. **2.** subject to controversy; debatable. **3.** given to controversy; disputatious. **—con′tro·ver′sial·ist,** *n.* **—con′tro·ver′-**
sial·ly, *adv.*

con·tro·ver·sy (kŏn′trə vûr′sY), *n., pl.* **-sies. 1.** dispute, debate, or contention; disputation concerning a
matter of opinion. **2.** a dispute or contention. [t. L: m.
s. *controversia* debate, contention] **—Syn. 1.** disagreement, altercation. **2.** quarrel, wrangle. See **argument.**

con·tro·vert (kŏn′trə vûrt′, kŏn′trə vûrt′), *v.t.* **1.** to
contend against in discussion; dispute; deny; oppose.
2. to contend about in discussion; debate; discuss.
—con′tro·vert′er, *n.* **—con′tro·vert′i·ble,** *adj.*
—con′tro·vert′i·bly, *adv.*

con·tu·ma·cious (kŏn′tyŏŏ mā′shəs, -tŏŏ-), *adj.* stubbornly perverse or rebellious; willfully and obstinately
disobedient. [f. m. CONTUMACY + -OUS] **—con′tu·ma′-**
cious·ly, *adv.* **—con′tu·ma′cious·ness,** *n.*

con·tu·ma·cy (kŏn′tyŏŏ mə sY, -tŏŏ-), *n., pl.* **-cies.**
stubborn perverseness or rebelliousness; willful and obstinate resistance or disobedience to authority. [ME
contumacie, t. L: m. *contumācia,* der. *contumax* stubborn]

con·tu·me·ly (kŏn′tyŏŏ mə lY, -tŏŏ-; kən tū′mə lY,
-tŏŏ-; *formerly* kŏn′tyŏŏ mē′lY), *n., pl.* **-lies. 1.** insulting manifestation of contempt in words or actions; contemptuous or humiliating treatment. **2.** a humiliating
insult. [ME *contumelie,* t. L: s. *contumēlia*] **—con-**
tu·me·li·ous (kŏn′tyŏŏ mē′lY əs, -tŏŏ-), *adj.* **—con′tu-**
me′li·ous·ly, *adv.* **—con′tu·me′li·ous·ness,** *n.*

con·tuse (kən tūz′, -tŏŏz′), *v.t.,* **-tused, -tusing.** to
injure as by a blow with a blunt instrument, without
breaking the skin; bruise. [t. L: m.s. *contūsus,* pp.,
beaten together] **—con·tu·sive** (kən tū′sŸv, -tŏŏ′-), *adj.*

con·tu·sion (kən tū′zhən, -tŏŏ′-), *n.* an injury as from
a blow with a blunt instrument, without breaking of the
skin; a bruise.

co·nun·drum (kə nŭn′drəm), *n.* **1.** a riddle the answer
to which involves a pun or play on words. **2.** anything
that puzzles. [orig. unknown]

con·va·lesce (kŏn′və lĕs′), *v.i.,* **-lesced, -lescing.** to
grow stronger after illness; make progress toward recovery of health. [t. L: m.s. *convalescere* grow strong]

con·va·les·cence (kŏn′və lĕs′əns), *n.* **1.** the gradual
recovery of health and strength after illness. **2.** the period during which one is convalescing.

con·va·les·cent (kŏn′və lĕs′ənt), *adj.* **1.** convalescing. **2.** of or pertaining to convalescence or convalescents. *—n.* **3.** a convalescent person.

con·val·lar·i·a·ceous (kŏn və lâr′Y ā′shəs), *adj.* belonging to the *Convallariaceae,* a family of plants including the lily of the valley, asparagus, etc. [f. s. NL Con-
valleria the lily-of-the-valley genus (der. L *convallis*
valley inclosed on all sides) + -ACEOUS]

con·vec·tion (kən vĕk′shən), *n.* **1.** *Physics.* the transference of heat by the circulation or movement of the
heated parts of a liquid or gas. **2.** *Meteorol.* a mechanical
process thermally produced involving the upward or
downward transfer of a limited portion of the atmosphere. Convection is essential to the formation of many
types of clouds. **3.** conveyance. [t. LL: s. *convectio,* der.
L *convehere* carry together] **—con·vec′tion·al,** *adj.*
—con·vec′tive, *adj.* **—con·vec′tive·ly,** *adv.*

con·ve·nance (kŏn′və näns′; *Fr.* kôN və näNs′), *n.* **1.**
suitability; expediency; propriety. **2.** (*pl.*) the proprieties or conventionalities. [t. F: agreement, propriety,
der. *convenir* agree, be fitting, g. L *convenīre* come to-
gether]

con·vene (kən vēn′), *v.,* **-vened, -vening.** *—v.i.* **1.** to
come together; assemble, usually for some public purpose. *—v.t.* **2.** to cause to assemble; convoke. **3.** to
summon to appear, as before a judicial officer. [late ME,
t. L: m.s. *convenīre* come together] **—con·ven′er,** *n.*
—Syn. 1. congregate, meet, collect, gather.

con·ven·ience (kən vēn′yəns), *n.* **1.** quality of being
convenient; suitability. **2.** a situation of affairs or a
time convenient for one: *to await one's convenience.*
3. advantage, as from something convenient: *a shelter for*
the convenience of travelers. **4.** anything convenient; an
advantage; an accommodation; a convenient appliance,
utensil, or the like.

con·ven·ient (kən vēn′yənt), *adj.* **1.** agreeable to the
needs or purpose; well-suited with respect to facility or
ease in use; favorable, easy, or comfortable for use.
2. at hand; easily accessible. **3.** *Obs.* fitting or appropriate. [ME, t. L: s. *conveniens,* ppr., agreeing, suiting]
—con·ven′ient·ly, *adv.* **—Syn. 1.** suitable, adapted,
serviceable.

con·vent (kŏn′vĕnt), *n.* **1.** a community of persons
devoted to religious life under a superior. **2.** a society of
monks, friars, or nuns. **3.** (in popular usage) a society of
nuns. **4.** the building or buildings occupied by such a
society; a monastery or nunnery. **5.** (in popular usage)
a nunnery. [t. L: s. *conventus* meeting, assembly, company, in ML convent; r. ME *covent,* t. AF]

con·ven·ti·cle (kən vĕn′tə kəl), *n.* **1.** a secret or unauthorized meeting, esp. for religious worship, as those
held by Protestant dissenters in England when they were
prohibited by law. **2.** a place of meeting or assembly,
esp. a nonconformist meetinghouse. **3.** *Obs.* a meeting
or assembly. [ME, t. L: m. s. *conventiculum,* dim. of *con-*
ventus meeting] **—con·ven′ti·cler,** *n.*

con·ven·tion (kən vĕn′shən), *n.* **1.** a meeting or assembly, esp., a formal assembly, as of representatives or
delegates, for action on particular matters. **2.** *U.S.*
Pol. a representative party assembly to nominate candidates, adopt platforms, and adopt party rules. **3.** an
agreement, compact, or contract. **4.** an international

agreement, esp. one dealing with a specific matter, as postal service, copyright, arbitration, etc. **5.** general agreement or consent; accepted usage, esp. as a standard of procedure. **6.** conventionalism. **7.** a rule, method, or practice established by general consent or usage. [t. L: s. *conventio* a meeting]
—**Syn. 1.** CONVENTION, ASSEMBLY, CONFERENCE, CONVOCATION name meetings for particular purposes. CONVENTION usually suggests a meeting of delegates representing political, church, social, or fraternal organizations. ASSEMBLY usually implies a meeting for a settled or customary purpose, as for discussion, legislation, or participation in a social function. CONFERENCE suggests a meeting for consultation and discussion about business or professional problems. CONVOCATION denotes a (church) assembly, the members of which have been summoned for a special purpose; chapel services at some colleges are called CONVOCATIONS. **7.** custom, precedent.

con·ven·tion·al (kən vĕn′shən əl), *adj.* **1.** conforming or adhering to accepted standards, as of conduct or taste. **2.** pertaining to convention or general agreement; established by general consent or accepted usage; arbitrarily determined: *conventional symbols*. **3.** formal, rather than spontaneous or original: *conventional phraseology*. **4.** *Art.* **a.** in accordance with accepted manner, model, or tradition. **b.** (of figurative art) represented in a generalized or simplified manner. **5.** of or pertaining to a convention, agreement, or compact. **6.** *Law.* resting on consent, express or implied. **7.** of or pertaining to a convention or assembly. —**con·ven′tion·al·ist**, *n.* —**con·ven′tion·al·ly**, *adv.* —**Syn. 1.** See **formal**.

con·ven·tion·al·ism (kən vĕn′shə nə lĭz′əm), *n.* **1.** adherence or the tendency to adhere to that which is conventional. **2.** something conventional.

con·ven·tion·al·i·ty (kən vĕn′shə năl′ə tĭ), *n., pl.* **-ties. 1.** conventional quality or character. **2.** adherence to convention. **3.** a conventional practice, principle, form, etc. **4. the conventionalities,** the conventional rules of propriety.

con·ven·tion·al·ize (kən vĕn′shən ə lĭz′), *v.t.*, **-ized, -izing. 1.** to make conventional. **2.** *Art.* to represent in a conventional manner. —**con·ven′tion·al·i·za′tion**, *n.*

con·ven·tu·al (kən vĕn′chŏŏ əl), *adj.* **1.** of, belonging to, or characteristic of a convent. —*n.* **2.** (*cap.*) one of an order of Franciscan friars which in the 15th century was separated from the Observants, and which follows a mitigated rule. **3.** an inmate of a convent. [late ME, t. ML: s. *conventuālis*, der. *conventus* CONVENT]

con·verge (kən vûrj′), *v.*, **-verged, -verging.** —*v.i.* **1.** to tend to meet in a point or line; incline toward each other, as lines which are not parallel. **2.** to tend to a common result, conclusion, etc. —*v.t.* **3.** to cause to converge. [t. LL: m.s. *convergere* incline together]

con·ver·gence (kən vûr′jəns), *n.* **1.** act or fact of converging. **2.** convergent state or quality. **3.** degree of convergence, or point of convergence. **4.** *Physiol.* a turning of the eyes inward to bear upon a near point. **5.** *Meteorol.* a condition brought about by a net flow of air into a given region. **6.** *Biol.* similarity of form or structure caused by environment rather than heredity. Also, **con·ver′gen·cy** for 1–3. —**con·ver′gent**, *adj.*

convergent evolution, the appearance of apparently similar structures in organisms of different lines of descent.

con·vers·a·ble (kən vûr′sə bəl), *adj.* **1.** that may be conversed with, esp. easily and agreeably. **2.** able or disposed to converse. **3.** pertaining to or proper for conversation. —**con·vers′a·ble·ness**, *n.* —**con·vers′a·bly**, *adv.*

con·ver·sant (kŏn′vər sənt, kən vûr′-), *adj.* **1.** familiar by use or study (fol. by *with*): *conversant with a subject*. **2.** having regular or frequent conversation; intimately associating; acquainted. [ME, t. L. s. *conversans*, ppr., associating with] —**con′ver·sance**, **con′ver·san·cy**, *n.* —**con′ver·sant·ly**, *adv.* —**Syn. 1.** versed, learned, skilled, practiced, well-informed; proficient.

con·ver·sa·tion (kŏn′vər sā′shən), *n.* **1.** informal interchange of thoughts by spoken words; a talk or colloquy. **2.** association or social intercourse; intimate acquaintance. **3.** *Obs.* familiar acquaintance from using or studying. **4.** *Archaic.* behavior, or manner of living. [ME, t. OF, t. L: s. *conversātio* frequent use, intercourse]

con·ver·sa·tion·al (kŏn′vər sā′shən əl), *adj.* **1.** of, pertaining to, or characteristic of, conversation. **2.** able, or ready to converse; given to conversation. —**con′ver·sa′tion·al·ly**, *adv.* —**Syn. 1.** See **colloquial.**

con·ver·sa·tion·al·ist (kŏn′vər sā′shən əl ĭst), *n.* one given to or excelling in conversation.

conversational quality, (in public speaking and reading) a manner of utterance which sounds like spontaneous, direct communication.

conversation piece, a type of painting esp. popular in England in the 18th century, showing a group of more or less fashionable people in an appropriate setting.

con·ver·sa·zi·o·ne (kŏn′vər sät′sĭ ō′nĭ; *It.* kŏn′vĕr sä tsyō′nĕ), *n., pl.* **-zi·o·nes** (-sĭ ō′nēz), *It.* **-zi·oni** (-tsyō′nē). *Italian.* a social gathering for conversation, etc., esp. on literary or scholarly subjects.

con·verse¹ (*v.* kən vûrs′; *n.* kŏn′vûrs), *v.*, **-versed, -versing**, *n.* —*v.i.* **1.** to talk informally with another;

interchange thought by speech. **2.** to hold inward communion (fol. by *with*). —*n.* **3.** familiar discourse or talk; conversation. **4.** inward communion. [ME *converse*(*n*), t. OF: m. *converser*, g. L *conversārī* dwell or associate with] —**con·vers′er**, *n.* —**Syn. 1.** talk, chat. See **speak.**

con·verse² (*adj.* kən vûrs′, kŏn′vûrs; *n.* kŏn′vûrs), *adj.* **1.** turned about; opposite or contrary in direction or action. —*n.* **2.** a thing which is the opposite or contrary of another. **3.** *Logic.* **a.** a proposition obtained from another proposition by conversion. **b.** the relation between one term and a second when the second term is related in a certain manner to the first. For example: the relation *descendant of* is the converse of *ancestor of*. **4.** a group of words correlative with a preceding group but having a significant pair of terms interchanged. Example: *hot in winter but cold in summer* is the converse of *cold in winter but hot in summer*. [t. L: m.s. *conversus*, pp., turned about] —**con·verse·ly** (kən vûrs′lĭ, kŏn′vûrs-), *adv.*

con·ver·sion (kən vûr′zhən, -shən), *n.* **1.** act of converting. **2.** state of being converted. **3.** change in character, form, or function. **4.** spiritual change from sinfulness to righteousness. **5.** change from one religion, party, etc., to another. **6.** *Math.* a change in the form or units of an expression. **7.** *Logic.* the transposition of the subject and the predicate of a proposition, in accordance with certain rules, so as to form a new proposition. For example: *no good man is unhappy* becomes by conversion *no unhappy man is good*. **8.** *Law.* **a.** unauthorized assumption and exercise of rights of ownership over personal property belonging to another. **b.** change from realty into personalty, or vice versa, as in sale or purchase of land, mining coal, etc. **9.** *Psychoanal.* the process by which a repressed psychic event, idea, feeling, memory, or impulse is represented by a bodily change or symptom, thus simulating physical illnesses or their symptoms. —**con·ver′sion·al**, **con·ver·sion·ar·y** (kən vûr′zhə nĕr′ĭ, -shə-), *adj.*

con·vert (*v.* kən vûrt′, *n.* kŏn′vûrt), *v.t.* **1.** to change into something of different form or properties; transmute; transform. **2.** *Chem.* to cause (a substance) to undergo a chemical change: *to convert sugar into alcohol*. **3.** to cause to adopt a different religion, party, opinion, etc., esp. one regarded as better. **4.** to change in character; cause to turn from an evil life to a righteous one. **5.** to turn to another or a particular use or purpose; divert from the proper or intended use. **6.** to appropriate wrongfully to one's own use. **7.** *Law.* to assume unlawful rights of ownership of (personal property). **8.** to invert or transpose. **9.** *Logic.* to transpose the subject and predicate of (a proposition) by conversion. **10.** to exchange for an equivalent: *to convert banknotes into gold*. **11.** *Finance.* to exchange voluntarily (a bond or preferred share) into another security, usually common stock, because of the greater value of the latter. —*v.i.* **12.** to be converted. —*n.* **13.** one who has been converted, as to a religion or an opinion. [ME *converte*(*n*), t. L: m. *convertere* turn about, change] —**Syn. 1.** See **transform. 13.** proselyte, neophyte, disciple.

con·vert·er (kən vûr′tər), *n.* **1.** one who or that which converts. **2.** one engaged in converting textile fabrics, esp. cotton cloths, from the raw state into the finished product ready for the market, as by bleaching, dyeing, etc. **3.** *Elect.* See **synchronous converter. 4.** an oval vessel in which molten pig iron is converted into steel by forcing air through the metal. Also, **con·ver′tor.**

con·vert·i·ble (kən vûr′tə bəl), *adj.* **1.** capable of being converted. **2.** *Auto.* having a folding top. —*n.* **3.** *Colloq.* a convertible automobile. —**con·vert′i·bil′i·ty**, **con·vert′i·ble·ness**, *n.* —**con·vert′i·bly**, *adv.*

con·vert·i·plane (kən vûr′tə plān′), *n.* a plane capable of both vertical flight (like a helicopter) or fast forward speed (like a conventional airplane).

con·vert·ite (kŏn′vər tīt′), *n.* *Archaic.* a convert.

con·vex (*adj.* kŏn vĕks′, kən-; *n.* kŏn′vĕks), *adj.* **1.** curved like a circle or sphere when viewed from without; bulging and curved. —*n.* **2.** a convex surface, part, or thing. [t. L: s. *convexus* vaulted, arched; appar. earlier var. of *convectus*, pp., carried together] —**con·vex′ly**, *adv.*

con·vex·i·ty (kən vĕk′sə tĭ), *n., pl.* **-ties. 1.** state of being convex. **2.** a convex surface or thing.

con·vex·o-con·cave (kən vĕk′sō-kŏn kāv′), *adj.* convex on one side and concave on the other.

con·vex·o-con·vex (kən vĕk′sō kŏn vĕks′), *adj.* convex on both sides.

con·vex·o-plane (kən vĕk′sō plān′), *adj.* plano-convex.

A. Convex or plano-convex lens; B. Convexo-concave lens; C. Convexo-convex lens

con·vey (kən vā′), *v.t.* **1.** to carry or transport from one place to another. **2.** to lead or conduct as a channel or medium; transmit. **3.** to communicate; impart; make known. **4.** *Law.* to transfer; pass the title to. **5.** *Obs.* to take away secretly. **6.** *Obs.* to steal. [ME *convey*(*n*), t. OF: m. *conveier*, f. con- CON- + *veier*, der. *veie*, g. L *via* way, journey] —**con·vey′a·ble**, *adj.* —**Syn. 1.** See **carry.**

con·vey·ance (kən vā′əns), *n.* **1.** act of conveying; transmission; communication. **2.** a means of conveyance, esp. a vehicle; a carriage, auto, etc. **3.** *Law.* **a.** the transfer of property from one person to another. **b.** the instrument or document by which this is effected.

ăct, āble, dâre, ärt; ĕbb, ēqual; Ỹf, īce; hŏt, ōver, ôrder, oil, bŏŏk, ōoze, out; ŭp, ūse, ûrge; ə = a in alone; ch, chief; g, give; ng, ring; sh, shoe; th, thin; ŧħ, that; zh, vision. See the full key on inside cover.

con·vey·anc·er (kən vā′ən sər), *n.* a person engaged in conveyancing.

con·vey·anc·ing (kən vā′ən sĭng), *n.* that branch of law practice consisting of examining titles, giving opinions as to their validity, and drawing of deeds, etc., for the conveyance of property from one person to another.

con·vey·or (kən vā′ər), *n.* **1.** one who or that which conveys. **2.** a contrivance for transporting material, as from one part of a building to another. Also, **con·vey′er.**

conveyor belt. See belt (def. 4b).

con·vict (*v., adj.* kən vĭkt′; *n.* kŏn′vĭkt), *v.t.* **1.** to prove or declare guilty of an offense, esp. after a legal trial: *to convict the prisoner of felony.* **2.** to impress with the sense of guilt. —*n.* **3.** a person proved or declared guilty of an offense. **4.** a person serving a prison sentence. —*adj.* **5.** *Archaic.* convicted. [ME, t. L: s. *convictus*, pp., overcome, convicted] —**con·vic′tive,** *adj.*

con·vic·tion (kən vĭk′shən), *n.* **1.** act of convicting. **2.** fact or state of being convicted. **3.** act of convincing. **4.** state of being convinced. **5.** a fixed or firm belief. —**con·vic′tion·al,** *adj.* —**Syn. 5.** See belief. —**Ant. 2.** doubt, uncertainty.

con·vince (kən vĭns′), *v.t.,* -vinced, -vincing. **1.** to persuade by argument or proof; cause to believe in the truth of what is alleged (often fol. by *of): to convince a man of his errors.* **2.** *Obs.* to prove or find guilty. **3.** *Obs.* to overcome; vanquish. [t. L: m.s. *convincere* overcome by argument or proof, convict of error or crime, prove] —**con·vince′ment,** *n.* —**con·vinc′er,** *n.* —**con·vin′ci·ble,** *adj.* —**con·vinc′ing·ly,** *adv.* —**con·vinc′ing·ness,** *n.* —**Syn. 1.** See persuade.

con·viv·i·al (kən vĭv′ī əl), *adj.* **1.** fond of feasting, drinking, and merry company; jovial. **2.** of or befitting a feast; festive. [t. L: s. *convīviālis* pertaining to a feast] —**con·viv′i·al·ist,** *n.* —**con·viv′i·al′i·ty,** *n.* —**con·viv′i·al·ly,** *adv.*

con·vo·ca·tion (kŏn′və kā′shən), *n.* **1.** act of convoking. **2.** fact or state of being convoked. **3.** a group of persons met in answer to a summons; an assembly. **4.** *Ch. of Eng.* one of the two provincial synods or assemblies of the clergy. **5.** *Prot. Episc. Ch.* **a.** an assembly of the clergy of part of a diocese. **b.** the area represented at such an assembly. [ME, t. L: s. *convocātio*] —**con′vo·ca′tion·al,** *adj.* —**Syn. 3.** See convention.

con·voke (kən vōk′), *v.t.,* -voked, -voking. to call together; summon to meet; assemble by summons. [t. L: m.s. *convocāre* call together] —**con·vok′er,** *n.*

con·vo·lute (kŏn′və lōōt′), *v.,* -luted, -luting, *adj.* —*v.t.* **1.** to coil up; form into a twisted shape. —*adj.* **2.** rolled up together, or one part over another. **3.** *Bot.* coiled up longitudinally, so that one margin is within the coil and the other without, as the petals of cotton. [t. L: m.s. *convolūtus,* pp., rolled together] —**con′vo·lute·ly,** *adv.*

con·vo·lu·tion (kŏn′və lōō′shən), *n.* **1.** a rolled up or coiled condition. **2.** a rolling or coiling together. **3.** a turn of anything coiled; whorl; sinuosity. **4.** *Anat.* one of the sinuous folds or ridges of the surface of the brain.

con·volve (kən vŏlv′), *v.t., v.i.,* -volved, -volv ng. to roll or wind together; coil; twist. [t. L: m.s. *convolvere* roll together]

con·vol·vu·la·ceous (kən vŏl′vyə lā′shəs), *adj.* belonging to the *Convolvulaceae,* or morning-glory family of plants, including the convolvuluses, ipomoeas, etc.

con·vol·vu·lus (kən vŏl′vyə ləs), *n., pl.* -luses, -li (-lī′). any plant of the genus *Convolvulus,* which comprises erect, twining, or prostrate herbs with trumpet-shaped flowers. See **morning-glory.** [t. L: bindweed]

con·voy (*v.* kən voi′, kŏn′voi; *n.* kŏn′voi), *v.t.* **1.** to accompany or escort, now usually for protection: *a merchant ship convoyed by a destroyer.* [ME, t. F: s. *convoyer,* earlier *conveier* CONVEY] —*n.* **2.** act of convoying. **3.** the protection afforded by an escort. **4.** an armed force, warship, etc., that escorts, esp. for protection. **5.** a formation of ships, a train of vehicles, etc., usually accompanied by a protecting escort. **6.** any group of military vehicles traveling together under the same orders. **7.** a drag or friction brake, as for a wagon. [t. F: m. *convoi,* der. *convoyer.* See v. above] —**Syn. 1.** See accompany.

con·vulse (kən vŭls′), *v.t.,* -vulsed, -vulsing. **1.** to shake violently; agitate. **2.** to cause to laugh violently. [t. L: m. s. *convulsus,* pp., shattered]

con·vul·sion (kən vŭl′shən), *n.* **1.** *Pathol.* contortion of the body caused by violent muscular contractions of the extremities, trunk, and head. **2.** violent agitation or disturbance; commotion. **3.** a violent fit of laughter.

con·vul·sion·ar·y (kən vŭl′shə něr′ī), *adj., n., pl.* -aries. —*adj.* **1.** pertaining to, of the nature of, or affected with convulsion. —*n.* **2.** one who is subject to convulsions.

con·vul·sive (kən vŭl′sĭv), *adj.* **1.** of the nature of or characterized by convulsions or spasms. **2.** producing or attended by convulsion: *convulsive rage.* —**con·vul′sive·ly,** *adv.* —**con·vul′sive·ness,** *n.*

co·ny (kō′nĭ, kŭn′ĭ), *n., pl.* -nies. **1.** the fur of a rabbit, esp. when dyed to simulate Hudson seal. **2.** the daman or some other animal of the same genus. **3.** the pika. **4.** *Archaic.* a rabbit. Also, **coney.** [ME *cunin,* t. OF: m. *conil,* g. L *cunīculus* rabbit]

coo (kōō), *v.,* cooed, cooing, *n.* —*v.i.* **1.** to utter the soft, murmuring sound characteristic of pigeons or doves,

or a similar sound. **2.** to murmur or talk fondly or amorously. —*v.t.* **3.** to utter by cooing. —*n.* **4.** a cooing sound. —*interj.* **5.** *Cockney.* an exclamation of surprise or amazement. [imit.] —**coo′er,** *n.* —**coo′ing·ly,** *adv.*

Co·o (kō′ō), *n.* Italian name of Cos.

Cooch Be·har (kōōch′ bə här′), *n.* **1.** a former state in NE India, in Bengal. Now a part of West Bengal. 671,158 (1950); 1334 sq. mi. **2.** a city in West Bengal. 33,242 (1951).

coo·ee (kōō′ī, kōō′ē), *n., v.* cooeed, cooeeing. —*n.* **1.** a prolonged, shrill, clear call or cry used as a signal by Australian aborigines and adopted by the settlers in the country. —*v.i.* **2.** to utter the call "cooee." Also, **coo·ey** (kōō′ī, kōō′ē), *n., pl.* cooeys, *v.,* cooeyed, cooeying. cooee.

cook (kōōk), *v.t.* **1.** to prepare (food) by the action of heat, as by boiling, baking, roasting, etc. **2.** to subject (anything) to the action of heat. **3.** *Colloq.* to concoct; invent falsely; falsify (often fol. by *up*). **4.** *Slang.* to ruin; spoil. —*v.i.* **5.** to prepare food by the action of heat. **6.** (of food) to undergo cooking. [v. use of n.] —*n.* **7.** one whose occupation is the preparation of food for the table; one who cooks (commonly used in England without *the*): *I'll tell (the) cook to prepare sandwiches.* [ME; OE *cōc,* t. LL: m.s. *cocus,* L *coquus*] —**cook′er,** *n.*

Cook (kōōk), *n.* **1. Captain James,** 1728–79, British navigator and explorer: expeditions to 8 Pacific, Antarctic oceans, and coasts of Australia and New Zealand. **2. Mount,** a mountain in New Zealand, on South Island. 12,349 ft. Also, **Aorangi.**

cook·book (kōōk′bōōk′), *n.* a book containing recipes and instructions for cooking. Also, *Brit.,* **cookery book.**

Cooke (kōōk), *n.* **Jay,** 1821–1905, U.S. financier.

cook·er·y (kōōk′ər ĭ), *n., pl.* -eries. **1.** the art or practice of cooking. **2.** a place for cooking.

Cook Islands, a group of islands in the 8 Pacific, belonging to New Zealand. 15,079 pop. (1951); 99 sq. mi.

Cook Strait, a strait between North and South Islands, in New Zealand.

cook·y (kōōk′ĭ), *n., pl.* **cookies. 1.** *U.S.* a small cake made from stiff sweet dough, dropped, rolled, or sliced, and then baked. **2.** *Scot.* a bun. Also, *U.S.,* **cook′ie.** [t. D: m. *koekie,* colloq. var. of *koekje,* dim. of *koek* cake]

cool (kōōl), *adj.* **1.** moderately col ; neither warm nor very cold. **2.** imparting or permitting a sensation of moderate coldness: *a cool dress.* **3.** not excited; calm; unmoved; not hasty; deliberate. **4.** deficient in ardor or enthusiasm. **5.** lacking in cordiality: *a cool reception.* **6.** calmly audacious or impudent. **7.** *Colloq.* (of a number or sum) without exaggeration or qualification: *a cool million dollars.* **8.** (of colors) with green, blue, or violet predominating. **9.** *Colloq.* coolly. —*adv.* **10.** that which is cool; the cool part, place, time, etc. **11.** coolness. —*v.i.* **12.** to become cool. **13.** to become less ardent, cordial, etc.; become more moderate. —*v.t.* **14.** to make cool; impart a sensation of coolness to. **15.** to lessen the ardor or intensity of; allay; calm; moderate. **16. cool one's heels,** to be kept waiting. [ME; OE *cōl;* akin to COLD, CHILL] —**cool′ly,** *adv.* —**cool′ness,** *n.* —**Syn. 1.** See cold. **3.** composed, collected; self-possessed. See calm. **5.** indifferent, lukewarm.

cool·ant (kōōl′ənt), *n.* a substance, usually a liquid or gas, used to reduce the temperature of a system below a specified value by conducting away the heat evolved in the operation of the system, as the liquid in an automobile cooling system. The coolant may be used to transfer heat to a power generator, as in a nuclear reactor. **2.** A lubricant which serves to dissipate the heat caused by friction. [f. COOL + -ANT]

cool·er (kōōl′ər), *n.* **1.** a container or apparatus for cooling or keeping cool: *a water cooler.* **2.** anything that cools or makes cool; refrigerant. **3.** *Slang.* a jail.

cool-head·ed (kōōl′hĕd′ĭd), *adj.* not easily excited; calm.

Cool·idge (kōōl′ĭj), *n.* **Calvin,** 1872–1933, 30th president of the U.S., 1923–29.

coo·lie (kōōl′ĭ), *n.* **1.** (in India, China, etc.) an unskilled native laborer. **2.** (elsewhere) such a laborer employed for cheap service. [prob. var. of *kōlī,* name of tribe of Gujarat, but cf. Tamil *kūli* hire, wages]

cool·ish (kōōl′ĭsh), *adj.* somewhat cool.

coo·ly (kōōl′ĭ), *n., pl.* -lies. coolie.

coomb (kōōm, kōm), *n.* combe. [OE *cumb* valley, c.d. G *Kwmm* trough; but cf. Welsh *cwm* valley]

coon (kōōn), *n.* **1.** raccoon. **2.** *U.S. Slang.* (in contemptuous use) a Negro.

coon·can (kōōn′kän′), *n.* a card game of the rummy family for two players.

coon's age, a long time.

coon·tie (kōōn′tĭ), *n.* **1.** the arrowroot plant of Florida, *Zamia integrifolia,* the only species of the *Cycadaceae* native in the U.S. **2.** the flour produced from its starch. [t. Seminole: m. *kunti* the flour]

coop (kōōp, kŏp), *n.* **1.** an enclosure, cage, or pen, usually with bars or wires on one side or more, in which fowls, etc., are confined for fattening, transportation, etc. **2.** any small or narrow place. **3.** *Slang.* a prison. **4. fly the coop,** *Slang.* to escape from a prison, etc. —*v.t.* **5.** to place in, or as in, a coop; confine narrowly (often fol. by *up* or *in*). [ME *coupe* basket, unexplained var. of *kipe,* ME *cupe,* OE *cype* basket, c. LG *kūpe*]

co·öp (kō′ŏp′, kō′ŏp), *n. Colloq.* a coöperative store or society. Also, **co-op′.**

coop·er (kōō'pər, kŏŏp'ər), n. 1. one who makes or repairs vessels formed of staves and hoops, as casks, barrels, tubs, etc. —v.t. 2. to make or repair (casks, barrels, etc.). 3. to furnish or fix (fol. by up). —v.i. 4. to work as a cooper. [ME couper, t. MD or MLG: m. kuper, t. VL: m. s. cūpārius, der. L cūpa cask]

Coo·per (kōō'pər, kŏŏp'ər), n. 1. Anthony Ashley. See Shaftesbury. 2. James Fenimore (fĕn'ə môr'), 1789–1851, U.S. novelist. 3. Peter, 1791–1883, U.S. inventor, manufacturer, reformer, and philanthropist.

coop·er·age (kōō'pər ĭj, kŏŏp'ər-), n. 1. the work or business of a cooper. 2. the place where it is carried on. 3. the price paid for coopers' work.

co·öp·er·ate (kōō ŏp'ə rāt'), v.i., -ated, -ating. 1. to work or act together or jointly; unite in producing an effect. 2. to practice economic coöperation. Also, co-op'er·ate', co-op'er·ate'. [t. LL: m.s. cooperātus, pp., having worked together.] —co·öp'er·a'tor, n.

co·öp·er·a·tion (kōō ŏp'ə rā'shən), n. 1. act or fact of coöperating; joint operation or action. 2. Econ. the combination of persons for purposes of production, purchase, or distribution for their joint benefit: producers' coöperation, consumers' coöperation. 3. Sociol. activity shared for mutual benefit. 4. Ecol. the conscious or unconscious behavior of organisms living together and producing a result which has survival value for them. Also, co-op'er·a'tion, co-op'er·a'tion. —co·öp'er·a'tion·ist, n.

co·öp·er·a·tive (kōō ŏp'ə rā'tĭv, -ŏp'rə tĭv), adj. 1. coöperating; of coöperation. 2. pertaining to economic coöperation: a coöperative store. 3. a coöperative society or store. Also, co-op'er·a'tive, co-op'er·a'tive. —co·öp'er·a·tive·ly, adv. —co·öp'er·a'tive·ness, n.

coöperative store, 1. a retail store owned and managed by consumer-customers who supply the capital and share in the profits by patronage dividends. 2. a store operated by a farmers' coöperative organization or by a coöperative chain.

coop·er·y (kōō'pər ĭ, kŏŏp'ər ĭ), n., pl. -eries. 1. the work of a cooper. 2. a cooper's shop. 3. articles made by a cooper.

co-öpt (kōō ŏpt'), v.t. to elect into a body by the votes of the existing members. Also, co-opt'. [t. L: s. cooptāre] —co·öp'ta'tion, n. —co·öp'ta·tive (kōō ŏp'tə tĭv), adj.

co·ör·di·nal (kōō ôr'də nəl), adj. Bot., Zool. belonging to the same order. Also, co-or'di·nal.

co·ör·di·nate (adj., n. kōō ôr'də nĭt, -nāt'; v. kōō ôr'də nāt'), adj., n., v., -nated, -nating. —adj. 1. of the same order or degree; equal in rank or importance. 2. involving coördination. 3. Math. using or pertaining to systems of coördinates. —n. 4. one who or that which is equal in rank or importance; an equal. 5. Math. any of the magnitudes which define the position of a point, line, or the like, by reference to a fixed figure, system of lines, etc. —v.t. 6. to place or class in the same order, rank, division, etc. 7. to place or arrange in due order or proper relative position. 8. to combine in harmonious relation or action. —v.i. 9. to become coördinate. 10. to assume proper order or relation. 11. to act in harmonious combination. Also, co-or'di·nate, co-or'di·nate. [f. co- + ORDINATE] —co·ör'di·nate·ly, adv. —co·ör'di·nate·ness, n. —co·ör'di·na'tive, adj. —co·ör'di·na'tor, n.

co·ör·di·na·tion (kōō ôr'də nā'shən), n. 1. act of coördinating. 2. state of being coördinated. 3. due ordering or proper relation. 4. harmonious combination. Also, co-or'di·na'tion, co-or'di·na'tion.

Coorg (kōōrg), n. a former province in SW India, now a part of Mysore state. 229,405 (1951). 1593 sq. mi. Cap.: Mercara.

Coos (kōōs), n. any of several Penutian languages of Oregon.

coot (kōōt), n. 1. any of the aquatic birds constituting the genus Fulica, characterized by lobate toes and short wings and tail, as the common coot (F. atra) of Europe. 2. any of various other swimming or diving birds, as the scoter. 3. Colloq. a fool; simpleton. [cf. D koet]

coot·ie (kōō'tĭ), n. Orig. Brit. Colloq. a louse.

cop¹ (kŏp), n., v., copped, copping. —n. 1. Colloq. a policeman. —v.t. 2. Slang. to catch. 3. Slang. to steal. [OE coppian lop, steal]

Coot, Fulica americana (15 in. long)

cop² (kŏp), n. 1. a conical mass of thread, etc., wound on a spindle. 2. Obs. or Dial. the top or crest, esp. of a hill. [OE cop, copp top, summit. Cf. G kopf head]

co·pai·ba (kō pā'bə, -pī'bə), n. an oleoresin obtained from various tropical (chiefly South American) trees of the caesalpiniaceous genus Copaiba, used esp. as a stimulant and diuretic. [t. Sp., t. Guarani: m. kupaiba]

co·pal (kō'pəl, -päl), n. a hard, lustrous resin yielded by various tropical trees, used chiefly in making varnishes. [t. Sp., t. Nahuatl: m. kopalli resin]

Co·pán (kō pän'), n. Santa Rosa de Copán.

co·par·ce·nar·y (kō pär'sə nĕr'ĭ), n. Law. a special kind of joint ownership, esp. arising under common law upon the descent of real property to several female heirs. Also, co·par·ce·ny (kō pär'sə nĭ).

co·par·ce·ner (kō pär'sə nər), n. a member of a coparcenary. [f. co- + PARCENER]

co·part·ner (kō pärt'nər), n. a partner; an associate. —co·part'ner·ship', n.

cope¹ (kōp), v., coped, coping. —v.i. 1. to struggle or contend, esp. on fairly even terms or with a degree of success (fol. by with). 2. Archaic. to have to do (fol. by with). —v.t. 3. Brit. Colloq. to cope with. 4. Obs. to meet in contest. [ME coupe(n), t. F: m. couper strike, der. coup stroke, blow. See COUP, n.]

cope² (kōp), n., v., coped, coping. —n. 1. a long mantle of silk or other material worn by ecclesiastics over the alb or surplice in processions and on other occasions. 2. any cloaklike or canopylike covering. 3. the vault of heaven; the sky. 4. Archit. a coping. —v.t. 5. to furnish with or as with a cope or coping. [ME; OE cāp (in cantel-cāp cope), t. ML: s. cāpa cope]

A. Cope; B. Crosier

co·peck (kō'pĕk), n. kopeck.

Co·pen·ha·gen (kō'pən hā'gən), n. a seaport in and the capital of Denmark, on the E coast of Zealand. 730,226 (est. 1959); with suburbs, 1,253,529 (est. 1959). Danish, København.

copenhagen blue, gray blue.

co·pe·pod (kō'pə pŏd'), n. 1. any of the Copepoda, a large order of (mostly) minute freshwater and marine crustaceans. —adj. 2. pertaining to the Copepoda. [f. m. Gk. kōpē handle, oar + -POD]

Co·per·ni·cus (kō pûr'nə kəs, kə-), n. Nicolaus (nĭk'-ə lā'əs), 1473–1543, Polish astronomer who promulgated the now accepted theory that the earth and the planets move about the sun (the Copernican system). Polish, Kopernik. —Co·per'ni·can, adj.

cope·stone (kōp'stōn'), n. 1. the top stone of a building or the like. 2. a stone used for or in coping. 3. the crown or completion.

cop·i·er (kŏp'ĭ ər), n. one who copies; a copyist.

co·pi·lot (kō'pī'lət), n. the assistant or second pilot in an aircraft.

cop·ing (kō'pĭng), n. the uppermost course of a wall or the like, usually made sloping so as to carry off water.

coping saw, a saw with a short, narrow blade held at both ends in a deeply recessed handle, for cutting curved shapes.

co·pi·ous (kō'pĭ əs), adj. 1. large in quantity or number; abundant. 2. having or yielding an abundant supply. 3. exhibiting abundance or fullness, as of thoughts or words. [ME, t. L: m. s. cōpiōsus plentiful] —co'pi·ous·ly, adv. —co'pi·ous·ness, n. —Syn. 1. plentiful, overflowing. See ample. —Ant. 1. scanty. 3. meager.

co·pla·nar (kō plā'nər), adj. Math. (of figures) in the same plane.

Cop·land (kōp'lənd), n. Aaron (âr'ən), born 1900, U.S. composer.

Cop·ley (kŏp'lĭ), n. John Singleton (sĭng'gəl tən), 1738–1815, U.S. historical and portrait painter.

co·pol·y·mer (kō pŏl'ə mər), n. Chem. a compound made by polymerizing different compounds together.

co·pol·y·mer·ize (kō pŏl'ə mə rīz'), v.t., v.i., -ized, -izing. to subject to or undergo a change analogous to polymerization but with a union of unlike molecules. —co·pol'y·mer·i·za'tion, n.

Cop·pée (kô pě'), n. François (frän swä'), 1842–1908, French poet, dramatist, and novelist.

cop·per¹ (kŏp'ər), n. 1. Chem. a malleable, ductile metallic element having a characteristic reddish-brown color. Symbol: Cu; at. wt.: 63.57; at. no.: 29; sp. gr.: 8.92 at 20°C. 2. a copper coin, as the English penny or halfpenny or the U.S. cent. 3. a container made of copper. 4. Brit. a large boiler, as for cooking on shipboard. 5. a metallic reddish brown. —v.t. 6. to cover, coat, or sheathe with copper. 7. Slang. to bet against. [ME coper, OE coper, copor (c. G kupfer), t. LL: m.s. cuprum, for L aes Cyprium Cyprian metal. See CYPRUS]

cop·per² (kŏp'ər), n. Slang. a policeman. [see COP¹]

cop·per·as (kŏp'ər əs), n. green vitriol, or ferrous sulfate, used in dyeing, medicine, photography, making ink, etc. [ME coperose. Cf. OF couperose, t. ML: m.s. (aqua) cuprōsa, der. LL cuprum. See COPPER¹]

cop·per·head (kŏp'ər hĕd'), n. 1. a venomous snake, Ancistrodon contortrix, of the U.S., having a copper-colored head and reaching a length of about 3 feet. 2. (cap.) a Northern sympathizer with the South during the U.S. Civil War.

Cop·per·mine (kŏp'ər mīn'), n. a river in the central Northwest Territories of Canada, flowing N to the Arctic Ocean. 525 mi.

cop·per·plate (kŏp'ər plāt'), n. 1. a plate of polished copper on which a writing, picture, or design is made by engraving or etching. 2. a print or an impression from such a plate. 3. engraving or printing of this kind.

copper pyrites, chalcopyrite.

cop·per·smith (kŏp'ər smĭth'), n. 1. a worker in copper; one who manufactures copper utensils. 2. the crimson-breasted barbet, Megalaema haemacephala, a common bird in India, etc.

copper sulfate, blue vitriol.

cop·per·y (kŏp'ər ĭ), adj. of, like, or containing copper.

cop·pice (kŏp'ĭs), n. Chiefly Brit. a wood or thicket of small trees or bushes. Also, copse (kŏps). [t. OF: m. copeiz, f. m.s. couper cut + -eiz (g. L -ātícium)]

cop·ra (kŏp′rə), *n.* the dried kernel or meat of the coconut, from which coconut oil is expressed. [t. Pg., t. Malayalam: m. *koppara*, in Hindi *khoprā* coconut]

cop·re·mi·a (kŏp′rē′mĭ·ə), *n. Pathol.* blood poisoning due to absorption of fecal matter. Also, **cop·rae′mi·a**. [f. *copr*(o)- (see COPROLITE) + -EMIA]

cop·ro·lite (kŏp′rə līt′), *n.* a roundish, stony mass consisting of petrified fecal matter of animals. [f. *copro*- (t. Gk.: m. *kopro*-, comb. form of *kópros* dung) + -LITE]

cop·roph·a·gous (kŏprŏf′ə gəs), *adj.* feeding on dung, as certain beetles. [f. *copro*- (see COPROLITE) + -PHAGOUS]

copse (kŏps), *n.* coppice.

Copt (kŏpt), *n.* **1.** one of the natives of Egypt descended from the ancient Egyptians. **2.** an Egyptian Christian of the sect of the Monophysites. [t. Ar.: m. *qibt, qubt* the Copts, t. Coptic: m. *gyptios,* aphetic var. of Gk. *Aigýptios* Egyptian]

'cop·ter (kŏp′tər), *n. Colloq.* helicopter.

Cop·tic (kŏp′tĭk), *n.* **1.** the extinct language of Egypt which developed from ancient Egyptian, used liturgically by Egyptian Christians. —*adj.* **2.** of the Copts.

Coptic Church, the native Christian church in Egypt, embracing about one twelfth of the population.

cop·u·la (kŏp′yə lə), *n., pl.* **-las, -lae** (-lē′). **1.** something that connects or links together. **2.** *Gram., Logic.* a word or set of words (in English the verb *be*) which acts as a connecting link between the subject and the predicate. [t. L: a band, bond] —**cop′u·lar,** *adj.*

cop·u·late (*v.* kŏp′yə lāt′; *adj.* kŏp′yə lĭt), *v.,* **-lated, -lating,** *adj.* —*v.i.* **1.** to unite in sexual intercourse. —*adj.* **2.** *Obs.* joined. [t. L: m.s. *copulātus,* pp., coupled]

cop·u·la·tion (kŏp′yə lā′shən), *n.* **1.** a joining together or coupling. **2.** sexual union or intercourse.

cop·u·la·tive (kŏp′yə lā′tĭv), *adj.* **1.** serving to unite or couple. **2.** involving or consisting of connected words or clauses. **3.** of the nature of a copula: *a copulative verb.* **4.** of or pertaining to copulation. —*n.* **5.** a copulative word. —**cop′u·la·tive·ly,** *adv.*

cop·y (kŏp′ĭ), *n., pl.* **copies,** *v.,* **copied, copying.** —*n.* **1.** a transcript, reproduction, or imitation of an original. **2.** that which is to be transcribed, reproduced, or imitated. **3.** written, typed, or printed matter, or art work, intended to be reproduced in print. **4.** one of the various examples or specimens of the same book, engraving, or the like. **5.** an example of penmanship to be copied by a pupil. **6.** *Brit. Colloq.* (in schools) a composition; a written assignment. —*v.t.* **7.** to make a copy of; transcribe; reproduce: *to copy out a set of figures.* **8.** to follow as a pattern or model; imitate. —*v.i.* **9.** to make a copy or copies. **10.** to make or do something in imitation of something else: *to copy after bad precedents.* [ME *copie,* t. F, t. L: m. *cōpia* plenty, ML transcript] —**Syn. 1.** duplicate. **8.** See **imitate.** —**Ant. 8.** originate.

cop·y·book (kŏp′ĭ bŏŏk′), *n.* **1.** a book in which copies are written or printed for learners to imitate. **2.** a book for or containing copies, as of documents.

copy desk, *Journalism.* the desk at which news stories, etc., are edited and prepared for printing.

cop·y·hold (kŏp′ĭ hōld′), *n. Law.* (formerly) a type of ownership of land in England, evidenced by a copy of the manor roll establishing the title.

cop·y·hold·er (kŏp′ĭ hōl′dər), *n.* **1.** one who or that which holds copy. **2.** a device for holding copy in its place, as on a printer's frame or on a typewriter. **3.** a proofreader's assistant who reads copy aloud, or follows it while proof is read, for the detection of deviations from it in proof. **4.** *Brit. Law.* one who holds an estate in copyhold.

cop·y·ist (kŏp′ĭ ĭst), *n.* **1.** a transcriber, esp. of documents. **2.** an imitator.

cop·y·read·er (kŏp′ĭ rē′dər), *n. Journalism.* one who edits and corrects material written by others.

cop·y·right (kŏp′ĭ rīt′), *n.* **1.** the exclusive right, granted by law for a certain term of years, to make and dispose of copies of, and otherwise to control, a literary, musical, or artistic work. —*adj.* **2.** protected by copyright. —*v.t.* **3.** to secure a copyright on. —**cop′y·right′a·ble,** *adj.* —**cop′y·right′er,** *n.*

Co·que·lin (kōk lăn′), *n.* **Benoit Constant** (bə nwá′ kôn stän′), 1841–1909, French actor.

co·quet (kōkĕt′), *v.,* **-quetted, -quetting,** *adj., n.* —*v.i.* **1.** to trifle in love; flirt; play the coquette. **2.** to act without seriousness; trifle; dally. —*adj.* **3.** coquettish. —*n.* **4.** *Obs.* a male flirt. [t. F, dim. of *coq* cock]

co·quet·ry (kō′kə trĭ, kōkĕt′rĭ), *n., pl.* **-ries. 1.** the behavior or arts of a coquette; flirtation. **2.** trifling.

co·quette (kō kĕt′), *n.* a woman who tries to gain the admiration and affections of men for mere self-gratification; a flirt. [t. F. See COQUET] —**co·quet′tish,** *adj.* —**co·quet′tish·ly,** *adv.* —**co·quet′tish·ness,** *n.*

co·quil·la nut (kōkēl′yə, -kē′yə), the elongated oval fruit or nut of a South American palm, *Attalea funifera,* having a very hard brown shell, used in turnery. [*coquilla,* t. Pg.: m. *coquilho,* dim. of *coco* coconut]

co·qui·na (kōkē′nə), *n.* a soft, whitish rock made up of fragments of marine shells and coral, used to some extent as a building material. [t. Sp.: shellfish, cockle]

co·qui·to (kōkē′tō), *n., pl.* **-tos.** a palm, *Jubaea spectabilis,* of Chile, bearing small edible nuts, which yield a sweet syrup. Also, **coquito palm.** [t. Sp., dim. of *coco* coconut]

cor (kôr), *interj. Brit. Slang.* exclamation of surprise.

cor-, var. of **com-** before *r,* as in *corrupt.*

Cor., **1.** Corinthians. **2.** Coroner.

cor., **1.** corner. **2.** corrected. **3.** correction. **4.** corresponding.

cor·a·ci·i·form (kôr′ə sĭ′ə fôrm′, kôr′-), *adj.* belonging or pertaining to the *Coraciiformes,* the order of birds that includes the kingfishers, motmots, rollers, bee eaters, and hornbills. [f. s. NL *Coracia* genus of birds (der. Gk. *kórax* raven) + -(I)FORM]

cor·a·cle (kôr′ə kəl, kŏr′-), *n. Brit.* (local to Wales and W England) a native boat nearly or quite as broad as long, made like a basket. [t. Welsh: m. *corwgl, cwrwgl,* der. *corwg, cwrwg* carcass, boat]

cor·a·coid (kôr′ə koid′, kŏr′-), *Anat., Zool.* —*adj.* **1.** pertaining to a bony process extending from the scapula toward the sternum in many *Vertebrata.* —*n.* **2.** a coracoid bone. [t. Gk.: m.s. *korakoeidēs* ravenlike]

cor·al (kôr′əl, kŏr′-), *n.* **1.** the hard, calcareous (red, white, black, etc.) skeleton of any of various, mostly compound, marine coelenterate animals, the individual polyps of which come forth by budding. **2.** such skeletons collectively, as forming reefs, islands, etc. **3.** an animal of this kind. **4.** something made of coral, as an ornament, child's toy, etc. **5.** a reddish yellow; light yellowish red; pinkish yellow. **6.** the unimpregnated roe or eggs of the lobster, which when boiled assume the color of red coral. —*adj.* **7.** made of coral: *a coral reef, coral ornament.* **8.** making coral: *a coral polyp.* **9.** resembling coral, esp. in color. [ME, t. OF, g. L *corallum, coralium,* t. Gk.: m. *korállion* red coral]

Cor·al Ga·bles (kôr′əl gā′bəlz, kŏr′-), a city in SE Florida, near Miami. 34,793 (1960).

cor·al·lif·er·ous (kôr′ə lĭf′ər əs, kŏr′-), *adj.* containing or bearing coral; producing coral.

cor·al·line (kôr′ə lĭn, -līn′, kŏr′-), *adj.* **1.** consisting of or containing deposits of calcium carbonate. **2.** corallike. **3.** coral-colored; reddish-yellow; light-yellowish red; pinkish-yellow. —*n.* **4.** any alga having a red color and impregnated with lime. **5.** any of various corallike animals, or calcareous algae.

cor·al·loid (kôr′ə loid′, kŏr′-), *adj.* having the form or appearance of coral. Also, **cor′al·loi′dal.**

coral root, any of the species of the orchidaceous genus *Corallorrhiza,* native to the Northern Hemisphere.

Coral Sea, a part of the S Pacific, partially enclosed by NE Australia, New Guinea, the Solomon Islands, and the New Hebrides: U.S. naval victory over the Japanese, May, 1942.

coral snake, any of the brilliantly colored venomous snakes of the genus *Micrurus,* often with alternating black, yellow, and red rings, including forms found in the southern and southwestern U.S.

co·ram po·pu·lo (kôr′ăm pŏp′yə lō′), *Latin.* before the public.

cor·ban (kôr′băn, kôr′bän′), *n.* (among the ancient Jews) an offering of any kind made to God, one kind being in fulfillment of a vow. [t. Heb.: m. *qorbān*]

cor·bel (kôr′bəl), *n., v.,* **-beled, -beling** or (*esp. Brit.*) **-belled, -belling.** *Archit.* —*n.* **1.** a supporting projection of stone, wood, etc., on the face of a wall. **2.** a short horizontal timber supporting a girder. —*v.t.* **3.** to furnish with or support by a corbel or corbels. [ME, t. OF, g. LL *corvellus,* dim. of L *corvus* raven]

cor·bel·ing (kôr′bəl ĭng), *n. Archit.* **1.** the construction of corbels. **2.** an overlapping arrangement of stones, etc., each course projecting beyond the one below. Also, *esp. Brit.,* **cor′bel·ling.**

cor·bie (kôr′bĭ), *n. Scot.* a raven or crow. [ME *corbin,* t. OF, dim. of *corb* raven, g. L *corvus*]

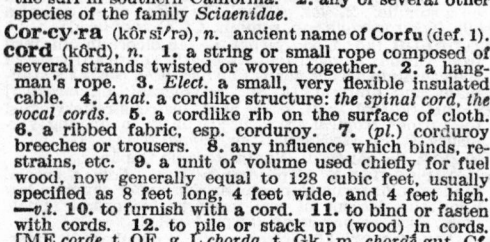

Corbel (def. 1)

corbie gable, a gable with corbiesteps.

cor·bie·step (kôr′bĭ stĕp′), *n.* one of a set of steplike projections on the sides of a gable.

cor·bi·na (kôr bī′nə), *n.* **1.** a fish, *Menticirrhus undulatus,* of the croaker family, the most prized game fish of the surf in southern California. **2.** any of several other species of the family *Sciaenidae.*

Cor·cy·ra (kôr sī′rə), *n.* ancient name of Corfu (def. 1).

cord (kôrd), *n.* **1.** a string or small rope composed of several strands twisted or woven together. **2.** a hangman's rope. **3.** *Elect.* a small, very flexible insulated cable. **4.** *Anat.* a cordlike structure: *the spinal cord, the vocal cords.* **5.** a cordlike rib on the surface of cloth. **6.** a ribbed fabric, esp. corduroy. **7.** (*pl.*) corduroy breeches or trousers. **8.** any influence which binds, restrains, etc. **9.** a unit of volume used chiefly for fuel wood, now generally equal to 128 cubic feet, usually specified as 8 feet long, 4 feet wide, and 4 feet high. —*v.t.* **10.** to furnish with a cord. **11.** to bind or fasten with cords. **12.** to pile or stack up (wood) in cords. [ME *corde,* t. OF, g. L *chorda,* t. Gk.: m. *chordē* gut. Cf. CHORD[1]]

cord·age (kôr′dĭj), *n.* **1.** cords or ropes collectively, esp. in a ship's rigging. **2.** a quantity of wood measured in cords.

cor·date (kôr′dāt), *adj.* **1.** heart-shaped, as a shell. **2.** (of leaves) heart-shaped with the attachment at the notched end. [t. NL: m.s. *cordātus*, der. *L cor* heart] —**cor′date·ly**, *adv.*

Cordate leaf

Cor·day **d'Ar·mont** (kôr dě′ dàr môN′), (**Marie Anne**) **Charlotte** (mả-rē′ án shàr lŏt′), 1768–93, French revolutionary heroine who assassinated Marat.

cord·ed (kôr′dĭd), *adj.* **1.** furnished with, made of, or in the form of cords. **2.** ribbed, as a fabric. **3.** bound with cords. **4.** (of wood) stacked up in cords.

Cor·de·lier (kôr′də lǐr′), *n.* **1.** a Franciscan friar (so called from his girdle of knotted cord). **2.** (*pl.*) a Parisian political club in the time of the French Revolution, which met in an old convent of the Cordeliers. [ME *cordilere*, t. F: m. *cordelier*, ult. der. *corde* CORD]

cor·dial (kôr′jəl), *adj.* **1.** hearty; warmly friendly. **2.** invigorating the heart; stimulating. **3.** *Obs.* of the heart. —*n.* **4.** anything that invigorates or exhilarates. **5.** a strong, sweetened, aromatic alcoholic liquor; a liqueur. **6.** a cordial or stimulating medicine. [ME, t. ML: s. *cordiālis*, der. *L cor* heart] —**cor′dial·ly**, *adv.* —**cor′dial·ness**, *n.*

cor·dial·i·ty (kôr jăl′ə tĭ or, esp. Brit., kôr′dĭ ăl′-), *n., pl.* -**ties**. **1.** cordial quality or feeling. **2.** an instance or expression of cordial feeling.

cor·di·er·ite (kôr′dĭ ər īt′), *n.* a blue mineral, consisting of a silicate of magnesium, aluminum, and iron.

cor·di·form (kôr′də fôrm′), *adj.* heart-shaped. [f. s. *L cor* heart + -(I)FORM]

cor·dil·le·ra (kôr′dĭl yâr′ə, kôr dĭl′ə rə), *n.* a chain of mountains, usually the principal mountain system or mountain axis of a large land mass. [t. Sp.: mountain chain, ult. der. *L chorda* rope] —**cor′dil·le′ran**, *adj.*

Cor·dil·le·ras (kôr′dĭl yâr′əz, kôr dĭl′ə rəz; *Sp.* kôr′dē yě′räs), *n. pl.* **1.** a mountain system in W South America: the Andes and its component ranges. **2.** a mountain system in W North America, including the Sierra Nevada, Coast Range, Cascade Range, Rocky Mountains, etc. **3.** the entire chain of mountain ranges parallel to the Pacific coast, extending from Cape Horn to Alaska. —**Cor′dil·le′ran**, *adj.*

cord·ite (kôr′dīt), *n.* a smokeless powder composed of 30–58% nitroglycerin, 65–37% nitrocellulose, and 5–6% mineral jelly. [f. CORD + -ITE[1]; so named from its cordlike or cylindrical form]

Cór·do·ba (kôr′dô bä), *n.* **1.** Also, **Cordova** (kôr′də-və). a city in S Spain, on the Guadalquiver river: the capital of Spain under Moorish rule; famous cathedral. 180,716 (est. 1955). **2.** a city in central Argentina. 369,886 (1947). **3.** (*l.c.*) **a.** the Nicaraguan monetary unit equivalent to the U.S. gold dollar. **b.** the Nicaraguan silver coin equivalent to this unit.

cor·don (kôr′dən), *n.* **1.** a cord or braid worn for ornament or as a fastening. **2.** a ribbon worn, usually diagonally across the breast, as a badge of a knightly or honorary order. **3.** a line of sentinels, military posts, or the like, enclosing or guarding a particular area. **4.** *Fort.* a projecting course of stones at the base of a parapet. **5.** *Archit.* a stringcourse. [t. F, der. *corde* CORD]

cor·don bleu (kôr dôN blœ′), **1.** the sky-blue ribbon worn as a badge by knights of the highest order of French knighthood under the Bourbons. **2.** some similar high distinction. **3.** one entitled to wear the cordon bleu. **4.** any person of great distinction in his field.

Cor·do·van (kôr′də vən), *adj.* **1.** of Córdoba, Spain. **2.** (*l.c.*) designating or made of a leather made orig. at Córdoba, first of goatskin tanned and dressed, but later also of split horsehide, etc. —*n.* **3.** a native or inhabitant of Córdoba, Spain. **4.** (*l.c.*) cordovan leather.

cor·du·roy (kôr′də roi′, kôr′də roi′), *n.* **1.** a cotton pile fabric with lengthwise cords or ridges. **2.** (*pl.*) trousers or breeches made of this. —*adj.* **3.** of or like corduroy. **4.** constructed of logs laid together transversely, as a road across swampy ground. —*v.t.* **5.** to form, as a road, by laying logs together transversely. **6.** to make a corduroy road over. [cf. obs. *duroy*, a kind of coarse woolen fabric]

cord·wain (kôrd′wān), *n.* *Archaic.* cordovan leather. [ME *corduan*, t. OF: m. *cordoan*, t. Sp.: m. *cordován*]

cord·wain·er (kôrd′wā nər), *n.* **1.** *Archaic.* a worker in cordovan leather. **2.** *Obs.* a shoemaker.

core (kôr), *n., v.*, **cored, coring.** —*n.* **1.** the central part of a fleshy fruit, containing the seeds. **2.** the central, innermost, or most essential part of anything. **3.** *Elect.* **a.** the piece of iron, bundle of iron wires, or the like, forming the central or inner portion of an electromagnet, induction coil, or the like. **b.** the armature core of a dynamo machine, consisting of the assembled armature laminations without the slot insulation or windings. **4.** *Founding.* a body of sand, usually dry, placed in a mold to form openings or give shape to a casting. **5.** the inside wood of a tree. **6.** the base to which veneer woods are attached, usually of a soft or inexpensive wood. —*v.t.* **7.** to remove the core of (fruit). **8.** to cut from the central part. [ME; orig. unknown] —**core′less**, *adj.*

CORE (kôr, kŏr), *n.* Congress of Racial Equality.

Co·re·a (kō rē′ə), *n.* Korea.

co·re·li·gion·ist (kō′rĭ lĭj′ən ĭst), *n.* an adherent of the same religion as another.

co·re·op·sis (kō′rĭ ŏp′sĭs), *n.* any plant of the composite genus *Coreopsis*, including familiar garden species with yellow, brownish, or parti-colored (yellow and red) flowers. [t. NL, f. m.s. Gk. *kóris* bug + -*opsis* -OPSIS; so called from the form of the seed]

cor·er (kôr′ər), *n.* a knife for coring apples, etc.

co·re·spond·ent (kō′rĭ spŏn′dənt, kôr′-), *n.* *Law.* a joint defendant, esp. in a divorce proceeding, where one charged with adultery is made a joint defendant.

corf (kôrf), *n., pl.* **corves** (kôrvz). *Brit.* a small wagon (formerly a wicker basket) for carrying ore, coal, etc., in mines. [t.MD,t.L:m.s.*corbis*basket]

Cor·fu (kôr′fū; *It.* kôr foo′), *n.* **1.** Ancient, **Corcyra.** one of the Ionian Islands, off the NW coast of Greece. 105,414 pop. (1951); 229 sq. mi. **2.** a seaport on this island. 30,739 (1951). Greek, **Kerkyra.**

Cor·gi (kôr′gĭ), *n.* See **Welsh Corgi.**

co·ri·a·ceous (kôr′ĭ ā′shəs, kŏr′-), *adj.* of or like leather. [t. LL: m. *coriāceus* leathern]

co·ri·an·der (kôr′ĭ ăn′dər, kŏr′-), *n.* **1.** a herbaceous plant, *Coriandrum sativum*, with aromatic seedlike fruit (coriander seeds) used in cookery and medicine. **2.** the fruit or seeds. [ME *coriandre*, t. F, t. L: m. *coriandrum*, t. Gk.: m. *koríandron*, var. of *koriannon*]

Cor·inth (kôr′ĭnth, kŏr′-), *n.* **1.** an ancient city in Greece, strategically located on the Isthmus of Corinth: famed for its luxury. **2. Gulf of**, an arm of the Ionian Sea, N of the Peloponnesus. Also, **Gulf of Lepanto**. **3. Isthmus of**, a narrow isthmus at the head of the Gulf of Corinth, connecting the Peloponnesus with central Greece: traversed by a ship canal.

Co·rin·thi·an (kə rĭn′thĭ ən), *adj.* **1.** of Corinth, noted in ancient times for its artistic adornment, luxury, and licentiousness. **2.** luxurious; licentious. **3.** ornate, as literary style. **4.** *Archit.* designating or pertaining to one of the three Greek orders, distinguished by a bell-shaped capital with rows of acanthus leaves and a continuous frieze. See diag. under **order.** —*n.* **5.** a native or inhabitant of Corinth. **6.** (*pl.*) the two books or epistles of the New Testament addressed by St. Paul to the Christian community at Corinth. **7.** a man of fashion.

Cor·i·o·la·nus (kôr′ĭ ə lā′nəs, kŏr′-), *n.* **1.** Gaius (or Gnaeus) **Marcius** (gā′əs, or nē′əs, mär′shĭ əs), a legendary Roman general of the 5th century B.C. who, in revenge for being exiled, led an army against Rome, but was turned back by the appeals of his mother and his wife. **2.** a tragedy (about 1608) by Shakespeare.

co·ri·um (kôr′ĭ əm), *n., pl.* **coria** (kôr′ĭ ə). *Anat.* the sensitive vascular layer of the skin, beneath the epidermis; the derma. [t. L: skin, hide, leather]

cork (kôrk), *n.* **1.** the outer bark of a species of oak, *Quercus Suber*, of Mediterranean countries, used for making stoppers of bottles, floats, etc. **2.** the tree itself. **3.** something made of cork. **4.** a piece of cork, or of other material (as rubber), used as a stopper for a bottle, etc. **5.** *Angling.* a small float to buoy up a fishing line or to indicate when a fish bites. **6.** *Bot.* an outer tissue of bark produced by and exterior to the phellogen. —*v.t.* **7.** to provide or fit with cork or a cork. **8.** to stop with, or as with, a cork (often fol. by *up*). **9.** to blacken with burnt cork. [t.Sp.: aphetic m. *alcorque* shoe with cork, t. Ar.: m. *al qorq*, t. L: m. *quercus* oak; ? b. with Sp. *corcho* cork, ult. g. L *cortex* bark] —**cork′like**, *adj.*

Cork (kôrk), *n.* **1.** county in S Ireland, in Munster province. 336,687 pop. (est. 1956); 2881 sq. mi. **2.** its county seat: a seaport. 79,945 (est. 1956).

cork·age (kôr′kĭj), *n.* a charge made by hotel keepers, etc., for serving liquor not supplied by the house.

cork cambium, *Bot.* phellogen.

corked (kôrkt), *adj.* **1.** stopped with a cork. **2.** (of wine) tasting of the cork; having the flavor spoiled by poor corking. **3.** blackened with burnt cork.

cork·er (kôr′kər), *n.* **1.** one who or that which corks. **2.** *Slang.* something that closes a discussion or settles a question. **3.** *Slang.* something striking or astonishing. **4.** *Slang.* something very good of its kind.

cork·ing (kôr′kĭng), *adj. Slang.* excellent; fine.

cork·screw (kôrk′skroo′), *n.* **1.** an instrument consisting of a metal spiral with a sharp point and a transverse handle, used to draw corks from bottles. —*adj.* **2.** resembling a corkscrew; helical; spiral. —*v.t., v.i.* **3.** to move in a spiral or zigzag course.

cork·wood (kôrk′wŏŏd′), *n.* **1.** a stout shrub or small tree, *Leitneria floridana*, with shining deciduous leaves, densely pubescent aments, and a drupaceous fruit. **2.** any of certain trees and shrubs having a light and porous wood, as the balsa.

cork·y (kôr′kĭ), *adj.*, **corkier, corkiest. 1.** of the nature of cork; corklike. **2.** *Colloq.* buoyant, lively, or skittish. **3.** (of wine) corked (def. 2). —**cork′i·ness**, *n.*

corm (kôrm), *n. Bot.* an enlarged, fleshy bulblike base of a stem, as in the crocus. [t. NL: s. *cormus*, t. Gk.: m. *kormós* tree trunk with boughs lopped off]

Corm of crocus

cor·mo·phyte (kôr′mə fīt′), *n.* any of the *Cormophyta*, an old primary division or group of plants having an axis differentiated into stem and root, and including all phanerogams and the higher cryptogams. [f. *cormo-* (comb. form of CORM) + -PHYTE] —**cor·mo·phyt·ic** (kôr′mə fĭt′ĭk), *adj.*

cor·mo·rant (kôr′mə rənt), *n.* **1.** any bird of the family *Phalacrocoracidae*, comprising large, voracious, totipalmate water birds with a long neck and a pouch under the beak in which they hold captured fish, as *Phalacrocorax carbo*, a common species of America, Europe, and Asia. **2.** a greedy or rapacious person. —*adj.* **3.** greedy; rapacious; insatiable. [ME *cormoraunte*, t. OF: m. *cormoran*, cormaran, f. *corp* raven + *marenc* marine (der. *mer* sea)]

Crested cormorant.
Phalacrocorax auritus
(2½ ft. long)

corn¹ (kôrn), *n.* **1.** maize; Indian corn. **2.** any edible grain, esp. wheat in England and oats in Scotland. **3.** a single seed of certain plants, esp. of cereal plants, as wheat, rye, barley, and maize; a grain. **4.** *U.S. Colloq.* whiskey made from Indian corn. —*v.t.* **5.** to granulate, as gunpowder. **6.** to preserve and season with salt in grains. **7.** to lay down in brine, as meat. **8.** to plant (land) with corn. **9.** to feed with corn. [ME and OE; c. G *korn*, akin to L *grānum* GRAIN]

corn² (kôrn), *n.* a horny induration or callosity of the epidermis, usually with a central core, caused by undue pressure or friction, esp. on the toes or feet. [t. OF: horn, g. L *cornū*]

cor·na·ceous (kôr nā′shəs), *adj.* belonging to the *Cornaceae*, a family of plants, mostly shrubs and trees, including the dogwood, etc. [f. NL *cornāce(ae)* (der. L *cornus* cornel) + -OUS]

Corn Belt, a region in the midwestern U.S., esp. Iowa, Illinois, and Indiana, excellent for raising corn and corn-fed livestock.

corn borer, the larva of a small moth, *Pyrausta nubilalis*, which feeds on corn and other grasses.

corn bread, a kind of bread made of corn meal.

corn cake, *U.S.* a cake made of corn meal.

corn·cob (kôrn′kŏb′), *n.* *U.S.* **1.** the elongated woody core in which the grains of an ear of maize are embedded. **2.** a tobacco pipe with a bowl made of this.

corn cockle, a caryophyllaceous annual, *Agrostemma Githago*, bearing red or white flowers, common as a weed among crops of grain.

corn color, light yellow. —**corn′-col′ored,** *adj.*

corn crake, the European land rail, *Crex crex*, a bird common in grain fields.

corn·crib (kôrn′krĭb′), *n.* a ventilated structure used for the storage of unshelled maize.

corn dodger, *U.S.* a kind of bread made of corn meal, fried or baked hard.

cor·ne·a (kôr′nĭ ə), *n.* *Anat.* the transparent anterior part of the external coat of the eye, covering the iris and the pupil, and continuous with the sclera. See diag. under eye. [t. L, fem. sing. of *corneus* horny] —**cor′·ne·al,** *adj.*

corn earworm, the larva of a noctuid moth, *Heliothis armigera*, destructive to corn, cotton, and other plants; bollworm.

corned (kôrnd), *adj.* preserved or cured with salt: *corned beef.*

Cor·neille (kôr nā′; *Fr.* kôr nĕ′y), *n.* **Pierre** (pyĕr), 1606–84, French dramatist and poet.

cor·nel (kôr′nəl), *n.* any of the trees or perennials constituting the genus *Cornus*, as *C. sanguinea*, the European dogwood, or *C. florida*, the flowering dogwood of America. [t. G, t. ML: m. *cornolius* cornel tree, ult. der. L *cornus*]

Cor·nel·ia (kôr nēl′yə), *n.* died after 121 B.C., the mother of Tiberius and Gaius Gracchus, champions of the rights of the Roman people.

cor·nel·ian (kôr nēl′yən), *n.* carnelian.

Cor·ne·li·us (kôr nē′lĭ ŏos′), *n.* **Peter von** (pā′tər fən), 1783–1867, German painter, esp. of historical frescoes.

Cor·nell (kôr nĕl′), *n.* **Ezra**, 1807–74, U.S. capitalist and philanthropist.

cor·ne·ous (kôr′nĭ əs), *adj.* consisting of a horny substance; horny. [t. L: m. *corneus* horny]

cor·ner (kôr′nər), *n.* **1.** the meeting place of two converging lines or surfaces. **2.** the space between two converging lines or surfaces near their intersection; angle. **3.** a projecting angle. **4.** the place where two streets meet. **5.** an end; margin; edge. **6.** any narrow, secluded, or secret place. **7.** an awkward or embarrassing position, esp. one from which escape is impossible. **8.** any part, even the least or the most remote. **9.** *Finance.* a monopolizing or a monopoly of the available supply of a stock or commodity, to a point permitting control of price (applied only when monopoly price is exacted). **10.** a region; quarter: *all the corners of the earth.* **11.** a piece to protect the corner of anything. —*v.t.* **12.** to furnish with corners. **13.** to place in, or drive into, a corner. **14.** *Chiefly U.S.* to force into an awkward or difficult position, or one from which escape is impossible. **15.** to form a corner in (a stock, etc.). —*v.i.* **16.** *U.S.* to meet in, or be situated on or at, a corner. **17.** to form a corner in a stock or commodity. [ME, t. AF, var. of OF *cornere*, ult. der. L *cornū* horn, corner]

cor·ner·stone (kôr′nər stōn′), *n.* **1.** a stone which lies at the corner of two walls, and serves to unite them.

2. a stone built into a corner of the foundation of an important edifice as the actual or nominal starting point in building, usually laid with formal ceremonies, and often hollowed out and made the repository of documents, etc. **3.** something of fundamental importance.

cor·ner·wise (kôr′nər wīz′), *adv.* **1.** with the corner in front. **2.** so as to form a corner. **3.** from corner to corner; diagonally. Also, **cor·ner·ways** (kôr′nər wāz′).

cor·net (kôr nĕt′ *for 1;* kôr′nĭt, kôr nĕt′ *for 2–7*), *n.* **1.** a wind instrument of the trumpet class, with valves or pistons. **2.** a little cone of paper twisted at the end, used for enclosing small wares. **3.** *Brit.* a cone, as for ice cream. **4.** the great white cap worn by Sisters of Charity. **5.** a headdress formerly worn by women. **6.** *Naut.* a signal pennant. **7.** (formerly) an officer in a troop of cavalry, who carried the colors. [ME *cornette*, t. OF: m. *cornet*, ult. der. L *cornū* horn] —**cor·net′ist, cor·net′tist,** *n.*

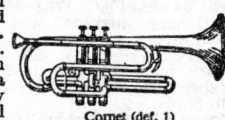
Cornet (def. 1)

cor·net-à-pis·tons (kôr nĕt′ə pĭs′tənz; *Fr.* kôr nĕ′à pēs tôN′), *n., pl.* **cornets-à-pistons** (kôr nĕts′; *Fr.* kôr nĕ′zà pēs tôN′). cornet. [t. F: cornet with pistons]

corn·flow·er (kôrn′flou′ər), *n.* **1.** any of several plants growing in grain fields, as *Centaurea cyanus*, a composite plant with blue (varying to white) flowers, growing wild in Europe and often cultivated for ornament; bluebottle. **2.** corn cockle. [f. *Brit.* cornstarch.

corn·husk (kôrn′hŭsk′), *n.* the husk of an ear of maize.

cor·nice (kôr′nĭs), *n., v.,* **-niced, -nicing.** —*n.* **1.** *Archit.* **a.** a horizontal molded projection which crowns or finishes a wall, building, etc. **b.** the uppermost division of an entablature, resting on the frieze. See diag. under **column. c.** the exposed exterior surface of a gutter. **2.** the molding or moldings between the walls and ceiling of a room. **3.** any of the various other ornamental horizontal moldings or bands, as for concealing hooks or rods from which curtains are hung or for supporting picture hooks. —*v.t.* **4.** to furnish or finish with, or as with, a cornice. [t. F, t. It., t. MGk.: m.s. *korōnis* summit, Gk. anything curved or bent]

cor·nic·u·late (kôr nĭk′yə lāt′, -lĭt), *adj.* resembling a small horn in appearance. [f. s. L *corniculus* little horn + -ATE¹]

Cor·nish (kôr′nĭsh), *adj.* **1.** of Cornwall (England), its inhabitants, or the language formerly spoken by them. —*n.* **2.** the old Celtic language of Cornwall. **3.** the dialect of English now spoken in Cornwall. —**Cor·nish·man** (kôr′nĭsh mən), *n.*

Corn Law, *Eng. Hist.* any one of a series of laws regulating the home and foreign grain trade, the last of which was repealed in 1846.

corn lily, any of several ornamental bulbous plants of the South African genus *Ixia*, family *Iridaceae*.

corn meal, **1.** meal made of corn or grain; Indian meal. **2.** *Scot.* oatmeal. —**corn′meal′,** *adj.*

corn picker, *U.S.* a machine for picking ears of corn from standing stalks and removing husks from the ears.

corn pit, an exchange devoted to trading in corn futures.

corn pone, *Southern U.S.* **1.** corn bread, esp. of a plain or simple kind. **2.** a cake or loaf of this.

corn poppy, the common Old World poppy, *Papaver rhoeas*, bearing bright-red flowers, now the symbol of fallen soldiers.

corn rose, **1.** the common red poppy, *Papaver rhoeas*. **2.** the corn cockle, *Agrostemma Githago*.

corn salad, any of several plants of the genus *Valerianella*, esp. *V. olitoria* and *V. eriocarpa*, sometimes found wild in grain fields, and used for salad.

corn shock, a stack of upright cornstalks.

corn silk, the fresh styles and stigmas of *Zea mays*, used in medicine as a diuretic.

corn smut, a fungus, *Ustilago zeae*, growing on Indian corn, formerly used medicinally.

corn·stalk (kôrn′stôk′), *n.* the stalk or stem of corn, esp. Indian corn.

corn·starch (kôrn′stärch′), *n.* a starch, or a starchy flour made from corn, used for making puddings, etc.

corn sugar, a sugar made from corn, being the common form of glucose.

corn syrup, the syrup prepared from corn.

cor·nu (kôr′nū), *n., pl.* **-nua** (-nyŏŏ ə). a horn, esp. a process of bone resembling a horn. [t. L. See HORN]

cor·nu·co·pi·a (kôr′nə kō′pĭ ə), *n.* **1.** the fabulous horn of the goat Amalthaea, which suckled Zeus, represented as overflowing with flowers, fruit, etc., and symbolizing plenty. **2.** an overflowing supply. **3.** a horn-shaped or conical receptacle or ornament. [t. LL, for L *cornū cōpiae* horn of plenty] —**cor·nu·co′pi·an,** *adj.*

cor·nus (kôr′nəs), *n.* a cornel. [t. L: dogwood tree]

cor·nut·ed (kôr nū′tĭd, -nŏŏ′-), *adj.* having horns.

Corn·wall (kôrn′wôl *or, esp. Brit.,* -wəl), *n.* a county in SW England. 345,442 pop. (1951); 1357 sq. mi. *Co. seat:* Bodmin.

Corn·wal·lis (kôrn wŏl′ĭs, -wôl′ĭs), *n.* **Charles, 1st Marquis,** 1738–1805, British general and statesman: surrendered to Washington at Yorktown, Virginia, October 19, 1781.

---

corn whiskey, whiskey made from corn.

corn·y (kôr′nĭ), *adj.,* **cornier, corniest. 1.** of or abounding in corn. **2.** *Colloq.* (of jazz) written or played with self-conscious emotionalism, lacking sophistication or spontaneity and enthusiasm. **3.** *Slang.* of poor quality: *corny radio programs.*

cor·o·dy (kôr′ə dĭ, kŏr′-), *n., pl.* **-dies.** *Chiefly Hist.* **1.** an allowance, as of food, etc., for one's maintenance. **2.** the right to this. [late ME, t. ML: m.s. *corrōdium,* var. of *corrēdium* provision. Cf. ARRAY]

co·rol·la (kə rŏl′ə), *n. Bot.* the internal envelop or floral leaves of a flower, usually of delicate texture and of some color other than green; the petals considered collectively. [t. L: dim. of *corōna* crown]

cor·ol·la·ceous (kôr′ə lā′shəs, kŏr′-), *adj. Bot.* having or resembling a corolla.

cor·ol·lar·y (kôr′ə lĕr′ĭ, kŏr′-, *or, esp. Brit.,* kə rŏl′ə rĭ), *n., pl.* **-laries. 1.** *Math.* a proposition incidentally proved in proving another. **2.** an immediate or easily drawn consequence. **3.** a natural consequence or result. [ME *corolarie,* t. LL: m. *corollārium* corollary, L gift, gratuity, orig. garland, der. L *corolla* garland]

Corollas
Polypetalous corollas: A, Unguiculate; B, Papilionaceous; C, Cruciate. Gamopetalous corollas: D, Personate; E, Ligulate; F, Labiate

Cor·o·man·del Coast (kôr′ə măn′dəl, kŏr′-), that part of the coastline of SE India extending from Point Calimere (opposite the N end of Ceylon) to the mouth of the Kistna river.

co·ro·na (kə rō′nə), *n., pl.* **-nas, -nae** (-nē). **1.** a white or colored circle of light seen round a luminous body, esp. the sun or moon (in meteorology, restricted to those circles due to the diffraction produced by thin clouds or mist). **2.** *Astron.* a faintly luminous envelope outside of the sun's chromosphere, the inner part consisting of highly ionized elements. **3.** *Archit.* that part of a cornice supported by and projecting beyond the bed molding. See diag. under **column. 4.** *Anat.* the upper portion or crown of a part, as of the head. **5.** *Bot.* a crownlike appendage, esp. one on the inner side of a corolla, as in the narcissus. **6.** *Elect.* a discharge, frequently luminous, at the surface of a conductor, or between two conductors of the same transmission line, accompanied by ionization of the surrounding atmosphere and power loss; brush discharge. [t. L: garland, CROWN]

Co·ro·na Aus·tra·lis (kə rō′nə ô strā′lĭs), the Southern Crown, a southern constellation touching the southern part of Sagittarius. [t. L]

Co·ro·na Bo·re·al·is (kə rō′nə bōr′ĭ ăl′ĭs, -ā′lĭs), the Northern Crown, a northern constellation between Hercules and Boötes. [t. L]

cor·o·nach (kôr′ə nəkh, kŏr′-), *n.* (in Scotland and Ireland) a song or lamentation for the dead; a dirge. [t. Gaelic: m. *corranach* outcry, dirge]

Co·ro·na·do (kôr′ə nä′dō; *Sp.* kô′rô nä′dô), *n.* **Francisco Vásquez de** (frän thēs′kô väs′kĕth dĕ), 1510–1554?, Spanish explorer in the SW part of the U.S.

cor·o·nal (*n.* kôr′ə nəl, kŏr′-; *adj.* kə rō′nəl, kôr′ə nəl, kŏr′-), *n.* **1.** *Anat.* the coronal suture. **2.** a crown; coronet. **3.** a garland. —*adj.* **4.** of or pertaining to a coronal. **5.** *Phonet.* retroflex. [t. LL: s. *coronālis*]

coronal suture, *Anat.* a suture extending across the skull between the frontal bone and the parietal bones. See diag. under **cranium.**

cor·o·nar·y (kôr′ə nĕr′ĭ, kŏr′-), *adj.* **1.** of or like a crown. **2.** *Anat.* **a.** encircling like a crown, as certain blood vessels. **b.** pertaining to the arteries which supply the heart tissues and which originate in the root of the aorta. [t. L: m.s. *coronārius*]

coronary thrombosis, *Pathol.* the occlusion of a coronary arterial branch by a blood clot within the vessel, usually at a site narrowed by arteriosclerosis.

cor·o·na·tion (kôr′ə nā′shən, kŏr′-), *n.* act or ceremony of investing a king, etc., with a crown.

cor·o·ner (kôr′ə nər, kŏr′-), *n.* an officer, as of a county or municipality, whose chief function is to investigate by inquest (often before a **coroner's jury**) any death not clearly due to natural causes. [ME, t. AF: m. *corouner* officer of the crown, der. *coroune.* See CROWN] —**cor′o·ner·ship′,** *n.*

cor·o·net (kôr′ə nĭt, -nĕt′, kŏr′-), *n.* **1.** a small or inferior crown. **2.** an insignia for the head, worn by peers or members of nobility. **3.** a crownlike ornament for the head, as of gold or jewels. **4.** the lowest part of the pastern of a horse, just above the hoof. [t. OF: m. *coronete,* dim. of *corone* CROWN]

cor·o·net·ed (kôr′ə nĭt′ĭd, -nĕt′ĭd, kŏr′-), *adj.* wearing, or entitled to wear, a coronet. Also, **cor′o·net′ted.**

Co·rot (kô rō′), *n.* **Jean Baptiste Camille** (zhän bȧ·tēst′ kȧ mē′y), 1796–1875, French landscape painter.

Corp., 1. Corporal. **2.** Corporation. Also, **corp.**

Corpl., Corporal.

cor·po·ra (kôr′pər ə), *n.* pl. of **corpus.**

cor·po·ral[1] (kôr′pər əl), *adj.* **1.** of the human body, bodily; physical: *corporal pleasure.* **2.** personal: *corporal possession.* **3.** *Zool.* of the body proper (as distinguished from the head and limbs). **4.** *Obs.* corporeal. [ME, t. L: s. *corporālis* bodily] —**cor′po·ral′i·ty,** *n.* —**cor′po·ral·ly,** *adv.* —**Syn. 1.** See **physical.**

cor·po·ral[2] (kôr′pər əl), *n.* **1.** (in the army) a noncommissioned officer of lowest rank. **2.** *Brit. Navy.* a petty officer whose duty is to assist the master-at-arms. [t. F, obs. var. of *caporal,* t. It.: m. *caporale,* der. *capo* (g. L *caput*) head] —**cor′po·ral·ship′,** *n.*

cor·po·ral[3] (kôr′pər əl), *n. Eccles.* a fine cloth, usually of linen, on which the consecrated elements are placed during the celebration of the Eucharist. [ME, t. ML: s. *corporālis, corporāle,* der. L *corpus* body]

corporal punishment, *Law.* physical injury inflicted on the body of one convicted of a crime, and including the death penalty, flogging, sentence to a term of years, etc.

cor·po·rate (kôr′pər ĭt, -prĭt), *adj.* **1.** forming a corporation. **2.** of a corporation. **3.** united in one body. **4.** pertaining to a united body, as of persons. [t. L: m.s. *corporātus,* pp., formed into a body] —**cor′po·rate·ly,** *adv.*

cor·po·ra·tion (kôr′pə rā′shən), *n.* **1.** an association of individuals, created by law or under authority of law, having a continuous existence irrespective of that of its members, and powers and liabilities distinct from those of its members. **2.** (*cap.*) (in England) the principal officials of a borough, etc. **3.** any group of persons united, or regarded as united, in one body. **4.** *Slang.* the abdomen, esp. when large and prominent.

cor·po·ra·tive (kôr′pə rā′tĭv), *adj. Pol. Econ.* of a political system under which the principal economic functions (banking, industry, labor, etc.) are organized as corporate unities.

cor·po·ra·tor (kôr′pə rā′tər), *n.* a member of a corporation, esp. one of the original members.

cor·po·re·al (kôr pōr′ĭ əl), *adj.* **1.** of the nature of the physical body; bodily. **2.** of the nature of matter; material; tangible: *corporeal property.* [f. s. L *corporeus* of the nature of body + -AL[1]] —**cor·po′re·al·i·ty, cor·po′re·al·ness,** *n.* —**cor·po·re·al·ly,** *adv.* —**Syn. 1.** See **physical.** —**Ant. 1.** spiritual. **2.** intangible.

cor·po·re·i·ty (kôr′pə rē′ə tĭ), *n.* material or physical nature or quality; materiality.

cor·po·sant (kôr′pə zănt′), *n.* a light, due to atmospheric electricity, sometimes seen on the mastheads, yardarms, etc., of ships and on church towers, treetops, etc. [t. Pg.: m. *corpo santo* holy body [L *corpus sanctum*]]

corps (kōr), *n., pl.* **corps** (kōrz). **1.** *Mil.* an organized military body consisting of officers and men, or of officers alone: *the U.S. Marine Corps, Corps of Cadets.* **b.** a military unit of ground combat forces consisting of two or more divisions and other troops. **2.** a group of persons associated or acting together: *the diplomatic corps.* **3.** *Obs.* corpse. [t. F. See CORPSE]

corps area, *Mil.* (formerly) one of the nine military subdivisions of the continental U.S.

corps de bal·let (kôr də bȧ lĕ′), *French.* the dancers in a ballet company who perform as a group and have no solo parts.

corpse (kôrps), *n.* **1.** a dead body, usually of a human being. **2.** *Obs.* a living body. [ME *corps, cors,* t. OF, g. L *corpus* body] —**Syn. 1.** See **body.**

corps·man (kôr′mən), *n., pl.* **-men. 1.** *U.S. Navy.* an enlisted man working as a pharmacist or hospital assistant. **2.** *U.S. Army.* an enlisted man of the Medical Department who accompanies combat troops into battle to give first aid, carry off the wounded, etc.

cor·pu·lence (kôr′pyə ləns), *n.* bulkiness or largeness of body; fatness; fleshiness; portliness. Also, **cor′pu·len·cy.** [late ME, t. F, t. L: m.s. *corpulentia*]

cor·pu·lent (kôr′pyə lənt), *adj.* large or bulky of body; portly; stout; fat. [ME, t. L: s. *corpulentus,* der. *corpus* body] —**cor′pu·lent·ly,** *adv.*

cor·pus (kôr′pəs), *n., pl.* **-po·ra** (-pər ə). **1.** the body of a man or animal. **2.** *Anat.* any of various bodies, masses, or parts of special character or function. **3.** a large or complete collection of writings, laws, etc. **4.** a principal or capital sum, as opposed to interest or income. [t. L]

cor·pus al·la·tum (kôr′pəs ə lā′təm), *pl.* **corpora allata** (kôr′pə rə ə lā′tə). *Entomol.* one of a pair of small ductless, hormone-secreting glands in the head of an insect behind the brain. [NL: added body]

cor·pus cal·lo·sum (kôr′pəs kə lō′səm), *pl.* **corpora callosa** (kôr′pə rə kə lō′sə). *Anat., Zool.* a great band of deeply situated transverse white fibers uniting the two halves of the cerebrum, peculiar to *Mammalia.* [NL: hard body]

cor·pus car·di·a·cum (kôr′pəs kär dī′ə kəm), *pl.* **corpora cardiaca** (kôr′pə rə kär dī′ə kə). *Entomol.* one of a pair of small cellular bodies associated with the corpora allata in the back of an insect's head, generally attached to the aorta, probably organs of hormone secretion.

Cor·pus Chris·ti (kôr′pəs krĭs′tĭ; *for 1 also* -tī). **1.** *Rom. Cath. Ch.* a festival in honor of the Eucharist, kept on the Thursday after Trinity Sunday. **2.** a seaport in S Texas, on **Corpus Christi Bay,** an inlet of the Gulf of Mexico. 167,690 (1960). [t. L: body of Christ]

ăct, āble, dâre, ärt; ĕbb, ēqual; ĭf, īce; hŏt, ōver, ôrder, oil, bŏŏk, ōōze, out; ŭp, ūse, ûrge; ə = a in alone; ch, chief; g, give; ng, ring; sh, shoe; th, thin; ŧh, that; zh, vision.   See the full key on inside cover.

cor·pus·cle (kôr′pəs əl, -pŭs əl), *n.* **1.** *Physiol.* one of the minute bodies which form a constituent of the blood (**blood corpuscles**, both red and white), the lymph (**lymph corpuscles**, white only), etc. **2.** a minute body forming a more or less distinct part of an organism. **3.** *Physics, Chem.* a minute or elementary particle of matter, as an electron, proton, or atom. **4.** a minute particle. Also, **cor·pus·cule** (kôr′pŭs′kŭl). [t. L: m. s. *corpusculum*, dim. of *corpus* body] —**cor·pus·cu·lar** (kôr pŭs′kyə lər), *adj.*

cor·pus de·lic·ti (kôr′pəs dĭ lĭk′tī), *Law.* the fact that a crime or offense has actually been committed. Except where the accused pleads guilty, corroboration of this fact by other evidence is usually required before he can be convicted. [t. L: body of the transgression]

cor·pus ju·ris (kôr′pəs jŏŏr′ĭs), a compilation of law or the collected law of a nation or state. [t. L]

Corpus Juris Ca·non·i·ci (kə nŏn′ə sī′), the collection of church law which remained in power until it was replaced in 1918 by the Codex Juris Canonici. [t. L]

Corpus Juris Ci·vi·lis (sĭ vī′lĭs), the collective title (since the 17th century) of the whole legislation of Justinian Code, promulgated in the 6th century, as the Digest, the Institutes, the Code, and the Novels. [t. L]

cor·pus lu·te·um (kôr′pəs lōō′tĭ əm), *pl.* **corpora lutea** (kôr′pə rə lōō′tĭ ə). **1.** *Anat.* a ductless gland developed within the ovary by the reorganization of a Graafian follicle following ovulation. **2.** *Pharm.* progesterone. [NL: yellow body]

cor·pus stri·a·tum (kôr′pəs strī ā′təm), *pl.* **corpora striata** (kôr′pə rə strī ā′tə). *Anat.* a mass of gray matter beneath the cortex and in front of the thalamus in each cerebral hemisphere. [NL: striped body]

cor·ral (kə rǎl′), *n., v.,* **-ralled, -ralling.** —*n.* **1.** a pen or enclosure for horses, cattle, etc. **2.** an enclosure formed of wagons during an encampment, for defense against attack. —*v.t.* **3.** to confine in, or as in, a corral. **4.** *U.S. Colloq.* to seize; capture. **5.** to form (wagons) into a corral. [t. Sp.: enclosed yard, der. *corro* a ring]

cor·rect (kə rěkt′), *v.t.* **1.** to set right; remove the errors or faults of. **2.** to point out or mark the errors in. **3.** to admonish or rebuke in order to improve. **4.** to counteract the operation or effect of (something hurtful). **5.** *Math., Physics, etc.* to alter or adjust so as to bring into accordance with a standard or with some required condition. —*adj.* **6.** conforming to fact or truth; free from error; accurate: *a correct statement.* **7.** in accordance with an acknowledged or accepted standard; proper: *correct behavior.* [ME *correcte*(*n*), t. L: m. s. *correctus,* pp., made straight, directed] —**cor·rect′ly,** *adv.* —**cor·rect′ness,** *n.* —**cor·rec′tor,** *n.*
—**Syn. 1.** rectify, amend, emend, reform, remedy. **3.** discipline. See **punish. 6.** faultless, perfect, exact. CORRECT, ACCURATE, PRECISE imply conformity to fact, standard, or truth. A CORRECT statement is one free from error, mistakes, or faults. An ACCURATE statement is one which, as a result of an active effort to comprehend and verify, shows careful conformity to fact, truth, or spirit. A PRECISE statement shows scrupulously strict and detailed (sometimes excessive) conformity to fact. —**Ant. 6.** faulty, inaccurate. **7.** unconventional

correcting plate, the thin lens used to correct incoming light rays in special forms of reflecting telescopes.

cor·rec·tion (kə rěk′shən), *n.* **1.** act of correcting. **2.** that which is substituted or proposed for what is wrong; an emendation. **3.** punishment; chastisement; discipline; reproof. **4.** *Math., Physics, etc.* a subordinate quantity that has to be applied in order to ensure accuracy, as in the use of an instrument or the solution of a problem. —**cor·rec′tion·al,** *adj.*

cor·rect·i·tude (kə rěk′tə tūd′, -tōōd′), *n.* correctness, esp. of manners and conduct. [f. CORRECT, v. + *-itude,* modeled on RECTITUDE]

cor·rec·tive (kə rěk′tĭv), *adj.* **1.** tending to correct; having the quality of correcting. —*n.* **2.** a corrective agent. —**cor·rec′tive·ly,** *adv.*

Cor·reg·gio (kô rěd′jō), *n.* **Antonio Allegri da** (än-tō′nyō äl lě′grē dä), 1494–1534, Italian painter.

Cor·reg·i·dor (kə rěg′ə dôr′; *Sp.* kôr rě′hē dôr′), *n.* a fortified island in Manila Bay, in the Philippine Islands: surrendered to the Japanese after heroic resistance, May 6, 1942. 2 sq. mi.

cor·re·late (kôr′ə lāt′, kôr′-), *v.,* **-lated, -lating,** *adj.,* *n.* —*v.t.* **1.** to place in or bring into mutual or reciprocal relation; establish in orderly connection. —*v.i.* **2.** to have a mutual or reciprocal relation; stand in correlation. —*adj.* **3.** mutually or reciprocally related; correlated. —*n.* **4.** either of two related things, esp. when one implies the other. [f. COR- + RELATE]

cor·re·la·tion (kôr′ə lā′shən, kôr′-), *n.* **1.** mutual relation of two or more things, parts, etc. **2.** act of correlating. **3.** state of being correlated. **4.** *Statistics.* the degree of relationship of two attributes or measurements on the same group of elements. **5.** *Physiol.* the interdependence or reciprocal relations of organs or functions.

correlation coefficient, *Statistics.* the measure of correlation, called *r,* having the value +1 for perfect positive linear correlation, −1 for perfect negative linear correlation, and a value of 0 for a complete lack of correlation.

correlation ratio, *Statistics.* a mathematical measure of the correlation between two sets of values not linearly correlated.

cor·rel·a·tive (kə rěl′ə tĭv), *adj.* **1.** so related that each implies or complements the other. **2.** being in correlation; mutually related. **3.** having a mutual relation; answering to or complementing one another, as *either* and *or, where* and *there.* **4.** *Biol.* (of a typical structure of an organism) found in correlation with another. —*n.* **5.** either of two things, as two terms, which are correlative. **6.** a correlative expression. —**cor·rel′a·tive·ly,** *adv.* —**cor·rel′a·tive·ness, cor·rel′a·tiv′i·ty,** *n.*

cor·re·spond (kôr′ə spŏnd′), *v.i.* **1.** to be in agreement or conformity (often fol. by *with* or *to*): *his words and actions do not correspond.* **2.** to be similar or analogous; be equivalent in function, position, amount, etc. (fol. by *to*): *the U.S. Congress corresponds to the British Parliament.* **3.** to communicate by exchange of letters. [t. ML: s. *correspondēre* f. L: *cor-* COR- + *respondēre* answer] —**cor·re·spond′ing·ly,** *adv.* —**Syn. 1.** harmonize, accord, match. See **agree.**

cor·re·spond·ence (kôr′ə spŏn′dəns, kôr′-), *n.* **1.** Also, **cor′re·spond′en·cy.** act or fact of corresponding. **2.** relation of similarity or analogy. **3.** agreement; conformity. **4.** communication by exchange of letters. **5.** letters that pass between correspondents.

correspondence course, the study materials issued by a correspondence school on a subject or topic.

correspondence school, a school which gives instruction by correspondence.

cor·re·spond·ent (kôr′ə spŏn′dənt, kôr′-), *n.* **1.** one who communicates by letters. **2.** one employed to contribute news, etc., regularly from a distant place. **3.** one who contributes letters to a newspaper. **4.** one who has regular business relations with another, esp. at a distance. **5.** a thing that corresponds to something else. —*adj.* **6.** corresponding; having a relation of correspondence. —**cor′re·spond′ent·ly,** *adv.*

cor·re·spon·sive (kôr′ə spŏn′sĭv, kôr′-), *adj.* responsive to effort or impulse; answering; corresponding.

cor·ri·dor (kôr′ə dər, -dôr′, kôr′-), *n.* **1.** a gallery or passage connecting parts of a building. **2.** a passage into which several rooms or apartments open. **3.** *Brit. Railroads.* a passageway on one side of a car into which the compartments open. **4.** a narrow tract of land forming a passageway, as one belonging to an inland country and affording an outlet to the sea: *the Polish Corridor.* [t. F: long passageway, t. It.: m. *corridore* covered way, t. Sp.: m. *corredor,* der. *correr* run, g. L *currere*]

cor·rie (kôr′ĭ, kŏr′ĭ), *n.* *Scot.* a circular hollow in the side of a hill or mountain. [t. Gaelic: m. *coire* caldron]

Cor·rie·dale (kôr′ĭ dāl′, kôr′-), *n.* a white-faced breed of sheep, orig. developed in New Zealand, noted for highquality wool and good market lambs of the mutton type.

Cor·ri·en·tes (kôr′ē ĕn′tĕs), *n.* a city in NE Argentina: a port on the Paraná River. 90,000 (est. 1952).

cor·ri·gen·dum (kôr′ə jĕn′dəm, kôr′-), *n., pl.* **-da** (-də). **1.** an error to be corrected, esp. an error in print. **2.** (*pl.*) a list of corrections of errors in a book, etc. [t. L, neut. gerundive of *corrigere* correct]

cor·ri·gi·ble (kôr′ə jə bəl, kôr′-), *adj.* **1.** capable of being corrected. **2.** submissive to correction. [t. LL: m.s. *corrigibilis,* der. L *corrigere* correct] —**cor′ri·gi·bil′i·ty,** *n.* —**cor′ri·gi·bly,** *adv.*

cor·ri·val (kə rī′vəl), *n., adj.* rival. [t. L: s. *corrīvālis* joint rival]

cor·rob·o·rant (kə rŏb′ə rənt), *adj.* **1.** corroborating; confirming. **2.** strengthening; invigorating. —*n.* **3.** something that corroborates or strengthens. **4.** *Obsolesc.* a strengthening medicine.

cor·rob·o·rate (*v.* kə rŏb′ə rāt′; *adj.* kə rŏb′ə rĭt), *v.,* **-rated, -rating,** *adj.* —*v.t.* **1.** to make more certain; confirm. —*adj.* **2.** *Archaic.* corroborated. [t. L: m. s. *corrōborātus,* pp., strengthened] —**cor·rob′o·ra·tive, cor·rob·o·ra·to·ry** (kə rŏb′ə rə tôr′ĭ), *adj.* —**cor·rob′o·ra·tive·ly,** *adv.* —**cor·rob′o·ra′tor,** *n.*

cor·rob·o·ra·tion (kə rŏb′ə rā′shən), *n.* **1.** act of corroborating. **2.** a corroboratory fact, statement, etc.

cor·rob·o·ree (kə rŏb′ə rĭ), *n.* **1.** a native Australian assembly of sacred, festive, or warlike character. **2.** *Australia.* any large or noisy gathering. **3.** a disturbance; an uproar. [t. native Australian]

cor·rode (kə rōd′), *v.,* **-roded, -roding.** —*v.t.* **1.** to eat away gradually as if by gnawing, esp. by chemical action. **2.** to impair; deteriorate: *jealousy corroded his character.* —*v.i.* **3.** to become corroded. [t. L: m. s. *corrōdere* gnaw away] —**cor·rod′i·ble,** *adj.* —**Syn. 1.** gnaw, eat, consume. **3.** canker, rust, crumble.

cor·ro·sion (kə rō′zhən), *n.* **1.** act or process of corroding. **2.** corroded condition. **3.** a product of corroding, as rust. [t. L: s. *corrōsio*]

cor·ro·sive (kə rō′sĭv), *adj.* **1.** having the quality of corroding, eating away, or consuming. —*n.* **2.** something corrosive, as an acid, drug, etc. —**cor·ro′sive·ly,** *adv.* —**cor·ro′sive·ness,** *n.*

corrosive sublimate, bichloride of mercury, $HgCl_2$, a strongly acrid, highly poisonous, white crystalline salt, prepared by sublimation, much used as an antiseptic.

cor·ru·gate (*v.* kôr′ə gāt′, kôr′-; *adj.* kôr′ə gĭt, kôr′-), *v.,* **-gated, -gating,** *adj.* —*v.t., v.i.* **1.** to draw or bend into folds or alternate furrows and ridges. **2.** to wrinkle, as the skin, etc. —*adj.* **3.** corrugated; wrinkled; furrowed. [t. L: m. s. *corrūgātus,* pp., wrinkled]

corrugated iron, a type of sheet iron or steel strengthened for use in construction by having a series

---

b., blend of, blended;   c., cognate with;   d., dialect, dialectal;   der., derived from;   f., formed from;   g., going back to; m., modification of;   r., replacing;   s., stem of;   t., taken from;   ?, perhaps.   See the full key on inside cover.

of alternating grooves and ridges forced into it, and usually galvanized for weather resistance.

or·ru·gat·ed paper, heavy paper with alternating ridges and grooves for protecting packages, etc.

or·ru·ga·tion (kôr'ə gā'shən, kor'-), *n.* 1. act of corrugating. 2. state of being corrugated. 3. a wrinkle; fold; furrow; ridge.

or·rupt (kə rŭpt'), *adj.* 1. dishonest; without integrity; guilty of dishonesty, esp. involving bribery: *a corrupt judge.* 2. debased in character; depraved; perverted; wicked; evil. 3. putrid. 4. infected; tainted. 5. made bad by errors or alterations, as a text. —*v.t.* 6. to destroy the integrity of; cause to be dishonest, disloyal, etc., esp. by bribery. 7. to lower morally; pervert; deprave. 8. to infect; taint. 9. to make putrid or putrescent. 10. to alter (a language, text, etc.) for the worse; debase. 11. *Archaic.* to mar; spoil. —*v.i.* 12. to become corrupt. [ME, t. L: s. *corruptus*, pp., broken in pieces, destroyed] —**cor·rupt'er,** *n.* —**cor·rup'tive,** *adj.* —**cor·rupt'ly,** *adv.* —**cor·rupt'ness,** *n.* —**Syn.** 1. CORRUPT, DISHONEST, VENAL apply to one, esp. in public office, who acts on mercenary motives, without regard to honor, right, or justice. A CORRUPT politician is one originally honest who has succumbed to temptation and begun questionable practices. A DISHONEST politician is one lacking native integrity and thoroughly untrustworthy. VENAL is a strongly opprobrious term; a VENAL politician is one so debased that he frankly sells his patronage. 6. demoralize, bribe. 7. debase. 8. contaminate, pollute.

or·rupt·i·ble (kə rŭp'tə bəl), *adj.* that may be corrupted. —**cor·rupt'i·bil'i·ty, cor·rupt'i·ble·ness,** *n.* —**cor·rupt'i·bly,** *adv.*

or·rup·tion (kə rŭp'shən), *n.* 1. act of corrupting. 2. state of being corrupt. 3. moral perversion; depravity. 4. perversion of integrity. 5. corrupt or dishonest proceedings. 6. bribery. 7. debasement, as of a language. 8. a debased form of a word. 9. putrefactive decay. 10. any corrupting influence or agency. —**Syn.** 4. baseness, dishonesty. 9. foulness, pollution.

or·sage (kôr säzh'), *n.* 1. a small bouquet worn by a woman at the waist, on the shoulder, etc. 2. the body or waist of a dress; bodice. [t. F, der. *cors* body. See CORSE]

or·sair (kôr'sâr), *n.* 1. a privateer, esp. one of the Barbary Coast. 2. a pirate. 3. a fast vessel used for piracy. [t. F: m. *corsaire,* t. It.: m. *corsaro,* a runner, g. LL *cursārius,* der. *cursus* COURSE]

orse (kôrs), *n. Archaic.* corpse. [ME *cors,* t. OF, g. L *corpus* body]

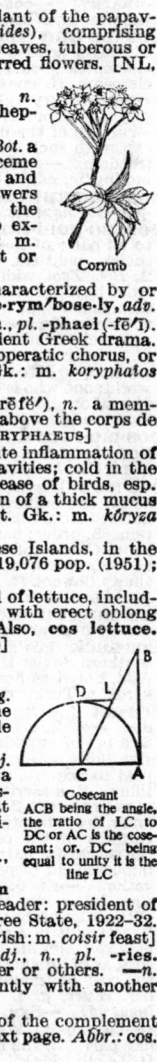

C, Corselet of German or Flemish pikeman (1600); M, morion

or·se·let (kôr'sə lĕt' *for 1;* kôrs'lĭt *for 2),* *n.* 1. a supporting undergarment with very few or no bones, worn by women. 2. armor for the body, esp. the breastplate and back piece together. Also, **corslet.** [t. F, dim. of OF *cors.* See CORSE]

or·set (kôr'sĭt), *n.* 1. (*often pl.*) a shaped, close-fitting inner garment stiffened with whalebone or the like and capable of being tightened by lacing, enclosing the trunk and extending for a distance above and below the waistline, worn, chiefly by women, to give shape and support to the body; stays. 2. *Obs.* a close-fitting outer body garment. [ME, t. F, dim. of OF *cors.* See CORSE]

or·si·ca (kôr'sə kə), *n.* an island in the Mediterranean, SE of and forming a department in France. 204,266 pop. (1954); 3367 sq. mi. *Cap.:* Ajaccio. French, **Corse** (kôrs). See map under Elba. —**Cor'si·can,** *adj., n.*

ors·let (kôrs'lĭt), *n.* corselet.

or·tege (kôr tăzh', -tĕzh'), *n.* 1. a train of attendants; retinue. 2. a procession. Also, *French.,* **cor·tège** (kôr tĕzh'). [t. F, t. It.: m. *corteggio,* der. *corte* COURT]

Cor·tes (kôr'tĭz; *Sp.* -tĕs), *n.* the two houses constituting the national legislative body of Spain, or those of Portugal. [t. Sp., Pg., pl of *corte.* See COURT]

Cor·tés (kôr tĕz'; *Sp.* kôr tĕs'), *n.* Hernando or Hernán (ĕr nän'dō *or* ĕr nän'), 1485–1547, Spanish conqueror of Mexico. Also, **Cor·tez'.**

cor·tex (kôr'tĕks), *n., pl.* **-tices** (-tə sēz'). 1. *Bot.* that portion of the stem between the epidermis and the vascular tissue; bark. 2. *Anat., Zool.* a. the rind of an organ, such as the outer wall of the kidney. b. the layer of gray matter which invests the surface of the cerebral hemispheres and the cerebellum. [t. L: bark, rind, shell]

cor·ti·cal (kôr'tə kəl), *adj.* 1. *Anat.* of, or of the nature of, cortex. 2. *Physiol., Pathol.* due to the function or condition of the cerebral cortex. 3. *Bot.* of the cortex. [t. NL: s. *corticālis.* See CORTEX] —**cor'ti·cal·ly,** *adv.*

cor·ti·cate (kôr'tə kĭt, -kāt'), *adj.* having a cortex. Also, **cor'ti·cat'ed.** [t. L: m.s. *corticātus* having bark]

cor·tin (kôr'tĭn), *n. Biochem.* a hormone essential to life, secreted by the adrenal glands. [f. CORT(EX) + -IN²]

cor·ti·sone (kôr'tə sōn', -zōn'), *n.* an adrenal-gland hormone, originally obtained by extraction from animal glands, now prepared synthetically from strophanthus or other plants: used in the treatment of arthritic ailments and many other diseases.

Co·ru·ña (kō rōō'nyä), *n.* La Coruña.

co·run·dum (kə rŭn'dəm), *n.* a common mineral, aluminum oxide, Al_2O_3, notable for its hardness (=9). Transparent varieties, including the ruby and sapphire, are prized gems; translucent varieties are used as abrasives. [t. Tamil: m. *kurundam,* in Skt. *kuruvinda* ruby]

cor·us·cate (kôr'ə skāt', kor'-), *v.i.,* **-cated, -cating.** to emit vivid flashes of light; sparkle; gleam. [t. L: m. s. *coruscātus,* pp., moved quickly, flashed]

cor·us·ca·tion (kôr'ə skā'shən, kor'-), *n.* 1. act of coruscating. 2. a flashing or a flash of light.

cor·vée (kôr vā'; *Fr.* kôr vě'), *n.* 1. labor, as on the repair of roads, exacted by a feudal lord. 2. an obligation imposed on inhabitants of a district to perform services, as repair of roads, etc., for little or no remuneration. [F, ult. der. L *corrogāre* bring together by entreaty]

corves (kôrvz), *n.* pl. of **corf.**

cor·vette (kôr vĕt'), *n.* 1. a warship of the old sailing class, having a flush deck and usually only one tier of guns. 2. *Brit.* a small, lightly armed, fast vessel, used mostly for convoy escort, ranging between a destroyer and a gunboat in size. Also, **cor·vet** (kôr vĕt', kôr'vĕt). [t. F, ult. g. L *corbita* ship of burden]

cor·vine (kôr'vīn, -vīn), *adj.* 1. pertaining to or resembling a crow. 2. belonging or pertaining to the *Corvidae,* a family of birds including the crows, ravens, jays, etc. [t. L: m. s. *corvīnus,* der. *corvus* raven]

Cor·vus (kôr'vəs), *n., gen.* **-vi** (-vī). a southern constellation between Virgo and Hydra. [t. L: a raven]

Cor·y·bant (kôr'ə bănt', kor'-), *n., pl.* **Corybantes** (kôr'ə băn'tēz, kor'-), **Corybants.** one of the spirits or secondary divinities fabled to form the train of the ancient goddess Cybele, following her over the mountains by torchlight with wild music and dancing. [t. L: s. *Corybās,* t. Gk.: m. *Korýbās*] —**Cor·y·ban·tian** (kôr'ə băn'shən, kor'-), **Cor'y·ban'tic, Cor·y·ban·tine** (kôr'ə băn'tīn, -tīn, kor'-), *adj.*

co·ryd·a·lis (kə rĭd'ə lĭs), *n.* any plant of the papaveraceous genus *Corydalis* (*Capnoides*), comprising erect or climbing herbs with divided leaves, tuberous or fibrous roots, and very irregular spurred flowers. [NL, t. Gk.: m. *korydallis* crested lark]

Cor·y·don (kôr'ə dən, -dŏn', kôr'-), *n.* (in pastoral literature) a name for a shepherd or rustic.

cor·ymb (kôr'ĭmb, -ĭm, kor'-), *n. Bot.* a form of inflorescence resembling a raceme but having a relatively shorter rachis and longer lower pedicles, so that the flowers form a flat-topped or convex cluster, the outermost flowers being the first to expand. [t. L: s. *corymbus,* t. Gk.: m. *kórymbos* head, top, cluster of fruit or flowers] —**cor'ymb·like',** *adj.*

Corymb

co·rym·bose (kə rĭm'bōs), *adj.* characterized by or growing in corymbs; corymblike. —**co·rym'bose·ly,** *adv.*

cor·y·phae·us (kôr'ə fē'əs, kor'-), *n., pl.* **-phaei** (-fē'ī). 1. the leader of the chorus in the ancient Greek drama. 2. (in modern use) the leader of an operatic chorus, or of any band of singers. [t. L, t. Gk.: m. *koryphaios* leader, head man]

cor·y·phée (kôr'ə fā', kôr'-; *Fr.* kô rē fě'), *n.* a member of a ballet company ranking just above the corps de ballet. [t. F, t. L: m.s. *coryphaeus* CORYPHAEUS]

co·ry·za (kə rī'zə), *n.* 1. *Pathol.* acute inflammation of the mucous membrane of the nasal cavities; cold in the head. 2. *Vet. Sci.* a contagious disease of birds, esp. poultry, characterized by the secretion of a thick mucus in the mouth and throat. [t. LL, t. Gk.: m. *kóryza* catarrh]

Cos (kŏs), *n.* one of the Dodecanese Islands, in the Aegean, off the SW coast of Turkey. 19,076 pop. (1951); 111 sq. mi. Also, **Kos.** Italian, **Coo.**

cos (kŏs, kôs), *n. Chiefly Brit.* a kind of lettuce, including the romaine and other varieties, with erect oblong heads and generally crisp leaves. Also, **cos lettuce.** [named after Cos whence it orig. came]

cos, cosine.

cosec, cosecant.

co·se·cant (kō sē'kənt, -kănt), *n. Trig.* the secant of the complement, or the reciprocal of the sine, of a given angle or arc.

co·seis·mal (kō sīs'məl, -sīz'-), *adj.* denoting, pertaining to, or being in a line, curve, etc., connecting or comprising points on the earth's surface at which an earthquake wave arrives simultaneously. Also, **co·seis'mic.**

Cosecant

ACB being the angle, the ratio of LC to DC or AC is the cosecant; or, DC being equal to unity it is the line LC

co·sey (kō'zĭ), *adj.,* **-sier, -siest,** *n., pl.* **-seys.** cozy.

Cos·grave (kŏz'grāv), *n.* **William Thomas,** born 1880, Irish political leader: president of the executive council of the Irish Free State, 1922–32.

cosh·er (kŏsh'ər), *v.t.* to pamper. [t. Irish: m. *coisir* feast]

co·sig·na·to·ry (kō sĭg'nə tôr'ĭ), *adj., n., pl.* **-ries.** —*adj.* 1. signing jointly with another or others. —*n.* 2. one who signs a document jointly with another or others.

co·sine (kō'sīn), *n. Trig.* the sine of the complement of a given angle or arc. See illus. on next page. *Abbr.:* cos.

cos lettuce, cos.

cosm-, var. of **cosmo-,** before vowels.

cos·met·ic (kŏz mĕt'ĭk), *n.* 1. a preparation for beautifying the complexion, skin, etc. —*adj.* 2. serving to beautify; imparting or improving beauty, esp. of the complexion. [t. Gk.: m. s. *kosmētikós* relating to adornment] —**cos·met'i·cal·ly,** *adv.*

cos·mic (kŏz/mĭk), *adj.* **1.** of or pertaining to the cosmos: *cosmic philosophy.* **2.** characteristic of the cosmos or its phenomena; immeasurably extended in time and space; vast. **3.** forming a part of the material universe, esp. outside of the earth. **4.** orderly or harmonious. [t. Gk.: m.s. *kosmikós* of the world] —**cos/mi·cal·ly,** *adv.*

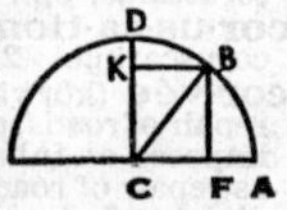

cosmic dust, *Astron.* matter in fine particles collected by the earth from space, like meteorites.

cosmic rays, rays of extremely high penetrating power that seem to originate beyond the earth's atmosphere, and that consist, partly, of particles moving in velocities nearly the speed of light.

[Diagram: labeled D, K, B, C, F, A with "Cosine" caption]

Cosine
ACB being the angle, the ratio of FC to BC or that of BK to CD, is the cosine: or, CD being equal to unity, it is the line BK

cos·mism (kŏz/mĭzəm), *n.* the philosophy of cosmic evolution. —**cos/mist,** *n.*

cosmo-, a word element representing **cosmos.**

cos·mog·o·ny (kŏz mŏg/ə nĭ), *n., pl.* **-nies.** a theory or story of the genesis or origination of the universe. [t. Gk.: m. s. *kosmogonía* creation of the world. See cosmo-, -gony] —**cos·mo·gon·ic** (kŏz/mə gŏn/ĭk), **cos/mo·gon/i·cal,** *adj.* —**cos·mog/o·nist,** *n.*

cos·mog·ra·phy (kŏz mŏg/rə fĭ), *n., pl.* **-phies. 1.** the science which describes and maps the main features of the heavens and the earth, embracing astronomy, geography, and geology. **2.** a description or representation of the universe in its main features. [t. Gk.: m. s. *kosmographía* description of the world. See cosmo-, -graphy] —**cos·mog/ra·pher,** *n.* —**cos·mo·graph·ic** (kŏz/mə grăf/ĭk), **cos/mo·graph/i·cal,** *adj.*

cos·mo·line (kŏz/mə lēn/), *n., v.,* **-lined, -lining.** —*n.* **1.** heavy grease used to preserve weapons from the elements. —*v.t.* **2.** to grease (weapons) against the elements. [f. cosm(etic) + -ol² + -ine²]

cos·mol·o·gy (kŏz mŏl/ə jĭ), *n.* the branch of philosophy that concerns itself with the origin and general structure of the universe, its parts, elements, and laws, esp. with such characteristics as space, time, causality, freedom. —**cos·mo·log·i·cal** (kŏz/mə lŏj/ə kəl), **cos/mo·log/ic,** *adj.* —**cos·mol/o·gist,** *n.*

cos·mo·naut (kŏz/mə nôt/), *n.* astronaut. [f. cosmo- + s. Gk. *nautílos,* sailor.]

cos·mo·pol·i·tan (kŏz/mə pŏl/ə tən), *adj.* **1.** belonging to all parts of the world; not limited to one part of the social, political, commercial, or intellectual world. **2.** *Bot., Zool.* widely distributed over the globe. **3.** free from local, provincial, or national ideas, prejudices, or attachments; at home all over the world. **4.** of or characteristic of a cosmopolite. —*n.* **5.** one who is free from provincial or national prejudices; a citizen of the world. [f. cosmopolite + -an] —**cos/mo·pol/i·tan·ism,** *n.*

cos·mop·o·lite (kŏz mŏp/ə līt/), *n.* **1.** a citizen of the world; one who is cosmopolitan in his ideas or life. **2.** an animal or plant of world-wide distribution. [t. Gk.: m. s. *kosmopolítēs* citizen of the world] —**cos·mop/o·lit/ism,** *n.*

cos·mo·ram·a (kŏz/mə răm/ə, -rä/mə), *n.* an exhibition of pictures of different parts of the world. [f. cosm- + m. Gk. *horáma* view] —**cos/mo·ram/ic,** *adj.*

cos·mos (kŏz/məs, -mŏs), *n.* **1.** the world or universe as an embodiment of order and harmony (as distinguished from *chaos*). **2.** a complete and harmonious system. **3.** order; harmony. **4.** any plant of the composite genus *Cosmos,* of tropical America, some species of which, as *C. bipinnatus* and *C. sulphureus,* are cultivated for their showy flowers. [t. NL, t. Gk.: m. *kósmos* order, form, the world or universe as an ordered whole, ornament]

cos·mo·tron (kŏz/mə trŏn/), *n. Physics.* a type of electro-nuclear machine.

Cos·sack (kŏs/ăk, -ək), *n.* one of a people of the southern Soviet Union in Europe and adjoining parts of Asia, noted as horsemen or light cavalry. [t. Russ.: m. *kazak,* t. Turk.: m. *quzzâq* adventurer, freebooter]

cos·set (kŏs/ĭt), *v.t.* **1.** to treat as a pet; pamper; coddle. —*n.* **2.** a lamb brought up by hand; a pet lamb. **3.** a pet of any kind. [cf. OE *cossetung* kissing]

cost (kôst, kŏst), *n., v.,* **cost, costing.** —*n.* **1.** the price paid to acquire, produce, accomplish, or maintain anything. **2.** a sacrifice, loss, or penalty: *to work at the cost of one's health.* **3.** outlay or expenditure of money, time, labor, trouble, etc. **4. at all costs,** or **at any cost,** regardless of the cost. **5.** (*pl.*) *Law.* the sums which the successful party is usually entitled to recover for reimbursement of particular expenses incurred in the litigation. —*v.i.* **6.** to require the expenditure of money, time, labor, etc., in exchange, purchase, or payment; be of the price of; be acquired in return for: *it cost five dollars.* **7.** to result in a particular sacrifice, loss, or penalty: *it may cost him his life.* **8.** to estimate or determine the cost, as of production. —*v.t.* **9.** to estimate or determine the cost of (manufactured articles, etc.). [ME, t. OF, der. *coster,* g. L *constāre* stand together.] —**cost/-less,** *adj.* —**Syn. 1.** charge, expense. See **price.**

cos·ta (kŏs/tə, kôs/-), *n., pl.* **-tae** (-tē). **1.** a rib or rib-like part. **2.** the midrib of a leaf in mosses. **3.** a ridge. [t. L: rib, side]

cost accounting, 1. an accounting system indicating the cost items involved in production. **2.** the operation of such an accounting system. —**cost accountant.**

cos·tal (kŏs/təl, kôs/təl), *adj. Anat.* pertaining to the ribs or the side of the body: *costal nerves.* [t. LL: s. *costālis*]

cos·tard (kŏs/tərd), *n.* **1.** a large English apple with prominent ribs. **2.** *Archaic and Humorous.* the head.

Cos·ta Ri·ca (kŏs/tə rē/kə, kôs/-, kōs/-), a republic in Central America between Panama and Nicaragua. 988,000 pop. (est. 1956); 19,238 sq. mi. *Cap.:* San José. —**Cos/ta Ri/can.**

cos·tate (kŏs/tāt, kôs/-), *adj.* **1.** *Anat.* bearing ribs. **2.** (of mosses) having a midrib or costa.

cos·ter·mon·ger (kŏs/tər mŭng/gər, kôs/-), *n. Chiefly Brit.* a hawker of fruit, vegetables, fish, etc. Also, **cos/ter.** [earlier *costardmonger,* f. costard + monger]

cos·tive (kŏs/tĭv, kôs/-), *adj.* **1.** suffering from constipation; constipated. **2.** slow in action or in expressing ideas, opinions, etc. [t. OF, g. L *constīpātus,* pp. See constipate] —**cos/tive·ly,** *adv.* —**cos/tive·ness,** *n.*

cost·ly (kôst/lĭ, kŏst/-), *adj.,* **-lier, -liest. 1.** costing much; of great price or value. **2.** *Archaic.* lavish; extravagant. —**cost/li·ness,** *n.* —**Syn. 1.** dear, high-priced, valuable, sumptuous. See **expensive.**

cost·mar·y (kôst/mâr/ĭ, kŏst/-), *n., pl.* **-maries.** a perennial plant, *Chrysanthemum balsamita,* with fragrant leaves, used in salads, etc. [f. OE *cost* (t. L: s. *costus,* t. Gk.: m. *kostos* kind of aromatic plant) + Mary]

costo-, *Anat., Zool.* a word element meaning "rib," as in *costoscapular.* [comb. form repr. L *costa*]

cos·to·cla·vic·u·lar (kŏs/tō klə vĭk/yə lər, kôs/-), *adj.* referring to both the ribs and the collarbone.

cost of living, the average cost of food, clothing, and other necessities paid by a person, family, etc.

cos·to·scap·u·lar (kŏs/tō skăp/yə lər, kôs/-), *adj. Anat.* pertaining to ribs and to the scapula.

cost-plus (kôst/plŭs/, kŏst/-), *n.* the cost of production plus an agreed rate of profit (often used as a basis of payment in government contracts).

cos·trel (kŏs/trəl), *n.* a bottle of leather, earthenware, or wood, often of flattened form and commonly having an ear or ears to suspend it by, as from the waist. [ME, t. OF: m. *costerel,* appar. orig. a flask hung at the side, der. *coste* rib, side, g. L *costa.* See -rel]

cos·tume (*n.* kŏs/tūm, -tōōm; *v.* kŏs tūm/, -tōōm/), *n., v.,* **-tumed, -tuming.** —*n.* **1.** the style of dress, including ornaments and the way of wearing the hair, esp. that peculiar to a nation, class, or period. **2.** dress or garb belonging to another period, place, etc., as worn on the stage, at balls, etc. **3.** a set of garments, esp. for a woman. **4.** fashion of dress appropriate to a particular occasion or season: *winter costume.* —*v.t.* **5.** to dress; furnish with a costume; provide appropriate dress for: *to costume a play.* [t. F, t. It.: habit, fashion, t. OF, g. L *consuētūdo* custom] —**Syn. 1.** See **dress.**

cos·tum·er (kŏs tū/mər, -tōō/-), *n.* one who makes or deals in costumes. Also, **cos·tum·i·er** (kŏs tū/mĭ ər, -tōō/-; *Fr.* kôs tȳ myě/).

co·sy (kō/zĭ), *adj.,* **-sier, -siest,** *n., pl.* **-sies.** cozy. [orig. uncert.] —**co/si·ly,** *adv.* —**co/si·ness,** *n.*

cot¹ (kŏt), *n.* **1.** a light portable bed, esp. one of canvas stretched on a frame. **2.** *Brit.* a crib for a child. **3.** a light bedstead. **4.** *Naut.* a swinging bed made of canvas. [t. Anglo-Ind., t. Hind.: m. *khāt*]

cot² (kŏt), *n.* **1.** a small house; cottage; hut. **2.** a small place of shelter or protection. **3.** a sheath; covering. [ME and OE; orig. unknown]

cot, cotangent.

co·tan·gent (kō tăn/jənt), *n. Trig.* the tangent of the complement, or the reciprocal of the tangent, of a given angle or arc. *Abbr.:* cot or ctn. —**co·tan·gen·tial** (kō/tăn jĕn/shəl), *adj.*

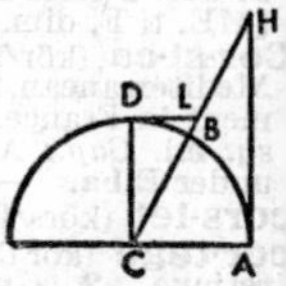

cote¹ (kōt), *n.* **1.** a shelter for sheep, pigs, pigeons, etc. **2.** *N. Eng.* a small house; cottage. [OE. See cot²]

cote² (kōt), *v.t.,* **coted, coting.** *Archaic.* to pass by; outstrip; surpass. [? var. of coast, v.]

Côte d'A·zur (kōt dá zyr/), French name for the Riviera of S France.

co·tem·po·ra·ne·ous (kō tĕm/pə rā/nĭ əs), *adj.* contemporaneous.

co·tem·po·rar·y (kō tĕm/pə rĕr/ĭ), *adj., n., pl.* **-raries,** contemporary.

co·ten·ant (kō tĕn/ənt), *n.* a tenant in common with another or others; a joint tenant. —**co·ten/an·cy,** *n.*

co·te·rie (kō/tə rĭ), *n.* **1.** a group of persons who associate closely, esp. for social purposes. **2.** a clique. [t. F: set, association of people, earlier cotters' tenure, der. OF *cotier* cotter. See cotter²] —**Syn. 1.** See **circle.**

co·ter·mi·nous (kō tûr/mə nəs), *adj.* conterminous.

co·thur·nus (kō thûr/nəs), *n., pl.* **-ni** (-nī). the high, thick-soled shoe worn by ancient Greek and Roman tragic actors, often symbolic of tragedy. Also, **co·thurn** (kō/thûrn, kō thûrn/). [t. L, t. Gk.: m. *kóthornos*]

co·tid·al (kō tī/dəl), *adj.* **1.** pertaining to a coincidence of tides. **2.** denoting a line connecting points where it is high tide at the same time.

[Diagram: labeled H, D, L, B, C, A with "Cotangent" caption]

Cotangent
ACB being the angle, the ratio of DL to DC, or that of AC to AH, is the cotangent; or DC being taken as unity, it is the line DL

co·til·lion (kō tĭl/yən, kə-), *n.* **1.** a lively French social dance, originated in the 18th century, for two, eight, or even more performers, and consisting of a variety of steps and figures. **2.** any of various dances of the quadrille kind. **3.** music arranged or played for these dances. **4.** *U.S.* a complex dance, or entertainment of dancing, consisting of picturesque or elaborate figures, with changing of partners and giving of favors; a german. Also, **co·til·lon** (kō tĭl/yən, kə-; *Fr.* kō tē yôn/). [t. m. *cotillon,* orig., petticoat, dim. of *cotte* coat]

Co·to·pax·i (kō′tə păk′sĭ; *Sp.* kô′tô pä′hē), *n.* a volcano in central Ecuador, in the Andes: the highest known active volcano in the world. 19,498 ft.

ot·quean (kŏt′kwēn), *n. Obs.* 1. a coarse hussy. 2. a man who busies himself with women's household affairs. [f. COT² + QUEAN]

Cots·wold (kŏts′wōld, -wəld), *n.* a breed of large sheep with long wool (so called from the Cotswolds).

Cots·wolds (kŏts′wōldz, -wəldz), *n.* a range of hills in SW England, in Gloucestershire: sheep herding.

ot·ta (kŏt′ə), *n. Eccles.* 1. a surplice. 2. a short surplice, with short sleeves or sleeveless, worn esp. by choristers. [t. ML. See COAT]

ot·tage (kŏt′ĭj), *n.* 1. a small, humble house. 2. a small country residence or detached suburban house. 3. *U.S.* a temporary residence at a vacation resort. [ME, var. of *cotage* (f. COT² + -AGE)]
—**Syn.** 1–3. COTTAGE, CABIN, LODGE, SHACK, HUT, SHANTY formerly meant small, simple, often crude dwellings. During recent years, the first four words have gained great currency as terms for the often elaborate structures visited by the well-to-do for recreational purposes. HUT and SHANTY, however, still have the former meaning as their most frequent one.

ottage cheese, *U.S.* a kind of soft white cheese made of skim milk curds without rennet.

ottage pudding, a pudding made by covering some plain cake with a sweet (often fruit) sauce.

ot·tag·er (kŏt′ĭ jər), *n.* 1. one who lives in a cottage. 2. *Brit.* a laborer in a village or on a farm. 3. *U.S.* a person having a private house at a vacation resort.

ot·ter¹ (kŏt′ər), *n.* 1. a pin, wedge, key, or the like, fitted or driven into an opening in order to secure something or hold parts together. 2. cotter pin. [orig. uncert.]

ot·ter² (kŏt′ər), *n.* 1. *Scot.* a person occupying a plot of land under a system similar to cottier tenure. 2. *Irish.* cottier. 3. a cottager. Also, **cot′tar.** [t. ML: m.s. *cotārius,* der. *cota,* Latinized form of COT²]

otter pin, *Mech.* a cotter having a split end which is spread after being pushed through a hole, to prevent the cotter from working loose.

Cot·ti·an Alps (kŏt′ĭ ən), a range of the Alps on the boundary between France and Italy. Highest peak, Monte Viso, 12,602 ft.

ot·ti·er (kŏt′ĭ ər), *n.* 1. an Irish peasant holding a portion of land directly from the owner, the amount of rent being fixed not by custom or private agreement but by public competition (**cottier tenure**). 2. a cottager (def. 1). [ME *cotier,* t. OF, der. *cote* cot, t. Gmc.]

ot·ton (kŏt′ən), *n.* 1. a soft, white, downy substance, consisting of the hairs or fibers attached to the seeds of plants of the malvaceous genus *Gossypium,* used in making fabrics, thread, wadding, guncotton, etc. 2. a plant yielding cotton, as *G. hirsutum* (**upland cotton**) or *G. barbadense* (**sea-island cotton**). 3. such plants collectively, as a cultivated crop. 4. cloth, thread, etc., made of cotton. 5. any soft, downy substance resembling cotton, but growing on some other plant. —*v.i.* 6. *Colloq.* to make friends. 7. *Colloq.* to become attached to; friendly (fol. by *to* or *with*). 8. *Colloq.* to get on together; agree. 9. *Obs.* to prosper or succeed. [ME *coton,* t. OF, t. It.: m. *cotone,* t. Ar.: m. *quṭn*]

Cot·ton (kŏt′ən), *n.* **John,** 1584–1652, U.S. clergyman, colonist, and author.

cotton belt, that part of the southern U.S. where cotton is grown.

cotton cake, *U.S.* a mass of compressed cottonseed after the oil has been extracted, used to feed cattle, etc.

cotton flannel, Canton flannel.

cotton gin, a machine for separating the fibers of cotton from the seeds.

cotton grass, any of the rushlike cyperaceous plants constituting the genus *Eriophorum,* common in swampy places and bearing spikes resembling tufts of cotton.

cot·ton·mouth (kŏt′ən mouth′), *n.* the water moccasin, a venomous snake of the southern U.S.

cotton picker, a machine for removing the ripe cotton fiber from the standing plant.

cot·ton·seed (kŏt′ən sēd′), *n., pl.* -seeds, (*esp. collectively*) -seed. the seed of the cotton plant, yielding an oil.

cottonseed meal, cotton cake.

cottonseed oil, a brown-yellow, viscid oil with a nutlike odor, obtained from the seed of the cotton plant, used in pharmacology and as an oil for salad dressing.

cotton stainer, any bug of the genus *Dysdercus* and related genera, which stains cotton an indelible reddish or yellowish color.

cot·ton·tail (kŏt′ən tāl′), *n.* the common rabbit, *Sylvilagus floridanus,* of the U.S., having a fluffy white tail.

cot·ton·weed (kŏt′ən wēd′), *n.* any of certain plants with stems and leaves covered with a soft, hoary pubescence, as those of the composite genus *Gnaphalium* or of various allied genera.

cot·ton·wood (kŏt′ən wŏŏd′), *n.* any of several American species of poplar, as *Populus deltoides,* with cottonlike tufts on the seeds.

Cottontail.
Sylvilagus floridanus
(14 to 15 in. long)

cotton wool, 1. cotton in its raw state, as on the boll or gathered for use. 2. *Brit.* absorbent cotton.

cot·ton·y (kŏt′ən ĭ), *adj.* 1. of or like cotton; soft. 2. covered with a down or nap resembling cotton.

cot·y·le·don (kŏt′ə lē′dən), *n. Bot.* the primary or rudimentary leaf of the embryo of plants. See diag. under **hypocotyl.** [t. L: navelwort (a plant), t. Gk.: m. *kotylēdōn* any cup-shaped hollow] —**cot′y·le·don·al,** *adj.* —**cot·y·le·don·ar·y** (kŏt′ə lē′də nĕr′ĭ), *adj.*

couch (kouch), *n.* 1. a bed or other place of rest; a lounge; any place used for repose. 2. the lair of a wild beast. 3. the frame on which barley is spread to be malted. 4. a coat of paint, etc. [ME *couche,* t. OF, der. *coucher,* v. See below]
—*v.t.* 5. to arrange or frame (words, a sentence, etc.); put into words; express. 6. to express indirectly. 7. to lower or bend down, as the head. 8. to lower (a spear, etc.) to a horizontal position, as for attack. 9. to lay or put down; cause to lie down; lay or spread flat. 10. to overlay; embroider with thread laid flat on a surface and caught down at intervals. 11. *Obs.* to place or lodge; conceal. 12. *Surg.* to remove (a cataract) by inserting a needle and pushing the opaque crystalline lens downward in the vitreous humor below the axis of vision; remove a cataract from (a person) in this manner. —*v.i.* 13. to lie at rest; repose; recline. 14. to crouch; bend; stoop. 15. to lie in ambush; lurk. 16. to lie in a heap for decomposition or fermentation, as leaves. [ME *couche(n),* t. OF: m. *coucher,* g. L *collocāre* lay in its place]

couch·ant (kou′chənt), *adj.* 1. lying down; crouching. 2. *Her.* lying down, as of a lion. [t. F, ppr. of *coucher* lie]

couch grass (kouch, kōōch), any of various grasses, esp. *Agropyron repens,* known chiefly as troublesome weeds, characterized by creeping rootstocks which spread rapidly; quitch. [var. of QUITCH GRASS]

couch·ing (kou′chĭng), *n.* 1. act of one who or that which couches. 2. a method of embroidering in which a thread, often heavy, laid upon the surface of the material, is caught down at intervals by stitches taken with another thread through the material. 3. work so made.

Cou·é (kōō ā′; *Fr.* kwĕ), *n.* **Émile** (ē mēl′), 1857–1926, French psychologist: advocate of autosuggestion.

cou·gar (kōō′gər), *n. Zool.* a large tawny feline, *Felis concolor,* of North and South America; the puma; panther; mountain lion. [t. F: m. *couguar,* t. NL: m. s. *cuguacuara,* repr. Tupi *çuaçu ara,* Guarani *guaçu ara*]

Cougar. *Felis concolor*
(Total length 8 ft.,
2½ ft. high at the shoulder)

cough (kôf, kŏf), *v.i.* 1. to expel the air from the lungs suddenly and with a characteristic noise. —*v.t.* 2. to expel by coughing (fol. by *up* or *out*). 3. **cough up,** *Slang.* a. to give; hand over. b. to blurt out. —*n.* 4. act or sound of coughing. 5. an illness characterized by frequent coughing. [ME *coghen,* back formation from OE *cohhetan* cough. Cf. G *keuchen* wheeze] —**cough′er,** *n.*

cough drop, a small medicinal lozenge for relieving a cough, sore throat, etc.

could (kŏŏd), *v.* pt. of **can¹.** [ME *coude,* OE *cūthe;* mod. *l* improperly inserted, after *would* and *should*]

could·n't (kŏŏd′nt), contraction of *could not.*

couldst (kŏŏdst), *v. Archaic or Poetic.* 2nd pers. sing. of **could.**

cou·lee (kōō′lĭ), *n.* 1. *Western North America.* a deep ravine or gulch, usually dry, which has been worn by running water. 2. a stream of lava. Also, *French,* **cou·lée** (kōō lē′). [t. F, der. *couler* flow, slide, g. L *colāre* strain]

cou·loir (kōō lwär′), *n.* a steep gorge or gully on the side of a mountain. [F, der. *couler.* See COULEE]

cou·lomb (kōō lŏm′), *n.* the usual unit of quantity of electricity; the quantity transferred by a current of one ampere in one second. [named after C. A. de *Coulomb,* 1736–1806, French physicist]

coul·ter (kōl′tər), *n.* colter.

Coul·ter (kōl′tər), *n.* **John Merle** (mûrl), 1851–1928, U.S. botanist.

cou·ma·rin (kōō′mə rĭn), *n.* a white crystalline substance, with a vanillalike odor, $C_9H_6O_2$, obtained from the tonka bean and certain other plants, or prepared synthetically, and used for flavoring and in perfumery. [t. F: m. *coumarine,* der. *coumarou,* repr. Guiana *kumarū* Tonka-bean tree]

coun·cil (koun′səl), *n.* 1. an assembly of persons summoned or convened for consultation, deliberation, or advice. 2. an ecclesiastical assembly for deciding matters of doctrine or discipline. 3. (in the New Testament) the Sanhedrin or other body of authorities. 4. a body of persons specially designated or selected to act in an advisory, administrative, or legislative capacity. 5. (in many of the British colonies) a body assisting the governor in either an executive or a legislative capacity, or in both. [ME *counceil,* t. OF: m. *concile,* t. L: m.s. *concilium* assembly, union, but with sense affected by L *consilium* COUNSEL]

Council Bluffs, a city in SW Iowa, across the Missouri river from Omaha, Nebraska. 34,361 (1960).

council house, *Brit.* a low-rent dwelling house built by the local governing authority (county council, urban district council, or rural district council).

coun·cil·man (koun′səl mən), *n., pl.* -men. a member of a council, esp. the local legislative body of a city.

coun·cil-man·ag·er plan (koun′səl măn′ə jər), a system of municipal government in which the administrative powers of the city are entrusted to a manager selected by the city council.

Council of the Reich, Reichsrath (def. 1).

Council of Trent, the council of the Roman Catholic Church which met at Trent intermittently from 1545 to 1563, condemning the Reformation and defining church doctrines.

council of war, 1. a conference of high-ranking military or naval officers, usually to discuss major war problems. **2.** any conference to make important plans.

coun·ci·lor (koun'sə lər), *n.* a member of a council. Also, *esp. Brit.,* **coun'cil·lor.** —**coun'ci·lor·ship',** *n.*

council school, *Brit.* a public school (in U.S. sense).

coun·sel (koun'səl). *n., v.,* **-seled, -seling** or (*esp. Brit.*) **-selled, -selling.** —*n.* **1.** advice; opinion or instruction given in directing the judgment or conduct of another. **2.** interchange of opinions as to future procedure; consultation; deliberation: *to take counsel with one's partners.* **3.** *Archaic.* wisdom; prudence. **4.** deliberate purpose; plan; design. **5.** a private or secret opinion or purpose; *to keep one's own counsel.* **6.** the advocates or advocate engaged in the direction of a cause in court; a legal adviser or counselor. **7.** *Theol.* one of the advisory declarations of Christ, considered as not universally binding but as given for aid in attaining greater moral perfection. —*v.t.* **8.** to give counsel to; advise. **9.** to urge the doing or adoption of; recommend (a plan, etc.). —*v.i.* **10.** to give counsel or advice. **11.** to take counsel. [ME *conseil,* t. OF, g. L *consilium* consultation, plan. Cf. COUNCIL] —**Syn. 1.** See **advice.**

coun·se·lor (koun'sə lər), *n.* **1.** one who counsels; an adviser. **2.** *Law.* a lawyer, esp. a trial lawyer. **3.** an adviser, esp. a legal adviser, of an embassy or legation. Also, *esp. Brit.,* **coun'sel·lor.** —**coun'se·lor·ship',** *n.*

count¹ (kount), *v.t.* **1.** to check over one by one (the individuals of a collection) in order to ascertain their total number; enumerate. **2.** to reckon up; calculate; compute. **3.** to list or name the numerals up to. **4.** to include in a reckoning; take into account. **5.** to reckon to the credit of another; ascribe; impute. **6.** to esteem; consider. **7. count out, a.** *Boxing.* to proclaim (one) a loser because of his inability to stand up after the referee has counted ten seconds. **b.** to disqualify (some ballots) illegally in counting, in order to control the election. —*v.i.* **8.** to count the items of a collection one by one in order to know the total. **9.** to list or name the numerals in order. **10.** to reckon numerically. **11.** to depend or rely (fol. by *on*). **12.** to have a numerical value (as specified). **13.** to be accounted or worth: *a book which counts as a masterpiece.* **14.** to enter into consideration: *every effort counts.* **15.** to be worth; amount (fol. by *for*). **16.** to divide into groups by calling off numbers in order (fol. by *off*). **17.** *Obs.* to take account (fol. by *of*). —*n.* **18.** act of counting; enumeration; reckoning; calculation. **19.** the number representing the result of a process of counting; the total number. **20.** an accounting. **21.** *Law.* a distinct charge or theory of action in a declaration or indictment. **22.** *Archaic.* regard; notice. [ME *counte(n),* t. OF. m. *conter,* g. L *computāre* calculate, reckon] —**count'a·ble,** *adj.*

count² (kount), *n.* (in some European countries) a nobleman corresponding in rank to the English earl. [t. AF: m. *counte,* g. L *comes* companion]

count down, the final check prior to the firing of a missile, detonation of an explosive, etc. With the precise moment of firing or detonation designated as zero, the days, hours, minutes, and seconds are counted backwards from the initiation of a project.

coun·te·nance (koun'tə nəns), *n., v.,* **-nanced, -nancing.** —*n.* **1.** aspect; appearance, esp. the look or expression of the face. **2.** the face; visage. **3.** composed expression of face. **4. out of countenance,** visibly disconcerted, or abashed. **5.** appearance of favor; encouragement; moral support. **6.** *Obs.* bearing; behavior. —*v.t.* **7.** to give countenance or show favor to; encourage; support. [ME, t. OF: m. *contenance* bearing, t. ML: m. s. *continentia* demeanor, L restraint] —**coun'te·nanc·er,** *n.* —**Syn. 2.** See **face.**

count·er¹ (koun'tər), *n.* **1.** a table or board on which money is counted, business is transacted, or goods are laid for examination. **2.** anything used in keeping account, as in games, esp. a round or otherwise shaped piece of metal, ivory, wood, or other material. **3.** an imitation coin or token. **4.** *Slang.* a piece of money. [ME, t. AF: m. *counteour* counting house, counting table, der. OF *conter* COUNT¹]

count·er² (koun'tər), *n.* **1.** one who counts. **2.** an apparatus for counting revolutions or other movements. [f. COUNT¹ + -ER¹]

coun·ter³ (koun'tər), *adv.* **1.** in the wrong way; contrary to the right course; in the reverse direction. **2.** contrary; in opposition (chiefly with *run* or *go*): *to run counter to the rules.* —*adj.* **3.** opposite; opposed; contrary. —*n.* **4.** that which is opposite or contrary to something else. **5.** a blow delivered in receiving and parrying another blow, as in boxing. **6.** *Fencing.* a circular parry. **7.** that portion of the stern of a boat or vessel extending from the water line to the full outward swell. **8.** the piece of stiff leather forming the back of a shoe or boot around the heel. **9.** that part of a horse's breast which lies between the shoulders and under the neck. —*v.t.* **10.** to go counter to; oppose; controvert. **11.** to meet or answer (a move, blow, etc.) by another

in return. —*v.i.* **12.** to make a counter or opposing move. **13.** to give a blow while receiving or parrying one, as in boxing. [t. F: m. *contre,* g. L *contrā,* adv. and prep., in opposition, against. Cf. COUNTER-]

coun·ter⁴ (koun'tər), *n., v.t. Obs.* encounter.

counter-, a first element of compounds of various parts of speech signifying opposition to the latter element, which it modifies, as military opposition (*counterattack*) logical opposition (*counterproof*), reversal (*counterclockwise*), complementary position (*counterpoise*), etc. [see COUNTER³]

coun·ter·act (koun'tər ăkt'), *v.t.* to act in opposition to; frustrate by contrary action. —**coun'ter·ac'tion,** *n.* —**coun'ter·ac'tive,** *adj.* —**Syn.** neutralize, thwart.

coun·ter·at·tack (*n.* koun'tər ə tăk'; *v.* koun'tər ə tăk'), *n.* **1.** an attack designed to counteract another attack; a responsive attack. **2.** *Mil.* an attack by a ground combat unit to stop and drive back an enemy attack. —*v.t., v.i.* **3.** to deliver a counterattack (to).

coun·ter·at·trac·tion (koun'tər ə trăk'shən), *n.* a rival or opposite attraction.

coun·ter·bal·ance (*n.* koun'tər băl'əns; *v.* koun'tər băl'əns), *n., v.,* **-anced, -ancing.** —*n.* **1.** a weight balancing another weight; an equal weight, power, or influence acting in opposition; counterpoise. —*v.i.* **2.** to weight or act against with an equal weight or force.

coun·ter·blast (koun'tər blăst', -blăst'), *n.* an opposing blast; a blast in opposition to another blast.

coun·ter·change (koun'tər chānj'), *v.t.,* **-changed, -changing. 1.** to cause to change places, qualities, etc.; interchange. **2.** to diversify; checker.

coun·ter·charge (*n.* koun'tər chärj'; *v.* koun'tər chärj'), *n., v.,* **-charged, -charging.** —*n.* **1.** a charge by an accused person against his accuser. **2.** *Mil.* a retaliatory charge. —*v.t.* **3.** to make an accusation against (one's accuser). **4.** *Mil.* to charge in retaliation.

coun·ter·check (*n.* koun'tər chĕk'; *v.* koun'tər chĕk'), *n.* **1.** a check that opposes or restrains. **2.** a check controlling or confirming another check. —*v.t.* **3.** to oppose or restrain (some obstacle, etc.) by contrary action. **4.** to control or confirm by a second check.

coun·ter·claim (*n.* koun'tər klăm'; *v.* koun'tər klăm'), *n.* **1.** a claim set up against another claim. —*v.i.* **2.** to set up a counterclaim. —**coun'ter·claim'ant,** *n.*

coun·ter·clock·wise (koun'tər klŏk'wīz'), *adj., adv.* in a direction opposite to that of the rotation of the hands of a clock.

coun·ter·cur·rent (koun'tər kûr'ənt), *n.* a current in an opposite direction.

coun·ter·dem·on·stra·tion (koun'tər dĕm'ən strā'shən), *n.* a demonstration intended to offset the effect of a preceding demonstration.

coun·ter·es·pi·o·nage (koun'tər ĕs'pĭ ə nĭj, -näzh'), *n.* the detection of enemy espionage.

coun·ter·feit (koun'tər fĭt), *adj.* **1.** made to imitate, and pass for, something else; not genuine: *counterfeit coin.* **2.** pretended: *counterfeit grief.* —*n.* **3.** an imitation designed to pass as an original; a forgery. **4.** *Archaic.* a copy. **5.** *Obs.* a likeness; portrait. **6.** *Obs.* an impostor. —*v.t.* **7.** to make a counterfeit of; imitate fraudulently; forge. **8.** to resemble. **9.** to simulate. —*v.i.* **10.** to make counterfeits, as of money. **11.** to feign; dissemble. [ME *counterfet,* t. OF: m. *contrefait,* pp. of *contrefaire* imitate, der. *contre* CONTRA- + *faire* do (g. L *facere*)] —**coun'ter·feit'er,** *n.* —**Syn. 1.** spurious. See **false. 2.** sham, feigned, simulated, fraudulent.

coun·ter·foil (koun'tər foil'), *n. Chiefly Brit.* a complementary part of a bank check, etc., which is retained by the issuer, and on which particulars are noted. See U.S. **stub.**

coun·ter·in·sur·gen·cy (koun'tər ĭn sûr'jən sī'), *n.* specialized tactics used in combating the indirect military activities of guerrilla raiders or fifth columnists.

coun·ter·ir·ri·tant (koun'tər ĭr'ə tənt), *n. Med.* an agent for producing irritation in one part to counteract irritation or relieve pain or inflammation elsewhere.

coun·ter·jump·er (koun'tər jŭmp'ər), *n. Slang.* a salesman at a counter.

coun·ter·mand (*v.* koun'tər mănd', -mänd'; *n.* koun'tər mănd', -mänd'), *v.t.* **1.** to revoke (a command, order, etc.). **2.** to recall or stop by a contrary order. —*n.* **3.** a command, order, etc., revoking a previous one. [ME *countermaund(en),* t. OF: m. *contremander,* f. *contre* CONTRA- + *mander* command, g. L *mandāre* enjoin]

coun·ter·march (*v.* koun'tər märch'; *n.* koun'tər märch'), *n.* **1.** a march back again. **2.** a complete reversal of conduct or measures. —*v.i.* **3.** to turn about and march back along the same route; execute a countermarch. —*v.t.* **4.** to cause to countermarch.

coun·ter·meas·ure (koun'tər mĕzh'ər), *n.* an opposing or retaliatory measure.

coun·ter·mine (*n.* koun'tər mīn'; *v.* koun'tər mīn'), *n., v.,* **-mined, -mining.** —*n.* **1.** *Mil.* a mine intended to intercept or destroy an enemy's mine. **2.** a counterplot. —*v.t.* **3.** to oppose by a countermine. —*v.i.* **4.** to make a countermine. **5.** *Mil.* to destroy enemy mines.

coun·ter·move (*n.* koun'tər mōōv'; *v.* koun'tər mōōv'), *n., v.,* **-moved, -moving.** —*n.* **1.** an opposing or retaliatory move. —*v.i., v.t.* **2.** to move in opposition or retaliation. —**coun'ter·move'ment** *n.*

coun·ter·of·fen·sive (koun'tər ə fĕn'sĭv), *n. Mil.* an attack by an army against an enemy force which has been and may still be attacking.

b., blend of, blended; **c.,** cognate with; **d.,** dialect, dialectal; **der.,** derived from; **f.,** formed from; **g.,** going back to; **m.,** modification of; **r.,** replacing; **s.,** stem of; **t.,** taken from; **?,** perhaps. See the full key on inside cover.

coun·ter·pane (koun'tər pān'), *n.* a quilt or coverlet for a bed. [var. of obs. *counterpoint* cover, t. OF]

coun·ter·part (koun'tər pärt'), *n.* 1. a copy; duplicate. 2. a part that answers to another, as each part of a document executed in duplicate. 3. one of two parts which fit each other; a thing that complements something else. 4. a person or thing closely resembling another.

coun·ter·plot (*n., v.* koun'tər plŏt'; *v. also* koun'tər plŏt'), *n., v.,* **-plotted, -plotting.** —*n.* 1. a plot directed against another plot. —*v.i.* 2. to devise a counterplot; plot in opposition. —*v.t.* 3. to plot against (a plot or plotter); frustrate by a counterplot.

coun·ter·point (koun'tər point'), *n.* *Music.* 1. the art of combining melodies. 2. the texture resulting from the combining of individual melodic lines. 3. a melody composed to be combined with another melody. [t. F: m. *contrepoint.* Cf. ML *punctum contrā punctum* note against note]

coun·ter·poise (koun'tər poiz'), *n., v.,* **-poised, -poising.** —*n.* 1. a counterbalancing weight. 2. any equal and opposing power or force. 3. the state of being in equilibrium. —*v.t.* 4. to balance by an opposing weight; counteract by an opposing force. 5. to bring into equilibrium. 6. *Archaic.* to weigh (one thing) against another. [ME *counterpeis,* t. OF, var. of *contrepois,* f. *contre* CONTRA- + *pois* weight (g. L *pensum*)]

coun·ter·poi·son (koun'tər poi'zən), *n.* 1. an agent for counteracting a poison; an antidote. 2. an opposite poison.

coun·ter·prop·a·gan·da (koun'tər prŏp'ə găn'də), *n.* propaganda to combat unfriendly or enemy propaganda.

coun·ter·ref·or·ma·tion (koun'tər rĕf'ər mā'shən), *n.* a reformation opposed to or counteracting a previous reformation.

Counter Reformation, the movement within the Roman Catholic Church which followed the Protestant Reformation of the 16th century.

coun·ter·rev·o·lu·tion (koun'tər rĕv'ə lōō'shən), *n.* a revolution opposed to a preceding one. —**coun·ter·rev·o·lu·tion·ar·y** (koun'tər rĕv'ə lōō'shə nĕr'Y), *adj.* —**coun'ter·rev'o·lu'tion·ist,** *n.*

coun·ter·scarp (koun'tər skärp'), *n.* *Fort.* 1. the exterior slope or wall of the ditch of a fort, supporting the covered way. 2. this slope with the covered way and glacis. [t. F: m. *contrescarpe,* t. It.: m. *contrascarpa,* f. *contra-* COUNTER- + *scarpa* slope of a wall]

coun·ter·shaft (koun'tər shăft', -shäft'), *n.* *Mach.* an intermediate shaft driven from a main shaft.

coun·ter·sign (*n., v.* koun'tər sīn'; *v. also* koun'tər sīn'), *n.* 1. *Mil.* a password given by authorized persons in passing through a guard. 2. a sign used in reply to another sign. 3. a signature added to another signature, esp. for authentication. —*v.t.* 4. to sign (a document) in addition to another signature, esp. in confirmation or authentication. [t. OF: m. *contresigne,* t. It.: m. *contrassegno*]

coun·ter·sink (*v., n.* koun'tər sĭngk'; *v. also* koun'tər sĭngk'), *v.,* **-sunk, -sinking,** *n.* —*v.t.* 1. to enlarge the upper part of (a hole or cavity), esp. by chamfering, to receive the cone-shaped head of a screw, bolt, etc. 2. to cause (the head of a screw, bolt, etc.) to sink into a depression made for it, so as to be flush with or below the surface. —*n.* 3. a tool for countersinking a hole. 4. a countersunk hole.

coun·ter·state·ment (koun'tər stāt'mənt), *n.* a statement made to deny or refute another.

coun·ter·stroke (koun'tər strōk'), *n.* a stroke or blow given in return.

coun·ter·tend·en·cy (koun'tər tĕn'dən sĭ), *n., pl.* **-cies.** an opposing tendency.

coun·ter·ten·or (koun'tər tĕn'ər), *n.* *Music.* 1. an adult male voice or voice part higher than the tenor. 2. a singer with such a voice; a high tenor.

coun·ter·thrust (koun'tər thrŭst'), *n.* a thrust made in opposition or return.

coun·ter·type (koun'tər tīp'), *n.* 1. a corresponding type. 2. an opposite type.

coun·ter·vail (koun'tər vāl'), *v.t.* 1. to act or avail against with equal power, force, or effect; counteract. 2. to furnish an equivalent of or a compensation for; offset. 3. *Archaic.* to equal. —*v.i.* 4. to be of equal force in opposition; avail. [ME *countrevaile(n),* t. AF: m. *countrevaloir,* f. *countre* against + *valoir* be strong, g. L *valēre*]

coun·ter·weight (koun'tər wāt'), *n.* a counterbalancing weight; a counterpoise. —**coun'ter·weight'ed,** *adj.*

coun·ter·work (*n.* koun'tər wûrk'; *v.* koun'tər wûrk'), *n.* 1. opposing work or action; a work in opposition to another work. —*v.t.* 2. to work in opposition to. —*v.i.* 3. to work in opposition to; hinder or frustrate. —**coun'ter·work'er,** *n.*

count·ess (koun'tĭs), *n.* 1. the wife or widow of a count in the nobility of continental Europe, or of an earl in the British peerage. 2. a woman having the rank of a count or earl in her own right. [ME *contesse,* t. OF, g. LL *comitissa,* fem. of L *comes.* See COUNT²]

counting house, *Chiefly Brit.* a building or office set aside for bookkeeping, etc., as in a factory.

counting room, a room used as a counting house.

count·less (kount'lĭs), *adj.* incapable of being counted; innumerable: *the countless stars of the unbounded heavens.*

count palatine, 1. (orig. in Germany) a count having supreme jurisdiction in his fief or province. 2. (formerly, in England) an earl, or other county proprietor, who exercised royal prerogatives within his county.

coun·tri·fied (kŭn'trĭ fīd'), *adj.* rustic or rural in appearance, conduct, etc.: *a countrified person, stretch of land, etc.* Also, **countryfied.**

coun·try (kŭn'trĭ), *n., pl.* **-tries,** *adj.* —*n.* 1. a tract of land considered apart from geographical or political limits; region; district. 2. any considerable territory demarcated by geographical conditions or by a distinctive population. 3. the territory of a nation. 4. a state. 5. the people of a district, state, or nation. 6. the public. 7. *Law.* the public at large, as represented by a jury. 8. the land of one's birth or citizenship. 9. rural districts (as opposed to cities or towns). —*adj.* 10. of the country; rural. 11. rude; unpolished: *country manners.* 12. of a country or one's own country. [ME *contree,* t. OF, g. LL *contrāta,* lit., what lies opposite, der. L *contrā* opposite to]

country club, a club in the country, often near a city, with a house, grounds, and facilities for outdoor sports, etc.

country cousin, a relative from the country to whom the sights and activities of a large city are novel and bewildering.

coun·try-dance (kŭn'trĭ dăns', -däns'), *n.* a dance of rural (or native) English origin, esp. one in which the partners stand facing each other in two lines.

coun·try·fied (kŭn'trĭ fīd'), *adj.* countrified.

country gentleman, a wealthy man living in his country home or estate.

country house, a house on a country estate.

coun·try·man (kŭn'trĭ mən), *n., pl.* **-men.** 1. a man of one's own country. 2. a native or inhabitant of a particular region. 3. a man who lives in the country. —**coun·try·wom·an** (kŭn'trĭ wŏŏm'ən), *n. fem.* —*Syn.* 1. compatriot, fellow citizen. 3. rustic, farmer.

coun·try·seat (kŭn'trĭ sēt'), *n.* *Chiefly Brit.* a country estate, esp. a fine one, often one used for only part of the year.

coun·try·side (kŭn'trĭ sīd'), *n.* 1. a particular section of a country, esp. rural. 2. its inhabitants.

coun·ty (koun'tĭ), *n., pl.* **-ties.** 1. the political unit next below the State in the U.S. 2. one of the chief administrative divisions of a country or state, as in Great Britain and Ireland. 3. one of the larger divisions for purposes of local administration, etc., in Canada, New Zealand, etc. 4. the inhabitants of a county. 5. *Obs. or Hist.* the domain of a count or an earl. [ME *counte,* t. AF, var. of OF *conte,* der. *conte* COUNT²]

county college, (in England) a part time continuation school with compulsory attendance for boys and girls from 15 to 18 years of age, created under the Education Act (1944).

county court, 1. *U.S.* a. an administrative board in counties in some States. b. a judicial tribunal in some States with jurisdiction extending over one or more counties. 2. *England.* a. the lowest civil tribunal, but unconnected with county. b. *Hist.* a primary assembly, with varying composition, of inhabitants of a county.

county seat, *U.S.* the seat of government of a county. Also, **county town.**

coup (kōō), *n., pl.* **coups** (kōōz; *Fr.* kōō). an unexpected and successful stroke. [t. F, in OF *coip,* g. LL *colpus* blow, for L *colaphus,* t. Gk.: m. *kólaphos*]

coup de grâce (kōō də gräs'), 1. a death blow, now usually a bullet in the head to make sure an executed person is dead. 2. a finishing stroke. [F: grace-stroke]

coup de main (kōō də măn'), a surprise attack. [F: hand-stroke]

coup d'é·tat (kōō dĕ tä'), a sudden and decisive measure in politics, esp. one effecting a change of government illegally or by force. [F: lit., stroke of state]

coup de thé·â·tre (kōō də tĕ ä'tr), *French.* 1. a theatrical hit. 2. a surprising or sensational trick.

coup d'oeil (kōō dœ'y), *French.* a quick glance.

cou·pé (kōō pā'; *for 1, also* kōōp), *n.* 1. Also, **coupe.** a closed two-door automobile with a body shorter than that of a sedan of the same model. 2. a short four-wheeled closed carriage with (usually) a single cross seat for two persons and with an outside seat for the driver. 3. the end compartment in a European diligence or railroad car. [t. F, prop. pp. of *couper* cut]

couped (kōōpt), *adj.* *Her.* cut off, as of a cross cut off so as not to touch the edge of the shield, or an animal, cut off at its chest.

Cou·pe·rus (kōō pā'rəs), *n.* **Louis** (lōō ē'), 1863–1923, Dutch author.

cou·ple (kŭp'əl), *n., v.,* **-pled, -pling.** —*n.* 1. a combination of two; a pair. 2. two of the same sort connected or considered together. 3. a man and a woman united by marriage or betrothal, associated as partners in a dance, etc. 4. *Mech.* a pair of equal, parallel forces acting in opposite directions and tending to produce rotation. 5. a leash for holding two hounds together. —*v.t.* 6. to fasten, link, or associate together in a pair or pairs. 7. to join; connect. 8. *Colloq.* to unite in matrimony. **9.** *Radio.* to join or associate by means of a coupler. —*v.i.* **10.** to join in a pair; unite. **11.** to copulate. [ME, t. OF: m. *cople,* g. L *copula* band, bond] —**Syn. 1.** See **pair.**

cou·pler (kŭp′lər), *n.* **1.** one who or that which couples, or links together. **2.** a device in an organ for connecting keys, manuals, or a manual and pedals, so that they are played together when one is played. **3.** *Radio.* a device for transferring electrical energy from one circuit to another, as a transformer which joins parts of a radio apparatus together by induction.

cou·plet (kŭp′lĭt), *n.* **1.** a pair of successive lines of verse, esp. such as rhyme together and are of the same length. **2.** a pair; couple. [t. F, dim. of *couple* COUPLE]

cou·pling (kŭp′lĭng), *n.* **1.** act of one who or that which couples. **2.** any mechanical device for uniting or connecting parts or things. **3.** a device used in joining railroad cars, etc. **4.** *Elect.* **a.** the association of two circuits or systems in such a way that power may be transferred from one to the other. **b.** a device or expedient to insure coupling. **5.** the part of the body between the tops of the shoulder blades and the tops of the hip joints in a dog, etc.

cou·pon (kōō′pŏn, kū′-), *n.* **1.** a separable part of a certificate, ticket, advertisement, etc., entitling the holder to something. **2.** one of a number of such parts calling for periodical payments on a bond. **3.** a separate ticket or the like, for a similar purpose. [t. F, der. *couper* cut]

cour·age (kûr′ĭj, kŭr′-), *n.* **1.** the quality of mind that enables one to encounter difficulties and danger with firmness or without fear; bravery. **2. have the courage of one's convictions,** to act consistently with one's opinions. **3.** *Obs.* heart; mind; disposition. [ME *corage,* t. OF, der. *cor* heart, g. L]
—**Syn. 1.** fearlessness, dauntlessness, intrepidity, fortitude, pluck, heroism, daring, hardihood. COURAGE, BRAVERY, VALOR, BRAVADO refer to qualities of spirit and conduct. COURAGE is that quality of mind which enables one to face dangers, difficulties, threats, pain, etc., without fear: *to take (or lose) courage.* BRAVERY implies true courage together with daring and an intrepid boldness: *bravery in a battle.* VALOR implies continuous, active bravery in the face of personal danger and a noble and lofty quality of courage: *valor throughout a campaign, in fighting for the right.* BRAVADO is now usually a boastful and ostentatious pretense of courage or bravery: *empty bravado.* —**Ant. 1.** cowardice.

cou·ra·geous (kə rā′jəs), *adj.* possessing or characterized by courage; brave; valiant. —**cou·ra′geous·ly,** *adv.* —**cou·ra′geous·ness,** *n.* —**Syn.** See **brave.**

cou·rante (kōō ränt′; *Fr.* kōō ränt′), *n.* **1.** an old-fashioned dance dating back to the 17th century characterized by a running or gliding step. **2.** a piece of music for or suited to this dance. **3.** *Music.* a movement in the classical suite, following the allemande. Also, **cou·rant′.** [t. F, prop. fem. of *courant,* ppr. of *courir* run]

Cour·bet (kōōr bě′), *n.* Gustave (gÿs tȧv′), 1819–77, French painter.

Cour·be·voie (kōōrb vwȧ′), *n.* a city in N France; a suburb of Paris. 59,730 (1954).

cour·i·er (kûr′ĭ ər, kōōr′-), *n.* **1.** a messenger sent in haste. **2.** a person hired by travelers to take charge of the arrangements of a journey. [t. F, t. It.: m. *corriere* runner, der. *corre* run, g. L *currere*; r. ME *corour,* t. OF: m. *coreor,* g. LL *curritor* runner]

cour·lan (kōōr′lən), *n.* a bird of the tropical American genus *Aramus,* comprising one species, *A. guarauna,* a large, long-billed, raillike bird notable for its peculiar cry. [t. F, appar. repr. native name]

Cour·land (kōōr′lənd), *n.* a former duchy on the Baltic: later a province of Russia, and in 1918 incorporated into Latvia. Also, **Kurland.**

course (kōrs), *n., v.,* **coursed, coursing.** —*n.* **1.** advance in a particular direction; onward movement. **2.** the path, route or channel along which anything moves: *the course of a stream, ship, etc.* **3.** the ground, water, etc., on which a race is run, sailed. etc. **4.** the continuous passage or progress through time or a succession of stages: *in the course of a year, a battle, etc.* **5.** customary manner of procedure; regular or natural order of events: *the course of a disease, argument, etc.,* a *matter of course.* **6.** a mode of conduct; behavior. **7.** a particular manner of proceeding: *try another course with him.* **8.** a systematized or prescribed series: *a course of studies, lectures, medical treatments, etc.* **9.** any one of the studies in such a series: *the first course in algebra.* **10.** a part of a meal served at one time: *the main course was steak.* **11.** *Naut.* **a.** the point of the compass toward which a ship sails. **b.** the lowest square sail on any mast of a square-rigged ship, identified as **fore course, main course,** etc. **12.** a continuous horizontal (or inclined) range of stones, bricks, or the like, in a wall, the face of a building, etc. **13.** *Knitting.* the row of stitches going across from side to side (as opposed to *wale*). **14.** (*often pl.*) the menses. **15.** a charge, as in tilting. **16.** pursuit of game with dogs. **17.** *Archaic.* a race. **18. in due course,** in the proper or natural order; at the right time. **19. of course, a.** certainly; obviously. **b.** in the natural order.
—*v.t.* **20.** to run through or over. **21.** to chase; pursue. **22.** to hunt (game) with hounds, esp. by sight and not by scent. **23.** to cause (dogs) to pursue game. —*v.i.* **24.** to follow a course; direct one's course. **25.** to run; move swiftly; race. **26.** to engage in coursing, in a hunt, a tilting match, etc. [t. F; r. ME *cors,* t. OF, g. L *cursus* a running] —**Syn.**

2. way, road, track, passage. **5.** process, career. **7.** method, mode. **8.** sequence, succession.

cours·er¹ (kōr′sər), *n.* **1.** one who or that which courses. **2.** a dog for coursing. [f. COURSE, v. + -ER²]

cours·er² (kōr′sər), *n.* *Chiefly Poetic.* a swift horse. [ME, t. F: m. *coursier,* der. *cours* COURSE]

cours·er³ (kōr′sər), *n.* any of certain swift-footed ploverlike birds constituting the genus *Cursorius,* of the desert regions of Africa and Asia, as *C. cursor,* occasionally found also in Europe. [t. L: m.s. *cursōrius* fitted for running]

cours·ing (kōr′sĭng), *n.* **1.** act of one who or that which courses. **2.** *Chiefly Brit.* the sport of pursuing hares, etc., with hounds, when the game is started in sight of the hounds.

court (kōrt), *n.* **1.** an open space wholly or partly enclosed by a wall, buildings, etc. **2.** a large building within such a space. **3.** *Chiefly Brit.* a stately dwelling. **4.** a short street. **5.** a smooth, level area on which to play tennis, handball, etc. **6.** one of the divisions of such an area. **7.** the residence of a sovereign or other high dignitary; palace. **8.** the collective body of persons forming his retinue. **9.** a sovereign and his councilors as the political rulers of a state. **10.** a formal assembly held by a sovereign. **11.** homage paid, as to a sovereign. **12.** assiduous attention directed to gain favor, affection etc.: *to pay court to a king, a pretty woman, etc.* **13.** *Law.* **a.** a place where justice is administered. **b.** a judicial tribunal duly constituted for the hearing and determination of cases. **c.** a session of a judicial assembly. **14.** the body of qualified members of a corporation, council, board, etc. **15.** a branch or lodge of a fraternal society. **16. out of court,** not entitled to a hearing. —*v.t.* **17.** to endeavor to win the favor of. **18.** to seek the affections of; woo. **19.** to attempt to gain (applause, favor, a decision, etc.). **20.** to hold out inducements to; invite. —*v.i.* **21.** to make love; woo. [ME, t. OF: m. *cort,* g. L *co(ho)rs* enclosure, also division of troops (see COHORT)]

court card, *Brit.* face card.

court dress, the formal costume worn at court, for men including silk knee breeches and stockings.

cour·te·ous (kûr′tĭ əs), *adj.* having or showing good manners; polite. [ME *curteis,* t. OF, der. *cort* COURT] —**cour′te·ous·ly,** *adv.* —**cour′te·ous·ness,** *n.* —**Syn.** See **civil.** —**Ant.** rude.

cour·te·san (kōr′tə zən, kûr′-), *n.* a prostitute. Also **cour′te·zan.** [t. F: m. *courtisane,* t. It.: m. *cortigiana* lewd woman, orig. woman of the court, der. *corte* COURT]

cour·te·sy (kûr′tə sĭ), *n., pl.* **-sies. 1.** excellence of manners or behavior; politeness. **2.** a courteous act or expression. **3.** favor; indulgence; consent: *a title by courtesy rather than by right.* **4.** a curtsy. [ME *cortesie,* t. OF, der. *corteis* COURTEOUS] —**Syn. 1.** courteousness, civility, urbanity.

courtesy title, *Brit.* a title allowed by custom, as to the children of dukes.

court hand, a style of handwriting formerly used in the English law courts.

court·house (kōrt′hous′), *n.* **1.** a building in which courts of law are held. **2.** *U.S.* a county seat.

cour·ti·er (kōr′tĭ ər), *n.* **1.** one in attendance at the court of a sovereign. **2.** one who seeks favor.

court·ly (kōrt′lĭ), *adj.* **-lier, -liest,** *adv.* —*adj.* **1.** polite; elegant; refined. **2.** flattering; obsequious. **3.** of the court of a sovereign. —*adv.* **4.** in the manner of courts; elegantly; flatteringly. —**court′li·ness,** *n.*

court-mar·tial (kōrt′mär′shəl), *n., pl.* **courts-martial,** *v.,* **-tialed, -tialing** or (*esp. Brit.*) **-tialled, -tialling.** —*n.* **1.** a court consisting of military or naval officers appointed by a commander to try charges of offense against military or naval law. —*v.t.* **2.** to arraign and try by court-martial.

Court of St. James's, the British royal court, so called from St. James's Palace, London, the former scene of royal receptions.

court plaster, cotton or other fabric coated on one side with an adhesive preparation, as of isinglass and glycerin, used for covering slight cuts, etc., on the skin.

Cour·trai (kōōr trě′), *n.* a city in W Belgium, on the Lys river: important medieval city. 40,657 (1947).

court·room (kōrt′rōōm′, -rŏŏm′), *n.* a room in which the sessions of a law court are held.

court·ship (kōrt′shĭp), *n.* **1.** the wooing of a woman. **2.** solicitation, esp. of favors. **3.** *Obs.* courtly manners.

court tennis, tennis (def. 1).

court·yard (kōrt′yärd′), *n.* a space enclosed by walls next to or within a castle, large house, etc.

cous·in (kŭz′ən), *n.* **1.** the son or daughter of an uncle or aunt. **2.** one related by descent in a diverging line from a known common ancestor. The children of brothers and sisters are called cousins, cousins-german, first cousins, or full cousins; children of first cousins are called second cousins, etc. Often, however, the term second cousin is loosely applied to the son or daughter of a cousin-german, more properly called a first cousin once removed. **3.** a kinsman or kinswoman. **4.** a person or thing related to another by similar natures languages, etc.: *our Canadian cousins.* **5.** a term of address from one sovereign to another or to a great noble. —*v.t.* **6.** to call "cousin"; claim kindred with. [t. F, g. L *consobrinus* mother's sister's child; r. ME *cosin,* t. OF] —**cous′in·hood,** **cous′in·ship,** *n.*

ou·sin (kŏŏz′ăn′), n. **Victor** (vēk′tôr′), 1792–1867, French philosopher and educational reformer.

ous·in·ger·man (kŭz′ən jûr′mən), n., pl. **cousins-german.** a first cousin. See **cousin** (def. 2). [t. F: m. *cousin-germain.* See GERMAN, adj.]

ous·in·ly (kŭz′ən lĭ), adj. **1.** like or befitting a cousin. —adv. **2.** in the manner of a cousin; as a cousin.

ou·teau (kŏŏ tō′), n., pl. **-teaux** (-tōz′; Fr. -tō′). a knife, esp. a large double-edged one formerly carried as a weapon. [F, in OF *coutel*, g. L *cultellus*, dim. of *culter* knife]

ou·tu·rier (kŏŏ tʏ ryē′), n. a dressmaker (man). [F, der. *couture* sewing] —**cou·tu·rière** (kŏŏ tʏ ryêr′), n. *fem.*

ou·vade (kŏŏ väd′; Fr. -väd′), n. a practice among some primitive peoples by which, at the birth of a child, the father takes to bed and performs other acts natural rather to the mother. [t. F, der. *couver* brood, incubate. See COVEY]

o·va·lence (kō vā′ləns), n. *Chem.* **1.** the number of electron pairs that an atom can share with those which surround it. **2.** the bond formed by the sharing of a pair of electrons by two atoms.

ove[1] (kōv), n., v., **coved, coving.** —n. **1.** a small indentation or recess in the shoreline of a sea, lake, or river. **2.** a sheltered nook. **3.** a hollow or recess in a mountain; cave; cavern. **4.** a narrow pass between mountains. **5.** a sheltered area, usually prairie, between woods or hills. **6.** *Archit.* a concavity; a concave molding or member. —v.t., v.i. **7.** to form into a cove. [ME; OE *cofa* chamber, c. Icel. *kofi* hut]

ove[2] (kōv), n. *Brit. Slang.* a person; a fellow. [said to be t. Romany: m. *kova* creature]

ov·e·nant (kŭv′ə nənt), n. **1.** an agreement between two or more persons to do or refrain from doing some act; a compact; a contract. **2.** an incidental clause of agreement in such an agreement. **3.** *Eccles.* a solemn agreement between the members of a church, as that they will act together in harmony with the precepts of the gospel. **4.** (cap.) one of certain bonds of agreement signed by the Scottish Presbyterians for the defense or promotion of their religion, esp. the **National Covenant** of 1638, or the **Solemn League and Covenant** of 1643 (entered into with England). **5.** (in Biblical usage) the agreement or engagement of God with man as set forth in the Old and the New Testament. **6.** *Law.* **a.** a formal agreement of legal validity, esp. one under seal. **b.** an early English form of action in suits involving sealed contracts. **7.** (cap.) in full, **Covenant of the League of Nations,** the "Constitution" of the League of Nations, included as the first 26 articles in the Treaty of Versailles. —v.i. **8.** to enter into a covenant. —v.t. **9.** to agree to by covenant; stipulate. [ME, t. OF, der. *covenir,* g. L *convenire* agree]

ov·e·nant·er (kŭv′ə nən tər; for 2, also Scot. kŭv′ə năn′tər), n. **1.** one who enters into a covenant. **2.** (cap.) adherent of the National Covenant. See **covenant,** def. 4.

:ov·e·nan·tor (kŭv′ə nən tər), n. *Law.* the party who is to perform the obligation expressed in a covenant.

Cov·ent Garden (kŭv′ənt), n. **1.** district in central London, England, noted for its vegetable and flower market. **2.** a theater in this district, first built in 1731, important in English theatrical history.

Cov·en·try (kŏv′ən trĭ, kŭv′-), n. **1.** a city in central England, in Warwickshire: heavily bombed, Nov., 1940. 272,600 (est. 1956). **2. send to Coventry,** to refuse to associate with.

:ov·er (kŭv′ər), v.t. **1.** to put something over or upon, as for protection or concealment. **2.** to be or serve as a covering for; extend over; occupy the surface of. **3.** to put a cover or covering on; clothe. **4.** to put one's hat on (one's head). **5.** to bring upon or invest (oneself): *to cover oneself with honors.* **6.** to shelter; protect; serve as a defense to. **7.** *Mil.* **a.** to be in line with by occupying a position directly before or behind. **b.** to protect (a soldier, force, or military position) during an expected period of ground combat by taking a position from which any hostile troops can be fired upon who might shoot at the soldier, force, or position. **8.** to hide from view; screen. **9.** to aim directly at, as with a pistol. **10.** to have within range, as a fortress does certain territory. **11.** to include; comprise; provide for; take in: *this book covers all common English words.* **12.** to suffice to defray or meet (a charge, expense, etc.); offset (an outlay, loss, liability, etc.). **13.** to deposit the equivalent of (money deposited), as in wagering; accept the conditions of (a bet, etc.). **14.** to act as reporter of (occurrences, performances, etc.), as for a newspaper, etc. **15.** to pass or travel over. **16.** (of a male animal) to copulate with. **17.** to brood or sit on (eggs or chicks). —n. **18.** that which covers, as the lid of a vessel, the binding of a book, the wrapper of a letter, etc. **19.** protection; shelter; concealment. **20.** woods, underbrush, etc., serving to shelter and conceal wild animals or game; a covert. **21.** *Ecol.* vegetation which serves to protect or conceal animals, such as birds, from excessive sunlight or drying, or predators. **22.** something which veils, screens, or shuts from sight. **23.** a set of articles (plate, knife, fork, etc.) laid at table for one person. **24.** *Finance.* funds to cover liability or secure against risk of loss. **25.** *Philately.* **a.** an envelope or outer wrapping for mail. **b.** a letter folded so that the address may be placed on the outside and the missive mailed.

26. under cover, a. secret. **b.** secretly. [ME *cover(en),* t. OF: m. *covrir,* g. L *cooperire*] —**cov′er·er,** n. —**cov′er·less,** adj.

—**Syn. 1.** overlay, overspread, envelop, enwrap. **8.** cloak, conceal. **12.** counterbalance, compensate for. **19.** COVER, PROTECTION, SCREEN, SHELTER mean a defense against harm or danger, and a provision for safety. The main idea in COVER is that of concealment, as in darkness, in a wood, behind something, etc.: *keep under cover, take cover, the ground troops were left without cover when the air force was withdrawn.* SCREEN refers specifically to something behind which one can hide: *a heavy fire formed a screen for ground operations.* PROTECTION and SHELTER emphasize the idea of a guard or defense, a shield against injury or death. A PROTECTION is any such shield: *in World War II, an "air cover" of airplanes acted as a protection for troops.* A SHELTER is something which covers over, and acts as a place of refuge: *an abandoned monastery acted as a shelter.*

cov·er·age (kŭv′ər ĭj), n. **1.** *Insurance.* the total extent of risk, or the total number of risks, as fire, accident, etc., covered in a policy of insurance. **2.** *Finance.* the value of funds held to back up or meet liabilities.

cov·er·all (kŭv′ər ôl′), n. (usually pl.) a loose-fitting work garment with sleeves.

cover charge, an amount charged by a restaurant, night club, etc., for service or entertainment.

cover crop, a crop, preferably leguminous, planted to keep nutrients from leaching, soil from eroding, and land from weeding over, as during the winter.

Cov·er·dale (kŭv′ər dāl′), n. **Miles,** 1488–1569, English divine: translator of the Bible into English, 1535.

covered wagon, *U.S.* **1.** a large wagon with a canvas top, esp. a prairie schooner. **2.** *Brit. Railroads.* a boxcar.

cov·er·ing (kŭv′ər ĭng), n. **1.** something laid over or wrapped about a thing, esp. for concealment, protection, or warmth. **2.** *Com.* the operation of buying securities, etc., that one has sold short, in order to return them to the person from whom they were borrowed.

cov·er·let (kŭv′ər lĭt), n. **1.** the outer covering of a bed; a bedspread. **2.** any covering or cover. Also, **cov·er·lid** (kŭv′ər lĭd). [ME *coverlite,* appar. f. COVER + m. F *lit* bed]

Cov·er·ley (kŭv′ər lĭ), n. **Sir Roger de,** a literary figure representing the ideal of the early 18th century squire in the *Spectator* by Addison and Steele.

cov·er·point (kŭv′ər point′), n. *Cricket, Lacrosse, etc.* a player who supports the player called *point.*

covers, covered sine.

co·versed sine (kō′vûrst), *Math.* the versed sine of the complement of an angle or arc.

cov·ert (kŭv′ərt), adj. **1.** covered; sheltered. **2.** concealed; secret; disguised. **3.** *Law.* under cover or protection of a husband. —n. **4.** a covering; cover. **5.** shelter; concealment; disguise; a hiding place. **6.** *Hunting.* a thicket giving shelter to wild animals or game. **7.** (pl.) *Ornith.* the smaller feathers that cover the bases of the large feathers of the wing and tail. **8.** covert cloth. [ME, t. OF, pp. of *covrir* COVER] —**cov′ert·ly,** adv. —**cov′ert·ness,** n.

covert cloth, a cotton or worsted fabric of twill weave. The warp is of ply yarns, one of which is white.

covert coat, *Brit.* a short, light overcoat; a duster.

cov·er·ture (kŭv′ər chər), n. **1.** a cover or covering; shelter; concealment. **2.** *Law.* the status of a married woman considered as under the protection and authority of her husband.

cov·et (kŭv′ĭt), v.t. **1.** to desire inordinately, or without due regard to the rights of others; desire wrongfully. **2.** to wish for, esp. eagerly. —v.i. **3.** to have an inordinate or wrongful desire. [ME *coveiten,* t. OF: m. *cuveitier,* ult. der. L *cupiditas* desire] —**cov′et·a·ble** adj. —**cov′et·er,** n. —**Syn. 1.** See **envy.**

cov·et·ous (kŭv′ə təs), adj. **1.** inordinately or wrongly desirous. **2.** eagerly desirous. [ME, t. OF: m. *coveitos,* ult. der. L *cupiditas* desire] —**cov′et·ous·ly,** adv. —**cov′et·ous·ness,** n. —**Syn. 1.** greedy, grasping, rapacious, avaricious.

cov·ey (kŭv′ĭ), n., pl. **-eys. 1.** a brood or small flock of partridges or similar birds. **2.** a company; a group. [ME, t. OF: m. *covee,* der. *cover,* incubate, g. L *cubāre* lie]

cov·in (kŭv′ĭn), n. **1.** *Obs. except Law.* a secret or collusive agreement between two or more to the prejudice of another. **2.** *Obs. or Archaic.* fraud. [ME, t. OF, ult. der. L *convenire* agree]

Cov·ing·ton (kŭv′ĭng tən), n. a city in N Kentucky, on the Ohio river. 60,376 (1960).

cow[1] (kou), n., pl. **cows,** (Archaic) **kine. 1.** the female of a bovine animal, esp. of the genus *Bos,* that has produced a calf and is usually over three years of age. **2.** the female of various other large animals, as the elephant, whale, etc. [ME; OE *cū,* c. G *kuh*]

cow[2] (kou), v.t. to frighten with threats, etc.; intimidate. [t. Scand.; cf. Icel. *kūga* cow, tyrannize over]

cow·age (kou′ĭj), n. cowhage.

cow·ard (kou′ərd), n. **1.** one who lacks courage to meet danger or difficulty; one who is basely timid. —adj. **2.** lacking courage; timid. **3.** proceeding from or expressive of fear or timidity: *a coward cry.* [ME, t. OF: m. *coart,* der. *coe* tail, g. L *cauda,* through comparison with animal with tail between legs] —**Syn. 1.** craven, poltroon, dastard, milksop.

Cow·ard (kou′ərd), n. **Noel** (nō′əl), born 1899, British author, actor, and composer.

cow·ard·ice (kou′ər dĭs), *n.* lack of courage to face danger, difficulty, opposition, etc. **—Syn.** poltroonery, dastardliness, pusillanimity, timidity.

cow·ard·ly (kou′ərd lĭ), *adj.* **1.** lacking courage; basely timid. **2.** characteristic of or befitting a coward. **—*adv.* 3.** like a coward. **—cow′ard·li·ness,** *n.*
—Syn. 1. craven, poltroon, dastardly, pusillanimous, timorous, faint-hearted, white-livered, chicken-hearted. Cowardly, timid refer to a lack of courage or self-confidence. Cowardly means weakly and basely fearful in the presence of danger: *the cowardly wretch deserted his comrades in battle.* Timid means lacking in boldness or self-confidence even when there is no danger present: *a timid person stands in the way of his own advancement.* **—Ant. 1.** brave, self-confident.

cow·bane (kou′bān′), *n.* any of several umbelliferous plants supposed to be poisonous to cattle, as the European water hemlock, *Cicuta virosa,* or an American swamp plant, *Oxypolis rigidior.*

cow·bell (kou′bĕl′), *n.* **1.** a bell hung round a cow's neck, to indicate her whereabouts. **2.** an American name of the bladder campion, *Silene latifolia.*

cow·ber·ry (kou′bĕr′ĭ), *n., pl.* **-ries. 1.** the berry or fruit of any of various shrubs, as *Vaccinium vitis-idaea,* that grow in pastures. **2.** any of these shrubs.

cow·bind (kou′bīnd′), *n.* either the black-berried white bryony, *Bryonia alba,* or the red-berried bryony, *B. dioica.*

cow·bird (kou′bûrd′), *n.* any of the American blackbirds of the genus *Molothrus,* esp. *M. ater* of North America (so called because they accompany cattle). Also, **cow blackbird, cow bunting.**

cow·boy (kou′boi′), *n. U.S.* **1.** a man employed in the care of the cattle of a ranch, doing his work largely on horseback. **2.** *Now Hist.* (during the Revolutionary War) a member of one of the Tory guerrilla bands that operated between the American and British lines near New York.

cow·catch·er (kou′kăch′ər), *n. U.S.* a triangular frame at the front of a locomotive, streetcar, etc., designed for clearing the track of obstructions.

cow·er (kou′ər), *v.i.* **1.** to crouch in fear or shame. **2.** to bend with the knees and back; stand or squat in a bent position. [ME *couren,* t. Scand.; cf. Icel. *kūra* sit moping, doze, c. G *kauern* cower, crouch]

Cowes (kouz), *n.* a seaport on the Isle of Wight, in S England: resort. 17,154 (1951).

cow·fish (kou′fĭsh′), *n., pl.* **-fishes,** (*esp. collectively*) **-fish. 1.** any of various marine fishes with hornlike projections over the eyes, as *Lactophrys tricornis,* found along the southern Atlantic coast of the U.S., to Panama, Brazil, etc. **2.** a sirenian, as the manatee. **3.** any of various small cetaceans, as a porpoise or dolphin or the grampus, *Grampus griseus.*

cow·girl (kou′gûrl′), *n.* a girl who assists in herding and handling cattle on a ranch.

cow·hage (kou′ĭj), *n.* **1.** the hairs on the pods of a tropical leguminous plant, *Stizolobium* (or *Mucuna*) *pruriens,* causing intense itching and sometimes used as a vermifuge. **2.** the pods. **3.** the plants. Also, **cowage.** [t. Hind.: m. *kawānch*]

cow hand, one employed on a cattle ranch; a cowboy.

cow·herd (kou′hûrd′), *n.* one whose occupation is the tending of cows.

cow·hide (kou′hīd′), *n., v.,* **-hided, -hiding. —*n.* 1.** the hide of a cow. **2.** the leather made from it. **3.** *U.S.* a strong, flexible whip made of rawhide or of braided leather. **—*v.t.* 4.** to whip with a cowhide.

cow killer, a wasp, *Dasymutilla occidentalis,* of the southern U.S., resembling a large ant.

cowl (koul), *n.* **1.** a hooded garment worn by monks. **2.** the hood of this garment. **3.** a hood-shaped covering for a chimney or ventilating shaft, to increase the draft. **4.** the forward part of the automobile body supporting the rear of the hood and the windshield, and housing the pedals and instrument panel. **5.** *Aeron.* a cowling. **6.** a wire netting fastened to the top of the smokestack of a locomotive, to prevent large sparks from being discharged; a spark arrester. **—*v.t.* 7.** to put a monk's cowl on. **8.** to make a monk of. **9.** to cover with, or as with, a cowl. [ME *couel,* OE *cūle, cug(e)le,* t. LL: m. *cuculla* cowl, var. of L *cucullus* hood]

cowled (kould), *adj.* **1.** wearing a cowl. **2.** shaped like a cowl; cucullate.

Cow·ley (kou′lĭ, kōō′lĭ), *n.* **Abraham,** 1618–67, British poet.

cow·lick (kou′lĭk′), *n.* a tuft of hair turned up, usually over the forehead.

cowl·ing (kou′lĭng), *n. Aeron.* a streamlined housing for an aircraft engine, usually forming a continuous line with the fuselage or wing.

cow·man (kou′mən), *n., pl.* **-men. 1.** *Western U.S.* an owner of cattle; a ranchman. **2.** *Brit.* a farm laborer who takes care of cows.

co-work·er (kō wûr′kər), *n.* fellow worker.

cow parsnip, any plant of the umbelliferous genus *Heracleum,* as *H. spondylium,* of Europe, or *H. lanatum,* of North America.

cow·pea (kou′pē′), *n.* **1.** an annual plant, *Vigna sinensis,* extensively grown in the southern U.S. for forage, soil improvement, etc., the seeds sometimes being used for hu.. an food. **2.** the seed.

Cow·per (kōō′pər, kou′pər), *n.* **William,** 1731–1800, British poet.

Cow·per's glands (kou′pərz, kōō′-), (in various animals) a pair of accessory prostate or urethral glands of lobulated or follicular structure, which during sexual excitement pour a mucous secretion into the urethra [named after Wm. *Cowper,* 1666–1709, British anatomist who discovered them]

cow pilot, a small fish, *Abudefduf saxatilis,* with dark bars, common in the West Indies and along both coasts of tropical America; pintano; sergeant major.

cow pony, *Western U.S.* a pony used in herding cattle.

cow·pox (kou′pŏks′), *n.* an eruptive disease appearing on the teats and udders of cows in which small pustules form which contain a virus used in the vaccination of man against smallpox.

cow·punch·er (kou′pŭn′chər), *n. U.S. Colloq.* a cowboy.

cow·rie (kou′rĭ), *n.* **1.** the shell of any of the marine gastropods constituting the genus *Cypraea,* as that of *C. moneta,* a small shell with a fine gloss, used as money in certain parts of Asia and Africa, or that of *C. tigris,* large, handsome shell often used as a mantel ornament. **2.** the animal itself. [t. Hind.: m. *kaurī*]

cow·ry (kou′rĭ), *n., pl.* **-ries.** cowrie.

cow·skin (kou′skĭn′), *n.* **1.** the skin of a cow. **2.** the leather made from it.

cow·slip (kou′slĭp), *n.* **1.** an English primrose, *Primula officinalis* (*P. veris*), bearing yellow flowers. **2.** *U.S.* the marsh marigold. [OE *cūslyppe* cowslime, var. of *cū-sloppe* (ME *couslop*) cow-slobber. Cf. oxlip]

cox (kŏks), *n.* **1.** *Colloq.* coxswain. **—*v.t., v.i.* 2.** to act as coxswain to (a boat).

cox·a (kŏk′sə), *n., pl.* **coxae** (kŏk′sē). **1.** *Anat.* **a.** the innominate bone. **b.** the joint of the hip. **2.** *Zool.* the first or proximal segment of the leg of insects and other arthropods. [t. L: hip] **— cox′al,** *adj.*

cox·al·gi·a (kŏk săl′jĭ ə), *n. Pathol.* pain in the hip. Also, **cox·al·gy** (kŏk′săl jĭ). [NL; f. cox(a) + -algia] **—cox·al′gic,** *adj.*

Leg of beetle (enlarged)
A, Coxa; B. Trochanter; C, Femur
D, Tibia; E. Tarsus

cox·comb (kŏks′kōm′), *n.* **1.** a conceited dandy. **2.** *Bot.* cockscomb. **3.** *Obs.* the cap, resembling a cock's comb formerly worn by professional fools. **4.** *Obs.* or *Humorous.* the head. [var. of *cock's comb*] **—cox·comb·i·cal** (kŏks kŏm′ə kəl, -kō′mə-). *adj.* **—Syn. 1.** fop, dude, exquisite, beau, popinjay, jackanapes.

cox·comb·ry (kŏks′kōm′rĭ), *n., pl.* **-ries. 1.** the manners or behavior of a coxcomb. **2.** a foppish trait.

cox·swain (kŏk′sən, -swān), *n.* **1.** the steersman of a boat. **2.** (on a ship) one who has charge of a boat and its crew. Also, **cockswain.** [f. *cock* ship's boat + swain servant]

coy (koi), *adj.* **1.** shy; modest (now usually of girls). **2.** affectedly shy or reserved. **3.** *Obs.* disdainful. **4.** *Obs.* quiet. **—*v.i.* 5.** *Archaic.* to act in a coy manner. **—*v.t.* 6.** *Obs.* to quiet; calm. **7.** *Obs.* to pat; caress. [ME, t. F: m. *coi,* earlier *quei,* g. L *quiētus* at rest] **—coy′ly,** *adv.* **—coy′-ness,** *n.* **—Syn. 1.** retiring, diffident, bashful, demure.

coy·o·te (kī ō′tĭ, kī′ōt), *n.* **1.** a wild animal of the wolf kind, *Canis latrans,* of western North America, noted for loud and prolonged howling at night; the prairie wolf. **2.** *Amer. Ind. Legend.* the culture hero and trickster of the American Indians of the West (sometimes human, sometimes animal). **3.** *U.S.* a contemptible person. [t. Mex. Sp., t. Nahuatl: m. *koyotl*]

Coyote. *Canis latrans* (3½ to 4 ft. long)

co·yo·til·lo (kō′yō tēl′yō, kĭ′ō-; *Sp.* kô′yô tē′yô), *n., pl.* **-los.** any plant of the rhamnaceous genus *Karwinskia,* native to Mexico and some parts of southern U.S. and bearing fruits reported to be injurious to man. [t. Mex. Sp. (dim.). See coyote]

coy·pu (koi′pōō), *n., pl.* **-pus,** (*esp. collectively*) **-pu.** a large South American aquatic rodent, *Myocastor* (or *Myopotamus*) *coypus,* yielding the fur nutria. [t. Amer. Sp.: m. *coipu,* t. Araucan: m. *koypu*]

Coypu. *Myocastor coypus* (Total length ab. 3 ft. tail 14 in.)

coz (kŭz), *n. Colloq.* cousin.

coze (kōz), *v.,* **cozed, cozing,** *n.* **—*v.i.* 1.** to converse in a friendly way; chat. **—*n.* 2.** a friendly talk; a chat. [t. F: m.s. *causer*]

coz·en (kŭz′ən), *v.t., v.i.* to cheat; deceive; beguile. [orig. obscure] **—coz′en·er,** *n.*

coz·en·age (kŭz′ən ĭj), *n.* **1.** the practice of cozening. **2.** the fact of being cozened. **3.** a fraud; a deception.

co·zy (kō′zĭ), *adj.,* **-zier, -ziest,** *n., pl.* **-zies. —*adj.* 1.** snug; comfortable. **—*n.* 2.** a padded covering for a teapot, etc., to retain the heat. Also, **cosy, co′zey, cosey.** [orig. Scot.; prob. t. Scand.; cf. Norw. *koselig*] **—co′zi·ly,** *adv.* **—co′zi·ness,** *n.*

cp., compare.
C.P., Common Prayer.

---

c.p., 1. candle power. 2. chemically pure.
C.P.A., 1. Certified Public Accountant. 2. Chartered Public Accountant. Also,
c.p.a.
Cpl, Corporal. Also, **cpl.**
c.p.o., chief petty officer.
Cr, *Chem.* chromium.
cr., 1. credit. 2. creditor.
crab[1] (krăb), *n., v.,* **crabbed, crabbing.** *—n.* 1. any of the stalk-eyed decapod crustaceans constituting the suborder **Brachyura** (**true crabs**), having a short, broad,

Crab, *Callinectes sapidus*
(3 in. long)

more or less flattened body, the abdomen or so-called tail being small and folded under the thorax. 2. any of various other crustaceans (as the **hermit crab**), or other animals (as the **horseshoe crab**), resembling the true crabs. 3. (*cap.*) the zodiacal constellation or sign Cancer. 4. an ill-tempered or grouchy person. 5. **catch a crab,** to make a faulty stroke in rowing, so that the oar strikes the water forcibly on the backstroke. 6. any of various mechanical contrivances for hoisting or pulling. 7. (*pl.*) a losing throw, as two aces, in the game of hazard. *—v.i.* 8. to catch crabs. [ME *crabbe*, OE *crabba*, c. G *krabbe*]
crab[2] (krăb), *n.* a crab apple (fruit or tree). [ME *crabbe*, ? var. of d. *scrab* crab apple. Cf. d. Sw. *skrabba*]
crab[3] (krăb), *v.,* **crabbed, crabbing.** *—v.i.* 1. (of hawks) to claw each other. 2. to find fault. *—v.t.* 3. to claw, as a hawk. 4. *Colloq.* to find fault with. 5. *Colloq.* to spoil. [cf. MD *krabben* scratch, quarrel; akin to CRAB[1]]
crab apple, 1. a small, sour wild apple. 2. any of various cultivated species and varieties of apple, small, sour, and astringent or slightly bitter, used for making jelly and preserves. 3. any tree bearing such fruit.
Crabb (krăb), *n.* George, 1778–1851, British author and philologist.
Crabbe (krăb), *n.* George, 1754–1832, British poet.
crab·bed (krăb′ĭd), *adj.* 1. perverse; contrary; grouchy; ill-natured; churlish; irritable. 2. perplexing; intricate: *a crabbed author, writings, etc.* 3. difficult to decipher, as handwriting. [ME; f. CRAB[1] + -ED[3]] **—crab′bed·ly,** *adv.* **—crab′bed·ness,** *n.*
crab·ber (krăb′ər), *n.* 1. one who catches crabs. 2. a boat used in catching crabs.
crab·by (krăb′ĭ), *adj.,* **-bier, -biest.** crabbed (def. 1).
crab grass, an annual grass, *Digitaria sanguinalis,* common in cultivated and waste grounds. It is a weedy pest in lawns.
crab·stick (krăb′stĭk′), *n.* 1. a stick, cane, or club made of wood, esp. of the crab tree. 2. an ill-tempered, crabbed person.
crab tree, a tree which bears crab apples.
crack (krăk), *v.i.* 1. to make a sudden, sharp sound in, or as in, breaking; snap, as a whip. 2. to break with a sudden, sharp sound. 3. to break without complete separation of parts; become fissured. 4. (of the voice) to break abruptly and discordantly, esp. into an upper register. 5. *Colloq.* to fail; give way. 6. *Now Chiefly Dial.* to brag; boast. 7. *Chiefly Scot.* to chat; gossip. 8. **crack down,** *U.S. Colloq.* to take severe measures, esp. in enforcing discipline. 9. **crack up, a.** to suffer a physical, mental, or moral breakdown. **b.** *Aeron.* to crash. *—v.t.* 10. *Colloq.* to cause to make a sudden, sharp sound; make a snapping sound with (a whip, etc.); strike with a sharp noise. 11. to break without complete separation of parts; break into fissures. 12. to break (a nut, etc.) with a sudden, sharp sound. 13. *Colloq.* to break into (a safe, vault, etc.). 14. to open and drink (a bottle of wine, etc.). 15. to damage (credit, etc.). 16. to make unsound mentally. 17. to make (the voice) harsh or unmanageable. 18. to break with grief; affect deeply. 19. to utter or tell, as a joke. 20. *Obs.* to boast. 21. to subject to the process of cracking in the distillation of petroleum, etc. 22. **crack up, a.** *Colloq.* to praise; extol. **b.** to crash: *to crack up a plane.* *—n.* 23. a sudden, sharp noise, as of something breaking. 24. the snap of a whip, etc. 25. *Colloq.* a shot, as with a rifle. 26. *Colloq.* a resounding blow. 27. a break without complete separation of parts; a fissure; a flaw. 28. an opening between floor boards or in the floor. 29. a slight opening, as one between door and doorpost. 30. a mental flaw. 31. a broken or changing tone of the voice. 32. *Colloq.* a try; an opportunity or chance. 33. *Slang.* a joke; gibe. 34. *Colloq.* one who or that which excels in some respect. 35. *Colloq.* a moment; instant: *he was on his feet again in a crack.* 36. *Slang.* a burglary. 37. *Slang.* a burglar. 38. *Scot.* conversation; chat. 39. *Now Chiefly Dial.* a boast; a lie. *—adj.* 40. *Colloq.* of superior excellence; first-rate. [unexplained var. of obs. *crake* creak, OE *cracian* resound. See CREAK, CROAK, all prob. imit. in orig.] **—Syn.** 23. snap, report. 27. crevice, cranny, chink, cleft, interstice.
crack·a·jack (krăk′ə jăk′), *n., adj.* crackerjack.
crack·brain (krăk′brān′), *n.* an insane person.
crack·brained (krăk′brānd′), *adj.* insane; crazy.
cracked (krăkt), *adj.* 1. broken. 2. broken without separation of parts; fissured. 3. damaged. 4. *Colloq.* mentally unsound. 5. broken in tone, as the voice.
crack·er (krăk′ər), *n.* 1. a thin, crisp biscuit. 2. a firecracker. 3. Also, **cracker bonbon,** a small paper roll containing an explosive, and usually a candy, etc.,

and which explodes when pulled sharply at both ends. 4. one of a class of poor whites in parts of the southeastern U.S. 5. *Obs. or Dial.* a boaster; a liar. 6. one who or that which cracks.
crack·er·jack (krăk′ər jăk′), *n. U.S. Slang.* 1. a person of marked ability; something exceptionally fine. *—adj.* 2. *Slang.* of marked ability; exceptionally fine. Also, **crackajack.**
crack·ing (krăk′ĭng), *n.* (in the distillation of petroleum or the like) the process of breaking down certain hydrocarbons into simpler ones of lower boiling points, by means of excess heat, distillation under pressure, etc., in order to give a greater yield of low-boiling products than could be obtained by simple distillation.
crack·le (krăk′əl), *v.,* **-led, -ling,** *n. —v.i.* 1. to make slight, sudden, sharp noises, rapidly repeated. *—v.t.* 2. to cause to crackle. 3. to break with a crackling noise. *—n.* 4. act of crackling. 5. a crackling noise. 6. a network of fine cracks, as in the glaze of some kinds of porcelain. 7. pottery ware with a network of fine cracks in the glaze. [freq. of CRACK]
crack·le·ware (krăk′əl wâr′), *n.* crackle (def. 7).
crack·ling (krăk′lĭng), *n.* 1. the making of slight cracking sounds rapidly repeated. 2. the crisp browned skin or rind of roast pork. 3. (*usually pl.*) *Dial.* the crisp residue left when fat, especially hogs' fat, is rendered.
crack·ly (krăk′lĭ), *adj.* apt to crackle.
crack·nel (krăk′nəl), *n.* 1. a hard, brittle cake or biscuit. 2. (*pl.*) small bits of fat pork fried crisp. [ME *crakenelle,* appar. t. F: m. *craquelin,* t. MD: m. *crakelinc*]
crack of doom, 1. the signal that announces the Day of Judgment. 2. the end of the world; doomsday.
crack·pot (krăk′pŏt′), *Slang. —n.* 1. an eccentric or insane person. *—adj.* 2. eccentric; insane.
cracks·man (krăks′mən), *n., pl.* **-men.** *Slang.* burglar.
crack-up (krăk′ŭp′), *n.* 1. a crash; collision. 2. *Colloq.* a breakdown in health. 3. collapse; defeat.
Cra·cow (krăk′ou, krä′kō; *Ger.* krä′kou), *n.* a city in S Poland, on the Vistula: the capital of Poland, 1320–1609. 435,000 (est. 1954). Polish, **Kraków.**
-cracy, a noun termination meaning "rule," "government," "governing body," as in *autocracy, bureaucracy.* [t. F: m. *-cratie,* ult. t. Gk.: m. *-kratía,* der. *krátos* rule, strength]
cra·dle (krā′dəl), *n., v.,* **-dled, -dling.** *—n.* 1. a little bed or cot for an infant, usually built on rockers. 2. the place where anything is nurtured during its early existence. 3. any of various contrivances similar to a child's cradle, as the framework on which a ship rests during construction or repair, or a frame or case for protecting a broken limb. 4. a flat, movable framework with swivel wheels, on which a mechanic can lie while working beneath an automobile. 5. *Agric.* a. a frame of wood with a row of long curved teeth projecting above and parallel to a scythe, for laying grain in bunches as it is cut. b. a scythe together with the cradle in which it is set. 6. a kind of box on rockers used by miners for washing auriferous gravel or sand to separate the gold. 7. a docklike structure in which a rigid or semirigid airship is built or supported during inflation. 8. an engraver's tool for laying mezzotint grounds. *—v.t.* 9. to place or rock in or as in a cradle. 10. to nurture during infancy. 11. to cut (grain) with a cradle. 12. to place in a ship's cradle. 13. to wash in a miner's cradle. 14. to receive or hold as a cradle. *—v.i.* 15. to lie in, or as in, a cradle. 16. to use in mowing. [ME *cradel,* OE *cradol.* Cf. G *kratte* basket] **—cra′dler,** *n.*
cra·dle·song (krā′dəl sông′, -sŏng′), *n.* a lullaby.
craft (krăft, kräft), *n.* 1. skill; ingenuity; dexterity. 2. skill or art applied to bad purposes; cunning; deceit; guile. 3. an art, trade, or occupation requiring special skill, esp. manual skill; a handicraft. 4. the members of a trade or profession collectively; a guild. 5. (*construed as pl.*) boats, ships, and vessels collectively. 6. a single vessel. 7. (*construed as pl.*) aircraft collectively. 8. a single aircraft. [ME; OE *cræft,* c. G *kraft*] **—Syn.** 2. craftiness, subtlety, artifice. See **cunning.**
crafts·man (krăfts′mən, kräfts′-), *n., pl.* **-men.** 1. one who practices a craft; an artisan. 2. an artist. [f. *crafts* (poss. of CRAFT) + MAN] **—crafts′man·ship′,** *n.* **—Syn.** 1. artificer, mechanic, handicraftsman.
craft union, a labor union composed only of people in the same craft.
craft·y (krăf′tĭ, kräf′-), *adj.,* **craftier, craftiest.** 1. skillful in underhand or evil schemes; cunning; deceitful; sly. 2. *Archaic.* skillful; ingenious; dexterous. **—craft′i·ly,** *adv.* **—craft′i·ness,** *n.* **—Syn.** 1. artful, wily, insidious, tricky, designing, scheming, plotting.
crag[1] (krăg), *n.* a steep, rugged rock; a rough, broken, projecting part of a rock. [ME, t. Celtic; cf. Welsh *craig* rock] **—crag′gy, crag·ged** (krăg′ĭd), *adj.* **—crag′gi·ness,** *n.*
crag[2] (krăg), *n. Scot. and N Eng.* the neck; the throat; the craw. [t. MFlem.: m. *krage*]
crags·man (krăgz′mən), *n., pl.* **-men.** one accustomed to or skilled in climbing crags.
Craig·a·von (krăg·ä′von, -ăv′ən), *n.* James Craig, 1st Viscount, 1871–1940, first prime minister of Northern Ireland, 1921–40.
Crai·gie (krā′gĭ), *n.* Sir William A., 1867–1957, British lexicographer.
Craik (krāk), *n.* Dinah Maria Mulock (mū′lŏk), 1826–87, British novelist.

ăct; āble, dâre, ärt; ĕbb, ēqual; ĭf, īce; hŏt, ōver, ôrder, oil, bŏŏk, ōōze, out; ŭp, ūse, ûrge; ə = a in alone; ch, chief; g, give; ng, ring; sh, shoe; th, thin; ŧ͟h, that; zh, vision. See the full key on inside cover.

Cra·io·va (krä yô′vä), *n.* a city in SW Rumania. 85,474 (1947).

crake (krāk), *n.* any of various European birds of the ra'l family, esp. short-billed, as the corn crake (*Crex crex*). [ME, t. Scand.; cf. Icel. *krāka* crow]

cram (krăm), *v.*, **crammed, cramming,** *n.* —*v.t.* 1. to fill (something) by force with more than it can conveniently hold. 2. to force or stuff (fol. by *into, down,* etc.). 3. to fill with or as with excess of food. 4. *Colloq.* to prepare (a person), as for an examination, by hastily storing his memory with facts. 5. *Colloq.* to get a knowledge of (a subject) by so preparing oneself. 6. *Slang.* to tell lies or exaggerated stories to. —*v.i.* 7. to eat greedily or to excess. 8. *Colloq.* to cram a person, as for an examination. —*n.* 9. *Colloq.* act or result of cramming. 10. a crammed state. 11. *Colloq.* a dense crowd. 12. *Colloq.* information acquired by cramming. [OE *crammian,* der. *crimman* insert] —**cram′mer,** *n.* —**Syn.** 2. stuff, crowd, pack, squeeze, compress, overcrowd.

Cram (krăm), *n.* **Ralph Adams,** 1863–1942, U.S. architect and writer.

cram·bo (krăm′bō), *n.* 1. a game in which one person or side must find a rhyme to a word or a line of verse given by another. 2. (in contemptuous use) rhyme.

cram·oi·sy (krăm′oi zĭ, -ə zĭ), *adj.* 1. *Archaic.* crimson. —*n.* 2. *Obs.* crimson cloth. Also, **cram′oi·sie.** [t. F: m. *cramoisi,* t. It.: m. *chermisi,* t. Ar.: m. *qirmizī* CRIMSON]

cramp¹ (krămp), *n.* 1. a sudden involuntary, persistent contraction of a muscle or a group of muscles, esp. of the extremities, sometimes associated with severe pain. 2. **writer's cramp,** a professional or occupational disease involving some muscles of the fingers and hands: 3. (*often pl.*) piercing pains in the abdomen. —*v.t.* 4. to affect with, or as with, a cramp. [ME *crampe,* t. MD]

cramp² (krămp), *n.* 1. a small metal bar with bent ends, for holding together timbers, masonry, etc. 2. a portable frame or tool with a movable part which can be screwed up to hold things together; clamp. 3. anything that confines or restrains. 4. a cramped state or part. —*v.t.* 5. to fasten or hold with a cramp. 6. to confine narrowly; restrict; restrain; hamper. 7. to steer; to turn the front wheel of a motor vehicle by means of the steering gear. 8. **cramp one's style,** to hinder from showing one's best abilities, etc. —*adj.* 9. hard to decipher or understand; difficult; knotty. 10. contracted; narrow. [t. MD: hook, clamp]

cramp·fish (krămp′fish′), *n., pl.* **-fishes,** (*esp. collectively*) **-fish.** an electric ray (fish).

cramp iron, a cramp, or piece of iron with bent ends, for holding together pieces of stone, etc.

cram·pon (krăm′pon), *n.* 1. a grappling iron, esp. one of a pair for raising heavy weights. 2. a spiked iron plate worn on the shoe to prevent slipping. Also, **crampoon** (krăm pōōn′). [t. F, der. *crampe* (t. Gmc. See CRAMP²)]

cran·ber·ry (krăn′ber′ĭ), *n., pl.* **-ries.** the red, acid fruit or berry of any plant of the ericaceous genus *Vaccinium,* as *V. oxycoccus* (**small cranberry or European cranberry**) or more commonly *V. macrocarpus* (**large cranberry or American cranberry**), used in making sauce, jelly, etc. 2. the plant itself. [t. LG: m. *kraanbere;* cf. G *kran(ich)beere* crane berry. See CRANE]

cranberry tree, a caprifoliaceous tree or shrub, *Viburnum Opulus,* bearing red berries and white cymose flowers, known in cultivated form as *snowball.* Also, **cranberry bush.**

crane (krān), *n., v.,* **craned, craning.** —*n.* 1. any of a group of large wading birds (family *Gruidae*) with very long legs, bill, and neck, and elevated hind toe. 2. (popularly) any of various similar birds of other families, as the great blue heron, *Ardea herodias.* 3. a device for moving heavy weights, having two motions, one a direct lift and the other a horizontal movement, and consisting in one of its simplest forms of an upright post turning on its vertical axis and bearing a projecting arm on which the hoisting tackle is fitted. 4. any of various similar devices, as a horizontally swinging arm by a fireplace, used for suspending pots, etc., over the fire. 5. (*pl.*) *Naut.* supports of iron or timber at a vessel's side for stowing boats or spars upon. —*v.t.* 6. to hoist, lower, or move by or as by a crane. 7. to stretch (the neck) as a crane does. —*v.i.* 8. to stretch out one's neck. 9. *Colloq.* to hesitate at danger, difficulty, etc. [ME; OE *cran,* c. G *kran*]

Crane (def. 1).
Grus americana
(Ab. 4½ ft. long)

Crane (krān), *n.* 1. **(Harold) Hart,** 1899–1932, U.S. writer. 2. **Ichabod** (ĭk′ə bŏd′), an awkward, superstitious schoolmaster in Irving's *Legend of Sleepy Hollow.* 3. **Stephen,** 1871–1900, U.S. novelist, poet, and short-story writer.

crane fly, any of the dipterous insects constituting the family *Tipulidae,* characterized by very long legs; the daddy-longlegs of Great Britain.

crane's-bill (krānz′bĭl′), *n.* any plant of the genus *Geranium* (see **geranium**) with long, slender, beaked fruit. Also, **cranes·bill′, crane·bill′.** [t. CRANE('s) + BILL²; 16th cent. trans. of D *kranebek* geranium]

cra·ni·al (krā′nĭ əl), *adj.* of or pertaining to the cranium or skull. —**cra′ni·al·ly,** *adv.*

cranial index, *Craniom.* the ratio of the greatest breadth of the skull to the greatest length from front to back, multiplied by 100.

cra·ni·ate (krā′nĭ ĭt, -āt′), *adj.* 1. having a cranium or skull. 2. belonging to the *Craniata,* a primary division of vertebrates, comprising those which possess a skull and brain, and including the mammals, birds, reptiles, amphibians, and fishes. —*n.* 3. a craniate animal.

cranio-, a combining form of **cranium.** Also, **crani-.**

cra·ni·ol·o·gy (krā′nĭ ŏl′ə jĭ), *n.* the science that deals with the size, shape, and other characteristics of skulls. —**cra·ni·o·log·i·cal** (krā′nĭ ə lŏj′ə kəl), *adj.* —**cra′ni·ol′o·gist,** *n.*

craniom., craniometry.

cra·ni·om·e·ter (krā′nĭ ŏm′ə tər), *n.* an instrument for measuring the external dimensions of skulls.

cra·ni·om·e·try (krā′nĭ ŏm′ə trĭ), *n.* the science of measuring skulls. —**cra·ni·o·met·ric** (krā′nĭ ə mĕt′rĭk), **cra′ni·o·met′ri·cal,** *adj.* —**cra′ni·o·met′rist,** *n.*

cra·ni·ot·o·my (krā′nĭ ŏt′ə mĭ), *n., pl.* **-mies.** *Surg.* the operation of opening the skull, usually for operations on the brain.

cra·ni·um (krā′nĭ əm), *n., pl.* **-niums, -nia** (-nĭ ə). 1. the skull of a vertebrate. 2. that part of the skull which encloses the brain. [t. ML, t. Gk.: m. *krānīon*]

crank¹ (krăngk), *n.* 1. a device for communicating motion, or for changing rotary motion into reciprocating motion, or vice versa, consisting in its simplest form of an arm projecting from, or secured at right angles at the end of, the axis or shaft which receives or imparts the motion. 2. *U.S. Colloq.* an ill-tempered, grouchy person. 3. *U.S. Colloq.* an eccentric or impracticable person. 4. an eccentric notion. 5. a turn of speech; a verbal conceit. 6. *Obs.* a bend. —*v.t.* 7. to bend into or make in the shape of a crank. 8. to furnish with a crank. 9. to cause (a shaft) to revolve by applying force to a crank; turn a crankshaft in (an automobile engine, etc.) to start the engine. —*v.i.* 10. to turn a crank, as in starting an automobile engine. 11. *Obs.* to twist, wind. —*adj.* 12. unstable; shaky; unsteady. 13. *Brit. Dial.* sickly. [ME *cranke,* OE *cranc,* in *crancstæf* weaving implement, crank]

Human cranium, (from above) F, P, O, frontal, parietal, and occipital bones; C, S, L, coronal, sagittal and lambdoidal sutures

crank² (krăngk), *adj.* liable to lurch or capsize, as a ship. [short for *crank-sided;* cf. D *krengd* careened]

crank³ (krăngk), *adj.* *Obs.* or *Dial.* lively; in high spirits; cheerful. [ME; orig. unknown]

crank·case (krăngk′kās′), *n.* (in an internal-combustion engine) the housing which encloses the crankshaft, connecting rods, and allied parts.

crank·le (krăng′kəl), *n., v.t., v.i.,* **-kled, -kling.** bend; turn. [freq. of CRANK¹, v.]

crank·ous (krăng′kəs), *adj.* *Scot.* irritated; cranky.

crank·pin (krăngk′pĭn′), *n.* *Mach.* a pin or cylinder at the outer end or part of a crank, as for holding a connecting rod.

crank·shaft (krăngk′shăft′, -shäft′), *n.* *Mach.* a shaft driving or driven by a crank.

crank·y¹ (krăng′kĭ), *adj.,* **crankier, crankiest.** 1. ill-tempered; cross. 2. eccentric; queer. 3. shaky; unsteady; out of order. 4. full of bends or windings; crooked. 5. *Brit. Dial.* sickly; infirm. —**crank′i·ly,** *adv.* —**crank′i·ness,** *n.* —**Syn.** 1. crotchety, cantankerous, perverse. —**Ant.** 1. good-natured.

crank·y² (krăng′kĭ), *adj.* liable to capsize.

Cran·mer (krăn′mər), *n.* **Thomas,** 1489–1556, first Protestant archbishop of Canterbury: a leader of the Protestant Reformation in England.

cran·nog (krăn′əg), *n.* an ancient Irish or Scottish lake dwelling, usually built on an artificial island. Also, **cran·noge** (krăn′əj). [t. Irish, der. *crann* tree, beam]

cran·ny (krăn′ĭ), *n., pl.* **-nies.** a small, narrow opening (in a wall, rock, etc.); a chink; crevice; fissure. [ME *crany,* f. F *cran* fissure (der. *crener* cut away, g. L *crēnāre*) + -y², dim. suffix] —**cran′nied,** *adj.*

cran·reuch (krăn′rəxh), *n.* *Scot.* hoarfrost.

Cran·ston (krăn′stən), *n.* a city in E Rhode Island, near Providence. 66,766 (1960).

crap (krăp), *n.* *U.S.* 1. (in craps) a losing throw, in which the total on the two dice is 2, 3, or 12. 2. craps.

crape (krāp), *n., v.t.,* **craped, craping.** crepe. (Anglicized sp. of CREPE]

crap·pie (krăp′ĭ), *n.* a small sunfish of the central U.S.: either the **black crappie,** *Pomoxis nigro-maculatus,* or the **white crappie,** *Pomoxis annularis.*

craps (krăps), *n.* *U.S.* a gambling game played with two dice, a modern and simplified form of hazard.

crap·shoot·er (krăp′shōō′tər), *n.* *U.S.* a person who plays the game of craps.

crap·u·lent (krăp′yōō lənt), *adj.* sick from gross excess in drinking or eating. [t. L: s. *crāpulentus* drunk] —**crap′u·lence,** *n.*

crap·u·lous (krăp′yōō ləs), *adj.* 1. given to or characterized by gross excess in drinking or eating. 2. suffering from or due to such excess. [t. LL: m.s. *crāpulōsus,* der. L *crāpula* intoxication] —**crap′u·lous·ness,** *n.*

crash¹ (krăsh), *v.t.* **1.** to break in pieces violently and noisily; shatter. **2.** to force or drive with violence and noise (fol. by *in*, *through*, *out*, etc.). **3.** *Colloq.* to come uninvited to (a party, etc.). **4.** *Colloq.* to enter without buying a ticket: *to crash the gate.* **5.** to cause (an aircraft) to make a landing in an abnormal manner, usually damaging or wrecking the apparatus. —*v.i.* **6.** to break or fall to pieces with noise. **7.** to make a loud, clattering noise, as of something dashed to pieces. **8.** to move or go with a crash; strike with a crash. **9.** *Aeron.* to land in an abnormal manner, usually damaging or wrecking the apparatus. —*n.* **10.** a breaking or falling to pieces with loud noise. **11.** the shock of collision and breaking. **12.** a sudden and violent falling to ruin. **13.** a sudden collapse of a financial enterprise or the like. **14.** a sudden loud noise, as of something dashed to pieces; the sound of thunder, loud music, etc. **15.** *Aeron.* act of crashing. —*adj.* **16.** *Colloq.* characterized by all-out, intensive effort, esp. to meet an emergency: *a crash program to produce vaccine.* [ME; b. CRAZE and MASH] —crash′er, *n.* —Syn. **1.** smash. **13.** failure, ruin.

crash² (krăsh), *n.* **1.** a fabric of plain weave, made of rough, irregular, or lumpy yarns. It may be used as linen or cotton toweling, rayon dress fabric, etc. **2.** *Bookbinding.* starched cotton fabric used to reinforce the spine of a bound book. [orig. unknown]

Crash·aw (krăsh′ô), *n.* **Richard**, 1613?–49, English religious poet.

crass (krăs), *adj.* **1.** gross; stupid: *crass ignorance.* **2.** thick; coarse. [t. L: s. *crassus* solid, thick, dense, fat] —crass′ly, *adv.* —crass′ness, *n.*

cras·si·tude (krăs′ə·tūd′, -tōōd′), *n.* **1.** gross ignorance or stupidity. **2.** thickness; grossness.

cras·su·la·ceous (krăs′yŏŏ·lā′shəs), *adj.* belonging to the *Crassulaceae* family of plants, mostly fleshy or succulent herbs, incl. houseleek, etc. [f. s. NL *Crassula* the typical genus, (der. L *crassus* thick) + -ACEOUS]

Cras·sus (krăs′əs), *n.* **Marcus Licinius** (mär′kəs lə·sĭn′ĭ·əs), c115–53 B.C., Roman general: member of the first triumvirate.

-crat, a noun termination meaning "ruler," "member of a ruling body," "advocate of a particular form of rule," as in *aristocrat*, *autocrat*, *democrat*, *plutocrat*. Cf. **-cracy**. [t. F: m. *-crate*, t. Gk.: m. *-kratēs* ruler]

cratch (krăch), *n. Archaic or Dial.* a crib to hold fodder; a manger. [ME *crecche*, t. OF: m. *cresche*, t. Gmc.]

crate (krāt), *n.*, *v.*, **crated**, **crating.** —*n.* **1.** a box or framework, usually made of wooden slats, for packing and transporting fruit, furniture, etc. **2.** a basket of wickerwork, for the transportation of crockery, etc. —*v.t.* **3.** to put in a crate. [t. L: m.s. *crātis* wickerwork]

cra·ter (krā′tər), *n.* **1.** the cup-shaped depression or cavity marking the orifice of a volcano. **2.** the hole or pit in the ground where a military mine or shell has exploded. **3.** a large vessel or bowl used by the ancient Greeks and Romans, orig. for mixing wine with water. **4.** (*cap.*) *Astron.* a small southern constellation. [t. L. Gk.: m. *krātēr*, orig., bowl for mixing wine and water]

Crater Lake, a lake in the crater of an extinct volcano in SW Oregon. 5–6 mi. across; 1996 ft. deep.

craunch (krônch, kränch), *v.t.*, *v.i.*, *n.* crunch. [var. of *scranch*, *cranch*. Cf. D *schranzen* break]

cra·vat (krə·văt′), *n.* **1.** *Orig. Brit. and still somewhat affected in U.S.* necktie. **2.** a scarf worn around the neck; neckcloth. [t. F: m. *cravate*; so called because adopted from the Croats (F *Cravates*)]

crave (krāv), *v.*, **craved**, **craving.** —*v.t.* **1.** to long for or desire eagerly. **2.** to need greatly; require. **3.** to ask earnestly for (something); beg for. **4.** to ask (a person) earnestly for something or to do something. —*v.i.* **5.** to beg or plead (fol. by *for*). **6.** to long (fol. by *for* or *after*). [ME *craven*, OE *crafian.* Cf. Icel. *krefja* demand] —crav′er, *n.* —crav′ing·ly, *adv.* —Syn. **1.** want, yearn for, hunger for. **4.** beg, beseech, entreat, implore.

cra·ven (krā′vən), *adj.* **1.** cowardly; pusillanimous; mean-spirited. **2.** *Obs.* defeated. —*n.* **3.** a coward. —*v.t.* **4.** to make cowardly. [ME *cravant*, f. OF: b. *crav(ante)* overthrown and (*recre*)*ant* RECREANT] —cra′ven·ly, *adv.* —cra′ven·ness, *n.* —Ant. **1.** brave.

Crav·en·ette (krăv′ə·nĕt′, krā′və-), *n. Trademark.* a finish for wool or cotton fabrics to render them waterrepellent. [der. *Craven*, proper name]

crav·ing (krā′vĭng), *n.* eager or urgent desire; longing; yearning. —Syn. See **desire.**

craw (krô), *n.* **1.** the crop of a bird or insect. **2.** the stomach of an animal. [ME *crawe*, c. D *kraag* neck]

craw·fish (krô′fĭsh′), *n.*, *pl.* **-fishes**, (*esp. collectively*) **-fish**, *v.* —*n.* **1.** any of numerous fresh-water decapod crustaceans of the suborder *Macrura*, closely related to the lobsters but smaller, as *Astacus fluviatilis*, of Europe, and various American species of the genus *Cambarus.* **2.** any of certain similar marine crustaceans. **3.** *U.S. Colloq.* one who backs out or retreats from a position or undertaking. —*v.i.* **4.** *U.S. Colloq.* to back out or retreat from a position or undertaking. Also, *esp. Brit.*, **crayfish** for 1, 2. [var. of CRAY-FISH]

Crawfish.
Cambarus diogenes
(3½ in. long)

Craw·ford (krô′fərd), *n.* **Francis Marion**, 1854–1909, U.S. novelist, long resident in Italy.

crawl¹ (krôl), *v.i.* **1.** to move slowly by dragging the body along the ground, as a worm. **2.** to progress slowly, laboriously, or timorously: *the work crawled.* **3.** to go stealthily or abjectly. **4.** to be, or feel as if, overrun with crawling things. —*n.* **5.** act of crawling; a slow, crawling motion. **6.** *Swimming.* a stroke in prone position characterized by alternate overarm movements and a continuous up and down kick. [ME, t. Scand.; cf. Dan. *kravle* creep] —crawl′er, *n.* —crawl′ing·ly, *adv.* —Syn. **1.** CRAWL, CREEP refer to methods of moving like reptiles or worms, or on all fours. They are frequently interchangeable, but CRAWL is used of a more prostrate movement than CREEP: *a dog afraid of punishment crawls toward his master.* CREEP expresses slow progress: *a baby creeps before walking.* —Ant. **1.** stride.

crawl² (krôl), *n.* an enclosure in shallow water on the seacoast, for confining fish, turtles, etc. [t. D.: m. *kraal*, t. Sp.: m. *corral* CORRAL]

crawl·y (krô′lĭ), *adj. Colloq.* creepy.

cray·fish (krā′fĭsh′), *n.*, *pl.* **-fishes**, (*esp. collectively*) **-fish.** *Chiefly Brit.* crawfish (defs. 1, 2). [ME *crevice*, t. OF, t. OHG: m. *krebiz* crab]

cray·on (krā′on, -ŏn), *n.*, *v.*, **-oned**, **-oning.** —*n.* **1.** a pointed stick or pencil of colored clay, chalk, etc., used for drawing. **2.** a drawing in crayons. —*v.t.* **3.** to draw with a crayon or crayons. **4.** to sketch out (a plan, etc.). [t. F, der. *craie*, g. L *crēta* chalk] —cray′on·ist, *n.*

craze (krāz), *v.*, **crazed**, **crazing**, *n.* —*v.t.* **1.** to impair in intellect; make insane. **2.** to make small cracks on the surface of (pottery, etc.); to crackle. **3.** *Archaic or Dial.* to weaken or impair (health, etc.). **4.** *Obs. or Dial.* to crack. **5.** *Obs.* to break; shatter. —*v.i.* **6.** to become insane. **7.** to become minutely cracked, as the glaze of pottery. **8.** *Obs.* to break. —*n.* **9.** a mania; a popular fashion, etc., usually short-lived; a rage. **10.** insanity; an insane condition. **11.** a minute crack in the glaze of pottery, etc. **12.** *Obs. or Dial.* a crack. [ME *crase(n)* break, t. Scand.; cf. Sw. *krasa*]

crazed (krāzd), *adj.* **1.** insane; demented. **2.** having small cracks in the glaze, as pottery.

cra·zy (krā′zĭ), *adj.*, **-zier**, **-ziest. 1.** demented; insane; mad. **2.** *Colloq.* too excited or enthusiastic. **3.** liable to break or fall to pieces. **4.** weak; infirm. —cra′zi·ly, *adv.* —cra′zi·ness, *n.* —Syn. **1.** crazed, deranged, lunatic. See **mad.** **3.** rickety, shaky, tottering.

crazy bone, *U.S.* funny bone.

crazy quilt, *U.S.* a patchwork quilt made of irregular patches combined with little or no regard to pattern.

cra·zy·weed (krā′zĭ·wēd′), *n.* locoweed.

creak (krēk), *v.i.* **1.** to make a sharp, harsh, grating, or squeaking sound. **2.** to move with creaking. —*v.t.* **3.** to cause to creak. —*n.* **4.** a creaking sound. [ME *creken.* Cf. OE *crǣcettan*, var. of *crǣcettan* CROAK]

creak·y (krē′kĭ), *adj.*, **creakier**, **creakiest.** creaking; apt to creak. —creak′i·ly, *adv.* —creak′i·ness, *n.*

cream (krēm), *n.* **1.** the fatty part of milk, which rises to the surface when the liquid is allowed to stand. **2.** something containing or resembling this substance, as a table delicacy, a cosmetic, etc. **3.** (*usually pl.*) a soft-centered confection of fondant or fudge coated with chocolate. **4.** a purée or soup containing cream sauce: *cream of tomato soup.* **5.** the best part of anything. **6.** yellowish white; light tint of yellow or buff. —*v.t.* **7.** to form cream. **8.** to froth; foam. —*v.i.* **9.** to work (butter and sugar, etc.) to a smooth, creamy mass. **10.** to prepare (chicken, oysters, vegetables, etc.) with cream, milk, or a cream sauce. **11.** to allow (milk) to form cream. **12.** to skim (milk). **13.** to separate as cream. **14.** to take the cream or best part of. **15.** to add cream to (tea, coffee, etc.). [ME *creme*, t. F, g. LL *chrisma* CHRISM]

cream cheese, a soft, white, smooth-textured, unripened cheese made of sweet milk and sometimes cream.

cream-col·ored (krēm′kŭl′ərd), *adj.* having a yellowish-white color. Also, *Brit.*, cream′-col′oured.

cream-cups (krēm′kŭps′), *n.*, *pl.* **-cups.** a papaveraceous plant, *Platystemon californicus*, of California, bearing small pale-yellow or cream-colored flowers.

cream·er (krē′mər), *n.* **1.** one who or that which creams. **2.** a small jug, pitcher, etc., for holding cream. **3.** a refrigerator in which milk is placed to facilitate the formation of cream. **4.** a vessel or apparatus for separating cream from milk.

cream·er·y (krē′mər·ĭ), *n.*, *pl.* **-eries. 1.** an establishment engaged in the production of butter and cheese. **2.** a place for the sale of milk and its products. **3.** a place where milk is set to form cream.

cream ice, *Brit.* ice cream.

cream of tartar, purified and crystallized potassium bitartrate, used as a baking powder ingredient, etc. See **tartar¹** (def. 3).

cream sauce, a sauce made of cream or milk, flour, butter, etc.

cream·y (krē′mĭ), *adj.*, **creamier**, **creamiest. 1.** containing cream. **2.** resembling cream, as in appearance or consistency; soft and smooth. **3.** cream-colored. —cream′i·ness, *n.*

crease¹ (krēs), *n.*, *v.*, **creased**, **creasing.** —*n.* **1.** a line or mark produced in anything by folding; a fold; a ridge; a furrow. **2.** *Cricket.* **a.** one of certain lines marked on the ground to define the positions of the bowler and the batsman. **b.** the space between such lines. —*v.t.* **3.** to make a crease or creases in or on; wrinkle. **4.** *U.S.* to wound or stun by a furrowing or superficial shot. —*v.i.* **5.** to become creased. [orig. unknown] —**creas'er,** *n.* —**creas'y,** *adj.*

crease² (krēs), *n.* creese.

crease-re·sist·ant (krēs'rĭ zĭs'tənt), *adj.* (of a fabric) able to resist normal wrinkling.

cre·ate (krē āt'), *v.,* **-ated, -ating,** *adj.* —*v.t.* **1.** to bring into being; cause to exist; produce. **2.** to evolve from one's own thought or imagination. **3.** to be the first to represent (a part or role). **4.** to make by investing with new character or functions; constitute; appoint: *to create a peer.* **5.** to be the cause or occasion of; give rise to. —*adj.* **6.** *Poetic.* created. [t. L: m.s. *creātus,* pp. of *creāre* bring into being] —**Syn. 1.** originate, invent.

cre·a·tine (krē'ə tēn', -tĭn), *n.* *Biochem.* an alkaloid or amino acid, $C_4H_9O_2N_3 + H_2O$, found in the muscles of vertebrates. Also, **cre·a·tin** (krē'ə tĭn). [f. m.s. Gk. *krěas* flesh + -INE²]

cre·a·tion (krē ā'shən), *n.* **1.** act of creating. **2.** fact of being created. **3. the Creation,** the original bringing into existence of the universe by the Deity. **4.** that which is created. **5.** the world; universe. **6.** creatures collectively. **7.** a product of inventive ingenuity; an original work, esp. of the imaginative faculty. —**cre·a'tion·al,** *adj.*

cre·a·tion·ism (krē ā'shə nĭz'əm), *n.* **1.** the doctrine that God immediately creates out of nothing a new human soul for each individual born. Cf. **traducianism. 2.** the doctrine that matter and all things were created, substantially as they now exist, by the fiat of an omnipotent Creator, and not gradually evolved or developed. —**cre·a'tion·ist,** *n.*

cre·a·tive (krē ā'tĭv), *adj.* **1.** having the quality or power of creating. **2.** originative; productive (fol. by *of*). —**cre·a'tive·ly,** *adv.* —**cre·a'tive·ness,** *n.*

cre·a·tor (krē ā'tər), *n.* **1.** one who or that which creates. **2. the Creator,** God. —**cre·a'tor·ship',** *n.*

crea·tur·al (krē'chər əl), *adj.* of, pertaining to, or of the nature of a creature or creatures.

crea·ture (krē'chər), *n.* **1.** anything created, animate or inanimate. **2.** an animate being. **3.** an animal, as distinct from man: applied in the U.S. esp. to cattle, horses, etc. **4.** a human being (often used in contempt, commiseration, or endearment). **5.** a person owing his rise and fortune to another, or subject to the will or influence of another. **6.** *Humorous.* intoxicating liquor; whiskey. [ME, t. OF, t. LL: m. *creātūra* a thing created]

creature comforts, things, esp. food, which minister to bodily comfort.

crea·ture·ly (krē'chər lĭ), *adj.* creatural.

crèche (krāsh; *Fr.* krĕsh), *n.* **1.** *Chiefly Brit.* a nursery where children are cared for while their mothers work. Cf. *U.S.* **day nursery. 2.** an asylum for foundlings. **3.** a tableau of Mary, Joseph, and others around the crib of Jesus in the stable at Bethlehem, often built for display at Christmas. [t. F, t. OHG: m. *kripja* crib]

Cré·cy (krĕs'ĭ; *Fr.* krĕ sē'), *n.* a village in N France: English victory over the French, 1346. Also, **Cressy.**

cre·dence (krē'dəns), *n.* **1.** belief: *to give credence to a statement.* **2.** something giving a claim to belief or confidence: *letter of credence.* **3.** Also, **credence table.** a small side table, shelf, or niche for holding articles used in the eucharist service. [ME, t. ML: m.s. *crēdentia* belief, credit, sideboard, der. L *crēdens,* ppr., believing]

cre·den·dum (krĭ dĕn'dəm), *n., pl.* **-da** (-də). that which is to be believed; an article of faith. [L, neut. of *crēdendus,* gerundive of *crēdere* believe]

cre·dent (krē'dənt), *adj.* **1.** believing. **2.** *Obs.* credible.

cre·den·tial (krĭ dĕn'shəl), *n.* **1.** that which gives a title to credit or confidence. **2.** (*usually pl.*) a letter or other testimonial attesting the bearer's right to confidence or authority. —*adj.* **3.** giving a title to belief or confidence. [f. s. ML *crēdentia* belief + -AL¹]

cre·den·za (krə dĕn'zə), *n.* a sideboard or buffet. [It., t. ML: m. *crēdentia.* See CREDENCE]

cred·i·ble (krĕd'ə bəl), *adj.* **1.** capable of being believed; believable. **2.** worthy of belief or confidence; trustworthy. [ME, t. L: m.s. *crēdibilis*] —**cred'i·bil'i·ty,** *and* **cred'i·ble·ness,** *n.* —**cred'i·bly,** *adv.*

cred·it (krĕd'ĭt), *n.* **1.** belief; trust. **2.** influence or authority resulting from the confidence of others or from one's reputation. **3.** trustworthiness; credibility. **4.** repute; reputation. **5.** favorable estimation. **6.** commendation or honor given for some action, quality, etc. **7.** a source of commendation or honor. **8.** the ascription or acknowledgment of something as due or properly attributable to a person, etc. **9.** *Educ.* a. official acceptance and recording of the work of a student in a particular course of study. **b.** a unit of a curriculum (short for **credit hour**): *he took the course for four credits.* **10.** time allowed for payment for goods, etc., obtained on trust. **11.** confidence in a purchaser's ability and intention to pay, displayed by entrusting him with goods, etc., without immediate payment. **12.** reputation of solvency and probity, entitling a person to be trusted in buying or borrowing. **13.** power to buy or borrow on trust. **14.** a sum of money due to a person; anything valuable standing on the credit side of an account. **15.** the balance in one's favor in an account. **16.** *Bookkeeping.* **a.** the acknowledgment or an entry of payment or value received, in an account. **b.** the side (right-

hand) of an account on which such entries are made (opposed to *debit*). **c.** an entry, or the total shown, on the credit side. **17.** any deposit or sum against which one may draw. —*v.t.* **18.** to believe; put confidence in; trust; have faith in. **19.** to reflect credit upon; do credit to; give reputation or honor to. **20.** to ascribe (something) to a person, etc.; make ascription of something to (a person, etc.; fol. by *with*). **21. a.** *Bookkeeping.* to enter upon the credit side of an account; give credit for or to. **b.** to give the benefit of such an entry to (a person, etc.) **22.** *Educ.* to award educational credits to: *credited with three hours in history.* [t. F, t. It.: m. *credito,* g. L *creditus,* pp., believed] —**Syn. 12.** CREDIT, REPUTE, REPUTATION, STANDING refer to one's status in the estimation of a community. CREDIT refers to business and financial status and the amount of money for which a man will be trusted: *his credit is excellent at all the stores.* REPUTE is particularly what is reported about someone, the favor in which he is held, etc.: *a man of fine repute among his acquaintances.* REPUTATION is the moral and other character commonly ascribed to someone: *of unblemished reputation.* STANDING is one's position in a community, or rank and condition in life: *a man of good standing and education.* —**Ant. 5.** disrepute.

cred·it·a·ble (krĕd'ĭt ə bəl), *adj.* bringing credit, honor, reputation, or esteem. —**cred'it·a·ble·ness,** *n.* —**cred'it·a·bly,** *adv.* —**Syn.** praiseworthy, meritorious, estimable, honorable, reputable, respectable.

credit memorandum, a record that the customer is entitled to an allowance or deduction. Also, **credit slip.**

cred·i·tor (krĕd'ĭ tər), *n.* **1.** one who gives credit in business transactions. **2.** one to whom money is due (opposed to *debtor*). **3.** *Bookkeeping.* credit (def. 16 b, c)

credit standing, reputation for meeting financial obligations.

credit union, a coöperative group making low interest rate loans to its members.

cre·do (krē'dō, krā'dō), *n., pl.* **-dos. 1.** the Apostles' or the Nicene Creed. **2.** a musical setting of the creed usually of the Nicene Creed. **3.** any creed or formula of belief. [t. L: I believe, the first word of the Apostles' and the Nicene Creeds in Latin]

cre·du·li·ty (krə dū'lə tĭ, -dōō'-), *n.* a disposition arising from weakness or ignorance, to believe too readily. [late ME *credulite,* t. L: m.s. *crēdulitas*]

cred·u·lous (krĕj'ə ləs), *adj.* **1.** ready or disposed to believe, esp. on weak or insufficient evidence. **2.** marked by or arising from credulity. [t. L: m. *crēdulus* apt to believe] —**cred'u·lous·ly,** *adv.* —**cred'u·lous·ness,** *n.* —**Syn. 1.** believing, trustful, unsuspecting, gullible.

Cree (krē), *n., pl.* **Cree, Crees. 1.** (*pl.*) an important North American Indian tribe belonging to the Algonquian linguistic stock, and located in Manitoba, Saskatchewan, etc. **2.** a member of this tribe. [short for F *Kristinaux,* m. *Kinistenoag,* given as one of their own names]

creed (krēd), *n.* **1.** an authoritative formulated statement of the chief articles of Christian belief, as the Apostles', the Nicene, or the Athanasian Creed. **2.** the Apostles' Creed. **3.** any formula of religious belief, as of a denomination. **4.** an accepted system of religious belief. **5.** any system of belief or of opinion. [ME *crede,* OE *crēda,* t. L: m. *crēdo* I believe. See CREDO] —**creed'al,** *adj.* —**creed'less,** *adj.*

creek (krēk, krĭk), *n.* **1.** *U.S., Canada, and Australia.* a small stream, as a branch of a river. **2.** *Chiefly Brit.* a narrow recess in the shore of the sea, a river, etc.; a small inlet or bay. **3.** *Obs.* a narrow or winding passage. [ME *creke,* appar. north. var. of *crike* (short vowel), t. Scand.; cf. Icel. *kriki* crack, nook]

Creek (krēk), *n.* **1.** (*pl.*) a powerful confederacy of Muskhogean Indians which in historic times occupied the greater part of Alabama and Georgia. **2.** an Indian of this confederacy. [so called because of numerous streams in Creek territory]

creel (krēl), *n.* **1.** a wickerwork basket, esp. one used by anglers for holding fish. **2.** a wickerwork trap to catch fish, lobsters, etc. **3.** a framework, esp. one for holding bobbins in a spinning machine. [ME *crele,* ? t. F: m. *creil,* ult. der. L *crātis* wickerwork. Cf. GRILLE]

creep (krēp), *v.,* **crept, creeping,** *n.* —*v.i.* **1.** to move with the body close to the ground, as a reptile or an insect, or a child on hands and knees. **2.** to move slowly, imperceptibly, or stealthily. **3.** to move or behave timidly or servilely. **4.** to slip or move along gradually, as a railroad track under traffic. **5.** to have a sensation as of something creeping over the skin. **6.** to grow along the ground, a wall, etc., as a plant, esp. a creeper (def. 3). —*v.t.* **7.** *Poetic.* to creep along or over. —*n.* **8.** act of creeping. **9.** (*usually pl.*) a sensation as of something creeping over the skin. [ME *crepen,* OE *crēopan* c. D. *kruipen*] —**Syn. 1.** See **crawl.**

creep·er (krē'pər), *n.* **1.** one who or that which creeps. **2.** (*pl.*) a loose garment, usually with attached pants, worn by infants. **3.** *Bot.* a plant which grows upon or just beneath the surface of the ground, or upon any other surface, sending out rootlets from the stem, as ivy and couch grass (often used in England where Americans say *vine*). **4.** any of various birds that creep or climb about on trees, esp. the several species of the family *Certhiidae* of Europe and North America, as the **tree creeper,** *Certhia familiaris.* **5.** one of a breed of domestic fowls with short legs. **6.** a grappling device for dragging a river, etc. **7.** a spiked piece of iron worn on the heel of the shoe to prevent slipping on ice, etc.

creep·ie (krē′pĭ′, krĭ′p′ĭ), n. Brit. Dial. a low stool.

creep·y (krē′pĭ′), adj., **creepier**, **creepiest**. **1.** that creeps, as an insect. **2.** having or causing a creeping sensation of the skin, as from horror: a creepy silence. —**creep′i·ness**, n.

creese (krēs), n. a short sword or heavy dagger with a wavy blade, used by the Malays. Also, **crease**, **kris**. [t. Malay: m. kris]

creesh (krēsh), n., v.t. Scot. grease. [t. OF: m. cresse, craisse, g. L crassa, fem. of crassus thick, fat]

Cre·feld (krā′fĕld; Ger. -fĕlt), n. Krefeld.

cre·mate (krē′māt), v.t., **-mated**, **-mating**. **1.** to reduce (a corpse) to ashes. **2.** to consume by fire; burn. [t. L: m. s. cremātus, pp., consumed by fire] —**cre·ma′tion**, n.

cre·ma·tion·ist (krĭ·mā′shən·ĭst), n. one who advocates cremation instead of burial of the dead.

cre·ma·tor (krē′mā′tər), n. **1.** one who cremates. **2.** a furnace for cremating dead bodies. **3.** an incinerator for garbage, etc.

cre·ma·to·ri·um (krē′mə·tōr′ĭ·əm, krĕm′ə-), n. Chiefly Brit. a crematory.

cre·ma·to·ry (krē′mə·tōr′ĭ, krĕm′-), adj., n., pl. **-ries**. —adj. **1.** of or pertaining to cremation. —n. **2.** a furnace or an establishment for cremating.

crème (krĕm), n. French. **1.** cream. **2.** one of various liqueurs. [F. See CREAM]

crème de ca·ca·o (krĕm′ də kȧ·kä′ō′), French. a liqueur flavored with cacao and vanilla beans.

crème de la crème (krĕm′ də lȧ krĕm′), French. cream of the cream; the very best; the flower.

crème de menthe (krĕm də mänt′), French. liqueur flavored with mint.

Cre·mo·na (krĭ′mō′nə; It. krĕ·mō′nä), n. **1.** a city in N Italy, on the Po river. 69,000 (est. 1954). **2.** one of a class of violins of superior quality made there during the 16th, 17th, and 18th centuries.

cre·nate (krē′nāt), adj. having the margin notched or scalloped so as to form rounded teeth, as a leaf. Also, **cre′nat·ed**. [t. NL: m.s. crēnātus, der. crēna notch] —**cre′nate·ly**, adv.

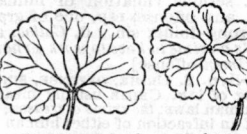

Crenate and doubly crenate leaves

cre·na·tion (krĭ′nā′shən), n. **1.** a rounded projection or tooth, as on the margin of a leaf. **2.** crenate state.

cre·na·ture (krē′nə·chər, krē′nə-), n. **1.** a rounded tooth, as of a crenate leaf. **2.** a notch between teeth.

cren·el (krĕn′əl), n., v., **-eled**, **-eling** or (esp. Brit.) **-elled**, **-elling**. —n. **1.** one of the open spaces between the merlons of a battlement. **2.** a crenature. —v.t. **3.** to crenelate. Also, **crenelle**. [late ME, t. MF, dim. of cren notch. See CRENULATE]

cren·el·ate (krĕn′ə·lāt′), v.t., **-ated**, **-ating**. **1.** to furnish with crenels or battlements. **2.** Archit. to form with square indentations, as a molding. Also, esp. Brit., **cren′el·late′**. [f. s. F creneler (der. crenel, dim. of cren notch) + -ATE¹] —**cren′el·at·ed**, adj.

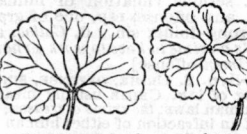

cren·el·a·tion (krĕn′ə·lā′shən), n. **1.** act of crenelating. **2.** state of being crenelated. **3.** a battlement. **3. a** notch; indentation. Also, esp. Brit., **cren′el·la′tion**.

cre·nelle (krĭ′nĕl′), n., v.t., **-nelled**, **-nelling**. crenel.

Crenelated molding

cren·u·late (krĕn′yə·lāt′, -lĭt), adj. having the edge cut into very small scallops, as some leaves. Also, **cren′u·lat′ed**. [t. NL: m.s. crēnulātus, der. crēnula, dim. of crena notch, t. OIt., g. L (unrecorded)]

cren·u·la·tion (krĕn′yə·lā′shən), n. **1.** a minute crenation. **2.** crenulate state.

cre·o·dont (krē′ə·dŏnt′), n. any of the Creodonta, a group of primitive carnivorous mammals, characterized by small brains. Certain creodonts are regarded as the ancestors of the modern carnivores. [t. NL: s. Creodonta (pl.), f. Gk.: m. kréas flesh + m.s. odoús tooth]

Cre·ole (krē′ōl), n. **1.** (in the West Indies and Spanish America) one born in the region but of European, usually Spanish, ancestry. **2.** (in Louisiana and elsewhere) a person born in the region but of French ancestry. **3.** a person born in a place but of foreign ancestry, as distinguished from the aborigines and half-breeds. **4.** the French language of Louisiana, especially that spoken by white persons in New Orleans. **5.** (l.c.) a person of mixed Creole and Negro ancestry speaking a form of French or Spanish. **6.** (l.c.) a native-born Negro, as distinguished from a Negro brought from Africa. —adj. **7.** of, pertaining to, or characteristic of a Creole or the Creoles. **8.** (l.c.) of, belonging to, or characteristic of the creoles: a creole dialect, creole French. **9.** bred or growing in a country, but of foreign origin, as an animal or plant. **10.** Cookery. denoting a sauce or dish made with stewed tomatoes, peppers, onions, etc. [t. F, f. Sp.: m. criollo native to the locality, t. Pg.: m. crioulo, der. criar bring up, g. L creāre create]

cre·o·lized (krē′ə·līzd′), adj. (of a language) having become a jargon and then passed into use as a native language, as the English used by many Negroes of Dutch Guiana.

Cre·on (krē′ŏn), n. Gk. Legend. king of Thebes, after the fall of Oedipus. See **Antigone**.

cre·o·sol (krē′ə·sōl′, -sŏl′), n. Chem. a colorless oily liquid, $C_8H_{10}O_2$, with an agreeable odor and burning taste, resembling carbolic acid: obtained from wood tar and guaiacum resin. [f. CREOS(OTE) + -OL²]

cre·o·sote (krē′ə·sōt′), n., v., **-soted**, **-soting**. —n. **1.** an oily liquid with a burning taste and a penetrating odor, obtained by the distillation of wood tar, and used as a preservative and antiseptic. **2.** coal-tar creosote. —v.t. **3.** to treat with creosote. [f. creo- (comb. form repr. Gk. kréas flesh) + m. Gk. sōtér savior] —**cre·o·sot·ic** (krē′ə·sŏt′ĭk), adj.

creosote bush, a zygophyllaceous evergreen shrub, Covillea tridentata (or Larrea mexicana), of northern Mexico and adjacent regions, bearing resinous foliage with a strong odor of creosote.

crepe (krāp), n., v., **creped**, **creping**. —n. **1.** a thin, light fabric of silk, cotton, or other fiber, with a finely crinkled or ridged surface. **2.** Also, **crepe paper**. thin paper wrinkled to resemble crepe. **3.** a black (or white) silk fabric, used for mourning veils, trimmings, etc. **4.** a band or piece of this material, as for a token of mourning. —v.t. **5.** to cover, clothe, or drape with crepe. Also, **crêpe**, **crape**. [t. F, g. L crispus curled]

crepe de Chine (krāp′ də shēn′), a light, soft, thin silk or rayon fabric with minute irregularities of surface. [t. F: china crape]

crêpe su·zette (krāp′ sōō·zĕt′), a thin dessert pancake usually rolled with hot orange or tangerine sauce, often flavored with curaçao or other liqueurs.

crep·i·tant (krĕp′ə·tənt), adj. crackling.

crep·i·tate (krĕp′ə·tāt′), v.i., **-tated**, **-tating**. to make a crackling sound; crackle; rattle. [t. L: m. s. crepitātus, pp.] —**crep′i·ta′tion**, n.

crept (krĕpt), v. pt. and pp. of **creep**.

cre·pus·cu·lar (krĭ′pŭs′kyə·lər), adj. **1.** of, pertaining to, or resembling twilight; dim; indistinct. **2.** Zool. appearing or flying in the twilight.

cre·pus·cule (krĭ′pŭs′kūl), n. twilight; dusk. [t. F, t. L: m. crepusculum]

cres., Music. crescendo (def. 3). Also, **cresc.**

cres·cat sci·en·ti·a vi·ta ex·co·la·tur (krĕs′kăt sĭ·ĕn′shĭ′ə vī′tə ĕks·kō′lā·tər), Latin. where knowledge increases life is ennobled.

cre·scen·do (krə·shĕn′dō, -sĕn′dō; It. krĕ·shĕn′dō), n., pl. **-dos** (-dōz), **-di** (-dē), adj., adv. —n. **1.** a gradual increase in force or loudness. **2.** Music. a crescendo passage. —adj., adv. **3.** gradually increasing in force or loudness. [It., ppr. of crescere increase, g. L crescere] —Ant. **2.** diminuendo.

cres·cent (krĕs′ənt), n. **1.** the convexo-concave figure of the moon in its first quarter, or the similar figure of the moon in its last quarter, resembling a bow terminating in points. See diag. under **moon**. **2.** a representation of this. **3.** the emblem of the Turkish Empire. **4.** the Turkish or Mohammedan power. **5.** any crescent-shaped object. **6.** a musical percussion instrument of Turkish origin used in military bands, consisting of a crescent-shaped metal plate hung with a set of little bells. **7.** Chiefly Brit. a curved street. —adj. **8.** shaped like the moon in its first quarter. **9.** increasing; growing. [t. L: s. crescens, ppr., increasing; r. ME cressant, t. OF: m. creissant (later croissant), ppr.]

cre·scit e·un·do (krĕs′ĭt ē·ŭn′dō), Latin. it grows as it goes (motto of New Mexico). Lucretius, De Rerum Natura VI, 341.

cres·cive (krĕs′ĭv), adj. increasing; growing.

cre·sol (krē′sōl, -sŏl), n. Chem. any one of three isomeric methyl phenols, $CH_3C_6H_4OH$, occurring in coal tar and wood tar. [var. of CREOSOL]

cress (krĕs), n. **1.** any of various plants of the mustard family with pungent-tasting leaves, often used for salad and as a garnish, esp. the water cress. **2.** any of various similar plants. [ME and OE cresse, c. G kresse]

cres·set (krĕs′ĭt), n. a metal cup often mounted on a pole or suspended from above, containing oil, pitch, etc., which is burned for light or as a beacon. [ME, t. OF]

Cres·si·da (krĕs′ə·də), n. a new character developed, in medieval redactions of the Troy story, out of Chryseis and Briseis and made the lover of the Trojan Troilus, who is deserted by her for the Greek Diomedes.

Cres·sy (krĕs′ĭ), n. Crécy.

cress·y (krĕs′ĭ), adj. abounding in cresses.

crest (krĕst), n. **1.** a tuft or other natural growth of the top of an animal's head, as the comb of a cock. **2.** anything resembling or suggesting such a tuft. **3.** the ridge of the neck of a horse, dog, etc. **4.** the mane growing from this ridge. **5.** a plume or other ornament on the top of a helmet. **6.** a helmet. **7.** the apex of a helmet. **8.** Her. a figure borne above the escutcheon in a coat of arms, and also used separately as a distinguishing device. **9.** the head or top of anything. **10.** the highest part of a hill or mountain range. **11.** a ridge or ridgelike formation. **12.** the foamy top of a wave.

Cresset

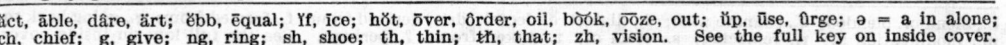

ăct, āble, dâre, ärt; ĕbb, ēqual; Ĭf, īce; hŏt, ōver, ôrder, oil, bŏŏk, ōōze, out; ŭp, ūse, ûrge; ə = a in alone; ch, chief; g, give; ng, ring; sh, shoe; th, thin; ŧħ, that; zh, vision. See the full key on inside cover.

13. the highest or best of the kind. **14.** pride; high spirit; courage; daring. **15.** *Archit.* a cresting. —*v.t.* **16.** to furnish with a crest. **17.** to serve as a crest for; crown or top. **18.** to reach the crest or summit of (a hill, etc.). —*v.i.* **19.** to form or rise into a crest, as a wave. [ME *creste*, t. OF, g. L *crista* tuft] —**crest′ed,** *adj.* —**crest′less,** *adj.*

crested auklet, a small diving bird, *Aethia cristatella,* found in various parts of the north Pacific Ocean.

crested flycatcher, a North American flycatcher, *Myiarchus crinitus,* famous for its use of castoff snakeskin as nest material.

crest·fall·en (krĕst′fô′lən), *adj.* **1.** dejected; dispirited; depressed. **2.** with drooping crest. —**crest′-fall·en·ly,** *adv.* —**crest′fall·en·ness,** *n.*

crest·ing (krĕs′tĭng), *n. Archit.* the ornamental part which surmounts a roof ridge, wall, etc.

cre·ta·ceous (krĭ tā′shəs), *adj.* **1.** of the nature of, resembling, or containing chalk. **2.** *(cap.) Stratig.* pertaining to a geological period or a system of rocks succeeding the Jurassic and preceding the Tertiary. —*n.* **3.** *(cap.) Stratig.* the period or system comprising the youngest or uppermost part of the Mesozoic. [t. L: m. *crētāceus* chalklike]

Cre·tan (krē′tən), *adj.* **1.** of or pertaining to the island of Crete or its inhabitants. —*n.* **2.** a native or inhabitant of Crete, esp. one of the indigenous Grecians.

Crete (krēt), *n.* a Greek island in the Mediterranean, SE of Greece. 462,124 pop. (1951); 3235 sq. mi. *Cap.:* Canea. Also, **Candia.**

cre·tin (krē′tĭn), *n.* a person afflicted with cretinism. [t. F, m. d. F. *crestin,* g. L *Christiānus* Christian] —**cre′tin·ous,** *adj.*

cre·tin·ism (krē′tə nĭz′əm), *n. Pathol.* a chronic disease, due to absence or deficiency of the normal thyroid secretion, characterized by physical deformity (often with goiter), dwarfism, and idiocy.

cre·tonne (krĭ tŏn′, krē′tŏn), *n.* a heavy cotton material in printed designs, used esp. for drapery and slip covers. [t. F, der. *Creton,* village in Normandy]

Cre·u·sa (krē ōō′sə), *n. Gk. Legend.* **1.** the bride of Jason, slain by the magic of the jealous Medea. **2.** a daughter of Priam and the wife of Aeneas, lost in the flight from Troy.

Creu·sot (krœ zō′), *n.* Le (lə). See Le Creusot.

cre·vasse (krə văs′), *n., v.,* **-vassed, -vassing.** —*n.* **1.** a fissure or deep cleft in the ice of a glacier. **2.** *U.S.a* breach in an embankment or levee. —*v.t.* **3.** to fissure with crevasses. [t. F. See CREVICE]

Crève·coeur (krĕv kœr′), *n.* **Michel Guillaume Jean de** (mē shĕl′ gē yŏm′ zhän də), *(J. Hector St. John Crèvecoeur)* 1735–1813, French writer and agriculturist who became an American citizen.

crev·ice (krĕv′ĭs), *n.* a crack forming an opening; a cleft; a rift; a fissure. [ME *crevace,* t. OF, der. *crever* burst, g. L *crepāre* crack] —**crev′iced,** *adj.*

crew[1] (krōō), *n.* **1.** a group of persons engaged upon a particular work: *a train crew.* **2.** *Naut.* **a.** the company of men who man a ship or boat. **b.** the common sailors of a ship's company. **c.** a particular gang of a ship's company. **3.** any force or band of armed men. **4.** (often in derogatory use) a company; crowd. [late ME *crue,* t. NF: m. *creue* increase, ult. der. L *crescere* grow]

crew[2] (krōō), *v.* pt. of **crow**[2].

crew cut, a very closely cropped haircut.

crew·el (krōō′əl), *n.* a kind of worsted yarn used for embroidery, etc. —**crew′el·work,** *n.*

crib (krĭb), *n., v.,* **cribbed, cribbing.** —*n.* **1.** a child's bed with enclosed sides. **2.** a stall or pen for cattle. **3.** a rack or manger for fodder, as in a stable or house for cattle. **4.** a small house. **5.** a small room. **6.** any confined space. **7.** *Thieves′ Slang.* a house, shop, etc. **8.** a wicker basket. **9.** any of various frameworks, as of logs or timbers, used in construction work. **10.** the wooden lining on the inside of a shaft. **11.** a bin for storing grain, salt, etc. **12.** *Colloq.* a petty theft, plagiarism, etc. **13.** *Brit. Colloq.* a translation or other illicit aid used by students. Cf. *U.S.* **pony** (def. 3). **14.** *Cribbage.* a set of cards made up by equal contributions from each player's hand, and belonging to the dealer. —*v.t.* **15.** to confine in, or as in, a crib. **16.** to provide with a crib or cribs. **17.** to line with timber or planking. **18.** *Colloq.* to pilfer or steal, as a passage from an author. —*v.i.* **19.** *Colloq.* to use a crib. **20.** to crib-bite. [ME *cribbe,* OE *crib(b),* c. G *krippe*]

crib·bage (krĭb′ĭj), *n.* a game at cards, basically for two, but also played by three, or four players, a characteristic feature of which is the crib. [f. CRIB + -AGE]

crib·ber (krĭb′ər), *n.* **1.** one who cribs. **2.** a horse that practices cribbing.

crib·bing (krĭb′ĭng), *n.* **1.** Also, **crib-biting.** wind sucking by horses, an injurious habit in which the animal bites his manger and in the process swallows air. **2.** *Mining.* **a.** timber lining, closely spaced, as in a shaft or raise. **b.** pieces of timber for lining a shaft, raise, etc.

crib-bite (krĭb′bīt′), *v.i.,* **-bit, -bitten** or **-bit, -biting.** to practice cribbing, as a horse. —**crib′-bit′er,** *n.*

crib·ri·form (krĭb′rə fôrm′), *adj.* sievelike. Also, **crib·rous** (krĭb′rəs). [f. s. L *crībrum* sieve + -(I)FORM]

crib·work (krĭb′wûrk′), *n.* structural work consisting of layers of logs or beams one above another, with the logs of each layer at right angles to those below.

Crich·ton (krī′tən), *n.* **James,** *("the Admirable Crichton")* 1560?–82, young Scottish scholar, poet, and adventurer who spoke many languages.

crick[1] (krĭk), *n.* **1.** a sharp, painful spasm of the muscles, as of the neck or back, making it difficult to move the part. —*v.t.* **2.** to give a crick or wrench to (the neck, etc.). [orig. uncert.]

crick[2] (krĭk), *n. U.S. Dial.* creek (def. 1).

crick·et[1] (krĭk′ĭt), *n.* any of the orthopterous insects comprising the family *Gryllidae,* characterized by their long antennae, ability to leap, and the ability of the males to produce shrill sounds by friction of their leathery fore wings. [ME *criket,* t. OF: m. *criquet;* ult. imit.]

House cricket, *Gryllus domesticus*

crick·et[2] (krĭk′ĭt), *n.* **1.** an open-air game played with ball, bats, and wickets, by two sides of eleven players each. **2.** *Colloq.* fair play. —*v.i.* **3.** to play cricket. [cf. OF *criquet* stick] —**crick′et·er,** *n.*

crick·et[3] (krĭk′ĭt), *n.* small, low stool. [orig. obscure]

cri·coid (krī′koid), *Anat.* —*adj.* **1.** having the shape of a seal ring: applied to a cartilage at the lower part of the larynx. —*n.* **2.** the cricoid cartilage. [t. Gk.: m.s. *krikoeidēs* ring-shaped]

cri·er (krī′ər), *n.* **1.** one who cries. **2.** a court or town official who makes public announcements. **3.** a hawker.

Crile (krīl), *n.* **George Washington,** 1864–1943, U.S. surgeon.

crim., criminal.

crime (krīm), *n.* **1.** an act committed or an omission of duty, injurious to the public welfare, for which punishment is prescribed by law, imposed in a judicial proceeding usually brought in the name of the state. **2.** serious violation of human law: *steeped in crime.* **3.** any offense, esp. one of grave character, **4.** serious wrong-doing; sin. **5.** *Colloq.* a foolish or senseless act: *it's a crime to have to work so hard.* [ME, t. OF, t. L: m. s. *crīmen* offense]

—**Syn. 2.** CRIME, OFFENSE, SIN agree in meaning a breaking of law. CRIME usually means any serious violation of human laws: *the crime of treason, of robbery.* OFFENSE is used of an infraction of either human or divine law, and does not necessarily mean a serious one: *an offense leading to a jail sentence, an offense against morals.* SIN means a serious breaking of moral or divine law: *the sin of hating one's neighbor.*

Cri·me·a (krī mē′ə, krī′-), *n.* **1.** a large peninsula in the SW Soviet Union, separating the Black Sea from the Sea of Azov. **2.** an autonomous republic of the Soviet Union coextensive with this peninsula. 1,126,824 pop. (1939); ab. 10,000 sq. mi. *Cap.:* Simferopol. Official name, **Crimean Autonomous Soviet Socialist Republic.** —**Cri·me′an,** *adj.*

Crime and Punishment, a novel (1866) by Feodor Dostoevski.

Crimean War, a war between Great Britain, France, Turkey, and Sardinia on one side, and Russia on the other, fought chiefly in the Crimea, 1853–56.

crim·i·nal (krĭm′ə nəl), *adj.* **1.** of or pertaining to crime or its punishment: *criminal law.* **2.** of the nature of or involving crime. **3.** guilty of crime. —*n.* **4.** a person guilty or convicted of a crime. [t. L: s. *crīminālis*] —**crim′i·nal·ly,** *adv.* —**Syn. 2.** felonious, unlawful, illegal, nefarious, flagitious, iniquitous, wicked, sinful, wrong. **4.** convict, malefactor, evildoer, transgressor, culprit. —**Ant. 2.** lawful. **3.** innocent.

criminal conversation, *Law.* adultery; illicit intercourse with a married woman, or, more recently, with a married man.

crim·i·nal·i·ty (krĭm′ə năl′ə tĭ), *n., pl.* **-ties. 1.** quality of being criminal. **2.** a criminal act or practice.

crim·i·nate (krĭm′ə nāt′), *v.t.,* **-nated, -nating. 1.** to charge with a crime. **2.** to incriminate. **3.** to censure (an act, etc.) as criminal; condemn. [t. L: m.s. *crīminātus,* pp., accused] —**crim′i·na′tion,** *n.*

crim·i·na·tive (krĭm′ə nā′tĭv), *adj.* tending to or involving crimination; accusatory. Also, **crim·i·na·to·ry** (krĭm′ə nə tôr′ĭ).

crim·i·nol·o·gy (krĭm′ə nŏl′ə jĭ), *n.* the science dealing with the causes and treatment of crimes and criminals. [f. s. L *crīmen* crime + -(o)LOGY] —**crim′i·no·log·i·cal** (krĭm′ə nə lŏj′ə kəl), *adj.* —**crim′i·nol′o·gist,** *n.*

crim·mer (krĭm′ər), *n.* krimmer.

crimp[1] (krĭmp), *v.t.* **1.** to press into small regular folds; make wavy. **2.** to bend (leather) into shape. **3.** *Cookery.* to gash (the flesh of a live fish or of one just killed) with a knife to make it more crisp when cooked. —*n.* **4.** act of crimping. **5.** crimped condition or form. **6.** *(usually pl.)* something crimped, as a lock of hair. **7.** the waviness of wool fibers as naturally grown on sheep. **8.** a crease formed in sheet metal or plate metal to make the material less flexible, or for fastening purposes. **9.** put a crimp in, *Colloq.* to hinder. [ME *crympe(n),* OE

gecrympan curl (der. *crump* crooked), c. LG *krümpen*, Dan. *krympe* shrink.] —**crimp'er,** *n.*

crimp² (krĭmp), *n.* 1. an agent who procures seamen, soldiers, etc., by inducing, swindling, or coercing them. —*v.t.* 2. to procure (seamen, soldiers, etc.) by such means. [special use of CRIMP¹]

crim·ple (krĭm'pəl), *v.i.*, *v.t.*, **-pled, -pling.** to wrinkle, crinkle, or curl. [freq. of CRIMP¹]

crimp·y (krĭm'pĭ), *adj.*, **crimpier, crimpiest.** of a crimped form or appearance.

crim·son (krĭm'zən), *adj.* 1. deep purplish-red. 2. sanguinary. —*n.* 3. a crimson color, pigment, or dye. —*v.t.* 4. to make crimson. [ME *cremesin*, t. early It.: m. *cremesino*, der. *chermisĭ*, or t. Sp.: m. *cremesin*, der. *carmesĭ*; both t. Ar.: m. *qirmizĭ*]

cringe (krĭnj), *v.*, **cringed, cringing,** *n.* —*v.i.* 1. to shrink, bend, or crouch, esp. from fear or servility; cower. 2. to fawn. —*n.* 3. servile or fawning obeisance. [ME *crengen*, der. OE *cringan* yield, fall (in battle). See CRINKLE, CRANK] —**cring'er,** *n.* —**cring'ing·ly,** *adj.*

crin·gle (krĭng'gəl), *n.* *Naut.* a ring or eye of rope or the like, esp. on the edge of a sail. It is usually made up around a metal thimble or grommet. [t. LG: m. *kringel*, dim. of *kring* circle, ring]

cri·nite¹ (krī'nīt), *adj.* 1. hairy. 2. *Bot., Entomol.* having long hairs, or tufts of long, weak hairs. [t. L: m. s. *crīnītus*, pp., provided with hair]

cri·nite² (krī'nīt, krĭn'īt), *n.* a fossil crinoid. [f. m. s. Gk. *krínon* lily + -ITE¹]

crin·kle (krĭng'kəl), *v.*, **-kled, -kling,** *n.* —*v.t.*, *v.i.* 1. to wind or turn in and out. 2. to wrinkle; crimple; ripple. 3. to make slight, sharp sounds; rustle. —*n.* 4. a turn or twist; a wrinkle; a ripple. 5. a crinkling sound. [ME; freq. of OE *crincan* bend, yield. See CRINGE, CRANK] —**crin'kly,** *adj.*

crin·kle·root (krĭng'kəl rōōt', -rŏŏt'), *n.* any of several species of the North American cruciferous perennials (genus *Dentaria*), esp. *Dentaria diphylla.*

crin·kum-cran·kum (krĭng'kəm krăng'kəm), *n.* *Colloq.* something full of twists and turns.

cri·noid (krī'noid, krĭn'oid), *adj.* 1. lilylike. —*n.* 2. one of the *Crinoidea.* [t. Gk.: m. s. *krinoeidḗs* lilylike]

Cri·noi·de·a (krĭ noi'dḯ ə, krī-), *n. pl. Zool.* a class of echinoderms with radiating arms usually borne mouthside up on an attached stalk, including the sea lilies, feather stars, and numerous fossil forms.

Unstalked crinoid, feather star, *Antedon rosacea*

crin·o·line (krĭn'ə lĭn, -lēn'), *n.* 1. a petticoat of haircloth or other stiff material, formerly worn by women under a full dress skirt. 2. a hoop skirt. 3. stiff coarse cotton material for interlining. [t. F, t. It.: m. *crinolino*, f. *crino* hair + *lino* thread]

cri·num (krī'nəm), *n.* any plant of the tropical and subtropical amaryllidaceous genus *Crinum*, comprising tall bulbous plants, usually with umbels of large, showy flowers. [NL, t. Gk.: m. s. *krínon* lily]

cri·o·sphinx (krī'ə sfĭngks'), *n.* a sphinx with the head of a ram. [f. m. Gk. *kriós* ram + *sphinx* sphinx]

crip·ple (krĭp'əl), *n., v.*, **-pled, -pling.** —*n.* 1. one who is partially or wholly deprived of the use of one or more of his limbs; a lame person. 2. *U.S. Dial.* a dense thicket in swampy or low land. —*v.t.* 3. to make a cripple of; lame. 4. to disable; impair. [ME *cripel*, OE *crypel*; akin to CREEP] —**crip'pler,** *n.*

—Syn. 3, 4. CRIPPLE, DISABLE mean to injure permanently or temporarily, to a degree which interferes with normal activities. To CRIPPLE is to injure in such a way as to deprive of the use of a member, particularly a leg or arm: *a broken arm cripples but does not disable a judge.* DISABLE, a more general word, implies such illness, injury, or impairment as makes a person incapable of engaging in his normal activities: *disabled by an attack of malaria, by a wound.*

Cripple Creek, a city in central Colorado, in the heart of one of the world's richest gold-producing areas: gold rush, 1891. 853 (1950); 9600 ft. high.

Cripps (krĭps), *n.* **Sir Stafford,** 1889–1952, British statesman and socialist leader.

cri·sis (krī'sĭs), *n., pl.* **-ses** (-sēz). 1. a decisive or vitally important stage in the course of anything; a turning point; a critical time or occasion: *a political crisis, a business crisis.* 2. the point in a play or story at which hostile elements are most tensely opposed to each other. 3. *Pathol.* **a.** the point in the course of a disease at which a decisive change occurs, leading either to recovery or to death. **b.** the change itself. [t. L, t. Gk.: m. *krísis* decision] —Syn. 1. climax, juncture, exigency, strait, pinch. See **emergency.**

crisp (krĭsp), *adj.* 1. hard but easily breakable; brittle: *crisp toast.* 2. firm and fresh: *crisp leaf of lettuce.* 3. brisk; sharp; decided: *crisp manner, reply, etc.* 4. lively; pithy; sparkling: *crisp repartee.* 5. bracing; invigorating: *crisp air.* 6. crinkled, wrinkled, or rippled, as skin or water. 7. in small, stiff or firm curls; curly. —*v.t., v.i.* 8. to make or become crisp. 9. to curl. —*n.* 10. *Brit.* a potato chip. [ME and OE, t. L: s. *crispus* curled] —**crisp'ly,** *adv.* —**crisp'ness,** *n.*

cris·pate (krĭs'pāt), *adj.* crisped or curled. Also, **cris'pat·ed.** [t. L: m. s. *crispātus*, pp., curled]

cris·pa·tion (krĭs pā'shən), *n.* 1. act of crisping or curling. 2. state of being crisped. 3. a slight contraction or undulation.

crisp·er (krĭs'pər), *n.* one who or that which crisps, corrugates, or curls.

Cris·pi (krēs'pē), *n.* **Francesco** (frän chĕ'skō), 1819–1901, prime minister of Italy, 1887–91, and 1893–96.

Cris·pin (krĭs'pĭn), *n.* 1. **Saint,** fl. 3rd century A.D., patron saint of shoemakers. 2. a shoemaker.

crisp·y (krĭs'pĭ), *adj.* **crispier, crispiest.** 1. brittle; crisp. 2. curly or wavy. 3. brisk.

cris·sal (krĭs'əl), *adj.* of or pertaining to the crissum.

criss·cross (krĭs'krôs', -krŏs'), *adj.* 1. in crossing lines; crossed; crossing; marked by crossings. —*n.* 2. a crisscross mark, pattern, etc. 3. tick-tack-toe. —*adv.* 4. in a crisscross manner; crosswise. —*v.t., v.i.* 5. to mark with or form crossing lines. [var. of CHRISTCROSS]

criss-cross-row (krĭs'krôs' rō', -krŏs'-), *n.* *Archaic or Dial.* christcross-row.

cris·sum (krĭs'əm), *n., pl.* **crissa** (krĭs'ə). *Ornith.* 1. the region surrounding the cloacal opening beneath the tail of a bird. 2. the feathers of this region collectively. [NL, der. L *crissāre* move the haunches]

cris·tate (krĭs'tāt), *adj.* 1. having a crest; crested. 2. forming a crest. Also, **cris'tat·ed.** [t. L: m. s. *cristātus*, der. *crista* CREST]

Cris·to·bal (krĭs tō'bəl; Sp. krēs tō'bäl), *n.* a seaport in the Canal Zone at the Atlantic end of the Panama Canal, adjacent to Colón. 417 (1950).

cri·te·ri·on (krī tĭr'ĭ ən), *n., pl.* **-teria** (-tĭr'ĭ ə), **-terions.** a standard of judgment or criticism; an established rule or principle for testing anything. [t. Gk.: m. *kritḗrion* test, standard] —Syn. See **standard.**

crit·ic (krĭt'ĭk), *n.* 1. a person skilled in judging the qualities or merits of some class of things, esp. of literary or artistic work. 2. one who judges captiously or with severity; one who censures or finds fault. 3. *Obs.* a critique. [t. L: s. *criticus*, t. Gk.: m. *kritikós* skilled in judging, decisive, critical (as n., a critic)] —Syn. 1. reviewer, censor, judge, connoisseur. 2. censurer, carper.

crit·i·cal (krĭt'ə kəl), *adj.* 1. inclined to find fault or to judge with severity. 2. occupied with or skilled in criticism. 3. involving skillful judgment as to truth, merit, etc.; judicial: *a critical analysis.* 4. of or pertaining to critics or criticism: *critical essays.* 5. pertaining to, or of the nature of, a crisis; of decisive importance with respect to the outcome; crucial: *the critical moment.* 6. involving suspense, risk, peril, etc.; dangerous: *a critical shortage.* 7. *Physics.* denoting a constant value, as of temperature, frequency, etc., at which one or more related properties of a substance undergo an abrupt change: *critical pressure.* 8. *Math.* indicating a point at which some transition or change takes place. —**crit'i·cal·ly,** *adv.* —**crit'i·cal·ness,** *n.* —Syn. 1. captious, censorious, carping, faultfinding, caviling. 3. discriminating, fastidious, nice, exact. 5. decisive, climacteric. 6. hazardous, precarious.

critical angle, 1. *Optics.* the limiting angle of incidence for total reflection. 2. *Aeron.* the angle of attack at which there is a sudden change in the airflow around an airfoil with subsequent decrease in lift and increase in drag.

critical constants, *Physics.* the critical temperature, pressure, density, and volume of a substance.

critical mass, *Physics.* the mass of nuclear fuel necessary for a chain reaction to take place.

critical pressure, *Physics.* the vapor tension of a liquid at the critical temperature.

critical temperature, *Physics.* the temperature above which a gas cannot be liquefied by pressure alone.

crit·i·cas·ter (krĭt'ĭk ăs'tər), *n.* an inferior or incompetent critic. [f. CRITIC + -ASTER¹]

crit·i·cism (krĭt'ə sĭz'əm), *n.* 1. act or art of criticizing, esp. of criticizing literary or artistic work. 2. act of passing judgment as to the merits of anything. 3. act of passing severe judgment; censure; faultfinding. 4. a critical comment, article, or essay; a critique. 5. investigation of the text, origin, etc., of literary, esp. Biblical, documents: *textual criticism.* —Syn. 3. stricture, animadversion, reflection. 4. See **review.**

crit·i·cize (krĭt'ə sīz'), *v.*, **-cized, -cizing.** —*v.i.* 1. to make judgments as to merits and faults. 2. to find fault. —*v.t.* 3. to judge or discuss the merits and faults of. 4. to find fault with. Also, *Brit.,* **crit'i·cise'.** —**crit'i·ciz'a·ble,** *adj.* —**crit'i·ciz'er,** *n.*

cri·tique (krĭ tēk'), *n.* 1. an article or essay criticizing a literary or other work; a review. 2. art or practice of criticism. [t. F, t. Gk.: m. *kritikḗ* the critical art, prop. fem. of *kritikós*]

crit·ter (krĭt'ər), *n.* *Dial.* creature.

croak (krōk), *v.i.* 1. to utter a low, hoarse, dismal cry, as a frog or a raven. 2. to speak with a low, hollow voice. 3. to talk despondingly; forebode evil; grumble. 4. *Slang.* to die. —*v.i.* 5. to utter or announce by croaking. 6. *Slang.* to kill. —*n.* 7. act or sound of croaking. [late ME; back formation from OE *crācettan.* Cf. CREAK]

croak·er (krō'kər), *n.* 1. one who or that which croaks. 2. any of various sciaenoid fishes that make a croaking noise, esp. *Micropogon undulatus*, a food fish common on the Atlantic coast of the southern U.S.

croak·y (krō'kĭ), *adj.* making a croaking sound.

Cro·at (krō′ăt), n. 1. a native or inhabitant of Croatia; a Croatian. 2. Croatian (def. 3).

Cro·a·tia (krō ā′shə, -shī′ə), n. a constituent republic of Yugoslavia, in the NW part: a medieval kingdom; now corresponding to the former Austrian crown land of **Croatia** and **Slavonia.** 4,043,000 pop. (est. 1956); 21,835 sq. mi. Cap.: Zagreb.

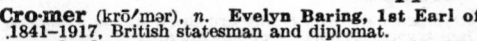

Cro·a·tian (krō ā′shan, -shī′ən), adj. 1. of or pertaining to Croatia, the Croats, or their language. —n. 2. a Croat. 3. Serbo-Croatian.

Cro·ce (krō′chě), n. **Benedetto** (bě′ně dět′tō), 1866–1952, Italian statesman, philosopher, and historian.

cro·ce·in (krō′sĭ′ĭn), n. any of several acid azo dyes producing orange or scarlet colors. [f. s. L croceus saffron-colored + -IN²]

cro·chet (krō shā′), n., v., -cheted (-shād′), -cheting (-shā′ĭng). —n. 1. a kind of needlework done with a needle having at one end a small hook for drawing the thread or yarn into intertwined loops. 2. the work or fabric so made. —v.t., v.i. 3. to form by crochet. [t. F: hooked implement, dim. of OF croche hook]

cro·cid·o·lite (krō sĭd′ə līt′), n. a mineral of the amphibole group, essentially a sodium iron silicate, occurring in fibers of a delicate blue color, and appearing in altered form as the (golden-brown) tiger's-eye. [f. crocido- (comb. form repr. Gk. krokís nap, wool) + -LITE]

crock¹ (krŏk), n. 1. an earthen pot, jar, or other vessel. 2. a vessel of metal. [ME crokke, OE croc(c), crocca pot. Cf. Icel. krukka jug]

crock² (krŏk), n. 1. an old ewe. 2. an old worn-out horse. 3. Brit. Slang. or Colloq. a worn-out superannuated person. —v.i. 4. Brit. Slang. to get injured (often fol. by up). [akin to CRACK, v.]

crock³ (krŏk), n. 1. soot; smut. 2. soil or marking from imperfectly dyed cloth. —v.t. 3. to soil with crock. —v.i. 4. to give off crock. [orig. uncert.]

crock·er·y (krŏk′ər′ĭ), n. crocks or earthen vessels collectively; earthenware.

crock·et (krŏk′ĭt), n. Archit. a medieval ornament in the form of leafage curled out over a knot or knob placed on the angles of the inclined sides of pinnacles, under cornices, etc. [ME croket, t. AF. See CROCHET]

Crock·ett (krŏk′ĭt), n. David, 1786–1836, U.S. frontiersman and political figure, killed in the Texan defense of the Alamo.

crock·ing (krŏk′ĭng), n. Textiles. the surface dye which rubs off.

croc·o·dile (krŏk′ə dīl′), n. 1. any of the large, thick-skinned reptiles, lizardlike in form, which constitute the genus Crocodylus (order Crocodilia), inhabiting the waters of tropical Africa, Asia, Australia, and America, esp. C. niloticus of the Nile. 2. any animal of the order Crocodilia, including the alligators of America and the gavial of India. 3. one who makes a hypocritical show of sorrow. 4. Brit. Colloq. a file of persons, usually school girls, out for a walk. [L: m. s. crocodilus, t. Gk.: m. krokódeilos lizard; r. ME cocodrille, t. OF]

Crocodile. Crocodylus niloticus (16 ft long)

crocodile bird, an African plover, Pluvianus aegyptius, which often sits upon basking crocodiles and feeds on their insect parasites.

Crocodile River, Limpopo.

crocodile tears, 1. false or insincere tears, as the tears fabled to be shed by crocodiles over those they devour. 2. hypocritical show of sorrow.

croc·o·dil·i·an (krŏk′ə dĭl′ĭ′ən), n. 1. any of the Crocodilia, an order of reptiles including the crocodiles, alligators, etc. —adj. 2. of or pertaining to the crocodile. 3. pertaining to the crocodilians. 4. hypocritical.

cro·co·ite (krō′kōĭt′), n. a mineral, lead chromate, PbCrO₄. [f. m. Gk. krokó(eis) saffron-colored + -ITE¹]

cro·cus (krō′kəs), n., pl. crocuses. 1. any of the small bulbous plants constituting the iridaceous genus Crocus, much cultivated for their showy, solitary flowers. 2. the flower or bulb of the crocus. 3. a deep yellow; orangish yellow; saffron. 4. a polishing powder consisting of iron oxide. [t. L, t. Gk.: m. krókos saffron]

Croe·sus (krē′səs), n. 1. died 546 B.C., king of Lydia, 560–546 B.C., noted for his great wealth. 2. a very rich man.

croft (krôft, krŏft), n. 1. Brit. or Scot. a small piece of enclosed ground for tillage, pasture, etc. 2. a very small agricultural holding, as one worked by a Scottish crofter. [ME and OE. Cf. MD kroft field on high land]

croft·er (krôf′tər, krŏf′-), n. one who rents and tills a croft, as in parts of Scotland or northern England.

croix de guerre (krwä də gěr′), a French military award for heroism in battle.

Cro-Mag·non (krō măg′nŏn; Fr. krō má nyôN′), adj. Anthropol. belonging to a prehistoric race of Europe, believed to be of the same species as modern man. Remains found in the cave of Cro-Magnon in Dordogne, France, were characterized by a very long head, low face and orbits, and tall stature.

Cro·mer (krō′mər), n. **Evelyn Baring, 1st Earl of,** 1841–1917, British statesman and diplomat.

crom·lech (krŏm′lěk), n. Archaeol. 1. a circle of upright stones or monoliths. 2. a dolmen. [t. Welsh, f. crom bent, bowed + llech flat stone]

Cromp·ton (krŏmp′tən), n. **Samuel,** 1753–1827, British inventor of the spinning mule.

Crom·well (krŏm′wəl, -wěl, krŭm′-), n. 1. **Oliver,** 1599–1658, British general, Puritan statesman, and Lord Protector of the Commonwealth, 1653–58. 2. his son, **Richard,** 1626–1712, British soldier, politician, Lord Protector of the Commonwealth, 1658–59. 3. **Thomas,** (Earl of Essex) 1485?–1540, British statesman.

crone (krōn), n. an old woman. [t. MD: m. croonje, t. north. F: m. carogne carcass]

Cron·jé (krôn′yā), n. **Piet Arnoldus** (pēt är nōl′dōōs), 1835?–1911, Boer general.

Cro·nus (krō′nəs), n. Gk. Myth. a Titan, son of Uranus and Gaea, who dethroned his father, and was dethroned by his own son Zeus. Saturn is his Roman counterpart. Also, **Cro·nos** (krō′nŏs), **Kronos.**

cro·ny (krō′nĭ), n., pl. -nies. an intimate friend or companion; a chum.

crook (krŏŏk), n. 1. a bent or curved implement, piece, appendage, etc.; a hook; the hooked part of anything. 2. an instrument or implement having a bent or curved part, as a shepherd's staff hooked at one end or as the crosier of a bishop or abbot. 3. Scot. a pothook. 4. act of crooking or bending. 5. any bend, turn, or curve. 6. Colloq. a dishonest person, esp. a sharper, swindler, or thief. 7. a device on some musical wind instruments for changing the pitch, consisting of a piece of tubing inserted into the main tube. —v.t. 8. to bend; curve; make a crook in. —v.i. 9. to bend; curve. [ME crok(e), t. Scand.; cf. Icel. krókr]

crook·back (krŏŏk′băk′), n. a humpback. —**crook-backed′,** adj.

crook·ed (krŏŏk′ĭd), adj. 1. bent; not straight; curved. 2. deformed. 3. not straightforward or honest. [OE gecrōcod] —**crook′ed·ly,** adv. —**crook′ed·ness,** n. —**Syn.** 1. winding, devious, sinuous, flexuous, tortuous, spiral, twisted, askew, awry. 2. misshapen. 3. dishonest, unscrupulous, knavish, tricky, fraudulent. —**Ant.** 1. straight. 3. honorable.

Crookes (krŏŏks), n. **Sir William,** 1832–1919, British chemist and physicist: discovered the element thallium and cathode rays.

Crookes space, Physics. the dark space in a vacuum tube between the cathode and the negative glow, occurring when pressure is very low. [named after Sir William CROOKES]

Crookes tube, a form of vacuum tube.

crook·neck (krŏŏk′něk′), n. U.S. a variety of squash with a long, recurved neck.

croon (krŏŏn), v.i. 1. to sing softly, esp. with exaggerated feeling. 2. to utter a low murmuring sound. 3. Scot. and N Eng. to bellow; roar. —v.t. 4. to sing softly, esp. with exaggerated feeling. —n. 5. act or sound of crooning. [late ME, t. MD: m. kronen murmur] —**croon′er,** n.

crop (krŏp), n., v., cropped, cropping. —n. 1. the cultivated produce of the ground, as grain or fruit, while growing or when gathered. 2. the yield of such produce for a particular season. 3. the yield of some other product in a season: the ice crop. 4. a supply produced. 5. the stock or handle of a whip. 6. a short riding whip with a loop instead of a lash. 7. an entire tanned hide of an animal. 8. act of cropping. 9. a mark produced by clipping the ears, as of an animal. 10. a style of wearing the hair cut short. 11. a head of hair so cut. 12. an outcrop of a vein or seam. 13. a special pouchlike enlargement of the gullet of many birds, in which food is held, and may undergo partial preparation for digestion. 14. a digestive organ in other animals; the craw. —v.t. 15. to cut off or remove the head or top of (a plant, etc.). 16. to cut off the ends or a part of. 17. to cut short. 18. to clip the ears, hair, etc., of. 19. to cause to bear a crop or crops. —v.i. 20. to bear or yield a crop or crops. 21. Mining. to come to the surface of the ground, as a vein of ore (usually fol. by up or out). 22. to appear unintentionally or unexpectedly (fol. by up or out): a new problem cropped up. [ME and OE, c. G kropf; orig. meaning protuberance. See CROUP²]

—**Syn.** 1. CROP, HARVEST, PRODUCE, YIELD refer to the return in food for men and animals obtained from land at the end of a season of growth. CROP, the term common in agricultural and commercial use, denotes the amount produced at one cutting or for one particular season: the wheat crop, potato crop. HARVEST denotes either the time of reaping and gathering, or the gathering, or that which is gathered: the season of harvest; to work in a harvest; a ripe harvest. PRODUCE esp. denotes household vegetables: produce from the fields and gardens was taken to market. YIELD emphasizes what is given by the land in return for expenditure of time and labor: there was a heavy yield of grain this year.

crop-eared (krŏp′ĭrd′), adj. 1. having the ears cropped. 2. having the hair cropped short, so that the ears are conspicuous.

crop·per (krŏp′ər), n. 1. one who or that which crops. 2. one who raises a crop. 3. one who cultivates land for its owner in return for part of the crop. 4. Colloq. a heavy fall, esp. from a horse: to come a cropper. 5. a failure; collapse. 6. a plant which furnishes a crop. 7. a cloth-shearing machine.

cro·quet (krō kā′; *Brit.* krō′kā, -kĭ), *n.*, *v.*, **-queted** (-kād′; *Brit.* -kād, -kĭd), **-queting** (-kā′ĭng; *Brit.* -kā-ĭng, -kĭ ĭng). **—n. 1.** an outdoor game played by knocking wooden balls through a series of iron arches by means of mallets. **2.** (in this game) act of driving away an opponent's ball by striking one's own when the two are in contact. **—v.t. 3.** to drive away (a ball) by a croquet. [t. d. F: hockey stick]

cro·quette (krō kĕt′), *n.* a small mass of minced meat or fish, or of rice, potato, or other material, often coated with beaten egg and bread crumbs, and fried in deep fat. [t. F, der. *croquer* crunch]

crore (krōr), *n. India.* ten millions; one hundred lacs: *a crore of rupees.* [t. Hind.: m. *k(a)rōr*, g. Prakrit *krodi*]

cro·sier (krō′zhər), *n.* **1.** the pastoral staff of a bishop or an abbot, hooked at one end like a shepherd's crook. See illus. under **cope. 2.** *Bot.* the circinate young frond of a fern. Also, **crozier.** [short for *crosier-staff* staff carried by the *crosier* crossbearer (t. F: m. *crosier* = ML *crociārius* crookbearer)]

cross (krôs, krŏs), *n.* **1.** a structure consisting essentially of an upright and a transverse piece, upon which persons were formerly put to death. **2. the Cross,** the cross upon which Jesus died. **3.** a figure of the cross as a Christian emblem, badge, etc. **4.** the cross as the symbol of Christianity. **5.** a small cross with a human figure attached to it, as a representation of Jesus crucified; a crucifix. **6.** the sign of the cross made with the right hand as an act of devotion. **7.** a structure or monument in the form of a cross, set up for prayer, as a memorial, etc. **8.** any of various conventional representations or modifications of the Christian emblem as used symbolically or for ornament, as in heraldry, art, etc.: *a Latin, Greek, St. George's, or Maltese cross.* **9.** the crucifixion of Jesus as the culmination of His redemptive mission. **10.** any suffering borne for Jesus' sake. **11.** the teaching of redemption gained by Jesus' death. **12.** Christian religion, or those who accept it; Christianity; Christendom. **13.** any object, figure, or mark resembling a cross, as two intersecting lines. **14.** such a mark made instead of a signature by a person unable to write. **15.** a fourway joint or connection used in pipe fitting, the connections being at right angles. **16.** a crossing. **17.** a place of crossing. **18.** an opposing; thwarting. **19.** any misfortune; trouble. **20.** a crossing of animals or plants; a mixing of breeds. **21.** an animal, plant, breed, etc. produced by crossing; a crossbreed. **22.** something intermediate in character between two things. **23.** *Slang.* a contest the result of which is dishonestly arranged beforehand. **24. the Southern Cross,** Crux, a constellation. **—v.t. 25.** to make the sign of the cross upon or over, as in devotion. **26.** to mark with a cross. **27.** to cancel by marking with a cross or with a line or lines. **28.** to place in the form of a cross or crosswise. **29.** to put or draw (a line, etc.) across. **30.** to set (a yard, etc.) in position across a mast. **31.** to lie or pass across; intersect. **32.** to move, pass, or extend from one side to the other side of (a street, river, etc.). **33.** to transport across something. **34.** to meet and pass. **35.** *Archaic.* to encounter. **36.** to oppose; thwart. **37.** *Biol.* to cause (members of different genera, species, breeds, varieties, or the like) to produce offspring; cross-fertilize. **—v.i. 38.** to lie or be athwart; intersect. **39.** to move, pass, extend from one side or place to another. **40.** to meet and pass. **41.** to interbreed. **—adj. 42.** lying or passing crosswise or across each other; athwart; transverse; *cross beams, streets, etc.* **43.** involving interchange; reciprocal. **44.** contrary; opposite. **45.** adverse; unfavorable. **46.** ill-humored; snappish: *a cross word.* **47.** crossbred; hybrid. **48.** *Slang.* dishonest. [ME and OE *cros*, t. OIrish, t. L: m. *crux* (Icel. *kross*, also, t. OIrish or ? t. OE)] **—cross′ly,** *adv.* **—cross′ness,** *n.*

—Syn. 36. baffle, frustrate, foil, contradict. **46.** petulant, fractious, irascible, waspish, crabbed, churlish, sulky, cantankerous. CROSS, ILL-NATURED, PEEVISH, SULLEN refer to being in a bad mood or ill temper. CROSS means temporarily in an irritable or fretful state, and sometimes somewhat angry: *a cross reply, cross and tired.* ILL-NATURED implies a more permanent condition, without definite cause, and means unpleasant, unkind, inclined to snarl or be spiteful: *an ill-natured dog, ill-natured spite.* PEEVISH means complaining and snappish: *a peevish and whining child.* SULLEN suggests a kind of glowering silent gloominess and means refusing to speak because of bad humor, anger, or a sense of injury or resentment: *sullen and vindictive.* **—Ant. 36.** aid. **46.** good-natured.

Cross (krôs, krŏs), *n.* **Wilbur Lucius,** 1862–1948, U.S. educator: governor of Connecticut, 1931–39.

cross-, a first element of compounds, modifying the second part, meaning: **1.** going across: *crossroad.* **2.** counter: *cross-examination.* **3.** marked with a cross: *hot cross buns.* **4.** cruciform: *crossbones,* etc.

cross·bar (krôs′bär′, krŏs′-), *n.* a transverse bar, line, or stripe.

cross·bed·ded (krôs′bĕd′ĭd, krŏs′-), *adj. Geol.* having irregular laminations, as strata of sandstone, inclining in various directions not coincident with the general stratification.

cross bench, *Brit.* a set of seats at the back of the halls of both houses of Parliament for those who belong neither to the government nor to opposition parties.

cross·bill (krôs′bĭl′, krŏs′-), *n.* any bird of the fringilline genus *Loxia,* characterized by mandibles curved so that the tips cross each other when the bill is closed.

cross·bones (krôs′bōnz′, krŏs′-), *n.pl.* two bones placed crosswise, usually below a skull, symbolizing death.

cross·bow (krôs′bō′, krŏs′-), *n.* an old weapon for shooting missiles, consisting of a bow fixed transversely on a stock having a groove or barrel to direct the missile. **—cross·bow·man** (krôs′bō′mən, krŏs′-), *n.*

cross·bred (krôs′brĕd′, krŏs′-), *adj.* **1.** produced by crossbreeding. **—n. 2.** an animal or group of animals produced by hybridization.

cross·breed (krôs′brēd′, krŏs′-), *v.,* **-bred, -breeding,** *n.* **—v.t. 1.** to produce (a hybrid) within a species, using two breeds or varieties. **—v.i. 2.** to undertake or engage in hybridizing, esp. within a single species. **—n. 3.** a crossbred.

cross bun, *Chiefly Brit.* a bun marked with a cross, eaten esp. on Good Friday.

cross-coun·try (krôs′kŭn′trĭ, krŏs′-), *adj.* **1.** directed across fields or open country; not following the roads or the great highways. **2.** from one end of the country to the other: *a cross-country flight.*

cross-cut (krôs′kŭt′, krŏs′-), *adj., n., v.,* **-cut, -cutting. —adj. 1.** made or used for cutting crosswise: *a crosscut saw.* **2.** cut across the grain or on the bias: *crosscut crepe.* **—n. 3.** a direct course between two points, as one diagonal to a main way. **4.** a transverse cut or course. **5.** *Mining.* an underground passageway, usually from shaft to a vein of ore or crosswise of a vein of ore. **—v.t. 6.** to cut across.

crosscut saw, a saw used for sawing lumber in a direction perpendicular to the axis of the tree.

crosse (krôs, krŏs), *n.* a long-handled racket used in the game of lacrosse. [t. F; of Gmc. orig.]

cross-ex·am·ine (krôs′ĭg zăm′ĭn, krŏs′-), *v.t.,* **-ined, -ining. 1.** to examine by questions intended to check a previous examination; examine closely or minutely. **2.** to examine (a witness called by the opposing side), as for the purpose of disproving his testimony. **—cross-ex·am·i·na·tion** (krôs′ĭg zăm′ə nā′shən, krŏs′-), *n.* **—cross′-ex·am′in·er,** *n.*

cross-eye (krôs′ī′, krŏs′-), *n.* strabismus, esp. the form in which both eyes turn toward the nose. **—cross′-eyed′,** *adj.*

cross-fer·ti·li·za·tion (krôs′fûr′tə lə zā′shən, krŏs′-), *n.* **1.** *Biol.* the fertilization of an organism by the fusion of an egg from one individual with a sperm (or male gamete) of a different individual. **2.** *Bot.* fertilization of one flower or plant by pollen from another (opposed to *self-fertilization*).

cross-fer·ti·lize (krôs′fûr′tə līz′, krŏs′-), *v.t.* **-lized, -lizing.** to cause the cross-fertilization of.

cross fire, *Mil.* lines of fire from two or more positions, crossing one another, or a single one of such lines.

cross-grained (krôs′grānd′, krŏs′-), *adj.* **1.** having the grain running transversely or diagonally, or having an irregular or gnarled grain, as timber. **2.** perverse.

cross hairs, fine wires, or strands of spider web or other material, crossing in a focal plane of an optical instrument, serving to define a line of sight.

cross·hatch (krôs′hăch′, krŏs′-), *v.t.* to hatch or shade with two or more intersecting series of parallel lines. **—cross′hatch′ing,** *n.*

cross·head (krôs′hĕd′, krŏs′-), *n.* **1.** *Print.* a title or heading filling a line or group of lines the full width of the column. **2.** the sliding and bearing member of a Diesel, steam, or gas engine, between the piston rod and the connecting rod.

cross·ing (krôs′ĭng, krŏs′ĭng), *n.* **1.** act of one who or that which crosses. **2.** a place where lines, tracks, etc., cross each other. **3.** the intersection of nave and transept in a cruciform church. **4.** a place at which a road, river, etc., may be crossed. **5.** act of opposing or thwarting; contradiction.

crossing over, *Biol.* the interchange of corresponding chromatid segments of homologous chromosomes with their linked genes.

cross·jack (krôs′jăk′, krŏs′-; *Naut.* krō′jĭk, krŏj′ĭk), *n. Naut.* a square sail on the lower yard of a mizzenmast. See illus. under **sail.**

cross-leg·ged (krôs′lĕg′ĭd, -lĕgd′, krŏs′-), *adj.* having the legs crossed; having one leg laid across the other.

cross·let (krôs′lĭt, krŏs′-), *n. Chiefly Heraldry.* a small cross.

cros·sop·te·ryg·i·an (krŏ sŏp′tə rĭj′ĭ ən), *n.* any fish of the group *Crossopterygii,* all fossil except *Latimeria chalumnae,* supposed to be ancestral to amphibians and other land vertebrates.

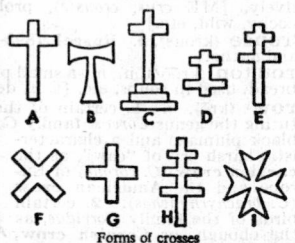

Forms of crosses

A. Latin cross; B. Tau cross or St. Anthony's cross; C. Cross of Calvary; D. Cross of Lorraine; E. Patriarchal cross; F. St. Andrew's cross; G. Greek cross, or St. George's cross; H. Papal cross; I. Maltese cross.

cross·o·ver (krôs′ō′vər, krŏs′-), n. Biol. 1. crossing over. 2. a genotype resulting from crossing over.

crossover network an audio circuit device in a radio or phonograph which sorts the impulses received and channels them into high- or low-frequency loudspeakers.

cross·patch (krôs′păch′, krŏs′-), n. Colloq. an ill-humored person.

cross·piece (krôs′pēs′, krŏs′-), n. a piece of any material placed across something; a transverse piece.

cross-pol·li·nate (krôs′pŏl′ə nāt′, krŏs′-), v.t., -nat-ed, -nating. cross-fertilize. —**cross′-pol′li·na′tion,** n.

cross-pur·pose (krôs′pûr′pəs, krŏs′-), n. 1. an opposing or counter purpose. 2. **be at cross-purposes,** to misunderstand another's, or each other's, purpose, or act under such a misunderstanding. 3. (pl.) a kind of conversational game in which words are taken in different senses.

cross-ques·tion (krôs′kwĕs′chən, krŏs′-), v.t. 1. to cross-examine. —n. 2. a question asked by way of cross-examination.

cross-re·fer (krôs′rĭ fûr′, krŏs′-), v.t., v.i., -ferred, -ferring. to refer by a cross reference.

cross reference, a reference from one part of a book, etc., to a word, item, etc., in another part.

cross relation, Music. a relationship between two successive tones in different voices which normally occurs in one voice; false relation.

cross·road (krôs′rōd′, krŏs′-), n. 1. a road that crosses another road, or one that runs transversely to main roads. 2. a by-road. 3. (often pl., construed as sing.) the place where roads intersect.

cross·ruff (krôs′rŭf′, krŏs′-), n. Whist, Bridge. a play in which each hand of a partnership trumps a different suit; a seesaw.

cross section, 1. a section made by a plane cutting anything transversely, esp. at right angles to the longest axis. See diag. under **section.** 2. a piece so cut off. 3. act of cutting anything across. 4. a typical selection; a sample showing all characteristic parts, etc.: a cross section of American opinion. 5. Survey. a vertical section of the ground surface taken at right angles to a survey line. —**cross′-sec′tion·al,** adj.

cross-stitch (krôs′stĭch′, krŏs′-), n. 1. a kind of stitching employing pairs of diagonal stitches of the same length crossing each other in the middle at right angles. —v.t., v.i. 2. to work in cross-stitch.

cross street, a street crossing another street, or one running transversely to main streets.

cross talk, 1. interference in a telephone or radio channel from one or more other telephone channels. 2. Brit. Parliament. an interchange of remarks across the hall between members of different parties.

cross-tie (krôs′tī′, krŏs′-), n. U.S. a timber placed transversely to form a foundation or support.

cross-town (krôs′toun′, krŏs′-), adj. U.S. that runs across the town: a cross-town bus.

cross-tree (krôs′trē′, krŏs′-), n. Naut. one of the horizontal transverse pieces of timber or metal fastened to the head of a lower mast or topmast in order to support the top, spread the shrouds, etc.

cross·way (krôs′wā′, krŏs′-), n. a cross-road.

cross wind, a wind blowing at right angles to the line of flight of an aircraft.

cross·wise (krôs′wīz′, krŏs′-), adv. 1. across; transversely. 2. in the form of a cross. 3. contrarily. Also, **cross·ways** (krôs′wāz′, krŏs′-).

C, Crosstree

cross·word puzzle (krôs′wûrd′, krŏs′-), a puzzle in which words corresponding to given meanings are to be supplied and fitted into a particular figure divided into spaces, the letters of the words being arranged across the figure, or vertically, or sometimes otherwise.

crotch (krŏch), n. 1. a forked piece, part, support, etc. 2. a forking or place of forking, as of the human body between the legs. [var. of CRUTCH] —**crotched** (krŏcht), adj.

crotch·et (krŏch′ĭt), n. 1. a small hook. 2. a hooklike device or part. 3. Entomol. a small hooklike process. 4. a curved surgical instrument with a sharp hook. 5. an odd fancy or whimsical notion. 6. Chiefly Brit. Music. a quarter note. See illus. under **note.** [ME crochet, t. OF. See CROCHET]

crotch·et·y (krŏch′ĭt ĭ), adj. 1. given to crotchets or odd fancies; full of crotchets. 2. of the nature of a crotchet. —**crotch′et·i·ness,** n.

cro·ton (krō′tən), n. 1. any of the chiefly tropical euphorbiaceous plants constituting the genus Croton, many species of which, as C. tiglium, have important medicinal properties. 2. (among florists) any plant of the related genus Codiaeum (or Phyllaurea) cultivated for the ornamental foliage. [NL, t. Gk.: m. krotōn a tick, also a plant having ticklike seeds]

Cro·ton bug (krō′tən), the common cockroach, Blatella germanica. [from the Croton Aqueduct water, introduced into New York City in 1842]

cro·ton·ic acid (krō tŏn′ĭk, -tō′nĭk), Chem. a colorless, crystalline compound, CH₃CHCHCOOH, used in organic synthesis.

croton oil, a powerful purgative oil from Croton

tiglium **(croton-oil plant),** a euphorbiaceous shrub or tree of the East Indies.

crouch (krouch), v.i. 1. to stoop or bend low. 2. to bend close to the ground, as an animal preparing to spring, or shrinking with fear. 3. to bow or stoop servilely; cringe. —v.t. 4. to bend low. —n. 5. act of crouching; a stooping or bending low. [ME crouche, t. OF: m. crochir become bent, der. croche hook]

croup¹ (krōōp), n. Pathol. any affection of the larynx or trachea characterized by a hoarse cough and difficult breathing. [f. n. use of croup, v. (now dial.) cry hoarsely, b. CROAK and WHOOP]

croup² (krōōp), n. the rump or buttocks of certain animals, esp. of a horse. [ME croupe, t. F, t. Gmc.; cf. CROP]

crou·pi·er (krōō′pĭ ər; Fr. krōō pyĕ′), n. 1. an attendant who collects and pays the money at a gaming table. 2. one who at a public dinner sits at the lower end of the table as assistant chairman. [t. F; orig., one who rides behind on the croup of another's horse]

croup·ous (krōō′pəs), adj. Pathol. pertaining to, of the nature of, or resembling croup.

croup·y (krōō′pĭ), adj. 1. pertaining to or resembling croup. 2. affected with croup.

crouse (krōōs), adj. Scot. and N. Eng. bold; brisk; lively. [ME crus, crous(e), prob. t. Fris.: m. krus cocky, wild, etc.]

Crouse (krous), n. Russel, 1893–1966, U. S. dramatist and author.

crou·ton (krōō′tŏn), n. a small piece of fried or toasted bread, used in soups, etc. [t. F, der. croûte. See CRUST]

crow¹ (krō), n. 1. certain of the oscine birds constituting the genus Corvus (family Corvidae), with lustrous black plumage and a characteristic harsh cry of "caw", as the **carrion crow** (C. corone) of Europe and the **American crow** (C. brachyrhynchos). 2. certain birds of the family Corvidae, as the chough, or **Cornish crow,** Pyrrhocorax graculus. 3. any of various similar birds of other families, as the **pied crow** of Australia. 4. Astron. the southern constellation Corvus. 5. a crowbar. 6. **as the crow flies,** in a straight line. 7. **eat crow,** to be forced to do or say something very unpleasant or humiliating. 8. **have a crow to pick with,** to have an unpleasant matter to discuss with. [ME; OE crāwe. See CROW², v.]

American crow, Corvus brachyrhynchos (17 to 19 in. long)

crow² (krō), v., crowed (or crew for 1), crowed, crowing, n. —v.i. 1. to utter the characteristic cry of a cock. 2. to utter an inarticulate cry of pleasure, as an infant does. 3. to exult loudly; boast. —n. 4. the characteristic cry of the cock. 5. an unarticulate cry of pleasure. [ME crowe(n), OE crāwan, c. D kraaien, G krähen; imit.]

Crow (krō), n. 1. a North American Indian Plains tribe, belonging to the Siouan linguistic stock, located in eastern Montana. 2. a member of this tribe. 3. a Siouan language closely related to Hidatsa. [trans. (through F gens de corbeaux) of their own name. Absaroke crow, sparrow-hawk, or bird people]

crow·bar (krō′bär′), n. a bar of iron, often with a wedge-shaped end, for use as a lever, etc.

crow·ber·ry (krō′bĕr′ĭ), n., pl. -ries. 1. the insipid black or reddish berry of an evergreen heathlike shrub, Empetrum nigrum, of northern regions. 2. the plant itself, of the family Empetraceae. 3. any of certain other fruits or the plants bearing them, as the bearberry.

crow blackbird, any of several North American birds of the genus Quiscalus (family Icteridae), as Q. quiscula, the purple grackle, noted for iridescent black plumage and trough-shaped tails.

crowd¹ (kroud), n. 1. a large number of persons gathered closely together; a throng. 2. any large number of persons. 3. people in general; the masses: far from the madding crowd's ignoble strife. 4. any group or set of persons: a jolly crowd. 5. a large number of things gathered or considered together. 6. Sociol. a group of persons acting together only through temporary stimulus, having no past or future continuity. [n. use of v.] —v.i. 7. to gather in large numbers; throng; swarm. 8. to press forward; advance by pushing. —v.t. 9. to push; shove. 10. to press closely together; force into a confined space. 11. to fill to excess; fill by crowding or pressing into. 12. Colloq. to urge; press by solicitation; annoy by urging: to crowd a debtor for immediate payment. 13. **crowd on sail,** Naut. to carry a press of sail. [ME crowde(n), OE crūdan, c. MD kruyden]

—**Syn.** 1. CROWD, MULTITUDE, SWARM, THRONG are terms referring to large numbers of people. CROWD suggests a jostling, uncomfortable, and possibly disordered company: a crowd gathered to listen to the speech. MULTITUDE emphasizes the great number of persons or things but suggests that there is space enough for all: a multitude of people at the market on Saturdays. SWARM as used of people is usually contemptuous, suggesting a moving, restless, often noisy, crowd: a swarm of dirty children played in the street. THRONG suggests a company that presses together or forward, often with some common aim: the throng pushed forward to see the cause of the excitement. 10. pack, cram, squeeze, cramp.

crowd² (kroud), n. an ancient Celtic musical instrument related to the kithara, but bowed. [ME crowde, t. Welsh: m. crwth]

crowd·ed (krou'dĭd), *adj.* **1.** filled to excess; filled with a crowd; packed: *crowded streets.* **2.** uncomfortably close together: *crowded passengers on a bus.* —**crowd'ed·ly,** *adv.* —**crowd'ed·ness,** *n.*

crow·foot (krō'fŏŏt'), *n., pl.* **-foots** for 1 and 2, **-feet** for 3 and 4. **1.** any plant of the genus *Ranunculus,* esp. one with divided leaves suggestive of a crow's foot; a buttercup. **2.** any of various other plants with leaves or other parts suggestive of a bird's foot, as certain species of the genus *Geranium.* **3.** caltrop. **4.** *Naut.* a device consisting of small diverging lines or cords rove through a block of wood, used for suspending awnings, etc.

crow·keep·er (krō'kē'pər), *n. Now Dial.* scarecrow.

crown (kroun), *n.* **1.** an ornamental wreath or garland for the head, conferred by the ancients as a mark of victory or distinction. **2.** honorary distinction; reward. **3.** a decorative fillet or covering for the head, worn as a symbol of sovereignty. **4.** the power or dominion of a sovereign. **5.** the Crown, the sovereign as head of the state, or the supreme governing power of a state under a monarchical government. **6.** any crownlike emblem or design, used in a heraldic crest, as a badge of rank in some armies, etc. **7.** a coin generally bearing a crown or a crowned head on the reverse. The English crown is worth five shillings. **8.** a krone or a krona. **9.** something having the form of a crown, as the corona of a flower. **10.** *Bot.* **a.** the leaves and living branches of a tree. **b.** the point at which the root of a seed plant joins the stem. **c.** a circle of appendages on the throat of the corolla, etc.; corona. **11.** the top or highest part of anything, as of the head, a hat, a mountain, etc. **12.** the head itself: *he broke his crown.* **13.** the crest, as of a bird. **14.** *Dentistry.* **a.** that part of a tooth which is covered by enamel. **b.** an artificial substitute, as of gold or porcelain, for the crown of a tooth. **15.** the highest or most perfect state of anything. **16.** an exalting or chief attribute. **17.** the acme or supreme source of honor, excellence, beauty, etc. **18.** crown glass. **19.** *Naut.* the part of an anchor where the arms join the shank. **20.** the part of a cut gem above the girdle. —*v.t.* **21.** to place a crown or garland upon the head of. **22.** to invest with a regal crown, or with regal dignity and power. **23.** to honor as with a crown; reward; invest with honor, dignity, etc. **24.** to surmount as with a crown; surmount as a crown does. **25.** to complete worthily; bring to a successful or effective conclusion. **26.** *Checkers.* to change (a checker) into a king after it has safely reached the last row by putting another piece on top of it. [ME *croune, coroune,* t. AF, g. L *corōna* garland, wreath, crown. Cf. CORONA] —**crown'er,** *n.*

crown colony, a colony in which the crown has the entire control of legislation and administration, as distinguished from one having a constitution and representative government.

crown·er (krou'nər, krōō'-), *n. Brit. Dial.* coroner.

crown glass, **1.** an optical glass of low dispersion and generally low refractive index. **2.** an old form of window glass formed by blowing a globe and whirling it into a disk: composed essentially of soda, lime, and silica.

crown graft, *Hort.* a graft in which the scion is inserted at the crown of the stock.

crown land, **1.** land belonging to the crown, the revenue of which goes to the reigning sovereign. **2.** Also, **crown'land'.** one of the provinces, or great administrative divisions of the former empire of Austria-Hungary.

crown·piece (kroun'pēs'), *n.* a piece or part forming or fitting the crown or top of anything.

Crown Point, a village in NE New York, on Lake Champlain: the site of a strategic fort in the French and Indian and Revolutionary wars.

crown prince, the heir apparent of a monarch.

crown princess, the wife of a crown prince.

crown saw, a rotary saw consisting of a hollow cylinder with teeth on its end or edge, as the surgeons' trephine.

crown wheel, *Horol.* a wheel next to the winding knob, having two sets of teeth, one at right angles to its plane.

crown·work (kroun'wûrk'), *n. Fort.* an outwork containing a central bastion with a curtain and demibastions, usually designed to cover some advantageous position.

crow's-foot (krōz'fŏŏt'), *n., pl.* **-feet. 1.** (*usually pl.*) a wrinkle at the outer corner of the eye. **2.** *Aeron.* a method by which one main cord exerts pressure or pull at several points simultaneously through smaller ropes. **3.** *Tailoring.* a three-pointed embroidered figure used as a finish, as at the end of a seam or opening.

crow's-nest (krōz'nĕst'), *n. Naut.* **1.** a box or shelter for the lookout man, secured near the top of a mast. **2.** a similar lookout station ashore.

Croy·don (kroi'dən), *n.* a city in SE England, near London: airport. 249,300 (est. 1956).

croze (krōz), *n.* **1.** the groove at the ends of the staves of a barrel, cask, etc., into which the edge of the head fits. **2.** a tool for cutting such a groove. [cf. F *creux* groove]

cro·zier (krō'zhər), *n.* crosier.

cru·ces (krōō'sēz), *n.* pl. of **crux.**

cru·cial (krōō'shəl), *adj.* **1.** involving a final and supreme decision; decisive; critical: *a crucial experiment.* **2.** severe; trying. **3.** of the form of a cross; cross-shaped.

[f. *cruci-* (t. L, comb. form of *cruz* cross) + -AL¹] —**cru'cial·ly,** *adv.*

cru·ci·ate (krōō'shĭ'ĭt, -āt'), *adj.* **1.** cross-shaped. **2.** *Bot.* having the form of a cross with equal arms, as the flowers of mustard, etc. **3.** *Entomol.* crossing each other diagonally in repose, as the wings of an insect. [t. NL: m. s. *cruciātus,* der. L *cruz* CROSS]

cru·ci·ble (krōō'sə bəl), *n.* **1.** a vessel of metal or refractory material employed for heating substances to high temperatures. **2.** (in a metallurgical furnace) the hollow part at the bottom, in which molten metal collects. **3.** a severe, searching test. [t. ML: m.s. *crucibulum* night lamp, melting pot; this ? m. *crucibolum* whale oil cruse (cf. L *bālaena* whale). See CRUSE]

Cruciate flower

crucible steel, steel made in a crucible, esp. a high-grade steel prepared by melting selected materials.

cru·ci·fer (krōō'sə fər), *n.* **1.** one who carries a cross, as in ecclesiastical processions. **2.** *Bot.* a cruciferous plant. [t. LL]

cru·cif·er·ous (krōō sĭf'ər əs), *adj.* **1.** bearing a cross. **2.** *Bot.* belonging or pertaining to the family *Cruciferae* or *Brassicaceae,* whose members bear flowers having a crosslike, four-petaled corolla; brassicaceous. [f. LL *crucifer* cross-bearing + -OUS]

cru·ci·fix (krōō'sə fĭks), *n.* **1.** a cross with the figure of Jesus crucified upon it. **2.** any cross. [ME, t. LL: s. *crucifixus,* pp., fixed to a cross]

cru·ci·fix·ion (krōō'sə fĭk'shən), *n.* **1.** act of crucifying. **2.** (*cap.*) the death of Jesus by exposure upon a cross. **3.** a picture or other representation of this.

cru·ci·form (krōō'sə fôrm'), *adj.* cross-shaped. [f. s. L *cruz* cross + -(I)FORM] —**cru'ci·form·ly,** *adv.*

cru·ci·fy (krōō'sə fī'), *v.t.* **-fied, -fying. 1.** to put to death by nailing or binding the body to a cross. **2.** to torment; treat with severity. **3.** to subdue (passion, sin, etc.). [ME *crucifien,* t. OF: m. *crucifier,* t. LL: m. *crucifigere* fix to a cross. See -FY]

crud (krŭd), *v.t., v.i.,* **crudded, crudding.** *Obs. or Dial.* to curd. [metathetic var. of CURD]

crude (krōōd), *adj.,* **cruder, crudest. 1.** in a raw or unprepared state; unrefined: *crude oil, sugar, etc.* **2.** unripe; not mature. **3.** lacking finish, polish, proper arrangement, or completeness: *a crude summary.* **4.** lacking culture, refinement, tact, etc.: *crude persons, behavior, speech, etc.* **5.** undisguised; blunt; bare: *a crude answer.* [ME, t. L: m. s. *crūdus* raw, crude, rough. Cf. CRUEL] —**crude'ly,** *adv.* —**crude'ness,** *n.* —**Syn. 1.** unfinished. See **raw. 2.** undeveloped. **3.** unpolished. **4.** uncouth, rough, rude, coarse, clumsy. —**Ant. 4.** cultivated.

cru·di·ty (krōō'də tĭ), *n., pl.* **-ties. 1.** state or quality of being crude. **2.** an instance of this; anything crude.

cru·el (krōō'əl), *adj.* **1.** disposed to inflict suffering; indifferent to, or taking pleasure in, the pain or distress of another; hard-hearted; pitiless. **2.** causing or marked by great pain or distress: *a cruel remark.* [ME, t. OF, g. L *crūdēlis* hard, cruel, akin to *crudus* CRUDE] —**cru'el·ly,** *adv.* —**cru'el·ness,** *n.* —**Syn. 1.** barbarous, bloodthirsty, ferocious, merciless, relentless, implacable. CRUEL, PITILESS, RUTHLESS, BRUTAL, SAVAGE imply readiness to cause pain to others, and being unmoved by their suffering. CRUEL implies willingness to cause pain, and indifference to suffering: *a cruel stepfather, cruel to animals.* PITILESS adds the idea of hard-heartedness and positive refusal to show compassion: *pitiless to captives, fate that seems pitiless.* RUTHLESS implies cruelty and unscrupulousness, letting nothing stand in one's way, and using any methods necessary: *ruthless in pressing an advantage, ruthless greed.* BRUTAL implies cruelty which takes the form of physical violence: *a brutal master.* SAVAGE suggests fierceness and brutality: *savage battles, jealousy.* —**Ant. 1.** kind, sympathetic, compassionate.

cru·el·ty (krōō'əl tĭ), *n., pl.* **-ties. 1.** state or quality of being cruel. **2.** cruel disposition or conduct. **3.** a cruel act. —**Syn. 1.** harshness, brutality, ruthlessness, barbarity, inhumanity, atrocity. —**Ant. 2, 3.** kindness.

cru·et (krōō'ĭt), *n.* a glass bottle, esp. one for holding vinegar, oil, etc., for the table. [ME, t. OF, dim. of *crue* pitcher, pot, t. Gmc.; cf. G *krug* pot]

Cruik·shank (krŏŏk'shăngk'), *n.* George, 1792–1878, British artist and caricaturist.

cruise (krōōz), *v.,* **cruised, cruising,** *n.* —*v.i.* **1.** to sail to and fro, or from place to place, as in search of hostile ships, or for pleasure. **2.** *Colloq.* to move hither and thither on land. **3.** *Aeron.* to fly at practical rather than high speed, esp. at the speed which permits maximum operating efficiency. **4.** *Colloq.* (of a car, plane, etc.) to move along easily at a moderate speed. —*v.t.* **5.** to cruise over. —*n.* **6.** act of cruising; a voyage made by cruising. [t. D: m. *kruisen* cross, cruise, der. *kruis* cross]

cruis·er (krōō'zər), *n.* **1.** one who or that which cruises, as a person or a ship. **2.** one of a class of warships of medium tonnage, designed for high speed and long cruising radius. **3.** a boat, usually power-driven, adapted for pleasure trips.

crul·ler (krŭl'ər), *n.* a light, sweet cake cut from a rolled dough and fried in deep hot fat, often having a ring-shaped or twisted form. Also, **kruller.** [f. m. LG *krull(koken)* + -ER¹]

crumb (krŭm), *n.* **1.** a small particle of bread, cake, etc., such as breaks or falls off. **2.** a small particle or portion of anything. **3.** the soft inner portion of a bread (distinguished from *crust*). —*v.t.* **4.** *Cookery.* to dress or prepare with bread crumbs; to bread. **5.** to break into crumbs or small fragments. Also, (formerly) **crum.** [ME *crumme*, OE *cruma*, akin to G *krume*]

crum·ble (krŭm′bəl), *v.*, **-bled, -bling,** *n.* —*v.t.* **1.** to break into small fragments or crumbs. —*v.i.* **2.** to fall into small pieces; break or part into small fragments. **3.** to decay; disappear piecemeal. —*n.* **4.** something crumbling or crumbled. **5.** *Now Dial.* a small or tiny crumb or fragment. [earlier *crimble*, freq. of OE *gecrymman* crumble (der. *cruma* crumb); assimilated in form to CRUMB]

crum·bly (krŭm′blĭ), *adj.,* **-blier, -bliest.** apt to crumble; friable.

crumb·y (krŭm′ĭ), *adj.,* **crumbier, crumbiest. 1.** full of crumbs. **2.** soft.

crum·mie (krŭm′ĭ, krŏŏm′ĭ), *n.* a cow with crooked horns. Also, **crummy.** [der. obs. *crum* crooked, OE *crumb*, c. G *krumm*]

crum·my[1] (krŭm′ĭ), *adj.,* **-mier, -miest.** *Slang.* very inferior, mean, or shabby.

crum·my[2] (krŭm′ĭ, krŏŏm′ĭ), *n., pl.* **-mies. crummie.**

crump (krŭmp, krŏŏmp), *v.t.* **1.** to crunch with the teeth. **2.** to strike heavily. —*v.i.* **3.** to make a crunching sound, as in walking over snow, or as snow when trodden on. —*n.* **4.** a crunching sound. **5.** a heavy blow. **6.** *Brit.* a soldiers' term for a large explosive shell.

crum·pet (krŭm′pĭt), *n. Chiefly Brit.* a kind of light, soft bread resembling a muffin, cooked on a griddle or the like, and often toasted. [short for *crumpet cake* curled cake, ME *crompid,* pp. of obs. *crump,* var. of CRIMP]

crum·ple (krŭm′pəl), *v.,* **-pled, -pling,** *n.* —*v.t.* **1.** to draw or press into irregular folds; rumple; wrinkle. —*v.i.* **2.** to contract into wrinkles; shrink; shrivel. **3.** *Colloq.* to collapse; give way. —*n.* **4.** an irregular fold or wrinkle produced by crumpling. [freq. of obs. *crump,* var. of CRIMP]

crunch (krŭnch), *v.t.* **1.** to crush with the teeth; chew with a crushing noise. **2.** to crush or grind noisily. —*v.i.* **3.** to chew with a crushing sound. **4.** to produce, or proceed with, a crushing noise. —*n.* **5.** act or sound of crunching. Also, **craunch.** [b. CRAUNCH and CRUSH]

cru·or (krŏŏ′ôr), *n.* coagulated blood, or that portion of the blood which forms the clot. [t. L: blood, gore]

crup·per (krŭp′ər, krŏŏp′-), *n.* **1.** a leather strap on the back of the saddle of a harness, and passing in a loop under a horse's tail, to prevent the saddle from slipping forward. See illus. under **harness. 2.** the rump or buttocks of a horse. [ME *cropere,* t. OF, der. *crope.* See CROUP[2]]

cru·ral (krŏŏr′əl), *adj.* **1.** of or pertaining to the leg or the hind limb. **2.** of or pertaining to the leg proper, or crus. [t. L: s. *crūrālis,* der. *crūs* leg]

crus (krŭs), *n., pl.* **crura** (krŏŏr′ə). **1.** *Anat., Zool.* **a.** that part of the leg or hind limb between the femur and thigh and the ankle or tarsus; the shank. **b.** a limb or process, as of a bone or other structure. **2.** any of various parts likened to a leg. [t. L: leg]

cru·sade (krŏŏ sād′), *n., v.,* **-saded, -sading.** —*n.* **1.** (*often cap.*) any of the military expeditions undertaken by the Christians of Europe in the 11th, 12th and 13th centuries for the recovery of the Holy Land from the Mohammedans. **2.** any war carried on under papal sanction. **3.** any vigorous, aggressive movement for the defense or advancement of an idea, cause, etc. —*v.i.* **4.** to go on or engage in a crusade. [b. earlier *crusada* (t. Sp.: m. *cruzada*) and *croisade* (t. F). See CROSS, -ADE[1]] —**cru·sad′er,** *n.*

cru·sa·do (krŏŏ sā′dō), *n., pl.* **-does, -dos.** an early Portuguese coin of gold or silver, bearing the figure of a cross. [t. Pg.: m. *cruzado,* prop. pp. of *cruzar* mark with a cross. Cf. CRUSADE]

cruse (krŏŏz, krŏŏs), *n.* an earthen pot, bottle, etc., for liquids. [t. MD]

crush (krŭsh), *v.t.* **1.** to press and bruise between two hard bodies; squeeze out of shape or normal condition. **2.** to break into small fragments or particles, as ore, stone, etc. **3.** to force out by pressing or squeezing. **4.** to drink (wine, etc.). **5.** to put down, overpower, or subdue completely; overwhelm. **6.** to oppress grievously. —*v.i.* **7.** to become crushed. **8.** to advance with crushing; press or crowd forcibly. —*n.* **9.** act of crushing. **10.** state of being crushed. **11.** *Colloq.* a great crowd; a crowded social gathering. [ME *crusch(en),* appar. t. OF: m. *croissir* crash, gnash, break, crush; prob. t. Gmc.] —**crush′er,** *n.* —Syn. **1.** crumple, rumple. **2.** shatter, pulverize, mash. See **break. 5.** quell, subdue, overcome.

Cru·soe (krŏŏ′sō), *n.* **Robinson,** the shipwrecked seaman in Defoe's novel *Robinson Crusoe* (1719), who lives adventurously for years on a small uninhabited island.

crust (krŭst), *n.* **1.** the hard outer portion of a loaf of bread (distinguished from *crumb*). **2.** a piece of this. **3.** the outside covering of a pie. **4.** any more or less hard external covering or coating. **5.** the hard outer shell or covering of an animal or plant. **6.** the exterior portion of the earth, accessible to examination. **7.** a scab or eschar. **8.** deposit from wine, as it ripens, on the interior of bottles, consisting of tartar and coloring matter. —*v.t.* **9.** to cover with or as with a crust; encrust. **10.** to form (something) into a crust. —*v.i.* **11.** to form or contract a crust. **12.** to form into a crust. [ME, t. L: s. *crusta* rind, r. ME *crouste,* t. OF]

Crus·ta·ce·a (krŭs tā′shĭ ə, -shə), *n.pl.* See **crustacean.** [NL, neut. pl. of *crustāceus* hard-shelled]

crus·ta·cean (krŭs tā′shən), *adj.* **1.** belonging to the Crustacea, a class of (chiefly aquatic) arthropods, including the lobsters, shrimps, crabs, barnacles, wood lice, etc., commonly having the body covered with a hard shell or crust. —*n.* **2.** a crustacean animal.

crus·ta·ceous (krŭs tā′shəs), *adj.* **1.** of the nature of or pertaining to a crust or shell. **2.** belonging to the Crustacea. **3.** having a hard covering or crust.

crus·tal (krŭs′təl), *adj.* of or pertaining to a crust, as that of the earth.

crust·y (krŭs′tĭ), *adj.,* **crustier, crustiest. 1.** of the nature of or resembling a crust; having a crust. **2.** harsh; surly; crabbed: *a crusty person, manner, remark, etc.* —**crust′i·ly,** *adv.* —**crust′i·ness,** *n.*

crutch (krŭch), *n.* **1.** a staff or support to assist a lame or infirm person in walking, now usually with a crosspiece at one end to fit under the armpit. **2.** any of various devices resembling this in shape or use. **3.** a forked support or part. **4.** a forked rest for the legs in sidesaddle. **5.** the crotch of the human body. **6.** *Naut.* a forked support for the booms, when the sails are stowed. —*v.t.* **7.** to support on crutches; prop; sustain. [ME *crucche,* OE *crycc,* c. D *kruk* and G *krücke.* Cf. CROOK]

crutched (krŭcht), *adj.* having or bearing a cross: *a crutched friar.*

crux (krŭks), *n., pl.* **cruxes, cruces** (krŏŏ′sēz). **1.** a vital, basic, or decisive point. **2.** a cross. **3.** something that torments by its puzzling nature; a perplexing difficulty. [t. L: cross, torment, trouble]

Crux (krŭks), *n., gen.* **Crucis** (krŏŏ′sĭs). *Astron.* the Southern Cross.

crux an·sa·ta (krŭks′ ăn sā′tə), a T-shaped cross with a loop at the top; ankh. [L: cross with a handle]

cru·zei·ro (krŏŏ zār′ō; *Port.* -zĕ′rŏ, -rŏō), *n., pl.* **-ros.** the gold unit of the Brazilian monetary system equivalent to a milreis, written Cr $1.00. [t. Pg., der. *cruz* cross]

cry (krī), *v.,* **cried, crying,** *n., pl.* **cries.** —*v.i.* **1.** to utter inarticulate sounds, esp. of lamentation, grief, or suffering, usually with tears. **2.** to weep; shed tears, with or without sound. **3.** to call loudly; shout. **4.** to give forth vocal sounds or characteristic calls, as animals; yelp; bark. —*v.t.* **5.** to utter or pronounce loudly; call out. **6.** to announce orally in public; sell by outcry. **7.** to beg for or implore in a loud voice. **8.** to disparage; belittle (fol. by *down*). **9.** to break a promise, agreement, etc. (fol. by *off*). **10.** to praise; extol (fol. by *up*). —*n.* **11.** act or sound of crying; any loud utterance or exclamation; a shout, scream, or wail. **12.** clamor; outcry. **13.** an entreaty; appeal. **14.** an oral proclamation or announcement. **15.** a call of wares for sale, etc., as by a street vendor. **16.** public report. **17.** an opinion generally expressed. **18.** a battle cry. **19.** a political or party slogan. **20.** a fit of weeping. **21.** the utterance or call of an animal. **22.** a pack of hounds. [ME *crie(n),* t. OF: m. *crier,* g. L *quirītāre*] —**cry′ing·ly,** *adv.* —Syn. **1.** wail, bewail, weep, sob, squall, blubber, whimper, mewl, pule. **3.** clamor, vociferate, exclaim, ejaculate, bawl, scream, howl, yell, yowl. CRY, SHOUT, BELLOW, ROAR refer to kinds of loud articulate or inarticulate sounds. CRY is the general word: *to cry out.* To SHOUT is to raise the voice loudly in uttering words or other articulate sound: *he shouted back to his companions.* BELLOW especially refers to the loud, deep cry of a bull, moose, etc., or, somewhat in deprecation, to human utterance which suggests such a sound: *the speaker bellowed his answer.* ROAR refers to a deep, hoarse, rumbling or vibrant cry; it often implies tumultuous volume: *the crowd roared approval.* **6.** hawk. **11.** roar, howl, yell, whoop.

cry·ba·by (krī′bā′bĭ), *n., pl.* **-bies.** one given to crying like a baby, or to weak display of injured feeling.

cry·ing (krī′ĭng), *adj.* **1.** that cries; clamorous; wailing; weeping. **2.** demanding attention or remedy: *a crying evil.* —Syn. **2.** flagrant, notorious, urgent.

cryo-, a word element meaning "icy cold," "frost." [t. Gk.: m. *kryo-,* comb. form of *krýos*]

cry·o·gen (krī′ə jən), *n.* a substance for producing low temperatures; a freezing mixture.

cry·o·gen·ics (krī′ə jĕn′ĭks), *n.* low temperature research. —**cry′o·gen′ic,** *adj.*

cry·o·hy·drate (krī′ō hī′drāt), *n.* a mixture of ice and another substance in definite proportions such that a minimum melting or freezing point is attained.

cry·o·lite (krī′ə līt′), *n.* a mineral, sodium aluminum fluoride, Na₃AlF₆, occurring in white masses, used as a flux in the electrolytic production of aluminum and as an insecticide.

cry·om·e·ter (krī ŏm′ə tər), *n.* a thermometer for the measurement of low temperatures, as one containing alcohol instead of mercury.

cry·os·co·py (krī ŏs′kə pĭ), *n.* **1.** the determination of the freezing points of liquids or solutions, or of the lowering of the freezing points by dissolved substances. **2.** *Med.* the determination of the freezing points of certain bodily fluids, as urine, for diagnosis.

cry·o·stat (krī′ə stăt′), *n.* an apparatus, usually automatic, maintaining a very low constant temperature.

cry·o·ther·a·py (krī′ō thĕr′ə pĭ), *n. Med.* treatment by means of applications of ice.

crypt (krĭpt), *n.* **1.** a subterranean chamber or vault, esp. one beneath the main floor of a church, used as a burial place, etc. **2.** *Anat.* a slender pit or recess; a small glandular cavity. [t. L: s. *crypta,* t. Gk.: m. *kryptē,* prop. fem. of *kryptós* hidden]

---

b., blend of, blended;   **c.,** cognate with;   **d.,** dialect, dialectal;   der., derived from;   f., formed from;   g., going back to;   **m.,** modification of;   r., replacing;   s., stem of;   t., taken from;   ?, perhaps.   See the full key on inside cover.

cryp·tic (krĭp′tĭk), *adj.* **1.** hidden; secret; occult. **2.** *Zool.* fitted for concealing. Also, **cryp′ti·cal.** —**cryp′-ti·cal·ly,** *adv.*

crypto-, a word element meaning "hidden," as in *cryptoclastic.* Also, before vowels, **crypt-.** [comb. form repr. Gk. *kryptós*]

cryp·to·clas·tic (krĭp′tō klăs′tĭk), *adj. Petrog.* composed of fragments invisible to the unaided eye.

cryp·to·crys·tal·line (krĭp′tō krĭs′tə lĭn, -lĭn′). *adj. Mineral.* indistinctly crystalline; having an indistinguishable crystalline structure.

cryp·to·gam (krĭp′tə găm′), *n. Bot.* **1.** any of the *Cryptogamia,* an old primary division of plants comprising those without true flowers and seeds, as the ferns, mosses, and thallophytes. **2.** a plant without a true seed (opposed to *phanerogam*). [back formation from NL *cryptogamia,* f. *crypto-* + Gk. *-gamia* married state] —**cryp′to·gam′ic, cryp·tog·a·mous** (krĭp tŏg′ə-məs), *adj.*

cryp·to·gen·ic (krĭp′tə jĕn′ĭk), *adj.* of obscure or unknown origin, as a disease.

cryp·to·gram (krĭp′tə grăm′), *n.* a message or writing in secret characters or otherwise occult; a cryptograph. —**cryp′to·gram′ic,** *adj.*

cryp·to·graph (krĭp′tə grăf′, -gräf′), *n.* **1.** a cryptogram. **2.** a system of secret writing; a cipher. **3.** a device for translating text into cipher.

cryp·tog·ra·phy (krĭp tŏg′rə fĭ), *n.* **1.** process or art of writing in secret characters or in cipher. **2.** anything so written. —**cryp·tog′ra·pher, cryp·tog′ra·phist,** *n.* —**cryp·to·graph·ic** (krĭp′tə grăf′ĭk), *adj.*

cryp·to·nym (krĭp′tə nĭm), *n.* a secret name. [f. CRYPT- + Gk. *ónym(a)* name]

cryp·ton·y·mous (krĭp tŏn′ə məs), *adj.* anonymous.

cryp·to·zo·ite (krĭp′tə zō′ĭt), *n. Parasitol.* the phase in the development of malaria parasites in their vertebrate hosts during which they live in cells other than red blood corpuscles.

cryst., crystallography. Also, **crystall.**

crys·tal (krĭs′təl), *n.* **1.** a clear, transparent mineral or glass resembling ice. **2.** the transparent form of crystallized quartz. **3.** *Chem., Mineral.* a solid body having a characteristic internal structure and enclosed by symmetrically arranged plane surfaces, intersecting at definite and characteristic angles. **4.** anything made of or resembling such a substance. **5.** a single grain or mass of a crystalline substance. **6.** glass of a high degree of brilliance. **7.** cut glass. **8.** the glass or plastic cover over the face of a watch. **9.** *Radio.* **a.** the piece of galena, carborundum, or the like, forming the essential part of a crystal detector. **b.** the crystal detector itself. **10.** a quartz crystal ground in the shape of a rectangular parallelepiped, which vibrates strongly at one frequency when electric voltages of that frequency are placed across opposite sides. It is used to control the frequency of an oscillator as, for example, the frequency of a radio transmitter. —*adj.* **11.** composed of crystal. **12.** resembling crystal; clear; transparent. **13.** *Radio.* pertaining to or employing a crystal detector. **14.** indicating the 15th event of a series, as a wedding anniversary. [ME *cristal,* t. OF; r. OE *cristalla,* t. L: m. *crystallum,* t. Gk.: m. *krýstallos* ice, crystal] —**crys′tal·like′,** *adj.*

crystal detector, *Radio.* a device for rectifying the alternating currents in a receiving apparatus, consisting essentially of a crystal, as of galena or carborundum, permitting a current to pass freely in one direction only.

crystal gazing, a steady staring at a crystal or glass ball or other clear object in order to arouse visual perceptions, as of distant happenings, the future, etc. —**crys·tal·gaz·er** (krĭs′təl gā′zər), *n.*

crystall., var. of **crystallo-,** used before vowels.

crystall., crystallography.

crys·tal·lif·er·ous (krĭs′tə lĭf′ər əs), *adj.* bearing, containing, or yielding crystals. Also, **crys·tal·lig·er·ous** (krĭs′tə lĭj′ər əs). [f. s. L *crystallum* crystal + -(I)FEROUS]

crys·tal·line (krĭs′tə lĭn, -lĭn′), *adj.* **1.** of or like crystal; clear; transparent. **2.** formed by crystallization. **3.** composed of crystals, as rocks. **4.** pertaining to crystals or their formation. [ult. t. Gk.: m. *krystállinos*]

crystalline lens, *Anat.* a doubly convex, transparent, lenslike body in the eye, situated behind the iris and serving to focus the rays of light on the retina. See diag. under **eye.**

crys·tal·lite (krĭs′tə lĭt′), *n. Mineral.* a minute body in igneous rocks, marking an incipient stage in crystallization. [f. CRYSTALL- + -ITE²]

crys·tal·li·za·tion (krĭs′tə lə zā′shən), *n.* **1.** act of crystallizing; the process of forming crystals. **2.** a crystallized body or formation.

crys·tal·lize (krĭs′tə līz′), *v.* -lized, -lizing. —*v.t.* **1.** to form into crystals; cause to assume crystalline form. **2.** to give definite or concrete form to. —*v.i.* **3.** to form crystals; become crystalline in form. **4.** to assume definite or concrete form. —**crys′tal·liz′a·ble,** *adj.*

crystallo-, a word element meaning "crystal," as in *crystallographic.* Also, **crystall-.** [t. Gk.: m. *krystallo-,* comb. form of *krýstallos*]

crys·tal·lo·graph·ic (krĭs′tə lə grăf′ĭk), *adj.* of or pertaining to crystallography. Also, **crys′tal·lo·graph′-i·cal.** —**crys′tal·lo·graph′i·cal·ly,** *adv.*

crys·tal·log·ra·phy (krĭs′tə lŏg′rə fĭ), *n.* the science

dealing with crystallization and the forms and structure of crystals. —**crys′tal·log′ra·pher,** *n.*

crys·tal·loid (krĭs′tə loid′), *adj.* **1.** resembling a crystal; of the nature of a crystalloid. —*n.* **2.** a substance (usually crystallizable) which, when dissolved in a liquid, will diffuse readily through vegetable or animal membranes (contrasted with *colloid*). **3.** *Bot.* one of certain minute crystallike granules of protein, found in the tissues of various seeds. [t. Gk.: m. s. *krystalloeidḗs.* See CRYSTAL, -OID] —**crys′tal·loi′dal,** *adj.*

crystal set, *Radio.* a tubeless receiving set with a crystal detector.

crystal violet, a dye derived from rosaniline, used as an indicator in medicine and in Gram's method in bacteriology.

crystal vision, 1. visual perception, as of distant happenings, the future, etc., supposed to be aroused by crystal gazing. **2.** that which seems to be perceived.

Cs, *Chem.* cesium.

C.S.A., Confederate States of America.

csc, cosecant.

C.S.T., Central Standard Time.

Ct., 1. Connecticut. **2.** Count.

ct., 1. cent. **2.** certificate. **3.** court.

cteno-, *Zool.* a word element referring to comblike scales, as in *ctenophore.* Also, before vowels, **cten-.** [t. Gk.: m. *kteno-,* comb. form of *kteís* comb]

cte·noid (tē′noid, tĕn′oid), *adj. Zool.* **1.** comblike or pectinate; rough-edged. **2.** having rough-edged scales. [t. Gk.: m.s. *kienoeidḗs* comb-shaped]

Cte·noph·o·ra (tĭ nŏf′ə rə), *n.pl.* a phylum of marine swimming invertebrates with rounded, oval or band-shaped gelatinous bodies and eight meridional rows of ciliated plates. —**cte·noph′o·ran,** *adj., n.*

cten·o·phore (tĕn′ə fōr′, tē′nə-), *n.* one of the Ctenophora or comb jellies.

Ctes·i·phon (tĕs′ə fŏn′), *n.* a ruined city in Iraq, on the Tigris, near Bagdad: an ancient capital of Parthia.

ctn, cotangent.

cts., 1. cents. **2.** certificates.

Cu, cuprum.

cu., cubic.

cuar·ta (kwär′tə), *n. Southwestern U.S.* a long rawhide whip.

cub (kŭb), *n.* **1.** the young of certain animals, as the fox, bear, etc. **2.** *Humorous or Contemptuous.* an awkward or uncouth youth. **3.** *Colloq.* cub reporter. **4.** a member of the junior division (ages 8–11) of the Boy Scouts. [var. of COB] —**cub′bish,** *adj.* —**cub′-bish·ness,** *n.*

Cu·ba (kū′bə; *Sp.* kōō′bä), *n.* a republic S of Florida: largest island in the West Indies. 5,829,029 pop. (est. 1953); 44,218 sq. mi. *Cap.:* Havana. —**Cu′ban,** *adj., n.*

Cu·ba li·bre (kū′bə lē′brə), a drink consisting of rum and a kola drink.

cu·ba·ture (kū′bə chər), *n.* **1.** the determination of the cubic contents of a thing. **2.** cubic contents. [der. L *cubus* cube, on model of QUADRATURE]

cub·by (kŭb′ĭ), *n., pl.* -bies. a snug, confined place; a cubbyhole. [der. *cub* shed; cf. LG *kübje* shed]

cub·by·hole (kŭb′ĭ hōl′), *n.* a small enclosed space.

cube (kūb), *n., v.,* **cubed, cubing.** —*n.* **1.** a solid bounded by six equal squares, the angle between any two adjacent faces being a right angle. **2.** a piece of anything of this form. **3.** *Arith., Alg.* the third power of a quantity: *the cube of 4 is $4 \times 4 \times 4$, or 64.* —*v.t.* **4.** to make into a cube or cubes. **5.** to measure the cubic contents of. **6.** to raise to the third power; find the cube of. [t. L: m.s. *cubus,* t. Gk.: m. *kýbos* die, cube]

cu·beb (kū′bĕb), *n.* the spicy fruit or drupe of an East Indian piperaceous climbing shrub, *Piper cubeba,* dried in an unripe but fully grown state, and used in the treatment of urinary and bronchial disorders. [ME *quibibe,* t. F: m. *cubèbe,* ult. t. Ar.: m. *kabāba*]

cube root, the quantity of which a given quantity is the cube: *4 is the cube root of 64.*

cu·bic (kū′bĭk), *adj.* **1.** of three dimensions; solid, or pertaining to solid content: *a cubic foot* (the volume of a cube whose edges are each a foot long). **2.** having the form of a cube. **3.** *Arith., Alg., etc.,* being of the third power or degree. **4.** *Crystall.* belonging or pertaining to the isometric system of crystallization. Also, **cu′bi·cal.** —**cu′bi·cal·ly,** *adv.* —**cu′bi·cal·ness,** *n.*

cu·bi·cle (kū′bə kəl), *n.* **1.** a bedroom, esp. one of a number of small ones in a divided dormitory, as in English public schools. **2.** any small space or compartment partitioned off. [t. L: m.s. *cubiculum* bedchamber]

cubic measure, 1. the measurement of volume in cubic units. **2.** a system of such units, esp. that in which 1728 cubic inches = 1 cubic foot, 27 cubic feet = 1 cubic yard.

cu·bic·u·lum (kū bĭk′yə ləm), *n., pl.* -la (-lə). *Archaeol.* a burial chamber, as in catacombs. [t. L: bedroom]

cu·bi·form (kū′bə fôrm′), *adj.* formed like a cube.

cub·ism (kū′bĭz əm), *n. Art.* one of the aspects of post-impressionism, which aims to express the artist's emotions through arrangements on his canvas of geometrical forms in various colors and textures. —**cub′ist,** *n., adj.* —**cu·bis′tic,** *adj.* —**cu·bis′ti·cal·ly,** *adv.*

cu·bit (kū′bĭt), *n.* an ancient linear unit based on the length of the forearm, varying in extent, but usually from 17 to 21 inches. [ME, t. L: s. *cubitum* elbow, ell]

ăct, āble, dâre, ärt; ĕbb, ēqual; Ĭf, īce; hŏt, ōver, ôrder, oil, bŏŏk, ōōze, out; ŭp, ūse, ûrge; ə = a in alone; ch, chief; g, give; ng, ring; sh, shoe; th, thin; ŧħ, that; zh, vision.   See the full key on inside cover.

cu·boid (kū′boid), *adj.* **1.** resembling a cube in form. **2.** *Anat.* noting or pertaining to the outermost bone of the distal row of tarsal bones. —*n.* **3.** *Math.* a rectangular parallelepiped. **4.** *Anat.* the cuboid bone. —**cu·boi′dal**, *adj.*

cub reporter, *Colloq.* a reporter without experience.

cuck·ing stool (kŭk′ĭng), a former instrument of punishment consisting of a chair in which an offender, esp. a common scold, was strapped, to be jeered at and pelted by the crowd, or, sometimes, to be ducked.

cuck·old (kŭk′ōld), *n.* **1.** the husband of an unfaithful wife. —*v.t.* **2.** to make a cuckold of (a husband). [ME *cokewold*; orig. uncert.]

cuck·old·ry (kŭk′əl drĭ), *n.* making a cuckold of one.

cuck·oo (kŏŏk′ōō), *n.*, *pl.* **-os**, *v.*, **-ooed**, **-ooing**, *adj.* —*n.* **1.** any bird of the family *Cuculidae*, esp. *Cuculus canorus*, a common European migratory bird noted for its characteristic call, and for its loss of the instinct to build a nest. The females lay their eggs in the nests of various "host species," which rear the young cuckoos. **2.** the call of the cuckoo, or an imitation of it. **3.** a fool; simpleton. —*v.i.* **4.** to utter the call of the cuckoo or an imitation of it. —*v.t.* **5.** to repeat monotonously. —*adj.* **6.** *U.S. Slang.* crazy; silly; foolish. [ME *cucu* (imit. of its call). Cf. F *coucou*, G *kuckuk*]

cuckoo clock, a clock which announces the hours by a sound like the call of the cuckoo.

cuck·oo·flow·er (kŏŏk′ōō flou′ər), *n.* any of various plants, as the lady's-smock or the ragged robin.

cuck·oo·pint (kŏŏk′ōō pĭnt′), *n.* a common European species of arum, *Arum maculatum*; wake-robin.

cuck·oo·spit (kŏŏk′ōō spĭt′), *n.* **1.** a frothy secretion found on plants, exuded as a protective covering by the young of certain insects, as the froghoppers. **2.** an insect secreting this.

cu·cu·li·form (kū kū′lə fôrm′), *adj.* pertaining to or resembling the order *Cuculiformes*, containing the cuckoos, road runners, anis, etc. [f. s. L *cuculus* cuckoo + -(ɪ)ғоʀм]

cu·cul·late (kū′kə lāt′, kū kŭl′āt), *adj.* **1.** cowled; hooded. **2.** resembling a cowl or hood. Also, **cu·cul·lat·ed** (kū′kə lā′tĭd, kū kŭl′ā tĭd). [t. LL: m.s. *cucullātus* hooded]

cu·cum·ber (kū′kŭm bər), *n.* **1.** a creeping plant, *Cucumis sativus*, occurring in many cultivated forms, yielding a long fleshy fruit which is commonly eaten green as a salad and used for pickling. **2.** the fruit of this plant. **3.** any of various allied or similar plants. **4.** its fruit. [t. F (obs.): m. *cocombre*, g. s. L *cucumis*; r. ME *cucumer*, t. L: s. *cucumis*]

cucumber tree, **1.** any of several American magnolias, esp. *Magnolia acuminata*. **2.** any of certain other trees, as an East Indian tree of the genus *Averrhoa*.

cu·cu·mi·form (kū kū′mə fôrm′), *adj.* shaped like a cucumber; approximately cylindrical, with rounded or tapering ends. [f. L *cucumi(s)* cucumber + -ғоʀм]

cu·cur·bit (kū kûr′bĭt), *n.* a gourd. **2.** any cucurbitaceous plant. [ME *cucurbite*, t. F, t. L: s. *cucurbita* gourd]

cu·cur·bi·ta·ceous (kū kûr′bə tā′shəs), *adj.* belonging to the *Cucurbitaceae*, or gourd family of plants which includes the pumpkin, squash, cucumber, muskmelon, watermelon, etc. [f. s. L *cucurbita* gourd + -ᴀᴄᴇᴏᴜꜱ]

cud (kŭd), *n.* the portion of food which a ruminating animal returns from the first stomach to the mouth to chew a second time. [ME; OE *cudu*, var. of *cwidu*. See QUID]

cud·bear (kŭd′bâr′), *n.* a violet coloring matter obtained from various lichens, esp. *Lecanora tartarea*.

cud·dle (kŭd′əl), *v.*, **-dled**, **-dling**, *n.* —*v.t.* **1.** to draw or hold close in an affectionate manner; hug tenderly; fondle. —*v.i.* **2.** to lie close and snug; nestle; curl up in going to sleep. —*n.* **3.** act of cuddling; a hug; an embrace. [f. *couth*, adj., comfortable, friendly (OE *cūth* familiar) + *-le*, freq. suffix. Cf. FONDLE] —**cud·dle·some** (kŭd′əl səm), *adj.* —**cud′dly**, *adj.*

cud·dy[1] (kŭd′ĭ), *n.*, *pl.* **-dies**. **1.** a small cabin on a ship or boat, esp. one under the poop. **2.** (in small vessels) the galley or pantry. **3.** a small room; a cupboard. [orig. unknown]

cud·dy[2] (kŭd′ĭ, kŏŏd′ĭ), *n.*, *pl.* **-dies**. *Chiefly Scot.* **1.** a donkey. **2.** a stupid fellow. [orig. unknown]

cudg·el (kŭj′əl), *n.*, *v.*, **-eled**, **-eling**, or (*esp. Brit.*) **-elled**, **-elling**. —*n.* **1.** a short, thick stick used as a weapon; a club. **2.** take up the cudgels, to engage in a contest. —*v.t.* **3.** to strike with a cudgel; beat. **4.** cudgel one's brains, to think hard. [ME *cuggel*, OE *cycgel*, akin to G *kugel* ball] —**cudg′el·er**, *n.*

cud·weed (kŭd′wēd′), *n.* **1.** any of the woolly herbs constituting the composite genus *Gnaphalium*. **2.** any of various plants of allied genera.

cue[1] (kū), *n.* **1.** anything said or done on or behind the stage that is followed by a specific line or action: *each line of dialogue is a cue to the succeeding line; an off-stage door slam was his cue to enter.* **2.** a hint; an intimation; a guiding suggestion. **3.** the part one is to play; a prescribed or necessary course of action. **4.** humor; disposition. [?sp. of abbr. *q.* or *qu.* for L *quando* when]

cue[2] (kū), *n.*, *v.*, **cued**, **cuing**. —*n.* **1.** a long tapering rod, tipped with a soft leather pad, used to strike the ball in billiards, pool, etc. **2.** a queue of hair. **3.** a queue or file, as of persons awaiting their turn. —*v.t.* **4.** to tie into a cue or tail. [var. of *queue*, t. F]

cue ball, *Billiards, etc.* the ball struck by the cue as distinguished from the other balls on the table.

Cuen·ca (kwĕng′kä), *n.* a city in SW Ecuador. 53,871 (est. 1954).

cues·ta (kwĕs′tə), *n.* *U.S.* a long low ridge presenting a relatively steep face or escarpment on one side and a long gentle slope on the other.

cuff[1] (kŭf), *n.* **1.** a fold, band, or variously shaped piece serving as a trimming or finish for the bottom of a sleeve. **2.** a turned-up fold at the bottom of trouser legs, etc. **3.** the part of a gauntlet or long glove that extends over the wrist. **4.** a separate or detachable band or piece of linen or other material worn about the wrist, inside or outside of the sleeve. [ME *cuffe*, *coffe* glove, mitten; orig. uncert.]

cuff[2] (kŭf), *v.t.* **1.** to strike with the open hand; beat; buffet. —*n.* **2.** a blow with the fist or the open hand; a buffet. **3.** a handcuff. [cf. Swed. *kuffa* thrust, push]

cuff button, the button for a man's shirt cuff.

cuff link, a link which fastens the cuff of a shirt.

cui bo·no (kwē′ bō′nō, wī′), *Latin*. **1.** for whose benefit? **2.** for what use? of what good?

cui·rass (kwĭ räs′), *n.* **1.** a piece of defensive armor for the body, combining a breastplate and a piece for the back. **2.** the breastplate alone. **3.** any similar covering, as the protective armor of a ship. **4.** *Zool.* a hard shell or other covering forming an indurated defensive shield. —*v.t.* **5.** to equip or cover with a cuirass. [t. F: m. *cuirasse*, b. *cuir*(*ie*) leather armor (der. *cuir*, g. L *corium* leather) and Pr. (*coir*)*assa* (g. LL *coriācea*, fem., made of leather)]

cui·ras·sier (kwĭr′ə sĭr′), *n.* a cavalry soldier wearing a cuirass. [t. F]

cui·sine (kwĭ zēn′), *n.* **1.** the kitchen; the culinary department of a house, hotel, etc. **2.** style of cooking; cookery. [t. F, g. L *cocina*, *coquina* kitchen. See KITCHEN]

cuisse (kwĭs), *n.* a piece of armor to protect the thigh. Also, **cuish** (kwĭsh). See illus. under **armor**. [t. F: thigh, g. L *coxa* hip]

cuit·tle (kĭ′təl), *v.t.*, **-tled**, **-tling**. *Scot.* to wheedle; cajole, or coax. Also, **cui′tle**.

Cul·bert·son (kŭl′bərt sən), **Ely** (ē′lĭ), 1893–1955, U.S. authority and writer on contract bridge.

culch (kŭlch), *n.* **1.** the stones, old shells, etc., forming an oyster bed and furnishing points of attachment for the spawn of oyster. **2.** the spawn. **3.** *Chiefly Dial.* rubbish; refuse. —*v.t.* **4.** to prepare (an oyster bed) with culch. Also, **cultch**. [cf. OF *culche* bed]

cul-de-sac (kŭl′də săk′, kŏŏl′-; *Fr.* kʏd săk′), *n.* **1.** a saclike cavity, tube, or the like, open only at one end, as the caecum. **2.** a street, lane, etc. closed at one end; blind alley. **3.** *Mil.* the situation of a military force hemmed in on all sides except behind. [t. F: bottom of sack]

-cule, a diminutive suffix of nouns, as in *animalcule*, *molecule*. Also, **-cle**. [t. F, or t. L: m. *-culus*, *-cula*, *-culum*]

Cu·le·bra Cut (kŏŏ lā′brə; *Sp.* kŏŏ lĕ′brä), former name of **Gaillard Cut**.

cu·let (kū′lĭt), *n.* **1.** the small flat face forming the bottom of a brilliant. **2.** the part of medieval armor protecting the back of the body below the waist. [t. F (obs.), dim. of *cul* bottom, g. L *culus*. Cf. F *culasse* culet]

cu·lex (kū′lĕks), *n.*, *pl.* **-lices** (-lə sēz′), any mosquito of the genus *Culex*, including the common house mosquito, *Culex pipiens*. [t. L: a gnat]

cu·lic·id (kū lĭs′ĭd), *n.* **1.** any of the dipterous family *Culicidae*; a mosquito. —*adj.* **2.** belonging or pertaining to the *Culicidae*.

cu·li·nar·y (kū′lə nĕr′ĭ), *adj.* pertaining to the kitchen or to cookery; used in cooking. [t. L: m. s. *culīnārius*, der. *culīna* kitchen]

Cu·lion (kŏŏ lyōn′). *n.* one of the Philippine Islands, in the W part of the group, N of Palawan: leper colony. 7328 pop. (1939); 150 sq. mi.

cull[1] (kŭl), *v.t.* **1.** to choose; select; pick; gather the choice things or parts from. **2.** to collect; gather; pluck. —*n.* **3.** act of culling. **4.** something culled; esp. something picked out and put aside as inferior. [ME *culle*(n), t. OF: m. *coillir*, g. L *colligere* COLLECT]

cull[2] (kŭl), *n.* *Slang.* a fool; a dupe. [? short for CULLY]

Cul·len (kŭl′ən), **Countee** (koun tā′), 1903–46, U.S. poet.

cul·len·der (kŭl′ən dər), *n.* a colander.

cul·let (kŭl′ĭt), *n.* broken or waste glass suitable for remelting.

cul·lion (kŭl′yən), *n.* *Obs.* a base or vile fellow. [ME *coillion*, t. F: m. *couillon*, der. L *cōleus* testicle]

cul·ly (kŭl′ĭ), *n.*, *pl.* **-lies**, *v.*, **-lied**, **-lying**. *Slang* or *Colloq.* —*n.* **1.** a dupe. **2.** a man or fellow. —*v.t.* **3.** to trick; cheat; dupe. [short for CULLION]

culm[1] (kŭlm), *n.* **1.** coal dust; slack. **2.** anthracite, esp. of inferior grade. **3.** (*cap.*) *Geol.* a series of Lower Carboniferous rocks, mainly developed in parts of Europe, mostly dark-colored and siliceous. [var. of *coom* soot]

culm[2] (kŭlm), *n.* **1.** a stem or stalk, esp. the jointed and usually hollow stem of grasses. —*v.i.* **2.** to grow or develop into a culm. [t. L: s. *culmus* stalk. Cf. HALM]

cul·mif·er·ous (kŭl mĭf′ər əs), *adj.* bearing culms.

cul·mi·nant (kŭl′mə nənt), *adj.* culminating; topmost.

b., blend of, blended; c., cognate with; d., dialect, dialectal; der., derived from; f., formed from; g., going back to; m., modification of; r., replacing; s., stem of; t., taken from; ?, perhaps. See the full key on inside cover.

cul·mi·nate (kŭl/mə nāt/), v.i. -nated, -nating. 1. to reach the highest point, the summit, or highest development (usually fol. by *in*). 2. *Astron.* (of a celestial body) to be on the meridian, or reach the highest or the lowest altitude. [t. LL: m.s. *culminātus*, pp., crowned]

cul·mi·na·tion (kŭl/mə nā/shən), n. 1. act or fact of culminating. 2. that in which anything culminates; the highest point; the acme. 3. *Astron.* the position of a celestial body when it is on the meridian. —Syn. 2. climax, zenith, peak.

cu·lottes (kŭ lŏts/; Fr. kʏ lŏt/), n.pl. a skirtlike garment, separated and sewn like trousers. [t. F]

cul·pa·ble (kŭl/pə bəl), adj. deserving blame or censure; blameworthy. [t. L: m.s. *culpābilis* blameworthy; r. ME *coupable*, t. OF] —**cul/pa·bil/i·ty**, **cul/pa·ble·ness**, n. —**cul/pa·bly**, adv. —Syn. censurable, reprehensible. —Ant. praiseworthy.

Cul·pep·er (kŭl/pĕp/ər), n. Thomas, died 1689, British governor of the colony of Virginia, 1680-83.

cul·prit (kŭl/prĭt), n. 1. a person arraigned for an offense. 2. one guilty of an offense or fault. [orig. uncert.]

cult (kŭlt), n. 1. a particular system of religious worship, esp. with reference to its rites and ceremonies. 2. an instance of an almost religious veneration for a person or thing, esp. as manifested by a body of admirers: *a cult of Napoleon.* 3. the object of such devotion. 4. *Sociol.* a group having an exclusive sacred ideology and a series of rites centering around their sacred symbols. [t. L: s. *cultus* care, worship]

cultch (kŭlch), n., v.t. culch.

cul·ti·va·ble (kŭl/tə və bəl), adj. capable of being cultivated. Also, **cul·ti·vat·a·ble** (kŭl/tə və̄/tə bəl). [t. F, der. *cultiver* cultivate] —**cul/ti·va·bil/i·ty**, n.

cul·ti·vate (kŭl/tə vāt/), v.t. -vated, -vating. 1. to bestow labor upon (land) in raising crops; till; improve by husbandry. 2. to use a cultivator on. 3. to promote or improve the growth of (a plant, etc.) by labor and attention. 4. to produce by culture. 5. to develop or improve by education or training; train; refine. 6. to promote the growth or development of (an art, science, etc.); foster. 7. to devote oneself to (an art, etc.). 8. to seek to promote or foster (friendship, etc.). 9. to seek the acquaintance or friendship of (a person). [t. ML: m. s. *cultīvātus*, pp. of *cultīvāre*, der. *cultīvus* tilled, der. L *cultus*, pp. of *colere* till] —Ant. 8. neglect. 9. ignore.

cul·ti·vat·ed (kŭl/tə vā/tĭd), adj. 1. subjected to cultivation. 2. produced or improved by cultivation, as a plant. 3. educated; refined; cultured.

cul·ti·va·tion (kŭl/tə vā/shən), n. 1. act or art of cultivating. 2. state of being cultivated. 3. culture.

cul·ti·va·tor (kŭl/tə vā/tər), n. 1. one who or that which cultivates. 2. an implement for loosening the earth and destroying weeds when drawn between rows of growing plants.

cul·trate (kŭl/trāt), adj. sharp-edged and pointed, as a leaf. Also, **cul/trat·ed**. [t. L: m.s. *cultrātus*, der. *culter* knife]

cul·tur·al (kŭl/chər əl), adj. of or pertaining to culture or cultivation. —**cul/tur·al·ly**, adv.

cultural change, culture change.

cultural lag, culture lag.

cul·ture (kŭl/chər), n., v., -tured, -turing. —n. 1. action or practice of cultivating the soil; tillage. 2. the raising of plants or animals, esp. with a view to their improvement. 3. the product or growth resulting from such cultivation. 4. development or improvement by education or training. 5. enlightenment or refinement resulting from such development. 6. a particular state or stage of civilization, as in the case of a certain nation or period: *Greek culture.* 7. *Sociol.* the sum total of ways of living built up by a group of human beings, which is transmitted from one generation to another. 8. *Biol.* a. the cultivation of microorganisms, as bacteria, or of tissues, for scientific study, medicinal use, etc. b. the product or growth resulting from such cultivation. —v.t. 9. to subject to culture; cultivate. 10. *Biol.* a. to develop (microorganisms, tissues, etc.) in an artificial medium. b. to introduce (living material) into a culture medium. [ME, t. F, t. L: m. *cultūra* tending, cultivation] —Syn. 5. See education.

culture area, *Sociol.* a region having a distinct pattern of culture.

culture change, *Sociol.* the process by which a culture is significantly modified for one or more various reasons, such as contact with another culture. Also, **cultural change**.

culture complex, *Sociol.* a group of culture traits all interrelated and dominated by one essential trait: *political nationalism is a culture complex.*

cul·tured (kŭl/chərd), adj. 1. cultivated. 2. enlightened; refined.

culture diffusion, *Sociol.* the spread of elements of culture from a point of origin.

culture factor, *Sociol.* the whole of a culture at a given time as it affects further cultural development.

culture lag, *Sociol.* a failure of one portion of culture of a group to keep abreast of the development of other portions of the culture. Also, **cultural lag**.

culture pattern, *Sociol.* a group of interrelated cultural traits of some continuity.

culture trait, *Sociol.* any fact in human activity acquired in social life and transmitted by communication.

cul·tur·ist (kŭl/chər ĭst), n. 1. a cultivator. 2. an advocate or devotee of culture.

cul·tus¹ (kŭl/təs), n. a cult. [t. L]

cul·tus² (kŭl/təs), n. a common marine food fish, *Ophiodon elongatus*, of the Pacific coast of the U.S. Also, **cultus cod**. [t. Chinook: worthless]

cul·ver (kŭl/vər), n. a dove; a pigeon. [ME *colfre*, OE *culfre*]

Culver City, a city in SW California, W of Los Angeles. 32,163 (1960).

cul·ver·in (kŭl/vər ĭn), n. 1. a medieval form of musket. 2. a kind of heavy cannon, used in the 16th and 17th centuries. [t. F: m. *couleverine*, der. *couleuvre*, g. L *colubra* serpent. Cf. COBRA]

Cul·ver's root (kŭl/vərz), 1. the root of a tall scrophulariaceous herb, *Veronica virginica*, used in medicine as a cathartic and emetic. 2. the plant.

cul·vert (kŭl/vərt), n. a drain or channel crossing under a road, etc.; a sewer; a conduit. [orig. uncert.]

cum (kŭm, kŏŏm), prep. 1. with; together with; including (used sometimes in financial phrases, as *cum dividend*, etc., which are often abbreviated simply *cum*). 2. *Brit.* closely related: *the dwelling-cum-workshop was nearby.* [t. L]

Cu·mae (kū/mē), n. an ancient city on the coast of Campania, in SW Italy: reputedly the earliest Greek colony in Italy or Sicily. —**Cu·mae/an**, adj.

Cumaean sibyl, one of the legendary women of antiquity whose authority in matters of divination was acknowledged by the Romans.

cum·ber (kŭm/bər), v.t. 1. to hinder; hamper. 2. to overload; burden. 3. to inconvenience; trouble. —n. 4. hindrance. 5. that which cumbers. 6. *Archaic.* embarrassment; trouble. [t.MFlem.: m. *comber*, c. G *kummer* trouble] —**cum/ber·er**, n.

Cum·ber·land (kŭm/bər lənd), n. 1. a county in NW England. 285,338 pop. (1951); 1520 sq. mi. *Co. seat*: Carlisle. 2. a city in NW Maryland, on the Potomac. 33,415 (1960). 3. a river flowing from SE Kentucky through N Tennessee into the Ohio near Paducah, Kentucky. 687 mi.

Cumberland Gap, a pass in the Cumberland Mountains at the junction of the Virginia, Kentucky, and Tennessee boundaries. 1315 ft. high.

Cumberland Mountains, a W plateau of the Appalachian Mountains, largely in Kentucky and Tennessee. Highest point, ab. 4000 ft. Also, **Cumberland Plateau**.

cum·ber·some (kŭm/bər səm), adj. 1. burdensome; troublesome. 2. unwieldy; clumsy. —**cum/ber·some·ly**, adv. —**cum/ber·some·ness**, n.

cum·brance (kŭm/brəns), n. 1. trouble. 2. encumbrance.

cum·brous (kŭm/brəs), adj. cumbersome. —**cum/brous·ly**, adv. —**cum/brous·ness**, n.

cum gra·no sa·lis (kŭm grā/no sā/lĭs), *Latin.* with a grain of salt (that is, not too seriously).

cum·in (kŭm/ən), n. 1. a small apiaceous plant, *cuminum cyminum*, bearing aromatic seed-like fruit used in cookery and medicine. 2. the fruit or seeds.

cum lau·de (kŭm lô/dē, kŏŏm lou/dĕ), *Latin.* with honor (used in diplomas to grant the lowest of three special honors for grades above the average). See **magna cum laude** and **summa cum laude**.

cum·mer (kŭm/ər), n. *Scot.* 1. a godmother. 2. a female companion. 3. a girl or woman. [Scot., ME *commare*, t. F: m. *commère*, g. LL *commāter*. See COM-, MATER]

cum·mer·bund (kŭm/ər bŭnd/), n. (in India and elsewhere) a shawl or sash worn as a belt. Also, **kummerbund**. [t. Hind., Pers.: m. *kamarband* loin band]

Cum·mings (kŭm/ĭngz), n. E(dward) E(stlin) (ĕst/-lĭn), 1894-1962, U. S. poet, writer, and painter.

cum·quat (kŭm/kwŏt), n. kumquat.

cum·shaw (kŭm/shô), n. (in Chinese ports) a present; gratuity; tip. [t. Chinese: m. Amoy *kamsiâ* for Mandarin *kan hsieh* grateful thanks]

cu·mu·late (v. kū/myə lāt/; adj. kū/myə lĭt, -lāt/), v., -lated, -lating, adj. —v.t. 1. to heap up; amass; accumulate. —adj. 2. heaped up. [t. L: m. s. *cumulātus*, pp., heaped up]

cu·mu·la·tion (kū/myə lā/shən), n. 1. act of cumulating; accumulation. 2. a heap; mass.

cu·mu·la·tive (kū/myə lā/tĭv), adj. 1. increasing or growing by accumulation or successive additions. 2. formed by or resulting from accumulation or the addition of successive parts or elements. 3. *Finance.* of or pertaining to a dividend or interest which accumulates if not paid when due, and must be paid before those with an inferior claim to earnings can be paid. —**cu/mu·la/tive·ly**, adv. —**cu/mu·la/tive·ness**, n.

cumulative evidence, 1. evidence of which the parts reinforce one another, producing an effect stronger than any part taken by itself. 2. testimony repetitive of testimony earlier given.

cumulative voting, a system which gives each voter as many votes as there are persons to be elected from one representative district, allowing him to accumulate them on one candidate or to distribute them.

cu·mu·li·form (kū/myə lə fôrm/), adj. having the appearance or character of cumulus clouds.

cu·mu·lo-nim·bus (kū/myə lō nĭm/bəs), n. *Meteorol.* a heavy, tall mass of cloud whose summits rise in the form of mountains or towers, the upper parts having a fibrous texture characteristic of high clouds formed of ice crystals. This cloud is characteristic of thunderstorm conditions.

cu·mu·lous (kū′myə ləs) *adj.* of the form of a cumulus (cloud); composed of cumuli.

cu·mu·lus (kū′myə ləs), *n.*, *pl.* **-li** (-lī′). **1.** a heap; pile. **2.** *Meteorol.* a cloud with summit domelike or made up of rounded heaps, and with flat base, seen in fair weather and usually a brilliant white with a smooth, well-outlined structure.

Cu·nax·a (kū nåk′sə), *n.* an ancient town in Babylonia, near the Euphrates: famous battle between Cyrus the Younger and Artaxerxes II, 401 B.C.

cunc·ta·tion (kŭngk tā′shən), *n.* delay. [t. L: s. *cunctātio*, der. *cunctāri* delay] —**cunc·ta·tive** (kŭngk′tə tĭv), *adj.*

cunc·ta·tor (kŭngk tā′tər), *n.* a delayer. [t. L] —**cunc·ta·tor·ship′**, *n.*

cu·ne·al (kū′nĭ əl), *adj.* wedgelike; wedge-shaped. [f. s.L *cuneus* wedge +-AL¹]

cu·ne·ate (kū′nĭ ĭt, -āt′), *adj.* **1.** wedge-shaped. **2.** (of leaves) triangular and tapering to a point at the base. Also, **cu′ne·at′ed.** [t. L: m.s. *cuneātus*, pp., made wedge-shaped]

Cuneate leaf

cu·ne·i·form (kū nē′ə fôrm′, kū′nĭ ə fôrm′), *adj.* **1.** having the form of a wedge; wedge-shaped, as the characters anciently used in writing in Persia, Assyria, etc. **2.** noting or pertaining to this kind of writing. **3.** *Anat.* denoting or pertaining to any of various wedge-shaped bones, as of the tarsus. —*n.* **4.** cuneiform characters or writing. **5.** a cuneiform bone. Also, **cu·ni·form** (kū′nə fôrm′). [f. s. L *cuneus* wedge + -(I)FORM]

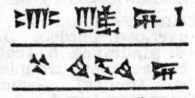

Assyrian cuneiform characters

cun·ner (kŭn′ər), *n.* a small labroid fish, *Tautogolabrus adopersus*, common on the North Atlantic coast of the U. S.

cun·ning (kŭn′ĭng), *n.* **1.** ability; skill; expertness. **2.** skill employed in a crafty manner; skillfulness in deceiving; craftiness; guile. —*adj.* **3.** exhibiting or wrought with ingenuity. **4.** artfully subtle or shrewd; crafty; sly. **5.** *U.S. Colloq.* quaintly pleasing or attractive, as a child or something little. **6.** *Archaic.* skillful; expert. [ME; var. of OE *cunnung*, der. *cunnan* know (how). See CAN¹] —**cun′ning·ly**, *adv.* —**cun′ning·ness**, *n.* —**Syn.** 2. shrewdness, artfulness, wiliness, trickery, finesse. *i*ntrigue CUNNING, ARTIFICE, CRAFT imply an inclination toward deceit, slyness, and trickery. CUNNING implies a shrewd, often instinctive skill in concealing or disguising the real purposes of one's actions: *not intelligence but a low kind of cunning.* An ARTIFICE is a clever, unscrupulous ruse, used to mislead others: *a successful artifice to conceal one's motives.* CRAFT suggests underhand methods and the use of deceptive devices and tricks to attain one's ends: *craft and deceitfulness in every act* 4. artful, wily, tricky, foxy.

cup (kŭp), *n.*, *v.*, cupped, cupping. —*n.* **1.** a small, open container, esp. of porcelain or metal, used mainly to drink from. **2.** an ornamental cup or other article, esp. of precious metal, offered as a prize for a contest. **3.** the containing part of a goblet or the like. **4.** a cup with its contents. **5** the quantity contained in a cup. **6.** a unit of capacity, equal to 8 fluid ounces, or 16 tablespoons. **7.** any of various beverages, as a mixture of wine and various ingredients: *claret cup.* **8.** the chalice used in the eucharist. **9.** the wine of the eucharist. **10.** something to be partaken of or endured, as suffering. **11.** (*pl.*) the drinking of intoxicating liquors. **12.** (*pl.*) a state of intoxication. **13.** any cuplike utensil, organ, part, cavity, etc. **14.** *Golf.* a. the metal receptacle within the hole. b. the hole itself. **15.** (*cap.*) *Astron.* the southern constellation Crater. **16.** a cupping glass. **17. in one's cups,** intoxicated; tipsy. —*v.t.* **18.** to take or place in or as in a cup: *He cupped his ear with the palm of his hand to hear better.* **19.** to use a cupping glass on. [ME and OE *cuppe*, t. LL: m. *cuppa* cup, var. of L *cūpa* tub, cask] —**cup′like′**, *adj.*

cup·bear·er (kŭp′bâr′ər), *n.* an attendant who fills and hands the cups in which drink is served.

cup·board (kŭb′ərd), *n.* **1.** a closet with shelves for dishes, etc. **2.** *Brit.* any small closet or cabinet, for clothes, etc. [ME, f. CUP + BOARD]

cupboard love, love inspired by considerations of good feeding.

cup·cake (kŭp′kāk′), *n.* a small cake baked in a cup-shaped pan.

cu·pel (kū′pəl, kū pĕl′), *n.*, *v.*, **-peled, -peling** or (*esp. Brit.*) **-pelled, -pelling.** *n.* **1.** a small cuplike porous vessel, usually made of bone ash, used in assaying, as for separating gold and silver from lead. **2.** a receptacle or furnace bottom in which silver is refined. —*v.t.* **3.** to heat or refine in a cupel. [t. F: m. *coupelle,* ult. der. LL *cuppa* CUP] —**cu·pel·la·tion** (kū′pə lā′shən), *n.*

cup·ful (kŭp′fŏŏl′), *n.*, *pl.* **-fuls.** a quantity sufficient to fill a cup.

Cu·pid (kū′pĭd), *n.* **1.** the Roman god of love, son of Venus, commonly represented as a winged boy with bow and arrows. See Eros. **2.** (*l.c.*) a similar winged being, or a representation of one, esp. as symbolical of love. [ME *Cupide,* t. L: m. *Cupīdo,* lit., desire, passion]

cu·pid·i·ty (kū pĭd′ə tĭ), *n.* eager or inordinate desire, esp. to possess something. [t. L: m. s. *cupiditas* passionate desire]

cup of tea, *Brit. Colloq.* a favored object: *that show wasn't my cup of tea.*

cu·po·la (kū′pə lə), *n.* **1.** a rounded vault or dome constituting, or built upon, a roof; a small domelike or towerlike structure on a roof. **2.** a dome of relatively small size, esp. when forming part of a minor or decorative element of a larger building. **3.** any of various domelike structures, organs, etc. **4.** *Metall.* a vertical, circular furnace for melting cast iron. It uses coke as a fuel, a flux, and a forced blast. [t. It.: dome, t. LL: s. *cūpula,* dim. of *cūpa* tub, cask]

cupped (kŭpt), *adj.* hollowed out like a cup; cup-shaped.

cup·per (kŭp′ər), *n.* one who performs the operation of cupping.

cup·ping (kŭp′ĭng), *n.* the process of drawing blood from the body by scarification and the application of a cupping glass, or by the application of a cupping glass without scarification, as for relieving internal congestion.

cupping glass, a glass vessel in which a partial vacuum is created, as by heat, used in cupping.

cupr-, a word element referring to copper. Also, before consonants, **cupri-, cupro-.** [t. L, comb. form of *cuprum*]

cu·pre·ous (kū′prĭ əs), *adj.* **1.** copper-colored; metallic reddish-brown. **2.** consisting of or containing copper; copperlike. [t. L: m. *cupreus* of copper]

cu·pric (kū′prĭk), *adj. Chem.* of or containing copper, esp. in the divalent state (Cu+²), as *cupric oxide,* CuO.

cu·prif·er·ous (kū prĭf′ər əs), *adj.* yielding copper.

cu·prite (kū′prīt), *n.* a mineral, cuprous oxide, Cu₂O, occurring in red crystals and granular masses: an ore of copper.

cu·pro·nick·el (kū′prə nĭk′əl), *Metall.* —*n.* **1.** an alloy of copper containing nickel. —*adj.* **2.** containing copper and nickel.

cu·prous (kū′prəs), *adj. Chem.* containing monovalent copper (Cu+¹), as *cuprous oxide,* Cu₂O.

cu·prum (kū′prəm), *n.* copper. *Chem. abbr.:* Cu [t. L]

cu·pule (kū′pūl), *n.* **1.** *Bot.* a cup-shaped involucre consisting of indurated, cohering bracts, as in the acorn. **2.** *Zool.* a small cup-shaped sucker or similar organ or part. [t. L: m.s. *cūpula,* dim. of *cūpa* tub, cup]

*Cupules (def. 1)
A, of acorn; B, of fungus*

cur (kûr), *n.* **1.** a snarling, worthless, or outcast dog. **2.** a low, despicable person. [ME *curre*; imit.]

cur·a·ble (kyŏŏr′ə bəl), *adj.* that may be cured. —**cur′a·bil′i·ty, cur′a·ble·ness,** *n.* —**cur′a·bly,** *adv.*

Cu·ra·çao (kyŏŏr′ə sō′, kŏŏ′rä sou′), *n.* **1.** the main island of the Netherlands Antilles, off the NW coast of Venezuela. 118,858 pop. (est. 1955); 173 sq. mi. *Cap.:* Willemstad. **2.** Netherlands Antilles. **3.** (*l.c.*) Also **cu′ra·çoa′.** a cordial or liqueur flavored with the peel of the (bitter) **Curaçao orange.**

cu·ra·cy (kyŏŏr′ə sĭ), *n.*, *pl.* **-cies.** the office or position of a curate.

cu·ragh (kûr′əкн, kûr′ə), *n.* currach.

cu·ra·re (kyŏŏ rä′rĭ), *n.* **1.** a blackish resinlike substance from *Strychnos toxifera* and other tropical plants of the genus *Strychnos,* and from *Chondodendron tomentosum,* used by South American Indians for poisoning arrows, and employed in physiological experiments, etc., for arresting the action of the motor nerves. **2.** a plant yielding it. Also, **cu·ra′ri.** [t. Carib: m. *kurare*]

cu·ra·rize (kyŏŏr′ə rīz′, kyŏŏ rä′rīz), *v.t.*, **-rized, -rizing.** to administer curare to, as in vivisection. —**cu′ra·ri·za′tion,** *n.*

cu·ras·sow (kyŏŏr′ə sō′, kyŏŏ răs′ō), *n.* any of various large, arboreal, gallinaceous South and Central American birds belonging to the family Cracidae, somewhat resembling the turkey and sometimes domesticated. [named after the island of Curaçao]

cu·rate (kyŏŏr′ĭt), *n.* **1.** *Chiefly Brit.* a clergyman employed as assistant or deputy of a rector or vicar. **2.** *Archaic.* any ecclesiastic entrusted with the cure of souls, as a parish priest. [ME *curat,* t. ML: s. *cūrātus,* der. *cūra.* See CURE, n.]

cu·ra·tive (kyŏŏr′ə tĭv), *adj.* **1.** serving to cure or heal; pertaining to curing or remedial treatment; remedial. —*n.* **2.** a curative agent; a remedy. —**cur′a·tive·ly,** *adv.* —**cur′a·tive·ness,** *n.* —Ant. 1. injurious.

cu·ra·tor (kyŏŏ rä′tər for 1, 2; kyŏŏr′ə tər for 3), *n.* **1.** the person in charge of a museum, art collection, etc.; a custodian. **2.** a manager; overseer; superintendent. **3.** a guardian, as of a minor, lunatic, etc. [t. L: overseer, guardian; r. ME *curatour,* t. AF] —**cu·ra·to·ri·al** (kyŏŏr′ə tôr′ĭ əl), *adj.* —**cu·ra′tor·ship′,** *n.*

curb (kûrb), *n.* **1.** a chain or strap attached to the upper ends of the branches of a bit and passing under the horse's lower jaw, used in restraining the horse. See diag. under harness. **2.** anything that restrains or controls; a restraint; a check. **3.** an enclosing framework or border. **4.** Also, *Brit.,* **kerb.** a line of joined stones, concrete, etc., at the edge of a street, wall, etc. **5.** the framework round the top of a well. **6.** the sidewalk or street as a market for the sale of securities: *the New York Curb Market was formerly a street market.* **7.** *Vet. Sci.* a swelling on the lower part of the back of the hock of a horse, often causing lameness. —*v.t.* **8.** to control as with a curb; restrain; check. **9.** to put a curb on (a horse). **10.** Also, *Brit.*, **kerb.** to furnish with, or protect by a curb. [late ME, t. F: m. *courbe* curved, g. L *curvus* bent, crooked] —**Syn. 8.** bridle, repress, control. See **check.**

curb bit, a bit for a horse, which, by slight effort, produces great pressure on the mouth to control the animal.

curb·ing (kûr′bĭng), *n.* the material forming a curb.

curb roof, a roof with two slopes to each face, the lower being the steeper.

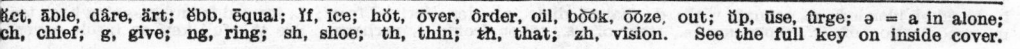

Diagram of a curb roof

curb·stone (kûrb′stōn′), *n.* one of the stones, or a range of stones, forming a curb, as along the outer edge of a sidewalk, etc. Also, *Brit.*, **kerbstone.**

curch (kûrch), *n.* a kerchief.

cur·cu·li·o (kûrkū′lĭ ō′), *n., pl.* **-lios.** any of certain snout beetles or weevils, as the **plum curculio,** *Conotrachelus nenuphar,* injurious to fruit. [t. L: weevil]

cur·cu·ma (kûr′kyŏŏ mə), *n.* any plant of the zingiberaceous genus *Curcuma,* of the East Indies, etc., as *C. longa* or *C. zedoaria,* the former yielding turmeric and the latter zedoary. [NL, t. Ar.: m. *kurkum* saffron, turmeric]

curd (kûrd), *n.* **1.** (*often pl.*) a substance consisting of casein, etc., obtained from milk by coagulation, used for making into cheese or eaten as food. **2.** any substance resembling this. —*v.t., v.i.* **3.** to turn into curd; coagulate; congeal. [ME *crud.* Cf. **crowd**]

curd cheese, *Chiefly Brit.* cottage cheese.

cur·dle (kûr′dəl), *v.t., v.i.* **-dled, -dling. 1.** to change into curd; coagulate; congeal. **2. curdle the blood,** to terrify with horror or fear. [freq. of **curd**]

curd·y (kûr′dĭ), *adj.* like curd; full of or containing curd; coagulated.

cure (kyŏŏr), *n., v.,* **cured, curing.** —*n.* **1.** a method or course of remedial treatment, as for disease. **2.** successful remedial treatment; restoration to health. **3.** a means of healing or curing; a remedy. **4.** act or a method of curing meat, fish, etc. **5.** spiritual charge of the people in a certain district. **6.** the office or district of one exercising such oversight. —*v.t.* **7.** to restore to health. **8.** to relieve or rid of something troublesome or detrimental, as an illness, a bad habit, etc. **9.** to prepare (meat, fish, etc.) for preservation, by salting, drying, etc. —*v.i.* **10.** to effect a cure. **11.** to become cured. [ME, t. OF, g. L *cūra* care, treatment, concern, ML an ecclesiastical cure] —**cure′less,** *adj.* —**cure′less·ly,** *adv.* —**cur′er,** *n.*
—**Syn. 8.** CURE, HEAL, REMEDY imply making well, whole, or right. CURE is especially applied to the eradication of disease or sickness: *to cure a fever, a headache.* HEAL suggests the making whole of wounds, sores, etc : *to heal a cut or a burn.* REMEDY is a more general word which includes both the others and applies also to making wrongs right: *to remedy a mistake, a misunderstanding.*

cu·ré (kyŏŏ rā′; *Fr.* kyrē′), *n.* (in French use) a parish priest. [t. F, g. VL *cūrātus.* See **curate**]

cure-all (kyŏŏr′ôl′), *n.* a cure for all ills; a panacea.

cu·ret·tage (kyŏŏr ĕt′ĭj, kyŏŏr′ə tāzh′), *n.* the process of curetting. [t. F]

cu·rette (kyŏŏ rĕt′), *n., v.,* **-retted, -retting.** —*n.* **1.** a scoop-shaped surgical instrument used for removing diseased tissue from body cavities such as the uterus, etc. —*v.t.* **2.** to scrape with a curette. [t. F, der. *curer* cleanse, g. L *cūrāre*]

cur·few (kûr′fū), *n.* **1.** the ringing of a bell at a fixed hour in the evening as a signal for covering or extinguishing fires, as practiced in medieval Europe. **2.** the ringing of an evening bell as later practiced. **3.** the ringing of a signal, esp. by a bell, at a certain hour in the evening, as for children to retire from the streets. **4.** the time of ringing such a bell. **5.** the bell itself. **6.** its sound. [ME *corfew,* t. AF: m. *coeverfu,* var. of OF *cuevreu* cover-fire]

cu·ri·a (kyŏŏr′ĭə), *n., pl.* **curiae** (kyŏŏr′ĭ ē′). **1.** one of the political subdivisions of each of the three tribes of ancient Roman citizens. **2.** the building in which such a division or group met, as for worship or public deliberation. **3.** the senate house in ancient Rome. **4.** the senate of ancient Italian towns. **5.** the Pope and those about him at Rome engaged in the administration of the papal authority (the **Curia Romana**). **6.** the papal court. [L and ML] —**cu′ri·al,** *adj.*

cu·rie (kyŏŏr′ē, kyŏŏ rē′), *n. Phys. Chem., Physics.* the unit of radioactivity equivalent to 3.70 × 10¹⁰ disintegrations per second. [named after Marie **Curie**]

Cu·rie (kyŏŏr′ē, kyŏŏ rē′; *Fr.* kyrē′), *n.* **1. Marie,** 1867-1934, Polish physicist and chemist, in France: with her husband, Pierre, discovered radium in 1898. **2. Pierre,** 1859-1906, French physicist and chemist.

Curie constant, *Physics.* the constant relating absolute temperature to the magnetic susceptibility of a given substance.

Curie point, *Physics.* the temperature at which a substance loses its magnetic susceptibility.

Curie's law, *Physics.* the law that the magnetic susceptibility of a substance is inversely proportional to the absolute temperature. [named after Pierre **Curie**]

cu·ri·o (kyŏŏr′ĭ ō′), *n., pl.* **curios.** any article, object of art, etc., valued as a curiosity. [short for **curiosity**]

cu·ri·o·sa (kyŏŏr′ĭ ō′sa), *n.pl.* books, pamphlets, etc., dealing with unusual subjects, esp. pornographic ones (a term used by booksellers and collectors). [t. L: curious (things)]

cu·ri·os·i·ty (kyŏŏr′ĭ ŏs′ə tĭ), *n., pl.* **-ties. 1.** the desire to learn or know about anything; inquisitiveness. **2.** curious or interesting quality, as from strangeness. **3.** a curious, rare, or novel thing. **4.** *Obs.* carefulness; fastidiousness. [t. L: m.s. *cūriōsitas*] —**Syn. 3.** curio, rarity, wonder, marvel, phenomenon, freak.

cu·ri·ous (kyŏŏr′ĭ əs), *adj.* **1.** desirous of learning or knowing; inquisitive. **2.** prying; meddlesome. **3.** *Archaic.* made or prepared with skill or art. **4.** marked by special care or pains, as an inquiry or investigation. **5.** exciting attention or interest because of strangeness or novelty. **6.** *Colloq.* odd; eccentric. **7.** (of books) indelicate, indecent, or obscene. **8.** *Obs.* careful; fastidious. **9.** *Obs.* marked by intricacy or subtlety. [ME, t. OF: m. *curios,* g. L *cūriōsus* careful, inquiring, inquisitive] —**cu′ri·ous·ly,** *adv.* —**cu′ri·ous·ness,** *n.*
—**Syn. 1, 2.** CURIOUS, INQUISITIVE, MEDDLESOME, PRYING refer to taking an undue (and petty) interest in others' affairs. CURIOUS implies a desire to know what is not properly one's concern: *curious about a neighbor's habits.* INQUISITIVE implies asking impertinent questions in an effort to satisfy curiosity: *inquisitive in asking about a neighbor's habits.* MEDDLESOME implies thrusting oneself into and taking an active part in other people's affairs (or handling their possessions) entirely unasked and unwelcomed: *a meddlesome aunt who tries to run the affairs of a family.* PRYING implies a meddlesome and persistent inquiring into others' affairs: *prying into the secrets of a business firm.* **5.** strange, unusual, singular, novel, rare.

Cu·ri·ti·ba (kōō′rē tē′ba), *n.* a city in S Brazil. 138,178 (1950). Also, **Cu′ri·ty·ba.**

cu·ri·um (kyŏŏr′ĭ əm), *n. Chem.* an element not found in nature, but discovered in 1945 among the products of the bombardment of uranium and plutonium by very energetic helium ions. *Symbol:* Cm; *at. no.:* 96.

curl (kûrl), *v.t.* **1.** to form into ringlets, as the hair. **2.** to form into a spiral or curved shape; coil. **3.** *Obs.* to adorn with, or as with, curls or ringlets. —*v.i.* **4.** to form curls or ringlets, as the hair. **5.** to coil. **6.** to become curved or undulated. **7.** *Scot.* to play at curling. —*n.* **8.** a ringlet of hair. **9.** anything of a spiral or curved shape. **10.** a coil. **11.** act of curling. **12.** state of being curled. **13.** any of various diseases of plants with which the leaves are distorted, fluted, or puffed because of unequal growth. [ME *crolled, crulled,* ppl. adj., t. MD or MFlem.]

curl·er (kûr′lər), *n.* **1.** one who or that which curls. **2.** a player at curling.

cur·lew (kûr′lōō), *n.* **1.** any of several shore birds of the genera *Numenius* and *Phaeopus,* with long slender downward curved bill, as the **common curlew** (*Numenius arquatus*) of Europe and the **Hudsonian curlew** (*Phaeopus hudsonicus*) of America. **2.** any of certain superficially similar birds. [ME *corlewe,* t. OF: m. *courlieu;* imit.]

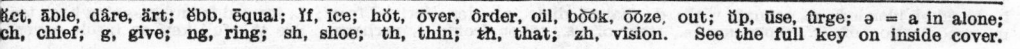

curl·i·cue (kûr′lĭ kū′), *n.* a fantastic curl or twist. Also, **curl′y·cue′.**

curl·ing (kûr′lĭng), *n.* a Scottish game played on the ice, in which large, smooth, rounded stones are slid toward a mark called the tee.

Long-billed curlew, Numenius americanus (26 in. long)

curling iron, a rod of iron to be used when heated for curling the hair, which is twined around it. Also, **curling irons, curling tongs.**

curl·pa·per (kûrl′pā′pər), *n.* a piece of paper on which a lock of hair is rolled up tightly, to remain until the hair has become fixed in a curl.

curl·y (kûr′lĭ), *adj.,* **curlier, curliest. 1.** curling or tending to curl: *curly blonde hair.* **2.** having curls: *curly-headed.* —**curl′i·ness,** *n.*

cur·mudg·eon (kər mŭj′ən), *n.* an irascible, churlish fellow. —**cur·mudg′eon·ly,** *adj.*

curn (kûrn), *n. Scot.* **1.** a grain. **2.** a small quantity or number. [? akin to **kernel**]

curr (kûr), *v.i.* to make a low, murmuring sound, like the purring of a cat. [cf. Icel. *kurra* murmur]

cur·rach (kŭr′əкн, kŭr′ə), *n. Scot., Irish.* a coracle. Also, **curagh, cur′ragh.** [t. Gaelic or Irish: m. *curach.* Cf. Welsh *corwg*]

cur·ra·jong (kŭr′ə jŏng′), *n.* the native name of *Plagianthus sidoides,* a malvaceous shrub or tree of Australia and Tasmania.

cur·rant (kûr′ənt), *n.* **1.** a small seedless raisin, produced chiefly in California and in the Levant, used in cookery, etc. **2.** the small, edible, acid, round fruit or berry of certain wild or cultivated shrubs of the genus *Ribes,* as *R. sativum* (**red currant** and **white currant**) and *R. nigrum* (**black currant**). **3.** the shrub itself. **4.** any of various similar fruits or shrubs. [ME (*raysons of*) *Coraunte,* t. AF: m. (*raisins de*) *Coraunlz* (raisins of) Corinth; so called because orig. from Corinth in Greece]

cur·ren·cy (kûr′ən sĭ), *n.*, *pl.* **-cies.** **1.** that which is current as a medium of exchange; the money in actual use. **2.** fact or quality of being passed on, as from person to person. **3.** general acceptance; prevalence; vogue. **4.** fact or state of passing in time. **5.** circulation, as of coin. **6.** *Obs. or Rare.* a running; flowing.

cur·rent (kûr′ənt), *adj.* **1.** passing in time, or belonging to the time actually passing: *the current month.* **2.** passing from one to another; circulating, as coin. **3.** publicly reported or known. **4.** prevalent. **5.** generally accepted; in vogue. **6.** *Now Rare.* running or flowing. **7.** *Obs.* genuine; authentic. —*n.* **8.** a flowing; flow, as of a river. **9.** that which flows, as a stream. **10.** a portion of a large body of water, or of air, etc., moving in a certain direction. **11.** *Elect.* **a.** a movement or flow of electricity. **b.** the rate of flow, in amperes. **12.** course, as of time or events; the main course; the general tendency. [t. L: s. *currens,* ppr., running; r. ME *corant,* t. OF] —**cur′rent·ly,** *adv.*
—**Syn. 4.** CURRENT, PRESENT, PREVAILING, PREVALENT, refer to something generally or commonly in use. That which is CURRENT is in general circulation or a matter of common knowledge or acceptance: *current usage in English.* PRESENT refers to that which is in general use now; it is more limited than CURRENT, as to time: *present customs.* That which is PREVAILING is that which has superseded others: *prevailing fashion.* That which is PREVALENT exists or is spread widely: *a prevalent idea.* **9.** See **stream.** —**Ant. 4.** obsolete. **5.** old-fashioned.

current assets, *Com.* assets readily convertible into cash without serious sacrifice.

current collector, *Elect.* (on a trolley, subway, etc.) any device, as a pantograph (def. 2), for maintaining electrical contact between a contact conductor and the electrical circuit of the vehicle on which the collector is mounted.

current density, *Elect.* the rate of flow in amperes per unit of cross-sectional area at a given place in a conductor.

current expenses, regularly continuing expenditures for the maintenance and the carrying on of business.

current liabilities, *Com.* indebtedness maturing within one year.

cur·ri·cle (kûr′ə kəl), *n.* a light, two-wheeled, open carriage drawn by two horses abreast. [t. L: m. s. *curriculum* a running, course, race, race chariot]

cur·ric·u·lum (kə rĭk′yə ləm), *n.*, *pl.* **-lums, -la** (-lə). **1.** the aggregate of courses of study given in a school, college, university, etc. **2.** the regular or a particular course of study in a school, college, etc. [t. L. See CURRICLE] —**cur·ric′u·lar,** *adj.*

cur·ri·er (kûr′ĭ ər), *n.* **1.** one who dresses and colors leather after it is tanned. **2.** one who curries (a horse, etc.). [ME *corier,* t. OF, g. L *coriārius* tanner]

Currier and Ives, the lithography firm of Nathaniel Currier and James Merritt Ives, founded originally by Currier (about 1834), which produced prints of American history, life, and manners.

cur·ri·er·y (kûr′ĭ ər ĭ), *n.*, *pl.* **-eries.** **1.** the occupation or business of a currier. **2.** the place where it is carried on.

cur·rish (kûr′ĭsh), *adj.* **1.** of or pertaining to a cur. **2.** curlike; snarling; quarrelsome. **3.** contemptible. —**cur′rish·ly,** *adv.* —**cur′rish·ness,** *n.*

cur·ry[1] (kûr′ĭ), *n.*, *pl.* **-ries,** *v.*, **-ried, -rying. 1.** an East Indian sauce or relish in many varieties, containing a mixture of spices, seeds, vegetables, fruits, etc., eaten with rice or combined with meat, fish, or other food. **2.** a dish prepared with a curry sauce or with curry powder. —*v.t.* **3.** to prepare (food) with a curry sauce or with curry powder. [t. Tamil: m. *kari* sauce]

cur·ry[2] (kûr′ĭ), *v.t.,* **-ried, -rying. 1.** to rub and clean (a horse, etc.) with a comb; currycomb. **2.** to dress (tanned hides) by soaking, scraping, beating, coloring, etc. **3.** to beat; thrash. **4. curry favor,** to seek favor by a show of kindness, courtesy, flattery, etc. [ME *cory,* t. OF: m. *coreer,* earlier *conreder* put in order, f. *con-* CON- + *-reder* make ready (ult. t. Gmc. See REDD)]

cur·ry·comb (kûr′ĭ kōm′), *n.* **1.** a comb, usually with rows of metal teeth, for currying horses, etc. —*v.t.* **2.** to rub or clean with such a comb.

curry powder, a powdered preparation of spices and other ingredients, notably turmeric, used for making curry sauce or for seasoning food.

curse (kûrs), *n.,* *v.,* **cursed** or **curst, cursing.** —*n.* **1.** the expression of a wish that evil, etc., befall another. **2.** an ecclesiastical censure or anathema. **3.** a profane oath. **4.** evil that has been invoked upon one. **5.** something accursed. **6.** the cause of evil, misfortune, or trouble. —*v.t.* **7.** to wish or invoke evil, calamity, injury, or destruction upon. **8.** to swear at. **9.** to blaspheme. **10.** to afflict with great evil. **11.** to excommunicate. —*v.i.* **12.** to utter curses; swear profanely. [ME *curs,* OE *cūrs,* der. *cūrsian,* v., curse, blame, reprove (whence ME *cursen*), t. OIrish: m.s. *cūrsagim* I blame] —**curs′er,** *n.*
—**Syn. 1.** imprecation, execration, fulmination, malediction. **6.** bane, scourge, plague, affliction, torment. **7–9.** CURSE, BLASPHEME, SWEAR are often interchangeable in the sense of using profane language. However, CURSE is the general word for the heartfelt invoking or violent or angry calling down of evil on another: *they called down curses on their enemies.* To BLASPHEME is to speak contemptuously or

with abuse of God or of sacred things: *to blaspheme openly.* To SWEAR is to use the name of God or of some holy person or thing as an exclamation to add force or show anger: *to swear in every sentence.* —**Ant. 7.** bless.

curs·ed (kûr′sĭd, kûrst), *adj.* **1.** under a curse; damned. **2.** deserving a curse; hateful; abominable. **3.** *Dial.* cantankerous; ill-tempered; cross. —**curs′ed·ly,** *adj.* —**curs′ed·ness,** *n.* —**Syn. 2.** damnable, execrable.

cur·sive (kûr′sĭv), *adj.* **1.** (of writing or printing type) in flowing strokes, with the letters joined together. —*n.* **2.** a cursive letter or printing type. [t. ML: m. s. *cursīvus,* der. L *cursus* a running] —**cur′sive·ly,** *adv.*

cur·so·ri·al (kûr sōr′ĭ əl), *adj. Zool.* **1.** adapted for running, as the feet and skeleton of dogs, horses, etc. **2.** having limbs adapted for running, as certain birds, insects, etc.

cur·so·ry (kûr′sə rĭ), *adj.* going rapidly over something, without noticing details; hasty; superficial. [t. L: m. s. *cursōrius* pertaining to a runner or a race] —**cur′so·ri·ly,** *adv.* —**cur′so·ri·ness,** *n.*

curst (kûrst), *v.* **1.** pt. and pp. of **curse.** —*adj.* **2.** cursed.

curt (kûrt), *adj.* **1.** short; shortened. **2.** brief in speech, etc. **3.** rudely brief in speech, manner, etc. [t. L: s. *curtus* cut short, clipped. Cf. SHORT] —**curt′ly,** *adv.* —**curt′ness,** *n.* —**Syn. 2.** See **blunt.**

cur·tail (kər tāl′), *v.t.* to cut short; cut off a part of; abridge; reduce; diminish. [var. (by assoc. with TAIL) of obs. *curtal,* v., dock. See CURTAL, adj.] —**cur·tail′er,** *n.* —**cur·tail′ment,** *n.* —**Syn.** lessen, dock. See **shorten.**

curtail step (kûr′tāl), the first or bottom step of a stair, when it is finished in a curved line at its outer end.

cur·tain (kûr′tən, -tĭn), *n.* **1.** a hanging piece of fabric used to shut out the light from a window, adorn a room, etc. **2.** anything that shuts off, covers, or conceals: *a curtain of artillery fire.* **3.** *Archit.* a flat portion of a wall, connecting two towers, projecting structures, or the like. **4.** *Fort.* the part of a wall or rampart connecting two bastions, towers, or the like. See diag. under **bastion.** —*v.t.* **5.** to provide, shut off, conceal, or adorn with, or as with, a curtain. [ME *curtine,* t. OF, g. LL *cortina* curtain]
—**Syn. 1.** drapery, portière, lambrequin, valance. CURTAIN, BLIND, SHADE, SHUTTER agree in being covers for a window, to shut out light or keep persons from looking in. CURTAIN, BLIND, and SHADE may mean a cover, usually of cloth, which can be rolled up and down inside the window. CURTAIN, however, may also refer to a drapery at a window; and a Venetian BLIND consists of slats mounted on tapes for drawing up or down and varying the pitch of the slats. BLIND and SHUTTER may mean a cover made of two wooden frames with movable slats, attached by hinges outside a window and pulled together or opened at will. SHUTTERS may mean also a set of panels (wooden or iron) put up outside small shops or stores at closing time.

curtain call, the appearance of performers at the conclusion of a performance in response to the applause of the audience.

curtain lecture, a private scolding, esp. one by a wife to her husband.

curtain raiser, a short play acted before a main play.

cur·tal (kûr′təl), *Obs. or Archaic.* —*adj.* **1.** wearing a short frock: *a curtal friar.* —*n.* **2.** anything docked or cut short. **3.** a 16th century bassoon. [t. F: m. *courtault,* der. *court* short, g. L *curtus*]

cur·te·sy (kûr′tə sĭ), *n.,* *pl.* **-sies.** *Law.* the life tenure formerly enjoyed by a husband in his wife's land inheritance after her death, provided they had issue able to inherit: *a tenancy by the curtesy.* [var. of COURTESY]

cur·ti·lage (kûr′tə lĭj), *n. Law.* the area of land occupied by a dwelling and its yard and outbuildings, actually enclosed or considered as enclosed. [ME, t. AF, der. OF *courtil* little court. See COURT]

Cur·tis (kûr′tĭs), *n.* **George William,** 1824–92, U.S. essayist, editor, and reformer.

Cur·tiss (kûr′tĭs), *n.* **Glenn Hammond,** 1878–1930, U.S. inventor: pioneer in aviation.

Cur·ti·us (kŏŏr′tsĭ ŏŏs), *n.* **Ernst** (ĕrnst), 1814–96, German archaeologist and historian.

curt·sey (kûrt′sĭ), *n.,* *pl.* **-seys,** *v.,* **-seyed, -seying.** curtsy.

curt·sy (kûrt′sĭ), *n.,* *pl.* **-sies,** *v.,* **-sied, -sying.** —*n.* **1.** a bow by women in recognition or respect, consisting of bending the knees and lowering the body. —*v.i.* **2.** to make a curtsy. [var. of COURTESY]

cu·rule (kyŏŏr′ŏŏl), *adj.* **1.** privileged to sit in a curule chair. **2.** of the highest rank.

curule chair, *Hist.* a folding seat with curved legs and no back, often ornamented with ivory, etc., used only by certain high officials of ancient Rome.

cur·va·ceous (kûr və′shəs), *adj. Colloq.* having a full figure. [f. CURVE + -ACEOUS]

cur·va·ture (kûr′və chər), *n.* **1.** act of curving. **2.** curved condition, often abnormal: *curvature of the spine.* **3.** degree of curving. **4.** something curved.

curve (kûrv), *n.,* *v.,* **curved, curving,** *adj.* —*n.* **1.** a continuously bending line, without angles. **2.** a curving. **3.** any curved outline, form, thing, or part. **4.** a curved ruler used by draftsmen. **5.** *Baseball.* **a.** the curved course (other than one due to the force of gravity) given to a ball by the pitcher; a curved ball. **b.** the deflection itself. **6.** *Math.* a collection of points whose coördinates are continuous functions of a single independent variable. —*v.t.,* *v.i.* **7.** to bend in a curve; take, or cause to take, the course of a curve. —*adj.* 8. curved. [t. L: m. s. *curvus* bent, curved] —**curv·ed·ly** (kûr'vĭd lĭ'), *adv.* —**curv'ed·ness**, *n.*

cur·vet (*n.* kûr'vĭt; *v.* kər vĕt', kûr'vĭt), *n., v.,* **-vetted, -vetting** or **-veted, -veting.** —*n.* 1. a leap of a horse in which the forelegs are raised together and equally advanced, and then, as they are falling, the hindlegs are raised with a spring, so that all the legs are off the ground at once. —*v.i.* 2. to leap in a curvet, as a horse; cause one's horse to do this. 3. to leap and frisk. —*v.t.* 4. to cause to make a curvet. [t. It.: m. *corvetta*, dim. of *corvo*, g. L *curvus* bent, curved]

curvi-, a combining form of **curve.**

cur·vi·lin·e·ar (kûr'və lĭn'ĭ ər), *adj.* 1. consisting of or bounded by curved lines: *a curvilinear figure.* 2. forming, or moving in, a curved line. 3. formed, or characterized by, curved lines. Also, **cur'vi·lin'e·al.**

Cur·zon of Ked·le·ston (kûr'zən ɔv kĕd'əl stən, kĕl'stən), George Nathaniel Curzon, 1st Marquis, 1859–1925, British statesman: viceroy of India, 1899–1905.

Cus·co (kōōs'kō), *n.* Cuzco.

Cush (kŭsh), *n. Bible.* 1. the eldest son of Ham. Gen. 10:6. 2. (probably) Upper Egypt and the neighboring country.

cush·at (kŭsh'ət, kōōsh'-), *n.* the wood pigeon or ringdove, *Columba palumbus*, of Europe. [OE *cuscote*]

cu·shaw (kə shô'), *n.* any of various long-necked squashes, esp. varieties of *Cucurbita moshcata*; cashaw.

Cush·ing (kōōsh'ĭng), *n.* 1. Caleb (kā'ləb), 1800–79, U.S. statesman and diplomat. 2. Harvey, 1869–1939, U.S. surgeon and author.

cush·ion (kōōsh'ən), *n.* 1. a soft bag of cloth, leather, or rubber, filled with feathers, air, etc., used to sit, kneel, or lie on. 2. anything similar in appearance or use. 3. a pillow used in lacemaking. 4. a pad worn under the hair by women. 5. the elastic raised rim encircling the top of a billiard table. 6. something to absorb or counteract a shock, jar, or jolt, as a body of air or steam. —*v.t.* 7. to place on or support by a cushion. 8. to furnish with a cushion or cushions. 9. to cover or conceal with, or as with, a cushion. 10. to check the motion of (a piston, etc.) by a cushion, as of steam. 11. to form (steam, etc.) into a cushion. 12. to suppress (complaints, etc.) quietly, as by ignoring. [ME *cushin*, t. OF: m. *coussin*, ? ult. der. L *culcita* cushion]
—**Syn.** 1. CUSHION, PILLOW agree in being cases filled with a material more or less resilient, intended to be used as supports for the body or parts of it. A CUSHION is a soft pad used to sit, lie, or kneel on, or to lean against: *a number of cushions on a sofa, cushions on pews in a church.* A PILLOW is a bag or case filled with feathers, down, or other soft material, usually to support the head: *to sleep with a pillow under one's head.*

Cush·it·ic (kə shĭt'ĭk), *n.* a group of Hamitic languages, including Somali and other languages of Somaliland and Ethiopia.

Cush·man (kōōsh'mən), *n.* 1. Charlotte Saunders, 1816–76, U. S. actress. 2. Robert, 1580?–1625, one of the Pilgrim founders of Plymouth, Massachusetts.

cush·y (kōōsh'ĭ), *adj.,* **cushier, cushiest.** *Chiefly Brit. Slang.* easy; pleasant. [f. CUSH(ION) + -Y¹]

cusk (kŭsk), *n., pl.* **cusks,** (*esp. collectively*) **cusk.** 1. an edible marine fish, *Brosmius brosme*, of both coasts of the northern Atlantic. 2. a similar fish, as the American burbot, *Lota lota maculosa.* [var. of *tusk* fish]

cusp (kŭsp), *n.* 1. a point; pointed end. 2. *Anat., Zool., Bot.* a point, projection, or elevation, as on the crown of a tooth. 3. *Geom.* a point where two branches of a curve meet, end, and are tangent. 4. *Archit., etc.* a point or figure formed by the intersection of two small arcs or curved members, as one of the pointed projections sometimes decorating the internal curve of an arch or a traceried window. 5. *Astron.* a point of a crescent, esp. of the moon. [t. L: m. *cuspis* point]

cusped (kŭspt), *adj.,* having a cusp or cusps; cusplike. Also, **cus·pate** (kŭs'pĭt, -pāt), **cus'pat·ed.**

cus·pid (kŭs'pĭd), *n.* a tooth with a single projection point or elevation; a canine tooth (*cuspid* is preferred for a human canine tooth). [t. L: s. *cuspis* point]

cus·pi·dal (kŭs'pə dəl), *adj.* of, like, or having a cusp; cuspidate.

cus·pi·date (kŭs'pə dāt'), *adj.* 1. having a cusp or cusps. 2. furnished with or ending in a sharp and stiff point or cusp: *cuspidate leaves, cuspidate tooth.* Also, **cus'pi·dat'ed.** [t. NL: m.s. *cuspidātus*, der. L *cuspis* point]

cus·pi·da·tion (kŭs'pə dā'shən), *n.* decoration with cusps, as in architecture.

cus·pi·dor (kŭs'pə dôr'), *n.* a bowl used as a receptacle for spit. [t. Pg.: spitter, spittoon, der. *cuspir*, g. L *conspuere* spit upon]

cuss (kŭs), *U.S. Colloq.* —*n.* 1. a curse. 2. a person or animal: *a queer but likable cuss.* —*v.t., v.i.* 3. to curse. [early var. of CURSE]

cuss·ed (kŭs'ĭd), *adj. Colloq.* 1. cursed. 2. obstinate; perverse. —**cuss'ed·ly,** *adv.* —**cuss'ed·ness,** *n.*

cus·tard (kŭs'tərd), *n.* a dish made of eggs and milk, sweetened and baked or boiled. [earlier *crustarde* (with loss of first -r- by dissimilation), a kind of patty, der. OE *croste* CRUST]

custard apple, 1. the fruit of any of a group of shrubs and trees, native in tropical America, and possessing soft edible pulp; often confined to the single species, *Annona reticulata.* 2. the tree itself. 3. some

related tree, as *Asimina triloba*, the North American papaw. 6. its fruit.

Cus·ter (kŭs'tər), *n.* George Armstrong, 1839–76, U.S. general and Indian fighter.

cus·to·di·al (kŭs tō'dĭ əl), *adj.* pertaining to custody.

cus·to·di·an (kŭs tō'dĭ ən), *n.* a person who has custody; a keeper; guardian. —**cus·to'di·an·ship',** *n.*

cus·to·dy (kŭs'tə dĭ), *n., pl.* **-dies.** 1. keeping; guardianship; care: *in the custody of her father.* 2. the keeping or charge of officers of the law: *the car was held in the custody of the police.* 3. imprisonment: *he was taken into custody.* [t. L: m.s. *custōdia*]
—**Syn.** 1, 2. safekeeping, charge, watch. CUSTODY, KEEPING, POSSESSION imply a guardianship or care for something. CUSTODY denotes a strict keeping, as by a formally authorized and responsible guardian or keeper: *in the custody of the sheriff.* KEEPING denotes having in one's care or charge, as for guarding or preservation: *in a bank for safekeeping.* POSSESSION means holding, ownership, or mastery: *leave it in possession of its owner.*

cus·tom (kŭs'təm), *n.* 1. a habitual practice; the usual way of acting in given circumstances. 2. habits or usages collectively; convention. 3. a long-continued habit which is so established that it has the force of law. 4. such habits collectively. 5. a customary tax, tribute, or service due by feudal tenants to their lord. 6. *Sociol.* a group pattern of habitual activity usually transmitted from one generation to another. 7. toll; duty. 8. (*pl.*) duties imposed by law on imported or, less commonly, exported goods. 9. (*pl.*) the government department that collects these duties. 10. habitual patronage of a particular shop, etc.; business patronage. 11. customers or patrons collectively. 12. the aggregate of customers. —*adj.* 13. made specially for individual customers: *custom shoes.* 14. dealing in things so made, or doing work to order: *a custom tailor.* [ME *custume*, t. OF, ult. g. L *consuētūdo* custom. See CONSUETUDE, Cf. COSTUME]
—**Syn.** 1, 2. CUSTOM, HABIT, PRACTICE mean an established way of doing things. CUSTOM, applied to a community or to an individual, implies a (more or less permanent) continuance of a social usage: *it is the custom to give gifts at Christmas time.* HABIT, applied particularly to an individual, implies such repetition of the same action as to develop a natural, spontaneous, or rooted tendency or inclination to perform it: *make a habit of reading the newspapers.* PRACTICE applies to a set of fixed habits or an ordered procedure in conducting activities: *it is his practice to verify all statements, secret practice of a cult.*

cus·tom·a·ble (kŭs'təm ə bəl), *adj.* subject to customs or duties; dutiable.

cus·tom·ar·y (kŭs'tə mĕr'ĭ), *adj., n., pl.* **-aries.** —*adj.* 1. according to or depending on custom; usual; habitual. 2. of or established by custom rather than law. 3. *Law.* defined by long continued practices: *the customary service due from land in a manor.* —*n.* 4. a book or document containing the legal customs or customary laws of a locality. 5. any body of such customs or laws. [t. ML: m. s. *customārius*, der. OF *custume* CUSTOM] —**cus'tom·ar'i·ly** or, for emphasis, **cus'tom·ar'i·ly,** *adv.* —**cus'tom·ar'i·ness,** *n.* —**Syn.** 1. wonted, accustomed, conventional. See **usual.** —**Ant.** 1. uncommon.

cus·tom-built (kŭs'təm bĭlt'), *adj.* made to individual order: *a custom-built limousine.*

cus·tom·er (kŭs'təm ər), *n.* 1. one who purchases goods from another; a buyer; a patron. 2. *Colloq.* a person one has to deal with; a fellow: *a queer customer.*

custom house, a government office, often at a seaport, for collecting customs, clearing vessels, etc.

cus·tom-made (kŭs'təm mād'), *adj.* made to individual order: *custom-made shoes.*

customs union, an arrangement between independent nations or tariff areas to remove customs barriers between them and to adopt a uniform tariff policy.

cus·tos (kŭs'tŏs), *n., pl.* **custodes** (kŭs tō'dēz). *Latin.* 1. a custodian. 2. a superior in the Franciscan order.

cus·tos mo·rum (kŭs'tŏs mōr'əm), *Latin.* a custodian or guardian of morals; censor.

cus·tu·mal (kŭs'chōō məl), *n.* customary. [t. ML: s. *custumālis*, Latinization of OF *costumel* customary]

cut (kŭt), *v.,* **cut, cutting,** *adj., n.* —*v.t.* 1. to penetrate with, or as with, a sharp-edged instrument: *he cut his finger.* 2. to strike sharply, as with a whip. 3. to wound severely the feelings of. 4. to divide with, or as with, a sharp-edged instrument; sever; carve: *to cut a rope, bread into slices, etc.* 5. to hew or saw down; fell: *to cut timber.* 6. to detach with, or as with, a sharp-edged instrument; separate from the main body; lop off. 7. to reap; mow; harvest: *to cut grain or hay.* 8. to trim by clipping, shearing, paring, or pruning: *to cut the hair or the nails.* 9. to intersect; cross: *one line cuts another at right angles.* 10. to abridge or shorten by omitting a part: *to cut a speech.* 11. to lower; reduce; diminish (sometimes fol. by *down*): *to cut rates.* 12. to dissolve; dilute; make less thick: *to cut phlegm.* 13. to make or fashion by cutting, as a statue, jewel, garment, etc. 14. to hollow out; excavate; dig: *cut a trench.* 15. *Colloq.* to renounce; give up. 16. *Colloq.* to refuse to recognize socially. 17. to perform or execute: *to cut a caper.* 18. *Colloq.* to absent oneself from. 19. *Cards.* a. to divide (a pack of cards) at random into two or more parts, by removing cards from the top. b. to take (a card) from a deck. 20. *Sports.* to hit (a ball) either with the hand or some instrument so as to change its course and often to cause it to spin. 21. *Cricket.* to strike and send off (a ball) in front of the batsman, and

parallel to the wicket.
—*v.i.* 22. to penetrate or divide something as with a sharp-edged instrument; make an incision: *the scissors cut well.* 23. to admit of being cut, or turn out upon being cut. 24. to pass, go, or come, esp. in the most direct way (fol. by *across, through, in,* etc.): *to cut across an empty lot.* 25. to strike sharply, as with a whip. 26. (of the teeth) to grow through the gums. 27. *Cards.* to cut the cards. 28. *Slang.* to run away; make off. 29. (of a horse) to interfere. 30. to interrupt (fol. by *in*). 31. Some verb phrases are:
cut back, 1. to shorten by cutting off the end. 2. (in a novel, movie, etc.) to return suddenly to earlier events. 3. *Football.* to reverse direction suddenly by moving in the diagonally opposite course.
cut off, 1. to intercept. 2. to interrupt. 3. to bring to a sudden end. 4. to shut out. 5. to disinherit.
cut out, 1. to omit; delete; excise. 2. to oust and replace; supplant (esp. a rival). 3. to be fit for. 4. to stop; cease. 5. to plan or arrange; prepare. 6. to fashion or shape; form; make. 7. to move suddenly out of the lane or path in which one has been driving.
cut teeth, to have the teeth grow through the gums.
cut up, *Colloq.* 1. to play pranks. 2. to behave badly.
—*adj.* 32. that has been subjected to cutting; divided into pieces by cutting; detached by cutting: *cut flowers.* 33. *Bot.* incised; cleft. 34. fashioned by cutting; having the surface shaped or ornamented by grinding and polishing: *cut glass.* 35. reduced by, or as by, cutting: *cut rates.* 36. castrated; gelded. 37. *Slang.* drunk. 38. **cut and dried,** a. fixed or settled in advance. b. lacking freshness or spontaneity.
—*n.* 39. act of cutting; a stroke or a blow as with a knife, whip, etc. 40. a piece cut off, esp. of meat. 41. *Butchering.* part of an animal usually cut as one piece. 42. *U.S. Colloq.* share: *his cut was 20%.* 43. quantity cut, esp. of lumber. 44. the result of cutting, as an incision, wound, etc.; a passage, channel, etc., made by cutting or digging. 45. manner or fashion in which anything is cut. 46. style; manner; kind. 47. a passage or course straight across: *a short cut.* 48. an excision or omission of a part. 49. a part excised or omitted. 50. a reduction in price, salary, etc. 51. an act, speech, etc., which wounds the feelings. 52. an engraved block or plate used for printing, or an impression from it. 53. *Colloq.* a refusal to recognize an acquaintance. 54. *Colloq.* an absence when attendance is required. 55. *Sports.* a. act of cutting a ball. b. the spin of the ball. 56. *Cards.* a cutting of the cards. 57. one of several pieces of straw, paper, etc., used in drawing lots. [ME *cutten, kytten, kitten;* akin to d. Sw. *kata* cut]
—**Syn.** 1. gash, slash, slit, lance. 4. cleave, sunder, bisect. CUT, CHOP, HACK, HEW, refer to giving a sharp blow or stroke. CUT is a general word for this: *to cut the grass.* To CHOP is to cut by giving repeated blows with something sharp, for example, an ax. To CHOP and to HEW are practically interchangeable, but CHOP may refer to a more or less undirected action; whereas HEW, more formal, suggests keeping to a definite purpose: *to chop or hew down a tree, to hew to a line.* To HACK is to cut or chop roughly and unevenly: *hack off a limb.* 44. gash, slash, slit.

cu·ta·ne·ous (kū tā'nĭ əs), *adj.* of, pertaining to, or affecting the skin. [t. ML: m. *cutāneus,* der. L *cutis* skin]

cut·a·way (kŭt'ə wā'), *adj.* 1. (of a coat) having the skirt cut away from the waist in front in a curve or slope. —*n.* 2. a cutaway coat.

cut·back (kŭt'băk'), *n.* 1. a return in the course of a story, motion picture, etc. to earlier events. 2. reduction to an earlier rate, as in production.

cutch (kŭch), *n.* catechu.

Cutch (kŭch), *n.* 1. a former state in western India, now part of Bombay State. 8461 sq. mi. *Former cap.:* Bhuj. Also, **Kutch.** 2. **Rann of** (rŭn), a large salt marsh NE of this state. ab. 9000 sq. mi.

cut·cher·ry (kə chĕr'ĭ), *n.* 1. *India.* a public administrative or judicial office. 2. any administrative office. Also, **cutch·er·y** (kŭch'ə rĭ). [t. Hind.: m. *kachĕri*]

cute (kūt), *adj.,* **cuter, cutest.** 1. *U.S. Colloq.* pleasingly pretty or dainty: *a cute child, hat, etc.* 2. *Archaic or Dial.* mentally keen; clever; shrewd. [aphetic var. of ACUTE] —**cute'ly,** *adv.* —**cute'ness,** *n.*

cut glass, glass ornamented or shaped by cutting or grinding with abrasive wheels. —**cut'glass',** *adj.*

cut-grass (kŭt'grăs', -gräs'), *n.* any of various grasses with blades having rough edges, esp. grasses of the genus *Homalocenchrus.*

Cuth·bert (kŭth'bərt), *n.* **Saint,** died A.D. 687, English monk and bishop.

cu·ti·cle (kū'tə kəl), *n.* 1. the epidermis. 2. a superficial integument, membrane, or the like. 3. the non-living epidermis which surrounds the edges of the finger nail or toenail. 4. *Bot.* a very thin hyaline film covering the surface of plants, and derived from the outer surfaces of the epidermal cells. [t. L: m.s. *cuticula,* dim. of *cutis* skin] —**cu·tic·u·lar** (kū tĭk'yə lər), *adj.*

cu·tic·u·la (kū tĭk'yə lə), *n., pl.* **-lae** (-lē'). the outer noncellular layer of the arthropod integument, composed of a mixture of chitin and protein, but commonly containing other hardening substances. [t. L: skin]

cu·tin (kū'tĭn), *n.* a transparent waxy substance constituting together with cellulose the cuticle of plants. [f. s. L *cutis* skin + -IN²]

cu·tin·ize (kū'tĭ nīz'), *v.t., v.i.,* **-ized, -izing.** to make into or become cutin. —**cu'tin·i·za'tion,** *n.*

cu·tis (kū'tĭs), *n. Latin.* the corium or true skin, beneath the epidermis. Also, **cutis ve·ra** (vĭr'ə).

cut·lass (kŭt'ləs), *n.* a short, heavy, slightly curved sword, formerly used esp. at sea. Also, **cut'las.** [t. F: m. *coutelas,* ult. der. L *cultellus* small knife]

cut·ler (kŭt'lər), *n.* one who makes, sells, or repairs knives and other cutting instruments. [ME *coteler,* t. F: m. *coutelier,* der. *coutel* small knife, g. L *cultellus*]

cut·ler·y (kŭt'lər ĭ), *n.* 1. art or business of a cutler. 2. cutting instruments collectively, esp. those for dinner table use. [t. F: m. *coutelerie.* See CUTLER]

cut·let (kŭt'lĭt), *n.* 1. a slice of meat for broiling or frying, orig. one, as of mutton, containing a rib, but now commonly one cut from the leg, esp. of veal or mutton. 2. a flat croquette of minced chicken, lobster, or the like. [t. F: m. *côtelette,* double dim. of *côte* rib, g. L *costa*]

cut·off (kŭt'ôf', -ŏf'), *n.* 1. a cutting off, or something that cuts off; a shorter passage or way. 2. a new and shorter channel formed for a river by the waters cutting across a bend in its course. 3. the arresting of the passage of steam or working fluid to the cylinder of an engine, or the mechanims effecting it.

cut·out (kŭt'out'), *n.* 1. something cut out from something else. 2. a valve in the exhaust pipe of an internal-combustion engine, which when open permits the engine to exhaust directly into the air ahead of the muffler.

cut·purse (kŭt'pûrs'), *n.* 1. one who stole by cutting purses from the girdle. 2. a pickpocket.

cut rate, *U.S.* a price, fare, or rate below the standard charge. —**cut'-rate',** *adj.*

cut·tage (kŭt'ĭj), *n.* the process of propagating plants from separate vegetative parts.

cut·ter (kŭt'ər), *n.* 1. one who or that which cuts. 2. a type of small sailing vessel with a deep hull, square stern, and sloop rig. 3. a medium-sized boat for rowing or sailing, or a launch, belonging to a warship. 4. a light-armed government vessel (**revenue cutter**), used to prevent smuggling and enforce the customs regulations. 5. a small, light, commonly single-seated sleigh, usually for one horse.

cut·throat (kŭt'thrōt'), *n.* 1. one who cuts throats; a murderer. —*adj.* 2. murderous. 3. relentless: *cutthroat competition.* 4. pertaining to a game participated in by three or more persons, each acting and scoring as an individual.

cut·ting (kŭt'ĭng), *n.* 1. act of one who or that which cuts. 2. something cut off. 3. *Hort.* a piece of plant, commonly a root, shoot, or leaf, cut from a plant to reproduce an entire new plant. 4. *Brit.* a clipping from a newspaper, etc. 5. *Now Brit.* something produced by cutting; an excavation through high ground, as in constructing a road, etc. —*adj.* 6. that cuts; penetrating or dividing by, or as by, a cut. 7. piercing, as a wind. 8. wounding the feelings severely; sarcastic. —**cut'ting·ly,** *adv.* —**Syn.** 7. sharp, kee incisive, trenchant. 8. caustic, biting, mordant.

cut·tle·bone (kŭt'l bōn'), *n.* the calcareous internal shell or plate of true cuttlefishes; used to make powder for polishing, and fed to canaries to supply the necessary lime, etc.

cut·tle·fish (kŭt'l fĭsh'), *n., pl.* **-fishes,** (*esp. collectively*) **-fish.** any of various decapod dibranchiate cephalopods, esp. of the genus *Sepia,* having sucker-bearing arms and the power of ejecting a black, inklike fluid when pursued. Also, **cut'tle.** [f. *cuttle* (ME *codulle,* OE *cudele* cuttlefish; akin to COD¹) + FISH]

cut·ty (kŭt'ĭ), *adj., n., pl.* **-ties.** *Chiefly Scot.* —*adj.* 1. cut short; short. 2. testy. —*n.* 3. a short spoon. 4. a short-stemmed tobacco pipe. 5. an improper girl or woman. [der. CUT, v.]

Cuttlefish. Sepia officinalis (5 in. long)

cutty stool, *Scot.* 1. a low stool. 2. a seat in old churches, where offenders against chastity, or other delinquents, sat and received public rebuke.

cut·up (kŭt'ŭp'), *n. Colloq.* a showoff or prankster.

cut·wa·ter (kŭt'wô'tər, -wŏt'ər), *n.* 1. the forepart of a ship's stem or prow, which cuts the water. 2. the sharp edge of a pier of a bridge, which resists the action of water or ice.

cut·work (kŭt'wûrk'), *n.* openwork embroidery in which the ground fabric is cut out about the pattern.

cut·worm (kŭt'wûrm'), *n.* any of various caterpillars of certain noctuid moths, which feed at night on the young plants of corn, cabbage, etc., cutting them off at or near the ground.

Cu·vi·er (kū'vĭ ā'; Fr. kʏ vyĕ'), *n.* **Georges Léopold Chrétien Frédéric Dagobert** (zhôrzh lĕ ō pōld' krĕ tyăn' frĕ dĕ rēk' dȧ gō bĕr'), **Baron,** 1769–1832, French naturalist: founder of the science of paleontology.

Cux·ha·ven (kōōks'hä'fən), *n.* a seaport in N West Germany at the mouth of the Elbe. 45,300 (1950).

Cu·ya·bá (kōō'yȧ bä'), *n.* a city in W Brazil: a port on the Cuyabá river. 23,745 (1950).

Cuy·a·hog·a Falls (kī'ə hŏg'ə; *older* -hō'gə), a city in NE Ohio, near Akron. 29,195 (1950).

Cuyp (koip), *n.* **Aalbert** (äl'bərt), 1620?–91, Dutch painter. Also, **Kuyp.**

Cuz·co (kōōs'kō), *n.* a city in S Peru: ancient Inca ruins. 58,400 (est. 1954). Also, **Cusco.**

c.w.o., cash with order.

cwt., hundredweight.

-cy, 1. a suffix of abstract nouns, paired usually with adjectives ending in *-t, -te, -tic*, especially *-nt* (like the pair *-ant, -ance*), as *democracy, accuracy, expediency, necromancy*, also paired with other adjectives, as *fallacy*, or with a noun, as *lunacy*, sometimes forming (in extended suffixes) action nouns, as *vacancy* (*vacate*), *occupancy* (*occupy*). 2. a suffix of nouns denoting a rank or dignity, sometimes attached to the stem of a word rather than the word itself, as *captaincy, colonelcy, magistracy*. [repr. F *-cie, -tie*, L *-cia, -tia*, Gk. *-kia, -keia, -tia, -teia*]

cyan-[1], var. of **cyano-**[1], usually before vowels and *h*, as in **cyanamide**.

cyan-[2], var. of **cyano-**[2], before vowels.

cyan-[3], var. of **cyano-**[3], before vowels.

cy·an·am·ide (sī′ə năm′īd, -ĭd, sī ăn′ə mīd′, -mĭd), *n. Chem.* 1. a white crystalline compound, H₂NCN, obtainable by the action of ammonia on cyanogen chloride or from calcium cyanamide. 2. an ester or salt of this substance. Also **cy·an·am·id** (sī′ə năm′ĭd, sī ăn′ə mĭd). [f. CYAN(O)-[1] + AMIDE]

cy·a·nate (sī′ə nāt′), *n. Chem.* a salt of cyanic acid.

cy·an·ic (sī ăn′ĭk), *adj.* blue (applied esp. to a series of colors in flowers, including the blues and colors tending toward blue). [f. CYAN(O)-[1] + -IC]

cyanic acid, *Chem.* a poisonous compound, HOCN, isomeric with fulminic acid, but unstable except at low temperatures.

cy·a·nide (sī′ə nīd′, -nĭd), *n., v.* **-nided, -niding.** —*n.* Also, **cy·a·nid** (sī′ə nĭd). 1. a salt of hydrocyanic acid, as *potassium cyanide*, KCN. —*v.t.* 2. to treat with a cyanide, as an ore in the process of extracting gold.

cy·a·nine (sī′ə nēn′, -nĭn), *n.* any of several groups of dyes which make silver halide photographic plates sensitive to a wider color range. Also, **cy·a·nin** (sī′ə nĭn).

cy·a·nite (sī′ə nīt′), *n.* a mineral aluminum silicate, Al₂SiO₅, occurring in blue or greenish bladed crystals, used as a refractory. Also, **kyanite**. [f. m.s. Gk. *kyanos* blue + -ITE[1]]

cyano-[1], a word element indicating dark-blue coloring. Also, **cyan-**[1]. [t. Gk.: m. *kyano-*, comb. form of *kyanos* dark blue]

cyano-[2], a combining form of cyanide. Also, **cyan-**[2].

cyano-[3], *Chem.* a word element referring to the cyanogen group, CN. Also, **cyan-**[3]. [comb. form repr. CYANOGEN]

cy·an·o·gen (sī ăn′ə jən), *n.* 1. a poisonous, inflammable gas, C₂N₂. 2. a univalent radical, CN. [f. CYANO-[3] + -GEN]

cy·a·no·hy·drin (sī′ə nō hī′drĭn), *n.* one of a class of organic compounds which have both the CN and the OH radicals linked to the same carbon atom.

cy·a·no·sis (sī′ə nō′sĭs), *n. Pathol.* blueness or lividness of the skin, as from imperfectly oxygenated blood. Also, **cy·a·nop·a·thy** (sī′ə nŏp′ə thĭ). [NL, t. Gk.: m. *kyanōsis* dark-blue color] —**cy·a·not·ic** (sī′ə nŏt′ĭk), *adj.*

cy·an·o·type (sī ăn′ə tīp′), *n.* 1. a process of photographic printing with ferric salts producing blue lines on a white background, used chiefly in printing tracings. 2. a print made by such a process. [f. CYANO-[1] + -TYPE]

cy·a·nu·ric acid (sī′ə nyŏŏr′ĭk, -nŏŏr′ĭk), *Chem.* a white, crystalline acid, C₃H₃O₃N₃·2H₂O, obtained by heating urea or by decomposing cyanogen chloride with water. [f. CYAN-[3] + URIC]

Cyb·e·le (sĭb′ə lē′), *n.* a great nature goddess of Phrygia and Asia Minor whose worship was carried to Greece and Rome ("the Great Mother of the Gods").

cy·ber·net·ics (sī′bər nĕt′ĭks), *n.* the scientific study of those methods of control and communication which are common to living organisms and machines, esp. as applied to the analysis of the operations of machines such as computers. [f. s. Gk. *kybernētēs* helmsman + -ICS] —**cy′ber·net′ic**, *adj.*

cy·cad (sī′kăd), *n.* any of the *Cycadales*, an order of gymnospermous plants intermediate in appearance between ferns and the palms, many species having a thick unbranched columnar trunk bearing a crown of large leathery pinnate leaves. [t. NL: s. *Cycas* the typical genus, t. Gk.: m. *kykas*, late spelling var. of *koikas*, acc. pl. of *koix* kind of palm]

cyc·a·da·ceous (sĭk′ə dā′shəs), *adj.* belonging or pertaining to the *Cycadales*. See **cycad**.

cycl-, a word element meaning "cycle," used especially in the chemical terminology of cyclic compounds, also in referring to wheel turns. Also, **cyclo-**. [t. Gk.: m. *kykl-*, comb. form of *kyklos* ring, circle, wheel]

Cyc·la·des (sĭk′lə dēz′), *n.pl.* a group of Greek islands in the S Aegean. 125,959 (est. 1950). 1023 sq. mi.

cyc·la·men (sĭk′lə mən, -mĕn′), *n.* any plant of the primulaceous genus *Cyclamen*, comprising low-growing herbs with tuberous rootstocks and nodding white, purple, pink, or crimson flowers with reflexed petals. [t. NL, t. Gk.: m.s. *kyklaminos*]

cy·cle (sī′kəl), *n., v.* **-cled, -cling.** —*n.* 1. a round of years or a recurring period of time, esp. one in which certain events or phenomena repeat themselves in the same order and at the same intervals. 2. any round of operations or events; a series which returns upon itself; any complete course or series. 3. any long period of years; an age. 4. a series of poetic or prose narratives about some mythical or heroic theme: *the Arthurian cycle*. 5. any group of poems about a central event,

figure, etc. 6. the aggregate of legendary or traditional matter with a common mythical or heroic theme. 7. a bicycle, tricycle, etc. 8. a period pertaining to the recurrence of astronomical phenomena. 9. *Physics.* a. a sequence of changes at the end of which the initial situation has been reëstablished. b. one of a succession of similar sequences of events or values. c. a complete or double alternation or reversal of an alternating electric current. —*v.i.* 10. to ride or travel by a bicycle, etc. 11. to move or revolve in cycles: pass through cycles. [t. L: m. s. *cyclus*, t. Gk.: m. *kyklos* ring, circle]

cy·cle·car (sī′kəl kär′), *n.* a light automobile, open like a motorcycle but having three or four wheels.

cy·clic (sī′klĭk, sĭk′lĭk), *adj.* 1. of or pertaining to a cycle or cycles; revolving or recurring in cycles; characterized by recurrence in cycles. 2. *Chem.* of or noting a compound whose structural formula contains a closed chain or ring of atoms. 3. *Bot.* a. arranged in whorls, as the parts of a flower. b. (of a flower) having the parts so arranged. Also, **cy′cli·cal**. [t. L: s. *cyclicus*, t. Gk.: m. *kyklikos* circular] —**cy′cli·cal·ly**, *adv.*

cy·clist (sī′klĭst), *n. Chiefly Brit.* one who rides or travels by a bicycle, tricycle, etc. Also, **cy′cler.**

cyclo-, var. of **cycl-**, before consonants, as in *cyclograph*.

cy·clo·graph (sī′klə grăf′, -gräf′), *n.* 1. arcograph. 2. *Photog.* a form of camera for obtaining a panoramic view of the periphery of an object, as a vase.

cy·clo·hex·ane (sī′klə hĕk′sān, sĭk′lə-), *n. Chem.* a colorless, hydrocarbon, ring compound, C₆H₁₂, composed of six methylene radicals (CH₂) united by single bonds. It is made by hydrogenation of benzene, and also occurs in some petroleum oils.

cy·cloid (sī′kloid), *adj.* 1. resembling a circle; circular. 2. (of fishes' scales) smooth-edged, more or less circular in form, with concentric striations. 3. having such scales, as a fish. —*n.* 4. a cycloid fish. 5. *Geom.* a curve generated by a point on the circumference of a circle which rolls, without slipping, on a straight line in its plane. [t. Gk.: m.s. *kykloeidēs* like a circle] —**cy·cloi′dal**, *adj.*

C. Cycloid; P. Point tracing cycloid on fixed circle

cy·clom·e·ter (sī klŏm′ə tər), *n.* 1. an instrument which measures circular arcs. 2. a device for recording the revolutions of a wheel and hence the distance traversed by a wheeled vehicle.

cy·clo·nal (sī klō′nəl), *adj.* of or like a cyclone.

cy·clone (sī′klōn), *n. Meteorol.* 1. an atmospheric pressure system characterized by relatively low pressure at its center, and by counterclockwise wind motion in the northern hemisphere, clockwise in the southern. 2. a tropical hurricane, esp. in the Indian Ocean. [t. Gk.: m.s. *kyklōn*, ppr., moving in a circle] —**cy·clon·ic** (sī klŏn′ĭk), **cy·clon′i·cal**, *adj.* —**cy·clon′i·cal·ly**, *adv.*

cyclone cellar, a cellar or underground place for refuge from tornadoes, etc.

cy·clo·no·scope (sī klō′nə skōp′), *n.* a device for determining the center of a cyclone.

Cy·clo·pe·an (sī′klə pē′ən), *adj.* 1. of or characteristic of the Cyclops. 2. (*sometimes l.c.*) gigantic; vast. 3. *Archit.* of, like, or noting an early style of masonry employing massive stones, more or less irregular in shape.

cy·clo·pe·di·a (sī′klə pē′dĭ ə), *n.* a book having articles on subjects from all or certain branches of knowledge; an encyclopedia. Also, **cy′clo·pae′di·a**. [aphetic var. of ENCYCLOPEDIA] —**cy′clo·pe′dist**, *n.*

cy·clo·pe·dic (sī′klə pē′dĭk), *adj.* like a cyclopedia in character or contents; broad and varied; exhaustive. Also, **cy′clo·pae′dic**. —**cy′clo·pe′di·cal·ly**, *adv.*

cy·clo·pen·tane (sī′klə pĕn′tān, sĭk′lə-), *n. Chem.* a colorless liquid, C₅H₁₀, derived from some petroleums.

cy·clo·ple·gi·a (sī′klə plē′jĭ ə, sĭk′lə-), *n. Pathol.* paralysis of the intraocular muscles.

cy·clo·pro·pane (sī′klə prō′pān, sĭk′lə-), *n. Chem.* a colorless gas, C₃H₆, used as an anesthetic.

Cy·clops (sī′klŏps), *n., pl.* **Cyclopes** (sī klō′pēz). *Gk. Myth.* one of a race of lawless giants with but one eye, which was circular and in the middle of the forehead, fabled to have forged thunderbolts for Zeus and to have assisted Hephaestus (Vulcan) in his workshops. [t. L, t. Gk.: m. *Kyklōps*, lit., round-eyed]

cy·clo·ram·a (sī′klə răm′ə, -rä′mə), *n.* a pictorial representation, in natural perspective, of a landscape, a battle, etc., on the inner wall of a cylindrical room or hall, the spectators occupying a position in the center. [f. CYCL- + Gk. (h)*orama* view] —**cy′clo·ram′ic**, *adj.*

cy·clo·stom·a·tous (sī′klə stŏm′ə təs, -stō′mə-, sĭk′lə-), *adj.* 1. having a circular mouth. 2. belonging or pertaining to the *Cyclostomata*. See **cyclostome**. Also, **cy·clos·to·mate** (sī klŏs′tə mĭt, -māt′).

cy·clo·stome (sī′klə stōm′, sĭk′lə-), *adj.* 1. belonging or pertaining to the *Cyclostomata*, a group or class of eellike aquatic vertebrates (the lampreys and hagfishes) characterized by pouchlike gills and a circular suctorial mouth without hinged jaws. 2. having a circular mouth. —*n.* 3. a cyclostome vertebrate; a lamprey or a hagfish. [f. CYCLO- + m. Gk. *stoma* mouth]

cy·clo·style (sī′klə stīl′, sĭk′lə-), *n.* a manifolding device consisting of a kind of pen with a small toothed wheel at the end which cuts minute holes in a specially prepared paper stretched over a smooth surface, thus forming a stencil from which copies are printed.

ăct, āble, dâre, ärt; ĕbb, ēqual; ĭf, īce; hŏt, ōver, ôrder, oil, bŏŏk, ōōze, out; ŭp, ūse, ûrge; ə = a in alone; ch, chief; g, give; ng, ring; sh, shoe; th, thin; ᵺ, that; zh, vision. See the full key on inside cover.

cy·clo·thy·mi·a (sī′klə thī′mǐ ə, sǐk′lə-), *n. Psychiatry.* a mild manic-depressive psychosis involving recurring cycles of exhilaration and depression. [f. CYCLO- + Gk. *-thymia* mindedness (der. *thymós* mind)] —**cy′clo·thy′mic,** *adj.*

cy·clo·thy·mi·ac (sī′klə thī′mǐ ǎk′, sǐk′lə-), *n.* a person affected with cyclothymia.

cy·clo·tron (sī′klə trŏn′, sǐk′lə-), *n. Physics.* a device for imparting very high speed to electrified particles by successive electric impulses at high frequency, space requirements and applied voltage being kept relatively low by causing the particles to move in spiral paths in a strong magnetic field.

cy·der (sī′dər), *n. Brit.* cider.

Cyd·nus (sǐd′nəs), *n.* a historic river of Cilicia, in SE Asia Minor, flowing through ancient Tarsus.

cyg·net (sǐg′nǐt), *n.* a young swan. [ME, f. s. L *cygnus* swan (t. Gk.: m. *kýknos*) + -ET]

Cyg·nus (sǐg′nəs), *n., gen.* **-ni** (-nī). *Astron.* a northern constellation containing the star Deneb. [t. L: swan]

cyl., cylinder.

cyl·in·der (sǐl′ǐn dər), *n.* **1.** *Geom.* a solid which may be conceived as generated by the revolution of a rectangle about one of its sides (**a right circular cylinder**). **2.** a similar solid in which the elements of the curved surface are oblique to the circular bases (**oblique circular cylinder**). **3.** any solid bounded by two parallel planes and a curved surface generated by a moving straight line which intersects a given curve and is always parallel to its original position. **4.** a curved surface generated in this manner. **5.** any cylinderlike object or part, whether solid or hollow. **6.** the rotating part of a revolver, which contains the chambers for the cartridges. **7.** the body of a pump. **8.** the chamber in an engine in which the working medium acts upon the piston. **9.** (in certain printing presses) **a.** a rotating cylinder which produces the impression, under which a flat form to be printed from passes. **b.** either of two cylinders, one carrying a curved form or plate to be printed from, which rotate against each other in opposite directions. **10.** *Archaeol.* a cylindrical or somewhat barrel-shaped stone or clay object, bearing a cuneiform inscription or a carved design, worn by the Babylonians, Assyrians, and kindred peoples as a seal and amulet. —*v.t.* **11.** to furnish with a cylinder or cylinders. **12.** to subject to the action of a cylinder or cylinders. [t. L: m. s. *cylindrus,* t. Gk.: m. *kýlindros* roller, cylinder] —**cyl′in·der-like′,** *adj.*

Right circular cylinder

cylinder head, a detachable portion of an engine fastened securely to the cylinder block containing all or a portion of the combustion chamber.

cy·lin·dri·cal (sǐ lǐn′drə kəl), *adj.* of, pertaining to, or of the form of a cylinder. Also, **cy·lin′dric.** —**cy·lin′dri·cal·ly,** *adv.*

cyl·in·droid (sǐl′ǐn droid′), *n.* **1.** a solid having the form of a cylinder with equal and parallel elliptical bases. —*adj.* **2.** resembling a cylinder. [t. Gk.: m. s. *kylindroeidēs* cylinderlike. See -OID]

cy·lix (sī′lǐks, sǐl′ǐks), *n., pl.* **cylices** (sǐl′ə sēz′). *Gk. Antiq.* a shallow drinking cup, usually with a stem and foot, and two handles; kylix. [t. Gk.: m. *kýlix*]

Cyl·le·ni·an (sǐ lē′nǐ ən), *adj.* pertaining to Mount Cyllene, in Arcadia, Greece, or to the god Hermes, reputed to have been born there.

cy·ma (sī′mə), *n., pl.* **-mae** (-mē). **1.** *Archit.* a projecting molding whose profile is a compound concavo-convex curve. It is called a **cyma recta** when the projecting part is concave and a **cyma reversa** when the projecting portion is convex. See diag. under **column. 2.** *Bot.* a cyme. [NL, t. Gk.: m. *kýma* something swollen, wave, waved molding, sprout]

cy·mar (sǐ mär′), *n.* simar.

cy·ma·ti·um (sǐ mā′shǐ əm), *n., pl.* **-tia** (-shǐ ə). *Archit.* the capping molding of a cornice, placed above the corona, commonly having a cyma recta as its most important feature. [t. L, t. Gk.: m. *kymátion,* dim. of *kýma* wave]

cym·bal (sǐm′bəl), *n.* one of a pair of concave plates of brass or bronze which are struck together to produce a sharp, ringing sound. [OE, t. L: s. *cymbalum,* t. Gk.: m. *kýmbalon,* der. *kýmbē* cup, bowl] —**cym′bal·ist,** *n.*

Cym·be·line (sǐm′bə lēn′), *n.* a romantic drama (about 1610) by Shakespeare.

cyme (sīm), *n. Bot.* **1.** an inflorescence in which the primary axis bears a single terminal flower which develops first, the inflorescence being continued by secondary, tertiary, and other axes. **2.** a flat or convex inflorescence of this type. [t. L: m. s. *cyma* sprout, t. Gk.: m. *kýma.* See CYMA.]

cy·mene (sī′mēn), *n. Chem.* a liquid hydrocarbon, $C_{10}H_{14}$, with a pleasant smell, occurring in the volatile oil of the common cumin, *Cuminum cyminum,* and existing in three isomeric forms, *ortho-, meta-,* and *para-cymene.* [f. *cym-* (comb. form repr. Gk. *kýminon* cumin) + -ENE]

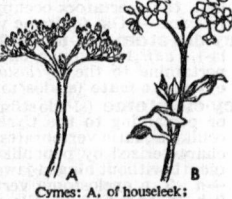

Cymes: A, of houseleek; B, of forget-me-not

cymo-, a word element meaning "wave." [t. Gk.: m. *kymo-,* comb. form of *kýma* wave, embryo, sprout]

cy·mo·gene (sī′mə jēn′), *n. Chem.* a mixture of very volatile inflammable hydrocarbons, constituting the fraction boiling at about 0° C. obtained in distilling crude petroleum, and containing a large percentage of butane. [f. *cymo-* (comb. form repr. Gk. *kýminon* cumin) + -GENE]

cy·mo·graph (sī′mə grăf′, -gräf′), *n.* kymograph.

cy·mom·e·ter (sī mǒm′ə tər), *n. Elect.* an instrument for measuring electromagnetic waves.

cy·mo·phane (sī′mə fān′), *n.* chrysoberyl.

cy·mo·scope (sī′mə skōp′), *n.* a device for detecting the presence of electromagnetic waves.

cy·mose (sī′mōs, sī mōs′), *adj. Bot.* **1.** bearing a cyme or cymes. **2.** of or of the nature of a cyme. [t. L: m. s. *cymōsus* full of shoots. See CYME] —**cy′mose·ly,** *adv.*

Cym·ric (kǐm′rǐk, sǐm′-), *adj.* **1.** pertaining to the Cymry. —*n.* **2.** Welsh (the language). Also, **Kymric.** [f. m. Welsh *Cymru* Wales or *Cymry* the Welsh + -IC]

Cym·ry (kǐm′rǐ), *n.pl.* the Welsh, or the branch of the Celtic race to which the Welsh belong, comprising also the Cornish people and the Bretons. Also, **Kymry.** [t. Welsh, pl. of *Cymro* Welshman. Cf. Welsh *cymru* Wales]

cyn·ic (sǐn′ǐk), *n.* **1.** a sneering faultfinder; one who doubts or denies the goodness of human motives, and who often displays his attitude by sneers, sarcasm, etc. **2.** (*cap.*) one of a sect of Greek philosophers founded by Antisthenes of Athens (born about 444 B.C.), who sought to develop the ethical teachings of Socrates. The chief doctrines of the Cynics were that virtue is the only good, that the essence of virtue is self-control, and that surrender to any external influence is beneath the dignity of man. —*adj.* **3.** cynical. **4.** (*cap.*) of or pertaining to the Cynics or their doctrines. **5.** of or pertaining to the Dog Star: *the cynic year.* [t. L: s. *cynicus,* t. Gk.: m. *kynikós* doglike, churlish, Cynic]

cyn·i·cal (sǐn′ə kəl), *adj.* **1.** like or characteristic of a cynic; distrusting the motives of others. **2.** (*cap.*) cynic (def. 4). —**cyn′i·cal·ly,** *adv.*

—**Syn. 1.** CYNICAL, PESSIMISTIC, SARCASTIC, SATIRICAL, imply holding a low opinion of mankind. CYNICAL suggests a disbelief in the sincerity of human motives: *cynical about honesty.* PESSIMISTIC implies a more or less habitual disposition to look on the dark side of things, and to believe that the worst will happen: *pessimistic as to the future.* SARCASTIC refers to sneering or making cutting jibes: *sarcastic about a profession of faith.* SATIRICAL suggests expressing scorn or ridicule by saying the opposite of what one means: *satirical about the way in which actions and protestations differ.* —**Ant. 1.** optimistic

cyn·i·cism (sǐn′ə sǐz′əm), *n.* **1.** cynical disposition or character. **2.** a cynical remark. **3.** (*cap.*) the doctrines or practices of the Cynics.

cy·no·sure (sī′nə shŏŏr′, sǐn′ə-), *n.* **1.** something that strongly attracts attention by its brilliance, etc.: *the cynosure of all eyes.* **2.** something serving for guidance or direction. **3.** (*cap.*) the constellation of the Little Bear (Ursa Minor). **4.** (*cap.*) the polestar. [t. L: m.s. *Cynosūra,* t. Gk.: m. *Kynósoura,* lit., dog's tail]

Cyn·thi·a (sǐn′thǐ ə), *n.* **1.** Artemis (Diana). **2.** *Poetic.* the moon, the emblem of Artemis (Diana).

cy·per·a·ceous (sī′pə rā′shəs, sǐp′ə-), *adj.* pertaining or belonging to, or resembling, the *Cyperaceae* or the sedge family of monocotyledonous plants, with solid, often triangular, stems and small, coriaceous, achenial fruit. [f. s. NL *Cyperus* the typical genus (t. Gk.: m. *kýpeiros* kind of marsh plant) + -ACEOUS]

cy·pher (sī′fər), *n., v.i., v.t.* cipher.

cy pres (sē′ prā′), *Law.* **1.** as near as practicable. **2.** doctrine of cy pres, an equitable doctrine (applicable only to cases of charitable trusts or donations) which, in place of an impossible or illegal condition, limitation, or object, allows the nearest practicable one to be substituted. Also, **cy′pres′.** [t. late AF: as nearly]

cy·press¹ (sī′prəs), *n.* **1.** any of the evergreen trees constituting the coniferous genus *Cupressus,* distinguished by dark-green scalelike, overlapping leaves, often a very slender tree with a durable wood. **2.** any of various other coniferous trees allied to the true cypress, as *Taxodium distichum* (**swamp,** or **bald cypress**) of the southern U. S., *Chamaecyparis,* etc. **3.** any of various other plants in some way resembling the true cypress, as *Gilia coronopifolia* (**standing cypress**), a tall, slender, herb of the U. S. **4.** the wood of these trees. [t. L: s. *cypressus,* t. Gk.: m. *kypárissos;* r. ME *cipres,* t. OF]

cy·press² (sī′prəs), *n. Obs.* a fine, thin fabric resembling lawn or crepe, which was formerly much used in black for mourning garments, etc. Also, **cyprus.** [ME *cipres,* prob. t. OF; appar. named from Cyprus]

cypress vine, a convolvulaceous garden plant, *Quamoclit pennata,* with finely parted leaves and scarlet or white tubular flowers.

Cyp·ri·an (sǐp′rǐ ən), *adj.* **1.** pertaining to Cyprus, famous as a center for the worship of Aphrodite (Venus). **2.** lewd; licentious. —*n.* **3.** a native or inhabitant of Cyprus. **4.** a lewd person, esp. a prostitute. [f. s. L *Cyprius* (t. Gk.: m. *Kýprios* of Cyprus) + -AN]

Cyp·ri·an (sǐp′rǐ ən), *n.* **Saint,** A.D. 200?-258, a bishop of Carthage, writer, and martyr.

cy·pri·nid (sī prī′nǐd, sǐp′rə nǐd), *n.* **1.** any fish belonging to the *Cyprinidae,* or minnow family. —*adj.* **2.** carplike in form or structure.

cy·prin·o·dont (sĭ´prĭn´ə·dŏnt´, sĭ´prĭ´nə-), *n.* any of the *Cyprinodontidae*, a family of small soft-finned fishes, mostly inhabiting the fresh and brackish waters of America, including the killifishes, certain top minnows, the guppy, etc. [f. s. Gk. *kyprīnos* carp + s. *odoús* tooth]

cyp·ri·noid (sĭp´rə·noid´, sĭ´prĭ´noid), *adj.* 1. resembling a carp; belonging to the *Cyprinoidea*, a group of fishes including the carps, suckers, loaches, etc. —*n.* 2. a cyprinoid fish. [f. s. Gk. *kyprīnos* carp + -OID]

Cyp·ri·ote (sĭp´rĭ·ōt´), *n.* 1. a native or inhabitant of Cyprus. 2. the Greek dialect of Cyprus. —*adj.* 3. Cyprian. Also, **Cyp·ri·ot** (sĭp´rĭ·ət). [t. Gk.: m. Kypriốtēs]

cyp·ri·pe·di·um (sĭp´rə·pē´dĭ·əm), *n.* any plant of the genus *Cypripedium*, comprising orchids having large flowers with a protruding saclike labellum; a lady's-slipper. [NL, f. L *Cypri(s)* Venus + s. L *pēs* foot + -IUM]

Cy·prus (sī´prəs), *n.* an island in the Mediterranean, S of Turkey, formerly a British colony: independent since 1960. 549,200 pop. (1959); 3572 sq. mi. *Cap.:* Nicosia.

cyp·re (sĭp´rəs), *n. Obs.* cypress².

cyp·se·la (sĭp´sə·lə), *n., pl.* **-lae** (-lē´). *Bot.* an achene with an adherent calyx, as in the composite plants. [NL, t. Gk.: m. *kypsélē* hollow vessel]

Cyr·e·na·ic (sĭr´ə·nā´ĭk, sī´rə-), *adj.* 1. of or pertaining to Cyrenaica, or its chief city, Cyrene. 2. noting or pertaining to a school of philosophy founded by Aristippus of Cyrene, who taught that pleasure is the only rational aim of life. —*n.* 3. a native or inhabitant of Cyrenaica. 4. a disciple of the Cyrenaic school of philosophy.

Cyr·e·na·i·ca (sĭr´ə·nā´ə·kə, sī´rə-), *n.* an ancient district in N Africa, W of Egypt. Also, **Barca**.

Cyrenaica, 550 B.C.

Cy·re·ne (sī·rē´nĭ), *n.* an ancient Greek city and colony in Cyrenaica, in N Africa.

Cyr·il (sĭr´əl), *n.* **Saint**, ("*Apostle of the Slavs*") A.D. 827–869, Greek missionary to the Moravians.

Cy·ril·lic (sĭ·rĭl´ĭk), *adj.* 1. of or pertaining to an old Slavic alphabet reputed to have been invented by St. Cyril, and its modern forms as used in Serbia, Bulgaria, and the Soviet Union. 2. of or pertaining to St. Cyril.

cyrto-, a word element meaning "curved." [t. Gk.: m. *kyrto-*, comb. form of *kyrtós*]

Cy·rus (sī´rəs), *n.* 1. ("*the Elder*" or "*the Great*") died 529 B.C., king of Persia, 558?–529 B.C.; founder of Persian Empire. 2. ("*The Younger*") died 401 B.C., Persian satrap: led army (including 10,000 Greeks) against his brother, Artaxerxes II, Persian king.

cyst (sĭst), *n.* 1. *Pathol.* a closed bladderlike sac formed in animal tissues, containing fluid or semifluid morbid matter. 2. a bladder, sac, or vesicle. 3. *Bot.* a. a sporelike cell with a resistant protective wall. b. a cell or cavity enclosing reproductive bodies, etc. 4. *Zool.* a. a sac, usually spherical, surrounding an animal that has passed into a dormant condition. b. such a sac plus the contained animal. c. a capsule or resistant covering. [t. NL: s. *cystis*, t. Gk.: m. *kýstis* bladder, bag, pouch]

cyst-, a combining form representing cyst. Also, **cysti-, cysto-**.

-cyst, a terminal combining form of cyst.

cys·tec·to·my (sĭs·tĕk´tə·mĭ), *n., pl.* **-mies**. *Surg.* excision of a cyst or bladder, usually the urinary bladder.

cys·te·ine (sĭs´tĭ·ēn´, -ĭn), *n. Biochem.* an amino acid, HSCH₂CH(NH₂)COOH, obtained from cystine and important for growth-stimulating characteristics.

cysti-, var. of cyst-, as in *cysticercoid*.

cyst·ic (sĭs´tĭk), *adj.* 1. pertaining to, of the nature of, or having a cyst or cysts; encysted. 2. *Anat.* belonging to or relating to the urinary bladder or the gall bladder.

cys·ti·cer·coid (sĭs´tə·sûr´koid), *n. Parasitol.* the larva of certain tapeworms, developing in insects, etc., in which a single head forms without a spacious bladder around it.

cys·ti·cer·cus (sĭs´tə·sûr´kəs), *n., pl.* **-cerci** (-sûr´sī). *Parasitol.* the bladderworm larva of certain tapeworms, with a single head (scolex) formed in a large bladder. [NL, f. Gk.: *cysti-* CYSTI- + m. *kérkos* tail]

cys·tine (sĭs´tēn, -tĭn), *n. Biochem.* one of the important sulfur-containing amino acids, C₆H₁₂O₄N₂S₂, found in proteins, esp. hair, wool, and horn. Also, **cystin** (sĭs´tĭn).

cys·ti·tis (sĭs·tī´tĭs), *n. Pathol.* inflammation of the urinary bladder.

cysto-, var. of cyst-, before consonants, as in *cystoscope*.

cys·to·carp (sĭs´tə·kärp´), *n.* the mass of carpospores formed as a result of fertilization in red algae (*Rhodophyta*), with or without a special envelope (pericarp).

cys·to·cele (sĭs´tə·sēl´), *n. Pathol.* hernia in which the urinary bladder protrudes into the vagina.

cyst·oid (sĭs´toid), *adj.* 1. resembling a cyst but having no enclosing capsule. —*n.* 2. a cystlike structure or formation.

cys·to·lith (sĭs´tə·lĭth), *n. Bot.* a mass of calcium carbonate on the cellulose wall.

cys·to·scope (sĭs´tə·skōp´), *n. Med.* a slender, cylindrical instrument for examining the interior of the urinary bladder and for the introduction of medication therein.

cys·tot·o·my (sĭs·tŏt´ə·mĭ), *n., pl.* **-mies**. *Surg.* the operation of cutting into the urinary bladder.

cy·tas·ter (sī·tăs´tər, sĭ·tăs´-), *n. Biol.* aster.

-cyte, a word element referring to cells or corpuscles, as in *leucocyte*. [comb. form repr. Gk. *kýtos* container]

Cy·the·ra (sĭ·thĭr´ə), *n.* a small island off S Greece, famous as a sanctuary of Aphrodite. Also, **Cerigo**.

Cyth·er·e·a (sĭth´ə·rē´ə), *n. Gk. Myth.* a surname of Aphrodite or Venus. —**Cyth·er·e·an**, *adj.*

cyto-, a word element referring to cells, as in *cytogenesis*. Also, before vowels, **cyt-**. [t. Gk.: m. *kyto-*, comb. form of *kýtos* container]

cy·to·gen·e·sis (sī´tō·jĕn´ə·sĭs), *n.* the genesis and differentiation of cells.

cy·to·ge·net·ics (sī´tō·jə·nĕt´ĭks), *n.* the part played by cells in causing phenomena of heredity, mutation, and evolution.

cy·to·ki·ne·sis (sī´tō·kĭ·nē´sĭs, -kĭ-), *n.* the changes in the cytoplasm during mitosis, meiosis, and fertilization.

cy·tol·o·gy (sī·tŏl´ə·jĭ), *n.* the scientific study of cells, esp. their formation, structure, and functions. —**cy·tol´o·gist,** *n.*

cy·tol·y·sis (sī·tŏl´ə·sĭs), *n. Physiol.* the dissolution or degeneration of cells.

cy·ton (sī´tŏn), *n.* the body of a nerve cell.

cy·to·plasm (sī´tə·plăz´əm), *n. Biol.* the living substance or protoplasm of a cell exclusive of the nucleus. Also, **cy·to·plast** (sī´tə·plăst´). —**cy·to·plas´mic,** *adj.*

Cyz·i·cus (sĭz´ĭ·kəs), *n.* an ancient city of Mysia, in NW Asia Minor, on a peninsula in the Sea of Marmara.

C.Z., Canal Zone (Panama).

czar (zär), *n.* 1. an emperor or king. 2. (*usually cap.*) the emperor of Russia. 3. (*often cap.*) an autocratic ruler or leader. Also, **tsar, tzar**. [t. Russ.: m. *tsar*, ult. t. L: m. *Caesar*] —**czar·dom** (zär´dəm), *n.*

czar·das (chär´däsh), *n.* a Hungarian national dance in two movements, one slow and the other fast.

czar·e·vitch (zär´ə·vĭch), *n.* 1. the son of a czar. 2. (later) the eldest son of a czar. Also, **tsarevitch, tzarevitch**. [t. Russ.: m. *tsarevich*]

cza·rev·na (zä·rĕv´nə), *n.* a daughter of a czar. Also, **tsarevna, tzarevna**. [t. Russ.: m. *tsarevna*]

cza·ri·na (zä·rē´nə), *n.* the wife of a czar; Russian empress. Also, **tsarina, tzarina**. [f. CZAR, TSAR + -*ina* (Latinization of G -*ina*, fem. suffix, as in *zarin* wife of czar)]

czar·ism (zär´ĭz·əm), *n.* dictatorship; autocratic government. Also, **tsarism, tzarism**.

cza·rit·za (zä·rĭt´sə), *n.* czarina. Also, **tsaritza, tzaritza**.

Czech (chĕk), *n.* 1. a member of the most westerly branch of the Slavs, comprising the Bohemians (or Czechs proper), the Moravians, and the Slovaks. 2. the language of Bohemia and Moravia, a Slavic language similar to Slovak. —**Czech´ic, Czech´ish,** *adj.*

Czech., Czechoslovakia. Also, **Czechosl**.

Czech·o·slo·vak (chĕk´ə·slō´văk, -väk), *n.* 1. a member of the branch of the Slavic race comprising the Czechs proper, the Slovaks, etc. —*adj.* 2. of or pertaining to the Czechoslovaks. Also, **Czech´o-Slo´vak**.

Czech·o·slo·va·ki·a (chĕk´ə·slō·vä´kĭ·ə, -väk´ĭ-), *n.* a republic in central Europe. 13,224,000 pop. (est. 1955); 49,379 sq. mi. (1938). *Cap.:* Prague. Also, **Czech´o-Slo·va´ki·a**. —**Czech´o·slo·vak´i·an,** *adj., n.*

Czer·no·witz (chĕr´nô·vĭts), *n.* Polish name of **Cernăuti**.

Cze·sto·cho·wa (chăн·stô·hô´vä), *n.* a city in S Poland. 144,000 (est. 1954).

D

D, d (dē), *n., pl.* **D's** or **Ds, d's** or **ds**. 1. the 4th letter of the English alphabet. 2. (used as a symbol) the fourth in order; the fourth in a series. 3. the lowest passing mark for school or college work. 4. *Music.* **a.** the second tone of the scale of C, or the fourth tone of the scale of A minor. **b.** a written or printed note representing this tone. **c.** a key, string, or pipe tuned to this note. **d.** (in solmization) the second note of the scale.

D, 1. Roman numeral for 500. 2. *Chem.* deuterium. 3. Dutch.

D., 1. December. 2. Democrat. 3. Democratic. 4. *Physics.* density. 5. *Chem.* dextro-. 6. Dutch.

d., 1. date. 2. daughter. 3. degree. 4. delete. 5. Brit. (L *denarius*) penny; (L *denarii*) pence: *3d = 6 cents.* 6. *Physics.* density. 7. *Chem.* dextro-. 8. dialect. 9. dialectal. 10. diameter. 11. died. 12. dime. 13. dividend. 14. dollar. 15. dose.

D.A., 1. District Attorney. 2. Delayed Action (bomb).

dab[1] (dăb), *v.*, **dabbed, dabbing,** *n.* —*v.t.* 1. to strike, esp. lightly, as with the hand. 2. to pat or tap gently, as with some soft or moist substance. 3. to apply (a substance) by light strokes. —*v.i.* 4. to strike lightly; peck. —*n.* 5. a quick or light blow; a pat, as with the hand or something soft. 6. a small moist lump or mass. 7. a small quantity. [ME. Cf. Norw. *dabba* tap with the foot, G *tappe* footprint]

dab[2] (dăb), *n.* 1. a European flatfish, *Limanda limanda.* 2. a sand dab or other flatfish. [orig. unknown]

dab·ber (dăb′ər), *n.* 1. one who or that which dabs 2. a cushionlike article used for applying ink, etc., as by printers and engravers.

dab·ble (dăb′əl), *v.* **-bled,** **-bling.** —*v.t.* 1. to wet slightly or repeatedly in or with a liquid; splash; spatter. —*v.i.* 2. to play in water, as with the hands. 3. to do anything in a slight or superficial manner: *to dabble in literature.* [t. Flem.: m. s. *dabbelen*] —**dab′bler,** *n.*

dab·chick (dăb′chĭk′), *n.* a small diving bird, esp. the little grebe, *Podiceps fluviatilis,* of Europe, or the pied-billed grebe, *Podilymbus podiceps,* of America.

dab·ster (dăb′stər), *n.* 1. *Brit. Dial.* an expert. 2. *Colloq.* a superficial worker; a dabbler.

da ca·po (dä kä′pō). *Music.* from the beginning (a direction to repeat). [It.]

Dac·ca (dăk′ə), *n.* the principal city of East Pakistan, in E Bengal. 276,033 (1951).

dace (dās), *n., pl.* **daces** (*esp. collectively*) **dace.** 1. a small fresh-water cyprinoid fish, *Leuciscus leuciscus,* of Europe, with a stout, fusiform body. 2. any of several similar or related fishes of the U.S. [ME *darse,* t. OF: m. *dars* DART]

Da·chau (dä′кнou), *n.* a Nazi concentration camp, scene of mass murders, in S Germany, near Munich.

dachs·hund (dăks′hŏŏnd′, dăsh′-; *Ger.* däks′hŏŏnt′), *n.* one of a German breed of small hounds with a long body and very short legs. [t. G: f. *dachs* badger + *hund* dog]

Dachshund (8 in. or more high at the shoulder)

Da·ci·a (dā′shĭ ə, -shə), *n.* an ancient kingdom and later a Roman province in S Europe between the Carpathian Mountains and the Danube, corresponding generally to modern Rumania and adjacent regions. —**Da·cian** (dā′shən), *adj, n.*

da·coit (də koit′), *n.* one of a class of robbers in India and Burma, who plunder in bands. [t. Hind.: m. *dākāit,* der. *dākā* gang robbery]

da·coit·y (də koi′tĭ), *n.* gang robbery in India and Burma. [t. Hind.: m. *dākāiti*]

Da·cron (dā′krŏn), *n.* *Trademark.* a synthetic textile fiber having outstanding wrinkle-resistance and strength.

dac·tyl (dăk′təl, -tĭl), *n.* *Pros.* a foot of three syllables, one long followed by two short, or, in modern verse, one accented followed by two unaccented (– ◡ ◡), as in "Gently ănd hūmănly." [ME *dactile,* t. L: m.s. *dactylus,* t. Gk.: m. *dáktylos* finger or toe, date (see DATE[2]), metrical foot]

dac·tyl·ic (dăk tĭl′ĭk), *adj.* 1. of or characterized by dactyls. 2. of a dactyl. —*n.* 3. a dactylic verse.

dac·ty·lol·o·gy (dăk′tə lŏl′ə jĭ), *n.* the art of communicating ideas by signs made with the fingers, as in a manual alphabet used by the deaf.

dad (dăd), *n.* (in childish or familiar use) father. [earlier *dadde,* nursery substitute for FATHER]

da·da·ism (dä′də ĭz′əm), *n.* a movement in art, literature, etc., which flourished during and just after World War I. It attempted to discredit all previous art by using the incongruous and the accidental. Also, **da·da** (dä′də). [t. F: m. *Dadaisme,* der. *Dada,* title of a review]

Daddy-longlegs, *Phalangium opilio*

dad·dy (dăd′ĭ), *n., pl.* **-dies.** a diminutive of dad.

dad·dy-long·legs (dăd′ĭ lông′lĕgz′, -lŏng′-), *n. sing. and pl.* 1. *U.S.* a harvestman. 2. *Brit. Dial.* a crane fly.

da·do (dā′dō), *n., pl.* **-does, -dos.** 1. *Archit.* the part of a pedestal between the base and the cornice or cap. 2. the lower broad part of an interior wall finished in wallpaper, a fabric, paint, etc. [t. It.: die, cube, pedestal, g. L *dātus.* See DIE[2]]

dae·dal (dē′dəl), *adj. Chiefly Poetic.* 1. skillful or ingenious. 2. showing skill or cunning. 3. diversified. [t. L: s. *daedalus* skillful, t. Gk.: m. *daídalos*]

Daed·a·lus (dĕd′ə ləs *or, esp. Brit.* dē′də-), *n. Gk. Myth.* an Athenian architect who built the labyrinth for Minos and made wings for himself and his son Icarus. [t. L, t. Gk.: m. *Daídalos,* lit., the cunning worker] —**Dae·da·li·an, Dae·da·le·an** (dĭ dā′lĭ ən, -dāl′yən), *adj.*

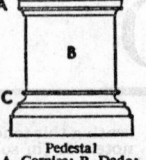

Pedestal
A. Cornice; B. Dado; C. Base

dae·mon (dē′mən), *n.* 1. *Gk. Myth.* a. a god. b. a subordinate deity, as the genius of a place or a man's attendant spirit. 2. a demon. Also, **daimon.** [t. L, t. Gk.: m. *daímōn*] —**dae·mon·ic** (dē mŏn′ĭk), *adj.*

daff[1] (dăf), *v.i. Scot.* to make sport; dally; play. [prop. play the fool, v. use of d. *daff* a fool; akin to DAFT]

daff[2] (dăf), *v.t.* 1. to turn or thrust aside. 2. *Obs.* to doff. [var. of DOFF]

daf·fo·dil (dăf′ə dĭl), *n.* 1. a plant, *Narcissus Pseudo-Narcissus,* of the genus *Narcissus,* with single or double yellow nodding flowers, blooming in the spring. 2. (formerly) any plant of this genus. 3. clear yellow; canary. [unexplained var. of ME *affodille,* t. VL: m. *affodillus,* var. of *asphodelus,* t. Gk.: m. *asphódelos*]

daf·fo·dil·ly (dăf′ə dĭl′ĭ), *n., pl.* **-lies.** *Poetic.* daffodil (def. 1, 2). Also, **daf·fa·down·dil·ly** (dăf′ə doun dĭl′ĭ), **daf′fy-down-dil′ly.**

daff·y (dăf′ĭ), *adj.,* **daffier, daffiest.** *U.S. Colloq. or Brit. Dial.* silly; weak-minded; crazy. [cf. DAFF[1]]

daft (dăft, däft), *adj.* 1. insane; crazy. 2. simple or foolish. 3. *Scot.* frolicsome. [ME *daffte,* OE *gedæfte* mild, meek. Cf. DEFT] —**daft′ly,** *adv.* —**daft′ness,** *n.*

dag (dăg), *n.* a daglock. [ME *dagge;* orig. uncert.]

da Gam·a (də găm′ə; *Port.* də gä′mə), **Vasco.** See Gama, Vasco da.

Da·gan (dā′găn), *n.* the Babylonian earth god.

Dag·en·ham (dăg′ən əm), *n.* a city in SE England, part of greater London. 114,588 (1951).

dag·ger (dăg′ər), *n.* 1. a short-edged and pointed weapon, like a small sword, used for thrusting and stabbing. 2. *Print.* a mark (†) used for references, etc.; the obelisk. —*v.t.* 3. to stab with a dagger. 4. *Print.* to mark with a dagger. [ME, der. obs. *dag* pierce, stab]

dag·gle (dăg′əl), *v.t., v.i.,* **-gled, -gling.** to drag or trail through mud, water, etc.; draggle. [freq. of d. *dag* bemire. See DAG]

dag·lock (dăg′lŏk′), *n.* a lock of wool on a sheep that hangs and drags in the wet. [see DAGGLE, LOCK[1]]

Da·go (dā′gō), *n., pl.* **-gos, -goes.** *U.S. Slang.* (in contemptuous use) 1. an Italian. 2. a Spaniard. 3. a Portuguese. [said to be t. Sp.: m. *Diego* James]

da·go·ba (dä′gə bə), *n.* a dome-shaped memorial alleged to contain relics of Buddha or a Buddhist saint.

Da·gon (dā′gŏn), *n.* the national god of the Philistines, represented as half man and half fish, originally a fish god and later the god of corn and grain. [t. L, t. Gk., t. Heb.: m. *dāghōn* little fish]

da·guerre·o·type (də gĕr′ə tīp′, -ĭ ə tīp′), *n., v.,* **-typed, -typing.** —*n.* 1. an early (1839) photographic process in which the impression was made on a silver surface sensitized to the action of light by iodine, and then developed by mercury vapor. 2. a picture so made. —*v.t.* 3. to photograph by this process. [named after L. J. M. *Daguerre* (1789–1851), French inventor. See -TYPE] —**da·guerre′o·typ′er, da·guerre′o·typ′ist,** *n.*

da·ha·be·ah (dä′hə bē′ə), *n.* a kind of houseboat or passenger boat, used on the Nile. Also, **da′ha·bee′yah, da′ha·bi′ya.** [t. Ar.: m. *dhahabīyah,* lit., the golden]

dahl·ia (dăl′yə, däl′- *or, esp. Brit.* dāl′-), *n.* 1. any plant of the composite genus *Dahlia,* native to Mexico and Central America, widely cultivated for its showy, variously colored flowers. 2. the flower or tuberous root of a dahlia. 3. a violet coal-tar color. [t. NL; named after A. *Dahl,* Swedish botanist]

Da·ho·mey (də hō′mĭ; *Fr.* dá á mě′), *n.* a republic in W Africa: independent member of the French Community: formerly part of French West Africa. 1,719,000 pop. (1959); 44,290 sq. mi. *Cap.:* Cotonou. —**Da·ho·man** (də hō′mən), *adj., n.*

Dail Eir·eann (dôl âr′ən; *Irish* tн̃ôl), the lower house of parliament of Ireland. See **Oireachtas.** Also, **Dail.** [Irish: *dail* assembly + *éireann,* gen. of *éire* Erin]

dai·ly (dā′lĭ), *adj., n., pl.* **-lies,** *adv.* —*adj.* 1. of, done, occurring, or issued each day or each weekday. —*n.* 2. a newspaper appearing each day or each weekday. 3. *Brit.* a servant who comes to work every day. —*adv.* 4. every day; day by day: *She phoned the hospital daily.*

dai·ly-bread·er (dā′lĭ brĕd′ər), *n. Brit.* commuter.

dai·men (dā′mĭn), *adj. Scot.* rare; occasional.

dai·mon (dī′mŏn), *n.* daemon. [see DEMON]

dai·myo (dī′myō), *n., pl.* **-myos, -myos.** 1. the class of greater nobles in Japanese feudalism. Often the daimyo were descendants of younger sons of emperors. 2. a member of this class. Also, **dai′mio.** [t. Jap.; f. Chinese: *dai* great + *mio* name]

Dai Nip·pon (dī′ nĭp′ŏn; *Jap.* dī′ nĕp′pŏn′), Greater Japan. Once the watchword of Japanese expansionists, it is now against the law to use *Dai Nippon* in Japan. See Japan.

dain·ty (dān′tĭ), *adj.,* **-tier, -tiest,** *n., pl.* **-ties.** —*adj.* 1. of delicate beauty or charm; exquisite. 2. pleasing to the palate; toothsome; delicious: *dainty food.* 3. particular in discrimination or taste; fastidious. 4. too particular; squeamish. —*n.* 5. something delicious to the taste; a delicacy. [ME *deinte,* t. OF, g. L *dignitas* worthiness] —**dain′ti·ly,** *adv.* —**dain′ti·ness,** *n.* —**Syn.** 1. See **delicate.** 3. See **particular.** 4. finical, overnice.

dai·qui·ri (dī′kə rĭ, dăk′ə-), *n., pl.* **-ris.** a vigorously shaken cocktail consisting of rum, lime juice, sugar, and ice.

Dai·ren (dī'rĕn'), *n.* a seaport in NE China: capital of the former Japanese leased territory of Kwantung in S Manchuria. Together with Port Arthur, 1,010,000 (est. 1954). Chinese, **Talien.** Formerly, **Dalny.**

dair·y (dâr'ĭ), *n., pl.* **dairies.** 1. a place, as a room or building, where milk and cream are kept and made into butter and cheese. 2. a shop or company that sells milk, butter, etc. 3. the business of producing milk, butter, and cheese. 4. a dairy farm. 5. the cows on a farm. [ME *deierie*, f. *dei* female servant, dairymaid (OE *dæge* breadmaker) + *-erie* -ERY]

dairy cattle, cows raised mainly for their milk.

dairy farm, a farm devoted chiefly to the production of milk and the manufacture of butter and cheese.

dair·y·ing (dâr'ĭ·ing), *n.* the business of a dairy.

dair·y·maid (dâr'ĭ mād'), *n.* a female servant employed in a dairy.

dair·y·man (dâr'ĭ mən), *n., pl.* **-men.** 1. an owner or manager of a dairy. 2. an employee in a dairy.

da·is (dā'ĭs, dās), *n.* a raised platform, as at the end of a room, for a throne, seats of honor, a lecturer's desk, etc. [ME *deis*, t. OF, g. LL *discus* table, L disk, dish. See DISCUS]

dai·sy (dā'zĭ), *n., pl.* **-sies,** *adj.* —*n.* 1. any of various composite plants, as *Chrysanthemum leucanthemum* (the common oxeye daisy of the U. S.) whose flower heads have a yellow disk and white rays, or *Bellis perennis* (the English daisy), etc. 2. *Slang.* something fine or first-rate —*adj.* 3. *Slang.* fine; first-class; excellent; first-rate [ME *dayesye*, OE *dægeséage* day's eye] —**dai'sied,** *adj.*

dai·sy-cut·ter (dā'zĭ kŭt'ər), *n. Colloq.* (in baseball, tennis, etc.) a batted or served ball that skims along near the ground.

dak (dôk, däk), *n.* (in the East Indies) 1. transportation by relays of men or horses. 2. the mail. Also, **dawk.** [t. Hind.]

Da·kar (dä kär'), *n.* a seaport in and the capital of Senegal; formerly capital of French West Africa. 234,500 pop. (1957); 68 sq. mi.

Da·kins solution (dā'-kĭnz), a liquid anti-septic, an approximately neutral solution containing about 0.5 percent of sodium hypochlorite, used in treating infected wounds. [named after H. D. *Dakin* (1880-1952), chemist, the originator]

Da·ko·ta (də kō'tə), *n.* 1. a former territory in the United States: divided into the States of North Dakota and South Dakota, 1889. 2. North Dakota or South Dakota. 3. a Sioux Indian. 4. a division of the Siouan stock of North American Indians, whose former habitat was in and near North and South Dakota. 5. any of several Siouan languages. — **Da·ko'tan,** *adj., n.*

Da·la·dier (dà là dyĕ'), *n.* Édouard (ĕ dwär'), born 1884, premier of France, 1933, 1934, and 1938-40.

Da·lai La·ma (dä lī' lä'mə), the Grand Lama, the chief pontiff and governmental ruler of Tibet. [f. Tibetan: *dalai* lit., ocean + *lama* priest]

dale (dāl), *n.* 1. a vale; valley. 2. *Phys. Geog.* a small, open, river valley partly enclosed by low hills. [ME; OE *dæl*, c. G *tal*]

Dale (dāl), *n.* Sir **Thomas,** died 1619, British governor of the colony of Virginia.

dales·man (dālz'mən), *n., pl.* **-men.** a person living in a dale or valley, esp. in the northern counties of England.

Dal·hou·sie (dăl hōō'zĭ, -hou'-), *n.* 1. George **Ramsay, Earl of,** 1770-1838, British general: governor of the Canadian colonies, 1819-28. 2. James **Andrew Brown Ramsay** (răm'zĭ), **1st Marquis and 10th Earl of,** 1812-60, British statesman: viceroy of India, 1848-56.

Da·li (dä'lē), *n.* Salvador (săl'və dôr'; *Sp.* säl'vä dôr'), born 1904. Spanish painter in U.S.

Dal·las (dăl'əs), *n.* a city in NE Texas. 679,684 (1960).

dalles (dălz), *n.pl. Western U.S.* 1. the precipice on either side of a deep ravine or canyon. 2. rapids flowing over a flat rock bottom in a narrowed portion of a river, esp. (*cap.*) the rapids of the Columbia river. [t. Canadian F, special use of F *dalle* gutter, t. Gmc; cf. OE *dæl* gorge, DALE]

dal·li·ance (dăl'ĭ əns), *n.* 1. a trifling away of time; dawdling. 2. amorous toying; flirtation.

dal·ly (dăl'ĭ), *v.,* **-lied, -lying.** —*v.i.* 1. to sport or play, esp. amorously. 2. to play mockingly; trifle: *dally with danger.* 3. to waste time; loiter; delay. —*v.t.* 4. to waste (time) (fol. by *away*). [ME *daly*(en), t. OF: m. *dalier* talk; ? of Gmc. orig.] —**dal'li·er,** *n.* —**dal'ly·ing·ly,** *adv.* —**Syn.** 3. See loiter. —**Ant.** 3. hasten.

Dal·ma·tia (dăl mā'shə), *n.* a region in W Yugoslavia, along the E coast of the Adriatic.

Dal·ma·tian (dăl mā'shən), *adj.* 1. of or pertaining to Dalmatia or its people. —*n.* 2. an inhabitant of Dalmatia, esp. a member of the native Slavic-

speaking race. 3. Also, **Dalmatian dog.** one of a breed of dogs resembling the pointer, and of a white color profusely marked with small black or liver-colored spots; coach dog.

dal·mat·ic (dăl măt'ĭk), *n.* an ecclesiastical vestment worn over the alb by the deacon, as at the celebration of the Mass, and worn by bishops on certain occasions, as at a coronation. [t. L: s. *dalmatica*, prop. fem. of L *Dalmaticus* Dalmatian]

Dalmatian
(19 to 23 in. high at the shoulder)

Dal·ny (däl'nĭ), *n.* former name of Dairen.

Dal·rym·ple (dăl rĭm'pəl, dăl'rĭm'-), *n.* **Sir James,** (*1st Viscount Stair*) 1619-95, British jurist.

dal se·gno (däl sĕ'nyō), *Music.* go back to the sign and repeat (a direction). [It.]

Dal·ton (dôl'tən), *n.* **John,** 1766-1844, British chemist and physicist.

dal·ton·ism (dôl'tə nĭz'əm), *n.* color blindness; esp., inability to distinguish red from green. [named after John DALTON, who was so afflicted]

Dalton System, a method of progressive education, whereby students contract to carry through on their own responsibility the year's work as divided up into monthly assignments. [from use in Dalton (Mass.) High Schools]

Da·ly (dā'lĭ), *n.* **John Augustin** (ô gŭs'tĭn), 1838-99, U.S. playwright, critic, and theatrical manager.

Da·ly City (dā'lĭ), a city in central California, S of San Francisco. 44,791 (1960).

dam¹ (dăm), *n., v.,* **dammed, damming.** —*n.* 1. a barrier to obstruct the flow of water, esp. one of earth, masonry, etc., built across a stream. 2. a body of water confined by a dam. 3. any barrier resembling a dam. —*v.t.* 4. to furnish with a dam; obstruct or confine with a dam. 5. to stop up; block up. [ME, c. G *damm*]

dam² (dăm), *n.* a female parent (used esp. of quadrupeds). [ME *dam*(*me*), var. of DAME]

dam·age (dăm'ĭj), *n., v.,* **-aged, -aging.** —*n.* 1. injury or harm that impairs value or usefulness. 2. (*pl.*) *Law.* the estimated money equivalent for detriment or injury sustained. 3. *Colloq.* cost; expense. —*v.t.* 4. to cause damage to; injure or harm; impair the usefulness of. —*v.i.* 5. to suffer damage. [ME, t. OF: f. *dam* (g. L *damnum* harm, loss) + *-age* -AGE] —**dam'age·a·ble,** *adj.* —**dam'ag·ing·ly,** *adv.* —**Syn.** 1. DAMAGE, DETRIMENT, HARM, MISCHIEF refer to injuries of various kinds. DAMAGE is the kind of injury (or the effect of injury) which directly impairs appearance, value, usefulness, soundness, etc.: *fire causes damage to property, property suffers damage.* DETRIMENT is a falling off from an original condition as the result of damage, depreciation, devaluation, etc.: *detriment to health because of illness, to property because of neglect.* HARM is the kind of injury which connotes sorrow or a sense of evil; it may denote either physical hurt or mental, moral, or spiritual injury: *bodily harm, harm to one's self-confidence.* MISCHIEF may be damage, harm, trouble, or misfortune caused by a person esp. if maliciously: *an enemy who would do one mischief.*

dam·an (dăm'ən), *n.* 1. a small mammal, *Procavia syriaca*, of the order *Hyracoidea*, inhabiting Syria, Palestine, etc. (the *cony* of the English Bible). 2. any hyrax. [t. Ar.: short for *daman isrāil* lamb of Israel]

Da·man·hur (dä'män hōōr'), *n.* a city in N Egypt, near Alexandria. 99,300 (est. 1952).

Da·mão (dä moun'), *n.* a seaport in Portuguese India, on the Arabian Sea. 10,000 (est. 1954); including district, 68,534 (1950). Also, **Da·man** (dä'män').

Da·ma·ra·land (dä mä'rə länd'), *n.* a region in the central part of South-West Africa.

Dam·a·scene (dăm'ə sēn', dăm'ə sēn'), *adj., n., v.,* **-scened, -scening.** —*adj.* 1. of or pertaining to the city of Damascus. 2. (*l.c.*) of or pertaining to the art of damascening. —*n.* 3. an inhabitant of Damascus. 4. (*l.c.*) work or patterns produced by damascening. —*v.t.* 5. (*l.c.*) to produce wavy lines on, as in the welding of iron and steel in the swords of Damascus. 6. (*l.c.*) to ornament (objects of iron and steel) by inlaying with precious metals, or by etching. Also, **damaskeen** for 5, 6. [ME, t. L: m.s. *Damascēnus*, t. Gk.: m. *Damaskēnós* of Damascus]

Da·mas·cus (də măs'kəs), *n.* the capital of Syria, in the SW part: reputed to be the oldest continuously existing city in the world. 383,239 (est. 1953).

Damascus steel, a kind of steel with a wavy or variegated pattern, originally made in the East, chiefly at Damascus, and used for making sword blades.

dam·ask (dăm'əsk), *n.* 1. a reversible fabric of linen, silk, cotton, or wool, woven with patterns. 2. the napery of this material. 3. Damascus steel. 4. the peculiar pattern or wavy appearance on its surface. 5. the pink color of the damask rose. —*adj.* 6. made of or like damask: *damask cloth.* 7. pink (like the damask rose). —*v.t.* 8. to damascene. 9. to weave or adorn with elaborate design, as in damask cloth. [ME *Damaske*, t. L: m. *Damascus*, t. Gk.: m. *Damaskós* Damascus]

dam·a·skeen (dăm'ə skēn'), *v.t.* damascene.

damask rose, a fragrant pink rose, *Rosa damascena.*

dame (dăm), *n.* 1. a form of address to any woman of rank or authority. 2. (in Great Britain) **a.** the legal title of the wife of a knight or baronet. **b.** (since 1917) the distinctive title employed before the name of a woman upon whom a dignity corresponding to that of a knight has been conferred. **3.** *U.S.* a married woman. **4.** *Slang.* a woman. **5.** *Archaic or Dial.* the mistress of a household. **6.** *Archaic.* a woman of rank or authority, as a female ruler. **7.** *Obsolesc.* the mistress of a school. [ME, t. OF, g. L *domina* mistress, lady]

Da·mien de Veus·ter (dä myăn′ də vœs těr′), **Joseph** (zhō zěf′), known as **Father Damien** (dā′mĭ ən), 1840–89, Belgian Roman Catholic missionary to the lepers of Molokai.

Dam·i·et·ta (dăm′ĭ ět′ə), *n.* a city in NE Egypt, in the Nile delta. 63,100 (est. 1952). Arabic, **Dumyat.**

dam·mar (dăm′ər), *n.* **1.** a copallike resin chiefly from dipterocarpaceous trees of southern Asia, esp. Malaya and Sumatra, much used for making colorless varnish. **2.** any of various similar resins from trees of other families. Also, **dam′mer.** [t. Malay: m. *damar* resin]

damn (dăm), *v.t.* **1.** to declare (something) to be bad, unfit, invalid, or illegal. **2.** to condemn as a failure: *damn a play.* **3.** to bring condemnation upon; ruin. **4.** to doom to eternal punishment, or condemn to hell. **5.** to swear at or curse, using the word "damn." —*v.i.* **6.** to use the word "damn": swear. —*n.* **7.** the utterance of "damn" in swearing or for emphasis. [ME *damne(n)*, t. OF: m. *damner*, t. L: m. *damnāre* condemn, doom]

dam·na·ble (dăm′nə bəl), *adj.* **1.** worthy of damnation. **2.** detestable, abominable, or outrageous. —**dam′na·ble·ness**, *n.* —**dam′na·bly**, *adv.*

dam·na·tion (dăm nā′shən), *n.* **1.** act of damning. **2.** state of being damned. **3.** a cause or occasion of being damned. **4.** *Theol.* sin as incurring or deserving eternal punishment. **5.** an oath expressing anger, disappointment, etc.

dam·na·to·ry (dăm′nə tôr′ĭ), *adj.* conveying or occasioning condemnation; damning.

damned (dămd), *adj.* **1.** condemned, esp. to eternal punishment. **2.** detestable. —*adv.* **3.** extremely; very.

dam·ni·fy (dăm′nə fī′), *v.t.* —**fied**, —**fying.** *Law.* to cause loss or damage to. [t. AF: m. *damnifier*, t. L: m. *damnificāre* injure]

damn·ing (dăm′ĭng, dăm′nĭng), *adj.* that damns or condemns; incriminating. —**damn′ing·ly**, *adv.*

Dam·o·cles (dăm′ə klēz′), *n. Gk. Legend.* a flatterer, who, having extolled the happiness of Dionysius, tyrant of Syracuse, was placed at a banquet with a sword suspended over his head by a single hair, to show him the perilous nature of that happiness. —**Dam·o·cle·an** (dăm′ə klē′ən), *adj.*

dam·oi·selle (dăm′ə zěl′), *n. Archaic.* damsel. Also **dam′o·sel′, dam′o·zel′.**

Da·mon (dā′mən), *n. Rom. Legend.* a Syracusan who barely escaped suffering the death penalty as voluntary hostage for his friend Pythias.

damp (dămp), *adj.* **1.** moderately wet; moist. **2.** *Archaic.* dejected. —*n.* **3.** moisture; humidity; moist air. **4.** a noxious or stifling vapor or gas, esp. in a mine. **5.** depression of spirits; dejection. **6.** a check or discouragement. —*v.t.* **7.** to make damp; moisten. **8.** to check or retard the energy, action, etc., of. **9.** to stifle or suffocate; extinguish. **10.** *Acoustics, Music.* to check or retard the action of (a vibrating string, etc.); dull; deaden. **11.** *Physics.* to cause a decrease in amplitude of (successive oscillations or waves). [ME *domp*, t. MFlem.: vapor, c. G *dampf* steam] —**damp′ish**, *adj.* —**damp′ly**, *adv.* —**damp′ness**, *n.*

—**Syn. 1.** DAMP, HUMID, MOIST mean slightly wet. DAMP usually implies slight and extraneous wetness, generally undesirable or unpleasant unless the result of intention: *a damp cellar, to put a damp cloth on a patient's forehead.* HUMID is a literary or scientific word, applied to that which is so permeated with moisture that the moisture seems a part of it, esp. unpleasant dampness in the air in either hot or cold weather: *the air is oppressively humid today.* MOIST denotes that which is slightly wet, naturally or properly: *moist ground, leather.* —**Ant. 1.** dry.

damp·en (dăm′pən), *v.t.* **1.** to make damp; moisten. **2.** to dull or deaden; depress. —*v.i.* **3.** to become damp. —**damp′en·er**, *n.*

damp·er (dăm′pər), *n.* **1.** one who or that which damps. **2.** a movable plate for regulating the draft in a stove, furnace, etc. **3.** *Music.* **a.** a device in stringed keyboard instruments to deaden the vibration of the strings. **b.** the mute of a brass instrument, as a horn. **4.** *Elect.* an attachment to keep the indicator of a measuring instrument from oscillating excessively, usually a set of vanes in an air space or fluid, or a short-circuited winding in a magnetic field.

Dam·pi·er (dăm′pĭ ər, dămp′yər), *n.* **William**, 1652–1715, British navigator, explorer, writer, and pirate.

Dam·rosch (dăm′rŏsh), *n.* **Walter Johannes** (jō′hän′əs), 1862–1950, U. S. musical conductor and composer, born in Germany.

dam·sel (dăm′zəl), *n.* a young woman; a girl; a maiden, originally one of gentle or noble birth. [ME *dameisele*, t. OF, ult. der. L *domina* mistress, lady. See DAME]

damsel fly, any of the more fragile, slow-flying insects of the order *Odonata*, distinguished from the dragonflies by having the wings closed while at rest.

dam·son (dăm′zən), *n.* **1.** the small dark-blue or purple fruit of a plum, *Prunus insititia*, introduced into Europe from Asia Minor. **2.** the tree bearing it. [ME *damascene*, repr. L (*prunum*) *damascēnum* (plum) of Damascus. See DAMASCENE]

Dan (dăn), *n.* **1.** one of the twelve sons of Jacob. Gen. 30:6. **2.** one of the twelve Hebrew tribes. Josh. 19:40. **3.** a city at the northern end of Palestine; hence, the common phrase **from Dan to Beersheba** (the two limits of Palestine). Judges 20:1. [t. Heb.]

Dan (dăn), *n. Archaic.* a title of honor, equivalent to *master* or *sir: Dan Chaucer, Dan Cupid.* [ME, t. OF, g. L *dominus* master, lord]

Dan., **1.** Daniel. **2.** Danish.

Da·na (dā′nə), *n.* **1. Charles Anderson**, 1819–97, U.S. journalist. **2. Edward Salisbury**, 1849–1935, U.S. mineralogist and physicist. **3.** his father, **James Dwight**, 1813–95, U.S. geologist and mineralogist. **4. Richard Henry**, 1815–82, U.S. lawyer and writer.

Dan·a·ë (dăn′ĭ ē′), *n. Gk. Legend.* a maiden imprisoned in a brazen tower by her father Acrisius, King of Argos. Visited by Zeus in the form of a shower of gold, she became the mother of Perseus.

Da·na·i·des (də nā′ə dēz′), *n.pl. Gk. Myth.* daughters of Danaüs, who for killing their husbands were condemned in Hades to pour water forever into a perforated or bottomless vessel. Also, **Da·na′i·des′.** —**Dan·a·id·e·an** (dăn′ĭ ĭd′ĭ ən, dăn′ĭ ə dē′ən), *adj.*

Dan·a·üs (dăn′ĭ əs), *n. Gk. Myth.* the ruler of Argos who married his daughters, the Danaides, to their fifty cousins, the sons of Ægyptus, but made them slay their husbands on the wedding night. Also, **Dan′a·us.**

Dan·bur·y (dăn′běr′ĭ, -bə rĭ), *n.* a city in SW Connecticut. 22,928 (1960).

dance (dăns, däns), *v.*, **danced**, **dancing**, *n.* —*v.i.* **1.** to move with the feet or body rhythmically, esp. to music. **2.** to leap, skip, etc., as from excitement or emotion; move nimbly or quickly. **3.** to bob up and down. —*v.t.* **4.** to perform or take part in (a dance). **5.** to cause to dance. **6.** to bring about or cause to be by dancing. **7. dance attendance**, to attend constantly or solicitously. —*n.* **8.** a successive group of rhythmical steps, generally executed to music. **9.** an act or round of dancing. **10.** a social gathering for dancing; ball. **11.** a piece of music suited in rhythm to a particular form of dancing. [ME *daunse(n)*, t. OF: m. *danser*; prob. of Gmc. orig.] —**danc′ing·ly**, *adv.*

dance of death. See macabre (def. 2).

danc·er (dăn′sər, dän′-), *n.* **1.** one who dances. **2.** one who dances professionally, as on the stage.

dan·de·li·on (dăn′də lī′ən), *n.* **1.** a common composite plant, *Taraxacum officinale*, abundant as a weed, characterized by deeply toothed or notched leaves and golden-yellow flowers. **2.** any other plant of the genus *Taraxacum.* [t. F: m. *dent de lion* lion's tooth (with allusion to the toothed leaves)]

dan·der (dăn′dər), *n. Colloq.* anger or temper. [? fig. use of *dander* DANDRUFF; or fig. use of *dander* ferment]

Dan·die Din·mont (dăn′dĭ dĭn′mŏnt), one of a breed of small terriers with a long body, short legs, and long pendulous ears. [from *Dandie* (Andrew) *Dinmont*, in Scott's "Guy Mannering," said to own the progenitors]

dan·di·fy (dăn′də fī′), *v.t.*, —**fied**, —**fying.** to make dandylike or foppish. —**dan′di·fi·ca′tion**, *n.*

dan·dle (dăn′dəl), *v.t.*, —**dled**, —**dling.** **1.** to move lightly up and down, as a child on the knees or in the arms. **2.** to pet; pamper. [? t. Scand.; cf. Faeroese *danda* dandle] —**dan′dler**, *n.*

dan·druff (dăn′drəf), *n.* a scurf which forms on the scalp and comes off in small scales. Also, **dan·driff** (dăn′drĭf). [orig. unknown]

dan·dy¹ (dăn′dĭ), *n., pl.* —**dies**, *adj.*, —**dier**, —**diest.** —*n.* **1.** a man who is excessively concerned about clothes and appearance; a fop. **2.** *Colloq.* something very fine or first-rate. **3.** *Naut. Brit.* **a.** a yawl with leg-of-mutton jigger. **b.** its small aftersail. —*adj.* **4.** foppish. **5.** *U.S. Colloq.* fine; first-rate. [? special use of *Dandy*, var. of *Andy* Andrew) —**dan′dy·ish**, *adj.* —**dan′dy·ism**, *n.*

dan·dy² (dăn′dĭ), *n.* (in the West Indies) dengue.

dandy roll, a roller used in making some kinds of paper and in impressing watermarks. Also, **dandy roller.**

Dane (dān), *n.* **1.** a native or inhabitant of Denmark. **2.** a person of Danish descent. **3.** a great Dane. [appar. back formation from OE *Dænemarc* Denmark; r. *Dene*, pl., the Danes; cf. Icel. *Danir*]

Dane·law (dān′lô′), *n.* **1.** the body of laws in force in that part of England to which the Danes were restricted in the ninth century. **2.** that part of England under this law. Also, **Dane·lagh** (dān′lô′). [f. DANE + LAW; r. OE *Denalagu* law of the Danes]

dan·ger (dān′jər), *n.* **1.** liability or exposure to harm or injury; risk; peril. **2.** an instance or cause of peril. **3.** *Obs.* power; jurisdiction; domain. [ME *daunger*, t. OF: m. *dangier*, g. LL deriv. of *dominium* lordship]

—**Syn. 1.** DANGER HAZARD, PERIL, JEOPARDY imply some evil or harm which one may encounter. DANGER is the general word for liability to all kinds of injury or evil consequences, either near at hand and certain, or remote and doubtful: *to be in danger of catching cold or of being killed.* HAZARD suggests a danger which one can foresee but cannot avoid: *an aviator is exposed to many hazards.* PERIL usually denotes great and imminent danger: *the passengers on the disabled ship were in great peril.* JEOPARDY, a less common word, has essentially the same meaning as PERIL, but emphasizes exposure to the chances of a situation: *to save his friend he put his life in jeopardy.* —**Ant. 1.** safety.

dan·ger·ous (dān′jər əs), *adj.* full of danger or risk; causing danger; perilous; hazardous; unsafe. —**dan′ger·ous·ly**, *adv.* —**dan′ger·ous·ness**, *n.*

---

b., blend of, blended; c., cognate with; d., dialect, dialectal; der., derived from; f., formed from; g., going back to; m., modification of; r., replacing; s., stem of; t., taken from; ?, perhaps. See the full key on inside cover.

dan·gle (dăng'gəl), v., **-gled, -gling,** n. · —v.i. **1.** to hang loosely with a swaying motion. **2.** to hang about or follow a person, as if seeking favor. —v.t. **3.** to cause to dangle; hold or carry swaying loosely. —n. **4.** act of dangling. **5.** something that dangles. [t. Scand; cf. Dan. *dangle* dangle, bob up and down] —**dan'gler,** n.

dangling participle, *Gram.* a participle separated from the word modified by intervening words, as *burning* in: *Burning with enthusiasm, the car brought us to Rome.*

Dan·iel (dăn'yəl), n. **1.** *Bible.* **a.** a Jewish captive and prophet living in Babylon. **b.** a canonical book in the Old Testament. **2. Samuel,** 1562–1619, English poet and historian. [t. Heb.: m. *Dāni'ēl*]

Dan·iels (dăn'yəlz), n. **Josephus** (jō sē'fəs), 1862–1948, U.S. editor and statesman.

Dan·ish (dā'nĭsh), adj. **1.** of or pertaining to the Danes, their country, or their language. —n. **2.** a Germanic language, the language of Denmark, closely related to Norwegian, Swedish, and Icelandic.

Danish West Indies, a former Danish colony in the Virgin Islands: purchased by the U. S., 1917.

Dan·ite (dăn'īt), n. **1.** *Bible.* a descendant of Dan. Judges 13:2. **2.** a member of an alleged secret order of Mormons supposed to have been formed about 1837.

dank (dăngk), adj. unpleasantly moist or humid; damp. [cf. Sw. *dank* marshy place, Icel. *dökk* pool] —**dank'ly,** adv. —**dank'ness,** n.

dan·ke schön (dăng'kə shœn'), *German.* thank you.

D'An·nun·zio (dän nōōn'tsyō), n. **Gabriele** (gä'brē-ā'lē), 1863–1938, Italian author and soldier.

Da·no-Nor·we·gian (dā'nō nôr wē'jən), n. a literary and urban language of Norway, based on Danish.

danse ma·ca·bre (däns mȧ kä'br), *French.* See **macabre** (def. 2).

dan·seuse (dän sœz'), n., pl. **-seuses** (-sœz'). a female ballet dancer. [t. F, fem. of *danseur* dancer, der. *danser* DANCE]

Dan·te (dăn'tĭ; *It.* dän'tĕ), n. (Dante Alighieri) 1265–1321, Italian poet: author of the *Divine Comedy.*

Dan·te·an (dăn'tĭ ən, dăn tē'ən), adj. **1.** of Dante or his writings. **2.** Dantesque.

Dan·tesque (dăn tĕsk'), adj. in the style of Dante; characterized by impressive elevation of style with deep solemnity or somberness of feeling.

Dan·ton (dăn'tən; *Fr.* dän tôn'), n. **Georges Jacques** (zhôrzh zhȧk), 1759–94, French Revolutionary leader.

Dan·ube (dăn'ūb), n. a river in Europe, flowing from SW West Germany E to the Black Sea. 1725 mi. German, **Donau.** Hungarian, **Duna.** —**Dan·u·bi·an** (dăn ū'bĭ ən), adj.

Dan·ville (dăn'vĭl), n. **1.** a city in E Illinois. 41,856 (1960). **2.** a city in S Virginia. 46,577 (1960).

Dan·zig (dăn'sĭg; *Ger.* dän'tsĭKH), n. **1.** a seaport in N Poland, on the **Bay of Danzig,** an inlet of the Baltic. 118,000 (1946). **2. Free City of,** a former self-governing territory including the seaport of Danzig, constituted by the treaty of Versailles, 1920: a part of Germany, 1939–1945; now in Poland. 202,000 (est. 1954); 754 sq. mi. Polish, **Gdansk.**

dap (dăp), v.i., **dapped, dapping. 1.** to fish by letting the bait fall lightly on the water. **2.** to dip lightly or suddenly into water. **3.** to bounce. [ME *dop*. Cf. DIP]

Daph·ne (dăf'nĭ), n. **1.** *Gk. Myth.* a nymph who, pursued by Apollo, was saved by being changed into a laurel tree. **2.** (l.c.) **a.** the laurel, *Laurus nobilis.* **b.** any plant of the thymelaeaceous genus *Daphne,* of Europe and Asia, comprising small shrubs of which some species, as *D. Mezereum,* are cultivated for their fragrant flowers. [t. L, t. Gk.: laurel]

Daph·nis (dăf'nĭs), n. *Gk. Myth.* a son of Hermes by a nymph: the inventor of pastoral poetry.

Daphnis and Chlo·ë (klō'ĭ), two lovers in pastoral literature, esp. in a Greek romance attributed to Longus.

dap·per (dăp'ər), adj. **1.** neat; trim; smart. **2.** small and active. [late ME *dapyr* pretty, elegant; cf. G *tapfer* brave.] —**dap'per·ly,** adv. —**dap'per·ness,** n.

dap·ple (dăp'əl), n., adj., v., **-pled, -pling.** —n. **1.** mottled marking, as of an animal's skin or coat. **2.** an animal with a mottled skin or coat. —adj. **3.** dappled; spotted: *a dapple horse.* —v.t., v.i. **4.** to mark or become marked with spots. [orig. uncert. Cf. Icel. *depill* spot, dot]

dap·pled (dăp'əld), adj. having spots of different colors or shades; spotted.

dap·ple-gray (dăp'əl grā'), adj. gray with ill-defined mottling of a darker shade.

D.A.R., Daughters of the American Revolution.

d Ar·blay (där'blā; *Fr.* där blĕ'), n. See **Burney.**

Dar·by and Joan (där'bĭ, jōn), the typical "old married couple" contentedly leading a life of placid, uneventful domesticity.

Dar·by·ites (där'bĭ īts'), n.pl. Plymouth Brethren.

Dar·dan (där'dən), adj., n. Trojan. Also, **Dar·da·ni·an** (där dā'nĭ ən). [f. s. L *Dardanius* (t. Gk.: m. *Dardánios*) + -AN]

Dar·da·nelles (där'də nĕlz'), n.pl. the strait between European and Asiatic Turkey, connecting the Aegean with the Sea of Marmara. 40 mi. long; 1–5 mi. wide. Ancient, Hellespont.

Dar·da·nus (där'də nəs), n. the mythical ancestor of the Trojans.

dare (dâr), v., **dared** or **durst, dared** (p. subj. often *dare*), **daring,** n. —v.i. **1.** to have the necessary courage or boldness for something; be bold enough. **2.** dare say, to assume as probable; have no doubt. —v.t. **3.** to have the necessary courage for; venture on. **4.** to meet defiantly. **5.** to challenge or provoke to action, esp. by doubting one's courage; defy: *to dare a man to fight.* —n. **6.** an act of daring; defiance; challenge. [ME *dar,* OE *dear(r),* 1st and 3d pers. sing. pres. ind. of *durran;* akin to OHG *giturran*] —**dar'er,** n.

—**Syn. 1.** DARE, VENTURE imply involvement in risks and dangers. DARE emphasizes the state of mind that makes one willing to meet danger: *he dared to do what he knew was right.* VENTURE emphasizes the act of doing something which involves risk: *he ventured into deep water.*

dare·dev·il (dâr'dĕv'əl), n. **1.** a recklessly daring person. —adj. **2.** recklessly daring.

dare·dev·il·try (dâr'dĕv'əl trĭ), n. recklessness; venturesomeness. Also, **dare·dev·il·ry** (dâr'dĕv'əl rĭ).

Dar es Sa·laam (där'ĕs sə läm'), n. a seaport in E Tanganyika and the capital of Tanzania. 128,742 (1957).

Dar·fur (där fōōr'), n. a province in the W Sudan. 1,005,600 (est. 1954); 191,650 sq. mi. *Cap.:* El Fasher.

darg (därg), n. *Scot. and N. Eng.* a day's work. [ME *dawerk,* OE *dægweorc* day-work]

dar·ic (dăr'ĭk), n. the gold coin unit of ancient Persia. [t. Gk.: m.s. *dāreikós;* from Pers.]

Dar·i·en (dâr'ĭ ĕn / dâr'ĭ ĕn / *Sp.* dä'rē ĕn'), n. **1. Gulf of,** an arm of the Caribbean between the NE coast of Panama and Colombia. **2. Isthmus of,** former name of the **Isthmus of Panama.**

dar·ing (dâr'ĭng), n. **1.** adventurous courage; boldness. —adj. **2.** that dares; bold; intrepid; adventurous. —**dar'ing·ly,** adv. —**dar'ing·ness,** n. —**Syn. 2.** dauntless, undaunted, venturesome, audacious. —**Ant. 1.** caution.

Da·ri·us I (də rī'əs), ("the Great," *Darius Hystaspes*) 558?–486? B.C., king of Persia, 521–486? B.C.

Dar·jee·ling (där jē'lĭng), n. a town in NE India, in W Bengal: mountain resort. 33,605 (1951).

dark (därk), adj. **1.** without light; with very little light: *a dark room.* **2.** radiating or reflecting little light: *a dark color.* **3.** approaching black in hue: *a dark brown.* **4.** not pale or fair: *a dark complexion.* **5.** gloomy; cheerless; dismal. **6.** sullen; frowning. **7.** morally or spiritually blind. **8.** destitute of knowledge or culture; unenlightened. **9.** hard to understand; obscure. **10.** hidden; secret: *a dark purpose.* **11.** silent; reticent. **12.** *Phonet.* (of *l* sounds) resembling a back vowel in quality: *English l is darker than French l.* —n. **13.** the absence of light; darkness. **14.** night; nightfall. **15.** a dark place. **16.** a dark color. **17.** obscurity. **18.** secrecy. **19.** ignorance. —v.t., v.i. *Obs.* **20.** to darken. [ME *derk,* OE *deorc.* Cf. MHG *terken*] —**dark'·ish,** adj.

—**Syn. 1.** DARK, DIM, GLOOMY, MURKY refer to absence or insufficiency of light. DARK implies a more or less complete absence of light: *a dark night.* DIM implies faintness of light or indistinctness of form (resulting from the lack of light or from imperfect vision): *a dim outline.* GLOOMY means cloudy, ill-lighted, dusky: *a gloomy hall.* MURKY implies a thick, cloudy, or misty darkness: *a murky cave.* **4.** dusky, swarthy, black. **9.** recondite, abstruse. —**Ant. 1.** lighted. **2.** bright. **5.** cheerful. **6.** pleasant. **9.** clear.

Dark Ages, 1. the time in history from about A.D. 476 to about A.D. 1000. **2.** (occasionally) the whole of the Middle Ages, from about A.D. 476 to the Renaissance.

Dark Continent, The, Africa: so called because it was formerly so little known.

dark·en (där'kən), v.t. **1.** to make dark or darker; make obscure. **2.** to make less white or clear in color. **3.** to make gloomy; sadden. **4.** to make blind. —v.i. **5.** to become dark or darker. **6.** to become obscure. **7.** to become less white or clear in color. **8.** to grow clouded, as with gloom or anger. **9.** to become blind.

dark·ey (där'kĭ), n., pl. **darkeys.** darky.

dark horse, 1. a race horse, competitor, etc., about whom little is known or who unexpectedly wins. **2.** a person unexpectedly nominated, esp. in a political convention.

dark lantern, a lantern whose light can be obscured by a dark slide or cover at the opening.

dar·kle (där'kəl), v.i., **-kled, -kling. 1.** to appear dark; show indistinctly. **2.** to grow dark, gloomy, etc. [back formation from DARKLING, adv., taken as ppr.]

dark·ling (där'lĭng), adv. **1.** in the dark. —adj. **2.** being or occurring in the dark; dark; obscure. [f. DARK + -LING²]

dark·ly (därk'lĭ), adv. **1.** so as to appear dark. **2.** mysteriously. **3.** *Archaic.* imperfectly; faintly.

dark·ness (därk'nĭs), n. **1.** state or quality of being dark. **2.** absence or deficiency of light. **3.** wickedness or evil. **4.** obscurity; concealment. **5.** blindness; ignorance.

dark·room (därk'rōōm', -rŏŏm'), n. *Photog.* a room from which the actinic rays of light have been excluded: used in making, handling, and developing film, etc.

dark·some (därk'səm), adj. dark; darkish.

dark·y (där'kĭ), n., pl. **darkies.** *Colloq.* (often offensive) a Negro. Also, **darkey.**

dar·ling (där′lĭng), n. **1.** a person very dear to another; person dearly loved. **2.** a person or thing in great favor. —adj. **3.** very dear; dearly loved. **4.** favorite. [ME derling, OE dēorling, f. dēore dear + -LING¹]

Dar·ling River (där′lĭng), a river in SE Australia, flowing into the Murray river. 1160 mi.

Dar·ling·ton (där′lĭng tən), n. a city in NE England, in Durham. 83,360 (est. 1956).

Darm·stadt (därm′stät; Ger. därm′shtät). n. a city in West Germany: former capital of Hesse. 124,393 (est. 1955).

darn¹ (därn), v.t. **1.** to mend (clothes, etc., or a rent or hole) with rows of stitches, sometimes with crossing and interwoven rows to fill up a gap. —n. **2.** a darned place in a garment, etc. **3.** act of darning. [? ME dernen, OE dernan hide] —darn′er, n. —Syn. 1. See mend.

darn² (därn), U.S. Colloq. —adj., adv. **1.** darned. —v.t. **2.** to confound (used as a mild imprecation). —n. **3.** not give a darn, to be utterly indifferent. [var. of DAMN]

darned (därnd), U.S. Colloq. —adj. **1.** confounded; blessed. —adv. **2.** extremely; remarkably.

dar·nel (där′nəl), n. an annual grass, Lolium temulentum, found as a weed in grain fields. [ME. Cf. d. F darnelle, prob. of Gmc. orig.]

darn·ing (där′nĭng), n. **1.** act of one who darns. **2.** the result produced. **3.** articles darned or to be darned.

darning needle, 1. a long needle with a long eye used in darning. **2.** a dragonfly.

Darn·ley (därn′lĭ), n. **Henry Stewart, Lord,** 1545–1567, the second husband of Mary, Queen of Scots; father of James I of England.

Dar·row (där′ō), n. **Clarence,** 1857–1938, American lawyer.

dart (därt), n. **1.** a long, slender, pointed, missile weapon propelled by the hand or otherwise. **2.** something resembling such a weapon, as the sting of an insect. **3.** act of darting; a sudden, swift movement. **4.** (pl.) a game in which a pointed missile is thrown at a scoring board. **5.** a seam that is used where a wedge-shaped piece has been cut out to adjust the fit of a garment. —v.i. **6.** to move swiftly; spring or start suddenly and run swiftly. **7.** to throw a dart or other missile weapon. —v.t. **8.** to throw or thrust suddenly and rapidly. **9.** to throw with a sudden thrust, as a dart. [ME, t. OF, t. OG] —dart′ing·ly, adv. —Syn. 6. dash, bolt.

dart·er (där′tər), n. **1.** one who or that which darts or moves swiftly. **2.** a snakebird or anhinga. **3.** any percoid fish of the American subfamily Etheostomatinae, small fresh-water fishes which dart quickly when disturbed.

dar·tle (där′təl), v.t., v.i., -tled, -tling. to dart or shoot forth repeatedly. [freq. of DART]

Dart·moor (därt′mŏŏr′, -mōr′), n. **1.** a rocky plateau in SW England, in Devonshire. ab. 25 mi. long. **2.** a famous prison located there.

Dar·win (där′wĭn), n. **1. Charles,** 1809–82, British naturalist. **2.** his grandfather, **Erasmus,** 1731–1802, British naturalist and poet. **3.** a city in N Australia, capital of Northern Territory. 8,071 (1954).

Dar·win·i·an (där wĭn′ĭ ən), adj. **1.** pertaining to Charles Darwin or his doctrines. —n. **2.** a follower of Charles Darwin; one who accepts Darwinism.

Dar·win·ism (där′wə nĭz′əm), n. the body of biological doctrine maintained by Charles Darwin respecting the origin of species as derived by descent, with variation, from parent forms, through the natural selection of those best adapted to survive in the struggle for existence. —Dar′win·ist, n., adj. —Dar·win·ite (där′wə nīt′), n.

dash (dăsh), v.t. **1.** to strike violently, esp. so as to break to pieces. **2.** to throw or thrust violently or suddenly. **3.** to splash violently; bespatter (with water, mud, etc.). **4.** to apply roughly as by splashing. **5.** to throw something into so as to produce a mixture; mix; adulterate: to dash wine with water. **6.** to ruin or frustrate (hopes, plans, etc.). **7.** to depress or dispirit. **8.** to confound or abash. **9.** to write, make, sketch, etc., hastily (usually fol. by off or down). **10.** Chiefly Brit. to damn (used as a mild imprecation). —v.i. **11.** to strike with violence. **12.** to move with violence; rush. —n. **13.** a violent and rapid blow or stroke. **14.** a check or discouragement. **15.** the throwing or splashing of water, etc., against a thing. **16.** the sound of the splashing. **17.** a small quantity of anything thrown into or mixed with something else: a dash of salt. **18.** a hasty stroke, esp. of a pen. **19.** a horizontal line (—) used in writing and printing as a mark of punctuation to note an abrupt break or pause in a sentence, to begin and end a parenthetic clause, as an indication of omission of letters, words, etc., as a dividing line between distinct portions of matter, and for other purposes. **20.** an impetuous movement; a rush; a sudden onset. **21.** Sports. a short race decided in one attempt, not in heats: a hundred-yard dash. **22.** spirited action; vigor in action or style. **23.** a dashboard. **24.** Teleg. a signal of longer duration than a dot, used in groups of dots and dashes to represent letters, as in Morse code. —interj. **25.** Chiefly Brit. a mild exclamation. [ME dasche(n), c. Dan. daske slap, flap] —Syn. 12. dart, bolt. See rush¹. 17. pinch, bit; touch, tinge.

dash·board (dăsh′bōrd′), n. **1.** the instrument board of an automobile. **2.** a board or leather apron on the front of a vehicle, to protect the occupants from mud, etc.

da·sheen (dă shēn′), n. the taro plant, Colocasia esculenta, native in tropical Asia, now cultivated in southern U.S. for its edible tubers. [t. F: m. de Chine of China]

dash·er (dăsh′ər), n. **1.** one who or that which dashes. **2.** plunger of a churn. **3.** Colloq. spirited person.

dash·ing (dăsh′ĭng), adj. **1.** impetuous; spirited; lively. **2.** brilliant; showy; stylish. —dash′ing·ly, adv.

dash·y (dăsh′ĭ), adj., dashier, dashiest. showy; stylish; dashing.

das·tard (dăs′tərd), n. **1.** a mean, sneaking coward. —adj. **2.** mean and sneaking; cowardly. [ME; f. dast (? var. of dazed, pp. of DAZE) + -ARD]

das·tard·ly (dăs′tərd lĭ), adj. cowardly; meanly base; sneaking. —das′tard·li·ness, n.

das·y·ure (dăs′ĭ yŏŏr′), n. **1.** any of the small, spotted, carnivorous marsupials constituting the genus Dasyurus and related genera, native in Australia, Tasmania, etc. **2.** any of several related animals, as the Tasmanian devil or ursine dasyure. [t. NL: m.s. Dasyūrus, f. dasy- (comb. form of Gk. dasýs shaggy) + -ūrus (m. Gk. ourá tail)]

dat., dative.

da·ta (dā′tə, dăt′ə, dä′tə), n. **1.** pl. of datum. **2.** facts, figures, etc., known or available; information.

da·ta·ry (dā′tə rĭ), n., pl. -ries. Rom. Cath. Ch. **1.** an officer, now cardinal, at the head of a certain office or department of the curia who investigates the fitness of candidates for benefices in the gift of the papal see. **2.** this office or department. [t. ML: m.s. datārius (the officer), datāria (the office), der. data DATE¹]

date¹ (dāt), n., v., dated, dating. —n. **1.** a particular point or period of time when something happens or happened. **2.** an inscription on a writing, coin, etc., that shows the time, or time and place, of writing, casting, delivery, etc. **3.** the time or period of an event or to which anything belongs. **4.** the time during which anything lasts; duration. **5.** U.S. Colloq. an appointment made for a particular time. **6.** U.S. Colloq. a person, usually of the opposite sex, with whom one has a social appointment. **7. down to date,** to the present time. **8. to date,** down to the present time. —v.i. **9.** to have a date: the letter dates from 1873. **10.** to belong to a particular period; have its origin. **11.** to reckon from some point in time. **12.** U.S. Colloq. to go out on dates (def. 5) with persons of the opposite sex. —v.t. **13.** to mark or furnish with a date. **14.** to ascertain or fix the date or time of; assign a date or time to. **15.** to make a date (def. 5) with. [ME, t. F, t. ML: m. data, prop. pp. fem. of L dare give] —dat′er, n.

date² (dāt), n. **1.** the oblong, fleshy fruit of the date palm, a staple food in northern Africa, Arabia, etc., and an important export. **2.** the date palm. [ME, t. OF, g. L dactylus, t. Gk.: m. dáktylos date, orig. finger]

dat·ed (dā′tĭd), adj. **1.** having or showing a date. **2.** out-of-date; old-fashioned.

date·less (dāt′lĭs), adj. **1.** without a date; undated. **2.** endless. **3.** so old as to be undatable. **4.** of permanent interest regardless of age.

date line, 1. a line in a letter, newspaper, article, or the like, giving the date (and often the place) of origin. **2.** a line, theoretically coinciding with the meridian of 180° from Greenwich, the regions on either side of which are counted as differing by one day in their calendar dates. It is occasioned by the difference in time between different points on the earth, due to the (apparent) movement of the sun.

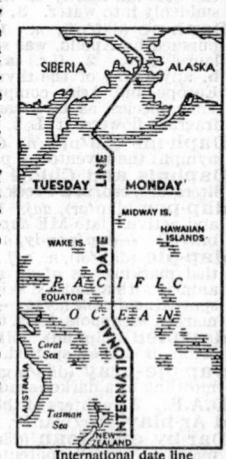

International date line

date palm, the species of palm, Phoenix dactylifera, which bears dates, having a stem up to 60 feet high terminating in a crown of pinnate leaves.

da·tive (dā′tĭv), Gram. —adj. **1.** denoting a case, in some inflected languages, having as one function indication of the indirect object of a verb. —n. **2.** the dative case. **3.** a word or form in that case, as regi in regi haec dicite meaning tell this to the king. [ME, t. L: m.s. datīvus of or belonging to giving] —da·ti·val (dā tī′vəl), adj. —da′tive·ly, adv.

da·to (dä′tō; Sp. -tô), n., pl. -tos (-tōz; Sp. -tôs). **1.** (in the Philippines) a native chief. **2.** the headman of a barrio or Malay tribe. Also, **dat′to.** [t. Malay: m. dátoq title of respect]

da·tum (dā′təm), n., pl. -ta (-tə). **1.** any proposition assumed or given, from which conclusions may be drawn. **2.** (often pl.) any fact assumed to be a matter of direct observation. [t. L: given (pp. neut.)]

datum plane, level, line, etc. Survey., Civ. Eng., etc. a plane, level, line, etc., from which heights and depths are calculated or measured.

da·tu·ra (də tyŏŏr′ə, -tŏŏr′ə), n. any plant of the solanaceous genus *Datura*, the species of which have funnel-shaped flowers, prickly pods, and narcotic properties. [NL, t. Hind.: m. *dhatūra*, native name of the plant]

dau., daughter.

daub (dôb), *v.t.* 1. to cover or coat with soft, adhesive matter, such as plaster, mud, etc. 2. to spread (plaster, mud, etc.) on or over something. 3. to smear, soil, or defile. 4. to paint unskillfully. —*v.i.* 5. to daub something. 6. to paint unskillfully. —*n.* 7. material, esp. of an inferior kind, for daubing walls, etc. 8. anything daubed on. 9. act of daubing. 10. a crude, inartistic painting. [ME *daube*(n), t. OF: m. *dauber*, g. L *dealbāre* whiten, plaster] —**daub′er,** *n.*

daub·er·y (dô′bərĭ), *n.* unskillful painting or work. Also, **daub·ry** (dô′brɪ).

Dau·bi·gny (dō bē nyē′), *n.* Charles François (shärl frän swä′), 1817–78, French landscape painter.

Dau·det (dō dě′), *n.* 1. Alphonse (ál fôns′), 1840–97, French novelist. 2. Léon (lě ôn′), 1867–1942, French journalist and novelist; son of Alphonse.

Dau·ga·va (dou′gä vä′), *n.* Lettish name of **Dvina.**

Dau·gav·pils (dou′gäf pĕls′), *n.* a city in the W Soviet Union, in the Latvian Republic. 50,000 (est. 1948). Russian, **Dvinsk.** German, **Dünaburg.**

daugh·ter (dô′tər), *n.* 1. a female child or person in relation to her parents. 2. any female descendant. 3. one related as if by the ties binding daughter to parent: *daughter of the church.* 4. anything (personified as female) considered with respect to its origin. [var. of ME *doughter*, OE *dohtor*, c. G *tochter*, Gk. *thygátēr*]

daugh·ter-in-law (dô′tər ĭn lô′), *n.*, *pl.* **daughters-in-law.** the wife of one's son.

daugh·ter·ly (dô′tər lǐ), *adj.* pertaining to, befitting, or like a daughter. —**daugh′ter·li·ness,** *n.*

Daughters of the American Revolution, The, a patriotic society of women descended from Americans of the Revolutionary period, organized in 1890.

Dau·mier (dō myě′), *n.* Honoré (ô nô rě′), 1808–1879, French lithographer and painter.

daunt (dônt, dänt), *v.t.* 1. to overcome with fear; intimidate. 2. to lessen the courage of; dishearten. [ME *daunte*(n), t. OF: m. *danter*, ult. der. L *domāre* tame, subdue] —**Syn.** 1. overawe. 2. discourage, dispirit.

daunt·less (dônt′lĭs, dänt′-), *adj.* not to be daunted; fearless; intrepid; bold. —**daunt′less·ly,** *adv.* —**daunt′less·ness,** *n.* —**Syn.** daring, courageous, indomitable.

dau·phin (dô′fĭn; *Fr.* dō făn′), *n.* the distinctive title of the eldest son of the king of France, from 1349 to 1830. [t. F, appar. orig. a proper name used as a surname; often identified with L *delphīnus* dolphin]

Dau·phine (dō fēn′), *n.* an old province in SE France.

dau·phin·ess (dô′fĭn ĭs), *n.* the wife of the dauphin. Also, **dau·phine** (dō′fēn; *Fr.* dō fēn′).

daut (dôt, dät), *v.t.* *Scot.* to fondle; caress. Also, **dawt.**

Da·vao (dä vou′), *n.* a seaport in the Philippine Islands, on Mindanao. 111,263 (1948).

D'Av·e·nant (dăv′ə nənt), *n.* Sir William, 1606–68, English dramatist and poet. Also, **Dav′e·nant.**

dav·en·port (dăv′ən pôrt′), *n.* 1. *U.S.* a kind of large sofa, often one convertible into a bed. 2. *Chiefly Brit.* a small writing table. [prob. from the maker's name]

Dav·en·port (dăv′ən pôrt′), *n.* 1. John, 1597–1670, Puritan clergyman: one of the founders of New Haven. 2. a city in E Iowa, on the Mississippi. 88,981 (1960).

Da·vid (dā′vĭd *for 1, 2;* dä vēd′ *for 3*), *n.* 1. fl. c1000 B.C., the second king of the Hebrews, successor to Saul: united tribes of Israel into a nation with the capital at Jerusalem. 2. **Saint,** (*Saint Dewi*) died A.D. 601?, Welsh bishop: patron saint of Wales. 3. **Jacques Louis** (zhäk lwē), 1748–1825, French painter. [t. Heb.: m. *Dāwīd*]

Da·vid I (dā′vĭd), 1084–1153, king of Scotland, 1124–1153.

David Cop·per·field (kŏp′ər fēld′), a novel (1850) by Charles Dickens.

Da·vid d'An·gers (dä vēd′ dän zhě′), (*Pierre Jean David*) 1788–1856, French sculptor.

Da·vid·son (dā′vĭd sən), *n.* Jo, 1883–1952, U.S. sculptor.

da Vi·gno·la (dä vē nyō′lä). See **Vignola.**

da Vin·ci (də vĭn′chǐ; *It.* dä vēn′chē). See **Vinci.**

Da·vis (dā′vĭs), *n.* 1. Jefferson, 1808–89, U.S. statesman: president of the Confederate States of America, 1861–65. 2. John, 1550?–1605, English navigator and explorer. 3. John William, 1873–1955, U.S. lawyer and diplomat: Democratic candidate for president of the U.S. in 1924. 4. Richard Harding, 1864–1916, U.S. journalist, novelist, and dramatist.

Da·vis·son (dā′və sən), *n.* Clinton Joseph, 1881–1958, U.S. physicist.

Davis Strait, a strait between Canada and Greenland, connecting Baffin Bay and the Atlantic. 200–500 mi. wide.

dav·it (dăv′ĭt, dā′vĭt), *n. Naut.* a projecting piece of wood or iron (frequently one of a pair) on the side or stern of a vessel, fitted with a tackle, etc., for raising, lowering, or suspending a small boat, anchor, or other weight. [ME *daviot*, t. AF, appar. dim. of *Davi* David]

D. Davit

Da·vout (dä vōō′), *n.* Louis Nicolas (lwē nē kō lä′) (*Duke of Auerstadt* and *Prince of Eckmühl*) 1770–1823, marshal of France: one of Napoleon's leading generals.

Da·vy (dā′vǐ), *n.* Sir Humphry, 1778–1829, British chemist.

Da·vy Jones (dā′vǐ jōnz′), *Naut.* the spirit of the sea; the sailors' devil.

Davy Jones's locker, 1. the ocean's bottom, esp. as the grave of all who perish at sea. 2. the ocean.

Davy lamp, an early safety lamp for miners.

daw (dô), *n.* 1. a jackdaw. 2. a simpleton. [ME *dawe.* Cf. OHG *tāha*]

daw·dle (dô′dəl), *v.t.*, **-dled, -dling.** —*v.i.* 1. to waste time; idle; trifle; loiter. —*v.t.* 2. to waste (time) by trifling (usually fol. by *away*). [? var. of *daddle* TODDLE] —**daw′dler,** *n.* —**Syn.** 1. See loiter.

Dawes (dôz), *n.* Charles Gates, 1865–1951, U.S. financier and diplomat: vice-president of the U.S., 1925–29.

dawk (dôk, däk), *n.* dak.

dawn (dôn), *n.* 1. the first appearance of daylight in the morning. 2. the beginning or rise of anything; advent. —*v. i.* 3. to begin to grow light in the morning. 4. to begin to open or develop. 5. to begin to be perceived (fol. by *on*): *the idea dawned on him.* [ME *dawen-*(in *dawening* dawn), appar. t. Scand.; cf. Icel. *dōgun* dawn] —**Syn.** 1. daybreak, sunrise.

Daw·son (dô′sən), *n.* 1. Sir John William, 1820–99, Canadian geologist and educator. 2. a town in NW Canada at the confluence of the Yukon and Klondike rivers: former capital of Yukon Territory. 783 (1951).

Dawson Creek, a village in W Canada at the SE terminus of the Alaska Highway, which extends from E British Columbia to Fairbanks, Alaska.

dawt (dôt, dät), *v.t. Scot.* daut.

Dax (däks), *n.* a city in SW France: mineral hot springs. 14,557 (1954).

day (dā), *n.* 1. the interval of light between two successive nights; the time between sunrise and sunset. 2. the light of day; daylight. 3. *Astron.* a. the period during which the earth (or a heavenly body) makes one revolution on its axis. b. the average length of this interval, twenty-four hours (mean solar day). c. the interval of time which elapses between two consecutive returns of the same terrestrial meridian to the sun (solar day). d. a period reckoned from midnight to midnight and equivalent in length to the mean solar day (civil day), as contrasted with a similar period reckoned from noon to noon (astronomical day). 4. the portion of a day allotted to labor: *an eight-hour day.* 5. a day as a point or unit of time, or on which something occurs. 6. a day assigned to a particular purpose or observance: *New Year's Day.* 7. a day of contest, or the contest itself: *to win the day.* 8. (*often pl.*) a particular time or period: *the present day, in days of old.* 9. (*often pl.*) period of life or activity. 10. period of power or influence. [ME; OE *dæg*, c. G *tag*]

day bed, a narrow bed convertible to a couch by day.

day blindness, nyctalopia (def. 2).

day·book (dā′bŏŏk′), *n.* 1. *Bookkeeping.* a book in which the transactions of the day are entered in the order of their occurrence. 2. a diary.

day·break (dā′brāk′), *n.* the first appearance of light in the morning; dawn.

day coach, *U.S.* an ordinary railroad passenger car, as distinguished from a sleeping car, parlor car, etc.

day·dream (dā′drēm′), *n.* 1. a visionary fancy indulged in while awake; reverie. —*v.i.* 2. to indulge in daydreams. —**day′dream′er,** *n.*

day·flow·er (dā′flou′ər), *n.* any plant of the genus *Commelina*, of the spiderwort family, mostly bearing cymes of small blue flowers.

day·fly (dā′flī′), *n., pl.* **-flies.** mayfly.

day laborer, an unskilled worker paid by the day.

day letter, a telegram sent during the day, usually longer and slower, but cheaper, than a regular telegram.

day·light (dā′līt′), *n.* 1. the light of day. 2. openness; publicity. 3. daytime. 4. daybreak.

day·light-sav·ing time (dā′līt′ sā′vĭng), time one or more hours later than the standard time for a country or community, usually used during summer months to give more hours of daylight to the working day.

day lily, 1. any plant of the liliaceous genus *Hemerocallis*, with yellow or orange flowers which commonly last only for a day. 2. any plant of the liliaceous genus *Niobe* (or *Funkia*), with white or blue flowers. 3. the flower of any of these plants.

day nursery, *U.S.* a nursery for the care of small children during the day, esp. while their mothers are at work.

Day of Atonement, a Jewish fast day, Yom Kippur.

Day of Judgment, the day of the Last Judgment, at the end of the world.

day school, 1. a school held on weekdays (distinguished from *Sunday school*). 2. a school held in the daytime (distinguished from *night school*). 3. a private school for pupils living outside the school (distinguished from *boarding school*).

days·man (dāz′mən), *n. Archaic.* an umpire; mediator. [f. *day's* (poss. of DAY) + MAN]

days of grace, days (commonly three) allowed by law or custom for payment after a bill or note falls due.

day·spring (dā′sprĭng′), *n. Poetic.* dawn; daybreak.

---

day·star (dā/stär/), *n.* **1.** the morning star. **2.** *Poetic.* the sun.

day·time (dā/tīm/), *n.* the time between sunrise and sunset.

Day·ton (dā/tən), *n.* a city in SW Ohio. 262,332 (1960).

Day·to·na Beach (dā tō/nə), a city in NE Florida: seaside resort. 37,395 (1960).

daze (dāz), *v.*, **dazed, dazing,** *n.* —*v.t.* **1.** to stun or stupefy with a blow, a shock, etc. **2.** to confuse; bewilder; dazzle. —*n.* **3.** a dazed condition. [ME *dase*(*n*), t. Scand.; cf. Dan. *dase* doze, mope] —**daz·ed·ly** (dā/-zĭd lĭ), *adv.*

daz·zle (dăz/əl), *v.*, **-zled, -zling,** *n.* —*v.t.* **1.** to overpower or dim (the vision) by intense light. **2.** to bewilder by brilliancy or display of any kind. —*v.i.* **3.** to be overpowered by light. **4.** to excite admiration by brilliance. —*n.* **5.** act or fact of dazzling. **6.** bewildering brightness. [freq. of DAZE] —**daz/zler**, *n.* —**daz/zling·ly**, *adv.*

db., decibel; decibels.

dbl., double.

DC, Dental Corps.

D.C., **1.** *Music.* da capo. **2.** *Elect.* direct current. **3.** District of Columbia.

d.c., *Elect.* direct current.

D.C.L., Doctor of Civil Law.

D.C.M., *Brit.* Distinguished Conduct Medal.

D.D., Doctor of Divinity.

D-day (dē/dā/), *n.* *Mil.* the day, usually unspecified, set for the beginning of a previously planned attack.

D.D.S., Doctor of Dental Surgery.

DDT, the symbol for a very powerful insecticide, p, p′-dichlorodiphenyl-trichloroethane.

de (də), *prep.* from; of: much used in French personal names, orig. to indicate place of origin. Also, **De.**

de-, a prefix meaning: **1.** privation and separation, as in *dehorn, dethrone, detrain.* **2.** negation, as in *demerit, derange.* **3.** descent, as in *degrade, deduce.* **4.** reversal, as in *detract.* **5.** intensity, as in *decompound.* [ME, t. L, repr. *de,* prep., from, away from, of, out of, etc.; in some words t. F, g. L *de-,* or g. L *dis-* (see DIS¹)]

dea·con (dē/kən), *n.* **1.** (in hierarchical churches) a member of the clerical order next below that of priest. **2.** (in other churches) an appointed or elected officer having variously defined duties. —*v.t.* **3.** *U.S. Colloq. or Dial.* to read out (a line of a psalm, hymn, etc.) before singing it. [ME *deacon, deken,* OE *dēacon, diacon,* t. LL: s. *diāconus,* t. Gk.: m. *diákonos* servant, minister, deacon] —**dea/con·ship,** *n.*

dea·con·ess (dē/kən ĭs), *n.* **1.** (in certain Protestant churches) one of an order of women who carry on educational, hospital, or social-service work. **2.** a woman elected by a church to assist the clergy.

dea·con·ry (dē/kən rĭ), *n., pl.* **-ries.** **1.** the office of a deacon. **2.** deacons collectively.

de·ac·ti·vate (dē ăk/tə vāt/), *v.t.,* **-vated, -vating.** to demobilize or disband (a military unit). —**de·ac/ti·va/-tion,** *n.*

dead (dĕd), *adj.* **1.** no longer living; deprived of life. **2.** not endowed with life; inanimate: *dead matter.* **3.** resembling death: *a dead sleep.* **4.** bereft of sensation; insensible; numb: *dead to all sense of shame.* **5.** no longer in existence or use: *dead languages.* **6.** *Law.* deprived of civil rights so that one is in the state of civil death, esp. deprived of the rights of property. **7.** without spiritual life or vigor. **8.** *Colloq.* very tired; exhausted. **9.** infertile; barren. **10.** deprived of or lacking animation, motion, force, vigor, or any other characteristic quality: *dead air, water, machinery, affections, etc.* **11.** extinguished: *a dead fire.* **12.** tasteless or flat, as liquor. **13.** not glossy, bright, or brilliant. **14.** without resonance: *a dead sound.* **15.** without resilience or bounce: *a dead tennis ball.* **16.** closed at one end: *a dead street.* **17.** dull or inactive: *a dead market.* **18.** complete; absolute: *dead loss, dead silence.* **19.** sure; unerring: *a dead shot.* **20.** direct; straight: *a dead line.* **21.** unproductive: *dead capital.* **22.** *Sports.* out of play: *a dead ball.* **23.** having been used or rejected, as type set up or copy for printing. **24.** *Elect.* **a.** free from any electric connection to a source of potential difference and from electric charge. **b.** not having a potential different from that of the earth. —*n.* **25.** one who is dead. **26.** (usually prec. by *the*) dead persons collectively. **27.** the period of greatest darkness, coldness, etc.: *the dead of night.* —*adv.* **28.** absolutely; completely: *dead right.* **29.** with abrupt and complete stoppage of motion, etc.: *he stopped dead.* **30.** directly; exactly; diametrically: *the wind was dead ahead.* [ME *deed,* OE *dēad,* c. G *tot;* orig. pp. See DIE] —**dead/ness,** *n.*

—**Syn.** **1.** DEAD, DECEASED, EXTINCT, LIFELESS refer to something which does not have (or appear to have) life. DEAD is usually applied to that which had life but from which life is now gone: *dead trees, animals; they recovered the dead bodies.* DECEASED, a more formal word than DEAD, is applied to human beings who no longer have life: *a deceased member of the church.* EXTINCT is applied esp. to a race, species, or the like, no member of which is any longer alive: *mastodons are now extinct.* LIFELESS is applied to what may or may not have had life but which does not have it (or appear to have it) now: *the lifeless body of a child was taken out of the water, minerals consist of lifeless materials.* **4.** unfeeling, indifferent, callous. **10.** still, motionless, inert, inoperative. —**Ant. 1.** living, alive.

dead-beat (dĕd/bēt/), *adj.* *Physics, etc.* **1.** free from oscillation or recoil. **2.** having an index needle that comes to a stop with little or no oscillation.

dead beat, **1.** *U.S. Colloq.* one who has a reputation for not paying his bills. **2.** *Slang.* a loafer; sponger.

dead-beat (dĕd/bēt/), *adj. Colloq.* very tired; exhausted.

dead center, **1.** (in a gasoline engine, etc.) either of two positions of the crank in which the connecting rod has no power to turn it, occurring when the crank and connecting rod are in the same plane, at each end of a stroke. **2.** *Mach.* a stationary center which holds the work, as the tailstock of a lathe.

D, Dead center

dead·en (dĕd/ən), *v.t.* **1.** to make less sensitive, active, energetic, or forcible; dull; weaken: *to deaden sound, the force of a ball, the senses.* **2.** to lessen the velocity of; retard. **3.** to make impervious to sound, as a floor. —*v.i.* **4.** to become dead. —**dead/en·er,** *n.*

dead end, a street, water pipe, etc., that is closed at one end. —**dead/-end/,** *adj.*

dead·en·ing (dĕd/ən ĭng), *n.* **1.** a device or material employed to deaden or render dull. **2.** a device or material preventing the transmission of sound.

dead·eye (dĕd/ī/), *n.* *Naut.* a round, laterally flattened block encircled by a rope or an iron band and pierced with three holes.

dead·fall (dĕd/fôl/), *n.* a trap, esp. for large game, in which a weight falls upon and crushes the prey.

dead hand, *Law.* mortmain.

dead·head (dĕd/hĕd/), *n.* *Colloq.* one who attends a theater, rides a streetcar, etc., without payment.

dead heat, a heat or race in which two or more competitors finish together.

dead letter, **1.** a law, ordinance, etc., which has lost its force, though not formally repealed or abolished. **2.** a letter which lies unclaimed for a certain time at a post office, or which, because of faulty address, etc., cannot be delivered. Such letters are sent to and handled in a special division or department (**dead-letter office**) of the general post office. —**dead/-let/ter,** *adj.*

Deadeyes

dead·light (dĕd/līt/), *n.* *Naut.* **1.** a strong wooden or iron shutter for a cabin window or porthole, to prevent water from entering. **2.** a thick pane of glass set in the hull or deck to admit light.

dead·line (dĕd/līn/), *n.* **1.** a line or limit that must not be passed. **2.** the latest time for finishing something.

dead load, a load that is permanent and immovable, as the weight of a bridge.

dead·lock (dĕd/lŏk/), *n.* **1.** state of affairs in which progress is impossible; complete standstill. —*v.t.* **2.** to bring to a deadlock. —*v.i.* **3.** to come to a deadlock.

dead·ly (dĕd/lĭ), *adj.,* **-lier, -liest,** *adv.* —*adj.* **1.** causing or tending to cause death; fatal: *a deadly poison.* **2.** aiming to kill or destroy; implacable: *a deadly enemy.* **3.** involving spiritual death: *a deadly sin.* **4.** like death: *a deadly pallor.* **5.** excessive: *deadly haste.* —*adv.* **6.** in a manner resembling or suggesting death: *deadly pale.* **7.** *Colloq.* excessively: *deadly dull.* —**dead/li·ness,** *n.* —**Syn. 1.** See fatal.

deadly nightshade, the belladonna.

deadly sins, pride, covetousness, lust, anger, gluttony, envy, and sloth.

dead march, a piece of solemn music for a funeral procession, esp. one played at a military funeral.

dead pan, *Slang.* **1.** a face completely lacking in expression. **2.** a person who assumes such a face, as a comedian. —**dead/-pan/,** *adj.*

dead point, dead center.

dead reckoning, *Naut.* **1.** the calculation of a ship's position without astronomical observations, by means of the distances sailed on the various courses as shown by the log and compass, with corrections for currents, etc. **2.** position as so calculated.

Dead Sea, a salt lake between Israel and Jordan: the lowest lake in the world. 46 mi. long; 10 mi. wide; 1293 feet below sea level.

dead-stick landing (dĕd/stĭk/), *Aeron.* a landing made with a dead engine.

dead weight, **1.** the heavy, unrelieved weight of anything inert. **2.** a heavy or oppressive burden. **3.** the weight of a railroad car, etc., as distinct from its load.

dead·wood (dĕd/wŏŏd/), *n.* **1.** the dead branches on a tree; dead branches or trees. **2.** anything useless.

deaf (dĕf; *now less often* dēf), *adj.* **1.** lacking or deprived of the sense of hearing, wholly or partially; unable to hear. **2.** refusing to listen; heedless of; inattentive: *deaf to advice, turn a deaf ear to a plea.* [ME *deef,* OE *dēaf,* c. G *taub*] —**deaf/ly,** *adv.* —**deaf/ness,** *n.*

deaf·en (dĕf/ən), *v.t.* **1.** to make deaf. **2.** to stun with noise. **3.** to render (a sound) inaudible, esp. by a louder sound. —**deaf/en·ing·ly,** *adv.*

deaf-mute (dĕf/mūt/), *n.* a person who is deaf and dumb, esp. one in whom inability to speak is due to congenital or early deafness.

deal[1] (dēl), v., dealt, dealing, n. —v.i. 1. to occupy oneself or itself (fol. by *with* or *in*): *deal with the first question, botany deals with the study of plants.* 2. to take action with respect to a thing or person (usually fol. by *with*): *law courts must deal with lawbreakers.* 3. to conduct oneself toward persons: *deal fairly.* 4. to trade or do business: *to deal with a firm, to deal in an article.* 5. to make a secret agreement or bargain (fol. by *with*). 6. to distribute, esp. the cards required in a game. —v.i. 7. to give to one as his share; apportion. 8. to distribute among a number of recipients, as the cards required in a game. 9. *Cards.* to give a player (a specific card) in dealing. 10. to deliver (blows, etc.). —n. 11. *Colloq.* a business transaction. 12. a bargain or arrangement for mutual advantage, as in commerce or politics, often a secret or underhand one. 13. treatment; arrangement: *a raw deal, a fair deal, a new deal.* 14. a quantity, amount, extent, or degree. 15. an indefinite but large amount or extent: *a deal of money.* 16. act of dealing or distributing. 17. *Cards.* a. the distribution to the players of the cards in a game. b. the set of cards in one's hand. c. the turn of a player to deal. d. the period of time during which a deal is played. 18. *Obs.* portion or share. [ME *delen*, OE *dǣlan* (c. G *teilen*, etc.), der. *dǣl* part (c. G *teil*)] —Syn. 7. allot, assign.

deal[2] (dēl), n. 1. a board or plank, esp. of fir or pine, in Britain usually more than 7 inches wide and 6 feet long, and less than 3 inches thick, in U. S. and Canada, 11 inches wide, 12 feet long, 2½ inches thick. 2. such boards collectively. 3. fir or pine wood. [ME *dele*, t. MLG or MD]

deal·er (dē′lər), n. 1. one who buys and sells articles without altering their condition; trader or merchant. 2. *Cards.* the player distributing the cards.

deal·fish (dēl′fĭsh′), n., pl. -fishes, (*esp. collectively*) -fish. any of the deep-sea fishes constituting the genus *Trachypterus*, characterized by a long, compressed, tapelike body. [f. DEAL² + FISH]

deal·ing (dē′lĭng), n. 1. (*usually pl.*) relations; trading: *business dealings.* 2. conduct in relation to others; treatment: *honest dealing.*

dealt (dĕlt), v. pt. and pp. of **deal**¹.

dean[1] (dēn), n. 1. *Educ.* a. the head of a faculty, or sometimes its registrar or secretary, in a university or college. b. the official in charge of undergraduate students at an English university. c. an official in an American college or university having charge of student personnel services, such as counseling or discipline: *the dean of men.* 2. *Eccles.* a. the head of the chapter of a cathedral or a collegiate church. b. any of various other ecclesiastical dignitaries, as the head of a division of a diocese. 3. the senior member, in length of service, of any body. [ME *deen*, t. OF: m. *deien*, g. LL *decānus* chief of ten] —**dean′ship**, n.

dean[2] (dēn), n. *Brit.* dene.

dean·er·y (dē′nə rĭ), n., pl. -eries. 1. the office, jurisdiction, or district of a dean. 2. the residence of a dean.

dear[1] (dĭr), adj. 1. beloved or loved: *a dear friend of mine.* 2. (in the salutation of a letter) highly esteemed: *Dear Sirs.* 3. precious in one's regard: *our dearest possessions.* 4. high-priced; expensive. 5. charging high prices. 6. high: *a dear price to pay.* 7. difficult to get. 8. *Obs.* worthy. —n. 9. one who is dear. 10. a beloved one (often used in direct address): *my dear.* —adv. 11. dearly; fondly. 12. at a high price. —interj. 13. an exclamation of surprise, distress, etc. [ME *dere*, OE *dēore*, c. G *teuer*] —**dear′ly**, adv. —**dear′ness**, n. —Syn. 4. See expensive. —Ant. 4. cheap.

dear[2] (dĭr), adj. *Archaic.* hard; grievous. Also, **dere.** [ME *dere*, OE *dēor*; cf. Icel. *dŷr* difficult, rigorous]

Dear·born (dĭr′bərn, -bôrn), n. 1. a city in SE Michigan, near Detroit. 112,007 (1960). 2. Fort, a former U.S. fort on the site of Chicago, 1803–37.

dearth (dûrth), n. 1. scarcity or scanty supply; lack. 2. scarcity and dearness of food; famine. [ME *derthe*. See DEAR², -TH¹]

dear·y (dĭr′ĭ), n., pl. dearies. darling. Also, **dear′ie.**

death (dĕth), n. 1. act of dying; the end of life; the total and permanent cessation of all the vital functions of an animal or plant. 2. (*often cap.*) the annihilating power personified, usually represented as a skeleton: *"O Death, where is thy sting?"* 3. state of being dead: *to lie still in death.* 4. extinction; destruction: *it will mean the death of our hopes.* 5. the time at which a person dies: *the letters may be published after my death.* 6. manner of dying: *a hero's death.* 7. loss or deprivation of civil life. 8. loss or absence of spiritual life. 9. bloodshed or murder. 10. a cause or occasion of death. 11. a pestilence: *the black death.* 12. do or put to death, to kill. [ME *deeth*, OE *dēath*, c. G *tod*] —Syn. 1. decease, demise, passing, departure.

death·bed (dĕth′bĕd′), n. 1. the bed on which a person dies. 2. the last few hours before death.

death bell, the bell that announces a death.

death·blow (dĕth′blō′), n. a blow causing death.

death camass, 1. a perennial liliaceous herb, *Zygadenus,* with several species in the southern and western U. S. and in Canada. 2. its root, poisonous to sheep and other animals.

death cup, 1. a poisonous mushroom of the genus *Amanita,* part of which persists around the base of the stipe as a definite membranous cup. 2. the cup.

death duty, *Brit. Law.* an inheritance tax.

death·ful (dĕth′fəl), adj. 1. fatal. 2. deathlike.

death house, a building or part of a prison in which persons condemned to death await execution.

death·less (dĕth′lĭs), adj. 1. not subject to death; immortal. 2. perpetual. —**death′less·ly,** adv. —**death′-less·ness,** n.

death·like (dĕth′līk′), adj. resembling death.

death·ly (dĕth′lĭ), adj. 1. causing death; deadly; fatal. 2. like death. 3. *Poetic.* of death. —adv. 4. in the manner of death. 5. very; utterly: *deathly afraid.* [ME *dethlich,* OE *dēathlīc*]

death mask, a cast of a person's face taken after death.

death rate, the number of deaths per unit (usually 1000) of population in a given place and time.

death's-head (dĕths′hĕd′), n. a human skull, esp. as a symbol of mortality.

deaths·man (dĕths′mən), n., pl. -men. *Archaic.* an executioner.

death·trap (dĕth′trăp′), n. a structure or situation involving imminent risk of death.

Death Valley, an arid basin in E California; lowest land in the Western Hemisphere. 276 ft. below sea level.

death warrant, 1. an official order authorizing the execution of the sentence of death. 2. anything which ends hope, expectation, etc.

death·watch (dĕth′wŏch′, -wôch′), n. 1. a vigil beside a dying or dead person. 2. a guard set over a condemned person before execution. 3. any of certain beetles of the family *Anobiidae* which infest timbers, esp. in Europe. The ticking sound caused by their heads tapping against wood was thought to presage death.

death·y (dĕth′ĭ), adj., adv. *Rare.* deathly.

Deau·ville (dō′vĭl; *Fr.* dō vēl′), n. a coastal resort in NW France, S of Le Havre. 5211 (1954).

deave (dēv), v.t. deaved, deaving. *Dial.* to make deaf; deafen. [ME *deve,* OE *dēafian*]

deb., debenture.

de·ba·cle (dā bä′kəl, -băk′əl, dĭ-), n. 1. a general breakup or rout; sudden overthrow or collapse. 2. a breaking up of ice in a river. 3. a violent rush of waters. [t. F, der. *débâcler* unbar, clear, f. *dé-* DIS-¹ + *bâcler* bar (der. L *baculum* stick, rod)]

de·bar (dĭ bär′), v.t. -barred, -barring. 1. to bar out or exclude from a place or condition. 2. to prevent or prohibit (an action, etc.). [t. F: m. s. *débarrer,* OF *desbarrer,* f. *des-* DIS-¹ + *barrer* BAR¹, v.] —**de·bar′ment,** n. —Syn. 1. See exclude. 2. interdict, hinder. —Ant. 1. admit. 2. permit.

de·bark (dĭ bärk′), v.t., v.i. to disembark. [t. F: m. s. *débarquer,* der. *dé-* DIS-¹ + *barque* BARK³] —**de·bar·ka·tion** (dē′bär kā′shən), n.

de·base (dĭ bās′), v.t., -based, -basing. 1. to reduce in quality or value; adulterate. 2. *Obs.* to lower in rank or dignity. [f. DE- + obs. *base* (aphetic var. of ABASE)] —**de·base′ment,** n. —**de·bas′er,** n. —**de·bas′ing·ly,** adv. —Syn. 1. lower, vitiate, corrupt, deteriorate.

de·bat·a·ble (dĭ bā′tə bəl), adj. 1. capable of being debated. 2. in dispute.

de·bate (dĭ bāt′), n., v., -bated, -bating. —n. 1. a discussion, esp. of a public question in an assembly. 2. deliberation; consideration. 3. a systematic contest of speakers in which two points of view of a proposition are advanced with proof. 4. *Obs.* strife; contention. —v.i. 5. to engage in discussion, esp. in a legislative or public assembly. 6. to deliberate; discuss or argue. 7. *Obs.* to fight; quarrel. —v.t. 8. to discuss or argue (a question), as in a public assembly. 9. to dispute about. 10. to deliberate upon; consider. 11. *Archaic.* to contend for or over. [ME *debaten*), t. OF: m. *debatre,* f. *de-* DE- + *batre* BEAT] —**de·bat′er,** n. —Syn. 1. argument, controversy, disputation. 6. See argue.

de·bauch (dĭ bôch′), v.t. 1. to corrupt by sensuality, intemperance, etc.; seduce. 2. to corrupt or pervert; deprave. 3. *Obs.* to lead away, as from allegiance or duty. —v.i. 4. to indulge in a debauch. —n. 5. a period of debauchery. 6. debauchery. [t. F: s. *débaucher,* OF *desbaucher* seduce from duty] —**de·bauch′er,** n. —**de·bauch′ment,** n.

deb·au·chee (dĕb′ô chē′, -shē′), n. one addicted to excessive indulgence in sensual pleasures; one given to debauchery. [t. F: m. *débauché,* pp. of *débaucher* DEBAUCH]

de·bauch·er·y (dĭ bô′chə rĭ), n., pl. -eries. 1. seduction from virtue or morality. 2. excessive indulgence in sensual pleasures; intemperance. 3. seduction from allegiance or duty.

de·ben·ture (dĭ bĕn′chər), n. 1. a certificate of indebtedness, as a debenture bond (more widely used in England, where it often takes the place of *bond*). 2. a certificate of drawback issued at a custom house. [t. L: m. *debentur* there are owing]

debenture bond, a corporation bond unsecured by any mortgage, dependent on the credit of the issuer.

de·bil·i·tate (dĭ bĭl′ə tāt′), v.t., -tated, -tating. to make weak or feeble; weaken; enfeeble. [t. L: m. s. *dēbilitātus,* pp., weakened] —**de·bil′i·ta′tion,** n. —**de·bil′i·ta′tive,** adj.

de·bil·i·ty (dĭ bĭl′ə tĭ), n., pl. -ties. 1. state of being weak or feeble; weakness. 2. *Pathol.* a condition of the body in which the vital functions are feebly discharged. [ME *debylite,* t. L: m.s. *dēbilitas* weakness]

deb·it (dĕb′ĭt), *n.* **1.** the recording or an entry of debt in an account. **2.** *Bookkeeping.* **a.** that which is entered in an account as a debt; a recorded item of debt. **b.** any entry, or the total shown, on the debit side. **c.** the side (left side) of an account on which such entries are made (opposed to *credit*). —*v.t.* **3.** to charge with a debt. **4.** to charge as a debt. **5.** *Bookkeeping.* to enter upon the debit side of an account. [t. L: s. *dēbitum* something owed. See DEBT]

deb·o·nair (dĕb′ə nâr′), *adj.* **1.** of pleasant manners; courteous. **2.** gay; sprightly. Also, **deb·o·naire′, deb′·on·naire′**. [ME *debonere*, t. OF: m. *debonaire*, orig. phrase *de bon aire* of good disposition] —**deb′o·nair′ly,** *adv.* —**deb′o·nair′ness,** *n.*

de bonne grâce (də bôn gräs′), *French.* graciously.

Deb·o·rah (dĕb′ə rə), *n. Bible.* a prophetess and judge of Israel. Judges 4, 5. [t. Heb.]

de·bouch (dĭ bōōsh′), *v.i.* **1.** to march out from a narrow or confined place into open country, as a body of troops. **2.** *Phys. Geog.* **a.** to emerge from a relatively narrow valley upon an open plain: *a river or glacier debouches on the plains.* **b.** to flow from a small valley into a larger one. **3.** to issue; emerge. —*n.* **4.** débouché. [t. F: m.s. *déboucher*, der. *dé-* DIS-¹ + *bouche* mouth (g. L *bucca* cheek, mouth)]

dé·bou·ché (dē bōō shē′), *n. French.* **1.** *Fort.* an opening in works for passing troops. **2.** an outlet; an exit.

de·bouch·ment (dĭ bōōsh′mənt), *n.* **1.** act or fact of debouching. **2.** a mouth or outlet, as of a river or pass.

De·bre·cen (dĕ′brĕ tsĕn′), *n.* a city in E Hungary. 113,248 (est. 1954).

de·brief (dē′brēf′), *v.t.* to interrogate immediately after a test flight (a test pilot, astronaut, etc.) in order to determine precisely his experiences and reactions. Also, **de′-brief′**.

de·bris (də brē′, dā′brē *or, esp. Brit.,* dĕb′rē), *n.* **1.** the remains of anything broken down or destroyed; ruins; fragments; rubbish. **2.** *Geol.* an accumulation of loose fragments of rock, etc. Also, **dé·bris′**. [t. F: m. *débris*, der. OF *debrisier* break down, f. *de-* DE-¹ + *brisier* break (cf. BRUISE)]

De Bro·glie (də brô glē′), **Louis Victor** (lwē vēk tōr′), born 1892, French physicist.

Debs (dĕbz), *n.* **Eugene Victor,** 1855–1926, U.S. labor leader; Socialist candidate for president 1900, 1904, 1908, 1912, and 1920.

debt (dĕt), *n.* **1.** that which is owed; that which one person is bound to pay to or perform for another. **2.** a liability or obligation to pay or render something. **3.** the condition of being under such an obligation. **4.** *Theol.* an offense requiring reparation; a sin; a trespass. [ME *det*, t. OF: m. *dete*, g. L *dēbitum* (thing) owed, prop. pp. neut.] —**Syn.** 1. obligation, duty, due.

debt of honor, a gambling debt.

debt·or (dĕt′ər), *n.* one who is in debt or under obligations to another (opposed to *creditor*).

de·bunk (dĭ bŭngk′), *v.t. U.S. Colloq.* to remove false sentiments, opinions, etc., about.

De·bus·sy (də bü′sē; *Fr.* də bü sē′), *n.* **Claude Achille** (klôd à shēl′), 1862–1918, French composer.

de·but (dē bū′, dā-; dā′bū *or, esp. Brit.,* dĕb′ōō), *n.* **1.** a first public appearance on a stage, over the radio, etc. **2.** a formal introduction and entrance into society. **3.** the beginning of a professional career, etc. Also, *French,* **début** (dē by′). [t. F, der. *débuter* make the first stroke in a game, make one's first appearance, der. *dé-* DE- + *but* goal, mark]

deb·u·tante (dĕb′yōō tänt′, dĕb′yə tänt′), *n.* a woman making a debut. [t. F, fem. ppr. of *débuter*. See DEBUT] —**deb′u·tant′,** *n. masc.*

dec-, var. of deca-.

Dec., December.

dec., **1.** deceased. **2.** decimeter. **3.** declension. **4.** decrease. **5.** decrescendo.

deca-, a word element meaning "ten," specialized in the metric system so that *deca-* (deka-) gives the multiplication by 10, *deci-* the division by 10; e.g., *decaliter* (610.25 cu. in.), *liter* (61.025 cu. in.), *deciliter* (6.10 cu. in.). Cf. deci-. [t. Gk.: m. *deka-*, comb. form of *dĕka* ten]

dec·ade (dĕk′ād), *n.* **1.** a period of ten years. **2.** a group, set, or series of ten. [t. F, t. L: m.s. *decas*, t. Gk.: m. *dekás* a group of ten]

de·ca·dence (dĭ kā′dəns, dĕk′ə-), *n.* act or process of falling into an inferior condition or state; decay; deterioration. Also, **de·ca·den·cy** (dĭ kā′dən sĭ, dĕk′ə-). [t. F, ult. der. L *dē-* DE- + *cadere* fall] —**Syn.** decline.

de·ca·dent (dĭ kā′dənt, dĕk′ə-), *adj.* **1.** falling off or deteriorating. **2.** of or like the decadents. —*n.* **3.** one who is decadent. **4.** one of a group of French (and other) writers and artists toward the end of the 19th century whose work was characterized by great refinement or subtlety of style with a marked tendency toward the artificial and abnormal. [der. DECADENCE] —**de·ca·dent·ly,** *adv.*

dec·a·gon (dĕk′ə gŏn′), *n. Geom.* a polygon having 10 angles and 10 sides. [t. ML: s. *decagōnum.* See DECA-, -GON] —**de·cag·o·nal** (dĭ kăg′ə nəl), *adj.*

dec·a·gram (dĕk′ə grăm′), *n. Metric System.* a unit of 10 grams, equivalent to 0.3527 ounce avoirdupois. Also, *esp. Brit.,* **dec′a·gramme′.** [t. F: m. *decagramme.* See DECA-, GRAM]

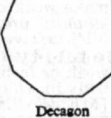

Decagon

dec·a·he·dron (dĕk′ə hē′drən), *n., pl.* **-drons, -dra** (-drə). *Geom.* a solid figure having 10 faces. —**dec·a·he·dral** (dĕk′ə hē′drəl), *adj.*

de·cal·ci·fy (dē kăl′sə fī′), *v.t.,* **-fied, -fying.** to deprive of lime or calcareous matter, as a bone. —**de·cal·ci·fi·ca·tion** (dē kăl′sə fə kā′shən), *n.*

de·cal·co·ma·ni·a (dĭ kăl′kə mā′nĭ ə), *n.* **1.** the art or process of transferring pictures or designs from specially prepared paper to wood, metal, china, glass, etc. **2.** the paper bearing such a picture or design. Also, **de·cal** (dē′kăl′). [t. F: m. *décalcomanie,* f. *décalco-* (repr. *décalquer* transfer a tracing of) + *manie* MANIA]

de·ca·les·cence (dē′kə lĕs′əns), *n.* (in the heating of iron) the sudden absorption of heat observed as it passes a certain temperature. —**de′ca·les′cent,** *adj.*

dec·a·li·ter (dĕk′ə lē′tər), *n. Metric System.* a unit of 10 lite rs equalent to 9.08 quarts U. S. dry measure, or 2.64 gallons U. S. liquid measure. Also, *esp. Brit.,* **dec′a·lit′re.** [t. F: m. *decalitre.* See DECA-, LITER]

Dec·a·logue (dĕk′ə lôg′, -lŏg′), *n.* the Ten Commandments. Ex. 20:2–17. Also *esp.* **Dec′a·log′, dec′a·log′.** [ME *decaloge,* t. LL: m.s. *decalogus,* t. Mk.: m. *dekálogos,* f. *dĕka* ten + *lógos* word]

De·cam·er·on (dĭ kăm′ər ən), *n.* **The,** a famous collection of 100 tales (1353) by Boccaccio.

dec·a·me·ter (dĕk′ə mē′tər), *n. Metric System.* a measure of length equal to 10 meters. Also *esp. Brit.,* **dec′a·me′tre.** [t. F: m. *décamètre.* See DECA-, METER]

de·camp (dĭ kămp′), *v.i.* **1.** to depart from a camp; break camp. **2.** to depart quickly, secretly, or unceremoniously. [t. F: m.s. *décamper,* f. *dé-* DIS-¹ + *camper* encamp] —**de·camp′ment,** *n.*

dec·ane (dĕk′ān), *n. Chem.* a hydrocarbon, $C_{10}H_{22}$, of the methane series, occurring in several isomeric forms.

de·cant (dĭ kănt′), *v.t.* **1.** to pour off gently, as liquor, without disturbing the sediment. **2.** to pour from one container into another. [t. ML: m.s. *decanthāre.* See DE-, CANT²] —**de·can·ta·tion** (dē′kăn tā′shən), *n.*

de·cant·er (dĭ kăn′tər), *n.* **1.** a bottle used for decanting. **2.** a vessel, usually an ornamental bottle, from which wine, water, etc., are served at table.

de·cap·i·tate (dĭ kăp′ə tāt′), *v.t.,* **-tated, -tating.** to cut off the head of; behead; kill by beheading. [t. ML: m.s. *decapitātus,* pp. of *decapitāre,* der. L *caput* head] —**de·cap′i·ta′tion,** *n.* —**de·cap′i·ta′tor,** *n.*

dec·a·pod (dĕk′ə pŏd′), *n.* **1.** any crustacean of the order *Decapoda,* including crabs, lobsters, crayfish, prawns, shrimps, etc., characterized by their five pairs of walking legs. **2.** any ten-armed dibranchiate cephalopod, as the cuttlefish, squid, etc. —*adj.* **3.** belonging to the *Decapoda.* **4.** having ten feet or legs. —**de·cap·o·dous** (dĭ kăp′ə dəs), *adj.*

de·car·bon·ate (dē kär′bə nāt′), *v.t.,* **-ated, -ating.** to deprive of carbon dioxide.

de·car·bon·ize (dē kär′bə nīz′), *v.t.,* **-ized, -izing.** decarburize. —**de·car′bon·i·za′tion,** *n.*

de·car·box·y·la·tion (dē′kär bŏk′sə lā′shən), *n. Chem.* the process of removing one or more carboxyl radicals, as carbon dioxide, from an organic acid.

de·car·bu·rize (dē kär′bə rīz′), *v.t.,* **-rized, -rizing.** to remove carbon from (molten steel, automobile cylinders, etc.). —**de·car′bu·ri·za′tion,** *n.*

dec·are (dĕk′âr, dĕ kâr′), *n. Metric System.* a unit of area equal to 10 ares.

de·car·te·lize (dē kär′tə līz), *v.t.,* **-lized, -lizing.** to break up or dissolve (a cartel, def. 1). —**de·car′te·li·za′tion,** *n.*

dec·a·stere (dĕk′ə stĭr′), *n. Metric System.* a unit of volume equal to 10 steres.

dec·a·syl·lab·ic (dĕk′ə sĭ lăb′ĭk), *adj.* having ten syllables: *a decasyllabic verse.*

dec·a·syl·la·ble (dĕk′ə sĭl′ə bəl), *n.* a line or verse of ten syllables.

de·cath·lon (dĭ kăth′lŏn), *n.* an athletic contest comprising ten different exercises or events, and won by the contestant having the highest total score. [f. DECA- + Gk. *āthlon* contest]

De·ca·tur (dĭ kā′tər), *n.* **1.** a city in Illinois. 78,004 (1960). **2.** **Stephen,** 1779–1820, U.S. naval officer.

de·cay (dĭ kā′), *v.i.* **1.** to fall away from a state of excellence, prosperity, health, etc.; deteriorate; decline. **2.** to become decomposed; rot. —*v.t.* **3.** to cause to decay. —*n.* **4.** a gradual falling into an inferior condition; progressive decline. **5.** loss of strength, health, intellect, etc. **6.** decomposition; rotting. **7.** *Obs.* a wasting disease, esp. consumption. [ME *decay(en),* t. OF: m.s. *decair,* f. *de-* DE-¹ + *cair* (g. L *cadere* fall)] —**Syn.** 2. DECAY, DECOMPOSE, DISINTEGRATE, ROT imply a deterioration or falling away from a sound condition. DECAY implies either entire or partial dissolution or deterioration by progressive natural changes: *teeth decay.* DECOMPOSE suggests the reducing of a substance, through natural change or human agency, to its component elements: *moisture makes some chemical compounds decompose.* DISINTEGRATE emphasizes the breaking up, going to pieces, or wearing away of anything, so that its original wholeness is impaired: *rocks disintegrate.* ROT is a stronger word than DECAY and is esp. applied to decaying vegetable matter, which may or may not emit offensive odors: *potatoes rot.* 4. deterioration, decadence, impairment, dilapidation.

Dec·can (dĕk′ən), *n.* **1.** the entire peninsula of India S of the Narbada river. **2.** the plateau region between the Narbada and Kistna rivers.

de·cease (dĭ sēs/), n., v., -ceased, -ceasing. —n. 1. departure from life; death. —v.i. 2. to depart from life; die. [ME deces, t. OF, t. L: m.s. dēcessus departure, death] —Syn. 2. See die[1].

de·ceased (dĭ sēst/), adj. 1. dead. —n. 2. the deceased, the dead person. —Syn. 1. See dead.

de·ce·dent (dĭ sē/dənt), n. Law. a deceased person. [t. L: s. dēcēdens, ppr., departing, withdrawing]

decedent estate, Law. the estate left by a decedent.

de·ceit (dĭ sēt/), n. 1. act or practice of deceiving; concealment or perversion of the truth for the purpose of misleading; fraud; cheating. 2. an act or device intended to deceive; a trick; stratagem. 3. deceiving quality; falseness. [ME deceite, t. OF, der. deceveir DECEIVE] —Syn. 1. DECEIT, GUILE, HYPOCRISY imply (usually) deliberate attempts to mislead someone. DECEIT is the habit or practice of intentionally concealing or perverting the truth for the purpose of misleading: honest and without deceit. GUILE implies craftiness in the use of deceit: using guile and trickery to attain one's ends. HYPOCRISY is the pretended possession of those qualities which would make others believe in one's sincerity, goodness, devotion, etc.: it was sheer hypocrisy for him to go to church. —Ant. 3. honesty, sincerity.

de·ceit·ful (dĭ sēt/fəl), adj. 1. full of deceit; given to deceiving. 2. misleading; fraudulent; deceptive. —de·ceit/ful·ly, adv. —de·ceit/ful·ness, n. —Syn. 1. insincere, disingenuous, false, hollow.

de·ceive (dĭ sēv/), v., -ceived, -ceiving. —v.t. 1. to mislead by a false appearance or statement; delude. 2. Obs. to beguile or while away (time, etc.). —v.i. 3. to practice deceit; act deceitfully. [ME deceyve(n), t. OF: m. deceveir, g. L dēcipere catch, ensnare, deceive] —de·ceiv/er, n. —de·ceiv/ing·ly, adv. —Syn. 1. See cheat. cozen, dupe, fool, gull, hoodwink, trick, defraud, outwit, entrap, ensnare, betray, bamboozle.

de·cel·er·ate (dē sĕl/ə rāt/), v.t., v.i., -ated, -ating. to decrease in velocity. [f. DE- + (AC)CELERATE] —de·cel/er·a/tion, n. —de·cel/er·a/tor, n.

De·cem·ber (dĭ sĕm/bər), n. the twelfth month of the year, containing 31 days. [t. L: the tenth month of the early Roman year; r. ME decembre, t. OF]

De·cem·brist (dĭ sĕm/brĭst), n. Russian Hist. a participant in the conspiracy and insurrection against the Emperor Nicholas on his accession, December, 1825.

de·cem·vir (dĭ sĕm/vər), n., pl. -virs, -viri (-və rī/). 1. a member of a permanent board or a special commission of ten members in ancient Rome, esp. the commission appointed to draw up Rome's first code of law. 2. a member of any council or ruling body of ten. [t. L, orig. pl., decemvirī, f. decem ten + virī men] —de·cem/vi·ral, adj.

de·cem·vi·rate (dĭ sĕm/vər rĭt, -rāt/), n. 1. a body of decemvirs. 2. the office or government of decemvirs.

de·cen·cy (dē/sən sĭ), n., pl. -cies. 1. state or quality of being decent. 2. conformity to the recognized standard of propriety, good taste, modesty, etc. 3. something decent or proper. 4. (pl.) the requirements or observances of decent life or conduct.

de·cen·na·ry (dĭ sĕn/ə rĭ), n., pl. -ries. a decennium. [f. s. L decennis of ten years + -ARY[1]]

de·cen·ni·al (dĭ sĕn/ĭ əl), adj. 1. of or for ten years. 2. occurring every ten years. —n. 3. a decennial anniversary. 4. its celebration. —de·cen/ni·al·ly, adv.

de·cen·ni·um (dĭ sĕn/ĭ əm), n., pl. -venniums, -cennia (-sĕn/ĭ ə). a period of ten years; a decade. [t. L, der. decennis of ten years]

de·cent (dē/sənt), adj. 1. fitting; appropriate. 2. conforming to the recognized standard of propriety, good taste, modesty, etc., as in behavior or speech. 3. respectable; worthy: a decent family. 4. of seemly appearance: decent clothes. 5. fair; tolerable; passable: a decent fortune. 6. Brit. Colloq. kind; obliging: thanks, that's frightfully decent of you. [t. L: s. dēcens, ppr., fitting] —de/cent·ly, adv. —de/cent·ness, n. —Syn. 2. seemly, proper, decorous.

de·cen·ter (dē sĕn/tər), v.t. 1. to put out of center. 2. to make eccentric. Also, Brit., decentre.

de·cen·tral·ize (dē sĕn/trə līz/), v.t., -ized, -izing. to undo the centralization of (administrative powers, etc.). —de·cen/tral·i·za/tion, n.

de·cen·tre (dē sĕn/tər), v.t., -tred, -tring. Brit. decenter.

de·cep·tion (dĭ sĕp/shən), n. 1. act of deceiving. 2. state of being deceived. 3. something that deceives or is intended to deceive; an artifice; a sham; a cheat. [ME decepcioun, t. LL: m. s. dēceptio, der. L dēcipere DECEIVE] —Syn. 3. imposture, treachery, subterfuge, stratagem, ruse, hoax, fraud. See trick.

de·cep·tive (dĭ sĕp/tĭv), adj. apt or tending to deceive. [t. NL: m.s. dēceptīvus] —de·cep/tive·ly, adv. —de·cep/tive·ness, n. —Syn. misleading, delusive, fallacious, specious, false.

de·cern (dĭ sûrn/), v.t. 1. Scot. Law. to decree by judicial sentence. 2. to discern. [t. L: s. dēcernere decide, decree]

deci-, a word element meaning "ten," specialized in the metric system so that deci- gives division by 10, e.g. deciliter (6.10 cu. in.), liter (61.025 cu. in.). See deca-. [comb. form repr. L decem ten, decimus tenth]

dec·i·bel (dĕs/ə bĕl/), n. Physics. the unit of power ratio equal to one tenth of a bel.

de·cide (dĭ sīd/), v., -cided, -ciding. —v.t. 1. to determine or settle (a question, controversy, struggle, etc.) by giving victory to one side. 2. to adjust or settle (anything in dispute or doubt). 3. to bring (a person) to a decision. —v.i. 4. to settle something in dispute or doubt. 5. to pronounce a judgment; come to a conclusion. [ME decide(n), t. L: m. dēcīdere cut off, determine] —de·cid/a·ble, adj. —Syn. 1. DECIDE, RESOLVE, DETERMINE imply settling upon a purpose and being able to adhere to it. To DECIDE is to make up one's mind promptly, clearly, and firmly as to what shall be done and the way to do it: he decided to go today. To RESOLVE is usually positively or actively to show firmness of purpose: he resolved to ask for a promotion. To DETERMINE is to make up one's mind and then doggedly, and sometimes obstinately, to stick to a fixed or settled purpose: determined to maintain his position at all costs.

de·cid·ed (dĭ sī/dĭd), adj. 1. free from ambiguity; unquestionable; unmistakable. 2. free from hesitation or wavering; resolute; determined. —de·cid/ed·ly, adv. —Syn. 1. undeniable, indisputable, positive, certain, emphatic, pronounced.

de·cid·u·a (dĭ sĭj/ŏŏ ə), n. Embryol. the inner mucosal lining of the uterus which in some mammals is cast off at parturition. [NL, prop. fem. of L dēciduus. See DECIDUOUS] —de·cid/u·al, adj.

de·cid·u·ous (dĭ sĭj/ŏŏ əs), adj. 1. shedding the leaves annually, as trees, shrubs, etc. 2. falling off or shedding at a particular season, stage of growth, etc., as leaves, horns, teeth, etc. 3. not permanent; transitory. [t. L: m. dēciduus falling down] —de·cid/u·ous·ly, adv. —de·cid/u·ous·ness, n.

dec·i·gram (dĕs/ə grăm/), n. Metric System. a unit of weight of one tenth of a gram, equivalent to 1.543 grains. Also, esp. Brit., dec/i·gramme/. [t. F: m. décigramme. See DECI-, GRAM]

dec·ile (dĕs/ĭl), n. Statistics. one of the values of a variable which divides the distribution of the variable into ten groups having equal frequencies. [f. L dec(em) ten + -ILE]

dec·i·li·ter (dĕs/ə lē/tər), n. Metric System. a unit of capacity of one tenth of a liter, equivalent to 6.102 cubic inches, or 3.381 U.S. fluid ounces. Also, esp. Brit., dec/i·li/tre. [t. F: m. décilitre. See DECI-, LITER]

de·cil·lion (dĭ sĭl/yən), n. 1. (in the U.S. and France) a cardinal number represented by one followed by 33 zeros. 2. (in England and Germany) a cardinal number represented by one followed by 60 zeros. —adj. 3. amounting to one decillion in number. [f. DECI- + (M)ILLION] —de·cil/lionth, adj., n.

dec·i·mal (dĕs/ə məl), adj. 1. pertaining to tenths, or to the number ten. 2. proceeding by tens: a decimal system. —n. 3. a decimal fraction. [f. s. L decimus tenth + -AL[1]] —dec/i·mal·ly, adv.

decimal fraction, a fraction whose denominator is some power of ten, usually indicated by a dot (the decimal point) written before the numerator: as 0.4 = 4/10; 0.126 = 126/1000.

dec·i·mal·ize (dĕs/ə mə līz/), v.t., -ized, -izing. to reduce to a decimal system. —dec/i·mal·i·za/tion, n.

decimal system, any system of counting or measurement whose units are powers of ten.

dec·i·mate (dĕs/ə māt/), v.t., -mated, -mating. 1. to destroy a great number or proportion of. 2. to select by lot and kill every tenth man of. 3. Obs. to take a tenth of or from. [t. L: m. s. decimātus, pp.] —dec/i·ma/tion, n. —dec/i·ma/tor, n.

dec·i·me·ter (dĕs/ə mē/tər), n. Metric System. a unit of length of one tenth of a meter. Also, esp. Brit., dec/i·me/tre. [t. F: m. décimètre. See DECI-, -METER]

de·ci·pher (dĭ sī/fər), v.t. 1. to make out the meaning of (poor or partially obliterated writing, etc.). 2. to discover the meaning of (anything obscure or difficult to trace or understand). 3. to interpret by the use of a key, as something written in cipher. 4. Obs. to depict. —de·ci/pher·a·ble, adj. —de·ci/pher·er, n. —de·ci/pher·ment, n.

de·ci·sion (dĭ sĭzh/ən), n. 1. act of deciding; determination (of a question or doubt). 2. a judgment, as one formally pronounced by a court. 3. a making up of one's mind. 4. that which is decided; a resolution. 5. the quality of being decided; firmness, as of character. [t. L: s. dēcīsio a cutting down, decision]

de·ci·sive (dĭ sī/sĭv), adj. 1. having the power or quality of determining; putting an end to controversy: a decisive fact, test, etc. 2. characterized by or displaying decision; resolute; determined. —de·ci/sive·ly, adv. —de·ci/sive·ness, n. —Syn. 1. conclusive, final.

dec·i·stere (dĕs/ə stĭr/), n. Metric System. a unit of volume equal to one tenth of a stere.

deck (dĕk), n. 1. a platform extending from side to side of a ship or of a part of a ship, forming a covering for the space below and itself serving as a floor. 2. a platform or part resembling this. 3. a pack of playing cards. [t. MD: m. dec covering, roof] —v.t. 4. to clothe or attire in something ornamental; array. 5. Naut. to furnish with or as with a deck, as a vessel. [t. MD: s. decken cover, c. G decken] —Syn. 4. bedeck, garnish, trim, bedizen.

deck·er (dĕk/ər), n. 1. one who or that which decks. 2. a ship, vehicle, etc., having a certain number of decks: a three-decker.

Deck·er (dĕk/ər), n. Thomas. See Dekker.

deck hand, a sailor or workman employed on the deck of a vessel.

deck·house (dĕk/hous/), n. a small house erected on the deck of a ship for any purpose.

deck·le (dĕk′əl), n. 1. (in paper making) a frame which forms the paper pulp, fixing the size of a sheet of paper. 2. deckle edge. Also, **deck′el**. [t. G: (m.) *deckel*, dim. of *decke* cover]

deckle edge, the untrimmed edge of handmade paper, often used for ornamental effect in fine books.

deck·le-edged (dĕk′əl ĕjd′), adj. having a deckle edge.

decl., declension.

de·claim (dĭ klām′), v.i. 1. to speak aloud rhetorically; make a formal speech. 2. to inveigh (fol. by *against*). 3. to speak or write for oratorical effect, without sincerity or sound argument. —v.t. 4. to utter aloud in a rhetorical manner. [ME *declame*(n), t. L: m. *dēclāmāre* cry aloud] —de·claim′er, n.

dec·la·ma·tion (dĕk′lə mā′shən), n. 1. act or art of declaiming. 2. an exercise in oratory or elocution. 3. speech or writing for oratorical effect. 4. *Music.* the proper enunciation of the words, as in recitative.

de·clam·a·to·ry (dĭ klăm′ə tôr′ĭ), adj. 1. pertaining to or characterized by declamation. 2. merely rhetorical; stilted.

dec·la·ra·tion (dĕk′lə rā′shən), n. 1. a positive, explicit, or formal statement, announcement, etc. 2. a proclamation: *a declaration of war*. 3. that which is proclaimed. 4. the document embodying the proclamation. 5. *Law.* a. the formal statement in which a plaintiff presents his claim in an action. b. a complaint. 6. *Cards.* a. *Bridge.* a bid, esp. the successful bid. b. the statement during the game of the points earned by a player, in bezique or other games. 7. a statement of goods, etc., liable to duty.

Declaration of Independence, *U.S. Hist.* 1. the public act by which the Second Continental Congress, on July 4, 1776, declared the colonies to be free and independent of Great Britain. 2. the document embodying it.

de·clar·a·tive (dĭ klăr′ə tĭv), adj. serving to declare, make known, or explain. Also, **de·clar·a·to·ry** (dĭ klăr′ə tôr′ĭ).

de·clare (dĭ klâr′), v., -clared, -claring. —v.t. 1. to make known, esp. in explicit or formal terms. 2. to announce officially; proclaim. 3. to state emphatically; affirm. 4. to manifest; reveal. 5. to make due statement of (dutiable goods, etc.). 6. to make (a dividend) payable. 7. *Bridge.* to signify (a certain suit) as trumps or to establish the bid at no-trump. —v.i. 8. to make a declaration. 9. to proclaim oneself. [ME *declar*(en), t. L: m. *dēclārāre* make clear] —de·clar′er, n.
—Syn. 3. DECLARE, AFFIRM, ASSERT, PROTEST imply making something known emphatically, openly, or formally. To DECLARE is to make known, sometimes in the face of actual or potential contradiction: *to declare someone the winner of a contest*. To AFFIRM is to make a statement based on one's reputation for knowledge or veracity, or so related to a generally recognized truth that denial is not likely: *to affirm the necessity of high standards*. To ASSERT is to state boldly, usually without other proof than personal authority or conviction: *to assert that the climate is changing*. To PROTEST is to affirm publicly, as if in the face of doubt: *to protest that a newspaper account is misleading*.

de·clared (dĭ klârd′), adj. avowed; professed. —**de·clar·ed·ly** (dĭ klâr′ĭd lĭ), adv.

de·class (dē klăs′, -kläs′), v.t. to remove or degrade from one's class (social or other).

dé·clas·sé (dē klä sē′), adj. fallen or lowered in social rank, class, etc. —**dé·clas·sée′,** adj. fem.

de·clen·sion (dĭ klĕn′shən), n. 1. act or fact of declining. 2. a bending, sloping, or moving downward. 3. deterioration; decline. 4. deviation, as from a standard. 5. *Gram.* a. the inflection of nouns, and of words similarly inflected, for categories such as case and number. Example (Latin): *puella, puellae, puellam, etc.* b. the whole set of inflected forms of such a word, or the recital thereof in a fixed order. c. a class of such words having similar sets of inflected forms, as the Latin *second declension*. [irreg. t. L: m.s. *dēclīnātio* a bending aside, inflection, prob. modeled on *dēscensio* descent] —**de·clen′sion·al** adj.

dec·li·na·tion (dĕk′lə nā′shən), n. 1. a bending, sloping, or moving downward. 2. deterioration; decline. 3. a swerving or deviating, as from a standard. 4. a polite refusal. 5. *Astron.* the angular distance of a heavenly body from the celestial equator, measured on a great circle passing through the celestial pole and the body. 6. the horizontal angle between the direction of true north and magnetic north at any place.

de·clin·a·to·ry (dĭ klī′nə tôr′ĭ), adj. expressing refusal; implying declination.

de·clin·a·ture (dĭ klī′nə chər), n. act of refusing.

de·cline (dĭ klīn′), v., -clined, -clining, n. —v.t. 1. to withhold consent to do, enter upon, or accept; refuse: *he declined to say more about it, he declined the offer with thanks.* 2. to cause to slope or incline downward. 3. *Gram.* a. to inflect (a noun, pronoun, or adjective). In Latin, *puella* is declined *puella, puellae, puellae, puellam, puellā* in the five cases of the singular. b. to recite or display all, or some subset, of the inflected

A Star:
DA. Declination of star;
N. North celestial pole;
S. South celestial pole;
CE. Celestial equator

forms of a noun, pronoun, or adjective in a fixed order. —v.i. 4. to express courteous refusal; refuse. 5. to bend or slant down; slope or trend downward; descend. 6. to draw toward the close, as the day. 7. to stoop (to an unworthy object); condescend. 8. to fail in strength, vigor, character, value, etc.; deteriorate. 9. *Gram.* to be characterized by declension. —n. 10. a downward incline or slope. 11. a failing or gradual loss, as in strength, character, value, etc.; deterioration; diminution. 12. progress downward or toward a close, as of the sun or the day. 13. a gradual diminution of the physical powers, as in later life or in disease. 14. the last part. [ME *decline*(n), t. OF: m. *decliner*, t. L: m. *dēclīnāre* bend from, avoid, inflect] —**de·clin′a·ble,** adj. —**de·clin′er,** n. —Syn. 1. reject. See refuse[1]. 8. degenerate, decay. 11. retrogression, degeneration.

dec·li·nom·e·ter (dĕk′lə nŏm′ə tər), n. an instrument for measuring declination. [f. *declino-* (comb. form repr. L *dēclīnāre* bend from) + -METER]

de·cliv·i·tous (dĭ klĭv′ə təs), adj. rather steep.

de·cliv·i·ty (dĭ klĭv′ə tĭ), n., pl. -ties. a downward slope, as of ground (opposed to *acclivity*). [t. L: m. s. *dēclīvitas* slope]

de·cli·vous (dĭ klī′vəs), adj. sloping downward.

de·coct (dĭ kŏkt′), v.t. to boil (a medicinal substance, etc.) in water, etc.; to extract the essence or principles. [t. L: s. *dēcoctus*, pp., boiled down]

de·coc·tion (dĭ kŏk′shən), n. 1. act of boiling in water, in order to extract the peculiar properties or virtues. 2. an extract obtained by decocting. 3. water in which a substance, usually animal or vegetable, has been boiled, and which thus contains the constituents or principles of the substance soluble in boiling water.

de·code (dē kōd′), v.t., -coded, -coding. to translate from code into the original language or form.

de·col·late (dĭ kŏl′āt), v.t., -lated, -lating. to behead; decapitate. [t. L: m. s. *dēcollātus*, pp., beheaded] —**de·col·la·tion** (dē′kə lā′shən), n. —**de·col·la′tor,** n.

dé·colle·tage (dā′kŏl tăzh′; Fr. dĕkôl tázh′), n. 1. the neckline of a dress cut low in the front and back and across the shoulders. 2. a décolleté garment or costume. [F, der. *décolleter*. See DECOLLETE.]

dé·colle·té (dā′kŏl tā′; Fr. dĕkôl tĕ′), adj. 1. (of a garment) low-necked. 2. wearing a low-necked garment. [t. F, pp. of *décolleter* bare the neck of, ult. der. *col* neck]

de·col·or (dē kŭl′ər), v.t. to deprive of color; bleach. Also, *Brit.,* **de·col′our.** [t. L: m. *dēcolōrāre* deprive of color] —**de′col·or·a′tion,** n.

de·col·or·ant (dē kŭl′ər ənt), adj. 1. having the property of removing color; bleaching. —n. 2. a decolorant substance or agent.

de·col·or·ize (dē kŭl′ər īz′), v.t., -ized, -izing. decolor. Also, *Brit.,* **de·col′our·ize′.** —**de·col′or·i·za′tion,** n. —**de·col′or·iz′er,** n.

de·com·pose (dē′kəm pōz′), v.t., v.i., -posed, -posing. 1. to separate or resolve into constituent parts or elements; disintegrate. 2. to rot; putrefy. [t. F: s. *décomposer*, f. *dé-* DIS-[1] + *composer* COMPOSE] —**de′com·pos′a·ble,** adj. —Syn. 2. See decay.

de·com·po·si·tion (dē′kŏm pə zĭsh′ən), n. 1. act or process of decomposing. 2. state of being decomposed; disintegration; decay.

de·com·pound (dē′kəm pound′), v.t. 1. to compound a second time or further, or of things already compound. 2. to decompose. —adj. 3. *Bot.* divided into compound divisions. 4. composed of things which are themselves compound.

de·con·tam·i·nate (dē′kən tăm′ə nāt′), v.t., -nated, -nating. to make (any object or area) safe for unprotected personnel by absorbing, making harmless, or destroying chemicals with which they have been in contact. —**de′con·tam′i·na′tion,** n.

de·con·trol (dē′kən trōl′), v., -trolled, -trolling, n. —v.t. 1. to remove controls, or from control. —n. 2. removal of control.

Decompound leaf

dé·cor (dā kôr′; Fr. dĕkôr′), n. 1. decoration in general. 2. a decoration. 3. *Theat.* scenic decoration; scenery. [F, der. *décorer* decorate, t. L: m. *decorāre*]

dec·o·rate (dĕk′ə rāt′), v.t., -rated, -rating. 1. to furnish or deck with something becoming or ornamental; embellish. 2. to confer distinction upon by a badge, a medal of honor, etc. [t. L: m. s. *decorātus*, pp.]

Decorated style, *Archit.* the second style of English pointed architecture, in use from the end of the thirteenth to the beginning of the fifteenth century.

dec·o·ra·tion (dĕk′ə rā′shən), n. 1. act of decorating. 2. adornment; embellishment. 3. a badge of an order, medal, etc., conferred and worn as a mark of honor.

Decoration Day, *U.S.* Memorial Day.

dec·o·ra·tive (dĕk′ə rā′tĭv, dĕk′rə tĭv), adj. serving or tending to decorate. —**dec′o·ra′tive·ly,** adv. —**dec′o·ra′tive·ness,** n.

dec·o·ra·tor (dĕk′ə rā′tər), n. 1. one who decorates. 2. one who professionally decorates houses or buildings, particularly their interior.

---

b., blend of, blended; c., cognate with; d., dialect, dialectal; der., derived from; f., formed from; g., going back to; m., modification of; r., replacing; s., stem of; t., taken from; ?, perhaps. See the full key on inside cover.

dec·o·rous (dĕk′ərəs, dĭ kōr′əs), *adj.* characterized by propriety in conduct, manners, appearance, character, etc. [t. L: m. *decōrus* becoming, seemly] —**dec′o·rous·ly,** *adv.* —**dec′o·rous·ness,** *n.* —**Syn.** proper, seemly, becoming, decent, sedate, conventional. —**Ant.** undignified.

de·cor·ti·cate (dē kôr′tə kāt′), *v.t.* **-cated, -cating.** to remove the bark, husk, or outer covering from. [t. L: m. s. *dēcorticātus,* pp.] —**de·cor′ti·ca′tion,** *n.* —**de·cor′ti·ca′tor,** *n.*

de·co·rum (dĭ kōr′əm), *n.* **1.** propriety of behavior, speech, dress, etc. **2.** that which is proper or seemly; fitness; congruity; propriety. **3.** an observance or requirement of polite society. [t. L, prop. neut. of *decōrus* DECOROUS] —**Syn. 1.** See etiquette.

de·coy (*n.* dĭ koi′, dē′koi; *v.* dĭ koi′), *n.* **1.** one who entices or allures, as into a trap, danger, etc. **2.** anything used as a lure. **3.** a trained bird or other animal used to entice game into a trap or within gunshot. **4.** an image of a bird used for the same purpose. **5.** a pond into which wild fowl are lured to permit their capture. —*v.t.* **6.** to lure by or as by a decoy. —*v.i.* **7.** to be decoyed. [var. of *coy* (now d.), both t. D: m. (*de*)*kooi* (the) cage, t. L: m. s. *cavea* CAGE] —**de·coy′er,** *n.*

de·crease (*v.* dĭ krēs′; *n.* dē′krēs, dĭ krēs′), *v.,* **-creased, -creasing,** *n.* —*v.i.* **1.** to diminish gradually in extent, quantity, strength, power, etc. —*v.t.* **2.** to make less; cause to diminish. —*n.* **3.** a process of growing less, or the resulting condition; gradual diminution. **4.** the amount by which a thing is lessened. [ME *decrese*(*n*), t. OF: m. *decreiss-,* g. L *dēcrescere* grow less] —**de·creas′ing·ly,** *adv.*
—**Syn. 1.** wane, lessen, fall off, decline, contract, abate. DECREASE, DIMINISH, DWINDLE, SHRINK imply becoming smaller or less in amount. DECREASE commonly implies a gradual and sustained reduction, esp. of bulk, size, volume, or quantity, often from some imperceptible cause or inherent process: *the swelling decreased daily.* DIMINISH usually implies the action of some external cause which keeps taking away: *disease caused the number of troops to diminish steadily.* DWINDLE implies an undesirable reduction by degrees, resulting in attenuation: *his followers dwindled to a mere handful.* SHRINK esp. implies contraction through an inherent property under specific conditions: *many fabrics shrink when wet.* **3.** abatement, reduction, decline. —**Ant. 1.** increase, expand.

de·cree (dĭ krē′), *n., v.,* **-creed, -creeing.** —*n.* **1.** an ordinance or edict promulgated by civil or other authority. **2.** *Law.* a judicial decision or order. **3.** *Theol.* one of the eternal purposes of God, by which events are foreordained. —*v.t., v.i.* **4.** to ordain or decide by decree. [ME *decre,* t. OF, var. of *decret,* t. L: s. *dēcrētum,* prop. pp. neut.]

decree ni·si (nī′sī), *Law.* a decree of divorce that will become absolute at a later date.

dec·re·ment (dĕk′rə mənt), *n.* **1.** the process or fact of decreasing; gradual diminution. **2.** the amount lost by diminution. **3.** *Math.* a negative increment.

de·crep·it (dĭ krĕp′ĭt), *adj.* broken down or weakened by old age; feeble; infirm. [t. L: s. *dēcrepitus,* lit., broken down] —**de·crep′it·ly,** *adv.* —**Syn.** See weak. —**Ant.** vigorous.

de·crep·i·tate (dĭ krĕp′ə tāt′), *v.,* **-tated, -tating.** —*v.t.* **1.** to roast or calcine (salt, etc.) so as to cause crackling or until crackling ceases. —*v.i.* **2.** to make a crackling noise, as salt in roasting. [t. NL: m.s. *dēcrepitātus* crackled down] —**de·crep′i·ta′tion,** *n.*

de·crep·i·tude (dĭ krĕp′ə tūd′, -tōōd′), *n.* decrepit condition; feebleness, esp. from old age.

de·cresc. *Music.* decrescendo.

de·cre·scen·do (dē′krə shĕn′dō, dā′-; *It.* dĕ′krĕ shĕn′dô), *adj., n., pl.* **-dos.** *Music.* —*adj.* **1.** gradually reducing force of loudness; diminuendo (opposed to *crescendo*). —*n.* **2.** a gradual reduction in force or loudness. **3.** a decrescendo passage. [t. It., ger. of *decrescere* DECREASE]

de·cres·cent (dĭ krĕs′ənt), *adj.* **1.** decreasing. **2.** waning, as the moon. [t. L: s. *dēcrescens,* ppr., decreasing]

de·cre·tal (dĭ krē′təl), *adj.* **1.** pertaining to, of the nature of, or containing a decree or decrees. —*n.* **2.** a papal document authoritatively determining some point of doctrine or church law. **3.** Decretals, the body or collection of such decrees as a part of the canon law. [ME *decretale,* t. ML, ult. der. L *dēcrētum* DECREE]

de·cre·tist (dĭ krē′tĭst), *n.* (in medieval universities) **1.** a student in the faculty of law. **2.** a student of the Decretals; one versed in the canon law.

de·cre·tive (dĭ krē′tĭv), *adj.* having the force of a decree; pertaining to a decree.

dec·re·to·ry (dĕk′rə tōr′Ĭ), *adj.* **1.** pertaining to or following a decree. **2.** established by a decree; judicial; definitive.

de·cri·al (dĭ krī′əl), *n.* act of crying down.

de·cry (dĭ krī′), *v.t.,* **-cried, -crying. 1.** to speak disparagingly of; censure as faulty or worthless. **2.** to condemn or depreciate by proclamation, as foreign or obsolete coins. [t. F: m. *décrier,* f. *dé-* DIS-[1] + *crier* CRY] —**de·cri′er,** *n.* —**Syn. 1.** belittle, disparage, discredit.

dec·u·man (dĕk′yōō mən), *adj.* **1.** large or immense, as a wave. **2.** every tenth in a series. [t. L: s. *decumānus,* var. of *decimānus* of the tenth, large (from the notion that every tenth wave is a large one)]

de·cum·bent (dĭ kŭm′bənt), *adj.* **1.** lying down; recumbent. **2.** *Bot.* (of stems, branches, etc.) lying or trail-

ing on the ground with the extremity tending to ascend. [t. L: s. *dēcumbens,* ppr.] —**de·cum′bence, de·cum′-ben·cy,** *n.* —**de·cum′bent·ly,** *adv.*

de·cu·ple (dĕk′yōō pəl), *adj., n., v.,* **-pled, -pling.** —*adj.* **1.** tenfold; ten times as great. —*n.* **2.** a tenfold quantity or multiple. —*v.t.* **3.** to make ten times as great. [t. F, t. L: m. *decuplus* tenfold]

de·cu·ri·on (dĭ kyŏŏr′Ĭ ən), *n.* **1.** *Rom. Hist.* the head of a decury. **2.** a member of the senate of an ancient Roman colony or municipality. [ME, t. L: s. *decurio*]

de·cur·rent (dĭ kûr′ənt), *adj. Bot.* extending down the stem below the place of insertion, as certain leaves. [t. L: s. *dēcurrens,* ppr., running down] —**de·cur′rent·ly,** *adv.*

de·cu·ry (dĕk′yŏŏrĬ), *n., pl.* **-ries. 1.** *Rom. Hist.* a division of a larger unit, nominally comprising ten persons, but frequently in excess of this number. **2.** a division, group, or class. [t. L: m. s. *decuria* a company of ten]

Decurrent leaf of thistle

de·cus·sate (*v.* dĭ kŭs′āt, dĕk′ə sāt′; *adj.* dĭ kŭs′āt, -Ĭt), *v.,* **-sated, -sating,** *adj.* —*v.t., v.i.* **1.** to cross in the form of the letter X; intersect. —*adj.* **2.** in the form of the letter X; crossed; intersected. **3.** *Bot.* (of leaves, etc.) arranged along the stem in pairs, each pair at right angles to the pair next above or below. [t. L: m. s. *decussātus,* pp., divided in the form of an X] —**de·cus·sa·tion** (dē′kə sā′shən, dĕk′ə-), *n.*

De·de A·gach (dĕ dĕ′ ä gäch′), *n.* former name of Alexandroupolis.

ded·i·cate (dĕd′ə kāt′), *v.,* **-cated, -cating,** *adj.* —*v.t.* **1.** to set apart and consecrate to a deity or to a sacred purpose. **2.** to give up wholly or earnestly, as to some person or end; set apart or appropriate. **3.** to inscribe or address (a book, piece of music, etc.) to a patron, friend, etc., as in testimony of respect or affection. —*adj.* **4.** *Archaic.* consecrated. [t. L: m. s. *dēdicātus,* pp., proclaimed, devoted] —**ded′i·ca′tor,** *n.*

Decussate leaf

ded·i·ca·tion (dĕd′ə kā′shən), *n.* **1.** act of dedicating. **2.** fact of being dedicated. **3.** an inscription prefixed or attached to a book, etc., dedicating it to some person.

ded·i·ca·to·ry (dĕd′ə kə tōr′Ĭ), *adj.* of or pertaining to dedication; serving as a dedication. Also, **ded·i·ca·tive** (dĕd′ə kā′tĬv).

de·duce (dĭ dūs′, -dōōs′), *v.t.,* **-duced, -ducing. 1.** to derive as a conclusion from something known or assumed; infer. **2.** to trace the derivation of; trace the course of. [t. L: m.s. *dēdūcere* lead down, derive] —**de·duc′i·ble,** *adj.*

de·duct (dĭ dŭkt′), *v.t.* to take away, as from a sum or amount. [t. L: s. *dēductus,* pp., led down, withdrawn] —**de·duct′i·ble,** *adj.* —**Syn.** See subtract.

de·duc·tion (dĭ dŭk′shən), *n.* **1.** act of deducting; subtraction; abatement. **2.** that which is deducted. **3.** the process of drawing a conclusion from something known or assumed. **4.** *Logic.* inference by reasoning from generals to particulars (opposed to *induction*).

de·duc·tive (dĭ dŭk′tĬv), *adj.* based on inference from accepted principles; reasoning by deduction. —**de·duc′tive·ly,** *adv.*
—**Syn.** DEDUCTIVE, INDUCTIVE, often confused, are not properly synonyms. They do agree in referring to processes of (formal or informal) reasoning, but the processes they describe are of opposite kinds. In DEDUCTIVE reasoning, an accepted general statement (true or false) is applied to an individual case; if formally, by the method of syllogism: *All dogs are animals; this is a dog; therefore this is an animal.* In INDUCTIVE reasoning, a set of individual cases is studied by the experimental method, and, from the observations made, a general principle is formed: *every metal I have tested expands when heated; therefore I can expect all metals to expand when heated.* When the general premise in deductive reasoning is true, the deduction from it will be certain for all possible instances. The principle formed in inductive reasoning is a workable theory but would be certain only when all possible instances had been examined.

Dee (dē), *n.* **1.** a river in NE Scotland, flowing into the North Sea at Aberdeen. **2.** a river in N Wales and W England, flowing into the Irish Sea.

deed (dēd), *n.* **1.** that which is done, performed, or accomplished; an act. **2.** an exploit or achievement. **3.** action or performance, often as contrasted with words. **4.** *Law.* a writing or document executed under seal and delivered to effect a conveyance, esp. of real estate. —*v.t.* **5.** to convey or transfer by deed. [ME *dede,* OE *dēd,* var. of *dæd,* c. G *tat.* See DO[1]] —**deed′less,** *adj.* —**Syn. 2.** See achievement.

deem (dēm), *v.i.* **1.** to form or have an opinion; judge; think. —*v.t.* **2.** to hold as an opinion; think; regard. [ME *demen,* OE *dēman,* c. Goth. *dōmjan.* See DOOM] —**Syn. 1.** See think[1].

deem·ster (dēm′stər), *n.* either of the two justices of the Isle of Man. Also, **dempster.** —**deem′ster·ship′,** *n.*

deep (dēp), *adj.* **1.** extending far downward, inward, or backward. **2.** having a specified dimension downward, inward, or backward: *a tank 8 feet deep.* **3.** situated far or a certain distance down, in, or back. **4.** extending to or coming from a depth: *a deep dive, a deep breath.* **5.** lying below the surface. **6.** difficult to penetrate or understand; abstruse. **7.** not superficial; profound. **8.** grave or serious. **9.** heartfelt: *deep sorrow or prayer.*

10. absorbing: *deep study.* **11.** great in measure; intense; extreme: *deep sleep, color, etc.* **12.** low in pitch, as sound. **13.** having penetrating intellectual powers. **14.** profoundly cunning or artful. **15.** much involved: *deep in debt.* **16.** absorbed: *deep in thought.* **17. go off the deep end, a.** *U.S.* to go to extremes. **b.** *Brit.* to get into a dither; to become hysterical. —*n.* **18.** the deep part of the sea, a river, etc. **19.** any deep space or place. **20.** the part of greatest intensity, as of winter. **21.** *Naut.* the depth in fathoms between two successive marks on a lead line. **22. the deep,** *Poetic.* the sea or ocean. [ME *depe,* OE *dēop,* c. G. *tief.* See DIP, v.] —*adv.* **23.** to or at a considerable or specified depth. **24.** far on (in time). **25.** profoundly; intensely. [ME *depe,* OE *dēope*] —**deep′ly,** *adv.* —**deep′ness,** *n.* —Syn. **6.** recondite, mysterious, obscure.

deep-dish (dēp′dĭsh′), *adj.* *Cookery.* baked in a deep dish, often with a pastry top, and usually in individual servings: *a deep-dish pie.*

deep·en (dē′pən), *v.t., v.i.* to make or become deep or deeper. —**deep′en·er,** *n.*

Deep-Freeze (dēp′frēz′), *n., v.,* **-freezed, -freezing.** *Trademark.* **1.** a locker or compartment in which foods are stored at a temperature of 0° F. —*v.t.* **2.** to store or freeze in a Deep-Freeze.

deep-fry (dēp′frī′), *v.t.,* **-fried, -frying.** to cook in a deep pan of fat.

deep-laid (dēp′lād′), *adj.* carefully, cunningly, or secretly made: *deep-laid plot.*

deep-root·ed (dēp′rōōt′ĭd, -rŏŏt′ĭd), *adj.* deeply rooted; firmly implanted.

deep-sea (dēp′sē′), *adj.* of, pertaining to, or in the deeper parts of the sea.

deep-seat·ed (dēp′sē′tĭd), *adj.* firmly implanted.

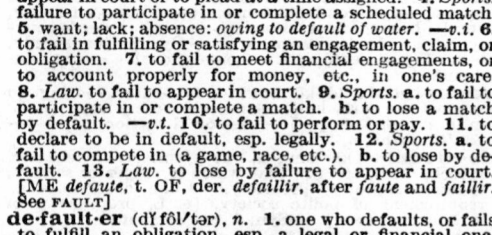

Virginia deer,
Odocoileus virginianus
(3½ ft. high at the shoulder,
total length ab. 6 ft.)

deer (dĭr), *n., pl.* **deer,** (*occasionally*) **deers.** **1.** any animal of the family *Cervidae,* comprising ruminants most of which have solid deciduous horns or antlers (usually in the male only), as *Cervus elaphus* (of Europe) or *Odocoileus virginianus* (of North America). **2.** any of the smaller species of this family, as distinguished from the moose, elk, etc. [ME *dere,* OE *dēor,* c. G *tier* beast]

deer fly, any of the blood-sucking flies of the genus *Chrysops* (family *Tabanidae*).

deer·hound (dĭr′hound′), *n.* a hound of a Scottish breed allied to and resembling the greyhound but larger and having a shaggy coat.

deer lick, *U.S.* a spot of ground, naturally or artificially salty, where deer come to nibble or lick the earth.

deer mouse, any of several species of mice (family *Cricetidae*), esp. the widely distributed white-footed mouse, *Peromyscus leucopus,* of North America.

Scottish deerhound
(2½ ft. high at the shoulder)

deer·skin (dĭr′skĭn′), *n.* **1.** the skin of a deer. **2.** leather made from this. **3.** a garment made of such leather.

deer·stalk·er (dĭr′stô′kər), *n.* one who stalks deer; one who hunts deer by stealing upon them unawares. —**deer′stalk′ing,** *n.*

def., 1. defective. **2.** defendant. **3.** deferred. **4.** defined. **5.** definite. **6.** definition.

de·face (dĭ fās′), *v.t.,* **-faced, -facing.** **1.** to mar the face or appearance of; disfigure. **2.** to blot out; obliterate; efface. [ME *deface(n),* t. F (obs.): m. *defacer,* earlier *desfacier,* der. des- DIS-1 + *face* FACE] —**de·face′a·ble,** *adj.* —**de·face′ment,** *n.* —**de·fac′er,** *n.* —Syn. **1.** See mar.

de fac·to (dē făk′tō), **1.** in fact; in reality. **2.** actually existing, whether with or without right. See de jure. [L: from the fact]

de·fal·cate (dĭ făl′kāt, -fôl′-), *v.i.,* **-cated, -cating.** *Law.* to be guilty of defalcation. [t. ML: m. s. *dēfalcātus,* pp.] —**de·fal′ca·tor,** *n.*

de·fal·ca·tion (dē′făl kā′shən, -fôl-), *n.* *Law.* **1.** misappropriation of money, etc., held by a trustee or other fiduciary. **2.** the sum misappropriated.

def·a·ma·tion (dĕf′ə mā′shən, dē′fə-), *n.* the wrong of injuring another's reputation without good reason or justification; calumny; slander or libel.

de·fam·a·to·ry (dĭ făm′ə tôr′ĭ), *adj.* containing defamation; injurious to reputation; slanderous.

de·fame (dĭ fām′), *v.t.,* **-famed, -faming.** **1.** to attack the good fame or reputation of, as by uttering or publishing maliciously anything injurious; slander; libel; calumniate. **2.** *Archaic.* to disgrace. **3.** *Obs.* to accuse. [ME *defamen,* t. ML: m. *dēfāmāre;* r. ME *diffamen,* t. OF: m. *diffamer,* t. L: m. *diffāmāre*] —**de·fam′er,** *n.*

de·fault (dĭ fôlt′), *n.* **1.** failure to act; neglect. **2.** failure to meet financial obligations. **3.** *Law.* failure to perform an act or obligation legally required, esp. to

appear in court or to plead at a time assigned. **4.** *Sports.* failure to participate in or complete a scheduled match. **5.** want; lack; absence: *owing to default of water.* —*v.i.* **6.** to fail in fulfilling or satisfying an engagement, claim, or obligation. **7.** to fail to meet financial engagements, or to account properly for money, etc., in one's care. **8.** *Law.* to fail to appear in court. **9.** *Sports.* **a.** to fail to participate in or complete a match. **b.** to lose a match by default. —*v.t.* **10.** to fail to perform or pay. **11.** to declare to be in default, esp. legally. **12.** *Sports.* **a.** to fail to compete in (a game, race, etc.). **b.** to lose by default. **13.** *Law.* to lose by failure to appear in court. [ME *defaute,* t. OF, der. *defaillir,* after *faute* and *faillir.* See FAULT]

de·fault·er (dĭ fôl′tər), *n.* **1.** one who defaults, or fails to fulfill an obligation, esp. a legal or financial one. **2.** *Brit.* a soldier convicted by court martial.

de·fea·sance (dĭ fē′zəns), *n.* *Law.* **1.** a rendering null and void. **2.** a condition on the performance of which a deed or other instrument is defeated or rendered void. **3.** a collateral deed or other writing embodying such a condition. [ME *defesance,* t. OF, der. *defesant,* ppr. of *de(s)faire* undo. See DEFEAT]

de·fea·si·ble (dĭ fē′zə bəl), *adj.* that may be annulled or terminated. —**de·fea′si·ble·ness, de·fea′si·bil′i·ty,** *n.*

de·feat (dĭ fēt′), *v.t.* **1.** to overcome in a contest, battle, etc.; vanquish; win over. **2.** to frustrate; thwart. **3.** to deprive of something expected. **4.** *Law.* to annul. —*n.* **5.** act of overcoming in a contest. **6.** an overthrow; vanquishment. **7.** a bringing to naught; frustration. **8.** *Obs.* undoing; destruction; ruin. [t. OF: m. *de(s)fait,* pp. of *desfaire* undo, f. *des-* DIS-1 + *faire* (L *facere* do)] —**de·feat′er,** *n.* —Syn. **1.** DEFEAT, CONQUER, OVERCOME, SUBDUE imply gaining a victory or control over an opponent. DEFEAT suggests temporarily, and often permanently, beating or frustrating: *to defeat an enemy in battle.* CONQUER, more formal, implies finally gaining control over, usually after a series of efforts or against systematic resistance: *to conquer a country, one's inclinations.* OVERCOME emphasizes surmounting difficulties in prevailing over an antagonist: *to overcome opposition, bad habits.* SUBDUE means to conquer so completely that the spirit of resistance is broken: *to subdue an uprising or a rebellious spirit.*

de·feat·ism (dĭ fē′tĭz əm), *n.* the attitude, policy, or conduct of those who admit or expect defeat, usually resulting from a premature decision that further struggle or effort is futile. —**de·feat′ist,** *n., adj.*

de·fea·ture (dĭ fē′chər), *n.* **1.** *Archaic.* disfigurement. **2.** *Obs.* defeat; ruin. [t. OF: m. *deffaiture.* See DEFEAT]

def·e·cate (dĕf′ə kāt′), *v.,* **-cated, -cating.** —*v.t.* **1.** to clear of dregs, impurities, etc.; purify; refine. —*v.i.* **2.** to become clear of dregs, impurities, etc. **3.** to void excrement. [t. L: m. s. *dēfaecātus,* pp., cleansed from dregs] —**def′e·ca′tion,** *n.* —**def′e·ca′tor,** *n.*

de·fect (dĭ fĕkt′, dē′fĕkt), *n.* **1.** a falling short; a fault or imperfection. **2.** want or lack, esp. of something essential to perfection or completeness; deficiency. [t. L: s. *dēfectus* want, defect] —Syn. **1.** DEFECT, BLEMISH, FLAW refer to faults which detract from perfection. DEFECT is the general word for any kind of shortcoming or imperfection, whether literal or figurative: *a defect in eyesight, in character, in a plan.* A BLEMISH is usually a defect on a surface, which mars the appearance: *a mole or scar on a cheek* (or *a scratch on a table*) *is a blemish.* FLAW is applied to a defect in quality, caused by imperfect structure (as in a diamond) or brought about during manufacture (as in texture of cloth, in tensile strength of metals, in clearness of glass, etc.).

de·fec·tion (dĭ fĕk′shən), *n.* **1.** a falling away from allegiance, duty, virtue, etc.; desertion; backsliding; apostasy. **2.** failure; lack. —Ant. **1.** loyalty.

de·fec·tive (dĭ fĕk′tĭv), *adj.* **1.** having a defect; faulty; imperfect. **2.** *Psychol.* characterized by subnormal intelligence or behavior. **3.** *Gram.* (of an inflected word or its inflection) lacking one or more of the inflected forms proper to most words of the same class in the language, as English *must* (which occurs only in the present tense). —*n.* **4.** one who or that which is defective. —**de·fec′tive·ly,** *adv.* —**de·fec′tive·ness,** *n.* —Ant. **1.** perfect, complete.

de·fence (dĭ fĕns′), *n.* *Brit.* defense.

de·fend (dĭ fĕnd′), *v.t.* **1.** to ward off attack from; guard against assault or injury (fol. by *from* or *against*). **2.** to maintain by argument, evidence, etc.; uphold. **3.** to contest (a legal charge, claim, etc.). —*v.i.* **4.** *Law.* to enter or make a defense. [ME *defende(n),* t. OF: m. *defendre,* g. L *dēfendere* ward off] —**de·fend′a·ble,** *adj.* —**de·fend′er,** *n.* —Syn. **1.** garrison, fortify, shield, shelter, screen. DEFEND, GUARD, PRESERVE, PROTECT all mean to keep safe. To DEFEND is to strive to keep safe by resisting attack: *to defend (a position) in battle, to defend one's country.* To GUARD is to watch over in order to keep safe: *to guard a camp, a secret.* To PRESERVE is to keep safe in the midst of danger, either in a single instance or continuously: *to preserve a unit, a spirit of conciliation.* To PROTECT is to keep safe by interposing a shield or barrier: *to protect books by means of heavy paper covers, the reputation of a friend.* —Ant. **1.** attack.

de·fend·ant (dĭ fĕn′dənt), *n.* **1.** *Law.* the party against whom a claim or charge is brought in a proceeding. —*adj.* **2.** *Obs.* defensive.

de·fen·es·tra·tion (dē fĕn′ə strā′shən), *n.* act of throwing out of a window. [f. DE- + s. L *fenestra* window + -ATION]

---

de·fense (dĭ fĕns´), *n.* **1.** resistance against attack; protection. **2.** something that defends, esp. a fortification. **3.** the defending of a cause or the like by speech, argument, etc. **4.** a speech, argument, etc., in vindication. **5.** *Law.* **a.** the denial or pleading of the defendant in answer to the claim or charge against him. **b.** the proceedings adopted by a defendant, or his legal agents, for defending himself. **c.** a defendant and his legal agents collectively. **6.** the practice or art of defending oneself or one's goal against attack, as in fencing or boxing, soccer, etc. Also, *Brit.*, **defence**. [ME, t. OF, t. LL: m. *dēfensa* prohibition, der. L *dēfendere* ward off; r. ME *defens*, t. OF, t. L: s. *dēfensum* (thing) forbidden, prop. pp. of *dēfendere*] **—de·fense´less,** *adj.* **—defense´less·ly,** *adv.* **—de·fense´less·ness,** *n.*

defense mechanism, 1. *Physiol.* organic activity, as the formation of an antitoxin, as a defensive measure. **2.** *Psychoanal.* a group of unconscious processes which oppose the entrance into consciousness or the acting out of unacceptable or painful ideas and impulses.

de·fen·si·ble (dĭ fĕn´sə bəl), *adj.* **1.** capable of being defended against assault or injury. **2.** capable of being defended in argument; justifiable. **—de·fen´si·bil´i·ty, de·fen´si·ble·ness,** *n.* **—de·fen´si·bly,** *adv.*

de·fen·sive (dĭ fĕn´sĭv), *adj.* **1.** serving to defend; protective: *defensive armor.* **2.** made or carried on for the purpose of resisting attack. **3.** of or pertaining to defense: *a defensive attitude.* *—n.* **4.** something that serves to defend. **5.** defensive position or attitude. **—de·fen´sive·ly,** *adv.* **—de·fen´sive·ness,** *n.*

de·fer¹ (dĭ fûr´), *v.*, **-ferred, -ferring.** *—v.t.* **1.** to put off (action, etc.) to a future time. *—v.i.* **2.** to put off action; delay. [ME *differe*(n), t. L: m. *differre* delay. See DIFFER] **—de·fer´rer,** *n.*
—Syn. 1. DEFER, DELAY, POSTPONE imply keeping something from occurring until a future time. To DEFER is to decide deliberately to do something later on: *to defer making a decision, a payment* To DELAY is sometimes equivalent to DEFER, but usually it is to act in a dilatory manner and thus lay something aside until some indefinite future time: *to delay one's departure, answering a letter.* To POSTPONE a thing is to defer it to (usually) some particular time in the future, with the intention of beginning or resuming it then; the word is esp. used of official business, formal meetings, or the like: *to postpone an election.* **—Ant. 1.** accelerate.

de·fer² (dĭ fûr´), *v.i.*, **-ferred, -ferring.** to yield in judgment or opinion (fol. by *to*). [t. F: s. *déférer*, t. L: m. *deferre* carry from or down, report, accuse]

def·er·ence (dĕf´ər əns), *n.* **1.** submission or yielding to the judgment, opinion, will, etc., of another. **2.** respectful or courteous regard: *in deference to his wishes.*

def·er·ent¹ (dĕf´ər ənt), *adj.* deferential. [t. L: s. *dēferens*, ppr., bringing down]

def·er·ent² (dĕf´ər ənt), *adj. Anat.* **1.** conveying away. **2.** pertaining to the vas deferens, the deferent duct of the testes. [see DEFERENT¹, DEFER²]

def·er·en·tial (dĕf´ə rĕn´shəl), *adj.* marked by or showing deference; respectful. **—def·er·en·tial·ly,** *adv.*

de·fer·ment (dĭ fûr´mənt), *n.* act of deferring or putting off; postponement.

de·ferred (dĭ fûrd´), *adj.* **1.** postponed or delayed, as property rights which do not vest until some future event has occurred. **2.** suspended or held back for a period: *deferred interest account of bondholders.*

de·fi·ance (dĭ fī´əns), *n.* **1.** a daring or bold resistance to authority or to any opposing force. **2.** open disregard: *in defiance of criticism.* **3.** a challenge to meet in combat or contest.

de·fi·ant (dĭ fī´ənt), *adj.* characterized by defiance, bold opposition, or antagonism. [t. F, ppr. of *défier* DEFY] **—de·fi´ant·ly,** *adv.* **—de·fi´ant·ness,** *n.* **—Syn.** insubordinate, contumacious, refractory, recalcitrant, rebellious, insolent. **—Ant.** obedient.

de·fi·cien·cy (dĭ fĭsh´ən sĭ), *n., pl.* **-cies. 1.** state or fact of being deficient; lack; incompleteness; insufficiency. **2.** the amount lacked; a deficit.

deficiency disease, an illness due to an insufficient supply of one or more essential dietary constituents.

deficiency judgment, *Law.* a judgment in favor of a creditor who has not satisfied the full amount of his claim against a debtor.

de·fi·cient (dĭ fĭsh´ənt), *adj.* **1.** lacking some element or characteristic; defective. **2.** insufficient; inadequate. [t. L: s. *dēficiens*, ppr., wanting] **—de·fi´cient·ly,** *adv.*

def·i·cit (dĕf´ə sĭt; *Brit.* also dĭ fĭs´ĭt), *n.* the amount by which a sum of money falls short of the required amount. [t. L: there is wanting] **—Ant.** surplus.

de fi·de (dē fī´dĭ), *Latin.* of the faith (used to describe a teaching of the Roman Catholic Church).

de·fi·er (dĭ fī´ər), *n.* one who defies.

def·i·lade (dĕf´ə lād´), *v.*, **-laded, -lading,** *n. Fort.* *—v.t.* **1.** to arrange the plan and profile of (a fortification) so as to protect its lines from enfilading fire and its interior from plunging or reverse fire. *—n.* **2.** act or operation of defilading. [t. F, der. *défiler*, orig., unthread, f. *dē-* DIS-¹ + (*en*)*filer* thread (ult. der. L *filum* a thread)]

de·file¹ (dĭ fīl´), *v.t.*, **-filed, -filing. 1.** to make foul, dirty, or unclean; pollute; taint. **2.** to violate the chastity of. **3.** to make ceremonially unclean; desecrate. **4.** to sully (a reputation, etc.). [alter. of *befile* (OE *befȳlan* befoul)] **—de·file´ment,** *n.* **—de·fil´er,** *n.*

de·file² (dĭ fīl´, dē´fīl´), *n., v.*, **-filed, -filing.** *—n.* **1.** any narrow passage, esp. between mountains. *—v.i.* **2.** to march in a line, or by files; file off. [t. F, n. use of pp. of *défiler* file off]

de·fine (dĭ fīn´), *v.t.*, **-fined, -fining. 1.** to state or set forth the meaning of (a word, phrase, etc.). **2.** to explain the nature or essential qualities of; describe. **3.** to determine or fix the boundaries or extent of. **4.** to make clear the outline or form of. **5.** to fix or lay down definitely; specify distinctly. [ME *deffyne*(n), t. F: m. *définir*, t. L: m. *dēfīnīre* limit, determine, explain, terminate] **—de·fin´a·ble,** *adj.* **—de·fin´a·bil´i·ty,** *n.* **—de·fin´a·bly,** *adv.* **—de·fin´er,** *n.*

def·i·nite (dĕf´ə nĭt), *adj.* **1.** clearly defined or determined; not vague or general; fixed; precise; exact. **2.** having fixed limits; bounded with precision. **3.** defining; limiting. **4.** *Bot.* (of an inflorescence) determinate. [t. L: m.s. *dēfīnītus*, pp., limited, determined] **—def´i·nite·ly,** *adv.* **—def´i·nite·ness,** *n.* **—Syn. 2.** certain, clear, express. **—Ant. 1.** confused.

definite article, the article (Eng. *the*) which classes as "identified" the noun it modifies.

def·i·ni·tion (dĕf´ə nĭsh´ən), *n.* **1.** act of defining, or making definite or clear. **2.** the formal statement of the meaning or signification of a word, phrase, etc. **3.** condition of being definite. **4.** *Optics.* sharpness of the image formed by an optical system. **5.** *Radio.* the accuracy of sound reproduction through a receiver, or picture reproduction in a television receiver.

de·fin·i·tive (dĭ fĭn´ə tĭv), *adj.* **1.** having the function of deciding or settling; determining; conclusive; final. **2.** serving to fix or specify definitely. **3.** having its fixed and final form. *—n.* **4.** a defining or limiting word, as an article, a demonstrative, or the like. **—de·fin´i·tive·ly,** *adv.* **—de·fin´i·tive·ness,** *n.*

de·fin·i·tude (dĭ fĭn´ə tūd´, -tōōd´), *n.* definiteness; exactitude; precision.

def·la·grate (dĕf´lə grāt´, dē´flə-), *v.t., v.i.,* **-grated, -grating.** to burn, esp. suddenly and violently. [t. L: m.s. *dēflagrātus*, pp.] **—def´la·gra´tion,** *n.*

de·flate (dĭ flāt´), *v.t.*, **-flated, -flating. 1.** to release the air or gas from (something inflated, as a balloon). **2.** to reduce (currency, prices, etc.) from an inflated condition. [t. L: m.s. *dēflātus*, pp., prop. blown off]

de·fla·tion (dĭ flā´shən), *n.* **1.** act of deflating. **2.** an abnormal decline in the level of commodity prices, esp. one not accompanied by an equal reduction in the costs of production. **—de·fla·tion·ar·y** (dĭ flā´shə nĕr´ĭ), *adj.*

de·flect (dĭ flĕkt´), *v.t., v.i.* to bend or turn aside; turn from a true course or right line; swerve. [t. L: s. *dēflectere*] **—de·flec´tor,** *n.*

de·flec·tion (dĭ flĕk´shən), *n.* **1.** act of deflecting. **2.** state of being deflected. **3.** amount of deviation. **4.** *Physics.* the deviation or swing of the indicator of an instrument from the position taken as zero. **5.** *Optics.* the bending of rays of light from a straight line. Also, *Brit.*, **de·flex´ion.**

de·flec·tive (dĭ flĕk´tĭv), *adj.* causing deflection.

def·lo·ra·tion (dĕf´lə rā´shən, dē´flə-), *n.* act of deflowering. [ME *defloracion*, t. LL: m.s. *dēflōrātiō*]

de·flow·er (dē flou´ər), *v.t.* **1.** to deprive or strip of flowers. **2.** to deprive (a woman) of virginity; ravish. **3.** to despoil of beauty, freshness, sanctity, etc. [f. DE- + FLOWER, r. ME *deflore*(n), t. OF: m. *desflorer* remove the flower(s) from, ravish] **—de·flow´er·er,** *n.*

de·flux·ion (dĭ flŭk´shən), *n. Pathol.* a copious discharge of fluid matter, as in catarrh.

De·foe (dĭ fō´), *n.* **Daniel,** 1661?–1731, British novelist and essayist.

de·fo·li·ate (dē fō´lĭ āt´), *v.*, **-ated, -ating.** *—v.t.* **1.** to strip or deprive (a tree, etc.) of leaves. *—v.i.* **2.** to lose leaves. [t. ML: m. s. *dēfoliātus*, pp., of *dēfoliāre*, der. L *folium* leaf] **—de·fo´li·a´tion,** *n.*

de·force (dĭ fōrs´), *v.t.*, **-forced, -forcing.** *Law.* to withhold (something) by force or violence, as from the rightful owner. [t. AF: s. *deforcer*, f. *de-* DE- + *forcer* FORCE, v.] **—de·force´ment,** *n.*

de·for·ciant (dĭ fōr´shənt), *n. Law.* one who deforces.

de·for·est (dē fōr´ĭst, -fŏr´-), *v.t.* to divest of forests or trees. **—de·for´est·a´tion,** *n.* **—de·for´est·er,** *n.*

De For·est (dĭ fōr´ĭst, fŏr´-), **Lee,** 1873–1961, U.S. inventor, esp. in the field of electronics.

de·form¹ (dĭ fôrm´), *v.t.* **1.** to mar the natural form or shape of; put out of shape; disfigure. **2.** to make ugly, ungraceful, or displeasing; mar the beauty of; spoil. **3.** to change the form of; transform. **4.** *Mech.* to subject to deformation. [ME, t. L: s. *dēformāre* disfigure] **—de·form´er,** *n.* **—Syn. 1.** See mar.

de·form² (dĭ fôrm´), *adj. Archaic.* deformed; ugly. [ME *defourme*, t. L: m. *dēformis* misshapen]

de·form·a·ble (dĭ fôr´mə bəl), *adj.* capable of being deformed. **—de·form·a·bil´i·ty,** *n.*

de·for·ma·tion (dē´fôr mā´shən, dĕf´ər-), *n.* **1.** act of deforming; distortion; disfigurement. **2.** result of deforming; change of form, esp. for the worse. **3.** *Mech.* a change in the shape or dimensions of a body, resulting from stress; strain. **4.** an altered form.

de·formed (dĭ fôrmd´), *adj.* **1.** having the form changed, with loss of beauty, etc.; misshapen; disfigured. **2.** hateful; offensive. **—Syn. 1.** malformed, crippled.

de·form·i·ty (dĭ fôr´mə tĭ), *n., pl.* **-ties. 1.** quality or state of being deformed, disfigured, or misshapen. **2.** *Pathol.* an abnormally formed part of the body, etc. **3.** a deformed person or thing. **4.** hatefulness; ugliness.

de·fraud (dǐ frôd′), *v.t.* to deprive of a right or property by fraud; cheat. [ME *defraude*(*n*), t. L: m. *defraudāre*. Cf. FRAUD] **—de·frau·da·tion**, *n.* **—de·fraud′er**, *n.*

de·fray (dǐ frā′), *v.t.* to bear or pay (the costs, expenses, etc.). [t. F: s. *défrayer*, OF *desfraier* pay costs, der. *des-* DIS-[1] + *frai* cost, of Gmc. origin] **—de·fray′a·ble**, *adj.* **—de·fray′er**, *n.*

de·fray·al (dǐ frā′əl), *n.* payment of charges or expenses. Also, **de·fray′ment.**

de·frock (dē frŏk′), *v.t.* to unfrock.

de·frost (dē frŏst′, -frôst′), *v.t.* to remove the frost or ice from. **—de·frost′er**, *n.*

deft (dĕft), *adj.* dexterous; nimble; skillful; clever. [ME; var. of DAFT] **—deft′ly**, *adv.* **—deft′ness**, *n.*

de·funct (dǐ fŭngkt′), *adj.* **1.** deceased; dead; extinct. **—n. 2.** the defunct, the dead person. [t. L: s. *defunctus*, pp., discharged, finished] **—de·funct′ness**, *n.*

de·func·tive (dǐ fŭngk′tǐv), *adj.* of or pertaining to the dead; funereal.

de·fy (*v.* dǐ fī′; *n.* dǐ fī′, dē′fī), *v.*, **-fied, -fying,** *n., pl.* **-fies.** *—v.t.* **1.** to challenge the power of; resist boldly or openly. **2.** to offer effective resistance to: *a fort which defies attacks.* **3.** to challenge (one) to do something deemed impossible. **4.** *Archaic.* to challenge to a combat or contest. **—n. 5.** *U.S. Slang.* a challenge; a defiance. [ME *defye*(*n*), t. OF: m. *defier,* f. *de-* DE- + *fier* (g. L *fīdere* trust)] **—Syn. 1.** dare, brave, flout, scorn.

deg., degree; degrees.

dé·ga·gé (dĕ gȧ zhě′), *adj.* *French.* unconstrained; easy, as in manner. [F, pp. of *dégager* disengage, put at ease]

de·gas (dǐ găs′), *v.t.,* **-gassed, -gassing. 1.** to free from gas. **2.** to treat with chemical agents to destroy a gas or its harmful properties. **3.** to complete the evacuation of gases in (a vacuum tube).

De·gas (də gäs′; *Fr.* də gä′), *n.* Hilaire Germain Edgar (ē lěr′ zhěr mǎn′ ěd gȧr′), 1834–1917, French painter.

De Gaulle (də gōl′), **Charles André Joseph Marie** (shȧrl ȧn drě′ zhō sěf′ mȧ rē′), born 1890, French general and statesman: president since 1959.

de·gauss·ing (dǐ gou′sǐng, -gō′zǐng), *n.* a demagnetizing process used esp. to neutralize a ship's magnetic field as a protection against magnetic mines. [f. DE- + *gauss* (from K. F. GAUSS) + -ING[1]]

de·gen·er·a·cy (dǐ jěn′ər ə sǐ), *n.* degenerate state or character; degeneration.

de·gen·er·ate (*v.* dǐ jěn′ə rāt′; *adj., n.* dǐ jěn′ər ǐt), *v.,* **-ated, -ating,** *adj., n.* *—v.i.* **1.** to decline in physical, mental, or moral qualities; deteriorate. **2.** *Biol.* to revert to a less highly organized or simpler type. *—adj.* **3.** having declined in physical or moral qualities; deteriorated; degraded: *a degenerate king.* **4.** having lost, or become impaired with respect to, the qualities proper to the race or kind: *a degenerate plant.* **5.** characterized by or associated with degeneracy: *degenerate times.* *—n.* **6.** one who has retrograded from a normal type or standard, as in morals or character. **7.** one exhibiting morbid physical and mental traits or tendencies, esp. from birth. [t. L: m. s. *dēgenerātus,* pp., departed from its race] **—de·gen′er·ate·ly,** *adv.* **—de·gen′er·ate·ness,** *n.*

de·gen·er·a·tion (dǐ jěn′ə rā′shən), *n.* **1.** process of degenerating. **2.** state of being degenerate. **3.** *Biol.* reversion to a less highly organized or a simpler type. **4.** *Pathol.* **a.** a process by which a tissue deteriorates, loses functional activity, and may become converted into or replaced by other kinds of tissue. **b.** the morbid condition produced by such a process.

de·gen·er·a·tive (dǐ jěn′ə rā′tǐv), *adj.* **1.** tending to degenerate. **2.** characterized by degeneration.

de·glu·ti·nate (dē glōō′tə nāt′), *v.t.,* **-nated, -nating.** to extract the gluten from. [t. L: m. s. *dēglūtinātus,* pp., unglued]

de·glu·ti·tion (dē′glōō tǐsh′ən), *n.* *Physiol.* act or process of swallowing. [der. *deglute* swallow down (now obs.), t. L: m.s. *dēglūtīre*]

deg·ra·da·tion (dĕg′rə dā′shən), *n.* **1.** act of degrading. **2.** state of being degraded. **3.** *Phys. Geog.* the wearing down of the land by the action of water, wind, or ice; erosion. **—Syn. 2.** humiliation, disgrace, dishonor, debasement.

de·grade (dǐ grād′), *v.t.,* **-graded, -grading. 1.** to reduce from a higher to a lower rank, degree, etc.; deprive of office, rank, or title as a punishment. **2.** to lower in character or quality; debase; deprave. **3.** to lower in dignity or estimation; bring into contempt. **4.** to reduce in amount, strength, intensity, etc. **5.** *Phys. Geog.* to wear down by erosion, as hills (opposed to *aggrade*). [ME *degrade*(*n*), t. ecclesiastical LL: m. *dēgradāre* reduce in rank, der. L *gradus* GRADE] **—de·grad′er,** *n.* **—Syn. 2.** demote, depose. **3.** humiliate, disgrace, dishonor. See **humble. —Ant. 1.** promote. **2.** uplift.

de·grad·ed (dǐ grā′dǐd), *adj.* debased; degenerate. **—de·grad′ed·ly,** *adv.* **—de·grad′ed·ness,** *n.*

de·grad·ing (dǐ grā′dǐng), *adj.* that degrades; debasing: *degrading obsequiousness.* **—de·grad′ing·ly,** *adv.* **—de·grad′ing·ness,** *n.*

de·gree (dǐ grē′), *n.* **1.** a step or stage in an ascending or descending scale, or in a course or process. **2.** *Genetics, etc.* a certain distance or remove in the line of descent, determining the proximity of blood. **3.** a stage in a scale of rank or dignity; relative rank, station, etc. **4.** a stage

in a scale of intensity or amount: *to the last degree.* **5.** *Geom., etc.* the 360th part of a complete angle or turn (often indicated by the sign °, as 45°). **6.** *Alg.* the sum of the exponents of the variables in an algebraic expression: x^3 and $2x^2y$ are terms of degree three. **7.** a unit in the measurement of temperature. **8.** a unit on an arbitrary scale of measurement. **9.** *Geog., Astron.* a line or point on the earth or in the celestial sphere whose position is fixed by its angular distance measured in degrees from the equator (equinoctial) or a given meridian. **10.** *Law.* a relative measure of criminality; *esp. U.S.,* a distinctive grade of crime: *murder in the first degree.* **11.** *Educ.* an academic title conferred by universities and colleges as an indication of the completion of a course of study, or as an honorary recognition of achievement. **12.** *Gram.* one of the three parallel formations (positive, comparative, and superlative) of adjectives and adverbs, showing differences in quality, quantity, or intensity in the attribute referred to, as English *low, lower, lowest.* **13.** *Music.* a tone, or step, of the scale. **14.** *Obs.* a step, as of a stair. **15.** by **degrees,** gradually. **16.** to a **degree,** to an undefined but considerable extent. [ME *degre,* t. OF, f. *de-* DE- + *gre,* g. L *gradus* step, degree, GRADE]

Degrees (def. 5) of a circle

de·gree-day (dǐ grē′dā′), *n.* a unit of mean daily outdoor temperature representing one degree of difference from a standard temperature, usually 65°, used in reckoning fuel consumption.

degrees of freedom, *Phys. Chem.* variance.

de·gres·sion (dǐ grěsh′ən), *n.* **1.** a going down; descent. **2.** the decrease in rate in degressive taxation.

de·gres·sive (dǐ grěs′ǐv), *adj.* pertaining to a form of taxation in which the rate diminishes gradually on sums below a certain fixed amount.

De Groot (də grōt′), **Huig** (hoȳкн). See **Grotius.**

de·gum (dē gŭm′), *v.t.,* **-gummed, -gumming.** to free from gum.

de·gust (dǐ gŭst′), *v.t., v.i.* *Rare.* to taste. [t. L: s. *dēgustāre*] **—de′gus·ta′tion,** *n.*

de gus·ti·bus non est dis·pu·tan·dum (dē gŭs′tə bŏs nŏn ěst dǐs′pyŏŏ tăn′dəm), *Latin.* there is no disputing about tastes.

de·hisce (dǐ hǐs′), *v.i.,* **-hisced, -hiscing.** to gape; burst open, as capsules of plants. [t. L: m.s. *dēhiscere*]

de·his·cence (dǐ hǐs′əns), *n.* **1.** *Bot.* the natural bursting open of capsules, fruits, anthers, etc., for the discharge of their contents. **2.** *Biol.* the release of materials by the splitting open of an organ or tissue.

de·his·cent (dǐ hǐs′ənt), *adj.* gaping open; characterized by dehiscence.

de·horn (dē hôrn′), *v.t.* to deprive (cattle) of horns. **—de·horn′er,** *n.*

de·hort (dǐ hôrt′), *v.t., v.i.* *Now Rare or Obs.* to seek to dissuade. [t. L: s. *dehortāri*] **—de·hor·ta′tion,** *n.* **—de·hor·ta·tive** (dǐ hôr′tə tǐv), **de·hor·ta·to·ry** (dǐ hôr′tə tōr′ǐ), *adj.* **—de·hort′er,** *n.*

de·hu·man·ize (dē hū′mə nīz′), *v.t.,* **-ized, -izing.** to deprive of human character. **—de·hu′man·i·za′tion,** *n.*

de·hu·mid·i·fy (dē′hū mǐd′ə fī′), *v.t.,* **-fied, -fying.** to remove moisture from. **—de·hu·mid′i·fi·ca′tion,** *n.*

de·hy·drate (dē hī′drāt), *v.,* **-drated, -drating.** *—v.t.* **1.** to deprive (a chemical compound) of water or the elements of water. **2.** to free (vegetables, etc.) from moisture for preservation. *—v.i.* **3.** to lose water or moisture. [f. DE- + HYDR- + -ATE[1]] **—Syn. 2.** See **evaporate.**

de·hy·dro·gen·ize (dē hī′drə jə nīz′), *v.t.,* **-ized, -izing.** *Chem.* to remove hydrogens from (a compound). **—de·hy·dro·gen·i·za·tion** (dē hī′drə jə nǐ zā′shən), *n.*

de·hyp·no·tize (dē hǐp′nə tīz′), *v.t.* **-tized, -tizing.** to bring out of the hypnotic state.

De·ia·ni·ra (dē′yə nī′rə), *n.* *Gk. Legend.* a sister of Meleager and wife of Hercules, whom she unwittingly killed by giving him the shirt of Nessus.

de·ic·er (dē i′sər), *n.* a mechanical or exhaust-heat device preventing or removing ice formation.

de·i·cide[1] (dē′ə sīd′), *n.* one who kills a god. [t. NL: m.s. *deicīda*] **—de′i·ci′dal,** *adj.*

de·i·cide[2] (dē′ə sīd′), *n.* the killing of a god. [f. s. L *deus* god + -(I)CIDE[2]] **—de′i·ci′dal,** *adj.*

de·ic·tic (dīk′tǐk), *adj.* **1.** *Logic.* proving directly. **2.** *Gram.* pointing; demonstrative. [t. Gk.: m.s. *deiktikós*] **—deic′ti·cal·ly,** *adv.*

de·if·ic (dē ǐf′ǐk), *adj.* making divine; deifying. [t. LL: s. *deificus* god-making, sacred]

de·i·fi·ca·tion (dē′ə fə kā′shən), *n.* **1.** act of deifying. **2.** state of being deified. **3.** a deified embodiment.

de·i·form (dē′ə fôrm′), *adj.* godlike; divine. [t. ML: s. *deiformis,* der. L *deus* god. See -FORM]

de·i·fy (dē′ə fī′), *v.t.,* **-fied, -fying. 1.** to make a god of; exalt to the rank of a deity. **2.** to adore or regard as a deity: *to deify prudence.* [ME *deify*(*en*), t. OF: m. *deifier,* t. LL: m. *deificāre*] **—de′i·fi′er,** *n.*

deign (dān), *v.i.* **1.** to think fit or in accordance with one's dignity; condescend. *—v.t.* **2.** to condescend to give or grant: *deigning no reply.* **3.** *Obs.* to condescend to accept. [ME *deine*(*n*), t. OF: m. *deignier,* g. L *dignārī* deem worthy]

De·i gra·ti·a (dē/ī grā/shĭ ə), *Latin.* by the grace of God.

deil (dēl), *n. Scot.* devil.

De·iph·o·bus (dē/ĭf/ə bəs), *n. Gk. Legend.* a son of Priam and Hecuba, who married Helen after the death of Paris and was slain by Menelaus.

Deir·dre (dĭr/drĭ; *Irish* dâr/drā), *n.* heroine of an Irish legend: raised to be the wife of King Conchobar of Ulster, she fell in love with one of the sons of Usnach and escaped with him and his brothers to Scotland. Conchobar had the brothers killed and Deirdre killed herself, fulfilling a prenatal prophecy that she would bring sorrow and death. Deirdre is often used as a symbol for Ireland.

de·ism (dē/ĭz əm), *n.* **1.** belief in the existence of a God on the evidence of reason and nature only, with rejection of supernatural revelation (distinguished from *theism*). **2.** belief in a God who created the world but has since remained indifferent to his creation (distinguished from *atheism, pantheism,* and *theism*). [f. s. L *deus* god + -ism]

de·ist (dē/ĭst), *n.* one who believes in deism. **—de·is/-tic, de·is/ti·cal, *adj.* —de·is/ti·cal·ly, *adv.*

de·i·ty (dē/ə tĭ), *n., pl.* **-ties. 1.** a god or goddess. **2.** divine character or nature. **3.** the estate or rank of a god. **4.** the character or nature of the Supreme Being. **5. the Deity,** God. [ME *deite,* t. OF, t. LL: m. s. *deitas*]

de·ject (dĭ jĕkt/), *v.t.* **1.** to depress the spirits of; dispirit; dishearten. **—adj. 2.** *Obs. or Archaic.* dejected; downcast. [t. L: s. *dējectus,* pp., thrown down]

de·jec·ta (dĭ jĕk/tə), *n. pl.* excrements. [NL, prop. neut. pl. of L *dējectus,* pp., thrown down]

de·ject·ed (dĭ jĕk/tĭd), *adj.* depressed in spirits; disheartened; low-spirited. **—de·ject/ed·ly, *adv.* —de·ject/ed·ness, *n.* —Syn.** discouraged, despondent, dispirited, downhearted. See **sad. —Ant.** gay.

de·jec·tion (dĭ jĕk/shən), *n.* **1.** depression or lowness of spirits. **2.** *Med., Physiol.* **a.** evacuation of the bowels; fecal discharge. **b.** excrement. **—Ant. 1.** exhilaration.

dé·jeu·ner (dā/zhə nā/; *Fr.* dĕ zhœ nĕ/), *n.* **1.** breakfast. **2.** (in Continental use) lunch. [F, orig. inf., OF *desjeuner* break one's fast, der. *des-* DIS-1 + *jeun* fasting, g. L *jējūnus* jejune]

de ju·re (dē jŏŏr/ĭ), *Latin.* by right; according to law.

dek-, var. of **dec-.**

deka-, var. of **deca-.**

De Kalb (dĭ kălb/), **Baron Johann** (yō/hän), 1721–1780, German general in the American Revolutionary Army.

dek·a·li·ter (dĕk/ə lē/tər), *n.* decaliter.

dek·a·me·ter (dĕk/ə mē/tər), *n.* decameter.

deki-, var. of **deci-.**

Dek·ker (dĕk/ər), *n.* **Thomas,** 1570?–1645?, English dramatist. Also, **Decker.**

De Ko·ven (dĭ kō/vən), **Henry Louis Reginald,** 1861–1920, U.S. composer.

De Kruif (də krīf/), **Paul,** born 1890, U.S. bacteriologist and author.

Del., Delaware.

del., delegate.

De·la·croix (də lå krwä/), *n.* **Ferdinand Victor Eugène** (fĕr dē nän/ vĕk tôr/ œ zhĕn/), 1798?–1863, French painter.

Del·a·goa Bay (dĕl/ə gō/ə), an inlet of the Indian Ocean in S Mozambique. 55 mi. long.

de·laine (də lān/), *n.* mousseline de laine.

de la Mare (də lə mâr/, dĕl/ə mâr/), **Walter John,** 1873–1956, British poet and novelist.

de·lam·i·nate (dē lăm/ə nāt/), *v.i.* **-nated, -nating.** to split into laminae or thin layers.

de·lam·i·na·tion (dē lăm/ə nā/shən), *n.* **1.** a splitting apart into layers. **2.** *Embryol.* the separation of a primitive blastoderm into two layers of cells.

De·land (dĭ lănd/), *n.* **Margaret,** (*Mrs. Margaretta Wade Campbell Deland*) 1857–1945, U.S. novelist.

De·la·roche (də lə rôsh/), *n.* **Hippolyte Paul** (ē pō lēt/ pōl), 1797–1856, French painter.

de·late (dĭ lāt/), *v.t.* **-lated, -lating. 1.** to inform against; denounce or accuse. **2.** to relate or report (an offense, etc.). [t. L: m. s. *dēlātus,* pp., carried from or down, reported, accused] **—de·la/tion, *n.* —de·la/-tor, *n.*

De·la·vigne (də lə vēn/y), *n.* **Jean François Casimir** (zhän frän swä/ kå zē mēr/), 1793–1843, French poet and dramatist.

Del·a·ware (dĕl/ə wâr/), *n.* **1.** a State in the eastern United States, on the Atlantic coast. 446,292 pop. (1960); 2057 sq. mi. *Cap.:* Dover. *Abbr.:* Del. **2.** a river flowing from SE New York along the boundary between Pennsylvania and New Jersey into Delaware Bay. 296 mi. **3.** (*pl.*) a group of North American Indians, formerly occupying the drainage basin of the Delaware river and the greater part of New Jersey. **4.** a member of this group. **5.** their language, of the Algonquian stock. **6.** See **De La Warr.** [named after Baron **DE LA WARR**] **—Del·a·war·e·an** (dĕl/ə wâr/ĭ ən), *adj., n.*

Delaware Bay, an estuary between E Delaware and S New Jersey. ab. 70 mi. long.

Delaware Water Gap, a scenic gorge cut by the Delaware river through the Appalachian Mountains, on the boundary between E Pennsylvania and NW New Jersey, near Stroudsburg, Pa. ab. 1400 ft. deep.

De La Warr (dĕl/ə wâr/; *Brit.* -wər), **Thomas West, Baron,** 1577–1618, first English colonial governor of Virginia. Also, **Del/a·ware/.**

de·lay (dĭ lā/), *v.t.* **1.** to put off to a later time; defer; postpone. **2.** to impede the progress of; retard; hinder. **—v.i. 3.** to put off action; linger; loiter: *Don't delay!* **—n. 4.** act of delaying; procrastination; loitering. **5.** fact of being delayed. [ME *delaie(n),* t. OF: m. *delaier* put off, b. L *dīlātāre* (freq. of L *differre* DEFER1) and L var. (unrecorded) of *dēliquāre* strain, clear off] **—de·lay/er, *n.* —Syn. 1.** See **defer. 5.** deferment, postponement, respite.

Del·cas·sé (dĕl kå sĕ/), *n.* **Théophile** (tĕ ô fēl/), 1852–1923, French statesman.

de·le (dē/lĭ), *v.t.,* **deled, deleing.** *Print.* (usually imperative) to take out; omit; delete (generally represented by a symbol). See "Proofreader's Marks" on page 1432. [t. L]

de·lec·ta·ble (dĭ lĕk/tə bəl), *adj.* delightful; highly pleasing; enjoyable. [ME, t. L: m. s. *dēlectābilis*] **—de·lec/ta·ble·ness, de·lec/ta·bil/i·ty, *n.* —de·lec/ta·bly, *adv.* —Ant.** disagreeable, distasteful.

de·lec·tate (dĭ lĕk/tāt), *v.t.* **-tated, -tating.** to please; charm; delight. [t. L: m. s. *dēlectātus,* pp. delighted]

de·lec·ta·tion (dē/lĕk tā/shən), *n.* delight.

De·led·da (dĕ lĕd/dä), *n.* **Grazia** (grä/tsyä), 1875–1936, Italian novelist.

del·e·ga·cy (dĕl/ə gə sĭ), *n., pl.* **-cies. 1.** the position or commission of a delegate. **2.** the sending or appointing of a delegate. **3.** a body of delegates. **4.** (at English universities) a standing committee for certain duties.

de·le·gal·ize (dē lē/gə līz/), *v.t.,* **-ized, -izing.** to revoke the statutory authorization of.

del·e·gate (n. dĕl/ə gət/, -gĭt; *v.* dĕl/ə gāt/), *n., v.,* **-gated, -gating. —n. 1.** one delegated to act for or represent another or others; a deputy; a representative, as in a political convention. **2.** *U.S. Govt.* **a.** the representative of a Territory in the House of Representatives of the U.S. **b.** a member of the lower house of the State legislatures of Maryland, Virginia, and West Virginia. **—v.t. 3.** to send or appoint (a person) as deputy or representative. **4.** to commit (powers, functions, etc.) to another as agent or deputy. [t. L: m. s. *dēlēgātus,* pp., sent, deputed] **—Syn. 4.** depute, entrust.

del·e·ga·tion (dĕl/ə gā/shən), *n.* **1.** act of delegating. **2.** fact of being delegated. **3.** the body of delegates chosen to represent a political unit in an assembly.

de·lete (dĭ lēt/), *v.t.,* **-leted, -leting.** to strike out or take out (anything written or printed); cancel; erase; expunge. [t. L: m. s. *dēlētus,* pp., done away with, destroyed] **—Syn.** See **cancel.**

del·e·te·ri·ous (dĕl/ə tĭr/ĭ əs), *adj.* **1.** injurious to health. **2.** hurtful; harmful; injurious. [t. NL: m. *dēlētērius,* t. Gk.: m. *dēlētērios*] **—del/e·te/ri·ous·ly, *adv.* —del/e·te/ri·ous·ness, *n.* —Ant. 2.** beneficial.

de·le·tion (dĭ lē/shən), *n.* **1.** act of deleting. **2.** fact of being deleted. **3.** a deleted passage. [t. L: s. *dēlētio*]

delft (dĕlft), *n.* **1.** a kind of glazed earthenware decorated in colors, esp. in blue, made at Delft. **2.** any pottery resembling this. Also, **delf** (dĕlf), **delft/ware/.**

Delft (dĕlft), *n.* a city in W Netherlands. 67,758 (est. 1954).

Del·ga·do (dĕl gä/dō), *n.* Cape, a cape at the NE extremity of Mozambique.

Del·hi (dĕl/ĭ), *n.* **1.** a centrally-administered territory in N India. 1,744,072 pop. (1951); 574 sq. mi. **2.** the capital of this province; former capital of the old Mogul Empire. Delhi was the administrative headquarters of British India from 1912 until 1929, when New Delhi became the capital. 914,790 (1951).

De·li·an (dē/lĭ ən), *adj.* **1.** pertaining to Delos. **—n. 2.** a native or inhabitant of Delos.

Delhi (def. 2)

de·lib·er·ate (*adj.* dĭ lĭb/ər It; *v.* dĭ lĭb/ə rāt/), *adj., v.,* **-ated, -ating. —adj. 1.** carefully weighed or considered; studied; intentional. **2.** characterized by deliberation; careful or slow in deciding. **3.** leisurely in movement or action; slow; unhurried. **—v.t. 4.** to weigh in the mind; consider: *to deliberate a question, a proposition, etc.* **—v.i. 5.** to think carefully or attentively; reflect. **6.** to consult or confer formally. [t. L: m. s. *dēlīberātus,* pp., weighed well] **—de·lib/er·ate·ly, *adv.* —de·lib/er·ate·ness, *n.* —de·lib/er·a/tor, *n.*
—Syn. 1. DELIBERATE, INTENTIONAL, PREMEDITATED, VOLUNTARY refer to something not happening by chance. DELIBERATE is applied to what is not done hastily but with full realization of what one is doing: *a deliberate attempt to evade justice.* INTENTIONAL is applied to what is definitely intended, or done on purpose: *an intentional omission.* PREMEDITATED is applied to what has been planned in advance: *a premeditated crime.* VOLUNTARY is applied to what is done by a definite exercise of the will and not because of outward pressures: *a voluntary enlistment.* **2.** thoughtful, circumspect, cautious. **3.** See **slow. 5.** weigh, ponder, cogitate. **—Ant. 1.** accidental. **2.** impulsive, precipitate.

de·lib·er·a·tion (dĭ lĭb/ə rā/shən), *n.* **1.** careful consideration before decision. **2.** formal consultation or discussion. **3.** deliberate quality; leisureliness of movement or action; slowness.

de·lib·er·a·tive (dĭ lĭb′ər ā/tĭv), *adj.* **1.** having the function of deliberating, as a legislative assembly. **2.** having to do with policy; dealing with the wisdom and expediency of a proposal: *a deliberative speech.* —**de·lib/er·a·tive·ly**, *adv.* —**de·lib/er·a/tive·ness**, *n.*

del·i·ca·cy (dĕl/ə kə sĭ), *n., pl.* **-cies. 1.** fineness of texture, quality, etc.; softness: *the delicacy of lace.* **2.** fineness of perception or feeling; sensitiveness. **3.** the quality of requiring or involving great care or tact: *negotiations of great delicacy.* **4.** nicety of action or operation; minute accuracy: *a surgeon's delicacy of touch.* **5.** fineness of feeling with regard to what is fitting, proper, etc. **6.** bodily weakness; liability to sickness. **7.** something delightful or pleasing, esp. to the palate. **8.** gratification; luxury. —Ant. 1, 2. coarseness.

del·i·cate (dĕl/ə kĭt), *adj.* **1.** fine in texture, quality, construction, etc. **2.** dainty or choice, as food. **3.** soft or faint, as color. **4.** so fine or slight as to be scarcely perceptible; subtle. **5.** easily damaged; fragile. **6.** requiring great care, caution, or tact. **7.** fine or exquisite in action or execution: *a delicate instrument.* **8.** regardful of what is becoming, proper, etc., or of the feelings of others. **9.** exquisite or refined in perception or feeling; sensitive. **10.** distinguishing subtle differences. **11.** *Obs.* fastidious. **12.** *Obs.* luxurious or voluptuous. —*n.* **13.** *Archaic.* a delicacy; a dainty. **14.** *Obs.* a luxury. [ME, t. L: m. s. *dēlicātus* delightful, luxurious, soft; akin to DELICIOUS] —**del/i·cate·ly**, *adv.* —**del/i·cate·ness,** *n.*
—**Syn. 1.** DELICATE, DAINTY, EXQUISITE imply beauty such as belongs to rich surroundings or which needs careful treatment. DELICATE, used of an object, suggests fragility, small size, and often very fine workmanship: *a delicate piece of carving.* DAINTY, in concrete references, suggests a smallness, gracefulness, and beauty which forbid rough handling; there is a connotation of attractiveness: *a dainty handkerchief;* of persons, it refers to fastidious sensibilities: *dainty in eating habits.* EXQUISITE suggests an outstanding beauty, daintiness, and elegance, or a discriminating sensitivity and ability to perceive fine distinctions: *an exquisite sense of humor.* **5.** tender, frail. **6.** critical, precarious. **7.** exact, precise, accurate. —Ant. 1-2. coarse.

del·i·ca·tes·sen (dĕl/ə kə tĕs/ən), *n.* **1.** (*construed as sing.*) a store selling foods that are ready or require little preparation for serving. **2.** (*construed as pl.*) the foods sold. [t. G, pl. of *delicatesse* delicacy, t. F]

de·li·cious (dĭ lĭsh/əs), *adj.* **1.** highly pleasing to the senses, esp. to taste or smell. **2.** pleasing in the highest degree; delightful. —*n.* **3.** (*cap.*) a variety of red eating apple, widely grown in the U.S. [ME, t. OF, t. LL: m. s. *dēliciōsus,* der. L *dēlicia* delight] —**de·li/cious·ly,** *adv.* —**de·li/cious·ness,** *n.*
—**Syn. 1.** DELICIOUS, LUSCIOUS refer to that which is especially agreeable to the senses. That which is DELICIOUS is highly agreeable to the taste (or sometimes to the smell): *a delicious meal.* LUSCIOUS implies such a luxuriant fullness or ripeness as to make an object sweet and rich, sometimes to excess; it is often used in transferred or humorous senses: *a luscious banana, a luscious beauty, luscious music.* —Ant. 1. tasteless, insipid.

de·lict (dĭ lĭkt′), *n.* **1.** *Civil Law.* a misdemeanor. **2.** *Rom. Law.* a civil wrong permitting compensation or punitive damages. [t. L: s. *dēlictum* fault, orig. pp. neut.]

de·light (dĭ līt′), *n.* **1.** a high degree of pleasure or enjoyment; joy; rapture. **2.** something that gives great pleasure. —*v.t.* **3.** to give great pleasure, satisfaction, or enjoyment to; please highly. —*v.i.* **4.** to have great pleasure; take pleasure (fol. by *in* or an infinitive). [erroneous 16th cent. sp., after *light,* r. ME *delit,* t. OF: der. *delitier,* g. L *dēlectāre,* freq. of *dēlicere* allure] —**de·light/er,** *n.* —Syn. 1. enjoyment, transport, delectation. See pleasure. —Ant. 1. distress. 2. disappointment.

de·light·ed (dĭ lī/tĭd), *adj.* **1.** highly pleased. **2.** *Obs.* delightful. —**de·light/ed·ly,** *adv.*

de·light·ful (dĭ līt/fəl), *adj.* affording delight; highly pleasing. —**de·light/ful·ly,** *adv.* —**de·light/ful·ness,** *n.* —Syn. pleasurable, enjoyable; charming, enchanting, delectable, agreeable. —Ant. obnoxious.

de·light·some (dĭ līt/səm), *adj.* delightful. —**de·light/some·ly,** *adv.* —**de·light/some·ness,** *n.*

De·li·lah (dĭ lī/lə), *n.* **1.** *Bible.* Samson's mistress, who betrayed him to the Philistines. Judges 16. **2.** a seductive and treacherous woman.

de·lim·it (dĭ lĭm/ĭt), *v.t.* to fix or mark the limits of; demarcate. [t. F: s. *délimiter,* t. L: m. *dēlimitāre*]

de·lim·i·tate (dĭ lĭm/ə tāt′), *v.t.,* **-tated, -tating.** delimit. —**de·lim/i·ta/tion,** *n.* —**de·lim/i·ta/tive,** *adj.*

de·lin·e·ate (dĭ lĭn/ĭ āt′), *v.t.,* **-ated, -ating. 1.** to trace the outline of; sketch or trace in outline; represent pictorially. **2.** to portray in words; describe. [t. L: m. s. *dēlīneātus,* pp., sketched out]

de·lin·e·a·tion (dĭ lĭn/ĭ ā/shən), *n.* **1.** act or process of delineating. **2.** a chart or diagram; a sketch; a rough draft. **3.** a description. —**de·lin/e·a/tive,** *adj.*

de·lin·e·a·tor (dĭ lĭn/ĭ ā/tər), *n.* **1.** one who or that which delineates. **2.** a tailor's pattern which can be adjusted for cutting garments of different sizes.

de·lin·e·a·vit (dĭ lĭn/ĭ ā/vĭt), *Latin.* he (or she) drew (this).

de·lin·quen·cy (dĭ lĭng/kwən sĭ), *n., pl.* **-cies. 1.** failure in or neglect of duty or obligation; fault; guilt. **2.** a shortcoming; a misdeed or offense.

de·lin·quent (dĭ lĭng/kwənt), *adj.* **1.** failing in or neglectful of a duty or obligation; guilty of a misdeed or

offense. **2.** of or pertaining to delinquents: *delinquent taxes.* —*n.* **3.** one who is delinquent. [t. L: s. *dēlinquens,* ppr.] —**de·lin/quent·ly,** *adv.*

del·i·quesce (dĕl/ə kwĕs′), *v.i.,* **-quesced, -quescing. 1.** to melt away. **2.** to become liquid by absorbing moisture from the air, as certain salts. **3.** *Bot.* to form many small divisions or branches. [t. L: m. s. *dēliquescere* melt away]

del·i·ques·cence (dĕl/ə kwĕs/əns), *n.* **1.** act or process of deliquescing. **2.** the liquid produced when something deliquesces. —**del/i·ques/cent,** *adj.*

del·i·ra·tion (dĕl/ə rā/shən), *n.* mental derangement; raving; delirium. [t. L: s. *dēlīrātio*]

de·lir·i·ous (dĭ lĭr/ĭ əs), *adj.* **1.** *Pathol.* affected with delirium. **2.** characteristic of delirium. **3.** wild with excitement, enthusiasm, etc. —**de·lir/i·ous·ly,** *adv.* —**de·lir/i·ous·ness,** *n.*

de·lir·i·um (dĭ lĭr/ĭ əm), *n., pl.* **-liriums, -liria** (-lĭr/ĭ ə). **1.** a more or less temporary disorder of the mental faculties, as in fevers, disturbances of consciousness, or intoxication, characterized by restlessness, excitement, delusions, hallucinations, etc. **2.** a state of violent excitement or emotion. [t. L, der. *dēlīrāre* be deranged, lit., go out of the furrow]

delirium tremens (trē/mənz), a violent restlessness due to excessive indulgence in alcohol, characterized by trembling, terrifying visual hallucinations, etc. [NL trembling delirium]

del·i·tes·cent (dĕl/ə tĕs/ənt), *adj.* concealed. [t. L: s. *dēlitescens,* ppr.] —**del/i·tes/cence,** *n.*

De·li·us (dē/lĭ əs, dēl/yəs), *n.* **Frederick,** 1862–1934, British composer.

de·liv·er (dĭ lĭv/ər), *v.t.* **1.** to give up or surrender; give into another's possession or keeping. **2.** to carry and turn over (letters, goods, etc.) to the intended recipients. **3.** *U.S. Colloq.* to bring (votes) to the support of a candidate or a cause. **4.** to give forth in words; utter or pronounce: *to deliver a verdict.* **5.** to give forth or emit; direct; cast. **6.** to set free; liberate. **7.** to release or save: *deliver us from evil.* **8.** to disburden (a woman) of a child in childbirth. **9.** to disburden (oneself) of thoughts, opinions, etc. **10.** *Obs.* to make known; assert. —*adj.* **11.** *Obs.* or *Archaic.* agile; active; quick. [ME *delivre(n),* t. F: m. *délivrer,* g. LL *dēlīberāre* set free] —**de·liv/er·a·ble,** *adj.* —**de·liv/er·er,** *n.* —Syn. **1.** hand over, transfer, cede. **4.** communicate, impart. **6.** free, emancipate. **7.** redeem, rescue.

de·liv·er·ance (dĭ lĭv/ər əns), *n.* **1.** act of delivering. **2.** fact of being delivered. **3.** a thought or judgment expressed; a formal or authoritative pronouncement.

de·liv·er·ly (dĭ lĭv/ər lĭ), *adv.* *Obs.* or *Archaic.* quickly; deftly.

de·liv·er·y (dĭ lĭv/ər ĭ), *n., pl.* **-eries. 1.** the delivering of letters, goods, etc. **2.** a giving up or handing over; surrender. **3.** the utterance or enunciation of words. **4.** vocal and bodily behavior during the presentation of a speech. **5.** act or manner of giving or sending forth, as of a ball by the pitcher in baseball. **6.** release or rescue. **7.** the being delivered of, or giving birth to a child; parturition. **8.** something delivered. **9.** *Com.* a shipment of goods from the seller to the buyer. **10.** *Law.* an act sometimes essential to a legally effective transfer of property: *a delivery of deed.*

dell (dĕl), *n.* *Literary in U.S.* a small valley; a vale. [ME *delle,* OE *dell;* akin to DALE]

del·la Rob·bia (dĕl/lä rôb/byä), **Luca** (lōō/kä). See **Robbia.**

de·lo·cal·ize (dē lō/kə līz′), *v.t.,* **-ized, -izing.** to remove from the proper or usual locality. —**de·lo/cal·i·za/tion,** *n.*

De·lorme (də lôrm′), *n.* **Philibert** (fē lē bĕr′), c1510–1570, French architect.

De·los (dē/lŏs), *n.* a tiny Greek island in the Cyclades, in the SW Aegean: the site of an oracle of Apollo.

de·louse (dē lous′, -louz′), *v.t.,* **-loused, -lousing.** to free of lice; remove lice from.

Del·phi (dĕl/fī), *n.* an ancient city in central Greece, in Phocis: the site of an oracle of Apollo.

Del·phic (dĕl/fĭk), *adj.* **1.** pertaining to Delphi, to the temple and oracle of Apollo there, or to Apollo himself. **2.** ambiguous. Also, **Del·phi·an** (dĕl/fĭ ən). [t. L: s. *Delphicus,* t. Gk.: m. *Delphikós*]

Delphic oracle, the oracle of the temple of Apollo at Delphi which often gave ambiguous answers.

del·phi·nine (dĕl/fə nēn′, -nĭn). *n. Chem.* a bitter, poisonous, crystalline alkaloid obtained from various species of larkspur, genus *Delphinium,* esp. *D. Staphisagria.* [f. DELPHIN(IUM) + -INE²]

del·phin·i·um (dĕl fĭn/ĭ əm), *n.* any of numerous garden varieties of ranunculaceous flowers, genus *Delphinium,* having handsome, usually blue, irregular flowers; larkspur. [t. NL, t. Gk.: m. *delphīnion* larkspur, dim. of *delphīn* dolphin; so called from the shape of the nectary]

Del·phi·nus (dĕl fī/nəs), *n., gen.* **-ni** (-nī). *Astron.* a northern constellation between Aquila and Pegasus. [t. L: dolphin]

Del·sarte (dĕl särt′; *Fr.* -sȧrt′), **François,** 1811–71, French musician and teacher.

Del·sar·ti·an (dĕl sär/tĭ ən), *adj.* pertaining to François Delsarte or to his system for developing bodily grace and improving musical and dramatic expression.

Del Sar·to (dĕl sär/tō), **Andrea** (än drĕ/ä). See **Sarto.**

---

b., blend of, blended; c., cognate with; d., dialect, dialectal; der., derived from; f., formed from; g., going back to; m., modification of; r., replacing; s., stem of; t., taken from; ?, perhaps.   See the full key on inside cover.

del·ta (dĕl′tə), *n.* **1.** the fourth letter (Δ, δ, = English *D*, *d*) of the Greek alphabet. **2.** anything triangular, like the Greek capital Δ. **3.** a nearly flat plain of alluvial deposit between diverging branches of the mouth of a river, often, though not necessarily, triangular: *the delta of the Nile.*

del·ta·ic (dĕl·tā′ĭk), *adj.* **1.** forming a delta. **2.** having a delta.

del·toid (dĕl′toid), *n.* **1.** a large triangular muscle covering the joint of the shoulder and serving to raise the arm away from the side of the body. —*adj.* **2.** triangular. [t. Gk.: m. s. *deltoeidēs* delta-shaped]

Deltoid leaf

de·lude (dĭ·lōōd′), *v.t.,* **-luded, -luding.** **1.** to mislead the mind or judgment of; deceive. **2.** *Obs.* to cheat the hopes of. **3.** *Obs.* to elude; evade. [t. L: m.s. *dēlūdere* play false] —**de·lud′er,** *n.* —**Syn. 1.** beguile, cozen, dupe, cheat, defraud.

del·uge (dĕl′ūj), *n., v.,* **-uged, -uging.** —*n.* **1.** a great overflowing of water; inundation; flood; downpour. **2.** anything that overwhelms like a flood. **3. the Deluge,** *Bible.* the great flood in the days of Noah. Gen. 7. —*v.t.* **4.** to flood; inundate. **5.** to overrun; overwhelm. [ME, t. OF, g. L *dīluvium*] —**Syn. 1.** See **flood.** —**Ant. 1.** drought. **2.** scarcity.

de·lu·sion (dĭ·lōō′zhən), *n.* **1.** act of deluding. **2.** fact of being deluded. **3.** a false belief or opinion. **4.** *Psychiatry.* a fixed, dominating, or persistent false mental conception resistant to reason with regard to actual things or matters of fact: *a paranoiac delusion.* —**de·lu′sion·al,** *adj.* —**Syn. 2.** See **illusion.**

de·lu·sive (dĭ·lōō′sĭv), *adj.* **1.** tending to delude; deceptive. **2.** of the nature of a delusion; false; unreal. Also, **de·lu·so·ry** (dĭ·lōō′sə·rĭ). —**de·lu′sive·ly,** *adv.* —**de·lu′sive·ness,** *n.*

de luxe (də lōōks′, lŭks′; *Fr.* də lyks′), of special elegance, sumptuousness, or fineness. [t. F: of luxury]

delve (dĕlv), *v.,* **delved, delving.** —*v.i.* **1.** to carry on intensive or thorough research for information, etc. **2.** *Archaic or Dial.* to dig, as with a spade. —*v.t.* **3.** *Archaic or Dial.* to dig. **4.** *Archaic.* to obtain by digging. [ME *delve(n),* OE *delfan,* c. D *delven*] —**delv′er,** *n.*

Dem., **1.** Democrat. **2.** Democratic.

de·mag·net·ize (dē·măg′nə·tīz′), *v.t.,* **-ized, -izing.** to remove magnetic properties from. —**de·mag′net·i·za′-tion,** *n.* —**de·mag′net·iz′er,** *n.*

dem·a·gog·ic (dĕm′ə·gŏj′ĭk, -gŏg′ĭk), *adj.* **1.** characteristic of a demagogue. **2.** of a demagogue. Also, **dem′a·gog′i·cal.**

dem·a·gogue (dĕm′ə·gŏg′, -gŏg′), *n.* **1.** a leader who uses the passions or prejudices of the populace for his own interests; an unprincipled popular orator or agitator. **2.** (historically) a leader of the people. Also, **dem′a·gog′.** [t. Gk.: m. s. *dēmagōgós,* f. s. *dēmos* people + *agōgós* leader]

dem·a·gogu·er·y (dĕm′ə·gŏg′ər·ĭ, -gŏg′ər·ĭ), *n. Chiefly U.S.* the methods or practices of a demagogue.

dem·a·gogu·ism (dĕm′ə·gŏg′ĭz·əm, -gŏg′ĭz·əm), *n.* demagoguery. Also, **dem′a·gog′ism.**

dem·a·go·gy (dĕm′ə·gŏj′ĭ, -gŏg′ĭ, -gŏg′ĭ), *n. Chiefly Brit.* **1.** demagoguery. **2.** the character of a demagogue. **3.** a body of demagogues.

de·mand (dĭ·mănd′, -mänd′), *v.t.* **1.** to ask for with authority; claim as a right: *to demand something of or from a person.* **2.** to ask for peremptorily or urgently. **3.** to call for or require as just, proper, or necessary: *a task which demands patience.* **4.** *Law.* **a.** to lay formal legal claim to. **b.** to summon, as to court. —*v.i.* **5.** to make a demand; inquire or ask. —*n.* **6.** act of demanding. **7.** that which is demanded. **8.** an urgent or pressing requirement: *demands upon one's time.* **9.** an inquiry or question. **10.** a requisition; a legal claim. **11.** the state of being in request for purchase or use: *an article in great demand.* **12.** *Econ.* **a.** the desire to purchase and possess, coupled with the power of purchasing. **b.** the quantity of any goods which buyers will take at a particular price. See **supply.** **13. on demand,** subject to payment upon presentation and demand. [t. F: s. *demander,* g. L *dēmandāre* give in charge, intrust, ML *demand*] —**de·mand′a·ble,** *adj.* —**de·mand′er,** *n.* —**Syn. 1.** DEMAND, CLAIM, REQUIRE imply making an authoritative request. To DEMAND is to ask in a bold, authoritative way: *to demand an explanation.* To CLAIM is to assert a right to something: *he claimed it as his due.* To REQUIRE is to ask for something as being necessary: *the Army requires absolute obedience of its soldiers.*

de·mand·ant (dĭ·măn′dənt, -män′-), *n. Law.* **1.** the plaintiff in a real action. **2.** any plaintiff.

demand bill, draft, or **note,** a bill of exchange, note, etc., payable on demand or presentation.

demand deposit, *Banking.* a deposit withdrawable at the will of the depositor without prior notice.

demand loan, call loan.

de·mar·cate (dĭ·mär′kāt, dē′mär·kāt′), *v.t.,* **-cated, -cating.** **1.** to mark off the boundaries of. **2.** to separate distinctly. [back formation from DEMARCATION]

de·mar·ca·tion (dē′mär·kā′shən), *n.* **1.** the marking off of the boundaries of something. **2.** separation by distinct boundaries. **3.** the defining of boundaries. Also, **de′mar·ka′tion.** [Latinization of Sp. *demarcación,* der. *demarcar* mark out the bounds of]

dé·marche (dā·märsh′), *n. French.* **1.** a plan or mode of procedure. **2.** a change in a course of action. [F, der. *démarcher* march]

de·ma·te·ri·al·ize (dē′mə·tǐr′ẽ·ə·līz′), *v.t., v.i.,* **-ized, -izing.** to deprive of or lose material character. —**de′ma·te′ri·al·i·za′tion,** *n.*

Dem·a·vend (dĕm′ə·vĕnd′), *n.* a mountain peak of the Elburz Mountains in N Iran. 18,606 ft.

deme (dēm), *n.* one of the administrative divisions of ancient Attica and of modern Greece. [t. Gk.: m. s. *dēmos* district, country, people, commons]

de·mean[1] (dĭ·mēn′), *v.t.* to lower in dignity or standing; debase. [f. DE- + MEAN[2], modeled on DEBASE]

de·mean[2] (dĭ·mēn′), *v.t.* to conduct or behave (oneself) in a specified manner. [ME *demene(n),* t. OF: m. *demener,* f. *de-* DE- + *mener* lead, g. L *mināre* drive]

de·mean·or (dĭ·mē′nər), *n.* conduct; behavior. Also, *Brit.,* **de·mean′our.** [ME *demenure,* der. *demene(n)* DEMEAN[2], v.]

de·ment (dĭ·mĕnt′), *v.t.* to make mad or insane. [t. L: s. *dēmentāre* deprive of mind]

de·ment·ed (dĭ·mĕn′tĭd), *adj.* out of one's mind; crazed; insane; affected with dementia. —**de·ment′-ed·ly,** *adv.* —**de·ment′ed·ness,** *n.*

de·men·tia (dĭ·mĕn′shə, -shĭ·ə), *n. Pathol., Psychiatry.* a state of mental disorder characterized by impairment or loss of the mental powers; commonly an end result of several mental or other diseases. [t. L: madness]

dementia prae·cox (prē′kŏks), *Pathol., Psychiatry.* a form of insanity usually occurring or beginning at puberty and characterized by introversion, dissociation, and odd, distorted behavior. [t. L: precocious insanity]

de·mer·it (dē·mĕr′ĭt), *n.* **1.** censurable or punishable quality; fault. **2.** a mark against a person for misconduct or deficiency. **3.** *Obs.* merit or desert. [t. L: s. *demeritum* (in ML, fault), prop. pp. neut. of *demerēri* deserve (esp. well)]

dem·e·rol (dĕm′ə·rōl′, -rŏl′), *n.* **1.** a synthetic drug used as an analgesic and sedative. **2.** (*cap.*) a trademark for this drug.

de·mesne (dĭ·mān′, -mēn′), *n.* **1.** possession (of land) as one's own. **2.** an estate possessed, or in the actual possession or use of the owner. **3.** the land attached to a manor house, reserved for the owner's use. **4.** the dominion or territory of a sovereign or state; a domain. **5.** a district; region. [ME *demeyne,* t. AF. See DOMAIN]

De·me·ter (dĭ·mē′tər), *n. Gk. Myth.* the goddess of the fruitful earth, protectress of social order and marriage, identified by the Romans with Ceres. [t. L, t. Gk.]

demi-, a prefix meaning: **1.** half, as in *demiquaver.* **2.** inferior, as in *demigod.* [t. F: repr. *demi,* adj. (also n. and adv.), g. L *dīmedius,* r. *dīmidius* half]

dem·i·bas·tion (dĕm′ĭ·băs′chən), *n. Fort.* a work consisting of half a bastion, and hence having one face and one flank.

dem·i·god (dĕm′ĭ·gŏd′), *n.* **1.** one partly divine and partly human; an inferior deity. **2.** a deified mortal. —**dem·i·god·dess** (dĕm′ĭ·gŏd′ĭs), *n. fem.*

dem·i·john (dĕm′ĭ·jŏn′), *n.* a large small-necked bottle, usually cased in wickerwork. [t. F: m. *dame-jeanne,* appar. a popular name, Dame Jane]

de·mil·i·ta·rize (dē·mĭl′ə·tə·rīz′), *v.t.,* **-rized, -rizing.** **1.** to deprive of military character; free from militarism. **2.** to place under civil instead of military control. —**de·mil′i·ta·ri·za′tion,** *n.*

dem·i·mon·daine (dĕm′ĭ·mŏn·dān′; *Fr.* də·mē·môN·dĕn′), *n.* a woman of the demimonde. [t. F]

dem·i·monde (dĕm′ĭ·mŏnd′; *Fr.* də·mē·môNd′), *n.* the world or class of women who have become socially declassed, or of doubtful reputation and standing. [t. F: lit., half-world]

dem·i·pique (dĕm′ĭ·pēk′), *n.* an 18th century saddle having a peak about half the height of earlier styles. [f. DEMI- + *pique* (pseudo-F sp. of PEAK)]

dem·i·re·lief (dĕm′ĭ·rĭ·lēf′), *n.* mezzo-rilievo.

dem·i·rep (dĕm′ĭ·rĕp′), *n.* a woman of doubtful or compromised reputation. [short for *demi-reputation*]

de·mise (dĭ·mīz′), *n., v.,* **-mised, -mising.** —*n.* **1.** death or decease. **2.** *Law.* **a.** a death or decease occasioning the transfer of an estate. **b.** a conveyance or transfer of an estate. **3.** *Govt.* transfer of sovereignty, as by the death or deposition of the sovereign. —*v.t.* **4.** *Law.* to transfer (an estate, etc.) for a limited time; lease. **5.** *Govt.* to transfer (sovereignty), as by the death or abdication of the sovereign. —*v.i.* **6.** *Law.* to pass by bequest, inheritance, or succession to the Crown. [t. OF, prop. pp. fem. of *desmettre* send or put away. See DEMIT] —**de·mis′a·ble,** *adj.*

dem·i·sem·i·qua·ver (dĕm′ĭ·sĕm′ĭ·kwā′vər), *n. Music.* a note having half the time value of a semiquaver; a thirty-second note. See illus. under **note.**

de·mis·sion (dĭ·mĭsh′ən), *n.* **1.** abdication. **2.** *Rare.* dismissal. [t. F. Cf. L *dīmissio* a sending away]

de·mit (dĭ·mĭt′), *v.,* **-mitted, -mitting.** *Chiefly Scot.* —*v.t.* **1.** to give up, as a dignity or office; resign. **2.** *Archaic.* to dismiss. —*v.i.* **3.** to resign. [b. F *démettre* send or put away and L *dīmittere* send away]

dem·i·tasse (dĕm′ĭ·tăs′, -täs′; *Fr.* də·mē·täs′), *n.* **1.** a small cup for serving black coffee after dinner. **2.** the coffee contained in such a cup. [t. F: half cup]

dem·i·urge (dĕm′ĭ·ûrj′), *n.* **1.** *Philos.* **a.** (in Platonic philosophy) the artificer of the world. **b.** (in the Gnostic and certain other systems) a supernatural being imagined as creating or fashioning the world in subordination to the Supreme Being, and sometimes regarded as the originator of evil. **2.** (in many states of ancient Greece) a public official or magistrate. [t. Gk.: m. s. *dēmiourgós* worker for the people, artificer, maker] —dem·i·ur·geous (dĕm′ĭ ûr′jəs), dem′i·ur′gic, *adj.* —dem′i·ur·gi·cal·ly, *adv.*

dem·i·volt (dĕm′ĭ vōlt′), *n.* a half turn made by a horse with the forelegs raised. Also, **dem′i·volte′**. [t. F: m. *demi-volte*. See DEMI-, VOLT[1]]

demo-, a word element meaning "people," "population," "common people." [t. Gk., comb. form of *dēmos*]

de·mob (dē mŏb′), *n., v.,* -mobbed, -mobbing. *Brit. Colloq.* —*n.* **1.** demobilization. **2.** one who has been discharged from the army. —*v.t.* **3.** to discharge (a soldier) from the army. [short for DEMOBILIZE]

de·mo·bi·lize (dē mō′bə līz′), *v.t.,* -lized, -lizing. to disband (an army, etc.). —**de·mo/bi·li·za/tion,** *n.*

de·moc·ra·cy (dĭ mŏk′rə sĭ), *n., pl.* -cies. **1.** government by the people; a form of government in which the supreme power is vested in the people and exercised by them or by their elected agents under a free electoral system. **2.** a state having such a form of government. **3.** (in a restricted sense) a state in which the supreme power is vested in the people and exercised directly by them rather than by elected representatives. See **republic. 4.** a state of society characterized by formal equality of rights and privileges. **5.** political or social equality; democratic spirit. **6.** the common people of a community as distinguished from any privileged class; the common people with respect to their political power. **7.** (*cap.*) *U.S. Pol.* **a.** the principles of the Democratic party. **b.** the members of this party collectively. [t. F: m. *démocratie,* ult. t. Gk.: m. s. *dēmokratía* popular government, f. *dēmo-* DEMO- + -*kratía* rule, authority]

dem·o·crat (dĕm′ə krăt′), *n.* **1.** an advocate of democracy. **2.** one who maintains the political or social equality of men. **3.** (*cap.*) *U.S. Pol.* **a.** a member of the Democratic party. **b.** *Obs.* a member of the old Democratic-Republican party.

dem·o·crat·ic (dĕm′ə krăt′ĭk), *adj.* **1.** pertaining to or of the nature of democracy or a democracy. **2.** pertaining to or characterized by the principle of political or social equality for all. **3.** advocating or upholding democracy. **4.** (*cap.*) *U.S. Pol.* **a.** of, pertaining to, or characteristic of the Democratic party. **b.** of, pertaining to, or belonging to the Democratic-Republican party. Also, **dem′o·crat′i·cal.** —**dem′o·crat′i·cal·ly,** *adv.*

Democratic party, one of the two major political parties in the U.S., founded in 1828.

Democratic-Republican party, *U.S. Hist.* a political party opposed to the old Federalist party.

de·moc·ra·tize (dĭ mŏk′rə tīz′), *v.t., v.i.,* -tized, -tizing. to make or become democratic. —**de·moc′ra·ti·za/tion,** *n.*

De·moc·ri·tus (dĭ mŏk′rə təs), *n.* ("*the Laughing Philosopher*") c460–c370 B.C., a Greek philosopher.

de·mod·ed (dē mō′dĭd), *adj.* no longer in fashion.

de·mod·u·late (dē mŏj′ə lāt′), *v.t.,* -lated, -lating. *Radio.* detect (def. 4).

de·mod·u·la·tion (dē mŏj′ə lā′shən), *n.* *Radio.* detection (def. 4b).

De·mo·gor·gon (dē′mə gôr′gən, dĕm′ə-), *n.* a vague, mysterious, infernal power or divinity of ancient mythology, variously represented, as an object of awe or fear. [t. LL, t. Gk. See DEMO-, GORGON]

de·mog·ra·phy (dĭ mŏg′rə fĭ), *n.* the science of vital and social statistics, as of the births, deaths, diseases, marriages, etc., of populations. —**de·mog′ra·pher, de·mog/ra·phist,** *n.* —**de·mo·graph·ic** (dē′mə grăf′ĭk), **de/mo·graph′i·cal,** *adj.* —**de/mo·graph′i·cal·ly,** *adv.*

dem·oi·selle (dĕm′wä zĕl′; *Fr.* də mwä zĕl′), *n.* **1.** a damsel. **2.** the Numidian crane, *Anthropoides virgo,* of northern Africa, Asia, and Europe, having long white plumes behind the eyes. **3.** any of various slender-bodied dragonflies. [F]

de·mol·ish (dĭ mŏl′ĭsh), *v.t.* **1.** to throw or pull down (a building, etc.); reduce to ruins. **2.** to put an end to; destroy; ruin utterly; lay waste. [t. F: m. *démoliss-*, t. L: m. *dēmōlīrī* throw down, destroy] —**de·mol′ish·er,** *n.* —**de·mol′ish·ment,** *n.* —**Syn. 2.** See destroy. —**Ant. 2.** restore.

dem·o·li·tion (dĕm′ə lĭsh′ən, dē′mə-), *n.* **1.** act of demolishing. **2.** state of being demolished; destruction.

demolition bomb, *Mil.* a bomb containing a relatively large charge used to destroy material objects.

de·mon (dē′mən), *n.* **1.** an evil spirit; a devil. **2.** an evil passion or influence. **3.** an atrociously wicked or cruel person. **4.** a person of great energy, etc. **5.** daemon. [(defs. 1–4) used for L *daemonium,* t. Gk.: m. *daimónion* thing of divine nature (in Jewish and Christian writers, evil spirit); (def. 5) t. L: m. *daemon* spirit, evil spirit, t. Gk.: m. *daímōn* tutelary divinity, evil spirit]

demon-, a word element meaning "demon." [t. Gk., comb. form of *daimōn*]

de·mon·e·tize (dē mŏn′ə tīz′, -mŭn′-), *v.t.,* -tized, -tizing. **1.** to divest of value, as the monetary standard. **2.** to withdraw from use as money. —**de·mon/e·ti·za/tion,** *n.*

de·mo·ni·ac (dĭ mō′nĭ ăk′), *adj.* Also, **de·mo·ni·a·cal** (dē′mə nī′ə kəl). **1.** of, pertaining to, or like a demon. **2.** possessed by an evil spirit; raging; frantic. —*n.* **3.** one

seemingly possessed by a demon or evil spirit. [ME *demoniak,* t. LL: m.s *daemoniacus,* t. Gk.: m. *daimoniakós*] —**de·mo·ni·a·cal·ly** (dē′mə nī′ĭk lĭ), *adv.* —**Ant.** angelic.

de·mo·ni·an (dĭ mō′nĭ ən), *adj.* pertaining to or of the nature of a demon.

de·mon·ic (dĭ mŏn′ĭk), *adj.* **1.** of, pertaining to, or of the nature of a demon. **2.** inspired as if by a demon, indwelling spirit, or genius. [t. L: m.s *daemonicus,* t. Gk.: m. *daimonikós*]

de·mon·ism (dē′mə nĭz′əm), *n.* **1.** belief in demons. **2.** worship of demons. **3.** demonology. —**de/mon·ist,** *n.*

de·mon·ize (dē′mə nīz′), *v.t.,* -ized, -izing. **1.** to turn into or make like a demon. **2.** to subject to the influence of demons.

demono-, var. of **demon-,** before consonants.

de·mon·ol·a·ter (dē′mə nŏl′ə tər), *n.* a demon worshiper.

de·mon·ol·a·try (dē′mə nŏl′ə trĭ), *n.* the worship of demons.

de·mon·ol·o·gy (dē′mə nŏl′ə jĭ), *n.* **1.** the study of demons or of beliefs about demons. **2.** the doctrine of demons. —**de/mon·ol′o·gist,** *n.*

de·mon·stra·ble (dĭ mŏn′strə bəl, dĕm′ən-), *adj.* capable of being demonstrated. —**de·mon/stra·bil/i·ty, de·mon/stra·ble·ness,** *n.* —**de·mon/stra·bly,** *adv.*

de·mon·strant (dĭ mŏn′strənt), *n.* demonstrator.

dem·on·strate (dĕm′ən strāt′), *v.,* -strated, -strating. —*v.t.* **1.** to make evident by arguments or reasoning; prove. **2.** to describe and explain with the help of specimens or by experiment. **3.** to manifest or exhibit. —*v.i.* **4.** to make, give, or take part in, a demonstration. **5.** *Mil.* to attack or make a show of force to deceive the enemy. [t. L: m. s. *dēmonstrātus,* pp., showed, proved]

dem·on·stra·tion (dĕm′ən strā′shən), *n.* **1.** the proving of anything conclusively, as by arguments, reasoning, evidence, etc. **2.** proof, or anything serving as a proof. **3.** a description or explanation, as of a process, given with the help of specimens or by experiment. **4.** act of exhibiting and explaining an article or commodity by way of advertising it. **5.** an exhibition, as of feeling; a display; manifestation. **6.** a public exhibition of sympathy, opposition, etc., as a parade or mass meeting. **7.** a show of military force or of offensive operations, made to deceive the enemy. **8.** *Math.* a logical presentation of the way in which given assumptions imply a certain result. —**dem/on·stra/tion·al,** *adj.* —**dem/on·stra/tion·ist,** *n.*

de·mon·stra·tive (dĭ mŏn′strə tĭv), *adj.* **1.** characterized by or given to open exhibition or expression of the feelings, etc. **2.** serving to demonstrate; explanatory or illustrative. **3.** serving to prove the truth of anything; indubitably conclusive. **4.** *Gram.* indicating or specifying the thing referred to. —*n.* **5.** *Gram.* a demonstrative word, as *this* or *there.* —**de·mon/stra·tive·ly,** *adv.* —**de·mon/stra·tive·ness,** *n.*

dem·on·stra·tor (dĕm′ən strā′tər), *n.* **1.** one who or that which demonstrates. **2.** Also, **demonstrant.** one who takes part in a public demonstration. **3.** one who explains or teaches by practical demonstrations.

de·mor·al·ize (dĭ mŏr′ə līz′, -mŏr′-), *v.t.,* -ized, -izing. **1.** to corrupt or undermine the morals of. **2.** to deprive (a person, a body of soldiers, etc.) of spirit, courage, discipline, etc. **3.** to reduce to a state of weakness or disorder. [t. F: m.s. *démoraliser*] —**de·mor/al·i·za/tion,** *n.* —**de·mor/al·iz/er,** *n.*

De Mor·gan (dĭ môr′gən), **William Frend,** 1839–1917, British novelist and artist in stained glass and ceramics.

de mor·tu·is nil ni·si bo·num (dē môr′chŏŏ′ĭs nĭl′ nĭ′sĭ bō′nəm). *Latin.* of the dead say nothing but good.

de·mos (dē′mŏs), *n.* **1.** the people or commons of an ancient Greek state. **2.** the common people; the populace. [t. Gk.: district, people]

De·mos·the·nes (dĭ mŏs′thə nēz′), *n.* 384?–322 B.C., Athenian statesman and orator.

de·mote (dĭ mōt′), *v.t.,* -moted, -moting. to reduce to a lower grade or class (opposed to *promote*). [f. DE- + -*mote,* modeled on PROMOTE]—**de·mo/tion,** *n.*

de·mot·ic (dĭ mŏt′ĭk), *adj.* **1.** of or pertaining to the common people; popular. **2.** noting or pertaining to the ancient Egyptian handwriting of ordinary life, a simplified form of the hieratic characters. [t. Gk.: m. s. *dēmotikós* popular, plebeian]

de·mot·ics (dĭ mŏt′ĭks), *n.* sociology.

de·mount (dē mount′), *v.t.* to remove from its mounting, setting, or place of support, as a gun. —**de·mount/a·ble,** *adj.*

demp·ster (dĕmp′stər), *n.* deemster.

de·mul·cent (dĭ mŭl′sənt), *adj.* **1.** soothing or mollifying, as a medicinal substance. —*n.* **2.** a demulcent (often mucilaginous) substance or agent, as for soothing or protecting an irritated mucous membrane. [t. L: s. *dēmulcens,* pprr., stroking down, softening]

de·mur (dĭ mûr′), *v.,* -murred, -murring, *n.* —*v.i.* **1.** to make objection; take exception; object. **2.** *Law.* to interpose a demurrer. **3.** *Obs.* to linger; hesitate. —*n.* **4.** act of making objection. **5.** an objection raised. **6.** *Obs., Law.* a demurrer. **7.** *Obs.* hesitation. [ME *demeore(n),* t. OF: m. *demeurer,* g. L *dēmorārī* linger] —**Ant. 1.** agree, accede.

de·mure (dĭ myŏŏr′), *adj.,* -murer, -murest. **1.** affectedly or unnaturally modest, decorous, or prim. **2.** sober;

serious; sedate; decorous. [ME. der. *mure* grave, discreet, t. OF: m. *meur*, g. L *mātūrus* MATURE] —**de-mure/ly**, *adv.* —**de-mure/ness**, *n.* —Syn. 1. See modest.

de-mur-rage (dĭ mûr/ĭj), *n.* Com. 1. the detention of a vessel, as in loading or unloading, beyond the time agreed upon. 2. the similar detention of a railroad car, etc. 3. a charge for such detention.

de-mur-ral (dĭ mûr/əl), *n.* act of demurring; demur.

de-mur-rer (dĭ mûr/ər), *n.* 1. one who demurs; an objector. 2. *Law.* a pleading in effect that even if the facts are as alleged by the opposite party, they do not sustain the contention based on them. 3. an objection or demur. [t. AF, var. of OF *demourer*. See DEMUR]

de-my (dĭ mī/), *n.*, *pl.* -**mies.** 1. a foundation scholar at Magdalen College, Oxford (so called because orig. receiving half the allowance of a fellow). 2. a particular size of paper, 16 × 21 inches in America, 17½ × 22 inches in Great Britain. [free form of DEMI-, with change of final *i* to *y* in accordance with rules of English spelling]

den (dĕn), *n.*, *v.*, **denned, denning.** —*n.* 1. a retired place, as a cave, serving as the habitation of a beast. 2. a cave as a place of shelter, concealment, etc. 3. a squalid or vile abode or place: *dens of misery.* 4. a cozy or retired room for personal use. —*v.i.* 5. to live in or as in a den. [ME; OE *denn* floor, cave, den, G *tenne* floor]

Den., Denmark.

de-nar-i-us (dĭ nâr/ĭ əs), *n.*, *pl.* -**narii** (-nâr/ĭ ī/). 1. a Roman silver coin of varying intrinsic value. 2. (in English monetary reckoning) a penny. [t. L, orig. adj., containing ten (asses). See DENARY]

den-a-ry (dĕn/ə rĭ, dē/nə-), *adj.* 1. containing ten; tenfold. 2. proceeding by tens; decimal. [t. L: m. s. *dēnārius* containing ten, der. *dēnī* ten at a time]

de-na-tion-al-ize (dē nāsh/ən ə līz/), *v.t.*, -**ized, -izing.** to deprive of national status, attachments, or characteristics. —**de-na/tion-al-i-za/tion,** *n.*

de-nat-u-ral-ize (dē nāch/ər ə līz/), *v.t.*, -**ized, -izing.** 1. to deprive of the original nature; make unnatural. 2. to deprive of the rights and privileges of citizenship or of naturalization. —**de-nat/u-ral-i-za/tion,** *n.*

de-na-ture (dē nā/chər), *v.t.*, -**tured, -turing.** 1. to deprive of its peculiar nature. 2. to render (alcohol, etc.) unfit for drinking or eating, as by adding an unwholesome substance, without altering the usefulness for other purposes. 3. *Biochem.* to treat, as a protein, by chemical or physical means so as to alter its original state. —**de-na/tur-ant,** *n.* —**de-na/tur-a/tion,** *n.*

de-na-tur-ize (dē nā/chə rīz/), *v.t.*, -**ized, -izing.** to denature. —**de-na/tur-i-za/tion,** *n.*

de-na-zi-fy (dē nā/tsə fī/, -nazə-), *v.t.*, -**fied, -fying.** to rid of Nazism or Nazi influences. —**de-na/zi-fi-ca/tion,** *n.*

Den-bigh-shire (dĕn/bĭ shĭr/, -shər), *n.* a county in N Wales. 170,726 pop. (1951); 669 sq. mi. *Co. seat:* Denbigh. Also, **Den/bigh.**

dendr-, var. of dendro-, before vowels.

den-dri-form (dĕn/drə fôrm/), *adj.* treelike in form. [DENDR- + -(I)FORM]

den-drite (dĕn/drīt), *n.* 1. *Geol.* a. a branching figure or marking, resembling moss or a shrub or tree in form, found on or in certain stones or minerals, and due to the presence of a foreign material. b. any arborescent crystalline growth. 2. *Anat., Physiol.* the branching portion of a neuron which picks up the stimulus and transmits it to the cyton. See diag. under neuron. [t. Gk.: m. s. *dendrītēs* of a tree]

Dendrite (def. 1a)

den-drit-ic (dĕn drĭt/ĭk), *adj.* 1. formed or marked like a dendrite. 2. of a branching form; arborescent. Also, **den-drit/i-cal.** —**den-drit/i-cal-ly,** *adv.*

dendro-, a word element meaning "tree," as in *dendrology.* [t. Gk., comb. form of *déndron*]

den-droid (dĕn/droid), *adj.* treelike; branching like a tree; arborescent. Also, **den-droi/dal.** [t. Gk.: m. s. *dendroeidēs* treelike]

den-drol-a-try (dĕn drŏl/ə trĭ), *n.* the worship of trees.

den-drol-o-gy (dĕn drŏl/ə jĭ), *n.* the part of botany that treats of trees and shrubs. —**den-dro-log-i-cal** (dĕn/drə lŏj/ə kəl), **den-drol-o-gous** (dĕn drŏl/ə gəs), *adj.* —**den-drol-o-gist** (dĕn drŏl/ə jĭst), *n.*

-dendron, a word element meaning "tree," as in *rhododendron.* [repr. Gk. *déndron* tree]

dene (dēn), *n. Brit.* a bare sandy tract or low sand hill near the sea. Also, **dean.** [ME; orig. uncert.]

Den-eb (dĕn/ĕb), *n. Astron.* a star of the first magnitude in the constellation Cygnus. [t. Ar.: m. *dhanab* tail]

den-e-ga-tion (dĕn/ə gā/shən), *n.* denial; contradiction. [t. LL: s. *dēnegātio*]

den-gue (dĕng/gā, -gĭ), *n. Pathol.* an infectious, eruptive, usually epidemic, fever of warm climates, characterized esp. by severe pains in the joints and muscles; breakbone fever. [t. Sp.; ? of African orig.]

Den-ham (dĕn/əm), *n.* **Sir John,** 1615–69, British poet, born in Ireland.

de-ni-al (dĭ nī/əl), *n.* 1. contradiction of a statement, etc. 2. refusal to believe a doctrine, etc. 3. disbelief in the existence or reality of a thing. 4. the refusal of a claim, request, etc., or of a person making a request. 5. refusal to recognize or acknowledge; a disowning or disavowal. 6. self-denial. [f. DENY + -AL³]

de-nic-o-tin-ize (dēnĭk/ə tĭ nīz/), *v.t.*, -**ized, -izing.** to remove nicotine from (tobacco).

de-ni-er¹ (dĭ nī/ər), *n.* one who denies. [ME; f. DENY + -ER¹]

de-nier² (də nĭr/; *Fr.* də nyĕ/), *n.* 1. a unit of weight used to indicate the fineness of silk, rayon, or nylon yarn. 2. an obsolete French coin varying in value with time and locality. [ME, t. OF, g. L *denārius* DENARIUS]

den-i-grate (dĕn/ə grāt/), *v.t.*, -**grated, -grating.** 1. to sully; defame. 2. to blacken. [t. L: m. s. *dēnigrātus*, pp., blackened] —**den/i-gra/tion,** *n.* —**den/i-gra/tor,** *n.*

De-ni-ker (dĕ nē kĕr/), *n.* **Joseph** (zhō zĕf/), 1852–1918, French anthropologist and naturalist.

den-im (dĕn/əm), *n.* 1. a heavy twilled cotton for overalls, playsuits, etc. 2. a similar fabric of a finer quality used to cover cushions, etc. [t. F: short for *serge de Nîmes* serge of Nimes, city in southern France]

Den-is (dĕn/ĭs; *Fr.* də nē/), *n.* **Saint,** died A.D. 280?, first bishop of Paris; patron saint of France. Also, **Denys.**

de-ni-trate (dē nī/trāt), *v.t.*, -**trated, -trating.** to free from nitric acid or nitrates; remove oxides of nitrogen from. —**de/ni-tra/tion,** *n.*

de-ni-tri-fy (dē nī/trə fī/), *v.t.*, -**fied, -fying.** to reduce (nitrates) to nitrites, ammonia, and free nitrogen, as in soil by microörganisms. —**de-ni/tri-fi-ca/tion,** *n.*

den-i-zen (dĕn/ə zən), *n.* 1. an inhabitant; resident. 2. *Brit.* an alien admitted to residence and to certain rights of citizenship in a country. 3. anything adapted to a new place, condition, etc., as a naturalized foreign word, or an animal or plant not indigenous to a place but successfully naturalized. —*v.t.* 4. to make a denizen of. [ME *deynseyn*, t. AF, m. *deinzein*, der. AF *deinz* within, g. L *de intus*]

Den-mark (dĕn/märk), *n.* a kingdom in N Europe, on Jutland peninsula and the adjacent islands. 4,439,000 pop. (est. 1955); 16,576 sq. mi. *Cap.:* Copenhagen.

Denmark Strait, a strait between Iceland and Greenland. 130 mi. wide.

Den-nis (dĕn/ĭs), *n.* **John,** 1657–1734, British critic and dramatist.

de-nom-i-nate (dĭ nŏm/ə nāt/), *v.t.*, -**nated, -nating.** to give a name to, esp. to call by a specific name. [t. L: m. s. *dēnōminātus*, pp.]

de-nom-i-na-tion (dĭ nŏm/ə nā/shən), *n.* 1. a name or designation, esp. one for a class of things. 2. a class or kind of persons or things distinguished by a specific name. 3. a religious sect. 4. act of denominating. 5. one of the grades or degrees in a series of designations of quantity, value, measure, weight, etc.: *money of small denominations.* —**de-nom/i-na/tion-al,** *adj.* —**de-nom/-i-na/tion-al-ly,** *adv.*

de-nom-i-na-tion-al-ism (dĭ nŏm/ə nā/shən ə lĭz/əm), *n.* denominational or sectarian spirit or policy; the tendency to divide into denominations or sects. —**de-nom/-i-na/tion-al-ist,** *n.*

de-nom-i-na-tive (dĭ nŏm/ə nā/tĭv, -nə tĭv), *adj.* 1. conferring or constituting a distinctive denomination or name. 2. *Gram.* (esp. of verbs) formed from a noun, as English *to man* from the noun *man.* —*n.* 3. *Gram.* a denominative verb or other word.

de-nom-i-na-tor (dĭ nŏm/ə nā/tər), *n.* 1. *Math.* that term of a fraction (usually under the line) which shows the number of equal parts into which the unit is divided; a divisor placed under a dividend. 2. one who or that which denominates or from which a name is derived.

de-no-ta-tion (dē/nō tā/shən), *n.* 1. the meaning of a term when it identifies something by naming it (distinguished from *connotation*). 2. act or fact of denoting; indication. 3. something that denotes; a mark; symbol. 4. *Logic.* a. the class of particulars to which a term is applicable. b. that which is represented by a sign.

de-no-ta-tive (dē nō/tə tĭv, dē/nō tā/tĭv), *adj.* having power to denote. —**de-no/ta-tive-ly,** *adv.*

de-note (dĭ nōt/), *v.t.*, -**noted, -noting.** 1. to be a mark or sign of; indicate: *a quick pulse often denotes fever.* 2. to be a name or designation for. 3. to represent by a symbol; stand as a symbol for. [t. F: m.s. *dénoter*, t. L: m. *dēnōtāre* mark out] —**de-not/a-ble,** *adj.*

de-noue-ment (dē/nōō mäN/), *n.* 1. the final disentangling of the intricacies of a plot, as of a drama or novel. 2. the place in the plot at which this occurs. 3. outcome; solution. Also, *French,* **dé-noue-ment** (dē-nōō mäN/). [t. F, der. *dénouer* untie, f. de- DE- + *nouer,* g. L *nōdāre* knot, tie]

de-nounce (dĭ nouns/), *v.t.*, -**nounced, -nouncing.** 1. to condemn openly; assail with censure. 2. to make formal accusation against; inform against. 3. to give formal notice of the termination of (a treaty, etc.). 4. *Archaic.* to announce or proclaim (something evil). 5. *Obs.* to portend. [ME *denounse(n),* t. OF: m. *denoncier,* g. L *dēnuntiāre* threaten] —**de-nounce/ment,** *n.* —**de-nounc/er,** *n.* —Ant. 1. praise.

de no-vo (dē nō/vō), *Latin.* from the beginning; anew.

dense (dĕns), *adj.*, **denser, densest.** 1. having the component parts closely compacted together; compact:

ăct, āble, dâre, ärt; ĕbb, ēqual; ĭf, īce; hŏt, ōver, ôrder, oil, boŏk, ōoze, out; ŭp, ūse, ûrge; ə = a in alone; ch, chief; g, give; ng, ring; sh, shoe; th, thin; ŧh, that; zh, vision. See the full key on inside cover.

a dense forest, dense population, dense style. **2.** thick-headed; obtuse; stupid. **3.** intense: *dense ignorance.* **4.** *Photog.* (of a developed negative) relatively opaque; transmitting little light. [t. L: m. s. *densus* thick, thickly set] **—dense′ly,** *adv.* **—dense′ness,** *n.*

den·si·tom·e·ter (děn′sə tŏm′ə tər), *n. Photog.* an instrument for measuring the denseness of negatives.

den·si·ty (děn′sə tĭ), *n., pl.* **-ties. 1.** state or quality of being dense; compactness; closely set or crowded condition. **2.** stupidity. **3.** *Physics.* the mass per unit of volume. **4.** *Elect.* **a.** the quantity of electricity per unit of volume at a point in space, or the quantity per unit of area at a point on a surface. **b.** current density.

dent¹ (děnt), *n.* **1.** a hollow or depression in a surface, as from a blow. **—v.t. 2.** to make a dent in or on; indent. **3.** to impress as a dent. **—v.i. 4.** to sink in, making a dent. **5.** to become indented. [ME *dente*; var. of DINT]

dent² (děnt), *n.* a toothlike projection, as a tooth of a gearwheel. [t. F, g. L *dens* tooth]

dent., 1. dentist. **2.** dentistry.

den·tal (děn′təl), *adj.* **1.** of or pertaining to the teeth. **2.** of or pertaining to dentistry. **3.** *Phonet.* **a.** with the tongue tip touching or near the upper front teeth, as French *t.* **b.** alveolar, as English alveolar *t.* **—n. 4.** *Phonet.* a dental sound. [t. ML: s. *dentālis,* der. L *dens* tooth]

den·tal·man (děn′təl mən), *n. U.S. Navy.* an enlisted man working as a dental assistant.

den·tate (děn′tāt), *adj. Bot., Zool.* having a toothed margin, or toothlike projections or processes. [t. L: m. s. *dentātus,* der. *dens* tooth] **—den′tate·ly,** *adv.*

den·ta·tion (děn tā′shən), *n. Bot., Zool.* **1.** dentate state or form. **2.** an angular projection of a margin.

denti-, a word element meaning "tooth," as in *dentiform.* Also, before vowels, **dent-** [t. L, comb. form of *dens*]

Dentate leaf

den·ti·cle (děn′tə kəl), *n.* a small tooth or toothlike part. [ME, t. L: m. s. *denticulus,* dim. of *dens* tooth]

den·tic·u·late (děn tĭk′yə lĭt, -lāt′), *adj.* **1.** *Bot., Zool.* finely dentate, as a leaf. **2.** *Archit.* having dentils. Also, **den·tic′u·lat·ed. —den·tic′u·late·ly,** *adv.*

den·tic·u·la·tion (děn tĭk′yə lā′shən), *n.* **1.** denticulate state or form. **2.** a denticle. **3.** a series of denticles.

den·ti·form (děn′tə fôrm′), *adj.* having the form of a tooth; tooth-shaped.

den·ti·frice (děn′tə frĭs), *n.* a powder, paste, or other preparation for cleaning the teeth. [t. F, t. L: m. s. *dentifricium* tooth powder. See DENTI-, FRICTION]

den·til (děn′təl, -tĭl), *n. Archit.* one of a series of small rectangular blocks arranged like a row of teeth, as in the lower part of a cornice. [t. F: m. *dentille* (obs.), fem. dim. of *dent* tooth]

den·ti·la·bi·al (děn′tə lā′bĭ əl), *adj., n.* labiodental.

den·ti·lin·gual (děn′tə lĭng′gwəl), *adj.* (of speech sounds) uttered with the tongue at the teeth, as the *th* in *thin* and *this.*

den·tin (děn′tĭn), *n. Anat.* the hard calcareous tissue beneath the enamel of the crown of the tooth and beneath the cementum of the root of the tooth. It contains less organic substance than cementum or bone and forms the greatest part of a tooth. Also, **den·tine** (děn′těn, -tĭn). [f. DENT- + -INE²] **—den′tin·al,** *adj.*

den·ti·phone (děn′tə fōn′), *n.* an instrument held against the teeth to assist hearing by transmitting sound vibrations to the auditory nerve.

den·tist (děn′tĭst), *n.* one whose profession is dentistry. [t. F: m. *dentiste,* der. *dent* tooth]

den·tist·ry (děn′tĭs trĭ), *n.* the science or art dealing with the prevention and treatment of oral disease, esp. in relation to the health of the body as a whole, and including such operations as the filling and crowning of teeth, the construction of artificial dentures, etc.

den·ti·tion (děn tĭsh′ən), *n.* the kind, number, and arrangement of the teeth of an animal, including man. [t. L: s. *dentītio* teething]

D'En·tre·cas·teaux Islands (dän trə kȧs tō′), a group of British islands in the Pacific, E of New Guinea.

den·ture (děn′chər), *n.* an artificial restoration of several teeth (**partial denture**) or of all the teeth of either jaw (**full denture**). [t. F, der. *dent* tooth]

den·u·date (v. děn′yŏŏ dāt′, dĭ nū′dāt, -nŏŏ′-; *adj.* dĭ nū′dāt -nŏŏ′-, děn′yŏŏ dāt′), v., **-dated, -dating,** *adj.* **—v.t. 1.** to denude. **—adj. 2.** denuded; bare.

den·u·da·tion (děn′yŏŏ dā′shən, dĭ nyŏŏ′-, -nŏŏ′-), *n.* **1.** act of denuding. **2.** denuded or bare condition. **3.** *Geol.* the laying bare of rock by erosive processes.

de·nude (dĭ nūd′, -nŏŏd′), v.t., **-nuded, -nuding. 1.** to make naked or bare; strip. **2.** *Geol.* to subject to denudation. [t. L: m. s. *dēnūdāre* lay bare]

de·nun·ci·ate (dĭ nŭn′sĭ āt′, -shĭ āt′), v.t., v.i., **-ated, -ating.** to denounce; condemn openly. [t. L: m. s. *dēnuntiātus,* pp.] **—de·nun′ci·a′tor,** *n.*

de·nun·ci·a·tion (dĭ nŭn′sĭ ā′shən, -shĭ-), *n.* **1.** a denouncing as evil; open and vehement condemnation. **2.** an accusation of crime before a public prosecutor or tribunal. **3.** notice of the termination of an international agreement or part thereof. **4.** announcement of impending evil; threat; warning.

de·nun·ci·a·to·ry (dĭ nŭn′sĭ ə tôr′ĭ, -shĭ-), *adj.* char-

acterized by or given to denunciation. Also, **de·nun·ci·a·tive** (dĭ nŭn′sĭ ā′tĭv, -shĭ-).

Den·ver (děn′vər), *n.* the capital of Colorado, in the central part. 493,887 (1960).

de·ny (dĭ nī′), v.t., **-nied, -nying. 1.** to assert the negative of; declare not to be true: *I deny the charge, I deny he has done it.* **2.** to refuse to believe (a doctrine, etc.); reject as false or erroneous. **3.** to refuse to grant (a claim, request, etc.): *he denied me this, I was denied this.* **4.** to refuse to recognize or acknowledge; disown; disavow; repudiate. **5.** to refuse access to (one visited). **6.** *Obs.* to refuse to accept. **7.** *Obs.* to refuse (to do something). **8. deny oneself,** to exercise self-denial. [ME *denye(n),* t. F: m. *dénier,* g. L *dēnegāre*] **—Syn. 1.** dispute, controvert, oppose, gainsay. DENY, CONTRADICT both imply objecting to or arguing against something. To DENY is to say that something is not true, or that it would not hold in practice: *to deny an allegation.* To CONTRADICT is to declare that the contrary is true: *to contradict a statement.* **—Ant. 1.** admit. **2.** accept. **3.** allow.

Den·ys (děn′ĭs; *Fr.* da nē′), *n.* Saint. See Denis.

de·o·dand (dē′ə dănd′), *n. Eng. Law.* (formerly) an animal or article which, having been the immediate occasion of the death of a human being, was forfeited to the crown to be applied to pious uses. [t. ML: s. *deōdandum* a thing to be given to God, f. L: dat. of *deus* god + neut. gerundive of *dare* give]

de·o·dar (dē′ə där′), *n.* a species of cedar, *Cedrus deodara,* a large Himalayan tree valued for its beauty and for its durable wood. [t. Hind., g. Skt. *devadāra* wood of the gods]

de·o·dor·ant (dē ō′dər ənt), *n.* **1.** an agent for destroying odors. **—adj. 2.** capable of destroying odors.

de·o·dor·ize (dē ō′də rīz′), v.t., **-ized, -izing.** to deprive of odor, esp. of the fetid odor arising from impurities. **—de·o′dor·i·za′tion,** *n.* **—de·o′dor·iz′er,** *n.*

De·o fa·ven·te (dē′ō fȧ věn′tĭ), *Latin.* God favoring (befriending; protecting).

De·o gra·ti·as (dē′ō grä′shĭ ăs), *Latin.* thanks be to God.

De·o ju·van·te (dē′ō jŏŏ văn′tĭ), *Latin.* God helping; if God gives aid.

de·on·tol·o·gy (dē′ŏn tŏl′ə jĭ), *n.* the science of duty or moral obligation; ethics. [f. Gk.: s. *dĕon* that which is binding or needful (prop. ppr. neut. of *dein* bind) + -(O)LOGY] **—de·on·to·log·i·cal** (dĭ ŏn′tə lŏj′ə kəl), *adj.* **—de′on·tol′o·gist,** *n.*

De·o vo·len·te (dē′ō vō lěn′tĭ), *Latin.* God willing (it); if God wills it.

de·ox·i·dize (dē ŏk′sə dīz′), v.t., **-dized, -dizing.** to remove oxygen from; reduce from the state of an oxide. **—de·ox′i·di·za′tion,** *n.* **—de·ox′i·diz′er,** *n.*

de·ox·y·gen·ate (dē ŏk′sə jə nāt′), v.t., **-ated, -ating.** to remove oxygen from. **—de·ox′y·gen·a′tion,** *n.*

de·ox·y·gen·ize (dē ŏk′sə jə nīz′), v.t., **-ized, -izing.** to deoxygenate.

dep., 1. department. **2.** departs. **3.** deponent. **4.** deputy.

de·part (dĭ pärt′), v.i. **1.** to go away, as from a place; take one's leave. **2.** to turn aside or away; diverge; deviate (fol. by *from*). **3.** to pass away, as from life or existence. **—v.i. 4.** to go away from or leave: *rare, except* in *to depart this life.* **—n. 5.** *Obs.* departure; death. [ME *departe(n),* t. OF: m. *departir,* f. *de-* DE- + *partir* leave (g. L *partīre*)] **—Syn. 1.** DEPART, RETIRE, RETREAT, WITHDRAW imply leaving a place. DEPART is a somewhat literary word, implying going away from a definite place: *to depart on a journey.* RETIRE emphasizes the reason or purpose for absenting oneself or drawing back from a place: *to retire from a position* (in battle). RETREAT implies a necessary withdrawal, esp. as a result of adverse fortune in war: *to retreat to secondary lines of defense.* WITHDRAW suggests leaving some specific place or situation, usually for some definite and often unpleasant reason: *to withdraw from a hopeless task.* **—Ant. 1.** arrive.

de·part·ed (dĭ pär′tĭd), *adj.* **1.** deceased; dead. **2.** gone; past. **—n. 3. the departed, a.** the dead person. **b.** the dead collectively.

de·part·ment (dĭ pärt′mənt), *n.* **1.** a distinct part of anything arranged in divisions; a division of a complex whole or organized system. **2.** a division of official business or duties or functions. **3.** one of the (large) districts into which a country, as France, is divided for administrative purposes. **4.** one of the principal branches of a governmental organization. **5.** one of the sections of a school or college dealing with a particular field of knowledge: *the department of English.* **6.** *Mil.* **a.** a permanent military area, corresponding to the limits of a territory: *the Hawaiian department.* **b.** (formerly) one of the large geographical divisions of the United States as divided for military purposes. **—de·part·men·tal** (dē′pärt měn′təl), *adj.* **—de′part·men′tal·ly,** *adv.*

department store, a large retail store handling several lines of goods, including dry goods, women's wear, etc., and organized in separate departments.

de·par·ture (dĭ pär′chər), *n.* **1.** a going away; a setting out or starting. **2.** divergence or deviation. **3.** *Naut.* **a.** the distance due east or west made by a ship when sailing on any course. **b.** the bearing or position of a point from which a vessel commences dead reckoning. **4.** *Archaic.* decease or death.

de·pas·ture (dē păs′chər, -päs′-), v., **-tured, -turing. —v.t. 1.** to consume the produce of (land) as pasture. **2.** to pasture (cattle). **—v.i. 3.** to graze.

b., blend of, blended of; **c.,** cognate with; **d.,** dialect, dialectal; **der.,** derived from; **f.,** formed from; **g.,** going back to; **m.,** modification of; **r.,** replacing; **s.,** stem of; **t.,** taken from; **?,** perhaps. See the full key on inside cover.

de·pend (dĭ pĕnd′), *v.i.* **1.** to rely; trust: *you may depend on the accuracy of the report.* **2.** to rely for support, maintenance, help, etc.: *children depend on their parents.* **3.** to be conditioned or contingent: *it depends upon himself, his efforts, his knowledge.* **4.** *Gram.* (of a word or other linguistic form) to be subordinate (to another linguistic form in the same construction). **5.** to hang down; be suspended. **6.** to be undetermined or pending. [ME *depend(en)*, t. OF: m. *dependre*, t. L: m. *dēpendere* hang upon]

de·pend·a·ble (dĭ pĕn′də bəl), *adj.* that may be depended on; reliable; trustworthy. —**de·pend′a·bil′i·ty, de·pend′a·ble·ness,** *n.* —**de·pend′a·bly,** *adv.*

de·pend·ence (dĭ pĕn′dəns), *n.* **1.** state of depending for aid, support, etc. **2.** reliance; confidence; trust. **3.** state of being conditional or contingent on something; natural or logical sequence. **4.** subordination or subjection: *the dependence of the church upon the state.* **5.** an object of reliance or trust. **6.** the condition, as of a lawsuit, of awaiting settlement. Also, **de·pend′ance.**

de·pend·en·cy (dĭ pĕn′dən sĭ), *n., pl.* **-cies. 1.** state of being dependent; dependence. **2.** something dependent or subordinate; an appurtenance. **3.** an outbuilding or annex. **4.** a subject territory which is not an integral part of the ruling country. Also, **de·pend′an·cy.**

de·pend·ent (dĭ pĕn′dənt), *adj.* **1.** depending on something else for aid, support, etc. **2.** conditioned; contingent. **3.** subordinate; subject. **4.** (of linguistic forms) not used in isolation; used only in connection with other forms. **5.** hanging down; pendent. —*n.* **6.** one who depends on or looks to another for support, favor, etc. **7.** *Obs.* a subordinate part. Also, **de·pend′ant.**

De·pew (də pū′), *n.* **Chauncey Mitchell** (chôn′sĭ, chăn′sĭ), 1834–1928, U.S. lawyer and politician.

de·phlo·gis·ti·cat·ed (dē′flə jĭs′tə kā′tĭd), *adj. Obs.* lacking phlogiston.

de·pict (dĭ pĭkt′), *v.t.* **1.** to represent by or as by painting; portray; delineate. **2.** to represent in words; describe. [t. L: s. *dēpictus,* pp., portrayed] —**de·pict′er,** *n.* —**de·pic′tion,** *n.*
—**Syn. 1, 2. DEPICT, PORTRAY, SKETCH** imply an actual reproduction of an object or scene by colors or lines, or by words. **DEPICT** emphasizes vividness of detail: *to depict the confusion of departure.* **PORTRAY** emphasizes faithful representation: *could not portray the anguish of the exiles.* **SKETCH** suggests a drawing in which only the outlines of the most prominent features or fundamental facts are given, often in a preparatory way: *to sketch a scene so that it can later be painted, to sketch the plans for a community development.*

de·pic·ture (dĭ pĭk′chər), *v.t.,* -tured, -turing. to picture; depict.

dep·i·late (dĕp′ə lāt′), *v.t.,* -lated, -lating. to remove the hair from. [t. L: m. s. *dēpilātus,* pp.] —**dep′i·la′tion,** *n.*

de·pil·a·to·ry (dĭ pĭl′ə tôr′ĭ), *adj., n., pl.* -ries. —*adj.* **1.** capable of removing hair. —*n.* **2.** a depilatory agent.

de pla·no (dē plā′nō), *Latin.* **1.** without argument. **2.** by manifest right; plainly. **3.** *Law.* out of court.

de·plete (dĭ plēt′), *v.t.,* -pleted, -pleting. **1.** to deprive of that which fills; decrease the fullness of; reduce the stock or amount of. **2.** *Med.* to empty or relieve (overcharged vessels, etc.), as by bloodletting or purging. [t. L: m. s. *dēplētus,* pp., emptied out] —**de·ple′tion,** *n.* —**de·ple′tive, de·ple·to·ry** (dĭ plē′tə rĭ), *adj.*

de·plor·a·ble (dĭ plôr′ə bəl), *adj.* **1.** lamentable. **2.** sad; calamitous; grievous; wretched. —**de·plor′a·ble·ness, de·plor·a·bil′i·ty,** *n.* —**de·plor′a·bly,** *adv.*

de·plore (dĭ plôr′), *v.t.,* -plored, -ploring. to feel or express deep grief for or in regard to; regret deeply. [t. L: m. s. *dēplōrāre* bewail] —**de·plor′er,** *n.* —**de·plor′ing·ly,** *adv.* —**Syn.** lament, bemoan, bewail.

de·ploy (dĭ ploi′), *Mil.* —*v.t.* **1.** to spread out (troops or military units) and form an extended front. —*v.i.* **2.** to spread out with extended front. [t. F: s. *déployer,* f. *dé*- DIS-¹ + *ployer,* g. L *plicāre* fold] —**de·ploy′ment,** *n.*

de·plume (dē plōōm′), *v.t.,* -plumed, -pluming. **1.** to deprive of feathers; pluck. **2.** to strip of honor, w alth, etc. [t. F: m.s. *déplumer,* der. *dé*- DIS-¹ + *plume* (g. L *plūma* feather)] —**de·plu·ma′tion,** *n.*

de·po·lar·ize (dē pō′lə rīz′), *v.t.,* -ized, -izing. to deprive of polarity or polarization. —**de·po′lar·i·za′tion,** *n.* —**de·po′lar·iz′er,** *n.*

de·pone (dĭ pōn′), *v.t.,v.i.,* -poned, -poning. to testify under oath; depose. [t. L: m. s. *dēpōnere* put away or down, ML testify. See DEPOSIT]

de·po·nent (dĭ pō′nənt), *adj.* **1.** *Gk.* and *Lat. Gram.* (of a verb) appearing only in the passive (or Greek middle) voice forms, but with active meaning. —*n.* **2.** *Law.* one who testifies under oath, esp. in writing. **3.** *Gk.* and *Lat. Gram.* a deponent verb: *a Latin form such as loqui is a deponent.* [t. L: s. *dēpōnens,* ppr., laying aside, depositing, ML testifying]

de·pop·u·late (*v.* dē pŏp′yə lāt′; *adj.* dē pŏp′yə lĭt, -lāt′), *v.,* -lated, -lating, *adj.* —*v.t.* **1.** to deprive of inhabitants, wholly or in part, as by destruction or expulsion. —*adj.* **2.** *Archaic.* depopulated. [t. L: m. s. *dēpopulātus,* pp., having laid waste] —**de·pop′u·la′tion,** *n.* —**de·pop′u·la′tor,** *n.*

de·port (dĭ pôrt′), *v.t.* **1.** to transport forcibly, as to a penal colony or a place of exile. **2.** to bear, conduct, or behave (oneself) in a particular manner. —*n.* **3.** *Obs.* deportment. [t. F: s. *déporter,* g. L *dēportāre* carry away, transport, banish oneself]

de·por·ta·tion (dē′pôr tā′shən), *n. Law.* an expulsion of undesired aliens and other persons from a state.

de·por·tee (dē′pôr tē′), *n.* **1.** one who is deported, as from a country. **2.** a person awaiting deportation. [f. DEPORT, v. + -EE]

de·port·ment (dĭ pôrt′mənt), *n.* demeanor; conduct; behavior. —**Syn.** see **behavior.**

de·pos·al (dĭ pō′zəl), *n.* deposition, as from office.

de·pose (dĭ pōz′), *v.,* -posed, -posing. —*v.t.* **1.** to remove from office or position, esp. high office. **2.** to declare or testify, esp. under oath, usually in writing. —*v.i.* **3.** to bear witness; give sworn testimony, esp. in writing. [ME *depose(n),* t. OF: m. *deposer* put down, f. *de*- DE- + *poser* POSE¹] —**de·pos′a·ble,** *adj.* —**de·pos′er,** *n.*

de·pos·it (dĭ pŏz′ĭt), *v.t.* **1.** to put or lay down; place; put. **2.** to throw down or precipitate: *soil deposited by a river.* **3.** to place for safekeeping or in trust. **4.** to give as security or in part payment. —*n.* **5.** anything laid or thrown down, as matter precipitated from a fluid; sediment. **6.** a coating of metal deposited by an electric current. **7.** an accumulation, or occurrence, of ore, oil, etc., of any form or nature. **8.** anything laid away or entrusted to another for safekeeping. **9.** money placed in a bank. **10.** anything given as security or in part payment. **11.** a depository (def. 1). [t. L: s. *dēpositus,* pp., put away or down, deposited, ML testified. See DEPONE] —**Syn. 5.** precipitate, deposition.

de·pos·i·tar·y (dĭ pŏz′ə tĕr′ĭ), *n., pl.* -taries. **1.** one to whom anything is given in trust. **2.** a depository.

dep·o·si·tion (dĕp′ə zĭsh′ən, dē′pə-), *n.* **1.** removal from an office or position. **2.** act of depositing. **3.** that which is deposited. **4.** *Law.* **a.** the giving of testimony under oath. **b.** the testimony so given. **c.** a statement under oath, taken down in writing, to be used in court in place of the production of the witness.

de·pos·i·tor (dĭ pŏz′ə tər), *n.* **1.** one who or that which deposits. **2.** one who deposits money in a bank.

de·pos·i·to·ry (dĭ pŏz′ə tôr′ĭ), *n., pl.* -ries. **1.** a place where anything is deposited or stored for safekeeping; a storehouse. **2.** a depositary; trustee.

de·pot (dē′pō; *Mil.* or *Brit.* dĕp′ō), *n.* **1.** *U.S.* a railroad station. **2.** *Mil.* **a.** a place to which supplies and materials are shipped and stored for distribution. **b.** (formerly) a place where recruits receive their first training. **3.** *Chiefly Brit.* a depository; storehouse. [t. F, g. L *dēpositum* DEPOSIT, n.] —**Syn. 1.** See **station.**

de·prave (dĭ prāv′), *v.t.,* -praved, -praving. **1.** to make bad or worse; vitiate; corrupt. **2.** *Obs.* to defame. [ME *deprave(n),* t. L: m. *dēprāvāre* pervert] —**dep·ra·va·tion** (dĕp′rə vā′shən), *n.* —**de·prav′er,** *n.*

de·praved (dĭ prāvd′), *adj.* corrupt or perverted, esp. morally; wicked. —**Syn.** See **immoral.**

de·prav·i·ty (dĭ prăv′ə tĭ), *n., pl.* -ties. **1.** state of being depraved. **2.** a depraved act or practice.

dep·re·cate (dĕp′rə kāt′), *v.t.,* -cated, -cating. **1.** to express earnest disapproval of; urge reasons against; protest against (a scheme, purpose, etc.). **2.** *Archaic.* to pray for deliverance from. [t. L: m. s. *dēprecātus,* pp., having prayed against] —**dep′re·cat′ing·ly,** *adv.* —**dep′re·ca′tion,** *n.* —**dep′re·ca′tor,** *n.*

dep·re·ca·tive (dĕp′rə kā′tĭv), *adj.* deprecatory. —**dep′re·ca′tive·ly,** *adv.*

dep·re·ca·to·ry (dĕp′rə kə tôr′ĭ), *adj.* of the nature of deprecation; expressing deprecation. —**dep′re·ca·to′ri·ly,** *adv.*

de·pre·ci·ate (dĭ prē′shĭ āt′), *v.,* -ated, -ating. —*v.t.* **1.** to reduce the purchasing value of (money). **2.** to lessen the value of. **3.** to represent as of little value or merit; belittle. —*v.i.* **4.** to decline in value. [t. LL: m. s. *dēpretiātus* (ML *dēpreciātus*) undervalued] —**de·pre′ci·at′ing·ly,** *adv.* —**de·pre′ci·a′tor,** *n.*

de·pre·ci·a·tion (dĭ prē′shĭ ā′shən), *n.* **1.** decrease in value due to wear and tear, decay, decline in price, etc. **2.** a decrease in the purchasing or exchange value of money. **3.** a lowering in estimation; disparagement.

de·pre·ci·a·to·ry (dĭ prē′shĭ ə tôr′ĭ), *adj.* tending to depreciate. Also, **de·pre·ci·a·tive** (dĭ prē′shĭ ā′tĭv).

dep·re·date (dĕp′rə dāt′), *v.,* -dated, -dating. —*v.t.* **1.** to prey upon; plunder; lay waste. —*v.i.* **2.** to prey; make depredations. [t. L: m. s. *dēpraedātus,* pp., having pillaged] —**dep′re·da′tor,** *n.* —**dep·re·da·to·ry** (dĕp′rə dā′tə rĭ, dĭ prĕd′ə tôr′ĭ), *adj.*

dep·re·da·tion (dĕp′rə dā′shən), *n.* a preying upon or plundering; robbery; ravage.

de·press (dĭ prĕs′), *v.t.* **1.** to lower in spirits; deject; dispirit. **2.** to lower in force, vigor, etc.; weaken; make dull. **3.** to lower in amount or value. **4.** to put into a lower position: *to depress the muzzle of a gun.* **5.** to press down. **6.** *Music.* to lower in pitch. [ME *depresse(n),* t. OF: m. *depresser,* der. L *dēpressus,* pp., pressed down] —**de·press′i·ble,** *adj.* —**de·press′ing·ly,** *adv.* —**Syn. 1.** See **oppress.** —**Ant. 4.** raise, elevate.

de·pres·sant (dĭ prĕs′ənt), *Med.* —*adj.* **1.** having the quality of depressing or lowering the vital activities; sedative. —*n.* **2.** a sedative.

de·pressed (dĭ prĕst′), *adj.* **1.** dejected; downcast. **2.** pressed down; lower than the general surface. **3.** lowered in force, amount, etc. **4.** *Bot., Zool.* flattened down; broader than high. —**Syn. 1.** See **sad.**

depressed area, *Brit.* a region where unemployment and a low standard of living prevail.

de·pres·sion (dĭ·prĕsh/ən), n. 1. act of depressing. 2. state of being depressed. 3. a depressed or sunken place or part; a hollow. 4. dejection of spirits. 5. *Psychiatry.* a morbid condition of emotional dejection and withdrawal; sadness greater and more prolonged than that warranted by any objective reason. 6. dullness or inactivity, as of trade. 7. period during which there is a decline in business. 8. *Pathol.* a low state of vital powers or functional activity. 9. *Astron., etc.* angular distance below the horizon. 10. *Survey.* the angle between the line from an observer to an object below him and a horizontal line. 11. *Meteorol.* an area of low atmospheric pressure. [ME, t. L: s. *dēpressio*] —**Syn.** 4. discouragement, despondency, gloom.

de·pres·sive (dĭ·prĕs/ĭv), adj. 1. tending to depress. 2. characterized by depression, esp. mental depression. —**de·pres/sive·ly,** adv. —**de·pres/sive·ness,** n.

de·pres·so·mo·tor (dĭ·prĕs/ō·mō/tər), adj. *Physiol., Med.* causing a retardation of motor activity: *depressomotor nerves.*

de·pres·sor (dĭ·prĕs/ər), n. 1. one who or that which depresses. 2. *Physiol., Anat.* a. a muscle that draws down a part. b. Also, **depressor nerve.** a nerve from the aorta to the centers controlling heart rate and blood pressure. 3. *Surg.* an instrument for pressing down a protruding part.

dep·ri·va·tion (dĕp/rə·vā/shən), n. 1. act of depriving. 2. fact of being deprived. 3. dispossession; loss. Also, **de·priv·al** (dĭ·prī/vəl).

de·prive (dĭ·prīv/), v.t., **-prived, -priving.** 1. to divest of something possessed or enjoyed; dispossess; strip; bereave. 2. to keep (a person, etc.) from possessing or enjoying something withheld. [ME *deprive(n),* t. OF: m. *depriver,* der. *priver,* g. L *prīvāre* deprive] —**de·priv/a·ble,** adj. —**de·priv/er,** n. —**Syn.** 1. See strip[1].

de pro·fun·dis (dē prō·fŭn/dĭs), *Latin.* out of the depths (of sorrow, despair, etc.).

dep·side (dĕp/sīd, -sĭd), n. *Chem.* any of a group of esters formed from two or more phenol carboxylic acid molecules. [f. s. Gk. *dēpsein* tan + -IDE]

dept., department.

Dept·ford (dĕt/fərd), n. a SE borough of London, England. 75,694 (1951).

depth (dĕpth), n. 1. measure or distance downward, inward, or backward. 2. deepness, as of water, suited to or safe for a person or thing. 3. abstruseness, as of a subject. 4. gravity; seriousness. 5. emotional profundity: *depth of woe.* 6. intensity, as of silence, color, etc. 7. lowness of pitch. 8. intellectual penetration, sagacity, or profundity. 9. a deep part or place, as of the sea. 10. an unfathomable space, or abyss. 11. the remotest or extreme part, as of space. 12. a deep or underlying region, as of feeling. 13. the part of greatest intensity, as of night or winter. [ME *depth(e),* f. dep- (OE *dēop* depth) + -TH[1]] —**Ant.** 2. shallowness. 8. superficiality.

depth bomb, a depth charge, esp. when dropped from an airplane.

depth charge, a bomb dropped or thrown into the water from a ship or airplane and which explodes on reaching a certain depth, used to destroy submarines, etc.

dep·u·rate (dĕp/yə·rāt/), v.t., v.i., **-rated, -rating.** to make or become free from impurities; purify; cleanse. [t. ML: m. s. *dēpūrātus,* pp.] —**dep/u·ra/tion,** n. —**dep/u·ra/tor,** n.

dep·u·ra·tive (dĕp/yə·rā/tĭv), adj. 1. serving to depurate; purifying. —n. 2. a depurative agent or substance.

dep·u·ta·tion (dĕp/yə·tā/shən), n. 1. appointment to represent or act for another or others. 2. the person or (usually) body of persons so appointed or authorized. Cf. *U.S.* **delegation** (def. 3).

de·pute (dĭ·pūt/), v.t., **-puted, -puting.** 1. to appoint as one's substitute or agent. 2. to assign (a charge, etc.) to a deputy. [ME *depute(n),* t. OF: m. *deputer,* t. LL: m. *dēputāre* destine, allot, in L count as, reckon]

dep·u·tize (dĕp/yə·tīz/), v., **-tized, -tizing.** —v.t. 1. to appoint as deputy. —v.i. 2. *Colloq.* to act as a deputy.

dep·u·ty (dĕp/yə·tĭ), n., pl. **-ties,** adj. —n. 1. a person appointed or authorized to act for another or others. 2. a person appointed or elected as assistant to a public official, serving as successor in the event of a vacancy. 3. a person representing a constituency in any of certain legislative bodies, as in the French Chamber of Deputies. —adj. 4. acting as deputy for another. [ME *depute,* t. OF, prop. pp. of *deputer* DEPUTE]

De Quin·cey (dĭ kwĭn/sĭ), Thomas, 1785-1859, British essayist.

der., 1. derivation. 2. derivative. 3. derived.

de·rac·in·ate (dĭ·răs/ə·nāt/), v.t., **-nated, -nating.** to pull up by the roots; uproot; extirpate; eradicate. [f. s. F *déraciner* (der. *dé-* DIS-[1] + *racine,* der. L *rādix* root) + -ATE[1]] —**de·rac/i·na/tion,** n.

de·raign (dĭ·rān/), v.t. 1. *Law.* a. to dispute or contest (a claim, etc., of another). b. to maintain or vindicate a claim to (something). 2. *Hist.* to dispose troops for (battle). [ME *dereyne(n),* t. OF: m. *deraisnier* render an account, f. de- DE- + *raisnier* discourse, der. *raison,* g. L *ratio* reckoning. Cf. ARRAIGN] —**de·raign/ment,** n.

de·rail (dē·rāl/), v.t. 1. to cause (a train, etc.) to run off the rails. —v.i. 2. (of a train, etc.) to run off the rails of a track. [t. F: m. *dérailler,* der. *dé-* DIS-[1] + *rail* rail, t. E. See RAIL[1]] —**de·rail/ment,** n.

De·rain (də·răN/), n. **André** (äN·drā/), 1880-1954. French painter.

de·range (dĭ·rānj/), v.t., **-ranged, -ranging.** 1. to throw into disorder; disarrange. 2. to disturb the condition, action, or functions of. 3. to unsettle the reason of; make insane. [t. F: m. s. *déranger,* OF *desrengier,* f. *des-* DIS-[1] + *rengier* RANGE, v.]

de·ranged (dĭ·rānjd/), adj. 1. disordered. 2. insane.

de·range·ment (dĭ·rānj/mənt), n. 1. act of deranging. 2. disarrangement; disorder. 3. mental disorder; insanity.

de·ray (dĭ·rā/), n. *Archaic or Dial.* disorderly merrymaking. [ME *derai,* t. OF: m. *desrei,* der. *desreer* put out of order, der. des- DIS-[1] + *rei* order. Cf. ARRAY, v.]

Der·bent (dĕr·bĕnt/), n. a seaport in the SE Soviet Union in Europe, on the Caspian Sea. 35,000 (est. 1948).

Der·by (dûr/bĭ; *Brit.* där/bĭ), n., pl. **-bies.** 1. a horse race in the United States, founded in 1875, run annually at Churchill Downs, Kentucky. 2. a horse race in England, founded 1780, run annually at Epsom Downs, near London. 3. some other important race, of horses, airplanes, foot runners, etc. 4. (*l.c.*) a stiff felt hat with rounded crown and narrow brim, worn chiefly by men. Cf. *Brit.* **bowler.**

Der·by (dûr/bĭ; *Brit.* där/bĭ), n. 1. a city in central England: the county seat of Derbyshire. 137,500 (est. 1956). 2. Derbyshire.

Der·by·shire (dûr/bĭ·shĭr/, -shər; *Brit.* där/bĭ-), n. a county in central England. 826,437 pop. (1951); 1006 sq. mi. *Co. seat:* Derby. Also, **Derby.**

dere (dĭr), adj. dear[2].

de rè·gle (də rĕ/gl), *French.* according to rule; following a pattern, principle, or law.

der·e·lict (dĕr/ə·lĭkt), adj. 1. left or abandoned, as by the owner or guardian (said esp. of a ship abandoned at sea). 2. neglectful of duty; delinquent; unfaithful. —n. 3. personal property abandoned or thrown away by the owner. 4. a ship abandoned at sea. 5. a person forsaken or abandoned, esp. by society. 6. one guilty of neglect of duty. 7. *Law.* land left dry by a change of the water line. [t. L: s. *dērelictus,* pp., forsaken utterly]

der·e·lic·tion (dĕr/ə·lĭk/shən), n. 1. culpable neglect, as of duty; delinquency; fault. 2. act of abandoning. 3. state of being abandoned. 4. *Law.* a. a leaving dry of land by recession of the water line. b. the land thus left dry. —**Syn.** 1. See neglect.

de·req·ui·si·tion (dē/rĕk/wə·zĭsh/ən), *Brit.* —n. 1. the return from military to civilian control. —v.t., v.i. 2. to return to civilian control.

de re·rum na·tu·ra (dē rĭr/əm nə·tyŏŏr/ə, -tŏŏr/ə), *Latin.* on the nature of things.

de·ride (dĭ·rīd/), v.t., **-rided, -riding.** to laugh at in contempt; scoff or jeer at; mock. [t. L: m. s. *dērīdēre* laugh] —**de·rid/er,** n. —**de·rid/ing·ly,** adv. —**Syn.** taunt, flout, gibe, banter, rally. See ridicule.

de ri·gueur (də rē·gœr/), *French.* strictly required, as by etiquette or usage.

de·ris·i·ble (dĭ·rĭz/ə·bəl), adj. subject to or worthy of derision.

de·ri·sion (dĭ·rĭzh/ən), n. 1. act of deriding; ridicule; mockery. 2. an object of ridicule. [t. L: s. *dērisio*]

de·ri·sive (dĭ·rī/sĭv), adj. characterized by derision; ridiculing; mocking. Also, **de·ri·so·ry** (dĭ·rī/sə·rĭ). —**de·ri/sive·ly,** adv. —**de·ri/sive·ness,** n.

deriv. 1. derivation. 2. derivative.

der·i·va·tion (dĕr/ə·vā/shən), n. 1. act of deriving. 2. fact of being derived. 3. origination or origin. 4. *Math.* (of a theorem) a. development. b. differentiation. 5. *Gram.* a. the process of composing new words by the addition of prefixes or suffixes to already existing root words, as *atomic* from *atom, hardness* from *hard.* b. the systematic description of such processes in a particular language, as contrasted with *inflection* which consists of adding prefixes, infixes, or suffixes to make a different form of the same word: *hardness* is an example of derivation; *harder* of inflection. c. such processes collectively or in general. —**der/i·va/tion·al,** adj.

de·riv·a·tive (dĭ·rĭv/ə·tĭv), adj. 1. derived. 2. not original or primitive; secondary. —n. 3. something derived or derivative. 4. *Gram.* a form derived from another: *atomic* is a derivative of *atom.* 5. *Chem.* a substance or compound obtained from, or regarded as derived from, another substance or compound. 6. *Math.* the limit of the ratio of the increment of a function to the increment of a variable in it, as the latter becomes 0. —**de·riv/a·tive·ly,** adv.

de·rive (dĭ·rīv/), v., **-rived, -riving.** —v.t. 1. to receive or obtain from a source or origin (fol. by *from*). 2. to trace, as from a source or origin. 3. to obtain by reasoning; deduce. 4. *Chem.* to produce (a compound) from another compound by replacement of elements or radicals. 5. *Obs.* to bring or direct (fol. by *to, on, upon,* etc.). —v.i. 6. to come from a source; originate. [t. F: m.s. *dériver,* t. L: m. *dērīvāre* lead off] —**de·riv/a·ble,** adj. —**de·riv/er,** n.

derived unit, *Physics, etc.* any unit derived from primary units of length, time, mass, etc.

-derm, a word element meaning "skin," as in *endoderm.* [t. Gk.: s. *-dermos,* etc., having skin, skinned]

der·ma (dûr/mə), n. *Anat., Zool.* 1. the corium or true skin, beneath the epidermis. 2. the skin in general. [NL, t. Gk.: skin] —**der/mal,** adj.

der·ma·ti·tis (dûr′mə tī′tĭs), *n.* *Pathol.* inflammation of the skin.

dermato-, a word element meaning "skin," as in *dermatology.* Also, **derm-, dermat-, dermo-**. [t. Gk., comb. form of *dérma*]

der·mat·o·gen (dər mǎt′ə jən, dûr′mə tō′jən), *n.* *Bot.* a thin layer of meristem in embryos and growing ends of stems and roots, which gives rise to the epidermis.

der·ma·toid (dûr′mə toid′), *adj.* resembling skin; skinlike.

der·ma·tol·o·gy (dûr′mə tŏl′ə jĭ), *n.* the science of the skin and its diseases. —**der·ma·to·log·i·cal** (dûr′mə tə lŏj′ə kəl), *adj.* —**der′ma·tol′o·gist,** *n.*

der·ma·to·phyte (dûr′mə tō fīt′), *n.* *Pathol.*, *Vet. Sci.* any fungus parasitic on the skin and causing a skin disease, as ringworm.

der·ma·to·plas·ty (dûr′mə tō plăs′tĭ), *n.* plastic surgery of the skin. See **skin grafting.**

der·mis (dûr′mĭs), *n.* *Anat.,* *Zool.* derma. [NL; abstracted from EPIDERMIS] —**der′mic,** *adj.*

der·moid (dûr′moid), *adj.* skinlike; dermatoid.

der·ni·er (dûr′nĭ ər; *Fr.* děr nyĕ′), *adj.* last; final; ultimate. [t. F]

der·nier cri (děr nyĕ krē′), *French.* 1. the latest word. 2. the latest fashion.

der·o·gate (*v.* děr′ə gāt′; *adj.* děr′ə gĭt, -gāt′), *v.,* **-gated, -gating,** *adj.* —*v.i.* 1. to detract, as from authority, estimation, etc. (fol. by *from*). 2. to fall away in character or conduct; degenerate (fol. by *from*). —*v.t.* 3. *Archaic.* to take away (something) from a thing so as to impair it. —*adj.* 4. *Obs.* or *Archaic.* debased. [t. L: m. s. *dērogātus,* pp., repealed, taken or detracted from] —**der′o·ga′tion,** *n.*

de·rog·a·tive (dĭ rŏg′ə tĭv), *adj.* lessening; belittling; derogatory. —**de·rog′a·tive·ly,** *adv.*

de·rog·a·to·ry (dĭ rŏg′ə tōr′ĭ), *adj.* tending to derogate or detract, as from authority or estimation; disparaging; depreciatory. —**de·rog′a·to′ri·ly,** *adv.* —**de·rog′a·to′ri·ness,** *n.*

der·rick (děr′ĭk), *n.* 1. any of various devices for lifting and moving heavy weights. 2. the towerlike framework over an oil well or the like. [named after *Derrick,* a hangman at Tyburn, London, about 1600]

der·ring-do (děr′ĭng dōō′), *n.* *Pseudoarchaic.* daring deeds; heroic daring. [ME *dorryng don* daring to do; erroneously taken as n. phrase by Spenser]

der·rin·ger (děr′ĭn jər), *n.* *U.S.* a short-barreled pistol of large caliber. [named after the inventor]

der·ris (děr′ĭs), *n.* an East Indian leguminous plant, *Derris elliptica* and allied species, the roots of which contain rotenone and are used as an insecticide.

Der·ry (děr′ĭ), *n.* Londonderry.

der·ry (děr′ĭ), *n.* a meaningless refrain or chorus in old songs. Also, **der·ry-down** (děr′ĭ doun′).

der Tag (děr täkʀ′), *German.* the day: used by German nationalists to refer to the day on which Germany would begin the "Drang nach Osten"; later, the day on which she would undertake a plan of conquest.

der·vish (dûr′vĭsh), *n.* a member of any of various Mohammedan ascetic orders, some of which carry on ecstatic observances, such as violent dancing and pirouetting (**dancing, spinning,** or **whirling dervishes**) or vociferous chanting or shouting (**howling dervishes**). [t. Turk., t. Pers.: m. *darvish* religious mendicant]

Der·went (dûr′wĕnt), *n.* 1. name of four rivers in England. 2. a river in Tasmania. ab. 130 mi.

De·saix de Vey·goux (dĕ zĕ′ də vĕ gōō′), **Louis Charles Antoine** (lwē shàrl ăn twàn′), 1768–1800, French general.

des·cant (*n.* děs′kănt; *v.* děs kănt′, dĭs-), *n.* 1. *Music.* **a.** a melody or counterpoint accompanying a simple musical theme and usually written above it. **b.** (in part music) the soprano. **c.** a song or melody. 2. a variation upon anything; comment on a subject. —*v.i.* 3. *Music.* to sing. 4. to make comments; discourse at length and with variety. Also, **discant.** [ME. t. ONF. f. *des-* DIS-[1] + *cant* (g. L *cantus* song)] —**des·cant′er,** *n.*

Des·cartes (dĕ kärt′), *n.* René (rə nĕ′), 1596–1650, French philosopher and mathematician.

de·scend (dĭ sĕnd′), *v.i.* 1. to move or pass from a higher to a lower place; go or come down; fall; sink. 2. to pass from higher to lower in any scale. 3. to go from generals to particulars. 4. to slope or tend downward. 5. to come down by transmission, as from ancestors. 6. to be derived by birth or extraction. 7. to come down in a hostile manner, as an army: *to descend upon the enemy.* 8. to come down from a certain intellectual, moral, or social standard: *he would never descend to baseness.* 9. *Astron.* to move toward the horizon, or toward the south, as a star. —*v.t.* 10. to move downward upon or along; go down (stairs, a hill, etc.). [ME *descend(en),* t. OF: m. *descendre,* g. L *dēscendere*]

de·scend·ant (dĭ sĕn′dənt), *n.* 1. one descended from an ancestor; an offspring, near or remote. —*adj.* 2. descendent. [t. F, ppr. of *descendre* DESCEND]

de·scend·ent (dĭ sĕn′dənt), *adj.* 1. descending; going or coming down. 2. descending from an ancestor. [t. L: s. *dēscendens,* ppr., descending]

de·scend·er (dĭ sĕn′dər), *n.* 1. one who or that which descends. 2. *Print.* the part of such letters as *p, q, j,* and *y* that goes below the body of most lower-case letters.

de·scend·i·ble (dĭ sĕn′də bəl), *adj.* capable of being transmitted by inheritance. Also, **de·scend′a·ble.**

de·scen·sion (dĭ sĕn′shən), *n.* *Now Rare.* descent.

de·scent (dĭ sĕnt′), *n.* 1. act or fact of descending. 2. a downward inclination or slope. 3. a passage or stairway leading down. 4. extraction; lineage. 5. any passing from higher to lower in degree or state. 6. a sudden incursion or attack. 7. *Law.* transmission of real property by intestate succession. [ME, t. OF: m. *descente,* der. *descendre* DESCEND] —**Syn.** 1. falling, sinking. 2. decline, grade, declivity.

Des·chutes (dā shōōt′), *n.* a river flowing from the Cascade Range in central Oregon N to the Columbia river. ab. 250 mi.

de·scribe (dĭ skrīb′), *v.t.,* **-scribed, -scribing.** 1. to set forth in written or spoken words; give an account of: *to describe a scene, a person, etc.* 2. *Geom.* to draw or trace, as an arc. [t. L: m.s. *dēscrībere* copy off, sketch off, describe] —**de·scrib′a·ble,** *adj.* —**de·scrib′er,** *n.* —**Syn.** 1. DESCRIBE, NARRATE agree in the idea of giving an account of something. To DESCRIBE is to convey an image or impression in words designed to reveal the appearance, nature, attributes, etc., of the thing described. The word applies primarily to what exists in space (by extension, to what occurs in time) and often implies the vividness of personal observation: *to describe a scene, a sensation, a character, a room.* To NARRATE is to recount the occurrence of something, usually by giving the details of an event or events in the order of their happening. NARRATE thus applies only to that which happens in time: *to narrate an incident.*

de·scrip·tion (dĭ skrĭp′shən), *n.* 1. representation by written or spoken words; a statement that describes. 2. sort; kind; variety: *persons of that description.* 3. *Geom.* act of describing a figure. [ME, t. L: s. *dēscrīptiō*]

de·scrip·tive (dĭ skrĭp′tĭv), *adj.* 1. having the quality of describing; characterized by description. 2. *Gram.* **a.** (of an adjective) expressing a quality of the noun it modifies (opposed to *limiting* or *demonstrative*), as *fresh* in *fresh milk.* **b.** (of any other expression) acting like such an adjective. —**de·scrip′tive·ly,** *adv.* —**de·scrip′tive·ness,** *n.*

descriptive clause, a relative clause, in English writing usually set off in commas, which describes or supplements, but does not identify, the antecedent; nonrestrictive clause. In "this year, *which has been dry,* is bad for crops" the italicized part is a descriptive clause.

descriptive geometry, 1. the theory of making projections of any accurately defined figure such that from them can be deduced not only its projective, but also its metrical properties. 2. geometry in general, treated by means of projections.

descriptive science, a science which classifies and describes the material in a particular field (usually opposed to *explanatory science,* which gives causes).

de·scry (dĭ skrī′), *v.t.,* **-scried, -scrying.** 1. to make out by looking; espy: *the lookout descried land.* 2. to discover; perceive; detect. [ME *descry(en),* appar. t. OF: m. *descrier* proclaim. See DECRY] —**de·scri′er,** *n.*

des·e·crate (děs′ə krāt′), *v.t.,* **-crated, -crating.** to divest of sacred or hallowed character or office; divert from a sacred to a profane purpose; treat with sacrilege; profane. [f. DE- + -*secrate,* modeled on CONSECRATE] —**des′e·crat′er, des′e·cra′tor,** *n.* —**des′e·cra′tion,** *n.*

de·seg·re·ga·tion (dē′sĕg′rĭ gā′shən), *n.* the process of elimi ati g racial segregation in schools, public places, railroads, the armed forces, etc. —**de·seg′re·gate′,** *v.*

de·sen·si·tize (dē sĕn′sə tīz′), *v.t.,* **-tized, -tizing.** 1. to lessen the sensitiveness of. 2. *Physiol.* to eliminate the natural or acquired reactivity or sensitivity of (an animal, organ, tissue, etc.) to an external stimulus, as an allergen. 3. *Photog.* to make less sensitive or wholly insensitive to light, as the emulsion on a film. —**de·sen′si·ti·za′tion,** *n.* —**de·sen′si·tiz′er,** *n.*

des·ert[1] (děz′ərt), *n.* 1. an area so deficient in moisture as to support only a sparse, widely spaced vegetation, or none at all. 2. any area in which few forms of life can exist because of lack of water, permanent frost, or absence of soil. —*adj.* 3. of, pertaining to, or like a desert; desolate; barren. [ME, t. OF, t. L (Eccl.): s. *dēsertum,* prop. neut. pp. of *dēserere* abandon, forsake] —**Syn.** 1. DESERT, WASTE, WILDERNESS refer to areas which are uninhabited. DESERT emphasizes lack of water; it refers to a dry, barren, treeless region, usually sandy: *an oasis in a desert, the Sahara Desert.* WASTE emphasizes lack of inhabitants and of cultivation; it is used of wild, barren land, but fig. the word is also applied to turbulent seas: *a desolate waste, a terrifying waste of water.* WILDERNESS emphasizes the difficulty of finding one's way, whether because of barrenness or of luxuriant vegetation; it is also applied to the ocean, especially in stormy weather: *a trackless wilderness.*

de·sert[2] (dĭ zûrt′), *v.t.* 1. to abandon or forsake; depart from: *he deserted his wife.* 2. (of a soldier or sailor) to leave or run away from (the service, duty, etc.) with the intention of never coming back. 3. to fail (one): *all hope deserted him.* —*v.i.* 4. (esp. of a soldier or sailor) to forsake one's duty, etc. [t. F: m. s. *déserter,* t. LL: m. *dēsertāre,* freq. of L *dēserere*] —**de·sert′er,** *n.* —**Syn.** 1. DESERT, ABANDON, FORSAKE mean to leave behind one persons, places, or things. DESERT implies intentionally violating an oath, formal obligation, or duty: *to desert campaign pledges.* ABANDON suggests giving up wholly and finally, whether of necessity, unwillingly, or through shirking responsibilities: *to abandon a hopeless task.* FORSAKE has emotional connotations, since it implies violating obligations of affection or association: *to forsake a noble cause.*

de·sert³ (dĭ zûrt/), n. 1. that which is deserved; a due reward or punishment. 2. worthiness of reward or punishment; merit or demerit. 3. the fact of deserving well; merit; a virtue. [ME, t. OF: m. *deserte*, der. *deservir* DESERVE] —Syn. 3. See merit.

de·ser·tion (dĭ zûr/shən), n. 1. act of deserting. 2. state of being deserted. 3. *Law*. willful abandonment, esp. of one's wife or husband without consent, in violation of legal or moral obligation.

de·serve (dĭ zûrv/), v., -served, -serving. —v.t. 1. to merit (reward, punishment, esteem, etc.) in return for actions, qualities, etc. —v.i. 2. to be worthy of recompense. [ME *deserve(n)*, t. OF: m. *deservir*, g. L *dēservīre* serve zealously] —de·serv/er, n.

de·serv·ed·ly (dĭ zûr/vĭd lĭ), adv. justly; according to desert, whether of good or evil.

de·serv·ing (dĭ zûr/vĭng), adj. worthy of reward or praise; meritorious (often fol. by *of*). —de·serv/ing·ly, adv. —de·serv/ing·ness, n.

des·ha·bille (dĕz/ə bēl/), n. dishabille. [t. F]

des·ic·cant (dĕs/ə kənt), adj. 1. desiccating or drying, as a medicine. —n. 2. a desiccant substance or agent.

des·ic·cate (dĕs/ə kāt/), v., -cated, -cating. —v.t. 1. to dry thoroughly; dry up. 2. to preserve by depriving of moisture, as foods. —v.i. 3. to become dry [t. L: m. s. *dēsiccātus*, pp., completely dried] —des/ic·ca/tion, n. —des/ic·ca/tive, adj., n.

des·ic·cat·ed (dĕs/ə kā/tĭd), adj. dehydrated or powdered: *desiccated milk or soup*.

des·ic·ca·tor (dĕs/ə kā/tər), n. 1. one who or that which desiccates. 2. an apparatus for drying fruit, milk, etc., or for absorbing the moisture present in a chemical substance, etc.

de·sid·er·a·ta (dĭ sĭd/ə rā/tə), n. pl. of desideratum.

de·sid·er·ate (dĭ sĭd/ə rāt/), v.t., -ated, -ating. to feel a desire for; long for; feel the want of. [t. L: m. s. *dēsiderātus*, pp., longed for] —de·sid/er·a/tion, n.

de·sid·er·a·tive (dĭ sĭd/ə rā/tĭv), adj. 1. having or expressing desire. 2. *Gram.* (of a verb derived from another) expressing desire to perform the action denoted by the underlying verb. Example: Sanskrit *vēda*, he knows; *vi-vid-is-ati*, he wishes to know. —n. 3. *Gram.* a desiderative verb.

de·sid·er·a·tum (dĭ sĭd/ə rā/təm), n., pl. -ta (-tə). something wanted or needed. [t. L, prop. pp. neut.]

de·sign (dĭ zīn/), v.t. 1. to prepare the preliminary sketch or the plans for (a work to be executed). 2. to plan and fashion artistically or skillfully. 3. to form or conceive in the mind; contrive; plan: *he is designing a plan to enlarge his garden*. 4. to assign in thought or intention; purpose: *he is designing that his son shall help him in the garden*. 5. *Obs*. to mark out, as by a sign; indicate. —v.i. 6. to make drawings, preliminary sketches, or plans. 7. to plan and fashion a work of art, etc. —n. 8. an outline, sketch, or plan, as of a work of art, an edifice, or a machine to be executed or constructed. 9. the combination of details or features of a picture, building, etc.; the pattern or device of artistic work. 10. the art of designing: *a school of design*. 11. a plan; a project; a scheme. 12. a hostile plan; crafty scheme. 13. the end in view; intention; purpose. 14. evil or selfish intention: *have designs on (or against) a person*. 15. adaptation of means to a preconceived end. 16. an artistic work. [t. F: s. *dēsigner* designate, t. L: m. *dēsignāre* mark out] —Syn. 4. See intend. 11. See plan.

des·ig·nate (v. dĕz/ĭg nāt/; adj. dĕz/ĭg nĭt, -nāt/), v., -nated, -nating, adj. —v.t. 1. to mark or point out; indicate; show; specify. 2. to name; entitle; style. 3. to nominate or select for a duty, office, purpose, etc.; appoint; assign. —adj. 4. designated. [t. L: m. s. *dēsignātus*, pp., marked out] —des/ig·na/tive, adj. —des/ig·na/tor, n.

des·ig·na·tion (dĕz/ĭg nā/shən), n. 1. act of designating. 2. fact of being designated. 3. that which designates; a name. 4. nomination; appointment.

de·sign·ed·ly (dĭ zī/nĭd lĭ), adv. by design; purposely.

de·sign·er (dĭ zī/nər), n. 1. one who devises or executes designs, as for works of art, decorative patterns, dresses, machines, etc. 2. a schemer or intriguer.

de·sign·ing (dĭ zī/nĭng), adj. 1. contriving schemes; artful. 2. showing forethought. —n. 3. act or art of making designs. —de·sign/ing·ly, adv. —Syn. 1. wily, cunning, crafty, tricky, sly.

de·sign·ment (dĭ zīn/mənt), n. designation; design.

des·i·nence (dĕs/ə nəns), n. 1. termination or ending, as a line of verse. 2. *Gram.* a termination, ending, or suffix of a word.

de·sir·a·ble (dĭ zīr/ə bəl), adj. 1. worthy to be desired; pleasing; excellent, or fine. —n. 2. one who or that which is desirable. —de·sir·a·bil/i·ty, de·sir/a·ble·ness, n. —de·sir/a·bly, adv.

de·sire (dĭ zīr/), v., -sired, -siring, n. —v.t. 1. to wish or long for; crave; want: *he desires a college education*. 2. to express a wish to obtain; ask for; request: *the king desired of him that he should return*. —n. 3. a longing or craving. 4. an expressed wish; a request. 5. something desired. 6. sensual appetite; lust. [ME *desire(n)*, t. OF: m. *desirer*, g. L *dēsīderāre* want] —de·sir/er, n. —Syn. 1. See wish. 1. DESIRE, CRAVING, LONGING, YEARNING suggest feelings which impel one to the attainment or possession of something. DESIRE is a strong feeling, worthy or unworthy, that impels to the attainment or possession of something which is (in reality or imagination) within

reach: *a desire for success*. CRAVING implies a deep and imperative wish for something, based on a sense of need and hunger (lit. or fig.): *a craving for food, companionship*. A LONGING is an intense wish, generally repeated or enduring, for something that is at the moment beyond reach but may be attainable at some future time: *a longing to visit Europe*. YEARNING suggests persistent, uneasy, and sometimes wistful or tender longing: *a yearning for one's native land*. —Ant. 3. indifference.

de·sir·ous (dĭ zīr/əs), adj. having or characterized by desire; desiring.

de·sist (dĭ zĭst/), v.i. to cease, as from some action or proceeding; stop. [t. OF: s. *desister*, t. L: m. *dēsistere* leave off] —de·sist/ance, de·sist/ence, n.

de Sit·ter (də sĭt/ər), Willem (vĭl/əm), 1872–1934, Dutch mathematician and astronomer.

desk (dĕsk), n. 1. a table specially adapted for convenience in writing or reading, sometimes made with a sloping top. 2. a frame for supporting a book from which the service is read in a church. 3. a pulpit. [ME *deske*, t. It.: m. *desco*, g. L *discus* disk, dish, ML table]

desk work, 1. work done at a desk. 2. habitual writing, as that of a clerk or a literary man.

D. ès L., (F *Docteur ès Lettres*) Doctor of Letters.

des·man (dĕs/mən), n., pl. -mans. either of two aquatic, insectivorous mammals, related to shrews, *Myogale moschata* of SE Russia, and *M. pyrenaica* of the Pyrenees. [t. Sw.: short for *desman-ratta* muskrat]

des·mid (dĕs/mĭd), n. any of the microscopic freshwater algae belonging to the family *Desmidiaceae*. [t. NL: m. s. *Desmidium*, typical genus, dim. of Gk. *desmós* band, chain] —des·mid/i·an, adj.

des·moid (dĕs/moid), adj. *Anat.* 1. resembling a fascia or fibrous sheet. 2. resembling a ligament; ligamentous. —n. 3. *Pathol.* a firm and tough tumor of woven fibrous tissue. [f. s. Gk. *desmós* band, chain, ligament+ -OID]

Des Moines (də moin/, moinz/), 1. the capital of Iowa, in the central part, on the Des Moines river. 208,982 (1960). 2. a river flowing from SW Minnesota, SE through Iowa to the Mississippi. ab. 450 mi.

Des·mou·lins (dā mōō lăN/), n. Lucie Simplice Camille Benoit (lȳ sē/ săN plēs/ kå mē/y bə nwä/), 1760–1794, one of the leaders of the French Revolution.

des·o·late (adj. dĕs/ə lĭt; v. dĕs/ə lāt/), adj., v., -lated, -lating. —adj. 1. barren or laid waste; devastated. 2. deprived or destitute of inhabitants; deserted. 3. left alone; lonely. 4. having the feeling of being abandoned by friends or by hope. 5. dreary; dismal. —v.t. 6. to lay waste; devastate. 7. to deprive of inhabitants; depopulate. 8. to make disconsolate. 9. to forsake or abandon. [ME, t. L: m. s. *dēsōlātus*, pp., left alone, forsaken] —des/o·lat/er, des/o·la/tor, n. —des/o·late·ly, adv. —des/o·late·ness, n. —Syn. 4. miserable, wretched, woebegone. DESOLATE, DISCONSOLATE, FORLORN suggest one who is in a sad and wretched condition. The DESOLATE person or place gives a feeling or impression of isolation or of being deprived of human consolation, relationships, or presence: *desolate and despairing*. The DISCONSOLATE person is aware of the efforts of others to console and comfort him, but is unable to be relieved or cheered by them: *she remained disconsolate even in the midst of friends*. The FORLORN person has the feeling or gives the impression of being lost, deserted, or forsaken by friends: *wretched and forlorn in a strange city*.

des·o·la·tion (dĕs/ə lā/shən), n. 1. act of desolating. 2. state of being desolated. 3. depopulation; devastation; ruin. 4. dreariness; barrenness. 5. deprivation of companionship or comfort; loneliness; disconsolateness. 6. a desolate place. [ME, t. L: m. s. *dēsōlātiō*]

De So·to (də sō/tō; *Sp.* dě sō/tō), Hernando or Fernando (ĕr nän/dō or fĕr nän/dō), 1500–42, Spanish soldier-explorer in America: reached the Mississippi river, 1541.

de·spair (dĭ spâr/), n. 1. loss of hope; hopelessness. 2. that which causes hopelessness; that of which there is no hope. —v.i. 3. to lose or give up hope; be without hope (fol. by *of*): *to despair of humanity*. —v.t. 4. *Archaic*. to give up hope of. [ME *despeir(en)*, t. OF: m. s. *desperer*, g. L *dēspērāre* be without hope] —Syn. 1. DESPAIR, DESPERATION, DESPONDENCY, DISCOURAGEMENT, HOPELESSNESS refer to a state of mind caused by circumstances which seem too much to cope with. DESPAIR suggests total loss or abandonment of hope, which may be passive or may drive one to furious efforts, even if at random: *in the depths of despair, courage born of despair*. DESPERATION is usually an active state, the abandonment of hope impelling to a furious struggle against adverse circumstances, with utter disregard of consequences: *an act of desperation when everything else had failed*. DESPONDENCY is usually a temporary state of deep gloom and disheartenment: *a spell of despondency*. DISCOURAGEMENT is a temporary loss of courage, hope, and ambition because of obstacles, frustrations, etc.: *his optimism resisted all discouragements*. HOPELESSNESS is a loss of hope so complete as to result in a more or less permanent state of passive despair: *a state of hopelessness and apathy*.

de·spair·ing (dĭ spâr/ĭng), adj. 1. given to despair or hopelessness. 2. indicating despair. —de·spair/ing·ly, adv. —Syn. 1. See hopeless. —Ant. 1. hopeful.

des·patch (dĭ spăch/), v.t., v.i., n. dispatch. —des·patch/er, n.

des·per·a·do (dĕs/pə rä/dō, -rā/dō), n., pl. -does, -dos. a desperate or reckless criminal; one ready for any desperate deed. [prob. refashioning of *desperate* after Sp. words in -ado. Cf. OSp. *desperado*, g. L *dēspērātus* DESPERATE]

b., blend of, blended; c., cognate with; d., dialect, dialectal; der., derived from; f., formed from; g., going back to; m., modification of; r., replacing; s., stem of; t., taken from; ?, perhaps. See the full key on inside cover.

des·per·ate (dĕs′pər ĭt), *adj.* **1.** reckless from despair; ready to run any risk. **2.** characterized by the recklessness of despair. **3.** leaving little or no hope; very serious or dangerous. **4.** extremely bad. **5.** extreme or excessive. **6.** having no hope. [late ME, t. L: m. s. *dēspērātus*, pp., given up] —**des′per·ate·ly,** *adv.* —**des′per·ate·ness,** *n.* —Syn. 3. See **hopeless.** —**Ant. 1.** cautious.

des·per·a·tion (dĕs′pə rā′shən), *n.* **1.** state of being desperate; the recklessness of despair. **2.** act or fact of despairing; despair. —Syn. 1. See **despair.**

des·pi·ca·ble (dĕs′pĭ kə bəl; *less often* dĕs pĭk′ə bəl), *adj.* that is to be despised; contemptible. [t. LL: m. s. *dēspĭcābilis*, der. L *dēspĭcārī* despise] —**des′pi·ca·bil′i·ty, des′pi·ca·ble·ness,** *n.* —**des′pi·ca·bly,** *adv.* —Syn. worthless, base, vile. —**Ant.** admirable.

de·spise (dĭ spīz′), *v.t.,* -**spised, -spising.** to look down upon, as in contempt; scorn; disdain. [ME *despise(n)*, t. OF: m. *despis-*, s. *despire*, g. L *dēspicere* look down upon, despise] —**de·spis′er,** *n.* —**Ant.** admire.

de·spite (dĭ spīt′), *prep., n., v.* -**spited, -spiting.** —*prep.* **1.** in despite of; notwithstanding. —*n.* **2.** contemptuous treatment; insult. **3. in despite of,** in contempt or defiance of; in spite of; notwithstanding. **4.** *Archaic.* malice, hatred, or spite. —*v.t.* **5.** *Obs.* to offend; vex; spite. [orig., *in despite of;* ME *despit*, t. OF, g. L *dēspectus* a looking down upon] —Syn. 1. See **notwithstanding.**

de·spite·ful (dĭ spīt′fəl), *adj. Archaic.* contemptuous; malicious; spiteful. —**de·spite′ful·ly,** *adv.* —**de·spite′ful·ness,** *n.*

des·pit·e·ous (dĕs pĭt′ĭ əs), *adj. Archaic.* **1.** malicious; spiteful **2.** contemptuous. —**des·pit′e·ous·ly,** *adv.*

Des Plaines (dĕs plānz′), a city in NE Illinois, near Chicago. 34,886 (1960).

de·spoil (dĭ spoil′), *v.t.* to strip of possessions; rob; plunder; pillage. [ME *despoile(n)*, t. OF: m. *despoil-lier*, g. L *dēspoliāre* plunder, rob] —**de·spoil′er,** *n.* —**de·spoil′ment,** *n.*

de·spo·li·a·tion (dĭ spō′lĭ ā′shən), *n.* **1.** act of despoiling. **2.** fact of being despoiled.

de·spond (dĭ spŏnd′), *v.i.* **1.** to lose heart, courage, or hope. —*n.* **2.** *Archaic.* despondency. [t. L: s. *dēspondēre* promise, give up, lose (heart)] —**de·spond′ing·ly,** *adv.*

de·spond·en·cy (dĭ spŏn′dən sĭ), *n.* a being despondent; depression of spirits from loss of courage or hope; dejection. Also, **de·spond′ence.** —Syn. discouragement, melancholy, gloom, desperation. See **despair.** —**Ant.** joy.

de·spond·ent (dĭ spŏn′dənt), *adj.* desponding; depressed or dejected. [t. L: s. *dēspondens*, ppr., giving up, despairing] —**de·spond′ent·ly,** *adv.* —Syn. discouraged, disheartened, downhearted, melancholy, low-spirited. See **hopeless.** —**Ant.** hopeful.

des·pot (dĕs′pət, -pŏt), *n.* **1.** an absolute ruler; an autocrat. **2.** a tyrant or oppressor. **3.** *Hist.* master or lord (a title of autocratic rulers, esp. the late Roman and Byzantine Emperors). [t. Gk.: s. *despótēs* master]

des·pot·ic (dĕs pŏt′ĭk), *adj.* of, pertaining to, or of the nature of a despot or despotism; autocratic; arbitrary; tyrannical. —**des·pot′i·cal·ly,** *adv.*

des·pot·ism (dĕs′pə tĭz′əm), *n.* **1.** the rule of a despot; the exercise of absolute authority. **2.** an absolute or autocratic government. **3.** a country ruled by a despot. **4.** absolute power or control; tyranny.

de·spu·mate (dĭ spū′māt, dĕs′pyŏŏ māt′), *v.,* -**mated, -mating.** —*v.t.* **1.** to skim. —*v.i.* **2.** to throw off froth, scum, or impurities. [t. L: m. s. *dēspūmātus*, pp., skimmed] —**des′pu·ma′tion,** *n.*

des·qua·mate (dĕs′kwə māt′), *v.i.,* -**mated, -mating.** *Pathol.* to come off in scales, as the skin in certain diseases; peel off. [t. L: m. s. *dēsquāmātus*, pp., scaled off] —**des′qua·ma′tion,** *n.*

D. ès S., (F. *Docteur ès Sciences*) Doctor of Sciences.

Des·sau (dĕs′ou), *n.* a city in East Germany, formerly capital of Anhalt. 88,139 (1946.)

des·sert (dĭ zûrt′), *n.* **1.** *U.S.* a final course including pies, puddings, etc. **2.** *Brit.* a serving of fruits, sweetmeats, etc., at the end of a meal. [t. F, der. *desservir* clear the table, f. *des-* DIS-¹ + *servir*, g. L *servīre* serve]

des·sert·spoon (dĭ zûrt′spŏŏn′, -spŏŏn′), *n.* a spoon intermediate in size between a tablespoon and a teaspoon. —**des·sert·spoon·ful** (dĭ zûrt′spŏŏn fŏŏl′, -spŏŏn-), *n.*

des·sia·tine (dĕs′yə tēn′), *n.* a Russian unit of land measure equal to 2.7 U.S. acres. [t. Russ.: m. *des-yatĭna*, lit., tithe, tenth]

de·ster·i·lize (dē stĕr′ə līz′), *v.t.,* -**lized, -lizing.** to utilize an idle fund or commodity, as when a nation issues currency against gold previously unused.

Des·ter·ro (dĕs tĕr′rŏŏ), *n.* former name of **Florianópolis.**

des·ti·na·tion (dĕs′tə nā′shən), *n.* **1.** the predetermined end of a journey or voyage. **2.** the purpose for which anything is destined; ultimate end or design.

des·tine (dĕs′tĭn), *v.t.,* -**tined, -tining. 1.** to set apart for a particular use, purpose, etc.; intend. **2.** to appoint or ordain beforehand, as by divine decree; foreordain; predetermine. [ME *destene(n)*, t. OF: m. *destiner*, t. L: m. *dēstĭnāre* make fast, establish, appoint]

des·tined (dĕs′tĭnd), *adj.* **1.** bound for a certain destination. **2.** designed; intended. **3.** foreordained; predetermined.

des·ti·ny (dĕs′tə nĭ), *n., pl.* -**nies. 1.** that which is to happen to a particular person or thing; one's lot or fortune. **2.** the predetermined course of events. **3.** the power or agency which determines the course of events. **4.** (*cap.*) this power personified or represented as a goddess. **5. the Destinies,** the Fates. [ME *destinee*, t. OF, der. *destiner* DESTINE] —Syn. 2. See **fate.**

des·ti·tute (dĕs′tə tūt′, -tŏŏt′), *adj.* **1.** bereft of means or resources; lacking the means of subsistence. **2.** deprived or devoid of (something) (fol. by *of*). **3.** *Obs.* abandoned or deserted. [ME, t. L: s. *dēstĭtūtus*, pp., put away, abandoned] —**des′ti·tute′ness,** *n.* —Syn. 1. needy, poor, indigent, penniless, poverty-stricken.

des·ti·tu·tion (dĕs′tə tū′shən, -tŏŏ′-), *n.* **1.** want of the means of subsistence; utter poverty. **2.** deprivation; want; absence. [ME, t. L: s. *dēstĭtūtiō*] —Syn. 1. See **poverty.** —**Ant. 1.** affluence.

des·tri·er (dĕs′trĭ ər, dĕs trĭr′), *n. Archaic.* a war horse; a charger. [ME *destrer*, t. AF, var. of OF *destrier*, g. LL *dextrārius*, lit., (horse) led at the right hand]

de·stroy (dĭ stroi′), *v.t.* **1.** to reduce to pieces or to a useless form; ruin; spoil; consume; demolish. **2.** to put an end to; extinguish. **3.** to kill; slay. **4.** to render ineffective; nullify; invalidate. [ME *destruy(en)*, t. OF: m. *destruire*, g. LL var. of L *dēstruere* pull down, destroy] —**de·stroy′a·ble,** *adj.* —Syn. 1. DESTROY, DEMOLISH, RAZE imply reducing a thing to uselessness. To DESTROY is to reduce something to nothingness or to take away its powers and functions so that restoration is impossible; the action is usually violent or sudden, but may be gradual and slow, esp. when it entails a reversal of natural processes: *fire destroys a building, disease destroys tissues.* To DEMOLISH is to destroy an organized body or structure by complete separation of parts: *to demolish a machine.* To RAZE is to level down to the ground: *to raze a fortress.* —**Ant. 1.** construct. **2.** establish. **3.** save. **4.** preserve.

de·stroy·er (dĭ stroi′ər), *n.* **1.** one who or that which destroys. **2.** a torpedo-boat destroyer.

de·struct·i·ble (dĭ strŭk′tə bəl), *adj.* that may be destroyed; liable to destruction. —**de·struct′i·bil′i·ty, de·struct′i·ble·ness,** *n.*

de·struc·tion (dĭ strŭk′shən), *n.* **1.** act of destroying. **2.** fact or condition of being destroyed; demolition; annihilation. **3.** a cause or means of destroying. [ME, t. L: s. *dēstructiō*] —Syn. 1. extinction, extermination. See **ruin.**

de·struc·tion·ist (dĭ strŭk′shən ĭst), *n.* an advocate of the destruction of an existing political institution or the like.

de·struc·tive (dĭ strŭk′tĭv), *adj.* **1.** tending to destroy; causing destruction (fol. by *of* or *to*). **2.** tending to overthrow, disprove, or discredit: *destructive criticism.* —**de·struc′tive·ly,** *adv.* —**de·struc′tive·ness, de·struc·tiv·i·ty** (dē′strŭk tĭv′ə tĭ), *n.* —Syn. 1. ruinous, baleful, pernicious, deleterious.

destructive distillation, *Chem.* the destruction or decomposition of a substance, as wood, coal, etc., by heat in a closed vessel, and the collection of the volatile matters evolved.

de·struc·tor (dĭ strŭk′tər), *n. Brit.* a furnace for the burning of refuse; an incinerator. [t. LL, der. L *dēstruere* destroy]

des·ue·tude (dĕs′wə tūd′, -tŏŏd′), *n.* state of being no longer used or practiced. [t. F, t. L: m. *dēsuētūdo*]

de·sul·fur (dē sŭl′fər), *v.t.* to free from sulfur; desulfurize.

de·sul·fu·rize (dē sŭl′fə rīz′), *v.t.,* -**rized, -rizing.** to free from sulfur. —**de·sul′fu·ri·za′tion,** *n.*

des·ul·to·ry (dĕs′əl tōr′ĭ), *adj.* **1.** veering about from one thing to another; disconnected, unmethodical, or fitful: *desultory reading or conversation.* **2.** random: *a desultory thought.* [t. L: m. s. *dēsultōrius* of a leaper, superficial] —**des′ul·to′ri·ly,** *adv.* —**des′ul·to′ri·ness,** *n.* —**Ant. 1.** methodical. **2.** pertinent.

de·tach (dĭ tăch′), *v.t.* **1.** to unfasten and separate; disengage; disunite. **2.** to send away (a regiment, ship, etc.) on a special mission: *men were detached to defend the pass.* [t. F: s. *détacher*, der. OF *tache* (g. Rom. *tacca*) nail. Cf. ATTACH.] —**de·tach′a·ble,** *adj.* —**de·tach′-a·bil′i·ty,** *n.* —**de·tach′er,** *n.*

de·tached (dĭ tăcht′), *adj.* **1.** standing apart; separate; unattached (usually applied to houses): *he lives in a detached house.* **2.** not interested; unconcerned.

de·tach·ment (dĭ tăch′mənt), *n.* **1.** act of detaching. **2.** condition of being detached. **3.** a state of aloofness, as from worldly affairs or from the concerns of others. **4.** freedom from prejudice or partiality. **5.** act of sending out a detached force of troops or naval ships. **6.** something detached, as a number of troops separated from a main force for some special combat or other task.

de·tail (*n.* dĭ tāl′, dē′tāl; *v.* dĭ tāl′), *n.* **1.** an individual or minute part; an item or particular. **2.** particulars collectively; minutiae. **3.** a dealing with or treating part by part or item by item. **4.** a narrative or report of particulars. **5.** a detail drawing. **6.** any small section of a larger structure considered as a unit. **7.** *Mil.* **a.** a detailing or telling off, as of a small force or an officer, for a special service. **b.** the party or person so selected. **c.** a particular assignment of duty. **8. in detail,** circumstantially; item by item. —*v.t.* **9.** to relate or report in particulars; tell fully and distinctly. **10.** *Mil.* to tell off or appoint for some particular duty, as a patrol, a guard, etc. [t. F, der. *détailler* cut in pieces, retail]

ăct, āble, dâre, ärt; ĕbb, ēqual; ĭf, īce; hŏt, ōver, ôrder, oil, bŏŏk, ōōze, out; ŭp, ūse, ûrge; ə = a in alone; ch, chief; g, give; ng, ring; sh, shoe; th, thin; ŧħ, that; zh, vision. See the full key on inside cover.

detail drawing, a drawing, at relatively large scale, of a part of a building, machine, etc., with dimensions or other information for use in construction.

de·tain (dĭ tān′), v.t. 1. to keep from proceeding; keep waiting; delay. 2. to keep under restraint or in custody. 3. to keep back or withhold, as from a person. [late ME detaine(n), t. OF: m. detenir, t. L: m. dētinēre keep back]

de·tain·er (dĭ tā′nər), n. Law. 1. the wrongful detaining or withholding of what belongs to another. 2. a writ for the further detention of a person already in custody. [t. AF: m. detener, var. of OF detenir]

de·tect (dĭ tĕkt′), v.t. 1. to discover or catch (a person) in the performance of some act: to detect someone in a dishonest act. 2. to find out the action or character of: to detect a hypocrite. 3. to discover the presence, existence, or fact of. 4. Radio. to subject to the action of a detector. [t. L: s. dētectus, pp., discovered, uncovered] —de·tect′a·ble, de·tect′i·ble, adj. —Syn. 3. See learn.

de·tec·tion (dĭ tĕk′shən), n. 1. act of detecting. 2. fact of being detected. 3. discovery, as of error or crime. 4. Radio. a. rectification of alternating currents in a radio receiver. b. the conversion of an alternating carrier wave or current into a direct pulsating current equivalent to the transmitted signal; demodulation.

de·tec·tive (dĭ tĕk′tĭv), n. 1. a member of the police force whose function it is to obtain information and evidence, as of offenses against the law. —adj. 2. pertaining to detection or detectives: a detective story.

de·tec·tor (dĭ tĕk′tər), n. 1. one who or that which detects. 2. Radio. a. a device for detecting electric oscillations or waves. b. a device, as a crystal detector or a vacuum tube, which rectifies the alternating currents in a radio receiver. [t. LL]

de·tent (dĭ tĕnt′), n. a piece of a mechanism which, when disengaged, releases the operating power, or by which the action is prevented or checked; a catch, as in a lock; a pawl. [t. F: m. détente, der. détendre relax, f. dé- DIS-1 + tendre (g. L tendere stretch)]

dé·tente (dā tänt′; Fr. de täNt′), n. a relaxing, esp. of international tension. [F]

de·ten·tion (dĭ tĕn′shən), n. 1. act of detaining. 2. state of being detained. 3. a keeping in custody; confinement. 4. the withholding of what belongs to or is claimed by another.

de·ter (dĭ tûr′), v.t., -terred, -terring. to discourage or restrain (one) from acting or proceeding through fear, doubt, etc. [t. L: m. s. dēterrēre frighten from] —de·ter′ment, n. —Syn. dissuade, hinder, prevent, stop.

de·terge (dĭ tûrj′), v.t., -terged, -terging. 1. to wipe away. 2. to cleanse by removing foul or morbid matter, as from a wound. [t. L: m. s. dētergēre wipe off]

de·ter·gen·cy (dĭ tûr′jən sĭ), n. cleansing or purging power. Also, **de·ter′gence.**

de·ter·gent (dĭ tûr′jənt), adj. 1. cleansing; clearing away foul matter, as a medicinal substance. —n. 2. a detergent substance or agent.

de·te·ri·o·rate (dĭ tĭr′ĭ ə rāt′), v.t., v.i., -rated, -rating. to make or become worse; make or become lower in character or quality. [t. L: m. s. dēteriōrātus, pp.] —de·te′ri·o·ra′tion, n. —de·te′ri·o·ra′tive, adj.

de·ter·mi·na·ble (dĭ tûr′mə nə bəl), adj. 1. capable of being determined. 2. Law. subject to termination.

de·ter·mi·nant (dĭ tûr′mə nənt), n. 1. a determining agent or factor. 2. Math. an algebraic expression in the elements of any square matrix used in solving linear systems of equations.

de·ter·mi·nate (dĭ tûr′mə nĭt), adj. 1. having defined limits; definite. 2. settled; positive. 3. determined upon; conclusive; final. 4. determined; resolute. 5. Bot. (of an inflorescence) having the primary and each secondary axis ending in a flower or bud, thus preventing further elongation. [ME, t. L: m. s. dēterminātus, pp., determined] —de·ter′mi·nate·ly, adv. —de·ter′mi·nate·ness, n.

de·ter·mi·na·tion (dĭ tûr′mə nā′shən), n. 1. act of coming to a decision; the fixing or settling of a purpose. 2. ascertainment, as after observation or investigation. 3. a result ascertained; a solution. 4. the settlement of a dispute, etc., by authoritative decision. 5. the decision arrived at or pronounced. 6. the quality of being determined or resolute; firmness of purpose. 7. a fixed purpose or intention. 8. the fixing or settling of amount, limit, character, etc. 9. fixed direction or tendency toward some object or end. 10. Chiefly Law. conclusion or termination. 11. Embryol. the fixation of the nature of morphological differentiation in a group of cells before actual, visible differentiation. 12. Logic. a. the rendering of a notion more definite by the addition of differentiating characters. b. the definition of a concept by citing its constituent elements.

de·ter·mi·na·tive (dĭ tûr′mə nā′tĭv), adj. 1. serving to determine; determining. —n. 2. something that determines. —de·ter′mi·na·tive·ly, adv. —de·ter′mi·na·tive·ness, n.

de·ter·mine (dĭ tûr′mĭn), v., -mined, -mining. —v.t. 1. to settle or decide (a dispute, question, etc.) by an authoritative decision. 2. to conclude or ascertain, as after reasoning, observation, etc. 3. Geom. to fix the position of. 4. to fix or decide causally; condition: demand determines supply. 5. to give direction or tendency to; impel. 6. Logic. to limit, as an idea, by adding differentiating characters. 7. Chiefly Legal. to put an end to; terminate. 8. to lead or bring (a person) to a

decision: it finally determined him to do it. 9. to decide upon. —v.i. 10. to come to a decision or resolution; decide. 11. Chiefly Legal. to come to an end. [ME determine(n), t. OF: m. determiner, t. L: m. dētermināre limit] —de·ter′min·er, n. —Syn. 1. See decide.

de·ter·mined (dĭ tûr′mĭnd), adj. resolute; unflinching; firm. —de·ter′mined·ly, adv. —de·ter′mined·ness, n. —Syn. stanch, inflexible, unfaltering, unwavering.

de·ter·min·ism (dĭ tûr′mə nĭz′əm), n. the doctrine that neither outer events nor human choices are uncaused, but are the results of antecedent conditions, physical or psychological. —de·ter′min·ist, n., adj. —de·ter′min·is′tic, adj.

de·ter·rent (dĭ tûr′ənt, -tĕr′-), adj. 1. deterring; restraining. —n. 2. something that deters. —de·ter′rence, n.

de·ter·sive (dĭ tûr′sĭv), adj. 1. detergent. —n. 2. a detersive agent or medicine.

de·test (dĭ tĕst′), v.t. to feel abhorrence of; hate; dislike intensely. [t. F: s. détester, t. L: m. dētestāri, lit., curse while calling a deity to witness] —de·test′er, n. —Syn. abhor, loathe, abominate. See hate.

de·test·a·ble (dĭ tĕs′tə bəl), adj. deserving to be detested; abominable; hateful. —de·test′a·bil′i·ty, de·test′a·ble·ness, n. —de·test′a·bly, adv. —Syn. execrable, abhorrent, loathsome, odious, vile.

des·tes·ta·tion (dē′tĕs tā′shən), n. 1. abhorrence; hatred. 2. a person or thing detested.

de·throne (dē thrōn′), v.t., -throned, -throning. to remove from the throne; depose. —de·throne′ment, n. —de·thron′er, n.

det·i·nue (dĕt′ə nū′, -nōō′), n. Law. an old common-law form of action to recover possession or the value of articles of personal property wrongfully detained. [t. OF: m. detenue detention, orig. pp. fem. of detenir DETAIN]

det·o·nate (dĕt′ə nāt′, dē′tə-), v.i., v.t., -nated, -nating. to explode, esp. with great noise, suddenness, or violence. [t. L: m. s. dētonātus, pp., thundered forth]

det·o·na·tion (dĕt′ə nā′shən, dē′tə-), n. 1. act of detonating. 2. an explosion.

det·o·na·tor (dĕt′ə nā′tər, dē′tə-), n. 1. a device, as a percussion cap or an explosive, used to make another substance explode. 2. something that explodes.

de·tour (dē′tŏŏr, dĭ tŏŏr′), n. 1. a roundabout or circuitous way or course, esp. one used temporarily instead of the main route. —v.i. 2. to make a detour; go by way of a detour. —v.t. 3. to cause to make a detour; send by way of a detour. Also, French, dé·tour (dē tŏŏr′). [t. F, der. détourner turn aside, f. dé- DIS-1 + tourner turn]

de·tract (dĭ trăkt′), v.t. 1. to take away (a part); abate (fol. by from). 2. to draw away or divert. —v.i. 3. to take away a part, as from quality, value, or reputation. [t. L: s. dētractus, pp., drawn away or down] —de·tract′ing·ly, adv. —de·trac′tor, n.

de·trac·tion (dĭ trăk′shən), n. act of detracting, or of disparaging or belittling the reputation or worth of a person. —Syn. defamation, vilification.

de·trac·tive (dĭ trăk′tĭv), adj. tending or seeking to detract; depreciative. Also, **de·trac·to·ry** (dĭ trăk′tə rĭ). —de·trac′tive·ly, adv.

de·train (dē trān′), v.i., v.t. Chiefly Brit. to discharge or alight from a railroad train. —de·train′ment, n.

det·ri·ment (dĕt′rə mənt), n. 1. loss, damage, or injury. 2. a cause of loss or damage. [t. L: s. dētrimentum loss, damage] —Syn. 1. harm, hurt, impairment, disadvantage, prejudice. See damage.

det·ri·men·tal (dĕt′rĭ mĕn′təl), adj. causing detriment; injurious; prejudicial. —det′ri·men′tal·ly, adv.

de·tri·tal (dĭ trī′təl), adj. composed of detritus.

de·tri·tion (dĭ trĭsh′ən), n. act of wearing away by rubbing.

de·tri·tus (dĭ trī′təs), n. 1. Geol. particles of rock or other material worn or broken away from a mass, as by the action of water or glacial ice. 2. any disintegrated material; debris. [t. L: a rubbing away]

De·troit (dĭ troit′), n. 1. a city in SE Michigan, on the Detroit river. 1,670,144 (1960). 2. a river flowing from Lake St. Clair into Lake Erie, forming a part of the boundary between the U.S. and Canada: the busiest inland waterway in the world. 25 mi.

de trop (də trō′), French. 1. too much; too many. 2. in the way; not wanted.

de·trude (dĭ trōōd′), v.t., -truded, -truding. 1. to thrust out or away. 2. to thrust or force down. [t. L: m. s. dētrūdere]

de·trun·cate (dĭ trŭng′kāt), v.t., -cated, -cating. to reduce by cutting off a part; cut down. [t. L: m. s. dētruncātus, pp.] —de′trun·ca′tion, n.

de·tru·sion (dĭ trōō′zhən), n. act of detruding. [t. LL: s. dētrūsio, der. L dētrūdere thrust away]

Deu·ca·li·on (dū kā′lĭ ən, dōō-), n. Gk. Legend. a son of Prometheus. He survived the deluge with his wife Pyrrha, and became the ancestor of the renewed human race.

deuce[1] (dūs, dōōs), n. 1. Cards, Dice. a card, or the side of a die, having two pips. 2. Tennis. a score in which each side has three points (the score 40) in a game, or five games in a set. [t. OF: m. deus, g. L duōs, acc. of duo two]

b., blend of, blended; c., cognate with; d., dialect, dialectal; der., derived from; f., formed from; g., going back to; m., modification of; r., replacing; s., stem of; t., taken from; ?, perhaps. See the full key on inside cover.

deuce² (dūs, dōōs), *n. Colloq.* bad luck; the mischief; the devil (used in mild imprecations and exclamations). [special use of *deuce*, prob. t. LG: m. *de duus!* the deuce, an unlucky throw at dice. Cf. G *der daus!*]

deu·ced (dū′sĭd, dōō′-; dūst, dōōst), *adj. Brit. Colloq.* confounded; excessive. —**deu′ced, deu/ced·ly,** *adv.*

de·us ex ma·chi·na (dē′əs ĕks măk′ə nə), *Latin.* a supernatural or unmotivated device for unraveling a plot, esp. in drama. [L: god from a machine]

De·us Mi·se·re·a·tur (dē′əs mĭz′ər ĭ ā′tər or, esp. in Church Latin, dā′ŏŏs mē′sä rā ä′tŏŏr), *Latin.* (May) God have mercy; God be merciful (title of Psalm 67).

De·us vult (dē′əs vŭlt′ or, esp. in Church Latin, dā′-ŏŏs vŏŏlt′), *Latin.* God wills (it) (cry of the Crusaders).

deut-, var. of deuto-, before vowels.

Deut., Deuteronomy.

deuter-, a form of deutero- (def. 1) before a vowel.

deu·te·ri·um (dū tĭr′ĭ əm, dōō-), *n. Chem.* an isotope of hydrogen, having twice the mass of ordinary hydrogen; heavy hydrogen. Symbol: D; *at. no.:* 1; *at. wt.:* 2.01. [NL, t. Gk.: m. *deutereîon*, neut. sing. of *deutereîos*, adj., having second place]

deuterium oxide, *Chem.* heavy water, D₂O.

deutero-, a word element: 1. meaning "second" or "later," as in *deuterogamy.* 2. *Chem.* indicating the presence of deuterium. [t. Gk., comb. form of *deúteros* second]

deu·ter·o·ca·non·i·cal books (dū′tər ō kə nŏn′ə-kəl, dōō′-), the books of the Bible regarded by the Roman Catholic Church as canonical but not universally acknowledged as such in the early church, including, in the Old Testament, most of the Protestant Apocrypha.

deu·ter·og·a·my (dū′tə rŏg′ə mĭ, dōō′-), *n.* 1. a second marriage, after the death or divorce of a first husband or wife. 2. the custom of contracting such marriage. [t. Gk.: m. s. *deuterogamía* second marriage] —**deu′ter·og′a·mist,** *n.*

deu·ter·on (dū′tər ŏn′, dōō′-), *n. Physics.* a deuterium nucleus, a particle with one positive charge.

Deu·ter·on·o·my (dū′tə rŏn′ə mĭ, dōō′-), *n. Bible.* the fifth book of the Pentateuch, containing a second statement of the Mosaic law. [t. LL: m. s. *Deuteronomium*, t. Gk.: m. *Deuteronómion* the second law]

deuto-, 1. var. of deutero-. 2. *Chem.* a prefix denoting the second in a series. Also, **deut-.**

deu·to·plasm (dū′tə plăz′əm, dōō′-), *n. Embryol.* that part of the ovocyte which furnishes the nourishment of the embryo.

Deut·sche mark (doi′chə), the monetary unit of West Germany since 1948, worth about 25 U.S. cents. *Abbr.:* DM

Deut·sches Reich (doi′chəs rīкн′), former official name of Germany.

Deutsch·land (doich′länt′), *n.* German for **Germany.**

de·va (dā′və), *n. Hindu Myth.* a god or divinity; one of an order of good spirits. [t. Skt.]

De Va·le·ra (dĕv′ə lâr′ə, -lĭr′ə; *Irish* dĕ vä lā′rä), **Ea·mon** (ā′mən), born 1882, Irish statesman: president of Executive Council of Irish Free State, 1932–37; prime minister of Ireland, 1937–48. and 1951–54.

de·val·u·ate (dē văl′yōō āt′), *v.t.,* **-ated, -ating.** 1. to deprive of value; reduce the value of. 2. to fix a lower legal value on (a currency). [f. DE- + VALUE, n. + -ATE¹] —**de·val′u·a′tion,** *n.*

de·val·ue (dē văl′ū), *v.t.,* **-valued, -valuing.** to devaluate.

De·va·na·ga·ri (dā′və nä′gə rē′), *n.* the syllabary invented for writing Sanskrit and widely employed for modern languages of India. [t. Skt.: lit., Nagari (an alphabet of India) of the gods]

dev·as·tate (dĕv′ə stāt′), *v.t.,* **-tated, -tating.** to lay waste; render desolate. [t. L: m.s. *dēvāstātus,* pp.] —**dev′as·tat′ing·ly,** *adv.* —**dev′as·ta′tor,** *n.*

dev·as·ta·tion (dĕv′ə stā′shən), *n.* 1. act of devastating; destruction. 2. devastated state; desolation.

de Ve·ga (dĕ vĕ′gä), **Lope** (lō′pĕ), (*Lope Félix de Vega Carpio*) 1562–1635, Spanish dramatist and poet.

dev·el (dĕv′əl), *n. Scot.* a heavy blow.

devel., development.

de·vel·op (dĭ vĕl′əp), *v.t.* 1. to bring out the capabilities or possibilities of; bring to a more advanced or effective state; cause to grow or expand; elaborate. 2. to make known; disclose; reveal. 3. to bring into being or activity; generate; evolve. 4. *Biol.* to cause to go through the process of natural evolution from a previous and lower stage, or from an embryonic state to a later and more complex or perfect one. 5. *Math.* to express in an extended form, as in a series. 6. *Music.* to unfold, by various technical means, the inherent possibilities of (a theme). 7. *Photog.* **a.** to render visible (the latent image) in the exposed sensitized film of a photographic plate, etc. **b.** to treat (a photographic plate, etc.) with chemical agents so as to bring out the latent image. —*v.i.* 8. to grow into a more mature or advanced state; advance; expand: *he is developing into a good citizen.* 9. to come gradually into existence or operation; be evolved. 10. to come out or be disclosed: *the plot of a novel develops.* 11. *Biol.* to undergo differentiation in ontogeny or progress in phylogeny. 12. to undergo developing, as a photographic plate. Also, **de·vel′ope.** [t. F: m.s. *développer.* f. *dé-* DIS¹ + m. *voluper* wrap. Cf. ENVELOP] —**de·vel′op·a·ble,** *adj.*

de·vel·op·er (dĭ vĕl′əp ər), *n.* 1. one who or that which develops. 2. *Photog.* the reducing agent or solution used to develop a photographic film or plate.

de·vel·op·ment (dĭ vĕl′əp mənt), *n.* 1. act of developing. 2. a developed state, form, or product. 3. *Music.* the part of a movement or composition in which a theme or themes are developed. 4. a large group of private houses or of apartment houses of similar design, constructed as a unified community. —**de·vel′op·men′tal,** *adj.* —**de·vel′op·men′tal·ly,** *adv.* —**Syn.** 1. expansion, elaboration, growth.

Dev·e·reux (dĕv′ə rōō′), *n.* **Robert.** See **Essex.**

de·vest (dĭ vĕst′), *v.t.* 1. *Law.* to divest. 2. *Obs.* to undress. [MF: s. *devester,* var. of OF *desvestir,* f. *des-* DIS¹ + *vestir,* g. L *vestīre* clothe. See DIVEST]

De·vi (dā′vē), *n. Hinduism.* a female deity. [t. Skt.]

de·vi·ate (dē′vĭ āt′), *v.,* **-ated, -ating.** —*v.i.* 1. to turn aside (from the way or course); depart or swerve (from a course of action or procedure); digress (from a line of thought or reasoning). —*v.t.* 2. to cause to swerve; turn aside. [t. LL: m.s. *dēviātus,* pp. of *dēviāre,* der. L *dē-* DE- + *via* way] —**de′vi·a′tor,** *n.*

—**Syn.** 1. DEVIATE, DIGRESS, DIVERGE, SWERVE imply turning or going aside from a path. To DEVIATE is to turn or wander, often by slight degrees, from what is considered the most direct or desirable approach to a given physical, intellectual, or moral end: *fear caused him to deviate from the truth.* To DIGRESS is primarily to wander from the main theme or topic in writing or speaking, esp. for explanation or illustration: *some authors digress to relate entertaining episodes.* Two paths DIVERGE when they proceed from a common point in such directions that the distance between them increases: *the sides of an angle diverge from a common point, their interests gradually diverged.* To SWERVE is to make a sudden or sharp turn from a line or course (and then, often, return to it): *the car swerved to avoid striking a pedestrian.*

de·vi·a·tion (dē′vĭ ā′shən), *n.* 1. act of deviating; divergence. 2. *Statistics.* the difference between one of a set of values and the mean of the set.

de·vi·a·tion·ism (dē′vĭ ā′shən ĭz əm), *n.* (in Communist ideology) departure from accepted party policies. —**de′vi·a′tion·ist,** *n.*

de·vice (dĭ vīs′), *n.* 1. an invention or contrivance. 2. a plan or scheme for effecting a purpose. 3. a crafty scheme; a trick. 4. an artistic figure or design used as a heraldic bearing (often accompanied by a motto), or as an emblem, badge, trademark, or the like. 5. a motto. 6. (*pl.*) will; desire; inclination: *left to his own devices.* 7. something artistically or fancifully designed. 8. *Archaic.* act or faculty of planning, contriving, or inventing.. [b. ME *devis* division, discourse and *devise* heraldic device, will, both t. OF, g. L *dīvisus, -a,* pp., divided] —**Syn.** 3. wile, ruse, artifice, shift.

dev·il (dĕv′əl), *n., v.,* **-iled, -iling** or (*esp. Brit.*) **-illed, -illing.** —*n.* 1. *Theol.* **a.** (*sometimes cap.*) the supreme spirit of evil; Satan. **b.** a subordinate evil spirit at enmity with God, and having power to afflict man both with bodily disease and with spiritual corruption. 2. an atrociously wicked, cruel, and ill-tempered person. 3. a person of great cleverness, energy, or recklessness. 4. the errand boy or the youngest apprentice in a printing office. 5. a fellow, esp. an unfortunate one. 6. any of various mechanical devices, as a machine for tearing rags, etc. 7. the devil, an emphatic expletive used in disgust, vexation, wonder, strong negation, etc. 8. **the devil to pay,** great mischief afoot or trouble to be faced. 9. **give the devil his due,** to do justice even to a bad person or one who is disliked. —*v.t.* 10. *Colloq.* to harass, torment, or plague. 11. to tear (rags, etc.) to pieces with a devil (def. 6). 12. *Cookery.* to prepare (food) with hot or savory seasoning. [ME *devel,* OE *deofol,* t. L: m.s. *diabolus,* t. Gk.: m. *diábolos* Satan, orig. slanderer]

devil dog, a nickname for a United States Marine.

dev·il·fish (dĕv′əl fĭsh′), *n., pl.* **-fishes,** (*esp. collectively*) **-fish.** 1. any of various marine animals, as the manta rays. 2. any of various large cephalopods, as the octopus.

Devilfish (def. 1), *Manta hamilton i* (Total length 20 ft., tail 6 ft. width 20 ft.)

dev·il·ish (dĕv′əl ĭsh, dĕv′lĭsh), *adj.* 1. of, like, or befitting a devil; diabolical; fiendish. 2. *Colloq.* excessive; very great. —*adv.* 3. *Colloq.* excessively; extremely. —**dev′il·ish·ly,** *adv.* —**dev′il·ish·ness,** *n.* —**Syn.** 1. satanic, demoniac, infernal.

dev·il·kin (dĕv′əl kĭn), *n.* a little devil; an imp.

dev·il·ment (dĕv′əl mənt), *n.* devilish action or conduct; mischief.

dev·il·ry (dĕv′əl rĭ), *n., pl.* **-ries.** deviltry.

devil's advocate, 1. an advocate of an opposing or bad cause. 2. *Rom. Cath. Ch.* a person appointed to present the arguments against a proposed canonization as a saint. [trans. of L *advocātus diabolī*]

devil's darning needle, dragonfly.

devil's food cake, a rich, chocolate cake.

Devil's Island, one of the Safety Islands, off the coast of French Guiana: former French penal colony. French, *Île du Diable.*

devil's tattoo, a meaningless beating or drumming with the hands or feet.

dev·il·try (dĕv′əl trĭ), *n., pl.* **-tries.** 1. wicked or reckless mischief. 2. extreme wickedness. 3. diabolic magic or art. 4. demonology. Also, **devilry.**

ăct, āble, dâre, ärt; ĕbb, ēqual; ĭf, īce; hŏt, ōver, ôrder, oil, bŏŏk, ōōze, out; ŭp, ūse, ûrge; ə = a in alone; ch, chief; g, give; ng, ring; sh, shoe; th, thin; ŧh, that; zh, vision. See the full key on inside cover.

dev·il·wood (děv′əl wŏod′), *n.* a small oleaceous tree, *Osmanthus americanus*, of the U.S., with a hard wood.

de·vi·ous (dē′vĭ əs), *adj.* 1. departing from the direct way; circuitous: *a devious course.* 2. turning aside from the way; swerving; straying: *a devious comet.* 3. erring. [t. L: m. *dēvius* out of the way] —**de′vi·ous·ly,** *adv.* —**de′vi·ous·ness,** *n.*

de·vis·a·ble (dĭ vī′zə bəl), *adj.* 1. capable of being invented or contrived. 2. *Law.* capable of being bequeathed or assigned by will.

de·vis·al (dĭ vī′zəl), *n.* act of devising; contrivance.

de·vise (dĭ vīz′), *v.,* -**vised,** -**vising,** *n.* —*v.t.* 1. to order or arrange the plan of; think out; plan; contrive; invent. 2. *Law.* to assign or transmit (property, formerly specif. real property) by will. 3. *Obs.* to conceive or imagine. —*v.i.* 4. to form a plan; contrive. —*n.* 5. *Law.* a. act of disposing of property, esp. real property, by will. b. a will or clause in a will disposing of property, esp. real property. c. the property disposed of. [ME *devise(n),* t. OF: m. *deviser,* g. LL freq. of L *dīvidere* separate] —**de·vis′er,** *n.* —**Syn.** 1. See **prepare.**

de·vi·see (dĭ vī′zē′, děv′ə zē′), *n. Law.* one to whom a devise is made.

de·vi·sor (dĭ vī′zər), *n. Law.* one who makes a devise.

de·vi·tal·ize (dē vī′tə līz′), *v.t.,* -**ized,** -**izing.** to deprive of vitality or vital properties; make lifeless or weak. —**de·vi′tal·i·za′tion,** *n.* —**Ant.** invigorate.

de·vit·ri·fy (dē vĭt′rə fī′), *v.t.,* -**fied,** -**fying.** to deprive, wholly or partly, of vitreous character or properties. —**de·vit′ri·fi·ca′tion,** *n.*

de·vo·cal·ize (dē vō′kə līz′), *v.t.,* -**ized,** -**izing.** *Phonet.* to deprive of vocal quality. —**de·vo′cal·i·za′tion,** *n.*

de·void (dĭ void′), *adj.* empty, void, or destitute (fol. by *of*). [orig. pp. of obs. *devoid,* v., t. OF: m. *desvuidier* empty out, f. *des-* DIS-¹ + *vuidier* empty, VOID, v.]

de·voir (də vwär′, děv′wär; *Fr.* də vwär′), *n.* 1. an act of civility or respect. 2. *(pl.)* respects or compliments. 3. *Archaic.* duty. [t. F, orig. inf., g. L *dēbēre* owe]

dev·o·lu·tion (děv′ə lōō′shən), *n.* 1. act or fact of devolving; passage onward from stage to stage. 2. the passing on to a successor of an unexercised right. 3. *Law.* the passing of property upon death. 4. *Biol.* degeneration; retrograde evolution (opposed to *evolution*).

de·volve (dĭ vŏlv′), *v.,* -**volved,** -**volving.** —*v.t.* 1. to transfer or delegate (a duty, responsibility, etc.) to or upon another; pass on. 2. *Archaic.* to roll downward; roll. —*v.i.* 3. to fall as a duty or responsibility on a person. 4. *Archaic.* to roll down. [t. L: m.s. *dēvolvere* roll down] —**de·volve′ment,** *n.*

Dev·on (děv′ən), *n.* 1. one of a breed of cattle, usually red, originating in Devonshire. 2. Devonshire.

De·vo·ni·an (də vō′nĭ ən), *adj. Stratig.* pertaining to a geological period or a system of rocks following the Silurian and preceding the Carboniferous or Mississippian. 2. of or pertaining to Devonshire, England. —*n.* 3. *Stratig.* the Devonian period or system.

Dev·on·shire (děv′ən shĭr′, -shər), *n.* a county in SW England. 797,738 pop. (1951); 2612 sq. mi. *Co. seat:* Exeter. Also, **Devon.**

de·vote (dĭ vōt′), *v.,* -**voted,** -**voting,** *adj.* —*v.t.* 1. to give up or appropriate to a particular pursuit, occupation, purpose, cause, person, etc.: *devoting himself to science, evenings devoted to reading.* 2. to appropriate by or as by a vow; set apart or dedicate by a solemn or formal act; consecrate. 3. *Rare.* to pronounce a curse upon; doom. —*adj.* 4. *Archaic.* devoted. [t. L: m. s. *dēvōtus,* pp., vowed] —**Syn.** 1. assign, apply.

de·vot·ed (dĭ vō′tĭd), *adj.* 1. zealous or ardent in attachment: *a devoted friend.* 2. dedicated; consecrated. 3. *Archaic.* accursed or doomed. —**de·vot′ed·ly,** *adv.* —**de·vot′ed·ness,** *n.*

dev·o·tee (děv′ə tē′), *n.* 1. one ardently devoted to anything. 2. one zealously or fanatically devoted to religion.

de·vote·ment (dĭ vōt′mənt), *n.* devotion; dedication.

de·vo·tion (dĭ vō′shən), *n.* 1. dedication; consecration. 2. earnest attachment to a cause, person, etc. 3. a giving over or appropriating to any purpose, cause, etc. 4. *Theol.* the ready will to perform what belongs to the service of God. 5. *(often pl.) Eccles.* religious observance or worship; a form of prayer or worship for special use. [ME, t. L: s. *dēvōtio*] —**Syn.** 2. See **love.**

de·vo·tion·al (dĭ vō′shən əl), *adj.* characterized by devotion; used in devotions. —**de·vo′tion·al·ly,** *adv.*

de·vour (dĭ vour′), *v.t.* 1. to swallow or eat up voraciously or ravenously. 2. to consume destructively, recklessly, or wantonly. 3. to swallow up or engulf. 4. to take in greedily with the senses or intellect. 5. to absorb or engross wholly: *devoured by fears.* [ME *devoure(n),* t. OF: m. *devorer,* t. L: m. *dēvorāre* swallow down] —**de·vour′er,** *n.* —**de·vour′ing·ly,** *adv.*

de·vout (dĭ vout′), *adj.* 1. devoted to divine worship or service; pious; religious. 2. expressing devotion or piety: *devout prayer.* 3. earnest or sincere; hearty. [ME, t. OF: m. *devot,* t. L: s. *dēvōtus,* pp., devoted] —**de·vout′·ly,** *adv.* —**de·vout′ness,** *n.* —**Syn.** 1. See **religious.**

De Vries (də vrēs′), **Hugo** (hy′gō), 1848–1935, Dutch botanist: proposed mutation theory of evolution.

dew (dū, dōō), *n.* 1. moisture condensed from the atmosphere, esp. at night, and deposited in the form of small drops upon any cool surface. 2. something likened to dew, as serving to refresh or as suggestive of morning or of youth. 3. moisture in small drops on a surface, as tears, perspiration, etc. —*v.t.* 4. to wet with or as with dew. [ME; OE *dēaw,* c. G *tau*] —**dew′less,** *adj.*

de·wan (dĭ wän′, -wŏn′), *n.* (in India) any of certain officials or servants. Also, **diwan.** [t. Hind.: minister (of state) t. Pers.: m. *dēvan* register. See DIVAN]

Dew·ar (dū′ər, dōō′-), *n.* **Sir James,** 1842–1923, Scottish chemist and physicist.

dew·ber·ry (dū′běr′ĭ, dōō′-), *n., pl.* -**ries.** 1. (in North America) the fruit of several species of running, trailing blackberries, principally *Rubus flagellaris.* 2. (in England) the fruit of *Rubus caesius.* 3. a plant bearing either fruit.

dew·claw (dū′klô′, dōō′-), *n.* 1. a functionless inner claw or digit in the foot of some dogs, not reaching the ground in walking. 2. an analogous false hoof of deer, hogs, etc.

dew·drop (dū′drŏp′, dōō′-), *n.* a drop of dew.

De Wet (də vět′), **Christian Rudolph** (krĭs′tĭ än′ rŭ′dŏlf), 1854–1922, Boer general.

Dew·ey (dū′ĭ, dōō′ĭ), *n.* 1. **George,** 1837–1917, U.S. admiral: defeated Spanish fleet in Manila Bay in the Spanish-American War. 2. **John,** 1859–1952, U.S. philosopher and educator. 3. **Melvil,** 1851–1931, U.S. librarian. 4. **Thomas Edmund,** born 1902, U.S. lawyer and political leader.

D, Dewclaw. Left forefoot of a terrier

Dewey decimal system, *Library Science.* a system of classifying books and other publications into ten main classes of knowledge with further subdivision in these classes by use of the numbers (**Dewey decimals**) of a decimal system, devised by Melvil Dewey in 1876 and used in most libraries in the United States.

De Witt (də vĭt′), **Jan** (yän), 1625–72, Dutch statesman.

dew·lap (dū′lăp′, dōō′-), *n.* 1. the pendulous fold of skin under the throat of cattle. 2. any similar part, as the loose skin under the throat of some dogs, the wattle of fowls, etc. [f. *dew,* of uncert. meaning + *lap,* OE *læppa* pendulous piece. Cf. Dan. *doglæp*] —**dew′-lapped′,** *adj.*

DEW line (dū, dōō), a 3,000-mile-long network of radar stations north of the Arctic Circle to provide advance warning of the approach of hostile planes, missiles, etc. [*d(istant) e(arly) w(arning)*]

dew plant, the ice plant.

dew point, the temperature of the air at which dew begins to be deposited; the temperature at which a given sample of air will have a relative humidity of 100%.

dew·y (dū′ĭ, dōō′ĭ), *adj.,* **dewier, dewiest.** 1. moist with or as with dew. 2. having the quality of dew: *dewy tears.* 3. *Poetic.* falling gently, or refreshing like dew: *dewy sleep.* 4. of dew. —**dew′i·ly,** *adv.* —**dew′i·ness,** *n.*

dex·ter (děk′stər), *adj.* 1. on the right side; right. 2. *Her.* situated to the right of the bearer and hence to the left of the spectator (opposed to *sinister*). 3. *Obs.* favorable. [t. L: right, favorable]

dex·ter·i·ty (děks těr′ə tĭ), *n.* 1. adroitness or skill in using the hands or body. 2. mental adroitness or skill; cleverness. 3. right-handedness. [f. DEXTER + -(I)TY²]

dex·ter·ous (děks′trəs, -tər əs), *adj.* 1. skillful or adroit in the use of the hands or body. 2. having mental adroitness or skill; clever. 3. done with dexterity. 4. right-handed. Also, **dextrous.** —**dex′ter·ous·ly,** *adv.* —**dex′ter·ous·ness,** *n.* —**Syn.** 1. adroit, deft, nimble, skillful. —**Ant.** 1. clumsy. 2. inept. 3. awkward.

dex·tral (děks′trəl), *adj.* 1. on the right-hand side; right. 2. right-handed. —**dex′tral·ly,** *adv.*

dex·tran (děks′trən), *n. Chem.* a white gummy material, produced from milk, molasses, etc., by bacterial action. [f. DEXTR(O)- + -AN(E)]

dex·trin (děks′trĭn), *n. Chem.* a soluble gummy substance formed from starch by the action of heat, acids, or ferments, occurring in various forms and having dextrorotatory properties, used as a substitute for gum arabic, as a mucilage, etc. Also, **dex·trine** (děks′trĭn, -trēn). [t. F: m. *dextrine,* der. L *dexter* right]

dex·tro (děks′trō), *adj. Chem.* turning clockwise.

dextro-, a word element meaning: 1. right. 2. *Chem.* turning clockwise. Also, **dextr-.** [t. L, comb. form of *dexter* right]

dex·tro·glu·cose (děks′trō glōō′kōs), *n. Chem.* d-glucose. See glucose.

dex·tro·gy·rate (děks′trō jī′rĭt, -rāt), *adj. Optics, Crystall., etc.* causing to turn toward the right hand: *a dextrogyrate crystal.*

dex·tro·ro·ta·tion (děks′trō rō tā′shən), *n. Optics, Chem., etc.* a turning of the plane of polarization of light to the right.

dex·tro·ro·ta·to·ry (děks′trō rō′tə tôr′ĭ), *adj. Optics, Chem., etc.* turning the plane of polarization of light to the right, as certain crystals and compounds. Also, **dex·tro·ro·ta·ry** (děks′trō rō′tə rĭ).

dex·trorse (děks′trôrs, děks trôrs′), *adj. Bot.* rising spirally from left to right (from a point of view at the center of the spiral), as a stem (opposed to *sinistrorse*). Also, **dex·tror′sal.** [t. L: m.s. *dextrorsum* toward the right] —**dex′trorse·ly,** *adv.*

Dextrorse stem

dex·trose (dĕks/trōs), *n. Chem.* dextroglucose, commercially obtainable from starch by acid hydrolysis. See glucose. [f. DEXTR(O)- + (GLUC)OSE]

dex·trous (dĕks/trəs), *adj.* dexterous. **—dex/trous·ly,** *adv.* **—dex/trous·ness,** *n.*

dey (dā), *n.* 1. the title of the governor of Algiers before the French conquest in 1830. 2. a title sometimes borne by the former rulers of Tunis and Tripoli. [t. F, t. Turk.: m. *dāī,* orig., maternal uncle]

Dezh·nev (dĕzh nyôf/), *n.* Cape, the NE tip of Asia, on Bering Strait. Also, **East Cape.**

de·zinc·i·fi·ca·tion (dē zĭng/kə fə kā/shən), *n. Metall.* a process of corrosion in which the zinc of copper-zinc alloys becomes absorbed by the environment.

D.F., 1. (L *Defensor Fidei*) Defender of the Faith. 2. Distrito Federal.

dg., decigram; decigrams.

d-glu·cose (dē/glōō/kōs), *n. Chem.* dextroglucose. See glucose.

Dhah·ran (dä rän/), *n.* a city in E Saudi Arabia; oil center. 75,000 (est. 1952).

dhar·ma (där/mə; *native* dŭr/-), *n.* (in Hinduism and Buddhism) 1. essential quality or character. 2. law, esp. religious law. 3. conformity to law; propriety. 4. virtue. 5. religion. [Skt.: decree, custom]

dhar·na (där/nə; *native* dŭr/-), *n.* the practice formerly common in India, etc., of fasting at a person's door until he complies with some demand. Also, **dhur·na** (dŭr/nə). [Hind.: placing]

Dhau·la·gi·ri (dou/lə gĭr/ĭ), *n.* a peak of the Himalayas, in Nepal. 26,826 ft.

dhole (dōl), *n.* the Asiatic wild dog, a fierce, red-coated species, *Cuon rutilus,* of Asia, hunting in packs, and capable of running down large game. [orig. unknown]

dho·ti (dō/tĭ), *n., pl.* **-tis.** a loincloth worn by men in India. Also, **dhoo·ti** (dōō/tĭ). [t. Hind.]

dhow (dou), *n.* an Arab coasting vessel, usually lateen-rigged, used in the Arabian Sea, etc.

di (dē), *n. Music.* a tone in the scale between do and re.

di-¹, a prefix of Greek origin, meaning "twice," "doubly," "two," freely used (like *bi-*) as an English formative, as in *dicotyledon, dipolar,* and in many chemical terms, as *diatomic, disulfide.* Also, **dis-².** Cf. **mono-.** [t. Gk., repr. *dís* twice, double; akin to Gk. *dýo* two. See BI-]

di-², var. of dis-¹, before b, d, l, m, n, r, s, and v, and sometimes g and j, as in *divide.*

di-³, var. of dia-, before vowels, as in *diocese, diorama.*

Di, *Chem.* didymium.

dia-, a prefix of learned words meaning: 1. passing through, as in *diathermy.* 2. thoroughly; completely, as in *diagnosis.* 3. going apart, as in *dialysis.* 4. opposed in moment, as in *diamagnetism.* Also, **di-³.** [t. Gk., repr. *diá,* prep., through, between, across, by, of; akin to *dýo* two, and *di-* DI-¹]

di·a·base (dī/ə bās/), *n.* 1. *U.S.* a dark igneous rock occurring as minor intrusives composed essentially of labradorite and pyroxene. 2. *Brit.* a dark-colored igneous rock consisting essentially of augite and feldspar, an altered dolerite. 3. *Obs.* diorite. [t. F, f. *dia-* (erron. for *di-* two) + *base* BASE¹] **—di/a·ba/sic,** *adj.*

di·a·be·tes (dī/ə bē/tĭs, -tēz), *n. Pathol.* 1. a disease in which the ability of the body to use sugar is impaired and sugar appears abnormally in the urine (**diabetes mellitus**). 2. a disease in which there is a persistent abnormal amount of urine (**diabetes insipidus**). [t. NL, t. Gk.: lit., a passer through]

di·a·bet·ic (dī/ə bĕt/ĭk, -bē/tĭk), *adj.* 1. of or pertaining to diabetes. 2. having diabetes. **—n.** 3. a person who has diabetes.

di·a·ble·rie (dĭ ä/blərĭ; *Fr.* dyä blə rē/), *n.* 1. diabolic magic or art; sorcery. 2. the domain or realm of devils. 3. the lore of devils; demonology. 4. reckless mischief; deviltry. [t. F, der. *diable* DEVIL]

di·a·ble·ry (dĭ ä/blə rĭ), *n., pl.* **-leries.** diablerie.

di·a·bol·ic (dī/ə bŏl/ĭk), *adj.* 1. having the qualities of a devil; fiendish; outrageously wicked: *a diabolic plot.* 2. pertaining to or actuated by the devil or a devil. Also, **di/a·bol/i·cal** (esp. for def. 1). [t. LL: s. *diabolicus,* t. Gk.: m. *diabolikós*] **—di/a·bol/i·cal·ly,** *adv.* **—di/a·bol/i·cal·ness,** *n.*

di·a·bo·lism (dī äb/ə lĭz/əm), *n.* 1. *Theol.* **a.** action aided or caused by the devil; sorcery; witchcraft. **b.** the character or condition of a devil. **c.** doctrine concerning devils; belief in or worship of devils. 2. action befitting the devil; deviltry. **—di·ab/o·list,** *n.*

di·a·bo·lize (dī äb/ə līz/), *v.t.,* **-lized, -lizing.** 1. to make diabolical or devilish. 2. to represent as diabolical. 3. to subject to diabolical influences.

di·a·caus·tic (dī/ə kôs/tĭk), *Math., Optics.* **—adj.** 1. denoting a caustic surface or curve formed by refraction of light. See **catacaustic.** **—n.** 2. a diacaustic surface or curve.

di·ach·y·lon (dī ăk/ə lŏn/), *n.* an adhesive plaster consisting essentially of lead oxide and oil. Also, **di·ach·y·lum** (dī ăk/ə ləm). [t. L, t. Gk.: m. *dià chýlōn* (something) made of juices; also Latinized as *diachylum,* whence E sp. with *-um;* r. ME *diaculon,* t. ML, and ME *diaquilon,* t. F, both g. L *diachýlōn*]

di·ac·id (dī ăs/ĭd), *adj. Chem.* 1. capable of combining with two molecules of a monobasic acid. 2. (of an acid or a salt) having two replaceable hydrogen atoms.

di·ac·o·nal (dī ăk/ə nəl), *adj.* pertaining to a deacon. [t. LL: s. *diāconālis,* der. *diāconus* DEACON]

di·ac·o·nate (dī ăk/ə nĭt, -nāt/), *n.* 1. the office or dignity of a deacon. 2. a body of deacons.

di·a·crit·ic (dī/ə krĭt/ĭk), *n.* . 1. a diacritical mark, point, or sign. **—adj.** 2. diacritical. 3. *Med.* diagnostic. [t. Gk.: m. s. *diakritikós* that separates or distinguishes]

di·a·crit·i·cal (dī/ə krĭt/ə kəl), *adj.* 1. distinctive. 2. capable of distinguishing. **—di/a·crit/i·cal·ly,** *adv.*

diacritical mark, point, or sign, a mark, point, or sign added or attached to a letter or character to distinguish it from another of similar form, to give it a particular phonetic value, to indicate stress, etc.

di·ac·tin·ic (dī/ăk tĭn/ĭk), *adj. Photog..* etc. capable of transmitting the actinic rays of light. **—di·ac/tin·ism,** *n.*

di·a·del·phous (dī/ə dĕl/fəs), *adj. Bot.* 1. (of stamens) united into two sets by their filaments. 2. (of plants) having the stamens so united. [f. DI-¹ + s. Gk. *adelphós* brother + -OUS]

di·a·dem (dī/ə dĕm/), *n.* 1. a crown. 2. a cloth headband, sometimes adorned with jewels, formerly worn by Oriental kings. 3. royal dignity or authority. **—v.t.** 4. to adorn with, or as if with, a diadem; crown. [t. L: m. *diadēma,* t. Gk.: fillet, band; r. ME *dyademe,* t. OF]

di·aer·e·sis (dī ĕr/ə sĭs), *n., pl.* **-ses** (-sēz/). dieresis. [t. L, t. Gk.: m. *diaíresis* division]

diag., diagram.

Dia·ghi·lev (dyä gĭ lĕf), *n.* **Sergei Pavlovich** (sĕr gĕ/ĭ pä vlô/vĭch), 1872–1929, Russian art critic, ballet master, and producer.

di·ag·nose (dī/əg nōs/, -nōz/), *v.t., v.i.,* **-nosed, -nosing.** to make a diagnosis of (a case, disease, etc.).

di·ag·no·sis (dī/əg nō/sĭs), *n., pl.* **-ses** (-sēz). 1. *Med.* **a.** the process of determining by examination the nature and circumstances of a diseased condition. **b.** the decision reached from such an examination. 2. *Biol.* scientific determination; a description which classifies precisely. 3. any analogous examination or analysis. [t. NL, t. Gk.: a distinguishing]

di·ag·nos·tic (dī/əg nŏs/tĭk), *adj.* 1. pertaining to a diagnosis. 2. having value in diagnosis. **—n.** 3. diagnosis (def. 1 a, b). 4. a symptom or characteristic of value in diagnosis. [t. Gk.: m. s. *diagnōstikós*] **—di/ag·nos/ti·cal·ly,** *adv.*

di·ag·nos·ti·cate (dī/əg nŏs/tə kāt/), *v.t., v.i.,* **-cated, -cating.** to diagnose.

di·ag·nos·ti·cian (dī/əg nŏs tĭsh/ən), *n.* an expert in making diagnoses.

di·ag·nos·tics (dī/əg nŏs/tĭks), *n.* the art or science of diagnosis. [pl. of DIAGNOSTIC]

di·ag·o·nal (dī ăg/ə nəl), *adj.* 1. *Math.* **a.** connecting, as a straight line, two nonadjacent angles or vertices of a quadrilateral, polygon, or polyhedron. **b.** extending, as a plane, from one edge of a solid figure to an opposite edge. 2. having an oblique direction. 3. having oblique lines, ridges, etc. **—n.** 4. a diagonal line or plane. 5. a diagonal row, plank, part, etc. 6. diagonal cloth. [t. L: s. *diagōnālis,* der. Gk. *diagōnios* from angle to angle] **—di·ag/o·nal·ly,** *adv.*

di·a·gram (dī/ə grăm/), *n., v.,* **-gramed, -graming** or (*esp. Brit.*) **-grammed, -gramming. —n.** 1. a figure, or set of lines, marks, etc., to accompany a geometrical demonstration, give the outlines or general features of an object, show the course or results of a process, etc. 2. a chart, plan, or scheme. **—v.t.** 3. to represent by a diagram; make a diagram of. [t. L: m. *diagramma,* t. Gk.: that which is marked out by lines]

di·a·gram·mat·ic (dī/ə grə măt/ĭk), *adj.* 1. in the form of a diagram. 2. pertaining to diagrams. Also, **di/a·gram·mat/i·cal.** **—di/a·gram·mat/i·cal·ly,** *adv.*

di·a·graph (dī/ə grăf/, -gräf/), *n.* 1. a device for drawing, used in reproducing outlines, plans, etc., mechanically on any desired scale. 2. a combined protractor and scale. [t. F: m. *diagraphe,* t. Gk.: m. *digraphē* marking out by lines. See DIAGRAM]

di·a·ki·ne·sis (dī/ə kĭ nē/sĭs, -kī-), *n. Biol.* the prophase of the first meiotic division of a spermatocyte or ovocyte. [NL, f. *dia-* DIA- + Gk. *kínēsis* movement]

di·al (dī/əl, dīl), *n., v.,* **dialed, dialing** or (*esp. Brit.*) **dialled, dialling. —n.** 1. a face upon which time is indicated by hands, pointers, or shadows. 2. a plate or disk with graduations or figures, as for the indication of pressure, number of revolutions, etc., as by the movements of a pointer. 3. a rotatable plate or disk used for tuning a radio station in or out. 4. a plate or disk with letters and numbers, used in making telephone connections. 5. *Mining.* a compass used for underground surveying. **—v.t.** 6. to measure with or as with a dial. 7. to indicate on a telephone dial. 8. to call by means of a telephone dial. 9. *Mining.* to survey with the aid of a dial (def. 5) or compass. **—v.i.** 10. to use a telephone dial. [ME, t. ML: s. *diālis* daily, der. L *dies* day]

dial., 1. dialect. 2. dialectal.

di·a·lect (dī/ə lĕkt/), *n.* 1. the language of a particular district or class, esp. as distinguished from the standard language, as a provincial or rural substandard form of a language. 2. a special variety or branch of a language, as Afrikaans if considered as a branch of Dutch. 3. a language considered as one of a number of related languages: *the Romance dialects.* 4. jargon.. [t. L: s. *dialectus,* t. Gk.: m. *diálektos* discourse, language, dialect] **—Syn.** 3. See **language.**

di·a·lec·tal (dī/ə lĕk/təl), *adj.* **1.** of a dialect. **2.** characteristic of a dialect. —**di·a·lec/tal·ly**, *adv.*

di·a·lec·tic (dī/ə lĕk/tĭk), *adj.* **1.** of, pertaining to, or of the nature of logical argumentation. **2.** dialectal. —*n.* **3.** the art or practice of logical discussion as employed in investigating the truth of a theory or opinion. **4.** logical argumentation. **5.** logic, or a branch of logic. [t. L: s. *dialectica*, t. Gk.: m. *dialektikē* (*technē*) argumentative (art); r. ME *dialetike*, t. OF]

di·a·lec·ti·cal (dī/ə lĕk/tə kəl), *adj.* **1.** dialectic. **2.** dialectal. —**di·a·lec/ti·cal·ly**, *adv.*

di·a·lec·ti·cian (dī/ə lĕk tĭsh/ən), *n.* **1.** one skilled in dialectic; a logician. **2.** one who studies dialects.

dia·lec·ti·cism (dī/ə lĕk/tə sĭz/əm), *n.* **1.** dialectal speech or influence. **2.** a dialectal word or expression.

di·a·lec·tics (dī/ə lĕk/tĭks), *n.* dialectic (def. 5).

di·a·lo·gism (dī ăl/ə jĭz/əm), *n.* the discussion of a subject in an imaginary dialogue. [t. Gk.: s. *dialogismós* consideration]

di·a·lo·gist (dī ăl/ə jĭst), *n.* **1.** a speaker in a dialogue. **2.** a writer of dialogue. —**di·a·lo·gis·tic** (dī/ə lō jĭs/tĭk), *adj.*

di·a·lo·gize (dī ăl/ə jīz/), *v.i.* **-gized, -gizing.** to carry on a dialogue. [t. Gk.: m.s. *dialogízesthai* converse]

di·a·logue (dī/ə lôg/, -lŏg/), *n., v.,* **-logued, -loguing.** —*n.* **1.** conversation between two or more persons. **2.** the conversation between characters in a novel, drama, etc. **3.** a literary work in the form of a conversation. —*v.i.* **4.** to carry on a dialogue; converse. —*v.t.* **5.** to put into the form of a dialogue. Also, **di/a·log/.** [t. F, t. L: m.s. *dialogus*, t. Gk.: m. *diálogos*; r. ME *dialoge*, t. OF] —**di/a·logu/er**, *n.*

dial telephone system, a system in which a connection between two telephones (**dial telephones**) is ordinarily made without the help of an operator.

dial tone, (in a dial telephone) a steady humming sound which indicates that the line is ready for dialing.

di·al·y·sis (dī ăl/ə sĭs), *n., pl.* **-ses** (-sēz/). *Phys. Chem.* the separation of crystalloids from colloids in a solution by diffusion through a membrane. [t. Gk.: separation, dissolution]

di·a·lyt·ic (dī/ə lĭt/ĭk), *adj.* **1.** pertaining to dialysis. **2.** characterized by dialysis. —**di/a·lyt/i·cal·ly**, *adv.*

di·a·lyze (dī/ə līz/), *v.t.* **-lyzed, -lyzing.** *Phys. Chem.* to subject to dialysis; separate or procure by dialysis. —**di/a·lyz/er**, *n.*

diam., diameter.

di·a·mag·net·ic (dī/ə măg nĕt/ĭk), *adj.* denoting or pertaining to a class of substances, as bismuth and copper, whose permeability is less than that of a vacuum. In a magnetic field their induced magnetism is in a direction opposite to that of iron (opposed to *paramagnetic* and *ferromagnetic*). —**di/a·mag·net/i·cal·ly**, *adv.* —**di·a·mag·net·ism** (dī/ə măg/nə tĭz/əm), *n.*

di·a·man·tif·er·ous (dī/ə măn tĭf/ər əs), *adj.* containing diamonds. [see DIAMOND, -FEROUS]

di·am·e·ter (dī ăm/ə tər), *n.* **1.** *Geom.* **a.** a straight line passing though the center of a circle or sphere and terminated at each end by the circumference or surface. **b.** a straight line passing from side to side of any figure or body, through its center. **2.** the length of such a line; thickness. [ME *diametre*, t. OF, t. L: m. s. *diametros*, t. Gk.: diagonal, diameter]

di·am·e·tral (dī ăm/ə trəl), *adj.* **1.** of a diameter. **2.** forming a diameter. —**di·am/e·tral·ly**, *adv.*

di·a·met·ri·cal (dī/ə mĕt/rə kəl), *adj.* **1.** pertaining to a diameter; along a diameter. **2.** direct; complete; absolute: *diametrical opposites.* Also, **di/a·met/ric.** —**di/a·met/ri·cal·ly**, *adv.*

di·am·ine (dī/ə mēn/, -mĭn, dī/ə mēn/), *n. Chem.* a compound containing two NH₂ radicals.

dia·mond (dī/mənd, dī/ə-), *n.* **1.** a pure or nearly pure form of carbon, crystallized in the isometric system, of extreme hardness and, when used as a precious stone, of great brilliancy. **2.** a piece of this stone. **3.** a tool provided with an uncut diamond, used for cutting glass. **4.** *Geom.* an equilateral quadrilateral, esp. as placed with its diagonals vertical and horizontal; a lozenge or rhombus. **5.** *Cards.* **a.** a red lozenge-shaped figure on a playing card. **b.** a card of the suit bearing such figures. **c.** (*pl.*) the suit. **6.** *Baseball.* **a.** the space enclosed by the home plate and three bases; the infield. **b.** the entire field. **7.** a printing type (4½ point) of a size between brilliant and pearl. —*adj.* **8.** made of or with a diamond or diamonds. **9.** indicating the 75th, or sometimes the 60th, event of a series, as of a wedding anniversary. —*v.t.* **10.** to adorn with or as with diamonds. [ME *diamant*, t. OF, t. LL: s. *diamas*, alter. of L *adamas* adamant, diamond. See ADAMANT]

Dia·mond (dī/mənd, dī/ə-), *n.* a Cape, a hill overlooking the St. Lawrence at Quebec, Canada.

dia·mond·back (dī/mənd băk/, dī/ə-), *n.* **1.** any of the rattlesnakes with diamond-shaped marking, as the **Florida diamondback**, *Crotalus adamanteus.* **2.** Also, **diamondback terrapin.** any of several terrapins of edible turtles of the genus *Malaclemmys,* living in the salt-water marshes of the eastern and southern U.S. and characterized by diamond-shaped markings on the back.

Diamond Head, a promontory at Honolulu, in the Hawaiian Islands.

Di·an·a (dī ăn/ə), *n.* **1.** an ancient Italian deity, goddess of the moon and of hunting, and protectress of women, identified by the Romans with the Greek Artemis. **2.** a young woman of fine physique and easy, graceful carriage. **3.** the moon.

di·an·drous (dī ăn/drəs), *adj. Bot.* **1.** (of a flower) having two stamens. **2.** (of a plant) having flowers with two stamens. [t. NL: m. *diandrus.* See DI-, ANDROUS]

di·a·no·et·ic (dī/ə nō ĕt/ĭk), *adj.* pertaining to thought or reasoning, esp. discursive reasoning. [t. Gk.: s. *dianoētikós* pertaining to thinking]

di·an·thus (dī ăn/thəs), *n.* any plant of the caryophyllaceous genus *Dianthus,* as the carnation or the sweet william. [NL, f. Gk.: *Di(ós)* of Zeus + m. *ánthos* flower]

di·a·pa·son (dī/ə pā/zən, -sən), *n. Music.* **1.** a melody or strain. **2.** the compass of a voice or instrument. **3.** a fixed standard of pitch. **4.** either of two principal timbres or stops of a pipe organ: **a.** the **open diapason,** giving full, majestic tones. **b.** the **stopped diapason,** giving powerful flutelike tones. **5.** any of several other organ stops. **6.** a tuning fork. [t. L, t. Gk., short for *dià pasōn chordōn symphōnia* concord through all notes (of the scale)] —**di·a·pa·son·ic** (dī/ə pā zŏn/ĭk, -sŏn/-), *adj.*

di·a·per (dī/ə pər), *n.* **1.** a piece of cloth which forms part of a baby's underclothing; a baby's breechcloth. **2.** a linen or cotton fabric with a woven pattern of small constantly repeated figures, as diamonds. **3.** such a pattern (originally used in medieval weaving of silk and gold). —*v.t.* **4.** to put a diaper on (a baby). **5.** to ornament with a diaperlike pattern. [ME *diapre,* t. OF, var. of *diaspre,* ult. t. MGk.: m. *díaspros* pure white]

di·a·pha·ne·i·ty (dī/ə fə nē/ə tĭ), *n.* transparency.

di·aph·a·nous (dī ăf/ə nəs), *adj.* transparent; translucent. [t. ML: m. *diaphanus,* t. Gk.: m. *diaphanēs*] —**di·aph/a·nous·ly**, *adv.* —**di·aph/a·nous·ness**, *n.*

di·a·pho·re·sis (dī/ə fə rē/sĭs), *n. Med.* perspiration, esp. when artificially produced. [t. LL, t. Gk.: a sweat]

di·a·pho·ret·ic (dī/ə fə rĕt/ĭk), *Med.* —*adj.* **1.** producing perspiration. —*n.* **2.** a diaphoretic medicine.

di·a·phragm (dī/ə frăm/), *n.* **1.** *Anat.* **a.** a muscular, membranous or ligamentous wall separating two cavities or limiting a cavity. **b.** the partition separating the thoracic cavity from the abdominal cavity in mammals. **2.** *Phys. Chem., etc.* **a.** a porous plate separating two liquids, as in a galvanic cell. **b.** a semipermeable membrane or the like. **3.** a vibrating membrane or disk, as in a telephone. **4.** *Optics.* a ring, or a plate pierced with a circular hole so arranged as to fall in the axis of the instrument, used in optical instruments to cut off marginal beams of light, as in a camera or a telescope. —*v.t.* **5.** to furnish or act upon with a diaphragm. [t. LL: m. *diaphragma,* t. Gk.: midriff, barrier]

di·a·phrag·mat·ic (dī/ə frăg măt/ĭk), *adj.* **1.** of the diaphragm. **2.** like a diaphragm. —**di/a·phrag·mat/i·cal·ly**, *adv.*

di·aph·y·sis (dī ăf/ə sĭs), *n., pl.* **-ses** (-sēz/). *Anat.* the shaft of a long bone. [NL, t, Gk.: a growing through] —**di·a·phys·i·al** (dī/ə fĭz/ĭ əl), *adj.*

di·a·poph·y·sis (dī/ə pŏf/ə sĭs), *n., pl.* **-ses** (-sēz/). *Anat., Zool.* the transverse process proper of a vertebra. [NL. See DI³-, APOPHYSIS] —**di·a·po·phys·i·al** (dī/ə pō-fĭz/ĭ əl), *adj.*

Di·ar·bek·r (dī är/bĕk/ər), *n.* Diyarbekir.

di·ar·chy (dī/är kĭ), *n., pl.* **-chies.** government or a government in which power is vested in two rulers or authorities. Also, **dyarchy.** [f. DI-¹ + m.s. Gk. *archía* rule]

di·a·rist (dī/ə rĭst), *n.* one who keeps a diary.

di·ar·rhe·a (dī/ə rē/ə), *n. Pathol.* an intestinal disorder characterized by morbid frequency and fluidity of fecal evacuations. Also, **di/ar·rhoe/a.** [t. LL: m. *diar-rhoea,* t. Gk.: m. *diárrhoia* a flowing through] —**di/ar·rhe/al, di/ar·rhe/ic,** *adj.*

di·ar·thro·sis (dī/är thrō/sĭs), *n., pl.* **-ses** (-sēz). *Anat.* a form of articulation which permits maximal motion, as the knee joint. [NL, t. Gk.: division by joints. See DIA-, ARTHROSIS] —**di·ar·thro·di·al** (dī/är thrō/dĭ əl), *adj.*

di·a·ry (dī/ə rĭ), *n., pl.* **-ries.** **1.** a daily record, esp. of the writer's own experiences or observations. **2.** a book for keeping such a record. [t. L: m. s. *diārium* daily allowance, journal]

Di·as (dē/əs; *Port.* dē/əsh), *n.* **Bartholomeu** (bär tô/-lô mĕ/ōō), c1450–1500, Portuguese navigator and discoverer of the Cape of Good Hope. Also, **Diaz.**

Di·as·po·ra (dī ăs/pə rə), *n.* **1.** the whole body of Jews living scattered among the Gentiles after the Babylonian captivity. **2.** (among the early Jewish Christians) the body of Jewish Christians outside Palestine. **3.** the dispersion of the Jews. [t. Gk.: a scattering]

di·a·spore (dī/ə spōr/), *n.* a mineral, aluminum hydroxide, HAlO₂, occurring in crystals, or more usually in lamellar or scaly masses.

di·a·stase (dī/ə stās/), *n. Biochem.* an enzyme present in germinated barley, potatoes, etc., which converts starch into dextrin and maltose. [t. F, t. Gk.: m. *diástasis* separation]

di·a·stat·ic (dī/ə stăt/ĭk), *adj. Biochem.* **1.** pertaining to diastase. **2.** having the properties of diastase: *diastatic action.* Also, **di·a·sta·sic** (dī/ə stā/sĭk). [t. Gk.: m. s. *diastatikós* separating]

di·as·ter (dī ăs/tər), *n. Biol.* a stage in mitosis at which the chromosomes, after their division and separation, are grouped near the poles of the spindle. [f. DI¹ + -ASTER²] —**di·as/tral**, *adj.*

di·as·to·le (dī ăs′tə lē′), *n.* **1.** *Physiol., etc.* the normal rhythmical dilatation of the heart, esp. that of the ventricles. **2.** *Pros.* the lengthening of a syllable regularly short, esp. before a pause or at the ictus. [t. LL, t. Gk.: a putting asunder, dilatation, lengthening]

di·as·tol·ic (dī′ə stŏl′ĭk), *adj.* pertaining to or produced by diastole.

di·as·tro·phism (dī ăs′trə fĭz′əm), *n.* *Geol.* **1.** the action of the forces which cause the earth's crust to be deformed, producing continents, mountains, changes of level, etc. **2.** any such deformation. [f. s. Gk. *diastrophḗ* distortion + -ISM] —**di·a·stroph·ic** (dī′ə strŏf′ĭk), *adj.*

di·a·tes·sa·ron (dī′ə tĕs′ə rŏn′), *n.* **1.** *Bible.* a harmony of the four Gospels, arranged to form a single narrative. **2.** *Gk. and Medieval Music.* the interval of a fourth. [t. L, t. Gk.: the interval of a fourth (lit., made of four, or through four)]

di·a·ther·man·cy (dī′ə thûr′mən sĭ), *n.* *Physics.* the property of transmitting radiant heat; quality of being diathermanous. [t. F: m. *diathermansie*, f. *dia-* DIA- + m. s. Gk. *thérmansis* heating]

di·a·ther·ma·nous (dī′ə thûr′mə nəs), *adj.* *Physics.* permeable to radiant heat.

di·a·ther·mic (dī′ə thûr′mĭk), *adj.* **1.** *Med.* pertaining to diathermy. **2.** *Physics.* diathermanous. [t. F: m. *diathermique*, f. *dia-* DIA- + s. Gk. *thérmē* heat + -*ique* -IC]

di·a·ther·my (dī′ə thûr′mĭ), *n.* *Med.* the production of heat in body tissues by high currents for therapeutic purposes. Also, **di·a·ther·mi·a** (dī′ə thûr′mĭ ə).

di·ath·e·sis (dī ăth′ə sĭs), *n., pl.* **-eses** (-ə sēz′). *Pathol.* a constitutional predisposition or tendency, as to a particular disease or affection. [NL, t. Gk.: arrangement, disposition] —**di·a·thet·ic** (dī′ə thĕt′ĭk), *adj.*

di·a·tom (dī′ə təm, -tŏm′), *n.* any of numerous microscopic, unicellular, marine or fresh-water algae having siliceous cell walls. [t. NL: m. *Diatoma*, a genus of diatoms, der. LGk. *diátomos*, verbal adj. of Gk. *diatémnein* cut through]

di·a·to·ma·ceous (dī′ə tə mā′shəs), *adj.* consisting of or containing diatoms or their fossil remains.

diatomaceous earth, a fine siliceous earth composed chiefly of cell walls of diatoms: used in filtration, as an abrasive, etc. Also, **di·at·o·mite** (dī ăt′ə mīt′).

di·a·tom·ic (dī′ə tŏm′ĭk), *adj.* *Chem.* **1.** having two atoms in the molecule. **2.** containing two replaceable atoms or groups; bivalent.

di·a·ton·ic (dī′ə tŏn′ĭk), *adj.* *Music.* involving only the tones, intervals, or harmonies of a major or minor scale without chromatic alteration. [t. LL: s. *diatonicus*, t. Gk.: m. *diatonikós*, for *diátonos*] —**di·a·ton′i·cal·ly**, *adv.*

di·a·tribe (dī′ə trīb′), *n.* a bitter and violent denunciation. [t. L: m. s. *diatriba*, t. Gk.: m. *diatribē* pastime, study, discourse]

di·at·ro·pism (dī ăt′rə pĭz′əm), *n.* *Bot.* the tendency of some plant organs to take a transverse position to the line of action of an outside stimulus. —**di·a·trop·ic** (dī′ə trŏp′ĭk), *adj.*

Di·az (dē′əs; *Port.* dē′əsh), *n.* **Bartholomeu.** See **Dias.**

Di·az (dē′äs), *n.* **Porfirio** (pŏr fē′ryō), 1830–1915, president of Mexico, 1877–80, 1884–1911.

di·a·zine (dī′ə zēn′, dī ăz′ēn, -ĭn), *n.* *Chem.* any of a group of three isomeric hydrocarbons, $C_4H_4N_2$, containing a ring of four carbon and two nitrogen atoms. Also, **di·a·zin** (dī′ə zĭn, dī ăz′ĭn).

diazo-, *Chem.* a combining form denoting a diazo compound. [f. DI-[1] + AZO-]

di·az·o compound (dī ăz′ō, -ä′zō), a compound containing a group of two nitrogen atoms, N_2, united with one hydrocarbon radical or with one hydrocarbon radical and another atom or group of atoms.

di·a·zole (dī′ə zōl′, dī ăz′ōl), *n.* *Chem.* any of a group of organic compounds containing three carbon and two nitrogen atoms arranged in a ring.

di·az·o·meth·ane (dī ăz′ō mĕth′ān, dī ä′zō-), *n.* *Chem.* an odorless, yellow gas, CH_2N_2, which is poisonous, used as a methylating agent in organic syntheses.

di·a·zo·ni·um compounds (dī′ə zō′nĭ əm), *Chem.* a series of aromatic compounds which have the **diazonium radical** (ArN ≡ N)+.

diazonium salts, a group of salts of the general formula ArN₂X (X being an acid radical): important intermediates in dye manufacture.

di·az·o·ti·za·tion (dī ăz′ə tə zā′shən), *n.* the preparation of a diazo compound, as by treating an amine with nitrous acid.

di·az·o·tize (dī ăz′ə tīz′), *v.t.,* **-tized, -tizing.** *Chem.* to treat so as to convert into a diazonium salt.

dib (dĭb), *v.i.* **dibbed, dibbing.** to fish by letting the bait bob lightly on the water. [b. DIP and BOB[1]]

di·bas·ic (dī bā′sĭk), *adj.* *Chem.* **1.** containing two replaceable or ionizable hydrogen atoms, as *dibasic acid.* **2.** having two univalent, basic atoms, as *dibasic sodium phosphate*, Na_2HPO_4.

dib·ber (dĭb′ər), *n.* a dibble.

dib·ble (dĭb′əl), *n., v.,* **-bled, -bling.** —*n.* **1.** an implement for making holes in the ground for planting seeds, bulbs, etc. —*v.t.* **2.** to make a hole in (the ground) with or as with a dibble. [? akin to DIB] —**dib′bler,** *n.*

di·bran·chi·ate (dī brăng′kĭ ĭt, -kĭ āt′), *Zool.*—*adj.* **1.** belonging or pertaining to the *Dibranchiata*, a subclass or order of cephalopods with two gills, including the decapods and octopods. —*n.* **2.** a dibranchiate cephalopod. [t. NL: m. s. *Dibranchiāta*, pl. See DI-[1], BRANCHIATE]

di·bro·mide (dī brō′mĭd, -mĭd), *n.* *Chem.* a compound containing two bromine atoms, as *ethylene dibromide.*

di·car·box·yl·ic acid (dī kär′bŏk sĭl′ĭk), *Chem.* any of the organic compounds which have two carboxyl radicals, -COOH.

di·cast (dī′kăst, dĭk′ăst), *n.* (in ancient Athens) one of 6000 citizens over 30 years old, eligible to be chosen by lot to sit as judges. [t. Gk.: s. *dikastḗs* juryman] —**di·cas′tic,** *adj.*

dice (dīs), *n. pl., sing.* **die,** *v.,* **diced, dicing.** —*n.* **1.** small cubes whose sides are marked with different numbers of spots, thrown from a box or the hand in gaming. **2.** the game played. **3.** any small cubes. —*v.t.* **4.** to cut into small cubes. **5.** to decorate with cubelike figures. —*v.i.* **6.** to play at dice. [see DIE[2]] —**dic′er,** *n.*

di·cen·tra (dī sĕn′trə), *n.* any of the plants constituting the genus *Dicentra* (or *Bikukulla*), characterized by racemes of drooping flowers, as the Dutchman's-breeches or the bleeding heart. [NL, t. Gk.: m. *dikentros* with two stings or points]

di·ceph·a·lous (dī sĕf′ə ləs), *adj.* having two heads. [t. Gk.: m. *dikḗphalos*]

di·cha·si·um (dī kā′zhĭ əm, -zĭ əm), *n., pl.* **-sia** (-zhĭ ə, -zĭ ə). *Bot.* a form of cymose inflorescence in which each axis produces a pair of lateral axes. [NL, f. s. Gk. *dichasis* division + -IUM] —**di·cha′si·al,** *adj.*

di·chlo·ride (dī klōr′ĭd, -ĭd), *n.* bichloride. *Dichloride* is more common in organic chemistry. Also, **di·chlo·rid** (dī klōr′ĭd).

di·chlo·ro·di·phen·yl·tri·chlor·o·eth·ane (dī klōr′ō dī fĕn′ĭl trī klōr′ō ĕth′ān), *n.* *Chem.* a white powdery compound having a faint, agreeable odor, used as a contact insecticide: commonly known as DDT.

dicho-, a word element meaning in "two parts," "in pairs." [t. Gk., comb. form of *dícha* in two, asunder]

di·chog·a·mous (dī kŏg′ə məs), *adj.* *Bot.* having the stamens and pistils maturing at different times (thus preventing self-fertilization), as a monoclinous flower (opposed to *homogamous*). Also, **di·cho·gam·ic** (dī′kō găm′ĭk).

di·chog·a·my (dī kŏg′ə mĭ), *n.* dichogamous condition.

di·chot·o·mize (dī kŏt′ə mīz′), *v.t., v.i.,* **-mized, -mizing. 1.** to divide or separate into two parts. **2.** to divide into pairs. —**di·chot′o·mist,** *n.* —**di·chot·o·mi·za′tion,** *n.*

di·chot·o·mous (dī kŏt′ə məs), *adj.* divided or dividing into two parts. Cf. **dichotomy.** Also, **di·ko·tom′ĭk** (dī′kō tŏm′ĭk). —**di·chot′o·mous·ly,** *adv.*

di·chot·o·my (dī kŏt′ə mĭ), *n., pl.* **-mies. 1.** division into two parts or into twos; subdivision into halves or pairs. **2.** *Logic.* classification by division, or by successive subdivision, into two groups or sections. **3.** *Bot.* a mode of branching by constant bifurcation as in some stems, in veins of leaves, etc. **4.** *Astron.* the phase of the moon, or of an inferior planet, when half of its disk is visible. [t. Gk.: m. s. *dichotomia* a cutting in two]

Dichotomy (def. 3)

di·chro·ic (dī krō′ĭk), *adj.* **1.** characterized by dichroism: *a dichroic crystal.* **2.** dichromatic. Also, **di·chro·it·ic** (dī′krō ĭt′ĭk). [f. s. Gk. *díchroos* of two colors + -IC]

di·chro·ism (dī′krō ĭz′əm), *n.* **1.** *Crystall.* a property possessed by many doubly refracting crystals of exhibiting different colors when viewed in different directions. **2.** *Chem.* the exhibition of essentially different colors by certain solutions in different degrees of dilution or concentration. [f. s. Gk. *díchroos* of two colors + -ISM]

di·chro·mate (dī krō′māt), *n.* *Chem.* a salt of a hypothetical acid, $H_2Cr_2O_7$, as *potassium dichromate*, $K_2Cr_2O_7$.

di·chro·mat·ic (dī′krō măt′ĭk), *adj.* **1.** having or showing two colors; dichromic. **2.** of or having dichromatism (def. 2). **3.** *Zool.* exhibiting two color phases within a species not due to age or season. [f. DI-[1] + m.s. Gk. *chrōmatikós* pertaining to color]

di·chro·mat·i·cism (dī′krō măt′ə sĭz′əm), *n.* dichromatism (def. 1).

di·chro·ma·tism (dī krō′mə tĭz′əm), *n.* **1.** dichromatic condition. **2.** dichromic condition.

di·chro·mic[1] (dī krō′mĭk), *adj.* of or embracing two colors only. [f. s. Gk. *díchrōmos* two-colored + -IC]

di·chro·mic[2] (dī krō′mĭk), *adj.* *Chem.* of a compound containing two atoms of chromium. [f. DI-[1] + CHROM-(IUM) + IC]

dichromic acid, *Chem.* the hypothetical acid, $H_2Cr_2O_7$, from which the dichromates (sometimes called bichromates) are derived.

dichromic vision, *Pathol.* color blindness in which only two of the three primary colors are perceived.

di·chro·scope (dī′krə skōp′), *n.* *Crystall.* an instrument for testing the dichroism (or pleochroism) of crystals. [f. s. Gk. *díchroos* of two colors + -SCOPE]

dick (dĭk), *n.* **1.** *U.S. Slang.* a detective. **2.** *Colloq.* a man. [application of the proper name]

dick·cis·sel (dĭk sĭs′əl), *n.* the black-throated bunting, *Spiza americana*, an open-country bird of the eastern and central U.S.

Dick·ens (dĭk'ĭnz), *n.* **Charles (John Huffam)** (hŭf'-əm), 1812–70, British novelist. —**Dick·en·si·an** (dĭ-kĕn'zĭ ən), *adj.*

dick·ens (dĭk'ĭnz), *n., interj.* (prec. by *the*) devil; deuce (used as a mild imprecation).

dick·er[1] (dĭk'ər), *Chiefly U.S.* —*v.i., v.t.* **1.** to trade by barter or by petty bargaining; haggle. **2.** *U.S. Pol.* to try to arrange matters by mutual bargaining. —*n.* **3.** a petty bargain; barter. **4.** *U.S. Pol.* a deal. [? v. use of DICKER[2]]

dick·er[2] (dĭk'ər), *n.* *Hist.* the number or quantity ten, esp. a lot of ten hides or skins. [ME *dyker*, c. G *decher*; ult. akin to DECURY]

dick·ey (dĭk'ĭ), *n., pl.* **-eys.** **1.** a waist for women, without sides or sleeves, to be worn under a dress or suit. **2.** a detachable shirt front. **3.** a linen shirt collar. **4.** a bib or pinafore worn by a child. **5.** a small bird. **6.** a donkey, esp. a male. **7.** (of a carriage) **a.** a rear seat for servants, etc. **b.** *Obsolesc.* the driver's seat on the outside. **8.** *Brit.* a rumble seat. Also, **dicky, dick'ie.** [application of *Dicky*, dim. of *Dick*, proper name]

dick·ey·bird (dĭk'ĭ bûrd'), *n.* dickey (def. 5).

Dick·in·son (dĭk'ĭn sən), *n.* **1. Emily,** 1830–86, U.S. poet. **2. John,** 1732–1808, U.S. statesman and publicist.

dick·y (dĭk'ĭ), *n., pl.* **dickies.** dickey.

di·cli·nous (dī'klə nəs, dī klī'-), *adj.* *Bot.* **1.** (of a plant species, etc.) having the stamens and the pistils in separate flowers, either on the same plant or on different plants; either monoecious or dioecious. **2.** (of a flower) having only stamens or only pistils; unisexual. [f. DI-[1] + m. s. Gk. *klīnē* bed + -OUS]

di·cot·y·le·don (dī kŏt'ə lē'dən, dī'kŏt-), *n.* **1.** a plant with two cotyledons. **2.** a member of the group *Dicotyledones,* one of the two subclasses of angiospermous plants, characterized by producing seeds with two cotyledons or seed leaves, and by an exogenous mode of growth. Cf. **monocotyledon.**

di·cot·y·le·don·ous (dī kŏt'ə lē'dən əs, -lĕd'ən-, dī'-kŏt-), *adj.* having two cotyledons; belonging or pertaining to the *Dicotyledones.* See **dicotyledon** (def. 2).

di·cou·ma·rin (dī koo'mə rĭn), *n.* a drug occurring in spoiled clover and also synthesized, used to prevent the coagulation of blood and in the treatment of arterial thrombosis.

di·crot·ic (dī krŏt'ĭk), *adj.* *Physiol.* **1.** having two arterial beats for one heartbeat, as certain pulses. **2.** pertaining to such a pulse. [f. m.s. Gk. *dikrotos* double-beating + -IC] —**di·cro·tism** (dī'krə tĭz'əm), *n.*

dict., **1.** dictation. **2.** dictator. **3.** dictionary.

dic·ta (dĭk'tə), *n.* a pl. of dictum.

Dic·ta·phone (dĭk'tə fōn'), *n.* *Trademark.* a phonographic instrument that records and reproduces dictation. [f. DICTA(TE) + -PHONE]

dic·tate (v. dĭk'tāt, dĭk tāt'; n. dĭk'tāt), *v.,* **-tated, -tating,** *n.* —*v.t.* **1.** to say or read aloud (something) to be taken down in writing or otherwise. **2.** to prescribe positively; command with authority. —*v.i.* **3.** to say or read aloud something to be taken down in writing. **4.** to give orders. —*n.* **5.** a positive order or command. [t. L: m. s. *dictātus,* pp., pronounced, dictated, composed, prescribed]

dic·ta·tion (dĭk tā'shən), *n.* **1.** act of dictating for reproduction in writing, etc. **2.** words dictated, or taken down as dictated. **3.** act of commanding positively or authoritatively. **4.** something commanded.

dic·ta·tor (dĭk'tā tər, dĭk tā'tər), *n.* **1.** a person exercising absolute power, esp. one who assumes absolute control in a government without hereditary right or the free consent of the people. **2.** (in ancient Rome) a person constitutionally invested with supreme authority during a crisis, the regular magistracy being subordinated to him until the crisis was met. **3.** a person who authoritatively prescribes conduct, usage, etc. **4.** one who dictates. [t. L] —**dic'ta·tor·ship',** *n.* —**dic·ta·tress** (dĭk tā'trĭs), *n. fem.*

dic·ta·to·ri·al (dĭk'tə tōr'ĭ əl), *adj.* **1.** of a dictator. **2.** like that of a dictator; absolute; unlimited. **3.** inclined to dictate or command; imperious; overbearing: *a dictatorial tone.* —**dic'ta·to'ri·al·ly,** *adv.* —**dic'ta·to'ri·al·ness,** *n.*

dic·tion (dĭk'shən), *n.* **1.** style of speaking or writing as dependent upon choice of words: *good diction, a Latin diction.* **2.** the degree of distinctness with which speech sounds are uttered; enunciation. [t. L: s. *dictio* saying] —**Syn. 1.** DICTION, PHRASEOLOGY, WORDING refer to the means and the manner of expressing ideas. DICTION usually implies a high level of usage; it refers chiefly to the choice of words, their arrangement, and the force, accuracy, and distinction with which they are used: *the speaker was distinguished for his excellent diction, poetic diction.* PHRASEOLOGY refers more to the manner of combining the words into related groups, and esp. to the peculiar or distinctive manner in which certain technical, scientific, and professional ideas are expressed: *legal phraseology.* WORDING refers to the exact words or phraseology used to convey thought: *the wording of a will.*

dic·tion·ar·y (dĭk'shə nĕr'ĭ), *n., pl.* **-aries. 1.** a book containing a selection of the words of a language, or of a particular class of words, usually arranged alphabetically, with explanations of their meanings and other information concerning them, expressed either in the same or in another language; a lexicon; a glossary. **2.** a book giving information on a particular subject, under alpha-

betically arranged headings: *a biographical dictionary.* [t. ML: m.s. *dictiōnārium,* lit., a wordbook, der. LL *dictio* word. See DICTION]

dic·to·graph (dĭk'tə gräf', -gräf'), *n.* **1.** a telephonic device with a highly sensitive transmitter obviating the necessity of a mouthpiece, much used for secretly listening to conversations or obtaining a record of them. **2.** (*cap.*) a trademark for this device. [f. s. L *dictum* something said + -(o)GRAPH; modeled on PHONOGRAPH]

dic·tum (dĭk'təm), *n., pl.* **-ta** (-tə), **-tums. 1.** an authoritative pronouncement; judicial assertion. **2.** a saying; maxim. **3.** obiter dictum. [t. L: something said, a saying, a command, prop. pp. neut. of *dicere* say]

di·cy·an·di·am·ide (dī sī'ən dī ăm'ĭd, -ĭd), *n.* *Chem.* a polymerization product of cyanamide, (H₂NCN)₂, used in the manufacture of plastics and resins and as a chemical intermediate.

did (dĭd), *v.* pt. of do.

Did·a·che (dĭd'ə kē'), *n.* a Christian treatise of the second century, called more fully "The Teaching of the Twelve Apostles." [t. Gk.: teaching]

di·dac·tic (dī dăk'tĭk), *adj.* **1.** intended for instruction; instructive: *didactic poetry.* **2.** inclined to teach or lecture others too much: *a didactic old lady.* [t. Gk.: m. s. *didaktikōs* apt at teaching] —**di·dac'ti·cal·ly,** *adv.* —**di·dac'ti·cism,** *n.*

di·dac·tics (dī dăk'tĭks), *n.* the art or science of teaching.

di·dap·per (dī'dăp'ər), *n.* a dabchick. [for *divedapper*]

did·dle[1] (dĭd'əl), *v.,* **-dled, -dling.** *Colloq.* —*v.t.* **1.** to cheat; swindle; victimize. —*v.i.* **2.** to waste time. [orig. uncert.] —**did'dler,** *n.*

did·dle[2] (dĭd'əl), *v.i., v.t.,* **-dled, -dling.** *Colloq.* to move rapidly up and down or backward and forward. [akin to DODDER]

Di·de·rot (dēd rō'), *n.* **Denis** (də nē'), 1713–84, French philosopher, critic, and encyclopedist.

didn't (dĭd'nt), contraction of *did not.*

Di·do (dī'dō), *n.* the legendary queen of Carthage who killed herself when abandoned by Aeneas. [t. L. t. Gk.]

di·do (dī'dō), *n., pl.* **-dos, -does.** (*often pl.*) *U.S. Colloq.* a prank; an antic. [orig. uncert.]

didst (dĭdst), *v.* *Archaic or Poetic.* 2nd pers. sing. pt. of do.

di·dy (dī'dĭ), *n., pl.* **-dies.** diaper (def. 1).

di·dym·i·um (dī dĭm'ĭ əm, dī-), *n.* *Chem.* a mixture of neodymium and praseodymium, formerly supposed to be an element and called the "twin brother of lanthanum". [NL, f. s. Gk. *dídymos* twin + -ium -IUM]

did·y·mous (dĭd'ə məs), *adj.* *Bot.* occurring in pairs; paired; twin. [t. Gk.: m. *dídymos* double, twin]

die[1] (dī), *v.i.,* **died, dying. 1.** to cease to live; suffer death: *to die by violence, from a wound.* **2.** to come to an end; pass out of existence: *the secret died with him.* **3.** to lose force, strength, or active qualities. **4.** to become less subject to: *to die to all sin.* **5.** to pass gradually; fade (fol. by *away, down, out,* etc.). **6.** *Theol.* to lose spiritual life. **7.** to sink; faint. **8.** to suffer as if dying. **9.** to pine with desire, love, etc. **10.** *Colloq.* to desire keenly or greatly: *he was dying to see her.* **11.** die hard, to resist or yield only after a bitter struggle. [early ME *deghen,* c. Icel. *deyja.* Cf. DEAD, DEATH] —**Syn 1, 2.** DIE, DECEASE, PASS AWAY (PASS ON), PERISH mean to relinquish life. To DIE is to become dead from any cause and in any circumstances. It is the simplest, plainest, and most direct word for this idea, and is used fig. of anything that has once displayed activity: *an echo, flame, storm, rumor dies.* DECEASE, now almost entirely a legal term, refers only to the death of a human being: *a person deceases.* PASS AWAY (or PASS ON) is a commonly used euphemism implying a continuation of life after death: *Grandpa has passed away (passed on).* PERISH, a more literary term, implies death under harsh circumstances such as hunger, cold, neglect, etc.; fig. PERISH connotes utter extinction: *hardship caused many pioneers to perish, ancient Egyptian civilization has perished.* —**Ant. 1.** live. **2.** continue.

die[2] (dī), *n., pl.* **dies** for 1, 2, 5, **dice** for 3, 4; *v.,* **died, dieing.** —*n.* **1.** *Mach.* **a.** any of various devices for cutting or forming material in a press. **b.** a hollow device of steel, often composed of several pieces to be fitted into a stock, for cutting the threads of bolts, etc. **c.** one of the separate pieces of such a device. **d.** a steel block or plate with small conical holes through which wire, plastic rods, etc., are drawn. **2.** an engraved stamp for impressing a design, etc., upon some softer material, as in coining money. **3.** a small cube or block whose sides are marked with different numbers of spots, thrown from a box or the hand in gaming. **4.** any small cube or square block. **5.** *Archit.* the dado of a pedestal, esp. when cubical. **6. the die is cast,** the decision has been irrevocably made. —*v.t.* **7.** to impress, shape, or cut with a die. [ME *de,* t. OF, g. L *datum,* orig. pp. neut., lit., given (appar. in sense of given by fortune)]

die casting, *Metall.* **1.** a process in which metal is forced into metallic molds under hydraulic pressure. **2.** an article made by this process. —**die'-cast'ing,** *n.*

di·e·cious (dī ē'shəs), *adj.* *Bot.* dioecious.

Die·fen·ba·ker (dē'fən bā'kər), *n.* **John George,** born 1895, prime minister of Canada 1957–1963.

die-hard (dī'härd'), *n.* **1.** one who resists vigorously to the last, esp. a conservative in politics. —*adj.* **2.** resisting vigorously to the last.

di·e·lec·tric (dī'ĭ lĕk'trĭk), *Elect.* —*adj.* **1.** nonconducting. **2.** conveying electric effects otherwise than

---

b., blend of, blended; c., cognate with; d., dialect, dialectal; der., derived from; f., formed from; g., going back to; m., modification of; r., replacing; s., stem of; t., taken from; ?, perhaps. See the full key on inside cover.

by conduction, as a medium through which electricity acts in the process of induction. —*n.* 3. a dielectric substance. [f. DI-³ + ELECTRIC] —**di·e·lec'tri·cal·ly,** *adv.*

di·en·ceph·a·lon (dī'ĕn sĕf'ə lŏn'), *n. Anat.* the posterior section of the prosencephalon; the interbrain or middle brain. [f. DI-³ + ENCEPHALON]

dienes, *Chem.* a suffix designating a compound containing two double bonds. [f. DI-¹ + -ENE + -s (pl.)]

Di·eppe (dī'ĕp'; *Fr.* dyĕp), *n.* a seaport in N France, on the English Channel: raided by an Allied expeditionary force, Aug., 1942. 26,427 (1954).

di·er·e·sis (dī'ĕr'ə sĭs), *n.*, *pl.* -ses (-sēz'). 1. the separation of two adjacent vowels. 2. a sign (··) placed over the second of two adjacent vowels to indicate separate pronunciation, as in coöperate. 3. *Pros.* the division made in a line or verse by coincidence of the end of a foot and the end of a word. Also, **diaeresis.** [t. L, t. Gk.: m. *diairesis* separation, division]

di·es (dī'ēz or, *esp. in Church Latin,* dē'ās), *n. sing. and pl. Latin.* day.

Die·sel (dē'zəl), *n.* 1. **Rudolf** (rōō'dŏlf), 1858–1913, German engineer who invented the Diesel engine. 2. a Diesel engine. 3. a locomotive, truck, ship, etc., driven by a Diesel engine.

Diesel cycle, *Mach.* an engine cycle, usually 4 strokes, as intake, compression, power, and exhaust, in which ignition occurs at constant pressure, and heat is rejected at constant volume.

Diesel engine, an ignition-compression type of internal-combustion engine in which fuel oil is sprayed into the cylinder after the air in it has been compressed to about 1000° F., thus causing the ignition of the oil, at substantially constant pressure. Also, **Diesel motor.** [named after Rudolf *Diesel*, of Munich, the inventor]

die-sink·er (dī'sĭngk'ər), *n.* an engraver of dies for stamping or embossing. —**die'sink'ing,** *n.*

Di·es I·rae (dī'ēz ī'rē or, *esp. in Church Latin,* dē'ās ē'rī), *Latin.* a famous medieval Latin hymn on the Day of Judgment (commonly ascribed to Thomas of Celano, a Franciscan of the first half of the 13th century), sung or recited in the Mass for the dead. [ML: day of wrath (the first words of the hymn)]

di·e·sis (dī'ə sĭs), *n.*, *pl.* -ses (-sēz'). *Print.* the mark ‡; double dagger. [t. L, t. Gk.: a sending through]

di·es non (dī'ēz nŏn'), *Law.* a day on which no courts can be held or no legal business transacted. [short for L *dies nōn jūridicus* a day not juridical]

die·stock (dī'stŏk'), *n. Mach.* a device for holding the dies used in cutting threads on a rod or pipe.

di·et¹ (dī'ət), *n.*, *v.*, -eted, -eting. —*n.* 1. food considered in relation to its quality and effects: *milk is a wholesome article of diet.* 2. a particular selection of food, esp. one prescribed to improve the physical condition or cure a disease. 3. manner of living as regards food. —*v.t.* 4. to regulate the food of, esp. to improve the physical condition. 5. to feed. —*v.i.* 6. to adhere to a particular diet. 7. to eat; feed. [ME *diete*, t. OF, t. L: m. *diaeta*, t. Gk.: m. *diaita* way of living, diet] —**di'et·er,** *n.*

di·et² (dī'ət), *n.* a formal assembly for discussing or acting upon public or state affairs, as the general assembly of the estates of the former Holy Roman Empire, the German Reichstag, Japan, etc. [late ME, t. ML: m. s. *dīēta*, *diaeta* public assembly, appar. the same word as L *diaeta* (see DIET¹), with sense affected by L *dies* day]

di·e·tar·y (dī'ə tĕr'ĭ), *adj.*, *n.*, *pl.* -taries. —*adj.* 1. pertaining to diet: *dietary laws.* —*n.* 2. a system or course of diet. 3. a regulated allowance of food.

di·e·tet·ic (dī'ə tĕt'ĭk), *adj.* pertaining to diet or to regulation of the use of food. Also, **di·e·tet'i·cal.** [t. L: m. s. *diaetēticus*, t. Gk.: m. *diaitētikós*] —**di·e·tet'i·cal·ly,** *adv.*

di·e·tet·ics (dī'ə tĕt'ĭks), *n.* the art or science concerned with the regulation of diet.

di·eth·yl·stil·bes·trol (dī'ĕth'əl stĭl bĕs'trōl, -trŏl), *n. Chem.* a synthetic substance, [HOC₆H₄C(C₂H₅)₂]₂, not itself an estrogen but having a more potent estrogenic activity than estrone: used in the treatment of menopausic symptoms, etc.

di·e·ti·tian (dī'ə tĭsh'ən), *n. Orig. U.S.* one versed in the regulation of diet, or in the planning or supervision of meals. Also, **di·e·ti·cian.** [der. DIET¹, modeled on PHYSICIAN]

diet kitchen, an establishment for preparing and dispensing suitable diet for invalids, esp. among the poor.

Dieu a·vec nous (dyœ à vĕk nōō'), *French.* God with us.

Dieu et mon droit (dyœ' ĕ môN drwä'), *French.* God and my right (motto on the royal arms of England).

diff., 1. difference. 2. different.

dif·fer (dĭf'ər), *v.i.* 1. to be unlike, dissimilar, or distinct in nature or qualities (fol. by *from*). 2. to disagree in opinion, belief, etc.; be at variance (fol. by *with* or *from*). 3. *Obs.* to dispute. [t. F: s. *différer*, t. L: m. *differre* bear apart, put off, delay (see DEFER¹), be different]

dif·fer·ence (dĭf'ər əns, dĭf'rəns), *n.*, *v.*, -enced, -encing. —*n.* 1. state or relation of being different; dissimilarity. 2. an instance or point of unlikeness or dissimilarity. 3. a distinguishing characteristic. 4. the degree in which one person or thing differs from another. 5. act of distinguishing; discrimination; distinction. 6. a disagreement in opinion; dispute; quarrel. 7. the amount by which one quantity is greater or less than

another. 8. *Logic.* a differentia. 9. *Her.* the descent of a younger branch from the main line of a family. 10. **make a difference, a.** to alter or affect the case; matter. **b.** to make a distinction; discriminate. 11. **split the difference, a.** to compromise. **b.** to divide the remainder equally. —*v.t.* 12. to cause or constitute a difference in or between; make different. 13. to perceive the difference in or between; discriminate.
—**Syn.** 1. DIFFERENCE, DISCREPANCY, DISPARITY, DISSIMILARITY imply perceivable unlikeness, variation, or diversity. DIFFERENCE refers to a complete or partial lack of identity or a degree of unlikeness: *a difference of opinion, a difference of six inches.* DISCREPANCY usually refers to the difference or inconsistency between things that should agree, balance, or harmonize: *a discrepancy between the statements of two witnesses.* DISPARITY implies inequality, often where a greater approximation to equality might reasonably be expected: *a great disparity between the ages of husband and wife.* DISSIMILARITY indicates an essential lack of resemblance between things in some respect comparable: *a dissimilarity between the customs in Asia and in America.* 5. See **distinction.** —**Ant.** 1. likeness, similarity.

dif·fer·ent (dĭf'ər ənt, dĭf'rənt), *adj.* 1. differing in character; having unlike qualities (unless used absolutely fol. by *from*, often *to*, sometimes *than;* use of *to* and *than* is considered improper by many, but the use of *to* is especially common in England): *these two things are different; this is different from that.* 2. not identical; separate; various; several: *three different answers.* 3. unusual; not ordinary. —**dif'fer·ent·ly,** *adv.* —**Syn.** 1. unlike, diverse, divergent, altered, changed. 2. sundry, divers, miscellaneous. See **various.**

dif·fer·en·ti·a (dĭf'ə rĕn'shĭ ə), *n.*, *pl.* -tiae (-shĭ ē'). *Logic.* the character or attribute by which one species is distinguished from all others of the same genus. [t. L: difference]

dif·fer·en·ti·a·ble (dĭf'ə rĕn'shĭ ə bəl), *adj.* capable of being differentiated.

dif·fer·en·tial (dĭf'ə rĕn'shəl), *adj.* 1. of or pertaining to difference or diversity. 2. constituting a difference; distinguishing; distinctive: *a differential feature.* 3. exhibiting or depending upon a difference or distinction. 4. *Physics, Mach., etc.* pertaining to or involving the difference of two or more motions, forces, etc.: *a differential gear.* 5. *Math.* pertaining to or involving differentials. —*n.* 6. *Mach.* an epicyclic train of gears designed to permit two or more shafts to revolve at different speeds, as a set of gears in an automobile permitting the rear wheels to revolve at different speeds when the car is turning. 7. *Elect.* a coil of wire in which the polar action produced is opposite to that of another coil. 8. *Math.* (of a function) a linear form whose coefficients are the derivatives of the function with respect to its arguments. 9. *Com.* **a.** the difference involved in a differential rate. **b.** differential rate. —**dif'fer·en'tial·ly,** *adv.*

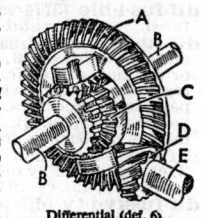

Differential (def. 6) A. Ring gear; B. Axle; C. Pinion gear; D. Drive shaft gear; E. Drive shaft

differential calculus, the branch of mathematics which treats of differentials and derivatives.

differential coefficient, *Math.* the derivative of a function with respect to one of its arguments.

differential equation, *Math.* an equation involving differentials or derivatives.

differential gear, *Mach.* 1. differential (def. 6). 2. any of various analogous arrangements of gears.

differential quotient, derivative (def. 6).

differential rate, a special lower rate, as one charged by one of two or more competing businesses.

differential windlass, *Mach.* a windlass with a barrel composed of two parts of different diameter, its power being determined by the difference in the two diameters.

dif·fer·en·ti·ate (dĭf'ə rĕn'shĭ āt'), *v.*, -ated, -ating. —*v.t.* 1. to mark off by differences; distinguish; alter; change. 2. to perceive the difference in or between; discriminate. 3. to make different by modification, as a biological species. 4. *Math.* to obtain the differential or the derivative of. —*v.i.* 5. to become unlike or dissimilar; change in character. 6. to make a distinction; discriminate. 7. *Biol.* (of cells or tissues) to change from relatively generalized to specialized kinds, during development. —**dif'fer·en'ti·a'tion,** *n.* —**dif'fer·en'ti·a'tor,** *n.* —**Syn.** 1. See **distinguish.**

dif·fi·cile (dĭf'ə sēl'; *Fr.* dē fē sēl'), *adj.* hard to deal with, get on with, please, or satisfy; difficult. [t. F, t. L: m. *difficilis* hard to do]

dif·fi·cult (dĭf'ə kŭlt', -kəlt), *adj.* 1. hard to do, perform, or accomplish; not easy; requiring much effort: *a difficult task.* 2. hard to understand or solve: *a difficult problem.* 3. hard to deal with or get on with. 4. hard to please or satisfy. 5. hard to persuade or induce. [earlier *difficul* (? t. L): -*t* from DIFFICULTY or *difficul·ting* making difficult] —**dif'fi·cult·ly,** *adv.* —**Syn.** 1. See **hard.** —**Ant.** 1. easy. 2. simple.

dif·fi·cul·ty (dĭf'ə kŭl'tĭ, -kəl tĭ), *n.*, *pl.* -ties. 1. fact or condition of being difficult. 2. an embarrassing situation, esp. of financial affairs. 3. a trouble. 4. a cause of trouble or embarrassment. 5. reluctance; unwillingness. 6. a demur; objection. 7. that which is hard to do, understand, or surmount. [ME *difficulte*, t. L: m.s. *difficultas*] —Syn. 2. dilemma, predicament, quandary.

dif·fi·dence (dĭf′ə dəns), *n.* lack of confidence in one's own ability, worth, or fitness; timidity; shyness.

dif·fi·dent (dĭf′ə dənt), *adj.* 1. lacking confidence in one's own ability, worth, or fitness; timid; shy. 2. *Rare.* distrustful. [t. L: s. *diffīdens*, ppr., mistrusting] —**dif′·fi·dent·ly,** *adv.* —Syn. 1. See shy[1]. —Ant. 1. self-confident.

dif·flu·ent (dĭf′lōō ənt), *adj.* tending to flow apart; readily dissolving. [t. L: s. *diffluens*, ppr., flowing away]

dif·fract (dĭ frăkt′), *v.t.* to break up by diffraction. [t. L: s. *diffractus*, pp., broken in pieces]

dif·frac·tion (dĭ frăk′shən), *n.* *Physics.* 1. a modification that light or other radiation undergoes when it passes by the edge of an opaque body, or is sent through small apertures, resulting in the formation of a series of light and dark bands, prismatic colors, or spectra. This effect is an interference phenomenon due to the wave nature of radiation. 2. the analogous modification produced upon sound waves when passing by the edge of a building or other large body.

diffraction grating, *Physics.* a band of equidistant parallel lines (from 10,000 to 30,000 or more to the inch), ruled on a surface of glass or polished metal, used for obtaining optical spectra.

dif·frac·tive (dĭ frăk′tĭv), *adj.* causing or pertaining to diffraction. —**dif·frac′tive·ly,** *adv.* —**dif·frac′tive·ness,** *n.*

dif·fuse (*v.* dĭ fūz′; *adj.* dĭ fūs′), *v.,* -**fused,** -**fusing,** *adj.* —*v.t.* 1. to pour out and spread, as a fluid. 2. to spread or scatter widely; disseminate. 3. *Physics.* to spread by diffusion. —*v.i.* 4. to spread. 5. *Physics.* to intermingle or pass by diffusion. [t. L: m. s. *diffūsus*, pp., poured out] —*adj.* 6. characterized by great length or discursiveness in speech or writing; wordy. 7. widely spread or scattered; dispersed. [ME, t. L: m. s. *diffūsus*, pp., poured out] —**dif·fuse·ly** (dĭ fūs′lĭ), *adv.* —**dif·fuse′ness,** *n.* —**dif·fus·er,** **dif·fu·sor** (dĭ fū′zər), *n.*

dif·fus·i·ble (dĭ fū′zə bəl), *adj.* capable of being diffused. —**dif·fus·i·bil·i·ty** (dĭ fū′zə bĭl′ə tĭ), *n.*

dif·fu·sion (dĭ fū′zhən), *n.* 1. act of diffusing. 2. state of being diffused. 3. diffuseness or prolixity of speech or writing. 4. *Physics.* a. the gradual permeation of any region by a fluid, owing to the thermal agitation of its particles or molecules. b. the process of being scattered. See **scatter** (def. 3). 5. *Anthropol., Sociol.* the transmission of elements from one culture to another.

dif·fu·sive (dĭ fū′sĭv), *adj.* 1. tending to diffuse. 2. characterized by diffusion. 3. diffuse; prolix. —**dif·fu′sive·ly,** *adv.* —**dif·fu′sive·ness,** *n.*

dif·fu·siv·i·ty (dĭf′yōō sĭv′ə tĭ), *n.* *Physics.* the property of a substance indicative of the rate at which a thermal disturbance will be transmitted.

dig (dĭg), *v.,* **dug** or **digged,** **digging,** *n.* —*v.i.* 1. to break up, turn over, or remove earth, etc., as with a spade; make an excavation. 2. to make one's way by, or as by, digging. 3. *Colloq.* to work hard, esp. at lessons (often fol. by *in*). 4. *Mil.* to dig a hole or trench for occupancy in a zone subject to the enemy's fire (fol. by *in*). —*v.t.* 5. to break up and turn over, or penetrate and loosen (the ground) with a spade, etc. (often fol. by *up*). 6. to make (a hole, tunnel, etc.) by removing material. 7. to obtain or remove by digging (often fol. by *up* or *out*). 8. to find or discover by effort or search. 9. to thrust, plunge, or force (fol. by *into*): *he dug his heel into the ground.* —*n. Colloq.* 10. a thrust; punch; poke. 11. a cutting, sarcastic remark. 12. *U.S.* a diligent student. 13. (*pl.*) *Brit.* lodgings. [ME *diggen,* prob. t. F: m. *diguer,* of Gmc. orig.]

dig., digest.

di·gam·ma (dī găm′ə), *n.* a letter of the Greek alphabet, but early in disuse, corresponding in form to *F* and having much the same sound as English *w.* [t. L, t. Gk.: f. di- DI-[1] + *gámma* gamma; from its likeness to two gammas (Γ) one above the other]

dig·a·my (dĭg′ə mĭ), *n.* second marriage; the practice of marrying again after the death of the first spouse. [t. LL: m. s. *digamia,* t. Gk.] —**dig′a·mous,** *adj.*

di·gas·tric (dī găs′trĭk), *adj.* *Anat.* having two fleshy bellies with an intervening tendinous part, as certain muscles. —*n.* 2. a muscle of the lower jaw (so called because in man it has two bellies).

di·gen·e·sis (dī jĕn′ə sĭs), *n.* *Zool.* alternation of generations.—**di·ge·net·ic** (dī′jə nĕt′ĭk), *adj.*

di·gest (*v.* dĭ jĕst′, dī-; *n.* dī′jĕst), *v.t.* 1. to prepare (food) in the alimentary canal for assimilation into the system. 2. to promote the digestion of (food). 3. to assimilate mentally; obtain mental nourishment or improvement from. 4. to arrange methodically in the mind; think over: *to digest a plan.* 5. to bear with patience; endure. 6. to arrange in convenient or methodical order; reduce to a system; classify. 7. *Chem.* to keep (a substance) in contact with a liquid to soften or to disintegrate it. —*v.i.* 8. to digest food. 9. to undergo digestion, as food. —*n.* 10. a collection or summary, esp. of literary, historical, legal, or scientific matter, often classified or condensed. 11. *Law.* a systematic abstract of some body of law. b. **the Digest,** a collection in fifty books, of excerpts compiled by order of Justinian in the sixth century, the largest part of the Corpus Juris Canonici; the Pandects. [ME, t. L: s. *dīgestus,* pp., separated, arranged, dissolved] —Syn. 10. See **summary.**

di·gest·ant (dĭ jĕs′tənt, dī-), *n.* *Med.* an agent that promotes digestion.

di·gest·er (dĭ jĕs′tər, dī-), *n.* 1. one who or that which digests. 2. an apparatus in which substances are reduced or prepared by moisture and heat, chemical action, etc.

di·gest·i·ble (dĭ jĕs′tə bəl, dī-), *adj.* capable of being digested; easily digested. —**di·gest′i·bil′i·ty, di·gest′·i·ble·ness,** *n.* —**di·gest′i·bly,** *adv.*

di·ges·tion (dĭ jĕs′chən, dī-), *n.* 1. the process by which food is digested. 2. the function or power of digesting food. 3. act of digesting. 4. the resulting state.

di·ges·tive (dĭ jĕs′tĭv, dī-), *adj.* 1. serving for or pertaining to digestion; having the function of digesting food. 2. promoting digestion. —*n.* 3. an agent or medicine promoting digestion. —**di·ges′tive·ly,** *adv.*

digestive biscuit, *Brit.* a graham cracker.

dig·ger (dĭg′ər), *n.* 1. a person or an animal that digs. 2. a tool, part of a machine, etc., for digging. 3. (*cap.*) any one of several Indian tribes of western North America, who subsist largely on roots dug from the ground. 4. *Colloq.* an Australian or New Zealand soldier (used also as a term of address).

digger wasp, any of the solitary wasps of the family *Sphecidae* which excavate holes in the ground and provision them with caterpillars, etc.

dig·gings (dĭg′ĭngz *for 1–3;* dĭg′ənz *for 4*), *n. pl.* 1. a place where digging is carried on. 2. a mining operation or locality. 3. that which is dug out. 4. *Chiefly Brit. Colloq.* living quarters; lodgings.

dight (dīt), *v.t.,* **dight** or **dighted, dighting.** *Archaic.* 1. to make ready; prepare. 2. to equip; furnish. 3. to dress; adorn. 4. *Dial.* to clean. [ME *dighte(n),* OE *dihtan* compose, arrange, t. L: m. *dictāre* DICTATE. Cf. G *dichten* compose, Icel. *dikta* to write Latin]

dig·it (dĭj′ĭt), *n.* 1. a finger or toe. 2. the breadth of a finger used as a unit of linear measure, usually equal to three fourths of an inch. 3. any of the Arabic figures 0, 1, . . . 9. [t. L: s. *digitus* finger, toe]

dig·it·al (dĭj′ə təl), *adj.* 1. of or pertaining to a digit. 2. resembling a digit or finger. 3. having digits or digitlike parts. —*n.* 4. one of the keys or finger levers of instruments of the organ or piano class.

digital computer. See **computer.**

dig·i·tal·in (dĭj′ə tăl′ĭn, -tā′lĭn), *n.* *Pharm.* 1. a glucoside obtained from digitalis. 2. any of several extracts or mixtures of glucosides obtained from digitalis.

dig·i·tal·is (dĭj′ə tăl′ĭs, -tā′lĭs), *n.* 1. any plant of the scrophulariaceous genus *Digitalis,* esp. the common foxglove, *D. purpurea.* 2. the dried leaves of the common foxglove, used in medicine, esp. as a heart stimulant. [NL, the genus name (after G name *fingerhut* thimble; from the shape of the corolla), special use of L *digitālis* pertaining to the finger]

dig·i·tal·ism (dĭj′ə tăl′ĭz′əm), *n.* *Pathol.* the morbid result of overconsumption of digitalis.

dig·i·tate (dĭj′ə tāt′), *adj.* 1. *Zool.* having digits or digitlike processes. 2. *Bot.* having radiating divisions or leaflets resembling the fingers of a hand. 3. like a digit or finger. Also, **dig′i·tat′ed.** —**dig′i·tate′ly,** *adv.*

dig·i·ta·tion (dĭj′ə tā′shən), *n. Biol.* 1. digitate formation. 2. a digitlike process or division.

Digitate leaf

dig·i·ti·form (dĭj′ə tə fôrm′), *adj.* fingerlike.

dig·i·ti·grade (dĭj′ə tə grād′), *adj.* *Zool.* walking on the toes, as most quadruped mammals. See **plantigrade.** [t. F, f. s. L *digitus* finger + -(i)*grade* -(I)GRADE]

dig·i·tox·in (dĭj′ə tŏk′sĭn), *n.* *Pharm.* a cardiac glucoside obtained from digitalis.

di·glot (dī′glŏt), *adj.* 1. bilingual. —*n.* 2. a bilingual book or edition. [t. Gk.: m. s. *díglōttos* speaking two languages] —**di·glot′tic,** *adj.*

dig·ni·fied (dĭg′nə fīd′), *adj.* marked by dignity of aspect or manner; noble; stately: *dignified conduct.* —**dig′ni·fied′ly,** *adv.* —Syn. stately, grave, august.

dig·ni·fy (dĭg′nə fī′), *v.t.,* -**fied,** -**fying.** 1. to confer honor or dignity upon; honor; ennoble. 2. to give high-sounding title or name to; confer unmerited distinction upon. [t. ML: m. s. *dignificāre,* f. L: *digni-* worthy + -*ficāre* make]

dig·ni·tar·y (dĭg′nə tĕr′ĭ), *n., pl.* -**taries.** one who holds a high rank or office, esp. in the church.

dig·ni·ty (dĭg′nə tĭ), *n., pl.* -**ties.** 1. nobility of manner or style; stateliness; gravity. 2. nobleness or elevation of mind; worthiness: *dignity of sentiments.* 3. honorable place; elevated rank. 4. degree of excellence, either in estimation or in the order of nature: *man is superior in dignity to brutes.* 5. relative standing; rank. 6. a high office or title. 7. the person holding it. 8. persons of high rank collectively. [t. L: m.s. *dignitas* worthiness, rank; r. ME *dignete,* t. OF]

di·graph (dī′grăf, -gräf), *n.* a pair of letters representing a single speech sound, as *ea* in *meat,* or *th* in *path.*

di·gress (dĭ grĕs′, dī-), *v.i.* 1. to deviate or wander away from the main purpose in speaking or writing, or from the principal line of argument, study, etc. 2. *Rare.* to turn aside. [t. L: s. *dīgressus,* pp., having departed] —**di·gress′er,** *n.* —Syn. 1. See **deviate.**

---

b., blend of, blended; c., cognate with; d., dialect, dialectal; der., derived from; f., formed from; g., going back to; m., modification of; r., replacing; s., stem of; t., taken from; ?, perhaps. See the full key on inside cover.

di·gres·sion (dĬ grĕsh′ən, dī-), *n.* **1.** act of digressing. **2.** a portion of a discourse, etc., deviating from the main theme. —**di·gres′sion·al**, *adj.*

di·gres·sive (dĬ grĕs′Ĭv), *adj.* tending to digress; departing from the main subject. —**di·gres′sive·ly**, *adv.* —**di·gres′sive·ness**, *n.*

di·he·dral (dĭ hē′drəl), *adj. Math.* **1.** having, or formed by, two planes: *a dihedral angle.* **2.** pertaining to or having a dihedral angle or angles. —*n.* **3.** Also, **dihedral angle.** *Math.* the figure made by two planes which intersect. **4.** *Aeron.* the angle at which the right and left wings of an airplane or the like are inclined upward or downward with reference to the center section. [f. DI-¹ + s. Gk. *hĕdra* seat, base + -AL¹]

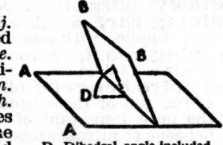

D, Dihedral angle included between planes AA and BB

Di·jon (dē zhôN′), *n.* a city in E France. 112,844 (1954).

dik-dik (dĬk′dĬk′), *n.* a diminutive antelope, genus *Madoqua*, native to eastern and southwestern Africa.

dike (dĭk), *n., v.,* **diked, diking.** —*n.* **1.** an embankment for restraining the waters of the sea or a river. **2.** a ditch. **3.** a ridge or bank of earth as thrown up in excavating. **4.** a causeway. **5.** *Brit. Dial.* a low wall or fence, esp. of earth or stone, for dividing or enclosing land. **6.** an obstacle; barrier. **7.** *Geol.* **a.** a long, narrow, cross-cutting mass of igneous or eruptive rock intruded into a fissure in older rock. **b.** a similar mass of rock composed of other kinds of material, as sandstone. —*v.t.* **8.** to furnish or drain with a dike. **9.** to enclose, restrain, or protect by a dike: *to dike a tract of land.* Also, **dyke.** [ME, t. Scand.; cf. Icel. *dĭk, dĭki* ditch; akin to DITCH] —**dik′er**, *n.*

di·ke·tone (dĭ kē′tōn), *n. Chem.* a compound containing two CO groups.

di·lac·er·ate (dĬ lăs′ə rāt′, dī-), *v.t.,* **-ated, -ating.** to rend asunder; tear in pieces. [t. L: m. s. *dīlacerātus*, pp.] —**di·lac′er·a′tion**, *n.*

di·lap·i·date (dĬ lăp′ə dāt′), *v.,* **-dated, -dating.** —*v.t.* **1.** to bring (a building, etc.) into a ruinous condition, as by misuse or neglect. **2.** to squander; waste. —*v.i.* **3.** to fall into ruin or decay. [t. L: m. s. *dīlapidātus*, pp., thrown away, lit., scattered (orig. referring to stones)] —**di·lap′i·da′tion**, *n.*

di·lap·i·dat·ed (dĬ lăp′ə dā′tĬd), *adj.* reduced to or fallen into ruin or decay.

di·lat·ant (dĬ lā′tənt, dī-), *adj.* dilating; expanding. —**di·lat′an·cy**, *n.*

dil·a·ta·tion (dĬl′ə tā′shən, dī′lə-), *n.* **1.** act of dilating. **2.** state of being dilated. **3.** a dilated formation or part. **4.** *Pathol.* **a.** an abnormal enlargement of an aperture or a canal of the body, or one made for the purposes of surgical or medical treatment. **b.** a restoration to normal potency of an abnormally small body opening or passageway, as the anus or esophagus.

di·late (dī lāt′, dĬ-), *v.,* **-lated, -lating.** —*v.t.* **1.** to make wider or larger; cause to expand. **2.** to enlarge upon. —*v.i.* **3.** to spread out; expand. **4.** to speak at length; expatiate (fol. by *upon* or *on* or used absolutely). [t. L: m.s. *dīlātāre* spread out] —**di·lat′a·ble**, *adj.* —**di·lat′a·bil′i·ty**, *n.* —**Syn. 1.** See **expand.** —**Ant. 1.** narrow.

di·la·tion (dī lā′shən, dĬ-), *n.* dilatation.

di·la·tive (dī lā′tĬv, dĬ-), *adj.* serving or tending to dilate.

dil·a·tom·e·ter (dĬl′ə tŏm′ə tər), *n.* an instrument for measuring the expansion of substances.

di·la·tor (dī lā′tər, dĬ-), *n.* **1.** one who or that which dilates. **2.** *Anat.* a muscle that dilates some cavity of the body. **3.** *Surg.* an instrument for dilating body canals, orifices, or cavities.

dil·a·to·ry (dĬl′ə tôr′Ĭ), *adj.* **1.** inclined to delay or procrastinate; slow; tardy; not prompt. **2.** intended to bring about delay, gain time, or defer decision: *a dilatory strategy.* [t. L: m. s. *dīlātōrius*, der. *dīlātor* delayer] —**dil′a·to′ri·ly**, *adv.* —**dil′a·to′ri·ness**, *n.*

di·lem·ma (dĬ lĕm′ə), *n.* **1.** a situation requiring a choice between equally undesirable alternatives; an embarrassing situation. **2.** *Logic.* a form of argument in which two or more alternatives (**the horns of the dilemma**) are presented, each of which is indicated to have consequences (sometimes unfavorable) for the one who must choose. [t. LL, t. Gk.: double proposition] —**dil·em·mat·ic** (dĬl′ə măt′Ĭk), *adj.* —**Syn. 1.** See **predicament.**

dil·et·tan·te (dĬl′ə tän′tĬ, -ə tänt′), *n.,* pl. **-tes, -ti** (-tē), *adj.* —*n.* **1.** one who pursues an art or science desultorily or merely for amusement; a dabbler. **2.** a lover of an art or science, esp. of a fine art. —*adj.* **3.** of or pertaining to dilettantes. [t. It., prop. ppr. of *dilettare*, g. L *dēlectāre* DELIGHT, v.] —**dil′et·tan′tish, dil′et·tan·te·ish**, *adj.*

dil·et·tant·ism (dĬl′ə tăn′tĬz əm, -tän′-), *n.* the practice or characteristics of a dilettante. Also, **dil·et·tan·te·ism** (dĬl′ə tăn′tĬ′zəm).

dil·i·gence¹ (dĬl′ə jəns), *n.* **1.** constant and earnest effort to accomplish what is undertaken; persistent exertion of body or mind. **2.** *Obs.* care; caution. [ME, t. L: m. *dīligentia*] —**Syn. 1.** application, industry, assiduity, perseverance or persistence.

dil·i·gence² (dĬl′ə jəns; *Fr.* dē lē zhäNs′), *n.* a public stagecoach, esp. in France. [t. F: short for *carrosse de diligence* speed coach]

Diligence

dil·i·gent (dĬl′ə jənt), *adj.* **1.** constant in effort to accomplish something; attentive and persistent in doing anything. **2.** pursued with persevering attention; painstaking. [ME, t. L: s. *dīligens*, prop. ppr., choosing, liking] —**dil′i·gent·ly**, *adv.* —**Syn. 1.** industrious, assiduous. See **busy.** **2.** persevering, indefatigable, untiring, unremitting.

dill (dĬl), *n.* **1.** an apiaceous plant, *Anethum graveolens*, bearing a seedlike fruit used in medicine and for flavoring pickles, etc. **2.** its aromatic seeds or leaves. [ME *dille, dile*, OE *dile-*; akin to G *dill(e)*, Sw. *dill*]

dill pickle, a cucumber pickle flavored by dill.

dil·ly-dal·ly (dĬl′Ĭ dăl′Ĭ), *v.i.,* **-lied, -lying.** to waste time, esp. by indecision; trifle; loiter.

dil·u·ent (dĬl′yŏŏ ənt), *adj.* **1.** diluting; serving for dilution. —*n.* **2.** a diluting substance, esp. one that dilutes the blood. [t. L: s. *dīluens*, ppr., washing away]

di·lute (dĬ lōōt′, dī-; *adj. also* dī′lōōt), *v.,* **-luted, -luting,** *adj.* —*v.t.* **1.** to make thinner or weaker by the addition of water or the like. **2.** to make (a color, etc.) fainter. **3.** to reduce the strength, force, or efficiency of by admixture. —*v.i.* **4.** to become diluted. —*adj.* **5.** reduced in strength, as a chemical by admixture; weak: *a dilute solution.* [t. L: m. s. *dīlūtus*, pp., washed to pieces, dissolved, diluted]

di·lu·tion (dĬ lōō′shən, dī-), *n.* **1.** act of diluting. **2.** state of being diluted. **3.** something diluted; a diluted form of anything.

di·lu·vi·al (dĬ lōō′vĬ əl), *adj.* **1.** pertaining to a deluge or flood. **2.** *Geol.* pertaining to or consisting of diluvium. Also, **di·lu′vi·an.** [t. L: s. *dīluviālis*]

di·lu·vi·um (dĬ lōō′vĬ əm), *n., pl.* **-via** (-vĬ ə). *Geol.* a coarse superficial deposit formerly attributed to a general deluge but now regarded as glacial drift. [t. L: deluge.]

dim (dĬm), *adj.,* **dimmer, dimmest,** *v.,* **dimmed, dimming.** —*adj.* **1.** not bright; obscure from lack of light; somewhat dark: *a dim room.* **2.** not clearly seen; indistinct: *a dim object.* **3.** not clear to the mind; vague: *a dim idea.* **4.** not brilliant; dull in luster: *a dim color.* **5.** faint: *a dim sound.* **6.** not seeing clearly: *eyes dim with tears.* **7.** not clearly understanding. **8.** disparaging; adverse: *to take a dim view.* —*v.t.* **9.** to make dim. —*v.i.* **10.** to become or grow dim. [ME *dim(e)*, OE *dim(m)*, c. O Fris. *dim*, Icel. *dimmr*] —**dim′ly**, *adv.* —**dim′ness**, *n.* —**Syn. 1.** See **dark.** **9.** darken, cloud. **10.** blur, dull, fade.

dim., **1.** diminuendo. **2.** diminutive. Also, **dimin.**

dime (dĭm), *n.* a silver coin of the U.S., of the value of 10 cents or ¹/₁₀ dollar. [ME, t. OF, var. of *disme*, g. L *decima* tenth part, tithe, prop. fem. of *decimus* tenth]

dime novel, *U.S.* a melodramatic story designed for juvenile intelligence.

di·men·sion (dĬ mĕn′shən), *n.* **1.** magnitude measured in a particular direction, or along a diameter or principal axis. **2.** (*usually pl.*) measure; extent; size; magnitude. [t. L: s. *dimensio* a measuring] —**di·men′sion·al**, *adj.* —**di·men′sion·less**, *adj.*

dim·er·ous (dĬm′ər əs), *adj.* **1.** consisting of or divided into two parts. **2.** *Bot.* (of flowers) having two members in each whorl. [f. s. Gk. *dimerēs* bipartite + -ous] —**dim′er·ism**, *n.*

Dimerous flower

dim·e·ter (dĬm′ə tər), *n. Pros.* a verse or line of two measures or feet. For example: *He is gone on the mountain,│He is lost to the forest.* [t. LL, t. Gk.: m. s. *dimetros* of two measures]

di·met·ric (dī mĕt′rĬk), *adj. Crystal.* tetragonal.

di·mid·i·ate (dĬ mĭd′Ĭ āt′, dī-), *v.,* **-ated, -ating,** *adj.* —*v.t.* **1.** to divide into halves; reduce to half. —*adj.* **2.** divided into halves. [t. L: m. s. *dīmidiātus*, pp., halved]

di·min·ish (dĬ mĬn′Ĭsh), *v.t.* **1.** to make, or cause to seem, smaller; lessen; reduce. **2.** *Archit.,* etc. to cause to taper. **3.** *Music.* to make smaller by a half step than the corresponding perfect or minor interval. **4.** *Archaic.* to detract from; disparage. —*v.i.* **5.** to lessen; decrease. [b. earlier *diminue* (t. ML: m.s. *dīminuere*, for L *dēminuere* make smaller) and MINISH] —**di·min′ish·a·ble**, *adj.* —**di·min′ish·ing·ly**, *adv.* —**Syn. 1.** See **decrease. 5.** subside, ebb, dwindle, shrink, abate.

diminishing returns, *Econ.* the fact, often stated as a law or principle, that as any factor in production (as labor, capital, etc.) is increased, the output per unit factor will eventually decrease.

di·min·u·en·do (dĬ mĬn′yōō ĕn′dō; *It.* dē mēnwĕn′dō), *adj., n., pl.* **-dos** (-dōz; *It.* -dōs). *Music.* —*adj.* **1.** gradually reducing in force or loudness; decrescendo (opposed to *crescendo*). —*n.* **2.** a gradual reduction of force or loudness. **3.** a diminuendo passage. *Symbol:* > [t. It., ppr. of *diminuire*. See DIMINISH]

dim·i·nu·tion (dĬm′ə nū′shən, -nōō′-), *n.* **1.** act, fact, or process of diminishing; lessening; reduction. **2.** *Music.* the repetition or imitation of a subject or theme in notes of shorter duration than those first used. [ME *dim-inucion*, t. AF: m. *diminucion*, t. L: m. s. *dīminūtio*]

di·min·u·tive (dĭ mĭn′yə tĭv), *adj.* **1.** small; little; tiny: *a diminutive house.* **2.** *Gram.* pertaining to or productive of a form denoting smallness, familiarity, affection, or triviality, as the suffix -*let*, in *droplet* from *drop.* —*n.* **3.** a small thing or person. **4.** *Gram.* a diminutive element or formation. [ME, t. ML: m.s. *dīminutīvus*, der. L *dī-*, *dēminutis*, pp., lessened] —**di·min′u·tive·ly**, *adj.* —**di·min′u·tive·ness**, *n.* —Syn. **1.** See little.

dim·is·so·ry letter (dĭm′ə sōr′ĭ, dĭ mĭs′ə rĭ), a letter issued by a bishop, abbot, etc., permitting a subject to be ordained by another bishop. Also, **dim′is·so′ri·al letter.** [ME *dymyssorie* (pl.), t. L: m. (*litterae*) *dimissōriae* dimissory (letter), der. *dīmissus*, pp., sent away]

dim·i·ty (dĭm′ə tĭ), *n.*, *pl.* -**ties.** a thin cotton fabric, white, dyed, or printed, woven with a stripe or check of heavier yarn. [late ME *demyt*, t. It.: m. *dimito* coarse cotton, t. Gk.: m. *dímitos* of double thread]

dim·mer (dĭm′ər), *n.* **1.** one who or that which dims. **2.** a rheostat, or similar device, by which the intensity of illumination, especially in stage lighting, is varied.

di·morph (dĭ′môrf), *n.* *Crystall.* either of the two forms assumed by a dimorphous substance.

di·mor·phism (dĭ môr′fĭz əm), *n.* **1.** *Zool.* the occurrence of two forms distinct in structure, coloration, etc., among animals of the same species. **2.** *Bot.* the occurrence of two different forms of flowers, leaves, etc., on the same plant or on distinct plants of the same species. **3.** *Crystall.* the property of some substances of crystallizing in two chemically identical but crystallographically distinct forms.

di·mor·phous (dĭ môr′fəs), *adj.* exhibiting dimorphism. Also, **di-mor′phic.** [t. Gk.: m. *dímorphos*]

Dimorphism (def. 2)
Submerged and floating
leaves of water shield,
genus *Calumba*

dim-out (dĭm′out′), *n.* a reduction or concealment of night lighting, as of a city, a ship, etc., to make it less visible from the air or sea.

dim·ple (dĭm′pəl), *n.*, *v.*, -**pled**, -**pling.** —*n.* **1.** a small natural hollow, permanent or transient, in some soft part of the human body, esp. one produced in the cheek in smiling. **2.** any slight depression like this. —*v.t.* **3.** to mark with, or as with, dimples; produce dimples in. —*v.i.* **4.** to form dimples. [ME *dympull*, c. MHG *tümpfil* pool] —**dim′ply**, *adj.*

dim-wit (dĭm′wĭt′), *n.* *Slang.* a stupid or slow-thinking person. —**dim′-wit′ted**, *adj.*

din (dĭn), *n.*, *v.*, **dinned**, **dinning.** —*n.* **1.** a loud, confused noise; a continued loud or tumultuous sound; noisy clamor. —*v.t.* **2.** to assail with din. **3.** to sound or utter with clamor or persistent repetition. —*v.i.* **4.** to make a din. [ME *din(e)*, OE *dyne*, *dynn*, c. Icel. *dynr*] —Syn. **1.** hubbub, uproar, racket. See **noise.**

di·nar (dĭ när′), *n.* **1.** any of certain Oriental coins, esp. gold coins of ancient Arab governments. **2.** a small monetary unit of Iran, equal to one hundredth part of a rial. **3.** a silver coin of Yugoslavia, worth about 19.3 U.S. cents. [t. Ar. and Pers., t. LGk.: m. s. *dēnárion*, t. L: m. *dēnārius* DENARIUS]

Di·nar·ic Alps (dĭ när′ĭk), a mountain range in W Yugoslavia: a part of the E Alpine system.

din·dle (dĭn′dəl, dĭn′əl), *v.t.*, *v.i.*, -**dled**, -**dling**, *n.* *Scot. and N. Eng.* tingle; thrill.

dine (dīn), *v.*, **dined**, **dining**, *n.* —*v.i.* **1.** to eat the principal meal of the day; take dinner. **2.** dine out, to eat dinner away from home. **3.** to take any meal. —*v.t.* **4.** to entertain at dinner. —*n.* **5.** *Obs.* dinner. [ME *dine(n)*, t. F: m. *dîner*, g. LL. *disjējūnāre* breakfast]

din·er (dī′nər), *n.* **1.** one who dines. **2.** *U.S.* a railroad dining car. **3.** a restaurant built like such a car.

Din·e·sen (dĭn′ə sən), *n.* Isak (ĭ′zək), [*Baroness Karen Blixen (Finecke)*], 1885–1962, Danish author.

di·nette (dī nĕt′), *n.* a small dining room.

ding (dĭng), *v.i.*, *v.t.* **1.** to sound, as a bell; ring, esp. with wearisome continuance. **2.** *Colloq.* to keep repeating; impress by reiteration. —*n.* **3.** the sound of a bell or the like. [imit.]

ding-dong (dĭng′dông′, -dŏng′), *n.* **1.** the sound of a bell. **2.** any similar sound of repeated strokes. —*adj.* **3.** repeated in succession or alternation. **4.** *Colloq.* vigorously fought: *a ding-dong contest.* [imit.]

din·gey (dĭng′gĭ), *n.*, *pl.* -**geys.** dinghy.

din·ghy (dĭng′gĭ), *n.*, *pl.* -**ghies.** **1.** a small boat used as a tender, as to a yacht. **2.** a small clinker-built rowboat carried by men-of-war. **3.** any of various boats for rowing or sailing used in the East Indies. Also, **dingey**, **dingy**, **dinky.** [t. Hind.: m. *dīngī*]

din·gle (dĭng′gəl), *n.* *Chiefly Poetic and Dial.* a deep, narrow cleft between hills; a shady dell.

din·go (dĭng′gō), *n.*, *pl.* -**goes.** a wolflike wild dog, *Canis dingo*, of Australia, believed to have been introduced by the aborigines. [native Australian name]

Dingo. *Canis dingo*
(Total length 3½ ft.
tail 14 in., 21 in. high
at the shoulder)

ding·us (dĭng′əs), *n.* *Slang.* gadget; thing in general. [t. S Afr. D, der. D *ding* thing]

din·gy[1] (dĭn′jĭ), *adj.*, -**gier**, -**giest.** of a dark, dull, or dirty color or aspect; lacking brightness or freshness. [orig. uncert.] —**din′gi·ly**, *adv.* —**din′gi·ness**, *n.*

din·gy[2] (dĭng′gĭ), *n.*, *pl.* -**gies.** dinghy.

dining car, a railroad car equipped as a restaurant and supplied with a kitchen, pantry, etc.

dining room, a room in which dinner and other meals are taken.

di·ni·tro·ben·zene (dī nī′trō bĕn′zēn, -bĕn zēn′), *n.* *Chem.* one of three isomeric compounds, $C_6H_4(NO_2)_2$, the most important of which is made by nitration of benzene or nitrobenzene and used in the manufacture of azo dyes.

dink (dĭngk), *Scot.* —*adj.* **1.** neatly dressed. —*v.t.* **2.** to deck; array. [? nasalized var. of *decked* adorned]

dink·ey (dĭngk′ĭ), *n.*, *pl.* **dinkeys.** anything small, esp. a small locomotive. Also, **dinky.**

dink·y (dĭngk′ĭ), *adj.*, **dinkier**, **dinkiest**, *n.*, *pl.* **dinkies.** —*adj.* **1.** *Colloq.* of small size. **2.** *Brit. Colloq.* neat; dainty; smart. —*n.* **3.** dinkey. **4.** dinghy.

din·ner (dĭn′ər), *n.* **1.** the main meal, esp. as taken about noon or (now) in the evening. **2.** a formal meal in honor of some person or occasion. [ME *diner*, t. F, orig. inf. See DINE] —**din′ner·less**, *adj.*

dinner coat or **jacket**, coat or jacket for semiformal wear by men; tuxedo.

dino-, a word element meaning "terrible," as in *dinothere*. [t. Gk.: m. *deino-*, comb. form of *deinós*]

Di·noc·er·as (dī nŏs′ər əs), *n.* *Paleontol.* an extinct genus comprising the huge horned ungulate mammals of the Eocene of North America. [NL, f. dino- DINO- + m. Gk. *kéras* horn]

di·no·saur (dī′nə sôr′), *n.* *Paleontol.* any member of extinct groups of Mesozoic reptiles, mostly of gigantic size, known in modern classifications as the *Saurischia* and the *Ornithischia.* [t. NL: s. *dinosaurus*. See DINO-, -SAUR]

Dinosaur, *Triceratops elatus*
(Ab. 24 ft. long)

di·no·sau·ri·an (dī′nə sôr′Ĭ ən), *adj.* **1.** pertaining to or of the nature of a dinosaur. —*n.* **2.** a dinosaur.

di·no·there (dī′nə thĭr′), *n.* *Paleontol.* any animal of the extinct genus *Dinotherium*, comprising elephantlike mammals of the later Tertiary of Europe and Asia, characterized by downward curving tusks in the lower jaw. [t. NL: m.s. *dinotherium*, f. dino- DINO- + m. Gk. *thēríon* wild beast]

dint (dĭnt), *n.* **1.** force; power: *by dint of argument.* **2.** a dent. **3.** *Obs.* a blow; stroke. —*v.t.* **4.** to make a dint or dints in. **5.** to impress or drive in with force. [ME; OE *dynt*, c. Icel. *dyntr*] —**dint′less**, *adj.*

Din·wid·die (dĭn wĭd′Ĭ, dĭn′wĭd′Ĭ), *n.* Robert, 1693?–1770, British official, lieutenant governor of Virginia.

di·o·ce·san (dī ŏs′ə sən, dī′ə sē′sən), *adj.* **1.** of or pertaining to a diocese. —*n.* **2.** one of the clergy or people of a diocese. **3.** the bishop in charge of a diocese.

di·o·cese (dī′ə sēs′, -sĭs), *n.* the district, with its population, falling under the pastoral care of a bishop. [ME *diocise*, t. OF, t. ML: m. *diocēsis*, for L *dioecēsis* district, t. Gk.: m. *dioíkēsis* housekeeping, administration, province, diocese]

Di·o·cle·tian (dī′ə klē′shən), *n.* A.D. 245–313, Roman emperor, A.D. 284–305.

di·ode (dī′ōd), *n.* *Electronics.* a device consisting of an anode and cathode whose volt-ampere characteristics are asymmetric. [f. DI-[1] + -ODE[2]]

di·oe·cious (dī ē′shəs), *adj.* *Biol.* (esp. of plants) having the male and female organs in separate and distinct individuals; having separate sexes. [f. s. NL *dioecia* genus name (f. Gk.: di- DI-[1] + m. s. *oîkíon* little house) + -OUS]

di·oes·trum (dī ĕs′trəm, -ēs′-), *n.* the period between the rutting periods, esp. of female animals. [NL. See DI[1]-, OESTRUM]

Di·og·e·nes (dī ŏj′ə nēz′), *n.* c412–c323 B.C., Greek Cynic philosopher.

di·oi·cous (dī oi′kəs), *adj.* *Biol.* dioecious.

Di·o·me·des (dī′ə mē′dēz), *n.* *Gk. Legend.* the son of Tydeus and the next in prowess to Achilles among the Greeks before Troy. Also, **Di·o·mede** (dī′ə mēd′), **Di·o·med** (dī′ə mĕd′). [t. L, t. Gk.]

Di·o·ny·si·a (dī′ə nĭsh′Ĭ ə, -nĭs′-), *n. pl. Gk. Antiq.* the orgiastic and dramatic festivals in honor of Dionysus or Bacchus, celebrated periodically in various parts of Greece, esp. those in Attica, out of which Greek comedy and tragedy developed. [t. L, t. Gk.]

Di·o·nys·i·ac (dī′ə nĭs′Ĭ ăk′), *adj.* pertaining to the Dionysia or to Dionysus; Bacchic. —**Di·o·ny·si·a·cal·ly** ((dī′ə nĭ sī′Ĭk lĭ), *adv.*

Di·o·ny·sian (dī′ə nĭsh′ən, -nĭs′Ĭ ən), *adj.* **1.** pertaining to Dionysus or Bacchus. **2.** (*l.c.*) wild; orgiastic.

Di·o·ny·si·us (dī′ə nĭsh′Ĭ əs, -nĭs′-), *n.* (*the Elder*) 430?–367 B.C., ruler of the ancient Greek city of Syracuse, on the island of Sicily.

Dionysius Ex·ig·u·us (ĕg zĭg′yŏŏ əs, ĕks′Ĭg′-), fl. A.D. 530, Roman monk and scholar: believed to have founded system of reckoning dates as before or after the birth of Christ.

•ionysius of Halicarnassus, died 7? B.C., Greek rhetorician and historian, in Rome.

•i·o·ny·sus (dī'ə nī'səs), n. Gk. Myth. the youthful and beautiful god of wine and the drama, identified with the Roman god Bacchus. Also, **Di'o·ny'sos.**

•i·op·side (dī ŏp'sīd, -sĭd), n. Mineral. a common variety of pyroxene, occurring in various colors, usually in crystals. [t. F, f. di- DI-¹ + m. s. Gk. ópsis appearance]

•i·op·tase (dī ŏp'tās), n. a mineral, hydrous copper silicate, CuSiO₃H₂O, occurring in emerald-green crystals. [t. F, f. Gk.: di- DI-³ + m.s. optasía view]

•i·op·ter (dī ŏp'tər), n. Optics. the refractive power of a lens whose focal length is one meter. [t. L: m. s. dioptra, t. Gk.: kind of leveling instrument]

•i·op·tom·e·ter (dī'ŏp tŏm'ə tər), n. an instrument for measuring the eye's refraction.

•i·op·tric (dī ŏp'trĭk), adj. 1. Optics. pertaining to dioptrics: dioptric images. 2. Ophthalm. assisting vision by refractive correction. Also, **di·op'tri·cal.** [t. Gk.: s. dioptrikós pertaining to the use of the dióptra. See DIOPTER] —**di·op'tri·cal·ly,** adv.

•i·op·trics (dī ŏp'trĭks), n. the branch of geometrical optics dealing with the formation of images by lenses.

•i·o·ram·a (dī'ə răm'ə, -rä'mə), n. 1. a miniature scene reproduced in three dimensions with the aid of lights, colors, etc. 2. a spectacular picture, partly translucent, for exhibition through an aperture, made more realistic by various illuminating devices. [t. F, f. di- DI-³ + Gk. (h)órama view] —**di'o·ram'ic,** adj.

•i·o·rite (dī'ə rīt'), n. a granular igneous rock consisting essentially of plagioclase feldspar and hornblende. [t. F, f. Gk. dior(izein) distinguish + -ite -ITE¹] —**di·o·rit·ic** (dī'ə rĭt'ĭk), adj.

)i·os·cu·ri (dī'ə skyŏŏr'ī), n.pl. Castor and Pollux.

•i·os·mose (dī'ŏs mōs, -ŏz'-), v.t., -mosed, -mosing. osmose. —**di·os·mo·sis** (dī'ŏs mō'sĭs, dī'ŏz-), n.

•i·ox·ane (dī ŏk'sān), n. Chem. a colorless liquid, a cyclic ether with a faint, pleasant odor, C₄H₈O₂, used in the varnish and silk industries and as a dehydrator in histology.

•i·ox·ide (dī ŏk'sīd, -sĭd), n. Chem. 1. an oxide containing two atoms of oxygen per molecule, as manganese dioxide, MnO₂. 2. (loosely) peroxide. Also, **di·ox·id** (dī ŏk'sĭd). [f. DI-¹ + OXIDE]

ip (dĭp), v., dipped or dipt, dipping, n. —v.t. 1. to plunge temporarily into a liquid, as to wet or to take up some of the liquid. 2. to raise or take up by a dipping action; lift by bailing or scooping: to dip water out of a boat. 3. to lower and raise: to dip a flag in salutation. 4. to baptize by immersion. 5. to immerse (a sheep, etc.) in a solution to destroy germs, parasites, or the like. 6. to make (a candle) by repeatedly dipping a wick into melted tallow. 7. to moisten or wet as if by immersion. —v.i. 8. to plunge into water or other liquid and emerge quickly. 9. to plunge the hand, a dipper, etc., into water, etc., esp. in order to remove something. 10. to sink or drop down, as if plunging into water. 11. to incline or slope downward. 12. to engage slightly in a subject. 13. to read here and there in a book. —n. 14. the act of dipping; a plunge into water, etc. 15. that which is taken up by dipping. 16. a liquid into which something is dipped. 17. a lowering momentarily; a sinking down. 18. downward extension, inclination, or slope. 19. the amount of such extension. 20. a hollow or depression in the land. 21. Geol., Mining. the downward inclination of a stratum or vein, referred to a horizontal plane. 22. Survey. the angular amount by which the horizon lies below the level of the eye. 23. the angle which a freely poised magnetic needle makes with the plane of the horizon. 24. a short downward plunge of an airplane or the like. 25. a candle made by repeatedly dipping a wick into melted tallow. 26. Gymnastics. an exercise on parallel bars in which a person bends his elbow until his chin is on a level with the bars, then elevates himself by straightening out his arms. [ME dippe(n), OE dyppan; akin to G taufen baptize, and DEEP]

—**Syn.** 1. DIP, IMMERSE, PLUNGE refer literally to putting something into water (or any liquid). To DIP is to put down into a liquid quickly or partially and lift out again: to dip a finger into water to test the temperature. IMMERSE denotes a gradual lowering into a liquid until covered by it, sometimes for a moment only (as in one mode of baptism): to immerse meat in salt water. PLUNGE adds a suggestion of force or suddenness to the action of dipping: to plunge a hen into boiling water before stripping off the feathers.

di·pet·al·ous (dī pĕt'əl əs), adj. Bot. bipetalous.

di·phase (dī'fāz'), adj. Elect. having two phases. Also, **di·phas·ic** (dī fā'zĭk).

di·phen·yl (dī fĕn'ĭl, -fē'nĭl), n. Chem. biphenyl.

di·phen·yl·a·mine (dī fĕn'ĭl ə mēn', -ăm'ĭn, -fē'nĭl-), n. Chem. an aromatic crystalline benzene derivative, (C₆H₅)₂NH, used in the preparation of various dyes, as a reagent for oxidizing agents, and as a stabilizer in nitrocellulose propellants.

di·phos·gene (dī fŏs'jĕn), n. Chem. a poison gas, ClCOOCCl₃, used in World War I.

diph·the·ri·a (dĭf thĭr'ĭ ə, dĭp-), n Pathol. a febrile infectious disease caused by a specific bacillus and characterized by the formation of a false membrane in the air passages, esp. the throat. [NL, f. s. Gk. diphthéra skin, leather + -ia, noun suffix]

diph·the·rit·ic (dĭf'thə rĭt'ĭk, dĭp'-), adj. Pathol. 1. pertaining to diphtheria. 2. affected by diphtheria. Also, **diph·the·ri·al** (dĭf thĭr'ĭ əl, dĭp-), **diph·ther·ic** (dĭf thĕr'ĭk, dĭp-).

diph·the·roid (dĭf'thə roid', dĭp'-), adj. Pathol. resembling diphtheria.

diph·thong (dĭf'thông, -thŏng, dĭp'-), n. 1. a composite speech sound made up of two vowels, one sonantal, the other consonantal, as ei in vein. 2. a digraph or ligature representing a vowel, as ae or æ. [t. LL: s. diphthongus, t. Gk.: m. díphthongos, lit., having two sounds] —**diph·thon'gal,** adj.

diph·thong·ize (dĭf'thông īz', -gīz', -thŏng-, dĭp'-), v., -ized, -izing. —v.t. 1. to change into or pronounce as a diphthong. —v.i. 2. to become a diphthong. —**diph'thong·i·za'tion,** n.

di·phyl·lous (dī fĭl'əs), adj. Bot. having two leaves.

diph·y·o·dont (dĭf'ĭ ō dŏnt'), adj. Zool. having two successive sets of teeth, as most mammals. [f. s. Gk. diphyès double + -ODONT]

di·plex (dī'plĕks), adj. noting or pertaining to a system of telegraphic or radio communication, for sending two messages simultaneously in the same direction over a single wire or communications channel. [f. DI-¹ + -plex, modeled on DUPLEX]

diplo-, a word element referring to pairs, doubles, as in diplocardiac. Also, before vowels, **dipl-.** [t. Gk., comb. form of diplóos twofold]

dip·lo·car·di·ac (dĭp'lə kär'dĭ ăk'), adj. Zool. pertaining to a condition whereby the right and left sides of the heart are somewhat or completely divided.

dip·lo·coc·cus (dĭp'lə kŏk'əs), n., pl. -cocci (-kŏk'sī). Bacteriol. any of certain bacterial species whose organisms occur in pairs, as in diplococcus pneumoniae, etc. [NL. See DIPLO-, COCCUS]

di·plod·o·cus (dī plŏd'ə kəs), n. Paleontol. any animal of the extinct genus Diplodocus, comprising gigantic dinosaurs of the upper Jurassic of western North America. [NL, f. diplo- DIPLO- + m. Gk. dokós beam]

dip·lo·ë (dĭp'lō ē'), n. Anat. the cancellate bony tissue between the hard inner and outer walls of the bones of the cranium. [t. Gk.: a fold]

dip·loid (dĭp'loid), adj. 1. double. 2. Biol. having two similar complements of chromosomes. —n. 3. Biol. an organism or cell with double the basic (haploid) number of chromosomes. 4. Crystall. a solid belonging to the isometric system, with 24 trapezoidal planes.

di·plo·ma (dĭ plō'mə), n., pl. -mas, L -mata (-mə tə), v., -maed, -maing. —n. 1. a document conferring some honor, privilege, or power, esp. one given by a university, etc., conferring a degree on a person or certifying to his qualifications. 2. a public or official document. —v.t. 3. to furnish with a diploma. [t. L, t. Gk.: paper folded double, letter of recommendation, license, etc.]

di·plo·ma·cy (dĭ plō'mə sĭ), n., pl. -cies. 1. the conduct by government officials of negotiations and other relations between states. 2. the science of conducting such negotiations. 3. skill in managing any negotiations; artful management. [t. F: m. diplomatie (with t pron. as s), der. diplomate diplomat]

dip·lo·mat (dĭp'lə măt'), n. one employed or skilled in diplomacy; a diplomatist.

dip·lo·mate (dĭp'lə măt'), n. one who has received a diploma; esp. a doctor, engineer, etc., who has been certified as a specialist by a board within his profession. [f. DIPLOM(A) + -ATE]

dip·lo·mat·ic (dĭp'lə măt'ĭk), adj. 1. of, pertaining to, or engaged in diplomacy. 2. skilled in diplomacy; tactful. —**dip'lo·mat'i·cal·ly,** adv.

—**Syn.** 2. DIPLOMATIC, POLITIC, TACTFUL imply ability to avoid offending others or hurting their feelings, esp. in situations where this is important. DIPLOMATIC suggests a smoothness and skill in handling others, usually in such a way as to attain one's own ends and yet avoid any unpleasantness or opposition: by diplomatic conduct he avoided antagonizing anyone. POLITIC emphasizes expediency or prudence in looking out for one's own interests, thus knowing how to treat people of different types and on different occasions: a truth which it is not politic to insist on. TACTFUL suggests a nice touch in the handling of delicate matters or situations, and, unlike the other two, often suggests a sincere desire not to hurt the feelings of others: a tactful wife. —**Ant.** 2. blunt, blundering, tactless.

diplomatic corps, the entire body of diplomats accredited to and resident at a court or capital. Also, **diplomatic body.**

dip·lo·mat·ics (dĭp'lə măt'ĭks), n. the phase of paleography devoted to ancient documents.

di·plo·ma·tist (dĭ plō'mə tĭst), n. 1. Brit. a diplomat. 2. one who is astute and tactful in any negotiation.

di·plo·pi·a (dĭ plō'pĭ ə), n. Ophthalm. a morbid condition of vision in which a single object appears double. [NL. See DIPL-, -OPIA] —**di·plop·ic** (dī plŏp'ĭk), adj.

dip·lo·pod (dĭp'lə pŏd'), adj. 1. of or pertaining to the Diplopoda. —n. 2. any member of the Diplopoda; a millipede. [f. DIPLO- + -POD]

Di·plop·o·da (dĭ plŏp'ə də), n.pl. Zool. a class of arthropods having tracheae, consisting of the millipedes.

di·plo·sis (dĭ plō'sĭs), n. Biol. the doubling of the chromosome number by the union of the haploid sets in the union of gametes. [t. Gk.: a doubling]

dip·lo·ste·mo·nous (dĭp'lə stē'mə nəs, -stĕm'ə-), adj. Bot. having two series of stamens, or twice as many stamens as petals.

äct, āble, dâre, ärt; ĕbb, ēqual; Yf, īce; hŏt, ōver, ôrder, oil, bŏŏk, ōōze, out; ŭp, ūse, ûrge; ə = a in alone; ch, chief; g, give; ng, ring; sh, shoe; th, thin; ŧħ, that; zh, vision.   See the full key on inside cover.

dip·no·an (dĭp′nō·ən), *adj.* **1.** belonging or pertaining to the *Dipnoi*, a class or group of fishes having both gills and lungs. **—n. 2.** a dipnoan fish. [f. NL: s. *Dipnoi*, pl., genus type (t. Gk.: m. *dípnoos* (sing.) having two breathing apertures) + -AN]

dip·o·dy (dĭp′ə·dĭ), *n., pl.* **-dies.** *Pros.* a group of two feet.

di·pole (dī′pōl′), *n. Physics, Phys. Chem.* **1.** a pair of equal and opposite electric charges or magnetic poles, forces, etc., as on the surface of a body or in a molecule. **2.** a molecule having the effective centers of the positive and negative charges separated. **—di·po′lar,** *adj.*

dip·per (dĭp′ər), *n.* **1.** one who or that which dips. **2.** a container with a handle, used to dip liquids. **3.** (*cap.*) *Astron.* **a.** Also, **Big Dipper.** the group of seven bright stars in Ursa Major resembling such a vessel in outline. **b.** Also, **Little Dipper.** a similar group in Ursa Minor. **4.** any of various diving birds, esp. of the genus *Cinclus,* as *C. aquaticus,* the common European water ouzel. **—dip·per·ful** (dĭp′ər·fōōl′), *n.*

dip·sa·ca·ceous (dĭp′sə·kā′shəs), *adj.* belonging to the *Dipsacaceae,* or teasel family of plants. [f. s. NL *Dipsacus,* typical genus (t. Gk.: m. *dípsakos* teasel) + -ACEOUS]

dip·so·ma·ni·a (dĭp′sə·mā′nĭ·ə), *n.* an irresistible, generally periodic, craving for intoxicating drink. [NL, f. Gk.: *dípso(s)* thirst + *manía* MANIA]

dip·so·ma·ni·ac (dĭp′sə·mā′nĭ·ăk′), *n.* one who suffers from an irresistible and insatiable craving for intoxicants. **—dip·so·ma·ni·a·cal** (dĭp′sə·mə·nī′ə·kəl), *adj.* **—Syn.** See **drunkard.**

dipt (dĭpt), *v.* pt. and pp. of **dip.**

dip·ter·al (dĭp′tər·əl), *adj.* **1.** *Archit.* having two rows of columns on all sides. **2.** *Biol.* dipterous.

dip·ter·an (dĭp′tər·ən), *adj.* **1.** dipterous. **—n. 2.** a dipterous insect.

dip·ter·o·car·pa·ceous (dĭp′tə·rō·kär·pā′shəs), *adj.* belonging to the *Dipterocarpaceae,* a family of trees, chiefly of tropical Asia.

dip·ter·on (dĭp′tər·ŏn′), *n.* a dipterous insect; a fly. [t. Gk., neut. of *dípteros* two-winged]

dip·ter·ous (dĭp′tər·əs), *adj.* **1.** *Entomol.* belonging or pertaining to the order *Diptera,* that includes the common houseflies, gnats, mosquitoes, etc., characterized typically by a single pair of membranous wings. **2.** *Bot.* having two winglike appendages, as seeds, stems, etc. [t. NL: m. *dípterus* two-winged, t. Gk.: m. *dípteros*]

dip·tych (dĭp′tĭk), *n.* **1.** a hinged two-leaved tablet used by the ancients for writing on with the stylus. **2.** a pair of pictures or carvings on two panels hinged together. [t. LL: s. *diptycha,* neut. pl., double-folded, t. Gk.]

Di·rac (dĭ′răk′), *n.* **Paul Adrien Maurice** (pôl ä′drĭ·ən môr′ĭs), born 1902, British physicist.

dir·dum (dĭr′dəm, dûr′-), *n. Scot. and N. Eng.* blame.

dire (dīr), *adj.,* **direr, direst.** causing or attended with great fear or suffering; dreadful; awful: *a dire calamity.* [t. L: m. s. *dīrus*] **—dire′ly,** *adv.* **—dire′ness,** *n.*

di·rect (dĭ·rĕkt′, dī-), *v.t.* **1.** to guide with advice; regulate the course of; conduct; manage; control. **2.** to give authoritative instructions to; command; order or ordain (something): *I directed him to do it, or that he do it.* **3.** to tell or show (a person) the way to a place, etc. **4.** to point or aim toward a place or an object; cause to move, act, or work toward a certain object or end. **5.** to address (words, etc.) to a person. **6.** to mark (a letter, etc.) as intended for or sent to a particular person. **—v.i. 7.** to act as a guide. **8.** to give commands or orders. **—adj. 9.** proceeding in a straight line or by the shortest course; straight; undeviating; not oblique. **10.** proceeding in an unbroken line of descent; lineal, not collateral. **11.** following the natural order, as in mathematics. **12.** without intervening agency; immediate; personal. **13.** going straight to the point; straightforward; downright. **14.** absolute; exact: *the direct contrary.* **15.** *Gram.* (of quotation or discourse) consisting exactly of the words originally used. Example: *He said "I am coming."* **16.** *Govt.* of or by action of voters, which takes effect without any intervening agency such as representatives. **17.** *Elect.* of or pertaining to direct current. **18.** *Astron.* **a.** moving in an orbit in the same direction as the earth in its revolution round the sun. **b.** appearing to move in the zodiac according to the natural order of the signs, or from west to east (opposed to *retrograde*). **19.** *Dyeing.* working without the use of a mordant; substantive. **—adv. 20.** in a direct manner; directly; straight. [ME *direct(en)*, t. L: s. *dīrectus,* pp.] **—di·rect′ness,** *n.* **—Syn. 1.** See **guide. 2.** DIRECT, ORDER, COMMAND mean to issue instructions. DIRECT suggests also giving explanations or advice; the emphasis is not on the authority of the director, but on steps necessary for the accomplishing of a purpose. ORDER connotes a personal relationship, in which one in a superior position imperatively instructs a subordinate (or subordinates) to do something. COMMAND, less personal and, often, less specific in detail suggests greater formality; and, sometimes, a more fixed authority on the part of the superior. **12.** DIRECT, IMMEDIATE imply relationships which are readily to be observed. A DIRECT result is one which is easily traceable to its cause or causes; there may be a number of steps in between, but the line from one to another is unbroken, simple, and quite evident. An IMMEDIATE result is one in which there is no medium or step (or practically none) intervening between cause and result; these are consecutive or side by side, so that it is possible to pass at once from one to the other. **—Ant. 13.** devious.

direct action, any method of directly pitting th[e] force of organized workers' strength against employe[r]s or capitalists, as strikes, picketing, sabotage, slowdow[n], etc. **—direct actionist.**

direct carving, *Sculpture.* the art of carvin[g] directly in stone or wood without a finished model as [a] guide.

direct current, *Elect.* a relatively steady current [in] one direction in a circuit; a continuous stream of ele[c]trons through a conductor. Cf. **alternating current.**

direct discourse, *Rhet.* discourse in which th[e] original words of a speaker are reported exactly (co[n]trasted with *indirect discourse*).

direct evidence, evidence of a witness who testifi[es] to the truth of the fact to be proved (contrasted wit[h] *circumstantial evidence*).

di·rec·tion (dĭ·rĕk′shən, dī-), *n.* **1.** act of directin[g,] pointing, aiming, etc. **2.** the line along which anythi[ng] lies, faces, moves, etc., with reference to the point [of] region toward which it is directed. **3.** the point o[r] region itself. **4.** a line of action, tendency, etc. **5.** guid[ance; instruction. **6.** order; command. **7.** managemen[t;] control. **8.** a directorate. **9.** the superscription on [a] letter, etc., giving the name and address of the intende[d] recipient. **10.** *Theat.* decisions in a stage or film pr[o]duction as to stage business, speaking of lines, lightin[g,] and general presentation. **11.** *Music.* a symbol [or] phrase in a score which indicates the proper temp[o,] style of performance, mood, etc. **—Syn. 4.** See ten[d]ency.

di·rec·tion·al (dĭ·rĕk′shən·əl, dī-), *adj.* **1.** of or per[]taining to direction in space. **2.** *Radio.* adapted f[or] determining the direction of signals received, or f[or] transmitting signals in a given direction: *a direction[al] antenna.*

direction finder, *Radio.* a contrivance on a receiv[er] usually based on a loop antenna rotating on a vertic[al] axis, which ascertains the direction of incoming rad[io] waves.

di·rec·tive (dĭ·rĕk′tĭv, dī-), *adj.* **1.** serving to direc[t;] directing. **—n. 2.** an authoritative instruction or d[i]rection.

di·rect·ly (dĭ·rĕkt′lĭ, dī-), *adv.* **1.** in a direct line, way or manner; straight. **2.** *Chiefly Brit.* without delay; im[]mediately. **3.** presently. **4.** absolutely; exactly; pr[e]cisely. **—conj. 5.** *Chiefly Brit.* as soon as: *directly he a[r]rived, he mentioned the subject.* **—Syn. 2.** See **immed[i]ately.**

direct object, (in English and some other language[s]) the person or thing upon which the action of the verb [is] expended or toward which it is directed, in English e[x]pressed by a noun or pronoun without a preposition an[d] generally coming after the verb. Example: *he hit th[e] horse* has the horse as the direct object.

Di·rec·toire (dē·rĕk·twär′), *n.* **1.** *French Hist.* th[e] French Directory. See **Directory. —adj. 2.** (of costume[)] in the style of the period of the French Directory.

di·rec·tor (dĭ·rĕk′tər, dī-), *n.* **1.** one who or tha[t] which directs. **2.** *Com.* one of a body of persons chose[n] to control or govern the affairs of a company or cor[]poration. **3.** the manager of the interpretive aspects [of] a stage or film production who supervises such element[s] as the acting, photography, etc. **4.** *Mil.* a mechanica[l] device that continuously calculates firing data for us[e] against an airplane or other moving target. **—di·rec[′]tor·ship,** *n.* **—di·rec·tress** (dĭ·rĕk′trĭs, dī-), *n. fem[.]*

di·rec·to·rate (dĭ·rĕk′tə·rĭt, dī-), *n.* **1.** the office of [a] director. **2.** a body of directors.

di·rec·to·ri·al (dĭ·rĕk′tōr′ĭ·əl, dī′rĕk-), *adj.* pertain[]ing to a director or directorate.

di·rec·to·ry (dĭ·rĕk′tə·rĭ, dī-), *n., pl.* **-ries,** *adj.* **—n[.] 1.** a book or billboard containing an alphabetical list [of] the names and addresses of people in a city, district[,] building, etc., or of a particular class of persons, etc[.] **2.** a book of directions. **3. the Directory,** *French Hist[.]* the body of five directors forming the executives [of] France from 1795 to 1799. **—adj. 4.** serving to direct[;] directing. [(defs. 1, 2, 4) t. L: m.s. *dīrectōrius* that direct[s] (ML *dīrectōrium,* n.); (def. 3) t. F: m. *Directoire,* t. L, etc[.]

direct primary, *Govt.* an election through which [a] political party nominates its candidates by direct vot[e.]

di·rec·trix (dĭ·rĕk′trĭks, dī-), *n., pl.* **directrixes** (d[ī·] rĕk′trĭk·sĭz, dī-), **directrices** (dī·rĕk·trī′sēz). **1.** *Math[.]* a fixed line used in the description of a curve or surface[.] See diag. under **parabola. 2.** a directress. [t. NL]

direct tax, *Govt.* a tax demanded from the very per[]sons who will bear the burden of it (not reimbursin[g] themselves at the expense of others), as a poll tax, [a] general property tax, or an income tax.

dire·ful (dīr′fəl), *adj.* dreadful; awful; terrible[.] **—dire′ful·ly,** *adv.* **—dire′ful·ness,** *n.*

dirge (dûrj), *n.* **1.** a funeral song or tune, or one ex[]pressing mourning. **2.** *Eccles.* the office of the dead, o[r] the funeral service as sung. [t. L, syncopated var. [of] *dīrige* (impv. of *dīrigere* direct), first word of the antiphon[] sung in the L office of the dead]

dir·hem (dĭr′hĕm′), *n.* a silver coin of the Mohammed[]ans, usually equal to 1/10 dinar.

dir·i·gi·ble (dĭr′ə·jə·bəl), *n.* **1.** a dirigible balloon; a[n] airship. **—adj. 2.** that may be directed, controlled, o[r] steered. [f. s. L. *dīrigere* DIRECT, v. + -IBLE] **—dir′i·gi·[]bil′i·ty,** *n.*

di·ri·go (dĭr′ĭ·gō′), *Latin.* I direct (motto of Maine).

---

b., blend of, blended;   c., cognate with;   d., dialect, dialectal;   der., derived from;   f., formed from;   g., going back to[;] m., modification of;   r., replacing;   s., stem of;   t., taken from;   ?, perhaps.   See the full key on inside cover.

dir·i·ment (dĭr′ə mənt), *adj.* **1.** that renders absolutely void; nullifying. **2.** *Rom. Cath. Ch.* rendering marriage null and void from the very beginning. [t. L: s. *dirimens*, ppr., separating, breaking off]

dirk (dûrk), *n.* **1.** a stabbing weapon; a dagger. —*v.t.* **2.** to stab with a dirk. [orig. unknown]

dirl (dûrl, dŭrl), *v.i.* *Scot.* to vibrate; shake.

dirn·dl (dûrn′dəl), *n.* **1.** a type of woman's dress with full skirt and close-fitting bodice, commonly of colorful and strikingly patterned material, derived from Tyrolean peasant use. **2.** a skirt in such a style. [t. G: girl]

dirt (dûrt), *n.* **1.** any foul or filthy substance, as dust, excrement, mud, etc. **2.** *U.S. and Brit. Dial.* earth or soil, esp. when loose. **3.** something vile, mean, or worthless. **4.** moral filth; vileness. **5.** abusive or scurrilous language. **6.** gossip. **7.** *Mining.* **a.** crude broken ore or waste. **b.** (in placer mining) the material from which the gold is separated by washing. [metathetic var. of ME *drit*, t. Scand.; cf. Icel. *drit* excrement]

dirt-cheap (dûrt′chēp′), *adj.* very inexpensive.

dirt·y (dûr′tĭ), *adj.*, **dirt·i·er, dirt·i·est; v., dirt·ied, dirty·ing.** —*adj.* **1.** soiled with dirt; foul; unclean. **2.** imparting dirt; soiling. **3.** vile; mean. **4.** morally unclean; indecent. **5.** (of devices capable of producing nuclear reactions) having the ability to generate unwanted radioactive by-products, as *a dirty bomb.* **6.** stormy; squally, as the weather: *it looks dirty to windward.* **7.** appearing as if soiled; dark-colored; dingy. —*v.t., v.i.* **8.** to make or become dirty. —**dirt′i·ly,** *adv.* —**dirt′i·ness,** *n.* —Syn. **1.** DIRTY, FILTHY, FOUL, SQUALID refer to that which is not clean. DIRTY is applied to that which is filled or covered with dirt so that it is unclean or defiled: *dirty streets, dirty clothes.* FILTHY is an emphatic word suggesting that which is offensively defiled or is excessively soiled or dirty: *a filthy hovel.* FOUL implies an uncleanness that is grossly offensive to the senses: *a foul odor.* SQUALID, applied usually to dwellings or surroundings, implies dirtiness that results from the slovenly indifference often associated with poverty: *a whole family living in one squalid room.* **4.** obscene, nasty.

Dis (dĭs), *n.* *Rom. Myth.* **1.** the god of the lower world, Pluto. **2.** the infernal world.

dis-¹, a prefix of Latin origin, meaning "apart," "asunder," "away," "utterly," or having a privative, negative, or reversing force (see **de-** and **un-²**), used freely, esp. with these latter significations, as an English formative, as in *disability, disaffirm, disbar, disbelief, discontent, disentangle, dishearten, disinfect, dislike, disown, disrelish.* Also, **di-.** [t. L (akin to L *bis,* Gk. *dís* twice); before *f, dif-* before some consonants, *di-;* often r. obs. *des-,* t. OF]

dis-², var. of **di-¹,** as in *dissyllable.*

dis·a·bil·i·ty (dĭs′ə bĭl′ə tĭ), *n., pl.* **-ties. 1.** lack of competent power, strength, or physical or mental ability; incapacity. **2.** legal incapacity; legal disqualification. —Syn. **1.** DISABILITY, INABILITY imply a lack of power or ability. A DISABILITY is some disqualifying deprivation or loss of power, physical or other: *excused because of a physical disability, a temporary disability.* INABILITY is a want of ability, usually because of an inherent lack of talent, power, etc.: *inability to talk, to do well in higher mathematics.*

disability clause, *Life Insurance.* a clause whereby a policy belonging to a totally and permanently disabled policyholder remains in full force and effect without payment of additional premiums, often providing for periodic payment of money to the assured during the period of disability.

dis·a·ble (dĭs ā′bəl), *v.t.,* **-bled, -bling. 1.** to make unable; weaken or destroy the capability of; cripple; incapacitate. **2.** to make legally incapable; disqualify. —**dis·a′ble·ment,** *n.* —Syn. **1.** See **cripple.**

dis·a·buse (dĭs′ə būz′), *v.t.,* **-bused, -busing.** to free from deception or error; set right. [f. DIS-¹ + ABUSE, v.]

di·sac·cha·ride (dī săk′ə rīd′, -rĭd), *n.* *Chem.* any of a group of carbohydrates, as sucrose or lactose, which hydrolyze into two simple sugars (monosaccharides). [f. DI-¹ + SACCHARIDE]

dis·ac·cord (dĭs′ə kôrd′), *v.i.* **1.** to be out of accord; disagree. —*n.* **2.** lack of accord; disagreement. [ME *disacorde(n),* t. OF: m. *desac(c)order,* f. *des-* DIS-¹ + *ac(c)order* ACCORD, v.]

dis·ac·cus·tom (dĭs′ə kŭs′təm), *v.t.* to cause to lose a habit.

dis·ad·van·tage (dĭs′əd văn′tĭj, -văn′-), *n., v.,* **-taged, -taging.** —*n.* **1.** absence or deprivation of advantage; any unfavorable circumstance or condition. **2.** injury to interest, reputation, credit, profit, etc.; loss. —*v.t.* **3.** to subject to disadvantage. —Syn. **1.** drawback, inconvenience, hindrance. **2.** detriment, hurt, harm, damage.

dis·ad·van·ta·geous (dĭs ăd′vən tā′jəs, dĭs′ăd-), *adj.* attended with disadvantage; unfavorable; detrimental. —**dis·ad·van·ta′geous·ly** *adv.* —**dis·ad·van·ta′geous·ness,** *n.*

dis·af·fect (dĭs′ə fĕkt′), *v.t.* to alienate the affection of; make ill-affected, discontented, or disloyal.

dis·af·fec·tion (dĭs′ə fĕk′shən), *n.* absence or alienation of affection or good will; estrangement; disloyalty.

dis·af·firm (dĭs′ə fûrm′), *v.t.* **1.** to deny; contradict. **2.** *Law.* to annul; reverse; repudiate. —**dis·af·firm′ance, dis·af·fir·ma·tion** (dĭs′ăf ər mā′shən), *n.*

dis·af·for·est (dĭs′ə fôr′ĭst, -fŏr′-), *v.t.* **1.** to reduce from the legal status of a forest to that of common land. **2.** to strip of forests. [t. ML: s. *disafforestāre*] —**dis·af·for·es·ta·tion, dis·af·for·est·ment,** *n.*

dis·a·gree (dĭs′ə grē′), *v.i.,* **-greed, -greeing. 1.** to fail to agree; differ (fol. by *with*): *the conclusions disagree with the facts.* **2.** to differ in opinion; dissent. **3.** to quarrel. **4.** to conflict in action or effect: *food that disagrees with one.*

dis·a·gree·a·ble (dĭs′ə grē′ə bəl), *adj.* **1.** contrary to one's taste or liking; unpleasant; offensive; repugnant. **2.** unpleasant in manner or nature; unamiable. —**dis·a·gree′a·ble·ness,** *n.* —**dis·a·gree′a·bly,** *adv.*

dis·a·gree·ment (dĭs′ə grē′mənt), *n.* **1.** act, state, or fact of disagreeing. **2.** lack of agreement; diversity; unlikeness. **3.** difference of opinion; dissent. **4.** dissension; quarrel. **5.** unwholesome action or effect, as of food.

dis·al·low (dĭs′ə lou′), *v.t.* **1.** to refuse to allow. **2.** to refuse to admit the truth or validity of. —**dis·al·low′ance,** *n.*

dis·an·nul (dĭs′ə nŭl′), *v.t.,* **-nulled, -nulling.** to annul utterly; make void. [f. DIS-¹ (intensive) + ANNUL] —**dis·an·nul′ment,** *n.*

dis·a·noint (dĭs′ə noint′), *v.t.* to invalidate the consecration of.

dis·ap·pear (dĭs′ə pĭr′), *v.i.* **1.** to cease to appear or be seen; vanish from sight. **2.** to cease to exist or be known; pass away; end gradually. —Syn. **1.** DISAPPEAR, FADE, VANISH suggest that something passes from sight. DISAPPEAR is used of whatever suddenly or gradually goes out of sight: *we watched him turn down a side street and then disappear.* FADE suggests a (complete or partial) disappearance that proceeds gradually and often by means of a blending into something else: *colors in the sky at sunrise quickly fade.* VANISH suggests complete, generally rapid, and often mysterious disappearance: *a mirage can vanish as suddenly as it appeared.*

dis·ap·pear·ance (dĭs′ə pĭr′əns), *n.* act of disappearing; a ceasing to appear or to exist.

dis·ap·point (dĭs′ə point′), *v.t.* **1.** to fail to fulfill the expectations or wishes of (a person): *his conduct disappointed us.* **2.** to defeat the fulfillment of (hopes, plans, etc.); thwart; frustrate. [t. OF: m. *desappointer,* f. *des-* DIS-¹ + *appointer* APPOINT] —**dis·ap·point′er,** *n.* —**dis·ap·point′ing·ly,** *adv.*

dis·ap·point·ment (dĭs′ə point′mənt), *n.* **1.** act or fact of disappointing: *he has lost hope because of frequent disappointments.* **2.** state or feeling of being disappointed: *great was his disappointment.* **3.** something that disappoints: *the play was a disappointment.* —Syn. **1.** failure, defeat, frustration. **2.** mortification, frustration.

dis·ap·pro·ba·tion (dĭs′ăp rə bā′shən), *n.* disapproval.

dis·ap·prov·al (dĭs′ə prōō′vəl), *n.* act or state of disapproving; a condemnatory feeling or utterance; censure. —Syn. disapprobation, dislike, condemnation.

dis·ap·prove (dĭs′ə prōōv′), *v.,* **-proved, -proving.** —*v.t.* **1.** to think wrong or reprehensible; censure or condemn in opinion. **2.** to withhold approval from; decline to sanction: *the court disapproved the verdict.* —*v.i.* **3.** to have an unfavorable opinion (fol. by *of*). —**dis·ap·prov′ing·ly,** *adv.* —Ant. **1.** praise.

dis·arm (dĭs ärm′), *v.t.* **1.** to deprive of arms. **2.** to deprive of means of attack or defense. **3.** to divest of hostility, suspicion, etc.; make friendly. —*v.i.* **4.** to lay down arms. **5.** (of a country) to reduce or limit the size, equipment, armament, etc., of the army, navy, or air forces. [t. OF: m.s. *desarmer,* f. *des-* DIS-¹ + *armer* ARM²] —**dis·arm′er,** *n.*

dis·ar·ma·ment (dĭs är′mə mənt), *n.* **1.** act of disarming. **2.** the reduction or limitation of the size, equipment, armament, etc., of the army, navy, or air forces.

dis·arm·ing (dĭs är′mĭng), *adj.* ingenuous. —**dis·arm′ing·ly,** *adv.*

dis·ar·range (dĭs′ə rānj′), *v.t.,* **-ranged, -ranging.** to disturb the arrangement of; disorder; unsettle. —**dis·ar·range′ment,** *n.* —**dis·ar·rang′er,** *n.*

dis·ar·ray (dĭs′ə rā′), *v.t.* **1.** to put out of array or order; throw into disorder. **2.** to undress. —*n.* **3.** disorder; confusion. **4.** disorder of apparel; disorderly dress.

dis·ar·tic·u·late (dĭs′är tĭk′yə lāt′), *v.t., v.i.,* **-lated, -lating.** to separate or come apart at the joints. —**dis·ar·tic′u·la′tion,** *n.* —**dis·ar·tic·u·la′tor,** *n.*

dis·as·sem·ble (dĭs′ə sĕm′bəl), *v.t.,* **-bled, -bling.** to take apart.

dis·as·sem·bly (dĭs′ə sĕm′blĭ), *n.* **1.** act of disassembling. **2.** state of being disassembled.

dis·as·so·ci·ate (dĭs′ə sō′shĭ āt′), *v.t.,* **-ated, -ating.** to dissociate. —**dis·as·so′ci·a′tion,** *n.*

dis·as·ter (dĭ zăs′tər, -zăs′-), *n.* **1.** any unfortunate event; esp. a sudden or great misfortune. **2.** *Obs.* an unfavorable aspect of a star or planet. [It.: m. *disastro,* der. *disastrato* not having a (lucky) star, f. *dis-* DIS-¹ + *astr(o)* star + *-ato,* prop., ppl. ending] —Syn. **1.** mischance, misfortune, misadventure, blow, reverse. DISASTER, CALAMITY, CATASTROPHE refer to adverse happenings occurring often suddenly and unexpectedly. A DISASTER may be caused by carelessness, negligence, bad judgment, and the like; or by natural forces, as a hurricane, flood, etc.: *a railway disaster.* CALAMITY suggests great affliction, either personal or general; the emphasis is on the grief or sorrow caused: *the calamity of losing a dear child.* CATASTROPHE refers esp. to the tragic outcome of a personal or a public situation; the emphasis is on the destruction or irreplaceable loss: *the catastrophe of a defeat in battle.*

dis·as·trous (dǐ zăs'trəs, -zäs'-), *adj.* **1.** causing great distress or injury; ruinous; unfortunate; calamitous. **2.** *Archaic.* foreboding disaster. **—dis·as'trous·ly,** *adv.* **—dis·as'trous·ness,** *n.*

dis·a·vow (dǐs'ə vou'), *v.t.* to disclaim knowledge of, connection with, or responsibility for; disown; repudiate. [ME *desavoue(n)*, t. OF: m. *desavouer*, f. *des-* DIS-¹ + *avouer* AVOW] **—dis·a·vow'er,** *n.*

dis·a·vow·al (dǐs'ə vou'əl), *n.* a disowning; repudiation; denial.

dis·band (dǐs bănd'), *v.t.* **1.** to break up or disorganize (a band or company); dissolve (a military force) by dismissing from service. **—v.i. 2.** to break up, as a band or company. [t. MF: m. *desbander*, f. *des-* DIS-¹ + *bander* tie] **—dis·band'ment,** *n.* **—Syn. 1.** demobilize, dissolve, disperse.

dis·bar (dǐs bär'), *v.t.,* **-barred, -barring.** *Law.* to expel from the legal profession or from the bar of a particular court. [f. DIS-¹ + BAR¹] **—dis·bar'ment,** *n.*

dis·bos·om (dǐs bŏŏz'əm, -bŏŏ'zəm), *v.t.* to make known; reveal; confess.

dis·bow·el (dǐs bou'əl), *v.t.,* **-eled, -eling** or (*esp. Brit.*) **-elled, -elling.** to disembowel.

dis·branch (dǐs brănch', -bränch'), *v.t.* **1.** to deprive of branches, as a tree. **2.** to cut or break off, as a branch.

dis·bur·den (dǐs bûr'dən), *v.t.* **1.** to remove a burden from; rid of a burden. **2.** to relieve of anything oppressive or annoying. **3.** to get rid of (a burden); discharge. **—v.i. 4.** to unload a burden. **—dis·bur'den·ment,** *n.*

dis·burse (dǐs bûrs'), *v.t.,* **-bursed, -bursing.** to pay out (money); expend. [t. OF: m. *desbourser,* f. *des-* DIS-¹ + *bourse* purse (g. LL *bursa.* See BURSA)] **—dis·burs'a·ble,** *adj.* **—dis·burs'er,** *n.* **—Syn.** See **spend.**

dis·burse·ment (dǐs bûrs'mənt), *n.* **1.** act of disbursing. **2.** that which is disbursed; money expended.

dis·bur·then (dǐs bûr'thən), *v.t., v.i. Archaic.* to disburden.

disc (dǐsk), *n.* **1.** disk. **2.** *Anat., Zool.* **a. interarticular disc,** a plate of cartilage interposed between the articulating ends of bones. **b. intervertebral disc,** the plate of fibrocartilage interposed between the bodies of adjacent vertebrae. [see DISK, DISCUS]

disc., 1. discount. **2.** discovered.

dis·calced (dǐs kălst'), *adj.* without shoes; unshod; barefooted: specif. applied to a branch of the Carmelite monks known as **Discalceati** (the barefooted). Also, **dis·cal·ce·ate** (dǐs kăl'sē ĭt, -āt').

dis·cant (*n.* dǐs'kănt; *v.* dǐs kănt'), *n., v.i., v.t.* descant.

dis·card (*v.* dǐs kärd'; *n.* dǐs'kärd), *v.t.* **1.** to cast aside; reject; dismiss, esp. from use. **2.** *Cards.* **a.** to throw out (a card or cards) from one's hand. **b.** to play (a card, not a trump, of a different suit from that of the card led). **—v.i. 3.** *Cards.* to discard a card or cards. **—n. 4.** act of discarding. **5.** one who or that which is cast out or rejected. **6.** *Cards.* the card or cards discarded. **—dis·card'er,** *n.* **—Syn. 1.** See **reject.** **—Ant. 1.** retain.

dis·case (dǐs kās'), *v.t.,* **-cased, -casing.** to take the case or covering from; uncase.

dis·cept (dǐ sĕpt'), *v.i.* to dispute. [t. L: s. *disceptāre* contend] **—dis·cep·ta'tion,** *n.*

dis·cern (dǐ zûrn', -sûrn'), *v.t.* **1.** to perceive by the sight or some other sense or by the intellect; see, recognize, or apprehend clearly. **2.** to distinguish mentally; recognize as distinct or different; discriminate: *he discerns good and bad, good from bad.* **—v.i. 3.** to distinguish or discriminate. [ME *discerne(n),* t. F: m. *discerner,* t. L: m. *discernere*] **—dis·cern'er,** *n.* **—Syn. 1.** See **notice.**

dis·cern·i·ble (dǐ zûr'nə bəl, -sûr'-), *adj.* capable of being discerned; distinguishable. **—dis·cern'i·ble·ness,** *n.* **—dis·cern'i·bly,** *adv.*

dis·cern·ing (dǐ zûr'nǐng, -sûr'-), *adj.* showing discernment; discriminating. **—dis·cern'ing·ly,** *adv.*

dis·cern·ment (dǐ zûrn'mənt, -sûrn'-), *n.* **1.** faculty of discerning; discrimination; acuteness of judgment. **2.** act of discerning.

dis·cerp·ti·ble (dǐ sûrp'tə bəl), *adj.* capable of being torn apart; divisible. **—dis·cerp'ti·bil'i·ty,** *n.*

dis·charge (*v.* dǐs chärj'; *n. also* dǐs'chärj), *v.,* **-charged, -charging,** *n.* **—v.t. 1.** to relieve of a charge or load; unload a ship, etc.). **2.** to remove, send forth, or get rid of (a charge, load, etc.). **3.** to fire; shoot: *discharge a gun, bow, bullet, etc.* **4.** to pour forth, as water. **5.** to relieve oneself of (an obligation, etc.). **6.** to relieve of obligation, responsibility, etc. **7.** to fulfill, perform, or execute (a duty, function, etc.). **8.** to relieve or deprive of office, employment, etc.; dismiss from service. **9.** to send away or allow to go (fol. by *from*). **10.** to pay (a debt). **11.** *Law.* to release, as bail or a defendant. **12.** *Elect.* to rid (something) of a charge of electricity. **13.** *Dyeing.* to free from a dye, as by chemical bleaching. **—v.i. 14.** to get rid of a burden or load. **15.** to deliver a charge or load. **16.** to come or pour forth. **17.** to blur; run. **18.** *Elect.* to lose, or give up, a charge of electricity. **—n. 19.** act of discharging a ship, load, etc. **20.** act of firing a missile weapon, as a bow by drawing and releasing the string, or a gun by exploding the charge of powder. **21.** a sending or coming forth, as of water from a pipe; ejection; emission. **22.** rate or amount of issue. **23.** something discharged or emitted. **24.** a relieving or ridding, or a getting rid, of something of

the nature of a charge. **25.** *Law.* **a.** acquittal or exoneration. **b.** annulment, as of a court order. **c.** freeing of one held under legal process. **26.** a relieving or being relieved of obligation or liability; the fulfilling of an obligation. **27.** the payment of a debt. **28.** release or dismissal from office, employment, etc. **29.** a certificate of release, as from obligation or liability. **30.** *Elect.* **a.** the withdrawing or transference of an electric charge. **b.** the equalization of the difference of potential between two terminals or the like. [ME *discharge(n),* t. OF: m. *deschargier.* See DIS-¹, CHARGE] **—dis·charge'a·ble,** *adj.* **—dis·charg'er,** *n.* **—Syn. 4.** eject, expel, emit, exude. **6.** See **release.** **7.** See **perform.** **10.** settle, liquidate. **26.** fulfillment, execution, performance.

disci-, a combining form of **disk.**

dis·ci·flo·ral (dǐs'ǐ flôr'əl), *adj. Bot.* having flowers in which the receptacle is expanded into a conspicuous disk.

dis·ci·ple (dǐ sī'pəl), *n., v.,* **-discipled, -discipling. 1.** one of the twelve personal followers of Jesus Christ. **2.** any follower of Christ. **3.** an adherent of the doctrines of another; a follower. **—v.t. 4.** to convert into a disciple. **5.** *Obs.* to teach; train. [ME, t. OF, t. L: m. s. *discipulus;* r. ME *deciple,* t. OF; r. OE *discipul,* t. L (as above)] **—dis·ci'ple·ship,** *n.* **—Syn. 3.** See **pupil¹.**

Disciples of Christ, a denomination of Christians, founded in the U.S. in the early part of the 19th century by Alexander Campbell (1788–1866), which seeking the unity of all Christians, rejects all creeds, accepts the Bible as a sufficient rule of faith and practice, and administers baptism by immersion.

dis·ci·plin·a·ble (dǐs'ə plǐn'ə bəl), *adj.* **1.** subject to or meriting correction. **2.** capable of being instructed.

dis·ci·pli·nal (dǐs'ə plǐ'nəl, dǐs'ə plǐn'əl), *adj.* of, pertaining to, or of the nature of discipline.

dis·ci·plin·ant (dǐs'ə plǐn'ənt), *n.* **1.** one who subjects himself to discipline. **2.** (*cap.*) *Eccles.* a member of a former Spanish religious order who scourged themselves publicly and inflicted upon themselves other severe tortures.

dis·ci·pli·nar·i·an (dǐs'ə plə när'ǐ ən), *n.* **1.** one who enforces or advocates discipline. **—adj. 2.** disciplinary.

dis·ci·pli·nar·y (dǐs'ə plə nĕr'ǐ), *adj.* of or for discipline; promoting discipline.

dis·ci·pline (dǐs'ə plǐn), *n., v.,* **-plined, -plining. —n. 1.** training to act in accordance with rules; drill: *military discipline.* **2.** instruction and exercise designed to train to proper conduct or action. **3.** punishment inflicted by way of correction and training. **4.** the training effect of experience, adversity, etc. **5.** subjection to rules of conduct or behavior; a state of order maintained by training and control: *good discipline in an army.* **6.** a set or system of rules and regulations. **7.** *Eccles.* the system of government regulating the practice of a church as distinguished from its doctrine. **8.** a branch of instruction or learning. **—v.t. 9.** to train by instruction and exercise; drill. **10.** to bring to a state of order and obedience by training and control. **11.** to subject to discipline or punishment; correct; chastise. [ME, t. L: m. *disciplīna* instruction] **—dis'ci·plin·er,** *n.* **—Syn. 11.** See **punish.**

dis·claim (dǐs klām'), *v.t.* **1.** to repudiate or deny interest in or connection with; disavow; disown: *disclaiming all participation.* **2.** *Law.* to renounce a claim or right to. **3.** to reject the claims or authority of. **—v.i. 4.** *Law.* to renounce or repudiate a legal claim or right. **5.** *Obs.* to disavow interest. [t. AF: s. *disclaimer, desclamer,* f. *des-* DIS-¹ + *clamer* CLAIM]

dis·claim·er (dǐs klā'mər), *n.* **1.** act of disclaiming; the renouncing, repudiating, or denying of a claim; disavowal. **2.** one who disclaims. [t. AF]

dis·cla·ma·tion (dǐs'klə mā'shən), *n.* act of disclaiming; renunciation; disavowal.

dis·close (dǐs klōz'), *v.,* **-closed, -closing,** *n.* **—v.t. 1.** to cause to appear; allow to be seen; make known; reveal: *to disclose a plot.* **2.** to uncover; lay open to view. **3.** *Obs.* to open up; unfold. **—n. 4.** *Obs.* disclosure. [ME *disclose(n), desclose(n),* t. OF: m. *desclos-, desclore* unclose, f. *des-* DIS-¹ + *clore* (g. L *claudere* CLOSE)] **—dis·clos'er,** *n.* **—Syn. 1.** See **reveal.**

dis·clo·sure (dǐs klō'zhər), *n.* **1.** act of disclosing; exposure; revelation. **2.** that which is disclosed; a revelation. **3.** (in a patent application) the descriptive information imparted by the specification claims, drawings, and models.

dis·cob·o·lus (dǐs kŏb'ə ləs), *n., pl.* **-li** (-lī'). **1.** *Class. Antiq.* a thrower of the discus. **2.** (*cap.*) a famous statue of a discus thrower by the Greek sculptor Myron (5th century B.C.). [t. L, t. Gk.: m. *diskobólos*]

dis·coid (dǐs'koid), *adj.* **1.** having the form of a discus or disk; flat and circular. **2.** *Bot.* (of a composite flower) consisting of a disk only, without rays. **—n. 3.** something in the form of a disk. [t. LL: s. *discoīdes,* t. Gk.: m. *diskoeidēs*]

dis·coi·dal (dǐs koi'dəl), *adj.* discoid.

dis·col·or (dǐs kǔl'ər), *v.t.* **1.** to change the color of; spoil the color of; stain. **—v.i. 2.** to change color; become faded or stained. Also, *Brit.,* **dis·col'our.** [ME *discolour(en),* t. OF: m. *descolorer,* der. L: *dis-* DIS-¹ + *color* color]

dis·col·or·a·tion (dǐs kǔl'ər ā'shən), *n.* **1.** act or fact of discoloring. **2.** state of being discolored. **3.** a discolored marking; a stain. Also, **dis·col'or·ment.**

dis·com·fit (dĭs·kŭm′fĭt), *v.t.* **1.** to defeat utterly; rout. **2.** to frustrate the plans of; thwart; foil. **3.** to throw into perplexity and dejection; disconcert. —*n.* **4.** *Obs.* rout; defeat. [ME, t. OF: m. *desconfit*, pp. of *desconfire*, f. *des-* DIS-¹ + *confire* make, accomplish (g. L *conficere*)]

dis·com·fi·ture (dĭs·kŭm′fĭ·chər), *n.* **1.** defeat in battle; rout. **2.** frustration of hopes or plans. **3.** disconcertion; confusion.

dis·com·fort (dĭs·kŭm′fərt), *n.* **1.** absence of comfort or pleasure; uneasiness; disturbance of peace; pain. **2.** anything that disturbs the comfort. —*v.t.* **3.** to disturb the comfort or happiness of; make uncomfortable or uneasy. [ME *discomfort(en)*, t. OF: m. *desconforter*, f. *des-* DIS-¹ + *conforter* COMFORT]

dis·com·fort·a·ble (dĭs·kŭm′fərt·ə·bəl), *adj.* **1.** uncomfortable; uneasy. **2.** *Archaic.* discomforting.

dis·com·mend (dĭs′kə·mĕnd′), *v.t.* **1.** to express disapproval of. **2.** to bring into disfavor. —**dis′com·mend′a·ble,** *adj.* —**dis·com·men·da·tion** (dĭs·kŏm·ən·dā′shən), *n.* —**dis′com·mend′er,** *n.*

dis·com·mode (dĭs′kə·mōd′), *v.t.,* -moded, -moding. to put to inconvenience; trouble; incommode. [f. DIS-¹ + m. s. L *commodāre* make fit]

dis·com·mod·i·ty (dĭs′kə·mŏd′ə·tĭ), *n.,* *pl.* -ties. **1.** inconvenience; disadvantageousness. **2.** a source of inconvenience or trouble; disadvantage.

dis·com·mon (dĭs·kŏm′ən), *v.t.* **1.** (at Oxford and Cambridge) to prohibit (a tradesman or townsman who has violated the regulations of the university) from dealing with the undergraduates. **2.** *Law.* to deprive of the character of a common, as by enclosing a piece of land. [f. DIS-¹ + obs. *common*, v, participate, associate]

dis·com·pose (dĭs′kəm·pōz′), *v.t.,* -posed, -posing. **1.** to bring into disorder; disarrange; unsettle. **2.** to disturb the composure of; agitate; perturb. —**dis′com·pos′ed·ly,** *adv.* —**dis′com·pos′ing·ly,** *adv.*

dis·com·po·sure (dĭs′kəm·pō′zhər), *n.* state of being discomposed; disorder; agitation; perturbation.

dis·con·cert (dĭs′kən·sûrt′), *v.t.* **1.** to disturb the self-possession of; confuse; perturb; ruffle. **2.** to throw into disorder or confusion; disarrange. —**dis′con·cert′ing·ly,** *adv.* —**dis′con·cert′ment,** *n.*

dis·con·cert·ed (dĭs′kən·sûr′tĭd), *adj.* confused; abashed. —**dis′con·cert′ed·ly,** *adv.* —**dis′con·cert′ed·ness,** *n.*

dis·con·form·i·ty (dĭs′kən·fôr′mə·tĭ), *n.,* *pl.* -ties. **1.** the lack of conformity; refusal or failure to conform. **2.** *Geol.* the surface of a division between parallel rock strata, indicating interruption of sedimentation.

dis·con·nect (dĭs′kə·nĕkt′), *v.t.* to sever or interrupt the connection of or between; detach.

dis·con·nect·ed (dĭs′kə·nĕk′tĭd), *adj.* **1.** disjointed; broken. **2.** incoherent. —**dis′con·nect′ed·ly,** *adv.* —**dis′con·nect′ed·ness,** *n.*

dis·con·nec·tion (dĭs′kə·nĕk′shən), *n.* **1.** act of disconnecting. **2.** state of being disconnected; lack of union. Also, *Brit.,* **dis′con·nex′ion.**

dis·con·sid·er (dĭs′kən·sĭd′ər), *v.t.* to discredit.

dis·con·so·late (dĭs·kŏn′sə·lĭt), *adj.* **1.** without consolation or solace; unhappy; inconsolable. **2.** characterized by or causing discomfort; cheerless; gloomy. [t. ML: m.s. *disconsōlātus*, f. *dis-* DIS-¹ + L *consōlātus*, pp., having consoled] —**dis·con′so·late·ly,** *adv.* —**dis·con·so·la·tion** (dĭs·kŏn′sə·lā′shən), **dis·con′so·late·ness,** *n.* —**Syn. 1.** See desolate.

dis·con·tent (dĭs′kən·tĕnt′), *adj.* **1.** not content; dissatisfied; discontented. —*n.* **2.** Also, **dis′con·tent′ment.** the lack of content; dissatisfaction. **3.** a malcontent. —*v.t.* **4.** to deprive of content; dissatisfy; displease. —**Syn. 2.** uneasiness, inquietude, restlessness, displeasure. See **dissatisfaction.**

dis·con·tent·ed (dĭs′kən·tĕn′tĭd), *adj.* uneasy in mind; dissatisfied; restlessly unhappy. —**dis′con·tent′ed·ly,** *adv.* —**dis′con·tent′ed·ness,** *n.*

dis·con·tin·u·ance (dĭs′kən·tĭn′yŏŏ·əns), *n.* **1.** lack of continued connection or cohesion of parts; lack of union; disruption. **2.** *Law.* the termination of a suit by the act of the plaintiff, as by notice in writing, or by neglect to take the proper adjournments to keep it pending.

dis·con·tin·u·a·tion (dĭs′kən·tĭn′yŏŏ·ā′shən), *n.* breach or interruption of continuity or unity.

dis·con·tin·ue (dĭs′kən·tĭn′yŏŏ), *v.,* -tinued, -tinuing. —*v.t.* **1.** to cause to cease; put an end to. **2.** to cease to take, use, etc.: *to discontinue a newspaper.* **3.** *Law.* to terminate or abandon (a suit, etc.). —*v.i.* **4.** to come to an end or stop; cease; desist. —**dis′con·tin′u·er,** *n.* —**Syn. 1.** See **interrupt.** —**Ant. 1.** resume.

dis·con·ti·nu·i·ty (dĭs′kŏn·tə·nū′ə·tĭ, -nŏŏ′-), *n.* lack of continuity, uninterrupted connection, or cohesion.

dis·con·tin·u·ous (dĭs′kən·tĭn′yŏŏ·əs), *adj.* not continuous; broken; interrupted; intermittent. —**dis′con·tin′u·ous·ly,** *adv.* —**dis′con·tin′u·ous·ness,** *n.*

dis·cord (*n.* dĭs′kôrd; *v.* dĭs·kôrd′), *n.* **1.** lack of concord or harmony between persons or things; disagreement of relations. **2.** difference of opinions. **3.** strife; dispute; war. **4.** *Music.* an inharmonious combination of musical tones sounded together. **5.** any confused or harsh noise; dissonance. —*v.i.* **6.** to disagree; be at variance. [ME *discord(en),* t. OF: m. *discorder,* t. L: m. *discordāre* be at variance]

dis·cord·ance (dĭs·kôr′dəns), *n.* discordant character; disagreement; discord. Also, **dis·cord′an·cy.**

dis·cord·ant (dĭs·kôr′dənt), *adj.* **1.** being at variance; disagreeing; incongruous: *discordant opinions.* **2.** disagreeable to the ear; dissonant; harsh. —**dis·cord′ant·ly,** *adv.*

dis·co·theque (dĭs′kō·tĕk′), *n.* a cabaret in which the patrons dance to recorded music played on high-fidelity equipment. Also, **dis′co·thèque′.**

dis·count (*v.* dĭs′kount, dĭs·kount′; *n.* dĭs′kount), *v.t.* **1.** to reckon off or deduct, as a certain amount in settling a bill; make a reduction of. **2.** to advance money with deduction of interest on (commercial paper not immediately payable). **3.** to purchase or sell (a bill or note) before maturity at a reduction based on the interest for the time it still has to run. **4.** to leave out of account; disregard. **5.** to make a deduction from; allow for exaggeration in (a statement, etc.). **6.** to take (an event, etc.) into account in advance, esp. with loss of value, effectiveness, etc. —*v.i.* **7.** to advance money after deduction of interest. —*n.* **8.** act of discounting. **9.** amount deducted for prompt payment or other special reason. **10.** any deduction from the nominal value. **11.** a payment of interest in advance upon a loan of money. **12.** the amount of interest obtained by one who discounts. **13.** at a discount, **a.** *Com.* below par. **b.** in low esteem or regard. **c.** not in demand. [t. OF: m. *desconter,* f. *des-* DIS-¹ + *conter* COUNT¹] —**dis′count·a·ble,** *adj.* —**dis′count·er,** *n.*

dis·coun·te·nance (dĭs·koun′tə·nəns), *v.,* -nanced, -nancing, *n.* —*v.t.* **1.** to put out of countenance; disconcert; abash. **2.** to show disapproval of; treat with disfavor. —*n.* **3.** disapproval. [t. F (obs.): m. *descontenancer,* f. *des-* DIS-¹ + *contenancer* COUNTENANCE, v.]

discount house, a store selling practically all of its merchandise at a price often considerably below the usual or advertised retail price.

discount rate, *Finance.* **1.** rate of interest charged in discounting commercial paper. **2.** rediscount rate.

dis·cour·age (dĭs·kûr′ĭj), *v.t.,* -aged, -aging. **1.** to deprive of courage; dishearten; dispirit. **2.** to dissuade (fol. by *from*). **3.** to obstruct by opposition or difficulty; hinder: *low prices discourage industry.* **4.** to express disapproval of: *to discourage the expression of enthusiasm.* [t. OF: m. *descoragier,* der. *des-* DIS-¹ + *corage* COURAGE] —**dis·cour′ag·er,** *n.* —**dis·cour′ag·ing·ly,** *adv.* —**Syn. 1.** daunt, depress, deject, overawe, cow, abash. DISCOURAGE, DISMAY, INTIMIDATE may imply the attempt to dishearten or frighten one so as to prevent some action, or any further action. To DISCOURAGE is to dishearten by expressing disapproval or by suggesting that a contemplated action or course will probably fail: *he was discouraged from giving up his job.* To DISMAY is to dishearten completely, by the disclosure of unsuspected facts, so that the action contemplated seems useless or dangerous: *to dismay a prosecutor by revealing his brother's connection with a crime.* To INTIMIDATE is to frighten, as by threats of force, violence, or dire consequences: *to intimidate a witness.* —**Ant. 1.** encourage.

dis·cour·age·ment (dĭs·kûr′ĭj·mənt), *n.* **1.** act of discouraging. **2.** state of being discouraged. **3.** something that discourages. —**Syn. 2.** depression, dejection, hopelessness. See **despair.** **3.** deterrent, damper.

dis·course (*n.* dĭs′kōrs, dĭs·kōrs′; *v.* dĭs·kōrs′), *n.,* *v.,* -coursed, -coursing. —*n.* **1.** communication of thought by words; talk; conversation. **2.** a formal discussion of a subject in speech or writing, as a dissertation, treatise, sermon, etc. —*v.i.* **3.** to communicate thoughts orally; talk; converse. **4.** to treat of a subject formally in speech or writing. —*v.t.* **5.** to utter or give forth (musical sounds). [ME *discours,* t. F, t. L: m.s. *discursus*]

dis·cour·te·ous (dĭs·kûr′tĭ·əs), *adj.* lacking courtesy; impolite; uncivil; rude. —**dis·cour′te·ous·ly,** *adv.* —**dis·cour′te·ous·ness,** *n.*

dis·cour·te·sy (dĭs·kûr′tə·sĭ), *n.,* *pl.* -sies. **1.** lack or breach of courtesy; incivility; rudeness. **2.** a discourteous or impolite act.

dis·cov·er (dĭs·kŭv′ər), *v.t.* **1.** to get knowledge of, learn of, or find out; gain sight or knowledge of (something previously unseen or unknown). **2.** *Archaic.* to act so as to manifest unconsciously or unintentionally; betray. **3.** *Archaic.* to make known; reveal. [ME *discover(en),* t. OF: m. *descovrir,* f. *des-* DIS-¹ + *covrir* COVER] —**dis·cov′er·a·ble,** *adj.* —**dis·cov′er·er,** *n.* —**Syn. 1.** detect, espy, descry, discern, ascertain, unearth, ferret out, notice. DISCOVER, INVENT, ORIGINATE suggest bringing to light something previously unknown. To DISCOVER may be to find something which had previously been in existence but had hitherto been unknown: *to discover a new continent, a planet, electricity;* it may also refer to devising a new use for something already known: *to discover how to make synthetic rubber.* To INVENT is to make or create something new, esp. something ingeniously devised to perform mechanical operations: *to invent a device for detecting radioactivity.* To ORIGINATE is to begin something new, esp. new ideas, methods, etc.: *to originate a religious or political movement, the use of deep-freezing units.* See **learn.**

dis·cov·ert (dĭs·kŭv′ərt), *adj.* *Law.* (of a woman) not covert; not under the protection of a husband. [t. OF: m. *descovert,* pp. of *descouvrir* DISCOVER]

dis·cov·er·y (dĭs·kŭv′ə·rĭ), *n.,* *pl.* -eries. **1.** act of discovering. **2.** something discovered. **3.** *Law.* compulsory disclosure, as of facts or documents.

Discovery Day, Columbus Day.

Discovery Inlet, inlet of the Ross Sea, Antarctica.

dis·cred·it (dĭs·krĕd′ĭt), *v.t.* **1.** to injure the credit or reputation of. **2.** to show to be undeserving of credit or belief; destroy confidence in. **3.** to give no credit to;

disbelieve: *the report is discredited.* —*n.* 4. loss or lack of belief, or confidence; disbelief; distrust. 5. loss or lack of repute or esteem; disrepute. 6. something that damages a good reputation. [f. DIS-¹ + CREDIT, v.]

dis·cred·it·a·ble (dĭs krĕd/ĭt ə bəl), *adj.* such as to bring discredit; disgraceful. —**dis·cred/it·a·bly,** *adv.*

dis·creet (dĭs krēt/), *adj.* wise or judicious in avoiding mistakes or faults; prudent; circumspect; cautious; not rash. [ME *discret,* t. OF, t. L: s. *discrētus,* pp., separated] —**dis·creet/ly,** *adv.* —**dis·creet/ness,** *n.* —**Syn.** See careful.

dis·crep·an·cy (dĭs krĕp/ən sĭ), *n., pl.* **-cies.** 1. state or quality of being discrepant; difference; inconsistency. 2. an instance of difference or inconsistency. Also, **dis·crep/ance.** —**Syn.** 1. See **difference.**

dis·crep·ant (dĭs krĕp/ənt), *adj.* differing; disagreeing; discordant; inconsistent. [t. L: s. *discrepans,* ppr., being discordant] —**dis·crep/ant·ly,** *adv.*

dis·crete (dĭs krēt/), *adj.* 1. detached from others; separate; distinct. 2. consisting of or characterized by distinct or individual parts; discontinuous. [t. L: m. s. *discrētus* separated] —**dis·crete/ly,** *adv.* —**dis·crete/ness,** *n.*

dis·cre·tion (dĭs krĕsh/ən), *n.* 1. power or right of deciding, or of acting according to one's own judgment; freedom of judgment or choice. 2. the quality of being discreet; discernment of what is judicious or expedient, esp. with reference to one's own actions or speech; prudence. 3. **at discretion,** as one wishes or decides.

dis·cre·tion·al (dĭs krĕsh/ən əl), *adj.* discretionary. —**dis·cre/tion·al·ly,** *adv.*

dis·cre·tion·ar·y (dĭs krĕsh/ə nĕr/ĭ), *adj.* 1. subject or left to one's discretion. 2. of or pertaining to discretion.

dis·crim·i·nate (*v.*dĭs krĭm/ə nāt/; *adj.* dĭs krĭm/ə nĭt), *v.,* **-nated, -nating,** *adj.* —*v.i.* 1. to make a distinction, as in favor of or against a person or thing: *discriminate against a minority.* 2. to note or observe a difference; distinguish accurately: *to discriminate between things.* —*v.t.* 3. to make or constitute a distinction in or between; differentiate: *to discriminate one thing from another.* 4. to note or distinguish as different. —*adj.* 5. marked by discrimination; making nice distinctions. [t. L: m. s. *discrīminātus,* pp., divided, distinguished] —**dis·crim/i·nate·ly,** *adv.* —**dis·crim/i·na/tor,** *n.* —**Syn.** 3. See **distinguish.**

dis·crim·i·nat·ing (dĭs krĭm/ə nā/tĭng), *adj.* 1. differentiating; distinctive. 2. noting differences or distinctions with nicety; possessing discrimination. 3. differential, as a tariff. —**dis·crim/i·nat/ing·ly,** *adv.*

dis·crim·i·na·tion (dĭs krĭm/ə nā/shən), *n.* 1. act of discriminating. 2. the resulting state. 3. the making of a difference in particular cases, as in favor of or against a person or thing. 4. the power of making nice distinctions; discriminating judgment. 5. *Rare.* something that serves to differentiate. 6. *Lexicog.* the attempt to distinguish between synonyms.

dis·crim·i·na·tive (dĭs krĭm/ə nā/tĭv), *adj.* 1. that marks distinction; constituting a difference; characteristic: *the discriminative features of men.* 2. making distinctions; discriminating. 3. (of a tariff, etc.) differential. Also, **dis·crim·i·na·to·ry** (dĭs krĭm/ə nə tōr/ĭ). —**dis·crim/i·na/tive·ly,** *adv.*

dis·crown (dĭs kroun/), *v.t.* to deprive of a crown.

dis·cur·sive (dĭs kûr/sĭv), *adj.* 1. passing rapidly or irregularly from one subject to another; rambling; digressive. 2. proceeding by reasoning or argument; not intuitive. —**dis·cur/sive·ly,** *adv.* —**dis·cur/sive·ness,** *n.*

dis·cus (dĭs/kəs), *n., pl.* **discuses, disci** (dĭs/ī). *Gymnastics.* 1. a circular stone or metal plate for throwing to a distance, as among the ancient Greeks and Romans. 2. the exercise or game of throwing it. [t. L, t. Gk.: m. *dískos* discus, disk, dish]

dis·cuss (dĭs kŭs/), *v.t.* 1. to examine by argument; sift the considerations for and against; debate; talk over. 2. (in humorous use) to try the quality of (food or drink) by consuming. 3. *Civil Law.* **a.** to collect a debt from (the person primarily liable) before proceeding against the person secondarily liable. **b.** to execute against the movable property of (a debtor) before proceeding against his immovable property, as land. 4. *Obs.* to make known; reveal. [ME *discusse(n),* t. L: m. s. *discussus,* pp., struck asunder] —**dis·cuss/er,** *n.* —**Syn.** 1. reason, deliberate. See **argue.**

dis·cus·sion (dĭs kŭsh/ən), *n.* act of discussing; critical examination by argument; debate.

dis·dain (dĭs dān/), *v.t.* 1. to look upon or treat with contempt; despise; scorn. 2. to think unworthy of notice, performance, etc.; consider beneath oneself. —*n.* 3. a feeling of contempt for anything regarded as unworthy; haughty contempt; scorn. [ME *desdaine(n),* t. OF: m. *desdeignier,* f. *des-* DIS-¹ + *deignier* DEIGN] —**Syn.** 3. contemptuousness, haughtiness, arrogance, superciliousness, contumely. See **contempt.**

dis·dain·ful (dĭs dān/fəl), *adj.* full of or showing disdain; scornful. —**dis·dain/ful·ly,** *adv.* —**dis·dain/ful·ness,** *n.* —**Syn.** contemptuous, haughty, supercilious, contumelious.

dis·ease (dĭ zēz/), *n., v.,* **-eased, -easing.** —*n.* 1. a morbid condition of the body, or of some organ or part; illness; sickness; ailment. 2. a similar disorder in plants. 3. any deranged or depraved condition, as of the mind,

affairs, etc. —*v.t.* 4. to affect with disease; make ill. [ME *disese,* t. OF: m. *desaise,* f. *des-* DIS-¹ + *aise* EASE] —**Syn.** 1. DISEASE, AFFECTION, DISORDER, MALADY imply a deviation of the body, or an organ of it, from health or normality. DISEASE and MALADY apply to organic deviations involving structural change. A DISEASE is a serious, active, prolonged, and deep-rooted condition. A MALADY is a lingering, chronic disease, usually painful and often fatal. An AFFECTION is a seriously abnormal state of body or mind, esp. one that interferes with their functions. A DISORDER is usually a physical or mental derangement, frequently a slight or transitory one. —**Ant.** 1. health. 4. cure.

dis·em·bark (dĭs/ĕm bärk/), *v.t., v.i.* to put or go on shore from a ship; land. —**dis·em·bar·ka·tion** (dĭs/ĕm/bär kā/shən), *n.*

dis·em·bar·rass (dĭs/ĕm băr/əs), *v.t.* 1. to free from embarrassment. 2. to relieve; rid. 3. to disentangle; extricate. —**dis/em·bar/rass·ment,** *n.*

dis·em·bod·y (dĭs/ĕm bŏd/ĭ), *v.t.,* **-bodied, -bodying.** to divest (a soul, etc.) of the body. —**dis/em·bod/i·ment,** *n.*

dis·em·bogue (dĭs/ĕm bōg/), *v.,* **-bogued, -boguing.** —*v.i.* 1. to empty or discharge by pouring forth the contents. 2. *Geol.* to debouch. —*v.t.* 3. to discharge; cast forth. [t. Sp.: m. *desembocar,* f. *des-* DIS-¹ + *embocar* enter by the mouth, f. *en-* in- + *boca* mouth (g. L *bucca*)] —**dis/em·bogue/ment,** *n.*

dis·em·bos·om (dĭs/ĕm bŏŏz/əm), *v.t.* 1. to reveal; divulge. 2. to relieve (oneself) of a secret.

dis·em·bow·el (dĭs/ĕm bou/əl), *v.t.,* **-eled, -eling** or (*esp. Brit.*) **-elled, -elling.** to remove the bowels or entrails from; eviscerate. —**dis/em·bow/el·ment,** *n.*

dis·em·broil (dĭs/ĕm broil/), *v.t.* to free from embroilment, entanglement, or confusion.

dis·en·a·ble (dĭs/ĕn ā/bəl), *v.t.,* **-bled, -bling.** to deprive of ability; make unable; prevent.

dis·en·chant (dĭs/ĕn chănt/, -chänt/), *v.t.* to free from enchantment; disillusion. —**dis/en·chant/er,** *n.* —**dis/en·chant/ment,** *n.*

dis·en·cum·ber (dĭs/ĕn kŭm/bər), *v.t.* to free from encumbrance; disburden.

dis·en·dow (dĭs/ĕn dou/), *v.t.* to deprive of endowment, esp. a church. —**dis/en·dow/er,** *n.* —**dis/en·dow/ment,** *n.*

dis·en·fran·chise (dĭs/ĕn frăn/chīz), *v.t.,* **-chised, -chising.** to disfranchise. —**dis/en·fran·chise·ment** (dĭs/ĕn frăn/chĭz mənt), *n.*

dis·en·gage (dĭs/ĕn gāj/), *v.,* **-gaged, -gaging.** —*v.t.* 1. to release from attachment or connection; loosen; unfasten. 2 to free from engagement, pledge, obligation, etc. 3. *Mil.* to break off action with (an enemy). —*v.i.* 4. to become disengaged; free oneself.

dis·en·gage·ment (dĭs/ĕn gāj/mənt), *n.* 1. act or process of disengaging, or state of being disengaged. 2. freedom from obligation or occupation; leisure.

dis·en·tail (dĭs/ĕn tāl/), *v.t. Law.* to free (an estate) from entail. —**dis/en·tail/ment,** *n.*

dis·en·tan·gle (dĭs/ĕn tăng/gəl), *v.t., v.i.,* **-gled, -gling.** to free or become free from entanglement; untangle; extricate (fol. by *from*). —**dis/en·tan/gle·ment,** *n.*

dis·en·thral (dĭs/ĕn thrôl/), *v.t.,* **-thralled, -thralling.** disenthrall. —**dis/en·thral/ment,** *n.*

dis·en·thrall (dĭs/ĕn thrôl/), *v.t.* to free from thralldom. —**dis/en·thrall/ment,** *n.*

dis·en·throne (dĭs/ĕn thrōn/), *v.t.,* **-throned, -throning.** to dethrone. —**dis/en·throne/ment,** *n.*

dis·en·ti·tle (dĭs/ĕn tī/təl), *v.t.,* **-tled, -tling.** to deprive of title or right.

dis·en·tomb (dĭs/ĕn tōōm/), *v.t.* to take from the tomb; disinter. —**dis/en·tomb/ment,** *n.*

dis·en·trance (dĭs/ĕn trăns/, -träns/), *v.t.,* **-tranced, -trancing.** to bring out of an entranced condition. —**dis/en·trance/ment,** *n.*

dis·en·twine (dĭs/ĕn twīn/), *v.t., v.i.,* **-twined, -twining.** to bring or come out of an entwined or intertwined state; untwine.

di·sep·a·lous (dī sĕp/ə ləs), *adj. Bot.* having two sepals.

dis·es·tab·lish (dĭs/ĕs tăb/lĭsh), *v.t.* 1. to deprive of the character of being established. 2. to withdraw exclusive state recognition or support from (a church). —**dis/es·tab/lish·ment,** *n.*

dis·es·teem (dĭs/ĕs tēm/), *v.t.* 1. to hold in low esteem; think slightingly of. —*n.* 2. lack of esteem; disregard.

di·seur (dē zœr/), *n.* a professional public entertainer who talks, recites, etc. [t. F: one who tells, says] —**di·seuse** (dē zœz/), *n. fem.*

dis·fa·vor (dĭs fā/vər), *n.* 1. unfavorable regard; displeasure; disesteem: *the minister incurred the king's disfavor.* 2. lack of favor; state of being regarded unfavorably: *in disfavor at court.* 3. an act of disregard, dislike, or unkindness: *to dispense disfavors.* —*v.t.* 4. to regard or treat with disfavor. Also, *Brit.,* **dis·fa/vour.**

dis·fea·ture (dĭs fē/chər), *v.t.,* **-tured, -turing.** to mar the features of; disfigure. —**dis·fea/ture·ment,** *n.*

dis·fig·ure (dĭs fĭg/yər), *v.t.,* **-ured, -uring.** 1. to mar the figure, appearance, or beauty of; deform; deface. 2. to mar the effect or excellence of. [ME *disfigure(n),* t. OF: m. *desfigurer,* f. *des-* DIS-¹ + *figurer,* der. *figure* FIGURE, n.] —**dis·fig/ur·er,** *n.* —**Syn.** 1. See **mar.**

dis·fig·ure·ment (dĭs fĭg/yər mənt), *n.* 1. act of disfiguring. 2. disfigured condition. 3. something that disfigures. Also, **dis·fig/ur·a/tion.**

---

b., blend of, blended; c., cognate with; d., dialect, dialectal; der., derived from; f., formed from; g., going back to; m., modification of; r., replacing; s., stem of; t., taken from; ?, perhaps. See the full key on inside cover.

dis·for·est (dĭs·fôr′ĭst, -fŏr′-), *v.t.* *Law.* to disafforest. —dis·for·es·ta′tion, *n.*

dis·fran·chise (dĭs·frăn′chīz), *v.t.*, -chised, -chising. 1. to deprive (persons) of rights of citizenship, as of the right to vote. 2. to deprive of a franchise, privilege, or right. —dis·fran·chise·ment (dĭs frăn′chĭz mənt), *n.*

dis·frock (dĭs·frŏk′), *v.t.* *Eccles.* to unfrock.

dis·fur·nish (dĭs·fûr′nĭsh), *v.t.* to deprive of something with which a person or thing is furnished; strip. —dis·fur′nish·ment, *n.*

dis·gorge (dĭs·gôrj′), *v.*, -gorged, -gorging. —*v.t.* 1. to eject or throw out from or as from the gorge or throat; vomit forth; discharge. 2. to give up unwillingly. —*v.i.* 3. to disgorge something. [late ME, t. OF: m. *desgorger*, f. *des-* DIS-¹ + *gorge* throat] —dis·gorge′ment, *n.* —dis·gorg′er, *n.*

dis·grace (dĭs·grās′), *n.*, *v.*, -graced, -gracing. —*n.* 1. state of being in dishonor; ignominy; shame. 2. a cause of shame or reproach; that which dishonors. 3. state of being out of favor; exclusion from favor, confidence, or trust. —*v.t.* 4. to bring or reflect shame or reproach upon. 5. to dismiss with discredit; put out of grace or favor; treat with disfavor. [t. F, t. It.: m. *disgrazia*. See DIS-¹, GRACE] —dis·grac′er, *n.* —**Syn.** 1. DISGRACE, DISHONOR, IGNOMINY, INFAMY imply a very low position in the opinion of others. DISGRACE implies the disfavor, with a greater or less degree of reproachful disapprobation, of others: *he brought disgrace on his family, to be in disgrace.* DISHONOR implies a stain on honor or honorable reputation; it relates esp. to the conduct of the person himself: *he preferred death to dishonor.* IGNOMINY is disgrace in which one's situation invites contempt: *the ignominy of being discovered cheating.* INFAMY is shameful notoriety, or baseness of action or character which is widely known and recognized: *the children never outlived the father's infamy.* —**Ant.** 1. honor.

dis·grace·ful (dĭs·grās′fəl), *adj.* bringing or deserving disgrace; shameful; dishonorable; disreputable. —dis·grace′ful·ly, *adv.* —dis·grace′ful·ness, *n.*

dis·grun·tle (dĭs·grŭn′təl), *v.t.*, -tled, -tling. to put into a state of sulky dissatisfaction; make discontent. [f. DIS-¹ + *gruntle*, freq. of GRUNT] —dis·grun′tle·ment, *n.*

dis·guise (dĭs·gīz′), *v.*, -guised, -guising, *n.* —*v.t.* 1. to change the guise or appearance of so as to conceal identity or to mislead; conceal the identity of by means of a misleading garb, etc. 2. to conceal or cover up the real state or character of by a counterfeit form or appearance; misrepresent: *to disguise one's intentions.* —*n.* 3. that which disguises; something that serves or is intended for concealment of identity, character, or quality; a deceptive covering, condition, manner, etc. 4. the make-up, mask, or costume of an entertainer. 5. act of disguising. 6. state of being disguised. [ME *desgise*(n), t. OF: m. *desguiser*, f. *des-* DIS-¹ + *guise* GUISE] —dis·guis′er, *n.*

dis·gust (dĭs·gŭst′), *v.t.* 1. to cause nausea or loathing in. 2. to offend the good taste, moral sense, etc. of; cause aversion or impatient dissatisfaction in. —*n.* 3. strong distaste; nausea; loathing. 4. repugnance caused by something offensive; strong aversion; impatient dissatisfaction. [t. MF: m. *desgouster*, f. *des-* DIS-¹ + *gouster* taste, relish] —dis·gust′ed·ly, *adv.* —**Syn.** 4. See dislike.

dis·gust·ful (dĭs·gŭst′fəl), *adj.* causing disgust; nauseous; offensive.

dis·gust·ing (dĭs·gŭs′tĭng), *adj.* causing disgust; offensive to the physical, moral, or aesthetic taste. —dis·gust′ing·ly, *adv.* —**Syn.** loathsome, sickening, nauseous, repulsive, revolting.

dish (dĭsh), *n.* 1. an open, more or less shallow container of pottery, glass, metal, wood, etc., used for various purposes, esp. for holding or serving food. 2. any container used at table. 3. that which is served or contained in a dish. 4. a particular article or preparation of food. 5. as much as a dish will hold; a dishful. 6. anything like a dish in form or use. 7. concave state, or the degree of concavity, as of a wheel. —*v.t.* 8. to put into or serve in a dish, as food: *to dish up food.* 9. to fashion like a dish; make concave. 10. *Slang.* to feat; frustrate; cheat. [ME; OE *disc* dish, plate, bowl (cf. G *tisch* table), t. L: *discus* dish, DISCUS]

dis·ha·bille (dĭs′ə bēl′), *n.* 1. undress or negligee. 2. a garment worn in undress. 3. a loose morning dress. Also, **deshabille.** [F: m. *déshabillé*, prop. pp. of *déshabiller* undress, f. *dés-* DIS-¹ + *habiller* dress]

dis·ha·bit·u·ate (dĭs′hə bĭch′ōō āt′), *v.t.*, -ated, -ating. to cause to be no longer habituated or accustomed.

dis·hal·low (dĭs·hăl′ō), *v.t.* to profane; desecrate.

dis·har·mo·ni·ous (dĭs′här mō′nĭ əs), *adj.* inharmonious; discordant.

dis·har·mo·nize (dĭs·här′mə nīz′), *v.t.*, *v.i.*, -nized, -nizing. to make or be inharmonious.

dis·har·mo·ny (dĭs·här′mə nĭ), *n.*, *pl.* -nies. 1. discord. 2. something discordant.

dish·cloth (dĭsh′klôth′, -klŏth′), *n.* a cloth for use in washing dishes. Also, **dish·clout** (dĭsh′klout′).

dis·heart·en (dĭs·här′tən), *v.t.* to depress the spirits of; discourage. —dis·heart′en·ing·ly, *adv.* —dis·heart′en·ment, *n.*

dished (dĭsht), *adj.* 1. concave: *a dished face.* 2. *Slang.* exhausted; worn out.

dis·helm (dĭs·hĕlm′), *v.t.*, *v.i.* *Archaic.* to divest of, or take off, the helmet.

dis·her·it (dĭs·hĕr′ĭt), *v.t.* *Obs.* or *Rare.* to disinherit.

di·shev·el (dĭ shĕv′əl), *v.t.*, -eled, -eling or (*esp. Brit.*) -elled, -elling. to let down (the hair); let hang in loose disorder. [ME *dischevelen*, t. OF: m. *descheveler*, der. *des-* DIS-¹ + *chevel* hair (g. L *capillus*)] —di·shev′el·ment, *n.*

di·shev·eled (dĭ shĕv′əld), *adj.* 1. hanging loosely or in disorder; unkempt: *disheveled hair.* 2. untidy; disarranged: *disheveled appearance.* Also, *esp. Brit.,* di·shev′elled.

dish gravy, juice from cooked meat.

dis·hon·est (dĭs·ŏn′ĭst), *adj.* 1. not honest; disposed to lie, cheat, or steal: *a dishonest person.* 2. proceeding from or exhibiting lack of honesty; fraudulent. —dis·hon′est·ly, *adv.* —**Syn.** 1. unscrupulous, knavish, thievish. See corrupt.

dis·hon·es·ty (dĭs·ŏn′ĭs tĭ), *n.*, *pl.* -ties. 1. lack of honesty; a disposition to lie, cheat, or steal. 2. a dishonest act; a fraud; theft.

dis·hon·or (dĭs·ŏn′ər), *n.* 1. lack of honor; dishonorable character or conduct. 2. disgrace; ignominy; shame. 3. an indignity; insult. 4. a cause of shame; a disgrace. 5. *Com.* failure or refusal of the drawee or acceptor of a bill of exchange or note to accept it, or, if it is accepted, to pay and retire it. —*v.t.* 6. to deprive of honor; disgrace; bring reproach or shame on. 7. *Com.* to fail or refuse to honor (a draft, etc.) by payment. Also, *Brit.,* dis·hon′our. [ME *dishonour*, t. OF: m. *deshonor*, f. *des-* DIS-¹ + *honor* honor (t. L)] —dis·hon′or·er, *n.* —**Syn.** 2. See disgrace.

dis·hon·or·a·ble (dĭs·ŏn′ər ə bəl), *adj.* 1. showing lack of honor; ignoble; base; disgraceful; shameful: *a dishonorable act.* 2. having no honor or good repute: *a dishonorable man.* Also, *Brit.,* dis·hon′our·a·ble. —dis·hon′or·a·ble·ness, *n.* —dis·hon′or·a·bly, *adv.* —**Syn.** 2. infamous, unscrupulous, unprincipled.

dish·pan (dĭsh′păn′), *n.* a pan in which dishes are washed.

dish·rag (dĭsh′răg′), *n.* dishcloth.

dish·tow·el (dĭsh′tou′əl), *n.* a towel for drying dishes.

dish·wa·ter (dĭsh′wô′tər, -wŏt′ər), *n.* water in which dishes are, or have been, washed.

dis·il·lu·sion (dĭs′ĭ lōō′zhən), *v.t.* 1. to free from illusion; disenchant. —*n.* 2. a freeing or a being freed from illusion; disenchantment. —dis′il·lu′sion·ment, *n.* —dis·il·lu·sive (dĭs′ĭ lōō′sĭv), *adj.*

dis·il·lu·sion·ize (dĭs′ĭ lōō′zhə nīz′), *v.t.*, -ized, -izing. to disillusion.

dis·im·pas·sioned (dĭs′ĭm păsh′ənd), *adj.* calm; dispassionate; passionless.

dis·im·pris·on (dĭs′ĭm prĭz′ən), *v.t.* to release from imprisonment. —dis′im·pris′on·ment, *n.*

dis·in·cli·na·tion (dĭs ĭn′klə nā′shən), *n.* the absence of inclination; averseness; distaste; unwillingness.

dis·in·cline (dĭs′ĭn klīn′), *v.t.*, *v.i.*, -clined, -clining. to make or be averse or indisposed.

dis·in·fect (dĭs′ĭn fĕkt′), *v.t.* to cleanse (rooms, clothing, etc.) from infection; destroy disease germs in. —dis′in·fec′tor, *n.*

dis·in·fect·ant (dĭs′ĭn fĕk′tənt), *n.* 1. any chemical agent that destroys bacteria. —*adj.* 2. disinfecting.

dis·in·fec·tion (dĭs′ĭn fĕk′shən), *n.* the process of disinfecting.

dis·in·gen·u·ous (dĭs′ĭn jĕn′ū əs), *adj.* not ingenuous; lacking in frankness, candor, or sincerity; insincere: *disingenuous persons.* —dis′in·gen′u·ous·ly, *adv.* —dis′in·gen′u·ous·ness, *n.*

dis·in·her·it (dĭs′ĭn hĕr′ĭt), *v.t.* 1. *Law.* to exclude from inheritance (an heir or a next of kin). 2. to deprive of the right to inherit. —dis′in·her′it·ance, *n.*

dis·in·te·grate (dĭs ĭn′tə grāt′), *v.*, -grated, -grating. —*v.t.* 1. to reduce to particles, fragments, or parts; break up or destroy the cohesion of: *rocks are disintegrated by frost and rain.* —*v.i.* 2. to separate into its component parts; break up. —dis·in·te·gra·ble (dĭs ĭn′tə grə bəl), *adj.* —dis·in′te·gra′tion, *n.* —dis·in′te·gra′tor, *n.* —**Syn.** 2. See decay.

dis·in·ter (dĭs′ĭn tûr′), *v.t.*, -terred, -terring. 1. to take out of the place of interment; exhume; unearth. 2. to bring from obscurity into view. —dis′in·ter′ment, *n.*

dis·in·ter·est (dĭs ĭn′tər ĭst, -trĭst), *n.* 1. absence of interest; indifference. —*v.t.* 2. to divest of interest or concern.

dis·in·ter·est·ed (dĭs ĭn′tər ĕs′tĭd, -trĭs tĭd), *adj.* 1. unbiased by personal interest or advantage; not influenced by selfish motives. 2. *U.S. Colloq.* not interested; indifferent. —dis·in′ter·est·ed·ly, *adv.* —dis·in′ter·est·ed·ness, *n.* —**Syn.** 1. DISINTERESTED, UNINTERESTED are not properly synonyms. DISINTERESTED today stresses lack of prejudice or of selfish interests: *a disinterested report.* UNINTERESTED suggests aloofness and indifference: *completely uninterested and taking no part in proceedings.* See fair¹.

dis·ject (dĭs jĕkt′), *v.t.* to cast asunder; scatter; disperse. [t. L: s. *disjectus*, pp., thrown asunder]

dis·jec·ta mem·bra (dĭs jĕk′tə mĕm′brə), *Latin.* scattered members; disjointed portions or parts.

dis·join (dĭs join′), *v.t.* 1. to undo or prevent the junction or union of; disunite; separate. —*v.i.* 2. to become disunited; separate. [ME *desjoyne*(n), t. OF: m. *desjoindre*, g. L *disjungere*]

dis·joint (dĭs joint′), *v.t.* **1.** to separate or disconnect the joints or joinings of. **2.** to put out of order; derange. —*v.i.* **3.** to come apart. **4.** to be dislocated; be put out of joint. —*adj.* **5.** *Obs.* disjointed; out of joint. [t. OF: m. *desjoint*, pp. of *desjoindre*, g. L *disjungere*]

dis·joint·ed (dĭs join′tĭd), *adj.* **1.** having the joints or connections separated: *a disjointed fowl.* **2.** disconnected; incoherent: *a disjointed discourse.* —**dis·joint′ed·ly,** *adv.* —**dis·joint′ed·ness,** *n.*

dis·junct (dĭs jŭngkt′), *adj.* **1.** disjoined; separated. **2.** *Music.* progressing melodically by intervals larger than a second. **3.** *Entomol.* having the head, thorax, and abdomen separated by deep constrictions. [t. L: s. *disjunctus*, pp., disjoined]

dis·junc·tion (dĭs jŭngk′shən), *n.* **1.** act of disjoining. **2.** state of being disjoined. **3.** *Logic.* **a.** a proposition in which two (or more) alternatives are asserted, only one of which can be true. **b.** the relation between the terms of such a proposition.

dis·junc·tive (dĭs jŭngk′tĭv), *adj.* **1.** serving or tending to disjoin; separating; dividing; distinguishing. **2.** *Gram.* **a.** syntactically setting two or more expressions in opposition to each other, as *but* in *poor but happy*, or expressing an alternative, as *or* in *this or that.* **b.** not syntactically dependent upon some particular expression. **3.** *Logic.* characterizing propositions which are disjunctions. —*n.* **4.** a statement, etc., involving alternatives. —**dis·junc′tive·ly,** *adv.*

dis·junc·ture (dĭs jŭngk′chər), *n.* **1.** act of disjoining. **2.** state of being disjoined.

dis·june (dĭs jo͞on′), *n.* *Scot. Obs.* breakfast.

disk (dĭsk), *n.* **1.** any thin, flat, circular plate or object. **2.** a round, flat area. **3.** the apparently flat surface of the sun, etc. **4.** a phonograph record. **5.** a discus. **6.** *Bot., Zool., etc.* any of various roundish, flat structures or parts. **7.** *Bot.* (in the daisy and other composite plants) the central portion of the flower head, composed of tubular florets. —*v.t.* **8.** to prepare (soil) with a disk harrow. Also, **disc.** [t. L: m. s. *discus* DISCUS]

disk harrow, a harrow having a number of sharp-edged concave disks set at such an angle that as the machine is drawn along they pulverize and turn the soil and destroy weeds.

disk jockey, a radio announcer on an all-record program.

disk wheel, a spokeless vehicular wheel, esp. on motor cars, having a heavy circular pressed-steel disk mounted on the wheel hub and supporting the tire rim on its outer edge.

dis·like (dĭs līk′), *v.*, **-liked, -liking,** *n.* —*v.t.* **1.** not to like; regard with displeasure or aversion: *I dislike him, I dislike his doing it, I dislike having to work.* —*n.* **2.** the feeling of disliking; distaste: *I have taken a strong dislike to him, of him, for him.* —**dis·lik′a·ble,** *adj.*
—**Syn. 2.** disrelish. DISLIKE, DISGUST, DISTASTE, REPUGNANCE imply antipathy toward something. DISLIKE is a general word, the strength of the feeling being indicated by the context. It expresses a positive (not necessarily strong), sometimes inherent or permanent feeling of antipathy for something: *to have a dislike for crowds, for someone, for noise.* DISGUST is a very strong word, expressing a feeling of loathing for what is offensive to the physical taste or to the feelings and sensibilities: *the taste of spoiled food fills one with disgust, to feel disgust at seeing snobbery and ostentation.* DISTASTE, though etymologically equal to DISGUST, is weaker; it implies a more or less settled dislike for what is naturally uncongenial or has been made so by association: *to have distaste for certain foods, for hard work, for unconventional art or music.* REPUGNANCE is a strong feeling of aversion for, and antagonism toward, something: *to feel repugnance for* (or *toward*) *low criminals, or a kind of conduct.*

dis·limn (dĭs lĭm′), *v.t.* *Archaic or Poetic.* to obliterate (a picture); efface.

dis·lo·cate (dĭs′lō kāt′), *v.t.*, **-cated, -cating. 1.** to put out of place; displace; put out of proper relative position. **2.** *Surg.* to put out of joint or out of position, as a limb or an organ. **3.** to throw out of order; derange; upset; disorder. [t. ML: m. s. *dislocātus*, pp. of *dislocāre*, f. L: *dis-* DIS-[1] + *locāre* place] —**dis′lo·ca′tion,** *n.*

dis·lodge (dĭs lŏj′), *v.*, **-lodged, -lodging.** —*v.t.* **1.** to remove or drive from a place of lodgment; drive from a position occupied. —*v.i.* **2.** to go from a place of lodgment. —**dis·lodg′ment;** *esp. Brit.*, **dis·lodge′ment,** *n.*

dis·loy·al (dĭs loi′əl), *adj.* not loyal; false to one's obligations or allegiance; faithless; treacherous. [t. OF: m. *desloial*, f. *des-* DIS-[1] + *loial* law-abiding (g. L *lēgālis*)] —**dis·loy′al·ly,** *adv.* —**Syn.** unfaithful, false, perfidious, traitorous, treasonable. —**Ant.** constant.

dis·loy·al·ty (dĭs loi′əl tĭ), *n.*, *pl.* **-ties. 1.** quality of being disloyal; unfaithfulness. **2.** violation of allegiance or duty, as to a government. **3.** a disloyal act.
—**Syn. 1.** DISLOYALTY, PERFIDY, TREACHERY, TREASON imply betrayal of trust, and esp. traitorous acts against one's country or its government. DISLOYALTY applies to any violation of loyalty, whether to a person, a cause, or one's country, and whether in thought or in deeds: *to suspect disloyalty in a friend.* PERFIDY implies deliberate breaking of faith or of one's pledges and promises, on which others are relying: *it is an act of perfidy to cheat innocent persons.* TREACHERY implies being secretly traitorous but seeming friendly and loyal: *in treachery deceit is added to disloyalty.* TREASON is definitely wishing harm to one's country or government, and performing overt acts to help its enemies: *acting to aid a hostile power is treason.*

dis·mal (dĭz′məl), *adj.* **1.** causing gloom or dejection; gloomy; dreary; cheerless; melancholy. **2.** terrible; dreadful. **3.** *Now Rare.* disastrous; calamitous. **4.** *Obs.* evil; unlucky. —*n.* **5.** (*usually pl.*) *Colloq.* gloom; melancholy; dumps: *in the dismals.* **6.** something dismal. **7.** any of certain tracts of swampy land along or near the southern Atlantic coast of the U.S. [ME *dismall;* orig. uncert.] —**dis′mal·ly,** *adv.* —**dis′mal·ness,** *n.* —**Ant. 1.** gay.

Dis·mal Swamp (dĭz′məl), an extensive swamp in SE Virginia and NE North Carolina. ab. 30 mi. long.

dis·man·tle (dĭs măn′təl), *v.t.*, **-tled, -tling. 1.** to deprive or strip of apparatus, furniture, equipments, defenses, etc.: *to dismantle a ship or a fortress.* **2.** to pull down; take apart; take to pieces. **3.** to divest of dress, covering, etc. [t. F (obs.): m. s. *desmanteler.* See DIS-[1], MANTLE] —**dis·man′tle·ment,** *n.*

dis·mast (dĭs măst′, -mäst′), *v.t.* to deprive of masts; break off the masts of. —**dis·mast′ment,** *n.*

dis·may (dĭs mā′), *v.t.* **1.** to break down the courage of utterly, as by sudden danger or trouble; dishearten utterly; daunt. —*n.* **2.** sudden or complete loss of courage; utter disheartenment. [ME *desmaien*, prob. t. OF; cf. OF *esmaier* dismay] —**Syn. 1.** appall, terrify, horrify, frighten, disconcert. See **discourage. 2.** consternation, terror, panic, horror, fear.

dis·mem·ber (dĭs mĕm′bər), *v.t.* **1.** to deprive of members or limbs; divide limb from limb. **2.** to separate into parts; divide and distribute the parts of (a kingdom, etc.). [ME *dismembre(n)*, t. OF: m. *desmembrer*, der. *des-* DIS-[1] + *membre* MEMBER] —**dis·mem′ber·er,** *n.* —**dis·mem′ber·ment,** *n.*

dis·miss (dĭs mĭs′), *v.t.* **1.** to direct or allow (an assembly of persons, etc.) to disperse. **2.** to bid or allow (a person) to go; give permission to depart. **3.** to send forth (a thing); let go. **4.** to discharge or remove, as from office or service. **5.** to discard or reject. **6.** to put off or away; lay aside; esp., to put aside from consideration. **7.** to have done with (a subject) after summary treatment. **8.** *Law.* to put out of court, as a complaint or appeal. [t. ML: m. s. *dismissus*, pp., sent away, for L *dīmissus*] —**dis·miss′i·ble,** *adj.* —**Syn. 2.** See **release.** —**Ant. 5.** accept.

dis·miss·al (dĭs mĭs′əl), *n.* **1.** act of dismissing. **2.** state of being dismissed. **3.** a spoken or written order of discharge. Also, **dis·mis·sion** (dĭs mĭsh′ən).

dis·mount (dĭs mount′), *v.i.* **1.** to get off or alight (from a horse, bicycle, truck, etc.). —*v.t.* **2.** to bring or throw down, as from a horse; unhorse. **3.** to remove (a thing) from its mounting, support, setting, etc. **4.** to take (a piece of mechanism) to pieces. —*n.* **5.** act or manner of dismounting. —**dis·mount′a·ble,** *adj.*

dis·na·ture (dĭs nā′chər), *v.t.*, **-tured, -turing.** to deprive of its proper nature; make unnatural.

Dis·ney (dĭz′nĭ), *n.* **Walt(er E.),** born 1901, U.S. motion-picture cartoon producer.

dis·o·be·di·ence (dĭs′ə bē′dĭ əns), *n.* lack of obedience; neglect or refusal to obey.

dis·o·be·di·ent (dĭs′ə bē′dĭ ənt), *adj.* neglecting or refusing to obey; refractory. —**dis′o·be′di·ent·ly,** *adv.* —**Syn.** insubordinate, contumacious, defiant.

dis·o·bey (dĭs′ə bā′), *v.t., v.i.* to neglect or refuse to obey. [ME *disobey(en)*, t. OF: m. *desobeir*, f. *des-* DIS-[1] + *obeir* OBEY] —**dis′o·bey′er,** *n.* —**Syn.** transgress, violate, disregard, defy.

dis·o·blige (dĭs′ə blīj′), *v.t.*, **-bliged, -bliging. 1.** to refuse or neglect to oblige; act contrary to the desire or convenience of; fail to accommodate. **2.** to give offense to; affront. **3.** *Obs. or Dial.* to incommode; put to inconvenience. —**dis′o·blig′ing,** *adj.* —**dis′o·blig′ing·ly,** *adv.* —**dis′o·blig′ing·ness,** *n.*

dis·op·er·a·tion (dĭs ŏp′ə rā′shən), *n.* *Ecol.* the conscious or unconscious behavior of organisms living together and producing a result which is disadvantageous or harmful to the organisms concerned.

dis·or·der (dĭs ôr′dər), *n.* **1.** lack of order or regular arrangement; disarrangement; confusion. **2.** an irregularity. **3.** breach of order; disorderly conduct; a public disturbance. **4.** a derangement of physical or mental health or functions. —*v.t.* **5.** to destroy the order or regular arrangement of; disarrange. **6.** to derange the physical or mental health or functions of.
—**Syn. 1.** disorderliness, disarray, jumble, litter, clutter. **3.** DISORDER, BRAWL, DISTURBANCE, UPROAR are disruptions or interruptions of a peaceful situation. DISORDER refers to unrest within a city or state, and to any scene in which there is confusion or fighting among individuals or groups: *the police went to a scene of disorder.* A BRAWL is a noisy, unseemly quarrel, usually in a public place: *a tavern brawl.* A DISTURBANCE is disorder of such size as to inconvenience many people: *to cause a disturbance.* An UPROAR is a tumult, a bustle and clamor of many voices, often because of a disturbance: *a mighty uproar.* **4.** ailment, malady. See **disease.**

dis·or·dered (dĭs ôr′dərd), *adj.* **1.** in confusion. **2.** mentally ill.

dis·or·der·ly (dĭs ôr′dər lĭ), *adj.* **1.** characterized by disorder; irregular; untidy; confused. **2.** unruly; turbulent; tumultuous. **3.** *Law.* violating, or opposed to, constituted order; contrary to public order or morality. —*adv.* **4.** without order, rule, or method; irregularly; confusedly. —**dis·or′der·li·ness,** *n.*

disorderly conduct, *Law.* any of various petty misdemeanors, generally including nuisances, breaches of the peace, offensive or immoral conduct in public, etc.

b., blend of, blended; c., cognate with; d., dialect, dialectal; der., derived from; f., formed from; g., going back to; m., modification of; r., replacing; s., stem of; t., taken from; ?, perhaps. See the full key on inside cover.

dis·or·der·ly house, 1. a house of prostitution; brothel. 2. a gambling place.

dis·or·der·ly per·son, *Law.* 1. a person guilty of disorderly conduct. 2. a person guilty of a separate offense including loitering in public, vagrancy, etc.

dis·or·gan·i·za·tion (dĭs ôr´gən ə zā´shən), *n.* 1. a breaking up of order or system; disunion or disruption of constituent parts. 2. the absence of organization or orderly arrangement; disarrangement; disorder. —**dis·or´gan·iz´er,** *n.*

dis·or·gan·ize (dĭs ôr´gə nīz´), *v.t.,* -ized, -izing. to destroy the organization, systematic arrangement, or orderly connection of; throw into confusion or disorder. —**dis·or´gan·iz´er,** *n.*

dis·own (dĭs ōn´), *v.t.* to refuse to acknowledge as belonging or pertaining to oneself; deny the ownership of or responsibility for; repudiate; renounce.

dis·par·age (dĭs păr´ĭj), *v.t.,* -aged, -aging. 1. to bring reproach or discredit upon; lower the estimation of. 2. to speak of or treat slightingly; depreciate; belittle. [ME *desparage(n),* t. OF: m. *desparagier* match equally, der. *des-* DIS-¹ + *parage* equality, der. *parer* equalize (g. L *pariāre*)] —**dis·par´ag·er,** *n.* —**dis·par´ag·ing·ly,** *adv.*

dis·par·age·ment (dĭs păr´ĭj mənt), *n.* 1. act of disparaging. 2. something that causes loss of dignity or reputation.

dis·pa·rate (dĭs´pə rĭt), *adj.* distinct in kind; essentially different; dissimilar; unlike; having no common genus. [t. L: m. s. *disparātus,* pp., separated] —**dis´pa·rate·ly,** *adv.* —**dis´pa·rate·ness,** *n.*

dis·par·i·ty (dĭs păr´ə tĭ), *n., pl.* -ties. lack of similarity or equality; inequality; difference: *a disparity in age, rank, condition, etc.* —**Syn.** See difference.

dis·part (dĭs pärt´), *v.t., v.i.* to part asunder; separate; divide into parts. [appar. t. It.: s. *dispartire* part, separate, divide, g. L] —**dis·part´ment,** *n.*

dis·pas·sion (dĭs păsh´ən), *n.* freedom from passion; unemotional state or quality.

dis·pas·sion·ate (dĭs păsh´ən ĭt), *adj.* free from or unaffected by passion; devoid of personal feeling or bias; impartial; calm: *a dispassionate critic.* —**dis·pas´sion·ate·ly,** *adv.* —**dis·pas´sion·ate·ness,** *n.*

dis·patch (dĭs păch´), *v.t.* 1. to send off; put under way: *to dispatch a messenger, telegram, etc.* 2. to dismiss (a person), as after an audience. 3. to put to death; kill. 4. to transact or dispose of (business, etc.) promptly or speedily; execute quickly; settle. —*v.i.* 5. *Archaic.* to hasten; be quick. 6. *Obs.* to settle a matter. —*n.* 7. the sending off of a messenger, letter, etc., to a destination. 8. dismissal of a person after the transaction of his business. 9. a putting to death; killing. 10. prompt or speedy transaction, as of business. 11. expeditious performance, promptitude, or speed: *proceed with all possible dispatch.* 12. *Com.* a. a method of effecting a speedy delivery of goods. b. a conveyance or organization for the expeditious transmission of merchandise, etc. 13. a written message sent in haste. 14. an official communication sent by special messenger. 15. **mentioned in dispatches,** *Brit.* named in military reports for special bravery or acts of service. 16. *Journalism.* a news account transmitted by a reporter to his newspaper or other agency. 17. a telegram. Also, **despatch.** [t. It.: m. *dispacciare* hasten, speed, or t. Sp.: m. *despachar*] —**dis·patch´er,** *n.*

dis·pel (dĭs pĕl´), *v.t.,* -pelled, -pelling. to drive off in various directions; scatter; disperse; dissipate: *to dispel vapors, fear, etc.* [t. L: m. s. *dispellere* drive asunder] —**dis·pel´ler,** *n.* —**Syn.** See scatter. —**Ant.** gather.

dis·pend (dĭs pĕnd´), *v.t.* *Obs.* or *Archaic.* to pay out; expend; spend. [ME *despende(n),* t. OF: m. *despendre,* g. L *dispendere* weigh out]

dis·pen·sa·ble (dĭs pĕn´sə bəl), *adj.* 1. that may be dispensed with or done without; unimportant. 2. capable of being dispensed or administered. 3. admitting of dispensation, as an offense or a law. 4. that may be declared not binding. —**dis·pen´sa·bil´i·ty,** *n.*

dis·pen·sa·ry (dĭs pĕn´sə rĭ), *n., pl.* -ries. 1. a place where something is dispensed, esp. medicines. 2. a charitable or public institution where medicines are furnished and medical advice is given gratuitously or for a small fee.

dis·pen·sa·tion (dĭs´pən sā´shən, -pĕn-), *n.* 1. act of dispensing; distribution; administration; management. 2. that which is distributed or given out. 3. a certain order, system, or arrangement. 4. *Theol.* a. the divine ordering of the affairs of the world. b. an appointment or arrangement, as by God. c. a divinely appointed order or system: *the old, Mosaic, or Jewish dispensation; the new, gospel, or Christian dispensation.* 5. a dispensing with, doing away with, or doing without something. 6. *Rom. Cath. Ch.* a. a relaxation of a law in a particular case granted by a competent superior or his delegate in laws which he has the power to make and enforce. b. the document containing this. —**dis´pen·sa´tion·al,** *adj.*

dis·pen·sa·tor (dĭs´pən sā´tər, -pĕn-), *n.* one who dispenses; a distributor; an administrator.

dis·pen·sa·to·ry (dĭs pĕn´sə tōr´ĭ), *n., pl.* -ries. 1. a book in which the composition, preparation, and uses of medicinal substances are described; a nonofficial pharmacopoeia. 2. a dispensary.

dis·pense (dĭs pĕns´), *v.,* -pensed, -pensing. —*v.t.* 1. to deal out; distribute: *to dispense justice, wisdom, etc.*

2. to administer (laws, etc.). 3. *Pharm.* to put up and distribute (medicine), esp. on prescription. 4. *Rom. Cath. Ch.* to grant a dispensation to, for, or from. —*v.i.* 5. to grant dispensation. 6. **dispense with,** a. to do without; forego. b. to do away with (a need, etc.). c. to grant exemption from (a law, promise, etc.). —*n.* 7. *Obs.* dispensation. [ME *dispense(n),* t. OF: m. *dispenser,* t. L: m. *dispensāre* weigh out, freq. of L *dispendere*] —**dis·pens´er,** *n.* —**Syn.** 1. See distribute.

dis·peo·ple (dĭs pē´pəl), *v.t.,* -pled, -pling. to deprive of people; depopulate.

dis·per·mous (dī spûr´məs), *adj.* *Bot.* two-seeded.

dis·per·sal (dĭs pûr´səl), *n.* dispersion (defs. 1 and 2).

dis·perse (dĭs pûrs´), *v.,* -persed, -persing. —*v.t.* 1. to scatter abroad; send or drive off in various directions. 2. to spread; diffuse: *the wise disperse knowledge.* 3. to dispel; cause to vanish: *the fog is dispersed.* —*v.i.* 4. to separate and move apart in different directions without order or regularity; become scattered: *the company dispersed at 10 o'clock.* 5. to be dispelled; be scattered out of sight; vanish. [t. F: m. s. *disperser,* ult. der. L *dispersus,* pp., scattered] —**dis·pers´ed·ly,** *adv.* —**dis·pers´er,** *n.* —**Syn.** 1. See scatter.

dis·per·sion (dĭs pûr´shən, -zhən), *n.* 1. act of dispersing. 2. state of being dispersed. 3. *Optics.* a. (of glass or other transparent substance) the variation of the refractive index with the wave length of light increasing as the wave length decreases. It is responsible for prism spectra. b. the separation of white or complex light into its constituent colors. 4. *Statistics.* the scattering of values of a variable around the mean or median of a distribution. 5. *Mil.* a scattered pattern of hits of bombs dropped under identical conditions, or of shots fired from the same gun with the same firing data.

dispersion error, *Mil.* the distance of one shot from the center of impact.

dis·per·sive (dĭs pûr´sĭv), *adj.* serving or tending to disperse.

dis·pir·it (dĭs pĭr´ĭt), *v.t.* to deprive of spirit; depress the spirits of; discourage; dishearten. —**dis·pir´it·ed,** *adj.* —**dis·pir´it·ed·ly,** *adv.* —**dis·pir´it·ed·ness,** *n.* —**dis·pir´it·ing,** *adj.* —**dis·pir´it·ing·ly,** *adv.*

dis·pit·e·ous (dĭs pĭt´ĭ əs), *adj.* *Chiefly Poetic.* malicious; cruel; pitiless.

dis·place (dĭs plās´), *v.t.,* -placed, -placing. 1. to put out of the usual or proper place: *to displace a wall.* 2. to take the place of; replace. 3. to remove from a position, office, or dignity. 4. *Obs.* to banish; remove. —**dis·place´a·ble,** *adj.* —**dis·plac´er,** *n.* —**Syn.** 1. DISPLACE, MISPLACE mean to put something in a different place from where it should be. To DISPLACE now often means to shift something solid and comparatively immovable, more or less permanently from its place: *the flood displaced houses from their foundations.* To MISPLACE is to put an object, usually an easily portable one, in a wrong place, so that it is difficult to find: *papers belonging in the safe were misplaced and temporarily lost.*

displaced person, (esp. in Europe) a person removed from his homeland for use as a slave laborer or driven from it by an invasion.

dis·place·ment (dĭs plās´mənt), *n.* 1. act of displacing. 2. state of being displaced. 3. *Physics.* a. the displacing or replacing of one thing by another, as of water by something immersed or floating in it. b. the weight or the volume of fluid displaced by a floating or submerged body, equivalent to the weight of the floating body or to the volume of the submerged body. 4. *Mach.* (of a cylinder) the volume swept out by the piston. 5. *Geol.* offset of rocks due to movement along a fault. 6. *Psychoanal.* the transfer of an emotion from the object about which it was originally experienced to another object.

displacement ton. See **ton**¹ (def. 4).

dis·plant (dĭs plănt´, -plänt´), *v.t.* *Obs.* 1. to dislodge. 2. to transplant.

dis·play (dĭs plā´), *v.t.* 1. to show; exhibit; make visible: *to display a flag.* 2. to reveal; betray: *to display fear.* 3. to unfold; open out; spread out: *to display a sail.* 4. to show ostentatiously. 5. *Print.* to give special prominence to (words, etc.) by choice and arrangement of type, etc. —*n.* 6. act of displaying; exhibition; show: *a display of radios, skill, etc.* 7. an ostentatious show: *a vulgar display of wealth.* 8. *Print.* a. the giving of prominence to particular words, etc., by the choice and arrangement of types and position, as in an advertisement, headline, or news story. b. printed matter thus displayed. [ME *desplay(en),* t. OF: m. *despleier, desploier* DEPLOY] —**dis·play´er,** *n.*

—**Syn.** 1. DISPLAY, EVINCE, EXHIBIT, MANIFEST mean to show or bring to the attention of another or others. To DISPLAY is literally to spread something out so that it may be most completely and favorably seen: *to display goods for sale.* To EXHIBIT is to put something in plain view and usually in a favorable position for particular observation: *to exhibit the best flowers at a special show.* They may both be used of showing (off) one's qualities or feelings: *he displayed his wit, his ignorance; he exhibited great surprise.* To EVINCE and to MANIFEST have only this latter reference, MANIFEST being the stronger word: *to evince or manifest surprise, interest, sympathy.* 4. flourish, flaunt, parade, air. 6. See show. —**Ant.** 1. conceal.

dis·please (dĭs plēz´), *v.,* -pleased, -pleasing. —*v.t.* 1. to cause dissatisfaction or dislike to; offend; annoy. —*v.i.* 2. to be unpleasant; cause displeasure. —**dis·pleas´ing·ly,** *adv.*

dis·pleas·ure (dǐs plĕzh′ər), *n.*, *v.*, **-ured, -uring.** —*n.* 1. dissatisfaction; annoyance; anger. 2. *Archaic.* discomfort, uneasiness, or pain. 3. *Archaic.* a cause of offense, annoyance, or injury. —*v.t.* 4. *Archaic.* to displease. —**Syn.** 1. See **dissatisfaction.**

dis·plode (dǐs plōd′), *v.t.*, *v.i.*, **-ploded, -ploding.** *Obs.* to explode. [t. L: m. s. *displōdere* burst asunder]

dis·plume (dǐs plōōm′), *v.t.*, **-plumed, -pluming.** 1. to strip of plumes; deplume. 2. to strip of honors.

dis·port (dǐs pōrt′), *v.t.* 1. to divert or amuse (oneself); exercise or display (oneself) in a sportive manner. —*v.i.* 2. to divert oneself; sport. —*n.* 3. diversion; amusement; play; sport. [ME *desporte(n)*, t. OF: m. *desporter, deporter,* f. *des-* DIS-1, *de-* DE- + *porter* carry (g. L *portāre*)]

dis·pos·a·ble (dǐs pō′zə bəl), *adj.* capable of being disposed of; subject to disposal; inclined.

dis·pos·al (dǐs pō′zəl), *n.* 1. act of disposing, or of disposing of, something; arrangement. 2. a disposing of as by gift or sale; bestowal or assignment. 3. power or right to dispose of a thing; control: *left at his disposal.*

dis·pose (dǐs pōz′), *v.*, **-posed, -posing.** —*v.t.* 1. to put in a particular or the proper order or arrangement; adjust by arranging the parts. 2. to put in a particular or suitable place. 3. to give a tendency or inclination to; incline. 4. *Archaic.* to make fit or ready; prepare. —*v.i.* 5. to arrange or decide matters. 6. *Obs.* to make terms. 7. **dispose of, a.** to deal with definitely; get rid of. **b.** to make over or part with, as by gift or sale. —*n.* 8. *Archaic.* disposition; habit. 9. *Obs.* arrangement; regulation; disposal. [ME *dispose(n)*, t. OF: m. *disposer,* f. *dis-* DIS-1 + *poser* POSE1, but assoc. with derivs. of L *dispōnere* (cf. DISPOSITION)] —**dis·pos′er,** *n.*

dis·posed (dǐs pōzd′), *adj.* inclined or minded, esp. favorably (usually fol. by *to* or infinitive).

dis·po·si·tion (dǐs′pə zǐsh′ən), *n.* 1. mental or moral constitution; turn of mind. 2. mental inclination; willingness. 3. physical inclination or tendency. 4. arrangement, as of troops or buildings. 5. final settlement of a matter. 6. regulation; appointment; dispensation. 7. bestowal, as by gift or sale. 8. power to dispose of a thing; control. [t. L: s. *dispositio*]
—**Syn.** 1. DISPOSITION, TEMPER, TEMPERAMENT refer to the aspects and habits of mind which one displays over a length of time. DISPOSITION is the natural or prevailing aspect of one's mind as shown in behavior and in relationships with others: *a happy disposition, a selfish disposition.* TEMPER sometimes denotes the essential quality of one's nature: *a temper of iron;* usually it has to do with propensity toward anger: *an even temper, a quick or hot temper.* TEMPERAMENT suggests the delicate balance of one's emotions, the disturbance of which determines one's moods: *an artistic temperament, an unstable temperament.*

dis·pos·sess (dǐs′pə zĕs′), *v.t.* to put (a person) out of possession, esp. of real property; oust. —**dis′pos·ses′- sion,** *n.* —**dis′pos·ses′sor,** *n.* —**dis·pos·ses·so·ry** (dǐs′pə zĕs′ə rǐ), *adj.* —**Syn.** See **strip1.**

dis·po·sure (dǐs pō′zhər), *n.* disposal; disposition.

dis·praise (dǐs prāz′), *v.*, **-praised, -praising,** *n.* —*v.t.* 1. to speak of as undeserving; censure; disparage. —*n.* 2. act of dispraising; censure. —**dis·prais′er,** *n.* —**dis·prais′ing·ly,** *adv.*

dis·pread (dǐs prĕd′), *v.t.*, *v.i.*, **-pread, -preading.** *Archaic.* to spread out; extend. Also, **disspread.**

dis·prize (dǐs prīz′), *v.t.*, **-prized, -prizing.** *Archaic.* to hold in small esteem; disdain.

dis·proof (dǐs prōōf′), *n.* act of disproving; proof to the contrary; refutation.

dis·pro·por·tion (dǐs′prə pōr′shən), *n.* 1. lack of proportion; want of due relation, as in size, number, etc. 2. something out of proportion. —*v.t.* 3. to make disproportionate. —**dis′pro·por′tion·a·ble,** *adj.* —**dis′- pro·por′tion·a·ble·ness,** *n.* —**dis′pro·por′tion·a·bly,** *adv.*

dis·pro·por·tion·al (dǐs′prə pōr′shə nəl), *adj.* disproportionate. —**dis′pro·por′tion·al·ly,** *adv.*

dis·pro·por·tion·ate (dǐs′prə pōr′shə nǐt), *adj.* not proportionate; out of proportion, as in size, number, etc. —**dis′pro·por′tion·ate·ly,** *adv.* —**dis′pro·por′tion- ate·ness,** *n.*

dis·pro·por·tion·a·tion (dǐs′prə pōr′shə nā′shən), *n. Chem.* the simultaneous oxidation and reduction of a substance reacting with itself, to form two dissimilar molecules, as $2C_2H_4 \rightarrow C_2H_6 + C_2H_2$.

dis·prove (dǐs prōōv′), *v.t.*, **-proved, -proving.** to prove (an assertion, claim, etc.) to be false or wrong; refute; invalidate. [ME *disprove(n)*, t. OF: m. *desprover,* f. *des-* DIS-1 + *prover* PROVE] —**dis·prov′a·ble,** *adj.* —**dis·prov′al,** *n.*

dis·put·a·ble (dǐs pū′tə bəl, dǐs′pyŏŏ tə bəl), *adj.* that may be disputed; liable to be called in question; questionable. —**dis·put′a·bil′i·ty,** *n.* —**dis·put′a·bly,** *adv.*

dis·pu·tant (dǐs pyŏŏ′tənt, dǐs pū′tənt), *adj.* 1. disputing. —*n.* 2. one who disputes; a debater.

dis·pu·ta·tion (dǐs′pyŏŏ tā′shən), *n.* 1. act of disputing or debating; verbal controversy; a discussion or debate. 2. an academic exercise consisting of the arguing of a thesis between its maintainer and his opponents. 3. *Obs.* conversation.

dis·pu·ta·tious (dǐs′pyŏŏ tā′shəs), *adj.* given to disputation; argumentative; contentious. Also, **dis·put·a·tive** (dǐs pū′tə tǐv). —**dis′pu·ta′tious·ly,** *adv.* —**dis′- pu·ta′tious·ness,** *n.*

dis·pute (dǐs pūt′), *v.*, **-puted, -puting,** *n.* —*v.i.* 1. to engage in argument or discussion. 2. to argue vehemently; wrangle or quarrel. —*v.t.* 3. to argue or debate about; discuss. 4. to argue against; call in question. 5. to quarrel or fight about; contest. 6. to strive against; oppose: *to dispute an advance.* —*n.* 7. argumentation; verbal contention; a debate or controversy; a quarrel. [ME, t. L: m. s. *disputāre;* r. ME *despute(n),* t. OF] —**dis·put′er,** *n.* —**Syn.** 7. See **argument.**

dis·qual·i·fi·ca·tion (dǐs kwǒl′ə fə kā′shən), *n.* 1. act of disqualifying. 2. state of being disqualified. 3. something that disqualifies.

dis·qual·i·fy (dǐs kwǒl′ə fī′), *v.*, **-fied, -fying.** —*v.t.* 1. to deprive of qualification or fitness; render unfit; incapacitate. 2. to deprive of legal or other rights or privileges; pronounce unqualified. 3. *Sports.* to deprive of the right to engage or compete in a match because the rules have been broken.

dis·qui·et (dǐs kwī′ət), *v.t.* 1. to deprive of quiet, rest, or peace; disturb; make uneasy: *disquieting news.* —*n.* 2. lack of quiet; disturbance; unrest; uneasiness. —*adj.* 3. *Rare.* unquiet; uneasy. —**dis·qui′et·ly,** *adv.*

dis·qui·e·tude (dǐs kwī′ə tūd′, -tōōd′), *n.* state of disquiet; uneasiness.

dis·qui·si·tion (dǐs′kwə zǐsh′ən), *n.* a formal discourse or treatise in which a subject is examined and discussed; a dissertation. [t. L: s. *disquīsītio* inquiry]

Dis·rae·li (dǐz rā′lǐ), *n.* **Benjamin,** *(Earl of Beaconsfield)* 1804–81, British statesman and novelist: prime minister, 1867, 1874–80.

dis·rate (dǐs rāt′), *v.t.*, **-rated, -rating.** *Naut.* to reduce to a lower rating, as a petty officer, or a noncommissioned officer of marines. Cf. **degrade.**

dis·re·gard (dǐs′rǐ gärd′), *v.t.* 1. to pay no attention to; leave out of consideration. 2. to treat without due regard, respect, or attentiveness. —*n.* 3. lack of regard or attention; neglect. 4. lack of due or respectful regard. —**dis′re·gard′er,** *n.* —**Syn.** 2. See **slight.**

dis·re·gard·ful (dǐs′rǐ gärd′fəl), *adj.* neglectful; careless.

dis·rel·ish (dǐs rĕl′ǐsh), *v.t.* 1. to have a distaste for; dislike. —*n.* 2. distaste; dislike.

dis·re·mem·ber (dǐs′rǐ mĕm′bər), *v.t.*, *v.i. Colloq.* to fail to remember; forget.

dis·re·pair (dǐs′rǐ pâr′), *n.* state of being out of repair; impaired condition.

dis·rep·u·ta·ble (dǐs rĕp′yə tə bəl), *adj.* 1. not reputable; having a bad reputation. 2. discreditable; dishonorable. —**dis·rep′u·ta·bil′i·ty, dis·rep′u·ta·ble- ness,** *n.* —**dis·rep′u·ta·bly,** *adv.*

dis·re·pute (dǐs′rǐ pūt′), *n.* ill repute; discredit (usually prec. by *in, into*): *that policy is in disrepute; this would bring the administration of justice into disrepute.* Also, *Archaic,* **dis·rep·u·ta·tion** (dǐs rĕp′yə tā′shən).

dis·re·spect (dǐs′rǐ spĕkt′), *n.* 1. lack of respect; disesteem; rudeness. —*v.t.* 2. to regard or treat without respect; regard or treat with contempt or rudeness.

dis·re·spect·a·ble (dǐs′rǐ spĕk′tə bəl), *adj.* not respectable. —**dis′re·spect′a·bil′i·ty,** *n.*

dis·re·spect·ful (dǐs′rǐ spĕkt′fəl), *adj.* characterized by disrespect; having or showing disrespect. —**dis′- re·spect′ful·ly,** *adv.* —**dis′re·spect′ful·ness,** *n.* —**Syn.** discourteous, uncivil, impolite, rude, impudent.

dis·robe (dǐs rōb′), *v.t.*, *v.i.*, **-robed, -robing.** to undress. —**dis·robe′ment,** *n.* —**dis·rob′er,** *n.*

dis·root (dǐs rōōt′, -rŏŏt′), *v.t.* to uproot; dislodge.

dis·rupt (dǐs rŭpt′), *v.t.* 1. to break or rend asunder; break up. —*adj.* 2. disrupted; rent asunder. [t. L: s. *disruptus,* pp.] —**dis·rupt′er, dis·rup′tor,** *n.*

dis·rup·tion (dǐs rŭp′shən), *n.* 1. forcible separation or division into parts. 2. a disrupted condition.

dis·rup·tive (dǐs rŭp′tǐv), *adj.* disrupting; pertaining to disruption.

disruptive discharge, *Elect.* the sudden and large increase in current through an insulating medium due to complete failure of the medium under electrostatic stress.

dis·rup·ture (dǐs rŭp′chər), *v.t.*, **-tured, -turing.** *Rare.* to disrupt.

dis·sat·is·fac·tion (dǐs′sǎt ǐs fǎk′shən), *n.* lack of satisfaction; state of not being satisfied. —**Syn.** DISSATISFACTION, DISCONTENT, DISPLEASURE imply a sense of dislike for, or unhappiness in, one's surroundings and a wish for other conditions. DISSATISFACTION results from contemplating what falls short of one's wishes or expectations, and is usually only temporary: *dissatisfaction with results of an afternoon's work.* DISCONTENT is a sense of lack, and a general feeling of uneasy dislike for the conditions of one's life, which colors one's entire outlook: *feeling a continual vague discontent.* DISPLEASURE, a more positive word, suggests a certain amount of anger as well as dissatisfaction: *displeasure at being kept waiting.*

dis·sat·is·fac·to·ry (dǐs′sǎt ǐs fǎk′tər ǐ), *adj.* causing dissatisfaction.

dis·sat·is·fied (dǐs sǎt′ǐs fīd′), *adj.* 1. discontented; not pleased; offended. 2. showing dissatisfaction: *a dissatisfied look.* —**dis·sat′is·fied′ly,** *adv.*

dis·sat·is·fy (dǐs sǎt′ǐs fī′), *v.t.*, **-fied, -fying.** to make ill-satisfied, ill-pleased, or discontented.

dis·seat (dǐs sēt′), *v.t.* to unseat.

dis·sect (dǐ sĕkt′), *v.t.* 1. to cut apart (an animal body, plant, etc.) to examine the structure, relation of parts, or the like. 2. to examine minutely part by part;

---

b., blend of, blended; c., cognate with; d., dialect, dialectal; der., derived from; f., formed from; g., going back to; m., modification of; r., replacing; s., stem of; t., taken from; ?, perhaps. See the full key on inside cover.

analyze. [t. L: s. *dissectus*, pp., cut asunder] —**dis·sec′ti·ble**, *adj.* —**dis·sec′tor**, *n.*

dis·sect·ed (dĭ sĕk′tĭd), *adj.* **1.** *Bot.* deeply cut into numerous segments, as a leaf. **2.** *Phys. Geog.* cut up by many closely spaced valleys, as a plateau.

dis·sec·tion (dĭ sĕk′shən), *n.* **1.** act of dissecting. **2.** something that has been dissected.

dis·seize (dĭs sēz′), *v.t.*, **-seized, -seizing.** *Law.* to deprive (a person) of seizin, or of the possession, of a freehold interest in land, esp. wrongfully or by force; oust. Also, **dis·seise.** [ME *disseyse(n)*, t. AF: m. *disseisir* dispossess, f. *dis-* DIS-¹ + *saisir* SEIZE] —**dis·seizor**, *n.*

dis·sei·zee (dĭs′sē zē′, dĭs sē′zē′), *n.* one who is disseized. Also, **dis′sei·see′.**

dis·sei·zin (dĭs sē′zĭn), *n.* *Law.* **1.** act of disseizing. **2.** state of being disseized. Also, **dis·sei′sin.** [ME *dysseysyne*, t. AF: m. *disseisine*, f. *dis-* DIS-¹ + *saisine* possession, SEIZIN]

dis·sem·blance¹ (dĭ sĕm′bləns), *n.* *Archaic.* dissimilarity; unlikeness. [t. OF: m. *dessemblance*, der. *dessembler* be unlike, f. *des-* DIS-¹ + *sembler* seem (g. L *simulāre*)]

dis·sem·blance² (dĭ sĕm′bləns), *n.* *Archaic.* dissembling; dissimulation. [f. DISSEMBLE + -ANCE]

dis·sem·ble (dĭ sĕm′bəl), *v.*, **-bled, -bling.** —*v.t.* **1.** to give a false semblance to; conceal the real nature of. **2.** to put on the appearance of; feign. **3.** to let pass unnoticed; ignore. —*v.i.* **4.** to conceal one's motives, etc., under some pretense; speak or act hypocritically. [f. DIS- + -*semble*, modeled on RESEMBLE] —**dis·sem′bler**, *n.* —**dis·sem′bling·ly**, *adv.*

dis·sem·i·nate (dĭ sĕm′ə nāt′), *v.t.*, **-nated, -nating.** to scatter, as seed in sowing; spread abroad; diffuse; promulgate. [t. L: m. s. *dissēminātus*, pp.] —**dis·sem′i·na′tion**, *n.* —**dis·sem′i·na′tor**, *n.*

dis·sen·sion (dĭ sĕn′shən), *n.* **1.** violent disagreement; discord; a contention or quarrel. **2.** difference in sentiment or opinion; disagreement.

dis·sent (dĭ sĕnt′), *v.i.* **1.** to differ in sentiment or opinion; disagree; withhold assent (fol. by *from*). **2.** to differ in religious opinion; reject the doctrines or authority of an established church. —*n.* **3.** difference in sentiment or opinion. **4.** separation from an established church, esp. that of England; nonconformity. [ME *dissente(n)*, t. L: m. *dissentīre* differ in opinion] —**dis·sent′ing**, *adj.* —**dis·sent′ing·ly**, *adv.*
—**Syn. 3.** DISSENT, DISSIDENCE mean disagreement with the majority opinion. DISSENT may express either withholding of agreement or open disagreement. DISSENTERS may withdraw from a group, but if so, they merely go their own way. DISSIDENCE, formerly much the same as DISSENT, has come to suggest not only strong dissatisfaction but a determined opposition. If dissidents withdraw, they continue actively to oppose the original group.

dis·sent·er (dĭ sĕn′tər), *n.* **1.** one who dissents, as from an established church. **2.** (*sometimes cap.*) a person, now esp. a Protestant, who dissents from the Church of England.

dis·sen·tient (dĭ sĕn′shənt), *adj.* **1.** dissenting, esp. from the opinion of the majority. —*n.* **2.** one who dissents. —**dis·sen′tience**, *n.*

dis·sen·tious (dĭ sĕn′shəs), *adj.* contentious; quarrelsome.

dis·sep·i·ment (dĭ sĕp′ə mənt), *n.* **1.** a partition or septum. **2.** *Bot.* one of the partitions formed within ovaries and fruits by the coherence of the sides of the constituent carpels. [t. L: m. s. *dissaepimentum* that which separates] —**dis·sep′i·men′tal**, *adj.*

D. Dissepiment

dis·sert (dĭ sûrt′), *v.i.* *Obs.* or *Rare.* to discourse on a subject. [t. L: s. *dissertus*, pp., examined, discussed]

dis·ser·tate (dĭs′ər tāt′), *v.i.*, **-tated, -tating.** to treat of a subject in discourse; make a dissertation. [t. L: m.s. *dissertātus*, pp., discussed] —**dis′ser·ta′tor**, *n.*

dis·ser·ta·tion (dĭs′ər tā′shən), *n.* **1.** a written essay, treatise, or thesis, esp. one written by a candidate for the Doctor's degree. **2.** a formal discourse.

dis·serve (dĭs sûrv′), *v.t.*, **-served, -serving.** to serve ill; do an ill turn to.

dis·serv·ice (dĭs sûr′vĭs), *n.* harm; injury; an ill turn.

dis·sev·er (dĭ sĕv′ər), *v.t.* **1.** to sever; separate. **2.** to divide into parts. —*v.i.* **3.** to part; separate. —**dis·sev′er·ance, dis·sev′er·ment, dis·sev′er·a′tion**, *n.*

dis·si·dence (dĭs′ə dəns), *n.* disagreement. See **dissent.**

dis·si·dent (dĭs′ə dənt), *adj.* **1.** differing; disagreeing; dissenting. —*n.* **2.** one who differs; a dissenter. [t. L: s. *dissidens*, ppr., differing, sitting apart]

dis·sil·i·ent (dĭ sĭl′ĭ ənt), *adj.* flying or bursting asunder. [t. L: s. *dissiliens*, ppr.] —**dis·sil′i·en·cy, dis·sil′i·ence**, *n.*

dis·sim·i·lar (dĭ sĭm′ə lər), *adj.* not similar; unlike; different. —**dis·sim′i·lar·ly**, *adv.*

dis·sim·i·lar·i·ty (dĭ sĭm′ə lâr′ə tĭ), *n.*, *pl.* **-ties. 1.** unlikeness; difference. **2.** a point of difference. —**Syn. 1.** See **difference.**

dis·sim·i·late (dĭ sĭm′ə lāt′), *v.t.*, **-lated, -lating.** *Phonet.* to change (a speech sound) so that it is less like another sound in a neighboring syllable: Americans who pronounce *er* as the *r*-like vowel may fail to do so in the second syllable of *Northerner* and thus avoid a sequence of three *r* syllables. —**dis·sim′i·la′tive**, *adj.*

dis·sim·i·la·tion (dĭ sĭm′ə lā′shən), *n.* **1.** a making or becoming unlike. **2.** *Phonet.* act or process of dissimilating speech sounds. **3.** *Biol.* catabolism.

dis·si·mil·i·tude (dĭs′sĭ mĭl′ə tūd′, -tōōd′), *n.* **1.** unlikeness; difference. **2.** a point of difference.

dis·sim·u·late (dĭ sĭm′yə lāt′), *v.*, **-lated, -lating.** —*v.t.* **1.** to disguise or conceal under a false semblance; dissemble. —*v.i.* **2.** to use dissimulation; dissemble. [t. L: m. s. *dissimulātus*, pp.] —**dis·sim′u·la′tive**, *adj.* —**dis·sim′u·la′tor**, *n.*

dis·sim·u·la·tion (dĭ sĭm′yə lā′shən), *n.* **1.** act of dissimulating; feigning; hypocrisy. **2.** *Psychiatry.* the ability or the tendency to appear mentally normal when actually suffering from disorder: a characteristic of the paranoiac. Cf. **simulation.**

dis·si·pate (dĭs′ə pāt′), *v.*, **-pated, -pating.** —*v.t.* **1.** to scatter in various directions; disperse; dispel; disintegrate. **2.** to scatter wastefully or extravagantly; squander. —*v.i.* **3.** to become scattered or dispersed; be dispelled; disintegrate. **4.** to indulge in extravagant, intemperate, or dissolute pleasure; practice dissipation. [t. L: m.s. *dissipātus*, pp., scattered, demolished] —**dis′si·pat′or, dis′si·pa′tor**, *n.* —**dis′si·pa′tive**, *adj.* —**Syn. 1.** See **scatter.**

dis·si·pat·ed (dĭs′ə pā′tĭd), *adj.* indulging in or characterized by excessive devotion to pleasure; intemperate; dissolute. —**dis′si·pat′ed·ly**, *adv.* —**dis′si·pat′ed·ness**, *n.*

dis·si·pa·tion (dĭs′ə pā′shən), *n.* **1.** act of dissipating. **2.** state of being dissipated; dispersion; disintegration. **3.** a wasting by misuse. **4.** mental distraction; a diversion. **5.** dissolute mode of living; intemperance.

dis·so·ci·a·ble (dĭ sō′shĭ ə bəl, -sha bəl), *adj.* **1.** capable of being dissociated; separable. **2.** unsociable. **3.** incongruous; not reconcilable.

dis·so·cial (dĭ sō′shəl), *adj.* unsocial; disinclined to or unsuitable for society.

dis·so·ci·ate (dĭ sō′shĭ āt′), *v.*, **-ated, -ating.** —*v.t.* **1.** to sever the association of; disunite; separate. **2.** *Chem.* to subject to dissociation. —*v.i.* **3.** to withdraw from association. **4.** *Chem.* to undergo dissociation. [t. L: m.s. *dissociātus*, pp.] —**dis·so′ci·a′tive**, *adj.*

dis·so·ci·a·tion (dĭ sō′sĭ ā′shən, -shĭ ā′/-), *n.* **1.** act of dissociating. **2.** state of being dissociated; disunion. **3.** *Phys. Chem.* **a.** the reversible resolution or decomposition of a complex substance into simpler constituents, due to variation in the physical conditions, as when water gradually decomposes into hydrogen and oxygen under great heat, in such a way that when the temperature is lowered the liberated elements recombine to form water. **b.** electrolytic dissociation. **4.** *Psychiatry.* the splitting off of certain mental processes from the main body of consciousness, with varying degrees of autonomy resulting.

dis·sol·u·ble (dĭ sŏl′yə bəl), *adj.* capable of being dissolved. —**dis·sol′u·bil′i·ty**, *n.*

dis·so·lute (dĭs′ə lōōt′), *adj.* indifferent to moral restraints; given over to dissipation; licentious. [t. L: m.s. *dissolūtus*, pp., loosened] —**dis′so·lute′ly**, *adv.* —**dis′so·lute′ness**, *n.*

dis·so·lu·tion (dĭs′ə lōō′shən), *n.* **1.** act of resolving into parts or elements. **2.** the resulting state. **3.** the undoing or breaking up of a tie, bond, union, etc. **4.** the breaking up of an assembly or organization; dismissal; dispersal. **5.** *Govt.* an order issued by the head of the state terminating a parliament and necessitating a new election. **6.** death or decease. **7.** a bringing or coming to an end; destruction. **8.** the legal termination of business activity, including the distribution of assets and the fixing of liabilities. **9.** *Chem.* solution in a liquid substance. —**dis′so·lu′tive**, *adj.*

dis·solve (dĭ zŏlv′), *v.*, **-solved, -solving.** —*v.t.* **1.** to make a solution of in a solvent. **2.** to undo (a tie or bond); break up (a connection, union, etc.). **3.** to break up (an assembly or organization); dismiss; disperse. **4.** *Govt.* to order the termination of a parliament, as in Great Britain, at five-year intervals (or less if the government is defeated). **5.** to bring to an end; destroy; dispel. **6.** to resolve into parts or elements; disintegrate. **7.** to destroy the binding power of: *dissolve a spell.* **8.** *Law.* to deprive of force; annul: *to dissolve a marriage or injunction.* —*v.i.* **9.** to become dissolved, as in a solvent. **10.** to break up or disperse. **11.** to lose force or strength; lose binding force. **12.** to disappear gradually; fade from sight or apprehension. **13.** *Motion Pictures.* to fade out one shot while simultaneously fading in the next shot, overlapping the two shots during the process. —*n.* **14.** *Motion Pictures.* a scene made by dissolving. [ME *dissolve(n)*, t. L: m. *dissolvere* loosen, disunite] —**dis·solv′a·ble**, *adj.* —**dis·solv′er**, *n.* —**dis·solv′ing**, *adj.* —**dis·solv′ing·ly**, *adv.* —**Syn. 1.** See **melt.**

dis·sol·vent (dĭ zŏl′vənt), *adj.*, *n.* solvent.

dissolving view, pictures thrown on a screen by a slide projector or magic lantern, which seem to dissolve one into another, without any interval between them.

dis·so·nance (dĭs′ə nəns), *n.* **1.** an inharmonious or harsh sound; discord. **2.** *Music.* a simultaneous combination of tones conventionally accepted as being in a state of unrest and needing completion (opposed to *consonance*). **3.** disagreement or incongruity. Also, **dis′so·nan·cy.**

dis·so·nant (dĭs'ə nənt), *adj.* **1.** disagreeing or harsh in sound; discordant. **2.** out of harmony; incongruous; at variance. [t. L: *s. dissonans*, ppr., disagreeing in sound] **—dis'so·nant·ly,** *adv.*

dis·spread (dĭs·prĕd'), *v.t., v.i.* dispread.

dis·suade (dĭ swād'), *v.t.,* **-suaded, -suading. 1.** to deter by advice or persuasion; persuade not to do something (fol. by *from*): *dissuade him from leaving home.* **2.** to advise or urge against (an action, etc.). [t. L: m.s. *dissuādēre* advise against] **—dis·suad'er,** *n.*

dis·sua·sion (dĭ swā'zhən), *n.* act of dissuading.

dis·sua·sive (dĭ swā'sĭv), *adj.* tending to dissuade. **—dis·sua'sive·ly,** *adv.*

dis·syl·la·ble (dĭ sĭl'ə bəl, dĭs'sĭl'-), *n.* disyllable. **—dis·syl·lab·ic** (dĭs'ĭ lăb'ĭk, dĭs'sĭ-), *adj.*

dis·sym·me·try (dĭ sĭm'ə trĭ), *n.* absence of symmetry. **—dis·sym·met·ric** (dĭs'ĭ mĕt'rĭk), **dis·sym·met'ri·cal,** *adj.*

dist., 1. distance. **2.** distinguish. **3.** distinguished. **4.** district.

dis·taff (dĭs'tăf, -täf), *n.* **1.** a staff with a cleft end, formerly used for holding the wool, flax, etc., from which the thread was drawn in spinning by hand. **2.** an analogous part of a spinning wheel, for holding flax to be spun. **3.** the female sex. **4.** a female heir; a woman. [ME *distaf,* OE *distæf,* f. dis-, akin to LG *diesse* bunch of flax on a distaff (cf. DIZEN) + *stæf* STAFF]

distaff side, the female side of a family.

dis·tain (dĭs tān'), *v.t. Archaic.* to discolor; stain; sully. [ME *disteyne(n)*, t. OF: m. *desteindre,* f. *des-* DIS-[1] + *teindre* wet, dye (g. L *tingere*)]

dis·tal (dĭs'təl), *adj.* situated away from the point of origin or attachment, as of a limb or bone; terminal (opposed to *proximal*). [f. DIST(ANT) + -AL[1]]

dis·tance (dĭs'təns), *n., v.,* **-tanced, -tancing. —n. 1.** the extent of space intervening between things or points. **2.** state or fact of being distant, as of one thing from another; remoteness. **3.** the interval between two points of time. **4.** remoteness in any respect. **5.** a distant point or place; the distant region. **6.** the distant part of a landscape, etc. **7.** reserve or aloofness; one's proper degree of aloofness: *to keep one's distance.* **8.** *Music.* interval (def. 7). **9.** *Sports.* the length, usually measured in furlongs (eighths of miles), to be run to the winning post on a race track. **10.** *Obs.* disagreement or dissension; a quarrel. **—v.t. 11.** to leave behind at a distance, as at a race; surpass. **12.** to place at a distance. **13.** to cause to appear distant.

dis·tant (dĭs'tənt), *adj.* **1.** far off or apart in space; not near at hand; remote (fol. by *from*). **2.** separate or apart in space: *a place a mile distant.* **3.** apart or far off in time. **4.** far apart in any respect: *a distant relative.* **5.** reserved; not familiar or cordial. **6.** to a distance: *a distant journey.* [t. F, t. L: *s. distans*, ppr., being distant, standing apart] **—dis'tant·ly,** *adv.*

dis·taste (dĭs tāst'), *n., v.,* **-tasted, -tasting. —n. 1.** dislike; disinclination. **2.** disrelish for food or drink. **—v.t. 3.** *Archaic.* to dislike. **—Syn. 1.** aversion, repugnance, disgust. See **dislike.**

dis·taste·ful (dĭs tāst'fəl), *adj.* **1.** causing dislike. **2.** unpleasant to the taste. **—dis·taste'ful·ly,** *adv.* **—dis·taste'ful·ness,** *n.* **—Syn. 1.** disagreeable, displeasing; offensive, repugnant, repulsive. **2.** unpalatable, unsavory.

Dist. Atty., District Attorney.

dis·tem·per[1] (dĭs tĕm'pər), *n.* **1.** *Vet. Sci.* **a.** a specific infectious disease of young dogs caused by a filterable virus. **b.** a disease of horses; strangles. **c.** (formerly) any of several diseases characterized by fever and catarrhal symptoms. **2.** deranged condition of mind or body; a disorder or disease. **3.** disorder or disturbance. **—v.t. 4.** to derange physically or mentally. [ME *distempre(n),* t. ML: m. *distemperāre.* See DIS-[1], TEMPER]

dis·tem·per[2] (dĭs tĕm'pər), *n.* **1.** a method of painting in which the colors are mixed with some binding medium, as egg mixed with water, usually executed upon a gesso ground, used for murals, scene painting, or the like. **2.** a painting executed by this method. **3.** *Brit.* calcimine. **—v.t. 4.** to paint in distemper. **5.** *Brit.* to calcimine. [t. OF: m. *destemprer,* f. *des-* DIS-[1] + *temprer* dilute, soak (g. L *temperāre*)]

dis·tem·per·a·ture (dĭs tĕm'pər ə chər), *n.* distempered or disordered condition; disturbance of health, mind, or temper.

dis·tend (dĭs tĕnd'), *v.t., v.i.* **1.** to stretch apart or asunder; stretch out. **2.** to expand by stretching, as something hollow or elastic. [t. L: *s. distendere*] **—Syn. 2.** See **expand.**

dis·ten·si·ble (dĭs tĕn'sə bəl), *adj.* capable of being distended. **—dis·ten'si·bil'i·ty,** *n.*

dis·tent (dĭs tĕnt'), *adj. Rare.* distended. [t. L: *s. distentus,* pp.]

dis·ten·tion (dĭs tĕn'shən), *n.* **1.** act of distending. **2.** state of being distended. Also, **dis·ten'sion.**

dis·tich (dĭs'tĭk), *n. Pros.* **1.** a group of two lines of verse, usually making complete sense; a couplet. **2.** a rhyming couplet. [t. L: *s. distichon,* t. Gk., neut. of *dístichos* of two rows or lines]

dis·tich·ous (dĭs'tĭk əs), *adj. Bot.* arranged alternately in two vertical rows on opposite sides of an axis, as leaves. See illus. under **alternate.** [t. L: m. *distichus* of two rows. See DISTICH] **—dis'tich·ous·ly,** *adv.*

dis·til (dĭs tĭl'), *v.t., v.i.,* **-tilled, -tilling.** *Chiefly Brit.* distill.

dis·till (dĭs tĭl'), *v.t.* **1.** to subject to a process of vaporization and subsequent condensation, as for purification or concentration. **2.** to extract the volatile components of by distillation; transform by distillation. **3.** to extract or obtain by distillation. **4.** to drive (*off* or *out*) by distillation. **5.** to let fall in drops; give forth in or as in drops. **—v.i. 6.** to undergo distillation. **7.** to become vaporized and then condensed in distillation. **8.** to drop, pass, or condense as a distillate. **9.** to fall in drops; trickle; exude. [ME *distille(n),* t. L: m. *distillāre,* var. of *dēstillāre* drip down] **—dis·till'a·ble,** *adj.*

dis·til·late (dĭs'tə lĭt, -lāt'), *n.* the product obtained from the condensation of vapors in distillation.

dis·til·la·tion (dĭs'tə lā'shən), *n.* **1.** the volatilization or evaporation and subsequent condensation of a liquid, as when water is boiled in a retort and the steam is condensed in a cool receiver. **2.** the purification or concentration of a substance; the obtaining of the essence or volatile properties contained in it, or the separation of one substance from another, by such a process. **3.** a product of distilling; a distillate. **4.** act or process of distilling. **5.** fact of being distilled. **—dis·til·la·to·ry** (dĭs tĭl'ə tôr'ĭ), *adj.*

dis·tilled (dĭs tĭld'), *adj.* obtained or produced by distillation.

dis·till·er (dĭs tĭl'ər), *n.* **1.** an apparatus for distilling, as a condenser, or esp., one for distillation of salt water at sea. **2.** one whose business it is to extract spirituous liquors by distillation.

dis·till·er·y (dĭs tĭl'ər ĭ), *n., pl.* **-eries.** a place or establishment where distilling, esp. the distilling of spirituous liquors, is carried on.

dis·till·ment (dĭs tĭl'mənt), *n.* **1.** act or process of distilling. **2.** the product of distilling. Also, *esp. Brit.,* **dis·til'ment.**

dis·tinct (dĭs tĭngkt'), *adj.* **1.** distinguished as not being the same; not identical; separate (fol. by *from* or used absolutely). **2.** different in nature or qualities; dissimilar. **3.** clear to the senses or intellect; plain; definite; unmistakable. **4.** distinguishing clearly, as the vision. **5.** *Poetic.* decorated or adorned. [ME, t. L: *s. distinctus,* pp., separated] **—dis·tinct'ness,** *n.* **—Syn. 1.** See **various.**

dis·tinc·tion (dĭs tĭngk'shən), *n.* **1.** a marking off or distinguishing as different. **2.** the recognizing or noting of differences; discrimination. **3.** a discrimination made between things as different. **4.** the condition of being different; a difference. **5.** a distinguishing characteristic. **6.** a distinguishing or treating with special attention or favor. **7.** a mark of special favor. **8.** marked superiority; note; eminence. **9.** distinguished appearance. **10.** division. **—Syn. 3.** DISTINCTION and DIFFERENCE may both refer to perceivable dissimilarities and, in this meaning, may be used interchangeably: *there is a distinction (difference) between the two.* DISTINCTION, however, usually suggests the perception of dissimilarity, as the result of analysis and discrimination (*a carefully made distinction between two treatments of the same theme*) whereas DIFFERENCE refers only to the condition of being dissimilar: *the differences between Gothic and Roman architecture.* "A distinction without a difference" is a way of referring to an artificial or false discrimination. **7.** See **honor.—Ant. 4.** resemblance.

dis·tinc·tive (dĭs tĭngk'tĭv), *adj.* distinguishing; serving to distinguish; characteristic. **—dis·tinc'tive·ly,** *adv.* **—dis·tinc'tive·ness,** *n.*

dis·tinct·ly (dĭs tĭngkt'lĭ), *adv.* **1.** in a distinct manner; clearly. **2.** without doubt; unmistakably. **—Syn. 1.** See **clearly.**

dis·tin·gué (dĭs'tăng gā', dĭs tăng'gā; *Fr.* dēs tăn gĕ'), *adj.* distinguished; having an air of distinction. [F, pp. of *distinguer* distinguish] **—dis'tin·guée',** *adj. fem.*

dis·tin·guish (dĭs tĭng'gwĭsh), *v.t.* **1.** to mark off as different (fol. by *from*). **2.** to recognize as distinct or different; discriminate. **3.** to perceive clearly by sight or other sense; discern; recognize. **4.** to serve to separate as different; be a distinctive characteristic of; characterize. **5.** to make prominent, conspicuous, or eminent: *to distinguish oneself in battle.* **6.** to divide into classes; classify. **7.** *Archaic.* to single out for or honor with special attention. **—v.i. 8.** to indicate or show a difference (fol. by *between*). **9.** to recognize or note differences; discriminate. [f. *s.* L *distinguere* separate, distinguish + -ISH[2], modeled on EXTINGUISH] **—dis·tin'guish·a·ble,** *adj.* **—dis·tin'guish·a·ble·ness,** *n.* **—dis·tin'guish·a·bly,** *adv.* **—dis·tin'guish·er,** *n.* **—dis·tin'guish·ing·ly,** *adv.*

—Syn. 2. DISTINGUISH, DIFFERENTIATE, DISCRIMINATE suggest a positive attempt to analyze characteristic features or qualities of things. To DISTINGUISH is to recognize the characteristic features belonging to a thing: *to distinguish a light cruiser from a heavy cruiser.* To DISCRIMINATE is to perceive the particular, nice, or exact differences between things, to determine wherein these differences consist, and to estimate their significance: *to discriminate prejudiced from unprejudiced testimony.* To DIFFERENTIATE is especially to point out exactly and in detail the differences (usually) between two things: *the symptoms of some diseases are so similar that it is hard to differentiate one from another.* **—Ant. 2.** confuse.

dis·tin·guished (dĭs tĭng'gwĭsht), *adj.* **1.** conspicuous; marked. **2.** noted; eminent, famous. **3.** having an air of distinction; distingué. **—Syn. 2.** See **famous.**

Dis·tin·guished Serv·ice Cross, *U.S. Army.* a bronze medal awarded to an officer or enlisted man for extraordinary heroism in military action against an armed enemy.

dis·tort (dĭs tôrt′), *v.t.* **1.** to twist awry or out of shape; make crooked or deformed. **2.** to pervert; misrepresent. [t. L: s. *distortus,* pp.] **—dis·tort′ed,** *adj.* **—dis·tort′ed·ly,** *adv.* **—dis·tort′ed·ness,** *n.* **—dis·tort′er,** *n.*

dis·tor·tion (dĭs tôr′shən), *n.* **1.** act of distorting. **2.** state of being distorted. **3.** anything distorted. **—dis·tor′tion·al,** *adj.*

dis·tract (dĭs trăkt′), *v.t.* **1.** to draw away or divert, as the mind or attention. **2.** to divide (the mind, attention, etc.) between objects. **3.** to disturb or trouble greatly in mind. **4.** to rend by disssension or strife. *—adj.* **5.** *Archaic.* distracted. [t. L: s. *distractus,* pp., pulled asunder. Cf. DISTRAUGHT] **—dis·tract′ed,** *adj.* **—dis·tract′ed·ly,** *adv.* **—dis·tract′er,** *n.* **—dis·tract′ing,** *adj.* **—dis·tract′ing·ly,** *adv.*

dis·trac·tion (dĭs trăk′shən), *n.* **1.** act of distracting. **2.** state of being distracted. **3.** violent disturbance of mind; mental derangement or madness. **4.** division or disorder due to dissention; tumult.

dis·trac·tive (dĭs trăk′tĭv), *adj.* tending to distract.

dis·train (dĭs trān′), *Law.* *—v.t.* **1.** to constrain by seizing and holding goods, etc., in pledge for rent, damages, etc., or in order to obtain satisfaction of a claim. **2.** to levy a distress upon. *—v.i.* **3.** to levy a distress. [ME *destreyne(n),* t. OF: m. *destreindre* constrain, g. L *distringere* draw asunder, detain, hinder] **—dis·train′a·ble,** *adj.* **—dis·train′ment,** *n.* **—dis·train′or, dis·train′er,** *n.*

dis·traint (dĭs trānt′), *n.* *Law.* act of distraining; a distress.

dis·trait (dĭs trā′; *Fr.* dĕs trĕ′), *adj.* abstracted in thought; absent-minded. [t. F, pp. of *distraire,* g. L *distrahere* pull asunder. See DISTRACT] **—dis·traite** (dĭs trāt′; *Fr.* dĕs trĕt′), *n. fem.*

dis·traught (dĭs trôt′), *adj.* **1.** distracted; bewildered; deeply agitated. **2.** crazed. [var. of obs. *distract,* adj., by assoc. with *straught,* pp. of STRETCH]

dis·tress (dĭs trĕs′), *n.* **1.** great pain, anxiety, or sorrow; acute suffering; affliction; trouble. **2.** a state of extreme necessity. **3.** the state of a ship requiring immediate assistance, as because of accident. **4.** *Law.* **a.** act of distraining; the legal seizure and detention of the goods of another as security or satisfaction for debt, etc. **b.** the thing seized in distraining. *—v.t.* **5.** to afflict with pain, anxiety, or sorrow; trouble sorely; worry; bother. **6.** to subject to pressure, stress, or strain; embarrass or exhaust by strain. **7.** to constrain. [ME *destresse,* t. OF: m. *destrece,* der. L *districtus,* pp., distrained] **—dis·tress′ing,** *adj.* **—dis·tress′ing·ly,** *adv.* **—Syn. 1.** grief, agony, anguish, misery. See **sorrow.**

dis·tressed ar·ea, *Brit.* a region where unemployment and a low standard of living prevail. Latterly called **special area.**

dis·tress·ful (dĭs trĕs′fəl), *adj.* **1.** causing or involving distress. **2.** full of distress; feeling or indicating distress. **—dis·tress′ful·ly,** *adv.* **—dis·tress′ful·ness,** *n.*

dis·tress mer·chan·dise, *Com.* goods sold quickly, usually at less than the prevailing price, to secure cash.

dis·trib·ute (dĭs trĭb′ūt), *v.t.,* **-uted, -uting. 1.** to divide and bestow in shares; deal out; allot. **2.** to disperse through a space or over an area; spread; scatter. **3.** to divide into parts of distinct character. **4.** to divide into classes: *these plants are distributed into 22 classes.* **5.** *Logic.* to employ (a term) so as to refer to all the individuals denoted by it: *the term men is distributed in "all men are mortal" but not in "some men are old."* [t. L: m. s. *distribūtus,* pp.] **—dis·trib′ut·a·ble,** *adj.* **—Syn. 1.** assign, mete, apportion. DISTRIBUTE, DISPENSE, apply to giving out something. DISTRIBUTE implies apportioned, individualized and, often, personal giving, esp. of something that is definite or limited in amount or number: *the prizes were distributed among ten winners.* DISPENSE formerly implied indiscriminate, general, and liberal giving, esp. of something that was more or less indefinite or unmeasured in amount: *to dispense largess.* It now applies chiefly to giving according to need or deserts, from an organized and official source: *to dispense medicines and food to the victims, justice to criminals.*

dis·trib·u·tee (dĭs trĭb′yŏŏ tē′), *n.* *Law.* a person who shares in a decedent's estate.

dis·tri·bu·tion (dĭs′trə bū′shən), *n.* **1.** act of distributing. **2.** state or manner of being distributed. **3.** arrangement; classification. **4.** that which is distributed. **5.** the places where things of any particular category occur: *the distribution of coniferous forests in the world.* **6.** *Econ.* **a.** the division of the aggregate income of any society among its members, or among the factors of production. **b.** the system of dispersing goods throughout a community. **7.** *Statistics.* a set of values or measurements of a set of elements, each measurement being associated with an element. **—dis′tri·bu′tion·al,** *adj.*

dis·tri·bu·tion curve, *Statistics.* the curve or line of a graph whose axes or data are based upon a specific frequency distribution. See **frequency distribution.**

dis·trib·u·tive (dĭs trĭb′yə tĭv), *adj.* **1.** that distributes; characterized by or pertaining to distribution. **2.** *Gram.* treating the members of a group individually,

as the adjectives *each* and *every.* **3.** *Logic.* (of a term) distributed in a given proposition. *—n.* **4.** a distributive word or expression. **—dis·trib′u·tive·ly,** *adv.* **—dis·trib′u·tive·ness,** *n.*

dis·trib·u·tor (dĭs trĭb′yə tər), *n.* **1.** one who or that which distributes. **2.** *Com.* one engaged in the general distribution or marketing of some article or class of goods. **3.** *Mach.* a device in a multicylinder engine which distributes the igniting voltage to the spark plugs in a definite sequence. Also, **dis·trib′u·ter.**

dis·trict (dĭs′trĭkt), *n.* **1.** a division of territory, as of a country, state, county, etc., marked off for administrative, electoral, or other purposes. **2.** a region or locality. *—v.t.* **3.** to divide into districts. [t. ML: s. *districtus* territory under jurisdiction, special use of L *districtus,* pp., constrained]

district at·tor·ney, an officer who acts as attorney for the people or government within a specified district.

district coun·cil, *Brit.* a unit of local government.

district court, *U.S. Law.* **1.** (in many States) the court of general jurisdiction. **2.** the federal trial court sitting in each district of the United States.

District of Co·lum·bia, a federal area in the E United States, on the Potomac, coextensive with the federal capital, Washington: governed by Congress. 763,957 pop. (1960); 69 sq. mi. *Abbr.:* D. C.

Dis·tri·to Fe·de·ral (dĕs trē′tŏ fĕ′dĕ räl′), Spanish name of Federal District. *Abbr.:* D.F.

dis·trust (dĭs trŭst′), *v.t.* **1.** to feel distrust of; regard with doubt or suspicion. *—n.* **2.** lack of trust; doubt; suspicion. **—dis·trust′er,** *n.* **—Syn. 2.** See **suspicion.**

dis·trust·ful (dĭs trŭst′fəl), *adj.* full of distrust; doubtful; suspicious. **—dis·trust′ful·ly,** *adv.* **—dis·trust′ful·ness,** *n.*

dis·turb (dĭs tûrb′), *v.t.* **1.** to interrupt the quiet, rest, or peace of. **2.** to interfere with; interrupt; hinder. **3.** to throw into commotion or disorder; agitate; disorder; disarrange; unsettle. **4.** to perplex; trouble. [t. L: s. *disturbāre* throw into disorder, disturb] **—dis·turb′er,** *n.* **—dis·turb′ing·ly,** *adv.*

dis·turb·ance (dĭs tûr′bəns), *n.* **1.** act of disturbing. **2.** state of being disturbed. **3.** an instance of this; a commotion. **4.** something that disturbs. **5.** an outbreak of disorder; a breach of public peace. **6.** *Geol.* a mountain-making crustal movement of moderate intensity and somewhat restricted in geographic extent. **—Syn. 2.** perturbation. See **agitation. 5.** confusion, tumult, riot. See **disorder.**

di·sul·fate (dī sŭl′fāt), *n.* **1.** *Chem.* a salt of pyrosulfuric acid, as *sodium disulfate,* Na₂S₂O₇. See pyro-. **2.** bisulfate. Also, **di·sul′phate.** [f. DI-¹ + SULFATE]

di·sul·fide (dī sŭl′fīd, -fĭd), *n.* *Chem.* a sulfide containing two atoms of sulfur, as *carbon disulfide,* CS₂. Also, **di·sul′phide.**

di·sul·fu·ric (dī′sŭl fyŏŏr′ĭk), *n.* *Chem.* pyrosulfuric. See pyro-. Also, **di′sul·phu′ric.**

dis·un·ion (dĭs ūn′yən), *n.* **1.** severance of union; separation; disjunction. **2.** lack of union; dissension.

dis·un·ion·ist (dĭs ūn′yən ĭst), *n.* *U.S. Pol.* (during the Civil War period) an advocate of the disruption of the U.S. **—dis·un′ion·ism,** *n.*

dis·u·nite (dĭs′ū nīt′), *v.,* **-nited, -niting.** *—v.t.* **1.** to sever the union of; separate; disjoin. **2.** to set at variance, or alienate. *—v.i.* **3.** to part; fall asunder.

dis·u·ni·ty (dĭs ū′nə tĭ), *n., pl.* **-ties.** lack of unity.

dis·use (*n.* dĭs ūs′; *v.* dĭs ūz′), *n., v.,* **-used, -using.** *—n.* **1.** discontinuance of use or practice. *—v.t.* **2.** to cease to use.

dis·u·til·i·ty (dĭs′ū tĭl′ə tĭ), *n.* the quality of causing inconvenience or harm; injuriousness.

dis·val·ue (dĭs văl′ū), *v.t.,* **-ued, -uing.** *Rare.* to depreciate; disparage.

dis·syl·la·ble (dĭ sĭl′ə bəl), *n.* a word of two syllables, as *virtue.* [t. L: m. s. *disyllabus,* t. Gk.: m. *disýllabos.* See SYLLABLE] **—dis·yl·lab·ic** (dĭs′ĭ lăb′ĭk), *adj.*

dis·yoke (dĭs yōk′), *v.t.,* **-yoked, -yoking.** to free from or as from a yoke.

di·tat De·us (dī′tăt dē′əs), *Latin.* God enriches (motto of Arizona).

ditch (dĭch), *n.* **1.** a long, narrow hollow made in the earth by digging, as one for draining or irrigating land; a trench. **2.** any open passage or trench, as a natural channel or waterway. *—v.t.* **3.** to dig a ditch or ditches in. **4.** to throw into or as into a ditch, as a railroad train. **5.** *Slang.* to get rid of; get away from. *—v.i.* **6.** *Slang.* to abandon a disabled plane. [ME *dich,* OE *dīc,* c. G *teich.* See DIKE] **—ditch′er,** *n.*

di·the·ism (dī′thē ĭz′əm), *n.* *Relig.* **1.** the doctrine of, or belief in, two supreme gods. **2.** belief in the existence of two independent antagonistic principles, one good and the other evil. [f. DI-¹ + s. Gk. *theós* god + ISM] **—di′the·ist,** *n.* **—di′the·is′tic,** *adj.*

dith·er (dĭth′ər), *n.* **1.** a trembling; vibration. **2.** *Colloq.* a state of trembling excitement or fear. *—v.i.* **3.** *Chiefly Dial.* to tremble with excitement or fear. [var. of *didder,* ME *diddir;* orig. obscure. Cf. DODDER]

di·thi·on·ous (dī′thī ŏn′əs, dĭ′th′Ī-), *adj.* *Chem.* hyposulfurous. [f. DI-¹ + m. Gk. *theîon* sulfur + -OUS]

dith·y·ramb (dĭth′ə răm′, -răm′b), *n.* **1.** a Greek choral song of vehement or wild character and usually irregular in form, orig. in honor of Dionysus or Bacchus.

---

2. any poem or other composition having similar characteristics. [t. L: s. *dīthyrambus*, t. Gk.: m. *dīthýrambos*]

dith·y·ram·bic (dĭth'/ə răm'/bĭk), *adj.* **1.** of, pertaining to, or of the nature of a dithyramb. **2.** wildly irregular in form. **3.** wildly enthusiastic.

Dit·mars (dĭt'/märz), *n.* Raymond Lee, 1876–1942, U. S. zoölogist and author.

dit·ta·ny (dĭt'/ə nĭ), *n., pl.* **-nies. 1.** a labiate plant, *Origanum dictamnus* (dittany of Crete), formerly in high repute for its alleged medicinal virtues. **2.** a labiate plant, *Cunila origanoides*, of North America, bearing clusters of purplish flowers. **3.** a rutaceous plant, *Dictamnus albus*, cultivated for its showy flowers. [ME *dittonye*, der. OF *ditan*, g. L *dictamnus*, t. Gk.: m. *dίktamnon*, said to be so called from Mount Dicte in Crete, where it abounded]

dit·tied (dĭt'/ĭd), *adj.* composed or sung as a ditty.

dit·to (dĭt'/ō), *n., pl.* **-tos,** *adv., v..* **-toed, -toing.** —*n.* **1.** the aforesaid; the same (used in accounts, lists, etc., to avoid repetition. *Symbol:* "; *abbr.:* do. **2.** the same thing repeated. **3.** *Colloq.* a duplicate or copy. —*adv.* **4.** as already stated; likewise. —*v.t.* **5.** to duplicate; copy. [t. L.: said, aforesaid, g. L *dictus*, pp., said]

dit·tog·ra·phy (dĭ tŏg'/rə fĭ), *n. Paleog.* **1.** unintentional repetition of one or more symbols in writing. **2.** the resulting passage or reading. [f. Gk. *dittó(s)* double + -GRAPHY] —**dit·to·graph·ic** (dĭt'/ə grăf'/ĭk), *adj.*

ditto marks, two small marks (") indicating the repetition of something, usually placed beneath the thing repeated.

dit·ty (dĭt'/ĭ), *n., pl.* **-ties. 1.** a poem intended to be sung. **2.** a short, simple song. [ME *dite*, t. OF, g. L *dictātum* thing composed or recited]

ditty bag, a bag used by sailors to hold sewing implements and other necessaries.

ditty box, a small box used like a ditty bag.

di·u·re·sis (dī'/yŏŏ rē'/sĭs), *n. Pathol.* excessive discharge of urine. [NL, f. Gk.: di- DI-² + *oúrēsis* urination]

di·u·ret·ic (dī'/yŏŏ rĕt'/ĭk), *Med. adj.* **1.** increasing the volume of the urine, as a medicinal substance. —*n.* **2.** a diuretic medicine or agent. [t. LL: s. *diūrēticus* promoting urine, t. Gk.: m. *diourētikόs*]

di·ur·nal (dī ûr'/nəl), *adj.* **1.** of or pertaining to each day; daily. **2.** of or belonging to the daytime. **3.** *Bot.* showing a periodic alteration of condition with day and night, as certain flowers which open by day and close by night. **4.** active by day, as certain birds and insects. —*n.* **5.** *Liturgy.* a service book containing the offices for the day hours of prayer. **6.** *Archaic.* a diary. **7.** *Archaic.* a daily or other newspaper. [t. LL: s. *diurnālis* daily] —**di·ur'nal·ly,** *adv.*

diurnal parallax. See **parallax** (def. 2).

div., **1.** divided. **2.** dividend. **3.** division. **4.** divisor.

di·va (dē'/vä), *n., pl.* **-vas, -ve** (-vĕ). a distinguished female singer; a prima donna. [t. It., t. L: goddess]

di·va·gate (dī'/və gāt/), *v.i.* **-gated, -gating. 1.** to wander; stray. **2.** to digress in speech. [t. L: m. s. *dīvagātus*, pp., having wandered] —**di'va·ga'tion,** *n.*

di·va·lent (dī vā'/lənt), *adj. Chem.* having a valence of two, as the ferrous ion, Fe⁺⁺.

di·van (dī'/văn, dī văn'), *n.* **1.** a sofa or couch. **2.** a long, cushioned seat against a wall, as in Oriental countries. **3.** a council of state in Turkey and other Oriental countries. **4.** any council, committee, or commission. **5.** (in the Orient) **a.** a council chamber, judgment hall, audience chamber, or bureau of state. **b.** a large building used for some public purpose, as a custom house. **6.** a smoking room, as in connection with a tobacco shop. [t. Turk., t. Pers.: m. *dēvān* (now *dīwān*)]

di·var·i·cate (*v.* dī văr'/ə kāt/, dī-; *adj.* dī văr'/ə kĭt, -kāt/, dī-), *v.,* **-cated, -cating,** *adj.* —*v.i.* **1.** to spread apart; branch; diverge. **2.** *Bot., Zool.* to branch at a wide angle. —*adj.* **3.** spread apart; widely divergent. **4.** *Bot., Zool.* branching at a wide angle. [t. L: m. s. *dīvāricātus*, pp., spread apart] —**di·var'i·cate·ly,** *adv.* —**di·var'i·ca'tion,** *n.* —**di·var'i·ca'tor,** *n.*

dive (dīv), *v.,* **dived** or *U.S. Colloq.* and *Brit. Dial.* **dove; dived; diving;** *n.* —*v.i.* **1.** to plunge, esp. head first, as into water. **2.** to go below the surface of the water, as a submarine. **3.** to plunge deeply. **4.** *Aeron.* (of an airplane) to plunge downward at a greater angle than when gliding. **5.** to penetrate suddenly into anything, as with the hand. **6.** to dart. **7.** to enter deeply into (a subject, business, etc.). —*n.* **8.** act of diving. **9.** *Colloq.* a disreputable place, as for drinking, gambling, etc. [ME *dive(n)* dive, dip, OE *dyfan*, v.t., dip (causative of *dūfan*, v.i., dive, sink), c. Icel. *dyfa* dip]

dive bomber, an airplane of the pursuit type which drops its bombs while diving at the target.

dive bombing, *Mil.* the releasing of a bomb load just before the bomber pulls out of a dive towards the target at an angle such that the pilot sights through his gun sights.

div·er (dī'/vər), *n.* **1.** one who or that which dives. **2.** one who makes a business of diving, as for pearl oysters, to examine sunken vessels, etc. **3.** any of various birds that habitually dive, as loons, grebes, etc.

di·verge (dī vûrj'/), *v.i.,* **-verged, -verging. 1.** to move or lie in different directions from a common point; branch off. **2.** to differ in opinion or character; deviate. [t. NL: m.s. *dīvergere,* f. L dī- DIS-¹ + *vergere* incline, VERGE²] —**Syn. 2.** See **deviate.**

di·ver·gence (dī vûr'/jəns, dĭ-), *n.* **1.** act, fact, or amount of diverging. **2.** *Meteorol.* a condition brought about by a net flow of air from a given region.

di·ver·gen·cy (dī vûr'/jən sĭ, dĭ-), *n., pl.* **-cies.** divergence.

di·ver·gent (dī vûr'/jənt, dĭ-), *adj.* **1.** diverging; deviating. **2.** pertaining to divergence. —**di·ver'gent·ly,** *adv.*

di·vers (dī'/vərz), *adj.* several; sundry (sometimes used pronominally): *divers of them.* [ME, t. OF, g. L *dīversus*, pp., lit., turned different ways]

di·verse (dī vûrs'/, dĭ-, dī'/vûrs), *adj.* **1.** of a different kind, form, character, etc.; unlike. **2.** of various kinds or forms; multiform. [var. of DIVERS, but now assoc. more directly with L *dīversus*] —**di·verse'ly,** *adv.* —**di·verse'ness,** *n.* —**Syn. 2.** See **various.**

di·ver·si·fied (dī vûr'/sə fīd/, dĭ-), *adj.* **1.** distinguished by various forms, or by a variety of objects. **2.** varied; distributed among several types: *diversified investments.*

di·ver·si·form (dī vûr'/sə fôrm/, dĭ-), *adj.* differing in form; of various forms. [f. s. L *dīversus* various + -(I)FORM]

di·ver·si·fy (dī vûr'/sə fī/, dĭ-), *v.t.,* **-fied, -fying. 1.** to make diverse, as in form or character; give variety or diversity to; variegate. **2.** to vary (investments); invest in different types of (securities). [t. F: m. *diversifier,* t. ML: m.s. *dīversificāre,* f. L *dīversi-* diverse + *-ficāre* make] —**di·ver'si·fi·ca'tion,** *n.*

di·ver·sion (dī vûr'/zhən, -shən, dĭ-), *n.* **1.** act of diverting or turning aside, as from a course. **2.** *Brit.* a detour around a stoppage in a road. **3.** distraction from business, care, etc.; recreation; entertainment; amusement; a pastime. **4.** *Mil.* a feint intended to draw off attention from the point of main attack.

di·ver·si·ty (dī vûr'/sə tĭ, dĭ-), *n., pl.* **-ties. 1.** the state or fact of being diverse; difference; unlikeness. **2.** variety; multiformity. **3.** a point of difference.

di·vert (dī vûrt'/, dĭ-), *v.t.* **1.** to turn aside or from a path or course; deflect. **2.** *Brit.* to set (traffic) on a detour. **3.** to draw off to a different object, purpose, etc. **4.** to distract from serious occupation; entertain or amuse. [t. OF: s. *divertir,* t. L: m. *dīvertere* turn aside, separate] —**di·vert'er,** *n.* —**di·vert'i·ble,** *adj.* —**Syn. 4.** See **amuse.**

di·ver·tic·u·lum (dī'/vər tĭk'/yə ləm), *n., pl.* **-la** (-lə). *Anat.* a blind tubular sac or process, branching off from a canal or cavity. [L: byway] —**di·ver·tic'u·lar,** *adj.*

di·ver·ti·men·to (dē vĕr'/tē mĕn'/tō), *n., pl.* **-ti** (-tē). *Music.* an instrumental composition in several movements, light and diverting in character, similar to a serenade. [It.]

di·vert·ing (dī vûr'/tĭng, dĭ-), *adj.* that diverts; entertaining; amusing. —**di·vert'ing·ly,** *adv.*

di·ver·tisse·ment (dē vĕr tēs män'/), *n.* **1.** a diversion or entertainment. **2.** *Music.* a divertimento. **3.** a short ballet or other performance given between or in the course of acts or longer pieces. **4.** a series of such performances. [F, der. *divertiss-,* s. of *divertir* DIVERT]

di·ver·tive (dī vûr'/tĭv, dĭ-), *adj.* diverting; amusing.

Di·ves (dī'/vēz), *n.* **1.** *Bible.* the rich man of the parable in Luke 16:19–31. **2.** any rich man. [L: rich, rich man]

di·vest (dī vĕst'/, dĭ-), *v.t.* **1.** to strip of clothing, etc.; disrobe. **2.** to strip or deprive of anything; dispossess. **3.** *Law.* to take away or alienate (property, etc.). [t. ML: s. *dīvestīre,* var. of *disvestīre* (Latinization of OF *desvestir*)] —**Syn. 2.** See **strip².**

di·ves·ti·ble (dī vĕs'/tə bəl, dĭ-), *adj.* capable of being divested, as an estate in land.

di·vest·i·ture (dī vĕs'/tə chər, dĭ-), *n.* **1.** act of divesting. **2.** state of being divested. Also, **di·vest'ment, di·ves·ture** (dī vĕs'/chər, dĭ-).

di·vid·a·ble (dī vī'/də bəl), *adj.* divisible.

di·vide (dī vīd'/), *v.,* **-vided, -viding,** *n.* —*v.t.* **1.** to separate into parts. **2.** to separate or part from each other or from something else; sunder; cut off. **3.** to deal out in parts; apportion; share. **4.** to separate in opinion or feeling; cause to disagree. **5.** to distinguish the kinds of; classify. **6.** *Math.* **a.** to separate into equal parts by the process of division. **b.** to be a divisor of, without a remainder. **c.** to graduate (a rule, etc.). **7.** *Brit. Govt.* to separate (a legislature, etc.) into two groups in ascertaining the vote on a question. —*v.i.* **8.** to become divided or separated. **9.** to share something with others. **10.** *Brit. Govt.* to vote by separating into two groups. —*n.* **11.** *Colloq.* act of dividing; a division. **12.** *Phys. Geog.* the line or zone separating the flow of water to either of two adjacent streams or drainage basins. [ME *divide(n),* t. L: m. *dīvidere* force asunder, cleave, part, distribute] —**Syn. 1.** See **separate.**

di·vid·ed (dī vī'/dĭd), *adj.* **1.** separated; separate; disunited; shared. **2.** *Bot.* (of a leaf) cut into distinct portions by incisions extending to the midrib or the base.

di·vi·de et im·pe·ra (dī'/və dē/ ĕt ĭm'/pə rä), *Latin.* divide and rule (political maxim of Machiavelli, etc.).

div·i·dend (dĭv'/ə dĕnd/), *n.* **1.** *Math.* a number to be divided by another number (the divisor). **2.** *Law.* a sum out of an insolvent estate to be divided among the creditors. **3.** *Finance.* **a.** a pro-rata share in an amount to be distributed. **b.** a sum of money paid to shareholders of a corporation out of earnings. **4.** *Insurance.* a profit distribution by a company to an assured. **5.** a share of anything divided. [t. L: s. *dīvidendum* (thing) to be divided, neut. ger. of *dīvidere* DIVIDE]

di·vid·er (dĭ vī′dər), n. 1. one who or that which divides. 2. (pl.) a pair of compasses as used for dividing lines, measuring, etc.

div·i·div·i (dĭv′ĭ dĭv′ĭ), n. 1. a shrub or small tree, *Caesalpinia coriaria*, of tropical America, the astringent pods of which are much used in tanning and dyeing. 2. the related species *C. tinctoria*. 3. the pods of either plant. [native Carib or Galibi name]

di·vid·u·al (dĭ vĭj′ṓō əl), adj. 1. divisible or divided. 2. separate; distinct. 3. distributed; shared. [f. s. L *dividuus* divisible + -AL¹] —**di·vid·u·al·ly**, adv.

div·i·na·tion (dĭv′ə nā′shən), n. 1. the discovering of what is obscure or the foretelling of future events, as by supernatural means. 2. augury; a prophecy. 3. instinctive prevision. [t. L: s. *divinatio*, der. *divinare* DIVINE, v.] —**di·vin·a·to·ry** (dĭ vĭn′ə tŏr′ĭ), adj.

di·vine (dĭ vīn′), adj., n., v., -vined, -vining. —adj. 1. of or pertaining to a god, esp. the Supreme Being. 2. addressed or appropriated to God; religious; sacred. 3. proceeding from God. 4. godlike; characteristic of or befitting a deity. 5. heavenly; celestial. 6. being a god, or God. 7. pertaining to divinity or theology. 8. of superhuman or surpassing excellence. —n. 9. one versed in divinity; a theologian. 10. a priest or clergyman. —v.t. 11. to discover or declare (something obscure or future), as by supernatural means; prophesy. 12. to perceive by intuition or insight; conjecture. 13. *Obs.* or *Archaic.* to portend. —v.i. 14. to use or practice divination; prophesy. 15. to have perception by intuition or insight; conjecture. [ME; L: m. s. *divinus*; r. ME *devine*, t. OF] —**di·vine′ly**, adv. —**di·vine′ness**, n.

di·vin·er (dĭ vī′nər), n. one who divines; a soothsayer; a prophet; a conjecturer.

divine right of kings, the right to rule derived directly from God, not from the consent of the people.

diving beetle, any of the predacious beetles that constitute the family *Dytiscidae*, adapted for swimming and diving.

diving bell, a hollow vessel filled with air under pressure, in which persons may work under water.

diving suit, a watertight garment, consisting of a rubber or metal body covering and a helmet with an air-supply line attached, worn by divers.

divining rod, a rod used in divining, esp. a forked stick, commonly of hazel, supposed to be useful in locating spots where water, metal, etc., is underground.

di·vin·i·ty (dĭ vĭn′ə tĭ), n., pl. -ties. 1. the quality of being divine; divine nature. 2. deity; godhood. 3. a divine being, or god. 4. **the Divinity**, the Deity. 5. a deity below God but above man. 6. the science of divine things; theology. 7. godlike character; supreme excellence. 8. a fluffy white confection made usually of sugar, corn syrup, egg whites and flavoring, often with nuts.

div·i·nize (dĭv′ə nīz), v.t., -nized, -nizing. to make divine; deify. —**div′i·ni·za′tion**, n.

di·vis·i·bil·i·ty (dĭ vĭz′ə bĭl′ə tĭ), n. *Math.* the capacity of being exactly divided, without remainder.

di·vis·i·ble (dĭ vĭz′ə bəl), adj. capable of being divided. —**di·vis′i·ble·ness**, n. —**di·vis′i·bly**, adv.

di·vi·sion (dĭ vĭzh′ən), n. 1. act of dividing; partition. 2. state of being divided. 3. *Math.* the operation inverse to multiplication; the finding of a quantity (the quotient) which, when multiplied by a given quantity (the divisor) gives another given quantity (the dividend). 4. something that divides; a dividing line or mark. 5. one of the parts into which a thing is divided; a section. 6. separation by difference of opinion or feeling; disagreement; dissension. 7. *Govt.* the separation of a legislature, etc., into two groups, in taking a vote. 8. one of the parts into which a country or an organization is divided for political, administrative, judicial, military, or other purposes. 9. *Mil.* a major administrative and tactical unit, larger than a regiment or brigade, and smaller than a corps. It is usually commanded by a major general. 10. *Zool.* any subdivision of a classificatory group or category. [t. L: s. *divisio*; r. ME *devisioun*, t. OF] —**di·vi′sion·al**, adj. —Syn. 1. separation, apportionment, allotment, distribution. DIVISION, PARTITION suggest the operation of dividing into parts or of one part from another. DIVISION usually means little more than the marking off or separation of a whole into parts. PARTITION often adds the idea of sharing, of an allotting or assigning of parts following division: *partition of an estate, of a country.*

division sign, the symbol (÷) placed between two expressions, denoting division of the first by the second.

di·vi·sive (dĭ vī′sĭv), adj. 1. forming or expressing division or distribution. 2. creating division or discord. —**di·vi′sive·ly**, adv. —**di·vi′sive·ness**, n.

di·vi·sor (dĭ vī′zər), n. *Math.* 1. a number by which another number (the dividend) is divided. 2. a number contained in another given number a certain number of times, without a remainder.

di·vorce (dĭ vōrs′), n., v., -vorced, -vorcing. —n. 1. *Law.* a. an absolute legal dissolution of the marriage bond (**absolute divorce**). b. a judicial separation of man and wife, or termination of cohabitation, without dissolution of the marriage bond (**limited divorce** or **divorce from bed and board**). c. a judicial declaration of the nullity of a supposed marriage. 2. any formal separation of man and wife according to established custom, as among uncivilized tribes. 3. a complete separation of any kind. —v.t. 4. to separate by divorce; put away (one's husband or wife) by divorce. 5. to

separate; cut off. [ME *divors*, t. F: m. *divorce*, g. L *divortium* separation, dissolution] —**di·vorce′a·ble**, adj. —**di·vorc′er**, n.

di·vor·cé (dĭ vōr′sā), n. a divorced man. [t. F, prop. pp. of *divorcer*] —**di·vor′cée**, n. fem.

di·vor·cee (dĭ vōr′sē), n. a divorced person.

di·vorce·ment (dĭ vōrs′mənt), n. divorce.

div·ot (dĭv′ət), n. 1. *Golf.* a piece of turf cut out with a club in making a stroke. 2. *Scot.* a piece of turf; a sod.

di·vul·gate (dĭ vŭl′gāt), v.t. -gated, -gating. to make publicly known; publish. [t. L: m. s. *divulgatus*, pp., divulged] —**di·vul′gat·er**, **di·vul′ga·tor**, n. —**div·ul·ga·tion** (dĭv′əl gā′shən), n.

di·vulge (dĭ vŭlj′), v.t., -vulged, -vulging. to disclose or reveal (something private, secret, or previously unknown). [t. L: m. s. *divulgare* make common] —**di·vulge′ment**, n. —**di·vulg′er**, n. —Syn. 1. See reveal.

di·vul·gence (dĭ vŭl′jəns), n. a divulging.

di·vul·sion (dĭ vŭl′shən), n. a tearing asunder; violent separation. [t. F, t. L: s. *divulsio*] —**di·vul·sive** (dĭ vŭl′sĭv), adj.

di·wan (dĭ wän′, -wŏn′), n. dewan. [see DIVAN]

Dix·ie (dĭk′sĭ), n. 1. Also, **Dixie Land**. the Southern States of the United States. 2. any of several songs with this name, esp. the minstrel song (1859) by D. D. Emmett, popular as a Confederate war song. [orig. uncert.]

Dix·ie·crat (dĭk′sĭ krăt), n. a member of a minority in the Democratic party consisting of Democrats living in the Southern States. Under the name of the States Rights party, the Dixiecrats nominated an independent ticket in the presidential election of 1948. [f. DIXIE + (DEMO)CRAT]

Dix·ie·land (dĭk′sĭ lănd′), n. *Jazz.* a style of composition and performance characterized by vigorous improvisation.

dix·it (dĭk′sĭt), n. an utterance. [t. L: he has said

Di·yar·be·kir (dē yär′bĕ kĭr′), n. a city in SE Turkey, on the Tigris river. 63,180 (prelim. 1955). Also, **Diarbekr**.

diz·en (dĭz′ən, dī′zən), v.t. to deck with clothes or finery; bedizen. [akin to *dis-* in DISTAFF] —**diz′en·ment**, n.

diz·zy (dĭz′ĭ), adj., -zier, -ziest, v., -zied, -zying. —adj. 1. affected with a sensation of whirling, with tendency to fall; giddy; vertiginous. 2. bewildered; confused. 3. causing giddiness: *a dizzy height.* 4. heedless; thoughtless. 5. *Colloq.* foolish or stupid. —v.t. 6. to make dizzy. [ME and OE *dysig* foolish, c. LG *düsig* stupefied] —**diz′zi·ly**, adv. —**diz′zi·ness**, n.

Dja·kar·ta (jə kär′tə), n. a seaport in and the capital of Indonesia, on the NW coast of Java. 1,800,000 (est. 1951). Also, **Jacarta**, **Jakarta**. Formerly, **Batavia**.

Dji·bou·ti (jē bōō′tē), n. a seaport in and the capital of French Somaliland, on the Gulf of Aden. 31,000 (est. 1954). Also, **Jibuti**.

Djok·ja·kar·ta (jŏk′yä kär′tə), n. Dutch name of **Jogjakarta**.

dl., deciliter.

D. Lit., (L *Doctor Literarum*) Doctor of Literature.

D. Litt., (L *Doctor Litterarum*) Doctor of Letters.

D.L.S., Doctor of Library Science.

dm., decimeter.

D. Mus., Doctor of Music.

Dne·pro·dzer·zhinsk (dnĕ′prŏ jĕr zĭnsk′), n. a city in SW Soviet Union, on the Dnieper. 163,000 (est. 1956).

Dne·pro·pe·trovsk (dnĕ′prŏ pĕ trôfsk′), n. a city in the SW Soviet Union, on the Dnieper. 576,000 (est. 1956). Formerly, **Ekaterinoslav**.

Dnie·per (nē′pər), n. a river in the W Soviet Union, flowing S to the Black Sea. ab. 1400 mi. Russian, **Dne·pr** (dnē′pər).

Dnies·ter (nē′stər), n. a river flowing from the Carpathian Mountains in the SW Soviet Union SE to the Black Sea. ab. 800 mi. Russian, **Dnes·tr** (dnĕs′tər). Rumanian, **Nistru**.

do¹ (dōō), v., pres. sing. 1 do, 2 do or (*Archaic*) doest or dost, 3 does or (*Archaic*) doeth or doth; pl. do; pt. did; pp. done; ppr. doing; n. —v.t. 1. to perform (acts, duty, penance, a problem, a part, etc.). 2. to execute (a piece or amount of work, etc.). 3. to accomplish; finish. 4. to put forth; exert: *do your best.* 5. to be the cause of (good, harm, credit, etc.); bring about; effect. 6. to render (homage, justice, etc.). 7. to deal with (anything) as the case may require: *to do* (cook) *meat, do* (wash) *the dishes.* 8. to cover; traverse: *we did thirty miles today.* 9. *Slang.* to cheat or swindle (often fol. by *out of*). 10. to serve; suffice for: *this will do us for the present.* 11. *Colloq.* to provide; prepare: *we do lunches here.* 12. fol. in, *Slang.* a. to ruin. b. to kill; murder. 13. **do up, a.** to wrap and tie up. **b.** to comb out and pin up (hair). **c.** to renovate; launder. **d.** *Colloq.* to tire out. —v.i. 14. to act, esp. effectively; be in action. 15. to behave or proceed (wisely, etc.). 16. to get along, or fare (well or ill); manage (with, without, etc.). 17. to be as to health: *how do you do?* 18. to serve or be satisfactory, as for the purpose; suffice, or be enough: *will this do?* 19. to deal with; treat (fol. by *by*): *to do well by a man.* 20. **do away with**, to put an end to; abolish. 21. **do for, a.** to accomplish defeat, ruin, death, etc., of. **b.** *Brit.* to cook and keep house for. **c.** to provide or manage for. 22. **make do**, to get along with what one has. 23. (used without special meaning in interrogative, negative, and inverted constructions; in imperatives

with *you* or *thou* expressed, and occasionally as a metrical expedient in verse): *do you think so? I don't agree.* 24. (used to lend emphasis to a principal verb): *do come!* 25. (used to avoid repetition of a verb or full verb expression): *I think as you do. Did you see him? I did.* —*n.* 26. *Brit. Dial.* ado; action; work. 27. *Slang.* a swindle. 28. *Colloq.* a festivity or treat: *we're having a big do next week.* [ME; OE *dōn*, c. D *doen*, G *tun*; akin to L *-dere*, Gk. *tithēnai*]
—**Syn.** 3. Do, ACCOMPLISH, ACHIEVE mean to bring some action to a conclusion. Do is the general word, carrying no implication of success or failure: *he did a great deal of hard work.* ACCOMPLISH and ACHIEVE both have a connotation of successful completion of an undertaking. ACCOMPLISH emphasizes attaining a desired purpose through effort, skill, and perseverance: *to accomplish what one has hoped for.* ACHIEVE emphasizes accomplishing something important, excellent, or great: *to achieve a beneficial service for mankind.*

do² (dō), *n. Music.* 1. the syllable used for the first tone or keynote of a diatonic scale. 2. (sometimes) the tone C. See **ut** and **sol-fa.** [see GAMUT]

do., ditto.

D.O., Doctor of Osteopathy.

D.O.A., dead on arrival.

do·a·ble (dōō′ə bəl), *adj.* that may be done.

do-all (dōō′ôl′), *n.* a factotum.

doat (dōt), *v.i.* dote.

dob·ber (dŏb′ər), *n. Local U.S.* a float for a fishing line; bob. [t. D]

dob·bin (dŏb′ĭn), *n.* 1. a name for a horse, esp. a quiet, plodding horse for farm work or family use. 2. a horse of this kind. [var. of *Robin,* familiar var. of *Robert,* man's name]

dob·by (dŏb′ĭ), *n., pl.* **-bies.** *Dial.* a sprite or goblin.

Do·ber·man pin·scher (dō′bər mən pĭn′shər), a breed of large smooth-coated terriers, usually black-and-tan or brown, with long forelegs, and wide hindquarters.

do·bie (dō′bĭ), *n., pl.* **-bies.** adobe.

do·bra (dō′brə), *n.* any of several former Portuguese coins, esp. a gold coin first issued by King John V and having twice the value of the johannes. [t. Pg., der. L *duplus* double]

Doberman pinscher
(24 to 27 in. high
at the shoulder)

Do·bru·ja (dō′brōō jə; *Bulg.* dô′brōō jä′), *n.* a region in SE Rumania and NE Bulgaria, between the Danube and the Black Sea. Rumanian part, 531,317 pop. (est. 1943); 6120 sq. mi. (1946); Bulgarian part, 356,730 pop. (1946); 2970 sq. mi. Rumanian, **Do·bro·gea** (dō′brô jä′).

dob·son (dŏb′sən), *n.* 1. a large, membranous-winged insect, *Corydalis cornutus,* possessing greatly elongated and hornlike mandibles. 2. its large aquatic larva, the hellgrammite. [orig. uncert.]

Dob·son (dŏb′sən), *n.* (Henry) **Austin,** 1840–1921, British poet, biographer, and essayist.

dobson fly, any insect of the family *Corydalidae* (order *Megaloptera*), as the dobson.

doc., *pl.* **docs.** document.

do·cent (dō′sənt; *Ger.* dō tsĕnt′), *n.* 1. Privatdocent. 2. a college or university lecturer. [t. L: s. *docens,* ppr., teaching. Cf. G *privatdocent*] —**do′cent·ship′,** *n.*

doc·ile (dŏs′əl; *Brit.* dō′sīl), *adj.* 1. readily trained or taught; teachable. 2. easily managed or handled; tractable. [late ME, t. L: m. s. *docilis*] —**doc′ile·ly,** *adv.* —**do·cil·i·ty** (dō sĭl′ə tĭ, dŏ-), *n.*

dock¹ (dŏk), *n.* 1. a wharf. 2. the space or waterway between two piers or wharves, as for receiving a ship while in port. 3. such a waterway, enclosed or open, together with the surrounding piers, wharves, etc. 4. See **dry dock.** —*v.t.* 5. to bring into a dock; lay up in a dock. 6. to put into a dry dock for repairs, cleaning, or painting. —*v.i.* 7. to come or go into a dock or dry dock. [cf. D *dok;* orig. uncert.]

dock² (dŏk), *n.* 1. the solid or fleshy part of an animal's tail, as distinguished from the hair. 2. the part of a tail left after cutting or clipping. —*v.t.* 3. to cut off the end of (a tail, etc.). 4. to deduct a part from (wages, etc.). 5. to cut short the tail of. 6. to deduct from the wages of. [ME *dok,* OE *-docca,* in *fingerdocca* finger muscle]

dock³ (dŏk), *n.* the place in a courtroom where a prisoner is placed during trial. [cf. Flem. *dok* cage]

dock⁴ (dŏk), *n.* 1. any of various plants of the polygonaceous genus *Rumex,* as *R. obtusifolius* (**bitter dock**) or *R. Acetosa* (**sour dock**), mostly troublesome weeds with long taproots. 2. any of various other plants, mostly coarse weeds. [ME *dokke,* OE *docce,* c. MD *docke*]

dock·age¹ (dŏk′ĭj), *n.* 1. a charge for the use of a dock. 2. docking accommodations. 3. act of docking a vessel. [f. DOCK¹ + -AGE]

dock·age² (dŏk′ĭj), *n.* 1. curtailment; deduction, as from wages. 2. waste material in wheat and other grains which is easily removed. [f. DOCK² + -AGE]

dock·er¹ (dŏk′ər), *n. Brit.* a dock laborer; a longshoreman. [f. DOCK¹ + -ER¹]

dock·er² (dŏk′ər), *n.* one who or that which docks, cuts short, or cuts off. [f. DOCK² + -ER¹]

dock·et (dŏk′ĭt), *n., v.,* **-eted, -eting.** —*n.* 1. a list of causes in court for trial, or the names of the parties who

have causes pending. 2. *Chiefly Brit.* an official memorandum or entry of proceedings in a legal cause, or a register of such entries. 3. *U.S.* the list of business to be transacted by court or assembly; the agenda; a list of projects or cases awaiting action. 4. a writing on a letter or document, stating its contents; any statement of particulars attached to a package, etc.; a label or ticket. —*v.t.* 5. Law. to make an abstract or summary of the heads of, as a document; abstract and enter in a book: *judgments regularly docketed.* 6. to endorse (a letter, etc.) with a memorandum. [ME *doket;* orig. obscure]

dock·mack·ie (dŏk′măk ĭ), *n.* a caprifoliaceous shrub, *Viburnum acerifolium,* of North America, with yellowish-white flowers and ovoid, almost black berries. [t. Amer. Ind. (Delaware): m. *dogekumak,* c. Ojibwa *takaiamagad* it is cool]

dock·wal·lop·er (dŏk′wŏl′əp ər), *n. Slang.* a casual laborer about docks or wharves.

dock·yard (dŏk′yärd′), *n.* 1. an enclosure containing docks, shops, warehouses, etc., where ships are repaired, fitted out, and built. 2. *Eng.* a navy yard.

doc·tor (dŏk′tər), *n.* 1. a person licensed to practice medicine, or some branch of medicine; a physician; a surgeon. In England, a surgeon is not called a doctor. 2. a person who has received the highest degree conferred by a faculty of a university. 3. the academic title possessed by such a person, orig. implying qualification to teach, now generally based on at least three years of advanced study and research beyond the bachelor's degree. 4. a man of great learning. 5. *Colloq.* a cook, as on shipboard. 6. any of various mechanical contrivances for particular purposes. 7. a kind of artificial fly for angling, such as silver doctor. 8. *Old Slang.* a false or loaded die. —*v.t.* 9. to treat medicinally. 10. *Colloq.* to repair or mend. 11. *Colloq.* to tamper with; falsify; adulterate. —*v.i.* 12. to practice medicine. 13. to take medicine; receive medical treatment. [t. L: teacher; r. ME *doctour,* t. OF] —**doc′tor·al,** *adj.* —**doc′tor·ship′,** *n.* —**doc·tress** (dŏk′trĭs), (*Rare*) *n.,* *fem.*

doc·tor·ate (dŏk′tər ĭt), *n.* the degree of doctor.

Doctors' Commons, a building in London, at one time the dining hall of the College of Doctors of Civil Law, and later housing ecclesiastical and Admiralty courts which applied primarily civil law.

Doctor s degree, *Colloq.* Ph.D.

doc·tri·naire (dŏk′trə nâr′), 1. one who tries to apply some doctrine or theory without a sufficient regard to practical considerations; an impractical theorist. —*adj.* 2. dogmatic about others' acceptance of one's ideas. 3. theoretic and unpractical. 4. of a doctrinaire. [t. F. der. *doctrine* DOCTRINE] —**doc′tri·nar′ism,** *n.* —**doc′tri·nar′i·an,** *n.*

doc·tri·nal (dŏk′trə nəl; *Brit. also* dŏk trī′nəl), *adj.* of, pertaining to, or concerned with, doctrine. —**doc′tri·nal·ly,** *adv.*

doc·trine (dŏk′trĭn), *n.* 1. a particular principle taught or advocated. 2. that which is taught; teachings collectively. 3. a body or system of teachings relating to a particular subject. [ME, t. F, t. L: m. *doctrina* teaching, learning] —**Syn.** 1. tenet, dogma, theory, precept, belief.

doc·u·ment (*n.* dŏk′yə mənt; *v.* dŏk′yə mĕnt′), *n.* 1. a written or printed paper furnishing information or evidence, a legal or official paper. 2. *Obs.* evidence: proof. —*v.t.* 3. to furnish with documents, evidence, or the like. 4. to support by documentary evidence. 5. *Obs.* to instruct. [ME, t. L: s. *documentum* lesson, example]

doc·u·men·ta·ry (dŏk′yə mĕn′tə rĭ), *adj., n., pl.* **-ries.** —*adj.* 1. Also, **doc·u·men·tal** (dŏk′yə mĕn′təl). pertaining to, consisting of, or derived from documents. —*n.* 2. *Motion Pictures.* a film, usually nonfiction, in which the elements of dramatic conflict are provided by ideas, political or economic forces, etc.

doc·u·men·ta·tion (dŏk′yə mĕn tā′shən), *n.* 1. the use of documentary evidence. 2. a furnishing with documents.

Dodd (dŏd), *n.* **William Edward,** 1869–1940, U.S. historian and diplomat.

dod·der¹ (dŏd′ər), *v.i.* to shake; tremble; totter. [cf. DITHER, TOTTER, etc.]

dod·der² (dŏd′ər), *n.* any of the leafless parasitic plants comprising the genus *Cuscuta,* with yellowish, reddish, or white threadlike stems that twine about clover, flax, etc. [ME *doder,* c. G *dotter*]

dod·dered (dŏd′ərd), *adj.* infirm; feeble.

dod·der·ing (dŏd′ər ĭng), *adj.* that dodders; shaking; tottering; senile.

dodeca-, a word element meaning "twelve." Also, before vowels, **dodec-.** [t. Gk.: m. *dōdeka,* comb. form of *dōdeka*]

do·dec·a·gon (dō dĕk′ə gŏn′, -gən), *n. Geom.* a polygon having twelve angles and twelve sides. [t. Gk.: s. *dōdekágōnon.* See DODECA-, -GON] —**do·de·cag·o·nal** (dō′də kăg′ə nəl), *adj.*

do·dec·a·he·dron (dō′dĕk ə hē′drən), *n., pl.* **-drons, -dra** (-drə). *Geom.* a solid figure having twelve faces. [t. Gk.: m. *dōdekáedron*] —**do′-dec·a·he′dral,** *adj.*

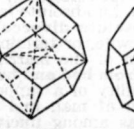

Rhombic   Pentagonal
dodecahedron   dodecahedron

b., blend of, blended; c., cognate with; d., dialect, dialectal; der., derived from; f., formed from; g., going back to; m., modification of; r., replacing; s., stem of; t., taken from; ?, perhaps. See the full key on inside cover.

Do·dec·a·nese Islands (dō·děk'ə·nēs', -něz', dō'-děk ə-), a group of twelve Greek islands in the Aegean, off the SW coast of Turkey: formerly belonging to Italy. 121,480 pop. (1951); 1035 sq. mi.

dodge (dŏj). v. **dodged, dodging,** n. —*v.i.* **1.** to move aside or change position suddenly, as to avoid a blow or to get behind something. **2.** to use evasive methods; prevaricate. —*v.t.* **3.** to elude by a sudden shift of position or by strategy. —*n.* **4.** an act of dodging; a spring aside. **5.** *Colloq.* an ingenious expedient or contrivance; a shifty trick. [orig. uncert.] —**Syn. 2.** equivocate, quibble. **3.** evade, elude.

Dodge City, a city in SW Kansas, on the Arkansas river: it was an important frontier town and railhead on the old Santa Fe route. 13,520 (1960).

dodg·er (dŏj'ər), n. **1.** one who dodges. **2.** a shifty person. **3.** *U.S.* a small handbill. **4.** *Southern U.S.* a corn dodger.

Dodg·son (dŏj'sən), n. **Charles Lutwidge** (lŭt'wĭj), ("*Lewis Carroll*") 1832–98, British mathematician and author of books for children.

do·do (dō'dō). n., pl. **-does, -dos. 1.** a clumsy flightless bird of the genera *Raphus* and *Pezophaps*, about the size of a goose, related to the pigeons, formerly inhabiting the islands of Mauritius, Réunion and Rodriguez, but extinct since the advent of European settlers. **2.** *Colloq.* an old fogy. [t. Pg.: m. *doudo* silly]

Dodo. *Raphus solitarius* (Ab. 3 ft. long)

Do·do·na (dō·dō'nə), n. an ancient town in NW Greece, in Epirus: the site of a famous oracle of Zeus. —**Do·do·nae·an, Do·do·ne·an** (dō'də·nē'ən), adj.

doe (dō), n. the female of the deer, antelope, goat, rabbit, and certain other animals. [ME *do*, OE *dā*. Cf. L *dāma, damma* deer]

Doe (dō), n. **John,** a name referring to an avowedly fictitious person, used esp. in law for the plaintiff in action of ejectment.

do·er (dōō'ər), n. one who or that which does something; a performer; an actor.

does (dŭz), v. 3rd pers. sing. pres. ind. of **do**[1].

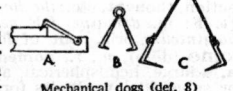

Doe of Virginia deer. *Odocoileus virginianus* (5 ft. long)

doe·skin (dō'skĭn'), n. **1.** the skin of a doe. **2.** leather made from this. **3.** (pl.) gloves made of sheepskin. **4.** a smoothly finished, closely woven, finely twilled woolen cloth.

does·n't (dŭz'ənt), contraction of *does not*.

do·eth (dōō'ĭth), aux. v. *Archaic.* (now only in poetic or solemn use) 3rd pers. sing. pres. of **do**[1].

doff (dŏf, dôf), v.t. **1.** to put or take off, as dress. **2.** to remove (the hat) in salutation. **3.** to throw off; get rid of. [contr. of *do off*. Cf. DON[2]] —**doff'er,** n.

dog (dôg, dŏg), n., v., **dogged, dogging.** —*n.* **1.** a domesticated carnivore, *Canis familiaris*, bred in a great many varieties. **2.** any animal belonging to the same family, *Canidae*, including the wolves, jackals, foxes, etc. **3.** the male of such an animal (opposed to *bitch*). **4.** any of various animals suggesting the dog, as the prairie dog. **5.** a despicable fellow. **6.** a fellow in general: *a gay dog.* **7.** (*cap.*) *Astron.* either of two constellations, Canis Major (**Great Dog**) and Canis Minor (**Little Dog**), situated near Orion. **8.** *Mech.* any of various mechanical devices, as for gripping or holding something. **9.** an andiron. **10.** *Meteorol.* a sundog or fogdog. **11.** go to the dogs, *Colloq.* to go to ruin. **12.** put on the dog, *U.S. Colloq.* to behave pretentiously; put on airs. —*v.t.* **13.** to follow or track like a dog, esp. with hostile intent; hound. **14.** to drive or chase with a dog or dogs. [ME *dogge*, OE *docga;* orig. unknown]

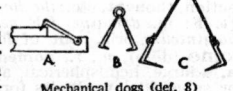

Mechanical dogs (def. 8)
A. Bench dog; B. Ring dog; C. Sling dog

dog·bane (dôg'bān', dŏg'-), n. any plant of the genus *Apocynum*, esp. *A. androsaemifolium*, a perennial herb abounding in an acrid milky juice and having an intensely bitter root that has been used in medicine.

dog·ber·ry (dôg'běr'ĭ, dŏg'-), n., pl. **-ries. 1.** the berry or fruit of any of various plants, as the European dogwood, *Cornus sanguinea*, the chokeberry, *Aronia arbutifolia*, or the mountain ash *Sorbus americana*. **2.** the plant itself. **3.** *Local and Eng.* any of several plants, esp. the dog rose, bearberry and guelder rose.

dog·cart (dôg'kärt', dŏg'-), n. **1.** a light, two-wheeled vehicle for ordinary driving, with two transverse seats back to back. **2.** a cart drawn by dogs.

dog days, a sultry part of the summer supposed to occur about the time of the heliacal rising of one of the Dog Stars, now often reckoned from July 3 to Aug. 11.

doge (dōj), n. the chief magistrate of the old republics of Venice and Genoa, who had no real power. [t. It. (Venetian), g. L *dux* leader] —**doge'ship,** n.

dog-ear (dôg'ĭr', dŏg'-), n. **1.** the corner of a page in a book folded over like a dog's ear, as by careless use or to mark a place. —*v.t.* **2.** to disfigure with dog-ears. Also, **dog's-ear.** —**dog'-eared',** adj.

dog fennel, mayweed.

dog·fight (dôg'fīt', dŏg'-), n. **1.** *Mil.* a violent engagement of war planes at close quarters, esp. of small and highly maneuverable planes. **2.** any rough and tumble physical battle.

dog·fish (dôg'fĭsh', dŏg'-), n., pl. **-fishes,** (esp. collectively) **-fish. 1.** any of various small sharks, as the spiny dogfish *Squalus acanthias*, common on both coasts of the northern Atlantic and destructive to food fishes, and the smooth dogfishes (genus *Mustelus*). **2.** any of various other fishes, as the bowfin.

dog fox, a male fox.

dog·ged (dôg'ĭd, dŏg'-), adj. having the pertinacity of a dog; obstinate. [f. DOG + -ED[3]. Cf. CRABBED] —**dog'ged·ly,** adv. —**dog'ged·ness,** n. —**Syn.** mulish, persistent, inflexible, unyielding. See **stubborn.**

dog·ger (dôg'ər, dŏg'-), n. a two-masted Dutch fishing vessel with a blunt bow, used in the North Sea. [ME *doggere.* Cf. Icel. *dugga* small fishing vessel]

Dog·ger Bank (dôg'ər, dŏg'-), an extensive shoal in the North Sea, ab. 70 mi. E of N England: fishing grounds; naval battle, 1915. 36–120 ft. deep. [said to be named from DOGGER or from MD *dogger* trawler]

dog·ger·el (dôg'ər·əl, dŏg'-), adj. **1.** (of verse) comic or burlesque, and usually loose or irregular in measure. **2.** rude; crude; poor. —*n.* **3.** doggerel verse. Also, **dog·grel** (dôg'rəl, dŏg'-). [ME; orig. uncert.]

dog·ger·y (dôg'ər·ĭ, dŏg'-), n., pl. **-geries. 1.** doggish behavior or conduct; mean or mischievous action. **2.** dogs collectively. **3.** rabble; canaille.

dog·gish (dôg'ĭsh, dŏg'-), adj. **1.** canine. **2.** surly. **3.** stylish and showy. —**dog'gish·ly,** adv. —**dog'gish·ness,** n.

dog·gy (dôg'ĭ, dŏg'ĭ), n., pl. **-gies,** adj., **-gier, -giest.** —*n.* **1.** a little dog. **2.** a pet term for any dog. —*adj.* **3.** of or pertaining to a dog. **4.** fond of dogs. **5.** pretentious; ostentatious. Also, **dog'gie.**

dog·house (dôg'hous', dŏg'-), n. **1.** a small shelter for a dog. **2. in the doghouse,** in disfavor.

do·gie (dō'gĭ), n. *Western U.S.* a motherless calf in a cattle herd.

dog in the manger, a person who, like the dog in the fable, churlishly keeps something of no particular use to himself so that others cannot use it.

dog Latin, mongrel or spurious Latin.

dog·ma (dôg'mə, dŏg'-), n., pl. **-mas, -mata** (-mə tə). **1.** a system of principles or tenets, as of a church. **2.** a tenet or doctrine authoritatively laid down, as by a church. **3.** prescribed doctrine. **4.** a settled opinion; a belief; a principle. [t. L, t. Gk.]

dog·mat·ic (dôg·măt'ĭk, dŏg·-), adj. **1.** of, pertaining to, or of the nature of a dogma or dogmas; doctrinal. **2.** asserting opinions in an authoritative, positive, or arrogant manner; positive; opinionated. Also, **dog·mat'·i·cal.** —**dog·mat'i·cal·ly,** adv.

dog·mat·ics (dôg·măt'ĭks, dŏg·-), n. the science which treats of the arrangement and statement of religious doctrines, esp. of the doctrines received in and taught by the Christian church; doctrinal theology.

dog·ma·tism (dôg'mə·tĭz'əm, dŏg'-), n. dogmatic character; authoritative, positive, or arrogant assertion of opinions.

dog·ma·tist (dôg'mə·tĭst, dŏg'-), n. **1.** one who asserts positively his own opinions; a dogmatic person. **2.** one who lays down dogmas.

dog·ma·tize (dôg'mə·tīz', dŏg'-), v., **-tized, -tizing.** —*v.i.* **1.** to make dogmatic assertions; speak or write dogmatically. —*v.t.* **2.** to assert or deliver as a dogma. [t. ML: m.s. *dogmatizāre,* t. Gk.: m. *dogmatizein*] —**dog'ma·ti·za'tion,** n. —**dog'ma·tiz'er,** n.

do-good·er (dōō'gŏŏd'ər), n. *Colloq.* a foolish, idealistic reformer.

dog rose, a species of wild rose, *Rosa canina,* having pale-red flowers, a common Old World plant.

dog's-ear (dôgz'ĭr', dŏgz'-), n., v.t. dog-ear. —**dog's-eared',** adj.

dog's-tail (dôgz'tāl', dŏgz'-), n. any grass of the Old World genus *Cynosurus,* the species of which have the spikes fringed on one side only, esp. *C. cristatus* (crested dog's-tail). Also, **dog's-tail grass.**

Dog Star, 1. the bright star Sirius, in Canis Major. **2.** the bright star Procyon, in Canis Minor.

dog's-tongue (dôgz'tŭng', dŏgz'-), n. hound's-tongue.

dog tag, 1. a small disk or strip attached to a dog's harness or collar stating owner, home, etc. **2.** *Colloq.* one of a pair of metal disks on a neckchain serving to identify men in the armed forces.

dog-tired (dôg'tīrd', dŏg'-), adj. very tired.

dog·tooth (dôg'tōōth', dŏg'-), n., pl. **-teeth** (-tēth'). **1.** a canine tooth. **2.** *Archit.* a toothlike medieval ornament, or a molding cut in projecting teeth.

dogtooth violet, 1. a bulbous liliaceous plant, *Erythronium dens-canis,* of Europe, bearing purple flowers. **2.** any of several American plants of the same genus, as *E. americanum,* bearing yellow flowers, or *E. albidum,* bearing pinkish-white flowers. Also, **dog's-tooth violet.**

dog·trot (dôg'trŏt', dŏg'-), n. a gentle trot, like that of a dog.

dog·vane (dôg'vān',dŏg'-), n. *Naut.* a small vane, composed of bunting or the like, set on the weather gunwale of a vessel to show the direction of the wind.

dog·watch (dôg'wŏch', -wôch', dŏg'-), *n. Naut.* either of two short watches on shipboard, from 4 to 6 P.M. and from 6 to 8 P.M.

dog·wood (dôg'wŏŏd', dŏg'-), *n.* **1.** any tree or shrub of the genus *Cornus*, esp. *C. sanguinea*, of Europe, or *C. florida* (**flowering dogwood**), an American ornamental tree with large white or pinkish flowers, widely planted. **2.** the wood of any such tree.

doiled (doild), *adj. Scot.* stupid; foolish; crazed.

doi·ly (doi'lĭ), *n., pl.* **-lies. 1.** a small ornamental napkin used at table at dessert, etc. **2.** any small ornamental mat, as of embroidery or lace. [named after a 17th century draper of London]

do·ing (dōō'ĭng), *n.* **1.** action; performance; execution. **2.** (*pl.*) deeds; proceedings.

doit (doit), *n.* **1.** a small copper coin formerly current among the Dutch. **2.** a bit or jot. [t. D: m. *duit*]

doit·ed (doi'tĭd, -tĭt), *adj. Scot.* enfeebled in mind, esp. by age; childish.

do-it-your·self (dōō'ĭt yŏor sĕlf'), *adj. Slang.* of or designed for use by amateurs without special training: *a do-it-yourself kit for building a radio.* —**do-'it-your'self'er,** *n.*

Dolabriform leaf

do·lab·ri·form (dō lăb'rə fôrm'), *adj. Bot., Zool.* shaped like an ax or a cleaver. [f. s. L *dolābra* pickax, ax + -(I)FORM]

dol·ce (dōl'chě), *Music.* —*adj.* **1.** sweet; soft. —*n.* **2.** an instruction to the performer that the music is to be executed softly and sweetly. **3.** a soft-toned organ stop. [It.: sweet, g. L *dulcis*]

dol·ce far nien·te (dōl'chě fär nyĕn'tě), *Italian.* pleasing inactivity. [It.: lit., sweet doing nothing]

dol·drum (dōl'drəm), *n.* **1.** a calm, windless area, esp. on the ocean. **2.** a becalmed state. **3.** (*pl.*) *Naut.* **a.** the region of relatively calm winds near the equator. **b.** the calms or weather variations characteristic of those parts. **4.** (*pl.*) dullness; low spirits. [orig. uncert.]

dole[1] (dōl), *n., v.,* **doled, doling.** —*n.* **1.** a portion of money, food, etc., given, esp. in charity or for maintenance. **2.** a dealing out or distributing, esp. in charity. **3.** a form of payment to the unemployed instituted by the British government in 1918. **4.** any similar payment by a government to an unemployed person. **5. go** or **be on the dole,** to receive such payments. **6.** *Archaic.* one's fate or destiny. —*v.t.* **7.** to distribute in charity. **8.** to give out sparingly or in small quantities (fol. by *out*). [ME; OE *dāl* part, portion. See DEAL[1]]

dole[2] (dōl), *n. Archaic.* grief or sorrow; lamentation. [ME *dol, doel,* t. OF, ult. der. L *dolēre* grieve]

dole·ful (dōl'fəl), *adj.* full of grief; sorrowful; gloomy. —**dole'ful·ly,** *adv.* —**dole'ful·ness,** *n.*

dol·er·ite (dōl'ə rīt'), *n.* **1.** a coarse-grained variety of basalt. **2.** any of various other igneous rocks, as diabase. **3.** *U.S.* any igneous rock resembling basalt whose composition cannot be determined without microscopic examination. [t. F, f. s. Gk. *dolerós* deceptive + -ITE[1]] —**dol·er·it·ic** (dōl'ə rĭt'ĭk), *adj.*

dole·some (dōl'səm), *adj. Archaic* or *Dial.* doleful.

dol·i·cho·cephal·ic (dŏl'ə kō sə făl'ĭk), *adj. Ceph·alom.* **1.** long-headed; having a breadth of head small in proportion to the length from front to back (opposed to *brachycephalic*). **2.** having a cephalic index of 76 and under. Also, **dol·i·cho·ceph·a·lous** (dŏl'ə kō sĕf'ə ləs). [f. Gk. *dolichó(s)* long + m.s. Gk. *kephalē* head + -IC] —**dol·i·cho·ceph·a·lism** (dŏl'ə kō sĕf'ə lĭz'əm), *n.* —**dol'·i·cho·ceph'a·ly,** *n.*

dol·i·cho·cra·nic (dŏl'ə kō krā'nĭk), *adj. Craniom.* **1.** long-skulled; having a breadth of skull small in proportion to length from front to back (opposed to *brachycranic*). **2.** having a cranial index of 75 and under.

doll (dŏl), *n.* **1.** a toy puppet representing a child or other human being; a child's toy baby. **2.** a pretty but expressionless or unintelligent woman. —*v.t., v.i.* **3.** *Slang.* to dress in a smart or showy manner (fol. by *up*). [from *Doll, Dolly,* for *Dorothy,* woman's name] —**doll'ish,** *adj.* —**doll'ish·ly,** *adv.* —**doll'ish·ness,** *n.*

dol·lar (dŏl'ər), *n.* **1.** the monetary unit of the U.S., equivalent to 100 cents. **2.** a gold coin of this value, or a silver coin or a paper note having a corresponding legal value. **3.** a corresponding unit, coin, or note elsewhere, as in Canada, China, etc. **4.** the English name for the German thaler, a large silver coin of varying value, current in various German states from the 16th century. **5.** any of various similar coins, as the Spanish or Mexican peso. **6.** Levant dollar. [earlier *daler,* t. LG, and early mod. D, c. HG *thaler,* for *Joachimsthaler* coin of Joachimsthal, Bohemian city where they were coined]

dol·lar-a-year man (dŏl'ər ə yîr'), a federal appointee serving for a token salary.

dollar diplomacy, a government policy of promoting the business interests of its citizens in other countries.

dol·lar·fish (dŏl'ər fĭsh'), *n., pl.* **-fishes,** (*esp. collectively*) **-fish. 1.** the butterfish. **2.** the moonfish.

Doll·fuss (dŏl'fŏŏs), *n.* **Engelbert** (ĕng'əl bĕrt'), 1892–1934, Austrian statesman: premier, 1932–34.

dol·lop (dŏl'əp), *n. Colloq.* a lump; a mass.

doll·y (dŏl'ĭ), *n., pl.* **dollies. 1.** a child's name for a doll. **2.** a low truck with small wheels for moving loads too heavy to be carried by hand. **3.** *Mach.* a tool for receiving and holding the head of a rivet while the other end is being headed. **4.** *Bldg. Trades.* an extension piece placed on the head of a pile while being driven. **5.** a small locomotive operating on narrow-gauge tracks, esp. in quarries, construction sites, etc. **6.** a primitive apparatus for jerking cloths about while washing.

Doll·y Var·den (dŏl'ĭ vär'dən), **1.** a style of gay-flowered print gown. **2.** a broad-brimmed, flower-trimmed hat, formerly worn by women. **3.** a species of trout or charr, *Salvelinus malma,* ranging from Alaska to California. [named after character in Dickens' "Barnaby Rudge"; applied to fish in allusion to its coloring]

dol·man (dōl'mən), *n., pl.* **-mans. 1.** a woman's mantle with capelike arm pieces instead of sleeves. **2.** a long outer robe worn by Turks. [ult. t. Turk.: m. *dōlāmān*]

Dolmen

dol·men (dōl'mĕn), *n. Archaeol.* a structure usually regarded as a tomb, consisting of two or more large upright stones set with a space between and capped by a horizontal stone. Cf. **cromlech.** [t. F, made up by F writers as if from Breton *taol, tol* table + *men* stone]

dol·o·mite (dŏl'ə mīt'), *n.* **1.** a very common mineral, calcium magnesium carbonate, $CaMg(CO_3)_2$, occurring in crystals and in masses (called **dolomite marble** when coarse-grained). **2.** a rock consisting essentially or largely of this mineral. [named after D. G. de *Dolomieu* (1750–1801), French geologist] —**dol·o·mit·ic** (dŏl'ə mĭt'ĭk), *adj.*

Dol·o·mites (dŏl'ə mīts'), *n.pl.* a mountain range in N Italy: a part of the Alpine system. Highest peak, Marmolada, 10,965 feet. Also, **Dolomite Alps.**

do·lor (dō'lər), *n. Now Chiefly Poetic.* sorrow or grief. Also, *Brit.,* **do'lour.** [ME *doloure,* t. OF: m. *dolour,* g. L *dolor* pain, grief]

do·lo·ro·so (dō'lō rō'sō), *adj. Music.* soft and pathetic; plaintive. [It.]

dol·or·ous (dŏl'ər əs, dō'lər-), *adj.* full of, expressing, or causing pain or sorrow; distressed; grievous; mournful. —**dol'or·ous·ly,** *adv.* —**dol'or·ous·ness,** *n.*

dol·phin (dŏl'fĭn), *n.* **1.** any of various cetaceans of the family *Delphinidae,* some of which are commonly called porpoises, esp. *Delphinus delphis,* which has a long, sharp nose and abounds in the Mediterranean and the temperate Atlantic. **2.** a large, thin-bodied ocean fish, *Coryphaena hippurus* or *C. equisetis,* notable for its rapid color change on death. **3.** *Naut.* a post, pile cluster, or buoy to which to moor a vessel. **4.** (*cap.*) *Astron.* the northern constellation Delphinus. [ME *dalphyne,* t. OF: m. *daulphin,* g. L *delphīnus,* t. Gk.: m.s. *delphís.* Cf. DAUPHIN]

Dolphin. *Delphinus delphis* (Ab. 7½ ft. long)

dolphin striker, *Naut.* a martingale (def. 2).

dolt (dōlt), *n.* a dull, stupid fellow; a blockhead. —**dolt'ish,** *adj.* —**dolt'ish·ly,** *adv.* —**dolt'ish·ness,** *n.*

-dom, a noun suffix meaning: **1.** domain, as in *kingdom.* **2.** collection of persons, as in *officialdom.* **3.** rank or station as in *earldom.* **4.** general condition, as in *freedom.* [OE *-dōm,* suffix, repr. *dōm,* n. See DOOM]

dom., **1.** domestic. **2.** dominion.

do·main (dō mān'), *n.* **1.** *Law.* ultimate ownership and control over the use of land. **2.** eminent domain. **3.** a territory under rule or influence; a realm. **4.** a field of action, thought, etc.: *the domain of commerce or of science.* [t. F: m. *domaine,* OF *demeine* (see DEMESNE), g. L *dominicum,* orig. neut. of *dominicus* of a lord]

dome (dōm), *n., v.,* **domed, doming.** —*n.* **1.** *Archit.* **a.** a large, hemispherical, approximately hemispherical, or spheroidal vault, its form produced by rotating an arch on its vertical radius. **b.** a roof of domical shape. **c.** a vault or curved roof on a polygonal plan, as an octagonal dome. **2.** *Poetic.* a large, impressive, or fanciful structure. **3.** anything shaped like a dome. **4.** *Crystall.* a form whose planes intersect the vertical axis but are parallel to one of the lateral axes. —*v.t.* **5.** to cover with or as with a dome. **6.** to shape like a dome. —*v.i.* **7.** to rise or swell as a dome. [t. L: m.s. *domus* house; partly through F *dôme* cathedral church, t. It.: m. *duomo* cupola, dome, t. Pr.: m. *doma* cupola, t. Gk.: house]

Domes·day Book (dōōmz'dā'), a record of a survey of the lands of England made by order of William the Conqueror about 1086, giving ownership, extent, value, etc., of the properties. Also, **Doomsday Book.**

do·mes·tic (də mĕs'tĭk), *adj.* **1.** of or pertaining to the home, the household, or household affairs. **2.** devoted to home life or affairs. **3.** living with man; tame: *domestic animals.* **4.** of or pertaining to one's own or a particular country as apart from other countries. **5.** belonging, existing, or produced within a country; not foreign: *domestic trade.* —*n.* **6.** a hired household servant. **7.** (*pl.*) home manufacturers or goods. [t. F; g. L *domesticus* belonging to the household] —**do·mes'ti·cal·ly,** *adv.*

do·mes·ti·cate (də mĕs'tə kāt'), *v.,* **-cated, -cating.** —*v.t.* **1.** to convert to domestic uses; tame. **2.** to attach to home life or affairs. **3.** to cause to be or feel at home; naturalize. —*v.i.* **4.** to be domestic. —**do·mes'ti·ca'·tion,** *n.* —**do·mes'ti·ca'tor,** *n.*

do·mes·tic·i·ty (dō'mĕs tĭs'ə tĭ), *n., pl.* **-ties.** state of being domestic; domestic or home life.

dom·i·cal (dō′mə kəl, dŏm′ə-), *adj.* **1.** domelike. **2.** having a dome or domes. —**dom′i·cal·ly,** *adv.*

dom·i·cile (dŏm′ə səl, -sīl′), *n., v.,* -ciled, -ciling. —*n.* Also, **dom′i·cil. 1.** a place of residence; an abode; a house or home. **2.** *Law.* a permanent legal residence. —*v.t.* **3.** to establish in a domicile. —*v.i.* **4.** to have one's domicile; dwell (fol. by *at, in,* etc.). [t. F, t. L: m.s. *domicilium* habitation, dwelling]

dom·i·cil·i·ar·y (dŏm′ə sĭl′ĭ ĕr′ĭ), *adj.* of or pertaining to a domicile.

dom·i·cil·i·ate (dŏm′ə sĭl′ĭ āt′), *v.t., v.i.,* -ated, -ating. domicile. —**dom·i·cil·i·a′tion,** *n.*

dom·i·nance (dŏm′ə nəns), *n.* **1.** rule; control; authority; ascendancy. **2.** the condition of being dominant. Also, **dom′i·nan·cy.**

dom·i·nant (dŏm′ə nənt), *adj.* **1.** ruling; governing; controlling; most influential. **2.** occupying a commanding position: *the dominant points of the globe.* **3.** *Genetics.* pertaining to or exhibiting a dominant, as opposed to a recessive. **4.** *Music.* pertaining to or based on the dominant: *the dominant chord.* —*n.* **5.** *Genetics.* a hereditary character resulting from a gene with a greater biochemical activity than another, termed the recessive. The dominant masks the recessive. **6.** *Music.* the fifth tone of a scale. [t. F, t. L: s. *dominans,* ppr.] —**dom′i·nant·ly,** *adv.*
—**Syn. 1.** prevailing, principal. DOMINANT, PREDOMINANT, PARAMOUNT, PREEMINENT describe something outstanding. DOMINANT describes that which is most influential or important: *the dominant characteristics of monkeys.* PREDOMINANT describes that which is dominant over all others, or is more widely prevalent: *curiosity is the predominant characteristic of monkeys.* PARAMOUNT applies to that which is first in rank or order: *safety is of paramount importance.* PREEMINENT applies to a prominence based on recognition of excellence: *his work was of preëminent quality.*

dominant tenement, *Law.* land in favor of which an easement or other servitude exists over another's land (the **servient tenement**). Also, **dominant estate.**

dom·i·nate (dŏm′ə nāt′), *v.,* -nated, -nating. —*v.t.* **1.** to rule over; govern; control. **2.** to tower above; overshadow. —*v.i.* **3.** to rule; exercise control; predominate. **4.** to occupy a commanding position. [t. L: m.s. *dominātus,* pp.] —**dom′i·na′tor,** *n.*

dom·i·na·tion (dŏm′ə nā′shən), *n.* **1.** act of dominating. **2.** rule or sway, often arbitrary. **3.** (*pl.*) an order of angels. See **angel.**

dom·i·na·tive (dŏm′ə nā′tĭv), *adj.* dominating; controlling.

dom·i·ne (dŏm′ə nĭ, dō′mə-), *n. Obs.* lord; master (used as a title of address). [vocative of L *dominus* master]

dom·i·ne, di·ri·ge nos (dŏm′ĭ nĭ, dĭr′ĭ jĭ nōs′), *Lat-in.* Master, guide us (motto of the City of London).

dom·i·neer (dŏm′ə nĭr′), *v.i., v.t.* **1.** to rule arbitrarily; tyrannize. **2.** to tower (over or above). [t. D: m.s. *domineren,* t. F: m. *dominer,* t. L: m. *dominārī* rule]

dom·i·neer·ing (dŏm′ə nĭr′ĭng), *adj.* inclined to domineer; overbearing; tyrannical. —**dom′i·neer′-ing·ly,** *adv.* —**dom′i·neer′ing·ness,** *n.*

Dom·i·nic (dŏm′ə nĭk), *n.* Saint, 1170–1221, Spanish priest: founder of the Dominican order.

Dom·i·ni·ca (dŏm′ə nē′kə, də mĭn′ə kə), *n.* a British colony in the Federation of the West Indies (British), in the Windward Island group. 57,017 pop. (est. 1952); 305 sq. mi. *Cap.:* Roseau.

do·min·i·cal (də mĭn′ə kəl), *adj.* **1.** of or pertaining to Jesus Christ as Lord. **2.** of or pertaining to the Lord's Day, or Sunday. [t. ML: s. *dominicālis* of or pertaining to the Lord or the Lord's Day (ML *dominica*), der. L *dominicus* belonging to a lord or (LL) the Lord]

dominical letter, that one of the seven letters *A* to *G* which is used in calendars to mark the Sundays throughout a particular year, and serving primarily to aid in determining the date of Easter.

Do·min·i·can (də mĭn′ə kən), *adj.* **1.** of or pertaining to St. Dominic (1170–1221), or to the mendicant religious order founded by him. **2.** of or pertaining to the Dominican Republic. —*n.* **3.** a member of the order of St. Dominic; a Black Friar. **4.** a native or inhabitant of the Dominican Republic. [t. Eccl. L: s. *Dominicānus,* der. *Dominicus,* Latin form of the name of Domingo de Guzmán, founder of the order]

Dominican Republic, a republic in the West Indies, occupying the E part of the island of Hispaniola. 3,007,941 (est. 1961); 19,129 sq. mi. *Cap.:* Santo Domingo. Also, **Santo Domingo.**

dom·i·nie (dŏm′ə nĭ, dō′mə-), *n.* **1.** *Chiefly Scot.* a schoolmaster. **2.** a clergyman, pastor, or parson (a title used specifically in the Reformed Church in America). [t. L: m. *domine,* vocative of *dominus* master, lord]

do·min·ion (də mĭn′yən), *n.* **1.** the power or right of governing and controlling; sovereign authority. **2.** rule or sway. **3.** control or influence. **4.** a territory, usually of considerable size, in which a single rulership holds sway. **5.** lands or domains subject to sovereignty or control. **6.** *Govt.* a territory constituting a self-governing commonwealth and being one of a number of such territories united in a community of nations, or empire (formerly applied to self-governing divisions of the British Empire, as Canada, New Zealand, etc.). **7.** the **Dominion,** Canada. **8.** (*pl.*) *Theol.* dominations (def. 3). [ME, t. F(obs.), der. L *dominium* lordship, ownership]

Dominion Day, (in Canada) a legal holiday, July 1,

celebrating the Dominion's formation on July 1, 1867.

do·min·i·um (də mĭn′ĭ əm), *n. Law.* complete power to use, to enjoy, and to dispose of property at will. [t. L. See DOMINION]

dom·i·no¹ (dŏm′ə nō′), *n., pl.* **-noes, -nos. 1.** a large, loose cloak, usually hooded, worn with a small mask by persons in masquerade. **2.** the mask. **3.** a person wearing such dress. [t. Sp., t. L, dative of *dominus* master]

dom·i·no² (dŏm′ə nō′), *n., pl.* **-noes. 1.** (*pl. construed as sing.*) any of various games played with flat, oblong pieces of ivory, bone, or wood, the face of which is divided into two parts, each left blank or marked with pips, usually from one to six. **2.** one of these pieces. [orig. unknown]

Do·mi·nus vo·bis·cum (dŏm′ĭ nəs vō bĭs′kəm), *Lat-in.* the Lord (be or is) with you.

Do·mi·tian (də mĭsh′ən, -ĭ ən), *n.* A.D. 51–96, Roman emperor, A.D. 81–96.

Dom·re·my-la-Pu·celle (dôn rə mē′ lä py sĕl′), *n.* a village in NE France: birthplace of Joan of Arc. Also, **Dom·re·my′.**

don¹ (dŏn), *n.* **1.** (*cap.*) Mr.; Sir (a Spanish title prefixed to a man's Christian name). **2.** a Spanish lord or gentleman. **3.** a person of great importance. **4.** *Colloq.* (in the English universities) a head, a fellow, or tutor of a college. [t. Sp., g. L *dominus* master, lord]

don² (dŏn), *v.t.,* donned, donning. to put on (clothing, etc.). [contr. of *do on.* Cf. DOFF]

Don (dŏn; *also for 1, Russ.* dôn), *n.* **1.** a river flowing from the central Soviet Union in Europe S through a wide arc to the Sea of Azov. ab. 1300 mi. **2.** a river in NE Scotland, in Aberdeen county, flowing E to the North Sea. 62 mi. **3.** a river in central England, in S Yorkshire, flowing NE to the Humber estuary. 60 mi.

do·na (dō′nə), *n.* Portuguese form of **doña.**

do·ña (dō′nyä), *n.* (in Spanish use) **1.** a lady. **2.** (*cap.*) a title of respect for a lady. [Sp., g. L *domina* lady, mistress. See DON¹]

Do·nar (dō′när), *n. German Myth.* the god of thunder. [OHG, c. OE *thunor,* Icel. *Thōr*]

do·nate (dō′nāt), *v.t.,* -nated, -nating. *Chiefly U.S.* to present as a gift; make a gift or donation of, as to a fund or cause. [t. L: m.s. *dōnātus,* pp.] —**do′na·tor,** *n.*

Don·a·tel·lo (dŏn′ə tĕl′ō; *It.* dô′nä tĕl′lō), *n.* c1386–1466, Italian sculptor. Also, **Do·na·to** (dô nä′tō).

do·na·tion (dō nā′shən), *n.* **1.** act of presenting something as a gift. **2.** a gift, as to a fund; a contribution. —**Syn. 2.** See **present².**

Don·a·tist (dŏn′ə tĭst), *n.* one of a Christian sect which arose in northern Africa in the year 311, and which maintained that it constituted the whole and only true church and that the baptisms and ordinations of the orthodox clergy were invalid. —**Don′a·tism,** *n.*

don·a·tive (dŏn′ə tĭv, dō′nə-), *n.* a gift or donation; a largess. [t. L: m.s. *dōnātīvum* gift, prop. neut. of *dōnātivus,* adj.]

Do·na·tus (dō nā′təs), *n.* fl. A.D. c315, bishop of Casae Nigrae in Numidia and leader of a heretical group of African Christians.

Do·nau (dō′nou), *n.* German name of the **Danube.**

Don·cas·ter (dŏng′kăs tər; *Brit.* -kəs tər), *n.* a city in central England, in S Yorkshire. 83,160 (est. 1956).

done (dŭn), *v.* **1.** pp. of do¹. —*adj.* **2.** executed; completed; finished; settled. **3.** cooked. **4.** worn out; used up. **5.** *Chiefly Brit.* in conformity with fashion and good taste: *it isn't done.*

do·nee (dō nē′), *n. Law.* **1.** one to whom a gift is made. **2.** one who has a power of appointment in property. [f. DON(OR) + -EE]

Don·e·gal (dŏn′ĭ gôl′, dŏn′ĭ gôl′), *n.* a county in N Ireland, in Ulster. 122,061 pop. (prelim. 1956); 1865 sq. mi. *Co. Seat:* Lifford.

Don·el·son (dŏn′əl sən), *n.* **Fort,** a Confederate fort in NW Tennessee, on the Cumberland river: captured by Union forces, 1862.

Do·nets (dō nĕts′), *n.* **1.** a river in the SW Soviet Union, flowing SE to the Don river. ab. 660 mi. **2.** Also, **Donets Basin,** an area S of this river, in the E Ukrainian Republic: important coal mining region and recently developed industrial area. 9650 sq. mi.

Do·netsk (dō nĕtsk′), *n.* a city in the SW Soviet Union, in the Donets Basin. 699,000 (est. 1959). Formerly, **Stalino, Yuzovka.**

Don·go·la (dŏng′gə lə), *n.* a former province in Sudan, now part of Northern Province.

Don·i·zet·ti (dŏn′ə zĕt′ĭ; *It.* dô′nē dzĕt′tē), *n.* **Gae-tano** (gä′ē tä′nō), 1797–1848, Italian operatic composer.

don·jon (dŭn′jən, dŏn′-), *n.* the inner tower, keep, or stronghold of a castle. [archaic var. of DUNGEON]

Don Ju·an (dŏn jōō′ən; *also for 1, 2, Sp.* dôn hwän′), **1.** a legendary Spanish nobleman of dissolute life. **2.** a libertine or rake. **3.** an incomplete romantic satirical poem (1819–24) by Byron.

don·key (dŏng′kĭ; *less often* dŭng′-), *n., pl.* **-keys. 1.** the ass. **2.** a stupid, silly, or obstinate person. [? familiar var. of *Duncan,* man's name.]

donkey engine, a small, usually subsidiary, steam engine.

donkey's years, *Brit. Colloq.* a long time.

don·na (dŏn′ə; *It.* dôn′nä), *n.* (in Italian use) **1.** a lady. **2.** (*cap.*) a title of respect for a lady. [It., g. L *domina* lady, mistress. See DON¹]

don·nard (dŏn'ərd), *adj. Chiefly Scot.* stunned; dazed. Also, **don·nered** (dŏn'ərd). [also *donnered*, f. Scot. v. *donner* stupefy (e. g., with a blow or loud noise) + -ED[2]]

Donne (dŭn), *n.* **John**, 1573–1631, English poet and clergyman.

don·nish (dŏn'ish), *adj.* resembling, or characteristic of, an English university don. —**don'nish·ness**, *n.*

Don·ny·brook Fair (dŏn'ĭ brŏŏk'), **1.** a fair which until 1855 was held annually at Donnybrook, County Dublin, Ireland, and which was famous for rioting and dissipation. **2.** any debauched or riotous occasion.

do·nor (dō'nər), *n.* **1.** one who gives or donates. **2.** *Med.* a person or animal furnishing blood for transfusion. **3.** *Law.* one who gives property by gift, legacy, or devise, or who confers a power of appointment. [ME *donour*, t. AF, der. *doner* give, g. L *dōnāre*]

Don Quix·ote (dŏn kwĭk'sət; *Sp.* dōn kē hō'tě), *Spanish.* **1.** the hero of Cervantes' romance who was inspired by lofty and chivalrous but impractical ideals. **2.** the romance itself (1605 and 1615).

don·sie (dŏn'sĭ), *adj. Scot.* unlucky. Also, **don'sy.**

don't (dōnt), contraction of *do not*.

don·zel (dŏn'zəl), *n. Archaic.* a young gentleman not yet knighted; a squire; a page. [t. It.: m. *donzello*, t. Pr.: m. *donsel*, g. LL *domnicellus*, dim. of L *dominus* master]

doo·dad (dōō'dăd), *n. Colloq.* any trifling ornament or bit of decorative finery.

doo·dle (dōō'dəl), *v.t., v.i.,* -dled, -dling. to draw or scribble idly.

doo·dle·bug[1] (dōō'dəl bŭg'), *n. Local U.S.* an ant lion larva. [f. *doodle* simpleton (cf. LG *dudeltopf*) + BUG]

doo·dle·bug[2] (dōō'dəl bŭg'), *n.* **1.** a divining rod or similar device supposedly useful in locating water, oil, minerals, etc., underground. **2.** *Brit. Colloq.* a buzz bomb. [appar. special uses of DOODLEBUG[1]]

Doo·lit·tle (dōō'lĭt'əl), *n.* **Hilda,** ("*H.D.*") 1886–1961, U.S. poet.

doo·ly (dōō'lĭ), *n., pl.* -lies. a kind of litter used in India. Also, **doo'lie.** [t. Hind.: m. *dōlī* litter]

doom (dōōm), *n.* **1.** fate or destiny, esp. adverse fate. **2.** ruin; death. **3.** a judgment, decision, or sentence, esp. an unfavorable one. **4.** the Last Judgment, at the end of the world. —*v.t.* **5.** to destine, esp. to an adverse fate. **6.** to pronounce judgment against; condemn. **7.** to ordain or fix as a sentence or fate. [ME *dome*, OE *dōm* judgment, sentence, law, authority, c. OHG *tuom*, Icel. *dōmr*, Goth. *dōms*, orig., that which is put or set; akin to DO, V., -DOM, suffix] —**Syn. 1.** See **fate.**

dooms (dōōmz), *adv. Scot.* and *N. Eng.* very; extremely.

dooms·day (dōōmz'dā'), *n.* **1.** the day of the Last Judgment, at the end of the world. **2.** any day of sentence or condemnation. [ME *domes dai*, OE *dōmes dæg* day of judgment]

Doomsday Book, Domesday Book.

Doon (dōōn), *n.* a river in SW Scotland, in Ayr county, flowing NW to the Firth of Clyde. ab. 30 mi.

door (dōr), *n.* **1.** a movable barrier of wood or other material, commonly turning on hinges or sliding in a groove, for closing and opening a passage or opening into a building, room, cupboard, etc. **2.** a doorway. **3.** the building, etc., to which a door belongs: *two doors down the street.* **4.** any means of approach or access, or of exit. [ME *dore*, OE *duru.* Cf. G *tür*, Icel. *dyrr*, also OE *dor* gate, c. G *tor*; akin to L *foris*, Gk. *thýra*]

door·bell (dōr'bĕl'), *n.* a bell at a door or connected with a door, rung by persons outside seeking admittance.

door·jamb (dōr'jăm'), *n.* a side or vertical piece of a door supporting the lintel.

door·keep·er (dōr'kē'pər), *n.* **1.** one who keeps or guards a door or entrance. **2.** *Brit.* janitor.

door·knob (dōr'nŏb'), *n.* the handle for opening a door.

door·man (dōr'măn', -mən), *n., pl.* -men (-mĕn', -mən). the door attendant of an apartment house, night club, etc., who performs minor duties for entering and departing guests.

Doorn (dōrn), *n.* a village in central Netherlands, SE of Utrecht: the residence of Wilhelm II of Germany after his abdication.

door·nail (dōr'nāl'), *n.* **1.** a large-headed nail formerly used for strengthening or ornamenting doors. **2. dead as a doornail,** dead beyond any doubt.

door·plate (dōr'plāt'), *n.* a plate on the door of a house or room, bearing a name, number, or the like.

door·post (dōr'pōst'), *n.* the jamb or upright sidepiece of a doorway.

door·sill (dōr'sĭl'), *n.* the sill of a doorway.

door·step (dōr'stĕp'), *n.* a step at a door, raised above the level of the ground outside; one of a series of steps leading from the ground to a door.

door·way (dōr'wā'), *n.* the passage or opening into a building, room, etc., closed and opened by a door.

door·yard (dōr'yärd'), *n.* a yard about the door of a house.

dope (dōp), *n., v.,* doped, doping. —*n.* **1.** any thick liquid or pasty preparation, as a sauce, lubricant, etc. **2.** an absorbent material used to absorb and hold a liquid, as in the manufacture of dynamite. **3.** *Aeron.* **a.** any of various varnishlike products for coating the cloth fabric of airplane wings or the like, in order to make it waterproof, stronger, etc. **b.** a similar product used to coat the fabric of a balloon to reduce gas leak-

age. **4.** *Slang.* the molasseslike preparation of opium used for smoking. **5.** *Slang.* any stupefying drug. **6.** *Slang.* a person under the influence, or addicted to the use, of drugs. **7.** *Slang.* a stimulating drug, as one wrongfully given to a race horse to induce greater speed. **8.** *Slang.* information or data. **9.** *U.S. Slang.* a stupid person. —*v.t.* **10.** *Slang.* to affect with dope or drugs. **11. dope out,** *Slang.* **a.** to work or make by calculation, inference, etc.: *to dope out a plan.* **b.** to deduce from information: *to dope out a story.* [t. D: m. *doop* a dipping, sauce, der. *doopen* dip, baptize. See DIP] —**dop'er,** *n.*

dope fiend, *Slang.* a person addicted to drugs.

dope·y (dō'pĭ), *adj.,* dopier, dopiest. *Slang.* affected by or as by a stupefying drug. Also, **dop'y.**

Dop·pel·gäng·er (dŏp'əl gĕng'ər), *n.* an apparitional double or counterpart of a living person. Also, **double-ganger.** [G: double-goer. Cf. D *dubbelganger*]

Dop·pler effect (dŏp'lər), *Physics.* the apparent change in frequency and wave length of a train of sound or light waves if the distance between the source and the receiver is changing.

dor[1] (dôr), *n.* a common European dung beetle, *Geotrupes stercorarius.* Also, **dorr, dor·bee·tle** (dôr'bē'təl), **dorrbeetle.** [ME *dor(r)e,* OE *dora*]

dor[2] (dôr), *n. Obs.* scoff; mockery. [cf. Icel. *dār* scoff]

Dor·cas (dôr'kəs), *n.* a Christian woman at Joppa who made clothing for the poor. Acts 9:36–41.

Dorcas society, a society of women of a church whose work it is to provide clothing for the poor.

Dor·ches·ter (dôr'chĕs'tər, -chĭs-), *n.* a town in S England: the county seat of Dorsetshire; named *Casterbridge* in Thomas Hardy's novels. 11,623 (1951).

Dor·dogne (dôr dōn'y), *n.* a river in SW France, flowing W to the Gironde estuary. ab. 300 mi.

Dor·drecht (dôr'drĕkнt), *n.* a city in SW Netherlands, on the Waal. 74,541(est. 1954). Also, **Dort.**

Dore (dôr), *n. Monts* (môN'), a group of mountains in central France. Highest peak, 6188 ft.

Do·ré (dō rě'), *n.* **Paul Gustave** (pōl gɥs tȧv'), 1832?–83, French illustrator and artist.

do·ré (dô rě'), *n. Canadian Dial.* the walleye or pike perch of North America.

Do·ri·an (dôr'ĭ ən), *adj.* **1.** of or pertaining to Doris, a division of ancient Greece, or the race named from it, one of the principal divisions of the ancient Greeks. —*n.* **2.** a Dorian Greek. [f. s. L *Dōrius* (t. Gk: m. *Dōrios* Dorian) + -AN]

Dor·ic (dôr'ĭk, dŏr'-), *adj.* **1.** of or pertaining to Doris, its inhabitants, or their dialect. **2.** rustic, as a dialect. **3.** *Archit.* noting or pertaining to the simplest of the three Greek orders, distinguished by low proportions, shaft without base, saucer-shaped capital (echinus) and frieze of metopes and triglyphs. See illus. under **order.** —*n.* **4.** a dialect of ancient Greek. [t. L: s. *Dōricus*, t. Gk.: m. *Dōrikós*]

Do·ris (dôr'ĭs), *n.* an ancient region in central Greece.

Dor·king (dôr'kĭng), *n.* a breed of domestic fowls characterized by a long, low, full body and having five toes on each foot, esp. valued for the table. [named after *Dorking*, town in Surrey, southeastern England]

dorm (dôrm), *n. Colloq.* a dormitory.

dor·man·cy (dôr'mən sĭ), *n.* state of being dormant.

dor·mant (dôr'mənt), *adj.* **1.** lying asleep or as if asleep; inactive as in sleep; torpid. **2.** in a state of rest or inactivity; quiescent; inoperative; in abeyance. **3.** (of a volcano) not erupting. **4.** *Bot.* temporarily inactive: *dormant buds, dormant seeds.* **5.** *Her.* (of an animal) lying down with its head on its fore paws, as if asleep. [ME, t. OF, ppr. of *dormir*, g. L *dormīre* sleep, be inactive] —**Syn. 1.** See **inactive.**

dor·mer (dôr'mər), *n.* **1.** Also, **dormer window,** a vertical window in a projection built out from a sloping roof. **2.** the whole projecting structure. [orig., a sleeping chamber; cf. OF *dormeor*, g. L *dormītōrium* DORMITORY]

Dormer (def. 1)

dor·mered (dôr'mərd), *adj.* having dormer windows.

dor·mi·ent (dôr'mĭ ənt), *adj.* sleeping; dormant. [t. L: s. *dormiens*, ppr.]

dor·mi·to·ry (dôr'mə tōr'ĭ), *n., pl.* -ries. **1.** *U.S.* a building containing a number of sleeping rooms. **2.** *Brit.* a sleeping apartment containing a number of beds. [t. L: m.s. *dormītōrium*, prop. neut. of *dormītōrius* of sleeping]

dor·mouse (dôr'mous'), *n., pl.* -mice (-mīs'). any of the small, furry-tailed Old World rodents which constitute the family *Gliridae*, resembling small squirrels in appearance and habits. [? f. DOR(MANT) + MOUSE]

dor·my (dôr'mĭ), *adj. Golf.* (of a player or side) being in the lead by as many holes as are still to be played.

dor·nick (dôr'nĭk), *n. Obs.* a stout linen cloth, esp. a damask linen. Also, **dor·nock** (dôr'nək).

dorp (dôrp), *n.* a village; a hamlet. [t. D. See THORP]

Dor·pat (dôr'păt), *n.* German name of **Tartu.**

Dormouse.
Muscardinus avellanarius
(Total length 5½ to 6 in.)

dorr (dôr), *n.* dor[1]. Also, **dorr·bee·tle** (dôr/bē′təl).

dor·sal[1] (dôr/səl), *adj.* **1.** *Zool.* of, pertaining to, or situated on the back, as of an organ or part: *dorsal nerves.* **2.** *Bot.* pertaining to the surface away from the axis, as of a leaf; abaxial. [t. ML: s. *dorsālis*, der. L *dorsum* back] —**dor/sal·ly**, *adv.*

dor·sal[2] (dôr/səl), *n.* dossal.

dorsal fin, the fin or finlike integumentary expansion generally developed on the back of aquatic vertebrates.

Dor·set (dôr/sĭt), *n.* **1.** Thomas Sackville, 1st Earl of 1536–1608, English statesman and poet. **2.** Dorsetshire.

Dorset Horn, one of an English breed of a large-horned sheep bearing medium-length wool of close texture. [named after DORSETSHIRE]

Dor·set·shire (dôr/sĭt shĭr′, -shər), *n.* a county in S England. 291,323 pop. (1951); 973 sq. mi. *Co. seat:* Dorchester. Also, **Dorset.**

dorsi-, a combining form of dorsal, dorsum, as in *dorsiferous.* Also, **dorso-.**

dor·sif·er·ous (dôr sĭf/ər əs), *adj. Bot.* borne on the back, as the sori on most ferns.

dor·si·ven·tral (dôr/sĭ vĕn/trəl), *adj.* **1.** *Bot.* having distinct dorsal and ventral sides, as most foliage leaves. **2.** *Zool.* dorsoventral.

dor·so·ven·tral (dôr/sō vĕn/trəl), *adj.* **1.** *Zool.* pertaining to the dorsal and ventral aspects of the body; extending from the dorsal to the ventral side: *the dorsoventral axis.* **2.** *Bot.* dorsiventral.

dor·sum (dôr/səm), *n., pl.* **-sa** (-sə). *Anat., Zool.* **1.** the back, as of the body. **2.** the back or outer surface of an organ, part, etc. [t. L]

Dort (dôrt), *n.* Dordrecht.

Dort·mund (dôrt/mənd; *Ger.* dôrt/mŏŏnt), *n.* a city in W West Germany. 618,305 (est. 1955).

dort·y (dôr/tĭ), *adj. Scot.* sullen; sulky.

do·ry[1] (dôr/ĭ), *n., pl.* **-ries.** a boat with a narrow, flat bottom, high ends, and flaring sides. [first used in W Indies; native Central Amer. name for a dugout]

do·ry[2] (dôr/ĭ), *n., pl.* **-ries.** **1.** a flattened, deep-bodied, spiny-rayed, marine food fish, *Zeus faber* (the John Dory), found both in European and in Australian seas. **2.** any of several related species. [ME *dore*, t. F: m. *dorée*, lit., gilded]

dos-à-dos (dō zà dō′; *n. in U.S. country dancing usually,* dō/sē dō′), *adv., n., pl.* **-dos** (-dōz′; *Fr.* -dō′). —*adv.* **1.** back to back. —*n.* **2.** *Dancing.* an evolution in reels, etc., in which two persons advance, pass around each other back to back, and return to their places. [F]

dos·age (dō/sĭj), *n.* **1.** the administration of medicine in doses. **2.** the amount of a medicine to be given. **3.** the sugar syrup added to champagne to produce secondary fermentation or to sweeten it.

dose (dōs), *n., v.* **dosed, dosing.** —*n.* **1.** a quantity of medicine prescribed to be taken at one time. **2.** a definite quantity of anything analogous to medicine, esp. of something nauseous or disagreeable. —*v.t.* **3.** to administer in or apportion for doses. **4.** to give doses to. [t. F, t. ML: m.s. *dosis*, t. Gk.: giving, portion, dose]

do·sim·e·ter (dō sĭm/ə tər), *n.* an apparatus for measuring minute quantities of liquid; a drop meter. [f. Gk. *dósi*(s) DOSE + -METER]

do·sim·e·try (dō sĭm/ə trĭ), *n.* the measurement of the doses of medicines. —**do·si·met·ric** (dō/sə mĕt/rĭk), *adj.*

Dos Pas·sos (dəs păs/əs), **John Roderigo** (rŏd rē/gō), born 1896, U.S. novelist and playwright.

doss (dŏs), *n. Brit. Slang.* **1.** a place to sleep, esp. in a cheap lodging house. **2.** sleep. [prob. t. F: m. *dos* back, through LL, g. L *dorsum*]

dos·sal (dŏs/əl), *n.* **1.** Also, **dorsal.** an ornamental hanging placed at the back of an altar or at the sides of the chancel. **2.** *Archaic.* dosser (def. 2). Also, **dos/sel.** [t. ML: s. *dossālis* for *dorsālis*, L *dorsuālis* of the back]

dos·ser (dŏs/ər), *n.* **1.** a basket for carrying objects on the back; a pannier. **2.** an ornamental covering for the back of a seat, esp. a throne, etc. **3.** a hanging sometimes richly embroidered for the walls of a hall or for the back or sides of a canopied structure. [ME *doser*, t. OF: m. *dossier*, der. *dos* back, g. L *dorsum*]

dos·si·er (dŏs/ĭ ā′, -ĭ ər; *Fr.* dô syĕ′), *n.* a bundle of documents on the same subject. [t. F. See DOSSER]

dost (dŭst), *v.* (now only in poetic or solemn use) 2nd pers. sing. pres. ind. of do[1].

Dos·to·ev·ski (dŏs/tə yĕf/skĭ; *Russ.* dô stô-), *n.* **Feodor Mikhailovich** (fyŏ/dôr mĭ hĭ/lō vĭch), 1821–81, Russian novelist, short-story writer. Also, **Dos/to·yev/sky.**

dot[1] (dŏt), *n., v.* **dotted, dotting.** —*n.* **1** a minute or small spot on a surface; a speck. **2.** a small, roundish mark made with or as with a pen. **3.** anything relatively small or specklike. **4.** *Music.* **a.** a point placed after a note or rest, to indicate that the duration of the note or rest is to be increased one half. A double dot further increases the duration by one half the value of the single dot. **b.** a point placed under a note to indicate that it is to be played staccato, i.e., shortened. **5.** *Telegraphy.* a signal of shorter duration than a dash, used in groups of dots, dashes, and spaces, to represent letters in a Morse or a similar code. —*v.t.* **6.** to mark with or as with a dot or dots. **7.** to stud or diversify, as dots do. **8.** to place like dots. —*v.i.* **9.** to make a dot or dots. [OE *dott* head of a boil. Cf. D *dot* kind of knot] —**dot/ter,** *n.*

dot[2] (dŏt; *Fr.* dôt), *n. Mod. Civil Law.* dowry. [t. F, t. L: s. *dōs*] —**do·tal** (dō/təl), *adj.*

dot·age (dō/tĭj), *n.* **1.** feebleness of mind, esp. resulting from old age; senility. **2.** excessive fondness; foolish affection. [f. DOTE, v. + -AGE]

do·tard (dō/tərd), *n.* one who is weak-minded, esp. from old age.

do·ta·tion (dō tā/shən), *n.* endowment.

dote (dōt), *v.i.,* **doted, doting. 1.** to bestow excessive love or fondness (fol. by *on* or *upon*). **2.** to be weak-minded, esp. from old age. Also, **doat.** [ME *doten,* c. MD *doten.* Cf. D *dūten* doze, dote, Icel. *dotta* nod from sleep, MHG *totzen* take a nap] —**dot/er,** *n.*

doth (dŭth), *v.* (now only in poetic or solemn use) 3rd per. sing. pres. ind. of do[1].

Do·than (dō/thən), *n.* a city in SE Alabama. 31,440 (1960).

dot·ing (dō/tĭng), *adj.* **1.** extravagantly fond. **2.** weak-minded, esp. from old age. —**dot/ing·ly,** *adv.*

dot·ter·el (dŏt/ər əl), *n.* **1.** a plover, *Eudromias morinellus,* of Europe and Asia, which allows itself to be approached and readily taken. **2.** *Dial.* a dotard or silly fellow. Also, **dot·trel** (dŏt/rəl). [f. DOTE + -REL]

dot·tle (dŏt/əl), *n.* the plug of half-smoked tobacco in the bottom of a pipe after smoking. Also, **dot/tel.**

dot·ty (dŏt/ĭ), *adj.,* **-tier, -tiest. 1.** *Chiefly Brit. Colloq.* crazy. **2.** *Colloq. or Dial.* feeble or unsteady in gait. **3.** marked with dots; placed like dots. [f. DOT, n.[1] + -Y[1]]

Dou (dou), *n.* **Gerard** (gā/rärt), 1613–75, Dutch painter. Also, **Dow.**

Dou·ai (dōō ā′; *Fr.* dwĕ), *n.* a city in N France. 43,380 (1954). Also, **Dou·ay/.**

Dou·a·la (dōō ä/lä), *n.* a seaport in Cameroun. 45,000 (est. 1950). Also, **Duala.**

Dou·ay Bible (dōō/ā), an English translation of the Bible, from the Latin Vulgate, prepared by Roman Catholic scholars, the Old Testament being published at Douay (Douai) in France, in 1609–10, and the New Testament at Rheims, in 1582. Also, **Douay Version.**

dou·ble (dŭb/əl), *adj., n., v.* **-bled, -bling,** *adv.* —*adj.* **1.** twice as great, heavy, strong, etc.: *double pay, a double portion.* **2.** twofold in form, size, amount, extent, etc.; of extra size or weight: *double blanket.* **3.** composed of two like parts or members; paired: *a double cherry.* **4.** *Bot.* (of flowers) having the number of petals largely increased. **5.** (of musical instruments) producing a tone an octave lower than the notes indicate. **6.** twofold in character, meaning, or conduct; ambiguous: *a double interpretation.* **7.** deceitful; hypocritical; insincere. **8.** duple, as time or rhythm. —*n.* **9.** a twofold size or amount; twice as much. **10.** a duplicate; a counterpart. **11.** a fold or plait. **12.** a sudden backward turn or bend. **13.** a shift or artifice. **14.** *Eccles.* one of the more important feasts of the year: so called because the antiphon is doubled, i.e., sung in full before each psalm as well as after (save for Little Hours). **15.** a substitute actor or singer ready to take another's place. **16.** *Motion Pictures.* a substitute who performs feats too hazardous or too difficult technically for a star to do. **17.** *Music. Rare.* a variation. **18.** *Mil.* double time. **19.** *Baseball.* a two-base hit. **20.** a game in which there are two players on each side. **21.** (in bridge or other card games) a challenge by an opponent that declarer cannot fulfill his contract, increasing the points to be won or lost. **22.** *Bridge.* **a.** a conventional bid informing partner that a player's hand is of certain strength. **b.** a hand which warrants such a challenge. —*v.t.* **23.** to make double or twice as great: *to double a sum, size, etc.* **24.** to be or have twice as much as. **25.** to bend or fold with one part upon another (often fol. by *over, up, back,* etc.). **26.** to clench (the fist). **27.** to sail or go round: *to double Cape Horn.* **28.** to couple; associate. **29.** *Music.* to reduplicate by means of a tone in another part, either at the unison or at an octave above or below. **30.** *Bridge.* **a.** to increase (the points) to be won or lost on a declaration. **b.** to make increased, as a bid. —*v.i.* **31.** to become double. **32.** to bend or fold (often fol. by *up*). **33.** to turn back on a course (often fol. by *back*). **34.** to share quarters, etc. (fol. by *up*). **35.** *Mil.* to march at the double-time pace. **36.** to serve in two capacities, as: **a.** *Theat.* to play two stage roles in a small company. **b.** *Music.* to play two instruments in a band. **37.** *Bridge.* to become increased, as a bid. —*adv.* **38.** twofold; doubly. [ME, t. OF: m. *duble,* g. L *duplus*] —**dou/ble·ness,** *n.* —**dou/bler,** *n.*

dou·ble-act·ing (dŭb/əl ăk/tĭng), *adj.* (of any reciprocating machine or implement) acting effectively in both directions (distinguished from *single-acting*).

double bar, *Music.* a double vertical line on a staff indicating the conclusion of a piece of music or a subdivision of it. See *illus.* under **bar.**

dou·ble-bar·reled (dŭb/əl băr/əld), *adj.* **1.** having two barrels, as a gun. **2.** serving a double purpose.

double bass, *Music.* **1.** Also, **double-bass viol.** the largest instrument of the violin family, now usually having 4 strings (sometimes 3), played resting vertically on the floor; the violone. **2.** contrabass.

double bassoon, *Music.* a bassoon an octave lower in pitch than the ordinary bassoon: the largest and deepest-toned instrument of the oboe class.

double boiler, a pair of interlocking pans, the bottom one containing water which while boiling gently heats the food in the upper pan.

ăct, āble, dâre, ärt; ĕbb, ēqual; ĭf, īce; hŏt, ōver, ôrder, oil, bŏŏk, ōoze, out; ŭp, ūse, ûrge; ə = a in alone; ch, chief; g, give; ng, ring; sh, shoe; th, thin; ŧh, that; zh, vision. See the full key on inside cover.

dou·ble-breast·ed (dŭb'əl brĕs'tĭd), *adj.* (of a garment) overlapping sufficiently to form two thicknesses of considerable width on the breast. See **single-breasted**.

dou·ble-check (dŭb'əl chĕk'), *v.t.*, *v.i.* to check twice or again; recheck. —**dou'ble-check'**, *n.*

double chin, a fold of fat beneath the chin.

double cloth, a fabric woven of two sets of yarns, as double-faced coating or Jacquard blanket.

double cross, 1. *Slang.* an act of treachery; betrayal. 2. *Slang.* a proving treacherous to a person with reference to some dishonest arrangement made with him, as concerning the outcome of a contest. 3. *Genetics.* the first generation hybrid between two single crosses of inbred lines, thus involving four inbred lines.

dou·ble-cross (dŭb'əl krôs', -krŏs'), *v.t. Slang.* to prove treacherous to; betray. —**dou'ble-cross'er**, *n.*

double dagger, a mark (‡) used for references, etc.; the diesis.

double date, *Colloq.* a social engagement or activity of two couples.

dou·ble-date (dŭb'əl dāt'), *v.i.*, -dated, -dating. (of two couples) to have a social engagement.

dou·ble-deal·ing (dŭb'əl dē'lĭng), *n.* 1. duplicity. —*adj.* 2. using duplicity; treacherous. —**dou'ble-deal'er**, *n.*

dou·ble-deck·er (dŭb'əl dĕk'ər), *n.* something with two decks, tiers, or the like, as two beds one above the other, a ship with two decks above the water line, or a streetcar having a second floor for passengers.

double eagle, a US gold coin worth two eagles, or $20.

dou·ble-edged (dŭb'əl ĕjd'), *adj.* 1. having two cutting edges. 2. acting both ways: *a double-edged charge.*

dou·ble-en·ten·dre (dōō blän tän'dr), *n.* 1. a double meaning. 2. a word or expression with two meanings, one often indelicate. [F (obs.)]

double entry, *Bookkeeping.* a method in which each transaction is entered twice in the ledger, once to the debit of one account, and once to the credit of another. Cf. **single entry**.

dou·ble-faced (dŭb'əl fāst'), *adj.* 1. practicing duplicity; hypocritical. 2. having two faces or aspects.

double first, (at Oxford University) one who gains first-class honors in final examinations in two subjects.

dou·ble-gang·er (dŭb'əl găng'ər), *n.* Doppelgänger.

dou·ble-head·er (dŭb'əl hĕd'ər), *n.* 1. the playing of two games, as of baseball, between the same teams on the same day in immediate succession. 2. a railroad train pulled by two locomotives.

dou·ble-joint·ed (dŭb'əl join'tĭd), *adj.* having unusually flexible joints which enable the appendages and spine to curve in extraordinary ways.

dou·ble-mind·ed (dŭb'əl mīn'dĭd), *adj.* wavering or undecided in mind. —**dou'ble-mind'ed·ness**, *n.*

dou·ble·ness (dŭb'əl nĭs), *n.* 1. the quality or condition of being double. 2. deception or dissimulation.

dou·ble-park (dŭb'əl pärk'), *v.t.*, *v.i.* to park a car alongside another, making a double row along the curb.

double play, *Baseball.* a play in which two put-outs are registered before the ball is again put into play.

dou·ble-quick (dŭb'əl kwĭk'), *adj.* 1. very quick or rapid. —*adv.* 2. in a quick or rapid manner. —*n.* 3. double time. —*v.t.*, *v.i.* 4. to double-time.

dou·ble-reed (dŭb'əl rēd'), *adj. Music.* of or pertaining to wind instruments producing sounds through two reeds fastened and beating together, as the oboe.

double refraction, *Physics.* the separation of a ray of light into two unequally refracted rays, as in passing through certain crystals.

dou·ble-rip·per (dŭb'əl rĭp'ər), *n.* a contrivance for coasting, consisting of two sleds, one behind the other, connected by a plank. Also, **dou'ble-run'ner**.

double salt, *Chem.* a salt which crystallizes as a single substance, but when dissolved ionizes as two distinct salts.

double standard, a moral code more lenient for men than for women.

double star, *Astron.* two stars so near to each other in the sky that they appear as one under certain conditions. **Optical double stars** are two stars at greatly different distances but nearly in line with each other and the observer. **Physical double stars** or **binary stars** are a physical system whose two components are at nearly the same distance from the earth.

double summer time, *Brit.* a setting of the clocks two hours ahead of Greenwich mean time.

dou·blet (dŭb'lĭt), *n.* 1. a close-fitting outer body garment, with or without sleeves, formerly worn by men. 2. a pair of like things; a couple. 3. one of a pair of like things; a duplicate. 4. one of two words in the same language, representing the same original, as the English *coy* and *quiet*, one taken from Old French, the other from Latin. 5. *Print.* an unintentional repetition in printed matter of proof. 6. (*pl.*) two dice on each of which the

Doublets (def. 1), Elizabethan period

same number of spots turns up at a throw. 7. *Jewelry.* a counterfeit gem made by the welding of two pieces of a different nature, usually a garnet top with a colored glass base. [ME, t. OF: f. *double* DOUBLE, adj. + *-et* -ET]

double tackle, a pulley having two grooved wheels.

double take, a second look, either literally or figuratively given to a person, event, etc., whose significance had not been completely grasped at first.

double talk, *Colloq.* 1. speech using nonsense syllables along with words in a rapid patter. 2. evasive or ambiguous language.

double time, 1. *U.S. Army.* the fastest rate of marching troops, a slow jog in which 180 paces, each of 3 feet, are taken in a minute. 2. a slow run by troops in step. 3. *Colloq.* a run at any speed.

dou·ble-time (dŭb'əl tīm'), *v.*, -timed, -timing. —*v.t.* 1. to cause to march in double time. —*v.i.* 2. to march in double time. 3. to move or run at double time.

dou·ble-tongue (dŭb'əl tŭng'), *v.i.*, -tongued, -tonguing. *Music.* (in playing the flute, cornet, etc.) to apply the tongue rapidly to the teeth and the hard palate alternately, so as to ensure a brilliant execution of a staccato passage.

dou·ble-tongued (dŭb'əl tŭngd'), *adj.* deceitful.

dou·ble·tree (dŭb'əl trē', -trĭ), *n.* (in a vehicle) a pivoted bar with a singletree attached to each end, used when two horses are harnessed abreast.

dou·bloon (dŭb lōōn'), *n.* a former Spanish gold coin, of varying value, orig. equal to 16 silver dollars, finally worth about $5. [t. F: m. *doublon*, or t. Sp.: m. *doblón*, aug. of *doble* DOUBLE, adj.]

dou·blure (dōō blyr'), *n.* an ornamental lining of a book cover. [F, der. *doubler* to line, DOUBLE]

dou·bly (dŭb'lĭ), *adv.* 1. in a double manner, measure, or degree. 2. in two ways. 3. *Obs.* or *Archaic.* with duplicity.

Doubs (dōō), *n.* a river in E France, flowing into the Saône river. ab. 270 mi.

doubt (dout), *v.t.* 1. to be uncertain in opinion about; hold questionable; hesitate to believe. 2. *Archaic* or *Prov.* to fear; suspect. —*v.i.* 3. to feel uncertainty as to something; be undecided in opinion or belief. —*n.* 4. undecidedness of opinion or belief; a feeling of uncertainty. 5. state of affairs such as to occasion uncertainty. 6. *Obs.* fear; dread. 7. **in doubt**, in uncertainty; in suspense. 8. **no doubt** or **without doubt**, without question; certainly. [ME *douten*, t. OF: m. *douter*, g. L *dubitāre* hesitate, doubt] —**doubt'a·ble**, *adj.* —**doubt'er**, *n.* —**doubt'ing·ly**, *adv.* —**Syn.** 1. distrust, mistrust, suspect, question. 4. faltering, indecision, irresolution.

doubt·ful (dout'fəl), *adj.* 1. admitting of or causing doubt; uncertain; ambiguous. 2. of uncertain issue. 3. of questionable character. 4. unsettled in opinion or belief; undecided; hesitating. —**doubt'ful·ly**, *adv.* —**doubt'ful·ness**, *n.*
—**Syn.** 2. undetermined, unsettled, indecisive, dubious. 4. irresolute, vacillating. DOUBTFUL, DUBIOUS, INCREDULOUS, SKEPTICAL imply reluctance or unwillingness to be convinced. To be DOUBTFUL about something is to feel that it is open to question or that more evidence is needed to prove it: *to be doubtful about the statements of witnesses.* DUBIOUS implies greater vacillation, vagueness, or suspicion: *dubious about suggested methods of manufacture, about future plans.* INCREDULOUS means actively unwilling or reluctant to believe, usually in a given situation: *incredulous at the good news.* SKEPTICAL implies a general disposition to doubt or question: *skeptical of human progress.* —**Ant.** 1. certain.

doubting Thomas, one who refuses to believe without proof. See *John* 20:24-29.

doubt·less (dout'lĭs), *adv.* 1. without doubt; unquestionably. 2. probably or presumably. —*adj.* 3. free from doubt or uncertainty. —**doubt'less·ly**, *adv.* —**doubt'less·ness**, *n.*

douce (dōōs), *adj. Scot.* and *N. Eng.* quiet, sedate, or modest. [ME, t. OF, g. L *dulcis* sweet] —**douce'ly**, *adv.*

dou·ceur (dōō scr'), *n.* 1. a gratuity, fee, or tip. 2. a conciliatory gift or bribe. 3. sweetness; agreeableness. [F, der. *douce* (fem.) sweet, g. L *dulcis*]

douche (dōōsh), *n.*, *v.*, douched, douching. —*n.* 1. a jet or current of water applied to a body part, organ, or cavity for medicinal purposes. 2. the application of such a jet. 3. an instrument for administering it. 4. a bath administered by such a jet. —*v.t.* 5. to apply a douche to; douse. —*v.i.* 6. to receive a douche. [t. F, t. It.: m. *doccia* conduit, shower, ult. der. L *dūcere* lead]

dough (dō), *n.* 1. flour or meal combined with water, milk, etc., in a mass for baking into bread, cake, etc.; paste of bread. 2. any soft, pasty mass. 3. *Slang.* money. [ME *dogh*, OE *dāh*, c. D *deeg*, G *teig*]

dough bird, the Eskimo curlew, *Numenius borealis*, of America.

dough·boy (dō'boi'), *n. U.S. Colloq.* an infantryman.

dough·nut (dō'nut, -nŭt'), *n.* a small cake of sweetened or, sometimes, of unsweetened dough fried in deep fat. [f. DOUGH + NUT, in allusion to the original shape]

dought (dout), *v.* pt. of dow.

dough·ty (dou'tĭ), *adj.*, -tier, -tiest. *Now Archaic, and/or Humorous.* strong; hardy; valiant. [ME; OE *dohtig*, unexplained var. of *dyhtig*, der. *dugan* be good, avail, c. G *tüchtig*] —**dough'ti·ly**, *adv.* —**dough'ti·ness**, *n.*

Dough·ty (dou'tĭ), *n.* **Charles Montagu** (mŏn'tə-gū'), 1843-1926, British traveler and author.

---

b., blend of, blended; c., cognate with; d., dialect, dialectal; der., derived from; f., formed from; g., going back to; m., modification of; r., replacing; s., stem of; t., taken from; ?, perhaps. See the full key on inside cover.

dough·y (dō'ĭ), *adj.*, **doughier, doughiest.** of or like dough; half-baked; soft and heavy; pallid and flabby.

Doug·las (dŭg'ləs). *n.* **1. Sir James,** (*"the Black Douglas"*) c1286–1330, Scottish military leader. **2. James,** c1358–88, Scottish military leader. **3. Stephen Arnold,** 1813–61, U.S. political leader who ran for president against Lincoln in 1860. **4. William Orville,** born 1898, associate justice of the U.S. Supreme Court since 1939. **5.** the capital of the Isle of Man: resort. 20,288 (1951).

Douglas fir, a coniferous tree, *Pseudotsuga taxifolia* (*P. mucronata* or *P. douglasii*), of western North America, often over 200 feet high, and yielding a strong, durable timber. Also, **Douglas pine, Douglas spruce.** [named after David *Douglas* (1798–1834), Scottish botanist and traveler]

Douglas-Home (dŭg'ləs hūm'), *n.* **Sir Alec,** born 1903, British prime minister and first lord of the treasury since 1963.

Doug·lass (dŭg'ləs), *n.* **Frederick,** 1817–95, U.S. Negro leader and orator who opposed slavery.

Dou·kho·bors (dōō'kŏ bôrz'), *n.* Dukhobors.

dou·ma (dōō'mä), *n.* duma.

Dou·mergue (dōō mĕrg'), *n.* **Gaston** (gȧs tôɴ'), 1863–1937, French statesman: president of France, 1924–31.

dour (dŏŏr, dour), *adj.* **1.** sullen; gloomy; sour. **2.** *Scot.* hard; severe; stern. **3.** *Scot.* obstinate; stubborn. [ME *dowre*, t. L: m.s. *dūrus* hard] —**dour′ly,** *adv.*

dou·ra (dŏŏr'ə), *n.* durra. Also, **dou′rah.**

dou·ri·cou·li (dŏŏr′ĭ kŏŏ′lē), *n.*, *pl.* **-lis.** a small nocturnal South American monkey, genus *Aotus*, with large owllike eyes.

dou·rine (dŏŏ rēn'), *n.* *Vet. Sci.* an infectious disease of horses, affecting chiefly the genitals and hind legs, caused by a protozoan parasite, *Trypanosoma equiperdum.* [t. F: m. *dourin*]

Dou·ro (dō'rŏŏ), *n.* a river flowing from N Spain W through N Portugal to the Atlantic. ab. 500 mi. Spanish, **Duero.**

douse (dous), *v.*, **doused, dousing.** —*v.t.* **1.** to plunge into water or the like; drench: *to douse someone with water.* **2.** *Slang.* to put out or extinguish (a light). **3.** *Colloq.* to take off or doff. **4.** *Naut.* to lower in haste, as a sail; slacken suddenly. —*v.i.* **5.** to plunge or be plunged into a liquid. —*n.* **6.** *Chiefly Dial.* a stroke or blow. Also, **dowse.** [orig. obscure] —**dous′er,** *n.*

douze·pers (dōōz'pärz'), *n.pl.*, *sing.* **douzeper** (dōōz'-pär'), **1.** the twelve peers or paladins represented in old French romances as attendants of Charlemagne. **2.** twelve great spiritual and temporal peers of France, taken to represent those of Charlemagne. [ME *dusze pers, duspers,* t. OF: m. *douze pers* twelve peers]

dove[1] (dŭv), *n.* **1.** any bird of the pigeon family (*Columbidae*), esp. certain small species of terrestrial habits, as the **ground dove,** *Columbigallina passerina,* of the southern U.S. and Mexico. **2.** (in literature) the symbol of innocence, gentleness, and tenderness. **3.** (*cap.*) *Theol.* the Holy Ghost. **4.** an innocent, gentle, or tender person. [ME *dūfe-*, c. D *duif,* G *taube,* Icel. *dūfa,* Goth. *dubō* dove, lit., diver; akin to DIVE, L.]

dove[2] (dōv), *v.* *U.S. Colloq. and Brit. Dial.* pt. of dive.

dove color (dŭv), warm gray with a slight purplish or pinkish tint. —**dove′-col′ored,** *adj.*

dove·cote (dŭv'kōt'), *n.* a structure, usually at a height above the ground, for domestic pigeons. Also, **dove·cot** (dŭv'kŏt').

dove·kie (dŭv'kĭ), *n.* **1.** the rotche, or little auk, *Plautus alle,* of Greenland, Novaya Zemlya, etc. **2.** a European name for the black guillemot. Also, **dove′key.** [dim. of DOVE]

Do·ver (dō'vər), *n.* **1.** a seaport in SE England, nearest to the coast of France. 35,217 pop. (1951). **2. Strait of,** a strait between England and France, connecting the English Channel with the North Sea. Least width, 20 mi. French, **Pas de Calais. 3.** the capital of Delaware, in the central part. 7,250 (1960).

Dover's powder, *Med.* a powder containing ipecac and opium, used as an anodyne, diaphoretic, and antispasmodic. [named after T. *Dover* (1660–1742), English physician]

dove·tail (dŭv'tāl'), *n.* **1.** *Carp.* a joint or fastening formed by one or more tenons and mortises spread in the shape of a dove's tail. —*v.t.*, *v.i.* **2.** *Carp.* to join or fit together by means of a dovetail or dovetails. **3.** to join or fit together compactly or harmoniously.

Dovetails
A. Common; B. Lapped

dow (dou, dō), *v.i.*, **dowed** or **dought** (dout), **dowing.** *Scot. and N. Eng.* **1.** to be able. **2.** to do well, or thrive. [ME *dowen, doghen,* OE *dugan,* c. G *taugen.* Cf. DOUGHTY]

Dow (dou), *n.* **Gerard** (gä'rärt). See **Dou.**

Dow., Dowager.

dow·a·ble (dou'ə bəl), *adj.* *Law.* entitled to dower.

dow·a·ger (dou'ə jər), *n.* **1.** a woman who holds some title or property from her deceased husband, esp. the widow of a king, duke, or the like. **2.** *Colloq.* a dignified elderly lady. [t. MF: m. *douagiere,* der. *douage* dower, der. *douer* endow, g. L *dōtāre*]

Dow·den (dou'dən), *n.* **Edward,** 1843–1913, British critic and poet.

dow·dy (dou'dĭ), *adj.*, **-dier, -diest,** *n.*, *pl.* **-dies.** —*adj.* **1.** ill-dressed; not trim, smart, or stylish. —*n.* **2.** an ill-dressed woman. **3.** a deep-dish pie with a fruit filling. See **pandowdy.** [earlier *dowd,* ME *doude*; orig. obscure] —**dow′di·ly,** *adv.* —**dow′di·ness,** *n.* —**dow′dy·ish,** *adj.* —Syn. **1.** frumpy, shabby.

dow·el (dou'əl), *n.*, *v.*, **-eled, -eling** or (*esp. Brit.*) **-elled, -elling.** *Carp.* —*n.* **1.** Also, **dowel pin.** a pin, usually round, fitting into corresponding holes in two adjacent pieces to prevent slipping or to align the two pieces. **2.** a piece of wood driven into a hole drilled in masonry wall to receive nails or skirtings, etc. —*v.t.* **3.** to reinforce with dowels; furnish with dowels. [cf. G *döbel* peg, plug, pin]

D. Dowel (def. [1])

dow·er (dou'ər), *n.* **1.** *Law.* the portion of a deceased husband's real property allowed by the law to his widow for her life. **2.** dowry (def. [1]). **3.** a natural gift or endowment. —*v.t.* **4.** to provide with a dower or dowry. **5.** to give as a dower or dowry. [ME, t. OF: m. *douaire,* g. LL *dōtārium,* der. L *dōs* dowry] —**dow′er·less,** *adj.*

dow·er·y (dou'ər ĭ), *n.*, *pl.* **-eries.** dowry.

dowf (douf, dōōf), *adj.* *Scot. and N. Eng.* dull; stupid.

dow·ie (dou'ĭ, dō'ĭ), *adj.* *Scot. and N. Eng.* dull; melancholy; dismal. Also, **dowy.**

dow·itch·er (dou'ĭch ər), *n.* a long-billed, snipelike American shore bird, *Limnodromus griseus.* [orig. uncert.]

Dow·met·al (dou'mĕt'əl), *n.* **1.** a trademark for any of many magnesium base alloys produced in the U.S. **2. dowmetals,** the alloys themselves.

down[1] (doun), *adv.* **1.** from higher to lower; in descending direction or order; into or in a lower position or condition. **2.** on or to the ground. **3.** to or in a position spoken of as lower, as the south, the country, a business district, etc. **4.** to or at a low point, degree, rate, pitch, etc. **5.** from an earlier to a later time. **6.** from a greater to a less bulk, degree of consistency, etc.: *to boil down syrup.* **7.** in due position or state: *to settle down to work.* **8.** on paper or in a book: *to write down.* **9.** in cash; at once: *to pay $40 down.* **10.** confined to bed with illness. **11.** *Colloq.* in a prostrate, depressed, or degraded condition. —*prep.* **12.** in a descending direction on, over, or along. —*adj.* **13.** downward; going or directed downward. **14.** downcast; dejected: *a down expression.* **15.** *Football.* pertaining to the ball which s not in play because it has stopped moving, or has been, halted by the referee for any reason, or because the ca'rrier shouts "down." **16.** *Games.* losing or behind an opp onent by a specified number of points, holes, etc. (opposed to *up*). **17. down and out, a.** without friends, money, or prospects. **b.** *Boxing.* completely knocked out. **18. down on,** *Colloq.* hostile to; disapproving of. —*n.* **19.** a downward movement; a descent. **20.** a reverse: *the ups and downs of fortune.* **21.** *Football.* one of a series of four plays during which a team must advance the ball at least ten yards to keep possession of it. **b.** the declaring of the ball as down or out of play, or the play immediately preceding this. —*v.t.* **22.** to put or throw down; subdue. **23.** *Brit. Colloq.* to drink down: *to down a tankard of ale.* —*v.i.* **24.** to go down; fall. [ME *doune,* late OE *dūne,* aphetic var. of *adūne,* earlier *of dūne* from (the) hill. See DOWN[3]]

down[2] (doun), *n.* **1.** the first feathering of young birds. **2.** the soft under plumage of birds as distinct from the contour feathers. **3.** a soft hairy growth as the hair on the human face when first beginning to appear. **4.** *Bot.* **a.** a fine soft pubescence upon plants and some fruits. **b.** the light feather pappus or coma upon seeds by which they are borne upon the wind, as in the dandelion and thistle. [ME *downe,* t. Scand.; cf. Icel. *dūnn*]

down[3] (doun), *n.* **1.** a hill; a sand hill or dune. **2.** (*usually pl., applied esp. in S and SE England*) open, rolling, upland country with fairly smooth slopes usually covered with grass. [ME; OE *dūn* hill, c. OD *dūna.* See DUNE. Not connected with OIrish *dūn* walled town]

Down (doun), *n.* a county in N Ireland, in SE Ulster. 241,181 pop. (1951). 952 sq. mi.

down-bow (doun'bō'), *n.* *Music.* (in bowing on a stringed instrument) a stroke bringing the tip of the bow towards the strings, indicated in scores by the symbol ⌐ (opposed to *up-bow*).

down·cast (doun'kȧst', -käst'), *adj.* **1.** directed downward, as the eyes. **2.** dejected in spirit; depressed. —*n.* **3.** overthrow or ruin. **4.** a downward look or glance. **5.** a shaft down which air passes, as into a mine.

down·come (doun'kŭm'), *n.* **1.** descent; downfall. **2.** a downcomer.

down·com·er (doun'kŭm'ər), *n.* a pipe, tube, or passage for conducting material downward.

down East, 1. New England. **2.** Maine.

down·fall (doun'fôl'), *n.* **1.** descent to a lower position or standing; overthrow; ruin. **2.** a fall, as of rain or snow. **3.** a kind of trap or deadfall, in which a weight or missile falls upon the prey. —**down′fall′en,** *adj.*

down·grade (doun'grād'), *n.*, *adj.*, *adv.*, *v.*, **-graded, -grading.** —*n.* **1.** a downward slope. **2.** on the downgrade, headed for poverty, ruin, etc. —*adj.*, *adv.* **3.** downhill. —*v.t.* **4.** to assign (a position) to a lower status with a smaller salary. —**down′grad′ing,** *n.*

down·haul (doun′hôl′), *n.* *Naut.* a rope for hauling down a sail.

down·heart·ed (doun′här′tĭd), *adj.* dejected; depressed; discouraged. **—down′heart′ed·ly,** *adv.* **— down′heart′ed·ness,** *n.* **—Syn.** downcast, despondent.

down·hill (doun′hĭl′), *adv.* **1.** down the slope of a hill; downward. **—adj.** **2.** going or tending downward on or as on a hill.

Down·ing Street (dou′nĭng), **1.** a short street in W central London, Eng.: usual residence of the prime minister at No. 10; other important government offices here. **2.** *Colloq.* the British prime minister and cabinet.

down·pour (doun′pōr′), *n.* a heavy, continuous fall of water, rain, etc.

down·right (doun′rīt′), *adj.* **1.** thorough; absolute; out-and-out. **2.** direct; straightforward. **3.** directed straight downward: *a downright blow.* **—adv. 4.** completely or thoroughly: *he is downright angry.* **—down′·right′ly,** *adv.* **—down′right′ness,** *n.*

Downs (dounz), *n.pl.* **The, 1.** low ridges in S and SE England. **2.** a roadstead in the Strait of Dover, between the SE tip of England and Goodwin Sands.

down·spout (doun′spout′), *n.* a pipe for conveying rain water from roofs to the drain or the ground.

down·stage (doun′stāj′), *adv.* *Theat.* at or toward the front of the stage.

down·stairs (doun′stârz′), *adv.* **1.** down the stairs. **2.** to or on a lower floor. **—adj. 3.** Also, **down′stair′.** pertaining to or situated on a lower floor. **—n. 4.** the lower floor of a house.

down·stream (doun′strēm′), *adv.* with or in the direction of the current of a stream.

down·throw (doun′thrō′), *n.* a throwing down or being thrown down; an overthrow.

down town, the business section of a city.

down·town (doun′toun′), *adv.* **1.** to or in the business section of a city. **—adj. 2.** of, pertaining to, or situated in the business section of a city.

down·trod·den (doun′trŏd′ən), *adj.* trodden down; trampled upon; tyrannized over. Also, **down′trod′.**

down under, Australia or New Zealand.

down·ward (doun′wərd), *adv.* **1.** Also, **down′wards.** from a higher to a lower place or condition; down from a head, source, or beginning. **—adj. 2.** moving or tending to a lower place or condition. **3.** descending from a head or beginning. **—down′ward·ly,** *adv.* **—down′·ward·ness,** *n.*

down·y (dou′nĭ), *adj.,* **downier, downiest. 1.** of the nature of or resembling down; fluffy; soft. **2.** made of down. **3.** covered with down. **4.** soft; soothing; calm. **—down′i·ness,** *n.*

downy woodpecker, a small North American woodpecker, *Dryobates pubescens.*

dow·ry (dou′rĭ), *n.,* *pl.* **-ries. 1.** the money, goods, or estate which a woman brings to her husband at marriage; dot. **2.** any gift or reward given to or for a bride by a man in consideration for the marriage. **3.** *Obs.* a widow's dower. **4.** a natural gift or endowment: *a noble dowry.* Also, **dowery.** [ME *dowerie,* t. AF. See DOWER]

dow·sa·bel (dou′sə·bĕl′), *n.* *Obs.* sweetheart. [var. of *Dulcibella,* woman's name]

dowse¹ (dous), *v.t., v.i.,* **dowsed, dowsing.** douse. **—dows′er,** *n.*

dowse² (douz), *v.i.,* **dowsed, dowsing.** to search for subterranean supplies of water, ore, etc., by the aid of a divining rod. [orig. unknown] **—dows′er,** *n.*

Dow·son (dou′sən), *n.* **Ernest,** 1867–1900, British poet.

dow·y (dō′ĭ), *adj.* dowie.

dox·ol·o·gy (dŏks·ŏl′ə·jĭ), *n.,* *pl.* **-gies.** a hymn or form of words containing an ascription of praise to God, as the Gloria in Excelsis (**great doxology** or **greater doxology**), the Gloria Patri (**lesser doxology**), or the metrical formula beginning "Praise God from whom all blessings flow." [t. ML: m. s. *doxologia,* t. Gk.: a praising] **—dox·o·log·i·cal** (dŏk′sə·lŏj′ə·kəl), *adj.* **—dox′o·log′i·cal·ly,** *adv.*

dox·y¹ (dŏk′sĭ), *n.,* *pl.* **doxies. 1.** opinion; doctrine. **2.** religious views. Also, **dox′ie.** [abstracted from ORTHODOXY, HETERODOXY, etc.]

dox·y² (dŏk′sĭ), *n.,* *pl.* **doxies.** *Slang.* a mistress or paramour; a prostitute. [f. MFlem. *docke* doll + -sy, affectionate dim. suffix]

doy·en (doi′ən; *Fr.* dwá yăN′), *n.* a dean; the senior member of a body, class, profession, etc. [F. See DEAN] **—doy·enne** (dwä yĕn′), *n. fem.*

Doyle (doil), *n.* **Sir Arthur Conan,** 1859–1930, British author of detective stories.

doz., dozen; dozens.

doze (dōz), *v.,* **dozed, dozing,** *n.* **—v.i. 1.** to sleep lightly or fitfully. **2.** to fall into a light sleep unintentionally (often fol. by *off*). **3.** to be dull or half asleep. **—v.t. 4.** to pass or spend (time) in drowsiness (often fol. by *away*). **—n. 5.** a light or fitful sleep. [cf. OE *dwæsian* become stupid, Dan. *dōse* make dull, heavy, drowsy] **—doz′er,** *n.*

doz·en¹ (dŭz′ən), *n.,* *pl.* **dozen, dozens.** a group of twelve units or things. [ME *dozein,* t. OF: m. *dozeine,* der. *douze* twelve, g. L *duodecim*]

doz·en² (dō′zən), *v.t.* *Scot.* to stun. [? akin to DOZE]

doz·enth (dŭz′ənth), *adj.* twelfth.

doz·y (dō′zĭ), *adj.,* **dozier, doziest.** drowsy. **—doz′i·ly,** *adv.* **—doz′i·ness,** *n.*

D.P., displaced person. Also, **DP**

dpt., 1. department. **2.** deponent.

D.P.W., Department of Public Works.

Dr., Doctor. Also, **Dr**

dr., 1. debtor. **2.** dram; drams. **3.** drawer.

drab¹ (drăb), *n., adj.,* **drabber, drabbest. —n. 1.** dull gray; dull brownish or yellowish gray. **—adj. 2.** having a drab color. **3.** dull; cheerless. [t. F: m. *drap* cloth. See DRAPE] **—drab′ly,** *adv.* **—drab′ness,** *n.*

drab² (drăb), *n., v.,* **drabbed, drabbing. —n. 1.** a dirty, untidy woman; a slattern. **2.** a prostitute. **—v.i. 3.** to associate with drabs. [cf. d. *drabbletail* slattern (with DRABBLE, v.) and its synonym *draggletail.* Cf. also Irish *drabog,* Gaelic *dragbag* slattern]

drab·bet (drăb′ĭt), *n.* a coarse drab linen fabric used for making men's smock-frocks, etc. [f. DRAB¹ + -ET]

drab·ble (drăb′əl), *v.t., v.i.,* **-bled, -bling.** to draggle; make or become wet and dirty. [ME *drabelen,* ? t. LG]

dra·cae·na (drə·sē′nə), *n.* **1.** any tree of the liliaceous genus *Dracaena,* natives of tropical regions. **2.** any tree of the closely related genus *Cordyline.* [NL, t. Gk.: m. *drákaina* she-dragon]

drachm (drăm), *n.* **1.** *Brit.; Archaic in U.S.* dram. **2.** drachma. [t. L: s. *drachma,* t. Gk.: m. *drachmḗ* an Attic weight and coin]

drach·ma (drăk′mə), *n., pl.* **-mas, -mae** (-mē). **1.** the monetary unit, or a silver coin, of modern Greece, equivalent to about U.S. \$.00007 at present. **2.** the principal silver coin of the ancient Greeks, varying in weight and value. **3.** a small ancient Greek weight, approximately corresponding to the U.S. and British apothecaries' dram. **4.** any of various modern weights, esp. a dram. [t. L, t. Gk.: m. *drachmḗ,* lit., handful]

Dra·co (drā′kō), *n., gen.* **Draconis** (drā·kō′nĭs). a northern circumpolar constellation between Ursa Major and Cepheus. [t. L, t. Gk.: m. *drákōn* serpent]

Dra·co (drā′kō), *n.* fl. 7th century B.C., Athenian statesman noted for the severity of his code of laws.

Dra·co·ni·an (drā·kō′nĭ·ən), *adj.* **1.** of, like, or befitting Draco. **2.** rigorous; severe. **—Dra·co′ni·an·ism,** *n.*

dra·co·ni·an (drā·kō′nĭ·ən), *adj.* draconic.

Dra·con·ic (drā·kŏn′ĭk), *adj.* *Hist.* Draconian. **—Dra·con′i·cal·ly,** *adv.*

dra·con·ic (drā·kŏn′ĭk), *adj.* of or like a dragon. [f. s. L *draco* DRAGON + -ic]

draff (drăf), *n.* refuse; lees; dregs. **—draff′y,** *adj.*

draft (drăft, dräft), *n.* (*Draft* is the common spelling for the following definitions. See also *draught.*) **1.** a drawing, sketch, or design. **2.** a first or preliminary form of any writing, subject to revision and copying. **3.** act of drawing; delineation. **4.** a current of air, esp. in a room, chimney, stove, or any enclosed space. **5.** act of drawing or pulling, or that which is drawn; a pull; haul. **6.** the taking of supplies, forces, money, etc., from a given source. **7.** a selection or drawing of persons from the general body of the people, by lot or otherwise, for military service; a levy; conscription. **8.** (formerly) a selection of persons already in service, to be sent from one post or organization to another, in either the army or the navy; a detachment. **9.** a written order drawn by one person upon another; a writing directing the payment of money on account of the drawer; a bill of exchange. **10.** a drain or demand made on anything. **11.** *Foundry.* the slight taper given to a pattern so that it may be drawn from the sand without injury to the mold. **12.** *Masonry.* a line or border chiseled at the edge of a stone, to serve as a guide in leveling the surfaces. **13.** the sectional area of the openings in a turbine wheel or in a sluice gate. **14.** *Obs.* an allowance for waste of goods sold by weight. **—v.t. 15.** to draw the outlines or plan of, or sketch. **16.** to draw up in written form, as a first draft. **17.** to draw or pull. **18.** to take by draft, as for military service. **19.** *Masonry.* to cut a draft on. **—adj. 20.** used or suited for drawing loads: *draft cattle.* [ME *draht,* later *draught, droft* (cf. OE *droht* pull, draught), verbal abstract of *draw* (OE *dragan*), c. G *tracht.* See DRAUGHT] **—draft′er,** *n.*

draft·ee (drăf·tē′, dräf-), *n.* one who is drafted, as for military service.

drafts·man (drăfts′mən, dräfts′-), *n., pl.* **-men. 1.** one who draws sketches, plans, or designs. **2.** one employed in making mechanical drawings, as of machines, structures, etc. **3.** one who draws up documents. **4.** draughtsman. **—drafts′man·ship′,** *n.*

draft tube, the flared passage leading vertically from a water turbine to its tailrace.

draft·y (drăf′tĭ, dräf′-), *adj.,* **draftier, draftiest.** characterized by or causing drafts (of air). Also, **draughty. —draft′i·ness,** *n.*

drag (drăg), *v.,* **dragged, dragging,** *n.* **—v.t. 1.** to draw with force, effort, or difficulty; pull heavily or slowly along; haul; trail. **2.** to search with a drag, grapnel, or the like. **3.** to break (land) with a drag or harrow. **4.** to bring (*in*) as by main force, as an irrelevant matter. **5.** to protract or pass tediously (often fol. by *out* or *on*). **—v.i. 6.** to be drawn or hauled along. **7.** to trail on the ground. **8.** to move heavily or with effort. **9.** to proceed or pass with tedious slowness. **10.** to use a drag or grapnel; dredge. **—n. 11.** *Naut.* a. something used by or for dragging, as a dragnet or a dredge. b. a grapnel, net, or other apparatus dragged through water in searching, as for dead bodies. **12.** *Agric.* a heavy harrow. **13.** a stout sledge or sled. **14.** a four-horse sporting and passenger coach with seats inside and on top. **15.** a metal shoe to receive a wheel of heavy wagons and serve as a wheel lock on steep grades. **16.** anything that retards progress. **17.** act of dragging. **18.** slow, laborious movement or procedure; retardation. **19.** *Aeron.* the force exerted on an airplane or airfoil or other aerodynamic body tending to reduce its forward motion, consisting partly of a component of the aerodynamic lift and partly of the effect of air eddies, friction, etc. **20.** *Hunting.* **a.** the scent or trail of a fox, etc. **b.** something, as aniseed, dragged over the ground to leave an artificial scent. **c.** a hunt with such a scent. **21.** *Angling.* **a.** a brake on a fishing reel. **b.** the sideways pull on a fishline as caused by a cross current. **22.** *Slang.* influence: *to have a drag.* [late ME; cf. MLG *dragge* grapnel] —**Syn. 1.** See **draw.**

dra·gée (drà zhě′), *n.* *French.* **1.** a sweetmeat in the form of a sugar-coated fruit or the like. **2.** a sugar-coated medicine.

drag·gle (drăg′əl), *v.*, **-gled, -gling.** —*v.t.* **1.** to soil by dragging over damp ground or in the mud. —*v.i.* **2.** to hang trailing; become draggled. **3.** to follow slowly; straggle. [b. DRAG and DRABBLE]

drag·gle·tail (drăg′əl tāl′), *n.* a bedraggled or untidy person; slut; slattern.

drag·gle·tailed (drăg′əl tāld′), *adj.* having the garments draggled as from trailing in the wet and dirt.

drag·hound (drăg′hound′), *n.* a hound trained to follow a drag or artificial scent.

drag hunt, a hunt with a drag or artificial scent.

drag·line (drăg′līn′), *n.* a dragrope (def. 2).

drag link, *Mach.* a link for connecting the cranks of two shafts.

drag·net (drăg′nĕt′), *n.* **1.** a net to be drawn along the bottom of a river, pond, etc., or along the ground, to catch something. **2.** anything that serves to catch or drag in, as a police system.

drag·o·man (drăg′ə mən), *n.*, *pl.* **-mans, -men.** (in the Orient) a professional interpreter. [t. F, t. LGk.: m. *dragoúmanos*, t. Ar.: m. *targumān* interpreter. Cf. TARGUM]

drag·on (drăg′ən), *n.* **1.** a fabulous monster variously represented, generally as a huge winged reptile with crested head and terrible claws, and often spouting fire. **2.** *Now Rare.* a huge serpent or snake. **3.** (in the Bible) a large serpent, a crocodile, a great marine animal, or a jackal. **4.** a name for Satan. **5.** a fierce, violent person. **6.** a severely watchful woman; a duenna. **7.** any of the small flying lizards of the East Indian region. **8.** *Bot.* any of various araceous plants, as the jack-in-the-pulpit, *Arisaema atrorubens* (*A. triphyllum*). **9.** a short musket, carried by a dragoon (def. 2) in the 16th and 17th centuries. **10.** (*cap.*) *Astron.* the northern constellation Draco. [ME, t. OF, g. L *draco*, t. Gk.: m. *drákōn* serpent] —**drag·on·ess** (drăg′ən ĭs), *n. fem.* —**drag·on·ish**, *adj.*

drag·on·et (drăg′ən ĭt), *n.* **1.** a little or young dragon. **2.** any fish of the genus *Callionymus*, comprising small shore fishes which are often brightly colored. [ME, t. OF dim. of *dragon* DRAGON]

drag·on·fly (drăg′ən flī′), *n.*, *pl.* **-flies.** any of the larger, harmless insects of the order Odonata, feeding on mosquitoes and other insects. Their immature forms are aquatic.

Common dragonfly,
Libellula trimaculata

drag·on·head (drăg′ən hĕd′), *n.* any mint of the genera *Dracocephalum* (or *Moldavica*), esp. *D. parviflora.*

drag·on·nade (drăg′ə nād′), *n.* **1.** one of a series of persecutions of French Protestants, under Louis XIV, by dragoons quartered upon them. **2.** any persecution with the aid of troops. [t. F, der. *dragon* DRAGOON]

dragon's blood, 1. a red resin exuding from the fruit of *Daemonorops* (or *Calamus*) *Draco*, a palm of the Malay Archipelago, formerly used in medicine, but now chiefly in the preparation of varnishes, etc. **2.** any of various similar resins from other trees.

dragon tree, a liliaceous tree, *Dracaena Draco*, of the Canary Islands, yielding a variety of dragon's blood.

dragon withe, (in the West Indies) a malpighiaceous climber, *Heteropteris* (*Banisteria*) *laurifolia*, one of a large genus resembling maples and bearing winged fruits.

dra·goon (drə gōōn′), *n.* **1.** a cavalryman of a particular type, as in the British army. **2.** *Obs.* a mounted infantryman armed with a short musket. —*v.t.* **3.** to set dragoons or soldiers upon; to persecute by armed force; to oppress; harass. **4.** to force by rigorous and oppressive measures; coerce. [t. F: m. *dragon* dragoon (orig., dragon), referring first to the hammer of a pistol, then to the firearm and then to the troops carrying it]

drag·rope (drăg′rōp′), *n.* **1.** a rope for dragging something, as a piece of artillery. **2.** a rope dragging from something, as the guide rope from a balloon.

drag sail, *Naut.* sea anchor. Also, **drag sheet.**

drain (drān), *v.t.* **1.** to draw off gradually, as a liquid; remove by degrees, as by filtration. **2.** to draw off or take away completely. **3.** to withdraw liquid gradually from; make empty or dry by drawing off liquid. **4.** to deprive of possessions, resources, etc., by gradual withdrawal; exhaust. —*v.i.* **5.** to flow off gradually. **6.** to become empty or dry by the gradual flowing off of moisture. —*n.* **7.** that by which anything is drained, as a pipe or conduit. **8.** *Surg.* a material or appliance for maintaining the opening of a wound to permit free exit of fluid contents. **9.** gradual or continuous outflow, withdrawal, or expenditure. **10.** act of draining. [OE *drēnian, dreahnian* drain, strain out; akin to DRY] —**drain′a·ble,** *adj.* —**drain′er,** *n.*

drain·age (drā′nĭj), *n.* **1.** act or process of draining. **2.** a system of drains, artificial or natural. **3.** drainage basin. **4.** that which is drained off. **5.** *Surg.* the draining of body fluids (bile, urine, etc.) or of pus and other morbid products from a wound.

drainage basin, the entire area drained by a river and all its tributaries. Also, **drainage area.**

drain·less (drān′lĭs), *adj.* *Poetic.* inexhaustible.

drain·pipe (drān′pīp′), *n.* a pipe receiving the discharge of waste pipes and soil pipes.

drake[1] (drāk), *n.* the male of any bird of the duck kind. [ME, c. d. G *draak*; orig. unknown]

drake[2] (drāk), *n.* *Obs.* **1.** a dragon. **2.** a small kind of cannon. [ME; OE *draca*, t. L: m. *draco* DRAGON]

Drake (drāk), *n.* **1.** Sir **Francis**, c1540–1596, English buccaneer, circumnavigator of the globe, and admiral. **2.** **Joseph Rodman**, 1795–1820, U.S. poet.

drake fly, a May fly used in angling.

Dra·kens·berg (drä′kənz bûrg′), *n.* a mountain range in the E part of the Union of South Africa. ab. 600 mi. long; highest peak, 10,988 ft.

dram (drăm), *n.*, *v.*, **drammed, dramming.** —*n.* **1.** a unit of apothecaries' weight, equal to 60 grains, ⅛ ounce. **2.** *Obs.* ℈ ounce, avoirdupois weight (27.34 grains). **3.** a fluid dram. **4.** a small drink of liquor. **5.** a small quantity of anything. —*v.i.* **6.** to drink drams; tipple. —*v.t.* **7.** to ply with drink. [ME *drame*, t. OF, g. L *drachma* DRACHMA]

dra·ma (drä′mə, drăm′ə), *n.* **1.** a composition in prose or verse presenting in dialogue or pantomime a story involving conflict or contrast of character, esp. one intended to be acted on the stage; a play. **2.** the branch of literature having such compositions as its subject; dramatic art or representation. **3.** that art which deals with plays from their writing to their final production. **4.** any series of events having dramatic interest or results. [t. LL: a play, t. Gk.: deed, play]

Dram·a·mine (drăm′ə mēn′), *n.* *Trademark. Pharm.* a synthetic antihistamine, used in the treatment of allergic disorders and as a preventive for seasickness and airsickness.

dra·mat·ic (drə măt′ĭk), *adj.* **1.** of or pertaining to the drama. **2.** employing the form or manner of the drama. **3.** characteristic of or appropriate to the drama; involving conflict or contrast. Also, *Rare,* **dra·mat′i·cal.** —**dra·mat′i·cal·ly,** *adv.*

dra·mat·ics (drə măt′ĭks), *n.* **1.** (*construed as sing. or pl.*) the art of producing or acting dramas. **2.** (*construed as pl.*) dramatic productions, esp. by amateurs. **3.** (*construed as pl.*) dramatic behavior.

dram·a·tis per·so·nae (drăm′ə tĭs pər sō′nē), *Latin.* the persons or characters in a drama.

dram·a·tist (drăm′ə tĭst), *n.* a writer of dramas or dramatic poetry; a playwright.

dram·a·ti·za·tion (drăm′ə tə zā′shən), *n.* **1.** act of dramatizing. **2.** construction or representation in dramatic form. **3.** a dramatized version, of another form of literature or of historic facts.

dram·a·tize (drăm′ə tīz′), *v.t.*, **-tized, -tizing. 1.** to put into dramatic form. **2.** to express or represent dramatically: *he dramatizes his woes.* —**dram′a·tiz′er,** *n.*

dram·a·turge (drăm′ə tûrj′), *n.* dramatist. Also, **dram′a·tur′gist.**

dram·a·tur·gy (drăm′ə tûr′jĭ), *n.* **1.** the science of dramatic composition. **2.** the dramatic art. **3.** dramatic representation. [t. Gk.: m. s. *dramatourgía* composition of dramas] —**dram′a·tur′gic, dram′a·tur′gi·cal,** *adj.*

dram. pers., dramatis personae.

dram·shop (drăm′shŏp′), *n.* a liquor saloon.

Drang nach Ost·en (dräng näkh ôs′tən), *German.* drive to the east: the German imperialistic foreign policy of extending influence to the east and south.

drank (drăngk), *v.* pt. and former pp. of **drink.**

drape (drāp), *v.*, **draped, draping,** *n.* —*v.t.* **1.** to cover or hang with cloth or some fabric, esp. in graceful folds; adorn with drapery. **2.** to adjust (hangings, clothing, etc.) in graceful folds. —*v.i.* **3.** to fall in folds, as drapery. —*n.* **4.** a draped curtain or hanging. **5.** manner or style of hanging: *the drape of a skirt.* [t. F: m. s. *draper,* der. *drap* cloth, g. LL *drappus*]

drap·er (drā′pər), *n.* *Eng.* a dealer in dry goods, etc. [ME, t. AF, var. of F *drapier*]

Dra·per (drā′pər), *n.* **1.** **Henry,** 1837–82, U.S. astronomer. **2.** his father, **John William,** 1811–82, U.S. chemist, physiologist, and historian.

dra·per·y (drā′pə rĭ), *n.*, *pl.* **-peries. 1.** coverings, hangings, clothing, etc., of some fabric, esp. as arranged in loose, graceful folds. **2.** the draping or arranging of hangings, clothing, etc., in graceful folds. **3.** *Art.* hangings, clothing, etc., so arranged as represented in sculpture or painting. **4.** cloths or textile fabrics collectively. **5.** *Brit.* the business of a draper. —**dra′per·ied,** *adj.*

dras·tic (drăs′tĭk), *adj.* acting with force or violence; violent. [t. Gk.: m. s. *drastikós* efficacious] —**dras′ti·cal·ly,** *adv.*

drat·ted (drăt′ĭd), *adj. Colloq.* or *Dial.* confounded.

draught (dräft, dräft), *n.* (Draught is the common spelling for the following definitions. See also *draft*.) 1. a current of air, esp. in a room, chimney, stove, or any enclosed space. 2. a device for regulating the flow of air or gas, as a damper in a stove. 3. the drawing of a liquid from its receptacle, as of ale from a cask: *ale on draught.* 4. drinking, or a drink or potion. 5. a take of fish, etc. 6. the depth a vessel sinks in water. 7. (*pl. construed as sing.*) the game of checkers. —*adj.* 8. being on draught; drawn as required: *draught ale.* [ME *draht*, c. D *dragt*, G *tracht*, Icel. *drāttr.* See DRAFT] —**draught′er,** *n.*

draughts·man (dräfts′mən, dräfts′-), *n., pl.* -**men.** 1. a checker. 2. draftsman. —**draughts′man·ship′,** *n.*

draught·y (dräf′tĭ, dräf′-), *adj.*, **draughtier, draughtiest.** drafty. —**draught′i·ness,** *n.*

Dra·va (drä′vä), *n.* a river flowing from S Austria, along a portion of the boundary between Hungary and SE Yugoslavia into the Danube. ab. 450 mi. Also, **Dra·ve** (drä′və). German, **Drau** (drou).

drave (dräv), *v. Archaic.* pt. of **drive.**

Dra·vid·i·an (drə vĭd′ĭən), *n.* 1. a great linguistic family of India, including Tamil, Telugu, Kanarese, and Malayalam, and, in Baluchistan, Brahui. It is wholly distinct from Indo-European. 2. a member of the Dravidian race. —*adj.* 3. Also, **Dra·vid′ic.** of or pertaining to this people or their language.

draw (drô), *v.*, **drew, drawn, drawing,** *n.* —*v.t.* 1. to cause to come in a particular direction as by a pulling force; pull; drag; lead (often fol. by *along, away, in, out, off,* etc.). 2. to bring or take out, as from a receptacle, or source: *to draw water, blood, tears, teeth.* 3. to bring toward oneself or itself, as by inherent force or influence; attract. 4. to sketch in lines or words; delineate; depict: *to draw a picture.* 5. to mark out; trace. 6. to write or draft (often fol. by *up*). 7. to frame or formulate, as a distinction. 8. to take in, as by sucking or inhaling. 9. to get; derive; deduce: *to draw a conclusion.* 10. to produce; bring in: *the deposits draw interest.* 11. to disembowel (a fowl, etc.). 12. to drain (a pond, etc.). 13. to pull out to full or greater length; stretch; make by attenuating, as wire. 14. to wrinkle or shrink by contraction. 15. *Med.* to digest and cause to discharge: *to draw an abscess by a poultice.* 16. *U.S. Army.* to obtain (rations, clothing, equipment, weapons, or ammunition) from an issuing agency, such as the quartermaster. 17. *Naut.* (of a boat) to displace (a certain depth of water). 18. *Games.* to leave (a contest) undecided. 19. *Billiards.* to cause to recoil after impact, as if pulled back. 20. *Chiefly Brit.* to search (cover) for game. 21. *Cricket.* to play (a ball) with a bat held at an angle in order to deflect the ball between the wicket and the legs. 22. *Curling.* to toss (the stone) gently. 23. (of tea) see **steep**² (def. 1). —*v.i.* 24. to exert a pulling, moving, or attracting force: *a sail draws by being filled with wind and properly trimmed.* 25. to be drawn; move as under a pulling force (often fol. by *on, off, out,* etc.): *the day draws near.* 26. to take out a sword, pistol, etc., for action (often fol. by *on*). 27. to use or practice the art of tracing figures; practice drawing. 28. to shrink or contract. 29. to make a draft or demand (fol. by *on* or *upon*): *to draw on one's imagination.* 30. to levy or call (*on*) for money, supplies, etc. 31. *Med.* to act as an irritant or to cause blisters. 32. to produce or have a draught of air, etc., as in a pipe or flue. 33. *Games.* to leave a contest undecided. 34. *Hunting.* **a.** (of a hound) to advance carefully toward the game, after indicating it by pointing. **b.** (of a hound) to follow the game animal by its scent. —*n.* 35. act of drawing. 36. something that draws or attracts. 37. that which is drawn, as a lot or the movable part of a drawbridge. 38. *Games.* a drawn or undecided contest. 39. *Phys. Geog.* small, natural drainway, usually the upper part of a stream valley. [ME *drawen*, OE *dragan*, c. Icel. *draga* draw, G *tragen* carry, bear. Cf. DRAG]

—**Syn.** 1. DRAW, DRAG, HAUL, PULL imply causing movement of an object toward one by exerting force upon it. To DRAW is to move by a force, in the direction from which the force is exerted: *a magnet draws iron to it, horses draw a wagon.* To DRAG is to draw with greater force, necessary to overcome friction between the object drawn and the surface on which it rests: *to drag a sled to the top of a hill, a heavy piece of furniture across a room.* To HAUL is slowly to transport a heavy object by mechanical force or with sustained effort: *to haul a piano up to the seventh floor, to haul a large boat across a portage.* To PULL is to draw or tug, exerting varying amounts of force according to the effort needed: *to pull out an eyelash, to pull fighting dogs apart.* —**Ant.** 1. push.

draw·back (drô′băk′), *n.* 1. a hindrance or disadvantage. 2. *Com.* an amount paid back from a charge made. 3. *Govt.* refund of tariff or other tax, as when imported goods are reexported. See **rebate**¹.

draw·bar (drô′bär′), *n. Railroads.* a metal rod or bar for connecting locomotive, tender, and railway cars.

draw·bore (drô′bôr′), *n. Carp.* a hole in a tenon so that when a pin (**drawbore pin**) is driven in, the mortised and tenoned parts are drawn snugly together.

draw·bridge (drô′brĭj′), *n.* a bridge of which the whole or a part may be drawn up or aside, to prevent access or to leave a passage open for boats, etc.

draw·ee (drô ē′), *n. Finance.* one on whom an order, draft, or bill of exchange is drawn.

draw·er (drôr for *1, 2;* drô′ər for *3–5*), *n.* 1. a sliding compartment, as in a piece of furniture, that may be

drawn out in order to get access to it. 2. (*pl.*) a garment for the lower part of the body, with a separate portion for each leg. 3. one who or that which draws. 4. *Finance.* one who draws an order, draft, or bill of exchange. 5. *Archaic.* a tapster.

draw·ing (drô′ĭng), *n.* 1. act of a person or thing that draws. 2. representation by lines; delineation of form without reference to color. 3. a sketch, plan, or design, esp. one made with pen, pencil, or crayon. 4. the art of making these.

drawing account, *Com.* 1. an account used by a partner or employee for cash withdrawals. 2. an account that is charged with advances of money for expenses, on salaries, against earnings, etc., esp. for salesmen.

drawing card, an entertainer, act, etc., which can be relied upon to produce a large audience.

drawing pin, *Brit.* a thumbtack.

drawing room, 1. a room for the reception of company. 2. *U.S.* a private compartment in a railway car. 3. *Brit.* a formal reception, esp. at court. [f. obs. *drawing* *withdrawing* + ROOM]

draw·knife (drô′nīf′), *n. Carp., etc.* a knife with a handle at each end at right angles to the blade used by drawing over a surface. Also, **drawing knife.**

Drawknife

drawl (drôl), *v.t., v.i.* 1. to say or speak with slow, lingering utterance. —*n.* 2. act or utterance of one who drawls. [appar. a freq. form connected with DRAW. Cf. D *dralen,* LG *drauelen* loiter] —**drawl′er,** *n.* —**drawl′ing·ly,** *adv.* —**drawl′y,** *adj.*

drawn (drôn), *v.* 1. pp. of **draw.** —*adj.* 2. eviscerated, as a fowl.

drawn butter sauce, *U.S.* a sauce of melted butter, flour, seasonings, and hot water.

drawn work, ornamental work done by drawing threads from a fabric, the remaining portions usually being formed into lacelike patterns by needlework.

draw·plate (drô′plāt′), *n. Mach.* a die plate with conical holes through which to draw wire and thus to regulate its size and shape.

draw·shave (drô′shāv′), *n. Carp., etc.* drawknife.

draw string, a string, cord, etc., which tightens or closes an opening, as of a bag, clothing, etc., when one or both ends are pulled.

draw·tube (drô′tūb′, -tōōb′), *n.* a tube sliding within another tube, as the tube carrying the eyepiece in a microscope.

dray (drā), *n.* 1. a low, strong cart without fixed sides, for carrying heavy loads. 2. a sledge or sled. —*v.t.* 3. to convey on a dray. [ME *draye* sled without wheels. Cf. OE *dræg-* in *drægnett* dragnet, der. OE *dragan* draw]

dray·age (drā′ĭj), *n.* 1. conveyance by dray. 2. a charge made for it.

dray·man (drā′mən), *n., pl.* -**men.** a man who drives a dray.

Dray·ton (drā′tən), *n.* **Michael,** 1563–1631, English poet.

dread (drĕd), *v.t.* 1. to fear greatly; be in shrinking apprehension or expectation of: *to dread death.* 2. *Obs.* to hold in respectful awe. —*v.i.* 3. to be in great fear. —*n.* 4. terror or apprehension as to something future; great fear. 5. deep awe or reverence. 6. a person or thing dreaded. —*adj.* 7. greatly feared; frightful; terrible. 8. held in awe; revered. [ME *drede(n),* OE *drædan,* aphetic var. of *adrædan, ondrædan,* c. OHG *intrātan* fear] —**Syn.** 4. See **fear.** —**Ant.** 1. welcome.

dread·ful (drĕd′fəl), *adj.* 1. causing great dread, fear, or terror; terrible: *a dreadful storm.* 2. venerable; awe-inspiring. 3. *Colloq.* extremely bad, unpleasant, ugly, great, etc. —*n. Brit.* 4. a cheap, lurid story, as of crime or adventure. 5. a periodical given to highly sensational matter. —**dread′ful·ly,** *adv.* —**dread′ful·ness,** *n.* —**Syn.** 1. frightful, dire.

dread·nought (drĕd′nôt′), *n.* 1. a type of battleship with the main battery consisting of heavy-caliber guns in turrets: so called from the British battleship, *Dreadnaught,* launched in 1906, the first of the type. 2. one who fears nothing. 3. an outer garment of heavy woolen cloth. 4. a thick cloth with a long pile. Also, **dread′naught′.**

dream (drēm), *n., v.,* **dreamed** or **dreamt, dreaming.** —*n.* 1. a succession of images or ideas present in the mind during sleep. 2. the sleeping state in which this occurs. 3. an object seen in a dream. 4. an involuntary vision occurring to one awake: *a waking dream.* 5. a vision voluntarily indulged in while awake; daydream; reverie. 6. a wild or vain fancy. 7. something of an unreal beauty or charm. —*v.i.* 8. to have a dream or dreams. 9. to indulge in daydreams or reveries. 10. to think or conceive of something in a very remote way (fol. by *of*). —*v.t.* 11. to see or imagine in sleep or in a vision. 12. to imagine as if in a dream; fancy; suppose. 13. to pass or spend (time, etc.) in dreaming (often fol. by *away*). [ME *dreem* dream, OE *drēam* mirth, noise; change of meaning prob. due to Scand. influence. Cf. Icel. *draumr* dream] —**dream′er,** *n.* —**dream′ful,** *adj.* —**dream′ing·ly,** *adv.* —**dream′less,** *adj.*

dream·land (drēm′lănd′), *n.* the land of imagination or fancy; the region of reverie.

dreamt (drĕmt), *v.* a pt. and pp. of **dream.**

dream world, the world of fancy, rather than of objective reality.

dream·y (drē'mĭ), *adj.*, **dreamier, dreamiest. 1.** full of dreams; characterized by or causing dreams. **2.** of the nature of or characteristic of dreams; visionary. **3.** vague; dim. **—dream'i·ly,** *adv.* **—dream'i·ness,** *n.*

drear·y (drĭr'ĭ), *adj.*, **drearier, dreariest. 1.** causing sadness or gloom. **2.** dull. **3.** *Archaic.* sad; sorrowful. Also, *Poetic,* **drear.** [ME *drery*, OE *drēorig* gory, cruel, sad] **—drear'i·ly,** *adv.* **—drear'i·ness,** *n.* **—drear·i·some** (drĭr'ĭsəm), *adj.* **—Syn. 1.** gloomy, dismal, drear, cheerless. **2.** tedious, monotonous, wearisome. **—Ant. 2.** interesting.

dredge¹ (drĕj), *n.*, *v.*, **dredged, dredging. —n. 1.** any of various powerful machines for dredging up or removing earth, etc., as from the bottom of a river, by means of a scoop, a series of buckets, a suction pipe, or the like. **2.** a dragnet or other contrivance for gathering material or objects from the bed of a river, etc. **—v.t. 3.** to clear out with a dredge; remove sand, silt, mud, etc., from the bottom of. **4.** to take, catch, or gather with a dredge; obtain or remove by a dredge. **—v.i. 5.** to use a dredge. [late ME *dreg*, akin to OE *dragan* DRAW]

dredge² (drĕj), *v.t.*, **dredged, dredging.** *Cookery.* to sprinkle or coat with some powdered substance, esp. flour. [appar. v. use of *dredge* mixed grain]

dredg·er¹ (drĕj'ər), *n.* *Brit.* **1.** dredge¹ (def. 1). **2.** one who uses a dredge. [f. DREDGE¹ + -ER¹]

dredg·er² (drĕj'ər), *n.* a container with a perforated top for sprinkling flour, etc. [f. DREDGE² + -ER¹]

dredging machine, dredge (def. 1).

dree (drē), *v.*, **dreed, dreeing,** *adj.* **—v.t. 1.** *Scot.* and *N. Eng.* to suffer; endure. **—adj. 2.** Also, **dreegh** (drēKH), **dreigh** (drēKH), **driegh.** *N. Eng.* tedious; dreary. [ME; OE *drēogan* endure].

dreg (drĕg), *n.* **1.** (*usually pl.*) the sediment of liquors; lees; grounds. **2.** any waste or worthless residue; refuse. **3.** a small remnant; any small quantity. [ME, t. Scand.; cf. Icel. *dreggjar* dregs] **—dreg'gy,** *adj.*

Drei·bund (drī'bŏŏnt'), *n.* **1.** the alliance between Germany, Austria-Hungary, and Italy, formed in 1882 and continuing until the withdrawal of Italy in May, 1915. **2.** (*l.c. or cap.*) a triple alliance. [G: f. *drei* three + *bund* alliance]

Drei·ser (drī'sər, -zər), *n.* **Theodore,** 1871–1945, U.S. novelist.

drench (drĕnch), *v.t.* **1.** to wet thoroughly; steep; soak: *garments drenched with rain, swords drenched in blood.* **2.** to cause to drink. **3.** *Vet. Sci.* to administer a draft of medicine to (an animal), esp. by force: *to drench a horse.* **—n. 4.** act of drenching. **5.** something that drenches: *a drench of rain.* **6.** a preparation for drenching or steeping. **7.** a large drink or draft. **8.** a draft of medicine, esp. one administered to an animal by force. [ME *drenche(n)*, OE *drencan,* causative of *drincan* drink] **—drench'er,** *n.* **—Syn. 1.** See wet.

Dres·den (drĕz'dən), *Ger.* drās'dən), *n.* **1.** a city in East Germany, on the Elbe. 496,548 (est. 1955). **2.** an expensive china originally from Dresden.

dress (drĕs), *n.*, *adj.*, *v.*, **dressed** or **drest, dressing. —n. 1.** the garment worn by women, consisting of a skirt and a waist, made either separately or together. **2.** clothing; apparel; garb. **3.** fine clothes; formal costume: *full dress.* **4.** outer covering, as the plumage of birds. **—adj. 5.** of or for a dress or dresses. **6.** of or for a formal occasion: *a dress suit.* [n., adj. uses of v.] **—v.t. 7.** to equip with clothing, ornaments, etc.; deck; attire. **8.** to put formal or evening clothes on. **9.** to put best clothes on (fol. by *up*). **10.** to trim; ornament; adorn; *to dress a store window.* **11.** to prepare (food, skins, fabrics, timber, stone, ore, etc.) by special processes. **12.** to comb out and do up (hair). **13.** to cultivate (land, etc.). **14.** to treat (wounds or sores). **15.** to make straight; bring (troops) into line: *to dress ranks.* **16.** *Colloq.* to scold; thrash (fol. by *down*). **17. dress ship, a.** to decorate a ship by hoisting lines of flags running the full length of the ship. **b.** *U.S. Navy.* to display the national ensigns at each masthead and a larger ensign on the flagstaff. **—v.i. 18.** to clothe or attire oneself, esp. in formal or evening clothes: *she is dressing.* **19.** to put on one's best clothing (fol. by *up*). **20.** to come into line, as troops. [ME *dres(en),* t. OF: m. *dresser* arrange, ult. der. L *directus* straight. See DIRECT v.] **—Syn. 1.** DRESS, COSTUME, GOWN refer to the outer garment of women. DRESS is the general term, esp. for a garment such as is used not only for covering but for adornment: *a black dress, a summer dress, a becoming dress.* COSTUME is used of the style of dress appropriate to some occasion, purpose, period, or character, esp. as used on the stage, at balls, at court, or the like: *an eighteenth-century costume, an appropriate costume for the country, costumes worn at an important social event.* GOWN is usually applied to a dress more expensive and elegant than the ordinary, to be worn on a special occasion: *a wedding gown, an evening gown* (or *dress*). **2.** raiment, vesture, clothes, garments, vestments. **7.** clothe, apparel, array, robe.

dress circle, a circular or curving division of seats in a theater, etc., usually the first gallery, orig. set apart for spectators in evening dress.

dress coat, a man's close-fitting evening coat, with open front and with the skirts cut away over the hips.

dress·er¹ (drĕs'ər), *n.* **1.** one who dresses. **2.** one employed to help dress actors, etc., at a theater. **3.** any of several tools or devices used in dressing materials. **4.** *Brit.* an assistant to a surgeon. [f. DRESS + -ER¹]

dress·er² (drĕs'ər), *n.* **1.** a dressing table or bureau. **2.** a sideboard or set of shelves for dishes and cooking utensils. **3.** *Obs.* a table or sideboard on which food is dressed for serving. [ME *dressour*, t. OF: m. *dresseur*, der. *dresser* DRESS]

dress goods, cloth or material for dresses.

dress·ing (drĕs'ĭng), *n.* **1.** act of one who or that which dresses. **2.** that with which something is dressed. **3.** a sauce for food: *salad dressing.* **4.** stuffing for a fowl. **5.** an application for a wound. **6.** manure, compost, or other fertilizers for land.

dress·ing-down (drĕs'ĭng doun'), *n.* *Colloq.* **1.** a severe reprimand; scolding. **2.** a thrashing; beating.

dressing gown, a loose gown or robe worn while making the toilet or when in dishabille.

dressing room, a room for use in getting dressed, esp. backstage in a theater.

dressing sack, *U.S.* a woman's sack or jacket for wearing while making the toilet or when in dishabille.

dressing station, *Mil.* a post or center close to the combat area, which gives first aid to the wounded.

dressing table, a table or stand, usually surmounted by a mirror, for use in making the toilet.

dress·mak·er (drĕs'mā'kər), *n.* one whose occupation is the making of women's dresses, coats, etc. **—dress'mak'ing,** *n.*

dress parade, the ceremony at which soldiers in their dress uniforms take formation under arms.

dress rehearsal, a rehearsal of a play in costume and with scenery, properties, and lights arranged and operated as for a performance; the final rehearsal.

dress shield, a pad worn under the arms beneath the clothing to keep perspiration from showing or staining.

dress suit, a man's suit of evening clothes, with dress coat and open-fronted waistcoat.

dress·y (drĕs'ĭ), *adj.*, **dressier, dressiest.** *Colloq.* **1.** showy in dress; stylish. **2.** fond of dress. **—dress'i·ness,** *n.*

drest (drĕst), *v.* a pt. and pp. of **dress.**

drew (drōō), *v.* pt. of **draw.**

Drew (drōō), *n.* **1. John,** 1827–62, U.S. actor, born in Ireland. **2.** his son **John,** 1853–1927, U.S. actor.

Drey·fus (drā'fəs, drī'-; *Fr.* drĕ'fŭs'), *n.* **Alfred** (ăl'frĭd; *Fr.* ăl frĕd'), 1859–1935, French army officer (Jewish) convicted of treason in 1894 and 1899, but proved innocent in 1906.

drib·ble (drĭb'əl), *v.*, **-bled, -bling,** *n.* **—v.i. 1.** to fall or flow in drops or small quantities; trickle. **2.** to drivel; slaver. **3.** (in men's basketball) to move about a court while bouncing the ball. **—v.t. 4.** to let fall in drops. **5.** *Sports.* **a.** (in men's basketball) to bounce (a basketball). **b.** (in some other games) to move (the ball) along by a rapid succession of short kicks or pushes. **—n. 6.** a small trickling stream, or a drop. **7.** a small quantity of anything. **8.** *Sports.* **a.** (in men's basketball) act of bouncing a basketball on the floor of the court as a player moves with the ball, it being a penalty to take more than two steps without such bouncing while in possession of the ball. **b.** (in some other games) act of dribbling. **9.** *Scot.* a drizzle. [freq. of obs. *drib* drip; in some senses influenced by DRIVEL] **—drib'bler,** *n.*

drib·let (drĭb'lĭt), *n.* **1.** a small portion or part. **2.** a small or petty sum. Also, **drib'blet.** [f. DRIBBLE + -ET]

dried (drīd), *v.* pt. and pp. of **dry.**

driegh (drēKH), *adj.* dree.

dri·er (drī'ər), *adj.* **1.** compar. of **dry.** **—n.** Also, **dryer. 2.** one who or that which dries. **3.** any substance added to paints, varnishes, etc., to make them dry quickly. **4.** mechanical contrivance or apparatus for removing moisture.

dri·est (drī'ĭst), *adj.* superl. of **dry.**

drift (drĭft), *n.* **1.** a driving movement or force; impulse; impetus; pressure. **2.** *Navig.* movement or course under the impulse of water currents, wind, etc. **3.** *Phys. Geog.* a broad and shallow current which advances at a rate of ten or fifteen miles a day, like that which crosses the middle Atlantic. **4.** *Naut.* the speed in knots of an ocean current. **5.** *Aeron.* deviation of an aircraft from a set course, due to cross winds. **6.** the course of anything; tendency; aim: *the drift of an argument.* **7.** something driven, or formed by driving. **8.** a heap of any matter driven together: *a drift of snow.* **9.** *Geol.* **a.** a deposit of detritus. **b.** the deposit of a continental ice sheet. **10.** state or process of being driven. **11.** overbearing power or influence. **12.** an implement for cleaning the vent of ordnance after discharge. **13.** *Mach.* a round, tapering piece of steel for enlarging holes in metal, or for bringing holes in line to receive rivets, etc. **14.** *Civ. Eng.* a secondary tunnel between two main tunnels or shafts. **15.** *Mining.* an approximately horizontal passageway in underground mining, etc. **—v.i. 16.** to be carried along by currents of water or air, or by the force of circumstances. **17.** to be driven into heaps: *drifting sand.* **—v.t. 18.** to carry along: *the current drifted the boat to sea.* **19.** to drive into heaps: *drifted snow.* [ME *drift* act of driving, verbal abstract from OE *drīfan* drive] **—drift'er,** *n.*

drift·age (drĭf'tĭj), *n.* **1.** action or amount of drifting. **2.** drifted matter. **3.** *Naut.* the amount of deviation from a ship's course due to leeway. **4.** windage.

drift anchor, a sea anchor or drag.

drift ice, detached floating ice in masses which drift with the wind or ocean currents, as in the polar seas.

drift meter, *Aeron.* an instrument for measuring the drift of aircraft.

drift tube, *Radio.* a conducting enclosure, usually cylindrical, held at a constant potential so that electrons or charged particles within will experience no force, and hence no change in velocity. See **klystron.**

drift·wood (drĭft′wŏŏd′), *n.* wood floating on, or cast ashore by, the water.

drift·y (drĭf′tĭ), *adj.* of the nature of, or characterized by, drifts.

drill[1] (drĭl), *n.* 1. a tool or machine for drilling or boring holes in metal, stone, or other hard substance. 2. *Mil.* **a.** training in formal marching or other precise military or naval movements. **b.** an exercise in such training: *gun drill.* 3. any strict, methodical training, instruction, or exercise. 4. a gastropod, *Urosalpinx cinera,* destructive to oysters. —*v.t.* 5. to pierce or bore a hole in (anything). 6. to make (a hole) by boring. 7. *Mil.* to instruct and exercise in formation marching and movement, the carrying of arms during formal marching, and the formal handling of arms for ceremonies and guard work. 8. to impart (knowledge) by strict training or discipline. —*v.i.* 9. to pierce or bore with a drill. 10. to go through exercise in military or other training. [t. D: m. *drillen* bore, drill] —**drill′a·ble,** *adj.* —**drill′er,** *n.* —**Syn.** 3. See **exercise.**

drill[2] (drĭl), *n.* 1. a small furrow made in the soil in which to sow seeds. 2. a machine for sowing in rows and for covering the seeds when sown. 3. a row of seeds or plants thus sown. —*v.t.* 4. to sow (seed) or raise (crops) in drills. 5. to plant (ground) in drills. —*v.i.* 6. to sow seed in drills. [orig. uncert.] —**drill′er,** *n.*

drill[3] (drĭl), *n.* strong twilled cotton for a variety of uses. [short for **DRILLING**[2], t. G: triplet, confused with *drillich* ticking (f. *dri* three + *-lich*), t. L: m. s. *trilix* with three threads, *tri-* being translated]

drill[4] (drĭl), *n.* a baboon, *Papio leucophaeus,* of western Africa, smaller than the mandrill. [appar. native name. See **MANDRILL**]

drill bit, *Mach.* a boring tool for making round holes in metal or other hard substance.

drill·ing[1] (drĭl′ĭng), *n.* act of a person or thing that drills. [f. **DRILL**[1], v. + **-ING**[1]]

drill·ing[2] (drĭl′ĭng), *n.* **drill**[3].

drill·mas·ter (drĭl′măs′tər, -mäs′tər), *n.* 1. one who trains others in anything, esp. in a mechanical manner. 2. *Mil.* one who instructs in marching drill.

drill press, *Mach.* a machine tool for boring holes with a drill or drills.

dri·ly (drī′lĭ), *adv.* dryly.

Drin (drĕn), *n.* a river flowing from S Yugoslavia through N Albania into the Adriatic. 180 mi.

Dri·na (drē′nä), *n.* a river in central Yugoslavia, flowing N to the Sava river. 160 mi.

drink (drĭngk), *v.,* **drank** (formerly also **drunk**); **drunk** (sometimes **drank,** formerly or as pred. adj. **drunken**); **drinking;** *n.* —*v.i.* 1. to swallow water or other liquid; imbibe. 2. to imbibe alcoholic liquors, esp. habitually or to excess; tipple. 3. to salute in drinking; drink in honor of (fol. by *to*). —*v.t.* 4. to swallow (a liquid). 5. to take in (a liquid) in any manner; absorb. 6. to take in through the senses, esp. with eagerness and pleasure. 7. to swallow the contents of (a cup, etc.). 8. to drink in honor of or with good wishes for. —*n.* 9. any liquid which is swallowed to quench thirst, for nourishment, etc.; a beverage. 10. alcoholic liquor. 11. excessive indulgence in alcoholic liquor. 12. a draft of liquid; a potion. [ME *drinke(n),* OE *drincan,* c. G *trinken*] —**Syn.** 1. DRINK, IMBIBE, SIP refer to swallowing liquids. DRINK is the general word: *to drink coffee.* IMBIBE is more formal and today is hardly used in reference to actual drinking except facetiously; it is used figuratively in the meaning to absorb: *to imbibe culture.* SIP implies drinking little by little, at short, succeeding intervals, often in a delicate, toying, or idle manner: *sip a cup of broth.*

drink·a·ble (drĭngk′ə bəl), *adj.* 1. that may be drunk; suitable for drinking. —*n.* 2. (*usually pl.*) something drinkable; a liquid for drinking.

drink·er (drĭngk′ər), *n.* 1. one who drinks. 2. one who drinks alcoholic liquors habitually or to excess.

Drink·wa·ter (drĭngk′wô′tər, -wŏt′ər), *n.* **John,** 1882–1937, British poet, dramatist, and critic.

drip (drĭp), *v.,* **dripped** or **dript, dripping,** *n.* —*v.i.* 1. to let fall drops; shed drops. 2. to fall in drops, as a liquid. —*v.t.* 3. to let fall in drops. —*n.* 4. act of dripping. 5. the liquid that drips. 6. *Archit.* a projecting part of a cornice or the like, so shaped as to throw off rain water and thus protect the parts below. **b.** a projecting metal strip having the same function. [ME *dryppe,* OE *dryppan,* der. OE *dropa* drop]

drip coffee, a beverage prepared in a vessel (**drip coffee maker**) in which boiling water filters from a top compartment through the coffee into a pot below.

drip·ping (drĭp′ĭng), *n.* 1. act of anything that drips. 2. (*often pl.*) the liquid that drips. 3. fat exuded from meat in cooking and used as shortening.

dripping pan, a pan used under roasting meat to receive the dripping. Also, **drip pan.**

drip·stone (drĭp′stōn′), *n.* 1. *Archit.* a projecting stone molding or cornice for throwing off rain water.

2. calcium carbonate, $CaCO_3$, occurring in the form of stalactites and stalagmites.

drive (drīv), *v.,* **drove** or (*Archaic*) **drave; driven; driving;** *n.* —*v.t.* 1. to send along, away, off, in, out, back, etc., by compulsion; force along: *to drive someone to desperation, out of one's senses, to do something.* 2. to overwork; overtask. 3. to cause and guide the movement of (an animal, vehicle, etc.). 4. to convey in a vehicle. 5. to keep (machinery) going. 6. to impel; constrain; urge; compel. 7. to carry (business, a bargain, etc.) vigorously through. 8. *Mining, etc.* to excavate horizontally (or nearly so). 9. *Baseball, Tennis, etc.* to knock or throw (the ball) very swiftly. 10. *Hunting.* **a.** to chase (game). **b.** to search (a district) for game. —*v.i.* 11. to go along before an impelling force; be impelled: *the ship drove before the wind.* 12. to rush or dash violently. 13. to make an effort to reach or obtain; aim (fol. by *at*): *the idea he was driving at, what is he driving at?* 14. to act as driver. 15. to go or travel in a driven vehicle: *to drive away, back, in, out, from, to, etc.* 16. let drive (at), to aim a blow, missile, etc., (at). —*n.* 17. the act of driving. 18. an impelling along, as of game, cattle, or floating logs, in a particular direction. 19. the animals, logs, etc., thus driven. 20. *Psychol.* a source of motivation: *the hunger drive.* 21. *Sports.* a propelling or forcible stroke. 22. a vigorous onset or onward course. 23. a strong military offensive. 24. a united effort to accomplish some purpose, esp. to raise money for a government loan or for some charity. 25. vigorous pressure or effort, as in business. 26. a trip in a driven vehicle. 27. a road for driving. 28. *Mach.* a driving mechanism, as of a motorcar: *gear drive, chain drive.* 29. *Auto.* point or points of power application to the roadway: *front drive, rear drive, four-wheel drive.* 30. *Trade Slang.* an attempt to force down the market price of a commodity by offering a quantity at a low price. 31. *Baseball, Tennis, etc.* the knocking of a ball very swiftly. [ME *driven,* OE *drīfan,* c. G *treiben*] —**Syn.** 1. push, force. 15. DRIVE, RIDE are used interchangeably to mean taking a trip in a private horse-drawn vehicle or an automobile. These two words are not synonyms in other connections. To DRIVE is to guide or steer the progress of a vehicle: *to drive a bus, a truck, an automobile, a horse, oxen.* To RIDE is to sit on the back of, and be carried about by, an animal; or to be carried as a passenger in a vehicle: *to ride a horse, in a train, on a bus, on a public conveyance.* 25. energy. —**Ant.** 1. lead.

drive-in (drīv′ĭn′), *n.* a motion-picture theater, refreshment stand, etc., catering to customers who remain in their automobiles.

driv·el (drĭv′əl), *v.,* **-eled, -eling** or (*esp. Brit.*) **-elled, -elling,** *n.* —*v.i.* 1. to let saliva flow from the mouth or mucus from the nose; slaver. 2. to issue like spittle. 3. to talk childishly or idiotically. 4. to act foolishly. —*v.t.* 5. to utter childishly or idiotically. 6. to waste foolishly. —*n.* 7. saliva flowing from the mouth, or mucus from the nose; slaver. 8. childish, idiotic, or silly talk; twaddle. [ME *dryvele, drevel(en),* OE *dreflian*] —**driv′el·er;** *esp. Brit.,* **driv′el·ler,** *n.*

driv·en (drĭv′ən), *v.* pp. of **drive.**

driv·er (drī′vər), *n.* 1. one who or that which drives. 2. one who drives an animal or animals, a vehicle, etc.; coachman, drover, chauffeur, etc. 3. *Brit.* a locomotive engineer. 4. *Mach.* a part that transmits force or motion. 5. *Golf.* a long-shafted, wooden-headed club, used for making long shots, as from the tee. —**driv′er·less,** *adj.*

driver ant, any of the ants of the subfamily *Dorylinae,* occurring in tropical Africa and America, which live in temporary nests and travel as vast armies in long files, preying on other animals, chiefly insects. See **army ant.**

drive·way (drīv′wā′), *n.* 1. a private road from a house to the street. 2. a road for driving on.

driv·ing (drī′vĭng), *adj.* 1. (of a person) effective in eliciting work from others; energetic. 2. relaying or transmitting power.

driving wheel, 1. *Mach.* a main wheel which communicates motion to others. 2. one of the propelling wheels of a locomotive; any wheel used to transform the force of the locomotive cylinder into tractive effort.

driz·zle (drĭz′əl), *v.,* **-zled, -zling,** *n.* —*v.i., v.t.* 1. to rain gently and steadily in fine drops; sprinkle. —*n.* 2. a very light rain; mist. 3. *Meteorol.* precipitation consisting of numerous, minute droplets of water less than ¹/₅₀ inch in diameter. [possibly dim. and freq. form of rare ME *dresen,* OE *drēosan* fall] —**driz′zly,** *adj.*

Drog·he·da (drŏ′hĭ də), *n.* a seaport in NE Ireland, near the mouth of the Boyne river: town captured and the inhabitants massacred by Cromwell, 1649. 16,779 (1951).

droit (droit; *Fr.* drwä), *n.* 1. a legal right or claim. 2. that to which one has a legal right or claim. 3. the body of rules constituting the law. 4. *Finance.* duty; custom. [t. F, g. Rom. *dērectum,* r. L *dīrectum* right, prop. neut. of L *dīrectus* straight. See **DIRECT,** adj.]

droll (drōl), *adj.* 1. amusingly queer; comical; waggish. —*n.* 2. a waggish fellow; a jester; a buffoon. —*v.i.* 3. to play the droll or buffoon; jest; joke. [t. F: m. *drôle,* t. MD: m. *drolle* little man] —**droll′ness,** *n.* —**droll′ly,** *adv.* —**Syn.** 1. See **amusing.**

droll·er·y (drō′lə rĭ), *n., pl.* **-eries.** 1. something amusingly queer or funny. 2. a jest; a facetious tale. 3. droll quality; humor. 4. the action or behavior of a buffoon or wag; jesting. 5. *Obs.* a comic picture. 6. *Obs.* a puppet show.

---

b., blend of, blended; **c.,** cognate with; **d.,** dialect, dialectal; **der.,** derived from; **f.,** formed from; **g.,** going back to; **m.,** modification of; **r.,** replacing; **s.,** stem of; **t.,** taken from; **?,** perhaps.   See the full key on inside cover.

drome, a word element meaning "running," "course," "race course," as in *hippodrome.* [comb. form repr. Gk. *drómos*]

rom·e·dar·y (drŏm′ə dĕr′Ĭ, drŭm′-), *n., pl.* **-daries.** the one-humped or Arabian camel, *Camelus dromedarius,* light swift types of which are bred for riding and racing. [ME *drome-darye,* t. LL: m. *dromedārius* (sc. *camēlus*), der. L *dromas* dromedary, t. Gk.: running]

rom·ond (drŏm′ənd, drŭm′-), *n.* a large, fast-sailing vessel of the Middle Ages. [ME *dromon,* t. LL: s. *dromo,* t. LGk.: m. *drŏmŏn* light vessel, der. Gk. *drŏmos* a running]

dromous, an adjective termination corresponding to **-drome.** [f. -DROME + -OUS]

Dromedary.
Camelus dromedarius
(6 ft. high at the shoulder,
7 to 8 ft. high at the hump)

rone¹ (drōn), *n.* **1.** the male of the honeybee and other bees, sting-less and making no honey. **2.** one who lives on the labor of others; an idler; a sluggard. **3.** a remotely controlled mechanism, as a radio-controlled airplane or boat. [earlier *dron(e), drowne,* early ME *dron,* var. of ME and OE *dran* (cf. G *drohne*) —**dron′ish,** *adj.*

rone² (drōn), *v.,* **droned, droning.** —*v.i.* **1.** to make a dull, continued, monotonous sound; hum; buzz. **2.** to speak in a monotonous tone. —*v.t.* **3.** to say in a dull, monotonous tone. —*n.* **4.** *Music.* **a.** a continuous low tone produced by the bass pipes or bass strings of musical instruments. **b.** the pipes (esp. of the bagpipe) or strings producing this tone. **c.** a bagpipe equipped with such pipes. **5.** a monotonous tone; a humming; a buzzing. **6.** a monotonous speaker. [cf. DRONE¹; akin to ME *droun* roar] —**dron′ing·ly,** *adv.*

ron·go (drŏng′gō), *n., pl.* **-gos.** any of the oscine passerine birds of the African and Asiatic family *Dicruridae,* usually black in color, with long forked tails, and insectivorous habits. [t. Malagasy]

rool (drōōl), *v., n. Colloq.* drivel. [contr. of DRIVEL]

roop (drōōp), *v.i.* **1.** to sink, bend, or hang down, as from weakness or exhaustion. **2.** *Poetic.* to sink; descend, as the sun. **3.** to fall into a state of physical weakness; flag; fail. **4.** to lose spirit or courage. —*v.t.* **5.** to let sink or droop. —*n.* **6.** a drooping. [ME *droupe(n),* t. Scand.; cf. Icel. *drúpa;* akin to DROP] —**droop′-ing·ly,** *adv.* —**droop′y,** *adj.* —**Syn. 1.** flag, languish.

rop (drŏp), *n., v.,* **dropped** or **dropt, dropping.** —*n.* **1.** a small quantity of liquid which falls or is produced in a more or less spherical mass; a liquid globule. **2.** the quantity of liquid contained in such a mass. **3.** a very small quantity of liquid. **4.** a minute quantity of anything. **5.** *(usually pl.)* liquid medicine given in drops. **6.** something like or likened to a drop. **7.** a lozenge (confection). **8.** a pendant. **9.** act of dropping; fall; descent. **10.** the distance or depth to which anything drops. **11.** a steep slope. **12.** that which drops or is used for dropping. **13.** a drop curtain. **14.** a trap door. **15.** gallows. **16.** a slit or aperture into which to drop mail, as a letter box. **17.** *Naut.* the vertical length of a course. See hoist. **18.** **get** or **have the drop on,** *Colloq.* **a.** to pull and aim a gun, etc., before an antagonist can. **b.** to get or have at a disadvantage. —*v.i.* **19.** to fall in globules or small portions, as water or other liquid: *rain drops from the clouds.* **20.** to fall vertically like a drop; have an abrupt descent. **21.** to sink to the ground as if inanimate. **22.** to fall wounded, dead, etc. **23.** to come to an end; cease; lapse: *there the matter dropped.* **24.** to withdraw; disappear (fol. by *out*). **25.** to squat or crouch, as a dog at the sight of game. **26.** to fall lower in condition, degree, etc.; sink: *the prices dropped sharply.* **27.** to pass without effort into some condition: *to drop asleep, drop into the habit of doing it.* **28.** to move down gently, as with the tide or a light wind. **29.** to fall or move (*back, behind, to the rear,* etc.). **30.** to come or go casually or unexpectedly into a place; to visit informally: *he dropped in on us occasionally.* **31.** to give birth. **32. drop astern,** to pass or move toward the stern; move back; let another vessel pass ahead. **33. drop off, a.** to decrease; decline: *sales have dropped off.* **b.** to fall asleep. —*v.t.* **34.** to let fall in drops or small portions: *drop a medicine.* **35.** *Archaic.* to sprinkle with or as with drops. **36.** to let fall; allow to sink to a lower position; lower: *to drop anchor.* **37.** to give birth to (young). **38.** to utter or express casually or incidentally, as a hint. **39.** to send (a note, etc.) in a casual or offhand manner: *drop me a line!* **40.** to bring to the ground by a blow or shot. **41.** to set down, as from a ship, car, etc. **42.** to omit (a letter or syllable) in pronunciation or writing: *he dropped his h's.* **43.** to lower (the voice) in pitch or loudness. **44.** to cease to keep up or have to do with: *I dropped the subject.* **45.** *U.S.* to cease to employ; to dismiss (from college, etc.). **46.** *Football.* to score (a goal) by a drop kick. **47.** *Naut.* to outdistance; pass out of sight of. **48.** *Cookery.* to poach. [ME *drope,* OE *dropa,* c. Icel. *dropi.*]

rop biscuit, a biscuit made by dropping baking powder biscuit dough from a spoon onto a pan for baking.

rop cooky, a cooky made by dropping batter from a spoon onto a greased cooky sheet for baking.

rop curtain, *Theat.* a curtain which is lowered into position from t he flies.

drop-forge (drŏp′fôrj′), *v.t.,* **-forged, -forging.** *Metall.* to forge by the impact of a falling mass or weight, the hot piece of metal usually being placed between dies and subjected to the blow of a drop hammer or the like.

drop forging, *Metal.* a drop-forged forging.

drop hammer, an apparatus for forging, etc., in which a heavy weight is made to drop on the metal to be worked, which is placed on an anvil or in dies.

drop kick, *Football.* a kick given the ball as it rises from the ground after being dropped by the kicker.

drop-kick (drŏp′kĭk′), *v.i., v.t. Football.* to give a drop kick. —**drop′-kick′er, n.**

drop leaf, *Furnit.* an extension attached to the end or side of a table and folded vertically when not needed. —**drop′-leaf′, adj.**

drop·let (drŏp′lĭt), *n.* a little drop.

drop letter, *U.S.* a letter to be delivered from or by the same post office in which it is posted.

drop·light (drŏp′līt′), *n.* a portable gas or electric lamp connected with a fixture above by a tube or wire.

drop·per (drŏp′ər), *n.* **1.** one who or that which drops. **2.** a glass tube with an elastic cap at one end and a small orifice at the other, for drawing in a liquid and expelling it in drops; medicine dropper.

drop·ping (drŏp′ĭng), *n.* **1.** act of one who or that which drops. **2.** that which drops or falls in drops. **3.** *(pl.)* dung of animals.

drop shipment, *Com.* an order shipped by a seller to the customer or his distributor, as a shipment by a manufacturer to a retailer that is billed to a wholesaler.

drop·si·cal (drŏp′sĭ kəl), *adj.* of, like, or affected with dropsy. —**drop′si·cal·ly, adv.**

drop·sy (drŏp′sĭ), *n. Pathol.* an excessive accumulation of serous fluid in a serous cavity or in the subcutaneous cellular tissue. [ME *(y)dropesie,* t. OF: m. *idropisie,* t. L: m.s. *hydrōpsis,* der. Gk. *hydrōps*] —**drop′sied** (drŏp′sĭd), *adj.*

dropt (drŏpt), *v.* pt. and pp. of **drop.**

drop-wort (drŏp′wûrt′), *n.* **1.** a European rosaceous herb, *Filipendula hexapetala,* bearing small, scentless, white or reddish flowers. **2.** any plant of the North American umbelliferous genus *Oxypolis (Tiedmania),* as *O. rigidior,* an herb of ditches and marshes.

drosh·ky (drŏsh′kĭ), *n., pl.* **-kies. 1.** a light, low, four-wheeled, open vehicle, used in Russia, in which the passengers sit astride or sideways on a long, narrow bench. **2.** any of various other vehicles, as the ordinary cab, used mainly in Russia. Also, **dros·ky** (drŏs′kĭ). [t. Russ.: m. *drozhki,* dim. of *drogi* wagon]

dro·soph·i·la (drō sŏf′ə lə), *n., pl.* **-lae** (-lē′). a fly of the genus *Drosophila.*

Dro·soph·i·la (drō sŏf′ə lə), *n.pl.* a genus of flies of the family *Drosophilidae,* one species of which, the vinegar fly, *D. melanogaster,* is very widely used in laboratory studies of inheritance. [NL, f. Gk.: *dróso(s)* dew + *phila,* fem. of *philos* loving]

dross (drôs, drŏs), *n.* **1.** *Metall.* a waste product taken off molten metal during smelting, essentially metallic in character. **2.** waste matter; refuse. [ME and OE *drōs,* c. MD *droes* dregs. Cf. G *drusen* dregs, husks] —**dross′y, adj.** —**dross′i·ness, n.**

drought (drout), *n.* **1.** dry weather; lack of rain. **2.** *Now Rare.* scarcity. **3.** *Dial.* thirst. Also, **drouth** (drouth). [ME *drought(h),* etc., OE *drūgath,* akin to *drȳge* dry]

drought·y (drou′tĭ), *adj.* **1.** dry. **2.** lacking rain. **3.** *Dial.* or *Prov.* thirsty. Also, **drouth·y** (drou′thĭ).

drouk (drōōk), *v.t. Scot.* to drench; wet thoroughly. [t. Scand.; cf. Icel. *drukna* be drowned]

drove¹ (drōv), *v.* pt. of **drive.**

drove² (drōv), *n., v.,* **droved, droving.** —*n.* **1.** a number of oxen, sheep, or swine driven in a group; herd; flock. **2.** a large crowd of human beings, esp. in motion. **3.** *Bldg. Trades.* **a.** Also, **drove chisel,** a stonemason's chisel, from two to four inches broad, used in making droved work. **b.** drove work. —*v.t., v.i.* **4.** to drive or deal in (cattle) as a drover. **5.** *Bldg. Trades.* to work or smooth (stone, etc.) as with a stonemason's drove. [ME; OE *drāf* act of driving, herd, company. See DRIVE] —**Syn. 1.** See **flock¹.**

dro·ver (drō′vər), *n.* **1.** one who drives cattle, sheep, etc., to market. **2.** a dealer in cattle.

drove work, *Bldg. Trades.* the surface of stone worked with a drove.

drown (droun), *v.i.* **1.** to be suffocated by immersion in water or other liquid. —*v.t.* **2.** to suffocate (a person, etc.) by immersion in water or other liquid. **3.** to destroy; get rid of. **4.** to flood; inundate. **5.** to overwhelm as by a flood; overpower. [var. of obs. *drunken,* OE *druncnian;* ME *drounne* shows loss of *c* between the nasals; length of nasal later shifted to vowel]

drowse (drouz), *v.,* **drowsed, drowsing,** *n.* —*v.i.* **1.** to be sleepy; be half-asleep. **2.** to be dull or sluggish. —*v.t.* **3.** to make sleepy. **4.** to pass or spend (time) in drowsing. —*n.* **5.** a sleepy condition; state of being half-asleep. [OE *drūsian* droop, become sluggish]

drow·si·head (drou′zĭ hĕd′), *n. Archaic.* drowsiness.

drow·sy (drou′zĭ), *adj.,* **-sier, -siest. 1.** inclined to sleep; half asleep. **2.** marked by or resulting from sleepiness. **3.** dull; sluggish. **4.** inducing sleepiness. —**drow′si·ly, adv.** —**drow′si·ness, n.**

ăct, āble, dâre, ärt; ĕbb, ēqual; Ĭf, īce; hŏt, ōver, ôrder, oil, bŏŏk, ōōze, out; ŭp, ūse, ûrge; ə = a in alone; ŭ, chief; g, give; ng, ring; sh, shoe; th, thin; ŧh, that; zh, vision. See the full key on inside cover.

drub (drŭb), v., **drubbed, drubbing,** n. —v.t. **1.** to beat with a stick or the like; cudgel; flog; thrash: *to drub something into or out of a person.* **2.** to defeat decisively. **3.** to stamp (the feet). —n. **4.** a blow with a stick or the like. [? t. Ar.: m. *ḍarb* stroke] —**drub′ber,** n.

drub·bing (drŭb′ĭng), n. **1.** a beating; a sound thrashing. **2.** a decisive defeat.

drudge (drŭj), n., v., **drudged, drudging.** —n. **1.** one who labors at servile or uninteresting tasks; a hard toiler. —v.i. **2.** to perform servile, distasteful, or hard work. [OE *Drycg*- bearer (in proper name); akin to DREE] —**drudg′er,** n. —**drudg′ing·ly,** adv.

drudg·er·y (drŭj′ər ĭ), n., pl. **-eries.** tedious, hard, or uninteresting work. —**Syn.** See work.

drug (drŭg), n., v., **drugged, drugging.** —n. **1.** a chemical substance given with the intention of preventing or curing disease or otherwise enhancing the physical or mental welfare of men or animals. **2.** a habit-forming medicinal substance; a narcotic. **3.** (formerly) any ingredient used in chemistry, pharmacy, dyeing, or the like. **4.** a commodity that is overabundant, or in excess of demand, in the market. —v.t. **5.** to mix (food or drink) with a drug, esp. a narcotic or poisonous drug. **6.** to stupefy or poison with a drug. **7.** to administer anything nauseous to; surfeit. [ME *drogges* (pl.), t. OF: m. *drogue,* ? t. D: m. *drog* dry thing]

drug·get (drŭg′ĭt), n. **1.** a rug from India made of coarse hair with cotton or jute. **2.** *Obs.* a fabric woven wholly or partly of wool, used for clothing. [t. F: m. *droguet,* der. *drogue* drug, cheap article]

drug·gist (drŭg′ĭst), n. *Scot. and U.S.* one who compounds or prepares drugs according to medical prescriptions; apothecary; pharmacist; dispensing chemist.

drug store, *U.S.* the place of business of a druggist or pharmacist, often also selling cosmetics, stationery, light meals, cigarettes, etc.

Dru·id (drōō′ĭd), n. (*often l.c.*) one of an order of priests or ministers of religion among the ancient Celts of Gaul, Britain, and Ireland. [t. L: m. *druide,* t. L: m. *druidae,* pl.] —**Dru·id·ess** (drōō′ĭd ĭs), n. fem. —**dru·id′ic,** adj. —**dru·id′i·cal,** adj.

dru·id·ism (drōō′ĭd ĭz′əm), n. the religion or rites of the Druids.

drum¹ (drŭm), n., v., **drummed, drumming.** —n. **1.** a musical instrument consisting of a hollow body covered at one or both ends with a tightly stretched membrane, or head, which is struck with the hand, a stick, or a pair of sticks. **2.** any hollow tree or similar device used in this way. **3.** the sound produced by either of these. **4.** any noise suggestive of it. **5.** one who plays the drum. **6.** a natural organ by which an animal produces a loud or bass sound. **7.** something resembling a drum in shape or structure, or in the noise it produces. **8.** *Anat., Zool.* **a.** the tympanum or middle ear. **b.** the eardrum or tympanic membrane. **9.** a cylindrical part of a machine. **10.** a cylindrical box or receptacle. **11.** drumfish. **12.** *Obs.* an assembly of fashionable people at a private house in the evening. —v.i. **13.** to beat or play a drum. **14.** to beat on anything rhythmically. **15.** to make a sound like that of a drum; resound. **16.** (of partridges and other birds) to produce a sound resembling drumming. —v.t. **17.** to beat rhythmically; perform (a tune) by drumming. **18.** to call or summon by, or as by, beating a drum. **19.** to drive or force by persistent repetition: *to drum an idea into someone.* **20.** to solicit or obtain (trade, customers, etc.) (often fol. by *up*). **21.** (formerly) to expel or dismiss in disgrace to the beat of a drum (fol. by *out*). [back formation from *drumslade* drummer, t. LG: m. *trommelslag drumbeat* (confused in E with *trommelslager* drummer); E *d-* ? by assoc. with *dub-a-dub* sound made in beating a drum]

drum² (drŭm), n. *Irish, Scot.* a long, narrow hill or ridge. [t. Irish and Gaelic: m. *druim* back, ridge]

drum·beat (drŭm′bēt′), n. the sound of a drum.

drum·ble (drŭm′bəl, drŭm′əl), v.i., **-bled, -bling.** *Obs.* or *Prov.* to move sluggishly.

drum corps, a body of drum players under the direction of a drum major or the like.

drum·fire (drŭm′fīr′), n. gunfire so heavy and continuous as to sound like the beating of drums.

drum·fish (drŭm′fĭsh′), n., pl. **-fishes,** (*esp. collectively*) **-fish.** any of various American sciaenoid fishes producing a drumming sound, as *Pogonias cromis* of the Atlantic coast of the United States, or the **fresh-water drumfish,** *Aplodinotus grunniens,* of the Great Lakes and the Mississippi valley.

drum·head (drŭm′hĕd′), n. **1.** the membrane stretched upon a drum. **2.** the top part of a capstan.

drumhead court-martial, a court-martial held (orig. round an upturned drum for a table) for the summary trial of charges of offenses committed during military operations.

drum·lin (drŭm′lĭn), n. *Geol.* a long narrow, or oval, smoothly rounded hill of unstratified glacial drift. [? var. of *drumling,* dim. of DRUM²]

drum·ly (drŭm′lĭ), adj. *Scot.* troubled; gloomy.

drum major, the leader of a drum corps or band in marching.

drum·mer (drŭm′ər), n. **1.** one who plays a drum. **2.** *U.S.* a commercial traveler or traveling salesman.

Drum·mond (drŭm′ənd), n. **1. Henry,** 1851–97, Scottish clergyman and writer. **2. William Henry,** 1854–1907, Canadian poet, born in Ireland.

Drummond light, the calcium light. [named after Capt. T. *Drummond,* R.E.]

drum·stick (drŭm′stĭk′), n. **1.** a stick for beating a drum. **2.** the lower part of the leg of a cooked chicken, duck, turkey, etc.

drunk (drŭngk), pred. adj. **1.** intoxicated with, or as with, strong drink: *drunk with joy, success.* —n. *Colloq.* **2.** a drunken person. **3.** a spree; a drinking party. —v. **4.** pp. and former pt. of **drink.**

drunk·ard (drŭngk′ərd), n. a person who is habitually or frequently drunk.
—**Syn.** toper, sot. DRUNKARD, INEBRIATE, DIPSOMANIAC are terms for a person who drinks hard liquors habitually. DRUNKARD connotes willful indulgence to excess. INEBRIATE, once a more formal word, is now applied only humorously. DIPSOMANIAC is the term for a person who, because of some psychological or physiological illness, has an irresistible craving for liquor. The dipsomaniac is popularly called an ALCOHOLIC.

drunk·en (drŭngk′ən), adj. **1.** intoxicated; drunk. **2.** given to drunkenness. **3.** pertaining to, proceeding from, or marked by intoxication: *a drunken quarrel.* —**drunk′en·ly,** adv. —**drunk′en·ness,** n. —**Syn. 1.** inebriated, tipsy, fuddled.

dru·pa·ceous (drōō pā′shəs), adj. *Bot.* **1.** resembling or relating to a drupe; consisting of drupes. **2.** producing drupes: *drupaceous trees.*

drupe (drōōp), n. *Bot.* a fruit, as the peach, cherry, plum, etc., consisting of an outer skin (epicarp), a (generally) pulpy and succulent layer (mesocarp), and a hard and woody inner shell or stone (endocarp) which incloses usually a single seed. [t. NL: m. s. *drūpa* drupe, L *drūpa, druppa* overripe olive, t. Gk.: m. *drȳppa*]

drupe·let (drōōp′lĭt), n. *Bot.* a little drupe, as one of the individual pericarps composing the blackberry.

Druse (drōōz), n. one of a fanatical and warlike people and religious sect of Syria. [t. Ar.: m. *Durūz,* pl.] —**Dru·si·an, Dru·se·an** (drōō′zĭ ən), adj.

Dru·sus (drōō′səs), n. **Nero Claudius** (nĭr′ō klô′dĭ-əs), ("*Germanicus*") 38 B.C.–9 B.C., Roman general.

dry (drī), adj., **drier, driest,** v., **dried, drying,** n., pl. **drys.** —adj. **1.** free from moisture; not moist; not wet. **2.** having little or no rain: *a dry climate or season.* **3.** characterized by absence, deficiency, or failure of natural or ordinary moisture. **4.** not under, in, or on water: *dry land.* **5.** not yielding water or other liquid: *a dry well.* **6.** not yielding milk: *a dry cow.* **7.** free from tears: *dry eyes.* **8.** wiped or drained away; evaporated: *a dry river.* **9.** desiring drink; thirsty. **10.** causing thirst: *dry work.* **11.** without butter or the like: *dry toast.* **12.** *Art.* hard and formal in outline, or lacking mellowness and warmth in color. **13.** plain; bald; unadorned: *dry facts.* **14.** dull; uninteresting: *a dry subject.* **15.** humorous or sarcastic in an unemotional or impersonal way: *dry humor.* **16.** indifferent; cold; unemotional: *a dry answer.* **17.** (of wines) not sweet. **18.** of or pertaining to nonliquid substances or commodities: *dry measure.* **19.** *U.S. Colloq.* characterized by or favoring prohibition of the manufacture and sale of alcoholic liquors for use as beverages. —v.t. **20.** to make dry; free from moisture: *dry your eyes.* —v.i. **21.** to become dry; lose moisture. **22. dry up, a.** to become completely dry. **b.** to become intellectually barren. **c.** *Colloq.* to stop talking. —n. **23.** *U.S. Colloq.* a prohibitionist. [ME *drie,* OE *drȳge,* akin to LG *drög,* G *trocken*] —**dry′ly, drily,** adv. —**dry′ness,** n.
—**Syn. 1.** DRY, ARID both mean without moisture. DRY is the general word indicating absence of water or freedom from moisture (which may be favorable): *dry well, dry clothes or land.* ARID suggests great or intense dryness in a region or climate, esp. such as results in bareness or in barrenness: *arid tracts of desert.* **20.** See evaporate. —**Ant. 1.** wet.

dry·ad (drī′əd, -ăd), n., pl. **-ads, -ades** (-ə dēz′). *Gk. Myth.* (*often cap.*) a deity or nymph of the woods; a nymph supposed to reside in trees or preside over woods. [t. L: s. *Dryas* (pl. *Dryades*), t. Gk., der. *drȳs* tree, oak] —**dry·ad·ic** (drī ăd′ĭk), adj.

dry-as-dust (drī′əz dŭst′), n. one who deals with dry, uninteresting subjects; a dull pedant. —**dry′-as-dust′,** adj.

dry battery, *Elect.* a dry cell, or voltaic battery consisting of a number of dry cells.

dry-bone ore (drī′bōn′), smithsonite.

dry cell, *Elect.* a cell in which the electrolyte exists in the form of a paste or is absorbed in a porous medium, or is otherwise restrained from flowing from its original position.

dry-clean (drī′klēn′), v.t. to clean (garments, etc.) with benzine, gasoline, etc., rather than water. —**dry cleaner.**

dry-cleanse (drī′klĕnz′), v.t., **-cleansed, -cleansing.** dry-clean.

Dry·den (drī′dən), n. **John,** 1631–1700, British poet, dramatist, and critic.

dry distillation, *Chem.* destructive distillation.

dry dock, 1. a basinlike structure from which the water can be removed after the entrance of a ship: used when making repairs on a ship's bottom, etc. **2.** a floating structure which may be partially submerged to permit a vessel to enter, and then raised to lift the vessel out of the water for repairs, etc.

dry-dock (drī′dŏk′), v.t. **1.** to place in a dry dock. —v.i. **2.** to go into dry dock.

dry·er (drī′ər), *n.* drier.

dry farming, a mode of farming practised in regions of slight or insufficient rainfall, depending largely upon tillage methods which render the soil more receptive of moisture and reduce evaporation. **—dry farmer.**

dry-fly fishing (drī′flī′), fishing with an artificial fly in such a manner that the fly floats on the surface of the water.

dry fog, *Meteorol.* a haze due principally to the presence of dust or smoke in the air.

dry goods, textile fabrics and related articles of trade, in distinction from groceries, hardware, etc.

dry ice, 1. solid carbon dioxide, having a temperature of 109° Fahr. below zero at atmospheric pressure. **2.** (*cap.*) a trademark for this substance.

dry kiln, an oven for the controlled drying of cut lumber, boards, etc.

dry law, *U.S.* a law prohibiting general use of intoxicating liquors.

dry measure, the system of units of capacity ordinarily used in measuring dry commodities, such as grain, fruit, etc. In the U.S. 2 pints = 1 quart; 8 quarts = 1 peck; 4 pecks = 1 bushel or 2150.42 cubic inches. In Great Britain, the gallon of 4 quarts and the quarter of 8 bushels are added, the bushel being 2219.36 cubic inches.

dry nurse, 1. a nurse who takes care of a child but does not suckle it. **2.** one who tutors and guides an inexperienced superior officer.

dry-nurse (drī′nûrs′), *v.t.*, **-nursed, -nursing.** to act as a dry nurse to.

dry plate, *Photog.* a glass plate coated with a sensitive emulsion of silver bromide and silver iodide in gelatin, upon which a negative or positive can be produced by exposure (as in a camera) and development.

dry point, 1. a stout, sharp-pointed needle used for ploughing into copper plates to produce furrows with raised edges that print with a fuzzy, velvety black. **2.** the process of engraving in this way. **3.** an engraving so made.

dry rot, 1. a decay of seasoned timber causing it to become brittle and to crumble to a dry powder, due to various fungi. **2.** any of various diseases of vegetables in which the dead tissue is dry. **3.** any concealed or unsuspected inward decay.

dry-shod (drī′shŏd′), *adj.* having or keeping the shoes dry.

Dry Tor·tu·gas (drī tôr tŏŏ′gəz), a group of ten small islands at the N entrance to the Gulf of Mexico: a part of Florida; the site of Fort Jefferson.

dry wash, clothes, etc., washed and dried, but unironed.

Ds, *Chem.* dysprosium.

D.S., 1. Doctor of Science. **2.** *Music.* dal segno.

d.s., 1. daylight saving. **2.** *Com.* days after sight.

D. Sc., Doctor of Science.

D.S.C., Distinguished Service Cross.

D.S.M., *U.S.* Distinguished Service Medal.

D.S.O., *Brit.* Distinguished Service Order.

D.S.T., Daylight Saving Time.

d.t., delirium tremens. Also, **d.t.'s.**

D. Th., Doctor of Theology. Also, **D. Theol.**

Du., 1. Duke. **2.** Dutch.

du·ad (dū′ăd, dŏŏ′-), *n.* a group of two. [b. DUAL and DYAD]

du·al (dū′əl, dŏŏ′-), *adj.* **1.** of or pertaining to two. **2.** composed or consisting of two parts; twofold; double: *dual ownership, dual controls on a plane.* **3.** *Gram.* (in some languages) designating a number category which implies two persons or things. **—n. 4.** *Gram.* **a.** the dual number. **b.** a form therein, as Greek *anthrópō* two men, nominative dual of *ánthropos* man, cf. *ánthropoi* three or more men, or Old English *git* 'you two' as contrasted with *ge,* 'you' referring to three or more. [t. L: s. *duālis* containing two] **—du′al·ly,** *adv.*

Du·a·la (dŏŏ ä′lä), *n.* Douala.

Dual Alliance, 1. the alliance formed in 1891–94 between France and Russia, lasting until the Bolshevik revolution in 1917. **2.** the alliance between Germany and Austria, 1879–1918, more frequently called the Austro-German alliance.

du·al·ism (dū′ə lĭz′əm, dŏŏ′-), *n.* **1.** state of being dual or consisting of two parts; division into two. **2.** *Philos.* a theory holding that there are two, and only two, basic and irreducible principles, as mind and body. **3.** *Theol.* **a.** the doctrine that there are two independent divine beings or eternal principles, one good and the other evil. **b.** the belief that man embodies two parts, such as body and soul. **—du′al·ist,** *n.*

du·al·is·tic (dū′ə lĭs′tĭk, dŏŏ′-), *adj.* **1.** of, pertaining to, or of the nature of dualism. **2.** dual. **—du′al·is′ti·cal·ly,** *adv.*

du·al·i·ty (dū ăl′ə tĭ, dŏŏ′-), *n.* dual state or quality.

du·al-pur·pose (dū′əl pûr′pəs, dŏŏ′-), *adj.* **1.** serving two functions. **2.** (of cattle) bred for two purposes, as beef and milk.

dub¹ (dŭb), *v.t.*, **dubbed, dubbing. 1.** to strike lightly with a sword in the ceremony of conferring knighthood; make, or designate as, a knight: *the King dubbed him a Knight.* **2.** to invest with any dignity or title; style; name; call: *he dubbed me quack.* **3.** to strike, cut, rub, etc., to make smooth, or of an equal surface: *to dub leather, timber.* **4.** to dress (a fly) for fishing. [ME *dubben,* OE *dubbian,* c. Icel. *dubba* equip, dub; akin to DOWEL]

dub² (dŭb), *n. Slang.* an awkward, unskilful person. [appar. akin to DUB¹]

dub³ (dŭb), *v.,* **dubbed, dubbing,** *n.* **—v.t., v.i. 1.** to thrust; poke. **—n. 2.** a thrust; poke. **3.** a drumbeat. [see DUB¹. Cf. LG *dubben* thrust, beat]

dub⁴ (dŭb), *v.,* **dubbed, dubbing,** *n. Motion Pictures.* **—v.t. 1.** to change the sound record on a film or to add sounds. **—n. 2.** the new sounds added. [shortened form of DOUBLE]

dub⁵ (dŭb), *n. Scot. and N. Eng.* a pool of water; a puddle. [orig. uncertain]

Du Bar·ry (dū băr′ĭ, dŏŏ; *Fr.* dy bà rē′), **Comtesse,** (born *Marie Jeanne Bécu*) 1746–93, mistress of Louis XV of France.

dub·bing (dŭb′ĭng), *n.* **1.** the conferring of knighthood; the accolade. **2.** the materials used for the body of an angler's fly.

du·bi·e·ty (dū bī′ə tĭ, dŏŏ-), *n., pl.* **-ties. 1.** doubtfulness; doubt. **2.** a matter of doubt. Also, **du·bi·os·i·ty** (dū′bī ŏs′ə tĭ, dŏŏ′-), *n.*

du·bi·ous (dū′bĭ əs, dŏŏ′-), *adj.* **1.** doubtful; marked by or occasioning doubt: *a dubious question.* **2.** of doubtful quality or propriety; questionable: *a dubious transaction, a dubious compliment.* **3.** of uncertain outcome: *in dubious battle.* **4.** wavering or hesitating in opinion; inclined to doubt. [t. L: m. s. *dubiōsus* doubtful] **—du′bi·ous·ly,** *adv.* **—du′bi·ous·ness,** *n.* **—Syn. 1.** See doubtful.

du·bi·ta·ble (dū′bə tə bəl, dŏŏ′-), *adj.* that may be doubted; doubtful; uncertain. **—du′bi·ta·bly,** *adv.*

du·bi·ta·tion (dū′bə tā′shən, dŏŏ′-), *n.* doubt. [t. L: s. *dubitātiō,* der. *dubitāre* doubt]

du·bi·ta·tive (dū′bə tā′tĭv, dŏŏ′-), *adj.* **1.** doubting; doubtful. **2.** expressing doubt. [t. LL: m. s. *dubitātīvus* doubtful] **—du′bi·ta′tive·ly,** *adv.*

Dub·lin (dŭb′lĭn), *n.* **1.** the capital of Ireland, in the E part. 537,878 (prelim. 1956). **2.** a county in E Ireland. 703,490 (prelim. 1956); 356 sq. mi. *Co. seat:* Dublin.

Du Bois (dŏŏ bois′), **William Edward Burghardt** (bûrg′härd), 1868–1963, U.S. educator and writer.

Du·brov·nik (dŏŏ′brôv nĭk), *n.* a seaport in SW Yugoslavia, on the Adriatic. 19,063 (1953). Italian, **Ragusa.**

Du·buque (də būk′), *n.* a city in E Iowa, on the Mississippi. 56,606 (1960).

duc (dyk), *n. French.* duke.

du·cal (dū′kəl, dŏŏ′-), *adj.* of or pertaining to a duke. [t. LL: s. *ducālis,* der. *dux* leader. See DUKE] **—du′cal·ly,** *adv.*

duc·at (dŭk′ət), *n.* **1.** any of various gold coins formerly in wide use in European countries, usually worth from $2.27 to $2.32. **2.** an old silver coin of varying value; an old Venetian money of account. **3.** (*pl.*) *Slang.* money; cash. **4.** *Slang.* ticket. [ME, t. F, t. It.: m. *ducato* a coin (orig. one issued in 1140 by Roger II of Sicily as duke of Apulia), also duchy, der. *duca* DUKE]

du·ce (dŏŏ′chě), *n.* **1.** leader. **2.** il Duce, the leader (applied esp. to Benito Mussolini as head of the Fascist Italian State). [It., g. L *dux* leader]

Du Chail·lu (dy shà yy′), **Paul Belloni** (pôl; *Fr.* pôl; bě lô nē′), 1835 or 1838–1903, U.S. explorer in Africa, traveler, and writer, born in France.

duch·ess (dŭch′ĭs), *n.* **1.** the wife or widow of a duke. **2.** *Hist.* a woman who holds in her own right the sovereignty or titles of a duchy. [ME *duchesse,* t. F, der. *duc* DUKE]

duch·y (dŭch′ĭ), *n., pl.* **duchies.** the territory ruled by a duke or duchess. [ME *duche,* t. OF, der. *duc* DUKE]

duck¹ (dŭk), *n.* **1.** any of numerous wild or domesticated web-footed swimming birds of the family *Anatidae,* esp. of the genus *Anas* and allied genera, characterized by a broad, flat bill, short legs, and depressed body. **2.** the female of this fowl, as distinguished from the male (or drake). **3.** the flesh of a duck, eaten as food. **4.** *Colloq.* a darling; pet. [ME *duk, doke,* OE *dūce,* lit., diver; akin to DUCK², v.]

duck² (dŭk), *v.i.* **1.** to plunge the whole body or the head momentarily under water. **2.** to stoop suddenly; bob. **3.** to avoid a blow, unpleasant task, etc. **—v.t. 4.** to plunge or dip in water momentarily. **5.** to lower (the head, etc.) suddenly. **6.** to avoid (a blow, unpleasant task, etc). **—n. 7.** act of ducking. [ME *duke, douke,* c. MLG *duken,* G *tauchen* dive] **—Syn. 1.** dive, dip, souse. **2.** bow, dodge.

duck³ (dŭk), *n.* **1.** heavy plain cotton fabric for tents, clothing, bags, mechanical uses, etc., in many weights and widths. **2.** (*pl.*) clothes esp. trousers, made of it. [t. D: m. *doek* cloth, c. G *tuch*]

duck⁴ (dŭk), *n.* (in World War II) a military truck for amphibious use. [from *DUKW,* its code name]

duck-bill (dŭk′bĭl′), *n.* a small, aquatic, egg-laying monotreme mammal *Ornithorhynchus anatinus,* of Australia and Tasmania, having webbed feet and the muzzle like the beak of a duck. Also, **duck′-billed′ platypus.**

Duckbill
Ornithorhynchus anatinus
(2 ft. long, tail 5½ in.)

ăct, āble, dâre, ärt; ĕbb, ēqual; ĭf, īce; hŏt, ōver, ôrder, oil, bŏŏk, ōoze, out; ŭp, ūse, ûrge; ə = a in alone; ch, chief; g, give; ng, ring; sh, shoe; th, thin; th, that; zh, vision. See the full key on inside cover.

duck board, a board, or a section or structure of boarding, laid as a floor or track over wet or muddy ground, as for military use.

duck call, *Hunting.* a tubular device into which a hunter blows to imitate the quack of a duck.

duck·er¹ (dŭk'ər), *n.* one who or that which ducks. [f. DUCK² + -ER¹]

duck·er² (dŭk'ər), *n.* 1. one who raises ducks. 2. one who hunts ducks. [f. DUCK¹ + -ER¹]

duck hawk, the American peregrine falcon, *Falco peregrinus anatum,* famous for its speed and audacity.

ducking stool, a stool or chair in which common scolds were formerly punished by being tied and plunged into water. See **cucking stool.**

Ducking stool

duck·ling (dŭk'lĭng), *n.* a young duck.

duck·pin (dŭk'pĭn'), *n.* 1. *Bowling.* a short pin of relatively large diameter, used in a game resembling tenpins, and bowled at with small balls. 2. (*pl. construed as sing.*) the game played with such pins.

ducks and drakes, 1. (*construed as sing.*) a pastime consisting in throwing shells, flat stones, etc., over the surface of water so as to strike and rebound repeatedly. 2. **make ducks and drakes of, play (at) ducks and drakes with,** to handle recklessly; squander.

duck·weed (dŭk'wēd'), *n.* any member of the family *Lemnaceae,* esp. of the genus *Lemna,* comprising small aquatic plants which float free on still water. [so called because it is eaten by ducks]

duck·y (dŭk'ĭ), *adj. Colloq.* dear; darling.

duct (dŭkt), *n.* 1. any tube, canal, or conduit by which fluid or other substances are conducted or conveyed. 2. *Anat., Zool.* a tube, canal, or vessel conveying a body fluid, esp. a glandular secretion or excretion. 3. *Bot.* a cavity or vessel formed by elongated cells or by many cells. 4. *Elect.* a single enclosed runway for conductors or cables. [t. L: s. *ductus* leading, conduct, conduit]

duc·tile (dŭk'tal, -tĭl), *adj.* 1. capable of being hammered out thin, as certain metals; malleable. 2. capable of being drawn out into wire or threads, as gold. 3. able to stand deformation under a load without fracture. 4. capable of being molded or shaped; plastic. 5. susceptible; compliant; tractable. [ME *ductil,* t. L: s. *ductilis* that may be led] —**duc·til'i·ty,** *n.*

duct·less gland, *Anat., Zool.* a gland which possesses no excretory duct, but whose secretion is absorbed directly into the blood or lymph, as the thyroid, adrenals, pituitary gland, and parathyroids.

dud¹ (dŭd), *n. Colloq.* 1. an article of clothing. 2. (*pl.*) clothes; (often) old or ragged clothes. 3. belongings in general. [ME *dudde,* akin to LG *dudel* a coarse sackcloth]

dud² (dŭd), *n. Colloq.* 1. any thing or person that proves a failure. 2. *Mil.* a shell that fails to explode after being fired. [? special use of DUD¹]

dud·dy (dŭd'ĭ), *adj. Scot.* ragged; tattered.

dude (dūd, dŏŏd), *n.* 1. an affected or fastidious man; fop. 2. *Slang.* a person raised in a large city. 3. *Western U.S.* an Easterner who vacations on a ranch. [orig. unknown] —**dud'ish,** *adj.*

du·deen (dŏŏdēn'), *n. Irish.* a short clay tobacco pipe.

dude ranch, a ranch operated also as a vacation resort.

Du·de·vant (dȳd văn'), *n.* **Madame Amandine Lucile Aurore** (à măn dēn' lȳ sēl' ō rôr'). See **Sand, George.**

dudg·eon¹ (dŭj'ən), *n.* a feeling of offense or resentment; anger: *we left in high dudgeon.* [orig. unknown]

dudg·eon² (dŭj'ən), *n.* 1. *Obs.* a kind of wood used esp. for the handles of knives, daggers, etc. 2. *Obs.* a handle or hilt made of this wood. 3. *Archaic.* a dagger having such a hilt. [t. AF: m. *digeon,* ult. orig. unknown]

Dud·ley (dŭd'lĭ), *n.* 1. **Robert,** (*Earl of Leicester*) 1532?–88, English statesman and favorite of Queen Elizabeth. 2. a city in central England, near Birmingham. 61,940 (est. 1946).

due (dū, dŏŏ), *adj.* 1. immediately payable. 2. owing, irrespective of whether the time of payment has arrived. 3. rightful; proper; fitting: *due care, in due time.* 4. adequate; sufficient: *a due margin for delay.* 5. attributable, as to a cause: *a delay due to an accident.* 6. under engagement as to time; expected to be ready, be present, or arrive. —*n.* 7. that which is due or owed. 8. (*chiefly pl.*) a payment due, as a charge, a fee, etc. 9. **give a person his due,** to treat fairly. —*adv.* 10. directly or straight: *a due east course.* 11. *Archaic.* duly. [ME *dew,* t. OF: m. *deü,* orig. pp. of *devoir,* g. L *dēbēre* owe]

due bill, a brief written acknowledgment of indebtedness, not payable to order.

du·el (dū'əl, dŏŏ'-), *n., v.,* **-eled, -eling** or (*esp. Brit.*) **-elled, -elling.** —*n.* 1. a prearranged combat between two persons, fought with deadly weapons according to an accepted code of procedure, esp. to settle a private quarrel. 2. any contest between two persons or parties. —*v.i., v.t.* 3. to fight in a duel. [t. ML: m.s. *duellum* a combat between two] —**du'el·er;** *esp. Brit.,* **du'el·ler,** *n.* —**du'el·ist;** *esp. Brit.,* **du'el·list,** *n.*

du·el·lo (dŏŏ ĕl'ō), *n., pl.* **-los.** 1. the practice or art of dueling. 2. the code of rules regula'ing it. [It.]

du·en·na (dū ĕn'ə, dŏŏ-), *n.* 1. (in Spain and Portugal) an older woman serving as escort or protector of a young lady. 2. a governess; chaperon. [t. Sp.: m. *dueña,* g. L *domina* mistress]

Due·ro (dwĕ'rō), *n.* Spanish name of **Douro.**

du·et (dū ĕt', dŏŏ-), *n. Music.* a composition for two voices or performers. [t. It.: m. *duetto,* dim. of *duo* two]

duff¹ (dŭf), *n.* a kind of organic surface consisting of matted peaty materials in forested soils. [fig. use of DUFF²]

duff² (dŭf), *n.* a flour pudding boiled, or sometimes steamed, in a bag. [var. of DOUGH]

duf·fel (dŭf'əl), *n.* 1. a sportman's or camper's outfit. 2. a coarse woolen cloth having a thick nap. Also, **duf'fle.** [named after *Duffel,* town near Antwerp]

duffel bag, a canvas bag used esp. by military personnel for transporting personal effects. Also, **duffle bag.**

duff·er (dŭf'ər), *n.* 1. *Brit. Colloq.* a plodding, stupid, or incompetent person. 2. *Slang.* anything inferior, counterfeit, or useless. 3. *Slang or Dial.* a peddler, esp. one who sells cheap, flashy goods as valuable.

Du·fy (dȳ fē'), *n.* **Raoul** (rä ŏŏl'), 1877–1953, French artist.

dug¹ (dŭg), *v.* pt. and pp. of **dig.**

dug² (dŭg), *n.* the mamma or the nipple of a female. [cf. Sw. *dägga,* Dan. *dægge* suckle]

du·gong (dŏŏ'gŏng), *n.* the only member of the sirenian genus *Dugong,* a large herbivorous aquatic mammal of the East Indian and other waters, characterized by a fishlike body, flipperlike forelimbs, no hind limbs, and a rounded, paddlelike tail. [t. Malay: m. *dúyong*]

Dugong. *Dugong australis* (8 ft. long)

dug·out (dŭg'out'), *n.* 1. a rough shelter or dwelling formed by an excavation in the ground or in the face of a bank. 2. a boat made by hollowing out a log. 3. *Baseball.* a low, three-walled enclosure from which players and other members of the squad watch the game.

Du Gues·clin (dȳ gĕklăn'), **Bertrand** (bĕr trän'), c1320–80, French military leader, constable of France.

dui·ker (dī'kər), *n.* any of the small African antelopes with spikelike horns (usually on the males only). They plunge through and under bushes instead of leaping over them. They are included in two genera, *Cephalophus,* and *Syloicapra.* Also, **dui·ker·bok** (dī'kər bŏk'). [t. S Afr. D: diver]

Duis·burg (dȳs'bŏŏrκн), *n.* a city in W West Germany at the junction of the Rhine and Ruhr rivers: the largest river port in Europe; formerly the two cities of Duisburg and Hamborn. 478,983 (est. 1955).

duke (dūk, dŏŏk), *n.* 1. a sovereign prince, the ruler of a small state called a duchy. 2. *Great Britain.* a nobleman of the highest rank after that of a prince and ranking next above a marquis. 3. a nobleman of corresponding rank in certain other countries. 4. (*chiefly pl.*) *Slang.* the hand or fist. [ME *duc,* t. OF, t. L: s. *dux* leader, ML *duke*]

duke·dom (dūk'dəm, dŏŏk'-), *n.* 1. the state or territory ruled by a duke. 2. the office or rank of a duke.

Du·kho·bors (dŏŏ'kō bôrz'), *n.pl.* a Russian Christian religious sect of peasants, dating from the 18th century. A number of them, under persecution, migrated to Canada in 1899. [t. Russ.: m. *Dukhobortsy* spirit wrestlers, contenders against the Holy Spirit]

dul·ce et de·co·rum est pro pa·tri·a mo·ri (dŭl'sĭ ĕt dĭ'kōr'əm ĕst prō pä'trĭ ə mōr'ĭ). *Latin.* sweet and fitting it is to die for one's country.

dul·cet (dŭl'sĭt), *adj.* 1. agreeable to the feelings, the eye, or, esp., the ear; pleasing; soothing; melodious. 2. *Archaic.* sweet to the taste or smell. —*n.* 3. an organ stop resembling the dulciana, but an octave higher. [ME *doucet,* t. OF, dim. of *dous* sweet, g. L *dulcis*]

dul·ci·an·a (dŭl'sĭ ăn'ə), *n.* an organ stop having metal pipes, and giving thin, incisive, somewhat stringlike tones. [NL, der. L *dulcis* sweet]

dul·ci·fy (dŭl'sə fī'), *v.t.* **-fied, -fying.** 1. to make more agreeable; mollify; appease. 2. to sweeten. [t. LL: m.s. *dulcificāre,* f. L: *dulci-* sweet + *-ficāre* make] —**dul'ci·fi·ca'tion,** *n.*

dul·ci·mer (dŭl'sə mər), *n. Music.* 1. a trapezoidal zither with metal strings struck by light hammers. 2. a modern folk instrument related to the guitar and plucked with the fingers. [late ME *dowcemer,* t. OF: m. *doulcemer,* var. of *doulcemele.* See DOUCE]

Dulcimer (def. 1)

dul·cin·e·a (dŭl sĭn'ĭ ə, dŭl'sə nē'ə; *Sp.* dŏŏl'thē nĕ'ä), *n.* a ladylove; a sweetheart. [from *Dulcinea* (der. Sp. *dulce,* g. L *dulcis* sweet), name given by Don Quixote, in Cervantes's romance, to his peasant ladylove]

du·li·a (dū lī'ə, dŏŏ-), *n. Rom. Cath. Theol.* veneration and invocation given to saints as the servants of God and friends of God. See **hyperdulia** and **latria.** [t. ML, t. Gk.: m. *douleia* servitude, service]

dull (dŭl), *adj.* 1. slow of understanding; obtuse; stupid. 2. lacking keenness of perception in the senses or feelings; insensible; unfeeling. 3. not intense or acute: *a dull pain.* 4. slow in motion or action; not brisk; sluggish. 5. listless; spiritless. 6. causing ennui or depression; tedious; uninteresting: *a dull sermon.* 7. not

harp; blunt: *a dull knife.* **8.** having very little depth of
olor; lacking in richness or intensity of color. **9.** not
right, intense, or clear; dim: *a dull day or sound.* —*v.t.,
.i.* **10.** to make or become dull. [ME *dul, dull;* akin to
)E *dol* foolish, stupid, G *toll* mad] —dull'ish, *adj.*
–dull'ness, dul'ness, *n.* —dul'ly, *adv.*
–**Syn. 1.** DULL, BLUNTED, SLOW, STUPID are applied figuratively to mental qualities. DULL implies obtuseness, inabil-
ty to receive clear impressions, lack of imagination: *a dull
hild.* BLUNTED implies loss of original keenness of intelli-
;ence through disease, sad experience, and the like: *blunted
its or faculties. SLOW applies to a sluggish intellect not able
apidly to take in or understand, though its eventual action
nay be good: *a slow mind.* STUPID implies slowness of mental
*rocesses, but also applies to lack of intelligence, wisdom,
*rudence, etc.: *a stupid person, thing to do.* **7.** DULL, BLUNT
*efer to the edge or point of an instrument, tool, or the like.
)ULL implies a lack or a loss of keenness or sharpness: *a
tull razor or saw. BLUNT may mean the same or may refer
o an edge or point not intended to be keen or sharp: *a
lunt or stub pen, a blunt foil. —**Ant. 1.** keen, **7.** sharp.
ull·ard (dŭl'ərd), *n.* a dull or stupid person. [f. DULL,
dj. + -ARD]

ul·les (dŭl'əs), *n.* **John Foster,** 1888–1959, U.S.
tatesman; Secretary of State, 1953–59.

ulse (dŭls), *n.* coarse, edible, red seaweed, *Rhody-
nenia palmata.* [t. Irish and Gaelic: m. *duileasg*]

u·luth (də looth', doo-), *n.* a city in E Minnesota: a
ort on Lake Superior. 106,884 (1960).

u·ly (dū'lĭ, doo'-), *adv.* **1.** in a due manner; properly;
tly. **2.** in due season; punctually. **3.** adequately.

u·ma (doo'mä), *n.* (in Russia prior to 1917) **1.** a
:ouncil or official assembly. **2.** (*cap.*) an elective legis-
ative assembly, constituting the lower house of parlia-
aent, which was established in 1905 by Nicholas II.
Also, **douma.** [t. Russ.]

u·mas (dy mä'), *n.* **1. Alexandre** (à lĕk sän'dr), (*Du-
nas père*) 1802–70. French novelist and dramatist.
2. his son, **Alexandre** (*Dumas fils*) 1824–95, French
lramatist and novelist.

u Mau·ri·er (dū môr'ĭ ā', doo; *Fr.* dy môr yě'),
George Louis Palmella Busson (päl měl'ə bы sôn'),
1834–96, British illustrator and novelist.

umb (dŭm), *adj.* **1.** without the power of speech.
2. bereft of the power of speech temporarily: *dumb with
stonishment. **3.** that does not speak, or is little addicted
:o speaking. **4.** made, done, etc., without speech.
5. lacking some usual property, characteristic, etc.:
lumb ague. **6.** *U.S. Colloq.* stupid; dull-witted. [OE,
:. G *dumm* stupid] —dumb'ly, *adv.* —dumb'ness, *n.*
–**Syn. 1, 2.** DUMB, MUTE, SPEECHLESS, VOICELESS describe
a condition in which speech is absent. DUMB was formerly
used to refer to persons unable to speak; it is now used
almost entirely of the inability of animals to speak: *dumb
beasts of the field. The term MUTE is now the one more often
applied to persons who, usually because of congenital
leafness, have never learned to talk: *with training most
mutes learn to speak well enough to be understood. Either of
the foregoing terms or SPEECHLESS may describe a temporary
nability to speak, caused by emotion, etc.: *dumb with
amazement, mute with terror, left speechless by surprise.
VOICELESS means literally having no voice, either from
natural causes or from injury: *fish are voiceless, an operation
o remove the larynx leaves one voiceless.

umb ague, an irregular form of intermittent
malarial fever, lacking the usual chill.

um·bar·ton (dŭm bär'tən), *n.* **1.** Also, **Dum·bar-
ton·shire** (dŭm bär'tən shĭr), **Dunbarton.** a county in
W Scotland. 169,900 (est. 1956); 241 sq. mi. **2.** its
county seat, near Clyde river: shipbuilding. 23,706 (1951).

umbarton Oaks, site in the District of Columbia
where conferences discussing proposals for the United
Nations organization were held Aug.–Oct., 1944.

umb·bell (dŭm'bĕl'), *n.* **1.** gymnasium hand apparatus made of wood or metal, consisting of two balls
joined by a barlike handle, used as weights, usually
in pairs. **2.** *U.S. Slang.* a stupid, dull person.

umb show, 1. a part of a dramatic representation
given in pantomime, common in the early English
drama. **2.** gesture without speech.

umb·wait·er (dŭm'wā'tər), *n.* **1.** *U.S.* a conveyor
of framework with shelves drawn up and down in a shaft.
2. *Brit.* a small stand placed near a dining table.

um·dum (dŭm'dŭm), *n.* a kind of hollow-nosed bullet
that expands on impact, inflicting a severe wound.
Also, **dumdum bullet.** [named after *Dum Dum,* town
near Calcutta, India, where ammunition is made]

um·found (dŭm found'), *v.t.* to strike dumb with
amazement. Also, **dumb·found'.** [appar. b. DUMB and
CONFOUND] —dum·found'er, *n.*

um·fries (dŭm frēs'), *n.* **1.** Also, **Dum·fries·shire**
(dŭm frēs'shĭr, -shər), a county in S Scotland. 87,500
pop. (est. 1956); 1074 sq. mi. **2.** its county seat: burial
place of Robert Burns. 26,320 (1951).

um·my (dŭm'ĭ), *n., pl.* -mies, *adj.* —*n.* **1.** an imitation or copy of something, as for display, to indicate appearance, exhibit clothing, etc. **2.** *Colloq.* a stupid person; dolt. **3.** one who has nothing to say or who takes no
active part in affairs. **4.** one put forward to act for
others while ostensibly acting for himself. **5.** a dumb
person; a mute. **6.** *Cards.* **a.** (in bridge) the dealer's
partner whose hand is exposed and played by the dealer.
b. the cards so exposed. **c.** a game so played. **d.** an imaginary player represented by an exposed hand which is
played by and serves as partner to one of the players.

7. *Railroads.* a type of steam switching locomotive
having boiler and running gear completely enclosed,
formerly used in city streets. **8.** *Print.* sheets folded
and made up to show the size, shape, form, sequence,
and general style of a contemplated piece of printing.
—*adj.* **9.** put forward to act for others while ostensibly
acting for oneself. **10.** counterfeit; sham; imitation.
11. *Cards.* played with a dummy. [f. DUMB + -Y³]

du·mor·ti·er·ite (dū môr'tĭ ə rīt', doo-), *n.* a mineral,
aluminum borosilicate, used in making refractories.
[named after M. Eugène *Dumortier.* See -ITE¹]

dump¹ (dŭmp), *v.t.* **1.** to throw down in a mass; fling
down or drop heavily. **2.** to empty out, as from a cart
by tilting. **3.** to empty out (a cart, etc.) by tilting or
overturning. **4.** *Com.* **a.** to put (goods) on the market in
large quantities and at a low price, esp. to a large or favored buyer. **b.** to market (goods) thus in a foreign country, as at a price below that charged in the home country.
—*v.i.* **5.** to fall or drop down suddenly. **6.** to unload.
7. to offer for sale at a low price, esp. to offer low prices to
favored buyers. —*n.* **8.** anything, as rubbish, dumped or
thrown down. **9.** a place where it is deposited. **10.** *Mil.*
a collection of ammunition, stores, etc., deposited at
some point, as near a battle front, to be distributed for
use. **11.** act of dumping. **12.** *Mining.* **a.** a runway
or embankment, equipped with tripping devices, from
which low-grade ore, rock, etc., are dumped. **b.** the pile
of ore so dumped. **13.** *U.S. Slang.* a place, house, or
town that is poorly kept up. —*adj.* **14.** (of a motor
truck or railroad car, or the body of such a vehicle)
equipped to haul loads of sand, coal, gravel, etc., and to
spill the load by inclining the body. [ME, t. Scand.; cf.
Dan. *dumpe* fall plump] —dump'er, *n.*

dump² (dŭmp), *n.* **1.** (*now only pl.*) *Colloq.* a dull,
gloomy state of mind. **2.** *Obs.* a plaintive melody.
3. *Obs.* a tune. **4.** *Obs.* a slow dance with a peculiar
rhythm. [orig. obscure. Cf. MD *domp* haze]

dump³ (dŭmp), *n.* a leaden counter used by
boys in games. [orig. uncert.; ? akin to DUMPY²]

dump·cart (dŭmp'kärt'), *n.* a cart the body of which
can be tilted, or the bottom opened downward, to discharge the contents.

dump·ish (dŭmp'ĭsh), *adj.* **1.** dull; stupid. **2.** depressed; sad. —dump'ish·ly, *adv.* —dump'ish·ness, *n.*

dump·ling (dŭmp'lĭng), *n.* **1.** a rounded mass of
steamed dough (often served with stewed meat, etc.).
2. a kind of pudding consisting of a wrapping of dough
enclosing an apple or other fruit, and boiled or baked.
3. *Colloq.* a short and stout person or animal. [history
obscure; ? orig. *lumpling* (f. LUMP¹ + -LING¹), with *d*- by
dissimilation]

dump·y¹ (dŭmp'ĭ), *adj.,* dumpier, dumpiest. dump-
ish; dejected; sulky. [f. DUMP² + -Y¹]

dump·y² (dŭmp'ĭ), *adj.,* dumpier, dumpiest. short
and stout; squat: *a dumpy woman.* [? akin to DUMPLING]
—dump'i·ly, *adv.* —dump'i·ness, *n.*

dumpy level, *Survey.* an instrument consisting of a
spirit level mounted under and parallel to a telescope,
the latter being rigidly attached to its supports.

dum spi·ro, spe·ro (dŭm spī'rō, spĭr'ō), *Latin.* while
I breathe, I hope (a second motto of South Carolina).

dum vi·vi·mus, vi·va·mus (dŭm vĭv'ĭ məs, vĭ vä'-
məs), *Latin.* while we are living, let us live (to the full).

Dum·yat (doom yät'), *n.* Arabic name of Damietta.

dun¹ (dŭn), *v.,* dunned, dunning, *v.* —*v.t.* **1.** to make
repeated and insistent demands upon, esp. for the payment of a debt. —*n.* **2.** one who duns; an importunate
creditor. **3.** a demand for payment, esp. a written one.
[special use of obs. *dun* din, t. Scand.; cf. Icel. *duna*
boom, roar]

dun² (dŭn), *adj.* **1.** dull- or grayish-brown. **2.** dark;
gloomy. —*n.* **3.** dun color. **4.** a May fly. **5.** a dun fly.
[ME *dun*(ne), OE *dunn,* c. OS *dun* reddish brown]

Du·na (doo'nö), *n.* Hungarian name of Danube.

Dü·na (dy'nä), *n.* German name of Dvina.

Dü·na·burg (dy'nä boorĸʜ'), *n.* German name of
Daugavpils.

Dun·bar (dŭn'bär *for def.* 1; dŭn bär' *for defs* 2, 3), *n.*
1. Paul Laurence, 1872–1906, U. S. poet. **2. William,**
1465?–1530?, Scottish poet. **3.** a town in SE Scotland
at the mouth of the Firth of Forth: Cromwell defeated
the Scots here, 1650. 4115 (1951).

Dun·bar·ton (dŭn bär'tən), *n.* Dumbarton.

Dun·can (dŭng'kən), *n.* **1. I,** died 1040, king of Scotland, 1034–40, murdered by Macbeth. **2. Isadora**
(Yz'ə dôr'ə), 1878–1927, U.S. dancer.

Duncan Phyfe (dŭng'kən fīf'), of or like the furniture designed by Duncan Phyfe.

dunce (dŭns), *n.* a dull-witted or stupid person; a dolt
[from John DUNS SCOTUS; his system was attacked as
foolish by the humanists] —**Syn.** dullard, numbskull,
blockhead, ignoramus, simpleton, nincompoop, ninny.

dunce cap, a tall paper cone put on the head of a slow
or lazy student. Also, **dunce's cap.**

dunch (dŭnsh), *n.* *Scot.* and *N. Eng.* a jog; shove.

Dun·ci·ad (dŭn'sĭ äd'), *n.* **The,** a poem (1728–42) by
Pope, satirizing various contemporary writers.

Dun·dee (dŭn dē'), *n.* a seaport in E Scotland, on the
Firth of Tay. 178,500 (est. 1956).

dun·der·head (dŭn'dər hĕd'), *n.* a dunce; blockhead. Also, **dun·der·pate** (dŭn'dər pāt'). —dun'der-
head'ed, *adj.*

ct, āble, dâre, ärt; ĕbb, ēqual; ĭf, īce; hŏt, ōver, ôrder, oil, bŏŏk, ōōze, out; ŭp, ūse, ûrge; ə = a in alone;
h, chief; g, give; ng, ring; sh, shoe; th, thin; ŧħ, that; zh, vision.　See the full key on inside cover.

dune (dūn, dōōn), *n.* a sand hill or sand ridge formed by the wind, usually in desert regions or near lakes and oceans. [t. F, t. MD, c. OE *dūn*. See DOWN³]

Dun·e·din (dŭn ē′dĭn), *n.* a seaport in New Zealand, on South Island. 71,000 (est. 1953).

Dun·ferm·line (dŭn fûrm′lĭn, -fĕrm′-), *n.* a city in E Scotland, in Fife county. 45,200 (est. 1956).

dun fly, *Angling.* a dun-colored artificial fly attached to the leader to mimic the larval stage of certain flies.

dung (dŭng), *n.* 1. manure; excrement, esp. of animals. —*v.t.* 2. to manure (ground) with, or as with, dung. [ME *dunge*, OE *dung*, c. G *dung*] —**dung′y,** *adj.*

dun·ga·ree (dŭng′gə rē′), *n.* 1. a coarse cotton fabric of East Indian origin, used esp. for sailors' clothing. 2. (*pl.*) work clothes, overalls, etc., made of this fabric. [t. Hind.: m. *dungrī*]

dung beetle, any of various scarabaeid beetles that feed upon or breed in dung, as the sacred Egyptian scarab *Scarabaeus sacer.*

dun·geon (dŭn′jən), *n.* any strong, close cell, esp. underground; donjon. [ME, t. OF: m. *donjon*, g. LL *dominio* dominion, tower, der. L *dominus* master, lord]

dung·hill (dŭng′hĭl′), *n.* 1. a heap of dung. 2. a mean or vile place, abode, condition, or person.

dun·ie·was·sal (dōō′nĭ wŏs′əl), *n.* a gentleman, esp. of secondary rank, among the Highlanders of Scotland; a cadet of a ranking family. [t. Gaelic: m. *duine uasal* gentleman. (f. *duine* man + *uasal* of good birth)]

dunk (dŭngk), *v.t., v.i.* to dip (doughnuts, etc.) into coffee, milk, etc. [t. G: s. *dunken*, var. of *tunken* dip]

dunk·er (dŭngk′ər), *n.* one who dunks.

Dunk·er (dŭngk′ər), *n.* a popular name for a member of the German Baptist Brethren, now located chiefly in America, characterized by their Baptist practices, opposition to legal oaths and military service and by simplicity of life. Also, **Dunk·ard** (dŭngk′ərd). [var. of *Tunker*, t. G, der. *tunken* dip; with reference to baptism by immersion]

Dun·kirk (dŭn′kûrk), *n.* a seaport in N France; scene of the evacuation under German fire of the British expeditionary force of over 330,000 men, May 29–June 4, 1940. 21,316 (1954). Also, French, **Dunkerque** (dœn kĕrk′).

dun·lin (dŭn′lĭn), *n.* a widely distributed sandpiper, *Erolia alpina,* which breeds in northern parts of the northern hemisphere. The American form is known as the **red-backed sandpiper,** *E. a. sakhalina.* [d. var. of *dunling,* f. DUN² + -LING¹]

Dun·more (dŭn môr′), *n.* a borough in NE Pennsylvania, near Scranton. 18,917 (1960).

dun·nage (dŭn′ĭj), *n.* 1. baggage or personal effects. 2. *Naut.* loose material laid beneath or wedged among cargo to prevent injury from water or chafing: *dried brush for dunnage.* [t. D: m. *dunnetjes* loosely together]

Dunne (dŭn), n. **Finley Peter,** 1867–1936, U.S. humorist.

dunn·ite (dŭn′īt), *n.* an ammonium picrate explosive (officially known as explosive D) used as a bursting charge for armor-piercing projectiles and in high-explosive shells. [named after Colonel B. W. *Dunn* (1860–1936), of the U.S. Army, the inventor. See -ITE¹]

dun·nock (dŭn′ək), *n.* the common hedge sparrow, *Prunella modularis,* of Europe. [f. DUN² + -OCK]

Du·nois (dʏ nwȧ′), *n.* **Jean** (zhäN), **Count de,** ("Bastard of Orleans") c1403–68, French military leader, relieved by Joan of Arc and her troops when besieged at Orleans.

Dun·sa·ny (dŭn sā′nĭ), *n.* **Edward John Moreton Drax Plunkett, 18th Baron,** 1878–1957, Irish dramatist and writer of tales.

Dun·si·nane (dŭn′sə nān′, dŭn′sə nān′), *n.* a hill in central Scotland, NE of Perth: a ruined fort on its summit is traditionally called Macbeth's Castle. 1012 ft.

Duns Sco·tus (dŭnz skō′təs), **John,** c1265–c1308, Irish or Scottish scholastic theologian in England.

Dun·stan (dŭn′stən), *n.* **Saint,** A.D. 925?–988, archbishop of Canterbury and statesman.

dunt (dŭnt), *n. Scot. Dial.* —*n.* 1. a hard blow making a dull sound. 2. a wound from such a blow. —*v.t., v.i.* 3. to strike or knock with a dull sound. [var. of DINT. Cf. Swed *dunt* dint]

du·o (dōō′ō), *n., pl.* **duos, dui** (dōō′ē). *Music.* a duet. [It., t. L: two]

duo-, a word element meaning "two," as in *duologue.* [t. L, comb. form of *duo*]

du·o·dec·i·mal (dū′ə dĕs′ə məl, dōō′-), *adj.* 1. pertaining to twelfths, or to the number twelve. 2. proceeding by twelves. —*n.* 3. one of a system of numerals the base of which is twelve. 4. one of twelve equal parts. [f. L: s. *duodecimus* twelfth + -AL¹] —**du′o·dec′i·mal·ly,** *adv.*

du·o·dec·i·mo (dū′ə dĕs′ə mō′), *n., pl.* **-mos,** *adj.* —*n.* 1. a book size (about 5 x 7½ inches) determined by printing on sheets folded to form twelve leaves or twenty-four pages. *Abbr.:* 12mo or 12°. —*adj.* 2. in duodecimo. [t. L: (*in*) *duodecimō* in twelfth]

duoden-, a combining form representing **duodenum,** as in **duodenitis.** Also, **duodeno-.**

du·o·de·nal (dū′ə dē′nəl, dōō′-), *adj.* of or pertaining to the duodenum.

du·o·den·a·ry (dū′ə dĕn′ə r̄ɪ, -dē′nə rɪ̄, dōō′-), *adj.* duodecimal. [t. L: m.s. *duodēnārius* containing twelve]

du·o·de·ni·tis (dū′ə dʏ nī′tɪ̄s, dōō′-), *n. Pathol.* inflammation of the duodenum.

du·o·de·num (dū′ə dē′nəm, dōō′-), *n. Anat., Zool.* the first portion of the small intestine, from the stomach to the jejunum. See diag. under **intestine.** [t. ML, der. L *duodēnī* twelve each; so called from its length, about twelve finger breadths]

du·o·logue (dū′ə lôg′, -lŏg′, dōō′-), *n.* 1. a conversation between two persons; a dialogue. 2. a dramatic performance or piece in the form of a dialogue limited to two speakers. [f. DUO- + -*logue*, modeled on MONOLOGUE]

duo·mo (dwô′mō), *n., pl.* **-mi** (-mē). *Italian.* cathedral. [see DOME]

dup (dŭp), *v.t.,* **dupped, dupping.** *Archaic or Eng. Dial.* to open (a door or gate). [contr. of *do up*]

dup., duplicate.

dupe (dūp, dōōp), *n., v.,* **duped, duping.** —*n.* 1. a person who is imposed upon or deceived; a gull. —*v.t.* 2. to make a dupe of; deceive; delude; trick. [t. F: m. *dupe*, hoopoe, g. L *upupa*] —**dup′a·ble,** *adj.* —**dup′a·bil′i·ty,** *n.* —**dup′er,** *n.*

dup·er·y (dū′pə rɪ̄, dōō′-), *n., pl.* **-eries.** 1. act or practice of duping. 2. state of one who is duped.

du·ple (dū′pəl, dōō′-), *adj.* double; twofold. [t. L: m.s. *duplus* double]

Du·pleix (dʏ plĕks′), *n.* **Joseph François** (zhō zĕf′ fräN swȧ′), **Marquis,** 1697–1763, French Colonial governor in India, 1742–1754.

Du·ples·sis-Mor·nay (dʏ plĕ sē′môr nĕ′), *n.* Mornay.

duple time, *Music.* characterized by two beats to the measure.

du·plex (dū′plĕks, dōō′-), *adj.* 1. twofold; double. 2. *Mach.* including two identical working parts in a single framework, though one could operate alone. —*n.* 3. duplex house. [t. L: f. *du(o)* two + -*plex,* der. *plicāre* fold] —**du·plex′i·ty,** *n.*

duplex apartment, an apartment, or suite of rooms, on two floors or stories.

duplex house, *U.S.* a house for two families.

duplex telegraphy, a system for sending two messages simultaneously over the same wire, esp. in opposite directions.

du·pli·cate (*adj., n.* dū′plə kɪ̄t, dōō′-; *v.* dū′plə kāt′, dōō′-), *adj., n., v.,* **-cated, -cating.** —*adj.* 1. exactly like or corresponding to something else. 2. double; consisting of or existing in two corresponding parts. 3. *Cards.* denoting a game in which a team tries for the best result on hands also played by competing partnerships: *duplicate bridge.* —*n.* 4. a copy exactly like an original. 5. anything corresponding in all respects to something else. 6. *Cards.* a duplicate game. 7. **in duplicate,** in two copies, exactly alike. —*v.t.* 8. to make an exact copy of; repeat. 9. to double; make twofold. [t. L: m.s. *duplicātus,* pp., doubled] —**du′pli·ca′tive,** *adj.* —**Syn.** 4. facsimile, replica, reproduction. 8. See imitate.

du·pli·ca·tion (dū′plə kā′shən, dōō′-), *n.* 1. act of duplicating. 2. state of being duplicated. 3. a duplicate. 4. a folding or doubling, as of a membrane.

du·pli·ca·tor (dū′plə kā′tər, dōō′-), *n.* a machine for making duplicates.

du·plic·i·ty (dū plĭs′ə tɪ̄, dōō-), *n., pl.* **-ties.** deceitfulness in speech or conduct; speaking or acting in two different ways concerning the same matter with intent to deceive; double-dealing. [t. LL: m.s. *duplicitas* doubleness, der. L *duplex.* See DUPLEX] —**Syn.** guile, hypocrisy, deception, dissimulation. —**Ant.** straightforwardness.

Du Pont (dū pŏnt′, dōō-, dū′pŏnt, dōō′-; *also Fr.* dʏ pôN′ *for 1*). 1. U.S. industrialist family, founded by **Éleuthère Irénée** (ē lœtr′ ēr e nē′), 1771–1834. 2. **Samuel Francis,** 1803–65, U.S. rear admiral in the Union Navy in the Civil War.

Du·pré (dʏ prē′), *n.* **Jules** (zhyl), 1812–89, French landscape painter.

Du·quesne (dū kān′, dōō-; *also for 1, Fr.* dʏ kĕn′), *n.* 1. **Abraham** (ȧ brȧ ȧm′), **Marquis,** 1610–88, French naval commander. 2. a city in SW Pennsylvania, on the Monongahela river. 15,019 (1960). 3. **Fort,** a French fort built on the site of Pittsburgh, 1754.

du·ra (dyŏŏr′ə, dôŏr′ə), *n.* dura mater. —**du′ral,** *adj.*

du·ra·ble (dyŏŏr′ə bəl, dôŏr′-), *adj.* having the quality of lasting or enduring; not easily worn out, decayed, etc. [ME, t. L: m.s. *dūrābilis* lasting. See DURE²] —**du′ra·bil′i·ty, du′ra·ble·ness,** *n.* —**du′ra·bly,** *adv.* —**Syn.** permanent. —**Ant.** weak, transitory.

durable finish, any finish, as shrink-resistant or water-repellent, which endures washing and dry cleaning.

du·ral·u·min (dyŏŏ răl′yə mĭn, dôŏr′-, dōō-), *n.* 1. an aluminum-base alloy containing copper, manganese, and, sometimes, magnesium. It may be hardened and strengthened by heat treatment and was one of the first successful lightweight high-strength alloys: originally used in aircraft construction. 2. (*cap.*) a trademark for this alloy. [f. s. L *dūrus* hard + ALUMIN(UM)]

du·ra ma·ter (dyŏŏr′ə mā′tər, dôŏr′ə), *Anat.* the tough, fibrous membrane forming the outermost of the three coverings of the brain and spinal cord. See **arachnoid** and **pia mater.** Also, **dura.** [t. ML: lit., hard mother]

---

b., blend of, blended; c., cognate with; d., dialect, dialectal; der., derived from; f., formed from; g., going back to; m., modification of; r., replacing; s., stem of; t., taken from; ?, perhaps. See the full key on inside cover.

du·ra·men (dyŏŏrā′mĭn, dŏŏ-), *n.* *Bot.* the hard central wood, or heartwood, of an exogenous tree. [t. L: hardness, a hardened vine branch]

dur·ance (dyŏŏr′əns, dŏŏr′-), *n.* **1.** forced confinement; imprisonment. **2.** *Archaic.* duration; endurance. [late ME, t. MF: duration, der. *durer*, g. L *dūrāre* last]

du·ran·go (dŏŏräng′gō), *n.* **1.** a state in N Mexico. 664,288 (est. 1952); 47,691 sq. mi. **2.** the capital of this state. 59,496 (1950).

du·ran·te vi·ta (dyŏŏ răn′tĭ vī′tə), *Latin.* during life.

du·ra·tion (dyŏŏ rā′shən, dŏŏ-), *n.* **1.** continuance in time. **2.** the length of time anything continues. [ME, t. LL: s. *dūrātio*, der. L *dūrāre* last]

dur·a·tive (dyŏŏr′ə tĭv, dŏŏr′-), *adj.* *Gram.* denoting a verb aspect, as in Russian, expressing incompleted, or continued, action, etc. Compare English *beat* which implies duration or continued action with *strike*, also *walk*, durative, with *step*.

du·raz·zo (dŏŏ rät′tsō), *n.* a seaport in W Albania, on the Adriatic: important ancient city. 14,031 (1945). Albanian, **Durrës.**

Dur·ban (dûr′bən), *n.* a seaport in the E part of the Republic of South Africa, in Natal. 430,946 (1951).

dur·bar (dûr′bär), *n.* (in India) **1.** the court of a native ruler. **2.** a public audience or levee held by a native prince or a British governor or viceroy; an official reception. **3.** the hall or place of audience. **4.** the audience itself. [t. Hind., Pers.: m. *darbār* court]

dure[1] (dyŏŏr, dŏŏr), *adj.* *Archaic.* hard; severe. [ME *dur*, t. OF, g. L *dūrus* hard. Cf. DOUR]

dure[2] (dyŏŏr, dŏŏr), *v.i., v.t.,* **dured, during.** *Archaic.* endure. [ME *dure(n),* t. F: m. *durer*, g. L *dūrāre* endure]

Dü·rer (dy′rər), *n.* **Albrecht** (äl′brĕкнt) or **Albert** (äl′bĕrt), 1471–1528, German painter and engraver.

du·ress (dyŏŏr′ĭs, dŏŏr′-, dyŏŏ rĕs′, dŏŏ-), *n.* **1.** constraint; compulsion. **2.** forcible restraint of liberty; imprisonment. **3.** *Law.* such constraint or coercion as will render void a contract or other legal act entered or performed under its influence. [ME *duresse*, t. OF, g. L *dūritia* hardness]

Dur·ham (dûr′əm), *n.* **1.** a county in NE England. 1,463,868 pop. (1951); 1015 sq. mi. **2.** its county seat. 19,283 pop. (1951). **3.** a city in N North Carolina. 78,302 (1960). **4.** one of a breed of beef cattle originating in Durham, England, at one time known as good milkers, but now bred largely for meat production.

du·ri·an (dŏŏr′Y ən), *n.* **1.** the edible fruit, with a hard, prickly rind, of a tree, *Durio zibethinus,* of southeastern Asia. It has extraordinary flavor and odor. **2.** the tree itself. Also, **du′ri·on.** [t. Malay, der. *duri* thorn]

dur·ing (dyŏŏr′Yng, dŏŏr′-), *prep.* **1.** throughout the continuance of. **2.** in the course of. [orig. ppr. of DURE[2]]

Durk·heim (dûrk′hĭm, *French* dyr kĕm′), *n.* **Émile** (ĕ mēl′). 1858–1917, French sociologist and philosopher.

dur·mast (dûr′măst, -mäst), *n.* a European oak, *Quercus petraea,* with a heavy, elastic wood highly valued by the builder and the cabinetmaker.

du·ro (dŏŏ′rō; *Sp.* -rō), *n., pl.* **-ros** (-rōz; *Sp.* -rōs). the Spanish silver dollar. [t. Sp., for *peso duro* hard piastre]

Du·roc (dyŏŏr′ŏk, dŏŏr′-), *n.* an American red hog of a breed developed for hardiness, weight, and quick growth. Also, **Du·roc-Jer·sey** (dyŏŏr′ŏk jûr′zĭ, dŏŏr′-).

dur·ra (dŏŏr′ə), *n.* a type of grain sorghum with slender stalks, cultivated in Asia, etc., and introduced into the U.S.; Indian millet; Guinea corn. Also, **doura, dourah.** [t. Ar.: m. *dhura*]

Dur·rës (dŏŏr′rəs), *n.* Albanian name of **Durazzo.**

durst (dûrst), *v.* a pt. of **dare.**

du·rum wheat (dyŏŏr′əm, dŏŏr′-), an important species or variety of wheat, *Triticum durum,* the flour from which is largely used for macaroni, etc. Also, **durum.** [i.e. hard wheat. See DURE[1]]

Du·se (dŏŏ′zĕ), *n.* **Eleonora** (ĕ′lĕ ō nō′rä), (*Signora Checchi*) 1859–1924, Italian actress.

dusk (dŭsk), *n.* **1.** partial darkness; a state between light and darkness; twilight; shade; gloom. **2.** the darker stage of twilight. —*adj.* **3.** dark; tending to darkness. —*v.t., v.i.* **4.** to make or become dusk; darken. [metathetic var. of OE *dux, dox* dark, c. L *fuscus* dark brown] —**dusk′ish,** *adj.*

dusk·en (dŭs′kən), *v.t., v.i.* *Rare.* to make or grow dusk; dim.

dusk·y (dŭs′kĭ), *adj.,* **duskier, duskiest. 1.** somewhat dark; dark-colored. **2.** deficient in light; dim. **3.** gloomy. —**dusk′i·ly,** *adv.* —**dusk′i·ness,** *n.*

—**Syn. 1.** DUSKY, SWARTHY both mean dark in color. They differ more in application than in meaning. DUSKY suggests shadiness or a veiled and dim light, as well as darkness of coloring: *dusky twilight shadows, a dusky grove, a dusky Ethiopian.* SWARTHY, which usually denotes a greater degree of darkness or blackness, is used only of the complexion: *a swarthy skin.*

dusky grouse, a gallinaceous game bird, *Dendragapus obscurus,* of western North America.

Düs·sel·dorf (dŏŏs′əl dôrf′; *Ger.* dys′əl-), *n.* a city in W West Germany: a port on the Rhine and capital of North Rhine-Westphalia. 645,486 (est. 1955).

dust (dŭst), *n.* **1.** earth or other matter in fine, dry particles. **2.** any finely powdered substance, as sawdust. **3.** a cloud of finely powdered earth or other matter in the air. **4.** that to which anything, as the human body, is reduced by disintegration or decay. **5.** a dead body.

6. *Now Rare.* a single particle or grain. **7.** *Brit.* ashes, refuse, etc. **8.** a low or humble condition. **9.** anything worthless. **10.** gold dust. **11.** *Slang.* money; cash. **12.** disturbance; turmoil. **13. bite the dust,** to be killed or wounded. **14. lick the dust, a.** to be killed or wounded. **b.** to grovel; humble oneself abjectly. **15. throw dust in one's eyes,** to mislead. —*v.t.* **16.** to free from dust; wipe the dust from: *to dust (or dust off) the table.* **17.** to sprinkle with dust or powder: *to dust plants with powder.* **18.** to strew or sprinkle as dust: *dust powder over plants.* **19.** to soil with dust; make dusty. —*v.i.* **20.** to wipe dust from a table, room, etc. **21.** to become dusty. [ME *doust,* OE *dūst,* c. G *dunst* vapor] —**dust′less,** *adj.*

dust bin, *Brit.* ash can; garbage can.

dust bowl, an area subject to dust storms.

dust cart, *Brit.* garbage truck.

dust devil, a miniature whirlwind of considerable intensity that picks up dust and rubbish and carries it some distance into the air.

dust·er (dŭs′tər), *n.* **1.** one who or that which dusts. **2.** cloth, brush, etc., for removing dust. **3.** an apparatus for sprinkling dust or powder on something. **4.** a long, light overgarment to protect clothing from dust.

dust jacket, book jacket.

dust·man (dŭst′măn′, -mən), *n., pl.* **-men** (-mĕn′, -mən). **1.** *Brit.* one employed to remove dust and refuse. **2.** a popular personification of sleep. See **sandman.**

dust·pan (dŭst′păn′), *n.* a utensil in which dust is collected and removed.

dust storm, a storm of wind which raises dense masses of dust into the air, as in a desert region.

dust·y (dŭs′tĭ), *adj.,* **dustier, dustiest. 1.** filled, covered, or clouded with dust. **2.** of the nature of dust; powdery. **3.** of the color of dust; gray. —**dust′i·ly,** *adv.* —**dust′i·ness,** *n.*

Dutch (dŭch), *adj.* **1.** of, pertaining to, or characteristic of the natives or inhabitants of the Netherlands or Holland, or their country or language. **2.** *Archaic or Slang.* German; Teutonic. **3. go Dutch,** *Colloq.* to have each person pay his own expenses. **4. in Dutch,** *Slang.* in trouble or disfavor. —*n.* **5. the Dutch, a.** the people of the Netherlands or Holland. **b.** the German people. **6.** Pennsylvania Dutch. **7.** a Germanic language, the language of the Netherlands. **8.** *Obs.* the German language. [t. M D: m. *dutsch* German, Dutch, c. G *deutsch* German, orig., popular, national, trans. of L *vulgāris* vernacular]

Dutch Belted, one of a breed of dairy cattle originating in the Netherlands, and having a broad white belt circling an otherwise black body.

Dutch Borneo, former name for the southern and larger part of the island of Borneo: now part of Indonesia.

Dutch cheese, 1. a small, globular, hard cheese made from skim milk. **2.** cottage cheese.

Dutch courage, courage inspired by liquor.

Dutch door, a door consisting of two units horizontally divided so that while the upper part is open the lower can be closed and act as a barrier.

Dutch East Indies, the former island possessions of the Netherlands in the Malay Archipelago, including Sumatra, Java, Celebes, parts of Borneo and New Guinea, the Moluccas, and other islands; received independence in Dec. 1949 as the U.S. of Indonesia. Also, **Netherlands Indies.**

Dutch gold, an alloy of copper and zinc in the form of thin sheets, used as a cheap imitation of gold leaf. Also, **Dutch foil, Dutch leaf, Dutch metal.**

Dutch Guiana, Surinam.

Dutch Harbor, a U.S. naval base in the Aleutian Islands, on Unalaska island.

Dutch·man (dŭch′mən), *n., pl.* **-men. 1.** a native or inhabitant of Holland. **2.** *Now Colloq.* a German. **3.** (*l.c.*) *Carp., etc.* a piece or wedge inserted to hide the fault in a badly made joint, stop an opening, etc.

Dutch·man's-breech·es (dŭch′mənz brĭch′ĭz), *n. sing. and pl.* a delicate herb, *Dicentra* (or *Bicuculla*) *Cucullaria,* with pale-yellow, two-spurred flowers.

Dutch·man's-pipe (dŭch′mənz pīp′), *n.* an aristolochiaceous climbing vine, *Aristolochia Sipho,* with large leaves and flowers of a curved form suggesting a tobacco pipe.

Dutchman's-pipe. *Aristolochia Sipho*

Dutch New Guinea. See **West Irian.** Also, **Netherlands New Guinea.**

Dutch oven, 1. a heavily constructed kettle with a close-fitting lid, used for pot roasts, stews, etc. **2.** a metal utensil open in front, for roasting meat, etc., before an open fire. **3.** a brick oven in which the walls are preheated for cooking.

Dutch treat, *U.S. Colloq.* a meal or entertainment in which each person pays for himself.

Dutch uncle, a person who criticizes or reproves with unsparing severity and frankness.

Dutch West Indies, former name of **Netherlands Antilles.**

du·te·ous (dū′tĭ əs, dŏŏ′-), *adj.* dutiful; obedient; submissive. —**du′te·ous·ly,** *adv.* —**du′te·ous·ness,** *n.*

du·ti·a·ble (dū'tǐ ə bəl, dōō'-), *adj.* subject to duty, as imported goods.

du·ti·ful (dū'tǐ fəl, dōō'-), *adj.* 1. performing the duties required of one; obedient: *a dutiful child.* 2. required by duty; proceeding from or expressive of a sense of duty: *dutiful attention.* —**du'ti·ful·ly,** *adv.* —**du'ti·ful·ness,** *n.* —**Syn.** 1. respectful, docile, submissive.

du·ty (dū'tǐ, dōō'-), *n., pl.* **-ties.** 1. that which one is bound to do by moral or legal obligation. 2. the binding or obligatory force of that which is morally right; moral obligation. 3. action required by one's position or occupation; office; function: *the duties of a soldier or clergyman.* 4. the conduct due to a superior; homage; respect. 5. an act of respect, or an expression of respectful consideration. 6. *Com.* a specific or ad valorem levy imposed by law on the import or export of goods. 7. a payment, service, etc., imposed and enforceable by law or custom. 8. *Mach.* **a.** the amount of work done by an engine per unit amount of fuel consumed. **b.** the measure of effectiveness of any machine. 9. *Agric.* the amount of water necessary to provide for the crop in a given area. 10. **off duty,** not at work. 11. **on duty.** at work. [ME *duete.* t. AF, der. *du, due* DUE]
—**Syn.** 1. DUTY, OBLIGATION refer to what one feels bound to do. DUTY is what one performs, or avoids doing, in fulfillment of the permanent dictates of conscience, piety, right, or law: *duty to one's country, one's duty to tell the truth, to raise children properly.* An OBLIGATION is what one is bound to do to fulfill the dictates of usage, custom, or propriety, and to carry out a particular, specific, and often personal promise or agreement: *financial or social obligations.*

du·ty-free (dū'tǐ frē', dōō'-), *adj.* free of customs duty.

du·um·vir (dū ŭm'vər, dōō-), *n., pl.* **-virs, -viri** (-vǐ rī'). *Rom. Hist.* one of two officers or magistrates jointly exercising the same public function. [t. L: man of two]

du·um·vi·rate (dū ŭm'və rǐt, dōō-), *n.* 1. a union of two men in the same office, as in ancient Rome. 2. the office or government of two such persons.

du·ve·tyn (dōō'və tēn'), *n.* a napped fabric, in a twilled or plain weave, of cotton, wool, silk, or rayon. Also, **du've·tine', du've·tyne'.** [f. *duvet* kind of quilt (t. F) + *-ine,* var. of *-INE*[2]]

Du·vi·da (dōō'vē də), *n.* **Río da** (rē'ōō də). See Roosevelt, Río.

D.V., Deo volente.

Dvi·na (dvǐ nä'), *n.* 1. Lettish, **Daugava.** German, **Düna.** a river in the W Soviet Union, flowing NW to the Baltic at Riga. ab. 640 mi. 2. **Northern,** a river in the N Soviet Union in Europe, flowing NW to **Dvina Bay** (Gulf of Archangel), an arm of the White Sea. ab. 470 mi.

Dvinsk (dvēnsk), *n.* Russian name of **Daugavpils.**

D.V.M., Doctor of Veterinary Medicine.

D.V.M.S., Doctor of Veterinary Medicine and Surgery.

Dvo·řák (dvôr'zhäk), *n.* **Anton** (än'tôn), 1841–1904, Czech composer.

dwarf (dwôrf), *n.* 1. a human being much below the ordinary stature or size; a pygmy. 2. an animal or plant much below the ordinary size of its kind or species. —*adj.* 3. of unusually small stature or size; diminutive. —*v.t.* 4. to cause to appear or seem small in size, extent, character, etc. 5. to make dwarf or dwarfish; prevent the due development of. —*v.i.* 6. to become stunted or smaller. [ME *dwerf,* OE *dweorg,* c. D *dwerg,* G *zwerg*] —**Syn.** 1. manikin, homunculus. DWARF, MIDGET, PYGMY are terms for a very small person. A DWARF is one checked in growth, or stunted; he usually has a large head or is in some way not properly formed: *in the past, dwarfs were considered very comical.* A MIDGET is one perfect in form and normal in function, but like a tiny replica of the ordinary species: *some midgets are like handsome dolls.* A PYGMY is properly a member of one of certain small-sized peoples of Africa and Asia, but the word is often used to mean dwarf or midget. 2. runt.

dwarf alder, the alder-leafed buckthorn (*Rhamnus alnifolia*).

dwarf cornel, the bunchberry, *Cornus canadensis,* a low herb bearing red berries, of the NE United States.

dwarf·ish (dwôr'fĭsh), *adj.* like a dwarf; below the ordinary stature or size; diminutive. —**dwarf'ish·ly,** *adv.* —**dwarf'ish·ness,** *n.* —**Syn.** pygmy, tiny, stunted, atrophied, runty.

dwarf mallow, a European herb, *Malva neglecta,* with roundish leaves and small pinkish-white flowers.

dwarf star, *Astron.* a star of moderate luminosity and mass, such as the sun.

dwell (dwĕl), *v.i.,* **dwelt or dwelled, dwelling.** 1. to abide as a permanent resident. 2. to continue for a time. 3. to linger over in thought, speech, or writing; to emphasize (often fol. by *on* or *upon*): *to dwell upon a subject, a point in argument.* [ME *dwellen* delay, tarry, abide, OE *dwellan, dwelian* lead astray, hinder, delay, c. Icel. *dvelja*] —**dwell'er,** *n.* —**Syn.** 1. stay, reside, live.

dwell·ing (dwĕl'ĭng), *n.* 1. a place of residence or abode; a house. 2. continued or habitual residence. —**Syn.** 1. See house.

dwelling house, a house occupied, or intended to be occupied, as a residence.

dwelling place, a place of residence or abode.

dwelt (dwĕlt), *v.* pt. and pp. of **dwell.**

dwin·dle (dwǐn'dəl), *v.,* **-dled, -dling.** —*v.i.* 1. to become smaller and smaller; shrink; waste away: *his vast fortune has dwindled away.* 2. to fall away, as in quality;

degenerate. —*v.t.* 3. to make smaller and smaller; cause to shrink: *failing health dwindles ambition.* [dim. of DWINE] —**Syn.** 1. diminish, decline. See **decrease.** —**Ant.** 1. increase. 2. magnify.

dwine (dwĭn), *v.i.,* **dwined, dwining.** *Archaic or Dial.* to waste away; fade. [OE *dwinan* languish]

dwt., pennyweight. [f. *d,* for DENARIUS (see def. 2) + *wt.* weight]

DX, *Radio.* distance; distant. Also, **D.X.**

Dy, *Chem.* dysprosium.

dy·ad (dī'ăd), *n.* 1. a group of two; a couple. 2. *Biol.* **a.** a secondary morphological unit, consisting of two monads: *chromosome dyad.* **b.** the double chromosomes resulting from the splitting of a tetrad. 3. *Chem.* an element, atom, or radical having a valence of two. —*adj.* 4. dyadic. [t. LL: s. *dyas,* t. Gk.: the number two]

dy·ad·ic (dī ăd'ǐk), *adj.* of two parts; pertaining to the number two.

Dy·ak (dī'ăk), *n.* a member of a wild inland people of Borneo, notorious as head-hunters, of the same stock as the Malays, who found them there on first coming to the island.

dy·ar·chy (dī'ärkǐ), *n., pl.* **-chies.** diarchy. [t. Gk.: m.s. *dyarchía* rule of two] —**dy·ar'chic, dy·ar'chi·cal,** *adj.*

dye (dī), *n., v.,* **dyed, dyeing.** —*n.* 1. a coloring material or matter. 2. a liquid containing coloring matter, for imparting a particular hue to cloth, etc. 3. color or hue, esp. as produced by dyeing. 4. **of the deepest or blackest dye,** of the worst kind. [ME *die,* OE *dēag*] —*v.t.* 5. to color or stain; treat with a dye; color (cloth, etc.) by soaking in a liquid containing coloring matter: *to dye cloth red.* 6. to impart (color) by means of a dye. —*v.i.* 7. to impart color, as a dye: *this brand dyes well.* 8. to become colored when treated with a dye: *this cloth dyes easily.* [ME *dien,* OE *dēagian*] —**dy'er,** *n.*

dyed-in-the-wool (dīd'ǐn thə wōōl'), *adj.* 1. dyed before weaving. 2. through-and-through; complete: *a dyed-in-the-wool Republican.*

dye·ing (dī'ǐng), *n.* process of coloring fibers, yarns, or fabrics.

dy·er's-weed (dī'ərz wēd'), *n.* any of various plants yielding dyes, as the weld, *Reseda Luteola,* or the dyeweed, *Genista tinctoria,* or the woad, *Isatis tinctoria.*

dye·stuff (dī'stŭf'), *n.* a material yielding, or used as, a dye.

dye·weed (dī'wēd'), *n.* a fabaceous shrub, *Genista tinctoria,* a native of the Old World, bearing yellow flowers and yielding a yellow dye.

dye·wood (dī'wōōd'), *n.* any wood yielding a coloring matter used for dyeing.

dy·ing (dī'ĭng), *adj.* 1. ceasing to live; approaching death: *a dying man.* 2. pertaining to or associated with death: *a dying hour.* 3. given, uttered, or manifested just before death: *dying words.* 4. drawing to a close: *the dying year.* —*n.* 5. death.

dyke (dīk), *n., v.,* **dyked, dyking.** dike.

dyn., dynamics. Also, **dynam.**

dyna-, a word element referring to power, as in *dynameter.* Also, **dynam-.** [t. Gk., comb. form of *dýnamis* power, *dýnasthai* be able]

dy·nam·e·ter (dī năm'ə tər), *n.* *Optics.* an instrument for determining the magnifying power of telescopes. [f. DYNA- + -METER; or shortened form of DYNAMOMETER]

dy·nam·ic (dī năm'ǐk), *adj.* 1. of or pertaining to force not in equilibrium (opposed to *static*) or to force in any state. 2. pertaining to dynamics. 3. pertaining to or characterized by energy or effective action; active; forceful. Also, **dy·nam'i·cal.** [t. Gk.: m. s. *dynamikós* powerful] —**dy·nam'i·cal·ly,** *adv.*

dy·nam·ics (dī năm'ǐks), *n.* 1. that branch of physics or mechanics which deals with force as producing or affecting motion (including kinetics but not statics), or, more comprehensively, with the action of force on bodies in motion or at rest (including kinetics and statics). 2. the science or principles of forces acting in any field. 3. (construed as *pl.*) the forces, physical or moral, at work in any field.

dynamic similarity, a principle whereby model airplanes, ships, and hydraulic structures are operated for test purposes under conditions exactly simulating full-scale performance.

dy·na·mism (dī'nə mǐz'əm), *n.* any of various doctrines or philosophical systems which seek to explain phenomena of nature by the action of force (opposed to *mechanism*). —**dy'na·mist,** *n.* —**dy'na·mis'tic,** *adj.*

dy·na·mite (dī'nə mīt'), *n., v.,* **-mited, -miting.** —*n.* 1. a high explosive consisting of nitroglycerin mixed with some absorbent substance such as kieselguhr. —*v.t.* 2. to blow up, shatter, or destroy with dynamite. 3. to mine or charge with dynamite. —**dy·na·mit·ic** (dī'nə mǐt'ǐk), *adj.*

dy·na·mit·er (dī'nə mī'tər), *n.* one who uses dynamite, esp. for revolutionary purposes. Also, **dy'na·mit'ist.**

dy·na·mo (dī'nə mō'), *n., pl.* **-mos.** any rotating machine in which either mechanical energy input may be converted into electrical energy output (a generator), or electrical input may be converted into mechanical output (a motor). The British use *dynamo* for the U.S. term *generator* as applied to an automobile. [short for *dynamoelectric machine*]

---

b., blend of, blended; c., cognate with; d., dialect, dialectal; der., derived from; f., formed from; g., going back to; m., modification of; r., replacing; s., stem of; t., taken from; ?, perhaps. See the full key on inside cover.

ynamo-, var. of **dyna-**, as in *dynamometer*.
y·na·mo·e·lec·tric (dī'nəmō Ĭlĕk'trĭk), *adj.* pertaining to the conversion of mechanical energy into electric power, or vice versa: *a dynamoelectric machine*. Also, **dy/na·mo·e·lec'tri·cal.**
y·na·mom·e·ter (dī'nəmŏm'ətər), *n.* a device for measuring force or power. [f. DYNAMO + -METER]
y·na·mom·e·try (dī'nəmŏm'ətrĭ), *n.* act or art of using the dynamometer. **—dy·na·mo·met·ric** (dī'nə-nōmĕt'rĭk), **dy/na·mo·met'ri·cal,** *adj.*
y·na·mo·tor (dī'nəmō'tər), *n.* a machine which combines both motor and generator action in one magnetic field either with two armatures or with one armature having two separate windings.
y·nast (dī'năst, -nəst; *Brit. also* dĭn'ăst), *n.* a ruler or potentate, esp. a hereditary ruler. [t. L: s. *dynastes,* t. Gk.: lord, chief]
y·nas·ty (dī'nəstĭ; *Brit. also* dĭn'əstĭ), *n., pl.* **-ties.** 1. a sequence of rulers from the same family or stock: *the Ming dynasty ruled China from 1368 to 1644.* 2. the rule of such a sequence. **—dy·nas·tic** (dī nȁs'tĭk), **dy·nas'ti·cal,** *adj.* **—dy·nas'ti·cal·ly,** *adv.*
y·na·tron (dī'nətrŏn'), *n. Electronics.* a vacuum tube consisting of three electrodes, in which as the plate voltage increases there is a decrease in the plate current because of emission of electrons from the plate. It is frequently used as an oscillator in radio.
yne (dīn), *n. Physics.* the unit of force in the centimeter-gram-second system, being that force which, acting on a body of mass of one gram for one second, gives it a velocity of one centimeter per second. [t. F, t. Gk.: m. *dŷnamis* power]
ys-, a prefix, esp. medical, indicating difficulty, poor condition, as in *dysphoria.* [t. Gk.: hard, bad, unlucky; akin to Skt. *dus-, dur-,* OE *tŏ-,* HG *zer-*]
ys·en·ter·y (dĭs'əntĕr'ĭ), *n. Pathol.* an infectious disease marked by inflammation and ulceration of the lower part of the bowels, with diarrhea that becomes mucous and hemorrhagic. [t. L: m.s. *dysenteria,* t. Gk.; r. ME *dissenterie,* t. OF] **—dys·en·ter'ic,** *adj.*
ys·func·tion (dĭs fŭngk'shən), *n. Med.* malfunctioning, as of a structure of the body.

dys·gen·ic (dĭs jĕn'ĭk), *adj.* pertaining to or causing degeneration in the type of offspring produced (opposed to *eugenic*).
dys·gen·ics (dĭs jĕn'ĭks), *n. Biol.* the study of the operation of factors that cause degeneration in offspring.
dys·lo·gis·tic (dĭs'lə jĭs'tĭk), *adj.* conveying disapproval or censure; opprobrious; not eulogistic. [f. DYS- + (EU)LOGISTIC] **—dys·lo·gis'ti·cal·ly,** *adv.*
dys·pep·sia (dĭs pĕp'shə, -sĭ ə), *n.* deranged or impaired digestion; indigestion (opposed to *eupepsia*). Also, **dys·pep·sy** (dĭs pĕp'sĭ). [t. L, t. Gk.]
dys·pep·tic (dĭs pĕp'tĭk), *adj.* 1. pertaining to, subject to, or suffering from dyspepsia. 2 morbidly gloomy or pessimistic. **—n. 3** a person subject to or suffering from dyspepsia. Also, **dys·pep'ti·cal. —dys·pep'ti·cal·ly,** *adv.*
dys·pha·gi·a (dĭs fā'jĭ ə), *n. Pathol.* difficulty in swallowing. **—dys·phag·ic** (dĭs făj'ĭk), *adj.*
dys·pho·ni·a (dĭs fō'nĭ ə), *n.* disturbance of the normal functioning in the production of sound. [NL, t. Gk.: roughness of sound] **—dys·phon·ic** (dĭs fŏn'ĭk), *adj.*
dys·pho·ri·a (dĭs fōr'ĭ ə), *n. Pathol.* a state of dissatisfaction, anxiety, restlessness, or fidgeting. [NL, t. Gk.: agitation]
dysp·ne·a (dĭsp nē'ə), *n. Pathol.* difficult or labored breathing (opposed to *eupnea*). Also, **dysp·noe·a.** [t. L: m. *dyspnoea,* t. Gk.: m. *dýspnoia* difficulty of breathing] **—dysp·ne'al, dysp·ne'ic,** *adj.*
dys·pro·si·um (dĭs prō'sĭ əm, -shĭ-), *n. Chem.* a rare-earth metallic element found in small amounts in certain minerals together with other rare earths. Symbol: Dy; *at. wt.:* 162.46; *at. no.:* 66. [NL, der. Gk. *dysprósitos* hard to get at]
dys·tro·phy (dĭs'trə fĭ), *n.* See *muscular dystrophy.*
dys·u·ri·a (dĭs yŏŏr'ĭ ə), *n. Pathol.* difficult or painful urination. [t. LL, t. Gk.: m. *dysouría*]
Dyu·sham·be (dyŏŏ shȁm'bĕ), *n.* former name of Stalinabad.
dz., dozen; dozens.
Dzher·zinsk (jĕr zĭnsk'), *n.* a city in the central Soviet Union in Europe. 147,000 (est. 1956).
Dzu·gash·vi·li (jŏŏ'gȁsh vē'lĕ), *n.* See **Stalin.**

E

e (ē), *n., pl.* **E's** or **Es, e's** or **es.** 1. the 5th letter of the English alphabet. 2. *Music.* **a.** the third tone in the scale of C major or the fifth in the relative minor scale of A minor. **b.** a printed or written note indicating this tone. **c.** a string, key, or pipe tuned to this note. **d.** (in solmization) the third tone of the scale, called *mi.* 3. (in medieval Roman numerals) 250.
-, var. of **ex-**, used in words of Latin orig. before consonants except *c, f, p, q, s,* and *t,* as in *emit.*
, 1. east. 2. eastern. 3. English. 4. Excellent.
, 1. *Math.* a transcendental constant equal to 2.7182818 . . . , used as the base of natural logarithms. 2. erg.
, 1. Earl. 2. east. 3. eastern. 4. English.
, 1. eldest. 2. entrance. 3. Baseball. errors.
a., each.
ach (ēch), *adj.* 1. every, of two or more considered individually or one by one: *each stone in the building.* **—pron.** 2. each one: *each went his way.* **—adv.** 3. apiece: *they cost a dollar each.* [ME *ech(e),* etc., OE *ǣlc,* etc., f. *ā* ever + (ge)*līc* like, c. OHG *ēo-gilīh*] **—Syn.** 1. EACH, EVERY are alike in having a distributive meaning. Of two or more members composing a (usually) definite aggregate, EACH directs attention to the separate members in turn: *each child* (of those considered and enumerated) *received a large apple.* EVERY emphasizes the idea of inclusiveness or universality: it is also used of an indefinite number, all being regarded singly and separately: *every child present received an apple* (no child was omitted); *every child* (of all in existence) *likes to play.*
ach other, each the other: *they struck each other;* that is, they struck, *each* striking the *other;* used also (like *one another*) as a compound reciprocal pronoun in oblique cases: *they struck at each other.*
ads (ēdz), *n.* **James B.,** 1820–87, U.S. engineer.
a·ger (ē'gər), *adj.* 1. keen or ardent in desire or feeling; impatiently longing: *I am eager for or about it, eager to do it.* 2. characterized by great earnestness: *an eager look.* 3. *Obs.* keen; sharp; biting. [ME *egre,* t. OF: m. *aigre,* g. L *ācer* sharp] **—ea'ger·ly,** *adv.* **—ea'ger·ness,** *n.* **—Syn.** 1. fervent, zealous, enthusiastic.
a·gle (ē'gəl), *n.* 1. any of certain large diurnal birds of prey of the falcon family, esp. the **golden eagle,** *Aquila chrysaëtos,* of the northern hemisphere, and the **bald eagle,** *Haliaeetus leucocephalus,* of North America, noted for their size, strength, powerful flight, and keenness of vision. 2. a figure or representation of an eagle, much used as an emblem: *the Roman eagle.* 3. (*pl.*) insignia of a colonel in the U.S. Army. 4. a standard, seal,

etc., bearing such a figure, esp. the standard of the ancient Roman army. 5. a gold coin of the United States, of the value of ten dollars, having a figure of an eagle on the reverse. 6. (*cap.*) *Astron.* the northern constellation Aquila. 7. *Golf.* a score two below par on any but par-three holes. [ME *egle,* t. OF, g. L *aquila*]
ea·gle-eyed (ē'gəl īd'), *adj.* sharp-sighted.
eagle owl, a large, rapacious owl, *Bubo bubo,* of Europe.
ea·glet (ē'glĭt), *n.* a young eagle. [t. F: m. *aiglette,* dim. of *aigle* EAGLE]
ea·gre (ē'gər, ā'gər), *n. Brit. Dial.* bore[3]. [f. OE: *ēa* river + *gār* storm]
eal·dor·man (ōl'dər mən), *n. Early Eng. Hist.* 1. a chief. 2. (later) the chief magistrate of a county or group of counties.
Ea·ling (ē'lĭng), *n.* a city in SE England, part of Greater London. 184,200 (est. 1956).
EAM, National Liberation Front, a Greek underground resistance movement of World War II and political coalition of various leftist groups.
ear[1] (ĭr), *n.* 1. the organ of hearing, in man and mammals usually consisting of three parts (**external ear, middle ear,** and **internal ear**). 2. the external part alone. 3. the sense of hearing. 4. nice perception of the differences of sound; esp. sensitiveness to the quality and correctness of musical sounds: *an ear for music.* 5. attention; heed; esp. favorable attention: *gain a person's ear.* 6. any object resembling or suggestive of the external ear, as the handle of a pitcher or the part of a bell by which it is hung. 7. *Journalism.* either of the small spaces or boxes in the upper corners of the

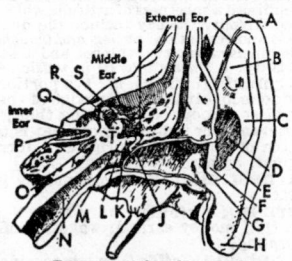

Transverse section of human ear
External ear: A. Helix; B. Fossa of antihelix; C. Antihelix; D. Concha; E. Antitragus; F. Tragus; G. External auditory meatus; H. Lobe. Middle ear: I. Incus; J. Tympanic membrane; K. Malleus; L. Tympanum; M. Stapes; N. Eustachian tube. Inner ear: O. Cochlea; P. Internal auditory meatus; Q. S. R. Anterior, posterior, external semicircular canals; T. Vestibule.

the front page of a newspaper, containing displayed matter, as an indication of the edition, a weather bulletin, etc. [ME *ere*, OE *ēare*, c. G *ohr*; akin to L *auris*, Gk. *oûs*] —*ear'less*, *adj.*

ear² (ĭr), *n.* **1.** that part of a cereal plant, as corn, wheat, etc., which contains the flowers and hence the fruit, grains, or kernels. —*v.i.* **2.** to form or put forth ears. [ME *ere*, OE *ēar*, c. G *ähre*]

ear·ache (ĭr'āk'), *n.* pain in the ear; otalgia.

ear·drop (ĭr'drŏp'), *n.* an earring with a pendant.

ear·drum (ĭr'drŭm'), *n.* **1.** the tympanic membrane. **2.** the tympanum, or middle ear.

eared (ĭrd), *adj.* having ears or earlike appendages, as eared owls (having earlike feathers), eared seals (having outer ears as contrasted with those which do not).

ear·flap (ĭr'flăp'), *n.* one of a pair of pieces attached to a cap, for covering the ears in cold weather.

ear·ing (ĭr'ĭng), *n.* a small rope attached to a cringle of a sail and used in reefing, etc. [appar. f. EAR¹ + -ING¹]

earl (ûrl), *n.* **1.** a British nobleman of a rank next below that of marquis and next above that of viscount. *Earl* is now a title unconnected with territorial jurisdiction. After the Norman Conquest earls were for a time called counts; the wife of an earl is a countess. **2.** (before the Norman Conquest) the governor of one of the great divisions of Wessex, Mercia, etc. [ME *erl*, OE *eorl* (c. Icel. *jarl* JARL), orig., man, warrior, esp. one of good birth (contrasted with *ceorl* simple freeman, CHURL).)]

ear·lap (ĭr'lăp'), *n.* **1.** earflap. **2.** the lobe of the ear. **3.** the withered ear.

earl·dom (ûrl'dəm), *n.* **1.** the rank or title of an earl. **2.** *Obs.* the territory or jurisdiction of an earl.

ear·ly (ûr'lĭ), *adv.*, **-lier, -liest,** *adj.* —*adv.* **1.** in or during the first part of some division of time, or of some course or series: *early in the year.* **2.** before the usual or appointed time; in good time: *come early.* **3.** far back in time. —*adj.* **4.** occurring in the first part of some division of time, or of some course or series: *an early hour.* **5.** occurring before the usual or appointed time: *an early dinner.* **6.** belonging to a period far back in time: *early English architecture.* **7.** occurring in the near future: *an early reply.* [ME *erli*, etc., OE *ærlīce* (f. *ær* soon + *-līce* -LY)] —*ear'li·ness,* *n.* —Ant. 1. late.

Ear·ly (ûr'lĭ), *n.* Jubal Anderson (jōō'bəl), 1816–94, Confederate general in the U.S. Civil War.

ear·mark (ĭr'märk'), *n.* **1.** a mark of identification made on the ear of an animal. **2.** any identifying or distinguishing mark or characteristic. —*v.t.* **3.** to mark with an earmark. **4.** to set aside for a specific purpose or use: *to earmark goods for export.*

ear·mind·ed (ĭr'mīn'dĭd), *adj.* responding strongly to auditory stimuli or showing a preference for them. —*ear'·mind'ed·ness, n.*

ear·muff (ĭr'mŭf'), *n.* *U.S.* one of a pair of adjustable coverings for protecting the ears in cold weather.

earn¹ (ûrn), *v.t.* **1.** to gain by labor or service: *to earn one's living.* **2.** to merit as compensation, as for service; deserve: *to receive more than one has earned.* **3.** to get as one's desert or due: *to earn a reputation for honesty.* **4.** to gain as due return or profit: *Savings bonds earn interest.* **5.** to bring or procure as deserved: *fair dealing earns confidence.* [ME *ernie(n),* OE *earnian;* akin to OHG *arnēn* earn] —*earn'er, n.* —Syn. 1. See gain¹.

earn² (ûrn), *v.i., v.t.* *Obs.* to yearn. [OE *eornian* murmur (? var. of *geornian*). See YEARN]

ear·nest¹ (ûr'nĭst), *adj.* **1.** serious in intention, purpose, or effort; sincerely zealous: *an earnest worker.* **2.** showing depth and sincerity of feeling: *earnest words.* **3.** having serious importance, or demanding serious attention: *"Life is real! Life is earnest!"* —*n.* **4.** seriousness, as of intention or purpose, as opposed to jest, play, or trifling: *in earnest.* [ME *erneste,* OE *eornost,* c. D and G *ernst*] —*ear'nest·ly, adv.* —*ear'nest·ness, n.* —Syn. 1. EARNEST, RESOLUTE, SERIOUS, SINCERE imply having qualities of depth, firmness, and stability. EARNEST implies having a purpose and being steadily and soberly eager in pursuing it: *an earnest student.* RESOLUTE adds somewhat more of a quality of determination; one who is resolute is very difficult to sway or to turn aside from a purpose: *resolute in defending the right.* SERIOUS implies having depth and a soberness of attitude which contrasts with gaiety and frivolity; it may include the qualities of both earnestness and resolution: *serious and thoughtful.* SINCERE suggests genuineness, trustworthiness, and absence of deceit or superficiality: *a sincere interest in music.* —Ant. 1. frivolous.

ear·nest² (ûr'nĭst), *n.* **1.** a portion of something, given or done in advance as a pledge of the remainder. **2.** *Law.* earnest money. **3.** anything that gives pledge, promise, assurance, or indication of what is to follow. [ME *ernes,* alter. of earlier *erres* (orig., a pl. form, t. OF; see ARLES), appar. by assoc. with suffix *-ness*]

earnest money, *Law.* money given to bind a contract.

earn·ing (ûr'nĭng), *n.* **1.** act of one who earns. **2.** (pl.) money earned; wages; profits. [ME *erning,* OE *earnung*]

ear·phone (ĭr'fōn'), *n.* a receiver in a headset.

ear·ring (ĭr'rĭng'), *n.* a ring or other ornament worn in or on the lobe of the ear.

ear shell, abalone.

ear·shot (ĭr'shŏt'), *n.* reach or range of hearing.

ear stone, an otolith.

earth (ûrth), *n.* **1.** the planet which we inhabit, the third in order from the sun, having an equatorial diam-

eter of 7926 miles. **2.** the inhabitants of this planet; *the whole earth rejoiced.* **3.** this planet as the habitation of man, often in contrast to heaven and hell. **4.** the surface of this planet. **5.** the solid matter of this planet; the dry land; the ground. **6.** the softer part of the land, as distinguished from rock; soil; dirt: *draw the earth up around the plant.* (The English often use this word where Americans say *dirt* or *ground.*) **7.** *Chiefly Brit.* the body of a burrowing animal. **8.** worldly matters, as distinguished from spiritual. **9.** *Chem.* any of certain difficultly reducible metallic oxides, as alumina, zirconia, yttria, etc. (the alkaline earths). **10.** *Elect.* a ground. **11.** *Obs.* a land or country. —*v.i.* **12.** *Brit. Elect.* to ground. [ME *erthe,* OE *eorthe,* c. G *erde*] —Syn. 3. EARTH, GLOBE, WORLD are terms applied to the planet on which we dwell. EARTH is used esp. in speaking of a condition of existence contrasted with that in heaven or hell: *those who are yet on earth.* GLOBE formerly emphasized merely the roundness of the earth: *to circumnavigate the globe.* It is now coming to be used more like WORLD, with especial application to the inhabitants of the earth and their activities, interests, and concerns. In this sense, both GLOBE and WORLD are more inclusive than EARTH and are used more abstractly: *the politics of the globe, the future of the world, One World.*

earth·born (ûrth'bôrn'), *adj.* **1.** born or sprung from the earth; of earthly origin. **2.** mortal.

earth·bound (ûrth'bound'), *adj.* **1.** firmly fixed in the earth. **2.** having only earthly interests.

earth·en (ûr'thən), *adj.* **1.** composed of earth. **2.** made of baked clay.

earth·en·ware (ûr'thən wâr'), *n.* **1.** earthen pottery; vessels, etc., of baked or hardened clay. **2.** the material of such vessels (usually the coarse, opaque varieties, the finer, translucent kinds being called *porcelain*).

earth inductor compass, *Aeron.* a compass actuated by induction from the earth's magnetic field.

earth·i·ness (ûr'thĭ nĭs), *n.* **1.** earthy nature or properties. **2.** earthliness.

earth·ling (ûrth'lĭng), *n.* **1.** an inhabitant of earth; a mortal. **2.** one attached to earthly or worldly things.

earth·ly (ûrth'lĭ), *adj.,* **-lier, -liest. 1.** of or pertaining to the earth, esp. as opposed to heaven; worldly. **2.** possible or conceivable: *no earthly use.* [ME *erthly,* OE *eorthlīc*] —*earth'li·ness, n.* —Syn. 1. EARTHLY, TERRESTRIAL, WORLDLY, MUNDANE refer to that which is concerned with the earth literally or figuratively. EARTHLY now almost always implies a contrast to that which is heavenly: *earthly pleasures, our earthly home.* TERRESTRIAL, the dignified Latin equivalent of EARTHLY, applies to the earth as a planet or to the land as opposed to the water, and is contrasted with that which is celestial: *terrestrial areas, the terrestrial globe.* WORLDLY is commonly used in the derogatory sense of being devoted to the vanities, cares, advantages, or gains of this present life to the exclusion of spiritual interests or the life to come: *worldly success, worldly standards.* MUNDANE, a formal Latin word, equivalent to WORLDLY, especially suggests that which is bound to the earth, is not exalted, and therefore is commonplace: *mundane affairs, pursuits, etc.*

earth·nut (ûrth'nŭt'), *n.* **1.** any of various roots, tubers, or underground growths, as the peanut and the truffle. **2.** any of the plants producing these.

earth·quake (ûrth'kwāk'), *n.* a vibration or movement of a part of the earth's surface, due to the faulting of rocks, to volcanic forces, etc.

earth·shine (ûrth'shīn'), *n.* *Astron.* the faint light on the part of the moon not illuminated by the sun, due to the light which the earth reflects on the moon.

earth·star (ûrth'stär'), *n.* a fungus of the genus *Geaster,* with an outer covering which splits into the form of a star.

earth·ward (ûrth'wərd), *adv.* **1.** Also, **earth'wards.** toward the earth. —*adj.* **2.** directed toward the earth.

earth·work (ûrth'wûrk'), *n.* **1.** the excavating and embanking of earth involved in engineering construction. **2.** *Mil.* a construction formed chiefly of earth, used in both defensive and offensive operations.

earth·worm (ûrth'wûrm'), *n.* **1.** any one of numerous annelid worms that burrow in soil and feed on soil and decaying organic matter. **2.** a mean or groveling person.

earth·y (ûr'thĭ), *adj.,* **earthier, earthiest. 1.** of the nature of or consisting of earth or soil. **2.** characteristic of earth: *an earthy smell.* **3.** worldly. **4.** coarse or unrefined. **5.** direct; robust; unaffected.

ear trumpet, a device for collecting and intensifying sounds, held to the ear as an aid in defective hearing.

ear·wax (ĭr'wăks'), *n.* cerumen.

ear·wig (ĭr'wĭg'), *n., v.* **-wigged, -wigging.** —*n.* **1.** any insect of the order *Dermaptera,* characterized by the forceps or pincers at the end of the abdomen. These harmless insects were popularly supposed to injure the human ear. —*v.t.* **2.** to fill the mind of with prejudice by insinuations. [ME *erwyge,* OE *ēarwicga* ear insect]

ease (ēz), *n., v.,* **eased, easing.** —*n.* **1.** freedom from labor, pain, or physical annoyance of any kind; tranquil rest; comfort: *to take one's ease.* **2.** freedom from concern, anxiety, or solicitude; a quiet state of mind: *be at ease.* **3.** freedom from difficulty or great labor; facility: *it can be done with ease.* **4.** freedom from stiffness, constraint, or formality; unaffectedness: *ease of manner, at ease with others.* **5.** **at ease,** *Mil.* a position of rest in which soldiers may relax, but may not leave their place or talk. —*v.t.* **6.** to give rest or relief to; make comfortable. **7.** to free from anxiety or care: *to ease one's*

mind. **8.** to mitigate, lighten, or lessen: *to ease the pain.* **9.** to release from pressure, tension, or the like: *to ease off a rope.* **10.** to render less difficult; facilitate. **11.** *Naut.* **a.** to bring (the helm) slowly toward midships. **b.** to give (a ship) leeward helm or trim sails so as to present the bow to a wave. —*v.i.* **12.** to reduce severity, pressure, tension, etc. (often fol. by *off* or *up*). **13.** to become less painful, burdensome, etc. [ME *eise*, t. OF: m. *aise*, g. LL *adjacens* near]
—**Syn. 1.** EASE, COMFORT refer to a sense of relaxation or of well-being. EASE implies a relaxed condition with an absence of effort or pressure: *a life of ease, ease after the day's work.* COMFORT suggests a sense of well-being, along with ease, which produces a quiet happiness and contentment: *comfort in one's old age.* **7.** tranquilize, soothe. **8.** alleviate, assuage, allay. —**Ant. 1.** discomfort. **2.** anxiety. **3.** effort.

ase·ful (ēz'fəl), *adj.* comfortable; quiet; peaceful; restful. —**ease'ful·ly,** *adv.* —**ease'ful·ness,** *n.*

a·sel (ē'zəl), *n.* a frame in the form of a tripod, for supporting an artist's canvas, a blackboard, or the like. [t. D: m. *ezel,* c. G *esel* beast, lit., ass; akin to EASE]

ase·ment (ēz'mənt), *n.* **1.** an easing; relief. **2.** something that gives ease; a convenience. **3.** *Law.* a right held by one person to make use of the land of another.

as·er (ē'zər), *n.* one who or that which eases.

as·i·ly (ē'zə lǐ, ēz'lǐ), *adv.* **1.** in an easy manner; with ease; without trouble. **2.** beyond question: *easily the best.*

as·i·ness (ē'zĭ nǐs), *n.* **1.** quality or condition of being easy. **2.** ease of manner; carelessness; indifference.

ast (ēst) *n.* **1.** a cardinal point of the compass (90 degrees to the right of North), corresponding to the point where the sun is seen to rise. **2.** the direction in which this point lies. **3.** (*l.c. or cap*) a quarter or territory situated in this direction. **4. the East, a.** the parts of Asia collectively (as lying east of Europe) where civilization has existed from early times, including Asia Minor, Syria, Arabia, India, China, etc.; the Orient. **b.** the whole eastern or Atlantic portion of the United States, esp. that north of Maryland. **c.** New England. [ME *est*, OE *ēaste*, c. OE *ōsten*] —*adj.* **5.** directed or proceeding toward the east. **6.** coming from the east: *an east wind.* **7.** lying toward or situated in the east: *the east side.* **8.** *Eccles.* toward the altar as situated with respect to the nave. —*adv.* **9.** toward or in the east: *he went east.* **10.** from the east. [ME *est.* OE *ēast,* c. MHG *ōst.* See EASTER]

ast An·gli·a (ǎng'gǐ|ə), an early English kingdom in SE Britain; modern Norfolk and Suffolk. See map under **Mercia.**

ast Bengal, a state in Pakistan, formerly part of the Indian province of Bengal; now coextensive with East Pakistan. See **Bengal.**

ast·bound (ēst'bound'), *adj.* **1.** traveling eastward. **2.** pertaining to eastward travel.

ast·bourne (ēst'bôrn, -bərn), *n.* a seaport in SE England, in Sussex. 51,820 (est. 1946).

ast by north, *Navig., Survey.* 11°15′ (one point) north of east; 78° 45′ from due north. *Abbr.:* E by N.

ast by south, *Navig., Survey.* 11° 15′ (one point) south of east; 101° 15′ from due east. *Abbr.:* E by S.

ast Cape. See Dezhnev, Cape.

ast Chicago, a city in NW Indiana, near Chicago: a port on Lake Michigan. 57,669 (1960).

ast China Sea, a part of the N Pacific, bounded by China, Korea, Japan, the Ryukyus, and Formosa. 37,991 (1960).

ast Cleveland, a city in NE Ohio, near Cleveland. 37,991 (1960).

ast End, a large, thickly settled, and impoverished part of London, England, in the E part.

ast·er (ēs'tər), *n.* **1.** an annual Christian festival in commemoration of the resurrection of Jesus Christ, observed on the first Sunday after the full moon that occurs on or next after March 21. **2.** the day on which this festival is celebrated. [ME *ester,* OE *ēastre,* pl. *ēastron,* (c. G *Ostern,* pl.), orig., name of goddess; akin to L *aurora* dawn, Gk. *eōs.* Cf. EAST]

aster egg, a colored egg, or imitation of one, used at Easter as a gift or decoration.

aster Island, an island in the S Pacific, ab. 2000 mi. W of and belonging to Chile: stone monuments. 45 sq. mi. Native name, **Rapa Nui.**

ast·er·ling (ēs'tər lǐng), *n.* a native of some country lying eastward of another.

ast·er·ly (ēs'tər lǐ), *adj.* **1.** moving, directed, or situated toward the east: *an easterly course.* **2.** coming from the east: *an easterly wind.* —*adv.* **3.** toward the east. **4.** from the east.

Easter Monday, the day after Easter.

ast·ern (ēs'tərn), *adj.* **1.** lying toward or situated in the east: *the eastern side of town.* **2.** directed or proceeding toward the east: *an eastern route.* **3.** coming from the east: *an eastern wind.* **4.** (*l.c. or cap.*) of or pertaining to the East: *the Eastern Church, an Eastern Congressman.* **5.** (*usually cap.*) Oriental. [ME *esterne,* OE *ēasterne*]

Eastern Church, 1. the church of the countries comprised in the Eastern Roman Empire. **2.** any body of Christians owing allegiance to the Greek Church and observing the Greek rite rather than the Roman.

East·ern·er (ēs'tər nər), *n.* a person of or from the eastern U.S.

Eastern Hemisphere, the part of the world lying E of the Greenwich Meridian, including Asia, Africa, Australia, and Europe.

east·ern·most (ēs'tərn mōst', -məst), *adj.* farthest east.

Eastern Roman Empire, the eastern division of the Roman Empire and, after A.D. 476, the Roman Empire with its capital at Constantinople. Also, **Eastern Empire.**

Eastern shore, that part of Maryland along the eastern shores of Chesapeake Bay, sometimes including Delaware and parts of Virginia east of Chesapeake Bay.

Eastern time. See standard time.

East·er·tide (ēs'tər tīd'), *n.* **1.** Easter time. **2.** the week ushered in by and following Easter. **3.** the fifty days between Easter and Whitsuntide.

East Germany, a country in central Europe, formed after World War II as the Russian Zone of occupation. 17,944,000 pop. (est. 1956); 41,535 sq. mi. *Cap.:* Berlin. Also called Soviet Zone. Official name, **German Democratic Republic.** See **Germany.**

East Ham, a city in SE England, near London. 114,400 (est. 1956).

East Indies, 1. a collective name of the two large peninsulas (India and Indochina) of SE Asia, together with the Malay Archipelago. **2.** the Malay Archipelago. See the map just below. Also, **East India.** —**East Indian.**

East Indies (def. 2)

east·ing (ēs'tǐng), *n.* **1.** the distance due east made by a ship on any course tending eastward; easterly departure. **2.** a shifting eastward; easterly direction.

East Lansing, a city in S Michigan. 30,198 (1960).

East Liverpool, a city in E Ohio, on the Ohio river. 22,306 (1960).

East London, a seaport in the Republic of South Africa, in SE Cape of Good Hope province. With suburbs, 90,606 (1951).

East Los Angeles, a seaport in SW California, near Los Angeles. 104,270 (1960).

East Lo·thi·an (lō'thǐ ən), a county in SE Scotland. 51,600 pop. (est. 1956); 267 sq. mi. *Co. seat:* Haddington. Also, **Haddington.**

East·man (ēst'mən), *n.* George, 1854–1932, U.S. inventor (in field of photography) and philanthropist.

east-north·east (ēst'nôrth'ēst'), *n. Navig.* that point of the compass midway between east and northeast: 67° 30′ from north. *Abbr.:* ENE.

Eas·ton (ēs'tən), *n.* a city in E Pennsylvania, on the Delaware. 31,955 (1960).

East Orange, a city in NE New Jersey, near Newark. 77,259 (1960).

East Pakistan, a part of Pakistan, north of the Bay of Bengal. 42,063,000 pop. (1951); 54,501 sq. mi. *Cap.:* Dacca. See *Pakistan.*

East Providence, a town in NE Rhode Island, near Providence. 41,955 (1960).

East Prussia, a former province in NE Germany: until 1939 it was an exclave separated from Germany by the Polish Corridor; now divided between Poland and the Soviet Union. (Prior to the annexation of the Polish Corridor) 2,186,413 (1939); 14,283 sq. mi. *Cap.:* Königsberg. German, **Ostpreussen.**

East Riding, an administrative county in Yorkshire, England. 510,904 (1951); 1172 sq. mi. *Co. seat:* Beverley.

East River, a strait in SE New York, separating Manhattan Island from Long Island, and connecting New York Bay and Long Island Sound.

east-south·east (ēst'south'ēst'), *n. Navig.* that point of the compass midway between east and southeast; 112° 30′ from north. *Abbr.:* ESE.

East St. Louis, a city in SW Illinois, across the Mississippi from St. Louis, Missouri. 81,712 (1960).

east·ward (ēst'wərd), *adv.* **1.** Also, **east'wards.** toward the east. —*adj.* **2.** moving, bearing, facing, or situated toward the east. —*n.* **3.** the eastward part, direction, or point. [ME *estwarde,* OE *eastewearde*]

east·ward·ly (ēst'wərd lǐ), *adj.* **1.** having an eastward direction or situation. **2.** coming from the east: *an eastwardly wind.* —*adv.* **3.** toward the east. **4.** from the east.

eas·y (ē'zǐ), *adj., easier, easiest, adv.* —*adj.* **1.** not difficult; requiring no great labor or effort: *easy to read, an easy victory.* **2.** free from pain, discomfort, worry, or care: *he is resting easier this morning, easy in one's mind.* **3.** conducive to ease or comfort: *an easy chair.* **4.** fond of or given to ease; easygoing. **5.** not harsh or strict; lenient: *an easy master.* **6.** not burdensome or oppressive: *easy terms.* **7.** not difficult to influence; compliant. **8.** free from formality, constraint, or embarrassment: *an easy style or manners.* **9.** not tight; fitting loosely: *an*

easy fit. 10. not forced or hurried; moderate: *an easy pace.* **11.** *Com.* **a.** (of a commodity) not difficult to obtain; in plentiful supply and (often) weak in price. **b.** (of the market) not characterized by eager demand. —*adv.* **12.** *Colloq.* in an easy manner; comfortably: *to go easy, take it easy.* [ME *aisie*, t. OF, pp. of *aisier* EASE, v.] —**Syn. 2.** tranquil, untroubled, comfortable, contented. **8.** smooth, unconstrained. —**Ant. 1.** difficult.

eas·y·go·ing (ē/zĭ·gō/ĭng), *adj.* **1.** taking matters in an easy way; comfortably unconcerned. **2.** going easily, as a horse.

eat (ēt), *v.,* **ate** (āt; *esp. Brit.* ĕt) or (*Archaic*) **eat** (ĕt, ĕt); **eaten** or (*Archaic*) **eat** (et, ēt); **eating**; *n.* —*v.t.* **1.** to take into the mouth and swallow for nourishment; esp. to masticate and swallow, as solid food. **2.** to consume by or as by devouring. **3.** to ravage or devastate. **4.** to wear or waste away; corrode. **5.** to make (a hole, passage, etc.) as by gnawing or corrosion. **6. eat one's words,** to take back what one has said. —*v.i.* **7.** to consume food; take a meal. **8.** to make a way as by gnawing or corrosion. —*n.* **9.** (*pl.*) *Slang.* food. [ME *eten,* OE *etan,* c. G *essen;* akin to L *edere,* Gk. *édein*] —**eat/er,** *n.*

eat·a·ble (ē/tə bal), *adj.* **1.** edible. —*n.* **2.** (*usually pl.*) an article of food.

eat·ing (ē/tĭng), *n.* **1.** act of one who or that which eats. **2.** food with reference to the quality perceived when eaten: *this fish is delicious eating.*

eau (ō), *n., pl.* **eaux** (ō), water. [F, g. L *aqua*]

Eau Claire (ō/ klâr/), a city in W Wisconsin. 37,987 (1960).

eau de Co·logne (ō/ də kə lōn/), **1.** cologne. **2.** (*cap.*) a trademark for a certain type of cologne. [t. F]

eau de Ja·velle (ō/ də zhä vĕl/), Javel water.

eau de vie (ō/ də vē/; *Fr.* ōd vē/), French. brandy, esp. the coarser and less purified varieties. [F: lit., water of life]

eaves (ēvz), *n.pl.* the overhanging lower edge of a roof. [ME *eves,* OE *efes,* c. OHG *obisa* hall]

eaves·drop (ēvz/drŏp/), *v.i.,* **-dropped, -dropping.** to listen clandestinely. [lit., be on the *eavesdrop* (of a house), earlier *eavesdrip* ground on which falls the drip from the eaves, OE *yfesdrype*] —**eaves/drop/per,** *n.*

ebb (ĕb), *n.* **1.** the reflux or falling of the tide (opposed to *flood* and *flow*). **2.** a flowing backward or away; decline or decay. **3.** a point of decline: *his fortunes were at a low ebb.* —*v.i.* **4.** to flow back or away, as the water of a tide (opposed to *flow*). **5.** to decline or decay; waste or fade away: *his life is ebbing.* [ME *ebbe,* OE *ebba,* c. D *ebbe, eb*] —**Syn. 4.** subside, abate. **5.** sink, wane.

ebb tide, the reflux of the tide; the retiring tide.

E·bert (ā/bərt), *n.* Friedrich (frē/drĭKH), 1871–1925, first president of Germany, 1919–25.

Eb·lis (ĕb/lĭs), *n. Mohammedan Myth.* an evil spirit or devil, the chief of the wicked jinn. [t. Ar.: m. *Iblīs,* t. Gk.: m. *diábolos* (see DEVIL); dropping of *di-* through confusion with Aram. *di-* of]

E-boat (ē/bōt/), *n. Brit.* a very fast unarmored motorboat armed with torpedoes and small guns. [short for *enemy boat*]

eb·on·ite (ĕb/ə nīt/), *n.* vulcanite. [f. EBON(Y) + -ITE[1]]

eb·on·ize (ĕb/ə nīz/), *v.t.,* **-ized, -izing.** to stain or finish in imitation of ebony.

eb·on·y (ĕb/ən/), *n., pl.* **-onies,** *adj.* —*n.* **1.** a hard, heavy, durable wood, most highly prized when black, from various tropical trees of the genus *Diospyros,* as *D. Ebenum* of southern India and Ceylon, used for cabinetwork, etc. **2.** any tree yielding such wood. **3.** any of various similar woods or trees. —*adj.* **4.** made of ebony. **5.** like ebony; black. Also, *Poetic,* **eb/on.** [ME *hebenyf,* irreg. t. L: m.s. *hebeninus,* t. Gk.: m. *ebéninos* made of ebony]

Eb·o·ra·cum (ĕb/ərā/kəm), *n.* ancient name of **York** (def. 4).

e·brac·te·ate (ē·brăk/tĭ āt/), *adj. Bot.* without bracts.

E·bro (ē/brō; *Sp.* ĕ/brō), *n.* a river flowing from N Spain SE to the Mediterranean. ab. 470 mi.

e·bul·lience (ĭ bŭl/yəns), *n.* a boiling over; overflow. Also, **e·bul/lien·cy.**

e·bul·lient (ĭ bŭl/yənt), *adj.* **1.** seething or overflowing with fervor, enthusiasm, excitement, etc. **2.** boiling up; bubbling up like a boiling liquid. [t. L: s. *ēbulliens,* ppr., boiling out or up] —**e·bul/lient·ly,** *adv.*

e·bul·li·tion (ĕb/ə lĭsh/ən), *n.* **1.** a seething or overflowing, as of passion or feeling; an outburst: *ebullition of feeling.* **2.** ebullient state. **3.** act or process of boiling up. **4.** a rushing forth of water, lava, etc., in a state of agitation. [t. L: s. *ēbullītio*]

e·bur·na·tion (ē/bər nā/shən, ĕb/ər-), *n. Pathol.* a morbid change in bone, by which it becomes hard and dense, like ivory. [f. s. L *eburnus* of ivory + -ATION]

ec-, var. of **ex-**[3], before consonants, as in *eccentric.*

ECA, Economic Coöperation Administration. Also, **E.C.A.**

é·car·té (ā/kär tā/; *Brit.* ā kär/tā; *Fr.* ĕ kår tĕ/), *n.* a game at cards for two persons. [t. F, prop. pp. of *écarter* discard]

Ec·bat·a·na (ĕk băt/ə na), *n.* an ancient city in W Asia, the capital of ancient Media. Modern, **Hamadan.**

ec·ce ho·mo (ĕk/sĭ hō/mō, ĕk/ē), *Latin.* **1.** "Behold the man!"—the words with which Pilate presented Christ, crowned with thorns, to his accusers. John 19:5. **2.** *Art.* a representation of Christ crowned with thorns.

ec·cen·tric (ĭk sĕn/trĭk, ĕk-), *adj.* **1.** deviating from

the recognized or usual character, practice, etc.; irregular; erratic; peculiar; odd; queer: *eccentric conduct, an eccentric person.* **2.** *Math.* not having the same center, as two circles or spheres of which one is within the other or which intersect; not concentric. **3.** not situated in the center, as an axis. **4.** *Mach.* having the axis or support away from the center, as a wheel. **5.** *Astron.* deviating from a circular form, as an orbit. —*n.* **6.** one who or that which is unusual, peculiar, odd. **7.** *Mach.* a device for converting circular into reciprocating rectilinear motion, consisting of a disk fixed somewhat out of center to a revolving shaft, and working freely in a surrounding collar (**eccentric strap**), to which a rod (**eccentric rod**) is attached. [t. LL: s. *eccentricus,* t. Gk.: m. *ékkentros* out of the center] —**ec·cen/tri·cal·ly,** *adv.* —**Ant. 1.** normal, ordinary.

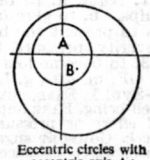

Eccentric circles with eccentric axis A; B, Center of large circle

ec·cen·tric·i·ty (ĕk/sən trĭs/ə tĭ, ĕk/sĕn-), *n., pl.* **-ties. 1.** an oddity or peculiarity, as of conduct. **2.** quality of being eccentric. **3.** the amount by which anything is eccentric. **4.** *Mach.* the throw of an eccentric. —**Syn. 2.** queerness, freakishness, aberration.

ec·ce sig·num (ĕk/sĭ sĭg/nəm, ĕk/ē), *Latin.* behold the sign (or proof).

ec·chy·mo·sis (ĕk/ə mō/sĭs), *n., pl.* **-ses** (-sēz). *Pathol.* a discoloration due to extravasation of blood, as in a bruise. [NL, t. Gk.: m. *ekchýmōsis,* der. *ekchymoûsthai* extravasate blood]

Eccl., Ecclesiastes. Also, **Eccles.**

eccl., ecclesiastical. Also, **eccles.**

Ec·cles (ĕk/əlz), *n.* **Marriner Stoddard,** born 1890, U. S. economist and banker.

ec·cle·si·a (ĭ klē/zhĭ ə, -zĭ ə), *n., pl.* **-siae** (-zhĭ ē/, -zĭ ē/). **1.** an assembly, esp. the popular assembly of ancient Athens. **2.** a congregation; a church. [t. L: assembly of the people, LL church, t. Gk.: m. *ekklēsía*]

Ec·cle·si·as·tes (ĭ klē/zĭ ăs/tēz), *n.* a book of the Old Testament traditionally ascribed to Solomon. [t. LL, t. Gk.: lit., preacher]

ec·cle·si·as·tic (ĭ klē/zĭ ăs/tĭk), *n.* **1.** a clergyman, or person in orders. —*adj.* **2.** ecclesiastical. [t. LL: s. *ecclēsiasticus,* t. Gk.: m. *ekklēsiastikós* of the assembly or church]

ec·cle·si·as·ti·cal (ĭ klē/zĭ ăs/tĭ kal), *adj.* of or pertaining to the church or the clergy; churchly; clerical; not secular; not lay: *ecclesiastical discipline, affairs, ecclesiastical courts.* —**ec·cle/si·as/ti·cal·ly,** *adv.*

ecclesiastical society, (in the Congregational churches of the U.S.) a legal corporation with power to sue and be sued, and to administer all of the temporalities of the church.

ec·cle·si·as·ti·cism (ĭ klē/zĭ ăs/tə sĭz/əm), *n.* **1.** ecclesiastical principles, practices, or spirit. **2.** devotion to the principles or interests of the church.

Ec·cle·si·as·ti·cus (ĭ klē/zĭ ăs/tə kəs), *n.* the book of the Apocrypha called also "The Wisdom of Jesus, the Son of Sirach." [t. LL. See ECCLESIASTIC]

ec·cle·si·ol·a·try (ĭ klē/zĭ ŏl/ə trĭ), *n.* worship of the church; excessive reverence for churchly forms and traditions. [f. ECCLESI(A) + -(O)LATRY]

ec·cle·si·ol·o·gy (ĭ klē/zĭ ŏl/ə jĭ), *n.* the science of church architecture and decoration. [f. ECCLES·(A) + -(O)LOGY] —**ec·cle·si·o·log·ic** (ĭ klē/zĭ ə lŏj/ĭk), **ec·cle/si·o·log/i·cal,** *adj.* —**ec·cle/si·ol/o·gist,** *n.*

Ecclus., Ecclesiasticus (Apocrypha).

ec·dy·sis (ĕk/də sĭs), *n., pl.* **-ses** (-sēz), the shedding or casting off of an outer coat or integument by snakes, crustaceans, etc. [NL, t. Gk.: m. *ékdysis* a getting out]

e·ce·sis (ĭ sē/sĭs), *n. Ecol.* the establishment of an immigrant plant in a new location. [NL, t. Gk.: m. *oíkēsis* an inhabiting]

ECG, electrocardiogram.

E·che·ga·ray (ĕ/chē gä rä/ē), *n.* José (hō sĕ/), 1833?–1916, Spanish dramatist and statesman.

ech·e·lon (ĕsh/ə lŏn/; *Fr.* ĕsh lôn/), *n.* **1.** a level of command: *in the higher echelons.* **2.** a formation of troops, ships, airplanes, etc., in which groups are disposed in parallel lines, each to the right or left of the one in front, so that the whole presents the appearance of steps. **3.** one of the groups of a command so disposed. —*v.t., v.i.* **4.** to form in echelon. [t. F: lit., round of a ladder, der. *échelle* ladder, g. L *scāla* SCALE]

e·chid·na (ĭ kĭd/na), *n., pl.* **-nas, -nae** (-nē) any of the spine-covered insectivorous monotreme mammals with claws and a slender snout, occurring in two genera, the curved-beaked echidna, *Zaglossus* (or *Proechidna*), of New Guinea, and the smaller, straight-beaked echidna, *Tachyglossus,* about 10 in. long, represented by several species in Australia, Tasmania, and southern New Guinea; spiny anteater. [NL, t. Gk.: viper]

Echidna, *Tachyglossus aculeatus* (Ab. 10 in. long)

ech·i·nate (ĕk/ə nāt/), *adj.* spiny; bristly. Also, **ech/i·nat/ed.**

---

b., blend of, blended; c., cognate with; d., dialect, dialectal; der., derived from; f., formed from; g., going back to; m., modification of; r., replacing; s., stem of; t., taken from; ?, perhaps. See the full key on inside cover.

e·chi·no·derm (ĭ kī′nə dûrm′, ĕk′ĭ nə-), *n.* any of the *Echinodermata*. [t. NL: m. *Echinodermata*. See ECHINUS, -DERM]

E·chi·no·der·ma·ta (ĭ kī′nə dûr′mə tə, ĕk′ĭ nə-), *n.pl.* a phylum of marine animals such as starfishes, sea urchins, sea cucumbers, etc., having a radiating arrangement of parts and a body wall stiffened by calcareous pieces that may protrude as spines.

e·chi·noid (ĭ kī′noid, ĕk′ə noid′). *adj.* **1.** belonging to the *Echinoidea*. **2.** resembling a sea urchin. —*n.* **3.** one of the *Echinoidea*; a sea urchin. [f. ECHIN(US) + -OID]

Ech·i·noi·de·a (ĕk′ə noi′dĭ′ə), *n.pl.* a class of echinoderms of rounded form covered with projecting spines, including the sea urchins, etc.

e·chi·nus (ĭ kī′nəs), *n.*, *pl.* **-ni** (-nī). **1.** a sea urchin of the genus *Echinus*. **2.** *Archit.* a rounded molding, as that supporting the abacus of a Doric capital. See diag. under **column**. [t. L, t. Gk.: m. *echinos*, orig., hedgehog]

ech·o (ĕk′ō), *n.*, *pl.* **echoes**, *v.*, **echoed**, **echoing**. —*n.* **1.** a repetition of sound, produced by the reflection of sound waves from an obstructing surface. **2.** a sound heard again near its source, after reflection. **3.** any repetition or close imitation, as of the ideas or opinions of another. **4.** one who reflects or imitates another. **5.** a sympathetic response, as to sentiments expressed. **6.** (*cap.*) **a.** the personification of echo. **b.** *Class. Myth.* a mountain nymph who pined away for love of the beautiful youth Narcissus until only her voice remained. **7.** *Music.* **a.** part (**echo organ**) or stop (**echo stop**) of a large organ for the production of echolike effects. **8.** *Cards.* (esp. in bridge or whist) a signal to a partner that the player wishes the suit continued. **9.** *Electronics.* the reflection of a radio wave such as is used in radar or the like. —*v.i.* **10.** to emit an echo; resound with an echo. **11.** to be repeated by or as by an echo. —*v.t.* **12.** to repeat by or as by an echo; emit an echo of: *the hall echoes even faint sounds.* **13.** to repeat or imitate the words, sentiments, etc., of (a person). [t. L, t. Gk.: sound, echo] —**ech′o·er,** *n.* —**Syn. 10, 12.** reverberate.

e·cho·ic (ĕ kō′ĭk), *adj.* **1.** echolike. **2.** onomatopoetic.

ech·o·ism (ĕk′ō ĭz′əm), *n.* onomatopoeia.

ech·o·la·tion (ĕk′ō lā′shən), *n. Electronics.* the general method of locating objects by determining the time for an echo to return and the direction from which it returns, as by radar and sonar.

Eck·hart (ĕk′härt), *n.* **Johannes** (yō hän′əs) ("*Meister Eckhart*"), c1260–1327? the founder of German mysticism.

é·clair (ā klâr′; *Fr.* ĕ klĕr′), *n.* a light, finger-shaped cake having a cream or custard filling and coated with an icing. [t. F: lit., lightning, der. *éclairer* lighten. Cf. L *exclārāre*]

é·clair·cisse·ment (ĕ klĕr sēs mäN′), *n. French.* a clearing up of something obscure; an explanation.

ec·lamp·si·a (ĕk lămp′sĭ ə), *n. Pathol.* a form of convulsions, esp. of a recurrent nature, as during pregnancy or parturition. [NL, der. Gk. *eklámpein* shine forth]

é·clat (ā klä′; *Fr.* ĕ klä′), *n.* brilliance of success, reputation, etc: *the éclat of a great achievement.* [t. F: fragment, also burst (of light, etc.)]

ec·lec·tic (ĕk lĕk′tĭk), *adj.* **1.** selecting; choosing from various sources. **2.** made up of what is selected from diverse sources. **3.** not following any one system, as of philosophy, medicine, etc., but selecting and using whatever is considered best in all systems. —*n.* **4.** one who follows an eclectic method, as in philosophy. [t. Gk.: m.s. *eklektikós* selective] —**ec·lec′ti·cal·ly,** *adv.*

ec·lec·ti·cism (ĕk lĕk′tə sĭz′əm), *n.* **1.** the use or advocacy of an eclectic method. **2.** an eclectic system.

e·clipse (ĭ klĭps′), *n.*, *v.*, **eclipsed**, **eclipsing.** —*n.* **1.** *Astron.* **a.** the obscuration of the light of a satellite by the intervention of its primary planet between it and the sun, as in a **lunar eclipse** when the moon is partially or wholly within the earth's shadow. **b.** **solar eclipse,** the interception of the light of the sun by the intervention of the moon between it and the observer. **c.** (in an eclipsing binary system) the partial or complete interception of the light of one component by the other. **2.** any obscuration of light. **3.** any obscuration or overshadowing; loss of brilliance or splendor. —*v.t.* **4.** to cause to suffer eclipse: *the moon eclipses the sun.* **5.** to cast a shadow upon; obscure; darken. **6.** to make dim by comparison; surpass. [ME, t. OF, t. L: m.s. *eclipsis*, t. Gk.: m. *ékleipsis*, lit., a failing]

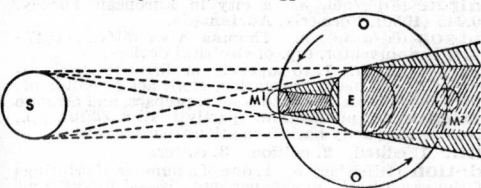

Diagram of eclipse
S, Sun; E, Earth; M¹, position of moon in a solar eclipse; M², position of moon in a lunar eclipse; O, Orbit of moon.

eclipsing variable, *Astron.* a variable star whose changes in brightness are caused by periodic eclipses of two stars in a binary system.

e·clip·tic (ĭ klĭp′tĭk), *n.* **1.** the great circle formed by the intersection of the plane of the earth's orbit with the celestial sphere; the apparent annual path of the sun in the heavens. **2.** an analogous great circle on a terrestrial globe. —*adj.* Also, **e·clip′ti·cal. 3.** pertaining to an eclipse. **4.** pertaining to the ecliptic. [t. L: s. *eclipticus*, t. Gk.: m. *ekleptikós* of or caused by an eclipse. See ECLIPSE] —**e·clip′ti·cal·ly,** *adv.*

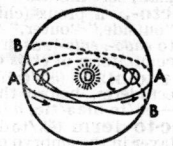

Diagram of ecliptic
A, Ecliptic; B, Celestial equator; C, Orbit of earth; D, Sun

ec·lo·gite (ĕk′lə jīt′), *n.* a rock consisting of granular aggregate of green pyroxene and red garnet, often also containing cyanite, silvery mica, quartz, and pyrite. [f. s. Gk. *eklogē* selection + -ITE¹]

ec·logue (ĕk′lôg, -lŏg), *n.* a short poem, esp. pastoral or idyllic. [t. L: m. *ecloga,* t. Gk.: m. *eklogē* a selection.

ecol., ecology.

é·cole (ĕ kôl′), *n. French.* a school.

e·col·o·gy (ĭ kŏl′ə jĭ), *n.* **1.** the branch of biology which treats of the relations between organisms and their environment; bionomics. **2.** the branch of sociology concerned with the spacing of people and of institutions and their resulting interdependency. [f. m. Gk. *oíko(s)* house + -LOGY] —**ec·o·log·i·cal** (ĕk′ə lŏj′ə kəl, ē′kə-), **ec′o·log′ic,** *adj.* —**ec′o·log′i·cal·ly,** *adv.* —**e·col·o·gist** (ĭ kŏl′ə jĭst), *n.*

econ., **1.** economic. **2.** economics. **3.** economy.

e·co·nom·ic (ē′kə nŏm′ĭk, ĕk′ə-), *adj.* **1.** pertaining to the production, distribution, and use of income and wealth. **2.** of or pertaining to the science of economics. **3.** pertaining to an economy, or system of organization or operation, esp. of the process of production. **4.** pertaining to the means of living; utilitarian: *economic entomology, botany, etc.* [t. L: m. s. *oeconomicus,* t. Gk.: m. *oikonomikós,* der. *oikonomía.* See ECONOMY]

e·co·nom·i·cal (ē′kə nŏm′ə kəl, ĕk′ə-), *adj.* **1.** avoiding waste or extravagance; thrifty. **2.** economic. —**Syn. 1.** saving, provident. ECONOMICAL, THRIFTY, FRUGAL imply careful and saving use of resources. ECONOMICAL implies prudent planning in the disposition of resources so as to avoid unnecessary waste or expense: *economical in budgeting household expenditures.* THRIFTY is a stronger word than ECONOMICAL, and adds to it the idea of industry and successful management: *a thrifty housewife looking for bargains.* FRUGAL emphasizes being saving, sometimes excessively saving, esp. in such matters as food, dress, or the like: *frugal almost to the point of being stingy.* —**Ant. 1.** wasteful, lavish.

e·co·nom·i·cal·ly (ē′kə nŏm′ĭk lĭ, ĕk′ə-), *adv.* **1.** with economy; with frugality or moderation. **2.** as regards the efficient use of income and wealth.

Economic Coöperation Administration, the U.S. government agency (established 1948) in charge of aid to foreign nations in their economic recovery.

e·co·nom·ics (ē′kə nŏm′ĭks, ĕk′ə-), *n.* the science treating of the production, distribution, and consumption of goods and services, or the material welfare of mankind; political economy.

e·con·o·mist (ĭ kŏn′ə mĭst), *n.* **1.** one versed in the science of economics. **2.** an economical person.

e·con·o·mize (ĭ kŏn′ə mīz′), *v.*, **-mized, -mizing.** —*v.t.* **1.** to manage economically; use sparingly or frugally. —*v.i.* **2.** to practice economy; avo'd waste or extravagance. Also, *Brit.,* **e·con′o·mise/.** —**e·con′o·miz′er,** *n.*

e·con·o·my (ĭ kŏn′ə mĭ), *n.*, *pl.* **-mies. 1.** thrifty management; frugality in the expenditure or consumption of money, materials, etc. **2.** an act or means of thrifty saving; a saving. **3.** the management, or science of management, of the resources of a community, etc., with a view to productiveness and avoidance of waste: *national economy.* **4.** the disposition or regulation of the parts or functions of any organic whole; an organized system or method. **5.** *Theol.* **a.** the divine plan for man, his creation, redemption, final beatitude. **b.** the method of divine administration, as at a particular time or for a particular race. **6.** *Archaic.* the management of household affairs. [t. L: m.s. *oeconomia,* t. Gk.: m. *oikonomía* management of a household or of the state] —**Syn. 1.** thriftiness, thrift, saving.

e·co·tone (ē′kə tōn′), *n.* the transition zone between two different plant communities, as that between forest and prairie. [f. Gk.: m. *oíko(s)* home + m.s. *tónos* stress]

é·cra·seur (ĕ krä zœr′), *n.* a surgical instrument used in an operation where hemorrhage is feared, as in removing certain types of tumors, by the gradual tightening of a chain or wire loop. [t. F, der. *écraser* crush]

ec·ru (ĕk′rōō, ā′krōō; *Fr.* ĕ krȳ′), *adj.* **1.** very light brown in color, as raw silk, unbleached linen, etc. —*n.* **2.** ecru color. Also, **é/cru.** [F: raw, unbleached, f. é- thoroughly (g. L *ex-* EX-¹) + *cru* raw, g. L *crūdus*]

ec·sta·sy (ĕk′stə sĭ), *n.*, *pl.* **-sies. 1.** overpowering emotion or exaltation; a sudden access of intense feeling. **2.** rapturous delight. **3.** the frenzy of poetic inspiration. **4.** mental transport or rapture from the contemplation of divine things. [ME *extasie,* t. ML: m. *extasis,* t. Gk.: m. *ékstasis* extension] —**Syn. 1.** rapture.

ec·stat·ic (ĕk stăt′ĭk), *adj.* **1.** of, pertaining to, or characterized by ecstasy. **2.** subject to or in a state of ecstasy; transported; rapturous. —*n.* **3.** one subject to fits of ecstasy. **4.** (*pl.*) ecstatic transports; raptures. —**ec·stat′i·cal·ly,** *adv.*

ec·thy·ma (ĕk′thə mə), *n. Vet. Sci.* a contagious virus disease of sheep and goats marked by vesicular and pustular lesions on the lips, and occasionally affecting man; sore mouth.

ecto-, a prefix (chiefly in biological words) meaning "outside," "outer," "external," "lying upon" (opposed to *endo-, ento-*), as in *ectoderm, Ectozoa.* [t. Gk.: m. *ekto-,* comb. form of *ektós* outside]

ec·to·blast (ĕk′tə blăst′), *n. Embryol.* the prospective ectoderm, before the separation of the germ layers. —**ec′to·blas′tic,** *adj.*

ec·to·derm (ĕk′tə dûrm′), *n. Embryol.* the outer germ layer in the embryo of any metazoan. —**ec′to·der′mal, ec′to·der′mic,** *adj.*

ec·to·mere (ĕk′tə mĭr′), *n. Embryol.* any one of the blastomeres which participates in the development of the ectoderm.

-ectomy, a combining form attached to the name of a part of the body and producing a word meaning an operation for the excision of that part. [f. *ec-* (t. Gk.: m. *ek-,* prefix form of *ek, ez-* out of) + -TOMY]

ec·to·par·a·site (ĕk′tō păr′ə sīt′), *n.* an external parasite (opposed to *endoparasite*).

ec·top·ic (ĕk tŏp′ĭk), *adj. Pathol.* in an abnormal position or place, as in pregnancy outside the womb, tallpes, etc. [f. Gk. *éktop(os)* displaced + -ic]

ec·to·plasm (ĕk′tə plăz′əm), *n.* 1. *Biol.* the outer portion of the cytoplasm in the cell of a protozoan or vegetable cell. 2. *Spiritualism.* the supposed emanation from the body of a medium. —**ec′to·plas′mic,** *adj.*

ec·to·sarc (ĕk′tə särk′), *n. Biol.* the ectoplasm of a protozoan (opposed to *endosarc*).

ec·tos·to·sis (ĕk′tŏs tō′sĭs), *n. Anat.* the ossification of cartilage proceeding from without inward. [NL; f. ECT(O)- + -*ostosis* as in EXOSTOSIS]

ec·type (ĕk′tīp), *n.* a reproduction or copy (opposed to *prototype*). [t. Gk.: m.s. *éktypos* wrought in relief, formed in outline] —**ec·ty·pal** (ĕk′tə pəl), *adj.*

é·cu (ĕ kY′), *n., pl.* **écus** (ĕ kY′). *French.* 1. the shield carried by a mounted man-at-arms in the middle ages. 2. any of several gold and silver coins of France from the 14th century onward. [F: orig., shield, g. L *scūtum*]

Ecua., Ecuador.

Ec·ua·dor (ĕk′wə dôr′), *n.* a republic in NW South America. 3,777,000 pop. (est. 1956); 104,510 sq. mi. *Cap.:* Quito. —**Ec′ua·do′ri·an,** *adj., n.*

ec·u·men·i·cal (ĕk′yŏŏ mĕn′ə kəl or, *esp. Brit.,* ē′kyŏŏ-), *adj.* 1. general; universal. 2. pertaining to the whole Christian church. Also, **œcumenical, ec′u·men′ic.** [f. (m.) s. LL *oecūmenicus* (t. LGk.: m. *oikoumenikós* general, universal) + -AL¹] —**ec′u·men′i·cal·ly,** *adv.*

ec·ze·ma (ĕk′sə mə, ĕg zē′-), *n. Pathol.* an inflammatory disease of the skin attended with itching and the exudation of serous matter. [t. NL, t. Gk.: a cutaneous eruption] —**ec·zem·a·tous** (ĕg zĕm′ə təs), *adj.*

-ed¹, a suffix forming the past tense, as in *he crossed the river.* [OE *-de, -ede, -ode, -ade*]

-ed², a suffix forming 1. the past participle, as in *he had crossed the river.* 2. participial adjectives indicating a condition or quality resulting from the action of the verb, as *inflated balloons.* [OE *-ed, -od, -ad*]

-ed³, a suffix serving to form adjectives from nouns, as *bearded, moneyed, tender-hearted.* [OE *-ede*]

ed., 1. edited. 2. edition. 3. (*pl.,* **eds.**) editor.

e·da·cious (ĭ dā′shəs), *adj.* devouring; voracious; consuming. [f. EDACI(TY) + -OUS]

e·dac·i·ty (ĭ dăs′ə tĭ), *n. Humorous.* good appetite. [t. L: m.s. *edācitas* gluttony]

E·dam cheese (ē′dăm, -dəm; *Du.* ā dăm′), a hard, round, fine-flavored yellow cheese, usually colored red on the outside. Also, **Edam.**

e·daph·ic (ĭ dăf′ĭk), *adj. Ecol.* due to soil or topography rather than climate. [f. s. Gk. *édaphos* bottom + -IC]

Ed.B., Bachelor of Education.

EDC, European Defense Community.

Ed.D., Doctor of Education.

Ed·da (ĕd′ə), *n., pl.* **Eddas.** 1. Elder or Poetic Edda, a collection of old Icelandic poems on mythical and religious subjects, erroneously ascribed to Saemund Sigfusson (about 1055–1133). 2. Younger or Prose Edda, an old Icelandic work, compiled and partly written by Snorri Sturluson (1179–1241), containing ancient myths and legends of Scandinavia, rules and theories of versemaking, poems, etc. [t. Icel.] —**Ed·da·ic** (ĕ dā′ĭk), **Ed′dic,** *adj.*

Ed·ding·ton (ĕd′ĭng tən), *n.* Sir Arthur Stanley, 1882–1944, British astronomer, physicist, and author.

ed·does (ĕd′ōz), *n.pl.* the edible roots of the taro, or of any several related plants; dasheen. [t. West Afr.]

ed·dy (ĕd′Y), *n., pl.* **-dies,** *v.,* **-died, -dying.** —*n.* 1. a current at variance with the main current in a stream of liquid or gas, esp. one having a rotary or whirling motion. 2. any similar current, as of air, dust, fog, etc. —*v.i., v.t.* 3. to move or whirl in eddies. [f. OE: *ed-* turning + *ēa* stream. Cf. Icel. *idha*]

Ed·dy (ĕd′Y), *n.* Mrs. Mary Baker, (*Mrs. Glover, Mrs. Patterson*), 1821–1910, U.S. religious leader: founder of the Christian Science Church.

Ed·dy·stone Rocks (ĕd′Y stən), dangerous rocks near the W end of the English Channel, SW of Plymouth, England: site of the Eddystone Lighthouse.

e·del·weiss (ā′dəl vīs′), *n.* a small composite herb,

Leontopodium alpinum, with white woolly leaves and flowers, growing in the high altitudes of the Alps. [t. G: f. *edel* noble + *weiss* white]

e·de·ma (Ĭ dē′mə), *n., pl.* **-mata** (-mə tə). *Pathol.* effusion of serous fluid into the interstices of cells in tissue spaces or into body cavities. [NL, t. Gk.: m. *oídēma* a swelling] —**e·dem·a·tous** (Ĭ dĕm′ə təs), **e·dem·a·tose** (Ĭ dĕm′ə tōs′), *adj.*

E·den (ē′dən), *n.* 1. the garden which was the first home of Adam and Eve. 2. any delightful region or abode. 3. a state of perfect happiness. [t. Heb.: lit., pleasure, delight]

E·den (ē′dən), *n.* (Robert) Anthony, (*Lord Avon*), born 1897, British foreign minister, 1935–38, 1940–45, 1951–55; prime minister, 1955–57.

e·den·tate (ē dĕn′tāt), *adj.* 1. belonging or pertaining to the *Edentata,* an order of New World mammals, comprising the armadillos, the sloths, and the South American anteaters. 2. toothless. —*n.* 3. an edentate mammal. [t. L: m.s. *ēdentātus,* pp., deprived of teeth]

EDES, Hellenic National Democratic army, a conservative Greek resistance coalition in World War II.

E·des·sa (Ĭ dĕs′ə), *n.* an ancient city in NW Mesopotamia, an early center of Christianity; the capital of a principality under the Crusaders. Modern, Urfa.

edge (ĕj), *n., v.,* **edged, edging.** —*n.* 1. the border or part adjacent to a line of division; a brim or margin: *the horizon's edge.* 2. a brink or verge: *the edge of a precipice.* 3. one of the narrow surfaces of a thin, flat object: *a book with gilt edges.* 4. the line in which two surfaces of a solid object meet: *the edge of a box.* 5. the thin, sharp side of the blade of a cutting instrument or weapon. 6. the sharpness proper to a blade. 7. sharpness or keenness of language, argument, appetite, desire, etc. 8. *Brit. Local.* a hill or cliff. 9. **have the edge,** to have the advantage (usually fol. by *on* or *over*). 10. **on edge, a.** acutely uncomfortable or sensitive: *nerves on edge, to set the teeth on edge.* **b.** eager or impatient. 11. *Poker.* the prerogative or duty of the player at the dealer's left to put up the first stake. —*v.t.* 12. to put an edge on; sharpen. 13. to provide with an edge or border; border. 14. to move edgewise; move or force gradually: *to edge one's way through a crowd.* —*v.i.* 15. to move edgewise; advance gradually. [ME *egge,* OE *ecg,* c. G *ecke,* Icel. *egg;* akin to L *aciēs* edge, point] —**edged,** *adj.* —**edge′less,** *adj.*

—**Syn.** 1. EDGE, BORDER, MARGIN refer to a boundary. An EDGE is the boundary line of a surface or plane: *the edge of a table.* BORDER is the boundary of a surface or the strip adjacent to it, inside or out: *a border of lace.* MARGIN is a limited strip, generally unoccupied, at the extremity of an area: *the margin of a page.*

edge tool, a tool with a cutting edge.

edge·wise (ĕj′wĭz′), *adv.* with the edge forward; in the direction of the edge. Also, **edge·ways** (ĕj′wāz′).

Edge·worth (ĕj′wûrth), *n.* Maria, 1767–1849, British novelist.

edg·ing (ĕj′Ĭng), *n.* 1. act of one who edges. 2. something that serves for an edge or border; trimming for edges.

edg·y (ĕj′Y), *adj.* 1. sharp-edged; sharply defined, as outlines. 2. on edge; irritable. —**edg′i·ness,** *n.*

edh (ĕth), *n.* eth.

ed·i·ble (ĕd′ə bəl), *adj.* 1. fit to be eaten as food; eatable; esculent. —*n.* 2. (*usually pl.*) anything edible; an eatable. [t. LL: m.s. *edibilis,* der. L *edere* eat] —**ed′i·bil′i·ty, ed′i·ble·ness,** *n.*

e·dict (ē′dĬkt), *n.* 1. a decree issued by a sovereign or other authority. 2. any authoritative proclamation or command. [t. L: s. *ēdictum,* prop. pp. neut., declared, proclaimed; r. ME *edit,* t. OF] —**e·dic′tal,** *adj.* —**e·dic′tal·ly,** *adv.*

ed·i·fi·ca·tion (ĕd′ə fə kā′shən), *n.* 1. act of edifying. 2. state of being edified. 3. moral improvement.

ed·i·fice (ĕd′ə fĭs), *n.* a building, esp. one of large size or imposing appearance: *a spacious edifice of brick.* [t. F, t. L: m.s. *aedificium* building] —**ed·i·fi·cial** (ĕd′ə-fĭsh′əl), *adj.* —**Syn.** See **building.**

ed·i·fy (ĕd′ə fī′), *v.t.,* **-fied, -fying.** to build up or increase the faith, morality, etc., of; instruct or benefit, esp. morally. [ME *edifie(n),* t. OF: m. *edifier,* t. L: m.s. *aedificāre* build] —**ed′i·fi′er,** *n.* —**ed′i·fy′ing·ly,** *adv.*

e·dile (ē′dĬl), *n.* aedile.

Ed·in·burgh (ĕd′ən bûr′ō; *or, esp. Brit.,* -brə), *n.* 1. the capital of Scotland, in the SE part. 467,000 (est. 1956). 2. former name of **Midlothian.**

E·dir·ne (ĕ dĕr′nĕ), *n.* a city in European Turkey. 30,245 (1950). Formerly, **Adrianople.**

Ed·i·son (ĕd′ə sən), *n.* Thomas Alva (ăl′və), 1847–1931, U.S. inventor, esp. of electrical devices.

ed·it (ĕd′Ĭt), *v.t.* 1. to supervise or direct the preparation of (a newspaper, magazine, etc.); act as editor of; direct the policies of. 2. to collect, prepare, and arrange (materials) for publication. [partly t. L: s. *ēditus,* pp., given forth; partly back formation from EDITOR]

edit., 1. edited. 2. edition. 3. editor.

e·di·tion (Ĭ dĬsh′ən), *n.* 1. one of a number of printings of the same book, newspaper, etc., issued at different times, and differing from another by alterations, additions, etc. (as distinguished from *impression*). 2. the format in which a literary work is published: *a one-volume edition of Shakespeare.* 3. the whole number of impressions or copies of a book, newspaper, etc., printed from one set of type at one time. [t. L: s. *ēditio*]

---

b., blend of, blended; c., cognate with; d., dialect, dialectal; der., derived from; f., formed from; g., going back to; m., modification of; r., replacing; s., stem of; t., taken from; ?, perhaps. See the full key on inside cover.

ed·i·tor (ĕd′ĭ tər), *n.* **1.** the supervising director of a newspaper, presenting the opinion or comment of the one. **2.** one who writes editorials. **3.** one who edits material for publication. [t. L] **—ed′i·tress,** *n. fem.*

ed·i·to·ri·al (ĕd′ə tôr′Ĭ əl), *n.* **1.** an article, as in a newspaper, presenting the opinion or comment of the periodical. **—adj. 2.** of or pertaining to an editor. **3.** written by an editor.

ed·i·to·ri·al·ize (ĕd′ə tôr′Ĭ ə līz′), *v.i.,* **-ized, -izing.** to set forth one's position or opinion on some subject in, or as if in, an editorial.

ed·i·to·ri·al·ly (ĕd′ə tôr′Ĭ ə lĭ), *adv.* **1.** in an editorial manner; as an editor does. **2.** in an editorial.

editor in chief, the policy-making executive or principal editor of a publishing house, publication, etc.

ed·i·tor·ship (ĕd′Ĭ tər shĭp′), *n.* **1.** the office or function of an editor. **2.** editorial direction.

Ed. M., Master of Education.

Ed·mon·ton (ĕd′mən tən), *n.* **1.** a city in SW Canada: the capital of Alberta. 159,631 (1951). **2.** a city in SE England, part of Greater London. 104,244 (1951).

E·dom (ē′dəm), *n.* **1.** Esau, the brother of Jacob. **2.** Greek, **Idumaea** or **Idumea.** an ancient region between the Dead Sea and the Gulf of Aqaba, bordering ancient Palestine. **3.** the nation living there.

E·dom·ite (ē′də mīt′), *n.* a descendant of Esau or Edom. Num. 20:14–21.

eds., editors.

Ed·sel Ford Range (ĕd′səl fôrd′), a mountain range in Antarctica, E of the Ross Sea.

E.D.T., Eastern daylight time. Also, **e.d.t.**

educ., **1.** educated. **2.** education. **3.** educational.

ed·u·ca·ble (ĕj′ŏŏ kə bəl), *adj.* capable of being educated.

ed·u·cate (ĕj′ŏŏ kāt′), *v.t.,* **-cated, -cating. 1.** to develop the faculties and powers of by teaching, instruction, or schooling; qualify by instruction or training for a particular calling, practice, etc.; train: *to educate someone for something or to do something.* **2.** to provide education for; send to school. **3.** to develop or train (the ear, taste, etc.). [t. L: m.s. *ēducātus,* pp., brought up, trained, educated] **—Syn. 1.** teach, instruct, school, drill, indoctrinate.

ed·u·cat·ed (ĕj′ŏŏ kā′tĭd), *adj.* **1.** having undergone education. **2.** characterized by or displaying qualities of culture and learning.

ed·u·ca·tion (ĕj′ŏŏ kā′shən), *n.* **1.** act or process of educating; the imparting or acquisition of knowledge, skill, etc.; systematic instruction or training. **2.** the result produced by instruction, training, or study. **3.** the science or art of teaching; pedagogics.

—Syn. 1. instruction, schooling, tuition. EDUCATION, TRAINING imply a discipline and development by means of study and learning. EDUCATION is the development of the special and general abilities of the mind (learning to know): *a liberal education.* TRAINING is practical education (learning to do) or practice, usually under supervision, in some art, trade, or profession: *training in art, teacher training.* **2.** learning, knowledge, enlightenment. EDUCATION, CULTURE are often used interchangeably to mean the results of schooling. EDUCATION, however, suggests chiefly the information acquired. CULTURE is a mode of thought and feeling encouraged by education (the process and the acquirement). It suggests an aspiration toward, and an appreciation of, high intellectual and esthetic ideals: *the level of culture in a country depends upon the education of its people.*

ed·u·ca·tion·al (ĕj′ŏŏ kā′shən əl), *adj.* **1.** pertaining to education. **2.** tending to educate. **—ed′u·ca′tion·al·ly,** *adv.*

ed·u·ca·tion·al·ist (ĕj′ŏŏ kā′shən əl ĭst), *n.* an expert in theories and methods of education. Also, **ed′u·ca′tion·ist.**

ed·u·ca·tive (ĕj′ŏŏ kā′tĭv), *adj.* **1.** serving to educate: *educative knowledge.* **2.** pertaining to education: *the educative process.*

ed·u·ca·tor (ĕj′ŏŏ kā′tər), *n.* one who or that which educates; a teacher. [t. L]

ed·u·ca·to·ry (ĕj′ŏŏ kə tôr′Ĭ), *adj.* serving to educate.

e·duce (Ĭ dūs′, Ĭ dōōs′), *v.t.,* **educed, educing.** to draw forth or bring out; elicit; develop. [t. L: m.s. *ēdūcere* lead forth, bring up] **—e·duc′i·ble,** *adj.*

e·duct (ē′dŭkt), *n.* **1.** something educed. **2.** *Chem.* one substance extracted unchanged from another (distinguished from a *product*). [t. L: s. *ēductus,* pp., educed]

e·duc·tion (Ĭ dŭk′shən), *n.* **1.** act of educing. **2.** something educed.

e·dul·co·rate (Ĭ dŭl′kə rāt′), *v.t.,* **-rated, -rating.** *Chem.* to free from acids, salts, or impurities by washing; to purify. [t. L: m.s. *ēdulcōrātus,* pp., sweetened.] **—e·dul′co·ra′tion,** *n.*

Ed·ward (ĕd′wərd), *n.* **1.** (*"the Black Prince"*), Prince of Wales, 1330–76; English military commander (son of Edward III). **2.** a lake in central Africa between Uganda and the Belgian Congo: a headwater of the Nile. ab. 830 sq. mi.

Edward I, (*"Edward Longshanks"*), 1239–1307, king of England, 1272–1307 (son of Henry III).

Edward II, 1284–1327, king of England, 1307–27 (son of Edward I).

Edward III, 1312–77, king of England, 1327–77 (son of Edward II).

Edward IV, 1442–83, king of England, 1461–70 and 1471–83 (successor of Henry VI, and son of Richard, Duke of York, and first king of the house of York).

Edward V, 1470–83, king of England in 1483; murdered in the Tower of London (son of Edward IV).

Edward VI, 1537–53, king of England and Ireland 1547–53 (son of Henry VIII and Jane Seymour).

Edward VII, (*Albert Edward*), 1841–1910, king of England, 1901–10 (son of Queen Victoria).

Edward VIII, (*Duke of Windsor*), born 1894, king of England in 1936 (son of George V and brother of George VI).

Ed·ward·i·an (ĕd wôr′dĬ ən), *adj.* pertaining to the time of Edward VII, a period often regarded latterly as ornate and overgenteel.

Ed·wards (ĕd′wərdz), *n.* **Jonathan,** 1703–58, colonial American clergyman and metaphysician.

Edward the Confessor, c1004–66, king of England, 1042–66.

-ee, a suffix of nouns denoting one who is the object of some action, or undergoes or receives s mething (often as opposed to the person acting), as in *assignee, donee, employee.* [t. F: m. *-ē,* pp. ending, g. L *-ātus* -ATE[1]]

E.E., Electrical Engineer.

e.e., errors excepted.

eel (ēl), *n.* **1.** an elongate, snakelike, apodal fish, esp. of the genus *Anguilla,* as *A. anguilla,* of European fresh waters, or the American eel, *A. bostoniensis.* **2.** any of several similar but unrelated fishes, as the lamprey. [ME *ele,* d. OE *ēl,* r. OE *ǣl,* c. D and G *aal*]

eel·grass (ēl′grăs′), *n.* *U.S.* any of several marine or sweet-water plants with ribbonlike leaves, as *Zostera marina* and *Vallisneria spiralis.*

eel·pout (ēl′pout′), *n.* **1.** any of the blennylike marine fishes constituting the family *Zoarcidae.* **2.** the burbot. [OE *ǣlepūte*]

eel·worm (ēl′wûrm′), *n.* any small nematode worm of the family *Anguillulidae,* including the minute vinegar eel, *Anguillula aceti.*

eel·y (ē′lĬ), *adj.* eellike; wriggling.

e′en (ēn), *adv. Poet.* or *Dial.* even.

e′er (âr), *adv. Poetic.* ever.

-eer, a suffix of nouns denoting one who is concerned with, or employed in connection with, or busies himself with something, as in *auctioneer, engineer, profiteer.* Also, **-ier.** [t. F: m. *-ier,* g. L *-ārius.* See -ARY[1] and -ER[2]]

ee·rie (ĭr′Ĭ), *adj.,* **-rier, -riest. 1.** inspiring fear; weird, strange, or uncanny. **2.** affected with superstitious fear. [ME *eri,* d. var. of obs. *argh,* OE *earg* cowardly, c. G *arg* bad] **—ee′ri·ly,** *adv.* **—ee′ri·ness,** *n.* **—Syn. 1.** See **weird.**

ee·ry (ĭr′Ĭ), *adj.,* **-rier, -riest.** eerie.

ef-, var. of **ex-** (by assimilation) before *f,* as in *efferent.*

ef·fa·ble (ĕf′ə bəl), *adj.* utterable; expressible.

ef·face (Ĭ fās′), *v.t.,* **-faced, -facing. 1.** to wipe out; destroy; do away with: *to efface a memory.* **2.** to rub out, erase, or obliterate (outlines, traces, inscriptions, etc.). **3.** to make inconspicuous or not noticeable: *to efface oneself.* [late ME, t. F: m.s. *effacer,* der. *ef-* (g. L *ex-* EX-[1]) + *face* FACE] **—ef·face′a·ble,** *adj.* **—ef·face′-ment,** *n.* **—ef·fac′er,** *n.*

ef·fect (Ĭ fĕkt′), *n.* **1.** that which is produced by some agency or cause; a result; a consequence: *the effect of heat.* **2.** power to produce results; efficacy; force; validity; weight: *of no effect.* **3.** state of being operative; operation or execution; accomplishment or fulfillment: *to bring a plan into effect.* **4.** a mental impression produced, as by a painting, speech, etc. **5.** the result intended; purport or intent; tenor or significance: *he wrote to that effect.* **6.** (*pl.*) goods; movables; personal property. **7. in effect, a.** in fact or reality. **b.** in operation, as a law. **8. take effect,** to operate or begin to operate. **—v.t. 9.** to produce as an effect; bring about; accomplish; make happen. **10.** to produce or make. [ME, t. L: s. *effectus,* der. *efficere* bring about] **—ef·fect′er,** *n.* **—ef·fect′i·ble,** *adj.*

—Syn. 1. EFFECT, CONSEQUENCE(S), RESULT refer to something produced by an action or a cause. An EFFECT is that which is produced, usually more or less immediately and directly: *the effect of morphine is to produce sleep,* or *morphine produces the effect of sleep.* A CONSEQUENCE, something that follows naturally or logically, as in a train of events or sequence of time, is less intimately connected with its cause than is an effect: *punishment is the consequence of disobedience, take the consequences.* A RESULT may be near or remote, and often is the sum of effects or consequences as making an end or final outcome: *the English language is the result of the fusion of many different elements.* **6.** See **property. 9.** accomplish, achieve, realize, fulfill. See **affect.**

ef·fec·tive (Ĭ fĕk′tĭv), *adj.* **1.** serving to effect the purpose; producing the intended or expected result: *effective measures; effective steps toward peace.* **2.** actually in effect: *the law becomes effective at midnight.* **3.** producing a striking impression; striking: *an effective picture.* **—n. 4.** a soldier or sailor fit for duty or active service. **5.** the effective total of a military force. **—ef·fec′tive·ly,** *adv.* **—ef·fec′tive·ness,** *n.*

—Syn. 1. capable, competent. EFFECTIVE, EFFECTUAL, EFFICACIOUS, EFFICIENT refer to that which is able to produce a (desired) effect. EFFECTIVE is applied to that which has the power to, or which actually does, produce an (often lasting) effect: *an effective action, remedy, speech.* EFFECTUAL is used esp. of that which produces the effect desired or intended, or a decisive result: *an effectual bombardment silenced the enemy.* EFFICACIOUS suggests the capability of achieving a certain end, a capability often manifested only when actually employed: *an efficacious plan, medicine.* EFFICIENT (applied also to persons) is the most active of these words, and implies the skillful use of energy or industry to accomplish desired results with little waste of effort: *efficient methods, an efficient manager.* **—Ant. 1.** futile.

ef·fec·tor (Ĭ fĕk′tər), *n.* **1.** *Physiol.* an organ tissue or cell that carries out a response to a nerve impulse, such as a muscle or gland. **2.** effecter. [t. L]

ef·fec·tu·al (Ĭ fĕk′chŏŏ əl), *adj.* **1.** producing, or capable of producing, an intended effect; adequate. **2.** valid or binding, as an agreement or document. [t. LL: s. *effectuālis*] **—ef·fec′tu·al′i·ty, ef·fec′tu·al-ness,** *n.* **—ef·fec′tu·al·ly,** *adv.* **—Syn. 1.** See effective.

ef·fec·tu·ate (Ĭ fĕk′chŏŏ āt′), *v.t.*, **-ated, -ating.** to bring about; effect. [f. s. F *effectuer* (der. L *effectus* EF-FECT) + -ATE¹] **—ef·fec′tu·a′tion,** *n.*

ef·fem·i·na·cy (Ĭ fĕm′ə nə sĭ), *n.* state or quality of being effeminate.

ef·fem·i·nate (Ĭ fĕm′ə nĬt), *adj.* **1.** soft or delicate to an unmanly degree in traits, tastes, habits, etc.; womanish. **2.** characterized by unmanly softness, delicacy, self-indulgence, etc.: *an effeminate life.* [t. L: m. s. *effēminātus,* pp., made womanish] **—ef·fem′i·nate·ly,** *adv.* **—ef·fem′i·nate·ness,** *n.* **—Syn. 1.** See female.

ef·fen·di (Ĭ fĕn′dĬ), *n., pl.* **-dis.** a Turkish title of respect for government officials, etc. [t. Turk.: m. *efendī,* t. Gk.: m. *authéntēs* master, actual doer. See AUTHENTIC]

ef·fer·ent (ĕf′ər ənt), *adj. Anat., Physiol.* carrying away (opposed to *afferent*): *efferent impulses from the brain.* [t. L: s. *efferens,* ppr., bringing out, raising]

ef·fer·vesce (ĕf′ər vĕs′), *v.i.,* **-vesced, -vescing. 1.** to give off bubbles of gas, as fermenting liquors; bubble and hiss. **2.** to issue forth in bubbles. **3.** to exhibit fervor, excitement, liveliness, etc. [t. L: m.s. *effervescere* boil up] **—ef′fer·ves′cence, ef′fer·ves′cen·cy,** *n.*

ef·fer·ves·cent (ĕf′ər vĕs′ənt), *adj.* **1.** effervescing; bubbling. **2.** gay; lively; sparkling.

ef·fete (Ĭ fēt′), *adj.* **1.** that has lost its vigor or energy; exhausted; worn out. **2.** unable to produce. [t. L:m.s. *effētus* exhausted] **—ef·fete′ness,** *n.*

ef·fi·ca·cious (ĕf′ə kā′shəs), *adj.* having or showing efficacy; effective as a means, measure, remedy, etc. [f. s. L *efficācia* efficacy + -OUS] **—ef′fi·ca′cious·ly,** *adv.* **—ef′fi·ca′cious·ness,** *n.* **—Syn.** See effective.

ef·fi·ca·cy (ĕf′ə kə sĬ), *n., pl.* **-cies.** capacity for serving to produce effects; effectiveness: *the efficacy of a means, measure, expedient, remedy, etc.* [t. L: m.s. *efficācia*]

ef·fi·cien·cy (Ĭ fĬsh′ən sĬ), *n., pl.* **-cies. 1.** fact or quality of being efficient; competency in performance. **2.** the ratio of the work done or energy developed by a machine, engine, etc., to the energy supplied to it.

ef·fi·cient (Ĭ fĬsh′ənt), *adj.* **1.** adequate in operation or performance; having and using the requisite knowledge, skill, and industry; competent; capable. **2.** producing an effect, as a cause; causative. [t. L: s. *efficiens,* ppr., accomplishing] **—ef·fi′cient·ly,** *adv.* **—Syn. 1.** effectual, competent, capable. See effective.

ef·fi·gies (ĕ fĬj′Ĭ ēz′), *n. Latin.* effigy. [L. See EFFIGY]

ef·fi·gy (ĕf′ə jĬ), *n., pl.* **-gies. 1.** a representation or image, esp. sculptured, as on a monument. **2.** a representation of an obnoxious person. **3. burn or hang in effigy,** to burn or hang an image of a person as an expression of public indignation, ridicule, or hatred. [t. F: m. *effigie,* t. L: m. *effigies* copy of an object]

ef·flo·resce (ĕf′lō rĕs′), *v.i.,* **-resced, -rescing. 1.** to burst into bloom; blossom. **2.** *Chem.* **a.** to change either throughout or on the surface to a mealy or powdery substance upon exposure to air, as a crystalline substance, through loss of water of crystallization. **b.** to become incrusted or covered with crystals of salt or the like through evaporation or chemical change. [t. L: m.s. *efflōrescere* blossom]

ef·flo·res·cence (ĕf′lō rĕs′əns), *n.* **1.** state or period of flowering. **2.** *Chem.* **a.** act or process of efflorescing. **b.** the resulting powdery substance or incrustation. **3.** *Pathol.* a rash or eruption.

ef·flo·res·cent (ĕf′lō rĕs′ənt), *adj.* **1.** efflorescing; blossoming. **2.** *Chem.* **a.** subject to efflorescence. **b.** covered with or forming an efflorescence. [t. L: s. *efflōrescens,* ppr.]

ef·flu·ence (ĕf′lŏŏ əns), *n.* **1.** outward flow; efflux. **2.** something that flows out; an emanation. [coinage modeled on *affluence.* See EFFLUENT]

ef·flu·ent (ĕf′lŏŏ ənt), *adj.* **1.** flowing out or forth. **—n. 2.** that which flows out or forth; outflow. **3.** a stream flowing out of another stream, a lake, etc. [t. L: s. *effluens,* ppr.]

ef·flu·vi·um (Ĭ flŏŏ′vĬ əm), *n., pl.* **-via** (-vĬ ə), **-viums.** a slight or invisible exhalation or vapor, esp. one that is disagreeable or noxious. [t. L: a flowing out] **—ef·flu′-vi·al,** *adj.*

ef·flux (ĕf′flŭks), *n.* **1.** outward flow, as of water. **2.** that which flows out; an effluence. [t. L: s. *effluxus,* der. *effluere* flow out]

ef·fort (ĕf′ərt), *n.* **1.** exertion of power, physical or mental: *an effort to reform.* **2.** a strenuous attempt. **3.** something done by exertion; an achievement, as in literature or art. **4.** *Brit.* a drive (for funds, etc.). **5.** *Mech.* a force independently exerted, opposed to the reaction arising in opposition to a force. [t. F, der. OF *esforcier,* der. es- (g. L *ex-* EX-¹) + *force* strength, ult. der. L *fortis* strong.]
—Syn. 1. EFFORT, APPLICATION, ENDEAVOR, EXERTION imply

actions directed or force expended toward a definite end. EFFORT is an expenditure of energy to accomplish some (usually single and definite) object: *he made an effort to control himself.* APPLICATION is continuous effort plus careful attention: *constant application to duties.* ENDEAVOR means a continued and sustained series of efforts to achieve some, often worthy and difficult, end: *a constant endeavor to be useful.* EXERTION is the vigorous and often strenuous expenditure of energy, frequently without conscious reference to a definite end: *out of breath from exertion.*

ef·fort·less (ĕf′ərt lĬs), *adj.* **1.** requiring or involving no effort; easy. **2.** making no effort; passive.

ef·fron·ter·y (Ĭ frŭn′tə rĬ), *n., pl.* **-teries.** shameless or impudent boldness; barefaced audacity. [t. F: m. *effronterie,* der. OF *esfront* shameless, f. *es-* (g. L *ex-* EX-¹) + *front* brow, g. s. L *frons*]

ef·fulge (Ĭ fŭlj′), *v.t., v.i.,* **-fulged, -fulging.** to shine or send forth brilliantly. [t. L: m.s. *effulgēre* shine forth]

ef·ful·gent (Ĭ fŭl′jənt), *adj.* shining forth brilliantly; radiant. **—ef·ful′gence,** *n.* **—ef·ful′gent·ly,** *adv.*

ef·fuse (*v.* Ĭ fūz′; *adj.* Ĭ fūs′), *v.,* **-fused, -fusing,** *adj.* **—v.t. 1.** to pour out or forth; shed; disseminate. **—v.i. 2.** to exude. **3.** *Physics.* (of gas) to flow gradually through porous material or one or more tiny apertures. **—adj. 4.** *Bot.* spread out loosely. **5.** (of certain shells) having the lips separated by a gap or groove. [t. L: m.s. *effūsus,* pp., poured forth]

ef·fu·sion (Ĭ fū′zhən), *n.* **1.** act of effusing or pouring forth. **2.** that which is effused. **3.** unrestrained expression of feelings, etc.: *poetic effusions.* **4.** *Pathol.* **a.** the escape of a fluid from its natural vessels into a body cavity. **b.** the fluid which escapes.

ef·fu·sive (Ĭ fū′sĬv), *adj.* **1.** unduly demonstrative; without reserve: *effusive emotion, an effusive person.* **2.** *Geol.* noting or pertaining to igneous rocks which have solidified near or on the surface of the earth (opposed to *plutonic*). **—ef·fu′sive·ly,** *adv.* **—ef·fu′sive-ness,** *n.*

eft (ĕft), *n.* **1.** *U.S.* the common newt in its land stage. **2.** *Obs.* a lizard or salamander. [ME *evete,* OE *efete.* See NEWT]

eft·soon (ĕft sŏŏn′), *adv.* *Archaic.* **1.** soon afterward. **2.** again. **3.** forthwith. Also, **eft·soons′.** [ME *eftsone,* OE *eftsōna,* f. *eft* again + *sōna* at once]

Eg., **1.** Egypt. **2.** Egyptian.

e.g., (L *exempli gratia*) for example.

e·gad (Ĭ găd′, ē-), *interj.* an expletive or mild oath: *egad, that's true.* [alter. of *a God oh* God!]

e·gal·i·tar·i·an (Ĭ găl′ə târ′Ĭ ən), *n.* asserting the equality of all men.

é·ga·li·té (ĕ gȧ lē tĕ′), *n. French.* equality.

Eg·bert (ĕg′bərt), *n.* died A.D. 839?, king of the West Saxons in England, A.D. 802–839: first overlord of England and Wales, A.D. 829–839.

E·ge·ri·a (Ĭ jĬr′Ĭ ə), *n.* **1.** *Rom. Legend.* a nymph who instructed King Numa in religious worship. **2.** a woman counselor.

e·gest (ē jĕst′), *v.t.* to discharge, as from the body; void (opposed to *ingest*). [t. L: s. *ēgestus,* pp., brought out] **—e·ges′tive,** *adj.*

e·ges·ta (ē jĕs′tə), *n.pl.* matter egested from the body, as excrement. [t. L, neut. pl. of *ēgestus,* pp., brought out]

e·ges·tion (ē jĕs′chən), *n.* the process of egesting; the voiding of the refuse of digestion.

egg¹ (ĕg), *n.* **1.** the roundish reproductive body produced by the female of animals, consisting of the female reproductive cell and its envelopes. The envelopes may be albumen, jelly, membranes, egg case, or shell, according to species. **2.** the body of this sort produced by birds, esp. the domestic hen. **3.** anything resembling a hen's egg. **4.** Also, **egg cell.** *Biol.* the ovum or female reproductive cell. **—v.t. 5.** to prepare (food) by dipping in beaten egg. [t. Scand. (cf. Icel. *egg*); r. ME *ey,* OE *ǣg,* c. G *ei.* Cf. L *ōvum,* Gk. *ōión*]

egg² (ĕg), *v.t.* to incite or urge; encourage (usually fol. by *on*). [t. Scand.; cf. Icel. *eggja,* der. *egg* EDGE]

egg and dart, egg and tongue, egg and anchor, an egg-shaped ornament alternating with a dart-like, tonguelike, or anchorlike ornament, used to enrich a molding.

egg cozy, *Brit.* a little hood to put over a boiled egg to keep it warm until it is eaten.

egg·er (ĕg′ər), *n.* a tent caterpillar.

Egg and dart molding

egg·head (ĕg′hĕd′), *n.* *Colloq.* an intellectual.

Eg·gle·ston (ĕg′əl stən), *n.* Edward, 1837–1902, U.S. author, editor, and clergyman.

egg·nog (ĕg′nŏg′), *n.* a drink made of eggs, milk, sugar, and, usually, wine or spirits. [f. EGG + *nog* strong ale]

egg·plant (ĕg′plănt′, -plänt′), *n.* **1.** a plant, *Solanum Melongena,* cultivated for its edible, more or less egg-shaped fruit, dark-purple (or sometimes white or yellow) in color. **2.** the fruit, used as a table vegetable.

egg-shaped (ĕg′shāpt′), *adj.* having elongated rounded (oval) form, esp. with one end broader than the other.

egg·shell (ĕg′shĕl′), *n.* **1.** the shell of an egg in birds, consisting of keratin fibers and calcite crystals. **—adj. 2.** like an eggshell; thin and delicate; very brittle.

eggshell china, very thin, translucent porcelain.

e·gis (ē′jĬs), *n.* aegis.

eg·lan·tine (ĕg′lən tĬn′, -tēn′), **1.** the sweetbrier,

Rosa eglanteria. 2. the Austrian brier, *Rosa foetida.* Also, *Archaic,* **eg·la·tere** (ĕg′lə tȳr′). [ME *eglentine,* t. F: m. *eglantine,* der. OF *aiglent* sweetbrier, ult. der. L *acus* needle]

e·go (ē′gō, ĕg′ō), *n., pl.* **egos.** 1. the "I" or self of any person; a person as thinking, feeling, and willing, and distinguishing itself from the selves of others and from objects of its thought. 2. (*often cap.*) *Philos.* **a.** the enduring and conscious element which knows experience. **b.** (in Scholasticism) the complete man comprising both body and soul. 3. *Psychoanal.* that part of the psychic apparatus which experiences the outside world and re-acts to it, thus mediating between the primitive drives of the Id and the demands of the social and physical environment. 4. *Colloq.* conceit; egotism. [t. L: I]

e·go·cen·tric (ē′gō sĕn′trĭk, ĕg′ō-), *adj.* 1. having or regarding self as the center of all things, esp. as applied to the known world. —*n.* 2. an egocentric person. —**e·go·cen·tric·i·ty** (ē′gō sĕn trĭs′ə tĭ, ĕg′ō-), *n.*

ego ideal, *Psychoanal.* a more or less conscious criterion of personal excellence toward which an individual strives. It is derived from a composite image of the characteristics of persons (initially the parents) with whom the individual identifies himself.

e·go·ism (ē′gō ĭz′əm, ĕg′ō-), *n.* 1. the habit of valuing everything only in reference to one's personal interest; pure selfishness. 2. egotism or self-conceit. 3. *Ethics.* the doctrine that the individual and his self-interest are the basis of all behavior. [f. EGO + -ISM] —**Syn.** 1. See egotism. —**Ant.** 1. altruism.

e·go·ist (ē′gō ĭst, ĕg′ō-), *n.* 1. a self-centered or selfish person. 2. an egotist. 3. an adherent of the meta-physical principle of the ego or self; a solipsist. [f. EGO + -IST] —**e·go·is′tic, e·go·is′ti·cal,** *adj.* —**e′go·is′ti·cal·ly,** *adv.*

e·go·ma·ni·a (ē′gō mā′nĭ ə, ĕg′ō-), *n.* morbid egotism.

e·go·tism (ē′gə tĭz′əm, ĕg′ə-), *n.* 1. the habit of talk-ing too much about oneself; self-conceit; boastfulness. 2. selfishness. [f. EGO + hiatus-filling -*t-* + -ISM]

—**Syn.** 1. EGOTISM, EGOISM refer to preoccupation with one's ego or self. EGOTISM is the common word for obtrusive and excessive reference to and emphasis upon oneself and one's own importance, in conversation and writing, often to the ex-tent of monopolizing attention and showing disregard for others' opinions: *his egotism alienated all his friends.* EGOISM, a less common word, is used especially in philosophy, ethics, or metaphysics, where it emphasizes the importance of self in relation to other things: *sufficient egoism to understand one's place in the universe.* —**Ant.** 1. humility.

e·go·tist (ē′gə tĭst, ĕg′ə-), *n.* 1. a conceited, boastful person. 2. an egoist. —**e′go·tis′tic, e′go·tis′ti·cal,** *adj.* —**e′go·tis′ti·cal·ly,** *adv.*

e·gre·gious (ĭ grē′jəs, -jĭ əs), *adj.* 1. remarkably or extraordinarily flagrant: *an egregious lie, an egregious fool.* 2. *Obs.* distinguished or eminent. [t. L: m. *ēgregius* distinguished, lit., (standing) out from the herd] —**e·gre′gious·ly,** *adv.* —**e·gre′gious·ness,** *n.*

e·gress (ē′grĕs), *n.* 1. act of going or passing out, esp. from an enclosed place. 2. a means or place of going out; an exit. 3. the right of going out. 4. *Astron.* the passing of a star, planet, or satellite (except the moon) out from behind or before the disk of the sun, the moon, or a planet. [t. L: s. *ēgressus,* der. *ēgredī* go out]

e·gres·sion (ĭ grĕsh′ən), *n.* a going out; egress.

e·gret (ē′grĭt, ĕg′rĭt), *n.* 1. any of various herons, as the great white heron, *Casmerodius albus,* of Europe and America and the **snowy egret,** *Leuco-phoyzt thula* of North America, bearing in the breeding season tufts of long plumes. 2. plume of an egret; aigrette. [ME *egrete,* t. OF, var. of *aigrette*]

American great white egret, *Casmerodius albus egretta* (38 in. long)

E·gypt (ē′jĭpt), *n.* a former kingdom in NE Africa; divided into **Lower Egypt** (the Nile delta) and **Upper Egypt** (from near Cairo S to the Sudan); now the only member of the United Arab Republic. 26,059,000 pop. (1960); 386,198 sq. mi. *Cap.:* Cairo.

Egypt., Egyptian.

E·gyp·tian (ĭ jĭp′shən), *adj.* 1. of or pertaining to Egypt or its people: *Egyptian architecture.* 2. of or per-taining to the Gypsies. —*n.* 3. a native or inhabitant of Egypt. 4. a Gypsy. 5. the language of the ancient Egyptians, an extinct Hamitic language.

E·gyp·tol·o·gy (ē′jĭp tŏl′ə jĭ), *n.* the science of Egyp-tian antiquities. —**E·gyp·to·log·i·cal** (ĭ jĭp′tə lŏj′ə kəl), *adj.* —**E′gyp·tol′o·gist,** *n.*

eh (ā, ĕ), *interj.* an interrogative utterance, sometimes expressing surprise or doubt: *wasn't it lucky, eh?*

Eh·ren·breit·stein (ā′rən brīt′shtīn), *n.* a famous Roman fortress overlooking the Rhine at Coblenz.

Eh·ren·burg (ā′rən bŏŏrkʜ′), *n.* **Ilya Grigorievich** (ĭl yä′ grĭ gōr′yə vĭch), born 1891, Russian author.

Ehr·lich (âr′lĭкʜ), *n.* **Paul** (poul), 1854–1915, German physician, bacteriologist, and chemist.

E.I., 1. East Indian. 2. East Indies.

ei·der (ī′dər), *n.* 1. eider duck. 2. eider down. [t. Sw. or G, ult. t. Icel. (see EIDER DOWN)]

eider down, 1. down or soft feathers from the breast of the eider duck. 2. *U.S.* a fabric of cotton with wool nap. 3. a heavy quilt or comfort, properly one filled with eider down (def. 1). [ult. t. Icel.: m. *ædardūn* (18th cent. spelling) down of the eider (gen. sing.); spelling *eider-* fol-lows (18th cent.) Sw. or G, repr. Icel. *æ* with *ei*]

eider duck, any of several large sea ducks of the genus *So-materia* and allied genera of the northern hemisphere, generally black and white, and yielding eider down.

Elder duck, *Somateria Mollssima* (Ab. 22 in. long)

ei·det·ic imagery (ī dĕt′ĭk), a vivid and persistent type of imagery, esp. during childhood.

ei·do·lon (ī dō′lən), *n., pl.* **-la** (-lə). an image; a phan-tom; an apparition. [t. Gk.: image. Cf. IDOL]

Eif·fel Tower (ī′fəl), a tower of skeletal iron con-struction in Paris, France: built for the exhibition of 1889. 984 ft. high.

eight (āt), *n.* 1. a cardinal number, seven plus one. 2. a symbol for this number, as 8 or VIII. 3. a set of this many persons or things, as the crew of an eight-oared racing shell. —*adj.* 4. amounting to eight in number. [ME *eighte, ehte,* OE *eahta,* c. D and G *acht;* akin to L *octō,* Gk. *oktō*]

eight·een (ā′tēn′), *n.* 1. a cardinal number, ten plus eight. 2. a symbol for this number, as 18 or XVIII. [ME *ehtetene,* OE *eahtatēne.* See EIGHT, -TEEN] —**eight-eenth** (ā′tēnth′), *adj., n.*

eight·een·mo (ā′tēn′mō), *n.* octodecimo.

eight·fold (āt′fōld′), *adj.* 1. comprising eight parts or members; eight times as great or as much. —*adv.* 2. in eightfold measure.

eighth (ātth), *adj.* 1. next after the seventh. 2. being one of eight equal parts. —*n.* 3. the eighth number of a series. 4. an eighth part. 5. *Music.* an octave.

eighth note, *Music.* a note having ⅛ of the time value of a whole note; a quaver. See illus. under **note.**

eight·y (ā′tĭ), *n., pl.* **eighties,** *adj.* —*n.* 1. a cardinal number, ten times eight. 2. a symbol for this number, as 80 or LXXX or XXC. —*adj.* 3. amounting to eighty in number. [ME *eighteti,* OE *eahtatig*] —**eight·i·eth** (ā′tĭ ĭth), *adj., n.*

eight·y-nin·er (ā′tĭ nī′nər), *n.* one who began home-steading in Oklahoma in 1889.

ei·kon (ī′kŏn), *n.* icon.

Eind·ho·ven (īnt′hō′vən), *n.* a city in S Netherlands. 149,460 (est. 1954).

Ein′ fes·te Burg ist un·ser Gott (īn fĕs′tə bŏŏrкʜ′ ĭst ŏŏn′zər gŏt′), *German.* a mighty fortress is our God (first line of a hymn by Luther).

Ein·stein (īn′stīn; *Ger.* -shtīn), *n.* **Albert** (ăl′bərt; *Ger.* äl′bĕrt), 1879–1955, German physicist who formulated the theory of relativity; became a U.S. citizen in 1940. —**Ein·stein′i·an,** *adj.*

ein·stein·i·um (īn stī′nĭ əm), *n.* *Chem.* a synthetic, radioactive, metallic element. *Symbol:* Es; *at. no.:* 99. [f. (ALBERT) EINSTEIN + -IUM]

Einstein theory. See relativity.

Eir·e âr′ə; *Gael.* ā′rə), *n.* former name (1937–49) of the Republic of Ireland; still its official Gaelic name.

Ei·sen·ach (ī′zə näкʜ′), *n.* a city in East Germany, in Thuringia. 50,038 (est. 1955).

Ei·sen·how·er (ī′zən hou′ər), *n.* **Dwight David,** born 1890, 34th president of the United States, 1953–1961: U.S. general, supreme commander of Allied Expedition-ary Forces, 1943–45, Chief of Staff, 1945–48; president of Columbia University, 1948–1953; supreme com-mander of Atlantic Pact forces 1950–1952.

Eisk (āsk), *n.* a seaport in the SW Soviet Union, on the Sea of Azov. 49,280 (est. 1946). Also, **Yeisk.**

eis·tedd·fod (ā stĕѳ′vŏd, ĭ-), *n., pl.* **eisteddfods, eisteddfodau** (ā′stĕѳ vŏd′ī, ĕs′tĕѳ-), a congress of Welsh bards and minstrels. [t. Welsh: session, der. *eistedd* sit]

ei·ther (ē′ѳər or, esp. Brit., ī′ѳər), *adj.* 1. one or the other of two: *you may sit at either end of the table.* 2. each of the two; the one and the other: *there are trees on either side of the river.* —*pron.* 3. one or the other: *take either; either will do.* —*conj.* 4. (used as one of two coördinate alternatives): *either come or write.* —*adv.* 5. (used after negative sentences coördinated by *and, or, nor*): *he is not fond of parties and I am not either (or nor I either), I am not going and nobody can prevent it either;* after a neg. sub. clause: *if you do not come, he will not come either.* [ME; OE *ægther,* contr. of *æghwæther* each of two, both, f. *ā* always + *gehwæther* each of two. See WHETHER]

e·jac·u·late (ĭ jăk′yə lāt′), *v.t.,* -lated, -lating. 1. to utter suddenly and briefly; exclaim. 2. to eject sud-denly and swiftly; discharge. [t. L: m.s. *ĕjaculātus,* pp., having cast out] —**e·jac′u·la′tor,** *n.*

e·jac·u·la·tion (ĭ jăk′yə lā′shən), *n.* 1. an abrupt, exclamatory utterance. 2. act of ejaculating. 3. *Physiol.* the rhythmic discharge of seminal fluid from the male passages; an emission.

e·jac·u·la·to·ry (ĭ jăk′yə lə tōr′ĭ), *adj.* 1. pertaining to or of the nature of an ejaculation or exclamatory utterance. 2. *Physiol.* pertaining to ejaculation.

ăct, āble, dâre, ärt; ĕbb, ēqual; ĭf, īce; hŏt, ōver, ôrder, oil, bŏŏk, ōōze, out; ŭp, ūse, ûrge; ə = a in alone; ch, chief; g, give; ng, ring; sh, shoe; th, thin; ѳ, that; zh, vision. See the full key on inside cover.

e·ject (v. ĭ jĕkt′; n. ē′jĕkt), v.t. **1.** to drive or force out; expel, as from a place or position. **2.** to dismiss, as from office, occupancy, etc. **3.** to evict, as from property. —n. **4.** Psychol. something whose existence is inferred as a reality, but which is outside of, and inaccessible to, the consciousness of the one making the inference. [t. L: s. ējectus, pp., thrown out]

e·jec·ta (ĭ jĕk′tə), n.pl. matter ejected, as from a volcano in eruption. [t. L, neut. pl. of ējectus. See EJECT]

e·jec·tion (ĭ jĕk′shən), n. **1.** act of ejecting. **2.** state of being ejected. **3.** something ejected, as lava.

e·jec·tive (ĭ jĕk′tĭv), adj. **1.** serving to eject. **2.** Phonet. (of a stop or fricative) produced with air compressed above the closed glottis. —n. **3.** Phonet. an ejective stop or fricative.

e·ject·ment (ĭ jĕkt′mənt), n. **1.** act of ejecting. **2.** Law. a possessory action wherein the title to real property may be tried and the possession recovered, wherever the party claiming has a right of entry.

e·jec·tor (ĭ jĕk′tər), n. **1.** one who or that which ejects. **2.** the mechanism in a firearm or gun which, after firing, throws out the empty cartridge or shell from the weapon.

E·ka·te·rin·burg (ĕ kä′tĕ rĕn bŏŏrкн′), n. former name of Sverdlovsk.

E·ka·te·ri·no·dar (ĕ kä′tĕ rē′nŏ där′), n. former name of Krasnodar.

E·ka·te·ri·no·slav (ĕ kä′tĕ rē′nŏ släf′), n. former name of Dnepropetrovsk.

eke¹ (ēk), v.t., eked, eking. **1.** eke out, **a.** to supply what is lacking to; supplement. **b.** to contrive to make (a living) or support (existence) by various makeshifts. **2.** Archaic or Dial. to increase; enlarge; lengthen. [var. of obs. èche, OE ēcan, with k from obs. n. eke addition (OE ēaca). Cf. èacen augmented. Akin to Icel. auka, Goth. aukan, L augēre increase]

eke² (ēk), adv., conj. Archaic. also. [ME eek, d. OE ēc; r. OE ēac, c. G auch]

el (ĕl), n. **1.** elevated railroad. **2.** ell¹.

EKG, electrocardiogram. [f. G Elektrokardiogramme]

e·lab·o·rate (adj. ĭ lăb′ə rĭt; v. ĭ lăb′ə rāt′), adj., v., -rated, -rating. —adj. **1.** worked out with great care and nicety of detail; executed with great minuteness: elaborate preparations, care, etc. —v.t. **2.** to work out carefully or minutely; work up to perfection. **3.** to produce or develop by labor. —v.i. **4.** to add details in writing, speaking, etc.; give additional or fuller treatment (fol. by on or upon): to elaborate upon a theme or an idea. [t. L: m.s. ēlăbŏrātus, pp., worked out] —e·lab′o·rate·ly, adv. —e·lab′o·rate·ness, n. —e·lab′o·ra·tive, adj. —e·lab′o·ra′tor, n.

—**Syn. 1.** perfected, painstaking. ELABORATE, LABORED, STUDIED apply to that which is worked out in great detail. That which is ELABORATE is characterized by great, sometimes even excessive, nicety or minuteness of detail: elaborate preparations for a banquet, an elaborate apology. That which is LABORED is marked by excessive, often forced or uninspired, effort: a labored explanation, style of writing. That which is STUDIED is accomplished with care and deliberation, and is done purposely, sometimes even having been rehearsed: a studied pose.—**Ant. 1.** simple.

e·lab·o·ra·tion (ĭ lăb′ə rā′shən), n. **1.** act of elaborating. **2.** state of being elaborated; elaborateness. **3.** something elaborated.

El·a·gab·a·lus (ĕl′ə găb′ə ləs, ē′lə-), n. (Varius Avitus Bassanius), A.D. 205?–222, Roman emperor, A.D. 218–222. Also, Heliogabalus.

E·laine (ĭ lān′), n. the name of several characters in Arthurian legends, notably: **1.** the "lily maid of Astolat" who pined and died for Lancelot. **2.** the half sister of Arthur and mother of his son Modred. **3.** the daughter of King Pelles and mother of Sir Galahad.

El A·la·mein (ĕl ä′lä mān′), a town on the N coast of Egypt, ab. 70 mi. W of Alexandria: decisive British victory, Oct., 1942.

E·lam (ē′ləm), n. an ancient country E of Babylonia and N of the Persian Gulf. Cap.: Susa. —E·lam·ite (ē′lə mīt′), n., adj.

é·lan (ā län′), n. dash; impetuous ardor. [F, der. élancer hurl, rush forth]

e·land (ē′lənd), n. a large, heavily built antelope, Taurotragus oryx, of southern and eastern Africa. [t. S Afr. D, special use of D eland elk, t. G: m. elend, said to be t. Lithuanian: m. elnis elk]

é·lan vi·tal (ā län vē täl′), French. (esp. in Bergsonian philosophy) the creative force within an organism, which is able to build physical form and to produce growth and necessary or desirable adaptations. [F: lit., living force]

Eland. Taurotragus oryx (6 ft. high at the shoulder, body 11½ ft. long, tail ab. 2 ft.)

e·lapse (ĭ lăps′), v.i., -lapsed, -lapsing. (of time) to slip by or pass away. [t. L: m.s. ēlapsus, pp.]

E.L.A.S., Hellenic People's Army of Liberation, the military organization of the EAM: powerful Greek resistance force in World War II. Also, Elas (ĕ′läs).

e·las·mo·branch (ĭ lăs′mə brăngk′, ĭ läz′-), adj. **1.** of the Elasmobranchii, the group of vertebrates including the sharks and rays, with cartilaginous skeletons and five to seven pairs of gill openings. —n. **2.** an elasmobranch fish. [t. NL: m.s. Elasmobranchiī, pl., f. Gk.: elasmŏ(s) metal plate + brănchia gills]

e·las·tic (ĭ lăs′tĭk), adj. **1.** having the property of recovering shape after deformation, as solids; spontaneously expansive, as gases. **2.** flexible, yielding, or accommodating: an elastic conscience. **3.** springing back or rebounding; springy: an elastic step. **4.** readily recovering from depression or exhaustion; buoyant: an elastic temperament. —n. **5.** webbing, or material in the form of a band, made elastic with strips of rubber. **6.** a piece of this material. **7.** rubber band. [t. NL: s. elasticus, t. Gk.: m. elastikós propulsive] —e·las′ti·cal·ly, adv.

e·las·tic·i·ty (ĭ lăs′tĭs′ə tĭ, ē′lăs-), n. **1.** state or quality of being elastic. **2.** flexibility: elasticity of meaning. **3.** buoyancy; ability to resist or overcome depression.

e·las·tin (ĭ lăs′tĭn), n. Biochem. a protein constituting the basic substance of elastic tissue. [f. ELAST(IC) + -IN²]

e·las·to·mer (ĭ lăs′tə mər), n. Chem. an elastic, rubberlike substance occurring naturally (natural rubber) or produced synthetically (butyl rubber, neoprene, etc.). [f. ELAST(IC) + -o- + Gk. mer(os) part] —e·las′to·mer′ic, adj.

e·late (ĭ lāt′), v., elated, elating, adj. —v.t. **1.** to put in high spirits; make proud. —adj. **2.** elated. [ME, t. L: m.s. ēlātus, pp., brought out, raised, exalted]

e·lat·ed (ĭ lā′tĭd), adj. in high spirits; proud; jubilant. —e·lat′ed·ly, adv. —e·lat′ed·ness, n.

el·a·ter (ĕl′ə tər), n. **1.** Bot. an elastic filament serving to disperse spores. **2.** Zool. elaterid. [NL, t. Gk.: driver]

e·lat·er·id (ĭ lăt′ər ĭd), n. any of the click beetles, constituting the family Elateridae, most of which have the power of springing up when laid on their backs.

e·lat·er·in (ĭ lăt′ər ĭn), n. Chem. a white crystalline substance obtained from and constituting the active principle of elaterium, used as a cathartic.

e·lat·er·ite (ĭ lăt′ə rīt′), n. a brownish, elastic, rubberlike, naturally occurring asphalt.

e·la·te·ri·um (ĕl′ə tēr′ĭ əm), n. a cathartic obtained from the juice of Ecballium elaterium, the squirting cucumber. [t. L, t. Gk.: m. elatērion an opening medicine]

e·la·tion (ĭ lā′shən), n. exaltation of spirit, as from joy or pride; exultant gladness; high spirits.

El·ba (ĕl′bə), n. an Italian island in the Mediterranean between Corsica and Italy: the scene of Napoleon's first exile, 1814–15. 29,462 pop. (1951); 94 sq. mi.

El·be (ĕl′bə), n. a river flowing from W Czechoslovakia NW through East Germany and West Germany to the North Sea near Hamburg. 725 mi.

El·ber·feld (ĕl′bər fĕlt′), n. See Wuppertal.

El·ber·ta (ĕl bûr′tə), n. Hort. a yellow, freestone peach widely grown in eastern U.S.

El·bert Peak (ĕl′bərt), a mountain in central Colorado, in the Sawatch range; second highest peak of the Rocky Mountains in the U.S. 14,431 ft.

El·blag (ĕl′bloung), n. a seaport in N Poland: formerly in Germany. 20,924 (1950). Also, El·bing (ĕl′bĭng).

el·bow (ĕl′bō), n. **1.** the bend or joint of the arm between upper arm and forearm. **2.** something bent like the elbow, as a sharp turn in a road or river, or a piece of pipe bent at an angle. **3.** at one's elbow, near at hand. **4.** out at elbows or out at the elbow, ragged or impoverished. **5.** up to the elbows in, very busy with; wholly engaged or engrossed in. —v.t. **6.** to push with or as with the elbow; jostle. **7.** to make (one's way) by so pushing. —v.i. **8.** to elbow one's way. [ME elbowe, OE elneboga, c. G ellenbogen, orig. arm bow. See ELL², BOW¹]

el·bow·room (ĕl′bō rŏŏm′, -rŏŏm′), n. ample room.

El·brus (ĕl′brŏŏs, ĕl′brŏŏs), n. a mountain in the S Soviet Union in Europe, in the Caucasus Mountains: the highest peak in Europe. 18,465 ft. Also, El′bruz.

El·burz Mountains (ĕl bŏŏrz′), a mountain range in N Iran, along the S coast of the Caspian Sea. Highest peak, Mt. Demavend, 18,606 ft.

El Cap·i·tan (ĕl kăp′ə tän′; Sp. ĕl kä′pē tän′), a peak of the Sierra Nevada Mountains in E California, with a precipice rising over 3300 ft. above Yosemite Valley.

El Cid Cam·pe·a·dor (ĕl thēd′ käm′pĕ ä dôr′). See Cid.

eld (ĕld), n. Archaic. **1.** age. **2.** old age. **3.** antiquity. [ME elde, OE eld(o), der. eald, old old]

eld·er¹ (ĕl′dər), adj. **1.** older. **2.** senior: an elder officer. **3.** earlier: in elder times. —n. **4.** a person who is older than oneself; one's senior. **5.** an aged person. **6.** one of the older and more influential men of a tribe or community, often a chief or ruler. **7.** a presbyter. **8.** (in certain Protestant churches) a governing officer, often with teaching or pastoral functions. **9.** (in the Mormon church) one holding the higher or Melchizedek priesthood. [ME; OE eldra, etc. (compar. of eald, eald old), c. G älter] —eld′er·ship′, n. —Syn. 1. See older.

el·der² (ĕl′dər), n. any plant of the caprifoliaceous genus Sambucus, which comprises shrubs and small trees bearing clusters of small white or light-colored flowers and a blackish or red fruit, Alnus glutinosa, of Europe. [ME eldre, elrene, ellerne, OE ellærn, c. MLG ellern, elderne]

el·der·ber·ry (ĕl'dər bĕr'ĭ), n., pl. -ries. 1. the drupaceous fruit of the elder, used in making wine, jelly, etc. 2. elder².

eld·er·ly (ĕl'dər lĭ), adj. 1. somewhat old; between middle and old age. 2. of or pertaining to persons in later life. —eld'er·li·ness, n. —Syn. 1. See old.

elder statesman, 1. an influential elderly citizen whose advice is sought, especially on major national problems. 2. (pl.) (in Japan) a group of senior statesmen, with no legal status, and no defined membership, who toward the end of the Meiji era were a powerful influence on government policy; the genro.

eld·est (ĕl'dĭst), adj. oldest: now surviving only in the eldest brother, sister, and eldest hand. [OE eldest(a), superl. of ald. eald OLD, c. G. ältest(e)]

eldest hand, Cards. the player on the dealer's left.

El Do·ra·do (ĕl dạ rä'dō, -rä'-; Sp. ĕl dô rä'dô), 1. a legendary treasure city of South America, sought by the early Spanish explorers. 2. any place of reputed fabulous wealth. [t. Sp.: the gilded]

el·dritch (ĕl'drĭch), adj. Orig. Scot. weird; unearthly.

E·le·a (ē'lĭ ə), n. an ancient Greek city on the coast of Lucania in SW Italy.

El·ea·nor of Aquitaine (ĕl'ə nər), 1122?-1204, queen of Henry II of England.

El·e·at·ic (ĕl'ĭ ăt'ĭk), adj. 1. pertaining to Elea. 2. pertaining to the philosophical system of Xenophanes, Parmenides, and others who lived there. —n. 3. a school of Greek philosophy founded by Xenophanes of Colophon, who resided in Elea, whose doctrines are developments of the conception of the universal unity of being. [t. L: s. Eleāticus, der. Elea, name of an ancient Greek city in SW Italy] —El·e·at/i·cism, n.

el·e·cam·pane (ĕl'ə kăm pān'), n. a composite plant, Inula Helenium, with large yellow flowers and aromatic leaves and root. [earlier elena (OE elene) campana, for ML enula (in L inula) campāna, prob., inula of the fields]

e·lect (ĭ lĕkt'), v.t. 1. to select by vote, as for an office. 2. to determine in favor of (a course of action, etc.). 3. to pick out or choose. 4. Theol. (of God) to select for divine mercy or favor, esp. for salvation. —adj. 5. selected for an office, but not yet inducted (usually after the noun): the governor-elect. 6. picked out; chosen. 7. select or choice. 8. Theol. chosen by God, esp. for eternal life. —n. 9. a person or the persons chosen or worthy to be chosen. 10. Theol. those chosen by God, esp. for eternal life. [late ME, t. L: s. électus, pp., chosen, picked out] —Syn. 3. See choose.

elect., 1. electric. 2. electrical. 3. electricity. Also, elec.

e·lec·tion (ĭ lĕk'shən), n. 1. the selection of a person or persons for office by vote. 2. a public vote upon a proposition submitted. 3. act of electing. 4. Theol. the choice by God of individuals, as for a particular work, or esp. for salvation of eternal life. —Syn. 3. choice.

e·lec·tion·eer (ĭ lĕk'shə nîr'), v.i. to work for the success of a candidate, party, ticket, etc., in an election. —e·lec'tion·eer'er, n.

e·lec·tive (ĭ lĕk'tĭv), adj. 1. pertaining to the principle of electing to office, etc. 2. appointed by election, as an officer. 3. bestowed by or derived from election, as an office. 4. having the power of electing to office, etc., as a body of persons. 5. open to choice; optional; not required: an elective subject in high school or college. 6. Chem. selecting for combination or action: elective attraction (tendency to combine with certain substances in preference to others). —n. 7. an optional study; a study which a student may select from among alternatives. —e·lec'tive·ly, adv. —e·lec'tive·ness, n.

e·lec·tor (ĭ lĕk'tər), n. 1. one who elects or may elect, esp. a qualified voter. 2. U.S. a member of the electoral college. 3. (usually cap.) (in the Holy Roman Empire) one of the princes entitled to elect the emperor.

e·lec·tor·al (ĭ lĕk'tər əl), adj. 1. pertaining to electors or election. 2. consisting of electors.

electoral college, a body of electors chosen by voters in the several states to elect the president and vice-president of the United States.

e·lec·tor·ate (ĭ lĕk'tər ĭt), n. 1. the body of persons entitled to vote in an election. 2. the dignity or territory of an elector of the Holy Roman Empire.

electr-, var. of electro-, before vowels, as in electrode.

E·lec·tra (ĭ lĕk'trə), n. Gk. Legend. the daughter of Agamemnon and Clytemnestra. She incited her brother Orestes to avenge the murder of his father.

Electra complex, Psychoanal. the unresolved desire of a daughter for sexual gratification from her father.

e·lec·tress (ĭ lĕk'trĭs), n. 1. a female elector. 2. the wife or widow of an elector of the Holy Roman Empire.

e·lec·tric (ĭ lĕk'trĭk), adj. 1. pertaining to, derived from, produced by, or involving electricity: an electric current, an electric shock. 2. producing, transmitting, or operated by electric currents: an electric bell. 3. electrifying; thrilling; exciting; stirring. —n. 4. a railroad operated by electricity. 5. a truck, etc., operated by electricity from storage batteries. [t. NL: s. électricus, der. L électrum, t. Gk.: m. ēlektron amber (as a substance that develops electricity under friction)]

e·lec·tri·cal (ĭ lĕk'trə kəl), adj. 1. electric. 2. concerned with electricity: an electrical engineer. —e·lec'tri·cal·ly, adv.

electrical transcription, 1. a radio broadcast

from a phonograph record made for the purpose. 2. the phonograph record itself.

electric chair, 1. an electrified chair used to execute criminals. 2. the electrocution.

electric eel, a fish. Electrophorus electricus, of eel-like form, having the power of giving strong electric discharges. It is found in the fresh waters of northern South America, and is sometimes over 6 feet long.

electric eye, a photoelectric cell.

electric field, a condition of space in the vicinity of an electric charge or a moving magnet which manifests itself as a force on an electric charge within that space.

electric furnace, a furnace in which the heat required is produced through electricity.

e·lec·tri·cian (ĭ lĕk'trĭsh'ən, ē'lĕk-), n. one who installs, operates, maintains, or repairs electrical devices.

e·lec·tric·i·ty (ĭ lĕk'trĭs'ə tĭ, ē'lĕk-), n. 1. an agency producing various physical phenomena, as attraction and repulsion, luminous and heating effects, shock to the body, chemical decomposition, etc., which were originally thought to be caused by a kind of fluid, but are now regarded as being due to the presence and movements of electrons and other particles. 2. the science dealing with this agency. 3. electric current: to install electricity, a machine run by electricity.

electric organ, an organ with an electrophonic, rather than a mechanical or a pneumatic, action.

electric ray, a ray of the family Torpedinidae which possesses a peculiar organ enabling it to stun its prey with electric shock.

e·lec·tri·fy (ĭ lĕk'trə fī'), v.t., -fied, -fying. 1. to charge with or subject to electricity; to apply electricity to. 2. to equip for the use of electric power, as a railroad. 3. to startle greatly; excite or thrill: to electrify an audience. [f. ELECTR(IC) + -(I)FY] —e·lec/tri·fi·ca'tion, n. —e·lec/tri·fi'er, n.

e·lec·trize (ĭ lĕk'trīz), v.t., -trized, -trizing. electrify (defs. 1, 2). —e·lec/tri·za'tion, n. —e·lec/triz·er, n.

e·lec·tro (ĭ lĕk'trō), n., pl. -tros. electrotype.

electro-, a word element meaning "pertaining to or caused by electricity," as in electromagnet, electrotype, electrochemistry, electrolysis, electrocute. Also, electr-. [t. Gk.: m. ēlektro-, comb. form of ēlektron amber]

e·lec·tro·a·nal·y·sis (ĭ lĕk'trō ə năl'ə sĭs), n. chemical analysis by electrolysis.

e·lec·tro·car·di·o·gram (ĭ lĕk'trō kär'dĭ ə grăm'), n. the graphic record produced by an electrocardiograph Also, cardiogram. [f. ELECTRO- + CARDIO- + -GRAM¹]

e·lec·tro·car·di·o·graph (ĭ lĕk'trō kär'dĭ ə grăf', -gräf'), n. a device which detects and records the minute differences in potential caused by heart action and occurring between different parts of the body: used in the diagnosis of heart disease. Also, cardiograph. [f. ELECTRO- + CARDIO- + -GRAPH]

e·lec·tro·chem·is·try (ĭ lĕk'trō kĕm'ĭs trĭ), n. the branch of chemistry that deals with the chemical changes produced by electricity and the production of electricity by chemical changes. —e·lec·tro·chem·i·cal (ĭ lĕk'-trō kĕm'ə kəl), adj. —e·lec/tro·chem/i·cal·ly, adv. —e·lec/tro·chem/ist, n.

e·lec·tro·cute (ĭ lĕk'trə kūt'), v.t., -cuted, -cuting. 1. to kill by electricity. 2. to execute (a criminal) by electricity. [f. ELECTRO- + -cute in EXECUTE] —e·lec/-tro·cu'tion, n.

e·lec·trode (ĭ lĕk'trōd), n. Elect. a conductor belonging to the class of metallic conductors, but not necessarily a metal, through which a current enters or leaves an electrolytic cell, arc generator, vacuum tube, gaseous discharge tube, or any conductor of the nonmetallic class. [f. ELECTR(O)- + -ODE²]

e·lec·tro·de·pos·it (ĭ lĕk'trō dĭ pŏz'ĭt), v.t. 1. to deposit (a metal, etc.) by electrolysis. —n. 2. a deposit, as of metal, produced by electrolysis.

e·lec·tro·dy·nam·ic (ĭ lĕk'trō dĭ năm'ĭk), adj. 1. pertaining to the force of electricity in motion. 2. pertaining to electrodynamics. Also, e·lec/tro·dy·nam/i·cal.

e·lec·tro·dy·nam·ics (ĭ lĕk'trō dĭ năm'ĭks), n. the branch of electricity that deals with the mutual action of electric currents and the interaction of currents and magnets.

e·lec·tro·dy·na·mom·e·ter (ĭ lĕk'trō dĭ'nə mŏm'ə tər), n. an instrument in which the mechanical reactions between two parts of the same circuit are used for detecting or measuring an electric current.

e·lec·tro·en·ceph·a·lo·gram (ĭ lĕk'trō ĕn sĕf'ə lə grăm'), n. a record of the electrical potentials of the brain.

e·lec·tro·graph (ĭ lĕk'trō grăf', -gräf'), n. 1. a curve automatically traced, forming a record of the indications of an electrometer. 2. an apparatus for engraving metal plates on cylinders used in printing. 3. an apparatus used to transmit pictures, etc., electrically. —e·lec/tro·graph/ic, adj. —e·lec·trog·ra·phy (ĭ lĕk'trŏg'rə fĭ, ē'lĕk-), n.

e·lec·tro·ki·net·ics (ĭ lĕk'trō kĭ nĕt'ĭks, -kī-), n. the branch of electricity that deals with currents. —e·lec/-tro·ki·net/ic, adj.

e·lec·tro·lier (ĭ lĕk'trə lîr'), n. a chandelier for electric lamps. [f. ELECTRO- + -lier in CHANDELIER]

e·lec·tro·lu·mi·nes·cence (ĭ lĕk'trō lōō'mə nĕs'əns), n. the property of emitting light on activation by an alternating current. —e·lec/tro·lu/mi·nes/cent, adj.

e·lec·trol·y·sis (Ĭlĕk/trŏl/ə sĭs), *n.* **1.** the decomposition of a chemical compound by an electric current. **2.** *Surg.* the destruction of tumors, hair roots, etc., by an electric current.

e·lec·tro·lyte (Ĭlĕk/trəlīt/), *n.* **1.** *Elect.* a conducting medium in which the flow of current is accompanied by the movement of matter. **2.** *Chem.* any substance which dissociates into ions when dissolved in a suitable medium or when melted, thus forming a conductor of electricity.

e·lec·tro·lyt·ic (Ĭlĕk/trəlĭt/Ĭk), *adj.* **1.** pertaining to or derived by electrolysis. **2.** pertaining to an electrolyte. Also, **e·lec/tro·lyt/i·cal.** —**e·lec/tro·lyt/i·cal·ly,** *adv.*

electrolytic cell. See cell (def. 9).

electrolytic dissociation, the separation of the molecule of an electrolyte into its constituent atoms.

e·lec·tro·lyze (Ĭlĕk/trə līz/), *v.t.,* -**lyzed,** -**lyzing.** to decompose by electrolysis. —**e·lec/tro·ly·za/tion,** *n.* —**e·lec/tro·lyz/er,** *n.*

e·lec·tro·mag·net (Ĭ lĕk/trō măg/nĭt), *n.* a device consisting of an iron or steel core which is magnetized by electric current in a coil which surrounds it.

e·lec·tro·mag·net·ic (Ĭ lĕk/trō măg nĕt/Ĭk), *adj.* **1.** pertaining to an electromagnet. **2.** pertaining to electromagnetism. —**e·lec/tro·mag·net/i·cal·ly,** *adv.*

electromagnetic tape, a ribbon of material, usually with a plastic base, coated on one side (**single tape**) or both (**double tape**) with a substance containing iron oxide pigment, thereby making it sensitive to impulses from an electromagnet.

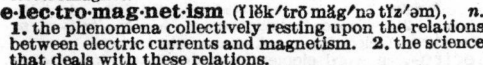

Electromagnet
C. Coil carrying current;
A. Armature; L. Load

e·lec·tro·mag·net·ism (Ĭlĕk/trō măg/na tĭz/əm), *n.* **1.** the phenomena collectively resting upon the relations between electric currents and magnetism. **2.** the science that deals with these relations.

e·lec·tro·met·al·lur·gy (Ĭlĕk/trō mĕt/ə lûr/jĭ, -mə tăl/ər jĭ), *n.* the refining of metals and ores by an electric current. —**e·lec/tro·met/al·lur/gi·cal,** *adj.* —**e·lec/tro·met/al·lur/gist,** *n.*

e·lec·trom·e·ter (Ĭlĕk/trŏm/ə tər, ō/lĕk-), *n.* an instrument for detecting or measuring a potential difference by means of the mechanical forces exerted between electrically charged bodies.

e·lec·tro·mo·tive (Ĭlĕk/trə mō/tĭv), *adj.* pertaining to, producing, or tending to produce a flow of electricity.

electromotive force, the amount of energy supplied to an electric circuit in one second by a voltaic cell, dynamo, or other source of electrical energy when one ampere of current flows in the circuit.

e·lec·tro·mo·tor (Ĭlĕk/trə mō/tər), *n.* electric motor.

e·lec·tron (Ĭlĕk/trŏn), *n.* *Physics, Chem.* an extremely small, negatively charged particle, having about one two-thousandth the mass of a hydrogen atom, supposed to be or to contain the unit of negative electricity. [t. Gk.: m. *ĕlektron.* See ELECTRUM] —**e·lec·tron·ic** (Ĭlĕk/trŏn/Ĭk, ō/lĕk-), *adj.*

e·lec·tro·neg·a·tive (Ĭlĕk/trō nĕg/ə tĭv), *adj. Physics, Chem.* **1.** containing negative electricity; tending to pass to the positive pole in electrolysis. **2.** assuming negative potential when in contact with a dissimilar substance. **3.** nonmetallic.

electron gun, *Television.* the cathode in a cathode-ray tube which emits electrons, and the surrounding electrostatic or electromagnetic apparatus which controls and focuses the electron stream.

e·lec·tron·ics (Ĭlĕk/trŏn/Ĭks, ō/lĕk-), *n.* the investigation and application of phenomena involving the movement of free electrons, as in radio, television, etc., now extended to include applications involving ions.

electron lens, a combination of static or varying electric and magnetic fields used to focus streams of electrons in a manner similar to that of an optical lens.

electron microscope, a microscope of extremely high power which uses beams of electrons focused by electron lenses instead of rays of light, the magnified image being formed on a fluorescent screen or recorded on a photographic plate. This magnification is substantially greater than that of any optical microscope.

electron tube, *Electronics.* a vacuum tube (def. 1), or a gas-filled discharge tube.

e·lec·tro·nu·cle·ar machine (Ĭ lĕk/trə nū/klĭ ər), a device for the production of very high energy beams of particles (protons, electrons, etc.) by acceleration in electric and magnetic fields. Examples are the cyclotron, synchrotron, bevatron, cosmotron, etc.

e·lec·tron-volt (Ĭlĕk/trŏn vōlt/), *n.* *Physics.* the energy acquired by an electron accelerating through a potential difference of one volt.

e·lec·tro·phon·ic (Ĭlĕk/trə fŏn/Ĭk), *adj.* (of musical instruments) based on oscillating electric currents.

e·lec·tro·pho·re·sis (Ĭlĕk/trō fə rē/sĭs), *n.* *Physics, Chem.* the motion of colloidal particles suspended in a fluid medium, under the influence of an electric field. [f. ELECTRO- + Gk. *phórēsis* a carrying]

e·lec·troph·o·rus (Ĭlĕk/trŏf/ə rəs, ō/lĕk-), *n., pl.* -**ri** (-rī/). an instrument for generating static electricity by means of induction. [NL. See ELECTRO-, -PHOROUS]

e·lec·tro·plate (Ĭlĕk/trə plāt/), *v.,* -**plated,** -**plating,** *n.* —*v.t.* **1.** to plate or coat with a metal by electrolysis. —*n.* **2.** electroplated articles or ware. —**e·lec/tro·plat/er,** *n.* —**e·lec/tro·plat/ing,** *n.*

e·lec·tro·pos·i·tive (Ĭlĕk/trə pŏz/ə tĭv), *adj. Physics, Chem.* **1.** containing positive electricity; tending to pass to the negative pole in electrolysis. **2.** assuming positive potential when in contact with another substance. **3.** basic, as an element or radical.

e·lec·tro·scope (Ĭlĕk/trə skōp/), *n.* a device for detecting the presence of electricity, and whether it is positive or negative, by means of electric attraction and repulsion. —**e·lec·tro·scop·ic** (Ĭlĕk/trə skŏp/Ĭk), *adj.*

e·lec·tro·shock (Ĭlĕk/trə shŏk/), *n.* *Psychiatry.* shock therapy administered by electrical means.

e·lec·tro·stat·ics (Ĭlĕk/trə stăt/Ĭks), *n.* the science of static electricity. —**e·lec/tro·stat/ic,** *adj.*

e·lec·tro·ther·a·peu·tics (Ĭlĕk/trō thĕr/ə pū/tĭks), *n.* therapeutics based upon the curative use of electricity. —**e·lec/tro·ther/a·peu/tic, e·lec/tro·ther/a·peu/ti·cal,** *adj.*

e·lec·tro·ther·a·pist (Ĭlĕk/trō thĕr/ə pĭst), *n.* one versed in electrotherapeutics. Also, **e·lec·tro·ther·a·peu·tist** (Ĭlĕk/trō thĕr/ə pū/tĭst).

e·lec·tro·ther·a·py (Ĭlĕk/trō thĕr/ə pĭ), *n.* treatment of diseases by means of electricity; electrotherapeutics.

e·lec·trot·o·nus (Ĭlĕk/trŏt/ə nəs, ō/lĕk-), *n.* *Physiol.* the altered state of a nerve during the passage of an electric current through it. [NL, f. Gk.: *ēlektro-* ELECTRO- + m. *tónos* tension] —**e·lec·tro·ton·ic** (Ĭlĕk/trə tŏn/Ĭk), *adj.*

e·lec·tro·type (Ĭlĕk/trə tīp/), *n., v.,* -**typed,** -**typing.** —*n.* **1.** a facsimile, for use in printing, of a block of type, an engraving, or the like, consisting of a thin shell of metal (copper or nickel), deposited by electrolytic action in a wax, lead, or plastic mold of the original and backed with lead alloy. **2.** electrotypy. —*v.t.* **3.** to make an electrotype or electrotypes of. —**e·lec/tro·typ/er,** *n.*

e·lec·tro·typ·y (Ĭlĕk/trə tī/pĭ), *n.* the electrotype process.

e·lec·trum (Ĭlĕk/trəm), *n.* an amber-colored alloy of gold and silver known to the ancients. [t. L. t. Gk.: m. *ēlektron* amber, also gold-silver alloy. See ELECTRIC]

e·lec·tu·ar·y (Ĭlĕk/chōō ĕr/Ĭ), *n., pl.* -**aries.** a medicine composed usually of a powder mixed into a pasty mass with syrup or honey. [ME, t. LL: m. s. *ēlectuārium.* Cf. Gk. *ekleiktón* electuary, der. *ekleíchein* lick up (in passive, be taken as an electuary)]

el·ee·mos·y·nar·y (ĕl/ə mŏs/ə nĕr/Ĭ, ĕl/Ĭ ə-), *adj.* **1.** of or pertaining to alms, charity, or charitable donations; charitable. **2.** derived from or provided by charity. **3.** dependent on or supported by charity. [t. ML: m.s. *eleēmosynārius,* der. LL *eleēmosyna* alms. See ALMS]

el·e·gance (ĕl/ə gəns), *n.* **1.** elegant quality: *elegance of dress.* **2.** something elegant; a refinement.

el·e·gan·cy (ĕl/ə gən sĭ), *n., pl.* -**cies.** elegance.

el·e·gant (ĕl/ə gənt), *adj.* **1.** tastefully fine or luxurious in dress, manners, etc.: *elegant furnishings.* **2.** gracefully refined, as in tastes, habits, literary style, etc. **3.** nice, choice, or pleasingly superior in quality or kind, as a contrivance, preparation, or process. **4.** *Colloq.* excellent; fine; superior. [t. L: s. *ēlegans* fastidious, nice, fine, elegant] —**el/e·gant·ly,** *adv.* —Syn. **1.** See fine[1].

el·e·gi·ac (ĕl/ə jī/ăk, -ək, Ĭlē/jĭ ăk/), *adj.* Also, **el·e·gi/a·cal. 1.** *Ancient Pros.* noting a distich the first line of which is a dactylic hexameter and the second a pentameter, or a verse differing from the hexameter by suppression of the arsis or metrically unaccented part of the third and the sixth foot. **2.** belonging to an elegy or to elegy; having to do with elegies. **3.** expressing sorrow or lamentation: *elegiac strains.* —*n.* **4.** an elegiac or distich verse. **5.** a poem or poems in such distichs or verses. [t. LL: s. *elegīacus,* t. Gk.: m. *elegeiakós*]

el·e·gist (ĕl/ə jĭst), *n.* the author of an elegy.

el·e·git (Ĭlē/jĭt), *n.* *Law.* a writ of execution against a judgment debtor's goods or property held by the judgment creditor until payment of the debt. [L: he has chosen]

el·e·gize (ĕl/ə jīz/), *v.,* -**gized,** -**gizing.** —*v.t.* **1.** to lament in or as in an elegy. —*v.i.* **2.** to compose an elegy.

el·e·gy (ĕl/ə jĭ), *n., pl.* -**gies. 1.** a mournful, melancholy, or plaintive poem, esp. a funeral song or a lament for the dead, as Milton's *Lycidas.* **2.** poetry or a poem written in elegiac meter. **3.** *Music.* a sad or funeral composition, vocal or instrumental, whether actually commemorative or not. [t. L: m.s. *elegia,* t. Gk.: m. *elegeta,* prop. neut. pl. of *elegetos* elegiac; der. *élegos* lament]

elem., **1.** elementary. **2.** elements.

el·e·ment (ĕl/ə mənt), *n.* **1.** a component or constituent part of a whole. **2.** the rudimentary principles of an art, science, etc.: *the elements of grammar.* **3.** one of the simple substances, usually earth, water, air, and fire, early regarded as constituting the material universe. **4.** one of these four substances regarded as the natural habitat of something. **5.** the sphere or environment adapted to any person or thing: *to be in one's element.* **6.** (*pl.*) atmospheric agencies or forces: *exposed to the elements.* **7.** one of a class of substances (of which 102 are now recognized) which cannot be separated into substances of other kinds, or, at least, have hitherto resisted analysis by any known chemical means. **8.** *Math.* **a.** an infinitesimal part of a given quantity, similar in nature

to it. **b.** any entity that satisfies the conditions of belonging to a class of objects, such as one of a number of objects arranged in a symmetrical or regular figure. **9.** *Geom.* one of the points, lines, planes, or other geometrical forms, of which a figure is composed. **10.** *Astron., etc.* one of the data required for the solution of a problem: *the elements of a planetary orbit,* which determine the orientation, size, and shape of the orbit, and the position of the planet in the orbit at any time. **11.** *Elect.* either of the two dissimilar substances which constitute a voltaic couple. **12.** *Radio.* one of the electrodes in a vacuum tube. **13.** *Gram.* any word, group of words, or part of a word, which recurs in various contexts in a language with relatively constant meaning. **14.** *(pl.)* the bread and wine used in the Eucharist. [ME, t. L: s. *elementum* a first principle, rudiment]
—**Syn. 1.** ELEMENT, COMPONENT, CONSTITUENT, INGREDIENT refer to the units which build up substances and compounds or mixtures. ELEMENT denotes a fundamental, ultimate part: *the elements of matter, of a discussion.* COMPONENT and CONSTITUENT denote that which goes into the making of a compound, COMPONENT suggesting one of a number of parts, and CONSTITUENT an active and necessary participation: *iron and carbon as components of steel; hydrogen and oxygen the constituents of water.* INGREDIENT denotes something essential or nonessential which enters into a mixture or compound: *the ingredients of a cake.*

el·e·men·tal (ĕl′ə mĕn′təl), *adj.* **1.** of the nature of an ultimate constituent; simple; uncompounded. **2.** pertaining to rudiments or first principles. **3.** of, pertaining to, or of the nature of the four elements or any one of them. **4.** pertaining to the agencies, forces, or phenomena of physical nature: *elemental gods, elemental worship.* **5.** comparable to the great forces of nature, as with reference to their power: *elemental grandeur.* **6.** pertaining to chemical elements. —**el′e·men′tal·ly,** *adv.*

el·e·men·ta·ry (ĕl′ə mĕn′tər ̇̈y, -trĭ), *adj.* **1.** pertaining to or dealing with elements, rudiments, or first principles: *elementary education, an elementary grammar.* **2.** of the nature of an ultimate constituent; simple or uncompounded. **3.** pertaining to the four elements or to the great forces of nature; elemental. —**el′e·men′ta·ri·ly,** *adv.* —**el′e·men′ta·ri·ness,** *n.*
—**Syn. 1.** ELEMENTARY, PRIMARY, RUDIMENTARY refer to what is basic and fundamental. ELEMENTARY refers to the introductory, simple, easy facts, steps, or parts of a subject which must necessarily be learned first in order to understand succeeding ones: *elementary facts about geography, elementary arithmetic.* PRIMARY may mean much the same as ELEMENTARY; however, it usually emphasizes the idea of what comes first even more than that of simplicity: *the primary grades in school.* RUDIMENTARY applies to what is undeveloped or imperfect: *a rudimentary form of government.*

elementary school, the lowest school giving formal instruction, teaching the rudiments of learning and extending variously from six to eight years.

el·e·mi (ĕl′ə mĭ), *n., pl.* **-mis.** any of various fragrant resins used in medicine, varnish making, etc. [cf. F *élémi,* Sp. *elemí,* t. Ar.: m. *allāmī*]

·len·chus (ĭ lĕng′kəs), *n., pl.* **-chi** (-kī). **1.** a logical refutation; an argument which refutes another argument by proving the contrary of its conclusion. **2.** a false refutation; a sophistical argument. [t. L, t. Gk.: m. *élenchos* cross-examination] —**e·lenc·tic** (ĭ lĕngk′tĭk), *adj.*

·le·op·tene (ĕl′ĭ ŏp′tēn), *n. Chem.* the liquid portion of volatile oils (opposed to the solid part, *stearoptene*). [f. Gk.: m. *élaio(n)* oil + m.s. *ptenós* winged, volatile]

·le·phant (ĕl′ə fənt), *n., pl.* **-phants,** *(esp. collectively)* **-phant. 1.** any of the large five-toed mammals, with long prehensile trunk or proboscis and long tusks of ivory, constituting the family *Eliphantidae,* comprising species of two existing genera, *Elephas* and *Loxodonta,* esp. *Elephas maximus,* of India and neighboring regions, with comparatively small ears, and *Loxodonta africana,* of Africa, with large, flapping ears. **2.** *U.S.* a representation of this animal as the emblem of the Republican party. **3.** a burdensome or perplexing possession. [t. L: s. *elephantus,* also s. *elephãs,* t. Gk.: m. *eléphas* elephant, ivory; r. ME *olifaunt,* t. OF: m. *olifant*]

African elephant.
Loxodonta africana
(10 ft. high at the shoulder)

Indian elephant. *Elephas maximus*
(9 ft. high at the shoulder)

·lephant Butte, a dam and irrigation reservoir in SW New Mexico, on the Rio Grande. Dam, 306 ft. high; reservoir, 40 mi. long.

·le·phan·ti·a·sis (ĕl′ə fən tī′ə sĭs, -făn-), *n. Pathol.* a chronic disease, due to lymphatic obstruction, characterized by enormous enlargement of the parts affected. [t. L, t. Gk., der. *eléphas* elephant]

·le·phan·tine (ĕl′ə făn′tĭn, -tīn, -tēn), *adj.* **1.** pertaining to or resembling an elephant. **2.** huge; ponderous; clumsy: *elephantine movements, elephantine humor.*

el·e·phant's-ear (ĕl′ə fənts ̇Yr′), *n.* the taro.
El·eu·sin·i·a (ĕl′yo͝o sĭn′ĭ ə), *n. Gk. Antiq.* the famous mysteries and festival celebrated at Eleusis, in honor of Demeter (Ceres). —**El′eu·sin′i·an,** *adj.*
E·leu·sis (ĭ lōō′sĭs), *n.* a city in ancient Greece, in Attica.
el·e·vate (ĕl′ə vāt′), *v.,* **-vated, -vating,** *adj.* —*v.t.* **1.** to move or raise to a higher place or position; lift up. **2.** to raise to a higher state or station; exalt. **3.** to raise the spirits; put in high spirits. —*adj.* **4.** *Poetic.* raised; elevated. [ME *elevat,* t. L: s. *ēlevātus,* pp.]
—**Syn. 2.** ELEVATE, ENHANCE, EXALT, HEIGHTEN mean to raise or make higher in some respect. To ELEVATE is to raise something up to a relatively higher level, position, or state: *to elevate the living standards of a group.* To ENHANCE is to add to the attractions or desirability of something: *landscaping enhances the beauty of the grounds, paved streets enhance the value of real estate.* To EXALT is to raise very high in rank, character, estimation, mood, etc.: *a king is exalted above his subjects.* To HEIGHTEN is to increase the strength or intensity: *to heighten one's powers of concentration.* —**Ant. 2.** lower.
el·e·vat·ed (ĕl′ə vā′tĭd), *adj.* **1.** raised up, esp. above the ground: *an elevated platform.* **2.** exalted or noble. *elevated thoughts.* —*n.* **3.** *Colloq.* an elevated railroad.
elevated railroad, a railway system operating on an elevated structure, as over streets. Also, **el.**
el·e·va·tion (ĕl′ə vā′shən), *n.* **1.** an elevated place; an eminence. **2.** the height to which anything is elevated. **3.** loftiness; grandeur or dignity; nobleness. **4.** act of elevating. **5.** state of being elevated. **6.** *Archit., etc.* a drawing or design which represents an object or structure as being projected geometrically on a vertical plane parallel to its chief dimension. **7.** *Survey.* the angle between the line from an observer to an object above him and a horizontal line. **8.** the ability of a dancer to stay in the air while executing a step. —**Syn. 2.** See **height.**
el·e·va·tor (ĕl′ə vā′tər), *n.* **1.** one who or that which elevates or raises. **2.** a moving platform or cage for conveying goods, persons, etc., from one level to another, as in a building. **3.** a mechanical device for raising articles. **4.** *U.S.* a building for storing grain, the grain being handled by means of mechanical elevating and conveying devices. **5.** a hinged horizontal plane on an airplane, etc., used to control the longitudinal inclination, generally placed at the tail end of the fuselage. [t. LL]
e·lev·en (ĭ lĕv′ən), *n.* **1.** a cardinal number, ten plus one. **2.** a symbol for this number, as 11 or XI. **3.** a set of this many persons or things, as a football team. —*adj.* **4.** amounting to eleven in number. [ME *elleven(e),* etc., OE *ellefne, endleofan,* etc., lit., one left (after counting ten). Cf. OHG *einlif,* MHG *eilf,* G *elf*] —**e·lev′enth,** *adj.*
eleventh hour, the last possible hour for doing something.
elf (ĕlf), *n., pl.* **elves** (ĕlvz). **1.** one of a class of imaginary beings, esp. from mountainous regions, with magical powers, given to capricious interference in human affairs, and usually imagined to be a diminutive being in human form; a sprite; a fairy. **2.** a dwarf or a small child. **3.** a small, mischievous person. [ME; repr. OE var. of *ælf,* c. G *alp* nightmare (def. 3), incubus] —**elf′-like′,** *adj.* —**Syn. 1.** See **fairy.**
El Fai·yum (ĕl fī yo͞om′), a city in N Egypt. 82,600 (est. 1952). Also, **El Fai·yûm′** or **El Fa·yûm′.**
El Fer·rol (ĕl fĕr rôl′), a seaport in NW Spain: naval arsenal and dockyard. 77,030 (1950). Also, **Ferrol.**
elf·in (ĕl′fĭn), *adj.* **1.** of or like elves. —*n.* **2.** an elf.
elf·ish (ĕl′fĭsh), *adj.* elflike; elfin; small and mischievous. Also, **elvish.** —**elf′ish·ly,** *adv.* —**elf′ish·ness,** *n.* —**Syn.** prankish, impish.
elf·lock (ĕl′lŏk′), *n.* a tangled lock of hair.
El·gar (ĕl′gər, -gär), *n.* Sir Edward, 1857–1934, British composer.
El·gin (ĕl′jĭn *for 1;* ĕl′gĭn *for 2*), *n.* **1.** a city in NE Illinois. 49,447 (1960). **2.** former name of **Moray.**
El Gi·za (ĕl gē′zə), a city in N Egypt, near Cairo: the pyramids and the Sphinx are located nearby. 135,100 (est. 1952). Also, **El Gi′zeh, Giza,** or **Gizeh.**
El·gon (ĕl′gŏn), *n.* an isolated volcanic mountain in E Africa, on the boundary between Uganda and Kenya. 14,176 ft.
El Gre·co (ĕl grā′kō, grĕk′ō; *Sp.* ĕl grĕ′kō), ("the Greek") (Domingo Theolocopouli 1548?–1614, painter, architect, and sculptor in Spain and Italy, born in Crete.
El Ha·sa (ĕl hä′sə), Hasa.
E·li (ē′lī), *n. Bible.* a Hebrew judge and high priest. I Sam. 1–3. [t. Heb.: m. 'Ēlī]
E·li·a (ē′lĭ ə), *n.* the pen name of Charles Lamb.
E·li·as (ĭ lī′əs), *n.* (in the New Testament) Elijah. Matt. 16:14, etc.
e·lic·it (ĭ lĭs′ĭt), *v.t.* to draw or bring out or forth; educe; evoke: *to elicit the truth.* [t. L: s. *ēlicitus,* pp.] —**e·lic′i·ta′tion,** *n.* —**e·lic′i·tor,** *n.*
e·lide (ĭ līd′), *v.t.,* **elided, eliding. 1.** to omit (a vowel or syllable) in pronunciation. **2.** to suppress. **3.** *Law.* to annul or quash. [t. L: m.s. *ēlīdere* crush out]
el·i·gi·bil·i·ty (ĕl′ə jə bĭl′ə tĭ), *n.* **1.** worthiness or fitness to be chosen. **2.** legal qualification for election or appointment.
el·i·gi·ble (ĕl′ə jə bəl), *adj.* **1.** fit or proper to be chosen; worthy of choice; desirable. **2.** legally qualified to be

elected or appointed to office. —*n.* 3. a person or thing that is eligible. [t. F. der. L *ēligere* pick out] —**el′i-gi·bly,** *adv.*

E·li·jah (Ĭ lī′jə), *n.* a great Hebrew prophet of the 9th century B.C. I Kings 17, II Kings 2.

e·lim·i·nate (Ĭ lĭm′ə nāt′), *v.t.*, **-nated, -nating.** 1. to get rid of; expel; remove: *to eliminate errors.* 2. to omit as irrelevant or unimportant; ignore. 3. *Physiol.* to void or expel from an organism. 4. *Math.* to remove (a quantity) from an equation by elimination. [t. L: m.s. *ēlimĭnātus,* pp., turned out of doors] —**e·lim′i·na′tive,** *adj.* —**e·lim′i·na′tor,** *n.* —**e·lim′i·na·to′ry,** *adj.* —**Syn.** 1. See **exclude.** —**Ant.** 2. include.

e·lim·i·na·tion (Ĭ lĭm′ə nā′shən), *n.* 1. act of eliminating. 2. state of being eliminated. 3. *Math.* the process of solving a system of linear equations by a procedure in which variables are successively removed.

El·i·ot (ĕl′Ĭ ət), *n.* 1. **Charles William,** 1834–1926, U.S. educator: president of Harvard University, 1869–1909. 2. **George,** (*Mary Ann Evans*) 1819–80, British novelist. 3. **John,** ("the Apostle of the Indians") 1604–1690, colonial American missionary. 4. **Sir John,** 1592–1632. British statesman. 5. **T**(**homas**) **S**(**tearns**) 1888–1965, British poet, critic, and essayist, born in the U. S.

E·lis (ē′lĭs), *n.* 1. an ancient country in W Greece, in the Peloponnesus: site of the ancient Olympic games. 2. the capital of this country.

E·li·sa·vet·grad (ĕ lē zä vĕt′grät), *n.* former name of Kirovograd.

E·li·sa·vet·pol (ĕ lē zä vĕt′pŏl′y), *n.* former name of Kirovabad.

E·li·sha (Ĭ lī′shə), *n.* a Hebrew prophet of the 9th century B.C., the successor of Elijah. II Kings 2.

e·li·sion (Ĭ lĭzh′ən), *n.* 1. the omission of a vowel in pronunciation. 2. (in verse) the omission of a vowel at the end of one word when the next word begins with a vowel, as *th′orient.* [t. L: s. *ēlisio* a striking out]

e·lite (Ĭ lēt′, ā-), *n.* the choice or best part, as of a body or class of persons. Also, *French,* **é·lite** (ĕ lēt′). [t. F, der. *élire* choose, g. L *ēligere.*]

e·lix·ir (Ĭ lĭk′sər), *n.* 1. an alchemic preparation for transmuting base metals into gold, or for prolonging life: *elixir vitae,* or *elixir of life.* 2. a sovereign remedy; panacea; cure-all. 3. the quintessence or absolute embodiment of anything. 4. *Pharm.* **a.** a tincture with more than one base, or some similar compound medicine. **b.** an aromatic, sweetened alcoholic liquid containing medicinal agents, or used as a vehicle for them. [ME, t. ML, t. Ar.: m. *el, al* the + *iksīr* philosopher's stone, prob. t. LGk.: m. *xērion* a drying powder for wounds]

E·liz·a·beth (Ĭ lĭz′ə bəth), *n.* 1. **I,** 1533–1603, queen of England 1558–1603 (successor of Mary I; daughter of Henry VIII and Anne Boleyn). 2. **II,** born 1926, queen of England since 1952; daughter of George VI. 3. ("*Carmen Silva*") 1843–1916, queen of Rumania, 1881–1914, and author. 4. (in the New Testament) the mother of John the Baptist. Luke 1:5–25. 5. a city in NE New Jersey. 107,698 (1960).

E·liz·a·be·than (Ĭ lĭz′ə bē′thən, -bĕth′ən), *adj.* 1. of or pertaining to Elizabeth I, queen of England, or to her times. —*n.* 2. one who lived in England during the Elizabethan period, esp. a poet or dramatist.

Elizabethan sonnet, a sonnet form rhyming *abab cdcd efef gg.*

elk (ĕlk), *n.*, *pl.* **elks,** (*esp. collectively*) **elk.** 1. the largest existing European and Asiatic deer, *Alces alces,* the male of which has large palmate antlers. See **moose.** 2. (in America) the **wapiti.** 3. a pliable leather used for sport shoes, made orig. of elk hide but now of calfskin or cowhide tanned and smoked to resemble elk hide. [appar. f. OE *ealh* elk (c. G *elch*) + -*k* suffix. Cf. OE *cranoc* crane (not dim.), L *alces,* Gk. *álkē* elk, of Gmc. orig.]

American elk, *Cervus canadensis* (5 ft high at the shoulder, total length 9½ft., female smaller)

European elk, *Alces alces* (Ab. 6 ft. high at the shoulder)

Elk·hart (ĕlk′härt′; *commonly* ĕl′kärt), *n.* a city in N Indiana. 40,274 (1960).

ell¹ (ĕl), *n.* an extension to a building, usually at right angles to one end. Also, **el.** [from the shape of the letter L]

ell² (ĕl), *n.* a measure of length, now little used, varying in different countries: in England and her colonies equal to 45 inches. [ME and OE *eln,* c. D, G *elle;* orig. meaning arm, forearm (see **ELBOW**), and akin to L *ulna,* Gk. *ōlénē*]

Elles·mere Island (ĕlz′mĭr), a large island in the Arctic Ocean, NW of Greenland: a part of the Canadian Northwest Territories. ab. 76,600 sq. mi.

El·lice Islands (ĕl′Ĭs), a group of islands in the central Pacific, S of the equator: a part of the British colony of Gilbert and Ellice islands. 4487 (1947); 16½ sq. mi. Also, **Lagoon Islands.**

el·lipse (Ĭ lĭps′), *n.* *Geom.* a plane curve such that the sums of the distances of each point in its periphery from two fixed points, the foci, are equal. It is a conic section formed by the intersection of a right circular cone by a plane which cuts obliquely the axis and the opposite sides of the cone. See diag. under **conic section.** [t. L: m.s. *ellipsis.* See **ELLIPSIS**]

el·lip·sis (Ĭ lĭp′sĬs), *n.*, *pl.* **-ses** (-sēz). 1. *Gram.* the omission from a sentence of a word or words which would complete or clarify the construction. 2. *Print.* a mark or marks as ——. . . . , * * * , to indicate an omission or suppression of letters or words. [t. L, t. Gk.: m. *élleipsis* omission]

Ellipse
F, G, foci. FM + GM equals FN + GN, M and N being any points in the curve

el·lip·soid (Ĭ lĭp′soid), *n.* *Geom.* a solid figure all plane sections of which are ellipses or circles.

el·lip·soi·dal (Ĭ lĭp′soi′dəl, ĕl lĬp′-), *adj.* pertaining to, or having the form of, an ellipsoid.

el·lip·ti·cal (Ĭ lĭp′tə kəl), *adj.* 1. pertaining to or having the form of an ellipse. 2. pertaining to or marked by grammatical ellipsis. Also, **el·lip′tic.**

el·lip·ti·cal·ly (Ĭ lĭp′tĬk lĬ), *adv.* 1. in the form of an ellipse. 2. in an elliptical manner; with an ellipsis.

el·lip·tic·i·ty (Ĭ lĬp′tĬs′ə tĬ, ĕl′Ĭp-), *n.* the degree of divergence of an ellipse from the circle.

El·lis (ĕl′Ĭs), *n.* 1. **Alexander John,** (orig. *Alexander John Sharpe*) 1814–90, British phonetician and mathematician. 2. (**Henry**) **Havelock** (hăv′lŏk), 1859–1939, British scientific and miscellaneous writer.

El·lis Island (ĕl′Ĭs), a small island in upper New York Bay: a former U.S. immigrant examination station.

Ells·worth (ĕlz′wûrth), *n.* **Lincoln,** 1880–1951, U.S. polar explorer.

elm (ĕlm), *n.* 1. any of the trees of the genus *Ulmus,* as *U. procera* (**English elm**), *U. americana* (**white** or **American elm**), *U. fulva* (**slippery elm**), etc., some of which are widely cultivated for shade and ornament. 2. the wood of such a tree. [ME and OE, c. OHG *elm;* akin to Icel. *âlmr,* L *ulmus*]

El·man (ĕl′mən), *n.* **Mischa** (mē′shə), born 1891, U.S. violinist, born in Russia.

Elm·hurst (ĕlm′hûrst′), *n.* a city in NE Illinois, W of Chicago. 36,991 (1960).

El·mi·ra (ĕl mī′rə), *n.* city in S New York. 46,517 (1960).

El Mis·ti (ĕl mēs′tē), a volcanic mountain in S Peru, in the Andes. 19,200 ft. Also, **Misti.**

elm leaf beetle, a beetle, *Galerucella xanthomelena,* of the family *Chrysomelidae,* a pest in the eastern U.S.

elm·y (ĕl′mĬ), *adj.* abounding in or consisting of elms.

el·o·cu·tion (ĕl′ə kū′shən), *n.* 1. manner of speaking or reading in public. 2. *Speech.* the study and practice of delivery, including both the management of voice and gesture. 3. (in a derogatory sense) a stilted, artificial manner of delivery. [t. L: s. *ēlocūtio* a speaking out] —**el·o·cu·tion·ar·y** (ĕl′ə kū′shə nĕr′Ĭ), *adj.* —**el′o·cu′tion·ist,** *n.* —**Syn.** 2. oratory, declamation.

E·lo·him (ĕ lō′hĬm), *n.* the Hebrew word for God, often used in Hebrew text of the Old Testament. [t. Heb.: m. *elōhim,* prop. pl. of *elōh* god, but often taken as sing.]

E·lo·hist (ĕ lō′hĬst), *n.* the writer (or writers) of one of the major strands or sources of the Hexateuch in which God is characteristically referred to as Elohim instead of Yahweh (Jehovah). See **Yahwist.** —**E·lo·his·tic** (ĕl′ō·hĬs′tĬk), *adj.*

e·loign (Ĭ loin′), *v.t.* to remove (oneself) to a distance. Also, **e·loin′.** [t. AF: m.s. *esloignier,* der. OF *es-* (See **EX-¹**) + *loign* far away (g. L *longē*)]

e·lon·gate (Ĭ lŏng′gāt, Ĭ lŏng′-), *v.,* **-gated, -gating,** *adj.* —*v.t.* 1. to draw out to greater length; lengthen; extend. —*v.i.* 2. to increase in length. 3. to be comparatively long. —*adj.* 4. elongated. [t. LL: m.s. *ēlongātus,* pp., removed, prolonged]

e·lon·ga·tion (Ĭ lŏng′gā′shən, Ĭ lŏng′-; ē′lŏng-, ĕ′lŏng-), *n.* 1. act of elongating. 2. state of being elongated. 3. that which is elongated; an elongated part.

e·lope (Ĭ lōp′), *v.i.,* **eloped, eloping.** 1. to run away with a lover. 2. to abscond or escape. [ME **alopen,* f. a-A³ + *lopen* LOPE. Cf. AF *aloper* ravish (a woman), elope (with a man)] —**e·lope′ment,** *n.* —**e·lop′er,** *n.*

el·o·quence (ĕl′ə kwəns), *n.* 1. the action, practice, or art of using language with fluency, power, and aptness. 2. eloquent language or discourse: *a flow of eloquence.*

el·o·quent (ĕl′ə kwənt), *adj.* 1. having or exercising the power of fluent, forcible, and appropriate speech: *an eloquent orator.* 2. characterized by forcible and appropriate expression: *an eloquent speech.* 3. movingly expressive: *eloquent looks.* [ME, t. L: s. *ēloquens,* ppr., speaking out] —**el′o·quent·ly,** *adv.*

El Pas·o (ĕl păs′ō), a city in W Texas, on the Rio Grande. 276,687 (1960).

El Sal·va·dor (ĕl săl′və dôr′; *Sp.* ĕl säl′vä dôr′), a republic in W Central America. 2,269,000 pop. (est. 1956); 13,176 sq. mi. *Cap.:* San Salvador. Also, **Salvador.**

else (ĕls), *adv.* **1.** (following as an appositive an indef. or interrog. pronoun) **a.** other than the person or the thing mentioned; instead: *somebody else; who else?* **b.** in addition: *what else shall I do? who else is going?* **2.** (following an indef. or interrog. pronoun and forming with it an indef. or compound pronoun with inflection at the end): *somebody else's child, nobody else's business, whose else* (older usage) or now usually *who else's child could it be?* **3.** otherwise: *run, else* (or *or else*) *you will be late, how else could I do it?* [ME and OE *elles* (c. OHG *elles*) adv. gen. of a pre-E word, c. L *alius* other]

Ixse·ne (ĕl′sə nə), *n.* Flemish name of **Ixelles.**

El·se·vier (ĕl′zə vîr′, -vər), *n., adj.* Elzevir.

else·where (ĕls′hwâr′), *adv.* somewhere else; in or to some other place.

El·si·nore (ĕl′sə nōr′), *n.* Helsingör.

e·lu·ci·date (ĭ lōō′sə dāt′), *v.t.,* **-dated, -dating.** to make lucid or clear; throw light upon; explain. [t. LL: m.s. *ēlūcidātus,* pp., made light] —**e·lu′ci·da′tion,** *n.* —**e·lu′ci·da′tive,** *adj.* —**e·lu′ci·da′tor,** *n.* —Syn. See **explain.**

e·lude (ĭ lōōd′), *v.t.,* **eluded, eluding. 1.** to avoid or escape by dexterity or artifice: *to elude pursuit.* **2.** to slip away from; evade: *to elude vigilance.* **3.** to escape the mind; baffle. [t. L: m.s. *ēlūdere* finish play, deceive] —**e·lud′er,** *n.* —Syn. **1.** shun, dodge. See **escape. 3.** foil, frustrate.

E·lul (ĕ lōōl′), *n.* (in the Jewish calendar) the twelfth month of the year. [t. Heb.]

e·lu·sion (ĭ lōō′zhən), *n.* act of eluding; evasion; clever escape. [t. ML: s. *ēlūsio.* See ELUDE]

e·lu·sive (ĭ lōō′sĭv), *adj.* **1.** eluding clear perception or complete mental grasp; hard to express or define. **2.** dexterously evasive. Also, **e·lu·so·ry** (ĭ lōō′sə rĭ). —**e·lu′sive·ly,** *adv.* —**e·lu′sive·ness,** *n.*

e·lu·tri·ate (ĭ lōō′trĭ āt′), *v.t.,* **-ated, -ating. 1.** to purify by washing and straining or decanting. **2.** to separate the light and heavy particles of by washing. [t. L: m.s. *ēlūtriātus,* pp.] —**e·lu′tri·a′tion,** *n.*

e·lu·vi·um (ĭ lōō′vĭ əm), *n., pl.* **-via** (-vĭ ə). *Geol.* a deposit of soil, dust, etc., originating in the place where found as through decomposition of rock (distinguished from *alluvium*). [NL, der. L *ēluere* wash out] —**e·lu′vi·al,** *adj.*

el·ver (ĕl′vər), *n.* a young eel, particularly when running up a stream from the ocean. [var. of *eel-fare* (f. EEL + FARE) passage of young eels up a river]

elves (ĕlvz), *n.* pl. of **elf.**

elv·ish (ĕl′vĭsh), *adj.* elfish. —**elv′ish·ly,** *adv.*

E·ly (ē′lĭ), *n.* **1.** Isle of, an administrative county in E England: formerly a part of Cambridgeshire. 89,049 pop. (1951); 375 sq. mi. *Co. seat:* March. **2.** a town in this county: famous cathedral. 9989 (1951).

El·y·ot (ĕl′ĭ ət, -yət), *n.* Sir Thomas, c1490–1546, English scholar and diplomat.

E·lyr·i·a (ĭ lĭr′ĭ ə), *n.* a city in N Ohio. 43,782 (1960).

E·ly·sée (ā lē zā′), *n.* a palace in Paris: the official residence of the president of France.

E·ly·sian (ĭ lĭzh′ən), *adj.* **1.** pertaining to, or resembling, Elysium. **2.** blissful; delightful.

E·ly·si·um (ĭ lĭzh′ĭ əm, ĭ lĭz′-, ĭ lĭzh′əm), *n.* **1.** Also, **Elysian fields.** *Gk. Myth.* the abode of the blessed after death. **2.** any similarly conceived abode or state of the dead. **3.** any place or state of perfect happiness. [t. L, t. Gk.: short for *Ēlýsion* (*pedŕon*) Elysian (plain or field)]

el·y·tra (ĕl′ə trə), *n.* pl. of **elytron, elytrum.**

el·y·troid (ĕl′ə troid′), *adj.* like an elytron.

el·y·tron (ĕl′ə trŏn′), *n., pl.* **-tra** (-trə). one of the pair of hardened forewings of certain insects, as beetles, forming a protective covering for the posterior wings. [NL, t. Gk.: cover, sheath]

el·y·trum (ĕl′ə trəm), *n., pl.* **-tra** (-trə). elytron.

El·ze·vir (ĕl′zə vîr′, -vər), *n.* **1.** Louis, c1540–1617, founder of a Dutch printing firm at Leyden, carried on by his son, **Bonaventure,** 1583–1652, and his grandson, **Abraham,** (nephew of Bonaventure) 1592–1652. **2.** a book produced by the Elzevir printing house. **3.** a style of printing type with firm hairlines and stubby serifs. —*adj.* **4.** of or pertaining to the Elzevir family, famous for their small editions of the classics. **5.** indicating the type originated by this family. Also, **Elsevier, El′ze·vi′er,** **El′se·vir·i·an** (ĕl′zə vîr′ĭ ən), *adj.*

em¹ (ĕm), *n., pl.* **ems. 1.** the letter M, m. **2.** *Print.* the square of any size of type (orig. the portion of a line occupied by the letter M), used as the unit of measurement for printed matter. **3.** **em pica,** about one sixth of an inch, generally used as the unit of measurement in printing. —*adj.* **4.** having the size of an em: *em quad.* [name of the letter M]

em² (əm), *pron., pl. Colloq.* them (occurs only in unstressed position). Also, **'em.** [ME *hem,* dat. and acc. pl. of HE; now taken for weak form of THEM]

em-¹, var. of **en-¹,** before *b, p,* and sometimes *m,* as in *embalm.* Cf. **im-¹.**

em-², var. of **en-²,** before *b, m, p, ph,* as in *embolism, emphasis.*

Em., *Chem.* emanation (def. 3).

e·ma·ci·ate (ĭ mā′shĭ āt′), *v.t.,* **-ated, -ating.** to make lean by a gradual wasting away of flesh. [t. L: m.s. *ēmaciātus,* pp.]

e·ma·ci·a·tion (ĭ mā′shĭ ā′shən, -sĭ-), *n.* abnormal thinness, caused by lack of nutrition or by disease.

em·a·nate (ĕm′ə nāt′), *v.i.,* **-nated, -nating.** to flow out, issue, or proceed as from a source or origin; come forth; originate. [t. L: m.s. *ēmānātus,* pp.] —**em′a·na′tive,** *adj.* —Syn. See **emerge.**

em·a·na·tion (ĕm′ə nā′shən), *n.* **1.** act or fact of emanating. **2.** something that emanates. **3.** *Chem.* a gaseous product of radioactive disintegration including radon, thoron, and actinon.

e·man·ci·pate (ĭ măn′sə pāt′), *v.t.,* **-pated, -pating. 1.** to free from restraint of any kind. **2.** *Roman and Civil Law.* **a.** to free (a slave). **b.** to terminate paternal control over. [t. L: m.s. *ēmancipātus,* pp.] —**e·man′ci·pa′tive,** *adj.*

e·man·ci·pa·tion (ĭ măn′sə pā′shən), *n.* **1.** act of emancipating. **2.** fact of being emancipated; freedom.

e·man·ci·pa·tor (ĭ măn′sə pā′tər), *n.* **1.** one who emancipates. **2.** the **Great Emancipator,** Abraham Lincoln. [t. LL]

e·mar·gi·nate (ĭ mär′jə nāt′), *adj.* **1.** notched at the margin. **2.** *Bot.* notched at the apex, as a petal or leaf. Also, **e·mar′gi·nat′ed.** [t. L: m.s. *ēmarginātus,* pp., deprived of an edge]

Emarginate leaves

e·mas·cu·late (*v.* ĭ măs′kyə lāt′; *adj.* ĭ măs′kyə lĭt, -lāt′), *v.,* **-lated, -lating,** *adj.* —*v.t.* **1.** to castrate. **2.** to deprive of strength or vigor; weaken; render effeminate. —*adj.* **3.** emasculated; effeminate. [t. L: m.s. *ēmasculātus,* pp.] —**e·mas′cu·la′tion,** *n.* —**e·mas′cu·la′tor,** *n.* —**e·mas·cu·la·to·ry** (ĭ măs′kyə lə tōr′ĭ), **e·mas′cu·la′tive,** *adj.*

em·balm (ĕm bäm′), *v.t.* **1.** to treat (a dead body) with balsams, spices, etc., or (now usually) with drugs or chemicals, in order to preserve from decay. **2.** to preserve from oblivion; keep in memory. **3.** *Poetic.* to impart a balmy fragrance to. [ME *enbaume(n),* t. F: m. *embaumer,* der. *em-* EM-¹ + *baume* BALM] —**em·balm′er,** *n.* —**em·balm′ment,** *n.*

em·bank (ĕm băngk′), *v.t.* to enclose, confine, or protect with a bank, mound, dike, or the like.

em·bank·ment (ĕm băngk′mənt), *n.* **1.** a bank, mound, dike, or the like, raised to hold back water, carry a roadway, etc. **2.** act of embanking.

em·bar·ca·tion (ĕm′bär kā′shən), *n.* embarkation.

em·bar·go (ĕm bär′gō), *n., pl.* **-goes,** *v.,* **-goed, -going.** —*n.* **1.** an order of a government prohibiting the movement of merchant vessels from or into its ports. **2.** an injunction from a government commerce agency to refuse freight for shipment, in case of insufficient facilities, congestion, etc. **3.** any restriction imposed upon commerce by law. **4.** a restraint or hindrance; a prohibition. —*v.t.* **5.** to impose an embargo on. [t. Sp., der. *embargar* restrain, ult. der. Rom. *barra* BAR¹]

em·bark (ĕm bärk′), *v.t.* **1.** to put or receive on board a ship. **2.** to involve (a person) in an enterprise; venture or invest (money, etc.) in an enterprise. —*v.i.* **3.** to board a ship, as for a voyage. **4.** to engage in an enterprise, business, etc. [t. F: m.s. *embarquer,* der. *em-* EM-¹ (g. L *in-*) + *barque* BARK³]

em·bar·ka·tion (ĕm′bär kā′shən), *n.* act or process of embarking. Also, **embarcation.**

em·bar·rass (ĕm băr′əs), *v.t.* **1.** to disconcert; abash; make uncomfortable, self-conscious, etc.; confuse. **2.** to make difficult or intricate, as a question or problem; complicate. **3.** to put obstacles or difficulties in the way of; impede. **4.** to beset with financial difficulties; burden with debt. [t. F: s. *embarrasser,* lit., block, obstruct, der. *embarras* obstacle] —**em·bar′rass·ing,** *adj.* —**em·bar′rass·ing·ly,** *adv.* —Syn. See **confuse. 3.** hamper, hinder.

em·bar·rass·ment (ĕm băr′əs mənt), *n.* **1.** embarrassed state; disconcertment; abashment. **2.** act of embarrassing. **3.** that which embarrasses. —Syn. **1.** perplexity, discomposure, mortification, chagrin.

em·bas·sa·dor (ĕm băs′ə dər), *n.* ambassador.

em·bas·sy (ĕm′bə sĭ), *n., pl.* **-sies. 1.** a body of persons entrusted with a mission to a sovereign or government; an ambassador and his staff. **2.** the official headquarters of an ambassador. **3.** the function or office of an ambassador. **4.** the sending of ambassadors. [var. of *ambassy,* t. MF: m. *ambassée,* ult. der. L *ambactia* office]

em·bat·tle¹ (ĕm băt′əl), *v.t.,* **-tled, -tling. 1.** to arrange in order of battle; prepare for battle; arm. **2.** to fortify (a town, etc.). [ME *embataile(n),* t. OF: m. *embataillier,* der. *em-* EM-¹ + *bataille* BATTLE¹]

em·bat·tle² (ĕm băt′əl), *v.t.,* **-tled, -tling.** to furnish with battlements. [EM-¹ + BATTLE²]

em·bay (ĕm bā′), *v.t.* to enclose in or as in a bay; surround or envelop.

em·bay·ment (ĕm bā′mənt), *n.* **1.** a bay. **2.** *Phys. Geog.* the process by which a bay is formed.

em·bed (ĕm bĕd′), *v.t.,* **-bedded, -bedding. 1.** to fix in a surrounding mass. **2.** to lay in or as in a bed. Also, **imbed.** —**em·bed′ment,** *n.*

em·bel·lish (ĕm bĕl′ĭsh), *v.t.* **1.** to beautify by or as by ornamentation; ornament; adorn. **2.** to enhance (a statement or narrative) with fictitious additions; embroider. [ME *embelyss(en),* t. OF: m. *embelliss-,* s. *embellir,* der. *em-* EM-¹ + *bel* handsome] —**em·bel′lish·er,** *n.* —Syn. **1.** decorate, garnish, bedeck, embroider.

ăct, āble, dâre, ärt; ĕbb, ēqual; Ĭf, Īce; hŏt, ōver, ôrder, oil, bŏŏk, ōōze, out; ŭp, ūse, ûrge; ə = a in alone; h, chief; g, give; ng, ring; sh, shoe; th, thin; ŧh, that; zh, vision. See the full key on inside cover.

em·bel·lish·ment (ĕm bĕl/ĭsh mənt), *n.* **1.** an ornament or decoration. **2.** a fictitious addition, as in a statement. **3.** act of embellishing. **4.** state of being embellished.

em·ber[1] (ĕm/bər), *n.* **1.** a small live coal, brand of wood, etc., as in a dying fire. **2.** (*pl.*) the smoldering remains of a fire. [ME *eemer, emeri,* OE *ǣmerge,* c. Icel. *eimyrja*]

em·ber[2] (ĕm/bər), *adj.* pertaining to the three-day period of prayer and fasting that comes once in each season. See **Ember days.** [ME *ymber* (attrib.), OE *ymbren,* special use of OE *ymbrene, ymbryne* circuit, course, f. *ymb* around + *ryne* a running]

Ember days, a quarterly season of fasting and prayer (the Wednesday, Friday, and Saturday after the first Sunday in Lent, after Whitsunday, after Sept. 14, and after Dec. 13) observed in the Roman Catholic and other Western churches.

em·bez·zle (ĕm bĕz/əl), *v.t.,* **-zled, -zling.** to appropriate fraudulently to one's own use, as money or property entrusted to one's possession. [ME *enbesyl(en),* t. AF: m. *enbesiler,* f. *en-* EM-[1] + *beseler* destroy, dissipate] **—em·bez/zle·ment,** *n.* **—em·bez/zler,** *n.*

em·bit·ter (ĕm bĭt/ər), *v.t.* to make bitter or more bitter. **—em·bit/ter·ment,** *n.*

em·bla·zon (ĕm blā/zən), *v.t.* **1.** to portray or inscribe on or as on a heraldic shield; to embellish or decorate. **2.** to proclaim; celebrate or extol. **—em·bla/zon·er,** *n.*

em·bla·zon·ment (ĕm blā/zən mənt), *n.* **1.** act of emblazoning. **2.** that which is emblazoned.

em·bla·zon·ry (ĕm blā/zən rĭ), *n.* **1.** act or art of emblazoning; heraldic decoration. **2.** brilliant representation or embellishment.

em·blem (ĕm/bləm), *n.* **1.** an object, or a representation of it, symbolizing a quality, state, class of persons, etc.; a symbol. **2.** an allegorical drawing or picture, often with explanatory writing. [t. L: m. *emblēma* inlaid work, ornamentation, t. Gk.: an insertion] **—Syn. 1.** token, sign, figure, image, device, badge.

em·blem·at·ic (ĕm/blə măt/ĭk), *adj.* pertaining to, of, the nature of, or serving as an emblem; symbolic. Also, **em/blem·at/i·cal. —em/blem·at/i·cal·ly,** *adv.*

em·blem·a·tist (ĕm blĕm/ə tĭst), *n.* a designer, maker, or user of emblems.

em·blem·a·tize (ĕm blĕm/ə tīz/), *v.t.,* **-tized, -tizing.** to serve as an emblem of; represent by an emblem.

em·ble·ments (ĕm/blə mənts), *n. pl. Law.* the products or profits of land which has been sown or planted. [t. AF: m. *emblaement,* der. *emblaer,* der. *em-* EM-[1] + *blé* grain (t. Gmc. Cf. MD *blaad,* OE *blǣd*)]

em·bod·i·ment (ĕm bŏd/ĭ mənt), *n.* **1.** act of embodying. **2.** state or fact of being embodied. **3.** that in which something is embodied; an incarnation. **4.** something embodied.

em·bod·y (ĕm bŏd/ĭ), *v.t.,* **-bodied, -bodying. 1.** to invest with a body, as a spirit; incarnate; make corporeal. **2.** to give a concrete form to; express or exemplify (ideas, etc.) in concrete form. **3.** to collect into or include in a body; organize; incorporate. **4.** to embrace or comprise.

em·bold·en (ĕm bōl/dən), *v.t.* to make bold or more bold; hearten or encourage.

em·bo·lec·to·my (ĕm/bə lĕk/tə mĭ), *n., pl.* **-mies.** the removal of an embolus from an artery, which it is obstructing, by surgery. [f. EMBOL(US) + -ECTOMY]

em·bol·ic (ĕm bŏl/ĭk), *adj.* **1.** *Pathol.* pertaining to an embolus or to embolism. **2.** *Embryol.* developing inwardly: related to a process of invagination.

em·bo·lism (ĕm/bə lĭz/əm), *n.* **1.** intercalation, as of a day in a year. **2.** a period of time intercalated. **3.** *Pathol.* the occlusion of a blood vessel by an embolus. [t. LL: s. *embolismus* intercalation, der. Gk. *embállein* throw in. See EMBLEM] **—em/bo·lis/mic,** *adj.*

em·bo·lus (ĕm/bə ləs), *n., pl.* **-li** (-lī/). *Pathol.* undissolved material carried by the blood current and impacted in some part of the vascular system, as thrombi or fragments of thrombi, tissue fragments, clumps of bacteria, protozoan parasites, fat globules, gas bubbles. [t. L: piston, t. Gk.: m. *émbolos* peg, stopper]

em·bon·point (äN bôN pwăN/), *n. French.* exaggerated plumpness; stoutness. [F: lit., in good condition]

em·bos·om (ĕm bo͝oz/əm, -bo͞o/zəm), *v.t.* **1.** to enfold, envelop, or enclose. **2.** to take into or hold in the bosom; embrace. **3.** to cherish; foster.

em·boss (ĕm bôs/, -bŏs/), *v.t.* **1.** to raise or represent surface designs in relief. **2.** to cause to bulge out; make protuberant. **3.** to raise a design on a fabric by pressing. [ME *embosse(n),* t. OF: m. *embocer* swell in protuberances, der. *em-* EM-[1] + *boce* swelling, BOSS[2]] **—em·boss/er,** *n.* **—em·boss/ment,** *n.*

em·bou·chure (äm/bo͞o sho͝or/; *Fr.* äN bo͞o shyr/), *n.* **1.** the mouth of a river. **2.** the opening out of a valley into a plain. **3.** *Music.* **a.** the mouthpiece of a wind instrument, esp. when of metal. **b.** the adjustment of a player's mouth to such a mouthpiece. [t. F, der. *emboucher* put into the mouth, discharge by a mouth or outlet, der. *em-* EM-[1] + *bouche* mouth (g. L *bucca* cheek, mouth)]

em·bow·el (ĕm bou/əl, -boul/), *v.t.,* **-eled, -eling** or (*esp. Brit.*) **-elling, -elling.** to disembowel.

em·bow·er (ĕm bou/ər), *v.t., v.i.* to shelter in or as in a bower; cover or surround with foliage.

em·brace (ĕm brās/), *v.,* **-braced, -bracing,** *n.* **—***v.t.* **1.** to take or clasp in the arms; press to the bosom; hug. **2.** to take or receive (an idea, etc.) gladly or eagerly; accept willingly. **3.** to avail oneself of (an opportunity, etc.). **4.** to adopt (a profession, a religion, etc.). **5.** to take in with the eye or the mind. **6.** to encircle; surround; enclose. **7.** to include or contain. **—***v.i.* **8.** to join in an embrace. **—***n.* **9.** act of embracing; a hug. [ME *enbrace(n),* t. OF: m. *embracier,* der. *em-* EM-[1] + *bras* arm (g. L *brāchium*)] **—em·brace/a·ble,** *adj.* **—em·brace/ment,** *n.* **—em·brac/er,** *n.* **—Syn. 2.** adopt, espouse. **7.** comprise, comprehend. See **include.**

em·branch·ment (ĕm brănch/mənt, -bränch/-), *n.* **1.** a branching or ramification. **2.** a branch.

em·bra·sure (ĕm brā/zhər), *n.* **1.** an opening in a wall or parapet through which a gun may be fired, constructed with sides which flare outward. See diag. under **bartizan. 2.** *Archit.* an enlargement of the aperture of a door or window, at the inside face of the wall, by means of splayed sides. [t. F, der. *embraser, ébraser* to splay (an opening)]

em·bro·cate (ĕm/brō kāt/), *v.t.,* **-cated, -cating.** to moisten and rub with a liniment or lotion. [t. ML: m.s. *embrocātus,* pp. of *embrocāre,* der. LL *embrocha,* t. Gk.: m. *embrochḗ* lotion]

em·bro·ca·tion (ĕm/brō kā/shən), *n.* **1.** act of embrocating a bruised or diseased part of the body. **2.** the liquid used for this; a liniment or lotion.

em·broi·der (ĕm broi/dər), *v.t.* **1.** to decorate with ornamental needlework. **2.** to produce or form in needlework. **3.** to adorn or embellish rhetorically, esp. with fictitious additions. **—***v.i.* **4.** to do embroidery. [appar. f. EM-[1] + BROIDER] **—em·broi/der·er,** *n.*

em·broi·der·y (ĕm broi/dərĭ), *n., pl.* **-deries. 1.** the art of working, with a needle, raised and ornamental designs in threads of silk, cotton, gold, silver, or other material, upon any woven fabric, leather, paper, etc. **2.** embroidered work or ornamentation.

em·broil (ĕm broil/), *v.t.* **1.** to bring into a state of discord; involve in contention or strife. **2.** to throw into confusion; complicate. [t. F: m. *embrouiller,* f. *em-* EM-[1] + *brouiller* BROIL[1]] **—em·broil/er,** *n.* **—em·broil/ment,** *n.*

em·brown (ĕm broun/), *v.t., v.i.* to make or become brown or dark.

em·brute (ĕm bro͞ot/), *v.t., v.i.* imbrute.

em·bry·ec·to·my (ĕm/brĭ ĕk/tə mĭ), *n., pl.* **-mies.** removal of an embryo by surgery. [f. EMBRY(O) + -ECTOMY]

em·bry·o (ĕm/brĭ ō/), *n., pl.* **-os. 1.** an organism in the earlier stages of its development, as before emergence from the egg or before metamorphosis. **2.** (among mammals and other viviparous animals) a young animal during its earlier stages within the mother's body (including, in man, the developmental stages up to the end of the seventh week). **3.** *Bot.* the rudimentary plant usually contained in the seed. **4.** the beginning or rudimentary stage of anything. **—***adj.* **5.** embryonic. [t. ML, t. Gk.: m. *émbryon*]

em·bry·og·e·ny (ĕm/brĭ ŏj/ə nĭ), *n.* the formation and development of the embryo, as a subject of scientific study. Also, **em·bry·o·gen·e·sis** (ĕm/brĭ ō jĕn/ə sĭs). [f. EMBRYO + -GENY] **—em·bry·o·ge·net·ic** (ĕm/brĭ ō jə nĕt/ĭk), *adj.*

embryol., embryology.

em·bry·ol·o·gy (ĕm/brĭ ŏl/ə jĭ), *n.* the science of the embryo, its genesis, development, etc. [f. EMBRYO + -LOGY] **—em·bry·o·log·i·cal** (ĕm/brĭ ə lŏj/ə kəl), **em/bry·o·log/ic,** *adj.* **—em/bry·ol/o·gist,** *n.*

em·bry·on·ic (ĕm/brĭ ŏn/ĭk), *adj.* **1.** pertaining to or in the state of an embryo. **2.** rudimentary; undeveloped. Also, **em·bry·o·nal** (ĕm/brĭ ə nəl), *adj.*

embryo sac, *Bot.* the megaspore of a seed-bearing plant, being situated within the ovule, giving rise to the endosperm or supposed female prothallium, and forming the cell in which the embryo is developed.

em·cee (ĕm/sē/), *n., v.i., v.t.,* **-ceed, -ceeing. —***n.* **1.** master of ceremonies. **—***v.i., v.t.* **2.** to act as master of ceremonies (for). [var. *M.C.* master of ceremonies]

Em·den (ĕm/dən), *n.* a seaport in NW West Germany. 41,200 (est 1953).

e·meer (ə mĭr/), *n.* emir.

e·mend (ĭ mĕnd/), *v.t.* **1.** to free from faults or errors; correct. **2.** to amend (a text) by removing errors. [t. L: s. *ēmendāre* correct] **—e·mend/a·ble,** *adj.*

e·men·date (ē/mən dāt/), *v.t.,* **-dated, -dating.** to emend (a text). **—e·men·da·tor** (ē/mən dā/tər, ĕm/-ən-), *n.*

e·men·da·tion (ē/mĕn dā/shən, ĕm/ən-), *n.* **1.** a correction. **2.** act of emending. **—e·mend/a·to/ry,** *adj.*

em·er·ald (ĕm/ər əld, ĕm/rəld), *n.* **1.** a rare green variety of beryl, highly valued as a gem. **2.** clear deep green. **3.** *Brit.* a printing type (6½ point) of a size between nonpareil and minion. **—***adj.* **4.** having a clear, deep-green color. [ME *emeraude,* t. OF, g. L *smaragdus* a green precious stone, t. Gk.: m. *smáragdos*]

Emerald Isle, Ireland.

e·merge (ĭ mûrj/), *v.i.,* **emerged, emerging. 1.** to rise or come forth from or as from water or other liquid. **2.** to come forth into view or notice, as from concealment or obscurity. **3.** to come up or arise, as a question or difficulty. [t. L: m.s. *ēmergere* rise out]
—Syn. 2. EMERGE, EMANATE, ISSUE mean to come forth from a place or source. EMERGE is used of coming forth from something that envelops or encloses, from a place shut off

from view, or from concealment, obscurity, retirement, or the like, into sight and notice: *the sun emerges from behind the clouds.* EMANATE is used esp. of intangible or immaterial things, as light, vapor, ideas, news, etc. spreading or streaming from a source: *rumors often emanate from irresponsible persons.* ISSUE is most often used of a number of persons, a mass of matter, or a volume of smoke, sound, or the like, coming forth through any outlet or outlets: *the crowd issued from the building.*

e·mer·gence (ĭ mûr′jəns), *n.* **1.** act or fact of emerging. **2.** an outgrowth, as a prickle, on the surface of an organ. **3.** *Biol., Philos.* the appearance of new properties in the course of development or evolution that could not have been foreseen in the earlier stage.

e·mer·gen·cy (ĭ mûr′jən sĭ), *n., pl.* **-cies.** an unforeseen occurrence; a sudden and urgent occasion for action. [t. L: m.s. *ēmergentia* a coming up]
—**Syn.** EMERGENCY, CRISIS, STRAITS refer to situations in which quick action and judgment are necessary, though they may not avert undesirable consequences. An EMERGENCY is a situation demanding immediate action: *a power failure created an emergency in transportation.* A CRISIS is a vital or decisive turning point in a condition or state of affairs, and everything depends on the outcome of it: *help arrived when affairs had reached a crisis.* STRAIT (usually plural) suggests a pressing situation, often one of need or want, which usually makes necessary some difficult alternative or choice: *the family was in desperate straits for food and clothing.*

e·mer·gent (ĭ mûr′jənt), *adj.* **1.** emerging; rising from a liquid or other surrounding medium. **2.** coming into view or notice; issuing. **3.** arising casually or unexpectedly. **4.** calling for immediate action; urgent. **5.** *Biol., Philos.* displaying emergence (def. 3).

emergent evolution, *Biol., Philos.* the origin of entirely new properties at certain critical stages or levels in the course of evolution, e.g. the origin of multicellular organisms, of nervous systems, psychic processes, etc.

e·mer·i·tus (ĭ mĕr′ə təs), *adj.* retired or honorably discharged from active duty because of age, infirmity, or long service, but retained on the rolls: *a professor emeritus.* [t. L: pp., having served out one's time]

e·mersed (ĭ mûrst′), *adj.* **1.** having emerged. **2.** *Bot.* risen or standing out of water, surrounding leaves, etc. [f. s. L *ēmersus,* pp., emerged + -ED²]

e·mer·sion (ĭ mûr′shən, -zhən), *n.* **1.** act or fact of emerging; emergence. **2.** *Astron.* the reappearance of a heavenly body after an eclipse or occultation.

Em·er·son (ĕm′ər sən), *n.* Ralph Waldo, 1803–82, U.S. essayist and poet. —**Em·er·so·ni·an** (ĕm′ər sō′nĭ ən), *adj.*

em·er·y (ĕm′ər ĭ, ĕm′rĭ), *n.* a granular mineral substance consisting typically of corundum mixed with magnetite or hematite, used powdered, crushed, or consolidated for grinding and polishing. [t. F: m. *émeri,* t. It.: m. *smeriglio,* der. Gk. *smēris*]

emery cloth, emery-coated cloth used as an abrasive.
emery wheel, a wheel for grinding or polishing consisting mostly of or faced with emery.

e·me·sis (ĕm′ə sĭs), *n. Pathol.* vomiting. [NL, t. Gk.]

e·met·ic (ĭ mĕt′ĭk), *adj.* **1.** inducing vomiting, as a medicinal substance. —*n.* **2.** an emetic medicine or agent. [t. L: s. *emeticus,* t. Gk.: m. *emetikós*]

em·e·tine (ĕm′ə tēn′, -tĭn), *n.* a colorless crystalline, or white powdery substance, C₂₉H₄₀N₂O₂, principal ingredient of ipecac, a specific against amoebic dysentery. Also, **em·e·tin** (-tĭn). [f. s. Gk. *emetos* vomiting + -INE²]

e·meu (ē′mū), *n.* emu.

E.M.F., electromotive force. Also, **e.m.f., emf**

-emia, *Med.* a suffix referring to the state of the blood, as in *hyperemia.* Also, **-aemia, -haemia, -hemia.** [NL: also *-hemia, -haemia,* t. Gk.: m. *-aimia* (as in *anaimía* want of blood), der. *haîma* blood]

em·i·grant (ĕm′ə grənt), *n.* **1.** one who emigrates, as from his native country. —*adj.* **2.** emigrating. [t. L: s. *ēmigrans,* ppr.]

em·i·grate (ĕm′ə grāt′), *v.i.* **-grated, -grating.** to leave one country or region to settle in another; migrate. [t. L: m.s. *ēmigrātus,* pp.] —**Syn.** See **migrate.**

em·i·gra·tion (ĕm′ə grā′shən), *n.* **1.** act of emigrating. **2.** a body of emigrants; emigrants collectively.

é·mi·gré (ĕm′ə grā′; Fr. ē mē grĕ′), *n., pl.* **-grés** (-grāz′; Fr. -grĕ′). **1.** an emigrant, esp. one who flees from his native land to escape political persecution. **2.** a person who fled from France because of opposition to or fear of the revolution that began in 1789. [F, pp. of *émigrer,* t. L: m. *ēmigrāre* emigrate]

E·mil·ia (ĕ mē′lyä), *n.* a department in N Italy. 3,546,086 pop. (est. 1952); 8547 sq. mi.

em·i·nence (ĕm′ə nəns), *n.* **1.** high station, rank, or repute. **2.** a high place or part; a hill or elevation; height. **3.** (*cap.*) *Rom. Cath. Ch.* the title of honor of a cardinal: *your Eminence.* —**Syn.** **1.** distinction, prominence, celebrity, renown.

em·i·nen·cy (ĕm′ə nən sĭ), *n., pl.* **-cies.** *Rare.* eminence.

em·i·nent (ĕm′ə nənt), *adj.* **1.** high in station, rank, or repute; distinguished. **2.** conspicuous, signal, or noteworthy: *eminent services, eminent fairness.* **3.** lofty; high. **4.** prominent; projecting; protruding. [t. L: s. *ēminens,* ppr., standing out] —**em′i·nent·ly,** *adv.* —**Syn.** **1.** prominent, celebrated, renowned, illustrious. See **famous.** **2.** noted; noteworthy. —**Ant.** **1.** unknown.

eminent domain, *Law.* the dominion of the sovereign power over all property within the state, by which it can appropriate private property for public use, compensation being given for it.

e·mir (ə mĭr′), *n.* **1.** an Arabian chieftain or prince. **2.** a title of honor of the descendants of Mohammed. Also, **emeer.** [var. of AMIR]

em·is·sar·y (ĕm′ə sĕr′ĭ), *n., pl.* **-saries,** *adj.* —*n.* **1.** an agent sent on a mission or errand. **2.** an agent sent on a mission of a secret nature. —*adj.* **3.** sent forth, as on a mission. **4.** pertaining to one so sent forth. [t. L: m.s. *ēmissārius* sent out (adj.), scout (n.)]

e·mis·sion (ĭ mĭsh′ən), *n.* **1.** act of emitting. **2.** that which is emitted; a discharge; an emanation. **3.** act of issuing (as of paper money). **4.** *Electronics.* a measure of the number of electrons emitted by the heated filament or cathode of a vacuum tube. [t. L: s. *ēmissio*]

e·mis·sive (ĭ mĭs′ĭv), *adj.* **1.** serving to emit. **2.** pertaining to emission.

em·is·siv·i·ty (ĕm′ə sĭv′ə tĭ), *n. Thermodynamics.* the relative ability of a surface to emit radiant energy compared to an ideal, black body at the same temperature and with the same area.

e·mit (ĭ mĭt′), *v.t.,* **emitted, emitting. 1.** to send forth; give out or forth (liquid, light, heat, sound, etc.); discharge. **2.** to issue, as an order or a decree. **3.** to issue formally for circulation, as paper money. **4.** to utter, as opinions. [t. L: m.s. *ēmittere* send out] —**e·mit′ter,** *n.* —**Syn. 1.** vent, exhale, exude, expel, eject.

Em·man·u·el (ĭ măn′yŏŏ əl), *n.* Christ. See **Immanuel.**

em·men·a·gogue (ə mĕn′ə gŏg′, -gŏg′, ə mē′nə-), *n.* a medicine that promotes the menstrual discharge. [f. Gk. *émmēn(a)* menses + -AGOGUE]

em·met (ĕm′ĭt), *n. Archaic or Dial.* an ant.

Em·met (ĕm′ĭt), *n.* Robert, 1778–1803, Irish patriot.

em·me·tro·pi·a (ĕm′ə trō′pĭ ə), *n.* the normal refractive condition of the eye, in which the rays of light are accurately focused on the retina. [NL, f. Gk.: s. *ēmmetros* in measure + -ōpia eye state] —**em·me·trop·ic** (ĕm′ə trŏp′ĭk), *adj.*

e·mol·lient (ĭ mŏl′yənt), *adj.* **1.** having the power of softening or relaxing living tissues, as a medicinal substance; soothing, esp. to the skin. —*n.* **2.** *Med.* an emollient medicine or agent. [t. L: s. *ēmolliens,* ppr.]

e·mol·u·ment (ĭ mŏl′yə mənt), *n.* profit arising from office or employment; compensation for services; salary or fees. [t. L: (m.) s. *ēmolumentum, ēmolimentum* profit]

e·mote (ĭ mōt′), *v.i.,* **emoted, emoting.** *Colloq.* **1.** to show or affect emotion. **2.** to behave theatrically; to act a part, esp. without talent. [back formation from EMOTION]

e·mo·tion (ĭ mō′shən), *n.* **1.** an affective state of consciousness in which joy, sorrow, fear, hate, or the like, is experienced (distinguished from cognitive and volitional states of consciousness). **2.** any of the feelings of joy, sorrow, fear, hate, love, etc. [t. L: s. *ēmōtio,* der. *ēmōtus,* pp., moved out, stirred up] —**e·mo′tion·less,** *adj.* —**Syn. 1.** See **feeling.**

e·mo·tion·al (ĭ mō′shən əl), *adj.* **1.** pertaining to emotion or the emotions. **2.** subject to or easily affected by emotion. **3.** appealing to the emotions. —**e·mo′tion·al·ly,** *adv.*

e·mo·tion·al·ism (ĭ mō′shən ə lĭz′əm), *n.* **1.** emotional character. **2.** appeal to the emotions. **3.** tendency to emotion, esp. morbid emotion. **4.** expression of emotion.

e·mo·tion·al·ist (ĭ mō′shən əl ĭst), *n.* **1.** one who appeals to the emotions, esp. unduly. **2.** one easily affected by emotion. **3.** *Philos.* one who bases conduct or the theory of conduct upon feelings.

e·mo·tion·al·i·ty (ĭ mō′shə năl′ə tĭ), *n.* emotional state or quality.

e·mo·tion·al·ize (ĭ mō′shən ə līz′), *v.t.* **-ized, -izing.** to make emotional; treat as a matter of emotion.

e·mo·tive (ĭ mō′tĭv), *adj.* **1.** characterized by or pertaining to emotion. **2.** exciting emotion. —**e·mo′tive·ly,** *adv.* —**e·mo′tive·ness, e·mo·tiv·i·ty** (ē′mō tĭv′ə tĭ), *n.*

Emp., **1.** Emperor. **2.** Empress.

em·pale (ĕm pāl′), *v.t.,* **-paled, -paling.** impale.

em·pan·el (ĕm păn′əl), *v.t.,* **-eled, -eling** or (*esp. Brit.*) **-elled, -elling.** impanel.

em·pa·thy (ĕm′pə thĭ), *n. Psychol.* mental entering into the feeling or spirit of a person or thing; appreciative perception or understanding; motor mimicry. [t. Gk.: m.s. *empátheia.* Cf. G *Einfühlung,* lit., infeeling] —**em·path·ic** (ĕm păth′ĭk), *adj.* —**em·path·i·cal·ly,** *adv.*

Em·ped·o·cles (ĕm pĕd′ə klēz′), *n.* c490–c430 B.C., Greek philosopher and statesman.

em·pen·nage (än pĕ näzh′), *n.* the rear part of an airplane or airship, usually comprising stabilizer, elevator, vertical fin, and rudder. [t. F, der. *empenner* feather, der. em- EM-¹ + *penne* (g. L *penna* feather)]

em·per·or (ĕm′pər ər), *n.* the sovereign or supreme ruler of an empire. [ME *emperour*(e), t. OF: m. *emperour,* g. L *imperātor* ruler] —**em′per·or·ship′,** *n.*

em·per·y (ĕm′pər ĭ), *n., pl.* **-peries.** *Poetic.* **1.** absolute dominion; empire. **2.** the territory of an emperor. [ME *emperie,* t. OF, der. *emperer* to rule, g. L *imperāre*]

em·pha·sis (ĕm′fə sĭs), *n., pl.* **-ses** (-sēz′). **1.** stress laid upon, or importance or significance attached to, anything. **2.** *Rhet.* **a.** special and significant stress of voice laid on particular words or syllables. **b.** stress laid on particular words, by means of position, repetition, or other indication. **3.** intensity or force of expression, action, etc. **4.** prominence, as of outline. [t. L, t. Gk.]

ăct, āble, dâre, ärt; ĕbb, ēqual; ĭf, īce; hŏt, ōver, ôrder, oil, bŏŏk, ōōze, out; ŭp, ūse, ûrge; ə = a in alone; ch, chief; g, give; ng, ring; sh, shoe; th, thin; ŧh, that; zh, vision.   See the full key on inside cover.

em·pha·size (ĕm′fə sīz′), *v.t.*, **-sized, -sizing.** to give emphasis to; lay stress upon; stress.

em·phat·ic (ĕm făt′Ĭk), *adj.* **1.** uttered, or to be uttered, with emphasis; strongly expressive. **2.** using emphasis in speech or action. **3.** forcibly significant; strongly marked; striking. [t. Gk.: m.s. *emphatikós*, var. of *emphantikós* expressive] —**em·phat′i·cal·ly,** *adv.* —Syn. **3.** positive, energetic, forcible, pronounced.

em·phy·se·ma (ĕm′fə sē′mə), *n. Pathol., Vet. Sci.* abnormal distention of an organ or a part of the body with air or other gas. [NL, t. Gk.: inflation] —**em·phy·sem·a·tous** (ĕm′fə sĕm′ə təs, -sē′mə-), *adj.*

em·pire (ĕm′pīr), *n.* **1.** an aggregate of nations or peoples ruled over by an emperor or other powerful sovereign or government; usually a territory of greater extent than a kingdom ruled by a single sovereign: *the Roman empire.* **2.** a government under an emperor: *the first French empire.* **3.** supreme power in governing; imperial power; sovereignty. **4.** supreme control; absolute sway. —*adj.* **5.** (*cap.*) developed or in vogue during the first French empire (1804–15): applied esp. to certain styles of interior decoration, furniture, etc., and of women's dress (implying esp. a high waistline, with undraped skirts hanging loosely). [ME, t. F, g. L *imperium* a command, authority, realm] —Syn. **3.** dominion, rule.

Empire Day, May 24, the anniversary of Queen Victoria s birth, observed throughout the British Empire.

Empire State, the State of New York.

em·pir·ic (ĕm pĭr′Ĭk),*n.* **1.** any one who follows an empirical method. **2.** a quack; a charlatan. —*adj.* **3.** empirical. [t. L: s. *empīricus*, t. Gk.: m. *empeirikós*, der. *empeiría* experience]

em·pir·i·cal (ĕm pĭr′ə kəl), *adj.* **1.** derived from or guided by experience or experiment. **2.** depending upon experience or observation alone, without using science or theory, esp. in medicine. —**em·pir′i·cal·ly,** *adv.*

empirical formula, *Chem.* See **formula.**

em·pir·i·cism (ĕm pĭr′ə sĭz′əm), *n.* **1.** empirical method or practice. **2.** *Philos.* the doctrine that all knowledge is derived from experience. **3.** undue reliance upon experience; quackery. **4.** an empirical conclusion. —**em·pir′i·cist,** *n., adj.*

em·place·ment (ĕm plās′mənt), *n.* **1.** *Fort.* the space, platform, or the like for a gun or battery and its accessories. **2.** a putting in place or position; location.

em·ploy (ĕm ploi′), *v.t.* **1.** to use the services of (a person); have or keep in one's service; keep busy or at work: *this factory employs thousands of men.* **2.** to make use of (an instrument, means, etc.); use; apply. **3.** to occupy or devote (time, energies, etc.): *I employ my spare time in reading.* —*n.* **4.** employment; service: *to be in someone's employ.* [t. F: s. *employer*, g. L *implicāre* enfold] —**em·ploy′a·ble,** *adj.* —Syn. **1.** engage, hire. —Ant. **1.** discharge.

em·ploy·ee (ĕm ploi′ē, ĕm′ploi ē′), *n.* a person working for another person or a business firm for pay. Also, **em·ploy′e, em·ploy′é.** [f. EMPLOY, v. + -EE; F. *employe*, t. F, pp. of *employer* employ] —Syn. See **servant.**

em·ploy·er (ĕm ploi′ər), *n.* one who employs, esp. for wages.

em·ploy·ment (ĕm ploi′mənt), *n.* **1.** act of employing. **2.** state of being employed; employ; services. **3.** that on which one is employed; work; occupation; business.

em·poi·son (ĕm poi′zən), *v.t.* **1.** to corrupt. **2.** *Obs.* to poison. [ME *empoyson(en)*, t. F: m. *empoisoner*, der. *em-* EM-¹ + *poison* POISON]

Em·po·ri·a (ĕm pōr′Ĭ ə), *n.* a city in E Kansas. 18,190 (1960).

em·po·ri·um (ĕm pōr′Ĭ əm), *n., pl.* **-poriums, -poria** (-pōr′Ĭ ə). **1.** a place, town, or city of important commerce, esp. a principal center of trade. **2.** a large store selling a great variety of articles. [t. L, t. Gk.: a trading place]

em·pov·er·ish (ĕm pŏv′ər Ĭsh, -pŏv′rĬsh), *v.t.* impoverish.

em·pow·er (ĕm pou′ər), *v.t.* **1.** to give power or authority to; authorize: *I empowered him to make the deal for me.* **2.** to enable or permit. —**em·pow′er·ment,** *n.* —Syn. **1.** warrant, commission, license, qualify.

em·press (ĕm′prĬs), *n.* **1.** a woman ruler of an empire. **2.** the consort of an emperor. **3.** a supreme or sovereign ruler: *empress of the seas.* [ME *empresse,* t. OF: (m.) *emper(er)esse,* r. *empereris,* g. L *imperātrīx*]

empress dowager, the widow of an emperor.

em·presse·ment (äN prĕs män′), *n. French.* display of cordiality.

em·prise (ĕm prīz′), *n. Archaic.* **1.** an adventurous enterprise. **2.** knightly daring or prowess. Also, **em·prize′.** [ME, t. OF, n. use of fem. pp. of *emprendre* undertake, f. *em-* EM-¹ + *prendre* take (g. L *prehendre*)]

emp·ty (ĕmp′tĬ), *adj.,* **-tier, -tiest,** *v.,* **-tied, -tying,** *n., pl.* **-ties.** —*adj.* **1.** containing nothing; void of the usual or appropriate contents: *an empty bottle.* **2.** vacant; unoccupied: *an empty house.* **3.** without burden or load: *an empty wagon.* **4.** destitute of some quality or qualities; devoid (fol. by *of*): *a life now as empty of happiness as it was full of it.* **5.** without force, effect, or significance; unsatisfactory; meaningless: *empty compliments, empty pleasures.* **6.** *Colloq.* hungry. **7.** without knowledge or sense; frivolous; foolish. —*v.t.* **8.** to make empty; deprive of contents; discharge the contents of: *to empty a bucket.* **9.** to discharge (contents): *empty the water out of a*

a *bucket.* —*v.i.* **10.** to become empty: *the room emptied rapidly after the lecture.* **11.** to discharge contents, as a river: *the river empties into the sea.* —*n.* **12.** *Colloq.* something empty, as a freight car, bottle, etc. [ME: OE *æmtig,* var. of *æmettig,* f. s. *æmetta* leisure + *-ig* -Y¹] —**emp′ti·ly,** *adv.* —**emp′ti·ness,** *n.* —Syn. **1.** EMPTY, VACANT, BLANK denote absence of content or contents. EMPTY means without appropriate or accustomed contents: *empty barrel, the house is empty* (has no furnishings). VACANT is usually applied to that which is temporarily unoccupied: *vacant chair, house* (uninhabited). BLANK applies to surfaces free from any marks or lacking appropriate markings, openings, etc.: *blank paper, wall.* **5.** hollow, delusive, vain. **8.** unload, unburden. —Ant. **1.** full.

emp·ty-hand·ed (ĕmp′tĬ hăn′dĬd), *adj.* having nothing in the hands; bringing or taking nothing.

emp·ty-head·ed (ĕmp′tĬ hĕd′Ĭd), *adj.* brainless; foolish.

em·pur·ple (ĕm pûr′pəl), *v.t.,* **-pled, -pling.** to tinge or color with purple.

em·py·e·ma (ĕm′pĬ ē′mə, -pī-), *n. Pathol.* a collection of pus in some cavity of the body, esp. in the pleural cavity. [NL, t. Gk.: suppuration] —**em′py·e′mic,** *adj.*

em·py·re·al (ĕm pĬr′Ĭ əl, ĕm′pə rē′əl, -pī-), *adj.* **1.** pertaining to the highest heaven; empyrean. **2.** pertaining to the sky; celestial. **3.** formed of pure fire or light. [f. s. LL *empyreus* (t. Gk.: m. *émpyros* fiery) + -AL¹]

em·py·re·an (ĕm′pə rē′ən, -pī-), *n.* **1.** the highest heaven, supposed by the ancients to contain the pure element of fire. **2.** the visible heavens; the firmament. —*adj.* **3.** empyreal.

e·mu (ē′mū), *n.* either of two large, flightless, three-toed Australian birds of the ratite genus *Dromiceius, D. novae* (or *n.*) *hollandiae* and *D. diemenianus,* closely related to the ostrich, but smaller. The latter species is now extinct. Also, **emeu.** [t. Moluccan: m. *emeu* cassowary]

em·u·late (*v.* ĕm′yə lāt′; *adj.* ĕm′yə lĬt), *v.,* **-lated, -lating,** *adj.* —*v.t.* **1.** to try to equal or excel; imitate with effort to equal or surpass. **2.** to rival with some degree of success. —*adj.* **3.** *Obs.* emulous. [t. L: m.s. *aemulātus,* pp., having rivaled] —**em′u·la′tive,** *adj.* —**em′u·la′tor,** *n.*

Emu.
Dromiceius novae hollandiae
(Total length ab. 6½ ft.)

em·u·la·tion (ĕm′yə lā′shən), *n.* **1.** effort or desire to equal or excel others. **2.** *Obs.* jealous rivalry. —Syn. **1.** competition, rivalry.

em·u·lous (ĕm′yə ləs), *adj.* **1.** desirous of equaling or excelling; filled with emulation. **2.** arising from or of the nature of emulation, as actions, etc. **3.** *Obs.* jealous; envious. [t. L: m. *aemulus*] —**em′u·lous·ly,** *adv.* —**em′u·lous·ness,** *n.*

e·mul·si·fy (Ĭ mŭl′sə fī′), *v.t.,* **-fied, -fying.** to make into an emulsion. —**e·mul′si·fi·ca′tion,** *n.* —**e·mul′si·fi′er,** *n.*

e·mul·sion (Ĭ mŭl′shən), *n.* **1.** a liquid preparation of the color and consistency of milk. **2.** *Phys. Chem.* any colloidal suspension of a liquid in another liquid. **3.** *Pharm.* a liquid preparation consisting of minute particles of an oily, fatty, resinous, or other substance held in suspension in an aqueous fluid by means of a gum or other viscous matter. **4.** *Photog.* the light sensitive layer on a photographic film, plate, or paper, consisting of one or more of the silver halides in gelatin. [t. NL: s. *ēmulsio,* der L *ēmulsus,* pp., milked out] —**e·mul′sive,** *adj.*

e·munc·to·ry (Ĭ mŭngk′tər Ĭ), *n., pl.* **-ries,** *adj.* —*n.* **1.** a part or organ of the body, as the skin, a kidney, etc., carrying off waste products. —*adj.* **2.** excretory. [t. NL: m.s. *ēmunctōrium,* L a pair of snuffers]

en (ĕn), *n.* **1.** the letter N, n. **2.** *Print.* half of the width of an em; N quad.

en-¹, a prefix meaning primarily "in," "into," first occurring in words from French, but now used freely as an English formative: **1.** with the old concrete force of putting the object into or on something or of bringing the object into the specified condition, often serving to form transitive verbs from nouns or adjectives, as in *enable, enact, endear, engulf, enshrine, enslave.* **2.** prefixed to verbs, to make them transitive, or, if already transitive, to give them the transitive sign, as in *enkindle, entwine, engild, engird, engrave, enshield.* Also, **em-¹.** Cf. **in-², im-¹.** [t. F, g. L *in-,* repr. *in,* prep., in, into, on, to]

en-², a prefix representing Greek *en-,* corresponding to **en-¹** and occurring chiefly in combinations chiefly formed in Greek, as *energy, enthusiasm.* Also, **em-².**

-en¹, a suffix, forming transitive and intransitive verbs from adjectives, as in *fasten, harden, sweeten,* or from nouns, as in *heighten, lengthen, strengthen.* [abstracted from old verbs like *fasten* (contrast *listen,* where *-en* has kept its nonmorphemic character]

-en², a suffix of [adjectives indicating "material," "appearance," as in *ashen, golden, oaken.* [OE]

-en³, a suffix used to mark the past participle in many strong and some weak verbs, as in *taken, proven.* [OE]

-en⁴, a suffix forming the plural of some nouns, as in *brethren, children, oxen,* and other words, now mostly archaic, as *eyen, hosen.* [ME; OE *-an,* case ending of

b., blend of, blended; c., cognate with; d., dialect, dialectal; der., derived from; f., formed from; g., going back to; m., modification of; r., replacing; s., stem of; t., taken from; ?, perhaps. See the full key on inside cover.

weak nouns, as in *oxan*, oblique sing. and nom. and acc. pl. of *oxa* ox]

-en⁵, a diminutive suffix, as in *maiden, kitten*, etc. [OE]

en·a·ble (ĕn ā'bəl), *v.t.*, **-bled, -bling.** 1. to make able; give power, means, or ability to; make competent; authorize: *this will enable him to do it.* 2. to make possible or easy: *aeronautics enables us to overcome great distances.*

enabling act or **statute**, an act or statute enabling a person or a corporation to do something otherwise illegal.

en·act (ĕn ăkt'), *v.t.* 1. to make into an act or statute. 2. to ordain; decree. 3. to represent on or as on the stage; act the part of: *to enact Hamlet.* —**en·act'a·ble**, *adj.* —**en·ac'tor**, *n.*

en·ac·tive (ĕn ăk'tĭv), *adj.* having power to enact or establish, as a law.

en·act·ment (ĕn ăkt'mənt), *n.* 1. act of enacting. 2. state or fact of being enacted. 3. that which is enacted; a law; a statute. 4. a single provision of a law.

en·ac·to·ry (ĕn ăk'tə rĭ), *adj. Law.* of or pertaining to an enactment which creates new rights and obligations.

e·nam·el (ĭ năm'əl), *n., v.*, **-eled, -eling** or (*esp. Brit.*) **-elled, -elling.** —*n.* 1. a glassy substance, usually opaque, applied by fusion to the surface of metal, pottery, etc., as an ornament or for protection. 2. enamelware. 3. any of various enamellike varnishes, paints, etc. 4. any enamellike surface with a bright luster. 5. an artistic work executed in enamel. 6. *Anat., Zool.* the hard, glossy, calcareous outer structure of the crowns of the teeth, containing only a slight amount of organic substance. 7. a coating applied to the skin to simulate a beautiful complexion. —*v.t.* 8. to inlay or overlay with enamel. 9. to form an enamellike surface upon: *to enamel cardboard.* 10. to decorate as with enamel; variegate with colors. [ME *enamayl*, t. AF, f. en- EN-¹ + *amayl*, OF *esmail*, c. It. *smalto* SMALT; akin to SMELT¹] —**e·nam'el·er**; *esp. Brit.*, **e·nam'el·ler**, *n.* —**e·nam'el·ist**; *esp. Brit.*, **e·nam'el·list**, *n.* —**e·nam'el·work'**, *n.*

e·nam·el·ing (ĭ năm'əl ĭng), *n.* 1. act or work of one who enamels. 2. a decoration or coating of enamel. Also, *esp. Brit.*, **e·nam'el·ling.**

e·nam·el·ware (ĭ năm'əl wâr'), *n.* metalware, as cooking utensils, covered with an enamel surface.

en a·mi (än nà mē'), *French.* as a friend.

en·am·or (ĕn ăm'ər), *v.t.* to inflame with love; charm; captivate (usually passive fol. by *of*): *to be enamored of a lady.* Also, *Brit.*, **en·am'our.** [ME *enamor(en)*, t. OF: m. *enamourer*, der. en- EN-¹ + *amour* (g. L *amor* love)] —*Syn.* fascinate, bewitch.

en ar·riè·re (än nà ryĕr'), *French.* backward.

en·ar·thro·sis (ĕn'är thrō'sĭs), *n., pl.* **-ses** (-sēz). *Anat.* a joint, as at the shoulder, in which a convex end of one bone is socketed in a concavity of another; a ball-and-socket joint. [NL, t. Gk.: jointing in]

en a·vant (än nà vän'), *French.* forward; onward.

en bloc (ĕn blŏk'; *Fr.* än blôk'), *French.* as a whole.

en bro·chette (än brō shĕt'), *French.* See **brochette** (def. 2).

enc., 1. enclosed. 2. enclosure.

en·cae·ni·a (ĕn sē'nyə, -nī'ə), *n.pl.* 1. festive ceremonies commemorating the founding of a city or the consecration of a church. 2. (*cap.*) ceremonies at Oxford University in honor of founders and benefactors. [t. L, t. Gk.: m. *enkaínia* consecration feast]

en·cage (ĕn kāj'), *v.t.*, **-caged, -caging.** to confine in or as in a cage; coop up. Also, **incage.**

en·camp (ĕn kămp'), *v.i., v.t.* to settle or lodge in a camp.

en·camp·ment (ĕn kămp'mənt), *n.* 1. act of encamping; lodgment in a camp. 2. the place or quarters occupied in camping; a camp.

en·car·nal·ize (ĕn kär'nə līz'), *v.t.*, **-ized, -izing.** to invest with a carnal or fleshly form.

en·case (ĕn kās'), *v.t.*, **-cased, -casing.** incase.

en cas·se·role (än kàs rôl'), *French.* See **casserole** (def. 5).

en·caus·tic (ĕn kôs'tĭk), *adj.* 1. painted with wax colors fixed with heat, or with any process in which colors are burned in. —*n.* 2. a work of art produced by an encaustic process. [t. L: s. *encausticus* of burning in, t. Gk.: m. *enkaustikós*]

-ence, a noun suffix equivalent to -ance, and corresponding to -ent in adjectives, as in *abstinence, consistence, dependence, difference.* [t. F, alter. of *-ance* -ANCE by etymological assoc. with L *-entia* noun suffix]

en·ceinte¹ (ĕn sānt'; *Fr.* än sănt'), *adj.* pregnant; with child. [F, g. LL *incincta*, pp. fem., ungirt]

en·ceinte² (ĕn sānt'; *Fr.* än sănt'), *n.* 1. a wall or enclosure, as of a fortified place. 2. the place enclosed. [F, der. *enceindre*, g. L *incingere* enclose, as with a girdle]

en·ce·phal·ic (ĕn'sə făl'ĭk), *adj.* of or pertaining to the encephalon or brain.

en·ceph·a·li·tis (ĕn sĕf'ə lī'tĭs), *n. Pathol.* inflammation of the substance of the brain. [NL; see ENCEPHAL(O)-, -ITIS] —**en·ceph·a·lit·ic** (ĕn sĕf'ə līt'ĭk), *adj.*

encephalitis le·thar·gi·ca (lĭ thär'jə kə), sleeping sickness.

encephalo-, a word element meaning "brain," as in *encephalomyelitis.* Also, **encephal-.** [t. Gk., m. *enkephalo-*, comb. form of *enképhalos*]

en·ceph·a·lo·ma (ĕn sĕf'ə lō'mə), *n., pl.* **-mata** (-mə tə). *Pathol.* 1. a brain tumor. 2. hernia of the brain.

en·ceph·a·lo·my·e·li·tis (ĕn sĕf'ə lō mī'ə lī'təs), *n. Pathol., Vet. Sci.* any of several inflammatory diseases of the brain.

en·ceph·a·lon (ĕn sĕf'ə lŏn'), *n., pl.* **-la** (-lə). the brain. [NL, t. Gk.: (neut.) within the head, as n., the brain]

en·chain (ĕn chān'), *v.t.* 1. to fasten with or as with a chain or chains; fetter; restrain. 2. to hold fast, as the attention. [ME *encheinen*, t. OF: m. *enchainer*, der. en- EN-¹ + *chaine* CHAIN] —**en·chain'ment**, *n.*

en·chant (ĕn chănt', -chänt'), *v.t.* 1. to subject to magical influence; cast a spell over; bewitch. 2. to impart a magic quality or effect to. 3. to delight in a high degree; charm. [ME *enchaunt(en)*, t. OF: m. *enchanter*, g. L *incantāre* chant a magic formula against] —*Syn.* fascinate, captivate, enrapture, transport.

en·chant·er (ĕn chăn'tər, -chän'-), *n.* 1. one who enchants. 2. a magician.

en·chant·ing (ĕn chăn'tĭng, -chän'-), *adj.* charming; bewitching. —**en·chant'ing·ly**, *adv.*

en·chant·ment (ĕn chănt'mənt, -chänt'-), *n.* 1. act or art of enchanting. 2. that which enchants. —*Syn.* 1. magic, sorcery, fascination, witchery. 2. spell, charm.

en·chant·ress (ĕn chăn'trĭs, -chän'-), *n.* 1. a woman who enchants; a sorceress. 2. a fascinating woman.

en·chase (ĕn chās'), *v.t.*, **-chased, -chasing.** 1. to place (gems) in an ornamental setting. 2. to decorate with inlay, embossing, or engraving. [t. F: m. *enchâsser*, der. en- EN-¹ + *châsse* shrine (g. L *capsa* box. See CASE²)]

en·chi·rid·i·on (ĕn'kī rĭd'ē ən, -kī'-), *n., pl.* **-ridions, -ridia** (-rĭd'ī ə). a handbook; a manual. [t. Gk.: f. en- EN-² + m. *cheir* hand + *-idion*, dim. suffix]

en·chon·dro·ma (ĕn'kən drō'mə), *n., pl.* **-mata** (-mə tə), **-dromas.** *Pathol.* a tumor which consists essentially of cartilage. [EN-² + s. Gk. *chóndros* cartilage + -OMA] —**en·chon·drom·a·tous** (ĕn'kən drŏm'ə təs, -drō'mə-), *adj.*

en·cho·ri·al (ĕn kōr'ē əl), *adj.* (esp. of demotic writing) belonging to or used in a particular country; native; domestic. Also, **en·chor·ic** (ĕn kōr'ĭk, -kŏr'-). [f. s. Gk. *enchōrios* in or of a country + -AL¹]

en·cir·cle (ĕn sûr'kəl), *v.t.*, **-cled, -cling.** 1. to form a circle round; surround; encompass. 2. to make a circling movement about; make the circuit of. —**en·cir'cle·ment**, *n.* —*Syn.* 1. environ, gird, enfold, enclose.

encl., 1. enclosed. 2. enclosure.

en·clasp (ĕn klăsp', -kläsp'), *v.t.* to hold in or as in a clasp or embrace. Also, **inclasp.**

en·clave (ĕn'klāv; *Fr.* än klàv'), *n.* a country, or, esp., an outlying portion of a country, entirely or mostly surrounded by the territory of another country. [t. F, der. *enclaver* shut in, g. Rom. *inclāvāre*]

en·clit·ic (ĕn klĭt'ĭk), *adj.* 1. (of a word) so closely connected with a preceding word as to have no independent accent. —*n.* 2. an enclitic word, as *que* (and) in Latin: *arma virumque*, arms and the man. [t. LL: s. *encliticus*, t. Gk.: m. *enklitikós*, lit., leaning on] —**en·clit'i·cal·ly**, *adv.*

en·close (ĕn klōz'), *v.t.*, **-closed, -closing.** 1. to shut in; close in on all sides. 2. to surround as with a fence or wall: *to enclose land.* 3. to insert in the same envelope, etc., with the main letter, etc.: *he enclosed a check.* 4. to contain (the thing transmitted): *his letter enclosed a check.* Also, **inclose.** [f. EN-¹ + CLOSE, v., after OF *enclos*, pp. of *enclore*] —*Syn.* 1. surround, encircle, encompass.

en·clo·sure (ĕn klō'zhər), *n.* 1. act of enclosing. 2. the separation and appropriation of land by means of a fence. 3. a tract of land surrounded by a fence. 4. that which encloses, as a fence or wall. 5. that which is enclosed, as a paper sent in a letter. Also, **inclosure.**

en·co·mi·ast (ĕn kō'mĭ ăst'), *n.* one who utters or writes an encomium; a eulogist. [t. Gk.: s. *enkōmiastēs*]

en·co·mi·as·tic (ĕn kō'mĭ ăs'tĭk), *adj.* eulogistic.

en·co·mi·um (ĕn kō'mĭ əm), *n., pl.* **-miums, -mia** (-mĭ ə). a formal expression of praise; a eulogy. [t. L, t. Gk.: m. *enkōmion* eulogy, prop. neut. of *enkōmios* belonging to a Bacchic revel]

en·com·pass (ĕn kŭm'pəs), *v.t.* 1. to form a circle about; encircle; surround. 2. to enclose; contain. 3. *Obs.* to outwit. —**en·com'pass·ment**, *n.*

en·core (äng'kōr, än'-), *interj. n., v.*, **-cored, -coring.** —*interj.* 1. again; once more (used by an audience in calling for a repetition of a song, etc., or for an additional number or piece). —*n.* 2. a demand, as by applause, for a repetition of a song, etc., or for an additional number or piece. 3. that which is given in response to such a demand. —*v.t.* 4. to call for a repetition of. 5. to call for an encore from (a performer). [t. F: still, yet, besides, g. L *hanc hōram* within this hour]

en·coun·ter (ĕn koun'tər), *v.t.* 1. to come upon; meet with, esp. unexpectedly. 2. to meet with or contend against (difficulties, opposition, etc.). 3. to meet (a person, military force, etc.) in conflict. —*v.i.* 4. to meet, esp. in conflict. —*n.* 5. a meeting with a person or thing, esp. casually or unexpectedly. 6. a meeting in conflict or opposition; a battle; a combat. 7. *Obs.* manner of meeting; behavior. [ME *encountre(n)*, t. OF: m. *encontrer*, g. LL *incontrāre*, der. L *in-* IN-² + *contrā* against] —*Syn.* 6. conflict, skirmish.

en·cour·age (ĕn kûr'ĭj), *v.t.*, **-aged, -aging. 1.** to inspire with courage, spirit, or confidence. **2.** to stimulate by assistance, approval, etc. [ME *encorage(n)*, t. OF: m. *encoragier*, der. *en-*¹ + *corage* COURAGE] —**en·cour'ag·er,** *n.* —**en·cour'ag·ing·ly,** *adv.* —**Syn. 1.** inspirit, embolden, hearten. **2.** urge, abet, second; foment, promote, advance, foster. —**Ant. 1.** dishearten.

en·cour·age·ment (ĕn kûr'ĭj mənt), *n.* **1.** act of encouraging. **2.** state of being encouraged. **3.** that which encourages. —**Ant. 1.** disapproval. **2.** depression.

en·crim·son (ĕn krĭm'zən), *v.t.* to make crimson.

en·cri·nite (ĕn'krə nīt'), *n.* **1.** a fossil crinoid. **2.** any crinoid. [f. EN-² + m.s. Gk. *krínon* lily + -ITE¹]

en·croach (ĕn krōch'), *v.i.* **1.** to advance beyond proper limits; make gradual inroads. **2.** to trespass upon the property or rights of another, esp. stealthily or by gradual advances. [ME *encroche(n)*, t. OF: m. *encrochier*, der. *en-* EN-¹ + *croc* hook] —**en·croach'er,** *n.* —**Syn. 1, 2.** See **trespass.**

en·croach·ment (ĕn krōch'mənt), *n.* **1.** act of encroaching. **2.** anything taken by encroaching.

en·crust (ĕn krŭst'), *v.t.* incrust. —**en'crus·ta'tion,** *n.*

en·cum·ber (ĕn kŭm'bər), *v.t.* **1.** to impede or hamper; retard; embarrass. **2.** to block up or fill with what is obstructive or superfluous. **3.** to burden with obligations, debt, etc. Also, **incumber.** [ME *encombre(n)*, t. OF: m. *encombrer*, der. *en-* EN-¹ + *combre* barrier (g. LL *combrus*, t. Gallic: m. *comberos* a bringing together)] —**Syn. 3.** oppress, overload.

en·cum·brance (ĕn kŭm'brəns), *n.* **1.** that which encumbers; something useless or superfluous; a burden; a hindrance. **2.** a dependent person, esp. a child. **3.** *Law.* a burden or claim on property, as a mortgage. Also, **incumbrance.**

en·cum·branc·er (ĕn kŭm'brən sər), *n. Law.* one who holds an encumbrance.

-ency, a noun suffix, equivalent to **-ence,** as in *consistency, dependency, exigency.* [t. L: m.s. *-entia*]

ency., encyclopedia. Also, **encyc.**

en·cyc·li·cal (ĕn sĭk'lə kəl, -sī'klə-), *n.* **1.** a letter addressed by the Pope to all the bishops of the world in communion with the Holy See. —*adj.* **2.** intended for wide or general circulation; general. Also, **en·cyc'lic.** [f. s. LL *encyclicus* (r. L *encyclios*, t. Gk.: m. *enkýklios* circular, general) + -AL¹]

en·cy·clo·pe·di·a (ĕn sī'klə pē'dĭ ə), *n.* **1.** a work treating separately various topics from all branches of knowledge, usually in alphabetical arrangement. **2.** a work treating exhaustively one art or science, esp. in articles arranged alphabetically; a cyclopedia. **3.** (*cap.*) the French work edited by Diderot and D'Alembert, published in the 18th century, distinguished by its advanced or radical character. Also, **en·cy'clo·pae'di·a.** [t. LL, t. pseudo-Gk. (occurring in mss. of Quintilian, Pliny, and Galen): m. *enkyklopaideia,* for *enkýklios paideía* general education, complete round or course of learning. See ENCYCLIC, CYCLOPEDIA]

en·cy·clo·pe·dic (ĕn sī'klə pē'dĭk), *adj.* pertaining to or of the nature of an encyclopedia; relating to all branches of knowledge. Also, **en·cy'clo·pae'dic, en·cy'clo·pe'di·cal.**

en·cy·clo·pe·dism (ĕn sī'klə pē'dĭz əm), *n.* **1.** encyclopedic learning. **2.** (*often cap.*) the doctrines and influence of the Encyclopedists. Also, **en·cy'clo·pae'dism.**

en·cy·clo·pe·dist (ĕn sī'klə pē'dĭst), *n.* **1.** a compiler of or contributor to an encyclopedia. **2.** (*often cap.*) one of the collaborators in the French Encyclopedia. Also, **en·cy'clo·pae'dist.**

en·cyst (ĕn sĭst'), *v.t.*, *v.i. Biol.* to enclose or become enclosed in a cyst. —**en·cyst'ment, en'cys·ta'tion,** *n.*

end¹ (ĕnd), *n.* **1.** an extremity of anything that is longer than it is broad: *the end of a street, rope, rod, etc.* **2.** an extreme or furthermost part of anything extended in space: *the ends of the earth.* **3.** anything that bounds an object at one of its extremities; a limit. **4.** act of coming to an end; termination. **5.** the concluding part. **6.** a purpose or aim: *to gain one's ends.* **7.** the object for which a thing exists: *the happiness of the people is the end of government.* **8.** issue or result. **9.** termination of existence; death. **10.** a cause of death, destruction, or ruin. **11.** a remnant or fragment: *odds and ends.* **12.** *Football, etc.* either of the players at the ends of the forward line. **13.** at loose ends, in disorder. **14. make both ends meet,** to keep within one's means. —*v.t.* **15.** to bring to an end, or natural conclusion. **16.** to put an end to by force. **17.** to form the end of. —*v.i.* **18.** to come to an end; terminate; cease: *he ended by settling down.* **19.** to issue or result: *extravagance ends in want.* [ME and OE *ende,* c. G *ende.* See AND] —**end'er,** *n.* —**Syn. 3.** tip, bound, limit, terminus. **4.** END, CLOSE, CONCLUSION, FINISH, OUTCOME refer to the termination of something. END implies a natural termination, completion of an action or process, or attainment of purpose: *the end of a day, of a race, to some good end.* CLOSE implies a planned rounding off of something in process: *the close of a conference.* CONCLUSION suggests a decision or arrangement: *all evidence leads to this conclusion, the conclusion of peace terms.* FINISH emphasizes completion of something begun: *a fight to the finish.* OUTCOME suggests the issue or something which was in doubt: *the outcome of a game.* **5.** finale, peroration. **6.** See **aim. 8.** outcome, consequence. **9.** destruction, extermination, annihilation, ruin. **15.** conclude, finish, complete, terminate. **16.** close, stop, discontinue. —**Ant. 4.** beginning. start. **15.** begin.

end² (ĕnd), *v.t. Now Dial.* to put (wheat, hay, etc.) into a barn, stack, etc. [? var. of *inn* to lodge, der. INN]

end-, var. of **endo-,** before vowels, as in *endamoeba.*

en·dam·age (ĕn dăm'ĭj), *v.t.*, **-aged, -aging.** damage.

en·da·moe·ba (ĕn'də mē'bə), *n.* a protozoan, genus *Endamoeba,* one species of which causes dysentery and liver abscess. Also, **en'da·me'ba.** [f. END- + AMOEBA]

en·dan·ger (ĕn dān'jər), *v.t.* to expose to danger; imperil. —**en·dan'ger·ment,** *n.*

end-blown (ĕnd'blōn'), *adj.* (of a flute) having a mouthpiece at the end of the tube, so that the player's breath is directed into the instrument.

en·dear (ĕn dĭr'), *v.t.* **1.** to make dear, esteemed, or beloved: *he endeared himself to his mother.* **2.** *Obs.* to make costly. —**en·dear'ing·ly,** *adv.*

en·dear·ment (ĕn dĭr'mənt), *n.* **1.** act of endearing. **2.** state of being endeared. **3.** action or utterance manifesting affection; a caress or an affectionate term.

en·deav·or (ĕn dĕv'ər), *v.i.* **1.** to exert oneself to do or effect something; make an effort; strive. —*v.t.* **2.** to attempt; try: *he endeavors to keep things nice about his place.* —*n.* **3.** a strenuous effort; an attempt. Also, *Brit.,* **en·deav'our.** [ME *endeveren,* der. EN-¹ + DEVOIR. Cf. F *en devoir* in duty] —**en·deav'or·er,** *n.* —**Syn. 1, 2.** struggle, labor, essay, undertake, seek, aim. See **try. 3.** exertion, struggle, essay. See **effort.**

en·dem·ic (ĕn dĕm'ĭk), *adj.* **1.** Also, **en·dem'i·cal.** peculiar to a particular people or locality, as a disease. —*n.* **2.** an endemic disease. [f. s. Gk. *éndēmos* belonging to a people + -IC] —**en·dem'i·cal·ly,** *adv.*

En·der·by Land (ĕn'dər bī), a part of the coast of Antarctica, in the central part of the **Enderby Quadrant** (the quadrant below Africa): discovered, 1831.

en·der·mic (ĕn dûr'mĭk), *adj.* acting through the skin, as a medicine. [f. EN-² + DERM(A) + -IC]

en dés·ha·bil·lé (än dĕ zà bē yĕ'), French. in dishabille or undress.

En·di·cott (ĕn'dĭ kət, -kŏt'), *n.* **John,** 1588?-1665, colonial governor of Massachusetts, born in England. Also **En'de·cott.**

end·ing (ĕn'dĭng), *n.* **1.** a bringing or coming to an end; termination; close. **2.** the final or concluding part. **3.** death. **4.** *Gram.* an inflexional morpheme at the end of a word form, as *-s* in *cuts.* **5.** (in popular use) any final word part, as the *-ow* of *widow.* [ME; OE *endung*]

en·dive (ĕn'dīv, än'dēv; *Fr.* än dēv'), *n.* **1.** *U.S.* a plant, *Cichorium endivia,* of two main types, one with finely divided, much curled leaves and one with broad, fleshy leaves, both used for salads. **2.** *Brit.* chicory (defs. 1, 2). [ME. t. F, t. ML: m.s. *endivia,* t. MGk.: m. *endivi,* t. L: m. *intibus, intibum*]

end·less (ĕnd'lĭs), *adj.* **1.** having no end, limit, or conclusion; boundless; infinite; interminable; incessant. **2.** made continuous, as by joining the two ends of a single length: *an endless chain or belt.* —**end'less·ly,** *adv.* —**end'less·ness,** *n.* —**Syn. 1.** limitless, illimitable, immeasurable, unending, unceasing, continuous, continual, perpetual, everlasting. See **eternal.**

end·long (ĕnd'lông', -lŏng'), *adv. Archaic or Dial.* **1.** lengthwise. **2.** on end. [ME *endelong,* r. OE *andlang* ALONG]

end man, 1. a man at one end of a row or line. **2.** a man at either end of the line of performers of a minstrel troupe, who plays on the bones or tambourine and carries on humorous dialogue with the interlocutor.

end·most (ĕnd'mōst'), *adj.* furthest.

endo-, a word element meaning "internal," as in *endocardial.* Also, **end-.** [t. Gk., comb. form of *éndon* within]

en·do·blast (ĕn'dō blăst'), *n. Embryol.* the prospective endoderm; the blastemic cells which are to form the endoderm. —**en'do·blas'tic,** *adj.*

en·do·car·di·al (ĕn'dō kär'dĭ əl), *adj.* **1.** within the heart; intracardiac. **2.** pertaining to the endocardium.

en·do·car·di·tis (ĕn'dō kär dī'tĭs), *n. Pathol.* inflammation of the endocardium. [NL; f. ENDOCARD(IUM) + -ITIS] —**en·do·car·dit·ic** (ĕn'dō kär dĭt'ĭk), *adj.*

en·do·car·di·um (ĕn'dō kär'dĭ əm), *n. Anat.* the delicate serous membrane which lines the cavities of the heart and aids in forming the valves by duplication. [NL; f. *endo-* ENDO- + *-cardium* (comb. form repr. Gk. *kardía* heart)]

en·do·carp (ĕn'dō kärp'), *n. Bot.* the inner layer of a pericarp, as the stone of certain fruits.

Fruit of peach
A. Endocarp; B. Epicarp; C. Mesocarp; ABC. Pericarp

en·do·cen·tric construction (ĕn'dō sĕn'trĭk), a grammatical construction which contains as one of its immediate constituents a word or other form (called the *head*) which belongs to the same form class and may play the same grammatical role as the construction itself (opposed to *exocentric construction*). Example: *cold water* (having the noun *water* as head), or *good work* where both constituents as a unit function as the word *work* would alone.

en·do·crine (ĕn'dō krĭn', -krĭn), *n.* **1.** an endocrine gland or organ. **2.** an internal secretion. —*adj.* **3.** of or pertaining to the endocrine glands or their secretions: *endocrine function.* [f. ENDO- + m.s. Gk. *krínein* separate] —**en·do·cri·nal** (ĕn'dō krī'nəl), **en·do·crin·ic** (ĕn'dō krĭn'ĭk), **en·doc·ri·nous** (ĕn dŏk'rə nəs), *adj.*

en·do·crine gland, any of various glands or organs (as the thyroid gland, suprarenal bodies, pituitary body, etc.) which produce certain important internal secretions (products given up directly to the blood or lymph) acting upon particular organs, and which, through improper functioning, may cause grave disorders or death.

en·do·cri·nol·o·gy (ĕn′dō krĭ nŏl′ə jĭ̆, -krĭ́-), *n.* the science that deals with the endocrine glands, and their relation to bodily changes. —**en′do·cri·nol′o·gist,** *n.*

en·do·derm (ĕn′dō dûrm′), *n. Embryol.* the inner germ layer in the embryo of a metazoan. Also, **entoderm.** —**en′do·der′mal, en′do·der′mic,** *adj.*

en·dog·a·mous (ĕn dŏg′ə məs), *adj.* **1.** marrying customarily within the tribe or other social unit. **2.** pertaining to such marriage (opposed to *exogamous*). Also, **en·do·gam·ic** (ĕn′dō găm′ĭk).

en·dog·a·my (ĕn dŏg′ə mĭ̆), *n.* marriage within the tribe or other social unit, a custom among some savage peoples (opposed to *exogamy*).

en·do·gen (ĕn′də jĕn), *n. Bot.* any plant of the obsolete class *Endogenae,* including the monocotyledons, whose stems were erroneously supposed to grow from within.

en·dog·e·nous (ĕn dŏj′ə nəs), *adj.* **1.** *Biol.* growing or proceeding from within; originating within. **2.** *Physiol., Biochem.* pertaining to the anabolic processes of a cell. **3.** *Anat.* autogenous. —**en·dog′e·nous·ly,** *adv.*

en·do·lymph (ĕn′dō lĭmf′), *n. Anat.* the fluid contained within the membranous labyrinth of the ear.

en·do·morph (ĕn′dō môrf′), *n. Mineral.* a mineral enclosed within another mineral (opposed to *perimorph*).

en·do·mor·phic (ĕn′dō môr′fĭk), *adj. Mineral.* **1.** occurring in the form of an endomorph. **2.** of or relating to endomorphs. **3.** taking place within a rock mass.

en·do·mor·phism (ĕn′dō môr′fĭzəm), *n. Mineral.* a change brought about within the mass of an intrusive igneous rock.

en·do·par·a·site (ĕn′dō păr′ə sīt′), *n.* an internal parasite (opposed to *ectoparasite*).

en·do·pe·rid·i·um (ĕn′dō pĭ rĭd′ĭ əm), *n. Bot.* See peridium (def. 1).

en·do·phyte (ĕn′dō fīt′), *n. Bot.* a plant living within an animal or another plant, usually as a parasite.

en·do·plasm (ĕn′dō plăz′əm), *n. Biol.* **1.** the inner portion of the cytoplasm in the cell of a protozoan. **2.** the granular inner layer of cytoplasm in a vegetable cell (opposed to *ectoplasm*). —**en′do·plas′mic,** *adj.*

end organ, *Physiol.* one of several specialized structures found at the peripheral end of sensory or motor nerve fibers.

en·dorse (ĕn dôrs′), *v.t.,* **-dorsed, -dorsing. 1.** to approve, support, or sustain: *to endorse a statement.* **2.** to write (something) on the back of a document, etc. **3.** to designate oneself as payee of (a check) by signing, usually on the reverse side of the instrument. **4.** to sign one's name on (a commercial document or other instrument). **5.** to designate another as payee by one's endorsement. **6.** to acknowledge (payment) by placing one's signature on a bill, draft, etc. Also, **indorse.** [partial Latinization of ME *endosse,* t. OF: m. *endosser,* der. *en-* on + *dos* (g. L *dorsum* back)] —**en·dors′a·ble,** *adj.* —**en·dors′er, en·dor′sor,** *n.*

en·dor·see (ĕn dôr′sē′, ĕn′dôr-), *n.* one to whom a negotiable document is endorsed. Also, **indorsee.**

en·dorse·ment (ĕn dôrs′mənt), *n.* **1.** approval or sanction. **2.** the placing of one's signature, etc., on a document. **3.** the signature, etc., placed on the reverse of a commercial document which assigns the interest therein to another. **4.** *Insurance.* a clause under which the stated coverage of an insurance policy may be altered. Also, **indorsement.**

en·do·sarc (ĕn′dō särk′), *n. Biol.* the endoplasm of a protozoan (opposed to *ectosarc*).

en·do·scope (ĕn′də skōp′), *n. Med.* a slender tubular instrument used to examine the interior of a body cavity or hollow viscus. —**en·dos·co·py** (ĕn dŏs′kə pĭ̆), *n.*

en·do·skel·e·ton (ĕn′dō skĕl′ə tən), *n. Anat.* the internal skeleton or framework of the body of an animal (opposed to *exoskeleton*). —**en′do·skel′e·tal,** *adj.*

en·dos·mo·sis (ĕn′dŏs mō′sĭs, -dŏz-), *n. Phys. Chem.* **1.** osmosis from without inward. **2.** (in osmosis) the flow of that fluid which passes with the greater rapidity into the other (opposed to *exosmosis*). [NL] —**en·dos·mot·ic** (ĕn′dŏs mŏt′ĭk, -dŏz-), *adj.*

en·do·sperm (ĕn′dō spûrm′), *n. Bot.* nutritive matter in seed plant ovules, derived from the embryo sac.

en·do·spore (ĕn′dō spōr′), *n.* **1.** *Bot.* the inner coat of a spore. **2.** *Bacteriol.* a spore formed within a cell of a rod-shaped organism. —**en′dos·por·ous** (ĕn′dŏs′pər əs, ĕn dŏs′pər-), *adj.*

en·do·spo·ri·um (ĕn′dō spōr′ĭ əm), *n., pl.* **-sporia** (-spōr′ĭ ə). *Bot.* endospore (def. 1). [NL]

en·dos·te·um (ĕn dŏs′tĭ əm), *n., pl.* **-tea** (-tĭ ə). *Anat.* the vascular membrane lining the medullary cavity of a bone. [NL, f. Gk.: *end-* END- + m. *ostéon* bone]

en·dos·to·sis (ĕn′dŏs tō′sĭs), *n. Anat.* bone formation beginning in the substance of cartilage. [f. END(o)- + OSTOSIS]

en·do·the·ci·um (ĕn′dō thē′shĭ əm, -sĭ əm), *n., pl.* **-cia** (-shĭ ə, -sĭ ə). *Bot.* **1.** the lining of the cavity of an anther. **2.** (in mosses) the central mass of cells in the

rudimentary capsule, from which the archespore is generally developed. **3.** (in bryophytes) the central mass of cells in the capsule, including the spores and columella. [NL, f. Gk.: *endo-* ENDO- + m. *thēkíon* little case]

en·do·the·li·al (ĕn′dō thē′lĭ əl), *adj.* pertaining to endothelium.

en·do·the·li·oid (ĕn′dō thē′lĭ oid′), *adj.* resembling endothelium.

en·do·the·li·o·ma (ĕn′dō thē′lĭ ō′mə), *n., pl.* **-mata** (-mə tə), **-mas.** *Pathol.* a tumor (malignant or benign) originating from the endothelium. [f. ENDOTHELI(UM) + -OMA]

en·do·the·li·um (ĕn′dō thē′lĭ əm), *n., pl.* **-lia** (-lĭ ə). *Anat.* the tissue which lines blood vessels, lymphatics, serous cavities, and the like: a form of epithelium (in the broad sense). [NL, f. Gk.: *endo-* ENDO- + s. *thēlē* nipple + m. *-ion*]

en·do·ther·mic (ĕn′dō thûr′mĭk), *adj.* noting or pertaining to a chemical change which is accompanied by an absorption of heat (opposed to *exothermic*).

en·do·tox·in (ĕn′dō tŏk′sĭn), *n.* the toxic protoplasm of an organism which is liberated and causes its toxic action when the organism dies and disintegrates, as in *Eberthella typhi,* the causative agent of typhoid fever.

en·dow (ĕn dou′), *v.t.* **1.** to provide with a permanent fund or source of income: *to endow a college.* **2.** to furnish, as with some gift, faculty, or quality; equip: *Nature has endowed him with great ability.* **3.** *Archaic.* to provide with dower. [ME *endow(en),* t. OF: m. *endouer,* f. *en-* EN-[1] + *douer,* g. L *dōtāre* endow] —**en·dow′er,** *n.* —**Syn. 2.** invest, clothe, endue.

en·dow·ment (ĕn dou′mənt), *n.* **1.** act of endowing. **2.** that with which an institution, person, etc., is endowed, as property or funds. **3.** (*usually pl.*) an attribute of mind or body; a gift of nature. —**Syn.** capacity, talent, faculties.

endowment insurance, a form of insurance providing for the payment of a fixed sum to the insured person at a specified time, or to his heirs, or a person designated, should he die before the time named.

end product, final or resulting product.

en·due (ĕn dū′, -dōō′), *v.t.,* **-dued, -duing. 1.** to invest or endow with some gift, quality, or faculty: *endued with life.* **2.** to put on; assume. **3.** to clothe (fol. by *with*). Also, **indue.** [ME *endew(en),* t. OF: m. *enduire,* g. L *indūcere* lead into, confused with L *induere* put on]

en·dur·a·ble (ĕn dyŏōr′ə bəl, -dōōr′-), *adj.* that may be endured. —**en·dur′a·bly,** *adv.* —**Syn.** bearable, tolerable.

en·dur·ance (ĕn dyŏōr′əns, -dōōr′-), *n.* **1.** fact or power of enduring or bearing anything. **2.** lasting quality; duration. **3.** something endured, as a hardship. —**Syn. 1.** See **patience.**

en·dure (ĕn dyŏōr′, -dōōr′), *v.,* **-dured, -during.** —*v.t.* **1.** to hold out against; sustain without impairment or yielding; undergo. **2.** to bear without resistance or with patience; tolerate: *I cannot endure to listen to that any longer.* —*v.i.* **3.** to continue to exist; last. **4.** to support adverse force or influence of any kind; suffer without yielding; suffer patiently. [ME *endure(n).* t. OF: m. *endurer,* g. L *indūrāre* harden, ML *endure*] —**Syn. 2.** experience, stand. See **bear**[1]. **3.** abide, remain, persist. See **continue.**

en·dur·ing (ĕn dyŏōr′ĭng, -dōōr′-), *adj.* that endures; lasting; permanent. —**en·dur′ing·ly,** *adv.* —**en·dur′ing·ness,** *n.*

end·ways (ĕnd′wāz′), *adv.* **1.** on end. **2.** with the end upward or forward. **3.** toward the ends or end; lengthwise. **4.** end to end. Also, **end·wise** (ĕnd′wīz′).

En·dym·i·on (ĕn dĭm′ĭ ən), *n. Gk. Myth.* a beautiful youth whom Selene caressed as he slept.

-ene, 1. a noun suffix used in chemistry, in names of hydro-carbons, as *anthracene, benzene, napthhalene,* specif. those of the olefine or ethylene series, as *butylene.* **2.** a generalized suffix used in trademarks for substances, often implying synthetic manufacture. [special use of *-ene,* adj. suffix (as in *terrene),* t. L: m. s. *-ēnus* (in Gk. *-ēnos*)]

ENE, east-northeast. Also, **E.N.E.**

en·e·ma (ĕn′ə mə), *n., pl.* **enemas, enemata** (ĕ nĕm′ə tə). *Med.* a fluid injected into the rectum. [t. Gk.: injection, clyster]

en·e·my (ĕn′ə mĭ̆), *n., pl.* **-mies,** *adj.* —*n.* **1.** one who cherishes hatred or harmful designs against another; an adversary or opponent. **2.** an armed foe; an opposing military force. **3.** a hostile nation or state. **4.** a subject of such a state. **5.** something harmful or prejudicial. —*adj.* **6.** belonging to a hostile power or to any of its nationals: *enemy property.* **7.** *Obs.* inimical; ill-disposed. [ME, t. OF: m. *enemi,* g. L *inimicus* unfriendly, hostile] —**Syn. 1.** ENEMY, FOE refer to a dangerous public or personal adversary. ENEMY emphasizes the idea of hostility: *to overcome the enemy, a bitter enemy.* FOE, a more literary word, may be used interchangeably with ENEMY, but emphasizes somewhat more the danger to be feared from such a one: *deadly foe, arch foe of mankind* (the Devil). —**Ant. 1.** friend. **2.** ally.

en·er·get·ic (ĕn′ər jĕt′ĭk), *adj.* **1.** possessing or exhibiting energy; forcible; vigorous. **2.** powerful in action or effect; effective. [t. Gk.: m.s. *energētikós* active] —**en′er·get′i·cal·ly,** *adv.* —**Syn. 1.** See **active.** —**Ant. 1.** listless.

en·er·get·ics (ĕn′ər jĕt′ĭks), *n.* the science of the laws of energy. [pl. of ENERGETIC. See -ICS]

en·er·gize (ĕn'ər jīz'), v., **-gized, -gizing.** —v.t. 1. to give energy to; rouse into activity. —v.i. 2. to be in operation; put forth energy. —**en'er·giz'er,** n.

en·er·gu·men (ĕn'ər gū'mən), n. 1. one possessed by an evil spirit; a demoniac. 2. a fanatical enthusiast. [t. LL: s. energūmenus, t. Gk.: m. energoúmenos, ppr. pass. of energein operate, influence]

en·er·gy (ĕn'ər jĭ), n., pl. **-gies.** 1. capacity or habit of vigorous activity. 2. the actual exertion of power; operation; activity. 3. power as exerted. 4. ability to produce action or effect. 5. vigor or forcefulness of expression. 6. Physics. the property of a system which diminishes, when the system does work on any other system, by an amount equal to the work so done. [t. LL: m.s. energīa, t. Gk.: m. enérgeia agency, force] —**Syn.** 1. vigor, force, potency, zeal, push.

en·er·vate (v. ĕn'ər vāt'; adj. ĭ nûr'vĭt), v., **-vated, -vating,** adj. —v.t. 1. to deprive of nerve, force, or strength; destroy the vigor of; weaken. —adj. 2. enervated. [t. L: m.s. ēnervātus, pp.] —**en'er·va'tion,** n. —**en'er·va'tor,** n.

en·face (ĕn fās'), v.t., **-faced, -facing.** 1. to write, print, or stamp something on the face of (a note, draft, etc.). 2. to write, print, or stamp (something) on the face of a note, draft, etc. —**en·face'ment,** n.

en fa·mille (än fà mē'y), French. in the family.

en·fants per·dus (än fän pĕr dȳ'), French. a suicide squad or rear guard of soldiers. [F: lit., lost children]

en·fant ter·ri·ble (än fän tĕ rē'bl), French. 1. a child that makes embarrassing remarks. 2. an indiscreet and irresponsible person. [F: lit., terrible child]

en·fee·ble (ĕn fē'bəl), v.t., **-bled, -bling.** to make feeble; weaken. [ME enfeble(n), t. OF: m. enfeblir, der. en- EN-¹ + feble FEEBLE] —**en·fee'ble·ment,** n. —**en·fee'bler,** n.

en·feoff (ĕn fĕf', -fēf'), v.t. 1. to invest with a fief or fee. 2. to give as a fief. 3. to surrender. [ME enfeoffe(n), t. AF: m. enfeoffer. See EN-¹, FIEF] —**en·feoff'ment,** n.

en fête (än fĕt'), French. in festivity; in gala attire.

en·fet·ter (ĕn fĕt'ər), v.t. to bind with or as with fetters.

En·field (ĕn'fēld'), n. a city in SE England, in Middlesex, near London. 110,458 (1951).

en·fi·lade (ĕn'fə lād'), n., v., **-laded, -lading.** Mil. —n. 1. a situation of works, troops, etc., making them subject to a sweeping fire from along the length of a line of troops, a trench, a battery, etc. 2. the fire thus directed. —v.t. 3. to attack with an enfilade. [t. F, der. enfiler to thread, string, go through, rake with fire, der. en- EN-¹ + fil a thread]

en·fin (än fän'), adv. French. in conclusion; finally.

en·fleu·rage (än flœ räzh'), n. a process of extracting perfumes by exposing inodorous oils or fats to the exhalations of flowers. [t. F, der. enfleurer impregnate with the scent of flowers, der. en- EN-¹ + fleur flower]

en·fold (ĕn fōld'), v.t. infold. —**en·fold'er,** n. —**en·fold'ment,** n.

en·force (ĕn fōrs'), v.t., **-forced, -forcing.** 1. to put or keep in force; compel obedience to: to enforce laws or rules. 2. to obtain (payment, obedience, etc.) by force or compulsion. 3. to impose (a course of action) upon a person; support (a demand, etc.) by force. 4. to impress or urge (an argument, etc.) forcibly; lay stress upon. [ME enforce(n), t. OF: m. enforcier, ult. der. L. in- IN-¹ + fortis strong] —**en·force'a·ble,** adj. —**en·for·ced·ly** (ĕn fōr'sĭd lĭ), adv. —**en·forc'er,** n.

en·force·ment (ĕn fōrs'mənt), n. 1. act or process of enforcing. 2. Archaic. that which enforces.

en·fran·chise (ĕn frăn'chīz), v.t., **-chised, -chising.** 1. to grant a franchise to; admit to citizenship, esp. to the right of voting. 2. to set free; liberate, as from slavery. [t. MF: m. enfranchiss-, s. enfranchir, der. en- EN-¹ + franc free, FRANK] —**en·fran·chise·ment** (ĕn frăn'chĭz mənt), n. —**en·fran'chis·er,** n.

Eng., 1. England. 2. English.

eng., 1. engine. 2. engineer. 3. engineering. 4. engraved. 5. engraver. 6. engraving.

En·ga·dine (ĕn'gə dēn'), n. the valley of the Inn river in E Switzerland: resorts. ab. 60 mi. long.

en·gage (ĕn gāj'), v., **-gaged, -gaging.** —v.t. 1. to occupy the attention or efforts of (a person, etc.): he engaged her in conversation. 2. to secure for aid, employment, use, etc.; hire: to engage a workman, to engage a room. 3. to attract and hold fast: to engage the attention, interest, etc. 4. to attract or please: his good nature engages everybody to him. 5. to bind as by pledge, promise, contract, or oath; make liable: he engaged, verbally or by writing, to do it. 6. to betroth (usually used in the passive). 7. to bring (troops) into conflict; enter into conflict with: our army engaged the enemy. 8. Mech. to cause to become interlocked; interlock with. 9. Archaic. to entangle or involve. 10. Archaic. to attach or secure. —v.i. 11. to occupy oneself; become involved: to engage in business, politics. 12. to take employment. 13. to pledge one's word; assume an obligation. 14. to cross weapons; enter into conflict. 15. Mech. to interlock. [t. F: s. engager, der. en- EN-¹ + gage pledge, GAGE¹] —**en·gag'er,** n. —**Ant.** 2. discharge. 8. release.

en·gaged (ĕn gājd'), adj. 1. busy or occupied; involved. 2. under engagement; pledged. 3. betrothed. 4. entered into conflict with. 5. Mech. a. interlocked. b. (of wheels) in gear with each other. 6. Archit. secured to, or (actually or apparently) partly sunk into, something else, as a column with respect to a wall.

en·gage·ment (ĕn gāj'mənt), n. 1. act of engaging. 2. state of being engaged. 3. a pledge; an obligation or agreement. 4. betrothal. 5. employment, or a period or post of employment. 6. an affair of business. 7. an encounter, conflict, or battle. 8. Mech. act or state of interlocking. 9. (pl.) Com. financial obligations. —**Syn.** 3. contract, promise.

en·gag·ing (ĕn gāj'ĭng), adj. winning; attractive; pleasing. —**en·gag'ing·ly,** adv. —**en·gag'ing·ness,** n.

en gar·çon (än gàr sôn'), French. as a bachelor.

en·gar·land (ĕn gär'lənd), v.t. encircle with a garland.

En·gels (ĕng'əls for 1; ĕng'gĕls for 2), n. 1. **Friedrich** (frē'drĭкн), 1820–95, German socialist writer in England, associated with Karl Marx. 2. a city in the E Soviet Union in Europe, on the Volga. 80,000 (est. 1948).

en·gen·der (ĕn jĕn'dər), v.t. 1. to produce, cause, or give rise to: hatred engenders violence. 2. to beget; procreate. —v.i. 3. to be produced or caused; come into existence. [ME engendre(n), t. OF: m. engendrer, g. L ingenerāre beget] —**en·gen'der·er,** n. —**en·gen'der·ment,** n. —**Syn.** 1. create, occasion, excite, stir up.

En·ghien (dän găn'; Belg. -gyän'), n. **Duc d',** (Louis Antoine Henry de Bourbon-Condé) 1772–1804, French prince, executed by Napoleon I.

engin., engineering.

en·gine (ĕn'jən), n. 1. any mechanism or machine designed to convert energy into mechanical work: a steam engine, internal-combustion engine, etc. 2. a railroad locomotive. 3. any mechanical contrivance. 4. a machine or instrument used in warfare, as a battering ram, catapult, piece of artillery, etc. 5. Obs. an instrument of torture, esp. the rack. [ME engin, t. OF, g. L ingenium nature, invention]

engine driver, Brit. an engineer on a locomotive.

en·gi·neer (ĕn'jə nīr'), n. 1. one versed in the design, construction, and use of engines or machines, or in any of the various branches of engineering: a mechanical engineer, an electrical, civil, etc., engineer. 2. one who manages a stationary or locomotive engine. 3. a member of the army or navy especially trained in engineering work. 4. a skillful manager. —v.t. 5. to plan, construct, or manage as an engineer. 6. to arrange, manage, or carry through by skillful or artful contrivance.

en·gi·neer·ing (ĕn'jə nīr'ĭng), n. 1. the art or science of making practical application of the knowledge of pure sciences such as physics, chemistry, biology, etc. 2. the action, work, or profession of an engineer. 3. skillful or artful contrivance; maneuvering.

engineer's chain. See chain (def. 9).

engine house, a building in which a fire engine is stationed.

en·gi·ne·ry (ĕn'jən rĭ), n. 1. engines collectively. 2. engines of war. 3. skillful or artful contrivance.

en·gird (ĕn gûrd'), v.t., **-girt** or **-girded, -girding.** to encircle; encompass.

en·gir·dle (ĕn gûr'dəl), v.t., **-dled, -dling.** to engird.

en·gla·cial (ĕn glā'shəl), adj. Geol. 1. within the ice of a glacier. 2. believed to have been formerly within the ice of a glacier: englacial debris.

Eng·land (ĭng'glənd), n. the largest division of the United Kingdom, occupying all of the island of Great Britain except Scotland and Wales. 44,090,000 pop. (est. 1953); 50,327 sq. mi. Cap.: London. Latin, **Anglia.** [ME Engeland, OE Englaland land of the English]

Eng·land·er (ĭng'glən dər), n. a native of England.

Eng·lish (ĭng'glĭsh), adj. 1. of, pertaining to, or characteristic of England or its inhabitants, institutions, etc. 2. belonging or pertaining to, or spoken or written in, the English language. —n. 3. the people of England collectively, esp. as distinguished from the Scotch, Welsh, and Irish. 4. the Germanic language of the British Isles, widespread and standard also in the U.S. and most of the British Empire, historically termed Old English or Anglo-Saxon (to 1150), Middle English (to 1450), and Modern English. 5. (l.c.) U.S. Billiards. a spinning motion imparted to a ball by a quick stroke on one side of its center. 6. a printing type (14 point) of a size between pica and Columbian. —v.t. 7. to translate into English. 8. to adopt (a foreign word) into English. 9. (l.c.) U.S. Billiards. to impart english to (a ball). [ME; OE Englisc, der. Engle, Angle the English. See ANGLE]

English Channel, an arm of the Atlantic between England and France, connected with the North Sea by the Strait of Dover. ab. 350 mi. long; 20–100 mi. wide.

English daisy, Chiefly U.S. the common European daisy, Bellis perennis.

English horn, the alto of the oboe family, richer in tone and a fifth lower in pitch than the oboe.

Eng·lish·ism (ĭng'glĭsh ĭz'əm), n. 1. a Briticism. 2. attachment to what is English.

English ivy. See ivy (def. 1).

Eng·lish·man (ĭng'glĭsh mən), n., pl. **-men.** 1. a native or a naturalized citizen of England. 2. an English ship.

Man playing an English horn

Englishman's tie, Naut. a method of tying two rope ends or pieces of gut together by making an overhand knot in each around the other.

b., blend of, blended; c., cognate with; d., dialect, dialectal; der., derived from; f., formed from; g., going back to; m., modification of; r., replacing; s., stem of; t., taken from; ?, perhaps. See the full key on inside cover.

Eng·lish·ness (ĭng′glĭsh nĭs), *n.* quality of being English.

English Pale. See **pale** (def. 6).

English Revolution, The, *Eng. Hist.* the convulsion of 1688–89 by which James II was expelled and the sovereignty conferred on William and Mary.

Eng·lish·ry (ĭng′glĭsh rĭ), *n.* **1.** state of being English. **2.** a population that is English or of English descent.

English setter, a type of setter dog, usually black and white, tan and white, or pure white, with a rangy body.

English setter
(23 to 25 in. high)

English sonnet, the Elizabethan or Shakespearean sonnet.

English sparrow, sparrow (def. 1).

English walnut, 1. a walnut tree, *Juglans regia.* **2.** the nut of this tree, widely used in cookery.

Eng·lish·wom·an (ĭng′glĭsh wŏŏm′ən), *n., pl.* **-wom·en.** a woman who is a native or citizen of England.

en·gorge (ĕn gôrj′), *v.t.,* **-gorged, -gorging. 1.** to swallow greedily; glut or gorge. **2.** *Pathol.* to congest with blood. [t. F: m.s. *engorger,* der. en- EN-¹ + gorge GORGE] **—en·gorge′ment,** *n.*

engr., 1. engineer. **2.** engraved. **3.** engraver.

en·graft (ĕn grăft′, -gräft′), *v.t.* to insert, as a scion of one tree or plant into another, for propagation: *to engraft a peach on a plum.* Also, **ingraft.**

en·grail (ĕn grāl′), *v.t.* to ornament the edge of with curved indentations. [ME *engrele(n),* t. OF: m. *engresler,* der. en- EN-¹ + *gresle* hail] **—en·grail′ment,** *n.*

en·grain (ĕn grān′), *v.t., adj.* ingrain. [ME, f. EN-¹ + GRAIN. Cf. F *en graine* where *graine* means cochineal dye]

en·gram (ĕn′grăm), *n.* **1.** *Biol.* the durable mark caused by a stimulus upon protoplasm. **2.** *Psychol.* trace¹ (def. 6).

en·grave (ĕn grāv′), *v.t.,* **-graved, -graving. 1.** to chase (letters, designs, etc.) on a hard surface, as of metal, stone, or the end grain of wood. **2.** to print from such a surface. **3.** to mark or ornament with incised letters, designs, etc. **4.** to impress deeply; infix. [f. EN-¹ + GRAVE³, v., modeled on F *engraver*] **—en·grav′er,** *n.*

en·grav·ing (ĕn grā′vĭng), *n.* **1.** the act or art of one that engraves. **2.** the art of forming designs by cutting, corrosion by acids, a photographic process, etc., on the surface of metal plates or of blocks of wood, etc., for purpose of taking off impressions or prints of the design so formed. **3.** the design engraved. **4.** an engraved plate or block. **5.** an impression or print from this.

en·gross (ĕn grōs′), *v.t.* **1.** to occupy wholly, as the mind or attention; absorb. **2.** to write or copy in a fair, large hand or in a formal manner, as a public document or record. **3.** to acquire the whole of (a commodity), in order to control the market; monopolize. [ME *engross-(en),* t. AF: m. *engrosser* write large; also t. OF, der. *en gros* in large quantities, g. L *in-* IN-² + LL *grossus* thick, GROSS] **—en·gross′er,** *n.*

en·gross·ing (ĕn grō′sĭng), *adj.* fully occupying the mind or attention; absorbing. **—en·gross′ing·ly,** *adv.*

en·gross·ment (ĕn grōs′mənt), *n.* **1.** act of engrossing. **2.** an engrossed copy of a document.

en·gulf (ĕn gŭlf′), *v.t.* to swallow up in or as in a gulf; submerge. Also, **ingulf. —en·gulf′ment,** *n.*

en·hance (ĕn hăns′, -häns′), *v.t.,* **-hanced, -hancing. 1.** to raise to a higher degree; intensify; magnify. **2.** to raise the value or price of. [ME *enhaunce(n),* t. AF: m. *enhauncier,* nasalized var. of OF *enhaucier,* f. en- EN-¹ + *haucier* raise. See HAWSER.] **—en·hance′ment,** *n.* **—en·hanc′er,** *n.* **—Syn. 2.** See **elevate. —Ant.** **1.** diminish. **2.** reduce.

en·har·mon·ic (ĕn′härmŏn′ĭk), *adj. Music.* having the same pitch in the tempered scale but written in different notation, as G-sharp and A-flat. [t. LL: s. *enharmonicus* in accord, t. Gk.: m. *enarmonikós*] **—en′har·mon′i·cal·ly,** *adv.*

E·nid (ē′nĭd), *n.* **1.** a city in N Oklahoma. 38,859 (1960). **2.** *Arthurian Romance.* the beautiful wife of Sir Geraint in Tennyson's *Idylls of the King.*

e·nig·ma (ĭ nĭg′mə), *n.* **1.** something puzzling or inexplicable. **2.** a saying, question, picture, etc., containing a hidden meaning; a riddle. [t. L: m. *aenigma,* t. Gk.: m. *ainigma* riddle] **—Syn. 1.** See **puzzle.**

en·ig·mat·ic (ĕn′ĭg măt′ĭk, ē′nĭg-), *adj.* resembling an enigma; perplexing; mysterious. Also, **en′ig·mat′i·cal. —en′ig·mat′i·cal·ly,** *adv.*

en·isle (ĕn īl′), *v.t.,* **-isled, -isling.** *Poetic.* **1.** to make an island of. **2.** to place on an island. **3.** to isolate.

en·jamb·ment (ĕn jăm′mənt, -jämb′-; *Fr.* än zhänb-mäN′), *n. Pros.* the running on of the thought from one line or couplet to the next. Also, **en·jambe′ment.** [t. F: m. *enjambement,* der. *enjamber* stride over, project, der. en- EN-¹ + *jambe* leg]

en·join (ĕn join′), *v.t.* **1.** to order or direct (a person, etc.) to do something; prescribe (a course of action, etc.) with authority or emphasis. **2.** *Law.* to prohibit or restrain by an injunction. [ME *enjoyn(en),* t. OF: m. *enjoindre,* g. L *injungere* join into or to, impose, enjoin] **—en·join′er,** *n.* **—en·join′ment,** *n.* **—Syn. 1.** charge.

en·joy (ĕn joi′), *v.t.* **1.** to experience with joy; take pleasure in. **2.** to have and use with satisfaction; have

the benefit of. **3.** to find or experience pleasure for (oneself). [ME *enjoye(n),* t. OF: m. *enjoir,* f. en- EN-¹ + *joir* JOY, v.] **—en·joy′er,** *n.*

en·joy·a·ble (ĕn joi′ə bəl), *adj.* that may be enjoyed; affording enjoyment. **—en·joy′a·ble·ness,** *n.* **—en·joy′a·bly,** *adv.*

en·joy·ment (ĕn joi′mənt), *n.* **1.** the possession, use, or occupancy of anything with satisfaction or pleasure. **2.** a particular form or source of pleasure. **3.** *Law.* the exercise of a right: *the enjoyment of an estate.* **—Syn. 1.** delight, delectation, gratification. See **pleasure.**

en·kin·dle (ĕn kĭn′dəl), *v.t., v.i.,* **-dled, -dling.** to kindle into flame, ardor, activity, etc. **—en·kin′dler,** *n.*

enl., enlarged.

en·lace (ĕn lās′), *v.t.* **-laced, -lacing. 1.** to bind or encircle as with a lace or cord. **2.** to interlace; intertwine. [ME *enlase(n),* t. F: m. *enlacer,* f. en- EN-¹ + *lacier* LACE, v.] **—en·lace′ment,** *n.*

en·large (ĕn lärj′), *v.,* **-larged, -larging. —v.t. 1.** to make larger; increase in extent, bulk, or quantity; add to. **2.** to increase the capacity or scope of; expand. **3.** *Photog.* to make (a print) larger than the negative, by projection printing. **—v.i. 4.** to grow larger; increase; expand. **5.** to speak or write at large; expatiate: *to enlarge upon a point.* [ME *enlargen,* t. OF: m. *enlarger,* der. en- EN-¹ + *large* LARGE] **—en·large′a·ble,** *adj.* **—en·larg′er,** *n.* **—Syn. 1.** extend, augment, amplify, dilate. See **increase. —Ant. 1.** diminish. **2.** contract.

en·large·ment (ĕn lärj′mənt), *n.* **1.** act of enlarging; increase; expansion; amplification. **2.** anything, as a photograph, that is an enlarged form of something else. **3.** anything that enlarges something else; an addition.

en·light·en (ĕn lī′tən), *v.t.* **1.** to give intellectual or spiritual light to; instruct; impart knowledge to. **2.** *Archaic and Poetic.* to shed light upon. **—en·light′en·er,** *n.* **—Syn. 1.** illumine, edify, teach, inform.

en·light·en·ment (ĕn lī′tən mənt), *n.* **1.** act of enlightening. **2.** state of being enlightened. **3. the Enlightenment,** an 18th century philosophical movement characterized by rationalism.

en·list (ĕn lĭst′), *v.i.* **1.** to engage for military or naval service by enrolling after mutual agreement. **2.** to enter into some cause, enterprise, etc. **—v.t. 3.** to engage for military or naval service: *to enlist men for the army.* **4.** to secure (a person, services, etc.) for some cause, enterprise, etc. **—en·list′er,** *n.*

enlisted man, any male member of the U. S. armed services who is not a commissioned officer or a warrant officer, nurse, or cadet.

en·list·ment (ĕn lĭst′mənt), *n.* **1.** the period of years for which a man or woman engages to serve in the armed forces of his country. **2.** act of enlisting.

en·liv·en (ĕn lī′vən), *v.t.* **1.** to make vigorous or active; invigorate. **2.** to make sprightly, gay, or cheerful; brighten. [f. obs. *enlive* enliven (der. EN-¹ + LIVE, adj.) + -EN¹] **—en·liv′en·er,** *n.* **—en·liv′en·ment,** *n.* **—Syn. 1.** animate, inspirit, vivify, stimulate, quicken. **2.** exhilarate, gladden. See **cheer. —Ant. 2.** depress.

en masse (ĕn măs′; *Fr.* än mås′), French. in a mass or body; all together.

en·mesh (ĕn mĕsh′), *v.t.* to catch, as in a net; entangle. Also, **immesh, inmesh.**

en·mi·ty (ĕn′mə tĭ), *n., pl.* **-ties.** a feeling or condition of hostility; hatred; ill will; animosity; antagonism. [ME *enemyte,* t. OF: m. *ennemistie,* der. L *inimicus* enemy]

en·ne·ad (ĕn′ĭ ăd′), *n.* **1.** a group of nine persons or things. **2.** *(cap.)* nine gods in Egyptian religion. [t. Gk.: s. *ennéas,* der. *ennéa* nine] **—en′ne·ad′ic,** *adj.*

En·ni·us (ĕn′ĭ əs), *n.* **Quintus** (kwĭn′təs), 239–169? B.C., Roman poet.

en·no·ble (ĕn nō′bəl), *v.t.,* **-bled, -bling. 1.** to elevate in degree, excellence, or respect; dignify; exalt. **2.** to confer a title of nobility on. **—en·no′ble·ment,** *n.* **—en·no′bler,** *n.*

en·nui (än′wē; *Fr.* än nwē′), *n.* a feeling of weariness and discontent resulting from satiety or lack of interest; boredom. [t. F, g. L *in odiō.* See ANNOY, n.]

E·noch (ē′nək), *n. Bible.* **1.** the father of Methuselah. Gen. 5: 18–24. **2.** the eldest son of Cain. Gen. 4:17, 18.

e·nol (ē′nōl, ē′nŏl), *n. Chem.* an organic compound containing a hydroxyl group attached to a doubly linked carbon atom as in C=C-OH. [appar. f. Gk. *(h)én* (neut. of *hets* one) + -OL¹] **—e·nol·ic** (ē nŏl′ĭk), *adj.*

e·nor·mi·ty (ĭ nôr′mə tĭ), *n., pl.* **-ties. 1.** outrageous or heinous character; atrociousness: *the enormity of his offenses.* **2.** something outrageous or heinous, as an offense. [t. L: m.s. *ēnormitas* hugeness, irregularity]

e·nor·mous (ĭ nôr′məs), *adj.* **1.** greatly exceeding the common size, extent, etc.; huge; immense. **2.** outrageous or atrocious: *enormous wickedness.* [t. L: m.s. *ēnormis* huge] **—e·nor′mous·ly,** *adv.* **—e·nor′mous·ness,** *n.* **—Syn. 1.** vast, colossal, gigantic, mammoth, prodigious, stupendous. See **huge.**

E·nos (ē′nŏs), *n. Bible.* the son of Seth. Gen. 5:6.

e·nough (ĭ nŭf′), *adj.* **1.** adequate for the want or need; sufficient for the purpose or to satisfy desire: *I've had enough of it, noise enough to wake the dead.* **—n. 2.** an adequate quantity or number; a sufficiency. **—adv. 3.** in a quantity or degree that answers a purpose or satisfies a need or desire; sufficiently. **4.** fully or quite: *ready enough.* **5.** tolerably or passably: *he sings well enough.* **—interj. 6.** it (or that) is enough! [ME *enogh,* OE *genōh,* c. G *genug*]

e·nounce (ĭ nouns′), *v.t.*, **enounced, enouncing. 1.** to announce, declare, or proclaim. **2.** to state definitely, as a proposition. **3.** to utter or pronounce, as words. [t. F: m.s. *énoncer*, t. L: n. *nuntiāre*] **—e·nounce′ment,** *n.*

e·now (ĭ nou′; *formerly* ĭ nō′), *adj., adv.* Archaic. enough. [ME; OE *genŏg(e)* enough]

en pas·sant (än pä säN′), *French.* **1.** in passing; by the way. **2.** Chess. a method of taking a pawn. When, on moving a pawn two squares, an adversary's pawn is in a position to take the pawn moved if it were moved but one square, the moving pawn may be taken *en passant.*

en·plane (ĕn plān′), *v.i.*, **-planed, -planing.** to enter an airplane.

en prise (äN prēz′), *French.* (in chess) in line for capture; likely to be captured.

en·quire (ĕn kwīr′), *v.t., v.i.*, **-quired, -quiring.** inquire.

en·quir·y (ĕn kwīr′ĭ), *n., pl.* **-quiries.** inquiry.

en·rage (ĕn rāj′), *v.t.*, **-raged, -raging.** to put into a rage; infuriate. [t. MF: m.s. *enrager,* der. en- EN-¹ + *rage* RAGE] **—en·rage′ment,** *n.*
—**Syn.** ENRAGE, INCENSE, INFURIATE imply stirring to violent anger. To ENRAGE is to provoke a display of wrath: *enrage him by deliberate and continual injustice.* To INCENSE is to inflame with indignation or anger; the connotation is serious provocation present or prolonged: *to incense one by making insulting remarks.* To INFURIATE is to arouse suddenly to fury or fierce and vehement anger: *infuriate him by a false accusation.* —**Ant.** appease, pacify.

en rap·port (äN rȧ pôr′), *French.* in sympathy or accord; in agreement; congenial.

en·rapt (ĕn răpt′), *adj.* rapt; transported; enraptured.

en·rap·ture (ĕn răp′chər), *v.t.*, **-tured, -turing.** to move to rapture; delight beyond measure.

en·reg·is·ter (ĕn rĕj′ĭs tər), *v.t.* to register; record.

en rè·gle (äN rĕ′gl), *French.* according to rule; in due form.

en·rich (ĕn rĭch′), *v.t.* **1.** to supply with riches, wealth, abundant or valuable possessions, etc.: *commerce enriches a nation.* **2.** to supply with abundance of anything desirable: *to enrich the mind with knowledge.* **3.** to make finer in quality as by supplying desirable elements or ingredients: *to enrich bread or soil.* [ME *enrich(en),* t. OF: m. *enrichir,* der. en- EN-¹ + *riche* RICH] **—en·rich′er,** *n.*

en·rich·ment (ĕn rĭch′mənt), *n.* **1.** act of enriching. **2.** state of being enriched. **3.** something that enriches.

en·robe (ĕn rōb′), *v.t.*, **-robed, -robing.** to dress; attire.

en·rol (ĕn rōl′), *v.t.*, **-rolled, -rolling.** enroll.

en·roll (ĕn rōl′), *v.t.* **1.** to write (a name), or insert the name of (a person), in a roll or register; place upon a list. **2.** to put in a record; record. **4.** to roll or wrap up. [ME *enroll(en),* t. OF: m. *enroller,* der. en- EN-¹ + *rolle* ROLL, n.] **—en·roll′er,** *n.*

en·roll·ment (ĕn rōl′mənt), *n.* **1.** act of enrolling; process of being enrolled. **2.** the number of persons enrolled, as for a course or in a school. Also, **en·rol′ment.**

en·root (ĕn rōōt′, -rŏŏt′), *v.t.* **1.** to fix by the root. **2.** to fix fast; implant deeply.

en route (än rōōt′; *Fr.* äN), on the way. [F]

ens (ĕnz), *n., pl.* **entia** (ĕn′shĭ ə). Metaphys. being, considered in the abstract. [t. LL, ppr. neut. of *esse* be]

Ens., Ensign.

en·sam·ple (ĕn săm′pəl), *n.* Archaic. example.

en·san·guine (ĕn săng′gwĭn), *v.t.*, **-guined, -guining.** to stain or cover with blood. [der. EN-¹ + SANGUINE]

En·sche·de (ĕn′sκHə dā′), *n.* a city in E Netherlands. 113,513 (est. 1954).

en·sconce (ĕn skŏns′), *v.t.*, **-sconced, -sconcing. 1.** to cover or shelter; hide securely. **2.** to settle securely or snugly: *ensconced in an armchair.* [der. EN-¹ + SCONCE²]

en·sem·ble (än säm′bəl; *Fr.* äN säN′bl), *n.* **1.** all the parts of a thing taken together, so that each part is considered only in relation to the whole. **2.** the entire costume of an individual, esp. when all the parts are in harmony. **3.** the general effect, as of a work of art. **4.** Music. **a.** the united performance of the full number of singers, musicians, etc. **b.** the group so performing: *a string ensemble.* —*adv.* **5.** together; all at once; simultaneously. [ME, t. F, g. LL *insimul* at the same time]

en·shrine (ĕn shrīn′), *v.t.*, **-shrined, -shrining. 1.** to enclose in or as in a shrine. **2.** to cherish as sacred. Also, **inshrine.** **—en·shrine′ment,** *n.*

en·shroud (ĕn shroud′), *v.t.* to shroud; conceal.

en·si·form (ĕn′sə fôrm′), *adj.* Biol. sword-shaped; xiphoid. [f. L *ensi(s)* sword + -FORM]

en·sign (ĕn′sīn; Mil. ĕn′sən), *n.* **1.** a flag or banner, as of a nation. **2.** a badge of office or authority. **3.** any sign, token, or emblem. **4.** U.S. Navy. the lowest commissioned officer, ranking next below a lieutenant (junior grade), and equal to a second lieutenant in the Army. **5.** a standard bearer, formerly one in the British Army. [ME *ensaigne,* t. OF: m. *enseigne,* g. L *insignia* insignia] **—en′sign·ship′,** *n.* **—en′sign·cy,** *n.*

en·si·lage (ĕn′sə lĭj), *n., v.*, **-laged, -laging.** —*n.* **1.** the preservation of green fodder in a silo or pit. **2.** fodder thus preserved. —*v.t.* **3.** ensile. [t. F, der. *ensiler* ENSILE]

en·sile (ĕn sīl′, ĕn′sīl), *v.t.*, **-siled, -siling. 1.** to preserve (green fodder) in a silo. **2.** to make into ensilage. [t. F: m.s. *ensiler,* t. Sp.: m. *ensilar,* der. en- EN-¹ + *silo* SILO]

en·slave (ĕn slāv′), *v.t.*, **-slaved, -slaving.** to make a slave of; reduce to slavery. **—en·slave′ment,** *n.* **—en·slav′er,** *n.*

en·snare (ĕn snâr′), *v.t.*, **-snared, -snaring.** to capture in, or involve as in, a snare. Also, **insnare.** **—en·snare′ment,** *n.* **—en·snar′er,** *n.* **—Syn.** entrap, entangle, enmesh. **—Ant.** release.

en·soul (ĕn sōl′), *v.t.* to endow with a soul. Also, **insoul.**

en·sphere (ĕn sfīr′), *v.t.*, **-sphered, -sphering.** to enclose in or as in a sphere. Also, **insphere.**

en·sta·tite (ĕn′stə tīt′), *n.* a mineral of the pyroxene group, occurring as an important constituent of basic igneous rocks. [f. s. Gk. *enstátēs* adversary + -ITE¹; so called because of its refractory nature]

en·sue (ĕn sōō′), *v.i.*, **-sued, -suing. 1.** to follow in order; come afterward, esp. in immediate succession. **2.** to follow as a consequence; result. [ME *ensew(en),* t. OF: m. *ensuivre,* g. L *insequī* follow close upon] **—Syn. 1, 2.** See follow. **—Ant. 2.** cause.

en suite (äN swēt′; *Fr.* äN), *French.* in succession; in a series or set.

en·sure (ĕn shŏŏr′), *v.t.*, **-sured, -suring. 1.** to secure, or bring surely, as to a person: *this letter will ensure you a hearing.* **2.** to make sure or certain to come, occur, etc.: *measures to ensure the success of an undertaking.* **3.** to make secure or safe, as from harm. **4.** Obsolesc. to insure. [ME *ensure(n),* t. AF: m. *enseurer,* der. en- EN-¹ + OF *seur* SURE]

en·swathe (ĕn swáth′), *v.t.*, **-swathed, -swathing.** to swathe. Also, **inswathe.** **—en·swathe′ment,** *n.*

-ent, a suffix equivalent to -ant, in adjectives and nouns, as in *ardent, dependent, different, expedient.* [t. L: stem ending of ppr. in vbs. of conjugations 2, 3, 4]

en·tab·la·ture (ĕn tăb′lə chər), *n.* **1.** that part of a classic architectural order which rests horizontally upon the columns and consists of the architrave, frieze, and cornice. See diag. under **column. 2.** a similar part in other constructions. [t. It.: m. *intavolatura,* der. *intavolare* board up]

en·tail (ĕn tāl′), *v.t.* **1.** to bring on or involve by necessity or consequences: *a loss entailing no regret.* **2.** to impose as a burden. **3.** to limit the inheritance of (a landed estate) to a specified line of heirs, so that it cannot be alienated, devised, or bequeathed. **4.** to cause (anything) to descend to a fixed series of possessors. —*n.* **5.** act of entailing. **6.** state of being entailed. **7.** any predetermined order of succession, as to an office. **8.** that which is entailed, as an estate. **9.** the rule of descent settled for an estate. [f. EN-¹ + TAIL²] **—en·tail′ment,** *n.*

en·tan·gle (ĕn tăng′gəl), *v.t.*, **-gled, -gling. 1.** to make tangled; complicate (usually used in the passive). **2.** to involve in anything like a tangle; ensnare; enmesh. **3.** to involve in difficulties; embarrass; perplex. **—en·tang′ler,** *n.* **—Syn. 3.** bewilder, confuse. See involve.

en·tan·gle·ment (ĕn tăng′gəl mənt), *n.* **1.** act of entangling. **2.** state of being entangled. **3.** that which entangles; a snare; an embarrassment; a complication.

en·ta·sis (ĕn′tə sĭs), *n.* Archit. the swelling or outward curve of the shaft of a column. [t. NL, t. Gk.: a stretching]

En·teb·be (ĕn tĕb′ē), *n.* formerly the capital of Uganda. See **Kampala.**

en·tel·e·chy (ĕn tĕl′ə kĭ), *n., pl.* **-chies. 1.** a realization or actuality as opposed to a potentiality. **2.** (in vitalist philosophy) the vital force or principle directing growth and life. [t. L: m.s. *entelechia,* t. Gk., der. en *télei échein* be in fulfillment or completion]

en·tel·lus (ĕn tĕl′əs), *n.* the sacred monkey or langur of India, *Semnopithecus entellus,* having a long tail, a beard, and a caplike growth of hair. [NL; appar. named after *Entellus,* character (elderly man) in "Aeneid"]

en·tente (än tänt′; *Fr.* äN tänt′), *n.* **1.** understanding. **2.** the parties to an understanding. [t. F]

en·tente cor·diale (än tänt′ kôr dyäl′), *French.* a friendly understanding, esp. between two governments.

en·ter (ĕn′tər), *v.i.* **1.** to come or go in. **2.** to make an entrance, as on the stage. **3.** to be admitted. **4.** to make a beginning (often fol. by *on* or *upon*). **5.** enter into, **a.** to take an interest or part in; engage in. **b.** to take up the consideration of (a subject). **c.** to sympathize with (a person's feelings, etc.). **d.** to assume the obligation of. **e.** to become a party to. **f.** to make a beginning in. **g.** to form a constituent part or ingredient of: *lead enters into the composition of pewter.* —*v.t.* **6.** to come or go into. **7.** to penetrate or pierce: *the bullet entered the flesh.* **8.** to put in or insert: *to enter a wedge.* **9.** to become a member of, or join. **10.** to cause to be admitted, as into a school, competition, etc. **11.** to make a beginning of or in, or begin upon; engage or become involved in. **12.** to make a record of; record or register. **13.** Law. **a.** to place in regular form before a court, as a writ. **b.** to occupy or to take possession of (lands); make an entrance, entry, ingress in, under claim of a right to possession. **c.** to file an application for (public lands). **14.** to report (a vessel, etc.) at the custom house. [ME *entre(n),* t. OF: m. *entrer,* g. L *intrāre* go into] **—en′ter·a·ble,** *adj.* **—en′ter·er,** *n.* **—Ant. 1.** leave. **8.** remove.

en·ter·ic (ĕn tĕr′ĭk), *adj.* **1.** pertaining to the enteron; intestinal. **2.** Brit. typhoid. [t. Gk.: m.s. *enterikós,* der. *énteron* intestine]

enteric fever, typhoid fever.

en·ter·i·tis (ĕn′tərī′tĭs), n. *Pathol.* inflammation of the intestines.

entero-, a word element meaning "intestine," as in *enterotoxemia.* [t. Gk., comb. form of *énteron*]

en·ter·on (ĕn′tərŏn′), n., pl. **-tera** (-tə rə). *Anat., Zool.* the alimentary canal; the digestive tract. [NL, t. Gk.: intestine]

en·ter·os·to·my (ĕn′tə rŏs′tə mĭ), n., pl. **-mies**. *Surg.* the making of an artificial opening into the small intestine, which opens onto the abdominal wall, for feeding or drainage.

en·ter·o·tox·e·mi·a (ĕn′tə rō tŏk sē′mĭ ə), n. *Vet. Sci.* a disease of sheep caused by severe systemic poisoning from bacterial toxins in the intestinal tract.

en·ter·prise (ĕn′tər prīz′), n. **1.** a project undertaken or to be undertaken, esp. one that is of some importance or that requires boldness or energy. **2.** engagement in such projects. **3.** boldness or readiness in undertaking, adventurous spirit, or energy. [ME, t. OF: m. *entreprise,* der. *entreprendre* take in hand, f. *entre* INTER- + *prendre* seize, take (g. L *prehendere*)] —Syn. **1.** plan, undertaking, venture.

en·ter·pris·ing (ĕn′tər prī′zĭng), adj. ready to undertake projects of importance or difficulty, or untried schemes; energetic in carrying out any undertaking. —en′ter·pris′ing·ly, adv. —Syn. See **ambitious**. —Ant. timid.

en·ter·tain (ĕn′tər tān′), v.t. **1.** to hold the attention of agreeably; divert; amuse. **2.** to receive as a guest, esp. at one's table; show hospitality to. **3.** to give admittance or reception to. **4.** to admit into the mind; consider. **5.** to hold in the mind; harbor; cherish. **6.** *Archaic.* to maintain or keep up. —v.i. **7.** to exercise hospitality; entertain company; provide entertainment for guests. [late ME *entertene(n),* t. F: m. *entretenir,* f. *entre-* INTER- + *tenir* (g. L *tenēre* hold)] —Syn. **1.** See **amuse.**

en·ter·tain·er (ĕn′tər tā′nər), n. **1.** one who entertains. **2.** a singer, reciter, or the like, who gives, or takes part in, public entertainments.

en·ter·tain·ing (ĕn′tər tā′nĭng), adj. affording entertainment; amusing; diverting. —en′ter·tain′ing·ly, adv. —en′ter·tain′ing·ness, n.

en·ter·tain·ment (ĕn′tər tān′mənt), n. **1.** act of entertaining; agreeable occupation for the mind, diversion, or amusement. **2.** something affording diversion or amusement, esp. an exhibition or performance of some kind. **3.** hospitable provision for the wants of guests. **4.** *Obs.* maintenance in service.

en·thet·ic (ĕn thĕt′ĭk), adj. introduced from without, as diseases propagated by inoculation. [t. Gk.: m.s. *enthetikós* fit for implanting]

en·thral (ĕn thrôl′), v.t., **-thralled, -thralling.** enthrall. —en·thral′ment, n.

en·thrall (ĕn thrôl′), v.t. **1.** to captivate; charm. **2.** to put or hold in thraldom; subjugate. Also, **inthrall, inthral.** —en·thrall′er, n. —en·thrall′ment, n.

en·throne (ĕn thrōn′), v.t., **-throned, -throning. 1.** to place on or as on a throne. **2.** to invest with sovereign or episcopal authority. **3.** to exalt. Also, **inthrone.** —en·throne′ment, en·thron·i·za·tion (ĕn thrō′nə zā′shən), n.

en·thuse (ĕn thōōz′), v., **-thused, -thusing.** *U.S. Colloq.* —v.i. **1.** to become enthusiastic; show enthusiasm. —v.t. **2.** to move to enthusiasm. [back formation from ENTHUSIASM]

en·thu·si·asm (ĕn thōō′zĭ ăz′əm), n. **1.** absorbing or controlling possession of the mind by any interest or pursuit; lively interest. **2.** *Archaic.* extravagant religious emotion. [t. LL: s. *enthūsiasmus,* t. Gk.: m. *enthousiasmós*] —Syn. **1.** eagerness, warmth, fervor, zeal, ardor. —Ant. **1.** indifference.

en·thu·si·ast (ĕn thōō′zĭ ăst′), n. **1.** one who is filled with enthusiasm for some principle, pursuit, etc.; a person of ardent zeal. **2.** a religious visionary or fanatic. —Syn. **1.** zealot, devotee.

en·thu·si·as·tic (ĕn thōō′zĭ ăs′tĭk), adj. **1.** full of or characterized by enthusiasm; ardent. **2.** pertaining to or of the nature of enthusiasm. —en·thu′si·as′ti·cal·ly, adv. —Syn. **1.** zealous, eager, fervent, passionate.

en·thy·meme (ĕn′thə mēm′), n. *Logic.* a syllogism in which one premise is unexpressed. [t. L: m.s. *enthýmēma,* t. Gk.: thought, argument]

en·tice (ĕn tīs′), v.t., **-ticed, -ticing.** to draw on by exciting hope or desire; allure; inveigle. [ME *entyce(n),* t. OF: m. *enticier* incite, der. L *titio* firebrand] —en·tic′er, n. —en·tic′ing·ly, adv. —Syn. lure, attract, decoy, tempt.

en·tice·ment (ĕn tīs′mənt), n. **1.** act or practice of enticing, esp. to evil. **2.** state of being enticed. **3.** that which entices; an allurement.

en·tire (ĕn tīr′), adj. **1.** having all the parts or elements; whole; complete. **2.** not broken, mutilated, or decayed; intact. **3.** unimpaired or undiminished. **4.** being wholly of one piece; undivided; continuous. **5.** *Bot.* without notches or indentations, as leaves. **6.** full or thorough: *entire freedom of choice.* **7.** not gelded: *an entire horse.* **8.** *Obs.* wholly of one kind; unmixed or pure. —n. **9.** the whole; entirety. **10.** an entire horse; a stallion. **11.** *Brit.* a kind of malt liquor; porter. [ME *enter,* t. OF: m. *entier,* g. L *integrum,* acc. of *integer* untouched, whole] —en·tire′ness, n. —Syn. **1.** See **complete.** —Ant. **1.** partial. **2.** defective.

en·tire·ly (ĕn tīr′lĭ), adv. **1.** wholly or fully; completely or unreservedly. **2.** solely or exclusively.

en·tire·ty (ĕn tīr′tĭ), n., pl. **-ties. 1.** state of being entire; completeness. **2.** that which is entire; the whole.

en·ti·tle (ĕn tī′təl), v.t., **-tled, -tling. 1.** to give (a person or thing) a title, right, or claim to something; furnish with grounds for laying claim. **2.** to call by a particular title or name; name. **3.** to designate (a person) by an honorary title. Also, **intitle.** [ME *entitle(n),* t. OF: m. *entituler,* t. LL: m. *intitulāre,* der. L *in-* IN-² + *titulus* TITLE] —Syn. **1.** empower, qualify.

en·ti·ty (ĕn′tə tĭ), n., pl. **-ties. 1.** something that has a real existence; a thing. **2.** being or existence. **3.** essential nature. [t. LL: m.s. *entitas*]

ento-, var. of **endo-**.

en·to·derm (ĕn′tō dûrm′), n. endoderm.

en·toil (ĕn toil′), v.t. *Archaic.* to take in toils; ensnare.

entom., entomological. Also, **entomol.**

en·tomb (ĕn tōōm′), v.t. **1.** to place in a tomb; bury; inter. **2.** to serve as a tomb for. Also, **intomb.** [t. OF: s. *entomber,* der. en- EN-¹ + *tombe* TOMB] —en·tomb′ment, n.

entomo-, a word element meaning "insect." Also, before vowels, **entom-.** [comb. form repr. Gk. *éntomos,* lit., cut up, in neut. pl., insects]

en·to·mol·o·gize (ĕn′tə mŏl′ə jīz′), v.i., **-gized, -gizing. 1.** to study entomology. **2.** to gather entomological specimens.

en·to·mol·o·gy (ĕn′tə mŏl′ə jĭ), n., the branch of zoology that treats of insects. —en·to·mo·log·i·cal (ĕn′tə mə lŏj′ə kəl), en′to·mo·log′ic, adj. —en′to·mol′o·gist, n.

en·to·moph·a·gous (ĕn′tə mŏf′ə gəs), adj. feeding on insects; insectivorous.

en·to·mos·tra·can (ĕn′tə mŏs′trə kən), adj. **1.** belonging to the *Entomostraca,* a subclass of mostly small crustaceans. —n. **2.** an entomostracan crustacean. [f. ENTOM(o)- + m.s. Gk. *óstrakon* shell + -AN]

en·to·phyte (ĕn′tō fīt′), n. *Bot.* a plant growing within an animal or another plant, usually as a parasite. [f. ento- (comb. form repr. Gk. *entós* within) + -PHYTE] —en·to·phyt·ic (ĕn′tō fĭt′ĭk), adj.

en·tou·rage (än′tōō räzh′; Fr. än tōō räzh′), n. **1.** attendants, as of a person of rank. **2.** surroundings; environment. [t. F, der. *entourer* surround. See EN-¹, TOUR]

en·tr'acte (än träkt′; Fr. än träkt′), n. **1.** the interval between two consecutive acts of a theatrical or operatic performance. **2.** a performance, as of music or dancing, given during such an interval. **3.** a piece of music or the like for such performance. [t. F: between-act]

en·trails (ĕn′trālz, -trəlz), n.pl. **1.** the internal parts of the trunk of an animal body. **2.** the intestines or bowels. **3.** the internal parts of anything. [ME *entraile,* t. F: m. *entrailles,* g. LL *intrālia* intestines, der. L *inter* within]

en·train (ĕn trān′), v.t., v.i. to put or go aboard a train. —en·train′ment, n.

en·trance¹ (ĕn′trəns), n. **1.** act of entering, as into a place or upon new duties. **2.** a point or place of entering; an opening or passage for entering. **3.** power or liberty of entering; admission. **4.** *Theat.* the moment, or place in the script, at which an actor comes on the stage. [t. OF, der. *entrer* ENTER] —Syn. **1.** entry, ingress. **3.** ENTRANCE, ADMITTANCE, ADMISSION refer to the possibility of entering a place. ENTRANCE suggests the possibility of entering without supervision or permission: *entrance is by way of the side door.* ADMITTANCE refers to the act of admitting or allowing entry: *to give admittance to a building.* ADMISSION suggests entering by permission, special right or privilege, by ticket, and the like: *admission to a concert, a game.*

en·trance² (ĕn träns′, -träns′), v.t., **-tranced, -trancing. 1.** to fill with delight or wonder; enrapture. **2.** to put into a trance. [f. EN-¹ + TRANCE, v.] —en·trance′ment, n. —en·tranc′ing·ly, adv.

en·trant (ĕn′trənt), n. **1.** one who enters. **2.** a new member, as of an association, a university, etc. **3.** a competitor in a contest. [t. F, ppr. of *entrer* ENTER]

en·trap (ĕn trăp′), v.t., **-trapped, -trapping. 1.** to catch in or as in a trap; ensnare. **2.** to bring unawares into difficulty or danger. **3.** to draw into contradiction or damaging admission. [t. OF: s. *entraper,* der. en- EN-¹ + *trape* trap] —en·trap′ment, n. —en·trap′per, n.

en·treas·ure (ĕn trĕzh′ər), v.t., **-ured, -uring.** to lay up in or as in a treasury.

en·treat (ĕn trēt′), v.t. **1.** to make supplication to (a person); beseech; implore: *to entreat a person for something.* **2.** to ask earnestly for (something). —v.i. **3.** to make an earnest request or petition. Also, **intreat.** [ME *entrete(n),* t. OF: m. *entraitier,* f. en- EN-¹ + *traitier* TREAT] —en·treat′ing·ly, adv. —Syn. **1.** See appeal.

en·treat·y (ĕn trē′tĭ), n., pl. **-treaties.** earnest request or petition; supplication. —Syn. appeal, suit, plea.

en·tre·chat (än trə shä′), n. (in ballet) a jump during which the dancer crosses his feet a number of times while in the air. [t. F, t. It: m. *(capriola) intrecciata* complicated (caper), der. in- IN-² + *treccia* tress, plait]

en·tre·côte (än trə kōt′), n. *French.* rib steak.

en·tree (än′trā; Fr. än trē′), n. **1.** *U.S.* any food other than a roast, served as the main course. **2.** a dish served at dinner before the main course or between the regular courses. **3.** the right or privilege of entering. Also, **en′trée.** [t. F. See ENTRY]

en·tre·mets (än'trə mā'/; *Fr.* än trə mĕ'), *n.*, *pl.* **-mets** (-māz'; *Fr.* -mĕ'). *French.* a dish served at dinner between the principal courses or with the roast; a side dish. [F: lit., between-dish]

en·trench (ĕn trĕnch'), *v.t.* **1.** to dig trenches for defensive purposes around (oneself, a military position, etc.). **2.** to establish in a strong position: *safely entrenched behind undeniable facts.* —*v.i.* **3.** to trench or encroach; trespass; infringe (fol. by *on* or *upon*): *to entrench on the domain or rights of another.* **4.** to verge (fol. by *on* or *upon*): *proceedings entrenching on impiety.* Also, **intrench.** —**en·trench'er,** *n.*

en·trench·ment (ĕn trĕnch'mənt), *n.* **1.** act of entrenching. **2.** an entrenched position. **3.** (*usually pl.*) an earth breastwork or ditch for protection against enemy fire. Also, **intrenchment.**

en·tre nous (än trə noo'), *French.* between ourselves; confidentially.

en·tre·pôt (än'trə pō'; *Fr.* än trə pō'), *n.* **1.** a warehouse. **2.** a commercial center to which goods are sent for distribution. [t. F, der. OF *entreposer* store up, f. *entre-* INTER- + *poser* place (g. L *pausāre* rest)]

en·tre·pre·neur (än'trə prə nûr'; *Fr.* än trə prə nœr'), *n.* **1.** an employer of productive labor; a contractor. **2.** one who undertakes to carry out any enterprise. [t. F, der. *entreprendre* undertake. See ENTERPRISE]

en·tre·sol (ĕn'tər sŏl', än'trə-; *Fr.* än trə sôl'), *n. Archit.* a low story between two other stories of greater height, usually one immediately above the chief or ground floor; a mezzanine. [t. F: between-floor]

en·tro·py (ĕn'trə pĭ), *n. Physics.* a measure of the unavailable energy in a thermodynamic system, commonly expressed in terms of its changes on an arbitrary scale, being zero for water at 32° F. [t. Gk.: m.s. *entropía* transformation]

en·trust (ĕn trŭst'), *v.t.* **1.** to invest with a trust or responsibility; charge with a specified office or duty involving trust. **2.** to commit (something) in trust (*to*); confide, as for care, use, or performance: *to entrust a secret, money, powers, or work to another.* **3.** to commit as if with trust or confidence: *to entrust one's life to a frayed rope.* Also, **intrust.**

en·try (ĕn'trĭ), *n.*, *pl.* **-tries. 1.** act of entering; entrance. **2.** a place of ingress or entrance, esp. an entrance hall or vestibule. **3.** act of entering or recording something in a book, register, list, etc. **4.** the statement, etc., so entered or recorded. **5.** one entered in a contest or competition. **6.** *Law.* act of taking possession of lands or tenements by entering or setting foot on them. **7.** the giving of an account of a ship's cargo at a custom house, to obtain permission to land the goods. **8.** *Bookkeeping.* **a.** See **double entry. b.** See **single entry.** [ME *entree*, t. F, der. *entrer* ENTER]

en·try·way (ĕn'trĭ wā'), *n.* a passage for affording entrance.

en·twine (ĕn twīn'), *v.t.*, *v.i.*, **-twined, -twining.** to twine with, about, around, or together. Also, **intwine.** —**en·twine'ment,** *n.*

en·twist (ĕn twĭst'), *v.t.* to twist together or about. Also, **intwist.**

e·nu·cle·ate (*v.* ĭ noo'klĭ āt', ĭ noo'-; *adj.* ĭ noo'klĭ ĭt, -āt', ĭ noo'-), *v.t.* **-ated, -ating,** *adj.* —*v.t.* **1.** *Biol.* to deprive of the nucleus. **2.** to remove (a kernel, tumor, eyeball, etc.) from its enveloping cover. **3.** to bring out; disclose. —*adj.* **4.** having no nucleus. [t. L: m.s. *ēnucleātus,* pp.] —**e·nu'cle·a'tion,** *n.*

e·nu·mer·ate (ĭ noo'mə rāt', ĭ noo'-), *v.t.*, **-ated, -ating. 1.** to mention separately as if in counting; name one by one; specify as in a list. **2.** to ascertain the number of; count. [t. L: m.s. *ēnumerātus,* pp., counted out] —**e·nu'mer·a'tive,** *adj.* —**e·nu'mer·a'tor,** *n.* —Syn. **1.** recapitulate, recount, rehearse.

e·nu·mer·a·tion (ĭ noo'mə rā'shən, ĭ noo'-), *n.* **1.** act of enumerating. **2.** a catalogue or list.

e·nun·ci·ate (ĭ nŭn'sĭ āt', -shĭ-), *v.t.*, *v.i.*, **-ated, -ating. 1.** to utter or pronounce (words, etc.), esp. in a particular manner: *he enunciates his words distinctly.* **2.** to state or declare definitely, as a theory. **3.** to announce or proclaim. [t. L: m.s *ēnuntiātus,* pp.] —**e·nun'ci·a'tive,** *adj.* —**e·nun'ci·a·to'ry,** *adj.* —**e·nun'ci·a'tive·ly,** *adv.* —**e·nun'ci·a·tor,** *n.*

e·nun·ci·a·tion (ĭ nŭn'sĭ ā'shən, -shĭ-), *n.* **1.** act or the manner of enunciating. **2.** utterance or pronunciation. **3.** announcement; statement.

en·ure (ĕn yoor'), *v.t.*, *v.i.*, **-ured, -uring.** inure.

en·u·re·sis (ĕn'yə rē'sĭs), *n. Pathol.* incontinence or involuntary discharge of urine; bed-wetting. [NL, der. Gk. *enourein* make water in]

en·vel·op (ĕn vĕl'əp), *v.*, **-oped, -oping,** *n.* —*v.t.* **1.** to wrap up in or as in a covering. **2.** to serve as a wrapping or covering for. **3.** to surround entirely. —*n.* **4.** envelope. [ME *envolupe(n),* t. OF: m. *envoluper,* f. *en-* EN-¹ + *voluper* wrap. Cf. DEVELOP] —**en·vel'op·er,** *n.* —Syn. **1.** enfold, cover, hide, conceal. **3.** encompass, enclose.

en·ve·lope (ĕn'və lōp', än'-), *n.* **1.** a cover for a letter or the like, usually so made that it can be sealed or fastened. **2.** that which envelops; a wrapper, integument, or surrounding cover. **3.** *Bot.* a surrounding or enclosing part, as of leaves. **4.** *Geom.* a curve or surface tangent to each member of a family of curves or surfaces. **5.** the fabric structure enclosing the gasbag of an aerostat. **6.** the gasbag itself. [t. F: m. *enveloppe*]

en·vel·op·ment (ĕn vĕl'əp mənt), *n.* **1.** act of enveloping. **2.** state of being enveloped. **3.** a wrapping or covering.

en·ven·om (ĕn vĕn'əm), *v.t.* **1.** to impregnate with venom; make poisonous. **2.** to embitter. [ME *envenime(n),* t. OF: m. *envenimer,* der. *en-* EN-¹ + *venim* VENOM]

en·vi·a·ble (ĕn'vĭ ə bəl), *adj.* that is to be envied; worthy to be envied. —**en'vi·a·ble·ness,** *n.* —**en'vi·a·bly,** *adv.*

en·vi·ous (ĕn'vĭ əs), *adj.* **1.** full of, feeling, or expressing envy: *envious of a person's success, an envious attack.* **2.** *Obs.* emulous. [ME, t. AF, var. of OF *envieus,* der. *envie* ENVY] —**en'vi·ous·ly,** *adv.* —**en'vi·ous·ness,** *n.*

en·vi·ron (ĕn vī'rən), *v.t.* to form a circle or ring round; surround; envelop. [ME *environ(en),* t. F: m. *environner,* der. *environ* around]

en·vi·ron·ment (ĕn vī'rən mənt), *n.* **1.** the aggregate of surrounding things, conditions, or influences. **2.** act of environing. **3.** state of being environed. **4.** that which environs. —**en·vi'ron·men'tal,** *adj.*

en·vi·rons (ĕn vī'rənz, ĕn'və rənz), *n.pl.* surrounding parts or districts, as of a city; outskirts; suburbs. [t. F]

en·vis·age (ĕn vĭz'ĭj), *v.t.*, **-aged, -aging. 1.** to contemplate; visualize. **2.** to look in the face of; face. [t. F: m.s. *envisager,* der. *en-* EN-¹ + *visage* VISAGE]

en·vi·sion (ĕn vĭzh'ən), *v.t.* to picture mentally, esp. some future event or events.

en·voy¹ (ĕn'voi), *n.* **1.** a diplomatic agent of the second rank, next in dignity after an ambassador, commonly called minister (title in full: **envoy extraordinary and minister plenipotentiary**). **2.** a diplomatic agent. **3.** any accredited messenger or representative. [t. F: m. *envoyé,* prop. pp. of *envoyer* send. See ENVOY²]

en·voy² (ĕn'voi), *n.* **1.** *Pros.* a short stanza concluding a poem in certain archaic metrical forms. **2.** a postscript to a poetical or prose composition, sometimes serving as a dedication. Also, **en'voi.** [ME *envoye,* t. OF, der. *envoier* send, der. *en voie* on the way]

en·vy (ĕn'vĭ), *n.*, *pl.* **-vies,** *v.*, **-vied, -vying.** —*n.* **1.** a feeling of discontent or mortification, usually with ill will, at seeing another's superiority, advantages, or success. **2.** desire for some advantage possessed by another. **3.** an object of envious feeling. **4.** *Obs.* ill will. —*v.t.* **5.** to regard with envy; be envious of. —*v.i.* **6.** *Obs.* to be affected with envy. [ME *envie,* t. OF, g. L *invidia*] —**en'vi·er,** *n.* —**en'vy·ing·ly,** *adv.* —Syn. **5.** ENVY, BEGRUDGE, COVET refer to one's attitude concerning the possessions or attainments of others. To ENVY is to feel resentful, spiteful, and unhappy because someone else possesses, or has achieved, what one wishes oneself to possess, or to have achieved: *to envy the wealthy, a girl's beauty, an honest man's reputation.* To BEGRUDGE is simply to be unwilling that another should have the possessions, honors, or credit he deserves: *to begrudge a man a reward for heroism.* To COVET is to long jealously to possess what someone else possesses: *I covet your silverware.*

en·weave (ĕn wēv'), *v.t.* inweave.

en·wind (ĕn wīnd'), *v.t.*, **-wound, -winding.** to wind or coil about; encircle. Also, **inwind.**

en·womb (ĕn woom'), *v.t.* to enclose in or as in the womb.

en·wrap (ĕn rŏp'), *v.t.*, **-wrapped, -wrapping. 1.** to wrap or envelop in something: *enwrapped in leaves.* **2.** to wrap in slumber, etc.: *enwrapped in fond desire.* **3.** to absorb or engross in thought, etc. Also, **inwrap.**

en·wreathe (ĕn rēth'), *v.t.*, **-wreathed, -wreathing.** to surround with or as if with a wreath: *peace enwreathes thy brow.* Also, **inwreathe.**

en·zo·öt·ic (ĕn'zō ŏt'ĭk), *adj.* **1.** (of diseases) prevailing among or afflicting animals in a particular locality. Cf. **endemic.** —*n.* **2.** an enzoötic disease. [f. EN-² + zo(o)- + -OTIC, modeled on EPIZOOTIC]

en·zy·mat·ic (ĕn'zī măt'ĭk, -zī-), *adj.* of or pertaining to an enzyme.

en·zyme (ĕn'zīm, -zĭm), *n.* any of various complex organic substances, as pepsin, originating from living cells, and capable of producing by catalytic action certain chemical changes, as digestion, in organic substances; unorganized ferment. Also, **en·zym** (ĕn'zĭm). [t. MGk.: m.s. *enzymos* leavened, f. *en-* EN-² + Gk. *zȳmē* leaven]

eo-, a word element meaning "early," "primeval," as in *Eocene.* [t. Gk., comb. form of *ēōs* dawn]

E·o·cene (ē'ə sēn'), *adj.* **1.** pertaining to the second principal subdivision of the Tertiary period or system. —*n.* **2.** an early Tertiary epoch or series succeeding Paleocene and preceding Oligocene.

E·o·gene (ē'ə jēn'), *adj. Geol.* **1.** pertaining to a division of the Tertiary period or system that comprises Paleocene, Eocene, and Oligocene. —*n.* **2.** the time or rocks representing the earlier half of the Tertiary period or system.

e·o·hip·pus (ē'ō hĭp'əs), *n.* a horse of a fossil genus, *Eohippus,* from the Lower Eocene of the western U.S., the oldest type of the family *Equidae,* about as large as a fox, with four complete toes on each forefoot and three hoofed toes on each hindfoot. [NL, f. Gk.: *ēō-* EO- + *hippos* horse]

E·o·li·an (ē ō'lĭ ən), *adj., n.* Aeolian.

E·ol·ic (ē ŏl'ĭk), *n., adj.* Aeolic.

e·o·lith (ē'ə lĭth), *n.* a rude stone implement characteristic of the earliest stage of human culture, shaped by, rather than for, use.

•o·lith·ic (ē'ə lĭth'ĭk), *adj.* noting or pertaining to the earliest stage of human culture, characterized by the use of amorphous stone implements.

•o.m., *Chiefly Com.* end of the month.

•on (ē'ən, ē'ŏn), *n.* **1.** an indefinitely long period of time; an age; aeon. **2.** the largest division of geologic time comprising two or more eras. [t. L: m. *aeon*, t. Gk.: m. *aiōn* lifetime, age]

·os (ē'ŏs), *n.* the Greek goddess of the dawn, identified with the Roman Aurora. [t. L, t. Gk.: personification of *ēōs* dawn. Cf. EAST]

·o·sin (ē'ə sĭn), **1.** a coal-tar product, C₂₀H₈O₅Br₄, used for dyeing silk, etc., rose-red. **2.** any of a variety of eosinlike dyes. Also, **e·o·sine** (ē'ə sĭn, -sēn'). [f. Gk. *ēōs* dawn + -IN²] —**e·o·sin·like/,** *adj.*

•o·sin·o·phil (ē'ə sĭn'ə fĭl), *n. Anat.* a cell containing granules staining with acid dyes, whose numbers increase in allergic diseases and certain parasitic infections. [f. EOSIN + -(o)PHIL(E)]

eous, var. of **-ous,** occurring in adjectives taken from Latin or (infrequently) derived from Latin nouns. [t. L: m. *-eus*]

:o·zo·ic (ē'ə zō'ĭk), *n.* a division of pre-Cambrian time and rocks characterized by the dawn of life on the earth. [f. EO- + zo(o)- + -IC]

·p-, var. of **epi-,** before vowels, as in *epaxial.*

·p., Epistle.

:P (ē'pē'), *adj.* **1.** denoting a phonograph record impressed with microgrooves that revolves at 45 r.p.m. —*n.* **2.** such a record. [initials of *extended play*]

·pact (ē'păkt), *n.* **1.** the excess in days of a solar year over a lunar year. **2.** the age in days of the calendar moon at the beginning of the year (Jan. 1). [t. LL: s. *epacta*, t. Gk.: m. *epaktē*, prop. fem. of *epaktós*, vbl. adj., added]

:pam·i·non·das (ĭ păm'ə nŏn'dəs), *n.* c418–362 B.C., general and statesman of ancient Thebes in Greece.

·p·arch (ĕp'ärk), *n.* **1.** the prefect or governor of an eparchy. **2.** any military prefect. [t. Gk.: s. *éparchos* commander]

·p·ar·chy (ĕp'är kĭ), *n., pl.* **-chies.** **1.** (in modern Greece) one of the administrative subdivisions of a province. **2.** (in ancient Greece) a province. **3.** *Gk. Ch.* a diocese or archdiocese. —**ep·ar'chi·al,** *adj.*

·p·au·let (ĕp'ə lĕt' -lĭt), *n.* an ornamental shoulder piece worn on uniforms, chiefly by military and naval officers. Also, **ep/au·lette/.** [t. F: m. *épaulette*, der. *épaule* shoulder, g. L *spatula* blade]

·pax·i·al (ĕp ăk'sĭ əl), *adj. Anat.* above or posterior to an axis. —**ep·ax/i·al·ly,** *adv.*

·pée (ā pā'; *Fr.* ĕ pē'), *n. Fencing.* a long narrow weapon with blunted edges and a sharp point. [F, g. L *spatha*, t. Gk.: m. *spáthē* blade]

·pée·ist (ā pā'ĭst), *n. Fencing.* one who uses an épée.

·p·ei·rog·e·ny (ĕp'ĭ rŏj'ə nĭ), *n. Geol.* vertical or tilting movement of the earth crust, generally affecting broad areas of a continent. Also, **epirogeny.** [f. Gk. *ēpeiro(s)* land, mainland, continent + -GENY] —**e·pei·ro·gen·ic** (ĭ pī'rō jĕn'ĭk), *adj.*

·p·en·ceph·a·lon (ĕp'ən sĕf'ə lŏn'), *n., pl.* **-la** (-lə), *Anat.* the hindbrain. —**ep·en·ce·phal·ic** (ĕp'ən sə făl'ĭk), *adj.*

·p·en·the·sis (ĕp ĕn'thə sĭs), *n., pl.* **-ses** (-sēz'). (in linguistic process) the insertion of one or more sounds in the middle of a word, as the schwa in the substandard pronunciation (ĕl'əm) of *elm.* [t. LL, t. Gk.: insertion] —**ep·en·thet·ic** (ĕp'ən thĕt'ĭk), *adj.*

·pergne (ĭ pûrn', ā pârn'), *n.* an ornamental piece for the center of a dinner table, often elaborate in design, for holding fruit, flowers, etc. [? t. F: m. *épargne* saving, treasury]

·p·ex·e·ge·sis (ĕp ĕk'sə jē'sĭs), *n. Rhet.* **1.** the addition of a word or words to explain a preceding word or sentence. **2.** the word or words so added. —**p·ex·e·get·ic** (ĕp ĕk'sə jĕt'ĭk), *adj.* of or like an epexegesis. Also, **ep·ex/e·get/i·cal.** —**ep·ex/e·get/ical·ly,** *adv.*

·ph-, var. of **epi-,** before an aspirate, as in *ephemera.*

·ph., Ephesians.

·phah (ē'fə), *n.* a Hebrew unit of dry measure, equal to about a bushel. Also, **e/pha.** [t. Heb.]

·phebe (ĭ fēb', ĕf'ēb), *n.* (among the ancient Greeks) a youth just entering upon manhood or just enrolled as a citizen. [t. Gk.: m. *ēphēbos*] —**e·phe/bic,** *adj.*

·phed·rine (ĭ fĕd'rĭn; *Chem.* ĕf'ə drēn', -drĭn), *n. Pharm.* a crystalline alkaloid, C₁₀H₁₅NO, found in species of Ephedra, used esp. for colds, asthma, and hay fever. Also, **e·phed·rin** (ĭ fĕd'rĭn; *Chem.* ĕf'ə drĭn). [t. S. NL *ephedra* (L horsetail, a plant, t. Gk.) + -INE²]

·phem·er·a (ĭ fĕm'ər ə), *n., pl.* **-erae** (-ə rē'), **-eras.** **1.** anything short-lived or transitory. **2.** an ephemerid. [t. NL, orig., pl. of *ephémeron* t. Gk., neut. sing of *ephēmeros* of or for only one day), but now treated as sing.]

·phem·er·al (ĭ fĕm'ər əl), *adj.* **1.** lasting but a day or a very short time; short-lived; transitory. —*n.* **2.** an ephemeral entity, as certain insects. —**e·phem/er·al·ly,** *adv.* —**Syn. 1.** fleeting, evanescent, transient.

·phem·er·id (ĭ fĕm'ər ĭd), *n.* a May fly. [t. NL: s. *Ephēmeridae.* See EPHEMERA]

·phem·er·is (ĭ fĕm'ər ĭs), *n., pl.* **ephemerides** (ĕf'ə mĕr'ə dēz'). **1.** a table showing the positions of a heavenly body on a number of dates in an orderly sequence. **2.** an astronomical almanac containing such tables.

3. *Obs.* an almanac or calendar. [t. L, t. Gk.: diary calendar, record]

e·phem·er·on (ĭ fĕm'ə rŏn', -ərən), *n., pl.* **-era** (-ərə), **-erons.** anything short-lived or ephemeral. [t. Gk.: a short-lived insect. See EPHEMERA]

Ephes.. Ephesians.

E·phe·sian (ĭ fē'zhən), *adj.* **1.** of or pertaining to Ephesus. —*n.* **2.** a native or inhabitant of Ephesus. **3.** (*pl.*) the book of the New Testament called in full *The Epistle of Paul the Apostle to the Ephesians.*

Eph·e·sus (ĕf'ə səs), *n.* an ancient city in W Asia Minor, S of Smyrna: famous temple of Artemis (Diana).

eph·od (ĕf'ŏd, ē'fŏd), *n.* a kind of Hebrew priestly vestment, esp. that worn by the high priest. [t. Heb.: in some passages appar. meaning "idol"]

eph·or (ĕf'ŏr, ĕf'ər), *n., pl.* **-ors, -ori** (-ə rī'). one of a body of magistrates in various ancient Dorian states, esp. at Sparta, where a body of five was annually elected by the people. [t. Gk.: s. *éphoros* overseer] —**eph/or·al,** *adj.*

E·phra·im (ē'frĭ əm), *n. Old Testament.* **1.** the younger son of Joseph. Gen. 41:52. **2.** the tribe of Israel traditionally descended from him. Gen. 48:1, etc. **3.** the Kingdom of Israel. [t. Heb.]

epi-, a prefix meaning "on," "to," "against," sometimes used as an English formative, chiefly in scientific words, as *epiblast, epicalyx, epiblem.* Also, **ep-, eph-.** [t. Gk., repr. *epí*, prep. and adv., *ep-* before vowel, *eph-* before rough breathing]

ep·i·blast (ĕp'ə blăst'), *n. Embryol.* the outer layer of a gastrula, consisting of ectoblast and various portions of mesoblast and endoblast, according to species. —**ep/i·blas/tic,** *adj.*

e·pib·o·ly (ĭ pĭb'ə lĭ), *n. Embryol.* the development of one part so that it surrounds another. [t. Gk.: m. *epibolē* a throwing on] —**ep·i·bol·ic** (ĕp'ə bŏl'ĭk), *adj.*

ep·ic (ĕp'ĭk), *n.* Also, **ep/i·cal. 1.** denoting or pertaining to poetic composition in which a series of heroic achievements or events, usually of a hero, is dealt with at length as a continuous narrative in elevated style: *Homer's Iliad is an epic poem.* **2.** resembling or suggesting such poetry; heroic; imposing. —*n.* **3.** an epic poem. **4.** any epiclike composition. **5.** something worthy to form the subject of an epic: *the epic defense of the Alamo.* [t. L: s. *epicus*, t. Gk.: m. *epikós*, der. *épos* EPOS] —**ep/i·cal·ly,** *adv.* —**ep/iclike/,** *adj.*

ep·i·ca·lyx (ĕp'ə kā'lĭks, -kăl'ĭks), *n., pl.* **-calyxes, -calyces** (-kăl'ə sēz', -kā'lə-). *Bot.* an involucre resembling an outer calyx, as in the mallow.

A. Epicalyx; B, Calyx

ep·i·car·di·um (ĕp'ə kär'dĭ əm), *n., pl.* **-dia** (-dĭ ə). *Anat.* the inner serous layer of the pericardium, lying directly upon the heart. [t. NL: f. *epi-* EPI- + *-cardium* (comb. form repr. Gk. *kardía* heart] —**ep/i·car/di·al,** *adj.*

ep·i·carp (ĕp'ə kärp'), *n. Bot.* the outermost layer of a pericarp, as the rind or peel of certain fruits. See diag. under endocarp.

ep·i·ce·di·um (ĕp'ə sē'dĭ əm, -sə dī'əm), *n., pl.* **-sedia** (-sē'dĭ ə, -sə dī'ə). a funeral song; a dirge. [t. L, t. Gk.: m. *epikédeion*, prop. neut. adj., of or for a funeral]

ep·i·cene (ĕp'ə sēn'), *adj.* **1.** belonging to or partaking of the characteristics of both sexes. **2.** (of Greek and Latin nouns) of the same gender class regardless of the sex of the being referred to, as Latin *vulpēs*, fox or vixen, always grammatically feminine. —*n.* **3.** epicene person [t. L: m. *epicoenus*, t. Gk.: m. *epíkoinos* common]

ep·i·cen·ter (ĕp'ə sĕn'tər), *n. Geol.* a point from which earthquake waves seem to go out, directly above the true center of disturbance. Also, *Brit.*, **ep·i·cen·trum** (ĕp'ə sĕn'trəm), **ep·i·cen/tre.** [t. NL: m. *epicentrum*, t. Gk.: m. *epíkentros* on the center] —**ep/i·cen/tral,** *adj.*

ep·i·cot·yl (ĕp'ə kŏt'əl, -ĭl), *n. Bot.* (in the embryo of a plant) that part of the stem above the cotyledons.

ep·i·crit·ic (ĕp'ə krĭt'ĭk), *adj. Physiol.* referring or pertaining to cutaneous nerve fibers perceiving fine sensational variations, or to such perception (opposed to *protopathic*). [t. Gk.: m. s. *epikritikós* determining]

Ep·ic·te·tus (ĕp'ĭk tē'təs), *n.* A.D. 60?–120?, Greek Stoic philosopher, who taught in Rome.

ep·i·cure (ĕp'ə kyŏŏr'), *n.* **1.** one who cultivates a refined taste in eating and drinking. **2.** one given up to sensual enjoyment, esp. in eating; a glutton. [orig. Anglicized form of EPICURUS] —**Syn. 1.** gastronome, gourmet, gourmand.

ep·i·cu·re·an (ĕp'ə kyŏŏ rē'ən), *adj.* **1.** given or adapted to luxury, or indulgence in sensual pleasures; of luxurious tastes or habits, esp. in eating and drinking. **2.** fit for an epicure. **3.** (*cap.*) of Epicurus or Epicureanism. —*n.* **4.** one devoted to the pursuit of pleasure or luxury; an epicure. **5.** (*cap.*) a disciple of Epicurus.

Ep·i·cu·re·an·ism (ĕp'ə kyŏŏ rē'ə nĭz'əm), *n.* **1.** the philosophical system of Epicurus, or attachment to his doctrines, the chief of which were that the external world resulted from a fortuitous concourse of atoms, and that the highest good in life is pleasure, which consists in freedom from disturbance or pain. **2.** (*l.c.*) epicurean indulgence or habits. Also, **Ep·i·cur·ism** (ĕp'ə kyŏŏ rĭz'əm, ĕp'ə kyŏŏr'ĭz əm).

Ep·i·cu·rus (ĕp'ə kyŏŏr'əs), *n.* 342?–270 B.C., Greek philosopher.

---

ct, āble, dâre, ärt; ĕbb, ēqual; ĭf, īce; hŏt, ōver, ôrder, oil, bŏŏk, ōōze, out; ŭp, ūse, ûrge; ə = a in alone; n, chief; g, give; ng, ring; sh, shoe; th, thin; t͟h, that; zh, vision. See the full key on inside cover.

ep·i·cy·cle (ĕp′ə sī′kəl), n. 1. a small circle the center of which moves round in the circumference of a larger circle, used in Ptolemaic astronomy to account for observed periodic irregularities in planetary motions. 2. *Math.* a circle which rolls (externally or internally), without slipping, on another circle, generating an epicycloid or a hypocycloid. [t. LL: m.s. *epicyclus*, t. Gk.: m. *epikýklos*]

ep·i·cy·clic (ĕp′ə sī′klĭk, -sĭk′lĭk), adj. of or pertaining to an epicycle. Also, **ep′i·cy′cli·cal.**

epicyclic train, *Mach.* any train of gears the axes of the wheels of which revolve around a common center.

ep·i·cy·cloid (ĕp′ə sī′kloid), n. *Geom.* a curve generated by the motion of a point on the circumference of a circle which rolls externally, without slipping, on a fixed circle. **—ep′i·cy·cloi′dal,** adj.

E. Epicycloid; P, Point tracing epicycloid on fixed circle

epicycloidal wheel, one of the wheels in an epicyclic train.

ep·i·deic·tic (ĕp′ə dīk′tĭk), adj. *Rhet.* displaying the skill of the speaker: *epideictic orations.* Also, **epidictic.** [t. Gk.: m.s. *epideiktikós* displaying]

ep·i·dem·ic (ĕp′ə dĕm′ĭk), adj. 1. Also, **ep/i·dem/i·cal.** affecting at the same time a large number of persons in a locality, and spreading from person to person, as a disease not permanently prevalent there. —n. 2. a temporary prevalence of a disease. [der. obs. *epidemy*, t. LL: m.s. *epidēmia*, t. Gk.: prevalence of an epidemic] **—ep/i·dem/i·cal·ly,** adv. **—ep·i·de·mic·i·ty** (ĕp′ə də-mĭs′ə tĭ), n.

ep·i·de·mi·ol·o·gy (ĕp′ə dē′mĭ ŏl′ə jĭ), n. the branch of medicine dealing with epidemic diseases. **—ep·i·de·mi·o·log·i·cal** (ĕp′ə dē′mĭ ə lŏj′ə kəl), adj. **—ep/i·de/mi·ol/o·gist,** n.

ep·i·der·mis (ĕp′ə dûr′mĭs), n. 1. *Anat.* the outer, nonvascular, nonsensitive layer of the skin, covering the true skin or corium (dermis). 2. *Zool.* the outermost living layer of an animal, usually composed of one or more layers of cells. 3. *Bot.* a thin layer of cells forming the outer integument of seed plants and ferns. [t. LL, t. Gk.: outer skin] **—ep/i·der/mal, ep/i·der/mic,** adj.

ep·i·der·moid (ĕp′ə dûr′moid), adj. resembling epidermis. Also, **ep/i·der·moi/dal.**

ep·i·dic·tic (ĕp′ə dĭk′tĭk), adj. epideictic.

ep·i·did·y·mis (ĕp′ə dĭd′ə mĭs), n., pl. -didymides (-dĭ dĭm′ə dēz/). *Anat.* an elongated organ applied to the posterior surface of the testis, in which the spermatozoa ripen: chiefly the convoluted beginning of the deferent duct. [NL, t. Gk.] **—ep/i·did/y·mal,** adj.

ep·i·dote (ĕp′ə dōt′), n. a mineral, calcium aluminum iron silicate, $Ca_2(Al,Fe)_3Si_3O_{12}(OH)$, occurring in yellowish-green prismatic crystals. [t. F, der. Gk. *epididónai* increase] **—ep·i·dot·ic** (ĕp′ə dŏt′ĭk), adj.

ep·i·fo·cal (ĕp′ə fō′kəl), adj. *Geol.* epicentral.

ep·i·gas·tric (ĕp′ə găs′trĭk), adj. *Anat.* lying upon, distributed over, or pertaining to, the abdomen or the stomach.

ep·i·gas·tri·um (ĕp′ə găs′trĭ əm), n. *Anat.* the upper and median part of the abdomen, lying over the stomach. [NL, t. Gk.: m. *epigástrion* (neut.) over the belly]

ep·i·ge·al (ĕp′ə jē′əl), adj. 1. *Entomol.* living near the surface of the ground, as on low herbs or on other surface vegetation. 2. *Bot.* epigeous. Also, **ep/i·ge/an.** [f. EPIGE(OUS) + -AL¹]

ep·i·gene (ĕp′ə jēn′), adj. *Geol.* formed or originating on the earth's surface (opposed to *hypogene*). [t. F, t. Gk.: m.s. *epigenēs* growing after or later]

ep·i·gen·e·sis (ĕp′ə jĕn′ə sĭs), n. *Biol.* 1. a theoretical concept of generation according to which the embryo is formed by a series of new formations or successive differentiations (opposed to *preformation*). 2. *Geol.* the processes of ore deposition effective during a period subsequent to the original formation of the enclosing rock. **—ep·i·ge·net·ic** (ĕp′ə jə nĕt′ĭk), adj.

e·pig·e·nous (ĭ pĭj′ə nəs), adj. *Bot.* growing on the surface, esp. the upper surface, as fungi on leaves.

ep·i·ge·ous (ĕp′ə jē′əs), adj. *Bot.* 1. growing on or close to the ground. 2. (of cotyledons) lifted above ground in germination. [t. Gk.: m. *epígeios* on earth]

ep·i·glot·tis (ĕp′ə glŏt′ĭs), n. *Anat.* a thin, valvelike cartilaginous structure that covers the glottis during swallowing, preventing the entrance of food and drink into the larynx. See diag. under **larynx.** [t. NL, t. Gk.]

E·pig·o·ni (ĭ pĭg′ə nī′), n.pl. See **Seven against Thebes.**

ep·i·gram (ĕp′ə grăm′), n. 1. any witty, ingenious, or pointed saying tersely expressed. 2. epigrammatic expression. 3. a short poem dealing concisely with a single subject, usually ending with a witty or ingenious turn of thought, and often satirical. [t. L: m. *epigramma*, t. Gk.: an inscription]

ep·i·gram·mat·ic (ĕp′ə grə măt′ĭk), adj. 1. of or like an epigram; terse and ingenious in expression. 2. given to epigrams. **—ep/i·gram·mat/i·cal·ly,** adv.

ep·i·gram·ma·tism (ĕp′ə grăm′ə tĭz′əm), n. epigrammatic character or style.

ep·i·gram·ma·tist (ĕp′ə grăm′ə tĭst), n. a maker of epigrams.

ep·i·gram·ma·tize (ĕp′ə grăm′ə tīz′), v.t., v.i., -tized, -tizing. to express by epigrams, or make epigrams.

ep·i·graph (ĕp′ə grăf′, -gräf′), n. 1. an inscription, esp. on a building, statue, or the like. 2. an apposite quotation at the beginning of a book, chapter, etc. [t. Gk.: s. *epigraphē*]

ep·i·graph·ic (ĕp′ə grăf′ĭk), adj. 1. pertaining to epigraphs. 2. pertaining to epigraphy. Also, **ep/i·graph/i·cal.** **—ep/i·graph/i·cal·ly,** adv.

e·pig·ra·phy (ĭ pĭg′rə fĭ), n. 1. the study or science of epigraphs or inscriptions. 2. inscriptions collectively. **—e·pig/ra·phist, e·pig/ra·pher,** n.

e·pig·y·nous (ĭ pĭj′ə nəs), adj. *Bot.* 1. (of flowers) having all floral parts conjoint and generally divergent from the ovary at or near its summit. 2. having stamens, etc., so arranged, as a flower. [f. EPI- + m.s. Gk. *gynē* woman, female + -OUS]

e·pig·y·ny (ĭ pĭj′ə nĭ), n. an epigynous condition.

Epigynous stamens

ep·i·lep·sy (ĕp′ə lĕp′sĭ), n. *Pathol.* a nervous disease usually characterized by convulsions and practically always by loss of consciousness. [t. LL: m.s. *epilēpsia*, t. Gk.: lit., a seizure]

ep·i·lep·tic (ĕp′ə lĕp′tĭk), adj. 1. pertaining to epilepsy: *epileptic state.* —n. 2. one affected with epilepsy.

ep·i·lep·toid (ĕp′ə lĕp′toid), adj. resembling epilepsy. Also, **ep·i·lep·ti·form** (ĕp′ə lĕp′tə fôrm′).

e·pil·o·gist (ĭ pĭl′ə jĭst), n. the writer or speaker of an epilogue.

ep·i·logue (ĕp′ə lôg′, -lŏg′), n. 1. a speech, usually in verse, by one of the actors after the conclusion of a play. 2. the person or persons speaking this. 3. a concluding part added to a literary work. Also, **ep/i·log/.** [t. F, t. L: m.s. *epilogus*, t. Gk.: m. *epílogos* a conclusion]

Ep·i·me·theus (ĕp′ə mē′thoos, -thĭ əs), n. *Gk. Myth.* the brother of Prometheus and husband of Pandora.

ep·i·mor·pho·sis (ĕp′ə môr fō′sĭs), n. *Zool.* a form of development in segmented animals in which body segmentation is completed before hatching.

ep·i·nas·ty (ĕp′ə năs′tĭ), n. *Bot.* (esp. of leaves) increased growth on the upper surface of an organ or part, causing it to bend downward. [f. EPI- + s. Gk. *nastós* pressed close, compact + -y³] **—ep/i·nas/tic,** adj.

ep·i·neph·rine (ĕp′ə nĕf′rĭn, -rēn), n. *Chem.* adrenalin. Also, **ep·i·neph·rin** (ĕp′ə nĕf′rĭn). [f. EPI- + s. Gk. *nephrós* kidney + -INE²]

ep·i·neu·ri·um (ĕp′ə nyŏor′ĭ əm, -nŏor′-), n., pl. -neuria (-nyŏor′ĭ ə, -nŏor′-). *Anat.* the dense sheath of connective tissue which surrounds the trunk of a nerve. [NL, t. Gk.: *epi-* EPI- + m. *neûron* sinew, tendon]

Epiph., Epiphany.

E·piph·a·ny (ĭ pĭf′ə nĭ), n., pl. -nies. 1. a Christian festival, observed on Jan. 6, commemorating the manifestation of Christ to the Gentiles in the persons of the Magi. 2. (*l.c.*) an appearance or manifestation. esp. of a deity. [ME *epiphanie*, t. LL: m. *epiphania*, t. LGk.: the Epiphany, ult. der. *epiphainein* manifest]

ep·i·phe·nom·e·nal·ism (ĕp′ə fə nŏm′ə nə lĭz′əm), n. *Philos.* automatism (def. 2).

ep·i·phe·nom·e·non (ĕp′ə fə nŏm′ə nŏn′, -nən), n., pl. -na (-nə). 1. *Pathol.* a secondary or additional symptom or complication arising during the course of a malady. 2. any secondary phenomenon.

e·piph·y·sis (ĭ pĭf′ə sĭs), n., pl. -ses (-sēz′). *Anat.* 1. a part or process of a bone which is separated from the main body of the bone by a layer of cartilage, and which finally becomes united with the bone through further ossification. 2. the pineal body of the brain. [NL, t. Gk.: an outgrowth] **—ep·i·phys·i·al** (ĕp′ə fĭz′ĭ əl), adj.

ep·i·phyte (ĕp′ə fīt′), n. *Bot.* a plant which grows upon another but does not get food, water, or minerals from it; an air plant or aerophyte. **—ep·i·phyt·ic** (ĕp′ə fĭt′ĭk), **ep/i·phyt/i·cal,** adj. **—ep/i·phyt/i·cal·ly,** adv.

ep·i·phy·tot·ic (ĕp′ə fī tŏt′ĭk), adj. (of a disease or parasite) epidemic on plants. [f. EPI- + -PHYTE + -OTIC]

ep·i·plo·ön (ĭ pĭp′lō ŏn), n. *Anat.* the great omentum.

ep·i·rog·e·ny (ĕp′ī rŏj′ə nĭ), n. epeirogeny. **—e·pi·ro·gen·ic** (ĭ pī′rō jĕn′ĭk), adj.

E·pi·rus (ĭ pī′rəs), n. 1. a country of ancient Greece, corresponding to what is now NW Greece and S Albania. 2. a modern region in NW Greece. 330,543 pop. (1951); 3573 sq. mi.

Epis., Episcopal. Also, **Episc.**

e·pis·co·pa·cy (ĭ pĭs′kə pə sĭ), n., pl. -cies. 1. government of the church by bishops; church government in which there are three distinct orders of ministers, namely bishops, priests or presbyters, and deacons. 2. the office or incumbency of a bishop. 3. the order of bishops.

e·pis·co·pal (ĭ pĭs′kə pəl), adj. 1. pertaining to a bishop. 2. (*sometimes cap.*) based on or recognizing a governing order of bishops: *the Methodist Episcopal Church.* 3. (*cap.*) designating the Anglican Church or some branch of it: *the Protestant Episcopal Church in the U.S.* [t. LL: s. *episcopālis*, der. *epíscopus* BISHOP] **—e·pis/co·pal·ly,** adv.

E·pis·co·pa·lian (ĭ pĭs′kə pāl′yən), adj. 1. pertaining or adhering to the Episcopal Church (of the Anglican communion). 2. (*l.c.*) pertaining or adhering to the episcopal form of church government. —n. 3. a member of the Episcopal Church. 4. (*l.c.*) an adherent of the episcopal system. **—E·pis/co·pa/lian·ism,** n.

---

b., blend of, blended; c., cognate with; d., dialect, dialectal; der., derived from; f., formed from; g., going back to; m., modification of; r., replacing; s., stem of; t., taken from; ?, perhaps. See the full key on inside cover.

e·pis·co·pal·ism (Ɩ pĭs′kə pə lĭz′əm), *n.* the theory of church polity according to which the supreme ecclesiastical authority is vested in the episcopal order as a whole, and not in any individual except by delegation.

e·pis·co·pate (Ɩ pĭs′kə pĭt, -pāt′), *n.* 1. the office and dignity of a bishop; a bishopric. 2. the order or body of bishops. 3. the incumbency of a bishop.

ep·i·sode (ĕp′ə sōd′, -zōd′), *n.* 1. an incident in the course of a series of events, in a person's life or experience, etc. 2. an incidental narrative or digression in the course of a story, poem, or other writing. 3. a part in an old Greek tragedy between two choric songs. 4. *Music.* an intermediate passage, esp. in a contrapuntal composition. [t. Gk.: m.s. *epeisódion* a parenthetic addition, prop. neut. of *epeisódios* coming in besides]

ep·i·sod·ic (ĕp′ə sŏd′Ĭk, -zŏd′-), *adj.* pertaining to or of the nature of an episode; incidental. Also, **ep/i·sod′i·cal.** —**ep/i·sod/i·cal·ly,** *adv.*

ep·i·spas·tic (ĕp′ə spăs′tĬk), *adj.* 1. raising a blister. —*n.* 2. a blistering agent; a vesicatory. [t. Gk.: m.s. *epispastikós*, lit., drawing towards]

e·pis·ta·sis (Ɩ pĬs′tə sĬs), *n. Genetics.* a form of interaction between nonallelic genes in which one combination of such genes exerts a dominant effect over other combinations. [t. Gk.] —**ep·i·stat·ic** (ĕp′ə stăt′Ĭk), *adj.*

ep·i·stax·is (ĕp′ə stăk′sĬs), *n. Pathol.* bleeding from the nose. [NL, der. Gk. *epistázein* drop on]

e·pis·te·mol·o·gy (Ɩ pĬs′tə mŏl′ə jĬ), *n.* the branch of philosophy which investigates the origin, nature, methods, and limits of human knowing. [f. s. Gk. *epistēmē* knowledge + -(o)LOGY] —**e·pis·te·mo·log·i·cal** (Ɩ-pĬs′tə mə lŏj′ə kəl), *adj.* —**e·pis′te·mo·log′i·cal·ly,** *adv.* —**e·pis′te·mol′o·gist,** *n.*

ep·i·ster·num (ĕp′ə stûr′nəm), *n., pl.* -**na** (-nə). 1. *Anat.* the manubrium. 2. *Entomol.* the principal anterior subdivision of a thoracic pleuron. —**ep′i·ster/nal,** *adj., n.*

e·pis·tle (Ɩ pĬs′əl), *n.* 1. a written communication; a letter, esp. one of formal or didactic character. 2. (*usually cap.*) one of the apostolic letters found in the New Testament. 3. (*often cap.*) an extract, usually from one of the Epistles of the New Testament, forming part of the Eucharistic service in certain churches. [ME; OE *epistol*, t. L: s. *epistola*, t. Gk.: m. *epistolē* message, letter]

e·pis·tler (Ɩ pĬs′lər, Ɩ pĬs′t′lər), *n.* 1. a writer of an epistle. 2. the one who reads the epistle in the Eucharistic service. Also, **e·pis·to·ler** (Ɩ pĬs′tə lər).

e·pis·to·lar·y (Ɩ pĬs′tə lĕr′Ĭ), *adj.* 1. contained in or carried on by letters. 2. of or pertaining to letters.

ep·i·style (ĕp′ə stĬl′), *n. Archit.* an architrave. [t. L: m.s. *epistylium*, t. Gk.: m. *epistylion*]

ep·i·taph (ĕp′ə tăf′, -täf′), *n.* 1. a commemorative inscription on a tomb or mortuary monument. 2. any brief writing resembling such an inscription. [ME *epitaphe*, t. L: m.s. *epitaphium*, t. Gk.: m. *epitáphion* funeral oration, neut. of *epitáphios* over or at a tomb] —**ep·i·taph·ic** (ĕp′ə tăf′Ĭk), *adj.* —**ep/i·taph′ist,** *n.*

e·pit·a·sis (Ɩ pĬt′ə sĬs), *n.* the part of an ancient drama (following the protasis) in which the action is developed, before the catastrophe. [NL, t. Gk.: an intensifying, a stretching]

ep·i·tha·la·mi·on (ĕp′ə thə lā′mĬ on), *n., pl.* -**mia** (-mĬ ə). epithalamium.

ep·i·tha·la·mi·um (ĕp′ə thə lā′mĬ əm), *n., pl.* -**miums, -mia** (-mĬ ə), a nuptial song or poem; a poem in honor of a bride and bridegroom. [t. L, t. Gk.: m. *epithalámion* (neut. adj.) nuptial]

ep·i·the·li·al (ĕp′ə thē′lĬ əl), *adj.* of epithelium.

ep·i·the·li·oid (ĕp′ə thē′lĬ oid′), *adj.* resembling epithelium.

ep·i·the·li·o·ma (ĕp′ə thē′lĬ ō′mə), *n., pl.* -**mata** (-mə tə), -**mas.** *Pathol.* a cancer or malignant growth consisting chiefly of epithelial cells. [NL; f. EPITHELI(UM) + -OMA]

ep·i·the·li·um (ĕp′ə thē′lĬ əm), *n., pl.* -**liums, -lia** (-lĬ ə). *Biol.* any tissue which covers a surface, or lines a cavity or the like, and which performs protective, secreting, or other functions, as the epidermis, the lining of blood vessels, etc. [NL, f. Gk.: *epi-* EPI- + m. *thēlē* nipple + m. -*ion*, dim. suffix]

ep·i·thet (ĕp′ə thĕt′), *n.* 1. an adjective or other term applied to a person or thing to express an attribute, as in Alexander *the Great*. 2. a meaningful name. [t. L: s. *epitheton*, t. Gk., prop. neut. of *epithetos* added] —**ep/i·thet/i·cal,** *adj.*

e·pit·o·me (Ɩ pĬt′ə mĬ), *n.* 1. a summary or condensed account, esp. of a literary work; an abstract. 2. a condensed representation of something: *the epitome of all mankind.* [t. L, t. Gk., der. *epitémnein* cut into, abridge]

e·pit·o·mist (Ɩ pĬt′ə mĬst), *n.* an epitomizer.

e·pit·o·mize (Ɩ pĬt′ə mĬz′), *v.t.* -**mized, -mizing.** 1. to make an epitome of. 2. to contain in small compass. —**e·pit′o·miz/er,** *n.*

ep·i·zo·ic (ĕp′ə zō′Ĭk), *adj. Zool.* externally parasitic.

ep·i·zo·ön (ĕp′ə zō′ŏn, -ən), *n., pl.* -**zoa** (-zō′ə). an external parasite; an ectozoön. [f. EPI- + ZOON]

ep·i·zo·öt·ic (ĕp′ə zō′ŏt′Ĭk), *Vet. Sci.* —*adj.* 1. (of diseases) prevalent temporarily among animals. —*n.* 2. an epizoötic disease. [f. EPI- + zo(o)- + -OTIC. Cf. F *épizoötique*]

ep·i·zo·ö·ty (ĕp′ə zō′ə tĬ), *n., pl.* -**ties.** an epizoötic disease.

e plu·ri·bus u·num (ē ploor′ə bəs ū′nəm), *Latin.* one out of many (motto of the United States).

ep·och (ĕp′ək *or, esp. Brit.*, ē′pŏk), *n.* 1. a particular period of time as marked by distinctive character, events, etc. 2. the beginning of any distinctive period in the history of anything. 3. a point of time distinguished by a particular event, or state of affairs. 4. *Geol.* the main division of a geological period, representing the time required for making a geological series. 5. *Astron.* **a.** an arbitrarily fixed instant of time or date (usually the beginning of a century or half century) used as a reference in giving the elements of a planetary orbit or the like. **b.** the mean longitude of a planet as seen from the sun at such an instant or date. [t. ML: s. *epocha*, t. Gk.: m. *epochē* check, pause, position, epoch]

ep·och·al (ĕp′ək əl), *adj.* 1. of or pertaining to an epoch or epochs. 2. of the nature of an epoch. 3. epochmaking.

ep·och-mak·ing (ĕp′ək mā′kĬng), *adj.* opening a new era, as in human history, thought, or knowledge: *an epoch-making discovery.*

ep·ode (ĕp′ōd), *n. Anc. Pros.* 1. a kind of lyric poem, invented by Archilochus (about 650 B.C.), in which a long verse is followed by a short one. 2. the part of a lyric ode following the strophe and antistrophe. [t. F, t. L: m.s. *epōdos*, t. Gk.: m. *epōidós* after song, incantation]

ep·o·nym (ĕp′ə nĭm), *n.* 1. a person, real or imaginary, from whom a tribe, place, institution, etc., takes, or is supposed to take, its name, as *Britons* from *Brut* (supposed to be the grandson of Aeneas). 2. any ancient official whose name was used to designate his year of office. [t. Gk.: s. *epōnymon* (neut.) named after] —**ep/o·nym′ic,** *adj.*

ep·on·y·mous (ĕ pŏn′ə məs), *adj.* giving one's name to a tribe, place, etc. [t. Gk.: m. *epōnymos*]

ep·on·y·my (ĕ pŏn′ə mĬ), *n.* the derivation of names from eponyms. [t. Gk.: m.s. *epōnymia* surname]

ep·o·pee (ĕp′ə pē′, ĕp′ə pē′), *n.* 1. an epic. 2. epic poetry. Also, **ep·o·poe·ia** (ĕp′ə pē′ə). [t. F, t. Gk.: m. *epopoiïa* epic poetry]

ep·os (ĕp′ŏs), *n.* 1. an epic. 2. epic poetry. [t. L, t. Gk.: word, tale, song, pl. epic poetry]

e·pox·y (ĕ pŏk′sĬ), *n., pl.* **epoxies,** *adj. Chem.* —*n.* 1. Also, **epoxy resin.** any of a class of substances derived by polymerization from certain viscous liquid or brittle solid compounds, used chiefly in adhesives, coatings, electrical insulation, solder mix, and in the casting of tools and dies. —*adj.* 2. containing an oxygen atom that bridges two connected atoms, as in *epoxyethane.* [f. EPI- + OXY-²]

Ep·ping Forest (ĕp′Ĭng), a former royal forest in E England, at one time nearly coextensive with Essex: now a park NE of London. 8¾ sq. mi.

ep·si·lon (ĕp′sə lŏn′, -lən *or, esp. Brit.*, ĕp sĬ′lən), *n.* the fifth letter (E, ε, English short E, e) of the Greek alphabet. [t. Gk.: m. *ē psilón* e simple]

Ep·som (ĕp′səm), *n.* a town in SE England, in Surrey, S of London: site of **Epsom Downs,** a famous race track where the annual Derby is held.

Epsom salt, (*often pl.*) hydrated magnesium sulfate, used as a cathartic, etc. [so called because first prepared from the water of the mineral springs at EPSOM]

Ep·stein (ĕp′stĬn), *n.* **Jacob,** born 1880, English sculptor, born in New York of Russian-Polish parents.

eq., 1. equal. 2. equation. 3. equivalent.

eq·ua·ble (ĕk′wə bəl, ē′kwə-), *adj.* 1. free from variations; uniform, as motion or temperature. 2. uniform in operation or effect, as laws. 3. tranquil, even, or not easily disturbed, as the mind [t. L: m.s. *aequābilis* that can be made equal] —**eq/ua·bil′i·ty, eq/ua·ble·ness,** *n.* —**eq/ua·bly,** *adv.* —Syn. 1, 3. See even.

e·qual (ē′kwəl), *adj., n., v.,* equaled, equaling or (*esp. Brit.*) equalled, equalling. —*adj.* 1. as great as another (fol. by *to* or *with*): *the velocity of sound is not equal to that of light.* 2. like or alike in quantity, degree, value, etc.; of the same rank, ability, merit, etc. 3. evenly proportioned or balanced: *an equal mixture, an equal contest.* 4. uniform in operation or effect: *equal laws.* 5. adequate or sufficient in quantity or degree: *the supply is equal to the demand.* 6. having adequate powers, ability, or means: *he was not equal to the task.* 7. level, as a plain. 8. *Archaic.* tranquil or undisturbed. 9. *Archaic.* impartial or equitable. —*n.* 10. one who or that which is equal. —*v.t.* 11. to be or become equal to; match. 12. to make or do something equal to. 13. to recompense fully. 14. *Archaic.* to make equal; equalize. [t. L: m.s. *aequālis* like, equal]

—Syn. 2. proportionate, commensurate, coördinate, correspondent. EQUAL, EQUIVALENT, TANTAMOUNT imply a correspondence between two or more things. EQUAL indicates a correspondence in all respects, unless a particular respect (or respects) is stated or implied: *a dime is equal to ten cents* (that is, in purchasing power, which is implied) EQUIVALENT indicates a correspondence in one or more respects, but not in all: *an egg is said to be the equivalent of a pound of meat* (that is, in nutritive value). TANTAMOUNT, a word of limited application, is used esp. of immaterial things which are equivalent to such an extent as to be practically identical: *the prisoner's refusal to answer was tantamount to an admission of guilt.* 4. even, uniform, regular, unvarying. 10. peer.

e·qual·i·tar·i·an (Ɩ kwŏl′ə târ′Ĭ ən), *adj.* 1. pertaining or adhering to the doctrine of equality among men. —*n.* 2. one who adheres to the doctrine of equality among men. —**e·qual/i·tar/i·an·ism,** *n.*

e·qual·i·ty (Ɩ kwŏl′ə tĬ), *n., pl.* -**ties.** 1. state of being equal; correspondence in quantity, degree, value, rank, ability, etc. **2.** uniform character, as of motion or surface.

e·qual·ize (ē/kwə līz′), v.t., **-ized, -izing. 1.** to make equal: *to equalize tax burdens.* **2.** to make uniform. —e/qual·i·za′tion, n.

e·qual·iz·er (ē/kwə lī/zər), n. **1.** one who or that which equalizes. **2.** any of various devices or appliances for equalizing strains, pressures, etc. **3.** *Elect.* an electrical connection established between two points in a network to secure some constant relation between the two points, as potential, impedance, etc.

e·qual·ly (ē/kwəl ī), adv. in an equal manner; to an equal degree.

e·qua·nim·i·ty (ē/kwə nĭm/ə tĭ, ĕk/wə-), n. evenness of mind or temper; calmness; composure. [t. L: m.s. *aequanimitas,* der. *aequanimis* of an even mind]

e·quate (ĭ kwāt′), v.t., **equated, equating. 1.** to state the equality of or between; put in the form of an equation. **2.** to reduce to an average; make such correction or allowance in as will reduce to a common standard of comparison. **3.** to regard, treat, or represent as equivalent. [t. L: m.s. *aequātus,* pp., made equal]

e·qua·tion (ĭ kwā′zhən, -shən), n. **1.** act of making equal; equalization. **2.** equally balanced state; equilibrium. **3.** *Math.* **a.** an expression of, or a proposition asserting, the equality of two quantities, employing the sign = between them. **b.** a mathematical formula interpreted as a question asking for what values of a variable two expressions in that variable are equal, as $3x^2 - 2x + 4 = 0$. **4.** *Chem.* a symbolic representation of a reaction. **5.** See **personal equation.** —e·qua′tion·al, adj.

e·qua·tor (ĭ kwā′tər), n. **1.** that great circle of a sphere or any heavenly body which has a center at each pole and lies equidistant between them, its plane being perpendicular to the axis of the sphere or heavenly body. **2.** the great circle of the earth, equidistant from the North and South Poles. **3.** a circle separating a surface into two congruent parts. [ME, t. LL: m. *aequātor,* lit., equalizer (of day and night, as when the sun is on the equator)]

e·qua·to·ri·al (ē/kwə tōr/ĭ əl, ĕk/wə-), adj. **1.** of, pertaining to, or near an equator, esp. the equator of the earth. **2.** of or like the regions at the earth's equator: *equatorial vegetation.* —n. **3.** a telescope mounting having two axes of motion, one parallel to the earth's axis, and one at right angles to it. —e/qua·to/ri·al·ly, adv.

eq·uer·ry (ĕk/wər ĭ), n., pl. **-ries. 1.** an officer of a royal or similar household, charged with the care of the horses. **2.** an officer who attends on the British sovereign. [t. F: m. *écurie,* OF *escuirie,* der. *escuier* SQUIRE]

e·ques·tri·an (ĭ kwĕs′trĭ ən), adj. **1.** of or pertaining to horsemen or horsemanship. **2.** mounted on horseback. **3.** of or pertaining to the Roman equites: *the equestrian order.* **4.** representing a person on horseback: *an equestrian statue.* **5.** pertaining to or composed of knights. —n. **6.** a rider or performer on horseback. [f. L *equestri(s)* of a horseman + -AN]

e·ques·tri·enne (ĭ kwĕs/trĭ ĕn′), n. a female rider or performer on horseback. [pseudo-F fem. of EQUESTRIAN]

equi-, a word element meaning "equal," as in *equidistant, equivalent.* [comb. form repr. L *aequus* equal]

e·qui·an·gu·lar (ē/kwĭ ăng/gyə lər), adj. having all the angles equal.

e·qui·dis·tance (ē/kwə dĭs′təns), n. equal distance.

e·qui·dis·tant (ē/kwə dĭs′tənt), adj. equally distant. —e/qui·dis′tant·ly, adv.

e·qui·lat·er·al (ē/kwə lăt′ər əl), adj. **1.** having all the sides equal. —n. **2.** a figure having all its sides equal. **3.** a side equivalent, or equal, to others. [t. LL: s. *aequilaterālis*] —e/qui·lat/er·al·ly, adv.

e·quil·i·brant (ĭ kwĭl/ə brənt), n. *Physics.* a counterbalancing force or system of forces.

Equilateral triangle

e·quil·i·brate (ē/kwə lī/brāt, ĭ kwĭl/ə- brāt′), v., **-brated, -brating.** —v.t. **1.** to balance equally; keep in equipoise or equilibrium. **2.** to be in equilibrium with; counterpoise. —v.i. **3.** to balance. [t. LL: m.s. *aequilibrātus* in equilibrium, f. L: *aequi-* EQUI- + *lībrātus* balanced] —e·quil·i·bra·tion (ē/kwə lī/brā′shən, ĭ kwĭl/ə-), n. —e·quil·i·bra·tor (ē/kwĭ lī/brā′tər), n.

e·quil·i·brist (ĭ kwĭl/ə brĭst), n. one who practices balancing in unnatural positions and hazardous movements, as a ropedancer. [f. EQUILIBR(IUM) + -IST] —e·quil/i·bris/tic, adj.

e·qui·lib·ri·um (ē/kwə lĭb/rĭ əm), n. **1.** a state of rest due to the action of forces that counteract each other. **2.** equal balance between any powers, influences, etc.; equality of effect. **3.** mental balance. **4.** *Chem.* the condition obtaining when a chemical reaction and its reverse reaction proceed at equal rates. [t. L: m. *aequilibrium,* f. *aequi-* EQUI- + s. *lībra* balance + *-ium* -IUM]

e·quine (ē/kwīn), adj. **1.** of or resembling a horse. —n. **2.** a horse. [t. L: m.s. *equīnus,* der. *equus* horse]

e·qui·noc·tial (ē/kwə nŏk/shəl), adj. **1.** pertaining to an equinox or the equinoxes, or to the equality of day and night. **2.** pertaining to the celestial equator. **3.** occurring at or about the time of an equinox: *an equinoctial storm.* **4.** *Bot.* (of a flower) opening regularly at a certain hour. —n. **5.** equinoctial line. **6.** a gale or storm at or near the time of an equinox. [ME, t. L: m.s. *aequinoctiālis,* der. *aequinoctium* EQUINOX]

equinoctial line, the celestial equator. Also, **equinoctial circle.**

equinoctial point, either of the two points in which the celestial equator and the ecliptic intersect each other, reached by the sun's center at the equinoxes.

e·qui·nox (ē/kwə nŏks′), n. **1.** the time when the sun crosses the plane of the earth's equator, making night and day all over the earth of equal length, occurring about March 21 (**vernal equinox**) and Sept. 22 (**autumnal equinox**). **2.** either of the equinoctial points. [t. ML: m.s. *equinoxium,* L *aequinoctium* equality between day and night]

e·quip (ĭ kwĭp′), v.t. **equipped, equipping. 1.** to furnish or provide with whatever is needed for service or for any undertaking; to fit out, as a ship. **2.** to dress out; array. [t. F: m. *équipper,* OF *esquiper,* prob. t. Scand.; cf. Icel. *skipa* put in order, arrange, man (a ship, etc.)] —e·quip′per, n. —Syn. 1. See **furnish.**

eq·ui·page (ĕk/wə pĭj), n. **1.** a carriage. **2.** a completely equipped carriage, with horses and servants. **3.** outfit, as of a ship, an army, or a soldier; equipment. **4.** a set of small household articles, as of china. **5.** a collection of articles for personal ornament or use.

e·quip·ment (ĭ kwĭp′mənt), n. **1.** anything used in or provided for equipping. **2.** act of equipping. **3.** state of being equipped. **4.** a person's knowledge and skill necessary for a task, etc.: *a man's equipment for the law, for medicine.* **5.** *Railroads.* rolling stock. —Syn. 1. apparatus, paraphernalia.

e·qui·poise (ē/kwə poiz′, ĕk/wə-), n. **1.** an equal distribution of weight; even balance; equilibrium. **2.** a counterpoise.

e·qui·pol·lent (ē/kwə pŏl/ənt), adj. **1.** equal in power, effect, etc.; equivalent. **2.** *Logic.* (of two propositions, etc.) logically deducible from each other, as "All men are mortal" and "No men are immortal." —n. **3.** an equivalent. [t. L: m.s. *aequipollens* of equal value] —e/qui·pol′lence, e/qui·pol/len·cy, n.

e·qui·pon·der·ance (ē/kwə pŏn/dər əns), n. equality of weight; equipoise. Also, **e/qui·pon/der·an·cy.** —e/qui·pon/der·ant, adj.

e·qui·pon·der·ate (ē/kwə pŏn/də rāt′), v.t., **-ated, -ating.** to equal or offset in weight, force, importance, etc.; counterbalance. [t. ML: m.s. *aequiponderātus,* pp. of *aequiponderāre,* f. L: *aequi-* EQUI- + *ponderāre* weigh]

e·qui·po·tent (ē/kwə pō′tənt), adj. equal in power.

e·qui·po·ten·tial (ē/kwə pō tĕn′shəl), adj. *Physics.* of the same potential.

e·qui·ro·tal (ē/kwə rō′təl), adj. having wheels all of the same size or diameter, as a vehicle.

eq·ui·se·tum (ĕk/wə sē′təm), n., pl. **-tums, -ta** (-tə). any plant of the genus *Equisetum;* a horsetail or scouring rush. [NL, m. L *equisaetum,* f. *equi-* horse + m. *saeta* bristle]

eq·ui·ta·ble (ĕk/wə tə bəl), adj. **1.** characterized by equity or fairness; just and right; fair; reasonable. **2.** *Law.* pertaining to or valid in equity, as distinguished from the common law. —**eq/ui·ta·ble·ness,** n. —**eq/ui·ta·bly,** adv.

eq·ui·tant (ĕk/wə tənt), adj. *Bot.* straddling or overlapping, as leaves whose bases overlap the leaves above or within them. [t. L: s. *equitans,* ppr., riding]

eq·ui·ta·tion (ĕk/wə tā′shən), n. horsemanship. [t. L: s. *equitātio,* der. *equitāre* ride]

eq·ui·tes (ĕk/wə tēz′), n. pl. **1.** (in ancient Rome) **a.** the mounted military units; the cavalry. **b.** the equestrian order of knights. **2.** (later) a privileged or imperial class. [t. L, pl. of *eques* a horseman, knight]

eq·ui·ty (ĕk/wə tĭ), n., pl. **-ties. 1.** the quality of being fair or impartial; fairness; impartiality. **2.** that which is fair and just. **3.** *Law.* **a.** the application of the dictates of conscience or the principles of natural justice to the settlement of controversies. **b.** a system of jurisprudence or a body of doctrines and rules developed in England and followed in the United States, serving to supplement and remedy the limitations and the inflexibility of the common law. **c.** an equitable right or claim. **d.** an equity of redemption. **4.** the interest of a shareholder as distinguished from that of a bondholder. [ME *equite,* t. L: m.s. *aequitas* equality, justice]

equity of redemption, 1. the right of a mortgagor or pledgor by absolute deed to redeem the property by paying the debt, even after forfeiture, but before sale under foreclosure or transfer of title, or before this right is barred by statutes of limitation. **2.** the interest of an owner of land which is subject to a mortgage.

equiv., equivalent.

e·quiv·a·lence (ĭ kwĭv/ə ləns), n. **1.** state or fact of being equivalent; equality in value, force, significance, etc. **2.** *Chem.* the quality of having equal valence. Also, **e·quiv/a·len·cy.**

e·quiv·a·lent (ĭ kwĭv/ə lənt), adj. **1.** equal in value, measure, force, effect, significance, etc. **2.** corresponding in position, function, etc. **3.** *Geom.* having the same extent, as a triangle and a square of equal area. **4.** *Chem.* having the same capacity to combine or react chemically. —n. **5.** that which is equivalent. [ME, t. LL: s. *aequivalens,* ppr., having equal power] —e·quiv/a·lent·ly, adv. —Syn. 1. See **equal.**

e·quiv·o·cal (ĭ kwĭv/ə kəl), adj. **1.** of uncertain significance; not determined; an *equivocal attitude.* **2.** of doubtful nature or character; questionable; dubious;

b., blend of, blended; c., cognate with; d., dialect, dialectal; der., derived from; f., formed from; g., going back to; m., modification of; r., replacing; s., stem of; t., taken from; ?, perhaps. See the full key on inside cover

suspicious. **3.** having different meanings equally possible, as a word or phrase; susceptible of double interpretation; ambiguous. [f. ME *equivoc* (t. LL: m.s. *aequivocus* ambiguous) + -AL¹] —**e·quiv'o·cal·ly**, *adv.* —**e·quiv'o·cal·ness**, *n.* —Syn. **3.** See **ambiguous**.

e·quiv·o·cate (ĭkwĭv'əkāt'), *v.i.*, **-cated, -cating.** to use equivocal or ambiguous expressions, esp. to mislead; prevaricate. [back formation from EQUIVOCATION] —**e·quiv'o·cat'ing·ly**, *adv.* —**e·quiv'o·ca'tor**, *n.*

e·quiv·o·ca·tion (ĭkwĭv'əkā'shən), *n.* **1.** the use of equivocal or ambiguous expressions, esp. in order to mislead; prevarication. **2.** *Logic.* a fallacy depending on the double meaning of a word. [ME, t. LL: m.s. *aequivocātiō*]

eq·ui·voque (ĕk'wəvōk', ē'kwə-), *n.* **1.** an equivocal term; an ambiguous expression. **2.** a play upon words; a pun. **3.** double meaning; ambiguity. Also, **eq'ui·voke'**. [t. F, r. ME *equivoc*. See EQUIVOCAL]

-er¹, a suffix: **a.** forming nouns designating persons from the object of their occupation or labor, as in *hatter*, *tiler*, *tinner*, *moonshiner*, or from their place of origin or abode, as in *Icelander*, *southerner*, *villager*, or designating either persons or things from some special characteristic or circumstance, as in *six-footer*, *three-master*, *teetotaler*, *fiver*, *tenner*. **b.** serving as the regular English formative of agent nouns (being attached to verbs of any origin), as in *bearer*, *creeper*, *employer*, *harvester*, *teacher*, *theorizer*. [OE *-ere*, c. G *-er*, etc.; akin to L *-ārius*]

-er², a suffix of nouns denoting persons or things concerned or connected with something, as in *butler*, *grocer*, *officer*, *garner*. [ME, t. AF, OF: *-er*, *-ier*, g. L *-ārius*, neut. *-ārium*. *Cf.* -ARY¹]

-er³, termination of certain nouns denoting action or process, as in *dinner*, *rejoinder*, *remainder*, *trover*. [t. F; orig. sign of inf.]

-er⁴, a suffix forming the comparative degree of adjectives, as in *harder*, *smaller*. [OE *-ra*, *-re*, c. G *-er*]

-er⁵, a suffix forming the comparative degree of adverbs, as in *faster*. [OE *-or*, c. OHG *-or*, G *-er*]

-er⁶, a suffix forming frequentative verbs, as *flicker*, *flutter*, *glimmer*, *patter*. [OE *-r-*, c. G *-(e)r-*]

Er, *Chem.* erbium.

E.R., **1.** East Riding (Yorkshire). **2.** East River (New York City). **3.** (L *Eduardus Rex*), King Edward.

e·ra (Yr'ə, ē'rə), *n.* **1.** a period of time marked by distinctive character, events, etc.: *an era of progress.* **2.** the period of time to which anything belongs or is to be assigned. **3.** a system of chronologic notation reckoned from a given date. **4.** a period during which years are numbered and dates reckoned from a particular point of time in the past: *the Christian era.* **5.** a point of time from which succeeding years are numbered, as at the beginning of a system of chronology. **6.** a date or an event forming the beginning of any distinctive period. **7.** *Geol.* a major division of geological time: *Paleozoic era.* [t. LL, var. of *aera* number or epoch by which reckoning is made, era, prob. the same word as L *aera* counters, pl. of *aes* copper, bronze] —Syn. **1.** See **age**.

e·ra·di·a·tion (Yrā'dY ā'shən), *n.* act or process of shooting forth (light rays, etc.); radiation.

e·rad·i·ca·ble (Yrăd'əkəbəl), *adj.* that may be eradicated.

e·rad·i·cate (Yrăd'əkāt'), *v.t.*, **-cated, -cating. 1.** to remove or destroy utterly; extirpate. **2.** to pull up by the roots. [t. L, m.s. *ērādīcātus*, pp. rooted out] —**e·rad'i·ca'tion**, *n.* —**e·rad'i·ca'tive**, *adj.* —**e·rad'i·ca'tor**, *n.* —Syn. **1.** See **abolish**.

e·rase (Y rās'), *v.t.*, **erased, erasing. 1.** to rub or scrape out, as letters or characters written, engraved, etc.; efface. **2.** to obliterate material recorded on an electromagnetic tape by demagnetizing it. [t. L: m.s. *ērāsus*, pp., scratched out] —**e·ras'a·ble**, *adj.* —Syn. expunge, obliterate. See **cancel**.

e·ras·er (Y rā'sər), *n.* an instrument, as a piece of rubber or cloth, for erasing marks made with pen, pencil, chalk, etc.

E·ras·mus (Yrăz'məs), *n.* **Desiderius** (dĕz'ədYr'Y əs), *(Gerhard Gerhards)* 1466?–1536, Dutch humanist, scholar, theologian, and satirist.

E·ras·tian (Yrăs'chən, -tY'ən), *adj.* **1.** pertaining to Thomas Erastus, or to his doctrines, advocating the supremacy of the state in ecclesiastical matters. —*n.* **2.** an advocate of the doctrines of Erastus. —**E·ras'tian·ism**, *n.*

E·ras·tus (Y răs'təs; *Ger.* ā räs'tŏŏs), *n.* **Thomas** (tŏm'əs; *Ger.* tō'mäs), 1524–83, a Swiss-German theologian.

e·ras·ure (Y rā'shər), *n.* **1.** act of erasing. **2.** a place where something has been erased.

E·ra·to (ĕr'ətō'), *n. Gk. Myth.* the Muse of love poetry. [t. L, t. Gk.: lit., lovesome]

Er·a·tos·the·nes (ĕr'ətŏs'thənēz'), *n.* 276?–195? B.C., Greek mathematician and astronomer, at Alexandria.

er·bi·um (ûr'bY əm), *n. Chem.* a rare-earth metallic element, having pink salts. *Symbol:* Er; *at. wt.:* 167.2; *at. no.:* 68. [t. NL: f. (*Ytt*)*erb*(*y*) (see YTTERBIUM) + *-ium* -IUM]

Erck·mann-Cha·tri·an (ĕrk măn' shà trē än'), *n.* the joint pen name of **Émile** (ĕ mēl') **Erckmann**, 1822–99, and **Alexandre** (å lĕk săn'dr) **Chatrian**, 1826–90, collaborating French novelists and dramatists.

ere (âr), *prep.* **1.** before (in time). —*conj.* **2.** before. **3.** sooner than; rather than. [ME; OE *ǣr*, *er* (c. G *eher*), comparative of OE *ār* soon, early, c. Goth. *air*. See ERST, EARLY]

Er·e·bus (ĕr'ə bəs), *n.* **1.** *Gk. Myth.* a place of nether darkness through which the shades of the dead pass on their way to Hades: *dark as Erebus.* **2. Mount,** a volcano on Ross Island, in Antarctica. ab. 13,370 ft.

Er·ech·the·um (ĕr'ək thē'əm), *n.* a temple of Ionic order on the Acropolis, built c420 B.C., and one of the most perfect examples of Greek architecture, notable for its porches of different height, supported by caryatides.

e·rect (Y rĕkt'), *adj.* **1.** upright in position or posture: *to stand or sit erect.* **2.** raised or directed upward: *a dog with ears erect.* **3.** *Bot.* vertical throughout; not spreading or declined: *an erect stem, an erect leaf or ovule.* —*v.t.* **4.** to build; construct; raise: *to erect a house.* **5.** to raise and set in an upright or perpendicular position: *to erect a telegraph pole.* **6.** *Geom.* to draw or construct (a line or figure) upon a given line, base, or the like. **7.** *Optics.* to change (an inverted image) to a normal position. **8.** to form (fol. by *into*): *to erect a territory into a state.* **9.** to set up or establish, as an institution; found. **10.** *Mach.* to assemble; make ready for use. [ME, t. L: s. *ērectus*, pp., set upright, built] —**e·rect'a·ble**, *adj.* —**e·rect'er**, *n.* —**e·rect'ly**, *adv.* —**e·rect'ness**, *n.* —Syn. **1.** standing, vertical. See **upright.** **5.** upraise.

e·rec·tile (Y rĕk'təl, -tŸl), *adj.* **1.** capable of being erected or set upright. **2.** *Anat.* susceptible of being distended with blood and becoming rigid, as tissue. —**e·rec·til·i·ty** (Y rĕk'tŸl'ə tŸ, ē'rĕk-), *n.*

e·rec·tion (Y rĕk'shən), *n.* **1.** act of erecting. **2.** state of being erected. **3.** something erected, as a building or other structure. **4.** *Physiol.* a turgid and rigid state of an organ or part containing erectile tissue.

e·rec·tive (Y rĕk'tŸv), *adj.* tending to erect.

e·rec·tor (Y rĕk'tər), *n.* **1.** erecter. **2.** *Anat.* a muscle which erects the body or one of its parts.

ere·long (âr lông', -lŏng'), *adv.* before long; soon.

er·e·mite (ĕr'ə mīt'), *n.* a religious solitary; a hermit. [ME, t. LL: m. *erēmīta*, t. Gk.: m. *erēmītēs* a hermit] —**er·e·mit·ic** (ĕr'ə mŸt'Ÿk), **er'e·mit'i·cal, er·e·mit·ish** (ĕr'ə mī'tŸsh), *adj.*

ere·now (âr nou'), *adv.* ere now; before this time.

er·e·thism (ĕr'ə thŸz'əm), *n. Physiol.* an unusual or excessive degree of irritability or stimulation in an organ or tissue. [t. Gk.: s. *erethismós* irritation]

ere·while (âr hwīl'), *adv. Archaic.* a while before; formerly.

Er·furt (ĕr'fŏŏrt), *n.* a city in East Germany. 188,112 (est. 1955).

erg (ûrg), *n. Physics.* the unit of work or energy in the cgs system, being the work done by a force of one dyne when its point of application moves through a distance of one centimeter. [t. Gk.: s. *érgon* work. See WORK, *n.*]

er·go (ûr'gō; *older* ĕr'gō), *conj.*, *adv. Latin.* therefore; accordingly; consequently.

er·gos·ter·ol (ər gŏs'tə rōl', -rŏl'), *n. Biochem.* a sterol derived from ergot and contained in yeast, converted into vitamin D by exposure to ultraviolet rays. [f. ERGO(T) + STEROL]

er·got (ûr'gət, -gŏt), *n.* **1.** a disease of rye and other cereals, due to a fungus (in rye, *Claviceps purpurea*) which replaces the grain by a long, hard, hornlike, dark-colored body. **2.** a body so produced. **3.** the sclerotium of *C. purpurea*, developed on rye plants, and used as a hemostatic, etc. [t. F, in OF *argot* cock's spur]

er·got·ine (ûr'gət Ÿn), *n.* any of various extracts of ergot (def. 3) used in medicine.

er·got·ism (ûr'gə tŸz'əm), *n.* a disease due to eating food prepared from rye, etc., affected with ergot.

erg-sec·ond (ûrg'sĕk'ənd), *n. Physics.* a unit of action: one erg per second.

Er·hard (âr'härt; *Ger.* är'härt), *n.* **Lud·wig** (lŏŏd'-vŸKH), born 1897, chancellor of the West German Federal Republic since 1963.

er·i·ca·ceous (ĕr'Y kā'shəs), *adj.* belonging to the *Ericaceae*, or heath family of plants, which includes the heath, arbutus, azalea, rhododendron, American laurel, etc. [f. m.s. NL *Ericāceae* (der. *Erica* the heath genus, t. Gk.: m. *ereíkē* heath) + -OUS]

Er·ic·son (ĕr'Ÿk sən), *n.* **Leif** (lēf; *Icel.* lāv), fl. A.D. 1000, a Scandinavian navigator (son of Eric the Red); probable discoverer of "Vineland" or Nova Scotia.

Er·ics·son (ĕr'Ÿk sən), *n.* **1. John**, 1803–89, a Swedish-American engineer and inventor. **2.** Ericson.

Er·ic the Red (ĕr'Ÿk), born about A.D. 950, Norseman who discovered Greenland about A.D. 982 and later colonized it. Also, **Eric.**

E·rie (Yr'Y), *n.* **1. Lake,** one of the five Great Lakes, between the U.S. and Canada: the southernmost and most shallow of the group: Commodore Perry's defeat of the British, 1813. 239 mi. long; 9940 sq. mi. **2.** a city in NW Pennsylvania: a port on Lake Erie. 138,440 (1960). **3.** a member of a tribe of American Indians formerly living along the southern shore of Lake Erie. The Senecas conquered (1653) and absorbed them.

Erie Canal, a canal in New York, from Albany to Buffalo, connecting the Hudson with Lake Erie: completed in 1825. See **New York State Barge Canal.**

ăct, āble, dâre, ärt; ĕbb, ēqual; Yf, īce; hŏt, ōver, ôrder, oil, bŏŏk, ōōze, out; ŭp, ūse, ûrge; ə = a in alone; ch, chief; g, give; ng, ring; sh, shoe; th, thin; ᵺ, that; zh, vision.   See the full key on inside cover.

e·rig·er·on (ĭ rĭj′ə rŏn′), *n.* any plant of the composite genus *Erigeron*, with flower heads resembling those of the asters but having narrower and usually more numerous (white or purple) rays. [t. L, t. Gk.: groundsel]

Er·in (âr′ĭn, ĭr′ĭn, ĕr′ĭn), *n. Poetic.* Ireland. [t. OIrish: m. *Erinn*, dat. of *Eriu*, later *Eire* Ireland]

e·ri·na·ceous (ĕr′ĭ nā′shəs), *adj.* of the hedgehog kind or family.

e·rin·go (ĭ rĭng′gō), *n.* eryngo.

E·rin·ys (ĭ rĭn′ĭs, ĭ rī′nĭs), *n., pl.* **Erinyes** (ĭ rĭn′ĭ ēz′). *Gk. Myth.* one of the Furies.

E·ris (ĭr′ĭs, ĕr′ĭs), *n. Gk. Myth.* the goddess of discord, sister of Ares. See **apple of discord.**

er·is·tic (ĕ rĭs′tĭk), *adj.* pertaining to controversy or disputation; controversial. [t. Gk.: m.s. *eristikós*, der *erizein* wrangle]

E·ri·tre·a (ĕr′ĭ trē′ə; *It.* ĕ′rē trĕ′ä), *n.* a former Italian colony in NE Africa, on the Red Sea: now an autonomous province federated with Ethiopia. 1,104,000 pop. (est. 1951); 47,076 sq. mi. *Cap.:* Asmara. —**Er′i·tre′an,** *adj., n.*

Er·i·van (ĕr′ĭ vän′y), *n.* a city in the S Soviet Union, in Caucasia: the capital of the Armenian Republic. 385,000 (est. 1956).

erl·king (ûrl′kĭng′), *n.* (in German and Scandinavian mythology) a spirit or personified natural power which works mischief, esp. to children. [repr. G *erlkönig* alderking, itself a mistrans. of Dan. *ellerkonge,* var. of *elverkonge* king of the elves]

er·mine (ûr′mĭn), *n., pl.* **-mines,** (*esp. collectively*) **-mine. 1.** an Old World weasel, *Mustela erminea,* which turns white in winter. The brown summer phase is called the stoat. **2.** *U.S.* any of a number of weasels that are white in winter. **3.** the lustrous white winter fur of the ermine, having a black tail tip. **4.** the office or dignity of a judge. [ME, t. OF: m. (h)*ermine,* t. Gmc.; cf. OHG *harmīn* pertaining to the ermine]

Ermine. *Mustela erminea*
(10 to 11 in. long, tail ab. 4 in.)

er·mined (ûr′mĭnd), *adj.* covered or adorned with ermine.

-ern, adj. suffix occurring in *northern,* etc. [ME and OE *-erne,* c. OHG *-rōni* (as in *nordrōni* northern)]

erne (ûrn), *n.* a sea eagle. Also, **ern.** [ME; OE *earn,* c. MLG *arn* eagle]

e·rode (ĭ rōd′), *v.t.,* **eroded, eroding. 1.** to eat out or away; destroy by slow consumption. **2.** to form (a channel, etc.) by eating or wearing away (used esp. in geology, to denote the action of all the forces of nature that wear away the earth's surface). [t. L: m.s. *ērōdere* gnaw off]

e·rod·ent (ĭ rō′dənt), *adj.* eroding; erosive: *the erodent power of wind.*

e·rog·e·nous (ĭ rŏj′ə nəs), *adj.* arousing or tending to arouse sexual desire.

E·ros (ĭr′ŏs, ĕr′ŏs), *n.* the Greek god of love, identified by the Romans with Cupid. [t. L, t. Gk.: lit., love]

e·rose (ĭ rōs′), *adj.* **1.** uneven as if gnawed away. **2.** *Bot.* having the margin irregularly incised as if gnawed, as a leaf. [t. L: m.s. *ērōsus,* pp., gnawed off]

e·ro·sion (ĭ rō′zhən), *n.* **1.** act of eroding. **2.** state of being eroded. **3.** the process by which the surface of the earth is worn away by the action of water, glaciers, winds, waves, etc.

e·ro·sive (ĭ rō′sĭv), *adj.* serving to erode; causing erosion.

Erosion
Section of stratified rock bent into a low anticline by erosion

e·rot·ic (ĭ rŏt′ĭk), *adj.* **1.** of or pertaining to sexual love; amatory. —*n.* **2.** an erotic poem. **3.** an erotic person. [t. Gk.: m.s. *erōtikós* pertaining to love. See **Eros**] —**e·rot′i·cal·ly,** *adv.*

e·rot·i·cism (ĭ rŏt′ə sĭz′əm), *n.* **1.** erotic character or tendency. **2.** *Psychoanal.* erotism.

er·o·tism (ĕr′ə tĭz′əm), *n. Psychoanal.* the arousal and satisfaction of sexual desire.

ERP, European Recovery Program. Also, **E.R.P.**

err (ûr), *v.i.* **1.** to go astray in thought or belief; be mistaken; be incorrect. **2.** to go astray morally; sin. **3.** to deviate from the true course, aim, or purpose. [ME *erre(n),* t. OF: m. *errer,* t. L: m. *errāre* wander]

er·rand (ĕr′ənd), *n.* **1.** a trip to convey a message or execute a commission; a short journey for a specific purpose: *he was sent on an errand.* **2.** a special business entrusted to a messenger; a commission. **3.** the purpose of any trip or journey: *his errand was to bribe the chieftain into releasing the captives.* [ME; OE *ærende,* c. OHG *ārunti.* Cf. OE *ār* messenger]

er·rant (ĕr′ənt), *adj.* **1.** journeying or traveling, as a medieval knight in quest of adventure; roving adventurously. **2.** deviating from the regular or proper course; erring. [ME *erraunte,* t. F: m. *errant,* prop. ppr. of *errer,* OF *esrer* travel (g. VL *iterāre* journey), but b. with F *errant,* ppr. of *errer* **ERR**] —**er′rant·ly,** *adv.*

er·rant·ry (ĕr′ən trĭ), *n., pl.* **-ries.** conduct or performance like that of a knight-errant.

er·ra·re hu·ma·num est (ĕr ä′rĭ hū mä′nəm ĕst′), *Latin.* to err is human.

er·ra·ta (ĭ rä′tə, ĭ rä′-), *n. pl.* of **erratum.**

er·rat·ic (ĭ răt′ĭk), *adj.* **1.** deviating from the proper or usual course in conduct or opinion; eccentric; queer. **2.** having no certain course; wandering; not fixed: *an erratic star* (a planet). **3.** *Geol.* **a.** (of boulders, etc.) transported from the original site to an unusual location, as by glacial action. **b.** pertaining to such boulders, etc. —*n.* **4.** an erratic or eccentric person. **5.** *Geol.* an erratic boulder or block of rock. [ME, t. L: s. *errāticus,* der. *errāre* wander, **ERR**] —**er·rat′i·cal·ly,** *adv.*

er·ra·tum (ĭ rä′təm, ĭ rä′-), *n., pl.* **-ta** (-tə). an error in writing or printing. [t. L: prop. pp. neut., erred]

er·rhine (ĕr′ĭn, ĕr′īn), *Med.* —*adj.* **1.** designed to be snuffed into the nose. **2.** occasioning discharges from the nose. —*n.* **3.** a medicine to be snuffed up the nostrils to promote sneezing and increased discharges. [t. NL: m.s. *errhīnum,* t. Gk.: m. *érrhīnon,* der. *en-* **EN-²** + *rhís* nose]

err·ing (ûr′ĭng, ĕr′-), *adj.* **1.** going astray; in error; wrong. **2.** sinning. —**err′ing·ly,** *adv.*

erron., 1. erroneous. **2.** erroneously.

er·ro·ne·ous (ə rō′nĭ əs, ĕ-), *adj.* **1.** containing error; mistaken; incorrect. **2.** *Obs. or Archaic.* straying from the right. [ME, t. L: m. *errōneus* straying] —**er·ro′ne·ous·ly,** *adv.* —**er·ro′ne·ous·ness,** *n.* —**Syn. 1.** inaccurate, wrong, untrue, false.

er·ror (ĕr′ər), *n.* **1.** deviation from accuracy or correctness; a mistake, as in action, speech, etc. **2.** the belief of what is not true. **3.** condition of believing what is not true: *in error about the date.* **4.** a moral offense; wrongdoing. **5.** *Math., etc.* the difference between the observed or approximately determined value and the true value of a quantity. **6.** *Baseball.* any faulty play (except certain misplays by the pitcher or catcher, as a wild pitch or a passed ball) which prolongs a batsman's time at bat or leaves a runner safe, or allows him to advance one or more bases when he should have been put out. [t. L; r. ME *errour,* t. OF] —**er′ror·less,** *adj.* —**Syn. 1.** blunder, slip, oversight. See **mistake.**

error of closure, *Survey.* **1.** the amount by which a closed traverse fails to satisfy the requirements of a true mathematical figure as the length of line joining the true and computed position of the same point. **2.** the ratio of this linear error to the perimeter of the traverse. **3.** (for angles) the amount by which the sum of the observed angles fails to equal the true sum.

er·satz (ĕr zäts′), *adj.* **1.** serving as a substitute: *an ersatz meat dish made of eggplant and oatmeal.* —*n.* **2.** a substitute. [t. G]

Erse (ûrs), *n.* **1.** Gaelic, esp. Scotch Gaelic. —*adj.* **2.** of or pertaining to the Celts in the Highlands of Scotland, or their language. [Scot. var. of **IRISH**]

Er·skine (ûr′skĭn), *n.* **1.** John, 1695–1768, Scottish writer on law. **2.** John, 1879–1951, U.S. author.

erst (ûrst), *adv. Archaic.* before the present time; formerly. [ME; OE *ǣrst,* syncopated var. of *ǣrest* (c. G *erst*), superl. of *ǣr.* See **ERE**]

erst·while (ûrst′hwīl′), *adj.* **1.** former: *erstwhile enemies.* —*adv.* **2.** *Archaic.* formerly; erst.

er·u·bes·cent (ĕr′ŏŏ bĕs′ənt), *adj.* becoming red or reddish; blushing. [t. L: s. *ērubescens,* ppr., reddening] —**er′u·bes′cence,** *n.*

e·ruct (ĭ rŭkt′), *v.t., v.i.* **1.** to belch forth, as wind from the stomach. **2.** to emit or issue violently, as matter from a volcano. [t. L: s. *ēructāre* belch forth]

e·ruc·tate (ĭ rŭk′tāt), *v.t., v.i.,* **-tated, -tating.** eruct. —**e·ruc·ta·tion** (ĭ rŭk′tā′shən, ē′rŭk-), *n.*

er·u·dite (ĕr′ŏŏ dīt′, ĕr′yŏŏ-), *adj.* characterized by erudition; learned or scholarly: *an erudite professor, an erudite commentary.* [t. L: m.s. *ērudītus,* pp., instructed] —**er′u·dite′ly,** *adv.* —**er′u·dite′ness,** *n.*

er·u·di·tion (ĕr′ŏŏ dĭsh′ən, ĕr′yŏŏ-), *n.* acquired knowledge, esp. in literature, languages, history, etc; learning; scholarship. —**Syn.** See **learning.**

e·rum·pent (ĭ rŭm′pənt), *adj.* **1.** bursting forth. **2.** *Bot.* prominent, as if bursting through the epidermis.

e·rupt (ĭ rŭpt′), *v.i.* **1.** to burst forth, as volcanic matter. **2.** (of a volcano, geyser, etc.) to eject matter. **3.** (of teeth) to break through surrounding hard and soft tissues and become visible in the mouth. —*v.t.* **4.** to cause to burst forth. **5.** (of a volcano, etc.) to eject (matter). [t. L: s. *ēruptus,* pp.]

e·rup·tion (ĭ rŭp′shən), *n.* **1.** an issuing forth suddenly and violently; an outburst; an outbreak. **2.** *Geol.* the ejection of molten rock, water, etc., as from a volcano, geyser, etc. **3.** *Pathol.* **a.** the breaking out of a rash or the like. **b.** a rash or exanthema. [t. L: s. *ēruptio*]

e·rup·tive (ĭ rŭp′tĭv), *adj.* **1.** bursting forth, or tending to burst forth. **2.** pertaining to or of the nature of an eruption. **3.** *Geol.* (of rocks) formed by the eruption of molten material. **4.** *Pathol.* causing or attended with an eruption or rash. —*n.* **5.** *Geol.* an eruptive rock.

-ery, a suffix of nouns denoting occupation, business, calling, or condition, place or establishment, goods or products, things collectively, qualities, actions, etc., as in *archery, bakery, cutlery, fishery, grocery, nunnery, pottery, finery, foolery, prudery, scenery, tracery, witchery, witchery.* [ME, t. OF: m. *-erie,* f. *-ier* -ER² + *-ie* -Y³]

Er·y·man·thi·an boar (ĕr′ə măn′thĭ ən), *Gk. Legend.* a savage beast fabled to have infested Arcadia and to have been caught by Hercules.

b., blend of, blended; c., cognate with; d., dialect, dialectal; der., derived from; f., formed from; g., going back to; m., modification of; r., replacing; s., stem of; t., taken from; ?, perhaps.   See the full key on inside cover.

e·ryn·go (ĭrĭng/gō), *n., pl.* **-goes.** any plant of the umbelliferous genus *Eryngium,* consisting of coarse herbs, esp. *E. maritimum,* the sea holly, whose root was formerly candied as a sweetmeat. Also, **eringo.** [? t. It.: m. *eringio,* der. L *ēryngion,* t. Gk., dim. of *ēryngos*]

er·y·sip·e·las (ĕr/ə sĭp/ə ləs, ĭr/ə-), *n. Pathol.* an acute, febrile, infectious disease, due to a specific streptococcus, and characterized by diffusely spreading, deep-red inflammation of the skin or mucous membranes. [t. L, t. Gk.; r. ME *herisipila,* etc., t. ML] **—er·y·si·pel·a·tous** (ĕr/ə sĭ pĕl/ə təs, ĭr/-), *adj.*

er·y·sip·e·loid (ĕr/ə sĭp/ə loid/, ĭr/ə-), *n. Pathol.* a disease of man contracted by contact with the swine erysipelas bacillus: characterized by a painful local ulcer, generally on one of the hands.

er·y·the·ma (ĕr/ə thē/mə), *n. Pathol.* abnormal redness of the skin due to local congestion, as in inflammation. [NL, t. Gk.: redness or flush] **—er·y·the·mat·ic** (ĕr/ə thĭ măt/ĭk), **er·y·them·a·tous** (ĕr/ə thĕm/ə təs, -thē/mə-), *adj.*

e·ryth·rin (ĭrĭth/rĭn), *n. Chem.* 1. a crystalline compound, $C_{20}H_{22}O_{10}$, obtained from certain lichens. 2. a coal-tar color used to dye silk a fluorescent red.

e·ryth·rism (ĭrĭth/rĭz əm), *n.* abnormal redness, as of plumage or hair. **—er·y·thris·mal** (ĕr/ə thrĭz/məl), *adj.*

e·ryth·rite (ĭrĭth/rīt), *n.* 1. cobalt bloom. 2. erythritol.

e·ryth·ri·tol (ĭrĭth/rə tōl/, -tōl/), *n. Chem.* a tetrahydric crystalline alcohol, $(CH_2OHCHOH)_2$ related to carbohydrates, derived from certain lichens.

erythro-, a word element meaning "red," as in *erythrocyte.* Also, **erythr-.** [t. Gk., comb. form of *erythrós*]

e·ryth·ro·blast (ĭrĭth/rō blăst/), *n. Anat.* a nucleated cell in the bone marrow from which red blood cells develop.

e·ryth·ro·cyte (ĭrĭth/rō sīt/), *n. Anat.* one of the red corpuscles of the blood.

e·ryth·ro·cy·tom·e·ter (ĭrĭth/rō sī tŏm/ə tər), *n.* an apparatus used to make a red blood cell count.

Erz Ge·bir·ge (ĕrts/ gə bĭr/gə), a mountain range on the boundary between East Germany and NW Czechoslovakia. Highest point, Keilberg, 4080 ft.

Er·zu·rum (ĕr/zə rŏŏm/), *n.* a city in NE Turkey. 69,499 (1955). Also, **Er/ze·rum/.**

es-. For words with initial **es-,** see also **aes-.**

E·sau (ē/sô), *n. Bible.* a son of Isaac and Rebecca, older brother of Jacob, to whom he sold his birthright. Gen. 25:21–25.

es·ca·drille (ĕs/kə drĭl/; *Fr.* ĕs kȧ drē/y), *n.* 1. a squadron or divisional unit of airplanes: *the Lafayette Escadrille of World War I.* 2. a small naval squadron. [t. F, t. Sp.: m. *escadrilla,* dim. of *escuadra* squadron, t. It.: m. *squadra* square, der. *squadrare* to square, g. L *exquadrāre*]

es·ca·lade (ĕs/kə lād/), *n., v.,* **-laded, -lading. —***n.* 1. a scaling or mounting by means of ladders, esp. in an assault upon a fortified place. **—***v.t.* 2. to mount, pass, or enter by means of ladders. [t. F, t. It.: m. *scalata,* der. *scalare* climb, der. *scala* steps, SCALE³] **—es/ca·lad/er,** *n.*

es·ca·la·tor (ĕs/kə lā/tər), *n.* 1. a moving inclined continuous stairway or runway used for raising or lowering passengers. 2. (*cap.*) a trademark for this device. [? b. ESCALADE and ELEVATOR]

escalator clause, a provision in a contract between a labor union and a company permitting wage increases or decreases under specified conditions.

es·cal·lop (ĕskŏl/əp, eskăl/-), *v.t.* 1. to bake (food, usually cut in pieces) in a sauce or other liquid, often with crumbs on top; scallop. 2. to bake (fish, etc.) in scallop shells. 3. to bake (as potatoes or fish) in a sauce. **—***n.* 4. scallop. Also, **es·cal/op.** [t. MF: m. *escalope* shell, of Gmc. orig.; cf. D *schelp* shell] **—es·cal/loped, adj.**

es·ca·pade (ĕs/kə pād/, ĕs/kə pād/), *n.* 1. a reckless proceeding; a wild prank. 2. an escape from confinement or restraint. [t. F, t. Sp.: m. *escapada,* der. *escapar* escape, or t. It.: m. *scappata* (der. *scappare*)]

es·cape (ĕskāp/), *v.,* **-caped, -caping,** *n.* **—***v.i.* 1. to slip or get away, as from confinement or restraint; gain or regain liberty. 2. to slip away from pursuit or peril; avoid capture, punishment, or any threatened evil. 3. to issue from a confining enclosure, as a fluid. 4. *Bot.* (of an introduced plant) to grow wild. **—***v.t.* 5. to slip away from or elude (pursuit, etc.); succeed in avoiding (any threatened or possible evil). 6. to elude (notice, search, etc., or one's memory); fail to be noticed or recollected by (a person). 7. to slip from (a person) inadvertently, as a remark. **—***n.* 8. act of escaping. 9. fact of having escaped. 10. a means of escape: *a fire escape.* 11. avoidance of reality. 12. leakage, as of water, gas, etc. 13. *Bot.* a plant originally cultivated, now growing wild. [ME *escape(n),* t. ONF: m. *escaper,* der. L: *ex-* EX-¹ + *cappa* cloak] **—es·cap/a·ble,** *adj.* **—es·cap/ee/,** *n.* **—es·cap/er,** *n.*

—Syn. 1. flee, abscond, decamp. 5. shun, fly. ESCAPE, ELUDE, EVADE mean to keep free of something. To ESCAPE is to succeed in keeping away from danger, pursuit, observation, etc. *to escape punishment.* To ELUDE implies slipping through an apparently tight net, thus avoiding, often by a narrow margin, whatever threatens: it implies, also, using vigilance, adroitness, dexterity, or slyness, so as to baffle

or foil: *a fox managed to elude the hounds.* To EVADE is to turn aside from or go out of reach of a person or thing (at least temporarily), usually by using artifice or stratagem to direct attention elsewhere: *to evade the police.* See **avoid.**

es·cape·ment (ĕskāp/mənt), *n.* 1. a way of escape; an outlet. 2. *Horol.* the portion of a watch or clock which measures beats and controls the speed of the time train. 3. a mechanism consisting of a notched wheel and ratchet for regulating the motion of a typewriter carriage.

escape wheel, *Horol.* a revolving toothed wheel which transmits impulses to a vibrating fork.

es·cap·ism (ĕskā/pĭz əm), *n.* the avoidance of reality by absorption of the mind in entertainment, or in an imaginative situation, activity, etc. **—es·cap/ist,** *adj.,* *n.*

Two forms of escapement (def. 2)

es·car·got (ĕskärgō/), *n. French.* an edible snail.

es·ca·role (ĕs/kə rōl/; *Fr.* ĕs kȧ rōl/), *n.* a broad-leaved kind of endive, used for salads. [t. F]

es·carp (ĕskärp/), *n.* 1. *Fort.* the inner slope or wall of the ditch surrounding a rampart. 2. any similar steep slope. **—***v.t.* 3. to make into an escarp; give a steep slope to; furnish with escarps. [t. F: m. *escarpe,* t. It.: m. *scarpa,* of Gmc. orig. See SHARP, and cf. SCARP]

es·carp·ment (ĕskärp/mənt), *n.* 1. a long, precipitous, clifflike ridge of land, rock, or the like, commonly formed by faulting or fracturing of the earth's crust. 2. ground cut into an escarp about a fortification or defensive position.

Es·caut (ĕskō/), *n.* French name of **Scheldt.**

-esce, a suffix of verbs meaning to begin to be or do something, become, grow, or be somewhat (as indicated by the rest of the word), as in *convalesce, putresce.* [t. L: m.s. *-escere,* with inchoative force]

-escence, a suffix of nouns denoting action or process, change, state, or condition, etc., and corresponding to verbs ending in *-esce* or adjectives ending in *-escent,* as in *convalescence, deliquescence, luminescence, recrudescence.* [t. L: m.s. *-escentia.* See **-ESCE, -ENCE**]

-escent, a suffix of adjectives meaning beginning to be or do something, becoming or being somewhat (as indicated), as in *convalescent, deliquescent, recrudescent:* often associated with verbs ending in *-esce* or nouns ending in *-escence.* [t. L: s. *-escens,* ppr. ending]

esch·a·lot (ĕsh/ə lŏt/, ĕsh/ə lŏt/), *n.* shallot.

es·char (ĕs/kär, -kər), *n. Pathol.* a hard crust or scab, as from a burn. [t. LL: s. *eschara,* t. Gk.: hearth, scar]

es·cha·rot·ic (ĕs/kə rŏt/ĭk), *Med.* **—***adj.* 1. producing an eschar, as a medicinal substance; caustic. **—***n.* 2. a caustic application. [t. LL: s. *escharōticus,* t. Gk.: m. *escharōtikós*]

es·cha·tol·o·gy (ĕs/kə tŏl/ə jĭ), *n. Theol.* 1. the doctrines of the last or final things, as death, the judgment, the future state, etc. 2. the branch of theology dealing with them. [f. Gk. *ēschato(s)* last + -LOGY] **—es·cha·to·log·i·cal** (ĕs/kə tə lŏj/ə kəl), *adj.* **—es/cha·tol/o·gist,** *n.*

es·cheat (ĕschēt/), *n. Law.* 1. the "return" of property to the state or some agency of the state, or, as in England, to the crown, when there is a failure of persons legally qualified to inherit or to claim. 2. property or a possession which reverts by escheat. 3. the right to take property subject to escheat. **—***v.i.* 4. to revert by escheat, as to the crown or the state. **—***v.t.* 5. to make an escheat of; confiscate. [ME *eschete,* t. OF, der. *escheoir* fall to one's share, f. es- EX-¹ + *cheoir* (g. L *cadere* fall)] **—es·cheat/a·ble,** *adj.*

es·cheat·age (ĕschē/tĭj), *n.* the right of succeeding to an escheat.

es·cheat·or (ĕschē/tər), *n.* an officer in charge of escheats.

es·chew (ĕschōō/), *v.t.* to abstain from; shun; avoid: *to eschew evil.* [ME *eschewen,* t. OF: m. *eschiver,* ult. t. Gmc.; cf. SHY and see SKEW] **—es·chew/al,** *n.* **—es·chew/er,** *n.*

es·clan·dre (ĕsklän/dr), *n. French.* a scandalous scene; unbecoming conduct.

Es·co·ri·al (ĕskôr/ĭ əl; *Sp.* ĕs/kō rē äl/), *n.* a famous building in central Spain, 27 miles NW of Madrid, containing a monastery, palace, church, and mausoleum of the Spanish sovereigns: erected 1563–84. Also, **Escurial.** [t. Sp.: lit., a refuse heap, der. *escoria,* t. L: m. *scōria*]

es·cort (*n.* ĕs/kôrt; *v.* ĕskôrt/), *n.* 1. a body of persons, or a single person, accompanying another or others for protection, guidance, or courtesy. 2. an armed guard. 3. protection, safeguard, or guidance on a journey. **—***v.t.* 4. to attend or accompany as an escort. [t. F: m. *escorta,* t. It.: m. *scorta,* der. *scorgere* guide, f. s- (g. L *ex-*) + *-corgere* (g. L *corrigere* correct)] **—Syn.** 4. conduct, usher, guard, convoy. See **accompany.**

es·cri·toire (ĕs/krĭ twär/), *n.* a writing desk. [t. F, g. LL *scriptōria,* for *scriptōrium.* See SCRIPTORIUM]

es·crow (ĕs/krō, ĕskrō/), *n. Law.* a contract, deed, bond, or other written agreement deposited with a third person, by whom it is to be delivered to the grantee or promisee on the fulfillment of some condition. [t. AF: m. *escrowe,* OF *escroe* piece of cloth, parchment, SCROLL; g. Gmc. orig.; akin to SHRED]

es·cu·age (ĕs/kyŏŏ yj), *n. Feudal Law.* scutage. [t. AF, der. OF *escu,* g. L *scūtum* shield]

es·cu·do (ěskōō′dō; *Port.* -dŏŏ; *Sp.* -dô), *n., pl.* **-dos** (-dōz; *Port., Sp.* -dôs). **1.** the gold monetary unit (established in 1911) of Portugal, divided into 100 centavos, and equivalent in value at that time to about $1.08. **2.** a Portuguese gold or silver coin having this value. **3.** any of various gold and silver coins of Spain, Chile, etc. [t. Sp., Pg., g. L *scūtum* shield. Cf. ECU, SCUDO]

es·cu·lent (ěs′kyələnt), *adj.* **1.** suitable for use as food; edible. —*n.* **2.** something edible, esp. a vegetable. [t. L: s. *esculentus* good to eat]

Es·cu·ri·al (ěskyŏŏr′ĭəl), *n.* Escorial.

es·cutch·eon (ěskŭch′ən), *n.* **1.** the shield or shield-shaped surface, on which armorial bearings are depicted; a hatchment. **2.** blot on the escutcheon, a stain on one's honor or reputation. **3.** a plate for protecting the keyhole of a door, or to which the handle is attached. **4.** the panel on a ship's stern bearing her name. [t. ONF: m. *escuchon*, ult. der. L *scūtum* shield] —**es·cutch′eoned**, *adj.*

Esd., Esdras (Apocrypha).

Es·dra·e·lon (ěs′drā ē′lŏn, ěz′-), *n.* a plain in N Palestine (now in Israel): the scene of many ancient battles. Also, **Plain of Jezreel.** See Megiddo.

Es·dras (ěz′drəs), *n.* either of the first two books of the Apocrypha.

-ese, a noun and adjective suffix referring to locality, nationality, language, literary style, etc., as in *Bengalese, Chinese, Johnsonese, journalese.* [t. OF: m. *-eis*, g. L *-ěnsis*]

ESE, east-southeast. Also, **E.S.E.**

es·ker (ěs′kər), *n.* Geol. a serpentine ridge of gravelly and sandy drift, believed to have been formed by streams under or in glacial ice. Also, **es·kar** (ěs′kär, -kər). [t. Irish: m. *eiscir*]

Es·ki·mo (ěs′kəmō′), *n., pl.* **-mos, -mo,** *adj.* —*n.* **1.** one of a race or people, characterized by short stature, muscular build, light-brown complexion, and broad, flat face, inhabiting the arctic coasts of America from Greenland to Alaska and a small part of the adjacent Asiatic coast. **2.** their language, of Eskimoan stock. —*adj.* **3.** of or pertaining to the Eskimos or their language. Also, **Esquimau.** [t. Dan., t. F: m. *Esquimaux* (pl.), t. N Amer. Ind.: m. Algonquian name for the people, meaning eaters of raw flesh; cf. Abnaki *eskimantsiš*, Ojibwa *aškimek.* Cf. *Innuit* men, name applied by Eskimos to themselves]

Es·ki·mo·an (ěs′kəmō′ən), *adj.* **1.** of or pertaining to the Eskimos or their language. —*n.* **2.** a linguistic stock including Eskimo and Aleut. Also, **Es′ki·mau′an.**

Eskimo dog, one of a breed of strong dogs used by the Eskimos to draw sledges.

Es·ki·şe·hir (ěs kē′shě hĭr′), *n.* a city in W Turkey. 122,725 (1955). Also, **Es·ki′she·hir′.**

e·so·phag·e·al (ē′sŏ făj′ĭ əl), *adj.* pertaining to the esophagus: *esophageal glands.* Also, **oesophageal.**

e·soph·a·gus (ē sŏf′əgəs), *n., pl.* **-gi** (-jī′). Anat., Zool. a tube connecting the mouth or pharynx with the stomach in invertebrate and vertebrate animals; gullet. Also, **oesophagus.** [t. NL: m. *oesophagus*, t. Gk.: m. *oisophágos*]

es·o·ter·ic (ěs′ə těr′ĭk), *adj.* **1.** understood by or meant for a select few; profound; recondite. **2.** belonging to the select few. **3.** private; secret; confidential. **4.** (of philosophical doctrine, etc.) intended to be communicated only to the initiated (orig. applied to certain writings of Aristotle, and afterward to the secret teachings of Pythagoras). [t. Gk.: m. s. *esōterikós* inner] —**es′o·ter′i·cal·ly,** *adv.*

ESP, extrasensory perception; perception or communication outside of normal sensory activity, as in telepathy and clairvoyance.

esp., especially.

es·pal·ier (ěs păl′yər), *n.* **1.** a trellis or framework on which fruit trees or shrubs are trained to grow flat. **2.** a tree or plants so trained. —*v.t.* **3.** to train on an espalier. **4.** to furnish with an espalier. [t. F, t. It.: m. *spalliera* support, der. *spalla* shoulder]

Es·pa·ña (ěs pä′nyä), *n.* Spanish name of Spain.

Es·par·te·ro (ěs′pär tě′rō), *n.* **Joaquín Baldomero** (hwä kēn′ bäl′dō mě′rō), 1792–1879, a Spanish general and statesman.

es·par·to (ěs pär′tō), *n.* any of several grasses, esp. *Stipa tenacissima,* of S Europe and N Africa, used for making paper, cordage, etc. Also, **esparto grass.** [t. Sp., g. L *spartum,* t. Gk.: m. *spárton* a rope made of *spártos* a broomlike plant]

espec., especially.

es·pe·cial (ěs pěsh′əl), *adj.* **1.** special; exceptional; outstanding: *of no especial importance, an especial friend.* **2.** of a particular kind, or peculiar to a particular one: *your especial case.* [ME, t. OF, t. L: m.s. *speciālis* pertaining to a particular kind]

es·pe·cial·ly (ěs pěsh′ə lĭ), *adv.* particularly; principally; unusually: *be especially watchful.*

—**Syn.** ESPECIALLY, CHIEFLY, PARTICULARLY, PRINCIPALLY refer to those cases of a class or kind which seem to be significant. ESPECIALLY and PARTICULARLY single out the most prominent case or example (often in order to particularize a general statement): *winter is especially severe on old people; corn grows well in the Middle West, particularly*

in Iowa. CHIEFLY and PRINCIPALLY imply that the general statement applies to a majority of the cases in question, and have a somewhat comparative force: *owls fly chiefly at night, crime occurs principally in large cities.*

es·per·ance (ěs′pər əns), *n.* Obs. hope. [ME *esper-aunce,* t. OF: m. *esperance,* der. *esperer,* g. L *spěrāre* hope]

Es·pe·ran·to (ěs′pə rän′tō, -rän′tō), *n.* an artificial language invented in 1887 by Dr. Zamenhof and intended for international auxiliary use. It is based on the commonest words in the most important European languages. [t. Sp.: m. *esperanza* hope, used by Zamenhof as a pseudonym] —**Es′pe·ran′tist,** *n., adj.*

es·pi·al (ěs pī′əl), *n.* **1.** act of spying. **2.** keeping watch.

es·piè·gle (ěs pyě′gl), *adj.* French. roguish; playful. [F, alter. of *Ulespiegel,* t. D: m. (*Till*) *Uilenspiegel,* name of famous trickster]

es·piè·gle·rie (ěs pyě glə rē′), *n.* French. a roguish or playful trick. [F., der. *espiègle* ESPIEGLE]

es·pi·o·nage (ěs′pĭ ənĭj, əspī′-, ěs′pĭ ənäzh′), *n.* **1.** practice of spying on others. **2.** the systematic use of spies by a government to discover the military and political secrets of other nations. [t. F: m. *espionnage,* der. *espionner* spy upon, der. *espion* spy, t. It.: m. *spione,* aug. of *spia,* t. Gmc.; cf. G *spähe* spying]

es·pla·nade (ěs′plə nād′, -näd′), *n.* any open, level space, esp. one serving for public walks or drives. [t. F, t. Sp.: m. *esplanada,* der. *esplanar,* g. L *explānāre* level]

es·pous·al (ěs pou′zəl), *n.* **1.** adoption or advocacy, as of a cause or principle. **2.** (*sometimes pl.*) a marriage (or sometimes an engagement) ceremony. [ME *es-pousaile,* t. OF, g. L *sponsālia,* neut. pl. of *sponsālis* pertaining to betrothal]

es·pouse (ěs pouz′), *v.t.* **-poused, -pousing. 1.** to make one's own, adopt, or embrace, as a cause. **2.** to take in marriage; marry. **3.** to give (a woman) in marriage. [t. MF: m.s. *espouser,* g. L *sponsāre* betroth, espouse] —**es·pous′er,** *n.*

es·pres·so (ěs prěs′ō), *n.,* a strong beverage made by forcing live steam through powdered coffee. [It.]

es·prit (ěs prē′), *n.* French. wit; sprightliness; lively intelligence. [F, t. L: m.s. *spiritus* SPIRIT]

es·prit de corps (ěs prē′ də kôr′), French. a sense of union and of common interests and responsibilities, as developed among a group of persons associated together.

es·py (ěs pī′), *v.t.* **-pied, -pying.** to see at a distance; catch sight of. [ME *espy(en),* t. OF: m. *espier,* ult. t. Gmc.; cf. G *spähen* spy] —**es·pi′er,** *n.* —**Syn.** discern, descry, discover, perceive, make out.

Esq., Brit., latterly borrowed in U.S. as an affectation. Esquire. *Henry Adams, Esq.* = Mr. Henry Adams.

-esque, an adjective suffix indicating style, manner, or distinctive character, as in *arabesque, picturesque, statuesque.* [t. F, t. It.: m. *-esco;* of Gmc. orig. Cf. -ISH¹]

Es·qui·line (ěs′kwə lĭn′), *n.* one of the seven hills on which ancient Rome was built. [t. L: m.s. *Esquilīnus* (sc. *mons* hill)]

Es·qui·mau (ěs′kə mō′), *n., pl.* **-maux** (-mō′, -mōz′), *adj.* Eskimo. [t. F.]

es·quire (ěs kwīr′), *n., v.* **-quired, -quiring.** —*n.* **1.** Brit. a polite title (usually abbreviated to *Esq.*) after a man's last name (*Mr.* or *Dr.* is omitted when it is used): *John Smith, Esq.* **2.** (in the Middle Ages) a squire, or aspirant to knighthood, attendant upon a knight. **3.** a man belonging to the order of English gentry ranking next below a knight. **4.** Archaic. an English country "squire." —*v.t.* **5.** to raise to the rank of esquire. **6.** to address as "Esquire." [ME *esquier,* t. OF, g. LL *scūtārius* shieldbearer, der. L *scūtum* shield]

ess (ěs), *n.* **1.** the letter S, s. **2.** something shaped like an S.

-ess, a suffix forming distinctively feminine nouns, as *countess, hostess, lioness.* [t. F. m. *-esse,* g. L *-issa,* t. Gk.]

es·say (*n.* ěs′ā for 1; ěs′ā, ě sā′ for 2, 3; *v.* ě sā′), *n.* **1.** a short literary composition on a particular subject. **2.** an effort to perform or accomplish something; an attempt. **3.** Obs. a tentative effort. —*v.t.* **4.** to try; attempt. **5.** to put to the test; make trial of. [t. MF: m. *essai,* g. LL *exagium* a weighing. Cf. ASSAY] —**es·say′er,** *n.*

es·say·ist (ěs′ā ĭst), *n.* **1.** a writer of essays. **2.** Rare. one who makes essays or trials.

es·se (ěs′ĭ), *n.* Latin. being; existence. [L: to be]

Es·sen (ěs′ən), *n.* a city in W West Germany: the chief city of the Ruhr; Krupp works. 630,905 (est. 1955).

es·sence (ěs′əns), *n.* **1.** that by which a thing is what it is; intrinsic nature; important elements or features of a thing. **2.** a substance obtained from a plant, drug, or the like, by distillation or other process, and containing its characteristic properties in concentrated form. **3.** an alcoholic solution of an essential oil. **4.** a perfume. **5.** Philos. the inward nature, true substance, or constitution of anything. **6.** something that is, esp. a spiritual or immaterial entity. [ME, t. L: m.s. *essentia*]

Es·sene (ěs′ēn, ě sēn′), *n.* one of an ascetic, celibate brotherhood of Jews in ancient Palestine, first appearing in the 2d century B.C. [sing. of *Essenes,* Anglicized form of L *Essēnī,* pl., t. Gk.: m. *Essēnoí*] —**Es·se·ni·an** (ě sē′nĭ ən), **Es·se·nic** (ě sēn′ĭk), *adj.*

es·sen·tial (ə sěn′shəl), *adj.* **1.** absolutely necessary; indispensable: *discipline is essential in an army.* **2.** pertaining to or constituting the essence of a thing. **3.** having the nature of an essence of a plant, etc. **4.** being such by its very nature, or in the highest sense: *es-*

b., blend of, blended; c., cognate with; d., dialect, dialectal; der., derived from; f., formed from; g., going back to; m., modification of; r., replacing; s., stem of; t., taken from; ?, perhaps. See the full key on inside cover.

Escutcheon
A, Dexter chief;
B, Middle chief;
C, Sinister chief;
D, Honor or col-
  or point;
E, Fess or heart
  point;
F, Nombril or
  navel;
G, Dexter base;
H, Middle base;
I, Sinister base

Dexter   Sinister

A   B   C
   D
   E
   F
G   H   I

sential happiness, essential poetry. **—n. 5.** an indispensable element; a chief point: *concentrate on essentials rather than details.* [ME, t. LL: s. *essentiālis.* See ES-SENCE] **—es·sen′tial·ly,** *adv.* **—es·sen′tial·ness,** *n.* **—Syn. 1.** fundamental, basic, inherent, intrinsic. See **necessary. 2.** ESSENTIAL, INHERENT, INTRINSIC refer to that which is in the natural composition of a thing. ESSENTIAL suggests that which is in the very essence or constitution of a thing: *oxygen and hydrogen are essential in water.* INHERENT means inborn or fixed from the beginning as a permanent quality or constituent of a thing: *properties inherent in iron.* INTRINSIC implies belonging to the nature of a thing itself, and comprised within it, without regard to external considerations or accidentally added properties: *the intrinsic value of diamonds.* **—Ant. 2.** accidental, extrinsic.

es·sen·ti·al·i·ty (ə sĕn′shĭ ăl′ə tĭ′), *n., pl.* **-ties. 1.** the quality of being essential; essential character. **2.** an essential element or point.

essential oil, any of a class of oils obtained from plants, possessing the odor and other properties of the plant, and volatilizing completely when heated: used in making perfumes, flavors, etc.

es·se quam vi·de·ri (ĕs′ĭ kwăm vĭ dâr′ī), *Latin.* to be rather than (merely) to seem (motto of North Carolina).

Es·se·qui·bo (ĕs′ĭ kē′bō), *n.* a river flowing from S British Guiana N to the Atlantic. ab. 550 mi.

Es·sex (ĕs′ĭks), *n.* **1.** a county in SE England. 2,044,-964 (1951). 1528 sq. mi. *Co. seat:* Chelmsford. **2. Robert Devereux** (dĕv′ə rōō′), **Earl of,** 1567–1601, British soldier; favorite of Queen Elizabeth I.

-est, a suffix forming the superlative degree of adjectives and adverbs, as in *warmest, fastest, soonest.* [OE *-est, -ost.* Cf. Gk. *-isto-*]

EST, Eastern Standard Time. Also, **E.S.T., e.s.t.**

est., **1.** established. **2.** estate. **3.** estimated. **4.** estuary.

estab., established.

es·tab·lish (ĕs tăb′lĭsh), *v.t.* **1.** to set up on a firm or permanent basis; institute; found: *to establish a government, a business, a university, etc.* **2.** to settle or install in a position, business, etc.: *to establish one's son in business.* **3.** to settle (oneself) as if permanently. **4.** to cause to be permanently accepted: *to establish a custom or a precedent.* **5.** to show to be valid or well grounded; prove: *to establish a fact, theory, claim, etc.* **6.** to appoint or ordain for permanence, as a law; fix unalterably. **7.** to set up or bring about permanently: *establish order.* **8.** to make (a church) a national or state institution. **9.** *Cards.* to obtain control of (a suit) so that one can win all the subsequent tricks in that suit. [ME *establisse(n),* t. OF: m. *establiss-,* s. *establir,* g. L *stabilīre* make stable] **—es·tab′lish·er,** *n.* **—Syn. 1.** form, organize. See **fix. 5.** verify, substantiate. **—Ant. 1.** abolish. **5.** disprove.

established church, a church recognized and sometimes partly supported by the state, as (*caps.*) the Church of England.

es·tab·lish·ment (ĕs tăb′lĭsh mənt), *n.* **1.** act of establishing. **2.** state or fact of being established. **3.** something established; a constituted order or system. **4.** a household; a place of residence with everything connected with it. **5.** the building and equipment occupied by a business concern. **6.** a permanent civil, military, or other force or organization. **7.** institution. **8.** the recognition by the state of a church as the state church. **9.** the church so recognized, esp. the Church of England. **10.** fixed or settled allowance or income.

Es·taing, d' (dĕs tăn′), **Charles Hector, Comte,** 1729–94, French admiral.

es·ta·mi·net (ĕs tä mē nĕ′), *n. French.* a taproom. [F, t. Walloon: m. *staminé,* der. *stamon* post, t. Gmc.; cf. G *stamm* STEM]

es·tan·cia (ĕs tän′syä), *n.* (in Spanish America) a landed estate; a stock farm.

es·tate (ĕs tāt′), *n., v.,* **-tated, -tating. —n. 1.** a piece of landed property, esp. one of large extent: *to have an estate in the country.* **2.** *Law.* **a.** property or possessions. **b.** the legal position or status of an owner, considered with respect to his property in land or other things. **c.** the degree or quantity of interest which a person has in land with respect to the nature of the right, its duration, or its relation to the rights of others. **d.** interest, ownership, or property in land or other things. **e.** the property of a deceased person, a bankrupt, etc., viewed as an aggregate. **3.** *Brit.* a housing development. **4.** period or condition of life: *to attain to man's estate.* **5.** a political or social group or class, as in France, the clergy, nobles, and commons, or in England, the lords spiritual, lords temporal, and commons (the three **estates of the realm**). **6.** condition or circumstances with reference to worldly prosperity, estimation, etc.; social status or rank. **7.** high rank or dignity. **8.** *Archaic.* pomp or state. **—v.t. 9.** *Now Rare or Obs.* to establish in or as in an estate. [ME, t. OF: m. *estat,* t. L: m.s. *status.* See STATE] **—Syn. 1.** See **property.**

estate agent, *Brit.* **1.** the steward or manager of a landed estate. **2.** a real-estate agent; a realtor.

Estates General, *French Hist.* the States-General.

es·teem (ĕs tēm′), *v.t.* **1.** to regard as valuable; regard highly or favorably: *I esteem him highly.* **2.** to consider as of a certain value; regard: *I esteem it worthless.* **3.** to set a value on; value: *to esteem lightly.* **—n. 4.** favorable opinion or judgment; respect or regard: *to hold a person or thing in high esteem.* **5.** opinion or judgment of merit

or demerit; estimation. [late ME *estyme(n),* t. MF: m. *estimer,* t. L: m. s. *aestimāre.* See ESTIMATE, and cf. AIM] **—Syn. 1.** prize, honor, revere. See **appreciate. 4.** favor, admiration, honor, reverence, veneration. See **respect.** **—Ant. 1.** disdain.

es·ter (ĕs′tər), *n. Chem.* a compound formed by the reaction between an acid and an alcohol with the elimination of a molecule of water. [coined by L. Gmelin (1788–1853), German chemist]

es·ter·ase (ĕs′tə rās′), *n. Biochem.* any ferment or enzyme which saponifies an ester.

es·ter·i·fy (ĕs tĕr′ə fī′), *v.t., v.i.,* **-fied, -fying.** *Chem.* to convert into an ester. **—es·ter′i·fi·ca′tion,** *n.*

Es·tes Park (ĕs′tĭz), a summer resort in N Colorado.

Esth., **1.** Esther. **2.** Esthonia.

Es·ther (ĕs′tər), *n.* one of the books of the Old Testament, named from its principal character. [t. L (Vulgate), t. Gk. (Septuagint), t. Heb. See ISHTAR]

es·the·sia (ĕs thē′zhə, -zhĭ′ə), *n.* sensitivity; feeling; perceptibility. Also, **aesthesia.** [NL, t. Gk.: m. *-aisthēsia* perceptive state]

es·the·sis (ĕs thē′sĭs), *n.* esthesia. Also, **aesthesis.** [t. Gk.: m. *aisthēsis* a perceiving]

es·thete (ĕs′thēt), *n.* aesthete.

es·thet·ic (ĕs thĕt′ĭk), *adj.* aesthetic.

es·thet·i·cal (ĕs thĕt′ə kəl), *adj.* aesthetical. **—es·thet′i·cal·ly,** *adv.*

es·the·ti·cian (ĕs′thə tĭsh′ən), *n.* aesthetician.

es·thet·i·cism (ĕs thĕt′ə sĭz′əm), *n.* aestheticism.

es·thet·ics (ĕs thĕt′ĭks), *n.* aesthetics.

Es·tho·ni·a (ĕs tō′nĭə, -thō′-), *n.* Estonia. **—Es·tho′ni·an,** *adj., n.*

Es·tienne (ĕs tyĕn′), *n.* a French printing firm famous for its scholarship, founded by **Henri** (än rē′), 1460?–1520, and carried on by his son **Robert** (rō bĕr′), 1503–1559, and by his grandson **Henri,** 1528–98.

es·ti·ma·ble (ĕs′tə mə bəl), *adj.* **1.** worthy of esteem; deserving respect. **2.** capable of being estimated. **—es′ti·ma·ble·ness,** *n.* **—es′ti·ma·bly,** *adv.* **—Syn. 1.** reputable, respectable, worthy, meritorious. **—Ant. 1.** contemptible.

es·ti·mate (*v.* ĕs′tə māt′; *n.* ĕs′tə mĭt, -māt), *v.,* **-mated -mating,** *n.* **—v.t. 1.** to form an approximate judgment or opinion regarding the value, amount, size, weight, etc., of; calculate approximately. **2.** to form an opinion of; judge. **—v.i. 3.** to submit approximate figures, as of the cost of work to be done. **—n. 4.** an approximate judgment or calculation, as of the value, amount, etc., of something. **5.** a judgment or opinion, as of the qualities of a person or thing; estimation or judgment. **6.** an approximate statement of what would be charged for certain work to be done, submitted by one ready to undertake the work. [t. L: m. s. *aestimātus,* pp., valued, rated. Cf. ESTEEM] **—es′ti·ma·tor,** *n.* **—Syn. 1.** compute, count, reckon, gauge.

es·ti·ma·tive (ĕs′tə mā′tĭv), *adj.* **1.** capable of estimating. **2.** based upon or pertaining to estimation.

es·ti·ma·tion (ĕs′tə mā′shən), *n.* **1.** judgment or opinion: *in my estimation.* **2.** esteem; respect: *to hold in high estimation.* **3.** approximate calculation; estimate: *to make an estimation of one's resources.* **—Syn. 2.** appreciation, regard, honor, veneration.

e·stip·u·late (ē stĭp′yə lĭt, -lāt′), *adj.* exstipulate.

es·ti·val (ĕs′tə val, ĕs tī′vəl), *adj.* pertaining or appropriate to summer. Also, **aestival.** [t. L: m.s. *aestivālis*]

es·ti·vate (ĕs′tə vāt′), *v.i.,* **-vated, -vating. 1.** to spend the summer. **2.** *Zool.* to pass the summer in a torpid condition. Also, **aestivate. —es′ti·va′tor,** *n.*

es·ti·va·tion (ĕs′tə vā′shən), *n.* **1.** *Zool.* act of estivating. **2.** *Bot.* the arrangement of the parts of a flower in the bud. Also, **aestivation.**

est mo·dus in re·bus (ĕst mō′dəs ĭn rē′bəs), *Latin.* there is a due measure in things. Horace, *Satires* I, 1, 106.

Es·to·ni·a (ĕs tō′nĭ ə), *n.* a *de facto* constituent republic of the Soviet Union, on the Baltic, S of the Gulf of Finland: an independent republic, 1918–40; annexed by the Soviet Union, 1940, 1,100,000 pop. (est. 1956); 18,300 sq. mi. *Cap.:* Tallinn. Also, **Esthonia.** Official name, **Estonian Soviet Socialist Republic.**

Es·to·ni·an (ĕs tō′nĭ ən), *adj.* **1.** of or pertaining to Estonia and its people. **—n. 2.** one of a Finnish people inhabiting Estonia, Livonia, and other districts of Russia. **3.** the Finno-Ugric language of Estonia, very closely related to Finnish. Also, **Esthonian.**

es·top (ĕs tŏp′), *v.t.,* **-topped, -topping. 1.** *Law.* to hinder or prevent by estoppel. **2.** *Archaic.* to stop. [t. OF: m. *estoper* stop up, AF *estopper* (in law), der. OF *estoupe,* g. L *stuppa* tow. Cf. STOP, v.]

es·to per·pe·tu·a (ĕs′tō pər pĕch′ŏŏ ə), *Latin.* may she endure (live) forever (motto of Idaho).

es·top·page (ĕs tŏp′ĭj), *n.* condition of being estopped.

es·top·pel (ĕs tŏp′əl), *n. Law.* a bar or impediment preventing a party from asserting a fact or a claim inconsistent with a position he previously took, either by conduct or words, esp. where a representation has been relied or acted upon by others. [cf. OF *estoupail* stopple, stopper, der. *estouper* ESTOP]

es·to·vers (ĕs tō′vərz), *n.pl. Law.* necessaries allowed by law, as wood and timber to a tenant, alimony to a wife, etc. [t. AF: necessities, prop. *estover,* inf., be necessary, g. Rom. *estopēre,* der. L *est opus* it is necessary]

es·trange (ĕs트rānj'), v.t., -tranged, -tranging. 1. to turn away in feeling or affection; alienate the affections of. 2. to remove to or keep (usually oneself) at a distance. 3. to divert from the original use or possessor. [late ME, t. MF: m. estrangier, g. L eztrăneăre, der. extrāneus foreign. See STRANGE] —es·trange'ment, n. —es·trang'er, n.

es·tray (ĕsトrā'), n. 1. anything strayed away. 2. Law. a domestic animal, as a horse or a sheep, found wandering or without an owner. —v.i. Archaic. 3. to stray. [t. AF. See STRAY, V.]

es·treat (ĕsトrēt'), Eng. Law. —n. 1. a true copy or extract of an original writing or record, as of a fine. —v.t. 2. to make an estreat of (a fine, etc.) for prosecution. 3. to levy (fines) under an estreat; exact (anything) by way of fine or levy. [t. AF: m. estrete, var. of estraite, prop. fem. pp. of estraire, g. L extrahere. See EXTRACT]

Es·tre·ma·du·ra (ĕsトrĕmädoo'rä), n. a region in W Spain, formerly a province. Spanish, **Extremadura.**

es·tri·ol (ĕs'トrīōl', -ōl'), n. Biochem. an estrogenic hormone, C₁₈H₂₁(OH)₃, occurring in pregnancy urine. Also, **oestriol.**

es·tro·gen (ĕs'トrə jən), n. Biochem. any one of a group of female hormones which induce estrus in immature, spayed mammals. Also, **oestrogen.**

es·tro·gen·ic (ĕs'トrə jĕn'ĭk), adj. Biochem. promoting or producing estrus.

es·trone (ĕs'トrōn), n. Biochem. an estrogenic hormone, C₁₈H₂₂O₂, manufactured by the ovarian follicles and found in pregnancy urine and placental tissue. Also, **oestrin.**

es·trous (ĕs'トrəs), adj. involving or pertaining to the estrus. Also, **oestrous.**

estrous cycle, Zool. a recurrent series of physiological changes in sexual and other organs extending from one rutting period to the next. Also, **oestrous cycle.**

es·trus (ĕs'トrəs), n. Zool. the estrous cycle in mammals, especially females. Also, **es·trum** (ĕs'トrəm), **oestrus.** [t. L: m. oestrus frenzy]

es·tu·a·rine (ĕs'チōō ə rĭn, -rīn'), adj. 1. formed in an estuary. 2. found in estuaries.

es·tu·ar·y (ĕs'チōō ĕr'ĭ), n., pl. -aries. 1. that part of the mouth or lower course of a river in which its current meets the sea's tides, and is subject to their effects. 2. an arm or inlet of the sea. [t. L: m.s. aestuārium, der. aestus a heaving motion, surge, tide] —es·tu·ar·i·al (ĕs'チōō är'ĭ əl), adj.

e·su·ri·ent (ĭ sōōr'ĭ ənt). adj. hungry; greedy. [t. L: s. ēsuriens, ppr., desiring to eat] —e·su'ri·ence, e·su'ri·en·cy, n. —e·su'ri·ent·ly, adv.

-et, a noun suffix having properly a diminutive force (now lost in many words), as in islet, bullet, facet, midget, owlet, plummet. [t. OF: -et masc., -ette, fem.]

e·ta (ā'トə, ē'トə), n. the seventh letter (H, η, English long E, e) of the Greek alphabet.

é·ta·gère (ā tả zhĕr'), n. French. a series of open shelves for bric-a-brac, etc.

et al., 1. (L et alibi) and elsewhere. 2. (L et alit) and others.

etc., et cetera.

et cet·er·a (ĕt sĕt'ər ə, -sĕt'トrə), Latin. and others; and so forth; and so on (used to indicate that more of the same sort or class might have been mentioned, but for shortness are omitted). Abbr.: etc. [L, et cētera (sometimes caetera) and the rest]

et·cet·er·a (ĕt sĕt'ər ə, -sĕt'トrə), n., pl. -ras. 1. other things or persons unspecified. 2. (pl.) extras or sundries.

etch (ĕch), v.t. 1. to cut, bite, or corrode with an acid or the like; engrave (metals, etc.) with an acid or the like, esp. to form a design in furrows which when charged with ink will give an impression on paper. 2. to produce or copy by this method, as on copper. —v.i. 3. to practice the art of etching. [t. D: m. etsen, t. G: m. ätzen feed, corrode, etch; akin to EAT] —etch'er, n.

etch·ing (ĕch'ĭng), n. 1. a process of making designs or pictures on a metal plate, glass, etc., by the corrosion of an acid instead of by a burin. 2. an impression, as on paper, taken from an etched plate.

E·te·o·cles (ĭ tē'ə klēz'), n. Gk. Legend. a son of Oedipus, and brother of Polynices, by whom he was slain. His breach of an agreement made with his brother led to the expedition of the Seven against Thebes.

e·ter·nal (ĭ tûr'nəl), adj. 1. lasting throughout eternity; without beginning or end: eternal life. 2. perpetual; ceaseless: eternal quarreling, chatter, etc. 3. enduring; immutable: eternal principles. 4. Metaphys. existing outside of all relations of time; not subject to change. —n. 5. that which is eternal. 6. the Eternal, God. [ME, t. LL: m.s. aeternālis, der. L aeternus. See ETERNE] —e·ter'nal·ly, adv. —e·ter'nal·ness, n.

—Syn. 1. ETERNAL, ENDLESS, EVERLASTING, PERPETUAL imply lasting or going on without ceasing. That which is ETERNAL is, by its nature, without beginning or ending: God, the eternal father. That which is ENDLESS never stops but goes on continually as if in a circle: an endless succession of years. That which is EVERLASTING will endure through all future time: a promise of everlasting life. PERPETUAL implies continuous renewal and lasting as far into the future as one can foresee: perpetual strife between nations. 3. timeless, immortal, deathless, undying. —Ant. 2. temporary.

Eternal City, the, Rome.

e·terne (ĭ tûrn'), adj. Archaic. eternal. [ME, t. OF, t. L: m.s. aeternus, for aeviternus eternal]

e·ter·ni·ty (ĭ tûr'nə tĭ), n., pl. -ties. 1. infinite time; duration without beginning or end. 2. eternal existence, esp. as contrasted with mortal life. 3. an endless or seemingly endless period of time. [ME eternite, t. OF, t. L: m.s. aeternitas, der. aeternus. See ETERNE]

e·ter·nize (ĭ tûr'nĭz), v.t., -nized, -nizing. 1. to make eternal; perpetuate. 2. to immortalize.

e·te·sian (ĭ tē'zhən), adj. recurring annually (applied to certain Mediterranean winds). [f. s. L etēsius (t. Gk.: m. etēsios, lit., annual) + -AN]

eth (ĕth), n. name of a letter formerly used in the English alphabet, and still used in Icelandic and in phonetic alphabets. It is a crossed d in form, and represents (1) in Old English, both surd and vibrant th; (2) in present use, the vibrant th only. See **thorn** (def. 5). Also, **edh.**

-eth,[1] an ending of the third person singular present indicative of verbs, now occurring only in archaic forms or used in solemn or poetic language, as in doeth or doth, hath, hopeth, sitteth. [OE -eth, -ath, -oth, -th; akin to L -t]

-eth,[2] the form of -th, the ordinal suffix, after a vowel, as in twentieth, thirtieth, etc. See **-th².**

Eth., Ethiopia.

eth·ane (ĕth'ān), n. Chem. an odorless, gaseous hydrocarbon, C₂H₆, of the methane series, present in illuminating gas and crude petroleum. [f. ETH(ER) + -ANE]

eth·a·nol (ĕth'ə nōl', -nōl'), n. Chem. ethyl alcohol. [f. ETHAN(E) + -OL¹]

Eth·el·red II (ĕth'əl rĕd'), ("the Unready") 968?–1016, king of the English, 978–1016.

e·ther (ē'ジər), n. 1. Chem. a. a highly volatile and inflammable colorless liquid (**ethyl ether**), (C₂H₅)₂O, obtained by the action of sulfuric acid on alcohol, and used as a solvent and anesthetic. b. one of a class of organic compounds in which any two organic radicals are attached directly to oxygen, having the general formula R₂O, as diethyl ether (C₂H₅)₂O. 2. the upper regions of space; the clear sky; the heavens. 3. the medium anciently supposed to fill the upper regions. 4. an all-pervading medium postulated for the transmission of light, heat, etc., by the older elastic solid theory. Also, **aether** (for defs. 2–4). [t. L: m. aether, t. Gk.: m. aithēr upper air, sky]

e·the·re·al (ĭ thēr'ĭ əl), adj. 1. light, airy, or tenuous. 2. extremely delicate or refined: ethereal beauty. 3. heavenly or celestial. 4. of the ether or upper regions of space. 5. Chem. pertaining to, containing, or resembling ethyl ether. Also, **aethereal** (for defs. 1–4). —e·the're·al·i·ty, e·the're·al·ness, n. —e·the're·al·ly, adv.

e·the·re·al·ize (ĭ thēr'ĭ ə līz'), v.t., -ized, -izing. to make ethereal. —e·the're·al·i·za'tion, n.

Eth·er·ege (ĕth'ər ĭj), n. Sir George, 1635?–91, British dramatist.

e·ther·i·fy (ĭ thĕr'ə fī', ē'thər ə fī'), v.t., -fied, -fying. Chem. to convert into ether or one of the ethers. —e·ther'i·fi·ca'tion, n.

e·ther·ize (ē'thə rīz'), v.t., -ized, -izing. Med. to put under the influence of ether. —e'ther·i·za'tion, n. —e'ther·iz'er, n.

eth·ic (ĕth'ĭk), adj. 1. pertaining to morals; ethical. —n. 2. Rare. ethics. [t. L: s. ēthicus, t. Gk.: m. ēthikós of morals, moral]

eth·i·cal (ĕth'ə kəl), adj. 1. pertaining to or dealing with morals or the principles of morality; pertaining to right and wrong in conduct. 2. in accordance with the rules or standards for right conduct or practice, esp. the standards of a profession: it is not considered ethical by physicians to advertise. 3. (of drugs) sold only upon medical prescription. —eth'i·cal·ly, adv. —eth'i·cal·ness, n.

eth·i·cize (ĕth'ə sīz'), v.t., -cized, -cizing. to make ethical; treat or regard as ethical.

eth·ics (ĕth'ĭks), n.pl. 1. the principles of morality, including both the science of the good and the nature of the right. 2. the rules of conduct recognized in respect to a particular class of human actions: medical ethics. 3. moral principles, as of an individual. 4. (usually construed as sing.) the science of the human character in its ideal state. —Syn. 2. See **moral.**

E·thi·op (ē'thĭ ŏp'), adj., n. Ethiopian. [t. L: s. Aethiops, t. Gk.: m. Aethiops]

E·thi·o·pi·a (ē'thĭ ō'pĭ ə), n. 1. Also, **Abyssinia.** a kingdom in E Africa: formerly a part of Italian East Africa, 1936–41. 15,000,000 pop. (est. 1951); 409,266 sq. mi. Present boundaries include Eritrea. Cap.: Addis Ababa. 2. an ancient region in NE Africa, bordering on Egypt and the Red Sea.

Ethiopia (def. 1)

E·thi·o·pi·an (ē'thĭ ō'pĭ ən), adj. 1. pertaining to Ethiopia or to its inhabitants. 2. Negro. 3. belonging to Africa south of the tropic of Cancer. —n. 4. a native of Ethiopia. 5. Ethnol. a member of the Ethiopian race, one of the five racial divisions originally recognized, including the African Negro and Negrito. 6. a Negro.

E·thi·op·ic (ē/thǐ ŏp/ĭk, -ō/pǐk), *adj.* **1.** Ethiopian. —*n.* **2.** the ancient Semitic language of Ethiopia.

eth·moid (ĕth/moid), *Anat.* —*adj.* **1.** designating or pertaining to a bone of the skull at the root of the nose, containing numerous perforations for the filaments of the olfactory nerve. —*n.* **2.** the ethmoid bone. [t. Gk.: m.s. *ethmoeidēs* sievelike] —**eth·moi/dal,** *adj.*

eth·narch (ĕth/närk), *n.* the ruler of a people, tribe, or nation. [t. Gk.: s. *ethnárchēs.* See ETHNO-, -ARCH]

eth·nar·chy (ĕth/när kǐ), *n., pl.* **-chies.** the government, office, or jurisdiction of an ethnarch.

eth·nic (ĕth/nǐk), *adj.* **1.** pertaining to or peculiar to a population, esp. to a speech group, loosely also to a race. **2.** referring to the origin, classification, characteristics, etc., of such groups. **3.** pertaining to nations not Jewish or Christian; heathen or pagan: *ancient ethnic revels.* Also, **eth/ni·cal.** [ME, t. LL: s. *ethnicus,* t. Gk.: m. *ethnikós* national, gentile, heathen, der. *éthnos* nation] —**eth/ni·cal·ly,** *adv.*

ethnic group, *Sociol.* a group of people, racially or historically related, having a common and distinctive culture, as an Italian or Chinese colony in a large American city.

ethno-, a word element meaning "race," "nation," as in *ethnology.* [t. Gk., comb. form of *éthnos*]

eth·no·cen·trism (ĕth/nō sĕn/trǐz əm), *n. Sociol.* the belief in the inherent superiority of one's own group and culture accompanied by a feeling of contempt for other groups and cultures. —**eth/no·cen/tric,** *adj.*

ethnog., ethnography.

eth·nog·e·ny (ĕth nŏj/ə nǐ), *n. Anthropol.* the branch of ethnology which studies the origin of distinctive populations or races.

eth·nog·ra·phy (ĕth nŏg/rə fǐ), *n.* **1.** the scientific description and classification of the various cultural and racial groups of mankind. **2.** ethnology, esp. as descriptive. —**eth·nog/ra·pher,** *n.* —**eth·no·graph·ic** (ĕth/nə grăf/ĭk), **eth/no·graph/i·cal,** *adj.* —**eth/no·graph/i·cal·ly,** *adv.*

ethnol., **1.** ethnological. **2.** ethnology.

eth·nol·o·gy (ĕth nŏl/ə jǐ), *n.* the science that treats of the distinctive subdivisions of mankind, their origin, relations, speech, institutions, etc. —**eth·no·log·i·cal** (ĕth/nə lŏj/ə kəl), **eth/no·log/ic,** *adj.* —**eth/no·log/i·cal·ly,** *adv.* —**eth·nol/o·gist,** *n.*

et hoc (or **id) ge·nus om·ne** (ĕt hŏk/ (or ĭd) jē/nəs ŏm/nē), *Latin.* and all this (or that) sort of thing.

e·thos (ē/thŏs), *n.* **1.** character or disposition. **2.** *Sociol.* the fundamental spiritual characteristics of a culture. **3.** *Art.* the inherent quality of a work which produces, or is fitted to produce, a high moral impression, noble, dignified, and universal (opposed to *pathos*). [t. NL, t. Gk.: character]

eth·yl (ĕth/əl), *n.* **1.** *Chem.* a univalent radical, C_2H_5, from ethane. **2.** a type of antiknock fluid, containing tetraethyl lead and other ingredients for a more even combustion. **3.** gasoline to which this fluid has been added. **4.** (*cap.*) a trademark for the antiknock fluid (def. 2) or the gasoline (def. 3). [f. ETH(ER) + -YL] —**e·thyl·ic** (ǐ thǐl/ǐk), *adj.*

ethyl alcohol. See **alcohol.**

eth·yl·ate (ĕth/ə lāt/), *v.,* -ated, -ating, *n. Chem.* —*v.t.* **1.** to introduce one or more ethyl radicals into (a compound). —*n.* **2.** a metallic derivative of ethyl alcohol, as potassium ethylate (KOC_2H_5).

eth·yl·ene (ĕth/ə lēn/), *n. Chem.* a colorless, inflammable gas, C_2H_4, with an unpleasant odor. the first member of the ethylene series.

ethylene glycol, *Chem.* glycol.

ethylene series, *Chem.* a series of unsaturated aliphatic hydrocarbons having one double bond, with the general formula, C_nH_{2n}.

ethyl ether. See **ether** (def. 1a).

e·ti·o·late (ē/tǐ ə lāt/), *v.,* -lated, -lating. —*v.t.* **1.** to cause (a plant) to whiten by excluding light. —*v.i.* **2.** (of plants) to whiten through lack of light. [f. s. F *étioler* blanch (der. *tiolé* many-colored, mosaiclike, der. *tieule* tile, g. L *tégula*) + -ATE¹] —**e/ti·o·la/tion,** *n.*

e·ti·ol·o·gy (ē/tǐ ŏl/ə jǐ), *n.* the study of the causes of diseases. Also, **aetiology.** [t. L: m.s. *aetiologia,* t. Gk.: m. *aitiologia,* der. *aitía* cause. See -LOGY] —**e·ti·o·log·i·cal** (ē/tǐ ə lŏj/ə kəl), *adj.* —**e/ti·o·log/i·cal·ly,** *adv.* —**e/ti·ol·o·gist,** *n.*

et·i·quette (ĕt/ə kĕt/), *n.* **1.** conventional requirements as to social behavior; proprieties of conduct as established in any class or community or for any occasion. **2.** a prescribed or accepted code of usage in matters of ceremony, as at a court or in official or other formal observances. [t. F, in OF *estiquette* TICKET, of Gmc. orig.; cf. STICK²]

—**Syn. 1.** ETIQUETTE, DECORUM, PROPRIETY imply observance of the formal requirements governing behavior in polite society. ETIQUETTE refers to conventional forms and usages: *the rules of etiquette.* DECORUM suggests dignity and a sense of what is becoming or appropriate for a person of good breeding: *a fine sense of decorum.* PROPRIETY (usually plural) implies established conventions of morals and good taste: *she never fails to observe the proprieties.*

Et·na (ĕt/nə), *n.* **1.** Also, **Aetna. Mount,** an active volcano in E Sicily. 10,758 ft. **2.** (*l.c.*) a small vessel for heating liquids, consisting of a cup for the liquid with a fixed saucer surrounding it in which alcohol is burned.

E·ton (ē/tən), *n.* a town in S England, on the Thames, W of London: the site of Eton College. 3250 (1951).

Eton collar, a broad stiff collar folded outside an Eton jacket.

Eton College, an educational establishment at Eton, England, founded in 1440 by Henry VI.

E·to·ni·an (ē tō/nǐ ən), *n.* **1.** one who is or has been a pupil at Eton College. —*adj.* **2.** of or pertaining to Eton College.

Eton jacket, 1. a boys' short jacket reaching to the waistline, as worn by students at Eton College, England. **2.** a similar short jacket worn by women.

Boy wearing an Eton jacket

E·tru·ri·a (ǐ trŏŏr/Ǐ ə), *n.* an ancient country in W Italy, centering between the Arno and the Tiber and roughly corresponding to modern Tuscany.

E·trus·can (ǐ trŭs/kən), *adj.* **1.** pertaining to Etruria, its inhabitants, civilization, art, or language. —*n.* **2.** an inhabitant of ancient Etruria. **3.** the extinct language of Etruria. Also, **E·tru·ri·an** (ǐ trŏŏr/Ǐ ən). [f. s. L *Etruscus* of Etruria + -AN]

et seq., *pl.* **et seqq., et sqq.** (L *et sequens*) and the following.

et seqq., (L *et sequentes, et sequentia*) and those following. Also, **et sqq.**

et sic de si·mi·li·bus (ĕt sǐk dē sǐ mǐl/ə bəs), *Latin.* and thus concerning (all) similar (ones).

-ette, a noun suffix, the feminine form of *-et,* occurring esp.: **1.** with the original diminutive force, as in *cigarette.* **2.** as a distinctively feminine ending, as in *coquette,* and various colloquial or humorous formations, such as *usherette, farmerette.* **3.** in trademarks of imitations or substitutes, as in *leatherette.* [t. F, fem. of *-et* -ET]

et tu, Bru·te! (ĕt tū brŏŏ/tǐ), *Latin.* and thou, Brutus! (reproachful exclamation of Julius Caesar on seeing his friend Brutus among his assassins).

é·tude (ā tūd/, ā tōōd/; *Fr.* ĕ tyd/), *n. Music.* **1.** a composition intended mainly for the practice of some point of technique. **2.** a composition performed for its aesthetic appeal which also embodies a specific technical exercise. [F. See STUDY, n.]

e·tui (ā twē/, ĕt/wē), *n., pl.* **etuis.** a small case, esp. one for small objects, as needles, toilet articles, etc. Also, **e·twee/.** [t. F, der. OF *etuier* keep, g. L *studiāre* care for]

etym., **1.** etymological. **2.** etymology. Also, **etymol.**

et·y·mol·o·gize (ĕt/ə mŏl/ə jīz/), *v.,* -gized, -gizing. —*v.t.* **1.** to trace the history of (a word). —*v.i.* **2.** to study etymology. **3.** to give or suggest the etymology of words.

et·y·mol·o·gy (ĕt/ə mŏl/ə jǐ), *n., pl.* **-gies. 1.** the study of historical linguistic change, esp. as applied to individual words. **2.** an account of the history of a particular word. **3.** the derivation of a word. [t. L: m.s. *etymologia,* t. Gk. See ETYMON. -LOGY] —**et·y·mo·log·i·cal** (ĕt/ə mə lŏj/ə kəl), **et/y·mo·log/ic,** *adj.* —**et/y·mo·log/i·cal·ly,** *adv.* —**et/y·mol/o·gist,** *n.*

et·y·mon (ĕt/ə mŏn/), *n., pl.* **-mons, -ma** -(mə). a primary linguistic form, from which derivatives are formed. [t. L, t. Gk.: the original sense, form, or element of a word, prop. neut. of *étymos* true, real]

Et·zel (ĕt/səl), *n. German Legend.* Attila.

eu-, a prefix meaning "good," "well," occurring chiefly in words of Greek origin, as in *eupepsia.* [t. Gk., comb. form of *eús,* adj., good, neut. *eû* (used as adv., well)]

Eu, *Chem.* europium.

Eu·boe·a (ū bē/ə), *n.* an island in the Aegean, off the E coast of, and belonging to, Greece. 164,542 pop. (1951); 1586 sq. mi. *Cap.:* Chalcis. Modern Greek, **Evvoia.** Also, **Negropont.** —**Eu·boe/an,** *adj.*

eu·caine (ū kān/), *n.* **1.** a crystalline organic compound used, in the form of a salt, as a local anesthetic (**alpha eucaine**). **2.** a similar but less used compound (**beta eucaine**); leucaine. [f. EU- + (CO)CAINE]

eu·ca·lyp·tol (ū/kə lǐp/tōl, -tŏl), *n.* cineole. [f. EUCALYPT(US) + -OL²]

eu·ca·lyp·tus (ū/kə lǐp/təs), *n., pl.* **-ti** (-tī), **-tuses.** any member of the myrtaceous genus *Eucalyptus,* including many tall trees, esp. the blue gum, *E. globulus,* native in and around Australia and cultivated elsewhere, which yields a valuable timber and bears leaves containing an oil used in medicine. Also, **eu·ca·lypt** (ū/kə lǐpt/). [t. NL, f. *eu-* EU- + m. Gk. *kalyptós* covered (with allusion to the cap covering the buds)]

eu·cha·ris (ū/kər ǐs), *n.* any of the amaryllidaceous plants constituting the South American genus *Eucharis,* some of which are cultivated for their large, fragrant white flowers. [NL, t. Gk.: pleasing]

Eu·cha·rist (ū/kə rǐst), *n.* **1.** the sacrament of the Lord's Supper; the communion; the sacrifice of the Mass. **2.** the consecrated elements of the Lord's Supper, esp. the bread. **3.** (*l.c.*) the giving of thanks; thanksgiving. [t. LL: m.s. *eucharistia,* t. Gk.: gratefulness, thanksgiving, the eucharist] —**Eu/cha·ris/tic, Eu/cha·ris/ti·cal,** *adj.* —**Eu/cha·ris/ti·cal·ly,** *adv.*

eu·chre (ū/kər), *n., v.,* -chred, -chring. —*n.* **1.** *Cards.* a game played usually by two, three, or four persons, with the 32 (or 28 or 24) highest cards in the pack. **2.** an instance of euchring or being euchred. —*v.t.* **3.** to get the better of (an opponent) in a hand at euchre by his failure to win three tricks after having made the trump. **4.** *U.S. Colloq.* to outwit; get the better of, as by scheming (usually fol. by *out*). [orig. uncert.]

ăct, āble, dâre, ärt; ĕbb, ēqual; Ĭf, īce; hŏt, ōver, ôrder, oil, bŏŏk, ōōze, out; ŭp, ūse, ûrge; ə = a in alone; ch, chief; g, give; ng, ring; sh, shoe; th, thin; ŧħ, that; zh, vision. See the full key on inside cover.

Euck·en (oi/kən), *n* **Rudolph Christoph** (rōō/dôlf krĭs/tôf), 1846–1926, German philosopher.

eu·clase (ū/klās), *n.* a green or blue mineral, beryllium aluminum silicate, HBeAl(SiO₅), occurring in prismatic crystals. [t. F, f. *eu-* EU- + m.s. Gk. *klásis* a breaking]

Eu·clid (ū/klĭd), *n* **1.** fl. c300 B.C., Greek geometer at Alexandria. **2.** the works of Euclid, esp. his treatise on geometry. **3.** Euclidean geometry. **4.** a city in NE Ohio, near Cleveland. 62,998 (1960).

Eu·clid·e·an (ū klĭd/ĭ ən), *adj.* of or pertaining to Euclid, or adopting his postulates: *Euclidean geometry.* Also, **Eu·clid/i·an.**

eu·de·mon (ū dē/mən), *n* a good demon or spirit. Also, **eu·dae/mon.** [f. EU- + m. Gk. *daímōn* DEMON]

eu·de·mo·ni·a (ū/dĭ mō/nĭ ə), *n.* **1.** happiness; welfare. **2.** (in Aristotelian philosophy) happiness as the result of an active life governed by reason. Also, **eu/dae·mo/ni·a.** [t. Gk.: m. *eudaimonía*]

eu·de·mon·ic (ū/dĭ mŏn/ĭk), *adj.* **1.** pertaining or conducive to happiness. **2.** pertaining to eudemonics. Also, **eu/dae·mon/ic.**

eu·de·mon·ics (ū/dĭ mŏn/ĭks), *n.* **1.** the science of happiness. **2.** eudemonism. Also, **eu/dae·mon/ics.**

eu·de·mon·ism (ū dē/mə nĭz/əm), *n.* the system of ethics which holds that the basis of moral obligations lies in their relation to the production of happiness. Also, **eu·dae/mon·ism.** [f. EUDEMON(IA) + -ISM] —**eu·de/mon·ist,** *n.* —**eu·de/mon·is/tic, eu·de/mon·is/ti·cal,** *adj.*

eu·di·om·e·ter (ū/dĭ ŏm/ə tər), *n* *Chem.* a graduated glass measuring tube for gas analysis. [f. Gk. *eúdio(s)* fine, clear, as weather + -METER] —**eu·di·o·met·ric** (ū/dĭ ə mĕt/rĭk), **eu·di·o·met/ri·cal,** *adj.* —**eu·di·o·met/ri·cal·ly,** *adv.*

eu·di·om·e·try (ū/dĭ ŏm/ə trĭ), *n.* *Chem.* the measurement and analysis of gases with the eudiometer.

Eu·gene (ū jēn/), *n.* a city in W Oregon. 50,977 (1960).

Eu·gène (œ zhĕn/), *n.* **Prince,** (*François Eugène de Savoie-Carignan*) 1663–1736, Austrian general, born in France.

eu·gen·ic (ū jĕn/ĭk), *adj.* **1.** of or bringing about improvement in the type of offspring produced. **2.** having good inherited characteristics. Also, **eu·gen/i·cal.** [f. s. Gk. *eugenḗs* well born + -IC] —**eu·gen/i·cal·ly,** *adv.*

eu·gen·i·cist (ū jĕn/ə sĭst), *n.* **1.** a specialist in eugenics. **2.** an advocate of eugenic measures. Also, **eu·gen·ist** (ū/jə nĭst).

eu·gen·ics (ū jĕn/ĭks), *n.* **1.** the science of improving the qualities of the human race, esp. the careful selection of parents. **2.** the science of improving offspring.

Eu·gé·nie (œ zhē nē/), *n.* **Empress,** (*Marie Eugénie de Montijo de Guzmán*) 1826–1920, empress of the French, born in Spain (wife of Napoleon III).

eu·ge·nol (ū/jə nōl/, -nōl/), *n.* *Chem.* a colorless, aromatic, oily compound, C₁₀H₁₂O₂, contained in certain essential oils, as that of cloves. [f. NL *Eugen(ia)* genus of myrtaceous plants + -OL²]

Eu·gle·na (ū glē/nə), *n.* a green type of flagellate protozoan with one flagellum and a red eyespot, much used for class and experimental study.

eu·he·mer·ism (ū hē/mə rĭz/əm, ū hĕm/ə-), *n.* **1.** the theory held by Euhemerus that polytheistic mythology arose out of the deification of dead heroes. **2.** mythological interpretation which reduces the gods to the level of distinguished men; the derivation of mythology from history. —**eu·he/mer·ist,** *n.* —**eu·he/mer·is/tic,** *adj.* —**eu·he/mer·is/ti·cal·ly,** *adv.*

eu·he·mer·ize (ū hē/mə rīz/, ū hĕm/ə-), *v.t., v.i.,* **-ized, -izing.** to treat or explain (myths) by euhemerism.

Eu·he·mer·us (ū hē/mər əs), *n.* fl. c300 B.C., Greek writer. See **euhemerism.**

eu·la·chon (ū/lə kŏn/), *n.* candlefish.

Eu·ler (oi/lər), *n.* **Leonhard** (lā/ōn härt/), 1707–83, Swiss mathematician.

eu·lo·gi·a (ū lō/jĭ ə), *n.* *Eccles.* the unconsecrated bread not needed in the Eucharist, but blessed and distributed among those members of the congregation who did not commune. This custom still exists in the Greek Church. [t. Eccl. L, t. Gk. See EULOGY]

eu·lo·gist (ū/lə jĭst), *n.* one who eulogizes.

eu·lo·gis·tic (ū/lə jĭs/tĭk), *adj.* pertaining to or containing eulogy; laudatory. Also, **eu/lo·gis/ti·cal.** —**eu/lo·gis/ti·cal·ly,** *adv.*

eu·lo·gi·um (ū lō/jĭ əm), *n., pl.* **-giums, -gia** (-jĭ ə). **1.** eulogy. **2.** eulogistic language. [t. ML. See EULOGY]

eu·lo·gize (ū/lə jīz/), *v.t.,* **-gized, -gizing.** to praise highly; speak or write a eulogy about. —**eu/lo·giz/er,** *n.* —**Syn.** extol, laud, commend, panegyrize.

eu·lo·gy (ū/lə jĭ), *n., pl.* **-gies. 1.** a speech or writing in praise of a person or thing, esp. a set oration in honor of a deceased person. **2.** high praise or commendation. [t. ML: m.s. *eulogium,* var. of L *eulogia* (t. Gk.: praise), by assoc. with *élogium* short saying]

Eu·men·i·des (ū mĕn/ə dēz/), *n.pl.* *Class. Myth.* a euphemistic name for the Furies or Erinyes. [t. L, t. Gk.: lit., the gracious goddesses]

eu·nuch (ū/nək), *n.* a castrated man, esp. one formerly employed as a harem attendant or officer of state by Oriental rulers. [ME *eunuchus,* t. L, t. Gk.: m. *eunoûchos* chamber attendant]

eu·on·y·mus (ū ŏn/ə məs), *n.* any of the widespread genus *Euonymus,* of shrubs and small trees, of northern temperate regions, usually bearing crimson or rose-colored capsules which on opening disclose the seed. Also, **evonymus.** [t. Gk.: m. *euṓnymos* spindle tree, lit., of good name]

eu·pa·to·ri·um (ū/pə tōr/ĭ əm), *n.* any plant of the large composite genus *Eupatorium,* mostly American, with heads of white or purplish flowers, as thoroughwort and joe-pye weed, and esp. a garden species, the mistflower. [NL, t. Gk.: m. *eupatórion;* named after Mithridates *Eupator,* king of Pontus (120?–63 B.C.)]

eu·pat·rid (ū păt/rĭd, ū/pə trĭd), *n.* **1.** one of the hereditary aristocrats of ancient Athens and other states of Greece, who at one time formed the ruling class. **2.** any aristocrat or patrician. [t. Gk.: s. *eupatrídēs*]

eu·pat·ri·dae (ū păt/rə dē/), *n.pl.* the eupatrids. [NL, t. Gk.: m. *eupatrídai,* pl. of *eupatrídēs* of noble family]

Eu·pen and Mal·mé·dy (oi/pən; mål mē dē/), two districts on the Belgian-German border: ceded to Belgium, 1919; reannexed to Germany, 1940; now in Belgium.

eu·pep·sia (ū pĕp/shə, -sĭ ə), *n.* good digestion (opposed to *dyspepsia*). [t. NL, t. Gk.: good digestion] —**eu·pep·tic** (ū pĕp/tĭk), *adj.*

eu·phe·mism (ū/fə mĭz/əm), *n.* *Rhet.* **1.** the substitution of a mild, indirect, or vague expression for a harsh or blunt one. **2.** the expression so substituted: *"To pass away" is a euphemism for "to die."* [t. Gk.: s. *euphēmismós,* der. *euphēmízein* use fair words] —**eu/phe·mist,** *n.* —**eu/phe·mis/tic, eu/phe·mis/ti·cal,** *adj.* —**eu/phe·mis/ti·cal·ly,** *adv.*

eu·phe·mize (ū/fə mīz/), *v..* **-mized, -mizing.** —*v.t.* **1.** to refer to by means of euphemism. —*v.i.* **2.** to employ euphemism.

eu·phon·ic (ū fŏn/ĭk), *adj.* pertaining to or characterized by euphony. Also, **eu·phon/i·cal.** —**eu·phon/i·cal·ly,** *adv.* —**eu·phon/i·cal·ness,** *n.*

eu·pho·ni·ous (ū fō/nĭ əs), *adj.* characterized by euphony; well-sounding; agreeable to the ear. —**eu·pho/ni·ous·ly,** *adv.* —**eu·pho/ni·ous·ness,** *n.*

eu·pho·ni·um (ū fō/nĭ əm), *n.* *Music.* a baritone tuba, used in bands. [t. NL, der. Gk. *euphōnos* well-sounding]

eu·pho·nize (ū/fə nīz/), *v.t.,* **-nized, -nizing.** to make euphonious.

eu·pho·ny (ū/fə nĭ), *n., pl.* **-nies. 1.** agreeableness of sound; pleasing effect to the ear, esp. of speech sounds as uttered or as combined in utterance. **2.** a tendency to change speech sounds for ease and economy of utterance: a former explanation of phonetic change. [t. LL: m.s. *euphōnia,* t. Gk., der. *euphōnos* well-sounding]

eu·phor·bi·a (ū fôr/bĭ ə), *n.* any of the plants of the widespread genus *Euphorbia,* which vary greatly, but consist mostly of herbs and shrubs with an acrid milky juice; a spurge. [ME *euforbia,* for L *euphorbea* an African plant; named after *Euphorbus,* a Greek physician]

eu·phor·bi·a·ceous (ū fôr/bĭ ā/shəs), *adj.* belonging to the *Euphorbiaceae,* or spurge family of plants, which includes the spurges, the cascarilla, castor oil, and cassava plants, several that yield rubber, and others.

eu·pho·ri·a (ū fōr/ĭ ə), *n.* *Psychol.* a feeling or state of well-being. [t. NL, t. Gk., der. *euphoros* bearing well] —**eu·phor·is·tic** (ū/fôr ĭs/tĭk), *adj.*

eu·phra·sy (ū/frə sĭ), *n.* eyebright, *Euphrasia officinalis.* [late ME, t. ML: m.s. *euphrasia,* t. Gk.: *delight*]

Eu·phra·tes (ū frā/tēz), *n.* a river flowing from E Turkey through Syria and Iraq, joining the Tigris to form the Shatt-al-Arab near the Persian Gulf. 1700 mi.

eu·phroe (ū/frō, ū/vrō), *n.* *Naut.* an oblong or oval piece of wood perforated with holes through which small lines are rove, forming a crowfoot, from which an awning is suspended. Also, **uphroe.** [t. D: pseudolearned spelling of *juffrouw,* lit., young woman]

Eu·phros·y·ne (ū frŏs/ə nē/), *n.* *Gk. Myth.* one of the Graces.

Eu·phu·es (ū/fū ēz/), *n.* the main character in John Lyly's works *Euphues, the Anatomy of Wit* (1579), and *Euphues and his England* (1580). [t. Gk.: well grown]

eu·phu·ism (ū/fū ĭz/əm), *n.* **1.** an affected style in imitation of that of Lyly (see **Euphues**), fashionable in England about the end of the 16th century, characterized chiefly by long series of antitheses, frequent similes relating to fabulous natural history, alliteration, etc. **2.** any similar ornate style of writing or speaking; highflown language. **3.** an instance of such style or language. —**eu/phu·ist,** *n.* —**eu/phu·is/tic, eu/phu·is/ti·cal,** *adj.* —**eu/phu·is/ti·cal·ly,** *adv.*

eu·plas·tic (ū plăs/tĭk), *adj.* *Physiol.* capable of being transformed into organized tissue. [f. s. Gk. *euplastos* easy to mold + -IC]

eup·ne·a (ūp nē/ə), *n.* *Pathol.* easy or normal breathing (opposed to *dyspnea*). Also, **eup·noe/a.** [NL, t. Gk.: m. *eúpnoia,* der. *eúpnōos* breathing well]

Eur., **1.** Europe. **2.** European.

Eur·a·sia (yŏŏ rā/zhə, -shə), *n.* Europe and Asia considered as a whole.

Eur·a·sian (yŏŏ rā/zhən, -shən), *adj.* **1.** pertaining to Europe and Asia taken together. **2.** of mixed European and Asiatic descent. —*n.* **3.** a person one of whose parents is European and the other Asiatic.

eu·re·ka (yŏŏ rē/kə), *interj.* **1.** I have found (it): the reputed exclamation of Archimedes when, after long study, he discovered a method of detecting the amount of alloy in the crown of the king of Syracuse. **2.** an exclamation of triumph at a discovery or supposed discovery (motto of California). [t. Gk.: m. *heúrēka*]

---

b., blend of, blended; c., cognate with; d., dialect, dialectal; der., derived from; f., formed from; g., going back to; m., modification of; r., replacing; s., stem of; t., taken from; ?, perhaps. See the full key on inside cover.

Eu·re·ka (yŏŏ rē/kə), n. a city on the N coast of California; most westerly in the U.S. 28,137 (1960).

eu·rhyth·mic (yŏŏ rĭ*th*/mĭk), adj. characterized by a pleasing rhythm; harmoniously ordered or proportioned. Also, **eurythmic.**

eu·rhyth·mics (yŏŏ rĭ*th*/mĭks), n. the art of interpreting in bodily movements the rhythm of musical compositions: applied to a method invented by Émile Jaques-Dalcroze, a Swiss composer, aiming to develop the sense of rhythm and symmetry. Also, **eurythmics.**

eu·rhyth·my (yŏŏ rĭ*th*/mĭ), n. rhythmical movement or order; harmonious proportion. Also, **eurythmy.** [t. Gk.: m.s. *eurhythmía* rhythmical order]

Eu·rip·i·des (yŏŏ rĭp/ə dēz/), n. 480?–406? B.C., Athenian tragic poet.

eu·ri·pus (yŏŏ rī/pəs), n., pl. **-pi** (-pī). a strait, esp. one in which the flow of water in both directions is violent, as (cap.) that between the island of Euboea and Boeotia in Greece. [t. L, t. Gk.: m. *eúripos*, f. *eu-* EU- + m. *rhīpé* impetus, rush]

Eu·roc·ly·don (yŏŏ rŏk/lə dŏn/), n. a stormy northeast or north-northeast wind. [t. Gk.: m. *euroklýdōn*]

Eu·ro·pa (yŏŏ rō/pə), n. Gk. Myth. sister of Cadmus, borne to Crete by Zeus disguised in the form of a white bull; the mother by him of Rhadamanthus, Minos, and Sarpedon. [t. L, t. Gk.: m. *Eurṓpē*]

Eu·rope (yŏŏr/əp), n. a continent in the W part of Eurasia, separated from Asia by the Ural Mountains on the E and the Caucasus Mountains and the Black and Caspian seas on the SE. In British usage, *Europe* sometimes contrasts with *England.* 411,000,000 pop. excluding the Soviet Union (1955); ab. 3,754,000 sq. mi.

Eu·ro·pe·an (yŏŏr/ə pē/ən), adj. **1.** pertaining to Europe or its inhabitants. **2.** native to or derived from Europe. —n. **3.** a native or inhabitant of Europe. **4.** a person of European descent or connections.

Eu·ro·pe·an·ism (yŏŏr/ə pē/ə nĭz/əm), n. **1.** European characteristics, ideas, methods, sympathies, etc. **2.** a European trait or practice.

Eu·ro·pe·an·ize (yŏŏr/ə pē/ə nīz/), v.t., **-ized, -izing.** to make European. —**Eu/ro·pe/an·i·za/tion,** n.

European plan, U.S. that method of conducting a hotel according to which the fixed charge per day covers only lodging and service.

European Recovery Program, a broad plan for aiding the European nations in economic recovery, first proposed by Secretary of State George C. Marshall in 1947

eu·ro·pi·um (yŏŏ rō/pĭ əm), n. Chem. a rare-earth metallic element with light-pink salts. Symbol: Eu; at. wt.: 152; at no.: 63. [t. NL, der. L *Eurṓpa* Europe]

Eu·rus (yŏŏr/əs), n. Class. Myth. the easterly or southeasterly wind personified. [t. L, t. Gk.: m. *Eûros*]

eury-, a word element meaning "broad," as in *eurypterid.* [t. Gk., comb. form of *eurýs*]

Eu·ry·a·le (ū rī/ə lē/), n. Gk. Leg. one of the Gorgons.

Eu·ryd·i·ce (yŏŏ rĭd/ə sē/), n. Gk. Myth. the wife of Orpheus, permitted by Pluto to follow her husband out of Hades, but lost to him because he disobediently looked back at her. See **Orpheus.**

eu·ryp·ter·id (yŏŏ rĭp/tər ĭd), n. Paleontol. any of the *Eurypterida,* a group of Paleozoic arthropods resembling in some respects the horseshoe crabs. [t. NL: s. *Eurypterida,* pl., f. Gk. *eury-* EURY- + s. Gk. *pterón* wing + *-ida* (see ID-²)]

Eu·rys·theus (yŏŏ rĭs/thē os, -thĭ əs), n. Gk. Legend. a king of Mycenae: imposed 12 labors upon Hercules.

eu·ryth·mic (yŏŏ rĭ*th*/mĭk), adj. eurhythmic. —**eu·ryth/mics,** n. —**eu·ryth/my,** n.

Eu·se·bi·us (ū sē/bĭ əs), n. (Eusebius Pamphili) A.D. 260?–340?, Christian bishop in Palestine and historian of the early Christian church. —**Eu·se/bi·an,** adj.

eu·spo·ran·gi·ate (ū/spô răn/jĭ āt/), adj. Bot. having sporangia derived from a group of cells.

Eu·sta·chi·an tube (ū stā/kĭ ən, -stā/shən), Anat. a canal extending from the middle ear to the pharynx; auditory canal. See diag. under **ear.** [Eustachian, f. EUSTACHI(O) + -AN]

Eu·sta·chio (ĕ/ōō stā/kyô), n. **Bartolomeo** (bär/tô-lôm mĕ/ô), (Eustachius), died 1574, Italian anatomist.

eu·tax·y (ū/tăk sĭ/), n. good or right order. [t. F: m. *eutaxie,* t. Gk.: m. *eutaxía* good arrangement]

eu·tec·tic (ū tĕk/tĭk), adj. Chem. **1.** of greatest fusibility: said of an alloy or mixture whose melting point is lower than that of any other alloy or mixture of the same ingredients. **2.** denoting or pertaining to such a mixture or its properties: *a eutectic melting point.* —n. **3.** a eutectic substance. [t. s. Gk. *eútēktos* easily melted + -IC]

eu·tec·toid (ū tĕk/toid), adj. **1.** resembling a eutectic. —n. **2.** eutectoid alloy. [f. EUTECT(IC) + -OID]

Eu·ter·pe (ū tûr/pĭ), n. Class. Myth. the Muse of music and lyric poetry. [t. L, t. Gk.: lit., well-pleasing]

eu·tha·na·sia (ū/thə nā/zhə), n. **1.** painless death. **2.** the putting of a person to death painlessly, esp. a person suffering from an incurable and painful disease. [t. NL, t. Gk.: an easy death]

eu·then·ics (ū thĕn/ĭks), n. the science of bettering the environment or living conditions, esp. to improve the race. [f. s. Gk. *euthēnía* plenty, well-being + -ICS]

eux·e·nite (ūk/sə nīt/), n. a brownish-black mineral of complex composition, containing yttrium, columbium, titanium, uranium, etc. [f. s. Gk. *eúxenos* hospitable (in allusion to its many constituents) + -ITE¹]

Eux·ine Sea (ūk/sĭn, -sīn), Black Sea.

e·vac·u·ant (Ĭ văk/yŏŏ ənt), Med. —adj. **1.** evacuating; promoting evacuation, esp. from the bowels. —n. **2.** an evacuant medicine or agent.

e·vac·u·ate (Ĭ văk/yŏŏ āt/), v., **-ated, -ating.** —v.t. **1.** to leave empty; vacate. **2.** Mil. **a.** to remove (troops, wounded soldiers, inhabitants, etc.) from a place. **b.** to withdraw from or quit (a town, fort, etc., which has been occupied). **3.** Physiol. to discharge or eject as through the excretory passages, esp. from the bowels. —v.i. **4.** to leave a town because of air raid threats, etc.: *they had evacuated into the country.* [t. L: m.s. *ēvacuātus,* pp., emptied out] —**e·vac/u·a/tor,** n.

e·vac·u·a·tion (Ĭ văk/yŏŏ ā/shən), n. **1.** act or process of evacuating. **2.** condition of being evacuated. **3.** a making empty of contents; expulsion, as of contents. **4.** Physiol. discharge, as of waste matter through the excretory passages, esp. from the bowels. **5.** that which is evacuated or discharged. **6.** Mil. **a.** clearance by removal of troops, etc. **b.** the withdrawal or removal of troops, wounded soldiers, inhabitants, etc.

e·vac·u·ee (Ĭ văk/yŏŏ ē/, Ĭ văk/yŏŏ ē/), n. a person who is withdrawn or removed from a place of danger.

e·vade (Ĭ vād/), v., **evaded, evading.** —v.t. **1.** to escape from by trickery or cleverness: *evade pursuit.* **2.** to get around by trickery: *evade the law, the rules.* **3.** to avoid doing or fulfilling: *evade a duty, obligation, etc.* **4.** to avoid answering directly: *evade a question.* **5.** to baffle; elude: *a word that evades definition, the solution evaded him.* —v.i. **6.** to practice evasion. [t. L: m.s. *ēvādere* pass over, go out] —**e·vad/a·ble, e·vad/i·ble,** adj. —**e·vad/er,** n. —**e·vad/ing·ly,** adv. —**Syn. 1.** avoid, shun, dodge. **3.** See **escape. 6.** prevaricate.

e·vag·i·nate (Ĭ văj/ə nāt/), v.t., **-nated, -nating.** to turn inside out, or cause to protrude by eversion, as a tubular organ. [t. L: m.s. *ēvāgīnātus,* pp., unsheathed] —**e·vag/i·na/tion,** n.

e·val·u·ate (Ĭ văl/yŏŏ āt/), v.t., **-ated, -ating. 1.** to ascertain the value or amount of; appraise carefully. **2.** Math. to ascertain the numerical value of. [f. s. F *évaluer* (der. OF *value,* pp., of *valoir* be worth, g. L *valēre*) + -ATE¹] —**e·val/u·a/tion,** n.

ev·a·nesce (ĕv/ə nĕs/), v.i. **-nesced, -nescing.** to disappear gradually; vanish; fade away. [t. L: m.s. *ēvānescere*] —**ev/a·nes/cence,** n.

ev·a·nes·cent (ĕv/ə nĕs/ənt), adj. **1.** vanishing; passing away; fleeting. **2.** tending to become imperceptible; scarcely perceptible. —**ev/a·nes/cent·ly,** adv.

Evang., Evangelical.

e·van·gel¹ (Ĭ văn/jəl), n. **1.** the good tidings of the redemption of the world through Jesus Christ; the Gospel. **2.** (usually cap.) any of the four Gospels. **3.** doctrine taken as a guide or regarded as of prime importance. [t. LL: m.s. *evangelium,* t. Gk.: m. *euangélion* good tidings; r. ME *evangile,* t. OF]

e·van·gel² (Ĭ văn/jəl), n. an evangelist. [t. Gk.: m.s. *euángelos* good messenger]

e·van·gel·i·cal (ē/văn jĕl/ə kəl, ĕv/ən-), adj. Also, **e/van·gel/ic. 1.** pertaining to or in keeping with the Gospel and its teachings. **2.** belonging to or designating those Christian churches which emphasize the teachings and authority of the Scriptures, esp. of the New Testament, in opposition to that of the church itself or of reason. **3.** pertaining to certain movements in the Protestant churches in the 18th and 19th centuries which stressed the importance of personal experience of guilt for sin, and of reconciliation to God through Christ. **4.** evangelistic. —n. **5.** an adherent of evangelical doctrines; a member of an evangelical church or party, as of the Low Church party of the Church of England. —**e/van·gel/i·cal·ly,** adv.

e·van·gel·i·cal·ism (ē/văn jĕl/ə kə lĭz/əm, ĕv/ən-), n. **1.** evangelical doctrines or principles. **2.** adherence to them, or to an evangelical church or party.

e·van·ge·lism (Ĭ văn/jə lĭz/əm), n. **1.** the preaching or promulgation of the Gospel; the work of an evangelist. **2.** evangelicalism.

e·van·ge·list (Ĭ văn/jə lĭst), n. **1.** a preacher of the Gospel. **2.** (cap.) any of the writers (Matthew, Mark, Luke, and John) of the four Gospels. **3.** one of a class of teachers in the early church, next in rank after apostles and prophets. **4.** a revivalist. **5.** an occasional or itinerant preacher. **6.** (cap.) Mormon Ch. a patriarch.

e·van·ge·lis·tic (Ĭ văn/jə lĭs/tĭk), adj. **1.** pertaining to evangelists, or preachers of the Gospel. **2.** evangelical. **3.** seeking to evangelize; striving to convert sinners. **4.** designed or fitted to evangelize. **5.** (often cap.) of or pertaining to the four Evangelists. —**e·van/ge·lis/ti·cal·ly,** adv.

e·van·ge·lize (Ĭ văn/jə līz/), v., **-lized, -lizing.** —v.t. **1.** to preach the gospel to. **2.** to convert to Christianity. —v.i. **3.** to preach the gospel; act as an evangelist. —**e·van/ge·li·za/tion,** n. —**e·van/ge·liz/er,** n.

e·van·ish (Ĭ văn/ĭsh), v.i. Poetic. **1.** to vanish or disappear. **2.** to cease to be.

Ev·ans (ĕv/ənz), n. **1. Sir Arthur John,** 1851–1941, British archaeologist. **2. Herbert McLean** (mə klān/), born 1882, U.S. embryologist. **3. Mary Ann** (Mrs. J. W. Cross). See **Eliot, George.**

Ev·ans·ton (ĕv/ən stən), n. a city in NE Illinois, on Lake Michigan, near Chicago. 79,283 (1960).

Ev·ans·ville (ĕv/ənz vĭl/), n. a city in SW Indiana, on the Ohio river. 141,543 (1960).

e·vap·o·ra·ble (Ĭ văp'ərəbəl), *adj.* capable of being converted to gas by evaporation. —**e·vap'o·ra·bil'i·ty,** *n.*

e·vap·o·rate (Ĭ văp'ərāt'), *v.,* **-rated, -rating.** —*v.i.* **1.** to turn to vapor; pass off in vapor. **2.** to give off moisture. **3.** to disappear; vanish; fade: *as soon as his situation became clear to him, his hopes quickly evaporated.* —*v.t.* **4.** to convert into a gaseous state or vapor; drive off or extract in the form of vapor. **5.** to extract moisture or liquid from, as by heat, so as to make dry or to reduce to a denser state: *to evaporate fruit.* [t. LL: m.s. *ēvapōrātus,* pp., dispersed in vapor] —**e·vap'o·ra'tive,** *adj.* —**e·vap'o·ra'tor,** *n.*
—**Syn. 5.** EVAPORATE, DEHYDRATE, DRY mean to abstract moisture from. To EVAPORATE is to remove moisture by means of heat, and thus to produce condensation or shriveling: *to evaporate milk, sliced apples.* To DEHYDRATE is to remove all vestiges of moisture by means of a mechanical process: *to dehydrate foods makes them easier to preserve and to transport.* To DRY may mean to wipe moisture off the surface or to withdraw moisture by exposure to air or heat; the object dried is left unchanged: *to dry a dish, clothes.*

evaporated milk, thick, unsweetened, canned milk made by removing some of the water from whole milk.

e·vap·o·ra·tion (Ĭ văp'ərā'shən), *n.* **1.** act or process of evaporating. **2.** state of being evaporated. **3.** matter, or the quantity of matter, evaporated or passed off in vapor. —**e·vap'o·ra'tive,** *adj.*

Ev·arts (ĕv'ərts), *n.* **William Maxwell,** 1818-1901, U.S. lawyer and statesman.

e·va·sion (Ĭ vā'zhən), *n.* **1.** act of escaping something by trickery or cleverness: *evasion of one's duty, responsibilities, etc.* **2.** the avoiding of an argument, accusation, question, or the like, as by a subterfuge. **3.** a means of evading; a subterfuge; an excuse or trick to avoid or get around something. [late ME, t. LL: s. *ēvāsio*] —**Syn. 1.** avoidance, dodging. **2.** prevarication, equivocation, quibbling.

e·va·sive (Ĭ vā'sĭv), *adj.* **1.** tending or seeking to evade; characterized by evasion: *an evasive answer.* **2.** elusive or evanescent. —**e·va'sive·ly,** *adv.* —**e·va'sive·ness,** *n.*

eve (ēv), *n.* **1.** the evening, or often the day, before a church festival, and hence before any date or event. **2.** the period just preceding any event, etc.: *the eve of a revolution.* **3.** *Chiefly Poetic.* the evening. [var. of EVEN²]

Eve (ēv), *n.* *Bible.* the first woman. Gen. 3:20. [ME; OE *Efe,* t. L: m. *Eva,* t. Gk. (Septuagint), t. Heb.: m. *hawwāh,* explained as "mother of the living" (*hāy*), but meaning uncert.]

e·vec·tion (Ĭ vĕk'shən), *n.* *Astron.* a periodic inequality in the moon's motion caused by the attraction of the sun. [t. L: s. *ēvectio,* der. *ēvehere* carry forth or up] —**e·vec'tion·al,** *adj.*

Eve·lyn (ĕv'əlĭn, ēv'lĭn), *n.* **John,** 1620-1706, British diarist.

e·ven¹ (ē'vən), *adj.* **1.** level; flat; without irregularities; smooth: *an even surface, even country.* **2.** on the same level; in the same plane or line; parallel: *even with the ground.* **3.** free from variations or fluctuations; regular: *even motion.* **4.** uniform in action, character, or quality: *an even color, to hold an even course.* **5.** equal in measure or quantity: *even quantities of two substances, letters of even date* (letters of the same date). **6.** divisible by 2: thus, 2, 8, and 12 are *even* numbers (opposed to *odd,* as 1, 3, etc.). **7.** denoted by such a number: *the even pages of a book.* **8.** exactly expressible in integers, or in tens, hundreds, etc., without fractional parts: *an even mile, an even hundred.* **9.** leaving no balance of debt on either side, as accounts; square, as one person with another. **10.** calm; placid; not easily excited or angered: *an even temper.* **11.** equitable, impartial, or fair: *an even bargain, an even chance.* —*adv.* **12.** evenly. **13.** still; yet (used to emphasize a comparative): *even more suitable.* **14.** (used to suggest that something mentioned as a possibility constitutes an extreme case, or one that might not be expected): *the slightest noise, even disturbs him; even if he goes, he may not take part.* **15.** just: *even now.* **16.** fully or quite: *even to death.* **17.** indeed (used as an intensive for stressing identity or truth of something): *he is willing, even eager, to do it.* **18.** *Archaic.* exactly or precisely: *it was even so.* **19. break even,** *Colloq.* to have one's profits equal one's losses. **20. get even,** to get one's revenge; square accounts. —*v.t.* **21.** to make even; level; smooth. **22.** to place in an even state as to claim or obligation; balance: *to even, or even up, accounts.* [ME; OE *efen,* c. G *eben*] —**e·ven·er,** *n.* —**e'ven·ly,** *adv.* —**e'ven·ness,** *n.*
—**Syn. 1.** See **level. 3.** EVEN, EQUABLE, UNIFORM imply a steady sameness. EVEN implies freedom from inequalities or irregularities: *even breathing, an even flow.* EQUABLE suggests the inherent quality of regularity or, in a nonmaterial reference, that of being well-balanced, not easily disturbed, and impartial in judgment: *an equable temperament.* UNIFORM emphasizes sameness and conformity to a standard: *uniform height or practice.* —**Ant. 1.** irregular, changeable.

e·ven² (ē'vən), *n.* *Archaic.* evening; eve. [ME; OE *ǣfen, ǣfen;* akin to G *abend*]

e·ven·fall (ē'vənfôl'), *n.* the beginning of evening.

e·ven-hand·ed (ē'vənhăn'dĭd), *adj.* impartial; equitable: *even-handed justice.* —**e'ven-hand'ed·ness,** *n.*

eve·ning (ēv'nĭng), *n.* **1.** the latter part of the day and early part of the night. **2.** the period from sunset to bedtime. **3.** *Southern U.S.* the time between noon and dark, including afternoon and twilight. **4.** any concluding or declining period: *the evening of life.* **5.** an evening's reception or entertainment. —*adj.* **6.** of or pertaining to evening. **7.** occurring or seen in the evening. [ME; OE *ǣfnung,* der. *ǣfnian* draw toward evening] —**Syn. 1.** eventide, dusk, twilight, gloaming, nightfall.

evening dress, formal evening clothes.

evening gown, a woman's formal dress.

evening primrose, 1. a plant, *Oenothera biennis,* family *Onagraceae,* with yellow flowers that open at nightfall. **2.** any of various plants of the same or related genera.

evening star, a bright planet seen in the west after sunset, esp. Venus.

e·ven-mind·ed (ē'vən mīn'dĭd), *adj.* not easily ruffled, disturbed, prejudiced, etc.; calm; equable. —**e'ven-mind'ed·ness,** *n.*

e·ven·song (ē'vən sông', -sŏng'), *n.* **1.** *Anglican Ch.* a form of worship appointed to be said or sung at evening. **2.** *Rom. Cath. Ch.* vespers. **3.** *Archaic.* evening. [ME; OE *ǣfensang,* f. *ǣfen* evening + *sang* song]

e·vent (Ĭ vĕnt'), *n.* **1.** anything that happens or is regarded as happening; an occurrence, esp. one of some importance. **2.** fact of happening (chiefly in the phrase *in the event of*). **3.** the outcome, issue, or result of anything (chiefly in the phrase *after the event*). **4.** *Philos.* something which occurs in a certain place during a particular interval of time. **5.** *Sports.* **a.** each of the items in a program of races, etc. **b.** something on the outcome of which money is at stake. **6. at all events** or **in any event,** whatever happens; in any case. [t. L: s. *ēventus* occurrence, issue] —**e·vent'less,** *adj.*
—**Syn. 1.** happening, affair, case, circumstance. EVENT, EPISODE, INCIDENT, OCCURRENCE are terms for a happening. An EVENT is usually an important happening, esp. one that comes out of and is connected with previous happenings: *historical events.* An EPISODE is one of a progressive series of happenings, frequently distinct from the main course of events but arising naturally from them and having a continuity and interest of its own: *an episode in one's life.* An INCIDENT is usually a happening which takes place in connection with an event or a series of events of greater importance: *an amusing incident in a play.* An OCCURRENCE is something (usually of an ordinary nature) that happens, having no particular connection with (or causation by) antecedent happenings: *his arrival was an unexpected occurrence.*

e·ven-tem·pered (ē'vən tĕm'pərd), *adj.* not easily ruffled or disturbed; calm.

e·vent·ful (Ĭ vĕnt'fəl), *adj.* **1.** full of events or incidents, esp. of a striking character: *an eventful period.* **2.** having important issues or results; momentous. —**e·vent'ful·ly,** *adv.* —**e·vent'ful·ness,** *n.*

e·ven·tide (ē'vən tīd'), *n.* *Now Poetic.* evening.

eventu-, a word element meaning "event." [comb. form repr. L *eventus*]

e·ven·tu·al (Ĭ vĕn'chŏŏ əl), *adj.* **1.** pertaining to the event or issue; consequent; ultimate. **2.** depending upon uncertain events; contingent.

e·ven·tu·al·i·ty (Ĭ vĕn'chŏŏ ăl'ətĭ), *n., pl.* **-ties. 1.** a contingent event; a possible occurrence or circumstance. **2.** state or fact of being eventual; contingent character.

e·ven·tu·al·ly (Ĭ vĕn'chŏŏ əlĭ), *adv.* finally; ultimately.

e·ven·tu·ate (Ĭ vĕn'chŏŏ āt'), *v.i.,* **-ated, -ating. 1.** to have issue; result. **2.** to be the issue or outcome; come about. —**e·ven'tu·a'tion,** *n.*

ev·er (ĕv'ər), *adv.* **1.** at all times: *he is ever ready to excuse himself.* **2.** continuously: *ever since then.* **3.** at any time: *did you ever see anything like it?* **4.** (with emphatic force, in various idiomatic constructions and phrases) in any possible case; by any chance; at all: *how did you ever manage to do it?* In England *ever* sometimes appears in an order strange to U.S.: *we must try as hard as ever we can, why ever not?* **5. ever and again** or **ever and anon,** every now and then; continually. **6. ever so,** to whatever extent or degree; greatly; exceedingly: *ever so long, be he ever so bold.* **7. for ever,** (*usually one word*) for eternity; eternally; always; continually. **8. for ever and a day,** forever; eternally. [ME; OE *ǣfre,* prob. akin to ā ever. See AY¹] —**Syn. 1.** eternally, perpetually, constantly. See **always.**

Ev·er·est *n.* (ĕv'ər ĭst), *n.* **Mount,** a peak of the Himalayas, in E Nepal: the highest mountain in the world. 29,028 ft.

Ev·er·ett (ĕv'ər ĭt), *n.* **1.** Edward, 1794-1865, U.S. statesman, orator, and writer. **2.** a city in E Massachusetts, near Boston. 43,544 (1960). **3.** a seaport in NW Washington, on Puget Sound. 40,304 (1960).

ev·er·glade (ĕv'ər glād'), *n.* *Southern U.S.* a tract of low, swampy land characterized by clumps of tall grass and numerous branching waterways.

Ev·er·glades (ĕv'ər glādz'), *n. pl.* a swampy and partly forested region in S Florida, mostly S of Lake Okeechobee. Over 5000 sq. mi.

ev·er·green (ĕv'ər grēn'), *adj.* **1.** (of trees, shrubs, tc.) having green leaves throughout the entire year, the leaves of the past season not being shed until after the new foliage has been completely formed. **2.** (of leaves) belonging to such a tree, shrub, etc. —*n.* **3.** an evergreen plant. **4.** (*pl.*) evergreen twigs or branches used for decoration.

ev·er·last·ing (ĕv′ər lǎs′tĭng, -läs′-), *adj.* **1.** lasting forever; eternal. **2.** lasting or continuing indefinitely. **3.** incessant; constantly recurring. **4.** wearisome: *to tire of someone's everlasting puns.* —*n.* **5.** eternal duration; eternity. **6.** the **Everlasting,** the Eternal Being; God. **7.** any of various plants or flowers which retain their shape, color, etc., when dried, as certain species of the asteraceous genus *Helichrysum,* and various species of the sudweed, genus *Gnaphalium.* —ev′er·last′ing·ly, *adv.* —ev′er·last′ing·ness, *n.* —**Syn. 1.** See eternal.

everlasting flower, *Brit.* the immortelle.

ev·er·more (ĕv′ər môr′), *adv.* **1.** always; forever; eternally (often prec. by *for*). **2.** at all times; continually.

e·ver·si·ble (ĭ vûr′sə bəl), *adj.* capable of being everted.

e·ver·sion (ĭ vûr′shən, -zhən), *n.* a turning or being turned outward, or inside out.

e·vert (ĭ vûrt′), *v.t.* to turn outward, or inside out. [t. L: s. *ēvertere* overturn]

e·ver·tor (ĭ vûr′tər), *n. Anat.* a muscle which turns a part toward the outside.

ev·er·y (ĕv′rĭ), *adj.* **1.** each (referring one by one to all the members of an aggregate): *we go there every day, be sure to remember every word he says.* **2.** all possible; the greatest possible degree of: *every prospect of success.* **3. every bit,** *Colloq.* in every respect; in all points: *every bit as good.* **4. every now and then** or **every now and again** or **every once in a while,** repeatedly; frequently; from time to time. **5. every other,** every second; every alternate. [ME *every, everich,* etc., OE *ǣfre ǣlc* EVER, EACH] —**Syn. 1.** See each.

ev·er·y·bod·y (ĕv′rĭ bŏd′ĭ), *pron.* every person.

ev·er·y·day (ĕv′rĭ dā′), *adj.* **1.** of or pertaining to every day; daily: *an everyday occurrence.* **2.** of or for ordinary days, as contrasted with Sundays or special occasions: *everyday clothes.* **3.** such as is met with every day; ordinary; commonplace: *an everyday scene.*

ev·er·y·man (ĕv′rĭ măn′), *n.* a 15th century English morality play translated from the Dutch *Elkerlijk.*

ev·er·y·one (ĕv′rĭ wŭn′, -wən), *pron.* every person; everybody. Also, **every one.**

ev·er·y·thing (ĕv′rĭ thĭng′), *pron.* **1.** every thing or particular of an aggregate or total; all. **2.** something extremely important: *this news means everything to us.*

ev·er·y·way (ĕv′rĭ wā′), *adv.* in every way; in every direction, manner, or respect.

ev·er·y·where (ĕv′rĭ hwâr′), *adv.* in every place or part; in all places.

Eve·sham (ēv′shəm, ēv′zəm), *n.* a town in W England, SE of Worcester: battle, 1265. 12,066 (1951).

e·vict (ĭ vĭkt′), *v.t.* **1.** to expel (a person, esp. a tenant) from land, a building, etc., by legal process. **2.** to recover (property, etc.) by virtue of superior legal title. [t. L: s. *ēvictus,* pp., overcome completely, (property) recovered by judicial decision] —**e·vic′tion,** *n.* —**e·vic′tor,** *n.*

ev·i·dence (ĕv′ə dəns), *n., v.,* -denced, -dencing. —*n.* **1.** ground for belief; that which tends to prove or disprove something; proof. **2.** something that makes evident; an indication or sign. **3.** *Law.* the data, in the form of testimony of witnesses, or of documents or other objects (such as a photograph, a revolver, etc.) identified by witnesses, offered to the court or jury in proof of the facts in issue. **4.** one who bears testimony or witness. **5. turn state's,** or **king's** or **queen's, evidence,** of an accomplice in a crime) to become a witness for the prosecution against the others involved. **6. in evidence,** in a situation to be readily seen; plainly visible; conspicuous. —*v.t.* **7.** to make evident or clear; show clearly; manifest. **8.** to support by evidence. —**Syn. 3.** information, deposition, affidavit. EVIDENCE, EXHIBIT, TESTIMONY, PROOF refer to information furnished in a legal investigation to support a contention. EVIDENCE is any information so given, whether furnished by witnesses or derived from documents or from any other source: *hearsay evidence is not admitted in a trial.* An EXHIBIT in law is a document or article which is presented in court as evidence: *the signed contract is Exhibit A.* TESTIMONY is usually evidence given by witnesses under oath: *the jury listened carefully to the testimony.* PROOF is evidence that is so complete and convincing as to put a conclusion beyond reasonable doubt: *proof of the innocence of the accused.*

ev·i·dent (ĕv′ə dənt), *adj.* plain or clear to the sight or understanding: *an evident mistake.* [t. L: s. *ēvidens*] —**Syn.** obvious, manifest, palpable, patent, unmistakable. See apparent.

ev·i·den·tial (ĕv′ə dĕn′shəl), *adj.* of or having the nature of, serving as, or based on evidence.

ev·i·dent·ly (ĕv′ə dənt lĭ, -dĕnt′-; *emph.* ĕv′ə dĕnt′lĭ), *adv.* obviously; apparently. —**Syn.** clearly.

e·vil (ē′vəl), *adj.* **1.** violating or inconsistent with the moral law; wicked: *evil deeds, an evil life.* **2.** harmful; injurious: *evil laws.* **3.** characterized or accompanied by misfortune or suffering; unfortunate; disastrous: *to be fallen on evil days.* **4.** due to (actual or imputed) bad character or conduct: *an evil reputation.* **5. the evil one,** the devil; Satan. —*n.* **6.** that which is evil; evil quality,

intention, or conduct: *to choose the lesser of two evils.* **7.** harm; mischief; misfortune: *to wish one evil.* **8.** anything causing injury or harm. **9.** a disease: *king's evil* (scrofula). —*adv.* **10.** in an evil manner; badly; ill: *it went evil with his house.* [ME; OE *yfel,* c. G *übel*] —**e′vil·ly,** *adv.* —**e′vil·ness,** *n.* —**Syn. 1.** sinful, iniquitous, depraved, vicious, corrupt, immoral. See bad¹. **6.** wickedness, depravity, iniquity, unrighteousness. **7.** disaster, calamity. —**Ant. 1.** righteous.

e·vil-do·er (ē′vəl dōō′ər), *n.* one who does evil. —**e·vil-do·ing** (ē′vəl dōō′ĭng), *n.*

evil eye, the power superstitiously attributed to certain persons of inflicting injury or bad luck by a look. —**e′vil-eyed′,** *adj.*

e·vil-mind·ed (ē′vəl mīn′dĭd), *adj.* **1.** having an evil mind; malignant. **2.** excessively sexminded.

e·vince (ĭ vĭns′), *v.t.,* **evinced, evincing. 1.** to show clearly; make evident or manifest; prove. **2.** to reveal the possession of (a quality, trait, etc.). [t. L: m.s. *ēvincere* overcome completely, prove, demonstrate] —**e·vin′ci·ble,** *adj.* —**Syn. 1.** See display.

e·vin·cive (ĭ vĭn′sĭv), *adj.* serving to evince; indicative.

e·vis·cer·ate (ĭ vĭs′ə rāt′), *v.,* -ated, -ating, *adj.* —*v.t.* **1.** to disembowel. **2.** to deprive of vital or essential parts. —*adj.* **3.** *Surg.* disemboweled, usually after a surgical operation on the abdomen when the wound breaks open due to a technical error or poor healing. [t. L: m.s. *ēvicerātus,* pp., disemboweled] —**e·vis′cer·a′tion,** *n.*

ev·i·ta·ble (ĕv′ə tə bəl), *adj.* avoidable. [t. L: m.s. *ēvitābilis* avoidable]

e·vite (ĭ vīt′), *v.t.,* **evited, eviting.** *Archaic.* to avoid; shun. [t. L: m.s. *ēvitāre*]

ev·o·ca·ble (ĕv′ə kə bəl), *adj.* that may be evoked.

ev·o·ca·tion (ĕv′ō kā′shən), *n.* **1.** act of evoking; a calling forth. **2.** *Civil Law.* the power of a higher court to decide finally on an entire case when it is appealed, even if the court below decided only incidental matters and even if the appeal is based merely on procedural errors. [t. L: s. *ēvocātio,* der. *ēvocāre* call forth]

e·voc·a·tive (ĭ vŏk′ə tĭv, -vō′kə-), *adj.* tending to evoke.

ev·o·ca·tor (ĕv′ə kā′tər), *n.* **1.** *Embryol.* a morphogenic substance, or a piece of tissue, generally not living, which contains morphogenic substances. **2.** one who evokes, esp., one who calls up spirits.

e·voke (ĭ vōk′), *v.t.,* **evoked, evoking. 1.** to call up, or produce (memories, feelings, etc.): *to evoke a memory, a smile, etc.* **2.** to call up; cause to appear; summon: *to evoke a spirit from the dead.* [t. L: m.s. *ēvocāre* call forth] —**e·vok′er** *n.*

ev·o·lute (ĕv′ə lōōt′), *n. Geom.* the locus of the centers of curvature of, or the envelope of the normals to, another curve (called the *involute*). [t. L: m.s. *ēvolūtus,* pp., rolled out]

ABC, Evolute of parabolic arc OPQ

ev·o·lu·tion (ĕv′ə lōō′shən; *Brit.* also ē′və-), *n.* **1.** any process of formation or growth; development: *the evolution of man, the drama, the airplane, etc.* **2.** something evolved; a product. **3.** *Biol.* the continuous genetic adaptation of organisms or species to the environment by the integrating agencies of selection, hybridization, inbreeding, and mutation. **4.** a movement, or one of a series of movements, of troops, ships, etc., as for disposition in order of battle or in line on parade. **5.** any similar movement, esp. in close-order drill. **6.** a motion incomplete in itself, but combining with coördinated motions to produce a single action, as in a machine. **7.** an evolving or giving off of gas, heat, etc. **8.** *Math.* the extraction of roots from powers (the inverse of *involution*). [t. L: s. *ēvolūtio,* der. *ēvolvere* roll out] —**ev′o·lu′tion·al,** *adj.* —**ev′o·lu′tion·al·ly,** *adv.*

ev·o·lu·tion·ar·y (ĕv′ə lōō′shə nĕr′ĭ; *Brit.* also ē′və-), *adj.* **1.** pertaining to evolution or development; developmental: *the evolutionary origin of species.* **2.** in accordance with the theory of evolution. **3.** pertaining to or performing evolutions (def. 4).

ev·o·lu·tion·ist (ĕv′ə lōō′shən ĭst; *Brit.* also ē′və-), *n.* a believer in the doctrine of evolution.

ev·o·lu·tion·is·tic (ĕv′ə lōō′shə nĭs′tĭk; *Brit.* also ē′və-), *adj.* **1.** tending to support the theory of evolution. **2.** tending to cause evolution.

e·volve (ĭ vŏlv′), *v.,* **evolved, evolving.** —*v.t.* **1.** to develop gradually: *to evolve a scheme, a plan, a theory, etc.* **2.** *Biol.* to develop, as by a process of differentiation, to a more highly organized condition. **3.** to give off or emit, as odors, vapors, etc. —*v.i.* **4.** to come forth gradually into being; develop; undergo evolution. [t. L: m.s. *ēvolvere* roll out, unroll, unfold] —**e·volv′a·ble,** *adj.* —**e·volve′ment,** *n.* —**e·volv′er,** *n.*

ev·on·y·mus (ĕv ŏn′ə məs), *n.* euonymus.

e·vul·sion (ĭ vŭl′shən), *n.* act of plucking or pulling out; forcible extraction. [t. L: s. *ēvulsio,* der. *ēvellere* pluck out]

Ev·voi·a (ĕv′vē ä′), *n.* modern Greek name of Euboea.

ewe (ū; *dial.* yō), *n.* a female sheep. [ME and OE, c. D *ooi;* akin to L *ovis,* Gk. *ŏïs,* Skt. *avi* sheep]

E·we (ā′vā), *n.* a language of western Africa, spoken in parts of Togoland.

Ew·ell (ū′əl), *n.* Richard Stoddert, 1817–72, Confederate lieutenant general in the U.S. Civil War.

ewe-neck (ū′nĕk′), *n.* a thin hollow neck, low in front of the shoulder, as of a horse or or other animal. —**ewe-necked** (ū′nĕkt′), *adj.*

ew·er (ū′ər), *n.* 1. a pitcher with a wide spout, esp. one to hold water for ablutions. 2. *Decorative Art.* a vessel having a spout and a handle; esp., a tall, slender vessel with a base. [ME, t. AF, g. L *aquāria* vessel for water]

Ewer and basin

E·wig-Weib·li·che (ā′vĭKH vīp′lĭ KHə), *n.* German. the eternal feminine (used in Goethe's *Faust*).

ex¹ (ĕks), *prep.* 1. *Finance.* without, not including, or without the right to have: *ex dividend, ex interest, ex rights.* 2. *Com.* out of; free out of: *ex elevator, ex ship, etc.* (free of charges until the time of removal out of the elevator, ship, etc.). 3. (in U.S. colleges and universities) from, but not graduated with, the class of: *ex ′47.* [t. L. See EX-¹]

ex² (ĕks), *n.* the letter X, x.

ex-¹, a prefix meaning "out of," "from," and hence "utterly," "thoroughly," and sometimes serving to impart a privative or negative force or to indicate a former title, status, etc.; freely used as an English formative, as in *exstipulate, exterritorial,* and esp. in such combinations as *ex-president* (former president), *ex-member, ex-wife;* occurring before vowels and *c, p, q, s, t.* Also, **e-, ef-.** [t. L, comb. form of *ex, ē,* prep., out of, from, beyond]

ex-², var. of **exo-**.

ex-³, a prefix identical in meaning with **ex-¹**, occurring before vowels in words of Greek orig., as in *exarch, exegis.* Also, **ec-.** [t. Gk., also before consonants *ek-* EC-; becoming *ec-* in L derivatives]

Ex., Exodus.

ex., 1. examination. 2. examined. 3. example. 4. except. 5. exception. 6. exchange. 7. excursion. 8. executed. 9. executive.

ex·ac·er·bate (ĭg zăs′ər bāt′, ĭk săs′-), *v.t.,* **-bated, -bating.** 1. to increase the bitterness or violence of (disease, ill feeling, etc.); aggravate. 2. to embitter the feelings of (a person); irritate; exasperate. [t. L: m.s. *exacerbātus,* pp., irritated] —**ex·ac′er·ba′tion,** *n.*

ex·act (ĭg zăkt′), *adj.* 1. strictly accurate or correct: *an exact likeness, description, or translation.* 2. precise, as opposed to approximate: *the exact sum due, the exact date.* 3. admitting of no deviation, as laws, discipline, etc.; strict or rigorous. 4. characterized by or using strict accuracy or precision: *exact instruments, an exact thinker.* —*v.t.* 5. to call for, demand, or require: *to exact obedience, respect.* 6. to force or compel the payment, yielding, or performance of: *to exact money, tribute, etc.* [t. L: s. *exactus,* pp., forced out, required, measured by a standard] —**ex·act′a·ble,** *adj.* —**ex·act′er, ex·ac′tor,** *n.* —**ex·act′ness,** *n.* —Syn. 3. rigid, severe. 4. methodical, careful, punctilious. 5. force, compel, 6. extort, wrest, wring. See **extract.**

ex·act·ing (ĭg zăk′tĭng), *adj.* 1. severe, or unduly severe, in demands or requirements, as a person. 2. requiring close application or attention, as a task. 3. given to or characterized by exaction; extortionate. —**ex·act′ing·ly,** *adv.* —**ex·act′ing·ness,** *n.*

ex·ac·tion (ĭg zăk′shən), *n.* 1. act of exacting; extortion. 2. something exacted.

ex·act·i·tude (ĭg zăk′tə tūd′, -tōōd′), *n.* the quality of being exact; exactness; preciseness; accuracy.

ex·act·ly (ĭg zăkt′lĭ), *adv.* 1. in an exact manner; precisely, according to rule, measure, fact, etc. accurately. 2. quite so; that's right.

exact science, a science (such as mathematics) which permits of accurate analysis.

ex ae·quo et bo·no (ĕks ē′kwō ĕt bō′nō), *Latin.* according to the principle of fairness and good.

ex·ag·ger·ate (ĭg zăj′ə rāt′), *v.,* **-ated, -ating.** —*v.t.* 1. to magnify beyond the limits of truth; overstate; represent disproportionately: *to exaggerate one's importance, the difficulties of a situation, the size of one's house, etc.* 2. to increase or enlarge abnormally. —*v.i.* 3. to employ exaggeration, as in speech or writing: *a person who is always exaggerating.* [t. L: m.s. *exaggerātus,* pp., heaped up] —**ex·ag′ger·at′ing·ly,** *adv.* —**ex·ag′ger·a′tor,** *n.* —Ant. 1. minimize.

ex·ag·ger·at·ed (ĭg zăj′ə rā′tĭd), *adj.* 1. unduly magnified: *to have an exaggerated opinion of oneself.* 2. abnormally increased or enlarged: *a heart greatly exaggerated by disease.* —**ex·ag′ger·at′ed·ly,** *adv.*

ex·ag·ger·a·tion (ĭg zăj′ə rā′shən), *n.* 1. act of exaggerating. 2. state of being exaggerated. 3. an exaggerated statement.

ex·ag·ger·a·tive (ĭg zăj′ə rā′tĭv), *adj.* given to or characterized by exaggeration. Also, **ex·ag·ger·a·to·ry** (ĭg zăj′ə rə tôr′ĭ).

ex·alt (ĭg zôlt′), *v.t.* 1. to elevate in rank, honor, power, character, quality, etc.: *exalted to the position of President.* 2. to praise; extol: *to exalt someone to the skies.* 3. to elate, as with pride or joy. 4. to stimulate, as the imagination. 5. to intensify, as a color. 6. *Archaic or Rare.* to raise up. [t. L: s. *exaltāre* lift up] —**ex·alt′er,** *n.* —Syn. 1. promote, dignify. See **elevate.** 2. glorify. —Ant. 1. humble. 2. depreciate.

ex·al·ta·tion (ĕg′zôl tā′shən), *n.* 1. act of exalting. 2. state of being exalted. 3. elation of mind, or feeling sometimes abnormal or morbid in character; rapture. 4. abnormal intensification of the action of an organ.

ex·alt·ed (ĭg zôl′tĭd), *adj.* 1. elevated, as in rank or character; of high station: *an exalted personage.* 2. noble or elevated, lofty: *an exalted style, mind, etc.* 3. rapturously excited. —**ex·alt′ed·ly,** *adv.* —**ex·alt′edness,** *n.* —Syn. 1. sublime, grand.

ex·am (ĭg zăm′), *n. Colloq.* an examination.

exam., 1. examination. 2. examined. 3. examinee 4. examinor.

ex·a·men (ĭg zā′mĕn), *n. Eccles.* an examination, as conscience. [t. L: a weighing, consideration]

ex·am·i·nant (ĭg zăm′ə nənt), *n.* an examiner.

ex·am·i·na·tion (ĭg zăm′ə nā′shən), *n.* 1. act of examining; inspection; inquiry; investigation. 2. state being examined. 3. act or process of testing pupils, candidates, etc., as by questions. 4. the test itself; list questions asked. 5. the statements, etc., made by one examined. 6. *Law.* formal interrogation. [t. L: s. *aminātio*] —**ex·am′i·na′tion·al,** *adj.* Syn. 1. EXAMINATION, INSPECTION, SCRUTINY refer to scanning of something. An EXAMINATION may mean a careful noting of details or may mean little more than a casual glance over something: *a thorough examination of the plumbing revealed a defective pipe.* An INSPECTION is a formal and official examination: *an inspection of records, a military inspection.* SCRUTINY implies a critical and minutely detailed examination: *the papers seemed to be in good order but they would not stand close scrutiny.* See **investigation.**

ex·am·ine (ĭg zăm′ĭn), *v.t.,* **-ined, -ining.** 1. to inspect or scrutinize carefully; inquire into or investigate. 2. to test the knowledge, reactions, or qualifications of (a pupil, candidate, etc.), as by questions or assigned tasks. 3. to subject to legal inquisition; put to question in regard to conduct or to knowledge of facts; interrogate: *examine a witness or a suspected person.* [ME *examine*(n), t. F: m. *examiner,* t. L: m. *exāmināre* weigh accurately, test] —**ex·am′in·a·ble,** *adj.* —**ex·am′in·er,** *n.* —Syn. 1. search, probe, explore. 2. catechize.

ex·am·i·nee (ĭg zăm′ə nē′), *n.* one who is examined.

ex·am·ple (ĭg zăm′pəl, -zäm′-), *n., v.,* **-pled, -pling.** —*n.* 1. one of a number of things, or a part of something taken to show the character of the whole. 2. something to be imitated; a pattern or model: *to set a good example.* 3. an instance serving for illustration; a specimen. 4. an instance illustrating a rule or method, as a mathematical problem proposed for solution. 5. an instance, esp. of punishment, serving for a warning; a warning. 6. a precedent; a parallel case: *an action without example.* —*v.t.* 7. to give or be an example of (chiefly in pp.). [ME, t. OF: m. *essample,* g. L *exempla,* pl. of *exemplum* —Syn. 1. EXAMPLE, SAMPLE, SPECIMEN refer to an individual phenomenon taken as representative of a type, or to a part representative of the whole. EXAMPLE is used of an object, activity, condition, etc., which is assumed to illustrate a certain principle, law, or standard: *a good example of baroque architecture.* SAMPLE, used mainly in a concrete reference refers to a small portion of a substance, or to a single representative of a group or type, which is intended to show what the rest of the substance, or the group, is like: *a sample of yarn.* SPECIMEN usually suggests that the "sample" chosen is intended to serve a scientific or technical purpose: *a blood specimen, zoölogical specimens.* 2. See **ideal.** 3. See **case.**

ex·an·i·mate (ĭg zăn′ə mĭt, -māt′), *adj.* 1. inanimate or lifeless. 2. spiritless; disheartened. [t. L: m.s. *exanimātus,* pp., deprived of breath, life, or spirit]

ex a·ni·mo (ĕks ăn′ə mō′), *Latin.* from the heart; sincerely.

ex·an·the·ma (ĕk′săn thē′mə), *n., pl.* **-themata** (-thĕm′ə tə, -thē′mə tə). 1. *Pathol.* an eruptive disease esp. one attended with fever, as smallpox or measles. 2. See **vesicular exanthema.** [t. LL, t. Gk.: a bursting into flower] —**ex·an·the·mat·ic** (ĕk′săn′thə măt′ĭk), **ex·an·them·a·tous** (ĕk′săn thĕm′ə təs), *adj.*

ex·arch (ĕk′särk), *n.* 1. (in the Eastern Church) a. a patriarch's deputy. b. (formerly) a bishop ranking below a patriarch and above a metropolitan. c. (originally) patriarch. 2. the ruler of a province in the Byzantine Empire. [t. LL: s. *exarchus,* t. Gk.: m. *éxarchos* leader]

ex·ar·chate (ĕk′sär kāt′, ĕk sär′kāt), *n.* the office, jurisdiction, or province of an exarch.

ex·as·per·ate (ĭg zăs′pə rāt′), *v.t.,* **-ated, -ating.** 1. to irritate to a high degree; annoy extremely; infuriate 2. to increase the intensity or violence of (disease, pain feelings, etc.). [t. L: m.s. *exasperātus,* pp., roughened —**ex·as′per·at′ed·ly,** *adv.* —**ex·as′per·at′er,** *n.* —**ex·as′per·at′ing·ly,** *adv.* —Syn. 1. exacerbate, incense, anger. See **irritate.** —Ant. 1. mollify.

ex·as·per·a·tion (ĭg zăs′pə rā′shən), *n.* 1. act of exasperating; provocation. 2. state of being exasperated irritation; extreme annoyance: *his exasperation was understandable.*

Exc., Excellency.

exc., 1. except. 2. exception. 3. excursion.

Ex·cal·i·bur (ĕks kăl′ə bər), *n.* the magic sword of King Arthur.

ex ca·the·dra (ĕks kə thē′drə, kăth′ĭ drə), *Latin.* from the seat of authority; with authority. [t. L: from the chair] —**ex′-ca·the′dra,** *adj.*

ex·cau·date (ĕks kô′dāt), *adj. Zool.* tailless; destitute of a tail or taillike process.

ex·ca·vate (ĕks′kə vāt′), v.t., **-vated, -vating. 1.** to make hollow by removing the inner part; make a hole or cavity in; form into a hollow, as by digging. **2.** to make a hole, tunnel, etc.) by removing material. **3.** to dig or scoop out (earth, etc.). **4.** to expose or lay bare by digging; unearth: *to excavate an ancient city.* [t. L: m.s. *excavātus*, pp., hollowed out]

ex·ca·va·tion (ĕks′kə vā′shən), n. **1.** act of excavating. **2.** a hole or cavity made by excavating. **—Syn.** t. See hole.

ex·ca·va·tor (ĕks′kə vā′tər), n. **1.** one who or that which excavates. **2.** a power-driven machine for digging, moving, or transporting loose gravel, sand, or soil.

ex·ceed (ĭk sēd′), v.t. **1.** to go beyond the bounds or limits of: *to exceed one's powers.* **2.** to go beyond in quantity, degree, rate, etc.: *to exceed the speed limit.* **3.** to surpass; be superior to; excel. **—v.i. 4.** to be greater, as in quantity or degree. **5.** to surpass others, excel, or be superior. [ME *excede(n)*, t. F: m. *excéder*, t. L: m. *excēdere* go out] **—ex·ceed′er,** n. **—Syn. 1.** overstep, transcend.

ex·ceed·ing (ĭk sē′dĭng), adj. **1.** extraordinary; excessive. **—adv. 2.** Archaic. exceedingly.

ex·ceed·ing·ly (ĭk sē′dĭng lĭ′), adv. to an unusual degree; extremely.

ex·cel (ĭk sĕl′), v., **-celled, -celling. —v.t. 1.** to surpass; be superior to; outdo. **—v.i. 2.** to surpass others or be superior in some respect. [t. L: m.s. *excellere*] **—Syn. 1.** outstrip, eclipse, transcend. EXCEL, OUTDO, SURPASS imply being better than others or being superior in achievement. To EXCEL is to be superior to others in some (usually) good or desirable quality, attainment, or performance: *to excel competitors at playing chess.* To OUTDO is to make more successful effort than others: *to outdo competitors in the high jump.* To SURPASS is to go beyond others (who are definitely pointed out) esp. in a contest as to quality or ability: *to surpass one's classmates in knowledge of corporation law.*

ex·cel·lence (ĕk′sə ləns), n. **1.** fact or state of excelling; superiority; eminence. **2.** an excellent quality or feature. **3.** (*usually cap.*) Excellency (def. 1). **—Syn. 1.** preëminence, transcendence. **2.** merit, virtue.

ex·cel·len·cy (ĕk′sə lən sĭ′), n., pl. **-cies. 1.** (*usually cap.*) a title of honor given to certain high officials, as governors and ambassadors. **2.** (*usually cap.*) a person so entitled. **3.** excellence. [t. L: m.s. *excellentia*]

ex·cel·lent (ĕk′sə lənt), adj. **1.** possessing excellence or superior merit; remarkably good. **2.** Obs. extraordinary; superior. [ME. t. L: s. *excellens*, ppr.] **—ex′cel·lent·ly,** adv. **—Syn. 1.** worthy, estimable, choice, fine, first-rate.

ex·cel·si·or (n. ĭk sĕl′sĭ ər; adj. -sĭ ôr′), n. **1.** a kind of fine wood shavings, used for stuffing, packing, etc. **2.** a printing type (3 point) smaller than brilliant. **—adj. 3.** Latin. higher (motto of New York State). [t. L, compar. of *excelsus* high, prop. pp., risen above others]

ex·cept¹ (ĭk sĕpt′), prep. **1.** with the exclusion of; excluding; save; but: *they were all there except me.* **—conj. 2.** with the exception (that): *parallel cases except that A is younger than B.* **3.** otherwise than; but (fol. by an adv., phrase, or clause): *well fortified except here.* **4.** Archaic. unless. [t. L: s. *exceptus*, pp., taken out] **—Syn. 1.** EXCEPT (more rarely EXCEPTING), BUT, SAVE point out something excluded from a general statement. EXCEPT emphasizes the excluding: *take any number except 12.* BUT merely states the exclusion: *we ate all but one.* SAVE is now mainly found in poetic use: *nothing in sight save sky and sea.*

ex·cept² (ĭk sĕpt′), v.t. **1.** to exclude; leave out: *present company excepted.* **—v.i. 2.** to object: *to except against a statement, a witness, etc.* [ME *excepte(n)*, t. F: m. *excepter*, der. L *exceptus*, pp.]

ex·cept·ing (ĭk sĕp′tĭng), prep. **1.** excluding; barring; saving; except. **—conj. 2.** Archaic. except; unless; save. **—Syn. 1.** See except¹.

ex·cep·tion (ĭk sĕp′shən), n. **1.** act of excepting. **2.** fact of being excepted. **3.** something excepted; an instance or case not conforming to the general rule. **4.** an adverse criticism, esp. on a particular point; opposition of opinion; objection; demurral: *a statement liable to exception.* **5. take exception, a.** to make objection; demur with respect to something (usually fol. by to). **b.** to take offense (often fol. by at). **6.** Law. **a.** an objection, as to a ruling of the court in the course of a trial. **b.** a notation that an objection is preserved for purposes of appeal: *saving an exception.* [t. L: s. *exceptio*]

ex·cep·tion·a·ble (ĭk sĕp′shən ə bəl), adj. liable to exception or objection; objectionable. **—ex·cep′tion·a·ble·ness,** n. **—ex·cep′tion·a·bly,** adv.

ex·cep·tion·al (ĭk sĕp′shən əl), adj. forming an exception or unusual instance; unusual; extraordinary. **—ex·cep′tion·al·ly,** adv. **—ex·cep′tion·al·ness,** n. **—Syn.** uncommon, peculiar, singular, superior. See irregular. **—Ant.** average.

ex·cep·tive (ĭk sĕp′tĭv), adj. **1.** that excepts; making an exception. **2.** disposed to take exception; objecting.

ex·cerpt (n. ĕk′sûrpt; v. ĭk sûrpt′), n. **1.** a passage taken out of a book or the like; an extract. **—v.t. 2.** to take out (a passage) from a book or the like; extract. [t. L: s. *excerptus*, pp. picked out] **—ex·cerp′tion,** n.

ex·cess (n. ĭk sĕs′; adj ĕk′sĕs, ĭk sĕs′), n **1.** the fact of exceeding something else in amount or degree. **2.** the amount or degree by which one thing exceeds another. **3.** an extreme or excessive amount or degree; superabundance: *have an excess of energy.* **4.** a going beyond ordinary or proper limits. **5.** immoderate indulgence; intemperance in eating and drinking. **—adj. 6.** more than or above what is necessary, usual, or specified; extra: *excess baggage, excess profits.* [ME *excesse*, t. L: m. *excessus* a departure] **—Syn. 3.** overplus, surplus, surplusage. **—Ant. 3.** deficiency.

ex·ces·sive (ĭk sĕs′ĭv), adj. exceeding the usual or proper limit or degree; characterized by excess: *excessive charges, excessive indulgence.* **—ex·ces′sive·ly,** adv. **—ex·ces′sive·ness,** n. **—Syn.** immoderate, extravagant, extreme, inordinate, exorbitant.

ex·cess-prof·its tax (ĕk′sĕs prŏf′ĭts), a tax on the profits of a business enterprise in excess of the average profits for a number of base years, or of a specified rate of return on capital.

exch., 1. exchange. **2.** exchequer.

ex·change (ĭks chānj′), v., **-changed, -changing,** n. **—v.t. 1.** to part with for some equivalent; to give up (something) for something else. **2.** to replace by another or something else; change for another: *to exchange a purchase.* **3.** to give and receive reciprocally; interchange: *to exchange blows, gifts, etc.* **4.** to part with in return for some equivalent; transfer for a recompense; barter: *to exchange goods with foreign countries.* **5.** Chess. to capture (an enemy piece) in return for a capture by the opponent generally of pieces of equal value. **—v.i. 6.** to make an exchange. **7.** to pass or be taken in exchange or as an equivalent. **—n. 8.** act or process of exchanging: *an exchange of gifts, prisoners of war, etc.* **9.** that which is given or received in exchange or substitution for something else: *the car was a fair exchange.* **10.** a place for buying and selling commodities, securities, etc.: typically open only to members. **11.** a central office or central station: *a telephone exchange.* **12.** the method or system by which debits and credits in different places are settled without the actual transference of money, by means of documents (bills of exchange) representing money values. **13.** the discharge of obligations in different places by the transfer of credits. **14.** the amount or percentage charged for exchanging money, collecting a draft, etc. **15.** the reciprocal transference of equivalent sums of money, as in the currencies of two different countries. **16.** the giving or receiving of a sum of money in one place for a bill ordering the payment of an equivalent sum in another. **17.** the varying rate or sum, in one currency, given for a fixed sum in another currency; rate of exchange. **18.** the amount of the difference in value between two or more currencies, or between the values of the same currency at two or more places. **19.** the checks, drafts, etc. exchanged at a clearinghouse. **20.** Brit. labor exchange. [ME *eschaunge*, t. AF, g. LL *excambium*] **—ex·chang′er,** n. **—Syn. 1.** interchange, commute, barter, trade, swap. **8.** interchange, trade, traffic.

ex·change·a·ble (ĭks chān′jə bəl), adj. that can be exchanged. **—ex·change′a·bil′i·ty,** n. **—Syn.** EXCHANGEABLE, INTERCHANGEABLE apply to something which may replace something else. That is EXCHANGEABLE which may be taken or sent back to the place at which it was purchased, to be exchanged for money, credit, or other purchases to the amount of the original purchase: *these dishes are exchangeable if you find they are not satisfactory.* INTERCHANGEABLE applies to those things which are capable of being reciprocally put in each other's place: *standard parts are interchangeable.*

ex·cheq·uer (ĭks chĕk′ər, ĕks′chĕk′ər), n. **1.** a treasury, as of a state or nation. **2.** (in Great Britain) **a.** (*often cap.*) the governmental department in charge of the public revenues. **b.** (formerly) an office which administered the royal revenues and determined all cases affecting them. **c.** (*cap.*) an ancient common law court of civil jurisdiction (**Court of Exchequer**) in which all cases affecting the revenues of the crown were tried, now merged in the King's Bench Division of the High Court. **3.** Colloq. funds; finances. [ME *escheker*, t. OF: m. *eschequier* chess board (so called with reference to the table cover marked with squares on which accounts were reckoned with counters). See CHECKER]

ex·cide (ĭk sīd′), v.t. **-cided, -ciding.** to excise.

ex·cip·i·ent (ĭk sĭp′ĭ ənt), n. Pharm. a more or less inert substance, as sugar, jelly, etc., used as the medium or vehicle for the administration of an active medicine. [t. L: s. *excipiens*, ppr., taking out]

ex·cis·a·ble (ĭk sī′zə bəl), adj. subject to excise duty.

ex·cise¹ (n. ĭk sīz′, ĕk′sīz; v. ĭk sīz′), n., v., **-cised, -cising. —n. 1.** an inland tax or duty on certain commodities, as spirits, tobacco, etc., levied on their manufacture, sale, or consumption within the country. **2.** a tax levied for a license to carry on certain employments, pursue certain sports, etc. **3.** Brit. that branch of the civil service which collects excise duties. **—v.t. 4.** to impose an excise on. [prob. t. MD: m. *excijs*, t. OF: m. *acceis* a tax, ult. der. LL *accēnsāre* tax] **—ex·ci·sion** (ĭk sĭzh′ən), n,

ex·cise² (ĭk sīz′), v.t., **-cised, -cising. 1.** to expunge, as a passage or sentence. **2.** to cut out or off, as a tumor. [t. L: m.s. *excīsus*, pp., cut out.]

ex·cise·man (ĭk sīz′mən), n., pl. **-men.** Brit. an officer who collects excise taxes and enforces excise laws.

ex·cit·a·bil·i·ty (ĭk sī′tə bĭl′ə tĭ), n. **1.** quality of being excitable. **2.** Physiol. irritability.

ex·cit·a·ble (ĭk sī′tə bəl), adj. capable of being excited; easily excited. **—ex·cit′a·ble·ness,** n. **—ex·cit′a·bly,** adv. **—Syn.** emotional, passionate, fiery. **—Ant.** placid.

ex·cit·ant (Yk sī′tənt, ĕk′sə tənt), *adj.* **1.** exciting; stimulating. —*n.* **2.** *Physiol.* something that excites; a stimulant.

ex·ci·ta·tion (ĕk′sī tā′shən), *n.* **1.** act of exciting. **2.** state of being excited. **3.** *Elect.* the relative strength of the magnetic field in a dynamo: *normal excitation.*

ex·cit·a·tive (Yk sī′tə tYv), *adj.* tending to excite. Also, **ex·cit·a·to·ry** (Yk sī′tə tōr′Y).

ex·cite (Yk sīt′), *v.t.,* **-cited, -citing. 1.** to arouse or stir up the feelings of: *to excite jealousy or hatred.* **2.** to cause; awaken: *to excite interest or curiosity.* **3.** to stir to action; stir up: *to excite a dog.* **4.** *Physiol.* to stimulate: *to excite a nerve.* **5.** *Elect.* to produce electric activity or a magnetic field in: *to excite a dynamo.* [ME *excite(n),* t. L: m.s. *excitāre,* freq. of *exciere* call forth, rouse] —**Syn. 1.** stir, arouse, awaken, stimulate, animate, kindle, inflame. **3.** provoke. —**Ant. 1.** soothe.

ex·cit·ed (Yk sī′tYd), *adj.* **1.** stirred emotionally; agitated. **2.** stimulated to activity; brisk. **3.** *Physics.* (of an atom or nucleus) in a state of higher energy than the normal state. —**ex·cit′ed·ly,** *adv.* —**Syn. 1.** ruffled, discomposed, stormy, perturbed, impassioned.

ex·cite·ment (Yk sīt′mənt), *n.* **1.** excited state or condition. **2.** something that excites. —**Syn. 1.** perturbation, commotion, ado. See **agitation.**

ex·cit·er (Yk sī′tər), *n.* **1.** one who or that which excites. **2.** *Elect.* an auxiliary generator which supplies energy for the excitation of another electric machine.

ex·cit·ing (Yk sī′tYng), *adj.* producing excitement; stirring. —**ex·cit′ing·ly,** *adv.*

ex·ci·tor (Yk sī′tər, -tôr), *n.* **1.** *Physiol.* a nerve whose stimulation excites greater action. **2.** exciter.

ex·claim (Yk sklām′), *v.i.* **1.** to cry out or speak suddenly and vehemently, as in surprise, strong emotion, protest, etc. —*v.t.* **2.** to cry out; say loudly or vehemently. [earlier *exclame,* t. L: m.s. *exclāmāre* call out —**ex·claim′er,** *n.*

exclam., 1. exclamation. **2.** exclamatory.

ex·cla·ma·tion (ĕks′klə mā′shən), *n.* **1.** act of exclaiming; an outcry; a loud complaint or protest. **2.** an interjection. —**Syn. 1.** cry, ejaculation.

exclamation point, a punctuation mark (!) used after an exclamation. Also, **exclamation mark.**

ex·clam·a·to·ry (Yk sklăm′ə tō′rY), *adj.* **1.** using, containing, or expressing exclamation. **2.** pertaining to exclamation.

ex·clave (ĕks′klāv), *n.* a part of a country separated from it geographically and surrounded by alien territory. West Berlin is an *exclave* of West Germany. [f. EX¹ + -*clave* of ENCLAVE]

ex·clude (Yk sklōōd′), *v.t.,* **-cluded, -cluding. 1.** to shut or keep out; prevent the entrance of. **2.** to shut out from consideration, privilege, etc. **3.** to expel and keep out; thrust out; eject. [ME *exclude(n),* t. L: m. *exclūdere*] —**ex·clud′a·ble,** *adj.* —**ex·clud′er,** *n.* —**Syn. 2.** EXCLUDE, DEBAR, ELIMINATE mean to remove from a certain place, or from consideration in a particular situation. To EXCLUDE is to set aside as unwanted, unusable, etc.: *wo rds excluded from polite conversation.* To DEBAR is to prohibit, esp. in a legal sense, from a place or from the enjoyment of privileges, rights, or the like: *to debar all candidates lacking the necessary preparation.* To ELIMINATE is to select and remove, esp. as irrelevant, unnecessary, or undesirable: *to eliminate such objections.* —**Ant. 2.** admit.

excluded middle, law of, *Logic.* the law which states that a proposition is either true or false, or that a thing either has or does not have a given property.

ex·clu·sion (Yk sklōō′zhən), *n.* **1.** act of excluding. **2.** state of being excluded. **3.** *Physiol.* a keeping apart; the blocking of an entrance. [t. L: s. *exclūsio*]

ex·clu·sion·ism (Yk sklōō′zhən Yz′əm), *n.* the principle, policy, or practice of exclusion, as from rights or privileges. —**ex·clu′sion·ist,** *n.*

ex·clu·sive (Yk sklōō′sYv), *adj.* **1.** not admitting of something else; incompatible: *mutually exclusive ideas.* **2.** excluding from consideration or account: *from 100 to 121 exclusive* (excluding 100 and 121, and including from 101 to 120). **3.** limited to the object or objects designated: *exclusive attention to business.* **4.** shutting out all others from a part or share: *an exclusive grant.* **5.** in which no others have a share: *exclusive information.* **6.** single or sole: *the exclusive means of communication between two places.* **7.** disposed to resist the admission of outsiders to association, intimacy, etc.: *an exclusive clique.* **8.** *Colloq.* fashionable: *an exclusive club.* **9.** *Logic.* excluding all except what is specified: *an exclusive proposition.* [t. ML: m.s. *exclūsīvus,* der. L *exclūsus,* pp., excluded] —**ex·clu′sive·ly,** *adv.* —**ex·clu′sive·ness,** *n.* —**Syn. 7.** select, narrow, clannish, snobbish.

exclusive representation, *Labor.* the right of a union chosen by a majority of the employees in a plant, craft, industry, or department of a shop or business, to represent all the employees in the unit, regardless of whether they are members of the union or not.

ex·cog·i·tate (ĕks kŏj′ə tāt′), *v.t.,* **-tated, -tating.** to think out; devise; invent. [t. L: m.s. *excōgitātus,* pp., found out by thinking] —**ex·cog′i·ta′tion,** *n.* —**ex·cog′i·ta′tive,** *adj.* —**ex·cog′i·ta′tor,** *n.*

ex·com·mu·ni·ca·ble (ĕks′kə mū′nə kə bəl), *adj.* **1.** liable or deserving to be excommunicated, as a person. **2.** punishable by excommunication, as an offense.

ex·com·mu·ni·cate (ĕks′kə mū′nə kāt′), *v.,* **-cated, -cating,** *n., adj.* —*v.t.* **1.** to cut off from communion or

membership, esp. from the sacraments and fellowship o the church by ecclesiastical sentence. —*n.* **2.** an excom municated person. —*adj.* **3.** excommunicated. [t. LL m.s. *excommūnicātus,* pp., lit., put out of the community —**ex′com·mu′ni·ca′tor,** *n.*

ex·com·mu·ni·ca·tion (ĕks′kə mū′nə kā′shən), *n.* **1** act of excommunicating. **2.** state of being excommu nicated. **3.** the ecclesiastical sentence by which a per son is excommunicated.

ex·com·mu·ni·ca·tive (ĕks′kə mū′nə kā′tYv), *adj* disposed or serving to excommunicate.

ex·com·mu·ni·ca·to·ry (ĕks′kə mū′nə kə tōr′Y), *adj* relating to or causing excommunication.

ex·co·ri·ate (Yk skōr′Y āt′), *v.t.,* **-ated, -ating. 1.** *Phys iol.* to strip off or remove the skin from. **2.** to flay ver bally; denounce; censure. [t. L: m.s. *excoriātus,* pp. o *excoriāre* strip off the hide]

ex·co·ri·a·tion (Yk skōr′Y ā′shən), *n.* **1.** act of ex coriating. **2.** state of being excoriated. **3.** an excoriate place on the body.

ex·cre·ment (ĕks′krə mənt), *n.* waste matter dis charged from the body, esp. the feces. [t. L: s. *excrē mentum* what is evacuated] —**ex·cre·men·tal** (ĕks′ krə mĕn′təl), *adj.*

ex·cre·men·ti·tious (ĕks′krə mĕn tYsh′əs), *adj.* of o like excrement.

ex·cres·cence (Yk skrĕs′əns), *n.* **1.** abnormal growtl or increase. **2.** an abnormal outgrowth, usually harm less, on an animal or vegetable body. **3.** a normal out growth, such as hair. **4.** any disfiguring addition.

ex·cres·cen·cy (Yk skrĕs′ən sY), *n., pl.* **-cies.** state o being excrescent.

ex·cres·cent (Yk skrĕs′ənt), *adj.* **1.** growing abnor mally out of something else; superfluous. **2.** *Phonet* added without grammatical or historical justification, a in the *t* often heard at the end of *once* or *twice.* [t. L: s *excrescens,* ppr., growing out]

ex·cre·ta (Yk skrē′tə), *n.pl.* excreted matters, a sweat, urine, etc. [t. L, neut. pl. of *excrētus,* pp., sepa rated] —**ex·cre′tal,** *adj.*

ex·crete (Yk skrēt′), *v.t.,* **-creted, -creting.** to sep arate and eliminate from an organic body; separate anc expel from the blood or tissues, as waste or harmfu matters. [t. L: m.s. *excrētus,* pp., sifted out, discharged] —**ex·cre′tive,** *adj.*

ex·cre·tion (Yk skrē′shən), *n.* **1.** act of excreting **2.** the substance excreted, as sweat or urine, or certain plant products.

ex·cre·to·ry (ĕks′krə tōr′Y, Yk skrē′tə rY), *adj.* per taining to or concerned in excretion; having the functior of excreting: *excretory organs.*

ex·cru·ci·ate (Yk skrōō′shY āt′), *v.t.,* **-ated, -ating.** tc inflict severe pain upon; torture. [t. L: m.s. *excruciātus* pp., tortured greatly]

ex·cru·ci·at·ing (Yk skrōō′shY ā′tYng), *adj.* extremely painful; causing extreme suffering; torturing. —**ex· cru′ci·at′ing·ly,** *adv.*

ex·cru·ci·a·tion (Yk skrōō′shY ā′shən), *n.* **1.** act of ex cruciating. **2.** state of being excruciated. **3.** an instance of this; torture.

ex·cul·pate (ĕks′kŭl pāt′, Yk skŭl′pāt), *v.t.,* **-pated, -pating.** to clear from a charge of guilt or fault; free from blame; vindicate. [f. EX¹ + s. L *culpa* fault, blame + -ATE¹] —**ex·cul·pa·ble** (Yk skŭl′pə bəl), *adj.* —**ex′ cul·pa′tion,** *n.*

ex·cul·pa·to·ry (Yk skŭl′pə tōr′Y), *adj.* tending to clear from a charge of fault or guilt.

ex·cur·rent (Yk skûr′ənt), *adj.* **1.** running out ol forth. **2.** *Zool.* giving passage outward; affording exit: *the excurrent canal of certain sponges.* **3.** *Bot.* **a.** having the axis prolonged so as to form an undivided main stem or trunk, as the stem of the spruce. **b.** projecting beyond the apex, as the midrib in certain leaves. [t. L: s. *ex currens,* ppr., running out]

ex·cur·sion (Yk skûr′zhən, -shən), *n.* **1.** a short jour ney or trip to some point for a special purpose, with the intention of speedy return: *a pleasure excursion, a scien tific excursion.* **2.** a trip on a train, ship, etc., at a re duced rate: *week-end excursions to seashore or mountain resorts.* **3.** the persons who make such a journey. **4.** de viation or digression. **5.** *Physics.* the departure of a body from its mean position or proper course. **6.** *Mach.* **a.** the range of stroke of any moving part. **b.** the stroke itself. **7.** *Obs.* a sally or raid. [t. L: s. *excursio* a running out] —**Syn. 2.** EXCURSION, JAUNT, JUNKET, TOUR are trips made primarily for pleasure. An EXCURSION is a short trip, often no more than a day's outing, made usually by a number of people, as a result of special inducements (low fare, a special event, etc.): *an excursion at reduced rates.* JAUNT is a familiar term for a short, agreeable trip, now esp. by automobile take *a little jaunt to the country, over to a cousin's house.* JUNKET, with a still stronger suggestion of pleasure-seeking is frequently applied to trips made ostensibly on official business, enjoyed at public expense: *the junket of a con gressional committee.* A TOUR is a planned trip to celebrated places, to see interesting scenery, etc.: *a tour of Europe.*

ex·cur·sion·ist (Yk skûr′zhən Yst, -shən-), *n.* one who goes on an excursion.

excursion ticket, a ticket to a particular point and back, at a reduced fare.

ex·cur·sive (Yk skûr′sYv), *adj.* **1.** given to making ex cursions; wandering; digressive. **2.** of the nature of an excursion; rambling; desultory. —ex·cur′sive·ly, adv. —ex·cur′sive·ness, n.

ex·cur·sus (ĕks kûr′səs), n., pl. -suses, -sus. a detailed discussion of some point in a book (usually added as an appendix). [t. L, der. excurrere run out]

ex·cus·a·to·ry (Yk skū′zə tōr′Y), adj. serving or intended to excuse.

ex·cuse (v. Yk skūz′; n. Yk skūs′), v., -cused, -cusing, n. —v.t. 1. to regard or judge with indulgence; pardon or forgive; overlook (a fault, etc.). 2. to offer an apology for; apologize for; seek to remove the blame or. 3. to serve as an apology or justification for; justify: ignorance of the law excuses no man. 4. to release from an obligation or duty: to be excused from attending a meeting. 5. to seek or obtain exemption or release for (oneself): to excuse oneself from duty. 6. to refrain from exacting; remit; dispense with: to excuse a fine. —n. 7. that which is offered as a reason for being excused; a plea offered in extenuation of a fault, or for release from an obligation, etc. 8. something serving to excuse; a ground or reason for excusing. 9. act of excusing. 10. a pretext or subterfuge. [ME excuse(n), t. L: m. excūsāre allege in excuse] —ex·cus′a·ble, adj. —ex·cus′a·ble·ness, n. —ex·cus′a·bly, adv. —ex·cus′er, n.
—Syn. 1. EXCUSE, FORGIVE, PARDON imply being lenient or giving up the wish to punish. EXCUSE means to overlook some (usually) slight offense, because of circumstance, realization that it was unintentional, or the like: to excuse bad manners. FORGIVE is applied to excusing more serious offenses; the person wronged not only overlooks the offense but harbors no ill feeling against the offender: to forgive and forget. PARDON usually applies to a specific act of lenience or mercy by an official or superior in remitting all or the remainder of the punishment that belongs to a serious offense or crime: the governor was asked to pardon the condemned criminal. 3. extenuate, palliate. 7. EXCUSE, APOLOGY both imply an explanation of some failure or failing. EXCUSE implies a desire to avoid punishment or rebuke. APOLOGY usually implies acknowledgment that one has been, at least seemingly, in the wrong: it may aim at setting matters right by either alleging extenuating circumstances, or expressing regret for an error. —Ant. 1. blame, punish.

exec., 1. executive. 2. executor.

ex·e·cra·ble (ĕk′sə krə bəl), adj. 1. deserving to be execrated; detestable; abominable. 2. Colloq. very bad: an execrable pun. —ex′e·cra·bly, adv.

ex·e·crate (ĕk′sə krāt′), v., -crated, -crating. —v.t. 1. to detest utterly; abhor; abominate. 2. to curse; imprecate evil upon. —v.i. 3. to utter curses. [t. L: m.s. ex(s)ecrātus, pp., having cursed] —ex′e·cra′tor, n.

ex·e·cra·tion (ĕk′sə krā′shən), n. 1. act of execrating. 2. a curse or imprecation. 3. the object execrated; a thing held in abomination.

ex·e·cra·tive (ĕk′sə krā′tYv), adj. 1. pertaining to or characterized by execration. 2. prone to execrate.

x·e·cra·to·ry (ĕk′sə krə tōr′Y, -krā′tər y), adj. 1. pertaining to execration. 2. having the nature of or containing an execration.

ex·e·cu·tant (Yg zĕk′yə tənt), n. one who executes or performs, esp. musically.

ex·e·cute (ĕk′sə kūt′), v.t., -cuted, -cuting. 1. to carry out; accomplish: to execute a plan or order. 2. to perform or do: to execute a maneuver or gymnastic feat. 3. to inflict capital punishment on; put to death according to law. 4. to produce in accordance with a plan or design: to execute a statue or a picture. 5. to perform or play (a piece of music). 6. Law. to give effect or force to (a law, decree, judicial sentence, etc.); carry out the terms of (a will). b. to transact or carry through (a contract, mortgage, etc.) in the manner prescribed by law; complete and give validity to (a legal instrument) by fulfilling the legal requirements, as by signing, sealing, etc. [ME execute(n), t. ML: m. executāre, der. L ex(s)ecūtus, pp., having followed out] —ex′e·cut·a·ble, adj. —ex′e·cut′er, n. —Syn. 2. See perform. 3. See kill¹. 6. a. administer, enforce.

ex·e·cu·tion (ĕk′sə kū′shən), n. 1. act or process of executing. 2. state or fact of being executed. 3. the infliction of capital punishment, or, formerly, of any legal punishment. 4. mode or style of performance; technical skill, as in music. 5. effective action, esp. of weapons. 6. effective work, or the result attained by it (generally after do): every shot did execution. 7. Law. a judicial writ directing the enforcement of a judgment.

ex·e·cu·tion·er (ĕk′sə kū′shən ər), n. 1. one who executes. 2. an official who inflicts capital punishment in pursuance of a legal warrant.

ex·ec·u·tive (Yg zĕk′yə tYv), adj. 1. suited for execution or carrying into effect; of the kind requisite for practical performance or direction: executive ability. 2. charged with or pertaining to execution of laws, or administration of affairs. —n. 3. a person or body charged with or skilled in administrative work. 4. the person or persons in whom the supreme executive power of a government is vested. 5. the executive branch of a government. —ex·ec′u·tive·ly, adv.

Executive Mansion, (in the U.S.) the official residence of the President at Washington, D.C. (the White House), or of the governor of one of the States.

executive order, (usually cap.) an order issued by the President of the U.S. to the army, navy, or other part of the executive branch of the Government.

ex·ec·u·tor (Yg zĕk′yə tər), n. 1. one who executes, or carries out, performs, fulfills, etc. 2. Law. a person

named by a decedent in his will to carry out the provisions of his will. [ME executour, t. AF, t. L: m.s. ex(s)ecūtor, lit., one who follows out]

ex·ec·u·to·ry (Yg zĕk′yə tōr′Y), adj. 1. executive. 2. Law. intended, or of such a nature as, to take effect on a future contingency.

ex·ec·u·trix (Yg zĕk′yə trYks′), n., pl. executrices (Yg zĕk′yə tri′sēz), executrixes. Law. a female executor.

ex·e·ge·sis (ĕk′sə jē′sYs), n., pl. -ses (-sēz). critical explanation or interpretation, esp. of Scripture. [t. NL, t. Gk.: explanation]

ex·e·gete (ĕk′sə jēt′), n. one skilled in exegesis.

ex·e·get·ic (ĕk′sə jĕt′Yk), adj. pertaining to exegesis; expository. Also, ex′e·get′i·cal. [t. Gk.: s. exēgētikós explanatory] —ex′e·get′i·cal·ly, adv.

ex·e·get·ics (ĕk′sə jĕt′Yks), n. the science of exegesis; exegetical theology.

ex·e·gi mo·nu·men·tum ae·re pe·ren·ni·us (ĕk sā′jī mŏn′yoŏ mĕn′təm Yr′Y pə rĕn′Y əs). Latin. I have made a monument more lasting than brass. Horace, Odes, III, 30.

ex·em·plar (Yg zĕm′plər, -plär), n. 1. a model or pattern to be copied or imitated. 2. an example; typical instance. 3. an original or archetype. [t. L: copy, model; r. ME exemplaire, t. OF]

ex·em·pla·ry (Yg zĕm′plə rY, ĕg′zəm plĕr′Y), adj. 1. worthy of imitation; commendable: exemplary conduct. 2. such as may serve for a warning: an exemplary penalty. 3. serving for a model or pattern. 4. serving for an illustration or specimen; illustrative; typical. —ex·em′pla·ri·ly, adv. —ex·em′pla·ri·ness, n.

ex·em·pli·fi·ca·tion (Yg zĕm′plə fə kā′shən), n. 1. act of exemplifying. 2. that which exemplifies; an illustration or example. 3. Law. an attested copy of a document, under official seal.

ex·em·pli·fi·ca·tive (Yg zĕm′plə fə kā′tYv), adj. serving to exemplify.

ex·em·pli·fy (Yg zĕm′plə fī′), v.t., -fied, -fying. 1. to show or illustrate by example. 2. to furnish, or serve as, an example of. 3. Law. to transcribe or copy; make an attested copy of (a document) under seal. [ME exemplyfy(en), t. ML: m.s. exemplificāre, f. L: exempli- example + -ficāre make] —ex·em′pli·fi′er, n.

ex·em·pli gra·ti·a (Yg zĕm′plī grā′shY ə). Latin. for the sake of example; for example. Abbr.: e.g.

ex·empt (Yg zĕmpt′), v.t. 1. to free from an obligation or liability to which others are subject; release: to exempt someone from military service, from an examination, etc. —adj. 2. released from, or not subject to, an obligation, liability, etc.: exempt from taxes. —n. 3. one who is exempt from, or not subject to, an obligation, duty, etc. [ME, t. L: s. exemptus, pp.]

ex·emp·tion (Yg zĕmp′shən), n. 1. act of exempting. 2. state of being exempted; immunity.
—Syn. 2. EXEMPTION, IMMUNITY, IMPUNITY imply special privilege or freedom from requirements imposed upon others. EXEMPTION implies release or privileged freedom from sharing with others some (usually arbitrarily imposed) duty, tax, etc.: exemption from military service. IMMUNITY implies freedom from a penalty or from some natural or common liability, esp. one that is disagreeable or threatening: immunity from disease. IMPUNITY (limited mainly to the fixed expression with impunity) primarily suggests freedom from punishment: the police force was so inadequate that crimes could be committed with impunity. —Ant. 2. liability.

ex·e·qua·tur (ĕk′sə kwä′tər), n. 1. a written recognition of a consul by the government of the state in which he is stationed authorizing him to exercise his powers. 2. an authorization granted by a secular ruler for the publication of papal bulls or other ecclesiastical enactments to give them binding force. [t. L: let him execute]

ex·e·quies (ĕk′sə kwYz), n.pl. Now Rare. a funeral rite or ceremony. [ME exequies (pl.), t. OF, t. L: m. exequiae funeral procession]

ex·er·cise (ĕk′sər sīz′), n., v., -cised, -cising. —n. 1. bodily or mental exertion, esp. for the sake of training or improvement. 2. something done or performed as a means of practice or training: exercises for the piano. 3. a putting into action, use, operation, or effect: the exercise of caution or care, the exercise of will power. 4. (often pl.) a ceremony: graduating exercises. 5. a religious observance or service. —v.t. 6. to put through exercises, or forms of practice or exertion, designed to train, develop, condition, etc.: to exercise troops, a horse, the voice, etc. 7. to put (faculties, rights, etc.) into action, practice, or use: to exercise one's strength, one's sight, etc. 8. to use or display in one's action or procedure: to exercise caution, patience, judgment. 9. to make use of (one's privileges, powers, etc.): to exercise one's rights. 10. to discharge (a function); perform: to exercise the duties of one's office. 11. to have as an effect: to exercise an influence on someone. 12. to worry; make uneasy; annoy: to be much exercised about one's health. —v.i. 13. to go through exercises; take bodily exercise. [ME exercise, t. OF, g. L exercitium] —ex′er·cis′a·ble, adj. —ex′er·cis′er, n.
—Syn. 2. EXERCISE, DRILL, PRACTICE refer to activities undertaken for training in some skill. An EXERCISE may be either physical or mental, and may be more or less irregular in time and varied in kind: an exercise in arithmetic. DRILL is disciplined repetition of set exercises, often performed in a group, directed by a leader: military drill. PRACTICE is methodical exercise, usually characterized by

ict, āble, dâre, ärt; ĕbb, ēqual; Yf, īce; hŏt, ōver, ôrder, oil, boŏk, ōōze, out; ŭp, ūse, ûrge; ə = a in alone; ch, chief; g, give; ng, ring; sh, shoe; th, thin; ŧħ, that; zh, vision. See the full key on inside cover.

much repetition, with a view to becoming perfect in some operation or pursuit and to acquiring further skills: *even great musicians require constant practice*. **3.** employment, application. **6.** discipline. **8.** employ, apply, exert.

ex·er·ci·ta·tion (ĭg zûr/sə tā/shən), *n.* **1.** exercise or exertion, as of faculties or powers. **2.** practice or training. **3.** a performance. **4.** a disquisition or discourse. [ME *exercitacion*, t. L: m.s. *exercitātio* exercise, practice]

ex·ergue (ĭg zûrg/, ĕk/sûrg), *n.* *Numismatics.* the space below the base line on a coin or medal. [t. F, f. Gk.: *ex-* ᴇx⁻³ + m.s. *ērgon* work]

ex·ert (ĭg zûrt/), *v.t.* **1.** to put forth, as power; exercise, as ability or influence; put into vigorous action. **2.** exert oneself, to put forth one's powers; use one's efforts; strive. [t. L: s. *ex(s)ertus*, pp.] —**ex·er/tive**, *adj.*

ex·er·tion (ĭg zûr/shən), *n.* **1.** vigorous action or effort. **2.** an effort. **3.** exercise, as of power or faculties. **4.** an instance of this. —**Syn. 1.** endeavor, struggle, attempt. See **effort.**

Ex·e·ter (ĕk/sə tər), *n.* a city in SW England, in Devonshire: cathedral. 77,000 (est. 1956).

ex·e·unt (ĕk/sĭ ənt), *Latin.* they (or the persons named) go out (instruction for actors in plays).

ex·e·unt om·nes (ĕk/sĭ ənt ŏm/nēz), *Latin.* all go out; all go offstage (used in plays).

ex·fo·li·ate (ĕks fō/lĭ āt/), *v.*, -ated, -ating. —*v.t.* **1.** to throw off in scales. **2.** to remove the surface of (a bone, etc.) in scales or laminae. —*v.i.* **3.** to throw off scales or flakes; peel off in thin fragments: *the exfoliating bark of a tree*. **4.** *Geol.* **a.** to split or swell into a scaly aggregate, as certain minerals when heated. **b.** to separate into rudely concentric layers or sheets, as certain rocks during weathering. **5.** *Surg.* to separate and come off in scales, as scaling skin or any structure separating in flakes. [t. LL: m.s. *exfoliātus*, pp., stripped of leaves] —**ex·fo/li·a·tive**, *adj.*

ex·fo·li·a·tion (ĕks fō/lĭ ā/shən), *n.* **1.** act or process of exfoliating. **2.** state of being exfoliated. **3.** that which is exfoliated, or scaled off.

ex·hal·ant (ĕks hā/lənt, ĭg zā/lənt), *adj.* **1.** exhaling; emitting. —*n.* **2.** that which exhales.

ex·ha·la·tion (ĕks/hə lā/shən, ĕg/zə-), *n.* **1.** act of exhaling. **2.** that which is exhaled; a vapor; an emanation.

ex·hale (ĕks hāl/, ĭg zāl/), *v.*, -haled, -haling. —*v.i.* **1.** to emit breath or vapor. **2.** to pass off as vapor; pass off as an effluence. —*v.t.* **3.** to breathe out; emit (air, etc.). **4.** to give off as vapor. **5.** to draw out as a vapor or effluence; evaporate. [ME *exale(n)*, t. F: m. *exhaler*, t. L: m. *exhālāre* breathe out] —**ex·hal/a·ble**, *adj.*

ex·haust (ĭg zôst/), *v.t.* **1.** to empty by drawing out the contents. **2.** to create a vacuum in. **3.** to draw out or drain off; draw or drain off completely. **4.** to use up or consume completely; expend the whole of. **5.** to drain of strength or energy, wear out, or fatigue greatly, as a person: *I have exhausted myself working*. **6.** to draw out all that is essential in (a subject, topic, etc.); treat or study thoroughly. **7.** to deprive wholly of useful or essential properties, possessions, resources, etc. **8.** to deprive of ingredients by the use of solvents, as a drug. —*v.i.* **9.** to pass out or escape, as spent steam from the cylinder of an engine. —*n.* **10.** *Mach.* **a.** the escape of the gases from the cylinder of an engine after expansion. **b.** the steam or gases ejected. **c.** the parts of an engine through which the exhaust is ejected. [t. L: s. *exhaustus*, pp., drained out] —**ex·haust/er**, *n.* —**ex·haust/i·ble**, *adj.* —**ex·haust/i·bil/i·ty**, *n.* —**Syn. 5.** tire, enervate, prostrate. See **tired**[1]. —**Ant. 5.** invigorate.

exhaust fan, the fan in a ventilation system used to remove vitiated or excess air.

ex·haus·tion (ĭg zôs/chən), *n.* **1.** act or process of exhausting. **2.** state of being exhausted. **3.** extreme weakness or fatigue. —**Syn. 3.** weariness, lassitude.

ex·haus·tive (ĭg zôs/tĭv), *adj.* **1.** exhausting a subject, topic, etc.; comprehensive; thorough. **2.** tending to exhaust or drain, as of resources or strength. —**ex·haus/tive·ly**, *adv.* —**ex·haus/tive·ness**, *n.*

ex·haust·less (ĭg zôst/lĭs), *adj.* inexhaustible. —**ex·haust/less·ly**, *adv.* —**ex·haust/less·ness**, *n.*

ex·hib·it (ĭg zĭb/ĭt), *v.t.* **1.** to offer or expose to view; present for inspection. **2.** to manifest or display: *to exhibit anger*. **3.** to place on show: *to exhibit paintings*. **4.** *Law.* to submit (a document, etc.) in evidence in a court of law; present (a petition, charge, etc.) for consideration. **5.** *Med.* to administer (a remedy, etc.). —*v.i.* **6.** to make or give an exhibition; present something to public view. —*n.* **7.** an exhibiting or exhibition. **8.** that which is exhibited. **9.** an object or a collection of objects shown in an exhibition, fair, etc. **10.** *Law.* a document or other object exhibited in court and referred to and identified in written evidence. [t. L: s. *exhibitus*, pp.] —**ex·hib/i·tor, ex·hib/it·er,** *n.* —**Syn. 1.** See **display.** **2.** evince, disclose, betray. **8, 10.** See **evidence.** —**Ant. 2.** conceal.

ex·hi·bi·tion (ĕk/sə bĭsh/ən), *n.* **1.** an exhibiting, showing, or presenting to view. **2.** a public display, as of works of art, manufactures, etc., or of feats of skill, etc. **3.** *Brit.* an exposition; a big fair of extended duration. **4.** *Med.* administration, as of a remedy. **5.** an allowance given to a student in an English college or university or school, usually upon the result of a competitive examination.

ex·hi·bi·tion·er (ĕk/sə bĭsh/ən ər), *n.* a student who receives an exhibition (def. 5).

ex·hi·bi·tion·ism (ĕk/sə bĭsh/ə nĭz/əm), *n.* **1.** a tendency to display one's abilities or to behave in such a way as to attract attention. **2.** *Psychiatry.* the attaining of sexual gratification by exhibiting and attracting attention to the genitals.

ex·hi·bi·tion·ist (ĕk/sə bĭsh/ən ĭst), *n.* **1.** one who desires to make an exhibition of himself or his powers, personality, etc. **2.** *Psychiatry.* one affected with the compulsions of exhibitionism. —**ex/hi·bi/tion·is/-tic,** *adj.*

ex·hib·i·tive (ĭg zĭb/ə tĭv), *adj.* serving for exhibition; tending to exhibit.

ex·hib·i·to·ry (ĭg zĭb/ə tôr/ĭ), *adj.* pertaining to or intended for exhibition or display.

ex·hil·a·rant (ĭg zĭl/ə rənt), *adj.* **1.** exhilarating. —*n.* **2.** something that exhilarates.

ex·hil·a·rate (ĭg zĭl/ə rāt/), *v.t.*, -rated, -rating. to make cheerful or merry. [t. L: m.s. *exhilarātus*, pp.] —**ex·hil/a·rat/ing,** *adj.* —**ex·hil/a·rat/ing·ly,** *adv.* —**ex·hil/a·ra/tor,** *n.* —**Syn.** cheer, gladden, enliven, animate, inspirit.

ex·hil·a·ra·tion (ĭg zĭl/ə rā/shən), *n.* **1.** exhilarated condition or feeling. **2.** act of exhilarating. —**Syn. 1.** animation, joyousness, gaiety, jollity, hilarity.

ex·hil·a·ra·tive (ĭg zĭl/ə rā/tĭv), *adj.* tending to exhilarate. Also, **ex·hil·a·ra·to·ry** (ĭg zĭl/ə rə tôr/ĭ).

ex·hort (ĭg zôrt/), *v.t.* **1.** to urge, advise, or caution earnestly; admonish urgently. —*v.i.* **2.** to make exhortation; give admonition. [ME *exhort(en)*, t. L: m. *exhortārī* urge, encourage] —**ex·hort/er,** *n.*

ex·hor·ta·tion (ĕg/zôr tā/shən, ĕk/sôr-), *n.* **1.** act or process of exhorting. **2.** an utterance, discourse, or address conveying urgent advice or recommendations.

ex·hor·ta·tive (ĭg zôr/tə tĭv), *adj.* **1.** serving or intended to exhort. **2.** pertaining to exhortation. Also, **ex·hor·ta·to·ry** (ĭg zôr/tə tôr/ĭ).

ex·hume (ĭg zūm/, ĕks hūm/), *v.t.*, -humed, -huming. to dig (something buried, esp. a dead body) out of the earth; disinter. [t. ML: m.s. *exhumāre*, der. L *ex-* ᴇx⁻¹ + *humus* earth, ground] —**ex·hu·ma·tion** (ĕks/hyŏŏ mā/shən), *n.* —**ex·hum/er,** *n.*

ex·i·geant (ĕk/sə jənt; *Fr.* ĕg zē zhäɴ/), *adj.* exacting; overdemanding. —**ex·i·geante** (ĕg zē zhäɴt/), *adj. fem.*

ex·i·gen·cy (ĕk/sə jən sĭ), *n.*, *pl.* -cies. **1.** exigent state or character; urgency. **2.** (*usually pl.*) a circumstance that renders prompt action necessary; a need, demand, or requirement. **3.** a case or situation which demands prompt action or remedy; an emergency. Also, **ex/i·gence.**

ex·i·gent (ĕk/sə jənt), *adj.* **1.** requiring immediate action or aid; urgent; pressing. **2.** requiring a great deal, or more than is reasonable. [t. L: s. *exigens*, ppr. requiring, lit., driving out] —**ex/i·gent·ly,** *adv.*

ex·i·gi·ble (ĕk/sə jə bəl), *adj.* that may be exacted; requirable.

ex·ig·u·ous (ĭg zĭg/yŏŏ əs, ĭk sĭg/-), *adj.* scanty; small; slender. [t. L: m. *exiguus*] —**ex·i·gu·i·ty** (ĕk/sə gū/ə tĭ), *n.* **ex·ig/u·ous·ness,** *n.*

ex·ile (ĕg/zīl, ĕk/sīl), *n.*, *v.*, -iled, -iling. —*n.* **1.** prolonged separation from one's country or home, as by stress of circumstances. **2.** any one separated from his country or home. **3.** expulsion from one's native land by authoritative decree. **4.** fact or state of such expulsion. **5.** a person banished from his native land. **6. the Exile,** the Babylonian captivity of the Jews in the 6th century ᴮ.ᴄ. —*v.t.* **7.** to separate from country, home, etc. **8.** to expel or banish (a person) from his country; expatriate. [ME *exil*, t. OF, t. L: m.s. *ex(s)ilium* banishment]

ex·il·ic (ĕg zĭl/ĭk, ĕk sĭl/ĭk), *adj.* pertaining to exile, as that of the Jews in Babylon. Also, **ex·il/i·an.**

ex·im·i·ous (ĕg zĭm/ĭ əs), *adj. Now Rare.* distinguished; eminent; excellent. [t. L: m. *eximius* select]

ex int., ex (without) interest.

ex·ist (ĭg zĭst/), *v.i.* **1.** to have actual being; be. **2.** to have life or animation; live. **3.** to continue to be or to live. **4.** to have being in a specified place or under certain conditions; be found; occur. [t. L: s. *existere* stand forth, arise, be]

ex·ist·ence (ĭg zĭs/təns), *n.* **1.** state or fact of existing; being. **2.** continuance in being or life; life: *a struggle for existence*. **3.** mode of existing. **4.** all that exists. **5.** something that exists, an entity, or a being.

ex·ist·ent (ĭg zĭs/tənt), *adj.* **1.** existing; having existence. **2.** now existing. —*n.* **3.** one who or that which exists.

ex·is·ten·tial (ĕg/zĭs tĕn/shəl, ĕk/sĭs-), *adj.* pertaining to existence. —**ex·is·ten/tial·ly,** *adv.*

ex·is·ten·tial·ism (ĕg/zĭs tĕn/shə lĭz/əm, ĕk/sĭs-), *n. Philos.* **1.** the doctrine that there is no difference between the external world and the internal world of the mind, and that the source and the elements of knowledge have their existence in states of the mind. **2.** a recent movement which claims to represent a middle way between the traditional materialism and idealism and stresses personal decision in the face of a universe without purpose.

ex·it (ĕg/zĭt, ĕk/sĭt), *n.* **1.** a way or passage out. **2.** a going out or away; a departure: *to make one's exit*. **3.** the departure of a player from the stage. —*v.* **4.** he (or she, or the person named) goes out (used in the text of plays, with reference to an actor). [special use of stage direction *exit* he goes out, influenced by assoc. with L *exitus* a going out]

x lib., ex libris.

x li·bris (ĕks lī′brĭs, lē′-), *pl.* **-bris** for 2. *Latin.* **1.** from the library (of) (a phrase inscribed in or on a book, before the name of the owner). **2.** an inscription in or on a book, to indicate the owner; a bookplate.

x·moor (ĕks′mŏŏr), *n.* a high moorland in SW England, in Somersetshire and Devonshire: the scene of Blackmore's *Lorna Doone.*

x ni·hi·lo ni·hil fit (ĕks nī′hÿ lō′ nī′hÿl fĭt′), *Latin.* (only) nothing is created from nothing; that is, all that exists has always existed.

xo-, a prefix meaning "external." Also, **ex-²**. [t. Gk.: outside]

x·o·carp (ĕk′sō kärp′), *n. Bot.* epicarp.

x·o·cen·tric construction (ĕk′sō sĕn′trĭk), *Ling.* a grammatical construction which as a unit does not function in the same manner as any one of its immediate constituents (opposed to *endocentric construction*): "*in the garden,*" "*for her,*" "*Tom played*" are exocentric constructions.

xod., Exodus.

x·o·der·mis (ĕk′sō dûr′mĭs), *n. Bot.* a temporary, protective layer of cells in some roots, as in certain orchids.

x·o·don·tia (ĕk′sō dŏn′shə, -shÿ ə), *n.* the branch of dentistry dealing with the extraction of teeth. [NL, f. Gk.: *ex-* **EX-³** + s. *odoús* tooth + *-ia* **-IA.** Cf. Gk. *exodontízomai* have one's tusks removed]

x·o·dus (ĕk′sə dəs), *n.* **1.** a going out; a departure or emigration, usually of a large number of people. **2.** (*often cap.*) the departure of the Israelites from Egypt under Moses. **3.** (*cap.*) the second book of the Old Testament, containing an account of this departure. [ME, t. L, t. Gk.: m. *éxodos* a going out]

x off., ex officio.

x of·fi·ci·o (ĕks ə fĭsh′ĭ ō′), by virtue of office or official position. **—ex′-of·fi′ci·o′,** *adj.* [t. L: from office]

x·og·a·my (ĕks ŏg′ə mÿ), *n.* **1.** the custom of marrying outside the tribe or blood group (opposed to *endogamy*). **2.** *Biol.* the union of gametes of unrelated parents. **—ex·og·a·mous** (ĕks ŏg′ə məs), **ex·o·gam·ic** (ĕk′sō găm′ĭk), *adj.*

x·o·gen (ĕk′sə jĕn), *n. Bot.* any plant of the obsolete class *Exogenae*, including the dicotyledons. [t. F: m. *exogène*. See **EXO-, -GEN**]

x·og·e·nous (ĕks ŏj′ə nəs), *adj.* **1.** having its origin external; derived externally. **2.** *Bot.* **a.** (of plants, as the dicotyledons) having stems which grow by the addition of an annual layer of wood to the outside beneath the bark. **b.** pertaining to plants having such stems. **c.** belonging to the exogens. **3.** *Physiol., Biochem.* of or denoting the metabolic assimilation of proteins, in which the elimination of nitrogenous catabolites is in direct proportion to the amount of protein taken in. [t. NL: m. *exógenus* growing on the outside. See **EXO-, -GENOUS**] **—ex·og′e·nous·ly,** *adv.*

E E
A
B C D

Parts of an Exogen
Section of a branch of three years' growth: A. Medulla or pith; B. Medullary sheath; C. Circles of annual growth; D. Bark; E. Medullary ray

x·on·er·ate (ÿg zŏn′ə rāt′), *v.t.,* **-ated, -ating. 1.** to clear, as of a charge; free from blame; exculpate. **2.** to relieve, as from an obligation, duty, or task. [t. L: m.s. *exonerātus,* pp., disburdened] **—ex·on′er·a′tion,** *n.* **—ex·on′er·a·tive,** *adj.* **—Syn. 1.** See **absolve.**

x·o·per·id·i·um (ĕks′ō pÿ rĭd′ÿ əm), *n. Bot.* See **peridium.**

x·oph·thal·mos (ĕk′sŏf thăl′mŏs), *n. Pathol.* protrusion of the eyeball from the orbit, caused by disease or injury. Also, **ex·oph·thal·mus** (ĕk′sŏf thăl′məs), **ex·oph·thal·mi·a** (ĕk′sŏf thăl′mÿ ə). [NL, t. Gk.: as adj. with prominent eyes] **—ex′oph·thal′mic,** *adj.*

x·o·ra·ble (ĕk′sə rə bəl), *adj.* susceptible of being persuaded or moved by entreaty. [t. L: m.s. *exōrābilis*] **—ex′o·ra·bil′i·ty,** *n.*

x·or·bi·tance (ÿg zôr′bə təns), *n.* quality of being exorbitant; excessiveness. Also, **ex·or′bi·tan·cy.**

x·or·bi·tant (ÿg zôr′bə tənt), *adj.* exceeding the bounds of custom, propriety, or reason, esp. in amount or extent: *to charge an exorbitant price for something.* [t. LL: s. *exorbitans,* ppr., going out of the track] **—ex·or′bi·tant·ly,** *adv.* **—Syn.** inordinate, excessive, extravagant, unreasonable, unconscionable. **—Ant.** fair.

x·or·cise (ĕk′sôr sīz′), *v.t.,* **-cised, -cising. 1.** to seek to expel (an evil spirit) by adjuration or religious or solemn ceremonies. **2.** to deliver (a person, place, etc.) from evil spirits or malignant influences. Also, **ex′or·cize′.** [t. LL: m.s. *exorcizāre,* t. Gk.: m. *exorkízein*] **—ex·or·cise′ment,** *n.* **—ex′or·cis′er,** *n.*

x·or·cism (ĕk′sôr sĭz′əm), *n.* **1.** act or process of exorcising. **2.** the ceremony or the formula used. **—ex·or·cist** (ĕk′sôr sĭst), *n.*

x·or·di·um (ÿg zôr′dÿ əm, ÿk sôr′-), *n., pl.* **-diums, -dia** (-dÿ ə). **1.** the beginning of anything. **2.** the introductory part of an oration or discourse. [t. L: a beginning] **—ex·or′di·al,** *adj.*

ex·o·skel·e·ton (ĕk′sō skĕl′ə tən), *n. Anat.* an external protective covering or integument, esp. when hard, as the shell of crustaceans, the scales and plates of fishes, etc. (opposed to *endoskeleton*).

ex·os·mo·sis (ĕk′sŏs mō′sÿs, ĕk′sŏz-), *n. Phys. Chem., etc.* **1.** osmosis from within outward. **2.** (in osmosis) the flow of that fluid which passes with the lesser rapidity into the other (opposed to *endosmosis*). Also, **ex·os·mose** (ĕk′sŏs mōs′, ĕk′sŏz-). [f. **EX-³** + **OSMOSIS**] **—ex·os·mot·ic** (ĕk′sŏs mŏt′ÿk, ĕk′sŏz-), **ex·os·mic** (ĕk-sŏs′mÿk, -sŏz′-), *adj.*

ex·o·spore (ĕk′sō spôr′), *n. Bot.* the outer coat of a spore.

ex·os·to·sis (ĕk′sŏs tō′sÿs), *n., pl.* **-ses** (-sēz). *Pathol.* the morbid formation of bone, or a morbid bony growth, on a bone. [NL, t. Gk.: outgrowth of bone]

ex·o·ter·ic (ĕk′sə tĕr′ÿk), *adj.* **1.** suitable for or communicated to the general public. **2.** not belonging or pertaining to the inner or select circle, as of disciples. **3.** popular; simple; commonplace. [t. LL: s. *exōtericus* external, t. Gk. m. *exōterikós*] **—ex/o·ter/i·cal·ly,** *adv.*

ex·o·ther·mic (ĕk′sō thûr′mÿk), *adj. Chem.* noting or pertaining to a chemical change which is accompanied by a liberation of heat (opposed to *endothermic*).

ex·ot·ic (ÿg zŏt′ÿk), *adj.* **1.** of foreign origin or character; not native; introduced from abroad, but not fully naturalized or acclimatized. **2.** *Colloq.* strikingly unusual or colorful in appearance or effect. **—n. 3.** anything exotic, as a plant. [t. L: s. *exōticus,* t. Gk.: m. *exōtikós* foreign, alien] **—ex·ot/i·cal·ly,** *adv.*

ex·ot·i·cism (ÿg zŏt′ə sÿz′əm), *n.* **1.** tendency to adopt what is exotic. **2.** exotic quality or character. **3.** anything exotic, as a foreign word or idiom.

ex·o·tox·in (ĕk′sō tŏk′sÿn), *n. Biochem.* a toxin secreted during the life of an organism, either in the body tissues or in food. The organism itself is nontoxic.

exp., **1.** expenses. **2.** expired. **3.** export. **4.** exportation. **5.** exported. **6.** exporter. **7.** express.

ex·pand (ÿk spănd′), *v.t.* **1.** to increase in extent, size, volume, scope, etc.: *heat expands metal.* **2.** to spread or stretch out; unfold: *a bird expands its wings.* **3.** to express in fuller form or greater detail; develop: *to expand a short story into a novel.* **—v.i. 4.** to increase or grow in extent, bulk, scope, etc.: *most metals expand with heat, the mind expands with experience.* **5.** to spread out; unfold; develop: *the buds had not yet expanded.* [t. L: s. *expandere* spread out] **—ex·pand′er,** *n.* **—Syn. 1.** extend, swell, enlarge. **EXPAND, DILATE, DISTEND, INFLATE** imply becoming larger and filling more space. To **EXPAND** is to spread out, usually in every direction, so as to occupy more space or have more capacity: *to expand one's chest.* To **DILATE** is esp. to increase the width or circumference, and applies to space enclosed within confines or to hollow bodies: *to dilate the pupils of the eyes.* To **DISTEND** is to stretch, often beyond the point of natural expansion: *to distend an artery.* To **INFLATE** is to blow out or swell a hollow body with air or gas of some kind: *to inflate a balloon.* **2.** spread, unfurl. **—Ant. 1.** contract.

ex·pand·ed (ÿk spăn′dÿd), *adj.* **1.** increased in area, bulk, or volume; enlarged. **2.** spread out; extended. **3.** (of printing type) wider than usual for its height.

ex·panse (ÿk spăns′), *n.* **1.** that which is expanded; an uninterrupted space or area; a wide extent of anything: *an expanse of water, of sky, etc.* **2.** expansion. [t. L: m.s. *expansum,* prop. pp. neut.]

ex·pan·si·ble (ÿk spăn′sə bəl), *adj.* capable of being expanded. **—ex·pan′si·bil′i·ty,** *n.*

ex·pan·sile (ÿk spăn′sÿl), *adj.* **1.** capable of expanding; such as to expand. **2.** pertaining to expansion.

ex·pan·sion (ÿk spăn′shən), *n.* **1.** act of expanding. **2.** state of being expanded. **3.** the amount or degree of expanding. **4.** an expanded, dilated, or enlarged portion or form of a thing. **5.** anything spread out; an expanse. **6.** *Math.* the development at length of an expression indicated in a contracted form. **7.** *Mach.* that part of the operation of an engine in which the volume of the working medium increases and its pressure decreases. [t. LL: s. *expansio*]

ex·pan·sion·ism (ÿk spăn′shə nÿz′əm), *n.* policy of expansion, as of territory or currency. **—ex·pan′sion·ist,** *n.*

ex·pan·sive (ÿk span′sÿv), *adj.* **1.** tending to expand or capable of expanding. **2.** having a wide range or extent; comprehensive; extensive. **3.** (of a person's character, or speech) effusive, unrestrained, free, or open. **4.** *Psychiatry.* marked by an abnormal euphorisic state and by delusions of grandeur. **—ex·pan′sive·ly,** *adv.* **—ex·pan′sive·ness,** *n.*

ex par·te (ĕks pär′tÿ), *Latin.* from or on one side only, as in a controversy; in the interest of one party.

ex·pa·ti·ate (ÿk spā′shÿ āt′), *v.i.,* **-ated, -ating. 1.** to enlarge in discourse or writing; be copious in description or discussion: *to expatiate upon a theme.* **2.** *Now Rare.* to move or wander about without restraint. [t. L: m.s. *ex(s)patiātus,* pp., extended, spread out] **—ex·pa′ti·a′tion,** *n.* **—ex·pa′ti·a′tor,** *n.*

ex·pa·tri·ate (*v.* ĕks pā′trÿ āt′; *adj., n.* ĕks pā′trÿ ÿt, -āt′), *v.,* **-ated, -ating,** *adj., n.* **—v.t. 1.** to banish (a person) from his native country. **2.** to withdraw (oneself) from residence in one's native country. **3.** to withdraw (oneself) from allegiance to one's country. **—adj. 4.** expatriated. **—n. 5.** an expatriated person. [t. LL: m.s. *expatriātus,* pp.] **—ex·pa′tri·a′tion,** *n.*

ex·pect (ÿk spĕkt′), *v.t.* **1.** to look forward to; regard as likely to happen; anticipate the occurrence or the

coming of: *I expect to do it, I expect him to come, that he will come.* **2.** to look for with reason or justification: *we cannot expect obedience; expect him to do that.* **3.** *Colloq.* to suppose or surmise. **4.** *Obs.* to await or wait for. [t. L: s. *ex(s)pectāre* look for]
—**Syn. 1.** EXPECT, ANTICIPATE, HOPE, AWAIT all imply looking to some future event. EXPECT implies confidently believing, usually for good reasons, that an event will occur: *to expect a visit from a friend.* ANTICIPATE is to look forward eagerly to an event and even to picture it: *to anticipate seeing a play.* HOPE implies a wish that an event may take place and an expectation that it will: *to hope for the best.* AWAIT (WAIT FOR) implies being alert and ready, whether for good or evil: *to await news after a cyclone.*

ex·pect·an·cy (Ĭk spĕk′tən sĭ′), *n., pl.* **-cies. 1.** quality or state of expecting; expectation; anticipatory belief or desire. **2.** state of being expected. **3.** an object of expectation; something expected. Also, **ex·pec′tance.**

ex·pect·ant (Ĭk spĕk′tənt), *adj.* **1.** having expectations; expecting. **2.** expecting the birth of a child: *an expectant mother or father.* **3.** characterized by expectations. **4.** expected or anticipated. —*n.* **5.** one who expects; one who waits in expectation. —**ex·pect′-ant·ly,** *adv.*

ex·pec·ta·tion (ĕk′spĕk tā′shən), *n.* **1.** act of expecting. **2.** state of expecting: *wait in expectation.* **3.** state of being expected. **4.** expectant mental attitude. **5.** something expected; a thing looked forward to. **6.** (*often pl.*) a prospect of future good or profit: *to have great expectations.* **7.** the degree of probability of the occurrence of something. —**Syn. 2., 4.** expectancy, anticipation, hope, trust.

expectation of life, the average duration of life beyond any age, of persons who have attained that age, as shown by mortality tables.

ex·pect·a·tive (Ĭk spĕk′tə tĭv), *adj.* **1.** of or pertaining to expectation. **2.** characterized by expectation.

ex·pec·to·rant (Ĭk spĕk′tə rənt), *Med.* —*adj.* **1.** promoting the secretion of fluid from the respiratory tract. —*n.* **2.** an expectorant medicine.

ex·pec·to·rate (Ĭk spĕk′tə rāt′), *v.,* **-rated, -rating.** —*v.t.* **1.** to eject or expel (phlegm, etc.) from the throat or lungs by coughing or hawking and spitting; spit. —*v.i.* **2.** to spit. [t. L: m.s. *expectorātus,* pp., banished from the breast] —**ex·pec′to·ra′tor,** *n.*

ex·pec·to·ra·tion (Ĭk spĕk′tə rā′shən), *n.* **1.** act of expectorating. **2.** matter that is expectorated.

ex pe·de Her·cu·lem (ĕks pē′dĭ hûr′kyōŏ lĕm), *Latin.* from the foot (we may know) Hercules; from a part or sample we may judge the whole.

ex·pe·di·en·cy (Ĭk spē′dĭ ən sĭ′), *n., pl.* **-cies. 1.** quality of being expedient; advantageousness; advisability. **2.** a regard for what is politic or advantageous rather than for what is right or just; a sense of self interest. **3.** something expedient. Also, **ex·pe′di·ence.**

ex·pe·di·ent (Ĭk spē′dĭ ənt), *adj.* **1.** tending to promote some proposed or desired object; fit or suitable for the purpose; proper under the circumstances: *it is expedient that you go.* **2.** conducive to advantage or interest, as opposed to right. **3.** acting in accordance with expediency. —*n.* **4.** a means to an end. **5.** a means devised or employed in an exigency; a resource; a shift: *to resort to expedients to achieve one's purpose.* [ME, t. L: s. *expediens,* ppr., despatching] —**ex·pe′di·ent·ly,** *adv.* —**Syn. 1.** advantageous, profitable, advisable. **5.** device, contrivance.

ex·pe·di·en·tial (Ĭk spē′dĭ ĕn′shəl), *adj.* pertaining to or regulated by expediency.

ex·pe·dite (ĕks′pə dīt′), *v.,* **-dited, -diting,** *adj.* —*v.t.* **1.** to speed up the progress of; hasten: *to expedite matters.* **2.** to accomplish promptly, as a piece of business; dispatch. **3.** to issue officially, as a document. —*adj.* **4.** ready; alert. [t. L: m.s. *expeditus,* pp., extricated, helped forward, sent off or dispatched] —**ex·pe·dit′er,** *n.* —**Syn. 1.** quicken, speed, push. —**Ant. 1.** delay.

ex·pe·di·tion (ĕks′pə dĭsh′ən), *n.* **1.** an excursion, journey, or voyage made for some specific purpose, as of war or exploration. **2.** the body of persons or ships, etc., engaged in it. **3.** promptness or speed in accomplishing something. —**Syn. 1.** See **trip. 3.** haste, quickness, dispatch.

ex·pe·di·tion·ar·y (ĕks′pə dĭsh′ə nĕr′ĭ), *adj.* pertaining to or composing an expedition: *an expeditionary force.*

ex·pe·di·tious (ĕks′pə dĭsh′əs), *adj.* characterized by expedition or prompt dispatch; quick. —**ex′pe·di′tious·ly,** *adv.* —**ex′pe·di′tious·ness,** *n.*

ex·pel (Ĭk spĕl′), *v.t.,* **-pelled, -pelling. 1.** to drive or force out or away; discharge or eject: *to expel air from the lungs, an invader from a country.* **2.** to cut off from membership or relations: *to expel a student from a college.* [ME *expelle(n),* t. L: m. *expellere* drive out] —**ex·pel′-la·ble,** *adj.* —**ex·pel′ler,** *n.* —**Syn. 2.** oust, dismiss.

ex·pel·lant (Ĭk spĕl′ənt), *adj.* **1.** expelling or having the power to expel. —*n.* **2.** an expellant medicine. Also, **ex·pel′lent.**

ex·pend (Ĭk spĕnd′), *v.t.* **1.** to use up: *to expend energy, time, care, etc., on something.* **2.** to pay out; disburse; spend. [t. L: s. *expendere* weigh out, pay out] —**ex·pend′a·ble,** *adj.* —**ex·pend′er,** *n.* —**Syn. 1.** See **spend.**

ex·pend·i·ture (Ĭk spĕn′dĭ chər), *n.* **1.** act of expending; disbursement; consumption. **2.** that which is expended; expense.

ex·pense (Ĭk spĕns′), *n.* **1.** cost or charge. **2.** a cause or occasion of spending: *owning a car is a great expense.* **3.** act of expending; expenditure. **4.** loss or injury due to any detracting cause (prec. by *at*): *quantity at the expense of quality.* **5.** (*pl.*) *Com.* **a.** charges incurred in the execution of an undertaking or commission. **b.** money paid as reimbursement for such charges: *to receive a salary and expenses.* [ME, t. AF, t. LL: m. *expensa,* prop, pp. fem., paid or weighed out] —**Syn. 1.** See **price.**

ex·pen·sive (Ĭk spĕn′sĭv), *adj.* entailing great expense; costly. —**ex·pen′sive·ly,** *adv.* —**ex·pen′sive·ness,** *n.*
—**Syn.** EXPENSIVE, COSTLY, DEAR apply to that which is higher in price than the average person's usual purchases. EXPENSIVE is applied to whatever entails (usually considerable) expense; it suggests a price beyond a thing's worth and beyond what the person can properly afford to pay: *an expensive automobile.* COSTLY implies that the price is a large sum, usually because of the fineness, preciousness, etc. of the object: *a costly jewel.* DEAR is commonly applied in England to that which is selling beyond its usual or just price. In the U. S., HIGH-PRICED is the usual equivalent: *buy cheap and sell dear.* —**Ant.** cheap.

ex·pe·ri·ence (Ĭk spĭr′ĭ əns), *n., v.,* **-enced, -encing.** —*n.* **1.** a particular instance of personally encountering or undergoing something: *a strange experience.* **2.** the process or fact of personally observing, encountering, or undergoing something: *business experience.* **3.** the observing, encountering, or undergoing of things generally as they occur in the course of time: *to learn from experience, the range of human experience.* **4.** knowledge or practical wisdom gained from what one has observed, encountered, or undergone: *men of experience.* **5.** *Philos.* the totality of the cognitions given by perception; all that is perceived, understood, and remembered. —*v.t.* **6.** to have experience of; meet with; undergo; feel. **7.** *Rare.* to learn by experience. [ME, t. OF, t. L: m.s. *experientia* trial, proof, knowledge]
—**Syn. 6.** EXPERIENCE, UNDERGO refer to encountering situations, conditions, etc. in life, or to having certain sensations, feelings. EXPERIENCE implies being affected by what one meets with (pleasant or unpleasant), so that to a greater or less degree one suffers a change: *to experience a change of heart, bitter disappointment.* UNDERGO usually refers to the bearing or enduring of something hard, difficult, disagreeable, or dangerous: *to undergo severe hardships, an operation.*

ex·pe·ri·enced (Ĭk spĭr′ĭ ənst), *adj.* **1.** having had experience. **2.** having learned through experience; taught by experience. **3.** wise or skillful through experience: *an experienced teacher, general, etc.* —**Syn. 3.** skilled, expert, practiced, veteran.

experience table, *Life Insurance.* actuarial tables. See **mortality table.**

ex·pe·ri·en·tial (Ĭk spĭr′ĭ ĕn′shəl), *adj.* pertaining to or derived from experience. —**ex′pe·ri·en′tial·ly,** *adv.*

ex·per·i·ment (*n.* Ĭk spĕr′ə mənt; *v.* -mĕnt′), *n.* **1.** a test or trial; a tentative procedure; an act or operation for the purpose of discovering something unknown or of testing a principle, supposition, etc.: *a chemical experiment.* **2.** the conducting of such operations; experimentation: *a product that is the result of long experiment.* **3.** *Obs.* experience. —*v.i.* **4.** to try or test in order to find something out: *to experiment with drugs in order to find a cure for a certain disease.* [ME, t. L: s. *experimentum* a trial, test] —**ex·per′i·ment′er,** *n.* —**Syn. 1.** See **trial.**

ex·per·i·men·tal (Ĭk spĕr′ə mĕn′təl), *adj.* **1.** pertaining to, derived from, or founded on experiment: *an experimental science.* **2.** based on or derived from experience; empirical: *experimental religion.* **3.** of the nature of an experiment; tentative. —**ex·per′i·men′tal·ist,** *n.* —**ex·per′i·men′tal·ly,** *adv.*

experimental evolution, the artificial production of new races and even species by experimental transformation of genes and genotypes and by hybridization.

ex·per·i·men·ta·tion (Ĭk spĕr′ə mĕn tā′shən), *n.* act or practice of making experiments; the process of experimenting.

experiment station, an establishment in which experiments in a particular line of research or activity, as agriculture or mining, are systematically carried on.

ex·pert (*n.* ĕks′pûrt; *adj.* Ĭk spûrt′, ĕks′pûrt), *n.* **1.** a person who has special skill or knowledge in some particular field; a specialist; authority: *a language expert, an expert on mining.* —*adj.* **2.** possessing special skill or knowledge; trained by practice; skillful or skilled (often fol. by *in* or *at*): *an expert driver, to be expert at driving a car.* **3.** pertaining to, coming from or characteristic of an expert: *expert work, expert advice.* [ME, t. L: s. *expertus,* pp., having tried] —**ex·pert′ly,** *adv.* —**ex·pert′ness,** *n.* —**Syn. 1.** authority, specialist, connoisseur, master. **2.** experienced, trained, proficient, dexterous, adroit. See **skillful.** —**Ant. 1.** novice. **2.** clumsy.

ex·per·to cre·di·te (ĕks pûr′tō krĕd′ə tē′), *Latin.* believe in the expert; trust one who has had experience.

ex·pi·a·ble (ĕks′pĭ ə bəl), *adj.* that may be expiated.

ex·pi·ate (ĕks′pĭ āt′), *v.t.,* **-ated, -ating.** to atone for; make amends or reparation for. [t. L: m.s. *expiātus,* pp.] —**ex′pi·a′tor,** *n.*

ex·pi·a·tion (ĕks′pĭ ā′shən), *n.* **1.** act of expiating. **2.** the means by which atonement or reparation is made.

ex·pi·a·to·ry (ĕks′pĭ ə tōr′ĭ), *adj.* able to make atonement or expiation; offered by way of expiation.

b., blend of, blended; c., cognate with; d., dialect, dialectal; der., derived from; f., formed from; g., going back to; m., modification of; r., replacing; s., stem of; t., taken from; ?, perhaps.   See the full key on inside cover.

x·pi·ra·tion (ĕk/spə rā/shən), *n.* **1.** a coming to an end; termination; close. **2.** act of expiring, or breathing out; emission of air from the lungs. **3.** *Obs.* death.

x·pir·a·to·ry (ĭk spīr/ə tōr/ĭ), *adj.* pertaining to the expiration of air from the lungs.

x·pire (ĭk spīr/), *v.,* **-pired, -piring.** —*v.i.* **1.** to come to an end; terminate. **2.** to die out, as a fire. **3.** to emit the last breath; die. —*v.t.* **4.** to breathe out; emit (air) from the lungs. **5.** to emit or eject. [ME *expire(n),* ‹ L: m. *ex(s)pīrāre* breathe out] —**ex·pir/er,** *n.*

x·pi·ry (ĭk spī/rĭ, ĕk/spə rĭ), *n., pl.* **-ries.** expiration.

x·plain (ĭk splān/), *v.t.* **1.** to make plain or clear; render intelligible: *to explain an obscure point.* **2.** to make known in detail: *to explain how to do something, to explain a process.* **3.** to assign a meaning to; interpret. **4.** to make clear the cause or reason of; account for. **5.** to dispel (difficulties, etc.) by explanation; nullify the significance, or the apparent significance, of (words, acts, occurrences, etc.) by explanation (fol. by *away*). —*v.i.* **6.** to give an explanation. [t. L: m.s. *explānāre* make plain, flatten out] —**ex·plain/a·ble,** *adj.* —**ex·plain/er,** *n.*

—**Syn. 1.** EXPLAIN, ELUCIDATE, EXPOUND, INTERPRET imply making the meaning of something clear or understandable. To EXPLAIN is to make plain, clear, or intelligible something that is not known or understood: *to explain a theory or a problem.* To ELUCIDATE is to throw light on what before was dark and obscure, usually by illustration and commentary and sometimes by elaborate explanation: *they asked him to elucidate his statement.* To EXPOUND is to give a methodical, detailed, scholarly explanation of something, usually Scriptures, doctrines, or philosophy: *to expound the doctrine of free will.* To INTERPRET is to give the meaning of something by paraphrase, by translation, or by an explanation (sometimes involving one's personal opinion and therefore original), which is often of a systematic and detailed nature: *to interpret a poem or a symbol.*

x·pla·na·tion (ĕk/splə nā/shən), *n.* **1.** act or process of explaining. **2.** that which explains; a statement made to clarify something and make it understandable; an exposition. **3.** a meaning or interpretation: *to find an explanation of a mystery.* **4.** a mutual declaration of the meaning of words spoken, actions, motives, etc., with a view to adjusting a misunderstanding or reconciling differences. [t. L: s. *explānātio*] —**Syn. 1.** elucidation, explication, exposition, definition, interpretation. **3.** solution, key, answer.

x·plan·a·to·ry (ĭk splăn/ə tōr/ĭ), *adj.* serving to explain. Also, **ex·plan/a·tive.** —**ex·plan/a·to/ri·ly,** *adv.*

x·plant (ĕks plănt/, -plänt/), *v.t.* **1.** to take living material from an animal or plant and place it in a culture medium. —*n.* **2.** a piece of explanted tissue. [f. EX-¹ + PLANT]

x·ple·tive (ĕks/plə tĭv), *adj.* **1.** Also, **ex·ple·to·ry** (ĕks/plə tōr/ĭ). added merely to fill out a sentence or line, give emphasis, etc. —*n.* **2.** an expletive syllable, word, or phrase. **3.** an interjectory word or expression, frequently profane; an exclamatory oath. [t. LL: m.s. *explētīvus* serving to fill out] —**ex/ple·tive·ly,** *adv.*

x·pli·ca·ble (ĕks/plĭ kə bəl), *adj.* capable of being explained.

x·pli·cate (ĕks/plə kāt/), *v.t.,* **-cated, -cating. 1.** to develop (a principle, etc.). **2.** to make plain or clear; explain; interpret. [t. L: m.s. *explĭcātus,* pp., unfolded]

x·pli·ca·tion (ĕks/plə kā/shən), *n.* **1.** act of explicating. **2.** an explanation; interpretation.

x·pli·ca·tive (ĕks/plə kā/tĭv, ĭk splĭk/ə tiv), *adj.* explanatory; interpretative. Also, **ex/pli·ca·to/ry.**

x·plic·it (ĭk splĭs/ĭt), *adj.* **1.** leaving nothing merely implied; clearly expressed; unequivocal: *an explicit statement, instruction, etc.* **2.** clearly developed or formulated: *explicit knowledge or belief.* **3.** definite and unreserved in expression; outspoken: *he was quite explicit on that point.* [t. L: s. *explicitus,* var. of *explicātus,* pp., unfolded] —**ex·plic/it·ly,** *adv.* —**ex·plic/it·ness,** *n.* —**Syn. 1.** express, definite, precise, exact, unambiguous. —**Ant. 1.** vague.

x·plode (ĭk splōd/), *v.,* **-ploded, -ploding.** —*v.i.* **1.** to expand with force and noise because of rapid chemical change or decomposition, as gunpowder, nitroglycerine etc. **2.** to burst, fly into pieces, or break up violently with a loud report, as a boiler from excessive pressure of steam. **3.** to burst forth violently, esp. with noise, laughter, violent speech, etc. *Phonet.* (of stop consonants) to end with an explosion so that the end of the consonant is audible, as *t* in *ten.* In *Where's my hat?* the *t* usually does not explode. —*v.t.* **5.** to cause (gunpowder, a boiler, etc.) to explode. **6.** to cause to be rejected, destroy the repute of; discredit or disprove: *to explode a theory.* **7.** *Phonet.* to end with an explosion (def. 6). **8.** *Obs.* to drive (a player, play, etc.) from the stage by loud expressions of disapproval. [t. L: m.s. *explōdere* drive out by clapping] —**ex·plod/er,** *n.*

x·ploit¹ (ĕks/ploit, ĭk sploit/), *n.* a striking or notable deed; a feat; a spirited or heroic act. [ME *esploit,* t. OF, ‹ L *explicitum,* pp. neut., unfolded] —**Syn.** See achievement.

x·ploit² (ĭk sploit/), *v.t.* **1.** to turn to practical account; utilize for profit. **2.** to use selfishly for one's own ends. [ME *exploiten,* t. F: m. *exploiter,* g. L freq. of *explicāre* unfold] —**ex·ploit/a·ble,** *adj.* —**ex·ploit·a·tive** (ĭk sploi/tə tĭv), *adj.*

x·ploi·ta·tion (ĕks/ploi tā/shən), *n.* **1.** utilization for profit. **2.** selfish utilization.

---

ex·ploit·er (ĭk sploi/tər), *n.* **1.** one who exploits. —*v.t.* **2.** exploit².

ex·plo·ra·tion (ĕks/plə rā/shən), *n.* **1.** act of exploring. **2.** the investigation of unknown regions.

ex·plor·a·to·ry (ĭk splôr/ə tōr/ĭ), *adj.* **1.** pertaining to or concerned with exploration. **2.** inclined to make explorations. Also, **ex·plor/a·tive.**

ex·plore (ĭk splōr/), *v.,* **-plored, -ploring.** —*v.t.* **1.** to traverse or range over (a region, etc.) for the purpose of discovery. **2.** to look into closely; scrutinize; examine. **3.** *Surg.* to investigate into, esp. mechanically, as with a probe. **4.** *Obs.* to search for; search out. —*v.i.* **5.** to engage in exploration. [t. L: m.s. *explōrāre*]

ex·plor·er (ĭk splôr/ər), *n.* **1.** one who or that which explores, esp., one who investigates unknown regions. **2.** any instrument used in exploring or sounding a wound, or a cavity in a tooth, etc.

ex·plo·sion (ĭk splō/zhən), *n.* **1.** act of exploding; a violent expansion or bursting with noise, as of gunpowder or a boiler. **2.** the noise itself. **3.** a violent outburst of laughter, anger, etc. **4.** any violent bursting forth. **5.** the burning of the fuel and air mixture in an internal-combustion engine. **6.** *Phonet.* the audible end of a stop consonant at break of closure. See **explode,** def. 4. [t. L: s. *explōsio* a driving off by clapping]

ex·plo·sive (ĭk splō/sĭv), *adj.* **1.** tending or serving to explode: *an explosive substance.* **2.** pertaining to or of the nature of an explosion. **3.** *Phonet.* (of stop consonants) ending with an explosion. See **explode** (def. 4). —*n.* **4.** an explosive agent or substance, as dynamite. **5.** *Phonet.* a stop consonant that ends with an explosion. —**ex·plo/sive·ly,** *adv.* —**ex·plo/sive·ness,** *n.*

ex·po·nent (ĭk spō/nənt), *n.* **1.** one who or that which expounds or explains. **2.** one who or that which stands as a representative, type, or symbol of something: *the exponent of Republican principles.* **3.** *Alg.* a symbol placed above and at the right of another symbol (the base), to denote to what power the latter is to be raised, as in X^3. [t. L: s. *expōnens,* ppr., putting forth]

ex·po·nen·tial (ĕks/pō nĕn/shal), *adj. Alg.* of or pertaining to an exponent or exponents.

ex·po·ni·ble (ĭk spō/na bəl), *adj. Logic.* (esp. of an obscure proposition) admitting or requiring exposition.

ex·port (*v.* ĭk spōrt/, ĕks/pōrt; *n.* ĕks/pōrt), *v.t.* **1.** to send (commodities) to other countries or places for sale, exchange, or gift. —*n.* **2.** act of exporting; exportation. **3.** that which is exported; an article exported. —*adj.* **4.** of or pertaining to exportation of goods or to exportable goods. [t. L: s. *exportāre* carry away] —**ex·port/a·ble,** *adj.* —**ex·port/er,** *n.*

ex·por·ta·tion (ĕks/pōr tā/shən), *n.* **1.** act of exporting; the sending of commodities out of a country, typically in trade. **2.** something exported.

ex·pos·al (ĭk spō/zəl), *n.* exposure.

ex·pose (ĭk spōz/), *v.t.,* **-posed, -posing. 1.** to lay open to danger, attack, harm, etc.: *to expose soldiers to gunfire, to expose one's character to attack.* **2.** to lay open to something specified: *to expose oneself to misunderstanding.* **3.** to uncover or bare to the air, cold, etc., to expose *one's head to the rain.* **4.** to present to view; exhibit; display: *the beggar who exposes his sores.* **5.** to make known, disclose, or reveal (intentions, secrets, etc.); unmask (crime, fraud, an imposter, etc.). **6.** to hold up to public reprehension or ridicule (fault, folly, a fool, etc.). **7.** to put out into an unsheltered or open place, as a child. **8.** to subject, as to the action of something: *to expose photographic plate to light.* [t. OF: m.s. *exposer,* f. *ex-* EX¹ + *poser* put (see POSE), but assoc. with deriv. of L *expōnere* set forth] —**ex·pos/er,** *n.* —**Syn. 1.** subject (to), endanger, imperil, jeopardize. **5.** uncover, unveil, betray. —**Ant. 2.** protect (*from*). **5.** conceal.

ex·po·sé (ĕks/pō zā/), *n.* an exposure, as of something discreditable. [t. F, orig. pp. of *exposer* expose]

ex·posed (ĭk spōzd/), *adj.* **1.** left or being without shelter or protection. **2.** laid open to view; unconcealed. —**ex·pos·ed·ness** (ĭk spō/zĭd nĭs), *n.*

ex·po·si·tion (ĕks/pə zĭsh/ən), *n.* **1.** an exhibition or show, as of the products of art and manufacture. **2.** act of expounding, setting forth, or explaining. **3.** a detailed statement or explanation; an explanatory treatise. **4.** the act of presenting to view; display. **5.** act of putting out or abandoning in an unsheltered place: *the exposition of children.* **6.** state of being exposed. —**Syn. 3.** explanation, elucidation, commentary.

ex·pos·i·tor (ĭk spŏz/ə tər), *n.* one who expounds, or gives an exposition. [t. L; r. ME *exposit(o)ur,* t. AF]

ex·pos·i·to·ry (ĭk spŏz/ə tōr/ĭ), *adj.* serving to expound, set forth, or explain. Also, **ex·pos/i·tive.**

ex post fac·to (ĕks/ pōst/ făk/tō), *Latin.* from or by subsequent action; subsequently; retrospectively.

ex post facto law, one passed after an alleged crime has been committed which, if applied in the case of an accused person, would work to his disadvantage.

ex·pos·tu·late (ĭk spŏs/chə lāt/), *v.i.,* **-lated, -lating.** to reason earnestly with a person against something he intends to do or has done; remonstrate (fol. by *about, for, on,* or *upon*): *to expostulate with him on (or about) the impropriety.* [t. L: m.s. *expostulātus,* pp.] —**ex·pos/tu·lat/ing·ly,** *adv.* —**ex·pos/tu·la/tor,** *n.*

ex·pos·tu·la·tion (ĭk spŏs/chə lā/shən), *n.* **1.** act of expostulating; remonstrance; earnest and kindly protest. **2.** an expostulatory remark or address.

---

t, āble, dâre, ärt; ĕbb, ēqual; Ĭf, īce; hŏt, ōver, ôrder, oil, bŏŏk, ōoze, out; ŭp, ūse, ûrge; ə = a in alone; n, chief; g, give; ng, ring; sh, shoe; th, thin; ŧh, that; zh, vision.   See the full key on inside cover.

ex·pos·tu·la·to·ry (Ĭk spŏs′chə lə tōr′Ĭ), *adj.* expostulating; conveying expostulation. Also, **ex·pos′tu·la′tive.**

ex·po·sure (Ĭk spō′zhər), *n.* **1.** act of exposing. **2.** disclosure, as of something private or secret; unmasking, as of crime, fraud, an impostor, etc. **3.** presentation to view, esp. in an open or public manner. **4.** a laying open or subjecting to the action or influence of something: *exposure to the weather, to danger, or to ridicule.* **5.** *Photog.* act of presenting a sensitive material as film, plate, or paper, to the action of the actinic rays of light: *the exposure was too long.* **6.** a putting out without shelter or protection, as of an abandoned child. **7.** state of being exposed. **8.** situation with regard to sunlight or wind; aspect: *a southern exposure.* **9.** something exposed, as to view; an exposed surface. [f. EXPOS(E) + -URE] —**Syn. 2.** divulgement, revelation, exposé.

exposure meter, *Photog.* an instrument which measures the light intensity and indicates the proper exposure for a given scene.

ex·pound (Ĭk spound′), *v.t.* **1.** to set forth or state in detail: *to expound theories, principles, etc.* **2.** to explain; interpret. [ME *expoune(n), expounde(n),* t. OF: m. *espondre,* g. L *exponere* put out, expose, set forth, explain] —**ex·pound′er,** *n.* —**Syn. 2.** See **explain.**

ex·pres·i·dent (ĕks′prĕz′ə dənt), *n.* a former president.

ex·press (Ĭk sprĕs′), *v.t.* **1.** to put (thought) into words: *to express an idea clearly.* **2.** to show, manifest, or reveal: *to express one's feeling.* **3.** **express oneself,** to set forth one's opinion, meaning, feeling, etc., in words. **4.** to represent by a symbol, character, figure, or formula, or as a symbol or the like does. **5.** *U.S.* to send express: *to express a package or merchandise.* **6.** to press or squeeze out: *to express the juice of grapes.* **7.** to exude or emit (a liquid, odor, etc.) as if under pressure. —*adj.* **8.** clearly indicated; distinctly stated (rather than implied); definite, explicit; plain. **9.** special: *an express purpose.* **10.** duly or exactly formed or represented: *an express image.* **11.** pertaining to an express: *an express agency.* **12.** specially direct or fast, as a train, highway, etc. —*adv.* **13.** by express: *to travel express.* **14.** specially; for a particular purpose. —*n.* **15.** an express train, bus, elevator, etc. **16.** a messenger or a message specially sent. **17.** a system or method of sending parcels, money, etc.: *to send a package by express.* **18.** a company engaged in this business. **19.** that which is sent by express. [ME *expresse,* t. L: m.s. *expressus,* pp., pressed out, described] —**ex·press′er,** *n.* —**ex·press′i·ble,** *adj.* —**Syn. 1.** utter, declare, state. **4.** indicate, designate. —**Ant. 1.** imply.

ex·press·age (Ĭk sprĕs′Ĭj), *n.* **1.** the business of transmitting parcels, money, etc., by express. **2.** the charge for such transmission.

express delivery, *Brit.* special delivery.

ex·pres·sion (Ĭk sprĕsh′ən), *n.* **1.** act of expressing or setting forth in words: *the expression of opinions, facts, etc.* **2.** a particular word, phrase, or form of words: *archaic expressions.* **3.** the manner or form in which a thing is expressed in words; wording; phrasing. **4.** power of expressing in words: *joy beyond expression.* **5.** indication of feeling, spirit, character, etc., as on the face, in the voice, or in artistic execution. **6.** a look or intonation as expressing feeling, etc.: *a sad expression.* **7.** quality or power of expressing feeling, etc.: *a face that lacks expression.* **8.** act of expressing or representing, as by symbols. **9.** *Math.* a symbol or a combination of symbols serving to express something. **10.** act of expressing or pressing out. —**ex·pres′sion·less,** *adj.* —**Syn. 1.** utterance, declaration, assertion, statement. **2.** phrase, term. **3.** language, diction, phraseology. **5.** manifestation, sign. **6.** aspect, air.

ex·pres·sion·ism (Ĭk sprĕsh′ə nĬz′əm), *n.* a theory of art originating in Europe about the time of World War I, which aimed at the free expression of the artist's emotional reactions rather than the representation of the natural appearance of objects. —**ex·pres′sion·ist,** *n., adj.* —**ex·pres′sion·is′tic,** *adj.*

ex·pres·sive (Ĭk sprĕs′Ĭv), *adj.* **1.** serving to express; indicative of power to express: *a look expressive of gratitude.* **2.** full of expression, as the face or voice. **3.** pertaining to or concerned with the expression. —**ex·pres′sive·ly,** *adv.* —**ex·pres′sive·ness,** *n.* —**Syn. 1.** EXPRESSIVE, MEANING, SIGNIFICANT, SUGGESTIVE imply the conveying of a thought, indicating an attitude of mind, or the like, by words or otherwise. EXPRESSIVE suggests conveying, or being capable of conveying a thought, intention, emotion, etc. in an effective or vivid manner: *an expressive shrug.* MEANING and SIGNIFICANT imply an underlying and unexpressed thought whose existence is plainly shown although its precise nature is left to conjecture. MEANING implies a more secret and intimate understanding between the persons involved: *meaning looks passed between them.* SIGNIFICANT suggests calling the attention of a person or persons to a happening which is important in some way to them or to others: *on hearing this statement, he gave the officers a significant glance.* SUGGESTIVE implies an indirect or covert conveying of a meaning, sometimes mentally stimulating, sometimes verging on impropriety or indecency: *a suggestive story or remark.*

express letter, *Brit.* special delivery letter.

ex·press·ly (Ĭk sprĕs′lĬ), *adv.* **1.** in an express manner; explicitly. **2.** for the express purpose; specially.

ex·press·man (Ĭk sprĕs′mən), *n., pl.* **-men.** **1.** one engaged in the express business. **2.** a man who makes collections or deliveries for an express company.

ex·press·way (Ĭk′sprĕs′wā), *n.* a highway designed for express traffic.

ex·pro·pri·ate (ĕks prō′prĬ āt′), *v.t.,* **-ated, -ating. 1.** to take or condemn, esp. for public use by the right of eminent domain, thus divesting the title of the private owner. **2.** to dispossess (a person) of ownership. [t. LL: m.s. *expropriātus,* pp., deprived of property, der. L *ex- EX-¹ + proprium* property] —**ex·pro′pri·a′tion,** *n.* —**ex·pro′pri·a′tor,** *n.*

ex·pul·sion (Ĭk spŭl′shən), *n.* **1.** act of driving out or expelling. **2.** state of being expelled. [t. L: s. *expulsio*] —**ex·pul′sive** (Ĭk spŭl′sĬv), *adj.* tending or serving to expel.

ex·punc·tion (Ĭk spŭngk′shən), *n.* act of expunging; an erasure. [f. s. L *expunctus,* pp., struck out + -ION]

ex·punge (Ĭk spŭnj′), *v.t.,* **-punged, -punging. 1.** to strike or blot out; erase; obliterate. **2.** to efface; wipe out or destroy. [t. L: m.s. *expungere* prick out, strike out] —**ex·pung′er,** *n.*

ex·pur·gate (ĕks′pər gāt′, Ĭk spûr′gāt), *v.t.,* **-gated, -gating. 1.** to amend by removing offensive or objectionable matter: *to expurgate a book.* **2.** to purge or cleanse. [t. L: m.s. *expurgātus,* pp., purged] —**ex·pur·ga′tion,** *n.* —**ex′pur·ga′tor,** *n.*

ex·pur·ga·to·ri·al (Ĭk spûr′gə tōr′Ĭ əl), *adj.* pertaining to an expurgator or to expurgation.

ex·pur·ga·to·ry (Ĭk spûr′gə tōr′Ĭ), *adj.* serving to expurgate; of or pertaining to expurgation.

Expurgatory Index. See *index* (def. 10).

ex·qui·site (ĕks′kwĬ zĬt, Ĭk skwĬz′Ĭt), *adj.* **1.** of peculiar beauty or charm, or rare and appealing excellence, as a face, a flower, coloring, music, poetry, etc. **2.** extraordinarily fine, admirable, or consummate. **3.** intense, acute, or keen, as pleasure, pain, etc. **4.** keenly or delicately sensitive or responsive: *an exquisite ear for music.* **5.** of rare excellence of production or execution, as works of art, workmanship, or the artist or worker. **6.** of peculiar refinement or elegance, as taste, manners, etc., or persons. **7.** *Obs.* carefully sought out, chosen, ascertained, devised, etc. —*n.* **8.** a person, esp. a man, who is overnice in dress, etc.; a dandy; a coxcomb. [ME, t. L: m.s. *exquisitus,* pp., sought out] —**ex′qui·site·ly,** *adv.* —**ex′qui·site·ness,** *n.* —**Syn. 1.** dainty, beautiful, elegant, rare. See **delicate. 2.** perfect, matchless. See **fine¹.** —**Ant. 1.** gross. **2.** ordinary.

exr., executor.

ex·san·guine (ĕks săng′gwĬn), *adj.* anemic.

ex·scind (ĕk sĬnd′), *v.t.* to cut out or off. [t. L: s. *exscindere*]

ex·sect (ĕk sĕkt′), *v.t.* to cut out. [t. L: s. *exsectus,* pp.] —**ex·sec′tion,** *n.*

ex·sert (ĕks sûrt′), *v.t.* **1.** to thrust out. —*adj.* **2.** exserted. [t. L: s. *exsertus,* pp., put forth] —**ex·ser′tion,** *n.*

ex·sert·ed (ĕks sûr′tĬd), *adj. Biol.* projecting beyond the surrounding parts, as a stamen.

ex·ser·tile (ĕks sûr′təl, -tĬl), *adj. Biol.* capable of being exserted or protruded.

ex·ser·vice·man (ĕks′-sûr′vĬs măn′), *n., pl.* **-men** (-mĕn′). one who has served in one of the armed services, esp. during wartime. Ex-serviceman has greater currency in England, where *veteran* is not used in this sense.

ex·sic·cate (ĕk′sə kāt′), *v.t.,* **-cated, -cating. 1.** to dry or remove the moisture from, as a substance. **2.** to dry up, as moisture. [t. L: m.s. *exsiccātus,* pp.] —**ex·sic·ca′tion,** *n.* —**ex′sic·ca′tive,** *adj.* —**ex′sic·ca′tor,** *n.*

ex·stip·u·late (ĕks stĬp′yŏŏ lĬt, -lāt′), *adj. Bot.* without stipules. Also, **estipulate.**

ext., **1.** extension. **2.** external. **3.** extinct. **4.** extra.

ex·tant (ĕks′tənt, Ĭk stănt′), *adj.* **1.** in existence; still existing; not destroyed or lost. **2.** *Archaic.* standing out; protruding. [t. L: s. *ex(s)tans,* ppr., standing out]

ex·tem·po·ral (Ĭk stĕm′pə rəl), *adj. Obs.* or *Archaic.* extemporaneous; extempore. [t. L: s. *extemporālis*]

ex·tem·po·ra·ne·ous (Ĭk stĕm′pə rā′nĬ əs), *adj.* **1.** done or spoken extempore; impromptu: *an extemporaneous speech.* **2.** speaking or performing extempore. **3.** made for the occasion, as a shelter. [t. LL: m. *extemporāneus,* r. L *extemporālis*] —**ex·tem′po·ra′ne·ous·ly,** *adv.* —**ex·tem′po·ra′ne·ous·ness,** *n.* —**Syn. 1.** EXTEMPORANEOUS (EXTEMPORARY, EXTEMPORE), IMPROMPTU, IMPROVISED are used of (artistic) expression given without preparation or based on only partial preparation. EXTEMPORANEOUS, though often used interchangeably with IMPROMPTU, is applied esp. to an unmemorized speech given from an outline or notes: *an extemporaneous discussion.* IMPROMPTU is applied to a speech (poem, song, etc.) delivered without preparation and at a moment's notice: *called upon without warning, she nevertheless gave an excellent impromptu speech.* IMPROVISED is applied to that which is composed (recited, sung, acted) on a particular occasion, and is made up, at least in part, as one goes along: *an improvised piano accompaniment.* —**Ant. 1.** memorized.

ex·tem·po·rar·y (Ĭk stĕm′pə rĕr′ĭ), *adj.* **1.** extemporaneous; extempore. **2.** *Obs.* sudden; unexpected. —**ex·tem′po·rar′i·ly,** *adv.* —**ex·tem′po·rar′i·ness,** *n.* —**Syn. 1.** See **extemporaneous.**

ex·tem·po·re (Ĭk stĕm′pə rĬ), *adv.* **1.** on the spur of the moment; without premeditation or preparation; offhand. **2.** without notes: *to speak extempore.* **3.** (of musical performance) by improvisation. —*adj.* **4.** extemporaneous. [t. L: *ex tempore,* lit., out of the time] —**Syn. 4.** See **extemporaneous.**

x·tem·po·rize (ĭk stĕm′pə rīz′), v., **-rized, -rizing.** —v.i. 1. to speak extempore. 2. to sing, or play on an instrument, composing the music as one proceeds; improvise. —v.t. 3. to make or devise for the occasion. 4. *Music.* to compose offhand; improvise. —**ex·tem′- po·ri·za′tion,** n. —**ex·tem′po·riz′er,** n.

x·tend (ĭk stĕnd′), v.t. 1. to stretch out; draw out to the full length. 2. to stretch, draw, or arrange in a given direction, or so as to reach a particular point, as a cord or a line of troops. 3. to stretch forth or hold out, as the arm or hand. 4. to place at full length, esp. horizontally, as the body, limbs, etc. 5. to increase the length or duration of; lengthen; prolong. 6. to stretch out in various or all directions; expand; spread out in area. 7. to enlarge the scope of, or make more comprehensive, as operations or influence. 8. to hold forth as an offer or grant; offer; grant; give. 9. *Finance.* to postpone (the payment of a debt) beyond the time originally agreed upon. 10. *Com.* to transfer (figures) from one column to another in bookkeeping; invoices, etc. 11. *Law.* a. to assess or value. b. to make a seizure or levy upon, as land, by a writ of extent. 12. *Obs.* to take by seizure. 13. *Obs.* to exaggerate. —v.i. 14. to be or become extended; stretch out; to be continued in length or duration, or in various or all directions. 15. to reach, as to a particular point. 16. to increase in length, area, scope, etc. [ME *extend*(en), t. L: m. *extendere*] —**ex·tend′i·ble,** adj. —Syn. 5. prolong, protract, continue. See **lengthen.** 6. spread, enlarge, widen. 8. bestow, impart.

x·tend·ed (ĭk stĕn′dĭd), adj. 1. stretched out. 2. continued or prolonged. 3. spread out. 4. widespread or extensive; having extension or spatial magnitude. 5. outstretched. 6. *Print.* (of type) expanded. —**ex·tend′ed·ly,** adv.

x·ten·si·ble (ĭk stĕn′sə bəl), adj. capable of being extended. —**ex·ten′si·bil′i·ty, ex·ten′si·ble·ness,** n.

x·ten·sile (ĭk stĕn′səl), adj. *Chiefly Zool., Anat.* capable of being extended; adapted for stretching out; extensible; protrusible.

x·ten·sim·e·ter (ĕks′tĕn sĭm′ə tər), n. extensometer.

x·ten·sion (ĭk stĕn′shən), n. 1. act of extending. 2. state of being extended. 3. that by which something is extended; a prolongation, as an addition to a house. 4. something extended; an extended object or space. 5. range of extending; degree of extensiveness; extent. 6. *Com.* a written engagement on the part of a creditor, allowing a debtor further time to pay a debt. 7. *Physics.,* etc. that property of a body by which it occupies a portion of space. 8. *Anat.* a. act of straightening a limb. b. the position which a limb assumes when it is straightened. 9. *Surg.* act of pulling the broken or dislocated part of a limb in a direction from the trunk, in order to bring the ends of the bone into their natural situation. 10. *Logic.* the class of things to which a term is applicable; denotation: *the extension of the term "man" consists of the class, of such individuals as "Socrates," "Plato," "Aristotle,"* etc. [t. L: s. *extensio*] —**ex·ten′sion·al,** adj. —Syn. 1. stretching, expansion, enlargement. —Ant. 1. contraction.

xtension courses, (in many universities and colleges) a program for persons not regularly enrolled as students, frequently provided through evening classes or classes in off-campus centers, or by correspondence.

x·ten·si·ty (ĭk stĕn′sə tĭ), n. 1. the quality of having extension. 2. *Psychol.* that attribute of sensation from which the perception of extension is developed.

x·ten·sive (ĭk stĕn′sĭv), adj. 1. of great extent; wide; broad: *an extensive area.* 2. far-reaching; comprehensive; thorough: *extensive knowledge, extensive inquiries.* 3. pertaining to a system of agriculture involving the use or cultivation of large areas of land (as where land is cheap) with a minimum of labor and expense (opposed to *intensive*). —**ex·ten′sive·ly,** adv. —**ex·ten′sive·ness,** n. —Syn. 1. extended, large, spacious, ample, vast. —Ant. 1. limited. 2. intensive.

x·ten·som·e·ter (ĕks′tĕn sŏm′ə tər), n. *Mach.* an apparatus for measuring minute degrees of expansion, contraction, or deformation. Also, **extensimeter.** [f. s. L *extensus*, pp., extended + (-o)METER]

x·ten·sor (ĭk stĕn′sər, -sôr), n. a muscle which serves to extend or straighten a part of the body (opposed to *flexor*). [t. LL: one who or that which stretches]

x·tent (ĭk stĕnt′), n. 1. the space or degree to which a thing extends; length, area, or volume: *the extent of a line, to the full extent of his power.* 2. something extended; an extended space; a particular length, area, or volume; something having extension. 3. *U.S. Law.* a writ, or a levy, by which a creditor has his debtor's lands valued and transferred to himself, absolutely or for a term of years. 4. *Eng. Law.* a. a writ to recover debts of record due to the crown, under which land, etc., may be seized. b. a seizure made under such a writ. 5. *Brit. Hist.* assessment or valuation, as of land. 6. *Logic.* extension. [ME *extente*, t. AF, ult. der. L *extendere* extend] —Syn. 1. magnitude, measure, amount, scope, compass, range, expanse, stretch, reach. See size.

x·ten·u·ate (ĭk stĕn′yōō āt′), v.t., **-ated, -ating.** 1. to represent (fault, offense, etc.) as less serious: *to extenuate a crime.* 2. to serve to make (fault, offense, etc.) seem less serious: *extenuating circumstances.* 3. to underestimate, underrate, or make light of. 4. *Archaic.* a. to

make thin, lean, or emaciated. b. to reduce the consistence or density of. [t. L: m.s. *extenuātus*, pp., made thin] —**ex·ten′u·at′ing·ly,** adv. —**ex·ten′u·a′tive,** adj. —**ex·ten′u·a′tor,** n.

ex·ten·u·a·tion (ĭk stĕn′yōō ā′shən), n. 1. act of extenuating 2. state of being extenuated. 3. that which extenuates; a partial excuse.

ex·ten·u·a·to·ry (ĭk stĕn′yōō ə tōr′ĭ), adj. tending to extenuate; characterized by extenuation.

ex·te·ri·or (ĭk stĭr′ĭ ər), adj. 1. outer; being on the outer side: *the exterior side or surface, exterior decorations.* 2. situated or being outside; pertaining to or connected with what is outside: *the exterior possessions of a country.* 3. *Geom.* (of an angle) outer, as an angle formed outside two parallel lines when cut by a third line. See diag. under **interior.** —n. 4. the outer surface or part; the outside. 5. (pl.) externals. [t. L, compar. of *exter, exterus* outer, outward] —**ex·te′ri·or·ly,** adv. —Syn. 1. outward, outside. 2. outlying, extraneous. —Ant. 1. interior.

ex·ter·mi·nate (ĭk stûr′mə nāt′), v.t., **-nated, -nating.** to get rid of by destroying; destroy totally; extirpate. [t. L: m.s. *extermīnātus*, pp., driven beyond the boundaries] —**ex·ter′mi·na′tion,** n. —**ex·ter′mi·na′tor,** n. —Syn. eradicate, abolish, annihilate.

ex·ter·mi·na·to·ry (ĭk stûr′mə nə tōr′ĭ), adj. serving or tending to exterminate. Also, **ex·ter·mi·na·tive** (ĭk stûr′mə nā′tĭv).

ex·tern (ĕks′tûrn, ĭk stûrn′), n. *Brit.* a person connected with an institution but not residing in it. [t. L: s. *externus* outward]

ex·ter·nal (ĭk stûr′nəl), adj. 1. of or pertaining to the outside or outer part; outer. 2. to be applied to the outside of a body, as a remedy. 3. situated or being outside of something; acting or coming from without. 4. pertaining to the outward or visible appearance or show: *external acts of worship.* 5. pertaining to or concerned with what is outside or foreign: *external commerce.* 6. *Zool., Anat.* on the side farthest away from the body, from the median line, or from the center of a radially symmetrical form. 7. *Metaphys.* belonging or pertaining to the world of things, considered as independent of the perceiving mind. —n. 8. the outside; outer surface. 9. that which is external. 10. (pl.) external features, circumstances, etc.: *the externals of religion.* [f. EXTERN + -AL¹] —**ex·ter′nal·ly,** adv.

ex·ter·nal-com·bus·tion (ĭk stûr′nəl kəm bŭs′chən), adj. of or pertaining to an engine in which the ignition of the fuel mixture takes place outside the engine cylinder (as distinct from an *internal-combustion engine*).

ex·ter·nal·ism (ĭk stûr′nə lĭz′əm), n. 1. attention or devotion to externals; undue regard to externals, esp. in religion. 2. *Philos.* realism. —**ex·ter′nal·ist,** n.

ex·ter·nal·i·ty (ĕk′stər năl′ə tĭ), n., pl.**-ties.** 1. state or quality of being external. 2. something external; an outward feature. 3. undue regard to externals.

ex·ter·nal·ize (ĭk stûr′nə līz′), v.t., **-ized, -izing.** to make external; embody in an outward form. —**ex·ter′nal·i·za′tion,** n.

ex·ter·o·cep·tive (ĕk′stər ə sĕp′tĭv), adj. *Physiol.* pertaining to exteroceptors, the stimuli impinging upon them, and the nerve impulses initiated by them. [f. *extero-* (comb. form of L *exterus* exterior) + *-ceptive,* as in RECEPTIVE]

ex·ter·o·cep·tor (ĕk′stər ə sĕp′tər), n. *Physiol.* a sense organ, as the nose, eyes, ears, or skin, responding to and conveying stimuli from the external environment. [f. *extero-* + -CEPTOR. See EXTEROCEPTIVE]

ex·ter·ri·to·ri·al (ĕks′tĕr ə tōr′ĭ əl), adj. extraterritorial. —**ex·ter·ri·to′ri·al·i·ty,** n. —**ex′ter·ri·to′- ri·al·ly,** adv.

ex·tinct (ĭk stĭngkt′), adj. 1. extinguished; quenched; having ceased eruption, as a volcano. 2. obsolete, as an institution. 3. having come to an end; without a living representative, as a species. [ME *extincte,* t. L: m.s. *extinctus,* pp., destroyed, put out] —Syn. 3. See **dead.**

ex·tinc·tion (ĭk stĭngk′shən), n. 1. act of extinguishing. 2. fact of being extinguished; condition of being extinct. 3. suppression; abolition; annihilation. 4. *Biol.* a becoming extinct; a coming to an end or dying out.

ex·tinc·tive (ĭk stĭngk′tĭv), adj. tending or serving to extinguish.

ex·tin·guish (ĭk stĭng′gwĭsh), v.t. 1. to put out (a fire, light, etc.); put out the flame of (something burning or lighted). 2. to put an end to or bring to an end; wipe out of existence: *to extinguish a hope, a life, etc.* 3. to obscure or eclipse, as by superior brilliancy. 4. *Law.* to discharge (a debt), as by payment. [f. s. L *ex*(s)*tinguere* put out, quench, destroy + -ISH²] —**ex·tin′guish·a·ble,** adj. —**ex·tin′guish·ment,** n.

ex·tin·guish·er (ĭk stĭng′gwĭsh ər), n. 1. one who or that which extinguishes. 2. any of various portable apparatuses for extinguishing fire: *a chemical extinguisher.*

ex·tir·pate (ĕk′stər pāt′, ĭk stûr′pāt), v.t., **-pated, -pating.** 1. to remove utterly; destroy totally; exterminate; do away with. 2. to pull up by the roots; root up. [t. L: m.s. *ex*(s)*tirpātus,* pp., rooted out] —**ex′tir·pa′tion,** n. —**ex′tir·pa′tive,** adj. —**ex′tir·pa′tor,** n.

ex·tol (ĭk stōl′, -stŏl′), v.t., **-tolled, -tolling.** to praise highly; laud; eulogize. Also, *esp. Brit.,* **ex·toll′.** [t. L: m.s. *extollere,* lit., lift out or up] —**ex·tol′ler,** n. —**ex·tol′ment,** n. —Syn. commend, glorify. —Ant. disparage.

ct, āble, dâre, ärt; ĕbb, ēqual; ĭf, īce; hŏt, ōver, ôrder, oil, bŏŏk, ōōze, out; ŭp, ūse, ûrge; ə = a in alone; ℏ, chief; g, give; ng, ring; sh, shoe; th, thin; ℏ, that; zh, vision. See the full key on inside cover.

ex·tort (ĭkstôrt′), *v.t.* **1.** *Law.* **a.** to wrest or wring (something) from a person by violence, intimidation, or abuse of authority; obtain (money, information, etc.) by force, torture, threat, or the like. **b.** to take illegally under cover of office. **2.** to charge excessively for. [t. L: s. *extortus*, pp., twisted or wrested out] —**ex·tort′er,** *n.* —**ex·tor′tive,** *adj.* —**Syn. 1.** See **extract.**

ex·tor·tion (ĭkstôr′shən), *n.* **1.** act of extorting. **2.** *Law.* the crime of obtaining money or other things of value under color of office, when none is due or not so much is due, or before it is due. **3.** oppressive or illegal exaction, as of excessive price or interest. **4.** anything extorted. [ME, t. L: s. *extortio*]

ex·tor·tion·ar·y (ĭkstôr′shə nĕr′ĭ), *adj.* characterized by or given to extortion.

ex·tor·tion·ate (ĭkstôr′shən ĭt), *adj.* **1.** exorbitant; grossly excessive: *extortionate prices.* **2.** characterized by extortion, as persons. —**ex·tor′tion·ate·ly,** *adv.*

ex·tor·tion·er (ĭkstôr′shən ər), *n.* one who practices extortion. Also, **ex·tor′tion·ist.**

ex·tra (ĕks′trə), *adj.* **1.** beyond or more than what is usual, expected, or necessary; additional: *an extra edition of a newspaper, an extra price.* **2.** larger or better than what is usual: *an extra binding.* —*n.* **3.** something extra or additional. **4.** an additional expense. **5.** an edition of a newspaper other than the regular edition or editions. **6.** something of superior quality. **7.** *Motion Pictures.* a person hired by the day to play a minor part, as a member of a mob or crowd. **8.** an additional worker. **9.** (*usually pl.*) *Cricket.* a score or run not made from the bat, as a bye or a wide. —*adv.* **10.** in excess of the usual or specified amount: *an extra high price.* **11.** beyond the ordinary degree; unusually; uncommonly: *done extra well.* [prob. orig. short for EXTRAORDINARY. Cf. EXTRA-]

extra-, a prefix meaning "outside," "beyond," "besides," freely used as an English formative, as in *extrajudicial, extraterritorial,* and many other words mostly self-explanatory, as *extra-atmospheric,* etc. Also, **extro-.** [t. L, comb. form of *extrā,* adv. and prep., outside (of), without]

ex·tra·bold (ĕks′trə bōld′), *n.* *Print.* unusually heavy boldface.

ex·tra·ca·non·i·cal (ĕks′trə kə nŏn′ə kəl), *adj.* *Eccles.* not included in the canon of Scripture.

ex·tra·cel·lu·lar (ĕks′trə sĕl′yə lər), *adj.* *Biol.* outside a cell or cells.

ex·tra·con·densed (ĕks′trə kən dĕnst′), *adj.* *Print.* (of type) having an extremely narrow face.

ex·tract (*v.* ĭkstrăkt′; *n.* ĕks′trăkt), *v.t.* **1.** to draw forth or get out by force: *to extract a tooth.* **2.** to deduce (a doctrine, principle, etc.). **3.** to derive or obtain (pleasure, comfort, etc.) from a particular source. **4.** to take or copy out (matter from a book, etc.), or make excerpts from (the book, etc.). **5.** to extort (information, money, etc.). **6.** to separate or obtain (a juice, ingredient, principle, etc.) from a mixture by pressure, distillation, treatment with solvents, or the like. **7.** *Math.* to determine (the root of a quantity). —*n.* **8.** something extracted. **9.** a passage taken from a book, etc.; an excerpt; a quotation. **10.** a solution or preparation containing the active principles of a drug, plant juice, or the like. **11.** a solid or viscid substance extracted from a drug, plant, or the like. [t. L: s. *extractus,* pp., drawn out] —**ex·tract′a·ble, ex·tract′i·ble,** *adj.* —**Syn. 1.** pull out, pry out. **5.** evoke, educe, draw out, elicit. EXTRACT, EXACT, EXTORT, WREST imply using force to remove something. To EXTRACT is to draw forth something as by pulling, importuning, and the like: *to extract a confession by using third degree methods.* To EXACT is to impose a penalty, or to obtain by force or authority, something to which one lays claim: *to exact payment, obedience.* To EXTORT is usually to wring something by intimidation or threats from an unwilling person: *to extort money by threats of blackmail.* To WREST is to take by force or violence in spite of active resistance: *the courageous minority wrested the power from their oppressors.* **6.** withdraw, distill.

ex·trac·tion (ĭkstrăk′shən), *n.* **1.** act of extracting. **2.** state or fact of being extracted. **3.** descent or lineage: *to be of foreign extraction.* **4.** something extracted; an extract.

ex·trac·tive (ĭkstrăk′tĭv), *adj.* **1.** tending or serving to extract. **2.** that may be extracted. —*n.* **3.** something extracted.

ex·trac·tor (ĭkstrăk′tər), *n.* **1.** a person or a thing that extracts. **2.** the mechanism in a firearm or cannon which, after firing, pulls an empty or unfired cartridge or shell case out of the chamber of the weapon and brings it into place for action by the ejector.

ex·tra·cur·ric·u·lar (ĕks′trə kə rĭk′yə lər), *adj.* **1.** outside the regular curriculum. **2.** referring, designating, or pertaining to those phases of school activities not taught in the classroom, though functioning under the guidance of the faculty, as sports, clubs, etc.

ex·tra·dit·a·ble (ĕks′trə dī′tə bəl), *adj.* subject to, or subjecting one to, extradition: *an extraditable offense.*

ex·tra·dite (ĕks′trə dīt′), *v.t.,* -dited, -diting. **1.** to give up (a fugitive or prisoner) to another nation or authority. **2.** to obtain the extradition of. [back formation from EXTRADITION]

ex·tra·di·tion (ĕks′trə dĭsh′ən), *n.* the surrender of a fugitive from justice or a prisoner by one state or authority to another. [t. F, f. L: *ex-* EX-¹ + s. *trāditio* a giving over]

ex·tra·dos (ĕks trā′dŏs), *n.* *Archit.* the exterior curve or surface of an arch or vault. See diag. under **arch.** [t. F, f. L *extra-* EXTRA- + F *dos* back (g. L *dorsum*)]

ex·tra·ju·di·cial (ĕks′trə jōō dĭsh′əl), *adj.* outside of judicial proceedings; beyond the action or authority of a court. —**ex′tra·ju·di′cial·ly,** *adv.*

ex·tra·mun·dane (ĕks′trə mŭn′dān), *adj.* beyond our world or the material universe.

ex·tra·mu·ral (ĕks′trə myŏŏr′əl), *adj.* outside the walls or boundaries, as of a city or town or a university.

ex·tra·ne·ous (ĭkstrā′nĭ əs), *adj.* introduced or coming from without; not belonging or proper to a thing; external; foreign. [t. L: m. *extrāneus* that is without, foreign] —**ex·tra′ne·ous·ly,** *adv.* —**ex·tra′ne·ous·ness,** *n.* —**Syn.** extrinsic, adventitious, alien.

ex·traor·di·nar·y (ĭkstrôr′də nĕr′ĭ, ĕks′trə ôr′də nĕr′ĭ), *adj.* **1.** beyond what is ordinary; out of the regular or established order: *extraordinary power or expenses.* **2.** exceptional in character, amount, extent, degree, etc.; unusual; remarkable: *extraordinary weather, weight, speed, an extraordinary man or book.* **3.** (of officials, etc.) outside of, additional to, or ranking below an ordinary one: *an extraordinary professor.* [t. L: m.s. *extrāordinārius* out of the common order] —**ex·traor′di·nar′i·ly,** *adv.* —**ex·traor′di·nar′i·ness,** *n.* —**Syn. 2.** uncommon, exceptional, singular, rare, phenomenal.

ex·trap·o·late (ĕks′trə pə lāt′, ĕks trăp′ə lāt′), *v.t., v.i.,* -lated, -lating. *Statistics.* to estimate a quantity which depends on one or more variables by extending the variables beyond their established ranges. —**ex·trap·o·la·tion** (ĕks′trə pō lā′shən, ĕks trăp′ə-), *n.*

ex·tra·pro·fes·sion·al (ĕks′trə prə fĕsh′ən əl), *adj.* outside ordinary limits of professional interest or duty.

ex·tra·sen·so·ry (ĕks′trə sĕn′sə rĭ), *adj.* outside of the normal sense perception.

ex·tra·ter·ri·to·ri·al (ĕks′trə tĕr′ə tōr′ĭ əl), *adj.* **1.** beyond local territorial jurisdiction, as the status of persons resident in a country but not subject to its laws. **2.** pertaining to such persons. Also, **exterritorial.** [t. NL *extrā territōri(um)* outside the domain + -AL¹] —**ex′tra·ter′ri·to′ri·al·ly,** *adv.*

ex·tra·ter·ri·to·ri·al·i·ty (ĕks′trə tĕr′ə tōr′ĭ ăl′ə tĭ), *n.* the possession or exercise of political rights by a foreign power within a state having its own government.

ex·tra·u·ter·ine (ĕks′trə ū′tər ĭn, -tə rīn′), *adj.* being beyond or outside of the uterus.

ex·trav·a·gance (ĭkstrăv′ə gəns), *n.* **1.** excessive expenditure or outlay of money. **2.** an instance of this. **3.** unrestrained or fantastic excess, as of actions, opinions, etc. **4.** an extravagant action, notion, etc. —**Syn. 2.** lavishness, profusion. —**Ant. 1.** frugality.

ex·trav·a·gan·cy (ĭkstrăv′ə gən sĭ), *n., pl.* -cies. extravagance.

ex·trav·a·gant (ĭkstrăv′ə gənt), *adj.* **1.** going beyond prudence or necessity in expenditure; wasteful: *an extravagant person.* **2.** exorbitant: *extravagant expenses or prices.* **3.** exceeding the bounds of reason, as actions, demands, opinions, passions, etc. **4.** *Obs.* wandering beyond bounds. [ME, t. ML: s. *extrāvagans,* ppr. of *extrāvagārī* wander beyond, f. L *extrā-* EXTRA- + *vagārī* wander] —**ex·trav′a·gant·ly,** *adv.* —**ex·trav′a·gant·ness,** *n.* —**Syn. 2.** immoderate, excessive, inordinate. **3.** fantastic, wild. —**Ant. 2.** reasonable.

ex·trav·a·gan·za (ĭkstrăv′ə găn′zə), *n.* a musical or dramatic composition, as comic opera or musical comedy, marked by wildness and irregularity in form and feeling and elaborateness in staging and costume. [b. EXTRAVAGANCE and It. *stravaganza* queer behavior]

ex·trav·a·gate (ĭkstrăv′ə gāt′), *v.i.,* -gated, -gating. **1.** to wander beyond bounds; stray; roam at will. **2.** to go beyond the bounds of propriety or reason.

ex·trav·a·sate (ĭkstrăv′ə sāt′), *v.,* -sated, -sating. —*v.t.* **1.** *Pathol.* to force out from the proper vessels, as blood, esp. so as to diffuse through the surrounding tissues. **2.** *Geol.* to pour forth, as lava from a subterranean source in a molten state. —*v.i.* **3.** *Pathol.* to be extravasated, as blood. **4.** *Geol.* to pour forth lava, etc. [f. EXTRA + L *vās* vessel + -ATE¹]

ex·trav·a·sa·tion (ĭkstrăv′ə sā′shən), *n.* **1.** act of extravasating. **2.** the matter extravasated.

ex·tra·vas·cu·lar (ĕks′trə văs′kyə lər), *adj.* *Anat.* situated outside of a blood vessel or vessels.

ex·tra·ver·sion (ĕks′trə vûr′zhən, -shən), *n.* *Psychol.* extroversion.

ex·tra·vert (ĕks′trə vûrt′), *n.* extrovert.

Ex·tre·ma·du·ra (ĕs′trĕ mä dōō′rä), *n.* Spanish name of Estremadura.

ex·treme (ĭkstrēm′), *adj.,* -tremer, -tremest, *n.* —*adj.* **1.** of a character or kind farthest removed from the ordinary or average: *an extreme case, extreme measures.* **2.** utmost or exceedingly great in degree: *extreme joy.* **3.** farthest from the center or middle; outermost; endmost. **4.** farthest, utmost, or very far in any direction. **5.** going to the utmost lengths, or exceeding the bounds of moderation: *extreme fashions.* **6.** going to the utmost or very great lengths in action, habit, opinion, etc.: *an extreme socialist.* **7.** last or final: *extreme unction.* —*n.* **8.** the utmost or highest degree, or a very high degree: *showy in the extreme, or to an extreme.* **9.** one of two things as remote or different from each other as possible: *the extremes of joy and grief.* **10.** the furthest or utmost length, or an excessive length, beyond the ordinary or average: *to go to extremes in dress.* **11.** *Math.*

---

b., blend of, blended; c., cognate with; d., dialect, dialectal; der., derived from; f., formed from; g., going back to; m., modification of; r., replacing; s., stem of; t., taken from; ?, perhaps. See the full key on inside cover.

the first or the last term, as of a proportion or series. **12.** *Logic.* the subject or the predicate of the conclusion of a syllogism; either of two terms which are separated in the premises and brought together in the conclusion. **13.** *Obs. or Rare.* the utmost point, or extremity, of something. [ME, t. L: m.s. *extrēmus*, superl. of *exter* outer, outward] **—ex·treme′ness,** *n.* **—Syn. 6.** immoderate, excessive, fanatical, uncompromising. See **radical. —Ant. 6.** lukewarm.

ex·treme·ly (ĭk strēm′lĭ), *adv.* in an extreme degree; exceedingly.

extreme unction, *Rom. Cath. Ch.* a sacrament in which a dying person is anointed with oil by a priest for the health of his soul and body.

ex·trem·ism (ĭk strē′mĭz əm), *n.* tendency or disposition to go to extremes.

ex·trem·ist (ĭk strē′mĭst), *n.* **1.** one who goes to extremes. **2.** a supporter of extreme doctrines or practices. **—adj. 3.** belonging or pertaining to extremists.

ex·trem·i·ty (ĭk strĕm′ə tĭ), *n.*, *pl.* **-ties. 1.** the extreme or terminal point, limit, or part of something. **2.** a limb of the body. **3.** (*chiefly pl.*) the end part of a limb, as a hand or foot. **4.** (*often pl.*) a condition, or circumstances, of extreme need, distress, etc. **5.** the utmost or any extreme degree: *the extremity of joy.* **6.** (*chiefly pl.*) an extreme measure: *to be forced to extremities.* **7.** extreme character, as of views. **8.** (*chiefly pl.*) a person's last moments. **—Syn. 1.** end, termination, extreme, verge, border, boundary.

ex·tri·ca·ble (ĕks′trə kə bəl), *adj.* that may be extricated.

ex·tri·cate (ĕks′trə kāt′), *v.t.*, **-cated, -cating. 1.** to disentangle; disengage; free: *to extricate one from a dangerous or embarrassing situation.* **2.** to liberate (gas, etc.) from combination, as in a chemical process. [t. L: m.s. *extrīcātus*, pp., disentangled] **—ex′tri·ca′tion,** *n.*

ex·trin·sic (ĕks trĭn′sĭk), *adj.* **1.** extraneous; not inherent; unessential. **2.** being outside of a thing; outward or external; operating or coming from without. **3.** *Anat.* (of certain muscles, nerves, etc.) originating outside the anatomical limits of a part. Also, **ex·trin′si·cal.** [f. EX-¹ + (IN)TRINSIC. Cf. F *extrinsèque*, adj., L *extrinsecus*, adv.] **—ex·trin′si·cal·ly,** *adv.*

extro-, var. of **extra-** (used to contrast with **intro-**).

ex·trorse (ĕks trôrs′), *adj. Bot.* turned or facing outward, as anthers which open toward the perianth. [t. LL: m.s. *extrorsus* in an outward direction] **—extrorse′ly,** *adv.*

ex·tro·ver·sion (ĕks′trō vûr′zhən, -shən), *n.* **1.** Also, **extraversion.** *Psychol.* interest directed outward or to things outside the self (opposed to *introversion*). **2.** *Pathol.* a turning inside out, as of the eyelids or of the bladder. **3.** act of extroverting. **4.** extroverted state.

ex·tro·vert (ĕks′trō vûrt′), *Psychol.* **—n. 1.** one characterized by extroversion; a person concerned chiefly with what is external or objective (opposed to *introvert*). **—adj. 2.** marked by extroversion. **—v.t. 3.** to direct (the mind, etc.) outward, or to things outside the self. Also, **extravert.** [f. EXTRO- + s. L *vertere* turn. See INTROVERT]

ex·trude (ĭk strōōd′), *v.,* **-truded, -truding. —v.t. 1.** to thrust out; force or press out; expel. **2.** (in molding or making metals, plastics, etc.) to form into a desired cross-sectional shape by ejecting through a shaped opening: *to extrude tubing.* **—v.i. 3.** to protrude. [t. L: m.s. *extrūdere* thrust out] **—ex·tru·sion** (ĭk strōō′zhən), *n.*

ex·tru·sive (ĭk strōō′sĭv), *adj.* **1.** tending to extrude. **2.** pertaining to extrusion. **3.** *Geol.* (of rocks) having been forced out in a molten or plastic condition at the surface of the earth.

ex·u·ber·ance (ĭg zōō′bər əns), *n.* **1.** Also, **ex·u′ber·an·cy.** state of being exuberant. **2.** an instance of this. **—Syn. 1.** superabundance, excess, copiousness, profusion, luxuriance, lavishness. **—Ant. 1.** scarcity.

ex·u·ber·ant (ĭg zōō′bər ənt), *adj.* **1.** lavish; effusive: *exuberant health; an exuberant welcome.* **2.** profuse in growth or production; luxuriant; superabundant: *exuberant vegetation.* [t. L: s. *exūberans*, ppr., being fruitful] **—ex·u′ber·ant·ly,** *adv.* **—Syn. 2.** copious, rank. **—Ant. 2.** sparse.

ex·u·ber·ate (ĭg zōō′bə rāt′), *v.i.,* **-ated, -ating.** to be exuberant; superabound; overflow.

ex·u·date (ĕks′yŏŏ dāt′), *n.* a substance exuded.

ex·u·da·tion (ĕks′yŏŏ dā′shən), *n.* **1.** act of exuding. **2.** that which is exuded. **3.** a sweatlike issue or discharge through pores or small openings. **—ex·u·da·tive** (ĕks ū̄′də tĭv), *adj.*

ex·ude (ĭg zōōd′, ĭk sōōd′), *v.,* **-uded, -uding. —v.i. 1.** to come out gradually in drops like sweat through pores or small openings; ooze out. **—v.t. 2.** to send out like sweat; emit through pores or small openings. [t. L: m.s. *ex(s)ūdāre*]

ex·ult (ĭg zŭlt′), *v.i.* **1.** to show or feel a lively or triumphant joy; rejoice exceedingly; be highly elated; be jubilant (fol. by *in, at, over,* or an infinitive): *he exulted to find that he had won.* **2.** *Obs.* to leap, esp. for joy. [t. L: s. *ex(s)ultāre,* freq. of *exsilīre* leap out or up] **—ex·ult′ing·ly,** *adv.*

ex·ult·ant (ĭg zŭlt′ənt), *adj.* exulting; highly elated; triumphant. **—ex·ult′ant·ly,** *adv.*

ex·ul·ta·tion (ĕg′zŭl tā′shən, ĕk′sŭl-), *n.* act of exulting; lively or triumphant joy, as over success or victory. Also, **ex·ult·an·cy** (ĭg zŭl′tən sĭ), **ex·ult′ance.**

ex·u·vi·ae (ĭg zōō′vĭ ē′, ĭk sōō′-), *n.pl.* the cast skins, shells, or other coverings of animals. [t. L: garments stripped off, skins of animals] **—ex·u′vi·al,** *adj.*

ex·u·vi·ate (ĭg zōō′vĭ āt′, ĭk sōō′-), *v.i., v.t.,* **-ated, -ating.** to cast off or shed (exuviae); to molt. **—ex·u′vi·a′tion,** *n.*

ex vo·to (ĕks vō′tō), *Latin.* from, or in pursuance of, a vow.

-ey¹, var. of **-y¹,** used esp. after *y,* as in *clayey.*

-ey², var. of **-y²,** used esp. after *y.*

e·ya·let (ā′yä lĕt′), *n.* vilayet.

ey·as (ī′əs), *n.* a nestling. [ME, var. of *nyas, nias* (*a nyas* being taken as *an eyas*), t. F: m. *niais* a nestling, der. L *nīdus* nest]

Eyck (īk), *n.* **1.** Hubert or Huybrecht van (hȳ′bərt or hoi′brĕкнt vän), 1366?-1426, Flemish painter. **2.** his brother, Jan van (yän vän), (*Jan van Brugge*) 1385?-1440, Flemish painter.

eye (ī), *n., pl.* **eyes,** (*Archaic*) **eyen,** *v.,* **eyed, eying** or **eyeing,** *interj.* **—n. 1.** the organ of sight or vision. **2.** all the structures situated within or near the orbit which assist the organ of vision. **3.** this organ with respect to the color of the iris: *blue eyes.* **4.** the region surrounding the eye: *a black eye.* **5.** sight; vision. **6.** power of seeing; appreciative or discriminating visual perception: *an eye for color.* **7.** (*often pl.*) look, glance, or gaze: *to cast one's eye on a thing.* **8.** (*often pl.*) attentive look, close observation, or watch: *to keep an eye on a person, to be all eyes.* **9.** regard, respect, view, aim, or intention: *to have an eye to one's own advantage, with an eye to win favor.* **10.** (*often pl.*) manner or way of looking at a thing, estimation, or opinion: *in the eyes of the law.* **11.** mental view: *in my mind's eye.* **12.** a center of light, intelligence, influence, etc. **13.** something resembling or suggesting the eye in appearance, shape, etc., as the bud of a tuber, the central spot of a target, one of the round spots on the tail feathers of a peacock, the hole of a needle, a hole pierced in a thing for the insertion of some object, a metal or other ring as for a rope to pass through, or the loop into which a hook is inserted (forming together with the hook a **hook and eye**). **14.** *Meteorol.* the central region of low pressure in a tropical hurricane, where calm conditions prevail, often with clear skies. **15.** **eye of the wind,** *Naut.* the precise direction from which the wind is blowing. **16. make eyes at,** to throw amorous or covetous glances at. **17. set** or **lay eyes on,** *Colloq.* to catch sight of; see. **—v.t. 18.** to fix the eyes upon; view. **19.** to observe or watch narrowly. **20.** to make an eye in: *to eye a needle.* **—v.i. 21.** *Obs.* to appear to the eye. **—interj. 22.** mild exclamation of contradiction or surprise: *my eye!* [ME; OE *ēge,* d. var. of *ēage,* c. G *auge.* Cf. L *oculus*]

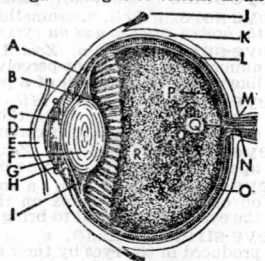

Human Eye

A, Ciliary muscle; B, Ciliary processes; C, Iris; D, Conjunctiva; E, Cornea; F, Crystalline lens; G, Anterior chamber; H, Posterior chamber; I, Suspensory ligament; J, Ocular muscles; K, Sclera; L, Choroid; M, Optic nerve; N, Retinal artery; O, Retina; P, Yellow spot; Q, Blind spot; R, Vitreous humor.

eye·ball (ī′bôl′), *n.* the ball or globe of the eye.

eye·beam (ī′bēm′), *n.* a beam or glance of the eye.

eye·bright (ī′brīt′), *n.* **1.** any of various scrophulariaceous herbs of the genus *Euphrasia,* as *E. officinalis* of Europe, formerly used for diseases of the eye. **2.** scarlet pimpernel.

eye·brow (ī′brou′), *n.* **1.** the arch or ridge forming the upper part of the orbit of the eye. **2.** the fringe of hair growing upon it.

eye·cup (ī′kŭp′), *n.* a device for applying lotions to the eye, consisting of a cup or glass with a rim shaped to fit snugly about the orbit of the eye. Also, **eye bath.**

eyed (īd), *adj.* **1.** having eyes. **2.** having eyelike spots.

eye·glass (ī′glăs′, ī′gläs′), *n.* **1.** (*pl.*) a device to aid defective vision, consisting usually of two glass lenses set in a frame which rests on the nose and is held in place by pieces passing over or around the ears. **2.** the eyepiece of an optical instrument; an ocular. **3.** an eyecup.

eye·hole (ī′hōl′), *n.* **1.** eye socket. **2.** a hole to look through, as in a mask or a curtain. **3.** a circular opening for the insertion of a pin, hook, rope, etc.

eye·lash (ī′lăsh′), *n.* one of the short, thick, curved hairs growing as a fringe on the edge of an eyelid.

eye·less (ī′lĭs), *adj.* **1.** lacking eyes. **2.** blind.

eye·let (ī′lĭt), *n.* **1.** a small, typically round hole, esp. one finished at the edge, as in cloth or leather, for the passage of a lace or cord; or in embroidery, for ornament. **2.** a metal ring for lining a small hole. **3.** an eyehole in a wall, mask, etc. **4.** a small eye. **—v.t. 5.** to make eyelets (holes) in. **6.** to insert metal eyelets in. [ME *oilet,* t. F: m. *œillet,* dim. of *œil* eye]

eye·let·eer (ī/lə tǐr/), *n.* a small pointed instrument for making eyelet holes.

eye·lid (ī/lǐd/), *n.* the movable lid of skin which serves to cover and uncover the eyeball.

ey·en (ī/ən), *n. Archaic.* pl. of eye.

eye opener, *U.S.* **1.** something that causes the eyes to open, as an enlightening or startling disclosure or experience. **2.** *Colloq.* a drink of liquor, esp. one taken early in the day.

eye·piece (ī/pēs/), *n.* (in an optical instrument) the lens or combination of lenses to which the eye is applied.

eye·serv·ant (ī/sûr/vənt), *n.* a servant or other who attends to his duty only when watched by his employer. Also, **eye/serv/er.**

eye·serv·ice (ī/sûr/vǐs), *n.* **1.** service performed only under the eye or watch of the employer. **2.** homage paid with the eyes; admiring looks.

eye·shot (ī/shŏt/), *n.* **1.** range of vision; view. **2.** a glance.

eye·sight (ī/sīt/), *n.* **1.** the power or faculty of seeing. **2.** action or fact of seeing. **3.** the range of the eye.

eye socket, the socket or orbit of the eye.

eye·some (ī/səm), *adj.* pleasant to look at.

eye·sore (ī/sōr/), *n.* something unpleasant to look at: *the broken window was an eyesore to the neighbors.*

eye·spot (ī/spŏt/), *n. Zool.* **1.** a sensory organ of lower animals, having a light-perceiving function. **2.** an eyelike spot, as on the tail of a peacock.

eyes right or **left**, *Mil.* the command given to turn the head and eyes to the right or to the left as a salute while marching at ceremonies.

eye·stalk (ī/stôk/), *n. Zool.* the stalk or peduncle upon which the eye is borne in lobsters, shrimps, etc.

eye·stone (ī/stōn/), *n.* a small calcareous body, flat on one side and convex on the other, passed between the eye and the eyelid to bring out cinders, etc.

eye·strain (ī/strān/), *n.* a sensation of discomfort produced in the eyes by their excessive or faulty use.

eye·tooth (ī/tōōth/), *n., pl.* **-teeth** (-tēth/). **1.** a canine tooth, esp. of the upper jaw (so named from its position under the eye). **2. cut one's eyeteeth**, to become old and experienced enough to understand things.

eye·wash (ī/wŏsh/, ī/wôsh/), *n.* **1.** Also, **eye·wa·ter** (ī/wô/tər, ī/wŏt/ər). a lotion for the eyes. **2.** *Slang.* deceitful excuse; applesauce.

eye·wink (ī/wǐngk/), *n.* **1.** a wink of the eye. **2.** a look or glance.

eye·wink·er (ī/wǐngk/ər), *n.* eyelash.

eye·wit·ness (ī/wǐt/nǐs), *n.* one who actually beholds some act or occurrence, and hence can give testimony concerning it.

eyne (īn), *n. Archaic.* pl. of eye.

ey·ot (ī/ət, āt), *n. Brit. Local.* a small island.

ey·ra (âr/ə, ī/rə), *n.* jaguarundi. [t. Tupi]

eyre (âr), *n.* **1.** a journey in a circuit. **2.** *Eng. Law.* **a.** a journey made by judges to hold court throughout a circuit, under royal commission, superseded prior to the time of Edward III by Commission of Assize. **b. justices in eyre**, the judges holding the commission. **c.** the court held by justices in eyre. [ME, t. OF: m. *eire* journey, circuit, der. *errer*, v., journey, g. LL *iterāre* FABLE]

Eyre (âr), *n.* Lake, a shallow salt lake in S Australia. ab. 4000 sq. mi.

Eyre Peninsula, a peninsula in S Australia, E of the Great Australian Bight. Also, **Eyre's Peninsula** (ârz).

ey·rie (âr/ǐ, ǐr/ǐ), *n.* aerie. Also, **ey/ry.**

Ez., Ezra. Also, **Ezr.**

Ezek., Ezekiel.

E·ze·ki·el (ǐ zē/kǐ əl), *n.* **1.** fl. 6th century B.C., one of the major Hebrew prophets. **2.** the 26th book of the Old Testament, written by him. **3. Moses Jacob,** 1844–1917, U.S. sculptor, in Rome. [t. Gk. (Septuagint): m. *Iezekiēl,* t. Heb.: m. *Yeḥezqēl;* r. *Ezechiel,* t. L (Vulgate)]

Ez·ra (ěz/rə), *n.* **1.** fl. 5th century B.C., Hebrew scribe and priest who with Nehemiah led the revival of Judaism in Palestine. **2.** a short book of chronicles of the Old Testament. [t.Heb.: m. *'Ezrā*]

F

F, f (ěf), *n., pl.* **F's** or **Fs, f's** or **fs. 1.** the sixth letter of the English alphabet. **2.** the sixth in order or in a series. **3.** *Music.* **a.** the fourth tone in the scale of C major or the sixth in the relative scale of A minor. **b.** a printed or written note indicating this tone. **c.** a string, key, or pipe tuned to this note. **d.** (in solmization) the fourth tone of the scale of C, called fa.

F, 1. failure (a grade or mark in school). **2.** *Elect.* farad. **3.** *Math.* field. **4.** *Genetics.* (with a subscript number following) a generation of filial offspring from a given parent: F_1 is the first generation of offspring, F_2 is the second, etc. **5.** *Chem.* fluorine. **6.** French. **7.** *Math.* function (of).

F, *Photog.* See F number. Also, **f, F:, f:, F/, f/.**

F., 1. Fahrenheit. **2.** February. **3.** French. **4.** Friday.

f., 1. *Music.* forte. **2.** *Math.* function (of). **3.** *Elect.* farad. **4.** farthing. **5.** fathom. **6.** female. **7.** feminine. **8.** fluid (ounce). **9.** (*pl.* **ff.**) folio. **10.** following. **11.** formed of. **12.** franc.

fa (fä), *n. Music.* the syllable used for the fourth tone of a scale. [see GAMUT]

fa·ba·ceous (fə bā/shəs), *adj. Bot.* belonging to the *Fabaceae,* or bean family of plants, sometimes included in the *Leguminosae,* including many herbs, shrubs, and trees, as the bean, pea, lentil, furze, broom, locust, etc., which bear seeds in pods or legumes. [t. L: m. *fabāceus,* der. *faba* bean]

Fa·bi·an (fā/bǐ ən), *adj.* **1.** avoiding battle; purposely delaying; cautiously dilatory: *Fabian policy.* See **Fabius Maximus. 2.** of the Fabian Society. **—n. 3.** a member of or sympathizer with the Fabian Society. **—Fa/bi·an·ism,** *n.* **—Fa/bi·an·ist,** *n., adj.*

Fabian Society, a socialist society founded in England in 1884 favoring the gradual spread of socialism by peaceful means.

Fa·bi·us Max·i·mus (fā/bǐ əs măk/sə məs), **Quintus** (kwǐn/təs), died 203 B.C., Roman general who harassed Hannibal's army without risking a pitched battle.

fa·ble (fā/bəl), *n., v.,* **-bled, -bling. —n. 1.** a short tale to teach a moral, often with animals or inanimate objects as characters; apologue: *the fable of the tortoise and the hare.* **2.** a story not founded on fact. **3.** a story about supernatural or extraordinary persons or incidents; a legend. **4.** legends or myths collectively: *Mohammedan fable.* **5.** an untruth; a falsehood. **6.** *Archaic.* the plot of an epic, a dramatic poem, or a play. **7.** *Archaic.* idle talk: *old wives' fables.* **—v.t. 8.** to tell or write fables. **9.** to speak falsely; lie. **—v.t. 10.** to invent (stories); talk about as if true. [ME, *fabul,* t. L: s. *fābula* narrative] **—fa/bler,** *n.* **—Syn. 1.** See **legend.**

fa·bled (fā/bəld), *adj.* **1.** celebrated in fables; mythical; legendary: *fabled goddess of the wood.* **2.** having no real existence; fictitious: *fabled chest of gold.*

fab·li·au (făb/lǐ ō/; Fr. fa blē ō/), *n., pl.* **-aux** (-ōz/; Fr. -ō/), one of the short metrical tales of the medieval French poets, usually rough and humorous. [t. F, orig., d., dim. of *fable* FABLE]

Fa·bre (fä/bər; Fr. fá/br), *n.* **Jean Henri** (zhän än rē/), 1823–1915, French entomologist and popular writer on insect life.

fab·ric (făb/rǐk), *n.* **1.** a cloth made by weaving, knitting, or felting fibers: *woolen fabrics.* **2.** the texture of the woven, knitted, or felted material: *cloths of different fabric.* **3.** framework; structure: *fabric of society.* **4.** a building; edifice. **5.** the method of construction. [late ME *fabrikue,* t. L: m.s. *fabrica* workshop, art, fabric]

fab·ri·cant (făb/rə kənt), *n.* a maker; artisan.

fab·ri·cate (făb/rə kāt/), *v.t.,* **-cated, -cating. 1.** to make by art and labor; construct. **2.** to make by assembling standard parts or sections. **3.** to devise or invent (a legend, lie, etc.). **4.** to fake; forge (a document). [t. L: m.s. *fabricātus,* pp., having made] **—fab/ri·ca/tor,** *n.* **—Syn. 1.** See **manufacture.**

fab·ri·ca·tion (făb/rə kā/shən), *n.* **1.** the process of fabricating; manufacture. **2.** something fabricated, esp. an untruthful statement. **—Syn. 2.** See **fiction.**

fab·ri·koid (făb/rə koid/), *n.* **1.** a waterproof fabric having a cloth foundation and a pyroxylin surface, used as a substitute for leather, cloth, etc. **2.** (*cap.*) a trademark for it. [f. m. FABRIC + -OID]

fab·u·list (făb/yə lǐst), *n.* **1.** a person who invents or relates fables. **2.** a liar.

fab·u·lous (făb/yə ləs), *adj.* **1.** almost unbelievable: *fabulous price.* **2.** told about in fables; not true or real: *the fabulous exploits of Hercules.* **3.** known about only through myths or legends: *the fabulous age in Greek history.* **4.** based on fables. [t. L: m.s. *fābulōsus*] **—fab/u·lous·ly,** *adv.* **—fab/u·lous·ness,** *n.* **—Syn. 1.** incredible, amazing, astonishing. **2.** fabled, fictitious, imaginary. **—Ant. 1.** moderate. **2.** historical.

fac., 1. facsimile. **2.** factor. **3.** factory.

fa·çade (fə säd/, fä-; Fr. fá sàd/), *n.* **1.** *Archit.* a face or front, or the principal face, of a building. **2.** the front part (of anything): *a façade of wealth.* [t. F, der. *face,* after It. *facciata,* der. *faccia* FACE]

face (fās), *n., v.,* **faced, facing.** —*n.* **1.** the front part of the head, from the forehead to the chin. **2.** sight; presence: *to one's face.* **3.** a look or expression on the face: *sad face.* **4.** an expression, indicating ridicule, disgust, etc.: *to make faces.* **5.** *Colloq.* boldness; impudence: *to have the face to ask.* **6.** outward appearance: *old problems with new faces.* **7.** outward show; pretense: *to put a good face on a matter.* **8.** good name; prestige: *to save one's face.* **9.** the amount specified in a bill or note, exclusive of interest. **10.** (of a document) the manifest sense or express terms. **11.** the geographic characteristics or general appearance (of a land surface). **12.** the surface: *face of the earth.* **13.** the side or part of a side upon which the use of a thing depends: *the face of a cloth, document, playing card, watch,* etc. **14.** the most important side; the front: *the face of a building, arch,* etc. **15.** the acting, striking, or working surface of an implement, tool, etc. **16.** *Geom.* any one of the bounding surfaces of a solid figure: *a cube has six faces.* **17.** *Mining.* the front or end of a drift or excavation, where the material is being or was last mined. **18.** *Print.* **a.** the working surface of a type, plate, etc. See diag. under **type.** **b.** the style or appearance of type: *broad or narrow face.* **19.** *Fort.* either of the two outer sides which form the salient angle of a bastion or the like. See diag. under **bastion.** **20. in (the) face of, a.** notwithstanding: *in the face of many obstacles.* **b.** when confronted with: *to keep up prices in the face of a falling market.* **c.** *Brit.* in front of: *in the face of the sea.* —*v.t.* **21.** to look toward: *face the light.* **22.** to front toward: *the statue faces the park.* **23.** to meet face to face; confront: *faced with a problem.* **24.** to confront with impudence: *to face a thing out.* **25.** to oppose confidently or defiantly: *to face fearful odds.* **26.** to cover or partly cover with a different material in front: *wooden house faced with brick.* **27.** to cover some part of (a garment) with another material. **28.** to turn the face of (a playing card) upwards. **29.** to dress or smooth the surface of (a stone, etc.). **30.** to cause (soldiers) to turn to the right, left, or in the opposite direction. —*v.i.* **31.** to be turned (often fol. by *to, toward*). **32.** to be placed (fol. by *on, to, toward*). **33.** to turn to the right, left, or in the opposite direction. [ME, t. F, g. VL *facia,* r. L *facies* form, face] —**face/-a·ble,** *adj.* —**face/less,** *adj.* —**Syn. 1.** FACE, COUNTENANCE, VISAGE refer to the front of the (usually human) head. The FACE is the combination of the features: *a face with broad cheekbones.* COUNTENANCE, a more formal word, denotes the face as it is affected by or reveals the state of mind, and hence often signifies the look or expression on the face: *an expressive countenance.* VISAGE, still more formal, refers to the face as seen in a certain aspect, esp. as revealing seriousness or severity: *a stern visage.*

face card, the king, queen, or jack of playing cards.

face-hard·en (fās/här/dən), *v.t.* to harden the face or surface of (steel or other metal or a metallic object) by chilling, case hardening, or the like. Cf. **caseharden.**

face lifting, plastic surgery on the face for the elimination of wrinkles, etc.

fac·er (fā/sər), *n.* **1.** one who or that which faces, esp. a cutter for smoothing a surface. See face (defs. 26, 29). **2.** *Colloq.* a blow in the face. **3.** *Chiefly Brit. Colloq.* a sudden and severe check.

face-sav·ing (fās/sā/vĭng), *adj.* that saves one's prestige.

fac·et (fās/ĭt), *n., v.,* **-eted, -eting** or (esp. Brit.) **-etted, -etting.** —*n.* **1.** one of the small plane polished surfaces of a cut gem. **2.** aspect; phase: *a facet of the mind.* **3.** *Archit.* a filled-in flute sometimes seen at the bottom of columnar shafts. **4.** *Zool.* one of the corneal lenses of a compound arthropod eye. —*v.t.* **5.** to cut facets on. [t. F: m. *facette,* dim. of *face* FACE]

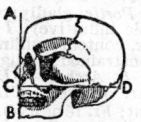

Compound eye of a housefly showing facets (highly magnified)

fa·cete (fə·sēt/), *adj. Archaic.* facetious; witty. [t. L: m.s. *facetus* fine, elegant, witty]

fa·ce·ti·ae (fə·sē/shĭ·ē/), *n.pl.* **1.** amusing writings or witty remarks. **2.** coarsely witty books. [t. L, pl. of *facētia* a witticism. See FACETE]

fa·ce·tious (fə·sē/shəs), *adj.* **1.** amusing; humorous: *a facetious remark.* **2.** trying to be amusing: *a facetious person.* [f. FACETI(AE) + -OUS] —**fa·ce/tious·ly,** *adv.* —**fa·ce/tious·ness,** *n.* —**Syn. 1.** See humorous.

face value, **1.** par value; the value printed on the face of a financial instrument or document. **2.** apparent value: *accept promises at face value.*

fa·cial (fā/shəl), *adj.* **1.** of the face: *facial expression.* **2.** for the face: *a facial cream.* —*n.* **3.** *Colloq.* a massage or treatment for the face. —**fa/cial·ly,** *adv.*

facial angle, *Craniom.* the angle formed by a line from nasion to prosthion at its intersection with the plane of the Frankfurt horizontal.

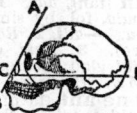

A
A
C
D
C
D
B
B
Orthognathous Skull   Prognathous Skull
ACD, Facial angle; AB, Axis of face; CD, Axis of the skull

facial index, *Craniom.* the ratio of the breadth of a face to its height.

-facient, a suffix forming adjectives meaning "that makes or causes (something)" and nouns meaning "one that makes or causes (something)," as in *absorbifacient,* n. and adj. [t. L: s. *faciens* ppr., doing, making]

fa·ci·es (fā/shĭ·ēz/), *n.* **1.** general appearance. **2.** *Geol.* the composite nature of sedimentary deposits reflecting the conditions and environment of their origin. [t. L]

fac·ile (fās/ĭl), *adj.* **1.** moving, acting, working, proceeding, etc., with ease: *a facile hand, tongue, pen,* etc., *facile expression.* **2.** easily done, performed, used, etc.: *a facile victory, method,* etc. **3.** easy or unconstrained, as manners or persons; affable, agreeable, or complaisant; easily influenced. [t. L: m.s. *facilis* easy to do, easy] —**fac/ile·ly,** *adv.* —**fac/ile·ness,** *n.*

fa·ci·le prin·ceps (fās/ə·lĭ prĭn/sĕps), *Latin.* easily the first or best.

fa·ci·lis de·scen·sus A·ver·ni (fās/ə·lĭs dĭ·sĕn/səs ə·vûr/nī), *Latin.* (the) descent to hell is easy; it is easy to take the downward path. Vergil, *Aeneid,* 6, 126.

fa·cil·i·tate (fə·sĭl/ə·tāt/), *v.t.,* **-tated, -tating.** **1.** to make easier or less difficult; help forward (an action, a process, etc.). **2.** to assist the progress of (a person).

fa·cil·i·ta·tion (fə·sĭl/ə·tā/shən), *n.* **1.** act or process of facilitating. **2.** *Psychol.* the tendency of a stimulus to reinforce another stimulus.

fa·cil·i·ty (fə·sĭl/ə·tĭ), *n., pl.* **-ties.** **1.** something that makes possible the easier performance of any action; advantage: *transportation facilities, to afford someone every facility for doing something.* **2.** freedom from difficulty; ease: *facility of understanding.* **3.** readiness because of skill or practice; dexterity: *compose with great facility.* **4.** an easy-flowing manner: *facility of style.* **5.** ready compliance. [t. L: m.s. *facilitas.* See FACILE]

fac·ing (fā/sĭng), *n.* **1.** a covering in front, for ornament, protection, etc., as an outer layer of different stone forming the face of a wall. **2.** material applied on the edge of a garment for ornament or protection. **3.** (pl.) coverings of a different color applied on the collar, cuffs, or other parts of a military coat. **4.** *Mil.* act of turning to face in a given direction in response to a command.

facing tool, a lathe tool for smoothing a plane surface at right angles to the axis of rotation.

fa·cin·o·rous (fə·sĭn/ə·rəs), *adj. Now Rare.* atrociously wicked. [t. L: m.s. *facinorōsus,* der. *facinus* (bad) deed]

facsim., facsimile.

fac·sim·i·le (făk·sĭm/ə·lĭ, -lē/). *n., adj., v.,* **-led, -leing.** —*n.* **1.** an exact copy. **2.** *Radio.* **a.** a method of transmitting pictures by radio telegraph. See **phototelegraphy.** **b.** a picture so sent. —*adj.* **3.** of a facsimile. **4.** producing facsimiles. —*v.t.* **5.** to reproduce in facsimile; make a fascimile of. [f. L: *fac,* impv., make + *simile* (neut.) like]

fact (făkt), *n.* **1.** what has really happened or is the case; truth; reality: *in fact rather than in theory, the fact of the matter is.* **2.** something known to have happened; a truth known by actual experience or observation: *scientists working with facts.* **3.** something said to be true or supposed to have happened: *the facts are as follows.* **4.** *Law.* **a.** an actual or alleged physical or mental event or existence, as distinguished from a legal effect or consequence. Thus, whether certain words were spoken is *a question of fact;* whether, if spoken, they constituted a binding promise, is usually *a question of law.* **b.** an evil deed (now only in certain legal phrases): *before the fact, after the fact.* **5. in fact,** really; indeed. [t. L: s. *factum* (thing) done, prop. pp. neut.]

fact-find·ing (făkt/fīn/dĭng), *adj.* engaged in determining facts.

fac·tice (făk/tĭs), *n.* a rubberlike substance produced by vulcanizing vegetable oils with sulfur or sulfur chloride. [t. F, t. L: m.s. *factītius* artificial]

fac·tion (făk/shən), *n.* **1.** a smaller group of people within a larger group, often one using unscrupulous methods to accomplish selfish purposes. **2.** party strife or intrigue: *faction has no regard for national interests.* [t. L: s. *factio* a doing or making, action, party]

fac·tion·al (făk/shən·əl), *adj.* of a faction or factions; self-interested; partisan. —**fac/tion·al·ism,** *n.*

fac·tious (făk/shəs), *adj.* **1.** inclined to act for party purposes: *factious opposition.* **2.** caused by party spirit or strife: *factious quarrels.* [t. L: m.s. *factiōsus*] —**fac/-tious·ly,** *adv.* —**fac/tious·ness,** *n.*

fac·ti·tious (făk·tĭsh/əs), *adj.* **1.** artificial; not spontaneous or natural: *a factitious value, factitious enthusiasm.* **2.** made; manufactured. [t. L: m. *factītius* made by art] —**fac·ti/tious·ly,** *adv.* —**fac·ti/tious·ness,** *n.*

fac·ti·tive (făk/tə·tĭv), *adj. Gram.* **1.** used to designate verbs which convey the idea of making or rendering according to order or specification; such verbs are accompanied not only by the direct object but by an additional word indicating the result of the process. For example: They *made* him their *ruler;* to *paint* the house red. **2.** pertaining to such a verb. [t. NL: m.s. *factītivus,* der. L *factitāre* declare (a person) to be, freq. of *facere* do, make] —**fac/ti·tive·ly,** *adv.*

fac·tor (făk/tər), *n.* **1.** one of the elements that contribute to bring about any given result. **2.** *Math.* one of two or more numbers, algebraic expressions, or the like, which when multiplied together produce a given product; a divisor: *6 and 3 are factors of 18.* **3.** *Biol.* a gene, allele, or determiner for hereditary characters. **4.** *Brit.* one who acts, or transacts business, for another. **5.** *Brit.* a commission merchant. **6.** *Brit.* an agent entrusted with the possession of goods for sale. **7.** *Law.* (in some of the United States) a person charged as a garnishee. **8.** *Now only Scot.* the steward or bailiff of an estate. —*v.t.* **9.** to express (a mathematical quantity) as a product of two or more quantities of like kind; thus: 30 = 2·3·5, or $x^2 - y^2$ = (x + y) (x − y). [t. L: doer, maker] —**fac′tor·ship′,** *n.*

fac·tor·age (făk′tər·Ĭj), *n.* **1.** the action or business of a factor. **2.** the allowance or commission paid to a factor.

fac·to·ri·al (făk·tōr′Ĭ·əl), *n.* **1.** *Math.* the product of an integer multiplied by all the lower integers: *the factorial of 4 (written 4! or |4) is* 4 × 3 × 2 × 1 = 24. —*adj.* **2.** *Math.* of or pertaining to factors or factorials. **3.** of or pertaining to a factor or a factory.

fac·tor·ing (făk′tər·Ĭng), *n.* *Com.* the business of purchasing and collecting accounts receivable.

fac·tor·ize (făk′tə·rīz′), *v.t.* **-ized, -izing. 1.** *Math.* to resolve into factors. **2.** *Law.* to garnish. —**fac′tor·i·za′tion,** *n.*

fac·to·ry (făk′tə·rĬ), *n., pl.* **-ries. 1.** a building or group of buildings, usually with equipment, where goods are manufactured. **2.** (formerly) an establishment for factors and merchants carrying on business in a foreign country. [t. ML: m.s. *factoria,* der. L *factor*] —**fac′to·ry·like′,** *adj.* —**Syn. 1.** manufactory, mill, workshop.

fac·to·tum (făk·tō′təm), *n.* one employed to do all kinds of work for another. [t. ML, f. L *fac,* impv., do + *totum* (neut.) all]

fac·tu·al (făk′chŏŏ·əl), *adj.* pertaining to facts; of the nature of fact; real. —**fac′tu·al·ly,** *adv.*

fac·ture (făk′chər), *n.* **1.** act, process, or manner of making anything; construction. **2.** the thing made. [ME, t. L: m. s. *factura,* der. *facere* do, make]

fac·u·la (făk′yə·lə), *n., pl.* **-lae** (-lē). *Astron.* one of the irregular patches on the sun's disk, brighter than the general surface. [t. L, dim. of *fax* torch] —**fac′u·lar,** *adj.*

fac·ul·ta·tive (făk′əl·tā′tĬv), *adj.* **1.** conferring a faculty, privilege, or permission, or the power of doing or not doing something: *a facultative enactment.* **2.** left to one's option or choice; optional. **3.** that may or may not take place; that may or may not assume a specified character. **4.** *Biol.* having the capacity to live under more than one specific set of environmental conditions, as an animal or plant that can lead either a parasitic or a nonparasitic life (opposed to *obligate*).

fac·ul·ty (făk′əl·tĬ), *n., pl.* **-ties. 1.** an ability, natural or acquired, for a particular kind of action. **2.** one of the powers of the mind, as memory, reason, speech, etc.: *the mental faculties, be in full possession of all one's faculties.* **3.** an inherent capability of the body: *the faculties of sight and hearing.* **4.** *U.S. Colloq.* executive ability; efficiency. **5.** *Educ.* **a.** one of the departments of learning, as theology, medicine, or law, in a university. **b.** the teaching body, sometimes with the students, in any of these departments. **c.** the entire teaching and administrative force of a university, college, or school. **6.** the members of a learned profession, esp. the medical profession. **7.** a power or privilege conferred. **8.** *Eccles.* a dispensation, license, or authorization. [ME *faculte,* t. L: m. s. *facultas* ability, means] —**Syn. 1.** capacity, capability, aptitude, knack, turn, talent. See **ability.**

fad (făd), *n.* a temporary, usually irrational, pursuit, fashion, etc. by numbers of people of some action that excites attention and has prestige. [n. use of d. *fad,* v., be busy about trifles, itself back formation from obs. *faddle,* v., fondle. Cf. FIDDLE v., and FIDDLE-FADDLE]

fad·dish (făd′Ĭsh), *adj.* **1.** fadlike. **2.** given to fads.

fad·dist (făd′Ĭst), *n.* one who has a fad or is given to fads.

fad·dy (făd′Ĭ), *adj.,* **-dier, -diest.** faddish.

fade (fād), *v.,* **faded, fading.** —*v.i.* **1.** to lose freshness, vigor, strength, or health: *the flower faded.* **2.** to lose brightness or vividness, as light or color. **3.** to disappear or die gradually (often fol. by *away* or *out*): *a fading smile, sound,* etc. **4.** *Motion Pictures.* to appear (**fade in**) or disappear (**fade out**) by gradually becoming lighter or darker. —*v.t.* **5.** to cause to fade: *sunshine faded the tapestry.* **6.** *Colloq.* (in dice throwing) to make a wager against (the caster). [ME *fade(n),* t. OF: m. *fader,* der. *fade* pale, weak, g. b. L *vapidus* flat and *fatuus* insipid] —**Syn. 1.** wither, droop, languish. **2.** blanch, bleach, pale. **3.** See **disappear.**

fade-in (fād′Ĭn′), *n.* a progressive lighting of a scene in a motion picture as it appears.

fade·less (fād′lĬs), *adj.* unfading. —**fade′less·ly,** *adv.*

fade-out (fād′out′), *n.* **1.** a progressive darkening of a scene in a motion picture as it disappears. **2.** a disappearance, esp. a gradual one.

fadge (făj), *v.i.,* **fadged, fadging.** *Obs. or Dial. Eng.* **1.** to fit; suit; agree. **2.** to succeed; thrive.

Fad·i·man (făd′ə·mən), *n.* **Clifton,** born 1904, U. S. writer and critic.

fae·ces (fē′sēz), *n.pl.* feces. —**fae·cal** (fē′kəl), *adj.*

Fa·en·za (fä·en′tsä), *n.* a city in N Italy, SE of Bologna. 48,061 (1951).

fa·e·rie (fā′ə·rĬ, fâr′Ĭ), *n.* **1.** fairyland. **2.** *Archaic.* a fairy. —*adj.* **3.** *Archaic.* fairy. [var. of FAIRY]

Faerie Queene (kwēn), a chivalric, allegorical romance in verse (1590–1609), by Edmund Spenser.

Faer·oe Is·lands (fâr′ō), a group of 21 islands in the N Atlantic between Great Britain and Iceland,

belonging to Denmark but having extensive home rule. 29,178 pop. (1945); 540 sq. mi. *Cap.:* Torshaven. Also, **the Faeroes** or **Faroe Islands.** Danish, **Færö·er·ne** (fĕr œ′ĕr nə).

fa·ër·y (fā′ə·rĬ, fâr′Ĭ), *n., pl.* **faëries,** *adj.* faërie.

Faf·nir (fäv′nĬr, fäf′-), *n.* (in the Icelandic version of the Siegfried story) the guardian dragon of the Nibelungs' hoard, slain by Sigurd. [Icel.]

fag (făg), *v.,* **fagged, fagging,** *n.* —*v.i.* **1.** *Brit.* to work till wearied; work hard: *to fag away at French.* **2.** *Brit.* to act as a fag. —*v.t.* **3.** to tire by labor; exhaust (often fol. by *out*): *we were fagged out.* **4.** *Brit.* to make a fag of. —*n.* **5.** drudgery; toil. **6.** *Brit. Colloq.* a younger pupil in English public schools required to perform certain services for an older pupil. **7.** a drudge. **8.** a fag end, as of cloth. **9.** *Chiefly Brit. Slang.* a cigarette. [special use of obs. *fag,* n., flap, which occurs only in expression *fag feathers,* ? for *wag feathers* by allit. assimilation; cf. FIELDFARE]

fa·ga·ceous (fa·gā′shəs), *adj.* belonging to the *Fagaceae,* or beech family of trees and shrubs, which includes the beech, chestnut, oak, etc. [f. m.s. NL *Fagaceae* = nus type (der. L *fagus* beech) + -ous]

fag end, 1. the last part or very end of something, esp. a remnant. **2.** the unfinished end of a piece of cloth.

Fa·gin (fā′gĬn), *n.* (in Dickens' *Oliver Twist*) a villainous old man who employs young boys as thieves.

fag·ot (făg′ət), *n.* **1.** a bundle of sticks, twigs, or small branches, etc. bound together, used for fuel, as a fascine, etc. **2.** a collection. **3.** a bundle of pieces of iron or steel to be welded. —*v.t.* **4.** to bind or make into a fagot. **5.** to ornament with fagoting. Also, *Brit.,* **fag′got.** [ME, t. OF; orig. uncert.]

fag·ot·ing (făg′ət·Ĭng), *n.* a type of decorative joining used to combine cloth or lace. Also, *Brit.,* **fag′got·ing.**

Fagoting

fahl·band (fäl′bänd / ; *Ger.* fäl′bänt′), *n.* *Mining.* a belt or zone of rock impregnated with metallic sulfides. [G: f. *fahl* ash-colored + *band* band, stripe]

Fahr., Fahrenheit (thermometer).

Fahr·en·heit (fär′ən·hīt / ; *Ger.* fär′-), *adj.* **1.** denoting or pertaining to a thermometric scale in which the melting point of ice is 32 degrees above the zero, and the boiling point of water 212 degrees above the zero. See illus. under **thermometer.** —*n.* **2. Gabriel Daniel** (gä′brē·ĕl / dä′nē·ĕl /), 1686–1736, German physicist who devised this scale and introduced the use of mercury in thermometers.

fa·ience (fīäns′, fā-; *Fr.* fȧ·yäNs′), *n.* glazed earthenware or pottery, esp. a fine variety with highly colored designs. [t. F, orig. pottery of Faenza]

fail (fāl), *v.i.* **1.** to come short or be wanting in action, detail, or result; disappoint or prove lacking in what is attempted, expected, desired, or approved: *the crop failed, the experiment failed of success, he failed in history.* **2.** to be or become deficient or lacking; fall short; be insufficient or absent: *our supplies failed.* **3.** to fall off; dwindle; pass or die away. **4.** to lose strength or vigor; become weaker. **5.** to become unable to meet one's engagements, especially one's debts or business obligations; become insolvent or bankrupt. —*v.t.* **6.** to neglect to perform or observe: *he failed to come.* **7.** to prove of no use or help to, as some expected or usual resource: *his friends failed him, words failed him.* **8.** to declare (a person) unsuccessful in a test, course of study, etc. —*n.* **9.** failure as to performance, occurrence, etc.: *pay him without fail.* [ME *faile(n),* t. OF: m. *faillir,* g. var. of L *fallere* deceive, disappoint] —**Syn. 4.** decline, sink, wane. **7.** desert, forsake. —**Ant. 4.** improve. **7.** support.

fail·ing (fā′lĬng), *n.* **1.** act or state of one who or that which fails; failure. **2.** a defect; shortcoming; weakness. —*prep.* **3.** in the absence or default of: *failing payment, we shall sue.* —**fail′ing·ly,** *adv.* —**Syn. 2.** See **fault.**

faille (fīl, fāl; *Fr.* fȧ′y), *n.* a soft, transversely ribbed silk or rayon fabric. [t. F]

fail-safe (fāl′sāf′), *adj.* insuring safety in the event of an accident: *a fail-safe system; a device that is fail-safe.*

fail·ure (fāl′yər), *n.* **1.** act of failing; a proving unsuccessful; lack of success: *his effort ended in failure, the campaign was a failure.* **2.** nonperformance of something due or required: *a failure to do what one has promised, a failure to appear.* **3.** running short; insufficiency: *failure of crops, of supplies.* **4.** loss of strength, vigor, etc.: *the failure of health.* **5.** condition of being bankrupt by reason of insolvency. **6.** a becoming insolvent or bankrupt: *the failure of a bank.* **7.** one who or that which proves unsuccessful. [t. AF: m. *failer,* orig. inf., var. of OF *faillir* FAIL] —**Syn. 2.** neglect, omission, dereliction.

fain (fān), *adv.* **1.** *Poetic.* gladly; willingly (only with *would,* fol. by simple infinitive): *I would fain be with you.* —*adj.* **2.** *Rare.* content; willing (fol. by an infinitive). **3.** *Rare.* constrained; obliged. **4.** *Archaic or Dial.* glad; pleased. **5.** *Archaic or Dial.* desirous; eager. [ME; OE *fægen,* var. of *fægen.* Cf. Icel. *feginn* glad]

fai·né·ant (fā′nĬ·ənt; *Fr.* fĕ·nāän′), *adj.* **1.** that does nothing; idle; indolent. —*n.* **2.** an idler. [t. F: f. s. *faire* do + *néant* nothing] —**fai′ne·an·cy,** *n.*

faint (fānt), *adj.* **1.** lacking brightness, vividness, clearness, loudness, strength, etc.: *a faint light, color, resemblance.* **2.** feeble; half-hearted: *faint resistance, faint* *praise.* **3.** feeling weak, dizzy, or exhausted; about to swoon: *faint with hunger.* **4.** lacking courage; cowardly; timorous: *faint heart.* —*v.i.* **5.** to lose consciousness temporarily; swoon. **6.** *Now Rare.* to lose brightness, vividness, etc. **7.** *Archaic.* to grow weak; lose spirit or courage. —*n.* **8.** temporary loss of consciousness; a swoon. [ME *faint, feint,* t. OF: feigned, hypocritical, sluggish, spiritless, pp. of *feindre* FEIGN] —**faint′er,** *n.* —**faint′ish,** *adj.* —**faint′ly,** *adv.* —**faint′ness,** *n.* —**Syn. 1.** indistinct, ill-defined, dim, faded. **2.** faltering, irresolute, weak. **3.** feeble, languid.

faint-heart-ed (fānt′här′tĭd), *adj.* lacking courage; cowardly; timorous. —**faint′-heart′ed·ly,** *adv.* —**faint′-heart′ed·ness,** *n.*

faints (fānts), *n.pl.* the impure spirit which comes over first and last in distilling whiskey, etc. Also, **feints.**

fair[1] (fâr), *adj.* **1.** free from bias, dishonesty, or injustice: *a fair decision or judge.* **2.** that is legitimately sought, pursued, done, given, etc.; proper under the rules: *fair game, stroke, hit,* etc. **3.** moderately good, large, or satisfactory; not undesirable, but not excellent: *a fair income, appearance, reputation.* **4.** marked by favoring conditions; likely; promising: *in a fair way to succeed.* **5.** *Meteorol.* **a.** (of the sky) bright; sunny; cloudless to half-cloudy. **b.** (of the weather) fine; with no aspect of rain, snow, or hail; not stormy. **6.** unobstructed; not blocked up. **7.** without irregularity or unevenness: *a fair surface.* **8.** free from blemish, imperfection, or anything that impairs the appearance, quality, or character: *a fair copy.* **9.** clear; easy to read: *fair handwriting.* **10.** of a light hue; not dark: *fair skin.* **11.** beautiful; pleasing in appearance; attractive. **12.** seemingly good or sincere but not so: *fair promises.* **13.** courteous; civil: *fair words.* —*adv.* **14.** in a fair manner: *he doesn't play fair.* **15.** straight; directly, as in aiming or hitting. **16.** favorably; auspiciously: *to bid fair.* **17.** *fair and square,* honestly; justly; straightforwardly. —*n.* **18.** *Archaic.* that which is fair. **19.** *Archaic.* a woman. **20.** *Archaic.* a beloved woman, sweetheart. —*v.t.* **21** *Obs.* to make fair. —*v.i.* **22.** *Brit. Dial. and U.S. Colloq.* (of the weather) to clear. [ME; OE *fæger,* c. OHG *fagar*] —**fair′ness,** *n.* —**Syn. 1.** unbiased, equitable, just, honest. FAIR, IMPARTIAL, DISINTERESTED, UNPREJUDICED refer to lack of bias in opinions, judgments, etc. FAIR implies the treating of all sides alike, justly and equitably: *fair play.* IMPARTIAL, like fair, implies showing no more favor to one side than another, but suggests particularly a judicial consideration of a case: *an impartial judge.* DISINTERESTED implies a fairness arising particularly from lack of desire to obtain a selfish advantage: *the motives of her guardian were entirely disinterested.* UNPREJUDICED means not influenced or swayed by bias, or by prejudice caused by irrelevant considerations: *an unprejudiced decision.* **3.** passable, tolerable, average, middling. **8.** clean, spotless, pure, untarnished, unsullied. **9.** legible, distinct. **10.** blond, pale. **11.** pretty, comely, lovely.

fair[2] (fâr), *n.* **1.** a competitive exhibition of farm products, live stock, etc. **2.** *Chiefly Brit.* a periodic gathering of buyers and sellers in an appointed place. **3.** an exhibition and sale of fancy articles to raise money, often for some charitable purpose. [ME *feire,* t. OF, g. L *fēria* holiday]

fair ball, *Baseball.* any batted ball other than a foul.

Fair·banks (fâr′băngks′), *n.* **1.** a town in central Alaska, on the Tanana river. 13,311 (1960). **2. Douglas,** 1883–1939, U.S. motion picture actor.

fair catch, *Football.* a catch of the kickoff, or of a punt, wherein the catcher signals that he will not advance the ball and is therefore not interfered with.

fair copy, 1. a copy of a document made after final correction. **2.** the condition of such a copy.

Fair Deal, the principles of the liberal wing of the Democratic party under the leadership of President Harry S. Truman, consisting largely of a continuation and development of the principles of the New Deal.

Fair·fax (fâr′făks), *n.* **1. Thomas, 3rd Baron,** 1612–1671, English general and commander in chief of the army of Parliament against Charles I in the English Civil War. **2. Thomas, 6th Baron,** 1692–1782, English colonist in Virginia.

fair green, *Golf.* fairway (def. 2).

fair·ground (fâr′ground′), *n.* (*often pl.*) a place where fairs, horse races, etc., are held.

fair-haired (fâr′hârd′), *adj.* **1.** having light-colored hair. **2.** favorite: *to be someone's fair-haired boy.*

fair·ing[1] (fâr′ĭng), *n.* an exterior part of an airplane, etc., which reduces eddying and resulting drag. [f. FAIR[1], adj. (def. 7) + -ING[1]]

fair·ing[2] (fâr′ĭng), *n. Archaic.* a gift, esp. one given at or bought at a fair. [f. FAIR[2] + -ING[1]]

fair·ish (fâr′ĭsh), *adj.* moderately good, large, or well.

fair-lead (fâr′lēd′), *n. Naut.* a fitting such as a ring, thimble, or block, or a strip of board with holes in it, through which running rigging is passed to be guided and kept clear of obstructions and chafing. Also, **fair′-lead′er.** [f. FAIR[1], adj. (def. 7) + LEAD[1]]

fair·ly (fâr′lĭ), *adv.* **1.** in a fair manner; justly; impartially. **2.** moderately; tolerably: *fairly good.* **3.** actually; completely: *the wheels fairly spun.* **4.** properly; legitimately. **5.** clearly; distinctly. **6.** *Obs.* softly. **7.** *Obs.* courteously.

fair-mind·ed (fâr′mīn′dĭd), *adj.* fair in mind or judgment; impartial; unprejudiced: *a wise and fair-minded judge.* —**fair′-mind′ed·ness,** *n.*

Fair·mont (fâr′mŏnt), *n.* a city in N West Virginia. 27,477 (1960).

Fair Oaks, a locality in E Virginia, near Richmond: battle (also called "Seven Pines"), 1862.

fair sex, women.

fair-spo·ken (fâr′spō′kən), *adj.* courteous, civil, or plausible in speech; smooth-tongued.

fair to middling, *U.S. Colloq.* tolerably good in appearance or quality; so so.

fair trade, *U.S.* (in some States) trade carried on under an agreement (**fair-trade agreement**) between a manufacturer and a retailer or retailers to sell a trademarked product at a minimum price.

fair-trade (fâr′trād′), *v.t.* **-traded, -trading,** to market (a product) under a fair-trade agreement.

fair·way (fâr′wā′), *n.* **1.** an unobstructed passage or way. **2.** *Golf.* that part of the links between tees and putting greens where the grass is kept short. **3.** *Naut.* **a.** (in a harbor, river, etc.) the navigable portion or channel for vessels. **b.** the usual course taken by vessels.

fair-weath·er (fâr′wĕth′ər), *adj.* **1.** for fair weather only. **2.** weakening or failing in time of trouble: *he was surrounded by fair-weather friends.*

Fair·weath·er (fâr′wĕth′ər), *n.* **Mount,** a mountain in SE Alaska. 15,292 ft.

fair·y (fâr′ĭ), *n., pl.* **fairies,** *adj.* —*n.* **1.** one of a class of supernatural beings, generally conceived as of diminutive human form, having magical powers capriciously exercised for good or evil in human affairs. **2.** such beings collectively. **3.** *Slang.* an effeminate male, usually a homosexual. —*adj.* **4.** having to do with fairies. **5.** of the nature of a fairy: fairylike. [ME, t. OF: m. *faerie,* der. *fae* FAY[1]] —**fair′y·like′,** *adj.* —**Syn. 1.** fay, fairy, leprechaun, nix, nixie. FAIRY, BROWNIE, ELF, SPRITE are terms for imaginary beings usually less than human size thought to be helpful or harmful to mankind. FAIRY is the most general name for such beings: *a good fairy as a godmother, misadventures caused by an evil fairy.* A BROWNIE is a good-natured tiny man who appears usually at night to do household tasks: *perhaps the brownies will come and help us tonight.* ELF suggests a young, mischievous or roguish fairy: *that child is a perfect little elf.* SPRITE suggests a fairy of pleasing appearance, older than an elf, to be admired for ease and lightness of movement; it may, however, be impish or even hostile: *a dainty sprite.*

fair·y·hood (fâr′ĭ·hŏŏd′), *n.* **1.** fairy state or nature. **2.** fairies collectively.

fair·y·ism (fâr′ĭ·ĭz′əm), *n.* **1.** fairylike quality. **2.** belief in fairies.

fair·y·land (fâr′ĭ·lănd′), *n.* **1.** the imaginary realm of the fairies. **2.** any enchanting, beautiful region.

fairy ring, a circle formed on the grass in a field by the growth of certain fungi, formerly supposed to be caused by fairies in their dances.

fairy tale, 1. a story about fairies. **2.** a statement or account of something imaginary, or incredible.

Fai·sal (fī′səl), *n.* **1.** 1885–1933, king of Syria in 1920, and king of Iraq, 1921–33. Also, **Feisal, Feisul. 2. II,** 1935–1958, king of Iraq, 1953–1958.

fait ac·com·pli (fĕ tà kôn plē′), *French.* an accomplished fact; a thing already done.

faith (fāth), *n.* **1.** confidence or trust in a person or thing. **2.** belief which is not based on proof. **3.** belief in the doctrines or teachings of religion. **4.** the doctrines which are or should be believed. **5.** a system of religious belief: *the Christian faith, the Jewish faith.* **6.** the obligation of loyalty or fidelity to a person, promise, engagement, etc.): *to keep or break faith with.* **7.** the observance of this obligation: *to act in good or bad faith.* **8.** *Theol.* that trust in God and in his promises as made through Christ by which man is justified or saved. —*interj.* **9. in faith,** *Archaic.* in truth; indeed. [ME, t. OF: m. *feit,* g. L *fidēs*] —**Syn. 5.** doctrine, tenet, creed, dogma, persuasion, religion.

faith cure, 1. a method of attempting to cure disease by prayer and religious faith. **2.** a cure thus effected.

faith·ful (fāth′fəl), *adj.* **1.** strict or thorough in the performance of duty. **2.** true to one's word, promises, vows, etc. **3.** full of or showing loyalty or fidelity. **4.** that may be relied upon, trusted, or believed. **5.** adhering or true to fact or an original: *a faithful account, a faithful copy.* **6.** *Obs.* full of faith; believing. —*n.* **7.** the body of loyal members of any party or group. **8. the faithful,** the believers, esp. **a.** the believing members of the Christian church or of some branch of it. **b.** the adherents of the Mohammedan faith. —**faith′-ful·ly,** *adv.* —**faith′ful·ness,** *n.* —**Syn. 1.** true, devoted, stanch. **3.** FAITHFUL, CONSTANT, LOYAL imply qualities of stability, dependability, and devotion. FAITHFUL implies long-continued and steadfast fidelity to whatever one is bound to by a pledge, duty, or obligation: *a faithful friend.* CONSTANT suggests firmness and steadfastness in attachment: *a constant affection.* LOYAL implies unswerving allegiance to a person, organization, cause, or idea: *loyal to one's associates, one's country.*

faith·less (fāth′lĭs), *adj.* **1.** not adhering to allegiance, promises, vows, or duty: *a faithless wife or servant.* **2.** that cannot be relied on or trusted: *faithless coward.* **3.** without trust or belief. **4.** without religious faith. **5.** (among Christians) without Christian faith. —**faith′less·ly,** *adv.* —**faith′less·ness,** *n.* —**Syn. 1.** false, inconstant, fickle; disloyal, perfidious, treacherous.

fake[1] (fāk), *v.,* **faked, faking,** *n., adj. Colloq.* —*v.t.* **1.** to get up, prepare, or make (something specious, deceptive, or fraudulent). **2.** to conceal the defects of, usually in order to deceive. **3.** to pretend; simulate: *to fake illness.* —*v.i.* **4.** to fake something; pretend. —*n.* **5.** something faked up; anything made to appear otherwise than it actually is. **6.** one who fakes. —*adj.* **7.** designed to deceive or cheat. [orig. obscure; ? var. of obs. *feak, feague*, t. D: m. *vegen* furbish up]

fake² (fāk), *n., v.,* **faked, faking.** *Naut.* —*n.* **1.** one of the rings or windings of a coiled cable or hawser. —*v.t.* **2.** to lay (a rope, cable, etc.) in a coil to prepare it for running. [orig. obscure]

fak·er (fā′kər), *n.* *Colloq.* **1.** one who fakes. **2.** a petty swindler. **3.** a peddler or street vendor.

fa·kir (fə kir′, fā′kər), *n.* **1.** a Mohammedan or Hindu religious ascetic or mendicant monk. **2.** a member of any Islamic religious order. Also, **fa·keer′.** [t. Ar.: m. *faqīr* poor]

fa·la (fä lä′), *n.* **1.** a text or refrain in old songs. **2.** an old kind of part song or madrigal. Also, **fal la.**

Fa·lange (fā′lănj; *Sp.* fä län′hě), *n.* the Fascist party in power in Spain since the Civil War of 1936–39.

Fa·lan·gist (fə lăn′jĭst), *n.* a member of the Falange.

fal·ba·la (făl′bə lə), *n.* a flounce; a furbelow. [t. F; orig. uncert.]

fal·cate (făl′kāt), *adj.* hooked; curved like a scythe or sickle; falciform: *a falcate part or organ.* [t. L: m.s. *fal-cātus,* der. *falx* sickle]

fal·chion (fôl′chən, -shən), *n.* **1.** a broad, short sword having a convex edge curving sharply to the point. **2.** *Poetic.* any sword. [t. It.: m. *falcione* (der. *falce* sickle, g. L *falx*); r. ME *fauchoun,* t. OF]

fal·ci·form (făl′sə fôrm′), *adj.* sickle-shaped; falcate. [f. s. L *falx* sickle + -(I)FORM]

fal·con (fôl′kən, fô′kən), *n.* **1.** any of various diurnal birds of prey of the family *Falconidae,* esp. of the genus *Falco,* as the peregrine falcon (*F. peregrinus*), having long, pointed wings and a notched bill, and taking its quarry as it moves. **2.** any of various hawks used in falconry, and trained to hunt other birds and game (properly, the female only, the male being known as a *tercel*). **3.** an old kind of cannon. [t. LL: s. *falco* (der. L *falx* sickle); r. ME *faucon,* t. OF]

Peregrine falcon.
Falco peregrinus
(16½ in. long)

fal·con·er (fôl′kən ər, fô′kən-), *n.* **1.** one who hunts with falcons; one who follows the sport of hawking. **2.** one who breeds and trains hawks for hunting.

fal·co·net¹ (fôl′kə nĕt′, fô′kə-), *n.* any of several very small Asiatic birds of prey principally of the genus *Microhierax.* [f. FALCON + -ET]

fal·co·net² (fôl′kə nĕt′, fô′kə-), *n.* an old kind of light cannon. [t. It.: m. *falconetto,* dim. of *falcone* FALCON]

fal·con·gen·tle (fôl′kən jĕn′təl, fô′kən-), *n.* **1.** the female of the peregrine falcon. **2.** any female falcon. [trans. of F *faucon gentil*]

fal·con·i·form (făl′kə nə fôrm′), *adj.* *Ornith.* of or belonging to the family *Falconidae,* which includes falcons, hawks, etc. [f. FALCON + -(I)FORM]

fal·con·ry (fôl′kən rĭ, fô′-), *n.* **1.** the art of training falcons to attack wild fowl or game. **2.** the sport of hawking.

fal·de·ral (făl′də răl′), *n.* **1.** meaningless syllables forming the refrain of various old songs. **2.** mere nonsense; foolish talk or ideas. **3.** a trifle; gimcrack; gewgaw. Also, **fal·de·rol** (făl′də rŏl′), **folderol.**

fald·stool (fôld′stōōl′), *n.* **1.** a chair or seat, orig. one capable of being folded, used by a bishop or other prelate when officiating in his own church away from the throne, or in a church not his own. **2.** a movable folding stool or desk at which worshipers kneel during certain acts of devotion. **3.** such a stool placed at the south side of the altar, at which the kings or queens of England kneel at their coronation. **4.** a desk at which the litany is said or sung. [OE *fealdestōl,* c. OHG *faltistuol* folding chair. See FOLD¹, STOOL]

Fa·li·e·ri (fä lyĕ′rē), *n.* **Marino** (mä rē′nō), c1278–1355, doge of Venice in 1354.

Fal·ken·hayn (fäl′kən hīn′), *n.* **Erich von** (ā′rĭкн fən), 1861–1922, German general of World War I.

Fal·kirk (fôl′kûrk, fô′kûrk), *n.* a city in central Scotland, in Stirling county: site of the defeat of the Scots under Wallace by the English, 1298. 37,000 (est. 1956).

Falk·land Islands (fôk′lənd) a group of about 200 islands in the S Atlantic, ab. 300 mi. E of the Strait of Magellan: a British crown colony; the British defeated the Germans in a naval battle near here, 1914. 2230 pop. (1953); with dependencies, 3630 (1953); 4618 sq. mi. *Cap.:* Stanley.

Falk·ner (fôk′nər), *n.* **William.** See Faulkner.

fall (fôl), *v.,* **fell, fallen, falling,** *n.* —*v.i.* **1.** to descend from a higher to a lower place or position through loss or lack of support; drop. **2.** to come down suddenly from a standing or erect position: *to fall*

on one's knees. **3.** to hang down; extend downward: *her hair falls from her shoulders.* **4.** to be cast down, as the eyes. **5.** to succumb to temptation. **6.** to lose high position, dignity, character, etc. **7.** to succumb to attack: *the city fell to the enemy.* **8.** to be overthrown, as a government. **9.** to drop down wounded or dead; be slain: *to fall in battle.* **10.** to pass into some condition or relation: *to fall asleep, in love, into ruin.* **11.** to become: *to fall sick, lame, vacant, due.* **12.** to come as if by dropping, as stillness, night, etc. **13.** to come by chance into a particular position: *to fall among thieves.* **15.** to come to pass; occur; happen: *Christmas falls on a Monday this year.* **16.** to have proper place; come by right: *the accent falls on the first syllable, the inheritance fell to the only surviving relative.* **17.** to become less or lower: *temperature, prices, values, tides fall, the voice falls.* **18.** to be naturally divisible (fol. by *into*). **19.** to lose animation, as the face. **20.** to slope, as land. **21.** to be directed, as light, sight, etc. on something. **22.** to come down in fragments, as a building. **23.** special meanings of the intransitive verb are:

fall away, 1. to withdraw support or allegiance. **2.** to decline; decay; perish. **3.** to lose flesh; become lean.

fall back, to recede; give way; retreat.

fall back on, 1. *Mil.* to retreat to. **2.** to have recourse to.

fall behind, to slacken in pace or progress; lag: *to fall behind in work, payments, etc.*

fall down, *Colloq.* to fail: *to fall down on the job.*

fall for, *Colloq.* **1.** to be deceived by. **2.** to fall in love with.

fall foul, 1. to come into collision, as ships; become entangled. **2.** to come into conflict; have trouble. **3.** to make an attack.

fall in, 1. to sink inward; fall to pieces inwardly. **2.** to take one's proper place in line, as a soldier. **3.** to come together; meet; agree.

fall off, 1. to drop off. **2.** to separate or withdraw. **3.** to become estranged; withdraw from allegiance. **4.** to decline in vigor, interest, etc. **5.** to decrease in number, amount, intensity, etc.; diminish. **6.** *Naut.* to deviate from the course to which the head of the ship was directed; fall to leeward.

fall on or upon, 1. to assault; attack. **2.** to light upon; chance upon.

fall out, 1. to drop out of one's place in line, as a soldier. **2.** to disagree; quarrel. **3.** to occur; happen; turn out.

fall short, 1. to fail to reach a particular amount, degree, standard, etc. **2.** to prove insufficient; give out.

fall through, to come to naught; fail; miscarry.

fall to, to betake or apply oneself; begin: *to fall to work, argument, blows, etc.*

fall under, to be classed as; be included in.

—*v.t.* **24.** to chop down or fell, as a tree.

—*n.* **25.** act of falling, or dropping from a higher to a lower place or position; descent, as of rain, snow, etc. **26.** the quantity that descends. **27.** *Chiefly U.S.* autumn. **28.** a becoming less; a lowering; a sinking to a lower level. **29.** the distance through which anything falls. **30.** (*usually pl.*) a cataract or waterfall: *Niagara Falls.* **31.** downward slope or declivity. **32.** a falling from an erect position, as to the ground: *to have a bad fall.* **33.** a hanging down; a dropping. **34.** a succumbing to temptation; lapse into sin. **35.** *Theol.* the lapse of mankind into a state of natural or innate sinfulness through the transgression of Adam and Eve: *the fall of man.* **36.** surrender or capture, as of a city. **37.** proper place: *the fall of an accent on a syllable.* **38.** *Wrestling.* a. the fact or a method of being thrown on one's back by an opponent. b. a bout: *to try a fall.* **39.** a loosely hanging veil. **40.** *Mach., etc.* the part of the rope of a tackle to which the power is applied in hoisting. **41.** (*pl.*) *Naut.* a. the apparatus used in lowering or hoisting a ship's boat, cargo, etc. b. the break in the line of a ship between decks of different levels. **42.** *Hunting.* a deadfall. [ME *falle(n),* OE *feallan* c. G *fallen*]

fal la, fa-la.

Fal·la (fä′lyä), *n.* **Manuel de** (mä nwĕl′ dě), 1876–1946, Spanish composer.

fal·la·cious (fə lā′shəs), *adj.* **1.** deceptive; misleading: *fallacious evidence.* **2.** containing a fallacy; logically unsound: *fallacious arguments, reasoning, etc.* **3.** disappointing; delusive: *a fallacious peace.* —**fal·la′cious·ly,** *adv.* —**fal·la′cious·ness,** *n.*

fal·la·cy (făl′ə sĭ), *n., pl.* **-cies. 1.** a deceptive, misleading, or false notion, belief, etc.: *a popular fallacy.* **2.** a misleading or unsound argument. **3.** deceptive, misleading, or false nature. **4.** *Logic.* any of various types of erroneous reasoning that render arguments logically unsound. **5.** *Obs.* deception. [ME *falacye,* t. L: m. *fallācia* deceit; r. ME *fallace,* t. OF]

fal·lal (făl′lăl′), *n.* **1.** a bit of finery; a showy article of dress. **2.** a piece of ribbon, worn with streaming ends as an ornament in the 17th century. —*adj.* **3.** finicky; foppish; trifling. [? var. of FALBALA]

fal·lal·er·y (făl′lăl′ə rĭ), *n.* fallals collectively; finery.

fall dandelion, a small scapose herb, *Leontodon autumnalis,* with yellow flowers, a native of Europe naturalized in the U.S.

fall·en (fô′lən), *v.* **1.** pp. of **fall.** —*adj.* **2.** that has dropped or come down from a higher place or level, or from an upright position. **3.** on the ground; prostrate;

---

b., blend of, blended; c., cognate with; d., dialect, dialectal; der., derived from; f., formed from; g., going back to; m., modification of; r., replacing; s., stem of; t., taken from; ?, perhaps.   See the full key on inside cover.

down flat. **4.** degraded: *a fallen woman.* **5.** overthrown; destroyed: *a fallen city.* **6.** dead: *fallen in battle.*

fall·er (fôl′ər), *n.* **1.** one who or that which falls. **2.** any of various devices that operate by falling.

fall·fish (fôl′fĭsh′), *n., pl.* **-fishes,** (*esp. collectively*) **-fish.** a large minnow, *Leucosomus corporalis,* of the eastern U.S.

fall guy, *U.S. Slang.* an easy victim; scapegoat.

fal·li·ble (făl′ə bəl), *adj.* **1.** liable to be deceived or mistaken; liable to err. **2.** liable to be erroneous or false. [t. ML: m.s. *fallibilis,* der. L *fallere* deceive] **—fal′li·bil′i·ty, fal′li·ble·ness,** *n.* **—fal′li·bly,** *adv.*

falling sickness, *Now Rare.* epilepsy.

falling star, an incandescent meteor; a shooting star.

Fal·lo·pi·an tubes (fə lō′pǐ ən). *Anat., Zool.* the uterine tubes, a pair of slender oviducts leading from the body cavity to the uterus, for transport and fertilization of ova. [named after *Fallopius,* Italian anatomist (1523–62)]

fall-out (fôl′out′), *n.* the descent of airborne particles of dust, soot, or, more particularly, of radioactive materials resulting from an atomic explosion.

fal·low¹ (făl′ō), *adj.* **1.** plowed and left unseeded for a season or more; uncultivated. **—n. 2.** land that has lain unseeded for a season or more after plowing and harrowing. **3.** the method of allowing land to lie for a season or more untilled in order to increase its productivity. **—v.t. 4.** to make (land) fallow for agricultural purposes. [ME *falwe,* OE *fealga,* pl., fallow land]

fal·low² (făl′ō), *adj.* pale-yellow; light-brown; dun. [ME *fal(o)we,* OE *fealu,* c. G *fahl, falb* fallow]

fallow deer, a Eurasian deer, *Dama dama,* with a fallow or yellowish coat.

Fall River, a seaport in SE Massachusetts, on an arm of Narragansett Bay. 99,942 (1960).

Fal·mouth (făl′məth), *n.* a seaport in SW England, in Cornwall. 17,036 (1951).

Fallow deer, *Dama dama* (3 ft. high at the shoulder, antlers ab. 2 ft. long)

false (fôls), *adj., falser, falsest.* **1.** not true or correct; erroneous: *a false statement or accusation.* **2.** uttering or declaring what is untrue: *false prophets, a false witness.* **3.** deceitful; treacherous; faithless: *a false friend.* **4.** deceptive; used to deceive or mislead: *false weights, to give a false impression.* **5.** not genuine: *a false signature, false diamonds, false teeth.* **6.** substitute or supplementary, esp. temporarily: *false supports for a bridge.* **7.** *Biol.* improperly so called, as from deceptive resemblance to something that properly bears the name: *the false acacia.* **8.** not properly adjusted, as a balance. **9.** inaccurate in pitch, as a musical note. [ME and OE *fals,* t. L: s. *falsus* feigned, deceptive, false, orig. pp] **—false′ly,** *adv.* **—false′ness,** *n.*
—Syn. 1. mistaken, incorrect, wrong, untrue. **2.** untruthful, lying, mendacious. **3.** insincere, hypocritical, disingenuous, disloyal, unfaithful, inconstant, recreant, perfidious, traitorous. **4.** misleading, fallacious. **5.** artificial, spurious, bogus, forged. FALSE, SHAM, COUNTERFEIT agree in referring to something that is not genuine. FALSE is used mainly of imitations of concrete objects; it often implies an intent to deceive: *false teeth, false hair.* SHAM is rarely used of concrete objects and has nearly always the suggestion of intent to deceive: *sham title, sham tears.* COUNTERFEIT always has the implication of cheating; it is used particularly of spurious imitation of coins, paper money, etc.

false bottom, a horizontal partition in the lower part of a box, trunk, etc., esp. one forming a secret section.

false cirrus, *Meteorol.* cirruslike clouds found over thunder clouds.

false colors, 1. another nation's flag. **2.** deceptive appearance; pretense.

false face, a mask.

false foxglove, any plant of the North American scrophulariaceous genus *Gerardia* (*Dasistoma, Aureolaria*), related to the foxglove.

false-heart·ed (fôls′här′tĭd), *adj.* having a false or treacherous heart; deceitful; perfidious.

false·hood (fôls′hŏŏd), *n.* **1.** lack of conformity to truth or fact. **2.** something false; an untrue idea, belief, etc. **3.** a false statement; a lie. **4.** act of lying or making false statements. **5.** *Rare.* falseness. **6.** *Obs.* deception.
—Syn. 3. FALSEHOOD, FIB, LIE, UNTRUTH refer to something untrue or incorrect. A FALSEHOOD is a statement that distorts or suppresses the truth, in order to deceive: *to tell a falsehood about one's ancestry, in order to escape punishment.* A FIB denotes a trivial falsehood, and is often used to characterize that which is not strictly true: *a polite fib.* A LIE is a vicious falsehood: *to tell a lie about one's neighbor.* An UNTRUTH is an incorrect statement, either intentionally misleading (less harsh, however, than falsehood or lie) or arising from misunderstanding or ignorance: *I'm afraid you are telling an untruth.* **4.** untruthfulness, inveracity, mendacity. **—Ant. 3.** truth.

false imprisonment, *Law.* the imprisonment of a person contrary to law.

false keel, a narrow extension of the keel, to protect a ship's bottom and reduce the leeway.

false pretenses, *Law.* the obtaining of title to money or property by the use of false representations, forged documents, or similar illegal device.

false relation, *Music.* cross relation.

false ribs, *Anat.* the five lower pairs of ribs, which are not attached to the sternum.

false step, 1. a stumble. **2.** an unwise act.

fal·set·to (fôl sĕt′ō), *n., pl.* **-tos,** *adj., adv.* **—n. 1.** an unnaturally or artificially high-pitched voice or register, esp. in a man. **2.** one who sings with such a voice. **—adj. 3.** of, or having the quality and compass of, such a voice. **4.** singing in a falsetto. **—adv. 5.** in a falsetto: *to speak falsetto.* [t. It., dim. of *falso* FALSE]

false vampire, a bat of any of the three Old World genera, *Megaderma, Macroderma,* and *Lyroderma,* large carnivorous forms erroneously reputed to suck blood.

fal·si·fy (fôl′sə fī), *v.,* **-fied, -fying. —v.t. 1.** to make false or incorrect, esp. so as to deceive. **2.** to alter fraudulently. **3.** to represent falsely; misrepresent. **4.** to show or prove to be false; disprove. **—v.i. 5.** to make false statements. [late ME *falsifie,* t. LL: m. *falsificāre,* der. L *falsificus* that acts falsely] **—fal·si·fi·ca·tion** (fôl′sə fə kā′shən), *n.* **—fal′si·fi′er,** *n.*

fal·si·ty (fôl′sə tĭ), *n., pl.* **-ties. 1.** the quality of being false; incorrectness; untruthfulness; treachery. **2.** something false; a falsehood. [t. L: m.s. *falsitas;* r. ME *falste,* t. OF: m. *falsete.*]

Fal·staff (fôl′stăf, -stäf), *n.* the jovial fat knight of brazen assurance and few scruples in Shakespeare's *Henry IV* and *Merry Wives of Windsor.* **—Fal·staff·i·an** (fôl stăf′ĭ ən), *adj.*

Fal·ster (fäl′stər), *n.* an island in SE Denmark. 45,665 pop. (1945); 198 sq. mi.

falt·boat (fält′bōt′), *n.* a folding boat similar to a kayak but more easily carried about. Also, **foldboat.** [t. G: m. *faltboot*]

fal·ter (fôl′tər), *v.i.* **1.** to hesitate or waver in action, purpose, etc.; give way. **2.** to speak hesitatingly or brokenly. **3.** to become unsteady in movement, as a person, an animal, or the legs, steps, etc.: *with faltering steps.* **—v.t. 4.** to utter hesitatingly or brokenly. **—n. 5.** act of faltering; an unsteadiness of gait, voice, action, etc. **6.** a faltering sound. [ME, ? t. Scand.; cf. Icel. *faltrask,* refl., be cumbered] **—fal′ter·ing·ly,** *adv.* **—Syn. 1.** vacillate. **2.** stammer, stutter.

F.A.M., Free and Accepted Masons. Also, **F. & A.M.**

fame (fām), *n., v.,* **famed, faming. —n. 1.** widespread reputation, esp. of a favorable character: *literary fame, to seek fame.* **2.** reputation; common estimation; opinion generally held. **—v.t. 3.** to spread the fame of; make famous: *a place famed throughout the world.* [ME, t. obs. F, t. L: m. *fāma* report, fame] **—fame′less,** *adj.*
—Syn. 1. repute, notoriety, celebrity, renown, eminence, honor, glory. **—Ant. 1.** obscurity; ignominy.

famed (fāmd), *adj.* famous.

Fa·meuse (fə mŭz′; *Fr.* fà mœz′), *n.* an American variety of red apple which ripens in the early winter. [t. F, fem. of *fameux* famous]

fa·mil·ial (fə mĭl′yəl), *adj.* **1.** of or pertaining to a family. **2.** appearing in individuals by heredity: *a familial disease.*

fa·mil·iar (fə mĭl′yər), *adj.* **1.** commonly or generally known or seen: *a familiar sight, a sight familiar to us all.* **2.** well-acquainted; thoroughly conversant: *to be familiar with a subject, book, method, tool, etc.* **3.** easy; informal; unceremonious; unconstrained: *to write in a familiar style.* **4.** closely intimate: *a familiar friend, to be on familiar terms.* **5.** unduly intimate; taking liberties; presuming. **6.** domesticated; tame. **7.** *Rare.* of or pertaining to a family or household. **—n. 8.** a familiar friend or associate. **9.** a familiar spirit. **10.** *Rom. Cath. Ch.* **a.** an officer of the Inquisition, employed to arrest accused or suspected persons. **b.** one who belongs to the household of the Pope or of a bishop, rendering domestic though not menial service. [t. L: s. *familiāris* belonging to a household, private; r. ME *familier,* t. OF] **—fa·mil′iar·ly,** *adv.*
—Syn. 1. common, well-known, frequent. **4.** close, friendly, fraternal. FAMILIAR, CONFIDENTIAL, INTIMATE suggest a long association between persons. FAMILIAR means well acquainted with another person: *a familiar friend.* CONFIDENTIAL suggests a sense of mutual trust which extends to the sharing of confidences and secrets: *a confidential advisor.* INTIMATE suggests close acquaintance or connection, often based on interest, sympathy, or affection: *intimate and affectionate letters.* **5.** free, forward, intrusive, bold. **—Ant. 1.** strange. **2.** unacquainted. **5.** well-bred.

fa·mil·i·ar·i·ty (fə mĭl′ĭ ăr′ə tĭ), *n., pl.* **-ties. 1.** close acquaintance; thorough knowledge of (a thing, subject, etc.). **2.** undue intimacy; freedom of behavior justified only by the most intimate friendly relations. **3.** (*often pl.*) an instance or manifestation of such freedom, as in action or speech. **4.** absence of formality or ceremony: *to be on terms of familiarity with someone.* **—Syn. 2.** liberty, disrespect. **4.** informality, unconstraint.

fa·mil·iar·ize (fə mĭl′yə rīz′), *v.t.,* **-ized, -izing. 1.** to make (a person) familiarly acquainted or conversant, as with something. **2.** to make (something) well-known; bring into common knowledge or use. **3.** *Rare.* to make familiar; establish (a person) in friendly intimacy. **—v.i. 4.** *Now Rare.* to associate in a familiar way. **—fa·mil′iar·i·za′tion,** *n.*

familiar spirit, a supernatural spirit or demon supposed to attend on or serve a person.

fam·i·ly (făm′ə lĭ, făm′lĭ), *n., pl.* **-lies. 1.** parents and their children, whether dwelling together or not. **2.** one's children collectively. **3.** any group of persons closely related by blood, as parents, children, uncles, aunts, and

ăct, āble, dâre, ärt; ĕbb, ēqual; ĭf, īce; hŏt, ōver, ôrder, oil, bŏŏk, ōōze, out; ŭp, ūse, ûrge; ə = a in alone; ch, chief; g, give; ng, ring; sh, shoe; th, thin; ŧħ, that; zh, vision. See the full key on inside cover.

cousins. **4.** all those persons descended from a common progenitor. **5.** *Chiefly Brit.* descent, esp. good or noble descent: *young men of family.* **6.** *Biol.* the usual major subdivision of an order or suborder, commonly comprising a plurality of genera: e.g. *Equidae* (horses), *Formicidae* (the ants), *Orchidaceae* (the orchids). Names of animal families end in *-idae,* of plant families in *-aceae.* **7.** the group of persons who form a household under one head, including parents, children, servants, etc. **8.** the staff, or body of assistants, of an official. **9.** a group of related things. **10.** (in the classification of languages) a number of languages all of which are more closely related to each other than any of them are to any language outside the group, usually a major grouping admitting of subdivisions: *English is of the Indo-European family.* [ME *familie,* t. L: m.s. *familia* the servants of a household, household, family]

family circle, 1. the closely related members of a family as a group: *a scandal known only within the family circle.* **2.** a gallery in a theater, etc., esp. the topmost one.

family name, 1. the hereditary surname of a family. **2.** a frequent Christian, or first name, in a family.

family skeleton, a secret or hidden source of shame to a family.

family tree, a genealogical chart showing the ancestry, descent, and relationship of all members of a family.

fam·ine (făm′ĭn), *n.* **1.** extreme and general scarcity of food. **2.** any extreme and general scarcity. **3.** extreme hunger; starvation. [ME, t. F, der. *faim* hunger, g. L *fames*]

fam·ish (făm′ĭsh), *v.t., v.i.* **1.** to suffer, or cause to suffer, extreme hunger; starve. **2.** to starve to death. [f. ME *fame(n)* famish (ult. der. L *fames* hunger) + -ISH²] —**fam′ish·ment,** *n.*

fam·ished (făm′ĭsht), *adj.* very hungry. —**Syn.** See **hungry.**

fa·mous (fā′məs), *adj.* **1.** celebrated in fame or public report; renowned; well-known: *a famous victory.* **2.** *Colloq.* first-rate; excellent. **3.** *Obs.* notorious (in an unfavorable sense). [ME, t. AF, t. L: m.s. *fāmōsus,* der. *fāma* fame] —**fa′mous·ly,** *adv.* —**fa′mous·ness,** *n.* —**Syn. 1.** famed, notable. FAMOUS, CELEBRATED, EMINENT, DISTINGUISHED refer to someone or something widely and favorably known. FAMOUS is the general word: *a famous lighthouse.* CELEBRATED originally referred to something commemorated, but now usually refers to someone or something widely known for conspicuous merit, services, etc.: *a celebrated writer.* EMINENT implies high standing among one's contemporaries, esp. in his own profession or craft: *an eminent physician.* DISTINGUISHED adds to *eminent* the idea of honors conferred more or less publicly: *a distinguished scientist.* —**Ant. 1.** unknown, obscure.

fam·u·lus (făm′yə ləs), *n., pl.* **-li** (-lī′). a servant or attendant, esp. of a scholar or a magician. [t. L]

fan¹ (făn), *n., v.,* **fanned, fanning.** —*n.* **1.** any device for causing a current of air by the movement of a broad surface or a number of such surfaces. **2.** an object of feathers, leaves, paper, cloth, etc., for causing a cooling current of air. **3.** anything resembling such an implement, as the tail of a bird. **4.** any of various devices consisting essentially of a series of radiating vanes or blades attached to and revolving with a central hublike portion, and used to produce a current of air. **5.** a series of revolving blades supplying air for winnowing or cleaning grain. —*v.t.* **6.** to move or agitate (the air) with, or as with, a fan. **7.** to cause air to blow upon, as from a fan; cool or refresh with, or as with, a fan. **8.** to stir to activity with, or as with, a fan: *fan a flame, emotions, etc.* **9.** (of a breeze, etc.) to blow upon, as if driven by a fan. **10.** to spread out like a fan. **11.** *Agric.* to winnow, esp. by an artificial current of air. **12.** *Baseball.* to strike out (a batter). —*v.i.* **13.** to spread out like a fan (fol. by *out*). **14.** *Baseball.* to strike out. [ME; OE *fann,* t. L: m.s. *vannus* fan for winnowing grain] —**fan′like′,** *adj.*

fan² (făn), *n. Colloq.* an enthusiastic devotee or follower: *a baseball fan, a movie fan.* [short for FANATIC]

fa·nat·ic (fə năt′ĭk), *n.* **1.** a person with an extreme and unreasoning enthusiasm or zeal, esp. in religious matters. —*adj.* **2.** fanatical. [t. L: s. *fānāticus* pertaining to a temple, inspired by a divinity, frantic]

fa·nat·i·cal (fə năt′ə kəl), *adj.* **1.** actuated or characterized by an extreme, unreasoning enthusiasm or zeal, esp. in religious matters. **2.** pertaining to or characteristic of a fanatic. —**fa·nat′i·cal·ly,** *adv.* —**Syn. 1.** See **intolerant. 2.** See **radical.**

fa·nat·i·cism (fə năt′ə sĭz′əm), *n.* fanatical character, spirit, or conduct.

fa·nat·i·cize (fə năt′ə sīz′), *v.,* **-cized, -cizing.** —*v.t.* **1.** to make fanatical. —*v.i.* **2.** to act with or show fanaticism.

fan·cied (făn′sĭd), *adj.* imaginary: *fancied grievances.*

fan·ci·er (făn′sĭ ər), *n.* **1.** a person having a liking for or interest in something, as some class of animals or plants. **2.** one who breeds and sells birds, dogs, etc. **3.** one who is under the influence of his fancy.

fan·ci·ful (făn′sĭ fəl), *adj.* **1.** exhibiting fancy; quaint or odd in appearance: *a fanciful design.* **2.** suggested by fancy; imaginary; unreal. **3.** led by fancy rather than by reason and experience; whimsical: *a fanciful mind.* —**fan′ci·ful·ly,** *adv.* —**fan′ci·ful·ness,** *n.*

fan·ci·less (făn′sĭ lĭs), *adj.* without fancy or imagination.

fan·cy (făn′sĭ), *n., pl.* **-cies,** *adj.,* **-cier, -ciest,** *v.,* **-cied, -cying,** *interj.* —*n.* **1.** imagination, esp. as exercised in a capricious or desultory manner. **2.** the faculty of creating illustrative or decorative imagery, as in poetical or literary composition, as distinct from the power of producing ideal creations consistent with reality (imagination). **3.** a mental image or conception. **4.** an idea or opinion with little foundation; a hallucination. **5.** a caprice; whim; vagary. **6.** capricious preference; inclination; a liking: *to take a fancy to something.* **7.** critical judgment; taste. **8.** the breeding of animals to develop points of beauty or excellence. **9.** *Obs.* love. —*adj.* **10.** adapted to please the taste or fancy; of superfine quality: *fancy goods, work, fruits, etc.* **11.** ornamental. **12.** imaginative. **13.** depending on fancy or caprice; whimsical; irregular. **14.** bred to develop points of beauty or excellence, as an animal. —*v.t.* **15.** to form a conception of; picture to oneself: *fancy living with him all your life!* **16.** to believe without being sure or certain. **17.** to take a liking to; like. **18.** to breed to develop a special type of animal. —*interj.* **19.** an expression of mild surprise. [contr. of FANTASY] —**Syn. 2.** FANCY, FANTASY, IMAGINATION refer to qualities in literary or other artistic composition. The creations of FANCY are casual, whimsical, and often amusing, being at once less profound and less inspirational than those of imagination: *letting one's fancy play freely on a subject, an impish fancy.* FANTASY now usually suggests an unrestrained or extravagant fancy, bordering on caprice: *the use of fantasy in art brings strange results.* The name and concept of creative IMAGINATION are less than two hundred years old; previously only the *reproductive* aspect had been recognized, hardly to be distinguished from memory. "Creative imagination" suggests that the memories of sights and experiences may so blend in the mind of the writer or artist as to produce something that has never existed before—often a hitherto unperceived vision of the realities of life: *to use imagination in portraying character and action.*

fancy ball, a ball at which costumes are worn.

fancy dress, dress chosen in accordance with the wearer's fancy, for wear at a ball or the like, as that characteristic of a particular period or place, class of persons, or historical or fictitious character.

fan·cy-free (făn′sĭ frē′), *adj.* free from any influence, esp. love.

fan·cy·work (făn′sĭ wûrk′), *n.* ornamental needlework.

fan·dan·go (făn dăng′gō), *n., pl.* **-gos. 1.** a lively Spanish or Spanish-American dance in triple time. **2.** a piece of music for such a dance or with its rhythm. **3.** a ball or dance. [t. Sp., from W Ind.]

fan delta, an alluvial cone, partially submerged.

fane (fān), *n. Archaic or Poetic.* **1.** a temple. **2.** a church. [t. L: m.s. *fānum* temple]

fa·ne·ga (fä nĕ′gä), *n.* **1.** a unit of dry measure in Spanish-speaking countries, equal in Spain to 1.58 U.S. bushels. **2.** a Mexican unit of land measure, equal to 8.81 acres. [t. Sp.]

fa·ne·ga·da (fä′nĕ gä′dä), *n.* a unit of land measure in Spanish-speaking countries varying from 1¼ to 1¾ acres. [t. Sp.]

Fan·euil (făn′əl, -yəl), *n.* **Peter,** 1700–43, colonial American merchant, founder of Faneuil Hall, in Boston.

Faneuil Hall, a market house and hall in Boston, Massachusetts, called "the Cradle of Liberty" because it was used as a meeting place by American patriots in the Revolutionary period.

fan·fare (făn′fâr), *n.* **1.** a flourish or short air played on trumpets or the like. **2.** an ostentatious flourish or parade. [t. F, der. *fanfarer* blow a fanfare, der. s. *fanfaron* FANFARON]

fan·fa·ron (făn′fə rŏn′), *n.* **1.** a braggart. **2.** a fanfare. [t. F, t. Sp.: m. *fanfarrón,* der. Ar. *farfār* talkative]

fan·fa·ron·ade (făn′fə rə nād′), *n.* bragging; bravado; bluster. [t. F: m. *fanfaronnade,* t. Sp.: m. *fanfarronada,* der. *fanfarrón* FANFARON]

fang (făng), *n.* **1.** one of the long, sharp, hollow or grooved teeth of a snake, by which venom is injected. **2.** a canine tooth. **3.** the root of a tooth. **4.** a doglike tooth. **5.** a pointed tapering part of a thing. **6.** *Mach.* a tang of a tool. [ME and OE, c. G *fang*] —**fanged** (făngd), *adj.* —**fang′less,** *adj.* —**fang′like′,** *adj.*

Head of rattlesnake F. Fangs; P. Poison sac; D. Poison duct; M. Muscle

fan·gle (făng′gəl), *n.* a fashion: *new fangles of dress.*

fan·light (făn′līt′), *n.* a fan-shaped or other window above a door or other opening. (In British usage *fanlight* often equals U.S. *transom.*)

fan·ner (făn′ər), *n.* one who or that which fans.

fanning mill, a machine for cleaning grain by the action of riddles and sieves and an air blast.

fan·on (făn′ən), *n. Eccles.* **1.** a maniple. **2.** a striped scarflike vestment worn by the pope over the alb when celebrating solemn pontifical mass. [ME, t. F, t. ML: s. *fano,* t. OHG: flag, cloth, c. VANE]

fan palm, any palm with fan-shaped leaves, as the talipot and numerous others.

fan·tail (făn′tāl′), *n.* **1.** a tail, end, or part shaped like a fan. **2.** a fancy breed of domestic pigeons with a fan-shaped tail. **3.** any of various small birds having fanlike tails, as the Old World flycatchers of the genus *Rhipidura* and the American wood warblers of the genus *Euthlypis*. **4.** an artificially bred variety of goldfish with double anal and caudal fins. **5.** an American fresh-water fish, a darter of the perch family, *Poecilichthys flabellaris*, or a related species. **6.** *Archit.* **a.** a member, or piece of a construction, having the shape of a fan. **b.** a substructure of radiating supports, as of an arch.

fan-tan (făn′tăn′), *n.* **1.** *Cards.* a game in which the cards are played in sequence, the winner being the player who first gets rid of his cards. **2.** a Chinese gambling game in which a pile of coins or counters is placed under a bowl and bets are made on what the remainder will be after they have been divided by four. [t. Chinese (Mandarin): m. *fan t'an* repeated divisions]

fan-ta-si-a (făn tā′zhI ə, -zhə, făn′tə zē′ə), *n.* **1.** *Music.* **a.** a composition in fanciful or irregular rather than strict form or style. **b.** a potpourri of well-known airs arranged with interludes and florid decorations. **2.** a literary work that is not curbed by a fixed plan. [t. It., g. L *phantasia*. See FANTASY]

fan-tasm (făn′tăzəm), *n.* phantasm.

fan-tas-ma-go-ri-a (făn tăz′mə gôr′I ə), *n.* phantasmagoria.

fan-tast (făn′tăst), *n.* a visionary.

fan-tas-tic (făn tăs′tĭk), *adj.* **1.** odd, quaint, eccentric, or grotesque in conception, design, character, movement, etc.: *fantastic ornaments.* **2.** fanciful or capricious, as persons or their ideas, actions, etc. **3.** imaginary; groundless; not real: *fantastic fears.* **4.** extravagantly fanciful; irrational: *fantastic reasons.* Also, **fan-tas′ti-cal.** [ME *fantastik*, t. ML: m.s. *fantasticus* imaginary, LL *phantasticus*, t. Gk.: m. *phantastikós* able to present (to the mind)] —**fan-tas′ti-cal-ly,** *adv.* —**fan-tas′-ti-cal-ness, fan-tas′ti-cal′i-ty,** *n.*

fan-ta-sy (făn′təsĭ, -zĭ), *n., pl.* **-sies. 1.** imagination, esp. when unrestrained. **2.** the forming of grotesque mental images. **3.** a mental image, esp. when grotesque. **4.** *Psychol.* an imaginative sequence fulfilling a psychological need; a daydream. **5.** a hallucination. **6.** a supposition based on no solid foundation; a visionary idea. **7.** caprice; whim. **8.** an ingenious or odd thought, design, or invention. **9.** *Music.* a fantasia. Also, **phantasy.** [ME *fantasie*, t. OF, t. L: m. *phantasia* idea, fancy, t. Gk.: impression, image] —**Syn. 1.** See **fancy.**

fan-toc-ci-ni (făn′tə chē′nĭ), *n.pl.* **1.** puppets operated by concealed wires or strings. **2.** dramatic representations in which they are used. [t. It., pl. of *fantoccino*, dim. of *fantoccio* puppet, der. *fante* boy, g. L *infans* child]

fan-tom (făn′təm), *n., adj.* phantom.

fan tracery, *Archit.* tracery which rises from a capital or a corbel and diverges like the folds of a fan, spreading over the surface of a vault.

fan vaulting, *Archit.* a complicated mode of roofing, in which the vault is covered by ribs and veins of tracery, diverging from a single point.

fan window, *Archit.* a fan-shaped window whose sash is formed with radial bars; a fanlight.

fan-wort (făn′wûrt′), *n.* a plant, *Cabomba caroliniana*, of the water-lily family, found in ponds, etc.

far (fär), *adv., adj.,* farther, farthest. —*adv.* **1.** at or to a great distance; a long way off; to a remote point: *far ahead.* **2.** very remote in time, degree, scope, purpose, desire, etc.: *far from successful.* **3.** to a great degree; very much: *far better, worse, different.* **4.** at or to a definite distance, point of progress, or degree. **5.** Some special adverb phrases are:
as far as, to the distance, extent, or degree that.
by far, very much.
far and away, very much.
far and wide, to great distances.
far be it from me, I do not wish or dare.
from far, from a distance.
go far, 1. to be successful; do much. **2.** to tend greatly.
how far, to what distance, extent, or degree.
in so far, to such an extent.
so far, 1. up to now. **2.** up to that point, extent, etc.
so far so good, no trouble yet.
—*adj.* **6.** at a great distance; remote. **7.** extending to a great distance. **8.** more distant of the two: *the far side.* **9.** greatly different or apart.
[ME *far, fer,* etc., OE *feor,* c. OHG *fer;* akin to Gk. *perā* further]

far-ad (făr′əd, -ăd), *n. Elect.* a unit of capacitance equal to the change in the number of coulombs of charge per volt of change of potential. [named after FARADAY]

Far-a-day (făr′ədĭ, -dā′), *n.* **1.** a unit of quantity used in electrolysis, equal to about 96,500 coulombs. **2.** Michael, 1791–1867, British physicist and chemist: discoverer of electromagnetic induction.

fa-rad-ic (fə răd′ĭk), *adj. Elect.* of or pertaining to induction or the phenomena connected with it. [var. of *faradaic,* der. FARADAY]

far-a-dism (făr′ə dĭz′əm), *n.* **1.** induced electricity. **2.** *Med.* its application for therapeutic purposes.

far-a-dize (făr′ə dīz′), *v.t.,* -dized, -dizing. *Med.* to stimulate or treat, as a muscle, with induced electric currents. —**far′a-di-za′tion,** *n.* —**far′a-diz′er,** *n.*

far-and (făr′ənd), *adj.* farrand.

far-an-dole (făr′ən dōl′; *Fr.* fȧ rän dôl′), *n.* **1.** a lively dance, of Provençal origin, in which all the dancers join hands and execute various figures. **2.** the music for this

dance. [t. F, t. Pr.: m. *farandoulo,* prob. f. *fa* make + *roundelo* round dance, ult. der. L *rotundus* round]

far-a-way (făr′ə wā′), *adj.* **1.** distant; remote. **2.** abstracted or dreamy, as a look.

farce (färs), *n., v.,* farced, farcing. —*n.* **1.** a play, light in tone, in which the plot depends upon situation rather than character. **2.** foolish show; mockery; a ridiculous sham. —*v.t.* **3.** to season (a speech or composition), as with scraps of wit. **4.** *Obs.* to stuff; cram. [ME *farse*(n), t. F: m. *farcir,* g. L *farcīre* stuff]

farce-meat (färs′mēt′), *n.* Cookery. forcemeat.

far-ceur (färsœr′), *n. French.* **1.** a writer or player of farces. **2.** a joker or wag.

far-ci (färsē′; *Fr.* făr-), *adj. Cookery.* stuffed. [t. F]

far-ci-cal (färsəkəl), *adj.* **1.** pertaining to or of the nature of farce. **2.** resembling farce; ludicrous; absurd. —**far′ci-cal′i-ty, far′ci-cal-ness,** *n.* —**far′ci-cal-ly,** *adv.*

far cry, a great distance.

far-cy (fär′sĭ), *n. Vet. Sci.* a form of the disease glanders chiefly affecting the superficial lymphatics and the skin of horses and mules. [var. of *farcin,* t. F, g. L *farcīminum* disease of horses]

farcy bud, *Vet. Sci.* an ulcerated swelling, produced in farcy. Also, **farcy button.**

far-del (fär′dəl), *n. Archaic.* a bundle; a burden. [ME, t. OF, dim. of *farde* pack, t. Ar.: m. *farda* bundle]

fare (fâr), *n., v.,* fared, faring. —*n.* **1.** the price of conveyance or passage. **2.** the person or persons who pay to be conveyed in a vehicle. **3.** food. **4.** *Archaic.* state of things. —*v.i.* **5.** to be entertained, esp. with food and drink. **6.** to experience good or bad fortune, treatment, etc.; get on: *he fared well.* **7.** to go; turn out; happen (used impersonally): *it fared ill with him.* **8.** *Archaic.* to go; travel. [ME *fare*(n), OE *faran,* c. G *fahren;* akin to Gk. *perān* pass, *póros* passage] —**far′er,** *n.* —**Syn. 3.** See food.

Far East, the countries of E and SE Asia: China, Japan, Korea, Thailand, etc.

Far Eastern Region, former name of **Khabarovsk** (def. 1).

fare-well (fâr′wĕl′), *interj.* **1.** may you fare well; good-by; adieu. —*n.* **2.** an expression of good wishes at parting. **3.** leave-taking; departure: *a fond farewell.* —*adj.* **4.** par ting; valedictory: *a farewell sermon or performance.* [o rig. two words, *fare well.* See FARE, v.]

Fare-well (fâr′wĕl′), *n.* Cape, the S tip of Greenland.

far-fetched (fär′fĕcht′), *adj.* remotely connected; forced; strained: *a far-fetched example.*

far-flung (fär′flŭng′), *adj.* flung or extending over a great distance: *our far-flung battle line.*

Far-go (fär′gō), *n.* a city in SE North Dakota. 46,662 (1960).

fa-ri-na (fə rē′nə), *n.* **1.** flour or meal made from cereal grains, cooked as cereal or used in puddings, etc. **2.** starch. [t. L, der. *far* spelt]

far-i-na-ceous (făr′ə nā′shəs), *adj.* **1.** consisting or made of flour or meal, as food. **2.** containing or yielding starch, as seeds. **3.** mealy in appearance or nature.

far-i-nose (făr′ə nōs′), *adj.* **1.** yielding farina. **2.** resembling farina. **3.** covered with a mealy powder.

far-kle-ber-ry (fär′kəl bĕr′Ĭ), *n., pl.* **-ries.** a shrub or small tree, *Vaccinium (Batodendron) arboreum,* of the southern U.S., bearing a black, many-seeded berry.

farl (färl), *n.* a thin circular cake of flour or oatmeal.

Far-ley (fär′lĭ), *n.* James Aloysius (ăl′ō Ĭsh′əs), born 1888, U.S. political leader.

farm (färm), *n.* **1.** a tract of land devoted to agriculture. **2.** a tract of land or water devoted to some other industry: *a chicken farm, an oyster farm.* **3.** the system, method, or act of collecting revenue by letting out a territory in districts. **4.** *Rare.* a country or district let out for the collection of revenue. **5.** a fixed amount accepted from a person in lieu of taxes or the like which he is authorized to collect. **6.** *Eng. Hist.* **a.** the rent or income from leased property or rights such as lands or revenues. **b.** the state of leased property or rights; a lease; possession under lease. **7.** *Obs.* a fixed yearly amount payable in the form of rent, taxes, or the like. —*v.t.* **8.** to cultivate (land). **9.** to take the proceeds or profits of (a tax, undertaking, etc.) on paying a fixed sum. **10.** to let or lease (taxes, revenues, an enterprise, etc.) to another for a fixed sum or a percentage (often fol. by *out*). **11.** to let or lease the labor or services of (a person) for hire. **12.** to contract for the maintenance of (a person, institution, etc.). —*v.i.* **13.** to cultivate the soil; operate a farm. [ME *ferme,* t. F, der. *fermer* fix, g. L *firmāre*]

farm-er (fär′mər), *n.* **1.** one who farms; one who cultivates land or operates a farm. **2.** one who undertakes some service, as the care of children, at a fixed price. **3.** one who undertakes the collection of taxes, etc., paying a fixed sum for the privilege of retaining them.

farm-er-ette (fär′mə rĕt′), *n. Colloq.* a girl or woman working on a farm.

farm-er-gen-er-al (fär′mər jĕn′ər əl), *n., pl.* **farm-ers-general.** (in France, under the old monarchy) a member of a company of capitalists that farmed certain taxes. [trans. of F *fermier-général*]

Farm-er-La-bor Party (fär′mər lā′bər), a political party in the U.S. attempting to unite farmers and industrial workers for the protection of their interests.

ăct, āble, dâre, ärt; ĕbb, ēqual; Ĭf, īce; hŏt, ōver, ôrder, oil, bŏŏk, ōoze, out; ŭp, ūse, ûrge; ə = a in alone. ch, chief; g, give; ng, ring; sh, shoe; th, thin; ŧh, that; zh, vision. See the full key on inside cover;

farmers' coöperative, an organization of farmers for marketing their products or buying supplies.

farm·er·y (fär′mər‑ĭ), n., pl. **-eries.** Brit. the buildings, yards, etc., of a farm.

farm hand, person who works on a farm.

farm·house (färm′hous′), n. a house on a farm.

farm·ing (fär′mĭng), n. 1. the business of operating a farm. 2. the practice of letting or leasing taxes, revenue, etc., for collection. 3. the business of collecting taxes. —adj. 4. of, for, or pertaining to farms: farming tools, land, etc.

farm·stead (färm′stĕd), n. Chiefly Brit. a farm with its buildings.

farm·yard (färm′yärd′), n. a yard or enclosure surrounded by or connected with farm buildings.

Far·ne·se (fär nĕ′sĕ), n. **Alessandro** (ä′lĕs sän′drō), (Duke of Parma) 1545–92, Italian general, statesman, and diplomat in the service of Philip II of Spain.

far·ne·sol (fär′nə sŏl′, ‑sōl′), n. Chem. an extract, $C_{15}H_{26}O$, from the flowers of the acacia, cassia oil, etc., used in the perfume industry.

far·o (fâr′ō), n. Cards. a gambling game in which the players bet on the cards of the dealer's or banker's pack. [alter. of PHARAOH]

Far·oe Islands (fâr′ō), Faeroe Islands.

Far·o·ese (fâr′ō ēz′, ‑ēs′), n., pl. **-ese.** 1. a native or an inhabitant of the Faeroes. 2. a Scandinavian dialect spoken in the Faeroes, closely related to Icelandic.

far-off (fär′ôf′, ‑ŏf′), adj. distant; remote.

fa·rouche (fà rōōsh′), adj. French. 1. fierce. 2. unsociable; shy. 3. sullen. [F, alter. of forasche, g. L forasticus foreign, der. foras outside]

Fa·rouk I (fä rōōk′). 1920–65, king of Egypt from 1936 to his abdication in 1952. Also, **Faruk.**

Far·quhar (fär′kwər, ‑kwär, ‑kər), n. **George,** 1678–1707, British writer of comedies.

far·rag·i·nous (fə răj′ə nəs), adj. Now Rare. formed of various materials. [f. s. L farrāgo mixed fodder + ‑ous]

far·ra·go (fə rā′gō, ‑rä′/‑), n., pl. **-goes.** a confused mixture; a hodgepodge; a medley: a farrago of doubts, fears, hopes, wishes. [t. L: mixed fodder, medley]

Far·ra·gut (făr′ə gət), n. **David Glasgow,** 1801–70, U.S. admiral: won the battles of New Orleans and Mobile Bay for the Union in the U.S. Civil War.

far·rand (făr′ənd), adj. having a (fair, ugly, evil, etc.) nature or appearance. Also, **farand.** [ME farand comely, orig. ppr. (North.) of FARE, v.]

Far·rar (fə rär′), n. **Geraldine** (Mrs. Lou Tellegen), born 1882, U.S. operatic soprano.

far-reach·ing (fär′rē′chĭng), adj. extending far in influence, effect, etc.

Far·rell (făr′əl), n. **James Thomas,** born 1904, U.S. novelist.

far·ri·er (făr′ĭ ər), n. Brit. 1. a blacksmith who shoes horses. 2. a doctor for horses; a veterinarian. [t. MF: m. ferrier, g. L ferrārius, der. ferrum iron]

far·ri·er·y (făr′ĭ ər ĭ), n., pl. **-eries.** the art or the establishment of a farrier.

far·row¹ (făr′ō), n. 1. a litter of pigs. —v.t. 2. (of swine) to bring forth (young). —v.i. 3. to produce a litter of pigs. [ME far, OE fearh; akin to G ferkel pig, L porcus]

far·row² (făr′ō), adj. (of a cow) not pregnant. [orig. uncert. Cf. Flem. verwekoe barren cow]

far-see·ing (fär′sē′ĭng), adj. 1. having foresight; sagacious; discerning. 2. able to see far; far-sighted.

far-sight·ed (fär′sī′tĭd), adj. 1. seeing to a great distance. 2. seeing objects at a distance more clearly than those near at hand; hypermetropic. 3. foreseeing future results wisely: a far-sighted statesman. —**far′-sight′-ed·ly,** adv. —**far′-sight′ed·ness,** n.

far·ther (fär′thər), compar. of far. —adv. 1. at or to a greater distance. 2. at or to a more advanced point. 3. to a greater degree or extent. 4. additionally. —adj. 5. more distant or remote. 6. extending or tending to a greater distance. 7. additional; further. [ME ferther; orig. var. of further, but now taken as an irreg. formed compar. (prop. farrer) of far, with superl. farthest]

Farther India, Indochina.

far·ther·most (fär′thər mōst′, ‑məst), adj. most distant or remote; farthest.

far·thest (fär′thĭst), superl. of far. —adj. 1. most distant or remote. 2. longest. —adv. 3. to or at the greatest distance. [ME ferthest, orig. var. of furthest. See FARTHER]

far·thing (fär′thĭng), n. 1. an English coin of bronze, worth one fourth of a penny, or about half a U.S. cent. 2. something of very small value. [ME ferthing, OE fēorthung, der. fēortha fourth]

far·thin·gale (fär′thĭng gāl′), n. a kind of hoop skirt or framework for expanding a woman's skirt, worn in the 16th and 17th centuries. [t. MF: m. verdugale, t. Sp.: m. verdugado, der. verdugo shoot, rod]

Fa·ruk I (fä rōōk′), Farouk I.

Far West, 1. the area of the Rocky Mountains and the Pacific Coast.

Farthingale.
Elizabethan period

2. U.S. Hist. the Middle West, esp. the area west of the Mississippi river. —**Far Western.**

F.A.S., free alongside ship (which see). Also, **f.a.s.**

fas·ces (făs′ēz), n.pl., sing. **fascis.** a bundle of rods containing an ax with the blade projecting, borne before Roman magistrates as an emblem of official power. [t. L, pl. of fascis bundle] —**fas·ci·al** (făsh′ĭ əl), adj.

fas·ci·a (făsh′ĭ ə), n., pl. **fasciae** (făsh′ĭ ē′). 1. a band or fillet. 2. Surg. a bandage. 3. Archit. **a.** a long, flat member or band. **b.** a triple horizontal division of an architrave in Ionic, Corinthian, and composite orders. See diag. under column. 4. Anat., Zool. **a.** a band or sheath of connective tissue investing, supporting, or binding together internal organs or parts of the body. **b.** tissue of this kind. 5. Zool. a distinctly marked band of color. [t. L: band] —**fas′ci·al,** adj.

Fasces

fas·ci·ate (făsh′ĭ āt′), adj. 1. bound with a band, fillet, or bandage. 2. Bot. **a.** compressed into a band or bundle. **b.** grown together, as stems. 3. Zool. **a.** composed of bundles. **b.** bound together in a bundle. **c.** marked with a band or bands. Also, **fas′ci·at′ed.** [t. L: m.s. fasciātus, pp., enveloped with bands]

fas·ci·a·tion (făsh′ĭ ā′shən), n. 1. act of binding up or bandaging. 2. the process of becoming fasciate. 3. resulting state.

fas·ci·cle (făs′ə kəl), n. 1. a small bundle. 2. a part of a printed work; a number of printed or written sheets bound together, as an installment for convenience in publication. 3. Bot. a close cluster, as of flowers or leaves. 4. Anat. a small bundle of fibers within a nerve or the central nervous system. [t. L: m.s. fasciculus, dim. of fascis bundle] —**fas′ci·cled,** adj.

fas·cic·u·lar (fə sĭk′yə lər), adj. pertaining to or forming a fascicle; fasciculate.

fas·cic·u·late (fə sĭk′yə lĭt, ‑lāt′), adj. arranged in a fascicle or fascicles. Also, **fas·cic′u·lat′ed.** —**fas·cic′u·late·ly,** adv.

fas·cic·u·la·tion (fə sĭk′yə lā′shən), n. fascicular condition.

fas·ci·cule (făs′ə kūl′), n. a fascicle, esp. of a book. [t. L: m.s. fasciculus little bundle]

fas·cic·u·lus (fə sĭk′yə ləs), n., pl. **-li** (‑lī′). 1. a fascicle, as of nerve or muscle fibers. 2. a fascicle of a book. [t. L: little bundle]

fas·ci·nate (făs′ə nāt′), v.t. **-nated, -nating.** 1. to attract and hold irresistibly by delightful qualities. 2. to deprive of the power of resistance, as through terror. 3. Obs. to bewitch. 4. Obs. to cast under a spell by a look. [t. L: m.s. fascinātus, pp., enchanted] —**Syn.** 1. bewitch, charm, enchant, entrance, enrapture, captivate, allure, infatuate, enamor. —**Ant.** 1. repel.

fas·ci·nat·ing (făs′ə nā′tĭng), adj. bewitching; enchanting; charming; captivating: a fascinating poem. —**fas′ci·nat′ing·ly,** adv.

fas·ci·na·tion (făs′ə nā′shən), n. 1. act of fascinating. 2. state of being fascinated. 3. fascinating quality; powerful attraction; charm.

fas·ci·na·tor (făs′ə nā′tər), n. 1. one who or that which fascinates. 2. a kind of scarf of crochet work, lace, etc., narrowing towards the ends, worn as a head covering by women.

fas·cine (fă sēn′, fə‑), n. 1. a fagot. 2. Fort. a long bundle of sticks bound together, used in building earthworks and batteries and in strengthening ramparts, etc. [t. F, t. L: m. fascina bundle of sticks]

fas·cis (făs′ĭs), n. sing. of fasces.

fas·cism (făsh′ĭz əm), n. 1. (often cap.) a governmental system with strong centralized power, permitting no opposition or criticism, controlling all affairs of the nation (industrial, commercial, etc.), emphasizing an aggressive nationalism, and (often) anticommunist. Fascism was established in Italy by Mussolini in 1922, whence its influence spread to Germany and elsewhere; it was dissolved in Italy in 1943. 2. (often cap.) the philosophy, principles, or methods of fascism. 3. (cap.) a fascist movement, esp. the one in Italy. Also, Italian, **Fa·scis·mo** (fä shēs′mō). [t. It.: m. Fascismo, der. fascio group, bundle, g. s. L fascis bundle (of sticks, an lictors' emblem). See FASCES]

fas·cist (făsh′ĭst), n. 1. anyone who believes in or sympathizes with fascism. 2. a member of a fascist movement or party, esp. (cap.) in Italy. —adj. 3. of or like fascism or fascists.

Fa·scis·ti (fə shĭs′tĭ; It. fä shē′stē), n.pl. Italian. Fascists.

fash (făsh), n., v.t., v.i. Scot. trouble; worry. [t. F: m.s. fâcher]

fash·ion (făsh′ən), n. 1. a prevailing custom or style of dress, etiquette, procedure, etc.: the latest fashion in hats. 2. conventional usage in dress, manners, etc., esp. of polite society, or conformity to it: dictates of fashion, out of fashion. 3. fashionable people collectively. 4. manner; way; mode: in a warlike fashion. 5. after or in a fashion, in some manner or other, but not particularly well. 6. the make or form of anything. 7. a kind; sort. 8. Obs. workmanship. 9. Obs. act or process of making. —v.t. 10. to give a particular shape or form to; make. 11. to accommodate; adapt: doctrines fashioned to the varying hour. 12. Obs. to contrive;

---

b., blend of, blended; c., cognate with; d., dialect, dialectal; der., derived from; f., formed from; g., going back to; m., modification of; r., replacing; s., stem of; t., taken from; ?, perhaps. See the full key on inside cover.

manage. [ME *facioun*, t. OF: m. *façon*, g. s. L *factio* a doing or making]
—Syn. 1. fad, rage, craze. FASHION, STYLE, VOGUE imply popularity or widespread acceptance of manners, customs, dress, etc. FASHION is that which characterizes or distinguishes the habits, manners, dress, etc., of a period or group: *the fashions of the eighteenth century*. STYLE is sometimes the equivalent of FASHION, but also denotes conformance to a prevalent standard: *to be in style, a chair in the Queen Anne style*. VOGUE suggests the temporary popularity of certain fashions: *this year's vogue in popular music*. **6.** shape, cut, pattern. **10.** frame, construct, mold.

fash·ion·a·ble (făsh′ən ə bəl), *adj.* **1.** observant of or conforming to the fashion. **2.** of, characteristic of, or patronized by the world of fashion. **—***n.* **3.** a fashionable person. **—fash′ion·a·ble·ness,** *n.* **—fash′ion·a·bly,** *adv.*

fash·ioned (făsh′ənd), *adj.* (of knitted garments) shaped: *full-fashioned hose*.

fash·ion·er (făsh′ən ər), *n.* **1.** one who fashions, forms, or gives shape to anything. **2.** *Obs.* a tailor or modiste.

fashion plate, 1. a pictorial design showing a prevailing or new mode of dress. **2.** *Colloq.* a person who wears the latest style in dress.

Fa·sho·da (fə shō′də), *n.* a town in the SE Sudan, on the White Nile: British and French colonial interests came into conflict here in the "Fashoda incident," 1898. Now called **Kodok.**

fast[1] (făst, fäst), *adj.* **1.** moving or able to move quickly; quick; swift; rapid: *a fast horse*. **2.** done in comparatively little time: *a fast race, fast work*. **3.** indicating a time in advance of the correct time, as a clock. **4.** adapted to or productive of rapid movement: *a fast track*. **5.** extremely energetic and active, esp. in pursuing pleasure immoderately or without restraint, as a person. **6.** characterized by such energy or pursuit of pleasure, as a mode of life. **7.** resistant: *acid-fast*. **8.** firmly fixed in place; not easily moved; securely attached. **9.** that cannot escape or be extricated. **10.** firmly tied, as a knot. **11.** closed and made secure, as a door. **12.** such as to hold securely: *to lay fast hold on a thing*. **13.** firm in adherence: *fast friends*. **14.** permanent; lasting: *a fast color*. **15.** deep or sound, as sleep. **16.** deceptive, insincere, inconstant, or unreliable. **17.** *Photog.* permitting very short exposure, as by having a wide shutter opening or high film sensitivity: *a fast lens or film*. **—***adv.* **18.** tightly: *to hold fast*. **19.** soundly: *fast asleep*. **20.** quickly, swiftly, or rapidly. **21.** in quick succession. **22.** in an energetic or dissipated way. **23.** *Archaic.* close; near: *fast by*. [ME; OE *fæst*, c. D *vast*, Icel. *fastr* fast, firm] **—Syn. 1, 2.** fleet, speedy. See **quick. 6.** dissipated, dissolute, profligate, immoral. **8.** secure, tight. **13.** loyal, faithful, steadfast. **18.** fixedly, firmly, tenaciously. **—Ant. 1, 2.** slow. **6.** well-behaved. **8.** loose.

fast[2] (făst, fäst), *v.i.* **1.** to abstain from all food. **2.** to eat only sparingly or of certain kinds of food, esp. as a religious observance. **—***n.* **3.** a fasting; an abstinence from food, or a limiting of one's food, esp. when voluntary and as a religious observance. **4.** a day or period of fasting. [ME *faste(n)*, OE *fæstan*, c. G *fasten*]

fast day, a day on which fasting is observed, esp. such a day appointed by some ecclesiastical or civil authority.

fas·ten (făs′ən, fäs′-), *v.t.* **1.** to make fast; fix firmly or securely in place or position; attach securely to something else. **2.** to make secure, as an article of dress with buttons, clasps, etc., or a door with a lock, bolt, etc. **3.** to enclose securely, as a person or an animal (fol. by *in*). **4.** to attach by any connecting agency: *to fasten a nickname or a crime upon one*. **5.** to direct (the eyes, thoughts, etc.) intently. **—***v.i.* **6.** to become fast, fixed, or firm. **7.** to take firm hold; seize (usually fol. by *on*). [ME *fasten(en)*, *fastne(n)*, OE *fæstnian*, der. *fæst*, adj., FAST] **—fas′ten·er,** *n.* **—Syn. 2.** attach, connect, link, hook, clasp, clinch, rivet, clamp, secure, bind, tie, tether.

fas·ten·ing (făs′ən ĭng, fäs′-), *n.* something that fastens, as a lock or clasp.

fas·tid·i·ous (făs tĭd′ĭ əs), *adj.* hard to please; excessively critical: *a fastidious taste*. [t. L: m.s. *fastīdiōsus*, der. *fastīdium* loathing, disgust] **—fas·tid′i·ous·ly,** *adv.* **—fas·tid′i·ous·ness,** *n.* **—Syn.** See **particular.**

fas·tig·i·ate (făs tĭj′ĭ ĭt, -āt′), *adj.* **1.** rising to a pointed top. **2.** *Zool.* joined together in a tapering adhering group. **3.** *Bot.* **a.** erect and parallel, as branches. **b.** having such branches. Also, **fas·tig′i·at′ed.** [f. s. L *fastīgium* gable top, summit, slope + -ATE[1]]

fast·ness (făst′nĭs, fäst′-), *n.* **1.** a secure or fortified place. **2.** state of being fixed or firm. **3.** state of being rapid. **4.** quality of being energetic or dissipated, as in behavior.

fat (făt), *adj.*, **fatter, fattest,** *n.*, *v.*, **fatted, fatting. —***adj.* **1.** having much flesh other than muscle; fleshy; plump. **2.** consisting of, resembling, or containing fat. **3.** abounding in a particular element: *fat pine* (pine rich in resin). **4.** fertile, as land. **5.** profitable, as an office. **6.** affording good opportunities: *a fat profit*. **7.** thick; broad; extended. **8.** plentiful. **9.** plentifully supplied. **10.** dull; stupid. **—***n.* **11.** any of several white or yellowish substances, greasy to the touch, forming the chief part of the adipose tissue of animals and also found in plants. When pure, the fats are odorless, tasteless, and colorless and may be either solid or liquid. They are insoluble in water or cold alcohol but easily soluble in ether, chloroform, or benzene. They are compound esters of various fatty acids with glycerol, the pure fats being composed of carbon, hydrogen, and oxygen. **12.** animal tissue containing much of this substance. **13.** the richest or best part of anything. **14.** especially profitable or advantageous work. **15.** action or lines in a dramatic part which permit an actor to display his abilities. **—***v.t., v.i.* **16.** to make or become fat. [ME; OE *fǣtt*, orig. pp., fatted, c. G *feist*] **—fat′less,** *adj.* **—fat′like′,** *adj.* **—Syn. 1.** corpulent, obese, adipose, chubby, pudgy. See **stout. 2.** oily, greasy. **5.** lucrative, remunerative. **—Ant. 1.** thin. **5.** ill-paying.

fa·tal (fā′təl), *adj.* **1.** causing death: *a fatal accident*. **2.** causing destruction or ruin: *an action that is fatal to the success of a project*. **3.** decisively important; fateful: *the fatal day finally arrived*. **4.** influencing fate: *the fatal sisters*. **5.** proceeding from or decreed by fate; inevitable. **6.** *Obs.* doomed. **7.** *Obs.* prophetic. [ME, t. L: s. *fātālis* of or belonging to fate] **—fa′tal·ness,** *n.*
—Syn. 1. FATAL, DEADLY, MORTAL refer to something which has caused or is capable of causing death. FATAL may refer to either the future or the past; in either case, it emphasizes inevitability and the inescapable—the disastrous, whether death or dire misfortune: *the accident was fatal, such a mistake would be fatal*. DEADLY looks to the future, and suggests that which is likely to cause death (though not inevitably so): *a deadly poison, disease*. MORTAL looks to the past, and refers to death which has actually occurred: *he received a mortal wound, the disease proved to be mortal*.

fa·tal·ism (fā′tə lĭz′əm), *n.* **1.** *Philos.* the doctrine that all events are subject to fate or inevitable predetermination. **2.** the acceptance of all things and events as inevitable; submission to fate. **—fa′tal·ist,** *n.* **—fa′tal·is′tic,** *adj.* **—fa′tal·is′ti·cal·ly,** *adv.*

fa·tal·i·ty (fā tăl′ə tĭ, fə-), *n.*, *pl.* **-ties. 1.** a disaster resulting in death; a calamity or misfortune. **2.** the quality of causing death or disaster; deadliness; a fatal influence. **3.** predetermined liability to disaster. **4.** the quality of being predetermined by or subject to fate. **5.** the fate or destiny of a person or thing. **6.** a fixed, unalterably predetermined course of things.

fa·tal·ly (fā′təlĭ), *adv.* **1.** in a manner leading to death or disaster. **2.** by a decree of fate or destiny; by inevitable predetermination.

Fa·ta Mor·ga·na (fä′tä môr gä′nä), **1.** a mirage seen esp. in the Strait of Messina, formerly attributed to fairy agency. **2.** Morgan le Fay. [t. It.: fairy Morgana. See FAY[1]]

fat cat, *U.S. Slang.* a wealthy person from whom large political campaign contributions are expected.

fate (fāt), *n.*, *v.*, **fated, fating. —***n.* **1.** fortune; lot; destiny. **2.** a divine decree or a fixed sentence by which the order of things is prescribed. **3.** that which is inevitably predetermined; destiny. **4.** a prophetic declaration of what must be. **5.** death, destruction, or ruin. **—***v.t.* **6.** to predetermine as by the decree of fate; destine (now only in the passive). [ME, t. L: m.s. *fātum* a prophetic declaration, fate, prop. pp. neut., (thing) said]
—Syn. 1. FATE, DESTINY, DOOM refer to the idea of a fortune, usually adverse, which is predetermined and unescapable. The three words are frequently interchangeable. FATE stresses the irrationality and impersonal character of events: *it was Napoleon's fate to be exiled*. The word is often lightly used, however: *it was my fate to meet him that very afternoon*. DESTINY emphasizes the idea of an unalterable course of events, and is often used of a propitious fortune: *a man of destiny; it was his destiny to save his nation*. DOOM esp. applies to the final ending, always unhappy or terrible, brought about by destiny or fate: *he met his doom bravely*.

fat·ed (fā′tĭd), *adj.* **1.** subject to, guided by, or predetermined by fate. **2.** destined. **3.** doomed.

fate·ful (fāt′fəl), *adj.* **1.** involving momentous consequences; decisively important. **2.** fatal, deadly, or disastrous. **3.** controlled by irresistible destiny. **4.** prophetic; ominous. **—fate′ful·ly,** *adv.* **—fate′ful·ness,** *n.*

Fates (fāts), *n.pl.* *Gk. and Roman Myth.* the three goddesses of destiny. Clotho spins the thread of life, Lachesis measures it, and Atropos severs it.

fat·head (făt′hĕd′), *n.* a stupid person. **—fat′head′ed,** *adj.*

fa·ther (fä′ᵺər), *n.* **1.** a male parent. **2.** any male ancestor, esp. the founder of a race, family, or line. **3.** *Colloq.* a father-in-law, stepfather, or adoptive father. **4.** one who exercises paternal care over another; a fatherly protector or provider: *a father to the poor*. **5.** a title of respect for an old man. **6.** *Chiefly Brit.* the oldest member of a society, profession, etc. Cf. *U.S.* **dean** (def. 3). **7.** one of the leading men of a city, etc. **8.** a person or thing who originates or establishes something. **9.** (*cap.*) *Theol.* the Supreme Being and Creator; God. **10. the Father,** the first person of the Trinity. **11.** *Ch. Hist.* any of the chief early Christian writers, whose works are the main sources for the history, doctrines, and observances of the church in the early ages. **12.** *Eccles.* **a.** (*often cap.*) a title of reverence, as for church dignitaries, officers of monasteries, monks, confessors, and priests. **b.** a person bearing this title. **13.** (*pl.*) *Rom. Hist.* conscript fathers. **—***v.t.* **14.** to beget. **15.** to originate; be the author of. **16.** to act as a father toward. **17.** to acknowledge oneself the father of. **18.** to assume as one's own; take the responsibility of. **19.** to charge with the begetting of. [ME *fader*, OE *fæder*, c. G *vater*; akin to L *pater*, Gk. *patḗr*]

Father Christmas, *Brit.* Santa Claus.

father confessor, *Eccles.* a confessor.

fa·ther·hood (fä′thər hŏŏd′), *n.* state of being a father.

fa·ther-in-law (fä′thər ĭn lô′), *n.*, *pl.* **fathers-in-law. 1.** the father of one's husband or wife. **2.** *Brit. Colloq.* a stepfather.

fa·ther·land (fä′thər lănd′), *n.* **1.** one's native country. **2.** the land of one's ancestors.

fa·ther·less (fä′thər lĭs), *adj.* **1.** without a living father. **2.** without a known or legally responsible father.

fa·ther·ly (fä′thər lĭ), *adj.* **1.** of, like, or befitting a father. —*adv.* **2.** in the manner of a father. —**fa′ther·li·ness,** *n.*
—**Syn. 1.** FATHERLY, PATERNAL refer to the relationship of a male parent to his children. FATHERLY has emotional connotations; it always suggests a kind, protective, tender, or forbearing attitude: *fatherly advice.* PATERNAL may suggest a kindly, more proprietary attitude: *paternal interest;* but it may also be used objectively, as a legal and official term: *his paternal grandmother, paternal estate.*

fath·om (făth′əm), *n.*, *pl.* **fathoms,** (*esp. collectively*) **fathom,** *v.* —*n.* **1.** a unit of length equal to 6 feet: used chiefly in nautical and mining measurements. —*v.t.* **2.** to reach in depth by measurement in fathoms; sound; try the depth of; penetrate to or find the bottom or extent of. **3.** to measure the depth of by sounding. **4.** to penetrate to the bottom of; understand thoroughly. [ME *fathme,* OE *fæthm,* c. G *faden;* akin to Gk. *petalos* spreading] —**fath′om·a·ble,** *adj.* —**fath′om·er,** *n.*

fath·om·less (făth′əm lĭs), *adj.* impossible to fathom. —**fath′om·less·ly,** *adv.*

fa·tid·ic (fā tĭd′ĭk, fə-), *adj.* prophetic. Also, **fa·tid′i·cal.** [t. L: s. *fātidicus* prophesying]

fat·i·ga·ble (făt′ə gə bəl), *adj.* easily fatigued or tired.

fa·tigue (fə tēg′), *n.*, *v.*, **-tigued, -tiguing,** *adj.* —*n.* **1.** weariness from bodily or mental exertion. **2.** a cause of weariness; labor; exertion. **3.** *Physiol.* temporary diminution of the excitability or functioning of organs, tissues, or cells after excessive exertion or stimulation. **4.** *Mech.* the weakening of material subjected to stress, esp. a continued series of stresses. **5.** Also, **fatigue duty.** *Mil.* **a.** labor of a generally nonmilitary kind done by soldiers, such as cleaning up an area, or digging drainage ditches, or raking up leaves. **b.** state of being engaged in such labor: *on fatigue.* **c.** (*pl.*) fatigue clothes. —*v.t.* **6.** to weary with bodily or mental exertion; exhaust the strength of. —*adj.* **7.** of or pertaining to fatigue: *fatigue detail.* [t. F, der. *fatiguer,* t. L: m. *fatīgāre* tire] —**fa·tigue′less,** *adj.*

fatigue clothes, a soldier's uniform for fatigue duty.

fa·tigued (fə tēgd′), *adj.* wearied. —**Syn.** See tired[1].

fatigue party, a group of soldiers on fatigue.

Fá·ti·ma (fä′tĭ mə), *n.* a shrine in central Portugal, north of Lisbon; renowned for miracles.

Fat·i·ma (făt′ĭ mə, fä′tĭ mä′), *n.* **1.** A.D. c606–632, daughter of Mohammed. **2.** the seventh and last wife of Bluebeard, popularly a symbol for feminine curiosity.

Fat·i·mid (făt′ə mĭd), *n.* **1.** caliph of the North African dynasty, 909–1171, claiming descent from Fatima (def. 1) and Ali. **2.** any descendant of Fatima and Ali. Also, **Fat·i·mite** (făt′ə mīt′).

fat·ling (făt′lĭng), *n.* a young animal, as a calf or a lamb, fattened for slaughter. [f. FAT + -LING[1]]

fat·ly (făt′lĭ), *adv.* **1.** in a fat manner; plumply. **2.** clumsily.

fat·ness (făt′nĭs), *n.* **1.** condition of being fat. **2.** corpulence. **3.** oiliness. **4.** richness; fertility.

Fat·shan (făt′shän′), *n.* Nanhai.

fat·sol·u·ble (făt′sŏl′yə bəl), *adj. Chem.* soluble in oils or fats.

fat·ten (făt′ən), *v.t.* **1.** to make fat. **2.** to feed for slaughter. **3.** to enrich; make fertile. **4.** *Poker.* to increase the number of chips in (a pot). —*v.i.* **5.** to grow fat. —**fat′ten·er,** *n.*

fat·ti ma·schi·i, pa·ro·le fe·mi·ne (fät′tē mä′skē ē′, pä rō′lĕ fĕ′mē nĕ), *Italian.* deeds (are) manly, words womanish (one of the mottoes of Maryland).

fat·tish (făt′ĭsh), *adj.* somewhat fat.

fat·ty (făt′ĭ), *adj.*, **-tier, -tiest. 1.** consisting of, containing, or resembling fat: *fatty tissue.* **2.** *Pathol.* characterized by overproduction or excessive accumulation of fat. —**fat′ti·ness,** *n.*

fatty acid, *Chem.* any of a class of aliphatic acids, esp. one such as palmitic, stearic, oleic, etc. present as glycerides in animal and vegetable fats and oils.

fatty degeneration, *Med.* deterioration of the cells of the body accompanied by the formation of fat globules within the diseased cells.

fatty tumor, lipoma.

fa·tu·i·tous (fə tū′ə təs, -tōō′-), *adj.* characterized by fatuity.

fa·tu·i·ty (fə tū′ə tĭ, -tōō′-), *n.*, *pl.* **-ties. 1.** foolishness; complacent stupidity. **2.** something foolish. [t. L: m.s. *fatuitas*]

fat·u·ous (făch′ŏŏ əs), *adj.* **1.** foolish, esp. in an unconscious, complacent manner; silly. **2.** unreal; illusory. [t. L: m. *fatuus*] —**fat′u·ous·ly,** *adv.* —**fat′u·ous·ness,** *n.* —**Syn. 1.** See foolish.

fat-wit·ted (făt′wĭt′ĭd), *adj.* dull; stupid.

fau·bourg (fō′bŏŏr. -bŏŏrg; *Fr.* fō bŏŏr′), *n.* a part of a city outside (or once outside) the walls; suburb. [t.F]

fau·cal (fô′kəl), *adj.* **1.** pertaining to the fauces or opening of the throat. **2.** *Phonet.* **a.** (of the explosion of a stop) produced by lowering the velum: the *t* of *button* has faucal explosion if no vowel is pronounced before the *n.* **b.** laryngeal. [f. s. L *fauces* throat + -AL[1]]

fau·ces (fô′sēz), *n.pl. Anat.* the cavity at the back of the mouth, leading into the pharynx. [t. L] —**fau·cial** (fô′shəl), *adj.*

fau·cet (fô′sĭt), *n.* any device for controlling the flow of liquid from a pipe or the like by opening or closing an orifice; a tap; a cock. [ME, t. OF: m. *fausset,* der. *fausser* force in, damage, g. L *falsāre* falsify]

faugh (fô), *interj.* an exclamation of disgust.

Faulk·ner (fôk′nər), *n.* William, 1897–1962, U.S. novelist, short-story writer, and poet. Also, **Falkner.**

fault (fôlt), *n.* **1.** a defect or imperfection; a flaw; a failing. **2.** an error or mistake. **3.** a misdeed or transgression. **4.** delinquency; culpability; cause for blame. **5.** *Geol., Mining.* a break in the continuity of a body of rock or of a vein, with dislocation along the plane of fracture. **6.** *Elect.* a partial or total local failure, in the insulation or continuity of a conductor, or in the functioning of an electric system. **7.** *Tennis, Rackets, etc.* **a.** a failure to serve the ball legitimately within the prescribed limits. **b.** a ball which when served does not land in the proper section of the opponent's court. **8.** *Hunting.* a break in the line of scent; a losing of the scent. **9.** *Obs.* lack; want. **10. at fault, a.** open to censure; blamable. **b.** puzzled; astray. **11. in fault,** open to censure; blamable. **12. find fault,** find something wrong; complain. **13. to a fault,** excessively. —*v.i.* **14.** *Geol.* to undergo a fault or faults. **15.** *Archaic.* to commit a fault. —*v.t.* **16.** *Geol.* to cause a fault in. **17.** *Now Rare or Dial.* to find fault with, blame, or censure. [ME *faute,* t. OF, g. LL *fallita,* der. L *fallere* deceive]

Section of strata displaced by a fault. F, Fault line; A and A, formerly a continuous mass of rock

—**Syn. 1.** FAULT, FAILING, FOIBLE, WEAKNESS, VICE imply moral shortcomings or imperfections in a person. FAULT is the common word used to refer to any of the average shortcomings of a person; when it is used, condemnation is not necessarily implied: *of his many faults the greatest is vanity.* FOIBLE, FAILING, WEAKNESS all tend to excuse the person referred to. Of these, FOIBLE is the mildest, suggesting a weak point that is slight and often amusing, manifesting itself in eccentricity rather than in wrongdoing: *the foibles of artists.* WEAKNESS suggests that the person in question is unable to control a particular impulse, and gives way to self-indulgence: *a weakness for pretty women.* FAILING is closely akin to FAULT, except that it is particularly applied to humanity at large, suggesting common, often venial, shortcomings: *procrastination and making excuses are common failings.* VICE (which may also apply to a sin in itself, apart from a person: *the vice of gambling*) is the strongest term, and designates a habit that is truly evil and corrupt: *he is very unruly, but he has no vices.* —**Ant. 1.** virtue, merit.

fault·find·er (fôlt′fīn′dər), *n.* one who finds fault; one who complains or objects.

fault·find·ing (fôlt′fīn′dĭng), *n.* **1.** act of pointing out faults; carping; picking flaws. —*adj.* **2.** given to finding fault; disposed to complain or object.

fault·less (fôlt′lĭs), *adj.* without fault or defect; perfect. —**fault′less·ly,** *adv.* —**fault′less·ness,** *n.*

fault plane, *Geol.* the plane of fracture in a fault.

fault·y (fôl′tĭ), *adj.*, **faultier, faultiest. 1.** having faults or defects: *faulty workmanship.* **2.** *Rare.* of the nature of a fault; morally blamable: *whatever is faulty with the Church.* **3.** *Obs.* culpable; at fault. —**fault′i·ly,** *adv.* —**fault′i·ness,** *n.* —**Syn. 1.** defective, imperfect, wrong, incomplete. **2.** blameworthy, reprehensible, censurable.

faun (fôn), *n. Rom. Myth.* one of a class of rural deities represented as men with the ears, horns, and tail, and later also the hind legs, of a goat. [ME. See FAUNUS] —**faun′like′,** *adj.*

fau·na (fô′nə), *n.* **1.** the animals of a given region or period, taken collectively (as distinguished from the plants or *flora*). **2.** a treatise on the animals of a given region or period. [NL, special use of *Fauna,* name of sister of FAUNUS] —**fau′nal,** *adj.*

Fau·nus (fô′nəs), *n. Rom. Relig.* a woodland deity, identified with Pan. [t. L]

Faust (foust), *n.* **1.** the chief character in a famous German story; he is represented as selling his soul to the devil for power or knowledge. **2.** a tragedy by Goethe (Part 1, 1808, Part 2, 1833). **3.** an opera (1859) by Gounod.

fau·teuil (fō′tĭl; *Fr.* fō tœ′y), *n. French.* an easy chair.

faux pas (fō pä′), *pl.* **faux pas** (fō päz′; *Fr.* pä′). *French.* a false step; a slip in manners or conduct; a breach of etiquette or propriety.

fa·ve·o·late (fə vē′ə lāt′), *adj.* honeycombed; alveolate; pitted. [f. s. NL *faveolus* (dim. of L *favus* honeycomb) + -ATE[1]]

fa·vo·ni·an (fə vō′nĭ ən), *adj.* **1.** of or pertaining to the west wind. **2.** mild; favorable; propitious. [t. L: s. *favōniānus,* der. *Favōnius,* the west wind]

fa·vor (fā′vər), *n.* **1.** a kind act; something done or granted out of good will, rather than from justice or for

remuneration: *ask a favor*. **2.** kindness; kind approval. **3.** state of being approved, or held in regard: *in favor, out of favor*. **4.** excessive kindness; unfair partiality: *show undue favor to someone*. **5.** a gift bestowed as a token of good will, kind regard, love, etc. **6.** a ribbon, badge, etc., worn in evidence of good will or loyalty. **7.** a letter. esp. a commercial one. **8.** (*pl.*) consent to sexual intimacy. **9.** in favor of, a. in support of; on the side of. **b.** to the advantage of. **c.** (of a check, etc.) payable to. —*v.t.* **10.** to regard with favor. **11.** to have a preference for; treat with partiality. **12.** to show favor to; oblige. **13.** to be favorable to; facilitate. **14.** *Now Rare.* to deal with gently: *favor a lame leg*. **15.** to aid or support. **16.** *Colloq.* to resemble. Also, *Brit.*, **fa′vour.** [ME, t. OF, g. L] —**fa′vor.er,** *n.* —**fa′vor.ing.ly,** *adv.*
—**Syn. 2.** FAVOR, GOOD WILL imply a kindly regard or friendly disposition shown by an individual or group. FAVOR may be merely an attitude of mind: *to look with favor on a proposal*. GOOD WILL is more active and leads often to outward manifestations of friendly approval: *by frequent applause the audience showed its good will toward the speaker.* —**Ant. 2.** animosity, malice.

fa.vor.a.ble (fā′vər ə bəl), *adj.* **1.** affording aid, advantage, or convenience: *a favorable position.* **2.** manifesting favor; inclined to aid or approve. **3.** (of an answer) granting what is desired. **4.** promising well: *the signs are favorable*. Also, *Brit.*, **fa′vour.a.ble.** —**fa′vor.able.ness,** *n.* —**fa′vor.a.bly,** *adv.*

fa.vored (fā′vərd), *adj.* **1.** regarded or treated with favor. **2.** enjoying special advantages. **3.** of specified appearance: *ill-favored*. Also, *Brit.*, **fa′voured.**

fa.vor.ite (fā′vər ĭt), *n.* **1.** a person or thing regarded with special favor or preference. **2.** *Sports.* a competitor considered likely to win. **3.** a person treated with special (esp. undue) favor by a prince, etc. —*adj.* **4.** regarded with particular favor or preference: *a favorite child*. Also, *Brit.*, **fa′vour.ite.** [t. F: m. *favorit*, var. of *favori*, t. It.: m. *favorito*, ult. der. *favore* favor, g. L *favor*]

fa.vor.it.ism (fā′vər ə tĭz′əm), *n.* **1.** the favoring of one person or group over others having equal claims. **2.** state of being a favorite. Also, *Brit.*, **fa′vour.it.ism.**

fa.vus (fā′vəs), *n.* *Pathol.* a skin disease, esp. of the scalp, characterized by dry incrustations due to the fungus *Achorion schonleinii*. [t. L: honeycomb]

Fawkes (fôks), *n.* Guy, 1570–1606, English conspirator and leader in the Gunpowder Plot to blow up the Houses of Parliament.

fawn¹ (fôn), *n.* **1.** a young deer. **2.** a buck or doe of the first year. **3.** a fawn color. —*adj.* **4.** light yellowish-brown. —*v.i.* **5.** (of deer) to bring forth young. [ME *foun*, t. OF: m. *faon*, ult. der. L *fētus* offspring, young] —**fawn′like′,** *adj.*

fawn² (fôn), *v.i.* **1.** to seek notice or favor by servile demeanor. **2.** to show fondness by crouching, wagging the tail, licking the hand, etc. (said esp. of dogs). [ME *fawne*(n), OE *fagnian*, var. of *fægnian* rejoice, *fawn*, der. *fægen* glad, fain] —**fawn′er,** *n.* —**fawn′ing.ly,** *adv.*

Fawn of Virginia deer.
Odocoileus virginianus

fay¹ (fā), *n.* a fairy. [ME, t. OF: m. *fae, fee*, g. L *fāta* the Fates, pl. of *fātum* FATE]

fay² (fā), *v.i., v.t.* to fit, esp. together closely, as timbers in shipbuilding. [ME *feien, fey*, OE *fēgan*, c. G *fügen*]

fay³ (fā), *n.* *Archaic.* faith. [ME *fei*, t. OF. See FAITH]

Fa.yal (fä yäl′), *n.* an island in the Azores, in the N Atlantic. 23,923 pop. (1950); 66 sq. mi.

fay.al.ite (fā′ə lĭt′, fī′lĭt), *n.* a black, greenish, or brownish mineral of the olivine group, ferrous orthosilicate, Fe₂SiO₄. [f. FAYAL + -ITE¹]

Fa.yette.ville (fā′ət vĭl), *n.* a city in S North Carolina. 47,106 (1960).

faze (fāz), *v.t.*, **fazed, faz.ing.** *U.S. Colloq.* to disturb; discomfit; daunt. [var. of FEEZE]

f.b., Football. fullback.

FBI, Federal Bureau of Investigation.

f.c., *Print.* follow copy.

FCC, Federal Communications Commission.

F clef, *Music.* a bass clef. See illus. under **clef.**

fcp., foolscap.

F.D., Fidei Defensor.

Fe, *Chem.* (L *ferrum*) iron.

feal (fēl), *adj.* *Archaic.* faithful; loyal. [back formation from FEALTY]

fe.al.ty (fē′əl tĭ), *n., pl.* **-ties. 1.** *Hist.* **a.** fidelity to a lord. **b.** the obligation or the engagement to be faithful to a lord, usually sworn to by the vassal. **2.** fidelity; faithfulness. [ME *feaute*, t. OF, g. s. L *fidēlitas* fidelity]

fear (fĭr), *n.* **1.** a painful feeling of impending danger, evil, trouble, etc.; the feeling or condition of being afraid. **2.** a specific instance of such a feeling. **3.** anxiety; solicitude. **4.** reverential awe, esp. toward God. **5.** a cause for fear. **6. for fear of,** in order to avoid or prevent. —*v.t.* **7.** to regard with fear; be afraid of. **8.** to have reverential awe of. **9.** *Archaic.* to be afraid (used reflexively). **10.** *Archaic and Dial.* to frighten. —*v.i.* **11.** to have fear; be afraid. [ME *fere*, OE *fǣr* sudden attack, sudden danger, c. OS *fār* ambush; akin to G *gefahr* danger] —**fear′er,** *n.*

—**Syn. 1.** apprehension, consternation, dismay, terror, fright, panic. FEAR, ALARM, DREAD all imply a painful emotion experienced when one is confronted by threatening danger or evil. ALARM implies an agitation of the feelings caused by awakening to imminent danger; it names a feeling of fright or panic: *he started up in alarm.* FEAR and DREAD usually refer more to a condition or state than to an event. FEAR is often applied to an attitude toward something which, when experienced, will cause the sensation of fright: *fear of falling.* DREAD suggests an attitude of anticipating something, usually a particular event, which, when experienced, will be disagreeable rather than frightening: *she lives in dread of losing her money.* (The same is often true of FEAR, when used in a negative statement: *she has no fear she'll lose her money.*)

Fear (fĭr), *n.* **Cape, 1.** a river in SE North Carolina. 202 mi. **2.** a cape at the mouth of this river.

fear.ful (fĭr′fəl), *adj.* **1.** causing, or apt to cause, fear. **2.** feeling fear, dread, apprehension, or solicitude: *I am fearful of his doing it, or lest he should do it.* **3.** full of awe or reverence. **4.** showing or caused by fear. **5.** *Chiefly Colloq.* extremely bad, large, etc. —**fear′ful.ly,** *adv.* —**fear′ful.ness,** *n.*

fear.less (fĭr′lĭs), *adj.* without fear; bold. —**fear′-less.ly,** *adv.* —**fear′less.ness,** *n.* —**Syn.** See **brave.**

fear.nought (fĭr′nôt′), *n.* a kind of stout woolen cloth. Also, **fear′naught′.**

fear.some (fĭr′səm), *adj.* **1.** causing fear. **2.** afraid; timid. —**fear′some.ly,** *adv.* —**fear′some.ness,** *n.*

fea.sance (fē′zəns), *n.* *Law.* doing or performance, as of a condition or duty. [t. AF: m. *fesance*, der. *faire* do]

fea.si.ble (fē′zə bəl), *adj.* **1.** capable of being done, effected, or accomplished: *a feasible plan.* **2.** suitable: *a road feasible for travel.* **3.** likely; probable: *a feasible theory.* [ME *fesable*, t. OF, der. *faire*, g. L *facere* do, make] —**fea′si.bil′i.ty, fea′si.ble.ness,** *n.* —**fea′si.bly,** *adv.* —**Syn. 1.** See **possible.**

feast (fēst), *n.* **1.** a periodical celebration, or day or time of celebration, of religious or other character, in commemoration of some event or person, or having some other special significance: *feasts of the church, the medieval feast of fools, the Chinese feast of lanterns.* **2.** a sumptuous entertainment or meal for many guests. **3.** any rich or abundant meal. **4.** something highly agreeable. —*v.i.* **5.** to have, or partake of, a feast; eat sumptuously. **6.** to dwell with gratification or delight, as on a picture. —*v.t.* **7.** to provide or entertain with a feast. **8.** to gratify; delight. [ME *feste*, t. OF, g. L *festa*, fem. sing. of *festus* festal] —**feast′er,** *n.*

—**Syn. 2.** FEAST, BANQUET imply large social events, with an abundance of food. A FEAST is a meal with a plenteous supply of food and drink for a large company: *to provide a feast for all company employees.* A BANQUET is an elaborate feast for a formal and ceremonious occasion: *the main speaker at a banquet.*

feast.ful (fēst′fəl), *adj.* festive; joyful.

Feast of Weeks, Pentecost (def. 2).

feat¹ (fēt), *n.* **1.** a noteworthy or extraordinary act or achievement, usually displaying boldness, skill, etc. **2.** an action; deed. [ME *fait*, t. OF, g. L *factum* (thing) done, prop. pp. neut.] —**Syn. 1.** See **achievement.**

feat² (fēt), *adj.* *Archaic or Dial.* **1.** apt; skillful; dexterous. **2.** suitable. **3.** neat. [ME *fete*, appar. t. OF: m. *fait*, pp. of *faire*, g. L *facere* do, make]

feath.er (fĕth′ər), *n.* **1.** one of the epidermal appendages which together constitute the plumage of birds, being typically made up of a hard, tubelike portion (the quill) attached to the body of the bird, which passes into a thinner, stemlike distal portion (the rachis) bearing a series of slender processes (barbs) which unite in a bladelike structure (web) on each side. **2.** plumage. **3.** attire. **4.** condition, as of health, spirits, etc.: *in fine feather, in high feather.* **5.** kind or character. **6.** something like a feather, as a tuft or fringe of hair. **7.** a featherlike flaw, as in a precious stone. **8.** *Archery.* **a.** a feather or feathers attached to the nock (rear) end of an arrow to direct its flight. **b.** the feathered end or string end of an arrow. **9.** something very light, weak, or small. **10.** *Rowing.* the act of feathering. **11. a feather in one's cap,** a mark of distinction; an honor. —*v.t.* **12.** to provide with feathers, as an arrow. **13.** to clothe or cover with, or as with, feathers. **14.** *Rowing.* to turn (an oar) after a stroke so that the blade becomes nearly horizontal, and hold it thus as it is moved back into position for the next stroke. **15. feather one's nest,** to provide for or enrich oneself. —*v.i.* **16.** to grow feathers. **17.** to be or become feathery in appearance. **18.** to move like feathers. **19.** *Rowing.* to feather an oar. [ME and OE *fether*, c. G *feder*; akin to Gk. *pterón* wing] —**feath′er.less,** *adj.* —**feath′er.like′,** *adj.*

feath.er.bed.ding (fĕth′ər bĕd′ĭng), *n.* a type of coercion of an employer by a labor union, in which the employer is forced to pay for services not performed, esp. by hiring unnecessary employees.

feath.er.bone (fĕth′ər bōn′), *n.* a substitute for whalebone, made from the quills of domestic fowls.

feath.er.brain (fĕth′ər brān′), *n.* a giddy or weakminded person. —**feath′er.brained′,** *adj.*

feath.ered (fĕth′ərd), *adj.* **1.** clothed, covered, or provided with feathers. **2.** winged; swift.

feath.er.edge (fĕth′ər ĕj′), *n.* **1.** an edge which thins out like a feather. **2.** the thinner edge of a wedge-shaped board or plank. **3.** the shallow edge of the furrow of a millstone, etc. —**feath′er.edged′,** *adj.*

ăct, āble, dâre, ärt; ĕbb, ēqual; ĭf, īce; hŏt, ōver, ôrder, oil, bŏŏk, ōoze, out; ŭp, ūse, ûrge; ə = a in alone; ch, chief; g, give; ng, ring; sh, shoe; th, thin; ŧh, that; zh, vision. See the full key on inside cover.

feather grass, any grass of the American genus *Stipa.*

feath·er·head (fĕth/ər hĕd/), *n.* **1.** a silly or light-headed person. **2.** a light or empty head. —**feath/er·head/ed,** *adj.*

feath·er·ing (fĕth/ər ĭng), *n. Music.* a very light and delicate use of the violin bow.

feather star, sea lily or crinoid.

feath·er·stitch (fĕth/ər stĭch/), *n.* **1.** an embroidery stitch producing work in which a succession of branches extend alternately on each side of a central stem. —*v.t.* **2.** to ornament by featherstitch.

feath·er·veined (fĕth/ər vānd/), *adj. Bot.* (of a leaf) having a series of veins branching from each side of the midrib toward the margin.

feath·er·weight (fĕth/ər wāt/), *n.* **1.** a boxer or other contestant lighter in weight than a lightweight. **2.** a fighter's weight when between 118 and 126 lbs. **3.** a very light or insignificant person or thing. —*adj.* **4.** belonging to the class of featherweights. **5.** trifling; slight.

feath·er·weight·ed (fĕth/ər wā/tĭd), *adj.* (of a race horse) assigned the least weight by the handicapper.

feath·er·y (fĕth/ər ĭ), *adj.* **1.** clothed or covered with feathers; feathered. **2.** resembling feathers; light; airy; unsubstantial. —**feath/er·i·ness,** *n.*

feat·ly (fēt/lĭ), *adv. Archaic* or *Dial.* **1.** in a feat manner; fitly. **2.** skillfully; nimbly. **3.** neatly; elegantly. [f. FEAT² + -LY] —**feat/li·ness,** *n.*

fea·ture (fē/chər), *n., v.,* **-tured, -turing.** —*n.* **1.** any part of the face, as the nose, chin, etc. **2.** (*pl.*) the face. **3.** the form or cast of the face. **4.** a prominent or conspicuous part or characteristic. **5.** the main picture in a movie program. **6.** a special article, column, cartoon, etc., in a newspaper or magazine. **7.** *Obs.* or *Archaic.* make, form, or shape. —*v.t.* **8.** to be a feature or distinctive mark of. **9.** to make a feature of, or give prominence to: *to feature a story or picture in a newspaper.* **10.** to delineate the features of; depict; outline. **11.** *Colloq.* to resemble in features; favor. [ME *feture,* t. OF, g. L *factūra* making, formation]

—**Syn. 4.** FEATURE, CHARACTERISTIC, PECULIARITY refer to a distinctive trait of an individual, or of a class. FEATURE suggests an outstanding or marked property which attracts attention: *complete harmony was a feature of the convention.* CHARACTERISTIC means a distinguishing mark or quality (or one of such) always associated in one's mind with a particular person or thing: *defiance is one of his characteristics, arrogance is a characteristic of bad consciences.* PECULIARITY means that distinct or unusual characteristic which marks off an individual in the class to which he (or it) belongs: (among flowers) *the arrangement of the petals is a peculiarity of pansies.*

fea·tured (fē/chərd), *adj.* **1.** made a feature of; given prominence to. **2.** having features, or a certain cast of features. **3.** *Obs.* formed; fashioned.

fea·ture·less (fē/chər lĭs), *adj.* without distinctive features; uninteresting.

feature story, *Journalism.* a story printed for reasons other than its news value.

feaze¹ (fēz), *v.t., v.i.,* **feazed, feazing.** to unravel. [t. LG: *m. fäsen.* Cf. OE *fæs* fringe]

feaze² (fēz, fāz), *n., v.i., v.t.,* **feazed, feazing.** feeze.

Feb., February.

febri-, a word element meaning "fever," as in *febrifuge.* [t. L, comb. form of *febris*]

fe·bric·i·ty (fĭ brĭs/ə tĭ), *n.* feverishness.

fe·bric·u·la (fĭ brĭk/yə lə), *n.* a slight and short fever, especially when of obscure causation. [t. L, dim. of *febris* fever]

feb·ri·fa·cient (fĕb/rə fā/shənt), *adj.* **1.** producing fever. —*n.* **2.** something that produces fever.

fe·brif·er·ous (fĭ brĭf/ər əs), *adj.* producing fever.

fe·brif·ic (fĭ brĭf/ĭk), *adj.* producing or marked by fever. [f. FEBRI- + -FIC]

fe·brif·u·gal (fĭ brĭf/yə gəl, fĕb/rə fū/gəl), *adj.* of or like a febrifuge.

feb·ri·fuge (fĕb/rə fūj/), *adj.* **1.** serving to dispel or reduce fever, as a medicine. —*n.* **2.** a febrifuge medicine or agent. **3.** a cooling drink. [t. F, t. L: m.s. *febrifugia,* f. *febri-* FEBRI- + *-fugia* -FUGE]

fe·brile (fē/brəl, fĕb/rəl), *adj.* pertaining to or marked by fever; feverish. [t. L: m.s. *febrilis* pertaining to fever]

Feb·ru·ar·y (fĕb/rŏŏ ĕr/ĭ, fĕb/yŏŏr/ĭ), *n.* the second month of the year, containing ordinarily 28 days, in leap years 29. [t. L: m.s. *Februārius,* der. *februa,* pl., the Roman festival of purification, celebrated Feb. 15; r. ME *feverer,* t. OF, and OE *Februarius,* t. L]

fec., fecit.

fe·ces (fē/sēz), *n. pl.* **1.** waste matter discharged from the intestines; excrement. **2.** dregs; sediment. Also, **faeces.** [t. L: m. *faecēs,* pl. of *faex* dregs] —**fe·cal** (fē/kəl), *adj.*

Fech·ner (fĕKH/nər), *n.* Gustav Theodor (gŏŏs/täf tā/ō dôr/), 1801–87, German physicist, psychologist, and philosopher.

fe·cit (fē/sĭt), *v. Latin.* he (or she) made (it, a work of art, etc.).

feck (fĕk), *n. Scot.* and *N. Eng.* **1.** effect; efficacy; value. **2.** amount. [var. of *fect,* aphetic var. of EFFECT]

feck·less (fĕk/lĭs), *adj. Orig. Scot.* and *N. Eng.* **1.** ineffective; feeble. **2.** spiritless; worthless. —**feck/less·ly,** *adv.* —**feck/less·ness,** *n.*

fec·u·la (fĕk/yə lə), *n., pl.* **-lae** (-lē). starch obtained by washing the comminuted roots, grains, or other parts of plants. [t. L: m. *faecula* crust of wine, dim. of *faex* dregs]

fec·u·lent (fĕk/yə lənt), *adj.* abounding in dregs or foul matter; turbid; muddy; foul. [t. L: s. *faeculentus* abounding in dregs, impure] —**fec/u·lence,** *n.*

fe·cund (fē/kŭnd, fĕk/ŭnd), *adj.* capable of producing offspring, or fruit. vegetation, etc., in abundance; prolific; fruitful; productive. [t. L: s. *fēcundus* fruitful; r. ME *fecounde,* t. OF: m. *fecond*]

fe·cun·date (fē/kən dāt/, fĕk/ən-), *v.t.,* **-dated, -dating.** **1.** to make prolific or fruitful. **2.** *Biol.* to impregnate. [t. L: m.s. *fēcundātus,* pp., made fruitful] —**fe/cun·da/tion,** *n.*

fe·cun·di·ty (fĭ kŭn/də tĭ), *n.* **1.** the quality of being fecund; the capacity, esp. in female animals, of producing young in great numbers. **2.** fruitfulness or fertility, as of the earth. **3.** capacity of abundant production: *fecundity of imagination.*

fed (fĕd), *v.* pt. and pp. **of feed.**

Fed., Federal.

fed·er·a·cy (fĕd/ər ə sĭ), *n.* a confederacy.

fed·er·al (fĕd/ər əl), *adj.* **1.** of or pertaining to a compact or a league, esp. a league between nations or states. **2.** *Govt.* **a.** pertaining to or of the nature of a union of states under a central government distinct from the individual governments of the separate states: *the federal government of the U.S.* **b.** favoring a strong central government in such a union. **c.** pertaining to such a central government: *federal offices.* **3.** (*cap.*) *U.S. Hist.* **a.** noting or pertaining to a party in early U.S. history advocating a strong central government. **b.** (in the Civil War) pertaining to or supporting the Union government. **c.** relating to, or adhering to, the support of the Constitution. —*n.* **4.** an advocate of federation or federalism. **5.** (*cap.*) *U.S. Hist.* **a.** a Federalist. **b.** an adherent of the Union government during the Civil War; a Unionist. **c.** a soldier in the Federal army. [earlier *foederal,* f. s. L *foedus* compact, league (akin to *fides* faith) +-AL¹] —**fed/er·al·ly,** *adv.*

Federal Bureau of Investigation, a federal agency charged with investigations for the attorney general of the U.S. and safeguarding national security.

Federal Capital Territory, former name of Australian Capital Territory.

Federal Constitution, the Constitution of the United States government. See **Constitution.**

Federal District, a district in which the national government of a country is located, esp. one in Latin America. Spanish, **Distrito Federal.**

fed·er·al·ism (fĕd/ər ə lĭz/əm), *n.* **1.** the federal principle of government. **2.** (*cap.*) *U.S. Hist.* the principles of the Federalist party.

fed·er·al·ist (fĕd/ər ə lĭst), *n.* **1.** an advocate of federalism. **2.** (*cap.*) *U.S. Hist.* **a.** a member or supporter of the Federalist party. **b. The,** a collection of essays written by Hamilton, Madison, and Jay supporting the adoption of the Constitution. —*adj.* **3.** Also, **fed/er·al·is/tic.** of federalism or the Federalists.

Federalist party, *U.S. Hist.* **1.** a political group that favored the adoption by the States of the Constitution. **2.** a political party in early U.S. history advocating a strong central government. Also, **Federal party.**

fed·er·al·ize (fĕd/ər ə līz/), *v.t.,* **-ized, -izing.** to make federal; unite in a federal union, as different states. —**fed/er·al·i·za/tion,** *n.*

Federal Republic of Germany. Official name of West Germany.

Federal Reserve System, a system of banks (**Federal Reserve Banks**) in the U.S., forming 12 districts under the control of a central board of governors (**Federal Reserve Board**) and 12 central banks, which regulate the making of loans, the amount of reserves, etc., of member banks, and, in general, attempt to adjust banking practices to the needs of the nation's industry and agriculture.

fed·er·ate (*v.* fĕd/ə rāt/; *adj.* fĕd/ər ĭt). *v.,* **-ated, -ating,** *adj.* —*v.t., v.i.* **1.** to unite in a league or federation. **2.** to organize on a federal basis. —*adj.* **3.** federated; allied: *federate nations.* [t. L: m.s. *foederātus,* pp., leagued together]

Federated Malay States, a former federation of four native states in British Malaya. See **Malaya.**

fed·er·a·tion (fĕd/ə rā/shən), *n.* **1.** act of federating, or uniting in a league. **2.** the formation of a political unity, with a central government, out of a number of separate states, etc., each of which retains control of its own internal affairs. **3.** a league or confederacy. **4.** a federated body formed by a number of states, societies, etc., each retaining control of its own internal affairs.

Federation of Rhodesia and Nyasaland. See **Rhodesia and Nyasaland, Federation of.**

Federation of the West Indies. See **West Indies, Federation of.**

fed·er·a·tive (fĕd/ə rā/tĭv), *adj.* **1.** pertaining to or of the nature of a federation. **2.** inclined to federate. —**fed/er·a/tive·ly,** *adv.*

fe·do·ra (fĭ dôr/ə), *n.* a soft felt hat with a curled brim, worn with the crown creased lengthwise. [said to be from *Fédora,* drama by Sardou]

Fed. Res. Bd., Federal Reserve Board.

Fed. Res. Bk., Federal Reserve Bank.

---

b., blend of, blended; c., cognate with; d., dialect, dialectal; der., derived from; f., formed from; g., going back to; m., modification of; r., replacing; s., stem of; t., taken from; ?, perhaps. See the full key on inside cover.

fee (fē), n., v., **feed, feeing.** —n. **1.** a payment for services: a doctor's fee. **2.** sum paid for a privilege: an admission fee. **3.** a gratuity; tip. **4.** a charge allowed by law for the service of a public officer. **5.** possession; ownership. **6.** Law. **a.** an estate of inheritance in land, either absolute and without limitation to any particular class of heirs (**fee simple**) or limited to a particular class of heirs (**fee tail**). **b.** an estate in land held of a feudal lord on condition of the performing of certain services. **c.** a territory held in fee. **7.** hold in fee, to have full ownership in (land). —v.t. **8.** to give a fee to. **9.** Chiefly Scot. to hire; employ. [ME, t. AF; of Gmc. orig.] —fee′less, adj.

fee·ble (fē′bəl), adj., **-bler, -blest. 1.** physically weak, as from age, sickness, etc. **2.** weak intellectually or morally: a feeble mind. **3.** lacking in volume, loudness, brightness, distinctness, etc.: a feeble voice, light. **4.** lacking in force, strength, or effectiveness: feeble resistance, arguments, barriers. [ME feble, t. OF, g. L flēbilis lamentable] —fee′ble·ness, n. —fee′blish, adj. —fee′bly, adv. —Syn. **1.** infirm, frail, sickly. See **weak.** —Ant. **1-4.** strong.

fee·ble-mind·ed (fē′bəl mīn′dĭd), adj. **1.** feeble in intellect; lacking the normal mental powers. **2.** lacking firmness of the mind. —fee′ble-mind′ed·ness, n.

feed (fēd), v., **fed, feeding,** n. —v.t. **1.** to give food to; supply with nourishment. **2.** to provide with the requisite materials for development, maintenance, or operation. **3.** to yield, or serve as, food for. **4.** to provide as food. **5.** to furnish for consumption. **6.** to satisfy; minister to; gratify. **7.** to supply for maintenance or to be operated upon, as to a machine. **8.** to use (land) as pasture. **9.** Colloq. to provide cues to (an actor, esp. a comedian). **10. be fed up,** Colloq. to have more than enough of something. —v.i. **11.** to take food; eat. **12.** to be nourished or gratified; subsist. —n. **13.** food, esp. for cattle, horses, etc. **14.** an allowance of such food. **15.** Colloq. a meal. **16.** act of feeding. **17.** the act or process of feeding a furnace, machine, etc. **18.** the material, or the amount of it, so fed or supplied. **19.** a feeding mechanism. **20.** Theat. Chiefly Brit. Colloq. a line spoken by one actor to which another actor responds with a line which causes a laugh. [ME fede(n), OE fēdan, der. fōda food] —Syn. **13.** FEED, FODDER, FORAGE, PROVENDER mean food for animals. FEED is the general word: pig feed, chicken feed. FODDER is esp. applied to dry or green feed, as opposed to pasturage, fed to horses, cattle, etc.: cornstalks are good fodder, fodder for winter feeding. FORAGE is food which an animal obtains (usually grass, leaves, etc.) by searching about for it: lost cattle can usually live on forage. PROVENDER denotes dry feed, such as hay, oats, or corn: a supply of provender in the haymow and corn cribs.

feed·back (fēd′bak′), adj. **1.** Electronics. denoting or pertaining to a system in which some of the energy of the plate circuit of a vacuum tube is returned (fed back) to the grid circuits. When this opposes the input, it is called inverse, when it aids the input it is called regenerative. —n. **2.** a feedback system.

feed·bag (fēd′bag′), n. a bag for feeding horses, placed before the mouth with straps around the head.

feed·er (fē′dər), n. **1.** one who or that which supplies food or feeds something. **2.** one who or that which takes food or nourishment. **3.** a lamb or sheep to be fed for fattening. **4.** a person or device that feeds a machine, printing press, etc. **5.** a tributary stream, a branch railroad, etc. **6.** Elect. a conductor, or group of conductors, connecting primary equipment in an electric power system. **7.** Brit. a bib.

feeder line, a branch line of an airline system.

feel (fēl), v., **felt, feeling,** n. —v.t. **1.** to perceive or examine by touch. **2.** to have a sensation (other than sight, hearing, taste, and smell) of. **3.** to find or pursue (one's way) by touching, groping, or cautious moves. **4.** to be or become conscious of. **5.** to be emotionally affected by: to feel one's disgrace keenly. **6.** to experience the effects of: the whole region felt the storm. **7.** to have a particular sensation or impression of (fol. by an adjunct or complement): to feel oneself slighted. **8.** to have a general or thorough conviction of. —v.i. **9.** to have perception by touch or by any nerves of sensation other than those of sight, hearing, taste, and smell. **10.** to make examination by touch; grope. **11.** have mental sensations or emotions. **12.** to be consciously, in emotion, opinion, etc.: to feel happy, angry, sure. **13.** to have sympathy or compassion (fol. by with or for). **14.** to have a sensation of being: to feel warm, free. **15.** to seem in the impression produced: how does it feel to be rich? —n. **16.** a quality of an object that is perceived by feeling or touching: a soapy feel. **17.** a sensation of something felt; a vague mental impression or feeling. **18.** the sense of touch: soft to the feel. [ME fele(n), OE fēlan, c. G fühlen]

feel·er (fē′lər), n. **1.** one who or that which feels. **2.** a proposal, remark, hint, etc., designed to bring out the opinions or purposes of others. **3.** Zool. an organ of touch, as an antenna or a tentacle.

feel·ing (fē′lĭng), n. **1.** the function or the power of perceiving by touch; physical sensation not connected with sight, hearing, taste, or smell. **2.** a particular sensation of this kind: a feeling of warmth, pain, or drowsiness. **3.** Psychol. consciousness itself without regard to thought or a perceived object, as excitement—calm, strain-relaxation. **4.** a consciousness or impression: a

feeling of inferiority. **5.** an emotion: a feeling of joy, sorrow, fear. **6.** capacity for emotion; pity. **7.** a sentiment; opinion: to have a feeling that something will succeed, the general feeling was in favor of the proposal. **8.** (pl.) sensibilities; susceptibilities: to hurt one's feelings. **9.** fine emotional endowment. **10.** Music., etc. **a.** emotional or sympathetic perception revealed by an artist in his work. **b.** the general impression conveyed by a work. **c.** sympathetic appreciation, as of music. —adj. **11.** that feels; sentient; sensitive, as nerves. **12.** accessible to emotion; sympathetic: a feeling heart. **13.** indicating emotion: a feeling retort. —feel′ing·ly, adv. —Syn. **5.** FEELING, EMOTION, PASSION, SENTIMENT refer to pleasurable or painful sensations experienced when one is stirred to sympathy, anger, fear, love, grief, etc. FEELING is a general term for a subjective point of view as well as for specific sensations: to be guided by feeling rather than by facts, a feeling of sadness, of rejoicing. EMOTION is applied to an intensified feeling: agitated by emotion. PASSION is strong or violent emotion, often so overpowering that it masters the mind or judgment: stirred to a passion of anger. SENTIMENT is a mixture of thought and feeling, esp. refined or tender feeling: recollections are often colored by sentiment.

fee simple. See fee (def. 6a).

feet (fēt), n. pl. of foot. —feet′less, adj.

fee tail. See fee (def. 6a).

feeze (fēz, fāz), n., v., **feezed, feezing.** Obs. or Dial. —n. **1.** U.S. a state of vexation or worry. **2.** a rush; a violent impact. —v.i. **3.** to fret; worry. —v.t. **4.** to disturb. **5.** to beat; flog. Also, **feaze.** [ME fese(n), OE fēs(i)an drive, c. Sw. fösa]

feign (fān), v.t. **1.** to invent fictitiously or deceptively, as a story or an excuse. **2.** to represent fictitiously; put on an appearance of: to feign sickness. **3.** to imitate deceptively: to feign another's voice. —v.i. **4.** to make believe; pretend: she feigns to be ill. [ME feigne(n), t. OF: m. feign-, s. feindre, g. L fingere form, conceive, devise] —feign′er, n. —feign′ing·ly, adv. —Syn. **4.** See **pretend.**

feigned (fānd), adj. **1.** pretended; sham; counterfeit. **2.** assumed, as a name. **3.** disguised, as a voice. **4.** fictitiously invented. —feign·ed·ly (fā′nĭd lĭ), adv.

feint (fānt), n. **1.** a movement made with the object of deceiving an adversary; an appearance of aiming at one part or point when another is the real object of attack. **2.** a feigned or assumed appearance. —v.i. **3.** to make a feint. [t. F: m. feinte, der. feindre FEIGN]

feints (fānts), n.pl. faints.

Fei·sal (fī′səl), n. Faisal. Also, **Fei′sul.**

feist (fīst), n. a small dog.

feld·spar (feld′spär′, fĕl′-), n. any of a group of minerals, principally aluminosilicates of potassium, sodium, and calcium, and characterized by two cleavages at nearly right angles. They are among the most important constituents of igneous rocks. Also, esp. Brit., **felspar.** [half-taken, half-translated from G feldspath] —feld·spath·ic (feld spăth′ĭk, fĕl′-), adj.

feld·spath·ose (feld′spăth ōs′, fĕl′-), adj. Mineral. of, pertaining to, consisting of, or containing feldspar.

fe·li·cif·ic (fē′lə sĭf′ĭk), adj. making happy; productive of happiness. [t. L: s. fēlicificus making happy]

fe·lic·i·tate (fĭ lĭs′ə tāt′), v., **-tated, -tating,** adj. —v.t. **1.** to compliment upon a happy event; congratulate: to felicitate a friend on his good fortune. **2.** Now Rare. to make happy. —adj. **3.** Obs. made happy. [t. LL: m.s. fēlicitātus, pp. of fēlicitāre make happy, der. L fēlix happy] —fe·lic′i·ta′tor, n.

fe·lic·i·ta·tion (fĭ lĭs′ə tā′shən), n. expression of good wishes; congratulation.

fe·lic·i·tous (fĭ lĭs′ə təs), adj. **1.** apt or appropriate, as action, manner, or expression. **2.** apt in manner or expression, as a person. —fe·lic′i·tous·ly, adv. —fe·lic′i·tous·ness, n.

fe·lic·i·ty (fĭ lĭs′ə tĭ), n., pl. **-ties. 1.** state of being happy, esp. in a high degree. **2.** an instance of this. **3.** a source of happiness. **4.** a skillful faculty: felicity of expression. **5.** an instance or display of this. **6.** Now Rare. good fortune. [ME felicite, t. L: m.s. fēlicitas happiness] —Syn. **1.** See **happiness.**

fe·lid (fē′lĭd), n. one of the cat family, Felidae.

fe·line (fē′līn), adj. **1.** belonging or pertaining to the cat family, Felidae, which includes, besides the domestic cat, the lions, tigers, leopards, lynxes, jaguars, etc. **2.** catlike; characteristic of animals of the cat family: feline softness of step. **3.** sly; stealthy; treacherous. —n. **4.** an animal of the cat family. [t. L: m.s. fēlinus of a cat] —fe′line·ly, adv. —fe′line·ness, fe·lin·i·ty (fĭ lĭn′ə tĭ), n.

feline agranulocytosis, Vet. Sci. a highly fatal, contagious virus disease of domestic cats characterized by fever, somnolence, and diarrhea.

fell[1] (fĕl), v. pt. of fall.

fell[2] (fĕl), v.t. **1.** to cause to fall; knock, strike, or cut down: to fell a moose, a tree, etc. **2.** Sewing. to finish (a seam) by sewing the edge down flat. —n. **3.** Lumbering. the timber cut down in one season. **4.** Sewing. a seam finished by felling. [ME felle(n), OE fellan, causative of feallan fall] —fell′er, n.

fell[3] (fĕl), adj. **1.** fierce; cruel; dreadful. **2.** destructive; deadly: fell poison or disease. [ME, t. OF: m. fel base. See **FELON**] —fell′ness, n.

fell[4] (fĕl), n. the skin or hide of an animal; a pelt. [ME and OE, c. G fell; akin to L pellis skin]

fell⁵ (fĕl), *n.* *Scot.* and *N. Eng.* a stretch of elevated waste land or pasture; a down. [ME, t. Scand.; cf. Icel. *fiall* mountain]

fell·a·ble (fĕl′ə bəl), *adj.* capable of being or fit to be felled.

fel·lah (fĕl′ə), *n., pl.* **fellahs**, *Ar.* **fellahin, fellaheen** (fĕl′ə hēn′). a native peasant or laborer in Egypt, Syria, etc. [t. Ar.: husbandman]

fell·mon·ger (fĕl′mŭng′gər), *n.* a dealer in skins or hides of animals, esp. sheepskins.

fel·loe (fĕl′ō), *n.* the circular rim, or a part of the rim of a wheel, into which the outer ends of the spokes are inserted. Also, **felly**. [ME *fely*, *felwe*, OE *felg*, c. G *felge*]

Wheel
F. Felloe: S. Spoke;
H. Hub

fel·low (fĕl′ō), *n.* **1.** a man; boy. **2.** *Colloq.* beau; suitor. **3.** *Colloq.* a person. **4.** a person of small worth or no esteem. **5.** a companion; comrade. **6.** one belonging to the same class; an equal; peer. **7.** one of a pair; a mate or match. **8.** *Educ.* **a.** a graduate student of a university or college, to whom an allowance is granted for special study. **b.** *Brit.* an incorporated member of a college, entitled to certain privileges. **c.** a member of the corporation or board of trustees of certain universities or colleges. **9.** a member of any of certain learned societies: *a fellow of the British Academy.* **10.** *Obs.* a partner. **11.** **hail fellow well met,** a boon companion. —*v.t.* **12.** to make, or represent as, equal with another. **13.** to produce a fellow to; match. —*adj.* **14.** belonging to the same class or group; united by the same occupation, interests, etc.; being in the same condition: *fellow students, citizens, etc., fellow sufferers.* [ME *felowe, felawe,* late OE *fēolaga,* t. Scand.; cf. Icel. *fēlagi* companion (f. *fē* money + *-lagi* one who lays (something) down)]

fellow creature, a creature produced by the same Creator (now used chiefly of human beings): *he was ashamed of his fellow creatures.*

fellow feeling, 1. sympathetic feeling; sympathy. **2.** sense of joint interest.

fellow servant rule, the common-law rule that the employer was not liable to a servant for injuries caused by the negligence of a fellow servant.

fellow servants, *Law.* workers engaged by the same employer.

fel·low·ship (fĕl′ō shĭp′), *n., v.,* **-shiped, -shiping** or (*esp. Brit.*) **-shipped, -shipping.** —*n.* **1.** the condition or relation of being a fellow. **2.** community of interest, feeling, etc. **3.** communion, as between members of the same church. **4.** friendliness. **5.** an association of persons having similar tastes, interests, etc. **6.** a company; a guild or corporation. **7.** *Educ.* **a.** the body of fellows in a college or university. **b.** the position or emoluments of a fellow of a university, etc., or the sum of money he receives. **c.** a foundation for the maintenance of a fellow in a college or university. —*v.t.* **8.** *Chiefly U.S.* to admit to fellowship, esp. religious fellowship. —*v.i.* **9.** *Chiefly U.S.* to join in fellowship, esp. religious fellowship.

fellow traveler, a nonmember who supports or sympathizes with a party, usually the Communist party.

fel·ly¹ (fĕl′ĭ), *n., pl.* **-lies.** felloe.

fel·ly² (fĕl′ĭ), *adv.* *Archaic.* in a fell manner; fiercely; ruthlessly. [f. FELL³ + -(L)Y]

fe·lo-de-se (fē′lō də sē′, fĕl′ō-), *n., pl.* **felones-de-se** (fĕl′ō nēz′də sē′) or **felos-de-se** (fē′lōz də sē′, fĕl′ōz-). *Latin.* **1.** one who commits suicide. **2.** suicide. [Anglo-L: a felon with respect to oneself]

fel·on¹ (fĕl′ən), *n.* **1.** *Law.* one who has committed a felony. **2.** *Obs.* a wicked person. —*adj.* **3.** wicked; malicious; treacherous. [ME *felun,* t. OF: m. *felon* base, der. L *fellāre* to suck (obscene)]

fel·on² (fĕl′ən), *n. Pathol.* an acute and painful inflammation of the deeper tissues of a finger or toe, usually near the nail; a form of whitlow. [orig. uncert.]

fe·lo·ni·ous (fĭ lō′nĭ əs), *adj.* **1.** *Law.* pertaining to, of the nature of, or involving a felony: *felonious homicide, felonious intent.* **2.** *Now Rare.* wicked; base; villainous. —**fe·lo′ni·ous·ly,** *adv.* —**fe·lo′ni·ous·ness,** *n.*

fel·on·ry (fĕl′ən rĭ), *n.* **1.** the whole body or class of felons. **2.** the convict population of a penal colony.

fel·o·ny (fĕl′ə nĭ), *n., pl.* **-nies.** *Law.* **1.** any of various offenses, as murder, burglary, etc., of graver character than those called misdemeanors, and commonly punished in the U.S. by death or imprisonment for more than a year. **2.** (in early English law) any crime punishable by loss of life or member and forfeiture of goods and chattels, and which could be prosecuted by appeal.

felony murder, a murder committed in conjunction with an independent felony, as robbery.

fel·site (fĕl′sīt), *n.* a dense, igneous rock consisting typically of feldspar and quartz, both of which may appear as phenocrysts. [f. FELS(PAR) + -ITE¹] —**fel·sit·ic** (fĕl sĭt′ĭk), *adj.*

fel·spar (fĕl′spär′), *n. Chiefly Brit.* feldspar.

felt¹ (fĕlt), *v.* pt. and pp. of **feel.**

felt² (fĕlt), *n.* **1.** a nonwoven fabric of wool, fur, or hair, matted together by pressure. **2.** any article of this material, as a hat. **3.** any matted fabric or material. —*adj.* **4.** pertaining to or made of felt. —*v.t.* **5.** to make

into felt; mat or press together. **6.** to cover with, or as with, felt. —*v.i.* **7.** to become matted together. [ME and OE; akin to G *filz.* See FILTER]

felt·ing (fĕl′tĭng), *n.* **1.** felted material. **2.** act or process of making felt. **3.** the materials of which felt is made.

fe·luc·ca (fĕ lŭk′ə), *n.* a long, narrow vessel propelled by oars or lateen sails, or both, used in the Mediterranean. [t. It., t. Ar.]

Felucca

fem., feminine.

fe·male (fē′māl), *n.* **1.** a human being of the sex which conceives and brings forth young; a woman or girl. **2.** any animal of corresponding sex. **3.** *Bot.* a pistillate plant. —*adj.* **4.** belonging to the sex which brings forth young, or any division or group corresponding to it. **5.** pertaining to or characteristic of this sex; feminine. **6.** *Bot.* **a.** designating or pertaining to a plant or its reproductive structure which produces or contains elements that need fertilization. **b.** (of seed plants) pistillate. **7.** *Mech.* designating some part, etc., into which a corresponding part fits: *a female outlet.* **8.** *Obs.* womanish; weakly. [ME *female* (a form due to assoc. with *male*), var. of *femelle,* t. OF, g. L *fēmella,* dim. of *fēmina* woman]

—**Syn. 1.** See **woman. 5.** FEMALE, EFFEMINATE, FEMININE refer to attributes of women. FEMALE, referring to anything not male, is the scientific word, and was once the general word, to designate one of the two sexes: *female organs in a plant or animal, a female seminary.* EFFEMINATE is applied reproachfully or contemptuously to qualities which, when possessed by men, are unmanly and weak, though these same qualities might be proper and becoming in women: *effeminate gestures, an effeminate voice.* FEMININE, corresponding to *masculine,* applies to the attributes particularly appropriate to women, esp. the softer and more delicate qualities. The word is seldom used merely to denote sex, and, if applied to men, suggests the delicacy and weakness of women: *a feminine figure, point of view, features.* —**Ant. 5.** male, masculine.

female rhyme, *Pros.* feminine rhyme.

female suffrage, woman suffrage.

feme (fĕm), *n. Law.* a woman or wife. [t. AF, g. L *fēmina* woman, wife; cf. F *femme*]

feme cov·ert (kŭv′ərt), *Law.* a married woman. [t. AF: a woman covered, i.e., protected]

feme sole (sōl), *Law.* **1.** an unmarried woman, whether spinster, widow, or divorcée. **2.** a married woman who is independent of her husband with respect to property. [t. AF: a woman alone]

feme-sole trader (fĕm′sōl′), *Law.* a married woman who is entitled to carry on business on her own account and responsibility, independently of her husband.

fem·i·ne·i·ty (fĕm′ə nē′ə tĭ), *n.* feminine nature; womanliness. Also, **fe·mal·i·ty** (fĭ măl′ə tĭ), **fem·i·nal·i·ty** (fĕm′ə năl′ə tĭ). [f. s. L *fēmineus* feminine + -ITY]

fem·i·nie (fĕm′ə nĭ), *n.* women collectively. [ME, t. OF, der. L *fēmina* woman]

fem·i·nin (fĕm′ə nĭn), *n. Biochem.* estrone.

fem·i·nine (fĕm′ə nĭn), *adj.* **1.** pertaining to a woman. **2.** like a woman; weak; gentle. **3.** effeminate. **4.** belonging to the female sex. **5.** *Gram.* denoting or pertaining to one of the three genders of Latin, Greek, German, etc., or one of the two of French, Spanish, etc. (so termed because many nouns denoting females belong to it). For example, in Latin, *puella* "girl" is feminine, but so is *stella* "star." In German, *Frau* "woman" is feminine, but so is *Zeit* "time." —*n.* **6.** *Gram.* **a.** the feminine gender. **b.** a noun of that gender. **c.** another element marking that gender, as *la* (the feminine article in French and Spanish). [ME, t. L: m.s. *fēminīnus,* der. *fēmina* woman] —**fem′i·nine·ly,** *adv.* —**fem′i·nine·ness,** *n.* —**Syn. 2.** See **female.**

feminine cadence, *Music.* a cadence in which the chord falls on a weak beat.

feminine ending, 1. *Pros.* an ending in which a line closes with an extra unaccented syllable in addition to the normal accented syllable. **2.** *Gram.* a termination or final syllable marking a feminine word: *"-ā" in Latin is a feminine ending for the ablative case in the singular.*

feminine rhyme, *Pros.* a rhyme of two syllables of which the second is unstressed: *motion, notion* (double rhyme), or of three syllables of which the second and third are unstressed: *fortunate, importunate* (triple rhyme).

fem·i·nin·i·ty (fĕm′ə nĭn′ə tĭ), *n.* **1.** the quality of being feminine; womanliness: *she kept her femininity even in greasy overalls.* **2.** women collectively. Also, **fe·min·i·ty** (fĭ mĭn′ə tĭ).

fem·i·nism (fĕm′ə nĭz′əm), *n.* **1.** the doctrine advocating extension of the activities of women in social and political life. **2.** feminine character. —**fem′i·nist,** *n., adj.* —**fem′i·nis′tic,** *adj.*

fem·i·nize (fĕm′ə nīz′), *v.t., v.i.,* **-nized, -nizing.** to make or become feminine. —**fem′i·ni·za′tion,** *n.*

femme de cham·bre (fäm də shäN′br), *French.* **1.** a lady's maid. **2.** a chambermaid.

fem·o·ral (fĕm′ə rəl), *adj.* of or pertaining to the thigh or femur. [f. s. L *femur* thigh + -AL¹]

fe·mur (fē′mər), *n., pl.* **femurs, femora** (fĕm′ə rə).
1. *Anat.* a bone in the limb of an animal, extending from the pelvis to the knee; the thigh bone. See diag. under **skeleton. 2.** *Entom.* the third segment of an insect's leg (counting from the base), situated between the trochanter and the tibia. See diag. under **coxa.** [t. L: thigh]

fen (fĕn), *n.* **1.** *Brit.* low land covered wholly or partially with water; boggy land; a marsh. **2. the Fens,** marshy region W and S of The Wash, in E England. [ME and OE, c. Icel. *fen* quagmire]

fence (fĕns), *n., v.,* **fenced, fencing. —n. 1.** an enclosure or barrier, as around or along a field, yard, etc. **2. on the fence,** *U.S. Colloq.* undecided or neutral. **3.** the act, practice, or art of fencing; swordplay. **4.** skill in argument, repartee, etc. **5.** a person who receives and disposes of stolen goods, or the place of business of such a person. **6.** *Mach.* a guard or guide, as for regulating the movements of a tool or machine. **7.** *Archaic.* a means of defense; a bulwark. **—v.t. 8.** to enclose by some barrier, thus asserting exclusive right to possession. **9.** to separate by, or as by, a fence or fences. **10.** *Archaic.* to ward off; keep out. **11.** to defend; protect; guard. **—v.i. 12.** to use a sword, foil, etc., in defense and attack, or in exercise or exhibition of skill in that art. **13.** to parry arguments; strive to evade giving direct answers. **14.** (of a horse) to leap over a fence. **15.** *Obs.* to raise a defense. [aphetic var. of DEFENCE] **—fence′less,** *adj.* **—fence′less·ness,** *n.* **—fence′-like′,** *adj.*

fenc·er (fĕn′sər), *n.* **1.** one who fences. **2.** one who practices the art of fencing with a sword, foil, etc. **3.** *Austral.* a person who makes or mends fences.

fen·ci·ble (fĕn′sə bəl), *n.* **1.** *Archaic.* a soldier enlisted for defensive service in his own country only. **—adj. 2.** *Scot.* capable of being defended or of making defense.

fenc·ing (fĕn′sĭng), *n.* **1.** act, practice, or art of using a sword, foil, etc., for defense and attack. **2.** a parrying of arguments; an evading of direct answers. **3.** an enclosure or railing. **4.** fences collectively. **5.** material for fences.

fend (fĕnd), *v.t.* **1.** to ward off (often fol. by *off*): *to fend off blows.* **2.** *Archaic.* to defend. **—v.i. 3.** to make defense; offer resistance. **4.** to parry. **5.** *Colloq.* to shift; provide: *to fend for oneself.* [aphetic var. of DEFEND]

fend·er (fĕn′dər), *n.* **1.** one who or that which wards something off. **2.** the pressed and formed sheet metal part mounted over the road wheel of an automobile, etc. **3.** *Chiefly Brit.* a device on the front of a locomotive, streetcar, or the like, for clearing the track of obstructions. **4.** a mudguard or splashboard on a horse-drawn vehicle. **5.** *Naut.* a piece of timber, bundle of rope, or the like, hung over the side of a vessel to lessen shock or prevent chafing. **6.** a low metal guard before an open fireplace, to keep back falling coals. [aphetic var. of DEFENDER]

Fé·ne·lon (fĕn lôN′), *n.* **François de Salignac de La Mothe** (fräN swä′ də så lē nyák′ də lá môt′), 1651–1715, French theologian and writer.

fen·es·tel·la (fĕn′ĭs tĕl′ə), *n., pl.* **-tellae** (-tĕl′ē). *Archit.* **1.** a small window or windowlike opening. **2.** a small windowlike niche in the wall on the south side of an altar, containing the piscina, and frequently also the credence. [t. L, dim. of *fenestra* window]

fe·nes·tra (fĭ nĕs′trə), *n., pl.* **-trae** (-trē). **1.** *Anat., Zool.* a small opening or perforation, as in a bone. **2.** *Entom.* a transparent spot in an otherwise opaque surface, as in the wings of certain butterflies and moths. **3.** *Archit.* a windowlike opening. [t. L: window] **—fe·nes′tral,** *adj.*

fe·nes·trat·ed (fĭ nĕs′trā tĭd), *adj. Archit.* having windows; windowed; characterized by windows. Also, **fe·nes′trate.** [f. m.s. L *fenestrātus,* pp., furnished with windows + -ED²]

fen·es·tra·tion (fĕn′ĭs trā′shən), *n.* **1.** *Archit.* the disposition of windows in a building. **2.** *Surg.* an operation which creates a small opening in the semicircular canal to relieve deafness caused by fused stapes. Also, **Lempert operation.**

Feng·tien (fŭng′tyĕn′), *n.* **1.** Mukden. **2.** former name of Liaoning.

Fe·ni·an (fē′nĭ ən, fĕn′yən), *n.* **1.** a member of an Irish revolutionary organization (Irish Republican Brotherhood) founded in New York in 1858, which had for its aim the establishment of an independent Irish republic. **2.** *Irish Hist.* a member of any of several bands of Scots and Picts (Fianna), fighting the Romans along Hadrian's Wall in Britain. **3.** *Later Irish Legend.* a member of a roving band of warriors, the center of numerous legends comparable to those of King Arthur and the Round Table. [appar. b. OIrish *fēn(e)* Irishman and OIrish *(f)iann* legendary band of warriors in service of Finn MacCool] **—Fe′ni·an·ism,** *n.*

fen·nec (fĕn′ĕk), *n.* a small North African fox, *Vulpes zerda,* of a pale-fawn color, and having large pointed ears. [t. Ar.: m. *fenek*]

fen·nel (fĕn′əl), *n.* **1.** an umbelliferous plant, *Foeniculum vulgare,* having yellow flowers, and bearing aromatic fruits used in cookery and medicine. **2.** the fruits (fennel seed) of this plant. **3.** any of various more or less similar plants, as *Ferula communis* (giant fennel), a tall ornamental apiaceous herb. [ME *fenel,* OE *fenol, finol, finugl,* t. VL: m.s. *fēnuclum,* var. of L *faeniculum* fennel, dim. of *faenum* hay]

fen·nel·flow·er (fĕn′əl flou′ər), *n.* **1.** any of the ranunculaceous herbs constituting the genus *Nigella,* esp. *N. sativa,* whose seeds are used in the East as a condiment and medicine. **2.** the flower of this plant.

fen·ny (fĕn′ĭ), *adj.* **1.** marshy; boggy. **2.** inhabiting, or growing in, fens. [ME; OE *fennig,* der. *fenn* fen]

Fen·rir (fĕn′rĭr), *n. Scand. Myth.* a gigantic wolflike water demon, son of Loki: slayer of Odin and slain by Vidar. Also, **Fen·ris** (fĕn′rĭs).

fen·u·greek (fĕn′yŏō grēk′), *n.* a plant, *Trigonella Foenum-Graecum,* indigenous to western Asia, but extensively cultivated elsewhere, chiefly for forage and for its mucilaginous seeds, which are used in medicine. [ME *fenegrek,* OE *fenogrǣcum,* t. L: m. *faenugraecum,* for *faenum graecum* Greek hay]

feod (fūd), *n.* feud². See fee (def. 6, 7).

feoff (fĕf *for 1;* fēf, fĕf *for 2*), *n.* **1.** a fief or fee. **—v.t. 2.** to invest with a fief or fee; enfeoff. [ME *feoff(en),* t. AF: m. *feoffer,* var. of OF *fefier, fieffer,* der. *fieu* FEE] **—feoff′ment,** *n.* **—feof′for, feof′fer,** *n.*

feoff·ee (fĕf ē′, fēf ē′), *n.* a person invested with a fief.

-fer, a noun suffix with a corresponding adjective in *-ferous,* as *conifer* (a coniferous tree). [t. L: bearing, der. *ferre* bear]

fe·ra·cious (fə rā′shəs), *adj.* fruitful; productive. [f. FERACI(TY) + -OUS]

fe·rac·i·ty (fə răs′ə tĭ), *n.* fruitfulness. [t. L: m.s. *ferācitas*]

fe·ral (fĭr′əl), *adj.* **1.** wild, or existing in a state of nature, as animals (or, sometimes, plants). **2.** having reverted to the wild state, as from domestication. **3.** of or characteristic of wild animals: *the feral state.* [f. s. L *fera* wild beast (prop. fem. of *ferus* wild) + -AL¹]

Fer·ber (fûr′bər), *n.* **Edna,** born 1887, U.S. novelist, short-story writer, and dramatist.

fer-de-lance (fĕr də läns′), *n.* a large, very venomous snake, *Trimeresurus atrox,* of tropical America. [F: lit., iron (head) of a lance]

Fer·di·nand I (fûr′dĭ nănd′; *Ger.* fĕr′dĭ nänt′), **1.** 1503–64, emperor of the Holy Roman Empire, 1558–64, and king of Bohemia and of Hungary, 1526–64 (brother of Emperor Charles V). **2.** (*Prince of Saxe-Coburg-Gotha*) born 1861, ruling prince of Bulgaria, 1887–1908, and tsar, 1908 until he abdicated in 1918. **3.** ("*Ferdinand the Great*"), died 1065, king of Castile, 1035?–65, and Leon, 1037–65; recognized as emperor of Spain, 1038–65.

Ferdinand II, **1.** 1578–1637, emperor of the Holy Roman Empire, 1619–37, king of Bohemia, 1617–37, and king of Hungary, 1618–37. **2.** 1452–1516, king of Aragon, 1479–1516 and of Sicily, 1468–1516. See **Ferdinand V.**

Ferdinand III, 1452–1516, king of Naples, 1502–16. See **Ferdinand V.**

Ferdinand V, ("*the Catholic*"), 1452–1516, Spanish king who founded the Spanish monarchy. He commissioned Christopher Columbus to make his voyages. (As **Ferdinand II,** king of Aragon, 1479–1516, and king of Sicily, 1468–1516; as **Ferdinand III,** king of Naples, 1502–16; as **Ferdinand V,** joint ruler of Castile with his wife Isabella I, 1474–1504, and sole ruler of United Spain, 1506–16).

fere (fĭr), *n. Obs.* a companion; a mate. [ME; OE *gefēra,* der. *fōr* journey; akin to FARE]

fer·e·to·ry (fĕr′ə tōr′ĭ), *n., pl.* **-ries. 1.** a shrine, usually portable, designed to hold the relics of saints. **2.** a room or chapel in which shrines were kept. [b. L *ferē-(trum)* bier and (REPOSI)TORY; r. ME *fertre,* t. OF]

fe·ri·al (fĭr′ĭ əl), *adj.* **1.** pertaining to a holiday. **2.** *Eccles.* pertaining to weekdays not set apart as festivals. [t. ML: s. *fēriālis,* der. L *fēria* holiday]

fe·rine (fĭr′īn, -ĭn), *adj.* feral. [t. L: m.s. *ferīnus*]

Fe·rin·gi (fə rĭng′gĭ), *n.* (in India, usually in contemptuous use) **1.** a European or a person of European descent. **2.** a Portuguese born in India. Also, **Fe·rin′ghee.** [ult. t. Pers.: m. *Farangī,* in Ar. *Faranjī,* lit., Frank]

fer·i·ty (fĕr′ə tĭ), *n.* **1.** wild, untamed, or uncultivated state. **2.** savagery; ferocity. [t. L: m.s. *feritas* wildness]

Fer·man·agh (fər măn′ə), *n.* a county in Northern Ireland, in SW Ulster. 53,044 pop. (1951); 653 sq. mi. *Co. seat:* Enniskillen.

fer·ment (*n.* fûr′mĕnt; *v.* fər mĕnt′), *n.* **1.** any of various agents or substances which cause fermentation, esp.: **a.** any of various living organisms (**organized ferments**), as yeasts, molds, certain bacteria, etc. **b.** any of certain complex substances derived from living cells (**unorganized ferments or enzymes**), as pepsin, etc. **2.** fermentation. **3.** agitation; excitement; tumult. **—v.t. 4.** to act upon as a ferment. **5.** to cause to undergo fermentation. **6.** to inflame; foment. **7.** to agitate; excite. **—v.i. 8.** to be fermented; undergo fermentation. **9.** to seethe with agitation or excitement. [t. L: s. *fermentum* leaven, agitation] **—fer·ment′a·ble,** *adj.*

fer·men·ta·tion (fûr′mĕn tā′shən), *n.* **1.** act or process of fermenting. **2.** *Chem.* a change brought about by a ferment, such as yeast enzymes which convert grape sugar into ethyl alcohol, etc. **3.** agitation; excitement.

fer·ment·a·tive (fər mĕn′tə tĭv), *adj.* **1.** tending to produce or undergo fermentation. **2.** pertaining to or of the nature of fermentation.

fer·mi (fûr'mǐ, *It.* fĕr'mē), *n.* a unit of length, 10⁻¹³ cm.

Fer·mi (fĕr'mē), *n.* **Enrico** (ĕn'rē'kō), 1901–1954, Italian physicist, in U.S. since 1939.

fer·mi·um (fûr'mǐ əm), *n. Chem.* a synthetic, radioactive element. *Symbol:* Fm; *at. no.:* 100. [f. (ENRICO) FERMI + -IUM]

fern (fûrn), *n. Bot.* any of the pteridophytes constituting the order *Filicales*, distinguished from other pteridophytes in having few leaves, large in proportion to the stems, and bearing sporangia on the undersurface or margin. [ME *ferne*, OE *fearn*, c. G *farn*; akin to Skt. *parna* feather] —**fern′like′,** *adj.*

Fer·nán·dez (far nän′dĕz; *Sp.* fĕr nän′dĕth), *n.* **Juan** (hwän), fl. c1570, Spanish navigator and explorer of the western coast of South America and islands of the Pacific.

Fer·nan·do (fĕr nän′dō), *n.* Spanish for **Ferdinand.**

Fer·nan·do de No·ron·ha (fĕr nän′dŏŏ də nô rō′nyə), an island in the S Atlantic, ab. 125 mi. E of the easternmost tip of Brazil: a Brazilian penal colony. 581 pop. (1950); 10 sq. mi.

Fer·nan·do Po (far nän′dō pō′), an island in the Bight of Biafra, near the W coast of Africa: a part of Spanish Guinea. 40,475 pop. (1950); ab. 800 sq. mi.

Fern·dale (fûrn′dāl′), *n.* a city in SE Michigan, near Detroit. 31,347 (1960).

fern·er·y (fûr′nə rǐ), *n., pl.* **-eries.** a place or a glass case in which ferns are grown for ornament.

fern seed, the spores of ferns, formerly supposed to have the power to make persons invisible.

fern·y (fûr′nǐ), *adj.* **1.** pertaining to, consisting of, or like ferns. **2.** abounding in or overgrown with ferns.

fe·ro·cious (fə rō′shəs), *adj.* savagely fierce, as a wild beast, person, action, aspect, etc.; violently cruel. [f. FEROCI(TY) + -OUS] —**fe·ro′cious·ly,** *adv.* —**fe·ro′cious·ness,** *n.* —Syn. see **fierce.**

fe·roc·i·ty (fə rŏs′ə tǐ), *n.* ferocious quality or state; savage fierceness. [t. L: m.s. *ferōcitas*]

-ferous, an adjective suffix meaning "bearing," "producing," "yielding," "containing," "conveying," as in *auriferous, coniferous, pestiferous.* [f. -FER producing, + -OUS]

Fer·ra·ra (fĕr rä′rä), *n.* a city in N Italy, near the Po: medieval university and cathedral. 140,000 (est. 1954).

fer·rate (fĕr′āt), *n. Chem.* a salt of the hypothetical ferric acid. [f. s. L *ferrum* iron + -ATE²]

Fer·re·ro (fĕr rĕ′rō), *n.* **Guglielmo** (gŏŏ lyĕl′mô), 1871–1942, Italian historian and sociologist.

fer·ret¹ (fĕr′ǐt), *n.* **1.** a domesticated, albinistic, red-eyed form of the polecat, employed in Europe for hunting the burrows of rabbits and rats. **2.** a wild species, *Mustela nigripes,* **(black-footed ferret)** yellowish-brown with the tip of the tail and the legs black, inhabiting the plains of Nebraska and Kansas, and feeding largely on prairie dogs. —*v.t.* **3.** to drive out by, or as by, means of a ferret. **4.** to hunt with ferrets. **5.** to search out or bring to light: *to ferret out the facts.* —*v.i.* **6.** to search about. [ME *fyrette,* t. OF: m. *fuiret,* der. L *fur* thief] —**fer′ret·er,** *n.*

Black-footed ferret. *Mustela nigripes* (21 to 23 in. long, tail 5 in.)

fer·ret² (fĕr′ǐt), *n.* a narrow tape or ribbon, as of silk or cotton, used for binding, etc. [t. It.: m. *fioretto,* dim. of *fiore,* g. L *flōs* flower; conformed to FERRET¹]

ferret badger, any of the small carnivores constituting the genus *Helictis,* of southern and eastern Asia.

ferri-, *Chem.* a word element meaning "iron," implying esp. combination with ferric iron. [var. of FERRO-]

fer·ri·age (fĕr′ǐ ǐj), *n.* **1.** conveyance by a ferryboat or the like. **2.** the price charged for ferrying.

fer·ric (fĕr′ǐk), *adj. Chem.* of or containing iron, esp. in the trivalent state (Fe+³). [f. FERR(I)- + -IC]

fer·ri·cy·a·nide (fĕr′ǐ sī′ə nīd′), *n. Chem.* a salt containing the radical Fe(CN)6⁻³, a complex of ferric iron and cyanide, as *potassium ferricyanide,* K₃Fe(CN)₆.

fer·rif·er·ous (fĕ rǐf′ərəs), *adj.* producing or yielding iron.

Fer·ris wheel (fĕr′ǐs), an amusement device consisting of a large upright wheel rotating about a fixed axis with seats suspended at intervals around its rim. [named after G.W.G. **Ferris** (1859–96), U.S. engineer]

fer·rite (fĕr′īt), *n.* **1.** *Chem.* a compound formed when ferric oxide is combined with a more basic metallic oxide, as NaFeO₂. **2.** *Metall.* the pure iron constituent of steel, etc., as distinguished from the iron carbides, etc. **3.** *Petrog.* any of certain indeterminable mineral substances (probably iron compounds) frequently observed in the microscopic examination of certain igneous rocks.

ferro-, a word element meaning "iron." In *Chem., ferro-* implies esp. combination with ferrous iron as opposed to ferric iron. Also, **ferri-.** [comb. form repr. L *ferrum* iron]

fer·ro·con·crete (fĕr′ō kŏn′krēt, -kŏn krēt′), *n.* reinforced concrete.

fer·ro·cy·a·nide (fĕr′ō sī′ə nīd′, -nǐd′), *n. Chem.* a salt containing the radical Fe(CN)6⁻⁴, a complex of ferrous iron and cyanide, as *potassium ferrocyanide,* K₄Fe(CN)₆.

Fer·rol (fĕr rōl′), *n.* El Ferrol.

fer·ro·mag·ne·sian (fĕr′ō măg nē′shən), *adj. Geol.* (of minerals and rocks) containing iron and magnesium.

fer·ro·mag·net·ic (fĕr′ō măg nĕt′ǐk), *adj. Physics.* paramagnetic to a high degree; behaving like iron in a magnetic field. —**fer·ro·mag·net·ism** (fĕr′ō măg′nə tǐz′əm), *n.*

fer·ro·type (fĕr′ō tīp′), *v.,* **-typed, -typing,** *n. Photog.* —*v.t.* **1.** to put a glossy surface on (a print) by pressing it while wet on a metal sheet (**ferrotype tin**). —*n.* **2.** a photograph taken on a sensitized sheet of enameled iron or tin; a tintype. **3.** the process itself.

fer·rous (fĕr′əs), *adj. Chem.* of or containing iron, esp. in the divalent state (Fe+²).

fer·ru·gi·nous (fĕ rŏŏ′jə nəs), *adj.* iron-bearing. [t. L: m. *ferrūginus,* der. *ferrūgo* iron rust]

fer·rule (fĕr′əl, -ōōl), *n., v.,* **-ruled, -ruling.** —*n.* **1.** a metal ring or cap put round the end of a post, cane, etc., for strength or protection. **2.** (in steam boilers) a bushing for expanding the end of a flue. —*v.t.* **3.** to furnish with a ferrule. Also, **ferule.** [late ME *vyrell,* t. OF: m. *virelle,* g. L *viriola,* dim. of *viriae* bracelets]

fer·ry (fĕr′ǐ), *n., pl.* **-ries,** *v.,* **-ried, -rying.** —*n.* **1.** an establishment with terminals and floating equipment, for transport from shore to shore across a body of water. **2.** a ferryboat. **3.** the legal right to ferry passengers, etc., and to charge toll for the service. —*v.t.* **4.** to carry or convey over water in a boat or plane. —*v.i.* **5.** to pass over water in a boat or by ferry. [ME *feri(en),* OE *ferian,* akin to *faran* fare]

fer·ry·boat (fĕr′ǐ bōt′), *n.* a boat used to convey passengers, vehicles, etc., across a river or the like.

fer·ry·man (fĕr′ǐ mən), *n., pl.* **-men.** one who owns or runs a ferry.

fer·tile (fûr′təl *or,* esp. *Brit.,* -tīl), *adj.* **1.** bearing or producing vegetation, crops, etc., abundantly, as land or soil. **2.** bearing offspring freely; prolific. **3.** abundantly productive: *a fertile imagination.* **4.** producing an abundance (fol. by *of* or in): *a land fertile of wheat.* **5.** conducive to productiveness: *fertile showers.* **6.** *Biol.* **a.** fertilized, as an egg or ovum; fecundated. **b.** capable of growth or development, as seeds or eggs. **7.** *Bot.* **a.** capable of producing sexual reproductive structures. **b.** capable of causing fertilization, as an anther with fully developed pollen. **c.** having spore-bearing organs, as a frond. **8.** *Obs.* produced in abundance. [ME, t. L: m.s. *fertilis* fruitful] —**fer′tile·ly,** *adv.* —**fer′tile·ness,** *n.* —Syn. **1.** See **productive.**

Fertile Crescent, 1. an arc-shaped region favorable for agriculture extending from the Levant to Iraq. **2.** an area in the Middle and Near East, once fertile but now partly desert, in which it is believed that man first practiced agriculture.

fer·til·i·ty (far tǐl′ə tǐ), *n.* **1.** state or quality of being fertile. **2.** *Biol.* the ability to produce offspring; power of reproduction. **3.** (of soil) the quality of supplying nutrients in proper amounts for plant growth when other factors are favorable.

fer·ti·li·za·tion (fûr′tə lə zā′shən), *n.* **1.** act or process of fertilizing. **2.** state of being fertilized. **3.** *Biol.* **a.** the union of male and female gametic nuclei. **b.** fecundation or impregnation of animals or plants. **4.** the enrichment of soil for the production of crops, etc.

fer·ti·lize (fûr′tə līz′), *v.t.,* **-lized, -lizing. 1.** *Biol.* **a.** to render (an egg, ovum, or female cell) capable of development by union with the male element, or sperm. **b.** to fecundate or impregnate (an animal or plant). **2.** to make fertile; enrich (soil, etc.) for crops, etc. **3.** to make productive. —**fer′ti·liz′a·ble,** *adj.*

fer·ti·liz·er (fûr′tə lī′zər), *n.* **1.** any material used to fertilize the soil, esp. a commercial or chemical manure. **2.** one who or that which fertilizes an animal or plant.

fer·u·la (fĕr′yŏŏ lə, fĕr′ŏŏ-), *n., pl.* **-lae** (-lē′). **1.** *Bot.* any plant of an umbelliferous genus, *Ferula,* chiefly of the Mediterranean region and central Asia, generally tall and coarse with dissected leaves, many of the Asiatic species yielding strongly scented, medicinal gum resins. **2.** a rod; a ferule. [t. L: rod, giant fennel]

fer·u·la·ceous (fĕr′yŏŏ lā′shəs, fĕr′ŏŏ-), *adj.* pertaining to reeds or canes; having a stalklike reed: *ferulaceous plants.* [t. L: m. *ferulāceus,* der. *ferula* giant fennel]

fer·ule¹ (fĕr′əl, -ōōl), *n., v.,* **-uled, -uling.** —*n.* **1.** a rod, cane, or flat piece of wood for the punishment of children, by striking them, esp. on the hand. —*v.t.* **2.** to punish with a ferule. [OE *ferele* rod, t. L: m. *ferula*]

fer·ule² (fĕr′əl, -ōōl), *n., v.t.,* **-uled, -uling.** ferrule.

fer·ven·cy (fûr′vən sǐ), *n.* warmth of feeling; ardor.

fer·vent (fûr′vənt), *adj.* **1.** having or showing great warmth and earnestness of feeling: *a fervent admirer, plea, etc.* **2.** hot; burning; glowing. [ME, t. L: s. *fervens,* ppr., boiling, glowing] —**fer′vent·ly,** *adv.* —**fer′vent·ness,** *n.* —Syn. **1.** fervid, fiery, ardent, eager, earnest, zealous, vehement, impassioned, passionate.

fer·vid (fûr′vǐd), *adj.* **1.** heated or vehement in spirit, enthusiasm, etc.: *a fervid orator.* **2.** burning; glowing; hot. [t. L: s. *fervidus* burning] —**fer′vid·ly,** *adv.* —**fer′vid·ness,** *n.*

fer·vor (fûr′vər), *n.* **1.** great warmth and earnestness of feeling: *to speak with great fervor.* **2.** intense heat. Also, *Brit.,* **fer′vour.** [ME, t. OF, t. L: heat, passion. —Syn. **1.** ardor, intensity, eagerness, enthusiasm.

Fes·cen·nine (fĕs′ə nīn′, -nǐn), *adj.* scurrilous; licentious; obscene: *Fescennine verse.* [t. L: m.s. *Fescennīnus* pertaining to *Fescennia* in Etruria]

fes·cue (fĕs′kū), *n.* **1.** any grass of the genus *Festuca,* some species of which are cultivated for pasture or

---

b., blend of, blended; c., cognate with; d., dialect, dialectical; der., derived from; f., formed from; g., going back to; m., modification of; r., replacing; s., stem of; t., taken from; ?, perhaps. See the full key on inside cover.

lawns. 2. a straw, slender twig, etc., used to point out the letters in teaching children to read. [ME *festue*, t. OF, g. L *festūca* stalk, straw]

ess (fĕs), *n.* *Her.* a wide horizontal band across the middle of an escutcheon. Also, **fesse.** [late ME *fesse*, t. AF, g. L *fascia* band]

'es·sen·den (fĕs'ən·dən), *n.* **William Pitt,** 1806–69, U.S. statesman.

ess point, *Her.* the central point of an escutcheon. See diag. under **escutcheon.**

ess·wise (fĕs'wīz'), *adv.* *Her.* in the manner of a fess; across the shield. Also, **fesse'wise'.**

es·ta (fĕs'ta), *n.* a feast, festival, or holiday. [It.]

es·tal (fĕs'tal), *adj.* pertaining to or befitting a feast, festival, or gala occasion. [late ME, t. OF, der. L *festum* a festival, feast] —**fes'tal·ly,** *adv.*

es·ter (fĕs'tər), *v.i.* 1. to generate purulent matter; suppurate. 2. to cause ulceration, or rankle, as a foreign body in the flesh. 3. to putrefy or rot. 4. to rankle, as a feeling of resentment. —*v.t.* 5. to cause to fester. —*n.* 6. an ulcer; a rankling sore. 7. a small, purulent, superficial sore. [ME *festre*, t. OF, g. L *fistula* ulcer]

'es·ti·na len·te (fĕs tī'na lĕn'tĭ), *Latin.* make haste slowly.

es·ti·na·tion (fĕs'ta nā'shən), *n.* *Pathol.* a type of gait marked by an involuntary hurrying in walking, observed in certain nervous diseases. [t. L: s. *festinātio* haste]

es·ti·val (fĕs'ta val), *n.* 1. a periodic religious or other feast: *the festival of Christmas, a Roman festival.* 2. any time of feasting; an anniversary for festive celebration. 3. any course of festive activities: *a music festival.* 4. *Archaic.* merrymaking; revelry. —*adj.* 5. of, pertaining to, or befitting a feast or holiday; festal. [ME, t. ML: s. *festivālis,* der. L *festivus* FESTIVE]

'es·tive (fĕs'tĭv), *adj.* pertaining to or suitable for a feast or festival. Also, *Rare,* **fes·ti·vous** (fĕs'tĭ vəs). [t. L: m.s. *festivus* merry, lively] —**fes'tive·ly,** *adv.* —**fes'tive·ness,** *n.*

es·tiv·i·ty (fĕs tĭv'ə tĭ), *n., pl.* **-ties.** 1. a festive celebration or occasion. 2. (*pl.*) festive proceedings. 3. festive character; festive gaiety or pleasure.

es·toon (fĕs tōōn'), *n.* 1. a string or chain of flowers, foliage, ribbon, etc., suspended in a curve between two points. 2. a decorative representation of this, as in architectural work or on pottery. —*v.t.* 3. to adorn with, or as with, festoons. 4. to form into festoons. 5. to connect by festoons. [t. F: m. *feston,* t. It.: m. *festone,* der. *festa* festival, FEAST]

estoon cloud, *Meteorol.* a mammato-cumulus.

es·toon·er·y (fĕs tōō'nər ĭ), *n.* 1. a decoration of festoons. 2. festoons collectively.

e·tal (fē'tal), *adj.* *Embryol.* of, pertaining to, or having the character of a fetus. Also, **foetal.**

e·ta·tion (fē tā'shən), *n.* *Embryol.* pregnancy; gestation. Also, **foetation.**

etch (fĕch), *v.t.* 1. to go and bring to the speaker, or to or from a particular place: *to fetch a book from another room.* 2. to cause to come to a particular place or condition; succeed in bringing: *to fetch a doctor.* 3. to bring (a price, etc.). 4. *Colloq.* to charm; captivate. 5. to take (a breath). 6. to utter (a sigh, groan, etc.). 7. to deal or deliver (a stroke, blow, etc.). 8. to perform or execute (a movement, step, leap, etc.). 9. *Chiefly Naut. or Dial.* to reach; arrive at. 10. *Hunting.* (as a command to a dog) to retrieve (game). 11. **fetch up,** to bring up a child, etc. —*v.i.* 12. to go and bring things. 13. *Chiefly Naut.* **a.** to move, go, or take a course: *to fetch about.* **b.** to reach; attain; get. 14. *Hunting.* to retrieve game. 15. **fetch and carry,** to do minor menial jobs. 16. to arrive; reach. —*n.* 17. act of fetching. 18. the distance of fetching. 19. the reach or stretch of a thing (specif. with reference to the traveling of waves of the sea). 20. a trick; dodge. 21. the apparition of a living person; a wraith. 22. *Archaic.* a stroke; effort: *a fetch of the imagination.* [ME *fecche(n), fet feccan,* prob. var. of *fetian*] —**fetch'er,** *n.* —**Syn.** 1. See **bring.**

etch·ing (fĕch'ĭng), *adj.* *Colloq.* charming; captivating. —**fetch'ing·ly,** *adv.*

ete (fāt; *Fr.* fĕt). *n., v.,* **feted, feting.** —*n.* 1. a feast or festival. 2. a festal day; a holiday. 3. a festive celebration or entertainment. —*v.t.* 4. to entertain at or honor with a fete. Also, **fête.** [t. F. See FEAST]

ête cham·pê·tre (fĕt shän pĕ'tr), *French.* an outdoor festival; a garden party.

ete day, a festival day.

fet·e·ri·ta (fĕt'ə rē'tə), *n.* a grain sorghum, a variety of *Sorghum vulgare,* cultivated for grain and forage. [prob. t. native African]

e·tial (fē'shəl), *adj.* 1. pertaining to fetiales. 2. concerned with declarations of war and treaties of peace: *fetial law.* 3. heraldic. —*n.* 4. one of the fetiales.

e·ti·a·les (fē'shĭ ā'lēz), *n.pl.* (in ancient Rome) a college of priests who acted as heralds and representatives of the people in disputes with foreign nations and in the declaration of war and the ratification of peace. [t. L]

e·tich·ism (fē'tĭsh ĭz'əm, fĕt'ĭsh-), *n.* fetishism. —**fe'tich·ist,** *n.* —**fe'tich·is'tic,** *adj.*

e·ti·cide (fē'tə sīd'), *n.* the destruction of the life of a fetus. Also, **foeticide.** [f. s. L *fētus* (see FETUS) + -(I)-CIDE²] —**fe'ti·cid'al,** *adj.*

fet·id (fĕt'ĭd, fē'tĭd), *adj.* having an offensive odor; stinking. Also, **foetid.** [t. L: s. *fētidus,* var. of *foetidus*] —**fet'id·ly,** *adv.* —**fet'id·ness, fe·tid'i·ty,** *n.*

fe·tish (fē'tĭsh, fĕt'ĭsh), *n.* 1. a material, commonly an inanimate object, regarded with awe as being the embodiment or habitation of a potent spirit, or as having magical potency because of the materials and methods used in compounding it. 2. any object of blind reverence. Also, **fe'tich.** [t. F: m. *fétich,* t. Pg.: m. *feitiço* orig. adj., artificial, g. L *facticius* factitious] —**fe'tish-like',** *adj.*

fe·tish·ism (fē'tĭsh ĭz'əm, fĕt'ĭsh-), *n.* 1. belief in or use of fetishes. 2. *Psychiatry.* the compulsive use of some inanimate object in attaining sexual gratification, such as a shoe, a lock of hair, stockings, underclothes, a neckpiece, etc. 3. blind devotion. Also, **fetichism.** —**fe'tish·is'tic,** *adj.*

fe·tish·ist (fē'tĭsh ĭst, fĕt'ĭsh-), *n.* a user of fetishes. Also, **fetichist.**

fet·lock (fĕt'lŏk), *n.* 1. a part of a horse's leg situated behind the joint between the cannon bone and the great pastern bone, and bearing a tuft of hair. See illus. under **horse.** 2. this tuft of hair. 3. the joint at this point (**fetlock joint**). [ME *fet(e)lok,* etc., c. G *fissloch*; orig. obscure]

fe·tor (fē'tər), *n.* any strong offensive smell; a stench. Also, **foetor.** [t. L]

fet·ter (fĕt'ər), *n.* 1. a chain or shackle placed on the feet. 2. (*usually pl.*) anything that confines or restrains. —*v.t.* 3. to put fetters upon. 4. to confine; restrain. [ME and OE *feter,* c. OHG *fezzera*; akin to FOOT]

fet·ter·bush (fĕt'ər bŏŏsh'), *n.* 1. an ericaceous evergreen shrub *Lyonia lucida,* of the southern U.S., with fragrant white flowers. 2. a similar shrub, *Pieris floribunda,* with white campanulate flowers. 3. any of several heathlike shrubs in the southern U.S.

fet·ter·less (fĕt'ər lĭs), *adj.* without fetters; unfettered.

fet·ter·lock (fĕt'ər lŏk'), *n.* fetlock.

fet·tle (fĕt'al), *n.* state; condition: *in fine fettle.* [n. use of *fettle* make ready, ME *fetlen,* der. OE *fetel* belt]

fet·tling (fĕt'lĭng), *n.* *Metall.* the material with which the hearth of a puddling furnace or the like is lined, as a substance rich in oxides of iron. [der. *fettle,* v. See FETTLE]

fe·tus (fē'təs), *n.* *Embryol.* the young of an animal in the womb or in the egg, esp. in its later stages. Also, **foetus.** [t. L: a bringing forth, offspring, young]

feu (fū), *n., v.t.* *Scot. Law.* fee (defs. 6, 7). [ME *few,* t. OF: m. *fieu.* See FEE]

feu·ar (fū'ər), *n.* *Scot. Law.* one who holds land in fee.

Feucht·wang·er (foiкнt'väng'ər), *n.* **Lion** (lē'ôn), 1884–1958, German novelist and dramatist.

feud¹ (fūd), *n.* 1. a bitter, continuous hostility, esp. between two families, clans, etc. 2. a quarrel or contention. [var. of *fead* (a being misread as ʃ), ME *fede,* t. OF: m. *fe(i)de,* t. OHG: m. *fēhida* (G *fehde*). c. OE *fæhth* enmity. Cf. FOE] —**Syn.** 2. See **quarrel¹.**

feud² (fūd), *n.* *Law.* fee (defs. 6, 7). Also, **feod.** [t. ML: s. *feudum,* var. of *feodum.* See FEE]

feu·dal (fū'dal), *adj.* 1. of, pertaining to, or of the nature of a fief or fee: *a feudal estate.* 2. of or pertaining to the holding of land in a fief or fee. 3. of or pertaining to the feudal system: *feudal law.* —**feu'dal·ly,** *adv.*

feudal investiture, (in the feudal system) the public grant of the land by the lord to the tenant.

feu·dal·ism (fū'dal ĭz'əm), *n.* the feudal organization, or its principles and practices. —**feu'dal·ist,** *n.* —**feu'dal·is'tic,** *adj.*

feu·dal·i·ty (fū dăl'ə tĭ), *n., pl.* **-ties.** 1. state or quality of being feudal. 2. the principles and practices of feudalism. 3. a fief or fee.

feu·dal·ize (fū'də līz'), *v.t.,* **-ized, -izing.** to make feudal; bring under the feudal system. —**feu'dal·i·za'-tion,** *n.*

feudal system, the organization in Europe during the Middle Ages, based on the holding of lands in fief or fee, and on the resulting relations between lord and vassal.

feu·da·to·ry (fū'də tōr'ĭ), *n., pl.* **-ries.** 1. one who holds his lands by feudal tenure; a feudal vassal. 2. a fief or fee.

feud·ist¹ (fū'dĭst), *n.* *U.S.* a person who fights in a feud. [f. FEUD¹ + -IST]

feud·ist² (fū'dĭst), *n.* a writer or authority on feudal law. [f. FEUD² + -IST]

Feuil·lant (fœ yän'), *n.* a member of a club of constitutional royalists in the French Revolution, which disintegrated as the Revolution grew radical, violent, and antimonarchical. [t. F]

feuil·le·ton (fœ yə tôN'), *n.* *French.* 1. a part of a newspaper (usually the bottom of one or more pages, marked off by a rule) devoted to light literature, fiction, criticism, etc. 2. an item printed in the feuilleton.

fe·ver (fē'vər), *n.* 1. a morbid condition of the body characterized by undue rise of temperature, quickening of the pulse, and disturbance of various bodily functions. 2. any of a group of diseases in which high temperature is a prominent symptom: *scarlet fever.* 3. intense nervous excitement. —*v.t.* 4. to affect with or as with fever. [ME; OE *fefer,* t. L: m.s. *febris*] —**fe'vered,** *adj.* —**fe'ver·less,** *adj.*

ăct, āble, dâre, ärt; ĕbb, ēqual; Yf, īce; hŏt, ōver, ôrder, oil, bŏŏk, ōōze, out; ŭp, ūse, ûrge; ə = a in alone; ch, chief; g, give; ng, ring; sh, shoe; th, thin; ŧħ, that; zh, vision. See the full key on inside cover.

fe·ver·few (fē/vər fū/), *n.* a perennial composite plant, *Chrysanthemum Parthenium*, bearing small white flowers, formerly used as a febrifuge. [ME *fevyrfue*, OE *feferfug(i)e*, t. LL: m. *febrifugia* kind of plant, f. L: *febri(s)* fever + *-fugia*. See -FUGE]

fever heat, 1. the heat of fever; bodily heat exceeding 98.6 degrees F. 2. feverish excitement.

fe·ver·ish (fē/vər ĭsh), *adj.* 1. excited or restless, as if from fever. 2. having fever, esp. a slight degree of fever. 3. pertaining to, of the nature of, or resembling fever. 4. infested with fever, as a region. 5. having a tendency to produce fever, as food. **—fe/ver·ish·ly,** *adv.* **—fe/ver·ish·ness,** *n.*

fe·ver·ous (fē/vər əs), *adj.* feverish. **—fe/ver·ous·ly,** *adv.*

fe·ver·root (fē/vər rōōt/, -rŏŏt/), *n.* a North American caprifoliaceous herb, *Triosteum perfoliatum*, having a purgative and emetic root.

fever sore, a cold sore.

fever tree, any of several trees which produce or are supposed to produce a febrifuge, as: 1. the blue gum (tree), which is supposed to prevent malaria. 2. a small rubiaceous tree, *Pinckneya pubens*, of the southeastern U.S., with a bark used as a tonic and febrifuge.

fe·ver·weed (fē/vər wēd/), *n.* any plant of the genus *Eryngium* used medicinally, esp. the *Eryngium foetidum* of the West Indies or the *Eryngium campestre* of Europe.

fe·ver·wort (fē/vər wûrt/), *n.* 1. the feverroot. 2. the thoroughwort or boneset.

few (fū), *adj.* 1. not many. **—***n.* 2. **the few,** the minority. 3. **quite a few,** *Colloq.* a fairly large number. [ME; OE *fēawe*, pl., c. OHG *fōhe*; akin to L *paucus*, Gk. *paûros* little, in pl., few] **—few/ness,** *n.*

few·er (fū/ər), *adj., comp. of* **few.** a smaller number of. **—Syn.** FEWER, LESS are sometimes confused because both imply a comparison with something larger (in number or in amount). FEWER applies only to number: *fewer sreet cars are running now than ten years ago.* LESS is used in various ways. It is commonly applied to material in bulk, in reference to amount: *less gasoline in the tank than we thought.* It is also used frequently with abstractions, esp. where the idea of amount is figuratively present: *less courage, less wealth.* LESS applies where such attributes as value, degree, etc. (but not size or number) are concerned: *a nickel is less than a dime* (in value); *a corporal is less than a sergeant* (in rank). **—Ant.** more.

fey (fā), *adj.* *Now Chiefly Scot.* 1. fated to die. 2. dying. 3. appearing to be under a spell. [ME; OE *fæge* doomed to die, timid, c. G *feige* cowardly]

fez (fĕz), *n., pl.* **fezzes.** a felt cap, usually of a red color, having the shape of a truncated cone, and ornamented with a long black tassel, formerly the national headdress of the Turks. [t. Turk.; named after the city of *Fez*]

Turkish fez

Fez (fĕz), *n.* a city in N Morocco, formerly one of the traditional capitals of the sultanate in the French Zone. 179,372 (1952).

Fez·zan (fĕz zän/), *n.* a region in SW Libya: a portion of the Sahara with numerous oases. 54,438 pop. (1954); ab. 280,000 sq. mi. *Chief town:* Murzuq.

ff., 1. folios. 2. and the following (pages, verses, etc.). 3. *Music.* fortissimo.

F.F.A., free from alongside (ship). Also, **f.f.a.**

FHA, Federal Housing Administration.

F.I., Falkland Islands.

fi·a·cre (fyä/kər; *Fr.* fyà/kr), *n.* a hackney coach. [t. F, named after the Hôtel de St. *Fiacre* in Paris]

fi·an·cé (fē/än sā/, fē än/sā; *Fr.* fē än sē/), *n.* a man engaged to be married; a man to whom a girl is engaged. [t. F, pp. of *fiancer* betroth, ult. der. *fier* trust, g. L *fidere*] **—fi/an·cée/,** *n. fem.*

Fi·an·na (fē/ə nə), *n.* the Fenians (def. 2).

Fianna Fail (foil/, fil/), an Irish nationalist party, organized in 1927 by Eamon De Valera, advocating establishment of an Irish Republic. [t. Irish: f. *Fianna* Fenians + *Fáil*, gen. sing. of *fál* sod]

fi·ar (fē/ər), *n. Scot. Law.* the owner of land in fee simple.

fi·as·co (fĭ äs/kō), *n., pl.* **-cos, -coes.** an ignominious failure. [t. It.: lit., bottle; sense development obscure]

fi·at (fī/ət, -ăt), *n.* 1. an authoritative decree, sanction, or order. 2. a formula containing the word *fiat*, by which a person in authority gave his sanction. [t. L: let it be done, or made]

fiat lux (fī/ăt lŭks/), *Latin.* let there be light.

fiat money, *U.S.* paper currency made legal tender by a fiat of the government, but not based on or convertible into coin.

fib¹ (fĭb), *n., v.,* **fibbed, fibbing. —***n.* 1. a trivial falsehood. **—***v.i.* 2. to tell a fib. [short for *fibble-fable*, redupl. of FABLE] **—fib/ber,** *n.* **—Syn.** 1. See falsehood.

fib² (fĭb), *v.t.,* **fibbed, fibbing.** *Slang.* to strike; beat. [orig. unknown]

fi·ber (fī/bər), *n.* 1. a fine threadlike piece, as of cotton, jute, or asbestos. 2. a slender filament. 3. filaments collectively. 4. matter composed of filaments. 5. fibrous structure. 6. character: *moral fiber.* 7. *Bot.* **a.** filamentous matter from the bast tissue or other parts of plants, used for industrial purposes. **b.** a slender, threadlike root of a plant. **c.** a slender, threadlike bast cell. 8. *Chem.* vulcanized fiber. Also, **fi/bre.** [ME *fibre,* t. F, t. L: m. *fibra* fiber, filament] **—fi/ber·less,** *adj.*

fi·ber·board (fī/bər bōrd/), *n.* 1. a building material made of wood or other plant fibers compressed and cemented into rigid sheets. 2. a sheet of fiberboard.

fiber glass, a material consisting of extremely fine filaments of glass which are combined in yarn and woven into fabrics, or are used in masses as an insulator. Also, **fi/ber·glass/.**

fibr-, a word element meaning "fiber," as in *fibrin.* Also, **fibri-, fibro-.** [comb. form repr. L *fibra*]

fi·bri·form (fī/brə fôrm/), *adj.* of the form of a fiber or fibers. [f. FIBRI- + -FORM]

fi·bril (fī/brəl), *n.* 1. a small or fine fiber. 2. *Bot.* one of the delicate hairs on the young roots of some plants. [t. NL: m.s. *fibrilla,* dim. of L *fibra* fiber]

fi·bril·lar (fī/brə lər), *adj.* of, pertaining to, or of the nature of fibrils.

fi·bril·li·form (fĭ brĭl/ə fôrm/), *adj.* of the form of a fibril.

fi·bril·lose (fī/brə lōs/), *adj.* composed of or furnished with fibrils.

fi·brin (fī/brĭn), *n.* 1. *Physiol.* a white, tough, strongly elastic, fibrous proteid, formed in the coagulation of blood. 2. *Bot.* a substance like fibrin found in some plants; gluten. [f. FIBR- + -IN²]

fibrino-, a word element representing **fibrin.**

fi·brin·o·gen (fĭ brĭn/ə jən), *n. Physiol.* a globulin occurring in blood and yielding fibrin in the coagulation of blood.

fi·brin·o·gen·ic (fī/brə nō jĕn/ĭk), *adj. Physiol.* producing fibrin. Also, **fi·bri·nog·e·nous** (fī/brə nŏj/ə nəs).

fi·brin·ous (fī/brə nəs), *adj.* containing, composed of, or of the nature of fibrin.

fibro-, var. of **fibr-,** before consonants.

fi·broid (fī/broid), *adj.* 1. resembling fiber or fibrous tissue. 2. composed of fibers, as a tumor. **—***n.* 3. *Pathol.* a tumor largely composed of smooth muscle.

fi·bro·in (fī/brō ĭn), *n. Biochem.* an indigestible protein, a principal component of spider webs and silk.

fi·bro·ma (fī brō/mə), *n., pl.* **-mata** (-mə tə), **-mas.** *Pathol.* a tumor consisting essentially of fibrous tissue. [NL: f. s. L *fibra* fiber + *-oma* -OMA]

fi·bro·sis (fī brō/sĭs), *n. Pathol.* the development in an organ of excess fibrous connective tissue. [NL: f. s. L *fibra* fiber + *-osis* -OSIS]

fi·brous (fī/brəs), *adj.* containing, consisting of, or resembling fibers. [t. NL: m.s. *fibrōsus,* der. L *fibra* fiber]

fib·ster (fĭb/stər), *n. Colloq.* one who tells fibs.

fib·u·la (fĭb/yə lə), *n., pl.* **-lae** (-lē), **-las.** 1. *Anat.* the outer and thinner of the two bones of the lower leg, extending from the knee to the ankle. See diag. under **skeleton.** 2. *Zool.* a corresponding bone (often rudimentary, or ankylosed with the tibia) of the leg or hind limb of other animals. 3. *Archaeol.* a clasp or brooch, usually more or less ornamented. [t. L: clasp, buckle, pin] **—fib/u·lar,** *adj.*

-fic, an adjective suffix meaning "making," "producing," "causing," as in *colorific, frigorific, horrific, pacific, prolific, soporific.* [t. L: s. *-ficus* making. Cf. F *-fique*]

-fication, a suffix of nouns of action or state corresponding to verbs ending in *-fy,* as in *deification, pacification.* [t. L: s. *-ficātio,* der. *-ficāre.* See -FY]

Fich·te (fĭкн/tə), *n.* **Johann Gottlieb** (yō/hän gŏt/lēp), 1762-1814, German philosopher. **—Fich·te·an** (fĭкн/tĭ ən, fĭк/-), *adj.*

fich·u (fĭsh/ōō; *Fr.* fē shy/), *n.* a kind of kerchief of muslin, lace, or the like, generally triangular in shape, worn about the neck by women, with the ends drawn together or crossed on the breast. [t. F, der. *ficher* to throw on in haste]

fick·le (fĭk/əl), *adj.* likely to change from caprice, irresolution, or instability. [ME *fikel,* OE *ficol* deceitful, treacherous, akin to *gefic* deceit, *befician* deceive, *ficung* fraud] **—fick/le·ness,** *n.* **—Syn.** unstable, unsteady, inconstant, changeable, variable, capricious, fitful.

fi·co (fē/kō), *n., pl.* **-coes.** 1. *Archaic.* the merest trifle. 2. *Obs.* fig¹ (def. 5). [t. It., g. L *ficus* fig]

fict., fiction.

fic·tile (fĭk/təl; *Brit.* -tīl), *adj.* 1. capable of being molded; plastic. 2. molded into form by art. 3. made of earth, clay, etc., by a potter. 4. having to do with pottery. [t. L: m.s. *fictilis,* der. *fingere* form]

fic·tion (fĭk/shən), *n.* 1. the branch of literature comprising works of imaginative narration, esp. in prose form. 2. works of this class, as novels or tales. 3. something feigned, invented, or imagined; a made-up story. 4. act of feigning, inventing, or imagining. 5. *Law.* an allegation that a fact exists which is known not to exist, made by authority of law to bring a case within the operation of a rule of law. [ME, t. L: s. *fictio* a making, fashioning, feigning] **—Syn.** 3. FICTION, FABRICATION, FIGMENT suggest a story which is without basis in reality. FICTION suggests a story invented and fashioned either to entertain or to deceive: *clever fiction, pure fiction.* FABRICATION applies particularly to a false but carefully invented statement or series of statements, in which some truth is sometimes interwoven, the whole usually intended to deceive: *fabrications to lure speculators.* FIGMENT applies to a tale, idea, or statement often made up to explain, justify, or glorify oneself: *his rich uncle was a figment of his imagination.* **—Ant.** 3. fact.

fic·tion·al (fĭk/shən əl), *adj.* of, pertaining to, or of the nature of fiction. **—fic/tion·al·ly,** *adv.*

b., blend of, blended; c., cognate with; d., dialect, dialectal; der., derived from; f., formed from; g., going back to; m., modification of; r., replacing; s., stem of; t., taken from; ?, perhaps. See the full key on inside cover.

fic·tion·ist (fĭk/shən ĭst), *n.* a writer of fiction.

fic·ti·tious (fĭk tĭsh/əs), *adj.* **1.** counterfeit; false; not genuine: *fictitious names.* **2.** pertaining to or consisting of fiction; imaginatively produced or set forth; created by the imagination: *a fictitious hero.* [t. L: m. *ficticius* artificial] —**fic·ti/tious·ly,** *adv.* —**fic·ti/tious·ness,** *n.*

fictitious person, *Law.* a legal entity or artificial person, as a corporation.

fic·tive (fĭk/tĭv), *adj.* **1.** fictitious; imaginary. **2.** pertaining to the creation of fiction. —**fic/tive·ly,** *adv.*

fid (fĭd), *n.* *Naut.* **1.** a square bar or support to hold in place a topmast, etc. **2.** a conical wooden pin used to open strands of rope in splicing. **3.** a bar or pin to support or steady something. [orig. obscure]

-fid, an adjective suffix meaning "divided," "lobed," as in *bifid, trifid, multifid, pinnatifid.* [t. L: s. *-fidus,* der. *findere* cleave]

fid·dle (fĭd/əl), *n., v.,* **-dled, -dling.** —*n.* **1.** a stringed musical instrument of the viol class, esp. a violin (now only in familiar or contemptuous use, or to denote bowed instruments of the Orient and the Middle Ages). **2.** *Naut.* a device to prevent things from rolling off the table in bad weather. **3.** **fit as a fiddle,** in excellent health. **4. play second fiddle,** to take a minor part. —*v.i.* **5.** *Colloq.* to play on the fiddle. **6.** to make aimless movements, as with the hands. **7.** to trifle. —*v.t.* **8.** *Colloq.* to play (a tune) on a fiddle. **9.** to trifle: *to fiddle time away.* [ME (and prob. OE) *fithele* (see **FIDDLER**), c. G *fiedel,* Icel. *fidhla.* Cf. ML *vitula, vidula* viol]

fiddle bow, a bow strung with horsehair with which the strings of the violin or a similar instrument are set in vibration.

fid·dle-de-dee (fĭd/əl dĭ dē/), *interj., n.* nonsense.

fid·dle-fad·dle (fĭd/əl făd/əl), *n., v.,* **-dled, -dling.** *Colloq.* —*n.* **1.** nonsense; something trivial. —*v.i.* **2.** to fuss with trifles. [redupl. of **FIDDLE,** v.]

fid·dle·head (fĭd/əl hĕd/), *n.* an ornament at the bow of a ship, containing a scroll somewhat like that at the head of a violin.

fid·dler (fĭd/lər), *n.* **1.** a violinist. **2.** one who trifles, etc. [ME and OE *fithelere,* c. Icel. *fithlari*]

fiddler crab, any small burrowing crab of the genus *Gelasimus,* the male of which has one greatly enlarged claw.

Fiddler crab, *Gelasimus annulipes*

fid·dle·stick (fĭd/əl stĭk/), *n.* **1.** a fiddle bow. **2.** a mere nothing.

fid·dle·sticks (fĭd/əl stĭks/), *interj.* nonsense.

fid·dle·wood (fĭd/əl wŏŏd/), *n.* **1.** the heavy, hard, durable wood of various West Indian and other trees. **2.** any of the trees.

fid·dling (fĭd/lĭng), *adj.* trifling; trivial.

fi·de·i·com·mis·sar·y (fĭ/dĭ ĭ kŏm/ə sĕr/ĭ), *n., pl.* **-saries,** *adj.* *Civil Law.* —*n.* **1.** the recipient of a fideicommissum. —*adj.* **2.** of, pertaining to, or resembling a fideicommissum. [t. L: m. s. *fidei commissārius.* See **-ARY¹**]

fi·de·i·com·mis·sum (fĭ/dĭ ĭ kə mĭs/əm), *n., pl.* **-mis·sa** (-mĭs/ə). *Civil Law.* a request by a testator that his heir convey a specified part of the estate to another person, or permit another person to enjoy such a part. [t. L, prop. neut. pp. of *fidei committere* entrust to faith]

Fi·de·i De·fen·sor (fĭ/dĭ ī/ dĭ fĕn/sôr), *Latin.* Defender of the Faith, one of the titles of English sovereigns.

Fi·de·lio (fĭ dā/lyō), *n.* an opera (1805) by Beethoven.

fi·del·i·ty (fĭ dĕl/ə tĭ, fə-), *n., pl.* **-ties.** **1.** strict observance of promises, duties, etc. **2.** loyalty. **3.** conjugal faithfulness. **4.** adherence to fact. **5.** *Radio.* the ability of a transmitter or receiver to produce radio waves or sound which reproduce its input accurately (often in combination): *a high-fidelity receiver.* [t. L: m.s. *fidēlitas* faithfulness] —**Syn. 2.** See **loyalty.**

fidge (fĭj), *v.i.* fidged, fidging, *n.* *Now Rare.* fidget. [var. of d. *fitch* v., c. Icel. *fikja* move restlessly, be eager]

fidg·et (fĭj/ĭt), *v.i.* **1.** to move about restlessly or impatiently; be uneasy. —*v.t.* **2.** to cause to fidget; make uneasy. —*n.* **3.** (*often pl.*) condition of restlessness or uneasiness. **4.** one who fidgets. [der. **FIDGE**]

fidg·et·y (fĭj/ə tĭ), *adj.* restless; uneasy. —**fidg/et·i·ness,** *n.*

fi·du·cial (fĭ dū/shəl, -dōō/-), *adj.* **1.** *Physics, etc.* accepted as a fixed basis of reference or comparison: *a fiducial point.* **2.** based on or having trust: *fiducial dependence upon God.* [t. ML: s. *fīdūciālis,* der. L *fīdūcia* trust] —**fi·du/cial·ly,** *adv.*

fi·du·ci·ar·y (fĭ dū/shĭ ĕr/ĭ, -dōō/-), *adj., n., pl.* **-aries.** —*adj.* **1.** *Law.* of or pertaining to the relation between a fiduciary and his principal: *a fiduciary capacity, a fiduciary duty.* **2.** depending on public confidence for value or currency, as fiat money. **3.** *Obs.* like or based on trust or reliance. —*n.* **4.** *Law.* a person to whom property is entrusted to hold, control, or manage for another.

Fi·dus A·cha·tes (fī/dəs ə kā/tēz), *Latin.* **1.** faithful Achates (the comrade of Aeneas). **2.** a devoted, trustworthy friend.

fie (fī), *interj.* an exclamation expressing: **1.** disgust, disapprobation, etc. **2.** humorous pretense of being shocked. [ME *fi,* t. OF, g. L *fī,* but cf. Icel. *fȳ*]

fief (fēf), *n.* **1.** a fee or feud, or estate in land held of a feudal lord; a tenure of land subject to feudal obligations. **2.** a territory held in fee. [t. F. See **FEE**]

field (fēld), *n.* **1.** a piece of open or cleared ground, esp. one suitable for pasture or tillage. **2.** *Sports.* **a.** a piece of ground devoted to sports or contests. **b.** sports played on it, collectively. **c.** all the contestants not individually favored in betting: *to bet on the field in a horse race.* **d.** the players on the field, in football: *to dodge through a broken field.* **3.** *Baseball.* **a.** that part of the ground on which the fielders play, and known as *infield, outfield, right, center,* and *left field,* according to the station or the corresponding players. **b.** the outfield. **4.** *Baseball, Cricket, etc.* the team in the field, as opposed to the one which is at bat. **5.** *Mil.* **a.** the scene or area of active military operations. **b.** a battleground. **c.** a battle. **d.** *Colloq.* (in the U.S. Army) the locations of the parts of the army not in Washington: *out in the field.* **6.** an expanse of anything: *a field of ice.* **7.** any region characterized by a particular feature or product: *a gold field.* **8.** the surface of a canvas, shield, etc., on which something is portrayed. **9.** (in a flag) the ground of each division. **10.** a sphere, or range of activity, interest, opportunity, etc. **11.** *Physics.* a region of space influenced by some agent: *electric field, temperature field.* **12.** *Optics.* the entire area visible through or projected by an optical instrument at a given time. **13.** *Elect.* **a.** the main magnetic field of an electric motor or generator. **b.** the structure in a dynamo designed to establish magnetic lines of force in an armature. **14.** *Math.* a number system which has the same properties relative to the operations of addition, subtraction, multiplication, and division as the number system of all real numbers: *the field of all rational numbers.* **15.** *Obs.* open country. —*v.t.* **16.** *Baseball, Cricket, etc.* **a.** to stop, or catch, and throw (the ball) as a fielder. **b.** to place (a player or group of players) into the field to play. —*v.i.* **17.** *Baseball, Cricket, etc.* **a.** to act as a fielder; field the ball. **b.** to take to the field. —*adj.* **18.** *Sports, etc.* of, or happening on, or competed on, a field rather than a track. **19.** *Mil.* of or pertaining to campaign and active combat service as distinguished from service in rear areas or at headquarters: *a field soldier.* [ME and OE *feld,* c. G *feld*]

Field (fēld), *n.* **1. Cyrus West,** 1819–92, U.S. capitalist; projector of first Atlantic cable. **2. Eugene,** 1850–95, U.S. poet and journalist.

field artillery, *Mil.* **1.** artillery mobile enough to accompany troops in the field. **2.** (*caps.*) a branch of the U.S. Army that is armed with various types of field guns and cannons.

field bag, *Mil.* a musette bag.

field battery, *Mil.* a battery of field guns.

field corn, maize or Indian corn grown for stock feed.

field day, **1.** a day devoted to outdoor sport or athletic contests. **2.** any day of unusual activity or display.

field·er (fēl/dər), *n.* **1.** *Baseball, Cricket, etc.* a player who fields the ball. **2.** *Baseball.* any of the players of the infield or the outfield, esp. an outfielder.

fielder's choice, *Baseball.* a fielder's attempt to put out a base runner rather than the batter, when a throw to first base would have put out the batter.

field·fare (fēld/fâr/), *n.* a large European thrush, *Turdus pilaris,* of reddish-brown color, with a blackish tail and ashy head. [ME *feldefare* (with two *f*'s by allit. assim.), late OE *feldeware* inhabitant of the fields]

field glass, a compact binocular telescope for use out-of-doors.

field goal, **1.** *Football.* a goal earned by a kick from the field. **2.** *Basketball.* a goal made while the ball is in play.

field gun, a cannon mounted on a carriage for service in the field.

field hockey, a hockey game which takes place on a field.

Field·ing (fēl/dĭng), *n.* **Henry,** 1707–54, British novelist.

field lark, either of two North American meadow larks, the eastern species, *Sturnella magna,* or the western, *S. neglecta.*

field magnet, a magnet for producing a magnetic field.

field marshal, an officer of the highest military rank in the British and certain other armies, and of the second highest rank in the French army.

field mouse, any of various short-tailed mice or moles inhabiting fields and meadows.

field music, *Mil.* **1.** trumpeters and drummers organized to play as a band. **2.** the music they play.

field officer, *Mil.* an officer above the rank of captain and below that of a brigadier general, as a colonel.

field of force, *Physics.* field (def. 11).

field of honor, the scene of a battle or duel.

field·piece (fēld/pēs/), *n.* *Mil.* a field gun.

field ration, *U.S. Army.* ration issued only in actual articles, not in money, and authorized for troops in the field.

fields·man (fēldz/mən), *n., pl.* **-men.** *Brit.* a fielder in cricket.

field sparrow, a common North American finch, *Spizella pusilla,* found in brushy pasture lands.

field trial, a trial of animals, as hunting dogs, in actual performance in the field.

field trip, an investigation away from the classroom.

field winding, *Elect.* the electrically conducting circuit, usually a number of coils wound on individual poles and connected in series, which produces excitation in a motor or generator.

field·work (fēld'wûrk'), *n. Fort.* a temporary fortification constructed in the field.

field work, work done in the field, as by a geologist.

fiend (fēnd), *n.* **1.** Satan; the devil. **2.** any evil spirit. **3.** a diabolically cruel or wicked person. **4.** *Colloq.* a person or thing that causes mischief or annoyance. **5.** *Colloq.* one who is hopelessly addicted to some pernicious habit: *an opium fiend.* **6.** *Colloq.* one who is excessively interested in some game, sport, etc.: *a bridge fiend.* [ME *feend,* OE *fēond,* c. G *feind,* all orig. ppr. of a verb meaning hate; cf. OE *fēo(ga)n*] **—fiend'like',** *adj.*

fiend·ish (fēn'dĭsh), *adj.* diabolically cruel and wicked. **—fiend'ish·ly,** *adv.* **—fiend'ish·ness,** *n.*

fierce (fîrs), *adj.,* **fiercer, fiercest. 1.** wild or vehement in temper, appearance, or action: *fierce animals, fierce looks.* **2.** violent in force, intensity, etc.: *fierce winds.* **3.** furiously eager or intense: *fierce competition.* **4.** *Slang.* extremely bad, unpleasant, etc. [ME *fers, fiers,* t. OF., g. L *ferus* wild, fierce, cruel] **—fierce'ly,** *adv.* **—fierce'ness,** *n.*

—Syn. 1. savage, cruel, fell, brutal; bloodthirsty, murderous. FIERCE, FEROCIOUS, TRUCULENT suggest vehemence and violence of manner and conduct. FIERCE suggests violence of temper, manner, or action: *fierce in repelling a foe.* FEROCIOUS implies fierceness or cruelty, esp. of a bloodthirsty kind, in disposition or action: *a ferocious glare, ferocious brutality toward helpless refugees.* TRUCULENT suggests an intimidating or bullying fierceness of manner or conduct: *his truculent attitude kept them terrified and submissive.* **—Ant. 1.** tame, mild.

fi·e·ri fa·ci·as (fī'ə rī' fā'shĭ ăs'), *Latin.* a writ commanding the sheriff to levy upon the goods, or the goods and lands, of a judgment debtor for the collection of the amount due. [L: lit., cause it to be done]

fier·y (fîr'ĭ, fī'ərĭ), *adj.,* **fierier, fieriest. 1.** consisting of, attended with, characterized by, or containing fire: *a fiery discharge.* **2.** intensely hot, as winds, desert sands, etc. **3.** like or suggestive of fire: *a fiery heat, a fiery red.* **4.** flashing or glowing, as the eye. **5.** intensely ardent, impetuous, or passionate: *fiery courage, zeal, speech, etc.* **6.** easily angered; irritable. **7.** inflammable, as gas in a mine. **8.** containing inflammable gas, as a mine. **9.** inflamed, as a tumor or sore. **10.** causing a burning sensation, as liquors or condiments. **—fier'i·ly,** *adv.* **—fier'i·ness,** *n.* **—Syn. 3.** flaming, glowing, burning. **5.** fervent, vehement, spirited, impassioned.

fiery cross, a burning cross, the emblem of several organizations, notably the Ku Klux Klan.

Fie·so·le (fyĕ'zō lĕ), *n.* **1.** a noted hill town in central Italy, near Florence. 5200 (1951). **2. Giovanni da** (jō vän'nē dä), **(Fra Angelico)** 1387-1455, Italian painter.

fi·es·ta (fĭ ĕs'tə; *Sp.* fyĕs'tä), *n.* Spanish. **1.** a religious celebration; a saint's day. **2.** a holiday or festival.

fife (fīf), *n., v.,* **fifed, fifing. —n. 1.** a high-pitched flute much used in military music. **—v.i., v.t. 2.** to play on a fife. [t. HG: m. *pfeife* PIPE] **—fif'er,** *n.*

Fife (fīf), *n.* a county in E Scotland. 316,700 pop. (est. 1956); 505 sq. mi. *Co. Seat:* Cupar. Also, **Fife·shire** (fīf'shĭr, -shər).

Man playing
a fife

fife rail, *Naut.* a rail round the lower part of a mast, for securing belaying pins.

fif·teen (fĭf'tēn'), *n.* **1.** a cardinal number, ten plus five. **2.** a symbol for this number, as 15 or XV. **—adj. 3.** amounting to fifteen in number. [ME and OE *fiftene,* f. *fif* FIVE + *-tēne* -TEEN]

fif·teenth (fĭf'tēnth'), *adj.* **1.** next after the fourteenth. **2.** being one of fifteen equal parts. **—n. 3.** a fifteenth part, esp. of one (1/15). **4.** the fifteenth member of a series.

fifth (fĭfth), *adj.* **1.** next after the fourth. **2.** being one of five equal parts. **—n. 3.** a fifth part, esp. of one (1/5). **4.** the fifth member of a series. **5.** a fifth part of a gallon of liquor or spirits; 4/5 of a quart. **6.** *Music.* **a.** a tone on the fifth degree from another tone (counted as the first). **b.** the interval between such tones. **c.** the harmonic combination of such tones. [earlier *fift,* ME *fifte,* OE *fifta;* mod. *-th* from *fourth,* etc.] **—fifth'ly,** *adv.*

Fifth Amendment, the section of the Constitution of the U.S. concerning certain criminal proceedings, double jeopardy, etc. It is sometimes invoked by witnesses at legislative hearings to avoid giving self-incriminating testimony.

fifth column, 1. a body of persons residing in a country who are in sympathy with its enemies, and who are serving enemy interests or are ready to assist an enemy attack. **2.** (originally) Franco sympathizers in Madrid during the civil war (in allusion to a statement in 1936 that the insurgents had four columns marching on Madrid and a fifth column of sympathizers in the city ready to rise and betray it). **—fifth columnist,** *n.*

fifth wheel, 1. a horizontal ring (or segment of a ring) consisting of two bands which slide on each other, placed above the front axle of a carriage and designed to support the forepart of the body while allowing it to turn freely in a horizontal plane. **2.** an extra wheel for a four-wheeled vehicle. **3.** any extra or superfluous thing or person.

fif·ty (fĭf'tĭ), *n., pl.* **-ties,** *adj.* **—n. 1.** a cardinal number, ten times five. **2.** a symbol for this number, as 50 or L. **—adj. 3.** amounting to fifty in number. [ME; OE *fiftig,* f. *fif* FIVE + *-tig* -TY[1]] **—fif'ti·eth,** *adj., n.*

fif·ty-fif·ty (fĭf'tĭ fĭf'tĭ), *adv., adj. Colloq.* with equality of shares, as of profits.

fig¹ (fĭg), *n.* **1.** any tree or shrub of the moraceous genus *Ficus,* esp. a small tree, *F. Carica,* native in southwestern Asia, bearing a turbinate or pear-shaped fruit which is eaten fresh or preserved or dried. **2.** the fruit of such a tree or shrub, or of any related species. **3.** any of various plants having a fruit somewhat resembling the fig. **4.** the value of a fig; the merest trifle; the least bit. **5.** a gesture of contempt; a fico. [ME *fige,* t. OF., t. OPr.: m. *figa,* ult. der. L *ficus*]

fig² (fĭg), *v.,* **figged, figging,** *n. Colloq.* **—v.t. 1.** to dress or array (fol. by *out*). **2.** to furbish (fol. by *up*). **—n. 3.** dress or array. **4.** condition. [orig. uncert.]

fig., **1.** figurative. **2.** figuratively. **3.** figure; figures.

fig-eat·er (fĭg'ē'tər), *n. Southern U.S.* a scarabaeid beetle, *Cotinis nitida.*

fight (fīt), *n., v.,* **fought, fighting. —n. 1.** a battle or combat. **2.** any contest or struggle. **3.** ability or inclination to fight: *there was no fight left in him, to show fight.* **4.** *Naval.* (formerly) a bulkhead or other screen for the protection of the men during a battle. **—v.i. 5.** to engage in battle or in single combat; attempt to defeat, subdue, or destroy an adversary. **6.** to contend in any manner; strive vigorously for or against something. **—v.t. 7.** to contend with in battle or combat; war against. **8.** to contend with or against in any manner. **9.** to carry on (a battle, duel, etc.). **10.** to maintain (a cause, quarrel, etc.) by fighting or contending. **11.** to make (one's way) by fighting or striving. **12.** to cause or set (a boxer, dog, etc.) to fight. **13.** to manage or maneuver (troops, ships, guns, planes, etc.) in battle. **14. fight it out,** to struggle till a decisive result is obtained. **15. fight shy of,** to keep carefully aloof from (a person, affair, etc.). [ME; OE *fe(o)htan,* c. G *fechten*] **—fight'a·ble,** *adj.*

—Syn. 1, 2. encounter, engagement, affray, fray; melee, scuffle, tussle. FIGHT, COMBAT, CONFLICT, CONTEST denote a struggle of some kind. FIGHT connotes a hand-to-hand struggle for supremacy, literally or in a figurative sense. COMBAT suggests an armed encounter, to settle a dispute. CONFLICT implies a bodily, mental, or moral struggle caused by opposing views, beliefs, etc. CONTEST applies to either a friendly or a hostile struggle for a definite prize or aim.

fight·er (fī'tər), *n.* **1.** one who fights. **2.** *Mil.* an aircraft designed to seek out and destroy enemy aircraft in the air, and to protect bomber aircraft.

fight·er-bomb·er (fī'tər bŏm'ər), *n. Mil.* an aircraft that combines the functions of a fighter and a bomber.

fighting chance, a possibility of success following a struggle.

fighting cock, 1. a gamecock. **2.** *Colloq.* a pugnacious person.

fighting fish, a small brilliantly colored aquarium fish, a species of *Betta,* noted for the fighting habits of the males.

fighting top, (in a warship) a platform on or near the top of a mast, from which rapid-fire guns, etc., are fired. It is also used for observation, lookouts, fire control, etc.

fig leaf, 1. the leaf of a fig tree, esp. in allusion to the first covering of Adam and Eve. Gen. 3:7. **2.** something designed to conceal what is shameful or indecorous.

fig marigold, any of various herbs of the genus *Mesembryanthemum,* with showy white, yellow, or pink flowers.

fig·ment (fĭg'mənt), *n.* **1.** a mere product of the imagination; a pure invention. **2.** a feigned, invented, or imagined story, theory, etc. [t. L: s. *figmentum* image, fiction, anything made] **—Syn. 2.** See fiction.

fig·u·line (fĭg'yōō lĭn), *n.* a piece of pottery. [t. L: m.s. *figulina,* fem. of *figulinus* of a potter]

fig·u·rant (fĭg'yōō rănt'; *Fr.* fēgÿrän'), *n.* a ballet dancer who dances only with others in groups or figures. [t. F, ppr. of *figurer,* t. L: m.s. *figurāre* form] **—fig·u·rante** (fĭg'yōō rănt'; *Fr.* fēgÿ·ränt'), *n. fem.*

fig·u·rate (fĭg'yər ĭt), *adj.* **1.** of a certain determinate figure or shape. **2.** *Music.* characterized by the use of passing notes or other embellishments; florid. [t. L: m.s. *figurātus,* pp., figured]

fig·u·ra·tion (fĭg'yə rā'shən), *n.* **1.** act of shaping into a particular figure. **2.** the resulting figure or shape. **3.** act of representing figuratively. **4.** a figurative representation. **5.** act of marking or adorning with designs. **6.** *Music.* **a.** the employment of passing notes or other embellishments. **b.** the figuring of a bass part.

fig·u·ra·tive (fĭg'yər ə tĭv), *adj.* **1.** of the nature of or involving a figure of speech, esp. a metaphor; metaphorical; not literal: *a figurative expression.* **2.** metaphorically so called: *this remark was a figurative boomerang.* **3.** abounding in or addicted to figures of speech. **4.** representing by means of a figure or likeness, as in drawing or sculpture. **5.** representing by a figure or emblem; emblematic. **—fig'ur·a·tive·ly,** *adv.* **—fig'ur·a·tive·ness,** *n.*

---

b., blend of, blended; c., cognate with; d., dialect, dialectal; der., derived from; f., formed from; g., going back to; m., modification of; r., replacing; s., stem of; t., taken from; ?, perhaps. See the full key on inside cover.

figure 451 **filibuster**

fig·ure (fĭg′yər; *Brit.* fĭg′ər), *n., v.,* **-ured, -uring.** —*n.* **1.** a written symbol other than a letter. **2.** a numerical symbol, esp. an Arabic numeral. **3.** an amount or value expressed in numbers. **4.** (*pl.*) the use of numbers in figuring: *poor at figures.* **5.** form or shape, as determined by outlines or exterior surfaces: *round, square, or cubical in figure.* **6.** the bodily form or frame: *a slender or graceful figure.* **7.** an individual bodily form, or a person with reference to form or appearance: *a tall figure stood in the doorway.* **8.** a person as he appears or as presented before the eyes of the world: *political figures.* **9.** a character or personage, esp. one of distinction: *a figure in society.* **10.** the appearance or impression made by a person, or sometimes a thing. **11.** a representation, pictorial or sculptured, of something, specif. of the human form. **12.** an emblem or type: *the dove is a figure of peace.* **13.** *Rhet.* a figure of speech. **14.** a device or pattern, as in cloth. **15.** a movement, pattern, or series of movements in skating. **16.** a distinct movement or division of a dance. **17.** *Music.* a short succession of musical notes, either as melody or as a group of chords, which produces a single, complete, and distinct impression. **18.** *Geom.* a combination of geometrical elements disposed in a particular form or shape: *the circle, square, and polygon are plane figures; the sphere, cube, and polyhedron are solid figures.* **19.** *Logic.* any of the forms of the syllogism with respect to the relative position of the middle term. **20.** *Optics.* the precise curve required on the surface of an optical element, esp. the mirror of a reflecting telescope. **21.** *Obs.* a phantasm or illusion. —*v.t.* **22.** to compute or calculate. **23.** to express in figures. **24.** to mark or adorn with figures, or with a pattern or design. **25.** to portray by speech or action. **26.** to represent or express by a figure of speech. **27.** to represent by a pictorial or sculptured figure, a diagram, or the like; picture or depict; trace (an outline, etc.). **28.** *Colloq.* to conclude or judge: *I figured she was jealous.* **29.** *Music.* **a.** to embellish with passing notes or other decorations. **b.** to write figures above or below (a bass part) to indicate accompanying chords. **30. figure out,** *Chiefly U.S. Colloq.* **a.** to make a calculation of. **b.** to solve; understand; make out. —*v.i.* **31.** to compute or work with numerical figures. **32.** to make a figure or appearance; be conspicuous: *his name figures in the report.* **33. figure on,** *Colloq.* **a.** to count or rely on. **b.** to take into consideration. [ME, t. F, t. L: m.s. *figūra* form, shape] —**fig′ure·less,** *adj.* —**fig′ur·er,** *n.* —**Syn. 5.** See **form.**

fig·ured (fĭg′yərd), *adj.* **1.** formed or shaped. **2.** represented by a pictorial or sculptured figure. **3.** ornamented with a device or pattern: *figured silk, figured wallpaper.* **4.** *Music.* **a.** florid. **b.** having the accompanying chords indicated by figures. **5.** figurative, as language.

fig·ure·head (fĭg′yər hĕd′), *n.* **1.** a person who is nominally the head of a society, community, etc., but has no real authority or responsibility. **2.** *Naut.* an ornamental figure, as a statue or bust, placed over the cutwater of a ship.

figure of eight, a kind of knot. See illus. under **knot.**

figure of speech, *Rhet.* a literary mode of expression, as a metaphor, simile, personification, antithesis, etc., in which words are used out of their literal sense, or out of ordinary locutions, to suggest a picture or image, or for other special effect; a trope.

fig·u·rine (fĭg′yə rēn′), *n.* a small ornamental figure of pottery, metalwork, etc.; statuette. [t. F, t. It.: m. *figurina,* dim. of *figura* FIGURE]

fig·wort (fĭg′wûrt′), *n.* **1.** any of numerous, usually coarse, herbs of the genus *Scrophularia.* **2.** any scrophulariaceous plant.

Fi·ji (fē′jē), *n.* **1.** a British colony in the S Pacific, N of New Zealand, comprising the Fiji Islands and a dependent group to the NW. 333,389 pop. (est. 1954); 7040 sq. mi. *Cap.:* Suva. See the map just below. **2.** a native of the Fiji Islands. —**Fi·ji·an** (fē′jĭ′ən, fĭ jē′in), *adj., n.*

fikh (fĭk), *n.* Mohammedan jurisprudence; the legal foundations of religious, political, and civil life.

fil·a·gree (fĭl′ə grē′), *n., adj., v.t.* filigree.

fil·a·ment (fĭl′ə mənt), *n.* **1.** a very fine thread or threadlike structure; a fiber or fibril. **2.** a single element of textile fiber (as silk), or mechanically produced fiber (as rayon or nylon). **3.** *Bot.* **a.** the stalklike portion of a stamen, supporting the anther. **b.** a long slender cell or series of attached cells, as in some algae, fungi, etc. **4.** *Ornith.* the barb of a down feather. **5.** *Elect.* (in an incandescent lamp) the threadlike conductor in the bulb which is raised to incandescence by the passage of current. **6.** *Electronics.* the heating element (sometimes also acting as a cathode) of a vacuum tube. It resembles an incandescent electric-lamp filament. **7.** *Pathol.* a threadlike substance sometimes contained in urine, or in fluids of inflammation. [t. LL: s. *filāmentum,* der. L *filum* thread]

fil·a·men·ta·ry (fĭl′ə mĕn′tər ĭ), *adj.* pertaining to or of the nature of a filament or filaments.

fil·a·men·tous (fĭl′ə mĕn′təs), *adj.* **1.** composed of or containing filaments. **2.** resembling a filament. **3.** bearing filaments. **4.** pertaining to filaments.

fi·lar (fī′lər), *adj.* **1.** of or pertaining to a thread or threads. **2.** having threads or the like. [f. s. L *filum* thread + -AR¹]

fi·lar·i·a (fĭ lâr′ĭ ə), *n., pl.* **-lariae** (-lâr′ĭ ē′). any of the slender, threadlike nematode worms (family *Filariidae*), parasitic as adults in the blood or tissues of vertebrates, and developing as larvae in insects, etc., which become infected by sucking the embryos from the blood. [NL, der. L *filum* thread]

fi·lar·i·al (fĭ lâr′ĭ əl), *adj.* **1.** belonging to the genus *Filaria* and allied genera of the family *Filariidae.* **2.** pertaining to infection by filariae: *filarial disease.*

fil·a·ri·a·sis (fĭl′ə rī′ə sĭs), *n.* *Pathol.* the presence of filarial worms in the blood and lymph channels, in the lymph glands, and other tissues. [t. NL. See FILARIA, -ASIS]

fil·a·ture (fĭl′ə chər), *n.* **1.** act of forming into threads. **2.** a reel for drawing off silk from cocoons. **3.** the reeling of silk from cocoons. **4.** an establishment for reeling silk. [t. F, der. LL *filāre* spin]

fil·bert (fĭl′bərt), *n.* **1.** the thick-shelled, edible nut of certain cultivated varieties of hazel, esp. of *Corylus avellana* of Europe. **2.** a tree or shrub bearing such nuts. [ME; short for *filbert nut,* nut of (St.) Philibert, so called because ripe about this saint's day, Aug. 22]

filch (fĭlch), *v.t., v.i.* to steal (esp. something of small value); pilfer. [orig. unknown] —**filch′er,** *n.*

file¹ (fīl), *n., v.,* **filed, filing.** —*n.* **1.** any device, as a cabinet, in which papers, etc., are arranged or classified for convenient reference. **2.** a collection of papers so arranged or classified; any orderly collection of papers, etc. **3.** a string or wire on which papers are strung for preservation and reference. **4. on file,** on or in a file, or in orderly arrangement for convenient reference, as papers. **5.** a line of persons or things arranged one behind another. **6.** *Mil.* **a.** a man in front of or behind another in a military formation. **b.** one step on a promotion list. **7.** one of the vertical lines of squares on a chessboard. **8.** a list or roll. —*v.t.* **9.** to arrange (papers, etc.) methodically for preservation and convenient reference. —*v.i.* **10.** to march in a file or line, one after another, as soldiers. **11.** to make application: *to file for a civil-service job.* [repr. F *fil* thread, string (g. L *filum*) and F *file* file, row, der. L *filum* thread] —**fil′er,** *n.*

file² (fīl), *n., v.,* **filed, filing.** —*n.* **1.** a metal (usually steel) tool of varying size and form, with numerous small cutting ridges or teeth on its surface, for smoothing or cutting metal and other substances. **2.** *Brit. Slang.* a cunning, shrewd, or artful person. —*v.t.* **3.** to reduce, smooth, cut, or remove with or as with a file. [ME; d. OE *fīl,* r. OE *fēol,* c. G *feile*] —**fil′er,** *n.*

file³ (fīl), *v.t.,* **filed, filing.** *Archaic or Dial.* defile. [ME; OE *fȳlan* befoul, defile, der. *fūl* foul]

file clerk, an employee who works primarily with office files.

file·fish (fīl′fĭsh′), *n., pl.* **-fishes,** (*esp. collectively*) **-fish.** **1.** any of various fishes with rough, granular skin, as *Alutera schoepfi* of the Atlantic coast of the U.S. and southward. **2.** triggerfish.

fi·let (fĭ lā′, fĭl′ā; *Fr.* fē lĕ′), *n., v.t.* fillet (defs. 6, 10).

fi·let de sole (fĭl′ā də sōl′; *Fr.* fē lĕ də sôl′), *French.* a fillet of any of certain flatfishes used for food.

filet lace, a square mesh net or lace, originally knotted by hand but now copied by machine.

fi·let mi·gnon (fĭl′ā′ mēn′yŏn; *Fr.* fē lĕ mē nyôn′), a round beef fillet to which pork or bacon is added before cooking. [t. F]

fil·i·al (fĭl′ĭ əl), *adj.* **1.** pertaining to or befitting a son or daughter: *filial obedience.* **2.** bearing the relation of a child to a parent. **3.** *Genetics.* indicating the sequence of generations from an original parent. First filial is shown as F₁, second filial as F₂, etc. [t. LL: s. *filiālis,* f. s. L *filius* son, *filia* daughter + -AL¹] —**fil′i·al·ly,** *adv.*

fil·i·ate (fĭl′ĭ āt′), *v.t.,* **-ated, -ating.** **1.** to affiliate. **2.** *Law.* to determine judicially the paternity of, as a bastard child. [t. LL: m.s. *filiātus,* pp. of *filiāre* have a child, der. L *filius* son, *filia* daughter. Cf. AFFILIATE]

fil·i·a·tion (fĭl′ĭ ā′shən), *n.* **1.** the fact of being the child of a certain parent. **2.** descent as if from a parent; derivation. **3.** *Law.* the judicial determination of the paternity of a child, especially of a bastard. **4.** the relation of one thing to another from which it is derived. **5.** act of filiating. **6.** state of being filiated. **7.** an affiliated branch, as of a society. [t. LL: s. *filiātio,* der. *filiāre* have a child]

fil·i·beg (fĭl′ə bĕg′), *n.* the kilt or plaited skirt worn by Scottish Highlanders. Also, **philibeg.** [t. Gaelic: m. *feileadh-beag* small kilt (as distinguished from the large one formerly worn)]

fil·i·bus·ter (fĭl′ə bŭs′tər), *n.* **1.** *U.S.* **a.** a member of a minority in a legislative assembly who resorts to irregular or obstructive tactics to prevent the adoption of a measure generally favored or to force a decision almost unanimously disliked. **b.** a course of legislative filibustering. **2.** an irregular military adventurer; a freebooter or buccaneer. **3.** one who engages in an unlawful military expedition into a foreign country to inaugurate or to aid a revolution. —*v.i.* **4.** *U.S.* to impede legislation by irregular or obstructive tactics. esp. by making long speeches. **5.** to act as a freebooter, buccaneer, or irregular military adventurer. [t. Sp.: m. *filibustero,* t. D: m. *vrijbuiter* freebooter] —**fil·i·bus/ter·er,** *n.*

fil·i·cide¹ (fĭl/ə sīd/), *n.* one who kills his son or daughter. [f. s. L *filius* son, *filia* daughter + -CIDE¹] —fil/i·cid/al, *adj.*

fil·i·cide² (fĭl/ə sīd/), *n.* act of killing one's son or daughter. [f. s. L *filius* son, *filia* daughter + -CIDE²] —fil/i·cid/al, *adj.*

fil·i·form (fĭl/ə fôrm/, fī/lə-), *adj.* threadlike; filamentous. [f. s. L *filum* thread + -(I)FORM]

fil·i·gree (fĭl/ə grē/), *n., adj., v.,* -greed, -greeing. —*n.* **1.** ornamental work of fine wires, esp. lacy jewelers' work of scrolls and arabesques. **2.** anything very delicate or fanciful. —*adj.* **3.** composed of or resembling filigree. —*v.t.* **4.** to adorn with or form into filigree. Also, **filagree, fillagree.** [var. of *filigrane,* t. F, t. It.: m. *filigrana.* See FILE¹, GRAIN] —fil/i·greed/, *adj.*

fil·i·greed (fĭl/ə grēd/), *adj.*having filigree decorations.

fil·ings (fī/lĭngz), *n.pl.* particles removed by a file.

Fil·i·pine (fĭl/ə pēn/), *adj.* Philippine.

Fil·i·pi·no (fĭl/ə pē/nō; *Sp.* fē/lē pē/nō), *n., pl.* -nos (-nōz; *Sp.* -nōs), *adj.* —*n.* **1.** a native of the Philippine Islands, esp. a member of a Christianized native tribe. —*adj.* **2.** Philippine. [t. Sp., der. *Felipe* Philip]

fill (fĭl), *v.t.* **1.** to make full; put as much as can be held into. **2.** to occupy to the full capacity: *water filled the basin, the crowd filled the hall.* **3.** to supply to fullness or plentifully: *to fill a house with furniture, to fill the hear with joy.* **4.** to satisfy, as food does. **5.** to put, as contents, into a receptacle. **6.** to be plentiful throughout: *fish filled the rivers.* **7.** to extend throughout; pervade completely: *the odor filled the room.* **8.** to furnish (a vacancy or office) with an occupant or incumbent. **9.** to execute (a business order). **10.** to supply (a blank space) with written matter, decorative work, etc. **11.** to meet (requirements, etc.) satisfactorily: *the book fills a longfelt want.* **12.** to make up or compound (a medical prescription). **13.** to stop up or close: *to fill a tooth or a crevice.* **14.** to occupy and perform the duties of (a vacancy, position, post, etc.). **15.** *Naut.* **a.** to distend (a sail) by pressure of the wind so as to impart headway to a vessel. **b.** to brace (a yard) so that the sail will catch the wind on its after side. **16.** to adulterate: *filled soaps.* **17.** *Civil Eng.* to build up with fill (def. 24): *to fill low ground with gravel, sand, or earth.* —*v.i.* **18.** to become full: *the hall filled rapidly, her eyes filled with tears.* **19.** to become distended, as sails with the wind. **20.** to fill a cup or other receptacle; pour out drink, as into a cup. **21.** Some special verb phrases are:
fill away, *Naut.* **1.** to fall off the wind and proceed on a board. **2.** to brace the yards, so that sails which have been aback will stand full.
fill in, 1. to fill (a hole, hollow, blank, etc.) with something put in. **2.** *Chiefly Brit.* to complete (a document, design, etc.) by filling blank spaces. **3.** to put in or insert so as to fill: *to fill in omitted names.*
fill out, 1. to complete (a document, list, etc.) by filling blanks, or fill (blanks) in a document, etc. **2.** to distend (sails, etc.). **3.** to round out (the cheeks, figure, etc.). **4.** to become rounded, as the cheeks, figure, etc.
fill the bill, *Colloq.* to satisfy the requirements of the case: be or do what is wanted.
fill up, to fill completely.
—*n.* **22.** a full supply; enough to satisfy want or desire: *to eat one's fill.* **23.** an amount of something sufficient for filling; a charge. **24.** a mass of earth, stones, etc., used to fill a hollow, etc. [ME *fille(n),* OE *fyllan,* c. G *füllen;* der. FULL¹]

fill·a·gree (fĭl/ə grē/), *n., adj., v.t.* filigree.

filled gold, a gold plate mechanically welded to a backing of brass or other base metal and rolled, in which the gold is ¹/₂₀ or more of the total weight.

filled milk, milk containing a substitute for the butter fat.

fill·er¹ (fĭl/ər), *n.* **1.** one who or that which fills. **2.** a thing or quantity of a material put in to fill something, or to fill out a gap. **3.** a liquid, paste, or the like used to coat a surface or to give solidity, bulk, etc., to a substance. **4.** the tobacco forming the body of a cigar, as distinguished from the wrapper. **5.** *Journalism.* something used to fill a vacant space. **6.** *Bldg. Trades, etc.* a sheet or plate inserted in a gap between two structural members. **7.** an implement used in filling, as a funnel. [f. FILL + -ER¹]

fil·lér² (fĕl/lâr), *n., pl.* -ler. a Hungarian minor bronze coin formerly equal to ¹/₁₀₀ of a pengő, and now equal to ¹/₁₀₀ of a forint. [t. Hung.]

fil·let (fĭl/ĭt; *usually* fĭl/ā *for* 6, 10), *n.* **1.** a narrow band of ribbon or the like bound round the head or hair. **2.** any narrow strip, as wood or metal. **3.** a strip of any material used for binding. **4.** *Bookbinding.* **a.** a decorative line impressed on a book's cover, usually at the top and bottom of the back. **b.** a rolling tool for impressing such lines. **5.** *Archit., etc.* **a.** a relatively narrow molding with a plane face, as between other moldings. **b.** the flat top of the ridge between two flutes of a column. **6.** *Cookery.* **a.** a strip or long (flat or thick) piece of meat or fish, esp. such as is easily detached from the bones or adjoining parts. **b.** a thick slice of meat, etc. **c.** a piece of

veal or other meat boned, rolled, and tied, for roasting. **7.** *Anat.* a band of fibers, esp. of white nerve fibers in the brain. **8.** a raised rim or ridge, as a ring on the muzzle of a gun. —*v.t.* **9.** to bind or adorn with or as with a fillet. **10.** *Cookery.* **a.** to cut or prepare (meat or fish) as a fillet. **b.** to cut fillets from. Also, filet for 6, 10. [ME *filet,* t. F, dim. of *fil* thread, string, g. L *filum*]

fill·ing (fĭl/ĭng), *n.* **1.** that which is put in to fill something: *the filling of a pie.* **2.** a substance in plastic form, as cement, amalgam, or gold foil, used to close a cavity in a tooth. **3.** act of one who or that which fills; a making or becoming full.

filling station, a place where gasoline and oil are retailed for automobiles.

fil·lip (fĭl/əp), *v.t.* **1.** to strike with the nail of a finger snapped from the end of the thumb. **2.** to tap or strike smartly. **3.** to drive by or as by a fillip. —*v.i.* **4.** to make a fillip with the fingers. —*n.* **5.** act or movement of filliping; a smart tap or stroke. **6.** anything that tends to rouse, excite, or revive; a stimulus. [appar. imit. Cf. FLIP]

fil·li·peen (fĭl/ə pēn/), *n. Games.* philopena.

fil·lis·ter (fĭl/ĭs tər), *n. Carp.* a rabbet or groove, as one on a window sash to hold the glass and putty.

fillister plane, *Carp.* a plane for cutting rabbets or grooves.

Fill·more (fĭl/môr), *n.* **Millard** (mĭl/ərd), 1800–74, 13th president of the United States, 1850–53.

fil·ly (fĭl/ĭ), *n., pl.* -lies. **1.** a female colt or foal; a young mare. **2.** *Colloq.* a lively young girl. [t. Scand.; cf. Icel. *fylja* female foal. See FOAL]

film (fĭlm), *n.* **1.** a thin layer or coating. **2.** a thin sheet of any material. **3.** *Photog.* **a.** the sensitive coating, as of gelatin and silver bromide, on a photographic plate. **b.** a strip or roll of cellulose nitrate or cellulose acetate composition coated with a sensitive emulsion, used instead of a photographic plate. **4.** *Motion Pictures.* **a.** the film strip containing the photographs exhibited in a motion-picture machine. **b.** a motion picture. **c.** (*pl.*) motion pictures collectively. **d.** (*pl.*) the motion-picture industry, or its productions, operations, etc. **5.** a thin skin or membrane. **6.** a delicate web of filaments or fine threads. —*v.t.* **7.** to cover with a film, or thin skin or pellicle. **8.** *Motion Pictures.* **a.** to photograph with a motion-picture camera. **b.** to reproduce in the form of motion pictures: *to film a novel.* —*v.i.* **9.** to become covered by a film. **10.** *Motion Pictures.* **a.** to be reproduced in a motion picture, esp. in a specified manner: *this story films easily.* **b.** to direct, make, or otherwise engage in the production of motion pictures. [ME *fylme,* OE *filmen;* akin to FELL⁴]

film library, *Library Sci.* an organized collection of films for private or public use, including reproductions of printed materials on film, slides, motion-picture reels, etc.

film pack, *Photog.* camera film so arranged in a stack that individual sheets can be brought successively in place.

film·y (fĭl/mĭ), *adj.,* **filmier, filmiest.** of the nature of, resembling, or covered with a film. —**film/i·ly,** *adv.* —**film/i·ness,** *n.*

fil·o·plume (fĭl/ə plōōm/, fī/lə-), *n. Ornith.* a degenerate feather with a shaft but few or no barbs.

fi·lose (fī/lōs), *adj.* **1.** threadlike. **2.** ending in a threadlike process. [f. s. L *filum* thread + -OSE¹]

fils (fēs), *n.* French. son: sometimes used after a name in meaning of *Jr.,* as in *Dumas fils.* Cf. *père.*

fil·ter (fĭl/tər), *n.* **1.** any device in which cloth, paper, porous porcelain, or a layer of charcoal or sand, is held and through which liquid is passed to remove suspended impurities or to recover solids. **2.** any of various analogous devices, as for removing dust from air or eliminating certain kinds of light rays. **3.** *Photog.* a screen of dyed gelatin or glass used to control the rendering of color or to diminish the intensity of light. **4.** *Physics.* a device for selecting waves or currents of certain frequencies only out of an aggregation including others. —*v.t.* **5.** to remove by the action of a filter. **6.** to act as a filter for. **7.** to pass through, or as through, a filter. —*v.i.* **8.** to percolate; pass through or as through a filter. [ME *filtre,* t. OF, t. ML: m.s. *feltrum* felt (used as a filter), ult. t. Gmc.; cf. FELT²] —**fil/ter·er,** *n.*

fil·ter·a·ble (fĭl/tər ə bəl), *adj.* **1.** capable of being filtered. **2.** *Bacteriol.* capable of passing through bacteria-retaining filters: *a filterable virus.* Also, **fil·tra·ble** (fĭl/trə bəl).

filter bed, a pond or tank having a false bottom covered with sand, and serving to filter river or pond waters.

filth (fĭlth), *n.* **1.** foul matter; offensive or disgusting dirt. **2.** foul condition. **3.** moral impurity, corruption, or obscenity. **4.** foul language. [ME; OE *fȳlth,* der. *fūl* foul]

filth·y (fĭl/thĭ), *adj.,* **filthier, filthiest. 1.** foul with, characterized by, or having the nature of filth; disgustingly dirty. **2.** vile; obscene. **3.** (as a general epithet of strong condemnation) highly offensive or objectionable. —**filth/i·ly,** *adv.* —**filth/i·ness,** *n.* —Syn. 1. See dirty.

fil·trate (fĭl/trāt), *v.,* -trated, -trating. —*v.t., v.i.* **1.** to filter. —*n.* **2.** liquid which has been passed through a filter. —**fil·tra/tion,** *n.*

fil·um (fī/ləm), *n., pl.* -la (-lə). *Latin.* a threadlike structure or part; a filament.

fim·ble (fĭm′bəl), *n.* the male or staminate plant of hemp, which is harvested before the female or pistillate plant. [t. LG: m. *fimel,* t. F: m. (*chanvre*) *femelle,* lit., female hemp]

fim·bri·a (fĭm′brĭ ə), *n., pl.* **-briae** (-brĭ ē′). (*often pl.*) *Bot., Zool.* a fringe or fringed border. [t. L: thread, fringe] —**fim′bri·al,** *adj.*

fim·bri·ate (fĭm′brĭ ĭt, -āt′), *adj. Bot., Zool.* fringed; bordered with hairs or with filiform processes. Also, **fim′bri·at′ed.**

fim·bri·a·tion (fĭm′brĭ ā′shən), *n. Bot., Zool.* 1. fimbriate or fringed condition. 2. a fringe or fringelike part.

fim·bril·late (fĭm brĭl′ĭt, -āt), *adj. Bot., Zool.* bordered with, or having, a small or fine fringe. [f. s. NL *fimbrilla* (dim. of L *fimbria* FIMBRIA) + -ATE]

Fimbriate petals

fin (fĭn), *n., v.,* **finned, finning.** —*n.* 1. a membranous winglike or paddlelike organ attached to any of various parts of the body of fishes and certain other aquatic animals, used for propulsion, steering, or balancing. 2. *Naut.* **a.** a fin-shaped plane on a submarine or boat. **b.** a fin keel. 3. *Aeron.* any of certain small, subsidiary planes on an aircraft, in general placed parallel to the plane of symmetry. 4. an external rib for cooling, used on radiators, the cylinders of air-cooled internal-combustion engines, etc. 5. any part, as of a mechanism, resembling a fin. 6. *Slang.* the arm or hand. —*v.t.* 7. to cut off the fins from (a fish); carve or cut up, as a chub. —*v.i.* 8. to move the fins; lash the water with the fins, as a whale when dying. [ME *finne,* OE *finn,* c. D *vin,* LG *finne.* Cf. L *pinna*] —**fin′less,** *adj.* —**fin′like′,** *adj.*

Fin., 1. Finland. 2. Finnish.

fin., financial.

fi·na·gle (fĭ nā′gəl), *v.,* **-gled, -gling.** *Colloq.* —*v.i.* 1. to practice deception or fraud. —*v.t.* 2. to trick or cheat (a person); get (something) by guile or trickery. 3. to wangle: *to finagle free tickets.* [var. of *fainaigue;* orig. uncert.] —**fi·na′gler,** *n.*

fi·nal (fī′nəl), *adj.* 1. pertaining to or coming at the end; last in place, order, or time. 2. ultimate: *the final goal.* 3. conclusive or decisive. 4. *Law.* **a.** precluding further controversy on the questions passed upon: *the decision of the Supreme Court is final.* **b.** determining completely the rights of the parties, so that no further decision upon the merits of the issues is necessary: *a final judgment or decree.* 5. constituting the end or purpose: *a final cause.* 6. pertaining to or expressing end or purpose: *a final clause.* 7. *Phonet.* coming at the end of a word or syllable: *"t" is final in the word "fit."* —*n.* 8. that which is last; that which forms an end or termination. 9. (*often pl.*) something final, as a decisive examination or contest after preliminary ones. 10. *Colloq.* the last edition of a newspaper during the day. [ME, t. LL: s. *finālis,* der. L *finis* end] —**Syn.** 1. See **last¹.**

final causes, *Philos.* the doctrine that the course of events in the universe is explicable mainly by reference to ends or purposes by which all events are controlled.

fi·na·le (fĭ nä′lĭ; *It.* fē nä′lē), *n.* 1. *Music.* the last piece, division, or movement of a concert, opera, or composition. 2. the concluding part of any performance, course of proceedings, etc. [t. It., adj. used as n. See FINAL]

fi·nal·ism (fī′nə lĭz′əm), *n. Philos.* the doctrine that nothing exists or was made except for a determinate end; the doctrine of final causes; teleology.

fi·nal·ist (fī′nə lĭst), *n.* one who is entitled to take part in the final trial or round, as of an athletic contest.

fi·nal·i·ty (fĭ năl′ə tĭ), *n., pl.* **-ties.** 1. state, quality, or fact of being final; conclusiveness or decisiveness. 2. something that is final; a final act, utterance, etc.

fi·na·lize (fī′nə līz′), *v.t.,* **-lized, -lizing.** *Colloq.* to put into final form.

fi·nal·ly (fī′nəl ĭ), *adv.* 1. at the final point or moment; in the end. 2. in a final manner; conclusively or decisively.

fi·nance (fĭ năns′, fī′năns), *n., v.,* **-nanced, -nancing.** —*n.* 1. the management of public revenues; the conduct or transaction of money matters generally, esp. such as affect the public, as in the fields of banking and investment. 2. (*pl.*) pecuniary resources, as of a sovereign, state, corporation, or an individual; revenues. —*v.t.* 3. to supply with means of payment; provide capital for; to obtain or furnish credit for. 4. to manage financially. —*v.i.* 5. to conduct financial operations; manage finances. [ME, t. OF: ending, payment, revenue, der. OF *finer* finish, settle, pay, der. *fin* end, settlement. See FINE²]

finance bill, *Govt.* a bill or act of a legislature to obtain public funds.

fi·nan·cial (fĭ năn′shəl, fī-), *adj.* 1. pertaining to monetary receipts and expenditures; pertaining or relating to money matters; pecuniary: *financial operations.* 2. of or pertaining to those commonly engaged in dealing with money and credit. —**fi·nan′cial·ly,** *adv.*

—**Syn** 1. FINANCIAL, FISCAL, MONETARY, PECUNIARY refer to matters concerned with money. FINANCIAL usually refers to money matters or transactions of some size or importance: *a financial wizard.* FISCAL is used esp. in connection with government funds, or those of any organization: *the end of the fiscal year.* MONETARY relates especially to money as such: *a monetary system or standard.* PECUNIARY refers to money as used in making ordinary payments: *a pecuniary obligation or reward.*

fin·an·cier (fĭn′ən sîr′, fī′nən-; *Brit.* fĭ năn′sĭ ər), *n.* 1. one skilled or engaged in financial operations, whether public, corporate, or individual. —*v.t.* 2. to finance. —*v.i.* 3. *Rare.* to act as a financier. [t. F, der. *finance* FINANCE]

fin·back (fĭn′băk′), *n.* any whalebone whale of the genus *Balaenoptera* having a prominent dorsal fin, as *B. musculus* of the northern Atlantic, or *B. physalus,* which attains a length of 60 or even 80 feet; a rorqual. Also, **finback whale.**

finch (fĭnch), *n.* 1. any of numerous small passerine birds of the family *Fringillidae,* including the buntings, sparrows, crossbills, linnets, grosbeaks, etc., most of which have heavy, conical, seed-cracking bills. 2. any of various nonfringilline birds. [ME; OE *finc,* c. D *vink,* G *fink*]

Purple finch,
Carpodacus purpureus
(6 in. long)

find (fīnd), *v.,* **found, finding,** *n.* —*v.t.* 1. to come upon by chance; meet with. 2. to learn, attain, or obtain by search or effort. 3. to discover. 4. to recover (something lost). 5. to gain or regain the use of: *to find one's tongue.* 6. to succeed in attaining; gain by effort: *find safety in flight, to find occasion for revenge.* 7. to discover by experience or to perceive: *to find something to be true, find something new to be developing.* 8. to ascertain by study or calculation: *to find the sum of several numbers.* 9. *Law.* **a.** to determine after judicial inquiry: *find a person guilty.* **b.** to pronounce as an official act (an indictment, verdict, or judgment). 10. to provide or furnish. 11. **find fault,** to find cause of blame or complaint; express dissatisfaction. 12. **find oneself,** to discover the right place or conditions for oneself. 13. **find out, a.** to discover in the course of time or experience; discover by search or inquiry; ascertain by study. **b.** to detect, as in an offense; discover the actions or character of; discover or detect (a fraud, imposture, etc.). **c.** to discover the identity of (a person). —*v.i.* 14. to determine an issue after judicial inquiry: *the jury found for the plaintiff.* 15. *Brit. Hunting.* to come upon game. —*n.* 16. act of finding; a discovery. 17. something found; a discovery, esp. a valuable or gratifying discovery: *our cook was a find.* [ME *finde(n),* OE *findan,* c. G *finden*] —**find′a·ble,** *adj.*

find·er (fīn′dər), *n.* 1. one who or that which finds. 2. *Photog.* a camera attachment enabling a photographer to determine what will be included in the picture. 3. *Astron.* a small telescope attached to a larger for the purpose of finding an object more readily.

fin de siè·cle (făn də syĕ′kl), *French.* 1. end of the century. 2. a period freed from social and moral traditions. —*attributive.* 3. (toward the close of the 19th century) **a.** modern; up-to-date. **b.** decadent.

find·ing (fīn′dĭng), *n.* 1. act of one who or that which finds; discovery. 2. that which is found or ascertained. 3. *Law.* a decision or verdict after judicial inquiry. 4. (*pl.*) tools, materials, etc., used by artisans.

Find·lay (fĭn′lĭ, fĭnd′-), *n.* a city in NW Ohio. 30,-344 (1960).

fine¹ (fīn), *adj.,* **finer, finest,** *adv., v.,* **fined, fining** —*adj.* 1. of the highest or of very high grade or quality; free from imperfections or impurities. 2. choice, excellent, or admirable: *a fine sermon.* 3. consisting of minute particles: *fine sand.* 4. very thin or slender: *fine thread.* 5. keen or sharp, as a tool. 6. delicate in texture: *fine linen.* 7. delicately fashioned. 8. highly skilled or accomplished: *a fine musician.* 9. trained down to the proper degree, as an athlete. 10. characterized by or affecting refinement or elegance: *a fine lady.* 11. polished or refined: *fine manners.* 12. affectedly ornate or elegant: *fine writing.* 13. delicate or subtle: *a fine distinction.* 14. showy or smart; smartly dressed. 15. good-looking or handsome. 16. (of gold, silver, etc.) having a high proportion of pure metal, or having the proportion as specified. —*adv.* 17. *Colloq.* in a fine manner; excellently or very well; elegantly; delicately; with nicety. 18. *Billiards, Pool.* in such a way that the driven ball barely touches the object ball in passing. —*v.i.* 19. to become fine or finer. —*v.t.* 20. to make fine or finer. 21. to clarify (wines or spirits) by filtration. [ME *fin,* t. OF, g. Common Rom. *fino,* back formation from L *finire* FINISH]

—**Syn.** 1. superior; finished, consummate, perfect. FINE, CHOICE, ELEGANT, EXQUISITE are terms of praise with reference to quality. FINE is a general term: *a fine horse, person, book.* CHOICE implies a discriminating selection of the object in question: *a choice piece of steak.* ELEGANT suggests a refined and graceful superiority as is generally associated with luxury and a cultivated taste: *elegant furnishings.* EXQUISITE suggests an admirable delicacy, finish, or perfection: *an exquisite piece of lace.* 3. powdered, pulverized. —**Ant.** 1. inferior.

fine² (fīn), *n., v.,* **fined, fining.** —*n.* 1. a sum of money exacted as a penalty for an offense or dereliction; a mulct. 2. *Law.* **a.** a fee paid by a feudal tenant to the landlord, as on the renewal of tenure. **b.** a sum of money paid by a tenant on the commencement of his tenancy so that his rent may be small or nominal. 3. *Eng. Law.* a conveyance of land through decree of a court, based upon a simulated law suit. 4. **in fine,** finally; in short. 5. *Archaic.* a penalty of any kind. —*v.t.* 6. to subject to a fine, or pecuniary penalty; punish by a fine. [ME *fin*, t. OF, g. L *finis* boundary, end, ML settlement, fine]

fi·ne³ (fē′nĕ). *n. Music.* **1.** the end of a repeated section, whether *da capo* or *dal segno.* **2.** the end of a composition comprising several movements. [It.: end]

fine arts, those arts which seek expression through beautiful or significant modes; specif., architecture, sculpture, painting, and engraving.

fine-cut (fīn′kŭt′), *adj.* (of tobacco) cut fine, and used for chewing or smoking.

fine-draw (fīn′drô′), *v.t.,* **-drew, -drawn, -drawing. 1.** *Sewing.* to sew together or up so finely or nicely that the joining is not noticeable. **2.** to draw out to extreme fineness, tenuity, or subtlety.

fine-drawn (fīn′drôn′), *adj.* drawn out to extreme fineness or thinness: *a fine-drawn wire or distinction.*

fine·ly (fīn′lĭ), *adv.* in a fine manner; excellently; elegantly; delicately; minutely; nicely; subtly.

fine·ness (fīn′nĭs). *n.* **1.** state or quality of being fine. **2.** the proportion of pure metal (gold or silver) in an alloy, often expressed by the number of parts in 1,000.

fin·er·y¹ (fī′nə rĭ), *n., pl.* **-er·ies. 1.** fine or showy dress, ornaments, etc. **2.** *Rare.* smartness or elegance. [f. FINE¹, adj. + -ERY]

fin·er·y² (fī′nə rĭ), *n., pl.* **-er·ies.** *Metall.* a hearth on which cast iron is converted into wrought iron. [t. F: m. *finerie,* der. *finer* FINE¹, v.]

fines herbes (fēn zĕrb′), *Cookery.* a combination of finely chopped herbs for flavoring soups, sauces, etc. [F]

fine-spun (fīn′spŭn′), *adj.* **1.** spun or drawn out to a fine thread. **2.** highly or excessively refined or subtle.

fi·nesse (fĭ nĕs′), *n., v.,* **-nessed, -nessing.** —*n.* **1.** delicacy of execution; subtlety of discrimination. **2.** artful management; craft; strategy; an artifice or stratagem. **3.** *Cards.* an attempt to win a trick with a card while holding a higher card not in sequence with it, in the hope that the card or cards between will not be played. —*v.i.* **4.** to use finesse or artifice. **5.** to make a finesse at cards. —*v.t.* **6.** to bring by finesse or artifice. **7.** to make a finesse with (a card). [t. F, der. *fin* FINE¹, adj.]

fin-foot (fĭn′fŏŏt′), *n., pl.* **-foots.** any of certain pinnatiped or lobately webbed aquatic birds, family *Heliornithidae,* of South America, Asia, and Africa, related to the rails and coots.

fin-foot·ed (fĭn′fŏŏt′ĭd), *adj. Ornith.* **1.** web-footed. **2.** having feet whose toes are separately furnished with flaps, as the finfoots and coots.

Fin·gal's Cave (fĭng′gəlz), an unusual cavern on the island of Staffa, in the Hebrides, Scotland. 227 ft. long; 42 ft. wide.

fin·ger (fĭng′gər), *n.* **1.** any of the terminal members of the hand, esp. one other than the thumb. **2.** a part of a glove made to receive a finger. **3.** the breadth of a finger as a unit of length; digit. **4.** the length of a finger, 4½ in., or approximately that. **5.** something like or likened to a finger, or serving the purpose of a finger: *the finger of a clock.* **6.** any of various projecting parts of machines. **7.** Some special noun phrases are:
burn one's fingers, to get hurt or suffer loss from meddling with or engaging in anything.
have a finger in the pie, to have a share in the doing of something.
lay or put one's finger on, to indicate exactly.
—*v.t.* **8.** to touch with the fingers; handle; toy or meddle with. **9.** to pilfer; filch. **10.** *Music.* **a.** to play on (an instrument) with the fingers. **b.** to perform or mark (a passage of music) with a certain fingering (def. 2b). —*v.i.* **11.** to touch or handle something with the fingers. **12.** *Music.* **a.** to have its keys arranged for playing with the fingers, as a piano, clarinet, etc. **b.** to use the fingers in playing. [ME and OE; c. G *finger;* akin to FIVE, FIST] —**fin′ger·er,** *n.* —**fin′ger·less,** *adj.*

finger board, 1. (in a violin, guitar, etc.) the strip of wood on the neck against which the strings are stopped by the fingers. **2.** (in a piano, organ, etc.) the keyboard.

finger bowl, a small bowl to hold water for rinsing the fingers at table.

fin·ger·ing (fĭng′gər ĭng), *n.* **1.** act of one who fingers. **2.** *Music.* **a.** the action or method of using the fingers in playing on an instrument. **b.** the indication of the way the fingers are to be used in performing a piece of music.

Finger Lakes, a series of elongated glacial lakes in central and W New York: a resort region.

fin·ger·ling (fĭng′gər lĭng), *n.* **1.** a young or small fish, esp. a very small salmon or a small trout. **2.** something very small. [f. FINGER + -LING¹. Cf. G *fingerling* thimble.]

finger mark, a mark, esp. a smudge or stain, made by a finger.

fin·ger·nail (fĭng′gər nāl′), *n.* the nail at the end of a finger.

finger post, a guidepost with an arm terminating in the shape of an index finger.

fin·ger·print (fĭng′gər prĭnt′), *n.* **1.** an impression of the markings of the inner surface of the last joint of the thumb or a finger. **2.** such an impression made with ink for purposes of identification. —*v.t.* **3.** to take the fingerprints of.

finger wave, *Hairdressing.* a wave set by impressing the fingers into hair dampened with lotion.

fin·i·al (fĭn′ĭ əl, fī′nĭ-), *n. Archit.* **1.** the ornamental termination of a pinnacle, gable, etc., usually foliated. **2.** a vertical termination; a cast, carved, or turned ornament capping another form. [ME. f. s. L *finis* end + -IAL]

fin·i·cal (fĭn′ə kəl), *adj.* **1.** overfastidious; too particular or fussy. **2.** (of things) overelaborate; containing too much unimportant detail. [f. FINE¹ + -ICAL] —**fin′i·cal′i·ty, fin′i·cal·ness,** *n.* —**fin′i·cal·ly,** *adv.*

fin·ick·y (fĭn′ə kĭ), *adj.* finical. Also, **fin·i·kin** (fĭn′ə kĭn), **fin·ick·ing** (fĭn′ə kĭng). [unexplained var. of FINICAL]

fin·ing (fī′nĭng), *n.* **1.** the process by which fused glass becomes free from undissolved gases. **2.** the process of clarifying or filtering a wine or spirit to render it brilliant in appearance. [der. FINE¹, v.]

fi·nis (fī′nĭs), *n. Latin.* end; conclusion (often used at the end of a book).

fin·ish (fĭn′ĭsh), *v.t.* **1.** to bring (action, speech, work, affairs, etc.) to an end or to completion. **2.** to come to the end of (a course, period of time, etc.). **3.** to use up completely: *to finish a plate of food.* **4.** *Colloq.* to overcome completely; destroy or kill. **5.** to complete and perfect in detail; put the final touches on. **6.** to perfect (a person) in education, accomplishments, social graces, etc. —*v.i.* **7.** to come to an end. **8.** to complete a course, etc. **9.** *Obs.* to die. —*n.* **10.** the end or conclusion; the last stage. **11.** the end of a hunt, race, etc. **12.** a decisive ending: *a fight to a finish.* **13.** the quality of being finished or completed with smoothness, elegance, etc. **14.** educational or social polish. **15.** the manner in which a thing is finished in preparation, or an effect imparted in finishing: *a soft or dull finish.* **16.** something used or serving to finish, complete, or perfect a thing. **17.** woodwork, etc., esp. in the interior of a building, not essential to the structure but used for purposes of ornament, neatness, etc. **18.** a final coat of plaster or paint. **19.** a material for application in finishing. [ME *finisch-* (en). t. F: m. *finiss-,* s. *finir,* g. L *finīre* bound, end] —**fin′ish·er,** *n.* —**Syn. 10.** See end¹.

fin·ished (fĭn′ĭsht), *adj.* **1.** ended or completed. **2.** completed or perfected in all details, as a product. **3.** polished to the highest degree of excellence: *a finished poem.* **4.** highly accomplished, as a person. —**Syn. 4.** talented, skilled, gifted; trained.

finishing school, a school for completing the education of young women and preparing them for entrance into society.

Fin·is·terre (fĭn′ĭs târ′; Sp. fē′nĕs tĕr′rĕ), *n.* **Cape,** a headland in NW Spain: the westernmost point of Spain.

fi·nite (fī′nīt), *adj.* **1.** having bounds or limits; not too great or too small to be measurable. **2.** *Math.* **a.** (of a class or integral number) capable of being completely counted. **b.** not infinite or infinitesimal. **3.** subject to limitations or conditions, as of space, time, circumstances, or the laws of nature: *finite existence.* —*n.* **4.** the finite, **a.** that which is finite. **b.** finite things collectively. [t. L: m.s. *finītus,* pp., bounded] —**fi′nite·ly,** *adv.* —**fi′nite·ness,** *n.*

finite verb, a verb limited by person, number, tense, mood, and aspect (opposed to the infinite forms: participle, infinitive, and gerund, which have only a few limitations).

fin·i·tude (fĭn′ə tūd′, -tōōd′, fī′nə-), *n.* state of being finite.

fink (fĭngk), *n. U.S. Slang.* **1.** a strikebreaker. **2.** a labor spy.

fin keel, *Naut.* a finlike projection extending downward from the keel of a sailboat, serving to prevent lateral motion and acting as additional ballast.

Fin·land (fĭn′lənd), *n.* **1.** Finnish, **Suomi.** a republic in N Europe: formerly a province of the Russian Empire. 4,289,000 pop. (est. 1956); ab. 130,000 sq. mi. (1945). *Cap.:* Helsinki. **2. Gulf of,** an arm of the Baltic, S of Finland. —**Fin′land·er,** *n.*

fin·let (fĭn′lĭt), *n.* a small detached finlike appendage in certain fishes, as the mackerel.

Finn (fĭn), *n.* **1.** an inhabitant or native of Finland. **2.** any native speaker of Finnish, as in America or Russia. **3.** *Rare.* a speaker of any Finnic language.

fin·nan had·die (fĭn′ən hăd′ĭ), smoked haddock. Also, **finnan haddock.** [lit., haddock of Findhorn, fishing port in Scotland].

finned (fĭnd), *adj.* having a fin or fins.

Finn·ic (fĭn′ĭk), *adj.* **1.** designating Finnish and the languages most closely related to it, as Estonian, Lapp, and some minor languages of the northwestern Soviet Union. **2.** designating all Finno-Ugric languages except the Ugric, or all except Ugric and Permian.

Finn·ish (fĭn′ĭsh), *n.* **1.** the principal language of Finland, a Finno-Ugric language, closely related to Estonian. —*adj.* **2.** of or pertaining to Finland or its inhabitants. **3.** Finnic.

Fin·no-U·gri·an (fĭn′ō ōō′grĭ ən), *adj.* pertaining to the Finns and the Ugrians.

Fin·no-U·gric (fĭn′ō ōō′grĭk), *n.* an important linguistic family of eastern Europe and western Siberia, including Finnish, Estonian, and Lapp, farther east the Zyrian and Votyak, and also the Ugric languages, such as Hungarian and Vogul. It is related to Samoyed.

fin·ny (fĭn′ĭ), *adj.* **1.** pertaining to or abounding in fish. **2.** having fins; finned. **3.** finlike.

Fin·ster·aar·horn (fĭn′stər är′hôrn), *n.* a mountain in S central Switzerland: the highest peak of the Bernese Alps. 14,026 ft.

fiord (fyôrd; *Nor.* fyŏr, fyŏŏr), *n.* a long, relatively narrow arm of the sea, bordered by steep cliffs, as on the coast of Norway. Also, **fjord.** [t. Norw. See FIRTH]

fip·pen·ny bit (fĭp′ə nĭ, fĭp′nĭ), *U.S.* the Spanish half real, the value of which was about 6 cents. Also, **fippenny piece.** [var. of *fivepenny bit*]

fip·ple (fĭp′əl), *n. Music.* a plug, stopping the upper end of a pipe.

fipple flute, *Music.* a flute equipped with a fipple.

fir (fûr), *n.* 1. any of the pyramidal coniferous trees constituting the genus *Abies*, as *A. balsamea*, the balsam fir. 2. the wood of such a tree. [ME *firr*(e), OE *fyrh*. Cf. OE *furh*(wudu) pine, Icel. *fura* fir; akin to L *quercus* oak]

Fir·dau·si (fĭr dou′sē), *n.* (*Abul Kasim Mansur*), A.D. c940–1020, Persian poet who wrote the greatest Persian epic poem. Also, **Fir·du·si** (fĭr dōō′sē).

fire (fĭr), *n., v.,* **fired, firing.** —*n.* 1. the active principle of burning or combustion, manifested by the evolution of light and heat. 2. a burning mass of material, as on a hearth or in a furnace. 3. the destructive burning of a building, town, forest, etc.; a conflagration. 4. a composition or device for producing a conflagration or a fiery display: *Greek fire.* 5. flashing light; luminous appearance. 6. brilliance, as of a gem. 7. burning passion; ardor; enthusiasm. 8. liveliness of imagination. 9. fever; inflammation. 10. severe trial or trouble. 11. exposure to fire by way of torture or ordeal. 12. heating quality, as of strong drink. 13. a spark or sparks. 14. the discharge of firearms: *to open fire.* 15. the effect of firing military weapons: *to place fire upon the enemy.* 16. *Archaic.* lightning, or a thunderbolt. 17. *Poetic.* a luminous object, as a star: *heavenly fires.* 18. Special noun phrases are:

between two fires, being attacked from both directions.
catch fire, to become ignited.
hang fire, 1. to be slow in exploding. 2. to be irresolute or slow in acting.
lay a fire, to arrange fuel to be lit.
miss fire, 1. to fail to explode or discharge. 2. to be unsuccessful; fail.
on fire, 1. ignited; burning. 2. eager; ardent; zealous.
play with fire, to meddle carelessly or lightly with a dangerous matter.
set fire to or **set on fire,** 1. to cause to burn. 2. to excite violently; inflame.
take fire, to become ignited.
under fire, 1. exposed to enemy fire. 2. under criticism or attack.
—*v.t.* 19. to set on fire. 20. to supply (a furnace, etc.) with fuel; attend to the fire of (a boiler, etc.). 21. to expose to the action of fire; subject to heat. 22. to apply heat in a kiln for baking or glazing; burn. 23. to heat very slowly for the purpose of drying, as tea. 24. to inflame, as with passion; fill with ardor. 25. to inspire. 26. to light or cause to glow as if on fire. 27. to discharge, as a gun. 28. to project (a missile) by discharging from a gun, etc. 29. to subject to explosion or explosive force, as a mine. 30. *Colloq.* to hurl; throw: *to fire a stone through a window.* 31. *Slang.* to eject or dismiss forcibly or peremptorily. 32. *Vet. Sci.* to apply a heated iron to (the skin) in order to create a local inflammation of the superficial structures, thus favorably affecting deeper inflammatory processes. 33. *Obs.* to drive out or away by, or as by, fire.
—*v.i.* 34. to take fire; be kindled. 35. to glow as if on fire. 36. to become inflamed with passion; become excited. 37. to go off, as a gun. 38. discharge a gun, etc.: *to fire at a fleeing enemy.* 39. *Colloq.* to hurl a missile. 40. (of grain crops) to lose green coloring and become yellow before ripening. [ME; OE *fȳr*, c. D *vuur*, G *feuer*; akin to Gk. *pȳr*]

fire alarm, 1. an alarm of fire. 2. an apparatus for giving the alarm.

fire·arm (fĭr′ärm′), *n.* 1. a gun from which a projectile is fired. 2. small arms.

fire·ball (fĭr′bôl′), *n.* 1. a ball filled with explosive or combustible material, used as a projectile, to injure the enemy by explosion or to set fire to their works. 2. a ball of fire, as the sun. 3. a luminous meteor, sometimes exploding. 4. lightning having the appearance of a globe of fire.

fire bay, *Brit. Fort.* that section of a fire trench occupied by riflemen, usually one squad to a bay.

fire beetle, any of the click beetles of the genus *Pyrophorus*, of tropical America, which emit reddish or greenish light from luminous spots.

fire·bird (fĭr′bûrd′), *n.* the Baltimore oriole.

fire·board (fĭr′bōrd′), *n.* a board used to close a fireplace.

fire·boat (fĭr′bōt′), *n.* a powered vessel fitted for fire fighting.

fire·box (fĭr′bŏks′), *n.* 1. the box or chamber in which the fire of a steam boiler, etc., is placed. 2. the furnace of a locomotive, where coal, oil, or other fuel is burned for the purpose of generating steam. 3. *Obs.* a tinderbox.

fire·brand (fĭr′brănd′), *n.* 1. a piece of burning wood or other material. 2. one who or that which kindles strife, inflames the passions, etc.

fire·break (fĭr′brāk′), *n. U.S.* a strip of ploughed or cleared land made to check the spread of a prairie or forest fire.

fire·brick (fĭr′brĭk′), *n.* a brick made of fire clay.

fire brigade, *Brit.* a company of firemen.

fire·bug (fĭr′bŭg′), *n. U.S. Colloq.* an incendiary.

fire clay, a kind of clay capable of resisting high temperature, used for making crucibles, firebricks, etc.

fire company, 1. a company of firemen. 2. a fire-insurance company.

fire control, *Mil.* technical supervision of artillery fire.

fire·crack·er (fĭr′krăk′ər), *n.* a paper or cardboard cylinder filled with an explosive and having a fuse that can be discharged to make a noise.

fire-cure (fĭr′kyōŏr′), *v.t.,* **-cured, -curing.** to cure (tobacco) by means of open fires, the smoke and flame imparting a creosotic flavor.

fire·damp (fĭr′dămp′), *n.* 1. a combustible gas, consisting chiefly of methane, formed esp. in coal mines, and dangerously explosive when mixed with certain proportions of atmospheric air. 2. the explosive mixture itself.

fire department, 1. the department of a municipal government charged with the prevention and extinction of fire. 2. the men in this department.

fire direction, *Mil.* tactical supervision of artillery fire.

fire·dog (fĭr′dôg′, -dŏg′), *n.* andiron.

fire·drake (fĭr′drāk′), *n.* a mythical fiery dragon. [OE *fȳrdraca*, f. *fȳr* fire + *draca* dragon]

fire drill, 1. a practice drill for a company of firemen, the crew of a ship, etc., to accustom them to their duties in case of fire. 2. a drill for pupils in a school, employees in a factory, etc., to train them in the manner of exit to be followed in case of fire.

fire-eat·er (fĭr′ē′tər), *n.* 1. a juggler who pretends to eat fire. 2. one who seeks occasion to fight or quarrel.

fire engine, a motor truck equipped for fire fighting, now usually having a motor-driven pump for shooting water from fire hydrants, etc., or chemical solutions at high temperature.

fire escape, an apparatus or structure used to escape from a burning building.

fire extinguisher, a portable apparatus, usually containing chemicals, for putting out a fire.

fire-flaught (fĭr′flôt′; *Scot.* -fläkħt′), *n. Chiefly Scot.* lightning. [f. FIRE, n. + *flaught* flash]

fire·fly (fĭr′flī′), *n., pl.* **-flies.** any of the soft-bodied, nocturnal beetles of the family *Lampyridae*, which possess abdominal light-producing organs. The luminous larvae or wingless females are called *glow-worms.*

fire-guard (fĭr′gärd′), *n.* a framework of wire placed in front of a fireplace as a protection.

fire·house (fĭr′hous′), *n.* a building where fire-fighting apparatus or firemen are stationed.

fire insurance, insurance covering loss or damage through fire.

fire·less (fĭr′lĭs), *adj.* 1. lacking fire; without a fire. 2. without life or animation.

Firefly,
Photuris pennsylvanica
A. Larva (line shows actual size); B. Adult beetle

fireless cooker, an insulated container which seals in heat for a long time to cook food.

fire·light (fĭr′līt′), *n.* the light from a fire, as on a hearth.

fire·lock (fĭr′lŏk′), *n.* 1. the flintlock musket, in whose lock the priming is ignited by sparks struck from flint and steel. 2. (formerly) a soldier armed with such a gun.

fire·man (fĭr′mən), *n., pl.* **-men.** 1. a man employed to extinguish or prevent fires. 2. a man employed to tend fires; a stoker. 3. *U.S. Navy.* an enlisted man assigned to the care and operation of a ship's machinery.

fire-new (fĭr′nū′, -nōō′), *adj. Archaic.* brand-new.

Fi·ren·ze (fē rĕn′tsĕ), *n.* Italian name of Florence.

fire opal, a red Mexican opal, often with a color play.

fire pink, a caryophyllaceous plant, *Silene virginica*, with brilliant scarlet flowers.

fire·place (fĭr′plās′), *n.* 1. that part of a chimney which opens into an apartment and in which fuel is burned. 2. any open structure, usually of masonry, for containing fire, as at a camp site.

fire·plug (fĭr′plŭg′), *n.* a hydrant for use in case of fire.

fire pot, that part of a household furnace in which the fire is made.

fire power, *Mil.* 1. the ability to deliver fire. 2. the amount of fire delivered by a unit or weapon.

fire·proof (fĭr′prōōf′), *adj.* 1. proof against fire; comparatively incombustible. —*v.t.* 2. to make fireproof.

fire·proof·ing (fĭr′prōō′fĭng), *n.* 1. act or process of rendering fireproof. 2. material for use in making anything fireproof.

fir·er (fĭr′ər), *n.* 1. one who fires, sets on fire, treats with fire or heat, discharges a firearm, etc. 2. a firearm with reference to its firing: *a single-firer, a rapid-firer.*

fire sale, *U.S.* a special sale of merchandise supposedly injured by fire.

fire screen, a metal screen placed in front of a fireplace for protection.

fire ship, a vessel freighted with combustibles and explosives and set adrift to destroy an enemy's ships, etc.

fire·side (fīr′sīd′), n. **1.** the space about a fire or hearth. **2.** home; home life.

fire step, *Fort.* a board or narrow ledge above the bottom of a fire trench from which men can fire, observe enemy movements, etc.

fire·stone (fīr′stōn′), n. a fire-resisting stone, esp. a kind of sandstone used in fireplaces, furnaces, etc. [OE fȳrstān, f. fȳr fire + stān stone]

fire·trap (fīr′trăp′), n. a building which, because of the material or arrangement of the structure, is especially dangerous in case of fire.

fire trench, *Fort.* a trench from which men can fire rifles and other small arms and in which they are relatively well protected.

fire wall, 1. a wall made of fireproof material to prevent the spread of a fire from one part of a building to another. **2.** *Aeron.* a wall made of stainless steel and asbestos to isolate the engine compartment from the rest of an aircraft.

fire·ward·en (fīr′wôr′dən), n. a person having authority in the prevention or extinguishing of fires, as in towns or camps.

fire·wa·ter (fīr′wô′tər, -wŏ′tər), n. *U.S.* strong liquor.

fire·weed (fīr′wēd′), n. any of various plants appearing in recently burned clearings or districts, as the willow herb, *Epilobium angustifolium*, or the composite weed, *Erechtites hieracifolia*, of North America.

fire·wood (fīr′wŏŏd′), n. wood for fuel.

fire·work (fīr′wûrk′), n. **1.** (*usually pl.*) a combustible or explosive device for producing a striking display of light or a loud noise, often also used in signaling at night, etc. **2.** (*pl.*) a pyrotechnic display.

fir·ing (fīr′ĭng), n. **1.** act of one who or that which fires. **2.** material for a fire; fuel.

firing battery, *Mil.* that part of a battery actually at the firing position when the battery is prepared for action.

firing data, *Mil.* precise calculations in set formula by which cannon are aimed and fired.

firing line, *Mil.* **1.** the positions at which troops are stationed to fire upon the enemy or targets. **2.** the troops firing from this line.

firing pin, *Ordn.* a plunger in the firing mechanism of a firearm or cannon that strikes the primer and thus ignites the propelling charge of a projectile.

firing squad, a military or naval detachment assigned to fire a salute at the burial of an honored person or to execute a condemned person.

fir·kin (fûr′kĭn), n. **1.** a unit of capacity, usually the fourth part of a barrel. **2.** a small wooden vessel for butter, etc. [ME *ferdekyn*, t. MD: m. *ferdelkijn*, dim. of *ferdel* firkin (lit., fourth part)]

firm¹ (fûrm), adj. **1.** comparatively solid, hard, stiff, or rigid: *firm ground, flesh, texture.* **2.** securely fixed in place. **3.** steady; not shaking or trembling: *a firm hand or voice.* **4.** fixed, settled, or unalterable, as a belief or conviction, a decree, etc. **5.** steadfast or unwavering, as persons or principles. **6.** indicating firmness: *a firm countenance.* **7.** not fluctuating or falling, as prices or the market. —*v.t., v.i.* **8.** to make or become firm. —*adv.* **9.** firmly: *stand firm.* [t. L: s. *firmus*; r. ME *erme*, t. OF] —**firm′ly,** adv. —**firm′ness,** n.
—**Syn. 1.** FIRM, HARD, SOLID, STIFF are applied to substances that tend to retain their form unaltered in spite of pressure or force. FIRM often implies that something has been brought from a more yielding state to a fixed or elastic one: *an increased amount of pectin makes jellies more firm.* HARD is applied to substances so resistant that it is difficult to make any impression upon their surface or to penetrate their interior: *as hard as a stone.* SOLID is applied to substances that without external support retain their form and resist pressure: *water in the form of ice is solid;* it sometimes denotes the opposite of hollow: *a solid block of marble.* STIFF implies rigidity that resists a bending force: *as stiff as a poker.* **5.** determined, immovable, resolute. —**Ant. 1.** yielding.

firm² (fûrm), n. **1.** a partnership or unincorporated association of two or more persons for carrying on a business. **2.** the name or title under which associated parties transact business: *the firm of Jones & Co.* [t. It., Sp.: m. *firma* signature, der. L *firmāre* confirm]

fir·ma·ment (fûr′mə mənt), n. the vault of heaven; the sky. [ME, t. LL: s. *firmāmentum* firmament, L a support, prop] —**fir′ma·men′tal,** adj.

fir·man (fûr′mən, fər män′), n., pl. **-mans.** an edict or administrative order issued by or in the name of an Oriental sovereign (formerly by an Ottoman Turkish sultan). [t. Pers.: m. *fermān*]

firm·er chisel (fûr′mər), a carpenter's chisel with a blade thin in proportion to its width, fixed to the handle by a tang, usually pushed by the hand and not driven with a mallet. [*firmer*, t. F: m. *fermoir*, b. *formoir* former (der. *former* form, t. L: m. *formāre*) and *fermer* make firm (g. L *firmāre*)]

firn (fĭrn), n. névé. [t. G: (prop. adj.) of last year]

fir·ry (fûr′ĭ), adj. **1.** of or pertaining to the fir. **2.** made of fir. **3.** abounding in firs.

first (fûrst), adj. **1.** being before all others with respect to time, order, rank, importance, etc. (used as the ordinal of *one*). **2.** *Music.* highest or chief among several voices or instruments of the same class: *first alto, first horn.* **3.** *Auto.* of or pertaining to low transmission gear ratio. **4. at first blush,** at the first view; on first consideration. **5. at first hand,** from the first or original source. —*adv.* **6.** before all others or anything else in time, order, rank, etc. **7.** before some other thing, event, etc. **8.** for the first time. **9.** in preference to something else; rather; sooner. **10.** in the first place; firstly. **11. first and last,** altogether; in all. **12. first off,** in the first place. **13. first or last,** at one time or another; sooner or later. —*n.* **14.** that which is first in time, order, rank, etc. **15.** the beginning. **16.** the first part; the first member of a series. **17.** *Music.* **a.** the voice or instrument that takes the highest or chief part in its class, especially in an orchestra or chorus. **b.** a leader of a part or group of performers. **18.** *Auto.* the lowest forward gear ratio, as in passenger cars. **19.** the first place in a race, etc. **20.** *Brit.* the highest class in an examination for honors: *he got a first in mathematics.* **21.** (*pl.*) the best quality of certain articles of commerce. **22. at (the) first,** at the beginning or outset. **23. from the first,** from the beginning or outset. [ME; OE *fyrst*, c. OHG *furist*, G *fürst* prince; a superl. form akin to FORE¹]

first aid, emergency aid or treatment given to persons suffering from accident, etc., before the services of a physician can be obtained.

first base, 1. *Baseball.* **a.** the first of the bases from the home plate. **b.** playing this position. **2. get to first base,** *Colloq.* to make a slight amount of progress.

first baseman, *Baseball.* the player stationed at first base.

first-born (fûrst′bôrn′), adj. **1.** first in the order of birth; eldest. —*n.* **2.** a first-born child. **3.** a first result or product.

first cause, 1. a cause which does not depend upon any other: *God is the first cause.* **2.** any prime mover.

first-class (fûrst′klăs′, -klăs′), adj. **1.** of the highest or best class or quality. **2.** best-equipped and most expensive: *a first-class coach.* —*adv.* **3.** by first-class conveyance: *to travel first-class.*

First day, Sunday (used by the Quakers).

first fruit, (*usually pl.*) **1.** the earliest fruit of the season. **2.** the first product or result of anything.

first-hand (fûrst′hănd′), adv. **1.** from the first or original source. —*adj.* **2.** of or pertaining to the first or original source. **3.** direct from the original source.

first lady, *U.S.* the wife of the president of the U.S., or of the governor of a State.

first lieutenant, *Mil.* an officer ranking next above a second lieutenant and next below a captain. See **lieutenant** (def. 1a).

first·ling (fûrst′lĭng), n. **1.** the first of its kind to be produced or to appear. **2.** first offspring. **3.** the first product or result.

first·ly (fûrst′lĭ), adv. in the first place; first.

first mortgage, a mortgage having priority over all other mortgages on property.

first-night·er (fûrst′nī′tər), n. one who makes a practice of attending the theater on the nights of the first public performance of plays.

first papers, *U.S.* the first documents of record in the naturalization of a foreigner.

first person, *Gram.* the class of a pronoun or verb in which the speaker is the subject. See **person** (def. 13a).

first-rate (fûrst′rāt′), adj. **1.** of the first rate or class. **2.** excellent; very good. —*adv.* **3.** *Colloq.* excellently.

First Reich. See **Reich** (def. 1).

first sergeant, *U.S. Army.* the senior noncommissioned officer of a company, squadron, etc., responsible for personnel and administration.

first speed, *Brit.* low gear.

first water, 1. the highest degree of fineness in a diamond or other precious stone. **2.** the highest rank.

firth (fûrth), n. *Chiefly Scot.* a long, narrow indentation of the seacoast. Also, **frith.** [t. Scand.; cf. Icel. *firdh-*, s. *fjördhr* firth. Cf. FIORD]

fisc (fĭsk), n. a royal or state treasury; an exchequer. [t. L: s. *fiscus* basket, purse, treasury]

fis·cal (fĭs′kəl), adj. **1.** of or pertaining to the public treasury or revenues. **2.** pertaining to financial matters in general. —*n.* **3.** (in some countries) an official having the function of public prosecutor. [t. L: s. *fiscālis* belonging to the state treasury] —**fis′cal·ly,** adv. —**Syn. 1.** See **financial.**

fiscal agent, a person or organization serving as another's financial agent.

fiscal year, any yearly period at the end of which a firm determines its financial condition without regard to the calendar year.

fish (fĭsh), n., pl. **fishes,** (*esp. collectively*) **fish.** (Note: In technical usage, *fishes* usually refers to several species, while *fish* refers to only one species.) **1.** any of various cold-blooded, completely aquatic vertebrates, having gills, commonly fins, and typically an elongated body usually covered with scales. **2.** any of various other aquatic animals. **3.** the flesh of fishes used as food. **4. other fish to fry,** *Colloq.* other matters requiring attention. **5. the Fishes,** *Astron.* the zodiacal constellation or sign Pisces. **6.** *Colloq.* (with an adjective) a person: *a queer fish, a poor fish.* **7.** a long strip of wood, iron, etc., used to strengthen a mast, joint, etc. —*v.t.* **8.** to catch or attempt to catch (fish or the like). **9.** to try to catch fish in (a stream, etc.). **10.** to draw as by fishing

b., blend of, blended; c., cognate with; d., dialect, dialectal; der., derived from; f., formed from; g., going back to; m., modification of; r., replacing; s., stem of; t., taken from; ?, perhaps. See the full key on inside cover.

(fol. by *up, out,* etc.). **11.** to search through as by fishing. **12.** *Naut.* **a.** to strengthen (a mast, joint, etc.) by a fish (def. 7). **b.** to hoist the flukes of (an anchor) up to the gunwale or rail by means of a tackle. **13. fish out, a.** to exhaust of fish by fishing. **b.** to obtain by careful search or by artifice. —*v.i.* **1.** to catch or attempt to catch fish, as by angling or drawing a net. **15.** to search for or attempt to catch onto something under water, in mud, etc., by the use of a dredge, rake, hook, or the like. **16.** to seek to obtain something by artifice or indirectly: *to fish for compliments, information, etc.* [ME; OE *fisc*, c. D *visch*, G *fisch*; akin to L *piscis*] —**fish′a·ble,** *adj.* —**fish′like′,** *adj.*

Fish (fĭsh), *n.* **Hamilton,** 1808–93, U.S. statesman; secretary of state, 1869–77.

fish and chips, *Chiefly Brit.* fried fish fillets and fried potatoes.

fish·bolt (fĭsh′bōlt′), *n.* a bolt that secures a fishplate to the rail in a railway track.

fish cake, a fried ball or cake of shredded fish, esp. salt codfish, and mashed potato. Also, **fish ball.**

fish crow, a North American crow, *Corvus ossifragus,* found along the entire Atlantic coast, fond of fish, mollusks, etc.

fish·er (fĭsh′ər), *n.* **1.** a fisherman. **2.** an animal that catches fish for food. **3.** a dark-brown or blackish, somewhat foxlike marten, *Martes pennanti,* of northern North America. **4.** its fur.

Fish·er (fĭsh′ər), *n.* **1. Dorothy Canfield,** (*Dorothea Frances Canfield,* Mrs. *Fisher*) 1879–1958, U.S. novelist. **2.** Irving, 1867–1947, U.S. political economist.

Fisher. Martes pennant (3 ft. long)

fish·er·man (fĭsh′ər mən), *n., pl.* **-men. 1.** one engaged in fishing, whether for profit or pleasure. **2.** a vessel employed in fishing.

fisherman's bend, a knot consisting of two round turns and a half hitch around them and the standing part, used commonly to bend a rope to an anchor or similar object.

Fisher of Kil·ver·stone (kĭl′vər stən), **John Arbuthnot** (är′bath nŏt, -nŏt′), **1st Baron,** 1841–1920, British admiral.

fish·er·y (fĭsh′ər ĭ), *n., pl.* **-eries. 1.** the occupation or industry of catching fish or taking other products of the sea or streams from the water. **2.** a place where such an industry is regularly carried on. **3.** a fishing establishment. **4.** *Law.* the right of fishing in certain waters.

fish hawk, osprey.

fish·hook (fĭsh′hŏŏk′), *n.* a hook used in fishing.

fish·ing (fĭsh′ĭng), *n.* **1.** the art or practice of catching fish. **2.** a place or facilities for catching fish.

fishing rod, a long, flexible pole supporting a line used in fishing.

fishing smack, any small vessel for deep-sea fishing.

fishing tackle, the equipment used to catch fish.

fish joint, a splice formed by fastening one or more fishplates to the sides of rails, beams, etc., which meet end to end: used esp. in connecting railroad rails.

fish·line (fĭsh′līn′), *n.* a line used in fishing.

fish louse, *Zool.* any of numerous small crustaceans, esp. certain copepods, parasitic on fish.

fish·mon·ger (fĭsh′mŭng′gər), *n. Chiefly Brit.* a dealer in fish.

fish·plate (fĭsh′plāt′), *n.* one of the splicing plates used in a fish joint.

Fishplate

fish·pound (fĭsh′pound′), *n. U.S.* a submerged net used by commercial fishermen for capturing fish.

fish slice, **1.** a broad-bladed kitchen implement with a long handle, for turning fish in frying. **2.** *Chiefly Brit.* a broad-bladed implement for serving fish at table.

fish spear, a spear or lance, often with several tines, for spearing fish through ice or from a boat or shore.

fish story, *Colloq.* an exaggerated or incredible story.

fish tackle, the tackle used for fishing an anchor.

fish·tail (fĭsh′tāl′), *Colloq.* —*v.i.* **1.** to slow an airplane by causing its tail to move rapidly from side to side. —*n.* **2.** such a maneuver.

fish·wife (fĭsh′wīf′), *n., pl.* **-wives. 1.** a woman who sells fish. **2.** a woman who uses abusive language.

fish·worm (fĭsh′wûrm′), *n.* an earthworm.

fish·y (fĭsh′ĭ), *adj.,* **fishier, fishiest. 1.** fishlike in shape, smell, taste, etc. **2.** consisting of fish. **3.** abounding in fish. **4.** *Colloq.* improbable, as a story. **5.** *Colloq.* of questionable character. **6.** dull and expressionless: *fishy eyes.* —**fish′i·ly,** *adv.* —**fish′i·ness,** *n.*

fish·y·back·ing (fĭsh′ĭ băk′ĭng), *n.* the transporting of loaded truck trailers by barge, ferry or similar vessel. —**fish′y-back′,** *adj.*

Fiske (fĭsk), *n.* **1. John,** (orig. *Edmund Fiske Green*) 1842–1901, U.S. historian and writer on philosophy and science. **2. Mrs.,** (*Minnie Davey,* known as *Minnie Maddern*), 1865–1932, U.S. actress.

fissi-, a word element meaning "cleft." [t. L. comb. form of *fissus,* pp.]

fis·sile (fĭs′əl), *adj.* capable of being split or divided; cleavable. [t. L: m.s. *fissilis*] —**fis·sil·i·ty** (fĭ sĭl′ə tĭ), *n.*

fis·sion (fĭsh′ən), *n.* **1.** act of cleaving or splitting into parts. **2.** *Biol.* the division of an organism into new organisms as a process of reproduction. **3.** *Physics.* the splitting of the nucleus of a heavy atom, as uranium, to form the nuclei of lighter atoms. [t. L: s. *fissio* a cleaving]

fis·sion·a·ble material (fĭsh′ən ə bəl), *Physics.* a substance capable of undergoing nuclear fission.

fis·sip·a·rous (fĭ sĭp′ə rəs), *adj.* reproducing by fission.

fis·si·ros·tral (fĭs′ĭ rŏs′trəl), *adj. Ornith.* **1.** having a broad, deeply cleft beak or bill, as the swallows and goatsuckers. **2.** (of the bill) deeply cleft.

Fissirostral bill of goatsucker. Caprimulgus europaeus

fis·sure (fĭsh′ər), *n., v.,* **-sured, -suring.** —*n.* **1.** a narrow opening produced by cleavage or separation of parts; a cleft. **2.** act of cleaving. **3.** state of being cleft; cleavage. **4.** *Surg., Anat.* a natural division or groove between adjoining parts of like substance. —*v.t.* **5.** to make fissures in; cleave; split. —*v.i.* **6.** to open in fissures; become split. [t. F, t. L: m.s. *fissūra* a cleft]

fist (fĭst), *n.* **1.** the hand closed tightly, with the fingers doubled into the palm. **2.** *Colloq.* the hand. **3.** *Colloq.* a person's handwriting. **4.** *Print.* the index sign (☞). —*v.t.* **5.** to strike with the fist. **6.** to grasp with the fist. [ME *fiste,* OE *fÿst,* c. G *faust*]

fist·ic (fĭs′tĭk), *adj.* of boxing; pugilistic: *fistic heroes.*

fist·i·cuff (fĭs′tə kŭf′), *n.* **1.** a cuff or blow with the fist. **2.** (*pl.*) combat with the fists. —*v.t., v.i.* **3.** to strike or fight with the fists. —**fist′i·cuff′er,** *n.*

fis·tu·la (fĭs′chŏŏ lə), *n., pl.* **-las, -lae** (-lē). **1.** *Pathol.* a narrow passage or duct formed by disease or injury, as one leading from an abscess to a free surface, or from one cavity to another. **2.** *Vet. Sci.* any of various suppurative inflammations, as in the withers of a horse, characterized by the formation of passages or sinuses through the tissues and to the surface of the skin. **3.** *Obs.* a pipe, as a flute. [t. L: pipe, tube, reed, ulcer. Cf. **FESTER**]

fis·tu·lous (fĭs′chŏŏ ləs), *adj.* **1.** *Pathol.* pertaining to or of the nature of a fistula. **2.** tubelike; tubular. **3.** containing tubes or tubelike parts. Also, **fis′tu·lar.**

fit¹ (fĭt), *adj.,* **fitter, fittest,** *v.,* **fitted, fitting,** *n.* —*adj.* **1.** well adapted or suited: *a fit choice or opportunity, fit to be eaten.* **2.** proper or becoming. **3.** qualified or competent, as for an office or function. **4.** worthy or deserving: *not fit to be seen.* **5.** prepared or ready: *crops fit for gathering.* **6.** in good physical condition, as an athlete, a race horse, military troops, etc. **7.** in good health. **8.** *U.S. Colloq.* in a condition; ready: *dressed up fit to kill; fit to be tied.* —*v.t.* **9.** to be adapted to or suitable for (a purpose, object, occasion, etc.). **10.** to be proper or becoming for. **11.** to be of the right size or shape for. **12.** to conform or adjust to something: *to fit a ring to the finger.* **13.** to make qualified or competent: *qualities that fit one for leadership.* **14.** to prepare: *this school fits students for college.* **15.** to put with nice adjustment (fol. by *in, into, on, over, together,* etc.). **16.** to provide; furnish; equip: *fit a door with a new handle.* **17. fit out** or **up,** to furnish with clothing, equipment, furniture, fixtures, or other requisites. —*v.i.* **18.** to be suitable or proper. **19.** to be of the right size or shape, as a garment for the wearer, or any object or part for a thing to which it is applied. —*n.* **20.** the manner in which a thing fits: *a perfect fit.* **21.** something that fits: *the coat is a poor fit.* **22.** the process or a process of fitting. [late ME *fyt;* orig. uncert.] —**fit′ness,** *n.*

fit² (fĭt), *n.* **1.** a sudden, acute attack or manifestation of a disease: *fit of epilepsy.* **2.** an excess, spell, or period of emotion or feeling, inclination, activity, idleness, etc. **3. by fits,** or **by fits and starts,** by irregular spells; fitfully; intermittently. [ME; OE *fitt* fight, struggle]

fit³ (fĭt), *n.* **1.** a song, ballad, or story. **2.** a division of a song, ballad, or story. [ME; OE *fitt*]

fitch (fĭch), *n.* **1.** the European polecat, *Mustela putorius.* **2.** its fur. Yellow fitch is often dyed to imitate other furs. Also, **fitch·et** (fĭch′ĭt), **fitch·ew** (fĭch′ōō). [t. MD: m. *vitsche* polecat]

Fitch (fĭch), *n.* **1. John,** 1743–98, American who invented a steamboat in 1790. **2. William Clyde,** 1865–1909, U.S. dramatist.

Fitch. Mustela putorius. (Total length 2 ft., tail 7 in.

Fitch·burg (fĭch′bûrg′), *n.* a city in N Massachusetts. 43,021 (1960).

fit·ful (fĭt′fəl), *adj.* coming, appearing, acting, etc., in fits or by spells; irregularly intermittent. [f. **FIT²** + **-FUL**] —**fit′ful·ly,** *adv.* —**fit′ful·ness,** *n.*

fit·ly (fĭt′lĭ), *adv.* **1.** in a fit manner. **2.** at a fit time.

fit·ter (fĭt′ər), *n.* **1.** one who or that which fits. **2.** one who fits garments. **3.** one who fits together or adjusts the parts of machinery. **4.** one who supplies and fixes fittings or fixtures. **5.** one who furnishes or equips with whatever is necessary for some purpose.

fit·ting (fĭt′ĭng), *adj.* **1.** suitable or appropriate; proper or becoming. —*n.* **2.** act of one who or that which fits. **3.** anything employed in fitting up. **4.** (*pl.*) furnishings, fixtures, etc. —**fit′ting·ly,** *adv.* —**fit′ting·ness,** *n.*

Fitz·Ger·ald (fĭts jĕr′əld), *n.* **Edward,** 1809–83, British poet who translated some of the poems of Omar Khayyam.

Fitz·ger·ald (fĭts jĕr′əld), *n.* **F(rancis) Scott (Key),** 1896–1940, U.S. novelist and short-story writer.

Fiu·me (fū′mĕ), *n.* former name for Rijeka.

five (fīv), *n.* **1.** a cardinal number, four plus one. **2.** a symbol for this number, as 5 or V. **3.** a set of this many persons or things. **4.** a playing card, etc., with five pips. —*adj.* **5.** amounting to five in number. [ME; OE *fīf*, c. D *vijf*, G *fünf*; akin to L *quīnque*, Gk. *pénte*]

five-and-ten (fīv′ən tĕn′), *n.* a store which carries a wide assortment of inexpensive items (formerly, costing 5 or 10 cents) for personal and household use. Also, **five′-and-dime′.** —**five′-and-ten′,** *adj.*

five-fin·ger (fīv′fĭng′gər), *n.* **1.** any of certain species of potentilla with leaves of five leaflets, as *Potentilla canadensis.* **2.** bird's-foot trefoil. **3.** oxlip. **4.** Virginia creeper.

five·fold (fīv′fōld′), *adj.* **1.** comprising five parts or members. **2.** five times as great or as much. —*adv.* **3.** in fivefold measure.

five hundred, a form of euchre in which a joker and a widow are included and in which 500 points win.

Five Nations, a confederacy of Iroquoian Indians: the Mohawks, Oneidas, Onondagas, Cayugas, and Senecas.

fiv·er (fī′vər), *n.* *Colloq.* **1.** a five-dollar bill or a five-pound note. **2.** anything that counts as five.

fives (fīvz), *n.* *Brit.* a game similar to handball.

fix (fĭks), *v.,* fixed or fixt, fixing, *n.* —*v.t.* **1.** to make fast, firm, or stable. **2.** to place definitely and more or less permanently. **3.** to settle definitely; determine: *to fix a price.* **4.** to direct (the eyes, the attention, etc.) steadily. **5.** to attract and hold (the eye, the attention, etc.). **6.** to make set or rigid. **7.** to put into permanent form. **8.** to put or place (responsibility, blame, etc.) on a person. **9.** to assign or refer to a definite place, time, etc. **10.** to repair. **11.** to put in order or in good condition; adjust or arrange (common in U.S., but not considered good usage in England). **12.** *Colloq.* to arrange matters with, or with respect to, esp. privately or dishonestly, so as to secure favorable action: *to fix a jury or a game.* **13.** *U.S.* to get (a meal); prepare (food). **14.** *Colloq.* to put in a condition or position to make no further trouble. **15.** *Colloq.* to get even with; get revenge upon. **16.** *Chem.* to make stable in consistence or condition; reduce from fluidity or volatility to a more permanent state. **17.** *Photog.* to remove the light-sensitive silver halides from (a photographic image), rendering it permanent. **18.** *Microscopy.* to kill, make rigid, and preserve for microscopic study. **19.** fix up, *U.S.* **a.** to clear up. **b.** to punish. —*v.i.* **20.** to become fixed. **21.** to become set; assume a rigid or solid form. **22.** to become stable or permanent. **23.** to settle down. **24.** fix on, to decide on. —*n.* **25.** *Colloq.* a position from which it is difficult to escape; a predicament. **26.** *Colloq.* the determining of a position, as of a plane, by mathematical, electronic, or other means. **27.** *Slang.* a shot of heroin. [late ME, t. ML: s. *fīxāre,* freq. of L *fīgere* fix] —**fix′a·ble,** *adj.* —**fix′er,** *n.* —**Syn. 1, 2.** Fix, ESTABLISH imply making firm or permanent. To FIX is to fasten in position securely or to make more or less permanent against change, esp. something already existing: *to fix a bayonet on a gun, fix a principle.* To ESTABLISH is to make firm or permanent something (usually newly) originated, created, or ordained: *to establish a business, a claim to property.*

fix·ate (fĭk′sāt), *v.,* -ated, -ating. —*v.t.* **1.** to fix; make stable, as a sensation. —*v.i.* **2.** to become fixed. [appar. back formation from FIXATION]

fix·a·tion (fĭk sā′shən), *n.* **1.** act of fixing. **2.** state of being fixed. **3.** *Chem.* **a.** reduction from a volatile or fluid to a stable or solid form. **b.** the process of converting atmospheric nitrogen into a useful compound, as a nitrate fertilizer. **4.** *Psychoanal.* a partial arrest of emotional and instinctual development at an early point in life, due to a severe traumatic experience or an overwhelming gratification. [ME, t. ML: s. *fixātio,* der. *fīxāre,* freq. of L *fīgere* fix]

fix·a·tive (fĭk′sə tĭv), *adj.* **1.** serving to fix; making fixed or permanent. —*n.* **2.** a fixative substance, esp.: **a.** a gummy liquid sprayed on a drawing or pastel to prevent blurring. **b.** a solution for killing, hardening, and preserving material for microscopic study.

fixed (fĭkst), *adj.* **1.** made fast or firm; firmly implanted. **2.** rendered stable or permanent, as color. **3.** set or intent upon something; steadily directed; set or rigid. **4.** definitely and permanently placed: *the fixed stars.* **5.** definite; not fluctuating or varying: *fixed charges.* **6.** put in order. **7.** *Colloq.* arranged with, or arranged, privately or dishonestly. **8.** *Chem.* **a.** (of an element) taken into a compound from its free state. **b.** nonvolatile, or not easily volatilized: *a fixed oil.* —**fix·ed·ly** (fĭk′sĭd lĭ), *adv.* —**fix′ed·ness,** *n.*

fixed charge, 1. an expense which must be met. **2.** periodic obligation, as taxes, interest on bonds, etc.

3. (*pl.*) such charges as depreciation, rent, interest, etc., arising out of the maintenance of fixed assets.

fixed idea, 1. a persistent or obsessing idea, often delusional, from which a person cannot escape. **2.** *Psychiatry.* a delusional idea which dominates the mind in certain forms of insanity.

fixed oil, *Chem.* a natural oil which is fixed (def. 8b), as lard oil, linseed oil, etc. Fixed oils occur in the cellular membranes, etc., of animals, and in the seeds, capsules, etc., of plants.

fixed star, *Astron.* any of the stars which apparently always retain the same position with respect to one another.

fix·ing (fĭk′sĭng), *n.* **1.** act of one who or that which fixes. **2.** (*pl.*) *U.S. Colloq.* appliances; trimmings.

fix·i·ty (fĭk′sə tĭ), *n., pl.* -ties. **1.** state or quality of being fixed; stability; permanence. **2.** something fixed.

fixt (fĭkst), *v.* a pt. and pp. of **fix.**

fix·ture (fĭks′chər), *n.* **1.** something securely fixed in position; a permanently attached part or appendage of a house, etc.: *an electric-light fixture.* **2.** a person or thing long established in the same place or position. **3.** *Mach.* a device for holding the work in a machine tool, esp. where the machining is to be done in straight surfaces, as in a planer or a milling machine. **4.** *Law.* a movable chattel (such as a machine, heating plant, etc.) which, by reason of (a) annexation to real property and (b) adaptation to continuing use in connection with the realty, is considered a part of the realty. **5.** *Rare.* act of fixing. [var. of *fixture* (t. LL: m.s. *fixūra*) modeled on MIXTURE] —**fix′ture·less,** *adj.*

fiz (fĭz), *v.i.,* fizzed, fizzing, *n.* flzz.

fiz·gig (fĭz′gĭg′), *n.* **1.** a frivolous, gadding girl or woman. **2.** a kind of hissing firework. **3.** a kind of whirling toy that makes a whizzing noise. **4.** a fish spear.

fizz (fĭz), *v.i.* **1.** to make a hissing or sputtering sound. —*n.* **2.** a hissing sound; effervescence. **3.** *U.S.* **a.** soda water or other effervescent water. **b.** an iced mixed drink made of liquor, lemon juice, sugar, and soda. **4.** *Brit.* champagne. [back formation from FIZZLE]

fiz·zle (fĭz′əl), *v.,* -zled, -zling, *n.* —*v.i.* **1.** to make a hissing or sputtering sound, esp. one that dies out weakly. **2.** *Colloq.* to fail ignominiously after a good start (often fol. by *out*). —*n.* **3.** a fizzling, hissing, or sputtering. **4.** *Colloq.* a fiasco; a failure. [f. obs. *fise* (t. Scand.; cf. Icel. *fīsa* break wind) +-*le,* freq. and dim. suffix]

fizz·y (fĭz′ĭ), *adj.,* fizzier, fizziest. that fizzes; fizzing.

fjeld (fyĕld; *Norw.* fyĕl), *n.* a high, bleak plateau on the Scandinavian peninsula. [t. Norw. See FELL²]

fjord (fyôrd; *Nor.* fyŏr, fyŏŏr), *n.* fiord.

Fl, *Chem.* fluorine.

fl., 1. florin. **2.** (L *floruit*) flourished. **3.** fluid.

Fla., Florida.

flab·ber·gast (flăb′ər găst′), *v.t. Colloq.* to overcome with surprise and bewilderment; astound. [? f. FLABB(Y) + AGHAST]

flab·by (flăb′ĭ), *adj.,* -bier, -biest. **1.** hanging loosely or limply, as flesh, muscles, etc. **2.** having such flesh. **3.** lacking firmness, as character, persons, principles, utterances, etc.; feeble. [cf. earlier *flappy* (f. FLAP + -Y¹) in same sense] —**flab′bi·ly,** *adv.* —**flab′bi·ness,** *n.*

fla·bel·late (flə bĕl′ĭt, -āt) *adj. Bot., Zool.* fan-shaped. Also, **fla·bel·li·form** (flə bĕl′ə fôrm′).

fla·bel·lum (flə bĕl′əm), *n., pl.* -bella (-bĕl′ə). **1.** a fan, esp. one used in religious ceremonies. **2.** a fan-shaped part. [t. L: fan]

flac·cid (flăk′sĭd), *adj.* soft and limber; flabby; limp; not firm: *flaccid muscles.* [t. L: s. *flaccidus*] —**flac·cid/i·ty, flac′cid·ness,** *n.* —**flac′cid·ly,** *adv.*

fla·con (flȧ kôn′), *n. French.* a small bottle or flask with a stopper.

flag¹ (flăg), *n., v.,* flagged, flagging. —*n.* **1.** a piece of cloth, commonly bunting, of varying size, shape, color, and device, usually attached by one edge to a staff or cord, and used as an ensign, standard, symbol, signal, etc. **2.** *Ornith.* the tuft of long feathers on the leg of falcons and most other hawks; the lengthened feathers on the crus or tibia. **3.** *Hunting.* the tail of a deer or of a setter dog. **4.** *Journalism.* the name or title of a newspaper as it appears on the first page. **5.** *Music.* hook (def. 12). —*v.t.* **6.** to place a flag or flags over or on; decorate with flags. **7.** to signal or warn (a person, etc.), or communicate (information) by, or as by, a flag. **8.** to decoy, as game, by waving a flag or the like to excite attention or curiosity. [appar. b. FLAP, n., and obs. *fag,* n., flap, flag; corresp. words in G, D, etc., t. E] —**flag′less,** *adj.*

flag² (flăg), *n.* **1.** any of various plants with long, sword-shaped leaves, as the sweet flag. **2.** the blue flag. **3.** the long, slender leaf of such a plant or of a cereal. [ME *flagge*; orig. uncert. Cf. D *vlag*]

flag³ (flăg), *v.i.,* flagged, flagging. **1.** to hang loosely or limply; droop. **2.** to fall off in vigor, energy, activity, interest, etc. [appar. b. FLAP, v., and FAG, v., in obs. sense of droop. See FLAG¹, n.]

flag⁴ (flăg), *n., v.,* flagged, flagging. —*n.* **1.** a flat slab of stone used for paving, etc. **2.** (*pl.*) a walk paved with such slabs. —*v.t.* **3.** to pave with flags. [late ME *flagge* turf, OE *flacg* poultice, plaster] —**flag′less,** *adj.*

Flag Day, June 14, the anniversary of the day (June 14, 1777) when Congress adopted the Stars and Stripes as the national emblem of the United States.

---

b., blend of, blended; c., cognate with; d., dialect, dialectal; der., derived from; f., formed from; g., going back to; m., modification of; r., replacing; s., stem of; t., taken from; ?, perhaps. See the full key on inside cover.

flag·el·lant (flăj′ə lənt, flə jĕl′ənt), *n.* **1.** one who flagellates. **2.** one who flagellates or scourges himself for religious discipline. **3.** (*often cap.*) one of a medieval European sect of fanatics that practiced scourging in public. —*adj.* **4.** flagellating. [t. L: *s. flagellans*, ppr.]

Flag·el·la·ta (flăj′ə lā′tə), *n.pl. Zool.* a class of *Protozoa* distinguished by having one or more long mobile filaments as locomotory organs.

flag·el·late (flăj′ə lāt′), *v.,* **-lated, -lating,** *adj., n.* —*v.t.* **1.** to whip; scourge; flog; lash. —*adj.* **2.** Also, **flag′el·lat′ed.** *Biol.* having flagella. See **flagellum. 3.** *Bot.* producing filiform runners or runnerlike branches, as the strawberry. —*n.* **4.** any of the *Flagellata.* [t. L: m.s. *flagellātus,* pp., whipped] —**flag′el·la′tion,** *n.* —**flag′el·la′tor,** *n.*

fla·gel·li·form (flə jĕl′ə fôrm′), *adj. Biol.* long, slender, and flexible, like the lash of a whip. [f. s. L *flagellum* a whip + -(I)FORM]

fla·gel·lum (flə jĕl′əm), *n.,* *pl.* **-gella** (-jĕl′ə), **-gellums. 1.** *Biol.* a long, lashlike appendage serving as an organ of locomotion in certain reproductive bodies, bacteria, protozoa, etc. **2.** *Bot.* a runner. **3.** a whip or lash. [t. L: whip, scourge]

flag·eo·let (flăj′ə lĕt′), *n.* a small end-blown flute with four finger holes in front and two in the rear. [t. F, dim. of OF *flajol* flute, ult. der. L *flāre* blow]

Flagg (flăg), *n.* **James Montgomery,** 1877–1960, U.S. painter and illustrator.

flag·ging[1] (flăg′ĭng), *adj.* drooping; failing. —**flag′ging·ly,** *adv.* [f. FLAG[3] + -ING[2]]

flag·ging[2] (flăg′ĭng), *n.* **1.** flagstones collectively. **2.** a pavement of flagstones. [f. FLAG[4] + -ING[1]]

flag·gy[1] (flăg′ĭ), *adj.* flagging; drooping; limp. [f. FLAG[3] + -Y[1]]

flag·gy[2] (flăg′ĭ), *adj.* consisting of or resembling flags or flagstone; laminate. [f. FLAG[4] + -Y[1]]

flag·gy[3] (flăg′ĭ), *adj.* abounding in, consisting of, or resembling the plants called flags. [f. FLAG[2] + -Y[1]]

Flag-eolet

fla·gi·tious (flə jĭsh′əs), *adj.* **1.** shamefully wicked, as persons, actions, times, etc. **2.** heinous or flagrant, as crime; infamous. [ME, t. L: m.s. *flāgitiōsus*] —**fla·gi′tious·ly,** *adv.* —**fla·gi′tious·ness,** *n.*

flag·man (flăg′mən), *n., pl.* **-men. 1.** one who has charge of or carries a flag. **2.** one who signals with a flag, as at a railroad crossing.

flag officer, 1. a naval officer, as an admiral, vice-admiral, or rear admiral, entitled to display a flag indicating his rank. **2.** an officer in command of a fleet, squadron, or group of ships.

flag of truce, *Mil.* a white flag displayed as an invitation to the enemy to confer, or carried as a sign of peaceful intention by one sent to deal with the enemy.

flag·on (flăg′ən), *n.* **1.** a large bottle for wine, etc. **2.** a vessel for holding liquids, as for use at table, esp. one with a handle, a spout, and usually a cover. [ME *flakon,* t. OF: m. *fla(s)con*; cf. ML *flasca* FLASK]

flag·pole (flăg′pōl′), *n.* a staff or pole on which a flag is displayed. Also, **flag·staff** (flăg′stăf′, -stäf′).

fla·grant (flā′grənt), *adj.* **1.** glaring; notorious; scandalous: *a flagrant crime, a flagrant offender.* **2.** *Rare.* blazing, burning, or glowing. [t. L: s. *flagrans,* ppr. blazing, burning] —**fla′gran·cy, fla′grance,** *n.* —**fla′grant·ly,** *adv.*

fla·gran·te de·lic·to (flə grăn′tĭ dĭ lĭk′tō), *Law.* while the crime is, or was, being committed. [L]

flag·ship (flăg′shĭp′), *n.* a ship which bears a flag officer of a fleet, squadron, or the like, and displays his flag.

Flag·staff (flăg′stăf′, -stäf′), *n.* a city in central Arizona. 18,214 (1960). ab. 6900 ft. high.

flag station, a railroad station where trains stop only when a flag or other signal is displayed or when one or more passengers are to be discharged.

flag·stone (flăg′stōn′), *n.* **1.** a flat slab of stone used for paving, etc. **2.** (*pl.*) a walk paved with such slabs. **3.** rock, such as sandstone, shale, etc., which can be split up into slabs for paving.

flail (flāl), *n.* **1.** an instrument for threshing grain by hand, consisting of a staff or handle to one end of which is attached a freely swinging stick or bar. **2.** *Mil.* an implement derived from the threshing flail used as a weapon of war in the Middle Ages. —*v.t.* **3.** to strike with, or as if with, a flail. [ME *flegl,* OE *flygel*; akin to FLY]

flair (flâr), *n.* **1.** talent; aptitude; keen perception. **2.** fondness; inclination; bent. **3.** *Hunting.* scent; sense of smell. [t. F, der. *flairer* smell, g. L *frāgrāre*]

flak (flăk), *n.* anti-aircraft fire, esp. as experienced by the crews of combat airplanes at which the fire is directed. [prop. *Fl.A.K.,* t. G, abbrev. of *flieger-abwehr-kanone* anti-aircraft cannon]

flake[1] (flāk), *n., v.,* **flaked, flaking.** —*n.* **1.** a small, flat, thin piece of anything. **2.** a small, detached piece or mass: *a flake of cloud.* **3.** a stratum or layer. —*v.i.* **4.** to peel off or separate in flakes. **5.** to fall in flakes, as snow. —*v.t.* **6.** to remove in flakes. **7.** to break flakes or chips from. **8.** to cover with or as with flakes. **9.** to form into flakes. [ME, appar. der. OE *flac-,* which occurs in *flac* or flying (said of arrows). Cf. also Icel. *flaka* be loose] —**flak′er,** *n.*

flake[2] (flāk), *n.* a frame, as for drying fish. [ME *flake, fleke.* Cf. Icel. *flaki, fleki* hurdle, wickerwork shield]

flake[3] (flāk), *n. Naut.* one fake of a cable or hawser laid in coils. [var. of FAKE[2]. Cf. G *flechte*]

flake white, a pigment made from pure white lead.

flak·y (flā′kĭ), *adj.,* **flakier, flakiest. 1.** of or like flakes. **2.** lying or cleaving off in flakes or layers. [f. FLAKE[1] + -Y[1]] —**flak′i·ly,** *adv.* —**flak′i·ness,** *n.*

flam (flăm), *n., v.,* **flammed, flamming.** *Dial. or Colloq.* —*n.* **1.** a falsehood. **2.** a deception or trick. —*v.t., v.i.* **3.** to deceive; delude; cheat. [see FLIMFLAM]

flam·beau (flăm′bō), *n., pl.* **-beaux** (-bōz), **-beaus. 1.** a flaming torch. **2.** a torch for use at night in illuminations, processions, etc. **3.** a large decorated candlestick, as of bronze. [t. F, der. OF *flambe* flame, earlier *flamble,* g. L *flammula,* dim. of *flamma* flame]

flam·boy·ant (flăm boi′ənt), *adj.* **1.** flaming; gorgeous: *flamboyant colors.* **2.** florid; ornate; showy: *flamboyant rhetoric.* **3.** *Archit.* characterized by wavy, flamelike tracery, as in windows and openwork: applied to the highly ornate style of French Late Gothic architecture of the 15th century. [t. F, ppr. of *flamboyer* to flame, flare, der. OF *flambe.* See FLAMBEAU] —**flam·boy′ance, flam·boy′an·cy,** *n.* —**flam·boy′ant·ly,** *adv.*

flame (flām), *n., v.,* **flamed, flaming.** —*n.* **1.** burning gas or vapor, as from wood, etc., undergoing combustion; a portion of ignited gas or vapor. **2.** (*often pl.*) state or condition of blazing combustion: *to burst into flames.* **3.** any flamelike condition; glow; inflamed condition. **4.** brilliant light; scintillating luster. **5.** bright coloring; a streak or patch of color. **6.** heat or ardor, as of zeal or passion. **7.** *Slang.* an object of the passion of love; sweetheart. —*v.i.* **8.** to burn with a flame or flames; burst into flames; blaze. **9.** to glow like flame; shine brilliantly; flash. **10.** to burn as with flame, as passion; break into open anger, indignation, etc. (often fol. by *out* or *up*). —*v.t.* **11.** to subject to the action of flame or fire. [ME, t. OF: m. *flamme,* g. L *flamma*] —**flame′less,** *adj.* —**flame·let** (flām′lĭt), *n.*

—**Syn. 1.** FLAME, BLAZE, CONFLAGRATION refer to the light and heat given off by combustion. FLAME is the common word, referring to a combustion of any size: *the light of a match flame.* BLAZE usually denotes a quick, hot, bright, and comparatively large flame: *the fire burst into a blaze.* CONFLAGRATION refers to destructive flames which spread over a considerable area: *a conflagration destroyed Chicago.*

flame color, bright reddish-orange. —**flame′-col′ored,** *adj.*

fla·men (flā′mĕn), *n., pl.* **flamens, flamines** (flăm′ə-nēz′). *Rom. Antiq.* a priest devoted to the service of one particular deity. [t. L; r. ME *flamin(e)*]

flame-out (flām′out′), *n.* the failure of a jet engine in flight or during take-off.

flame thrower, *Mil.* an apparatus, either portable or mounted on a tank, that throws a spray of oil that ignites in the air.

flam·ing (flā′mĭng), *adj.* **1.** emitting flames; blazing; fiery. **2.** glowing; brilliant. **3.** violent; vehement; passionate. —**flam′ing·ly,** *adv.*

fla·min·go (flə mĭng′gō), *n., pl.* **-gos, -goes.** any of the aquatic birds constituting the family *Phoenicopteridae,* with very long neck and legs, webbed feet, bills bent downward, and pinkish to scarlet plumage. [t. Pg., t. Sp.: m. *flamenco,* t. Pr.: m. *flamenc,* f. *flama* (g. L *flamma* FLAME) + suffix *-enc* (t. Gmc.: m. *-ing*)]

Florida flamingo,
Phoenicopterus ruber
(Ab. 4 ft. long)

Fla·min·i·an Way (flə mĭn′Y ən), an ancient Roman road extending from Rome N to Ariminum (Rimini) on the Adriatic coast. 215 mi.

Fla·min·i·us (flə mĭn′Y əs), *n.* **Ga·ius** (gā′əs), died 217 B.C., Roman general and statesman, defeated by Hannibal.

flam·ma·ble (flăm′ə bəl), *adj.* easily set on fire; combustible; inflammable. —**flam′ma·bil′i·ty,** *n.*

flam·y (flā′mĭ), *adj.* of or like flame.

flan (flän; *Fr.* fläN), *n.* **1.** a cheese-, cream-, or fruit-filled cake. **2.** a piece of metal shaped ready to form a coin, but not yet stamped by the die. **3.** the metal of which a coin is made, as distinct from its design. [t. F]

Flan·ders (flăn′dərz), *n.* a medieval county in W Europe, extending along the North Sea from the Strait of Dover to the mouth of the Scheldt river: the corresponding modern regions include the provinces of **East Flanders** and **West Flanders** in W Belgium, and the adjacent parts of N France and SW Netherlands.

flange (flănj), *n., v.,* **flanged, flanging.** —*n.* **1.** a projecting rim, collar, edge, ridge, or the like, on an object, for keeping it in place, attaching it to another object, strengthening it, etc. See illus. in col. 1 of next page. **2.** the horizontal portion or portions of steel shapes, such as the top and bottom flange of an I-beam. **3.** a device or tool for making flanges. —*v.i.* **4.** to project like, or take the form of, a flange. [var. of *flanch,* n., from *flanch,* v., t. OF: s. *flanchir* bend, b. *flanc* FLANK and *flechier* (g. Rom. *flecticāre,* der. L *flectere*)] —**flange′less,** *adj.*

flank (flăngk), *n.* **1.** the side of an animal or a human being between the ribs and hip. **2.** the thin piece of flesh constituting this part. **3.** a slice of meat from the flank. **4.** the side of anything, as of a building. **5.** *Mil., Naval.* the extreme right or left side of an army or fleet, or a subdivision of an army or fleet. **6.** *Fort.* **a.** the right or left side of a work or fortification. **b.** a part of a work that defends another work by a fire along the outside of its parapet. **c.** the part of a bastion which extends from the curtain to the face and protects the curtain, opposite face, etc. See diag. under **bastion**. —*v.t.* **7.** to stand or be placed or posted at the flank or side of. **8.** to defend or guard at the flank. **9.** to pass round or turn the flank of. —*v.i.* **10.** to occupy a position at the flank or side. **11.** to present the flank or side. [ME *flanke*, OE *flanc*, t. OF, t. Gmc.; cf. OHG *hlancha*]

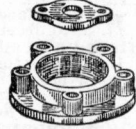

Three forms of flanges (def. 1)

flank·er (flăngk′ər), *n.* **1.** one who or that which flanks. **2.** *Mil.* one of a body of soldiers employed on the flank of an army to guard a line of march. **3.** *Fort.* a fortification projecting so as to defend another work, or to command the flank of an assailing body.

flan·nel (flăn′əl), *n., v.,* **-neled, -neling** or (*esp. Brit.*) **-nelled, -nelling.** —*n.* **1.** a warm, soft fabric of wool or blends of wool and cotton, wool and rayon, or cotton warp with wool filling. **2.** (*pl.*) an outer garment, esp. trousers, made of flannel. **3.** (*pl.*) woolen undergarments. —*v.t.* **4.** to cover or clothe with flannel. **5.** to rub with flannel. [orig. uncert.]

flannel cake, a tender, thin pancake.

flan·nel·et (flăn′ə lĕt′), *n.* a cotton fabric, plain or printed, napped on one side. Also, **flan′nel·ette′.**

flan·nel·ly (flăn′əl ĭ), *adj.* made of or resembling flannel.

flap (flăp), *v.,* **flapped, flapping,** *n.* —*v.i.* **1.** to swing or sway about loosely, esp. with noise: *a curtain or flag flaps in the wind.* **2.** to move up and down, as wings; flap the wings, or make similar movements. **3.** to strike a blow with something broad and flexible. —*v.t.* **4.** to move (wings, etc.) up and down. **5.** to cause to swing or sway loosely, esp. with noise. **6.** to strike with something broad and flexible. **7.** *Colloq.* to toss, fold, shut, etc., smartly, roughly, or noisily. —*n.* **8.** a flapping motion. **9.** the noise produced by something that flaps. **10.** a blow given with something broad and flexible. **11.** something broad and flexible, or flat and thin, that hangs loosely, attached at one side only. **12.** *Surg.* a portion of skin or flesh partially separated from the body which may subsequently be transposed by grafting. [ME *flappe(n)*, prob. of imit. orig.; cf. G *flappen* clap] —**flap′less,** *adj.*

flap·doo·dle (flăp′dōō′dəl), *n. Slang.* nonsense; bosh.

flap·drag·on (flăp′drăg′ən), *n.* **1.** an old game in which the players snatch raisins, plums, etc., out of burning brandy, and eat them. **2.** the object so caught and eaten.

flap·jack (flăp′jăk′), *n.* griddlecake.

flap·per (flăp′ər), *n.* **1.** something broad and flat for striking with, or for making a noise by striking. **2.** broad, flat, hinged or hanging piece; flap. **3.** a young bird just learning to fly. **4.** *Colloq.* a young, half-grown girl, often one who tries to appear sophisticated. **5.** *Slang.* the hand.

flare (flâr), *v.,* **flared, flaring,** *n.* —*v.i.* **1.** to burn with an unsteady, swaying flame, as a torch or candle in the wind. **2.** to blaze with a sudden burst of flame (often fol. by *up*). **3.** to start up or burst out in sudden fierce activity, passion, etc. (usually fol. by *up* or *out*). **4.** to shine or glow. **5.** to spread gradually outward as the end of a trumpet, or a ship's sides or bows. —*v.t.* **6.** to cause (a candle, etc.) to burn with a swaying flame. **7.** to display conspicuously or ostentatiously. **8.** to signal by flares of fire or light. **9.** to cause (something) to spread gradually outward in form. **10.** *Metall.* to heat (a high-zinc brass) to such a high temperature that the zinc vapors begin to burn. —*n.* **11.** a flaring or swaying flame or light, as of torches in the wind. **12.** a sudden blaze or burst of flame. **13.** a sudden blaze of fire or light used as a signal or for illumination or guidance, or a substance burned to produce such a blaze. **14.** a sudden burst, as of zeal or of temper. **15.** a gradual spread outward in form; outward curvature: *the flare of a skirt.* **16.** something that spreads out. **17.** *Optics.* light reflected by the surfaces of an optical system. [orig. meaning spread out, display; b. FLY[1] and BARE[1], but cf. Norw. *flara* blaze]

flare·back (flâr′băk′), *n.* **1.** a blast of flame that sometimes issues from the breech of a large gun or cannon when it is opened after firing. **2.** an outburst of something coming back: *a flareback of winter.*

flare-up (flâr′ŭp′), *n.* **1.** a sudden flaring up of flame or light. **2.** *Colloq.* a sudden outburst of anger.

flar·ing (flâr′ĭng), *adj.* **1.** that flares; flaming. **2.** glaringly bright or showy. **3.** spreading gradually outward in form. —**flar′ing·ly,** *adv.*

flash (flăsh), *n.* **1.** a sudden, transitory outburst of flame or light: *a flash of lightning.* **2.** a sudden, brief outburst or display of joy, wit, etc. **3.** the time occupied by a flash of light; an instant: *to do something in a flash.*

4. ostentatious display. **5.** *Journalism.* a brief telegraphic dispatch, usually transmitting preliminary news of an important story or development. **6.** *Colloq.* the cant or jargon of thieves, vagabonds. etc. **7.** *Naut., etc.* **a.** an extra volume or rush of water, as that produced by a dam or sluiceway, utilized to float a boat over shoals or for other purposes. **b.** the device, as a lock or sluice, used for this purpose. —*v.i.* **8.** to break forth into sudden flame or light, esp. transiently or intermittently (often used as a copula): *he flashed crimson with anger.* **9.** to gleam. **10.** to burst suddenly into view or perception: *the answer flashed into his mind.* **11.** to move like a flash. **12.** to break into sudden action. **13.** *Colloq.* or *Slang.* to make a flash or sudden display. **14.** *Rare.* to dash or splash, as the sea or waves. —*v.t.* **15.** to emit or send forth (fire or light) in sudden flashes. **16.** to cause to flash, as powder by ignition or a sword by waving. **17.** to send forth like a flash. **18.** to communicate instantaneously, as by telegraph. **19.** *Colloq.* to make a sudden or ostentatious display of: *to flash one's diamonds.* **20.** to increase the flow of water in (a river, etc.). **21.** *Rare.* to dash or splash (water). **22.** *Glassmaking.* **a.** to coat (plain glass or a glass object) with a film of colored, opal, or white glass. **b.** to apply (such a coating). **23.** *Bldg. Trades.* to protect by flashing (def. 1). —*adj.* **24.** showy or ostentatious. **25.** counterfeit or sham. **26.** belonging or pertaining to sporting men. **27.** *Colloq.* belonging to or connected with thieves, vagabonds, etc., or their cant or jargon. [ME *flasche(n)* rise and dash (said of tidal waters); FLOW (or FLOOD) and WASH] —**flash′er,** *n.* —**Syn. 8.** FLASH, GLANCE, GLINT, GLITTER mean to send forth a sudden gleam (or gleams) of bright light. To FLASH is to send forth light with a sudden, transient brilliancy: *a shooting star flashed briefly.* To GLANCE is to emit a brilliant flash of light as a reflection from a smooth surface: *sunlight glanced from the glass windshield.* GLINT suggests a hard bright gleam of reflected light as from something polished or burnished: *light glints from silver or from burnished copper.* To GLITTER is to reflect (intermittently) from a hard surface flashes of light like bright coins: *ice glitters in moonlight.*

flash·back (flăsh′băk′), *n.* a representation, during the course of a novel, motion picture, etc., of some event or scene occurring at a previous time.

flash·board (flăsh′bôrd′), *n. Civ. Eng.* a board, or one of a series of boards, as on a milldam, used to increase the depth of the impounded water.

flash bulb, *Photog.* a glass bulb filled with oxygen and thin sheet magnesium or aluminum, giving a momentary bright light when ignited, used as a light source.

flash flood, *Phys. Geog.* a sudden, destructive rush of water down a narrow gully or over a sloping surface in desert regions, due to heavy rains in the mountains or foothills. —**Syn.** See **flood.**

flash gun, *Photog.* a device which simultaneously discharges a flash bulb and operates the camera shutter.

flash·ing (flăsh′ĭng), *n.* **1.** *Bldg. Trades.* pieces of sheet metal, etc., used to cover and protect certain joints and angles, as where a roof comes in contact with a wall or chimney. **2.** act of creating an artificial flood in a conduit or stream, as in a sewer for cleansing it.

flash·light (flăsh′lĭt′), *n.* **1.** a small portable electric lamp powered by dry batteries or a tiny generator. **2.** a flash of light, or a light that flashes. **3.** any source of artificial light as used in flashlight photography.

flashlight photography, the process of picture making which uses a brilliant flash of artificial light as the source of illumination.

flash·o·ver (flăsh′ō′vər), *Elect.* —*n.* **1.** a disruptive discharge around or over the surface of a solid or liquid insulator. —*v.i.* **2.** to establish a flashover.

flash point, the lowest temperature at which a volatile oil will give off explosive or ignitable vapors.

flash·y (flăsh′ĭ), *adj.,* **flashier, flashiest. 1.** sparkling or brilliant, esp. in a superficial way or for the moment. **2.** pretentiously smart; showy; gaudy. **3.** *Rare.* flashing with light. —**flash′i·ly,** *adv.* —**flash′i·ness,** *n.* —**Syn. 2.** See **gaudy[1].**

flask[1] (flăsk, fläsk), *n.* **1.** a bottle-shaped container made of glass, metal, etc.: *a flask of oil, a brandy flask.* **2.** an iron container for shipping mercury. It holds 76 lbs. **3.** *Foundry.* a container of sand in which sand is rammed to form a mold. [OE *flasce, flaxe.* Cf. FLAGON]

flask[2] (flăsk, fläsk), *n. Ordn.* **1.** the armored plates making up the sides of a gun-carriage trail. **2.** *Obs.* the bed of a gun carriage. [t. d. F: m. *flasque* cheek of a gun carriage, g. LL *flasca* FLASK[1], t. Gmc. See FLAGON]

flask·et (flăs′kĭt, fläs′-), *n.* **1.** a small flask. **2.** a long, shallow basket. [ME *flaskett,* t. OF: m. *flasquet* small flask, der. *flasque* FLASK[1]]

flat[1] (flăt), *adj.,* **flatter, flattest,** *n., v.,* **flatted, flatting,** *adv.* —*adj.* **1.** horizontally level: *a flat roof.* **2.** level, even, or without inequalities of surface, as land, areas, surfaces, etc. **3.** comparatively lacking in projection or depression of surface: *a broad, flat face.* **4.** lying at full length, as a person. **5.** lying wholly on or against something: *a ladder flat against a wall.* **6.** thrown down, laid low, or level with the ground, as fallen trees or buildings. **7.** having a generally level shape or appearance; not deep or thick: *a flat plate.* **8.** spread out, as an unrolled map, the open hand, etc. **9.** collapsed; deflated: *a flat tire.* **10.** without qualification; unqualified,

downright, or positive: *a flat denial*. **11.** without modification: *a flat price*. **12.** uninteresting, dull, or tedious. **13.** having lost its flavor, sharpness, or life, as wine, beer, etc.; stale; tasteless or insipid, as food. **14.** pointless, as a remark, joke, etc. **15.** commercially dull, as trade or the market. **16.** lacking relief, contrast, or shading, as a painting. **17.** *Painting.* without gloss; mat. **18.** not clear, sharp, or ringing, as sound, a voice, etc. **19.** *Music.* **a.** (of a tone) lowered a half step in pitch: *B flat.* **b.** below an intended pitch, as a note; too low (opposed to *sharp*). **c.** (of an interval) diminished. **20. flat a,** the *a* sound in *glad*. **21.** *Gram.* derived without change in form, as English *to brush* from the noun *brush* and adverbs which do not add *-ly* to the adjective form as *fast, cheap, slow*, etc. **22.** *Naut.* (of a sail) **a.** cut with little or no fullness. **b.** trimmed as nearly fore-and-aft as possible, for sailing to windward.
—*n.* **23.** something flat. **24.** a flat surface, side, or part of anything: *the flat of a blade, the flat of the hand*. **25.** flat or level ground; a flat area. **26.** a marsh; a shallow. **27.** *Music.* **a.** (in musical notation) the character *♭*, which when attached to a note or to a staff degree lowers its significance one chromatic half step. **b.** a tone one chromatic half step below another: *the flat of B is B flat.* **c.** (on keyboard instruments, with reference to any given key) the key next below or to the left. **28.** *Theat.* a piece of scenery consisting of a wooden frame, usually rectangular, covered with lightweight board or fabric. **29.** *Colloq.* a deflated automobile tire. —*v.t.* **30.** to make flat. **31.** *Music.* to lower (a pitch) esp. one half step.
—*v.i.* **32.** to become flat.
—*adv.* **33.** in a flat position; horizontally; levelly. **34.** in a flat manner; positively; absolutely. **35.** exactly. **36.** *Music.* below the true pitch. **37.** *Finance.* without interest. **38. brace a yard flat aback,** *Naut.* to set a yard so that the wind is nearly at right angles to the forward surface of the sail. **39. fall flat,** to fail completely; fail to succeed in attracting interest, purchasers, etc.
[ME, t. Scand.; cf. Icel. *flatr*, Sw. *flat*; akin to OE *flet* floor. See FLAT²] —**flat/ly,** *adv.* —**flat/ness,** *n.* —**flat/tish,** *adj.* —Syn. 1. See level.

flat² (flăt), *n.* **1.** a floor, or a suite of rooms on one floor, forming a complete residence, as for a family. **2.** *Chiefly Brit.* a floor or story of a building. [var. of obs. *flet*, OE *flet* floor, house, hall; akin to FLAT¹]

flat·boat (flăt/bōt/), *n.* a large flat-bottomed boat for use in shallow water, esp. for floating down a river.

flat·car (flăt/kär/), *n.* *U.S.* a railroad car consisting of a platform without sides or top; a platform car.

flat-cyl·in·der press (flăt/sĭl/ĭn dər). See press¹ (def. 30a).

flat·fish (flăt/fĭsh/), *n., pl.* **-fishes,** (*esp. collectively*) **-fish.** any of a group of fishes (often considered as constituting the suborder *Heterosomata*), including the halibut, flounder, sole, etc., having a greatly compressed body, and swimming on one side, and (in the adult) having both eyes on the upper side.

flat·foot (flăt/fŏŏt/), *n., pl.* **-feet. 1.** *Pathol.* **a.** a condition in which the arch of the foot is flattened so that the entire sole rests upon the ground. **b.** a foot with such an arch. **2.** *Slang.* a policeman.

flat-foot·ed (flăt/fŏŏt/ĭd), *adj.* **1.** having flat feet. **2.** *Colloq.* taking or showing an uncompromising stand in a matter; firm and explicit. —**flat/-foot/ed·ly,** *adv.* —**flat/-foot/ed·ness,** *n.*

Flat·head (flăt/hĕd/), *n.* **1.** one of a tribe of Salishan Indians of northwest Montana. **2.** a Chinook Indian.

flat·i·ron (flăt/ī/ərn), *n.* an iron with a flat face, for smoothing cloth.

flat knot, reef knot.

flat·ling (flăt/lĭng), *Archaic or Dial.* —*adv.* **1.** in a flat position; with the flat side, as of a sword. **2.** flatly or positively. —*adj.* **3.** dealt with the flat side.

flat silver, flatware (def. 2).

flat·ten (flăt/ən), *v.t., v.i.* **1.** to make or become flat. **2. flatten out,** *Aeron.* to fly into a horizontal position, as after a dive. —**flat/ten·er,** *n.*

flat·ter¹ (flăt/ər), *v.t.* **1.** to seek to please by complimentary speech or attentions; compliment or praise insincerely. **2.** to represent too favorably, as in portrayal. **3.** to play upon the vanity or susceptibilities of; cajole, wheedle, or beguile. **4.** to gratify by compliments or attentions, or as a compliment does: *to feel flattered by an invitation.* **5.** to beguile with hopes; encourage (hopes); please (oneself) with the thought or belief (fol. by *that* and a clause): *he flattered himself (that) he might become the head of the school.* —*v.i.* **6.** to use flattery. [ME *flat(t)eren* float, flutter, fawn upon, OE *floterian* float, flutter; for sense development, cf. E *flicker*, Icel. *fladhra* flatter; not connected with F *flatter* flatter] —**flat/ter·er,** *n.* —**flat/ter·ing·ly,** *adv.*

flat·ter² (flăt/ər), *n.* **1.** one who or that which makes something flat. **2.** a hammer with a broad face, used by smiths. **3.** a drawplate with a flat orifice for drawing flat metal strips, as for watch springs, etc. [f. FLAT¹, v. + -ER¹]

flat·ter·y (flăt/ərĭ), *n., pl.* **-teries. 1.** act of flattering. **2.** a flattering compliment or attention; excessive, insincere praise. [ME *flaterie*, t. OF, der. *flatere* a flatterer, der. *flater*. Cf. FLATTER¹]

flat·top (flăt/tŏp/), *n.* *U.S. Navy.* an aircraft carrier.

flat·u·lent (flăch/ə lənt), *adj.* **1.** generating gas in the alimentary canal, as food. **2.** attended with or caused by, or suffering from, such an accumulation of gas. **3.** pretentious; empty. [t. F, der. L *flātus* a blowing] —**flat/u·lence, flat/u·len·cy,** *n.* —**flat/u·lent·ly,** *adv.*

fla·tus (flā/təs), *n.* an accumulation of gas in the stomach, intestines, or other body cavity. [t. L: a blowing]

flat·ware (flăt/wâr/), *n.* **1.** vessels for the table, or for other use, that are more or less flat, as plates, saucers, etc. (distinguished from *hollowware*). **2.** silver utensils, knives, forks, etc.

flat·wise (flăt/wīz/), *adv.* with the flat side (not the edge) foremost or in contact. Also, **flat·ways** (flăt/wāz/).

flat·worm (flăt/wûrm/), *n.* any platyhelminth.

Flau·bert (flō bĕr/), *n.* **Gustave** (gЎstȧv/), 1821–80, French novelist.

flaunt (flônt), *v.i.* **1.** to parade or display oneself conspicuously or boldly. **2.** to wave conspicuously in the air. —*v.t.* **3.** to parade or display ostentatiously. —*n.* **4.** act of flaunting. **5.** *Obs.* something flaunted. [t. Scand.; cf. Norw. *flanta* gad about, der. *flana* roam; akin to Gk. *plánē* roaming (see PLANET)] —**flaunt/er,** *n.* —**flaunt/ing·ly,** *adv.* —**flaunt/y,** *adj.*

flau·tist (flô/tĭst), *n.* a flutist. [t. It.: m. *flautista*, der. *flauto* flute]

fla·ves·cent (flə vĕs/ənt), *adj.* turning yellow; yellowish. [t. L: s. *flāvescens*, ppr.]

fla·vin (flā/vĭn), *n. Chem.* **1.** a complex heterocyclic ketone which is common to the nonprotein part of several important yellow enzymes, the flavoproteins. **2.** quercetin. [f. s. L *flāvus* yellow + -IN²]

-flavin, *Chem.* a word element indicating any of a number of natural derivatives of flavin, as *riboflavin*.

flavo-, a word element meaning "yellow," as in *flavoprotein*. Also, before vowels, **flav-.** [comb. form repr. L *flāvus*]

fla·vone (flā/vōn), *n. Chem.* **1.** an organic compound, $C_{15}H_{10}O_2$, the parent substance of various yellow dyes. **2.** a derivative of this compound.

fla·vo·pro·te·in (flā/vō prō/tʲ ən, -tēn), *n. Biochem.* an enzyme, containing riboflavin and linked chemically with a protein, active in the oxidation of foods in animal cells.

fla·vo·pur·pu·rin (flā/vō pûr/pyər ĭn), *n. Chem.* a yellowish crystalline compound, $C_{14}H_8O_5$ (isomeric with purpurin), used in dyeing.

fla·vor (flā/vər), *n.* **1.** taste, esp. a characteristic taste, or a noticeable element in the taste, of a thing. **2.** a flavoring substance or extract. **3.** the characteristic quality of a thing: *a book which has the flavor of the sea.* **4.** a particular quality noticeable in a thing: *language with a strong nautical flavor.* **5.** smell, odor, or aroma. —*v.t.* **6.** to give flavor. Also, *Brit.*, **fla/vour.** [ME, t. OF: m. *flaur*, ult. der. L *frāgrāre* emit an odor] —**fla/vor·er,** *n.* —**fla/vor·less,** *adj.* —Syn. 1. See taste.

fla·vor·ing (flā/vər ĭng), *n.* something that gives flavor; a substance or preparation used to give a particular flavor to food or drink. Also, *Brit.*, **fla/vour·ing.**

fla·vor·ous (flā/vər əs), *adj.* **1.** full of flavor. **2.** pleasant to the smell or taste.

flaw¹ (flô), *n.* **1.** a marring feature; a defect; a fault. **2.** a defect impairing legal soundness or validity: *flaw in a lease or a will.* **3.** a crack, break, breach, or rent. —*v.t.* **4.** to produce a flaw in. —*v.i.* **5.** to contract a flaw; become cracked or defective. [ME, t. Scand.; cf. Sw. *flaga* flake, flaw] —**flaw/less,** *adj.* —**flaw/less·ly,** *adv.* —**flaw/less·ness,** *n.* —Syn. 1. See defect.

flaw² (flô), *n.* **1.** a sudden gust or brief sharp storm of wind. **2.** a short spell of rough weather. **3.** *Obs.* a burst of feeling, fury, etc. [t. Scand.; cf. Sw. *flaga* gust]

flaw·y (flô/ĭ), *adj.* characterized by gusts, as wind.

flax (flăks), *n.* **1.** any plant of the genus *Linum*, esp. *L. usitatissimum*, a slender, erect annual plant with narrow, lance-shaped leaves and blue flowers, much cultivated for its fiber and seeds. **2.** the fiber of this plant, manufactured into linen yarn for thread or woven fabrics. **3.** any of various plants resembling flax. [ME; OE *fleax*, c. D and LG *vlas*, *G flachs*]

flax·en (flăk/sən), *adj.* **1.** made of flax. **2.** resembling flax. **3.** pertaining to flax. **4.** of the pale-yellowish color of dressed flax. Also, **flax/y.**

flax·seed (flăks/sēd/), *n.* the seed of flax, yielding linseed oil; linseed.

flay (flā), *v.t.* **1.** to strip off the skin or outer covering of. **2.** to criticise or reprove with scathing severity. **3.** to strip of money or property; fleece. [ME *flen*, etc., OE *flēan*, c. MD *vlaen*, Icel. *flā*] —**flay/er,** *n.*

flea (flē), *n.* **1.** any of numerous small, wingless, blood-sucking insects of the order *Siphonaptera*, parasitic upon mammals and birds, and noted for their powers of leaping. **2.** any of various small beetles and crustaceans which leap like a flea, or swim in a jumpy manner, as the water flea and beach flea. **3. flea in one's ear,** a discomfiting rebuke or rebuff; a sharp hint. [ME *fle*, OE *flēah*, *flēa*, c. G *floh*; akin to FLEE]

flea·bane (flē/bān/), *n.* any of various composite plants, as *Pulicaria dysenterica* of Europe or *Erigeron philadelphicus* of the U.S., reputed to destroy or drive away fleas.

*Dog flea.
Ctenocephalus canis
(Line shows actual length)*

ăct, āble, dâre, ärt; ĕbb, ēqual; ĭf, īce; hŏt, ōver, ôrder, oil, bŏŏk, ōōze, out; ŭp, ūse, ûrge; ə = a in alone; ch, chief; g, give; ng, ring; sh, shoe; th, thin; ᵺ, that; zh, vision. See the full key on inside cover.

flea beetle, any of certain leaf beetles, noted for their ability to leap.

flea·bite (flē′bīt′), *n.* **1.** the bite of a flea. **2.** the red spot caused by it. **3.** a trifling wound, annoyance, etc.

flea-bit·ten (flē′bĭt′ən), *adj.* **1.** bitten by a flea or fleas. **2.** (of a horse, etc.) having small reddish spots or streaks upon a lighter ground.

fleam (flēm), *n. Surg.* a kind of lancet, as for opening veins. [t. OF: m. *flieme,* ult. der. LL *phlebotomus* lancet, t. Gk.: m. *phlebotómos* opening veins. Cf. PHLEBOTOMY]

flea-wort (flē′wûrt′), *n.* **1.** a rough-leaved composite herb of Europe, *Inula Conyza.* **2.** a European plantain, *Plantago Psyllium,* whose seeds resemble fleas and are used in medicine.

flèche (flāsh; *Fr.* flĕsh), *n.* **1.** *Archit.* **a.** a spire, esp. a small light spire decorating a roof. **b.** a slender spire rising from the junction of the nave and transepts of a church, or sometimes crowning the apse. **2.** *Fort.* a fieldwork consisting of two faces forming a salient angle, open at the gorge. [t. F: arrow, prob. t. Gmc.; cf. FLY[1]]

flé·chette (flā shĕt′; *Fr.* flĕ-), *n. Mil.* a steel dart thrown from an airplane, used chiefly in World War I in personnel strafing. [t. F, dim. of *flèche* arrow]

fleck (flĕk), *n.* **1.** a spot or mark on the skin, as a freckle. **2.** any spot or patch of color, light, etc. **3.** a speck; a small bit. [n. use of FLECK, v., or back formation from *flecked,* ppl. adj., ME *flekked;* cf. G *fleck* spot] —*v.t.* **4.** to mark with a fleck or flecks; spot; dapple. [t. Scand.; cf. Icel. *flekka*]

fleck·less (flĕk′lĭs), *adj.* without flecks or spots.

flec·tion (flĕk′shən), *n.* **1.** act of bending. **2.** state of being bent. **3.** a bend; a bent part. **4.** *Anat.* flexion. **5.** *Gram.* inflection. Also, *esp. Brit.,* **flexion** for 1–3. [t. L: m.s. *flexio* a bending] —**flec′tion·al,** *adj.* —**flec′tion·less,** *adj.*

fled (flĕd), *v.* pt. and pp. of **flee.**

fledge (flĕj), *v.,* **fledged, fledging,** —*v.t.* **1.** to bring up (a young bird) until it is able to fly. **2.** to furnish with or as with feathers or plumage; feather (an arrow). —*v.i.* **3.** (of a young bird) to acquire the feathers necessary for flight. —*adj.* **4.** (of young birds) able to fly; having the wings developed for flight. [ME *flegge,* OE *-fligge,* in *unfligge* unfledged]

fledg·ling (flĕj′lĭng), *n.* **1.** a young bird just fledged. **2.** an inexperienced person. Also, *esp. Brit.,* **fledge·ling.**

fledg·y (flĕj′ĭ), *adj. Rare.* feathered or feathery.

flee (flē), *v.,* **fled, fleeing.** —*v.i.* **1.** to run away, as from danger, pursuers, etc.; take flight. **2.** to move swiftly; fly; speed. —*v.t.* **3.** to run away from (a place, person, etc.). [ME *flee(n),* OE *flēon,* c. G *fliehen*]

fleece (flēs), *n., v.,* **fleeced, fleecing.** —*n.* **1.** the coat of wool that covers a sheep or some similar animal. **2.** the wool shorn from a sheep at one time. **3.** something resembling a fleece: *a fleece of hair.* **4.** a fabric with a soft, silky pile, used for warmth, as for lining garments. **5.** the soft nap or pile of such a fabric. —*v.t.* **6.** to deprive (a sheep) of the fleece. **7.** to strip of money or belongings; plunder; swindle. **8.** to overspread as with a fleece; fleck with fleecelike masses. [ME *flees,* OE *flēos,* c. G *fliess*] —**fleece′a·ble,** *adj.* —**fleeced** (flēst), *adj.* —**fleece′less,** *adj.* —**fleec′er,** *n.*

fleec·y (flē′sĭ), *adj.,* **fleecier, fleeciest.** covered with, consisting of, or resembling a fleece or wool. —**fleec′i·ly,** *adv.* —**fleec′i·ness,** *n.*

fleer[1] (flĭr), *Dial.* —*v.i.* **1.** to grin or laugh coarsely or mockingly. —*v.t.* **2.** to fleer at; deride. —*n.* **3.** a fleering look; a jeer or gibe. [ME *flery(e), flire.* Cf. Norw. *flire* grin] —**fleer′ing·ly,** *adv.*

fle·er[2] (flē′ər), *n.* one who flees. [f. FLEE + -ER[3]]

fleet[1] (flēt), *n.* **1.** the largest organized unit of naval ships grouped for tactical or other purposes. **2.** the largest organization of warships under the command of a single officer (usually called the Commander in Chief). **3.** a number of naval vessels, or vessels carrying armed men. **4.** a large number of vessels of a commercial steamship company. **5.** a number of airplanes, automobiles, etc., moving or operating in company. [ME *flete,* OE *flēot* ship, craft, der. *flēotan* float]

fleet[2] (flēt), *adj.* **1.** swift; rapid: *fleet of foot, a fleet horse.* [adj. use of v. Cf. Icel. *fliótr*] —*v.i.* **2.** to move swiftly; fly. **3.** *Naut.* to change position; shift. **4.** *Archaic.* to glide away like a stream. **5.** *Archaic.* to fade; vanish. **6.** *Obs.* to float; drift. **7.** *Obs.* to swim; sail. —*v.t.* **8.** to cause (time) to pass lightly or swiftly. **9.** *Naut.* to change the position of; shift. [ME *flete(n),* v., OE *flēotan* float, G *fliessen* flow] —**fleet′ly,** *adv.* —**fleet′ness,** *n.*

fleet[3] (flēt), *n.* **1.** *Dial.* or in *Place Names.* an arm of the sea; an inlet; a creek. **2.** the **Fleet,** a former London prison, long used for debtors. [ME *flete,* OE *flēot* flowing water, c. G *fliess* brook]

Fleet Admiral, *U.S. Navy.* the highest ranking naval officer, ranking next above admiral (equivalent to *General of the Army* of the U.S. Army).

fleet-foot·ed (flēt′fŏŏt′ĭd), *adj.* swift of foot.

fleet·ing (flē′tĭng), *adj.* gliding swiftly away; passing swiftly; transient; transitory. —**fleet′ing·ly,** *adv.* —**fleet′ing·ness,** *n.*

Fleet Street, a famous old street in central London, now the location of many newspaper offices: often used figuratively for the English newspaper world.

Flem·ing (flĕm′ĭng), *n.* **1.** a native of Flanders. **2.** a Flemish-speaking Belgian.

Flem·ing (flĕm′ĭng), *n.* **Sir Alexander,** 1881–1955, British bacteriologist; discoverer of penicillin, 1929.

Flem·ish (flĕm′ĭsh), *adj.* **1.** of or pertaining to Flanders, its people, or their language. —*n.* **2.** the people of Flanders, the Flemings. **3.** one of the official languages of Belgium, a Germanic language very similar to Dutch.

flense (flĕns), *v.t.,* **flensed, flensing. 1.** to strip the blubber or the skin from (a whale, seal, etc.). **2.** to strip off (blubber or skin). Also, **flench** (flĕnch), **flinch.** [t. D]

flesh (flĕsh), *n.* **1.** the soft substance of an animal body, consisting of muscle and fat. **2.** muscular tissue. **3.** fatness; weight: *to put on flesh.* **4.** such substance of animals as an article of food, usually excluding fish and sometimes fowl; meat. **5.** the body, esp. as distinguished from the spirit or soul. **6.** man's physical or animal nature, as distinguished from his moral or spiritual nature. **7.** mankind. **8.** living creatures generally. **9.** one's kindred or family, or a member of it. **10.** *Bot.* the soft pulpy portion of a fruit, vegetable, etc., as distinguished from the core, skin, shell, etc. **11.** the surface of the body, esp. with respect to color. **12.** flesh color; pinkish white with a tinge of yellow; pinkish cream. **13. in the flesh, a.** alive. **b.** in bodily form; in person. —*v.t.* **14.** to plunge (a weapon) into the flesh. **15.** *Hunting.* to feed (a hound or hawk) with flesh in order to make it more eager for the chase. **16.** to incite and accustom (persons) to bloodshed or battle by an initial experience. **17.** to inflame the ardor or passions of by a taste of indulgence. **18.** to feed full with flesh, and hence with fleshly enjoyments, spoil, etc. **19.** to clothe (a skeleton, etc.) with flesh; make fleshy. **20.** to remove adhering flesh from (hides), for leather and for manufacture. [ME; OE *flǣsc,* c. G *fleisch*] —**flesh′less,** *adj.*

flesh and blood, 1. offspring or relatives: *one's own flesh and blood.* **2.** human nature: *more than flesh and blood can endure.*

flesh color, a pinkish-white color with a tinge of yellow; a pinkish-cream color. —**flesh′-col′ored,** *adj.*

flesh·er (flĕsh′ər), *n.* **1.** one who fleshes hides. **2.** a tool for fleshing hides.

flesh fly, any fly of the dipterous family *Sarcophagidae* which deposits its larvae in the flesh of living animals.

flesh·hook (flĕsh′hŏŏk′), *n.* **1.** a hook for use in lifting meat, as from a pot. **2.** a hook to hang meat on.

flesh·ings (flĕsh′ĭngz), *n.pl.* flesh-colored tights.

flesh·ly (flĕsh′lĭ), *adj.,* -**lier,** -**liest. 1.** of or pertaining to the flesh or body; bodily, corporeal, or physical. **2.** carnal; sensual. **3.** worldly, rather than spiritual. **4.** *Obs.* having much flesh; fleshy. —**flesh′li·ness,** *n.*

flesh·pot (flĕsh′pŏt′), *n.* **1.** a pot or vessel containing flesh or meat. **2.** (*pl.*) good living; luxuries.

flesh wound, a wound which does not extend beyond the flesh; a slight wound.

flesh·y (flĕsh′ĭ), *adj.,* **fleshier, fleshiest. 1.** having much flesh; plump; fat. **2.** consisting of or resembling flesh. **3.** *Bot.* consisting of fleshlike substance; pulpy, as a fruit; thick and tender, as a leaf. —**flesh′i·ness,** *n.*

fletch (flĕch), *v.t.* **1.** to provide (an arrow) with a feather. —*n.* **2.** (*pl.*) the feathers on an arrow.

fletch·er (flĕch′ər), *n. Archaic.* one who makes or deals in arrows, or bows and arrows. [t. OF: m. *flechier,* der. *flèche* arrow]

Fletch·er (flĕch′ər), *n.* **1. John,** 1579–1625, English dramatist who collaborated with Francis Beaumont. **2. John Gould,** 1886–1950, U.S. poet.

Fletch·er·ism (flĕch′ə rĭz′əm), *n.* the practice of chewing food until it is reduced to a finely divided, liquefied mass, as advocated by Horace Fletcher (1849–1919) as a nutritional measure.

Fletch·er·ize (flĕch′ə rīz′), *v.i., v.t.,* -**ized,** -**izing.** to masticate (food) thoroughly.

fleur-de-lis (flœr′də lē′), *n., pl.* **fleurs-de-lis** (flœr′-də lēz′). **1.** a heraldic device somewhat resembling three petals or floral segments of an iris tied by an encircling band. **2.** the distinctive bearing of the royal family of France. **3.** the iris (flower or plant). [t. F: lily flower; r. ME *flour-de-lys,* t. OF]

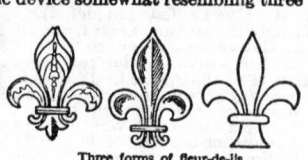

Three forms of fleur-de-lis

Fleu·ry (flœ rē′), *n.* **1. André Hercule de** (än drė′ ėr kyl′ də), 1653–1743, French cardinal and statesman. **2. Claude** (klōd), 1640–1723, French ecclesiastical historian.

flew[1] (flŏŏ), *v.* pt. of **fly**[1].

flew[2] (flŏŏ), *n.* flue[3].

flews (flŏŏz), *n.pl.* the large pendulous upper lip of certain dogs, as bloodhounds.

flex (flĕks), *v.t., v.i.* to bend, as a part of the body. [t. L: s. *flexus,* pp.]

flex·i·ble (flĕk′sə bəl), *adj.* **1.** capable of being bent; easily bent. **2.** susceptible of modification or adaptation; adaptable. **3.** willing or disposed to yield. [t. L: m.s. *flexibilis*] —**flex′i·bil′i·ty, flex′i·ble·ness,** *n.* —**flex′i·bly,** *adv.*

—**Syn. 1.** FLEXIBLE, LIMBER, PLIANT refer to that which bends easily. FLEXIBLE refers to that which is capable of being bent and adds sometimes the idea of compressibility or expansibility: *a flexible piece of rubber hose.* LIMBER is esp. applied to the body to refer to ease of movement; it also resembles FLEXIBLE except that there is an idea of even greater ease in bending: *a young and limber body, a limber willow wand.* PLIANT stresses an inherent quality or tendency to bend which does not require force or pressure from the outside; it may mean merely adaptable or may have a derogatory sense: *a pliant mind, character.* —**Ant. 1.** stiff.

flex·ile (flĕk′sĭl), *adj.* flexible; pliant; tractable; adaptable. [t. L: m.s. *flexilis*]

flex·ion (flĕk′shən), *n.* **1.** *Anat.* **a.** the motion of a joint which brings the connected parts continually nearer together; the action of any flexor muscle (opposed to *extension*). **b.** state of a part so moved. **2.** Chiefly *Brit.* flection (defs. 1, 2, 3). [t. L: s. *flexio* a bending] —**flex′ion·al,** *adj.* —**flex′ion·less,** *adj.*

Flex·ner (flĕks′nər), *n.* **1. Abraham,** 1866–1959, U.S. educator. **2.** his brother, **Simon,** 1863–1946, U.S. physician.

flex·or (flĕk′sər), *n. Anat.* a muscle which serves to flex or bend a part of the body. [NL. See FLEX, -OR²]

flex·u·os·i·ty (flĕk′shŏŏ ŏs′ə tĭ), *n.* quality or condition of being flexuous.

flex·u·ous (flĕk′shŏŏ əs), *adj.* full of bends or curves; winding; sinuous. Also, **flex·u·ose** (flĕk′shŏŏ ōs′). [t. L: m.s. *flexuōsus,* der. *flexus* a bending] —**flex′u·ous·ly,** *adv.*

flex·ure (flĕk′shər), *n.* **1.** act of flexing or bending. **2.** state of being flexed or bent. **3.** the part bent; a bend; a fold. [t. L: m.s. *flexūra* a bending] —**flex′ur·al,** *adj.*

flib·ber·ti·gib·bet (flĭb′ər tĭ jĭb′ĭt), *n.* **1.** a chattering or flighty person, usually a woman. **2.** (*cap.*) *Obs.* the name of a fiend.

flic·flac (flĭk′flăk′), *n.* a step in dancing in which the feet strike rapidly together. [t. F; imit. of the sound]

flick (flĭk), *n.* **1.** a sudden light blow or stroke, as with a whip or the finger. **2.** the sound thus made. **3.** something thrown off with or as with a jerk: *a flick of spray.* **4.** (*usually pl.*) *Brit. Slang.* motion pictures. —*v.t.* **5.** to strike lightly with a whip, the finger, etc. **6.** to remove with such a stroke: *to flick dust from one's coat,* to flick away a crumb. **7.** to move (something) with a sudden stroke or jerk. —*v.i.* **8.** to move with a jerk or jerks. **9.** to flutter. [late ME *flykke;* appar. imit.]

flick·er¹ (flĭk′ər), *v.i.* **1.** to burn unsteadily; shine with a wavering light. **2.** to wave to and fro; vibrate; quiver. **3.** to flutter. —*v.t.* **4.** to cause to flicker. —*n.* **5.** an unsteady flame or light. **6.** a flickering; flickering movement. **7.** a brief spark: *a flicker of hope.* [ME *flickeren,* OE *flicorian* flutter] —**flick′er·ing·ly,** *adv.*

flick·er² (flĭk′ər), *n.* any of several North American woodpeckers of the genus *Colaptes* with bright wing and tail linings, esp. *C. auratus,* of eastern parts of the continent. [imit. of the bird's note]

fli·er (flī′ər), *n.* **1.** something that flies, as a bird or insect. **2.** one who or that which moves with great speed. **3.** an aviator. **4.** some part of a machine having a rapid motion. **5.** a flying jump or leap. **6.** *U.S. Colloq.* a financial venture outside of one's ordinary business. **7.** *Archit.* a single step or a straight flight of steps or stairs. **b.** (*pl.*) stairs of straight flights (opposed to *winding stairs*). **8.** *U.S.* a small handbill. Also, **flyer.**

flight¹ (flīt), *n.* **1.** act, manner, or power of flying. **2.** the distance covered or the course pursued by a flying object. **3.** a number of beings or things flying or passing through the air together: *a flight of swallows.* **4.** a journey by air, esp. by airplane. **5.** a scheduled trip on an air line. **6.** the basic tactical unit of military air forces, consisting of two or more aircraft. **7.** act, principles, or art of flying an airplane. **8.** swift movement in general, as of a missile. **9.** a soaring above or transcending ordinary bounds: *a flight of fancy.* **10.** *Archit.* **a.** the series of steps or stairs between two adjacent landings. **b.** a series of steps, etc., ascending without change of direction. **11.** *Archery.* **a.** a light arrow for long-distance shooting. **b.** a contest with such arrows. —*v.i.* **12.** (of wild fowl) to fly in flights (def. 3). [ME; OE *flyht,* c. D *vlucht;* akin to FLY, v.]

flight² (flīt), *n.* **1.** act of fleeing; hasty departure. **2.** put to flight, to force to flee; rout. **3. take (to) flight,** to flee. [ME; c. G *flucht;* akin to FLEE]

flight arrow, *Archery.* **1.** an arrow having a conical or pyramidal head without barbs. **2.** a long and light arrow in general; a shaft or arrow for the longbow, as distinguished from the bolt.

flight deck, *Naval.* the upper deck of an aircraft carrier, constructed and equipped for the landing and take-off of aircraft.

flight feather, *Ornith.* one of the large, stiff feathers which form most of the extent of a bird's wing, and which are essential to flight.

flight formation, two or more airplanes flying in some set arrangement.

flight·less (flīt′lĭs), *adj.* incapable of flying.

flight·y (flī′tĭ), *adj.* **flightier, flightiest. 1.** given to flights or sallies of fancy, caprice, etc.; volatile; frivolous. **2.** slightly delirious; light-headed; mildly crazy. **3.** *Rare.* swift or fleet. [f. FLIGHT¹ + -Y¹] —**flight′i·ly,** *adv.* —**flight′i·ness,** *n.*

flim-flam (flĭm′flăm′), *n., v., -flammed, -flamming. Colloq.* —*n.* **1.** a piece of nonsense; mere nonsense.

2. a trick or deception; humbug. —*v.t.* **3.** to trick; delude; humbug; cheat. [cf. Icel. *flimska* mockery] —flim/flam/mer, *n.*

flim·sy (flĭm′zĭ), *adj.,* **-sier, -siest,** *n., pl.* **-sies.** —*adj.* **1.** without material strength or solidity: *a flimsy material,* a flimsy structure. **2.** weak; inadequate; not carefully thought out: *a flimsy excuse or argument.* —*n.* **3.** a thin kind of paper, esp. for use in making several copies of a writing, telegraphic dispatch, etc., at once, as in newspaper work. **4.** *Brit.* a copy of a report or dispatch on such paper. **5.** *Slang.* a bank note. [f. FILM (by metathesis) + -sy, adj. suffix] —**flim′si·ly,** *adv.* —**flim′si·ness,** *n.*

flinch¹ (flĭnch), *v.i.* **1.** to draw back or shrink from what is dangerous, difficult, or unpleasant. **2.** to shrink under pain; wince. **3.** *Croquet.* to let the foot slip from the ball in the act of croqueting. —*v.t.* **4.** to draw back or withdraw from. —*n.* **5.** act of flinching. **6.** *Cards.* a game in which the cards are accumulated on the table. [? nasalized var. of d. *flitch* flit, shift (one's) position] —**flinch′er,** *n.* —**flinch′ing·ly,** *adv.*

flinch² (flĭnch), *v.t.* flense. [var. of FLENSE]

flin·ders (flĭn′dərz), *n. pl.* splinters; small pieces or fragments. [cf. Norw. *flindra* splinter]

fling (flĭng), *v.,* **flung, flinging,** *n.* —*v.t.* **1.** to throw, cast, or hurl; throw with force or violence; throw with impatience, disdain. etc. **2.** to put suddenly or violently: *to fling one into jail.* **3.** to send forth suddenly and rapidly: *to fling fresh troops into a battle.* **4.** to throw aside or off. **5.** to throw to the ground, as in wrestling or from horseback. —*v.i.* **6.** to move with haste or violence; rush; dash. **7.** to fly into violent and irregular motions, as a horse; throw the body about, as a person. **8.** to utter harsh or abusive language (usually fol. by *out*). —*n.* **9.** act of flinging. **10.** a spell of unrestrained indulgence of one's impulses: *to have one's fling.* **11.** an attack upon or attempt at something, as in passing. **12.** a severe or contemptuous remark or gibe. **13.** a lively Scotch dance characterized by flinging movements of the legs and arms (commonly called **Highland fling**). [ME. Cf. Sw. *flänga* fly, race] —**fling′er,** *n.*

flint (flĭnt), *n.* **1.** a hard kind of stone, a form of silica resembling chalcedony but more opaque, less pure, and less lustrous. **2.** a piece of this, esp. as used for striking fire. **3.** something very hard or obdurate. —*v.t.* **4.** to furnish with flint. [ME and OE, c. MD *vlint,* Dan. *flint.* Cf. PLINTH.]

Flint (flĭnt), *n.* **1.** a city in SE Michigan. 196,940 (1960). **2.** Flintshire. **3. Austin,** 1812–1886, U.S. physician. **4.** his son, **Austin,** 1836–1915, U.S. physiologist and physician.

flint corn, a variety of maize, *Zea mays indurata,* having very hard-skinned kernels not subject to shrinkage.

flint glass, 1. an optical glass of high dispersion and relatively high index of refraction. **2.** a glass containing alkalis, lead oxide, and silica, with or without other bases. **3.** a colorless glass.

flint·head (flĭnt′hĕd′), *n.* the wood ibis (*Mycteria americana*) of North and South America (so named because the naked head is hard in appearance).

flint·lock (flĭnt′lŏk′), *n.* **1.** a gunlock in which a piece of flint striking against steel produces sparks which ignite the priming. **2.** a firearm with such a lock.

Flintlock fowling piece
A. Steel struck by flint; B. Powder pan; C. Touchhole; D. Flint; E. Cock

Flint·shire (flĭnt′shĭr, -shər), *n.* a county in NE Wales. 145,297 pop. (1951); 256 sq. mi. *Co. seat:* Mold. Also, **Flint.**

flint·y (flĭn′tĭ), *adj.,* **flintier, flintiest. 1.** composed of, containing, or resembling flint; hard as flint. **2.** obdurate; cruel; unmerciful: *a flinty heart.* —**flint′i·ly,** *adv.* —**flint′i·ness,** *n.*

flip¹ (flĭp), *v.,* **flipped, flipping,** *n.* —*v.t.* **1.** to toss or put in motion with a snap of a finger and thumb; fillip; flick. **2.** to move (something) with a jerk or jerks. —*v.i.* **3.** to make a fillip; strike smartly at something. **4.** to move with a jerk or jerks. **5.** flip up, to toss a coin. —*n.* **6.** a fillip; a smart tap or strike. **7.** a sudden jerk. [prob. imit.]

flip² (flĭp), *n.* a mixed drink made with liquor or wine, sugar, and egg, powdered with nutmeg. [? n. use of FLIP¹]

flip³ (flĭp), *adj.,* **flipper, flippest.** *Colloq.* smart; pert; flippant. [adj. use of FLIP¹]

flip·pant (flĭp′ənt), *adj.* **1.** smart or pert in speech. **2.** characterized by a shallow or disrespectful levity. **3.** *Obs.* voluble; talkative. **4.** *Obs. or Dial.* nimble, limber, or pliant. [orig. obscure; but cf. Icel. *fleipa* babble] —**flip′pan·cy, flip′pant·ness,** *n.* —**flip′pant·ly,** *adv.*

flip·per (flĭp′ər), *n.* **1.** a broad, flat limb, as of a seal, whale, etc., especially adapted for swimming. **2.** *Slang.* the hand.

flirt (flûrt), *v.i.* **1.** to trifle in love; play at love; coquet. **2.** to trifle or toy (with an idea, etc.). **3.** to move with a jerk or jerks; dart about. —*v.t.* **4.** to give a sudden or brisk motion to; wave smartly, as a fan. **5.** to throw or propel with a toss or jerk; fling suddenly. —*n.* **6.** a person (woman or man) given to flirting. **7.** a quick throw or toss; a sudden jerk; a darting motion. [imit.] —flirt′er, n. —flirt′ing·ly, adv.

flir·ta·tion (flŭr tā′shən), n. **1.** act or practice of flirting; coquetry. **2.** a love affair which is not serious.

flir·ta·tious (flŭr tā′shəs), adj. **1.** given to flirtation. **2.** pertaining to flirtation. Also, **flirt′y.** —flir·ta′-tious·ly, adv. —flir·ta′tious·ness, n.

flit (flĭt), v., **flitted, flitting,** n. —v.i. **1.** to move lightly and swiftly; fly, dart, or skim along. **2.** to flutter, as a bird. **3.** to pass away quickly, as time. **4.** Chiefly Scot. and N. Eng. **a.** to depart or die. **b.** to change one's residence. —v.t. **5.** Archaic. to remove; transfer; oust or dispossess. —n. **6.** a light, swift movement; a flutter. **7.** Chiefly Scot. and N. Eng. a removal. [ME flitten, t. Scand.; cf. Icel. flytja carry, convey] —Syn. **1.** See fly¹.

flitch (flĭch), n. **1.** the side of a hog (or, formerly, some other animal) salted and cured: a flitch of bacon. **2.** a steak cut from a halibut. —v.t. **3.** to cut into flitches. [ME flicche, OE flicce, c. MLG vlike, Icel. flikki]

flite (flīt), v., **flited, fliting,** n. Now Scot. and N. Eng. —v.i. **1.** to dispute; wrangle; scold; jeer. —n. **2.** a dispute or wrangle; a scolding. Also, **flyte.** [ME flite(n), OE flītan strive, contend]

flit·ing (flī′tĭng), n. **1.** contention. **2.** war of words, in versified dialogue.

flit·ter¹ (flĭt′ər), v.i., v.t. to flutter. [freq. of FLIT]

flit·ter² (flĭt′ər), n. one who or that which flits. [f. FLIT, v. + -ER¹]

flit·ter·mouse (flĭt′ər mous′), n., pl. **-mice.** Obs. a bat (animal). [f. FLITTER¹ + MOUSE. Cf. G fledermaus]

flit·ting (flĭt′ĭng), adj. moving lightly and swiftly; passing quickly; fluttering. —flit′ting·ly, adv.

fliv·ver (flĭv′ər), n. **1.** Slang. something of unsatisfactory quality or inferior grade, as an automobile. **2.** Humorous. any automobile. [orig. meaning a failure; ? b. flopper (der. FLOP) and fizzler (der. FIZZLE)]

float (flōt), v.i. **1.** to rest on the surface of a liquid; be buoyant. **2.** to move gently on the surface of a liquid; drift along. **3.** to rest or move in a liquid, the air, etc. **4.** to move or hover before the eyes or in the mind. **5.** to pass from one to another, as a rumor. **6.** to move or drift about free from attachment. **7.** to be launched or floated, as a company, scheme, etc. **8.** Com. to be in circulation, as an acceptance; be awaiting maturity. —v.t. **9.** to cause to float. **10.** to cover with water; flood; irrigate. **11.** to launch (a company, scheme, etc.); set going. **12.** to sell on the market, as a stock or a bond **13.** to make smooth or level, as the surface of plaster —n. **14.** something that floats, as a raft. **15.** something for buoying up. **16.** an inflated bag to sustain a person in water; a life preserver. **17.** Plumbing, Mach., etc. (in certain apparatus, cisterns, etc.) a device, as a hollow ball, which through its buoyancy automatically regulates the level, supply, or outlet of a liquid. **18.** Naut. a floating platform fastened to a wharf or the shore, from which to embark in or land from boats, as a landing place at a ferry. **19.** Aeron. a hollow, boatlike part under the wing or fuselage of an airplane enabling it to float on water. **20.** Angling. a piece of cork for supporting a baited line in the water and showing by its movement when a fish bites. **21.** Zool. an inflated organ that supports an animal in the water. **22.** a platform on wheels, bearing a display, and drawn in a procession. **23.** a low-bodied dray for transporting heavy goods. **24.** any of various tools for smoothing, leveling, or the like, as a kind of file, a plasterer's trowel, etc. **25.** the loose yarn on the back of cloth due to a figure weave or brocading. **26.** Banking. uncollected checks and commercial paper in process of transfer from bank to bank. **27.** (pl.) Theat. the footlights. [ME flotie(n), OE flotian, c. Icel. flota, MD vloten. See FLEET², v.]

float·a·ble (flō′tə bəl), adj. **1.** capable of floating; that may be floated. **2.** that can be floated on, as a river.

float·age (flō′tĭj), n. flotage.

float·a·tion (flō tā′shən), n. Brit. flotation.

float·er (flō′tər), n. **1.** one who or that which floats. **2.** Colloq. one who is continually changing his place of abode, employment, etc. **3.** U.S. a voter not attached to any party, esp. one whose vote may be purchased. **4.** U.S. one who fraudulently votes, usually for pay, in different places in the same election.

float-feed (flōt′fēd′), adj. Mach. equipped with a float to control the feed.

float·ing (flō′tĭng), adj. **1.** that floats. **2.** free from attachment, or having but little attachment. **3.** Pathol. away from its proper position, esp. in a downward direction: a floating kidney. **4.** not fixed or settled in a definite place or state: floating population. **5.** Finance. **a.** in circulation or use, or not permanently invested, as capital. **b.** composed of sums due within a short time and not requiring frequent renewal or refinancing: a floating debt. **6.** Mach. having a vibration-free suspension; working smoothly. —float′ing·ly, adv.

floating dock, a floating structure which may be lowered in the water to admit a ship and then raised to leave the ship dry for repairs, etc.; a floating dry dock.

floating heart, any of certain perennial aquatic herbs of the genus Nymphoides, esp. N. lacunosum, with floating, more or less heart-shaped leaves.

floating island, 1. a dish consisting of boiled custard

with portions of meringue or whipped cream, and often bits of jelly, etc., floating upon it. **2.** a floating, islandlike mass of earth and partly decayed vegetation held together by interlacing roots, sometimes built artificially on wooden platforms as in the Orient, or resulting naturally from the accumulation of plant litter on a water surface.

floating ribs, Anat. the two lowest pairs of ribs in man, which are attached neither to the sternum nor to the cartilages of other ribs.

floating stock, stock not held for permanent investment and hence available for speculation; stock held by brokers and speculators rather than investors.

floating supply, the aggregate supply of ready-to-market goods or securities.

floating vote, U.S. the voters collectively who are not permanently attached to any political organization, and whose votes therefore cannot be counted upon by party managers.

float·y (flō′tĭ), adj. **1.** able to float; buoyant. **2.** (of a boat) drawing little water.

floc (flŏk), n. a tuftlike mass, as in a chemical precipitate. Also, **flock.** [short for FLOCCULE]

floc·cil·la·tion (flŏk′sə lā′shən), n. Pathol. a delirious picking of the bedclothes, etc., by the patient, as in certain fevers. [f. s. *floccillus (assumed dim. of L floccus flock of wool) + -ATION]

floc·cose (flŏk′ōs), adj. **1.** Bot. consisting of or bearing woolly tufts or long soft hairs. **2.** flocculent. [t. LL: m.s. floccōsus, der. L floccus flock of wool]

floc·cu·late (flŏk′yə lāt′), v., **-lated, -lating.** —v.t. **1.** to form into flocculent masses. —v.i. **2.** to form flocculent masses, as cloud, a chemical precipitate, etc.; form aggregated or compound masses of particles. —floc′cu·la′tion, n.

floc·cule (flŏk′ūl), n. **1.** something resembling a small flock or tuft of wool. **2.** a bit of flocculent matter, as in a liquid. [t. NL: m.s. flocculus. See FLOCCULUS]

floc·cu·lent (flŏk′yə lənt), adj. **1.** like a flock or flocks of wool; covered with a soft woolly substance. **2.** consisting of or containing loose woolly masses. **3.** flaky. —floc′cu·lence, n. —floc′cu·lent·ly, adv.

flocculent precipitate, Chem. a woolly-looking precipitate, like that of aluminum hydroxide, from the solution of an aluminum salt to which ammonia is added.

floc·cu·lus (flŏk′yə ləs), n., pl. **-li** (-lī′). **1.** floccule. **2.** Astron. one of the bright or dark patches which mottle the sun's chromosphere, visible in spectroheliograms. [NL, dim. of L floccus flock of wool]

floc·cus (flŏk′əs), n., pl. **flocci** (flŏk′sī). a small tuft of woolly hairs. [t. L]

flock¹ (flŏk), n. **1.** a number of animals of one kind keeping, feeding, or herded together, now esp. of sheep or goats, or of birds. **2.** a crowd; large number of people. **3.** (in New Testament and ecclesiastical use) **a.** the Christian church in relation to Christ. **b.** a single congregation in relation to its pastor. **4.** Now Rare. a band or company of persons. —v.i. **5.** to gather or go in a flock, company, or crowd. [ME; OE flocc, c. Icel. flokkr] —flock′less, adj.
—Syn. **1, 2.** bevy, covey, flight, gaggle; brood, hatch, litter; shoal, school, swarm. FLOCK, DROVE, HERD, PACK refer to a company of animals, often under the care or guidance of someone. FLOCK is the popular term, which applies to groups of animals, esp. of sheep or goats, and companies of birds: this lamb is the choicest of the flock, a flock of wild geese flew overhead. DROVE is esp. applied to a number of oxen, sheep, or swine when driven in a group: a drove of oxen was taken to market, a large drove of swine filled the roadway. HERD is usually applied to large animals such as cattle, originally under the charge of someone; but by extension, to other animals feeding or driven together: a buffalo herd, a herd of elephants. PACK applies to a number of animals kept together; or herding together for offense or defense: a pack of hounds kept for hunting, a pack of wolves. As applied to crowds of people, DROVE, HERD, and PACK carry a contemptuous implication.

flock² (flŏk), n. **1.** a lock or tuft of wool, hair, etc. **2.** (pl. or sing.) wool refuse, shearings of cloth, old cloth torn to pieces, etc., used for stuffing mattresses, upholstering furniture, etc. **3.** (sing. or pl.) finely powdered wool, cloth, etc., used in making wallpaper. **4.** floc. —v.t. **5.** to stuff with flock, as a mattress. **6.** to cover or coat with flock, as wallpaper. [ME flokke, appar. t. OF: m. floc, g. L floccus flock of wool. Cf. OHG floccho]

flock dot, a pattern of dots or figures not woven but fastened to cloth with adhesive.

flock·y (flŏk′ĭ), adj. like flocks or tufts; flocculent.

Flod·den (flŏd′ən), n. a hill in NE England, in Northumberland county: the invading Scots were disastrously defeated here by the English in a famous battle, 1513.

floe (flō), n. **1.** a field of floating ice formed on the surface of the sea, etc. **2.** a detached floating portion of such a field. [? t. Norw.: m. flo. Cf. Icel. flō]

flog (flŏg, flôg), v.t., **flogged, flogging.** to beat hard with a whip, stick, etc.; whip. [? b. FLAY and jog, var. of JAG¹, v., prick, slash (but cf. FLAGELLATE)] —flog′ger, n.

flog·ging (flŏg′ĭng, flôg′ĭng), n. punishment by beating or whipping.

flood (flŭd), n. **1.** a great flowing or overflowing of water, esp. over land not usually submerged. **2.** the Flood, the universal deluge recorded as having occurred in the days of Noah. Gen. 7. **3.** Poetic. the sea; a river;

a lake; any large body of water in general. **4.** any great outpouring or stream: *a flood of words, tears, light, lava, etc.* **5.** the flowing in of the tide (opposed to *ebb*). —*v.t.* **6.** to overflow in or cover with a flood; fill to overflowing. **7.** to cover as with a flood. **8.** to overwhelm with an abundance of something. —*v.i.* **9.** to flow or pour in or as in a flood. **10.** to rise in a flood; overflow. **11.** *Med.* **a.** to suffer uterine hemorrhage, esp. in connection with parturition. **b.** to have an excessive menstrual flow. [ME; OE *flōd*, c. G *flut*] —**flood/a·ble,** *adj.* —**flood/-er,** *n.* —**flood/less,** *adj.*

—**Syn. 1.** FLOOD, FLASH FLOOD, DELUGE, FRESHET, INUNDATION refer to the overflowing of normally dry areas, usually after heavy rains. FLOOD is usually applied to the overflow of a great body of water, as for example a river, though it may refer to any water which overflows an area: *a flood along the river, a flood in a basement.* A FLASH FLOOD is one which comes so suddenly that no preparation can be made against it; it is usually destructive, but begins almost at once to subside: *a flash flood caused by a downpour.* DELUGE suggests a great downpouring of water, usually with much destruction: *the rain came down in a deluge.* FRESHET suggests a small, quick overflow such as that caused by heavy rains: *a freshet in an abandoned watercourse.* INUNDATION, a literary word, suggests the covering of a great area of land by water: *the inundation of thousands of acres.*

flood control, *Civ. Eng.* the technique of controlling river flow with dams, dikes, artificial channels, etc., so as to minimize the occurrence of floods.

flood·gate (flŭd/gāt/), *n.* **1.** *Civ. Eng.* a gate designed to regulate the flow of water. **2.** anything serving to control indiscriminate flow or passage.

flood·light (flŭd/līt/), *n.* **1.** an artificial light so directed or diffused as to give a comparatively uniform illumination over a given area. **2.** a floodlight lamp or projector. —*v.t.* **3.** to illuminate with floodlight.

floodlight projector, a powerful lamp having a reflector curved to produce a floodlight.

flood plain, *Phys. Geog.* a nearly flat plain along the course of a stream that is naturally subject to flooding at high water.

flood tide, the inflow of the tide; the rising tide.

floor (flōr), *n.* **1.** that part of a room or the like which forms its lower enclosing surface, and upon which one walks. **2.** a story of a building. **3.** a level supporting surface in any structure: *the floor of a bridge.* **4.** a platform or prepared level area for a particular use: *a threshing floor.* **5.** the flat bottom of any more or less hollow place: *the floor of the ocean.* **6.** a flat extent of surface. **7.** the part of a legislative chamber, etc., where the members sit, and from which they speak. **8.** the right of one member to speak from such a place in preference to other members: *to get or have the floor.* **9.** the main part of an exchange or the like, in distinction from galleries, etc. **10.** *Mining.* **a.** the bottom of a horizontal passageway. **b.** an underlying stratum, as of ore, usually flat. **11.** *Naut.* that part of the bottom of a vessel on each side of the keelson which is most nearly horizontal. **12.** the bottom, base, or minimum charged or paid: *a price or wage floor.* —*v.t.* **13.** to cover or furnish with a floor. **14.** to bring down to the floor or ground; knock down. **15.** *Colloq.* to beat or defeat. **16.** *Colloq.* to confound or nonplus: *to be floored by a problem.* [ME *flore,* OE *flōr,* c. G *flur*] —**floor/less,** *adj.*

floor·age (flōr/ĭj), *n.* floor space.

floor·cloth (flōr/klôth/, -klŏth/), *n.* **1.** a cloth for washing or wiping floors. **2.** a piece of cloth, as crash, drugget, linoleum, etc., used with or without a carpet for covering a floor.

floor·er (flōr/ər), *n.* **1.** one who lays floors. **2.** a person or thing, as a blow, that knocks to the floor. **3.** *Colloq.* something that beats, overwhelms, or confounds.

floor·ing (flōr/ĭng), *n.* **1.** a floor. **2.** floors collectively. **3.** materials for making floors.

floor leader, *U.S. Govt.* the party member in either the Senate or the House who directs the activities of his party on the floor.

floor show, an entertainment given in a night club or cabaret, usually consisting of a series of singing, dancing, and/or comic episodes.

floor·walk·er (flōr/wô/kər), *n.* a person employed in a store to direct customers, supervise salespeople, etc.

flop (flŏp), *v.,* **flopped, flopping,** *n.* —*v.i.* **1.** to fall or plump down suddenly, esp. with noise; drop or turn with a sudden bump or thud. **2.** to change suddenly, as from one side or party to another (often fol. by *over*). **3.** to yield or break down suddenly; fail. **4.** to flap, as in the wind. —*v.t.* **5.** to drop, throw, etc., with a sudden bump or thud. **6.** to flap clumsily and heavily, as wings. —*n.* **7.** act of flopping. **8.** the sound of flopping; a thud. **9.** a failure. [var. of FLAP] —**flop/per,** *n.*

flop·house (flŏp/hous/), *n.* a cheap hotel, usually for men only.

flop·py (flŏp/ĭ), *adj.,* **-pier, -piest.** *Colloq.* tending to flop. —**flop/pi·ly,** *adv.* —**flop/pi·ness,** *n.*

flor., (L *floruit*) flourished.

flo·ra (flōr/ə), *n., pl.* **floras, florae** (flōr/ē). **1.** the plants of a particular region or period, listed by species. **2.** a work systematically describing such plants. **3.** (*cap.*) the Roman goddess of flowers. [t. L, der. *flōs* flower]

flo·ral (flōr/əl), *adj.* **1.** pertaining to or consisting of flowers. **2.** (*cap.*) of or pertaining to the goddess Flora. [t. L: s. *Flōrālis* (def. 2)] —**flo/ral·ly,** *adv.*

floral envelope, *Bot.* the calyx and corolla of a flower.

Flo·re·al (flô rē äl/), *n.* (in the calendar of the first French republic) the eighth month of the year, extending from April 20 to May 19.

flo·re·at·ed (flōr/ĭ ā/tĭd), *adj.* floriated.

Flor·ence (flôr/əns, flŏr/-), *n.* **1.** a city in central Italy, on the Arno river: capital of the former grand duchy of Tuscany. 393,000 (est. 1954). Italian, *Firenze.* **2.** a city in NW Alabama, on Tennessee river. 31,649 (1960).

Flor·en·tine (flôr/ən tēn/, flôr/-; *less often* -tīn/), *adj.* **1.** of or pertaining to Florence, Italy: *the Florentine painters.* —*n.* **2.** a native or inhabitant of Florence.

Flo·res (flô/rĕs *for 1;* flō/rĭsh *for 2*), *n.* **1.** one of the Lesser Sunda Islands in Indonesia, separated from Celebes by the **Flores Sea.** With adjacent islands, 717,300 pop. (1930); 7753 sq. mi. **2.** the westernmost island of the Azores, in the N Atlantic. 7832 pop. (1950); 55 sq. mi.

flo·res·cence (flô rĕs/əns), *n.* act, state, or period of flowering; bloom. [t. NL: m.s. *flōrescentia,* der. L *flōrescens,* ppr., beginning to flower] —**flo·res/cent,** *adj.*

flo·ret (flōr/ĭt), *n.* **1.** a small flower. **2.** *Bot.* one of the closely clustered small flowers that make up the flower head of a composite flower, as the daisy. [cf. OF *florete,* dim. of *flor,* g. L *flōs* flower]

Flo·ri·a·nóp·o·lis (flōr/ĭ ə nŏp/ə lĭs; *Pg.* flôr/yə nô/-pŏō lēs/), *n.* a seaport on an island off the S coast of Brazil. 48,264 (1950). Formerly, **Desterro.**

flo·ri·at·ed (flōr/ĭ ā/tĭd), *adj.* decorated with floral ornamentation: *floriated columns.* Also, **floreated.**

flo·ri·cul·ture (flōr/ə kŭl/chər), *n.* the cultivation of flowers or flowering plants, esp. under glass. [f. L *flōri-* (comb. form of *flōs* flower) + CULTURE] —**flo/ri·cul/-tur·al,** *adj.* —**flo/ri·cul/tur·ist,** *n.*

flor·id (flôr/ĭd, flŏr/-), *adj.* **1.** high-colored or ruddy, as complexion, cheeks, persons, etc. **2.** flowery; excessively ornate; showy: *a florid prose style, florid music.* **3.** *Archit.* abounding in decorative features, as in baroque or rococo styles. **4.** *Archaic or Rare.* abounding in or consisting of flowers. [t. L: s. *flōridus* flowery] —**flo·rid·i·ty** (flô rĭd/ə tĭ), **flor/id·ness,** *n.* —**flor/id·ly,** *adv.*

Flor·i·da (flôr/ə də, flŏr/-), *n.* a State in the SE United States between the Atlantic and the Gulf of Mexico. 4,951,560 pop. (1960); 58,560 sq. mi. *Cap.:* Tallahassee. *Abbr.:* Fla. —**Flo·rid·i·an** (flô rĭd/ĭ ən), **Flor/i·dan,** *adj., n.*

Florida Keys, a chain of small islands and reefs off S Florida. ab. 225 mi. long.

Florida moss, a bromeliaceous epiphytic plant, *Tillandsia usneoides,* of the southern U.S., growing in long festoons which drape the branches of trees; Spanish moss.

Florida Strait, a strait separating Florida from Cuba and the Bahama Islands and connecting the Gulf of Mexico with the Atlantic.

flo·rif·er·ous (flô rĭf/ər əs), *adj.* flower-bearing. [f. L *flōrifer* bearing flowers + -OUS]

flor·in (flôr/ĭn, flŏr/-), *n.* **1.** an English silver coin worth 2 shillings, first minted in 1849. **2.** the gulden or florin of the Netherlands. **3.** a former gold coin weighing about 54 grains, first issued at Florence in 1252. **4.** a former English gold coin of Edward III, worth 6 shillings. [ME, t. F, t. It.: m. *fiorino* a Florentine coin stamped with a lily, der. *fiore,* g. L *flōs* flower]

Flo·ri·o (flōr/ĭ ō/), *n.* **John,** 1553?-1625, English lexicographer and translator.

flo·rist (flôr/ĭst, flōr/-), *n.* one who cultivates flowers, esp. for sale; a dealer in flowers.

flo·ris·tic (flô rĭs/tĭk), *adj.* pertaining to a flora.

-florous, an adjectival suffix meaning "flower," as in *uniflorous.* [t. L: m. *flōrus* flowered]

flos fer·ri (flŏs/ fĕr/ĭ), *Mineral.* a coralloid variety of aragonite. [t. L: flower of iron]

floss (flôs, flŏs), *n.* **1.** the cottony fiber yielded by the silk-cotton trees. **2.** silk filaments with little or no twist, used in weaving as brocade or in embroidery. **3.** any silky filamentous matter, as the silk of maize. Also, **floss silk.** [t. Scand.; cf. Icel. *flos* shag of velvet]

floss·y (flôs/ĭ, flŏs/ĭ), *adj.,* **flossier, flossiest.** made of or resembling floss.

flo·tage (flō/tĭj), *n.* **1.** act of floating. **2.** state of floating. **3.** floating power; buoyancy. **4.** *Colloq.* anything that floats; flotsam. **5.** the ships, etc., afloat on a river. **6.** the part of a ship above the water line. Also, **floatage.** [f. FLOAT, n. + -AGE. Cf. F *flottage*]

flo·ta·tion (flō tā/shən), *n.* **1.** act of floating. **2.** the floating or launching of a commercial venture, a loan, etc. **3.** *Metall.* a process for separating the different crystalline phasos in a mass of powdered ore based on their ability to sink in, or float on, a given liquid. **4.** the science of floating bodies. **5.** state of floating. Also, *Brit.,* **floatation.** [var. of *floatation.* Cf. F *flottaison* (see FLOTSAM)]

flo·til·la (flō tĭl/ə), *n.* **1.** number of small naval vessels; a subdivision of a fleet. **2.** a small fleet. [t. Sp., dim. of *flota* fleet, t. F: m. *flotte,* t. OE: m. *flota*]

Flo·tow (flō/tō), *n.* **Friedrich von** (frē/drĭKH fən), 1812-83, German operatic composer.

flot·sam (flŏt/səm), *n.* such part of the wreckage of a ship and its cargo as is found floating on the water. Cf. **jetsam.** [t. AF: m. *floteson,* der. *floter* float, t. OE: m. *flotian*]

flotsam and jetsam, **1.** the wreckage of a ship and its cargo found either floating upon the sea or washed ashore. **2.** odds and ends.

flounce[1] (flouns), *v.,* **flounced, flouncing,** *n.* —*v.i.* **1.** to go with an impatient or angry fling of the body (fol. by *away, off, out,* etc.): *to flounce out of a room in a rage.* **2.** to throw the body about, as in floundering or struggling; twist; turn; jerk. —*n.* **3.** action of flouncing; a flouncing movement. [t. Scand.; cf. Norw. *flunsa* hurry]

flounce[2] (flouns), *n., v.,* **flounced, flouncing.** —*n.* **1.** a strip of material, wider than a ruffle, gathered and attached at one edge and with the other edge left hanging: used for trimming, esp. on women's skirts. —*v.t.* **2.** to trim with a flounce or flounces. [var. of FROUNCE]

flounc·ing (floun′sÏng), *n.* **1.** material for flounces. **2.** trimming consisting of a flounce.

floun·der[1] (floun′dər), *v.i.* **1.** to struggle with stumbling or plunging movements (fol. by *along, on, through,* etc.). **2.** to struggle clumsily or helplessly in embarrassment or confusion. —*n.* **3.** action of floundering; a floundering movement. [? b. FLOUNCE[1] and FOUNDER[2]]

floun·der[2] (floun′dər), *n., pl.* **-ders,** *(esp. collectively)* **-der.** **1.** a European marine flatfish, *Platichthys flesus,* widely caught for food. **2.** any of a number of similar or closely related non-European flatfishes. **3.** any flatfish other than soles. [ME, t. AF: m. *floundre,* t. Scand.; cf. Norw. *flundra*]

flour (flour), *n.* **1.** the finely ground meal of grain, esp. the finer meal separated by bolting. **2.** the finely ground and bolted meal of wheat. **3.** any fine, soft powder: *flour of emery.* —*v.t.* **4.** to make (grain, etc.) into flour; grind and bolt. **5.** to sprinkle or dredge with flour, as food or utensils in cookery. **6.** *Mining.* to break up (mercury, in amalgamation) into fine globules, which, owing to some impurity, do not unite with a precious metal. [ME; special use of FLOWER. Cf. F *fleur de farine* the flower or finest part of the meal] —**flour′less,** *adj.*

flour·ish (flûr′Ïsh), *v.i.* **1.** to be in a vigorous state; thrive; prosper; be successful: *during this period art flourished.* **2.** to be in its or one's prime; be at the height of fame or excellence. **3.** to grow luxuriantly, or thrive in growth, as a plant. **4.** to make strokes or flourishes with a brandished weapon or the like. **5.** to make a parade or ostentatious display. **6.** to add embellishments or flourishes to writing, letters, etc. **7.** to speak or write in flowery or pretentious language. **8.** *Music.* **a.** to play a showy passage. **b.** to play in a showy manner. **c.** to sound a trumpet call or fanfare. —*v.t.* **9.** to brandish or wave (a sword, a stick, the limbs, etc.) about in the air. **10.** to parade, flaunt, or display ostentatiously: *to flourish one's wealth.* **11.** to embellish (writing, etc.) with sweeping or fanciful curves or lines. **12.** to adorn with decorative designs, color, etc. —*n.* **13.** a brandishing or waving, as of a sword, a stick, or the like. **14.** a parade or ostentatious display. **15.** a decoration or embellishment in writing. **16.** *Rhet.* a parade of fine language; an expression used merely for effect. **17.** *Music.* **a.** an elaborate passage or addition largely for display. **b.** a trumpet call or fanfare. **18.** *Rare.* the condition of flourishing or thriving: *in full flourish.* **19.** *Obs.* state of flowering. [ME *florish(en),* t. OF: m. *floriss-,* s. *florir,* ult. der. L *flōrēre* bloom] —**flour′ish·er,** *n.* —**Syn. 2.** See succeed.

flour·ish·ing (flûr′Ïsh Ïng), *adj.* that flourishes; vigorous in growth; thriving; prosperous. —**flour′ish·ing·ly,** *adv.*

flour mill, a mill for making flour.

flour·y (flour′Ï), *adj.* **1.** of, pertaining to, or resembling flour. **2.** covered or white with flour.

flout (flout), *v.t.* **1.** to mock; scoff at; treat with disdain or contempt. —*v.i.* **2.** to mock, gibe, or scoff (often fol. by *at*). —*n.* **3.** a flouting speech or action; a mocking insult; a gibe. [ME *floute(n),* var. of FLUTE, v. Cf. D *fluiten* play the flute, mock, impose upon] —**flout′er,** *n.* —**flout′ing·ly,** *adv.*

flow (flō), *v.i.* **1.** to move along in a stream, as a liquid; circulate, as the blood. **2.** to stream or well forth; issue or proceed from a source; discharge a stream, as of blood. **3.** to come or go as in a stream, as persons or things. **4.** to proceed continuously and smoothly, like a stream, as thought, speech, or verse. **5.** to fall or hang loosely at full length, as hair. **6.** to overflow or abound with something: *a land flowing with milk and honey.* **7.** to rise and advance, as the tide (opposed to *ebb*). —*v.t.* **8.** to cause or permit to flow. **9.** to cover with water or other liquid; flood. —*n.* **10.** act of flowing. **11.** movement in or as in a stream; any continuous movement, as of thought, speech, trade, etc., like that of a stream of water. **12.** the rate of flowing. **13.** the volume of fluid that flows through a passage of any given section in a unit of time. **14.** that which flows; a stream. **15.** an outpouring or discharge of something, as in a stream: *a flow of blood.* **16.** an overflowing. **17.** the rise of the tide (opposed to *ebb*). [ME *flowen,* OE *flōwan,* c. LG *flojen,* Icel. *flōa*]
—**Syn. 1.** FLOW, GUSH, SPOUT, SPURT refer to certain of the movements characteristic of fluids. FLOW is the general term: *water flows, a steam of blood flows.* To GUSH is to rush forth copiously from a cavity, in as large a volume as can issue therefrom, as the result of some strong impelling force: *the water will gush out if the main breaks.* SPOUT and SPURT both imply the ejecting of a liquid from a cavity by some internal impetus given to it. SPOUT implies a rather steady,

possibly well-defined, jet or stream, not necessarily of long duration but always of considerable force: *a whale spouts.* SPURT implies a forcible, possibly sudden, spasmodic, or intermittent issue or jet: *the liquid spurted out suddenly when the bottle cap was pushed in, juice is likely to spurt from oranges or grapefruit.* SPOUT applies only to liquids; the other terms apply also to gases.

flow·age (flō′Ïj), *n.* **1.** act of flowing; flow; state of being flooded. **2.** the flowing or overflowing liquid. **3.** *Mech.* gradual internal motion or deformation, without fracture, of a viscous solid such as asphalt.

flow·er (flou′ər), *n.* **1.** the blossom of a plant. **2.** *Bot.* **a.** that part of a seed plant comprising the reproductive organs and their envelopes (if any), esp. when such envelopes are more or less conspicuous in form and color. **b.** an analogous reproductive structure in other plants, as the mosses. **3.** a plant considered with reference to its blossom or cultivated for its floral beauty. **4.** state of efflorescence or bloom: *plants in flower.* **5.** an ornament representing a flower. **6.** any ornament or adornment. **7.** a figure of speech. **8.** the finest or most flourishing state or period, as of life or beauty. **9.** the best or finest member or part of a number, body, or whole. **10.** the finest or choicest product or example. **11.** (*pl.*) *Chem.* a substance in the form of a fine powder, esp. as obtained by sublimation: *flowers of sulfur.* —*v.i.* **12.** to produce flowers, or blossom, as a plant; to come to full bloom. **13.** to abound in flowers. **14.** to come out into full development or display (often fol. by *out*). —*v.t.* **15.** to cover or deck with flowers. **16.** to decorate with a floral design. [ME *flour,* t. OF, g. L *flōs*]

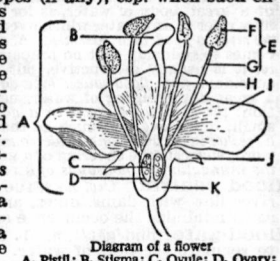

Diagram of a flower
A. Pistil; B. Stigma; C. Ovule; D. Ovary; E. Stamen; F. Anther; G. Filament; H. Style; I. Petal; J. Sepal; K. Receptacle

flow·er·age (flou′ər Ïj), *n.* **1.** flowers collectively. **2.** floral ornament or decoration. **3.** *Rare.* the process or state of flowering.

flow·er-de-luce (flou′də lōōs′), *n.* the iris (flower or plant). [old var. of *fleur-de-lis,* influenced by FLOWER]

flow·ered (flou′ərd), *adj.* **1.** having flowers. **2.** decorated with flowers, or a floral pattern.

flow·er·er (flou′ər ər), *n.* a plant that flowers at a specific time, etc.: *a late flowerer, an abundant flowerer.*

flow·er·et (flou′ər Ït), *n.* a small flower; a floret.

flower girl, *Brit.* a woman of any age who sells flowers in the streets.

flower head, *Bot.* an inflorescence consisting of a dense cluster of sessile florets; a capitulum.

flow·er·ing (flou′ər Ïng), *adj.* bearing flowers.

flowering dogwood, a North American tree, *Cornus florida,* widely planted, bearing in the spring a profusion of white or pale pink flowers.

flowering maple, any member of the malvaceous genus *Abutilon,* shrubs with large bright-colored flowers; abutilon.

flow·er·less (flou′ər lÏs), *adj.* **1.** without flowers. **2.** *Bot.* without a true seed; cryptogamic.

flow·er·pot (flou′ər pŏt′), *n.* a pot to hold earth for a plant to grow in.

flow·er·y (flou′ər Ï), *adj.,* **-erier, -eriest. 1.** abounding in or covered with flowers. **2.** containing highly ornate language: *a flowery style.* **3.** decorated with floral designs. —**flow′er·i·ly,** *adv.* —**flow′er·i·ness,** *n.*

flow·ing (flō′Ïng), *adj.* **1.** that flows; moving in or as in a stream: *flowing water.* **2.** proceeding smoothly or easily: *flowing language.* **3.** smoothly and gracefully continuous throughout the length: *flowing lines or curves.* **4.** falling or hanging loosely at full length: *flowing hair, draperies,* etc. —**flow′ing·ly,** *adv.*

flown[1] (flōn), *v.* pp. of fly[1].

flown[2] (flōn), *adj.* **1.** decorated by means of color freely blended or flowed, as a glaze. **2.** *Archaic.* filled to excess. **3.** *Obs.* swollen, as a river in flood. [ME *flowen,* OE *flōwen,* pp. of *flōwan* flow]

flow sheet, (in a factory, etc.) a detailed diagram or chart of the operations and equipment through which material passes.

fl. oz., fluid ounce; fluid ounces.

flu (flōō), *n. Colloq.* influenza.

flub·dub (flŭb′dŭb′), *n. Colloq.* pretentious nonsense or show; airs.

fluc·tu·ant (flŭk′chōō ənt), *adj.* fluctuating; varying. [t. L: s. *fluctuans,* ppr., undulating]

fluc·tu·ate (flŭk′chōō āt′), *v.,* **-ated, -ating. 1.** to change continually, as by turns, from one course, position, condition, amount, etc., to another, as the mind, opinion, policy, prices, temperature, etc.; vary irregularly; be unstable. **2.** to move in waves or like waves. —*v.t. Rare.* **3.** to cause to fluctuate. [t. L: m.s. *fluctuātus,* pp., undulated] —**Syn. 1.** See waver.

fluc·tu·a·tion (flŭk′chōō ā′shən), *n.* **1.** continual change from one course, position, condition, etc., to another; alternating variation; vacillation; wavering; instability. **2.** wavelike motion. **3.** *Biol.* a body variation which is not inherited.

ue¹ (flōō), *n.* **1.** the smoke passage in a chimney. **2.** any duct or passage for air, gases, or the like. **3.** (in certain steam boilers) any of the pipes or tubes through which hot gases, etc., are conveyed in order to heat surrounding or adjacent water. **4.** *Music.* **a.** a flue pipe. **b.** the air passage in a flue pipe between the blowing end and the lateral hole. [earlier *flew,* ? repr. OE *flēwsa* a blowing, the form *flews* being taken for a plural]

ue² (flōō), *n.* downy matter; fluff. [? OE *flug-* in *flugol* swift, fleeting (akin to FLY, v.). Cf. LG *flug*]

ue³ (flōō), *n.* a kind of fishing net. Also, **flew.** [ME *lowe.* Cf. MD *vluwe* fishing net]

ue⁴ (flōō), *n.* **1.** a barb of a feather. **2.** the fluke of an anchor. [orig. obscure. Cf. Sw. *fly*]

u·ent (flōō′ənt), *adj.* **1.** flowing smoothly and easily: *o speak fluent French.* **2.** able to speak or write readily: *a fluent speaker.* **3.** easy; graceful: *fluent motion, curves, tc.* **4.** flowing, as a stream. **5.** *Rare.* capable of flowing, or fluid, as liquids or gases. **6.** *Rare.* not fixed or stable n form. [t. L: s. *fluens,* ppr., flowing] —**flu′en·cy, flu′ent·ness,** *n.* —**flu′ent·ly,** *adv.*
—**Syn. 1.** FLUENT, GLIB, VOLUBLE may refer to a flow of words. FLUENT suggests an easy and ready flow and is usually a term of commendation: *a fluent and interesting speech.* GLIB implies an excessive fluency divorced from sincerity or profundity; it often suggests talking smoothly and hurriedly to cover up or deceive, not giving the audience a chance to stop and think; it may also imply a plausible, prepared, and well-rehearsed lie: *he had a glib answer for everything.* VOLUBLE implies the overcopious, and often rapid flow of words, characteristic of a person who loves to talk and will spare his audience no details: *she overwhelmed him with her voluble answer.* —**Ant. 1.** hesitant.

ue pipe, *Music.* an organ pipe in which a current of air striking a mouth or aperture produces the tone.

ue stop, *Music.* an organ stop whose sound is produced by flue pipes: a generic name for all but reed stops.

uff (flŭf), *n.* **1.** light, downy particles, as of cotton. **2.** a downy mass; something downy or fluffy. —*v.t.* **3.** to make into fluff; shake or puff out (feathers, hair, etc.) into a fluffy mass. —*v.i.* **4.** to become fluffy; move, float, or settle down like fluff. [? b. FLUE² and PUFF]

uff·y (flŭf′ĭ), *adj.,* **fluffier, fluffiest.** of, like, or covered with fluff. —**fluff′i·ly,** *adv.* —**fluff′i·ness,** *n.*

u·id (flōō′ĭd), *n.* **1.** a substance, as a liquid or a gas, which is capable of flowing, and which usually does not resist forces tending to change its shape but not its volume. —*adj.* **2.** capable of flowing; liquid or gaseous. **3.** consisting of or pertaining to fluids. **4.** changing readily; shifting; not fixed, stable, or rigid. [t. L: s. *fluidus,* der. *fluere* flow] —**flu·id′ic,** *adj.* —**flu·id′i·ty, flu′id·ness,** *n.* —**flu′id·ly,** *adv.* —**Syn. 1.** See liquid.

uid dram, the eighth part of a fluid ounce. Also, **fluid drachm.**

u·id·ex·tract (flōō′ĭd·ěks′trăkt), *n.* *Pharm.* an alcoholic solution of a vegetable drug when one cc. of the preparation is equivalent, in activity, to one gram of the drug in powdered form.

uid mechanics, an applied science embodying the basic principles of both gaseous and liquid flow.

uid ounce, *n.* a measure of capacity equal to ¹⁄₁₆ pint in the U.S., and to ¹⁄₂₀ of an imperial pint in Great Britain.

uid pressure, *Physics, etc.* pressure within a fluid or at the confines of a restrained fluid.

uke¹ (flōōk), *n.* **1.** the flat triangular piece at the end of each arm of an anchor, which catches in the ground. **2.** a barb, or the barbed head, of a harpoon, etc. **3.** either half of the triangular tail of a whale. [? special use of FLUKE³]

uke² (flōōk), *n., v.,* **fluked, fluking.** —*n.* **1.** any accidental advantage; a lucky chance. **2.** an accidentally successful stroke in billiards or other sports. —*v.t.* **3.** *Colloq.* to hit, make, or gain by a fluke. [orig. unknown. Cf. d. E *fluke* a guess]

uke³ (flōōk), *n.* **1.** the flounder, *Platichthys flesus.* **2.** any flounder. **3.** a trematode. [ME, var. of *flook,* OE *flōc*]

uk·ey (flōō′kĭ), *adj.,* **flukier, flukiest.** fluky.

uk·y (flōō′kĭ), *adj.,* **flukier, flukiest. 1.** *Colloq.* obtained by chance rather than skill. **2.** uncertain, as a wind. [f. FLUKE² + -Y¹] —**fluk′i·ness,** *n.*

ume (flōōm), *n., v.,* **flumed, fluming.** —*n.* **1.** a deep, narrow defile, esp. one containing a mountain torrent. **2.** an artificial channel or trough for conducting water, as one in which logs, etc., are transported. —*v.t.* **3.** to transport, as lumber, in a flume. **4.** to divert (a river, etc.) by a flume. [ME., t. OF: m. *flum,* g. L. *flūmen* stream]

lum·mer·y (flŭm′ərĭ), *n., pl.* **-meries. 1.** oatmeal or flour boiled with water until thick. **2.** any of various dishes made of flour, milk, eggs, sugar, etc. **3.** agreeable humbug; empty compliment. [t. Welsh: m. *llymru*]

lum·mox (flŭm′əks), *v.t.* *Slang.* to bewilder; confuse.

lump (flŭmp), *Colloq.* —*v.i., v.t.* **1.** to plump down suddenly or heavily; flop. —*n.* **2.** act or sound of flumping. [b. FALL and PLUMP²]

lung (flŭng), *v.* pt. and pp. of **fling.**

lunk (flŭngk), *U.S. Colloq.* —*v.i.* **1.** to fail, as a student in a recitation or examination. **2.** to give up; back out (fol. by *out*). —*v.t.* **3.** to fail in (a recitation, etc.). **4.** to remove (a student) as unqualified from a school, course, etc. —*n.* **5.** a failure, as in a recitation or examination. [? akin to FLINCH¹, FUNK]

flun·key (flŭng′kĭ), *n., pl.* **-keys.** flunky.

flun·ky (flŭng′kĭ), *n., pl.* **-kies. 1.** (in contemptuous use) a male servant in livery; a lackey. **2.** a servile follower; a toady. [? alter. of FLANKER] —**flun′ky·ism,** *n.*

flu·o·phos·phate (flōō′ə·fŏs′fāt), *n.* a substance containing both fluorine and phosphorus.

flu·or (flōō′ôr), *n.* fluorite. [t. L: a flowing (so called from its use as a flux)]

fluor-¹, a word element indicating the presence of fluorine. [comb. form of FLUORINE]

fluor-², a word element indicating fluorescence. [comb. form of FLUORESCENCE]

flu·o·resce (flōō′ə·rěs′), *v.i.,* **-resced, -rescing.** to exhibit the phenomena of fluorescence.

flu·o·res·ce·in (flōō′ə·rěs′ĭ·ĭn), *n.* *Chem.* an orange-red water-insoluble compound, $C_{20}H_{12}O_5$, whose solutions in alkalis produce an orange color and a green fluorescence. It is used as an indicator and in dyes. Also, **flu·o·res·ce·ine.**

flu·o·res·cence (flōō′ə·rěs′əns), *n.* *Physics, Chem.* **1.** the property possessed by certain substances of emitting light upon exposure to external radiation or bombardment by a stream of particles. **2.** the light or luminosity so produced.

flu·o·res·cent (flōō′ə·rěs′ənt), *adj.* possessing the property of fluorescence; exhibiting fluorescence.

fluorescent lamp, an electric discharge lamp in which light is produced by passage of electricity through a metallic vapor or gas enclosed in a tube or bulb.

flu·or·ic (flōō·ôr′ĭk, -ŏr′-), *adj.* **1.** *Chem.* pertaining to or obtained from fluorine. **2.** *Mineral.* pertaining to or obtained from fluor. [t. F: m. *fluorique,* der. *fluor* fluid acid, t. L: a flowing]

fluor·i·da·tion (flōō′ôr·ĭ·dā′shən), *n.* the addition of certain chemicals, such as sodium fluoride, to the public water supply to reduce tooth decay. —**fluor′i·date′,** *v.t.*

flu·o·ride (flōō′ə·rīd′), *n.* *Chem.* a compound, usually of two elements, one of which is fluorine, as *sodium fluoride,* NaF. Also, **flu·o·rid** (flōō′ə·rĭd).

flu·o·rine (flōō′ə·rēn′ -rĭn), *n.* *Chem.* a nonmetallic element, a pale yellow corrosive gas, occurring combined, esp. in fluorite, cryolite, phosphate rock, and other minerals. Symbol: F; at. wt.: 19.0; at. no.: 9. Also, **flu·o·rin** (flōō′ə·rĭn).

flu·o·rite (flōō′ə·rīt′), *n.* a common mineral, calcium fluoride, CaF₂, occurring in colorless, green, blue, purple, and yellow crystals, usually in cubes: the principal source of fluorine. It is also used as a flux in metallurgy and for ornamental purposes. Also, **fluor, fluorspar.**

flu·o·ro·car·bon (flōō′ə·rə·kär′bən), *n.* *Chem.* any of a class of compounds made by substituting fluorine for hydrogen in a hydrocarbon, and characterized by great chemical stability. They are used as lubricants, fire extinguishers, and in industrial applications in which resistance to heat, radioactivity, etc., is essential.

fluor·o·scope (flōō′ôr·ə·skōp′, flōō′ərə-), *n.* a tube or box, fitted with a screen coated with a fluorescent substance, used for viewing objects exposed to x-rays or other radiation directed to, or focused upon, the screen. [f. FLUOR-² + -(o)SCOPE]

fluor·o·scop·ic (flōō′ôr·ə·skŏp′ĭk, flōō′ərə-), *adj.* pertaining to the fluoroscope or to fluoroscopy. —**fluor′o·scop′i·cal·ly,** *adv.*

fluor·os·co·py (flōō′ôr·ŏs′kə·pĭ, flōō′ərŏs′-), *n.* the act of using the fluoroscope, or of examining by means of a fluorescent screen, the shadows of bodies being examined by means of x-rays.

flu·or·spar (flōō′ôr·spär′, -ər-), *n.* fluorite. Also, **fluor spar.**

flur·ry (flûr′ĭ), *n., pl.* **-ries,** *v.,* **-ried, -rying.** —*n.* **1.** a sudden gust of wind. **2.** a light gusty shower or snowfall. **3.** commotion; sudden excitement or confusion; nervous hurry. **4.** *Stock Exchange.* a brief agitation in prices. —*v.t.* **5.** to put (a person) into a flurry; make nervous; confuse; fluster. [b. FLUTTER and HURRY]

flush¹ (flŭsh), *n.* **1.** a blush; a rosy glow. **2.** a rushing or overspreading flow, as of water. **3.** a rush of emotion; elation: *the first flush of success, of victory.* **4.** glowing freshness or vigor: *the flush of youth.* **5.** the hot stage of a fever. —*v.t.* **6.** to redden; cause to blush or glow. **7.** to flood with water, as for cleansing purposes; wash out (a sewer, etc.). **8.** to animate or elate. —*v.i.* **9.** to blush; redden. **10.** to flow with a rush; flow and spread suddenly. [b. FLASH and GUSH; in some senses further blended with BLUSH] —**flush′er,** *n.*

flush² (flŭsh), *adj.* **1.** even or level, as with a surface; in one plane. **2.** well-supplied, as with money; affluent; prosperous. **3.** abundant or plentiful, as money. **4.** flushed with color; blushing. **5.** full of vigor; lusty. **6.** quite full; full to overflowing. **7.** *Naut.* (of a deck) unbroken by deckhouses, etc., and having an even surface fore and aft or from stem to stern. **8.** *Print.* even or level with the right or left margins of the type page; without an indentation. —*adv.* **9.** so as to be flush or even. **10.** to make flush or even. —*v.t.* **11.** to send out shoots, as plants in spring. —*n.* **12.** a fresh growth, as of shoots and leaves. [? adj. use of FLUSH¹]

flush³ (flŭsh), *Hunting.* —*v.t.* **1.** to rouse and cause to start up or fly off: *to flush a woodcock.* —*v.i.* **2.** to fly out or start up suddenly. —*n.* **3.** a flushed bird, or flock of birds. [ME *flussh,* orig. uncert.]

flush[4] (flŭsh), *Cards.* —*adj.* **1.** consisting entirely of cards of one suit: *a flush hand.* —*n.* **2.** a hand or set of cards all of one suit. See **royal flush, straight flush.** [cf. F (obs.) *flus,* var. of *flux* flow, flush (cf. E *run* of cards), t. L: s. *fluxus* FLUX]

Flush·ing (flŭsh'ĭng), *n.* a seaport in SW Netherlands, on Walcheren island. 25,745 (1948). Dutch, **Vlissingen.**

flus·ter (flŭs'tər), *v.t.* **1.** to confuse; make nervous. **2.** to excite and confuse with drink. —*v.i.* **3.** to become confused; become agitated or flurried. —*n.* **4.** confusion; flurry; nervous excitement. [cf. Icel. *flaustr* hurry, bustle and cf. BLUSTER]

flus·trate (flŭs'trāt), *v.t.,* **-trated, -trating.** fluster. —**flus·tra'tion,** *n.*

flute (floot), *n., v.,* **fluted, fluting.** —*n.* **1.** a musical wind instrument consisting of a tube with a series of finger holes or keys, in which the wind is directed against a sharp edge, either directly, as in the modern transverse flute, or through a flue, as in the re-corder.

Flute

2. an organ stop with wide flue pipes, having a flutelike tone. **3.** *Archit., etc.* a channel or furrow with a rounded section, as in a pillar. **4.** a groove in any material, as in a woman's ruffle. —*v.i.* **5.** to produce or utter flutelike sounds. **6.** to play on a flute. —*v.t.* **7.** to utter in flutelike tones. **8.** to form longitudinal flutes or furrows in. [ME *flowte,* t. OF: m. *fleüte,* t. Pr.: m. *flauta,* ult. der. L *flātus,* pp., blown] —**flute'like',** *adj.*

flut·ed (floo'tĭd), *adj.* **1.** fine, clear, and mellow; flute-like: *fluted notes.* **2.** having flutes or grooves, as a pillar.

flut·er (floo'tər), *n.* **1.** one who makes flutings. **2.** *Rare.* a flutist.

flut·ing (floo'tĭng), *n.* **1.** act of playing on the flute. **2.** the sound made by such playing; a flutelike sound. **3.** fluted work. **4.** act of making flutes. **5.** a flute, groove, or furrow.

fluting iron, a specially shaped iron for pressing ruffles, etc., into a fluted form.

flut·ist (floo'tĭst), *n.* a flute player. Also, **flautist.** [cf. F *flûtiste*]

flut·ter (flŭt'ər), *v.i.* **1.** to toss or wave in air, as a flag. **2.** (of birds, etc.) to flap the wings, or fly with flapping movements. **3.** to move in quick, irregular motions. **4.** to beat fast and irregularly, as the heart. **5.** to be tremulous or agitated. **6.** to go with irregular motions or aimless course. —*v.t.* **7.** to cause to flutter; vibrate; agitate. **8.** to confuse; throw into a state of nervous excitement, mental agitation, or tremulous excitement. —*n.* **9.** a fluttering movement. **10.** a state of nervous excitement or mental agitation. **11.** sensation; stir: *to cause or make a flutter.* **12.** *Swimming.* flutter kick. **13.** a rapid variation in pitch fidelity resulting from fluctuations in the speed of a recording. [ME *floteren,* OE *floterian,* freq. of *flotian* float] —**flut'ter·er,** *n.* —**flut'ter·ing·ly,** *adv.* —**Syn. 2.** See **fly**[1].

flutter kick, *Swimming.* the up-and-down movements of the legs in the crawl.

flut·ter·y (flŭt'ər·ĭ), *adj.* fluttering; apt to flutter.

flut·y (floo'tĭ), *adj.* flutelike, as in tone.

flu·vi·al (floo'vĭ·əl), *adj.* of, pertaining to, or produced by a river. [t. L: s. *fluviālis,* der. *fluvius* river]

flu·vi·a·tile (floo'vĭ·ə·tĭl; *Brit.* -tĭl), *adj.* pertaining to or peculiar to rivers; found in or near rivers. [t. L: m.s. *fluviātilis,* der. *fluvius* river]

flux (flŭks), *n.* **1.** a flowing or flow. **2.** the flowing in of the tide. **3.** continuous passage; continuous change: *to be in a state of flux.* **4.** *Pathol.* **a.** an abnormal or morbid discharge of blood or other matter from the body. **b.** dysentery (**bloody flux**). **5.** *Physics.* **a.** the rate of flow of a fluid, heat, or the like. **b.** luminous flux. **c.** magnetic flux. **6.** *Chem. Metall., etc.* **a.** a substance, as borax or fluorspar, used to promote the fusion of metals or minerals. **b.** a nonmetallic substance, as a salt or mixture of salts, used to protect the surface of molten metal from oxidation. **c.** (in the refining of scrap or other metal) a salt or mixture of salts which combines with nonmetallic impurities, causing them to float or coagulate. **7.** fusion. —*v.t.* **8.** to melt; fuse; make fluid. **9.** *Obs.* to purge. —*v.i.* **10.** to flow. [ME, t. L: s. *fluxus* a flowing]

flux density, *Physics.* the magnetic or electric flux per unit of cross-sectional area.

flux·ion (flŭk'shən), *n.* **1.** act of flowing; a flow or flux. **2.** *Math. Obs.* the derivative relative to the time. —**flux'ion·al, flux·ion·ar·y** (flŭk'shə·nĕr'ĭ), *adj.* —**flux'ion·al·ly,** *adv.*

flux·me·ter (flŭks'mē'tər), *n.* *Physics.* an instrument for measuring magnetic flux.

fly[1] (flī), *v.,* **flew** or (for def. 8) **flied; flown; flying;** *n., pl.* **flies.** —*v.i.* **1.** to move through the air on wings, as a bird. **2.** to be borne through the air by the wind or any other force or agency. **3.** to float or flutter in the air, as a flag, the hair, etc. **4.** to travel through the air in an aircraft or as an aircraft does. **5.** to move or pass swiftly; move with a start or rush. **6.** *Archaic.* to attack by flying, as a hawk does. **7.** *Baseball.* to bat a fly ball: *he flied into right field.* —*n.* **8.** a strip sewn along one edge of a garment, to aid in concealing the buttons or other fasteners. **9.** a flap forming the door of a tent. **10.** a piece of canvas ex-tending over the ridgepole of a tent and forming an outer roof. **11.** act of flying; a flight. **12. on the fly,** during flight, before reaching the ground. **13.** the course of a flying object, as a ball. **14.** *Baseball and Cricket.* a ball knocked high in the air. **15.** *Brit.* a light public carriage for passengers. **16.** *Mach.* a flywheel. **17.** *Horol.* a regulating device for chime and striking mechanisms, consisting of an arrangement of vanes on a revolving axis. **18.** *Print.* **a.** a contrivance for receiving and delivering separately printed sheets from a press. **b.** (formerly) one who removed printed matter from a press. **19.** the extent of a flag from the staff to the outer end, or the outer end itself. **20.** (*pl.*) *Theat.* the space and apparatus above the stage. [ME *flien,* OE *flēogan,* c. D *vliegen,* G *fliegen*] —**Syn. 1.** FLY, FLIT, FLUTTER, HOVER, SOAR refer to moving through the air as on wings. FLY is the general term: *birds fly, airplanes fly.* To FLIT is to make short rapid flights from place to place: *a bird flits from tree to tree.* To FLUTTER is to agitate the wings tremulously, either without flying or in flying only short distances: *a young bird flutters out of a nest and in again.* To HOVER is to linger in the air, or to move over or about something within a narrow area or space: *hovering clouds, a hummingbird hovering over a blossom.* To SOAR is to (start to) fly upward to a great height usually with little advance in any other direction, or else to (continue to) fly at a lofty height without visible movement of the wings: *above our heads great birds were soaring.*

fly[2] (flī), *n., pl.* **flies. 1.** any of the two-winged insects constituting the order *Diptera* (**true flies**), especially one of the family *Muscidae,* as the common housefly, *Musca domestica.* **2.** any of a number of other winged insects, as the May fly or firefly. **3.** *Angling.* a fishhook dressed with silk, tinsel, etc., to resemble an insect. [ME *flye,* OE *flēoge, flȳge,* c. G *fliege*] —**fly'less,** *adj.*

fly[3] (flī), *adj. Slang.* knowing; sharp; smart. [? special use of FLY[1]]

fly agaric, a very poisonous mushroom, *Amanita muscaria,* sometimes used for making a poison for flies.

fly·a·way (flī'ə·wā'), *adj.* **1.** fluttering; streaming. **2.** flighty; volatile; frivolous.

fly·blow (flī'blō'), *v.t.* **1.** to deposit eggs or larvae on (meat). —*n.* **2.** the egg or young larva (maggot) of a blowfly, deposited on meat, etc.

fly·blown (flī'blōn'), *adj.* **1.** tainted with flyblows. **2.** spoiled; corrupt.

fly·boat (flī'bōt'), *n.* a fast vessel. [t. D: m. *vlieboot*]

fly book, *Angling.* a booklike case for artificial flies.

fly-by-night (flī'bī·nīt'), *adj.* **1.** irresponsible; unreliable. —*n.* **2.** a person who leaves secretly at night in order to avoid paying his debts.

fly·catch·er (flī'kăch'ər), *n.* any of numerous small, insectivorous birds of the Old World family *Muscicapidae,* (as the **spotted flycatcher,** *Muscicapa grisola,* of Europe) or of the American family *Tyrannidae* (as the kingbird).

fly·er (flī'ər), *n.* flier.

fly-fish (flī'fĭsh'), *v.i. Angling.* to fish with artificial flies as bait. —**fly'-fish'er,** *n.* —**fly'-fish'ing,** *n.*

fly·ing (flī'ĭng), *adj.* **1.** that flies; making flight or passing through the air: *a flying insect, a flying boat.* **2.** floating, fluttering or waving, or hanging or moving freely, in the air: *flying banners, flying hair.* **3.** extending through the air. **4.** moving swiftly. **5.** made while moving swiftly: *a flying start.* **6.** hasty: *a flying trip.* **7.** designed for swiftness: *a flying squad.* **8.** fleeing, running away, or taking flight. **9.** *Naut.* (of a sail) having none of its edges bent to spars or stays. —*n.* **10.** act of moving through the air on wings; flight.

flying boat, an aircraft whose main body consists of a single hull or boat.

flying buttress, (in Gothic architecture) a segmental arch which carries the thrust of the nave wall over the aisle to a solid pier buttress. See illus. under **buttress.**

flying circus, a squadron of airplanes operating together, esp. any of several squadrons of famous World War I aviators.

flying column, *Mil.* (formerly) a force of troops equipped and organized to move swiftly and independently of a principal unit to which it is attached.

Flying Dutchman, 1. a legendary spectral Dutch ship supposed to be seen at sea, esp. near the Cape of Good Hope. **2.** the captain of this ship, supposed to have been condemned to sail the sea, beating against the wind, till the day of judgment.

flying field, *Aeron.* a small landing field with short runways and facilities for servicing airplanes on a lesser scale than an airport.

flying fish, any of certain fishes with winglike pectoral fins which help them to glide for some distance through the air after leaping from the water, esp. of the family *Exocoetidae,* as *Exocoetus volitans.*

flying fox, any large fruit-eating bat of the family *Pteropodidae,* esp. of the genus *Pteropus,* as *P. edulis,* of Old World tropical regions, having a foxlike head.

flying gurnard, any of several fishes of the family *Dactylopteridae,* esp. *Dactylopterus volitans,* having winglike pectoral fins, though apparently not able to fly.

flying jib, a triangular sail set outside of the jib. See illus. under **sail.**

flying lemur, a lemurlike mammal having a broad fold of skin on each side of the body to act as a wing in gliding from tree to tree. The species *Cynocephalus temminckii* is distributed over SE Asia and the East Indies, *Cynocephalus volans* in the Philippine area. They are the only representatives of the order *Dermoptera*.

flying lizard, any of the arboreal lizards of the genus *Draco* of southeastern Asia and the East Indies, with extensible membranes along the sides by means of which they make long gliding leaps from tree to tree.

flying machine, a contrivance which sustains itself in, and propels itself through, the air; an airplane or the like.

flying mare, *Wrestling.* a method of attack in which a wrestler grasps the wrist of his opponent, turns in the opposite direction, and throws him over his shoulder and down.

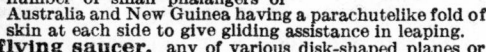

Flying phalanger.
Schoinobates volans
(Total length 3 ft.,
tail 1½ ft.)

flying phalanger, any of a number of small phalangers of Australia and New Guinea having a parachutelike fold of skin at each side to give gliding assistance in leaping.

flying saucer, any of various disk-shaped planes or missiles allegedly seen flying at high speeds and altitudes.

flying squirrel, a squirrellike animal, esp. of the genus *Glaucomys,* as *G. volans* of the eastern U.S., with folds of skin connecting the fore and hind legs, enabling it to take long gliding leaps.

Flying squirrel. *Glaucomys volans*
(Total length 9 to 9½ in., tail 3½ to 4 in.)

fly in the ointment, a trifle that spoils or lessens the pleasure or value of something else.

fly·leaf (flī'lēf'), *n., pl.* **-leaves** (-lēvz'). a blank leaf in the front or the back of a book.

fly loft, the portion of a theater building above the stage into which scenery may be raised.

fly·man (flī'mən), *n., pl.* **-men.** *Theat.* a stagehand, esp. one who operates the apparatus in the flies.

fly net, a fringe or net to protect a horse from flies.

fly·pa·per (flī'pā'pər). *n.* paper prepared to destroy flies by poisoning them or by catching them on its sticky surface.

Fly River (flī). a river flowing from central New Guinea SE to the Gulf of Papua. ab. 800 mi.

fly·speck (flī'spĕk'), *n.* 1. a speck or tiny stain from the excrement of a fly. 2. a minute spot. —*v.t.* 3. to mark with flyspecks.

flyte (flīt), *v.i.,* **flyted, flyting,** *n.* Now *Scot.* and *N. Eng.* flite.

fly·trap (flī'trăp'), *n.* 1. any of various plants which entrap insects, esp. Venus's-flytrap. 2. a trap for flies.

fly·weight (flī'wāt'), *n.* a boxer of 112 pounds or less, lighter than a featherweight and a bantamweight.

fly·wheel (flī'hwēl'), *n.* *Mach.* 1. a heavy wheel which by its momentum tends to equalize the speed of machinery with which it is connected. 2. a wheel used to carry the piston over dead center.

FM, *Radio.* frequency modulation.

fm., 1. fathom. 2. from.

F number, *Photog.* the focal distance divided by the effective diameter of the lens aperture; the relative aperture. It is a numerical indication of the relative exposure required by a lens, used to number diaphragm openings.

F.O., 1. Field Officer. 2. *Brit.* Foreign Office.

foal (fōl), *n.* 1. the young of the horse, ass, or any allied animal; a colt or filly. —*v.t., v.i.* 2. to bring forth (a foal). [ME *fole,* OE *fola,* c. OHG *folo*]

foam (fōm), *n.* 1. an aggregation of minute bubbles formed on the surface of a liquid by agitation, fermentation, etc. 2. the froth of perspiration formed on the skin of a horse or other animal from great exertion. 3. froth formed in the mouth, as in epilepsy and rabies. —*v.i.* 4. to form or gather foam; emit foam; froth. —*v.t.* 5. to cause to foam. [ME *fome,* OE *fām,* c. G *feim*] —**foam'ing·ly,** *adv.* —**foam'less,** *adj.*

foam-flow·er (fōm'flou'ər), *n.* a North American saxifragaceous herb, *Tiarella cordifolia,* which bears white flowers in the spring.

foam rubber, rubber so processed that it is light, firm, and spongy, used for mattresses, in furniture, for protective cushioning, etc.

foam·y (fō'mĭ), *adj.,* **foamier, foamiest.** 1. covered with or full of foam. 2. consisting of foam. 3. resembling foam. 4. pertaining to foam. —**foam'i·ness,** *n.*

fob[1] (fŏb), *n.* 1. a small pocket just below the waistline in trousers or breeches, to hold a watch, etc. 2. a short chain or ribbon with a seal or the like, attached to a watch and worn hanging from the pocket. [orig. unknown. Cf. d. HG *fuppe* pocket, *fuppen* to pocket stealthily]

fob[2] (fŏb), *v.t.,* **fobbed, fobbing.** 1. to palm off (fol. by *off*): *to fob off an inferior watch on a person.* 2. to put off (fol. by *off*): *to fob one off with promises.* 3. *Archaic.* to cheat; deceive. [akin to FOB[1]. Cf. G *foppen* deceive]

F.O.B., free on board (a price F.O.B. does not include carriage costs from the seller to the buyer). Also, **f.o.b.**

fo·cal (fō'kəl), *adj.* of or pertaining to a focus. —**fo'cal·ly,** *adv.*

focal distance, *Optics.* 1. (of a mirror or lens) the distance from a point near its center to the focal point. 2. (of a telescope) the distance between the object glass and the focal plane. Also, **focal length.**

focal infection, *Pathol., Dentistry.* an infection in which the bacteria are localized in some region, as the tissue around a tooth or a tonsil. from which they often spread to some other organ or structure of the body.

fo·cal·ize (fō'kə līz'), *v.t.,* **-ized, -izing.** focus. —**fo'cal·i·za'tion,** *n.*

focal plane, *Optics.* the transverse plane in a telescope where the real image of a distant view is in focus.

Foch (fôsh), *n.* **Ferdinand** (fĕr dē nän'), 1851–1929, French marshal.

fo·cus (fō'kəs), *n., pl.* **-cuses, -ci** (-sī), *v.,* **-cused, -cusing** or (*esp. Brit.*) **-cussed, -cussing.** —*n.* 1. *Physics.* a point at which rays of light, heat, or other radiation. meet after being refracted or reflected. 2. *Optics.* **a.** a point from which diverging rays appear to proceed, or a point at which converging rays would meet if they could be prolonged in the same direction (**virtual focus**). **b.** the focal distance of a lens. **c.** clear and sharply defined condition of an image. **d.** the position of a viewed object, or the adjustment of an optical device, necessary to produce a clear image: *in focus, out of focus.* 3. a central point, as of attraction, attention, or activity. 4. *Geom.* one of the points from which the distances to any point of a given curve are in a linear relation. See diag. under **parabola.** 5. *Seismology.* the point where an earthquake starts. 6. *Pathol.* the primary center from which a disease develops or in which it localizes. —*v.t.* 7. to bring to a focus or into focus. 8. to concentrate: *to focus one's thoughts.* —*v.i.* 9. to become focused. [t. L: hearth, fireplace] —**fo'cus·er,** *n.*

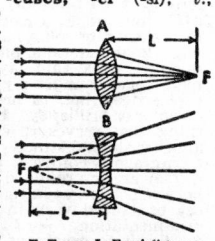

F. Focus; L. Focal distance;
A. Convex lens; B. Concave lens

fod·der (fŏd'ər), *n.* 1. coarse roughages used as feed for livestock, composed of entire plants, including leaves, stalks, and grain, of such forages as corn (maize) and sorghum. —*v.t.* 2. to feed with or as with fodder. [ME, OE *fodder, fōdor,* c. G *futter;* akin to FOOD] —**Syn. 1.** See **feed.**

fodg·el (fŏj'əl), *adj.* *Scot.* fat; stout; plump.

foe (fō), *n.* 1. one who entertains enmity, hatred, or malice against another; an enemy. 2. an enemy in war; hostile army. 3. one belonging to a hostile army or nation. 4. an opponent in a game or contest. 5. a person who is opposed in feeling, principle, etc., to something: *a foe to progress.* 6. a thing that is opposed to or destructive of: *cleanliness is a foe to infection.* [ME *foo,* OE (ge)*fā*(h) enemy (absolute use of adj. meaning hostile). See FEUD[1]] —**Syn. 1.** See **enemy.**

F.O.E., Fraternal Order of Eagles.

foehn (fān; *Ger.* fœn), *n.* *Meteorol.* föhn.

foe·man (fō'mən), *n., pl.* **-men.** *Archaic.* an enemy in war.

foe·ta·tion (fē tā'shən), *n.* fetation.

foe·ti·cide (fē'tə sīd'), *n.* feticide.

foe·tid (fē'tĭd, fĕt'ĭd), *adj.* fetid.

foe·tor (fē'tər), *n.* fetor.

foe·tus (fē'təs), *n.* fetus. —**foe'tal,** *adj.*

fog[1] (fŏg, fôg), *n., v.,* **fogged, fogging.** —*n.* 1. *Meteorol.* a cloudlike mass or layer of minute globules of water in the air near the earth's surface; thick mist. 2. any darkened state of the atmosphere, or the diffused substance which causes it. 3. a state of mental confusion or obscurity: *a fog of doubt.* 4. *Photog.* a darkening of the whole or of parts of a developed plate or print from sources other than image-forming light in the camera. 5. *Phys. Chem.* a colloidal system consisting of liquid particles dispersed in a gaseous medium. —*v.t.* 6. to envelop with, or as with, fog. 7. *Photog.* to affect (a negative or print) by fog. 8. to confuse; perplex; bewilder. —*v.i.* 9. to become enveloped or obscured with, or as with, fog. 10. *Photog.* to be affected by fog. [back formation from FOGGY. See FOG[2]] —**fog'less,** *adj.* —**Syn. 3.** See **cloud.**

fog[2] (fŏg, fôg), *n.* 1. a second growth of grass, as after mowing. 2. long grass left standing in fields during the winter. [ME *fogge,* t. Scand.; cf. Norw. *fogg* long grass on damp ground, and obs. E *foggy* marshy]

fog bank, a stratum of fog as seen from a distance.

fog·bound (fŏg'bound', fôg'-), *adj.* *Naut.* unable to navigate due to heavy fog.

fog-dog (fŏg'dôg', -dŏg', fôg'-), *n.* a bright spot sometimes seen in a fog bank.

fo·gey (fō'gĭ), *n., pl.* **-geys.** fogy.

fog-gage (fŏg'ĭj), *n. Chiefly Dial.* fog[2].

Fog·gia (fŏd'jä), *n.* a city in S Italy. 109,000 (est. 1954).

fog·gy (fŏg'ĭ, fôg'ĭ), *adj.,* **-gier, -giest.** 1. abounding in or thick with fog; misty. 2. resembling fog; dim; obscure. 3. *Photog.* affected by fog. [der. FOG[2]; orig. meaning marshy, thick, murky] —**fog'gi·ly,** *adv.* —**fog'gi·ness,** *n.*

ăct, āble, dâre, ärt; ĕbb, ēqual; ĭf, īce; hŏt, ōver, ôrder, oil, bŏŏk, ōōze, out; ŭp, ūse, ûrge; ə = a in alone; ch, chief; g, give; ng, ring; sh, shoe; th, thin; ŧh, that; zh, vision.   See the full key on inside cover.

fog·horn (fŏg′hôrn′, fŏg′-), *n.* **1.** a horn for sounding warning signals, as to vessels, in foggy weather. **2.** a deep, loud voice.

fo·gy (fō′gĭ), *n., pl.* **-gies. 1.** an old-fashioned or excessively conservative person: *the old fogy.* **2.** a slow or dull person. **—fo′gy·ish,** *adj.* **—fo′gy·ism,** *n.*

föhn (fān; *Ger.* fœn), *n. Meteorol.* a warm, dry wind descending a mountain, in the valleys on the north side of the Alps. Also, **foehn.** [t. G, t. Romansh: m. *favugn,* g. L *Favōnius*]

foi·ble (foi′bəl), *n.* **1.** a weak point or whimsy; a weakness or failing of character. **2.** the weaker part of a sword blade, between the middle and the point. [t. F, obs. form of *faible* FEEBLE] **—Syn. 1.** See **fault.**

foil¹ (foil), *v.t.* **1.** to frustrate (a person, an attempt, a purpose); baffle; balk. **2.** *Archaic.* to defeat; repulse; check. **—n. 3.** *Archaic.* a defeat; check; repulse. [ME *foile*(n), t. OF: m. *fuler* trample, full (cloth). See FULL²]

foil² (foil), *n.* **1.** a metallic substance formed into very thin sheets by rolling and hammering: *gold, tin, or lead foil.* **2.** the metallic backing applied to glass to form a mirror. **3.** a thin layer of metal placed under a gem in a closed setting, to improve its color or brilliancy. **4.** anything that serves to set off another thing distinctly or to advantage by contrast. **5.** *Archit.* an arc or a rounded space between cusps, as in the tracery of a window or in other ornamentation. **—v.t. 6.** to cover or back with foil. **7.** *Archit.* to ornament with foils. **8.** to set off by contrast. [ME *foile,* t. OF: m. *foil,* g. L *folium* leaf; akin to Gk. *phýllon*]

foil³ (foil) *n.* **1.** a blunt sword with a button at the point, for use in fencing. **2.** (*pl.*) the art of exercise or fencing with such swords. [orig. uncert.]

foils·man (foilz′mən), *n., pl.* **-men.** one who is expert at fencing with foils.

foin (foin), *Obs. or Archaic.* **—n. 1.** a thrust with a weapon. **—v.i. 2.** to thrust with a weapon; lunge. [appar. t. OF: m. *foine* fish spear, g. L *fuscina*]

foi·son (foi′zən), *n. Archaic.* **1.** abundance; plenty. **2.** abundant harvest. [ME, t. OF, ult. der. L *fūsio* a pouring out]

foist (foist), *v.t.* **1.** to palm off or impose fraudulently or unwarrantably (fol. by *on* or *upon*): *to foist inferior goods on a customer.* **2.** to bring or put surreptitiously or fraudulently (fol. by *in* or *into*). [prob. t. D: m. *vuisten* to take in hand]

Fo·kine (*Fr.* fô kēn′; *Russ.* fô′kĭn), *n.* **Michel** (mē-shĕl′), 1880–1942, U.S. choreographer, born in Russia.

Fok·ker (fŏk′ər), *n.* **1.** an airplane manufactured by, or according to the designs of, A. H. G. Fokker. **2.** trademark for such craft. **3. Anthony Herman Gerard** (än tō′nē hĕr′män gā′rärt), 1890–1939, Dutch airplane designer and builder.

fol., 1. folio. 2. following. 3. followed.

fold¹ (fōld), *v.t.* **1.** to double or bend (cloth, paper, etc.) over upon itself. **2.** to bring into a compact form, or shut, by bending and laying parts together (often fol. by *up*): *to fold up a map.* **3.** to bring together (the arms, hands, legs, etc.) with one around or within another: *to fold one's arms on one's chest.* **4.** to bend or wind (fol. by *about, round, etc.*): *to fold one's arms about a person's neck.* **5.** to bring (the wings) close to the body, as a bird on alighting. **6.** to enclose; wrap: *to fold something in paper.* **7.** to clasp or embrace: *to fold someone in one's arms.* **8.** *Cookery.* to mix (*in*), as beaten egg whites added to a batter or the like, by gently turning one part over another with a spoon, etc. **9.** *Poetic.* to be disposed about, surround, or cover. **—v.i. 10.** to be folded or be capable of folding: *the doors fold back.* **11. fold up, a.** to collapse. **b.** to fail in business. **—n. 12.** a part that is folded; pleat; layer: *to wrap something in folds of cloth.* **13.** a hollow made by folding: *to carry something in the fold of one's dress.* **14.** a hollow place in undulating ground: *a fold of the hills or mountains.* **15.** *Geol.* a portion of strata which is folded or bent (as an anticline or syncline), or which connects two horizontal or parallel portions of strata of different levels (as a monocline). **16.** a coil of a serpent, string, etc. **17.** act of folding or doubling over. [ME *folde*(n), d. OE *faldan,* r. OE *fealdan,* c. G *falten*]

fold² (fōld), *n.* **1.** an enclosure for domestic animals, esp. sheep. **2.** the sheep contained in it. **3.** a flock of sheep. **4.** the church, or a particular church. **—v.t. 5.** to confine (sheep, etc.) in a fold. [ME *folde,* OE *fald, falod,* c. LG *falt* enclosure, yard]

-fold, a suffix attached to numerals and other quantitative words or stems to denote multiplication by or division into a certain number, as in *twofold, manifold.* [ME; d. OE *-fald,* r. OE *-feald,* c. G *-falt;* akin to Gk. *-paltos,* as in *dípaltos* double]

fold·boat (fōld′bōt′), *n.* faltboat.

fold·er (fōl′dər), *n.* **1.** one who or that which folds. **2.** a folded printed sheet, as a circular or a timetable. **3.** an outer cover, usually a folded sheet of light cardboard, for papers.

fol·de·rol (fŏl′də rŏl′), *n.* falderal.

folding doors, a set of doors hinged together to fold flat against one another when opened.

fo·li·a (fō′lĭ ə), *n. pl.* of **folium.**

fo·li·a·ceous (fō′lĭ ā′shəs), *adj.* **1.** of the nature of a leaf; leaflike. **2.** bearing leaves or leaflike parts. **3.** pertaining to or consisting of leaves. **4.** consisting of leaflike plates or laminae; foliated. [t. L: m. *foliāceus* leafy]

fo·li·age (fō′lĭ ĭj), *n.* **1.** the leaves of a plant, collectively; leafage. **2.** leaves in general. **3.** the representation of leaves, flowers, and branches in architectural ornament, etc. [t. F: alter. (to conform to L *folium*) of *feuillage,* der. *feuille,* g. L *folium* leaf] **—fo′li·aged,** *adj.*

fo·li·ar (fō′lĭ ər), *adj.* of, pertaining to, or having the nature of a leaf or leaves.

fo·li·ate (*adj.* fō′lĭ ĭt, -āt′; *v.* fō′lĭ āt′), *adj., v.,* **-ated, -ating. —adj. 1.** having or covered with leaves. **2.** leaflike. **—v.i. 3.** to put forth leaves. **4.** to split into thin leaflike layers or laminae. **—v.t. 5.** to shape like a leaf or leaves. **6.** to decorate with foils or foliage. **7.** to form into thin sheets. **8.** to spread over with a thin metallic backing. **9.** to number leaves (not pages) of (a book). [t. L: m. s. *foliātus* leafy]

fo·li·at·ed (fō′lĭ ā′tĭd), *adj.* **1.** shaped like a leaf or leaves. **2.** *Crystall.* consisting of thin and separable laminae.

fo·li·a·tion (fō′lĭ ā′shən), *n.* **1.** act of foliating or putting forth leaves. **2.** state of being in leaf. **3.** *Bot.* the arrangement of leaves within the bud. **4.** leaves or foliage. **5.** the consecutive numbering of the leaves (not pages) of a book or manuscript. **6.** the total number of such leaves. **7.** *Geol.* the splitting up or the arrangement of certain rocks, or certain kinds of rocks, in leaflike layers. **8.** ornamentation with foliage, or an arrangement of foliage. **9.** *Archit.* ornamentation with foils, or tracery so formed. **10.** formation into thin sheets. **11.** the application of foil to glass.

fo·li·a·ture (fō′lĭ ə chər), *n.* a cluster of leaves; foliage.

fo·lic acid (fō′lĭk), *Biochem.* a synthetic form of one of the B complex of vitamins, said to be especially effective in curing anemia. [f. L FOL(IUM) leaf + -IC]

fo·li·o (fō′lĭ ō′), *n., pl.* **-lios,** *adj., v.,* **-lioed, -lioing. —n. 1.** a sheet of paper folded once to make two leaves (four pages) of a book. **2.** a volume having pages of the largest size, esp. one more than 30 cm. in height. **3.** a leaf of a manuscript or book numbered only on the front side. **4.** *Print.* the page number of a book. **5.** *Bookkeeping.* a page of an account book or a left-hand page and a right-hand page facing each other and having the same serial number. **6.** *Law.* a certain number of words (in the U.S. generally 100) taken as a unit for computing the length of a document. **—adj. 7.** pertaining to or having the format of a folio: *a folio volume.* **—v.t. 8.** to number the leaves of (a book) on one side only. **9.** *Law.* to mark each folio in (a pleading, etc.) with the proper number. [t. L, abl. of *folium* leaf]

fo·li·o·late (fō′lĭ ə lāt′, fō lĭ′ə lĭt, -lāt′), *adj. Bot.* pertaining to or consisting of leaflets (often used in compounds, as *bifoliolate, trifoliolate,* etc.). [t. NL: m. s. *foliolātus,* der. *foliolum* a leaflet, dim. of L *folium* leaf]

fo·li·ose (fō′lĭ ōs′), *adj. Bot.* leafy. Also, **fo·li·ous** (fō′-lĭ əs). [t. L: m.s. *foliōsus*]

-folious, *Bot.* an adjective suffix meaning "leafy." [t. L: m.s. *foliōsus*]

fo·li·um (fō′lĭ əm), *n., pl.* **-lia** (-lĭ ə). **1.** a thin leaflike stratum or layer; a lamella. **2.** *Geom.* a loop; part of a curve terminated at both ends by the same node. [t. L: leaf. See FOIL²]

folk (fōk), *n., pl.* **folk, folks,** *adj.* **—n. 1.** (*often pl.*) people in general. **2.** (*usually pl.*) people of a specified class or group: *poor folks.* **3.** (*pl.*) *Colloq.* the persons of one's own family; one's relatives. **4.** *Archaic.* a people or tribe. **—adj. 5.** originating among the common people. [ME; OE *folc,* c. D and G *volk,* Sw. and Dan. *folk* people]

folk dance, **1.** a dance which originated among, and has been transmitted through, the common people. **2.** a piece of music for such a dance.

Folke·stone (fōk′stən), *n.* a seaport in SE England, on the Strait of Dover. 44,900 (est. 1956).

Fol·ke·ting (fŏl′kə tĭng′), *n.* the lower house of the Danish parliament or Rigsdag.

folk etymology, a type of pseudolearned modification of linguistic forms according to a falsely assumed etymology, as in *Welsh rarebit* from *Welsh rabbit.*

folk·lore (fōk′lōr′), *n.* **1.** the lore of the common people; the traditional beliefs, legends, customs, etc., of a people. **2.** the study of such lore. **—folk′lor·ist,** *n.* **—folk′lor·is′tic,** *adj.*

folk·moot (fōk′mōōt′), *n.* (formerly, in England) a general assembly of the people of a shire, town, etc. Also, **folk·mote** (fōk′mōt′), **folk′mot′.** [ME; OE *folcmōt* folk meeting]

folk music, music, usually of simple character, originating and handed down among the common people.

folk·right (fōk′rīt′), *n.* *Early Eng. Hist.* the right of the people under the customary law.

folk·say (fōk′sā′), *n.* informal verbal expressions, such as proverbs and exclamations, among a relatively unsophisticated group of people, as *Was I ever* instead of *I certainly was.*

folk song, **1.** a song, usually of simple or artless character, originating and handed down among the common people. **2.** a song in imitation of this type.

---

b., blend of, blended; c., cognate with; d., dialect, dialectal; der., derived from; f., formed from; g., going back to; m., modification of; r., replacing; s., stem of; t., taken from; ?, perhaps. See the full key on inside cover.

folk·sy (fōk'sĭ), *adj.* sociable.

folk tale, a tale or legend originating and handed down among the common people. Also, **folk story.**

folk·ways (fōk'wāz'), *n.pl. Sociol.* the ways of living and acting in a human group, built up without conscious design but serving as compelling guides of conduct.

oll., following.

ol·li·cle (fŏl'ə kəl), *n.* **1.** *Bot.* a dry one-celled seed vessel consisting of a single carpel, and dehiscent only by the ventral suture, as the fruit of larkspur. **2.** *Anat.* a small cavity, sac, or gland. [t. L: m.s. *folliculus,* dim. of *follis* bellows, bag]

ol·lic·u·lar (fə lĭk'yə lər), *adj.* **1.** pertaining to, consisting of, or resembling a follicle or follicles; provided with follicles. **2.** *Pathol.* affecting or originating in a follicle or follicles. Also, **fol·lic·u·late** (fə lĭk'yə lāt'), **fol·lic'u·lat'ed.**

ol·lic·u·lin (fə lĭk'yə lĭn), *n.* **1.** estrone. **2.** *(cap.)* a trademark for it.

Follicle of larkspur

ol·low (fŏl'ō), *v.t.* **1.** to come after in natural sequence, order of time, etc.; succeed. **2.** to go or come after; move behind in the same direction: *go on ahead and I'll follow you.* **3.** to accept as a guide or leader; accept the authority or example of, or adhere to, as a person. **4.** to conform to, comply with, or act in accordance with: *to follow a person's advice.* **5.** to move forward along (a path, etc.). **6.** to come after as a result or consequence; result from: *it follows from this that he must be innocent.* **7.** to go after or along with (a person, etc.) as a companion. **8.** to go in pursuit of: *to follow an enemy.* **9.** to endeavor to obtain or to attain to. **10.** to engage in or be concerned with as a pursuit: *to follow the sea.* **11.** to watch the movements, progress, or course of. **12.** to keep up with and understand (an argument, etc.): *do you follow me?* **13.** follow suit, **a.** *Cards.* to play a card of the same suit as that first played. **b.** to follow the example of another. **14. follow up, a.** to pursue closely. **b.** to pursue to a conclusion. **c.** to prosecute with energy. **d.** to increase the effect of by further action. —*v.i.* **15.** to come next after something else in natural sequence, order of time, etc. **16.** to happen or occur after something else; come next as an event. **17.** to attend. **18.** to go or come after a person or thing in motion: *go on ahead and I'll follow.* **19.** to result as an effect; occur as a consequence. —*n.* **20.** act of following. **21.** *Billiards.* a stroke causing the player's ball to roll after the ball struck by it. [ME *folwe(n),* OE *folgian,* c. G *folgen*] —**fol'low·a·ble,** *adj.*

—**Syn. 8.** pursue, chase; trail, track, trace. **15.** FOLLOW, ENSUE, RESULT, SUCCEED imply coming after something else, in a natural sequence. FOLLOW is the general word: *we must wait to see what follows, a detailed account follows.* ENSUE implies a logical sequence, what might be expected normally to come after a given act, cause, etc., and indicates some duration: *when the power lines were cut, a paralysis of transportation ensued.* RESULT emphasizes the connection between a cause or event and its effect, consequence, or outcome: *the accident resulted in injuries to those involved.* SUCCEED implies coming after in time, particularly coming into a title, office, etc.: *a son often succeeds to his father's title.* —**Ant. 1.** precede. **19.** cause.

fol·low·er (fŏl'ō ər), *n.* **1.** one who or that which follows. **2.** one who follows another in regard to his ideas or belief; disciple or adherent. **3.** an attendant or servant. **4.** *Brit. Colloq.* a male admirer, esp. of a maidservant. **5.** *Mach.* a part of a machine that receives motion from, or follows the motion of, another part.

—**Syn. 2.** FOLLOWER, ADHERENT, PARTISAN refer to one who demonstrates allegiance to a person, a doctrine, a cause, and the like. FOLLOWER often has an implication of personal relationship or of slavish acquiescence. ADHERENT, a more formal word, has also implications of more active championship of a person or a point of view. PARTISAN, ordinarily meaning a person prejudiced and unreasoning in adherence to a party, during World War II took on the meaning of a member of certain groups in occupied countries of Europe, who carried on underground resistance to Fascists.

fol·low·ing (fŏl'ō ĭng), *n.* **1.** a body of followers, attendants, adherents, etc. **2. the following,** things, lines, pages, etc., that follow. —*adj.* **3.** that follows. **4.** that comes after or next in order or time: *the following day.* **5.** that is now to follow; now to be mentioned, described, related, or the like.

fol·low-through (fŏl'ō thrōō'), *n. Sports.* **1.** the completion of a motion, as in the stroke of a tennis racket. **2.** the portion of such a motion after the ball has been hit.

fol·low-up (fŏl'ō ŭp'), *n.* **1.** act of following up. **2.** a letter or circular sent to a person to increase the effectiveness of a previous one, as in advertising. —*adj.* **3.** (of business letters, etc.) sent to a prospective customer to obtain an additional order or offer.

fol·ly (fŏl'ĭ), *n., pl.* **-lies. 1.** state or quality of being foolish; lack of understanding or sense. **2.** a foolish action, practice, idea, etc.; an absurdity. **3.** a costly but foolish undertaking, structure, etc. **4.** *(pl.)* a theatrical revue. **5.** *Obs.* wickedness; wantonness. [ME *folie,* t. OF, der. *fol* mad. See FOOL[1]]

Fol·som man (fŏl'səm), a member of a hypothetical New World prehistoric people which may have inhabited North America during the most recent (Pleistocene) glacial epoch. [so named from Folsom, New Mexico, where implements were discovered in 1925]

fo·ment (fō mĕnt'), *v.t.* **1.** to promote the growth or development of; instigate or foster (discord, rebellion, etc.). **2.** to apply warm water or medicated liquid, cloths dipped in such liquid, or the like, to (the surface of the body). [t. LL: s. *fōmentāre,* der. L *fōmentum* a warm application] —**fo·ment'er,** *n.*

fo·men·ta·tion (fō'mĕn tā'shən), *n.* **1.** instigation; encouragement of discord, rebellion, etc. **2.** the application of warm liquid, etc., to the surface of the body. **3.** the liquid, etc., so applied.

fond¹ (fŏnd), *adj.* **1.** liking (fol. by *of*): *fond of children, fond of drink.* **2.** loving: *give someone a fond look.* **3.** foolishly tender; overaffectionate; doting: *a fond parent.* **4.** cherished with strong or unreasoning affection: *nourish fond hopes.* **5.** foolishly credulous or trusting. **6.** *Archaic or Dial.* foolish or silly. [ME *fonned,* pp. of *fonnen* be foolish; orig. uncert. Cf. FUN]

fond² (fŏnd; *Fr.* fôN), *n.* **1.** a background or groundwork, esp. of lace. **2.** *Obs.* fund; stock. [F. See FUND]

fon·dant (fŏn'dənt; *Fr.* fôN dän'), *n.* a thick, creamy sugar paste, the basis of many candies. [t. F, prop. ppr. of *fondre* melt]

Fond du Lac (fŏn' də lăk', jōō lăk'), a city in E Wisconsin, on Lake Winnebago. 32,179 (1960).

fon·dle (fŏn'dəl), *v.,* **-dled, -dling.** —*v.t.* **1.** to handle or touch fondly; caress. **2.** *Obs.* to treat with fond indulgence. —*v.i.* **3.** to show fondness, as by manner, words, or caresses. [freq. of obs. *fond,* v.] —**fon'dler,** *n.*

fond·ly (fŏnd'lĭ), *adv.* **1.** in a fond manner; lovingly or affectionately. **2.** with complacent credulity.

fond·ness (fŏnd'nĭs), *n.* **1.** state or quality of being fond. **2.** affectionateness or tenderness. **3.** doting affection. **4.** complacent credulity. **5.** instinctive liking.

fon·due (fŏn'dōō, fŏn dōō'; *Fr.* fôN dY'), *n.* a baked dish composed of grated cheese melted with butter, eggs, etc. [t. F, fem. pp. of *fondre* melt]

font¹ (fŏnt), *n.* **1.** a receptacle, usually of stone, in a baptistery or church, for the water used in baptism. **2.** a receptacle for holy water; stoup. **3.** the reservoir for oil in a lamp. **4.** *Archaic.* a fountain. [ME and OE, t. L: s. *fons* baptismal font, spring, fountain]

font² (fŏnt), *n. Print.* a complete assortment of type of one style and size. Also, *esp. Brit.,* **fount.** [t. F: m. *fonte,* der. *fondre* melt, cast. See FOUND[3]]

Baptismal font

Fon·taine·bleau (fŏn'tĭn blō'; *Fr.* fôN tĕn blō'), *n.* a town in N France, SE of Paris: site of a famous palace, long a favorite residence of French kings, and an extensive forest. 19,915 (1954).

Fontainebleau School, a group of painters, many of them Italian and Flemish, who worked on the decorations of the palace of Fontainebleau in the sixteenth century.

font·al (fŏn'təl), *adj.* **1.** pertaining to or issuing as from a fount or spring. **2.** pertaining to or being the source of something. **3.** of or pertaining to a font, as of baptism.

fon·ta·nel (fŏn'tə nĕl'), *n.* **1.** *Anat.* one of the spaces, closed by membrane, between the bones of the fetal or young skull. **2.** *Pathol. Obs.* an opening for the discharge of pus. Also, **fon'ta·nelle'.** [t. F: m. *fontanelle,* dim. of *fontaine* FOUNTAIN]

Fon·tanne (fŏn tăn'), *n.* **Lynn,** born 1887?, U.S. actress, born in England.

Foo·chow (fōō'chou'; *Chin.* -jō'), *n.* a seaport in SE China: the capital of Fukien province. 500,000 (est. 1954). Also, **Minhow.**

food (fōōd), *n.* **1.** what is eaten, or taken into the body, for nourishment. **2.** more or less solid nourishment (as opposed to *drink*). **3.** a particular kind of solid nourishment: *a breakfast food.* **4.** whatever supplies nourishment to organic bodies: *the food of plants.* **5.** anything serving as material for consumption or use. [ME *fode,* OE *fōda.* Cf. FEED, FODDER, FOSTER] —**food'less,** *adj.*

—**Syn. 1.** FOOD, FARE, PROVISIONS, RATION(s) refer to nutriment for any organism, whether of man, animal, or plant. FOOD is the general word: *breakfast foods have become very popular, many animals prefer grass as food.* FARE refers to the whole range of foods which may nourish person, animal, or plant: *an extensive bill of fare, the fare of some animals is limited in range.* PROVISIONS is applied to a store or stock of necessary things, esp. food, prepared beforehand: *provisions for a journey.* RATION implies an allotment or allowance of provisions: *a daily ration for each man of a company.* RATIONS often mean food in general: *to be on short rations.*

food chain, *Ecol.* a series of organisms interrelated in their feeding habits, the smallest being fed upon by a larger one, which in turn feeds a still larger one, etc.

food·stuff (fōōd'stŭf'), *n.* a substance or material suitable for food.

food web, *Ecol.* a series of organisms related by predator-prey activities; a series of interrelated food chains.

fool¹ (fōōl), *n.* **1.** one who lacks sense; a silly or stupid person. **2.** a professional jester, formerly kept by a person or rank for amusement. **3.** one who is made to appear a fool; one who has been imposed on by others: *to make a fool of someone.* **4.** a weak-minded or idiotic person. —*v.t.* **5.** to make a fool of; impose on; trick; deceive. **6.** to spend foolishly, as time or money (fol. by *away*). —*v.i.* **7.** to act like a fool; joke; play. **8.** to potter aimlessly; waste time: *to fool around with minor details.* **9.** to play or meddle foolishly (fol. by *with*): *to fool with a loaded gun.* **10.** to jest; make believe: *I was only fooling.* [ME *fol*, t. OF (n. and adj.), ? g. L *follis* bellows, LL bag] —**Syn. 1.** simpleton, dolt, dunce, blockhead, numskull, ignoramus, dunderhead, ninny, nincompoop, booby, saphead, sap. **2.** buffoon, droll. **5.** delude, hoodwink, trick, cheat, gull, hoax, cozen. **8.** play, trifle, toy, dally, idle, dawdle, loiter, tarry.

fool² (fōōl), *n.* *Brit. Cookery.* a dish made of fruit scalded or stewed, crushed, and mixed with cream, etc.: *gooseberry fool.* [prob. special use of FOOL¹]

fool·er·y (fōōl/lərĭ). *n.*, *pl.* **-eries.** **1.** foolish action or conduct. **2.** a foolish action, performance, or thing.

fool·har·dy (fōōl/här/dĭ), *adj.* **-dier, -diest.** bold without judgment; foolishly rash or venturesome. —**fool/har·di·ly,** *adv.* —**fool/har/di·ness,** *n.*

fool hen, *U.S.* a grouse which is confiding, hence easily killed, esp. the blue grouse, *Dendragapus obscurus,* and spruce grouse, *Canachites canadensis.*

fool·ish (fōō/lĭsh), *adj.* **1.** silly; without sense: *a foolish person.* **2.** resulting from or evidencing folly; ill-considered; unwise: *a foolish action, speech, etc.* **3.** *Obs.* or *Archaic.* trifling, insignificant, or paltry. —**fool/ish·ly,** *adv.* —**fool/ish·ness,** *n.*
—**Syn. 1, 2.** FOOLISH, FATUOUS, SILLY, STUPID imply weakness of intellect and of judgment. FOOLISH implies lack of common sense or good judgment or, sometimes, weakness of mind: *a foolish decision, the child seems foolish.* FATUOUS implies being foolish, dull, and vacant in mind, but complacent and highly self-satisfied: *fatuous and self-important, fatuous answers.* SILLY denotes extreme and conspicuous foolishness; it may also refer to pointlessness of jokes, remarks, etc.: *silly and senseless behavior, a perfectly silly statement.* STUPID implies natural slowness or dullness of intellect, or, sometimes, a benumbed or dazed state of mind; it is also used to mean foolish or silly: *well-meaning but stupid, rendered stupid by a blow, it is stupid to do such a thing.* —**Ant. 1.** wise, intelligent.

fool·proof (fōōl/prōōf/), *adj.* *Colloq.* **1.** involving no risk or harm, even when tampered with. **2.** never-failing: *a foolproof method.*

fools·cap (fōōlz/kăp/), *n.* **1.** writing paper, usually folded, varying in size from 12 x 15 to 12½ x 16 inches. **2.** an English printing paper size, 13½ x 17 inches (so called from its former watermark, the outline of a fool's cap). **3.** fool's cap.

fool's cap, 1. a kind of cap or hood, usually hung with bells, formerly worn by professional jesters. **2.** a conical paper cap sometimes worn by dunces at school as punishment.

fool's errand, an absurd or useless errand.

fool's gold, iron pyrites, sometimes mistaken for gold.

fool's paradise, state of illusory happiness; enjoyment based on false beliefs or hopes.

fool's-pars·ley (fōōlz/pärs/lĭ), *n.* a fetid, poisonous umbelliferous herb, *Aethusa Cynapium,* resembling parsley.

foot (fŏŏt), *n.*, *pl.* **feet** or (often for def. 17) **foots;** *v.* —*n.* **1.** (in vertebrates) the terminal part of the leg, below the ankle joint, on which the body stands and moves. **2.** (in invertebrates) any part similar in position or function. **3.** such a part considered as the organ of locomotion. **4.** a unit of length derived from the length of the human foot. In English-speaking countries it is divided into 12 inches and equal to 30.48 centimeters. **5.** infantry. **6.** walking or running motion. **7.** step; pace. **8.** any thing or part resembling a foot, as in function. **9.** the part of a stocking, etc., covering the foot. **10.** the lowest part, or bottom, as of a hill, ladder, page, etc. **11.** the part of anything opposite the top or head. **12.** the end of a bed, grave, etc., toward which the feet are placed. **13.** *Print.* the part of the type body which forms the sides of the groove, at the base. **14.** the last, as of a series. **15.** that which is written at the bottom, as the total of an account. **16.** *Pros.* a group of syllables constituting a metrical unit of a verse. **17.** (often in *pl.* **foots**) sediment or dregs. **18.** Some special noun phrases are:
have one foot in the grave, to be near death.
on foot, 1. on one's feet, rather than riding or sitting. **2.** in motion; astir. **3.** in active existence or operation.
put one's best foot forward, 1. to make as good an impression as possible. **2.** to do one's very best. **3.** to walk as fast as possible.
put one's foot down, to take a firm stand.
put one's foot in it, to make an embarrassing blunder. —*v.i.* **19.** to walk; go on foot (often fol. by indefinite *it*). **20.** to move the feet to measure or music, or dance (often fol. by indefinite *it*). **21.** to total, as an account (fol. by *up*). **22.** (esp. of vessels) to move. —*v.t.* **23.** to set foot on; walk or dance on. **24.** to traverse on foot. **25.** to make or attach a foot to: *to foot a stocking.* **26.** *Colloq. and Dial.* to add, as a column of figures, and set the sum at the foot (fol. by *up*). **27.** *Colloq.* to pay or settle, as a bill. **28.** to seize with talons, as a hawk. **29.** to establish. **30.** *Obs.* to kick. [ME; OE *fōt,* c. G *fuss;* akin to L *pēs,* Gk. *poús*]

foot·age (fŏŏt/ĭj), *n.* **1.** length or extent in feet: *the footage of lumber, motion-picture film, etc.* **2.** *Mining.* **a.** payment by the running foot of work done. **b.** amount so paid.

foot-and-mouth disease (fŏŏt/ən mouth/), *Vet. Sci.* a contagious virus disease of cattle and other cloven-footed animals, characterized by a vesicular eruption about the hoofs and mouth. The disease very rarely affects man.

foot·ball (fŏŏt/bôl/), *n.* **1.** a game played with a large, inflated leather ball on a field at either end of which there is a goal post. Each team, consisting of eleven players, tries to score touchdowns by running or passing the ball to its opponents' goal line and field goals by kicking the ball over the crossbars of the opponents' goal post. **2.** the ball itself. **3.** *Brit.* Rugby football. **4.** *Brit.* soccer; association football. **5.** any thing or person treated roughly, casually, etc.

foot·board (fŏŏt/bôrd/), *n.* **1.** a board or small platform on which to support the foot or feet. **2.** an upright piece across the foot of a bedstead. **3.** a treadle.

foot·boy (fŏŏt/boi/), *n.* a boy in livery employed as a servant; page; lackey.

foot brake, a brake which is applied by pressure on a foot pedal.

foot·bridge (fŏŏt/brĭj/), *n.* a bridge intended for pedestrians only.

foot·can·dle (fŏŏt/kăn/dəl), *n.* *Photom.* a unit of illumination equivalent to that produced by a standard candle at the distance of one foot.

foot·cloth (fŏŏt/klôth/, -klŏth/), *n.* **1.** a carpet or rug. **2.** *Obs.* a richly ornamented caparison for a horse, hanging down to the ground.

foot·ed (fŏŏt/ĭd), *adj.* provided with a foot or feet: *a four-footed animal.*

foot·er (fŏŏt/ər), *n.* **1.** one who goes on foot; a walker. **2.** (with a numeral prefixed) a person or thing of the height or length in feet indicated: *a six-footer.*

foot·fall (fŏŏt/fôl/), *n.* **1.** a footstep. **2.** the sound of footsteps.

foot·gear (fŏŏt/gĭr/), *n.* covering for the feet, as shoes, boots, etc.

foot·hill (fŏŏt/hĭl/), *n.* a minor elevation at the base of a mountain or mountain range.

foot·hold (fŏŏt/hōld/), *n.* **1.** a hold or support for the feet; a place where one may stand or tread securely. **2.** firm footing; secure position.

foot·ing (fŏŏt/ĭng), *n.* **1.** secure position; foothold. **2.** the basis or foundation on which anything is established. **3.** place or support for the feet; surface to stand on. **4.** act of one that foots, or moves on foot, as in walking or dancing. **5.** a firm placing or stable position of the feet. **6.** the part of the foundation of wall, column, etc. that is in direct contact with the ground. **7.** position or status assigned to a person, etc., in estimation or treatment. **8.** mutual standing; reciprocal relation: *to be on a friendly footing with someone.* **9.** entrance into a new position or relationship. **10.** a fee demanded from a person upon his entrance into a trade, society, etc. **11.** act of putting a foot to anything, as a stocking. **12.** that which is added as a foot. **13.** act of adding up a column of figures. **14.** the amount of such a column as footed up.

foot·le (fŏŏt/əl), *v.*, **-led, -ling,** *n.* —*v.i.* **1.** to talk or act in a silly way. —*n.* **2.** nonsense; silliness. [orig. obscure. Cf. FOOTY]

foot·less (fŏŏt/lĭs), *adj.* **1.** without a foot or feet. **2.** unsupported or unsubstantial. **3.** *Colloq.* awkward, helpless, or inefficient.

foot·lights (fŏŏt/līts/), *n.pl.* **1.** *Theat.* a row of lights at the front of the stage, nearly on a level with the feet of the performers. **2.** the stage; acting profession.

foot·ling (fŏŏt/lĭng), *adj.* *Colloq.* foolish; silly; trifling. [f. FOOTLE, v. + -ING²]

foot·loose (fŏŏt/lōōs/), *adj.* free to go or travel about; not confined by responsibilities.

foot·man (fŏŏt/mən), *n.*, *pl.* **-men. 1.** a male servant in livery who attends the door or the carriage, waits at table, etc. **2.** a metal stand before a fire, to keep something hot.

foot·mark (fŏŏt/märk/), *n.* a footprint.

foot·note (fŏŏt/nōt/), *n.* a note or comment at the foot of a page, referring to a specific part of the text on the page.

foot·pace (fŏŏt/pās/), *n.* **1.** a walking pace. **2.** a raised portion of a floor. **3.** a landing or resting place at the end of a short flight of steps.

foot·pad (fŏŏt/păd/), *n.* a highwayman who robs on foot.

foot·path (fŏŏt/păth/, -päth/), *n.* **1.** a path for pedestrians only. **2.** *Brit.* a sidewalk.

foot·pound (fŏŏt/pound/), *n.* *Mech.* a unit of energy or work, the equivalent to that produced by a force of one pound moving through a distance of one foot.

foot·pound·al (fŏŏt/poun/dəl), *n.* *Mech.* a unit of energy equivalent to that produced by a force of one poundal moving through a distance of one foot.

foot-pound-sec·ond system (fŏŏt/pound/sĕk/-ənd), a system of units employed in science, based on the foot, pound, and second as the fundamental units of length, mass, and time.

foot·print (fŏŏt/prĭnt/), *n.* a mark left by the foot.

foot·rest (fŏŏt/rĕst/), *n.* a short bench or stool used to support one's feet.

foot·rope (fŏŏt/rōp/), *n.* *Naut.* **1.** the portion of the boltrope to which the lower edge of a sail is sewn. **2.** a rope extended under a yard, for the men to stand on while reefing or furling.

foot rot, *Vet. Sci.* an infection of the feet of sheep, causing inflammatory changes of the toes and lameness.

foot soldier, an infantryman.

foot-sore (fŏŏt/sôr/), *adj.* having sore or tender feet, as from much walking.

foot-stalk (fŏŏt/stôk/), *n. Bot., Zool.* a pedicel; peduncle.

foot-stall (fŏŏt/stôl/), *n.* **1.** the stirrup of a woman's sidesaddle. **2** *Archit.* the plinth or base of a pillar.

foot-step (fŏŏt/stĕp/), *n.* **1.** a step or tread of the foot, or the sound produced by it; footfall. **2.** the distance traversed by the foot in stepping; a pace. **3.** a footprint. **4.** follow in one's footsteps, to succeed or imitate another. **5.** a step by which to ascend or descend.

foot-stone (fŏŏt/stōn/), *n.* a stone placed at the foot of a grave.

foot-stool (fŏŏt/stōōl/), *n.* a low stool upon which to rest one's feet.

foot-ton (fŏŏt/tŭn/), *n. Mech.* a unit of work equivalent to the energy expended in raising a ton of 2,240 pounds one foot.

foot-wall (fŏŏt/wôl/), *n. Mining.* the top of the rock stratum underlying a vein or bed of ore.

foot warmer, any of various contrivances for keeping the feet warm.

foot-way (fŏŏt/wā/), *n.* **1.** a way or path for pedestrians only. **2.** *Brit.* a sidewalk.

foot-wear (fŏŏt/wâr/), *n.* articles for wearing on the feet, esp. shoes, slippers, gaiters, etc.

foot-work (fŏŏt/wûrk/), *n.* the use of the feet, as in tennis, boxing, etc.

foot-worn (fŏŏt/wôrn/), *adj.* **1.** worn by the feet: *a footworn pavement.* **2.** footsore.

foo-ty (fōō/tĭ), *adj.,* **-tier, -tiest.** *Dial.* or *Colloq.* poor; worthless; paltry. [der. FOOT (def. 17)]

foo-zle (fōō/zəl), *v.,* **-zled, -zling,** *n.* —*v.t., v.i.* **1.** to bungle; play clumsily: *to foozle a stroke in golf.* —*n.* **2.** act of foozling, esp. a bad stroke in golf. [cf. d. G *fuseln* work badly]

fop (fŏp), *n.* a man who is excessively concerned about his manners and appearance. [orig. uncert. Cf. FOB²]

fop-per-y (fŏp/ərĭ), *n., pl.* **-peries. 1.** the manners actions, dress, etc., of a fop. **2.** something foppish.

fop-pish (fŏp/ĭsh), *adj.* resembling or befitting a fop. —**fop/pish-ly,** *adv.* —**fop/pish-ness,** *n.*

for (fôr; *unstressed* fər), *prep.* **1.** with the object or purpose of: *to go for a walk.* **2.** intended to belong to, suit the purposes or needs of, or be used in connection with: *a book for children, a box for gloves.* **3.** in order to obtain: *a suit for damages.* **4.** with inclination or tendency toward: *to long for a thing, to have an eye for beauty.* **5.** in consideration of, or in return for: *three for a dollar, to be thanked for one's efforts.* **6.** appropriate or adapted to: *a subject for speculation.* **7.** with regard or respect to: *pressed for time, too warm for April.* **8.** during the continuance of: *for a long time.* **9.** in favor of, or on the side of: *to stand for honest government.* **10.** in place of, or instead of: *a substitute for butter.* **11.** in the interest of: *to act for a client.* **12.** as an offset to: *blow for blow.* **13.** in honor of: *to give a dinner for a person.* **14.** with the purpose of reaching: *to start for London.* **15.** conducive to: *for the advantage of everybody.* **16.** in order to save: *to flee for one's life.* **17.** in order to become: *to go for a soldier.* **18.** in assignment or attribution to: *an engagement for this evening, it is for you to decide.* **19.** to allow of; to require: *too many for separate mention.* **20.** such as results in: *his reason for going.* **21.** as affecting the interests or circumstances of: *bad for one's health.* **22.** in proportion or with reference to: *tall for his age.* **23.** in the character of, or as being: *to know a thing for a fact.* **24.** by reason of, or because of: *to shout for joy, famed for its beauty.* **25.** in spite of: *for all that.* **26.** to the extent or amount of: *to walk for a mile.* **27.** (sometimes used to govern a noun or pronoun followed by an infinitive, in a construction equivalent to a clause with *that* and the auxiliary *should,* etc.): *it is time for him to go, or that he should go.* —*conj.* **28.** seeing that; since. **29.** because. [ME and OE; c. OS *for;* akin to *fore,* adv. and prep.] —**Syn. 29.** See **because.**

for-, a prefix meaning "away," "off," "to the uttermost," "extremely," "wrongly," or imparting a negative or privative force, occurring in words of Old or Middle English origin, many of which are now obsolete or archaic, as in *forswear, forbid.* [ME and OE. Cf. G *ver-,* Gk. *peri-,* L *per-*]

for., 1. foreign. **2.** forestry.

F.O.R., free on rails. Also, **f.o.r.**

for-age (fôr/ĭj, fŏr/-), *n., v.,* **-aged, -aging.** —*n.* **1.** food for horses and cattle; fodder; provender. **2.** the seeking or obtaining such food. **3.** act of searching for provisions of any kind. **4.** a raid. —*v.i.* **5.** to wander in search of supplies. **6.** to hunt or search about. **7.** to make a raid. —*v.t.* **8.** to collect forage from; strip of supplies; plunder. **9.** to supply with forage. **10.** to obtain by foraging. [ME, t. F: m. *fourrage,* der. OF *fuerre* fodder, t. Gmc. (see FODDER)] —**for/ag-er,** *n.* —**Syn. 1.** See **feed.**

forage cap, *Brit.* a small, low, undress military cap.

For-a-ker (fôr/ə kər, fŏr/-), *n.* Mount, a peak in central Alaska, near Mt. McKinley. ab. 17,000 ft.

fo-ra-men (fō rā/mən), *n., pl.* **-ramina** (-răm/ə nə). an opening, orifice, or short passage, as in a bone or in the integument of the ovule of a plant. [t. L: hole]

foramen mag-num (măg/nəm), *Latin.* the great hole in the occipital bone forming the passage from the cranial cavity to the spinal canal. [L: lit., great hole]

fo-ram-i-nate (fō răm/ə nĭt, -nāt/), *adj. Rare.* full of holes or foramina.

fo-ra-min-i-fer (fôr/ə mĭn/ə fər, fŏr/-), *n.* any of the *Foraminifera,* an extensive order of small, mostly marine rhizopods commonly having a calcareous shell perforated in many species by small holes or pores. [f. s. L *forāmen* hole + -(I)FER] —**fo-ram-i-nif-er-al** (fō răm/ə nĭf/ər-əl), **fo-ram/i-nif/er-ous,** *adj.*

for-as-much (fôr/az mŭch/), *conj.* in view of the fact that; seeing that; since (fol. by *as*).

for-ay (fôr/ā, fŏr/ā), *n.* **1.** a raid for the purpose of taking plunder. —*v.i.* **2.** to make a raid; forage; pillage. —*v.t.* **3.** to ravage in search of plunder. [ME *forrei*(en), back formation from *forrayer* FORAYER]

for-ay-er (fôr/ā ər, fŏr/-), *n.* a marauder. [ME *forreier,* t. OF: m. *forrier forager*]

forb (fôrb), *n.* any herb that is not a grass or grasslike.

for-bade (fər băd/), *v.* pt. of **forbid.** Also, **for-bad/.**

for-bear¹ (fôr bâr/), *v.,* **-bore, -borne, -bearing.** —*v.t.* **1.** to refrain from; desist from; cease. **2.** to refrain from using, etc.; keep back; withhold. **3.** *Archaic.* to endure. —*v.i.* **4.** to refrain; hold back. **5.** to be patient; show forbearance. [ME *forbere*(n), OE *forberan.* See FOR-, BEAR¹] —**for-bear/er,** *n.* —**for-bear/ing-ly,** *adv.*

for-bear² (fôr/bâr/), *n.* forebear.

for-bear-ance (fôr bâr/əns), *n.* **1.** act of forbearing; a refraining from something. **2.** forbearing conduct or quality; patient endurance; lenity. **3.** an abstaining from the enforcement of a right. **4.** a creditor's giving of indulgence after the day originally fixed for payment.

Forbes-Rob-ert-son (fôrbz/rŏb'ərt sən), *n.* Sir **Johnston,** 1853–1937, British actor and theater manager.

for-bid (fər bĭd/), *v.t.,* **-bade** or **-bad, -bidden** or **-bid, -bidding. 1.** to command (a person, etc.) not to do, have, use, etc., something, or not to enter some place. **2.** to put an interdiction against (something); prohibit **3.** to hinder or prevent; make impossible. **4.** to exclude; repel. [ME *forbede*(n), OE *forbēodan*] —**for-bid/der,** *n.*

—**Syn. 1.** FORBID, INHIBIT, PROHIBIT, TABOO indicate a command to refrain from some action. FORBID, a common and familiar word, usually denotes a direct or personal command of this sort: *I forbid you to go, to forbid children to play in the park.* INHIBIT, besides indicating ecclesiastical prohibition, implies a checking or hindering of impulses by the mind: *to inhibit one's desires.* PROHIBIT, a formal or legal word, means usually to forbid by official edict, enactment, or the like: *to prohibit the sale of liquor.* TABOO, primarily associated with primitive superstition, means to prohibit by common disapproval and by social custom: *to taboo a subject in polite conversation.* —**Ant. 1.** permit.

for-bid-dance (fər bĭd/əns), *n. Rare.* **1.** act of forbidding. **2.** state of being forbidden.

for-bid-den (fər bĭd/ən), *v.* **1.** pp. of **forbid.** —*adj.* **2.** prohibited.

forbidden fruit, unlawful pleasure.

for-bid-ding (fər bĭd/ĭng), *adj.* **1.** causing dislike or fear: *a forbidding countenance.* **2.** repellent; dangerous-looking: *forbidding cliffs, clouds, etc.* —**for-bid/ding-ly,** *adv.* —**for-bid/ding-ness,** *n.*

for-bore (fôr bōr/), *v.* pt. of **forbear**¹.

for-borne (fôr bōrn/), *v.* pp. of **forbear**¹.

for-by (fôr bī/), *prep., adv. Now Chiefly Scot. and Dial.* **1.** close by; near. **2.** besides. Also, **for-bye/.** [f. FOR- + BY]

force (fōrs), *n., v.,* **forced, forcing.** —*n.* **1.** strength; impetus; intensity of effect. **2.** might, as of a ruler or realm; strength for war. **3.** strength or power exerted upon an object; physical coercion; violence: *to use force in order to do something, to use force on a person.* **4.** *Law.* violence offered to persons or things, as the use of force in breaking into a house. **5.** power to influence, affect, or control; power to convince: *the force of an argument, the force of circumstances.* **6.** mental or moral strength; power of effective action or of overcoming resistance. **7.** (*often pl.*) a large body of armed men; an army. **8.** any body of persons combined for joint action: *a police force, an office force.* **9.** operation: *a law now in force.* **10.** *Physics.* **a.** an influence which produces or tends to produce motion or change of motion. **b.** the intensity of such an influence. **11.** any influence or agency analogous to physical force: *social forces.* **12.** binding power, as of an agreement. **13.** value; significance; meaning.

—*v.t.* **14.** to compel; constrain; or oblige (oneself or someone) to do something: *force someone to confess.* **15.** to drive or propel against resistance. **16.** to bring about or effect by force; bring about of necessity or as a necessary result: *force a passage, to force a smile, etc.* **17.** to put or impose (something) forcibly on or upon a person: *force something on someone's attention.* **18.** to compel by force; overcome the resistance of. **19.** to obtain or draw forth by or as by force; extort: *force a confession.* **20.** to overpower; enter or take by force. **21.** to break open (a door, lock, etc.). **22.** to cause plants, fruits, etc.) to grow or mature at an increased rate by artificial means. **23.** to press, urge, or exert to violent effort or to the utmost. **24.** to use force upon.

25. *Baseball.* **a.** to retire (a base runner) who has had to leave his base to make room for an advancing runner, or for a batter who has not been given a base on balls. **b.** (of a pitcher) to allow a score by walking (a batter) with the bases full which automatically brings home the runner on third. **26.** *Cards.* **a.** to compel (a player) to trump by leading a suit of which he has no cards. **b.** to compel a player to play (a particular card). **c.** to compel (a player) to play so as to make known the strength of his hand. **27.** *Obs.* to enforce (a law, etc.). **28.** *Obs.* to give force to; strengthen; reinforce. —*v.i.* **29.** *Rare.* to make one's way by force. [ME, t. F, g. VL *fortia*, der. L *fortis* strong] —**force′-less,** *adj.* —**forc′er,** *n.* —**Syn. 1.** See **strength.**

forced (fôrst), *adj.* **1.** enforced or compulsory: *forced labor.* **2.** strained, unnatural, or affected: *a forced smile.* **3.** subjected to force. **4.** emergency: *forced landing of an airplane.* —**forc·ed·ly** (fôr′sĭd lĭ), *adv.*

forced march, *Mil.* any march longer than troops are usually expected to travel, and maintained with little time for resting or for servicing vehicles.

force feed, a means of lubrication used on most internal-combustion engines, characterized by the use of a pressure pump.

force·ful (fôrs′fəl), *adj.* **1.** full of force; powerful; vigorous; effective. **2.** acting or driven with force. —**force′ful·ly,** *adv.* —**force′ful·ness,** *n.*

force ma·jeure (fôrs mȧ zhœr′), *French.* **1.** a superior force. **2.** *Law.* **a.** an unexpected and disruptive event operating to excuse a party from a contract. **b.** (of a clause) providing that a party to a contract shall be excused in case of war, strikes, etc.

force·meat (fôrs′mēt′), *n.* *Cookery.* meat chopped fine and seasoned, used as stuffing, etc. Also, **farcemeat.** [f. *force,* var. of obs. *farce* stuffing + MEAT]

for·ceps (fôr′səps), *n.,* *pl.* **-ceps, -cipes** (-sə pēz′), an instrument, as pincers or tongs, for seizing and holding objects, as in surgical operations. [t. L] —**for′ceps-like′,** *adj.*

force pump, any pump which delivers a liquid under pressure, so as to eject it forcibly (opposed to *lift pump*).

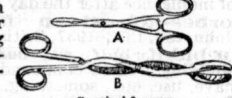

Surgical forceps A. For compression of an artery to control hemorrhage; B. For removing a stone from the bladder in lithotomy

for·ci·ble (fôr′sə bəl), *adj.* **1.** effected by force. **2.** having force; producing a powerful effect; effective. **3.** convincing, as reasoning. **4.** characterized by the use of force or violence. —**for′ci·ble·ness,** *n.* —**for′ci·bly,** *adv.*

ford (fôrd), *n.* **1.** a place where a river or other body of water may be crossed by wading. —*v.t.* **2.** to cross (a river, etc.) by a ford. [ME and OE, c. G *furt*; akin to FARE, PORT] —**ford′a·ble,** *adj.* —**ford′less,** *adj.*

Ford (fôrd), *n.* **1. Ford Madox** (fôrd măd′əks). (*Ford Madox Hueffer*) 1873–1939, British author. **2. Henry,** 1863–1947, U.S. automobile manufacturer. **3. John,** 1586–1640?, English dramatist.

for·do (fôr dōō′), *v.t.,* **-did, -done, -doing.** *Archaic.* **1.** to do away with; kill; destroy. **2.** to ruin; undo. Also, **foredo.** [ME *fordon,* OE *fordon.* See FOR-, DO]

for·done (fôr dŭn′), *adj.* *Archaic.* exhausted with fatigue; worn-out.

fore[1] (fôr), *adj.* **1.** situated at or toward the front, as compared with something else. **2.** first in place, time, order, rank, etc.; forward; earlier. —*adv.* **3.** *Naut.* at or toward the bow. **4.** *Dial.* before. **5.** *Dial.* forward. —*n.* **6.** the forepart of anything; the front. **7.** *Naut.* the foremast. **8. to the fore, a.** to or at the front; to or in a conspicuous place or position. **b.** ready at hand. **c.** still alive. —*prep. and conj.* **9.** *Now Only Dial.* before. [special use of FORE-, detached from words like *forepart, forefather,* etc.]

fore[2] (fôr), *interj.* *Golf.* a cry of warning to persons on a course who are liable to be struck by the ball. [prob. aphetic var. of BEFORE]

fore-, a prefix form of **before** meaning "front" (*forehead, forecastle*), "ahead of time" (*forecast, foretell*), "superior" (*foreman*), etc. [ME and OE *for(e)*]

fore and aft, *Naut.* in, at, or to both ends of a ship.

fore-and-aft (fôr′and ăft′), *adj.* *Naut.* **1.** in a line with the keel of a ship: *a fore-and-aft rig.* **2.** denoting a rig in which the principal sails are set on gaffs, stays, or masts, on the center line of the vessel.

fore-and-af·ter (fôr′and ăf′tər), *n.* *Naut.* a vessel with fore-and-aft sails, as a schooner.

fore-and-aft sail, *Naut.* any sail not set on a yard, usually bent to a gaff or set on a stay in the center line. See **sail** (def. 1).

fore·arm[1] (fôr′ärm′), *n.* the part of the arm between the elbow and the wrist. [f. FORE- + ARM[1]]

fore·arm[2] (fôr ärm′), *v.t.* to arm beforehand. [f. FORE- + ARM[2]]

fore·bear (fôr′bâr′), *n.* (*usually pl.*) an ancestor; forefather. Also, **forbear.** [ME (Scot.); f. FORE- + *bear* being (var. of *beer,* f. BE, v. + -ER[1])]

fore·bode (fôr bōd′), *v.,* **-boded, -boding.** —*v.t.* **1.** to foretell or predict; portend; be an omen of; indicate beforehand: *clouds that forebode a storm.* **2.** to have a presentiment of (esp. evil). **3.** to prophesy. **4.** to have a presentiment. —**fore·bod′er,** *n.*

fore·bod·ing (fôr bō′dĭng), *n.* **1.** a prediction; portent. **2.** a presentiment. —*adj.* **3.** that forebodes, esp. evil. —**fore·bod′ing·ly,** *adv.*

fore·brain (fôr′brān′). *n.* *Anat.* **1.** that portion of the adult brain which develops from the prosencephalon. **2.** the prosencephalon. **3.** the telencephalon.

fore·cast (fôr′kăst′, -käst′), *v.,* **-cast** or **-casted, -casting,** *n.* —*v.t.* **1.** to conjecture beforehand; predict. **2.** to make a forecast of (the weather, etc.). **3.** to serve as a forecast of; foreshadow. **4.** to cast, contrive, or plan beforehand; prearrange. —*v.i.* **5.** to conjecture beforehand; make a forecast. **6.** to plan or arrange beforehand. —*n.* **7.** a conjecture as to something in the future. **8.** a prediction, esp. as to the weather. **9.** act, practice, or faculty of forecasting. **10.** foresight in planning. —**fore′cast′er,** *n.* —**Syn. 1.** See **predict.**

fore·cas·tle (fōk′səl, fôr′kăs′əl), *n.* *Naut.* **1.** the seamen's quarters in the forward part of a merchant vessel. **2.** that part of the upper deck forward of the foremast. **3.** Also, **forecastle deck** or **head,** a short raised deck in the forepart of a ship.

fore·cit·ed (fôr′sī′tĭd), *adj.* previously cited.

fore·close (fôr klōz′), *v.,* **-closed, -closing.** —*v.t.* **1.** *Law.* **a.** to deprive (a mortgagor or pledgor) of the right to redeem his property. **b.** to take away the right to redeem (a mortgage or pledge). **2.** to shut out; exclude or bar. **3.** to hinder or prevent, as from doing something. **4.** to establish an exclusive claim to. **5.** to close, settle, or answer beforehand. —*v.i.* **6.** to foreclose a mortgage or pledge. [ME *forclose(n),* OF: m. *forclos,* pp. of *forclore* exclude, f. *for-* out + *clore* shut, g. L *claudere*] —**fore·clos′a·ble,** *adj.*

fore·clo·sure (fôr klō′zhər), *n.* *Law.* act of foreclosing a mortgage or pledge.

fore·course (fôr′kōrs′), *n.* *Naut.* the course set on the foremast (the foresail in a square-rigged vessel).

fore·date (fôr′dāt′), *v.t.* **-dated, -dating.** antedate.

fore·deck (fôr′dĕk′), *n.* *Naut.* the forward part of the spar deck.

fore·do (fôr dōō′), *v.t.,* **-did, -done, -doing.** fordo.

fore·doom (*v.* fôr dōōm′; *n.* fôr′dōōm′), *v.t.* **1.** to doom beforehand. —*n.* **2.** a doom ordained beforehand.

fore edge, the front outer edge of a book, opposite the bound edge.

fore·fa·ther (fôr′fä′thər), *n.* an ancestor.

Forefathers' Day, the anniversary of the day (Dec. 21, 1620, in Old Style Dec. 11) on which the Pilgrims landed at Plymouth, Massachusetts. Owing to an error in changing the date from the Old Style to the New, it is generally observed on Dec. 22.

fore·feel (fôr fēl′), *v.,* **-felt, -feeling,** *n.* —*v.t.* **1.** to feel or perceive beforehand; have a presentiment of. —*n.* **2.** a feeling beforehand.

fore·fend (fôr fĕnd′), *v.t.* forefend.

fore·fin·ger (fôr′fĭng′gər), *n.* the first finger, next to the thumb.

fore·foot (fôr′fŏŏt′), *n., pl.* **-feet** (-fēt′). **1.** *Zool.* one of the front feet of a quadruped, or of an insect, etc. **2.** *Naut.* the forward end of the keel.

fore·front (fôr′frŭnt′), *n.* the foremost part or place.

fore·gath·er (fôr găth′ər), *v.i.* forgather.

fore·go[1] (fôr gō′), *v.t., v.i.* **-went, -gone, -going.** to go before; precede. [OE *foregān* go before, f. *fore-* FORE- + *gān* go] —**fore·go′er,** *n.*

fore·go[2] (fôr gō′), *v.t.,* **-went, -gone, -going.** forgo. —**fore·go′er,** *n.*

fore·go·ing (fôr gō′ĭng), *adj.* going before; preceding: *the foregoing passage.*

fore·gone (fôr gôn′, -gŏn′, fôr′gôn′, -gŏn′), *adj.* that has gone before; previous; past. —**fore·gone′ness,** *n.*

foregone conclusion, 1. an inevitable conclusion or result. **2.** a conclusion, opinion, or decision formed in advance.

fore·ground (fôr′ground′), *n.* the ground or parts situated, or represented as situated, in the front; the nearer portion of a scene (opposed to *background*).

fore·gut (fôr′gŭt′), *n.* *Embryol., Zool.* the upper part of the embryonic digestive canal from which the pharynx, esophagus, stomach, and part of the duodenum develop.

fore·hand (fôr′hănd′), *adj.* **1.** made to the right side of the body (when the player is right-handed). **2.** being in front or ahead. **3.** foremost or leading. **4.** done beforehand; anticipative; given or made in advance, as a payment. —*n.* **5.** position in front or above; superior position; advantage. **6.** *Tennis, etc.* **a.** a forehand stroke. **b.** that type of playing, or the stance taken when making such strokes. **7.** the part of a horse which is in front of the rider.

fore·hand·ed (fôr′hăn′dĭd), *adj.* **1.** forehand, as a stroke in tennis, etc. **2.** providing for the future; prudent; thrifty. **3.** in easy circumstances; well-to-do. —**fore′hand·ed·ness,** *n.*

fore·head (fôr′ĭd, fŏr′-, fôr′hĕd′), *n.* **1.** the fore or front upper part of the head; the part of the face above the eyes; the brow. **2.** the fore or front part of anything. [ME *forehe(v)ed*, OE *forhēafod*, f. *for(e)-* FORE- + *hēafod* head]

or·eign (fôr′ĭn, fŏr′-), *adj.* **1.** pertaining to, characteristic of, or derived from another country or nation; not native or domestic. **2.** pertaining to relations, or dealings with other countries. **3.** external to one's own country or nation: *a foreign country.* **4.** carried on abroad, or with other countries: *foreign trade.* **5.** belonging to or coming from another district, province, society, etc. **6.** situated outside a district, province, etc. **7.** *Law.* outside the legal jurisdiction of the state; alien. **8.** belonging to or proceeding from other persons or things: *a statement supported by foreign testimony.* **9.** not belonging to the place or body where found: *a foreign substance in the eye.* **10.** not related to or connected with the thing under consideration: *foreign to our discussion.* **11.** alien in character; irrelevant or inappropriate; remote. **12.** strange or unfamiliar. [ME *forene*, t. OF: m. *forain*, ult. der. L *foras* out of doors, outside] —**for′eign·ness**, *n.*

foreign affairs, international relations; activities of a nation arising from its dealings with other nations.

for·eign·er (fôr′ĭn ər, fŏr′-), *n.* **1.** a person not native or naturalized in the country or jurisdiction under consideration; an alien. **2.** a thing produced in or brought from a foreign country. **3.** *Naut.* a foreign vessel. —**Syn. 1.** See **stranger.**

foreign exchange, **1.** the process of striking a balance in commercial transactions between businessmen of different nations. **2.** commercial paper drawn on a person or corporation in a foreign nation.

for·eign·ism (fôr′ĭnĭz′əm, fŏr′-), *n.* **1.** a foreign custom, etc. **2.** any trait or deviation from accepted speech standards that comes from the influence of a foreign language. **3.** imitation of anything foreign. **4.** foreign quality.

foreign legion, **1.** a military body in the service of a state, consisting of foreign volunteers. **2.** (*caps.*) a military body in the French Army, consisting of foreigners of all nationalities, including Frenchmen, used mainly for military operations and duties in northern Africa.

foreign office, *Brit.* the department of a government concerned with the conduct of international relations.

fore·judge[1] (fôr jŭj′), *v.t.*, **-judged, -judging.** to judge beforehand; prejudge. [f. FORE- + JUDGE, v.]

fore·judge[2] (fôr jŭj′), *v.t.*, **-judged, -judging.** forjudge.

fore·know (fôr nō′), *v.t.*, **-knew, -known, -knowing.** to know beforehand. —**fore·know′a·ble**, *adj.*

fore·knowl·edge (fôr nŏl′ĭj, fôr nŏl′ĭj), *n.* knowledge of a thing before it exists or happens; prescience: *had you any foreknowledge of the banquet?*

fore·la·dy (fôr′lā′dĭ), *n.*, *pl.* **-dies.** forewoman.

fore·land (fôr′lănd′), *n.* **1.** a cape, headland, or promontory. **2.** land or territory lying in front.

fore·leg (fôr′lĕg′), *n.* one of the front legs of a quadruped, or of an insect, etc.

fore·limb (fôr′lĭm′), *n.* a front limb of an animal.

fore·lock[1] (fôr′lŏk′), *n.* **1.** the lock of hair that grows from the fore part of the head. **2.** a prominent or somewhat detached lock above the forehead. [f. FORE- + LOCK[2]]

fore·lock[2] (fôr′lŏk′), *n.* a round or flat wedge of iron passed through a hole in the inner end of a bolt to prevent its withdrawal when a strain is placed on it. [f. FORE- + LOCK[1]]

fore·man (fôr′mən), *n.*, *pl.* **-men.** **1.** a man in charge of a group of workers. **2.** the chairman of a jury. —**fore′man·ship**, *n.*

fore·mast (fôr′măst′, -mäst′; *Naut.* -məst), *n. Naut.* the mast nearest the bow of a ship.

fore·most (fôr′mōst′, -məst), *adj., adv.* first in place, order, rank, etc. [f. FORE, adj. + -MOST, r. ME and OE *formest*, f. *forma* first (var. of *frum(a)*. Cf. L *primus*) + -EST]

fore·name (fôr′nām′), *n.* a name that precedes the family name or surname; a first name.

fore·named (fôr′nāmd′), *adj.* named before; mentioned before in the same writing or discourse.

fore·noon (*n.* fôr′nōōn′; *adj.* fôr′nōōn′), *n.* **1.** the period of daylight before noon. **2.** the latter part of the morning, esp. the part ordinarily employed in transacting business. —*adj.* **3.** of or pertaining to the forenoon.

fo·ren·sic (fə rĕn′sĭk), *adj.* **1.** pertaining to, connected with, or used in courts of law or public discussion and debate. **2.** adapted or suited to argumentation; argumentative. [f. L *forens(is)* of the forum + -IC] —**fo·ren′si·cal·ly**, *adv.*

fore·or·dain (fôr′ôr dān′), *v.t.* to ordain or appoint beforehand; predestinate. —**fore′or·dain′ment**, *n.*

fore·or·di·na·tion (fôr′ôr də nā′shən), *n.* previous ordination or appointment; predestination.

fore·part (fôr′pärt′), *n.* the fore, front, or early part.

fore·peak (fôr′pēk′), *n. Naut.* the part of the hold in the angle formed by the bow.

fore·quar·ter (fôr′kwôr′tər), *n.* (in cutting meat) the forward end of half of a carcass.

fore·reach (fôr rēch′), *v.i.* **1.** to gain, as one ship on another. —*v.t.* **2.** to gain upon; overhaul and pass.

fore·run (fôr rŭn′), *v.t.*, **-ran, -run, -running.** **1.** to run in front of; precede; be the precursor of. **2.** to anticipate or forestall. **3.** to outrun or outstrip.

fore·run·ner (fôr′rŭn′ər, fôr rŭn′ər), *n.* **1.** a predecessor; ancestor. **2.** one who or that which foreruns; a herald or harbinger. **3.** a prognostic or portent. **4. the Forerunner**, John the Baptist.

fore·said (fôr′sĕd′), *adj.* forementioned; aforesaid.

fore·sail (fôr′sāl′; *Naut.* -səl), *n. Naut.* **1.** the sail bent to the foreyard of a square-rigged vessel. See illus. under **sail. 2.** the principal sail on the foremast of a schooner. **3.** the forestaysail of a sloop, cutter, etc.

fore·see (fôr sē′), *v.*, **-saw, -seen, -seeing.** —*v.t.* **1.** to see beforehand; have prescience of; foreknow. —*v.i.* **2.** to exercise foresight. [ME *foresēon*, f. *fore-* FORE- + *sēon* SEE[1]] —**fore·see′a·ble**, *adj.* —**fore·se′er**, *n.* —**Syn. 1.** See **predict.**

fore·shad·ow (fôr shăd′ō), *v.t.* to shadow or indicate beforehand; prefigure. —**fore·shad′ow·er**, *n.*

fore·sheet (fôr′shēt′), *n. Naut.* **1.** a sheet of a foresail. **2.** (*pl.*) the forward part of an open boat.

fore·shore (fôr′shôr′), *n.* **1.** the forepart of the shore; the part of the shore between the ordinary high-water mark and low-water mark. **2.** the ground between the water's edge and the land cultivated or built upon.

fore·short·en (fôr shôr′tən), *v.t. Drawing.* to reduce the length of (a line, part, object, or the like, which lies in a plane not perpendicular to the line of sight) in order to give the proper impression to the eye by means of perspective.

fore·show (fôr shō′), *v.t.*, **-showed, -shown, -showing.** to show beforehand; foretell; foreshadow. [ME *forescewen*, OE *forescēawian*, f. *fore-* FORE- + *scēawian* show]

fore·side (fôr′sīd′), *n.* **1.** the front side or part. **2.** the upper side. **3.** *U.S.* a stretch of land fronting the sea.

fore·sight (fôr′sīt′), *n.* **1.** care or provision for the future; provident care. **2.** act or power of foreseeing; prevision; prescience. **3.** act of looking forward. **4.** perception gained by or as by looking forward; prospect; a view into the future. **5.** *Survey.* **a.** a sight or reading taken on a forward point. **b.** (in leveling) a rod reading on a point the elevation of which is to be determined. **6.** a sight on the muzzle of a gun. —**fore′sight′ed**, *adj.* —**fore′sight′ed·ness**, *n.* —**Syn. 1.** See **prudence.**

fore·skin (fôr′skĭn′), *n. Anat.* the prepuce.

for·est (fôr′ĭst, fŏr′-), *n.* **1.** a large tract of land covered with trees; an extensive wood. **2.** the trees alone: *to cut down a forest.* **3.** *Eng. Law.* a tract of woody grounds and pastures, generally belonging to the sovereign, set apart for game. —*v.t.* **4.** to cover with trees; convert into a forest. [ME, t. OF, g. VL *forestis* an unenclosed wood (as opposed to a park), der. L *foris* outside. See FOREIGN] —**for′est·ed**, *adj.* —**for′est·less**, *adj.* —**for′est·like′**, *adj.*

—**Syn. 1.** FOREST, GROVE, WOOD refer to an area covered with trees. A FOREST is an extensive wooded area, preserving some of its primitive wildness and usually having game or wild animals in it: *Sherwood Forest, the Black Forest.* A GROVE is a group or cluster of trees, usually not very large in area and cleared of underbrush; it may consist of fruit or nut trees: *a shady grove, a grove of pines, an orange grove, a walnut grove.* A WOOD (WOODS) is a wooded tract smaller than a forest and resembling one, but less wild in character and nearer to civilization: *a wood covering several acres, lost in the woods.*

fore·stall (fôr stôl′), *v.t.* **1.** to prevent, hinder, or thwart by action in advance; take measures concerning or deal with (a thing) in advance. **2.** to deal with, meet, or realize in advance of the natural or proper time; be beforehand with or get ahead of (a person, etc.) in action. **3.** to buy up (goods) in advance, in order to enhance the price. **4.** to prevent sales at (a fair, market etc.) by buying up or diverting goods. [ME *forstalle*, der. OE *foresteall* intervention (to defeat justice), waylaying. See FORE-, STALL[2]] —**fore·stall′er**, *n.* —**fore·stall′ment, fore·stal′ment**, *n.*

for·es·ta·tion (fôr′ĭs tā′shən, fŏr′-), *n.* the planting of forests.

fore·stay (fôr′stā′), *n. Naut.* a strong rope (now generally of wire) extending forward from the head of the foremast to the knightheads or stem to support the mast.

fore·stay·sail (fôr′stā′sāl′; *Naut.* -səl), *n. Naut.* a triangular sail set on the forestay, being the first sail in front of the forward (or single) mast.

for·est·er (fôr′ĭs tər, fŏr′-), *n.* **1.** one who practices, or is versed in, forestry. **2.** an officer having charge of a forest. **3.** *Zool.* an animal of the forest. **4.** the great gray kangaroo, *Macropus canguru.* **5.** any of various moths of the family *Zygaenidae*, as *Alypia octomaculata,* the eight-spotted forester, a moth whose larva devours grapevines.

For·est·er (fôr′ĭs tər, fŏr′-), *n.* **Cecil Scott**, 1899–1966, British novelist.

forest reserve, *U.S.* an area of forest set aside by the government as a reserve.

for·est·ry (fôr′ĭs trĭ, fŏr′-), *n.* **1.** the science of planting and taking care of forests. **2.** act of establishing and managing forests. **3.** forest land.

fore·taste (*n.* fôr′tāst′; *v.* fôr tāst′), *n., v.,* **-tasted, -tasting.** —*n.* **1.** a taste beforehand; anticipation. —*v.t.* **2.** to taste beforehand; enjoy by anticipation.

fore·tell (fôr tĕl′), *v.*, **-told, -telling.** —*v.t.* **1.** to tell of beforehand; predict or prophesy. **2.** (of things) to

foreshow. —*v.i.* **3.** to utter a prediction or a prophecy. —**fore·tell′er,** *n.*

fore·thought (fôr′thôt′), *n.* **1.** provident care; prudence. **2.** a thinking of something beforehand; previous consideration; anticipation. —**Syn. 1.** See **prudence.**

fore·thought·ful (fôr′thôt′fəl), *adj.* full of or having forethought; provident. —**fore·thought′ful·ly,** *adv.* —**fore·thought′ful·ness,** *n.*

fore·time (fôr′tīm′), *n.* former or past time; the past.

fore·to·ken (*n.* fôr′tō′kən; *v.* fôr tō′kən), *n.* **1.** a premonitory token or sign. —*v.t.* **2.** to foreshadow. [ME *foretokne,* OE *foretācn,* f. *fore-* FORE- + *tācn* token]

fore·top (fôr′tŏp′; *for 1 also Naut.* -təp), *n.* **1.** *Naut.* a platform at the head of a foremast. **2.** the front seat on the top of a vehicle. **3.** the forelock of an animal, esp. a horse. **4.** *Obs.* a human forelock, or a lock of hair on the front of a wig.

fore-top·gal·lant (fôr′tŏp gǎl′ənt; *Naut.* -təgǎl′-), *adj. Naut.* (of a mast, sail, yard, etc.) next above the fore-topmast. See illus. under **sail.**

fore-topgallant mast, *Naut.* the mast next above the fore-topmast.

fore-top·mast (fôr′tŏp′mǎst′, -mäst′; *Naut.* -məst), *n. Naut.* the mast erected at the head of the foremast, above the foretop.

fore-top·sail (fôr′tŏp′sāl′; *Naut.* -səl), *n. Naut.* the sail set on the fore-topmast. See illus. under **sail.**

for·ev·er (fôr ĕv′ər), *adv.* **1.** eternally; without ever ending: *to last forever, go away forever.* **2.** continually; incessantly: *he's forever complaining.* [prop. phrase]

for·ev·er·more (fôr ĕv′ər môr′), *adv.* for ever hereafter.

fore·warn (fôr wôrn′), *v.t.* to warn beforehand.

fore·wom·an (fôr′wŏom′ən), *n., pl.* **-women. 1.** a woman in charge of a group of workwomen. **2.** the chairlady of a jury.

fore·word (fôr′wûrd′), *n.* a preface or introductory statement in a book, etc. —**Syn.** See **introduction.**

fore·worn (fôr wôrn′), *adj. Archaic.* forworn.

fore·yard (fôr′yärd′), *n. Naut.* the lower yard on the foremast.

For·far (fôr′fər, -fär), *n.* former name of **Angus.**

for·feit (fôr′fĭt), *n.* **1.** a fine; a penalty. **2.** act of forfeiting; forfeiture. **3.** something to which the right is lost by the commission of a crime or misdeed, the neglect of a duty, a breach of contract, etc. **4.** an article deposited in a game because of a mistake and redeemable by a fine or penalty. **5.** (*pl.*) a game so played. —*v.t.* **6.** to lose as a forfeit. **7.** to lose, or become liable to lose, in consequence of crime, fault, breach of engagement, etc. —*adj.* **8.** forfeited. [ME *forfet,* t. OF, pp. of *forfaire,* f. *for-* outside, wrongly + *faire* do] —**for′feit·a·ble,** *adj.* —**for′feit·er,** *n.*

for·fei·ture (fôr′fĭ chər), *n.* **1.** act of forfeiting. **2.** that which is forfeited; a fine or mulct.

for·fend (fôr fĕnd′), *v.t.* **1.** to defend, secure, or protect. **2.** *Archaic.* to fend off, avert, or prevent. Also, **forefend.** [ME; f. FOR- + FEND]

for·fi·cate (fôr′fə kĭt, -kāt′), *adj.* deeply forked, as the tail of certain birds. [f. s. L *forfex* scissors + -ATE[1]]

for·gat (fôr gǎt′), *v. Archaic.* pt. of **forget.**

for·gath·er (fôr gǎth′ər), *v.i.* **1.** to gather together; convene; assemble. **2.** to encounter or meet, esp. by accident. **3.** to associate or fraternize (fol. by *with*). Also, **foregather.**

for·gave (fôr gāv′), *v.* pt. of **forgive.**

forge[1] (fôrj), *n., v.,* **forged, forging.** —*n.* **1.** the special fireplace, hearth, or furnace in which metal is heated before shaping. **2.** a smithy. —*v.t.* **3.** to form by heating and hammering; beat into shape. **4.** to form or make in any way. **5.** to invent (a fictitious story, a lie, etc.). **6.** to imitate (a signature, etc.) fraudulently; fabricate by false imitation. —*v.i.* **7.** to commit forgery. **8.** to work at a forge. [ME, t. OF, ult. g. L *fabrica* workshop] —**forge′a·ble,** *adj.* —**forg′er,** *n.*

forge[2] (fôrj), *v.i.,* **forged, forging.** to move ahead slowly, with difficulty, or by mere momentum (usually fol. by *ahead*). [orig. uncert.]

for·ger·y (fôr′jər ĭ), *n., pl.* **-geries. 1.** the making of a fraudulent imitation of a thing, or of something spurious which is put forth as genuine, as a coin, a work of art, a literary production, etc. **2.** something, as a coin, a work of art, a writing, etc., produced by forgery. **3.** *Law.* the false making or alteration of a writing by which the legal rights or obligations of another person are apparently affected; simulated signing of another person's name to any such writing (whether or not it is also the forger's name). **4.** act of fabricating or producing falsely. **5.** *Now Poetic.* fictitious invention; deception or artifice.

for·get (fôr gĕt′), *v.,* **-got** or (*Archaic*) **-gat; -gotten** or **-got; -getting.** —*v.t.* **1.** to cease to remember; fail to remember; be unable to recall. **2.** to omit or neglect unintentionally (to do something). **3.** to omit to take; leave behind inadvertently: *to forget one's keys.* **4.** to omit to mention; leave unnoticed. **5.** to omit to think of; take no note of. **6.** to neglect willfully; overlook, disregard, or slight. **7. forget oneself, a.** to say or do something improper. **b.** to fail to remember one's station, position, or character. **c.** to neglect or slight oneself. **d.** to become absent-minded. **e.** to lose conscious-

ness, as in sleep. —*v.i.* **8.** to cease or omit to think of something. [f. FOR- + GET; r. ME *foryete*(*n*), OE *forg*(*i*)*etan*] —**for·get′a·ble,** *adj.* —**for·get′er,** *n.*

for·get·ful (fôr gĕt′fəl), *adj.* **1.** apt to forget; that forgets: *a forgetful person.* **2.** heedless or neglectful (often fol. by *of*): *to be forgetful of others.* **3.** *Poetic.* causing to forget. —**for·get′ful·ly,** *adv.* —**for·get′ful·ness,** *n.*

for·ge·tive (fôr′jə tĭv), *adj. Archaic.* inventive; creative. [? b. FORGE[1], v. and CREATIVE]

for·get-me-not (fôr gĕt′mĭ nŏt), *n.* **1.** a small boraginaceous Old World plant, *Myosotis palustris,* bearing a light-blue flower commonly regarded as an emblem of constancy and friendship. **2.** any of several other plants of the same genus. **3.** any of various similar plants.

forg·ing (fôr′jĭng), *n.* **1.** something forged; a piece of forged work in metal. **2.** (in horses) the act of striking and injuring the forelegs with the shoes of the hind legs while racing.

for·give (fôr gĭv′), *v.,* **-gave, -given, -giving.** —*v.t.* **1.** to grant free pardon for or remission of (an offense, debt, etc.); pardon. **2.** to give up all claim on account of; remit (a debt, etc.). **3.** to grant free pardon to (a person). **4.** to cease to feel resentment against: *to forgive one's enemies.* —*v.i.* **5.** to pardon an offense or an offender. [f. FOR- + GIVE; r. ME *foryiven,* OE *forgiefan*] —**for·giv′a·ble,** *adj.* —**for·giv′er,** *n.* —**Syn. 1.** See **excuse.**

for·give·ness (fôr gĭv′nĭs), *n.* **1.** act of forgiving. **2.** state of being forgiven. **3.** disposition or willingness to forgive.

for·giv·ing (fôr gĭv′ĭng), *adj.* that forgives; disposed to forgive; indicating forgiveness. —**for·giv′ing·ly,** *adv.* —**for·giv′ing·ness,** *n.*

for·go (fôr gō′), *v.t.,* **-went, -gone, -going. 1.** to abstain or refrain from; do without; give up, renounce, or resign. **2.** *Archaic.* to neglect or overlook. **3.** *Archaic.* to quit or leave. **4.** *Obs.* to go or pass by. Also, **forego.** [ME *forgon,* OE *forgān.* See FOR-, GO] —**for·go′er,** *n.*

for·got (fôr gŏt′), *v.* pt. and pp. of **forget.**

for·got·ten (fôr gŏt′ən), *v.* pp. of **forget.**

for·int (fôr′ĭnt), *n.* the standard monetary unit of Hungary, equal to about $.085.

for·judge (fôr jŭj′), *v.t.,* **-judged, -judging.** *Law.* to exclude, expel, dispossess, or deprive by a judgment. Also, **forejudge.** [ME *forjuge*(*n*), t. OF: m. *forjugier,* f. *for-* out + *jugier* JUDGE, v.]

fork (fôrk), *n.* **1.** an instrument having two or more prongs or tines, for holding, lifting, etc., as any of various agricultural tools, or an implement for handling food at table or in cooking. **2.** something resembling or suggesting this in form. **3.** a tuning fork. **4.** a forking, or dividing into branches. **5.** the point or part at which a thing, as a river or a road, divides into branches. **6.** each of the branches into which a thing forks. **7.** *Chiefly U.S.* a principal tributary of a river. **8.** *Obs.* the barbed head of an arrow. —*v.t.* **9.** to make fork-shaped. **10.** to pierce, raise, pitch, dig, etc., with a fork. **11.** *Chess.* to assail (two pieces) at the same time. **12.** *Slang.* to hand (fol. by *over* or *out*). —*v.i.* **13.** to form a fork; divide into branches. [ME *forke,* OE *forca,* t. L: m. *furca*] —**fork′less,** *adj.* —**fork′like′,** *adj.*

forked (fôrkt, fôr′kĭd), *adj.* **1.** having a fork or forking branches. **2.** zigzag, as lightning. Also, **fork′y.** —**fork·ed·ly** (fôr′kĭd lĭ), *adv.* —**fork′ed·ness,** *n.*

For·lì (fôr lē′), *n.* a city in N Italy. 81,000 (est. 1954).

for·lorn (fôr lôrn′), *adj.* **1.** abandoned, deserted, or forsaken (sometimes fol. by *of*). **2.** desolate or dreary; unhappy or miserable, as in feeling, condition, or appearance. **3.** desperate or hopeless. **4.** bereft (fol. by *of*). [var. of *forlore*(*n*), pp. of (obs.) *forlese,* v., OE *forlēosan* lose, destroy. See FOR-, LORN] —**for·lorn′ly,** *adv.* —**for·lorn′ness,** *n.* —**Syn. 1.** See **desolate.**

forlorn hope, 1. a vain hope; an undertaking almost certain to fail. **2.** a perilous or desperate enterprise. **3.** a group of soldiers for some unusually perilous service. [t. D: alter. of *verloren hoop,* lit., lost troop]

form (fôrm), *n.* **1.** definite shape; external shape or appearance considered apart from color or material; configuration. **2.** the shape of a thing or person. **3.** a body, esp. that of a human being. **4.** something that gives or determines shape; a mold. **5.** a particular structural condition, character, or mode of being exhibited by a thing: *water in the form of ice.* **6.** the manner or style of arranging and coördinating parts for a pleasing or effective result, as in literary or musical composition. **7.** any assemblage of similar things constituting a component of a group, especially of a zoölogical group. **8.** *Crystall.* the combination of all the like faces possible on a crystal of given symmetry. **9.** due or proper shape; orderly arrangement of parts; good order. **10.** *Philos.* **a.** the structure, pattern, organization, or essential nature of anything. **b.** form or pattern considered in distinction from matter. **c.** (in Platonic use) an idea (def. 7c). **d.** (in Aristotelian use) that which gives to a thing its particular species or kind. **11.** *Logic.* the abstract relations of terms in a proposition, and of propositions to one another. **12.** a set, prescribed, or customary order or method of doing something. **13.** a set order of words, as for use in religious ritual or in a legal document. **14.** a document with blank spaces to be filled in with particulars before it is executed: *a tax form.* **15.** a typical document to be used as a guide in framing others for like cases: *a form for a deed.* **16.** a conventional method of procedure or behavior. **17.** a formality or ceremony, often with implication of absence of real meaning. **18.** procedure, according to a set order or method. **19.** formality; ceremony; conformity to the usages of society. **20.** mere outward formality or ceremony; conventional observance of social usages. **21.** procedure or conduct, as judged by social standards. **22.** manner or method of performing something. **23.** condition, esp. good condition, with reference to fitness for performing. **24.** *Gram.* **a.** any word, part of a word, or group of words arranged in a construction, which recurs in various contexts in a language with relatively constant meaning. **b.** a particular shape of a form (def. 24a) when it occurs in several: in *I'm*, *'m* is a form of *am*. **c.** a word with a particular inflectional ending or other modification, as *goes* is a form of *go*. **25.** *Brit.* a grade or class of pupils in a school. **26.** *Brit.* a bench or long seat. **27.** Also, *Brit.*, **forme.** an assemblage of types, etc., secured in a chase to print from. —*v.t.* **28.** to construct or frame. **29.** to make or produce. **30.** to serve to make up, or compose; serve for, or constitute. **31.** to place in order; arrange; organize. **32.** to frame (ideas, opinions, etc.) in the mind. **33.** to contract (habits, friendships, etc.). **34.** to give form or shape to; shape; fashion. **35.** to give a particular form to, or fashion in a particular manner. **36.** to mold by discipline or instruction. **37.** *Gram.* to stand in relation to (a particular derivative or other form) by virtue of the absence or presence of an affix or other grammatical element or change: *"man" forms its plural by the change of -a- to -e-.* **38.** *Mil.* to draw up in lines or in formation. —*v.i.* **39.** to take or assume form. **40.** to be formed or produced. **41.** to take a particular form or arrangement. [ME *forme*, t. OF, t. L: m. *forma* form, figure, model, mold, sort, ML seat]

—**Syn. 1.** FORM, FIGURE, OUTLINE, SHAPE refer to an appearance which can be recognized. FORM, FIGURE, and SHAPE are often used to mean recognizable lines as contrasted with color and material; SHAPE is more colloquial than the others. OUTLINE refers to the line which delimits a form, figure, or shape: *the outline of a hill.* FIGURE always refers to a concrete object, but FORM and SHAPE may also be applied to abstractions: *the figure of a man, the shape of a cow, of the future.* FORM is the most widely applied to physical objects, mental images, methods of procedure, etc.: *the form of a cross, of a ceremony, of a poem* —**Ant. 1.** substance.

-form, a suffix meaning "having the form of," as in *cruciform.* [t. L: s. *-formis*]

for·mal (fôr′məl), *adj.* **1.** being in accordance with conventional requirements; conventional. **2.** marked by form or ceremony: *a formal occasion.* **3.** observant of form, as persons; ceremonious. **4.** excessively ceremonious. **5.** being a matter of form only; perfunctory. **6.** made or done in accordance with forms ensuring validity: *a formal authorization.* **7.** being in accordance with prescribed or customary forms: *a formal siege.* **8.** academic; rigorously methodical. **9.** excessively regular or symmetrical. **10.** *Speech.* denoting language whose grammar and syntax are correct, and speech whose sounds are carefully formed without sounding stilted: *the language and speech of formal occasions.* See **informal** (def. 3). **11.** *Philos.* **a.** pertaining to form. **b.** (in Aristotelian use) not material; essential. **12.** pertaining to the form, shape, or mode of being of a thing, esp. as distinguished from the matter. **13.** being such in form, esp. in mere outward form. —**for′mal·ness,** *n.*

—**Syn. 2.** FORMAL, ACADEMIC, CONVENTIONAL may have either favorable or unfavorable implications. FORMAL may mean in proper form, or may imply excessive emphasis on empty form. In the favorable sense, ACADEMIC applies to scholars or higher institutions of learning; it may, however, imply slavish conformance to mere rules, or to belief in impractical theories. CONVENTIONAL, in a favorable sense, applies to desirable conformity with accepted conventions or customs; but it may apply to arbitrary, forced, or superficial conformance.

form·al·de·hyde (fôr·măl′də·hīd′), *n. Chem.* a gas, CH₂O, used most often in the form of a 40% aqueous solution, as a disinfectant and preservative, and in the manufacture of various resins and plastics. Also, **form·al′de·hyd′.** [f. FORM(IC) + ALDEHYDE]

for·ma·lin (fôr′mə·lĭn), *n. Chem.* an aqueous solution of formaldehyde.

for·mal·ism (fôr′mə·lĭz′əm), *n.* **1.** strict adherence to, or observance of, prescribed or customary forms. **2.** (in religion) excessive attachment to external forms and observances. —**for′mal·ist,** *n.* —**for′mal·is′tic,** *adj.*

for·mal·i·ty (fôr·măl′ə·tĭ), *n., pl.* **-ties. 1.** condition or quality of being formal; accordance with prescribed, customary, or due forms; conventionality. **2.** rigorously methodical character. **3.** excessive regularity or stiffness. **4.** observance of form or ceremony. **5.** marked or excessive ceremoniousness. **6.** an established order or mode of proceeding: *the formalities of judicial process.* **7.** a formal act or observance. **8.** something done merely for form's sake; a requirement of custom or etiquette.

for·mal·ize (fôr′mə·līz′), *v.,* **-ized, -izing.** —*v.t.* **1.** to make formal. **2.** to give a definite form or shape to. —*v.i.* **3.** to be formal; act with formality. —**for′mal·i·za′tion,** *n.*

formal logic, the branch of logic concerned exclusively with the principles of deductive reasoning, and in consequence with the forms (as distinct from the content) of propositions.

for·mal·ly (fôr′mə·lĭ), *adv.* **1.** in a formal manner. **2.** as regards form; in form.

for·mat (fôr′măt), *n.* **1.** the shape and size of a book as determined by the number of times the original sheet has been folded to form the leaves. See **folio** (def. 2), **quarto, octavo, duodecimo,** etc. **2.** the general physical appearance of a book, such as the type face, binding, quality of paper, margins, etc. [t. F, t. L: s. (*liber*) *formātus* (a book) formed (in a certain way)]

for·mate (fôr′māt), *n. Chem.* a salt or ester of formic acid. [f. FORM(IC) + -ATE²]

for·ma·tion (fôr·mā′shən), *n.* **1.** act or process of forming. **2.** state of being formed. **3.** the manner in which a thing is formed; disposition of parts; formal structure or arrangement. **4.** *Mil.* **a.** a particular disposition of troops, as in columns, squares, etc. **b.** any required assembling of the soldiers of a unit. **5.** something formed. **6.** *Geol.* **a.** a body of rocks classed as a unit for geologic mapping. **b.** the process of depositing rock or mineral of a particular composition or origin.

form·a·tive (fôr′mə·tĭv), *adj.* **1.** giving form or shape; forming; shaping; fashioning; molding. **2.** pertaining to formation or development: *the formative period of a nation.* **3.** *Biol.* **a.** capable of developing new cells or tissue by cell division and differentiation: *formative tissue.* **b.** concerned with the formation of an embryo, organ, or the like. **4.** *Gram.* pertaining to a formative. —*n.* **5.** *Gram.* a derivational affix, particularly one which determines the part of speech of the derived word, such as *-ness,* in *loudness, hardness,* etc. —**form′a·tive·ly,** *adv.* —**form′a·tive·ness,** *n.*

formative element, *Gram.* **1.** a morpheme which serves as an affix, not as a base (or root) in word formation. **2.** any noninflectional morpheme, whether base or affix.

form class, *Gram.* a class of words or forms in a language with one or more grammatical features in common, as (in Latin) all masculine nouns in the nominative singular, or all masculine singular nouns, or all masculine nouns, or all singular nouns, or all nouns.

form drag, *Hydraulics, etc.* that portion of the resisting force encountered by a body moving through a fluid which is due to irregularity of shape and hence can be reduced to a minimum by streamlining.

forme (fôrm), *n. Brit.* form (def. 27).

for·mer¹ (fôr′mər), *adj.* **1.** preceding in time; prior or earlier. **2.** past, long past, or ancient. **3.** preceding in order; being the first of two. **4.** being the first mentioned of two. **5.** having held a particular office in the past: *a former president.* [ME, f. obs. *forme* (OE *forma* first) + -ER⁴. Cf. ME and OE *formest* foremost]

form·er² (fôr′mər), *n.* one who or that which forms or serves to form. [f. FORM + -ER¹]

for·mer·ly (fôr′mər·lĭ), *adv.* **1.** in time past; heretofore; of old. **2.** *Obs.* in time just past; just now.

For·mi·ca (fôr′mə·kə, fôr·mī′kə), *n. Trademark.* a thermosetting plastic usually used in transparent or printed sheets as a chemical-proof and heatproof covering for furniture, wall panels, etc.

for·mic acid (fôr′mĭk), *Chem.* a colorless irritant liquid, HCOOH, once obtained from ants and other insects, but now manufactured synthetically. [*formic,* irreg. f. L: s. *formīca* ant]

for·mi·car·i·um (fôr′mə·kâr′Y·əm), *n., pl.* **-caria** (-kâr′Y·ə). formicary. [t. ML, der. L *formīca* ant]

for·mi·car·y (fôr′mə·kĕr′Y), *n., pl.* **-caries.** an ants' nest.

for·mi·cate (fôr′mə·kāt′), *v.i.,* **-cated, -cating.** to swarm with moving beings, as ants. [t. L: m.s. *formīcātus,* pp. of *formīcāre* creep like ants]

for·mi·da·ble (fôr′mĭ·də·bəl), *adj.* **1.** that is to be feared or dreaded, esp. in encounters or dealings. **2.** of alarming strength, size, difficulty, etc. **3.** such as to inspire apprehension of defeat or failure. [t. F, t. L: m.s. *formīdābilis* causing fear] —**for′mi·da·ble·ness,** **for′mi·da·bil′i·ty,** *n.* —**for′mi·da·bly,** *adv.* —**Syn. 1.** dread, dreadful, appalling, threatening, menacing.

form·less (fôrm′lĭs), *adj.* wanting form or shape; shapeless; without a determinate or regular form. —**form′less·ly,** *adv.* —**form′less·ness,** *n.*

form letter, a letter, printed, processed, or typed, copies of which are sent to a number of readers.

For·mo·sa (fôr·mō′sə), *n.* a Chinese island separated from the SE coast of China by **Formosa Strait**: a possession of Japan, 1895–1945; part of China 1945–49; homeland of Nationalist China since 1949. 8,438,016 (1953); 13,885 sq. mi. *Cap.:* Taipeh. Also, **Taiwan.**

for·mu·la (fôr′myə·lə), *n., pl.* **-las, -lae** (-lē′). **1.** a set form of words, as for stating or declaring something definitely or authoritatively, for indicating procedure to be followed, or for prescribed use on some ceremonial occasion. **2.** *Math.* a rule or principle frequently expressed in algebraic symbols. **3.** *Chem.* an expression of the constituents of a compound by symbols and figures, as an **empirical formula,** which merely indicates the number of each kind of atom in the molecule, as CH₂O, or a **structural formula,** which represents diagrammatically the linkage of each atom in the molecule, as H—O—H. **4.** a recipe or prescription. **5.** a formal statement of religious doctrine. [t. L, dim. of *forma* FORM. *n.*]

for·mu·lar·ize (fôr′myə lə rīz′), v.t., -ized, -izing. formulate. —for′mu·lar·i·za′tion, n.

for·mu·lar·y (fôr′myə lĕr′ĭ), n., pl. -laries, adj. —n. 1. a collection or system of formulas. 2. a set form of words; formula. 3. Pharm. a book listing pharmaceutical substances, formulas, and prescriptions. 4. Eccles. a book containing prescribed forms used in the services of a church. —adj. 5. of or pertaining to a formula or formulas. 6. of the nature of a formula.

for·mu·late (fôr′myə lāt′), v.t., -lated, -lating. 1. to express in precise form; state definitely or systematically. 2. to reduce to or express in a formula. —for′mu·la′tion, n. —for′mu·la′tor, n.

for·mu·lism (fôr′myə lĭz′əm), n. 1. adherence to or systematic use of formulas. 2. a system of formulas. —for′mu·lis′tic, adj.

for·mu·lize (fôr′myə līz′), v.t., -lized, -lizing. formulate. —for′mu·li·za′tion, n. —for′mu·liz′er, n.

for·myl (fôr′mĭl), n. Chem. the radical, HCO, derived from formic acid. [f. FORM(IC) + -YL]

for·ni·cate (fôr′nə kāt′), v.i., -cated, -cating. to commit fornication. [t. LL: m.s. fornicātus, pp. of fornicārī, der. L fornix (underground) brothel, arch, vault] —for′ni·ca′tor, n.

for·ni·ca·tion (fôr′nə kā′shən), n. 1. voluntary sexual intercourse on the part of an unmarried person with a person of the opposite sex. 2. Bible. a. adultery. b. idolatry.

for·nix (fôr′nĭks), n., pl. -nices (-nə sēz′). Anat. any of various arched or vaulted structures, as an arching fibrous formation in the brain. [t. L: arch, vault]

For·rest (fôr′ĭst, fôr′-), n. 1. Edwin, 1806–72, U.S. actor. 2. John, Baron, 1847–1918, Australian explorer and statesman. 3. Nathan Bedford, 1821—77, Confederate cavalry general in the U.S. Civil War.

for·sake (fôr sāk′), v.t., -sook, -saken, -saking. 1. to quit or leave entirely; desert: forsake one's friends. 2. to give up or renounce (a habit, way of life, etc.). [ME forsake(n), OE forsacan deny, give up, f. for- FOR- + sacan dispute] —Syn. 1. See desert².

for·sak·en (fôr sā′kən), v. 1. pp. of forsake. —adj. 2. deserted; abandoned; forlorn. —for·sak′en·ly, adv.

For·se·ti (fôr′sĕ tē′), n. Scand. Myth. the god of justice, son of Balder.

for·sook (fôr sŏŏk′), v. pt. of forsake.

for·sooth (fôr sŏŏth′), adv. in truth; in fact; indeed (now commonly used ironically or derisively). [ME forsoth(e), OE forsoth for sooth]

for·spend (fôr spĕnd′), v.t., -spent, -spending. to spend or use up completely, as strength; wear out or exhaust, as with exertion (occurs chiefly in pp.). [ME forspend(en), OE forspendan. See FOR-, SPEND.]

For·ster (fôr′stər), n. Edward Morgan, born 1879, British novelist.

for·ster·ite (fôr′stə rīt′), n. a mineral of the olivine group, a silicate of magnesium, Mg₂SiO₄, occurring usually as white, greenish, or yellowish grains in basic igneous rocks.

for·swear (fôr swâr′), v., -swore, -sworn, -swearing. —v.t. 1. to reject or renounce upon oath or with protestations. 2. to deny upon oath or with strong asseveration. 3. to perjure (oneself). —v.i. 4. to swear falsely; commit perjury. [ME forsweren, OE forswerian; see FOR-, SWEAR] —for·swear′er, n.

for·sworn (fôr swôrn′), v. 1. pp. of forswear. —adj. 2. perjured.

for·syth·i·a (fôr sĭth′ĭ ə, -sī′thĭ ə), n. any shrub of the oleaceous genus Forsythia, native in China and southeastern Europe, species of which are much cultivated for their showy yellow flowers, appearing in early spring before the leaves. [NL, named after W. Forsyth (1737–1804), British horticulturist.]

fort (fôrt), n. 1. a strong or fortified place; any armed place surrounded by defensive works and occupied by troops; a fortification; a fortress. 2. (in North America) a trading post. [t. F, g. L fortis strong]

Fort, for forts, see under the second word, as Sumter, Fort; when "Fort" is a part of the name of a city, see under the first word, as Fort Worth.

fort., 1. fortification. 2. fortified.

For·ta·le·za (fôr′tä lĕ′zə), n. a seaport in E Brazil. 213,604 (est. 1952). Also, Ceará.

for·ta·lice (fôr′tə lĭs), n. 1. a small fort; an outwork. 2. Obs. a fortress. [ME, t. ML: m.s. fortalitia, fortalitium, der. L fortis strong]

Fort-de-France (fôr də fräns′), n. a seaport in and the capital of Martinique, in the French West Indies. 60,648 (1954).

Fort Dodge (dŏj), a city in central Iowa, on the Des Moines river. 28,399 (1960).

forte¹ (fôrt), n. 1. a strong point, as of a person; that in which one excels. 2. the stronger part of a sword blade between the middle and the hilt (opposed to foible). [t. F: m. fort, n. use of fort, adj. See FORT]

for·te² (fôr′tĕ), Music. —adj. 1. loud; with force (opposed to piano). —adv. 2. loudly. —n. 3. a passage that is loud and forcible, or is intended to be so. [It., g. L fortis strong]

forth (fôrth), adv. 1. forward; onward or outward in place or space. 2. onward in time, in order, or in a se-

ries: from that day forth. 3. out, as from concealment or inaction; into view or consideration. 4. away, as from a place or country; abroad. 5. and so forth, and so on; and others; et cetera. —prep. 6. Archaic. out of; forth from. [ME and OE, c. G fort; akin to FURTHER]

forth·com·ing (fôrth′kŭm′ĭng), adj. 1. coming forth, or about to come forth; about to appear; approaching in time. 2. ready or available when required or expected. —n. 3. a coming forth; appearance.

Forth (fôrth), n. Firth of, an arm of the North Sea, in SE Scotland: the estuary of the Forth river, traversed by a railroad bridge, 5330 ft. long. 48 mi. long.

forth·right (adj., n. fôrth′rīt′; adv. fôrth′rīt′, fôrth′rīt′), adj. 1. going straight to the point; outspoken. 2. proceeding in a straight course; direct; straightforward. —adv. 3. straight or directly forward; in a direct manner. 4. straightway; at once; immediately. —n. 5. Archaic. a straight course or path. —forth′right′ness, n.

forth·with (fôrth′wĭth′, -wĭth′), adv. 1. immediately; at once; without delay. 2. as soon as can reasonably be expected.

for·ti·eth (fôr′tĭ ĭth), adj. 1. next after the thirty-ninth. 2. being one of forty equal parts. —n. 3. a fortieth part, esp. of one (1/40). 4. the fortieth member of a series.

for·ti·fi·ca·tion (fôr′tə fə kā′shən), n. 1. act of fortifying or strengthening. 2. that which fortifies or protects. 3. art or science of constructing defensive military works. 4. a military work constructed for the purpose of strengthening a position; fortified place; fort; castle. —Syn. 4. fortress, citadel, stronghold.

for·ti·fy (fôr′tə fī′), v., -fied, -fying. —v.t. 1. to strengthen against attack; surround with defenses or standing strain, wear, etc. 3. to make strong; impart strength or vigor to, as the body. 4. to strengthen mentally or morally. 5. to confirm or corroborate. 6. to add alcohol to (wines, etc.). —v.i. 7. to set up defensive works; erect fortifications. [ME fortifie(n), t. F: m. fortifier, t. LL: m. fortificāre, f. forti- strong + -ficāre make] —for′ti·fi′a·ble, adj. —for′ti·fi′er, n.

for·tis (fôr′tĭs), adj., n., pl. -tes (-tēz). —adj. 1. Phonet. pronounced with considerable muscular tension and breath pressure, resulting in a strong fricative or explosive sound: f and p are fortis, as compared to lenis v and b. —n. 2. a fortis consonant. [t. L: strong]

for·tis·si·mo (fôr tĭs′ə mō′; It. fôr tēs′sē mô′), Music. —adj. 1. very loud. —adv. 2. very loudly. [t. It., superl. of forte. See FORTE²]

for·ti·tude (fôr′tə tūd′, -tŏŏd′), n. patient courage under affliction, privation, or temptation; moral strength or endurance. [t. L: m. fortitūdo] —Syn. See patience.

Fort Lau·der·dale (lô′dər dāl′), a city in SE Florida: a seaside resort. 83,648 (1960).

fort·night (fôrt′nīt′, -nĭt), n. Chiefly Brit. in U.S. literary only. the space of fourteen nights and days; two weeks. [ME fourtenight, contr. of OE fēowertēne niht fourteen nights]

fort·night·ly (fôrt′nīt′lĭ), adj., adv., n., pl. -lies. —adj. 1. occurring or appearing once a fortnight. —adv. 2. once a fortnight. —n. 3. a periodical issued every two weeks.

for·tress (fôr′trĭs), n. 1. a large fortified place; a fort or group of forts, often including a town. 2. any place of security. —v.t. 3. to furnish with or defend by a fortress: the city is heavily fortressed. [ME forterresse, t. OF. der. fort strong]

Fort Smith, a city in W Arkansas, on the Arkansas river. 56,312 (1955).

for·tu·i·tism (fôr tū′ə tĭz′əm, -tŏŏ′-), n. Philos. the doctrine or belief that adaptations in nature come about by chance, and not by design. —for·tu′i·tist, n., adj.

for·tu·i·tous (fôr tū′ə təs, -tŏŏ′-), adj. happening or produced by chance; accidental. [t. L: m. fortuītus casual] —for·tu′i·tous·ly, adv. —for·tu′i·tous·ness, n. —Syn. See accidental.

for·tu·i·ty (fôr tū′ə tĭ, -tŏŏ′-), n., pl. -ties. 1. fortuitous character; the fact of being accidental or casual. 2. accident or chance. 3. an accidental occurrence.

For·tu·na (fôr tū′nə, -tŏŏ′-), n. Rom. Myth. the goddess of fortune and chance, the counterpart of the Greek Tyche.

for·tu·nate (fôr′chə nĭt), adj. 1. having good fortune; receiving good from uncertain or unexpected sources; lucky. 2. bringing or presaging good fortune; resulting favorably; auspicious. [ME, t. L: m.s. fortūnātus, pp., made prosperous or happy] —for′tu·nate·ly, adv. —for′tu·nate·ness, n.

—Syn. 1, 2. FORTUNATE, HAPPY, LUCKY refer to persons who enjoy, or events which produce, good fortune. FORTUNATE implies that the success is obtained by the operation of favorable circumstances more than by direct effort; it is usually applied to grave or large matters (esp. those happening in the ordinary course of things): fortunate in one's choice of a wife, a fortunate investment. HAPPY emphasizes a pleasant ending or something which happens by chance at just the right moment: by a happy accident I received the package on time. LUCKY, a more colloquial word, is applied to situations of minor moment that turn out well by chance: lucky at cards, my lucky day.

---

b., blend of, blended; c., cognate with; d., dialect, dialectal; der., derived from; f., formed from; g., going back to; m., modification of; r., replacing; s., stem of; t., taken from; ?, perhaps. See the full key on inside cover.

for·tune (fôr'chən), *n.*, *v.*, **-tuned, -tuning.** —*n.*
1. position in life as determined by wealth: *to make one's fortune, a man of fortune.* **2.** amount or stock of wealth. **3.** great wealth; ample stock of wealth. **4.** a person of wealth, esp. a woman; an heiress. **5.** chance; luck. **6.** (*often pl.*) that which falls or is to fall to one as his portion in life or in any particular proceeding. **7.** lot; destiny. **8.** (*often cap.*) chance personified, commonly regarded as a goddess distributing arbitrarily or capriciously the lots of life. **9.** good luck; success; prosperity. —*v.t.* **10.** to endow with a fortune. —*v.i.* **11.** *Rare.* to chance or happen; come by chance. [ME, t. F, t. L: m.s. *fortūna* chance, luck, fortune] **—for'tune·less,** *adj.*

fortune hunter, one who seeks to win a fortune, esp. through marriage. **—for'tune-hunt'ing,** *adj.*

for·tune-tell·er (fôr'chən tĕl'ər), *n.* one who professes to tell people what will happen in the future. **—for'tune-tell'ing,** *adj.*, *n.*

Fort Wayne (wān), a city in NE Indiana. 161,776 (1960).

Fort William, a city in S Canada, in Ontario: a port on Lake Superior. With suburbs, 71,191 (1951).

Fort Worth (wûrth), a city in N Texas. 356,268 (1960).

for·ty (fôr'tĭ), *n.*, *pl.* **-ties,** *adj.* —*n.* **1.** a cardinal number, ten times four. **2.** a symbol for this number, as 40 or XL or XXXX. **3.** amounting to forty in number. [ME *fourti,* OE *fēowertig,* f. *fēower* four + *-tig* -TY¹]

for·ty-nin·er (fôr'tĭ nī'nər), *n.* (*sometimes cap.*) *U.S. Hist.* one of those who went to California in 1849, during the gold rush, in search of fortune.

Forty Thieves, The, one of the tales of the *Arabian Nights' Entertainments,* often called *Ali Baba and the Forty Thieves.* See Ali Baba.

forty winks, a short nap, esp. in the daytime.

fo·rum (fôr'əm), *n.*, *pl.* **forums, fora** (fôr'ə). **1.** the market place or public square of an ancient Roman city, the center of judicial and other business and a place of assembly for the people. **2.** a court or tribunal: *he forum of public opinion.* **3.** an assembly for the discussion of questions of public interest. [t. L]

for·ward (fôr'wərd), *adv.* Also, **forwards. 1.** toward or at a place, point, or time in advance; onward; ahead: *to move forward, from this day forward, to look forward.* **2.** towards the front. **3.** out; forth; into view or consideration: *to come or bring forward.* —*adj.* **4.** directed toward a point in advance; moving ahead; onward: *a forward motion.* **5.** being in a condition of advancement; well-advanced. **6.** ready, prompt, or eager. **7.** presumptuous, pert, or bold. **8.** situated in the front or forepart. **9.** lying in advance; fore. **10.** of or pertaining to the future: *forward buying.* **11.** radical or extreme, as persons or opinions. —*n.* **12.** *Sports.* a player stationed in advance of others on his team: **a.** *Football.* any player in the forward line. **b.** *Basketball.* one of two (or in women's rules, three) offensive players on a team. —*v.t.* **13.** to send forward; transmit, esp. to a new address: *to forward a letter.* **14.** to advance or help onward; hasten; promote. **15.** *Bookbinding.* to prepare (a book) for the finisher. See **forwarding** (def. 1). [ME and OE *for(e)ward.* See FORE¹, WARD] **—for'ward·ly,** *adv.*
—Syn. 1. FORWARD, ONWARD both imply a direction toward the front or a movement in a frontward direction. FORWARD applies to any movement toward what is or is conceived to be the front or a goal: *to face forward, to move forward in the aisles.* ONWARD applies to any movement in continuance of a course: *to march onward toward a goal.* **7.** See **bold.** **—Ant. 4.** backward.

forward delivery, *Com.* delivery at a future date.

for·ward·er (fôr'wər dər), *n.* **1.** one who forwards or sends forward. **2.** one who undertakes to see that the goods of another are transported, without himself incurring the liability of a carrier to deliver.

for·ward·ing (fôr'wər dĭng), *n.* **1.** *Bookbinding.* a stage which involves stitching, fitting the back, pasting, etc., just before the pages are placed in the completed book cover. **2.** *Engraving.* the process of starting a copper plate by etching and of finishing with a graver.

for·ward·ness (fôr'wərd nĭs), *n.* **1.** overreadiness to push oneself forward; presumption; boldness; lack of due modesty. **2.** cheerful readiness; promptness; eagerness. **3.** condition of being forward or in advance.

forward pass, *Football.* a pass in which the ball is thrown towards the opponent's goal.

forward quotation, *Com.* the price quoted on a forward delivery.

for·wards (fôr'wərdz), *adv.* forward. [f. FORWARD + adv. genitive *-s*]

for·worn (fôr wôrn'), *adj.* *Archaic.* worn-out; exhausted. Also, **foreworn.**

for·zan·do (fôr tsän'dō). *adv.* *Music.* sforzando. [It., ger. of *forzare* force]

Fos·dick (fŏz'dĭk), *n.* **Harry Emerson,** born 1878, U.S. preacher and author.

fos·sa (fŏs'ə), *n.*, *pl.* **fossae** (fŏs'ē). *Anat.* a pit, cavity, or depression in a bone, etc. [t. L: ditch, trench]

fosse (fôs, fŏs), *n.* **1.** a moat or defensive ditch in a fortification, usually filled with water. **2.** any ditch, trench, or canal. Also, **foss.** [ME, t. F, g. L *fossa* ditch]

fos·sette (fŏ sĕt'), *n.* a little hollow; a depression; a dimple. [t. F, dim. of *fosse* FOSSE]

fos·sick (fŏs'ĭk), *Australia.* —*v.i.* **1.** *Mining.* to undermine another's digging; search for waste gold in relinquished workings, washing places, etc. **2.** to search for any object by which to make gain: *to fossick for clients.* —*v.t.* **3.** to dig; hunt. [cf. d. *fossick* troublesome person, *fussick* bustle about, appar. f. FUSS + *-ick,* var. of -OCK] **—fos'sick·er,** *n.*

fos·sil (fŏs'əl), *n.* **1.** any remains, impression, or trace of an animal or plant of a former geological age, as a skeleton or a footprint. **2.** *Colloq.* an outdated or old-fashioned person or thing. **3.** *Obs.* anything dug out of the earth. —*adj.* **4.** of the nature of a fossil: *fossil insects.* **5.** dug out of the earth, or obtained by digging: *fossil fuel.* **6.** belonging to a past epoch or discarded system; antiquated. [t. L: s. *fossilis* dug up; r. earlier *fossile,* t. F] **—fos'sil·like',** *adj.*

fos·sil·if·er·ous (fŏs'ə lĭf'ər əs), *adj.* bearing or containing fossils, as rocks or strata.

fos·sil·ize (fŏs'ə līz'), *v.*, **-ized, -izing.** —*v.t.* **1.** *Geol.* to convert into a fossil; replace organic substances with mineral in the remains of an organism. **2.** to change as if into mere lifeless remains or traces of the past. **3.** to make rigidly antiquated, as persons, ideas, etc. —*v.i.* **4.** to become a fossil. **—fos'sil·i·za'tion,** *n.*

fos·so·ri·al (fŏ sôr'ĭ əl), *adj.* *Zool.* **1.** digging or burrowing. **2.** adapted for digging, as the hands, feet, and skeleton of moles, armadillos, and aardvarks. [f. s. LL *fossōrius* (der. L *fossor* digger) + -AL¹]

fos·ter (fŏs'tər, fôs'-), *v.t.* **1.** to promote the growth or development of; further; encourage: *to foster foreign trade.* **2.** to bring up or rear, as a foster child. **3.** to care for or cherish. **4.** *Obs.* to feed or nourish. —*n.* **5.** a cherisher. **6.** nourishment. [ME; OE *fóster* nourishment, *fóstrian* nourish; akin to FOOD] **—fos'ter·er,** *n.* **—Syn. 3.** See **cherish.**

Fos·ter (fŏs'tər, fôs'-), *n.* **1. Stephen Collins,** 1826–64, U.S. song writer and composer of "Old Folks at Home" and other popular songs. **2. William Z.,** 1881–1961, U.S. Communist party leader and labor organizer.

fos·ter·age (fŏs'tər ĭj, fôs'-), *n.* **1.** act of fostering or rearing another's child as one's own. **2.** condition of being a foster child. **3.** act of promoting or encouraging.

foster brother, a boy brought up with another child of different parents.

foster child, a child raised by someone not its own mother or father.

foster daughter, a girl raised like one's own daughter, though not such by birth.

foster father, one who takes the place of a father in raising a child.

fos·ter·ling (fŏs'tər lĭng, fôs'-), *n.* a foster child. [ME; OE *fóstorling.* See FOSTER, n., -LING¹]

foster mother, 1. a woman who takes the place of the mother in raising a child. **2.** a nurse.

foster parent, a foster father or foster mother.

foster sister, a girl brought up with another child of different parents.

foster son, a boy raised like one's own son, though not such by birth.

fos·tress (fŏs'trĭs, fôs'-), *n.* a woman who fosters.

Foth·er·ing·hay (fŏth'ər ĭng gā'), *n.* a village in E England, near Peterborough: Mary, Queen of Scots, was imprisoned and executed (1587) in the castle here.

Fou·cault (fōō kō'), *n.* **Jean Bernard Léon** (zhäN bĕr när' lĕ ôN'), 1819–68, French physicist.

fou·droy·ant (fōō droi'ənt; *Fr.* fōō drwä yäN'), *adj.* **1.** striking as with lightning; sudden and overwhelming in effect; stunning; dazzling. **2.** *Pathol.* (of disease) beginning in a sudden and severe form. [t. F, ppr. of *foudroyer* strike with lightning, der. *foudre* lightning, g. L *fulgur*]

fought (fôt), *v.* pt. and pp. of **fight.**

fought·en (fô'tən), *adj.* *Archaic.* that has been the scene of fighting: *a foughten field.*

foul (foul), *adj.* **1.** grossly offensive to the senses; disgustingly loathsome; noisome: *a foul smell.* **2.** charged with or characterized by offensive or noisome matter: *foul air.* **3.** filthy or dirty, as places, vessels, or clothes. **4.** muddy, as a road. **5.** clogged or obstructed with foreign matter: *a foul chimney.* **6.** unfavorable or stormy, as weather. **7.** contrary, as the wind. **8.** grossly offensive in a moral sense. **9.** abominable, wicked, or vile, as deeds, crime, slander, etc. **10.** scurrilous, profane, or obscene, as language. **11.** contrary to the rules or established usages, as of a sport or game; unfair. **12.** *Baseball.* pertaining to a foul ball or a foul line. **13.** in collision or obstructing contact: *a ship foul of a rock.* **14.** entangled, caught, or jammed: *a foul anchor.* **15.** abounding in errors or in marks of correction, as a printer's proof. **16.** *Dial.* not fair; ugly or unattractive. **17.** *Obs.* disfigured. —*adv.* **18.** in a foul manner; foully; unfairly. —*n.* **19.** that which is foul. **20.** a collision or entanglement. **21.** a violation of the rules of a sport or game. **22.** *Baseball.* a foul ball. —*v.t.* **23.** to make foul; defile; soil. **24.** to clog or obstruct, as a chimney or the bore of a gun. **25.** to collide with. **26.** to cause to become entangled or caught, as a rope. **27.** to defile; dishonor; disgrace. **28.** *Naut.* to encumber (a ship's bottom) with seaweed, barnacles, etc. —*v.i.* **29.** to become foul. **30.** *Naut.* to come into collision, as two boats. **31.** to become entangled or clogged:

the rope fouled. **32.** *Sports.* to make a foul play; give a foul blow. **33.** *Baseball.* to knock a foul ball, etc. **34. foul out,** *Baseball.* to be retired, through the catching of a foul ball by one of the opposite nine. [ME; OE *fūl*, c. G *faul*; akin to L *pūs* pus, *pūtere* to stink] **—foul′ly,** *adv.* **—Syn. 3.** See **dirty.**

fou·lard (fōō lärd′, fə-), *n.* a soft lightweight silk or rayon of twill weave with printed design, for neckties, trimmings, etc. [t. F, prob. a var. of Swiss F: m. *foulat* fulled cloth, c. F *fouler* to full, g. L *fullāre*]

foul ball, *Baseball.* a ball struck so that it falls outside of the foul lines.

foul line, 1. *Baseball.* either of two lines connecting the "home" with the first and third bases respectively, or their continuation. **2.** *Basketball.* a line 15 feet from the backboard from which free throws are made.

foul-mind·ed (foul′mīn′dĭd), *adj.* having unclean thoughts. **—foul′-mind′ed·ness,** *n.*

foul-mouthed (foul′mou′t̶hd′, -moutht′), *adj.* using scurrilous, profane, or obscene language; given to filthy or abusive speech.

foul·ness (foul′nĭs), *n.* **1.** state or quality of being foul. **2.** that which is foul; foul matter; filth. **3.** wickedness. [ME; OE *fūlness.* See FOUL, adj., -NESS]

foul play, 1. any unfair or treacherous dealing, often such as involves murder. **2.** unfair conduct in a game.

fouls (foulz), *n.* *Vet. Sci.* an infection of the feet of cattle causing a foul-smelling inflammation between the toes and around the coronary band.

foul shot, *Basketball.* **1.** a free throw given a member of one team after a penalty has been called against an opponent. **2.** a score of one point.

foul tip, *Baseball.* a ball that glances off the bat directly into the catcher's glove. The player is out on such a play if he has two strikes on him.

found[1] (found). *v.* pt. and pp. **of find.** [ME; OE *funde, fundon* p.t., *funden* pp.]

found[2] (found), *v.t.* **1.** to set up or establish on a firm basis or for enduring existence: *to found a dynasty.* **2.** to lay the lowest part of, fix, or build (a structure) on a firm base or ground: *a house founded upon a rock.* **3.** to base or ground (fol. by *on* or *upon*): *a story founded on fact.* **4.** to afford a basis or ground for. **—v.i. 5.** to be founded or based (fol. by *on* or *upon*). **6.** to base one's opinion (fol. by *on* or *upon*). [ME *founde(n),* t. OF: m. *fonder,* g. L *fundāre* lay the bottom of, found]

found[3] (found), *v.t.* **1.** to melt and pour (metal, etc.) into a mold. **2.** to form or make (an article) of molten material in a mold; cast. [ME *fond(en),* t. OF: m. *fondre* melt, cast, g. L *fundere* pour, melt, cast]

foun·da·tion (foun dā′shən), *n.* **1.** that on which something is founded. **2.** the basis or ground of anything. **3.** the natural or prepared ground or base on which some structure rests. **4.** the lowest division of a building, wall, or the like, usually of masonry and partly or wholly below the surface of the ground. **5.** act of founding, setting up, establishing, etc. **6.** state of being founded. **7.** a donation or legacy for the support of an institution; an endowment. **8.** an endowed institution. **—Syn. 3.** See **base**[1].

Foundation Day, a legal holiday in Australia, usually January 26, to commemorate the British landings in 1788.

found·er[1] (foun′dər), *n.* one who founds or establishes. [f. FOUND[2] + -ER[1]]

foun·der[2] (foun′dər), *v.i.* **1.** to fill with water and sink, as a ship. **2.** to fall or sink down, as buildings, ground, etc. **3.** to suffer wreck, or fail utterly. **4.** to stumble, break down, or go lame, as a horse. **5.** *Vet. Sci.* (of a horse) to suffer from founder. **—v.t. 6.** to cause to fill with water and sink, as a ship. **7.** *Vet. Sci.* to cause (a horse, etc.) to break down, go lame, or suffer from founder. **8.** *Golf.* to drive (the ball) into the ground. **—n. 9.** *Vet. Sci.* laminitis. [ME *foundren,* t. OF: m. *fondrer,* ult. der. L *fundus* bottom]

found·er[3] (foun′dər), *n.* one who founds or casts metal, etc. [f. FOUND[3] + -ER[1]]

foun·der·ous (foun′dər əs), *adj.* *Now Chiefly Dial.* miry; swampy.

founders' shares, *Finance.* shares of stock given, at least nominally, for consideration to the organizers or original subscribers of a corporation, sometimes carrying special voting privileges, but likely to receive dividends after other classes of stock.

found·ling (found′lĭng), *n.* an infant found abandoned; a child without a parent or guardian. [ME *found(e)ling,* f. *founde(n),* pp. of FIND, v. + -LING[1]]

found·ry (foun′drĭ), *n., pl.* **-ries. 1.** an establishment for the production of castings, in which molten metal is poured into molds to shape the castings. **2.** the founding of metal, etc. **3.** things made by founding; castings. **4.** *Obs.* the casting of metals. [t. F: m. *fonderie,* der. *fondre* FOUND[3]]

foundry proof, *Print.,* a proof pulled for a final checking before printing plates are made.

fount[1] (fount), *n.* **1.** a spring of water; fountain. **2.** a source or origin. [short for FOUNTAIN]

fount[2] (fount, fŏnt), *n.* *Print., Chiefly Brit.* font[2].

foun·tain (foun′tən), *n.* **1.** a spring or source of water; the source or head of a stream. **2.** the source or origin of anything. **3.** a jet or stream of water (or other liquid) made by mechanical means to spout or rise from an opening or structure, as to afford water for use, or to cool the air, or to serve for ornament. **4.** a structure for discharging such a jet or a number of jets, often an elaborate or artistic work with basins, sculptures, etc. **5.** a soda fountain. **6.** a reservoir for a liquid to be supplied gradually or continuously. [late ME *fontaine,* OF: m. *fontaine,* g. LL *fontāna,* prop. fem. of L *fontānus* of or from a spring] **—foun′tain·less,** *adj.* **—foun′tain-like′,** *adj.*

foun·tain·head (foun′tən hĕd′), *n.* **1.** a fountain or spring from which a stream flows; the head or source of a stream. **2.** a primary source.

Fountain of Youth, a mythical spring, sought in the Bahama Islands and Florida by Ponce de Leon, Narváez, De Soto, and others. Indians of Central America believed that it was to the northward, and that its waters would cure ills and renew youth.

fountain pen, a writing pen with a reservoir for supplying ink continuously.

Fou·qué (fōō kā′), *n.* **Friedrich Heinrich Karl** (frē′drĭ҃кн hīn′rĭ҃кн kärl), (*Baron de La Motte-Fouqué*) 1777–1843, German novelist and poet.

Fou·quet (fōō kĕ′), *n.* **Nicolas** (nē kô lä′), (*Marquis de Belle-Isle*) 1615–80, French minister under Louis XIV.

Fou·quier-Tin·ville (fōō kyĕ′tăn vēl′), *n.* **Antoine Quentin** (än twän′/kän tăn′), 1747?–95, French revolutionist: prosecutor during the Reign of Terror.

four (fōr), *n.* **1.** a cardinal number, three plus one. **2.** a symbol of this number, 4 or IV or IIII. **3.** a set of this many persons or things. **4.** a playing card, etc., with four pips. **5. on all fours,** on the hands and feet (or knees). **—adj. 6.** amounting to four in number. [ME; OE *fēower,* c. D and G *vier* four; akin to L *quattuor,* Gk. *téttares*]

four·chette (fōōr shĕt′), *n.* **1.** *Anat.* the fold of skin which forms the posterior margin of the vulva. **2.** *Ornith.* the furcula or united clavicles of a bird; the wishbone of a fowl. **3.** *Zool.* the frog of an animal's foot. **4.** a strip of leather or fabric joining front and back sections of a glove finger. [t. F, dim. of *fourche,* g. L *furca* fork]

four-cy·cle (fōr′sī′kəl), *n.* (in an internal-combustion engine) a cycle in which one piston stroke out of every four is a power stroke.

four-di·men·sion·al (fōr′dĭ mĕn′shən əl), *adj.* *Math.* of a space having points, or a set having elements, which require four coördinates for their unique determination.

Four·drin·i·er (fōōr drĭn′ĭ ər), *n.* **Henry,** 1766–1854, British inventor (of papermaking machinery).

four flush, (in poker) **1.** four cards of a possible flush, which, with one card of a different suit, make up a hand. **2.** an imperfect flush.

four-flush (fōr′flŭsh′), *v.i.* *Slang.* to act as a four-flusher.

four-flush·er (fōr′flŭsh′ər), *n.* *Slang.* one who makes pretensions that he cannot or does not bear out.

four·fold (fōr′fōld′), *adj., adv.* four times as great or as much.

four-foot·ed (fōr′fŏŏt′ĭd), *adj.* having four feet.

four freedoms, freedom of speech, freedom of worship, freedom from want, and freedom from fear: listed by Franklin D. Roosevelt.

four·gon (fōōr gôN′), *n.* *French.* a long covered wagon for carrying baggage, goods, military supplies, etc.; a van or tumbril. [F, ? identical with *fourgon* oven fork, der. OF *forgier* search, ult. der. L *forāre* bore]

four-hand·ed (fōr′hăn′dĭd), *adj.* **1.** involving four hands or players, as a game at cards. **2.** intended for four hands, as a piece of music for the piano. **3.** having four hands, or four feet adapted for use as hands; quadrumanous.

four hundred, the, *U.S.* the exclusive social set.

Fou·rier (fōō ryĕ′), *n.* **1. François Marie Charles** (frän swà′ mà rē′ shärl), 1772–1837, French socialist, writer, and reformer. **2. Jean Baptiste Joseph** (zhän bȧ tēst′ zhō zĕf′), 1768–1830, French mathematician and physicist.

Fou·ri·er analysis (fōōr′ĭ ā′, -ĭ ər), *Physics.* the decomposition of any periodic function such as a complex sound or electromagnetic wave form into the sum of a number of sine and cosine functions.

Fou·ri·er·ism (fōōr′ĭ ə rĭz′əm), *n.* the communistic system propounded by François Marie Charles Fourier, under which society was to be organized into phalanxes or associations, each large enough for all industrial and social requirements. **—Fou′ri·er·ist, Fou′ri·er·ite** (fōōr′ĭ ə rīt′), *n.* **—Fou′ri·er·is′tic,** *adj.*

four-in-hand (fōr′ĭn hănd′), *n.* **1.** a long scarf or necktie to be tied in a slipknot with the ends left hanging. **2.** a vehicle drawn by four horses and driven by one person. **3.** a team of four horses. **—adj. 4.** having to do with a four-in-hand.

four-mast·ed (fōr′măs′tĭd, -mäs′-), *adj.* *Naut.* carrying four masts.

four-o'clock (fōr′ə klŏk′), *n.* **1.** a common nyctaginaceous garden plant, *Mirabilis jalapa,* with red, white, yellow, or variegated flowers which open late in the afternoon. **2.** a similar red-flowered plant, *M. laevis,* common in California. **3.** any plant of the same genus. **4.** the Australian friarbird.

four·pence (fōr′pəns), *n.* *Brit.* **1.** a sum of money of the value of four English pennies, or about 8 U.S. cents. **2.** a silver coin of this value.

b., blend of, blended; c., cognate with; d., dialect, dialectal; der., derived from; f., formed from; g., going back to; m., modification of; r., replacing; s., stem of; t., taken from; ?, perhaps. See the full key on inside cover.

four·pen·ny (fôr′pĕn′ĭ, -pə nĭ), *adj.* *Brit.* of the amount or value of fourpence.

four-post·er (fôr′pōs′tər), *n.* a bed with four posts, as for supporting curtains.

four·ra·gère (fōō rá zhĕr′), *n.* (in French and U.S. military use) **1.** an ornament of cord worn on the shoulder. **2.** such a cord awarded as an honorary decoration, as to members of a regiment or other unit that has received a requisite number of citations. [F]

four-score (fôr′skôr′), *adj.* four times twenty; eighty.

four·some (fôr′səm), *n.* **1.** *Golf, etc.* a match played by four persons, two on each side. **2.** a company or set of four. —*adj.* **3.** consisting of four; performed by four persons together. [f. FOUR + -SOME²]

four-square (fôr′skwâr′), *adj.* **1.** square. **2.** firm; steady. **3.** frank; blunt. —*adv.* **4.** without equivocation.

four·teen (fôr′tēn′), *n.* **1.** a cardinal number, ten plus four. **2.** a symbol for this number, as 14 or XIV or XIIII. —*adj.* **3.** amounting to fourteen in number. [ME *fourtene*, OE *fēowertēne*. See FOUR, -TEEN]

Fourteen Points, The, a statement of the war aims of the Allies, made by President Wilson on January 8, 1918.

four·teenth (fôr′tēnth′), *adj.* **1.** next after the thirteenth. **2.** being one of fourteen equal parts. —*n.* **3.** a fourteenth part, esp. of one (¹/₁₄). **4.** the fourteenth member of a series.

fourth (fôrth), *adj.* **1.** next after the third. **2.** being one of four equal parts. —*n.* **3.** a fourth part, esp. of one (¼). **4.** the fourth member of a series. **5.** *Music.* **a.** a tone on the fourth degree from a given tone (counted as the first). **b.** the interval between such tones. **c.** the harmonic combination of such tones. **6. the Fourth,** the Fourth of July. [ME; OE *fēo(we)rtha.* See FOUR, -TH²]

fourth-class matter (fôrth′klās′, -kläs′), (in the U. S. postal system) mail matter consisting of merchandise, not written or printed matter.

fourth dimension, *Math.* an assumed dimension in addition to length, breadth, and thickness.

fourth estate, the public press, the newspapers, or the body of journalists.

fourth·ly (fôrth′lĭ), *adv.* in the fourth place.

Fourth of July, *U.S.* the date of the adoption of the Declaration of Independence, in 1776, observed as a legal holiday.

four-wheel (fôr′hwēl′), *adj.* **1.** having four wheels. **2.** functioning on or by four wheels: *a four-wheel drive.*

fou·ter (fōō′tər), *n.* a word formerly used in expressions of contemptuous indifference: "*a fouter for the world!*" Also, **fou′tre.** [t. F: m. *(se) foutre (de)* care nothing for, g. L *futuere* have sexual intercourse with]

fo·ve·a (fō′vĭ ə), *n., pl.* **-veae** (-vĭ ē′). *Biol.* a small pit or depression in a bone or other structure. [t. L: small pit] —**fo′ve·al,** *adj.*

fovea cen·tra·lis (sĕn trā′lĭs), *Anat.* a small pit or depression at the back of the retina forming the point of sharpest vision. [L]

fo·ve·ate (fō′vĭ ĭt, -āt′), *adj.* *Biol.* having foveae; pitted.

fo·ve·o·la (fō vē′ə lə), *n., pl.* **-lae** (-lē′). *Biol.* a small fovea; a very small pit or depression. [NL., dim. of L *fovea.* See FOVEA]

fo·ve·o·late (fō′vĭ ə lāt′), *adj.* *Biol.* having foveolae, or very small pits. Also, **fo′ve·o·lat′ed.**

fowl (foul), *n., pl.* **fowls,** (*esp. collectively*) **fowl,** *v.* —*n.* **1.** the domestic or barnyard hen or rooster (**domestic fowl**), a gallinaceous bird (often designated as *Gallus domesticus*) of the pheasant family, descended from wild species of *Gallus* (**jungle fowl**). **2.** any of various other gallinaceous or similar birds, as the turkey or duck. **3.** (in market and household use) a full-grown domestic fowl for food purposes (as distinguished from a chicken, or young fowl). **4.** the flesh or meat of a domestic fowl. **5.** any bird (now chiefly in combination): *waterfowl, wild fowl.* —*v.i.* **6.** to hunt or take wild fowl. [ME *foule,* OE *fugel,* c. D and G *vogel*] —**fowl′er,** *n.*

fowl cholera, a specific, acute, diarrheal disease of fowls, especially chickens, caused by a bacterium, *Pasteurella multocida.*

fowl·ing (fou′lĭng), *n.* the practice or sport of shooting or snaring birds.

fowling piece, a shotgun for shooting wild fowl.

fowl pox, a virus disease of chickens and other birds characterized by warty excrescences on the comb and wattles, and often by diphtherialike changes in the mucous membranes of the head.

fox (fŏks), *n.* **1.** any of certain carnivores of the dog family (*Canidae*), esp. those constituting the genus *Vulpes,* smaller than the wolves, characterized by pointed muzzle, erect ears, and long, bushy tail. **2.** a cunning or crafty person. **3.** *Naut.* a seizing made by twisting several rope yarns together and rubbing them down. **4.** (*cap.*) **a.** a tribe of North American Algonquian Indians,

Red fox. *Vulpes fulva*
(Total length 3½ ft., tail 16 in.)

formerly in Wisconsin, later merged with the Sac tribe. **b.** a member of this tribe. **5.** *Bible.* (sometimes) the jackal. —*v.t.* **6.** *Colloq.* to deceive or trick. **7.** to intoxicate or befuddle. **8.** to cause (papers, etc.) to discolor with reddish-brown spots of mildew. **9.** to make sour, as beer. **10.** to repair or make (a shoe) with leather or other material applied so as to cover or form part of the upper front. —*v.i.* **11.** to act cunningly or craftily. **12.** (of papers, etc.) to become foxed. [ME and OE, c. G *fuchs.* See VIXEN] —**fox′like′,** *adj.*

Fox (fŏks), *n.* **1. Charles James,** 1749–1806, British statesman and orator. **2. George,** 1624–91, British preacher and writer, founder of the Society of Friends. **3. John.** See **Foxe.**

Foxe (fŏks), *n.* **John,** 1516–87, English clergyman and writer.

fox·glove (fŏks′glŭv′), *n.* any plant of the scrophulariaceous genus *Digitalis,* esp. *D. purpurea* (the common foxglove), a native of Europe, bearing drooping, tubular, purple or white flowers, and leaves that are used as digitalis in medicine. [ME *foxes glove,* OE *foxes glōfa*]

fox grape, either of two species of grape, *Vitis labrusca* of the northern U.S. or *V. rotundifolia* of the southern U.S., from which various cultivated varieties have been derived.

fox·hole (fŏks′hōl′), *n.* a small pit, usually for one or two men, used for cover in a battle area.

fox·hound (fŏks′hound′), *n.* one of a breed of fleet, keen-scented hounds trained to hunt foxes.

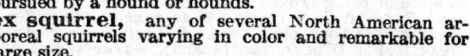
English foxhound
(23 in. high at the shoulder, 27½ in. long)

fox hunt, a sport in which the hunters follow a fox that is being pursued by a hound or hounds.

fox squirrel, any of several North American arboreal squirrels varying in color and remarkable for large size.

fox·tail (fŏks′tāl′), *n.* **1.** the tail of a fox. **2.** any of various grasses with soft, brushlike spikes of flowers.

foxtail millet, an annual grass, *Cetaria italica,* of numerous varieties, introduced into the U.S. from Europe and Asia, and grown chiefly for emergency hay crops.

fox terrier, one of a breed of small, active terriers, sometimes used for driving foxes from their holes, but kept chiefly as pets.

fox trot, 1. a social dance, in ⁴/₄ time, performed by couples, characterized by various combinations of short, quick steps. **2.** a pace, as of a horse, consisting of a series of short steps, as in slackening from a trot to a walk.

Fox terrier
(15 in. high at the shoulder)

fox-trot (fŏks′trŏt′), *v.i.,* **-trotted, -trotting.** to dance a fox trot.

fox·y (fŏk′sĭ), *adj.,* **foxier, foxiest. 1.** foxlike; cunning or crafty. **2.** discolored or foxed. **3.** yellowish- or reddish-brown; of the color of the common red fox. **4.** impaired or defective in quality. **5.** (of wines) having the pronounced flavor natural to native American grape varieties, as that of Concord grapes. —**fox′i·ly,** *adv.* —**fox′i·ness,** *n.*

foy (foi), *n.* *Dial.* **1.** a feast, gift, etc., given by or to a person about to start on a journey. **2.** a feast held on some special occasion, as at the end of the harvest. [t. MD: m. *foye,* prob. t. OF: m. *voie,* g. L *via* way]

foy·er (foi′ər, foi′ā; *Fr.* fwå yě′), *n.* **1.** the lobby of a theater or hotel. **2.** an entrance hall in a house. [t. F: hearth, fireside (orig. a room to which theater audiences went for warmth between the acts), g. Rom. *focārium,* der. L *focus* hearth]

F.P., foot-pound. Also, **f.p.**

f.p., freezing point.

f.p.s. system, foot-pound-second system.

Fr., **1.** Father. **2.** France. **3.** frater¹. **4.** French. **5.** Friar. **6.** Friday.

fr., **1.** fragment. **2.** (*pl.* **fr., frs.**) franc. **3.** from.

Fra (frä), *n.* brother (a title of a friar): *Fra Giovanni.* [t. It., abbr. of *frate* brother]

fra·cas (frā′kəs; *Brit.* fräk′ä), *n.* a disorderly noise, disturbance, or fight; uproar. [t. F, t. It.: m. *fracasso,* der. *fracassare* smash, f. *fra-* (g. L *infrā* among) completely + *cassare* (ult. g. L *quassāre* to shake)]

frac·tion (frāk′shən), *n.* **1.** *Math.* **a.** one or more aliquot parts of a unit or whole number; the ratio between any two numbers. **b.** a ratio of algebraic quantities analogous to the arithmetical vulgar fraction and similarly expressed. **2.** a part as distinct from the whole of anything: *only a fraction of the regiment came back.* **3.** a piece broken off; fragment or bit. **4.** act of breaking. —*v.t.* **5.** to divide into fractions. [ME, t. LL: s. *fractio,* der. L *frangere* break]

frac·tion·al (frāk′shən əl), *adj.* **1.** pertaining to fractions; comprising a part or the parts of a unit; constituting a fraction: *fractional numbers.* **2.** partial, inconsiderable, or insignificant. **3.** *Chem.* of or denoting a process, as distillation, crystallization, or oxidation, by which the component substances of a mixture are separated according to differences in certain of their properties, as boiling point, critical temperature, solubility, etc. Also, **frac·tion·ar·y** (frăk′shə nĕr′ĭ) for 1, 2. —**frac′tion·al·ly,** *adv.*

fractional currency, coins or paper money of a smaller denomination than the monetary unit.

frac·tion·ate (frăk′shə nāt′), *v.t.,* -**ated,** -**ating.** **1.** to separate (a mixture) into its ingredients, or into portions having different properties, as by distillation or crystallization; subject to fractional distillation, crystallization, or the like. **2.** to obtain by such a process. —**frac′tion·a′tion,** *n.*

frac·tion·ize (frăk′shə nīz′), *v.t., v.i.,* -**ized,** -**izing.** to divide into fractions.

frac·tious (frăk′shəs), *adj.* **1.** cross, fretful, or peevish. **2.** refractory or unruly. [f. FRACTI(ON) (in obs. sense of discord) + -OUS, modeled on CAPTIOUS, etc.] —**frac′tious·ly,** *adv.* —**frac′tious·ness,** *n.*

fracto-, a word element meaning "broken." [comb. form repr. L *fractus,* pp.]

frac·to·cu·mu·lus (frăk′tō kū′myə ləs), *n., pl.* -**li** (-lī′). *Meteorol.* very low, ragged clouds, slightly cumuliform, which often appear beneath nimbo-stratus clouds during active precipitation.

frac·to·stra·tus (frăk′tō strā′təs), *n., pl.* -**ti** (-tī) *Meteorol.* very low, ragged clouds of stratiform appearance which often appear beneath nimbo-stratus clouds during active precipitation; scud clouds.

frac·ture (frăk′chər), *n., v.,* -**tured,** -**turing.** —*n.* **1.** the breaking of a bone, cartilage, etc., or the resulting condition (in a bone, called *simple* when the bone does not communicate with the exterior, and *compound* when there is also a laceration of the integuments permitting communication with the exterior). **2.** the characteristic manner of breaking. **3.** the characteristic appearance of a broken surface, as of a mineral. **4.** act of breaking. **5.** state of being broken. **6.** a break, breach, or split. —*v.t.* **7.** to break or crack. **8.** to cause or to suffer a fracture in (a bone, etc.). —*v.i.* **9.** to undergo fracture; break. [t. F, t. L: m. *fractūra* breach] —**frac′tur·al,** *adj.*

frae (frā), *prep., adv.* *Scot.* from.

frae·num (frē′nəm), *n., pl.* -**na** (-nə). *Anat., Zool.* frenum.

frag·ile (frăj′əl; *Brit.* frăj′īl), *adj.* easily broken, shattered, or damaged; delicate; brittle; frail. [t. L: m.s. *fragilis*] —**frag′ile·ly,** *adv.* —**fra·gil·i·ty** (frə jĭl′ə tĭ), **frag′ile·ness,** *n.* —**Syn.** See frail[1].

frag·ment (frăg′mənt), *n.* **1.** a part broken off or detached: *scattered fragments of rock.* **2.** a portion that is unfinished or incomplete: *fragments of a letter.* **3.** an odd piece, bit, or scrap. [t. L: s. *fragmentum*]

frag·men·tal (frăg mĕn′təl), *adj.* **1.** fragmentary. **2.** *Geol.* clastic.

frag·men·tar·y (frăg′mən tĕr′ĭ), *adj.* composed of fragments; broken; disconnected; incomplete: *fragmentary evidence, remains, etc.* —**frag′men·tar′i·ly,** *adv.* —**frag′men·tar′i·ness,** *n.*

frag·men·ta·tion (frăg′mən tā′shən), *adj.* *Mil.* denoting a bomb, grenade, etc., that scatters fragments of its case or contents over a wide area.

frag·ment·ed (frăg′mənt ĭd), *adj.* reduced to fragments.

Fra·go·nard (frä gô när′), *n.* **Jean Honoré** (zhän ô nô rĕ′), 1732–1806, French painter.

fra·grance (frā′grəns), *n.* fragrant quality or odor; sweet scent. —**Syn.** See **perfume.**

fra·gran·cy (frā′grən sĭ), *n., pl.* -**cies.** fragrance.

fra·grant (frā′grənt), *adj.* **1.** having a pleasant odor; sweet-smelling; sweet-scented. **2.** delightful; pleasant: *fragrant memories.* [t. L: s. *frāgrans,* ppr., emitting an odor, smelling sweet] —**fra′grant·ly,** *adv.* —**Syn.** perfumed, odorous, redolent.

frail[1] (frāl), *adj.* **1.** weak; not robust; having delicate health. **2.** easily broken or destroyed; fragile. **3.** morally weak; not strong against temptation. [ME *frele,* t. OF, var. of *fraile,* g. L *fragilis* fragile] —**frail′ly,** *adv.* —**frail′ness,** *n.*

—**Syn.** 1, 2. FRAIL, BRITTLE, FRAGILE imply a delicacy or weakness of substance or construction. FRAIL applies particularly to health, and immaterial things: *a frail constitution, frail hopes.* BRITTLE implies a hard outside finish but delicate material which snaps or breaks to pieces easily: *brittle as glass.* FRAGILE implies that the object must be handled carefully to avoid breakage or damage: *fragile bric-à-brac.* —**Ant. 1.** sturdy.

frail[2] (frāl), *n.* **1.** a flexible basket made of rushes, used esp. for dried fruits, as dates, figs, or raisins. **2.** a certain quantity of raisins, about 75 pounds, contained in such a basket. [ME *frayel,* t. OF: m. *fraiel*]

frail·ty (frāl′tĭ), *n., pl.* -**ties.** **1.** quality or state of being frail. **2.** moral weakness; liability to yield to temptation. **3.** a fault proceeding from moral weakness.

fraise (frāz), *n.* **1.** *Fort.* a defense consisting of pointed stakes projecting from the ramparts in a horizontal or an inclined position. **2.** a ruff worn around the neck in the 16th century. [t. F, der. *fraiser* to frizzle, curl, t. Pr.: m. *frezar,* ult. der. a Gmc. word; cf. OE *frīs* curled]

Frak·tur (frăk tŏŏr′), *n.* *Print.* German text, a style of type.

fram·be·sia (frăm bē′zhə), *n.* *Pathol.* a contagious disease resembling syphilis, prevalent in certain tropical regions, characterized by an eruption of raspberrylike excrescences; yaws. Also, **fram·boe′sia.** [NL: Latin-

ization of F *framboise* raspberry, g. Rom. *frambosia,* contr. of *frāga ambrosia* ambrosia strawberry]

frame (frām), *n., v.,* **framed, framing.** —*n.* **1.** an enclosing border or case, as for a picture. **2.** anything composed of parts fitted and joined together; a structure. **3.** the sustaining parts of a structure fitted and joined together; framework or skeleton. **4.** the body, esp. the human body, with reference to its make or build. **5.** a structure for admitting or enclosing something. **6.** any of various machines operating on or within a framework. **7.** a particular state, as of the mind: *an unhappy frame of mind.* **8.** form, constitution, or structure in general; system; order. **9.** *Shipbuilding.* **a.** one of the transverse structural members of a ship's hull, extending from the gunwale to the bilge or to the keel. **b. square frame,** a frame set perpendicularly to the vertical plane of the keel. **c. cant frame,** a frame set at an acute angle to the vertical plane of the keel. **10.** *Colloq.* (in baseball) an inning. **11.** *American Bowling.* a turn to bowl, each player usually having ten turns, of two (or, if a strike is made, three) shots each, in a game. **12.** *Pool.* **a.** the triangular form used to set up the balls for a game. **b.** the balls as so set up. **c.** the period of play required to pocket them. **13.** *Movies.* one of the successive small pictures on a strip of film.

—*v.t.* **14.** to form or make, as by fitting and uniting parts together; construct. **15.** to contrive, devise, or compose, as a plan, law, poem, etc. **16.** to conceive or imagine, as ideas, etc. **17.** to fashion or shape. **18.** to shape or to adapt to a particular purpose. **19.** *Colloq.* to contrive or prearrange fraudulently or falsely, as a plot, a race, etc. **20.** *Colloq.* to incriminate unjustly by a plot, as a person. **21.** to provide with or put into a frame, as a picture. **22.** *Obs.* to direct, as one's steps.

—*v.i.* **23.** to betake oneself, or resort. **24.** to prepare, attempt, give promise, or manage to do something. [ME *frame*(n), OE *framian* avail, profit, der. *fram* forward] —**frame′less,** *adj.* —**fram′er,** *n.*

frame house, *U.S.* a house constructed with a skeleton frame of timber, as the ordinary wooden house.

frame-up (frām′ŭp′), *n.* *Orig. U.S. Slang.* **1.** that which is framed, as a plot, or a contest whose result is fraudulently prearranged. **2.** act of framing up.

frame·work (frām′wûrk′), *n.* **1.** a structure composed of parts fitted and united together. **2.** one designed to support or enclose something; frame or skeleton. **3.** frames collectively. **4.** work done in, on, or with a frame.

fram·ing (frā′mĭng), *n.* **1.** act, process, or manner of constructing anything. **2.** act of providing with a frame. **3.** framed work; a frame or a system of frames.

Fram·ing·ham (frā′mĭng hăm′), *n.* a town in E Massachusetts. 44,526 (1960).

franc (frăngk; *Fr.* frän), *n.* **1.** a French monetary unit and coin, equal at present to 20 U.S. cents. **2.** the corresponding coin and unit of Switzerland and Belgium. **3.** either of two old coins and units of France, one of gold and the other of silver. [ME *frank,* t. OF: m. *franc,* so called from the ML legend *Francōrum rex* king of the Franks (or French), on the first coin]

France (frăns, fräns), *n.* a republic in W Europe. 43,600,000 (est. 1956); 212,736 sq. mi. *Cap.:* Paris.

France (fräns), *n.* **Anatole** (à nà tôl′), (*Jacques Anatole Thibault*) 1844–1924, French novelist and essayist.

Fran·ces·ca (frän chĕs′kä), *n.* **Piero della** (pyĕ′rô dĕl′lä), (*Piero de' Franceschi*) c1420–92, Italian painter.

Franche-Com·té (fränsh kôn tĕ′), *n.* a former province in E France: once a part of Burgundy.

fran·chise (frăn′chīz), *n.* **1.** the right to vote. **2.** a privilege arising from the grant of a sovereign or government, or from prescription, which presupposes a grant. **3.** a privilege of a public nature conferred on an individual or body of individuals by a governmental grant: *a franchise for a street railway.* **4.** permission granted by a manufacturer to a distributor or retailer to sell his products. **5.** the district or jurisdiction to which the privilege of an individual or corporation extends. **6.** (orig.) a legal immunity or exemption from a particular burden, exaction, or the like. [ME, t. OF, der. *franc* free, FRANK]

Fran·cis (frăn′sĭs, fräN′-), *n.* **Saint,** (*Francis of Assisi*) 1181?–1226, Italian friar: founded Franciscan order.

Francis I, **1.** 1494–1547, king of France, 1515–47. **2.** title of Francis II as emperor of Austria.

Francis II, 1768–1835, last emperor of the Holy Roman Empire, 1792–1806. As Francis I, he was the first emperor of Austria, 1804–35.

Fran·cis·can (frăn sĭs′kən), *adj.* **1.** of or pertaining to St. Francis of Assisi or the mendicant religious order founded by him (authorized by the Pope in 1209; formally ratified in 1223). —*n.* **2.** a member of this order.

Francis Ferdinand, 1863–1914, Archduke of Austria, heir to the thrones of Austria and Hungary, nephew of Francis Joseph I. His assassination on June 28, 1914, led to the outbreak of World War I.

Francis Joseph I, 1830–1916, emperor of Austria, 1848–1916, and king of Hungary and Bohemia.

Francis of Pau·la (pä′ŏŏ lä′), **Saint,** 1416–1507, Italian monk: founder of order of Minims.

Francis of Sales (sālz; *Fr.* sàl), **Saint,** 1567–1622, French Roman Catholic bishop of Geneva, Switzerland.

Francis Xa·vi·er (zā′vĭ ər, zăv′ĭ-). See **Xavier**.

fran·ci·um (frăn′sĭ əm), *n.* a radioactive element of the alkali metal group. *Symbol:* Fr; *at. no.:* 87. [f. FRANC(E), where first identified + -IUM]

Franck (fräNk), *n.* **César Auguste** (sĕ zȧr′ ō gyst′), 1822–1890, French composer, born in Belgium.

Fran·co (fräng′kō), *n.* **Francisco** (frän thēs′kō), born 1892, Spanish chief of state, 1939–47; regent of the kingdom of Spain since 1947.

Franco-, a word element meaning "French" or "France," as in *Franco-American.* [comb. form repr. ML *Francus* a Frank, a Frenchman]

fran·co·lin (frăng′kə lĭn), *n.* any of numerous Old World gallinaceous birds of the genus *Francolinus* and allied genera, esp. *F. vulgaris,* a species formerly common in southern Europe but now chiefly confined to Asia. [t. F, t. It.: m. *francolino*]

Fran·co·ni·a (frăng kō′nĭ ə), *n.* a medieval duchy in Germany, largely in the valley of the Main river.

Fran·co·phile (frăng′kə fĭl′), *adj.* **1.** friendly to France or the French. —*n.* **2.** one who is friendly to France or the French. Also, **Fran·co·phil** (frăng′kə fĭl).

Fran·co·phobe (frăng′kə fōb′), *adj.* **1.** fearing or hating France. —*n.* **2.** one who fears or hates France.

franc·ti·reur (frän tē rœr′), *n., pl.* **francs-tireurs** (frän tē rœr′). a sharpshooter in the French Army. [F: lit., free shooter]

fran·gi·ble (frăn′jə bəl), *adj.* capable of being broken; breakable. [ME *frangebyll,* t. OF: m. *frangible,* der. L *frangere* break] —**fran′gi·bil′i·ty,** *n.*

fran·gi·pane (frăn′jə pān′), *n.* **1.** a kind of pastry cake, filled with cream, almonds and sugar. **2.** frangipani. [t. F; said to be from *Frangipani,* the inventor]

fran·gi·pan·i (frăn′jĭ păn′ĭ, -pä′nĭ), *n., pl.* **-panis.** **1.** a perfume prepared from, or imitating the odor of, the flower of the red jasmine, *Plumeria ruba,* an apocynaceous tree or shrub of tropical America. **2.** the tree or shrub itself. [said to be named after the inventor]

frank (frăngk), *adj.* **1.** open or unreserved in speech; candid or outspoken; sincere. **2.** undisguised; avowed; downright: *frank mutiny.* **3.** *Rare.* liberal or generous. **4.** *Obs.* free. —*n.* **5.** a signature or mark affixed by special privilege to a letter, package, or the like, to ensure its transmission free of charge, as by mail. **6.** the privilege of franking letters, etc. **7.** a franked letter, package, etc. —*v.t.* **8.** to mark (a letter, package, etc.) for transmission free of the usual charge, by virtue of official or special privilege; send free of charge, as mail. **9.** to facilitate the coming of (a person); convey (a person) free of charge. **10.** to enable to pass or go freely. **11.** to secure exemption for. [ME, t. OF: m. *franc,* g. LL *francus* free, orig. Frank] —**frank′a·ble,** *adj.* —**frank′er,** *n.*

—**Syn. 1.** FRANK, CANDID, OPEN, OUTSPOKEN imply a freedom and boldness in speaking. FRANK is applied to one unreserved in expressing the truth and his real opinions and sentiments: *a frank disagreement.* CANDID suggests one (sometimes unpleasantly) sincere and truthful or impartial and fair in judgment: *a candid expression of opinion.* OPEN implies a lack of reserve or of concealment: *open antagonism.* OUTSPOKEN applies to one who expresses himself freely, even when this is inappropriate: *outspoken disapproval.*

Frank (frăngk), *n.* **1.** a member of a group of ancient Germanic peoples dwelling in the regions of the Rhine, one division of whom, the Salians, conquered Gaul about A.D. 500, founded an extensive kingdom, and gave origin to the name *France.* **2.** (in the Levant) any native or inhabitant of western Europe. [ME *Franke,* OE *Franca,* c. OHG *Franko;* usually said to be from the name of the national weapon. Cf. OE *franca* spear, javelin. See FRANK]

Frank·en·stein (frăngk′ən stīn′), *n.* **1.** one who creates a monster or a destructive agency that he cannot control or that brings about his own ruin. **2.** the monster or destructive agency itself. [from the hero of Mary Shelley's novel, "Frankenstein," a student who created such a monster]

Frank·fort (frăngk′fərt), *n.* the capital of Kentucky, in the N part. 11,916 (1950).

Frankfort on the Main (mān), a city in central West Germany, on the Main river. 639,976 (est. 1955). German, **Frank·furt am Main** (frăngk′fŏŏrt äm mīn′), **Frankfurt.**

Frankfort on the O·der (ō′dər), a city in East Germany, on the Oder. 51,577 (1946). German, **Frankfurt an der O·der** (frăngk′fŏŏrt än dər ō′dər), **Frankfurt.**

frank·furt·er (frăngk′fər tər), *n.* a reddish variety of sausage made of beef and pork, commonly cooked by steaming or boiling. Also, **frank′furt.** [t. G: Frankfurt (sausage)]

Frank·furt·er (frăngk′fər tər), *n.* **Felix,** 1882–1964, U.S. jurist: associate justice U.S. Supreme Court 1939–62, born in Austria.

Frankfurt horizontal (frăngk′fərt), **1.** *Craniom.* the plane established when right and left poria and left orbitale are in the same horizontal plane. **2.** *Cephalom.* the plane established when right and left tragia and left orbitale are in the same horizontal plane.

frank·in·cense (frăngk′ĭn sĕns′), *n.* an aromatic gum resin from various Asiatic and African trees of the genus *Boswellia,* esp. *B. carteri:* used chiefly for burning as incense or ceremonially. [ME *franke ensens,* t. OF: m. *franc encens* pure incense. See FRANK, INCENSE²]

Frank·ish (frăngk′ĭsh), *adj.* **1.** of or pertaining to the Franks. —*n.* **2.** the language of the Franks (def. 1).

Frank·lin (frăngk′lĭn), *n.* **1. Benjamin,** 1706–90, American statesman, diplomat, author, scientist, and inventor. **2. Sir John,** 1786–1847, British explorer. **3.** a district in extreme N Canada, in the Northwest Territories, including Baffin Island, other Arctic islands, and Boothia and Melville peninsulas. 549,253 sq. mi.

frank·lin (frăngk′lĭn), *n.* (in the late Middle Ages) a non-noble freeholder of the middle class. [ME *frankeleyn,* ult. der. ML *francus* free, FRANK]

frank·lin·ite (frăngk′lĭ nīt′), *n.* a mineral of the spinel group, an oxide of zinc, manganese, and iron, occurring in black octahedral crystals or in masses: an ore of zinc. [named after *Franklin,* N. J., where it is found. See -ITE¹]

Franklin stove, U.S. **1.** a type of iron fireplace designed by Benjamin Franklin. **2.** an open stove of various types.

frank·ly (frăngk′lĭ), *adv.* in a frank manner; freely; openly; unreservedly; candidly; plainly.

frank·ness (frăngk′nĭs), *n.* plainness of speech; candor; openness.

frank·pledge (frăngk′plĕj′), *n. Early Eng. Law.* **1.** a system by which the inhabitants of a community were divided into groups of ten or more, whose members had to produce one of their number charged with a breach of the law or pay a fine. **2.** a member of such a group. **3.** the group itself. [t. AF: m. *franc plege,* mistranslation of OE *frithborg* peace pledge]

fran·tic (frăn′tĭk), *adj.* **1.** wild with excitement, passion, fear, pain, etc.; frenzied; characterized by or pertaining to frenzy. **2.** *Archaic.* insane or mad. [ME *frentik,* t. OF: m. *frenetique,* t. L: m. *phreneticus* delirious, t. Gk.: m. *phrenētikós*] —**fran′ti·cal·ly, fran′tic·ly,** *adv.* —**fran′tic·ness,** *n.*

Franz Jo·sef Land (fränts′ yō′zĕf), an archipelago in the Arctic Ocean, E of Spitzbergen and N of Novaya Zemlya, belonging to the Soviet Union. Also, **Fridtjof Nansen Land.**

frap (frăp), *v.t.,* **frapped, frapping.** *Naut.* to bind securely. [ME *frap*(en), t. OF: m. *fraper* strike.]

frap·pé (frȧ pā′; *Fr.* frȧ pĕ′), *n.* U.S. **1.** a fruit juice mixture frozen to a mush, to be sipped as an appetizer. —*adj.* **2.** chilled; iced; frozen. [t. F, pp. of *frapper* ice (drinks), orig., beat, t. Gmc.; cf. RAP]

Fra·ser (frā′zər), *n.* a river in SW Canada, flowing S through British Columbia to the Pacific. 695 mi.

frat (frăt), *n.* U.S. *College Slang.* a fraternity (def. 1).

fra·ter¹ (frā′tər), *n.* a brother; comrade. [L: brother]

fra·ter² (frā′tər), *n. Obs. except Hist.* the refectory of a religious house. [ME *freitur,* t. OF: m. *fraitur,* short for *refreitor,* repr. ML *refectórium* REFECTORY]

fra·ter·nal (frə tûr′nəl), *adj.* **1.** of or befitting a brother or brothers; brotherly. **2.** of or being a society of men associated in brotherly union, as for mutual aid or benefit: *a fraternal society.* [f. s. L *fráternus* brotherly + -AL¹] —**fra·ter′nal·ism,** *nr.* —**fra·ter′nal·ly,** *adv.*

fraternal insurance, insurance underwritten by a fraternal society, under either a legal reserve plan or an assessment plan.

fra·ter·ni·ty (frə tûr′nə tĭ), *n., pl.* **-ties. 1.** U.S. a student society organized for social and other purposes, commonly composed of affiliated branches or chapters in various institutions and designated by two or more letters of the Greek alphabet: commonly applied to men's or to coeducational organizations, women's organizations being called sororities. **2.** a body of persons associated as by ties of brotherhood. **3.** any body or class of persons having common purposes, interest, etc.: *the medical fraternity.* **4.** an organization of laymen for pious or charitable purposes. **5.** the relation of persons associated on the footing of brothers: *liberty, equality, and fraternity.* **6.** the relation of a brother or between brothers; brotherhood. [ME *fraternite,* t. L: m.s. *frāternitas* brotherhood]

fraternity house, a house occupied by a fraternity.

frat·er·nize (frăt′ər nīz′), *v.,* **-nized, -nizing.** —*v.i.* **1.** to associate in a fraternal or friendly way. **2.** to associate intimately with citizens of an enemy or conquered country. —*v.t.* **3.** to bring into fraternal association or sympathy. —**frat·er·ni·za′tion,** *n.* —**frat′er·niz′er,** *n.*

frat·ri·cide¹ (frăt′rə sīd′, frā′trə-), *n.* one who kills his or her brother. [t. L: m.s. *frātricīda*] —**frat′ri·cid′al,** *adj.*

frat·ri·cide² (frăt′rə sīd′, frā′trə-), *n.* act of killing one's own brother. [t. L: m.s. *frātricīdium*] —**frat′ri·cid′al,** *adj.*

Frau (frou), *n., pl.* **Fraus** (frouz), *Ger.* **Frauen** (frou′ən). *German.* a married woman; a wife; a lady (as title, equivalent to Mrs.).

fraud (frôd), *n.* **1.** deceit, trickery, sharp practice, or breach of confidence, by which it is sought to gain some unfair or dishonest advantage. **2.** a particular instance of such deceit or trickery: *election frauds.* **3.** any deception, artifice, or trick. **4.** U.S. *Colloq.* a person who makes deceitful pretenses; impostor. [ME *fraude,* t. OF, t. L: m.s. *fraus* cheating, deceit] —**Syn. 1.** See **trick.**

fraud·u·lent (frô′jə lənt), *adj.* **1.** given to or using fraud, as a person; cheating; dishonest. **2.** characterized by, involving, or proceeding from fraud, as actions, enterprise, methods, gains, etc. [ME, t. L: s. *fraudulentus* cheating] —**fraud′u·lence, fraud′u·len·cy,** *n.* —**fraud′u·lent·ly,** *adv.*

ăct, āble, dâre, ärt; ĕbb, ēqual; ĭf, īce; hŏt, ōver, ôrder, oil, bŏŏk, ōoze, out; ŭp, ūse, ûrge; ə = a in alone; ch, chief; g, give; ng, ring; sh, shoe; th, thin; ŧħ, that; zh, vision.   See the full key on inside cover.

fraught (frôt), *adj.* **1.** involving; attended (with); full (of): *an undertaking fraught with danger, a heart fraught with grief.* **2.** Archaic or Poetic. filled or laden (with): *ships fraught with precious wares.* —*n.* **3.** *Obs. or Scot.* a load; cargo; freight (of a ship). [ME, t. MD or MLG: m. *vracht* freight money, FREIGHT. Cf. OHG *frēht* earnings]

Fräu·lein (froi′līn), *n.*, *pl.* **Fräuleins,** *Ger.* **Fräulein.** German. an unmarried woman; a young lady (as a title, equivalent to *Miss*).

Fraun·ho·fer (froun′hō′fər), *n.* **Joseph von** (yō′zĕf fən), 1787–1826, German optician and physicist.

Fraunhofer lines, the dark lines of the solar spectrum. [named after Joseph von FRAUNHOFER]

frax·i·nel·la (frăk′sənĕl′ə), *n.* dittany (def. 3). [NL, dim. of L *fraxinus* ash tree]

fray[1] (frā), *n.* **1.** a noisy quarrel; brawl; fight, skirmish, or battle. **2.** *Obs. or Scot.* fright. —*v.t.* **3.** *Archaic.* to frighten. —*v.i.* **4.** *Archaic or Dial.* to fight; brawl. [aphetic var. of AFFRAY]

fray[2] (frā), *v.t.* **1.** to wear (cloth, rope, etc.) to loose, raveled threads or fibers at the edge or end; cause to ravel out. **2.** to rub. **3.** to wear by rubbing (sometimes fol. by *through*). —*v.i.* **4.** to become frayed, as cloth, etc.; ravel out. **5.** to rub against something. —*n.* **6.** a frayed part, as in cloth. [t. F: s. *frayer*, g. L *fricāre* rub]

Fra·zer (frā′zər), *n.* **Sir James George,** 1854–1941, British anthropologist.

fraz·zle (frăz′əl), *v.*, **-zled, -zling,** *n.* *Chiefly U.S.* —*v.i.*, *v.t.* **1.** to fray; wear to threads or shreds. **2.** to weary; tire out. —*n.* **3.** state of being frazzled or worn-out. **4.** a remnant; shred. [b. FRAY[2] and *fazzle*, ME *faselin* unravel, c. G *faseln*]

FRC, Federal Radio Commission.

freak[1] (frēk), *n.* **1.** a sudden and apparently causeless change or turn of the mind; a capricious notion; a whim. **2.** capriciousness. **3.** any abnormal product or curiously unusual object; monstrosity. **4.** a person or animal on exhibition as an example of some strange deviation from nature. —*adj.* **5.** unusual; odd; irregular: *a freak copy of a book.* [? akin to OE *frician* dance]

freak[2] (frēk), *v.t.* **1.** to fleck, streak, or variegate. —*n.* **2.** a fleck or streak of color. [? v. use of FREAK[1]; appar. coined by Milton]

freak·ish (frē′kĭsh), *adj.* **1.** given to or full of freaks; whimsical; capricious. **2.** resembling a freak; queer; odd; grotesque. —**freak′ish·ly,** *adv.* —**freak′ish·ness,** *n.*

freak·y (frē′kĭ), *adj.*, **freakier, freakiest.** freakish. —**freak′i·ness,** *n.*

Fré·chette (frē shĕt′), *n.* **Louis Honoré** (lwē ônō-rē′), 1839–1908, Canadian poet and journalist.

freck·le (frĕk′əl), *n.*, *v.*, **-led, -ling.** —*n.* **1.** a small brownish-yellow spot in the skin, esp. on the face, neck, or arms. **2.** any small spot or discoloration. —*v.t.* **3.** to cover with freckles or produce freckles on. —*v.i.* **4.** to become freckled. [b. obs. *frecken* freckle (t. Scand.; cf. Icel. *freknur*, pl.) and SPECKLE, n.] —**freck′led,** *adj.*

freck·ly (frĕk′lĭ) *adj.* full of freckles.

Fred·er·ick I (frĕd′ərĭk, frĕd′rĭk), **1.** Frederick Barbarossa. **2.** 1657–1713, first king of Prussia, 1701–13.

Frederick II, 1. 1194–1250, German king, king of Sicily, and emperor of the Holy Roman Empire, 1218–1250. **2.** Frederick the Great.

Frederick III, ("the Wise") 1463–1525, elector of Saxony, 1486–1525: protector of Martin Luther.

Frederick IX, b. 1899, king of Denmark since 1947.

Frederick Bar·ba·ros·sa (bär′bərŏs′ə), (*Frederick I*) c1123–1190, German king and emperor of the Holy Roman Empire, 1152–90.

Fred·er·icks·burg (frĕd′rĭksbûrg′), *n.* a city in NE Virginia, on the Rappahannock river: scene of a Confederate victory in the Civil War, 1862. 12,158 (1950).

Frederick the Great, (*Frederick II*) 1712–86, king of Prussia, 1740–86.

Frederick William, 1. ("the Great Elector") 1620–1688, elector of Brandenburg who increased the power and importance of Prussia. **2.** 1882–1951, former crown prince of Germany, 1888–1918; German general (son of William II of Germany).

Frederick William I, 1688–1740, king of Prussia, 1713–40.

Frederick William II, 1744–97, king of Prussia, 1786–97.

Frederick William III, 1770–1840, king of Prussia, 1797–1840.

Frederick William IV, 1795–1861, king of Prussia, 1840–61.

Fred·er·ic·ton (frĕd′ərĭk tən), *n.* a city in SE Canada, on the St. John river: the capital of New Brunswick. 16,018 (1951).

Fred·er·iks·borg (frĕth′ərĕksbôrkн′), *n.* a city in E Denmark, near Copenhagen. 153,115 (est. 1954).

free (frē), *adj.*, **freer, freest,** *adv.*, *v.*, **freed, freeing.** —*adj.* **1.** enjoying personal rights or liberty, as one not in slavery. **2.** pertaining to or reserved for those who enjoy personal liberty: *free soil.* **3.** possessed of, characterized by, or existing under civil liberty as opposed to arbitrary or despotic government, as a country or state, or its citizens, institutions, etc. **4.** enjoying political liberty or independence, as a people or country not under foreign rule. **5.** exempt from external authority, interference, restriction, etc., as a person, the will,

thought, choice, action, etc.; independent; unfettered. **6.** at liberty, permitted, or able at will (to do something): *free to choose.* **7.** not subject to special regulation or restrictions, as trade: *free trade.* **8.** not literal, as a translation. **9.** not subject to rules, set forms, etc.: *the free song of a bird, free verse.* **10.** clear of obstructions or obstacles, as a corridor. **11.** exempt or released from something specified that controls, restrains, burdens, etc. (fol. by *from* or *of*): *free from matrimonial ties, free of taxes.* **12.** having immunity or being safe (usually fol. by *from*): *free from criticism.* **13.** uncombined chemically: *free oxygen.* **14.** open (fol. by *to* or *for*): *a race free for all competitors, a free port.* **15.** general: *a free fight.* **16.** unimpeded, as motion or movements; easy, firm, or swift in movement: *a free step.* **17.** loose, or not held fast or attached: *to get one's arm free.* **18.** not joined to or in contact with something else: *a free surface.* **19.** acting without self-restraint or reserve: *too free with one's tongue.* **20.** frank and open; unconstrained, unceremonious, or familiar. **21.** unrestrained by decency; loose or licentious. **22.** ready in giving, liberal, or lavish: *to be free with one's advice.* **23.** given readily or in profusion, or unstinted. **24.** given without consideration of a return, as a gift. **25.** provided without, or not subject to, a charge or payment: *free schools.* **26.** admitted to entry and enjoyment at will (fol. by *of*): *to be free of a friend's house.* **27.** easily worked, as stone or land. **28.** *Naut.* (of a wind) blowing so that a boat can sail with sheets eased or yards squared; fair. **29.** *Phonet.* **a.** (of a vowel) situated in an open syllable. **b.** belonging to a class of vowels which need not be followed by a consonant: the vowel of *see* is one of the English free vowels. **30. free and clear,** *Law.* denoting real property without any encumbrance, such as a mortgage, on it. **31. make free with,** to treat or use too familiarly; take liberties with. —*adv.* **32.** in a free manner; freely. **33.** without cost or charge. **34.** *Naut.* further from the wind than when close-hauled: *to sail free.* —*v.t.* **35.** make free; set at liberty; release from bondage, imprisonment, or restraint. **36.** to exempt or deliver (fol. by *from*). **37.** to relieve or rid (fol. by *of*). **38.** to disengage (fol. by *from* or *of*). [ME; OE *frēo*, c. G *frei*, orig., dear, favored. Cf. FRIEND] —**Syn.** 35. See **release.**

free alongside ship, a term of sale meaning that the seller agrees to deliver the merchandise alongside ship without extra charge to buyer.

free·board (frē′bôrd′), *n.* *Naut.* the part of a ship's side between the water line and the deck or gunwale.

free·boot (frē′bōot′), *v.i.* to act as a freebooter.

free·boot·er (frē′bōo′tər), *n.* one who goes about in search of plunder; a pirate or buccaneer. [t. D: Anglicization of *vrijbuiter*, f. *vrij* free + *buit* booty + *-er* -ER[1]]

free·born (frē′bôrn′), *adj.* **1.** born free, rather than in slavery, bondage, or vassalage. **2.** pertaining to or befitting persons born free.

free city, a city having an independent government and forming a sovereign state by itself.

free coinage, the unrestricted coinage of bullion, or of a specified metal, as silver, into money for any person bringing it to the mint, either with or without charge for expenses of minting.

free companion, a member of a band of mercenary soldiers of the Middle Ages.

free company, a band of free companions.

free delivery, *U.S.* the delivery of mail matter without charge.

freed·man (frēd′mən), *n.*, *pl.* **-men.** a man who has been freed from slavery. —**freed′wom′an,** *n. fem.*

free·dom (frē′dəm), *n.* **1.** civil liberty, as opposed to subjection to an arbitrary or despotic government. **2.** political or national independence. **3.** a particular immunity or other privilege enjoyed, as by a city or corporation. **4.** personal liberty, as opposed to bondage or slavery. **5.** state of being at liberty rather than in confinement or under physical restraint. **6.** exemption from external control, interference, regulation, etc. **7.** power of determining one's or its own action. **8.** *Philos.* the condition of the will as the volitional instigator of human actions; relative self-determination. **9.** absence or release from ties, obligations, etc. **10.** exemption or immunity: *freedom from taxation.* **11.** exemption from the presence of anything specified (fol. by *from*): *freedom from fear.* **12.** ease or facility of movement or action. **13.** frankness of manner or speech. **14.** absence of ceremony or reserve; familiarity. **15.** a liberty taken. **16.** the right of enjoying all the privileges or peculiar rights of citizenship, membership, or the like: *the freedom of the city.* **17.** the right of frequenting, enjoying, or using at will: *to have the freedom of a friend's library.* [ME; OE *frēodōm.* See FREE, -DOM] —**Syn.** 1. FREEDOM, INDEPENDENCE, LIBERTY refer to an absence of undue restrictions and an opportunity to exercise one's rights and powers. FREEDOM emphasizes the large opportunity given for the exercise of one's rights, powers, desires, or the like: *freedom of speech or conscience, freedom of movement.* INDEPENDENCE implies not only lack of restrictions but also the ability to stand alone, unsustained by anything else: *independence of thought promotes invention and discovery.* LIBERTY, though often interchanged with FREEDOM, is commonly used to refer to past or possible restriction, confinement, or subjection: *give me liberty or, give me death.* —**Ant.** 1. oppression.

freedom of the press, the right of printing and publishing whatever is desired, without governmental permission or censorship.

freedom of the seas, *Internat. Law.* the doctrine that ships of neutral countries may sail anywhere on the high seas without interference by warring powers.

free energy, *Physics.* that portion of the energy of a system which is the maximum available for doing work.

free enterprise, the doctrine or practice of a minimum amount of government control of private business and industry.

free-for-all (frē′fər ôl′), *n.* a fight, game, contest, etc., open to everyone.

free form, a linguistic form which occurs sometimes or always by itself, not having the limitation of a bound form (which see), as *fire.*

free gold, 1. *U.S.* treasury gold, including the legal reserve, not restricted to the redemption of gold certificates or other specific uses. **2.** *Mining.* gold found in a pure state in nature, as in placer mining.

free-hand (frē′hănd′), *adj.* done by the hand without guiding instruments, measurements, or other aids.

free hand, unrestricted authority.

free-hand-ed (frē′hăn′dĭd), *adj.* **1.** open-handed; generous; liberal. **2.** having the hands free.

free-heart-ed (frē′här′tĭd), *adj.* having a free heart; light-hearted; spontaneous; frank; generous.

free-hold (frē′hōld′), *n.* *Law.* an estate in fee simple, in fee tail, or for life.

free-hold-er (frē′hōl′dər), *n.* the owner of a freehold.

free lance, 1. a contributor to periodicals, etc., who is not regularly employed by them. **2.** one who contends in a cause, or in a succession of various causes, as he chooses, without personal attachment or allegiance. **3.** a mercenary soldier or military adventurer of the Middle Ages, often of knightly rank, who offered his services to any state, party, or cause.

free-lance (frē′lăns′, -läns′), *v.i.,* **-lanced, -lancing.** to act or work as a free lance.

free list, *U.S. Com.* a list or register of articles that may be brought into a country duty-free.

free liver, one who in his mode of life freely indulges his appetites. —**free′-liv′ing,** *adj.*

free-load-er (frē′lō′dər), *n.* *Colloq.* one who imposes on others for free food, entertainment, etc. —**free′-load′,** *v.*

free love, the doctrine or practice of free choice in sexual relations, without restraint of legal marriage or of any continuing obligations independent of one's will.

free lunch, *U.S.* (formerly) food given without charge in a saloon, to attract customers.

free-ly (frē′lĭ), *adv.* in a free manner.

free-man (frē′mən), *n., pl.* **-men. 1.** a man who is free; a man who enjoys personal, civil, or political liberty. **2.** one who enjoys or is entitled to citizenship, franchise, or other peculiar privilege: *a freeman of a city.*

Free-man (frē′mən), *n.* **1. Douglas Southall** (sou′-thôl), 1886–1953, U.S. journalist and biographer. **2. Edward Augustus,** 1823–92, British historian. **3. Mary Wilkins,** 1862–1930, U.S. writer.

free-mar-tin (frē′mär′tən), *n.* a generally sterile heifer calf twinborn with a bull. [orig. uncert.]

Free-ma-son (frē′mā′sən, frē′mā′-), *n.* **1.** a member of a widely distributed secret order (**Free and Accepted Masons**), having for its object mutual assistance and the promotion of brotherly love among its members. **2.** (*l.c.*) *Hist.* **a.** one of a class of skilled stoneworkers of the Middle Ages, possessed of secret signs and passwords. **b.** a member of a society composed of such workers, with honorary members (known as *accepted masons*) who were not connected with the building trades. —**free-ma-son-ic** (frē′mə sŏn′ĭk), *adj.*

free-ma-son-ry (frē′mā′sən rĭ), *n.* **1.** secret or tacit brotherhood; instinctive sympathy. **2.** (*cap.*) the principles, practices, and institutions of Freemasons.

free-ness (frē′nĭs), *n.* state or quality of being free.

free on board, *Com.* a term of sale meaning that the seller agrees to deliver the merchandise aboard the carrier without extra charge to buyer.

free port, 1. a port open under equal conditions to all traders. **2.** a part or all of a port not included in customs territory so as to expedite transshipment of what is not to be imported.

Free-port (frē′pôrt′), *n.* **1.** a city in NW Illinois. 26,628 (1960). **2.** a village in SE New York, on Long Island. 34,419 (1960).

free radical, *Chem.* an organic compound in which an atom utilizes less than its normal valence, as CH_3-, the methyl radical in which carbon has a valence of three instead of four.

free-si-a (frē′zhĭ ə, -sĭ ə), *n.* any plant of the iridaceous genus *Freesia,* native in South Africa, esteemed for its fragrant white, yellow, or sometimes rose-colored, tubular flowers. [NL; named after E.M. *Fries* (1794–1878), Swedish botanist]

free silver, *Econ.* the free coinage of silver, esp. at a fixed ratio with gold.

free-soil (frē′soil′), *U.S. Hist.* —*adj.* **1.** pertaining to or in favor of the nonextension of slavery into the Territories, or those parts of the country not yet elected into states. —*n.* **2.** (*cap.*) a political party supporting this principle, active 1848–56. —**free′-soil′er,** *n.*

free-spo-ken (frē′spō′kən), *adj.* given to speaking freely or without reserve. —**free′-spo′ken-ness,** *n.*

Free State, 1. *U.S.* any nonslavery State prior to the Civil War. **2.** Irish Free State.

free-stone (frē′stōn′), *n.* **1.** any stone, as sandstone, which can be freely worked or quarried, esp. one which cuts well in all directions without splitting. **2.** a freestone fruit, esp. a peach or plum. —*adj.* **3.** having a stone from which the pulp is easily separated.

free-swim-mer (frē′swĭm′ər), *n.* *Zool.* an animal, as a fish, that swims about freely.

free-swim-ming (frē′swĭm′ĭng), *adj.* *Zool.* (of aquatic animals) not fixed or attached; capable of swimming about freely.

free-think-er (frē′thĭngk′ər), *n.* one who forms his opinions independently of authority or tradition, esp. in matters of religion. —**free′think′ing,** *n., adj.*

free thought, thought unrestrained by deference to authority, esp. in matters of religion.

free throw, *Basketball.* **a.** a throw from the foul line given a player after a penalty has been called against an opponent for a foul. **2.** a score of one point.

Free-town (frē′toun′), *n.* a seaport in and the capital of Sierra Leone, in W Africa. 100,000 (est. 1956).

free trade, 1. trade between different countries, free from governmental restrictions or duties. **2.** international trade free from protective duties, etc., and subject only to such tariffs as are needed for revenue. **3.** the system, principles, or maintenance of such trade.

free-trad-er (frē′trā′dər), *n.* **1.** an advocate of free trade. **2.** *Obs.* a smuggler. Also, **free trader.**

free verse, *Pros.* verse unhampered by fixed metrical forms, in extreme instances consisting of little more than rhythmic prose in lines of irregular length.

free-way (frē′wā′), *n.* an express highway, usually having traffic routed on and off cloverleaves.

free-wheel (frē′hwēl′), *n.* **1.** an overrunning clutch device in connection with the transmission gear box of a motor vehicle which automatically disengages the drive shaft whenever it tends to rotate more rapidly than the shaft driving it. **2.** a form of rear bicycle wheel which has a device freeing it from the driving mechanism, as when the pedals are stopped in coasting.

free will, 1. free choice; voluntary decision. **2.** the doctrine that the conduct of human beings expresses personal choice and is not simply determined by physical or divine forces.

free-will (frē′wĭl′), *adj.* **1.** made or done freely or of one's own accord; voluntary: *a freewill offering.* **2.** of or pertaining to the metaphysical doctrine of the freedom of the will: *the freewill controversy.*

freeze (frēz), *v.,* **froze, frozen, freezing,** *n.* —*v.i.* **1.** to become hardened into ice or into a solid body; to change from the liquid to the solid state by loss of heat. **2.** to become hard or rigid because of loss of heat, as objects containing moisture. **3.** to become obstructed by the formation of ice, as pipes. **4.** to become fixed to something by or as by the action of frost. **5.** to be of the degree of cold at which water freezes: *it is freezing tonight.* **6.** to suffer the effects of intense cold; have the sensation of extreme cold. **7.** to die of frost or cold. **8.** to lose warmth of feeling; be chilled with fear, etc. —*v.t.* **9.** to congeal; harden into ice; change from a fluid to a solid form by loss of heat. **10.** to form ice on the surface of, as a river or pond. **11.** to obstruct or close by the formation of ice, as pipes (often fol. by *up*). **12.** to fix fast in ice (fol. by *in* or *up*). **13.** to harden or stiffen by cold, as objects containing moisture. **14.** to cause to suffer the effects of intense cold; produce the sensation of extreme cold in. **15.** to kill by frost or cold. **16.** to congeal as if by cold; chill with fear; dampen the enthusiasm of. **17.** *U.S. Colloq.* to exclude, or compel to withdraw, from society, business, etc., as by chilling behavior, severe competition, etc. (fol. by *out*). **18.** *Finance, Colloq.* to render impossible of liquidation or collection: *bank loans are frozen in business depressions.* **19.** to fix (rents, prices, etc.) at a specific amount, usually by government order. **20.** to make insensitive (a part of the body) by artificial freezing, as for surgery. —*n.* **21.** act of freezing. **22.** state of being frozen. **23.** a frost. [ME *frese(n)*, OE *frēosan,* c. G *frieren*]

freeze-dry (frēz′drī′), *v.t.,* **-dried, -drying.** to dry (food, blood, serum, etc.) while frozen and under high vacuum, as for prolonged storage; lyophilize.

freez-er (frē′zər), *n.* **1.** one who or that which freezes or chills. **2.** a machine containing cold brine, etc., for freezing ice-cream mix or the like. **3.** a refrigerator or cabinet held at or below zero degrees Centigrade.

freezing point, the temperature at which a liquid freezes: *the freezing point of water is 32°F., 0°C.*

free zone, a free port area.

Frei-burg (frī′boŏrKH), *n.* **1.** a city in SW West Germany. 128,978 (est. 1955). **2.** German name of **Fribourg.**

freight (frāt), *n.* **1.** the ordinary conveyance or means of transport of goods afforded by common carriers (as opposed to *express*). **2.** the price paid for such transportation. **3.** the cargo, or any part of the cargo, of a vessel. **4.** *U.S. and Canada.* **a.** cargo or lading carried for pay either by water, land, or air. **b.** a train of cars for transporting goods or merchandise. **5.** transportation of goods by water or (esp. in the U.S. and Canada) by land. —*v.t.* **6.** to load; burden. **7.** to load or lade with goods or merchandise for transportation. **8.** to transport

ăct, āble, dâre, ärt; ĕbb, ēqual; ĭf, īce; hŏt, ōver, ôrder, oil, bŏŏk, ōōze, out; ŭp, ūse, ûrge; ə = a in alone; ch, chief; g, give; ng, ring; sh, shoe; th, thin; ᵺ, that; zh vision. **See the full key on inside cover.**

as freight; send by freight. [ME *freyght*, t. MD or MLG: m. *vrecht*, var. of *vracht*. See FRAUGHT, n.] —**freight/less,** *adj.* —**Syn. 4a.** FREIGHT, CARGO, SHIPMENT refer to goods being transported from place to place. FREIGHT usually applies only to goods carried on land or in the air: *to send freight from New York to New Orleans.* CARGO is the term used for goods carried by ship: *to send a cargo to Europe.* SHIPMENT is a quantity of goods destined for a particular place, no matter how sent: *a shipment of potatoes.*

freight·age (frā/tĭj), *n.* **1.** the transportation of goods. **2.** the price for this. **3.** freight, cargo, or lading.

freight car, a railroad car for carrying freight, commonly a boxcar.

freight engine, *U.S.* a locomotive used for drawing freight trains.

freight·er (frā/tər), *n.* **1.** a vessel engaged chiefly in the transportation of goods. **2.** one whose occupation it is to receive and forward freight. **3.** one for whom freight is transported.

freight house, *U.S.* depot or storage place for freight.

freight ton. See ton[1] (def. 2).

freight train, *U.S.* a train of freight cars.

Fre·ling·huy·sen (frē/lĭng hī/zən), *n.* **Frederick Theodore,** 1817–85, U. S. statesman.

Fre·man·tle (frē/măn/tal), *n.* a seaport in SW Australia, near Perth. 22,787 (1951).

fremd (frĕmd, frāmd), *adj. Dial.* **1.** foreign; strange. **2.** unfriendly. [ME and OE *fremde*, c. G *fremd*]

frem·i·tus (frĕm/ĭ təs), *n., pl.* **-tus.** *Pathol.* palpable vibration, as of the walls of the chest. [t. L: a roaring, murmuring]

Fré·mont (frē/mŏnt), *n.* **John Charles,** 1813–90, U. S. explorer, general, and political leader; first presidential candidate of the Republican Party, in 1856.

French (frĕnch) *adj.* **1.** of, pertaining to, or characteristic of France, its inhabitants, or their language. —*n.* **2.** the people of France and their immediate descendants elsewhere, collectively. **3.** a Romance language, the language of France, official also in Belgium, Switzerland, and Canada. [ME; OE *Frencisc,* der. *Franca* FRANK]

French (frĕnch), *n.* **1. Daniel Chester,** 1850–1931, U.S. sculptor. **2. Sir John Denton Pinkstone,** (*1st Earl of Ypres*) 1852–1925, British field marshal in World War I.

French Academy, an association of forty scholars and men of letters, formally established in 1635 by Cardinal Richelieu for the purpose of controlling the French language and regulating literary taste.

French and Indian War, the war between France and England in America, 1754–60, in which the French were aided by Indian allies.

French chalk, a talc for marking lines on cloth, etc.

French Chamber of Deputies, the second (or lower) house of the national assembly of France.

French Community, a group of autonomous nations linked by multilateral and bilateral agreements: the French Republic, Central African Republic, Chad, Congo, Dahomey, Gabon, Ivory Coast, Malagasy Republic, Mali, Mauritania, Niger, Senegal, Upper Volta.

French doors, a pair of doors hinged to the doorjambs and opening in the middle.

French dressing, salad dressing prepared from oil, vinegar, salt, spices, etc.

French Equatorial Africa, a former federation of French territories, in central Africa: Chad, Gabon, Middle Congo, and Ubangi-Shari.

French fried potatoes, thin strips of potatoes fried in deep fat.

French Gui·an·a (gĭ ăn/ə, gĭ ä/nə), an overseas department of France on the NE coast of South America; formerly a colony. 27,863 (1954); 7720 sq. mi. (with the dependent territory of Inini, 34,740 sq. mi.). *Cap.:* Cayenne. See map under **Guiana.**

French Guin·ea (gĭn/ē), a former overseas territory of French West Africa. See **Guinea** (def. 2).

French horn, a mellow-toned brass-wind instrument derived from the hunting horn and consisting of a long, coiled tube ending in a flaring bell. Illus. under **horn.**

French·i·fy (frĕn/chə fī/), *v.t.* **-fied, -fying.** to make French; imbue with French qualities. Also, **french/i·fy/.**

French India, (formerly) the five small French provinces of Chandernagor, Karikal, Mahé, Pondichéry, and Yanaon, along or near the coast of India: now part of India.

French Indochina, a territory in SE Asia, formerly a French colonial federation of Cochin-China, the protectorates of Annam, Cambodia, Tonkin, and Laos, and the leased territory of Kwangchowan: now (1958) it comprises the three independent states of Vietnam (divided into North Vietnam and South Vietnam), Cambodia, and Laos, Kwangchowan having reverted to the Chinese. Its capital was Hanoi.

French leave, departure without ceremony, permission, or notice.

French·man (frĕnch/mən), *n., pl.* **-men. 1.** a man belonging to the French nation. **2.** a French ship. —**French·wom·an** (frĕnch/wŏŏm/ən), *n., fem.*

French Morocco. See **Morocco.**

French Oceania, former name of French Polynesia.

French pancake, a light pancake which has been rolled and covered with sugar, eaten as a dessert.

French pastry, pastry made from the shortened

paste used for pie crusts and filled with rich creams, preserves, etc.

French Polynesia, a French overseas territory in the S Pacific, including the Society Islands, Marquesas Islands, and other widely-scattered island groups. 62,678 (1951); 1544 sq. mi. *Cap.:* Papeete. Formerly, **French Oceania.**

French Revolution, *French Hist.* the movement that, beginning in 1789, overthrew the absolute monarchy of the Bourbons and the system of class privilege, and ended in the seizure of power by Napoleon in 1799.

French seam, *Sewing.* a seam in which the edges of the cloth are sewn first on the right side, then on the wrong, so as to be completely covered.

French Somaliland, an overseas territory of France in E Africa, on the Gulf of Aden. 65,000 (est. 1953); 8492 sq. mi. *Cap.:* Djibouti.

French Sudan, a former overseas territory in French West Africa: now independent. See **Mali.**

French telephone, a telephone with the receiver and transmitter at the ends of a handle.

French toast, bread covered with an egg-and-milk mixture and sautéed.

French Union, a former administrative division of France (under the 1946 constitution), having jurisdiction over the French territories overseas, as the departments, colonies, protectorates, territories, etc.

French West Africa, a former federation of eight overseas territories in W Africa: Dahomey, French Guinea, French Sudan, Ivory Coast, Mauretania, Niger, Senegal, Dakar, and Upper Volta.

French West Indies, the French islands in the West Indies, comprising Guadeloupe and dependencies, and Martinique administered as two overseas departments. 468,250 pop.; 1114 sq. mi.

French window, a long window having two sashes hinged at the sides and opening in the middle.

French·y (frĕn/chĭ), *adj.* **Frenchier, Frenchiest,** *n. Colloq.* —*adj.* **1.** characteristic or suggestive of the French. —*n.* **2.** a Frenchman.

Fre·neau (frĭ nō/), *n.* **Philip,** 1752–1832, American poet and editor.

fre·net·ic (frə nĕt/ĭk), *adj.* frantic; frenzied. Also, **phrenetic.** [var. of PHRENETIC] —**fre·net/i·cal·ly,** *adv.*

fren·u·lum (frĕn/yə ləm), *n., pl.* **-la (-lə). 1.** *Anat., Zool.* a small frenum. **2.** *Entomol.* a strong spine or group of bristles on the hind wing of moths and butterflies, projecting beneath the forewing and serving to hold the two wings together in flight. [NL, dim. of L *frēnum* curb]

fre·num (frē/nəm), *n., pl.* **-na (-nə).** *Anat., Zool.* a little fold of membrane which checks or restrains the motion of a part, as the one which binds down the under side of the tongue. Also, **fraenum.** [t. L: bridle, curb]

fren·zied (frĕn/zĭd), *adj.* wildly excited or enthusiastic; frantic. Also, **phrensied.**

fren·zy (frĕn/zĭ), *n., pl.* **-zies,** *v.,* **-zied, -zying.** —*n.* **1.** violent mental agitation; wild excitement or enthusiasm. **2.** the violent excitement of a paroxysm of mania; mental derangement; delirium. —*v.t.* **3.** to drive to frenzy; make frantic. Also, **phrensy.** [ME *frenesie,* t. OF, t. LL: m. *phrenēsis,* t. LGK., r. Gk. *phrenîtis.* See PHRENITIS] —**Syn. 2.** madness, rage.

Fre·on (frē/ŏn), *n. Trademark.* an odorless, colorless gas, CCl₂F₂, boiling at −29° C., used as a refrigerant.

freq., **1.** frequent. **2.** frequentative. **3.** frequently.

fre·quen·cy (frē/kwən sĭ), *n., pl.* **-cies. 1.** Also, **fre/quence.** state or fact of being frequent; frequent occurrence. **2.** rate of recurrence. **3.** *Physics.* **a.** the number of periods or regularly recurring events of any given kind in unit time, usually in one second; the reciprocal of the period. **b.** (of an alternating current) the number of cycles, or completed alternations, per second. **4.** *Math.* the number of times an event occurs. **5.** *Statistics.* the number of items occurring in a given category. See **relative frequency.** [t. L: m.s. *frequentia*]

frequency distribution, *Statistics.* the set of frequencies associated with the different categories, intervals, or values to which items or variates in a group belong.

frequency modulation, *Electronics.* a broadcasting system, relatively free from static, in which the frequency of the transmitted wave is modulated or varied in accordance with the amplitude and pitch of the signal (distinguished from *amplitude modulation*).

fre·quent (*adj.* frē/kwənt; *v.* frĭ kwĕnt/), *adj.* **1.** happening or occurring at short intervals: *to make frequent trips to a place.* **2.** constant, habitual, or regular: *a frequent guest.* **3.** at short distances apart: *a coast with frequent lighthouses.* —*v.t.* **4.** to visit often; go often to; be often in. [t. L: s. *frequens* crowded] —**frequent/er,** *n.*

fre·quen·ta·tion (frē/kwən tā/shən), *n.* the practice of frequenting; habit of visiting often.

fre·quen·ta·tive (frĭ kwĕn/tə tĭv), *Gram.* —*adj.* **1.** (of a derived verb, or of an aspect of verb inflection) expressing repetition of the action denoted by the underlying verb. —*n.* **2.** a frequentative or iterative verb. **3.** the frequentative or iterative aspect. **4.** a verb therein, as *wrestle* from *wrest.*

fre·quent·ly (frē/kwənt lĭ), *adv.* often; many times; at short intervals. —**Syn.** See **often.**

frère (frĕr), *n., pl.* **frères** (frĕr). *French.* **1.** brother; fellow member of an organization. **2.** friar; monk.

fres·co (frĕs′kō), *n., pl.* **-coes, -cos,** *v.,* **-coed, -coing.**
—*n.* 1. a method of painting on a wall, ceiling, or the like, made before the plaster is dry so that the colors become incorporated (**true fresco**), or, less properly, after the plaster has dried (**dry fresco**). 2. a picture or design so painted. —*v.t.* 3. to paint in fresco. [t. It.: cool, FRESH; t. Gmc.] —**fres′co·er,** *n.*

fresh (frĕsh), *adj.* 1. newly made, arrived, obtained, etc.: *fresh footprints.* 2. new; not previously known, met with, etc.; novel. 3. additional or further: *fresh supplies.* 4. not salt, as water. 5. retaining the original properties unimpaired; not deteriorated. 6. not preserved by pickling, salting, drying, etc. 7. not fatigued; brisk; vigorous. 8. not faded, worn, obliterated, etc. 9. looking youthful and healthy. 10. pure, cool, or refreshing, as air. 11. *Meteorol.* (of wind) moderately strong or brisk; blowing at a velocity within the range of 19–24 miles per hour. 12. inexperienced. 13. *Slang.* forward or presumptuous. 14. (of a cow) having recently given birth to a calf. —*n.* 15. the fresh part or time. 16. a freshet. —*v.t., v.i.* 17. *Obs.* to make or become fresh. —*adv.* 18. freshly. [ME; OE *fersc,* c. G *frisch*] —**fresh′ly,** *adv.* —**fresh′ness,** *n.* —**Syn.** 1. See **new.** 12. artless, untrained, raw, green. —**Ant.** 1. old. 12. sophisticated.

fresh·en (frĕsh′ən), *v.t.* 1. to make fresh; refresh, revive, or renew. 2. to remove saltiness from. 3. *Naut.* to relieve, as a rope, by altering the position of a part exposed to friction. —*v.i.* 4. to become or grow fresh. 5. to give birth to a calf. —**fresh′en·er,** *n.*

fresh·et (frĕsh′ĭt), *n.* 1. a sudden rise in the level of a stream, or a flood, due to heavy rains or the rapid melting of snow and ice. 2. a fresh-water stream flowing into the sea. [dim. of FRESH, used as n.] —**Syn.** 1. See **flood.**

fresh·man (frĕsh′mən), *n., pl.* **-men.** 1. a student in the first year of the course at a university, college, or school. 2. a novice. Also, *Brit. Slang.,* **fresh′er.**

fresh-wa·ter (frĕsh′wô′tər, -wŏt′ər), *adj.* 1. of or living in water that is fresh, or not salt (opposed to *salt-water* or *marine*). 2. accustomed to fresh water only, and not to the sea. 3. of little experience. 4. *U.S.* small or little known: *a fresh-water college.*

Fres·no (frĕz′nō), *n.* a city in central California. 133,929 (1960).

fret¹ (frĕt), *v.,* **fretted, fretting,** *n.* —*v.i.* 1. to give oneself up to feelings of irritation, resentful discontent, regret, worry, or the like. 2. to cause corrosion; gnaw. 3. to make a way by gnawing or corrosion. 4. to become eaten, worn, or corroded. 5. to move in agitation or commotion, as water. —*v.t.* 6. to torment; irritate, annoy, or vex. 7. to wear away or consume by gnawing, friction, rust, corrosives, etc. 8. to form or make by wearing away a substance. 9. to agitate (water). —*n.* 10. an irritated state of mind; annoyance; vexation. 11. erosion; corrosion; gnawing. 12. a worn or eroded place. [ME *frete(n),* OE *fretan,* c. G *fressen*] —**Syn.** 6. worry, harass. —**Ant.** 6. soothe.

fret² (frĕt), *n., v.,* **fretted, fretting.** —*n.* 1. an interlaced, angular design; fretwork. 2. an angular design of bands within a border. —*v.t.* 3. to ornament with a fret or fretwork. [ME *frette,* of uncert. orig.; cf. OF *frete* interlaced work, OE *frettewian,* var. of *fretwian, frætwian* adorn]

fret³ (frĕt), *n., v.,* **fretted, fretting.** —*n.* 1. any of the ridges of wood, metal, or string, set across the finger board of a lute or similar instrument which help the fingers to stop the strings at the correct points. —*v.t.* 2. to provide with frets. [orig. uncert.]

Greek frets

fret·ful (frĕt′fəl), *adj.* disposed to fret; irritable or peevish. —**fret′ful·ly,** *adv.* —**fret′ful·ness,** *n.* —**Syn.** petulant, querulous, impatient. —**Ant.** patient.

fret saw, a long, narrow-bladed saw used to cut ornamental work from thin wood.

fret·ted (frĕt′ĭd), *adj.* ornamented with frets.

fret·work (frĕt′wûrk′), *n.* 1. ornamental work consisting of interlacing parts, esp. work in which the design is formed by perforation. 2. any pattern of dark and light, such as that of perforated fretwork.

Freud (froid; *Ger.* froit), *n.* **Sigmund** (sĭg′mənd; *Ger.* zĕKH′mŏont), 1856–1939, Austrian physician and psychoanalyst.

Freud·i·an (froi′dĭ ən), *adj.* 1. of or pertaining to Sigmund Freud or his doctrines, esp. in respect to the causes and treatment of neurotic and psychopathic states, the interpretation of dreams, etc. —*n.* 2. an adherent of the essential doctrines of Freud. —**Freud′i·an·ism,** *n.*

Frey (frā), *n. Scand. Myth.* god of earth's fruitfulness and dispenser of wealth. [t. Icel.: m. *Freyr*]

Frey·a (frā′ə), *n. Scand. Myth.* goddess of fruitfulness and sexual love; the daughter of Njord and sister of Frey. [t. Icel.: m. *Freyja*]

Frey·tag (frī′täKH), *n.* **Gustav** (gōos′täf), 1816–95, German novelist and dramatist.

F.R.G.S., Fellow of the Royal Geographical Society.

Fri., Friday.

fri·a·ble (frī′ə bəl), *adj.* easily crumbled or reduced to powder; crumbly: *friable rock.* [t. L: m.s. *friābilis*] —**fri·a·bil′i·ty, fri′a·ble·ness,** *n.*

fri·ar (frī′ər), *n. Rom. Cath. Ch.* a brother or member of one of certain religious orders, esp. the mendicant orders of Franciscans (**Gray Friars**), Dominicans (**Black Friars**), Carmelites (**White Friars**), and Augustinians (**Austin Friars**). [ME *frere,* t. OF, g. L *fräter* brother] —**Syn.** See **monk.**

fri·ar-bird (frī′ər bûrd′), *n.* any of various Australasian honey eaters (*Meliphagidae*), esp. of genus *Philemon.*

friar's lantern, the ignis fatuus or will-o'-the-wisp.

fri·ar·y (frī′ə rĭ), *n., pl.* **-aries.** 1. a convent of friars. 2. a brotherhood of friars.

frib·ble (frĭb′əl), *v.,* **-bled, -bling,** *n.* —*v.i.* 1. to act in a trifling or frivolous manner. —*v.t.* 2. to waste foolishly. —*n.* 3. a trifler. 4. anything trifling or frivolous. 5. frivolousness. [orig. uncert.]

Fri·bourg (frē bōōr′), *n.* a city in W Switzerland. 29,005 (1950). German, **Freiburg.**

fric·an·deau (frĭk′ən dō′), *n.* veal or other meat larded, stewed, and served with a sauce. [t. F]

fric·as·see (frĭk′ə sē′), *n., v.,* **-seed, -seeing.** —*n.* 1. meat, as chicken or veal, cut up, (sometimes browned), stewed, and served in a sauce made of its own gravy. —*v.t.* 2. to prepare as a fricassee. [t. F, der. *fricasser* to sauté and serve with sauce, t. Pr.: m. *fricassá,* der. *fricar* fry, g. Rom. *frigicāre,* intensive of L *frīgere*]

fric·a·tive (frĭk′ə tĭv), *Phonet.* —*adj.* 1. (of consonants) characterized by a noise produced by air being forced through an opening, as in *f, v, s,* etc. —*n.* 2. a fricative consonant. [t. NL: m.s. *fricātīvus,* der. L *fricāre* rub]

Frick (frĭk), *n.* **Henry Clay,** 1849–1919, U.S. manufacturer and philanthropist.

fric·tion (frĭk′shən), *n.* 1. *Mech., Physics.* the resistance to the relative motion (sliding or rolling) of surfaces of bodies in contact. 2. the rubbing of the surface of one body against that of another. 3. clashing or conflict, as of opinions, etc. [t. L: s. *frictio* a rubbing] —**fric′tion·less,** *adj.*

fric·tion·al (frĭk′shən əl), *adj.* 1. of, pertaining to, or of the nature of friction. 2. moved, worked, or produced by friction. —**fric′tion·al·ly,** *adv.*

friction match, a kind of match tipped with a compound that ignites by friction.

Fri·day (frī′dĭ), *n.* 1. the sixth day of the week, following Thursday. 2. the native companion of Defoe's Robinson Crusoe. 3. a devoted or servile follower. [ME; OE *Frigedæg* Freo's day, f. *Frige,* gen. sing. of *Frēo* (OE goddess identified with Venus) + *dæg* day; *Frēo* is identical with OE adj. *frēo* free]

Fridt·jof Nan·sen Land (frĭt′yŏf nän′sən), Franz Josef Land.

fried (frīd), *adj.* 1. cooked in fat. —*v.* 2. pt. and pp. of *fry¹.*

fried-cake (frīd′kāk′), *n.* a kind of small cake, cooked in deep fat, esp. a doughnut.

friend (frĕnd), *n.* 1. one attached to another by feelings of personal regard. 2. a well-wisher, patron, or supporter. 3. one who is on good terms with another; one not hostile. 4. a member of the same nation, party, etc. 5. (*cap.*) a member of the Society of Friends, the Christian sect opposed to taking oaths and to war, founded by George Fox about 1650; Quaker. [ME; OE *frēond,* c. D *vriend,* G *freund,* Goth. *frijōnds,* all orig. ppr. of a verb meaning love (in OE, *frēogan*). Cf. FRIDAY, FREE] —**friend′less,** *adj.* —**friend′less·ness,** *n.* —**Syn.** 1. companion, comrade, chum, crony. See **acquaintance.**

friend at court, a friend who is in a position to further one's interests with others.

friend·ly (frĕnd′lĭ), *adj.,* **-lier, -liest,** *adv.* —*adj.* 1. characteristic of or befitting a friend; showing friendship: *a friendly greeting.* 2. like a friend; kind. 3. favorably disposed; inclined to approve, help, or support. 4. not hostile or at variance; amicable. —*adv.* 5. in a friendly manner; like a friend. [ME *frendly,* OE *frēondlīc*] —**friend′li·ly,** *adv.* —**friend′li·ness,** *n.* —**Syn.** 3. amiable, cordial, genial, kindly.

Friendly Islands, Tonga Islands.

friend·ship (frĕnd′shĭp), *n.* 1. friendly feeling or disposition. 2. state of being a friend; association as friends. 3. a friendly relation or intimacy.

fri·er (frī′ər), *n.* fryer.

Frie·sian (frē′zhən), *adj., n.* Frisian. Also, **Fries·ic** (frē′zĭk).

Fries·land (frēz′lənd; *Du.* frēs′länt′), *n.* a province in N Netherlands. 469,943 pop. (est. 1954); 1431 sq. mi. *Cap.:* Leeuwarden.

frieze¹ (frēz), *n.* 1. that part of an entablature between the architrave and the cornice, commonly ornamented with sculpture. See diag. under **column.** 2. any similar decorative band or feature, as on a wall. [t. F: m. *frise,* ult. orig. uncert.]

frieze² (frēz), *n.* heavy, napped woolen cloth for coats. [t. MD: m. *frise* coarse, hairy cloth. Cf. FRAISE, FRIZZ]

frig·ate (frĭg′ĭt), *n.* an old type of sailing war vessel, designed for high speed and used primarily for scouting. [t. F: m. *frégate,* t. It.: m. *fregata*]

frigate bird, either of two species of rapacious totalpalmate marine birds, *Fregata aquila* and *F. minor,* noted for their powers of flight; man-o'-war bird.

Frigg (frĭg), *n. Scand. Myth.* wife of Odin and queen of the gods (often confused with Freya). Also, **Frig·ga** (frĭg′ə). [t. Icel.]

fright (frīt), *n.* **1.** sudden and extreme fear; a sudden terror. **2.** a person or thing of shocking, grotesque, or ridiculous appearance. —*v.t.* **3.** *Poetic.* to frighten. [ME *frighte,* OE *fryhto,* metathetic var. of *fyrhto;* akin to G *furcht*] —**Syn. 1.** dismay, consternation. See **terror.**

fright·en (frī′tən), *v.t.* **1.** to throw into a fright; terrify; scare. **2.** to drive (fol. by *away, off,* etc.) by scaring. —**fright′en·er,** *n.* —**fright′en·ing·ly,** *adv.*
—**Syn. 1.** FRIGHTEN, ALARM, SCARE, TERRIFY, APPALL mean to arouse fear in a person or animal. To FRIGHTEN is to shock with sudden, startling, but usually short-lived fear, especially that arising from the apprehension of physical harm: *to frighten someone by a sudden noise.* To ALARM is to arouse the feelings through the realization of some imminent or unexpected danger: *to alarm someone by a scream.* To SCARE is to frighten into a loss of poise or dignity, often in fun: *a sudden noise may scare anyone.* To TERRIFY is to strike with violent, overwhelming, or paralyzing fear: *to terrify a city by lawless acts.* To APPALL is to overcome or confound by dread, dismay, or horror: *the suffering caused by the earthquake appalled him.*

fright·ened (frī′tənd), *adj.* **1.** thrown into a fright. **2.** afraid (fol. by *of*). —**Syn. 2.** See **afraid.**

fright·ful (frīt′fəl), *adj.* **1.** such as to cause fright; dreadful, terrible, or alarming. **2.** horrible, shocking, or revolting. **3.** *Colloq.* unpleasant; disagreeable: *we had a frightful time.* **4.** *Colloq.* very great. —**fright′-ful·ly,** *adv.* —**fright′ful·ness,** *n.* —**Syn. 1.** fearful, awful. **2.** hideous. —**Ant. 1.** reassuring.

frig·id (frĭj′ĭd), *adj.* **1.** very cold in temperature: *a frigid climate.* **2.** without warmth of feeling; without ardor or enthusiasm. **3.** stiff or formal. [t. L: s. *frīgidus*] —**fri·gid′i·ty, frig′id·ness,** *n.* —**frig′id·ly,** *adv.*

Frigid Zone, the regions between the poles and the polar circles.

frig·o·rif·ic (frĭg′ərĭf′ĭk), *adj.* causing or producing cold. [t. L: s. *frīgorĭficus* cooling]

fri·jol (frē′hōl; *Sp.* frē·hōl′), *n., pl.* **frijoles** (frē′hōlz; *Sp.* frē·hō′lĕs). a cultivated bean of the genus *Phaseolus,* much used for food in Mexico, etc. Also, **fri·jo·le** (frē·hō′lĭ; *Sp.* frē·hō′lĕ). [t. Sp.]

frill (frĭl), *n.* **1.** a trimming consisting of a strip of cloth or lace, gathered at one edge and left loose at the other; a ruffle. **2.** something resembling such a trimming, as the fringe of hair on the chest of some dogs. **3.** *Colloq.* affectation of manner, style, etc. **4.** *Photog.* a loosening of the gelatin on a negative or positive, usually the result of high temperature in developing, fixing, etc. —*v.t.* **5.** to trim or ornament with a frill or frills. **6.** to form into a frill. [? t. Flem.: m. *frul* frill (of a collar), *frullen* have frills] —**frill′y,** *adj.*

frill·ing (frĭl′ĭng), *n.* frilled edging.

Fri·maire (frē·mĕr′), *n.* (in the calendar of the first French republic) the third month of the year, from Nov. 21 to Dec. 20. [t. F, der. *frimas* hoarfrost, der. OF *frim,* t. Gmc. See RIME²]

fringe (frĭnj), *n., v.,* **fringed, fringing,** *adj.* —*n.* **1.** an ornamental bordering having projecting lengths of thread, cord, etc., either loose or variously arranged or combined. **2.** anything resembling or suggesting this: *a fringe of trees about a field.* **3.** *Optics.* one of the alternate light and dark bands produced by diffraction or interference. —*v.t.* **4.** to furnish with or as with a fringe. **5.** to serve as a fringe for. —*adj.* **6.** accessory; supplementary: *fringe benefits.* [ME *frenge,* t. OF, g. LL *fimbria* border, fringe] —**fringe′less,** *adj.* —**fringe′like′,** *adj.* —**fring′y,** *adj.*

fringed gentian, a gentian of eastern North America, *Gentiana crinita,* with a blue fringed corolla.

fringed orchis, one of several species of American orchid, genus *Blephariglottis,* with cut fringed lip.

fringe tree, an oleaceous shrub or small tree, *Chionanthus virginicus,* of the southern U.S., bearing panicles of white flowers with long, narrow petals.

frin·gil·line (frĭn·jĭl′īn, -ĭn), *adj.* belonging or pertaining to the *Fringillidae,* the finch family, which includes the sparrows, canaries, linnets, etc., as well as various finches. [f. s. L *fringilla* kind of bird + -INE¹]

frip·per·y (frĭp′ərĭ), *n., pl.* **-peries. 1.** finery in dress, esp. when tawdry. **2.** empty display; ostentation. **3.** trifles. [t. F: m. *friperie,* OF *freperie,* der. *frepe* rag]

Fris., Frisian.

Frisch·es Haff (frĭsh′əs häf′), a lagoon on the Baltic coast of Poland. 52 mi. long; 4–12 mi. wide.

Fris·co (frĭs′kō), *n. Colloq.* San Francisco.

fri·sé (frĭ·zā′), *n.* a rug or upholstery fabric made with pile in uncut loops or in a combination of cut and uncut.

fri·sette (frĭ·zĕt′), *n.* a fringe of curled or frizzed hair, esp. artificial, worn on the forehead by women. Also, **frizette.** [t. F: little curl, frizz, der. *friser* to curl]

fri·seur (frē·zœr′), *n. French.* a hairdresser.

Fri·sian (frĭzh′ən), *adj.* **1.** of or pertaining to Friesland, its inhabitants, or their language. —*n.* **2.** one of the people of Friesland. **3.** the Germanic language most closely related to English, spoken in Friesland and nearby islands. Also, **Friesian, Friesic.**

frisk (frĭsk), *v.i.* **1.** to dance, leap, skip, or gambol, as in frolic. —*v.t.* **2.** *Slang.* to search (a person) for concealed weapons, etc., by feeling his clothing. **3.** *Slang.* to steal something from (someone) in this way. —*n.* **4.** a leap, skip, or caper. **5.** a frolic. [orig. adj.: t. OF: m. *frisque,* t. Gmc.; cf. G *frisch* lively] —**frisk′er,** *n.*

frisk·y (frĭs′kĭ), *adj.* **friskier, friskiest.** lively; frolicsome; playful. —**frisk′i·ly,** *adv.* —**frisk′i·ness,** *n.*

frit (frĭt), *n., v.,* **fritted, fritting.** —*n.* **1.** *Ceramics.* **a.** a fused or partially fused material used as a basis for glazes or enamels. **b.** the composition from which artificial soft porcelain is made. **2.** (in medieval glassmaking) fused or calcined material, ready to serve as part of the batch for glassmaking. —*v.t.* **3.** to fuse (materials) in making a frit. Also, **fritt.** [t. F: m. *fritte,* t. It.: m. *fritta,* der. *friggere* (g. L *frīgere*) roast, fry]

frit fly, a minute fly, *Oscinosoma frit,* whose larva is an injurious pest to wheat and other cereals.

frith (frĭth), *n. Chiefly Scot.* a firth. [metathetic var. of FIRTH]

frit·il·lar·i·a (frĭt′ə·lâr′ĭ·ə), *n.* any plant of the liliaceous genus *Fritillaria,* comprising bulbous herbs with drooping, bell-shaped flowers, as *F. imperialis,* the crown imperial.

frit·il·lar·y (frĭt′ə·lĕr′ĭ), *n., pl.* **-laries.** any of several orange-brown butterflies which are silver-spotted beneath, of the genus *Argynnis* and allies. [t. NL: m.s. *fritillāria,* der. L *fritillus* dicebox]

frit·ter¹ (frĭt′ər), *v.t.* **1.** to disperse or squander piecemeal, or waste little by little (usually fol. by *away*): *to fritter away one's money.* **2.** to break or tear into small pieces or shreds. —*n.* **3.** a small piece, fragment, or shred. [earlier *fitter,* der. *fit* part] —**frit′ter·er,** *n.*

frit·ter² (frĭt′ər), *n.* a small cake of batter, sometimes containing fruit, clams, or some other ingredient, fried in deep fat or sautéed in a frying pan. [ME *frytour,* t. OF: m. *friture,* der. *frire* FRY]

Fri·u·li·an (frĭ·ōō′lĭ·ən), *n.* a Rhaeto-Romanic language spoken by about half a million people in NE Italy.

Fri·u·li-Ve·ne·zi·a Giu·lia (frē·ōō′lē vě·nĕ′tsyä jōō′lyä), a region in NE Italy, formerly part of Venezia Giulia, most of which was ceded to Yugoslavia. 937,000 (est. 1954); 2947 sq. mi. *Cap.:* Trieste.

friv·ol (frĭv′əl), *v.,* **-oled, -oling** or (*esp. Brit.*) **-olled, -olling.** *Colloq.* —*v.i.* **1.** to behave frivolously; trifle. —*v.t.* **2.** to spend frivolously (fol. by *away*). [back formation from FRIVOLOUS] —**friv′ol·er;** *esp. Brit.* **friv′ol·ler,** *n.*

fri·vol·i·ty (frĭ·vŏl′ə·tĭ), *n., pl.* **-ties. 1.** quality or state of being frivolous. **2.** a frivolous act or thing.

friv·o·lous (frĭv′ə·ləs), *adj.* **1.** of little or no weight, worth, or importance; not worthy of serious notice: *a frivolous objection.* **2.** characterized by lack of seriousness or sense: *frivolous conduct.* **3.** given to trifling or levity, as persons. [t. L: m. *frivolus* silly, trifling, paltry] —**friv′o·lous·ly,** *adv.* —**friv′o·lous·ness,** *n.* —**Syn. 1.** trifling, petty, paltry, trivial. **3.** idle, silly, foolish. —**Ant. 1.** weighty. **3.** serious.

friz (frĭz), *v.,* **frizzed, frizzing,** *n., pl.* **frizzes.** —*v.t., v.i.* **1.** to form into small, crisp curls or little tufts. —*n.* **2.** state of being frizzed. **3.** something frizzed; frizzed hair. Also, **frizz.** [back formation from FRIZZLE¹]

fri·zette (frĭ·zĕt′), *n.* frisette.

friz·zle¹ (frĭz′əl), *v.,* **-zled, -zling,** *n.* —*v.t., v.i.* **1.** to friz. —*n.* **2.** a short, crisp curl. [orig. obscure. Cf. OE *fris* curled] —**friz′zler,** *n.*

friz·zle² (frĭz′əl), *v.,* **-zled, -zling.** —*v.i.* **1.** to make a sizzling or sputtering noise in frying or the like. —*v.t.* **2.** to crisp (meat, etc.) by frying. [b. FRY and FIZZLE]

friz·zly (frĭz′lĭ), *adj.* curly; *frizzly* hair. Also, **friz′zy.**

fro (frō), *adv.* **1.** from; back. **2.** to and fro, **a.** back and forth. **b.** hither and thither. [ME, earlier *frā,* t. Scand.; cf. Icel. *frā,* c. OE *fram* from]

Fro·bish·er (frō′bĭsh·ər, frŏb′ĭsh-), *n.* **Sir Martin,** 1535?–94 English navigator and explorer.

frock (frŏk), *n.* **1.** a gown or dress. **2.** a loose outer garment worn by peasants and workmen; smock. **3.** a coarse outer garment with large sleeves, worn by monks. **4.** a frock coat. —*v.t.* **5.** to provide with or clothe in a frock. **6.** to invest with priestly or clerical office. [ME *froke,* t. OF: m. *froc;* ult. orig. uncert.] —**frock′less,** *adj.*

frock coat, a man's close-fitting coat, usually double-breasted, extending to about the knees.

froe (frō), *n. Chiefly U.S.* frow.

Froe·bel (frœ′bəl), *n.* **Friedrich** (frē′drĭKH), 1782–1852, German educational reformer; founder of the kindergarten system.

frog¹ (frŏg, frôg), *n., v.,* **frogged, frogging.** —*n.* **1.** any of various tailless amphibians (order *Salientia*), esp. of the web-footed aquatic species constituting the genus *Rana* and allied genera. **2.** any of various froglike amphibians. **3.** a slight hoarseness due to mucus on the vocal cords: *a frog in the throat.* **4.** (*cap.*) *Contemptuous.* Frenchman. **5.** a small, heavy holder placed in a bowl or vase to hold flower stems in position. —*v.i.* **6.** to catch, or search for, frogs. [ME *frogge,* OE *frogga;* akin to G *frosch*] —**frog′like′,** *adj.*

Bullfrog. *Rana catesbelana* (7½ in. long)

frog² (frŏg, frôg), *n.* **1.** an ornamental fastening for the front of a coat, consisting of a button and a loop through which it passes. **2.** a device at the intersection of two railway tracks to permit the wheels and flanges on one track to cross or branch from the other. [? t. Pg.: m. *froco,* g. L *floccus* FLOCK²]

Ornamental frog (def. 1)

frog³ (frŏg, frôg), *n.* a triangular mass of elastic, horny substance in the middle of the sole of the foot of a horse or related animal. [special use of FROG[1]]

frog·eye (frŏg′ī′, frôg′ī′), n. a disease, attributed to a fungus, which affects tobacco leaves, producing small white spots.

frog·fish (frŏg′fĭsh′, frôg′-), n., pl. -fishes, (esp. collectively) -fish. 1. any of the anglers (def. 3) constituting the family Antennariidae, characterized by a wide froglike mouth and broad limblike fins. 2. an angler (def. 2).

frog·hop·per (frŏg′hŏp′ər, frôg′-), n. any of various small, leaping, homopterous insects (family Cercopidae) whose young live in a spittlelike secretion on plants.

frog kick, Swimming. a type of kick in which the legs are bent at the knees, extended outward, and then brought together forcefully.

frog lily, a yellow water lily.

frog·man (frŏg′măn′), n., pl. -men. a swimmer specially equipped for underwater demolition, salvage, scientific exploration, etc.

frog·mouth (frŏg′mouth′, frôg′-), n. any of the Australian and East Indian goatsuckers (birds) constituting the family Podargidae, or, according to some classifications, the subfamily Podarginae: so called from their wide, flat, froglike mouth.

frog spit, any of several filamentous fresh-water green algae forming floating masses. Also, **frog spittle.**

Froh·man (frō′mən), n. Charles, 1860-1915, U.S. theatrical producer.

Frois·sart (froi′särt′; Fr. frwȧ·sȧr′), n. Jean (zhäɴ), c1337-c1410, French historian and poet.

frol·ic (frŏl′ĭk), n., v., -icked, -icking, adj. —n. 1. merry living; gay prank; gaiety; fun. 2. a merrymaking. —v.i. 3. to play merrily; have fun; play merry pranks. —adj. 4. gay; merry; full of mirth or pranks; full of fun. [t. D: m. vrolijk joyful (c. G fröhlich), f. vro glad + lijk like] —**frol′ick·er,** n.

frol·ic·some (frŏl′ĭk·səm), adj. merrily playful; full of fun. —**frol′ic·some·ly,** adv. —**frol′ic·some·ness,** n.

from (frŭm; unstressed frəm), prep. a particle specifying a starting point, and hence used to express removal or separation in space, time, order, etc.; discrimination or distinction, source or origin, instrumentality, and cause or reason: a train running west from New York, from that time onward, to wander from one's purpose, to refrain from laughing, sketches drawn from nature. [ME and OE, var. of fram, prep., from, as adv., forward, forth, c. OHG and Goth. fram, prep. and adv., Icel. frā, prep. (cf. FRO), fram, adv.]

fro·men·ty (frō′mən·tĭ), n. Chiefly Brit. frumenty.

frond (frŏnd), n. Bot. 1. a finely divided leaf, often large, (properly applied to the ferns and some of the palms). 2. a leaflike expansion not differentiated into stem and foliage, as in lichens. [t. L: s. frons leafy branch] —**frond′ed,** adj. —**frond′less,** adj.

Fronde (frōɴd), n. French. 1. a parliamentary and aristocratic rebellion against the court party and Cardinal Mazarin during the minority of Louis XIV of France. 2. the groups which waged this rebellion.

fron·des·cence (frŏn·dĕs′əns), n. 1. the process or period of coming into leaf. 2. foliage. [t. NL: m.s. frondescentia, der. s. L frondescens, ppr. of frondescere, freq. of frondēre put forth leaves] —**fron·des′cent,** adj.

frons (frŏnz), n. the facial area of an insect's head above or behind the clypeus.

front (frŭnt), n. 1. the foremost part or surface of anything. 2. the part or side of anything, as a house, which seems to look out or be directed forward. 3. any side or face, as of a house. 4. a place or position directly before anything. 5. Front! U.S. ellip. command meaning (come to the) front, (come) forward, which a hotel clerk calls out to a bellhop. 6. Mil. a. the foremost line or part of an army, etc. b. a line of battle. c. the place where active operations are carried on. 7. land facing a road, river, etc. 8. Brit. a promenade along a seashore. 9. Colloq. a distinguished person listed as an official of an organization, for the sake of prestige, and usually inactive. 10. Colloq. outward impression of rank, position, or wealth. 11. bearing or demeanor in confronting anything: a calm front. 12. cool assurance, or impudence. 13. the forehead, or the entire face. 14. a coalition or movement to achieve a particular end, usually political: people's front. 15. something attached to or worn at the forepart, as a shirt front, a dicky, etc. 16. a necktie or cravat. 17. Meteorol. a surface of discontinuity separating two dissimilar air masses. 18. Theat. the auditorium. —adj. 19. of or pertaining to the front. 20. situated in or at the front. 21. Phonet. pronounced with the tongue relatively far forward in the mouth: the vowels of "beet" and "gait" are front vowels. —v.t. 22. to have the front toward; face: our house fronts the lake. 23. to meet face to face; confront. 24. to face in opposition, hostility, or defiance. 25. to furnish or supply with a front. 26. to serve as a front to. —v.i. 27. to have or turn the front in some specified direction: our house fronts on the lake. [ME, t. L: s. frons forehead, front] —**front′less,** adj.

front·age (frŭn′tĭj), n. 1. the front of a building or lot. 2. the lineal extent of this front. 3. the direction it faces. 4. land abutting on a river, street, etc. 5. the space lying between a building and the street, etc.

fron·tal (frŭn′təl), adj. 1. of, in, or at the front: a frontal attack. 2. noting or pertaining to the bone (or pair of bones) forming the forehead, or to the forehead in general. —n. 3. Eccles. a movable cover or hanging for the front of an altar. 4. Anat. a bone of the forehead; frontal bone. See diag. under **cranium.** [t. LL: s. frontālis, der. L frons front; r. ME frountel, t. OF: m. frontel] —**front′al·ly,** adv.

front bench, Brit. (in Parliament) the seats near the Speaker, on which the leaders of the parties sit.

Fron·te·nac (frŏn′tə·năk′, Fr. frôɴt·nȧk′), n. **Louis de Buade de** (lwē də bÿ·ȧd′ də), c1620-98, French governor of Canada.

front foot, U.S. a foot measured along the front of a lot.

fron·tier (frŭn·tîr′, frŏn′tîr′), n. 1. that part of a country which borders another country; the border. 2. U.S. that part of a country which forms the border of its settled or inhabited regions. 3. the incompletely developed region of a field of knowledge, feeling, etc.: frontiers of philosophy. —adj. 4. of or on the frontier: a frontier town. [ME frountere, t. OF: m. frontiere, der. front in sense of opposite side]

fron·tiers·man (frŭn·tîrz′mən), n., pl. -men. a man who lives on the frontier.

fron·tis·piece (frŭn′tĭs·pēs′, frŏn′-), n. 1. an illustrated leaf preceding the title page of a book. 2. Archit. a. the most richly decorated and usually central portion of the principal face of a building. b. the pediment over a door, gate, etc. [alter. (conformed to piece) of earlier frontispice. t. F, t. ML: m.s. frontispicium, f. L fronti- front + -spicium look]

front·let (frŭnt′lĭt), n. 1. the forehead of an animal. 2. Ornith. the forehead when marked by a different color or texture of the plumage. 3. something worn on the head. 4. (among the Jews) a phylactery worn on the head. [ME frontlette, t. OF: m. frontelet, dim. of frontel FRONTAL, n.]

front matter, U.S. Printing. all matter in a book that precedes the text proper.

front-page (frŭnt′pāj′), adj. of consequence; worth putting on the first page of a newspaper.

Front Range, the easternmost range of the Rocky Mountains, extending from central Colorado to S Wyoming. Highest peak, Grays Peak, 14,274 ft.

frore (frōr), adj. 1. Archaic. frozen. 2. Poetic. frosty; intensely cold. [old pp. of FREEZE]

frost (frôst, frŏst), n. 1. a state of the temperature which occasions the freezing of water. 2. Brit. degrees of frost, degrees below the freezing point: we had ten degrees of frost (i.e., 22° F.). 3. a covering of minute ice needles, formed from the atmosphere at night upon the ground and exposed objects when these have cooled by radiation below the dew point, and when the dew point is below the freezing point (**white frost or hoarfrost**). 4. act or process of freezing. 5. coldness of manner or temperature. 6. Colloq. a coolness between persons. 7. Slang. a failure. —v.t. 8. to cover with frost. 9. to give a frostlike surface to (glass, etc.). 10. to ice (a cake, etc.). 11. to kill or injure by frost. [ME and OE frost, forst, c. D vorst, G and Icel. frost; akin to FREEZE] —**frost′less,** adj. —**frost′like′,** adj.

Frost (frôst, frŏst), n. Robert, 1874-1963, U.S. poet.

frost·bite (frôst′bīt′, frŏst′-), n., v., -bit, -bitten, -biting. —n. 1. the inflamed, gangrenous effect of excessive exposure to extreme cold. —v.t. 2. to injure by frost or extreme cold.

frost·bit·ten (frôst′bĭt′ən, frŏst′-), adj. injured by frost or extreme cold.

frost·fish (frôst′fĭsh′, frŏst′-), n., pl. -fishes, (esp. collectively) -fish. the tomcod, Microgadus tomcod, which appears on the northeastern coast of North America as frost sets in.

frost·flow·er (frôst′flou′ər, frŏst′-), n. 1. a liliaceous plant, Milla biflora, of the southwestern U.S. and Mexico. 2. its waxy-white, starlike flower. 3. any aster.

frost·ing (frôs′tĭng, frŏs′-), n. 1. a preparation of confectioner's sugar beaten together with egg whites or cream, etc., or a cooked preparation of sugar, water, etc., used for covering cakes, etc. 2. a lusterless finish, as of metal or glass. 3. a material used for decorative work, as signs, etc., made from coarse, powdered glass flakes.

frost·work (frôst′wûrk′, frŏst′-), n. 1. the delicate tracery formed by frost, esp. on glass. 2. similar ornamentation, as on metal.

frost·y (frôs′tĭ, frŏs′-), adj., frostier, frostiest. 1. attended with or producing frost; freezing; very cold: frosty weather. 2. consisting of or covered with a frost. 3. lacking warmth of feeling. 4. resembling frost; white or gray, as hair. 5. of or characteristic of old age. —**frost′i·ly,** adv. —**frost′i·ness,** n. —**frost′i·est,** adj.

froth (frôth, frŏth), n. 1. an aggregation of bubbles, as on a fermented liquid or at the mouth of a hard-driven horse; foam. 2. a foam of saliva or fluid resulting from disease. 3. something unsubstantial or evanescent, as idle talk; trivial ideas. —v.t. 4. to cover with froth. 5. to cause to foam. 6. to emit like froth. —v.i. 7. to give out froth; foam. [ME frothe, ? t. Scand.; cf. Icel. frodha. Cf. also OE āfrēothan form froth]

froth·y (frôth′ĭ, frŏth′ĭ), adj., frothier, frothiest. 1. of, like, or having froth; foamy. 2. unsubstantial; trifling; shallow. —**froth′i·ly,** adv. —**froth′i·ness,** n.

Froude (frood), *n.* **James Anthony,** 1818–94, British historian.

frou·frou (frōō′frōō′), *n.* a rustling, particularly the rustling of silk, as in a woman's dress. [t. F]

frounce (frouns), *n., v.,* **frounced, frouncing.** —*n.* 1. *Archaic.* affectation; empty show. —*v.t.* 2. to curl the hair of. 3. *Obs.* to pleat. —*v.i.* 4. *Obs.* to frown. [ME *fronce*(n), t. OF: m. *froncier,* der. *fronce* a wrinkle, fold, t. Gmc.; cf. Icel. *hrukka,* G *runzel* wrinkle]

frouz·y (frou′zĭ), *adj.,* **frouzier, frouziest.** frowzy.

frow (frō), *n.* *U.S.* a cleaving, tool having a wedged-shaped blade, with a handle set at right angles to it. Also, **froe.** [special use of FROW(ARD) turned away from]

fro·ward (frō′wərd, frō′ərd), *adj.* perverse; willfully contrary; refractory; not easily managed. [ME. See FRO, -WARD] —**fro′ward·ly,** *adv.* —**fro′ward·ness,** *n.* —Syn. obstinate, willful, disobedient. —Ant. docile.

frown (froun), *v.i.* 1. to contract the brow as in displeasure or deep thought; scowl. 2. to look displeased; have an angry look. 3. to look disapprovingly (fol. by *on* or *upon*): *to frown upon a scheme.* —*v.t.* 4. to express by a frown. —*n.* 5. a frowning look; scowl. 6. any expression or show of disapproval. [ME *froune*(n), t. OF: m. *froignier,* der. *froigne* surly expression; of Celtic orig.] —**frown′er,** *n.* —**frown′ing·ly,** *adv.*

frowst·y (frous′tĭ), *adj.* *Brit. Dial.* and *Colloq.* ill-smelling; musty.

frowz·y (frou′zĭ), *adj.,* **frowzier, frowziest.** 1. dirty and untidy; slovenly. 2. ill-smelling; musty. Also, **frows′y, frouzy.** [akin to FROWSTY] —**frowz′i·ly,** *adv.* —**frowz′i·ness,** *n.*

froze (frōz), *v.* pt. of **freeze.**

fro·zen (frō′zən), *v.* 1. pp. of **freeze.** —*adj.* 2. congealed by cold; covered with ice, as a stream. 3. frigid; very cold. 4. injured or killed by frost or cold. 5. obstructed by ice, as pipes. 6. chilly or cold in manner; unfeeling: *a frozen stare.* 7. *Finance, Colloq.* rendered impossible of liquidation, as by business conditions: *frozen loans.* [pp. of FREEZE] —**fro′zen·ly,** *adv.* —**fro′zen·ness,** *n.*

F.R.S., Fellow of the Royal Society.

frt., freight.

Fruc·ti·dor (fryktēdôr′), *n.* (in the calendar of the first French republic) the twelfth month of the year, extending from Aug. 18 to Sept. 16. [t. F, f. L *fructidor* fruit + s. Gk. *dōron* gift]

fruc·tif·er·ous (frŭktĭf′ərəs), *adj.* fruit-bearing; producing fruit. [f. L *fructifer* fruit-bearing + -OUS]

fruc·ti·fi·ca·tion (frŭk′təfəkā′shən), *n.* 1. act of fructifying; the fruiting of a plant. 2. the fruit of a plant. 3. the organs of fruiting.

fruc·ti·fy (frŭk′təfī′), *v.,* **-fied, -fying.** —*v.i.* 1. to bear fruit. —*v.t.* 2. to make fruitful or productive; fertilize. [ME *fructifie*(n), t. F: m. *fructifier,* t. L: m. *fructificāre* bear fruit]

fruc·tose (frŭk′tōs), *n.* *Chem.* a levorotatory ketose sugar, $C_6H_{12}O_6$, known also as levulose. It is an intensely sweet carbohydrate occurring in honey and invert sugar. [f. s. L *fructus* fruit + -OSE[2]]

fruc·tu·ous (frŭk′chōōəs), *adj.* fruitful; profitable.

fru·gal (frōō′gəl), *adj.* 1. economical in use or expenditure; prudently saving or sparing. 2. entailing little expense; costing little. [t. L: s. *frūgālis* economical] —**fru·gal·i·ty** (frōō găl′ə tĭ), **fru′gal·ness,** *n.* —**fru′gal·ly,** *adv.* —Syn. 1. self-denying, thrifty, chary, provident. See **economical.** —Ant. 1. extravagant.

fruit (frōōt), *n.* 1. any product of vegetable growth useful to men or animals. 2. *Bot.* **a.** the developed ovary of a seed plant with its contents and accessory parts, as the pea pod, nut, tomato, pineapple, etc. **b.** the edible part of a plant developed from a flower, with any accessory tissues, as the peach, mulberry, banana, etc. **c.** the spores and accessory organs of a cryptogam. 3. anything produced or accruing; product, result, or effect; return or profit. —*v.i., v.t.* 4. to bear or bring to bear fruit. [ME, t. OF, g. L *fructus* enjoyment, proceeds, fruit] —**fruit′like′,** *adj.*

fruit·age (frōō′tĭj), *n.* 1. the bearing of fruit. 2. fruits collectively. 3. product or result.

fruit cake, a rich cake containing raisins, nuts, citron, etc.

fruit cup, an assortment of fruits served in a glass or a cup as an appetizer or dessert.

fruit·er (frōō′tər), *n.* 1. a ship employed in transporting fruit. 2. a fruit grower.

fruit·er·er (frōō′tərər), *n.* *Chiefly Brit.* a dealer in fruit.

fruit fly, 1. any small fly of the dipterous family *Trypetidae,* which includes many seriously destructive pests, as the Mediterranean fruit fly. 2. any member of the genus *Drosophila,* the vinegar flies.

fruit·ful (frōōt′fal), *adj.* 1. abounding in fruit, as trees or other plants; bearing fruit abundantly. 2. conducing to abundance of fruit, as soil or showers. 3. productive of results; profitable: *fruitful investigations.* —**fruit′ful·ly,** *adv.* —**fruit′ful·ness,** *n.* —Syn. 2, 3. prolific, fertile. See **productive.** —Ant. 3. barren.

fru·i·tion (frōō ĭsh′ən), *n.* 1. attainment of anything desired; realization of results: *the fruition of one's labors.* 2. enjoyment, as of something attained or realized. 3. state of bearing fruit. [ME, t. LL: s. *fruitio* enjoyment]

fruit jar, a large-mouthed bottle, usually with an air-tight cap, for preserving fruit.

fruit·less (frōōt′lĭs), *adj.* 1. useless; unproductive; vain; without results. 2. without fruit; barren. —**fruit′less·ly,** *adv.* —**fruit′less·ness,** *n.* —Syn. 1. ineffective, abortive, unprofitable, bootless, futile.

fruit ranch, a farm where fruit is the main produce.

fruit sugar, *Chem.* fructose.

fruit tree, a tree bearing edible fruit.

fruit·y (frōō′tĭ), *adj.,* **fruitier, fruitiest.** resembling fruit; having the taste or flavor of fruit.

fru·men·ta·ceous (frōō′mən tā′shəs), *adj.* of the nature of or resembling wheat or other grain. [t. LL: m. *frūmentāceus* of grain]

fru·men·ty (frōō′mən tĭ), *n.* *Chiefly Brit. Dial.* hulled wheat boiled in milk and seasoned with sugar, etc. Also, **fromenty, furmenty, furmety.** [ME *frumentee,* t. OF, der. *frument,* g. L *frūmentum* grain]

frump (frŭmp), *n.* a dowdy, sometimes cross, woman. [orig. unknown]

frump·ish (frŭmp′ĭsh), *adj.* dowdy, and sometimes cross. —**frump′ish·ly,** *adv.* —**frump′ish·ness,** *n.*

frump·y (frŭmp′ĭ), *adj.,* **frumpier, frumpiest.** frumpish. —**frump′i·ly,** *adv.* —**frump′i·ness,** *n.*

Frun·ze (frōōn′zĕ), *n.* a city in the SW Soviet Union in Asia: capital of Kirghiz Republic. 190,000 (est. 1956).

frus·trate (frŭs′trāt), *v.,* **-trated, -trating,** *adj.* —*v.t.* 1. to make (plans, efforts, etc.) of no avail; defeat; baffle; nullify. 2. to disappoint or thwart (a person). —*adj.* 3. *Archaic.* frustrated. [t. L: m.s. *frustrātus,* pp., having disappointed or deceived] —Syn. 1. balk, foil, circumvent. See **thwart.** —Ant. 1. assist.

frus·tra·tion (frŭs trā′shən), *n.* state or quality of being frustrated; nullification.

frus·tule (frŭs′chōōl), *n.* *Bot.* the siliceous cell wall of a diatom. [t. LL: m.s. *frustulum,* dim. of *frustum* piece, bit.]

frus·tum (frŭs′təm), *n., pl.* **-tums, -ta** (-tə). *Geom.* 1. the part of a conical solid left after cutting off a top portion by a plane parallel to the base. 2. the part of a conical solid between two cutting planes. [t. L: piece, bit]

F. Frustum of a cone

fru·tes·cent (frōō tĕs′ənt), *adj.* *Bot.* tending to be shrublike; shrubby. [irreg. f. L *frut*(ex) shrub, bush + -ESCENT] —**fru·tes′cence,** *n.*

fru·ti·cose (frōō′tə kōs′), *adj.* *Bot.* having the form of a shrub; shrublike. [t. L: m.s. *fruticōsus* bushy]

fry[1] (frī), *v.,* **fried, frying,** *n., pl.* **fries.** —*v.t.* 1. to cook in fat, usually over direct heat. —*v.i.* 2. to undergo cooking in fat. —*n.* 3. a dish of something fried. 4. *U.S.* an occasion at which the chief food is fried, frequently outdoors: *a fish fry.* [ME *frye*(n), t. F: m. *frire,* g. L *frigere*]

fry[2] (frī), *n., pl.* **fry.** 1. the young of fishes, or of some other animals, as frogs. 2. young or small fishes or other young creatures, as children, collectively. [ME; cf. Icel. *frjō,* Sw. *frö,* Goth. *fraiw* seed]

fry·er (frī′ər), *n.* 1. one who or that which fries. 2. something, as a young chicken, for frying. Also, **frier.**

frying pan, a shallow pan with a long handle, in which food is fried.

f.s., foot-second.

ft., 1. feet. 2. foot. 3. fort. 4. fortification.

FTC, Federal Trade Commission.

fth., fathom. Also, **fthm.**

ft-lb., foot-pound.

Fu·ad I (fōō äd′), (*Ahmed Fuad*) 1868–1936, king of Egypt, 1922–36.

fuch·sia (fū′shə), *n.* 1. any plant of the onagraceous genus *Fuchsia,* which includes many varieties cultivated for their handsome drooping flowers. 2. Also, **California fuchsia,** a herbaceous shrub, *Zauschneria californica,* with large crimson flowers. 3. bright purplish-red. [NL, named after Leonhard *Fuchs* (1501–66), German botanist. See -IA]

fuch·sin (fōōk′sĭn), *n.* a coal-tar dye obtained by oxidizing a mixture of aniline and the toluidines; magenta. The dye is a greenish solid which forms deep-red solutions. Also, **fuch·sine** (fōōk′sĭn, -sēn). [f. FUCHS(IA) + -IN[2]; so named from its likeness to the flower in color]

fu·coid (fū′koid), *adj.* 1. resembling, or allied to, seaweeds of the genus *Fucus.* See **fucus.** —*n.* 2. a fucoid seaweed. [f. FUC(US) + -OID]

fu·cus (fū′kəs), *n., pl.* **-ci** (-sī), **-cuses.** any seaweed of the genus *Fucus,* olive-brown algae with branching fronds and often air bladders. [t. L: rock lichen]

fud·dle (fŭd′əl), *v.,* **-dled, -dling.** —*v.t.* 1. to intoxicate. 2. to muddle or confuse. —*v.i.* 3. to tipple.

fudge[1] (fŭj), *n.* a kind of candy (often homemade) composed of sugar, butter, milk, chocolate, or the like. [orig. uncert.]

fudge[2] (fŭj), *n., v.,* **fudged, fudging.** —*n.* 1. nonsense or bosh (sometimes used as a contemptuous interjection). —*v.i.* 2. to talk nonsense. [orig. unknown]

fudge[3] (fŭj), *n., v.,* **fudged, fudging.** —*n.* 1. a small stereotype or a few lines of specially prepared type which may replace a detachable part of the page plate of a newspaper in order to admit a late bulletin without replating the whole page. 2. the bulletin thus printed, often in color. 3. a machine or attachment for printing such a bulletin. —*v.t.* 4. to adjust or perform clumsily, perfunctorily, or dishonestly; make or get (*up*). [var. of FADGE]

Fu·e·gi·an (fū·ē'jῐ'ən, fwā'jῐ'ən), *adj.* **1.** of or belonging to Tierra del Fuego or its indigenous Indians. —*n.* **2.** a native or inhabitant of Tierra del Fuego.

fu·el (fū'əl), *n., v.,* **-eled, -eling** or (*esp. Brit.*) **-elled, -elling.** —*n.* **1.** combustible matter used to maintain fire, as coal, wood, oil, etc. **2.** means of sustaining or increasing passion, ardor, etc. —*v.t.* **3.** to supply with fuel. —*v.i.* **4.** to procure or take in fuel. [ME *fuelle*, t. OF: m. *feuille*, ult. der. L *focus* hearth, fireplace]

fuel oil, an oil used for fuel, esp. one used as a substitute for coal, as crude petroleum.

fu·ga·cious (fū·gā'shəs), *adj.* **1.** *Bot.* falling or fading early. **2.** fleeting; transitory. [f. obs. *fugacy* flight + -OUS] —**fu·gac·i·ty** (fū·găs'ə tῐ), *n.*

fu·gal (fū'gəl), *adj. Music.* of or pertaining to a fugue, or composed in the style of a fugue. —**fu'gal·ly,** *adv.*

fu·gate (fū'gāt), *n. Music.* a piece composed in fugue style, but not according to strict rules.

-fuge, a word element referring to "flight," as in *refuge.* [comb. form repr. L -*fugia,* der. *fugāre* put to flight]

fu·gi·tive (fū'jə tῐv), *n.* **1.** a person who is fleeing; a runaway. —*adj.* **2.** having taken flight, or run away: *a fugitive slave.* **3.** fleeting; transitory. **4.** dealing with subjects of passing interest, as writings; ephemeral. **5.** wandering, roving, or vagabond. [t. L: m.s. *fugitivus* fleeing; r. ME *fugitif,* t. F] —**fu'gi·tive·ly,** *adv.* —**fu'gi·tive·ness,** *n.*

fu·gle·man (fū'gəl mən), *n., pl.* **-men. 1.** a well-drilled soldier placed in front of a military company as a model for the others. **2.** anyone serving as an example. [t. G: m. *flügelmann,* lit., wing man]

fugue (fūg), *n. Music.* a polyphonic composition based upon one, two, or even more themes, which are enunciated by the several voices or parts in turn, subjected to contrapuntal treatment, and gradually built up into a complex form having somewhat distinct divisions or stages of development and a marked climax at the end. [t. F, t. It.: m. *fuga,* g. L *fuga* flight] —**fugue'like,** *adj.*

Füh·rer (fy'rər), *n.* German. **1.** leader. **2.** der (dĕr) Füh·rer, the leader (applied esp. to Adolf Hitler).

Fu·ji (fōō'jē), *n.* an extinct volcano in central Japan, on Honshu island: it is the highest mountain in Japan and is renowned for its beautiful symmetry. 12,395 ft. Also, **Fu·ji·ya·ma** (fōō'jē yä'mä) or **Fu·ji·san** (fōō'jē-sän').

Fu·kien (fōō'kyĕn'), *n.* a maritime province in SE China. 13,142,721 (1953); 45,845 sq. mi. *Cap.:* Foochow.

Fu·ku·o·ka (fōō'kōō ō̄'kä), *n.* a city in SW Japan, on Kyushu island. 392,649 (1950).

Ful (fōōl), *n.* a language of Senegal related to Wolof.

-ful, a suffix meaning **1.** full or of characterized by: *shameful, beautiful, careful, thoughtful.* **2.** tending or able to: *wakeful, harmful.* **3.** as much as will fill: *spoonful, handful.* [ME and OE -*ful,* -*ful,* repr. *full, ful* FULL¹]

Fu·lah (fōō'lä), *n., pl.* **-lah.** an African people, probably of mixed Berber and Negro origin, scattered through the Sudan from Senegal eastward. Also, **Fu'la.**

ful·crum (fŭl'krəm), *n., pl.* **-crums, -cra** (-krə). **1.** the support, or point of rest, on which a lever turns in moving a body. **2.** a prop. [t. L: bedpost]

ful·fil (fŏŏl fῐl'), *v.t.,* **-filled, -filling, fulfill.**

ful·fill (fŏŏl fῐl'), *v.t.* **1.** to carry out, or bring to to consummation, as a prophecy, promise, etc. **2.** to perform or do, as duty; obey or follow, as commands. **3.** to satisfy (requirements, etc.). **4.** to bring to an end, finish, or complete, as a period of time. [ME *fulfill(en),* OE *fullfyllan,* f. *full,* adj., full + *fyllan,* v., fill] —**ful·fill'er,** *n.* —Syn. 2. execute, discharge.

F. Fulcrum; L, Lever

ful·fill·ment (fŏŏl fῐl'mənt), *n.* a fulfilling or carrying out; performance; completion. Also, **ful·fil'ment.**

ful·gent (fŭl'jənt), *adj.* shining brightly; resplendent. [ME, t. L: s. *fulgens,* ppr.] —**ful'gent·ly,** *adv.*

ful·gu·rant (fŭl'gyə rənt), *adj.* flashing like lightning. [t. L: s. *fulgurans,* ppr]

ful·gu·rate (fŭl'gyə rāt'), *v.,* **-rated, -rating.** —*v.i.* **1.** to flash or dart like lightning. —*v.t.* **2.** *Med.* to destroy (esp. an abnormal growth) by electricity. [t. L: m.s. *fulgurātus,* pp.] —**ful'gu·ra'tion,** *n.*

ful·gu·rat·ing (fŭl'gyə rā'tῐng), *adj. Med.* (of pains) sharp and piercing, like lightning.

ful·gu·rite (fŭl'gyə rīt'), *n.* a tube formed in sand or rock by lightning. [f. L *fulgur* lightning + -ITE¹]

ful·gu·rous (fŭl'gyə rəs), *adj.* lightninglike.

fu·lig·i·nous (fū lῐj'ə nəs), *adj.* **1.** sooty; smoky. **2.** dull or brownish dark-gray. [t. LL: m.s. *fulīginōsus* full of soot]

full¹ (fŏŏl), *adj.* **1.** filled; containing all that can be held; filled to utmost capacity: *a full cup.* **2.** complete; entire; maximum: *a full supply.* **3.** of the maximum size, amount, extent, volume, etc.: *a full mile, full pay, the full moon.* **4.** (of garments, etc.) wide, ample, or having ample folds. **5.** abundant; well-supplied: *a pocket full of money.* **6.** filled or rounded out, as in form.

7. *Music.* ample and complete in volume or richness of sound. **8.** (of wines) having considerable body. **9.** in full cry, in hot pursuit, as dogs in the chase. —*adv.* **10.** fully, completely, or entirely. **11.** exactly or directly: *the blow struck him full in the face.* **12.** Chiefly Poetic. very: *full well.* —*v.t.* **13.** Sewing. to bring (the cloth) on one side of a seam to a little greater fullness than on the other by gathering or tucking very slightly. —*v.i.* **14.** to become full. —*n.* **15.** in full, a. without reduction; to or for the full amount: *a receipt in full.* b. without abbreviation or contraction. **16.** to the full, in full measure; to the utmost extent. **17.** (of the moon) the stage of complete illumination. See diag. under **moon.** [ME and OE *full, ful,* c. G *voll;* akin to L *plēnus,* Gk. *plērēs*] —**full'ness,** *n.* —**ful'ly,** *adv.*

full² (fŏŏl), *v.t.* **1.** to cleanse and thicken (cloth, etc.) by special processes in manufacture. —*v.i.* **2.** (of cloth, etc.) to become compacted or felted. [ME *fulle(n),* back formation from FULLER¹]

full-back (fŏŏl'băk'), *n. Football.* the player usually farthest behind the line of scrimmage.

full binding, a complete binding of a volume in any one material, generally leather.

full blood, 1. an individual of unmixed ancestry; a purebred. **2.** relationship through both parents.

full-blood·ed (fŏŏl'blŭd'ῐd), *adj.* **1.** of unmixed ancestry; thoroughbred. **2.** vigorous; virile; hearty.

full-blown (fŏŏl'blōn'), *adj.* **1.** in full bloom: *a full-blown rose.* **2.** completely developed.

full-bod·ied (fŏŏl'bŏd'ῐd), *adj.* with all the flavor and strength possible.

full dress, 1. a ceremonial style of dress. **2.** the formal attire customarily worn in the evening.

full·er¹ (fŏŏl'ər), *n.* one who fulls cloth. [ME; OE *fullere,* f. L *full(o)* fuller + -*ere* -ER¹]

full·er² (fŏŏl'ər), *n.* a half-round set hammer used for grooving and spreading iron. [appar. f. *full,* v., to make full + -ER¹]

Ful·ler (fŏŏl'ər), *n.* **1.** Melville Weston, 1833–1910, chief justice of the U.S. Supreme Court, 1888–1910. **2. (Sarah) Margaret,** (*Marchioness Ossoli*) 1810–50, U.S. author and literary critic. **3. Thomas,** 1608–61, British clergyman and historian.

fuller's earth, an absorbent clay, used for removing grease from cloth, etc., in fulling, as a filter and, in medicine, as a dusting powder.

fuller's teasel, the teasel, *Dipsacus fullonum.*

Ful·ler·ton (fŏŏl'ər tən), *n.* a city in SW California, SE of Los Angeles. 56,180 (1960).

full-faced (fŏŏl'fāst'), *adj.* **1.** having a plump or round face. **2.** facing squarely toward the spectator or in a given direction. **3.** *Printing.* (of type) bold-faced.

full-fash·ioned (fŏŏl'făsh'ənd), *adj.* knitted in the shape of the foot or leg.

full-fledged (fŏŏl'flĕjd'), *adj.* **1.** fully developed. **2.** of full rank or standing: *a full-fledged professor.*

full gainer, *Swimming.* a type of dive in which the diver takes off facing forward and performs a complete back somersault before entering the water.

full-grown (fŏŏl'grōn'), *adj.* fully grown; mature.

full house, *Poker.* a hand consisting of three of a kind and a pair, as three queens and two tens.

full moon, the moon when the whole of its disk is illuminated. See **moon** (def. 2c).

fullness of time, the proper or destined time.

full-rigged (fŏŏl'rῐgd'), *adj.* **1.** *Naut.* carrying complete rigging. **2.** having all equipment.

full stop, a period.

ful·mar (fŏŏl'mər), *n.* any of certain oceanic birds of the petrel family, esp. *Fulmarus glacialis,* a gull-like arctic species. [? lit., foul gull (with allusion to its stench), t. Scand; cf. Icel. *fúll* foul, *mār* gull]

ful·mi·nant (fŭl'mə nənt), *adj.* **1.** fulminating. **2.** *Pathol.* developing or progressing suddenly: *fulminant plague.* [t. L: s. *fulminans,* ppr., lightening]

ful·mi·nate (fŭl'mə nāt'), *v.,* **-nated, -nating.** —*v.i.* **1.** to explode with a loud noise; detonate. **2.** to issue denunciations or the like (fol. by *against*). —*v.t.* **3.** to cause to explode. **4.** to denounce vehemently. —*n.* **5.** *Chem.* one of a group of unstable, explosive compounds derived from fulminic acid; esp. the mercury salt of fulminic acid which is a powerful detonating agent. [t. L: m.s. *fulminātus,* pp., lightened] —**ful'mi·na'tor,** *n.*

fulminating compound, *Chem.* a fulminate.

fulminating powder, *Chem.* **1.** powder which explodes by percussion. **2.** a fulminate.

ful·mi·na·tion (fŭl'mə nā'shən), *n.* **1.** a violent denunciation or censure. **2.** violent explosion.

ful·min·ic acid (fŭl mῐn'ῐk), *Chem.* an acid, HONC, an isomer of cyanic acid, found only in its salts, the fulminates.

ful·ness (fŏŏl'nῐs), *n.* fullness.

ful·some (fŏŏl'səm, fŭl'-), *adj.* **1.** offensive to good taste, esp. as being excessive; gross: *fulsome praise.* **2.** disgusting. [ME *fulsum,* f. FULL¹ + -SOME¹; evidence of assoc. with FOUL] —**ful'some·ly,** *adv.* —**ful'some·ness,** *n.*

Ful·ton (fŏŏl'tən), *n.* **Robert,** 1765–1815, American inventor: built the first profitable steamboat.

ful·vous (fŭl'vəs), *adj.* tawny; dull yellowish-gray or brown. [t. L: m. *fulvus* deep yellow]

act, āble, dâre, ärt; ĕbb, ēqual; ῐf, īce; hŏt, ōver, ôrder, oil, bŏŏk, ōōze, out; ŭp, ūse, ûrge; ə = a in alone; ch, chief; g, give; ng, ring; sh, shoe; th, thin; t̴h, that; zh, vision. See the full key on inside cover.

fu·mar·ic acid (fū măr′ĭk). *Chem.* a dibasic acid, $C_2H_2(COOH)_2$, isomeric with maleic acid and occurring in several plants.

fu·ma·role (fū′mə rōl′), *n.* a hole in or near a volcano, from which vapor issues. [t. F: m. *fumerolle*, g. LL *fūmāriolum*, dim. of L *fūmārium* smoke chamber]

um·ble (fŭm′bəl), *v.*, **-bled, -bling**, *n.* —*v.i.* **1.** to fee or grope about clumsily (fol. by *at, with, after, for*). **2.** *Sports.* to fumble the ball. —*v.t.* **3.** to handle clumsily. **4.** *Sports.* to fail to catch and hold (a ball). —*n.* **5.** act of fumbling. [cf. Sw. *fumla* grope] —**fum′bler**, *n.* —**fum′bling**, *adj.* —**fum′bling·ly**, *adv.*

fume (fūm), *n., v.*, **fumed, fuming.** —*n.* **1.** (*often pl.*) any smokelike or vaporous exhalation from matter or substances. **2.** an odorous exhalation, as from flowers. **3.** an irritable or angry mood: *to be in a fume.* —*v.t.* **4.** to send forth as fumes. **5.** to disperse or drive away in vapors; send up as vapor. **6.** to treat with fumes. —*v.i.* **7.** to rise, or pass off, as fumes. **8.** to emit fumes. **9.** to show irritation or anger. [ME, t. OF: m. *fum*, g. L *fūmus* smoke, steam, fume] —**fume′less**, *adj.* —**fume′like′**, *adj.* —**fum′ing·ly**, *adv.* —Syn. **9.** chafe, fret, rage.

fumed (fūmd), *adj.* darkened or colored by exposure to ammonia fumes, as oak and other wood.

fu·mi·gate (fū′mə gāt′), *v.t.*, **-gated, -gating.** to expose to smoke or fumes, as in disinfecting. [t. L: m.s. *fūmigātus*, pp., smoked] —**fu′mi·ga′tion**, *n.*

fu·mi·ga·tor (fū′mə gā′tər), *n.* **1.** one who or that which fumigates. **2.** a structure in which plants are fumigated to destroy insects.

fu·mi·to·ry (fū′mə tōr′ĭ), *n., pl.* **-ries.** any plant of the genus *Fumaria*, of the family *Fumariaceae*, esp. a delicate herb, *F. officinalis*, with finely dissected leaves and racemes of purplish flowers. [ME *fumeter*, t. OF: m. *fumeterre*, t. ML: m. *fūmus terrae* smoke of the earth]

fum·y (fū′mĭ), *adj.*, **fumier, fumiest.** full of fumes; fumelike.

fun (fŭn), *n., v.*, **funned, funning.** —*n.* **1.** mirthful sport or diversion; merry amusement; joking; playfulness. **2.** for or in fun, as a joke; playfully; not seriously. **3.** make fun of, to ridicule. —*v.i.* **4.** *Colloq.* to make fun; joke. [? d. var of obs. *fon*, v., befool. See FOND]

fu·nam·bu·list (fū năm′byə lĭst), *n.* a tightrope walker. [f. s. L *fūnambulus* ropedancer + -IST] —**fu·nam′bu·lism**, *n.*

Fun·chal (fōōn shäl′), *n.* a seaport in and the capital of the Madeira Islands: winter resort. 37,215 (1950).

func·tion (fŭngk′shən), *n.* **1.** the kind of action or activity proper to a person, thing, or institution. **2.** any ceremonious public or social gathering or occasion. **3.** *Math.* a mathematical quantity whose value depends upon the values of other quantities, called the arguments or independent variables of the function. **4.** *Gram.* **a.** the grammatical role which a linguistic form plays, or the position which it occupies in a particular construction. **b.** the grammatical roles or the positions of a linguistic form or form class collectively. —*v.i.* **5.** to perform a function, or one's or its functions; act; serve; operate; carry out normal work, activity, or processes. **6.** *Gram.* to have or exercise a function: *in earlier English the present tense often functioned as the future.* [t. L: s. *functio* performance] —**func′tion·less**, *adj.*

func·tion·al (fŭngk′shən əl), *adj.* **1.** of or pertaining to a function or functions. **2.** designed or adapted primarily to perform some operation or duty: *a functional building.* **3.** capable of operating or functioning. **4.** pertaining to an algebraical operation: *a functional symbol.* —**func′tion·al·ly**, *adv.*

functional disease, *Pathol.* a disease in which there is a morbid change in the function of an organ, but no structural alteration in the tissues involved (opposed to *organic disease*).

func·tion·al·ism (fŭngk′shən əl ĭz′əm), *n.* the doctrine or practice in furniture design, architecture, etc., under which such factors as material and form are determined primarily by functional considerations.

func·tion·ar·y (fŭngk′shə něr′ĭ), *n., pl.* **-aries.** an official.

fund (fŭnd), *n.* **1.** a stock of money or pecuniary resources, as for some purpose. **2.** a store or stock of something, now often of something immaterial: *a fund of knowledge.* **3.** (*pl.*) money in hand; pecuniary resources. —*v.t.* **4.** to provide a fund to pay the interest or principal of (a debt). **5.** to convert (general outstanding debts) into a more or less permanent debt or loan, represented by interest-bearing bonds. [t. L: s. *fundus* bottom, estate; r. FOND² in most of its meanings]

fun·da·ment (fŭn′də mənt), *n.* **1.** the physical characteristics of a geographical region, as land forms, drainage, climate, soils, etc. **2.** the buttocks. [t. L: s. *fundā-mentum* foundation; r. ME *fondement*, t. OF]

fun·da·men·tal (fŭn′də měn′təl), *adj.* **1.** serving as, or being a component part of, a foundation or basis; basic; underlying: *fundamental principles.* **2.** of or affecting the foundation or basis: *a fundamental change.* **3.** original. **4.** *Music.* (of a chord) having its root as its lowest note. —*n.* **5.** a leading or primary principle, rule, law, or the like, which serves as the groundwork of a system; essential part. **6.** Also, **fundamental note** or **tone.** *Music.* **a.** the root of a chord. **b.** the generator of a series of harmonics. **7.** *Physics.* the component of lowest frequency in a composite wave. [t. NL: s.

fundāmentālis, der. L *fundāmentum* foundation] —**fun′da·men·tal′i·ty**, *n.* —**fun·da·men′tal·ly**, *adv.*

funbamental bass, *Music.* a bass consisting of the roots of the chords employed.

funb·a·men·tal·ism (fŭn′də měn′tə lĭz′əm), *n.* **1.** a movement in American Protestantism which stresses the inerrancy of the Bible not only in matters of faith and morals but also as literal historical record and prophecy, e. g., of creation, the virgin birth of Christ, his second advent, etc. (opposed to *modernism*). **2.** the faith in the Bible so stressed. —**fun·da·men′tal·ist**, *n., adj.*

fundamental unit, *Physics.* one of the units (esp. those of mass, length, and time) taken as a basis for a system of units.

fun·dus (fŭn′dəs), *n. Anat.* the base of an organ, or the part opposite to or remote from an aperture. [t. L: bottom]

Fun·dy (fŭn′dĭ), *n.* **Bay of,** a deep inlet of the Atlantic in SE Canada between New Brunswick and Nova Scotia: noted for its swift tidal currents, sometimes rising 70 ft.

Fü·nen (fʏ′nən), *n.* German name of Fyn.

fu·ner·al (fū′nər əl), *n.* **1.** the ceremonies connected with the disposition of the body of a dead person; obsequies. **2.** a funeral procession. [ME, t. ML: m.s. *fūnerālia*, neut. pl. of the adj.] —*adj.* **3.** of or pertaining to a funeral. [ME, t. ML: s. *fūnerālis*, der. L *fūnus* funeral, death]

fu·ner·ar·y (fū′nə rěr′ĭ), *adj.* of or pertaining to a funeral or burial: *a funerary urn.*

fu·ne·re·al (fū nĭr′ĭ əl), *adj.* **1.** of or pertaining to a funeral. **2.** mournful; gloomy; dismal. [f. s. L *funereus* of a funeral + -AL¹] —**fu·ne′re·al·ly**, *adv.*

Fünf·kir·chen (fʏnf′kĭr′ĸʜən), *n.* German name of Pécs.

fun·gal (fŭng′gəl), *adj.* **1.** fungous. —*n.* **2.** a fungus.

fun·gi (fŭn′jī), *n. pl.* of fungus.

fun·gi·ble (fŭn′jə bəl), *Law.* —*adj.* **1.** of such a nature that one instance or portion may be replaced by another in respect of function, office, or use: usually confined to goods. —*n.* **2.** a fungible thing, as money or grain. [t. ML: m.s. *fungibilis*, der. L *fungī* fulfill the office of]

fun·gi·cide (fŭn′jə sīd′), *n.* an agent, such as a spray or dust, used for destroying fungi. [f. *fungi-* (comb. form of FUNGUS) + -CIDE¹] —**fun′gi·cid′al**, *adj.*

fun·gi·form (fŭn′jə fôrm′), *adj.* having the form of a fungus or mushroom. [f. *fungi-* (comb. form of FUNGUS) + -FORM]

fun·go (fŭng′gō), *n., pl.* **-goes.** *Baseball.* a ball tossed into the air by the batter himself and struck as it comes down. [orig. uncert.] —**fun′go**, *adj.*

fun·goid (fŭng′goid), *adj.* **1.** resembling a fungus; of the nature of a fungus. **2.** *Pathol.* characterized by funguslike morbid growths.

fun·gous (fŭng′gəs), *adj.* **1.** of, pertaining to, or caused by fungi; fungal. **2.** of the nature of or resembling a fungus. [ME, t. L: m.s. *fungōsus*, der. *fungus* sponge, mushroom, fungus]

fun·gus (fŭng′gəs), *n., pl.* **fungi** (fŭn′jī), **funguses,** *adj.* —*n.* **1.** any of the *Fungi*, a group of thallophytes including the mushrooms, molds, mildews, rusts, smuts, etc., characterized chiefly by absence of chlorophyll and by subsisting upon dead or living organic matter. **2.** *Pathol.* a spongy morbid growth, as proud flesh formed in a wound. —*adj.* **3.** of or pertaining to. [t. L: mushroom, fungus] —**fun′gus·like′**, *adj.*

fu·ni·cle (fū′nə kəl), *n. Bot.* the stalk of an ovule or seed. [t. L: m.s. *fūniculus*, dim. of *fūnis* rope]

fu·nic·u·lar (fū nĭk′yə lər), *adj.* **1.** of or pertaining to a rope or cord, or its tension. **2.** worked by a rope or the like. [r. s. L *fūniculus* little rope + -AR¹]

funicular railway, a railway system of short length operating up steep grades, in which cable-linked trains move up and down simultaneously, thus minimizing the pull of gravity.

fu·nic·u·late (fū nĭk′yə lĭt, -lāt′), *adj. Bot.* having a funicle.

fu·nic·u·lus (fū nĭk′yə ləs), *n., pl.* **-li** (-lī′). **1.** *Anat.* a conducting cord such as a nerve cord, umbilical cord, etc. **2.** *Bot.* a funicle. [t. L, dim. of *fūnis* rope]

funk (fŭngk), *Colloq.* —*n.* **1.** cowering fear; state of fright or terror. —*v.t.* **2.** to be afraid of. **3.** to frighten. **4.** to shrink from; try to shirk. —*v.i.* **5.** to shrink or quail in fear. [cf. OF *funicle* terrible; g. L *phrenēticus.* See FRANTIC]

fun·nel (fŭn′əl), *n., v.*, **-neled, -neling** or (*esp. Brit.*) **-nelled, -nelling.** —*n.* **1.** a cone-shaped utensil with a tube at the apex, for conducting liquid, etc., through a small opening, as into a bottle. **2.** a smokestack, esp. of a steamship or a locomotive. **3.** a flue, tube, or shaft, as for ventilation. —*v.t.* **4.** to converge or concentrate: *to funnel all one's energies into a job.* [ME *fonel*, t. OF. ult. g. LL *fundibulum*, L *infundibulum*] —**fun′nel·like′**, *adj.*

fun·nies (fŭn′ĭz), *n.pl. U.S. Colloq.* **1.** comic strips. **2.** the section of a newspaper containing them.

fun·ny (fŭn′ĭ), *adj.*, **-nier, -niest.** **1.** affording fun; amusing; comical. **2.** *Colloq.* curious; strange; queer; odd. [f. FUN, *n.* + -Y¹] —**fun′ni·ly**, *adv.* —**fun′ni·ness**, *n.* —Syn. **1.** comic, farcical, absurd, ridiculous, droll, witty, facetious, humorous. FUNNY, LAUGHABLE, LUDICROUS refer to that which excites laughter. FUNNY and LAUGHABLE are both applied to that which provokes laughter or deserves to be laughed at; FUNNY is a colloquial term loosely applied

---

b., blend of, blended; c., cognate with; d., dialect, dialectal; der., derived from; f., formed from; g., going back to; m., modification of; r., replacing; s., stem of; t., taken from; ?, perhaps. See the full key on inside cover.

and in popular use is commonly interchangeable with the other terms: *a funny story, scene, joke, a laughable incident, mistake.* That which is LUDICROUS excites laughter by its incongruity and foolish absurdity: *the monkey's attempts to imitate the woman were ludicrous.* —**Ant. 1.** solemn, serious.

funny bone, the part of the elbow where the ulnar nerve passes by the internal condyle of the humerus, which when struck causes a peculiar, tingling sensation in the arm and hand; the crazy bone.

Fun·ston (fŭn′stən), *n.* Frederick, 1865–1917, U.S. general.

fur (fûr), *n., v.,* **furred, furring.** —*n.* **1.** the skin of certain animals (as the sable, ermine, beaver, etc.), covered with a fine, soft, thick, hairy coating, used for lining or trimming garments or for entire garments. **2.** (*usually pl.*) an article of apparel made of or with such material, as a fur scarf or tippet. **3.** any coating resembling or suggesting fur, as one of morbid matter on the tongue. —*v.t.* **4.** to line, face, or trim (a garment, etc.) with fur. **5.** to clothe (a person) with fur. **6.** to coat with foul or deposited matter. [ME *furre,* t. OF: m. *forrer* line with fur, orig. encase, der. *forre* sheath, t. Gmc.; cf. G *futter* sheath] —**fur′less,** *adj.*

fu·ran (fyŏŏr′ăn, fyŏŏ răn′), *n. Chem.* a colorless liquid, C_4H_4O, an unsaturated five-membered ring compound derived from furfural. [short for *furfurane,* t. G: m. *furfuran,* f. L *furfur* bran + -*an* -ANE]

fur·be·low (fûr′bə lō′), *n.* **1.** a pleated or gathered trimming on a woman's gown or the like; flounce. **2.** any bit of showy trimming or finery. —*v.t.* **3.** to ornament with or as with furbelows. [var. of FALBALA]

fur·bish (fûr′bĭsh), *v.t.* **1.** to restore to freshness of appearance or condition (often fol. by *up*). **2.** to rub or scour (armor, weapons, etc.) to brightness; polish; burnish. [ME *furbish*(en), t. OF: m. *forbiss-,* s. *forbir* polish, clean, t. Gmc.; cf. OHG *furban*] —**fur′bish·er,** *n.*

fur·cate (*adj.* fûr′kāt, -kĭt; *v.* fûr′kāt), *adj., v.,* -**cated,** -**cating.** —*adj.* **1.** forked. —*v.i.* **2.** to form a fork; divide into branches. [t. ML: m.s. *furcātus* cloven, der. L *furca* fork]

fur·cu·la (fûr′kyə lə), *n., pl.* -**lae** (-lē′). the forked clavicular bone of a bird; wishbone. [t. L, dim. of *furca* fork]

fur·cu·lum (fûr′kyə ləm), *n., pl.* -**la** (-lə). furcula. [NL, incorrectly formed dim. of L *furca* fork]

fur·fu·ra·ceous (fûr′fyə rā′shəs), *adj.* **1.** branlike. **2.** scaly; scurfy. [t. LL: m. *furfurāceus*]

fur·fur·al (fûr′fə răl′), *n. Chem.* an oily liquid aldehyde, $C_5H_4O_2$, with an aromatic odor, obtained by distilling bran, sugar, wood, corncobs, etc., with dilute sulfuric acid: used in the manufacture of plastics and in refining lubricating oils. [f. L *furfur* bran + AL-(DEHYDE)]

Fu·ries (fyŏŏr′ĭz), *n.pl. Class. Myth.* See **fury** (def. 3).

fu·ri·ous (fyŏŏr′ĭəs), *adj.* **1.** full of fury, violent passion, or rage. **2.** intensely violent, as wind, storms, etc. **3.** of unrestrained energy, speed, etc.: *furious activity.* [ME, t. L: m.s. *furiōsus* raging] —**fu′ri·ous·ly,** *adv.* —**fu′ri·ous·ness,** *n.*

furl (fûrl), *v.t.* **1.** to draw into a compact roll, as a sail against a spar or a flag against its staff. —*v.i.* **2.** to become furled. —*n.* **3.** act of furling. **4.** a roll resulting from being furled. [cf. F *ferler,* OF *ferlier,* f. *fer* firm (g. L *firmus*) + *lier* to bind (g. L *ligāre*)]

furl., furlough.

fur·long (fûr′lông, -lŏng), *n.* a unit of distance, equal to 220 yards or ⅛ mi. [ME; OE *furlang,* f. *furh* furrow + *lang* long]

fur·lough (fûr′lō), *Mil.* —*n.* **1.** vacation granted to an enlisted man (in the U.S. Army, one month per year). —*v.t.* **2.** to grant a furlough to. [var. of *furloff,* t. D: m. *verlof* leave, furlough. Cf. G *verlaub* leave, permission; current pronunciation due to assoc. with *dough, though*]

fur·men·ty (fûr′mən tĭ), *n.* frumenty. Also, **fur·me·ty** (fûr′mə tĭ).

fur·nace (fûr′nĭs), *n.* **1.** a structure or apparatus in which to generate heat, as for heating houses, smelting ores, producing steam, etc. **2.** a place of burning heat. **3.** a place of severe trial. [ME *furneise,* t. OF: m. *fornais, fornaise,* g. s. L *fornax* oven] —**fur′nace·like′,** *adj.*

Fur·ness (fûr′nĭs), *n.* Horace Howard, 1833–1912, U.S. literary scholar.

fur·nish (fûr′nĭsh), *v.t.* **1.** to provide or supply. **2.** to fit up (a house, room, etc.) with necessary appliances, esp. furniture. [ME *furnisshe*(n), t. OF: m. *furniss-,* s. *furnir* accomplish, furnish, t. Gmc.; cf. OHG *frumjan* provide] —**fur′nish·er,** *n.*
—**Syn. 1, 2.** FURNISH, APPOINT, EQUIP all refer to providing something necessary. FURNISH emphasizes the idea of providing necessary or customary services or appliances in living quarters: *to furnish board, a room.* APPOINT (now found only in WELL-APPOINTED) means to furnish completely with all requisites or accessories or in an elegant style: *a well-appointed house.* EQUIP means to supply with necessary materials or apparatus for some service, action, or undertaking; it emphasizes preparation: *to equip a vessel, a soldier.*

fur·nish·ing (fûr′nĭsh ĭng), *n.* **1.** that with which anything is furnished. **2.** (*pl.*) fittings, appliances, articles of furniture, etc., for a house or room. **3.** (*pl.*) accessories of dress: *men's furnishings.*

furnit., furniture.

fur·ni·ture (fûr′nə chər), *n.* **1.** the movable articles, as tables, chairs, bedsteads, desks, cabinets, etc., required for use or ornament in a house, office, or the like.

2. fittings, apparatus, or necessary accessories for something. **3.** *Print.* pieces of wood or metal, less than type-high, set in and about pages of type to fill them out and hold the type in place. [t. F: m. *fourniture,* der. *fournir* FURNISH]

Fur·ni·vall (fûr′nə vəl), *n.* Frederick James, 1825–1910, British philologist and editor.

fu·ror (fyŏŏr′ôr), *n.* **1.** a general outburst of enthusiasm or excitement. **2.** a prevailing mania or craze. **3.** fury; rage; madness. [t. L: a raging; r. late ME *fureur,* t. F]

furred (fûrd), *adj.* **1.** having fur. **2.** made with or of fur, as garments. **3.** clad in fur or furs, as persons. **4.** coated with morbid matter, as the tongue.

fur·ri·er (fûr′ĭər), *n.* a dealer in or dresser of furs.

fur·ri·er·y (fûr′ĭ ə rĭ), *n., pl.* -**eries.** **1.** furs in general. **2.** the business or trade of a furrier.

fur·ring (fûr′ĭng), *n.* **1.** act of lining, trimming, or clothing with fur. **2.** the fur used. **3.** the formation of a coating of matter on something, as on the tongue. **4.** *Bldg. Trades.* **a.** the nailing on of thin strips of board, as to furnish a level surface for lathing or plastering, to provide air space between a wall and plastering, etc. **b.** materials so used.

fur·row (fûr′ō), *n.* **1.** a narrow trench made in the ground, esp. by a plow. **2.** a narrow, trenchlike depression in any surface: *the furrows of a wrinkled face.* —*v.t.* **3.** to make a furrow or furrows in; plow (land, etc.). **4.** to make wrinkles in (the face, etc.). [ME *forwe, furgh*(e), OE *furh,* c. G *furche;* akin to L *porca* ridge between furrows] —**fur′row·er,** *n.* —**fur′row·less,** *adj.* —**fur′row·like′,** *adj.* —**fur′row·y,** *adj.*

fur·ry (fûr′ĭ), *adj.,* -**rier,** -**riest.** **1.** made of or with fur. **2.** covered with fur; wearing fur. **3.** consisting of or resembling fur. —**fur′ri·ness,** *n.*

Northern fur seal,
Callorhinus alascanus
(Male 7 ft. long,
female ab. 4 ft.)

fur seal, any of various species of eared seal, as *Callorhinus alascanus,* which have under the outer hair a thick coat of fur of great commercial value (distinguished from *hair seal*).

Fürth (fyrt), *n.* a city in S West Germany, near Nuremberg. 101,615 (est. 1955).

fur·ther (fûr′thər), *compar. adv. and adj.,* superl. **furthest,** *v.* —*adv.* **1.** at or to a greater distance; farther. **2.** at or to a more advanced point; to a greater extent. **3.** in addition; moreover. —*adj.* **4.** more distant or remote; farther. **5.** more extended. **6.** additional; more. —*v.t.* **7.** to help forward (a work, undertaking, cause, etc.); promote; advance; forward. [ME *further*(e), *furthra,* c. G *vordere* more advanced] —**fur′ther·er,** *n.*

fur·ther·ance (fûr′thər əns), *n.* act of furthering; promotion; advancement.

fur·ther·more (fûr′thər mōr′), *adv.* moreover; besides; in addition.

fur·ther·most (fûr′thər mōst′), *adj.* most distant.

fur·thest (fûr′thĭst), *adj., adv.* superl. of **further.** [ME, coined as a superl. of FURTHER. Cf. FARTHEST]

fur·tive (fûr′tĭv), *adj.* **1.** taken, done, used, etc., by stealth; secret: *a furtive glance.* **2.** sly; shifty: *a furtive manner.* [t. L: m.s. *furtīvus* stolen] —**fur′tive·ly,** *adv.* —**fur′tive·ness,** *n.*

fu·run·cle (fyŏŏr′ŭng kəl), *n.* a boil or inflammatory sore. [t. L: m. *furunculus* a petty thief, a boil]

fu·run·cu·lo·sis (fyŏŏ rŭng′kyə lō′sĭs), *n. Pathol.* the morbid state characterized by the presence of furuncles.

fu·ry (fyŏŏr′ĭ), *n., pl.* -**ries.** **1.** frenzied or unrestrained violent passion, esp. anger. **2.** violence; vehemence; fierceness. **3.** (*cap.*) one of the avenging deities of classical mythology (in female form, with serpents twined in their hair), in later accounts three in number and called Alecto, Megaera, and Tisiphone. **4.** a fierce and violent person, esp. a woman. **5.** like fury, *Colloq.* furiously; violently. [ME, t. L: m.s. *furia* rage, madness] —**Syn. 1.** furor, frenzy, rage, ire, wrath. See **anger.**

furze (fûrz), *n.* any plant of the leguminous genus *Ulex,* esp. *U. europaeus,* a low, much-branched, spiny shrub with yellow flowers, common on waste lands in Europe; gorse. [ME *furse, firse,* OE *fyrs*]

fur·zy (fûr′zĭ), *adj. Brit.* **1.** of or pertaining to furze. **2.** overgrown with furze.

fu·sain (fū zăn′; *Fr.* fy zăN′), *n.* **1.** a fine charcoal used in drawing, made from the wood of the spindle tree. **2.** a drawing made with it. [t. F: spindle tree, charcoal made from its wood, der. L *fūsus* spindle]

Fu·san (fōō′sän′), *n.* former name of Pusan.

Furze,
Ulex europaeus

fus·cous (fŭs′kəs), *adj.* dark brownish-gray; dark; dusky. [t. L: m. *fuscus* dark]

fuse¹ (fūz), *n., v.,* **fused, fusing.** —*n.* **1.** *Elect.* an overcurrent protective device, with a circuit-opening fusible member directly heated and destroyed by the passage of overcurrent through it. **2.** a tube, ribbon, or the like, filled or saturated with combustible matter, for igniting an explosive. **3.** fuze. —*v.i.* **4.** *Chiefly Brit.* to blow a fuse. [t. L: m. *fuso,* g. L *fūsus* spindle] —**fuse′less,** *adj.* —**fuse′like′,** *adj.*

fuse² (fūz), v., **fused, fusing.** —v.t. 1. to combine or blend by melting together; melt. 2. to unite or blend into a whole, as if by melting together. —v.i. 3. to become liquid under the action of heat; melt. 4. to become united or blended, as if by melting together. [t. L: m.s. *fūsus*, pp., poured, melted, cast] —**Syn.** 1. See **melt.** 2. amalgamate, merge, liquefy, dissolve, smelt.

fu·see (fū zē′), n. 1. a kind of match with a large head, for igniting by friction. 2. a red flare light, used on a railroad as a warning signal to approaching trains. 3. *Horology.* a spirally grooved, conical pulley and chain arrangement for counteracting the diminishing power of the uncoiling mainspring. 4. a fuse. Also, **fuzee.** [t. F: spindleful, der. OF *fus* spindle, g. L *fūsus*]

fu·se·lage (fū′zə lĭj, fū′zə läzh′, -sə-), n. the framework of the body of an airplane. [t. F, der. *fuselé* spindle-shaped, der. *fuseau* spindle, der. L *fūsus*]

fuse link, *Elect.* an element, made of fusible wire or cast from fusible metal, inserted in a fuse receptacle.

fu·sel oil (fū′zəl, -səl), a mixture of amyl alcohols obtained as a by-product in the fermentation of grains. [*fusel*, t. G: inferior liquor or spirits]

fu·si·bil·i·ty (fū′zə bĭl′ə tĭ), n. 1. quality of being fusible, or convertible from a solid to a fluid state by heat. 2. the degree to which a substance is fusible.

fu·si·ble (fū′zə bəl), adj. capable of being fused or melted. —**fu′si·ble·ness,** n.

fusible metal, *Metall.* any of various alloys, as one of bismuth, lead, and tin, which melt at comparatively low temperatures, and hence can be used for making various safety devices. Also, **fusible alloy.**

fu·si·form (fū′zə fôrm′), adj. spindle-shaped; rounded and tapering from the middle toward each end, as some roots. [t. s. L *fūsus* spindle + -(I)FORM]

fu·sil (fū′zəl, -sĭl), n. a light flintlock musket. [t. F, in OF *foisil* steel for striking fire, ult. der. L *focus* hearth]

fu·sil·ier (fū′zə lĭr′), n. 1. a term used in the names of certain British regiments. 2. a soldier armed with a fusil. Also, **fu′sil·eer′.** [t. F, der. *fusil* musket]

fu·sil·lade (fū′zə lād′), n., v., **-laded, -lading.** —n. 1. a simultaneous or continuous discharge of firearms. 2. a general discharge or outpouring of anything: *a fusillade of questions.* —v.t. 3. to attack or shoot by a fusillade. [t. F, der. *fusiller* shoot, der. *fusil* FUSIL]

fu·sion (fū′zhən), n. 1. act or process of fusing. 2. state of being fused. 3. that which is fused. 4. *Pol.* a. the coalition of parties or factions. b. the body resulting from such coalition. 5. *Physics.* a thermonuclear reaction in which nuclei of light atoms join to form nuclei of heavier atoms, as the combination of deuterium atoms to form helium atoms. [t. L: s. *fūsio* a pouring out]

fu·sion·ism (fū′zhə nĭz′əm), n. *Pol.* the principle, policy, or practice of fusion. —**fu′sion·ist,** n., adj.

fuss (fŭs), n. 1. an excessive display of anxious activity; needless or useless bustle. 2. a person given to fussing. —v.i. 3. to make a fuss; make much ado about trifles. —v.t. 4. to put into a fuss; disturb with trifles; bother. [orig. unknown] —**fuss′er,** n. —**Syn.** 1. pother, to-do, stir, commotion.

fuss-budg·et (fŭs′bŭj′ĭt), n. *Colloq.* a fussy person.

fuss·y (fŭs′ĭ), adj., **fussier, fussiest.** 1. excessively busy with trifles; anxious or particular about petty details. 2. (of clothes, etc.) elaborately made or trimmed. 3. full of details, especially when excessively so. —**fuss′i·ly,** adv. —**fuss′i·ness,** n.

fus·tian (fŭs′chən), n. 1. a stout fabric of cotton and flax. 2. a stout twilled cotton fabric with a short nap or pile. 3. inflated or turgid language in writing or speaking; bombast; rant; claptrap. —adj. 4. made of fustian. 5. pompous or bombastic, as language. 6. worthless; cheap. [ME, t. OF: m. *fustaigne,* g. LL *fustāneum* (der. L *fustis* cudgel), translation of Gk. *xỹlinon,* der. *xỹlon* wood]

fus·tic (fŭs′tĭk), n. 1. the wood of a large moraceous tree, *Chlorophora tinctoria,* of tropical America, yielding a light-yellow dye. 2. the tree itself. 3. the dye. 4. any of several other dyewoods. [t. F: m. *fustoc,* t. Sp., t. Ar.: m. *fustuq;* akin to Gk. *pistákē* pistachio tree; from Pers.]

fus·ti·gate (fŭs′tə gāt′), v.t., **-gated, -gating.** to cudgel; beat. [t. L: m.s. *fustīgātus,* pp., cudgeled to death] —**fus′ti·ga′tion,** n. —**fus′ti·ga′tor,** n.

fust·y (fŭs′tĭ), adj., **fustier, fustiest.** 1. moldy; musty; having a stale smell; stuffy. 2. old-fashioned; fogyish. 3. stubbornly old-fashioned and out-of-date.

[der. *fust,* n., t. OF: wine cask, log, g. L *fustis* cudgel] —**fust′i·ly,** adv. —**fust′i·ness,** n.

fut., future.

fu·thorc (foo′thôrk), n. the runic alphabet. Also, **fu′thork, fu·tharc** (foo′thärk), **fu′thark.**

fu·tile (fū′təl, -tĭl; *Brit.* fū′tīl), adj. 1. incapable of producing any result; ineffective; useless; not successful. 2. trifling; not important. [t. L: m.s. *fut(t)ilis* untrustworthy, vain, lit., that easily pours out] —**fu′tile·ly,** adv. —**fu′tile·ness,** n. —**Syn.** 1. ineffectual, unavailing, vain, idle, profitless, unprofitable, bootless. See **useless.** 2. trivial, frivolous. —**Ant.** 1. effectual.

fu·til·i·tar·i·an (fū tĭl′ə târ′ĭ ən), adj. 1. believing that human hopes are vain and human strivings unjustified. —n. 2. one who holds this belief. [der. FUTILITY, modeled on UTILITARIAN]

fu·til·i·ty (fū tĭl′ə tĭ), n., pl. **-ties.** 1. quality of being futile; ineffectiveness; uselessness. 2. unimportance. 3. a futile act or event.

fut·tock (fŭt′ək), n. *Naut.* one of the curved timbers which form the middle sections of a compound rib in a ship. [said to be for *foothook*]

futtock plates, *Naut.* iron plates at the top of a lower mast, into which are fastened the upper ends of the futtock shrouds.

futtock shrouds, *Naut.* the short iron rods extending from the futtock plates to an iron band on the mast.

fu·ture (fū′chər), n. 1. time that is to be or come hereafter. 2. what will exist or happen in future time. 3. a future condition, esp. of success or prosperity. 4. *Gram.* a. the future tense. b. another future formation or construction. c. a form therein, as *he will come.* 5. (usually pl.) a speculative purchase or sale of commodities for future receipt or delivery. —adj. 6. that is to be or come hereafter: *future events, at some future day.* 7. pertaining to or connected with time to come: *one's future prospects, future hopes.* 8. *Gram.* designating a tense, or other verb formation or construction, which refers to events or states in time to come. [ME *futur,* t. L: s. *futūrus,* future participle of *esse*]

fu·ture·less (fū′chər lĭs), adj. without a future; having no prospect of future betterment or prosperity.

future life, a form of life which follows mortal death.

future perfect, *Gram.* 1. perfect with respect to a temporal point of reference in the future. 2. designating a tense, or other verb formation or construction, with such meaning. 3. a. the future perfect tense. b. another verb formation or construction with future perfect meaning. c. a form therein, as *he will have come.*

fu·tur·ism (fū′chər ĭz′əm), n. a relatively recent artistic doctrine or movement (orig. Italian) requiring complete abandonment of traditional usage and reconstruction of art and life on the basis of the dynamic, revolutionary, mechanical present and the future.

fu·tur·ist (fū′chər ĭst), adj. 1. of or pertaining to work of futurism. —n. 2. a futurist artist or writer. —**fu′tur·is′tic,** adj.

fu·tu·ri·ty (fū tyŏŏr′ə tĭ, -tŏŏr′-), n., pl. **-ties.** 1. future time. 2. a future state or condition; a future event. 3. quality of being future. 4. a futurity race.

futurity race, *U.S. Racing.* a race, as for horses, for which the entries are nominated long before the running.

futurity stakes, *U.S. Racing.* 1. the stakes in a futurity race. 2. a futurity race.

fuze (fūz), n. 1. a mechanical or electronic device to detonate an explosive charge. 2. fuse¹.

fu·zee (fū zē′), n. fusee.

fuzz (fŭz), n. 1. loose, light, fibrous or fluffy matter. 2. a mass or coating of such matter. [cf. D *voos* spongy]

fuzz·y (fŭz′ĭ), adj., **fuzzier, fuzziest.** 1. of the nature of or resembling fuzz. 2. covered with fuzz. 3. indistinct; blurred. —**fuzz′i·ly,** adv. —**fuzz′i·ness,** n.

f.v., (L *folio verso*) on the back of the page.

fwd., forward.

-fy, a suffix meaning: 1. to make; cause to be; render: *simplify, beautify.* 2. to become; be made: *liquefy.* Also, **-ify.** [t. F: m. s. *-fier,* g. L *-ficāre* do, make]

fyke (fīk), n. a bag-shaped fish trap. [t. D: m. *fuik*]

fyl·fot (fĭl′fŏt), n. swastika. [? var. of *fill-foot* foot filler]

Fyn (fyn), n. an island in S Denmark. 402,335 pop. (est. 1954); 1149 sq. mi. German, **Fünen.**

Fyz·a·bad (fī′zä bäd′), n. a city in N India, in Uttar Pradesh 76,582 (1951).

G

G, g (jē), n., pl. **G's** or **Gs, g's** or **gs.** 1. the 7th letter of the English alphabet. 2. *Music.* a. the fifth tone in the scale of C major or the seventh in the relative minor scale of A minor. b. a printed or written note indicating this tone. c. a string, key, or pipe tuned to this note. d. (in the fixed system of solmization) the 5th tone of the scale, called *sol.* 3. (in medieval Roman numerals) 400.

G, German.

g, 1. *Psychol.* general intelligence. 2. *Physics, etc.* a. (acceleration of) gravity. b. a unit of acceleration equal to 32 ft. per second per second.

---

b., blend of, blended; c., cognate with; d., dialect, dialectal; der., derived from; f., formed from; g., going back to; m., modification of; r., replacing; s., stem of; t., taken from; ?, perhaps. See the full key on inside cover.

G., 1. German. 2. (specific) gravity. 3. Gulf.

g., 1. *Elect.* conductance. 2. gauge. 3. gender. 4. genitive. 5. going back to. 6. gram. 7. *Brit.* guinea.

Ga, *Chem.* gallium.

Ga., Georgia.

G.A., 1. General Agent. 2. General Assembly.

g.a., general average.

gab (găb), *v.,* **gabbed, gabbing,** *n. Collop.* —*v.i.* 1. to talk idly; chatter. —*n.* 2. idle talk; chatter. 3. glib speech: *the gift of gab.* [var. of *gob* mouth, t. Gaelic or Irish]

gab·ar·dine (găb′ər dēn′, găb′ər dēn′), *n.* 1. firm, woven fabric of worsted, cotton, or spun rayon, with steep twill. 2. a man's long, loose cloak or frock, worn in the Middle Ages. Also, **gab′er·dine′.** [t. Sp.: m. *gabardina,* ult. der. MHG *wallevart* pilgrimage]

gab·ble (găb′əl), *v.,* **-bled, -bling,** *n.* —*v.i.* 1. to talk rapidly and unintelligibly; jabber. 2. (of geese, etc.) to cackle. —*v.t.* 3. to utter rapidly and unintelligibly. —*n.* 4. rapid, unintelligible talk. [freq. of GAB] —**gab′·bler,** *n.*

gab·bro (găb′rō), *n., pl.* **-bros.** *Petrog.* a granular igneous rock composed essentially of labradorite and augite. [t. It.]

gab·by (găb′ĭ), *adj.,* **-bier, -biest.** loquacious.

ga·belle (gə bĕl′), *n.* 1. a tax; an excise. 2. (in France before 1790) a tax on salt. [t. F. t. Pr.: m. *gabela,* t. It.: m. *gàbella* tax, t. Ar.: m. (*al-*)*qabāla* the impost]

Ga·bès (gä′bĕs), *n.* Gulf of, a gulf of the Mediterranean on the E coast of Tunisia.

ga·bi·on (gā′bĭ ən), *n.* 1. a cylinder of wickerwork filled with earth, used as a military defense. 2. a cylinder filled w th stones and sunk in water, used in laying the foundations of a dam or jetty. [t. F. t. It.: m. *gabbione,* aug. of *gabbia,* g. L *cavea* cage]

ga·bi·on·ade (gā′bĭ ə nād′), *n.* 1. a work formed of or with gabions. 2. a row of gabions sunk in a stream to control the current. [t. F: m. *gabionnade.* See GABION]

ga·ble (gā′bəl), *n., v.,* **-bled, -bling.** *Archit.* —*n.* 1. the end of a ridged roof cut off at its extremity in a vertical plane, together with the triangular expanse of wall from the level of the eaves to the apex of the roof. 2. a similar end, as of a gambrel roof, not triangular. 3. an architectural member resembling the triangular end of a roof. 4. an end wall. —*v.t.* 5. to build with a gable or gables; form as a gable (chiefly in **gabled,** *pp.*). [ME, prob. t. Scand.; cf. Icel. *gafl.* Cf. also OHG *gabala,* G *gabel* fork] —**ga′ble·like′,** *adj.*

Gables (def. 1)

gable end, (in a gabled building) the triangular wall space between the eaves level and the ridge, or the decorative wall carried up past the ends of a gable roof, and sloped, stepped, or scrolled to follow at a higher level its approximate shape.

gable roof, a ridged roof terminating at one or both ends in a gable.

gable window, 1. a window in or under a gable. 2. a window having its upper part shaped like a gable.

Ga·bon (gä bôN′), *n.* 1. a republic in SW equatorial Africa: independent member of the French Community, formerly part of French Equatorial Africa. 403,000 pop. (est. 1959); 102,290 sq. mi. *Cap.:* Libreville. 2. an estuary in this republic. Also, **Ga·bun** (gä bōōn′).

Ga·bo·riau (gä bŏ ryō′), *n.* Émile (ē mēl′), 1833 or 1835–73, French novelist.

Ga·bri·el (gā′brĭ əl), *n.* one of the archangels, appearing usually as a divine messenger. Dan. 8:16, 9:21. Luke, 1: 19, 26. [t. Heb.: m. *Gabri′ēl* the man of God]

Ga·bri·lo·witsch (gä′brĭ lŭ′vĭch; *Russ.* gä vrĭ′lô′vĭch), *n.* Ossip (ô′sĭp), 1878–1936, Russian pianist and conductor, in America.

ga·by (gā′bĭ), *n., pl.* **-bies.** *Colloq.* a fool. [orig. uncert.]

gad (găd), *v.,* **gadded, gadding,** *n.* —*v.i.* 1. to move restlessly or idly about. —*n.* 2. act of gadding. [? special use of GAD²] —**gad′der,** *n.*

gad² (găd), *n., v.,* **gadded, gadding.** —*n.* 1. a goad for driving cattle. 2. a pointed mining tool for breaking up rock, coal, etc. —*v.t.* 3. to break up with a mining gad. [ME, t. Scand.; cf. Icel. *gaddr* spike]

Gad (găd), *n., interj. Archaic.* a euphemistic form of *God* used as a mild oath. Also, **gad.**

Gad (găd), *n.* 1. son of Jacob by Zilpah. Gen. 30:11, etc. 2. a Hebrew prophet and chronicler ot the court of David. 2 Sam. 24:11–19. 3. one of the twelve tribes of Israel. 4. its territory east of the Jordan.

gad·a·bout (găd′ə bout′), *n. Colloq.* one who gads, esp. for curiosity or gossip.

gad·fly (găd′flī′), *n., pl.* **-flies.** any fly that goads or stings domestic animals, as many voracious, blood-sucking flies of the dipterous family *Tabanidae.* [f. GAD² + FLY]

Gadfly. *Tabanus ruficornis* (Ab. 1 in. long)

gadg·et (găj′ĭt), *n. Colloq.* a mechanical contrivance or device; any ingenious article. [orig. uncert. Cf. F *gâchette*]

Ga·dhel·ic (gə dĕl′ĭk, -dē′lĭk), *adj., n.* Goidelic.

---

ga·did (gā′dĭd), *n.* a fish of the cod family, *Gadidae.* [f. s. NL *gadus* cod + -ID²]

ga·doid (gā′doid), *adj.* 1. belonging to or resembling the *Anacanthini,* an order of soft-finned fishes including the cod, haddock, etc. —*n.* 2. a gadoid fish. [f. s. NL *gadus* cod (t. Gk.: m. *gados* kind of fish) + -OID]

gad·o·lin·ite (găd′ə lĭn′nīt′), *n.* a silicate ore from which the rare-earth metals gadolinium, holmium, and rhenium are extracted. [named after J. *Gadolin* (1760–1852), Finnish chemist. See -ITE¹]

gad·o·lin·i·um (găd′ə lĭn′ĭ əm), *n. Chem.* a rare-earth metallic element. *Symbol:* Gd; *at. wt.:* 156.9; *at. no.:* 64. [f. GADOLIN(ITE) + -IUM]

ga·droon (gə drōōn′), *n.* 1. *Archit.* an elaborately carved or indented convex molding. 2. a decorative series of curved inverted flutings, or of convex and concave flutings, as on silversmith's work. Also, **godroon.** [t. F: m. *godron,* der. *goder* crease, pucker] —**ga·drooned′,** *adj.*

Gads·den (gădz′dən), *n.* 1. **James,** 1788–1858, U.S. railroad promoter and diplomat. 2. a city in NE Alabama. 58,088 (1960).

Gadsden Purchase, The, a tract of 45,535 sq. mi., now contained in New Mexico and Arizona, purchased from Mexico for $10,000,000 in 1853, the treaty being negotiated by James Gadsden.

Gadsden Purchase. 1853

gad·wall (găd′wôl), *n., pl.* **-walls,** (*esp. collectively*) **-wall.** a wild duck, *Anas st epera,* found in temperate parts of the Northern Hemisphere.

Gae·a (jē′ə), *n. Gk. Myth.* earth goddess who bore Oceanus, Cronus, and the Titans. [t. Gk.: m. *Gaia*]

Gaek·war (gīk′wär), *n.* title of the ruler of Baroda. Also, **Gaikwar.** [t. Marathi: lit., cowherd]

Gael (gāl), *n.* 1. a Scottish Celt or Highlander. 2. *Rare.* Irish Celt. [t. Scot. Gaelic: m. *Gaidheal,* O Irish *Gaidel*]

Gael, Gaelic.

Gael·ic (gā′lĭk), *n.* 1. the Celtic language of ancient Ireland and any of the languages that developed from it (Irish, Scotch Gaelic, and Manx). 2. Goidelic. —*adj.* 3. of or pertaining to the Gaels or their language.

gaff¹ (găf), *n.* 1. a strong hook with a handle, used for landing large fish. 2. a metal spur for a gamecock. 3. **stand the gaff,** *U.S. Slang.* to endure hardship or strain. 4. *Naut.* the spar extending the upper edge of a fore-and-aft sail. —*v.t.* 5. to hook or land with a gaff. [ME *gaffe,* t. OF: boat hook, prob. of Celtic orig.]

G. Gaff (def. 4)

gaff² (găf), *n. Brit. Slang.* a cheap place of amusement. [? orig., a place of outcry or humbug, special use of d. *gaff* loud, rude talk (OE *gaf* in *gafspræc* foolish speech, scurrility)]

gaf·fer (găf′ər), *n. Brit.* 1. a rustic title or term for an old man. 2. an overseer or foreman. [var. of late ME *godfar* (contracted form of GODFATHER)]

gaff-top·sail (găf′tŏp′sāl′; *Naut.* -səl), *n. Naut.* a light triangular sail above a gaff, which extends its foot.

gag¹ (găg), *v.,* **gagged, gagging,** *n.* —*v.t.* 1. to stop up the mouth so as to prevent sound or speech. 2. to restrain by force or authority from freedom of speech. 3. to fasten open the jaws of, as in surgical operations. 4. to cause to heave with nausea. —*v.i.* 5. to heave with nausea. —*n.* 6. something thrust into the mouth to prevent speech. 7. any violent or authoritative suppression of freedom of speech. 8. a surgical instrument for holding the jaws open. [prob. imit. of the sound made in choking] —**gag′ger,** *n.*

gag² (găg), *v.,* **gagged, gagging,** *n.* —*v.t. Slang.* 1. to introduce interpolations into (an actor's stage part) (fol. by *up*). 2. to deceive; hoax. —*v.i. Slang.* 3. to introduce interpolations or gags in acting. 4. to play on one's credulity by false stories, etc. —*n.* 5. *U.S. Colloq.* a joke; an interpolation introduced by an actor into his part. **b.** any contrived piece of wordplay or horseplay. [cf. Icel. *gagg* yelp] —**gag′ger,** *n.*

gage¹ (gāj), *n., v.,* **gaged, gaging.** —*n.* 1. something, as a glove, thrown down in token of challenge to combat. 2. a challenge. 3. a pledge or pawn; security. —*v.t.* 4. *Archaic.* to pledge, stake, or wager. [ME, t. OF: pledge, security; of Gmc. orig. Cf. WAGE]

gage² (gāj), *n., v.,* **gaged, gaging.** gauge. —*v.t.* gauge.

gage³ (gāj), *n.* any of several plums, varieties of *Prunus domestica.* [short for GREENGAGE]

Gage (gāj), *n.* **Thomas,** 1721–87, British general in America, 1763–76.

gag·gle (găg′əl), *v.,* **-gled, -gling,** *n.* —*v.i.* 1. to cackle. —*n.* 2. a flock of geese. 3. a cackle. [imit.]

gag·root (găg′rōōt′, -rŏŏt′), *n.* a plant, *Lobelia inflata,* with emetic properties; Indian tobacco.

gahn·ite (gä′nīt), *n.* a dark-green to black mineral of the spinel group, zinc aluminate, $ZnAl_2O_4$. [named after J. G. *Gahn* (1745–1818), Swed. chemist. See -ITE¹]

ăct, āble, dâre, ärt; ĕbb, ēqual; ĭf, īce; hŏt, ōver, ôrder, oil, bŏŏk, ōōze, out; ŭp, ūse, ûrge; ə = a in alone; ch, chief; g, give; ng, ring; sh, shoe; th, thin; ᵺ, that; zh, vision. See the full key on inside cover.

gai·e·ty (gā´ə tĭ), *n.*, *pl.* **-ties.** **1.** state of being gay or cheerful; gay spirits. **2.** (*often pl.*) merrymaking or festivity: *the gaieties of the New Year season.* **3.** showiness; finery: *gaiety of dress.* Also, **gayety.** [t. F: m. *gaieté, gaîté,* der. *gai* GAY] **—Syn. 1.** merriment, mirth, glee, jollity, joyousness, liveliness, sportiveness, hilarity, vivacity. **—Ant. 1.** sadness.

Gaik·war (gīk´wär), *n.* Gaekwar.

Gail·lard Cut (gĭl yärd´, gä´lärd), an artificial defile excavated for the Panama Canal, 10 mi. NW of the city of Panama. ab. 8 mi. long. Formerly, *Culebra Cut.*

gail·lar·di·a (gə lär´dĭ ə), *n.* any plant of the American composite genus *Gaillardia,* several species of which are cultivated for their showy flowers. [NL: named after M. *Gaillard* de Marentonneau]

gai·ly (gā´lĭ), *adv.* **1.** merrily. **2.** showily. Also, **gayly.**

gain[1] (gān), *v.t.* **1.** to obtain; secure (something desired); acquire: *gain time.* **2.** to win; get in competition: *gain the prize.* **3.** to acquire as an increase or addition: *to gain weight, speed, etc.* **4.** to obtain as a profit: *he gained ten dollars by this deal.* **5.** to reach by effort; get to; arrive at: *to gain a good harbor.* **—v.i. 6.** to improve; make progress; advance. **7.** to get nearer, as in pursuit (fol. by *on* or *upon*). **—n. 8.** profit; advantage. **9.** (*pl.*) profits; winnings. **10.** an increase or advance. **11.** act of gaining; acquisition. **12.** the volume of sound emanating from a radio, phonograph, etc. [t. F: m. *gagner,* of Gmc. orig.] **gain´a·ble,** *adj.* **—Syn. 1.** GAIN, ATTAIN, EARN, WIN imply obtaining a reward or something advantageous. GAIN carries the least suggestion of method or of effort expended. ATTAIN emphasizes the reaching of a goal. EARN emphasizes the exertions and labor expended which deserve reward. WIN emphasizes attainment in spite of competition or opposition. **10.** addition, increment, acquisition. **—Ant. 1.** lose.

gain[2] (gān), *n.* **1.** a notch or dado cut across the edge of a board, usually made to support a cross board. **—v.t. 2.** to make a gain or gains in. [? akin to obs. *gane,* OE *ganian,* c. Icel. *gana* gape]

gain·er (gā´nər), *n.* **1.** one who or that which gains. **2.** a type of dive in which the diver takes off facing forward, and jumps upward and backward to enter the water facing the board.

Gaines·ville (gānz´vĭl), *n.* a city in N Florida. 29,701 (1960).

gain·ful (gān´fəl), *adj.* profitable; lucrative. **—gain´ful·ly,** *adv.* **—gain´ful·ness,** *n.*

gain·ly (gān´lĭ), *adj. Obs.* or *Dial.* agile; handsome. [der. *gain,* obs. adj., t. Scand.; cf. Icel. *gegn* straight, favorable, c. OE *gegn-,* in *gegnum,* adv., straight on, *gegnunga,* adv., directly] **—gain´li·ness,** *n.*

gain·say (gān´sā´), *v.t.,* **-said, -saying. 1.** to deny. **2.** to speak or act against. [f. gain- against + SAY]

Gains·bor·ough (gānz´bûr´ō; *Brit.* -bərə), *n.* **Thomas,** 1727–88, British painter, esp. of portraits and landscapes.

'gainst (gĕnst *or, esp. Brit.,* gänst), *prep., conj.* against. Also, **gainst.**

gait (gāt), *n.* **1.** the manner of walking or stepping, esp. of a horse, as the walk, trot, canter, gallop, single-foot, etc. **—v.t. 2.** to teach a uniform gait to. [Scot. and N Eng. sp. of GATE in various senses, incl. those above]

gait·ed (gā´tĭd), *adj.* having a specified gait: *slow-gaited, heavy-gaited oxen.*

gai·ter (gā´tər), *n.* **1.** a covering of cloth, leather, etc., for the ankle and instep, and sometimes also the lower leg, worn over the shoe, etc. **2.** a cloth or leather shoe with elastic insertions at the sides. [t. F: m. *guêtre*]

Ga·ius (gā´əs), *n.* A.D. c110–c180, Roman jurist.

gal (găl), *n. Slang.* girl.

Gal., Galatians.

gal., gallon; gallons.

ga·la (gā´lə, gäl´ə; *Brit.* gä´lə), *adj.* **1.** festive; festal; showy: *his visits were always gala occasions.* **—n. 2.** a celebration; festive occasion. **3.** festal pomp or dress. [t. F, t. It.: festal pomp, finery, t. OF: m. *gale* joy, pleasure, t. MD: m. *wale* riches]

ga·lac·ta·gogue (gə lăk´tə gŏg´, -gŏg´), *adj.* **1.** increasing the amount of milk collected, either with or without increasing the amount secreted. **—n. 2.** a galactagogue agent or medicine. [f. Gk.: m. *galakt-* milk (s. *gála*) + m.s.-*agōgós* bringing]

ga·lac·tic (gə lăk´tĭk), *adj. Astron.* pertaining to the Galaxy or Milky Way. [t. Gk.: m.s. *galaktikós* milky]

galactic circle, *Astron.* that great circle which most nearly coincides with the middle of the Milky Way.

galactic latitude. See latitude (def. 3).

galactic poles, the two opposite points of the heavens situated at 90° from the galactic circle.

ga·lac·to·poi·et·ic (gə lăk´tə poi ĕt´ĭk), *adj.* **1.** increasing the secretion of milk, though not necessarily the amount collected. **—n. 2.** a galactopoietic agent or medicine. [f. Gk.: m. *galakto-* milk (comb. form of *gála*) + m.s. *poiētikós* making]

ga·lac·tose (gə lăk´tōs), *n. Chem.* a hexose sugar, $C_6H_{12}O_6$, either levorotatory or dextrorotatory, the latter being derived from milk sugar by hydrolysis. [f. m.s. Gk. *gála* milk + OSE[2]]

Gal·a·had (găl´ə hăd´), *n.* **Sir, 1.** *Arthurian Romance.* the noblest and purest knight of the Round Table, son of Lancelot and Elaine and fated to retrieve the Holy Grail. **2.** a man of ideal purity of heart and life.

ga·lan·gal (gə lăng´gəl), *n.* the aromatic, medicinal rhizome of certain plants of the ginger family, esp. *Alpinia officinarum,* of China and the East Indies. [see GALINGALE]

Ga·lá·pa·gos Islands (gə lä´pə gŏs´; *Sp.* gä lä´pä gōs´), an archipelago on the equator in the Pacific, ab. 600 mi. W of and belonging to Ecuador: many unique species of animal life. 1346 (1950); 3029 sq. mi. Ecuadorian, **Archipélago de Colon.**

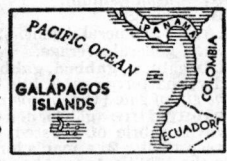

gal·a·te·a (găl´ə tē´ə), *n.* a strong striped cotton fabric used for clothing. [from the name of a British man-of-war]

Gal·a·te·a (găl´ə tē´ə), *n. Gk. Legend.* an ivory statue of a maiden, brought to life by Aphrodite in response to the prayers of the sculptor, Pygmalion, who had fallen in love with his work.

Ga·la·ţi (gä läts´), *n.* a city in E Rumania: a port on the Danube, 80,411 (1948). Also, **Ga·latz** (gä´läts).

Ga·la·tia (gə lā´shə, -shĭ ə), *n.* an ancient country in central Asia Minor: later a Roman province. **—Ga·la´tian,** *adj., n.*

Ga·la·tians (gə lā´shənz), *n. pl.* the book of the New Testament called in full "The Epistle of Paul the Apostle to the Galatians."

gal·a·vant (găl´ə vănt´), *v.i.* gallivant.

ga·lax (gā´lăks), *n.* an evergreen herb, *Galax aphylla,* of southeastern U.S., with small white flowers. [NL, der. Gk. *gála* milk; so called from the white flowers]

gal·ax·y (găl´ək sĭ), *n., pl.* **-axies. 1.** *Astron.* **a.** (*usually cap.*) the Milky Way. **b.** any galactic system including those outside of the Milky Way. **2.** any brilliant or splendid assemblage. [ME *galaxye,* t. ML: m. *galaxia,* var. of *galaxias,* t. Gk., der. *gála* milk]

Gal·ba (găl´bə), *n.* **Servius Sulpicius** (sûr´vĭ əs sŭl pĭsh´əs), 5? B.C.–A.D. 69, Roman emperor, A.D. 68–69.

gal·ba·num (găl´bə nəm), *n.* a gum resin with a peculiar disagreeable odor, obtained from certain Asiatic plants of the apiaceous genus *Ferula:* used in medicine and the arts. [t. L (Vulgate); answering to Gk. *chalbánē* (Septuagint), rendering Heb. *ḥelbĕnāh*]

gale[1] (gāl), *n.* **1.** a strong wind. **2.** *Meteorol.* a wind with a velocity between about 30 and about 65 miles per hour. **3.** *Colloq.* a noisy outburst: *a gale of laughter.* **4.** *Poetic.* a gentle breeze. [orig. uncert.]

gale[2] (gāl), *n.* a shrub, *Myrica gale,* with a pleasant aromatic odor, growing in marshy places; sweet gale. [ME *gayl,* OE *gagel,* c. D and G *gagel*]

Gale (gāl), *n.* **Zona** (zō´nə), 1874–1938, U.S. novelist.

ga·le·a (gā´lĭ ə), *n., pl.* **-leae** (-lĭ ē´). *Bot.* any part of the calyx or corolla in the form of a helmet, as the upper lip of the corolla of the monkshood. [t. L: helmet]

ga·le·ate (gā´lĭ āt´), *adj. Bot.* having a galea. Also, **ga/le·at/ed.**

ga·le·i·form (gə lē´ə fôrm´), *adj.* helmet-shaped; resembling a galea. [f. s. L *galea* helmet + -(i)FORM]

Ga·len (gā´lən), *n.* **1.** **Claudius** (klô´dĭ əs), A.D. c130–c200, Greek physician and writer on medicine. **2.** (in humorous use) a physician.

ga·le·na (gə lē´nə), *n.* a very common heavy (sp. gr. 7.6) mineral, lead sulfide, PbS, occurring in lead-gray crystals, usually cubes, and cleavable masses: the principal ore of lead. Also, **ga·le·nite** (gə lē´nīt). [t. L: lead ore]

Ga·len·ic (gā lĕn´ĭk, -lē´nĭk), *adj.* of or pertaining to Galen, or his principles, or his methods.

Ga·len·ism (gā´lə nĭz´əm), *n.* the medical system or principles of Galen. **—Ga´len·ist,** *n.*

Gales·burg (gālz´bûrg), *n.* a city in NW Illinois. 37,243 (1960).

Ga·li·cia (gə lĭsh´ə, -lĭsh´ĭ ə), *n.* **1.** a former crown land of Austria, included in S Poland after World War I, and now partly in the Soviet Union. ab. 30,500 sq. mi. **2.** a maritime region in NW Spain: a former kingdom, and later a province. 11,256 sq. mi. **—Ga·li´cian,** *adj., n.*

Gal·i·le·an (găl´ə lē´ən), *adj.* **1.** of or pertaining to Galilee. **—n. 2.** a native or inhabitant of Galilee. **3.** a Christian. **4. the Galilean,** Jesus. [f. GALILE(E) + · AN]

Gal·i·le·an (găl´ə lē´ən), *adj.* of or pertaining to Galileo: *the Galilean telescope.* [f. GALILE(O) + -AN]

Gal·i·lee (găl´ə lē´), *n.* **1.** an ancient Roman province in what is now N Israel. **2. Sea of,** a lake in NE Israel through which the river Jordan flows. 14 mi. long; 682 ft. below sea level. Also, **Sea of Tiberias.**

gal·i·lee (găl´ə lē´), *n.* a porch or vestibule, often on the ground floor of a tower, at the entrance of some English churches. [t. MF, t. ML: m.s. *galilaea,* a galilee, orig. (L) the province of Galilee; said to refer to the "Galilee of the Gentiles" in Matt. 4:15]

Gal·i·le·o (găl´ə lē´ō; *It.* gä´lē lĕ´ō), *n.* (*Galileo Galilei*) 1564–1642, Italian physicist and astronomer.

gal·i·ma·ti·as (găl´ə mā´shĭ əs, -măt´ĭ əs), *n.* confused or unintelligible talk; gibberish. [t. F: m. *Galli* term

---

b., blend of, blended; c., cognate with; d., dialect, dialectal; der., derived from; f., formed from; g., going back to; m., modification of; r., replacing; s., stem of; t., taken from; ?, perhaps.   See the full key on inside cover.

applied to doctoral candidates + m. Gk. *-matheia* knowledge, a humorous 16th cent. formation]

gal·in·gale (găl/ĭngāl/). *n.* any sedge of the genus *Cyperus*, esp. *C. longus*, an English plant with aromatic roots. [ME, t. OF: m. *galingal*, t. Ar.: m. *khalanjān*, said to be (through Pers.) from Chinese *Ko-liang-kiang*, lit., wild ginger from Ko, a prefecture in Canton province]

gal·i·ot (găl/Yət). *n.* a small galley propelled by both sails and oars. Also, **galliot**. [ME *galiote*, t. OF, dim. of *galie* GALLEY]

gal·i·pot (găl/əpŏt/). *n.* a kind of turpentine exuded on the stems of certain species of pine. Also, **gallipot**. [t. F, earlier *garipot* resin. prob. t. D: m. *harpuis*, c. MLG *harpois* boiled and skimmed resin]

gall¹ (gôl), *n.* 1. something very bitter or severe. 2. bitterness of spirit; rancor. 3. bile, esp. that of the ox. 4. *Anat.* gall bladder. 5. *U.S. Slang.* impudence; effrontery. [ME; d. OE *galla*, r. OE *gealla*, c. G *galle*; akin to L *fel*, Gk. *cholē* gall, bile]

gall² (gôl), *v.t.* 1. to make sore by rubbing; chafe severely. 2. to vex; irritate: *galled by sarcasm.* —*v.i.* 3. to be or become chafed. —*n.* 4. a sore on the skin, esp. of a horse, due to rubbing; excoriation. 5. something irritating. 6. a state of irritation. [special use of GALL¹]

gall³ (gôl), *n.* any abnormal vegetable growth or excrescence on plants, caused by various agents, including insects, nematodes, fungi, bacteria, viruses, chemicals, and mechanical injuries. [ME *galle*, t. F, g. L *galla* the oak apple]

gal·lant (*adj.* găl/ənt for 1–3; gəlănt/, găl/ənt *for* 4, 5; *n.* găl/ənt, gəlănt/), *adj.* 1. brave, high-spirited, or chivalrous. 2. stately: *a gallant sight.* 3. gay or showy, as in dress. 4. polite and attentive to women; courtly. 5. amorous. —*n.* 6. a man of spirit or mettle. 7. a gay and dashing man. 8. a man particularly attentive to women. 9. a suitor or lover. 10. a paramour. [ME *galaunt*, t. OF: m. *galant*, der. *gale* GALA] —**gal/lant·ly,** *adv.* —**gal/lant·ness,** *n.* —**Syn.** 1. valiant, courageous, heroic. See **brave.** —**Ant.** 1. cowardly, craven.

gal·lant·ry (găl/əntrY), *n., pl.* -**ries.** 1. dashing courage; heroic bravery. 2. gallant or courtly attention to women. 3. a gallant action or speech. —**Syn.** 1. bravery, valor, heroism. 2. chivalry, courtliness.

Gal·la·tin (găl/ətYn), *n.* **Albert,** 1761–1849, U.S. statesman, Secretary of the Treasury, 1801–13.

gall bladder, *Anat.* a vesicle attached to the liver which receives bile from the hepatic ducts, concentrates it, and discharges it after meals. See diag. under **stomach.**

Galle (găl), *n.* a seaport in SW Ceylon. 55,874 (1953).

gal·le·ass (găl/Yăs/), *n.* a large war galley formerly used in the Mediterranean, generally with three masts and rowed by slaves. Also, **galliass.** [t. MF: m. *galeace,* t. It.: m. *galeazza,* aug. of *galea* GALLEY]

gal·le·on (găl/Yən, găl/yən), *n.* a kind of large sailing vessel formerly used by the Spaniards and others. [t. Sp.: m. *galeón,* aug. of *galea* GALLEY]

gal·ler·y (găl/ərY, găl/rY). *n., pl.* -**leries.** 1. a covered walk or promenade. 2. *Southern U.S.* a piazza or portico; veranda. 3. a long narrow apartment; corridor. 4. a raised platform or passageway along the outside or inside of the wall of a building; balcony. 5. a platform projecting from the interior walls of a church, theater, etc., to provide seats or room for a part of the audience. 6. the highest of such platforms in a theater. 7. the occupants of such a platform in a theater. 8. any body of spectators or auditors, as the spectators of a golf match. 9. a room, series of rooms, or building devoted to the exhibition of works of art. 10. a collection of art for exhibition. 11. a room or building in which to take pictures, practice shooting, etc. 12. *Naut.* a balconylike structure or platform at the stern or quarters of old ships. 13. a passageway made by an animal. 14. *Fort.* an underground or covered passage to another part of a fortified position or to a mine. 15. *Mining.* a level or drift. [t. It.: m.s. *galleria,* t. ML: m. *galilaea* GALILEE]

gal·ley (găl/Y), *n., pl.* -**leys.** 1. an early sea-going vessel propelled by oars or by oars and sails. 2. a large rowboat. 3. the kitchen of a ship. 4. *Print.* **a.** a long, narrow tray, usually of metal, for holding type which has been set. **b.** galley proof. **c.** a rough unit of measurement for type composition (about 22 inches). [ME *galeie,* t. ML: m. *galeia,* t. LGk.: m. *galata*]

galley proof, *Print.* proof from type on a galley.

galley slave, 1. a person condemned to work at the oar on a galley. 2. an overworked person; drudge.

galley west, *U.S. Colloq.* out completely: *knock galley west.* [alter. of d. *collywest* (Brit.)]

gall·fly (gôl/flī/), *n., pl.* -**flies.** a gall wasp.

gal·liard (găl/yərd), *n.* 1. a spirited dance for two dancers in triple rhythm, common in the 16th and 17th centuries. —*adj.* 2. *Archaic.* lively or gay. [ME, t. OF, prob. der. Celtic *galli-* might, ability]

gal·li·ass (găl/Yăs/), *n.* galleass.

Gal·lic (găl/Yk), *adj.* 1. pertaining to the Gauls or Gaul. 2. pertaining to the French or France. [t. L: s. *Gallicus,* der. *Gallus* a Gaul]

gal·lic¹ (găl/Yk), *adj.* *Chem.* of or containing gallium, esp. in the trivalent state (Ga+3). [f. GALL(IUM) + -IC]

gal·lic² (găl/Yk), *adj.* pertaining to or derived from plant galls: *gallic acid.* [f. GALL³ + -IC]

gallic acid, *Chem.* an acid, $C_6H_2(OH)_3CO_2H$, a white or yellowish crystalline powder found in nutgalls, mangoes, and other plants.

Gal·li·can (găl/əkən), *adj.* 1. Gallic. 2. *Eccles.* **a.** pertaining to the Roman Catholic Church in France. **b.** pertaining to a school or party of French Roman Catholics, before 1870, advocating restricting papal authority in favor of the authority of general councils, the bishops, and temporal rulers.

Gal·li·can·ism (găl/əkənYz/əm), *n.* *Eccles.* a religious opinion peculiar to France opposing the Papal authority in favor of that of the bishops and the temporal order.

Gallican liberties, parliamentary form of Gallicanism which augmented the rights of the state to the prejudice of the church.

Gal·li·ce (găl/əsY), *adv.* in French. [ML]

Gal·li·cism (găl/əsYz/əm), *n.* 1. a French linguistic peculiarity. 2. a French idiom or expression used in another language. Also, **gal/li·cism.**

Gal·li·cize (găl/əsīz/), *v.t., v.i.,* -**cized,** -**cizing.** to make or become French in language, character, etc. Also, **gal/li·cize/.**

Gal·li-Cur·ci (găl/Ykûr/chY; *It.* găl/lēkŏŏr/chē), *n.* **Amelita** (ä/mělē/tä), 1889–1963, Italian soprano in the U.S.

gal·li·gas·kins (găl/əgăs/kYnz), *n.pl.* 1. a kind of loose hose or breeches worn in the 16th and 17th centuries. 2. loose breeches in general. 3. leggings or gaiters of leather. [appar. alter. of F *garguesque,* metathetic var. of *greguesque,* t. It.: m. *grechesa,* from *alla grechesa* in the Greek manner]

gal·li·mau·fry (găl/Ymô/frY), *n., pl.* -**fries.** 1. a hodgepodge; jumble; confused medley. 2. a ragout or hash. [t. F: m. *galimafree,* orig. unknown]

gal·li·na·cean (găl/ənā/shən), *n.* 1. a gallinaceous bird. —*adj.* 2. gallinaceous.

gal·li·na·ceous (găl/ənā/shəs), *adj.* 1. pertaining to or resembling the domestic fowls. 2. belonging to the group or order *Galliformes,* which includes the domestic fowls, pheasants, grouse, partridges, etc. [t. L: m.s. *gallīnāceus* pertaining to poultry]

Gal·li·nas (gä yē/näs), *n.* **Punta** (pōōn/tä), a cape in NE Colombia: northernmost point of South America.

gall·ing (gô/lYng), *adj.* that galls; chafing; irritating; exasperating. —**gall/ing·ly,** *adv.*

gal·li·nip·per (găl/ənYp/ər), *n.* a large American mosquito, *Psorophora ciliata.* [orig. uncert.]

gal·li·nule (găl/ənūl/, -nŏōl/), *n.* any of certain long-toed aquatic birds of the rail family, as the **Florida gallinule,** *Gallinula chloropus cachinnans,* and the European moor hen, *G. c. chloropus.* [t. NL: m.s. *Gallīnula,* the typical genus (LL: chicken), dim. of L *gallīna* hen]

gal·li·ot (găl/Yət), *n.* galiot.

Gal·lip·o·li Peninsula (gə lYp/əlī), a peninsula in European Turkey between the Dardanelles and the Aegean: the scene of a disastrous British naval and land campaign, 1915–16. ab. 60 mi. long.

gal·li·pot¹ (găl/əpŏt/), *n.* a small glazed pot used by druggists for medicines, etc. [? f. GALLEY + POT¹ (as if brought or imported in galleys)]

gal·li·pot² (găl/əpŏt/), *n.* galipot.

gal·li·um (găl/Yəm), *n.* *Chem.* a rare, bluish-white, easily fusible trivalent metallic element, used in high temperature thermometers on account of its high boiling point (1700°C.) and low melting point (30°C.). *Sym.* Ga; *at. wt.:* 69.72; *at. no.:* 31; *sp. gr.:* 5.91 at 20°C. [NL, said to be der. L *gallus* cock, trans. of F *coq,* from the name of the discoverer, *Lecoq* de Boisbaudran]

gal·li·vant (găl/əvănt/), *v.i.* to gad gaily or frivolously. Also, **galavant.** [? humorous alter. of GALLANT]

gall midge, any small fly of the family *Cecidomyidae* which makes galls on plants.

gall·nut (gôl/nŭt/), *n.* a nutlike gall on plants.

Gallo-, a word element meaning "Gallic." [t. L, comb. form of *Gallus* a Gaul]

gal·lon (găl/ən), *n.* a common unit of capacity (= 4 quarts) in English-speaking countries, the U.S. standard gallon being equal to 231 cu. in. (3.7853 liters), and the British imperial gallon 277.42 cu. in. (4.546 liters). [ME *galun,* t. ONF, ult. der. Gallic *galla* vessel, bowl]

gal·loon (gəlōōn/), *n.* a braid or trimming of worsted, silk or rayon tinsel, gold or silver, etc. [t. F: m. *galon,* der. *galonner* trim with *galloon,* orig. adorn (the head or hair) with bands or ribbons, der. OF *gale* GALA]

gal·loot (gəlōōt/), *n.* *U.S. Slang.* galoot.

gal·lop (găl/əp), *v.i.* 1. to ride a horse at a gallop; ride at full speed. 2. to run rapidly by leaps, as a horse; go at a gallop. 3. to go fast, race, or hurry, as a person, the tongue, time, etc. —*v.t.* 4. to cause (a horse, etc.) to gallop. —*n.* 5. a fast gait of the horse (or other quadruped) in which in the course of each stride all four feet are off the ground at once. 6. a run or ride at this gait. 7. a rapid rate of going, or a course of going at this rate. [t. F: m.s. *galoper,* t. OLG: m. *wala hlōpan* run well] —**gal/lop·er,** *n.*

gal·lo·pade (găl/əpād/), *n.* 1. a sprightly kind of dance. 2. the music for it. [t. F: m. *galopade,* der. *galoper* GALLOP]

Gallo-Rom., Gallo-Romance.

Gal·lo-Ro·mance (găl/ō rō măns/), *n.* the vernacular language, a development from Latin, spoken in France from about A.D. 600–900.

gal·ious (găl/əs), *adj. Chem.* containing divalent gallium (Ga+²).

Gal·lo·way (găl/ə wā/), *n.* **1.** a region in SW Scotland, comprising the counties of Wigtown and Kircudbright. **2.** one of a breed of beef cattle originating in this region, with a coat of curly black hair. **3.** one of a breed of small strong horses first raised in Galloway, Scotland.

gal·lows (găl/ōz, -əz), *n., pl.* **-lowses, -lows. 1.** a wooden frame, consisting of a cross beam on two uprights, on which condemned persons are executed by hanging. **2.** a similar structure, as for suspending something or for gymnastic exercise. [ME *galwes*, OE *galgan*, pl. of *g(e)alga* gallows, c. G *galgen*]

gallows bird, *Colloq.* one who deserves to be hanged.

gallows bitts, *Naut.* a frame on the deck of a ship for supporting spare topmasts, etc.

gall·stone (gôl/stōn/), *n. Pathol.* a calculus or stone formed in the bile or gall passages.

Gal·lup (găl/əp), *n.* **George Horace**, born 1901, U.S. statistician.

gal·lus·es (găl/əs ĭz), *n.pl. Chiefly Dial.* suspenders for trousers.

gall wasp, an insect of the hymenopterous family *Cynipidae*, whose larvae cause galls on plants.

ga·loot (gə lōōt/), *n. U.S. Slang.* an awkward, silly fellow. Also, **galloot.**

gal·op (găl/əp), *n.* **1.** a lively round dance in duple time. **2.** music for, or in the rhythm of, this dance. [t. F]

ga·lore (gə lōr/), *adv.* **1.** in abundance. —*n.* **2.** *Obs. or Rare.* abundance. [t. Irish: m. *go leōr* (Gaelic *guleōr*) to sufficiency]

ga·losh (gə lŏsh/), *n.* (*usually pl.*) an overshoe or rubber. Also, **ga·loshe/, golosh.** [ME *galoche*, t. F, prob. g. L *gallicula* Gallic (sandal), b. *gallica* Gallic and *caligula* soldier's boot]

gals., gallons.

Gals·wor·thy (gôlz/wûr/thĭ, gălz/-), *n.* **John**, 1867–1933, British novelist, dramatist, and short-story writer.

Gal·ton (gôl/tən), *n.* **Sir Francis**, 1822–1911, British scientist and writer. —**Gal·to·ni·an** (gôl tō/nĭ ən), *adj.*

Gal·va·ni (gäl vä/nē), *n.* **Luigi** (lōō ē/jē), 1737–98, an Italian physiologist whose experiments led to the discovery that electricity may result from chemical action.

gal·van·ic (găl văn/ĭk), *adj.* **1.** pertaining to or produced by galvanism; producing or caused by an electric current. **2.** affecting or affected as if by galvanism. [f. GALVAN(I) + -IC] —**gal·van/i·cal·ly,** *adv.*

galvanic battery, a voltaic battery.

galvanic cell, *Elect.* an electrolytic cell capable of producing electric energy by electrochemical action.

gal·va·nism (găl/və nĭz/əm), *n.* **1.** *Elect.* electricity, esp. as produced by chemical action. **2.** *Med.* the therapeutic application of electricity to the body.

gal·va·nize (găl/və nīz/), *v.t.* **-nized, -nizing. 1.** to stimulate by or as by a galvanic current. **2.** to startle into sudden activity. **3.** to coat (metal, esp. iron or steel) with zinc. Also, *esp. Brit.,* **gal/va·nise/.** —**gal/va·ni·za/tion,** *n.* —**gal/va·niz/er,** *n.*

galvanized iron, iron coated with zinc to prevent rust.

galvano-, a combining form representing **galvanic, galvanism,** as in *galvanocautery.*

gal·va·no·cau·ter·y (găl/və nō kô/tər ĭ, găl văn/ō-), *n., pl.* **-teries.** *Med.* **1.** a cautery heated by a galvanic current. **2.** cauterization by such means.

gal·va·nom·e·ter (găl/və nŏm/ə tər), *n.* an instrument for detecting the existence and determining the strength and direction of an electric current.

gal·va·nom·e·try (găl/və nŏm/ə trĭ), *n.* art or process of determining the strength of electric currents. —**gal·va·no·met·ric** (găl/və nō mĕt/rĭk, găl văn/ō-), *adj.*

gal·va·no·plas·tic (găl/və nō plăs/tĭk, găl văn/ō-), *adj.* pertaining to reproduction by electrotypy.

gal·va·no·plas·ty (găl/və nō plăs/tĭ, găl văn/ō-), *n.* electrotypy. Also, **gal/va·no·plas/tics.**

gal·va·no·scope (găl/və nə skōp/, găl văn/ə-), *n.* an instrument for detecting the existence and determining the direction of an electric current. —**gal·va·no·scop·ic** (găl/və nə skōp/ĭk, găl văn/ə-), *adj.*

gal·va·not·ro·pism (găl/və nŏt/rə pĭz/əm), *n. Bot.* the movements in growing organs induced by the passage of electric currents.

Gal·ves·ton (găl/vəs tən), *n.* a seaport in SE Texas, on an island at the mouth of **Galveston Bay**, an inlet of the Gulf of Mexico. 67,175 (1960).

Gal·way (gôl/wā), *n.* **1.** a county in W Ireland, in Connaught, 155,441 (prelim. 1956); 2293 sq. mi. **2.** its county seat: a seaport. 21,316 (1951).

gam (găm), *n.* **1.** (in whalers' speech) a herd or school of whales. **2.** *U.S. Local.* a social meeting, visit, or the like, as between vessels at sea. [var. of GAME¹]

Ga·ma (găm/ə; *Port.* gä/mə), *n.* **Vasco da** (väs/kō də; *Port.* väsh/kŏō), c1469–1524, Portuguese navigator and discoverer of the sea route from Portugal around the continent of Africa to India.

ga·ma grass (gä/mə), a tall, stout grass, *Tripsacum dactyloides,* one of the largest grasses in the U.S.

gam·ba·do (găm bā/dō), *n., pl.* **-dos, -does. 1.** one of a pair of large protective boots or gaiters fixed to a saddle instead of stirrups. **2.** any long gaiter or legging. [f. It. *gamba* leg + suffix *-ado.* See GAMBOL]

gam·be·son (găm/bə sən), *n.* a medieval military garment of linen, padded, and worn under mail, but also worn as the principal garment of defense. [ME *gambisoune,* t. OF: m. *gambison,* of Gmc. orig.]

Gam·bet·ta (găm bĕt/ə; *Fr.* găⁿ bĕ tä/), *n.* **Léon** (lĕ ōⁿ/), 1838–82, French statesman.

Gam·bi·a (găm/bĭ ə), *n.* **1.** a large river in W Africa, flowing W to the Atlantic. ab. 500 mi. **2.** an independent state extending inland along both sides of this river: member of the Brit. Commonwealth; formerly a British colony. 290,000 pop. (est. 1954); 4003 sq. mi. *Cap.:* Bathurst.

gam·bier (găm/bĭr), *n.* an astringent extract obtained from the leaves and young shoots of *Uncaria Gambir,* a tropical Asiatic rubiaceous shrub: used in medicine, dyeing, tanning, etc. [t. Malay: m. *gambir*]

gam·bit (găm/bĭt), *n. Chess.* an opening in which the player seeks by sacrificing a pawn or piece to obtain some advantage. [t. F, t. Pr.: m. *cambi* an exchange]

gam·ble (găm/bəl), *v.,* **-bled, -bling,** *n.* —*v.i.* **1.** to play at any game of chance for stakes. **2.** to stake or risk money, or anything of value, on the outcome of something involving chance: *gamble on the result of a race.* —*v.t.* **3.** to lose or squander by betting (usually fol. by *away*). —*n.* **4.** *Colloq.* any matter or thing involving risk or uncertainty. **5.** *Colloq.* a venture in or as in gambling. [?. d. var. of ME *gamenen,* OE *gamenian* to sport, play] —**gam/bler,** *n.* —**gam/bling,** *n.*

gam·boge (găm bōj/, -bōōzh/), *n.* **1.** Also, **cambogia.** a gum resin from various trees of the genus *Garcinia,* esp. *G. Hanburyi,* of Cambodia, Siam, etc.: used as a yellow pigment and as a cathartic. **2.** yellow or yellow orange. [t. NL: m.s. *gambogium,* der. *Camboja, Cambodia,* in Indochina]

gam·bol (găm/bəl), *v.,* **-boled, -boling** or (*esp. Brit.*) **-bolled, -bolling,** *n.* —*v.i.* **1.** to skip about, as in dancing or playing; frolic. —*n.* **2.** a skipping or frisking about; frolic. [earlier *gambald,* t. F: m. *gambade* a leap, t. It.: m. *gambata* a kick, der. *gamba* leg]

gam·brel (găm/brəl), *n.* the hock of an animal, esp. of a horse. [t. OF (Norman): m. **gamberel* butcher's gambrel, der. *gambe,* g. LL *gamba* hoof, leg]

gambrel roof, a roof whose ends are cut off in a vertical plane, and whose sides have two slopes (likened to a horse's gambrel), the lower one being the steeper. See diag. under **roof.** —**gam/brel-roofed/,** *adj.*

Gam·bri·nus (găm brī/nəs), *n.* mythical Flemish king, reputed inventor of beer.

game¹ (gām), *n., adj., gamer, gamest, v., gamed, gaming.* —*n.* **1.** an amusement or pastime: *children's games.* **2.** the apparatus employed in playing any of certain games: *a store selling toys and games.* **3.** a contest for amusement in the form of a trial of chance, skill, or endurance, according to set rules: *games of golf, etc.* **4.** a single contest at play, or a definite portion of play in a particular game: *a rubber of three games at bridge.* **5.** the number of points required to win a game. **6.** a particular manner or style of playing a game. **7.** a proceeding carried on like a game: *the game of diplomacy.* **8.** a trick; strategy: *to see through someone's game.* **9.** fun; sport of any kind; joke: *to make game of a person.* **10.** wild animals, including birds and fishes, such as are hunted or taken for sport or profit. **11.** the flesh of wild animals or game, used for food. **12.** any object of pursuit or attack; prey. **13.** fighting spirit; pluck. —*adj.* **14.** pertaining to animals hunted or taken as game. **15.** having the fighting spirit of a gamecock; plucky: *a game sportsman.* **16.** *Colloq.* having the spirit or will (fol. by *for* or an infinitive): *game to play.* —*v.i.* **17.** to play games of chance for stakes; gamble. —*v.t.* **18.** to squander in gaming (fol. by *away*). [ME; OE *gamen,* c. OHG *gaman* glee] —**game/ly,** *adv.* —**game/ness,** *n.* —**Syn.** **1.** sport, contest; diversion. See **play.** **8.** scheme, artifice, stratagem. **10.** prey, quarry.

game² (gām), *adj. Colloq.* lame: *a game leg.* [orig. uncert.]

game bird, a bird hunted for sport or profit, or protected by law.

game·cock (gām/kŏk/), *n.* a cock bred and trained for fighting, or one of a fighting breed.

game fish, an edible fish capable of affording sport to the angler in its capture.

game fowl, 1. a fowl of any species regarded as game or the object of hunting. **2.** a domestic fowl of a breed much used for fighting.

game·keep·er (gām/kē/pər), *n. Chiefly Brit.* a person employed, as on an estate, to take care of game, prevent poaching, etc.

game law, a law enacted for the preservation of game, as by restricting open seasons and the manner of taking.

game·some (gām/səm), *adj.* full of play; frolicsome. —**game/some·ly,** *adv.* —**game/some·ness,** *n.*

game·ster (gām/stər), *n.* a person who gambles habitually; gambler. [f. GAME¹ + -STER]

gam·e·tan·gi·um (găm/ə tăn/jĭ əm), *n., pl.* **-gia** (-jĭ ə). *Bot.* an organ or body producing gametes. [NL, f. Gk.: s. *gametē* wife, *gametēs* husband, + m. *angeion* vessel]

gam·ete (găm/ēt, gə mēt/), *n. Biol.* either of the two germ cells which unite to form a new organism; a mature reproductive cell. [t. NL: m.s. *gameta,* t. Gk.: m.

gametĕ wife or m. *gametĕs* husband] —**ga·met·ic** (gə-mĕt′ĭk), *adj.*

gam·e·to·gen·e·sis (găm′ə tō jĕn′ə sĭs), *n.* Biol. the development of gametes.

ga·me·to·phore (gə mē′tə fōr′), *n.* Bot. a part or structure producing gametes.

ga·me·to·phyte (gə mē′tə fīt′), *n.* Bot. the sexual form of a plant in the alternation of generations (opposed to *sporophyte*).

game warden, an official who enforces game laws.

gam·ic (găm′ĭk), *adj.* Biol. sexual (opposed to *agamic*). [t. Gk.: m.s. *gamikós* of or for marriage]

gam·in (găm′ĭn; *Fr* gȧ măn′), *n.* a neglected boy left to run about the streets; street Arab [t. F; orig. uncert.]

gam·ing (gā′mĭng), *n.* gambling.

gam·ma (găm′ə), *n.* 1. the third letter (Γ, γ. = English G, g) of the Greek alphabet. 2. the third of any series (used esp. in scientific classification). 3. a unit of weight equal to one microgram.

gam·ma·di·on (gə mā′dĭ ŏn), *n.*, *pl.* **-dia** (-dĭ ə) an ornamental figure consisting of combinations of the Greek capital gamma, esp. in the form of a swastika or fylfot, or of a voided Greek cross. [t. MGk., var. of *gammátion*, dim. of Gk. *gámma* gamma]

gamma globulin, a protein component of blood plasma containing antibodies effective against certain microörganisms, as in measles, infectious hepatitis, and poliomyelitis.

gamma rays, Physics. rays similar to x-rays, but of higher frequency and penetrating power, forming part of the radiation of radioactive substance.

gam·mer (găm′ər), *n.* Brit. an old woman. [var. of late ME *godmor* (contr. of GODMOTHER)]

gam·mon¹ (găm′ən). *n.* 1. the game of backgammon. 2. Backgammon. a victory in which the winner throws off all his men before his opponent throws off any. —*v.t.* 3. Backgammon. to win a gammon over. [? special use of ME and OE *gamen*. See GAME¹]

gam·mon² (găm′ən). *n.* 1. a smoked or cured ham. 2. the lower end of a side of bacon. [ME *gambon*, t. ONF: ham, der. *gambe* hoof, leg, g. LL *gamba*]

gam·mon³ (găm′ən), Brit. Colloq. —*n.* 1. deceitful nonsense; bosh. —*v.i.* 2. to talk gammon. 3. to make pretense. —*v.t.* 4. to humbug. [see GAMMON¹]

gam·mon⁴ (găm′ən), *v.t.* Naut. to fasten (a bowsprit) to the stem of a ship. [? akin to GAMMON²]

gamo-, Biol. a word element meaning "sexual union." [comb. form repr. Gk. *gámos* marriage]

gam·o·gen·e·sis (găm′ə jĕn′ə sĭs), *n.* Biol. sexual reproduction. —**gam·o·ge·net·ic** (găm′ō jə nĕt′ĭk), *adj.* —**gam·o·ge·net′i·cal·ly,** *adv.*

gam·o·pet·al·ous (găm′ə pĕt′əl əs), *adj.* Bot. having the petals united.

gam·o·phyl·lous (găm′ə fĭl′əs), *adj.* Bot. having leaves united by their edges.

gam·o·sep·al·ous (găm′ə sĕp′əl əs), *adj.* Bot. having the sepals united. See illus. under **calyx.**

-gamous, an adjectival word element corresponding to the noun element **-gamy,** as in *polygamous.* [t. Gk.: m. *-gamos* marrying]

Gamopetalous flower

gamp (gămp), *n.* Chiefly Brit. (in humorous use) an umbrella. [said to be from the umbrella of Mrs. Sarah *Gamp* in Dickens' "Martin Chuzzlewit"]

gam·ut (găm′ət), *n.* 1. the whole scale or range. 2. Music. **a.** the whole series of recognized musical notes. **b.** the major scale. [t. ML: contr. of *gamma ut,* f. *gamma,* used to represent the first or lowest tone (G) in the medieval scale + *ut* (later *do*); the notes of the scale being named from a L hymn to St. John: *Ut queant laxis resonare fibris, Mira gestorum famuli tuorum, Solve polluti labi reatum, Sancte Iohannes.* See GUIDO D'AREZZO]

gam·y (gā′mĭ), *adj.,* **gamier, gamiest.** 1. having the flavor of game, esp. game kept uncooked until slightly tainted, as preferred by connoisseurs: *the meat had a gamy flavor.* 2. plucky. —**gam′i·ly,** *adv.* —**gam′i·ness,** *n.*

-gamy, 1. a word element meaning "marriage," as in *polygamy.* 2. Biol. a word element meaning "sexual union," as in *allogamy.* [t. Gk.: m.s. *-gamía,* der. *-gamos* marrying, married]

gan (găn), *v.* Archaic and Poetic. began.

Gand (gän), *n.* French name of Ghent.

gan·der (găn′dər), *n.* the male of the goose. [ME; OE *gan(d)ra,* c. MLG *ganre,* D *gander,* g. Vernerian var. of Gmc. *gans-* goose]

Gan·der (găn′dər), *n.* an airport in NE Newfoundland: used by transatlantic aircraft as a fuel stop.

Gan·dhi (gän′dē), *n.* **Mohandas Karamchand** (mō′-hən däs′ kür′əm chŭnd′), (*Mahatma Gandhi*) 1869–1948, Hindu religious and political leader and social reformer.

Gand·zha (gänd′zhä), *n.* former name of Kirovabad.

gang¹ (găng), *n.* 1. a band or group: *a gang of boys.* 2. a group of persons working together; squad; shift: *a gang of laborers.* 3. a group of persons associated for a particular purpose (used esp. in a contemptuous sense of disreputable persons): *a gang of thieves.* 4. a set of tools, etc., arranged to work together or simultaneously. [ME and OE; orig. "a going"; sense of "group" from OE *gang* in *gangdæg* processional day] —*v.t.* 5. to arrange in gangs; form into a gang. 6. Colloq.

to attack in a gang. —*v.i.* 7. Colloq. to form or act as a gang (often fol. by *up*): *to gang up on Sam and Ned.* 8. Brit. Dial. to walk; go. [ME *gong(e), gang(en).* OE *gongan, gangan,* c. OHG *gangan*] —**Syn.** 1. company, crowd, crew.

gang² (găng), *n.* gangue.

gang cultivator, a cultivator having several shares or shovels mounted to be operated as a gang.

Gan·ges (găn′jēz), *n.* a river flowing from the Himalayas in N India SE to the Bay of Bengal: sacred to the Hindus. ab. 1500 mi.

gang hook, Angling. a hook made by joining back-to-back the shanks of two or three hooks.

gan·gli·a (găng′glĭ ə), *n.* pl. of **ganglion.**

gan·gli·at·ed (găng′glĭ ā′tĭd), *adj.* having ganglia. Also, **gan·gli·ate** (găng′glĭ ĭt, -āt′).

gan·gling (găng′glĭng), *adj.* awkwardly tall and spindly; lank and loosely built. Also, **gan′gly.** [akin to obs. *gangrel* gangling person, der. GANG¹]

gan·gli·on (găng′glĭ ən), *n.*, *pl.* **-glia** (-glĭ ə), **-glions.** 1. Anat. gray matter outside the brain and spinal cord. 2. Pathol. a cyst or enlargement in connection with the sheath of a tendon, usually at the wrist. 3. a center of intellectual or industrial force, activity, etc. [t. LL: kind of swelling, t. Gk.: tumor under the skin, on or near a tendon] —**gan·gli·on·ic** (găng′glĭ ŏn′ĭk), *adj.*

gan·gli·on·ec·to·my (găng′glĭ ə nĕk′tə mĭ), *n.,* *pl.* **-mies.** Surg. the excision of a ganglion.

gang·plank (găng′plăngk′), *n.* a plank, often with cleats, or a long, narrow, flat structure, used as a temporary bridge in passing into and out of a ship, etc.

gang plow, 1. a plow with several bottoms. 2. a combination of plows in one frame.

gan·grene (găng′grēn, găng grēn′), *n.,* *v.,* **-grened, -grening.** Pathol. —*n.* 1. the dying of tissue, as from interruption of circulation; mortification. —*v.t.,* *v.i.* 2. to affect or become affected with gangrene. [t. L: m.s. *gangraena,* t. Gk.: m. *gángraina* an eating sore] —**gan·gre·nous** (găng′grə nəs), *adj.*

gang·ster (găng′stər), *n.* Colloq. a member of a gang of criminals.

gangue (găng), *n.* the stony or earthy minerals occurring with the metallic ore in a vein or deposit. Also, **gang.** [t. F, t. G: m. *gang* mineral vein, lode]

gang·way (găng′wā′), *n.* 1. a passageway. 2. Naut. **a.** any of various passageways on a ship, as that between the rail and the cabins or houses on the deck. **b.** an opening or removable section of a ship's rail for the gangplank. **c.** a platform and ladder or stairway slung over the side of a ship. 3. Brit. **a.** an aisle in a theater, restaurant, etc. **b.** an aisle in Parliament separating the responsible members of the parties from the younger or uncertain members. 4. Mining. a main passage or level. 5. the ramp up which logs are moved into a sawmill. —*interj.* 6. Chiefly Naut. clear the way! [OE *gangweg*]

Gan·is (găn′ĭs), *n.* **Bors de.** See Bors (def. 1).

gan·is·ter (găn′ĭs tər), *n.* a highly refractory, siliceous rock, used to line furnaces, sometimes artificially made by mixing ground quartz with a bonding material. [orig. uncert.]

gan·net (găn′ĭt), *n.* any of several large totipalmate pelagic birds of the family *Sulidae,* which includes the boobies; esp., the common gannet, *Moris bassana,* of the Atlantic coasts of North America and Europe. [ME and OE *ganet,* akin to D *gent* gander]

gan·oid (găn′oid), *adj.* 1. belonging or pertaining to the *Ganoidei,* a composite and artificial grouping of fishes, many of which have hard, smooth scales, as the sturgeons, etc. 2. (of fish scales) having a smooth, shining surface. [f. s. Gk. *gános* brightness + -OID]

gant·let¹ (gänt′lĭt, gônt′-), *n.* 1. a former punishment, chiefly military, in which the offender ran between two rows of men who struck at him with switches or other weapons as he passed: *to run the gantlet.* 2. an attack from both or all sides; trying conditions. 3. a section of two-way railroad track, as through a tunnel or over a bridge, in which the inner rails overlap, so as to narrow the roadbed without switching to a single track. —*v.t.* 4. to lay down as a gantlet: *to gauntlet tracks.* Also, **gauntlet.** [earlier *gantlope,* t. Sw.: m. *gatlopp,* lit., lane run, f. *gata* way, lane + *lopp* a running course]

Gantlet (def. 3)

gant·let² (gänt′lĭt, gônt′-), *n.* gauntlet¹.

gant·line (gänt′lĭn′), *n.* Naut. a rope temporarily made fast or rove through a block, as for hoisting rigging, raising a man to the rigging, etc. [alter. of *girtline*]

gan·try (găn′trĭ), *n.,* *pl.* **-tries.** 1. a spanning framework, as a bridgelike portion of certain cranes. 2. a frame supporting a barrel or cask. Also, **gauntry.** [f. *gaun* (contr. of GALLON) + m. *-tree* supporting frame]

Gan·y·mede (găn′ə mēd′), *n.* 1. Class. Myth. a Trojan youth carried off (according to one legend, by an eagle) to become cupbearer to Zeus. 2. (in humorous use) a young waiter. 3. Astron. one of the satellites of Jupiter.

ăct, āble, dâre, ärt; ĕbb, ēqual; ĭf, īce; hŏt, ōver, ôrder, oil, bŏŏk, ōōze, out; ŭp, ūse, ûrge; ə = a in alone; ch, chief; g, give; ng, ring; sh, shoe; th, thin; ŧħ, that; zh, vision.   See the full key on inside cover.

gaol (jāl), *n.*, *v.t.* *Brit.* jail. [ME *gay(h)ole*, *gaile*, t. ONF: m. *gaiole*, *gaole*, ult. der. L *cavea* cavity, cage] —**gaol′er**, *n.*

gap (găp), *n.*, *v.*, **gapped, gapping.** —*n.* **1.** a break or opening, as in a fence, wall, or the like; breach. **2.** a vacant space or interval. **3.** a wide divergence. **4.** a deep, sloping ravine or cleft cutting a mountain ridge. **5.** *Aeron.* the distance between one supporting plane of an airplane and another above or below it. —*v.t.* **6.** to make a gap, opening, or breach in. [ME, t. Scand.; cf. Sw. *gap* opening chasm, *gapa* GAPE] —**gap′less**, *adj.*

gape (gāp, găp), *v.*, **gaped, gaping,** *n.* —*v.i.* **1.** to open the mouth involuntarily or as the result of hunger, sleepiness, or absorbed attention. **2.** to stare with open mouth, as in wonder. **3.** to open as a gap; split or become open wide. —*n.* **4.** a breach or rent; wide opening. **5.** act of gaping. **6.** a stare, as with open mouth. **7.** astonishment. **8.** *Zool.* the width of the open mouth. [ME *gapen*, t. Scand.; cf. Icel. and Sw. *gapa* open the mouth, c. G *gaffen*] —**gap′er**, *n.* —**gap′ing·ly**, *adv.* —**Syn.** **2.** See **gaze.**

gapes (gāps, găps), *n.pl.* **1.** a disease of poultry and other birds, attended with frequent gaping, due to infestation of the trachea and bronchi with gapeworms. **2.** a fit of yawning.

gape·worm (gāp′wûrm′, găp′-), *n.* a nematode worm, *Syngamus trachea,* which causes gapes.

gar (gär), *n.*, *pl.* **gars,** (*esp. collectively*) **gar.** **1.** a predaceous fish of the genus *Lepisosteus* (including several species, all of North American fresh waters), covered with very hard diamond-shaped ganoid scales and having a beak armed with large teeth. **2.** needlefish (def. 1). [short for GARFISH]

G.A.R., Grand Army of the Republic.

ga·rage (gəräzh′, -räj′ *or*, *esp. Brit.*, găr′Yj), *n.*, *v.*, **-raged, -raging.** —*n.* **1.** a building for sheltering, cleaning, or repairing motor vehicles. —*v.t.* **2.** to put or keep in a garage. [t. F, der. *garer* put in shelter. t. Pr.: m. *garar* keep, heed, t. Gmc.; cf. OHG *warôn* heed]

Gar·a·mond (găr′əmŏnd′), *n.* a kind of type designed in 1540 by Claude Garamond, French type founder.

Gar·and rifle (găr′ənd, gərănd′), a semiautomatic, gas-operated, clip-fed rifle, having a caliber of .30 inch and weighing 8.56 pounds. It is standard in the U. S. Army.

garb (gärb), *n.* **1.** fashion or mode of dress, esp. of a distinctive kind. **2.** clothes. **3.** covering, semblance, or form. —*v.t.* **4.** to dress; clothe. [t. F: m. *garbe*, t. It., m. *garbo* grace, t. Gmc.; cf. MHG *garwe* GEAR] —**Syn.** **2.** dress, costume, attire, apparel, habiliments, garments.

gar·bage (gär′bYj), *n.* **1.** refuse animal and vegetable matter from a kitchen. **2.** any foul refuse; vile or worthless matter. [ME; prob. der. Rom. root *garb*- mess]

gar·ble (gär′bəl), *v.*, **-bled, -bling,** *n.* —*v.t.* **1.** to make unfair or misleading selections from (facts, statements, writings, etc.); corrupt: *a garbled account.* **2.** *Rare.* to take out the best of. —*n.* **3.** the process of garbling. [t. It.: m. *garbellare*, t. Ar.: m. *gharbala* sift, ? t. LL: m. *crêbellâre*, der. *cêrbellum* little sieve] —**gar′bler**, *n.*

gar·board (gär′bôrd′), *n.* *Shipbuilding.* the strake of planks laid next to the keel. Also, **garboard strake.** [t. D: m. *gaarboord*]

Gar·cí·a Lor·ca (gär sē′ä lôr′kä), Federico (fĕ′dĕ rē′kō), 1899–1936, Spanish poet, dramatist, essayist and theatrical director.

gar·çon (gär sôn′), *n.*, *pl.* **-çons** (-sôn′). *French.* **1.** a boy; young unmarried man. **2.** a male employee or servant. **3.** a waiter, esp. at a public table.

Gar·da (gär′dä), *n.* **Lago di** (lä′gō dē), a lake in N Italy: largest of Italian lakes. 35 mi. long; 143 sq. mi.

gar·den (gär′dən), *n.* **1.** a plot of ground devoted to the cultivation of useful or ornamental plants. **2.** a piece of ground, or other space, commonly with ornamental plants, trees, etc., used as a place of public resort: *a botanical garden, a roof garden.* **3.** a fertile and delightful spot or region. —*adj.* **4.** pertaining to or produced in a garden. —*v.i.* **5.** to lay out or cultivate a garden. —*v.t.* **6.** to cultivate as a garden. [ME *gardin*, t. ONF, of Gmc. orig.; cf. G *garten*] —**gar′den·like′**, *adj.*

Gar·den (gär′dən), *n.* **Mary,** born 1877, U.S. soprano.

garden cress. See **peppergrass.**

gar·den·er (gärd′nər), *n.* **1.** a person employed to take care of a garden. **2.** one who gardens.

gar·de·nia (gär dē′nyə, -nY ə), *n.* any of the evergreen trees and shrubs of the rubiaceous genus *Gardenia,* native in the warmer parts of the Eastern Hemisphere, including species, as *G. jasminoides,* the Cape jasmine, cultivated for their fragrant, waxlike, white flowers. [NL; named after Dr. Alexander *Garden* (1730–91)]

gar·den·ing (gärd′nYng), *n.* **1.** act of cultivating a garden. **2.** the work or art of a gardener.

garden warbler, any of various small birds esteemed in Italy as a table delicacy, as the warblers of the family *Sylviidae,* esp. *Sylvia hortensis.*

Gar·di·ner (gär′dY nər, gärd′nər), *n.* **Samuel Rawson,** 1829–1902, British historian.

Gard·ner (gärd′nər), *n.* a city in N Massachusetts. 19,038 (1960).

Gar·eth (găr′Yth), *n.* *Arthurian Romance.* nephew of King Arthur.

Gar·field (gär′fēld), *n.* **1.** **James Abram** (ā′brəm), 1831–81, twentieth president of the United States, in 1881. **2.** a city in NE New Jersey. 29,253 (1960).

gar·fish (gär′fYsh′), *n.*, *pl.* **-fishes,** (*esp. collectively*) **-fish. gar.** [ME *garfysshe*, f. *gar* (OE *gār* spear) + *fysshe* FISH]

gar·ga·ney (gär′gənY), *n.* a small Old World species of duck, *Anas querquedula.* [erroneous var. of It. *garganello*, der. Rom. root *garg*- throat]

Gar·gan·tu·a (gär găn′chōō ə), *n.* the amiable giant and king, of enormous capacity for eating and drinking, in Rabelais' *Gargantua and Pantagruel.*

Gar·gan·tu·an (gär găn′chōō ən), *adj.* gigantic; enormous; prodigious.

gar·get (gär′gYt), *n.* *Vet. Sci.* inflammation of the udder of cows, etc., caused by bacteria; mastitis. [ME, t. OF: m. *gargate* throat, der. Rom. root *garg*-]

gar·gle (gär′gəl), *v.*, **-gled, -gling,** *n.* —*v.t.* **1.** to wash or rinse (the throat or mouth) with a liquid held in the throat and kept in motion by a stream of air from the lungs. —*v.i.* **2.** to gargle the throat or mouth. —*n.* **3.** any liquid used for gargling. [t. F: m. *gargouiller*, der. *gargouille* throat. Cf. L *gurgulio* gullet]

gar·goyle (gär′goil), *n.* a spout, often terminating in a grotesque head (animal or human) with open mouth, projecting from the gutter of a building for carrying off rain water. [ME *gargulye*, t. OF: m. *gargouille*, *gargoule*, appar. the same word as *gargouille* throat. See GARGLE]

Gargoyle, 13th century

Gar·i·bal·di (găr′ə bôl′dY; *It.* gä′rē bäl′dē), *n.* **Giuseppe** (jōō sĕp′pĕ), 1807–82, Italian patriot and general. —**Gar·i·bal′di·an**, *adj.*

gar·i·bal·di (găr′ə bôl′dY), *n.* a loose waist worn by women and children in mid-19th century, made in imitation of the red shirts worn by the soldiers of Garibaldi.

gar·ish (gâr′Ysh), *adj.* **1.** glaring, or excessively bright. **2.** crudely gay or showy, as dress, etc. **3.** excessively ornate, as structures, writings, etc. [earlier *gaurish*, der. obs. *gaure* stare, freq. of ME *gawe* stare] —**gar′ish·ly**, *adv.* —**gar′ish·ness**, *n.* —**Syn.** **2.** See **gaudy**[1].

gar·land (gär′lənd), *n.* **1.** a wreath or string of flowers, leaves, or other material, worn for ornament or as an honor, or hung on something as a decoration. **2.** a representation of such a wreath or festoon. **3.** a collection of short literary pieces, usually poems and ballads; a miscellany. **4.** *Naut.* a band, collar, or grommet, as of rope, for various purposes. —*v.t.* **5.** to crown with a garland; deck with garlands. [ME *garlande*, t. OF]

Gar·land (gär′lənd), *n.* **Hamlin** (hăm′lYn), 1860–1940, U.S. novelist, short-story writer, and poet.

gar·lic (gär′lYk), *n.* **1.** a hardy liliaceous plant, *Allium sativum,* whose strong-scented, pungent bulb is used in cookery and medicine. **2.** any of various other species of the same genus. **3.** the bulb of any such plant. [ME *garlec*, OE *gārlēac*, f. *gār* spear + *lēac* leek]

gar·lick·y (gär′lYk′Y), *adj.* like or containing garlic.

gar·ment (gär′mənt), *n.* **1.** any article of clothing. **2.** outer covering; outward appearance. —*v.t.* **3.** to clothe. [ME, t. OF: m. *garnement*, der. *garnir* equip. See GARNISH] —**gar′ment·less,** *adj.*

gar·ner (gär′nər), *v.t.* **1.** to collect or deposit in or as in a garner; hoard. [v. use of GARNER, n.] —*n.* **2.** a granary. **3.** a store of anything. [ME, t. OF: m. *gernier, grenier,* g. L *grānārium* GRANARY]

Gar·ner (gär′nər), *n.* **John Nance,** born 1869, vice-president of the United States, 1933–41.

gar·net[1] (gär′nYt), *n.* **1.** any of a group of hard, vitreous minerals, silicates of calcium, magnesium, iron, or manganese with aluminum or iron, varying in color. A deep-red transparent variety is used as a gem and as an abrasive (**garnet paper**). **2.** deep red, as of a garnet. [ME *gernet,* t. OF: m. *grenat,* t. ML: m. s. *grānâtum* garnet, also pomegranate, prop. neut. of *grānātus* having grains or seeds] —**gar′net·like′,** *adj.*

gar·net[2] (gär′nYt), *n.* *Naut.* a form of hoisting tackle. [orig. uncert. Cf. D *granaat*]

gar·ni·er·ite (gär′nY ə rīt′), *n.* a mineral, hydrous nickel magnesium silicate, occurring in earthy, green masses: an important ore of nickel. [named after Jules *Garnier,* French geologist. See -ITE[1]]

gar·nish (gär′nYsh), *v.t.* **1.** to fit out with something that adorns or decorates. **2.** to decorate (a dish) for the table. **3.** *Law.* **a.** to warn; give notice. **b.** to summon in, so as to take part in litigation already pending between others. **c.** to attach, as money due or property belonging to a debtor, while it is in the hands of a third person, by warning the latter not to pay it over or surrender it. —*n.* **4.** something placed around or added to a dish for decorative effect or relish. **5.** adornment or decoration. [ME *garnisshe(n),* t. OF: m. *garniss-,* s. *garnir* prepare, WARN; of Gmc. orig.] —**gar′nish·er,** *n.* —**Syn.** **1.** embellish, ornament, beautify, trim.

gar·nish·ee (gär′nY shē′), *v.*, **-nisheed, -nisheeing,** *n.* *Law.* —*v.t.* **1.** to attach (money or property) by garnishment. **2.** to make (a person) a garnishee. —*n.* **3.** a person served with a garnishment.

gar·nish·ment (gär′nYsh mənt), *n.* **1.** adornment; decoration. **2.** *Law.* **a.** a warning or notice. **b.** a summons to appear in litigation pending between others; **c.** a warning served on a person, at the suit of a creditor plaintiff, to hold, subject to the court's direction, money or property of the defendant in his possession.

---

b., blend of, blended; c., cognate with; d., dialect, dialectal; der., derived from; f., formed from; g., going back to; m., modification of; r., replacing; s., stem of; t., taken from; ?, perhaps. See the full key on inside cover.

gar·ni·ture (gär′nĭ chər), *n.* anything that garnishes; decoration; adornment. [t. F, der. *garnir*. See GARNISH]

Ga·ronne (gȧ rôn′), *n.* a river in SW France, flowing from the Pyrenees NW to the Gironde. ab. 350 mi.

ga·rote (gə rōt′, -rŏt′), *n.*, *v.t.*, **-roted, -roting.** garrote. Also, **ga·rotte′.**

gar pike, a gar.

gar·ret (găr′ĭt), *n.* attic (def. 1). [ME *garite*, t. OF: watchtower, der. *garir* defend. See GARRISON]

gar·ret·eer (găr′ə tǐr′), *n.* a person living in a garret, esp. a literary hack.

Gar·rick (găr′ĭk), *n.* **David,** 1717–79, British actor and theatrical manager.

gar·ri·son (găr′ə sən), *n.* **1.** a body of troops stationed in a fortified place. **2.** the place where they are stationed. —*v.t.* **3.** to provide (a fort, town, etc.) with a garrison. **4.** to occupy (a fort, post, station, etc.). **5.** to put on duty in a fort, post, station, etc. [ME *garison*, t. OF: defense, der. *garir* defend, of Gmc. orig.]

Gar·ri·son (găr′ə sən), *n.* **William Lloyd,** 1805–79, U.S. leader in the abolition movement.

garrison cap, U.S. military dress headgear of felt, or woolen or cotton cloth, with leather visor.

gar·rot (găr′ət), *n.* the goldeneye (duck). [t. F]

gar·rote (gə rōt′, -rŏt′), *n.*, *v.*, **-roted, -roting.** —*n.* **1.** a Spanish mode of capital punishment, orig. by means of an instrument causing death by strangulation, later by one injuring the spinal column at the base of the brain. **2.** the instrument used. **3.** strangulation or throttling, esp. for the purpose of robbery. —*v.t.* **4.** to execute by the garrote. **5.** to throttle, esp. for the purpose of robbery. Also, **garote, garotte, gar·rotte′.** [t. Sp.: orig. a stick (formerly used in drawing cord tight), t. Pr.: m. *garrot* cudgel, stick for tightening the cord about a pack, der. Celtic *garra* leg] —**gar·rot′er,** *n.*

gar·ru·li·ty (gə rōō′lə tĭ), *n.* the quality of being garrulous; talkativeness; loquacity.

gar·ru·lous (găr′ə ləs, -yə ləs), *adj.* **1.** given to much talking, esp. about trifles. **2.** wordy or diffuse, as speech. [t. L: m. *garrulus* talkative] —**gar′ru·lous·ly,** *adv.* —**gar′ru·lous·ness,** *n.* —Syn. **1.** See talkative.

gar·ter (gär′tər), *n.* **1.** a fastening, often in the form of a band passing round the leg, to keep up the stocking. **2.** *Brit.* the badge of the **Order of the Garter,** the highest order of knighthood. **3.** *Brit.* membership in the order. **4.** (*cap.*) *Brit.* the order itself. —*v.t.* **5.** to fasten with a garter. [ME, t. ONF: m. *gartier*, der. *garet* the bend of the knee, der. Celtic *garra* leg]

garter snake, any of various harmless snakes of the genus *Thamnophis,* usually with three light stripes on body and tail.

garth (gärth), *n.* **1.** the open court enclosed by a cloister (in full, **cloister garth**). **2.** *Archaic.* or *Dial.* a yard or garden. [ME, t. Scand.; cf. Icel. *gardhr,* c. YARD²]

Gar·y (gâr′ĭ), *n.* **1.** a city in NW Indiana: a port on Lake Michigan. 178,320 (1960). **2. Elbert Henry,** 1846–1927, U.S. financier.

gas (găs), *n., pl.* **gases,** *v.,* **gassed, gassing.** —*n.* **1.** *Physics.* a substance possessing perfect molecular mobility and the property of indefinite expansion. **2.** any such fluid or mixture of fluids except air, as laughing gas, or some combustible fluid burned for illumination and heating. **3.** *U.S. Colloq.* gasoline. **4.** *Coal Mining.* an explosive mixture of firedamp with air. **5.** an aeriform fluid, or a mistlike assemblage of fine particles suspended in air, used in warfare to asphyxiate, poison, or stupefy the enemy. **6.** *Slang.* empty talk. —*v.t.* **7.** to supply with gas. **8.** to affect, overcome, or asphyxiate with gas or fumes. **9.** to singe (yarns or fabrics) with a gas flame to remove superfluous fibers. **10.** to treat or impregnate with gas. **11.** *Slang.* to talk nonsense or falsehood to. —*v.i.* **12.** to give off gas, as a storage battery being charged. **13.** *Slang.* to indulge in empty talk idly. [coined by J. B. van Helmont, (1577–1644), Flemish chemist; suggested by Gk. *cháos* chaos] —**gas′less,** *adj*

gas attack, an attack in which asphyxiating or poisonous gases are employed, as by liberating the gases. and allowing the wind to carry the fumes, or by gas shells.

gas·bag (găs′băg′), *n.* **1.** a bag for holding gas, as in a balloon or dirigible, or for the use of dentists. **2.** *Slang.* an empty, voluble talker; a windbag.

gas black, the soot of a natural gas flame, used in paints; fine carbon.

gas burner, the tip, jet, or endpiece of a gas fixture, from which the gas issues to be ignited.

Gas·con (găs′kən), *n.* **1.** a native of Gascony, the inhabitants of which were noted for their boastfulness. **2.** (*l.c.*) a boaster or braggart. —*adj.* **3.** pertaining to Gascony and its people. [t. F, g. s. L *Vasco* Basque]

gas·con·ade (găs′kə nād′), *n., v.,* **-aded, -ading.** —*n.* **1.** extravagant boasting; boastful talk. —*v.i.* **2.** to boast extravagantly; bluster. [t. F: m. *gasconnade,* der. *gascon* GASCON]

Gas·co·ny (găs′kə nĭ), *n.* a former province in SW France. French, **Gas·cogne** (gȧs kôn′y).

gas engine, an internal-combustion engine operated by illuminating gas, natural gas, or other gas from without.

gas·e·ous (găs′ĭ əs), *adj.* having the nature of, in the form of, or pertaining to gas. —**gas′e·ous·ness,** *n.*

gas fitter, one whose business is the fitting up of buildings with apparatus for the use of gas.

gas fitting, 1. the work or business of a gas fitter. **2.** (*pl.*) fittings for the employment of gas for illuminating and heating purposes.

gas fixture, a permanent fixture attached to a gas pipe in the ceiling or wall of a room, as a more or less ornamental pipe (without or with branches) bearing a burner (or burners) and regulating devices.

gas gangrene, a gangrenous infection developing in wounds, esp. deep wounds with closed spaces, due to bacteria which form gases in the subcutaneous tissues.

gash (găsh), *n.* **1.** a long, deep wound or cut, esp. in the flesh; a slash. —*v.t.* **2.** to make a long, deep cut in; slash. [earlier *garsh,* t. ONF: m.s. *garser* scarify]

gas helmet, *Mil.* a type of gas mask.

gas·i·form (găs′ə fôrm′), *adj.* gaseous.

gas·i·fy (găs′ə fī′), *v.t., v.i.,* **-fied, -fying.** to convert into or become a gas. —**gas′i·fi·ca′tion,** *n.*

Gas·kell (găs′kəl), *n.* **Mrs.,** (*Elizabeth Cleghorn Stevenson Gaskell*) 1810–65, British novelist.

gas·ket (găs′kĭt), *n.* **1.** anything used as a packing, as a rubber or metal ring or disk. **2.** *Naut.* one of several bands or lines used to bind a furled sail to a yard, etc. [orig. uncert. Cf. It. *gassetta* gasket]

gas·light (găs′līt′), *n.* **1.** light produced by the combustion of illuminating gas. **2.** a gas burner.

gas mask, a masklike device worn to protect against noxious gases, fumes, etc., as in warfare or in certain industries, the air inhaled by the wearer being filtered through charcoal and chemicals.

gas meter, an apparatus for measuring and recording the amount of gas produced or consumed.

gas·o·line (găs′ə lēn′, găs′ə lēn′), *n.* a volatile, inflammable, liquid mixture of hydrocarbons, obtained in the distillation of petroleum, and used as a solvent, as fuel for internal-combustion engines, etc. Also, **gas′o·lene′.** [f. GAS + -OL² + -INE²]

gas·om·e·ter (găs ŏm′ə tər), *n.* **1.** an apparatus for measuring or storing gas. **2.** *Brit.* a tank for storing gas. [t. F: m. *gazomètre.* See GAS METER]

gasp (găsp, gäsp), *n.* **1.** a sudden, short breath; convulsive effort to breathe. **2.** a short, convulsive utterance. —*v.i.* **3.** to catch the breath, or struggle for breath, with open mouth; breathe convulsively. **4.** to long with breathless eagerness; desire; crave (fol. by *for* or *after*). —*v.t.* **5.** to utter with gasps (often fol. by *out, forth, away,* etc.). **6.** to breathe or emit with gasps (often fol. by *away*). [ME *gaspe(n), gayspe(n),* t. Scand.; cf. Icel. *geispa,* metathetic var. of *geipsa* yawn; akin to OE *gipian* yawn, *gipung* open mouth] —Syn. **3.** See **pant.**

Gas·pé Peninsula (găs pā′; *Fr.* gȧs pě′), a peninsula in SE Canada, in Quebec province, between New Brunswick and the St. Lawrence.

gas·per (găs′pər, gäs′-), *n.* *Brit. Slang.* a cheap cigarette.

gas range, a cooking range using gas as fuel.

gas·ser (găs′ər), *n.* **1.** one who or that which gasses. **2.** a well or boring yielding natural gas.

gas shell, *Mil.* an explosive shell containing a liquid or other material which, when the shell bursts, is converted into an asphyxiating or poisonous gas or vapor.

gas·sing (găs′ĭng), *n.* **1.** act of one who or that which gasses. **2.** an affecting or overcoming with gas or fumes, as in battle. **3.** the evolution of gases during electrolysis. **4.** a process by which a material is gassed.

gas station, filling station.

gas·sy (găs′ĭ), *adj.,* **-sier, -siest. 1.** full of or containing gas. **2.** like gas.

gas·ter·o·pod (găs′tər ə pŏd′), *n.* gastropod.

gas thermometer, a device for measuring temperature by observing the change in either pressure or volume of an enclosed gas.

gas·tight (găs′tīt′), *adj.* **1.** not penetrable by a gas. **2.** not admitting a given gas under a given pressure.

Gas·to·ni·a (găs tō′nĭ ə), *n.* a city in S North Carolina, W of Charlotte. 37,276 (1960).

gastr-, var. of gastro-, before vowels, as in *gastralgia.*

gas·tral·gi·a (găs trăl′jĭ ə), *n.* *Pathol.* **1.** neuralgia of the stomach. **2.** any stomach pain. [f. GASTR- + -ALGIA]

gas·trec·to·my (găs trĕk′tə mĭ), *n., pl.* **-mies.** *Surg.* the excision of a portion of the stomach.

gas·tric (găs′trĭk), *adj.* pertaining to the stomach.

gastric juice, *Biochem.* the digestive fluid secreted by the glands of the stomach, and containing pepsin and other enzymes.

gastric ulcer, *Pathol.* an erosion of the stomach's inner wall, caused in part by the corrosive action of the gastric juice upon the mucous membrane.

gas·trin (găs′trĭn), *n.* *Biochem.* a hormone which stimulates the secretion of gastric juice.

gas·tri·tis (găs trī′tĭs), *n.* *Pathol.* inflammation of the stomach, esp. of its mucous membrane. [f. GASTR- + -ITIS] —**gas·trit·ic** (găs trĭt′ĭk), *adj.*

gastro-, a word element meaning "stomach," as in *gastropod.* Also, **gastr-.** [comb. form of *gastēr*]

gas·tro·en·ter·i·tis (găs′trō ĕn′tər ī′tĭs), *n.* *Pathol.* inflammation of the stomach and intestines. [f. GASTRO- + ENTER(O)- + -ITIS]

gastroentero-, a combining form meaning "gastric and enteric," as in *gastroenterology.* [f. GASTRO- + ENTERO-]

gas·tro·en·ter·ol·o·gy (găs/trŏĕn/tə rŏl/ə jĭ), *n.* the study of the structure and diseases of digestive organs.

gas·tro·en·ter·os·to·my (găs/trŏĕn/tə rŏs/tə mĭ), *n.*, *pl.* **-mies.** *Surg.* the making of a new opening between the stomach and the small intestine.

gas·tro·lith (găs/trə lĭth), *n.* *Pathol.* a calculus or stony concretion in the stomach.

gas·trol·o·gy (găs trŏl/ə jĭ), *n.* the study of the structure, functions, and diseases of the stomach.

gas·tro·nome (găs/trə nōm/), *n.* a gourmet; epicure. Also, **gas·tron·o·mer** (găs trŏn/ə mər). [t. F, der. *gastronomie* GASTRONOMY]

gas·tron·o·my (găs trŏn/ə mĭ), *n.* the art or science of good eating. [t. F: m. *gastronomie*, t. Gk.: m.s. *gastronomía*] **—gas·tro·nom·ic** (găs/trə nŏm/ĭk), **gas/·tro·nom/i·cal,** *adj.* **—gas/tro·nom/i·cal·ly,** *adv.* **—gas·tron/o·mist,** *n.*

gas·tro·pod (găs/trə pŏd/), *n.* any of the Gastropoda. Also, **gasteropod.** [t. NL: s. *Gastropoda,* pl. See GASTRO-, -POD]

Gas·trop·o·da (găs trŏp/ə də), *n.pl.* a class of mollusks comprising the snails, having a shell of a single valve, usually spirally coiled, and a ventral muscular foot on which they glide about. [NL]

gas·tro·scope (găs/trə skōp/), *n.* *Med.* an instrument for inspecting the interior of the stomach. **—gas·tro·scop·ic** (găs/trə skŏp/ĭk), *adj.*

gas·tros·co·py (găs trŏs/kə pĭ), *n.* *Med.* examination with a gastroscope to detect disease.

gas·tros·to·my (găs trŏs/tə mĭ), *n.*, *pl.* **-mies.** *Surg.* the operation of cutting into the stomach and leaving a more or less permanent opening for feeding or drainage.

gas·trot·o·my (găs trŏt/ə mĭ), *n.*, *pl.* **-mies.** *Surg.* the operation of cutting into the stomach.

gas·tro·vas·cu·lar (găs/trō văs/kyə lər), *adj.* *Zool.* serving for digestion and circulation, as a cavity.

gas·tru·la (găs/trŏŏ lə), *n.*, *pl.* **-lae** (-lē/). *Embryol.* a metazoan embryo, consisting in typical cases of a cup-like body (formed from the blastula) with a wall formed by two layers of cells, the epiblast and hypoblast. [NL, dim. of Gk. *gastḗr* belly,stomach] **—gas/tru·lar,** *adj.*

gas·tru·late (găs/trŏŏ lāt/), *v.i.*, **-lated, -lating.** *Embryol.* to undergo gastrulation.

gas·tru·la·tion (găs/trŏŏ lā/shən), *n.* *Embryol.* **1.** the formation of a gastrula. **2.** any process (as that of invagination) by which a blastula or other form of embryo is converted into a gastrula.

gas turbine. See **turbine** (def. 2).

gat¹ (găt), *v.* *Archaic.* pt. **of get.**

gat² (găt), *n.* *Slang.* a gun, pistol, or revolver. [abbr. of GATLING GUN]

gate (gāt), *n.*, *v.*, **gated, gating.** **—n.** **1.** the movable barrier, as a swinging frame, often of openwork, in a fence or wall, or to close any passageway. **2.** an opening for passage into an enclosure such as a fenced yard or walled city. **3.** a structure built about such an opening and containing the barrier. **4.** any narrow means of access or entrance. **5.** a device for regulating the passage of water, steam, or the like, as in a dam, pipe, etc.; valve. **6.** the number of persons who pay for admission to an athletic contest or other exhibition. **7.** gate money. **8.** a sash or frame for a saw or gang of saws. **9.** *Metall.* a channel or opening in a mold through which molten metal enters the mold cavity to form a casting. **—v.t.** **10.** (at British universities) to punish by restricting (a student) within the college gates. [ME *gat, gate,* OE *gatu* gates, pl. of *geat* opening in a wall, c. LG and D *gat* hole, breach] **—gate/less,** *adj.* **—gate/like/,** *adj.* **—gate/man,** *n.*

gâ·teau (gä tō/), *n.*, *pl.* **-teaux** (-tō/). *French.* a cake.

gate·house (gāt/hous/), *n.* **1.** a house at or over a gate, used as the keeper's quarters, a fortification, etc. **2.** a house or structure at the gate of a dam, reservoir, etc., with apparatus for regulating the flow of water.

gate·keep·er (gāt/kē/pər), *n.* one in charge of a gate.

gate-leg table (gāt/lĕg/), a table having drop leaves which are supported when open by legs which swing out and are usually connected by crosspieces. Also, **gate-legged table.**

gate money, the receipts taken in for admission to an athletic contest or other exhibition.

gate·post (gāt/pōst/), *n.* the post on which a gate is hung, or the one against which it is closed.

Gates (gāts), *n.* **Horatio,** 1728–1806, American Revolutionary general, born in England.

Gates·head (gāts/hĕd/), *n.* a seaport in NE England, on the Tyne opposite Newcastle. 111,900 (est. 1956).

gate·way (gāt/wā/), *n.* **1.** a passage or entrance which is closed or may be closed by a gate. **2.** a frame or arch in which a gate is hung; structure built at or over a gate. **3.** any means of entering or leaving a place.

gath·er (găth/ər), *v.t.* **1.** to bring (persons, animals, or things) together into one company or aggregate. **2.** to get together from various places or sources; collect gradually. **3.** to learn or infer from observation: *I gather that he'll be leaving.* **4.** to pick (any crop or natural yield) from its place of growth or formation: *to gather grain, fruit, or flowers.* **5.** to take: *to gather a person into one's arms.* **6.** **be gathered to one's fathers,** to die. **7.** to take by selection from among other things; sort out; cull. **8.** to assemble or collect (one's energies or oneself) as for an effort (often fol. by *up*). **9.** to contract (the brow) into wrinkles. **10.** to draw up (cloth) on a thread in fine folds or puckers by means of even stitches. **11.** *Bookbinding.* to assemble (the printed sheets of a book) in their proper sequence to be bound. **12.** *Naut.* to gain (way) from a dead stop or extremely slow speed. **—v.i.** **13.** to come together or assemble: *to gather around a fire, to gather in crowds.* **14.** to collect or accumulate. **15.** to grow as by accretion; increase. **16.** to become contracted into wrinkles, as the brow. **17.** to come to a head, as a sore in suppurating. **—n.** **18.** a drawing together; contraction. **19.** (*usually pl.*) a fold or pucker in gathered cloth, etc. [ME *gader(en),* OE *gaderian,* der. *geador* together, akin to *gæd* fellowship. Cf. TOGETHER, GOOD] **—gath/er·a·ble,** *adj.* **—gath/er·er,** *n.*

—Syn. 2. GATHER, ASSEMBLE, COLLECT, MUSTER, MARSHAL imply bringing or drawing together. GATHER expresses the general idea usually with no implication of arrangement: *to gather seashells.* ASSEMBLE is used of objects or facts brought together preparatory to arranging them: *to assemble data for a report.* COLLECT implies purposeful accumulation to form an ordered whole: *to collect evidence.* MUSTER, primarily a military term, suggests thoroughness in the process of collection: *to muster all his resources.* MARSHAL, another term primarily military, suggests rigorously ordered, purposeful arrangement: *to marshal facts for effective presentation.* **3.** deduce, conclude, assume. **4.** pluck, crop, reap, glean, garner, harvest. **—Ant. 1.** disperse.

gath·er·ing (găth/ər ĭng), *n.* **1.** act of one who or that which gathers. **2.** that which is gathered together. **3.** an assembly or meeting; a crowd. **4.** a collection or assemblage of anything. **5.** an inflamed and suppurating swelling. **6.** *Bookbinding.* a section in a book, usually a sheet cut into several leaves. **—Syn. 3.** assemblage, assembly, convocation, congregation, concourse, company, throng. **5.** boil, abscess, carbuncle.

Gat·ling gun (găt/lĭng), an early type of machine gun consisting of a revolving cluster of barrels around a central axis, each barrel being automatically loaded and fired during every revolution of the cluster. [named after R. J. *Gatling* (1818–1903), American inventor]

Ga·tun (gä tōōn/), *n.* **1.** a town in the N Canal Zone. 2477 (1950). **2.** a large dam near this town. 1½ mi. long.

Gatun Lake, an artificial lake in the Canal Zone, created by Gatun dam. 164 sq. mi.

gauche (gōsh), *adj.* awkward; clumsy; tactless: *her reply was typically gauche.* [t. F. See GAUCHERIE]

gau·che·rie (gō/shə rē/; Fr. gōsh rē/), *n.* **1.** awkwardness; clumsiness; tactlessness. **2.** an awkward or tactless movement, act, etc. [t. F, der. *gauche* awkward, lit., left (hand)]

Gau·cho (gou/chō; Sp. -chō), *n.*, *pl.* **-chos** (-chōz; Sp. -chōs). a native of the South American pampas, of mixed Spanish and Indian descent. [t. Sp.]

gaud (gôd), *n.* a showy ornament. [ME *gaude,* ? t. AF, der. *gaudir* rejoice, jest, t. L: m. *gaudēre*]

gaud·er·y (gô/də rĭ), *n.*, *pl.* **-eries.** **1.** ostentatious show. **2.** finery; fine or showy things: *she stood in the doorway resplendent in her gaudery.*

gaud·y¹ (gô/dĭ), *adj.*, **gaudier, gaudiest.** **1.** brilliant; excessively showy. **2.** showy without taste; vulgarly showy; flashy. [orig. attributive use of GAUDY² large bead of rosary, feast; later taken as der. GAUD, n.] **—gaud/i·ly,** *adv.* **—gaud/i·ness,** *n.*

—Syn. 2. tawdry. GAUDY, FLASHY, GARISH, SHOWY agree in the idea of conspicuousness and, often, bad taste. That which is GAUDY challenges the eye, as by brilliant colors or evident cost, and is not in good taste: *a gaudy hat.* FLASHY suggests insistent and vulgar display, in rather a sporty manner: *a flashy necktie.* GARISH suggests a glaring brightness, or crude vividness of color, and too much ornamentation: *garish decorations.* SHOWY applies to that which is strikingly conspicuous, but not necessarily offensive to good taste: *a garden of showy flowers, a showy dress.* **—Ant. 2.** modest, sober.

gaud·y² (gô/dĭ), *n.*, *pl.* **gaudies.** *Brit.* a festival or merrymaking, esp. an annual college feast. [ME, t. L: m.s. *gaudium* joy]

gauf·fer (gō/fər, gôf/ər), *n.*, *v.t.* goffer.

gauge (gāj), *v.*, **gauged, gauging,** *n.* **—v.t.** **1.** to appraise, estimate, or judge. **2.** to determine the dimensions, capacity, quantity, or force of; measure, as with a gauge. **3.** to make conformable to a standard. **4.** *Plastering.* to prepare (plaster) in a certain gauge, as for hardness. **5.** to cut or rub (bricks or stones) to a uniform size or shape. **—n.** **6.** a standard of measure; standard dimension or quantity. **7.** a means of estimating or judging; criterion; test. **8.** extent; scope; capacity. **9.** *Ordn.* the internal diameter of a gun bore. **10.** the distance between the rails of a railroad. In the United States the **standard gauge** is 4 feet 8½ inches; **broad gauge** is wider, and **narrow gauge** narrower, than this. **11.** the position of one ship with reference to another and to the wind. **12.** *Plastering.* the quantity of plaster of Paris mixed with common plaster to accelerate its setting. Also, **gage.** [late ME, t. ONF: m.s. *gauger,* ult. der. *gal-* measuring rod; of Celtic orig.] **—gauge/a·ble,** *adj.*

gaug·er (gā/jər), *n.* **1.** one who or that which gauges. **2.** an officer who ascertains the contents of casks, etc. **3.** an exciseman. Also, **gager.**

Gau·guin (gō găN/), *n.* **Paul** (pōl), 1848–1903, French painter.

Gaul (gôl), n. **1.** a vast ancient region in W Europe, including what is now N Italy, France, Belgium, and parts of the Netherlands, Germany, and Switzerland: divided by the Alps into **Cisalpine Gaul** (N Italy) and **Transalpine Gaul. 2.** an inhabitant of this country. **3.** a Frenchman. [t. F: m. *Gaule*, t. Gmc. (cf. OHG *walh* foreigner, esp. Gaul), b. with L *Gallus, Gallia* Gaul]

Gau·lei·ter (gou'lī'tər), n. a Nazi official, head of a political district.

Gaul·ish (gô'lĭsh), n. the extinct language of ancient Gaul, a Celtic language.

gaul·the·ri·a (gôl thĭr'ĭ ə), n. any of the aromatic evergreen shrubs constituting the ericaceous genus *Gaultheria*, as *G. procumbens*, the American wintergreen. [NL; named after Dr. *Gaultier*, Canadian physician]

gaunt (gônt), adj. **1.** abnormally thin; emaciated; haggard. **2.** bleak, desolate, or grim, as places or things. [ME, t. d. F: m. *gaunet* yellowish] —**gaunt'ly**, adv. —**gaunt'ness**, n. —**Syn.** 1. lean, spare, scrawny, lank; angular, bony, raw-boned. See **thin.** —**Ant.** 1. stout.

Gaunt (gônt, gänt), n. **John of,** (*Duke of Lancaster*) 1340–99, English soldier and statesman; fourth son of Edward III and founder of the royal house of Lancaster.

gaunt·let[1] (gônt'lĭt, gänt'-), n. **1.** a medieval glove, as of mail or plate, to protect the hand. **2.** a glove with a cufflike extension for the wrist. **3.** the cuff itself. **4. the gauntlet,** a challenge. Also, **gantlet.** [ME, t. OF: m. *gantelet*, dim. of *gant* glove, t. Gmc.; cf. OSw. *wante*]

gaunt·let[2] (gônt'lĭt, gänt'-), n., v.t. gantlet[1].

gaun·try (gôn'trĭ), n., pl. **-tries.** gantry.

gauss (gous), n. *Physics.* **1.** a unit of magnetic induction such that an induction of one gauss will result in one volt per centimeter of length in a linear conductor moved perpendicularly across the induction at a speed of one centimeter per second. **2.** *Obs.* oersted (def. 1). [named after K. F. GAUSS]

Gauss (gous), n. **Karl Friedrich** (kärl frē'drĭкн, 1777–1855, German mathematician. —**Gauss·i·an** (gou'sĭ ən), adj.

Gau·ta·ma (gô'tə mə, gou'-), n. 563?–483? B.C., Buddha. Also, **Siddhartha, Gotama.**

Gau·tier (gō tyě'), n. **Théophile** (tĕ ô fēl'), 1811–72, French poet, novelist, and critic of art and literature.

gauze (gôz), n. **1.** any thin transparent fabric made from any fiber in a plain or leno weave. **2.** some similar open material, as of wire. **3.** a thin haze. [t. F: m. *gaze* named after city of *Gaza* in Palestine] —**gauze'like'**, adj.

gauz·y (gô'zĭ), adj., **gauzier, gauziest.** like gauze; thin as gauze. —**gauz'i·ness**, n.

ga·vage (gə väzh'; *Fr.* gȧ väzh'), n. forced feeding, as of poultry or human beings, as by a flexible tube and a force pump. [t. F, der. *gaver* to gorge]

gave (gāv), v. pt. of **give.**

gav·el (găv'əl), n. a small mallet used by a presiding officer to signal for attention or order. [back formation from *gavelock*, OE *gafeluc* spear]

gav·el·kind (găv'əl kīnd'), n. *Early Eng. Law.* **1.** a customary system of land tenure, whose chief feature was equal division of inherited land among the heirs. **2.** a tenure of land in which the tenant was liable for money rent rather than labor or military service. **3.** the land so held. [ME *gavelkynde, gavelikind,* f. OE *gafol* tax, tribute + *gecynd* KIND[2]]

ga·vi·al (gā'vĭ əl), n. a large crocodilian, *Gavialis gangeticus*, with elongated jaws, found in India. [t. F, t. Hind.: m. *ghariyāl*]

ga·votte (gə vŏt'), n. **1.** an old French dance in moderately quick ¾ time. **2.** a piece of music for, or in the rhythm of, this dance, often forming one of the movements in the classical suite, usually following the saraband. Also, **ga·vot'.** [t. F, t. Pr.: m. *gavoto* dance of the Gavots (Alpine mountaineers), fem. of *gavot* hillbilly, der. pre-Rom. *gav-* mountain stream]

Head of gavial, *Gavialis gangeticus* (Total length ab. 20 ft.)

Ga·wain (gä'wĭn, gô'-), n. *Arthurian Romance.* one of the knights of the Round Table.

gawk (gôk), n. **1.** an awkward, foolish person. —v.i. **2.** *Colloq.* to act like a gawk; stare stupidly. [appar. repr. OE word meaning fool, f. *gagol* foolish + *-oc* -OCK; used attributively in *gawk hand, gallock hand* left hand]

gawk·y (gô'kĭ), adj., **gawkier, gawkiest.** awkward; ungainly; clumsy. —**gawk'i·ly**, adv. —**gawk'i·ness**, n.

gay (gā), adj., **gayer, gayest. 1.** having or showing a joyous mood: *gay spirits, music, scenes, etc.* **2.** bright or showy: *gay colors, flowers, ornaments, etc.* **3.** given to or abounding in social or other pleasures: *a gay social season.* **4.** dissipated; licentious: *to lead a gay life.* ME, t. OF: m. *gai*; orig. uncert.] —**gay'ness**, n. —**Syn. 1.** gleeful, jovial, glad, joyous, light-hearted; lively, vivacious, frolicsome, sportive, hilarious. GAY, JOLLY, JOYFUL, MERRY describe a happy or light-hearted mood. GAY suggests a lightness of heart or liveliness of mood that is openly manifested: *when hearts were young and gay.* JOLLY indicates a good-humored, natural, expansive gaiety of mood or disposition: *a jolly crowd at a party.* JOYFUL suggests gladness, happiness, rejoicing: *joyful over the good news.* MERRY is often interchangeable with GAY: *a merry disposition, a merry party*; it suggests, even more than the latter, convivial animated enjoyment. —**Ant. 1.** solemn. **2.** sedate, sober.

Gay (gā), n. **John,** 1685–1732, British poet and dramatist.

Ga·ya (gä'yə, gī'ə), n. a city in NE India: a famous place of Hindu pilgrimage. 133,700 (1951).

gay·e·ty (gā'ə tĭ), n., pl. **-ties.** gaiety.

Gay-Lus·sac (gĕ lȳ sȧk'), n. **Joseph Louis** (zhô zĕf' lwē), 1778—1850, French chemist.

gay·ly (gā'lĭ), adv. gaily.

Gay-Pay-Oo (gā'pā'ōō'; *Russ.* gĕ'pĕ'ōō'), n. *U.S.S.R.* the secret service from 1922, when Cheka was reorganized, until 1935, when the N.K.V.D., the official state police, was formed; the Ogpu. [attempt to give the names of the Russian letters transliterated as *G.P.U.*]

gay·wings (gā'wĭngz'), n. the fringed milkwort, *Polygala paucifolia*, whose aerial flowers have paired, large, usually pink-purple petals.

gaz., **1.** gazette. **2.** gazetteer.

Ga·za (gā'zə, gä'zə), n. a seaport adjacent to SW Israel; now under Egyptian administration: ancient trade route center. 37,820 (est. 1952).

Gaza Strip, a coastal area formerly in the Palestine mandate; now provisionally administered by Egypt.

gaze (gāz), v., **gazed, gazing,** n. —v.i. **1.** to look steadily or intently; look with curiosity, wonder, etc. —n. **2.** a steady or intent look. [ME, t. Scand.; cf. d. Sw. *gasa* gape, stare] —**gaz'er**, n. —**Syn. 1.** GAZE, STARE, GAPE suggest looking fixedly at something. To GAZE is to look steadily and intently at something: esp. at that which excites admiration, curiosity, or interest: *to gaze at scenery, at a scientific experiment.* To STARE is to gaze with eyes wide open, as from surprise, wonder, alarm, stupidity, or impertinence: *to stare unbelievingly or rudely.* GAPE is a word with uncomplimentary connotations; it suggests open-mouthed, often ignorant or rustic wonderment or curiosity: *to gape at a high building, at a circus parade.*

ga·ze·bo (gə zē'bō), n., pl. **-bos, -boes.** a structure commanding an extensive prospect, esp. a pavilion or summerhouse. [? f. GAZE, v. + L (*vid*)*ebo* I shall see]

gaze·hound (gāz'-hound'), n. a hound that hunts by sight rather than scent.

ga·zelle (gə zĕl'), n. any of various small antelopes of the genus *Gazella* and allied genera, noted for their graceful movements and lustrous eyes. [t. F, t. Ar.: m. *ghazāl*] —**gazelle'like'**, adj.

Gazelle, *Gazella dama ruficollis* (3 ft. high at the shoulder)

ga·zette (gə zĕt'), n., v., **-zetted, -zetting.** —n. **1.** a newspaper (now common only in newspaper titles). **2.** an official government journal, esp. in Great Britain, containing lists of government appointments and promotions, bankruptcies, etc. —v.t. **3.** *Chiefly Brit.* to publish, announce, or list in a gazette. [t. F, t. It.: m. *gazzetta*, var. of Venetian *gazeta*, orig. a Venetian coin (the price of the gazette), dim. of *gaza* magpie]

gaz·et·teer (găz'ə tĭr'), n. **1.** a geographical dictionary. **2.** a journalist, esp. one appointed and paid by the government. [t. F (obs.): m. *gazettier*]

Ga·zi·an·tep (gä'zĭ än tĕp'), n. a city in S Turkey. 97,144 (1955). Also, **Aintab.**

G.B., Great Britain.

G.C.D., greatest common divisor. Also, **g.c.d.**

G.C.F., greatest common factor. Also, **g.c.f.**

G clef, *Music.* treble clef. See illus. under **clef.**

G.C.M., greatest common measure. Also, **g.c.m.**

Gd, *Chem.* gadolinium.

Gdansk (gdȧnsk), n. Polish name of **Danzig.**

gds., goods.

Gdy·nia (gdĭ'nyä), n. a seaport in N Poland, on the Bay of Danzig. 117,000 (est. 1954).

Ge, *Chem.* germanium.

ge·an·ti·cli·nal (jē'ăn tĭ klī'nəl), *Geol.* —adj. **1.** pertaining to an anticlinal fold extending over a relatively large part of the earth's surface. —n. **2.** a geanticline. [f. Gk. *gē* earth + ANTICLINAL]

ge·an·ti·cline (jē ăn'tə klīn'), n. *Geol.* a geanticlinal fold. [f. Gk. *gē* earth + ANTICLINE]

gear (gĭr), n. **1.** *Mach.* **a.** a mechanism for transmitting or changing motion, as by toothed wheels. **b.** a toothed wheel which engages with another wheel or part. **c.** the connection or engagement of toothed wheels with each other: *in gear, out of gear, in high gear, in low gear.* **d.** a group of parts in a complex machine that operates for a single purpose. **e.** the diameter of an imaginary wheel whose circumference is equal to the distance traversed by a bicycle during a single revolution of the pedals. **2.** implements, tools, or apparatus, esp. as used for a particular occupation: *harness; tackle.* **3.** *Naut.* **a.** the ropes, blocks, etc., belonging to a particular sail or spar. **b.** the tools and equipment used on a ship. **c.** a sailor's personal baggage. **4.** *Archaic.* property. **5.** *Archaic.*

Gears
A. Bevel gears; B. Herringbone gears; C. Spur gears

armor or arms. —*v.t.* **6.** to provide with gearing; connect by gearing; put (machinery) into gear. **7.** to provide with gear; supply; fit; harness. —*v.i.* **8.** to fit exactly, as one part of gearing into another; come into or be in gear. [ME *gere*, t. Scand.; cf. Icel. *gervi*, *görvi* gear, apparel; akin to OE *gearwe*, pl., equipment, *gearu* ready] —**gear′less,** *adj.*

gear·box (gîr′bŏks′), *n.* *Brit.* transmission (def. 4b).

gear·ing (gîr′ĭng), *n.* **1.** the parts collectively by which motion is transmitted in machinery, esp. a train of toothed wheels. **2.** act of equipping with gears. **3.** the method of installation of such gears.

gear·shift (gîr′shĭft′), *n.* a device for selecting or connecting gears for transmitting power. Also, *Brit.,* **gear lever.**

gear·wheel (gîr′hwēl′), *n.* a wheel having teeth or cogs which engage with those of another wheel or part; cogwheel. Also, **gear wheel.**

geb., (Ger. *geboren*) born.

geck·o (gĕk′ō), *n., pl.* **geckos, geckoes,** a small, harmless lizard of the family Geckonidae, mostly nocturnal, many with adhesive pads on the toes. [t. Malay: m. *gēkoq;* imit.]

Burmese gecko. *Gecko gecko*
(10 in. long)

Ged·des (gĕd′ēz), *n.,* **Norman Bel,** 1893–1958, U.S. industrial and stage designer and architect.

gee (jē), *interj., n., v.,* **geed, geeing.** —*interj.* **1.** a word of command to horses, etc., directing them to turn to the right or (fol. by *up*) to go faster. —*v.i.* **2.** to turn to the right. —*v.t.* **3.** to turn (something) to the right. **4.** to evade. [orig. uncert.]

Gee·long (jĭ-lông′), *n.* a seaport in SE Australia, in Victoria. 20,034 (1954); 44,561 with suburbs (1947).

Geel·vink Bay (KHāl′vĭngk), a large bay on the NW coast of New Guinea.

geese (gēs), *n.* pl. of **goose.**

geest (gēst), *n.* *Geol.* old deposits produced by flowing water. [t. LG: dry or sandy soil]

gee·zer (gē′zər), *n.* *Slang.* a queer character. [var. of *guiser* (f. GUISE (def. 6) + -ER¹), repr. d. pronunciation]

Ge·hen·na (gĭ-hĕn′ə), *n.* **1.** *Old Test.* the valley of Hinnom, near Jerusalem, regarded as a place of abomination (II Kings 23:10), and used as a dumping place for refuse, with fires kept burning to prevent pestilence. **2.** *New Test. and Rabbinical literature.* hell. **3.** any place of extreme torment or suffering. [t. LL, t. Gk.: m. *Géenna,* t. Heb.: m. *Gē-Hinnōm* hell, short for *gē ben Hinnōm,* lit., valley of son of Hinnom. See Jer. 19:5]

Gei·ger counter (gī′gər), an instrument for detecting and counting ionizing particles, consisting of a tube which conducts electricity when the gas within is ionized by such a particle. It is used in measuring the degree of radioactivity in an area left by the explosion of an atom bomb, in investigations of cosmic rays, etc.

Gei·kie (gē′kĭ), *n.* **Sir Archibald,** 1835–1924, Scottish geologist.

gei·sha (gā′shə), *n., pl.* **-sha, -shas.** a Japanese singing and dancing girl. [t. Jap.]

Geiss·ler tube (gīs′lər), a sealed glass tube with platinum connections at the ends, containing rarefied gas made luminous by an electrical discharge. [named after H. Geissler (1814–79), the (German) inventor]

gel (jĕl), *n., v.,* **gelled, gelling.** *Phys. Chem.* —*n.* **1.** a semirigid colloidal dispersion of a solid with a liquid or gas, as jelly, glue, or silica gel. —*v.i.* **2.** to form or become a gel. [short for GELATIN]

gel·a·tin (jĕl′ə-tĭn), *n.* **1.** a brittle, nearly transparent, faintly yellow, odorless, and almost tasteless organic substance, obtained by boiling in water the ligaments, bones, skin, etc., of animals, and forming the basis of jellies, glues, and the like. **2.** any of various similar substances, as vegetable gelatin. **3.** a preparation or product in which gelatin (defs. 1 or 2) is the essential constituent. Also, **gel′a·tine.** [t. F: (m.) *gélatine,* t. It.: m. *gelatina,* der. *gelata* jelly, g. L *gelāta,* pp. fem., frozen, congealed]

ge·lat·i·nize (jĭ-lăt′ə-nīz′), *v.,* **-nized, -nizing.** —*v.t.* **1.** to make gelatinous. **2.** to coat with gelatin, as paper. —*v.i.* **3.** to become gelatinous. —**ge·lat′i·ni·za′tion,** *n.*

ge·lat·i·noid (jĭ-lăt′ə-noid′), *adj.* **1.** resembling gelatin; gelatinous. —*n.* **2.** a gelatinoid substance.

ge·lat·i·nous (jĭ-lăt′ə-nəs), *adj.* **1.** having the nature of jelly; jellylike. **2.** pertaining to or consisting of gelatin. —**ge·lat′i·nous·ly,** *adv.* —**ge·lat′i·nous·ness,** *n.*

ge·la·tion (jĭ-lā′shən), *n.* solidification by cold; freezing. [t. L: s. *gelātio* freezing]

geld¹ (gĕld), *v.t.,* **gelded** or **gelt, gelding.** to castrate (esp. animals). [ME *gelde(n),* t. Scand.; cf. Icel. *gelda*]

geld² (gĕld), *n.* *Eng. Hist.* **1.** a payment; tax. **2.** a tax paid to the crown by landholders under the Saxon and Norman kings. [t. ML: s. *geldum,* t. OE: m. *geld, gield, gyld* payment, tribute, c. D and G *geld* money; akin to YIELD, v.]

Gel·der·land (gĕl′dər-lănd′), *n.* Du. KHĕl′dər-länt′), *n.* a province in E Netherlands. 1,149,102 pop. (est. 1954); 1965 sq. mi. *Cap.:* Arnhem. Also, **Guelders.**

geld·ing (gĕl′dĭng), *n.* a castrated animal, esp. a horse. [ME, t. Scand.; cf. Icel. *geldingr*]

Ge·lée (zhə-lā′), *n.* **Claude** (klōd). See **Lorrain.**

---

gel·id (jĕl′ĭd), *adj.* very cold; icy. [t. L: s. *gelidus* icy cold] —**ge·lid′i·ty, gel′id·ness,** *n.* —**gel′id·ly,** *adv.*

gel·se·mi·um (jĕl-sē′mĭ-əm), *n.* **1.** a twining shrub of the loganiaceous genus *Gelsemium,* esp. the yellow jasmine, *G. sempervirens,* of the southern U.S. **2.** the root of the yellow jasmine, or the tincture from it, used as a drug. [NL, der. It. *gelsomino* JASMINE]

Gel·sen·kir·chen (gĕl′zən-kĭr′KHən), *n.* a city in W West Germany, in the Ruhr. 371,693 (est. 1955).

gelt (gĕlt), *v.* pt. and pp. of **geld.**

gem (jĕm), *n., v.,* **gemmed, gemming.** —*n* **1.** a stone used in jewelry, fashioned to bring out its beauty. **2.** something likened to, or prized as, a gem because of its beauty or worth, esp. something small: *the gem of the collection.* **3.** *Cookery.* a kind of muffin. **4.** *Brit.* a printing type (4 point) between brilliant and diamond. —*v.t.* **5.** to adorn with or as with gems. [ME, t. F: m. *gemme,* g. L *gemma* bud, jewel; r. OE *gim* (c. OHG *gimma*), ult. t. L] —**gem′like′,** *adj.*

Ge·ma·ra (gə-mä′rä, -mô′rä), *n.* *Jewish Lit.* a commentary on the Mishnah; the Talmud. [t. Aram.: completion]

gem·i·nate (*adj.* jĕm′ə-nĭt, -nāt′; *v.* jĕm′ə-nāt′), *v.,* **-nated, -nating,** *adj.* —*v.t., v.i.* **1.** to make or become double or paired. —*adj.* **2.** twin; combined in pairs; coupled. [t. L: m.s. *geminātus,* pp., doubled] —**gem′i·nate·ly,** *adv.*

gem·i·na·tion (jĕm′ə-nā′shən), *n.* **1.** a doubling; duplication; repetition. **2.** *Phonetics.* the doubling of an originally single consonant. **3.** *Rhet.* the immediate repetition of a word, phrase, etc., for rhetorical effect.

Gem·i·ni (jĕm′ə-nī′), *n.pl., gen.* Geminorum (jĕm′ə-nôr′əm). **1.** *Astron.* the Twins, a zodiacal constellation containing the bright stars Castor and Pollux. **2.** the third sign of the zodiac. See diag. under ZODIAC. [t. L, pl. of *geminus* twin]

gem·ma (jĕm′ə), *n., pl.* **gemmae** (jĕm′ē). *Bot.* **1.** a cell or cluster of cells, or a leaf- or budlike body, which separates from the parent plant and forms a new plant, as in mosses, liverworts, etc. **2.** a bud, esp. a leaf bud. [t. L: bud, germ. Cf. GEM]

gem·mate (jĕm′āt), *adj., v.,* **-mated, -mating.** *Bot.* —*adj.* **1.** having buds; increasing by budding. —*v.i.* **2.** to put forth buds; increase by budding. [t. L: m. s. *gemmātus,* pp., increased by budding, set with gems]

gem·ma·tion (jĕm·ā′shən), *n.* *Bot.* the process of reproduction by gemmae.

gem·mule (jĕm′ūl), *n.* **1.** *Bot.* gemma. **2.** *Zool.* an asexually produced mass of cells that will develop into an animal. **3.** *Biol.* one of the hypothetical living units conceived by Darwin as the bearers of the hereditary attributes. [t. L: m. *gemmula,* dim. of *gemma* bud]

ge·mot (gə-mōt′), *n.* *Early Eng. Hist.* a meeting or an assembly, as for judicial purposes. Also, **ge·mote′.** [OE *gemōt,* f. ge- together + *mōt* meeting. Cf. MOOT]

gems·bok (gĕmz′bŏk′), *n.* a large antelope, *Oryx gazella,* of South Africa, having long, straight horns and a long, tufted tail. [t. S Afr. D: chamois buck]

Gemsbok, *Oryx gazella*
(4 ft. high at the shoulder)

-gen, a suffix meaning: **1.** something produced, or growing: *acrogen, endogen, exogen.* **2.** something that produces: *hydrogen, oxygen.* [t. F: m. *-gène,* ult. t. Gk.: m. *-genēs* born, produced, der. *gen-* bear, produce]

Gen., 1. *Mil.* General. **2.** Genesis. **3.** Geneva.

gen., 1. gender. **2.** general. **3.** genitive. **4.** genus.

gen·darme (zhän′därm; *Fr.* zhäɴ-dårm′), *n., pl.* **-darmes** (-därmz; *Fr.* -därm′). one of a corps of military police, esp. in France. [t. F, formed as sing. from *gens d'armes* men of arms]

gen·dar·me·rie (zhän-där′mə-rē′), *n.* gendarmes collectively. Also, **gen·darm·er·y** (zhän där′mə-rĭ).

gen·der (jĕn′dər), *n.* **1.** *Gram.* **a.** (in many languages) a set of classes which together include all nouns, membership in a particular class being shown by the form of the noun itself or by the form or choice of words that modify, replace, or otherwise refer to the noun; e.g., in Eng., the choice of *he* to replace *the man,* of *she* to replace *the woman,* of *it* to replace *the table,* of *it* or *she* to replace *the ship.* The number of genders in different languages varies from two to more than twenty; often the classification correlates in part with sex or animateness. The most familiar sets of genders are of three classes (e.g. Latin and German, *masculine, feminine, neuter*) or of two (e.g. French and Spanish, *masculine* and *feminine;* Dutch, *common* and *neuter*). **b.** one class of such a set. **c.** such classes or sets collectively or in general. **2.** *Colloq.* sex. **3.** *Obs.* kind, sort, or class. [ME *gendre,* t. OF, t. L: s. *genus* race, kind, sort, gender. Cf. GENUS, GENRE] —**gen′der·less,** *adj.*

gene (jēn), *n.* *Biol.* the unit of inheritance, probably biochemical in nature, which is located on and transmitted by the chromosome, and which develops into a hereditary character as it reacts with the environment and with the other genes. [t. Gk.: s. *geneá* breed, kind]

---

genealogical tree, family tree.

ge·ne·al·o·gy (jē'nĭ ăl'ə jĭ, jĕn'Y-, -ŏl'-), *n., pl.* **-gies.**
1. an account of human family pedigrees of ancestors or relatives. 2. the investigation of pedigrees as a department of knowledge. [ME, t. LL: m.s. *genealógia*, t. Gk.: tracing of descent] —**ge·ne·a·log·i·cal** (jē'nĭ ə lŏj'ə-kəl, jĕn'Y-), **ge'ne·a·log'ic,** *adj.* —**ge'ne·a·log'i·cal·ly,** *adv.* —**ge·ne·al·o·gist** (jē'nĭ ăl'ə jĭst, jĕn'Y-, -ŏl'-), *n.* —**Syn.** 2. See **pedigree.**

gen·er·a (jĕn'ər ə), *n.* pl. of **genus.**

gen·er·al (jĕn'ər əl), *adj.* 1. pertaining to, affecting, including, or participated in by all members of a class or group; not partial or particular: *a general election.* 2. common to many or most of a community; prevalent; usual: *the general practice.* 3. not restricted to one class or field; miscellaneous: *the general public.* 4. not limited to a detail of application; not specific or special: *general instructions.* 5. indefinite or vague: *to refer to a matter in a general way.* 6. having extended command, or superior or chief rank (often follows noun): *a general officer, governor general.* —*n.* 7. *Mil.* **a.** *U.S. Army.* brigadier general, major general, lieutenant general, general, general of the army, or general of the armies. **b.** *U.S. Army.* an officer with the rank between lieutenant general and general of the army (or armies), a full general. **c.** (in numerous foreign armies) an officer in the second or third highest rank, as in Great Britain, where he ranks just below a field marshal. 8. *Eccles.* the chief of a religious order. 9. a general statement or principle. 10. **in general, a.** with respect to the whole class referred to. **b.** as a general rule; commonly. 11. *Archaic.* the general public. [ME, t. L: s. *generãlis,* of or belonging to a (whole) race, kind, the opposite of *specialis* special, particular. See **GENUS**] —**gen'er·al·ness,** *n.*
—**Syn.** 1, 2. customary, regular, ordinary. **GENERAL, COMMON, POPULAR, UNIVERSAL** agree in the idea of being nonexclusive and widespread. **GENERAL** means belonging to, or prevailing throughout, a whole class or body collectively, irrespective of individuals: *a general belief.* **COMMON** means shared by all, and belonging to one as much as another: *a common fund, interests.* **POPULAR** means belonging to, or adapted for, or favored by the people or the public generally, rather than by a particular (esp. a superior) class: *the popular conception, a popular candidate.* **UNIVERSAL** means found everywhere, and with no exceptions: *a universal longing.* —**Ant.** 1. special, limited.

General American Speech, the pronunciation of English typical of American speakers not native to New England, New York City, or the South.

General Assembly, the legislature in certain States of the United States.

General Court, *U.S.* a State legislature, which, during colonial administration, had judicial authority: now used only in Massachusetts and New Hampshire.

gen·er·al·is·si·mo (jĕn'ər ə lĭs'ə mō'), *n., pl.* **-mos.**
1. (in certain foreign armies) the supreme commander of several armies acting together. 2. (in China and U.S. S.R.) the supreme commander of all the forces of the country. [t. It., superl. of *generale* general, der. L *generãlis.* See **GENERAL**]

gen·er·al·i·ty (jĕn'ər ăl'ə tĭ), *n., pl.* **-ties.** 1. a general or vague statement: *to speak in vague generalities.* 2. general principle; general rule or law. 3. the greater part or majority: *the generality of people.* 4. state or quality of being general.

gen·er·al·i·za·tion (jĕn'ər əl ə zā'shən), *n.* 1. act or process of generalizing. 2. a result of this process; general statement, idea, or principle. 3. *Logic.* **a.** a proposition asserting something to be true either of all members of a certain class or of an indefinite part of that class. **b.** the process of obtaining such propositions.

gen·er·al·ize (jĕn'ər əl īz'), *v.,* **-ized, -izing.** —*v.t.*
1. to give a general (rather than specific or special) character to. 2. to infer (a general principle, etc.) from facts, etc. 3. to make general; bring into general use or knowledge. —*v.i.* 4. to form general notions. 5. to deal in generalities. 6. to make general inferences.

gen·er·al·ly (jĕn'ər ə lĭ), *adv.* 1. with respect to the larger part, or for the most part: *a claim generally recognized.* 2. usually; commonly; ordinarily: *he generally comes at noon.* 3. without reference to particular persons or things: *generally speaking.* —**Syn.** 2. See **often.**

General of the Armies, *U.S. Army.* a special rank held by John J. Pershing, equivalent to General of the Army.

General of the Army, *U.S. Army.* the highest ranking military officer; the next rank above general (equivalent to *Fleet Admiral* of the U.S. Navy).

general paralysis, *Pathol.* a syphilitic brain disorder characterized by chronic inflammation and degeneration of cerebral tissue, resulting in mental and physical deterioration. Also, **general paresis.**

gen·er·al·pur·pose (jĕn'ər əl pûr'pəs), *adj.* of broad usage; not restricted in function, as a horse.

gen·er·al·ship (jĕn'ər əl shĭp'), *n.* 1. skill as commander of a large military force or unit. 2. management or tactics. 3. the rank or functions of a general.

general staff, *Mil.* a group of officers without command, whose duties are to assist high commanders in planning and carrying out orders in peace and war.

general strike, a mass strike in all or many trades and industries in a section or in all parts of a country.

gen·er·ate (jĕn'ə rāt'), *v.t.,* **-ated, -ating.** 1. to bring into existence; cause to be: *to generate electricity.* 2. to

produce; procreate. 3. *Math.* to trace out (a figure) by the motion of another figure. [t. L: m. s. *generãtus,* pp., begotten]

gen·er·a·tion (jĕn'ə rā'shən), *n.* 1. the whole body of individuals born about the same time: *the rising generation.* 2. the age or average lifetime of a generation; term of years (commonly 30) accepted as the average difference of age between one generation of a family and the next. 3. a single step in natural descent, as of human beings, animals, or plants. 4. act or process of generating; procreation. 5. the fact of being generated. 6. production by natural or artificial processes; evolution, as of heat or sound. 7. the offspring of a given parent or parents, considered as a single step in descent. 8. *Biol.* a form or phase of a plant or animal, with reference to the manner of its reproduction. 9. *Math.* the production of a geometrical figure by the motion of another figure. [ME, t. L: s. *generãtio*]

gen·er·a·tive (jĕn'ə rā'tĭv), *adj.* 1. pertaining to the production of offspring. 2. capable of producing.

gen·er·a·tor (jĕn'ə rā'tər), *n.* 1. a machine which converts mechanical energy into electrical energy; dynamo. 2. *Chem.* an apparatus for producing a gas or vapor. 3. one who or that which generates. [t. L]

gen·er·a·trix (jĕn'ə rā'trĭks), *n., pl.* **gen·er·a·tri·ces** (jĕn'ə rə trī'sēz). *Math.* an element generating a figure. [t. L]

ge·ner·ic (jĭ nĕr'ĭk), *adj.* 1. pertaining to a genus. 2. applicable or referring to all the members of a genus or class. Also, **ge·ner'i·cal.** [f. s. L *genus* kind + -IC. Cf. F *générique*] —**ge·ner'i·cal·ly,** *adv.*

gen·er·os·i·ty (jĕn'ə rŏs'ə tĭ), *n., pl.* **-ties.** 1. readiness or liberality in giving. 2. freedom from meanness or smallness of mind or character. 3. a generous act. —**Syn.** 1. munificence. 2. nobleness. —**Ant.** 1. stinginess.

gen·er·ous (jĕn'ər əs), *adj.* 1. munificent or bountiful; unselfish: *a generous giver or gift.* 2. free from meanness or smallness of mind or character. 3. furnished liberally; abundant: *a generous portion.* 4. rich or strong, as wine. 5. fertile, as soil. [t. L: m. s. *generõsus* of noble birth] —**gen'er·ous·ly,** *adv.* —**gen'er·ous·ness,** *n.* —**Syn.** 1. liberal, open-handed, free. 2. high-minded, noble. 3. ample, plentiful. —**Ant.** 1. selfish. 2. mean. 3. meager.

Gen·e·see (jĕn'ə sē'), *n.* a river flowing from N Pennsylvania through W New York into Lake Ontario. 144 mi.

Gen·e·sis (jĕn'ə sĭs), *n.* the first book of the Old Testament, telling of the beginnings of the world and of man. [special use of Gk. *génesis* origin, creation]

gen·e·sis (jĕn'ə sĭs), *n., pl.* **-ses** (-sēz'). origin; production; creation. [ME, t. L, t. Gk.: origin, creation]

gen·et[1] (jĕn'ĭt, jĭ nĕt'), *n.* 1. any of the small Old World carnivores constituting the genus *Genetta,* esp. *G. vulgaris,* allied to the civets but without a scent pouch, yielding a soft fur. 2. the fur. Also, **ge·nette'.** [ME *genete,* t. OF, t. Sp.: m. *gineta,* t. Ar.: m. *jarnaiţ*]

gen·et[2] (jĕn'ĭt), *n.* jennet.

ge·net·ic (jə nĕt'ĭk), *adj.* 1. *Biol.* pertaining or according to genetics. 2. pertaining to genesis or origin. Also, **ge·net'i·cal.** [t. Gk.: m. s. *genetikós* generative] —**ge·net'i·cal·ly,** *adv.*

ge·net·i·cist (jĭ nĕt'ə sĭst), *n.* one versed in genetics.

ge·net·ics (jĭ nĕt'ĭks), *n.* *Biol.* the science of heredity, dealing with resemblances and differences of related organisms flowing from the interaction of their genes and the environment. [pl. of **GENETIC** (def. 2). See -ICS]

Ge·ne·va (jə nē'və), *n.* 1. a city in SW Switzerland, on the Lake of Geneva: seat of the League of Nations, 1920–46. 151,400 (est. 1952). 2. **Lake of.** Also, **Lake Leman.** a lake between SW Switzerland and France. 45 mi. long; 225 sq. mi. French, **Ge·nève** (zhə nĕv').

ge·ne·va (jə nē'və), *n.* Hollands gin. [t. D: m. *genever,* t. OF: m. *genevre,* g. L *jūniperus* juniper]

Geneva bands, two bands, or pendent strips, worn at the throat as part of a clerical garb: worn orig. by the Swiss Calvinist clergy.

Geneva Convention, *Mil.* an international agreement establishing rules for the treatment during war of the sick, the wounded, and prisoners of war.

Geneva cross, a red Greek cross on a white ground, displayed in war, etc., to distinguish ambulances, hospitals, and persons serving them; red cross.

Geneva gown, a loose, large-sleeved, black preaching gown worn by Protestant clergymen: so named from its use by the Genevan Calvinist clergy.

Ge·ne·van (jə nē'vən), *adj.* 1. of or pertaining to Geneva. 2. Calvinistic. —*n.* 3. a native or inhabitant of Geneva. 4. a Calvinist.

Gen·e·vieve (jĕn'ə vēv'; *Fr.* zhən vyĕv'), *n.* **Saint,** A.D. c422–512, French nun, patron saint of Paris.

Gen·ghis Khan (jĕng'gĭs kän'), 1162–1227, Mongol conqueror of most of Asia and of E Europe to the Dnieper river. Also, **Jenghis Khan, Jenghiz Khan.**

gen·ial[1] (jēn'yəl), *adj.* 1. sympathetically cheerful; cordial: *a genial disposition, a genial host.* 2. enlivening; supporting life; pleasantly warm, or mild. 3. *Rare.* characterized by genius. [t. L: s. *geniãlis* festive, jovial, pleasant, lit., pertaining to generation or to marriage] —**gen'ial·ly,** *adv.* —**gen'ial·ness,** *n.* —**Syn.** 1. friendly hearty, pleasant, agreeable. —**Ant.** 1. sullen.

ge·ni·al[2] (jə nī'əl), *adj.* *Anat., Zool.* of or pertaining to the chin. [f. m. s. Gk. *géneion* chin + -AL[1]]

ge·ni·al·i·ty (jē'nĭ ăl'ə tĭ), *n.* genial quality; sympathetic cheerfulness or kindliness.

gen·ic (jĕn'ĭk), *adj. Biol.* of, relating to, resembling, or arising from a gene or genes.

ge·nic·u·late (jə nĭk'yə lĭt, -lāt'), *adj. Biol.* 1. having kneelike joints or bends. 2. bent at a joint like a knee. [t. L: m. s. *geniculātus* knotted]

ge·nic·u·la·tion (jə nĭk'yə lā'shən), *n.* 1. geniculate state. 2. a geniculate formation. [t. LL: s. *geniculātio* a bending of the knee]

ge·nie (jē'nĭ), *n.* a jinni or spirit of Mohammedan mythology. [t. F, t. L: m. *genius*. See GENIUS]

ge·ni·i (jē'nĭ ī'), *n.* pl. of genius (defs. 5, 6, 8).

gen·i·pap (jĕn'ə păp'), *n.* 1. the edible fruit of a tropical American rubiaceous tree, *Genipa americana*, about the size of an orange. 2. the plant. [t. Pg.: m. *genipapo*; of Tupian orig.]

gen·i·tal (jĕn'ə təl), *adj.* pertaining to generation or the organs of generation. [t. L: s. *genitālis*]

gen·i·ta·lia (jĕn'ə tāl'yə), *n.pl.* the genitals. [t. L]

gen·i·tals (jĕn'ə təlz), *n.pl.* the reproductive organs, esp. the external organs.

gen·i·tive (jĕn'ə tĭv), *Gram. —adj.* 1. (in some inflected languages) denoting the case of nouns generally used to modify other nouns, often indicating possession, but used also in expressions of measure, origin, characteristic: *Examples: John's hat, man's fate, week's vacation, duty's call.* 2. denoting the affix or other element characteristic of this case, or a word containing such an element. 3. similar to such a case form in function or meaning. —*n.* 4. the genitive case. 5. a word in that case. 6. a construction of similar meaning. [ME, t. L: m.s. *genitīvus*, lit., pertaining to generation] —**gen·i·ti·val** (jĕn'ə tĭ'vəl), *adj.* —**gen'i·ti'val·ly,** *adv.*

gen·i·to·u·ri·nar·y (jĕn'ə tō yŏŏr'ə nĕr'ĭ), *adj. Anat., Physiol.* noting or pertaining to the genital and urinary organs; urogenital. [f. *genito-* (comb. form of GENITAL) + URINARY]

gen·ius (jēn'yəs), *n., pl.* **geniuses** for 1–4, 7, **genii** (jē'nĭ ī') for 5, 6, 8. 1. exceptional natural capacity for creative and original conceptions. 2. a person having such capacity. 3. natural ability or capacity: *a task suited to one's genius.* 4. distinctive character or spirit, as of a nation, period, language, etc. 5. the guardian spirit of a place, institution, etc. 6. either of two mutually opposed spirits, one good and the other evil, supposed to attend a person throughout his life. 7. a person who strongly influences the character, conduct, or destiny of another: *an evil genius.* 8. any demon or spirit, esp. a genie or jinni (now chiefly or only in *pl.*). [t. L: tutelary spirit, any spiritual being, disposition, orig. a male generative or creative principle. Cf. GENIAL¹, GENITAL, GENUS, GENESIS, KIN] —**Syn.** 3. gift, talent, aptitude, faculty.

ge·ni·us lo·ci (jē'nĭ əs lō'sī), *Latin.* 1. guardian of a place. 2. the peculiar character of a place with reference to the impression that it makes on the mind.

Genl., General.

Gen·o·a (jĕn'ə wə), *n.* a seaport in NW Italy. 680,000 (est. 1954). Italian, **Ge·no·va** (jē'nō vä').

gen·o·cide (jĕn'ə sīd'), *n.* extermination of a national or racial group as a planned move. [f. Gk. *géno(s)* race +-CIDE²; coined by Dr. Raphael Lemkin, 1944] —**gen'o·cid'al,** *adj.*

Gen·o·ese (jĕn'ō ēz', -ēs'), *adj., n. pl.* **-ese.** —*adj.* 1. of Genoa. —*n.* 2. a native or inhabitant of Genoa.

gen·o·type (jĕn'ə tīp'), *n. Genetics.* 1. the fundamental hereditary constitution of an organism. 2. its breeding formula of genes. 3. a group of organisms with a common heredity. [f. Gk. *géno(s)* origin, race + -TYPE] —**gen·o·typ·ic** (jĕn'ə tĭp'ĭk), *adj.* —**gen'o·typ'i·cal·ly,** *adv.*

-genous, an adjective suffix derived from nouns in -gen and -geny. [-GEN + -OUS]

gen·re (zhäN'r), *n.* 1. genus; kind; sort; style. 2. *Painting,* etc. the category in which scenes from ordinary life are represented (as distinguished from landscapes, etc.). —*adj.* 3. of or pertaining to genre (def. 2). [t. F: kind. See GENDER]

gen·ro (gĕn'rō'), *n., pl.* **-ros.** elder statesman (def. 1). [t. Jap.: old man]

gens (jĕnz), *n., pl.* **gentes** (jĕn'tēz). 1. a group of families in ancient Rome claiming descent from a common ancestor and united by a common name and common religious rites. 2. *Anthropol.* a group tracing descent in the male line. [t. L: also race, people]

Gen·san (gĕn'sän'), *n.* a seaport in E North Korea. 112,952 (1949). Japanese, **Wŏnsan.**

Gen·ser·ic (jĕn'sər ĭk, gĕn'-), *n.* A.D. c390–477, king of the Vandals, conqueror in northern Africa and Italy.

gent (jĕnt), *n.* (often in humorous use) gentleman.

Gent (KHĕnt), *n.* Flemish name of Ghent.

Gent., gentleman; gentlemen. Also, **gent.**

gen·teel (jĕn tēl'), *adj.* 1. belonging or suited to polite society. 2. well-bred or refined; polite; elegant; stylish. 3. affected in manner. [t. F: m. *gentil.* See GENTLE] —**gen·teel'ly,** *adv.* —**gen·teel'ness,** *n.*

gen·tian (jĕn'shən), *n.* 1. any plant of the large genus *Gentiana*, comprising herbs having commonly blue flowers, less frequently yellow, white, or red; esp. *G. crinita* (one of the *fringed gentians*), of eastern North America, with blue, delicately fringed corolla, and *G. lutea*, a yellow-flowered European species. 2. any of various plants

resembling the gentian. 3. the root of *G. lutea*, or a preparation of it, used as a tonic. [ME *gencian*, t. L: m. s. *gentiana*; said to be named after *Gentius*, an Illyrian king]

gen·ti·a·na·ceous (jĕn'shĭ ə nā'shəs), *adj.* belonging to the *Gentianaceae*, or gentian family of plants.

gentian violet, crystal violet.

gen·tile (jĕn'tīl), *adj.* 1. of or pertaining to any people not Jewish. 2. Christian as distinguished from Jewish. 3. heathen or pagan. 4. (of a linguistic expression) expressing nationality or local extractions. —*n.* 5. a person who is not Jewish, esp. a Christian. 6. (among Mormons) one not a Mormon. 7. a heathen or pagan. Also, **Gen'tile.** [ME *gentil,* t. L: s. *gentīlis* belonging to a people, national, LL foreign]

gen·til·i·ty (jĕn tĭl'ə tĭ), *n., pl.* **-ties.** 1. superior refinement or elegance, possessed or affected. 2. (*usually pl.*) an instance of this. 3. gentle birth.

gen·tle (jĕn'təl), *adj.,* **-tler, -tlest,** *v.,* **-tled, -tling.** —*adj.* 1. mild, kindly, or amiable: *gentle words.* 2. not severe, rough, or violent: *a gentle wind, a gentle tap.* 3. moderate; gradual: *gentle heat, a gentle slope.* 4. of good birth or family; wellborn. 5. characteristic of good birth; honorable; respectable. 6. easily handled or managed: *a gentle animal.* 7. soft or low: *a gentle sound.* 8. polite; refined. 9. *Archaic.* noble; chivalrous: *a gentle knight.* —*v.t.* 10. *Colloq.* to tame; render tractable. 11. *Rare.* to mollify (a person). 12. *Obs.* to ennoble; dignify. [ME *gentil,* t. OF: of good family, noble, excellent, t. L *gentīlis.* See GENTILE] —**gen'tle·ness,** *n.* —**gen'tly,** *adv.*

—**Syn.** 1. soft, bland, peaceful, pacific, soothing; kind, tender, humane, lenient, merciful. GENTLE, MEEK, MILD, refer to an absence of bad temper or belligerence. GENTLE has reference esp. to disposition and behavior, and often suggests a deliberate or voluntary kindness or forbearance in dealing with others: *a gentle pat, gentle with children.* MEEK implies a submissive spirit, and may even indicate undue submission in the face of insult or injustice: *meek and even servile or weak.* MILD suggests absence of harshness or severity, rather because of natural character or temperament than conscious choice: *a mild rebuke, a mild manner.* —**Ant.** 1. arrogant.

gentle breeze, *Meteorol.* a wind of Beaufort scale #3, i.e. one within the range of 8–12 miles per hour.

gen·tle·folk (jĕn'təl fōk'), *n.pl.* persons of good family and breeding. Also, **gen'tle·folks'.**

gen·tle·man (jĕn'təl mən), *n., pl.* **-men.** 1. a man of good breeding, education, and manners. 2. (as a polite form of speech) any man. 3. a male personal servant, or valet, esp. of a man of social position. 4. a man of good social standing by birth. 5. *Hist.* a man above the rank of yeoman. —**gen'tle·man·like',** *adj.*

gen·tle·man-at-arms (jĕn'təl mən ət ärmz'), *n., pl.* **gentlemen-at-arms.** (in England) one of a guard of forty gentlemen with their officers who attend the sovereign on state occasions.

gen·tle·man-com·mon·er (jĕn'təl mən kŏm'ən ər), *n., pl.* **gentlemen-commoners.** a member of a class of commoners enjoying special privileges, formerly but no longer, at Oxford University.

gen·tle·man·ly (jĕn'təl mən lĭ), *adj.* like or befitting a gentleman; well-bred. —**gen'tle·man·li·ness,** *n.*

gentlemen's agreement, an agreement binding as a matter of honor alone, not enforceable at law.

gentle reader, courteous or kind reader: used in writing by the author in addressing the reader.

gentle sex, women.

gen·tle·wom·an (jĕn'təl wŏŏm'ən), *n., pl.* **-women.** 1. a woman of good family or breeding; a lady. 2. a woman who attends upon a lady of rank. —**gen'tle·wom'an·ly,** *adj.* —**gen'tle·wom'an·li·ness,** *n.*

gen·try (jĕn'trĭ), *n.* 1. wellborn and well-bred people. 2. (in England) the upper middle class. 3. (in humorous use) people; folks. [ME, f. *gent* noble + -RY]

ge·nu (jē'nū, -nōō), *n., pl.* **genua** (jĕn'yŏŏ ə). *Anat., Zool.* 1. the knee. 2. a kneelike part or bend. [L]

gen·u·flect (jĕn'yŏŏ flĕkt'), *v.i.* to bend the knee or knees in reverence. [t. ML: s. *genūflectere,* f. L *genū* knee + *flectere* bend] —**gen'u·flec'tor,** *n.*

gen·u·flec·tion (jĕn'yŏŏ flĕk'shən), *n.* act of bending the knee or knees in worship. Also, *esp. Brit.,* **gen'u·flex'ion.** [t. ML: m. s. *genūflexio,* der. ML *genūflectere* bend the knee]

gen·u·ine (jĕn'yŏŏ ĭn), *adj.* 1. being truly such; real; authentic: *genuine regret, genuine worth.* 2. properly so called: *genuine leprosy.* 3. sincere; free from pretense or affectation: *a genuine person.* 4. proceeding from the original stock; pure in breed: *a genuine Celtic people.* [t. L: m. s. *genuīnus* native, natural, authentic, genuine] —**gen'u·ine·ly,** *adv.* —**gen'u·ine·ness,** *n.*

ge·nus (jē'nəs), *n., pl.* **genera** (jĕn'ər ə), **genuses.** 1. a kind; sort; class. 2. *Biol.* the usual major subdivision of a family or subfamily, usually consisting of more than one species, essentially very similar to one another and regarded as phylogenetically very closely related. The genus designation is the first part of the scientific name of a species, as in *Lynx canadensis,* the Canadian lynx. 3. *Logic.* a class or group of individuals including subordinate groups called *species.* [t. L: race, stock, kind, sort, gender (c. Gk. *génos*)]

-geny, a suffix meaning "origin," as in *phylogeny.* [t. Gk.: m. s. *-geneia,* der. *-genēs* born, produced. See -GEN]

geo-, a word element meaning "the earth," as in *geocentric.* [t. Gk., comb. form of *gē*]

Geo., George.

ge·o·cen·tric (jē'ō sĕn'trĭk), *adj.* **1.** *Astron.* as viewed or measured from the center of the earth: *the geocentric altitude of a star.* **2.** having or representing the earth as a center: *a geocentric theory of the universe.* Also, **ge'o·cen'tri·cal.** —**ge'o·cen'tri·cal·ly,** *adv.*

geocentric parallax. See **parallax** (def. 2).

ge·o·chem·is·try (jē'ō kĕm'ĭs trĭ), *n.* the science dealing with the chemical changes in, and the composition of, the earth's crust. —**ge·o·chem·i·cal** (jē'ō-kĕm'ə kəl), *adj.* —**ge'o·chem'ist,** *n.*

geod., **1.** geodesy. **2.** geodetic.

ge·ode (jē'ōd), *n.* *Geol.* a hollow concretionary or nodular stone frequently lined with crystals. [t. F, t. L: m. s. *geōdēs* precious stone, t. Gk.: adj., earthlike]

ge·o·des·ic (jē'ə dĕs'ĭk, -dē'sĭk), *adj.* **1.** Also, **ge'o·des'i·cal.** pertaining to the geometry of curved surfaces, in which geodesic lines take the place of the straight lines of plane geometry. —*n.* **2.** a geodesic line.

geodesic line, *Math.* the shortest line lying on a given surface and connecting two given points.

ge·od·e·sy (jē'ŏd'ə sĭ), *n.* that branch of applied mathematics which determines the shape and area of large tracts of country, the exact position of geographical points, and the curvature, shape and dimensions of the earth. Also, **ge·o·det·ics** (jē'ə dĕt'ĭks). [t. NL: m. s. *geōdaesia,* t. Gk.: m. *geōdaisia* art of mensuration] —**ge·od'e·sist,** *n.*

ge·o·det·ic (jē'ə dĕt'ĭk), *adj.* **1.** pertaining to geodesy. Also, **ge·o·det'i·cal.** —**ge'o·det'i·cal·ly,** *adv.*

Geof·frey of Monmouth (jĕf'rĭ), 1100?–1154, English chronicler.

geog., **1.** geographer. **2.** geographic; geographical. **3.** geography.

ge·og·no·sy (jĭ ŏg'nə sĭ), *n.* that branch of geology which treats of the constituent parts of the earth, its envelope of air and water, its crust, and the condition of its interior. [f. GEO- + m. s. Gk. *-gnōsía* knowledge]

ge·og·ra·pher (jĭ ŏg'rə fər), *n.* one who specializes in the study and writing of geography.

ge·o·graph·i·cal (jē'ə grăf'ə kəl), *adj.* **1.** of or pertaining to geography. **2.** referring to or characteristic of a certain locality, esp. in reference to its location in relation to other places. Also, **ge'o·graph'ic.** —**ge'o·graph'i·cal·ly,** *adv.*

geographical mile. See **mile** (def. 1b).

geographic determinism, *Sociol.* the doctrine which regards geographical conditions as the determining or molding agency of group life.

geographic environment, *Sociol.* the entire natural surroundings of man, independent of his activity but conditioning it.

ge·og·ra·phy (jĭ ŏg'rə fĭ), *n., pl.* **-phies.** **1.** the study of the areal differentiation of the earth surface, as shown in the character, arrangement, and interrelations over the world of elements such as climate, relief, soil, vegetation, population, land use, industries, or states, and of the unit areas formed by the complex of these individual elements. **2.** the topographical features of a region, usually of the earth, but sometimes of Mars, the moon, etc. [t. L: m. s. *geōgraphia,* t. Gk.]

ge·oid (jē'oid), *n.* **1.** an imaginary surface which coincides with the mean sea level over the ocean and its extension under the continents. **2.** the geometrical figure formed by this surface, an ellipsoid flattened at the poles. [t. Gk.: m.s. *geōeidēs* earthlike]

geol., **1.** geologic; geological. **2.** geologist. **3.** geology.

ge·o·log·ic (jē'ə lŏj'ĭk), *adj.* of or pertaining to geology. Also, **ge'o·log'i·cal.** —**ge'o·log'i·cal·ly,** *adv.*

ge·ol·o·gize (jĭ ŏl'ə jīz'), *v.,* **-gized, -gizing.** —*v.i.* **1.** to study geology. —*v.t.* **2.** to examine geologically.

ge·ol·o·gy (jĭ ŏl'ə jĭ), *n., pl.* **-gies.** the science which treats of the earth, the rocks of which it is composed, and the changes which it has undergone or is undergoing. [t. NL: m. s. *geōlogia.* See GEO-, -LOGY] —**ge·ol'o·gist,** *n.*

geom., **1.** geometric. **2.** geometrical. **3.** geometry.

ge·o·mag·net·ic (jē'ō măg nĕt'ĭk), *adj.* of or pertaining to terrestrial magnetism.

ge·o·man·cer (jē'ə măn'sər), *n.* one versed in or practicing geomancy.

ge·o·man·cy (jē'ə măn'sĭ), *n.* divination by means of the figure made by a handful of earth thrown down at random, or, by figures or lines formed by means of dots made at random. [ME *geomancie,* t. ML: m. *geōmantia,* f. Gk. (see GEO-, -MANCY)]

ge·om·e·ter (jĭ ŏm'ə tər), *n.* geometrician. [t. L: m. s. *geōmetra, geōmetrēs,* t. Gk.: (m.) *geōmétrēs* land measurer, geometer]

ge·o·met·ric (jē'ə mĕt'rĭk), *adj.* **1.** of or pertaining to geometry; according to the principles of geometry. **2.** resembling or employing the lines or figures in geometry. **3.** of or pertaining to painting, sculpture, or ornamentation of predominantly geometrical characteristics or figures. Also, **ge'o·met'ri·cal.** —**ge'o·met'ri·cal·ly,** *adv.*

ge·om·e·tri·cian (jĭ ŏm'ə trĭsh'ən, jē'ə mə-), *n.* an expert in geometry.

geometric mean, *Math.* the means of n positive numbers obtained by taking the nth root of the product of the numbers: *the geometric mean of 6 and 24 is 12.*

geometric progression, *Math.* a sequence of

terms in which the ratio of any term to its predecessor is a constant; e.g., 1, 3, 9, 27, 81 and 243; 144, 12, 1, $^1/_{12}$.

geometric ratio, *Math.* the ratio of consecutive terms in a geometric progression.

ge·o·met·rid (jĭ ŏm'ə trĭd), *adj.* **1.** of or relating to the moths of the family *Geometridae,* the larvae of which are called measuring worms. —*n.* **2.** a geometrid moth. [t. NL: s. *Geōmetridae,* der. L *geōmetra* GEOM-ETER]

Geometrid
A. Larva; B. Moth
(Slightly enlarged)

ge·om·e·trize (jĭ ŏm'ə trīz'), *v.,* **-trized, -trizing.** —*v.i.* **1.** to work by geometrical methods. —*v.t.* **2.** to put into geometric form.

ge·om·e·try (jĭ ŏm'ə trĭ), *n.* that branch of mathematics which deduces the properties of figures in space from their defining conditions. by means of assumed properties of space. [ME *geometrie,* t. L: m. *geōmetria,* t. Gk.]

ge·o·mor·phic (jē'ə môr'fĭk), *adj.* **1.** of or pertaining to the figure of the earth, or the forms of its surface. **2.** resembling the earth in form.

ge·o·mor·phol·o·gy (jē'ə môr fŏl'ə jĭ), *n.* the study of the characteristics, origin, and development of land forms.

ge·oph·a·gy (jĭ ŏf'ə jĭ), *n.* the practice of eating earthy matter, esp. clay or chalk. [f. GEO- + -PHAGY]

ge·oph·i·lous (jĭ ŏf'ə ləs), *adj.* *Bot., Zool.* terrestrial, as certain snails, or any plant fruiting underground.

ge·o·phys·ics (jē'ō fĭz'ĭks), *n.* the physics of the earth, dealing esp. with the study of inaccessible portions of the earth by instruments and apparatus such as the torsion balance, seismograph, and magnetometer. —**ge'o·phys'i·cal,** *adj.* —**ge'o·phys'i·cist,** *n.*

ge·o·phyte (jē'ə fīt'), *n.* *Bot.* a plant with underground buds.

ge·o·pol·i·tics (jē'ō pŏl'ə tĭks), *n.* the application of political and economic geography to the external political problems of states, notably problems of national power, frontiers, and possibilities for expansion.

ge·o·pon·ic (jē'ə pŏn'ĭk), *adj.* of or pertaining to tillage or agriculture; agricultural. [t. Gk.: m. s. *geōponikós*]

ge·o·pon·ics (jē'ə pŏn'ĭks), *n.* the art or science of agriculture.

ge·o·ram·a (jē'ō răm'ə, -rä'mə), *n.* a large hollow globe on the inside of which is depicted a map of the earth's surface, to be viewed by a spectator within the globe. [t. F, f. Gk.: *gê* earth + (*h*)*órama* view]

George (jôrj), *n.* **1. David Lloyd.** See **Lloyd George.** **2. Henry,** 1839–97, U.S. economist, advocate of a single tax. **3. Saint,** died A.D. 303? Christian martyr, patron saint of England. **4. Lake,** a lake in E New York: "Lake Horicon" of Cooper's novels. 36 mi. long.

George I, **1.** 1660–1727, king of England, 1714–27; first king of the House of Hanover. **2.** 1845–1913, king of Greece, 1863–1913.

George II, **1.** 1683–1760, king of England, 1727–60 (son of George I). **2.** 1890–1947, king of Greece, 1922–1923 and 1935–47.

George III, 1738–1820, king of England, 1760–1820 (grandson of George II).

George IV, 1762–1830, king of England, 1820–30 (son of George III).

George V, 1865–1936, king of England, 1910–36 (son of Edward VII).

George VI, 1895-1952, king of England, 1936-1952 (second son of George V; brother of Edward VIII).

George·town (jôrj'toun'), *n.* a seaport in and the capital of Guyana. 91,529 (est. 1953).

George Town, a seaport in and the capital of the state of Penang, Malaya. 189,068 (1947). Also, **Georgetown** or **Penang.**

Geor·gette (jôr jĕt'), *n.* sheer silk or rayon crepe of dull texture. Also, **Georgette crepe.** [named after Mme. *Georgette,* French modiste]

Geor·gia (jôr'jə), *n.* **1.** a State in the SE United States. 3,943,116 pop. (1960); 58,876 sq. mi. *Cap.:* Atlanta. *Abbr.:* Ga. **2.** Official name, **Georgian Soviet Socialist Republic.** a constituent republic of the Soviet Union in Caucasia, bordering on the Black Sea: it was an independent kingdom for ab. 2000 years. 4,000,000 (est. 1956); ab. 26,800 sq. mi. *Cap.:* Tiflis. **3. Strait of,** an inlet of the Pacific in SW Canada between Vancouver Island and the mainland of British Columbia.

[map]
SOVIET UNION
CAUCASUS MTS.
GEORGIA
ARMENIA
AZERBAIJAN
TURKEY
IRAN
Caspian Sea
Black Sea
Georgia (def. 2)

Geor·gian (jôr'jən), *adj., n.* **1.** pertaining to the four Georges, kings of England (1714–1830), or the period of their reigns. **2.** pertaining to George V (1910–36), or the period of his reign. **3.** of or pertaining to the State of Georgia in the U.S. **4.** pertaining to Georgia in the Soviet Union. —*n.* **5.** a person, esp. a writer, of either of the Georgian periods in England. **6.** the styles or character of a Georgian period. **7.** a native or inhabitant of the State of Georgia. **8.** a native or inhabitant of Georgia in the Soviet Union. **9.** the most important South Caucasian language.

Georgian Bay, the NE part of Lake Huron, in Ontario, Canada. ab. 6000 sq. mi.

Georgia pine, longleaf pine.

geor·gic (jôr′jĭk), *adj.* **1.** agricultural. —*n.* **2.** a poem on agricultural matters. [t. L: s. *geōrgicus* agricultural, t. Gk.: m. *geōrgikós*]

ge·o·syn·cli·nal (jē′ō sĭn klī′nəl), *adj. Geol.* **1.** pertaining to a synclinal fold which involves a relatively large part of the earth's surface. —*n.* **2.** a geosyncline.

ge·o·syn·cline (jē′ō sĭn′klīn), *n. Geol.* a portion of the earth's crust subjected to downward warping during a large fraction of geologic time; a geosynclinal fold.

ge·o·tax·is (jē′ō tăk′sĭs), *n. Biol.* a movement of an organism toward or away from a gravitational force.

ge·o·tec·ton·ic (jē′ō tĕk tŏn′ĭk), *adj.* pertaining to the structure of the earth's crust or to the arrangement and form of its constituents.

ge·o·therm·al (jē′ō thûr′məl), *adj.* of or pertaining to the internal heat of the earth.

ge·o·trop·ic (jē′ə trŏp′ĭk), *adj. Biol.* taking a particular direction with reference to the earth: **a. positively geotropic,** directed downward. **b. negatively geotropic,** directed upward. **c. transversely geotropic,** directed horizontally. —**ge′o·trop′i·cal·ly,** *adv.*

ge·ot·ro·pism (jĭ ŏt′rə pĭz′əm), *n. Biol.* a tropism oriented with respect to gravitation, as the direction of growth of plants or the ability of some animals to avoid an upside-down position in the air.

Ger., **1.** German. **2.** Germany.

ger., **1.** gerund. **2.** gerundive.

ge·rah (gē′rə), *n.* a Hebrew weight and coin, equal to ¹/₂₀ of a shekel. [t. Heb.: m. *gērāh,* t. Akkadian: m. *girū*]

Ge·raint (jĭ rānt′), *n. Arthurian Romance.* one of the knights of the Round Table, husband of Enid.

ge·ra·ni·a·ceous (jĭ rā′nĭ ā′shəs), *adj.* belonging to the *Geraniaceae,* or geranium family of plants.

ge·ra·ni·al (jĭ rā′nĭ əl), *n. Chem.* citral.

ge·ra·ni·um (jĭ rā′nĭ əm), *n.* **1.** any of the plants of the genus *Geranium,* most of which have pink or purple flowers, and some of which, as *G. maculatum,* have an astringent root used in medicine; crane's-bill. **2.** a plant of the allied genus *Pelargonium,* of which many species are well known in cultivation for their showy flowers (as the **scarlet geraniums**) or their fragrant leaves (as the **rose geraniums**). [t. L, t. Gk.: m. *gerānion* crane's-bill]

ger·a·tol·o·gy (jĕr′ə tŏl′ə jĭ), *n.* the study of the decline of life, as in old age or in animals approaching extinction. [f. s. Gk. *géras* old age + -(o)LOGY]

ger·bil (jûr′bĭl), *n.* any of numerous jerboalike rodents (genus *Gerbillus,* etc.) of Asia, Africa, and southern Russia, belonging to the mouse family, and forming the subfamily *Gerbillinae.* Also, **ger′bille.** [t. F: m. *gerbille,* t. NL: m. s. *gerbillus,* dim. of *gerbo* JERBOA]

ge·rent (jĭr′ənt), *n.* a ruling power; manager. [t. L: s. *gerens,* ppr. bearing, conducting, managing]

ger·fal·con (jûr′fôl′kən, -fô′-), *n.* any of various large arctic and subarctic falcons, as the **white gerfalcon,** *Falco rusticolus obsoletus.* Also, **gyrfalcon.** [ME, t. OF: m. *gerfaucon;* of Gmc. orig.]

ger·i·at·rics (jĕr′ĭ ăt′rĭks), *n.* the science of the medical and hygienic care of, or the diseases of, aged persons. —**ger·i·a·tri·cian** (jĕr′ĭ ə trĭsh′ən), **ger′i·at′rist,** *n.*

Ger·la·chov·ka (gĕr′lä hôf′kä), *n.* See Carpathian Mountains.

Gerfalcon.
Falco rusticolus
(21 in. long)

germ (jûrm), *n.* **1.** a microörganism, esp. when disease-producing; microbe. **2.** that from which anything springs as if from a seed. **3.** *Embryol.* **a.** a bud, offshoot, or seed. **b.** the rudiment of a living organism; an embryo in its early stages. **4.** *Biol.* the initial stage in development or evolution, as a germ cell or ancestral form. [t. F: m. *germe,* g. L *germen* sprout] —**germ′less,** *adj.*

Ger·man (jûr′mən), *adj.* **1.** of or pertaining to Germany, its inhabitants, or their language. —*n.* **2.** a native or inhabitant of Germany; a High German or a Low German. **3.** a Germanic language, the language of Germany and Austria and an official language of Switzerland. **4.** *Ling.* High German. **5.** (*l.c.*) an elaborate kind of dance; cotillion. **6.** (*l.c.*) a party at which only the german is danced. [t. L: s. *Germānus;* orig. uncert.]

ger·man (jûr′mən), *adj.* **1.** sprung from the same father and mother (always placed after the noun): *a brother-german.* **2.** sprung from the brother or sister of one's father or mother, or from brothers or sisters: *a cousin-german.* **3.** germane. [t. L: s. *germānus* having the same father (and mother); r. ME *germain,* t. OF]

German Baptist Brethren. See Dunker.

German Democratic Republic, official name of East Germany. See Germany.

ger·man·der (jər măn′dər), *n.* **1.** any of the herbs or shrubs constituting the labiate genus *Teucrium,* as *T. Chamaedrys,* a purple-flowered European species, and *T. canadense,* an American species. **2.** a species of speedwell (**germander speedwell**). See **speedwell.** [t. ML: m. s. *germandra,* t. LGk.: m. *chamándra,* alter. of Gk. *chamáidrÿs,* lit., ground oak]

ger·mane (jər mān′), *adj.* closely related; pertinent: *a remark germane to the question.* [var. of GERMAN]

German East Africa, a former German territory in E Africa: now the independent republics of Tanganyika, Rwanda, and Burundi.

Ger·man·ic (jər măn′ĭk), *adj.* **1.** of the Teutonic race, the peoples belonging to it, or the group of languages spoken by these peoples; Teutonic. **2.** of the Germans; German. —*n.* **3.** a group of Indo-European languages, including English, German, Dutch, Gothic, and the Scandinavian languages. [t. L: s. *Germānicus*]

ger·man·ic (jər măn′ĭk), *adj. Chem.* of or containing germanium, esp. in the tetravalent state (Ge +⁴). [f. GERMAN(IUM) + -IC]

Ger·man·i·cus Caesar (jər măn′ĭ kəs), 15 B.C.–A.D. 19, Roman general.

Ger·man·ism (jûr′mə nĭz′əm), *n.* **1.** a German characteristic, usage, or idiom. **2.** German modes of thought, action, etc. **3.** attachment to what is German.

ger·ma·ni·um (jər mā′nĭ əm), *n. Chem.* a rare metallic element, normally tetravalent, with a grayish-white color. *Symbol:* Ge; *at. wt.:* 72.6; *at. no.:* 32; *sp. gr.:* 5.36 at 20⁰C. [NL, der. L *Germānia* country of the Germans]

Ger·man·ize (jûr′mə nīz′), *v.t., v.i.,* **-ized, -izing. 1.** to make or become German in character, sentiment, etc. **2.** to translate into German. —**Ger′man·i·za′tion,** *n.*

German measles, *Pathol.* a contagious disease, usually mild, accompanied by fever, often some sore throat, and a rash resembling that of scarlet fever; rubella.

German Ocean, the North Sea.

ger·man·ous (jər măn′əs), *adj. Chem.* containing divalent germanium (Ge+²).

German shepherd dog, police dog (def. 1).

German silver, a white alloy of copper, zinc, and nickel, used for making utensils, drawing instruments, etc.

German Southwest Africa, a former German protectorate, now under mandate to the Union of South Africa. See **South-West Africa.**

Ger·man·town (jûr′mən toun′), *n.* the NW part of Philadelphia, Pa.: American defeat by British, 1777.

Ger·ma·ny (jûr′mə nĭ), *n.* a country in central Europe; traditional capital: Berlin; German name, **Deutschland.** After World War II, Germany was divided into four zones of occupation: British, French, U.S., and Russian; it is now divided into **(a) West Germany** (the British, French, and U.S. Zones combined); 50,595,000 pop. (est. 1956); 94,905 sq. mi. *Provisional capital:* Bonn. Official name, **Federal Republic of Germany; (b) East Germany** (the Soviet Zone); 17,944,000 pop. (est. 1956); 41,535 sq. mi. *Cap.:* East Berlin. Official name, **German Democratic Republic; (c)** the section of East Germany east of the Oder-Neisse line, under provisional Polish and Russian administration.

germ cell, *Biol.* the sexual reproductive cell at any stage from the primordial cell to the mature gamete.

germ·i·cide (jûr′mə sīd′), *n.* an agent that kills germs or microörganisms. [f. GERM + -(I)CIDE¹] —**ger′mi·cid′al,** *adj.*

Ger·mi·nal (jûr′mə nəl; *Fr.* zhĕr mē nàl′), *n.* (in the calendar of the first French Republic) the seventh month of the year, extending from Mar. 21 to Apr. 19. [F, t. NL: m. *germinālis,* der. L *germen, germinis* sprout]

ger·mi·nal (jûr′mə nəl), *adj.* **1.** pertaining to a germ or germs. **2.** of the nature of a germ or germ cell. **3.** in the earliest stage of development: *germinal ideas.*

germinal disk, *Embryol.* blastodisc.

germinal vesicle, *Embryol.* the large, vesicular nucleus of an ovum before the polar bodies are formed.

ger·mi·nant (jûr′mə nənt), *adj.* germinating.

ger·mi·nate (jûr′mə nāt′), *v.,* **-nated, -nating.** —*v.i.* **1.** to begin to grow or develop. **2.** *Bot.* **a.** to develop into a plant or individual, as a seed, or as a spore, bulb, or the like. **b.** to sprout; put forth shoots. —*v.t.* **3.** to cause to develop; produce. [t. L: m.s. *germinātus,* pp.] —**ger′mi·na′tion,** *n.* —**ger′mi·na′tor,** *n.*

ger·mi·na·tive (jûr′mə nā′tĭv), *adj.* capable of germinating or developing; pertaining to germination.

Ger·mis·ton (jûr′mĭs tən), *n.* a city in the NE Republic of South Africa, in Transvaal. 114,215 (1951).

germ layer, one of the three primary embryonic cell layers, i.e., ectoderm, endoderm, and mesoderm.

germ plasm, the protoplasm of the germ cells containing the units of heredity (chromosomes and genes).

germ theory, **1.** *Biol.* the theory that living matter cannot be produced by evolution or development from nonliving matter, but is necessarily produced from germs or seeds; the doctrine of biogenesis. **2.** *Pathol.* the theory that infectious diseases, etc., are due to the agency of germs or microörganisms.

Gé·rôme (zhĕ rōm′), *n.* **Jean Léon** (zhän lĕ ôn′), 1824–1904, French painter and sculptor.

Ge·ron·i·mo (jĭ rŏn′ə mō′), *n.* c1834–1909, Apache Indian chief.

ger·on·toc·ra·cy (jĕr′ŏn tŏk′rə sĭ), *n., pl.* **-cies. 1.** government by old men. **2.** a governing body consisting of old men. [f. s. Gk. *gérōn* old man + -(o)CRACY]

ger·on·tol·o·gy (jĕr′ŏn tŏl′ə jĭ), *n.* the science that treats of the decline of life. —**ger′on·tol′o·gist′,** *n.*

-gerous, a combining form meaning "bearing" or "producing," as in *setigerous.* [f. L *-ger* bearing + -OUS]

Ger·ry (gĕr′ĭ), *n.* **Elbridge** (ĕl′brĭj), 1744–1814, vice-president of the U.S., 1813–14.

ger·ry·man·der (gĕr′ĭmăn′dər, jĕr′-), *v.t.* **1.** *U.S. Pol.* to subject (a State, county, etc.) to a gerrymander. **2.** to manipulate unfairly. —*n.* **3.** *U.S.Pol.* an arbitrary arrangement of the political divisions of a State, county, etc., made so as to give one party an unfair advantage in elections. [f. Gerry (gov. one party an unfair advantage in 1812 redistricted Massachusetts) + (*sala*)*mander* (from a fancied resemblance of the map of Essex Co., Mass., to this animal, after the redistricting)]

Gersh·win (gûrsh′wĭn), *n.* George, 1898–1937, U.S. composer.

ger·und (jĕr′ənd), *n.* *Gram.* **1.** (in Latin and some other languages) a derived noun form of verbs, having (in Latin) all case forms but the nominative. *Example:* Latin *dicendī* gen., *dicendō*, dat., abl., *dicendum*, acc., "saying." No nominative form occurs. **2.** *Gram.* (sometimes, from similarity of meaning) the English *-ing* form of a verb (*loving*) when in nominal function. *Hunting* and *writing* are gerunds in the sentences "Hunting is good exercise" and "writing is easy." **3.** (sometimes, in other languages) a form similar to the Latin gerund in meaning or function. [t. LL: m. s. *gerundium*, der. L *gerundum*, var. of *gerendum*, ger. of L *gerere* bear, conduct] —**ge·run·di·al** (jĭrŭn′dĭ əl), *adj.*

ge·run·dive (jĭrŭn′dĭv), *n.* **1.** (in Latin) the future passive participle, similar to the gerund in formation. *Example: Haec dicendum est* "This must be said." —*adj.* **2.** resembling a gerund. [t. LL: m. s. *gerundīvus*, der. *gerundium* GERUND] —**ger·un·di·val** (jĕr′ən dī′vəl), *adj.* —**ge·run′dive·ly**, *adv.*

Ge·ry·on (jĭr′ĭ ən, gĭr′ĭ-), *n.* *Class. Legend.* a monster king of Cadiz, whose cattle Hercules carried off.

ges·so (jĕs′ō), *n.* **1.** gypsum, or plaster of Paris, prepared with glue for use as a surface for painting. **2.** any plasterlike preparation to fit a surface for painting, gilding, etc. **3.** a prepared surface of plaster or plasterlike material for painting, etc. [t. It., g. L *gypsum* GYPSUM]

gest (jĕst), *n.* *Archaic.* **1.** a metrical romance or history. **2.** a story or tale. **3.** a deed or exploit. Also, **geste.** [ME *geste*, t. OF, t. L: m. *gesta* deeds, prop. pp. neut. pl.]

Ge·stalt (gəshtält′), *n., pl.* -**stalten** (-shtäl′tən). *Psychol.* an organized configuration or pattern of experiences or of acts: *the Gestalt of a melody is distinct from the separate tones.* [t. G: form]

Gestalt psychology, a school of psychology which believes that experiences and conduct do not occur through the summation of reflexes or other individual elements but through configurations called *Gestalten*, which operate individually or interact mutually.

Ge·sta·po (gə stä′pō; *Ger.* -shtä′-), *n.* Secret State Police of Nazi Germany. [G: *ge(heime) Sta(ats) po(lizei)*]

Ges·ta Ro·ma·no·rum (jĕs′tə rō′mə nôr′əm), a popular collection of stories in Latin, compiled late in the 13th century.

ges·tate (jĕs′tāt), *v.t.,* -**tated,** -**tating.** to carry in the womb during the period from conception to delivery. [t. L: m. s. *gestātus*, pp., carried]

ges·ta·tion (jĕs tā′shən), *n.* act or period of gestating. [t. L: s. *gestātio* a carrying]

ges·tic (jĕs′tĭk), *adj.* pertaining to bodily motions, esp. dancing. Also, **ges′ti·cal.** [f. L *gestus* gesture + -IC]

ges·tic·u·late (jĕs tĭk′yə lāt′), *v.i.,* -**lated,** -**lating.** **1.** to make or use gestures, esp. in an animated or excited manner with or instead of speech. —*v.t.* **2.** to express by gesturing. [t. L: m.s. *gesticulātus*, pp., having made mimic gestures] —**ges·tic′u·la′tor,** *n.*

ges·tic·u·la·tion (jĕs tĭk′yə lā′shən), *n.* **1.** act of gesticulating. **2.** an animated or excited gesture.

ges·tic·u·la·to·ry (jĕs tĭk′yə lə tōr′ĭ), *adj.* characterized by or making gesticulations. Also, **ges·tic′u·la′tive.**

ges·ture (jĕs′chər), *n., v.,* -**tured,** -**turing.** —*n.* **1.** movement of the body, head, arms, hands, or face expressive of an idea or an emotion: *the gestures of an orator, a gesture of impatience.* **2.** any action or proceeding intended for effect or as a formality; demonstration: *a gesture of friendship.* —*v.i.* **3.** to make or use gestures. —*v.t.* **4.** to express by gestures. [ME, t. ML: m. *gestūra*, der. L *gerere* bear, conduct] —**ges′tur·er,** *n.*

Ge·sund·heit (gə zŏŏnt′hīt), *n.* *German.* soundness; health (used after a person has sneezed or as a toast).

get (gĕt), *v.,* **got** or (*Archaic*) **gat; got** or **gotten; getting;** *n.* —*v.t.* **1.** to obtain, gain, or acquire by any means: *to get favor by service, get a good price.* **2.** to obtain by labor: *earn: to get one's living, get coal.* **3.** to acquire a mental grasp or command of; learn: *get a lesson.* **4.** to cause to be or do: *to get a friend appointed, get one's hair cut, get the fire to burn.* **5.** to capture; seize upon. **6.** *Colloq.* to be under an obligation to; be obliged to: *you have got to go.* **7.** to prevail on: *get him to speak.* **8.** to prepare; get ready: *to get dinner.* **9.** to beget (now usually of animals). **10.** *Slang.* to hit: *the bullet got him in the leg.* **11.** *Colloq.* to kill. **12.** *Colloq.* to puzzle; irritate: *that gets me.* **13.** *Chiefly U.S. Colloq.* to understand: *I get you.* —*v.i.* **14.** to come to or arrive: *to get home.* **15.** to become; grow: *to get tired.* **16.** to succeed in coming or going (fol. by *away, in, into, out, over, through,* etc.). **17.** to earn money; gain. **18.** to bribe; influence by surreptitious means (fol. by *at*). **19.** Some special verb phrases are:
get across, to make understood.
get along, 1. to go; go off. **2.** See **get on.**
get even with, to square accounts with.

get off, 1. to escape; evade consequences. **2.** to start a journey; leave. **3.** to dismount from (a horse or train). **4.** to say or express (a joke).
get on or along, 1. to make progress; proceed; advance. **2.** to succeed; manage well. **3.** to agree with.
get over, 1. to overcome (a difficulty, etc.). **2.** to recover from: *to get over a shock or illness.*
get round, 1. to outwit. **2.** to cajole.
get up, 1. to arise; sit up or stand. **2.** to rise from bed. **3.** to ascend or mount. **4.** (to a horse) go! go ahead! go faster! **5.** to prepare, arrange, or organize. **6.** to acquire a knowledge of: *to get up a subject.* **7.** to do up: *to get up the linen.* **8.** to produce in a specified style, as a book. **9.** to work up (a feeling, etc.).
—*n.* **20.** (in tennis, etc.) a return of a stroke which would normally be a point for the opponent.
[ME *geten*, t. Scand.; cf. Icel. *geta*, c. OE *gietan* (G *-gessen* in *vergessen* forget): akin to L *-hendere* in *prehendere* seize, take, and to Gk. *chandānein* hold, contain] —**get′ta·ble, get′a·ble,** *adj.* —**get′ter,** *n.*
—**Syn. 1–3.** GET, OBTAIN, ACQUIRE, PROCURE, SECURE imply gaining possession of something. GET may apply to coming into possession in any manner, and either voluntarily or not. OBTAIN suggests putting forth effort to gain possession, and ACQUIRE stresses the possessing after an (often prolonged) effort. PROCURE suggests the method of obtaining as that of search or choice. SECURE, considered in bad taste as a would-be-elegant substitute for GET, is, however, when used with discrimination, a perfectly proper word. It suggests making possession sure and safe, after obtaining something by competition or the like.

get·a·way (gĕt′ə wā′), *n.* *Colloq.* **1.** a getting away; an escape. **2.** the start of a race.

Geth·sem·a·ne (gĕth sĕm′ə nĭ), *n.* **1.** a garden east of Jerusalem, near the brook Kedron: the scene of Christ's agony and betrayal. Matt. 26: 36, etc. **2.** (*l.c.*) a scene or occasion of suffering.

Get·tys·burg (gĕt′ĭz bûrg′), *n.* a borough in S Pennsylvania: the Confederate forces were defeated in a crucial battle of the Civil War fought near here, July, 1, 2, and 3, 1863; national cemetery and military park. 7,960 (1960).

get·up (gĕt′ŭp′), *n.* *Colloq.* **1.** style of production; appearance: *getup of a book.* **2.** style of dress; costume.

gew·gaw (gū′gô), *n.* **1.** a bit of gaudy or useless finery. —*adj.* **2.** showy, but without value.

gey·ser (gī′zər, -sər *for 1;* gā′zər *for 2*), *n.* **1.** a hot spring which intermittently sends up fountainlike jets of water and steam into the air. **2.** *Brit.* a hot-water heater. [t. Icel.: m. *Geysir,* i.e. gusher, name of a hot spring in Iceland, der. *geysa* rush furiously, gush]

gey·ser·ite (gī′zə rīt′), *n.* a variety of opaline silica deposited about the orifices of geysers and hot springs.

g.gr., great gross.

Gha·na (gä′nə, găn′ə), *n.* a nation in West Africa comprising the former colonies of the Gold Coast and Ashanti, the protectorate of the Northern Territories, and the U.N. trusteeship of British Togoland: member of the British Commonwealth of Nations since 1957. 4,620,000 pop. (est. 1957); 91,843 sq. mi. *Cap.:* Accra.

ghast·ly (găst′lĭ, gäst′-), *adj.,* -**lier,** -**liest,** *adv.* —*adj.* **1.** frightful; dreadful; horrible: *a ghastly murder.* **2.** deathly pale: *a ghastly look.* **3.** *Colloq.* bad; unpleasant; shocking: *a ghastly failure.* —*adv.* **4.** in a ghastly manner; horribly. **5.** with a deathlike aspect: *ghastly pale.* [ME *gastly,* OE *gāstlic* spectral, f. *gāst* spirit + *lic* -LY] —**ghast′li·ness,** *n.* —**Syn.** 1. hideous, grisly.

ghat (gôt), *n.* (in India) **1.** a passage or stairway descending to a river. **2.** a mountain pass. **3.** a mountain range. Also, **ghaut.** [t. Hind.]

Ghats (gôts), *n. pl.* two low mountain ranges in S India, along the E and W margins of the Deccan plateau: the **Eastern Ghats,** parallel to the coast of the Bay of Bengal, and the **Western Ghats,** bordering on the Arabian Sea.

gha·zi (gä′zē), *n., pl.* -**zis.** **1.** a Mohammedan warrior fighting against non-Mohammedans. **2.** (*cap.*) a title given in Turkey to a victorious sultan or president. [t. Ar., ppr., of *ghazā* fight]

ghee (gē), *n.* (in the East Indies) a kind of liquid butter, clarified by boiling, made from the milk of cows and buffaloes. [t. Hind.: m. *ghī*]

Ghent (gĕnt), *n.* a city in NW Belgium: a port at the confluence of the Scheldt and Lys rivers: treaty, 1814. 164,713 (est. 1952). French, **Gand.** Flemish, **Gent.**

gher·kin (gûr′kĭn), *n.* **1.** the small, immature fruit of some common variety of cucumber, used in pickling. **2.** the small, spiny fruit of a cucurbitaceous vine, *Cucumis Anguria,* of the West Indies, the southern U.S., etc., used in pickling. **3.** the plant yielding it. [var. of *gurchen* (t. G), with substitution of -KIN for G dim. -*chen.* Cf. D *gurkje,* Pol. *ogurek,* etc., ult. der. LGk. *angoúrion* watermelon]

ghet·to (gĕt′ō), *n., pl.* **ghettos, ghetti** (gĕt′ē). **1.** any quarter inhabited chiefly by Jews. **2.** a quarter in a city in which Jews were formerly required to live. [t. It. (Venetian): b. Heb. *ghēt* separation and It. *ge(t)to* foundry (der. *getar* cast, ult. der. L *jacere* throw), as name of Jewish quarter in Venice in the 16th cent.]

Ghib·el·line (gĭb′əlῐn, -lēn′), n. **1.** a member of the imperial and aristocratic party of medieval Italy, opposed to the Guelphs. —adj. **2.** of or pertaining to the Ghibellines. [t. It.: m. *Ghibellino*, t. G: m. *Waiblingen*, name of an estate belonging to the imperial family]

Ghi·ber·ti (gē bĕr′tē), n. **Lorenzo** (lō rĕn′tsō), 1378?–1455, Florentine sculptor.

Ghir·lan·da·io (gēr′län dä′yō), n. (*Domenico di Tommaso Curradi di Doffo Bigordi*) 1449–94, Italian painter.

ghost (gōst), n. **1.** the soul of a dead person, a disembodied spirit imagined as wandering among or haunting living persons. **2.** a mere shadow or semblance: *ghost of a chance.* **3.** (*cap*.) a spiritual being: *Holy Ghost.* **4.** spirit; principle of life. **5. give up the ghost,** to die. **6.** *Colloq.* ghost writer. **7.** *Optics, Television.* a bright spot or secondary image, from a defect of the instrument. **8.** a red blood corpuscle with no hemoglobin, rendering it colorless. —v.t. **9.** to write for someone else who is publicly known as the author. **10.** to haunt. [ME *goost*, OE *gāst*, c. G *geist* spirit. Cf. GHASTLY] —**ghost′like′**, *adj.* —**Syn. 1.** apparition, phantom, phantasm, wraith, revenant; shade, spook. GHOST, SPECTER, SPIRIT all refer to the disembodied soul of a person. A GHOST is the soul or spirit of a deceased person, which appears or otherwise makes its presence known to man: *the ghost of a drowned child.* A SPECTER is a ghost or apparition of more or less weird, unearthly, or terrifying aspect: *a frightening specter.* SPIRIT is often interchangeable with GHOST but may mean a supernatural being, usually with an indication of good or malign intent toward man: *the spirit of a friend, an evil spirit.*

ghost dance, a religious movement of western North American Indian tribes, originating in connection with a Messianic doctrine which was put forth about 1888 and led to serious disturbances in 1890, and which prophesied the return of the dead and the extinction of the whites.

ghost·ly (gōst′lῐ), *adj.*, **-lier, -liest. 1.** of a ghost; spectral. **2.** *Archaic or Literary.* spiritual. —**ghost′li-ness,** *n.*

ghost writer, one who does literary work for someone else who takes the credit.

ghoul (gōōl), n. **1.** an evil demon of Oriental legend, supposed to feed on human beings, and esp. to rob graves, prey on corpses, etc. **2.** grave robber. **3.** one who revels in what is revolting. [t. Ar.: m. *ghūl*] —**ghoul′-ish,** *adj.* —**ghoul′ish·ly,** *adv.* —**ghoul′ish·ness,** *n.*

G.H.Q., *Mil.* General Headquarters.

gi., gill; gills.

G.I., *Colloq.* **1.** an enlisted man in any of the U.S. armed services. **2.** *U.S. Army,* government issue. —*attributive.* **3.** of or standardized by the Army: *G.I. shoes.* **4.** according to the letter of military regulations.

gi·ant (jῑ′ənt), n. **1.** one of a race of beings in Greek mythology, of more than human size and strength, who were subdued by the Olympian gods. **2.** an imaginary being of human form but superhuman size, strength, etc. **3.** a person or thing of unusually great size, endowments, importance, etc.: *an intellectual giant.* —*adj.* **4.** gigantic; huge: *the giant cactus.* **5.** great or eminent above others. [ME *geant,* t. OF; r. OE *gīgant,* t. L: s. *gigās,* t. Gk.] —**gi·ant·ess** (jῑ′ən tῐs), *n. fem.*

gi·ant·ism (jῑ′ən tῑz′əm), *n. Pathol.* gigantism.

giant panda, panda (def. 2).

giant powder, a form of dynamite composed of nitroglycerin and kieselguhr.

giant star, *Astron.* a star of great luminosity and mass, such as Arcturus or Betelgeuse.

giaour (jour), n. a Turkish word for an unbeliever or non-Mohammedan, esp. a Christian. [t. Turk.: m. *giaur,* t. Pers.: m. *gaur,* var. of *gabr*]

gib·ber (jῐb′ər, gῐb′-), v.i. **1.** to speak inarticulately; chatter. —n. **2.** gibbering utterance. [? freq. of obs. *gib* v., caterwaul, behave like a cat; sense devel. and pronunciation influenced by assoc. with *jabber*]

gib·be·rel·lic acid (jῐb′ə rĕl′ῐk), the acid metabolic product of the fungus *Gibberella fujikuroa* that stimulates plant growth.

gib·ber·ish (jῐb′ər ῐsh, gῐb′-), n. rapid, unintelligible talk. [f. GIBBER + -ISH¹ (modeled on *English*)]

gib·bet (jῐb′ῐt), n., v., **-beted, -beting.** —n. **1.** gallows with a projecting arm at the top, from which formerly the bodies of criminals were hung in chains and left suspended after execution. —v.t. **2.** to hang on a gibbet. **3.** to put to death by hanging on a gibbet. **4.** to hold up to public scorn. [ME *gibet,* t. OF, appar. dim. of *gibe* staff]

gib·bon (gῐb′ən), n. any of the small, slender, long-armed anthropoid apes, genus *Hylobates,* of arboreal habits, found in the East Indies and southern Asia. [t. F, appar. from a dialect of India]

Gib·bon (gῐb′ən), n. **Edward,** 1737–94, British historian.

gib·bos·i·ty (gῐ bŏs′ə tῐ), n., pl. **-ties. 1.** state of being gibbous. **2.** a protuberance or swelling.

gib·bous (gῐb′əs), *adj.* **1.** humpbacked. **2.** (of a heavenly body) so viewed as to appear convex on both margins, as the moon when more than half-full but less than full. See under **moon.** Also, **gib·bose** (gῐb′ōs). [t. L: m.s. *gibbōsus* humped] —**gib′-bous·ly,** *adv.* —**gib′bous·ness,** *n.*

Gibbon. *Hylobates lar* (3½ft. high)

Gibbs (gῐbz), n. **Josiah Willard,** 1839–1903, U.S. mathematical physicist.

gibbs·ite (gῐbz′ῑt), n. a mineral, hydrated aluminum oxide, Al₂O₃·3H₂O, occurring in whitish or grayish crystals and masses, an important constituent of bauxite ore. [named after G. Gibbs, U.S. mineralogist. See -ITE¹]

gibe (jῑb), v., **gibed, gibing,** n. —v.i. **1.** to utter mocking words; scoff; jeer. —v.t. **2.** to taunt; deride; flout. —n. **3.** a taunting or sarcastic remark. Also, **jibe.** [? t. OF: m.s. *giber,* handle roughly, shake. der. *gibe* staff, bill hook] —**gib′er,** n. —**gib′ing·ly,** *adj.*

Gib·e·on (gῐb′ῑ ən), n. an ancient town in Palestine, (now in Jordan) near Jerusalem. Josh. 9:3, etc.

Gib·e·on·ite (gῐb′ῑ ə nῑt′), n. *Bible.* one of the inhabitants of Gibeon, who were condemned by Joshua to be hewers of wood and drawers of water for the Israelites. Joshua 9.

gib·let (jῐb′lῐt), n. (*usually pl.*) the heart, liver, or gizzard from a fowl, often cooked separately. [ME *gibelet,* t. OF: dish of game]

Gi·bral·tar (jῐ brôl′tər), n. **1.** a British crown colony comprising a fortress and seaport located on a narrow promontory near the S tip of Spain. 24,736 pop. (est. 1953); 1⅞ sq. mi. **2. Rock of,** a long, precipitous mountain nearly coextensive with this colony: one of the Pillars of Hercules. 1396 ft. high; 2½ mi. long. **3. Strait of,** a strait between Europe and Africa at the Atlantic entrance to the Mediterranean. 8½–23 mi. wide.

Gib·son (gῐb′sən), n. **Charles Dana** (dā′nə), 1867–1944, U.S. artist and illustrator.

gid (gῐd), n. *Vet. Sci.* staggers in sheep, etc., due to infestation of the brain with larvae of the tapeworm, *Multiceps multiceps.* [back formation from GIDDY, adj.]

gid·dy (gῐd′ῐ), *adj.,* **-dier, -diest,** v., **-died, -dying.** —*adj.* **1.** frivolously light; impulsive; flighty: *a giddy mind, a giddy girl.* **2.** affected with vertigo; dizzy. **3.** attended with or causing dizziness: *a giddy climb.* —v.t., v.i. **4.** to make or become giddy. [ME *gidy,* OE *gydig* mad, der. *god;* orig. sense presumably godpossessed, in a state of divine frenzy] —**gid′di·ly,** *adv.* —**gid′di·ness,** *n.* —**Syn. 1.** unstable, volatile. **2.** light-headed, vertiginous. —**Ant. 1.** steady, stable.

Gide (zhēd), n. **André** (än drĕ′), 1869–1951, French novelist, essayist, and critic.

Gid·e·on (gῐd′ῑ ən), n. *Bible.* Hebrew liberator and religious leader, conqueror of the Midianites and judge in Israel for forty years. Judges 6–8. [var. of *Gedeon* (Septuagint), t. Heb.: m. *Gid′ōn*]

gift (gῐft), n. **1.** something given; a present. **2.** act of giving. **3.** the power or right of giving. **4.** a quality or special ability; natural endowment; talent. —v.t. **5.** to present with as a gift; bestow gifts upon; endow with. [ME, t. Scand.; cf. Icel. *gift,* c. OE *gift* husband's gift to wife at marriage, G *gift* poison, etc.; akin to GIVE, v.] —**Syn. 1.** donation, contribution, offering, boon, alms, gratuity. See present².

gift·ed (gῐf′tῐd), *adj.* endowed with natural gifts; talented: *a gifted artist.*

Gi·fu (gē′fōō′), n. a city in central Japan, on Honshu island. 211,845(1950).

gig¹ (gῐg), n., v., **gigged, gigging.** —n. **1.** *Naut.* a. a long, fast-pulling boat used esp. for racing. b. the boat reserved for a ship's captain. **2.** a light, two-wheeled one-horse carriage. —v.i. **3.** to ride in a gig. [orig. uncert.]

gig² (gῐg), n., v., **gigged, gigging.** —n. **1.** a device, commonly four hooks secured back to back, for dragging through a school of fish to hook them through the body. —v.t., v.i. **2.** to catch (fish) with a gig. [short for *fizgig,* t. Sp.: m. *fisga* harpoon]

Gig

gi·gan·te·an (jῑ′gǎn tē′ən), *adj.* gigantic. [f. s. L *gigantēus* + -AN. See GIANT]

gi·gan·tesque (jῑ′gǎn tĕsk′), *adj.* of a gigantic kind; suited to a giant. [t. F, t. It.: m. *gigantesco,* der. *gigante,* t. L: m.s. *gigās* GIANT]

gi·gan·tic (jῑ gǎn′tῐk), *adj.* **1.** of, like, or befitting a giant. **2.** very large; huge. [f. s. L *gigās* GIANT + -IC] —**gi·gan′ti·cal·ly,** *adv.* —**gi·gan′tic·ness,** *n.* —**Syn. 2.** enormous, immense, prodigious, herculean, cyclopean, titanic. GIGANTIC, COLOSSAL, MAMMOTH, MONSTROUS are used of whatever is physically or metaphorically of great magnitude. GIGANTIC refers to the size of a giant: *a gigantic stalk of corn.* COLOSSAL to that of a colossus: *a colossal skeleton of a brontosaurus.* MAMMOTH to that of the animal of that name: *a mammoth jaw of a prehistoric animal.* MONSTROUS means unusual or out of the normal in some striking way, as in size: *a monstrous blunder.* —**Ant. 2.** tiny.

gi·gan·tism (jῑ gǎn tῑz′əm, jῑ gǎn′tῑz-), n. *Pathol.* abnormally great development in size or stature of the whole body, or of parts of the body, most often due to dysfunction of the pituitary gland. Also, **giantism.**

gi·gan·to·ma·chi·a (jῑ gǎn′tō mā′kῑ ə), n. **1.** a war of giants, esp. the war of the giants of Greek mythology against the Olympian gods. **2.** a representation of this, as in sculpture. [t. LL, t. Gk.: the battle of the giants]

---

b., blend of, blended; c., cognate with; d., dialect, dialectal; der., derived from; f., formed from; g., going back to; m., modification of; r., replacing; s., stem of; t., taken from; ?, perhaps. See the full key on inside cover.

gig·gle (gĭg'əl), v., **-gled, -gling,** n. —v.i. 1. to laugh in a silly undignified way, as from youthful spirits or ill-controlled amusement; titter. —n. 2. a silly, spasmodic laugh; a titter. [appar. back formation from obs. *giglet* giddy, laughing girl, der. obs. *gig* flighty, giddy girl. Cf. D *gigelen,* G *gickeln* giggle] —**gig'gler,** n.

gig·gly (gĭg'lY), adj. inclined to giggle.

gig·o·lo (jĭg'əlō'), n., pl. **-los.** 1. a man supported by a woman. 2. a male professional dancing partner. [t. F]

gig·ot (jĭg'ət), n. 1. a leg-of-mutton sleeve. 2. a leg of mutton. [t. F, dim. of d. F *gigue* leg, der. *giguer* hop, dance, der. OF *gigue* fiddle, t. Gmc.; cf. G *geige*]

gigue (zhēg), n. 1. *Dance.* jig (def. 1). 2. *Music.* a jig (def. 2), often forming the concluding movement in the classical suite. [t. F. See JIG]

G.I. Joe, Colloq. an enlisted U.S. Army soldier.

Gi·jon (gē hôn'), n. a city in N Spain; seaport. 115,877 (est. 1955).

Gi·la (hē'lə), n. a river flowing from SW New Mexico W across S Arizona to the Colorado river. 630 mi.

Gila monster, a large, venomous lizard, *Heloderma suspectum,* of the southwestern U.S., having the skin studded with yellow- or orange-and-black headlike tubercles. [named after the *Gila* river, in Arizona]

Gila monster.
Heloderma suspectum

Gila woodpecker, a dull-colored woodpecker, *Centurus uropygialis,* of the southwestern United States and Mexico.

gil·bert (gĭl'bərt), n. *Elect.* the c. g. s. unit of magnetomotive force, equal to .7958 ampere turns. [named after W. *Gilbert* (1540–1603), English scientist]

Gil·bert (gĭl'bərt), n. 1. **Cass,** 1859–1934, U.S. architect. 2. **Sir Humphrey,** 1539?–83, English soldier, navigator, and colonizer in America. 3. **Sir William Schwenck,** 1836–1911, British dramatist, humorist, and poet; collaborator with Sir Arthur Sullivan.

Gilbert and El·lice Islands (ĕl'Ys), a British colony in the central Pacific, comprising the Gilbert and Ellice groups and other widely scattered islands. 36,000 pop. (1947); 203 sq. mi. *Cap.:* Ocean Island.

gild¹ (gĭld), v.t., **gilded** or **gilt, gilding.** 1. to coat with gold, gold leaf, or gold-colored substance. 2. to give a bright, pleasing, or specious aspect to. 3. *Obs.* to make red, as with blood. [ME *gilden,* OE *gyldan,* der. GOLD]

gild² (gĭld), n. guild. —**gilds·man** (gĭldz'mən), n.

gild·er¹ (gĭl'dər), n. one who or that which gilds. [f. GILD¹ + -ER¹]

gil·der² (gĭl'dər), n. guilder.

gild·hall (gĭld'hôl'), n. guildhall.

gild·ing (gĭl'dYng), n. 1. the application of gilt. 2. the gold leaf or other material with which anything is gilded. 3. the golden surface produced. 4. any deceptive coating or aspect used to give a fine appearance.

Gil·e·ad (gĭl'Yəd), n. 1. an ancient district of Palestine, E of the Jordan, in present Jordan. 2. **Mount, a** mountain in NW Jordan. 3596 ft.

Gil·ga·mesh (gĭl'gə mĕsh'), n. a mythical Babylonian king who is the hero of a Babylonian epic.

gill¹ (gĭl), n. 1. an aquatic respiratory organ, either external or internal, usually feathery, platelike, or filamentous. 2. one of the radiating vertical plates on the underside of the cap of an agaric. 3. the ground ivy. —v.t. 4. to catch (fish) by the gills in a gill net. 5. to gut or clean (fish). [ME *gile,* t. Scand.; cf. Sw. *gäl,* Dan. *gælle*] —**gilled,** adj. —**gill'-like',** adj.

gill² (jYl), n. a unit of liquid measure equal to ¼ pint. [ME *gille,* t. OF: wine measure. Cf. GALLON]

gill fungus, an agaricaceous fungus.

gil·lie (gĭl'Y), n. *Scot.* 1. a sportsman's attendant. 2. a male attendant on a Highland chieftain. [t. Gaelic: m. *gille* lad, servant]

gill net (gĭl), a curtainlike net, suspended vertically in the water, with meshes of such a size as to catch by the gills a fish that has thrust its head through.

gil·ly (gĭl'Y), n., pl. **-lies.** *Scot.* gillie.

gil·ly·flow·er (jĭl'Y flou'ər), n. 1. the name for various flowers, as for example, the wallflower, *Cheiranthus Cheiri,* the common stock gillyflower, *Matthiola incana,* etc. 2. *Archaic* or *Dial.* the clove pink. Also, **gil'li-flow'er.** [alter. of ME *gilofre,* t. OF: clove, g. L *caryophyllon,* t. Gk.: m. *karyóphyllon* clove tree]

Gil·man (gĭl'mən), n. **Daniel Coit,** 1831–1908, U.S. educator.

gil·son·ite (gĭl'sə nīt'), n. an extremely pure asphalt particularly valuable for the manufacture of paints and varnishes, the chief deposits being in Utah; uintaite. [named after S. H. *Gilson* of Salt Lake City. See -ITE¹]

gilt¹ (gĭlt), v. 1st pt. and pp. of gild. —adj. 2. gilded; golden in color. —n. 3. the gold or other material applied in gilding; gilding.

gilt² (gĭlt), n. a female swine that has not produced pigs and that has not reached an evident stage of pregnancy. [ME *gilte,* t. Scand.; cf. Icel. *gylta*]

gilt-edged (gĭlt'ĕjd'), adj. 1. having the edges gilded: *gilt-edged paper.* 2. of the highest order or quality: *gilt-edged securities.*

gim·bals (jĭm'bəlz, gĭm'-), n. a contrivance for keeping a suspended object, as a ship's compass, horizontal. [pl. of *gimbal* (now used only adjectively in composition), var. of *gimmal,* ME *gemel,* t. OF: twin]

gim·crack (jĭm'krăk'), n. 1. a showy, useless trifle; gewgaw. —adj. 2. showy but useless. [orig. uncert.]

gim·let (gĭm'lYt), n. 1. a small tool for boring holes, consisting of a shaft with a pointed screw at one end and a handle at the other. —v.t. 2. to pierce with or as with a gimlet. [ME *gymlet,* t. OF: m. *guimbelet,* dim. of unrecorded *guimbel* WIMBLE]

Gimlet

gim·mick (gĭm'Yk), n. *U.S. Slang.* 1. a device by which a magician or carnival pitchman works a trick. 2. any tricky device or means. [? b. *gimmer* trick finger ring and MAGIC]

gimp (gĭmp), n. a flat trimming of silk, wool, or other cord, sometimes stiffened with wire, for garments, curtains, etc. [appar. t. D; ult. orig. unknown]

gin¹ (jYn), n. an alcoholic beverage obtained by redistilling spirits with flavoring agents, esp. juniper berries, orange peel, angelica root, etc. [short for GENEVA]

gin² (jYn), n., v., **ginned, ginning.** —n. 1. a machine for separating cotton from its seeds, as a cotton gin. 2. a trap or snare for game, etc. —v.t. 3. to clear (cotton) of seeds with a gin. 4. to catch (game, etc.) in a gin. [ME, aphetic var. of OF *engin* ENGINE] —**gin'ner,** n.

gin³ (gYn), v.i., v.t., **gan, gun, ginning.** *Archaic or Poetic.* begin. [ME *ginnen,* OE *ginnan,* aphetic var. of *onginnan.* Cf. OE *beginnan* BEGIN]

gin⁴ (jYn), n. *Cards.* a rummy game in which a player with a total of 10 unmatched points or less may end the game. [? a pun: *gin* = *rum*]

gin·gal (jYn'gôl), n. jingal. Also, **gin'gall.**

gin·ge·li (jYn'jəlY), n. gingili. Also, **gin'gel·ly.**

gin·ger (jYn'jər), n. 1. the pungent, spicy rhizome of any of the reedlike plants of the genus *Zingiber,* esp. of *Z. officinale,* variously used in cookery and medicine. 2. any of these plants, native in the East Indies, but now cultivated in most tropical countries. 3. a dull-yellowish or tawny color. In England often used for red, especially for the color of the hair. 4. *Colloq.* piquancy; animation. —v.t. 5. to treat or flavor with ginger. 6. *Colloq.* to impart spiciness or piquancy to; make lively. [ME *gingivere,* OE *gingifere,* t. LL: m. *gingiber,* L *zingiberi,* t. Gk.: m. *zingiberis* ginger, appar. t. Prakrit: m. *singabēra*]

ginger ale, a drink similar to ginger beer.

ginger beer, a nonalcoholic effervescing drink of water, sugar or molasses, yeast, etc., flavored with ginger.

gin·ger·bread (jYn'jər brĕd'), n. 1. a kind of cake flavored with ginger and molasses. 2. a rolled cookie similarly flavored, often cut in fanciful shapes, and sometimes frosted. 3. something showy but unsubstantial and inartistic. —adj. 4. showy but unsubstantial and inartistic. [alter. of ME *gingimbrat* preserved ginger, t. ML: s. **gingimbratum,* der. *gingiber* GINGER]

gingerbread tree, a tree, *Parinarium macrophyllum,* of western Africa, with a large, edible, farinaceous fruit (**gingerbread plum**).

gin·ger·ly (jYn'jərlY), adv. 1. with extreme care or caution; warily. 2. *Obs.* mincingly; daintily. —adj. 3. cautious or wary. —**gin'ger·li·ness,** n.

gin·ger·snap (jYn'jər snăp'), n. a small, thin, brittle cookie spiced with ginger.

gin·ger·y (jYn'jərY), adj. 1. gingerlike; pungent; spicy. 2. of the color of ginger.

ging·ham (gYng'əm), n. yarn-dyed, plain-weave cotton fabric, usually striped or checked. [t. F: m. *guingan,* ult. t. Malay: m. *ginggang,* lit., striped]

gin·gi·li (jYn'jəlY), n., pl. **-lis.** 1. the sesame (plant). 2. its oil. Also, **gingeli, gingelly.** [t. Hind.: m. *jinjali,* ult. t. Ar.: m. *juljulān*]

gin·gi·val (jYn jī'vəl, jYn'jə vəl), adj. 1. of or pertaining to the gums. 2. *Phonet.* made at the gums. [f. s. L *gingiva* gum + -AL¹]

gin·gi·vi·tis (jYn'jə vī'tYs), n. *Pathol.* inflammation of the gums.

gink·go (gYngk'gō, jYngk'gō), n., pl. **-goes.** a large, ornamental, gymnospermous tree, *Ginkgo biloba,* native to China, with fan-shaped leaves, fleshy fruit, and edible nuts. Also, **ging'ko.** [t. Jap.]

gin·ner·y (jYn'ərY), n., pl. **-neries.** a mill for ginning cotton.

gin rummy, gin⁴.

gin·seng (jYn'sĕng), n. 1. either of two araliaceous plants, *Panax schinseng* of China, Korea, etc., and *P. quinquefolium* of North America, yielding an aromatic root which is extensively used in medicine by the Chinese. 2. the root itself. 3. a preparation made from it. [t. Chinese (Mandarin): m. *jên shên,* f. *jên* man + *shên,* of obscure meaning]

Gior·gio·ne (jôr jō'nĕ), n. (Giorgione da Castelfranco, Giorgio Barbarelli) 1478?–1511, Italian painter.

Giot·to (jŏt'ō; *It.* jôt'tô), n. c1266–1337, Florentine painter and architect.

gip (jYp), v.t., **gipped, gipping,** n. gyp¹. —**gip'per,** n.

Gip·sy (jYp'sY), n., pl. **-sies,** adj. *Chiefly Brit.* Gypsy.

gi·raffe (jərăf'), n. 1. a tall, long-necked, spotted ruminant, *Giraffa camelopardalis,* of Africa, the tallest of existing quadrupeds. See illus. on next page. 2. *(cap.) Astron.* the northern constellation Camelopard. [t. F (now *girafe*), t. Ar.: m. *zarāfah,* prob. of African orig.]

gir·an·dole (jYr'əndōl'), n. 1. a rotating and radiating firework. 2. *Fort.* a group of connected mines. 3. an ornate branched support for candles or other lights. Also, **gi·ran·do·la** (jĭ'răn'də lə). [t. F, t. It.: m. *girandola*, der. *girare* turn, g. L *gȳrāre*. See GYRATE.]

Gi·rard (jə·rärd'), *n.* **Stephen**, 1750–1831, American merchant, banker, and philanthropist.

gir·a·sol (jĭr'ə·sŏl', -sōl'), *n.* **1.** a variety of opal which reflects a floating luminous glow. **2.** Jerusalem artichoke. Also, **gir·a·sole'**, **girosol**. [t. F, t. It.: m. *girasole*, f. *gira(re)* turn + *sole* sun, in imitation of Gk. *hēliotrópion*]

Gi·raud (zhē·rō'), *n.* **Henri Honoré** (än rē' ō nō rē'), 1879–1949, French general.

gird[1] (gûrd), *v.t.*, **girt** or **gird·ed**, **gird·ing**. **1.** to encircle with a belt or girdle. **2.** to surround; hem in. **3.** to prepare (oneself) mentally for action (often fol. by *up*). **4.** to endue. [ME *girde(n)*, OE *gyrdan*, c. G *gürten*]

gird[2] (gûrd), *v.i.* **1.** to gibe; jeer (fol. by *at*). —*v.t.* **2.** *Obs.* to gibe or jeer at; taunt. —*n.* **3.** *Archaic.* a gibe. [ME; orig. obscure]

Giraffe.
Giraffa camelopardalis
(17 to 19 ft. high)

gird·er (gûr'dər), *n.* **1.** (in structural work) any main horizontal supporting member or beam, as of wood or iron. **2.** one of the principal horizontal timbers which support the joists in certain floors. [f. GIRD[1] + ER[1]]

gir·dle (gûr'dəl), *n., v.,* **-dled, -dling.** —*n.* **1.** a belt, cord, sash, or the like, worn about the waist. **2.** a lightweight undergarment which supports the abdominal region of the body. **3.** any encircling band; compass; limit. **4.** *Gems.* the edge about a brilliant or other cut stone at the junction of the upper and lower faces. **5.** *Anat.* the bony framework which unites the upper or lower extremities to the axial skeleton. **6.** a ring made about a tree trunk, etc., by cutting the bark. —*v.t.* **7.** to encircle with a belt; gird. **8.** to encompass; enclose; encircle. **9.** to cut away the bark in a ring about (a tree, branch, etc.), thus causing death. [ME; OE *gyrdel*, der. *gyrdan* gird[1]] —**gir·dle·like'**, *adj.* —**gir'dler**, *n.*

G, Steel girder; C, Cross section of girder

Gir·gen·ti (jēr·jĕn'tē), *n.* former name of **Agrigento**.

girl (gûrl), *n.* **1.** a female child or young person. **2.** a young unmarried woman. **3.** a female servant. **4.** *Colloq.* a sweetheart. **5.** *Colloq.* a woman. [ME *gurle*, *girle* child, young person, OE *gyrl-* in *gyrlgyden* virgin goddess. Cf. LG *gör*(*e*) young person]

girl guide, a member of an organization of girls (**Girl Guides**) in England and elsewhere: a sister organization of the Girl Scouts.

girl·hood (gûrl'hŏŏd), *n.* **1.** state or time of being a girl. **2.** girls collectively.

girl·ish (gûr'lĭsh), *adj.* of, like, or befitting a girl: *girlish laughter.* —**girl'ish·ly**, *adv.* —**girl'ish·ness**, *n.*

girl scout, a member of an organization of girls (**Girl Scouts**), founded in the U.S. in 1912, to develop health, citizenship, character, and homemaking ability.

gi·ro (jĭ'rō), *n., pl.* **-ros.** autogiro.

Gi·ronde (jə·rŏnd'; *Fr.* zhē·rônd'), *n.* **1.** an estuary in SW France, formed by the junction of the Garonne and Dordogne rivers. ab. 45 mi. long. **2. the Gironde**, the party of the Girondists taken collectively.

Gi·ron·dist (jə·rŏn'dĭst), *n.* a member of a French political party of moderate republicans (1791–1793), whose leaders were deputies from the department of Gironde, in SW France.

gir·o·sol (jĭr'ə·sŏl', -sōl'), *n.* girasol.

girt[1] (gûrt), *v.* pt. and pp. of **gird**[1].

girt[2] (gûrt), *v.t.*, **gird**[1] (def. 1).

girth (gûrth), *n.* **1.** the measure around anything; circumference. **2.** a band passed under the belly of a horse, etc., to secure a saddle or pack on its back. **3.** a band or girdle. —*v.t.* **4.** to bind or fasten with a girth. **5.** to girdle; encircle. [ME *girth*, *garth*, t. Scand.; cf. Icel. *gjördh* girdle, hoop; akin to GIRD[1]]

gi·sarme (gĭ·zärm'), *n.* a medieval shafted weapon with a scythelike cutting blade from the back edge of which emerges a long slender blade with a sharp point. [ME *gisharme*(*e*), t. OF: m. *g(u)isarme*; orig. uncert.]

Gis·sing (gĭs'ĭng), *n.* **George Robert**, 1857–1903, British novelist.

gist (jĭst), *n.* **1.** the substance or pith of a matter; essential part: *the gist of an argument.* **2.** the ground on which a legal action rests. [t. OF, 3rd pers. sing. pres. ind. of *gesir* lie, rest, g. L *jacēre*]

git·tern (gĭt'ərn), *n.* cittern. [ME *gitern*(*e*), t. OF: m. *guiterne*. Cf. GUITAR.]

Giu·ba (jōō'bä), *n.* Italian name of **Juba**.

Giu·lio Ro·ma·no (jōōl'yō rō·mä'nō), (*Giulio Pippi*) 1492?–1546, Italian painter and architect.

give (gĭv), *v.,* **gave, given, giving,** *n.* —*v.t.* **1.** to deliver freely; bestow; hand over: *give someone a present.* **2.** to deliver to another in exchange for something; pay. **3.** to grant permission or opportunity to; enable; assign; award. **4.** to set forth or show; present; offer. **5.** to assign as a basis of calculation or reasoning; suppose; assume: *given these facts.* **6.** to furnish or provide;

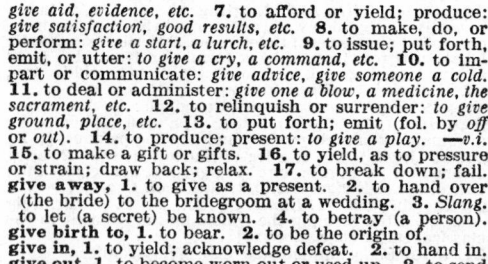

give aid, evidence, etc. **7.** to afford or yield; produce: *give satisfaction, good results, etc.* **8.** to make, do, or perform: *give a start, a lurch, etc.* **9.** to issue; put forth, emit, or utter: *to give a cry, a command, etc.* **10.** to impart or communicate: *give advice, give someone a cold.* **11.** to deal or administer: *give one a blow, a medicine, the sacrament, etc.* **12.** to relinquish or surrender: *to give ground, place, etc.* **13.** to put forth; emit (fol. by *off* or *out*). **14.** to produce; present: *to give a play.* —*v.i.* **15.** to make a gift or gifts. **16.** to yield, as to pressure or strain; draw back; relax. **17.** to break down; fail.

give away, 1. to give as a present. **2.** to hand over (the bride) to the bridegroom at a wedding. **3.** *Slang.* to let (a secret) be known. **4.** to betray (a person).

give birth to, 1. to bear. **2.** to be the origin of.

give in, 1. to yield; acknowledge defeat. **2.** to hand in.

give out, 1. to become worn out or used up. **2.** to send out; emit. **3.** to distribute; issue.

give rise to, to give origin to; cause; result in.

give up, 1. to lose all hope. **2.** to abandon as hopeless. **3.** to desist from; forsake: *give up a task.* **4.** to surrender. **5.** to devote entirely.

—*n.* **18.** act or fact of yielding to pressure; elasticity. [ME, t. Scand. (cf. Dan. *give*); r. ME *yeve*(*n*), *yive*(*n*), OE *gefan, gi(e)fan*, c. D *geven*, G *geben*, Goth. *giban*. Cf. GIFT] —**giv'er**, *n.*

—**Syn. 1.** offer, vouchsafe, impart, accord, furnish, provide, supply, donate, contribute. GIVE, CONFER, GRANT, PRESENT may mean that something concrete or abstract is bestowed on one person by another. GIVE is the general word: *to give someone a book, permission, etc.* CONFER usually means to give an honor or a favor; it implies courteous and gracious giving: *to confer a degree.* GRANT is limited to the idea of acceding to a request; it may apply to the bestowal of privileges, or the fulfillment of an expressed wish: *to grant a charter, a prayer, permission, etc.* PRESENT, a more formal word than GIVE, usually implies a certain ceremony in the giving: *to present a citation to a regiment.*

give-and-take (gĭv'ən tāk'), *n.* **1.** a method of dealing by compromise or mutual concession; coöperation. **2.** good-humored exchange of talk, ideas, etc.

give·a·way (gĭv'ə wā'), *Colloq.* —*n.* **1.** a betrayal, usually unintentional. **2.** a premium given with various articles to promote sales, etc. **3.** an unscrupulous deal, esp. one which benefits some while defrauding others. —*adj.* **4.** (of a radio program, etc.) characterized by the awarding of prizes, money, etc., to recipients chosen, usually, through a question-and-answer contest.

giv·en (gĭv'ən), *adj.* **1.** stated, fixed, or specified: *at a given time.* **2.** addicted or disposed (often fol. by *to*): *given to drink.* **3.** bestowed as a gift; conferred. **4.** assigned as a basis of calculation, reasoning, etc.: *given A and B, C follows.* **5.** *Math.* known or determined: *a given magnitude.* **6.** (on official documents) executed and delivered as of the date given.

given name, the name given to one, not inherited; first name.

Gi·za (gē'zə), *n.* El Giza. Also, **Gi'zeh.**

giz·zard (gĭz'ərd), *n.* the grinding or muscular stomach of birds, the organ in which food is triturated after leaving the glandular stomach; ventriculus. [ME *giser*, t. OF, ult. g. L *gigēria* cooked entrails of poultry]

Gk., Greek.

Gl, *Chem.* glucinum.

gla·bel·la (glə bĕl'ə), *n., pl.* **-bellae** (-bĕl'ē). *Anat.* the flat area of bone between the eyebrows, used as a craniometric point. [NL, prop. fem. of L *glabellus* smooth, hairless, dim. of *glaber*. See GLABROUS]

gla·bel·lum (glə bĕl'əm), *n., pl.* **-bella.** glabella.

gla·brate (glā'brāt, -brĭt), *adj.* **1.** *Zool.* smooth; glabrous. **2.** *Bot.* becoming glabrous; somewhat glabrous.

gla·brous (glā'brəs), *adj.* *Zool., Bot.* smooth; having a surface devoid of hair or pubescence. [f. s. L *glaber* smooth, hairless + -OUS]

gla·cé (glà sē'), *adj.* **1.** frozen. **2.** frosted or iced, as cake. **3.** candied, as fruits. **4.** finished with a gloss, as kid or silk. [F, pp. of *glacer*, der. *glace* ice, ult. g. L *glacies*]

gla·cial (glā'shəl), *adj.* **1.** characterized by the presence of ice in extensive masses or glaciers. **2.** due to or associated with the action of ice or glaciers. **3.** of or pertaining to glaciers or ice sheets. **4.** cold as ice; icy. **5.** *Chem.* of or tending to assume an icelike form, as certain acids. [t. L: s. *glaciālis* icy] —**gla'cial·ly**, *adv.*

glacial acetic acid, a 99.5% concentration of acetic acid.

glacial epoch, 1. the geologically recent Pleistocene epoch, during which much of the northern hemisphere was covered by great ice sheets. **2.** any one of the Eocene, Permian, Carboniferous, Cambrian, and Pre-Cambrian glaciations.

gla·cial·ist (glā'shəl ĭst), *n.* one who studies geological phenomena involving the action of ice.

gla·ci·ate (glā'shĭ āt'), *v.t.*, **-ated, -ating. 1.** to cover with ice or glaciers. **2.** to affect by glacial action. —**gla·ci·a·tion** (glā'sĭ ā'shən, -shĭ-), *n.*

gla·cier (glā'shər), *n.* an extended mass of ice formed from snow falling and accumulating over the years and moving very slowly, either descending from high mountains, as in valley glaciers, or moving outward from centers of accumulation, as in continental glaciers. [t. F, der. *glace* ice, ult. g. L *glacies*] —**gla'ciered**, *adj.*

Glacier National Park, a scenic mountain and forest reserve in NW Montana, with numerous glaciers and lakes. 1534 sq. mi.

---

b., blend of, blended; c., cognate with; d., dialect, dialectal; der., derived from; f., formed from; g., going back to; m., modification of; r., replacing; s., stem of; t., taken from; ?, perhaps. See the full key on inside cover.

la·cis (glā'sĭs, glăs'ĭs), *n.* **1.** a gentle slope. **2.** *Fort.* a bank of earth in front of the counterscarp or covered way of a fort, having an easy slope toward the field or open country. [t. F: orig., icy or slippery place, der. OF *glacier* slip. See GLACE]

lad (glăd), *adj.*, **gladder, gladdest. 1.** delighted or pleased (fol. by *of, at,* etc., or an infinitive or clause): *to be glad at the news, glad to go, glad that one has come.* **2.** characterized by or showing cheerfulness, joy, or pleasure, as looks, utterances, etc. **3.** attended with or causing joy or pleasure: *a glad occasion, glad tidings.* —*v.t.* **4.** *Archaic.* to make glad. [ME; OE *glæd,* c. Icel. *gladhr* bright, glad, D *glad* and G *glatt* smooth; akin to L *glaber* smooth] —**glad'ly,** *adv.* —**glad'ness,** *n.* —**Syn. 1.** elated, delighted, gratified. —**Ant.** sad.

lad·den (glăd'ən).*v.t.* **1.** to make glad. —*v.i.* **2.** *Obs.* to be glad. —**glad'den·er,** *n.* —**Syn. 1.** See cheer.

lade (glăd), *n.* an open space in a forest. [akin to GLAD (in obs. sense "bright")]

lad·i·ate (glăd'ĭ·ĭt, -āt', glā'dĭ-), *adj. Bot.* sword-shaped. [f. s. L *gladius* sword + -ATE¹]

lad·i·a·tor (glăd'ĭ·ā'tər), *n. Rom. Hist.* a person, often a slave or captive, who fought in public with a sword or other weapon to entertain the people. [t. L]

lad·i·a·to·ri·al (glăd'ĭ·ə·tôr'ĭ·əl), *adj.* pertaining to gladiators or their combats.

lad·i·o·la (glăd'ĭ·ō'lə, glə·dī'ə·lə), *n.* gladiolus. [t. L, neut. pl. treated as if fem. sing. See GLADIOLUS]

lad·i·o·lus (glăd'ĭ·ō'ləs *for the plant*; glə·dī'ə·ləs *for the lens*), *n.*, *pl.* **-lus, -li** (-lī), **-luses.** any plant of the iridaceous genus *Gladiolus,* native esp. in South Africa, with erect, gladiate leaves, and spikes of variously colored flowers. [t. L, dim. of *gladius* sword]

lad·some (glăd'səm), *adj.* **1.** making joyful; delightful. **2.** glad. —**glad'some·ly,** *adv.* —**glad'some·ness,** *n.*

lad·stone (glăd'stōn, -stən), *n.* **1. William Ewart** (ū'ərt), 1809–98, British statesman: prime minister four times between 1868 and 1894. **2.** a Gladstone bag. **3.** a four-wheeled pleasure carriage with a calash top, two inside seats, and driver and dickey seats.

ladstone bag, a light traveling bag hinged to open into two compartments. [named after W. E. *Gladstone*]

lair (glâr), *n.* **1.** the white of an egg. **2.** a glaze or size made of it. **3.** any viscous substance like egg white. [ME *glaire,* t. OF, ult. der. L *clārus* clear]

lair·y (glâr'ĭ), *adj.* **1.** of the nature of glair; viscous. **2.** covered with glair. Also, **glair·e·ous** (glâr'ĭ·əs). —**glair'i·ness,** *n.*

laive (glāv), *n. Archaic.* a sword or broadsword. [ME *gleyve,* t. OF: m. *glaive* lance, sword, g. L *gladius* sword]

la·mor·gan·shire (glə·môr'gən·shĭr', -shər), *n.* a county in SE Wales. 1,202,581 pop. (1951); 816 sq. mi. *Co. seat:* Cardiff. Also, **Gla·mor'gan.**

lam·or·ize (glăm'ə·rīz'), *v.t.,* **-rized, -rizing.** to make glamorous.

lam·or·ous (glăm'ər·əs), *adj.* full of glamour or charm. Also, **glam'our·ous.** —**glam'or·ous·ly,** *adv.*

lam·our (glăm'ər), *n.* **1.** alluring and often illusory charm; fascination. **2.** magic or enchantment; spell; witchery. Also, **glam'or.** [earlier *glammar,* dissimilated var. of GRAMMAR in sense of "occult learning," "magic"]

lance¹ (glăns, gläns), *v.*, **glanced, glancing.** —*v.i.* **1.** to look quickly or briefly. **2.** to gleam or flash. **3.** to go off in an oblique direction from an object struck: *a missile glances away.* **4.** to allude briefly in passing. —*v.t.* **5.** to cast a glance or brief look at; catch a glimpse of. **6.** to cast or reflect, as a gleam. —*n.* **7.** a quick or brief look. **8.** a gleam or flash of light. **9.** a glancing off, as of a missile after striking. **10.** a reference in passing. **11.** *Cricket.* a stroke in which the ball is allowed to glance off the bat. [late ME; nasalized var. of ME *glacen* strike a glancing blow, t. OF: m. *glacer* slip] —**Syn. 2.** See flash.

lance² (glăns, gläns), *n. Mining, Mineral.* any of various minerals having a luster which indicates their metallic nature. [t. G: m. *glanz,* lit., brightness, luster]

land (glănd), *n.* **1.** *Anat.* **a.** an organ by which certain constituents are separated from the blood for use in the body or for ejection from it, or by which certain changes are produced in the blood or lymph. **b.** any of various organs or structures likened to true glands. **2.** *Bot.* a secreting organ or structure, esp. one on or near a surface. [t. F: m. *glande,* m. OF *glandre,* g. L *glandula,* dim. of *glans* acorn] —**gland'less,** *adj.* —**gland'like',** *adj.*

lan·dered (glăn'dərd), *adj.* affected with glanders.

lan·ders (glăn'dərz), *n. Vet. Sci.* a contagious disease of horses, mules, etc., communicable to man, due to a microörganism (*Bacillus mallei*), and characterized by swellings beneath the jaw and a profuse mucous discharge from the nostrils. [late ME, t. OF: m. *glandres,* g. L *glandulae* (swollen) glands] —**glan'der·ous,** *adj.*

lan·du·lar (glăn'jə·lər), *adj.* **1.** consisting of, containing, or bearing glands. **2.** of, pertaining to, or resembling a gland.

landular fever, *Pathol.* an acute infectious disease characterized by sudden fever, a benign swelling of lymph nodes, and increase in leucocytes having only one nucleus in the blood stream; infectious mononucleosis.

lan·du·lous (glăn'jə·ləs), *adj.* glandular. [t. L: m. s. *glandulōsus*]

glans (glănz), *n., pl.* **glandes** (glăn'dēz). *Anat.* the head of the penis (**glans penis**) or of the clitoris (**glans clitoridis**). [t. L: lit., acorn]

glare¹ (glâr), *n., v.,* **glared, glaring.** —*n.* **1.** a strong, dazzling light; brilliant luster. **2.** dazzling or showy appearance; showiness. **3.** a fierce or piercing look. —*v.i.* **4.** to shine with a strong, dazzling light. **5.** to be too brilliantly ornamented. **6.** to be intensely bright in color. **7.** to be conspicuous. **8.** to look with a fierce or piercing stare. —*v.t.* **9.** to express with a glare. [ME *glaren,* c. MD and MLG *glaren;* akin to GLASS (cf. OE *glæren* glassy)] —**Syn. 4.** See shine. **8.** GLARE, GLOWER, GLOAT all have connotations of emotion which accompany an intense gaze. To GLARE is to look piercingly or angrily: *a tiger glares at its victims.* To GLOWER is to look fiercely and threateningly; as from wrath; it suggests a scowl along with a glare: *to glower at a persistently mischievous child.* To GLOAT meant originally to look with exultation, avaricious or malignant, on something or someone: *a tyrant gloating over the helplessness of his victim.* Today, however, it may simply imply inner exultation.

glare² (glâr), *n.* **1.** a bright, smooth surface, as of ice. —*adj.* **2.** bright and smooth; glassy: *glare ice.* [special uses of GLARE¹]

glar·ing (glâr'ĭng), *adj.* **1.** that glares; brilliant; dazzling. **2.** excessively bright; garish. **3.** very conspicuous: *glaring defects.* **4.** staring fiercely. —**glar'ing·ly,** *adv.* —**glar'ing·ness,** *n.*

glar·y¹ (glâr'ĭ), *adj.* brilliant; glaring. [f. GLARE¹ + -Y¹]

glar·y² (glâr'ĭ), *adj. U.S.* smooth and slippery, as ice. [early mod. E *glarie* icy. Cf. OE *glæren* glassy]

Glas·gow (glăs'gō, -kō, gläs'-), *n.* a seaport in SW Scotland, on the Clyde; shipyards. 1,085,000 (est. 1956).

Glas·gow (glăs'gō), *n.* **Ellen Anderson Gholson** (gōl'sən), 1874–1945, U.S. novelist.

glass (glăs, gläs), *n.* **1.** a hard, brittle, more or less transparent substance produced by fusion, usually consisting of mutually dissolved silica and silicates (the ordinary variety used for windows, bottles, and the like, containing silica, soda, and lime). See **crown glass** and **flint glass. 2.** any artificial or natural substance having similar properties and composition, as fused borax, obsidian, etc. **3.** something made of glass, as a window, mirror, lens, barometer, etc. **4.** (*pl.*) eyeglasses. **5.** things made of glass, collectively; glassware. **6.** a glass container for drinking water, etc. **7.** quantity or contents of a drinking glass; glassful. —*adj.* **8.** made of glass. **9.** furnished or fitted with panes of glass; glazed. —*v.t.* **10.** to fit with panes of glass; cover with or encase in glass. **11.** *Poetic.* to reflect: *trees glass themselves in the lake.* [ME *glas,* OE *glæs,* c. D and G *glas*] —**glass'-less,** *adj.*

Glass (glăs, gläs), *n.* **Carter,** 1858–1946, U.S. statesman.

glass blowing, **1.** the art or process of forming glass into ware by blowing by mouth or mechanically. **2.** the operation of working glass in a flame, starting with tubing, rod, or cane, and forming laboratory apparatus, ornaments, or knickknacks. —**glass blower.**

glass·ful (glăs'fool, gläs'-), *n., pl.* **-fuls.** as much as a glass holds.

glass harmonica, an instrument consisting of a series of glass bowls graduated in size which can be played by the friction of the moistened finger.

glass·house (glăs'hous', gläs'-), *n.* **1.** an establishment where glass is made. **2.** *Chiefly Brit.* a greenhouse.

glass·ine (glă·sēn'), *n.* a glazed, semitransparent paper, used for book jackets, etc.

glass·mak·ing (glăs'māk'ĭng, gläs'-), *n.* the art of making glass or glassware.

glass·man (glăs'mən, gläs'-), *n., pl.* **-men.** one who makes or sells glass. **2.** a glazier.

glass snake, **1.** a limbless, snakelike lizard, *Ophisaurus ventralis,* of the southern U.S., having an extremely fragile tail. **2.** any of certain similar lizards of Europe and Asia.

glass tank, a reverberatory furnace in which glass is melted directly under the flames.

glass·ware (glăs'wâr', gläs'-), *n.* articles of glass.

glass·work (glăs'wûrk', gläs'-), *n.* **1.** the manufacture of glass and glassware. **2.** the fitting of glass; glazing. **3.** articles of glass collectively; glassware.

glass·work·er (glăs'wûr'kər, gläs'-), *n.* one who works in glass.

glass·works (glăs'wûrks', gläs'-), *n. pl. or sing.* glasshouse (def. 1).

glass·wort (glăs'wûrt', gläs'-), *n.* **1.** any of the herbs with succulent leafless stems constituting the chenopodiaceous genus *Salicornia,* and formerly much used (when burned to ashes) as a source of soda for glassmaking. **2.** the saltwort, *Salsola Kali* (**prickly glasswort**).

glass·y (glăs'ĭ, gläs'ĭ), *adj.,* **glassier, glassiest. 1.** resembling glass, as in transparency, smoothness, etc. **2.** having a fixed, unintelligent stare. **3.** of the nature of glass; vitreous. —**glass'i·ly,** *adv.* —**glass'i·ness,** *n.*

Glau·ber salt (glou'bər), sodium sulfate, used as a cathartic, etc. Also, **Glau'ber's salt.** [named after J. R. Glauber (1604–68), German chemist]

glau·co·ma (glô·kō'mə), *n. Pathol.* a disease of the eye, characterized by increased pressure within the eyeball with progressive loss of vision. [t. Gk.: m. *glaukōma* opacity of the crystalline lens. See GLAUCOUS] —**glau·co·ma·tous** (glô·kō'mə·təs, -kŏm'ə-), *adj.*

glau·co·nite (glô′kə nīt′), *n.* a greenish micaceous mineral, essentially of a hydrous silicate of potassium, aluminum, and iron, and occurring in greensand, clays, etc. [f. m. Gk. *glaukōn*, neut. adj., bluish-green + -ITE[1]]

glau·cous (glô′kəs), *adj.* **1.** light bluish-green or greenish-blue. **2.** *Bot.* covered with a whitish bloom, as a plum. [t. L: m. *glaucus*, t. Gk.: m. *glaukós* gleaming, silvery, gray, bluish-green]

glaucous gull, a large white and pale-gray gull, *Latus hyperboreus*, of arctic regions.

glaze (glāz), *v.*, **glazed, glazing,** *n.* **—*v.t.* 1.** to furnish or fit with glass; cover with glass. **2.** to produce a vitreous or glossy surface on (pottery, biscuit, etc.). **3.** to cover with glaze. **4.** *Painting.* to cover (a painted surface or parts of it) with a thin layer of transparent color in order to modify the tone. **5.** to cover with a smooth lustrous coating; give a glassy surface to, as by polishing. **—*v.i.* 6.** to become glazed or glassy. **—*n.* 7.** a smooth, glossy surface or coating. **8.** the substance for producing it. **9.** *Ceramics.* **a.** the vitreous or glossy surface or coating on glazed pottery. **b.** the substance or material used to produce such a surface. **10.** *Painting.* a thin layer of transparent color, spread over a painted surface. **11.** *Cookery.* **a.** something used to coat a food, esp. sugar or sugar syrup. **b.** stock cooked down to a thin paste, for applying to the surface of meats. **12.** *U.S. Weather Bureau.* a smooth coating of ice on terrestrial objects due to the freezing of rain. [ME *glasen*, der. *glas* GLASS] **—glaz′er,** *n.* **—glaz′y,** *adj.*

gla·zier (glā′zhər), *n.* one who fits windows, etc., with glass. [ME *glasier*, f. *glas* GLASS + -IER]

gla·zier·y (glā′zhə rĭ), *n.* glaziers' work.

glaz·ing (glā′zĭng), *n.* **1.** act of furnishing or fitting with glass; business of a glazier. **2.** glass set, or to be set, in frames, etc. **3.** act of applying a glaze. **4.** the glassy surface of anything glazed.

gleam (glēm), *n.* **1.** a flash or beam of light. **2.** dim or subdued light. **3.** a brief or slight manifestation: *a gleam of hope.* **—*v.i.* 4.** to send forth a gleam or gleams. **5.** to appear suddenly and clearly, like a flash of light. **—*v.t.* 6.** *Rare.* to send forth in gleams. [ME *glem(e)*, OE *glǣm*, c. OHG *gleimo* glowworm; akin to OS *glīmo* brightness, etc. See GLIMMER, GLIMPSE]
—Syn. 1. GLEAM, RAY, GLIMMER are terms for a stream of light. GLEAM denotes a not very brilliant, and often intermittent, stream of light: *the distant gleam from a lighted window.* RAY usually implies a smaller amount of light than a beam; a single line of light: *a ray through a pinprick in a window shade.* GLIMMER indicates a feeble, unsteady light: *a faint glimmer of moonlight.*

glean (glēn), *v.t.* **1.** to gather slowly and laboriously in bits. **2.** to gather (grain, etc.) after the reapers or regular gatherers. **—*v.i.* 3.** to collect or gather anything little by little or slowly. **4.** to gather what is left by reapers. [ME *glene(n)*, t. OF: m. *glener*, g. LL *glenāre*, of Celtic orig.] **—glean′er,** *n.*

glean·ing (glē′nĭng), *n.* **1.** act of one who gleans. **2.** (*usually pl.*) that which is gleaned.

glebe (glēb), *n.* **1.** *Poetic.* soil; field. **2.** *Brit.* the cultivable land owned by a parish church or ecclesiastical benefice. [ME, t. L: m.s. *glēba*, *glaeba* clod, soil, land]

glede (glēd), *n.* the common European kite, *Milvus ictinus.* Also, **gled** (glĕd). [ME; OE *glida*, c. Icel. *gledha*; akin to GLIDE]

glee (glē), *n.* **1.** demonstrative joy; exultation. **2.** a kind of unaccompanied part song, grave or gay, for three or more voices. [ME; OE *glēo*, c. Icel. *glȳ*] **—Syn. 1.** merriment, jollity, hilarity. See **mirth.**

glee club, a club or group for singing choral music.

glee·ful (glē′fəl), *adj.* full of glee; merry; exultant. **—glee′ful·ly,** *adv.* **—glee′ful·ness,** *n.*

glee·man (glē′mən), *n.*, *pl.* **-men.** *Archaic.* a strolling professional singer or minstrel. [OE *glēomann*]

glee·some (glē′səm), *adj.* gleeful. **—glee′some·ly,** *adv.* **—glee′some·ness,** *n.*

gleet (glēt), *n.* *Pathol.* **1.** a thin, morbid discharge, as from a wound. **2.** a persistent or chronic gonorrhea. [ME *glette*, t. OF: slime, mucus, pus, foul matter]

glen (glĕn), *n.* a small, narrow, secluded valley. [ME, t. Gaelic: m. *gle(a)nn*, c. Welsh *glyn*] **—glen′like′,** *adj.*

Glen·dale (glĕn′dāl′), *n.* a city in SW California, near Los Angeles. 199,422 (1960).

Glen·dow·er (glĕn dou′ər, glĕn′dou ər), *n.* **Owen,** 1359?–1416?, Welsh rebel against Henry IV of England.

glen·gar·ry (glĕn găr′ĭ), *n.*, *pl.* **-ries.** a Scotch cap, with straight sides, a crease along the top, and sometimes short ribbon streamers at the back, worn by Highlanders as part of military dress. [named after *Glengarry*, valley in Invernesshire, Scotland]

gle·noid (glē′noid), *adj.* *Anat.* **1.** shallow or slightly cupped, as the articular cavities of the scapula and the temporal bone. **2.** pertaining to such a cavity. [t. Gk.: m.s. *glēnoeidēs* like a shallow joint socket. See -OID]

glib (glĭb), *adj.*, **glibber, glibbest. 1.** ready and fluent, often thoughtlessly or insincerely so: *glib speakers, a glib tongue.* **2.** easy, as action or manner. [back formation from obs. *glibbery* slippery, t. D: m. *glibberig*] **—glib′ly,** *adv.* **—glib′ness,** *n.* **—Syn. 1.** See **fluent.**

glide (glīd), *v.*, **glided, gliding,** *n.* **—*v.i.* 1.** to move smoothly along, as if without effort or difficulty, as a flying bird, a boat, a skater, etc. **2.** to pass by gradual or insensible change (often fol. by *along, away, by,* etc.). **3.** to go quietly or unperceived; slip (fol. by *in, out,* etc.). **4.** *Aeron.* to move in the air, esp. at an easy angle downward, by the action of gravity or by virtue of momentum already acquired. **5.** *Music.* to pass from tone to tone without a break; slur. **—*v.t.* 6.** to cause to glide. **—*n.* 7.** a gliding movement, as in dancing. **8.** a dance in which such movements are employed. **9.** *Music.* a slur (def. 8a). **10.** *Phonet.* **a.** a transitional sound produced while passing from the articulation required by one speech sound to that required by the next, such as the "y" sound often heard between the *i* and *e* of *quiet.* **b.** a semivowel, such as *w* in *wet.* [ME *glide(n)*, OE *glīdan*, c. G *gleiten*] **—glid′ing·ly,** *adv.* **—Syn. 1.** See **slide.**

glid·er (glī′dər), *n.* **1.** one who or that which glides. **2.** *Aeron.* a motorless heavier-than-air craft for gliding from a higher to a lower level by the action of gravity, or from a lower to a higher level by the action of air currents. **3.** a swing made of an upholstered seat suspended from a steel framework by links or springs.

glim·mer (glĭm′ər), *n.* **1.** a faint or unsteady light; gleam. **2.** a dim perception; inkling. **—*v.i.* 3.** to shine faintly or unsteadily; twinkle; flicker. **4.** to appear faintly or dimly. [ME *glemer(en)* gleam, c. G *glimmern.* Cf. OE *gleomu* splendor] **—Syn. 1.** See **gleam.**

glim·mer·ing (glĭm′ər ĭng), *n.* **1.** a faint or unsteady light; a glimmer. **2.** a faint glimpse; inkling. **—*adj.* 3.** that glimmers. **—glim′mer·ing·ly,** *adv.*

glimpse (glĭmps), *n.*, *v.*, **glimpsed, glimpsing. —*n.* 1.** a momentary sight or view. **2.** a momentary or slight appearance. **3.** a vague idea; inkling. **4.** *Archaic.* a gleam, as of light. **—*v.t.* 5.** to catch a glimpse of. **—*v.i.* 6.** to look briefly, or glance (fol. by *at*). **7.** *Poetic.* to come into view; appear faintly. [ME *glymsen*, c. MHG *glimsen* glow; akin to GLIMMER] **—glimps′er,** *n.*

Glin·ka (glĕn′kä), *n.* **Mikhail Ivanovich** (mĭ hä ēl′ ĭ vä′nŏ vĭch), 1803?–57, Russian composer.

glint (glĭnt), *n.* **1.** a gleam or glimmer; flash. **2.** glinting brightness; luster. **—*v.i.* 3.** to gleam or flash. **4.** to move suddenly; dart. **—*v.t.* 5.** to cause to glint; reflect. [ME *glynt*, var. of obs. *glent*, t. Scand.; cf. d. Sw. *glänta, glinta* slip, shine] **—Syn. 3.** See **flash.**

gli·o·ma (glī ō′mə), *n.*, *pl.* **-mata** (-mə tə), **-mas.** *Pathol.* a tumor arising from and consisting largely of neuroglia. [NL, f. s. Gk. *glía* glue + *-ōma* -OMA] **—gli·o·ma·tous** (glī ō′mə təs, -ŏm′ə-), *adj.*

glis·sade (glĭ säd′, -sād′), *n.*, *v.*, **-saded, -sading. —*n.* 1.** a skillful glide over snow or ice in descending a mountain. **2.** *Dancing.* a sliding or gliding step. **—*v.i.* 3.** to perform a glissade. [t. F, der. *glisser* slip, slide, b. OF *glacier* slip and *glier* slide (t. Gmc.; cf. GLIDE)]

glis·san·do (glĭ sän′dō), *adj.*, *n.*, *pl.* **-di** (-dē). **—*adj.* 1.** performed with a gliding effect by sliding one finger rapidly over the keys of a piano or strings of a harp. **—*n.* 2.** a glissando passage. **3.** (in string playing) a slide. [pseudo-It., t. F: m. *glissant*, ppr. of *glisser* slide]

glis·ten (glĭs′ən), *v.i.* **1.** to shine with a sparkling light or a faint intermittent glow. **—*n.* 2.** a glistening; sparkle. [ME *glis(t)nen*, OE *glisnian*, der. *glisian* glitter. See -EN[1]] **—glis′ten·ing·ly,** *adv.*
—Syn. 1. GLISTEN, SHIMMER, SPARKLE refer to different ways in which light is reflected from surfaces. GLISTEN refers to a lustrous light as from something sleek or wet, or it may refer to myriads of tiny gleams reflected from small surfaces: *wet fur glistens, snow glistens in the sunlight.* SHIMMER refers to the changing play of light on a (generally moving) surface, as of water or silk: *moonbeams shimmer on water, silk shimmers in a high light.* To SPARKLE is to give off sparks or small ignited particles, or to send forth small but brilliant gleams: *a diamond sparkles as with numerous points of light.*

glis·ter (glĭs′tər), *v.i.* **1.** *Archaic.* to glisten; glitter. **—*n.* 2.** *Archaic or Dial.* a glistening; glitter. [ME; freq. of obs. v. *glist* glitter, var. of GLISTEN (? back formation)]

glit·ter (glĭt′ər), *v.i.* **1.** to shine with a brilliant, sparkling light or luster. **2.** to make a brilliant show: *glittering scenes of a court.* **—*n.* 3.** glittering light or luster; splendor. [ME, t. Scand.; cf. Icel. *glitra*, freq. of *glita* shine; cf. OE *glitenian*, G *gleissan* shine, glitter] **—glit′ter·ing·ly,** *adv.* **—Syn. 1.** See **flash.**

glit·ter·y (glĭt′ə rĭ), *adj.* glittering; sparkling.

gloam·ing (glō′mĭng), *n.* *Poetic.* twilight; dusk. [ME *gloming*, OE *glōmung*, der. *glōm* twilight; mod. *-oa-* (instead of *-oo-*) presumably by contam. with GLOW]

gloat (glōt), *v.i.* to gaze with exultation; dwell mentally upon something with intense (and usually evil) satisfaction: *to gloat over another's misfortunes.* [cf. Icel. *glotta* grin, smile scornfully, d. Sw. *glotta* peep, G *glotzen* stare] **—gloat′er,** *n.* **—gloat′ing·ly,** *adv.* **—Syn.** See **glare**[1].

glob·al (glō′bəl), *adj.* **1.** spherical; globe-shaped. **2.** pertaining to the whole world. **—glob′al·ly,** *adv.*

glo·bate (glō′bāt), *adj.* shaped like a globe. Also, **glo′bat·ed.** [t. L: m.s. *globātus*, pp., formed into a ball]

globe (glōb), *n.*, *v.*, **globed, globing. —*n.* 1.** the earth (usually prec. by *the*). **2.** a planet or other celestial body. **3.** a sphere on which is depicted a map of the earth (**terrestrial globe**) or of the heavens (**celestial globe**). **4.** a spherical body; sphere. **5.** anything more or less spherical, as a lamp shade or a glass fish bowl. **6.** *Hist.* a golden ball borne as an emblem of sovereignty. **—*v.t.* 7.** to form into a globe. **—*v.i.* 8.** to take the form of a globe. [t. F, t. L: m. *globus* round body or mass, ball, globe] **—globe′like′,** *adj.* **—Syn. 1.** See **earth. 4.** See **ball**[1].

globe·fish (glōb′fĭsh′), *n.*, *pl.* **-fishes,** (*esp. collectively*) **-fish.** a puffer (def. 2).

globe·flow·er (glōb′flou′ər), *n.* **1.** a ranunculaceous plant, *Trollius europaeus*, of Europe, having pale-yellow globelike flowers. **2.** an American species, *T. laxus.*

globe·trot·ter (glōb′trŏt′ər), n. Colloq. one who travels widely, esp. for sightseeing. —**globe′trot′ting,** n., adj.
lo·big·er·i·na (glō bĭj′ə rī′nə), n., pl. **-nae** (-nē). a marine protozoan belonging to the Foraminifera, the shell of which, falling to the ocean floor upon death, forms a mud known as the **globigerina ooze**.
lo·bin (glō′bĭn), n. Biochem. a protein contained in hemoglobin. [f. s. L globus GLOBE + -IN²]
lo·boid (glō′boid), adj. 1. approximately globular. —n. 2. a globoid figure or body.
lo·bose (glō′bōs, glō bōs′), adj. globelike; globe-shaped, or nearly so. Also, **glo·bous** (glō′bəs). [t. L: m.s. globōsus round as a ball] —**glo′bose·ly,** adv. —**glo·bos·i·ty** (glō bŏs′ə tĭ), n.
lob·u·lar (glŏb′yə lər), adj. 1. globe-shaped; spherical. 2. composed of globules. —**glob′u·lar·i·ty,** n. —**glob′u·lar·ly,** adv.
lob·ule (glŏb′ūl), n. a small spherical body. [t. F, t. L: m. globulus, dim. of globus GLOBE]
lob·u·lin (glŏb′yə lĭn), n. Biochem. any of a group of proteins insoluble in pure water. [f. GLOBULE + -IN²]
lock·en·spiel (glŏk′ən spēl′; Ger. glŏk′ən shpēl′), n. Music. 1. a set of steel bars mounted in a frame and struck with hammers, used by military bands. 2. a small keyboard instrument, imitating the sound of bells. 3. a set of bells; carillon. [t. G: f. glocken-, comb. form of glocke bell + spiel play]
lom·er·ate (glŏm′ər ĭt), adj. compactly clustered. [t. L: m. s. glomerātus, pp., wound or formed into a ball]
lom·er·a·tion (glŏm′ə rā′shən), n. 1. glomerate condition; conglomeration. 2. a glomerate mass.
lom·er·ule (glŏm′ər ōōl′), n. Bot. a cyme condensed into a headlike cluster. [t. F, t. NL: m. s. glomerulus, dim. of L glomus ball (of yarn, thread, etc.)]
lo·mer·u·lus (glō mĕr′yōō ləs, -ōō ləs), n., pl. **-li** (-lī′). Anat. a compact cluster of capillaries. [NL. See GLOM-ERULE]
lon·o·in (glŏn′ō ĭn), n. nitroglycerin: esp. so called in medicine. Also, **glon·o·ine** (glŏn′ō ĭn, -ēn′). [said to be f. GL(YCERIN) + chemical symbols O (oxygen) and NO₃ (nitric anhydride) + -IN²]
loom¹ (glōōm), n. 1. darkness; dimness. —v.i. 2. to appear or become dark or gloomy. —v.t. 3. to make dark or somber. [OE glōm twilight. See GLOAMING, GLOW]. —Syn. 1. shadow, shade. —Ant. 1. brightness.
loom² (glōōm), n. 1. a state of melancholy or depression; low spirits. 2. a despondent look or expression. —v.i. 3. to look dismal or dejected; frown. —v.t. 4. to fill with gloom; make gloomy or sad. [ME gloum(b)e, glomme frown, lower. See GLUM] —Syn. 1. dejection, despondency. —Ant. 1. cheerfulness.
loom·y¹ (glōō′mĭ), adj., **gloomier, gloomiest.** dark; deeply shaded. [f. GLOOM¹ + -Y¹] —Syn. See **dark.**
loom·y² (glōō′mĭ), adj., **gloomier, gloomiest.** 1. causing gloom; depressing: a gloomy prospect. 2. affected with or expressive of gloom; melancholy. [f. GLOOM² + -Y¹] —**gloom′i·ly,** adv. —**gloom′i·ness,** n. —Syn. 2. dejected, downcast, downhearted, sad, despondent.
loos·cap (glōōs′kăp), n. a divinity or legendary hero among the northeastern Algonquian Indians.
lo·ri·a (glōr′ĭ ə), n. 1. (in Christian liturgical worship) the great, or greater, doxology beginning "Gloria in excelsis Deo" (Glory be to God on high), the lesser doxology beginning "Gloria Patri" (Glory be to the Father), or the response "Gloria tibi, Domine" (Glory be to thee, O Lord). 2. (l.c.) a repetition of one of these. 3. (l.c.) a musical setting for one of these, esp. the first. 4. (l.c.) a halo, nimbus, or aureole, or an ornament in imitation of one. 5. (l.c.) a silk and wool (or cotton) fabric for umbrellas, dresses, etc. [t. L: glory]
lo·ri·a in Ex·cel·sis De·o (glōr′ĭ ə ĭn ĕk sĕl′sĭs dē′ō), the hymn beginning, in Latin, "Gloria in Excelsis Deo" (Glory in the highest to God), and, in the English version, "Glory be to God on high."
lo·ri·a Pa·tri (glōr′ĭ ə pät′rĭ), the short hymn "Glory be to the Father, and to the Son, and to the Holy Ghost. As it was in the beginning, is now, and ever shall be, world without end. Amen."
lo·ri·fi·ca·tion (glōr′ə fə kā′shən), n. 1. act of glorifying; exaltation to the glory of heaven. 2. state of being glorified. 3. Colloq. a celebration or jubilation. 4. Colloq. a glorified or more splendid form of something.
lo·ri·fy (glōr′ə fī′), v.t., **-fied, -fying.** 1. to magnify with praise; extol. 2. to transform into something more splendid. 3. to make glorious; invest with glory. 4. to promote the glory of (God); ascribe glory and praise in adoration to (God). [ME glorify(en), t. OF: m. glorifier, t. LL: m. glōrificāre. See GLORY, -FY] —**glo′ri·fi′a·ble,** adj. —**glo′ri·fi′er,** n.
lo·ri·ole (glōr′ĭ ōl′), n. a halo, nimbus, or aureole. [t. F, t. L: m. s. glōriola, dim. of glōria GLORY, n.]
lo·ri·ous (glōr′ĭ əs), adj. 1. admirable; delightful: to have a glorious time. 2. conferring glory: a glorious victory. 3. full of glory; entitled to great renown: England is glorious in her poetry. 4. brilliantly beautiful: the glorious heavens. [ME, t. AF, t. L: m.s. glōriōsus full of glory] —**glo′ri·ous·ly,** adv. —**glo′ri·ous·ness,** n. —Syn. 3. famous, renowned; illustrious.
lo·ry (glōr′ĭ), n., pl. **glories,** v., **gloried, glorying.** —n. 1. exalted praise, honor, or distinction, accorded by common consent: paths of glory. 2. something that makes honored or illustrious; a distinguished ornament;

an object of pride. 3. adoring praise or thanksgiving: give glory to God. 4. resplendent beauty or magnificence: the glory of God. 5. state of splendor, magnificence, or greatest prosperity. 6. the splendor and bliss of heaven; heaven. 7. a ring, circle, or surrounding radiance of light represented about the head or the whole figure of a sacred person, as Christ, a saint, etc.; a halo, nimbus, or aureole. —v.i. 8. to exult with triumph; rejoice proudly. 9. to be boastful; exult arrogantly (fol. by in). [ME, t. OF: m. glorie, t. L: m. glōria glory, fame, vainglory, boasting] —Syn. 1. fame, eminence. 5. grandeur, pomp. —Ant. 1. disgrace.
gloss¹ (glŏs, glôs), n. 1. a superficial luster: gloss of satin. 2. an external show; specious appearance. —v.t. 3. to put a gloss upon. 4. to give a specious appearance to (often fol. by over). [t. Scand.; cf. Icel. glossi spark] —**gloss′er,** n. —**gloss′less,** adj. —Syn. 1. sheen, polish, glaze. See **polish.**
gloss² (glŏs, glôs), n. 1. an explanation, by means of a marginal or interlinear note, of a technical or unusual expression in a manuscript text. 2. a series of verbal interpretations of a text. 3. an artfully misleading interpretation. —v.t. 4. to insert glosses on; annotate. 5. to give a specious interpretation of; explain away (often fol. by over): to gloss over a mistake. —v.i. 6. to make glosses. [t. L: s. glossa (explanation of) hard word, t. Gk.: lit., tongue. Cf. GLOZE] —**gloss′er,** n.
gloss., glossary.
Glos·sa (glŏs′ə), n. Cape, a promontory in SW Albania.
glos·sal (glŏs′əl, glôs′əl), adj. of or pertaining to the tongue.
glos·sa·ry (glŏs′ə rĭ, glôs′ə-), n., pl. **-ries.** a list of basic technical, dialectal, and difficult terms in a subject or field, with definitions. [t. L: m.s. glossārium, der. glossa GLOSS²] —**glos·sar·i·al** (glŏ sâr′ĭ əl, glô-), adj. —**glos′sa·rist,** n.
glos·sa·tor (glŏ sā′tər, glô-), n. one of the early medieval interpreters (not later than 1250) of the Roman and canon laws. [t. ML, ult. der. L glossa GLOSS²]
glos·sec·to·my (glŏ sĕk′tə mĭ, glô-), n., pl. **-mies.** Surg. the removal of all or of a portion of the tongue.
glos·si·tis (glŏ sī′tĭs, glô-), n. Pathol. inflammation of the tongue. [f. glosso- (see GLOSSOLOGY) + -ITIS]
glos·sol·o·gy (glŏ sŏl′ə jĭ, glô-), n. Obs. linguistics. [f. glosso- (t. Gk., comb. form of glōssa tongue) + -LOGY]
gloss·y (glŏs′ĭ, glôs′ĭ), adj., **glossier, glossiest.** 1. having a glossy; lustrous. 2. having a specious appearance; plausible. [f. GLOSS¹, n. + -Y¹] —**gloss′i·ly,** adv. —**gloss′i·ness,** n. —Syn. 1. shining, polished, glazed; smooth, sleek. —Ant. 1. dull.
glost (glŏst, glôst), n. Ceramics. glaze or glazed ware.
-glot, a suffix indicating proficiency in language, as in polyglot. [t. Gk.: m.s. glōtta tongue]
glot·tal (glŏt′əl), adj. 1. pertaining to the glottis. 2. Phonet. articulated in the glottis.
glottal stop, Phonet. stop consonant made by closing the glottis so tightly that no breath can pass through, as in yep yes, nope no.
glot·tic (glŏt′ĭk), adj. 1. pertaining to the glottis; glottal. 2. Obs. linguistic.
glot·tis (glŏt′ĭs), n. the opening at the upper part of the larynx, between the vocal cords. [t. NL, t. Gk.: the mouth of the windpipe]
glot·tol·o·gy (glŏ tŏl′ə jĭ), n. Obs. linguistics. [f. glotto- (t. Gk., comb. form of glōtta tongue) + -LOGY] —**glot·to·log·ic** (glŏt′ə lŏj′ĭk), **glot′to·log′i·cal,** adj. —**glot·tol′o·gist,** n.
Glouces·ter (glŏs′tər, glôs′-), n. 1. a city in SW England: port on Severn. 67,300 (est. 1956). 2. a seaport in NE Massachusetts. 25,789 (1960). 3. Gloucestershire.
Glouces·ter (glŏs′tər, glôs′-), n. Duke of, 1. See **Humphrey.** 2. See **Richard III.** 3. See **Thomas of Woodstock.**
Glouces·ter·shire (glŏs′tər shĭr′, -shər, glôs′-), n. a county in SW England. 939,433 pop. (1951); 1255 sq. mi. Co. seat: Gloucester. Also, **Gloucester.**
glove (glŭv), n., v., **gloved, gloving.** —n. 1. a covering for the hand, now made with a separate sheath for each finger and for the thumb. 2. a boxing glove. —v.t. 3. to cover with or as with a glove; provide with gloves. 4. to serve as a glove for. [ME; OE glōf, c. Icel. glōfi] —**glove′less,** adj. —**glove′like′,** adj.
glov·er (glŭv′ər), n. one who makes or sells gloves.
Glov·ers·ville (glŭv′ərz vĭl′), n. a city in E New York. 23,634 (1950).
glow (glō), n. 1. light emitted by a substance heated to luminosity; incandescence. 2. brightness of color. 3. a state of bodily heat. 4. warmth of emotion or passion; ardor. —v.i. 5. to emit bright light and heat without flame; be incandescent. 6. to shine like something intensely heated. 7. to exhibit a strong, bright color; be lustrously red or brilliant. 8. to be excessively hot. 9. to be animated with emotion. [ME glowe(n), OE glōwan, akin to G glühen, Icel. glōa]
glow·er (glou′ər), v.i. 1. to look angrily; stare with sullen dislike or discontent. —n. 2. a glowering look; frown. [freq. of obs. glow stare, of uncert. orig.] —**glow′er·ing·ly,** adv. —Syn. 1. See **glare¹.**
glow·ing (glō′ĭng), adj. 1. incandescent. 2. rich and warm in coloring: glowing colors. 3. exhibiting the glow of health, excitement, etc. 4. ardent or impassioned: a glowing account. —**glow′ing·ly,** adv.

glow·worm (glō′wûrm′), n. 1. any of the fireflies of the family *Lampyridae* or their larvae. 2. a European beetle, *Lampyris noctiluca*, the wingless female of which emits a greenish light from the end of the abdomen.

glox·in·i·a (glŏk·sĭn′ĭ·ə), n. the garden name of tuberous-rooted plants of the genus *Sinningia*, esp. a widely cultivated species, *S. speciosa*, having large white, red, or purple bell-shaped flowers. [NL; named after B. P. *Gloxin*, German botanist]

gloze (glōz), v., **glozed, glozing,** n. —v.t. 1. to explain away; extenuate; gloss over (usually fol. by *over*). 2. to palliate with specious talk. —v.i. 3. *Obs.* to make glosses; comment. —n. 4. *Rare.* flattery or deceit. 5. *Obs.* a specious show. [ME *glose*, t. OF. See GLOSS²]

glu·ci·num (glōō·sī′nəm), n. *Chem.* beryllium. *Sym.:* Gl. Also, **glu·cin·i·um** (glōō·sĭn′ĭ·əm). [NL, der. Gk. *glykýs* sweet (some of the salts having a sweet taste)]

Gluck (glŏŏk), n. 1. **Alma,** (*Reba Fiersohn,* Mme. *Efrem Zimbalist*) 1884–1938, U.S. operatic soprano, born in Rumania. 2. **Christoph Willibald von** (krĭs′-tôf vĭl′ĭ·bält′ fən), 1714–87, German operatic composer.

glu·co·pro·te·in (glōō′kō·prō′tĭ·ĭn, -tēn), n. glycoprotein.

glu·cose (glōō′kōs), n. 1. *Chem.* a sugar, C₆H₁₂O₆, having several optically different forms, the common or dextrorotatory form (d-glucose) occurring in many fruits, animal tissues and fluids, etc., and having a sweetness about one half that of ordinary sugar. The levorotatory form (l-glucose) is rare and not naturally occurring. 2. *Com.* a syrup containing dextrose, maltose, and dextrine, obtained by the incomplete hydrolysis of starch. [t. F, f. m.s. Gk. *glykýs* sweet + *-ose* -OSE²]

glu·co·side (glōō′kə·sīd′), n. *Chem.* one of an extensive group of compounds which yield glucose and some other substance or substances when treated with a dilute acid or when decomposed by a ferment or enzyme. [f. GLUCOS(E) + -IDE]

glu·co·su·ri·a (glōō′kō·sŏŏr′ĭ·ə), n. *Pathol.* glycosuria.

glue (glōō), n., v., **glued, gluing.** —n. 1. an impure gelatin obtained by boiling skins, hoofs, and other animal substances in water, and used for various purposes in the arts, esp. as an adhesive medium in uniting substances. 2. any of various preparations of this substance. 3. any similar adhesive material. —v.t. 4. to join or fasten with glue. 5. to fix or attach firmly, as if with glue; make adhere closely. [ME, t. OF: m. *glu*, g. LL *glus*. Cf. GLUTEN] —**glue′like′,** adj. —**glu′er,** n.

glue·y (glōō′ĭ), adj., **gluier, gluiest.** 1. like glue; viscid; sticky. 2. full of or smeared with glue.

glum (glŭm), adj., **glummer, glummest.** gloomily sullen or silent; dejected. [cf. LG *glum* turbid, muddy; akin to GLOOM²] —**glum′ly,** adv. —**glum′ness,** n.

glu·ma·ceous (glōō·mā′shəs), adj. 1. glumelike. 2. consisting of or having glumes.

glume (glōōm), n. *Bot.* one of the characteristic bracts of the inflorescence of grasses, sedges, etc., esp. one of the pair of bracts at the base of a spikelet. [t. L: m.s. *gluma* hull or husk (of grain)] —**glume′like′,** adj.

glut (glŭt), v., **glutted, glutting.** —v.t. 1. to feed or fill to satiety; sate: *to glut the appetite.* 2. to feed or fill to excess; cloy. 3. **glut the market,** to overstock the market; furnish a supply of any article largely in excess of the demand, so that the price is unusually low. 4. to choke up: *glut a channel.* —v.i. 5. to eat to satiety. —n. 6. a full supply. 7. a surfeit. 8. act of glutting. 9. state of being glutted. [ME *glotye(n),* appar. der. obs. *glut,* n., glutton, t. OF: adj., greedy. See GLUTTON¹]

glu·tam·ic acid (glōō·tăm′ĭk), *Chem.* a colorless solid, HOOCCH₂CH₂CH(N₂H)COOH, found in the proteins of seeds and beets.

glu·ta·mine (glōō′tə·mēn′, -mĭn), n. *Chem.* a crystalline amino acid, HOOCCH(N₂H)CH₂CH₂CONH₂, related to glutamic acid. [f. GLUT(EN) + -AMINE]

glu·ta·thi·one (glōō′tə·thī′ōn, -thī·ōn′), n. *Biochem.* a peptide found in blood and animal tissues, in embryos and germinating seedlings: important in metabolic actions.

glu·te·al (glōō·tē′əl, glōō′tĭ·əl), adj. *Anat.* pertaining to buttock muscles or the buttocks. [f. GLUTE(US) + -AL¹]

glu·te·lins (glōō′tə·lĭnz), n.pl. *Biochem.* a group of simple proteins of vegetable origin, esp. from wheat.

glu·ten (glōō′tən), n. 1. the tough, viscid nitrogenous substance remaining when the flour of wheat or other grain is washed to remove the starch. 2. glue, or some gluey substance. [t. L: glue, akin to LL *glus* GLUE]

gluten bread, bread made from gluten flour.

gluten flour, wheat flour from which a large part of the starch has been removed, thus increasing the proportion of gluten.

glu·te·nous (glōō′tə·nəs), adj. 1. like gluten. 2. containing gluten, esp. in large amounts.

glu·te·us (glōō·tē′əs), n., *pl.* **-tei** (-tē′ī). *Anat.* any of several muscles of the buttocks. [NL, der. Gk. *gloutós* rump, pl. buttocks]

glu·ti·nous (glōō′tə·nəs), adj. of the nature of glue; gluey; viscid; sticky. [t. L: m. s. *glūtinōsus* gluey, viscous] —**glu′ti·nous·ly,** adv. —**glu′ti·nous·ness,** n. **glu·ti·nos·i·ty** (glōō′tə·nŏs′ə·tĭ), n.

glu·tose (glōō′tōs), n. an ingredient of the syrupy mixture obtained by the action of alkali on levulose, and in the unfermentable reducing portion of cane molasses.

glut·ton¹ (glŭt′ən), n. 1. one who eats to excess; a

gormandizer. 2. one who indulges in something excessively. [ME *glutun,* t. OF: m. *glouton,* g. L *glūto, glutto*]

glut·ton² (glŭt′ən), n. *Zool.* a thick-set, voracious mammal, *Gulo luscus,* of the weasel family, measuring from 2 to 3 feet in length, and inhabiting northern regions. The kind found in America is usually called the **wolverine,** and is practically identical with that of Europe and Asia. [ult. t. Sw.: trans. of *fjällfräs* (through G *vielfrass*), whence also NL name of animal, *gulo*]

glut·ton·ize (glŭt′ə·nīz′), v., **-ized, -izing.** —v.i. 1. to eat like a glutton. —v.t. 2. to feast gluttonously on.

glut·ton·ous (glŭt′ən·əs), adj. 1. given to excessive eating; voracious. 2. greedy; insatiable. —**glut′tonous·ly,** adv. —**glut′ton·ous·ness,** n.

glut·ton·y (glŭt′ə·nĭ), n., *pl.* **-tonies.** excess in eating.

gly·cer·ic (glĭ·sĕr′ĭk, glĭs′ər·ĭk), adj. *Chem.* pertaining to or derived from glycerin.

glyceric acid, *Chem.* a colorless, syrupy fluid CH₂OHCHOHCOOH, produced during the fermentation of alcohol.

glyc·er·ide (glĭs′ə·rīd′, -ər·ĭd), n. *Chem.* one of a group of esters obtained from glycerol in combination with acids. [f. GLYCER(IN) + -IDE]

glyc·er·in (glĭs′ər·ĭn), n. glycerol. Also, **glyc·er·ine** (glĭs′ər·ĭn, -ə·rēn′). [t. F: m.s. *glycérine,* f. m.s. Gk. *glykerós* sweet + *-ine* -INE²]

glyc·er·ol (glĭs′ə·rōl′, -rŏl′), n. *Chem.* a colorless, odorless, liquid alcohol, HOCH₂CHOHCH₂OH, of syrupy consistency and sweet taste, obtained by the saponification of natural fats and oils, and used in the arts, in medicine, etc.

glyc·er·yl (glĭs′ər·ĭl), adj. *Chem.* denoting or pertaining to the trivalent radical (C₃H₅) derived from glycerin. [f. GLYCER(IN) + -YL]

gly·cine (glī′sēn, glī·sēn′), n. *Chem.* a sweet-tasting colorless, crystalline compound, H₂NCH₂COOH, the simplest amino acid, obtained by hydrolysis of proteins. [f. m. Gk. *glyk(ýs)* sweet + -INE²]

gly·co·gen (glī′kə·jən), n. *Biochem.* a white, tasteless, polysaccharide (C₆H₁₀O₅)ₓ, usually stored in the liver, and easily hydrolyzed into glucose. [f. m.s. Gk. *glykýs* sweet + -GEN]

gly·co·gen·ase (glī′kə·jə·nās′), n. *Biochem.* a liver enzyme which changes glycogen to glucose, **gly·co·genol·y·sis** (glī′kō·jə·nŏl′ə·sĭs), or which imitates the reverse process, **gly·co·gen·e·sis** (glī′kə·jĕn′ə·sĭs), depending on conditions.

gly·co·gen·ic (glī′kə·jĕn′ĭk), adj. *Biochem.* of or pertaining to glycogen.

gly·col (glī′kōl, -kŏl), n. *Chem.* 1. a colorless, sweet-tasting liquid, CH₂OHCH₂OH, used as an antifreeze in automobiles. 2. any of a group of alcohols containing two hydroxyl groups. [b. GLYC(ERIN) and (ALCOH)OL]

gly·col·ic (glī·kōl′ĭk), adj. *Chem.* pertaining to or derived from glycol, as **glycolic acid,** HOCH₂COOH.

gly·co·pro·te·in (glī′kō·prō′tĭ·ĭn, -tēn), n. *Biochem.* any of a group of complex proteins containing a carbohydrate combined with a simple protein, as mucin, etc. Also, **glucoprotein.** [f. m.s. Gk. *glykýs* sweet + PROTEIN]

gly·co·su·ri·a (glī′kō·sŏŏr′ĭ·ə), n. *Pathol.* excretion of glucose in the urine, as in diabetes. Also, **glucosuria.** [NL, f. F *glycose* GLUCOSE + -*uria* -URIA] —**gly′cosu′ric,** adj.

gly·ox·a·lin (glī·ŏk′sə·lĭn), n. *Chem.* imidazole.

glyph (glĭf), n. 1. *Archit.* an ornamental channel or groove, usually vertical, as in a Doric frieze. 2. a sculptured figure. 3. *Archaeol.* a pictograph or hieroglyph. [t. Gk.: s. *glyphé* carving] —**glyph′ic,** adj.

glyp·tic (glĭp′tĭk), adj. of or pertaining to carving or engraving, esp. on precious stones. [t. Gk.: m.s. *glyptikós* of engraving]

glyp·tog·ra·phy (glĭp·tŏg′rə·fĭ), n. 1. the description or study of engraved gems, etc. 2. the art or process of engraving on gems or the like. [f. Gk. *glyptó(s)* carved + -GRAPHY]

gm., gram; grams.

G.M., 1. Grand Marshal. 2. Grand Master.

G-man (jē′măn′), n. an agent for the FBI.

Gmc., Germanic.

gnar (när), v.i., **gnarred, gnarring.** to snarl; growl.

gnarl (närl), n. 1. a knotty protuberance on a tree; knot. —v.t. 2. to twist. [back formation from GNARLED]

gnarled (närld), adj. 1. (of trees) full of or covered with gnarls. 2. (of persons) a. having a rugged, weatherbeaten appearance. b. cross-grained; perverse; cantankerous. Also, **gnarl′y.** [var. of KNURLED]

gnash (năsh), v.t. 1. to grind (the teeth) together, esp in rage or pain. 2. to bite with grinding action. —v.i. 3. to gnash the teeth. —n. 4. act of gnashing. [unexplained var. of obs. *gnast,* t. Scand.; cf. Icel. *gnastan* gnashing of teeth]

gnat (năt), n. 1. any of certain small flies, esp. the biting gnats or punkies (*Ceratopogonidae*), the midges (*Chironomidae*), and the buffalo gnats or black flies (*Simuliidae*). 2. *Eng.* any of certain small dipterous insects (mosquitoes) of the family *Culicidae,* esp. *Culex pipiens.* [ME; OE *gnæt(t),* c. d. G *gnatze*] —**gnat′like′,** adj.

Gnat (def. 2). *Culex pipiens* (Small figure shows natural size)

nat·catch·er (năt/kăch/ər), *n.* any of various small American insectivorous birds of the genus *Polioptila*, as the blue-gray gnatcatcher, *P. caerulea*.

nath·ic (năth/ĭk), *adj.* of or pertaining to the jaw. [f. s. Gk. *gnáthos* jaw + -ic]

nathic index, *Craniol.* the ratio of the distance from basion to prosthion to the distance from basion to nasion, expressed in per cent of the latter.

na·thi·on (nā/thĭ·ŏn', năth/ĭ-), *n. Craniol.* the lowest point on the anterior margin of the lower jaw in the mid-sagittal plane. [NL, dim. of Gk. *gnáthos* jaw]

gnathous, an adjectival word element referring to the jaw, as in *prognathous*. [f. s. Gk. *gnáthos* jaw + -ous]

naw (nô), *v.,* **gnawed, gnawed** or **gnawn, gnawing.** —*v.t.* 1. to wear away or remove by persistent biting. 2. to make by gnawing. 3. to corrode; consume. 4. to consume with passion; torment. —*v.i.* 5. to bite persistently. 6. to cause corrosion. 7. to act as if by corrosion. [ME *gnawe(n)*, OE *gnagan*, c. G *nagen*]

naw·ing (nô/ĭng), *n.* 1. act of one who or that which gnaws. 2. a persistent pain suggesting gnawing: *the gnawings of hunger.* —**gnaw'ing·ly,** *adv.*

neiss (nīs), *n.* a metamorphic rock, generally made up of bands which differ in color and composition, some bands being rich in feldspar and quartz, others rich in hornblende or mica. [t. G] —**gneiss'ic,** *adj.*

neiss·oid (nī/soid), *adj.* resembling gneiss.

nome[1] (nōm), *n.* one of a species of diminutive beings fabled to inhabit the interior of the earth and to act as guardians of its treasures, usually thought of as shriveled little old men; a troll. [t. F, t. NL (Paracelsus): m.s. *gnomus*] —**gnom'ish,** *adj.* —**Syn.** See **goblin, sylph.**

nome[2] (nōm), *n.* a short, pithy expression of a general truth; aphorism. [t. Gk.: judgment, opinion, maxim]

no·mic (nō/mĭk, nŏm/ĭk), *adj.* 1. like or containing gnomes or aphorisms. 2. of, pertaining to, or denoting a writer of aphorisms, esp. certain Greek poets. Also, **gno/mi·cal.** [t. Gk.: m.s. *gnōmikós*] —**gno/mi·cal·ly,** *adv.*

no·mist (nō/mĭst), *n.* a writer of aphorisms.

no·mon (nō/mŏn), *n.* 1. a vertical shaft, column, obelisk, or the like, used (esp. by the ancients) as an astronomical instrument for determining the altitude of the sun, the position of a place, etc., by noting the length of the shadow cast at noon. 2. the vertical triangular plate of a sundial. 3. *Geom.* the part of a parallelogram which remains after a similar parallelogram has been taken away from one of its corners. [t. L, t. Gk.: one who knows, an indicator]

EFGBCD Gnomon (def. 3)

no·sis (nō/sĭs), *n.* a knowledge of spiritual things; mystical knowledge. [NL, t. Gk.: knowledge]

gnosis, a suffix referring to recognition, esp. of a morbid condition, as in *prognosis*. [t. Gk.: knowledge]

nos·tic (nŏs/tĭk), *adj.* Also, **gnos'ti·cal.** 1. pertaining to knowledge. 2. possessing knowledge, esp. esoteric knowledge of spiritual things. 3. (*cap.*) pertaining to or characteristic of the Gnostics. —*n.* 4. (*cap.*) a member of any of certain sects among the early Christians who claimed to have superior knowledge of spiritual things, and explained the world as created by powers or agencies arising as emanations from the Godhead. [t. LL: s. *Gnosticus*, t. Gk.: m. *gnōstikós* pertaining to knowledge] —**Gnos'ti·cism,** *n.*

nos·ti·cize (nŏs/tə·sīz'), *v.,* -**cized, -cizing.** —*v.i.* 1. to adopt or maintain Gnostic views. —*v.t.* 2. to explain or on Gnostic principles; give a Gnostic coloring to.

nu (noo, nū), *n., pl.* **gnus, (esp. collectively) gnu.** any of several African antelopes constituting the genus *Connochaetes*, characterized by an oxlike head, curved horns, and a long, flowing tail; a wildebeest. [t. Kaffir: m. *nqu*]

Brindled gnu,
Connochaetes taurinus
(4¼ ft. high at the shoulder)

o (gō), *v.,* **went, gone, going,** *n., pl.* **goes.** —*v.i.* 1. to move or pass along; proceed. 2. to move away or out; depart (opposed to *come* or *arrive*). 3. to keep or be in motion; act, work, or run. 4. to become; assume another state or condition: *to go mad.* 5. to continue; be habitually: *to go in rags.* 6. to move toward a point or a given result or in a given manner; proceed; advance. 7. to be known: *to go by a name.* 8. to reach or extend: *this road goes to the city.* 9. (of time) to pass; elapse. 10. to be awarded, transferred, or applied to a particular recipient or purpose. 11. to be sold: *the property went for a song.* 12. to conduce or tend: *this only goes to prove the point.* 13. to turn out; result: *how did the game go?* 14. to belong; have a place: *this book goes on the top shelf.* 15. (of colors, etc.) to harmonize; be compatible; be suited. 16. to act or operate with sound, as a bell or a gun; make a certain sound: *the gun goes bang.* 17. to be discharged, or explode (fol. by *off*). 18. to be phrased: *how do the words go?* 19. to resort; have recourse: *to go to court.* 20. to get the facts; find out (fol. by *behind*). 21. to be given up; be worn out; be lost or ended. 22. to die. 23. to fail; give way. 24. to be

overwhelmed; be ruined (fol. by *under*). 25. to begin; come into action: *here goes!* 26. to attack (fol. by *at*). 27. to be contained (fol. by *into*): *4 goes into 12.* 28. to contribute in amount or quantity; be requisite: *16 ounces go to the pound.* 29. to share equally (fol. by a complementary substantive): *to go partners.* 30. to contribute to a result: *the items which go to make up a total.* 31. to be about, intending, or destined (used in the pres. part. fol. by an infinitive): *he is going to write.* 32. *Naut.* to change course by tacking or wearing (fol. by *about*). —*v.t.* 33. *Colloq.* to endure or tolerate: *I can't go his preaching.* 34. *Colloq.* to risk or wager. 35. Some special verb phrases are:

go around, 1. to move about; circulate. **2.** to be enough for all.

go back on, *Colloq.* **1.** to fail (someone); let (someone) down. **2.** to fail to keep (one's word, promise, etc.).

go by, 1. to pass. **2.** to be guided by.

go down, 1. to descend; slope down. **2.** to be defeated. **3.** *Brit.* to leave the University at the end of the term or permanently (according to context).

go in for, to make a (thing) one's particular interest.

go on, 1. to go ahead; proceed. **2.** to manage; do. **3.** to behave; act.

go out, 1. to come to a stop; end: *the light went out.* **2.** to go to social affairs, etc.

go over, 1. to read or reread. **2.** to repeat. **3.** to scan.

go through with, to complete; bring to a finish.

go up, 1. to rise or ascend; advance. **2.** *Brit.* to go to the University at the beginning of term.

go with, *Colloq.* **1.** to harmonize with. **2.** to frequent the society of.

—*n.* 36. act of going: *the come and go of the seasons.* 37. *Colloq.* energy, spirit, or animation: *to be full of go.* 38. *Eng.* the first or preliminary examination at Cambridge University for the degree of A.B. 39. *Colloq.* a try at something; attempt: *to have a go at something.* 40. *Colloq.* something that goes well; a success: *to make a go of something.* 41. *Colloq.* a bargain: *it's a go!* 42. **on the go,** *Colloq.* constantly going; very active. —*adj.* 43. *U.S.* **a.** ready. **b.** functioning properly: *All instruments are go.* [ME *go(n)*, OE *gán*; akin to D *gaan*, MLG *gān*, OHG *gān*, *gēn*, G *gehen.* Cf. **GANG**[2], v.] —**go'er,** *n.* —**Syn.** 1. walk, run, ride, travel, advance. —**Ant.** 1. stay.

G.O., general order.

go·a (gō/ə), *n.* the black-tailed gazelle, *Procapra picticaudata,* of the Tibetan plateau. [t. Tibetan: m. *dgoba*]

Gō·a (gō/ə), *n.* a district of Portuguese India, on the Arabian Sea, ab. 250 mi. S of Bombay. 551,397 pop. (1950); 1394 sq. mi. *Cap.:* Panjim.

Goa, *Procapra picticaudata*
(2 ft. high at the shoulder)

goad (gōd). *n.* 1. a stick with a pointed end, for driving cattle, etc. 2. anything that pricks or wounds like such a stick; a stimulus. —*v.t.* 3. to prick or drive with or as with a goad; incite. [ME *gode*, OE *gád*, c. Langobardic *gaida* arrowhead] —**goad'like',** *adj.* —**Syn.** 3. spur.

goal (gōl), *n.* 1. that toward which effort is directed; aim or end. 2. the terminal point in a race. 3. a pole or other object by which this is marked. 4. a bound or structure toward which the players strive to advance the ball, etc. 5. act of throwing or kicking the ball through or over the goal. 6. the score made by accomplishing this. [ME *gol* boundary, limit. Cf. OE *gǽlan* hinder, impede] —**goal'less,** *adj.*

goal·ie (gō/lĭ), *n.* the goalkeeper on a hockey team.

goal·keep·er (gōl/kē/pər), *n. Sports.* a player whose special duty it is to prevent the ball from going through or over the goal.

goal line, *Sports.* the line which bounds the goal.

goal post, either of the two posts which support a bar across them, and form the football or soccer goal.

goat (gōt), *n.* 1. any animal of the genus *Capra* (family *Bovidae*), comprising various agile hollow-horned ruminants closely related to the sheep, found native in rocky and mountainous regions of the Old World, and including domesticated forms common throughout the world. 2. any of various allied animals, as *Oreamnos montanus* (**Rocky Mountain goat**), a ruminant of western North America. 3. (*cap.*) *Astron.* the zodiacal constellation or sign Capricorn. 4. *U.S. Slang.* the scapegoat; one who is the butt of a joke. 5. **get one's goat,** *U.S. Slang.* to make one lose his temper. [ME *gote, goot,* OE *gát,* c. G *geiss;* akin to L *haedus* kid] —**goat'-like',** *adj.*

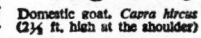

Domestic goat. *Capra hircus*
(2½ ft. high at the shoulder)

goat antelope, 1. a goatlike antelope of the genus *Naemorhedus,* as the goral, *N. goral,* or *N. crispus* of Japan. **2.** any antelope of the tribe *Rupicaprini,* a subdivision of the sheep and goat family, and including the chamois, goral serow, and Rocky Mountain goat.

goat·ee (gō·tē/), *n.* a man's beard trimmed to a tuft.

goat·fish (gōt′fĭsh′), *n., pl.* **-fishes**, (*esp. collectively*) **-fish.** any fish of the tropical and subtropical marine family *Mullidae*, having a pair of long barbels below the mouth, and including species highly esteemed as a delicacy by the ancient Romans; surmullet; red mullet.

goat god, any deity with the legs and feet of a goat, as Pan or the satyrs.

goat·herd (gōt′hûrd′), *n.* one who tends goats.

goat·ish (gō′tĭsh), *adj.* like a goat; lustful. —**goat′-ish·ly,** *adv.* —**goat′ish·ness,** *n.*

goats·beard (gōts′bîrd′), *n.* **1.** a composite plant, *Tragopogon pratensis.* **2.** a rosaceous herb, *Aruncus sylvester,* with long, slender spikes of small flowers.

goat·skin (gōt′skĭn′), *n.* **1.** the skin or hide of a goat. **2.** leather made from it.

goat's-rue (gōts′rōō′), *n.* **1.** an American leguminous herb, *Telphrosia virginiana.* **2.** a European leguminous herb, *Galega officinalis,* formerly used in medicine.

goat·suck·er (gōt′sŭk′ər), *n.* **1.** a nonpasserine nocturnal bird, *Caprimulgus europaeus,* of Europe, with flat head and wide mouth, formerly supposed to suck the milk of goats. **2.** any of the group of chiefly nocturnal or crepuscular birds to which this species belongs, usually regarded as including two families, the *Caprimulgidae* (**true goatsuckers**) and the *Podargidae* (**frogmouths**).

gob[1] (gŏb), *n.* a mass or lump. [ME *gobbe* lump, mass, appar. t. OF: m. *go(u)be,* ult. of Gallic derivation]

gob[2] (gŏb), *n. Slang.* a seaman in the U.S. naval service. [appar. akin to GOB[1]]

gob·bet (gŏb′ĭt), *n.* **1.** a fragment or hunk, esp. of raw flesh. **2.** *Archaic or Dial.* a lump or mass. [ME *gobet,* t. OF, dim of *gobe* GOB[1]]

gob·ble[1] (gŏb′əl), *v.,* **-bled, -bling.** —*v.t.* **1.** to swallow hastily in large pieces; gulp. **2.** *U.S. Slang.* to seize upon greedily or eagerly. —*v.i.* **3.** to eat hastily. [der. GOB[1]] —**gob′bler,** *n.* —**Syn. 1.** bolt. devour.

gob·ble[2] (gŏb′əl), *v.,* **-bled, -bling,** *n.* —*v.i.* **1.** to make the characteristic throaty cry of a turkey cock. —*n.* **2.** this sound. [var. of GABBLE, taken as imit. of the cry]

gob·ble·de·gook (gŏb′əl dĭ gŏŏk′), *n. Colloq.* language characterized by circumlocution and jargon: *the gobbledegook of government reports.* [intentionally grotesque coinage by Rep. Maury Maverick, 1895–1954), modeled on HOBBLEDEHOY. Final element *gook* may be slang word for tramp, var. of GOWK. Cf. GOBBLE, GOO]

gob·bler (gŏb′lər), *n.* a male turkey.

Gob·e·lin (gŏb′əlĭn; *Fr.* gô blăN′), *adj.* **1.** made at the tapestry factory of the Gobelins in Paris. **2.** resembling the tapestry made at the Gobelins.

go-be·tween (gō′bə twēn′), *n.* one who acts as agent between persons or parties.

Go·bi (gō′bĭ), *n.* a desert in E Asia, mostly in Mongolia. ab. 500,000 sq. mi. Chinese, **Shamo.**

go·bi·oid (gō′bĭ oid′), *adj.* **1.** of or resembling a goby. —*n.* **2.** a gobioid fish.

gob·let (gŏb′lĭt), *n.* **1.** a drinking glass with a foot and stem. **2.** *Archaic.* a bowl-shaped drinking vessel. [ME *gobelet,* t. OF, dim. of *gobel* cup; ult. of Celtic orig.]

gob·lin (gŏb′lĭn), *n.* a grotesque, mischievous sprite or elf. [ME *gobelin,* t. F (obs.), t. MHG: m. *kobold* goblin] —**Syn.** GOBLIN, GNOME, GREMLIN refer to imaginary beings, thought to be malevolent to man. GOBLINS are demons of any size, usually in human or animal forms, which are supposed to assail, afflict, and even torture human beings: "*Be thou a spirit of health or goblin damn'd, . . .*" (Shak. Hamlet I, iv). GNOMES are small beings, like ugly little old men, who live in the earth, guarding mines, treasures, etc. They are mysteriously malevolent and terrify human beings by causing dreadful mishaps to occur. GREMLINS are invisible beings who were said by pilots in World War II to cause all sorts of things to go wrong with airplanes.

go·by (gō′bĭ), *n., pl.* **-bies,** (*esp. collectively*) **-by. 1.** any member of the *Gobiidae,* a family of marine and freshwater fishes, mostly small and having the pelvic fins united to form a suctorial disk that enables them to cling to rocks, as *Baleosoma basci,* common on the South Atlantic coast of the U.S. **2.** any member of the closely related family, *Eleotridae,* in which the pelvic fins are separate. [t. L: m. s. *gōbius, cōbius,* t. Gk.: m. *kōbiós* kind of fish]

go-by (gō′bĭ′), *n. Colloq.* a going by without notice; intentional passing by: *to give one the go-by.*

go·cart (gō′kärt′), *n.* **1.** a small, wheeled vehicle for small children to ride in. **2.** a small framework with casters, in which children learn to walk. **3.** a handcart.

God (gŏd), *n.* **1.** the one Supreme Being, the creator and ruler of the universe. **2.** the Supreme Being considered with reference to a particular attribute: *the God of justice.* **3.** (*l.c.*) a deity, esp. a male deity, presiding over some portion of worldly affairs. **4.** (*cap. or l.c.*) a supreme being according to some particular conception: *the God of pantheism.* **5.** (*l.c.*) an image of a deity; an idol. **6.** (*l.c.*) any deified person or object. [ME and OE, c. D *god,* G *gott,* Icel. *godh,* Goth. *guth*]

Go·da·va·ri (gō dä′və rē′), *n.* a river flowing from W India SE to the Bay of Bengal. ab. 900 mi.

god·child (gŏd′chīld′), *n., pl.* **-children.** one for whom a person (godparent) stands sponsor at baptism.

god·daugh·ter (gŏd′dô′tər), *n.* a female godchild.

god·dess (gŏd′ĭs), *n.* **1.** a female god or deity. **2.** a woman of surpassing beauty. **3.** an adored woman. —**god′dess·hood′, god′dess·ship′,** *n.*

Go·de·froy de Bouil·lon (gôd frwa′ də bōō yôN′), c1060–1100, French crusader.

go-dev·il (gō′dĕv′əl), *n.* **1.** a movable-jointed apparatus forced through a pipe line to free it from obstructions. **2.** a dart dropped into a well to explode a charge of dynamite or nitroglycerin previously placed in a desired position. **3.** *Railway Slang.* a handcar.

god·fa·ther (gŏd′fä′thər), *n.* **1.** a man who stands sponsor for a child at baptism or confirmation. —*v.t.* **2.** to act as godfather to; be sponsor for.

God·head (gŏd′hĕd′), *n.* **1.** the essential being of God; the Supreme Being. **2.** (*l.c.*) godhood or godship. **3.** (*l.c.*) *Rare.* a deity; god or goddess.

god·hood (gŏd′hŏŏd), *n.* divine character; godship.

Go·di·va (gō dī′və), *n.* wife of Leofric, Earl of Mercia (11th century). According to legend, she rode naked through the streets of Coventry, England, to win relief for the people from a burdensome tax.

god·less (gŏd′lĭs), *adj.* **1.** having or acknowledging no God. **2.** wicked. —**god′less·ly,** *adv.* —**god′less·ness,** *n.*

god·like (gŏd′līk′), *adj.* like or befitting a god, or God. —**god′like′ness,** *n.*

god·ly (gŏd′lĭ), *adj.,* **-lier, -liest. 1.** conforming to God's laws; pious. **2.** *Archaic.* coming from God; divine. —**god′li·ly,** *adv.* —**god′li·ness,** *n.* —**Syn. 1.** devout, religious; saintly. —**Ant. 1.** wicked, ungodly.

god·moth·er (gŏd′mŭth′ər), *n.* **1.** a woman who sponsors a child at baptism. **2.** a female sponsor. —*v.t.* **3.** to act as godmother to; sponsor.

Go·dol·phin (gō dŏl′fĭn), *n.* **Sidney, 1st Earl of,** 1645–1712, British statesman and financier.

go·down (gō doun′), *n.* (in India and eastern Asia) a warehouse. [t. Malay: m. *godong*]

god·par·ent (gŏd′pâr′ənt), *n.* a godfather or godmother.

go·droon (gō drōōn′), *n.* gadroon.

God's acre, a burial ground; cemetery.

god·send (gŏd′sĕnd′), *n.* something unexpected but particularly welcome and timely, as if sent by God. [earlier *God's send,* var. (under influence of *send,* v.) of *God's sond* or *sand,* OE *sond, sand* message, service]

god·ship (gŏd′shĭp), *n.* the rank or character of a god.

god·son (gŏd′sŭn′), *n.* a male godchild.

God·speed (gŏd′spēd′), *n.* God speed you: a wish of success to one setting out on a journey or undertaking.

Go·du·nov (gŏ dŏŏ nôf′), *n.* **Boris Fëdorovich** (bŏ rēs′ fyô′dô rô′vĭch), 1552–1605, Russian regent and czar, 1598–1605.

God·ward (gŏd′wərd), *adv.* **1.** Also, **God′wards.** toward God. —*adj.* **2.** directed toward God.

God·win (gŏd′wĭn), *n.* **1.** (*Earl of Wessex*) died 1053, English statesman. **2. Mrs.,** (*Mary Wollstonecraft*) 1759–97, British writer (wife of William). **3. William,** 1756–1836, British political philosopher and writer.

God·win Aus·ten (gŏd′wĭn ôs′tĭn). See K2.

god·wit (gŏd′wĭt′), *n.* any of several large New and Old World shore birds of the genus *Limosa,* all with long, slightly upcurved bills, as the Hudsonian godwit, *L. haemastica,* of America.

Goeb·bels (gœb′əls), *n.* **Paul Joseph** (poul yō′zĕf) 1897–1945, German Nazi propaganda leader.

Goe·ring (gœ′rĭng), *n.* **Hermann** (hĕr′män), 1893–1946, German field marshal and Nazi party leader.

goes (gōz), *v.* **1.** 3rd pers. sing. pres. of go. —*n.* **2.** pl. of go.

Goe·thals (gō′thəlz), *n.* **George Washington,** 1858–1928, U.S. major general and army engineer, in charge of building the Panama Canal.

Goe·the (gœ′tə), *n.* **Johann Wolfgang von** (yō′hän vôlf′gäng fən), 1749–1832, German poet, dramatist, novelist, and philosopher.

goe·thite (gō′thīt, gœ′tīt), *n.* a very common mineral, iron hydroxide, FeO(OH), occurring in crystals, but more commonly in yellow or brown earthy masses, an ore of iron. Also, **göthite.** [named after the poet GOETHE. See -ITE[1]]

gof·fer (gŏf′ər), *n.* **1.** an ornamental plaiting used for the frills and borders of women's caps, etc. —*v.t.* **2.** to flute (a frill, etc.), as with a heated iron. **3.** to impress (book edges, etc.) with an ornamental pattern. Also, **gauffer.** [t. F: m. *gauffer* stamp cloth, paper, etc., der. *gaufre* honeycomb, waffle, t. D: m. *wafel.* See WAFER]

go-get·ter (gō′gĕt′ər), *n. U.S. Colloq.* an enterprising aggressive person.

gog·gle (gŏg′əl), *n., v.,* **-gled, -gling.** —*n.* **1.** (*pl.*) spectacles so devised as to protect the eyes from injury. **2.** a goggling look. —*v.i.* **3.** to roll the eyes; stare. **4.** (of the eyes) to roll; bulge and stare. —*v.t.* **5.** to roll (the eyes). [ME *gogelen* look aside; orig. uncert.]

gog·gle-eyed (gŏg′əl īd′), *adj.* having prominent rolling eyes, esp. as a mark of astonishment.

Gogh (gō, gôкн; *Du.* кнôкн), *n.* **Vincent van** (văn; *Du* vĭn sĕnt′ vän), 1853–90, Dutch painter.

gog·let (gŏg′lĭt), *n.* (in India, etc.) a long-necked vessel, usually of porous earthenware to permit evaporation, used as a water cooler. [earlier *gurglet,* t. Pg.: m. *gorgoleta,* ult. der. L *gurga,* abyss, throat]

Go·gol (gō′gôl), *n.* **Nikolai Vasilievich** (nyĭ kŏ lī′ və sē′lyə vĭch), 1809–52, Russian novelist, short-story writer, and dramatist.

---

oi·del·ic (goi děl′ĭk), *adj.* **1.** of or pertaining to the Gaels or their language. **—n. 2.** *Ling.* the Gaelic subgroup of Celtic. Also, **Gadhelic.** [f. m. OIrish *Goídeal* + Gael + -ic]

o·ing (gō′ĭng), *n.* **1.** a going away; departure: *a safe going and return.* **2.** condition of surfaces and roads for walking or driving: *the going was bad.* **3.** (*usually pl.*) way; deportment. **—adj. 4.** moving or working, as machinery. **5.** that goes; in existence. **6.** continuing to do business: *a going concern.* **7.** having to do with a going business: *the going value of a company.* **8.** departing. **9.** going on, nearly: *it is going on four o'clock.*

oings on, *Colloq.* actions; conduct; behavior (used chiefly with depreciative force): *The dean disapproved of all the goings on at the class dance.*

oi·ter (goi′tər), *n. Pathol.* an enlargement of the thyroid gland, on the front and sides of the neck. Also, **goi′tre.** [t. F: (m.) *goitre,* ult. der. L *guttur* throat]

oi·trous (goi′trəs), *adj.* pertaining to or affected with goiter.

ol·con·da (gŏl kŏn′də), *n.* **1.** an ancient city of India, the ruins of which are near the capital city of Hyderabad state: once the capital of a powerful Mohammedan kingdom, it was renowned for its wealth and diamond cutting. **2.** (*often l.c.*) a mine or source of wealth.

old (gōld), *n.* **1.** a precious yellow metal, highly malleable and ductile, and free from liability to rust. *Sym.:* Au; *at. wt.:* 197.2; *at. no.:* 79; *sp. gr.:* 19.3 at 20°C. **2.** coin made of it. **3.** money; wealth. **4.** something likened to this metal in brightness, preciousness, etc.: *a heart of gold.* **5.** bright metallic yellow sometimes tending toward brown. **—adj. 6.** consisting of gold. **7.** pertaining to gold. **8.** like gold. **9.** of the color of gold. [ME and OE, c. G *gold;* akin to Russ. *zoloto*]

old basis, adaptation of prices to a gold standard.

oldbeater's skin, the prepared outside membrane of the large intestine of the ox, used by goldbeaters to lay between the leaves of the metal while they beat it.

old beating, art or process of beating out gold into gold leaf. **—gold′beat′er,** *n.*

old beetle, any of certain beetles characterized by a golden luster, as *Coptocycla aurichalcea,* a small beetle which feeds on plants. Also, **gold bug.**

old brick, *Colloq.* **1.** a brick-shaped mass of gold, or an imitation of it, sold by a swindler who then delivers a spurious substitute. **2.** *Colloq.* anything of supposed value which turns out to be worthless. **3.** a loafer.

old-brick (gōld′brĭk′), *Colloq.* **—v.t. 1.** to swindle. **—v.i. 2.** to loaf on the job or evade responsibility. **—gold′-brick′er,** *n.*

old certificate. See **certificate** (def. 4).

old Coast, a former British territory in W Africa; received independence within British Commonwealth of Nations in 1957. See **Ghana.**

old digger, 1. one who digs or seeks for gold in a gold field. **2.** *Colloq.* a woman who uses her feminine arts to extract profit from men.

old digging, 1. the work of digging for gold. **2.** (*pl.*) a region where digging or seeking for gold, esp. by placer mining, is carried on.

old dust, gold in fine particles.

old·en (gōl′dən), *adj.* **1.** of the color of gold; yellow; bright, metallic, or lustrous like gold. **2.** made or consisting of gold: *golden keys.* **3.** resembling gold in value; most excellent: *a golden opportunity.* **4.** flourishing; joyous: *the golden hours.* **5.** indicating the 50th event of a series, as a wedding anniversary. **—gold′en·ly,** *adv.* **—gold′en·ness,** *n.*

olden age, 1. (in Greek and Roman mythology) the first and best age of the world, when mankind lived in innocence and happiness. **2.** the most flourishing period in the history of a nation, literature, etc.

olden aster, any plant of a North American genus, *Chrysopsis,* of asterlike composites with bright goldenyellow flowers, esp., a wild flower species, *C. mariana,* abundant in eastern U.S.

olden buck, a dish consisting of Welsh rabbit topped by a poached egg.

olden calf, *Bible.* **1.** a golden idol set up by Aaron. Ex. 32. **2.** either of the two similar idols set up by Jeroboam. I Kings, 12:28,29.

olden chain, laburnum.

olden Delicious, *Hort.* a variety of yellow apple grown in the U.S.

olden eagle, a large eagle, *Aquila chrysaëtos,* of both the eastern and western hemispheres (so called because of the golden-brown feathers on the back of the neck).

old·en·eye (gōl′dən ī′), *n., pl.* **-eyes,** (*esp. collectively*) **-eye.** a diving duck of the subfamily *Aythyinae* and genus *Glaucionetta* with bright-yellow eyes, as G. *clangula,* of Europe and America; whistler; garrot.

olden Fleece, *Gk. Legend.* the fleece of gold taken from the ram on which Phrixus was carried to Colchis, recovered from King Aeëtes by the Argonautic expedition under Jason. See **Medea.**

olden Gate, a strait in W California between San Francisco Bay and the Pacific: spanned by the **Golden Gate Bridge,** whose channel span of 4200 ft. is the longest single span in the world.

golden glow, a tall coneflower, *Rudbeckia laciniata,* with abundant yellow flowers and a yellow conical disk.

golden goose, *Gk. Legend.* a goose which laid one golden egg a day and was killed by its impatient owner who wanted all the gold immediately.

Golden Horn, an inlet of the Bosporus in European Turkey, which forms the inner port of Istanbul.

golden mean, the happy medium between extremes; moderate course of action. [trans. of L *aurea mediocritas* (Horace)]

golden pheasant, an Asiatic pheasant, *Chrysolophus pictus,* with rich yellow and orange tones in the head and neck plumage of the male.

golden plover, either of two plovers with yellow spotting above; the European species is *Pluvialis apricaria;* the American, *P. dominica.*

golden robin, Baltimore oriole.

gold·en·rod (gōl′dən rŏd′), *n.* **1.** any plant of the composite genus *Solidago,* most species of which bear numerous small yellow flowers. **2.** any of various related composite plants, as *Brachychaeta sphacelata* (false goldenrod).

Dwart goldenrod.
Solidago nemoralis
(2 ft. high)

golden rule, the rule of conduct: *Whatsoever ye would that men should do to you, do ye even so to them.* Matt. 7:12.

gold·en·seal (gōl′dən sēl′), *n.* **1.** a ranunculaceous herb, *Hydrastis canadensis,* with a thick yellow rootstock. **2.** the rhizomes and roots of this plant, formerly much used in medicine.

golden wattle, 1. a broad-leafed Australian acacia, *Acacia pycnantha,* yielding useful gum and tanbark. Its yellow flower is the unofficial Australian Commonwealth flower. **2.** any similar acacia, esp. *A. longifolia,* of Australia and Tasmania.

golden wedding, the fiftieth anniversary of a wedding.

gold-ex·change standard (gōld′ĭks chānj′), a monetary system whose monetary unit is kept at a fixed relation with that of a country on the gold standard.

gold·eye (gōld′ī′), *n., pl.* **-eyes,** (*esp. collectively*) **-eye.** a silvery, herringlike fish, *Amphiodon alosoides,* of the fresh waters of central North America, of some note as a game fish.

gold field, a district in which gold is mined.

gold-filled (gōld′fĭld′), *adj.* containing a filling of cheaper metal within a layer of gold.

gold·finch (gōld′fĭnch′), *n.* **1.** a European fringilline songbird, *Carduelis carduelis,* having a crimson face and wings marked with yellow. **2.** any of certain small American finches, esp. *Spinus tristis,* the male of which has yellow body plumage in summer. [ME; OE *goldfinc.* See GOLD, FINCH]

gold·fish (gōld′fĭsh′), *n., pl.* **-fishes,** (*esp.collectively*) **-fish.** a small fish, *Carassius auratus,* of the carp family and orig. native in China, prized for aquariums and pools because of its golden coloring and odd form (produced by artificial selection).

gold foil, gold beaten into thin sheets (many times thicker than gold leaf), esp. for the use of dentists.

gold·i·locks (gōl′dĭ lŏks′), *n.* **1.** a person with golden hair. **2.** an Old World species of buttercup, *Ranunculus auricomus.* **3.** a European plant, *Linosyris vulgaris,* resembling goldenrod, with small heads of yellow flowers. [f. obs. *goldy* golden + LOCK(s)²]

gold leaf, gold beaten into a very thin sheet, used for gilding, etc.

Gold·mark (gōld′märk), *n.* **Karl,** 1830–1915, Hungarian composer.

gold mine, 1. a mine yielding gold. **2.** a source of great wealth.

gold note, *U.S.* a bank note payable in gold coin.

gold-of-pleas·ure (gōld′əv plĕzh′ər), *n.* a brassicaceous herb, *Camelina sativa,* with small yellowish flowers.

Gol·do·ni (gŏl dō′nē), *n.* **Carlo** (kär′lō), 1707–93, Italian dramatist.

gold point, the point at which it is equally expensive to buy (or sell), exchange, or export (or import) gold in adjustment of foreign claims (or counterclaims).

gold reserve, that part of the U.S. federal gold supply held to maintain the value of governmental promissory notes.

gold rush, a large-scale emigration of people to a region where gold has been discovered, as that to California in 1849.

gold·smith (gōld′smĭth′), *n.* one who makes or sells articles of gold (down to the 18th cent., often acting also as a banker). [ME and OE]

Gold·smith (gōld′smĭth′), *n.* **Oliver,** 1728–74, British poet, novelist, and dramatist.

goldsmith beetle, a brilliant golden scarabaeid beetle of Europe, *Cetonia aurata.*

gold standard, a monetary system with gold of specified weight and fineness as the unit of value.

gold stick, (in England) **1.** the gilded rod carried on state occasions by certain members of the royal household. **2.** the bearer of it.

gold·stone (gōld′stōn′), *n.* aventurine (def. 1).

gold·thread (gōld′thrĕd′), *n.* **1.** a white-flowered ranunculaceous herb, *Coptis groenlandica*, with a slender yellow root. **2.** the root itself, used in medicine.

go·lem (gō′lĕm), *n.* **1.** *Jewish Legend.* a figure constructed to represent a human being, and endowed with life, by human agency. **2.** an automaton. [t. Heb.]

golf (gŏlf, gôlf; *Brit.* gŏf), *n.* **1.** an outdoor game, in which a small resilient ball is driven with special clubs into a series of holes, distributed at various distances over a course having natural or artificial obstacles, the object being to get the ball into each hole in as few strokes as possible. —*v.i.* **2.** to play golf. [ME (Scot.); orig. uncert.] —**golf′er**, *n.*

golf club, **1.** any of the various implements for striking the ball in golf. **2.** an organization of golf players. **3.** *Brit.* a country club.

golf links, (*pl. sometimes construed as sing.*) the ground or course over which golf is played. Also, **golf course**.

Gol·go·tha (gŏl′gə thə), *n.* **1.** Calvary. **2.** a place of suffering or sacrifice. [t. L (Vulgate), t. Gk. (N.T.), t. Aram.: m. *goghaltā*, Heb. *gulgōleth* skull; see John 19:17]

gol·iard (gōl′yərd), *n.* one of a class of wandering students in Germany, France, and England, chiefly in the 12th and 13th centuries, noted for their rioting and intemperance, and as the authors of satirical Latin verse. [late ME, t. OF: lit., glutton, der. *gole*, g. L *gula* throat, palate, gluttony] —**gol·iar·dic** (gōl yär′dĭk), *adj.*

gol·iar·der·y (gōl yär′dər ĭ) *n.* the poems of the goliards.

Go·li·ath (gə lī′əth), *n.* the giant champion of the Philistines whom David is reputed to have killed with a stone from a sling. I Sam. 17:4. Cf. II Sam. 21:19 and I Chron. 20:5. [t. L (Vulgate), t. Gk. (Septuagint), repr. Heb. *Golyath*]

gol·ly (gŏl′ĭ), *interj.* *Colloq.* a mild expletive expressing surprise, etc. [a euphemistic var. of *God!*]

go·losh (gə lŏsh′), *n.* galosh.

Goltz (gōlts), *n.* **Baron Colmar von der** (kōl′mär fən dər), 1843–1916, German field marshal.

gom·bo (gŭm′bō), *n.* gumbo.

gom·broon (gŏm brōon′), *n.* a type of Persian pottery ware. [named after a town on the Persian Gulf]

Go·mel (gô′mĕl), *n.* a city in the W Soviet Union, on a tributary of the Dnieper. 144,000 (est. 1956).

gom·er·el (gŏm′ər əl), *n.* *Scot. and N. Eng.* a fool. Also, **gom·er·al**, **gom·er·il** (gŏm′ər əl). [f. obs. *gome* man (OE *guma*, c. L *homo*) + -REL]

Go·mor·rah (gə môr′ə, -mŏr′ə), *n.* **1.** an ancient city destroyed (with Sodom) for the wickedness of its inhabitants. Gen. 18–19. **2.** any extremely wicked place. Also, **Go·mor′rha**.

Gom·pers (gŏm′pərz), *n.* **Samuel**, 1850–1924, U.S. labor leader; one of the founders of the American Federation of Labor and its president, 1886–94, 1896–1924.

gom·pho·sis (gŏm fō′sĭs), *n.* *Anat.* an immovable articulation in which one bone or part is received in a cavity in another, as a tooth in its socket. [NL, t. Gk.: a bolting together]

go·mu·ti (gə mōo′tĭ) *n., pl.* -**tis. 1.** Also, **gomuti palm.** a sago palm, *Arenga pinnata*, of the East Indies: source of palm sugar. **2.** a black, horsehairlike fiber obtained from it, used for making cordage, etc. [t. Malay]

-gon, a suffix denoting geometrical figures having a certain number or kind of angles, as in *polygon*, *pentagon*. [t. Gk.: m. -*gōnos* (neut. -*gōnon*) -angled, -angular]

gon·ad (gŏn′ăd), *n.* *Anat.* the sex gland, male or female, in which germ cells develop and appropriate sex hormones are produced. [t. NL: s. *gonār* womb] —**gon′ad·al**, **go·na·di·al** (gō nā′dĭ əl), **go·nad·ic** (gō nǎd′ĭk), *adj.*

gon·a·do·trop·ic (gŏn′ə dō trŏp′ĭk, gə nǎd′ō-), *adj.* *Biochem.* pertaining to substances formed in the hypophysis or the placenta which affect the activity of the ovary or testis. Also, **gon·a·do·troph·ic** (gŏn′ə dō trŏf′ĭk, gə nǎd′ō-).

Gon·court (gôN kōor′), *n.* **Edmond Louis Antoine Huot de** (ĕd môN′ lwē ăN twàN′ y ō′ də), 1822–96, and his brother, **Jules Alfred Huot de** (zhyl ǎl frĕd′), 1830–1870, French art critics, historians, and novelists, who collaborated in writing novels until the death of Jules.

Gond (gŏnd), *n.* one of an aboriginal nationality of Dravidian stock in central India and the Deccan.

Gon·dar (gŏn′där), *n.* a city in N W Ethiopia, N of Lake Tana: a former capital. 15,000 (est. 1948).

gon·do·la (gŏn′də lə), *n.* **1.** a long, narrow boat with a high peak at each end and often a small cabin near the middle, used on the Venetian canals and usually propelled at the stern by a single oar or pole. **2.** *U.S.* (locally) a heavy boat. **3.** the car of a dirigible. [t. It. (Venetian), der. *gondolar*, *gondolarsi*, ult. der. Rom. root *dond-* to rock]

Venetian gondola

gondola car, *U.S.* a railway freight car with sides but no top, used for transporting bulk commodities.

gon·do·lier (gŏn′də lĭr′), *n.* a man who rows or poles a gondola. [t. F, t. It.: m. *gondoliere*, der. *gondola*]

Gon·do·mar (gôn′dō mär′), *n.* **Diego Sarmiento de**

Acuña (dyĕ′gô sär myĕn′tô dĕ ä kōo′nyä), **Count of,** 1567–1626, Spanish diplomat.

Gond·wa·na (gŏnd wä′nə), *n.* *Geol.* a great land mass in the Southern Hemisphere that in Paleozoic and part of Mesozoic time joined South America, Africa, southern Asia, and Australia.

gone (gôn, gŏn), *v.* **1.** pp. of **go.** —*adj.* **2.** departed left. **3.** lost or hopeless. **4.** that has departed or passed away; dead. **5.** weak and faint: *a gone feeling*. **6.** far gone, **a.** much advanced; deeply involved. **b.** dying. **7.** gone on, *Colloq.* very much in love with.

gone·ness (gôn′nĭs, gŏn′-), *n.* sinking sensation; faintness.

gon·er (gôn′ər, gŏn′ər), *n.* *Colloq.* a person or thing that is dead, lost, or past recovery.

gon·fa·lon (gŏn′fə lən), *n.* **1.** a banner suspended from a crossbar, often with several streamers or tails. **2.** the standard used esp. by the medieval Italian republics [t. It.: m. *gonfalone*, t. OHG: m. *gundfano*, lit., war flag]

gon·fa·lon·ier (gŏn′fə lə nĭr′), *n.* **1.** the bearer of a gonfalon. **2.** chief magistrate or some other elected official in certain medieval Italian republics. [t. It.: m. *gonfaloniere*]

gong (gông, gŏng), *n.* *Music.* **1.** an oriental bronze disk with the rim turned up, to be struck with a soft-headed stick. **2.** a saucer-shaped bell sounded by a hammer. [t. Malay] —**gong′like′**, *adj.*

Gon·go·ra y Ar·go·te (gông gô′rä ē är gô′tĕ), **Luis de** (lōo ēs′dĕ), 1561–1627, Spanish poet.

Gon·go·rism (gông′gə rĭz′əm), *n.* affected elegance of style introduced into Spanish literature in imitation of the Spanish poet, Gongora y Argote.

go·nid·i·um (gə nĭd′Yəm), *n., pl.* -**nidia** (-nĭd′Yə). *Bot.* (among algae): **1.** any one-celled asexual reproductive body, as a tetraspore or zoöspore. **2.** an algal cell, or a filament of an alga, growing within the thallus of a lichen. [NL, f. Gk.: s. *gón s* offspring, seed + m. -*idion*, -IDION] —**go·nid′i·al**, *ado*

go·ni·om·e·ter (gō′nĭ ŏm′ə tər), *n.* an instrument for measuring solid angles, as of crystals. [t. F: m. *gonio métre*, f. Gk. *gōnio*-angle + *métre* METER] —**go·ni·o·met·ric** (gō′nĭ ə mĕt′rĭk), **go·ni·o·met′ri·cal**, *adj.* —**go·ni·om′e·try**, *n.*

go·ni·on (gō′nĭ ŏn′), *n., pl.* -**nia** (-nĭ′ə). *Craniol.* the point on either side of the lower jaw at the mandibular angle, marked by the intersection of a plane tangent to the lower border of the body and the posterior border of the ascending ramus. [NL, der. Gk. *gōnía* angle]

go·ni·um (gō′nĭ əm), *n., pl.* -**nia** (-nĭ′ə). *Biol.* a germ cell during the phase marked by mitosis. [NL]

-gonium, *Bot., Biol.* a word element referring to reproductive cells. [t. NL, t. Gk.: m. -*gonia*, comb. form repr. *goneía* generation]

gono-, a word element meaning "sexual" or "reproductive," as in *gonococcus*. [t. Gk., comb. form of *gónos*, *goné* seed, generation, etc.]

gon·o·coc·cus (gŏn′ə kŏk′əs), *n., pl.* -**cocci** (-kŏk′sī). a cell of the micrococcus found in the pus cells of the gonorrheal discharge. [NL. See GONO-, -COCCUS]

gon·o·cyte (gŏn′ə sīt′), *n.* *Biol.* a germ cell, esp. during the maturation phase; oöcyte; spermatocyte.

gon·o·phore (gŏn′ə fōr′), *n.* **1.** *Zool.* an asexually produced bud in hydrozoans that gives rise to a medusa or its equivalent. **2.** *Bot.* a prolongation of the axis of a flower above the perianth, bearing the stamens and pistil.

gon·or·rhe·a (gŏn′ə rē′ə), *n.* *Pathol.* a contagious purulent inflammation of the urethra or the vagina, due to the gonococcus. Also, *esp.* *Brit.*, **gon′or·rhoe′a** [t. LL: m. *gonorrhoea*, t. Gk.: m. *gonórrhoia*, f. gono- GONO- + *rhoía* a flow] —**gon′or·rhe′al**, **gon′or·rhoe′al**, *adj.*

-gony, a word element meaning "production," "genesis," "origination," as in *cosmogony*, *theogony*. [t. L: m. s. -*gonia*, t. Gk. See -GONIUM and cf. -GENY]

goo (gōo), *n.* *U.S. Slang.* sticky matter. [short for BURGOO]

goo·ber (gōo′bər), *n.* *U.S.* the peanut. Also, **goober pea.** [t. Angolan: m. *nguba*]

good (gōod), *adj.*, **better, best**, *n.*, *interj.*, *adv.* —*adj.* **1.** morally excellent; righteous; pious: *a good man*. **2.** satisfactory in quality, quantity, or degree; excellent: *good food, good health*. **3.** right; proper; qualified; fit: *do whatever seems good to you, his credit is good*. **4.** well-behaved: *a good child*. **5.** kind, beneficent, or friendly: *to do a good turn*. **6.** honorable or worthy; in good standing: *a good name, Mr. Hood and his good lady*. **7.** reliable; safe: *good securities*. **8.** genuine; sound or valid: *good judgment, good reasons*. **9.** agreeable; pleasant; genial: *have a good time*. **10.** satisfactory for the purpose; advantageous: *a good day for fishing*. **11.** sufficient or ample: *a good supply*. **12.** full: *a good day's journey*. **13.** competent or skillful; clever: *a good manager, good at arithmetic*. **14.** fairly great: *a good deal*. **15. as good as**, in effect; practically: *he as good as promised it to me*. —*n.* **16.** profit; worth; advantage; benefit: *what good will that do? to work for the common good*. **17.** excellence or merit; righteousness; kindness: *to be a power for good, do good*. **18.** a good, commendable, or desirable thing. **19.** (*pl.*) possessions, esp. movable effects or personal chattels. **20.** (*pl.*) articles of trade; wares; esp. in England, freight. **21.** (*pl.*) *U.S. Colloq.* what has been promised or is expected: *to deliver the goods*. **22.** (*pl.*) *U.S.*

Colloq. the genuine article. **23.** (*pl.*) *U.S. Colloq.* evidence of guilt, as stolen articles: *to catch with the goods.* **24.** (*pl.*) *U.S.* cloth or textile material: *will these goods wash well?* **25. for good** or **for good and all**, finally and permanently; forever: *to leave a place for good (and all).* **26. make good, a.** to make recompense for; pay for. **b.** to keep to an agreement; fulfill. **c.** to be successful. **d.** to prove the truth of; substantiate. —*interj.* **27.** an expression of approval or satisfaction. —*adv.* **28.** *Colloq.* well. [ME; OE *gōd,* c. D *goed,* G *gut,* Icel. *gōdhr,* Goth. *gōths* good; ? orig. meaning fitting, suitable, and akin to GATHER] —**Syn. 1.** pure, moral, virtuous; conscientious, meritorious, worthy, exemplary. **2.** commendable, admirable. **10.** favorable, auspicious, propitious, fortunate; profitable, useful. **11.** full, adequate. **13.** efficient, proficient, capable, dexterous, adroit, apt. **19.** See **property.** —**Ant. 1.** bad, evil.

Good Book, the Bible.

good-by (good'bī'), *interj., n., pl.* **-bys.** —*interj.* **1.** farewell: a conventional expression used at parting. —*n.* **2.** a farewell. [contr. of *God be with you (ye)*]

good-bye (good'bī'), *interj., n., pl.* **-byes.** good-by.

good cheer, 1. cheerful spirits; courage: *to be of good cheer.* **2.** feasting and merrymaking: *to make good cheer.* **3.** good fare or food; feasting: *to be fond of good cheer.*

good form, *Chiefly Brit.* good or proper conduct.

good-for-noth·ing (good'fər nŭth'ing), *adj.* **1.** worthless. —*n.* **2.** a worthless person.

Good Friday, the Friday before Easter, a holy day of the Christian church, observed as the anniversary of the crucifixion of Jesus.

good-heart·ed (good'här'tĭd), *adj.* kind; considerate. —**good'-heart'ed·ly,** *adv.* —**good'-heart'ed·ness,** *n.*

Good Hope, Cape of. See **Cape of Good Hope.**

good humor, a cheerful or amiable mood.

good-hu·mored (good'hū'mərd, -ū'mərd), *adj.* having or showing a pleasant, amiable mood: *good-humored man, a good-humored remark.* —**good'-hu'mored·ly,** *adv.* —**good'-hu'mored·ness,** *n.*

good·ish (good'ĭsh), *adj.* rather good; fairly good.

good-look·ing (good'look'ing), *adj.* of good appearance; handsome.

good looks, handsome personal appearance.

good·ly (good'lī), *adj.,* **-lier, -liest. 1.** of a good quality: *a goodly gift.* **2.** of good or fine appearance. **3.** of good size or amount: *a goodly sum.* —**good'li·ness,** *n.*

good·man (good'mən), *n., pl.* **-men.** *Archaic or Dial.* **1.** the master of a household; husband. **2.** title of respect used for those below the rank of gentleman, esp. a farmer or yeoman.

good nature, pleasant disposition; cheerful nature.

good-na·tured (good'nā'chərd), *adj.* having or showing good nature or a pleasant or complaisant disposition or mood; good-humored. —**good'-na'tured·ly,** *adv.* —**good'-na'tured·ness,** *n.*

Good Neighbor Policy, a diplomatic policy of the U.S., first presented in 1933 by President Roosevelt for the encouragement of friendly relations and mutual defense by the nations of the Western Hemisphere.

good·ness (good'nĭs), *n.* **1.** moral excellence; virtue. **2.** kindly feeling; kindness; generosity. **3.** excellence of quality: *goodness of workmanship.* **4.** the best part of anything; essence; strength. **5.** (used in various exclamatory or emphatic expressions): *thank goodness!* —**Syn. 1.** GOODNESS, MORALITY, VIRTUE refer to qualities of character or conduct which entitle the possessor to approval and esteem. GOODNESS is the simple word for the general quality recognized in character or conduct: *many could tell of her goodness and kindness.* MORALITY implies conformity to the recognized standards of right conduct: *a citizen of the highest morality.* VIRTUE is a rather formal word, and suggests usually GOODNESS that is consciously or steadily maintained, often in spite of temptations or evil influences: *of unassailable virtue, firm and of unwavering virtue.* —**Ant. 1.** badness, evil, vice.

good Samaritan, a person who is compassionate and helpful to one in distress. See Luke 10: 30–37.

Good Shepherd, Jesus Christ.

good-sized (good'sīzd'), *adj.* of ample size; largish.

good speed, good fortune, or success: *to wish a person good speed.*

goods train, *Brit.* a freight train.

good-tem·pered (good'těm'pərd), *adj.* good-natured; amiable. —**good'-tem'pered·ly,** *adv.*

good use, (in a language) standard use or usage.

good·wife (good'wīf'), *n., pl.* **-wives** (-wīvz'). *Archaic or Dial.* **1** the mistress of a household. **2.** a title of respect for a woman.

good will, 1. friendly disposition; benevolence; favor. **2.** cheerful acquiescence. **3.** *Com.* an intangible, salable asset arising from the reputation of a business and its relations with its customers, distinct from the value of its stock, etc. Also, **good·will** (good'wĭl'). **Syn. 1.** See **favor.**

Good·win Sands (good'wĭn), a dangerous line of shoals at the N entrance to the Strait of Dover, ab. 6 mi. off the SE coast of England. ab. 10 mi. long.

good·y¹ (good'ī), *n., pl.* **goodies,** *adj., interj. Colloq.* —*n.* **1.** (*pl.*) sweet food; candy. —*adj.* **2.** weakly or sentimentally good; affecting goodness. —*interj.* **3.** wonderful! how nice! [f. GOOD, adj. + -Y¹]

good·y² (good'ī), *n., pl.* **goodies.** a polite term for-

merly applied to a woman in humble life. [var. of GOODWIFE]

Good·year (good'yĭr), *n.* **Charles,** 1800–60, U.S. inventor (of vulcanized rubber).

good·y-good·y (good'ī good'ī), *adj., n., pl.* **-goodies.** —*adj.* **1.** goody. —*n.* **2.** a goody person.

goo·ey (goo'ī), *adj.,* **gooier, gooiest.** *Slang.* like goo; sticky; viscid.

goof (goof), *Slang.* —*n.* **1.** a foolish or stupid person. —*v.i.* **2.** to blunder; slip up. [appar. var. of obs. *goff* dolt, t. F: m. *goffe*] —**goof'y,** *adj.* —**goof'i·ly,** *adv.* —**goof'i·ness,** *n.*

goo·gly (goo'glī), *n., pl.* **-glies.** *Cricket.* a bowled ball that swerves first one way and then breaks in the other.

goo·gol (goo'gŏl), *n.* a number, usually 1, followed by 100 zeros. [fanciful, coined by Edward Kasner, 1878–1955, American mathematician.]

goon (goon), *n. U.S. Slang.* **1.** a stupid person. **2.** a hired thug used by one side or the other in a labor dispute. **3.** a roughneck.

goop (goop), *n. U.S. Slang.* a bad-mannered person.

goos·an·der (goo săn'dər), *n.* **1.** a saw-billed fish-eating duck, *Mergus merganser,* of Europe and North America. **2.** any merganser.

goose (goos), *n., pl.* **geese** for 1–4, 6; **gooses** for 5. **1.** any of numerous wild or domesticated web-footed birds of the family *Anatidae,* most of them larger and with a longer neck than the ducks: the principal genera are *Anser, Branta,* and *Chen.* **2.** the female of this bird, as distinguished from the male (or gander). **3.** the flesh of the goose. **4.** a silly or foolish person; simpleton. **5.** a tailors' smoothing iron with a curved handle. **6.** *Obs.* a game played with counters. [ME *gos(e), goos,* OE *gōs* (pl. *gēs*), c. D and G *gans,* Icel. *gās* goose; akin to L *anser,* Gk. *chēn*] —**goose'like',** *adj.*

Goose Bay, an airport on the coast of Labrador, used by transatlantic aircraft as a fuel stop.

goose·ber·ry (goos'bĕr'ī, gooz'-, -bə rī'), *n., pl.* **-ries. 1.** the small, edible, acid, globular fruit or berry of certain prevailingly prickly shrubs of the genus *Ribes,* esp. *R. Grossularia.* **2.** the shrub itself.

goose flesh, a rough condition of the skin, resembling that of a plucked goose, induced by cold or fear.

goose·foot (goos'foot'), *n., pl.* **-foots. 1.** any plant of the genus *Chenopodium,* containing many widely distributed herbs and shrubs with minute green flowers. **2.** any chenopodiaceous plant.

goose grass, cleavers.

goose grease, the melted fat of the goose, used in domestic medicine as an ointment.

goose·herd (goos'hûrd'), *n.* one who tends geese.

goose·neck (goos'něk'), *n.* something curved like the neck of a goose, as an iron hook for attaching a boom to a mast, or a flexible stand for a desk lamp.

goose pimples, goose flesh. Also, **goose skin.**

goose step, 1. a military exercise in which the body is balanced on one foot (without advancing) while the other foot is swung forward and back. **2.** marching step of the German and other foreign infantry, in which the legs are swung high with straight, stiff knees.

goose-step (goos'stĕp'), *v.i.,* **-stepped, -stepping.** *Colloq.* to walk in a goose step.

G.O.P., the "Grand Old Party," an epithet for the Republican party since 1880.

go·pher (gō'fər), *n.* **1.** any of various ground squirrels of western North America, as *Citellus* (or *Spermophilus*) *tridecemlineatus* (a destructive rodent common in the prairie states), and *Citellus* (or *Spermophilus*) *richardsoni,* a similar species prevalent in North Dakota. **2.** any of various burrowing rodents of the genera *Geomys, Thomomys,* etc. (family *Geomyidae*), of western and southern North America and Central America, with large external fur-lined cheek pouches (also called *pocket gopher* and *pouched rat*). **3.** an edible, burrowing land tortoise, *Gopherus* (or *Testudo*) *polyphemus,* of the southeastern U.S. **4.** Also, **gopher snake.** a burrowing snake, *Compsosoma corais,* of the southern U.S. **5.** (*cap.*) a nickname for a Minnesotan. [? t. F: m. *gaufre* honeycomb. See GOFFER]

Common pocket gopher,
Geomys bursarius
(10½ to 11½ in. long)

go·pher·wood (gō'fər wood'), *n.* **1.** yellowwood. **2.** an unidentified wood used in building Noah's ark. See Gen. 6:14. [f. *gopher,* a tree (t. Heb.) + wood¹]

go·ral (gōr'əl), *n.* a goat antelope, *Naemorhedus goral,* of mountainous southeastern Asia, having small horns shorter than the distance apart at their bases.

gor·cock (gôr'kŏk'), *n.* the moor cock, or male red grouse, *Lagopus scoticus,* of Great Britain. [orig. obscure]

Gor·di·an (gôr'dī ən), *adj.* **1.** pertaining to Gordius, ancient king of Phrygia, who tied a knot (the **Gordian knot**) which was to be undone only by one who should rule Asia, and which was summarily cut by Alexander the Great. **2.** resembling the Gordian knot; intricate. **3. cut the Gordian knot,** to devise and use instantly a drastic way out of a difficulty.

Gor·don (gôr'dən), *n.* **Charles George,** ("*Chinese Gordon*") 1833–85, British general and administrator in China and Egypt.

Gordon setter, a black, long-haired variety of setter dog with red or tan marks on the muzzle, neck, and legs.

gore[1] (gōr), *n.* blood that is shed, esp. when clotted. [ME; OE *gor* dung, dirt, c. D *goor*, OHG *gor* filth]

gore[2] (gōr), *v.t.*, **gored, goring.** (of an animal) to pierce with the horns or tusks. [ME *goren*. Cf. GORE[3]]

gore[3] (gōr), *n., v.*, **gored, goring.** —*n.* **1.** a triangular piece of cloth, etc., inserted in a garment, a sail, etc., to give greater width or secure the desired shape or adjustment. **2.** one of the breadths (mostly tapering, or shaped) of a woman's skirt. —*v.t.* **3.** to make or furnish with a gore or gores. [ME; OE *gāra* corner (c. G *gehre* gusset), der. *gār* spear] —**gored,** *adj.* —**gor′ing,** *n.*

Gor·gas (gôr′gəs), *n.* William Crawford, 1854–1920, surgeon general in the U.S. Army; chief sanitation expert in the building of the Panama Canal.

gorge (gôrj), *n., v.*, **gorged, gorging.** —*n.* **1.** a narrow cleft with steep, rocky walls, esp. one through which a stream runs. **2.** a gorging or gluttonous meal. **3.** that which is swallowed; contents of the stomach. **4.** strong disgust; repulsion: *one's gorge rises in resentment.* **5.** a choking mass. **6.** *Fort.* the rear entrance or part of a bastion or similar outwork. See diag. under **bastion. 7.** *Archaic.* the throat; gullet. —*v.t.* **8.** to stuff with food (mainly reflexive and passive): *gorged with food, he gorged himself.* **9.** to swallow, esp. greedily. **10.** to choke up (mainly passive). —*v.i.* **11.** to eat greedily. [ME, t. OF: throat, g. LL *gurga*, b. L *gurges* stream, abyss and *gula* throat] —**gorg′er,** *n.* —**Syn. 8.** glut, stuff. **9.** bolt, gulp, gobble.

gor·geous (gôr′jəs), *adj.* sumptuous; magnificent; splendid in appearance or coloring. [late ME, t. OF: m. *gorgias* fashionable, gay; orig. uncert.] —**gor′geous·ly,** *adv.* —**gor′geous·ness,** *n.* —**Syn.** rich, superb, grand; brilliant, resplendent. See **magnificent.**

gor·ger·in (gôr′jər ĭn), *n.* *Archit.* the necklike portion of a capital of a column, or a feature forming the junction between a shaft and its capital. [t. F, der. *gorge* throat]

gor·get (gôr′jĭt), *n.* **1.** a piece of armor for the throat. **2.** a form of wimple, or neck and chest covering, worn by women in the Middle Ages. **3.** a patch on the throat of a bird or other animal, distinguished by its color or otherwise. [late ME, t. OF: m. *gorgete,* dim. of *gorge* throat]

G. Gorget (def. 1), 15th century
A. Attached to the brigandine
B. Worn over mail

Gor·gon (gôr′gən), *n.* **1.** *Gk. Legend.* any of three sisters, Stheno, Euryale, and Medusa, whose heads were covered with snakes instead of hair, and whose glance turned the beholder to stone. **2.** (*l.c.*) a terrible or repulsive woman. —**Gor·go·ni·an** (gôr gō′nĭ ən), *adj.*

gor·go·nei·on (gôr′gə nē′ŏn), *n., pl.* **-neia** (-nē′ə). a representation of the head of a Gorgon, esp. that of Medusa. [t. Gk.]

Gor·gon·zo·la (gôr′gən zō′lə), *n.* a strongly flavored, Italian, semihard variety of milk cheese veined with mold. [named after *Gorgonzola,* a town in N Italy]

gor·hen (gôr′hĕn′), *n.* the female red grouse. [cf. GORCOCK]

go·ril·la (gə rĭl′ə), *n.* **1.** the largest of the anthropoid apes, *Gorilla gorilla,* ground-living and vegetarian, of western equatorial Africa and the Kivu highlands. **2.** an ugly, brutal fellow. [t. NL, t. Gk.; said to be of African orig.] —**go·ril′la·like′,** *adj.*

Gorilla (def. 1), *Gorilla gorilla*
(6 ft. high; standing height 5½ ft.)

Gö·ring (gœ′rĭng), *n.* Hermann (hĕr′män), Goering.

Go·ri·zia (gō rē′tsyä), *n.* a city in NE Italy, on the Isonzo river, N of Trieste. 42,000 (est. 1954). German, **Görz** (gœrts).

Gor·ki (gôr′kĭ), *n.* **1.** Maxim (mäk sēm′), (*Aleksyey Maksimovich Pyeshkov*) 1868–1936, Russian novelist, short-story writer, and dramatist. **2.** Formerly, **Nizhni Novgorod.** a city in the central Soviet Union in Europe, on the Volga. 876,000 (est. 1956).

Gör·litz (gœr′lĭts), *n.* a city in East Germany, on the Neisse river (the Polish boundary). 96,147 (est. 1955).

Gor·lov·ka (gôr lôf′kä), *n.* a city in the SW Soviet Union. 240,000 (est. 1956).

gor·mand (gôr′mənd), *n.* gourmand.

gor·mand·ize (gôr′mən dīz′), *v.*, **-ized, -izing,** *n.* —*v.i., v.t.* **1.** to eat like a glutton. [v. use of n.] —*n.* **2.** *Rare.* the habits of a glutton. [t. F: m. *gourmandise* gluttony] —**gor′mand·iz′er,** *n.*

gorse (gôrs), *n.* *Chiefly Brit.* furze. [ME *gorst,* OE *gors(t);* akin to G *gerst,* L *hordeum* barley] —**gors′y,** *adj.*

gor·y (gōr′ĭ), *adj.*, **gorier, goriest. 1.** covered or stained with gore; bloody. **2.** resembling gore. —**gor′i·ly,** *adv.* —**gor′i·ness,** *n.*

gosh (gŏsh), *interj.* an exclamation or mild oath. [a euphemistic var. of *God!*]

gos·hawk (gŏs′hôk′), *n.* any of various powerful, short-winged hawks formerly much used

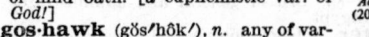

Goshawk.
Accipiter gentilis
(20 to 23 in. long)

in falconry, as *Accipiter gentilis* of Europe and America. [ME *goshawke,* OE *gōshafoc* goosehawk]

Go·shen (gō′shən), *n.* **1.** a pastoral region in Lower Egypt, colonized by the Israelites before the Exodus. Gen. 45:10, etc. **2.** a land or place of plenty and comfort.

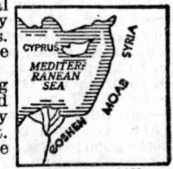

Goshen (def. 1), 1450 B.C.

gos·ling (gŏz′lĭng), *n.* **1.** a young goose. **2.** a foolish, inexperienced person. [ME *goselyng,* var. (by assoc. with GOOSE) of *geslyng,* t. Scand.; cf. Icel. *gǣslingr,* f. *gās* goose + *-lingr,* dim. suffix (see -LING[1])]

gos·pel (gŏs′pəl), *n.* **1.** the body of doctrine taught by Christ and the apostles; Christian revelation. **2.** glad tidings, esp. concerning salvation and the kingdom of God as announced to the world by Christ. **3.** the story of Christ's life and teachings, esp. as contained in the first four books of the New Testament. **4.** (*usually cap.*) one of these books. **5.** (*often cap.*) *Eccles.* an extract from one of the four Gospels, forming part of the Eucharistic service in certain churches. **6.** *Colloq.* something regarded as true and implicitly believed: *to take for gospel.* **7.** a doctrine regarded as of prime importance: *political gospel.* —*adj.* **8.** pertaining to the gospel. **9.** in accordance with the gospel; evangelical. [ME *go(d)spel,* OE *gōdspel,* f. *gōd* GOOD + *spell* tidings (SPELL[2]), trans. of L *ēvangelium.* See EVANGEL]

gos·pel·er (gŏs′pəl ər), *n.* *Eccles.* one who reads or sings the Gospel (def. 5). Also, *esp. Brit.,* **gos′pel·ler.**

Gos·plan (gŏs plän′), *n.* *U.S.S.R.* official planning organization, which draws up plans embracing trade and industry, agriculture, education, and popular health. [f. *gos(udar)* national + *plan* PLAN]

gos·sa·mer (gŏs′ə mər), *n.* **1.** a fine filmy cobweb, seen on grass and bushes, or floating in the air in calm weather, esp. in autumn. **2.** a thread or a web of this substance. **3.** an extremely delicate variety of gauze. **4.** any thin, light fabric. **5.** a thin, waterproof outer garment, esp. for women. —*adj.* **6.** Also, **gos·sa·mer·y** (gŏs′ə mə rĭ). of or like gossamer; thin and light. [ME *gos(e)-somer.* See GOOSE, SUMMER; possibly first used as name for late mild autumn (Indian summer), time when goose was a favorite dish (cf. G *gänsemonat* November), then transferred to the filmy matter also frequent at that time of year]

Gosse (gôs, gŏs), *n.* Sir Edmund William, 1849–1928, British critic and poet.

gos·sip (gŏs′əp), *n., v.*, **-siped, -siping.** —*n.* **1.** idle talk, esp. about the affairs of others. **2.** light, familiar talk or writing. **3.** a person, esp. a woman, given to tattling or idle talk. **4.** *Archaic.* a friend, esp. a woman. **5.** *Archaic or Dial.* a godparent. —*v.i.* **6.** to talk idly, esp. about the affairs of others; go about tattling. —*v.t.* **7.** to repeat like a gossip. **8.** *Archaic.* to stand godparent to. [ME *gossib,* ME *godsibb,* orig., godparent, f. *god* GOD + *sibb* related (see SIB[1], adj.] —**gos′sip·er,** *n.* —**gos′-sip·ing,** *n.* —**gos′sip·ing·ly,** *adv.*

—**Syn. 1.** GOSSIP, SCANDAL apply to idle talk and newsmongering about the affairs of others. GOSSIP is light chat or talk: *gossip about the neighbors.* SCANDAL is rumor or general talk that is damaging to reputation; it is usually more or less malicious: *a scandal involving bribes.*

gos·sip·mon·ger (gŏs′əp mŭng′gər), *n.* one especially addicted to gossiping.

gos·sip·y (gŏs′ə pĭ), *adj.* **1.** given to or fond of gossip. **2.** full of gossip.

gos·soon (gŏ sōōn′), *n.* *Anglo-Irish.* **1.** a boy. **2.** a male servant. [alter. of GARCON]

got (gŏt), *v.* pt. and pp. of GET.

Go·ta·ma (gō′tə mə, gō′-), *n.* Buddha. See **Gautama.**

Gö·te·borg (yœ′tə bôr′y), *n.* a seaport in SW Sweden, on the Kattegat. 367,579 (est. 1953). Also, **Goth·enburg** (gŏt′ən bûrg′).

Goth (gŏth), *n.* **1.** one of a Teutonic people who, in the 3rd to 5th century, invaded and settled in parts of the Roman Empire. **2.** a barbarian; rude person. [ME *Gothe,* t. LL: m.s. *Gothī,* pl.; r. OE *Gotan,* pl. (*Gota,* sing.), c. Goth. *Gut-* in *Gut-thiuda* Goth people]

Goth., Gothic.

Go·tha (gō′tä), *n.* a city in East Germany, in Thuringia, 57,639 (est. 1955).

Goth·am (gŏth′əm, gō′thəm *for 1;* gŏt′əm *for 2), n.* **1.** the city of New York. **2.** an English village, proverbial for the foolishness of its inhabitants.

Goth·ic (gŏth′ĭk), *adj.* **1.** *Archit.* denoting or pertaining to a style originating in France and spreading over western Europe from the 12th to the 16th century, characterized by a design emphasizing skeleton construction, the elimination of wall planes, the comparatively great height of the buildings, the pointed arch, rib vaulting, and the flying buttress. **2.** (orig. in derogatory use) denoting all European art of this period. **3.** (sometimes in disparagement) pertaining to the Middle Ages; barbarous; rude. **4.** (esp. in literature) stressing irregularity and details, usually of a grotesque or horrible nature: *a Gothic novel.* —*n.* **5.** Gothic architecture, sculpture, or decoration. **6.** an extinct Germanic language, preserved especially in Ulfilas' Bible (4th cent.). **7.** *Brit.* black letter. **8.** (*l.c.*) *U.S.* a square-cut printing type, without serifs or hairlines. [t. LL: *Gothicus*] —**Goth′i·cal·ly,** *adv.*

---

b., blend of, blended;   c., cognate with;   d., dialect, dialectal;   der., derived from;   f., formed from;   g., going back to;   m., modification of;   r., replacing;   s., stem of;   t., taken from;   ?, perhaps.   See the full key on inside cover

Goth·i·cism (gŏth'ə sĭz'əm), *n.* 1. conformity or devotion to the Gothic style of architecture. 2. a mixture of the elevated and the bizarre, often with many details, as distinct from the unity and simplicity of classicism. 3. adherence to aspects of Gothic culture. 4. (*also l.c.*) barbarism; rudeness. 5. a Gothic idiom.

Goth·i·cize (gŏth'ə sīz'), *v.t.,* **-cized, -cizing.** 1. to make Gothic, as in style. 2. to make pseudomedieval.

Go·thite (gœ'tīt), *n.* goethite.

Got·land (gŏt'lənd; *Swed.* gôt'lünd, gôl'lünd), *n.* an island in the Baltic, forming a province of Sweden. 58,129 pop. (est. 1953). 1212 sq. mi. *Cap.:* Visby. Also, **Gott'land.**

got·ten (gŏt'ən), *v.* a pp. of get.

Göt·ter·däm·mer·ung (gœt'ər dĕm'ə rŏŏng'), *n.* See **Ring of the Nibelung.** [G: twilight of the gods]

Göt·tin·gen (gœt'ĭng ən), *n.* a city in central West Germany. 79,700 (est. 1955).

Gott mit uns (gŏt' mĭt ŏŏns'), *German.* God is (or be) with us.

gouache (gwȧsh), *n.* 1. a method of painting with opaque water colors prepared with gum. 2. an opaque color used in painting a gouache. 3. a work executed in this medium. [F, t. It.: m. *guazzo* puddle, spray of water, g. L *aquātio* a watering, der. *aqua* water]

Gou·da (gou'də; *Du.* ᴋʜou'dä), *n.* a city in W Netherlands, NE of Rotterdam: noted for its cheese. 40,104 (est. 1954).

Gouda cheese, a cheese made in Holland from whole milk or partly skimmed milk, colored with saffron, and marketed in bladders or in colored wax skins. Also, **Gouda.**

gou·dy (gou'dĭ), *n.* **Frederic William,** 1865–1947, U.S. designer of printing types.

gouge (gouj), *n., v.,* **gouged, gouging.** —*n.* 1. a chisel whose blade has a concavo-convex cross section, the bevel being ground on either the inside or the outside of the cutting end of the tool. 2. *U.S. Colloq.* act of gouging. 3. a groove or hole made by gouging. 4. *U.S. Colloq.* an imposition or swindle. —*v.t.* 5. to scoop out or turn with or as with a gouge: *gouge a channel, gouge holes.* 6. to dig or force out with or as with a gouge: *to gouge out an eye.* 7. *U.S. Colloq.* to impose upon or swindle. [t. F, g. LL *gu(l)bia* (of Celtic orig.] —**goug'er,** *n.*

Carpenter's gouges

gou·lash (gŏŏ'läsh, -läsh), *n.* a stew of beef, veal, vegetables, etc., with paprika or other seasoning. [t. Hung.: m. *gulyas,* short for *gulyas hus* herdsman's meat]

gould (gŏŏld), *n.* **Jay,** 1836–92, U.S. financier and capitalist.

gou·nod (gŏŏ'nō; *Fr.* gŏŏ nō'), *n.* **Charles François** (shȧrl frȧn swä'), 1818–93, French composer.

gou·ra·mi (gŏŏr'ə mĭ), *n., pl.* **-mis.** 1. a large, air-breathing, nest-building, fresh-water Asiatic fish, *Osphronemus goramy,* highly prized for food. 2. any of a number of smaller, air-breathing, nest-building, Asiatic fishes (genera *Trichogaster, Colisa,* and *Trichopsis*) widely cultivated in home aquaria in the U.S., as the **dwarf gourami,** *Colisa lalia.*

gourd (gōrd, gŏŏrd), *n.* 1. the fruit of any of various cucurbitaceous plants, esp. that of *Lagenaria Siceraria* (**bottle gourd**), whose dried shell is used for bottles, bowls, etc., or that of certain forms of *Cucurbita Pepo* sometimes cultivated for ornament. 2. a plant bearing such a fruit. 3. a dried and excavated gourd shell used as a bottle, dipper, flask, etc. 4. a gourd-shaped, small-necked bottle or flask. [ME, t. F: m. *gourde,* g. L *cucurbita*] —**gourd'like',** *adj.* —**gourd-shaped** (gōrd'-shäpt', gŏŏrd'-), *adj.*

gourde (gŏŏrd), *n.* the monetary unit of Haiti since 1920, equal to 20 cents in U.S. [t. F, fem. of *gourd* numb, slow, heavy, g. L *gurdus* dull, obtuse]

gour·mand (gŏŏr'mənd; *Fr.* gŏŏr män'), *n.* one fond of good eating. Also, **gormand.** [late ME, t. F: glutton-ous, der. *gourmet* ɢOURMET]

gour·met (gŏŏr'mā; *Fr.* gŏŏr mĕ'), *n.* a connoisseur in the delicacies of the table; an epicure. [t. F, in OF also *groumet* wine taster, wine merchant's man. Cf. ɢROOM]

Gour·mont (gŏŏr môn'), *n.* **Remy de** (rə mē' də), 1858–1915, French critic and novelist.

gout (gout), *n.* 1. a constitutional disease characterized by painful inflammation of the joints (chiefly those in the feet and hands, and esp. in the great toe), and by excess of uric acid in the blood. 2. *Archaic or Poetic.* a drop, splash, or spot, esp. of blood. [ME *goute,* t. OF, g. L *gutta* a drop, ML gout]

goût (gŏŏ), *n. French.* taste; perception. [F, g. L *gustus* taste]

gout·y (gou'tĭ), *adj.,* **goutier, goutiest.** 1. pertaining to or having the nature of gout. 2. causing gout. 3. diseased with or subject to gout. 4. swollen as if from gout. —**gout'i·ly,** *adv.* —**gout'i·ness,** *n.*

gou·ver·nante (gŏŏ vĕr nänt'), *n. French.* 1. a chaperon. 2. a governess.

gov., governor.

gov., 1. governor. 2. government.

gov·ern (gŭv'ərn), *v.t.* 1. to rule by right of authority, as a sovereign does: *to govern a state.* 2. to exercise a directing or restraining influence over; guide: *the motives governing a decision.* 3. to hold in check: *to govern one's temper.* 4. to serve as or constitute a law for: *the principles governing a case.* 5. *Gram.* to be accompanied by

(a particular form) as in *"they helped us,"* not *"they helped we,"* the verb *"helped"* is said to govern the objective case of the pronoun. —*v.i.* 6. to exercise the function of government. 7. to have predominating influence. [ME *governe(n),* t. OF: m. *governer,* g. L *gubernāre,* t. Gk.: m. *kybernān* steer, guide, govern] —**gov'ern·a·ble,** *adj.* —**Syn.** 1. See rule.

gov·ern·ance (gŭv'ər nəns), *n.* 1. government; exercise of authority; control. 2. method or system of government or management.

gov·ern·ess (gŭv'ər nĭs), *n.* a woman who directs the education of children, generally in their own homes.

gov·ern·ment (gŭv'ərn mənt, -ər-), *n.* 1. the authoritative direction and restraint exercised over the actions of men in communities, societies, and states; direction of the affairs of a state, etc.; political rule and administration: *government is necessary to the existence of society.* 2. the form or system of rule by which a state, community, etc., is governed: *monarchical government, episcopal government.* 3. the governing body of persons in a state, community, etc.; the executive power; the administration: *the government was* (or in England, *were*) *defeated in the last election.* 4. direction; control; rule: *the government of one's conduct.* 5. the district governed; a province. 6. *Gram.* the established usage which requires that one word in a sentence should cause another to be of a particular form. —**gov·ern·men·tal** (gŭv'ərn mĕn'təl, -ər-), *adj.* —**gov'ern·men'tal·ly,** *adv.*

gov·er·nor (gŭv'ər nər), *n.* 1. the executive head of a State in the U.S. 2. *Chiefly Brit.* one charged with the direction or control of an institution, society, etc.: *governors of a bank, governor of a prison.* 3. the representative of the crown in a British colony or dependency. 4. a ruler or chief magistrate appointed to govern a province, town, fort, or the like. 5. *Mach.* a device for regulating a supply of fuel for ensuring uniform speed regardless of the load. 6. *Chiefly Brit. Colloq.* a. master or employer. b. one's father. [ME *governour,* t. OF: m. *governeor,* g. L *gubernātor* steersman, director]

governor general, *pl.* **governors general.** a governor who has under him subordinate or deputy governors. Also, *esp. Brit.,* **governor-general.** —**gov'er·nor·gen'er·al·ship',** *n.*

gov·er·nor·ship (gŭv'ər nər shĭp'), *n.* a governor's duties, term in office, etc.

Governors Island, a small island in New York Bay at the S end of the East river: U.S. military post.

Govt., government. Also, **govt.**

gow·an (gou'ən), *n. Scot. and N. Eng.* any of various yellow or white field flowers, esp. the English daisy. [? var. of obs. *gollan,* t. Scand.; cf. Icel. *gullinn* golden]

Gow·er (gou'ər, gōr), *n.* **John,** c1325–1408, English poet.

gowk (gouk, gōk), *n.* 1. the cuckoo. 2. a fool or simpleton. [ME *goke,* t. Scand.: cf. Icel. *gaukr,* c. OE *gēac* cuckoo, G *gauch* cuckoo, fool]

gown (goun), *n.* 1. a woman's dress or robe, comprising waist and skirt (either joined or separate). 2. a loose, flowing, outer garment in various forms, worn by men or women as distinctive of office, profession, or status: *a judge's gown, an academic gown.* 3. the student and teaching body in British university towns, as contrasted to the town, or townfolk. —*v.t., v.i.* 4. to dress in, or put on, a gown. [ME *goune,* t. OF, g. LL *gunna;* of uncert. orig.] —**Syn.** 1. See **dress.**

gowns·man (gounz'mən), *n., pl.* **-men.** a man who wears a gown indicating his office, profession, or status.

Go·ya (gō'yä), *n.* **Francisco de** (frän thēs'kō dě), (*Francisco José de Goya y Lucientes*) 1746–1828, Spanish painter and etcher.

G.P., 1. Gloria Patri. 2. Graduate in Pharmacy. 3. *Chiefly Brit.* General Practitioner.

GPO, Government Printing Office.

G.P.O., General Post Office.

G.P.U., Gay-Pay-Oo.

Gr., 1. Grecian. 2. Greece. 3. Greek.

gr., 1. grade. 2. grain; grains. 3. gram; grams. 4. gross.

G.R., *Brit.* Georgius Rex.

Graaf·i·an follicle (grä'fĭən), *Anat.* one of many small vesicles within the ovary which, at the time of ovulation, discharge an ovum. Also, **Graafian vesicle.** [der. name of R. de *Graaf,* Dutch anatomist (1641–73)]

grab (grăb), *v.,* **grabbed, grabbing.** —*v.t.* 1. to seize suddenly and eagerly; snatch. 2. to take illegal possession of; seize forcibly or unscrupulously: *to grab land.* —*n.* 3. a sudden, eager grasp or snatch. 4. seizure or acquisition by violent or unscrupulous means. 5. that which is grabbed. 6. a mechanical device for gripping objects. [c. MD and MLG *grabben,* Sw. *grabba*] —**grab'ber,** *n.*

grab bag, *n. U.S. Colloq.* a receptacle from which one draws without knowing what he is getting.

grab·ble (grăb'əl), *v.i.,* **-bled, -bling.** 1. to feel or search with the hands; grope. 2. to sprawl; scramble. [freq. of ɢRAB.·. Cf. D *grabbelen*]

gra·ben (grä'bən), *n.* a portion of the earth's crust, bounded on at least two sides by faults, that has been moved downward in relation to adjacent portions. [t. G: ditch]

grab rope, *Naut.* any of certain lines or ropes on a ship for taking hold of, as one for boatmen to hold on to when coming alongside. Also, **grab line.**

Grac·chi (grăk'ī), *n.pl.* Gaius and Tiberius Gracchus.

Grac·chus (gräk′əs), *n.* **1.** **Gaius Sempronius** (gā′əs sĕm prō′nĭ əs), 153?–121 B.C., Roman political reformer and orator. **2.** his brother, **Tiberius Sempronius** (tī bĭr′ĭ əs), 163?–133 B.C., Roman reformer and orator.

grace (grās), *n., v.,* **graced, gracing.** —*n.* **1.** elegance or beauty of form, manner, motion, or act. **2.** a pleasing or attractive quality or endowment. **3.** favor or good will. **4.** manifestation of favor, esp. as by a superior. **5.** mercy; clemency; pardon. **6.** favor shown in granting a delay or temporary immunity. **7.** *Law.* an allowance of time to a debtor before suit can be brought against him after his debt has by its terms become payable: *days of grace.* **8.** *Theol.* **a.** the free, unmerited favor and love of God. **b.** the influence or spirit of God operating in man to regenerate or strengthen. **c.** a virtue or excellence of divine origin: *the Christian graces.* **9.** state of grace, *Theol.* **a.** condition of being in God's favor. **b.** condition of being one of the elect. **10.** moral strength: *the grace to perform a duty.* **11.** a short prayer before or after a meal, in which a blessing is asked and thanks are given. **12.** (*usually cap.*) a formal title used in addressing or mentioning a duke, duchess, or archbishop, and formerly also a sovereign (prec. by *your, his,* etc.). **13.** (*cap.*) *Class. Myth.* one of three sister goddesses, commonly given as **Aglaia** (brilliance), **Euphrosyne** (joy), and **Thalia** (bloom), presiding over all beauty and charm in nature and humanity. **14.** *Music.* an embellishment consisting of a note or notes not essential to the harmony or melody, as an appoggiatura, an inverted mordent, etc. —*v.t.* **15.** to lend or add grace to; adorn. **16.** to favor or honor: *to grace an occasion with one's presence.* **17.** *Music.* to add grace notes, cadenzas, etc., to. [ME, t. OF, t. L: m. s. *grātia* favor, gratitude, agreeableness] —**Syn. 1.** attractiveness, charm, gracefulness. **4.** kindness. **5.** lenity. **15.** embellish, beautify; honor, enhance.

grace cup, **1.** a cup, as of wine, passed round at the end of the meal for the final health or toast. **2.** the drink.

grace·ful (grās′fəl), *adj.* characterized by grace of form, manner, movement, or speech; elegant; easy or effective. —**grace′ful·ly,** *adv.* —**grace′ful·ness,** *n.*

grace·less (grās′lĭs), *adj.* **1.** wanting grace, pleasing elegance, or charm. **2.** without any sense of right or propriety. —**grace′less·ly,** *adv.* —**grace′less·ness,** *n.*

grace note, *Music.* a note not essential to the harmony or melody, added as an embellishment, esp. an appoggiatura.

grac·ile (grās′ĭl), *adj.* **1.** gracefully slender. **2.** slender; thin. [t. L: m. s. *gracilis* slender] —**gra·cil′i·ty,** *n.*

gra·ci·o·so (grä′shĭ ō′sō; *Sp.* grä thyō′sō), *n., pl.* **-sos.** **1.** a character in Spanish comedy, resembling the English clown. **2.** a low comic character. **3.** *Obs.* a favorite. [Sp., der. *gracia* wit, grace, t. L: m. *grātia*]

gra·cious (grā′shəs), *adj.* **1.** disposed to show grace or favor; kind; benevolent; courteous. **2.** indulgent or beneficent in a condescending or patronizing way, esp. to inferiors. **3.** merciful or compassionate. **4.** *Obs.* fortunate or happy. —*interj.* **5.** an exclamation of surprise, etc. [ME, t. OF, t. L: m.s. *grātiōsus* enjoying or showing favor] —**gra′cious·ly,** *adv.* —**gra′cious·ness, gra·ci·os·i·ty** (grā′shĭ ŏs′ə tĭ), *n.* —**Syn. 1.** kindly, benign. See **kind**[1]. —**Ant. 1.** churlish, surly.

grack·le (gräk′əl), *n.* any of various birds of the Old World family *Sturnidae* (starlings), or of the American family *Icteridae* (American starlings, blackbirds, etc.), as the crow blackbird or **purple grackle** (*Guiscalus quiscula*). [t. L: m.s. *grāculus* jackdaw]

grad., **1.** graduate. **2.** graduated.

gra·date (grā′dāt), *v.,* **-dated, -dating.** —*v.i.* **1.** to pass by insensible degrees, as one color into another. —*v.t.* **2.** to cause to gradate. **3.** to arrange in grades.

gra·da·tion (grā dā′shən), *n.* **1.** any process or change taking place through a series of stages, by degrees, or gradually. **2.** (*usually pl.*) a stage, degree, or grade in such a series. **3.** the passing of one tint or shade of color to another, or one surface to another, by very small degrees, as in painting, sculpture, etc. **4.** act of grading. **5.** ablaut (def.2). —**gra·da′tion·al,** *adj.* —**gra·da′tion·al·ly,** *adv.*

grade (grād), *n., v.,* **graded, grading.** —*n.* **1.** a degree in a scale, as of rank, advancement, quality, value, intensity, etc. **2.** a class of persons or things of the same relative rank, quality, etc. **3.** a step or stage in a course or process. **4.** a single division of a school classified according to the progress of the pupils (American public schools commonly being divided into eight grades below the high school division). **5.** *U.S.* the pupils themselves in such a division. **6.** (*pl.*) *U.S.* the divisions of an elementary school or the school itself. **7.** *U.S.* a number, letter, etc., indicating the relative quality of a student's work in a course, examination, or special assignment. **8.** inclination with the horizontal of a road, railroad, etc., usually expressed by stating the vertical rise or fall as a percentage of the horizontal distance. **9.** at grade, on the same level: *a railroad crosses a highway at grade.* **10.** an animal resulting from a cross between a parent of common stock and one of a pure breed. —*v.t.* **11.** to arrange in a series of grades; class; sort. **12.** to determine the grade of. **13.** to cause to pass by degrees, as from one color or shade to another. **14.** to reduce to a level or to practicable degrees of inclination: *to grade a road.* **15.** to cross (a nondescript animal or a low grade one) with one of a pure breed. —*v.i.* **16.** to be graded. **17.** to be of a particular grade or quality. [t. F, t. L: m. s. *gradus* step, stage, degree]

-grade, a word element meaning "walking," "moving," "going," as in *retrograde.* [comb. form repr. L *gradus* step, or *gradī,* v., walk. See GRADE, GRADIENT]

grade crossing, a crossing of a railroad and a highway or another railroad at grade.

grade labeling, a method of giving information on a label about the quality of the merchandise.

grad·er (grā′dər), *n.* **1.** one who or that which grades. **2.** *Orig. U.S.* a pupil of a certain grade at school: *a fourth grader.* **3.** *U.S.* a machine for grading.

grade school, an elementary school that has its pupils grouped or classified into grades according to their advancement. Also, **graded school.**

gra·di·ent (grā′dĭ ənt), *n.* **1.** the degree of inclination, or the rate of ascent or descent, in a railroad, etc.; grade. **2.** an inclined surface; grade; ramp. **3.** *Physics.* **a.** change in a variable quantity, as temperature or pressure, per unit distance. **b.** curve representing such a rate of change. —*adj.* **4.** rising or descending by regular degrees of inclination. **5.** progressing by walking as an animal; gressorial. **6.** of a type suitable for walking, as some birds' feet. [t. L: s. *gradiens,* ppr., walking, going]

gra·din (grā′dĭn; *Fr.* grȧ dăn′), *n.* **1.** one of a series of steps or seats raised one above another. **2.** *Eccles.* a shelf or one of a series of shelves behind and above an altar. Also, **gra·dine** (grə dēn′). [t. F, t. It.: m. *gradino,* der. *grado* GRADE]

grad·u·al (grăj′ōō əl), *adj.* **1.** taking place, changing, moving, etc., by degrees or little by little: *gradual improvement in health.* **2.** rising or descending at an even, moderate inclination: *a gradual slope.* —*n.* **3.** *Eccles.* **a.** an antiphon sung between the epistle and the gospel in the eucharistic service. **b.** a book containing the words and music of the parts of the liturgy which are sung by the choir. [t. ML: s. *graduālis* (as n., *graduāle*), der. L *gradus* step, grade] —**grad′u·al·ly,** *adv.* —**grad′u·al·ness,** *n.* —**Syn. 1.** See **slow.**

grad·u·ate (*adj., n.* grăj′ōō ĭt, -āt′; *v.* grăj′ōō āt′), *n., adj., v.,* **-ated, -ating.** —*n.* **1.** one who has received a degree or diploma on completing a course of study, as in a university, college, or school. **2.** a student who holds the first or bachelor's degree and is studying for an advanced degree. **3.** a cylindrical or tapering graduated vessel of glass, for measuring. —*adj.* **4.** that has been graduated: *a graduate student.* **5.** of or pertaining to graduates: *a graduate school.* —*v.i.* **6.** to receive a degree or diploma on completing a course of study. **7.** to pass by degrees; change gradually. —*v.t.* **8.** to confer a degree upon, or to grant a diploma to, at the close of a course of study, as in a university, college, or school. **9.** to arrange in grades or gradations; establish graduation in. **10.** to divide into or mark with degrees or other divisions, as the scale of a thermometer. [t. ML: m.s. *graduātus,* pp. of *graduāre* admit to an academic degree, der. L *gradus* step, grade] —**grad′u·a·tor,** *n.*

grad·u·a·tion (grăj′ōō ā′shən), *n.* **1.** act of graduating. **2.** state of being graduated. **3.** ceremony of conferring degrees or diplomas, as at a college or school. **4.** marks or a mark on an instrument or a vessel for indicating degree, quantity, etc.

gra·dus (grā′dəs), *n.* *Music.* a work consisting wholly, or in part, of exercises of increasing difficulty. [t. L: short for *gradus ad Parnassum* step to Parnassus]

Grae·ae (grē′ē), *n.pl.* *Gk. Myth.* three old sea deities, who had but one eye and one tooth among them and were the protectresses of the Gorgons, their sisters. Also, **Graiae.**

Grae·ci·a Mag·na (grē′shĭ ə măg′nə), Magna Graecia.

Grae·cize (grē′sīz), *v.t., v.i.,* **-cized, -cizing.** *Chiefly Brit.* Grecize. —**Grae′cism,** *n,*

Graeco-, *Chiefly Brit.* var. of **Greco-.**

Graf (gräf), *n., pl.* **Grafen** (grä′fən). a count; a title of nobility in Germany, Austria, and Sweden, which corresponds to English earl and French comte. [cf. BURGRAVE, LANDGRAVE, MARGRAVE]

graf·fi·to (grə fē′tō), *n., pl.* **-ti** (-tē). *Archaeol.* an ancient drawing or writing scratched on a wall or other surface. [t. It., der. *graffio* a scratch, ult. der. Gk. *graphein* mark, draw, write]

graft[1] (gräft, gräft), *n.* **1.** *Hort.* **a.** a shoot or part of a plant (the scion) inserted in a groove, slit, or the like in another plant or tree (the stock) so as to become nourished by and united with it. **b.** the plant or tree (the united stock and scion) resulting from such an operation. **c.** the place where the scion is inserted. **2.** *Surg.* a portion of living tissue surgically transplanted from one part of an individual to another, or from one individual to another, with a view to its adhesion and growth. **3.** act of grafting. —*v.t.* **4.** to insert (a graft) into a plant or tree; insert a scion of (one plant) into another plant. **5.** to cause (a plant) to reproduce through grafting. **6.** *Surg.* to transplant (a portion of living tissue) as a graft. **7.** to insert as if by grafting: *to graft a pagan custom upon*

Types of grafting
A. Splice; B. Saddle; C. Cleft;
D, E. Whip or tongue

b., blend of, blended; c., cognate with; d., dialect, dialectal; der., derived from; f., formed from; g., going back to; m., modification of; r., replacing; s., stem of; t., taken from; ?, perhaps. See the full key on inside cover.

graft

Christian institutions. —v.i. 8. to insert scions from one tree, or kind of tree, into another. 9. to become graft-ed. [earlier graff, ME grafe, t. OF: orig., stylus, pencil, t. LL: m.s. graphium, t. Gk.: m. grapheion stylus] —graft′er, n. —graft′ing, n.

graft² (gråft, gräft), U.S. Colloq. —n. 1. the acquisition of gain or advantage by dishonest, unfair, or sordid means, esp. through the abuse of one's position or influence in politics, business, etc. 2. a particular instance, method, or means of thus acquiring gain. 3. the gain or advantage acquired. —v.i. 4. to obtain by graft. —v.i. 5. to practice graft. [cf. prov. Eng. or slang graft work, a job or trade, ? identical with graft in expression spade(s) graft. var. of spade(s)-graff, lit., spade's digging (depth of earth thrown up at a single spading), OE græf trench. See GRAVE¹] —graft′er, n.

graft·age (gråf′tÏj, gräf′-), n. the art of inserting a part of one plant into another plant in such a way that the two will unite and continue their growth.

gra·ham (grā′əm), adj. made of graham flour.

graham flour, unbolted wheat flour, containing all of the wheat grain; whole-wheat flour. [named after S. Graham (1794–1851), U.S. reformer of dietetics]

Gra·ham Land (grā′əm), Palmer Peninsula.

Gra·iae (grā′ē, grī′ē), n.pl. Graeae.

grail (grāl), n. a cup (also taken as a chalice) which according to medieval legend was used by Jesus at the Last Supper, and in which Joseph of Arimathea received the last drops of Jesus' blood at the cross: used often as a symbol for a lost, pure kind of Christianity; Holy Grail. [ME grayle, t. OF: m. graal, t. ML: m. s. gradāle plate, or der. L crātēr bowl, t. Gk.: m. krātēr]

grain (grān), n. 1. a small hard seed, esp. a seed of one of the cereal plants: wheat, rye, oats, barley, maize, or millet. 2. the gathered seeds of cereal plants in the mass. 3. the plants themselves, whether standing or gathered. 4. any small, hard particle, as of sand, gold, pepper, gunpowder, etc. 5. the smallest unit of weight in most systems, originally determined by the weight of a plump grain of wheat. In the U.S. and British systems —avoirdupois, troy, and apothecaries' —the grain is identical. In an avoirdupois ounce there are 437.5 grains; in the troy and apothecaries' ounces there are 480 grains. 6. the smallest possible amount of anything: a grain of truth. 7. with a grain of salt, with some reserve; without wholly believing. 8. the arrangement or direction of fibers in wood, or the resulting appearance or markings. 9. the side of leather from which the hair has been removed. 10. a stamped pattern to imitate natural grain of leather: used either on leather to simulate a different type of natural leather, or on coated cloth. 11. the fibers or yarn in a piece of fabric as differentiated from the fabric itself. 12. lamination or cleavage of stone, coal, etc. 13. Gems. unit of weight for pearls equal to 50 mg. or ¼ carat. 14. (in diamond polishing) the cleavage directions. 15. the size of constituent particles of any substance; texture: sugar of fine grain. 16. granular texture or appearance: a stone of coarse grain. 17. state of crystallization: boiled to the grain. 18. temper or natural character: to go against the grain. 19. Obs. color or hue. —v.t. 20. to form into grains, granulate. 21. to give a granular appearance to. 22. to paint in imitation of the grain of wood, stone, etc. 23. Tanning. to remove the hair from (skins); soften and raise the grain of (leather). [coalescence of two ME words: ME greyn, t. OF: m. grain, g. L grānum grain, seed; and ME grayne red dye, t. OF: m. graine, g. L grāna, pl. of grānum grain]. —grain′er, n. —grain′less, adj.

grain alcohol, alcohol made from grain; ethyl alcohol

grain elevator, a building where grain is stored.

Grain·ger (grān′jər), n. Percy Aldridge (ōl′drĬj), 1882-1961, Australian pianist and composer.

grains (grānz), n.pl. (often construed as sing.) an iron instrument with barbed prongs, for spearing or harpooning fish. [earlier also grainse, t. Icel.: m. grein division, branch; cf. Sw. gren]

grains of paradise, the pungent, peppery seeds of either of two zingiberaceous plants, Aframomum Melegueta and A. granum-paradisi, of Africa: used to strengthen cordials, etc., and in veterinary medicine.

grain·y (grā′nĬ), adj., grainier, grainiest. 1. grainlike or granular. 2. full of grains or grain. 3. resembling the grain of wood, etc. —grain′i·ness, n.

gral·la·to·ri·al (grăl′ə tōr′Ĭəl), adj. belonging or pertaining to the wading birds, as the snipe, cranes, storks, herons, etc., many species of which have very long legs. [f. L grallātor one who goes on stilts + -IAL]

gram¹ (grăm), n. a metric unit of mass, equal to 15.432 grains; one thousandth of a kilogram. Also, esp. Brit., gramme. [t. F: m. gramme. t. LL: m. gramma, t. Gk.: a small weight, orig. something drawn]

gram² (grăm), n. 1. (in the Orient) the chick-pea, there used as a food for man and cattle. 2. any of various other plants, as Phaseolus aureus (green gram) and P. mungo (black gram), beans cultivated in India as a food crop. [t. Pg.: m. grao, g. L grānum GRAIN¹]

-gram¹, a word element meaning something drawn or written, as in diagram, epigram, telegram, monogram. [t. Gk.: m. -gramma something drawn or written, or m. -grammon pertaining to a stroke or line]

-gram², a word element meaning grams; of or per-

taining to a gram, as in kilogram. [t. Gk.: m. grámma small weight]

gram., 1. grammar. 2. grammatical.

gra·ma grass (grä′mə), any range grass of the western and southwestern U.S. of the genus Bouteloua, as B. gracilis (blue grama), the commonest species. [grama, t. Sp.: kind of grass, g. L grāmen grass]

gram·a·rye (grăm′ə rĬ), n. Archaic. occult learning; magic. Also gram′a·ry. [ME grammarie, gramarye, t. OF: GRAMMAR, magic]

gram atom, Chem. that quantity of an element whose weight in grams is numerically equal to the atomic weight of the element.

gram calorie. See calorie (def. 1a).

gra·mer·cy (grə mûr′sĬ), interj. Archaic. 1. many thanks. 2. an exclamation of surprise or sudden feeling. [ME, t. OF: m. grant merci. See GRAND, MERCY]

gra·min·e·ous (grə mĬn′Yəs), adj. 1. grasslike. 2. pertaining or belonging to the Gramineae (or Poaceae) family, the grass family of plants. [t. L: m. grāmineus pertaining to grass]

gram·i·niv·o·rous (grăm′ə nĬv′ərəs), adj. 1. feeding on seeds or like food. 2. adapted for feeding on grain, as the jaws, teeth, etc., of gophers and other rodents.

gram·mar (grăm′ər), n. 1. the features of a language (sounds, words, formation and arrangement of words, etc.) considered systematically as a whole, especially with reference to their mutual contrasts and relations: English grammar. 2. an account of the preceding. 3. a similar account comparing two or more languages, or different stages of the same language. 4. speech or writing in accordance with standard usage: he knows his grammar. 5. the elements of any science, art, or subject. 6. a book treating them. [ME grammer, t. OF: m. grammaire, t. L: m. grammatica, t. Gk.: m. grammatikē grammar, prop. fem. of grammatikós pertaining to letters or literature] —gram′mar·less, adj.

gram·mar·i·an (grə mâr′Ĭən), n. 1. a specialist in the study of grammar. 2. a person who claims, or is reputed to establish, standards of usage in a language.

grammar school, 1. U.S. a graded school intermediate between a primary school and a high school. 2. Brit. a secondary school corresponding to an American high school. 3. a secondary school in which Latin and Greek are among the principal subjects taught.

gram·mat·i·cal (grə măt′ə kəl), adj. 1. of or pertaining to grammar: grammatical analysis. 2. conforming to standard usage: grammatical speech. —gram·mat′i·cal·ly, adv. —gram·mat′i·cal·ness, n.

gramme (grăm), n. Chiefly Brit. gram¹.

gram molecule, Chem. that quantity of a substance whose weight in grams is numerically equal to the number which expresses the molecular weight of the substance. Also, gram′-mo·lec′u·lar weight.

Gra·mont (grä mŏn′), n. Philibert de (fēlē bĕr′ də) 1621-1707, French courtier, soldier, and adventurer

gram·o·phone (grăm′ə fōn′), n. 1. a phonograph 2. (cap.) a trade name for this. [inverted var. of PHONO GRAM. See PHONO-, -GRAM¹]

Gram·pi·ans (grăm′pĬ ənz), n.pl. The, a range of low mountains in central Scotland, separating the Highlands from the Lowlands. Highest peak, Ben Nevis, 4406 ft. Also, Gram′pi·an Hills.

gram·pus (grăm′pəs), n. 1. a cetacean, Grampus griseus, of the dolphin family, widely distributed in northern seas. 2. any of various related cetaceans, as the killer, Orca orca. [earlier graundepose, alter. of grapays, t. OF: m. graspeis, g. ML crassus piscis fat fish]

Grampus, Grampus griseus (10 to 13 ft. long)

Gram's method (grămz), a method of bacterial staining in which the film is first stained with crystal violet and then with Gram's iodine solution. It permits the classification of bacteria, Gram-positive species keeping the violet dye, and Gram-negative species being decolorized. [named after H. C. J. Gram, Danish physician (1853–1938)]

Gra·na·da (grə nä′də; Sp. grä nä′dä), n. 1. a medieval kingdom along the Mediterranean coast of S Spain. See map under Castile. 2. a city in S Spain: the capital of this former kingdom and last stronghold of the Moors in Spain; site of the Alhambra. 163,393 (est. 1955).

gran·a·dil·la (grăn′ə dĬl′ə), n. 1. the edible fruit of certain species of passionflower, esp. Passiflora edulis (purple granadilla) and P. quadrangularis (giant granadilla). 2. any of the plants yielding these fruits. [t. Sp., dim. of granada pomegranate. See GRENADE]

gran·a·ry (grăn′ə rĬ, grā′nə-), n., pl. -ries. 1. a storehouse or repository for grain, esp. after it has been threshed or husked. 2. a region abounding in grain. [t. L: m. s. grānārium]

Gran Ca·na·ri·a (grän kä nä′rĬ ä′), one of the Canary Islands. 303,839 pop. (1950); 650 sq. mi. Cap.: Las Palmas. Also, Grand Canary.

Gran Cha·co (grän chä′kō), an extensive subtropical region in Argentina, Bolivia, and Paraguay. ab. 300,000 sq. mi. See Chaco.

grand (grănd), adj. 1. imposing in size or appearance or general effect: grand mountain scenery. 2. stately, majestic, or dignified. **3.** lofty: *grand ideas.* **4.** magnificent or splendid: *a grand palace, display, etc.* **5.** noble or fine: *a grand old man.* **6.** highest, or very high, in rank or official dignity: *a grand jury.* **7.** main or principal; chief: *the grand staircase.* **8.** of great importance, distinction, or pretension: *grand personages.* **9.** complete or comprehensive: *a grand total.* **10.** *Colloq.* first-rate; very good; splendid: *to have a grand time, grand weather.* **11.** *Music.* **a.** written on a large scale or for a large ensemble: *a grand fugue.* **b.** applied to compositions which contain all the regular parts or movements in a complete form. **12.** *Genealogy.* one degree more remote in ascent or descent (used in compounds), as in *grandaunt, grandchild, etc.* [ME *graunt,* t. OF, g. L *grandis* large, full-grown, great, grand] **—grand′ly,** *adv.* **—grand′ness,** *n.* **—Syn. 4.** great, large, palatial. **—Ant. 1.** insignificant.

Grand Army of the Republic, a society, founded in 1866, composed of men who served in the U.S. army or navy during the Civil War.

grand·aunt (grănd′ănt′, -änt′), *n.* a great-aunt.

Grand Banks, an extensive shoal SE of Newfoundland: one of the world's greatest fishing grounds. ab. 300 mi. long; ab. 40,000 sq. mi. Also, **Grand Bank.**

Grand Canal, 1. a canal in E China, extending from Tientsin S to Hangchow. ab. 900 mi. **2.** a large canal in Venice, Italy, forming the main thoroughfare.

Grand Canary, Gran Canaria.

Grand Canyon, a gorge of the Colorado river in N Arizona. Over 200 mi. long; 2000 to 6000 ft. deep.

Grand Canyon National Park, a national park in N Arizona, including a part of the Grand Canyon and the area around it. 1009 sq. mi.

grand·child (grănd′chīld′), *n., pl.* **-children.** a child of one's son or daughter.

Grand Cou·lee (kōō′lē), **1.** a dry canyon in central Washington, cut by the Columbia river in the glacial period. 52 mi. long; over 400 ft. deep. **2.** a dam on the Columbia river at the N end of this canyon: the largest concrete dam in the world. 550 ft. high.

grand·daugh·ter (grănd′dô′tər), *n.* a daughter of one's son or daughter.

grand duchess, 1. the wife or widow of a grand duke. **2.** a woman who governs a grand duchy in her own right. **3.** a daughter of a czar or of a czar's son.

grand duchy, a territory ruled by a grand duke or grand duchess.

grand duke, 1. the sovereign of a territory called a grand duchy, ranking next below a king. **2.** a son of a czar or of a czar's son.

Gran·de (*Texas* rĕ′ō grän′dā, rĕ′ō gränd′; *Brazil* rĕ′ōō grän′də), *n.* **Rio.** See **Rio Grande.**

grande dame (gränd dåm′), *French.* a great lady.

gran·dee (grăn dē′), *n.* a Spanish nobleman of the highest rank. [t. Sp., Pg.: m. *grande* great (person). See GRAND]

gran·deur (grăn′jər, -jōōr), *n.* state or quality of being grand; imposing greatness; exalted rank, dignity, or importance. [t. F, der. *grand* GRAND] **—Syn.** stateliness, majesty, sublimity; pomp, splendor. state.

Grand Falls, a great waterfall of the Hamilton river, in Labrador. ab. 200 ft. wide; 316 ft. high.

grand·fa·ther (grănd′fä′thər), *n.* **1.** the father of one's father or mother. **2.** a forefather.

grandfather clause, *U.S. Hist.* a state constitutional clause disfranchising Negroes, held void in 1915.

grand·fa·ther·ly (grănd′fä′thər lĭ), *adj.* **1.** of, or in the manner of, a grandfather. **2.** indulgent; kindly.

Grand Forks, a town in E North Dakota. 34,451 (1960).

Grand Island, a city in S Nebraska. 25,742 (1960).

gran·dil·o·quence (grăn dĭl′ə kwəns), *n.* lofty speech; bombast. [f. s. L *grandiloquus* speaking loftily + -ENCE]

gran·dil·o·quent (grăn dĭl′ə kwənt), *adj.* speaking or expressed in a lofty or pompous style; bombastic. **—gran·dil′o·quent·ly,** *adv.* **—Ant.** simple, sincere.

gran·di·ose (grăn′dĭ ōs′), *adj.* **1.** grand in an imposing or impressive way. **2.** affectedly grand or stately; pompous. [t. F, t. It.: m. *grandioso,* der. L *grandis* GRAND. See -OSE¹] **—gran′di·ose′ly,** *adv.* **—gran·di·os·i·ty** (grăn′dĭ ŏs′ə tĭ),*n.*

grand jury, a jury of (usually) 12 to 23 persons designated to inquire into alleged violations of the law in order to ascertain whether the evidence is sufficient to warrant trial by a petty jury.

Grand Lama. See **Dalai Lama.**

grand larceny. See larceny.

grand·ma (grănd′mä′, grăn′mä′, grăm′ə), *n.* grandmother.

grand·mam·ma (grănd′mə mä′, -mä′mə), *n.* grandmother.

Grand Ma·nan (mə năn′), a Canadian island at the entrance to the Bay of Fundy: a part of New Brunswick; summer resort. 2457 pop. (1941); 57 sq. mi.

grand monde (grän mônd′), *French.* the fashionable world; the best society. [F: lit., the great world]

grand·moth·er (grănd′mŭth′ər), *n.* **1.** the mother of one's father or mother. **2.** an ancestress.

grand·moth·er·ly (grănd′mŭth′ər lĭ), *adj.* **1.** of or in the manner of a grandmother. **2.** like a grandmother.

Grand Mufti, the head of the Moslem Arab community in Jerusalem, long chosen from the Husseini family.

grand·neph·ew (grănd′nĕf′ū, -nĕv′ū), *n.* a son of one's nephew or niece.

grand·niece (grănd′nēs′), *n.* a daughter of one's nephew or niece.

Grand Old Party. See **G.O.P.**

grand opera, a drama interpreted by music, the text being sung throughout.

grand·pa (grănd′pä′, grăm′pä′, grăm′pə), *n.* grandfather.

grand·pa·pa (grănd′pə pä′, -pä′pə), *n.* grandfather.

grand·par·ent (grănd′pâr′ənt), *n.* a parent of a parent.

grand piano. See piano (def. 2).

Grand Pré (grän prě′), a village in central Nova Scotia, on Minas Basin: locale of Longfellow's "Evangeline."

grand prix (grän prě′), *French.* a great prize.

Grand Rapids, city in SW Michigan. 177,313 (1960).

Grand River, 1. former name of the Colorado above its junction with the Green river. ab. 350 mi. **2.** a river in SW Michigan, flowing W to Lake Michigan. 260 mi. **3.** Hamilton (def. 10).

grand·sire (grănd′sīr′), *n. Archaic.* **1.** a grandfather. **2.** a forefather. **3.** an old man.

grand·son (grănd′sŭn′), *n.* a son of one's son or daughter.

grand·stand (grănd′stănd′), *n.* the principal stand for spectators at a racecourse, athletic field, etc.

grand tour, an extended tour on the continent of Europe, esp. as the finishing course in the education of British young men of good family.

grand·un·cle (grănd′ŭng′kəl), *n.* an uncle of one's father or mother; a great-uncle.

grand vizier, the chief officer of state of various Moslem countries, as in the former Turkish Empire.

grange (grānj), *n.* **1.** a farm. **2.** *Chiefly Brit.* a country dwelling house with its various farm buildings; dwelling of a yeoman or gentleman farmer. **3.** (formerly) an outlying farmhouse with barns, etc., belonging to a feudal manor or a religious establishment, where crops and tithes in kind were stored. **4.** (*cap.*) *U.S.* a lodge or local branch of the "Patrons of Husbandry," an association for promoting the interests of agriculture. **5. the Grange,** the association itself. [ME *graunge,* t. AF, var. of OF *grange,* g. LL *grānica,* der. L *grānum* grain]

grang·er (grän′jər), *n.* **1.** a farmer. **2.** a farm steward. **3.** (*cap.*) *U.S.* a member of a Grange.

grang·er·ize (grän′jə rīz′), *v.t.,* **-ized, -izing. 1.** to augment the illustrative content of (a book) by inserting additional prints, drawings, engravings, etc., not included in the original volume. **2.** to mutilate (books) in order to get illustrative material for such a purpose. [der. J. *Granger,* whose "Biographical History of England" (1769) was arranged for such illustration]

gran·ite (grăn′ĭt), *n.* **1.** a granular igneous rock composed chiefly of feldspar (orthoclase) and quartz, usually with one or more other minerals, as mica, hornblende, etc.: much used in building, and for monuments, etc. **2.** great hardness or firmness. [t. It.: m. *granito,* orig. pp., grained, of *granire,* der. *grano,* g. L *grānum* grain] **—gran′ite·like′,** *adj.* **—gra·nit′ic,** *adj.*

Granite City, a city in SW Illinois, near St. Louis, Missouri. 40,073 (1960).

gran·ite·ware (grăn′ĭt wâr′), *n.* **1.** a kind of ironware with a gray, stonelike enamel. **2.** pottery with a speckled appearance like granite. **3.** a semivitreous white pottery somewhat harder than earthenware.

gran·it·ite (grăn′ī tīt′), *n.* a granite rich in biotite.

gra·niv·o·rous (grə nĭv′ə rəs), *adj.* feeding on grain and seeds.

Gran·jon (grän′jon), *n. Print.* a style of type originally cut by the French designer Robert Granjon.

gran·ny (grăn′ĭ), *n., pl.* **-nies.** *Colloq.* **1.** a grandmother. **2.** an old woman. **3.** a fussy person. **4.** *Southern U.S.* a nurse or midwife. **5.** granny's knot. Also, **gran′nie.**

granny's knot, *Naut.* a reef or square knot in which the second part is crossed the wrong way: derided by seamen because it is difficult to untie when jammed, yet likely to slip under strain. See illus. under **knot.**

gran·o·phyre (grăn′ə fīr′), *n.* a fine-grained or porphyritic granitic rock with a micrographic intergrowth of the minerals of the groundmass. [t. G: m. *granophyr,* f. *grano-* (comb. form of *granit* GRANITE) + (*por*)*phyr* porphyry] **—gran·o·phyr′ic,** *adj.*

grant (grănt, gränt), *v.t.* **1.** to bestow or confer, esp. by a formal act: *to grant a right.* **2.** to give or accord: *to grant permission.* **3.** to agree or accede to: *to grant a request.* **4.** to admit or concede; accept for the sake of argument: *I grant that point.* **5.** to transfer or convey, esp. by deed or writing: *to grant property.* **—n. 6.** that which is granted, as a privilege or right, a sum of money, or a tract of land. **7.** act of granting. **8.** *Law.* an instrument which conveys property. **9.** a geographical unit in Vermont, Maine, and New Hampshire, originally a grant of land to a person or group of people. [ME *grant(en),* t. AF: m. *granter* promise, authorize, confirm, approve, ult. der. L *crēdens,* ppr., of *crēdere* trust, believe] **—grant′a·ble,** *adj.* **—grant′er,** *n.* **—Syn. 2.** See give.

Grant (grănt), *n.* Ulysses Simpson, 1822–85, Union general in the Civil War and 18th president of the U.S., 1869–77.

b., blend of, blended; c., cognate with; d., dialect, dialectal; der., derived from; f., formed from; g., going back to; m., modification of; r., replacing; s., stem of; t., taken from; ?, perhaps. See the full key on inside cover.

gran-tee (grăn tē′, grän-), *n. Law.* one to whom a grant is made.

Granth (grŭnt), *n.* the sacred scripture of the Sikhs.

grant-or (grăn′tər, grän tôr′, grän-), *n. Law.* one who makes a grant.

gran-u-lar (grăn′yə lər), *adj.* **1.** of the nature of granules. **2.** composed of or bearing granules or grains. **3.** showing a granulated structure. —**gran′u-lar′-i-ty,** *n.* —**gran′u-lar-ly,** *adv.*

gran-u-late (grăn′yə lāt′), *v.,* -**lated,** -**lating.** —*v.t.* **1.** to form into granules or grains. **2.** to raise in granules; make rough on the surface. —*v.i.* **3.** to become granular. **4.** *Pathol.* to form granulation tissue. [f. GRANUL(E) + -ATE¹] —**gran′u-la′tor,** *n.*

gran-u-la-tion (grăn′yə lā′shən), *n.* **1.** act or process of granulating. **2.** granulated condition. **3.** one of the grains of a granulated surface. **4.** *Pathol.* **a.** the formation of granulation tissue, esp. in healing. **b.** granulation tissue. **5.** *Astron.* one of the small short-lived features of the solar surface which in the aggregate give it a mottled appearance when viewed with a telescope.

granulation tissue, tissue formed in ulcers and in early wound healing and repair, composed largely of newly growing capillaries and so called from its irregular surface in open wounds; proud flesh.

gran-ule (grăn′ūl), *n.* **1.** a little grain. **2.** a small particle; pellet. **3.** a corpuscle; sporule. [t. LL: m. s. *gränulum,* dim. of L *gränum* GRAIN]

gran-u-lite (grăn′yə līt′), *n. Petrog.* a metamorphic rock composed of granular minerals of uniform size, such as quartz, feldspar, or pyroxene, and showing a definite banding. —**gran-u-lit-ic** (grăn′yə līt′ĭk), *adj.*

gran-u-lo-ma (grăn′yə lō′mə), *n. Pathol.* a section of inflamed tissue characterized by the red granules which occur at the base of an ulcer. [m. L GRANUL(UM) small grain + -OMA]

gran-u-lose (grăn′yə lōs′), *n.* that portion of the starch granule acted upon by diastase and the saliva.

Gran-ville (grăn′vĭl), *n.* **John Carteret, Earl of,** 1690-1763, British statesman.

Gran-ville-Bar-ker (grăn′vĭl bär′kər), *n.* **Harley,** 1877-1946, British dramatist, actor, and critic.

grape (grāp), *n.* **1.** the edible, pulpy, smooth-skinned berry or fruit which grows in clusters on vines of the genus *Vitis,* and from which wine is made. **2.** any vine bearing this fruit. **3.** dull, dark purplish-red. **4.** (*pl.*) *Vet. Sci.* a morbid growth on the fetlock of a horse, resembling a bunch of grapes. **5.** *Archaic.* grapeshot. [ME, t. OF, var. of *crape* cluster of fruit or flowers, orig. hook; of Gmc. orig. (cf. G *krapf* hook). Cf. GRAPNEL, GRAPPLE] —**grape′less,** *adj.* —**grape′like′,** *adj.*

grape-fruit (grāp′frōōt′), *n.* **1.** a large, roundish, yellow-skinned edible citrus fruit with a juicy, acid pulp, grown mainly in the U. S. **2.** the tropical or semitropical rutaceous tree, *Citrus paradisi,* yielding it.

grape hyacinth, any plant of the liliaceous genus *Muscari,* as *M. botryoides,* a species whose globular blue flowers resemble tiny grapes.

grap-er-y (grā′pə rĭ), *n., pl.* -**eries. 1.** a building where grapes are grown. **2.** a plantation of grapevines.

grape-shot (grāp′shŏt′), *n. Archaic.* a cluster of small cast-iron balls used as a charge for a cannon.

grape sugar, dextrose.

grape-vine (grāp′vīn′), *n.* **1.** a vine that bears grapes. **2.** *U.S. Colloq.* **a.** Also, **grapevine telegraph.** a person-to-person method of relaying secret reports which cannot be had through regular channels. **b.** an unauthenticated report.

graph (grăf, gräf), *n.* **1.** a diagram representing a system of connections or interrelations among two or more things by a number of distinctive dots, lines, bars, etc. **2.** *Math.* a curve as representing a given function. —*v.t.* **3.** to draw (a curve) as representing a given function. [short for *graphic formula.* See GRAPHIC] —**Syn. 1.** See map.

graph-, var. of **grapho-** before vowels.

-graph, a word element meaning: **1.** drawn or written, as in *autograph.* **2.** something drawn or written, as in *lithograph, monograph.* **3.** an apparatus for drawing, writing, recording, etc., as in *phonograph.* [t. Gk.: s. *-graphos* (something) drawn or written, also one who draws or writes. See GRAPHIC]

graph-ic (grăf′ĭk), *adj.* **1.** lifelike; vivid: *a graphic description of a scene.* **2.** pertaining to the use of diagrams, graphs, mathematical curves, or the like; diagrammatic. **3.** pertaining to writing: *graphic symbols.* **4.** *Geol.* possessing that kind of texture produced

in a rock when certain constituents crystallize in such a way as to appear like written characters on the surfaces or sections of the rock. **5.** *Math.* pertaining to the determination of values, solving of problems, etc., by direct measurement on diagrams instead of by ordinary calculations. **6.** of the graphic arts. Also, **graph′i-cal.** [t. L: s. *graphicus,* t. Gk.: m. *graphikós,* der. *graphē* drawing, writing] —**graph′i-cal-ly, graph′ic-ly,** *adv.* —**graph′i-cal-ness,** *n.* —**Syn. 1.** See picturesque.

graphic accent, *Gram.* **1.** any mark written above a letter, esp. one indicating stress in pronunciation, as in Spanish *rápido.* **2.** any of the written or printed signs used as diacritics to indicate an accent, esp. the acute accent used to mark stress.

graphic arts, drawing, engraving, etching, painting, and other arts involving the use of lines and strokes to express or convey ideas in terms of forms.

graph-ics (grăf′ĭks), *n.* **1.** the art of drawing, esp. as concerned with mathematics, engineering, etc. **2.** the science of calculating by diagrams. [f. GRAPH + -ICS]

graph-ite (grăf′īt), *n.* a very common mineral, soft native carbon, occurring in black to dark-gray foliated masses with metallic luster and greasy feel: used in "lead" pencils, as a lubricant, for making crucibles and other refractories, etc.; plumbago; black lead. [t. G: m. *graphit,* f. s. Gk. *gráphein* mark, draw, write + -*it* -ITE¹] —**gra-phit-ic** (grə fĭt′ĭk), *adj.*

graph-i-tize (grăf′ə tīz′), *v.t.,* -**tized,** -**tizing. 1.** to convert into graphite. **2.** to cover (the surface of an object) with graphite. —**graph′i-ti-za′tion,** *n.*

grapho-, a word element meaning "writing," as in *graphology.* Also, **graph-.** [t. Gk., comb. form of *graphē*]

graph-ol-o-gy (grǎ fŏl′ə jĭ), *n.* the study of handwriting, esp. as regarded as an expression of the writer's character. —**graph-ol′o-gist,** *n.*

graph-o-ma-ni-a (grăf′ə mā′nĭ ə), *n.* a mania for writing.

graph-o-mo-tor (grăf′ō mō′tər), *adj. Med.* pertaining to the muscular movements in writing.

-graphy, a combining form denoting some process or form of drawing, representing, writing, recording, describing, etc., or an art or science concerned with some such thing, as in *biography, choreography, geography, orthography, photography.* [t. Gk.: m.s. *graphia,* der. *gráphos.* See -GRAPH, Y³]

grap-nel (grăp′nəl), *n.* **1.** a device consisting essentially of one or more hooks or clamps, for grasping or holding something; a grapple; grappling iron. **2.** a small anchor with three or more flukes. Also, *Naut.,* **grap-lin** (grăp′lĭn), **grap′line.** [ME *grapenel,* dim. of OF *grapin* kind of hook, dim. of *grape* hook. See GRAPE]

Grapnel (def. 2)

grap-ple (grăp′əl), *n., v.,* -**pled,** -**pling.** —*n.* **1.** a hook or an iron instrument by which one thing, as a ship, fastens on another; a grapnel. **2.** a seizing or gripping. **3.** a grip or close hold in wrestling or hand-to-hand fighting. —*v.t.* **4.** to seize, hold, or fasten with or as with a grapple. **5.** to engage in a struggle or close encounter with. —*v.i.* **6.** to hold or make fast to something as with a grapple. **7.** to use a grapple. **8.** to seize another, or each other, in a firm grip, as in wrestling; clinch. **9.** to try to overcome or deal (fol. by *with*): *to grapple with a problem.* [appar. a freq. of OE *gegræppian* seize, assoc. with, grapnel] —**grap′pler,** *n.*

grap-pling (grăp′lĭng), *n.* **1.** that by which anything is seized and held. **2.** a grapnel.

grappling iron, a grapnel. Also, **grappling hook.**

grap-y (grā′pĭ), *adj.* of, like, or composed of grapes.

Gras-mere (grăs′mĭr, gräs′-), *n.* **1.** a lake in NW England, in Westmoreland. 1 mi. long. **2.** a village on this lake: Wordsworth's home, 1799-1808.

grasp (grăsp, gräsp), *v.t.* **1.** to seize and hold by or as by clasping with the fingers. **2.** to seize upon; hold firmly. **3.** to lay hold of with the mind; comprehend; understand. —*v.i.* **4.** to make the motion of seizing; seize something firmly or eagerly. **5.** to catch at; try to seize (fol. by *at*): *a drowning man grasps at a straw.* —*n.* **6.** a grasping or gripping; grip of the hand. **7.** power of seizing and holding; reach: *to have a thing within one's grasp.* **8.** hold, possession, or mastery: *to wrest power from the grasp of a usurper.* **9.** mental hold or comprehension: *a subject beyond one's grasp.* **10.** broad or thorough comprehension: *a good grasp of a subject.* [ME *graspen, grapsen* c. LG *grapsen* seize] —**grasp′a-ble,** *adj.* —**grasp′er,** *n.*

—**Syn. 1.** grip, clutch; grab. See **catch. 6, 9.** GRASP, REACH refer to the power of seizing, either concretely or figuratively. GRASP suggests actually seizing and closing the hand upon something (or figuratively thoroughly comprehending something) and therefore refers to something within one's possession or immediate possibility of possession: *a good grasp of a problem, immense mental grasp.* REACH suggests a stretching out of (usually) the hand to touch, strike, or if possible, seize something; it therefore refers to a potentiality of possession which requires an effort. Figuratively, it implies perhaps a faint conception of something still too far beyond one to be definitely and clearly understood. —**Ant. 1.** release.

grasp-ing (grăs′pĭng, gräs′-), *adj.* **1.** that grasps. **2.** greedy. —**grasp′ing-ly,** *adv.* —**grasp′ing-ness,** *n.*

Line graph

Bar graph

(Y-axis: POPULATION, 5,000 / 10,000 / 15,000 / 20,000 / 25,000; X-axis: YEAR, 1900 / 1910 / 1920 / 1930 / 1940)

grass (grås, gräs), *n.* **1.** any plant of the family *Gramineae* (or *Poaceae*), characterized by jointed stems, sheathing leaves, flower spikelets, and fruit consisting of a seedlike grain or caryopsis (**true grasses**). **2.** herbage in general, or the plants on which grazing animals pasture or which are cut and dried as hay. **3.** the grass-covered ground. **4.** pasture: *half of the farm is grass, to put animals to grass.* **5.** (*pl.*) stalks or sprays of grass: *filled with dried grasses.* **6.** the season of the new growth of grass. —*v.i.* **7.** to cover with grass or turf. **8.** to feed with growing grass; pasture. **9.** to lay on the grass, as for the purpose of bleaching. —*v.i.* **10.** to feed on growing grass; graze. **11.** to produce grass; become covered with grass. [ME *gras*, OE *græs*, c. D, G, Icel. and Goth. *gras*; akin to GROW and GREEN] —**grass/less,** *adj.* —**grass/like/,** *adj.*

Grasse (gräs), *n.* **1.** Francois Joseph Paul, Count de (frän swà/ zhò zěf/ pôl), (*Marquis de Grasse-Tilly*) 1722–1788, French admiral. **2.** a city in S France, near the coast; tourist center; perfume industry. 22,187 (1954).

grass finch, 1. the vesper sparrow, *Poœcetes gramineus,* of North America. **2.** any of various Australian weaverbirds, esp. of the genus *Poëphila.*

grass-green (grås/grēn/, gräs/-), *adj.* yellowish-green.

grass·hop·per (grås/hŏp/ər, gräs/-), *n.* any of numerous orthopterous insects which are terrestrial, herbivorous, and have their hind legs fitted for leaping. Many are very destructive to vegetation, as the locusts, certain katydids, etc.

Red-legged grasshopper, *Melanoplus femur-rubrum*

grass·land (grås/lǎnd/, gräs/-), *n.* an area in which the natural vegetation consists largely of perennial grasses, whereas trees are either limited to stream valleys or are widely spotted, characteristic of subhumid and semiarid climates.

grass-of-Par·nas·sus (grås/əv pär nǎs/əs, gräs/-), *n.* any of the genus *Parnassia* (family *Saxifragaceae* or *Parnassiaceae*) of perennials of marshy areas, having broad, smooth leaves and single pale flowers.

grass·quit (grås/kwĭt/, gräs/-), *n.* any of several small fringilline birds, esp. of the genus *Tiaris,* as the **melodious grassquit,** *Tiaris canora,* of Cuba.

grass-roots (grås/rōōts/, -rŏŏts/, gräs/-), *adj.* *U.S. Colloq.* close to, or emerging spontaneously from, the people.

grass snipe, the pectoral sandpiper.

grass tree, 1. any member of the Australian liliaceous genus *Xanthorrhoea,* comprising plants with a stout woody stem bearing a tuft of long grasslike leaves and a dense flower spike. **2.** any of various similar plants of Australasia.

grass widow, a woman who is separated, divorced, or lives apart from her husband.

grass widower, a man who is separated, divorced, or lives apart from his wife.

grass·y (grås/ĭ, gräs/ĭ), *adj.,* **grassier, grassiest. 1.** covered with grass. **2.** pertaining to or consisting of grass; grasslike. —**grass/i·ness,** *n.*

grate[1] (grāt), *n., v.,* **grated, grating.** —*n.* **1.** a frame of metal bars for holding fuel when burning, as in a fireplace or furnace. **2.** a framework of parallel or crossed bars used as a partition, guard, cover, or the like. **3.** a fireplace. —*v.t.* **4.** to furnish with a grate or grates. [ME, ult. t. It., g. L *crātis* wickerwork, hurdle. Cf. CRATE] —**grate/less,** *adj.* —**grate/like/,** *adj.*

grate[2] (grāt), *v.,* **grated, grating.** —*v.i.* **1.** to have an irritating or unpleasant effect on the feelings. **2.** to make a sound of rough scraping. **3.** to sound harshly; jar: *to grate on the ear.* **4.** to scrape or rub with rough or noisy friction, as one thing on or against another. —*v.t.* **5.** to rub together with a harsh, jarring sound: *to grate the teeth.* **6.** to reduce to small particles by rubbing against a rough surface or a surface with many sharp-edged openings: *to grate a nutmeg.* **7.** *Archaic.* to wear down or away by rough friction. [ME, t. OF: m. *grater*; of Gmc. orig. (cf. G *kratzen* scratch)] —**grat/er,** *n.* —**grat/ing,** *adj.* —**grat/ing·ly,** *adv.*

grate·ful (grāt/fəl), *adj.* **1.** warmly or deeply appreciative of kindness or benefits received; thankful: *I am grateful to you for your kindness.* **2.** actuated by or betokening gratitude: *a grateful letter.* **3.** pleasing to the mind or senses; agreeable or welcome; refreshing: *grateful slumber.* [f. obs. *grate* pleasing, thankful (t. L: m.s. *grātus*) +-FUL] —**grate/ful·ly,** *adv.* —**grate/ful·ness,** *n.* —**Syn. 1.** GRATEFUL, THANKFUL describe an appreciative attitude for what one has received. GRATEFUL indicates a warm or deep appreciation of personal kindness as shown to one: *grateful for favors. grateful to one's neighbors for help in time of trouble.* THANKFUL indicates a disposition to express gratitude by giving thanks, as to a benefactor or to a merciful Providence; there is often a sense of deliverance as well as of appreciation: *thankful that one's life was spared in an accident, thankful for the comfort of one's general situation.*

Gra·ti·an (grā/shĭ ən, -shən), *n.* (*Flavius Gratianus*) A.D. 359–383, Roman emperor, A.D. 375–383.

grat·i·fi·ca·tion (grăt/əfəkā/shən), *n.* **1.** state of being gratified; great satisfaction. **2.** something that gratifies; source of pleasure or satisfaction. **3.** act of gratifying. **4.** *Archaic.* a reward, recompense, or gratuity.

grat·i·fy (grăt/əfī/), *v.t.,* **-fied, -fying. 1.** to give pleasure to (persons) by satisfying desires or humoring inclinations or feelings. **2.** to satisfy; indulge; humor: *to gratify desires or appetites.* **3.** *Obs.* to reward; remuner-

ate. [t. F: m. s. *gratifier,* t. L: m. *grātificārī* do a favor to, oblige, gratify] —**grat/i·fi/er,** *n.* —**Syn. 1.** See humor.

gra·ti·fy·ing (grăt/əfī/ĭng), *adj.* that gratifies; pleasing; satisfying. —**grat/i·fy/ing·ly,** *adv.* —**Syn.** See interesting.

grat·in (grăt/ăn; *Fr.* grà tăn/), *n.* See au gratin. [F, der. *gratter,* earlier *grater* scrape. See GRATE[2]]

grat·ing (grā/tĭng), *n.* **1.** a partition or frame of parallel or crossing bars; open latticework of wood or metal serving as a cover or guard, but admitting light, air, etc. **2.** *Physics.* a diffraction grating.

gra·tis (grā/tĭs, grăt/ĭs), *adv.* **1.** for nothing; gratuitously. —*adj.* **2.** free of cost; gratuitous. [t. L]

grat·i·tude (grăt/ə tūd/, -tōōd/), *n.* quality or feeling of being grateful or thankful. [t. LL: m. *grătitūdo,* der. L *grātus* pleasing, thankful]

Grat·tan (grăt/ən), *n.* Henry, 1746–1820, Irish statesman and orator.

grat·toir (grà twär/; *Fr.* grà twàr/), *n.* *Archaeol.* a chipped stone implement used for working wood or leather; scraper. [t. F, der. *gratter* scrape]

gra·tu·i·tous (grə tū/ə təs, -tōō/-), *adj.* **1.** freely bestowed or obtained; free. **2.** being without reason, cause, or justification: *a gratuitous insult.* **3.** *Law.* given without receiving any return value. [t. L: m. *grātuītus* free, spontaneous] —**gra·tu/i·tous·ly,** *adv.* —**gra·tu/i·tous·ness,** *n.*

gra·tu·i·ty (grə tū/ə tĭ, -tōō/-), *n., pl.* **-ties. 1.** a gift of money, over and above payment due for service; tip. **2.** that which is given without claim or demand. **3.** *Chiefly Brit.* a bounty given to soldiers.

grat·u·late (grăch/əlāt/), *v.,* **-lated, -lating.** *Obs.* or *Archaic.* —*v.t.* **1.** to hail with joy; express joy at. **2.** to congratulate. —*v.i.* **3.** to express joy. [t. L: m.s. *grătulātus,* pp., having expressed joy, congratulated, or thanked] —**grat·u·la·to·ry** (grăch/ələ tōr/ĭ), *adj.*

grat·u·la·tion (grăch/əlā/shən), *n.* *Archaic.* **1.** a feeling of joy. **2.** the expression of joy.

Grau·bün·den (grou/byn/dən), *n.* German name of Grisons.

grau·pel (grou/pəl), *n.* a snow pellet. [t. G]

gra·va·men (grə vā/měn), *n., pl.* **-vamina** (-văm/ĭ nə). *Law.* **1.** that part of an accusation which weighs most heavily against the accused; the burden or substantial part of a charge or complaint. **2.** a grievance. [t. LL, der. L *gravāre* load, weigh down. Cf. GRIEVE]

grave[1] (grāv), *n.* **1.** an excavation made in the earth to receive a dead body in burial. **2.** any place of interment; a tomb or sepulcher. **3.** any place that becomes the receptacle of what is dead, lost, or past: *the grave of dead reputations.* **4.** death: *O grave, where is thy victory?* [ME; OE *græf,* c. G *grab.* See GRAVE[3]]

grave[2] (grāv), *adj.,* **graver, gravest.** *n.* —*adj.* **1.** dignified; sedate; serious; earnest; solemn: *a grave person, grave thoughts, grave ceremonies.* **2.** weighty, momentous, or important: *grave responsibilities.* **3.** important or critical; involving serious issues: *a grave situation.* **4.** *Phonet.* **a.** unaccented. **b.** spoken on a low pitch or falling pitch because of musical accent. **c.** noting or having a particular accent (`) indicating orig. a comparatively low pitch (as in ancient Greek); later, quality of sound (as in the French *père*), distinct syllabic value (as in *beloved*), etc. **5.** *Rare.* (of colors) dull; somber. —*n.* **6.** the grave accent. [t. F, t. L: m.s. *gravis* heavy] —**grave/ly,** *adv.* —**grave/ness,** *n.* —**Syn. 1.** GRAVE, SOBER, SOLEMN refer to the condition of being serious in demeanor or appearance. GRAVE indicates a weighty dignity, or the character, aspect, demeanor, speech, etc., of one conscious of heavy responsibilities or cares, or of threatening possibilities: *the jury looked grave while studying the evidence.* SOBER (from its original sense of freedom from intoxication, and hence temperate, staid, sedate) has come to indicate absence of levity, gaiety, or mirth, and thus to be akin to serious and grave: *as sober as a judge, a sober expression on one's face.* SOLEMN implies an impressive seriousness and deep earnestness: *the minister's voice was solemn as he announced the text.* —**Ant. 1.** gay, frivolous.

grave[3] (grāv), *v.t.,* **graved, graved or graven, graving. 1.** to incise or engrave. **2.** to impress deeply: *graven on the mind.* [ME *grave(n),* OE *grafan,* c. G *graben.* Cf. GRAVE, GROOVE, and GRAVURE] —**grav/er,** *n.*

grave[4] (grāv), *v.t.,* **graved, graving.** *Naut.* to clean (a ship's bottom or a ship) by burning or scraping off accretions and paving it over with pitch. [orig. obscure]

gra·ve[5] (grä/vě), *Music.* —*adj.* **1.** slow; solemn. —*adv.* **2.** slowly; solemnly. [It., g. L *gravis* GRAVE[2]]

grave-clothes (grāv/klōz/, -klōthz/), *n.pl.* the clothes in which a dead body is interred; cerements.

grav·el (grăv/əl), *n., v.,* **-eled, -eling** or (*esp. Brit.*) **-elled, -elling.** —*n.* **1.** small stones and pebbles, or a mixture of these with sand. **2.** *Pathol.* **a.** multiple small calculi formed in the kidneys. **b.** the disease characterized by such concretions. —*v.t.* **3.** to cover with gravel. **4.** to bring to a standstill from perplexity; puzzle. **5.** *U.S. Colloq.* to be a cause of irritation to. **6.** *Obs.* to run (a vessel) aground, as on a beach. [ME, t. OF: m. *gravele,* dim. of *grave* sandy shore; of Celtic orig.]

grav·el-blind (grăv/əl blīnd/), *adj.* more blind or dim-sighted than sand-blind and less than stone-blind.

grav·el·ly (grăv/ə lĭ), *adj.* **1.** abounding in gravel. **2.** consisting of or resembling gravel.

gra·ve·men·te (grä/vě měn/tě), *adv.* *Italian.* gravely.

grav·en (grā/vən), *v.* **1.** pp. of **grave**[3]. —*adj.* **2.** deeply impressed; firmly fixed. **3.** *Archaic.* carved; engraved.

Gra·ven·ha·ge (sкнrä′vən hä′кнə), *n.* **'s,** Dutch name of The Hague.

graven image, an idol.

Gra·ven·stein (grä′vən stīn′, gräv′ən stēn′), *n.* a large yellowish-red apple maturing in the autumn. [named after *Gravenstein* in Holstein, Germany]

grav·er (grā′vər), *n.* 1. any of various tools for chasing, engraving, etc., as a burin. 2. *Archaic.* an engraver.

Graves (grävz), *n.* Robert Ranke (räng′kə), born 1895, British poet, novelist, and critic.

Graves (grävz, grävz; *Fr.* grâv), *n.pl.* a class of red and white Bordeaux wines, esp. the white.

Graves' disease (grävz), *Pathol.* a disease characterized by an enlarged thyroid, rapid pulse, and increased basal metabolism due to excessive thyroid secretion. [named after R. J. *Graves,* 1796–1853, Irish physician]

Graves·end (grävz/end′), *n.* a seaport in SE England, in Kent, on the Thames. 45,043 (1951).

grave·stone (grāv′stōn′), *n.* a stone marking a grave.

grave·yard (grāv′yärd′), *n.* cemetery; burial ground.

grav·id (grav′ĭd), *adj.* pregnant. [t. L: s. *gravidus*] **—gra·vid·i·ty** (grə vĭd′ə tĭ), *n.*

grav·i·met·ric (grăv′ə mĕt′rĭk), *adj.* 1. of or pertaining to measurement by weight. 2. *Chem.* denoting a method of analyzing compound bodies by finding the weight of their elements (opposed to *volumetric*). Also, **grav′i·met′ri·cal. —grav′i·met′ri·cal·ly,** *adv.*

gra·vim·e·try (grə vĭm′ə trĭ), *n.* the measurement of weight or density. [f. L *gravi*(s) heavy + -METRY]

grav·ing dock (grā′vĭng), a dry dock.

grav·i·tate (grăv′ə tāt′), *v.i.,* **-tated, -tating.** 1. to move or tend to move under the influence of gravitational force. 2. to tend toward the lowest level; sink; fall. 3. to have a natural tendency or be strongly attracted (fol. by *to* or *toward*). [t. NL: s. *gravitātus,* pp., der. L *gravis* heavy]

grav·i·ta·tion (grăv′ə tā′shən), *n.* 1. *Physics.* **a.** that force of attraction between all particles or bodies, or that acceleration of one toward another, of which the fall of bodies to the earth is an instance. **b.** an act or process caused by this force. 2. a sinking or falling. 3. natural tendency toward some point or object of influence: *the gravitation of people toward suburbs.* **—grav′i·ta′tion·al,** *adj.* **—grav′i·ta′tion·al·ly,** *adv.*

grav·i·ta·tive (grăv′ə tā′tĭv), *adj.* 1. of or pertaining to gravitation. 2. tending or causing to gravitate.

grav·i·ty (grăv′ə tĭ), *n., pl.* **-ties.** 1. the force of attraction by which terrestrial bodies tend to fall toward the center of the earth. 2. heaviness or weight: *the center of gravity, specific gravity.* 3. gravitation in general. 4. seriousness; dignity; solemnity: *to preserve one's gravity.* 5. serious or critical character: *the gravity of the situation.* 6. lowness in pitch, as of sounds. [t. L: m.s. *gravitas* heaviness]

gravity fault, *Geol.* a fault along an inclined plane in which the upper side or hanging wall appears to have moved downward with respect to the lower side or footwall (opposed to *thrust fault*).

gra·vure (grə vyŏŏr′, grā′vyər), *n.* 1. a process of photomechanical printing, such as photogravure or rotogravure. 2. a plate or print produced by gravure. 3. the metal or wooden plate used in photogravure. [t. F: engraving, der. *graver* engrave, t. Gmc.; cf. GRAVE³]

gra·vy (grā′vĭ), *n., pl.* **-vies.** the fat and juices that drip from cooking meat, often made into a dressing for meat, etc. [ME *grave,* t. OF: kind of dressing]

gravy boat, a small boat-shaped (or other) vessel for serving gravy or sauce.

gray (grā), *adj.* 1. of a color between white and black, having no definite hue; ash-colored; technically, of an achromatic color. 2. dark, dismal, or gloomy. 3. gray-haired. 4. pertaining to old age; mature. 5. old or ancient. **—n.** 6. any achromatic color; any color with zero chroma from white to black. 7. something of this color. 8. gray material or clothing: *to dress in gray.* 9. an unbleached and undyed condition. **—v.t., v.i.** 10. to make or become gray. Also, *esp. Brit.,* **grey.** [ME; OE *grǣg,* c. G *grau*] **—gray′ly,** *adv.* **—gray′ness,** *n.*

Gray (grā), *n.* 1. Asa (ā′sə), 1810–88, U.S. botanist. 2. Thomas, 1716–71, British poet.

gray·back (grā′băk′), *n.* 1. any of various animals, as a bird, the knot *Tringa canutus,* and a whale, *Rhachianectes glaucus,* of the northern Pacific. 2. *U.S. Colloq.* a Confederate soldier. Also, *Brit.,* **grey′back′.**

gray·beard (grā′bîrd′), *n.* a man whose beard is gray; old man; sage. Also, *Brit.,* **grey′beard′.**

gray duck, any of several ducks in which certain immature or female plumages are predominantly gray, as the gadwall, *Anas strepera,* and the pintail, *A. acuta.* Also, *Brit.,* **grey duck.**

gray·fish (grā′fĭsh′), *n., pl.* **-fishes,** (*esp. collectively*) **-fish** a market name for several American sharks, esp. the dogfish (genus *Squalus*) and fishes of the genera *Cynias, Mustelus,* and related genera, often sold for food.

Gray Friar, a Franciscan friar.

gray-head·ed (grā′hĕd′ĭd), *adj.* 1. having gray hair. 2. of or pertaining to old age or old men. 3. old. Also, *Brit.,* **grey′-head′ed.**

gray·hound (grā′hound′), *n.* greyhound.

gray·ish (grā′ĭsh), *adj.* having a tinge of gray: *the sky was full of dark grayish clouds.* Also, *esp. Brit.,* **greyish.**

gray·lag (grā′lăg′), *n.* the common gray wild goose, *Anser anser,* of Europe. Also, *Brit.,* **grey′lag′.**

gray·ling (grā′lĭng), *n.* 1. any of the fresh-water fishes constituting the genus *Thymallus,* allied to the trout, but having a longer and higher dorsal fin of resplendent color. 2. any of certain somber gray moths of the family *Satyridae.*

gray matter, 1. *Anat.* nervous tissue, esp of the brain and spinal cord, containing both fibers and nerve cells, and of a dark reddish-gray color. 2. *Colloq.* brains or intellect.

gray plover, a large plover, *Squatarola squatarola,* of both the New and the Old World, called "gray plover" in Europe because it is gray in winter plumage, "black-bellied plover" in America because of the strikingly black under parts of the breeding plumage.

Gray's Inn (grāz), *Brit.* See Inns of Court.

Gray·son (grā′sən), *n.* David, pen name of Ray Stannard Baker.

gray squirrel, a gray American squirrel, *Sciurus carolinensis,* common in city parks.

gray·wacke (grā′wăk′, -wăk′ə), *n.* *Geol.* a dark-colored sandstone or grit, containing fragments of various rocks such as slate and schist. Also, *Brit.,* **grey′-wacke/.** [half trans., half adoption of G *grauwacke.* See WACKE]

Graz (gräts), *n.* a city in SE Austria. 226,453 (1951).

graze¹ (grāz), *v.,* **grazed, grazing. —v.i.** 1. to feed on growing herbage, as cattle, sheep, etc., do. **—v.t.** 2. to feed on (growing grass). 3. to put cattle, sheep, etc., to feed on (grass, lands, etc.). 4. to tend (cattle, sheep, etc.) while at pasture. [ME *grase*(n), OE *grasian,* der. *grӕs* GRASS] **—graz′er,** *n.*

graze² (grāz), *v.,* **grazed, grazing, n. —v.t.** 1. to touch or rub lightly in passing. 2. to scrape the skin from; abrade. **—v.i.** 3. to touch or rub something lightly, or so as to produce slight abrasion, in passing. **—n.** 4. a grazing; a touching or rubbing lightly in passing. 5. a slight scratch in passing; abrasion. [orig. uncert.]

gra·zier (grā′zhər), *n.* *Chiefly Brit.* one who grazes cattle for the market.

graz·ing (grā′zĭng), *n.* pasture land; a pasture.

Gr. Br., Great Britain. Also, **Gr. Brit.**

grease (*n.* grēs; *v.* grēs, grēz), *n., v.,* **greased, greasing. —n.** 1. the melted or rendered fat of animals, esp. when in a soft state. 2. fatty or oily matter in general; lubricant. 3. Also, **grease wool.** wool, as shorn, before being cleansed of the oily matter. 4. *Vet. Sci.* inflammation of a horse's skin in the fetlock region, attended with an oily secretion. **—v.t.** 5. to put grease on; lubricate: *he greased the axle but it did no good.* 6. to smear with grease. 7. to cause to run easily. 8. *Slang.* to bribe. [ME *grese,* t. OF: m. *graisse,* g. L *crassus* fat] **—grease′-less,** *adj.* **—greas′er,** *n.*

grease paint, 1. a mixture of tallow or hard grease and a pigment, used by actors for painting their faces. 2. theatrical make-up.

grease·wood (grēs′wŏŏd′), *n.* 1. a chenopodiaceous shrub, *Sarcobatus vermiculatus,* of the alkaline regions of the western U.S., containing a small amount of oil and used for fuel. 2. any of various similar shrubs. Also, **grease-bush** (grēs′bŏŏsh′).

greas·y (grē′sĭ, -zĭ), *adj.,* **greasier, greasiest. 1.** smeared or soiled with grease. 2. composed of or containing grease; oily: *greasy food.* 3. greaselike in appearance or to the touch; slippery. 4. *Vet. Sci.* affected with grease. **—greas′i·ly,** *adv.* **—greas′i·ness,** *n.*

great (grāt), *adj.* 1. unusually or comparatively large in size or dimensions: *a great house, lake, or fire.* 2. large in number; numerous: *a great many, in great detail.* 3. unusual or considerable in degree: *great pain.* 4. notable or remarkable: *a great occasion.* 5. distinguished; famous: *Alexander the Great.* 6. of much consequence; important: *great issues.* 7. chief or principal: *the great seal.* 8. of high rank, official position, or social standing: *a great noble.* 9. of noble or lofty character: *great thoughts.* 10. much in use or favor: "*humor*" *was a great word with the old physiologists.* 11. being such in an extreme degree: *great friends, a great talker.* 12. of extraordinary powers; having unusual merit; very admirable: *a great statesman.* 13. *Colloq.* much addicted; skillful or expert (fol. by *to* or *at*). 14. *Colloq.* first-rate; very good; fine: *we had a great time.* 15. one degree more remote in direct ascent or descent than a specified relationship: *great-grandfather.* 16. *Archaic.* pregnant. [ME *greet,* OE *grēat,* c. D *groot,* G *gross*] **—great′ness,** *n.*

—Syn. 1. immense, enormous, gigantic. GREAT, BIG, LARGE refer to size, extent, and degree. In reference to the size and extent of concrete objects, BIG is the most general and most colloquial word, LARGE is somewhat more formal, and GREAT is highly formal and even poetic, suggesting also that the object is notable or imposing: *a big tree, a large tree, a great oak; a big field, a large field, great plains.* When the reference is to degree or a quality, GREAT is the usual word: *great beauty, great mistake, great surprise,* though BIG sometimes alternates with it in colloquial style: *a big mistake, a big surprise;* LARGE is not used in reference to degree, but may be used in a quantitative reference: *a large number* (*great number*). 5. eminent, renowned, illustrious. 6. weighty, serious, momentous. **—Ant.** 1. little, small.

great auk, a large, flightless sea bird, *Plautus impennis,* of the North Atlantic, now extinct.

great-aunt (grāt/ănt′, -änt′), *n.* a father's or mother's aunt; a grandaunt.

Great Australian Bight, a wide, open bay in S Australia.

Great Barrier Reef, a coral reef parallel to the coast of Queensland, in NE Australia. ab. 1250 mi. long.

Great Basin, a region without drainage to the ocean, in the W United States, including most of Nevada and parts of Utah, California, Oregon, and Idaho. ab. 210,-000 sq. mi.

Great Bear, *Astron.* Ursa Major.

Great Bear Lake, a large lake in NW Canada, in the Northwest Territories. ab. 11,800 sq. mi.

Great Britain, an island of NW Europe, separated from the mainland by the English Channel and the North Sea: since 1707 the name has applied politically to England, Scotland, and Wales. 50,753,600 pop. (est. 1953); 88,139 sq. mi. See **United Kingdom.**

great circle, 1. a circle on a sphere the plane of which passes through the center of the sphere. Cf. **small circle.** 2. the line of shortest distance between two points on the surface of the earth.

great-circle sailing, navigation along a great circle of the earth, usually by a series of rhumb lines.

great·coat (grāt/kōt′), *n. Chiefly Brit.* a heavy overcoat.

Great Dane, one of a breed of large, powerful, short-haired dogs, somewhat resembling the mastiff.

Great Dane
(30 in. or more high
at the shoulder)

Great Divide, 1. the continental divide of North America: the Rocky Mountains. 2. any similar continental divide. 3. separation between life and death: *across the Great Divide.* 4. a crucial stage; crisis.

Great Dog. See **dog** (def. 7).

great·en (grā/tən), *Archaic.* —*v t.* 1. to make greater; enlarge; increase. —*v.i.* 2. to become greater.

Greater Antilles. See **Antilles.**

greater yellowlegs, a large American shore bird, *Totanus melanoleucus,* with bright yellow legs and feet.

greatest common divisor. See **common divisor.**

Great Falls, a city in central Montana, on the Missouri. 55,357 (1960).

great-grand·child (grāt/grănd′chīld′), *n., pl.* **-children.** a grandchild of one's son or daughter.

great-grand·daugh·ter (grāt/grănd′dô/tər), *n.* a granddaughter of one's son or daughter.

great-grand·fa·ther (grāt/grănd′fä/ᵗħər), *n.* a parent's grandfather.

great-grand·moth·er (grāt/grănd′mŭᵗħ/ər), *n.* a parent's grandmother.

great-grand·par·ent (grāt/grănd′pâr/ənt), *n.* a grandfather or grandmother of one's father or mother.

great-grand·son (grāt/grănd′sŭn′), *n.* a son's or daughter's grandson.

great-heart·ed (grāt/här/tĭd), *adj.* 1. having or showing a generous heart; magnanimous. 2. highspirited; courageous; fearless. —**great/-heart′ed·ness,** *n.*

great horned owl, a large, rapacious, American owl, *Bubo virginianus,* found from the tree limit in the north southward into South America.

Great Lakes, a series of five large lakes between the United States and Canada, connected with the Atlantic by the St. Lawrence: Lakes Erie, Huron, Michigan, Ontario, and Superior.

great·ly (grāt/lĭ), *adv.* 1. in or to a great degree; much. 2. in a great manner.

Great Mogul, 1. an emperor of the Mongol or Mogul empire of India, which flourished 1526 to 1761 and continued nominally until 1857. 2. *(l.c.)* an important or distinguished person.

great-neph·ew (grāt/nĕf′ū, -nĕv′ū), *n.* a grandnephew; nephew's or niece's son.

great-niece (grāt/nēs′), *n.* a grandniece; nephew's or niece's daughter.

Great Plains, a semiarid region E of the Rocky Mountains in the United States and Canada.

great rhododendron, the tall pink- or whiteflowering rhododendron, *Rhododendron maximum,* common in the eastern U.S. Also, **great rosebay.**

Great Russians, the main stock of the Russian people, dwelling chiefly in the northern and central parts of the Soviet Union in Europe.

greats (grāts), *n.pl. Brit. Colloq.* 1. the course in classics or *Literae Humaniores* at Oxford University. 2. the final examination for the B.A. in this subject.

Great Salt Lake, a shallow salt lake in NW Utah. ab. 2300 sq. mi.; ab. 80 mi. long; maximum depth, 60 ft.

great seal, 1. the principal seal of a government or state. 2. *(caps.) Brit.* the keeper of the great seal, the Lord Chancellor.

Great Slave Lake, a large lake in NW Canada, in the Northwest Territories. ab. 10,700 sq. mi.

Great Smoky Mountains, a mountain range in North Carolina and Tennessee: a part of the Appalachian

system. Highest peak, Clingman's Dome, 6642 ft. Also, **Smoky Mountains** or **Great Smokies.**

great-un·cle (grāt/ŭng/kəl), *n.* a granduncle.

Great Wall of China, a system of walls constructed as a defense for China against the nomads of the regions that are now Mongolia and Manchuria: completed in the third century B.C., but later repeatedly modified and rebuilt. ab. 1400 mi. long.

Great War, World War I.

Great Week, *Eastern Ch.* Holy Week.

great white heron, 1. a large white heron, *Ardea occidentalis,* of Florida and the Florida Keys. 2. a large white egret, *Casmerodius albus,* of southeastern Europe, tropical Africa, Asia, New Zealand, and America.

great white trillium, a trillium, *Trillium grandiflorum,* of the eastern and central U.S., the flowers having large white petals that turn rose color.

Great White Way, the theater district along Broadway, near Times Square in New York City, brilliantly lighted at night.

great willow herb, the willow herb.

Great Yar·mouth (yär/math), a seaport in E England, in Norfolk. 51,500 (est. 1956).

greave (grēv), *n.* armor for the leg from knee to ankle, usually of front and back plates. [ME *greves* (pl.), t. OF; orig. obscure]

greaves (grēvz), *n.pl.* the sediment of melted tallow or animal fat, used as dog food, fish bait, etc.

grebe (grēb), *n.* any of several diving birds of the order *Colymbiformes,* related to the loons, but having lobate rather than webbed toes and a rudimentary tail, as the **great crested grebe,** *Colymbus cristatus,* of Europe, and the **piedbilled grebe,** *Podilymbus podiceps,* of America. [t. F, orig. uncert.]

Great crested grebe,
Colymbus cristatus
(14 in. long)

Gre·cian (grē/shən), *adj.* 1. Greek. —*n.* 2. a Greek. 3. an expert in the Greek language or literature.

Gre·cism (grē/sĭzəm), *n.* 1. the spirit of Greek thought, art, etc. 2. adoption or imitation of this. 3. an idiom or peculiarity of Greek. Also, *esp. Brit.,* **Graecism.**

Gre·cize (grē/sīz), *v.,* **-cized, -cizing.** —*v.t.* 1. to impart Greek characteristics to. 2. to translate into Greek. —*v.i.* 3. to conform to what is Greek; adopt Greek speech, customs, etc. Also, *esp. Brit.,* **Graecize.** [t. L: m.s. *Graecizāre,* der. *Graecus* Greek. See **-IZE**]

Gre·co (grĕk/ō; *It.* grĕ/kō), *n.* El (ĕl). See **El Greco.**

Greco-, a word element meaning "Greek." Also, *esp. Brit.,* **Graeco-.** [t. L: m. *Graeco-,* comb. form of *Graecus*]

gree¹ (grē), *n. Archaic* and *Scot.* 1. superiority, mastery, or victory. 2. the prize for victory. [ME *gre,* t. OF, g. L *gradus* step]

gree² (grē), *n. Obs.* or *Archaic.* 1. favor; good will. 2. satisfaction, as for an injury. [ME *gre,* t. OF, g. L *grātum,* adj. neut., pleasing, grateful]

gree³ (grē), *v.t., v.i.,* **greed, greeing.** *Scot.* and *Brit. Dial.* to bring or come into accord. [apheric var. of AGREE. Cf. F *gréer*]

Greece (grēs), *n.* a kingdom in S Europe at the S end of the Balkan peninsula. 7,973,000 pop. (est. 1955); 50,147 sq. mi. *Cap.:* Athens. Ancient Greek, **Hellas.**

greed (grēd), *n.* inordinate or rapacious desire, esp. for wealth. [OE *grǣd* (only in dat. pl.), c. Icel. *grādhr* hunger, greed, Goth. *grēdus* hunger] —**greed/less,** *adj.* —**Syn.** avidity, avarice, cupidity, covetousness. GREED, GREEDINESS denote an excessive, extreme desire for something, often more than one's proper share. GREED means avid desire for gain or wealth (unless some other application is indicated) and is definitely uncomplimentary in implications: *his greed drove him to exploit his workers.* GREEDINESS, when unqualified, suggests a craving for food; it may, however, be applied to all avid desires, and need not be always uncomplimentary: *greediness for knowledge, fame, praise.*

greed·y (grē/dĭ), *adj.,* **greedier, greediest.** 1. very eager for wealth; avaricious. 2. greatly desiring food or drink. 3. keenly desirous; eager (often fol. by *of*): *greedy of praise.* [ME *gredy,* d. OE *grēdig,* r. OE *grǣdig.* See GREED] —**greed/i·ly,** *adv.* —**greed/i·ness,** *n.* —**Syn.** 1. grasping, rapacious. 2. ravenous, voracious, gluttonous.

gree·gree (grē/grē′), *n.* grigri.

Greek (grēk), *adj.* 1. of or pertaining to Greece, the Greeks, or their language. 2. pertaining to the Greek Church. [adj. use of n.] —*n.* 3. a native inhabitant of Greece. 4. the language of the ancient Greeks and any of the languages which have developed from it, such as Hellenistic Greek, Biblical Greek, the Koine, and Modern Greek. 5. anything unintelligible, as speech, etc.: *it's Greek to me.* 6. a member of the Greek Church. 7. the group of Indo-European languages to which Greek belongs; Hellenic. [ME *Grekes* (pl.), OE *Grēcas,* learned var. of *Crēcas* (pl.), ult. t. L: m. *Graeci,* pl. of *Graecus* a Greek, t. Gk.: m. *Graikós,* orig. adj.]

Greek Catholic, 1. a communicant of any Greek Orthodox Church. 2. a Greek or Byzantine acknowledging allegiance to the Pope and to the faith of the

Western Church but disagreeing in forms of liturgy and ritual; a Uniat.

Greek cross, a cross consisting of an upright crossed in the middle by a horizontal piece of the same length. See illus. under **cross**.

Greek fire, an incendiary used by the Byzantine Greeks to set fire to enemy ships, etc.

Greek Orthodox Church, 1. the Christian church of the countries in communion or doctrinal agreement with the patriarch of Constantinople, comprising the former Eastern (Roman) Empire and countries evangelized from it, as Russia. **2.** Also, **Greek Church.** that part of this church which constitutes the established church in Greece.

Gree·ley (grē′lĭ), n. **1. Horace,** 1811–72, U.S. journalist and politician; a founder of the Republican Party. **2.** a city in N Colorado. 26,314 (1960).

Gree·ly (grē′lĭ), n. **Adolphus Washington,** 1844–1935, U.S. general, Arctic explorer, and meteorologist.

green (grēn), adj. **1.** of the color of growing foliage, between yellow and blue in the spectrum. **2.** covered with herbage or foliage; verdant: *green fields.* **3.** characterized by the presence of verdure. **4.** full of life and vigor. **5.** unseasoned; not dried or cured: *green timber.* **6.** not fully developed or perfected in growth or condition; unripe; not properly aged. **7.** immature in age or judgment; untrained; inexperienced: *a green hand.* **8.** simple; gullible; easily fooled. **9.** fresh, recent, or new: *a green wound.* **10.** pale; sickly; wan: *green with fear.* **11.** freshly killed: *green meat.* **12.** not fired, as bricks or pottery. **13.** *Metall.* (in molding) the moist condition of the sand used in founding. —n. **14.** green color. **15.** green coloring matter, paint, etc. **16.** green material or clothing. **17.** grassy land; a plot of grassy ground. **18.** *Golf.* **a.** the whole course or links on which golf is played. **b.** a putting green alone. **19.** a piece of grassy ground constituting a town or village common. **20.** (pl.) **a.** fresh leaves or branches of trees, shrubs, etc., used for decoration; wreaths. **b.** the leaves and stems of plants, as spinach (or esp. in England, cabbage), used for food. —v.i., v.t. **21.** to become or make green. [ME and OE *grēne*, c. G *grün;* akin to GROW, GRASS] **—green′ness,** n.

Green (grēn), n. **1. John Richard,** 1837–83, British historian. **2. William,** 1873–1952, U.S. labor leader; president of the AFL 1924–1952.

green algae, *Bot.* algae belonging to the class *Chlorophyceae,* grass-green in color.

green·back (grēn′băk′), n. a United States legal-tender note, usually printed in green on the back, originally issued against the credit of the country and not against gold or silver on deposit.

Greenback party, *U.S. Hist.* a former political party, organized in 1874, opposed to the retirement or reduction of greenbacks and favoring their increase as the only paper currency. **—Green′back′er,** n.

Green Bay, 1. an arm of Lake Michigan, in NE Wisconsin. ab. 90 mi. long. **2.** a port in E Wisconsin at the S end of this bay. 62,888 (1960).

green belt, an area of parks and unoccupied ground surrounding a town.

green·bri·er (grēn′brī′ər), n. **1.** a climbing liliaceous plant, *Smilax rotundifolia,* of the eastern U.S., with prickly stem and thick leaves. **2.** any plant of this genus.

green corn, sweet corn (def. 2).

green dragon, an American araceous herb, *Arisaema Dracontium,* with a greenish or whitish spathe.

Greene (grēn), n. **1. Nathanael,** 1742–86, American Revolutionary general. **2. Robert,** c1560–92, English dramatic poet and pamphleteer.

green·er·y (grē′nər ĭ), n., pl. **-eries. 1.** green foliage or vegetation; verdure. **2.** a place where green plants are reared or kept.

green-eyed (grēn′īd′), adj. jealous.

green·finch (grēn′fĭnch′), n. a European finch, *Chloris chloris,* with green and yellow plumage.

green·gage (grēn′gāj′), n. one of several varieties of light-green plums. [f. GREEN + *Gage,* named after Sir Wm. *Gage,* who introduced it into England c1725]

green gland, *Zool.* one of the pair of excretory organs in the head region of decapod crustaceans.

green·gro·cer (grēn′grō′sər), n. *Brit.* a retailer of fresh vegetables and fruit. **—green′gro′cer·y,** n.

green·head (grēn′hĕd′), n. a male mallard.

green·heart (grēn′härt′), n. **1.** a South American lauraceous tree, *Ocotea* (or *nectandra) Rodiaei,* whose hard durable wood is often used for wharves, bridges, and in shipbuilding, and whose bark yields bebeerine; bebeeru. **2.** any of certain other timber trees of tropical America. **3.** their valuable greenish wood.

green heron, a small American heron, *Butorides virescens,* with glossy green wings.

green·horn (grēn′hôrn′), n. *Colloq.* **1.** a raw, inexperienced person. **2.** a person easily imposed upon. [orig. applied to an ox with green or young horns]

green·house (grēn′hous′), n. a building, usually chiefly of glass and kept at a constant temperature, for the cultivation or protection of tender plants.

green·ing (grē′nĭng), n. any variety of apple the skin of which is green when ripe. [f. GREEN, adj. + -ING¹]

green·ish (grē′nĭsh), adj. somewhat green; having a tinge of green.

Green·land (grēn′lənd), n. an integral part of the Danish Realm NE of North America: the largest island in the world. 26,000 pop. (est. 1955); ab. 840,000 sq. mi. (over 700,000 sq. mi. ice-capped).

green·let (grēn′lĭt), n. vireo.

green light, a green lamp, used as a traffic signal to mean "go."

green·ling (grēn′lĭng), n. any of the acanthopterygian fishes constituting the genus *Hexagrammos,* found about rocks and kelp in the north Pacific Ocean.

green manure, *Agric.* **1.** a green crop, esp. clover and other nitrogen-fixing plants, plowed under for fertilizer. **2.** manure which has not undergone decay.

green monkey, a monkey, *Cercopithecus aethiops sabaeus,* of West Africa, with a greenish-gray back and yellow tail.

Green Mountains, a mountain range in Vermont: a part of the Appalachian system. Highest peak, Mt. Mansfield, 4393 ft.

Green·ock (grē′nŏk, grĕn′ək), n. a seaport in SW Scotland, on the Firth of Clyde. 77,500 (est. 1956).

Green·ough (grē′nō), n. **Horatio,** 1805–52, U.S. sculptor.

green pepper, 1. the fruit of the bell or sweet pepper, *Capsicum frutescens* var. *grossum.* **2.** the mild, unripe fruit of any of the garden peppers, *Capsicum frutescens,* used as a green vegetable.

green plover, lapwing.

Green River, a river flowing from W Wyoming S through E Utah to the Colorado. 730 mi.

green·room (grēn′rōōm′, -rŏŏm′), n. a retiring room in a theater, for the use of the actors and actresses when not required on the stage.

green·sand (grēn′sănd′), n. a sandstone containing much glauconite, which gives it a greenish hue.

Greens·bor·o (grēnz′bŭr′ō), n. a city in N North Carolina. 119,574 (1960).

green·shank (grēn′shăngk′), n. a common European shore bird, *Glottis nebularia,* with green legs.

green·sick·ness (grēn′sĭk′nĭs), n. chlorosis (def. 2).

green soap, a soap made chiefly from potassium hydroxide and linseed oil, used in treating skin diseases.

green·stone (grēn′stōn′), n. any of various altered basaltic rocks having a dark-green color caused by the presence of chlorite, epidote, etc.

green·sward (grēn′swôrd′), n. turf green with grass.

green tea, a tea subjected to a heating process without previous special withering and fermenting.

green vegetables, vegetables useful for the part grown above the ground; leafy vegetables.

Green·ville (grēn′vĭl), n. **1.** a city in NW South Carolina. 66,188 (1960). **2.** a city in W Mississippi, on the Mississippi river. 41,502 (1960).

green vitriol, ferrous sulfate, $FeSO_4 7H_2O$, in the form of bluish-green crystals; copperas.

Green·wich (grĭn′ĭj, grēn′-, -ĭch), n. a SE borough of London, England: Royal Observatory; the prime meridian passes through here. 91,492 (1951).

Greenwich Time, the standard of time as designated at the Observatory in Greenwich, England used in England and as a basis of calculation elsewhere.

Green·wich Village (grĕn′ĭch), a section of New York City in Manhattan: artists' and writers' center.

green-winged teal, a small fresh-water duck of America, *Anas carolinense,* and Europe, *A. crecca,* having a shining green speculum in the wing.

green·wood (grēn′wŏŏd′), n. a wood or forest when green, as in summer.

greet[1] (grēt), v.t. **1.** to address with some form of salutation; welcome. **2.** to receive with demonstrations of welcome or expression of pleasure. **3.** to manifest itself to: *music greets the ear.* —v.i. **4.** to give salutations on meeting. [ME *grete(n),* OE *grētan,* c. G *grüssen*] **—greet′er,** n. **—Syn. 1.** hail, accost.

greet[2] (grēt), *Archaic, Scot., and N. Eng.* —v.i. **1.** to weep; lament; grieve. —v.t. **2.** to lament; bewail. [ME *grete,* OE *grētan,* north. var. of *grǣtan,* c. Icel. *grāta*]

greet·ing (grē′tĭng), n. **1.** act or words of one who greets. **2.** (usually pl.) a friendly message: *send greetings.*

greg·a·rine (grĕg′ə rĭn′, -rĭn), n. **1.** a type of sporozoan parasite that inhabits the digestive and other cavities of various invertebrates and produces cysts filled with spores. —adj. **2.** having the characteristics of or pertaining to a gregarine or gregarines. [t. NL: m.s. *Gregarīna,* der. L *gregārius* GREGARIOUS]

gre·gar·i·ous (grĭ gâr′ĭ əs), adj. **1.** living in flocks or herds, as animals. **2.** *Bot.* growing in open clusters; not matted together. **3.** fond of company; sociable. **4.** pertaining to a flock or crowd. [t. L: m. *gregārius*] **—gre·gar′i·ous·ly,** adv. **—gre·gar′i·ous·ness,** n.

Gregg (grĕg), n. **John Robert,** 1867–1948, U.S. inventor of a shorthand system.

gre·go (grē′gō, grā′-), n., pl. **-gos.** a short coarse jacket or cloak with a hood, worn by the Greeks and the Levantines. [?t. Pg., g. L *Graecus* Greek, adj.]

Gre·go·ri·an (grĭ gôr′ĭ ən), adj. of or pertaining to any of the popes named Gregory.

Gregorian calendar, the reformed Julian calendar now in use, according to which the ordinary year consists of 365 days, and a leap year of 366 days occurs in every year whose number is exactly divisible by 4 except centenary years whose numbers are not exactly divisible by 400, as 1700, 1800, and 1900.

ăct, āble, dâre, ärt; ĕbb, ēqual; ĭf, īce; hŏt, ōver, ôrder, oil, bŏŏk, ōōze, out; ŭp, ūse, ûrge; ə = a in alone; ch, chief; g, give; ng, ring; sh, shoe; th, thin; ŧh, that; zh, vision. See the full key on inside cover.

Gregorian chant, 1. the plain song or cantus firmus used in the ritual of the Roman Catholic Church (named after Pope Gregory I). **2.** a melody in this style.

Gregorian telescope, a telescope similar to the Cassegrainian telescope, but less common.

Greg·o·ry (grĕg′ər), *n.* **Lady Augusta,** (*Augusta Persse*) 1852–1932, Irish dramatist, poet, and writer.

Greg·o·ry I (grĕg′ər), **Saint,** ("*Gregory the Great*") A.D. c540–604, Italian cleric; pope, A.D. 590–604.

Gregory VII, **Saint,** (*Hildebrand*) c1020–1085, Italian ecclesiastic; pope, 1073–85.

Gregory XIII, (*Ugo Buoncompagni*) 1502–85, Italian ecclesiastic; pope, 1572–85: devised modern calendar.

Gregory of Nys·sa (nĬs′ə), **Saint,** A.D. c335–c395, Christian bishop and theologian of Asia Minor.

Gregory of Tours, **Saint,** A. D. 538?–594, Frankish bishop and historian.

grei·sen (grī′zən), *n.* an altered rock of granitic texture composed chiefly of quartz and mica, common in the tin mines of Saxony. [t. G]

gre·mi·al (grē′mĬəl), *n.* a cloth placed on a bishop's lap when he sits in celebrating Mass or in conferring orders. [t. LL: s. *gremiālis* (as n., ML *gremiāle*) der. L *gremium* lap, bosom]

grem·lin (grĕm′lĬn), *n.* a mischievous invisible being, said by airplane pilots in World War II to cause engine trouble and mechanical difficulties. **—Syn.** See goblin.

Gre·na·da (grĭ nā′də), *n.* a British colony in the Windward Islands; a member of the Federation of the West Indies, consisting of the island of Grenada and the S part of the Grenadines. 81,070 (est. 1952); 133 sq. mi. *Cap.*: St. George's.

gre·nade (grĭ nād′), *n.* **1.** a small explosive shell thrown by hand or fired from a rifle. **2.** a glass missile for scattering chemicals. [t. F, s. Sp.: m. *granada* pomegranate, der. *granado* having grains, g. L *grānātus*]

gren·a·dier (grĕn′ə dĭr′), *n.* **1.** (in the British army) a member of the first regiment of household infantry (**Grenadier Guards**). **2.** a tall foot soldier. **3.** (formerly) a soldier who threw grenades. **4.** a fish, *Coryphaenoides fabricii* or *C. rupestris*, of the deep water of the North Atlantic, the tail part of which ends in a sharp point. **5.** any other fish of the family *Coryphaenoididae* (*Macuouridae*). [t. F. der. *grenade* GRENADE]

gren·a·dine[1] (grĕn′ə dēn′, grĕn′ə dēn′), *n.* a thin dress fabric of leno weave in silk, rayon, or wool. [t. F, ? named after *Granada*, in Spain]

gren·a·dine[2] (grĕn′ə dēn′, grĕn′ə dēn′), *n.* a syrup made from pomegranate juice. [t. F, dim. of *grenade* pomegranate. See GRENADE]

Gren·a·dines (grĕn′ə dēnz′, grĕn′ə dēnz′), *n.pl.* a chain of ab. 600 islands: a part of the Windward Islands in the (British) Federation of the West Indies.

Gren·fell (grĕn′fĕl), *n.* **Sir Wilfred Thomason,** 1865–1940, British physician and missionary in Labrador and Newfoundland.

Gre·no·ble (grə nō′bəl; Fr. grə nō′bl), *n.* a city in SE France, on the Isère river. 116,440 (1954).

Gren·ville (grĕn′vĬl), *n.* **1. George,** 1712–70, British statesman. **2. Sir Richard,** c1541–91, English naval commander.

Gresh·am (grĕsh′əm), *n.* **Sir Thomas,** 1519?–1579, English merchant and financier.

Gresham's law, *Econ.* the tendency of the inferior of two forms of currency to circulate more freely than, or to the exclusion of, the superior, because of the hoarding of the latter. [named after T. GRESHAM]

gres·so·ri·al (grĕ sōr′Ĭəl), *adj.* *Zool.* adapted for walking, as the feet of some birds. [f.s. NL *gressōrius* + -AL]

Gret·na Green (grĕt′nə), a village in S Scotland, near the English border, to which many runaway English couples formerly eloped.

Greuze (grœz), *n.* **Jean Baptiste** (zhän bȧ tēst′), 1725–1805, French painter.

Grev·ille (grĕv′Ĭl), *n.* **Fulke,** 1554–1628, English poet and statesman.

grew (grōō), *v.* pt. of grow.

grew·some (grōō′səm), *adj.* gruesome.

grey (grā), *adj., n., v.* Chiefly Brit. gray. **—grey′ly,** *adv.* **—grey′ness,** *n.*

Grey (grā), *n.* **1. Charles,** (*2nd Earl Grey*) 1764–1845, British statesman; prime minister, 1830–34. **2. Sir Edward,** (*Viscount Fallodon*) 1862–1933, British statesman. **3. Lady Jane,** (*Lady Jane Dudley*) 1537–54, descendant of Henry VII of England; executed as usurper of the crown.

grey·hound (grā′hound′), *n.* **1.** one of a breed of tall, slender dogs, notable for keen sight and for fleetness. **2.** a swift ship, esp. a fast ocean liner. Also, **grayhound.** [ME *gre(i)hound,* appar. t. Scand.; cf. Icel. *greyhundr,* f. *grey* dog, bitch + *hundr* HOUND[1]; r. OE *grīghund*]

Greyn·ville (grĕn′vĬl), *n.* Sir Richard. See Grenville.

grib·ble (grĬb′əl), *n.* a small marine isopod crustacean, *Limnoria,* which destroys submerged timber by boring into it. [? akin to GRUB]

Greyhound
(28 in. high at the shoulder)

grid (grĬd), *n.* **1.** a grating of crossed bars; gridiron. **2.** *Elect.* a metallic framework employed in a storage cell or battery for conducting the electric current and supporting the active material. **3.** *Brit.* the system of electrical distribution (esp. the high-tension wires) throughout a country. **4.** *Electronics.* the electrode in an electron tube, usually made of parallel wires, a helix or coil of wire, or a screen, and controlling the electron flow between the other electrodes. See **vacuum tube.** [back formation from GRIDIRON]

grid circuit, *Electronics.* that part of a circuit which contains the cathode and the grid of an electron tube.

grid condenser, *Electronics.* a condenser arranged in series with the grid circuit.

grid current, *Electronics.* the current which moves within the electron tube from the grid to the cathode.

grid·dle (grĬd′əl), *n., v.,* -dled, -dling. **—n. 1.** a handled frying pan with only a slight ledge at the edge, for cooking pancakes, etc., over direct heat. **—v.t. 2.** to cook on a griddle. [ME *gredil,* t. OF: *gridiron.* See GRILL[1]]

grid·dle·cake (grĬd′əl kāk′), *n.* a thin cake of batter cooked on a griddle; flapjack; pancake.

gride (grĬd), *v.,* grided, griding, *n.* **—v.i. 1.** to grate; grind; scrape harshly; make a grating sound. **—v.t. 2.** to pierce or cut. **—n. 3.** a griding or grating sound. [metathetic var. of GRID[2]]

grid·i·ron (grĬd′Ī′ərn), *n.* **1.** a utensil consisting of parallel metal bars to broil meat, etc., on. **2.** any framework or network resembling a gridiron. **3.** *Football.* the field of play, so called on account of the transverse white lines crossing it every five yards. **4.** a structure above the stage of a theater, from which hung scenery, etc., is manipulated. [ME *gredirne,* etc., r. ME *gredire,* assimilated var. of *gredile* GRIDDLE; variants in *-irne, -iron* show pop. etymological assoc. with ME *ire, irne* iron]

grid leak, *Electronics.* a high-resistance device which permits excessive charges on the grid to leak off or escape.

grief (grēf), *n.* **1.** keen mental suffering or distress over affliction or loss; sharp sorrow; painful regret. **2. come to grief,** to come to a bad end; turn out badly. **3.** a cause or occasion of keen distress or sorrow. [ME, t. OF, der. *grever* GRIEVE] **—grief′less,** *adj.* **—Syn. 1.** anguish, heartache, woe; sadness. See **sorrow.**

grief-strick·en (grēf′strĬk′ən), *adj.* stricken or smitten with grief or sorrow; afflicted.

Grieg (grēg; *Norw.* grĬg), *n.* **Edvard** (ĕd′värt), 1843–1907, Norwegian composer.

griev·ance (grē′vəns), *n.* **1.** a wrong, real or fancied, considered as grounds for complaint: *a popular grievance.* **2.** resentment or complaint, or the grounds for complaint, against an unjust act: *to have a grievance against someone.* **—Syn. 1.** injustice, injury.

grieve (grēv), *v.,* grieved, grieving. **—v.i. 1.** to feel grief; sorrow. **—v.t. 2.** to distress mentally; cause to feel grief or sorrow. **3.** *Obs.* to oppress or wrong. [ME *greve(n),* t. OF: m. *grever,* ult. g. L *gravāre* weigh down] **—griev′er,** *n.* **—griev′ing·ly,** *adv.* **—Syn. 1.** lament, weep. GRIEVE, MOURN imply showing suffering caused by sorrow. GRIEVE is the stronger word, implying deep mental suffering often endured alone and in silence but revealed by one's aspect: *to grieve over the loss (or death) of a friend.* MOURN usually refers to manifesting sorrow outwardly, either with or without sincerity: *to mourn publicly and wear black.*

griev·ous (grē′vəs), *adj.* **1.** causing grief or sorrow: *grievous news.* **2.** flagrant; atrocious: *a grievous fault.* **3.** full of or expressing grief; sorrowful: *a grievous cry.* **4.** *Archaic.* burdensome or oppressive. [ME *grevous,* t. OF, der. *grever* GRIEVE] **—griev′ous·ly,** *adv.* **—griev′ous·ness,** *n.* **—Syn. 2.** deplorable, lamentable, calamitous, heinous.

griffe[1] (grĬf), *n.* *U.S. Dial.* **1.** the offspring of a Negro and a mulatto. **2.** a person of mixed Negro and American Indian blood. **3.** a mulatto, esp. a woman. [t. F. Cf. Sp. *grifo* a griffin]

griffe[2] (grĬf), *n.* *Archit.* an ornament at the base of a column, projecting from the torus toward a corner of the plinth. [t. F: claw; of Gmc. orig.]

Griffe[2]

grif·fin[1] (grĬf′Ĭn), *n.* *Gk. Myth.* a fabulous monster, usually having the head and wings of an eagle and the body of a lion. Also, **griffon, gryphon.** [ME *griffon,* t. OF: m. *grifon,* der. L *grȳphus,* var. of *grȳps,* t. Gk.]

grif·fin[2] (grĬf′Ĭn) *n.* (in India and the East) a newcomer. [orig. uncert.]

Grif·fith (grĬf′Ĭth), *n.* **David Wark,** 1880–1948, U.S. motion-picture director and producer.

grif·fon[1] (grĬf′ən), *n.* a vulture of the genus *Gyps,* esp. *G. fulvus* of southern Europe. [t. F. See GRIFFIN[1]]

Griffin

grif·fon[2] (grĬf′ən), *n.* **1.** a small, wiry-haired pet dog of Belgian origin. **2.** one of a breed of coarse-haired hunting dogs combining the qualities of the pointer and the setter. [t. F; akin to GRIFFIN[1]]

grif·fon[3] (grĬf′ən), *n.* griffin[1].

grift·er (grĬf′tər), *n.* one who manages a side show at a circus, fair, etc.

grig (grĬg), *n.* *Dial.* **1.** a cricket or grasshopper. **2.** a small or young eel. **3.** a lively person. [orig. uncert.]

gri·gri (grē′grē), *n., pl.* **-gris.** an African charm, amulet, or fetish. Also, **greegree.**

grill¹ (grĭl), *n.* **1.** a grated utensil for broiling meat, etc., over a fire; gridiron. **2.** a dish of grilled meat, etc. **3.** grillroom. **4.** *Philately.* a series of small pyramidal impressions in parallel rows impressed or embossed on a stamp. *—v.t.* **5.** to broil on a gridiron or other apparatus over or before a fire. **6.** to torment with heat. **7.** to mark with a series of parallel bars like those of a grill. **8.** *U.S. Colloq.* to subject to severe and persistent crossexamination or questioning. *—v.i.* **9.** to undergo broiling. [t. F: m. *gril* gridiron, ult. g. L *crātĭculum,* dim. of *crātis* wickerwork, hurdle. Cf. GRILLE] **—grill′er,** *n.*

grill² (grĭl), *n.* grille.

gril·lage (grĭl′ĭj), *n.* a framework of crossing beams used for spreading heavy loads over large areas. [t. F, der. *grille.* See GRILL¹]

grille (grĭl), *n.* **1.** a grating or openwork barrier, as for a gate, usually of metal and often of decorative design. **2.** *Court Tennis.* a square-shaped opening in the far corner of the court, on the side of the hazard. Also, **grill.** [t. F: grating. See GRILL¹] **—grilled,** *adj.*

Grill·par·zer (grĭl′pär′tsər), *n.* **Franz** (fränts), 1791–1872, Austrian poet and dramatist.

grill·room (grĭl′room′, -room′), *n.* a room or restaurant where meats, etc., are grilled and served.

grilse (grĭls), *n., pl.* **grilse.** a salmon which has ceased to be a smolt and is ready to return, or has returned, from the sea to the river for the first time. [ME; orig. unknown]

grim (grĭm), *adj.,* **grimmer, grimmest.** **1.** stern; unrelenting; merciless; uncompromising: *grim necessity.* **2.** of a sinister or ghastly character; repellent: *a grim joke.* **3.** of a fierce or forbidding aspect: *a grim countenance.* **4.** fierce, savage, or cruel: *grim warrior.* [ME and OE, c. OS, OHG *grim,* Icel. *grimmr*] **—grim′ly,** *adv.* **—grim′ness,** *n.* **—Syn. 1.** harsh, unyielding. **3.** severe, stern, harsh, hard. **—Ant. 3.** gentle.

gri·mace (grĭ′mās′, grĭ′məs), *n., v.,* **-maced, -macing.** *—n.* **1.** a wry face; facial contortion; ugly facial expression. *—v.i.* **2.** to make grimaces. [t. F, t. Sp.: m. *grimazo* panic, fear, der. *grima* fright, t. Goth.] **—grimac′er,** *n.*

Gri·mal·di (grĭ mäl′dĭ), *n.* **Joseph,** 1779–1837, British mimic and clown.

gri·mal·kin (grĭ măl′kĭn, -môl′-), *n.* **1.** a cat. **2.** an old female cat. **3.** an ill-tempered old woman. [appar. f. m. GRAY + *malkin,* dim. of *Maud,* proper name]

grime (grīm), *n., v.,* **grimed, griming.** *—n.* **1.** dirt or foul matter, esp. on or ingrained in a surface. *—v.t.* **2.** to cover with dirt; soil; make very dirty. [appar. special use of OE *grīma* mask, to denote layer of dust, etc., that forms on the face and elsewhere. Cf. Flem. *grym*]

Grimes Golden (grīmz), a yellow eating apple maturing in late autumn. [named after Thomas P. *Grimes* of W. Va.]

Grimm (grĭm), *n.* **Jakob Ludwig Karl** (yä′kôp lōōt′vĭкн kärl), 1785–1863, or his brother, **Wilhelm Karl** (vĭl′hĕlm kärl), 1786–1859, German philologists and collectors of fairy tales.

Grimm's law (grĭmz), *Ling.* the statement of a system of consonant changes from primitive Indo-European into the Germanic languages, especially as differently reflected in Low and High German, formulated by Jakob Grimm (1820–22) and independently recognized by Rasmus Rask (1818).

Grims·by (grĭmz′bĭ), *n.* a seaport in E England at the mouth of the Humber estuary. 95,400 (est. 1956).

grim·y (grī′mĭ), *adj.,* **grimier, grimiest.** covered with grime; dirty. **—grim′i·ly,** *adv.* **—grim′i·ness,** *n.*

grin (grĭn), *v.,* **grinned, grinning,** *n.* *—v.i.* **1.** to smile broadly, or with a wide distention of the mouth. **2.** to draw back the lips so as to show the teeth, as a snarling dog or a person in pain. *—v.t.* **3.** to express or produce by grinning. *—n.* **4.** act of grinning; broad smile. **5.** act of withdrawing the lips and showing the teeth. [ME *grin(en),* OE *grennian*] **—grin′ner,** *n.* **—grin′ning·ly,** *adv.* **—Syn. 1.** See **laugh.**

grind (grīnd), *v.,* **ground** or (*Rare*) **grinded, grinding,** *n.* *—v.t.* **1.** to wear, smooth, or sharpen by friction; whet: *to grind a lens, an ax, etc.* **2.** to reduce to fine particles, as by pounding or crushing; bray, triturate, or pulverize. **3.** to oppress or torment. **4.** to rub harshly or gratingly; grate together; grit: *to grind one's teeth.* **5.** to operate by turning a crank: *to grind a hand organ.* **6.** to produce by pulverizing, turning a crank, etc.: *to grind flour.* *—v.i.* **7.** to perform the operation of reducing to fine particles. **8.** to rub harshly; grate. **9.** to be or become ground. **10.** to be polished or sharpened by friction. **11.** *Colloq.* to work or study laboriously. *—n.* **12.** act of grinding. **13.** a grinding sound. **14.** *Colloq.* laborious work; close or laborious study. **15.** *College Slang.* a student who works hard at his studies. [ME *grind(en),* OE *grindan.* Cf. L *frendere* gnash the teeth, grind to pieces] **—grind′ing·ly,** *adv.* **—Syn. 2.** crush, powder, comminute. **3.** harass, persecute.

grin·de·li·a (grĭn dē′lĭ ə), *n.* **1.** any of the coarse, yellow-flowered asteraceous herbs constituting the genus *Grindelia.* **2.** the dried leaves and tops of certain species of this plant, used in medicine. [NL; named after D. H. *Grindel* (1777–1836), Russian scientist]

grind·er (grīn′dər), *n.* **1.** one who or that which grinds. **2.** a sharpener of tools. **3.** a molar tooth.

grind·stone (grīnd′stōn′), *n.* **1.** a rotating solid stone wheel used for sharpening, shaping, etc. **2.** a millstone.

grin·go (grĭng′gō), *n., pl.* **-gos.** (among Spanish Americans) a foreigner, esp. an Anglo-Saxon. [Mex. Sp. use of Sp. *gringo* gibberish]

grip (grĭp), *n., v.,* **gripped** or **gript, gripping.** *—n.* **1.** act of grasping; a seizing and holding fast; firm grasp: *the grip of a vise.* **2.** the power of gripping. **3.** a grasp, hold, or control. **4.** *U.S.* a small suitcase. **5.** mental or intellectual hold. **6.** a special mode of clasping hands. **7.** something which seizes and holds, as a clutching device on a cable car. **8.** a handle or hilt. **9.** a sudden, sharp pain; spasm of pain. **10.** grippe. **11.** *Theat. Slang.* a stagehand, esp. one who works on the stage floor. *—v.t.* **12.** to grasp or seize firmly; hold fast. **13.** to take hold on; hold the interest of: *to grip the mind.* **14.** to attach by a grip or clutch. *—v.i.* **15.** to take firm hold; hold fast. **16.** to take hold on the mind. [ME and OE *gripe* grasp, c. G *griff,* OE *gripa* handful, sheaf. See GRIPE, v.] **—grip′per,** *n.* **—grip′ping·ly,** *adv.*

gripe (grīp), *v.,* **griped, griping,** *n.* *—v.t.* **1.** to seize and hold firmly; grip; grasp; clutch. **2.** to distress or oppress. **3.** to produce pain in (the bowels) as if by constriction. *—v.i.* **4.** to grasp or clutch, as a miser at cash. **5.** to suffer pain in the bowels. **6.** *U.S. Colloq.* to complain constantly; grumble. **7.** *Naut.* to tend to come up into the wind. *—n.* **8.** act of griping, grasping, or clutching. **9** a firm hold; clutch. **10.** a grasp; hold; control. **11.** that which grips or clutches; a claw or grip. **12.** (*pl.*) *Naut.* lashing by which a boat is secured on the deck or on the davits of a ship. **13.** a handle, hilt, etc. **14.** (*usually pl.*) *Pathol.* an intermittent spasmodic pain in the bowels. [ME *gripe(n),* OE *grīpan,* c. D *grijpen,* G *greifen* gripe, seize. Cf. GRIP, GROPE] **—grip′er** *n.*

grippe (grĭp), *n.* influenza. [t. F, der. *gripper* seize, b. with Russ. *khrip* hoarseness] **—grippe′like′,** *adj.*

grip·sack (grĭp′săk′), *n.* *U.S.* a traveling bag; grip.

gript (grĭpt), *v.* pt. and pp. of **grip.**

Gri·qua (grē′kwə, grĭk′wə), *n.* a South African halfbreed.

gri·saille (grĭ zāl′; *Fr.* grē zä′y), *n.* **1.** monochromatic painting in shades of gray, usually simulating sculpture. **2.** a painting, a stained-glass window, etc., executed in this way. [t. F, der. *gris* gray. See GRIZZLE]

Gri·sel·da (grĭ zĕl′də), *n.* a woman of exemplary meekness and patience. [a character in Boccaccio, Chaucer, and elsewhere]

gris·e·ous (grĭs′ĭ əs, grĭz′-), *adj.* gray; pearl-gray. [t. ML: m. *griseus*]

gri·sette (grĭ zĕt′), *n.* a French working girl or shopgirl. [t. F: orig., a common gray fabric worn by working girls, der. *gris* gray. See GRIZZLE]

gris·ly (grĭz′lĭ), *adj.,* **-lier, -liest.** **1.** such as to cause a shuddering horror; gruesome: *a grisly monster.* **2.** formidable; grim: *a grisly countenance.* [ME; late OE *grislic* horrible. Cf. OE *āgrīsan* shudder] **—gris′li·ness,** *n.*

gri·son (grī′sən, grĭz′ən), *n.* a musteline carnivore, *Grison vittata,* of South and Central America, having the upper surface of the body grayish-white and the lower dark-brown. [t. F, der. *gris* gray]

Gri·sons (grē zōN′), *n.* a canton in E Switzerland. 139,800 pop. (est. 1952); 2747 sq. mi. *Cap.:* Chur. German, **Graubünden.**

grist (grĭst), *n.* **1.** grain to be ground. **2.** ground grain; meal produced from grinding. **3.** a quantity of grain for grinding at one time; the amount of meal from one grinding. **4.** *U.S. Colloq.* a quantity or lot. [ME; OE *grist,* der. *grindan* GRIND]

gris·tle (grĭs′əl), *n.* cartilage. [ME and OE; c. OFris. and MLG *gristel.* Cf. OE *grost* cartilage]

gris·tly (grĭs′lĭ), *adj.* of the nature of, containing, or pertaining to gristle; cartilaginous.

grist·mill (grĭst′mĭl′), *n.* a mill for grinding grain, esp. the customer's own grain.

grit (grĭt), *n., v.,* **gritted, gritting.** *—n.* **1.** fine, stony, or hard particles such as are deposited like dust from the air or occur as impurities in food, etc. **2.** a coarsegrained siliceous rock, usually with sharp, angular grains. **3.** *U.S.* firmness of character; indomitable spirit; pluck. *—v.t.* **4.** to grate or grind: *to grit the teeth.* *—v.i.* **5.** to give forth a grating sound, as of sand under the feet; grate. [ME *gre(e)t,* OE *grēot,* c. G *greiss.* Cf. GRITS] **—grit′less,** *adj.* **—Syn. 2.** sand, gravel. **3.** resolution, fortitude, courage.

grits (grĭts), *n.pl.* **1.** grain, hulled and often coarsely ground. **2.** *U.S.* coarsely ground hominy. [ME *gryttes,* OE *gryttan* (pl.), c. G *grütze*]

grit·ty (grĭt′ĭ), *adj.,* **-tier, -tiest.** **1.** consisting of, containing, or resembling grit; sandy. **2.** *U.S.* resolute and courageous; plucky. **—grit′ti·ly,** *adv.* **—grit′ti·ness,** *n.*

griv·et (grĭv′ĭt), *n.* a small Abyssinian monkey, *Cercopithecus aethiops,* with a grayish back, gray tail, black face, and dark extremities. [orig. unknown]

griz·zle (grĭz′əl), *v.,* **-zled, -zling,** *adj., n.* *—v.i., v.t.* **1.** to become or make gray. *—adj.* **2.** gray; devoid of hue. *—n.* **3.** gray hair. **4.** a gray wig. [ME *grisel,* t. OF, der. *gris* gray; of Gmc. orig. (cf. G *greis* gray, hoary)]

griz·zled (grĭz′əld), *adj.* gray-haired. **2.** gray.

griz·zly (grĭz′lĭ), *adj.,* **-zlier, -zliest,** *n., pl.* **-zlies.** *—adj.* **1.** somewhat gray; grayish. **2.** gray-haired. *—n.* **3.** a grizzly bear.

grizzly bear, a large, ferocious bear, *Ursus horribilis,* of western North America, varying in color from grayish to brownish.

gro., gross; 144 articles.

groan (grōn), *n.* **1.** a low, mournful sound uttered in pain or grief. **2.** a deep murmur uttered in derision or disapprobation. —*v.i.* **3.** to utter a deep inarticulate sound expressive of grief or pain; moan. **4.** to make a sound resembling a groan; resound harshly. **5.** to be overburdened or overloaded. **6.** to suffer lamentably (fol. by *beneath, under, with*). —*v.t.* **7.** to utter or salute with groans. [ME *grone(n)*, OE *grānian*, akin to G *greinen* whine] —**groan′er,** *n.* —**groan′ing,** *n., adj.* —**groan′ing.ly,** *adv.*

Grizzly bear.
Ursus horribilis
(6 to 8½ ft. long, 3 to 3½ ft. high at the shoulder)

—**Syn. 1.** GROAN, MOAN refer to sounds indicating deep suffering. A GROAN is a brief, strong, deep-throated sound emitted involuntarily under pressure of pain or suffering: *the wounded man groaned when they lifted him.* A MOAN is a prolonged, more or less continuous, low, inarticulate sound indicative of suffering, either physical or mental: *she was moaning after the operation, she did not weep but moaned softly.*

groat (grōt), *n.* an English silver coin, issued 1351–1662, worth fourpence. [ME *groot,* t. MD: lit., thick (coin)]

groats (grōts), *n.pl.* **1.** hulled and crushed (or whole) grain, as wheat. **2.** the parts of oat kernels used as food. [ME *grotes,* OE *grotan* coarse meal. Cf. OE *grot* particle]

gro.cer (grō′sər), *n.* a dealer in general supplies for the table, as flour, sugar, coffee, etc., and in other articles of household use. [ME *grosser,* t. OF: m. *grossier,* ult. der. LL *grossus* gross]

gro.cer.y (grō′sə rĭ), *n., pl.* **-ceries. 1.** *U.S.* a grocer's store. **2.** (*usually pl.*) a commodity sold by grocers. **3.** the business of a grocer.

Grod.no (grôd′nō), *n.* a city in the W Soviet Union, on the Niemen river: formerly Polish. 60,000 (est. 1948).

grog (grŏg), *n.* **1.** a mixture of alcoholic liquor and water. **2.** strong drink. [said to be from "Old *Grog,*" nickname of the British Admiral Vernon (with allusion to his *grogram* cloak), who in 1740 ordered the mixture to be served, instead of pure spirits, to sailors]

grog.ger.y (grŏg′ə rĭ), *n., pl.* **-geries.** *U.S. Slang.* a saloon.

grog.gy (grŏg′ĭ), *adj.,* **-gier, -giest.** *Colloq.* **1.** staggering, as from exhaustion or blows. **2.** drunk; intoxicated. —**grog′gi.ly,** *adv.* —**grog′gi.ness,** *n.*

grog.ram (grŏg′rəm), *n.* a coarse fabric of silk, of silk and mohair or wool, or of wool, formerly in use. [t. F: m. *gros grain.* See GROSGRAIN]

grog.shop (grŏg′shŏp′), *n. Brit.* (in contemptuous use) a saloon.

groin (groin), *n.* **1.** *Anat.* the fold or hollow on either side of the body where the thigh joins the abdomen. **2.** *Archit.* the curved line or edge formed by the intersection of two vaults. —*v.t.* **3.** *Archit.* to form with groins. [earlier *gryne,* ME *grynde.* Cf. OE *grynde* abyss, akin to *grund* bottom, GROUND]

A. A. Groins,
in early 12th
century vaulting

Gro.li.er (grō′lĭ ər; *Fr.* grô lyē′), *adj. Bookbinding.* **1.** referring to **Grolier design,** decorative bookbinding consisting of bands interlaced in geometrical forms. **2.** of or pertaining to **Jean Grolier de Servières** (1479–1565), French bibliophile noted for his decorative leather bindings.

grom.met (grŏm′ĭt), *n.* **1.** *Mach.* a ring or eyelet of metal, etc. **2.** *Naut.* an eyelet of rope, metal, or the like, as on the edge of a sail. Also, **grummet.** [t. F: m. *grommette* (obs.) curb of bridle, ult. der. LL *grumus* throat]

grom.well (grŏm′wəl), *n.* any plant of the boraginaceous genus *Lithospermum,* comprising hairy herbs with varicolored flowers and smooth, stony nutlets. [ME *gromyl,* t. OF: m. *gromil,* g. L *gruīnum milium* crane millet]

Gro.my.ko (grō mē′kō; *Russ.* grŏ mȳ′kŏ), *n.* **Andrei Andreievich** (än drā′ än drā′yə vĭch), born 1909, Russian diplomat.

Gro.ning.en (grō′nĭng ən; *Du.* KHRŌ′-), *n.* a city in NE Netherlands. 140,456 (est. 1954).

groom (grōōm, grŏŏm), *n.* **1.** a man or boy in charge of horses or the stable. **2.** a man newly married, or about to be married; bridegroom. **3.** any of several officers of the English royal household. **4.** *Archaic.* a manservant. —*v.t.* **5.** to tend carefully as to person and dress; make neat or tidy. **6.** to tend (horses). **7.** *U.S.* to prepare for a position, election, etc.: *groom a political candidate.* [ME *grom(e)* boy, man, groom; cf. D *grom* offspring; appar. akin to GROW]

groom's cake, a fruit cake in layers of graduated sizes, served at a wedding.

grooms.man (grōōmz′mən, grŏŏmz′-), *n., pl.* **-men.** a best man at a wedding.

Groot (grōt), *n.* **Gerhard** (gĕr′härt), (*Gerhardus Magnus*) 1340–84, Dutch religious reformer and founder of a monastic order ("Brothers of the Common Life").

groove (grōōv), *n., v.,* **grooved, grooving.** —*n.* **1.** a furrow or channel cut by a tool. **2.** a rut, furrow, or channel formed by any agency. **3.** a fixed routine: *to get into a groove.* **4.** *Print.* the furrow at the bottom of a piece of type. See diag. under **type. 5. in the groove,** *Jazz.* played in such a way as to arouse enthusiasm in the listener. —*v.t.* **6.** to cut a groove in; furrow. **7.** to fix in a groove. [ME *grofe, groof* mining shaft, OE *grōf* ditch, sewer, c. G *grube* ditch, pit; akin to GRAVE[1], GRAVE[3]] —**groove′less,** *adj.* —**groove′like′,** *adj.*

grope (grōp), *v.,* **groped, groping.** —*v.i.* **1.** to feel about with the hands; feel one's way. **2.** to search blindly or uncertainly. —*v.t.* **3.** to seek by or as by feeling. [ME *grop(i)en,* OE *grāpian,* der. *grāp,* n., grasp; akin to GRIPE, v.] —**grop′er,** *n.* —**grop′ing.ly,** *adv.*

Gro.pi.us (grō′pĭ əs; *Ger.* -pē ōōs′), *n.* **Walter** (wôl′tər; *Ger.* väl′-), born 1883, German architect, now in U.S.

Gros (grō), *n.* **Antoine Jean** (än twän′ zhän), **Baron,** 1771–1835, French painter.

gros.beak (grōs′bēk′), *n.* any of various finches having a large, stout conical bill, as the pine grosbeak, *Pinicola enucleator.* [t. F: m. *grosbec* large beak]

gro.schen (grō′shən), *n., pl.* **-schen. 1.** a former small German silver coin. **2.** *Colloq.* the 10-pfennig German nickel coin. **3.** (in Austria) a bronze coin valued at one hundredth of a schilling. [t. G, f. MHG *grosse,* lit., thick (coin) + *-chen* dim. suffix. See GROSS]

gros de Lon.dres (grō′ də lôn′dr), *French.* a crossribbed, silk dress fabric with ribs alternating in color or in coarse and fine yarn.

gros.grain (grō′grān′), *n.* heavy, corded, silk or rayon ribbon or cloth. [t. F: m. *gros grain* large grain. Cf. GROGRAM]

gross (grōs), *adj., n., pl.* **grosses** for 6, **gross** for 8, 9; *v.* —*adj.* **1.** whole, entire, or total, esp. without having been subjected to deduction, as for charges, loss, etc.: *gross profits.* **2.** glaring or flagrant: *gross injustice.* **3.** morally coarse; indelicate, or indecent: *gross tastes.* **4.** large, big, or bulky. **5.** thick; dense; heavy: *gross vegetation.* —*n.* **6.** the main body, bulk, or mass. **7. in the gross, a.** taken as a whole; in bulk. **b.** wholesale. **8.** a unit consisting of twelve dozen, or 144. **9. a great gross,** twelve gross, or 144 dozen. —*v.t.* **10.** to make a gross profit of; earn a total of. [ME, t. OF: m. *gros* large (as n., *grosse* twelve dozen), g. LL *grossus* thick] —**gross′ly,** *adv.* —**gross′ness,** *n.* —**Syn. 2.** shameful, outrageous, heinous. **3.** low, animal, sensual.

gross ton, 2,240 lbs.

gros.su.lar.ite (grŏs′yə lə rīt′), *n.* a mineral, calcium aluminum garnet, $Ca_3Al_2Si_3O_{12}$, occurring in crystals. [f. s. NL *grossulāria* gooseberry + -ITE[1]]

Gross.war.dein (grōs′vär dīn′), *n.* German name of Oradea.

gross weight, total weight without deduction for tare, tret, or waste.

Grosz (grōs), *n.* **George,** 1893–1959, German painter, in U.S. since 1932.

grot (grŏt), *n. Poetic.* a grotto. [t. F: m. *grotte,* t. It.: m. *grotta.* See GROTTO]

Grote (grōt), *n.* **George,** 1794–1871, British historian.

gro.tesque (grō tĕsk′), *adj.* **1.** fantastic in the shaping and combination of forms, as in decorative work combining incongruous human and animal figures with scrolls, foliage, etc. **2.** odd or unnatural in shape, appearance, or character; fantastically ugly or absurd; bizarre. —*n.* **3.** any grotesque object or thing. [t. F, t. It.: m. *grottesco* (as n., *grottesca* grotesque decoration, such appar. as was found in ancient excavated dwellings) der. *grotta.* See GROTTO] —**gro.tesque′ly,** *adv.* —**gro.tesque′ness,** *n.*

Italian grotesque
work.
16th century

gro.tes.quer.y (grō tĕs′kər ĭ), *n., pl.* **-queries. 1.** grotesque character. **2.** something grotesque. **3.** grotesque work. Also, **gro.tes′quer.ie.**

Gro.ti.us (grō′shĭ əs). *n.* **Hugo,** (*Huig De Groot*) 1583–1645, Dutch jurist, statesman, and writer.

grot.to (grŏt′ō), *n., pl.* **-toes, -tos. 1.** a cave or cavern. **2.** an artificial cavernlike recess or structure. [t. It.: m. *grotta,* g. VL *crupta,* in L *crypta* subterranean passage or chamber, crypt, t. Gk.: m. *krȳptē* vault]

grouch (grouch), *U.S. Colloq.* —*v.i.* **1.** to be sulky or morose; show discontent; complain. —*n.* **2.** a sulky or morose person. **3.** a sulky or morose mood. [var. of obs. *grutch,* t. OF: m. *groucher* grumble]

grouch.y (grou′chĭ), *adj.,* **grouchier, grouchiest.** *U.S. Colloq.* sullenly discontented; sulky; morose; ill-tempered. —**grouch′i.ly,** *adv.* —**grouch′i.ness,** *n.*

Grou.chy (grōō shē′), *n.* **Emmanuel** (ĕ mä ny ĕl′), **Marquis de,** 1766–1847, French general.

ground[1] (ground), *n.* **1.** the earth's solid surface; firm or dry land: *fall to the ground.* **2.** earth or soil: *stony ground.* **3.** land having a special character: *rising ground.* **4.** (*often pl.*) a tract of land occupied, or appropriated to a special use: *baseball grounds.* **5.** (*often pl.*) the foundation or basis on which a theory or action rests; motive; reason: *grounds for a statement.* **6.** the underlying or main surface, or background, in painting, decorative work, lace, etc. **7.** (*pl.*) dregs or sediment: *coffee grounds.* **8.** *Elect.* **a.** a conducting connection between an electric circuit or equipment and the earth or some similarly conducting body. **b.** the terminal to which the grounding lead is attached. **9.** *Music.* a ground bass. **10.** *Naut.* the solid bottom under water. **11.** *Com.* groundage. **12.** Some special noun phrases are: **break ground, 1.** to plow. **2.** to begin the construction of a building. **3.** to begin the execution of any plan. **cover ground, 1.** to go across a certain area. **2.** to go from place to place. **3.** to make a certain amount of progress in a piece of work, etc. **from the ground up,** thoroughly. **gain ground, 1.** to advance; make progress. **2.** to gain acceptance. **give ground,** to give up some of one's position; give way. **hold** or **stand one's ground,** to maintain one's position; not yield or give way. **lose ground, 1.** to lose what one has gained; retreat; give way. **2.** to become less well-known or accepted. **shift one's ground,** to take another position or defense in an argument or situation. —*adj.* **13.** situated on or at, or adjacent to, the surface of the earth: *the ground floor.* **14.** pertaining to the ground. —*v.t.* **15.** to lay or set on the ground. **16.** to place on a foundation; found; fix firmly; settle or establish. **17.** to instruct in elements or first principles. **18.** to furnish with a ground or background on decorative work, etc. **19.** *Elect.* to establish a ground for (a circuit, device, etc.). **20.** *Naut.* to run aground. —*v.i.* **21.** to come to or strike the ground. [ME and OE *grund,* c. D *grond,* G *grund* bottom, ground] —**Syn. 2.** land, mold, loam, dirt. **5.** premise.

ground² (ground), *v.* **1.** pt. and pp. of **grind.** —*adj.* **2.** reduced to fine particles or dust by grinding. **3.** having the surface abraded or roughened by or as by grinding: *ground glass.* [see GRIND]

ground·age (groun′dǐj), *n. Brit.* a tax levied on vessels stopping at a port.

ground alert, *Mil.* state of waiting for orders in or near combat airplanes ready to take to the air at once.

ground bait, bait dropped to the bottom of the water.

ground bass (bās), *Music.* a short fundamental bass part continually repeated throughout a whole movement.

ground beetle, any of the numerous beetles of the family *Carabidae,* most of which are terrestrial.

ground cherry, an American plant of the genus *Physalis,* as *P. peruviana,* the edible Cape gooseberry.

ground connection, *Elect.* the conductor used to establish a ground.

ground crew, *Mil.* ground personnel connected with air operations, as maintenance technicians.

ground·er (groun′dər), *n. Baseball, etc.* a ball knocked or thrown along the ground and not rising into the air.

ground floor, *U.S. Colloq.* the most advantageous position or relationship in a business matter or deal.

ground glass, glass whose polished surface is made hazy, as by grinding, so as to diffuse light.

ground hog, woodchuck.

ground-hog day (ground′hŏg′, -hôg′), Candlemas, Feb. 2, from the legend that the ground hog first emerges after hibernation on that day, and, if he sees his shadow, retires for six more weeks of winter.

ground ivy, a trailing labiate herb, *Glecoma hederacea,* bearing blue flowers.

ground·less (ground′lǐs), *adj.* without basis or reason: *groundless fears.* —**ground′less·ly,** *adv.* —**ground′less·ness,** *n.*

ground·ling (ground′lǐng), *n.* **1.** a plant or animal that lives on or close to the ground. **2.** any of various fishes that live at the bottom of the water. **3.** a spectator, reader, or other person of crude or uncultivated tastes; an uncritical or uncultured person. **4.** *obs.* a spectator in the pit of a theater which formerly was literally on the ground, having neither floor nor benches.

ground loop, *Aviation.* a sharp horizontal loop performed, usually involuntarily, while touching the ground.

ground·mass (ground′măs′), *n.* the crystalline, granular, or glassy base or matrix of a porphyry, in which the more prominent crystals are embedded.

ground·nut (ground′nŭt′), *n.* **1.** any of various plants with edible underground portions, as the peanut, *Arachis hypogaea,* and the American climbing leguminous vine, *Apios tuberosa,* which has an edible tuberous root. **2.** its edible tuber, pod, or the like.

ground owl, burrowing owl.

ground pine, 1. a European labiate herb, *Ajuga Chamaepitys,* having a resinous odor. **2.** any of several species of club moss, particularly *Lycopodium obscurum* and *L. complanatum.*

ground pink, 1. an annual herb, *Gilia dianthoides,* of southern California. **2.** the moss pink.

ground plan, 1. the plan of a floor of a building. **2.** first or fundamental plan.

ground plate, 1. *Elect.* a metal plate used for making a ground connection to earth. **2.** a groundsill.

ground plum, 1. a leguminous plant, *Astragalus caryocarpus,* of the American prairie regions. **2.** its plum-shaped fruit.

ground rent, *Chiefly Brit.* the rent at which land is let to a tenant for a long term or perpetually.

ground robin, the towhee or chewink, *Pipilo erythrophthalmus,* of North America.

ground·sel¹ (ground′səl), *n. Chiefly Brit.* any plant of the genus *Senecio* of the aster family, as *S. vulgaris,* a weed bearing small yellow flowers. [ME *grundeswilie,* etc., OE g(r)undeswelge, etc., appar. f. *gund* pus + *swelgan* swallow (from its use in medicine); or f. *grund* ground + *swelgan* (from its speed in spreading)]

ground·sel² (ground′səl), *n.* groundsill.

ground·sill (ground′sǐl′), *n.* the lowest horizontal timber of a frame or building lying next to the ground. [ME *gronsel,* etc., f. GROUND¹, n. + SILL]

ground speed, the speed of an aircraft in reference to the ground (in contrast to *air speed*).

ground squirrel, any of various terrestrial rodents of the squirrel family, as of the genus *Tamias* (chipmunks) and of the genus *Citellus* (or *Spermophilus*).

ground swell, a broad, deep swell or rolling of the sea, due to a distant storm or gale.

ground water, the water beneath the surface of the ground, consisting largely of surface water that has seeped down; the source of water in springs and wells.

ground wire, a lead from electrical apparatus to the ground or to a grounded connection.

ground·work (ground′wûrk′), *n.* the foundation, base, or basis.

group (grōōp), *n.* **1.** any assemblage of persons or things; cluster; aggregation. **2.** a number of persons or things ranged or considered together as being related in some way. **3.** *Ethnol.* a classification more limited than a branch. **4.** *Chem.* a number of atoms in a molecule connected or arranged together in some special manner; a radical: *the hydroxyl group,* =OH. **5.** *Linguistics.* **a.** a subdivision of a family, usually the greatest. **b.** any grouping of languages, whether geographically, on the basis of relationship, or otherwise. **6.** *Geol.* a division of stratified rocks comprising two or more formations. **7.** *U.S. Army.* **a.** a military unit of supporting troops, such as artillery or engineers, consisting of two or more battalions and a headquarters and headquarters troops. **b.** an administrative and tactical unit of the Army Air Forces, smaller than a wing and composed of two or more squadrons. **8.** *Music.* a section of an orchestra, comprising the instruments of the same class. **9.** *Art.* a number of figures or objects arranged together. —*v.t.* **10.** to place in a group, as with others. **11.** to arrange in or form into a group or groups. —*v.i.* **12.** to form a group. **13.** to be part of a group. [t. F: m. *groupe,* t. It: m. *gruppo;* ult. of Gmc. orig.]

group·er (grōō′pər), *n., pl.* -ers, (*esp. collectively*) -er. any of various serranoid fishes, esp. of the genus *Epinephelus,* as *E. morio* (**red grouper**), an important food fish of the southern Atlantic coast of the U.S., West Indies, etc. [t. Pg.: m. *garupa,* appar. repr. some S Amer. name]

group insurance, life, accident, or sickness insurance written on groups of lives, without medical examination.

group marriage, a form of marriage in which a group of males are united with a group of females to form a single conjugal unit.

group representation, *Govt.* representation in a governing body on the basis of interests rather than by geographical location.

grouse¹ (grous), *n., pl.* **grouse.** any of numerous gallinaceous birds of the family *Tetraonidae,* including such important game species as the **red grouse** (*Lagopus scoticus*) of Great Britain, **black grouse** (*Lyrurus tetrix*) and **capercaillie** or **wood grouse** (*Tetrao urogallus*) of Europe, and **spruce grouse** (*Canachites canadensis*) and **ruffed grouse** (*Bonasa umbellus*) of North America. [orig. uncert.] —**grouse′like′,** *adj.*

Ruffed grouse,
Bonasa umbellus
(16½ in. long)

grouse² (grous), *v.,* **groused, grousing,** *n. Slang.* —*v.i.* **1.** to grumble; complain. —*n.* **2.** a complaint. [orig. unknown. Cf. GROUCH] —**grous′er,** *n.*

grout (grout), *n.* **1.** a thin coarse mortar poured into the joints of masonry and brickwork. **2.** a finishing or setting coat of plaster for walls and ceilings. **3.** (*usually pl.*) lees or grounds. **4.** coarse meal or porridge. **5.** (*pl.*) groats. —*v.t.* **6.** to fill up, form, or finish the spaces between stones with grout. **7.** to use as grout. [OE *grūt;* akin to GRITS, GROATS, and GRIT]

grove (grōv), *n.* a small wood or plantation of trees. [ME; OE *gráf*] —**Syn.** See **forest.**

grov·el (grŭv′əl, grŏv′-), *v.i.,* **-eled, -eling** or (*esp. Brit.*) **-elled, -elling. 1.** to humble oneself or act in an abject manner, as in fear or in mean servility. **2.** to lie or move with the face downward and the body prostrate, esp. in abject humility, fear, etc. **3.** to take pleasure in mean or base things. [back formation from *groveling,* adv. (f. obs. *grufe* face down (t. Scand.) + -LING²), taken for ppr.] —**grov′el·er;** *esp. Brit.,* **grov′el·ler,** *n.* —**grov′el·ing·ly;** *esp. Brit.,* **grov′el·ling·ly,** *adv.*

grow (grō), *v.,* **grew, grown, growing.** —*v.i.* **1.** to increase by natural development, as any living organism or part by assimilation of nutriment; increase in size or substance. **2.** to arise or issue as from a germ, stock, or originating source. **3.** to increase gradually; become greater. **4.** to increase in influence or effect (fol. by *on* or *upon*): *a habit that grows on one.* **5.** to become gradually attached or united by or as by growth. **6.** to come to be, or become, by degrees: *to grow old.* **7. grow up, a.** to increase in growth; attain maturity. **b.** to spring up; arise. —*v.t.* **8.** to cause to grow: *he grows corn.* **9.** to allow to grow: *to grow a beard.* **10.** to cover with a growth (used in the passive): *a field grown with corn.* [ME *growe(n)*, OE *grōwan*, akin to D *groeien*, OHG *gruwan*, Icel. *grōa.* Cf. GRASS, GREEN]

grow·er (grō/ər), *n.* **1.** one who grows anything. **2.** a plant that grows in a certain way: *a quick grower.*

growing pains, 1. dull, indefinite pains in the limbs during childhood and adolescence, often popularly associated with the process of growing. **2.** difficulties attending any new project.

growing season, the period between the last killing frost in spring and the first killing frost in fall.

growl (groul), *v.i.* **1.** to utter a deep guttural sound of anger or hostility: *a dog growls.* **2.** to murmur or complain angrily; grumble. **3.** to rumble: *the thunder growled.* —*v.t.* **4.** to express by growling. —*n.* **5.** act or sound of growling. [ME *groule* rumble (said of the bowels), c. G *grollen* rumble] —**growl/ing·ly,** *adv.* —**Syn. 2.** See complain.

growl·er (grou/lər), *n.* **1.** one who or that which growls. **2.** *U.S. Slang.* a pitcher, pail, or other vessel brought by a customer for beer. **3.** *Brit. Slang.* a four-wheeled hansom cab.

grown (grōn), *adj.* **1.** advanced in growth: *a grown boy.* **2.** arrived at full growth or maturity; adult: *a grown man.* —*v.* **3.** pp. of **grow.**

grown-up (grōn/ŭp/), *n.* a grown-up person; an adult.

grown-up (grōn/ŭp/), *adj.* **1.** having reached the age of maturity. **2.** characteristic of or suitable for adults.

growth (grōth), *n.* **1.** act, process, or manner of growing; development; gradual increase. **2.** something that has grown or developed by or as by a natural process; a product: *a growth of weeds.* **3.** *Pathol.* a morbid mass of tissue, as a tumor. **4.** source; production: *a story of English growth.* —**Syn. 1.** augmentation, expansion.

Groz·ny (grōz/nĭ), *n.* a city in the S Soviet Union in Europe, in Caucasia. 226,000 (est. 1956).

grub (grŭb), *n., v.,* **grubbed, grubbing.** —*n.* **1.** the bulky larva of certain insects, esp. of scarabaeid and other beetles. **2.** a dull, plodding person; drudge. **3.** *Slang.* food or victuals. —*v.t.* **4.** to dig; clear of roots, etc. **5.** to dig up by the roots; uproot (often fol. by *up* or *out*). **6.** *Slang.* to supply with food. —*v.i.* **7.** to dig; search for or by as by digging. **8.** to lead a laborious or groveling life; drudge. **9.** to make laborious research; study closely. **10.** *Slang.* to take "grub" or food. [ME *grubbe(n)* dig. Cf. G *grübeln* grub, rake, rack (the brains), Icel. *gryfja* hole, pit; prob. akin to GRAVE[1]] —**grub/ber,** *n.*

grub·by (grŭb/ĭ), *adj.,* **-bier, -biest. 1.** dirty; slovenly. **2.** infested with or affected by grubs or larvae. [f. GRUB, n. + -Y[1]] —**grub/bi·ly,** *adv.* —**grub/bi·ness,** *n.*

grub hoe, a heavy hoe for grubbing up roots, etc.

grub·stake (grŭb/stāk/), *n., v.,* **-staked, -staking.** *U.S.* —*n.* **1.** provisions, outfit, etc., furnished to a prospector on condition of participating in the profits of his discoveries. —*v.t.* **2.** to furnish with a grubstake.

Grub Street, 1. a London street (now Milton Street) much inhabited by needy, inferior writers. **2.** petty and needy authors, or literary hacks, collectively.

grub·street (grŭb/strēt/), *adj.* **1.** hack; poor: *grub-street book.* —*n.* **2.** Grub Street (def. 2).

grudge (grŭj), *n., v.,* **grudged, grudging.** —*n.* **1.** a feeling of ill will or resentment excited by some special cause, as a personal injury or insult, etc. —*v.t.* **2.** to give or permit with reluctance; submit to unwillingly. **3.** to be dissatisfied at seeing the good fortune of (another). —*v.i.* **4.** to feel dissatisfaction or ill will. [earlier *grutch,* ME *gruche(n),* t. OF: m. *gruchier, groucier* murmur, grumble; orig. uncert. Cf. GROUCH] —**grudge/less,** *adj.* —**grudg/er,** *n.* —**grudg/ing·ly,** *adv.* —**Syn. 1.** GRUDGE, MALICE, SPITE refer to ill will held against another or others. A GRUDGE is a feeling of resentment harbored because of some real or fancied wrong: *to hold a grudge because of jealousy, she has a grudge against him.* MALICE is the state of mind which delights in doing harm, or seeing harm done, to others, whether expressing itself in an attempt seriously to injure or merely in sardonic humor: *malice in watching someone's embarrassment, to tell lies about someone out of malice.* SPITE is petty, and often sudden, resentment that manifests itself usually in trifling retaliations: *to reveal a secret out of spite, to build a high fence between properties out of spite.* **3.** begrudge, envy.

gru·el (grōō/əl), *n., v.,* **-eled, -eling** or (*esp. Brit.*) **-elled, -elling.** —*n.* **1.** a light, usually thin, cooked cereal made by boiling meal, esp. oatmeal, in water or milk. **2.** any similar substance. —*v.t.* **3.** to punish or use severely; exhaust; disable. [ME, t. OF: meal, g. dim. of ML *grūtum,* t. Gmc. Cf. GROUT]

gru·el·ing (grōō/əl Yng, grōōl/-), *adj.* **1.** exhausting; very tiring; severe. —*n.* **2.** any trying or exhausting procedure or experience. Also, *esp. Brit.,* **gru/el·ling.**

grue·some (grōō/səm), *adj.* such as to make one shudder; inspiring horror; revolting. Also, **grewsome.** [f. *grue,* v., shudder (c. G *grauen,* Dan. *grue*) + -SOME[1]. Of. G *grausam* horrible] —**grue/some·ly,** *adv.* —**grue/some·ness,** *n.*

gruff (grŭf), *adj.* **1.** low and harsh; hoarse: *a gruff voice.* **2.** rough; surly: *a gruff manner.* [earlier *grof,* t. D, f. *ge-* prefix (c. OE *ge-*) + *rof,* akin to OE *hrēof* rough]

—**gruff/ly,** *adv.* —**gruff/ness,** *n.* —**Syn. 1.** harsh. **2.** grumpy, brusque. —**Ant. 1.** pleasant. **2.** courteous.

grum·ble (grŭm/bəl), *v.,* **-bled, -bling,** *n.* —*v.i.* **1.** to murmur in discontent; complain ill-humoredly. **2.** to utter low, indistinct sounds; growl. **3.** to rumble: *the thunder grumbled.* —*v.t.* **4.** to express or utter with murmuring or complaining. —*n.* **5.** an ill-humored complaining; murmur; growl. **6.** (*pl.*) a grumbling, discontented mood. **7.** a rumble. [? freq. of OE *grymman* wail, mourn. Cf. OE *grymettan* grunt, roar, rage, G *grummeln* rumble, F *grommeter* mutter] —**grum/bler,** *n.* —**grum/bling·ly,** *adv.* —**Syn. 1.** See complain.

grum·met (grŭm/ĭt), *n.* grommet.

gru·mous (grōō/məs), *adj. Bot.* formed of clustered grains, granules, etc., as certain roots. Also, **gru·mose** (grōō/mōs). [f. *grume* (t. L: m. s. *grūmus* little heap, hillock) + -OUS]

grump·y (grŭm/pĭ), *adj.,* **grumpier, grumpiest.** surly; ill-tempered. [f. *grump* the sulks (b. GRUNT and DUMP) + -Y[1]] —**grump/i·ly,** *adv.* —**grump/i·ness,** *n.*

Grun·dy (grŭn/dĭ), *n.* **Mrs.,** society in regard to its censorship of personal conduct. [a character in Thomas Morton's play *Speed the Plough* (1798)]

grun·ion (grŭn/yən), *n.* a small slender food fish, *Leuresthes tenuis,* of southern California.

grunt (grŭnt), *v.i.* **1.** to utter the deep guttural sound characteristic of a hog. **2.** to utter a similar sound. **3.** to grumble, as in discontent. —*v.t.* **4.** to express with a grunt. —*n.* **5.** the sound of grunting. **6.** any of various marine fishes of the genus *Haemulon* and allied genera, which can emit a grunting sound. [ME *grunten,* OE *grunnettan,* freq. of *grunian* grunt. Cf. G *grunzen,* L *grunnīre*] —**grunt/ing·ly,** *adv.*

grunt·er (grŭn/tər), *n.* **1.** a hog. **2.** any animal or person that grunts. **3.** grunt (def. 6).

grutch (grŭch), *n., v.t., v.i. Brit. Dial.* grudge.

Gru·yère cheese (grĭ yâr/, grōō-; *Fr.* grᵪyĕr/), a firm, pale-yellow variety of French and Swiss cheese containing many holes. [named after *Gruyère,* district in Switzerland]

gryph·on (grĭf/ən), *n.* griffin.

G-string (jē/strĭng/), *n.* **1.** a loincloth or breechcloth. **2.** a similar covering, usually decorated, worn by women in a strip tease. [orig. uncert.]

gt., 1. great. **2.** (*pl.* **gtt.**) gutta.

Gt. Br., Great Britain. Also, **Gt. Brit.**

g.t.c., 1. good till canceled. **2.** good till countermanded.

gtd., guaranteed.

gua·cha·ro (gwä/chä rō/), *n., pl.* **-ros.** a nocturnal fruit-eating South American bird, *Steatornis caripensis,* valued by the natives for the oil produced from the fat of the young. [t. Sp., t. Araucanian: m. *uachar* cave]

gua·co (gwä/kō), *n., pl.* **-cos. 1.** a climbing asteraceous plant, *Mikania Guaco,* of tropical America. **2.** its medicinal leaves, or a substance obtained from them, used as an antidote for snake bites. **3.** a tropical American plant, *Aristolochia maxima,* also used for snake bites. [t. Sp.; from native name]

Gua·da·la·ja·ra (gwä/dä lä hä/rä), *n.* a city in W Mexico: the capital of Jalisco. 379,401 (est. 1951).

Gua·dal·ca·nal (gwä/dəl kə näl/, -däl kä näl/), *n.* one of the Solomon Islands, in the S Pacific: U.S. victory over the Japanese, 1942–43. 140,000 (est. 1951); ab. 2500 sq. mi.

Gua·dal·qui·vir (gwä/däl kē vēr/), *n.* a river in S Spain, flowing W to the Gulf of Cádiz. 374 mi.

Gua·da·lupe Hi·dal·go (gwä/da lōōp/ hĭ däl/gō; *Sp.* gwä/dä lōō/pĕ ē däl/gō), a city in the Federal District of Mexico: famous shrine; peace treaty, 1848. 60,239 (1950). Official name, **Gustavo A. Madero.**

Gua·de·loupe (gwä/da lōōp/), *n.* two islands separated by a narrow channel in the Leeward Islands of the West Indies: together with five dependencies they form a department of France. 229,120 pop. (1955); 687 sq. mi. *Cap.:* Basse-Terre.

Gua·di·a·na (gwä/dē ä/nä), *n.* a river from central Spain S through SE Portugal to the Gulf of Cádiz. 515 mi.

guai·a·col (gwī/ə kōl/, -kōl/), *n. Chem.* a colorless liquid, $CH_3OC_6H_4OH$, resembling creosote, obtained by distillation from guaiacum resin, and in other ways: used to treat phthisis, bronchitis, etc. [f. GUAIAC(UM) + -OL[2]]

guai·a·cum (gwī/ə kəm), *n.* **1.** any of the hard-wooded tropical American trees and shrubs constituting the zygophyllaceous genus *Guaiacum,* esp. *G. officinale* of the West Indies and South America, and *G. sanctum* of the West Indies and Florida. **2.** the hard, heavy wood of such a tree. See **lignum vitae** (def. 1). **3.** a greenish-brown resin obtained from such a tree, used as a stimulant and alterative, and as a remedy for rheumatism, cutaneous eruptions, etc. Also, **gua/o·cum, gui·ac** gwī/ăk). [NL, der. Sp. *guayaco;* from Haitian]

Guai·ra (gwī/rä), *n.* **La** (lä). See **La Guaira.**

Guam (gwäm), *n.* an island belonging to the U.S. in the N Pacific, E of the Philippine Islands: the largest of the Marianas group; U.S. naval station. 59,498 pop. (1950); 206 sq. mi. *Cap.:* Agaña.)

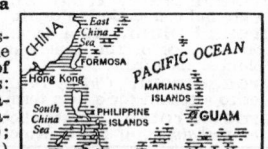

guan (gwän), *n.* any of various large gallinaceous birds constituting the subfamily *Penelopinae* (family *Cracidae*), chiefly of Central and South America, allied to the curassows. [? of W. Ind.orig.]

gua·na·co (gwä·nä′kō), *n., pl.* **-cos.** a wild South American ruminant, *Lama guanicoe*, of which the llama and alpaca are thought to be domesticated varieties, related to the camels. [t. Sp., t. Kechua: m. *huanacu*]

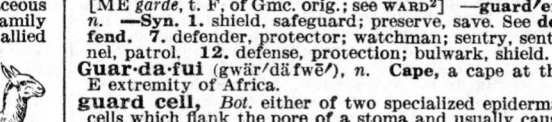
Guanaco, *Lama guanicoe* (3 ft. high at the shoulder)

Gua·na·jua·to (gwä′nä hwä′tō), *n.* 1. a state in central Mexico. 1,394,-157 (est. 1952); 11,805 sq. mi. 2. the capital of this state: center of a silver-mining region. 23,389 (1950).

gua·nase (gwä′nās), *n. Biochem.* an enzyme found in thymus, adrenals, and pancreas which converts guanine into xanthine. [f. GUAN(INE) + -ASE]

guan·i·dine (gwän′ə dēn′, -dĭn, gwä′nə-), *n.* a strongly caustic substance, $C(NH)(NH_2)_2$, forming crystalline salts and a wide variety of organic derivatives: used in the manufacture of plastics, resins, rubber accelerators, explosives, etc. Also, **guan·i·din** (gwän′ə dĭn, gwä′nə-). [der. GUANINE with infixed -ID³]

gua·nine (gwä′nēn, gōō′ə nēn′), *n. Chem.* a white crystalline substance, $C_5H_5N_5O$, found in guano, in the liver and pancreas of animals, in the scales of fishes, etc., and as a decomposition product of nucleic acids. Also, **gua·nin** (gwä′nĭn, gōō′ə-). [f. GUAN(O) + -INE²]

gua·no (gwä′nō), *n., pl.* **-nos.** 1. a natural manure composed chiefly of the excrement of sea birds, found esp. on islands near the Peruvian coast. 2. any similar substance, as an artificial fertilizer made from fish. [t. Sp., t. Kechua: m. *huanu dung*]

Guan·tá·na·mo (gwän tä′nä mô′), *n.* a city in SE Cuba. 83,684 (1953).

Guantánamo Bay, a bay on the SE coast of Cuba: U.S. naval station.

Gua·po·ré (gwä′pô rē′), *n.* a river forming part of the boundary between Brazil and Bolivia, flowing NW to the Mamoré river. ab. 900 mi.

Gua·ra·ni (gwä′rä nē′), *n., pl.* **-ni** (-nē′), **-nis** (-nēz′). 1. an important central South American tribe of Tupian family and affiliation. 2. a member of this tribe. 3. the Tupian language of the Guarani tribe.

guar·an·tee (găr′ən tē′), *n., v.,* **-teed, -teeing.** —*n.* 1. a warrant, pledge, or formal assurance given by way of security. 2. one who warrants, or gives a formal assurance or guaranty, as for the fulfillment of obligations. 3. one to whom a guarantee is made. 4. that which is taken or presented as security. 5. something that has the force or effect of a guaranty: *wealth is no guarantee of happiness.* —*v.t.* 6. to secure, as by giving or taking security. 7. to make oneself answerable for in behalf of one primarily responsible: *to guarantee the carrying out of a contract.* 8. to undertake to secure to another, as rights or possessions. 9. to serve as a warrant or guaranty for. 10. to engage (to do something). 11. to engage to protect or indemnify (fol. by *from, against,* or *in*): *to guarantee one against loss.* [appar. for GUARANTY] —Syn. 1. guaranty, surety. 11. See **warrant**.

guar·an·tor (găr′ən tôr′, -tər), *n.* one who makes or gives a guarantee.

guar·an·ty (găr′ən tĭ), *n., pl.* **-ties,** *v.,* **-tied, -tying.** —*n.* 1. a warrant, pledge, or promise given by way of security. 2. act of giving security. 3. one who acts as a guarantee. —*v.t.* 4. to guarantee. [t. AF: m. *guarantie,* der. *guarant, warant* WARRANT]

guard (gärd), *v.t.* 1. to keep safe from harm; protect; watch over. 2. to keep under close watch in order to prevent escape, outbreaks, etc.: *to guard a prisoner.* 3. to keep in check, from caution or prudence: *to guard the tongue.* 4. to provide with some safeguard or protective appliance, etc. —*v.i.* 5. to take precautions (fol. by *against*): *to guard against errors.* 6. to give protection; keep watch; be watchful. —*n.* 7. one who guards, protects, or serves protecting or restraining watch. 8. one who keeps watch over prisoners or others under restraint. 9. a body of men, esp. soldiers, charged with guarding a place from disturbance, theft, fire, etc. 10. restraining watch, as over a prisoner or other person under restraint: *to be kept under close guard.* 11. a contrivance, appliance, or attachment designed for guarding against injury, loss, etc. 12. something intended or serving to guard or protect; a safeguard. 13. a posture of defense or readiness, as in fencing, boxing, bayonet drill, etc. 14. *Football.* either of two players holding a position of defense at the right and the left of the center, in the forward line. 15. *Basketball.* one of the defensive players on a team. 16. **off one's guard,** unprepared to meet a sudden attack; unwary. 17. **on one's guard,** watchful or vigilant against attack; cautious; wary. 18. *Brit.* the conductor of a railroad train, etc. 19. (*cap., pl.*) the name of certain bodies of troops in the British army

guard, [ME *garde,* t. F, of Gmc. orig.; see WARD²] —**guard′er,** *n.* —Syn. 1. shield, safeguard; preserve, save. See **defend.** 7. defender, protector; watchman; sentry, sentinel, patrol. 12. defense, protection; bulwark, shield.

Guar·da·fui (gwär′dä fwē′), *n.* **Cape,** a cape at the E extremity of Africa.

guard cell, *Bot.* either of two specialized epidermal cells which flank the pore of a stoma and usually cause it to open and close.

guard·ed (gär′dĭd), *adj.* 1. cautious; careful: *to be guarded in one's speech.* 2. protected or watched, as by a guard. —**guard′ed·ly,** *adv.* —**guard′ed·ness,** *n.*

guard duty, military duties equivalent in general to those of civilian police, but including the watching over of military prisoners at work.

guard·house (gärd′hous′), *n.* 1. a military jail in which soldiers are confined for misconduct, or while awaiting trial for serious offenses. 2. the headquarters and quarters of the guard.

guard·i·an (gär′dē ən), *n.* 1. one who guards, protects, or preserves. 2. *Law.* one who is entrusted by law with the care of the person or property, or both, of another, as of a minor or of some other person legally incapable of managing his own affairs. —*adj.* 3. guarding; protecting: *a guardian angel.* [ME *gardein,* t. AF, der. *g(u)arde* GUARD, n.] —**guard′i·an·ship′,** *n.* —Syn. 1. protector, defender. 2. trustee, warden, keeper.

guards·man (gärdz′mən), *n., pl.* **-men.** 1. a man who acts as a guard. 2. *Chiefly Brit.* a member of any body of troops called "Guards." 3. *U.S.* a member of the National Guard.

Guar·ne·ri (gwär nĕ′rē), *n.* **Giuseppe Antonio** (jōō-zĕp′pĕ än tō′nyō), (*Joseph Guarnerius*) 1683–1745, Italian violinmaker.

Guar·ne·ri·us (gwär när′ĭ əs), *n.* a violin made by Guarneri or by a member of his family.

Guat., Guatemala.

Gua·te·ma·la (gwä′tə mä′lə; *Sp.* -tĕ mä′lä), *n.* 1. a republic in Central America. 3,258,000 (est. 1955); 42,-042 sq. mi. 2. Also, **Guatemala City,** the capital of this republic. 319,922 (est. 1953). —**Gua′te·ma′lan,** *adj., n.*

gua·va (gwä′və), *n.* 1. any of various trees or shrubs of the myrtaceous genus *Psidium,* esp. *P. Guajava,* natives of tropical or subtropical America, with a fruit used for jelly, etc. 2. the fruit, used for making jam, jelly, etc. [t. Sp.: m. *guayaba;* from S Amer. name]

Guay·a·quil (gwä′yä kēl′), *n.* a seaport in W Ecuador, on the **Gulf of Guayaquil,** an arm of the Pacific. 258,966 (1950).

gua·yu·le (gwä yōō′lĕ), *n.* 1. a rubber-yielding bushlike composite plant, *Parthenium argentatum,* of northern Mexico, etc. 2. the rubber obtained from this plant. [t. Sp.; from native name]

gu·ber·na·to·ri·al (gū′bər nə tōr′ĭ əl), *adj. Chiefly U.S.* pertaining to a governor. [f. L *gubernātor* steersman, governor + -IAL]

gu·ber·ni·ya (gōō bĕr′nĭ yä′), *n.* 1. (in the Soviet Union) an administrative division of the volosts, smaller than a district. 2. (in Russia before 1917) an administrative division equivalent to the province.

gude (gyd), *adj., adv., n. Scot. and Brit. Dial.* good.

Gude (gyd), *n. Scot. and Brit. Dial.* God.

gudg·eon (gŭj′ən), *n.* 1. a small European freshwater fish, *Gobio gobio,* of the minnow family, with a threadlike barbel at the corner of the mouth: easily caught, and much used for bait. 2. any of certain related fish. 3. one who is easily duped or cheated. 4. a bait or allurement. —*v.t.* 5. to dupe; cheat. [ME *gogen,* t. OF: m. *goujon,* g. s. L. *gōbio,* var. of *gōbius* GOBY]

Gud·run (gōōd′rōōn), *n.* 1. (in the Volsunga saga) daughter of the king of the Nibelungs; wife of Sigurd and later of Atli. 2. the heroine of the Middle High German epic poem called by her name. Also, **Kudrun.**

guel·der-rose (gĕl′dər rōz′), *n.* the European snowball, a cultivated variety of the European high-bush cranberry, *Viburnum Opulus* var. *roseum.* [named after *Geldern,* German town, or *Gelder(land),* Dutch province of which Geldern was formerly capital]

Guel·ders (gĕl′dərz), *n.* Gelderland.

Guelph (gwĕlf), *n.* 1. a member of the papal and popular party in medieval Italy, opposed to the Ghibellines. 2. a member of a secret society in Italy in the early 19th century, opposed to foreign rulers and reactionary ideas. Also, **Guelf.** [t. It.: m. *Guelfo,* t. G: m. *Welf,* name of founder of a princely German family] —**Guelph′ic,** *adj.*

gue·non (gə nôn′), *n.* any of the agile, long-tailed African monkeys, of the genus *Cercopithecus,* with their hairs many-banded, giving a speckled coloration. [t. F]

guer·don (gûr′dən), *Poetic.* —*n.* 1. a reward, recompense, or requital. —*v.t.* 2. to give a guerdon to; reward. [ME, t. OF, var. of *werdoun,* t. ML: m. s. *widerdonum,* alter. (prob. by assoc. with L *dōnum* gift), of OHG *widarlōn,* f. *widar* again, back + *lōn* reward, g. OE *witherlēan*]

Guern·sey (gûrn′zĭ), *n.* **Isle of,** one of the Channel Islands, in the English Channel. 41,149 (est. 1956); 24½ sq. mi.

Guern·sey (gûrn′zĭ), *n., pl.* **-seys.** 1. one of a breed of dairy cattle of average size, originating on Isle of Guernsey in the English Channel, giving a good supply of rich, golden-colored milk. 2. (*l.c.*) a close-fitting knitted woolen shirt much worn by seamen.

guer·ril·la (gə·rĭl′ə), *n.* **1.** a member of a small independent band of soldiers which harasses the enemy by surprise raids, attacks on communication and supply lines, etc. —*adj.* **2.** pertaining to such fighters or their warfare. Also, **gue·ril′la.** [t. Sp., dim. of *guerra* WAR]

Guesde (gĕd), *n.* **Jules** (zhyl), (*Mathieu Basile*) 1845–1922, French socialist leader, editor, and writer.

guess (gĕs), *v.t.* **1.** to form an opinion at random or from evidence admittedly uncertain: *to guess the age of a woman.* **2.** to estimate or conjecture correctly: *to guess a riddle.* **3.** to think, believe, or suppose: *I guess I can get there in time.* —*v.i.* **4.** to form an estimate or conjecture (often fol. by *at*): *to guess at the height of a building.* **5.** to estimate or conjecture correctly. —*n.* **6.** a notion, judgment, or conclusion gathered from mere probability or imperfect information; conjecture; surmise. [ME *gessen,* prob. t. Scand.; cf. MDan. *getze, gitse* (Dan. *gisse*) f. *get-* guess + *-s,* consol; cf. MD *gessen,* MLG *gissen*] —**guess′er,** *n.* —**guess′ing·ly,** *adv.*
—**Syn. 1, 2, 4.** suppose. GUESS, GUESS AT, CONJECTURE, SURMISE imply attempting to form an opinion as to the probable. To GUESS is to risk an opinion regarding something one does not know about; or, wholly or partly by chance, to arrive at the correct answer to a question: *to guess the outcome of a game.* GUESS AT implies more haphazard or random guessing: *to guess at the solution of a crime.* To CONJECTURE is to make inferences in the absence of sufficient evidence to establish certainty: *to conjecture the circumstances of the crime.* SURMISE implies making an intuitive conjecture which may or may not be correct: *to surmise the motives which led to it.* —**Ant. 3.** know.

guess-rope (gĕs′rōp′), *n.* guest-rope.

guess·work (gĕs′wûrk′), *n.* work or procedure based on or consisting in guessing; conjecture.

guest (gĕst), *n.* **1.** a person entertained at the house or table of another. **2.** one who receives the hospitality of a club, a city, or the like. **3.** a person who pays for lodging, and sometimes food, at a hotel, etc. **4.** *Zool.* a commensal (chiefly of insects living in other insects' nests). —*v.i.* **5.** *Rare.* to entertain as a guest. —*v.i.* **6.** *Rare.* to be a guest. [ME *gest*(*e*), t. Scand. (cf. Icel. *gestr*); r. OE *g*(*i*)*est,* c. D and G *gast*; akin to L *hostis* stranger, enemy] —**guest′less,** *adj.* —**Syn. 1, 3.** See **visitor.**

Guest (gĕst), *n.* Edgar Albert, 1881–1959, U.S. poet.

guest room, a room for the lodging of guests.

guest-rope (gĕst′rōp′), *n.* **1.** a line along a ship's side or from a boom for boats to make fast alongside. **2.** a line, in addition to the towrope, to steady a boat in tow. Also, **guess-rope.**

guf·faw (gŭ·fô′), *n.* **1.** a loud, coarse burst of laughter. —*v.i.* **2.** to laugh loudly and boisterously.

Gui., Guiana.

Gui·an·a (gē·ăn′ə, -ä′nə; Sp. gyä′nä), *n.* **1.** a vast tropical region in NE South America, bounded by the Orinoco, Río Negro, Amazon, and the Atlantic. ab. 690,000 sq. mi. **2.** a coastal portion of this region, including Guyana, French Guiana, and Surinam. 1,004,000 pop. (est. 1963); 175,275 sq. mi.

Guiana (def. 2)

guid·ance (gī′dəns), *n.* **1.** act of guiding; leadership; direction. **2.** something that guides.

guide (gīd), *v.,* **guided, guiding.** —*v.t.* **1.** to lead or conduct on the way, as to a place or through a region; show the way to. **2.** to direct the movement or course of: *to guide a horse.* **3.** to lead or direct in any course or action. —*n.* **4.** one who guides, esp. one employed to guide travelers, tourists, hunters, etc. **5.** a mark or the like to direct the eye. **6.** guidebook. **7.** guidepost. **8.** a contrivance for regulating progressive motion or action: *a sewing-machine guide.* **9.** a spirit believed to direct the utterances of a medium. [ME *guide*(*n*), t. OF: m. *guider,* t. Gmc.; cf. OE *witan* look after] —**guid′a·ble,** *adj.* —**guide′less,** *adj.* —**guid′er,** *n.*
—**Syn. 1.** pilot, steer. GUIDE, CONDUCT, DIRECT, LEAD imply showing the way or pointing out or determining the course to be taken. GUIDE implies continuous presence or agency in showing or indicating a course: *to guide a traveler.* To CONDUCT is to precede or escort to a place, sometimes with a degree of ceremony: *to conduct a guest to his room.* To DIRECT is to give information for guidance, or instructions or orders for a course of procedure: *to direct someone to the station.* To LEAD is to bring onward in a course, guiding by contact or by going in advance; hence, fig., to influence or induce to some course of conduct: *to lead a procession, to lead astray.* —**Ant. 3.** follow.

guide·board (gīd′bōrd′), *n.* a board on a guidepost containing directions to travelers.

guide·book (gīd′bŏok′), *n.* a book of directions and information for travelers, tourists, etc.

guided missile, an aerial missile, such as a rocket, steered during its flight by radio signals, clockwork controls, etc.

guide·post (gīd′pōst′), *n.* a post, usually mounted on the roadside or at the intersection of two or more roads, bearing a sign for the guidance of travelers.

guide rope, 1. *Aeron.* a long rope hung downward from a balloon and trailing along the ground, used to regulate the altitude automatically and to act as a brake. **2.** rope fastened, usually at an angle, to a hoisting or towing line, to guide the object being moved.

Gui·do d'A·rez·zo (gwē′dō dä·rĕt′tsō), A.D. c990–c1050, Italian or French monk, reformer of musical notation, who added lines to the staff and wrote notes on both spaces and lines.

gui·don (gī′dən), *n.* *Mil.* **1.** a small flag or streamer carried as a guide, for marking or signaling, or for identification. **2.** the soldier carrying it. [t. F, t. It.: m. *guidone,* b. *guidare* GUIDE and *gonfalone* GONFALON]

Gui·do Re·ni (gwē′dō rē′nē), 1575–1642, Italian painter.

Gui·enne (gwē·yĕn′), *n.* a former province in SW France. Also, **Guyenne.**

guild (gĭld), *n.* **1.** an organization of persons with common professional or cultural interests formed for mutual aid and protection. **2.** *Hist.* one of the associations, numerous in the middle ages, formed for mutual aid and protection or for a common purpose, most frequently by persons associated in trade or industry. **3.** *Bot.* all of the plants, such as parasites, having a similar habit of growth and nutrition. Also, **gild.** [ME *gild*(*e*), t. Scand. (cf. Icel. *gildi* guild, payment); r. OE *gegyld* guild; akin to G *geld* money, Goth. *gild* tribute]

guil·der (gĭl′dər), *n.* gulden. Also, **gilder.** [early mod. E *gildren,* var. of ME *guldren,* both t. D: m. (with intrusive *-r-*) *gulden*]

guild·hall (gĭld′hôl′), *n.* **1.** *Brit.* the hall built or used by a guild or corporation for its assemblies; town hall. **2.** *Hist.* a guild assembly hall. Also, **gildhall.**

guilds·man (gĭldz′mən), *n.,* *pl.* **-men.** a member of a guild. Also, **gildsman.**

guild socialism, a kind of English socialism by which workers' guilds manage and control government-owned industry.

guile (gīl), *n.* insidious cunning; treachery. [ME, t. OF; of Gmc. orig., and akin to WILE] —**Syn.** See **deceit.**

guile·ful (gīl′fəl), *adj.* full of guile; wily; deceitful; treacherous. —**guile′ful·ly,** *adv.* —**guile′ful·ness,** *n.*

guile·less (gīl′lĭs), *adj.* free from guile; sincere; honest; frank. —**guile′less·ly,** *adv.* —**guile′less·ness,** *n.*

guil·le·mot (gĭl′ə·mŏt′), *n.* any of several relatively narrow-billed northern oceanic birds of the genera *Cepphus* and *Uria,* as the **black guillemot,** *Cepphus grylle,* and **common guillemot,** *Uria aalge.* [t. F, appar. dim. of *Guillaume* William]

guil·loche (gĭ·lōsh′), *n.* an ornamental band or field with paired ribbons or lines flowing in interlaced curves. [t. F: graining tool, der. MF *goie* a kind of sickle, d. var. of F *gouge* GOUGE, n.]

Ionic guilloche

guil·lo·tine (*n.* gĭl′ə·tēn′; *v.* gĭl′ə·tēn′), *n., v.,* **-tined, -tining.** —*n.* **1.** a machine for beheading persons by means of a heavy blade falling in two grooved posts. **2.** an instrument for cutting the tonsils. —*v.t.* **3.** to behead by the guillotine. [t. F; named after J. I. Guillotin (1738–1814), French physician, who urged its use] —**guil′lo·tin′er,** *n.*

guilt (gĭlt), *n.* **1.** fact or state of having committed an offense or crime; grave culpability, as for some conscious violation of moral or penal law. **2.** guilty conduct. [ME *gilt,* OE *gylt* offense] —**Syn. 1.** guiltiness. **2.** criminality. —**Ant. 1.** innocence.

Guillotine
A. Knife; B. Cord, which releases knife; C. Board, to which victim is tied; D. Hole, for head of victim; E. Basket

guilt·less (gĭlt′lĭs), *adj.* **1.** free from guilt; innocent. **2.** having no knowledge or experience (fol. by *of*). **3.** destitute or devoid (fol. by *of*). —**guilt′less·ly,** *adv.* —**guilt′less·ness,** *n.* —**Syn. 1.** See **innocent.**

guilt·y (gĭl′tĭ), *adj.,* **guiltier, guiltiest. 1.** having incurred guilt or grave culpability, as by committing an offense or crime; justly chargeable with guilt (often fol. by *of*): *guilty of murder.* **2.** characterized by, connected with, or involving guilt: *guilty intent.* **3.** affected with or showing a sense of guilt: *a guilty conscience.* [ME *gilti,* OE *gyltig*] —**guilt′i·ly,** *adv.* —**guilt′i·ness,** *n.*

guimpe (gĭmp, gămp), *n.* a kind of chemisette or yoke of lace, embroidery, or other material, worn with a dress cut low at the neck. [earlier *gimp,* c. D *gimp*]

Guin., Guinea.

Guin·ea (gĭn′ĭ), *n.* **1.** a coastal region in W Africa, of indefinite extent, but generally considered as extending from the Gambia river to the Gabon estuary. **2.** an independent republic in W Africa, on the Atlantic coast. 2,800,000 pop. (est. 1959); ab. 96,900 sq. mi. *Cap.* Conakry. Formerly, **French Guinea. 3.** Gulf of, a large open bay in the angle of W Africa. **4.** (*l.c.*) a British gold coin issued from 1663 to 1813, at first of a nominal value of 20 shillings, but having since 1717 a fixed value of 21 shillings. **5.** (*l.c.*) *Colloq.* guinea fowl.

Guinea corn, durra.

guinea fowl, any member of an African gallinaceous bird family, the *Numididae,* which has (usually) dark-gray plumage with small white spots, one species of which is now domesticated throughout the world and valued for its flesh and eggs.

Common guinea fowl
Numida meleagris
(25 in. long)

guinea hen, 1. the female of the guinea fowl. **2.** any guinea fowl.

Guinea pepper, pepper pods, esp. of *Capsicum frutescens* var. *longum*, from which cayenne is ground.

guinea pig, a short-eared, short-tailed rodent of the genus *Cavia*, usually white, black, and tawny, much used in scientific experiments, commonly regarded as the domesticated form of one of the South American wild species of cavy. [f. GUINEA + PIG; reason for associating animal with Guinea unknown]

Guinea pig. *Cavia porcellus* (9 to 10 in. long)

Guinea worm, a long, slender, nematode worm, *Dracunculus medinensis,* parasitic under the skin of man and other animals, common in parts of India and Africa.

Guin·e·vere (gwĭn′ə vĭr′), *n.* *Arthurian Romance.* wife of King Arthur, and mistress of Lancelot. Also, **Guin·e·ver** (gwĭn′ə vər).

gui·pure (gĭ pyŏŏr′; *Fr.* gē pyr′), *n.* **1.** any of various laces, often heavy, made of linen, silk, etc., with the pattern connected by brides (rather than by a net ground). **2.** any of various laces or trimmings formerly in use, made with cords or heavy threads, metal, etc. [t. F, der. *guiper* cover or whip with silk, etc., t. Gmc.; cf. WIPE, WHIP]

Guis·card (gēs kär′), *n.* **Robert** (rô bĕr′), (*Robert de Hauteville*) c1015–85, Norman conqueror in Italy.

guise (gīz), *n.*, *v.*, **guised, guising.** —*n.* **1.** external appearance in general; aspect or semblance: *an old principle in a new guise.* **2.** assumed appearance or mere semblance: *under the guise of friendship.* **3.** Archaic. style of dress: *in the guise of a shepherdess.* **4.** Obs. manner; mode. —*v.t.* **5.** Archaic. to dress; attire. —*v.i.* **6.** *Scot. and N. Eng.* to go in disguise. [ME, t. OF, t. Gmc.; cf. WISE²] —**Syn. 1.** See **appearance.**

Guise (gēz), *n.* **1. François de Lorraine** (frän swä′ də lô rĕn′), **2nd Duc de,** 1519–63, French general and statesman. **2. Henri I de Lorraine** (äN rē′), **Duc de,** 1550–88, French general and leader of opposition to the Huguenots.

gui·tar (gĭ tär′), *n.* a musical stringed instrument with a long fretted neck and a flat, somewhat violinlike body. The strings, usually six in number, are plucked or twanged with the fingers. [t. Sp.: m. *guitarra,* t. Gk.: m. *kithára* cithara] —**gui·tar·ist,** *n.* —**gui·tar·like′,** *adj.*

Man playing a guitar

gui·tar·fish (gĭ tär′fĭsh′), *n., pl.* **-fishes,** (*esp. collectively*) **-fish.** a sharklike ray of the family *Rhinobatidae* inhabiting warm seas; specif., *Rhinobatus productus.*

Gui·try (gē trē′), *n.* **Sacha** (sä shä′), 1885–1957, French actor and dramatist, born in Russia.

Gui·zot (gē zō′), *n.* **François Pierre Guillaume** (frän swä′ pyĕr′ gē yōm′), 1787–1874, French historian and statesman.

Gu·ja·rat (gŏŏj′ə rät′), *n.* a level region in W India, N of the Narbada river: formerly a kingdom.

Gu·ja·ra·ti (gŏŏj′ə rä′tĭ), *n.* an Indic language of western India.

gulch (gŭlch), *n.* *U.S.* a deep narrow ravine, esp. one marking the course of a stream or torrent. [orig. uncert.]

gul·den (gŏŏl′dən), *n., pl.* **-dens, -den. 1.** the gold monetary unit of the Netherlands, equal to 26.3 U.S. cents. **2.** a Dutch silver coin of this value (also called *florin*). **3.** the Austrian florin. **4.** one of several gold coins formerly current in Germany from the 14th century, and in the Low Countries from the 15th century. Also, **guilder, gild r.** [t. D and G: lit., golden]

Gü·lek Bo·gaz (gy lĕk′ bō gäz′), Turkish name of the Cilician Gates.

gules (gūlz), *n.* *Her.* red. [ME *goules,* t. OF: m. *gueules* red fur neckpiece, ult. der. *gole* throat, g. L *gula*]

gulf (gŭlf), *n.* **1.** a portion of an ocean or sea partly enclosed by land. **2.** a deep hollow; chasm or abyss. **3.** any wide separation, as in station, education, etc. **4.** something that engulfs or swallows up. —*v.t.* **5.** to swallow like a gulf, or as in a gulf; engulf. [ME *goulf,* t. OF: m. *golfe,* t. It.: m. *golfo,* t. LGk.: m. *kólpos,* Gk. *kólpos* bosom, gulf] —**gulf′like′,** *adj.*

Gulf States, those States of the U.S. bordering on the Gulf of Mexico: Florida, Alabama, Mississippi, Louisiana, and Texas.

Gulf Stream, a warm oceanic current issuing from the Gulf of Mexico, flowing northward along the U.S. coast and thence northeasterly toward the British Isles.

gulf·weed (gŭlf′wēd′), *n.* **1.** a coarse olive-brown seaweed, *Sargassum bacciferum,* found in the Gulf Stream and elsewhere, characterized by numerous berrylike air vessels. **2.** any seaweed related to it.

gull¹ (gŭl), *n.* any of numerous long-winged, web-footed, aquatic birds constituting the subfamily *Larinae* (family *Laridae*), esp. of the genus *Larus,* usually white with gray back and wings. [ME *gull(e),* ? repr. OE word (unrecorded) akin to OE *giellan* yell]

gull² (gŭl), *v.t.* **1.** to deceive; trick; cheat. —*n.* **2.** one easily deceived or cheated; a dupe. [? akin to obs. *gull,* v., swallow, guzzle]

Herring gull. *Larus argentatus-smithsonianus* (22 to 25 in. long)

Gul·lah (gŭl′ə), *n.* **1.** a member of a Negro people settled as slaves on the sea islands and coastal region of Georgia and South Carolina. **2.** their English dialect.

gul·let (gŭl′ĭt), *n.* **1.** the esophagus, or tube by which food and drink swallowed pass to the stomach. **2.** the throat or pharynx. **3.** something like the esophagus. **4.** a channel for water. **5.** a gully or ravine. **6.** a preparatory cut in excavations. [ME *golet,* t. OF: m. *goulet,* ult. der. L *gula* throat]

gul·li·ble (gŭl′ə bəl), *adj.* easily deceived or cheated. —**gul′li·bil′i·ty,** *n.* —**gul′li·bly,** *adv.*

Gul·li·ver's Travels (gŭl′ə vərz), a social and political satire (1726) by Swift, narrating the voyages of Lemuel Gulliver to four imaginary regions: Lilliput, Brobdingnag, Laputa, and the land of the Houyhnhnms.

gul·ly (gŭl′ĭ), *n., pl.* **-lies,** *v.,* **-lied, -lying.** —*n.* **1.** a small valley or canyon cut by running water. **2.** a ditch or gutter. —*v.t.* **3.** to make gullies in. **4.** to form (channels) by the action of water. [appar. var. of GULLET, with substitution of -y³ for F -*et*]

gulp (gŭlp), *v.i.* **1.** to gasp or choke as when taking large drafts of liquids. —*v.t.* **2.** to swallow eagerly, or in large drafts or pieces (usually fol. by *down*). **3.** to take in, as by swallowing eagerly; choke back: *to gulp down a sob.* —*n.* **4.** act of gulping. **5.** the amount swallowed at one time; mouthful. [ME *gulpe(n).* Cf. D *gulpen* gulp, Norw. *glupa* swallow] —**gulp′er,** *n.*

gum¹ (gŭm), *n., v.,* **gummed, gumming.** —*n.* **1.** any of various viscid, amorphous exudations from plants, hardening on exposure to air, and soluble in, or forming a viscid mass with, water. **2.** any of various similar exudations, as resin or the like. **3.** a preparation of such a substance, as for use in the arts, etc. **4.** chewing gum. **5.** mucilage; glue. **6.** rubber. **7.** a gum tree. **8.** *Philately.* See **original gum. 9.** (*usually pl.*) *U.S. Local.* a rubber overshoe. —*v.t.* **10.** to smear, stiffen, or stick together with gum. **11.** to clog with or as with some gummy substance. —*v.i.* **12.** to exude or form gum. **13.** to become gummy; become clogged with some gummy substance. [ME *gomme,* t. OF, g. var. of L *gummi,* t. Gk.: m. *kómmi*] —**gum′like′,** *adj.*

gum² (gŭm), *n.* (*often pl.*) the firm, fleshy tissue covering the alveolar parts of either jaw and enveloping the necks of the teeth. [ME *gome,* OE *gōma* palate, inside of the mouth; akin to Icel. *gōmr,* G *gaumen* palate]

gum ammoniac, a medicinal gum resin from the umbelliferous plant, *Dorema ammoniacum,* of Persia, etc.

gum arabic, a gum obtained from *Acacia Senegal* and other species of acacia: used in calico printing, in making mucilage, ink, and the like, in medicine, etc.

gum benzoin, a resin obtained from *Styrax Benzoin* in Siam, containing benzoic acid, vanillin, and essential oils, used in the perfume and cosmetic industries.

gum·bo (gŭm′bō), *n., pl.* **-bos. 1.** the okra plant. **2.** its mucilaginous pods. **3.** a soup, usually chicken, thickened with okra pods. **4.** a silty soil, chiefly in the southern and western U.S., becoming very sticky when wet. Also, **gombo.** [from Angola name]

gum·boil (gŭm′boil′), *n.* a small abscess on the gum.

gum·bo·til (gŭm′bə tĭl), *n.* *Geol.* a sticky clay formed by the thorough weathering of glacial drift, the thickness of the clay furnishing means for comparing relative lengths of interglacial ages.

gum·drop (gŭm′drŏp′), *n.* *U.S.* a droplike confection of gum arabic, gelatin, or the like, sweetened and flavored.

gum elastic, rubber.

gum·ma (gŭm′ə), *n., pl.* **gummata** (gŭm′ə tə), **gummas.** *Pathol.* the rubbery, tumorlike lesion of tertiary syphilis. [NL, der. L *gummi* GUM¹]

gum·ma·tous (gŭm′ə təs), *adj.* **1.** of the nature of or resembling a gumma. **2.** pertaining to a gumma.

gum·mite (gŭm′īt), *n.* a yellow to red alteration product of pitchblende, having a greasy luster, and occurring in gumlike masses, a minor ore of uranium.

gum·mo·sis (gŭ mō′sĭs), *n.* *Bot.* an abnormal condition of certain plants such as the cherry, plum, sugar cane, cotton, etc., which causes the excessive formation of gum. [NL, f. L *gumm*(i) + -osis. See GUM¹]

gum·my (gŭm′ĭ), *adj.,* **-mier, -miest. 1.** of the nature of gum; viscid. **2.** covered with or clogged by gum or sticky matter. **3.** exuding gum. —**gum′mi·ness,** *n.*

gum plant, a plant of the composite genus *Grindelia,* of the western U.S., covered with a viscid secretion.

gump·tion (gŭmp′shən), *n.* *Colloq.* **1.** initiative; resourcefulness. **2.** shrewd, practical sense. [orig. Scot.]

gum·shoe (gŭm′shōō′), *n., v.,* **-shoed, -shoeing.** —*n.* **1.** a shoe made of gum elastic or India rubber; rubber overshoe. **2.** (*pl.*) sneakers. **3.** *U.S. Slang.* a. one who goes about softly, as if wearing rubber shoes. **b.** a policeman or detective. —*v.i.* **4.** *U.S. Slang.* to go softly as if wearing rubber shoes; move or act stealthily.

gum tree, 1. any tree that exudes gum, as a eucalyptus, the sour gum, the sweet gum, etc. **2.** any of various other gum-yielding trees, as the sapodilla.

gum·wood (gŭm′wŏŏd′), *n.* the wood of a gum tree, esp. the wood of the eucalyptus of Australia, or a gum tree of western U.S.

gun¹ (gŭn), *n., v.,* **gunned, gunning.** —*n.* **1.** a metallic tube, with its stock or carriage and attachments, from which heavy missiles are thrown by the force of gunpowder, etc.; a piece of ordnance. **2.** any portable firearm except a pistol or revolver, as a rifle. **3.** a long-

ăct, āble, dâre, ärt; ĕbb, ēqual; ĭf, īce; hŏt, ōver, ôrder, oil, bŏŏk, ōoze, out; ŭp, ūse, ûrge; ə = a in alone; ch, chief; g, give; ng, ring; sh, shoe; th, thin; ŧħ, that; zh, vision. See the full key on inside cover.

barreled cannon, having a flat trajectory. **4.** *U.S. Colloq.* a pistol or revolver. **5.** any similar device for projecting something: *an air gun, cement gun.* **6.** *Brit.* a member of a shooting party. —*v.i.* **7.** to hunt with a gun. **8.** to shoot with a gun. **9.** to seek with intent to kill (fol. by *for*). **10.** to seek; try to obtain (fol. by *for*): *to gun for support.* —*v.t.* **11.** *U.S. Colloq.* to shoot with a gun. **12.** *Aviation Slang.* to cause to increase in speed very quickly. **13.** to feed gas to, suddenly and quickly: *to gun an engine.* [ME *gunne, gonne,* appar. short for *Gunilda* (L), *gonnyld* (ME), name for engine of war, ult. t. Scand.; cf. Icel. *Gunna,* short for *Gunnhildr,* woman's name] —**gun′less,** *adj.*

gun² (gŭn), *v.* *Archaic and Poetic.* pp. of **gin³.**

gun·boat (gŭn′bōt′), *n.* **1.** a small vessel carrying mounted guns. **2.** a small, armed war vessel of light draft, used for visiting shallow-water ports, etc.

gun carriage, the carriage or structure on which a gun is mounted or moved, and on which it is fired.

gun·cot·ton (gŭn′kŏt′ən), *n.* a highly explosive cellulose nitrate, made by digesting clean cotton in a mixture of 1 part nitric acid and 3 parts sulfuric acid.

gun dog, a trained dog which accompanies hunters when they shoot game, esp. game birds.

gun·fire (gŭn′fīr′), *n.* **1.** the firing of a gun or guns. **2.** *Mil.* the tactical use of firearms, esp. cannon, as distinguished from other weapons, as bayonets or torpedoes, and from shock or charge tactics.

gun·flint (gŭn′flĭnt′), *n.* the flint in a flintlock.

gung ho (gŭng′hō′), *Chinese.* work together (a slogan of U.S. Marines under General Carlson in World War II.

gun·lock (gŭn′lŏk′), *n.* the mechanism of a firearm by which the charge is exploded.

gun·man (gŭn′mən), *n., pl.* **-men. 1.** *U.S.* a man armed with, or expert with, a gun, esp. one ready to use a gun unlawfully for hire. **2.** one who makes guns.

gun metal, 1. any of various alloys or metallic substances with a dark-gray or blackish color or finish, used for chains, belt buckles, etc. **2.** a dark gray with bluish or purplish tinge. **3.** a bronze formerly much employed for cannon. —**gun′-met′al,** *adj.*

Gun·nar (gŏŏn′när), *n.* brother of Gudrun and husband of Brünhild in the *Völsunga Saga.* [Icel.]

gun·nel¹ (gŭn′əl), *n.* any of certain elongate blennies (fishes) esp. the butterfish, *Pholis gunnellus,* which is found in the northern Atlantic. [orig. uncert.]

gun·nel² (gŭn′əl), *n.* gunwale.

gun·ner (gŭn′ər), *n.* **1.** one who works a gun or cannon. **2.** *U.S. Army.* a rating in the artillery. **3.** *U.S. Navy.* one skilled in handling ammunition and gunnery equipment. **4.** *U.S. Marines.* a warrant officer who may be given any one of a number of assignments. **5.** *Brit.* a man assigned to the artillery. **6.** a hunter with a gun.

gun·ner·y (gŭn′ərĭ), *n.* **1.** the art and science of constructing and managing guns, esp. large guns. **2.** the firing of guns. **3.** guns collectively.

gun·ning (gŭn′ĭng), *n.* **1.** act, practice, or art of shooting with guns. **2.** hunting of game with guns.

gun·ny (gŭn′ĭ), *n., pl.* **-nies. 1.** a strong, coarse material made commonly from jute, used for bagging, etc. **2.** Also, **gunny bag** or **sack.** a bag or sack made of this material. [t. Hind.: m. *gŏni*]

gun·pa·per (gŭn′pā′pər), *n.* *Mil.* a type of paper treated with nitric acid so that it has a composition similar to that of guncotton.

gun·pow·der (gŭn′pou′dər), *n.* **1.** an explosive mixture of saltpeter (potassium nitrate), sulfur, and charcoal, used esp. in gunnery. **2.** a fine variety of green China tea, each leaf of which is rolled into a little ball.

Gunpowder Plot, *Eng. Hist.* an unsuccessful plot to blow up King James I, the Lords, and the Commons assembled in Parliament on Nov. 5, 1605, in revenge for the laws against Roman Catholics.

gun room, 1. a room in which guns are kept. **2.** *Brit.* a room for the use of junior naval officers.

gun·run·ning (gŭn′rŭn′ĭng), *n.* the smuggling of guns, etc., into a country. —**gun′run′ner,** *n.*

gun·shot (gŭn′shŏt′), *n.* **1.** a shot fired from a gun. **2.** the range of a gun: *out of gunshot.* **3.** the shooting of a gun. —*adj.* **4.** made by a gunshot.

gun·shy (gŭn′shī′), *adj.* frightened at gunshot.

gun·smith (gŭn′smĭth′), *n.* one who makes or repairs firearms.

gun·stock (gŭn′stŏk′), *n.* the stock or support in which the barrel of a shoulder weapon is fixed.

Gun·ter (gŭn′tər), *n.* **Edmund,** 1581–1626, English mathematician and inventor of the sector and scale.

Gun·ter's chain (gŭn′tərz). See **chain** (def. 9).

Gun·ther (gŏŏn′tər), *n.* (in the Nibelungen epic) a Burgundian king, brother of Kriemhild and husband of Brunhild.

gun·wale (gŭn′əl), *n.* *Naut.* **1.** the upper edge of a vessel's or boat's side. **2.** the uppermost wale of a ship, next below the bulwarks. Also, **gunnel.** [f. GUN + *wale* a plank; so called because guns were set upon it]

gup·py (gŭp′ĭ), *n., pl.* **-pies.** a live-bearing top minnow, *Lebistes reticulatus,* of the family *Poeciliidae,* common in home aquaria.

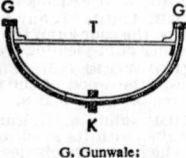

G. Gunwale;
K. Keel; T. Thwart

gur·gi·ta·tion (gûr′jətā′shən), *n.* surging rise and fall; ebullient motion, as of water. [f. s. LL *gurgitātus,* pp., engulfed + -ION]

gur·gle (gûr′gəl), *v.,* **-gled, -gling,** *n.* —*v.i.* **1.** to flow in a broken, irregular, noisy current: *water gurgles from a bottle.* **2.** to make a sound as of water doing this (often used of birds or of human beings). —*v.t.* **3.** to utter with a gurgling sound. —*n.* **4.** act or noise of gurgling. [? imit. Cf. G *gurgeln* GARGLE] —**gur′gling·ly,** *adv.*

Gur·kha (gŏŏr′kä), *n.* a member of a warlike Rajput people, Hindu in religion, living in Nepal.

gur·nard (gûr′nərd), *n., pl.* **-nards,** (esp. collectively) **-nard. 1.** any of various marine acanthopterygian fishes, esp. of the genus *Trigla* of Europe and the genus *Prionotus* of America, having a spiny head with mailed cheeks, and three pairs of free, fingerlike pectoral rays. **2.** any of various similar fishes. See **flying gurnard.** [ME, t. OF: m. *gornard,* prob. lit., grunter, der. Pr. *gourgna* grunt, ult. der. L *grunnīre* grunt]

gush (gŭsh), *v.i.* **1.** to issue with force, as a fluid from confinement; flow suddenly and copiously. **2.** *Colloq.* to express oneself extravagantly or emotionally; talk effusively. **3.** to have a copious flow of something, as of blood, tears, etc. **4.** to emit suddenly, forcibly, or copiously. —*v.t.* **5.** a sudden and violent emission of a fluid. **6.** the fluid emitted. **7.** *Colloq.* gushing or effusive language. [ME *gusche,* ? ult. f. *gus-* (see GUST) + -*k,* suffix. Cf. Icel. *gusa*] —**gush′ing·ly,** *adv.* —**Syn. 1.** pour, stream, spurt. See **flow.**

gush·er (gŭsh′ər), *n.* **1.** *Chiefly U.S.* a flowing oil well, usually of large capacity. **2.** a person who gushes.

gush·y (gŭsh′ĭ), *adj.,* **gushier, gushiest.** given to or marked by gush or effusiveness. —**gush′i·ness,** *n.*

gus·set (gŭs′ĭt), *n.* **1.** an angular piece of material inserted in a shirt, etc., usually under the armhole. **2.** a metallic plate used for connections, as in a steel truss connecting the members framing into a joint. **3.** *Armor.* **a.** a mail strips in the armpit region sewn to cloth sleeves. **b.** a narrow articulated plate of breastplate adjacent to the arm. [ME, t. OF: m. *gousset,* der. *gousse* pod, husk]

gust (gŭst), *n.* **1.** a sudden, strong blast of wind. **2.** a sudden rush or burst of water, fire, smoke, sound, etc. **3.** an outburst of passionate feeling. [t. Scand.; cf. Icel. *gustr* a gust, blast, f. *gus-* (akin to *gjōsa, gusa* gush) + -*t,* suffix] —**Syn. 1.** See **wind¹.**

gus·ta·to·ry (gŭs′tətōr′ĭ), *adj.* of taste or tasting.

Gus·ta·vo A. Ma·de·ro (gŏŏs tä′vō, mä dĕ′rō), official name of Guadalupe Hidalgo.

Gus·ta·vus I (gŭs tä′vəs), (*Gustavus Vasa*) 1496–1560, king of Sweden, 1523–60.

Gustavus V, 1858–1950, king of Sweden, 1907–50.

Gustavus VI, born 1882, king of Sweden since 1950.

Gustavus A·dol·phus (ə dŏl′fəs), 1594–1632, king of Sweden, 1611–32. Also, **Gustavus II.**

gus·to (gŭs′tō), *n., pl.* **-tos. 1.** keen relish or hearty enjoyment, as in eating, drinking, or in action or speech generally: *to tell a story with gusto.* **2.** individual taste or liking. [t. It., g. L *gustus* taste, relish]

gust·y (gŭs′tĭ), *adj.,* **gustier, gustiest. 1.** blowing or coming in gusts, as wind, rain, storms, etc. **2.** affected or marked by gusts of wind, etc.: *gusty day.* **3.** occurring or characterized by sudden bursts or outbursts, as sound, laughter, etc. —**gust′i·ly,** *adv.* —**gust′i·ness,** *n.*

gut (gŭt), *n., v.,* **gutted, gutting.** —*n.* **1.** the alimentary canal between the pylorus and the anus, or some portion of it. **2.** (*pl.*) the bowels or entrails. **3.** (*pl.*) *Slang.* courage; stamina; endurance: *to have guts.* **4.** the substance forming the case of the intestine; intestinal tissue or fiber: *sheep's gut.* **5.** a preparation of the intestines of an animal used for various purposes, as for violin strings, tennis rackets, fishing lines, etc. **6.** the silken substance taken from a silkworm killed when about to spin its cocoon, used in making snells for fishhooks. **7.** a narrow passage, as a channel of water or a defile between hills. —*v.t.* **8.** to take out the guts or entrails of; disembowel. **9.** to plunder of contents. **10.** to destroy the interior of: *fire gutted the building.* [ME; OE *guttas,* pl., akin to *gēotan pour*] —**Syn. 3.** pluck.

gut·buck·et (gŭt′bŭk′ĭt), *adj.* *Jazz.* in a low-down, primitive style.

Gu·ten·berg (gŏŏ′tən bûrg′; *Ger.* -bĕrкн′), *n.* **Johannes** (yō hän′ĕs), (*Johann Gensfleisch*) c1398–1468, German printer.

Gutenberg Bible, an edition of the Vulgate printed at Mainz before 1456, ascribed to Gutenberg and others: prob. the first large book printed with movable type.

Guth·rie (gŭth′rĭ), *n.* a city in central Oklahoma: the former state capital. 10,113 (1950).

gut·ta (gŭt′ə), *n., pl.* **guttae** (gŭt′ē). **1.** a drop, or something resembling one. **2.** *Archit.* one of a series of pendent ornaments, generally in the form of a frustum of a cone, attached to the underside of the mutules, etc., of the Doric entablature. [t. L: a drop]

gut·ta-per·cha (gŭt′ə pûr′chə), *n.* the concrete milky juice, nearly white when pure, of various Malaysian sapotaceous trees, esp. *Palaquium Gutta,* variously used in the arts, medicine, and manufactures, as for insulating electric wires. [f. Malay: m. *getah* gum, balsam + *percha* kind of tree producing the substance]

gut·ter (gŭt′ər), *n.* **1.** a channel at the side (or in the middle) of a road or street, for leading off surface water. **2.** any channel, trough, or the like for carrying off fluid. **3.** a channel at the eaves or on the roof of a building, for

---

b., blend of, blended; c., cognate with; d., dialect, dialectal; der., derived from; f., formed from; g., going back to; m., modification of; r., replacing; s., stem of; t., taken from; ?, perhaps.   See the full key on inside cover.

carrying off rain water.   **4.** a furrow or channel made by running water.   **5.** the abode or resort of the lowest class of persons in the community: *the language of the gutter.* —*v.i.* **6.** to flow in streams: *the candles guttered down.* **7.** to form gutters, as water does. —*v.t.* **8.** to make gutters in; channel.   **9.** to furnish with a gutter or gutters: *to gutter a house or shed.* [ME *goter*, t. OF: m. *goutiere*, ult. der. L *gutta* a drop] —**gut'ter·like',** *adj.*

gut·ter·snipe (gŭt'ərsnīp'), *n.* *Colloq.* a street child of the lowest class; street Arab; gamin.

gut·tur·al (gŭt'ərəl), *adj.* **1.** pertaining to the throat. **2.** harsh; throaty.   **3.** *Phonet.* pertaining to sounds articulated in the back of the mouth, esp. the velars. —*n.* **4.** a guttural sound. [t. NL: s. *gutturālis*, der. L *guttur* throat] —**gut'tur·al·ly,** *adv.* —**gut'tur·al·ness,** *n.*

guy[1] (gī), *n., v.,* **guyed, guying.** —*n.* **1.** *Slang.* a fellow or person: *he's a nice guy.* **2.** *Brit.* a person of grotesque appearance; a fright.   **3.** a grotesque effigy of Guy Fawkes, the leader of the Gunpowder Plot, carried about and burned on Guy Fawkes Day. —*v.t.* **4.** *Slang.* to jeer at or make fun of; ridicule. [from *Guy Fawkes*]

guy[2] (gī), *n., v.,* **guyed, guying.** —*n.* **1.** a rope or appliance used to guide and steady a thing being hoisted or lowered, or to secure anything liable to shift its position. —*v.t.* **2.** to guide, steady, or secure with a guy or guys. [ME *gye,* t. OF: m. *guie* a guide, der. *guier* GUIDE]

Guy·a·na (gē an'ə, -ä'nə; *Sp.* gyä'nä), *n.* a nation on the NE coast of South America; a former British protectorate; 628,000 pop. (est. 1964); 82,978 sq. mi. *Cap.*: Georgetown. Formerly, **British Guiana.** See map under Guiana.

Guy·enne (gwē·yĕn'), *n.* Guienne.

Guy Fawkes Day (gī' fôks'), *Brit.* Nov. 5, celebrated by fireworks, etc. See **Gunpowder Plot.**

guz·zle (gŭz'əl), *v.i., v.t.,* **-zled, -zling.** to drink frequently and greedily: *They sat there all evening guzzling their beer.* —**guz'zler,** *n.*

Gwa·li·or (gwä'lĭ ôr'), *n.* **1.** a former state in central India, now part of Madhya Pradesh.   **2.** a city in N Madhya Pradesh. 241,577 (1951).

Gwyn (gwĭn), *n.* Nell, 1650–87, British actress and mistress of Charles II.

gybe (jīb), *v.i., v.t., n.* *Naut.* jibe[1].

gym (jĭm), *n.* gymnasium.

gym·kha·na (jĭm kä'nə), *n.* *Chiefly Brit.* **1.** a series of athletic contests, esp. in racing.   **2.** the place where this is held. [t. Hind.: m. *gendkhāna,* lit., ball house]

gym·na·si·a (jĭm nā'zĭ ə), *n.* pl. of **gymnasium.**

gym·na·si·arch (jĭm nā'zĭ ärk'), *n.* a magistrate who superintended the gymnasia and certain public games in ancient Athens. [t. L: s. *gymnasiarchus,* t. Gk.: m. *gymnasiarchos*]

gym·na·si·um (jĭm nā'zĭ əm), *n.,* pl. **-siums, -sia** (-zĭ ə).   **1.** a building or room designed and equipped for physical education activities.   **2.** a place where Greek youths met for exercise and discussion. [t. L, t. Gk.: m. *gymnāsion* (see def. 2)]

Gym·na·si·um (jĭm nā'zĭ əm; *Ger.* gĭm nä'zĭ ŏŏm', gĭm-), *n.* (in continental Europe, esp. Germany) a classical school preparatory to the universities. [G, t. L. See GYMNASIUM]

gym·nast (jĭm'năst), *n.* one skilled in, or a teacher of, gymnastics. [t. Gk.: s. *gymnastēs* trainer of athletes]

gym·nas·tic (jĭm năs'tĭk), *adj.* pertaining to exercises which develop flexibility, strength, and agility. —**gym·nas'ti·cal·ly,** *adv.*

gym·nas·tics (jĭm năs'tĭks), *n.* **1.** (*construed as pl.*) gymnastic exercises.   **2.** (*construed as sing.*) the practice or art of gymnastic exercises.

gym·no·sperm (jĭm'nə spûrm'), *n.* *Bot.* a plant having its seeds exposed or naked, not enclosed in an ovary (opposed to **angiosperm**). [t. NL: s. *gymnospermus,* t. Gk.: m. *gymnóspermos*]

gym·no·sper·mous (jĭm'nə spûr'məs), *adj.* *Bot.* of the gymnosperm class; having naked seeds.

gyn-, var. of **gyno-,** before vowels, as in *gynarchy.*

gy·nae·ce·um (jī'nə sē'əm, jĭn'ə-), *n.,* pl. **-cea** (-sē'ə). **1.** *Bot.* gynoecium.   **2.** (among the Greeks) that part of a dwelling used by women. Also, **gy·nae·ci·um** (jī'nə-sī'əm, jĭn'ə-).

gy·nae·ce·o·mor·phous (jī nē'kō môr'fəs, jĭn'ə kō-), *adj.* gynecomorphous.

gy·nan·drous (jī năn'drəs, jĭ-), *adj.* *Bot.* having the stamens borne on the pistil and united in a column, as in orchids. [t. Gk.: m. *gýnandros* of doubtful sex]

gy·nar·chy (jī'närkĭ, jĭn'ər-), *n.,* pl. **-chies.** government by a woman or women.

gy·ne·ci·um (jī nē'sĭ əm, jĭn'-), *n.,* pl. **-cia** (-sĭ ə). gynoecium.

gy·ne·coc·ra·cy (jī'nə kŏk'rə sĭ, jĭn'ə-), *n.,* pl. **-cies.** government by a woman or women. Also, **gy·nae·coc'ra·cy.** [t. Gk.: m.s. *gynaikokratia*]

gy·ne·col·o·gy (jī'nə kŏl'ə jĭ, jĭn'ə-), *n.* that department of medical science which deals with the functions and diseases peculiar to women. Also, **gy'nae·col'o·gy.** [f. m. Gk. *gynaiko-* (comb. form of *gynē* woman) + -LOGY] —**gy·ne·co·log·i·cal** (gī'nə kə lŏj'ə kəl, jĭn'ə-), *adj.* —**gy·ne·col'o·gist,** *n.*

gy·ne·co·mor·phous (jī'nə kō môr'fəs, jĭn'ə kō-), *adj.* *Biol.* having the form, appearance, or attributes of a female. Also, **gynaecomorphous.** [t. Gk.: m. *gynai-kómorphos* in the shape of a woman]

gy·ne·pho·bi·a (jī'nə fō'bĭ ə, jĭn'ə-), *n.* a neurotic fear of women. [f. Gk. *gynē* woman + -PHOBIA]

gy·ni·a·trics (jī'nĭ ăt'rĭks, jĭn'ĭ-), *n.* the treatment of diseases of women. [f. Gk. *gyn(ē)* woman + -IATRIC(S)]

gyno-, a word element meaning "woman," "female," as in *gynogenic.* Also, **gyn-.** [t. Gk., comb. form of *gynē* woman]

gy·noe·ci·um (jī nē'sĭ əm, jī-), *n., pl.* **-cia** (-sĭ ə). *Bot.* the pistil, or the pistils collectively, of a flower. Also, **gynaeceum, gynaecium, gynecium.** [t. NL, f. *gyn-* GYN- + m. Gk. *oikíon* house]

gy·no·gen·ic (jī'nə jĕn'ĭk, jĭn'ə-), *adj.* *Embryol.* female-producing or feminizing (opposite to *androgenic*).

gy·no·phore (jī'nə fôr', jĭn'ə-), *n.* *Bot.* the elongated pedicel or stalk bearing the pistil in some flowers.

-gynous, 1. an adjective combining form referring to the female sex, as in *androgynous.*   **2.** a suffix meaning "woman." [t. Gk.: m. *-gynos,* der. *gynē* woman]

gyp[1] (jĭp), *v.,* **gypped, gypping,** *n.* *U.S. Slang.* —*v.t.* **1.** to swindle; cheat; defraud or rob by some sharp practice.   **2.** to obtain by swindling or cheating; steal. —*n.* **3.** a swindle.   **4.** a swindler or cheat. Also, **gip.** [orig. uncert.] —**gyp'per,** *n.*

gyp[2] (jĭp), *n.* *Brit. Colloq.* a male college servant, as at Cambridge, England. [? short for GYPSY]

gyp·soph·i·la (jĭp sŏf'ə lə), *n.* any of the genus *Gypsophila* of slender, graceful herbs, chiefly Mediterranean, allied to the pinks and having small panicled flowers. [NL, f. Gk.: *gýpso(s)* chalk + *phila,* neut. pl. of *phílos,* adj., fond of]

gyp·sum (jĭp'səm), *n.* a very common mineral, hydrated calcium sulfate, $CaSO_4.2H_2O$, occurring in crystals and in masses, soft enough to be scratched by the fingernail: used to make plaster of Paris, as an ornamental material, as a fertilizer, etc. [t. L, t. Gk.: m. *gýpsos* chalk, gypsum]

Gyp·sy (jĭp'sĭ), *n., pl.* **-sies.** **1.** one of a nomadic Caucasian minority race of Hindu origin.   **2.** Romany; the language of the Gypsies.   **3.** (*l.c.*) a person who resembles or lives like a Gypsy.   **4.** (*l.c.*) a gypsy winch. —*adj.* **5.** of or pertaining to the Gypsies. Also, *esp. Brit.,* **Gipsy.** [back formation from *gipcyan,* aphetic var. of *Egyptian*] —**gyp'sy·like',** *adj.*

gypsy moth, a moth, *Lymantria dispar,* introduced from Europe, whose caterpillar is destructive to trees.

gypsy winch, *Naut.* a small winch or crab.

gy·rate (*adj.* jī'rāt; *v.* jī'rāt, jī rāt'), *v.,* **-rated, -rating,** *adj.* —*v.i.* **1.** to move in a circle or spiral, or around a fixed point; whirl. —*adj.* **2.** *Zool.* having convolutions. [t. L: m. s. *gyrātus,* pp., wheeled round, turned]

gy·ra·tion (jī rā'shən), *n.* act of gyrating; circular or spiral motion; revolution; rotation; whirling.

gy·ra·to·ry (jī'rə tôr'ĭ), *adj.* moving in a circle or spiral; gyrating.

gyre (jīr), *n.* *Poetic.* **1.** a ring or circle.   **2.** a circular course or motion.

gyr·fal·con (jûr'fôl'kən, -fô'kən), *n.* gerfalcon.

gy·ro (jī'rō), *n., pl.* **-ros.** **1.** gyrocompass.   **2.** gyroscope. [short for GYROCOMPASS, GYROSCOPE]

gyro-, a word element meaning: **1.** "ring"; "circle." **2.** "spiral." [t. Gk., comb. form of *gýros* ring, circle]

gy·ro·com·pass (jī'rō kŭm'pəs), *n.* a device used like the ordinary compass for determining directions, but employing a continuously driven gyroscope instead of a magnetized needle or bar, the gyroscope being so mounted that its axis constantly maintains its position with reference to the geographical north, thus dealing with true geographical meridians used in navigation instead of magnetic meridians.

gy·ro·plane (jī'rə plān'), *n.* an airplane having lifting airfoils arranged in vanes rotated by the forward motion of the craft.

gy·ro·scope (jī'rə skōp'), *n.* an apparatus consisting of a rotating wheel so mounted that its axis can turn freely in certain or all directions, and capable of maintaining the same absolute direction in space in spite of movements of the mountings and surrounding parts. It is based on the principle that a body rotating steadily about an axis will tend to resist changes in the direction of the axis, and is used to maintain equilibrium, as in an airplane or ship, to determine direction, etc. [t. F. See GYRO-, -SCOPE] —**gy·ro·scop·ic** (jī'rə skŏp'ĭk), *adj.*

Gyroscope

gy·ro·sta·bi·liz·er (jī'rō stā'bə lī'zər), *n.* a device for stabilizing a seagoing vessel by counteracting its rolling motion from side to side, consisting essentially of a rotating gyroscope weighing about 1 percent of the displacement of the vessel.

gy·ro·stat (jī'rə stăt'), *n.* a modified gyroscope, consisting of a rotating wheel pivoted in a rigid case.

gy·ro·stat·ic (jī'rə stăt'ĭk), *adj.* pertaining to the gyrostat or to gyrostatics. —**gy·ro·stat'i·cal·ly,** *adv.*

gy·ro·stat·ics (jī'rə stăt'ĭks), *n.* *Mech.* the science which deals with the laws of rotating bodies.

gy·rus (jī'rəs), *n., pl.* **gyri** (jī'rī). *Anat.* a convolution, esp. of the brain. [t. L. t. Gk.: m. *gýros* ring, circle]

gyve (jīv), *n., v.,* **gyved, gyving.** —*n.* **1.** (*usually pl.*) a shackle, esp. for the leg; fetter. —*v.t.* **2.** to shackle. [ME *gives, gyves* (pl.); orig. uncert.]

H

H, h (āch), *n., pl.* **H's** or **Hs, h's** or **hs.** **1.** a consonant, the 8th letter of the English alphabet. **2.** (as a symbol) the eighth in a series. **3.** *Med. Roman Numerals.* 200.

H, **1.** *Elect.* henry. **2.** *Chem.* hydrogen. **3.** *Physics.* intensity of magnetic field.

h., **1.** harbor. **2.** hard. **3.** hardness. **4.** height. **5.** high. **6.** *Baseball.* hits. **7.** hour. **8.** husband.

ha (hä), *interj.* an exclamation of surprise, interrogation, suspicion, triumph, etc. Also, **hah.**

ha., hectare.

h. a., (L *hoc anno*) in this year.

Haa·kon VII (hô′kŏŏn), 1872–1957, king of Norway 1905–1957; exiled in England, 1940–45.

Haar·lem (här′ləm), *n.* a city in W Netherlands, W of Amsterdam. 165,142 (est. 1954).

Hab., Habakkuk.

Ha·bak·kuk (hə băk′ək, hăb′ə kŭk′), *n.* **1.** a Hebrew prophet and poet. **2.** his book of prophecies, the eighth of the minor prophets of the Old Testament.

Ha·ba·na (ä bä′nä), *n.* Spanish name of **Havana.**

ha·be·as cor·pus (hā′bĭ əs kôr′pəs), *Law.* a writ requiring the body of a person to be brought before a judge or court, esp. for investigation of a restraint of the person's liberty. [t. L: you shall have the body]

hab·er·dash·er (hăb′ər dăsh′ər), *n.* **1.** *U.S.* a dealer in men's furnishings, as shirts, ties, gloves, etc. **2.** *Chiefly Brit.* a dealer in small wares, as buttons, needles, etc. [orig. obscure. Cf. Anglo-F *hapertas* kind of fabric]

hab·er·dash·er·y (hăb′ər dăsh′ər ĭ), *n., pl.* **-eries.** **1.** a haberdasher's shop. **2.** the goods sold there.

hab·er·geon (hăb′ər jən), *n.* **1.** a short hauberk. **2.** any hauberk. Also, **haubergeon.** [ME *haubergeon,* t. OF, dim. of *hauberc* HAUBERK]

hab·ile (hăb′ĭl), *adj.* skillful; dexterous. [t. F, t. L: m. *habilis* fit, apt]

hab·il·i·ment (hə bĭl′ə mənt), *n.* **1.** (*pl.*) clothes or garments. **2.** dress; attire. [ME *habylement,* t. OF: m. *habillement,* der. *habiller* dress, der. *habile* (see HABILE)] —**ha·bil′i·ment′ed,** *adj.*

ha·bil·i·tate (hə bĭl′ə tāt′), *v.t.,* **-tated, -tating.** **1.** *Western U.S.* to furnish money or means to work (a mine). **2.** *Rare.* to clothe or dress. [t. ML: m.s. *habilitātus,* pp. of *habilitāre,* der. L *habilitas* ability]

hab·it (hăb′ĭt), *n.* **1.** a disposition or tendency, constantly shown, to act in a certain way **2.** such a disposition acquired by frequent repetition of an act. **3.** a particular practice, custom, or usage: *the habit of smoking.* **4.** customary practice or use: *to act from force of habit.* **5.** the mental character or disposition: *habit of mind.* **6.** characteristic bodily or physical condition: *habit of body.* **7.** the characteristic form, aspect, mode of growth, etc., of an animal or plant: *a twining habit.* **8.** garb of a particular rank, profession, religious order, etc.: *monk's habit.* **9.** a woman's riding dress. —*v.t.* **10.** to clothe; array. **11.** *Obs.* to dwell in. —*v.i.* **12.** *Obs.* to dwell. [t. L: s. *habitus* condition, appearance, dress; r. ME *abit,* t. OF] —**Syn. 2.** See **custom.**

hab·it·a·ble (hăb′ə tə bəl), *adj.* capable of being inhabited. —**hab′it·a·bil′i·ty, hab′it·a·ble·ness,** *n.* —**hab′it·a·bly,** *adv.*

hab·it·ant (hăb′ə tənt; *for 2 also Fr.* ȧ bē tän′), *n.* **1.** an inhabitant. **2.** a French settler in Canada or Louisiana, or a descendant of one, esp. one of the farming class. [late ME, t. F, t. L: s. *habitans,* ppr., dwelling]

hab·i·tat (hăb′ə tăt′), *n.* **1.** the kind of place where a given animal or plant naturally lives or grows, as warm seas, mountain tops, fresh waters, etc. **2.** place of abode; habitation. [t. L: it inhabits]

hab·i·ta·tion (hăb′ə tā′shən), *n.* **1.** a place of abode; dwelling. **2.** act of inhabiting; occupancy by inhabitants. —**Syn. 1.** residence, domicile, quarters.

ha·bit·u·al (hə bĭch′ŏŏ əl), *adj.* **1.** of the nature of a habit, or fixed by or resulting from habit: *habitual courtesy.* **2.** being such by habit: *a habitual drunkard.* **3.** commonly used (by a given person): *she took her habitual place at the table.* [t. LL: s. *habituālis*] —**ha·bit′u·al·ly,** *adv.* —**ha·bit′u·al·ness,** *n.* —**Syn. 2.** confirmed, inveterate. **3.** See **usual.** —**Ant. 2.** occasional. **3.** unaccustomed.

ha·bit·u·ate (hə bĭch′ŏŏ āt′), *v.t.,* **-ated, -ating.** **1.** to accustom (a person, the mind, etc.), as to something; make used (*to*). **2.** *U.S. Colloq.* to frequent. [t. LL: m.s. *habituātus,* pp. of *habituāre* bring into a condition, der. L *habitus* HABIT] —**ha·bit′u·a′tion,** *n.* —**Syn. 1.** familiarize; inure, harden, acclimatize, acclimate.

hab·i·tude (hăb′ə tūd′, -tŏŏd), *n.* **1.** customary condition, character, or habit. **2.** *Rare.* a habit or custom. **3.** *Obs.* relationship. [t. F, t. L: m. *habitūdo* condition]

ha·bit·u·é (hə bĭch′ŏŏ ā′; *Fr.* ȧ bē twē′), *n.* a habitual frequenter of a place. [t. F, pp. of *habituer* HABITUATE]

Habs·burg (hăps′bûrg; *Ger.* häps′bŏŏrКН), *n.* Hapsburg.

ha·chure (*n.* hă shŏŏr′, hăsh′ŏŏr; *v.* hă shŏŏr′), *n., v.,* **-chured, -churing.** —*n.* **1.** (in drawing, engraving, etc.) hatching. **2.** (on a map) shading used to indicate relief features, consisting of lines drawn parallel to the slopes and varying in width with the degree of slope. —*v.t.* **3.** to mark or shade with, or indicate by, hachures. [t. F, der. *hacher* HATCH³]

ha·ci·en·da (hä′sĭ ěn′də; *Sp.* ä syěn′dä), *n.* *Spanish American.* **1.** a landed estate; country house. **2.** a stock-raising, mining, or manufacturing establishment in the country. [t. Sp.: landed property, estate, g. L *facienda* things to be done, neut. pl. ger. of *facere* do]

hack¹ (hăk), *v.t.* **1.** to cut, notch, or chop irregularly, as with heavy blows. **2.** to break up the surface of (the ground). **3.** *Basketball.* to strike the arm of (a player). **4.** *Brit.* to kick the shins of intentionally, as in Rugby football. —*v.i.* **5.** to make rough cuts or notches; deal cutting blows. **6.** to emit short, frequently repeated coughs. **7.** *Brit.* to kick an opponent's shins intentionally, as in Rugby football. —*n.* **8.** a cut, gash, or notch. **9.** a tool, as an ax, hoe, pick, etc., for hacking. **10.** an act of hacking; a cutting blow. **11.** a short, broken cough. **12.** a hesitation in speech. **13.** *Basketball.* a personal foul. **14.** *Brit.* a gash in the skin produced by a kick, as in Rugby football. [ME *hacke(n),* OE (*tō*)*haccian* hack to pieces, c. D *hakken,* G *hacken*] —**hack′er,** *n.* —**Syn. 1.** See **cut.**

hack² (hăk), *n.* **1.** *Brit.* a horse kept for common hire, or adapted for general work, esp. ordinary riding. **2.** *Brit.* a saddle horse for the road. **3.** an old or worn-out horse; a jade. **4.** a person who hires himself out for general work, esp. literary work. **5.** *U.S.* a coach or carriage kept for hire; a hackney. **6.** *Colloq.* a taxi. —*v.t.* **7.** to make a hack of; let out for hire. **8.** to make trite or stale by frequent use; hackney. —*v.i.* **9.** *Brit.* to ride on the road at an ordinary pace, as distinguished from cross-country or military riding. **10.** *Colloq.* to drive a taxi. —*adj.* **11.** hired; of a hired sort: *hack work.* **12.** hackneyed; trite. [short for HACKNEY]

hack·a·more (hăk′ə môr′), *n.* **1.** a coil of rope which passes through the horse's mouth and about his neck, used to break a horse. **2.** *Western U.S.* any of several forms of halter used esp. for breaking horses.

hack·ber·ry (hăk′běr′ĭ), *n., pl.* **-ries.** **1.** the small, edible, cherrylike fruit of American trees of the ulmaceous genus *Celtis.* **2.** a tree bearing this fruit. **3.** its wood. [var. of HAGBERRY]

hack·but (hăk′bŭt), *n.* harquebus. [t. MF: m. *haquebute,* b. *buter* to butt and MF *haquebusche* (t. MD: m. *hakebus,* lit., a hook gun)]

Hack·en·sack (hăk′ən săk′), *n.* a city in NE New Jersey, near New York City. 30,521 (1960).

hack hammer, an adzlike tool for dressing stone.

hack·le¹ (hăk′əl), *n., v.,* **-led, -ling.** —*n.* **1.** one of the long, slender feathers on the neck or saddle of certain birds, as the domestic rooster, much used in making artificial flies for anglers. **2.** the whole neck plumage of the domestic rooster, etc. **3.** *Angling.* **a.** an artificial fly's legs made with hackles (def. 1). **b.** a hackle fly. **4.** a comb for dressing flax or hemp. —*v.t.* **5.** *Angling.* to supply with a hackle. **6.** to comb, as flax or hemp. [ME *hakell.* See HECKLE] —**hack′ler,** *n.*

hack·le² (hăk′əl), *v.t.,* **-led, -ling.** to cut roughly; hack; mangle. [freq. of HACK¹, c. MD *hakkelen*]

hack·le·back (hăk′əl băk′), *n.* the shovel-nosed sturgeon, *Scaphirhynchus platorynchus,* of the Mississippi Valley.

hackle fly, an artificial fly made with hackles, usually without wings.

hack·ly (hăk′lĭ), *adj.* rough or jagged. [f. HACKLE² + -Y¹]

hack·man (hăk′mən, -măn′), *n., pl.* **-men** (-mən, -měn′). *U.S.* the driver of a hack.

hack·ma·tack (hăk′mə tăk′), *n.* **1.** the tamarack, *Larix laricina,* an American larch. **2.** its wood. [t. N Amer. Ind.]

hack·ney (hăk′nĭ), *n., pl.* **-neys,** *adj., v.,* **-neyed, -neying.** —*n.* **1.** a horse for ordinary riding or driving. **2.** a horse kept for hire. **3.** a carriage kept for hire. —*adj.* **4.** let out, employed, or done for hire. —*v.t.*

5. to make common, stale, or trite by frequent use. **6.** to use as a hackney. [ME *hakeney;* orig. uncert.]

hack·neyed (hăk′nĭd), *adj.* **1.** made commonplace or trite; stale. **2.** habituated. —Syn. **1.** See **commonplace.**

hack·saw (hăk′sô′), *n.* a saw used for cutting metal, consisting typically of a narrow, fine-toothed blade fixed in a frame.

Hacksaw

had (hăd), *v.* pt. and pp. of **have.**

Had·ding·ton (hăd′ĭng tən), *n.* former name of **East Lothian.**

had·dock (hăd′ək), *n., pl.* **-docks,** (*esp. collectively*) **-dock. 1.** a food fish, *Melanogrammus aeglefinus,* of the northern Atlantic, related to but smaller than the cod. **2.** the rosefish. [ME *haddoc;* orig. unknown]

hade (hād), *n., v.,* **haded, hading.** *Geol.* —*n.* **1.** the angle between a fault plane and a vertical plane striking parallel to the fault. —*v.i.* **2.** to incline from a vertical position. [orig. uncert.]

Ha·des (hā′dēz), *n.* **1.** *Gk. Myth.* **a.** the gloomy subterranean abode of departed spirits or shades over which Pluto ruled. **b.** Pluto; the lord of the underworld. **2.** (in the Revised Version of the New Testament) the abode or state of the dead. **3.** (*l.c.*) *Colloq.* hell. [t. Gk.: m. *Haidēs* (orig. *aidēs*)] —**Ha·de·an** (hā dē′ən, hā′dĭ ən), *adj.*

Had·field (hăd′fēld′), *n.* **Sir Robert Abbott,** 1858–1940, British scientist and metallurgist.

Ha·dhra·maut (hä′drä môt′), *n.* a region along the S coast of the Arabian peninsula, in the Aden protectorate. Also, **Ha′dra·maut′.**

hadj (hăj), *n.* hajj.

hadj·i (hăj′ĭ), *n., pl.* **hadjis** hajji.

Had·ley (hăd′lĭ), *n.* **Henry Kimball,** 1871–1937, U.S. composer.

Ha·dri·an (hā′drĭ ən), *n.* A.D. 76–138, Roman emperor, A.D. 117–138. Also, **Adrian.**

Hadrian's Wall, a wall of defense for the Roman province of Britain, constructed by Hadrian between Solway Firth and the mouth of the Tyne.

Hadrian's Wall in A.D. 410

hae (hā, hä), *v.t. Scot.* have.

Haeck·el (hĕk′əl), *n.* **Ernst Heinrich** (ĕrnst hīn′rĭKH), 1834–1919, German biologist and philosopher.

haem-, var. of **hem-.** For words beginning in **haem-, haema-, haemo-,** see preferred spelling under **hem-, hema-, hemo-.**

hae·ma·tox·y·lin (hē′mə tŏk′sə lən, hĕm′ə-), *n.* **1.** a leguminous plant of a genus *Haematoxylon,* of which only one species, *H. campechianum,* the logwood tree, is known. **2.** the wood of the logwood. **3.** the dyestuff, hematoxylin. [f. s. NL *haematoxylum* logwood (f. Gk.: *haimato-* HEMATO- + m. *xylon* wood) + -IN²]

-haemia, var. of **-emia.**

haemo-, var. of **hemo-.** Also, **haem-.** For words beginning in **haemo-,** see preferred spelling under **hemo-.**

hae·res (hĭr′ēz), *n., pl.* **haeredes** (hĭ rē′dēz). heres.

ha·fiz (hä′fĭz), *n.* a title of a Mohammedan who knows the Koran by heart. [t. Ar.: *hāfiz* a guard, one who keeps (in memory)]

Ha·fiz (hä′fĭz′), *n.* died c1389, Persian poet.

haf·ni·um (hăf′nĭ əm, häf′-), *n. Chem.* a metallic element with a valence of four, found in zirconium ores. *Symbol:* Hf; *at. wt.:* 178.6; *at. no.:* 72; *sp. gr.:* 12.1. [f. *Hafn*(ia), L name of Copenhagen + -IUM]

haft (hăft, häft), *n.* **1.** a handle, esp. of a knife, sword, dagger, etc. —*v.t.* **2.** to furnish with a haft or handle; set in a haft. [ME; OE *hæft,* c. D and G *heft*]

haf·ta·rah (hăf′tä rä′, häf tôr′ä), *n.* haphtarah.

hag¹ (hăg), *n.* **1.** a repulsive, often vicious or malicious, old woman. **2.** a witch. **3.** a hagfish. [ME *hagge, hegge;* appar. a familiar short form (with hypocoristic gemination) of OE *hægtesse* fury, witch; akin to G *hexe* witch] —**hag′like′,** *adj.*

hag² (hăg, häg), *n. Scot. and Dial.* **1.** a soft spot in boggy land. **2.** a firm spot in a bog. [ME *hag* chasm, t. Scand.; cf. Icel. *högg* a cut, ravine]

Hag., Haggai.

Ha·gar (hā′gär, -gər), *n. Bible.* Egyptian concubine of Abraham, mother of Ishmael. Gen. 16.

hag·ber·ry (hăg′bĕr′ĭ), *n., pl.* **-ries.** the American hackberry. [t. Scand.; cf. Dan. *hæggebær*]

hag·but (hăg′bŭt), *n.* harquebus.

hag·don (hăg′dən), *n.* any of various oceanic birds along the North Atlantic coasts of Europe and America, esp. the greater shearwater, *Puffinus gravis.*

Ha·gen (hä′gən), *n.* (in the *Nibelungenlied*) the slayer of Siegfried. [G, c. OE *Hagena*]

Ha·gers·town (hā′gərz toun′), *n.* a city in NW Maryland. 36,660 (1960).

hag·fish (hăg′fĭsh′), *n., pl.* **-fishes,** (*esp. collectively*) **-fish.** any of the eellike marine cyclostomes (order or suborder *Hyperotreta*) with a round sucking mouth, notable esp. for their

circular suctorial mouth and their habit of boring into the bodies of fishes.

Hag·ga·da (hə gä′də), *n., pl.* **-doth** (-dōth). Haggadah.

Hag·ga·dah (hə gä′də), *n., pl.* **-doth** (-dōth). *Jewish Lit.* **1.** the nonlegal part of Jewish traditional literature. **2.** the free exposition or illustration, chiefly homiletic, of the Scripture. **3.** the ritual used on the first two nights of Passover. **4.** a book containing it. [t. Heb.: (m.) *haggādāh* narrative, der. *higgīd* tell] —**hag·gad·ic** (hə găd′ĭk, -gä′dĭk), **hag·gad′i·cal,** *adj.*

Atlantic hagfish
Myxine glutinosa
(1½ ft. long)

hag·ga·dist (hə gä′dĭst), *n.* **1.** a writer of Haggadoth. **2.** a student of the Haggadah. —**hag·ga·dis·tic** (hăg′ə dĭs′tĭk), *adj.*

Hag·ga·i (hăg′ĭ ī, hăg′ī), *n.* **1.** fl. B.C. 520, the tenth of the minor prophets of Israel. **2.** his book in the Old Testament.

hag·gard (hăg′ərd), *adj.* **1.** wild-looking, as from prolonged suffering, anxiety, exertion, want, etc.; careworn; gaunt. **2.** *Falconry.* wild or untamed, esp. of a hawk caught after it has assumed adult plumage. [orig. uncert. Cf. F *hagard* (? t. E)] —**hag′gard·ly,** *adv.* —**hag′gard·ness,** *n.* —Syn. **1.** emaciated, drawn; hollow-eyed. —Ant. **1.** unstrained.

Hag·gard (hăg′ərd), *n.* **Henry Rider,** 1856–1925, British novelist.

hagged (hăgd, hăg′ĭd), *adj. Dial.* **1.** haglike. **2.** haggard (def. 1).

hag·gis (hăg′ĭs), *n. Chiefly Scot.* a dish made of the heart, liver, etc., of a sheep, etc., minced with suet and oatmeal, seasoned, and boiled in the stomach of the animal. [? f. *hag* chop + *es,* OE *æs* food, meat]

hag·gish (hăg′ĭsh), *adj.* of or like a hag; old and ugly. —**hag′gish·ly,** *adv.* —**hag′gish·ness,** *n.*

hag·gle (hăg′əl), *v.,* **-gled, -gling,** *n.* —*v.i.* **1.** to bargain in a petty and tedious manner. **2.** to wrangle, dispute, or cavil. —*v.t.* **3.** to harass with wrangling or haggling. **4.** to mangle in cutting; hack. —*n.* **5.** act of haggling; wrangle or dispute over terms. [freq. of *hag,* v., cut, hew, hack, t. Scand.; cf. Icel. *höggva* strike, hack, c. OE *hēawan* hew] —**hag′gler,** *n.* —Syn. **1.** chaffer, higgle; negotiate.

hagio-, a word element meaning "saint." Also, **hagi-.** [t. Gk., comb. form of *hágios* sacred, holy]

hag·i·oc·ra·cy (hăg′ĭ ŏk′rə sĭ, hā′jĭ-), *n., pl.* **-cies.** government by a body of persons esteemed as holy.

Hag·i·og·ra·pha (hăg′ĭ ŏg′rə fə, hā′jĭ-), *n. pl.* the third of the three Jewish divisions of the Old Testament, variously arranged, but usually comprising the Psalms, Proverbs, Job, Canticles, Ruth, Lamentations, Ecclesiates, Esther, Daniel, Ezra, Nehemiah, and Chronicles. [t. LL, f., Gk.: *hagio-* HAGIO- + *grapha* (for *gráphia*) writings]

hag·i·og·ra·pher (hăg′ĭ ŏg′rə fər, hā′jĭ-), *n.* **1.** one of the writers of the Hagiographa. **2.** a writer of lives of the saints; a hagiologist. Also, **hag′i·og′ra·phist.**

hag·i·og·ra·phy (hăg′ĭ ŏg′rə fĭ, hā′jĭ-), *n., pl.* **-phies.** the writing and critical study of the lives of the saints; hagiology. —**hag·i·o·graph·ic** (hăg′ĭ ə grăf′ĭk, hā′jĭ-), **hag′i·o·graph′i·cal,** *adj.*

hag·i·ol·a·try (hăg′ĭ ŏl′ə trĭ, hā′jĭ-), *n.* the veneration of saints. [f. HAGIO- + *-latry* (see LATRIA)] —**hag′i·ol′a·ter,** *n.* —**hag′i·ol′a·trous,** *adj.*

hag·i·ol·o·gy (hăg′ĭ ŏl′ə jĭ, hā′jĭ-), *n., pl.* **-gies. 1.** that branch of literature which deals with the lives and legends of the saints. **2.** a work on these. **3.** a collection of such lives or legends. —**hag·i·o·log·ic** (hăg′ĭ ə lŏj′ĭk, hā′jĭ-), **hag′i·o·log′i·cal,** *adj.* —**hag′i·ol′o·gist,** *n.*

hag·rid·den (hăg′rĭd′ən), *adj.* worried or tormented, as by a witch.

Hague (hāg), *n.* **The,** a city in W Netherlands, near the North Sea: seat of the government, royal residence, and Permanent Court of International Justice. 590,755 (est. 1954). Dutch, **'s Gravenhage.**

Hague Tribunal, The, the permanent court of arbitration for the peaceful settlement of international disputes, established at The Hague by the international peace conference of 1899, whose panel of jurists nominates a list of persons from which members of the United Nations International Court of Justice are elected.

hah (hä), *interj.* ha.

ha-ha¹ (hä′hä′), *interj., n.* an imitation of the sound of laughter.

ha-ha² (hä′hä′), *n.* a barrier consisting of a trench or ditch; a sunk fence. [t. F: m. *haha*]

Hahn (hän), *n.* **Otto** (ŏt′ō), born 1879, German physicist.

Hah·ne·mann (hä′nə mən; *Ger.* -män′), *n.* **Samuel** (săm′yōō əl; *Ger.* zä′mōō ĕl′), (*Christian Fredrich Samuel*) 1755–1843, German physician: founder of homeopathy. —**Hah·ne·mann·i·an** (hä′nə măn′ĭ ən, -mä′nĭ-), *adj.* —**Hah′ne·mann′ism,** *n.*

Hai·da (hī′də), *n.* **1.** an American Indian language of southeastern Alaska. 2. a linguistic stock of the Na-Dene phylum, including Haida (def. 1).

Hai·dar A·li (hī'dər ä'lē, ä lē'), Hyder Ali.

Hai·duk (hī'dŏŏk), n. 1. one of a class of mercenary soldiers in 16th century Hungary. 2. a patriotic brigand in the Slav portions of the Balkan Peninsula. 3. a male servant or attendant dressed in Hungarian semimilitary costume. Also, **Heyduck, Heyduke, Heyduc, Heiduc, Heiduk.** [repr. Hung. *hajduk* (pl. of *hajdu*) kind of foot soldiers, and Polish *hajduk* retainers, ult. t. Turk.: m. *haidud* marauder, brigand]

Hai·fa (hī'fə), n. a seaport in NW Israel. 154,500 (est. 1954).

Haig (hāg), n. **Douglas, 1st Earl,** 1861–1928, British field marshal: commander in chief of the British forces in France from 1915–18.

haik (hīk, hāk), n. an oblong cloth used as an outer garment by the Arabs. [t. Ar.: m. *hayk,* der. *hāk* weave]

hai·kwan (hī'kwän'), n. maritime customs in China. [t. Chinese (Mandarin): f. *hai* sea + *kuan* gateway]

haikwan tael (tāl), 1. the customs unit in China, which is the basis for other local taels, equal to 1.20666 troy ounces of fine silver. 2. a liang.

hail¹ (hāl), v.t. 1. to salute or greet; welcome. 2. to salute or name as: *to hail one victor.* 3. to call out to, in order to attract attention: *to hail a person.* —v.i. 4. to call out in order to greet, attract attention, etc. 5. **hail from,** to belong to as the place of residence, point of departure, etc. —n. 6. a shout or call to attract attention. 7. act of hailing. 8. a salutation or greeting. 9. **within hail,** within reach of the voice. —interj. 10. *Poetic and Literary.* an exclamation of salutation or greeting. [ME *haile*(n), der. obs. *hail,* n. and adj., health(y), t. Scand.; cf. Icel. *heill* health, healthy, c. OE *hǣl* (n.), *hāl* (adj.). Cf. **wassail**] —**hail'er,** n.

hail² (hāl), n. 1. pellets or small, usually rounded, masses of ice falling from the clouds in a shower. 2. a shower or storm of such masses. 3. a shower of anything: *a hail of bullets.* —v.i. 4. to pour down hail; fall as hail. —v.t. 5. to pour down as or like hail. [ME *hail*(e), OE *hægl,* c. D and G *hagel*]

Hai·le Se·las·sie (hī'lĭ sə läs'ĭ, -läs'ĭ), born 1890, emperor of Ethiopia, 1930–36 and since 1941; exiled in England, 1936–41.

hail fellow, on familiar terms: often in the form *hail fellow well met.*

Hail Mary, Ave Maria.

hail·stone (hāl'stōn'), n. a pellet of hail. [ME, f. **hail²** + **stone**; r. ME *hawelstone.* OE *hagolstān*]

hail·storm (hāl'stôrm'), n. a storm with hail.

Hai·nan (hī'nän'), n. an island in the South China Sea, separated from the mainland of S China by **Hainan Strait** (15 mi. wide): a part of Kwangtung province. 2,700,000 pop. (est. 1956); ab. 13,200 sq. mi.

Hai·naut (ĕ nō'), n. a medieval county in territory now in SW Belgium and N France.

hain't (hānt), contraction of *have not* or *has not* (not regarded as good usage).

Hai·phong (hī'fŏng'), n. a seaport in NE Indochina, in North Vietnam, near the Gulf of Tonkin. 188,000 (est. 1953).

hair (hâr), n. 1. the natural covering of the human head. 2. the aggregate of hairs which grow on an animal. 3. one of the numerous fine, usually cylindrical filaments growing from the skin and forming the coat of most mammals. 4. a similar fine, filamentous outgrowth from the body of insects, etc. 5. *Bot.* a filamentous outgrowth of the epidermis. 6. cloth made of hair from such animals as camel and alpaca. 7. a very small magnitude, measure, degree, etc.: *he lost the race by a hair.* 8. **split hairs,** to make fine or unnecessary distinctions. [ME *ha*(*i*)*re,* t. Scand.; cf. Icel. *hār*); r. ME *her*(*e*), OE *hǣr,* c. D and G *haar*] —**hair'like',** adj.

Section of skin, showing the roots of two hairs (highly magnified): A. Cuticle; B. Deeper root parts of skin; C. A hair; D. Erecting muscle; E. Sebaceous glands

Hairs (highly magnified): Longitudinal section: A. Man; B. Sable; C. Mouse. External view: D. Mouse; E. Indian bat

hair·breadth (hâr'brĕdth'), n., adj. hair's-breadth

hair·brush (hâr'brŭsh'), n. a brush for dressing the hair.

hair·cloth (hâr'klôth', -klŏth'), n. cloth woven of hair from horses' tails and manes with cotton warp for interlinings of clothes, etc.

hair·cut (hâr'kŭt'), n. act or style of cutting the hair.

hair·do (hâr'dōō'), n., pl. **-dos.** 1. any method of arranging a woman's hair. 2. hair so dressed.

hair·dress·er (hâr'drĕs'ər), n. one who arranges or cuts hair, esp. women's hair. —**hair'dress'ing,** n., adj.

hair follicle, *Anat.* a small cavity from which a hair develops.

hair·less (hâr'lĭs), adj. without hair; bald. —**hair'less·ness,** n.

hair·line (hâr'līn'), n. 1. a very slender line. 2. worsted fabric woven with very fine lines or stripes. 3. *Print.* **a.** a very thin line on the face of a type. **b.** a style of type consisting entirely of such lines.

hair·pin (hâr'pĭn'), n. 1. a slender U-shaped piece of wire, shell, etc., used by women to fasten up the hair or hold a headdress. —adj. 2. (of a road, track, etc.) doubling back in a U-shape.

hair·rais·ing (hâr'rā'zĭng), adj. terrifying.

hair's-breadth (hârz'brĕdth'), n. 1. a very small space or distance. —adj. 2. extremely narrow or close. Also, **hairs'breadth', hairbreadth.**

hair seal, any of various seals with coarse hair and no soft underlying fur (distinguished from *fur seal*).

hair shirt, a garment of coarse haircloth, worn next the skin by ascetics and penitents.

hair space, *Print.* the thinnest metal space used to separate words, etc.

hair·split·ter (hâr'splĭt'ər), n. one who makes fine or unnecessary distinctions. —**hair'split'ting,** n., adj.

hair·spring (hâr'sprĭng'), n. a fine, spiralled spring in a timepiece for regulating the motion of the balance.

hair·streak (hâr'strēk'), n. any of certain small dark butterflies of the family *Lycaenidae,* distinguished by one or two thin tails on each of the hind wings.

hair stroke, a fine line in writing or printing.

hair trigger, a trigger that allows the firing mechanism of a firearm to be operated by very slight pressure.

hair·worm (hâr'wûrm'), n. any of a number of small, slender worms of the family *Trichostrongylidae,* parasitic in the alimentary canals of various animals.

hair·y (hâr'ĭ), adj., **hairier, hairiest.** 1. covered with hair; having much hair. 2. consisting of or resembling hair. —**hair'i·ness,** n.

Hai·ti (hā'tĭ), n. 1. a republic in the West Indies, occupying the W part of the island of Hispaniola. 3,305,000 pop. (est. 1955); 10,714 sq. mi. *Cap.:* Port-au-Prince. 2. former name of **Hispaniola.** —**Hai·ti·an** (hā'tĭ·ən, -shən), adj., n.

hajj (hăj), n. the pilgrimage to Mecca, which every good Mohammedan is supposed to make at least once in his lifetime. Also, **hadj.** [t. Ar.: m. *ḥajj* pilgrimage]

haj·ji (hăj'ĭ), n., pl. **-jis.** 1. a Mohammedan who has performed his hajj to Mecca. 2. a Greek or Armenian who has visited the Holy Sepulcher at Jerusalem. Also, **hadji.** [t. Turk.: m. *ḥājī,* t. Ar.: m. *ḥājj* pilgrim]

hake (hāk), n., pl. **hakes,** (*esp. collectively*) **hake.** 1. any of several marine gadoid fishes of the genus *Merluccius,* related to the cod, as *M. bilinearis* (**silver hake**) of the New England coast. 2. any of various related marine fishes, esp. of the genus *Urophycis,* or allied genera, as *U. tenius* (**white hake**) of the New England coast. [ME, special use of OE *haca* hook. Cf. MLG *haken* kipper salmon.]

ha·kim¹ (hä kēm'), n. (in Mohammedan countries) 1. a wise or learned man. 2. a physician. Also, **ha·keem** (hä kēm'). [t. Ar.: m. *ḥakīm* wise, wise man]

ha·kim² (hä'kēm), n. (in Mohammedan countries) a ruler; governor; judge. [t. Ar.: m. *ḥākim* governor]

Hak·luyt (hăk'lōōt, -lĭt), n. **Richard,** 1552?–1616, English geographer and editor of explorers' narratives.

Ha·ko·da·te (hä'kō dä'tĕ), n. a seaport in N Japan at the S end of Hokkaido island. 228,994 (1950).

hal-, var. of halo- before vowels, as in **halite.**

Hal, *Chem.* halogen.

Ha·la·kah (hä'lä кнä', hä lä'кнä), n. the legal part of Jewish traditional literature. Also, **Ha·la·cha** (hä'lä кнä', hä lä'кнä). [t. Heb.: m. *halākāh* rule to go by]

ha·la·tion (hä lā'shən, hä-), n. *Photog.* the blurring in a negative or print of very light areas (as a window in an interior view) caused by the reflection of light from the back of the support on which the emulsion is coated. [f. **hal**(o) + **-ation**]

hal·berd (hăl'bərd; *formerly* hôl'-, hŏ'-), n. a shafted weapon with an axlike cutting blade, beak, and apical spike, used esp. in the 15th and 16th centuries. Also, **hal·bert** (hăl'bərt; *formerly* hôl'-, hŏ'-). [late ME *haubert,* t. MF: m. *hallebarde,* t. MHG: m. *helmbarde*]

hal·berd·ier (hăl'bər dĭr'), n. a soldier, guard, or attendant armed with a halberd.

hal·cy·on (hăl'sĭ ən), n. 1. a bird, usually identified with the kingfisher, fabled by the ancients to breed about the time of the winter solstice in a nest floating on the sea, and to have the power of charming winds and waves into calmness. 2. any of various kingfishers, esp. of the genus *Halcyon.* —adj. 3. calm, tranquil, or peaceful. 4. of or pertaining to the halcyon or kingfisher. [t. L. pseudo-etymological var. of *alcyon,* t. Gk.: m. *alkyōn* kingfisher]

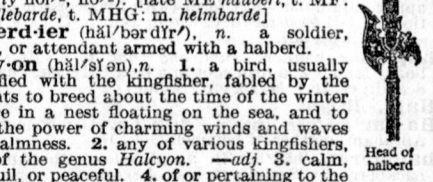

Head of halberd

halcyon days, 1. days of fine and calm weather about the winter solstice, when the halcyon was anciently believed to brood; esp., the seven days before and as many after the winter solstice. 2. days of peace and tranquillity.

Hal·dane (hôl'dān), n. 1. **John Burdon Sanderson,** 1892–1964, British biologist and writer on science. 2. his father, **John Scott,** 1860–1936, British physiologist and writer on science. 3. **Richard Burdon,** (*Viscount*

Haldane of Cloan) 1856–1928, British statesman and jurist (brother of John Scott Haldane).

hale[1] (hāl), *adj.*, **haler, halest. 1.** free from disease or infirmity; robust; vigorous. **2.** *Scot. and N. Eng.* free from injury or defect. [ME; OE *hāl*, c. Icel. *heill* hale, whole] —**hale′ness,** *n.* —**Syn. 1.** sound, healthy, hearty. See **strong.** —**Ant. 1.** sickly.

hale[2] (hāl), *v.t.*, **haled, haling. 1.** to haul, pull, or draw with force. **2.** to drag, or bring as by dragging: *to hale a man into court.* [ME *hale(n),* t. OF: m. *haler* hale, haul, t. Gmc.; cf. OHG *halōn,* G *holen* fetch] —**hal′er,** *n.*

Hale (hāl), *n.* **1.** Edward Everett, 1822–1909, U.S. clergyman and author. **2.** Sir Matthew, 1609–76, British jurist: Lord Chief Justice, 1671–76. **3.** Nathan, 1755–76, American soldier hanged as spy by British.

Ha·le·a·ka·la (hä′lĕ ä′kä lä′), *n.* an extinct volcano in the Hawaiian Islands, on the island of Maui. Crater, 19 sq. mi.; ab. 2000 ft. deep; 10,032 ft. high.

Ha·lé·vy (á lĕ vē′), *n.* Jacques François Fromental Elie (zhäk frän swä′ frō män tál′ ĕ lē′), 1799–1862, French composer and teacher of music.

half (hăf, häf), *n., pl.* **halves** (hăvz, hävz), *adj., adv.* —*n.* **1.** one of the two equal (or approximately equal) parts into which anything is or may be divided. **2.** *Sports.* either of the two periods of a game. **3.** *Football.* a halfback. **4.** *Golf.* an equal score (with the opponent) either on a hole or a round. —*adj.* **5.** being one of the two equal (or approximately equal) parts into which anything is or may be divided. **6.** being equal to only about half of the full measure: *half speed.* **7.** partial or incomplete. —*adv.* **8.** to the extent or measure of half: *a bucket half full of water.* **9.** in part; partly. **10.** to some extent. [ME and OE, c. MD and MLG *halve* side, half]

half-and-half (hăf′ən hăf′, häf′ən häf′), *adj.* **1.** half one thing and half another. —*adv.* **2.** in two equal portions. —*n.* **3.** a mixture of two things. **4.** *Chiefly Brit.* a mixture of two malt liquors, esp. porter and ale.

half·back (hăf′băk′, häf′-), *n.* *Football, etc.* one of the players behind the forward line.

half-baked (hăf′bākt′, häf′-), *adj.* **1.** insufficiently cooked. **2.** not completed: *a half-baked scheme.* **3.** lacking mature judgment or experience: *half-baked theorists.*

half·beak (hăf′bēk′, häf′-), *n.* any of certain marine fishes constituting the genus *Hemirhamphus* and allied genera, having a long protruding lower jaw.

half binding, a book having a leather binding on the back and corners, and paper or cloth sides.

half blood, the relation between persons having only one of their parents in common.

half-blood (hăf′blŭd′, häf′-), *n.* **1.** a half-breed. **2.** a person related by half blood.

half-blood·ed (hăf′blŭd′ĭd, häf′-), *adj.* having parents of different breeds, races, or the like.

half boot, a boot reaching about halfway to the knee.

half-bound (hăf′bound′, häf′-), *adj.* bound in half binding.

half-breed (hăf′brēd′, häf′-), *n.* **1.** the offspring of parents of different races; one who is half-blooded. **2.** the offspring of a white person and an American Indian.

half brother, a brother by one parent only.

half cadence, *Music.* a cadence ending with dominant harmony.

half-caste (hăf′kăst′, häf′käst′), *n.* **1.** a person of mixed race. **2.** one of mixed European and Hindu or Mohammedan parentage.

half cock, the position of the hammer of a firearm when held halfway by mechanism so that it will not operate. **2. go off at half cock,** to act prematurely.

half crown, an English silver coin worth 2*s*.6*d*.

half dollar, a silver coin of the United States worth 50 cents, weighing 385.8 grains to the dollar, 0.900 fine.

half eagle, a gold coin of the United States worth $5.

half gainer, *Swimming.* a type of dive in which the diver takes off facing forward and performs a back dive either with or without a jackknife.

half-heart·ed (hăf′här′tĭd, häf′-), *adj.* having or showing little enthusiasm. —**half′-heart′ed·ly,** *adv.* —**half′-heart′ed·ness,** *n.* —**Syn.** indifferent, perfunctory. —**Ant.** enthusiastic.

half hitch, a hitch formed by passing the end of a rope round its standing part and bringing it up through the bight. See illus. under **knot.**

half hose, short hose; socks.

half-hour (hăf′our′, häf′-), *n.* **1.** a period of thirty minutes. **2.** the mid point between the hours.

half-hour·ly (hăf′our′lĭ, häf′-), *adj.* **1.** of or lasting a half-hour. **2.** occurring once every half-hour. —*adv.* **3.** during a half-hour.

half leather, *Bookbinding.* half binding.

half-length (hăf′length′, häf′-), *n.* **1.** a portrait showing only the upper part of the body, including the hands. —*adj.* **2.** of or denoting such a portrait.

half life, *Physics, etc.* the time required for one half of a sample of unstable material to undergo chemical change, as the disintegration of radioactive material, the chemical change of free radicals, etc.

half-mast (hăf′măst′, häf′mäst′), *n.* **1.** a position approximately halfway below the top of a mast, staff, etc. —*v.t.* **2.** to place (a flag) at half-mast (as a mark of respect for the dead, or as a signal of distress).

half moon, 1. See **moon** (def. 2b). **2.** something of the shape of a half moon or crescent.

half mourning, 1. a mourning garb less somber than full mourning. **2.** the period during which it is worn.

half nelson, *Wrestling.* a method of attack, usually from behind, in which the wrestler pushes his arm under his opponent's arm and places the hand on the nape of his opponent's neck.

half note, *Music.* a note, formerly the shortest in use, but now equivalent in time value to one half of a semibreve. See illus. under **note.**

half pay, 1. half the full wages or salary. **2.** a reduced allowance paid to a British army or navy officer when not in actual service or after retirement.

half-pen·ny (hā′pə nĭ, hāp′nĭ), *n., pl.* **halfpennies** (hā′pə nĭz, hāp′nĭz) for 1; **halfpence** (hā′pəns) for 2; *adj.* —*n.* **1.** a British bronze coin of half the value of a penny. **2.** the sum of half a penny. —*adj.* **3.** of the price or value of a halfpenny. **4.** of trifling value.

half sister, a sister by one parent only.

half sole, that part of the sole of a boot or shoe which extends from the shank to the end of the toe.

half-sole (hăf′sōl′, häf′-), *v.t.*, **-soled, -soling.** to repair by putting on a new half sole.

half sovereign, a British gold coin worth 10 shillings and weighing about 61.6372 grains troy.

half step, 1. *Music.* a semitone. **2.** *Mil.* a step fifteen inches long in quick time and eighteen inches long in double time.

half tide, the state of the tide when halfway between high water and low water.

half-tim·bered (hăf′tĭm′bərd, häf′-), *adj.* (of a house or building) having the frame and principal supports of timber, but with the interstices filled in with masonry, plaster, or the like.

half title, 1. the short title of a book at the head of the first page of the text. **2.** the title of any subdivision of a book that immediately precedes that subdivision, when printed on a full page and in one line.

half-tone (hăf′tōn′, häf′-), *n.* **1.** *Painting, Photog., etc.* a value intermediate between high light and deep shade. **2.** *Photoengraving.* **a.** a process in which gradation of tone is obtained by a system of minute dots produced by a screen, placed in the camera a short distance in front of the sensitized plate. **b.** the metal plate made by photoengraving for reproduction by letterpress printing. **c.** a print from it. —*adj.* **3.** pertaining to, using, or used in, the half-tone process.

half tone, *Music.* a semitone.

half-track (hăf′trăk′, häf′-), *n.* a motor vehicle with its driving wheels on caterpillar treads.

half-truth (hăf′trōōth′, häf′-), *n.* a proposition or statement only partly true.

half volley, *Tennis, etc.* a delivered ball or its return, hit the moment after it bounces from the ground.

half-vol·ley (hăf′vŏl′ĭ, häf′-), *v.t., v.i.*, **-leyed, -ley·ing.** to hit or play (a half volley).

half·way (hăf′wā′, häf′-), *adv.* **1.** half over the way: *to go halfway to a place.* **2.** to or at half the distance: *the rope reaches only halfway.* —*adj.* **3.** midway, as between two places or points. **4.** going to or covering only half the full extent; partial: *halfway measures.*

half-wit (hăf′wĭt′, häf′-), *n.* one who is feebleminded.

half-wit·ted (hăf′wĭt′ĭd, häf′-), *adj.* feeble-minded. —**half′-wit′ted·ly,** *adv.* —**half′-wit′ted·ness,** *n.*

hal·i·but (hăl′ə bət, hŏl′-), *n., pl.* **-buts,** (esp. collectively) **-but. 1.** either of two species of large flatfishes, *Hippoglossus hippoglossus* of the North Atlantic and *H. stenolepis* of the North Pacific; the largest of the flatfishes and widely used for food. **2.** any of various other similar flatfishes. Also, **holibut.** [ME *halybutte,* appar. f. *haly* (OE *hālig* holy) + *butte* kind of fish; so called because eaten on holy days. Cf. LG *heilbutt*]

Hal·i·car·nas·sus (hăl′ə kär năs′əs), *n.* an ancient city of Caria, in SW Asia Minor: site of the Mausoleum, one of the seven wonders of the ancient world.

hal·ide (hăl′īd, hā′līd), *Chem.* —*n.* **1.** a compound, usually of two elements only, one of which is a halogen. —*adj.* **2.** of the nature of, or pertaining to, a halide; haloid. Also, **hal·id** (hăl′īd, hā′līd). [f. HAL(OGEN) + -IDE]

Hal·i·fax (hăl′ə făks′), *n.* **1.** a seaport in SE Canada: the capital of Nova Scotia. 85,589 (1951). **2.** a city in central England, in SW Yorkshire. 96,440 (est. 1956).

Hal·i·fax (hăl′ə făks′), *n.* Earl of, *(Edward Frederick Lindley Wood)* 1881–1959, British statesman.

hal·ite (hăl′īt, hā′līt), *n.* rock salt. [f. HAL- + -ITE[1]]

hal·i·to·sis (hăl′ə tō′sĭs), *n.* bad or offensive breath. [NL: f. s. L *hālitus* breath + -ōsis -OSIS]

hal·i·tus (hăl′ə təs), *n.* the breath. [t. L: breath]

hall (hôl), *n.* **1.** *U.S.* a corridor or passageway in a building. **2.** the entrance room or vestibule of a house or building. **3.** a large and impressive room of public nature. **4.** a large building for residence, instruction, or other purposes, as in a university or college. **5.** the occupants of such a building. **6.** (in English colleges) **a.** a large room in which the members and students dine. **b.** dinner in such a room. **7.** *Chiefly Brit.* the proprietor's residence on a large landed estate. **8.** the chief room in a medieval castle or similar structure, used for eating, sleeping, and entertaining. **9.** the house of a medieval chieftain or noble. [ME and OE, c. OHG *halla*, akin to OE *helan* cover, hide, L *cēlāre* hide, Gk. *kalýptein* cover]

Hall (hôl), *n.* **1.** Charles Francis, 1821–1871, U.S. Arctic explorer. **2.** Charles Martin, 1863–1914, U.S. chemist and inventor. **3.** Granville Stanley, 1846–1924, U.S. psychologist and educator.

Hal·lam (hăl′əm), *n.* **1.** Arthur Henry, 1811–33, British poet and essayist: subject of Tennyson's *In Memoriam*. **2.** Henry, 1777–1859, British historian.

Hal·le (hăl′ə), *n.* a city in East Germany. 289,680 (est. 1955).

Hal·leck (hăl′ĭk, -ək), *n.* **1.** Fitz-Greene, 1790–1867, U.S. poet. **2.** Henry Wager, 1815–72, Union general in the U.S. Civil War and writer on military subjects.

hal·lel (hə lāl′, häl′ĕl), *n. Jewish Rel.* a hymn of praise consisting of Psalms 113–118 or of Psalm 136. [t. Heb.: m. *hallēl* praise]

hal·le·lu·jah (hăl′ə lōō′yə), *interj.* **1.** Praise ye the Lord! **—n. 2.** an exclamation of "hallelujah!" **3.** a musical composition wholly or principally based upon the word *hallelujah*. Also, **hal′le·lu·iah.** [t. Heb.: m. *hallelūyah* praise ye Jehovah]

Hal·ley (hăl′ĭ), *n.* Edmund, 1656–1742, British astronomer: first to predict the return of the comet now known as Halley's Comet.

hal·liard (hăl′yərd), *n.* halyard.

hall·mark (hôl′märk′), *n.* **1.** an official mark or stamp indicating a standard of purity, used in marking gold and silver articles assayed by the Goldsmith's Company of London. **2.** any mark or special indication of genuineness, good quality, etc. [from Goldsmiths' *Hall* (in London), the seat of the Goldsmiths' Company]

hal·lo (hə lō′), *interj., n., v.* hollo. Also, **hal·loa** (hə lō′).

Hall of Fame, a colonnade at New York University having tablets and busts in honor of famous Americans.

hal·loo (hə lōō′), *interj., n., pl. -loos, v. —interj.* **1.** an exclamation used to attract attention, to incite the dogs in hunting, etc. **—n. 2.** the cry "halloo!" **—v.i. 3.** to call with a loud voice; shout; cry, as after dogs. **—v.t. 4.** to incite or chase with shouts and cries of "halloo!" **5.** to cry aloud to. **6.** to utter with shouts. [var. of HOLLO]

hal·low[1] (hăl′ō), *v.t.* **1.** to make holy; sanctify; consecrate. **2.** to honor as holy. [ME *halow(e)*, OE *hālgian* der. *hālig* HOLY]

hal·low[2] (hə lō′), *interj., n., v.* halloo. [var. of HALLOO]

hal·lowed (hăl′ōd; *in liturgical use often* hăl′ō′ĭd), *adj.* **1.** made holy; sacred; consecrated. **2.** honored or observed as holy. **—hal′lowed·ness,** *n.* **—Syn. 1.** See holy.

Hal·low·een (hăl′ō ēn′, hŏl′-), *n.* the evening of Oct. 31; the eve of All Saints' Day. Also, **Hal′low·e′en′.** [f. *hallow* saint + *een*, var. of *even* EVE]

Hal·low·mas (hăl′ō məs, -măs′), *n. Archaic.* the feast of Allhallows or All Saints' Day, on Nov. 1.

Hall·statt·i·an (häl stät′ĭ ən), *adj.* pertaining to a variously dated pre-Christian stage of culture in central Europe, characterized by the use of bronze, the introduction of iron, artistic work in pottery, jewelry, etc., as shown by the contents of a burial ground of the period found near Hallstatt, a village in central Austria.

hal·lu·cal (hăl′yə kəl), *adj. Anat.* referring to the great toe. [f. s. NL *hallux* (see HALLUX) + -AL[1]]

hal·lu·ci·nate (hə lōō′sə nāt′), *v.t.,* -nated, -nating. to affect with hallucination. [t. L: m.s. *hallūcinātus,* pp. of (h)*allūcinārī* wander in mind, dream]

hal·lu·ci·na·tion (hə lōō′sə nā′shən). *n.* **1.** an apparent perception, as by sight or hearing, for which there is no real external cause. **2.** a suffering from illusion or false notions. **—Syn. 1.** See illusion.

hal·lu·ci·na·to·ry (hə lōō′sə nə tōr′ĭ), *adj.* pertaining to or characterized by hallucination.

hal·lu·ci·no·sis (hə lōō′sə nō′sĭs), *n. Psychiatry.* a psychosis or state characterized and produced by hallucinations. [f. HALLUCIN(ATION) + -OSIS]

hal·lux (hăl′əks), *n., pl. -luces* (-yə sēz′). *Anat., Zool.* the innermost of the five digits normally present in the hind foot of air-breathing vertebrates, as (in man) the great toe. **b.** (in birds) the hind toe. [NL, m. L (h)*allex* great toe, with -*u-* by contam. with (h)*allus* thumb]

hall·way (hôl′wā′), *n.* U.S. **1.** a corridor, as in a building. **2.** an entrance hall.

halm (hôm), *n. Brit.* haulm.

Hal·ma·he·ra (häl′mä hĕ′rä), *n.* an island in Indonesia: the largest of the Moluccas. 83,700 pop. (1930); 6928 sq. mi. Also, **Jilolo.**

ha·lo (hā′lō), *n., pl. -los, -loes, v., -loed, -loing. —n.* **1.** a radiance surrounding the head in the representation of a sacred personage. **2.** an ideal glory investing an object viewed with feeling or sentiment: *the halo around Shakespeare's plays.* **3.** *Meteorol.* a circle of light appearing around the sun or moon, caused by the refraction of light in suspended ice crystals. **—v.t. 4.** to surround with a halo. **—v.i. 5.** to form a halo. [t. L: m. *halōs,* t. Gk.: disk, halo, threshing floor (on which the oxen trod out a circular path)] **—ha′lo·like′,** *adj.*

halo-, a word element meaning "salt," as in **halogen.** [t. Gk., comb. form of *hăls*]

hal·o·gen (hăl′ə jən, hā′lə-), *n. Chem.* any of the negative elements fluorine, chlorine, iodine, bromine, and astatine, which form binary salts by direct union with metals.

hal·o·gen·a·tion (hăl′ə jə nā′shən, hā′lə-), *n.* the introduction of a halogen into an organic compound.

hal·oid (hăl′oid, hā′loid), *adj.* **1.** denoting any halogen derivative. **—n. 2.** a haloid salt or derivative.

hal·o·phyte (hăl′ə fīt′), *n.* a plant which grows in salty or alkaline soil. **—hal·o·phyt·ic** (hăl′ə fĭt′ĭk), *adj.*

Hals (häls), *n.* Frans (fräns), 1580?–1666, Dutch portrait painter.

Hal·sey (hôl′zĭ), *n.* William Frederick, 1882–1959, U.S. admiral.

Häl·sing·borg (hĕl′sĭng bôr′y), *n.* a seaport in SW Sweden, opposite Helsingör. 72,660 (est. 1953).

halt[1] (hôlt), *v.i.* **1.** to make a temporary stop, as in marching, etc. **—v.t. 2.** to cause to halt. **—n. 3.** temporary stop. [t. G: stoppage] **—Syn. 2.** See stop.

halt[2] (hôlt), *v.i.* **1.** to proceed in a faulty way, as in speech, reasoning, etc. **2.** to be in doubt; waver; hesitate. **3.** *Archaic.* to be lame; walk lamely; limp. **—adj. 4.** *Archaic.* lame; limping. **—n. 5.** *Archaic.* lameness; a limp. [ME; OE *h(e)alt,* c. OHG *halz*] **—halt′ing,** *adj.* **—halt′ing·ly,** *adv.* **—halt′ing·ness,** *n.*

hal·ter[1] (hôl′tər), *n.* **1.** a rope or strap with a noose or headstall, for leading or fastening horses or cattle. **2.** a rope with a noose for hanging criminals. **3.** death by hanging. **4.** a woman's sports waist, tied behind the neck and across the back, leaving the arms and back bare. **—v.t. 5.** to put a halter on; restrain as by a halter. **6.** to hang (a person). [ME; OE *hælftre,* c. G *halfter*] **—hal′ter·like′,** *adj.*

hal·ter[2] (hăl′tər), *n., pl.* **halteres** (hăl tĭr′ēz). one of a pair of slender, club-shaped appendages attached to the body of a fly (order *Diptera*) near the wings, used for balancing in flight; balancer. [t. L, t. Gk.: usually pl. (*haltēres*) leaping weights]

halt·er[3] (hôl′tər), *n.* one who halts or hesitates. [f. HALT[2] + -ER[1]]

halt·er[4] (hôl′tər), *n.* one who halts or stops. [f. HALT[1] + -ER[1]]

halve (hăv, häv), *v.t.,* **halved, halving. 1.** to divide in halves; share equally. **2.** to reduce to half. **3.** *Golf.* to play (a hole, match, etc.) in the same number of strokes, as two opponents. [ME *halven,* der. HALF]

halves (hăvz, hävz), *n.* **1.** pl. of **half. 2. by halves,** *a.* incompletely. *b.* half-heartedly.

hal·yard (hăl′yərd), *n.* a rope or tackle used to hoist or lower a sail, yard, flag, etc. Also, **halliard.** [ME *halier, hallyer* that which hales or hauls (f. HALE[2] + -IER); influenced by YARD-]

ham (hăm), *n., v.,* **hammed, hamming. —n. 1.** one of the rear quarters of a hog, esp. the heavy-muscled part, between hip and hock. **2.** the meat of this part. **3.** the part of the leg back of the knee. **4.** (*often pl.*) the back of the thigh, or the thigh and the buttock together. **5.** *Theat. Slang.* **a.** an actor who overacts. **b.** overacting. **6.** *Slang.* an amateur: *a radio ham.* **—v.i. 7.** *Theat. Slang.* to act with exaggerated expression of emotion; overact. [ME *hamme,* OE *hamm,* c. OHG *hamma* angle of the knee. Cf. LL *camba* bend of leg]

Ham (hăm), *n. Bible.* second son of Noah. Gen. 10:1.

Ham·a·dan (hăm′ə dän′; *Persian* häm′ə dän′), *n.* a city in W Iran. 123,931 (est. 1950). See **Ecbatana.**

ham·a·dry·ad (hăm′ə drī′ad, -ăd), *n., pl. -ads, -ades** (-ə dēz′). *Class. Myth.* a wood nymph fabled to live and die with the tree which she inhabited. [t. L: s. *Hamadryas,* t. Gk.: f. *hăma* together + *dryás* wood nymph]

Ha·ma·mat·su (hä′mä mät′sōō), *n.* a city in central Japan, on Honshu island. 152,028 (1950).

ham·a·me·li·da·ceous (hăm′ə me lĭ dā′shəs, -mĕl′ə-), *adj.* belonging to the *Hamamelidaceae,* a family of shrubs and trees including the witch hazel, etc. [f. s. NL *hamamēlis* (t. Gk.: a kind of medlar) + -ACEOUS]

Ha·man (hā′mən), *n. Bible.* (in the Book of Esther) an enemy of the Jews who was hanged with his plot for their destruction was exposed.

ha·mate (hā′māt), *adj. Anat.* **1.** hook-shaped. **2.** having a hooklike process. [t. L: m. *hāmātus*]

Ham·ble·to·ni·an (hăm′bəl tō′nĭ ən), *n.* **1.** a superior strain of American trotting horses descended from Hambletonian (foaled 1849, died 1876). **2.** the principal annual harness race for three-year-old trotters, held at DuQuoine, Illinois.

ham·burg·er (hăm′bûr′gər), *n.* **1.** Hamburg steak. **2.** ground beef from which Hamburg steaks are made. **3.** a roll or bun containing such meat, often with relish.

Ham·burg (hăm′bûrg; *Ger.* häm′bŏŏrKH), *n.* **1.** a state in N West Germany. 1,792,936 pop. (1956); 288 sq. mi. **2.** the capital of this state, on the Elbe: the largest seaport in continental Europe. 1,781,524 (1955).

ham·born (häm′bôrn), *n.* See **Duisburg-Hamborn.**

ham·burg (häm′bûrg), *n.* hamburger.

Ham·burg steak (hăm′bûrg), (*sometimes l.c.*) chopped beef, seasoned, and fried or broiled in cakes.

hame (hām), *n.* either of two curved pieces lying upon the collar in the harness of an animal, to which the traces are fastened. See illus. under **harness.** [ME; akin to G *hamen* fishhook, dragnet, OE *hamele* rowlock]

Ha·meln (hä′məln), *n.* a city in N West Germany, on the Weser river: scene of the legend of the Pied Piper of Hamelin. 49,800 (est. 1953). Also, **Ham·e·lin** (hăm′ə lĭn).

Ha·mil·car Bar·ca (hə mĭl′kär bär′kə, hăm′ĭl kär′), died 228? B.C., Carthaginian general: Hannibal's father.

Ham·il·ton (hăm′əl tən), *n.* **1.** Alexander, 1757–1804, American statesman and writer on government. **2.** Lady Emma, (*Amy,* or *Emily, Lyon*) 1765?–1815, mistress of Viscount Nelson. **3.** Sir Ian Standish Monteith (ē′ən *or* ī′ən, mŏn tēth′), 1853–1947, British general.

4. Sir William, 1788–1856, Scottish philosopher. **5. Sir William Rowan,** 1805–65, British mathematician and astronomer. **6.** a city in SE Canada: a port near the W end of Lake Ontario. 208,321 (1951). **7.** a city in SW Ohio. 72,354 (1960). **8.** a city in S Scotland, SE of Glasgow. 41,000 (est. 1956). **9.** the capital of Bermuda. 2816 (1950). **10.** Also, **Grand River,** a river flowing ab. 600 mi. through S Labrador into **Hamilton Inlet,** an arm (ab. 150 mi. long) of the Atlantic. See **Grand Falls. 11. Mount,** a mountain of the Coast Range in California, near San Francisco: site of Lick Observatory. 4209 ft.

Ham·il·to·ni·an (hăm′əl tō′nĭ ən), *adj.* pertaining to or holding the political doctrines of Alexander Hamilton (strong central government, protective tariff, etc.).

Ham·ite (hăm′ īt), *n.* **1.** a descendant of Ham. Gen. 10: 1, 6–20. **2.** a member of any of various nations of Africa, as the ancient Egyptians and modern Berbers.

Ham·it·ic (hă mĭt′ĭk, ha-), *adj.* **1.** of or pertaining to the Hamites or their speech. **—n. 2.** a family of languages related to the Semitic, spoken in North Africa, including ancient Egyptian and modern Berber.

ham·let (hăm′lĭt), *n.* **1.** a small village. **2.** a little cluster of houses in the country. **3.** *Brit.* a village without a church of its own, but belonging to the parish of another village or a town. [ME *hamelet,* t. OF, dim. of *hamel* hamlet, dim. of *ham,* t. Gmc.; cf. OE *hamm* enclosed land] **—Syn. 1.** See **community.**

Ham·let (hăm′lĭt), *n.* **1.** a tragedy (first printed, 1603) by Shakespeare. **2.** its hero.

Ham·lin (hăm′lĭn), *n.* **Hannibal,** 1809–1901, U.S. statesman: vice-president of the U.S.; 1861–65.

Ham·mar·skjöld (hăm′ər shöld; *Sw.* häm′är shŭld), *n.* **Dag** (däg; *Sw.* dä) **Hjalmar Agne,** 1905–61, Swedish statesman; secretary general of United Nations, 1953–1961.

ham·mer (hăm′ər), *n.* **1.** an instrument consisting of a solid head, usually of metal, set crosswise on a handle, used for beating metals, driving nails, etc. **2.** any of various instruments or devices resembling a hammer in form, action, or use. **3.** *Firearms.* that part of the lock which by its fall or action causes the discharge, as by exploding the percussion cap; the cock. **4.** one of the padded levers by which the strings of a piano are struck. **5.** *Athletics.* a metal ball attached to a long, flexible handle, used in certain throwing contests. **6.** *Anat.* the malleus. **7.** come or go under the hammer, to be sold at auction. **—v.t. 8.** to beat or drive with or as with a hammer. **9.** to form with a hammer (often fol. by *out*). **10.** to fasten by or as by using a hammer. **11.** to contrive or work out laboriously (often fol. by *out*). **—v.i. 12.** to strike blows with or as with a hammer. **13.** to make persistent or laborious attempts. [ME *hamer,* OE *hamor,* c. G *hammer*] **—ham′mer·er,** *n.* **—ham′mer·less,** *adj.* **—ham′mer·like′,** *adj.*

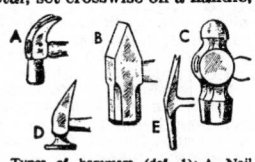

Types of hammers (def. 1): A. Nail hammer; B. Engineer's hammer; C, Machinist's hammer; D, Shoemaker's hammer; E. Carpenter's hammer

hammer and tongs, *Colloq.* with great noise, vigor, or violence.

hammered work, metalwork formed by the hammers, anvils, punches, etc., of craftsmen.

Ham·mer·fest (hăm′ər fĕst′), *n.* a seaport in N Norway: the northernmost town in Europe. 4282 (1950).

ham·mer·head (hăm′ər hĕd′), *n.* any of the sharks constituting the genus *Sphyrna,* characterized by a head expanded laterally so as to resemble a double-headed hammer, esp. *S. zygaena,* a widely distributed species.

Hammerhead, *Sphyrna zygaena* (15 ft. long)

hammer lock, *Wrestling.* a hold whereby the opponent's arm is twisted and pushed behind his back.

Ham·mer·stein (hăm′ər stīn′), *n.* **1. Oscar,** 1847?–1919, U.S. theatrical manager, born in Germany. **2.** his grandson, **Oscar, II,** 1895–1960, U.S. lyricist and librettist.

ham·mock (hăm′ək), *n.* a kind of hanging bed or couch made of canvas, netted cord, or the like. [t. Sp.: m. *hamaca.* of W Ind. orig.] **—ham′mock·like′,** *adj.*

Ham·mond (hăm′ənd), *n.* a city in NW Indiana, near Chicago. 111,698 (1960).

Hammond organ, 1. a musical instrument, resembling in shape an upright piano, with two keyboards, electronic tone generation, and a great variety of tone colors. **2.** a trademark for this instrument.

Ham·mu·ra·bi (hä′mŏŏ rä′bĭ, hăm′ŏŏ-), *n.* fl. c2100 B.C., king of Babylonia: famous code of laws made in his reign.

Hamp·den (hămp′dən, hăm′dən), *n.* **1. John,** 1594–1643, British statesman who defended the rights of the House of Commons against Charles I. **2. Walter,** (*Walter Hampden Dougherty*) 1879–1955, U.S. actor.

ham·per[1] (hăm′pər), *v.t.* **1.** to impede; hinder; hold back. **—n. 2.** *Naut.* articles which, while necessary to a ship's equipment, are often in the way. [ME *hampren,* orig. uncert.] **—Syn. 1.** obstruct, encumber, trammel. **See prevent. —Ant. 1.** assist.

ham·per[2] (hăm′pər), *n.* a large basket or wickerwork receptacle, usually with a cover. [ME *hampere;* syncopated var. of HANAPER]

Hamp·shire (hămp′shĭr, -shər), *n.* **1.** Also, **Hants.** a county in S England, including the administrative counties of Southampton and Isle of Wight. 1,197,170 (1951); 1650 sq. mi. **2.** an English breed of sheep of the mutton type, noted for the rapid growth of its lambs, popular in the U.S.

Hamp·stead (hămp′stĭd), *n.* a NW borough of London: residences of artists and writers. 95,073 (est. 1951).

Hamp·ton (hămp′tən), *n.* **Wade,** 1818–1902, Confederate general: U.S. senator, 1879–91.

Hampton Roads, a channel in SE Virginia between the mouth of the James river and Chesapeake Bay: battle between the Monitor and the Merrimac, 1862.

ham·ster (hăm′stər), *n.* **1.** any of a number of short-tailed, stout-bodied, burrowing rodents, having large cheek pouches, and inhabiting parts of Europe and Asia, as *Cricetus cricetus.* **2.** the fur of such an animal. [t. G]

Hamster, *Cricetus cricetus* (Ab. 10 in. long)

ham·string (hăm′strĭng′), *n.,* *v.,* **-strung** or (*Rare*) **-stringed, -stringing. —n. 1.** (in man) any of the tendons which bound the ham, or hollow of the knee. **2.** (in quadrupeds) the great tendon at the back of the hock. **—v.t. 3.** to cut the hamstring or hamstrings of and thus disable. **4.** to cripple or disable.

Ham·sun (häm′sŏŏn), *n.* **Knut** (knŏŏt), 1859–1952, Norwegian novelist.

Ham·tramck (hăm trăm′ĭk), *n.* a city in SE Michigan, within the city limits of Detroit. 34,137 (1960).

ham·u·lus (hăm′yə ləs), *n., pl.* **-li** (-lī′). *Anat., Zool., Bot., etc.* a small hook or hooklike process. [t. L, dim. of *hāmus* a hook]

Han (hä n), *n.* **1.** Chinese dynasty, 206 B.C.–A.D. 220, with an interregnum, A.D. 9–25, known as the **Earlier** or **Western Han** before the interregnum and as the **Later** or **Eastern Han** afterwards. The Han was distinguished for the revival of letters and the beginnings of Buddhism; its bureaucracy became a model for later dynasties. **2.** a river flowing from central China into the Yangtze at Hankow. ab. 900 mi.

han·a·per (hăn′ə pər), *n.* a wicker receptacle for documents. [ME *hanypere,* t. OF: m. *hanapier* case for holding a cup, der. *hanap* cup, t. Gmc.; cf. OS *hnapp* cup]

hance (häns, häns), *n.* **1.** *Naut.* a curved rise to a higher part, as of the bulwarks from the waist to the quarter-deck. **2.** *Archit.* **a.** the sharply curving portion nearest the impost at either side of an elliptical or similar arch. **b.** the haunch of an arch. [n. use of *hance,* v., raise (now obs.), aphetic var. of ENHANCE]

Han Cities (hän), Wuhan.

Han·cock (hăn′kŏk), *n.* **1. John,** 1737–93, American statesman: first signer of the Declaration of Independence. **2. Winfield Scott,** 1824–86, Union general in the U.S. Civil War.

hand (hănd), *n.* **1.** (in man) the terminal, prehensile part of the arm, consisting of the palm and five digits. **2.** the corresponding part of the forelimb in any of the higher vertebrates. **3.** the terminal part of any limb when prehensile, as the hind foot of a monkey, the chela of a crustacean, or (in falconry) the foot of a hawk. **4.** something resembling a hand in shape or function: *the hands of a clock.* **5.** a sign used in writing or printing to draw attention to something. **6.** a person employed in manual labor; worker; laborer: *a factory hand.* **7.** a person who does a specified thing: *a book by several hands.* **8.** the persons of any company or number: *all hands gave assistance, all hands on deck.* **9.** (*often pl.*) possession or power; control, custody, or care: *to have someone's fate in one's hands.* **10.** agency; active cooperation in doing something: *a helping hand.* **11.** side: *on every hand.* **12.** a side of a subject, question, etc.: *on the other hand.* **13.** a person considered as a source, as of information or of supply: *at first hand.* **14.** style of handwriting. **15.** a person's signature. **16.** skill; execution; touch: *a painting that shows a master's hand.* **17.** a person, with reference to action, ability, or skill: *a poor hand at writing letters.* **18.** a round or outburst of applause for a performer: *to get a hand.* **19.** a pledge of marriage. **20.** a lineal measure used in giving the height of horses, etc., equal to four inches. **21.** *Cards.* **a.** the cards dealt to or held by each player at one time. **b.** the person holding the cards. **c.** a single part of a game, in which all the cards dealt at one time are played. **22.** *Rom. Law.* the husband's control over the wife. **23.** skill or knack at manipulating the reins. **24.** a bundle of tobacco leaves tied together. **25.** Some special noun phrases are: **a heavy hand,** severity or oppression. **a high hand,** dictatorial manner or arbitrary conduct. **at hand, 1.** within reach; near by. **2.** near in time. **3.** ready for use. **at the hand** or **hands of,** from the action or agency of. **by hand,** by the use of the hands (as opposed to any other means): *to make pottery by hand.* **come to hand,** to be received; come within one's reach. **from hand to hand,** from one person to another. **from hand to mouth, 1.** by eating at once whatever one gets. **2.** with attention to immediate wants only.

hand and glove or **hand in glove**, very intimate.
hand in hand, 1. with hands mutually clasped. **2.** conjointly or concurrently.
hands off, keep off; refrain from blows or touching.
hand to hand, in close combat; at close quarters.
have a hand in, to have a part or concern in doing.
have one's hands full, to be fully occupied.
in hand, 1. under control. **2.** in immediate possession: *cash in hand.* **3.** in process: *keep to the matter in hand.*
off one's hands, out of one's responsible charge or care.
on hand, 1. in immediate possession: *cash on hand.* **2.** before one for attention. **3.** *U.S.* present.
on or **upon one's hands**, under one's care, management, or responsibility.
out of hand, 1. beyond control: *to let one's temper get out of hand.* **2.** at once; without delay. **3.** no longer in process; over and done with.
to hand, 1. within reach; at hand. **2.** into one's immediate possession.
wash one's hands of, to have nothing more to do with.
—v.t. 26. to deliver or pass with the hand. **27.** to help or conduct with the hand. **28.** *Naut.* to furl, as a sail. **29.** to pass on; transmit (fol. by *on*). **30. hand down, a.** to deliver the decision of a court. **b.** to transmit from the higher to the lower, in space or time: *to hand down to posterity.* **31. hand over, a.** to deliver into another's keeping. **b.** to give up or yield control of.
—adj. 32. of or belonging to the hand. **33.** done or made by hand. **34.** that may be carried in, or worn on, the hand. **35.** operated by hand.
[ME and OE, c. G *hand*] **—hand′less**, *adj.* **—hand′like′**, *adj.*

Hand (hănd), *n.* **Learned** (lûr′nĭd), 1872–1961. American jurist.

hand·bag (hănd′băg′), *n.* a bag for carrying in the hand, as a small valise or a woman's bag for carrying money, small purchases, toilet articles, etc.

hand·ball (hănd′bôl′), *n.* **1.** a game in which a small ball is batted against a wall with the (usually gloved) hand. **2.** the kind of ball used in this game.

hand·bar·row (hănd′băr′ō), *n.* **1.** a frame with handles at each end by which it is carried. **2.** a handcart.

hand·bill (hănd′bĭl′), *n.* a small printed bill or announcement, usually for distribution by hand.

hand·book (hănd′book′), *n.* **1.** a small book or treatise serving for guidance, as in an occupation or study: *handbook of radio.* **2.** a guidebook for travelers.

hand brake, a brake operated by a hand lever.

hand·breadth (hănd′brĕdth′), *n.* a unit of linear measure from 2½ to 4 inches. Also, **hand's-breadth**.

hand·car (hănd′kär′), *n.* *U.S.* a light car propelled by a mechanism worked by hand, used on some railroads for inspecting tracks and transporting workmen.

hand·cart (hănd′kärt′), *n.* a small cart drawn or pushed by hand.

hand·cuff (hănd′kŭf′), *n.* **1.** a ring-shaped shackle for the wrist, usually one of a pair connected by a short chain or linked bar. **—v.t. 2.** to put handcuffs on.

hand·ed (hăn′dĭd), *adj.* **1.** having a hand or hands. **2.** having a hand characterized in some specified manner: *right-handed.* **3.** done by hand in a specified way: *open-handed rowing.* **4.** done by a specified number of hands: *a double-handed game.*

Han·del (hăn′dəl), *n.* **George Frederick,** (*Georg Friedrich Händel*) 1685–1759, German composer.

hand·ful (hănd′fool′), *n., pl.* **-fuls. 1.** as much or as many as the hand can grasp or contain. **2.** a small quantity or number: *a handful of men.* **3.** *Colloq.* a thing or a person that is as much as one can manage.

hand glass, 1. a small mirror with a handle. **2.** a magnifying glass for holding in the hand.

hand grenade, 1. a grenade or explosive shell which is thrown by hand and exploded either by impact or by means of a fuse. **2.** a grenade or glass missile containing a chemical, for extinguishing fire.

hand·grip (hănd′grĭp′), *n.* **1.** a grasping with the hand; a grip, as in greeting. **2.** (*pl.*) hand-to-hand combat. **3.** a handle. [ME; OE *handgripe*]

hand·i·cap (hăn′dĭ kăp′), *n., v.,* **-capped, -capping. —n. 1.** a race or other contest in which certain disadvantages or advantages of weight, distance, time, etc., are placed upon competitors to equalize their chances of winning. **2.** the disadvantage or advantage itself. **3.** any encumbrance or disadvantage that makes success more difficult. **—v.t. 4.** to serve as a handicap or disadvantage to: *his age handicaps him.* **5.** to subject to a disadvantageous handicap, as a competitor of recognized superiority. **6.** to assign handicaps to (competitors). [orig. *hand i' cap* (with *i'* for *in* before a consonant); reason for this name uncert.] **—hand′i·cap′per**, *n.*

hand·i·craft (hăn′dĭ krăft′, -kräft′), *n.* **1.** manual skill. **2.** a manual art or occupation. [alter. of earlier *handcraft*, OE *handcræft*, modeled on HANDIWORK]

hand·i·crafts·man (hăn′dĭ krăfts′mən, -kräfts′-), *n., pl.* **-men.** a person skilled in a handicraft; craftsman.

hand·i·ly (hăn′də lĭ), *adv.* **1.** dexterously; expertly. **2.** conveniently.

hand·i·ness (hăn′dĭ nĭs), *n.* **1.** state or character of being handy or expert. **2.** quality of being easily handled; convenience.

hand·i·work (hăn′dĭ wûrk′), *n.* **1.** work done or a thing or things made by the hands. **2.** the labor or action of a particular doer or maker: *the handiwork of man.* **3.** the result of one's action or agency. [ME *handiwerk*, OE *handgeweorc*]

hand·ker·chief (hăng′kər chĭf, -chēf′), *n.* **1.** a small piece of linen, silk, or other fabric, usually square, carried about the person for wiping the face, nose, etc. **2.** a neckerchief or a kerchief. [f. HAND + KERCHIEF]

han·dle (hăn′dəl), *n., v.,* **-dled, -dling. —n. 1.** a part of a thing which is intended to be grasped by the hand in using or moving it. **2.** that by which anything may be held. **3.** something that may be taken advantage of in effecting a purpose. **—v.t. 4.** to touch or feel with the hand; use the hands on, as in picking up. **5.** to manage in use with the hands; manipulate. **6.** to wield, employ, or use: *to handle one's fists well in a fight.* **7.** to manage, direct, or control: *to handle troops.* **8.** to deal with or treat, as a matter or subject. **9.** to deal with or treat in a particular way: *to handle a person with tact.* **10.** to deal or trade in (goods, etc.). [ME *handlen*, OE *handlian* (c. G *handeln*), der. *hand* HAND] **—han′dled**, *adj.* **—han′dle·less**, *adj.*

handle bar, (*often pl.*) the curved steering bar of a bicycle, etc., in front of the rider.

han·dler (hăn′dlər), *n.* **1.** a person or thing that handles. **2.** *Boxing.* a person who assists in the training of a fighter or is his second during the fight. **3.** the individual who manages and arouses a dog, etc., in a contest.

han·dling (hănd′lĭng), *n.* **1.** a touching, grasping, or using with the hands. **2.** management; treatment.

hand·made (hănd′mād′), *adj.* made by hand, rather than by machine.

hand·maid (hănd′mād′), *n.* a female serv nt or personal attendant. Also, **hand′maid′en.**

hand-me-down (hănd′mĭ doun′, hăn′-), *n.* Now *U.S. Colloq.* **1.** an article of clothing handed down or acquired at second hand. **2.** a cheap, ready-made garment.

hand organ, a portable barrel organ played by means of a crank turned by hand.

hand·out (hănd′out′), *n.* *U.S. Slang.* a portion of food or the like given to a beggar.

hand-pick (hănd′pĭk′), *v.t.* **1.** to pick by hand **2.** to select carefully. **3.** to select for ulterior purposes: *to hand-pick a candidate for office.* **—hand′-picked′**, *adj.*

hand·rail (hănd′rāl′), *n.* a rail serving as a support or guard at the side of a stairway, platform, etc.

hand·saw (hănd′sô′), *n.* a saw used with one hand.

hand's-breadth (hăndz′brĕdth′), *n.* handbreadth.

hand·sel (hăn′səl), *n., v.,* **-seled, -seling** or (*esp. Brit.*) **-selled, -selling. —n. 1.** a gift or token for good luck or as an expression of good wishes, as at the beginning of the new year, or at entering upon a new state, situation, or enterprise. **2.** a first installment of payment. **3.** the first use or experience of anything; foretaste. **—v.t. 4.** to give a handsel to. **5.** to inaugurate auspiciously. **6.** to use, try, or experience for the first time. Also, **hansel.** [ME *handselne*, OE *handselen*, lit., hand gift; akin to Icel. *handsal* the binding of a bargain by joining hands]

hand·set (hănd′sĕt′), *n.* a part of a telephone combining both the receiver and the transmitter in one structure which can be held to the face of the speaker.

hand·some (hăn′səm), *adj.,* **-somer, -somest. 1.** of fine or admirable appearance; comely; tastefully or elegantly fine: *a handsome person.* **2.** considerable, ample, or liberal in amount: *a handsome fortune.* **3.** gracious; generous: *a handsome gift.* **4.** *U.S. Colloq.* dexterous; graceful: *a handsome speech.* [ME *handsom*, f. HAND + -SOME[1]; orig., easy to handle] **—hand′some·ly**, *adv.* **—hand′some·ness**, *n.* **—Syn. 1.** See beautiful.

hand·spike (hănd′spīk′), *n.* a bar used as a lever. [t. D: m. *handspeck* hand bar, assimilated to *spike*]

hand·spring (hănd′sprĭng′), *n.* a kind of somersault in which the body is supported upon one or both hands while turning in the air.

hand-to-hand (hănd′tə hănd′), *adj.* in close combat; at close quarters.

hand-to-mouth (hănd′tə mouth′), *adj.* precarious; unsettled.

hand·work (hănd′wûrk′), *n.* work done by hand, as distinguished from that done by machine.

hand·writ·ing (hănd′rī′tĭng), *n.* **1.** writing done with the hand. **2.** a kind or style of writing.

hand·y (hăn′dĭ), *adj.,* **handier, handiest. 1.** ready to hand; conveniently accessible: *to have aspirins handy.* **2.** ready or skillful with the hands; deft; dexterous. **3.** convenient to handle; easily manipulated or maneuvered: *a handy ship.* **4.** convenient or useful: *a handy tool.*

handy man, a man hired to do various kinds of work.

hang (hăng), *v.,* **hung** or (esp. for capital punishment and suicide) **hanged; hanging;** *n.* **—v.t. 1.** to fasten or attach (a thing) so that it is supported only from above; suspend. **2.** to suspend so as to allow free movement, as on a hinge. **3.** to fasten or suspend (a person) on a cross, gallows, or the like, as a mode of capital punishment; to suspend by the neck until dead. **4.** to let droop or bend downward: *to hang one's head in shame.* **5.** to furnish or decorate with something suspended: *to hang a room with pictures.* **6.** to fasten into position; fix at a proper angle: *to hang a scythe.* **7.** to attach (paper, etc.) to walls. **8.** (used in maledictions and

emphatic expressions): *I'll be hanged if I do.* **9.** to keep (a jury) from rendering a verdict, as one juror by refusing to agree with the others. —*v.i.* **10.** to be suspended; dangle. **11.** to swing freely, as on a hinge. **12.** to be suspended from a cross or gallows; suffer death in this way as punishment. **13.** to bend forward or downward; lean over; incline downward. **14.** to be conditioned or contingent; be dependent. **15.** to hold fast, cling, or adhere; rest for support (fol. by *on* or *upon*). **16.** to be doubtful or undecided; waver or hesitate; remain unfinished. **17.** to loiter or linger: *to hang about a place.* **18.** to rest, float, or hover in the air. **19.** to impend; be imminent. **20.** to remain in attention or consideration: *to hang upon a person's words.* **21.** to fail to agree, as a jury. **22.** Some special verb phrases are:
hang back, to resist advance; be reluctant to proceed.
hang in the balance, to be in doubt or suspense: *for days his life hung in the balance.*
hang out, 1. to lean through an opening. **2.** *Slang.* to live at or frequent a particular place. **3.** to suspend in open view; display: *to hang out a banner.*
hang together, 1. to hold together; remain united. **2.** to be consistent: *his statements do not hang together.*
hang up, 1. to suspend on a hook or peg. **2.** to put into or hold in abeyance; keep back; delay. **3.** to break off telephonic communication.
—*n.* **23.** the way in which a thing hangs: *the hang of a drape.* **24.** *U.S. Colloq.* the precise manner of doing, using, etc., something: *to get the hang of a tool.* **25.** *U.S. Colloq.* meaning or force: *to get the hang of a subject.* **26.** the least degree of care, concern, etc. (in mild expletives): *not to give a hang.*
[fusion of three verbs: (1) ME and OE *hōn* (orig., v.t.), now obs.; (2) ME *hang(i)en,* OE *hangian* (orig., v.i.); (3) ME *heng(e), hing,* t. Scand. (cf. Icel. *hengja* cause to hang)]
—**Syn. 3.** HANG, LYNCH through a widespread misconception have been thought of as synonyms. They do have in common the meaning of "to put to death," but lynching is not always by hanging. HANG, in the sense of "execute," is in accordance with a legal sentence, the method of execution being to suspend by the neck until dead. To LYNCH, however, implies the summary putting to death, by any method, of someone charged with a flagrant offense (though guilt may not have been proved). Lynching is done by private persons, usually a mob, without legal authority.

hang·ar (hăng′ər), *n.* **1.** a shed or shelter. **2.** a shed for airplanes or airships. [t. F, ? t. Gmc.]

hang·bird (hăng′bûrd′), *n.* a bird that builds a hanging nest, esp. the Baltimore oriole.

Hang·chow (hăng′chou′; *Chin.* häng′jō′), *n.* a seaport in and the capital of Chekiang province in E China, on Hangchow Bay, a funnel-shaped bay of the East China Sea. 518,000 (est. 1950).

hang·dog (hăng′dôg′, -dŏg′), *adj.* **1.** (of persons) having a mean or sneaking appearance. **2.** mean; sneaking: *a hangdog look.* —*n.* **3.** a degraded, contemptible person.

hang·er (hăng′ər), *n.* **1.** a contrivance that hangs things. **2.** a shaped support for a coat or other garment when not in use. **3.** something by which a thing is hung, as a loop on a garment. **4.** *Auto.* a double-hinged device linking the chassis with each of the springs. **5.** a light sabre of the 17th and 18th centuries, often worn at sea. **6.** one who hangs something.

hang·er-on (hăng′ər ŏn′), *n., pl.* **hangers-on.** one who clings to a service, place, or connection; follower.

hang·ing (hăng′ĭng), *n.* **1.** capital punishment by suspension with strangulation on a gallows. **2.** (*often pl.*) something that hangs or is hung on the walls of a room, as a drapery, tapestry, etc. **3.** act of one who or that which hangs; suspension. —*adj.* **4.** deserving punishment by hanging. **5.** punishable by, or inclined to inflict, death by hanging: *a hanging crime.* **6.** that hangs; pendent; overhanging. **7.** situated on a steep slope or at a height: *a hanging garden.* **8.** directed downward: *a hanging look.* **9.** made for hanging an object on.

hanging indention, *Print., etc.* an indentation of uniform amount at the beginning of each line except the first, which is of full width.

hang·man (hăng′mən), *n., pl.* **-men.** one who hangs persons condemned to death; public executioner.

hang·nail (hăng′nāl′), *n.* a small piece of partly detached skin at the side or base of the fingernail. [aspirated var. of *angnail,* OE *angnægl-* the aspirated form became standard by popular etymology (assoc. with *hang*)]

hang·out (hăng′out′), *n.* *Slang.* a place where one lives or frequently visits.

hang·o·ver (hăng′ō′vər), *n.* *U.S. Colloq.* **1.** something remaining behind from a former period or state of affairs. **2.** the effect on a person after excessive indulgence in alcoholic liquor.

hank (hăngk), *n.* **1.** a skein, as of thread or yarn. **2.** a definite length of thread or yarn: *a hank of cotton yarn measures 840 yards.* **3.** a coil, knot, or loop: *a hank of hair.* **4.** *Naut.* a ring, as of iron or wood, round a stay, to which a sail is attached. [ME, t. Scand.; cf. Icel. *hönk* hank, coil, skein]

han·ker (hăng′kər), *v.i.* to have a restless or incessant longing (often fol. by *after, for,* or an infinitive). [cf. d. D *hankeren*] —**han′ker·er,** *n.*

han·ker·ing (hăng′kər ĭng), *n.* a longing; craving.

Han·kow (hăn′kou′; *Chin.* häng′kō′), *n.* a city in E China, in Hupeh province; a port at the head of ocean navigation on Yangtze. 1,090,000 (est. 1952). See **Wuhan.**

han·ky (hăng′kĭ), *n.* a handkerchief.

han·ky-pan·ky (hăng′kĭ păng′kĭ), *n. Brit. Slang.* **1.** trickery. **2.** jugglery or legerdemain.

Han·na (hăn′ə), *n.* **Marcus Alonzo,** (*Mark Hanna*) 1837–1904, U.S. politician and senator, 1897–1904.

Han·ni·bal (hăn′ə bəl), *n.* **1.** 247–183? B.C., Carthaginian general who crossed the Alps and invaded Italy. **2.** a city in NE Missouri: a port on the Mississippi; Mark Twain's boyhood home. 20,008 (1960).

Han·no·ver (hä nō′vər), *n.* **Hanover** (defs. 1, 2).

Ha·noï (hä′noi′), *n.* a city in NE Indochina on the Songka river: capital of North Vietnam. 297,000 (est. 1953).

Ha·no·taux (à nō tō′), *n.* **Gabriel Albert Auguste** (gà brē ĕl′ àl bĕr′ ō gyst′), 1853–1944, French statesman and historian.

Han·o·ver (hăn′ō vər), *n.* **1.** German, **Hannover.** a former province in N West Germany; now a district in Lower Saxony. 14,944 sq. mi. **2.** German, **Hannover.** capital of Lower Saxony. 532,247 (est. 1955). **3.** the name of the English royal family from 1714 to 1901. **4.** a college town in W New Hampshire, on the Connecticut river. 4999 (1950).

Han·o·ve·ri·an (hăn′ō vĭr′ĭ ən), *adj.* **1.** of or pertaining to the former ruling house of Hanover. —*n.* **2.** *Brit. Pol.* a supporter of the house of Hanover.

Han·sard (hăn′sərd), *n.* the official stenographic reports of British Parliamentary debates, so called after a family of former compilers.

hanse (hăns), *n.* **1.** a company or guild of merchants. **2.** a fee paid to a medieval trading guild. **3.** (*cap.*) Also, **Hanse Towns.** Hanseatic League. [ME, t. OF, t. MHG: company (of merchants)]

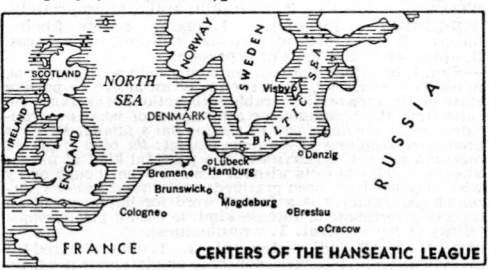

CENTERS OF THE HANSEATIC LEAGUE

Han·se·at·ic League (hăn′sĭ ăt′ĭk), a medieval league of towns of northern Germany and adjacent countries for the promotion and protection of commerce.

han·sel (hăn′səl), *n., v.t.* **-seled, -seling** or (*esp. Brit.*) **-selled, -selling.** handsel.

Han·sen's disease (hăn′sənz), *Pathol.* leprosy. [named after Gerhard Henrik Armauer *Hansen* (1841–1912), Norw. physician who discovered leprosy-causing *Mycobacterium leprae*]

han·som (hăn′səm), *n.* a low-hung, two-wheeled, covered vehicle drawn by one horse, for two passengers, the driver being mounted on an elevated seat behind, and the reins running over the roof. [named after J. A. *Hansom,* British patentee (1834)]

Han·son (hăn′sən), *n.* **Howard (Harold),** born 1896, U.S. composer.

Hants (hănts), *n.* Hampshire (def. 1).

Hansom

Ha·nuk·kah (hä′nŏŏ kä′; *Heb.* кнä′-), *n.* the Feast of the Dedication, a Jewish festival in commemoration of the victory of the Maccabees, lasting eight days (mostly in December). [t. Heb.: m. *ḥanukkäh* dedication]

Han·u·man (hŭn′ŏŏ män′), *n. Hindu Myth.* a monkey chief who is a conspicuous figure in the Ramayana. [t. Hind.: lit., the one with a jaw, the jawed one]

Han·yang (hän′yäng′), *n.* a city in E China at the junction of the Han and Yangtze rivers. 70,000 (1947).

hap (hăp), *n., v.* **happed, happing.** *Archaic.* —*n.* **1.** one's luck or lot. **2.** an occurrence, happening, or accident. —*v.i.* **3.** to happen: *if it so hap.* [ME, t. Scand.; cf. Icel. *happ* hap, chance, good luck. Cf. OE *gehæp,* adj., fit, convenient]

hap·haz·ard (*adj., adv.* hăp′hăz′ərd; *n.* hăp′hăz′ərd), *adj.* **1.** determined by or dependent on mere chance: *a haphazard remark.* —*adv.* **2.** in a haphazard manner; at random; by chance. —*n.* **3.** mere chance; accident: *to proceed at haphazard.* [f. HAP + HAZARD] —**hap′-haz′ard·ly,** *adv.* —**hap′haz′ard·ness,** *n.*

haph·ta·rah (häf′tä rä′, häf′tō rō′), *n., pl.* **-roth** (-rōth′, -ōth). a portion of the Prophets read immediately after a portion of the Pentateuch in the Jewish synagogue on Sabbaths and festivals. Also, **haftarah.** [t. Heb.: conclusion]

hap·less (hăp′lĭs), *adj.* luckless; unfortunate; unlucky. —**hap′less·ly,** *adv.* —**hap′less·ness,** *n.*

hap·lite (hăp′lĭt), *n. Geol.* aplite.

haplo-, a word element meaning "single," "simple." [t. Gk., comb. form of *haplóos*]

hap·loid (hăp′loid), *adj.*, Also, **hap·loi′dic.** **1.** single; simple. **2.** *Biol.* pertaining to a single set of chromosomes. —*n.* **3.** *Biol.* an organism or cell having only one complete set of chromosomes, ordinarily half the normal diploid number.

hap·lol·o·gy (hăp lŏl′ə jĭ), *n.* *Gram.* the syncope of a syllable within a word, as *syllabi(fi)cation.* [f. HAPLO- + -LOGY]

hap·lo·sis (hăp lō′sĭs), *n.* *Biol.* the production of haploid chromosome groups during meiosis.

hap·ly (hăp′lĭ), *adv.* *Archaic.* perhaps; by chance.

hap·pen (hăp′ən), *v.i.* **1.** to come to pass, take place, or occur. **2.** to come to pass by chance; occur without apparent reason or design; chance. **3.** to have the fortune or lot (to do or be as specified): *I happened to see him.* **4.** to befall, as to a person or thing. **5.** to come by chance (fol. by *on* or *upon*): *to happen on a clue to a mystery.* **6.** to be, come, or go (as specified) by chance: *to happen in to see a friend.* [ME *happene(n), hapnen;* f. HAP, n. + -EN[1]]

—Syn. 1. HAPPEN, CHANCE, OCCUR refer to the taking place of an event. HAPPEN, which originally denoted the taking place by hap or chance, is now the most general word for coming to pass: *an accident has happened.* CHANCE suggests the fortuitousness of an event: *it chanced to rain that day.* OCCUR is often interchangeable with HAPPEN, but is more formal, and is usually more specific as to time and event.

hap·pen·ing (hăp′ən ĭng, hăp′nĭng), *n.* **1.** an occurrence; event. **2.** a dramatic or similar performance consisting chiefly of a series of discontinuous events often characterized by violent action.

hap·pi·ly (hăp′ə lĭ), *adv.* **1.** in a happy manner; with pleasure. **2.** luckily. **3.** with skill; aptly; appropriately.

hap·pi·ness (hăp′ĭ nĭs), *n.* **1.** quality or state of being happy. **2.** good fortune; pleasure, content, or gladness. **3.** aptness or felicity, as of expression.

—Syn. 1. beatitude, blessedness, contentedness. HAPPINESS, BLISS, CONTENTMENT, FELICITY imply an active or passive state of pleasure or pleasurable satisfaction. HAPPINESS results from the possession or attainment of what one considers good: *the happiness of visiting one's family.* BLISS is unalloyed happiness or supreme delight: *the bliss of perfect companionship.* CONTENTMENT is a peaceful kind of HAPPINESS in which one rests without desires, even though every wish may not have been gratified: *contentment in one's surroundings.* FELICITY is a formal word for happiness of an especially fortunate or intense kind: *to wish a young couple felicity in life.* **—Ant. 1.** wretchedness.

hap·py (hăp′ĭ), *adj.*, **-pier, -piest.** **1.** characterized by or indicative of pleasure, content, or gladness: *a happy mood.* **2.** delighted, pleased, or glad, as over a particular thing: *to be happy to see a person.* **3.** favored by fortune; fortunate or lucky: *a happy event.* **4.** apt or felicitous, as actions, utterances, ideas, etc. [ME; f. HAP[1], n. + -Y[1]] **—Syn. 1.** joyous, joyful, glad, blithe, cheerful. **3.** favorable, propitious. See **fortunate.**

hap·py-go-luck·y (hăp′ĭ gō lŭk′ĭ), *adj.* **1.** trusting cheerfully to luck. —*adv.* **2.** haphazard; by mere chance.

Haps·burg (hăps′bûrg; *Ger.* häps′bŏŏrkh), *n.* a German princely family, prominent since the 11th century, which has furnished sovereigns to the Holy Roman Empire, Austria, Spain, etc. Also, **Habsburg.** [var. of *Habsburg*, shortening of *Habichtsburg* (hawk's castle) name of a castle in Aargau, Switzerland]

ha·ra-ki·ri (hä′rə kĭr′ĭ), *n.* suicide by ripping open the abdomen with a dagger or knife: national form of honorable suicide in Japan, formerly practiced by higher classes when disgraced or sentenced to death. Also, **ha·ra·ka·ri** (hä′rə kä′rĭ), **hari-kari.** [t. Jap.; belly cut]

ha·rangue (hə răng′), *n.*, *v.*, **-rangued, -ranguing.** —*n.* **1.** a passionate, vehement speech; noisy and intemperate address. **2.** any long, declamatory or pompous speech. —*v.t.* **3.** to address in a harangue. —*v.i.* **4.** to deliver a harangue. [t. F, t. Gmc.; cf. OE and OHG *hring* RING[1]] —**ha·rangu′er,** *n.* **—Syn. 1.** See **speech.**

Ha·rar (hä′rər), *n.* a city in Ethiopia. 45,000 (est. 1951).

har·ass (hăr′əs, hə răs′), *v.t.* **1.** to trouble by repeated attacks, incursions, etc., as in war or hostilities; harry; raid. **2.** to disturb persistently; torment, as with troubles, cares, etc. [t. F: s. *harasser*, der. OF *harer* set a dog on] —**har′ass·er,** *n.* —**har′ass·ing·ly,** *adv.* —**har·ass·ment** (hăr′əs mənt, hə răs′mənt), *n.* **—Syn. 2.** badger, vex, pester, plague. See **worry.**

Har·bin (här′bēn′, -bĭn), *n.* a city in NE China, in central Manchuria. 1,000,000 (est. 1954). Also, **Pinkiang.**

har·bin·ger (här′bĭn jər), *n.* **1.** one who goes before and makes known the approach of another. **2.** *Obs.* one sent in advance of troops, a royal train, etc., to provide or secure lodgings and other accommodations. —*v.t.* **3.** to act as harbinger to; herald the coming of. [ME *herbergere*, t. OF: m. *herbergeor*, der. *herbergier* provide lodging for, der. *herberge* lodging, t. OG. See HARBOR]

har·bor (här′bər), *n.* **1.** a portion of a body of water along the shore deep enough for ships, and so situated with respect to coastal features, whether natural or artificial, as to provide protection from winds, waves, and currents. **2.** any place of shelter or refuge. —*v.t.* **3.** to give shelter to: *to harbor fugitives.* **4.** to conceal; give a place to hide: *to harbor smuggled goods.* **5.** to entertain in the mind; indulge (usually unfavorable or evil feelings): *to harbor suspicion.* **6.** to shelter (a ship) in a harbor or haven. —*v.i.* **7.** (of a ship, etc.) to take shelter in a harbor. Also, *Brit.*, **harbour.** [ME *herber(we), hereberge*, OE *herebeorg* lodgings, quarters, f. *here* army + (*ge*)*beorg* refuge; c. G *herberge*] —**har′bor·er,** *n.* —**har′bor·less,** *adj.*

—Syn. 1. HARBOR, HAVEN, PORT indicate a shelter for ships. A HARBOR may be natural or artificially constructed or improved: *a fine harbor on the eastern coast.* A HAVEN is usually a natural harbor which can be utilized by ships as a place of safety; the word is common in poetic use: *a haven in time of storm, a haven of refuge.* A PORT is a HARBOR viewed esp. in its commercial relations, though it is frequently applied in the meaning of HARBOR or HAVEN, also: *a thriving port, any old port in a storm.* **5.** See **cherish.**

har·bor·age (här′bər ĭj), *n.* **1.** shelter for ships, as in a harbor. **2.** shelter or lodging. **3.** a place of shelter. Also, *Brit.*, **har′bour·age.**

harbor master, an officer in charge of the mooring and berthing of ships and other harbor regulations.

harbor seal. See **seal**[2] (def. 1).

har·bour (här′bər), *n.*, *v.t.*, *v.i.* *Brit.* harbor.

hard (härd), *adj.* **1.** solid and firm to the touch; not soft. **2.** firmly formed; tight: *a hard knot.* **3.** difficult to do or accomplish; fatiguing; troublesome: *a hard task.* **4.** difficult or troublesome with respect to an action specified: *hard to please.* **5.** difficult to deal with, manage, control, overcome, or understand: *a hard problem.* **6.** carried on or performed with great exertion, energy, or persistence: *hard work.* **7.** carrying on work in this manner: *a hard worker.* **8.** vigorous or violent; severe: *a hard rain.* **9.** oppressive; harsh; rough: *hard treatment.* **10.** harsh or severe in dealing with others: *a hard master.* **11.** incapable of being denied or explained away: *hard facts.* **12.** harsh or unfriendly; not easily moved: *hard feelings.* **13.** harsh or unpleasant to the eye, ear, or aesthetic sense. **14.** severe or rigorous in terms: *a hard bargain.* **15.** not swayed by sentiment or sophistry; shrewd: *to have a hard head.* **16.** *Colloq.* incorrigible; disreputable: *a hard character.* **17.** *Chiefly Dial.* niggardly; stingy. **18.** in coin rather than in paper currency, or as distinguished from other property: *hard cash.* **19.** *U.S.* strong; spirituous or intoxicating: *hard liquors.* **20.** (of water) containing mineral salts which interfere with the action of the soap. **21.** *Agric.* noting wheats with high gluten content, milled for a bread flour as contrasted with pastry flour. **22.** *Phonet.* **a.** (of consonants) fortis. **b.** (of *c* and *g*) pronounced as in *come* and *go.* **c.** (of consonants in Slavic languages) not palatalized. **23. hard of hearing,** partly deaf. **24. hard up,** *Colloq.* urgently in need of money. —*adv.* **25.** with great exertion; with vigor or violence: *to work hard.* **26.** earnestly or intently: *to look hard at a thing.* **27.** harshly or severely; gallingly: *it goes hard.* **28.** so as to be solid or firm: *frozen hard.* **29. hard put to it,** in great perplexity or difficulty. **30.** *Naut.* closely, fully, or to the extreme limit: *hard aport.* [ME; OE *heard*, c. G *hart*]

—Syn. 1. inflexible, rigid, unyielding, resisting, adamantine, flinty, impenetrable. See **firm**[1]. **3.** toilsome, burdensome, wearisome, exhausting. HARD, DIFFICULT both describe something resistant to one's efforts or one's endurance. HARD is the general word: *hard times, it was hard to endure the severe weather.* DIFFICULT means not easy, and particularly denotes that which requires special effort or skill: *a difficult task.* **5.** perplexing, puzzling, intricate, knotty, tough. **6.** arduous, onerous, laborious. **9.** severe, rigorous, grinding, cruel, merciless, unsparing. **10.** stern, austere, strict, exacting. HARD, CALLOUS, UNFEELING, UNSYMPATHETIC imply a lack of interest in, feeling for, or sympathy with others. HARD implies insensibility, either natural or acquired, so that the plight of others makes no impression on one: *a hard taskmaster.* CALLOUS may mean the same, or that one is himself insensitive to hurt, as the result of continued repression and indifference: *a callous answer, callous to criticism.* UNFEELING implies natural inability to feel with and for others: *an unfeeling and thoughtless remark.* UNSYMPATHETIC implies an indifference which makes no attempt to pity, etc.: *unsympathetic toward distress.*

hard and fast, **1.** strongly binding; not to be set aside or violated: *hard and fast rules.* **2.** firmly and securely: *bound hard and fast.*

hard-bit·ten (härd′bĭt′ən), *adj.* tough; stubborn.

hard·board (härd′bōrd′), *n.* a material made from wood fibers compressed into sheets, having many household and industrial uses.

hard-boiled (härd′boild′), *adj.* **1.** boiled until hard, as an egg. **2.** *Colloq.* hardened by experience: *a hard-boiled person.* **3.** *Slang.* rough or tough.

hard cider, cider which has fermented.

hard coal, anthracite.

Har·de·ca·nute (här′də kə nūt′, -nōōt′), *n.* c1019–42. king of Denmark, 1035–42, and king of England, 1040–42.

hard·en (här′dən), *v.t.* **1.** to make hard or harder. **2.** to make obdurate or unyielding; make unfeeling or pitiless: *to harden one's heart.* **3.** to strengthen or confirm with respect to any element of character; toughen. **4.** to make hardy, robust, or capable of endurance. —*v.i.* **5.** to become hard or harder. **6.** to become obdurate, unfeeling, or pitiless. **7.** to become inured or toughened. **8.** *Com.* (of prices, the market, etc.) **a.** to become higher; rise. **b.** to cease to fluctuate. **—Syn. 1.** solidify, indurate; petrify, ossify. **3.** fortify, steel, brace, nerve. **—Ant. 1.** soften. **3.** weaken. **4.** debilitate.

Har·den·berg (här′dən bĕrkh′), *n.* **Friedrich von** (frē′drĭkh fən), ("*Novalis*") 1772–1801, German author.

hard·ened (här′dənd), *adj.* **1.** made hard; indurated; inured. **2.** obdurate; unfeeling.

hard·en·er (här/dən ər), *n.* **1.** a person or thing that hardens. **2.** one who hardens a specified thing. **3.** a substance mixed with paint or other protective covering to make the finish harder or more durable.

hard·en·ing (här/dən Yng), *n.* **1.** a material which hardens another, as an alloy added to iron to make steel. **2.** the process of becoming hard or rigid.

hard-fa·vored (härd/fā/vərd), *adj.* having a hard, unpleasant countenance.

hard-fist·ed (härd/fĭs/tĭd), *adj.* **1.** niggardly; stingy. **2.** having hard or strong hands, as a laborer.

hard·hack (härd/hăk/), *n.* a woolly-leaved rosaceous shrub, *Spiraea tomentosa,* of North America, having terminal panicles of rose-colored or white flowers.

hard-hand·ed (härd/hăn/dYd), *adj.* **1.** having hands hardened by toil. **2.** ruling with a strong or cruel hand.

hard·head (härd/hĕd/), *n.* **1.** a shrewd, practical person. **2.** a blockhead.

hard-head·ed (härd/hĕd/Yd), *adj.* **1.** not easily moved or deceived; practical; shrewd. **2.** obstinate; stubborn; willful. —**hard/-head/ed·ly,** *adv.* —**hard/-head/ed·ness,** *n.*

hard-heart·ed (härd/här/tYd), *adj.* unfeeling; unmerciful; pitiless. —**hard/-heart/ed·ly,** *adv.* —**hard/-heart/ed·ness,** *n.*

har·di·hood (här/dY hŏŏd/), *n.* hardy spirit or character; boldness or daring.

har·di·ly (här/də lY), *adv.* in a hardy manner.

har·di·ness (här/dY nYs), *n.* **1.** robustness; capability of endurance; strength. **2.** hardihood; audacity.

Har·ding (här/dYng), *n.* **Warren Gamaliel** (gə mā/lY-əl), 1865–1923, 29th president of the U.S., 1921–23.

hard·ly (härd/lY), *adv.* **1.** barely; almost not at all: *hardly any, hardly ever.* **2.** not quite: *that is hardly true.* **3.** with little likelihood: *he will hardly come now.* **4.** with trouble or difficulty. **5.** harshly or severely.
—**Syn.** HARDLY, BARELY, SCARCELY imply a narrow margin by which performance was, is, or will be achieved. HARDLY, though often interchangeable with SCARCELY and BARELY, usually emphasizes the idea of the difficulty involved: *we could hardly endure the winter.* BARELY emphasizes the narrowness of the margin of safety, "only just and no more": *we barely succeeded.* SCARCELY implies a very narrow margin, below satisfactory performance: *we can scarcely read.*

hard maple, *U.S.* the sugar maple, *Acer saccharum.*

hard·ness (härd/nYs), *n.* **1.** state or quality of being hard. **2.** an instance of this quality. **3.** that quality in impure water which is imparted by the presence of dissolved salts, especially calcium sulfate. **4.** *Mineral.* the comparative capacity of a substance to scratch another or be scratched by another. See **Mohs scale.**

hard·pan (härd/păn/), *n.* *Chiefly U.S.* **1.** any layer of firm detrital matter, as of clay, underlying soft soil. **2.** hard, unbroken ground. **3.** solid foundation; hard underlying reality. **4.** the lowest level.

hard rubber, rubber vulcanized with a large amount of sulfur, usually 25–35%, to render it stiff and comparatively inflexible.

hards (härdz), *n.pl.* the refuse or coarser parts of flax or hemp, separated in hackling. Also, **hurds.** [ME *herdes,* OE *heordan*]

hard sauce, a creamed mixture of butter and confectioners' sugar, often with flavoring and cream, used on warm puddings, pies, etc.

hard sell, a method of advertising or selling which is direct, forceful, and insistent; high-pressure salesmanship. See **soft sell.**

hard-set (härd/sĕt/), *adj.* **1.** in a difficult position. **2.** firmly or rigidly set. **3.** determined; obstinate.

hard-shell (härd/shĕl/), *adj.* **1.** having a firm, hard shell, as a crab in its normal state, not having recently molted. **2.** *U.S. Colloq.* rigid or uncompromising.

hard·ship (härd/shYp/), *n.* **1.** a condition that bears hard upon one; severe toil, trial, oppression, or need. **2.** an instance of this; something hard to bear.
—**Syn.** **1.** HARDSHIP, PRIVATION, AUSTERITY are terms for something hard to endure. HARDSHIP applies to a circumstance in which excessive and painful effort of some kind is required, as enduring acute discomfort from cold, battling over rough terrain, and the like. PRIVATION has particular reference to lack of food, clothing, and other necessities or comforts. AUSTERITY, not only includes the ideas of privation and hardship but also implies deliberate control of emotional reactions to these. —**Ant.** **1.** ease.

hard-spun (härd/spŭn/), *adj.* (of yarn) compactly twisted in spinning.

hard·tack (härd/tăk/), *n.* a kind of hard biscuit much used by sailors and soldiers. [f. HARD + *tack* taste]

hard·top (härd/tŏp/), *n.* a style of car having a rigid metal top and no center posts between windows. —**hard/top/,** *adj.*

hard·ware (härd/wâr/), *n.* **1.** metalware, as tools, locks, hinges, cutlery, etc. **2.** *Colloq.* the mechanical equipment necessary for conducting an activity, usually distinguished from the theory and design which make the activity possible.

hard·wood (härd/wŏŏd/), *n.* **1.** the hard, compact wood or timber of various trees, as the oak, cherry, maple, mahogany, etc. **2.** a tree yielding such wood.

har·dy¹ (här/dY), *adj.,* **-di·er, -di·est. 1.** fitted for enduring fatigue, hardship, exposure, etc.: *hardy animals.* **2.** (of plants) able to withstand the cold of winter in the open air. **3.** requiring great physical endurance: *the*

hardiest sports. **4.** bold or daring; courageous, as persons, actions, etc. **5.** unduly bold; presumptuous; foolhardy. [ME *hardi,* t. OF, pp. of *hardir* harden, t. Gmc.; akin to HARD] —**Syn. 1.** vigorous, sturdy, robust, hale.

har·dy² (här/dY), *n., pl.* **-dies.** a chisel or fuller with a square shank for insertion into a square hole (**hardy hole**) in a blacksmith's anvil. [appar. der. HARD]

Har·dy (här/dY), *n.* **Thomas,** 1840–1928, British novelist and poet.

hare (hâr), *n., pl.* **hares,** (*esp. collectively*) **hare,** *v.,* **hared, haring.** —*n.* **1.** any rodentlike mammal of the genus *Lepus* (family *Leporidae*), with long ears, divided upper lip, short tail, and lengthened hind limbs adapted for leaping. **2.** any of the larger species of this genus, as distinguished from certain of the smaller ones known as rabbits. **3.** any of various similar animals of the same family. **4.** the person chased or pursued in the game of hare and hounds. —*v.i.* **5.** *Chiefly Brit.* to run fast. [ME; OE *hara,* c. Dan. *hare;* akin to G *hase.* Cf. OE *hasu* gray] —**hare/like/,** *adj.*

hare and hounds, an outdoor sport in which certain players (**hares**) start off in advance on a long run, scattering small pieces of paper (**scent**), the other players (**hounds**) following the trail so marked in an effort to catch the hares before they reach home.

hare·bell (hâr/bĕl/), *n.* **1.** a low campanulaceous herb, the bluebell of Scotland, *Campanula rotundifolia,* with blue, bell-shaped flowers. **2.** a liliaceous plant, *Scilla nonscripta,* with bell-shaped flowers.

hare·brained (hâr/brānd/), *adj.* giddy; reckless.

hare·lip (hâr/lYp/), *n.* a congenitally deformed lip, usually the upper one, in which there is a vertical fissure causing it to resemble the cleft lip of a hare. **2.** the deformity itself. —**hare/lipped/,** *adj.*

har·em (hâr/əm, hăr/-), *n.* **1.** that part of an Oriental palace or house reserved for the residence of women. **2.** the women in an Oriental household: mother, sisters, wives, concubines, daughters, entertainers, servants, etc. [t. Ar.: m. *harim,* lit., (something) forbidden]

Har·greaves (här/grēvz), *n.* **James,** died 1778, British inventor (of spinning machinery).

har·i·cot (här/ə kō/), *n.* *Chiefly Brit.* **1.** a plant of the genus *Phaseolus,* esp. *P. vulgaris,* the common kidney bean. **2.** its seed. [t. F, identical with *haricot* ragout]

ha·ri-ka·ri (hä/rY kä/rY), *n.* hara-kiri.

hark (härk), *v.i.* **1.** to listen; harken (used chiefly in the imperative). **2. hark back, a.** to return to a previous point or subject. as in discourse or thought; revert. **b.** (of hounds) to return along the course in order to regain a lost scent. —*v.t.* **3.** *Archaic.* to listen; hear. —*n.* **4.** a hunter's cry to hounds. [ME *herk(i)en,* c. OFris. *herkia.* Cf. HARKEN]

hark·ee (här/kē), hark ye.

hark·en (här/kən), *v.i. Poetic.* **1.** to listen; to give heed or attend to what is said. —*v.t.* **2.** *Archaic.* to listen to; hear. Also, **hearken.** [ME *herken,* OE *he(o)rcnian;* akin to HARK] —**hark/en·er,** *n.*

Har·lem (här/ləm), *n.* **1.** the chief Negro section of New York City, in the NE part of Manhattan. **2.** a tidal river in New York City, separating the boroughs of Manhattan and the Bronx and (with Spuyten Duyvil creek) connecting the Hudson and East rivers. 8 mi.

Har·le·quin (här/lə kwYn, -kYn), *n.* **1.** (*sometimes l.c.*) a droll character in comedy (orig. the early Italian) and pantomime, usually masked, dressed in particolored spangled tights, and bearing a wooden sword or magic wand. **2.** (*l.c.*) a buffoon. **3.** (*l.c.*) any one of various small, handsomely marked snakes. —*adj.* **4.** (*l.c.*) fancifully varied in color, decoration, etc. [t. F; OF *Harlequin, Herlequin,* t. ME: m. *Herle King* King Herla (mythical figure); modern meaning from It. *arlecchino,* t. F: m. *Harlequin*]

har·le·quin·ade (här/lə kwY nād/, -kY-), *n.* **1.** a pantomime or similar play in which the harlequin plays the principal part. **2.** buffoonery. [t. F: m. *arlequinade*]

harlequin duck, a small North American diving duck, *Histrionicus histrionicus,* in which the male is bluish-gray, marked with black, white, and chestnut.

har·le·quin·esque (här/lə kwY nĕsk/, -kY-), *adj.* in the style or manner of a harlequin.

Har·ley (här/lY), *n.* **Robert.** See **Oxford, 1st Earl of.**

Harley Street, a street in London, England, noted for the doctors who have offices there.

har·lot (här/lət), *n.* **1.** a lewd woman; prostitute; strumpet. —*adj.* **2.** pertaining to or like a harlot; low. [ME, t. OF: rogue, knave; orig. uncert.]

har·lot·ry (här/lə trY), *n., pl.* **-ries. 1.** the practice or trade of prostitution. **2.** a harlot.

harm (härm), *n.* **1.** injury; damage; hurt: *to do him bodily harm.* **2.** moral injury; evil; wrong. —*v.t.* **3.** to do harm to; injure; damage; hurt. [ME; OE *hearm,* c. G *harm.* Cf. Russ. *sram* shame] —**harm/er,** *n.* —**Syn. 1, 2.** See **damage.**

har·mat·tan (här/mə tăn/), *n.* a dry, parching land wind, charged with dust, on the west coast of Africa. [t. W. African (Fanti or Tshi)]

harm·ful (härm/fəl), *adj.* fraught with or doing harm. —**harm/ful·ly,** *adv.* —**harm/ful·ness,** *n.* —**Syn.** injurious, hurtful, detrimental. —**Ant.** beneficial.

harm·less (härm/lYs), *adj.* **1.** without power or tendency to harm: *harmless play.* **2.** *Rare.* unharmed. —**harm/less·ly,** *adv.* —**harm/less·ness,** *n.*

har·mon·ic (härmŏn′ĭk), *adj.* **1.** pertaining to harmony, as distinguished from melody and rhythm. **2.** marked by harmony; in harmony; concordant; consonant. **3.** *Physics.* denoting an integral multiple of a given frequency, thus 256, 512, 768, cycles per second are the *first, second,* and *third harmonics* of 256 cycles per second. **4.** *Math.* having relations resembling those of musical concords: *a harmonic progression is a series of numbers the reciprocals of which are in arithmetical progression.* —*n.* **5.** an overtone. [t. L: s. *harmonicus,* t. Gk.: m. *harmonikós* skilled in music] —**har·mon′i·cal·ly,** *adv.*

har·mon·i·ca (härmŏn′ə kə), *n.* **1.** a musical instrument having a set of small metallic reeds mounted in a case and played by the breath; a mouth organ. **2.** any of various percussion instruments which use graduated bars of metal or other hard material as sounding elements. [t. L. n. use of fem. of *harmonicus* HARMONIC]

harmonic mean, *Statistics.* the mean of *n* positive numbers obtained by taking the reciprocal of the average of the reciprocals of the numbers.

harmonic minor, *Music.* the minor scale from which chords are formed, having the sixth degree a semitone above the dominant and the seventh degree a semitone below the tonic.

har·mon·i·con (härmŏn′ə kən), *n.* any of various musical instruments, as a harmonica or an orchestrion. [t. Gk.: m. *harmonikón* (neut.) harmonic]

har·mon·ics (härmŏn′ĭks), *n. Music.* **1.** the science of musical sounds. **2.** (*construed as pl.*) the partials or overtones of a fundamental. Cf. **harmonic** (def. 2). **3.** (*construed as pl.*) the flageoletlike tones of a string (as a violin string) made to vibrate so as to bring out an overtone. [pl. of HARMONIC. See -ICS]

harmonic tone, *Music.* a tone produced by suppressing the fundamental tone and bringing into prominence one of its overtones.

har·mo·ni·ous (härmō′nĭ əs), *adj.* **1.** marked by agreement in feeling or action: *a harmonious group.* **2.** forming a pleasingly consistent whole; congruous. **3.** agreeable to the ear; tuneful; melodious. —**har·mo′ni·ous·ly,** *adv.* —**har·mo′ni·ous·ness,** *n.* —**Syn. 1.** amicable, congenial; sympathetic. **2.** concordant, congruent, consonant, consistent. —**Ant. 1, 3.** discordant.

har·mo·nist (här′mə nĭst), *n.* **1.** one skilled in harmony. **2.** one who makes a harmony, as of the Gospels.

har·mo·nis·tic (här′mə nĭs′tĭk), *adj.* **1.** pertaining to harmonistics or harmony. **2.** pertaining to the collation and harmonizing of parallel passages, as of the Gospels. —**har′mo·nis′ti·cal·ly,** *adv.*

har·mo·ni·um (härmō′nĭ əm), *n.* a reed organ, esp. one in which the air is forced outward through the reeds. [t. F, der. *harmonie,* t. L: m. *harmonia* HARMONY]

har·mo·nize (här′mə nīz′), —*nized,* —*nizing.* —*v.t.* **1.** to bring into harmony, accord, or agreement: *to harmonize the views.* **2.** *Music.* to accompany with appropriate harmony. —*v.i.* **3.** to be in agreement in action, sense, or feeling. **4.** *Colloq.* to sing in harmony. Also, *esp. Brit.,* **har′mo·nise′.** —**har′mo·ni·za′tion,** *n.* —**har′mo·niz′er,** *n.*

har·mo·ny (här′mə nĭ), *n., pl.* —**nies. 1.** agreement; accord; harmonious relations. **2.** a consistent, orderly, or pleasing arrangement of parts; congruity. **3.** *Music.* **a.** any simultaneous combination of tones. **b.** the simultaneous combination of tones; chordal structure, as distinguished from melody and rhythm. **c.** the science of the structure, relations, and practical combination of chords. **4.** an arrangement of the contents of the Gospels (either of all four or of the first three) designed to show their parallelism, mutual relations, and differences. [ME *harmonie,* t. F, t. L: m. *harmonia,* t. Gk.: a joining, concord, music] —**Syn. 1.** concord, unity, peace, amity, friendship. **2.** consonance, conformity, correspondence, consistency. **3.** HARMONY, MELODY in music suggest a combination of sounds from voices or musical instruments. HARMONY is the blending of simultaneous sounds of different pitch or quality, making chords: *harmony in part singing, harmony between violins and horns.* MELODY is the rhythmical combination of successive sounds of various pitch, making up the tune or air: *a tuneful melody to accompany cheerful words.* —**Ant. 1.** discord. **3.** dissonance.

har·ness (här′nĭs), *n.* **1.** the combination of straps, bands, and other parts forming the working gear of a horse or other draft animal (except the ox). See the illus. in the next column. **2.** routine of work: *to die in harness.* **3.** *Archaic.* armor for men or horses (or other animals), or a suit of armor. —*v.t.* **4.** to put harness on (a horse, etc.); attach by a harness, as to a vehicle. **5.** to bring under conditions for working: *to harness water power.* **6.** *Archaic.* to array in armor or equipments of war. [ME, t. OF: m. *harneis,* ? t. OHG; cf. OE *herenet* corselet] —**har′ness·er,** *n.* —**har′ness·less,** *adj.* —**har′ness·like′,** *adj.*

harness hitch, *Naut.* a knot of various uses which forms an eye in the bight of a line.

Har·ney Peak (här′nĭ), the highest peak in the Black Hills, in SW South Dakota. 7242 ft.

Har·old I (här′əld), (surnamed *Harefoot*) died 1040, king of England, 1035–40 (son of Canute).

Harold II, c1022–1066, king of England in 1066 (successor of Edward the Confessor and son of Earl Godwin); defeated by William the Conqueror in Battle of Hastings.

harp (härp), *n.* **1.** a musical instrument consisting of a triangular frame (comprising a soundboard, a pillar, and a curved neck) and strings stretched between soundboard and neck and plucked with the fingers. —*v.i.* **2.** to play on a harp. **3.** to dwell persistently or tediously in speaking or writing (fol. by *on* or *upon*). —*v.t.* **4.** *Poetic.* to bring, put, etc., by playing on a harp. **5.** *Archaic.* to give voice or utterance to. [ME *harp(e),* OE *hearpe,* c. D *harp,* G *harfe,* Icel. *harpa*] —**harp′er,** *n.* —**harp′like′,** *adj.*

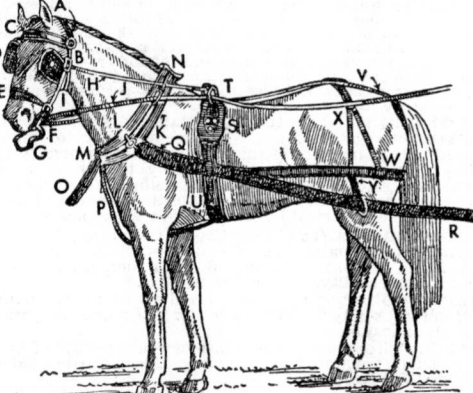

Modern harp
A. Pedestal; B. Pedals; C. Back; D. Soundboard; E. Neck; F. Pillar

Har·pers Ferry (här′pərz), a town in NE West Virginia at the confluence of the Shenandoah and Potomac rivers: John Brown's raid, 1859. Also, **Harper's Ferry.**

harp·ings (här′pĭngz), *n.pl. Naut.* the stout wales about the bow of a ship. Also, **harp·ins** (här′pĭnz).

harp·ist (här′pĭst), *n.* one who plays on the harp, esp. professionally.

har·poon (härpōōn′), *n.* **1.** a barbed, spearlike missile attached to a rope, and thrown by hand or shot from a gun, used in capturing whales and large fish. —*v.t.* **2.** to strike, catch, or kill with or as with a harpoon. [t. D: m. *harpoen,* t. F: m. *harpon,* der. *harper* grapple, of Gmc. orig.] —**har·poon′er,** *n.* —**har·poon′like′,** *adj.*

harp·si·chord (härp′sĭ kôrd′), *n.* a keyboard instrument, precursor of the piano, in common use from the 16th to the 18th century, and revived in the 20th, in which the strings are plucked by leather or quill points connected with the keys. [t. F. (obs.): m. *harpechorde,* f. *harpe* (of Gmc. orig.) harp + *chorde* string (see CHORD[1])]

Harness of a horse: A. Crown; B. Cheekpiece; C. Front; D. Blinds; E. Noseband; F. Bit; G. Curb; H. Checkrein; I. Throatlatch; J. Rein; K. Collar; L. Hame; M. Hame link; N. Hame strap; O. Pole strap; P. Martingale; Q. Trace tug; R. Trace; S. Saddle; T. Terret; U. Bellyband; V. Crupper; W. Breeching; X. Hip strap; Y. Tracebearer

Har·py (här′pĭ), *n., pl.* —**pies. 1.** *Gk. Myth.* a ravenous, filthy monster having a woman's head and a bird's body. **2.** (*l.c.*) a rapacious, grasping person. [t. L: m. s. *harpyia,* t. Gk.: lit., snatcher]

harpy eagle, a large, powerful, crested bird of prey, *Thrasaetus harpyia,* of tropical America.

har·que·bus (här′kwə bəs), *n.* a light hand gun with matchlock or wheel-lock mechanism. Also, **arquebus.** [t. F: m. *(h)arquebuse,* t. It. (obs.): m. *arcobuso,* t. D: m. *haakbus*]

har·que·bus·ier (här′kwə bə sĭr′), *n.* a soldier armed with a harquebus.

har·ri·dan (här′ə dən), *n.* a disreputable violent woman; vicious old hag. [cf. F *haridelle* sorry horse, jade]

har·ri·er[1] (här′ĭ ər), *n.* **1.** one who or that which harries. **2.** any of several hawks of the genus *Circus* (family *Falconidae*), all of which course back and forth over meadowlands searching for the small birds and mammals on which they feed. [f. HARRY, v., + -ER[1]]

har·ri·er[2] (här′ĭ ər), *n.* **1.** a breed of small hounds employed in hunting the hare. **2.** a cross-country runner. [special alter. of HARRIER[1], by assoc. with HARE]

Har·ri·man (här′ə mən), *n.* **William Averell,** born 1891, U.S. diplomat; governor of New York 1954–1958.

Har·ris (här′ĭs), *n.* **1. Joel Chandler** (jō′əl), 1848–1908, U.S. author: creator of Uncle Remus. **2. Roy,** born 1898, U.S. composer.

Har·ris·burg (här′ĭs bûrg′), *n.* capital of Pennsylvania, in the S part, on the Susquehanna. 79,697 (1960).

Har·ri·son (här′ə sən), *n.* **1. Benjamin,** 1833–1901, 23rd president of the U.S. 1889–93. **2.** his grandfather, **William Henry,** 1773–1841, U.S. general: 9th president of the U.S., in 1841.

Har·ro·vi·an (hə rō′vĭ ən), *adj.* of or pertaining to Harrow. See **Harrow-on-the-Hill.**

har·row (hăr′ō), *n.* **1.** a wheelless agricultural implement set with teeth, upright disks, etc., usually of iron, drawn over plowed land to level it, break clods, etc. —*v.t.* **2.** to draw a harrow over (land, etc.); break or tear with a harrow. **3.** to disturb keenly or painfully; distress the mind, feelings, etc. —*v.i.* **4.** to be broken up by harrowing, as soil, etc. [ME *haru, harwe.* Cf. Icel. *herfi* harrow, MLG *harke* rake]　—**har′row·er,** *n.* —**har′row·ing,** *adj.* —**har′row·ing·ly,** *adv.*

Har·row-on-the-Hill (hăr′ō ŏn ᵺə hĭl′), *n.* an urban district in SE England, near London: the seat of **Harrow,** a famous boys' school (founded 1571). 219,463 (1951).

har·ry (hăr′ĭ), *v.*, **-ried, -rying.** —*v.t.* **1.** to harass by forced exactions, rapacious demands, etc.; torment; worry. **2.** to ravage, as in war; devastate. —*v.i.* **3.** to make harassing incursions. [ME *herien,* OE *her(g)ian* ravage (der. *here* army), c. G *(ver)heeren* harry, lay waste]　—**Syn. 2.** plunder, strip, rob.

harsh (härsh), *adj.* **1.** rough to the touch or to any of the senses: *a harsh surface, a harsh voice.* **2.** ungentle and unpleasant in action or effect: *harsh treatment.* **3.** jarring upon the esthetic sense; inartistic: *his painting was full of harsh lines and clashing colors.* [unexplained doublet of ME *harsk.* Cf. Dan. *harsk* rancid, G *harsch* harsh, rough, hard]　—**harsh′ly,** *adv.* —**harsh′ness,** *n.* —**Syn. 2.** severe, austere; brusque, rough; hard, unfeeling, unkind, brutal. See **stern**[1]. **3.** discordant, dissonant, inharmonious. —**Ant. 2.** mild. **3.** pleasing.

hart (härt), *n.*, *pl.* **harts,** (*esp. collectively*) **hart.** a male of the deer, commonly the red deer, *Cervus elaphus,* esp. after its fifth year. [ME *hert,* OE *heort,* c. G *hirsch;* akin to L *cervus* stag]

Hart (härt), *n.* **Moss,** 1904–1961, U.S. dramatist and writer of librettos.

har·tal (här täl′), *n.* (in India) a day of mourning: a form of passive resistance including the closing of shops. [t. Hind.: m. *hathtal* market stoppage]

Harte (härt), *n.* **(Francis) Bret,** 1839–1902, U.S. author, esp. of short stories.

har·te·beest (här′tə bēst′, härt′bēst′), *n.* **1.** a large South African antelope of the genus *Alcephalus,* as *A. caama,* of a red color, having a long face with naked muzzle. **2.** any of various allied African antelopes, as some species of the genus *Damaliscus.* [t. S Afr. D: hart beast]

Hartebeest, Alcephalu sbuselaphus (4 to 4½ ft. high at the shoulder)

Hart·ford (härt′fərd), *n.* the capital of Connecticut, in the central part: a port on the Connecticut river. 162,178 (1960).

Hart·ley (härt′lĭ), *n.* **David,** 1705–57, British physician and philosopher.

harts·horn (härts′hôrn′), *n.* **1.** the antler of the hart, formerly much used as a source of ammonia. **2.** *Old Chem., Pharm.* ammonium carbonate; sal volatile. [var. of *hart's horn*]

hart's-tongue (härts′tŭng′), *n.* a fern, *Phyllitis Scolopendrium,* which has long simple fronds. Also, **harts′tongue′.**

har·um-scar·um (hâr′əm skâr′əm), *adj.* **1.** reckless; rash. —*adv.* **2.** recklessly; wildly. —*n.* **3.** a reckless person. **4.** reckless conduct. [? var. of *hare 'em scare 'em* (with obs. *hare* harry, scare)]

Ha·run-al-Ra·shid (hä rōōn′äl rä shēd′; *Arab.* är′räshēd′), *n.* A.D. 763?–809, caliph of Bagdad, A.D. 786–809. One of the greatest Abbasides, he was made almost a legendary hero in the *Arabian Nights.*

ha·rus·pex (hə rŭs′pĕks, hăr′ə spĕks′), *n.*, *pl.* **haruspices** (hə rŭs′pə sēz′). (in ancient Rome) one of a class of minor priests who practiced divination, esp. from the entrails of animals killed in sacrifice. [t. L]

Har·vard (här′vərd), *n.* **John,** 1607–38, British nonconformist minister who settled in America and was a principal benefactor of Harvard College.

har·vest (här′vĭst), *n.* **1.** the gathering of crops. **2.** the season of gathering ripened crops, esp. of grain. **3.** a crop or yield, as of grain. **4.** a supply of anything gathered at maturity and stored up: *a harvest of nuts.* **5.** the product or result of any labor or process. —*v.t.* **6.** to gather, as a crop. **7.** to gather the crop from: *to harvest the fields.* —*v.i.* **8.** to gather a crop; reap. [ME; OE *hærfest,* c. G *herbst* autumn]　—**har′vest·ing,** *n.* —**har′vest·less,** *adj.* —**Syn. 3.** See **crop.**

har·vest·er (här′vĭs tər), *n.* **1.** one who harvests; a reaper. **2.** any of various machines for harvesting or gathering field crops, such as grain, flax, potatoes, etc.

harvest fly, any of certain cicadas, as *Tibicen linnei,* noted for its shrill, noisy song in late summer.

harvest home, 1. the bringing home of the harvest. **2.** the time of doing it. **3.** an English festival celebrated at the close of the harvest.

har·vest·man (här′vĭst mən), *n.*, *pl.* **-men.** **1.** a man engaged in harvesting. **2.** any of the arachnids of the order *Opiliones* (or *Phalangida*), comprising spiderlike creatures with small rounded body and usually very long legs; daddy-longlegs.

harvest moon, the moon at and about the period of fullness which is nearest to the autumn equinox.

harvest tick, any of various acarids in an immature stage, common in late summer and autumn, which attach themselves to the skin of man and animals.

Har·vey (här′vĭ), *n.* **William,** 1578–1657, British physician, discoverer of the circulation of the blood.

Harz Mountains (härts), a range of low mountains in central Germany between the Elbe and Weser rivers. Highest peak, Brocken, 3745 ft.

has (hăz), *v.* 3rd pers. sing. pres. indic. of **have.**

Harvest ticks (magnified)
A. "*Leptus*" *irritans;*
B. *Trombidium americanum*

Ha·sa (hä′sə), *n.* a region in E Saudi Arabia, on the Persian Gulf. Also, **El Hasa.**

Ha·san (hä′sən), *n.* a son of Ali by Fatima, daughter of Mohammed.

has-been (hăz′bĭn′), *n. Colloq.* a person or thing that is no longer effective, successful, popular, etc.

Has·dru·bal (hăz′drŏŏ bəl, hăz drōō′-), *n.* **1.** died 207 B.C., Carthaginian general (brother of Hannibal). **2.** died 221 B.C., Carthaginian general (brother-in-law of Hannibal).

hash (hăsh), *n.* **1.** a dish of chopped meat and potatoes, usually sautéed in a frying pan. **2.** a mess, jumble, or muddle. **3.** any preparation of old material worked over. —*v.t.* **4.** to chop into small pieces; mince; make into a hash. [t. F: m.s. *hacher,* der. *hache* ax. See HATCHET, and cf. HATCH[3]]

Hash·e·mite Kingdom of Jordan (hăsh′ə mīt), official name of Jordan.

hash·ish (hăsh′ēsh, -ĭsh), *n.* **1.** the flowering tops, leaves, etc., of Indian hemp, smoked, chewed, or otherwise used in the Orient as a narcotic and intoxicant. **2.** any of certain preparations made from this plant.

has·let (hăs′lĭt, hăz′-), *n.* the heart, liver, etc., of a hog or other animal, as used for food. [ME *hastelet,* t. OF: roasted bit of meat, der. *haste* spit, g. L *hasta* spear]

has·n't (hăz′ənt), contraction of *has not.*

hasp (hăsp, häsp), *n.* **1.** a clasp for a door, lid, etc., esp. one passing over a staple and fastened by a pin or a padlock. —*v.t.* **2.** to fasten with or as with a hasp. [ME *hasp(e),* OE *hæsp, hæpse,* c. G *haspe;* akin to Icel. *hespa*]

Has·sam (hăs′əm), *n.* **Childe,** 1859–1935, U.S. artist.

has·sle (hăs′əl), *n. U.S. Slang.* quarrel; squabble.

has·sock (hăs′ək), *n.* **1.** a thick, firm cushion used as a footstool or for kneeling. **2.** a rank tuft of coarse grass or sedge, as in a bog. [ME; OE *hassuc* coarse grass]

hast (hăst), *v. Poetic or Solemn.* 2nd pers. sing. pres. indic. of **have.**

has·tate (hăs′tāt), *adj. Bot.* (of a leaf) triangular or shaped like a halberd, with two spreading lobes at the base. [t. L: m. s. *hastātus* armed with a spear]

haste (hāst), *n.*, *v.*, **hasted, hasting.** —*n.* **1.** energetic speed in motion or action. **2.** need, or sense of need, of speed: *to be in great haste.* **3.** make haste, a. to exert oneself to do something quickly. b. (with adjunct) to go with haste. **4.** thoughtless or rash speed: *haste makes waste.* —*v.t., v.i.* **5.** *Poetic.* to hasten. [ME, t. OF, t. Gmc.; cf. OE *hǣst* violence]　—**Syn. 1.** swiftness, celerity, quickness; rapidity. **2.** hurry, flurry, bustle.

Hastate leaf

has·ten (hā′sən), *v.i.* **1.** to move or act with haste; proceed with haste; hurry: *to hasten to a place.* —*v.t.* **2.** to cause to hasten; accelerate. —**has′ten·er,** *n.* —**Syn. 2.** urge, press; expedite, quicken, precipitate. —**Ant. 1.** lag. **2.** delay.

Has·tings (hās′tĭngz), *n.* **1. Warren,** 1732–1818, British statesman: first governor-general of India, 1773–85. **2.** a seaport in SE England, in Sussex: William the Conqueror defeated the Saxons near here (on Senlac Hill) 1066. 64,550 (est. 1956). **3.** a city in S Nebraska. 21,412 (1960).

Hastings, A.D. 1066

hast·y (hās′tĭ), *adj.*, **hastier, hastiest. 1.** moving or acting with haste; speedy; quick; hurried. **2.** made or done with haste or speed: *a hasty visit.* **3.** unduly quick in movement or action; precipitate; rash: *hasty temper.* **4.** done with or characterized by thoughtless or angry haste: *hasty words.* **5.** easily excited to anger; quick-tempered; irascible. [ME, t. OF: m. *hastif,* der. *haste* HASTE]　—**hast′i·ly,** *adv.* —**hast′i·ness,** *n.* —**Syn. 1.** swift; rapid, fast. **3.** foolhardy, reckless. —**Ant. 1.** slow. **3.** deliberate.

hasty pudding, 1. a dish made of flour or oatmeal stirred into seasoned boiling water or milk and quickly cooked. **2.** *U.S.* corn-meal mush.

hat (hăt), *n.*, *v.*, **hatted, hatting.** —*n.* **1.** a shaped covering for the head, usually with a crown and a brim, worn outdoors. **2. pass (round) the hat, a.** to receive contributions, as at a public meeting. **b.** to ask for money for charitable use or some purpose of common interest. **3.** *Rom. Cath. Ch.* **a.** the distinctive red head covering of a cardinal. **b.** the office or dignity of cardinal. —*v.t.* 4. to provide with a hat; put a hat on. [ME; OE *hæt* head covering, c. Icel. *höttr* hood; akin to HOOD] —**hat′less**, *adj.* —**hat′like′**, *adj.*

hat·a·ble (hā′tə bəl), *adj.* capable or worthy of being hated. Also, **hateable.**

hat·band (hăt′bănd′), *n.* 1. a band or ribbon placed about the crown of a hat, just above the brim. 2. a black band similarly worn as a sign of mourning.

hat·box (hăt′bŏks′), *n.* a case or box for a hat.

hatch¹ (hăch), *v.t.* 1. to bring forth (young) from the egg. 2. to cause young to emerge from (the egg). 3. to contrive; devise; concoct: *to hatch a plot.* —*v.i.* 4. to be hatched. —*n.* 5. act of hatching. 6. that which is hatched, as a brood. [ME *hacche,* akin to G *hecken*] —**hatch′er,** *n.* —**Syn.** 1. incubate, brood.

hatch² (hăch), *n.* 1. a cover for an opening in a ship's deck, a floor, a roof, or the like. 2. (*often pl.*) a hatchway. 3. a ship's deck: *under hatches.* 4. an opening in the floor or roof of a building. 5. the cover over such an opening. 6. the lower half of a divided door. [ME *hacche,* OE *hæc* grating, hatch]

hatch³ (hăch), *v.t.* 1. to mark with lines, esp. closely set parallel lines, as for shading in drawing or engraving. —*n.* 2. a shading line in drawing or engraving. [t. F: m. *hacher* chop, hash, hatch. See HASH]

Hatch Acts, two Congressional acts, passed 1939 and 1940, regulating expenditures, contributions, and procedures in political campaigns.

hatch·el (hăch′əl), *n., v., -eled, -eling* or (*esp. Brit.*) -elled, -elling. —*n.* 1. an instrument for cleaning flax; heckle. —*v.t.* 2. to heckle. [phonetic doublet of HACKLE¹. Cf. HECKLE] —**hatch′el·er,** *esp. Brit.* **hatch′el·ler,** *n.*

hatch·er·y (hăch′ər ĭ), *n., pl.* -eries. a place for hatching eggs of hens, fish, etc.

hatch·et (hăch′ĭt), *n.* 1. a small, short-handled ax for use with one hand. 2. a tomahawk. 3. **bury the hatchet,** to make peace. 4. **dig up the hatchet,** to prepare for war. [ME, t. F: m. *hachette,* dim. of *hache* ax, t. Gmc.; cf. HACK¹] —**hatch′et·like′,** *adj.*

hatchet face, a sharp, narrow face. —**hatch′et-faced′,** *adj.*

hatch·ing (hăch′ĭng), *n.* a series of lines, generally parallel, used in shading or modeling. [f. HATCH³ + -ING¹]

hatch·ment (hăch′mənt), *n. Chiefly Brit.* a square tablet, set diagonally, bearing the arms of a deceased person. [aspirated var. of *atch(e)ment,* syncopated form of ACHIEVEMENT]

Hatchment of an esquire

hatch·way (hăch′wā′), *n.* 1. an opening (covered by a hatch) in a ship's deck, for passage to parts below. 2. the opening of any trap door, as in a floor, ceiling, or roof.

hate (hāt), *v., hated, hating, n.* —*v.t.* 1. to regard with a strong or passionate dislike; detest. 2. to dislike; be unwilling: *I hate to do it.* —*v.i.* 3. to feel hatred. —*n.* 4. hatred; strong dislike. 5. the object of hatred. [ME *hat(i)en,* OE *hatian,* c. G *hassen*] —**hat′er,** *n.*

—**Syn.** 1. loathe, execrate, despise. HATE, ABHOR, DETEST, ABOMINATE imply feeling intense dislike or aversion toward something. HATE, the simple and general word, suggests passionate dislike and a feeling of enmity: *to hate autocracy.* ABHOR expresses a deep-rooted horror, and a sense of repugnance: *to abhor cruelty.* DETEST implies intense, even vehement, dislike and antipathy, besides a sense of disdain: *to detest a combination of ignorance and arrogance.* ABOMINATE expresses a strong feeling of disgust and repulsion toward something thought of as unworthy, unlucky, and the like: *to abominate treachery.*

hate·a·ble (hā′tə bəl), *adj.* hatable.

hate·ful (hāt′fəl), *adj.* 1. exciting hate; detestable; odious. 2. *Archaic.* full of hate; malignant; malevolent. —**hate′ful·ly,** *adv.* —**hate′ful·ness,** *n.*

Syn. 1. abominable, execrable, abhorrent, repugnant; invidious, loathsome. HATEFUL, OBNOXIOUS, ODIOUS, OFFENSIVE refer to that which causes strong dislike or annoyance. HATEFUL implies actually causing hatred or extremely strong dislike: *the sight of him is hateful to me.* OBNOXIOUS emphasizes causing annoyance or discomfort by objectionable qualities: *his persistence made him seem obnoxious, his piggish manners made him obnoxious to his companions.* ODIOUS emphasizes the disagreeable or displeasing: *an odious little man, odious servility.* OFFENSIVE emphasizes the distaste and resentment caused by something which may be either displeasing or insulting: *an offensive odor, remark.* —**Ant.** 1. likable, pleasant, agreeable.

hath (hăth), *v. Archaic.* 3rd pers. sing. pres. indic. of **have.**

Hath·a·way (hăth′ə wā′), *n.* **Anne,** 1557–1623, the wife of William Shakespeare.

Hath·or (hăth′ôr), *n. Egypt. Myth.* the goddess of love and joy, often represented with the head, horns, or ears of a cow.[t. Egyptian: the castle of Hor]

Ha·thor·ic (hə thôr′ĭk, -thŏr′-), *adj.* 1. of or pertaining to Hathor. 2. *Archit.* decorated with a face or head assumed to represent this goddess, as the capital of a column.

ha·tred (hā′trĭd), *n.* the feeling of one who hates; intense dislike; detestation. [ME *hatered(en),* f. *hate* hate + -*reden,* OE -*ræden* suffix making abstract nouns] —**Syn.** aversion, animosity.

hat·ter (hăt′ər), *n.* a maker or seller of hats.

Hat·ter·as (hăt′ər əs), *n.* **Cape,** a promontory on an island off the E coast of North Carolina: dangerous to shipping.

Hat·ties·burg (hăt′ĭz bûrg′), *n.* a city in SE Mississippi. 34,989 (1960).

hat tree, a stand with spreading arms or pegs on which hats, coats, etc., may be hung. Also, **hat rack.**

hau·ber·geon (hô′bər jən), *n.* habergeon.

hau·berk (hô′bûrk), *n.* a piece of armor originally intended for the protection of the neck and shoulders, but early developed into a long coat of mail reaching below the knees. [ME, t. OF: m. *hauberc,* t. Gmc.; cf. OHG *halsberg* neck protection]

haugh·ty (hô′tĭ), *adj., -tier, -tiest.* 1. disdainfully proud; arrogant; supercilious. 2. *Archaic.* exalted; lofty, or noble. [extended form of *haught,* orig. *haut,* t. F: high, in OF *halt,* g. L *altus,* b. with OG *hauh* (later *höh*) high] —**haugh′ti·ly,** *adv.* —**haugh′ti·ness,** *n.* —**Syn.** 1. lordly, disdainful, contemptuous. See **proud.** —**Ant.** 1. humble, unpretentious, unassuming.

Hauberk, 12th and 13th centuries

haul (hôl), *v.t.* 1. to pull or draw with force; move or transport by drawing. 2. **haul up,** *Colloq.* a. to bring up, as before a superior, for reprimand; call to account. b. to change the course of (a ship), esp. so as to sail closer to the wind. —*v.i.* 3. to pull or tug. 4. to change one's course of procedure or action; go in a given direction. 5. *Naut.* to sail, as in a particular direction. 6. (of the wind) to change direction, shift, or veer (often fol. by *round* or *to*). 7. **haul off,** a. *Naut.* to change the course of a ship so as to get further off from an object. b. to draw off or away. c. to draw back the arm in preparation for a blow. —*n.* 8. act of hauling; a strong pull or tug. 9. that which is hauled. 10. the distance through which anything is hauled. 11. *Fishing.* a. the quantity of fish taken at one draft of the net. b. the draft of a fishing net. c. the place where a seine is hauled. 12. *Colloq.* the taking or acquisition of anything, or that which is taken. [earlier *hall,* phonetic var. of HALE²] —**haul′er,** *n.* —**Syn.** 1. See **draw.**

haul·age (hô′lĭj), *n.* 1. act or labor of hauling. 2. the amount of force expended in hauling. 3. a charge made by a railroad for hauling cars, equipment, or commodities.

haulm (hôm), *n. Brit.* 1. stems or stalks collectively, as of grain or of peas, beans, hops, etc., esp. as used for litter or thatching. 2. a single stem or stalk. Also, **halm.** [ME *halm,* OE *healm,* c. D and G *halm*]

haunch (hônch, hänch), *n.* 1. the hip. 2. the fleshy part of the body about the hip. 3. a hind quarter of an animal. 4. the leg and loin of an animal, as used for food. 5. *Archit.* a. either side of an arch, extending from the vertex or crown to the impost. b. the part of a beam projecting below a floor or roof slab. [ME *hanche,* t. OF, t. Gmc.; cf. MD *hancke*]

haunch bone, the ilium or hipbone.

haunt (hônt; *for 9 sometimes also* hänt), *v.t.* 1. to reappear frequently to after death; visit habitually as a supposed spirit or ghost. 2. to intrude upon continually; recur to persistently: *memories that haunt one.* 3. to resort to much; visit frequently. 4. to frequent the company of; be often with. —*v.i.* 5. to reappear continually, as a disembodied spirit. 6. to resort habitually. 7. to associate, as with a person. —*n.* 8. (*often pl.*) a place of frequent resort: *to revisit one's old haunts.* 9. *Dial.* a ghost. [ME *haunten,* t. OF: m. *hanter* haunt, dwell, t. OE: m. *hämettan* shelter, der. *hām* home] —**haunt′er,** *n.* —**haunt′ing·ly,** *adv.*

haunt·ed (hôn′tĭd, hän′-), *adj.* 1. frequented or visited by ghosts: *a haunted house.* 2. much resorted to.

Haupt·mann (houpt′män), *n.* **Gerhart** (gĕr′härt), 1862–1946, German dramatist, novelist, and poet.

Hau·sa (hou′sä), *n.* 1. a prominent Negro stock in northern Nigeria and the Sudan. 2. their language, used widely in Africa as a language of commerce.

Haus·frau (hous′frou′), *n. German.* a housewife.

haus·tel·lum (hô stĕl′əm), *n., pl.* **haustella** (hô stĕl′ə). (in certain crustaceans and insects) an organ or part of the proboscis adapted for sucking blood or plant juices. [NL, dim. of L *haustrum* machine for drawing water]

haus·to·ri·um (hô stôr′ĭ əm), *n., pl.* **haustoria** (hô stôr′ĭ ə). *Bot.* an intracellular feeding organ of a parasite which does not kill the host cells but lives with them. [NL, der. *haustor* drinker]

haut·boy (hō′boi, ō′boi), *n.* oboe. [t. F: m. *hautbois,* f. *haut* high + *bois* wood; named with reference to the high notes]

hau·teur (hō tûr′; *Fr.* ō tœr′), *n.* haughty manner or spirit; haughtiness. [t. F, der. *haut* high. See HAUGHTY]

haut monde (ō mônd′), *French.* high society.

Ha·van·a (hə văn′ə), *n.* 1. Spanish, **Habana.** a seaport in and the capital of Cuba, on the NW coast. 785,455 (1953). 2. a cigar made in Cuba or of Cuban tobacco.

have (hăv), *v., pres.* 1 **have,** 2 **have** or **hast,** 3 **has** or **hath,** *pl.* **have;** *pt. and past part.* **had;** *pres. part.* **having.** —*v.t.* 1. to possess; own; to hold for use; contain: *to have property, the work has an index.* 2. to hold or possess in some other relation, as of kindred, relative position, etc.: *to have one's opponent down.* 3. to get, receive, or take: *to have no news.* 4. to be required, compelled, or under obligation (fol. by an infinitive): *I*

have to stop now. **5.** to experience, enjoy, or suffer: *to have a pleasant time.* **6.** to hold in mind, sight, etc.: *to have doubts.* **7.** to require or cause (to do something, be done, or as specified): *have him come here at five.* **8.** to show or exhibit in action: *to have a care.* **9.** to engage in or perform: *to have a talk.* **10.** to permit or allow: *I will not have it.* **11.** to assert or maintain: *rumor has it so.* **12.** to know or understand: *to have neither Latin nor Greek.* **13.** to give birth to: *to have a baby.* **14.** to wear (fol. by *on*). **15.** *Colloq.* to hold at a disadvantage: *he has you there.* **16.** *Chiefly Brit. Slang.* to outwit, deceive, or cheat: *a person not easily had.* **17. have it in for,** to hold a grudge against. **18. have it out,** to come to a final understanding by discussion. **19. have rather,** to consider as preferable: *I had much rather he go.* —*aux. v.* **20.** (used with the past participle of a verb to form a compound or perfect tense): *they have gone* [ME *have*(*n*), OE *habban,* c. D *hebben,* G *haben,* Icel. *hafa,* Goth. *haban;* akin to L *capere* take] —**Syn. 1.** HAVE, HOLD, OCCUPY, OWN mean to be, in varying degrees, in the possession of something. HAVE, being the most general word, admits of the widest range of application: *to have money, rights, discretion, a disease, a glimpse, an idea; to have a friend's umbrella.* To HOLD is to have in one's grasp or one's control, but not necessarily as one's own: *to hold stakes.* To OCCUPY is to hold and use, but not necessarily by any right of ownership: *to occupy a chair, a house, a position.* To OWN is to have the full rights of property in a thing, which, however, another may be holding or enjoying: *to own a house which is rented to tenants.* —**Ant. 1.** lack.

have·lock (hăv′lŏk), *n.* a cap cover with a flap hanging over the back of the neck, for protection from the sun. [named after H. *Havelock* (1795–1857),Brit. general]

ha·ven (hā′vən), *n.* **1.** a harbor or port. **2.** any place of shelter and safety. —*v.t.* **3.** to shelter as in a haven. [ME; OE *hæfen,* c. G *hafen*] —**ha′ven·less,** *adj.* —**Syn.** See **harbor.**

have·n't (hăv′ənt), contraction of *have not.*

Hav·er·ford (hăv′ərfərd), *n.* a township in SE Pennsylvania, near Philadelphia. 54,019 (1960).

Ha·ver·hill (hā′vər ĭl, -vrəl), *n.* a city in NE Massachusetts, on the Merrimack river. 46,346 (1960).

hav·er·sack (hăv′ər săk), *n.* **1.** a soldier's bag for rations. **2.** any bag used for provisions. [t. F: m. *havresac,* t. LG: m. *habersack,* lit., oat sack]

Ha·ver·sian canal (hə vûr′shən), a microscopic channel in bone, through which a blood vessel runs. [named after C. *Havers,* British anatomist, 1650–1702]

hav·oc (hăv′ək), *n., v.* -ocked, -ocking. —*n.* **1.** devastation; ruinous damage. **2. play havoc with,** to ruin; destroy. **3.** *Archaic.* a word used as the signal for pillage in warfare: *to cry havoc.* —*v.t.* **4.** to work havoc upon. —*v.i.* **5.** to work havoc. [ME *havok,* t. AF, var. of OF *havot,* used esp. in phrase *crier havot* cry havoc, give the call for pillaging; prob. from Gmc.] —**hav′ock·er,** *n.* —**Syn. 1.** See **ruin.**

Ha·vre (hä′vər), *n.* See **Le Havre.**

haw[1] (hô), *n.* the fruit of the Old World hawthorn, *Crataegus Oxyacantha,* or of other species of the same genus. [ME; OE *haga,* c. D *haag*]

haw[2] (hô), *interj.* **1.** an utterance marking hesitation in speech. **2.** the utterance "haw." —*v.i.* **3.** to use "haw," as in hesitation. [imit.]

haw[3] (hô), *interj.* **1.** a word of command to horses, etc., usually directing them to turn to the left. —*v.t., v.i.* **2.** to turn to the left (said of horses and cattle). [appar. orig. the same as *haw,* impv., look!, ME *hawen,* OE *hāwian*]

haw[4] (hô), *n.* the nictitating membrane of a horse, dog, etc., formerly only when inflamed. [orig. uncert.]

Ha·wai·i (hə wī′ē, -wä′yə), *n.* **1.** Hawaiian Islands. **2.** the largest of the Hawaiian Islands. 61,332 pop. (1960); 4021 sq. mi.

Ha·wai·ian (hə wī′yən, -wä′-), *adj.* **1.** of or pertaining to Hawaii. —*n.* **2.** a native or inhabitant of Hawaii or the Hawaiian Islands. **3.** the aboriginal language of Hawaii, a Polynesian language.

Hawaiian Islands, a group of islands in the N Pacific, 2090 mi. SW of San Francisco, forming a State of the United States. 632,772 pop. (1960); 6454 sq. mi. *Cap.:* Honolulu. Also, **Hawaii.** Formerly, **Territory of Hawaii, Sandwich Islands.**

Hawaii National Park, a large park that includes the active volcanoes Kilauea and Mauna Loa on the island of Hawaii and the extinct crater Haleakala on Maui. 343 sq. mi.

haw·finch (hô′fĭnch′), *n.* a European grosbeak, *Coccothraustes coccothraustes.*

haw-haw (hô′hô′), *n.* **1.** a word representing the sound of a loud, boisterous laugh. **2.** a guffaw.

hawk[1] (hôk), *n.* **1.** any of numerous diurnal birds of prey of the family *Falconidae,* as the falcons, buzzards, kites, harriers, etc., esp. the short-winged, long-tailed accipiters, as the goshawk. **2.** any of certain nonfalconiform birds, as the nighthawk. **3.** a person who preys on others, as a sharper. —*v.i.* **4.** to fly, or hunt on the wing, like a hawk. **5.** to hunt with hawks trained to pursue game. [ME *hauk*(*e*), OE *hafoc,* c. G *habicht*] —**hawk′ish,** *adj.*

Red-tailed hawk,
Buteo borealis
(19 to 22½ in. long)

hawk[2] (hôk), *v.t.* **1.** to offer for sale by outcry in a street or from door to door. —*v.i.* **2.** to carry wares about; peddle. [back formation from HAWKER[2]]

hawk[3] (hôk), *v.i.* **1.** to make an effort to raise phlegm from the throat; clear the throat noisily. —*v.t.* **2.** to raise by hawking: *to hawk up phlegm.* —*n.* **3.** a noisy effort to clear the throat. [imit.]

hawk[4] (hôk), *n.* a small square board with a handle underneath, used by plasterers to hold small quantities of mortar. [orig. uncert.]

hawk·bill (hôk′bĭl′), *n.* hawksbill.

hawk·er[1] (hô′kər), *n.* a falconer. [f. HAWK[1], v. + -ER[1]]

hawk·er[2] (hô′kər), *n.* one who offers goods for sale by outcry in the streets; peddler. [appar. t. MLG: m. *hoker.* Cf. G *höker,* D *heuker* retail dealer. See HUCKSTER]

hawk-eyed (hôk′īd′), *adj.* having very keen eyes.

hawk·ing (hô′kĭng), *n.* falconry.

Haw·kins (hô′kĭnz), *n.* **Sir John,** 1532–95, English slave trader and rear admiral. Also, **Hawkyns.**

hawk moth, any of certain moths of the family *Sphingidae,* noted for their very swift flight and ability to hover while sipping nectar from flowers.

hawk·nose (hôk′nōz′), *n.* a nose curved like the beak of a hawk. —**hawk′-nosed′,** *adj.*

hawk owl, a strikingly barred gray and white owl, *Surnia ulula,* of northern parts of the northern hemisphere, so named because it is diurnal.

hawk's-beard (hôks′bĭrd′), *n.* any herb of the composite genus *Crepis,* having yellow or orange flowers.

hawks·bill (hôks′bĭl′), *n.* a marine turtle, *Eretmochelys imbricata,* yielding tortoise shell and having a mouth shaped like the bill of a hawk. Also, **hawk′s-′bill′, hawkbill, hawksbill turtle.**

hawk's-eye (hôks′ī′), *n.* a dark-green chatoyant quartz formed like tiger's-eye by the silicification of an asbestos and used for ornamental purposes.

hawk·shaw (hôk′shô′), *n.* a detective.

hawk·weed (hôk′wēd′), *n.* **1.** any herb of the composite genus *Hieracium,* with yellow, orange, or red flowers. **2.** any of various related plants.

Haw·kyns (hô′kĭnz), *n.* Hawkins.

hawse (hôz, hôs), *n.* **1.** the part of a ship's bow having holes for the cables to pass through. **2.** a hawsehole. **3.** the space between a ship at anchor and her anchors. **4.** the situation of a ship's cables when she is moored with both bow anchors: *a clear hawse.* [ME *halse,* prob. t. Scand.; cf. Icel. *hāls* part of ship's bow, front sheet of sail, lit., neck, c. OE *hals* neck]

hawse·hole (hôz′hōl′, hôs′-), *n.* a hole in the bow of a ship, through which a cable is passed.

haw·ser (hô′zər, -sər), *n. Naut.* a small cable or large rope used in warping, mooring, towing, etc. [ME *haucer,* der. OF *haucier* raise, ult. der. L *altus* high]

hawser bend, a knot uniting the ends of two lines.

haw·ser-laid (hô′zər lād′, -sər-), *adj.* **1.** made of three small ropes laid up into one. **2.** cable-laid.

haw·thorn (hô′thôrn′), *n.* **1.** any species of the rosaceous genus *Crataegus,* usually small trees with stiff thorns, cultivated in hedges for their white or pink blossoms and bright-colored fruits. **2.** a thorny shrub, *Crataegus Oxyacantha,* native in the Old World, but introduced in the U.S. [ME; OE *haguthorn.* See HAW[1]]

Haw·thorne (hô′thôrn′), *n.* **1. Nathaniel,** 1804–64, U.S. novelist and short-story writer. **2.** a city in California, SW of Los Angeles. 33,035 (1960).

hay[1] (hā), *n.* **1.** grass cut and dried for use as fodder. **2.** grass mowed or intended for mowing. **3. make hay, a.** to cut and cure grass for fodder. **b.** to scatter everything in disorder. —*v.t.* **4.** to convert (grass) into hay. **5.** to furnish (horses, etc.) with hay. [ME; OE *hēg, hīeg,* c. G *heu*]

hay[2] (hā), *n.* a kind of old country dance with winding movements. [t. F (15th cent.): m. *haye* kind of dance]

Hay (hā), *n.* **John Milton,** 1838–1905, U.S. statesman and author.

hay·cock (hā′kŏk′), *n. Chiefly Brit.* a small conical pile of hay thrown up in a hayfield, while the hay is awaiting removal to a barn.

Hay·dn (hā′dən; *Ger.* hī′dən), *n.* **Franz Joseph** (fränts yō′zěf), 1732–1809, Austrian composer.

Hayes (hāz), *n.* **1. Helen,** born 1900, U.S. actress. **2. Rutherford Birchard** (bûr′chərd), 1822–93, 19th president of the U.S., 1877–81.

hay fever, a catarrhal affection of the mucous membranes of the eyes and respiratory tract, attacking susceptible persons (usually) during the summer, and due to the action of the pollen of certain plants.

hay·field (hā′fēld′), *n.* a field in which grass is grown for making into hay, or from which hay is being cut.

hay·fork (hā′fôrk′), *n.* a fork used for turning or lifting hay, operated either by hand or machine.

hay·loft (hā′lôft′, -lŏft′), *n.* a loft in a stable or barn, for the storage of hay.

hay·mak·er (hā′mā′kər), *n.* **1.** one who makes hay. **2.** one who tosses and spreads hay to dry after it has been mowed. **3.** *Boxing.* a swinging, knockout blow.

Hay·mar·ket (hā′mär′kĭt), *n.* a famous London market (1644–1830), now the theatrical center.

hay·mow (hā′mou′), *n.* **1.** a mow or mass of hay stored in a barn. **2.** the place in a barn where hay is stored. **3.** a rick or stack of hay.

hay·rack (hā′răk′), *n.* **1.** a rack for holding hay for feeding horses or cattle. **2.** a rack or framework mounted on a wagon, for use in carrying hay, straw, etc. **3.** the wagon and rack together.

hay·seed (hā′sēd′), *n.* **1.** grass seed, esp. that shaken out of hay. **2.** small bits of the chaff, etc., of hay. **3.** *U.S. Slang.* a countryman or rustic.

hay·stack (hā′stăk′), *n.* a stack of hay with a conical or ridged top, built up in the open air for preservation, and sometimes thatched or covered. Also, *esp. Brit.,* **hay·rick** (hā′rĭk′).

hay·ward (hā′wôrd′), *n.* *Obs.* an officer having charge of hedges and fences, esp. to keep cattle from breaking through, and to impound strays. [ME *heiward.* See HAY¹, WARD²]

Hay·ward (hā′wərd), *n.* a city in central California, SE of Oakland. 72,700 (1960).

hay·wire (hā′wīr′), *n.* **1.** wire used to bind bales of hay. —*adj.* **2.** *Slang.* in disorder; out of order. **3.** *Slang.* out of control; crazy: *to go haywire.*

haz·ard (hăz′ərd), *n.* **1.** exposure to danger or harm; risk; peril: *at all hazards.* **2.** chance, or a chance. **3.** *Golf.* an obstacle, as a bunker, road, bush, water, or the like, on the course. **4.** the uncertainty of the result in throwing a die. **5.** a game played with two dice; an earlier and more complicated form of modern craps. **6.** something risked or staked. **7.** *Court Tennis.* **a.** any of certain openings in the walls of the court, the striking of a ball into which scores the striker a point. **b.** that side of the court into which the ball is served (**hazard side**). **8.** *English Billiards.* a stroke by which the player pockets the object ball (**winning hazard**), or his own ball after contact with another ball (**losing hazard**). —*v.t.* **9.** to venture to offer (a statement, conjecture, etc.). **10.** to put to the risk of being lost; to expose to risk. **11.** to take or run the risk of (a misfortune, penalty, etc.). **12.** to venture upon (anything of doubtful issue). [ME *hasard,* t. OF, t. Ar.: m. *az-zahr* the die] —**haz′ard·a·ble,** *adj.* —**haz′ard·er,** *n.* —**haz′ard·less,** *adj.* —**Syn. 1.** See **danger.** —**Ant. 1.** safety.

haz·ard·ous (hăz′ər dəs), *adj.* **1.** full of risk; perilous; risky. **2.** dependent on chance: *a hazardous contract.* —**haz′ard·ous·ly,** *adv.* —**haz′ard·ous·ness,** *n.*

haze¹ (hāz), *n.* **1.** an aggregation of minute suspended particles of vapor, dust, etc., near the surface of the earth, causing an appearance of thin mist in the atmosphere. **2.** obscurity or vagueness of the mind. [orig. obscure] —**Syn. 2.** See **cloud.**

haze² (hāz), *v.t.,* **hazed, hazing. 1.** to subject (freshmen or newcomers) to abusive or ridiculous tricks. **2.** *Chiefly Naut.* to harass with unnecessary or disagreeable tasks. [cf. MF *haser* irritate, annoy] —**haz′er,** *n.*

ha·zel (hā′zəl), *n.* **1.** any of the shrubs or small trees of the betulaceous genus *Corylus,* which bear edible nuts, as *C. Avellana* of Europe or *C. americana* and *C. cornuta* of America. **2.** any of certain other shrubs or trees (as *Pomaderris apetala,* a rhamnaceous shrub of Australia, etc.), or their wood. **3.** the hazelnut or filbert. **4.** the wood of a hazel. **5.** light reddish brown of a hazelnut. —*adj.* **6.** of or pertaining to the hazel. **7.** made of the wood of the hazel. **8.** having a hazel color. [ME *hasel*(*l*), OE *hæs*(*e*)*l,* c. G *hasel*; akin to L *corylus* hazel shrub]

ha·zel·nut (hā′zəl nŭt′), *n.* the nut of the hazel.

haz·ing (hā′zĭng), *n.* act or practice of one who hazes.

Ha·zle·ton (hā′zəl tən), *n.* a city in E Pennsylvania. 32,056 (1960).

Haz·litt (hăz′lĭt), *n.* **William,** 1778–1830. British critic and essayist.

ha·zy (hā′zĭ), *adj.,* **-zier, -ziest. 1.** characterized by the presence of haze; misty: *hazy weather.* **2.** lacking distinctness; vague; confused: *a hazy proposition.* —**ha′zi·ly,** *adv.* —**ha′zi·ness,** *n.*

haz·zan (hä zän′, hä′zän), *n.* chazzan.

H.B.M., His (or Her) Britannic Majesty.

H-bomb, hydrogen bomb.

H.C., House of Commons.

H.C.F., highest common factor. Also, **h.c.f.**

h.c.l., *Colloq.* high cost of living.

hd., **1.** hand. **2.** head.

hdqrs., headquarters.

he (hē; *unstressed* ē, ĭ), *pron., nom.,* **he;** *gen.,* **his, of him, of his;** *dat. and acc.,* **him;** *pl. nom.,* **they;** *gen.,* **theirs, their, of them, of theirs;** *acc.,* **them;** *n., pl.* **hes. 1.** the male being in question or last mentioned. **2.** anyone; that person: *he who hesitates is lost.* —*n.* **3.** a man or any male person (correlative to *she*). **4.** a male, esp. of an animal. [ME *he,* OE *hē* (gen. *his,* dat. *him,* acc. *hine*), c. OS *he, hi,* OFris. *hi, he.* Cf. SHE, HER, IT, HENCE, HERE HITHER]

He, *Chem.* helium.

H.E. 1. His Eminence. **2.** His Excellency.

head (hĕd), *n.* **1.** the upper part of the human body, joined to the trunk by the neck. **2.** the corresponding part of an animal's body. **3.** the head considered as the seat of thought, memory, understanding, etc.: *to have a head for mathematics.* **4.** the position of leadership; chief command; greatest authority. **5.** one to whom others are subordinate; a leader or chief. **6.** that part of anything which forms or is regarded as forming the top, summit, or upper end: *head of a pin, head of a page.* **7.** the foremost part or end of anything; a projecting part: *head of a procession, head of a rock.* **8.** a person considered with reference to his mind, disposition, attributes, etc.: *wise heads, crowned heads.* **9.** a person or animal considered merely as one of a number (often with *pl.* **head**): *ten head of cattle, to charge so much a head.* **10.** culmination or crisis; conclusion: *to bring matters to a head.* **11.** the hair covering the head: *to comb someone's head.* **12.** something resembling a head in form: *a head of lettuce.* **13.** a rounded or compact part of a plant, usually at the top of the stem, as of leaves (as in the cabbage or lettuce), leafstalks (as in the celery), flower buds (as in the cauliflower), sessile florets, etc. **14.** the maturated part of an abscess, boil, etc. **15.** a projecting point of a coast, esp. when high, as a cape, headland, or promontory. **16.** the obverse of a coin, as bearing a head or other principal figure (opposed to *tail*). **17.** one of the chief points of divisions of a discourse; topic. **18.** strength or force gradually attained; progress. **19.** the source of a river or stream. **20.** froth or foam. **21.** the headline or group of headlines at the top of a newspaper article. **22.** *Naut.* **a.** the forepart of a ship, etc. **b.** the upper edge (or corner) of a sail. **23.** *Gram.* **a.** that member of an endocentric construction which belongs to the same form class and may play the same grammatical role as the construction itself. **b.** the member upon which another depends and to which it is subordinate, e.g., in *the first president, first president* is head and *the* is attribute, and in *first president,* the head is *president* and the attribute is *first.* **24.** the stretched membrane covering the end of a drum or similar instrument. **25.** *Coal Mining.* a level or road driven into the solid coal for proving or working a mine. **26.** the height of the free surface of a liquid above a given level. **27.** *Mach.* a device on turning and boring machines, esp. lathes, holding one or more cutting tools to the work. **28.** the pressure of a confined body of steam, etc., per unit of area. **29.** the height of a column of fluid required for a certain pressure. **30.** the part or parts of a tape-recorder which come into direct contact with the tape and serve to record, reproduce or erase electromagnetic impulses on it. **31.** Some special noun phrases are:

by, or **down by, the head,** *Naut.* so loaded as to draw more water forward than aft.

go to one's head, 1. to make one confused or dizzy. **2.** to make one conceited.

lay heads together, to come together to scheme.

make head or tail of, to understand; figure out.

out of one's head or **mind,** *Chiefly U.S.* demented; delirious.

over one's head, 1. passing over one having a prior claim or a superior position. **2.** beyond one's comprehension.

—*adj.* **32.** situated at the top or front: *the head division of a parade.* **33.** being in the position of leadership or superiority. **34.** coming from in front: *a head wind.* —*v.t.* **35.** to go at the head of or in front of; lead, precede: *to head a list.* **36.** to outdo or excel. **37.** to be the head or chief of. **38.** to turn the head or front of in a specified direction: *to head one's boat for the shore.* **39.** to go round the head of (a stream, etc.). **40.** to furnish or fit with a head. **41.** to take the head of (an animal) off. **42.** to poll (a tree). —*v.i.* **43.** to move forward toward a point specified; direct one's course; go in a certain direction. **44.** to come or grow to a head; form a head. **45.** *Chiefly U.S.* (of a river or stream) to have the head or source where specified.

[ME *he*(*v*)*ed,* OE *hēafod,* c. D *hoofd,* G *haupt,* Icel. *höfudh,* Goth. *haubith*] —**head′like′,** *adj.* —**Syn. 5.** commander, director. **33.** cardinal, foremost, first. —**Ant. 33.** subordinate.

-head, a suffix denoting state, condition, character, etc.: *godhead,* and other words, now mostly archaic or obsolete, many being superseded by forms in **-hood.** [ME *-hede, -hed,* der. *hede* rank, condition, character; akin to OE *hād,* whence the suffix -HOOD]

head·ache (hĕd′āk′), *n.* a pain located in the head.

head·band (hĕd′bănd′), *n.* **1.** a band worn around the head; a fillet. **2.** *Print.* a band for decorative effect at the head of a chapter or of a page in a book. **3.** a band sewn to the head and tail of the back of the book to protect and strengthen the binding.

head·board (hĕd′bōrd′), *n.* a board forming the head of anything, esp. of a bed.

head·cheese (hĕd′chēz′), *n.* a preparation of parts of the head and feet of hogs cut up, cooked, and seasoned, and forming when cold a jellied mass or loaf.

head·dress (hĕd′drĕs′), *n.* **1.** a covering or decoration for the head. **2.** an arrangement of the hair.

head·ed (hĕd′ĭd), *adj.* **1.** having a heading. **2.** shaped or grown into a head.

head·ed, a suffix meaning: **1.** having a specified kind of head: *long-headed, wrong-headed.* **2.** having a specified number of heads: *two-headed.*

head·er (hĕd′ər), *n.* **1.** one who or an apparatus which removes or puts a head on something. **2.** a form of reaping machine which cuts off and gathers only the heads of the grain. **3.** a chamber to which the ends of a number of tubes are connected so that water or steam may pass freely from one tube to the other. **4.** *Building.* **a.** a brick or stone laid with its length across the thickness of a wall. **b.** a timber or beam in the framing about an opening in a floor or roof, placed so as to fit between two long beams and support the ends of short ones. **5.** *Colloq.* a plunge or dive headforemost, as into water.

head·first (hĕd′fûrst′), *adv.* **1.** with the head in front or bent forward; headlong. **2.** rashly; precipitately. Also, **head·fore·most** (hĕd′fōr′mōst′, -məst).

head gate, 1. a control gate at the upstream end of a canal or lock. **2.** a floodgate of a race, sluice, etc.

head·gear (hĕd′gîr′), *n.* **1.** any covering for the head. **2.** the parts of a harness about the animal's head.

head·hunt·ing (hĕd′hŭn′tĭng), *n.* (among certain savage tribes) the practice of making incursions for procuring human heads as trophies or for use in religious ceremonies. **—head′·hunt′er,** *n.*

head·ing (hĕd′ĭng), *n.* **1.** something that serves as a head, top, or front. **2.** a title or caption of a page, chapter, etc. **3.** a section of a subject of discourse; a topic. **4.** a horizontal passage in the earth, as for an intended tunnel, for working a mine, for ventilation or drainage, etc.; a drift. **5.** the end of such a passage. **6.** *Aeron.* the compass point towards which a craft is flying.

head·land (hĕd′lənd *for 1;* hĕd′lănd′ *for 2*), *n.* **1.** a promontory extending into a large body of water, such as a sea or lake. **2.** a strip of unplowed land at the ends of furrows or near a fence or border.

head·less (hĕd′lĭs), *adj.* **1.** having no head; deprived of the head. **2.** without a leader or chief. **3.** foolish; stupid. [ME *he(ve)dles,* OE *hēafodlēas.* See -LESS]

head·light (hĕd′līt′), *n.* a lamp equipped with a reflector, on the front of an automobile, locomotive, etc.

head·line (hĕd′līn′), *n., v.,* **-lined, -lining.** *—n.* **1.** a display line over an article, etc., as in a newspaper. **2.** the line at the top of a page, containing the title, pagination, etc. *—v.t.* **3.** to furnish with a headline.

head·lin·er (hĕd′lī′nər), *n.* **1.** *Theat. Slang.* a performer whose name appears at the head of a bill, or in larger letters than other names on the bill. **2.** *Journalism.* one who writes headlines.

head·lock (hĕd′lŏk′), *n.* *Wrestling.* a hold in which a wrestler locks his arm around his opponent's head.

head·long (hĕd′lông′, -lŏng′), *adv.* **1.** headforemost: *to plunge headlong.* **2.** hastily. **3.** rashly; without deliberation. *—adj.* **4.** done or going with the head foremost. **5.** hasty. **6.** rash; impetuous. **7.** steep; precipitous. [late ME *hedlong,* f. *hed* HEAD + *long,* adv. suffix; r. *headling,* ME *hedlyng.* See -LING²]

head·man (hĕd′mən), *n., pl.* **-men.** a chief man; a chief or leader. [ME *hevedmon,* OE *hēafodman*]

head·mas·ter (hĕd′măs′tər, -mäs′tər), *n.* *Chiefly Brit.* the principal master of a school or seminary. Also, **head master.** **—head′mas′ter·ship′,** *n.* **—head·mis·tress** (hĕd′mĭs′trĭs), *n. fem.*

head money, 1. a tax of so much per head or person. **2.** a reward paid for each person captured or brought in. **3.** a reward for the head of an outlaw or enemy.

head·most (hĕd′mōst′), *adj.* foremost; most advanced.

head-on (hĕd′ŏn′, -ôn′), *adj.* with the head foremost: *a head-on collision.*

head·phone (hĕd′fōn′), *n.* (*often pl.*) a headset.

head·piece (hĕd′pēs′), *n.* **1.** armor for the head: a helmet. **2.** any covering for the head. **3.** a headset. **4.** the head as the seat of the intellect; judgment. **5.** the top piece or part of any of various things. **6.** *Print.* a decorative piece at the head of a page, chapter, etc.

head pin, *Tenpins.* the kingpin.

head·quar·ters (hĕd′kwôr′tərz), *n.pl. or sing.* **1.** any center from which official orders are issued: *police headquarters.* **2.** any center of operations. **3.** the offices of a military commander, the place where a commander customarily issues his orders. **4.** a military unit consisting of the commander, his staff, and other assistants. **5.** the building occupied by a headquarters.

head·race (hĕd′rās′), *n.* the race, flume, or channel leading to a water wheel or the like.

head resistance, *Aeron.* the drag inherent in the shape of an airplane and not due to a component of the aerodynamic lift.

head·rest (hĕd′rĕst′), *n.* a rest or support of any kind for the head.

head·sails (hĕd′sālz′; *Naut.* -səlz), *n.pl. Naut.* sails set forward of the foremast.

head·set (hĕd′sĕt′), *n.* *Radio, Teleph., etc.* a device

consisting of one or two telephone receivers, with attachments for holding them over the ears.

head·ship (hĕd′shĭp), *n.* the position of head or chief; chief authority; leadership; supremacy.

heads·man (hĕdz′mən), *n., pl.* **-men.** one who beheads condemned persons; a public executioner.

head·spring (hĕd′sprĭng′), *n.* **1.** the fountainhead or source of a stream. **2.** the source of anything.

head·stall (hĕd′stôl′), *n.* that part of a bridle or halter which encompasses the head.

head·stock (hĕd′stŏk′), *n.* the part of a machine containing the working members, as the assembly supporting and driving the live spindle in a lathe.

head·stone (hĕd′stōn′), *n.* a stone set at the head of a grave.

head·strong (hĕd′strông′, -strŏng′), *adj.* **1.** bent on having one's own way; willful. **2.** proceeding from willfulness: *a headstrong course.* **—head′strong′ness,** *n.* **—Syn. 1.** stubborn, obstinate. See **willful.**

head tone, *Music.* a vocal tone so produced as to bring the cavities of the nose and head into sympathetic vibration.

head·wa·ters (hĕd′wô′tərz, -wŏt′ərz), *n.pl.* the upper tributaries of a river.

head·way (hĕd′wā′), *n.* **1.** motion forward or ahead; advance. **2.** progress in general. **3.** rate of progress. **4.** the interval between two trains, etc., traveling in the same direction over the same route. **5.** clear space in height, as in a doorway or under an arch.

head·work (hĕd′wûrk′), *n.* mental labor; thought. **—head′work′er,** *n.*

head·y (hĕd′ĭ), *adj.,* **headier, headiest. 1.** rashly impetuous. **2.** intoxicating. [ME *he(ve)di.* See HEAD, *n.,* -Y¹] **—head′i·ly,** *adv.* **—head′i·ness,** *n.*

heal (hēl), *v.t.* **1.** to make whole or sound; restore to health; free from ailment. **2.** to free from anything evil or distressing; amend: *to heal a quarrel.* **3.** to cleanse or purify. *—v.i.* **4.** to effect a cure. **5.** to become whole or sound; get well (often fol. by *up* or *over*). [ME *hele(n),* OE *hǣlan,* der. *hǣl* hale, WHOLE] **—heal′er,** *n.* **—heal′ing,** *n.* **—heal′ing·ly,** *adv.* **—Syn. 1.** See **cure.**

heal·ing (hē′lĭng), *adj.* **1.** that heals; curing; curative. **2.** growing sound; getting well.

health (hĕlth), *n.* **1.** soundness of body; freedom from disease or ailment. **2.** the general condition of the body or mind with reference to soundness and vigor: *good health.* **3.** a polite or complimentary wish for a person's health, happiness, etc., esp. as a toast. [ME *helthe,* OE *hǣlth,* der. *hǣl* hale, whole. See WHOLE, -TH¹]

health·ful (hĕlth′fəl), *adj.* **1.** conducive to health; wholesome, or salutary: *healthful diet.* **2.** healthy. **—health′ful·ly,** *adv.* **—health′ful·ness,** *n.* **—Syn. 2.** See **healthy.**

health insurance, insurance which indemnifies the insured against loss of time occasioned by illness.

health·y (hĕl′thĭ), *adj.,* **healthier, healthiest. 1.** possessing or enjoying health: *healthy body or mind.* **2.** pertaining to or characteristic of health: *a healthy appearance.* **3.** conducive to health, or healthful: *healthy recreations.* **—health′i·ly,** *adv.* **—health′i·ness,** *n.* **—Syn. 1.** hale, hearty, robust, vigorous, strong; sound, well. **2.** nutritious, nourishing; hygienic, salubrious; invigorating, bracing. HEALTHY, HEALTHFUL, SALUTARY, WHOLESOME refer to that which promotes health. HEALTHY, while applied esp. to what possesses health, is also used of what is conducive to health: *a healthy climate, not a healthy place to be.* HEALTHFUL is applied chiefly to what is conducive to health: *healthful diet or exercise.* SALUTARY is applied to that which is conducive to well-being generally, as well as beneficial in preserving or in restoring health: *salutary effects, to take salutary measures.* It is used also of what is morally beneficial: *to have a salutary fear of consequences.* WHOLESOME has connotations of attractive freshness and purity; it applies to what is good for one, physically, morally, or both: *wholesome food or air, wholesome influences or advice.* **—Ant. 1.** sick, ill. **3.** injurious.

heap (hēp), *n.* **1.** an assemblage of things lying one on another; a pile: *a heap of stones.* **2.** *Colloq.* a great quantity or number; a multitude. *—v.t.* **3.** to gather, put, or cast in a heap; pile (often fol. by *up, on, together,* etc.). **4.** to accumulate or amass (often fol. by *up*): *to heap up riches.* **5.** to cast or bestow in great quantity: *to heap blessings or insults upon a person.* **6.** to load or supply abundantly with something: *to heap a person with favors.* *—v.i.* **7.** to become heaped or piled, as sand snow, etc.; rise in a heap or heaps. [ME *heep,* OE *hēap* heap, multitude, troop, c. LG *hōp;* akin to G *haufe*] **—heap′er,** *n.* **—Syn. 1.** mass, stack; accumulation.

hear (hĭr), *v.,* **heard** (hûrd), **hearing.** *—v.t.* **1.** to perceive by the ear. **2.** to listen to: *to refuse to hear a person.* **3.** to learn by the ear or by being told; be informed of: *to hear news.* **4.** to be among the audience at or of: *to hear an opera.* **5.** to give a formal, official, or judicial hearing to, as a sovereign, a teacher, an assembly, or a judge does. **6.** to listen to with favor, assent, or compliance. *—v.i.* **7.** to have perception of sound by the ear; have the sense of hearing. **8.** to listen or take heed (in imperative, "hear! hear!", used, chiefly in Britain, to applaud or endorse a speaker). **9.** to receive information by the ear or otherwise: *to hear from a friend.* **10.** to listen with favor or assent; *he would not hear of it.* [ME *here(n),* OE *hēran,* c. G *hōren*] **—hear′er,** *n.* **—Syn. 1. 2.** HEAR, LISTEN apply to the perception of sound. To HEAR is to have such perception by means of the auditory sense: *to hear distant bells.* To LISTEN is to give attention in order to hear and understand the meaning of a sound or sounds: *to listen to what is being said, to listen for a well-known footstep.* —Ant. 6. disregard.

hear·ing (hĭr′ĭng), *n.* 1. the faculty or sense by which sound is perceived. 2. act of perceiving sound. 3. opportunity to be heard: *to grant a hearing.* 4. *Law.* a presentation of testimony and arguments, as in a suit at law. 5. earshot: *their conversation was beyond my hearing.*

hearing aid, a compact, inconspicuous amplifier worn to improve one's hearing.

heark·en (här′kən), *v.i., v.t.* harken.

Hearn (hûrn), *n.* Lafcadio (lăf′kăd′ĭ ō′), 1850–1904, U.S. author who became a Japanese citizen.

hear·say (hĭr′sā′), *n.* gossip; rumor.

hearsay rule, *Law.* the rule which excludes out-of-court statements, oral or written, when offered as evidence (**hearsay evidence**).

hearse (hûrs), *n.* 1. a funeral vehicle for conveying a dead person to the place of burial. 2. a triangular frame for holding candles, used at the service of Tenebrae in Holy Week. [ME *herse,* t. OF: m. *herce* harrow, frame, ult. g. L *hirpex, irpex* large rake used as harrow]

Hearst (hûrst), *n.* **William Randolph,** 1863–1951, U.S. editor and publisher.

heart (härt), *n.* 1. a hollow muscular organ which by rhythmic contractions and relaxations keeps the blood in circulation throughout the body. 2. this organ considered as the seat of life or vital powers, or of thought, feeling, or emotion: *to die of a broken heart.* 3. the seat of emotions and affections (often in contrast to the *head* as the seat of the intellect): *to win a person's heart.* 4. feeling; sensibility; capacity for sympathy: *to have no heart.* 5. spirit, courage, or enthusiasm: *to take heart.* 6. the innermost or middle part of anything. 7. the vital or essential part; core: *the very heart of the matter.* 8. the breast or bosom: *to clasp a person to one's heart.* 9. a person, esp. in expressions of praise or affection: *dear heart.* 10. a figure or object with rounded sides meeting in an obtuse point at the bottom and curving inward to a cusp at the top. 11. *Cards.* **a.** a playing card of a suit marked with heart-shaped figures in red. **b.** the suit of cards bearing this symbol. **c.** (*pl. construed as sing.*) a game in which the players try to avoid taking tricks containing hearts. 12. *Bot.* the core of a tree; the solid central part without sap or albumen. 13. good condition for production, growth, etc., as of land or crops. 14. Some special noun phrases are:

Section of human heart A. Vena cava; B. Right auricle; C. Right ventricle; D. Aorta; E. Pulmonary artery; F. Left auricle; G. Left ventricle

Heart (def. 10)

at heart, in one's heart, thoughts, or feelings; in reality. **break the heart of,** 1. to disappoint grievously in love. 2. to crush with sorrow or grief. **from one's heart,** sincerely. **have at heart,** to have as an object, aim, etc. **have the heart,** 1. to have enough courage. 2. (in negative sentences) to be unfeeling enough. **heart and soul,** completely; wholly. **take to heart,** 1. to think seriously about. 2. to be deeply affected by; grieve over. **with all one's heart,** with all willingness; heartily. —*v.t. Archaic.* 15. to encourage. 16. to fix in the heart. [ME *herte,* OE *heorte,* c. G *herz*]

heart·ache (härt′āk′), *n.* mental anguish; sorrow.

heart·beat (härt′bēt′), *n. Physiol.* a pulsation of the heart, including one complete systole and diastole.

heart·break (härt′brāk′), *n.* great sorrow or grief.

heart·break·ing (härt′brā′kĭng), *adj.* causing heart-break. —**heart′break′er,** *n.*

heart·bro·ken (härt′brō′kən), *adj.* crushed with sorrow or grief. —**heart′bro′ken·ly,** *adv.* —**heart′-bro′ken·ness,** *n.*

heart·burn (härt′bûrn′), *n.* 1. an uneasy, burning sensation in the stomach, often extending toward the esophagus; cardialgia. 2. envy; bitter jealousy.

heart·burn·ing (härt′bûr′nĭng), *n.* rankling discontent, esp. from envy or jealousy; a grudge.

heart cherry, a heart-shaped kind of cherry with soft, sweet flesh.

heart disease, any condition of the heart which impairs its functioning.

heart·ed (här′tĭd), *adj.* having a specified kind of heart: *hard-hearted, sad-hearted.*

heart·en (här′tən), *v.t.* to give courage to; cheer.

heart·felt (härt′fĕlt′), *adj.* deeply or sincerely felt; earnest; sincere: *heartfelt joy or words.*

heart-free (härt′frē′), *adj.* not in love.

hearth (härth), *n.* 1. that part of the floor of a room on which the fire is made or above which is a stove, fireplace, furnace, etc. 2. the fireside; home. 3. *Metall.* **a.** the lower part of a blast furnace, cupola, etc., in which the molten metal collects and from which it is tapped out. **b.** the part of an open hearth, reverberatory furnace, etc., upon which the charge is placed and melted down or refined. 4. *Soldering.* a brazier, chafing dish, or box for charcoal. [ME *herth(e),* OE *he(o)rth,* c. G *herd;* akin to L *carbo* charcoal]

hearth·stone (härth′stōn′), *n.* 1. a stone forming a hearth. 2. the fireside; home. 3. a soft stone, or a preparation of powdered stone and clay, used to whiten or scour hearths, steps, floors, etc.

heart·i·ly (här′tə lĭ′), *adv.* 1. in a hearty manner; sincerely; cordially. 2. eagerly; enthusiastically. 3. with a hearty appetite. 4. thoroughly; completely.

heart·less (härt′lĭs), *adj.* 1. without heart or feeling; unfeeling; cruel: *heartless words.* 2. without courage or enthusiasm: *a heartless mood.* —**heart′less·ly,** *adv.* —**heart′less·ness,** *n.*

heart point, the mid point of an escutcheon. See diag. under **escutcheon.**

heart-rend·ing (härt′rĕn′dĭng), *adj.* causing acute mental anguish. —**heart′-rend′ing·ly,** *adv.*

hearts (härts), *n.* See **heart** (def. 11c).

hearts·ease (härts′ēz′), *n.* 1. peace of mind. 2. the pansy, or some other plant of the genus *Viola.* 3. (in some parts of the U.S.) the common persicary. Also, **heart's′-ease′.** [ME HEARTE, EASE]

heart-shaped (härt′shāpt′), *adj.* having the shape of a heart; cordate.

heart·sick (härt′sĭk′), *adj.* 1. sick at heart; grievously depressed or unhappy. 2. characterized by or showing grievous depression. —**heart′sick′ness,** *n.*

heart·sore (härt′sōr′), *adj.* 1. sore at heart; grieved. 2. showing grief.

heart·strick·en (härt′strĭk′ən), *adj.* deeply affected with grief, etc. Also, **heart-struck** (härt′strŭk′).

heart·strings (härt′strĭngz′), *n.pl.* the deepest feelings; the strongest affections: *to pull at one's heartstrings.*

heart·throb (härt′thrŏb′), *n.* a passionate or sentimental emotion.

heart-to-heart (härt′tə härt′), *adj.* frank; sincere.

heart-whole (härt′hōl′), *adj.* 1. having the heart untouched by love. 2. wholehearted; sincere.

heart·wood (härt′wŏŏd′), *n.* the hard central wood of the trunk of an exogenous tree; the duramen.

heart·worm (härt′wûrm′), *n.* a filarial worm living in the heart and pulmonary arteries of dogs.

heart·y (här′tĭ), *adj.,* **heartier, heartiest,** *n., pl.* **hearties.** —*adj.* 1. warm-hearted; affectionate; cordial; friendly: *a hearty welcome.* 2. heartfelt; genuine; sincere: *hearty approval or dislike.* 3. enthusiastic or zealous; vigorous: *a hearty laugh.* 4. physically vigorous; strong and well: *hale and hearty.* 5. substantial or satisfying: *a hearty meal.* 6. enjoying or requiring abundant food: *a hearty appetite.* 7. (of soil) fertile. —*n.* 8. a brave or good fellow. 9. a sailor. —**heart′i·ness,** *n.* —Syn. 1. warm, genial. 4. healthy, hale.

heat (hēt), *n.* 1. the quality or condition of being hot. 2. degree of hotness; temperature. 3. the sensation of hotness or warmth; heated bodily condition. 4. *Psychol.* a blended sensation, caused by stimulating the warmth and cold receptors on the skin. 5. a form of energy resident in the random motion of molecules, which will raise the temperature of a body to which it is added. 6. hot condition of the atmosphere or physical environment; hot season or weather. 7. warmth or intensity of feeling: *the heat of an argument.* 8. a fit of passion. 9. the height or greatest intensity of any action: *to do a thing at white heat.* 10. a single intense effort. 11. a single course in or division of a race or other contest. 12. a single operation of heating, as of metal in a furnace, in the heat treating and melting of metals. 13. *Zool.* **a.** sexual excitement in animals, esp. females. **b.** the period or duration of such excitement. —*v.t.* 14. to make hot or warm. 15. to excite in mind or feeling; inflame with passion. —*v.i.* 16. to become hot or warm. 17. to become excited in mind or feeling. [ME *hete,* OE *hǣtu;* akin to G *hitze*] —**heat′less,** *adj.* —Syn. 1. hotness, warmth, caloric. 6. caloricity. 7. ardor, fervor; vehemence, rage. —Ant. 1. cold. 7. indifference.

heat barrier, thermal barrier.

heat capacity, *Physics.* the heat required to raise the temperature of a unit mass of a substance one degree C.

heat·ed (hē′tĭd), *adj.* inflamed; vehement; angry. —**heat′ed·ly,** *adv.*

heat engine, an engine which transforms heat energy into mechanical energy.

heat·er (hē′tər), *n.* 1. an apparatus for heating, as a furnace. 2. *Electronics.* that element of an electron tube which carries the current for heating a cathode.

heath (hēth), *n.* 1. *Brit.* a tract of open and uncultivated land; waste land overgrown with shrubs. 2. any of various low evergreen ericaceous shrubs common on waste land, as *Calluna vulgaris,* the common heather of England and Scotland with small pinkish-purple flowers. 3. any plant of the genus *Erica,* or of the family *Ericaceae.* See **ericaceous.** 4. any of several heathlike but not ericaceous shrubs, as *Frankenia lævis* (**sea heath**) of the European coasts. [ME; OE *hǣth,* c. D and G *heide*] —**heath′like′,** *adj.*

heath aster, a pasture weed, *Aster ericoides,* with small white heads, very abundant in the eastern U.S.

heath·ber·ry (hēth′bĕr′ĭ), *n., pl.* **-ries.** 1. crowberry. 2. any berry found on heaths, esp. the bilberry.

heath·bird (hēth′bûrd′), *n.* the black grouse.

heath cock, the male heathbird.

hea·then (hē′thən), *n., pl.* **-thens, -then,** *adj.* —*n.* 1. an unconverted individual of a people which does not acknowledge the God of the Bible; a Gentile or

pagan. **2.** an irreligious or unenlightened person. —*adj.*
3. pagan; pertaining to the heathen. **4.** irreligious or unenlightened. [ME *hethen*, OE *hæthen*, n., adj., c. D *heiden*, n., G *heide*, n., Icel. *heidhinn*, adj.; commonly explained as meaning orig. heath dweller. See HEATH¹, and cf. PAGAN] —**hea'then·ness**, *n.*
—Syn. **4.** HEATHEN, PAGAN are both applied to peoples who are not Christian, Jewish, or Moslem. HEATHEN is often distinctively applied to unenlightened or barbaric idolaters, such as the tribes of Africa: *heathen rites, idols.* PAGAN, though applying to any of the more civilized peoples not worshiping according to the three religions mentioned above, is almost exclusively used in speaking of the ancient Greeks and Romans: *a pagan poem, a pagan civilization.*

hea·then·dom (hē'thən dəm), *n.* **1.** heathenism; heathen worship or customs. **2.** heathen lands or people.

hea·then·ish (hē'thən ish), *adj.* **1.** pertaining to the heathen. **2.** like or befitting the heathen; barbarous. —**hea'then·ish·ly**, *adv.* —**hea'then·ish·ness**, *n.*

hea·then·ism (hē'thə nĭz'əm), *n.* **1.** the condition, belief, or practice of heathen. **2.** pagan worship; irreligion. **3.** barbaric morals or behavior; barbarism.

hea·then·ize (hē'thə nīz'), *v.*, **-ized**, **-izing.** —*v.t.* **1.** to make heathen or heathenish. —*v.i.* **2.** to become heathen or heathenish. **3.** to practice heathenism.

hea·then·ry (hē'thən rĭ), *n.* **1.** heathenism. **2.** heathen people; the heathen.

heath·er (hĕth'ər), *n.* any of various heaths, esp. *Calluna vulgaris* (Scotch heather). See heath (def. 2). [b. HEATH and obs. *hadder* heather (orig. uncert.)]

heath·er·y (hĕth'ər ĭ), *adj.* **1.** of or like heather. **2.** abounding in heather. Also, **heath·y** (hē'thĭ).

heath grass, a European grass, *Sieglingia decumbens*, growing in spongy, wet, cold soils. Also, **heather grass.**

heath hen, 1. an extinct American bird, *Tympanuchus cupido cupido*, closely related to the prairie chicken (*T. c. pinnatus*). **2.** the female black grouse.

heat lightning, flashes of light near the horizon on summer evenings, reflections of more distant lightning.

heat of fusion, the heat required to melt a unit mass of a solid, already at the melting temperature.

heat of vaporization, the heat required to convert a unit mass of liquid into a vapor, without a rise in temperature.

heat pump, a device which, by means of a compressible refrigerant, transfers heat from a body (the atmosphere, the earth, a lake, etc.) and then either pumps it back into the body (for heating) or elsewhere (for cooling).

heat·stroke (hēt'strōk'), *n.* collapse or fever caused by exposure to excessive heat.

heat wave, 1. an air mass of high temperature, covering an extended area and moving relatively slowly. **2.** a prolonged period of excessively warm weather.

heaume (hōm), *n.* a large supplemental medieval headpiece reaching to the shoulders and worn over an inner helmet. [t. F. See HELMET]

heave (hēv), *v.*, **heaved** or (*esp. Naut.*) **hove**; **heaving**; *n.* —*v.t.* **1.** to raise or lift with effort or force; hoist. **2.** to lift and throw, often with effort or force: *to heave an anchor overboard.* **3.** *Naut.* to haul, draw, or pull, as by a cable. **4.** to utter laboriously or painfully: *to heave a sigh.* **5.** to cause to rise and fall with or as with a swelling motion. **6.** to raise or force up in a swelling movement; force to bulge. **7.** *Geol.* to cause a horizontal displacement in (a stratum, vein, etc.). See heave (def. 18). **8. heave to,** to stop the headway of (a vessel), esp. by bringing the head to the wind and trimming the sails so that they act against one another. —*v.i.* **9.** to rise and fall with or as with a swelling motion. **10.** to breathe with effort; pant. **11.** to vomit; retch. **12.** to rise as if thrust up, as a hill; swell or bulge. **13.** *Naut.* **a.** to haul or pull, as at a cable; to push, as at the bar of a capstan. **b.** to move a ship, or move as a ship does, by such action. **c.** to move or go (fol. by *about, ahead*, etc.). **14. heave in sight,** to rise into view as from below the horizon, as a ship. **15. heave to,** *Naut.* to heave a vessel to. —*interj.* **16. heave ho!,** an exclamation used by sailors when heaving the anchor up, etc. —*n.* **17.** act of heaving. **18.** *Geol.* the horizontal component of the apparent displacement resulting from a fault, measured in a vertical plane perpendicular to its strike. **19.** (*pl. construed as sing.*) a disease of horses, similar to asthma in man, characterized by difficult breathing; broken wind. [ME *heve(n)*, OE *hebban* (pret. *hōf, hefde*, pp. *hafen*), c. G *heben*; akin to L *capere* take] —Syn. **1.** See raise.

heav·en (hĕv'ən), *n.* **1.** the abode of God, the angels, and the spirits of the righteous after death; the place or state of existence of the blessed after the mortal life. **2.** (*cap., often pl.*) the celestial powers; God. **3.** a euphemistic term for God in various emphatic expressions: *for heaven's sake.* **4.** (*chiefly pl.*) the sky or firmament, or expanse of space surrounding the earth. **5.** a place or state of supreme bliss: *a heaven on earth.* **6.** See seventh heaven. [ME *heven*, OE *hefen, heofon* (c. MLG *heven*), appar. akin to Goth. *himins*, Icel. *himinn*]

heav·en-born (hĕv'ən bôrn'), *adj.* **1.** very talented; born with a special aptitude. **2.** of heavenly birth.

heav·en·ly (hĕv'ən lĭ), *adj.* **1.** resembling or befitting heaven; blissful; beautiful: *a heavenly spot.* **2.** of or in the heavens: *the heavenly bodies.* **3.** of, belonging to, or coming from the heaven of God, the angels, etc. **4.** celestial or divine: *heavenly peace.* —**heav'en·li·ness**, *n.* —Syn. **4.** blessed, beatific. —Ant. **4.** infernal, hellish.

heav·en·ward (hĕv'ən wərd), *adv.* **1.** Also, **heav'en·wards.** toward heaven. —*adj.* **2.** directed toward heaven.

heav·er (hē'vər), *n.* **1.** one who or that which heaves. **2.** *Naut.* a staff, generally from two to three feet long, used for twisting or heaving tight rope or strap.

heaves (hēvz), *n.* See heave (def. 19).

heav·i·er-than-air (hĕv'ĭ ər than âr'), *adj. Aeron.* **1.** of greater specific gravity than the air, as airplanes. **2.** of or pertaining to such aircraft.

heav·i·ly (hĕv'ə lĭ), *adv.* **1.** with great weight or burden: *a heavily loaded wagon.* **2.** in an oppressive manner: *cares weigh heavily upon him.* **3.** severely; intensely: *to suffer heavily.* **4.** densely; thickly; *heavily wooded.* **5.** laboriously; sluggishly: *he walked heavily across the room.*

heav·i·ness (hĕv'ĭ nĭs), *n.* state or quality of being heavy; weight; burden; gravity.

Heav·i·side (hĕv'ĭ sīd'), *n.* **Oliver,** 1850–1925, British physicist.

Heaviside layer, the lower region, or regions, of the ionosphere chiefly responsible for the reflection of radio waves of certain frequencies, thus making long-distance short-wave radio communication possible; Kennelly-Heaviside layer. [named after Oliver HEAVISIDE]

heav·y (hĕv'ĭ), *adj.*, **heavier, heaviest**, *n.*, *pl.* **heavies**, *adv.* —*adj.* **1.** of great weight; hard to lift or carry: *a heavy load.* **2.** of great amount, force, intensity, etc.: *a heavy vote.* **3.** bearing hard upon; burdensome; harsh; distressing: *heavy taxes.* **4.** having much weight in proportion to bulk; being of high specific gravity: *a heavy metal.* **5.** broad, thick, or coarse; not delicate: *heavy lines.* **6.** of more than the usual, average, or specified weight: *heavy freight.* **7.** *Mil.* **a.** heavily armed or equipped. **b.** of the larger sizes: *heavy weapons.* **8.** serious; intense: *a heavy offense.* **9.** hard to deal with; trying; difficult: *a heavy task.* **10.** being such in an unusual degree: *a heavy buyer.* **11.** weighted or laden: *air heavy with moisture.* **12.** depressed with trouble or sorrow; showing sorrow: *a heavy heart.* **13.** overcast or cloudy: *heavy sky.* **14.** clumsy; slow in movement or action. **15.** without vivacity or interest; ponderous; dull: *a heavy style.* **16.** loud and deep: *a heavy sound.* **17.** exceptionally dense in substance; insufficiently raised or leavened; thick: *heavy bread.* **18.** not easily digested: *heavy food.* **19.** pregnant. **20.** *Theat.* sober, serious, or somber: *a heavy part.* **21.** *Chem.* referring to that isotope of greater atomic weight: *heavy hydrogen.* —*n.* **22.** *Theat.* **a.** a villainous part or character. **b.** an actor who plays villainous parts or characters. **23.** *Mil.* a gun of great weight or large caliber. —*adv.* **24.** heavily. [ME *hevi*, OE *hefig*, der. *hefe* weight; akin to HEAVE,V.]
—Syn. **1.** ponderous, massive. **8.** HEAVY, MOMENTOUS, WEIGHTY refer to anything having a considerable amount of figurative weight. HEAVY suggests the carrying of a figurative burden: *words heavy with menace.* MOMENTOUS emphasizes the idea of great and usually serious consequences: *a momentous occasion, statement.* WEIGHTY, seldom used literally, refers to something heavy with importance, often concerned with public affairs, which may require deliberation and careful judgment: *a weighty matter, problem.* **12.** serious, grave; gloomy, sad. —Ant. **1.** light. **12.** cheerful.

heav·y-armed (hĕv'ĭ ärmd'), *adj.* (formerly) equipped with heavy arms or armor, as troops.

heav·y-du·ty (hĕv'ĭ dū'tĭ, -dōō'-), *adj.* **1.** sturdy; durable. **2.** having a high import or export tax rate.

heavy earth, baryta.

heav·y-hand·ed (hĕv'ĭ hăn'dĭd), *adj.* **1.** oppressive; harsh. **2.** clumsy. —**heav'y-hand'ed·ness**, *n.*

heav·y-heart·ed (hĕv'ĭ här'tĭd), *adj.* sorrowful; melancholy; dejected. —**heav'y-heart'ed·ness**, *n.*

heavy hydrogen, *Chem.* **1.** any of the heavy isotopes of hydrogen. **2.** deuterium, one of these isotopes, occurring in minute quantities in ordinary water. *Symbol:* D or H²; *at. no.:* 1; *at. wt.:* 2.014; *sp. gr.:* 1.1056.

heav·y-lad·en (hĕv'ĭ lā'dən), *adj.* **1.** laden with a heavy burden. **2.** very weary or troubled.

heavy spar, barite.

heavy water, water in which hydrogen atoms have been replaced by deuterium, used mainly as a source of deuterons for experiments in nuclear physics. *Symbol:* D₂O; *sp. gr.:* 1.1056 at 25°C.

heav·y·weight (hĕv'ĭ wāt'), *n.* **1.** one of more than average weight. **2.** a boxer or other contestant in the heaviest group; a fighter of more than 175 pounds. **3.** *Colloq.* a very intelligent or influential person.

Heb., 1. Hebrew. **2.** Hebrews.

heb·do·mad (hĕb'də măd'), *n.* **1.** the number seven. **2.** seven days; a week. [t. L: s. *hebdomas*, t. Gk.]

heb·dom·a·dal (hĕb dŏm'ə dəl), *adj.* weekly. Also, **heb·dom·a·dar·y** (hĕb dŏm'ə dĕr'ĭ). [t. LL: s. *hebdomadālis*] —**heb·dom'a·dal·ly**, *adv.*

He·be (hē'bĭ), *n.* *Gk. Myth.* the goddess of youth and spring, cupbearer (before Ganymede) of Olympus, and wife of Hercules. [t. L, t. Gk.: youth, youthful prime]

he·be·phre·ni·a (hē'bə frē'nĭ ə), *n.* *Psychiatry.* a form of dementia praecox incident to the age of puberty, characterized by childish behavior, hallucinations, and emotional deterioration. [f. Gk.: *hēbē* youth + *phrēn* mind + *-ia* -IA]

He·ber (hē'bər), *n.* **Reginald,** 1783–1826, British bishop and hymn writer.

ăct, āble, dâre, ärt; ĕbb, ēqual; ĭf, īce; hŏt, ōver, ôrder, oil, bŏŏk, ōōze, out; ŭp, ūse, ûrge; ə = a in alone; ch, chief; g, give; ng, ring; sh, shoe; th, thin; th, that; zh, vision. See the full key on inside cover.

heb·e·tate (hĕb′ə tāt′), v., **-tated, -tating,** adj. —v.t., v.i. **1.** to make or become blunt. —adj. **2.** Bot. having a blunt, soft point, as awns. [t. L: m.s. hebetātus, pp., blunted, dulled] —**heb′e·ta′tion,** n.

he·bet·ic (hĭ bĕt′ĭk), adj. Physiol. pertaining to or occurring in puberty. [t. Gk.: m.s. hēbētikós youthful]

heb·e·tude (hĕb′ə tūd′, -tōōd′), n. state of being dull; lethargy. [t. LL: m. hebetūdo, der. L hebes dull]

He·bra·ic (hĭ brā′ĭk), adj. Hebrew. [t. LL: s. Hebraicus, t. Gk.: m. Hebraïkós; r. OE Ebrēisc] —**He·bra′i·cal·ly,** adv.

He·bra·ism (hē′brā ĭz′əm, -brĭ′-), n. **1.** a Hebrew idiom. **2.** Hebrew character, spirit, thought, or practice.

He·bra·ist (hē′brā ĭst, -brĭ′-), n. **1.** one versed in Hebrew learning. **2.** a specialist in Hebrew philology. **3.** one imbued with the Hebrew spirit.

He·bra·is·tic (hē′brā ĭs′tĭk, -brĭ′-), adj. pertaining to Hebraists or Hebraism. Also, **He′bra·is′ti·cal.**

He·bra·ize (hē′brā īz′, -brĭ′-), v., **-ized, -izing.** —v.t. **1.** to make Hebrew. —v.i. **2.** to become Hebrew. **3.** to conform to the Hebrew usage or type. **4.** to use a Hebrew idiom or manner of speech. [t. Gk.: s. hebraízein speak Hebrew]

He·brew (hē′brōō), n. **1.** a member of that branch of the Semitic race descended from the line of Abraham; an Israelite; a Jew. **2.** a Semitic language, the language of the ancient Hebrews, which although not a vernacular after 100 B.C. was retained as the scholarly and liturgical language of Jews and now is used as the language of Israeli Jews. —adj. **3.** of or pertaining to the Hebrews or their language. [ME Ebreu, t. OF, t. ML: m.s. Ebreus, L Hebraeus, t. Gk.: m. Hebraîos, t. Aram.: m. ʿEbhrāyā, t. Heb.: m. ʾIbhrī, said to mean "one from beyond"; r. OE Ebrēas (pl.), t. ML: m. Ebrēi]

He·brews (hē′brōōz), n. a New Testament epistle, preserved among the Epistles of Paul.

Heb·ri·des (hĕb′rə dēz′), n.pl. a group of islands off the W coast of and belonging to Scotland. 61,800 pop. (1931); ab. 2900 sq. mi. Also, **Western Islands.** —**Heb′ri·de′an,** adj.

He·bron (hē′brən), n. a city in Jordan. 35,983 (1952).

Hec·a·te (hĕk′ə tĭ; in Shak. hĕk′ĭt), n. Gk. Myth. a goddess of the moon, earth, and infernal regions, also associated with sorcery and witchcraft. Also, **Hekate.** [t. L, t. Gk.: m. Hekátē, prop. fem. of hékatos far-darting (epithet of Apollo)]

hec·a·tomb (hĕk′ə tōm′, -tōōm′), n. **1.** a great public sacrifice, orig. of a hundred oxen, as to the Greek gods. **2.** any great slaughter. [t. L: m. hecatombē, t. Gk.: m. hekatómbē]

Hecht (hĕkt), n. **Ben,** 1894–1964, U.S. writer.

heck·le (hĕk′əl), v., **-led, -ling,** n. —v.t. **1.** Also, **hatchel.** to badger or torment; harass, esp. a public speaker, with questions and jibes. **2.** to cut (flax or hemp) with a hatchel. [der. HECKLE, n.] —n. **3.** hatchel. [late ME hechele, n., phonetic var. of hechele; akin to HACKLE¹, HATCHEL] —**heck′ler,** n. —**heck′ling,** n.

hec·tare (hĕk′târ), n. a surface measure, the common unit of land measure in the metric system, equal to 100 ares, or 10,000 square meters, equivalent to 2.471 acres. Also, **hektare.** [t. F. See HECTO-, ARE²]

hec·tic (hĕk′tĭk), adj. **1.** characterized by great excitement, passions, etc.: hectic pleasures. **2.** marking a particular habit or condition of body, as the fever of phthisis (**hectic fever**) when this is attended by flushed cheeks (**hectic flush**), hot skin, and emaciation. **3.** pertaining to or affected with such fever; consumptive. —n. **4.** a hectic fever. **5.** a hectic flush. **6.** a consumptive person. [t. LL: s. hecticus, t. Gk.: m. hektikós habitual, hectic] —**hec′ti·cal·ly,** adv.

hecto-, a word element meaning "hundred," used in the metric system to indicate the multiplication of the unit by 100. [comb. form representing Greek hekatón]

hec·to·cot·y·lus (hĕk′tə kŏt′ə ləs), n., pl. **-li** (-lī′). Zool. a modified arm of the male of certain cephalopods which is used to transfer sperm into the female. [NL, f. hecto- HECTO- + m. Gk. kotýlē cup]

hec·to·gram (hĕk′tə grăm′), n. Metric System. a unit of 100 grams, equivalent to 3.527 ounces avoirdupois. Also, **hektogram;** esp. Brit., **hec′to·gramme′.**

hec·to·graph (hĕk′tə grăf′, -gräf′), n. **1.** a process for making copies of a writing, etc., from a prepared gelatin surface to which the original writing has been transferred. **2.** the apparatus used. —v.t. **3.** to copy with the hectograph.

hec·to·li·ter (hĕk′tə lē′tər), n. Metric System. a unit of capacity of 100 liters, equivalent to 2.8378 bushels, or 26.418 U.S. gallons. Also, **hektoliter;** esp. Brit., **hec′to·li′tre.**

hec·to·me·ter (hĕk′tə mē′tər), n. Metric System. a measure of length equal to 100 meters, or 328.08 ft. Also, esp. Brit., **hec′to·me′tre.**

Hec·tor (hĕk′tər), n. **1.** the eldest son of Priam and husband of Andromache: the noblest of Homer's heroes, slain by Achilles. **2.** (l.c.) a blustering, domineering fellow; a swashbuckler; a bully. —v.t. **3.** (l.c.) to treat with insolence; bully; torment. —v.i. **4.** (l.c.) to act in a blustering, domineering way; be a bully.

Hec·u·ba (hĕk′yŏŏ bə), n. Gk. Legend. the wife of Priam.

he'd (hēd; unstressed ēd, ĭd), contraction of: **1.** he had. **2.** he would.

hed·dle (hĕd′əl), n. (in a loom) one of the sets of vertical cords or wires, forming the principal part of the harness which guides the warp threads. [metathetic var. of heald, OE hefeld thread (for weaving)]

hedge (hĕj), n., v., **hedged, hedging.** —n. **1.** a row of bushes or small trees planted close together, esp. when forming a fence or boundary. **2.** any barrier or boundary. **3.** an act or a means of hedging a bet or the like. —v.t. **4.** to enclose with or separate by a hedge (often fol. by in, off, about, etc.): to hedge a garden. **5.** to surround, as with a hedge; hem in (often fol. by in). **6.** to surround so as to prevent escape or hinder free movement; obstruct (often fol. by in or up): to be hedged by difficulties. **7.** to protect (a bet, etc.) by taking some offsetting risk. —v.i. **8.** to turn aside; swerve; avoid an open or decisive course. **9.** to protect a bet, speculation, etc., by taking some offsetting risk. **10.** Finance. to enter transactions that will protect against loss through a compensatory price movement. **11.** to hide as in a hedge; skulk. [ME hegge, OE hegge (oblique case), c. G hecke. Cf. HAW¹, HAY¹]

hedge garlic, an erect cruciferous herb, Sisymbrium officinale, with a garliclike odor.

hedge·hog (hĕj′hŏg′, -hôg′), n. **1.** an insectivorous mammal frequenting hedges and gardens, having spiny hairs on the back and sides, and found esp. in Europe but not in America (not to be confused with the porcupine). **2.** U.S. the porcupine.

Hedgehog,
Erinaceus europaeus
(10 to 11 in. long)

hedge·hop (hĕj′hŏp′), v.i. to fly an airplane at a very low altitude, as for spraying crops, bombing in warfare, etc. —**hedge′hop′per,** n. —**hedge′hop′ping,** n., adj.

hedge hyssop, 1. any of the low herbs constituting the scrophulariaceous genus Gratiola, as G. officinalis, a medicinal species of Europe. **2.** any of certain similar plants, as Scutellaria minor, an English skullcap.

hedg·er (hĕj′ər), n. Brit. **1.** one who makes or repairs hedges. **2.** one who hedges in betting, etc.

hedge·row (hĕj′rō′), n. a row of bushes or trees forming a hedge.

hedge sparrow, a small European passerine bird, Prunella modularis, which frequents hedges.

hedg·y (hĕj′ĭ), adj. abounding in hedges.

He·din (hĕ dēn′), n. **Sven Anders** (svĕn än′dərs), 1865–1952, Swedish explorer in Asia.

He·djaz (hē jăz′; Arab. hĕ zhäz′), n. Hejaz.

he·don·ic (hē dŏn′ĭk), adj. **1.** pertaining to or consisting in pleasure. **2.** pertaining to hedonism or hedonics. [t. Gk.: m.s. hēdonikós pleasurable] —**he·don′i·cal·ly,** adv.

he·don·ics (hē dŏn′ĭks), n. Psychol. the study of pleasurable and painful states of consciousness.

he·don·ism (hē′də nĭz′əm), n. **1.** the doctrine that pleasure or happiness is the highest good. **2.** devotion to pleasure. —**he′do·nist,** n., adj. —**he′do·nis′tic,** adj. —**he′do·nis′ti·cal·ly,** adv.

-hedron, a combining form denoting geometrical solid figures having a certain number of faces, as in polyhedron. [t. Gk.: etymological m. -edron, neut. of -edros, adj., having bases, -sided, der. hédra seat, base]

heed (hēd), v.t. **1.** to give attention to; regard; notice. —v.i. **2.** to give attention; have regard. —n. **3.** careful attention; notice; observation (usually with give or take). [ME hede(n), OE hēdan, c. G hüten attend to; mind; akin to HOOD, n.] —**heed′er,** n. —Syn. **1.** note, observe, consider. **3.** consideration, care.

heed·ful (hēd′fəl), adj. attentive; mindful: heedful of others. —**heed′ful·ly,** adv. —**heed′ful·ness,** n.

heed·less (hēd′lĭs), adj. careless; thoughtless; unmindful. —**heed′less·ly,** adv. —**heed′less·ness,** n.

hee·haw (hē′hô′), n. **1.** the braying sound made by an ass. **2.** rude laughter. —v.i. **3.** to bray. [imit.]

heel¹ (hēl), n. **1.** (in man) the back part of the foot, below and behind the ankle. **2.** an analogous part in other vertebrates. **3.** either hind foot or hoof of some animals, as the horse. **4.** the foot as a whole: small fauns with cloven heel. **5.** the part of a stocking, shoe, or the like, covering the heel. **6.** a solid part of wood, rubber, etc., attached to the sole of a shoe, under the heel. **7.** something resembling the human heel in position, shape, etc.: heel of bread. **8.** the latter or concluding part of anything: heel of a session. **9.** Naut. **a.** the after end of a ship's keel. **b.** the lower part of a mast, a boom, a sternpost, a rafter, etc. **10.** the crook in the head of a golf club. **11.** Some special noun phrases are: **at one's heels,** close behind one. **down at the heels, 1.** having the shoe heels worn down. **2.** shabby. **3.** slipshod or slovenly. **take to one's heels,** to run off or away. **to heel, 1.** close behind: the dog followed the hunter to heel. **2.** subservient. —v.t. **12.** to follow at the heels of; chase closely. **13.** to furnish with heels, as shoes. **14.** to perform (a dance) with the heels. **15.** Golf. to strike the (ball) with the heel of the club. **16.** to arm (a gamecock) with spurs. —v.i. **17.** to follow at one's heels. **18.** to use the heels, as in dancing. [ME; OE hēl(a), appar. der. hōh HOCK. Cf. D hiel, Icel. hæll] —**heel′less,** adj.

heel[2] (hēl), *v.i.* **1.** (of a ship, etc.) to lean to one side; cant; tilt. —*v.t.* **2.** to cause to lean or cant. —*n.* **3.** a heeling movement; a cant. [earlier *heeld,* ME *helde*(n), OE *h*(*i*)*eldan* bend, incline, der. *heald,* adj., sloping]

heel[3] (hēl), *n. Colloq.* a cad; a low character. [special use of HEEL[1]. See HEELER]

heel-and-toe (hēl′ən tō′), *adj.* denoting a pace, as in walking contests, in which the heel of the front foot touches ground before the toes of the rear one leave it.

heel·er (hē′lər), *n.* **1.** one who heels. **2.** *U.S. Slang.* a servile follower or hanger-on of a political boss: *ward heeler.* [see HEEL[1], sec. 11: TO HEEL, def. 2]

heel·piece (hēl′pēs′), *n.* **1.** a piece serving as or fitted to a heel of a shoe or stocking. **2.** a terminal piece or part of anything.

heel·post (hēl′pōst′), *n.* a post made to withstand strain, forming or fitted to the heel or end of something, as the post on which a gate or door is hinged.

heel·tap (hēl′tăp′), *n.* **1.** a layer of leather or the like in a shoe heel; a lift. **2.** a small portion of liquor left in a glass after drinking.

heft (hĕft), *n.* **1.** *U.S. and Brit. Dial.* weight; heaviness. **2.** *U.S. Colloq.* the bulk or main part. —*v.t.* **3.** to try the weight of by lifting. **4.** *U.S. Colloq. and Brit. Dial.* to heave or lift. [der. HEAVE]

heft·y (hĕf′tĭ), *adj.,* **heftier, heftiest.** *Colloq.* **1.** heavy; weighty. **2.** big and strong; powerful; muscular.

He·gel (hā′gəl), *n.* Georg Wilhelm Friedrich (gā ōr KH′ vĭl′hĕlm frē′drĭKH), 1770–1831, German philosopher.

He·ge·li·an (hā gā′lĭ ən, hĭ jē′-), *adj.* **1.** of or pertaining to Hegel or to Hegelianism. —*n.* **2.** one who accepts the philosophical opinions of Hegel.

He·ge·li·an·ism (hā gā′lĭ ən ĭz′əm, hĭ jē′-), *n.* the philosophical system of Hegel, which during the second quarter of the 19th century was the leading system of metaphysical thought in Germany. It is characterized by the **Hegelian dialectic,** the scheme of which is *thesis, antithesis, synthesis* (i.e., an original tendency, its opposing tendency, and their unification in a new movement).

he·gem·o·ny (hĭ jĕm′ə nĭ, hĕj′ə mō′nĭ), *n., pl.* **-nies.** **1.** leadership or predominant influence exercised by one state over others, as in a confederation. **2.** leadership; predominance. [t. Gk.: m.s. *hēgemonia*]

he·gi·ra (hĭ jī′rə, hĕj′ə rə), *n.* **1.** the flight of Mohammed from persecutions in Mecca to his successes in Medina. The date, A.D. 622, is the starting point in the Mohammedan calendar. **2.** the Mohammedan era itself. **3.** (*l.c.*) a flight similar to Mohammed's. Also, Hejira. [t. ML, t. Ar.: m. *hijra* departure, migration]

he·gu·men (hĭ gū′mĕn), *n. Gk. Orth. Ch.* the head of a monastery. Also, **he·gu·me·nos** (hĭ gū′mə nŏs′). [t. ML: s. *hēgumenus,* t. Gk.: m. *hēgoúmenos,* prop. ppr. of *hēgeîsthai* lead]

Hei·del·berg (hī′dəl bûrg′; *Ger.* hī′dəl bĕr KH′), *n.* a city in SW West Germany, in Baden-Württemberg. 128,250 (est. 1955).

Heidelberg jaw, *Anthropol.* a lower jaw supposed to belong to a very early human species, found in 1907 near Heidelberg, Germany.

Heidelberg man, the primitive man reconstructed from the Heidelberg jaw.

hei·duc (hī′dŏŏk), *n.* Haiduk. Also, **Hei′dku.**

heif·er (hĕf′ər), *n.* a cow that has not produced a calf and is under three years of age. [ME *hayfre,* OE *hēa*(*h*)*f*(*o*)*re, hēahfru.* f. *hēah* HIGH (i.e. grown) + -*fore,* fem. equivalent of *fearr* bull. Cf. Gk. *póris* young cow]

hei·fetz (hī′fĭts), *n.* Jascha (yä′shə), born 1901, a Russian-born violinist in the U.S.

heigh (hā, hī), *interj.* an exclamation used to call attention, give encouragement, etc.

heigh-ho (hī′hō′, hā′-), *interj.* an exclamation of surprise, exultation, melancholy, or weariness.

height (hīt), *n.* **1.** state of being high. **2.** extent upward; altitude; stature; distance upward; elevation: *height of an object above the ground.* **3.** considerable or great altitude or elevation. **4.** a high place or level; a hill or mountain. **5.** the highest part; the top; apex. **6.** the highest or culminating point; utmost degree: *the height of the season.* **7.** high degree, as of a quality. [ME; OE *hīehtho, hēahthu.* See HIGH, -TH[1]] —Syn. **2.** HEIGHT, ALTITUDE, ELEVATION refer to distance above a level. HEIGHT denotes extent upward (as from foot to head) as well as any measurable distance above a given level: *the tree has a height of 10 feet; they climbed to a great height.* ALTITUDE usually refers to the distance, determined by instruments, above a given level: *altitude of an airplane.* ELEVATION implies a distance to which something has been raised or uplifted above a level: *a hill's elevation above sea level.* **5.** summit. **6.** zenith, culmination. —Ant. **2.** depth.

height·en (hī′tən), *v.t.* **1.** to increase the height of; make higher. **2.** to increase the intensity of, as in a drawing: *to heighten a picture with highlights of Chinese white.* —*v.i.* **3.** to become higher. **4.** to increase; augment. —**height′en·er,** *n.* —Syn. **1.** See elevate.

height-to-pa·per (hīt′tə pā′pər), *n. Print.* the standard height of type, in the U.S. 0.9186 of an inch.

heil (hīl), *interj. German.* hail! (a greeting).

Heil·bronn (hīl′brŏn), *n.* a city in SW West Germany, in Baden-Württemberg. 73,100 (est. 1953).

Hei·lung·kiang (hā′lŏŏng′jyäng′), *n.* a province in NE China, in Manchuria. 11,897,309 pop. (1953). 108,880 sq. mi.

Heim·dall (hām′däl), *n. Scand. Myth.* a god of light, the guardian against the giants of the bridge of the gods; the slayer of Loki. [t. Icel.: s. *Heimdallr*]

Hei·ne (hī′nə), *n.* Heinrich (hīn′rĭKH), 1797–1856, German lyric and satiric poet, journalist, and critic.

hei·nous (hā′nəs), *adj.* hateful; odious; gravely reprehensible: *a heinous offense.* [ME *heynous,* t. OF: m. *hainos,* der. *haine* hatred, der. *haïr* hate; of Gmc. orig. and akin to HATE] —**hei′nous·ly,** *adv.* —**hei′nous·ness,** *n.* —Syn. wicked, infamous. —Ant. trivial.

heir (âr), *n.* **1.** *Anglo-American Law.* one who inherits, or has a right of inheritance in, the (real) property of an intestate person. **2.** *Civil Law.* one who inherits the property of a deceased person, testate or intestate, and is liable for the payments of the debts of the deceased and of the legacies. **3.** one to whom something falls or is due. —*v.t.* **4.** to inherit; succeed to. [ME, t. OF, g. L *hēres*] —**heir′less,** *adj.*

heir apparent, *pl.* **heirs apparent.** an heir whose right is indefeasible, provided he survives the ancestor.

heir·dom (âr′dəm), *n.* heirship; inheritance.

heir·ess (âr′ĭs), *n.* **1.** a female heir. **2.** a woman inheriting or expected to inherit great wealth.

heir·loom (âr′lŏŏm′), *n.* **1.** any family possession transmitted from generation to generation. **2.** *Law.* a chattel that because of its close connection with the mansion house descends to the heir, as a portrait of an ancestor, etc. [f. HEIR + LOOM[1], orig. tool or implement]

heir presumptive, an heir whose expectation may be defeated by the birth of a nearer heir.

heir·ship (âr′shĭp), *n.* the position or rights of an heir; right of inheritance; inheritance.

He·jaz (hē jăz′; *Arab.* hĕ zhäz′), *n.* a former independent kingdom in W Arabia, bordering on the Red Sea, now forming a part of Saudi Arabia: the holy cities of Islam, Mecca and Medina, are in Hejaz. ab. 2,000,000 pop.; ab. 150,000 sq. mi. *Cap.:* Mecca. Also, **Hedjaz.**

He·ji·ra (hĭ jī′rə, hĕj′ə rə), *n.* Hegira.

Hek·a·te (hĕk′ə tĭ; *in Shak.* hĕk′ĭt), *n.* Hecate.

hek·tare (hĕk′târ), *n.* hectare.

hek·to·gram (hĕk′tə grăm′), *n.* hectogram.

hek·to·li·ter (hĕk′tə lē′tər), *n.* hectoliter.

Hel (hĕl), *n. Scand. Myth.* the goddess of Niflheim, the realm of the dead: the daughter of Loki. [t. Icel.]

held (hĕld), *v.* pt. and pp. of **hold.**

Hel·en (hĕl′ən), *n.* the beautiful daughter of Zeus and Leda, and wife of Menelaus of Sparta. Her abduction by Paris caused the Trojan war. See **apple of discord.**

Hel·e·na (hĕl′ə nə), *n.* the capital of Montana, in the W part. 20,227 (1960).

Hel·go·land (hĕl′gō länt′), *n.* a German island in the North Sea: its heavy fortifications were destroyed, 1947; British naval victory in nearby **Helgoland Bight,** 1914. 148 pop. (1953). ¼ sq. mi. Also, **Heligoland.**

heli-, var. of **helio-,** before vowels, as in *helianthus.*

he·li·a·cal (hĭ lī′ə kəl), *adj. Astron.* pertaining to or occurring near the sun, esp. applied to such risings and settings of a star as are most nearly coincident with those of the sun while yet being visible. Also, **he·li·ac** (hē′lĭ ăk′). [f. s. LL *hēliacus* (t. Gk.: m. *hēliakós* of the sun) + -AL[1]] —**he·li′a·cal·ly,** *adv.*

he·li·an·thus (hē′lĭ ăn′thəs), *n.* a sunflower. [NL, f. Gk.: s. *hēlios* sun + m. *ánthos* flower]

hel·i·cal (hĕl′ə kəl), *adj.* pertaining to or having the form of a helix. [f. s. L *helix* HELIX + -AL[1]] —**hel′i·cal·ly,** *adv.*

hel·i·ces (hĕl′ə sēz′), *n.* pl. of **helix.**

hel·i·coid (hĕl′ə koid′; *Aeronaut.* often hē′lə-), *adj.* **1.** coiled or curving like a helix; spiral. —*n.* **2.** *Geom.* a warped surface generated by a straight line so moving as always to cut or touch a fixed helix. [t. Gk.: m.s. *helikoeidēs* of spiral form] —**hel′i·coi′dal,** *adj.* —**hel′i·coi′dal·ly,** *adv.*

Hel·i·con (hĕl′ə kŏn′, -kən), *n.* **1.** a mountain in S Greece, in Boeotia. 5738 ft. **2.** *Gk. Myth.* this mountain regarded as the source of poetry and poetic inspiration. From it flowed the fountains of Aganippe and Hippocrene, associated with the Muses. **3.** (*l.c.*) a tuba in coiled form to be carried over the shoulder in cavalry bands. —**Hel·i·co·ni·an** (hĕl′ə kō′nĭ ən), *adj.*

hel·i·cop·ter (hĕl′ə kŏp′tər; *Aeronaut.* often hē′lə-), *n.* any of a class of heavier-than-air craft which are lifted and sustained in the air by helicoid surfaces or propellers turning on vertical axes by virtue of power supplied from an engine. [t. F: m. *hélicoptère,* f. *hélico-* (comb. form. See HELIX) + m.s. Gk. *pterón* wing]

Hel·i·go·land (hĕl′ə gō länd′), *n.* Helgoland.

helio-, a word element meaning "sun," as in *heliocentric.* Also, **heli-.** [t. Gk., comb. form of *hēlios*]

he·li·o·cen·tric (hē′lĭ ō sĕn′trĭk), *adj. Astron.* **1.** as viewed or measured from the center of the sun. **2.** having or representing the sun as a center.

heliocentric parallax. See parallax (def. 3).

He·li·o·gab·a·lus (hē′lĭ ə găb′ə ləs), *n.* Elagabalus.

he·li·o·gram (hē′lĭ ə grăm′), *n.* a heliographic message. [b. HELIO(GRAPH) and (TELE)GRAM]

he·li·o·graph (hē′lĭ ə grăf′, -gräf′), *n.* **1.** a device for signaling by means of a movable mirror which flashes beams of light to a distance. **2.** an apparatus for photographing the sun. —*v.t., v.i.* **3.** to communicate by heliograph. —**he·li·og·ra·pher** (hē′lĭ ŏg′rə fər), *n.* —**he·li·o·graph′ic,** *adj.* —**he·li·og′ra·phy,** *n.*

He·li·op·o·lis (hē′lĭ ŏp′ə lĭs), *n.* 1. Biblical, **On.** an ancient ruined city in N Egypt, on the Nile delta. 2. ancient Greek name of **Baalbek.**

He·li·os (hē′lĭ ŏs′), *n. Gk. Myth.* the sun god, son of Hyperion, represented as driving a chariot across the heavens. [t. Gk.: the sun, the sun god]

he·li·o·stat (hē′lĭ ə stăt′), *n.* an instrument consisting of a mirror moved by clockwork, for reflecting the sun's rays in a fixed direction.

he·li·o·tax·is (hē′lĭ ə tăk′sĭs), *n.* a phototaxis in response to sunlight. **—he·li·o·tac·tic** (hē′lĭ ə tăk′tĭk), *adj.*

he·li·o·ther·a·py (hē′lĭ ə thĕr′ə pĭ), *n.* treatment of disease by means of sunlight.

he·li·o·trope (hē′lĭ ə trōp′, hĕl′yə- or, *esp. Brit.*, hĕl′yə-), *n.* 1. *Bot.* any plant that turns toward the sun. 2. any herb or shrub of the boraginaceous genus *Heliotropium*, esp. *H. arborescens* (*peruvianum*), a garden plant with small, fragrant purple flowers. 3. the medicinal valerian (*Valeriana officinalis*). 4. light tint of purple; reddish lavender. 5. bloodstone. [t. F, t. L: m.s. *hēliotropium*, t. Gk.: m. *hēliotrópion* sundial, plant, bloodstone]

he·li·o·trop·ic (hē′lĭ ə trŏp′ĭk, -trō′pĭk), *adj. Bot.* growing towards the light. **—he′li·o·trop′i·cal·ly,** *adv.*

he·li·ot·ro·pism (hē′lĭ ŏt′rə pĭz′əm), *n.* heliotropic habit of growth.

he·li·o·type (hē′lĭ ə tīp′), *n., v.,* **-typed, -typing. —n.** 1. a picture or print produced by a photomechanical process in which the impression in ink is taken directly from a prepared gelatin film which has been exposed under a negative. 2. Also, **he·li·o·typ·y** (hē′lĭ ə tī′pĭ). the process itself. **—v.t.** 3. to make a heliotype of. **—he·li·o·typ·ic** (hē′lĭ ə tĭp′ĭk), *adj.*

he·li·o·zo·an (hē′lĭ ə zō′ən), *n.* one of the *Heliozoa,* an order of protozoans, distinguished by a spherical body and radiating pseudopods.

hel·i·port (hĕl′ə pôrt), *n.* a landing place for helicopters, often the roof of a building.

he·li·um (hē′lĭ əm), *n. Chem.* an inert gaseous element present in the sun's atmosphere, certain minerals, natural gas, etc., and also occurring as a radioactive decomposition product, used as a substitute for inflammable gases in dirigible balloons. *Symbol:* He; *at. wt.:* 4.003; *at. no.:* 2; *density:* 0.1785 at 0°C. and 760 mm. pressure. [NL, der. Gk. *hēlios* sun]

he·lix (hē′lĭks), *n., pl.* **helices** (hĕl′ə sēz′), **helixes.** 1. any spiral. 2. a spiral object or part. 3. *Archit.* **a.** a spiral ornament. **b.** a volute under the abacus of the Corinthian capital. 4. *Geom.* the curve assumed by a straight line drawn on a plane when that plane is wrapped round a cylindrical surface of any kind, especially a right circular cylinder, as the curve of a screw thread. 5. *Anat.* the curved fold forming most of the rim of the external ear. See diag. under **ear.** [t. L, t. Gk.: anything of spiral shape]

H. Helix.
in a Corinthian capital (def. 3b)

hell (hĕl), *n.* 1. the place or state of punishment of the wicked after death; the abode of and condemned spirits; Gehenna or Tartarus. 2. any place or state of torment or misery: *a hell on earth.* 3. the powers of evil. 4. anything that causes torment. 5. the abode of the dead; Sheol or Hades. 6. a gambling house. 7. a receptacle into which a tailor throws his shreds or a printer his type. [ME *helle,* OE *hel*(*l*), c. G *hölle.* Cf. HALL.] **—Syn.** 2. inferno, Abaddon, pandemonium, Avernus. **—Ant.** 2. paradise.

he'll (hĕl; *unstressed* hĭl, ĭl), contraction of: 1. he will. 2. he shall.

Hel·las (hĕl′əs), *n.* ancient and modern Greek name of Greece.

hell·bend·er (hĕl′bĕn′dər), *n.* a large aquatic salamander, *Cryptobranchus alleganiensis,* of the Ohio and certain other American rivers.

Hellbender.
Cryptobranchus alleganiensis
(Ab. 18 in. long)

hell·broth (hĕl′brŏth′, -brôth′), *n.* a magical broth prepared for an infernal purpose.

hell·cat (hĕl′kăt′), *n.* 1. an evil-tempered, unmanageable woman. 2. a hag or witch.

hell·div·er (hĕl′dĭ′vər), *n.* a grebe, esp. the American pied-billed grebe.

hel·le·bore (hĕl′ə bōr′), *n.* 1. any plant of the ranunculaceous genus *Helleborus,* esp. *H. niger* (**black hellebore**), a European herb with showy flowers. 2. any of the coarse herbs constituting the melanthaceous genus *Veratrum,* as *V. album* (**European white hellebore**) and *V. viride* (**American white hellebore**). 3. the powdered root of American white hellebore used to kill lice and caterpillars. [t. Gk.: m.s. *hellēboros;* r. earlier *elebor*(*e*), ME *el*(*l*)*bre,* etc., t. L: m. *elleborus*]

Hel·len (hĕl′ən), *n. Gk. Legend.* a king of Phthia (in Thessaly), eponymous ancestor of the Hellenes.

Hel·lene (hĕl′ēn), *n.* a Greek. [t. Gk.: m. *Héllēn*]

Hel·len·ic (hĕ lĕn′ĭk, -lē′nĭk), *adj.* 1. pertaining to the Greeks. **—n.** 2. a group of Indo-European languages, including Greek. 3. Greek, especially Modern Greek.

Hel·len·ism (hĕl′ə nĭz′əm), *n.* 1. ancient Greek culture or ideals. 2. the character or spirit of the Greeks. 3. adoption of Greek speech, ideas, or customs.

Hel·len·ist (hĕl′ən ĭst), *n.* 1. one who adopts the Greek speech, ideas, or customs. 2. one who admires or studies Greek civilization. [t. Gk.: s. *Hellēnistēs*]

Hel·len·is·tic (hĕl′ə nĭs′tĭk), *adj.* 1. pertaining to Hellenists. 2. following or resembling Greek usage. 3. pertaining to the Greeks or their language, culture, etc., after the time of Alexander the Great when Greek characteristics were modified by foreign elements.

Hel·len·ize (hĕl′ə nīz′), *v.,* **-ized, -izing. —v.t.** 1. to make Greek in character. **—v.i.** 2. to adopt Greek ideas or customs. [t. Gk.: m.s. *Hellēnizein*] **—Hel·len·i·za·tion,** *n.* **—Hel′len·iz′er,** *n.*

hel·ler (hĕl′ər), *n., pl.* **heller.** 1. a small German coin formerly current, generally worth half a pfennig. 2. a copper Austrian coin equal to one hundredth of a krone. 3. Czechoslovakian money of account equal to one hundredth of a koruna. [G]

Hel·les (hĕl′ēs), *n.* **Cape,** a cape in European Turkey at the S end of Gallipoli Peninsula.

Hel·les·pont (hĕl′ə spŏnt′), *n.* ancient name of the **Dardanelles.** [t. Gk.: m. *Hellēspontos* sea of HELLE]

hell·fire (hĕl′fīr′), *n.* 1. the fire of hell. 2. punishment in hell.

Hell Gate, a narrow channel in the East River, in New York City.

hell·gram·mite (hĕl′grə mīt′), *n.* the aquatic larva of the dobson, used as a bait by anglers.

hell·hound (hĕl′hound′), *n.* 1. a hound of hell; a demon. 2. a fiendish person. [ME *hellehound,* OE *hellehund* hell's hound]

hell·ion (hĕl′yən), *n. Colloq.* a troublesome, mischief-making person.

hell·ish (hĕl′ĭsh), *adj.* of, like, or befitting hell; infernal; wicked. **—hell′ish·ly,** *adv.* **—hell′ish·ness,** *n.*

hel·lo (hĕ lō′, hə-, hĕl′ō), *interj., n., pl.* **-los,** *v.,* **-loed, -loing. —interj.** 1. an exclamation to attract attention or express greeting. 2. an exclamation of surprise, etc. **—n.** 3. the call "hello." **—v.i.** 4. to call "hello." Also, **hullo.** [var. of HALLO]

helm¹ (hĕlm), *n.* 1. the tiller or wheel by which the rudder of a vessel is controlled. 2. the entire steering apparatus. 3. a moving of the helm. 4. the place or post of control: *the helm of affairs.* **—v.t.** 5. to steer; direct. [ME *helme,* OE *helma;* akin to MHG *helm* handle, Icel. *hjálm* rudder] **—helm′less,** *adj.*

helm² (hĕlm), *n.* 1. *Archaic.* a helmet. **—v.t.** 2. to furnish or cover with a helmet. [ME and OE, c. D and G *helm.* See HELMET]

Hel·mand (hĕl′mənd), *n.* a river flowing from N Afghanistan SW to a lake in E Iran. ab. 650 mi.

hel·met (hĕl′mĭt), *n.* 1. a defensive covering for the head: **a.** any of various forms of protective head covering worn by soldiers, firemen, divers, etc. **b.** medieval armor for the head. **c.** *Fencing, Singlestick, etc.* a protective device for the head and face consisting of reinforced wire mesh. 2. anything resembling a helmet in form or position. [ME, t. OF, dim. of *helme* helm, helmet, t. Gmc. See HELM²] **—hel′met·ed,** *adj.*

Helmets: A. Medieval B. Modern

Helm·holtz (hĕlm′hōlts), *n.* Hermann Ludwig Ferdinand von (hĕr′män lōōt′vĭKH fĕr′dĭ nänt′ fən), 1821-94, German physiologist and physicist.

hel·minth (hĕl′mĭnth), *n.* a worm, especially a parasitic worm. [t. Gk.: s. *hélmins*]

hel·min·thi·a·sis (hĕl′mĭn thī′ə sĭs), *n. Pathol.* a condition characterized by worms in the body. [NL, f. s. Gk. *helminthiān* suffer from worms + -(*i*)*āsis* -(*i*)ASIS]

hel·min·thic (hĕl mĭn′thĭk), *adj.* 1. pertaining to worms. 2. expelling intestinal worms.

hel·min·thol·o·gy (hĕl′mĭn thŏl′ə jĭ), *n.* the science of worms, especially of parasitic worms.

helms·man (hĕlmz′mən), *n., pl.* **-men.** the man at the helm who steers a ship; a steersman.

Hé·lo·ïse (ē lō ēz′), *n.* pupil, mistress, and wife of Abélard, later an abbess. See **Abélard.**

hel·ot (hĕl′ət, hē′lət), *n.* 1. one of the serfs in ancient Sparta, owned by the state and under allotment to landowners. 2. (*l.c.*) a serf or slave; a bondman.

hel·ot·ism (hĕl′ə tĭz′əm, hē′lə-), *n.* serfdom.

hel·ot·ry (hĕl′ə trĭ, hē′lət-), *n.* 1. serfdom; slavery. 2. helots collectively.

help (hĕlp), *v.,* **helped** or (*Archaic*) **holp; helped** or (*Archaic*) **holpen; helping;** *n.* **—v.t.** 1. to coöperate effectively with a person; aid; assist: *to help a man in his work.* 2. to furnish aid to; contribute strength or means to; assist in doing: *remedies that help digestion.* 3. to succor; save. 4. to relieve (someone) in need, sickness, pain, or distress. 5. to refrain from; avoid (with *can* or *cannot*): *he can't help doing it.* 6. to remedy, stop, or prevent: *nothing will help now.* 7. to serve food to at table (fol. by *to*): *to help her to a salad.* 8. **help oneself to,** to take or appropriate at will. **—v.i.** 9. to give aid;

be of service or advantage: *every little bit helps.* —*n.*
10. act of helping; aid or assistance; relief or succor.
11. a person or thing that helps. **12.** a hired helper.
13. a body of such helpers. **14.** *U.S.* a domestic servant or a farm laborer **15.** means of remedying, stopping, or preventing *the thing is done, and there is no help
for it now.* **16.** *Rare or Dial.* a helping (def. 2). [ME
helpe(n), OE *helpan.* c. G *helfen*] —**help′a·ble,** *adj.*
—**Syn. 1.** encourage, befriend; support, second, uphold,
back, abet. HELP, AID, ASSIST, SUCCOR agree in the idea of
furnishing another with something needed, especially when
the need comes at a particular time. HELP implies furnishing
anything that furthers his efforts or relieves his wants or
necessities. AID and ASSIST, somewhat more formal, imply
especially a furthering or seconding of another's efforts.
AID implies a more active helping; ASSIST implies less need
and less help. To SUCCOR is to give timely help and relief
in difficulty or distress. **2.** facilitate, further, promote,
foster. **4.** ameliorate, alleviate, remedy, cure heal. **10.**
support, backing. —**Ant. 1.** hinder. **4.** afflict.
help·er (hĕl′pər), *n.* a person or thing that helps.
—*Syn.* aid, assistant; supporter, backer, auxiliary, ally.
help·ful (hĕlp′fəl), *adj.* giving or affording help; useful.
—**help′ful·ly,** *adv.* —**help′ful·ness,** *n.* —*Syn.* useful,
convenient; beneficial, advantageous.
help·ing (hĕl′pĭng), *n.* **1.** act of one who or that which
helps. **2.** a portion served to a person at one time.
—**help′ing·ly,** *adv.*
help·less (hĕlp′lĭs), *adj.* **1.** unable to help oneself;
weak or dependent: *a helpless invalid.* **2.** without help,
aid, or succor. **3.** incapable, inefficient, or shiftless.
4. *Rare.* affording no help. —**help′less·ly,** *adv.*
—**help′less·ness,** *n.*
help·mate (hĕlp′māt′), *n.* **1.** a companion and helper.
2. a wife or husband. [f. HELP + MATE. Cf. HELPMEET]
help·meet (hĕlp′mēt′), *n.* helpmate. [erroneously
from Gen. 2:18, 20, "an help meet for him"]
Hel·sing·ör (hĕl′sĭng œr′), *n.* a seaport in NE Denmark, on Zealand island: the scene of Shakespeare's
Hamlet. 22,607 (est. 1954). Also, **Elsinore.**
Hel·sin·ki (hĕl′sĭng kē), *n.* a seaport in and the capital
of Finland, on the S coast, 394,511 (est. 1953). Swedish,
Hel·sing·fors (hĕl′sĭng fôrz′, -fôrs′).
hel·ter-skel·ter hĕl′tər skĕl′tər), *adv.* **1.** in headlong, disorderly haste: *to run helter-skelter.* —*n.* **2.** tumultuous haste or disorder. **3.** a helter-skelter flight,
course, or performance. —*adj.* **4.** confused; disorderly;
carelessly hurried. [imit.]
helve (hĕlv), *n., v.,* **helved, helving.** *Chiefly Brit.* —*n.*
1. the handle of an ax, hatchet, hammer, or the like.
—*v.t.* **2.** to furnish with a helve. [ME; OE *h*(*i*)*elfe*]
Hel·vel·lyn (hĕl vĕl′ĭn), *n.* a mountain in NW England. 3118 ft.
Hel·ve·tia (hĕl vē′shə), *n.* **1.** an Alpine region in Roman times, corresponding to the W and N parts of
modern Switzerland. **2.** *Poetic.* Switzerland.
Hel·ve·tian (hĕl vē′shən), *adj.* **1.** of or pertaining to
Helvetia or the Helvetii. **2.** Swiss. —*n.* **3.** one of the
Helvetii. **4.** a Swiss. [f. s. L *Helvētius* + -AN]
Hel·vet·ic (hĕl vĕt′ĭk), *n.* **1.** a Swiss Protestant; a
Zwinglian. —*adj.* **2.** Helvetian.
Hel·ve·ti·i (hĕl vē′shĭ ī′), *n.pl.* the ancient inhabitants
of Helvetia in the time of Julius Caesar. [L]
Hel·ve·tius (hĕl vē′shəs; *Fr.* ĕl vĕ syYs′), *n.* **Claude
Adrien** (klôd ȧ drĕ ăN′). 1715-71, French philosopher.
hem¹ (hĕm), *v.,* **hemmed, hemming,** *n.* —*v.t.* **1.** to enclose or confine (fol. by *in, around,* or *about*): *hemmed in
by enemies.* **2.** to fold back and sew down the edge of
(cloth, a garment, etc.). **3.** to form an edge or border
to or about. —*n.* **4.** the edge made by folding back the
margin of cloth and sewing it down. **5.** the edge or
border of a garment, etc. **6.** the edge, border, or margin
of anything. [ME *hemm*(*e*), OE *hem,* prob. akin to
hamm enclosure]
hem² (hĕm), *interj., n., v.,* **hemmed, hemming.** —*interj.*
1. an utterance resembling a slight clearing of the throat,
used to attract attention, express doubt, etc. —*n.* **2.** the
utterance or sound of "hem." —*v.i.* **3.** to utter the
sound "hem." **4.** to hesitate in speaking. [imit.]
hem-, var. of hemo-, before vowels, as in *hemal.* Also,
haem-. Cf. haemat-.
hema-, var. of hemo-.
he·ma·chrome hē′mə krōm′, hĕm′ə-), *n.* the red
coloring matter of the blood. Also, **haemachrome.**
he·mal (hē′məl), *adj.* **1.** of or pertaining to the blood
or blood vessels. **2.** *Zool.* noting, pertaining to, or on
the side of the body ventral to the spinal axis, containing the heart and great blood vessels. Also, **haemal.**
Hem·ans (hĕm′ənz, hē′mənz), *n.* **Mrs.,** (*Felicia Dorothea Browne*) 1793-1835, British poet.
hemat-, a prefix equivalent to hemo-, as in *hematin.*
Also, **haemat-.**
he·mat·ic (hē măt′ĭk), *adj.* **1.** of or pertaining to
blood; hemic. **2.** acting on the blood, as a medicine.
—*n.* **3.** a hematic medicine. Also, **haematic.** [t. Gk.: m.s.
haimatikós of the blood]
hem·a·tin (hĕm′ə tĭn, hē′mə-), *n.* a pigment containing iron, produced in the decomposition of hemoglobin.
Also, **haematin, hem·a·tine** (hĕm′ə tĭn, -tĭn′, hē′mə-).
hem·a·tin·ic (hĕm′ə tĭn′ĭk, hē′mə-), *n.* **1.** a medicine,
as a compound of iron, which tends to increase the
amount of hematin or hemoglobin in the blood. —*adj.*
2. of or obtained from hematin. Also, **haematinic.**

hem·a·tite (hĕm′ə tīt′, hē′mə-), *n.* a very common
mineral, iron oxide, Fe_2O_3, occurring in steel-gray to
black crystals and in red earthy masses, the principal
ore of iron. Also, **haematite.** [t. L: m.s. *haematites*
hematite, t. Gk.: m. *haimatîtēs* bloodlike] —**hem·a·tit-
ic** (hĕm′ə tĭt′ĭk, hē′mə-), *adj.*
hemato-, a prefix equivalent to hemo-, as in *hemato-
genesis.* Also, **hemat-, haemato-.**
hem·a·to·cele (hĕm′ə tō sēl′, hē′mə-), *n.* *Pathol.* (usually) a hemorrhage imprisoned in membranous tissue.
Also, **haematocele.**
hem·a·toc·ry·al (hĕm′ə tŏk′rĭ əl, -tō krĭ′əl, hē′mə-),
adj. cold-blooded. Also, **haematocryal.**
hem·a·to·gen·e·sis (hĕm′ə tō jĕn′ə sĭs, hē′mə-), *n.*
the formation of blood. Also, **haematogenesis.**
hem·a·tog·e·nous (hĕm′ə tŏj′ə nəs, hē′mə-), *adj.* **1.**
originating in the blood. **2.** blood-producing. Also,
haematogenous.
he·ma·toid (hē′mə toid′, hĕm′ə-), *adj.* bloodlike. Also,
haematoid. [t. Gk.: m.s. *haimatoeidḗs* bloodlike]
he·ma·tol·o·gy (hē′mə tŏl′ə jĭ), *n.* *Med.* the study of
the nature, function, and diseases of the blood. Also,
haematology. [f. HEMATO- + -LOGY]
he·ma·to·ma (hē′mə tō′mə, hĕm′ə-), *n., pl.* **-mata**
(-mə tə), **-mas.** *Pathol.* a swelling filled with extravasated blood. Also, **haematoma.**
hem·a·to·poi·e·sis (hĕm′ə tō poi ē′sĭs, hē′mə-), *n.* the
formation of blood. Also, **haematopoiesis.** [t. NL: m.
haematopoiēsis, f. Gk.: m. *haimato-* HEMATO- + *poíēsis* a
making] —**hem·a·to·poi·et·ic** (hĕm′ə tō poi ĕt′ĭk, hē′-
mə-), *adj.*
he·ma·to·sis (hē′mə tō′sĭs, hĕm′ə-), *n.* **1.** the formation of blood. **2.** *Physiol.* the conversion of venous into
arterial blood; oxygenation in the lungs. Also, **haematosis.** [t. NL: m. *haematosis,* t. Gk.: m. *haimátōsis,* der.
haimatoûn make into blood]
hem·a·to·ther·mal (hĕm′ə tō thûr′məl, hē′mə-), *adj.*
warm-blooded. Also, **haematothermal.**
he·ma·tox·y·lin (hē′mə tŏk′sə lĭn, hĕm′ə-), *n.* **1.** a
colorless or pale-yellow crystalline compound, $C_{16}H_{14}O_6·
3H_2O$, the coloring material of logwood, used as a mor-
dant dye and as an indicator. **2.** haematoxylin. Also,
haematoxylin.
hem·a·to·zo·ön (hĕm′ə tō zō′ŏn, -ən, hē′mə-), *n., pl.*
-zoa (-zō′ə). an animal parasite, usually protozoan,
living in the blood. Also, **haematozoön.** [t. NL: m.
haematozoön. See HEMATO-, -ZOON] —**hem′a·to·zo′ic,**
adj.
hem·e·ly·tron (hē mĕl′ə trŏn′), *n., pl.* **-tra** (-trə).
Entomol. one of the forewings of hemipterous and especially heteropterous insects, coriaceous at the base
and membranous at the tip. Also, **hemielytron.** [var. of
hemielytron, f. HEMI- + ELYTRON]
hem·er·a·lo·pi·a (hĕm′ərə lō′pĭ ə), *n.* day blindness.
hemi-, a prefix meaning "half," as in *hemialgia.* Cf.
semi-. [t. Gk.]
-hemia, var. of -emia.
hem·i·al·gi·a (hĕm′ĭ ăl′jĭ ə), *n.* *Pathol.* pain or neuralgia involving only one side of the body or head.
he·mic (hē′mĭk, hĕm′ĭk), *adj.* hematic. Also, **haemic.**
hem·i·cel·lu·lose (hĕm′ĭ sĕl′yə lōs′), *n.* *Chem.* any of
a group of gummy polysaccharides, intermediate in
complexity between sugar and cellulose, which hydrolyze to monosaccharides more readily than cellulose.
Hem·i·chor·da·ta (hĕm′ĭ kôr dā′tə), *n.pl.* a chordate
subphylum that comprises a large number of small,
widely distributed marine animals.
hem·i·chor·date (hĕm′ĭ kôr′dāt), *adj.* denoting or
pertaining to the *Hemichordata.*
hem·i·cra·ni·a (hĕm′ĭ krā′nĭ ə), *n.* *Pathol.* migraine.
[t. LL, t. Gk.: m. *hēmikrania* a pain on one side of the
head]
hem·i·cy·cle (hĕm′ĭ sī′kəl), *n.* **1.** a semicircle. **2.** a
semicircular structure. [t. F, t. L: m.s. *hēmicyclium,* t.
Gk.: m. *hēmikýklion*]
hem·i·dem·i·sem·i·qua·ver (hĕm′ĭ dĕm′ĭ sĕm′ĭ
kwā′vər), *n. Chiefly Brit. Music.* a sixty-fourth note.
See illus. under **note.**
hem·i·el·y·tron (hĕm′ĭ ĕl′ə trŏn′), *n., pl.* **-tra** (-trə).
hemelytron.
hem·i·he·dral (hĕm′ĭ hē′drəl), *adj.* (of a crystal)
having only half the planes or faces required by the
maximum symmetry of the system to which it belongs.
[f. HEMI- + s. Gk. *hédra* seat, base + -AL¹]
hem·i·hy·drate (hĕm′ĭ hī′drāt), *n. Chem.* a hydrate
in which there are two molecules of the compound for
each molecule of water.
hem·i·mor·phic (hĕm′ĭ môr′fĭk), *adj.* (of a crystal)
having the two ends of an axis unlike in their planes or
modifications; lacking a center of symmetry.
hem·i·mor·phite (hĕm′ĭ môr′fĭt), *n. Brit.* calamine.
he·min (hē′mĭn), *n.* the typical, reddish-brown crystals, of microscopic size, resulting when a sodium chloride crystal, a drop of glacial acetic acid, and some blood
are heated on a slide: used to identify the blood of different species. [f. HEM- + -IN²]
Hem·ing·way (hĕm′ĭng wā′), *n.* **Ernest,** 1898-1961,
U.S. novelist and short-story writer.
hem·i·ple·gi·a (hĕm′ĭ plē′jĭ ə), *n. Pathol.* paralysis of
one side of the body, resulting from a disease of the brain
or of the spinal cord.
he·mip·ter·ous (hĭ mĭp′tər əs), *adj.* belonging or pertaining to insects of the order *Hemiptera,* including the

true bugs (*Heteroptera*), whose forewings are in part thickened and leathery, and the cicadas, leaf hoppers. aphids, etc. (*Homoptera*), whose wings are entirely membranous. [f. HEMI- + s. Gk. *pterón* wing + -OUS]

hem·i·sphere (hĕm′ə·sfïr′), *n.* **1.** half of the terrestrial globe or celestial sphere. **2.** a map or projection of either of these. **3.** the half of a sphere. **4.** *Anat.* either of the lateral halves of the cerebrum. [t. L: m.s. *hēmisphaerium*, t. Gk.: m. *hēmisphaírion*; r. ME *emysperie*, t. OF: m. *emispere*]

hem·i·spher·i·cal (hĕm′ə·sfĕr′ə·kəl), *adj.* **1.** of or pertaining to a hemisphere. **2.** in the form of a hemisphere. Also, **hem′i·spher′ic.** —**hem′i·spher′i·cal·ly,** *adv.*

hem·i·spher·oid (hĕm′ə·sfïr′oid), *n.* half of a spheroid. —**hem′i·spher·oi′dal,** *adj.*

hem·i·stich (hĕm′ə·stĭk′), *n. Pros.* **1.** the exact or approximate half of a stich, or poetic verse or line, esp. as divided by a caesura or the like. **2.** an incomplete line, or a line of less than the usual length. [t. L: m.s. *hemistichium,* t. Gk.: m. *hēmistíchion*]

hem·i·ter·pene (hĕm′ĭ·tûr′pēn), *n.* one of a group of hydrocarbon isomers of the general formula C₅H₈, related to, and half the molecular weight of, the terpenes.

hem·i·trope (hĕm′ə·trōp′), *adj., n. Crystall.* twin. [t. F. See HEMI-, -TROPE] —**hem·i·trop·ic** (hĕm′ə·trŏp′-ĭk), *adj.*

hem·lock (hĕm′lŏk), *n.* **1.** *Chiefly Brit.* a poisonous umbelliferous herb, *Conium maculatum,* with spotted stems, finely divided leaves, and small white flowers, used medicinally as a powerful sedative. **2.** a poisonous drink made from this herb. **3.** any of various other apiaceous herbs, esp. species of the genus *Cicuta* (**water hemlock**). **4.** *U.S.* **a.** the hemlock spruce. **b.** its wood. [ME *hemeluc,* OE *hemlic, hym*(*e*)*lic*(*e*), ? f. *hymele* hop plant + -*k* suffix (see -OCK). Note that hemlock and hops agree in having a sedative effect]

hemlock spruce, any of the trees of the coniferous genus *Tsuga,* esp. a tree of eastern North America, *T. canadensis,* whose bark is used in tanning.

hem·mer (hĕm′ər), *n.* **1.** one who or that which hems. **2.** a sewing-machine attachment for hemming edges.

hemo-, a word element meaning "blood," as in *hemolysis.* Also, **hem-, haem-, haemo-.** Cf. **hema-, haema-, haemat-, haemato-.** [t. Gk.: m. *haimo-,* comb. form of *haima*]

he·mo·glo·bin (hē′mə·glō′bĭn, hĕm′ə-), *n.* the protein coloring matter of the red blood corpuscles, which serves to convey oxygen to the tissues: occurring in reduced form (**reduced hemoglobin**) in venous blood, and in combination with oxygen (**oxyhemoglobin**) in arterial blood. Also, **haemoglobin.** [short for *hematoglobulin,* f. *hemato-* (for HEMATIN) + GLOBULIN]

he·moid (hē′moid), *adj.* bloodlike. Also, **haemoid.**

he·mo·leu·co·cyte (hē′mə·lōō′kə·sīt′, hĕm′ə-), *n. Anat.* any white blood cell that circulates in the blood. Also, **haemoleucocyte, he′mo·leu′ko·cyte′.**

he·mo·ly·sin (hē′mə·lī′sĭn, hĕm′ə-, hī′mŏl′ə-), *n. Immunol.* an antibody which, in coöperation with a material in fresh blood, causes dissolution of the red blood corpuscles. Also, **haemolysin.**

he·mol·y·sis (hī·mŏl′ə·sĭs), *n. Immunol.* the breaking down of the red blood cells with liberation of hemoglobin. Also, **haemolysis.** —**he·mo·lyt·ic** (hē′mə·lĭt′ĭk, hĕm′ə-), *adj.*

Hé·mon (ĕ·môN′), *n.* **Louis** (lwē), 1880–1913, French-Canadian novelist.

he·mo·phil·i·a (hē′mə·fĭl′ĭ·ə, hĕm′ə-), *n. Pathol.* a morbid condition, usually congenital, characterized by a tendency to bleed immoderately, as from an insignificant wound, caused by improper coagulation of the blood. Also, **haemophilia.** [NL: m. *haemophilia,* f. Gk.: m. *haimo-* HEMO- + *philía* affection, fondness]

he·mo·phil·i·ac (hē′mə·fĭl′ĭ·ăk′, hĕm′ə-), *n.* a person or organism which has hemophilia. Also, **haemophiliac.**

he·mo·phil·ic (hē′mə·fĭl′ĭk, hĕm′ə-), *adj.* **1.** affected by hemophilia. **2.** *Biol.* (of bacteria) developing best in a culture containing blood, or in blood itself. Also, **haemophilic.**

he·mop·ty·sis (hī·mŏp′tə·sĭs), *n. Pathol.* the expectoration of blood or bloody mucus. [t. NL: m. *haemoptysis,* f. Gk.: m. *haimo-* HEMO- + *ptýsis* spitting]

hem·or·rhage (hĕm′ə·rĭj, hĕm′rĭj), *n.* a discharge of blood, as from a ruptured blood vessel. Also, **haemorrhage.** [t. L: m.s. *haemorrhagia,* t. Gk.: m. *haimorrhagía* a violent bleeding] —**hem·or·rhag·ic** (hĕm′ə·răj′ĭk), *adj.*

hemorrhagic septicemia, *Vet. Sci.* an acute infectious disease of animals, marked by fever, catarrhal symptoms, pneumonia, and general blood infection.

hem·or·rhoid (hĕm′ə·roid′, hĕm′roid), *n. Pathol.* a dilation of the veins under the skin of the anus; a pile. Also, **haemorrhoid.** [t. L: m.s. *haemorrhoida* piles, t. Gk.: m.s. *haimorrhoís*] —**hem′or·rhoi′dal,** *adj.*

hem·or·rhoid·ec·to·my (hĕm′ə·roi·dĕk′tə·mī), *n., pl.* -**mies.** *Surg.* the operation for removal of hemorrhoids.

he·mo·stat (hē′mə·stăt′, hĕm′ə-), *n.* an instrument or agent used to compress or treat bleeding vessels in order to arrest hemorrhage. Also, **haemostat.**

he·mo·stat·ic (hē′mə·stăt′ĭk, hĕm′ə-), *adj.* **1.** arresting hemorrhage, as a drug; styptic. **2.** pertaining to stagnation of the blood. —*n.* **3.** a hemostatic agent or substance. Also, **haemostatic.**

hemp (hĕmp), *n.* **1.** a tall, annual moraceous herb,

Cannabis sativa, native in Asia, but cultivated in many parts of the world. **2.** the tough fiber of this plant, used for making coarse fabrics, ropes, etc. **3.** an East Indian variety, *Cannabis sativa indica* (or *Cannabis indica*), of common hemp, yielding hashish, bhang, cannabin, etc. **4.** any of various plants resembling hemp. **5.** any of various fibers similar to hemp. **6.** a narcotic drug obtained from Indian hemp. [ME; OE *henep, hænep,* c. G *hanf,* Gk. *kánnabis*]

hemp agrimony, a European composite herb, *Eupatorium cannabinum,* with dull purplish flowers.

hemp·en (hĕm′pən), *adj.* **1.** made of hemp- **2.** of or pertaining to hemp. **3.** resembling hemp.

hemp nettle, 1. a coarse labiate weed, *Galeopsis Tetrahit,* likened to the hemp from its general appearance, and to the nettle from its bristly hairs. **2.** any plant of the same genus.

hemp·seed (hĕmp′sēd′), *n.* the seed of hemp, used as a food for cage birds.

Hemp·stead (hĕmp′stĕd), *n.* a village in SE New York, on Long Island. 34,641 (1960).

hem·stitch (hĕm′stĭch′), *v.t.* **1.** to hem along a line from which threads have been drawn out, stitching the cross threads into a series of little groups. —*n.* **2.** the stitch used or the needlework done in hemstitching. [f. HEM, n. + STITCH¹, v.]

hen (hĕn), *n.* **1.** the female of the domestic fowl. **2.** the female of any bird, esp. of a gallinaceous bird. [ME and OE *hen*(*n*) (der. OE *hana* cock), c. G *henne*]

hen-and-chick·ens (hĕn′ən·chĭk′ənz), *n.* **1.** any of several herbs, esp. those having offshoot or runner plants growing around the parent. **2.** a species of houseleek, *Sempervivum globiferum,* native of Europe. **3.** the ground ivy, *Glecoma hederacea.*

hen·bane (hĕn′bān′), *n.* a solanaceous Old World herb, *Hyoscyamus niger,* bearing sticky, hairy foliage of a disagreeable odor, and yellowish-brown flowers, and possessing narcotic and poisonous properties: esp. destructive to domestic fowls. [ME. See HEN, BANE]

hen·bit (hĕn′bĭt′), *n.* a labiate weed, *Lamium amplexicaule,* with small purplish flowers.

hence (hĕns), *adv.* **1.** as an inference from this fact; for this reason; therefore: *of the best quality and hence satisfactory.* **2.** from this time onward; henceforth. **3.** at the end of a given period: *a month hence.* **4.** from this source or origin. **5.** from this place; away from here. —*interj.* **6.** depart! [ME *hen*(*ne*)*s,* f. *hen* hence (OE *heona, heonan*) + -(*e*)*s,* adv. suffix]

hence·forth (hĕns′fōrth′), *adv.* from this time forth; from now on. Also, **hence·for·ward** (hĕns′fōr′wərd).

hench·man (hĕnch′mən), *n., pl.* -**men. 1.** a trusty attendant or follower. **2.** a servile and unscrupulous follower. **3.** *Obs.* a squire or page. [ME *henchemanne, henztman,* prob. orig. meaning groom, and appar. f. OE *hengest* stallion + *mann* man]

hen·dec·a·gon (hĕn·dĕk′ə·gŏn′), *n.* a polygon having eleven angles and eleven sides. [f. m. Gk. *héndeka* eleven + -GON] —**hen·de·cag·o·nal** (hĕn′də·kăg′ə·nəl), *adj.*

hen·dec·a·syl·la·ble (hĕn′dĕk·ə·sĭl′ə·bəl), *n. Pros.* a metrical line of eleven syllables. [t. L: m. *hendecasyllabus* (conformed to *syllable*), t. Gk.: m. *hendekasýllabos*] —**hen·dec·a·syl·lab·ic** (hĕn′dĕk·ə·sĭ·lăb′ĭk), *adj., n.*

hen·di·a·dys (hĕn·dī′ə·dĭs), *n. Rhet.* a figure in which a complex idea is expressed by two words connected by a copulative conjunction: "to look with eyes and envy" instead of "with envious eyes." [t. LL, der. Gk. phrase *hèn dià dyoîn* one through two]

Hen·don (hĕn′dən), *n.* a city in SE England, in Middlesex, near London. 155,835 (1951).

hen·e·quen (hĕn′ə·kĭn), *n.* the fiber of an agave, *Agave fourcroydes,* of Yucatan, used for making ropes, coarse fabrics, etc. Also, **hen′e·quin.** [t. Sp.: m. *jeniquén;* from native name]

Hen·gist (hĕng′gĭst, hĕn′jĭst), *n.* died A.D. 488, chief of the Jutes; joint founder with his brother Horsa of the English kingdom of Kent.

Hen·ley (hĕn′lĭ), *n.* **William Ernest,** 1849–1903, British poet, critic, and editor.

Hen·ley-on-Thames (hĕn′lĭ·ŏn·tĕmz′), *n.* a city in S England, on the Thames: annual regatta. 7970 (1951).

hen·na (hĕn′ə), *n.* **1.** a shrub or small tree, *Lawsonia inermis,* of Asia and the Levant. **2.** a reddish-orange dye or cosmetic made from the leaves of this plant. **3.** reddish or orangish brown. —*v.t.* **4.** to tint or dye with henna. [t. Ar.: m. *ḥinnā′*]

Hen·ne·pin (hĕn′ə·pĭn; *Fr.* ĕn·păN′), *n.* **Louis** (lwē), 1640–1701?, Belgian Catholic missionary in America.

hen·ner·y (hĕn′ə·rĭ), *n., pl.* -**neries.** a place where fowls are kept.

hen·o·the·ism (hĕn′ə·thē′ĭz·əm), *n.* **1.** the worship of some one particular divinity among others existent, in contrast with monotheism which teaches that there exists only one God. **2.** ascription of supreme divine attributes to whichever one of several gods is at the time addressed. [f. *heno-* (comb. form repr. Gk. neut. *hén* one) + THEISM] —**hen′o·the′ist,** *n.* —**hen′o·the·is′tic,** *adj.*

hen·peck (hĕn′pĕk′), *v.t.* (of a wife) to domineer over (her husband). —**hen′pecked′,** *adj.*

hen·ry (hĕn′rĭ), *n., pl.* -**ries, -rys.** *Elect.* the practical unit of inductance, equivalent to the inductance of a circuit in which an electromotive force of one volt is pro-

---

duced by a current in the circuit which varies at the rate of one ampere per second. [named after Joseph HENRY]

Hen·ry (hĕn'rĭ), n. **1. Joseph**, 1797–1878, U.S. physicist. **2. O.**, (*William Sidney Porter*) 1862–1910, U.S. short-story writer. **3. Patrick**, 1736–99, American patriot, orator, and statesman. **4. Cape**, a cape in SE Virginia at the mouth of Chesapeake Bay. **5. Fort**, a fort in NW Tennessee, on the Tennessee river: Union victory, 1862.

Henry I, **1.** 1068–1135, king of England, 1100–35 (brother of William II). **2.** 1008?–1060, king of France, 1031–60.

Henry II, **1.** (*of Anjou*) 1133–89, king of England, 1154–89 (successor of Stephen and 1st king of Plantagenet line). **2.** 1519–59, king of France, 1547–59.

Henry III, **1.** (*of Winchester*) 1207–72, king of England, 1216–72 (son of John). **2.** 1551–89, king of France, 1574–89.

Henry IV, **1.** 1050–1106, emperor of Holy Roman Empire, 1056–1106. **2.** (*of Bolingbroke*) 1367–1413, king of England, 1399–1413 (successor of Richard II, son of John of Gaunt, and 1st king of house of Lancaster). **3.** (*of Navarre*) 1553–1610, king of France, 1589–1610.

Henry V, (*of Monmouth*) 1387–1422, king of England, 1413–22 (son of Henry IV).

Henry VI, (*of Windsor*) 1421–71, king of England, 1422–61 and 1470–71 (son of Henry V).

Henry VII, 1457–1509, king of England, 1485–1509 (successor of Richard III and 1st king of house of Tudor).

Henry VIII, 1491–1547, king of England, 1509–47, and of Ireland, 1541–47 (son of Henry VII).

Henry of Portugal, (*"the Navigator"*) 1394–1460, prince of Portugal, promoter of geographic exploration.

Hens·lowe (hĕnz'lō), n. **Philip**, died 1616, English theater manager.

Hen·ty (hĕn'tĭ), n. **George Alfred**, 1832–1902, British author of boys' stories.

hep (hĕp), adj. *U.S. Slang.* having inside knowledge, or being informed (fol. by *to*): *to be hep to swing music*.

hep·a·rin (hĕp'ərĭn), n. a glucoside produced in the liver which prevents the coagulation of the blood, and is used in the treatment of thrombosis.

he·pat·ic (hĭ păt'ĭk), adj. **1.** of or pertaining to the liver. **2.** acting on the liver, as a medicine. **3.** livercolored; dark reddish-brown. **4.** *Bot.* belonging or pertaining to the liverworts. —n. **5.** a medicine acting on the liver. **6.** a liverwort. [t. L: s. *hēpaticus*, t. Gk.: m. *hēpatikós* of the liver]

he·pat·i·ca (hĭ păt'ə kə), n., pl. **-cas**, **-cae** (-sē'). any of the ranunculaceous herbs, with three-lobed leaves and delicate purplish, pink, or white flowers constituting the genus *Hepatica*. [NL, prop. fem. of L *hēpaticus* HEPATIC]

hep·a·ti·tis (hĕp'ə tī'tĭs), n. *Pathol.* inflammation of the liver. [NL, f. s. Gk. *hēpar* liver + *-itis* -ITIS]

hep·a·tize (hĕp'ə tīz'), v.t. **-tized**, **-tizing**. *Pathol.* to convert (a lung, etc.) into liverlike tissue by engorgement. —**hep'a·ti·za'tion**, n.

hep-cat (hĕp'kăt'), n. *Jazz Slang.* an expert performer, or a knowing admirer, of jazz.

He·phaes·tus (hē fĕs'təs), n. *Gk. Myth.* the god of fire and metalworking. [t. Gk.: m. *Hēphaistos*]

Hep·ple·white (hĕp'əl hwīt'), n. **1. George**, died 1786, British furniture designer and cabinetmaker. —adj. **2.** in the style of Hepplewhite.

hepta-, a prefix meaning "seven." Also, before vowels, **hept-**. [t. Gk., comb. form of *heptá*]

hep·tad (hĕp'tăd), n. **1.** the number seven. **2.** a group of seven. **3.** *Chem.* an element, atom, or radical having a valence of seven. [t. LL: s. *heptas*, t. Gk.: the number seven]

hep·ta·gon (hĕp'tə gŏn'), n. a polygon having seven angles and seven sides. [t. Gk.: s. *heptá-gōnos* seven-cornered] —**hep-tag·o·nal** (hĕp täg'ə nəl), adj.

hep·ta·he·dron (hĕp'tə hē'drən), n., pl. **-drons**, **-dra** (-drə). a solid figure having seven faces. —**hep'ta·he'dral**, adj.

Regular   Irregular

Heptagons

hep·tam·er·ous (hĕp tăm'ər əs), adj. **1.** consisting of or divided into seven parts. **2.** *Bot.* (of flowers) having seven members in each whorl.

hep·tam·e·ter (hĕp tăm'ə tər), n. *Pros.* a verse of seven metrical feet. [t. LL: m. *heptametrum*, t. Gk.: m. *heptámetron*] —**hep·ta·met·ri·cal** (hĕp'təmĕt'rə kəl), adj.

hep·tane (hĕp'tān), n. any of nine isomeric hydrocarbons, C₇H₁₆, of the methane series, some of which are obtained from petroleum: used in fuels, as solvents, and as chemical intermediates.

hep·tan·gu·lar (hĕp tăng'yə lər), adj. having seven angles.

hep·tar·chy (hĕp'tär kĭ), n., pl. **-chies**. **1.** a government by seven persons. **2.** a group of seven states or kingdoms, each under its own ruler. **3.** (*often cap.*) the seven principal concurrent early English kingdoms. [f. HEPT- + -ARCHY] —**hep'tarch**, n. —**hep·tar'chic**, adj.

hep·ta·stich (hĕp'tə stĭk'), n. *Pros.* a strophe, stanza, or poem consisting of seven lines or verses. [f. HEPTA- + s. Gk. *stíchos* row, line]

Hep·ta·teuch (hĕp'tə tūk', -tōōk'), n. the first seven books of the Old Testament. [t. LL: s. *Heptateuchos*, t. Gk.: seven-volume (work)]

her (hûr; *unstressed* hər), pron. **1.** the objective case of *she*. —adj. **2.** the possessive form of *she*, used before a noun (cf. **hers**). **3.** of, belonging to, or having to do with a female person or personified thing. [ME *her(e)*, OE *hire*, gen. and dat. of *hēo* she (fem. of *hē* he)]

her., **1.** heraldic. **2.** heraldry.

He·ra (hĭr'ə), n. *Gk. Myth.* a goddess, wife and sister of Zeus and queen of heaven. Also, **Here**. [t. L, t. Gk.]

Her·a·cle·a (hĕr'ə klē'ə), n. an ancient city in S Italy, near the Gulf of Taranto: Roman defeat, 280 B.C.

Her·a·cles (hĕr'ə klēz'), n. Greek name of **Hercules**. Also, **Her'a·kles'**. —**Her'a·cle'an**, adj.

Her·a·clid (hĕr'ə klĭd), n., pl. **Her·a·cli·dae** (hĕr'ə klī'dī). a descendant of Hercules, esp. one of the Dorian aristocracy of Sparta, who claimed descent from him. Also, **Her'a·klid**. —**Her·a·cli·dan** (hĕr'ə klī'dən), adj.

Her·a·cli·tus (hĕr'ə klī'təs), n. (*"the Weeping Philosopher"*) c535–c475 B.C., Greek philosopher.

Her·a·cli·us (hĕr'ə klī'əs, hĭ răk'lĭ əs), n. A.D. c575–641, Byzantine emperor, A.D. 610–641.

He·ra·klei·on (ē rä'klē ŏn'), n. Greek name of **Candia**.

her·ald (hĕr'əld), n. **1.** a messenger; forerunner or harbinger. **2.** one who proclaims or announces (often used as the name of a newspaper). **3.** a royal or official proclaimer or messenger. **4.** an officer who arranged tournaments and other medieval functions, announced challenges, marshaled combatants, etc., later employed also to arrange tourneys, processions, funerals, etc., and to regulate the use of armorial bearings. —v.t. **5.** to give tidings of; proclaim. **6.** to usher in. [t. ML: s. *heraldus* (of Gmc. orig.); r. ME *heraud*, t. OF: m. *herau(l)t*]

he·ral·dic (hĕ răl'dĭk), adj. of or pertaining to heralds or heraldry. —**he·ral'di·cal·ly**, adv.

her·ald·ry (hĕr'əl drĭ), n., pl. **-ries**. **1.** the science of armorial bearings. **2.** the art of blazoning armorial bearings, of settling the right of persons to bear arms or to use certain bearings, of tracing and recording genealogies, of recording honors, and of deciding questions of precedence. **3.** the office or duty of a herald. **4.** a heraldic device, or a collection of such devices. **5.** a coat of arms; armorial bearings. **6.** heraldic symbolism. **7.** *Poetic.* heraldic pomp or ceremony.

Heralds' College, a royal corporation in England, instituted in 1483, occupied chiefly with armorial bearings, genealogies, honors, and precedence.

He·rat (hĕ rät'), n. a city in NW Afghanistan. 75,000 (est. 1953).

herb (ûrb, hûrb), n. **1.** a flowering plant whose stem above ground does not become woody and persistent. **2.** such a plant when valued for its medicinal properties, flavor, scent, or the like. **3.** *Rare.* herbage. [ME (*h*)*erbe*, t. F, g. L *herba* vegetation, grass, herb] —**herb'less**, adj. —**herb'like'**, adj.

her·ba·ceous (hûr bā'shəs), adj. **1.** of, pertaining to, or of the nature of an herb; herblike. **2.** (of plants or plant parts) not woody. **3.** (of flowers, sepals, etc.) having the texture, color, etc., of an ordinary foliage leaf.

herb·age (ûr'bĭj, hûr'-), n. **1.** nonwoody vegetation. **2.** the succulent parts (leaves and stems) of herbaceous plants. **3.** *Brit.* vegetation grazed by animals; pasturage. [ME, t. F, der. *herbe* grass. See HERB]

herb·al (hûr'bəl, ûr'-), adj. **1.** of, pertaining to, or consisting of herbs. —n. **2.** a treatise on herbs or plants. **3.** a herbarium.

herb·al·ist (hûr'bəl ĭst, ûr'-), n. **1.** one who collects or deals in herbs, esp. medicinal herbs. **2.** (formerly) an expert in herbs or plants.

her·bar·i·um (hûr bâr'ĭ əm), n., pl. **-bariums**, **-baria** (-bâr'ĭə). **1.** a collection of dried plants systematically arranged. **2.** a room or building in which an herbarium is kept. [t. LL, der. L *herba* HERB. Cf. ARBOR¹]

Her·bart (hĕr'bärt), n. **Johann Friedrich** (yō'hän frē'drĭKH), 1776–1841, German philosopher.

Her·bar·ti·an (hûr bär'tĭ ən), adj. **1.** of or pertaining to Herbart's system of philosophy. —n. **2.** one who accepts the doctrines of Herbart. —**Her·bar'ti·an·ism**, n.

herb bennet, a European perennial rosaceous herb, *Geum urbanum*, having yellow flowers and an aromatic, tonic, and astringent root.

Her·bert (hûr'bərt), n. **1. George**, 1593–1633, British poet. **2. Victor**, 1859–1924, U.S. composer and orchestra conductor, born in Ireland.

her·biv·o·rous (hûr bĭv'ə rəs), adj. feeding on plants. [t. NL: m. *herbivorus* herb-eating. See HERB, -VOROUS]

herb Paris, a European liliaceous herb, *Paris quadrifolia*, formerly used in medicine.

herb Robert, a species of geranium, *Geranium Robertianum*, with reddish-purple flowers.

herb·y (ûr'bĭ, hûr'-), adj. **1.** abounding in herbs or grass. **2.** pertaining to or like herbs.

Her·ce·go·vi·na (hĕr'tsĕ gō'vĭ nä), n. Serbian name of **Herzegovina**.

Her·cu·la·ne·um (hûr'kyə lā'nĭ əm), n. a buried city at the foot of Mt. Vesuvius, in SW Italy: destroyed along with Pompeii by an eruption, A.D. 79.

her·cu·le·an (hûr kū'lĭ ən, hûr'kyə lē'ən), adj. **1.** requiring the strength of a Hercules; very hard to perform: *a herculean task*. **2.** prodigious in strength, courage, or size. **3.** (*cap.*) of or relating to Hercules.

Her·cu·les (hûr'kyə lēz'), n. **1.** Also, *Greek*, **Heracles**, **Herakles**. *Class. Myth.* a celebrated hero of great

ăct, āble, dâre, ärt; ĕbb, ēqual; ĭf, īce; hŏt, ōver, ôrder, oil, bŏŏk, ōōze, out; ŭp, ūse, ûrge; ə = a in alone; ch, chief; g, give; ng, ring; sh, shoe; th, thin; th, that; zh, vision. See the full key on inside cover.

strength and courage who performed twelve extraordinary tasks: also known as Alcides. **2.** a northern constellation, between Lyra and Corona Borealis. [t. L, t. Gk.: m. *Hēraklēs*, lit., having the glory of Hera]

Her·cu·les'-club (hûr′kyə lēz klŭb′), *n.* **1.** a prickly rutaceous tree, *Zanthoxylum Clava-Herculis*, with a medicinal bark and berries. **2.** a prickly araliaceous shrub, *Aralia spinosa*, with medicinal bark and root.

herd[1] (hûrd), *n.* **1.** a number of animals, kept, feeding, or traveling together; drove; flock. **2.** a large company of people (now in a disparaging sense). **3.** the herd, the common people; the rabble. —*v.i.* **4.** to unite or go in a herd; to assemble or associate as a herd. —*v.t.* **5.** to form into or as if into a herd. [ME; OE *heord*, c. G *herde*] —**Syn. 1.** See **flock**[1].

herd[2] (hûrd), *n.* **1.** a herdsman (usually in composition): *cowherd.* —*v.t.* **2.** to tend, drive, or lead a herd of cattle, sheep, etc. [ME; OE *heorde*, c. G *hirte*; der. Gmc. stem represented by **herd**[1]]

herd·er (hûr′dər), *n.* **1.** a herdsman. **2.** *Chiefly U.S.* a person in charge of a herd of cattle or a flock of sheep.

Her·der (hĕr′dər), *n.* **Johann Gottfried von** (yō′hän gôt′frēt fən), 1744–1803, German philosopher and poet.

her·dic (hûr′dĭk), *n.* a low-hung carriage with two or four wheels, having the entrance at the back and the seats at the side. [named after P. *Herdic*, the inventor]

herd's-grass (hûrdz′gräs′, -gräs′), *n.* any of certain grasses used for pasture or hay, as timothy or redtop.

herds·man (hûrdz′mən), *n., pl.* **-men.** **1.** *Chiefly Brit.* the keeper of a herd. **2.** (*cap.*) *Astron.* the northern constellation Boötes.

here (hĭr), *adv.* **1.** in this place; in this spot or locality (opposed to *there*): *put it here.* **2.** to or toward this place; hither: *come here.* **3.** at this point; at this juncture: *here the speaker paused.* **4.** (often used in pointing out or emphasizing some person or thing present): *my friend here knows the circumstances.* **5.** present (used in answer to roll call, etc.). **6.** in the present life or state. **7.** Some special adverb phrases are:
here and there, 1. in this place and in that; in various places; at intervals. **2.** hither and thither; to and fro.
here goes! an exclamation to show one's resolution on the beginning of some bold or unpleasant act.
here's to, a formula in offering a toast: *here's to you!*
here we (or **you**) **are,** *Colloq.* here is what we (or you) want, or are looking for.
neither here nor there, 1. irrelevant; unimportant. **2.** neither in this place nor in that.
—*n.* **8.** this place. **9.** this world; this life.
[ME; OE *hēr*, c. D and G *hier*, Icel. and Goth. *hēr*; from the demonstrative stem represented by **he**]

He·re (hĭr′ē), *n.* Hera.

here-, a word element meaning "this (place)," "this (time)," etc., used in combination with certain adverbs and prepositions. [special use of **here**]

here·a·bout (hĭr′ə bout′), *adv.* about this place; in this neighborhood. Also, **here′a·bouts′.**

here·af·ter (hĭr äf′tər, -äf′-), *adv.* **1.** after this in time or order; at some future time; farther along. **2.** in the world to come. —*n.* **3.** a future life; the world to come. **4.** time to come; the future. [ME *hereafter*, OE *hēræfter* f. *hēr* **here** + *æfter* **after**]

here·at (hĭr ăt′), *adv.* **1.** at this time; when this happened. **2.** by reason of this; because of this.

here·by (hĭr bī′), *adv.* **1.** by this; by means of this; as a result of this. **2.** *Archaic.* near by.

he·red·i·ta·ble (hĭ rĕd′ə tə bəl), *adj.* heritable. [t. F (obs.), der. LL *hērēditāre* inherit, der. L *hēres* heir] —**he·red′i·ta·bil′i·ty,** *n.* —**he·red′i·ta·bly,** *adv.*

her·e·dit·a·ment (hĕr′ə dĭt′ə mənt), *n.* *Law.* any inheritable estate or interest in property. [t. ML: s. *hērēditāmentum*, der. LL *hērēditāre.* See **hereditable**]

he·red·i·tar·y (hĭ rĕd′ə tĕr′ĭ), *adj.* **1.** passing, or capable of passing, naturally from parents to offspring: *hereditary traits.* **2.** pertaining to inheritance or heredity: *hereditary descent.* **3.** being such through feelings, etc., derived from predecessors: *a hereditary enemy.* **4.** *Law.* **a.** descending by inheritance. **b.** transmitted or transmissible in the line of descent by force of law. **c.** holding a title, etc., by inheritance: *a hereditary proprietor.* [t. L: s. *hērēditārius* of an inheritance] —**he·red′i·tar′i·ly,** *adv.* —**he·red′i·tar′i·ness,** *n.*

he·red·i·tist (hĭ rĕd′ə tĭst), *n.* one who maintains that the whole personality is determined by heredity.

he·red·i·ty (hĭ rĕd′ə tĭ), *n., pl.* **-ties.** **1.** *Biol.* the transmission of genetic characters from parents to progeny; the protoplasmic or biochemical fixation of genetic units (genes) as the result of continuous selection in nature or by man. **2.** the genetic characteristics transmitted to an individual by its parents. [t. L: m.s. *hērēditas* heirship, inheritance]

Her·e·ford (hĕr′ə fərd, hûr′fərd), *n.* **1.** one of a breed of beef cattle originating in Herefordshire, characterized by a red body, white face, and other white markings. **2.** a city in W England: cathedral. 32,490 (1951).

Her·e·ford·shire (hĕr′ə fərd shĭr′, -shər), *n.* a county in W England. 127,159 pop. (1951); 842 sq. mi. *Co. seat:* Hereford. Also, **Hereford.**

here·in (hĭr ĭn′), *adv.* **1.** in or into this place. **2.** in this fact, circumstance, etc.; in view of this. [ME and OE *hērinne.* f. *hēr* **here** + *inne* **in,** adv.]

here·in·af·ter (hĭr′ĭn ăf′tər, -äf′-), *adv.* afterward in this document, statement, etc.

here·in·be·fore (hĭr′ĭn bĭ fôr′), *adv.* before in this document, statement, etc.

here·in·to (hĭr ĭn′tōō), *adv.* **1.** into this place. **2.** into this matter or affair.

here·of (hĭr ŏv′), *adv.* **1.** of this: *upon the receipt hereof.* **2.** concerning this: *more hereof later.*

here·on (hĭr ŏn′, -ôn′), *adv.* hereupon.

he·res (hĭr′ēz), *n., pl.* **heredes** (hĭ rē′dēz). *Civil Law.* an heir. Also, **haeres.** [L]

he·re·si·arch (hĭ rē′sĭ ärk′, hĕr′ə-), *n.* a leader in heresy; the chief of a heretical sect. [t. LL: m.s. *haeresiarcha,* t. Gk.: m. *hairesiárchēs* leader of a school]

her·e·sy (hĕr′ə sĭ), *n., pl.* **-sies.** **1.** opinion or doctrine at variance with the orthodox or accepted doctrine, esp. of a church or religious system. **2.** the maintaining of such an opinion or doctrine. [ME *(h)eresie,* t. OF, der. L *haeresis,* t. Gk.: m. *hairesis* a taking, choice]

her·e·tic (hĕr′ə tĭk), *n.* **1.** a professed believer who maintains religious opinions contrary to those accepted by his church or rejects doctrines prescribed by his church. —*adj.* **2.** heretical. [ME *heretyke,* t. F: *hérétique,* t. LL: m.s. *haereticus,* adj., n., t. Gk.: m. *hairetikós* heretical, able to choose]

he·ret·i·cal (hə rĕt′ə kəl), *adj.* of, pertaining to, or like heretics or heresy. —**he·ret′i·cal·ly,** *adv.*

here·to (hĭr tōō′), *adv.* to this place, thing, document, circumstance, proposition, etc.: *attached hereto.* Also, **here·un·to** (hĭr ŭn′tōō′, hĭr′ŭntōō′).

here·to·fore (hĭr′tə fôr′), *adv.* before this time.

here·un·der (hĭr ŭn′dər), *adv.* **1.** under this; subsequently set down. **2.** under authority of this.

here·up·on (hĭr′ə pŏn′, -pôn′), *adv.* upon this; following immediately upon this.

here·with (hĭr wĭth′, -wĭth′), *adv.* **1.** along with this. **2.** by means of this.

Her·ges·hei·mer (hûr′gəs hī′mər), *n.* **Joseph,** 1880–1954, U.S. novelist.

He·ring (hā′rĭng), *n.* **Ewald** (ā′vält), 1834–1918, German physiologist and psychologist.

her·i·ot (hĕr′ĭət), *n.* *Eng. Law.* a feudal service or tribute, orig. of military equipment, etc., due to the lord on the death of a tenant. [ME; OE *heregeatwa* war gear, f. *here* army + *geatwa,* pl., equipment]

her·it·a·ble (hĕr′ə tə bəl), *adj.* **1.** capable of being inherited; inheritable; hereditary. **2.** capable of inheriting. [ME, t. OF, der. *heriter.* See **heritage**] —**her′it·a·bil′i·ty,** *n.* —**her′it·a·bly,** *adv.*

her·it·age (hĕr′ə tĭj), *n.* **1.** that which comes or belongs to one by reason of birth; an inherited lot or portion. **2.** something reserved for one: *the heritage of the righteous.* **3.** *Law.* **a.** that which has been or may be inherited by legal descent or succession. **b.** any property, esp. land, that devolves by right of inheritance. **4.** *Bible.* God's chosen people; the Israelites. **5.** the Christian church. [ME *(h)eritage,* t. OF, der. *heriter* inherit, g. LL *hērēditāre*] —**Syn. 1.** See **inheritance.**

her·it·ance (hĕr′ə təns), *n.* *Archaic.* inheritance.

her·i·tor (hĕr′ə tər), *n.* inheritor. [ME *heriter,* t. AF, g. L *hērēditārius* **hereditary**] —**her′i·tress** (hĕr′ə trĭs), *n. fem.*

Her·ki·mer (hûr′kə mər), *n.* **Nicholas,** 1715?–77, American Revolutionary general.

herl (hûrl), *n.* **1.** a barb, or the barbs, of a feather, much used in dressing anglers' flies. **2.** a fly so dressed.

her·ma (hûr′mə), *n., pl.* **-mae** (-mē), **-mai** (-mī). *Gk. Antiq.* a kind of monument or statue, common in ancient Athens, consisting of a head, usually that of the god Hermes, supported on a quadrangular pillar corresponding roughly in mass to the absent body. Also, **herm, hermes.** [t. L, also *Hermēs,* t. Gk.]

her·maph·ro·dite (hûr măf′rə dīt′), *n.* **1.** an animal or a flower having normally both the male and the female organs of generation. **2.** a person or thing in which two opposite qualities are combined. —*adj.* **3.** of or like a hermaphrodite. **4.** combining two opposite qualities. **5.** *Bot.* monoclinous. [ME, t. L: m.s. *hermaphrodītus,* t. Gk.: m. *hermaphrodītos.* As proper name, son of Hermes and Aphrodite, who became united in body with the nymph Salmacis while bathing in her fountain] —**her·maph·ro·dit·ic** (hûr măf′rə dĭt′ĭk), *adj.* —**her·maph′ro·dit′i·cal·ly,** *adv.*

hermaphrodite brig, *Naut.* a two-masted vessel square-rigged on the foremast and schooner-rigged on the mainmast.

her·maph·ro·dit·ism (hûr măf′rə dīt′ĭz′əm), *n.* the condition of a hermaphrodite.

her·me·neu·tic (hûr′mə nū′tĭk, -nōō′-), *adj.* interpretative; explanatory. [t. Gk.: m.s. *hermēneutikós* of interpreting] —**her′me·neu′ti·cal·ly,** *adv.*

her·me·neu·tics (hûr′mə nū′tĭks, -nōō′-), *n.* **1.** the science of interpretation, esp. of the Scriptures. **2.** that branch of theology which treats of the principles of Biblical exegesis.

Her·mes (hûr′mēz), *n.* **1.** *Gk. Myth.* a deity, herald and messenger of the gods, and god of roads, commerce, invention, cunning, and theft. **2.** (*l.c.*) *Gk. Antiq.* herma.

Upper part of a
double herma

Hermes Tris·me·gis·tus (trĭs′mə jĭs′təs), a name given by Neoplatonists and others to the Egyptian god Thoth, who was to some extent identified with the Grecian Hermes, and to whom were attributed various works embodying mystical, theosophical, astrological, and alchemical doctrines. [t. Gk.: m. *Hermēs trismēgistos* thrice greatest Hermes]

her·met·ic (hûr mĕt′ĭk), *adj.* **1.** made airtight by fusion or sealing. **2.** pertaining to occult science. esp. alchemy. **3.** (*cap.*) of Hermes Trismegistus or the writings, etc., ascribed to him. Also, **her·met′i·cal.** [t. ML: s. *hermēticus*, der. L *Hermēs*, t. Gk.]

her·met·i·cal·ly (hûr mĕt′ĭk lĭ), *adv.* so as to be airtight: *hermetically sealed.*

Her·mi·o·ne (hûr mī′ə nĭ), *n.* the daughter of Menelaus and Helen: wife of Orestes.

her·mit (hûr′mĭt), *n.* **1.** one who has retired to a solitary place for a life of religious seclusion. **2.** any person living in seclusion. **3.** *Zool.* an animal of solitary habits. **4.** a spiced molasses cooky, often containing raisins or nuts. **5.** *Obs.* a beadsman. [ME (h)ermite, t. OF, t. LL: m. *erēmīta*, t. Gk.: m. *erēmītēs* a hermit, prop. adj., of the desert] —**her·mit′ic, her·mit′i·cal,** *adj.* —**her·mit′i·cal·ly,** *adv.* —**her′mit·like′,** *adj.*

her·mit·age (hûr′mə tĭj), *n.* **1.** the habitation of a hermit. **2.** any secluded habitation. **3.** (*cap.*) a full-bodied wine produced in SE France.

hermit crab, any of numerous decapod crustaceans of the genera *Pagurus, Eupagurus,* etc., which protect their soft uncovered rear by occupying the castoff shell of a univalve mollusk.

hermit thrush, a North American thrush, *Turdus aonalaschkae* (or *Hylocichla guttata*).

Her·mon (hûr′mən), *n.* **Mount,** a mountain in SW Syria, in the Anti-Lebanon range. ab. 9200 ft.

hern (hûrn), *n.* *Archaic.* or *Dial.* heron.

her·ni·a (hûr′nĭ ə), *n., pl.* **-nias, -niae** (-nĭ ē′). *Pathol.* the protrusion of an organ or tissue through an opening in its surrounding walls, esp. in the abdominal region. [ME, t. L] —**her′ni·al,** *adj.*

her·ni·or·rha·phy (hûr′nĭ ôr′ə fĭ, -ŏr′-), *n., pl.* **-phies.** *Surg.* the operation for repair of a hernia.

he·ro (hĭr′ō), *n., pl.* **heroes. 1.** a man of distinguished valor or performance, admired for his noble qualities. **2.** one invested with heroic qualities in the opinion of others. **3.** the principal male character in a story, play, etc. **4.** (in early mythological antiquity) a being of god-like prowess and beneficence, often a "culture hero," who came to be honored as a divinity. **5.** (in the Homeric period) a warrior chieftain of special strength, courage, or ability. **6.** (in later periods of antiquity) an immortal being intermediate in nature between gods and men. [back formation from ME *heroes,* pl., t. L, t. Gk.]

Hero and Le·an·der (lĭ ăn′dər), *Gk. Legend.* two lovers in a late Greek poem. Leander, a youth of Abydos, swam the Hellespont nightly to visit Hero. On a stormy night the guiding lamp in her tower at Sestos was extinguished and he was drowned. Hero, finding his body, hurled herself to the rocks beside it.

Her·od (hĕr′əd), *n.* (*the Great*) died 4 B.C., king of the Jews from 37 to 4 B.C.

Herod A·grip·pa (ə grĭp′ə), 10 B.C.–A.D. 44, king of Judea, A.D. 41–44.

Herod An·ti·pas (ăn′tĭ păs′), died after A.D. 39, ruler of Galilee, A.D. 4–39; executed John the Baptist and presided at the trial of Jesus.

He·ro·di·an (hĭ rō′dĭ ən), *adj.* pertaining to Herod the Great, his family, or its partisans.

He·ro·di·as (hĭ rō′dĭ əs), *n. Bible.* the wife of Herod Antipas and mother of Salome. She was responsible for the death of John the Baptist. See **Salome.**

He·rod·o·tus (hĭ rŏd′ə təs), *n.* 484?–425? B.C., Greek historian.

he·ro·ic (hĭ rō′ĭk), *adj.* Also, **he·ro′i·cal. 1.** of or pertaining to heroes. **2.** suitable to the character of a hero; daring; noble. **3.** having or displaying the character or attributes of a hero; intrepid; determined: *a heroic explorer.* **4.** having or involving recourse to bold, daring, or extreme measures. **5.** dealing with or applicable to heroes, as in literature. **6.** of or pertaining to the heroes of antiquity: *the heroic age.* **7.** used in heroic poetry. See **heroic verse. 8.** resembling heroic poetry in language or style; magniloquent; grand. **9.** (of style or language) high-flown; extravagant; bombastic. **10.** *Arts.* of a size larger than life and (usually) less than colossal. —*n.* **11.** (*usually pl.*) heroic verse. **12.** (*pl.*) extravagant language or sentiment; bombast. —**he·ro′i·cal·ly,** *adv.* —**he·ro′i·cal·ness, he·ro′ic·ness,** *n.* —**Syn. 1.** intrepid, valiant, dauntless, gallant. —**Ant. 1.** cowardly.

heroic age, the time when the heroes of Greek antiquity are supposed to have lived.

heroic verse, a form of verse adapted to the treatment of heroic or exalted themes: in classical poetry, the hexameter; in English, German, and Italian, the iambic of ten syllables; and in French, the Alexandrine (which see). The following is an example of English heroic verse: *Achilles' wrath, to Greece the direful spring Of woes unnumbered, heavenly goddess, sing!*

her·o·in (hĕr′ō ĭn), *n. Pharm.* **1.** a derivative of morphine, $C_{21}H_{23}NO_5$, used (usually in the form of a hydrochloride) as a sedative, etc., and constituting a dangerous habit-forming drug. **2.** (*cap.*) a trademark for this drug. [t. G, f. Gk. *hērō(s)* HERO + -*in* -IN[2]]

her·o·ine (hĕr′ō ĭn), *n.* **1.** a woman of heroic character; a female hero. **2.** the principal female character in a story, play, etc. [t. L, t. Gk., der. *hērōs* hero]

her·o·ism (hĕr′ō ĭz′əm), *n.* **1.** the qualities of a hero or heroine: *a heroic trait.* **2.** heroic conduct; valor. —**Syn. 1.** intrepidity, valor, prowess, gallantry. —**Ant. 2.** timidity.

her·on (hĕr′ən), *n.* **1.** any of numerous long-legged, long-necked, long-billed wading birds constituting the subfamily *Ardeinae* (**true herons**), as the **gray heron** (*Ardea cinerae*) of Europe or **great blue heron** (*A. herodias*) of America. **2.** any bird of the family *Ardeidae,* as the egret, bittern, or boatbill. [ME *heiroun,* t. OF: m. *hairon,* ult. t. Gmc.; cf. OHG *heiger*]

He·ron (hĭr′ŏn), *n.* fl. A.D. 1st cent. or earlier, Greek mathematician and mechanician, of Alexandria.

her·on·ry (hĕr′ən rĭ), *n., pl.* **-ries.** a place where a colony of herons breeds.

Great blue heron,
Ardea herodias
(38 in. long)

hero worship, 1. profound reverence for great men or their memory. **2.** the worship of deified heroes, as practiced by the ancients. —**hero worshiper.**

herp., herpetology. Also, **herpet.**

her·pes (hûr′pēz), *n. Pathol.* any of certain inflammatory infections of the skin or mucous membrane, characterized by clusters of vesicles which tend to spread. [t. L, t. Gk.: lit., a creeping] —**her·pet·ic** (hərpĕt′ĭk), *adj.*

herpes fa·ci·a·lis (fā′shĭ ā′lĭs), *Pathol.* cold sore. Also, **herpes la·bi·a·lis** (lā′bĭ ā′lĭs). [L]

herpes sim·plex (sĭm′plĕks), *n. Pathol.* cold sore.

herpes zos·ter (zŏs′tər), *Pathol.* shingles.

her·pe·tol·o·gy (hûr′pə tŏl′ə jĭ), *n.* the branch of zoölogy that treats of reptiles and amphibians. [f. Gk. *herpetó(n)* reptile + -LOGY] —**her·pe·to·log·i·cal** (hûr′pə tə lŏj′ə kəl), *adj.* —**her′pe·tol′o·gist,** *n.*

Herr (hĕr), *n., pl.* **Herren** (hĕr′ən). *German.* Mr.

Her·ren·volk (hĕr′ən fōlk′), *n. German.* the master race.

Her·re·ra (ĕr rĕ′rä), *n.* **Francisco de** (frän thĕs′kō dĕ), 1576–1656, Spanish painter.

Her·rick (hĕr′ĭk), *n.* **Robert,** 1591–1674, British poet.

her·ring (hĕr′ĭng), *n., pl.* **-rings,** (*esp. collectively*) **-ring. 1.** an important food fish, *Clupea harengus,* of the north Atlantic, occurring in enormous shoals in the North Sea and on the northern American coast. **2.** the north Pacific representative, *Clupea pallasii,* of the Atlantic herring, of similar appearance, size, and habits. **3.** any fish of the family *Clupeidae,* which includes the herring, shad, sardine, etc. [ME *hering,* OE *hæring,* c. G *häring*]

her·ring·bone (hĕr′ĭng bōn′), *n.* **1.** a pattern of parallel lines, set obliquely, with each successive line slanting away from the other, used in masonry, textiles, embroidery, etc. **2.** an embroidery stitch resembling cross-stitch. —*adj.* **3.** having or resembling herringbone: *herringbone tweed.*

Herringbone pattern

herring gull, a common large gull, *Larus argentatus,* virtually world-wide in distribution.

Her·ri·ot (ĕ ryō′), *n.* **Édouard** (ĕ dwär′), 1872–1957, French statesman, political leader, and author.

hers (hûrz), *pron.* **1.** form of the possessive *her,* used predicatively or without a noun following: *hers was the fault.* **2.** the person(s) or thing(s) belonging to her: *herself and hers, a friend of hers.*

Her·schel (hûr′shəl), *n.* **1. Sir John Frederick William,** 1792–1871, British astronomer and philosopher. **2.** his father, **Sir William** (*Friedrich Wilhelm Herschel*) 1738–1822, German-born British astronomer.

her·self (hər sĕlf′), *pron.* **1.** an emphatic form of *her* or *she.* **2.** a reflexive form of *her.*

Hert·ford·shire (här′fərd shĭr′, -shər, härt′-), *n.* a county in SE England. 609,775 pop. (1951); 632 sq. mi. *Co. seat:* Hertford. Also, **Hert′ford, Herts.**

Her·to·gen·bosch (sĕr′tō кнən bôs′), *n.* **'s.** See **'s Hertogenbosch.**

Hertz (hĕrts), *n.* **Heinrich Rudolph** (hĭn′rʏнE rōō′dôlf), 1857–94, German physicist. —**Hertz·i·an** (hĕrt′sĭ ən), *adj.*

hertzian wave, an electromagnetic wave, artificially produced as a means of transmission in radio telegraphy: first fully investigated by Hertz.

Her·tzog (hĕr′tsōкн), *n.* **James Barry Munnik** (mœn′ək), 1866–1942, South African statesman and general: prime minister, 1924–39.

Her·ze·go·vi·na (hĕr′tsə gō vē′nə), *n.* a former Turkish province in S Europe: a part of Austria-Hungary, 1878–1914; now a part of Bosnia and Herzegovina, Serbian, Hercegovina. —**Her′ze·go·vi′ni·an,** *adj., n.*

Herzl (hĕr′tsl), *n.* **Theodor** (tā′ō dōr), 1860–1904, Hungarian-born leader of modern Zionism.

he's (hēz; *unstressed* hĭz), contraction of *he is.*

Hesh·van (hĕsh′vän), *n.* (in the Jewish calendar) the second month of the year. Also, **Hesh′wan.**

He·si·od (hē′sĭ əd, hĕs′ĭ-), *n.* fl. 8th? cent. B.C., Greek poet. —**He·si·od·ic** (hē′sĭ ŏd′ĭk, hĕs′ĭ-), *adj.*

He·si·o·ne (hĭ sī′ə nē′), n. Gk. Legend. daughter of Laomedon, King of Troy, rescued from a sea monster by Hercules.

hes·i·tan·cy (hĕz′ə tən sĭ′), n., pl. -cies. hesitation; indecision. Also, **hes·i·tance**. [t. L: m.s. haesitantia stammering]

hes·i·tant (hĕz′ə tənt), adj. 1. hesitating; undecided. 2. lacking readiness of speech. —**hes′i·tant·ly**, adv.

hes·i·tate (hĕz′ə tāt′), v.i., -tated, -tating. 1. to hold back in doubt or indecision: to hesitate to believe. 2. to have scrupulous doubts; be unwilling. 3. to pause. 4. to falter in speech; stammer. [t. L: m.s. haesitātus, pp., stuck fast] —**hes′i·tat′er**, **hes′i·ta′tor**, n. —**hes′i·tat′ing**, adj. —**hes′i·tat′ing·ly**, adv. —**Syn.** 1. waver, vacillate, falter. 3. demur, delay. —**Ant.** 1. decide. 3. hasten.

hes·i·ta·tion (hĕz′ə tā′shən), n. 1. act of hesitating; a delay from uncertainty of mind: to be lost by hesitation. 2. a state of doubt. 3. a halting or faltering in speech. —**Syn.** 1. hesitancy, indecision, irresolution, vacillation.

hes·i·ta·tive (hĕz′ə tā′tĭv), adj. characterized by hesitation; hesitating. —**hes′i·ta·tive·ly**, adv.

Hes·pe·ri·an (hĕs pĭr′ĭ ən), adj. western. [f. s. L Hesperius (t. Gk.: m. hespérios at evening, western) + -AN]

Hes·per·i·des (hĕs pĕr′ə dēz′), n.pl. Gk. Myth. certain nymphs, variously given as from three to seven, fabled to guard, with the aid of a fierce serpent, a garden at the western extremity of the world in which grew golden apples, the wedding gift of Gaea to Hera. [t. L, t. Gk., prop. pl. of hesperis western] —**Hes·per·id·i·an** (hĕs′pə rĭd′ĭ ən), adj.

hes·per·i·din (hĕs pĕr′ə dĭn), n. a crystallizable glucoside found in the spongy envelope of oranges and lemons. [f. s. Gk. Hesperídes, a class of plants including the orange + -IN²]

hes·per·id·i·um (hĕs′pə rĭd′ĭ əm), n., pl. -peridia (-pə rĭd′ĭ ə). Bot. the fruit of a citrus plant, as an orange.

Hes·per·us (hĕs′pər əs), n. the evening star, esp. Venus. [t. L, t. Gk.: m. Hésperos the evening star, orig. adj., of or at evening, western]

Hes·se (hĕs for 1; hĕs′ə for 2), n. 1. a state in West Germany. 4,603,100 (est. 1956); 8150 sq. mi. Cap.: Wiesbaden. German, **Hes·sen** (hĕs′ən). 2. **Hermann**, 1877-1962, German novelist and poet: Nobel Prize, 1946.

Hesse-Nas·sau (hĕs′ nås′ō), n. a former state in W Germany; now a part of Hesse. German, **Hes·sen-Nas·sau** (hĕs′ən nås′ou).

Hes·sian (hĕsh′ən), adj. 1. of or pertaining to Hesse or its inhabitants. —n. 2. a native or inhabitant of Hesse. 3. U.S. a Hessian mercenary used by England during the American Revolution. 4. a hireling or ruffian.

Hessian boots, high tasseled boots fashionable in England during the early 19th century.

Hessian fly, a small dipterous insect, Phytophaga destructor, whose larva is one of the most destructive pests of wheat.

hes·so·nite (hĕs′ə nīt′), n. a yellowish or brownish variety of garnet, sometimes used in jewelry. [f. Gk. hésson less, inferior + -ITE¹]

hest (hĕst), n. Archaic. behest. [ME hest(e), OE hǽs, akin to hātan bid]

Hessian fly,
Phytophaga destructor
A. Larva; B. Pupa; C. Adult

Hes·ti·a (hĕs′tĭ ə), n. Gk. Myth. goddess of the hearth and hearth fire.

Hes·ton and I·sle·worth (hĕs′tən, ī′zəl wûrth′), a municipal borough in SE England, in Middlesex, near London. 106,636 (1951).

Hes·y·chast (hĕs′ə kăst′), n. one of a sect of mystics which originated in the 14th century among the monks on Mt. Athos, Greece. [t. Gk.: s. hésychastés a recluse] —**Hes·y·chast′ic**, adj.

he·tae·ra (hĭ tĭr′ə), n., pl. -taerae (-tĭr′ē). a female paramour or concubine, esp. in ancient Greece. [t. Gk.: m. hetaíra, fem. of hetaíros companion]

he·tai·ra (hĭ tī′rə), n., pl. -tairai (-tī′rī). hetaera.

hetero-, a word element meaning "other" or "different," as in heterocercal. Also, before vowels, **heter-**. [t. Gk., comb. form of héteros]

het·er·o·cer·cal (hĕt′ə rə sûr′kəl), adj. Ichthyol. 1. having an unequally divided tail or caudal fin, the backbone usually running into a much larger upper lobe. 2. denoting such a tail or caudal fin (cf. homocercal). [f. HETERO- + m.s. Gk. kérkos tail + -AL¹]

het·er·o·chro·mat·ic (hĕt′ər ə krō măt′ĭk), adj. 1. of, having, or pertaining to more than one color. 2. having a pattern of mixed colors.

Heterocercal tail

het·er·o·chro·ma·tin (hĕt′ə rə krō′mə tĭn), n. Biol. chromatin which remains compact during mitosis. Sex chromosomes may consist entirely of heterochromatin.

het·er·o·chro·mo·some (hĕt′ər ə krō′mə sōm′), n. Biol. a sex chromosome.

het·er·o·chro·mous (hĕt′ər ə krō′məs), adj. of different colors. [t. Gk.: m. heteróchrōmos]

het·er·o·clite (hĕt′ər ə klīt′), adj. 1. exceptional or anomalous. 2. Gram. irregular in inflection. —n. 3. a person or thing that deviates from the ordinary rule or form. 4. Gram. a heteroclite word. [t. F, t. LL: m.s. heteroclitus, t. Gk.: m. heteróklitos irregularly inflected]

het·er·o·cy·clic (hĕt′ər ə sī′klĭk, -sĭk′lĭk), adj. Chem. 1. referring to organic chemistry as dealing with ring compounds with both carbon atoms and atoms of other elements in the ring. 2. denoting such compounds.

het·er·o·dox (hĕt′ər ə dŏks′), adj. 1. not in accordance with established or accepted doctrines or opinions, esp. in theology. 2. holding unorthodox doctrines or opinions. [t. Gk.: s. heteródoxos of another opinion]

het·er·o·dox·y (hĕt′ər ə dŏk′sĭ), n., pl. -doxies. 1. heterodox state or quality. 2. a heterodox opinion, etc.

het·er·o·dyne (hĕt′ər ə dīn′), adj., v., -dyned, -dyning. Radio. —adj. 1. denoting or pertaining to a method of receiving continuous-wave radiotelegraph signals by impressing upon the continuous radiofrequency oscillations another set of radiofrequency oscillations of a slightly different frequency, the interference resulting in fluctuations or beats of audio frequency. —v.i. 2. to produce a heterodyne effect.

het·er·oe·cious (hĕt′ə rē′shəs), adj. Biol. pertaining to or characterized by heteroecism. [f. HETER- + m.s. Gk. oikía house + -OUS]

het·er·oe·cism (hĕt′ə rē′sĭzəm), n. Biol. the development of different stages of a parasitic species on different host plants, as in fungi.

het·er·o·ga·mete (hĕt′ər ə gə mēt′), n. Biol. a gamete of different character from one of the opposite sex (opposed to isogamete).

het·er·og·a·mous (hĕt′ə rŏg′ə məs), adj. 1. Biol. having unlike gametes, or reproducing by the union of such gametes (opposed to isogamous). 2. Bot. having flowers or florets of two sexually different kinds (opposed to homogamous).

het·er·og·a·my (hĕt′ə rŏg′ə mĭ), n. heterogamous state.

het·er·o·ge·ne·i·ty (hĕt′ər ə jə nē′ə tĭ), n., pl. -ties. the character or state of being heterogeneous; composition from dissimilar parts; disparateness.

het·er·o·ge·ne·ous (hĕt′ə rə jē′nĭ əs), adj. 1. different in kind; unlike; incongruous. 2. composed of parts of different kinds; having widely unlike elements or constituents; not homogeneous. [t. ML: m. heterogeneus, t. Gk.: m. heterogenés of different kinds] —**het′er·o·ge′ne·ous·ly**, adv. —**het′er·o·ge′ne·ous·ness**, n.

het·er·og·e·nous (hĕt′ə rŏj′ə nəs), adj. Biol., Pathol. having its source or origin outside the organism; having a foreign origin.

het·er·og·o·nous (hĕt′ə rŏg′ə nəs), adj. 1. Bot. noting or pertaining to monoclinous flowers of two or more kinds occurring on different individuals of the same species, the kinds differing in the relative length of stamens and pistils (opposed to homogonous). 2. Zool. heterogynous.

het·er·og·o·ny (hĕt′ə rŏg′ə nĭ), n. Biol. a. the alteration of dioecious and hermaphrodite individuals in successive generations, as in certain nematodes. b. (in more recent usage) the alternation of parthenogenetic and sexual generations.

het·er·og·ra·phy (hĕt′ə rŏg′rə fĭ), n. spelling different from that in current use. —**het·er·o·graph·ic** (hĕt′ə rə grăf′ĭk), adj.

het·er·og·y·nous (hĕt′ə rŏj′ə nəs), adj. Zool. having females of two different kinds, one sexual and the other abortive or neuter, as ants.

het·er·ol·o·gous (hĕt′ə rŏl′ə gəs), adj. 1. having a different relation; not corresponding. 2. Pathol. consisting of tissue unlike the normal tissue, as a tumor.

het·er·ol·o·gy (hĕt′ə rŏl′ə jĭ), n. 1. Biol. the lack of correspondence of organic structures as the result of unlike origins of constituent parts. 2. Pathol. abnormality; structural difference from a type or normal standard.

het·er·ol·y·sis (hĕt′ə rŏl′ə sĭs), n. Biochem. dissolution of the cells of one organism by the lysins of another.

het·er·om·er·ous (hĕt′ə rŏm′ər əs), adj. having or consisting of parts which differ in quality, number of elements, or the like: a heteromerous flower.

het·er·o·mor·phic (hĕt′ər ə môr′fĭk), adj. 1. Biol. dissimilar in shape, structure, or magnitude. 2. Entomol. undergoing complete metamorphosis; possessing varying forms. —**het′er·o·mor′phism**, n.

het·er·on·o·mous (hĕt′ə rŏn′ə məs), adj. 1. subject to or involving different laws. 2. pertaining to, or characterized by, heteronomy. 3. Biol. characterizing an organism which is metameric, or segmented, most or all of whose segments are specialized in different ways. [f. HETERO- + s. Gk. nómos law + -OUS]

het·er·on·o·my (hĕt′ə rŏn′ə mĭ), n. condition of being under the rule of another (opposed to autonomy).

het·er·o·nym (hĕt′ə rə nĭm′), n. a word having a different sound and meaning from another, but the same spelling, as lead (to conduct) and lead (a metal).

het·er·on·y·mous (hĕt′ə rŏn′ə məs), adj. 1. pertaining to or of the nature of a heteronym. 2. having different names, as a pair of correlatives. 3. Optics. denoting or pertaining to the images formed in a kind of double vision in which the image seen by the right eye is on the left side and vice versa. [t. Gk.: m. heterónymos having a different name]

---

b., blend of, blended; c., cognate with; d., dialect, dialectal; der., derived from; f., formed from; g., going back to; m., modification of; r., replacing; s., stem of; t., taken from; ?, perhaps. See the full key on inside cover.

Het·er·o·ou·si·an (hĕt/ər ō ōō/sĬ ən, -ou/sĬ ən), *n.* **1.** *Eccles.* one who believes the Father and Son to be unlike in substance or essence; an Arian (opposed to *Homooöusian*). —*adj.* **2.** of or pertaining to the Heteroöusians or their doctrine. [f. s. LGk. *heterooúsios* of different nature + -AN]

het·er·o·phyl·lous (hĕt/ər ə fĬl/əs), *adj.* *Bot.* having different kinds of leaves on the same plant. [f. HETERO- + s. Gk. *phýllon* leaf + -OUS] —**het/er·o·phyl/ly,** *n.*

het·er·o·plas·ty (hĕt/ər ə plăs/tĬ), *n.* *Surg.* the repair of lesions with tissue from another individual.

het·er·op·ter·ous (hĕt/ə rŏp/tər əs), *adj.* pertaining to the true bugs, *Heteroptera,* which constitute a suborder of the order *Hemiptera.* [f. s. NL *Heteroptera,* class name (f. *hetero-* HETERO- + Gk. *pterá* wings) + -OUS]

het·er·o·sex·u·al (hĕt/ər ə sĕk/shōō əl), *adj.* **1.** *Biol.* pertaining to the other sex or to both sexes. **2.** pertaining to or exhibiting heterosexuality.

het·er·o·sex·u·al·i·ty (hĕt/ər ə sĕk/shōō ăl/ə tĬ), *n.* sexual feeling for a person (or persons) of opposite sex.

het·er·o·sis (hĕt/ə rō/sĬs), *n.* *Genetics.* the increase in growth, size, fecundity, function, yield, or other characters in hybrids over those of the parents. [t. LGk.: alteration]

het·er·os·po·rous (hĕt/ə rŏs/pə rəs, hĕt/ər ə spōr/əs), *adj.* *Bot.* having more than one kind of spores.

het·er·os·po·ry (hĕt/ə rŏs/pər Ĭ), *n.* *Bot.* the production of both microspores and megaspores.

het·er·o·tax·is (hĕt/ər ə tăk/sĬs), *n.* abnormal or irregular arrangement, as of parts of the body, geological strata, etc. (opposite of *homotaxis*). Also, **het/er·o·tax/y.** —**het·er·o·tax/ic,** *adj.*

het·er·o·thal·lic (hĕt/ər ə thăl/Ĭk), *adj.* *Bot.* having mycelia of two unlike types both of which must participate in the sexual process (opposite of *homothallic*). [f. HETERO- + s. Gk. *thallôs* shoot, sprout + -IC]

het·er·o·to·pi·a (hĕt/ər ə tō/pĬ ə), *n.* *Pathol.* **1.** misplacement or displacement, as of an organ. **2.** the formation of tissue in a part where it is abnormal. Also, **het·er·o·to·py** (hĕt/ə rŏt/ə pĬ). [NL, f. Gk.: *hetero-* HETERO- + *-topia* (der. *tópos* place)] —**het·er·o·top·ic** (hĕt/ər ə tŏp/Ĭk), **het·er·ot·o·pous** (hĕt/ə rŏt/ə pəs), *adj.*

het·er·o·troph·ic (hĕt/ər ə trŏf/Ĭk), *adj.* *Biol.* incapable of synthesizing proteins and carbohydrates, as animals and dependent plants (opposite of *autotrophic*).

het·er·o·typ·ic (hĕt/ər ə tĬp/Ĭk), *adj.* *Biol.* applying meiotic division which reduces the chromosome number during the development of the reproductive cells. Also, **het/er·o·typ/i·cal.**

het·er·o·zy·gote (hĕt/ər ə zī/gōt, -zĬg/ōt), *n.* *Genetics.* a hybrid containing genes for two unlike characteristics; an organism which will not breed true to type. —**het·er·o·zy·gous** (hĕt/ər ə zī/gəs), *adj.*

het·man (hĕt/mən), *n.,* *pl.* **-mans.** a Cossack chief. [t. Pol., said to be t. G: m. *hauptmann* captain]

heu·ris·tic (hyōō rĬs/tĬk), *adj.* **1.** serving to find out; furthering investigation. **2.** (of a teaching method) encouraging the student to discover for himself. [appar. b. Gk. *heurís(kein)* find and obs. *(heure)tic* inventive (t. Gk.: m.s. *heuretikós*)] —**heu·ris/ti·cal·ly,** *adv.*

Heus·sler alloys (hūs/lər; *Ger.* hois/-), alloys of manganese and other nonferromagnetic metals which exhibit ferromagnetism.

he·ve·a (hē/vĬ ə), *n.* Pará rubber.

hew (hū), *v.,* **hewed, hewed** or **hewn, hewing.** —*v.t.* **1.** to strike forcibly with an ax, sword, or the like; chop; hack. **2.** to make or shape with cutting blows: *to hew a passage.* **3.** to sever (a part) from a whole, by means of cutting leaves (fol. by *away, off, out, from,* etc.). **4.** to cut down; fell: *to hew down trees.* —*v.i.* **5.** to deal cutting blows; to cut: *hew to the line, let the chips fall where they may.* [ME *hewe(n),* OE *hēawan,* c. G *hauen*] —**hew/er,** *n.* —Syn. 1. See cut.

hewers of wood and drawers of water, menial workers. Joshua 9:21.

Hew·lett (hū/lĬt), *n.* **Maurice,** 1861–1923, British author.

hex (hĕks), *v.t.* *U.S. Colloq. or Dial.* **1.** to bewitch; practice witchcraft on. [v. use of n.] —*n.* **2.** a witch. **3.** a spell. [t. G: m. *hexe* witch. See HAG¹]

hexa-, a prefix meaning "six," as in *hexagon.* Also, before vowels, **hex-.** [t. Gk., comb. form of *héx*]

hex·a·chord (hĕk/sə kôrd/), *n.* *Music.* a diatonic series of six tones, having (in medieval music) a half step between the third and fourth tones and whole steps between the others. [t. LGk.: s. *hexáchordos*]

hex·ad (hĕk/săd), *n.* **1.** the number six. **2.** a group or series of six. [t. LL: s. *hexas,* t. Gk.: six] —**hex·ad/ic,** *adj.*

hex·a·gon (hĕk/sə gŏn/, -gən), *n.* a polygon having six angles and six sides.

hex·ag·o·nal (hĕks ăg/ə nəl), *adj.* **1.** of, pertaining to, or having the form of a hexagon. **2.** having a hexagon as a base or cross section. **3.** divided into hexagons, as a surface. **4.** *Crystall.* noting or pertaining to the hexagonal system. Also, **hex.** —**hex·ag/o·nal·ly,** *adv.*

Regular hexagon

hexagonal system, *Crystall.* a system of crystallization characterized by three equal lateral axes intersecting at angles of 60° and a vertical axis of hexagonal symmetry and of different length at right angles to them.

hex·a·gram (hĕk/sə grăm/), *n.* **1.** a six-pointed starlike figure formed of two equilateral triangles placed concentrically with their sides parallel, and on opposite sides of the center: **2.** *Geom.* a figure of six lines.

Hexagram (def. 1)

hex·a·he·dron (hĕk/sə hē/drən), *n., pl.* **-drons, -dra** (-drə). a solid figure having six faces. —**hex/a·he/dral,** *adj.*

hex·am·er·ous (hĕks ăm/ər əs), *adj.* **1.** consisting of or divided into six parts. **2.** *Zool.* having a radially symmetrical arrangement of organs in six groups. **3.** *Bot.* having six members in each whorl.

hex·am·e·ter (hĕks ăm/ə tər), *n.* **1.** *Pros.* the dactylic verse of six feet, of Greek and Latin epic and other poetry **(dactylic hexameter),** in which the first four feet are dactyls or spondees, the fifth is ordinarily a dactyl, and the last is a trochee or spondee with a caesura usually following the long syllable in the third foot. **2.** any hexameter verse. —*adj.* **3.** consisting of six metrical feet. [t. L, t. Gk.: m. *hexámetros* of six measures] —**hex·a·met·ric** (hĕk/sə mĕt/rĬk), **hex/a·met/ri·cal,** *adj.*

hex·a·meth·yl·ene·tet·ra·mine (hĕk/sə mĕth/əlēn tĕt/rə mēn/), *n.* *Chem.* a colorless crystalline compound, $C_6H_{12}N_4$, used as a urinary antiseptic, an accelerator, an absorbent in gas masks, and in the manufacture of synthetic resins. Also **hex·a·meth/yl·enetet/ra·min** (-tĕt/rə mĬn).

hex·ane (hĕk/sān), *n.* *Chem.* any of the five isomeric saturated hydrocarbons, C_6H_{14}, derived from the fractional distillation of petroleum. [f. Gk. *héx* six (with reference to the atoms of carbon) + -ANE]

hex·an·gu·lar (hĕks ăng/gyə lər), *adj.* having six angles.

hex·a·pla (hĕk/sə plə), *n.* an edition of the Old Testament containing six versions in parallel columns, as one compiled by Origen. [t. Gk., prop. neut. pl. of *hexaplóos* sixfold] —**hex/a·plar,** *adj.*

hex·a·pod (hĕk/sə pŏd/), *n.* **1.** one of the *Hexapoda;* insect. —*adj.* **2.** having six feet. [t. Gk.: s. *hexápous* sixfooted] —**hex·ap·o·dous** (hĕks ăp/ə dəs), *adj.*

hex·a·po·dy (hĕks ăp/ə dĬ), *n., pl.* **-dies.** *Pros.* a line or verse consisting of six metrical feet.

hex·ar·chy (hĕk/sär kĬ), *n., pl.* **-chies.** a group of six states or kingdoms, each under its own ruler.

hex·a·stich (hĕk/sə stĬk), *n.* *Pros.* a strophe, stanza, or poem consisting of six lines or verses. Also, **hex·asti·chon** (hĕks ăs/tə kŏn/). [t. Gk.: s. *hexástichos* of six rows or lines]

Hex·a·teuch (hĕk/sə tūk/, -tōōk/), *n.* the first six books of the Old Testament. [f. HEXA- + s. Gk. *teûchos* book] —**Hex/a·teuch/al,** *adj.*

hex·one (hĕk/sōn), *n.* *Chem.* any of various organic ketones which contain six atoms of carbon in the molecule. [f. Gk. *héx* six + -ONE, after G *hexon*]

hex·o·san (hĕk/sə săn/), *n.* any of a group of hemicelluloses which hydrolyze to hexoses. [f. HEXOS(E) + -AN]

hex·ose (hĕk/sōs), *n.* *Chem.* any of a class of sugars containing six atoms of carbon, as glucose and fructose.

hex·yl (hĕk/sĬl), *n.* *Chem.* the univalent radical, C_6H_{13}, derived from hexane.

hex·yl·res·or·cin·ol (hĕk/sĬl rə zôr/sə nōl/, -nŏl/), *n.* a colorless, crystalline antiseptic, $C_{12}H_{18}O_2$, which is less toxic and more powerful than phenol.

hey (hā), *interj.* an exclamation to express pleasure, surprise, bewilderment, etc., or to call attention.

hey·day (hā/dā/), *n.* **1.** the stage or period of highest vigor or fullest strength. **2.** high spirits. —*interj.* **3.** an exclamation of cheerfulness, surprise, wonder, etc.

Hey·duck (hī/dŏŏk), *n.* Haiduk. Also, **Hey/duke.**

Hey·se (hī/zə), *n.* **Paul Johann Ludwig von** (poul yō/hän lōōt/vĬKH fən), 1830–1914, German writer.

Hey·ward (hā/wərd), *n.* **DuBose** (də bōz/), 1885–1940, U.S. author and dramatist.

Hey·wood (hā/wŏŏd), *n.* **1. John,** 1497?–1580?, English dramatist and epigrammatist. **2. Thomas,** died c1650, English dramatist, actor, and poet.

Hez·e·ki·ah (hĕz/ə kī/ə), *n.* a king of Judah of the 8th–7th centuries B.C. II Kings 18, etc.

Hf, *Chem.* hafnium.

HG, 1. High German. **2.** *Brit.* Home Guard.

Hg, (L *hydrargyrum*) *Chem.* mercury.

H.G., 1. His, or Her, Grace. **2.** High German.

H.H., 1. His, or Her, Highness. **2.** His Holiness.

hhd., hogshead.

H-hour (āch/our/), *n.* *Mil.* the time set for an attack.

hi (hī), *interj.* an exclamation, esp. of greeting.

H.I., Hawaiian Islands.

Hi·a·le·ah (hī/ə lē/ə), *n.* a city in SE Florida, near Miami; racetrack. 66,972 (1960).

hi·a·tus (hī ā/təs), *n., pl.* **-tuses, -tus. 1.** a break, with a part missing; an interruption; lacuna: *a hiatus in a manuscript.* **2.** a gap or opening. **3.** *Gram.* and *Pros.* a break or slight pause due to the coming together without contraction of two vowels in successive words or syllables. **4.** *Anat.* a natural fissure, cleft, or foramen in a bone or other structure. [t. L: gap]

Hi·a·wath·a (hī/ə wŏth/ə, -wô/thə, hē/ə-), *n.* the central figure of *The Song of Hiawatha* (1855), a poem by Longfellow.

ăct, āble, dâre, ärt; ĕbb, ēqual; Ĭf, īce; hŏt, ōver, ôrder, oil, bŏŏk, ōōze, out; ŭp, ūse, ûrge; ə = a in alone; ch, chief; g, give; ng, ring; sh, shoe; th, thin; ŧh, that; zh, vision.   See the full key on inside cover.

hi·ba·chi (hĭ bä/chē), *n.* a portable brazier for broiling foods, consisting of a heavy wire grill over a pot-shaped container for burning charcoal. [t. Jap.]

hi·ber·nac·u·lum (hĭ/bər năk/yə ləm), *n., pl.* **-la** (-lə). **1.** a protective case or covering for winter, as of an animal or a plant bud. **2.** Also, **hi·ber·nac·le** (hĭ/bər năk/əl). winter quarters, as of a hibernating animal. [t. L: winter residence]

hi·ber·nal (hī bûr/nəl), *adj.* of or pertaining to winter; wintry. [t. LL: s. *hĭbernālis* wintry]

hi·ber·nate (hī/bər nāt/), *v.i.,* **-nated, -nating. 1.** to spend the winter in close quarters in a dormant condition, as certain animals. **2.** to remain in seclusion. [t. L: m.s. *hĭbernātus,* pp., wintered] —**hi/ber·na/tion,** *n.*

Hi·ber·ni·a (hī bûr/nĭ ə), *n.* Latin or literary name of Ireland. [t. L]

Hi·ber·ni·an (hī bûr/nĭ ən), *adj.* **1.** Irish. —*n.* **2.** a native of Ireland. [f. s. L *Hibernia* Ireland + -AN]

Hi·ber·ni·cism (hī bûr/nə sĭz/əm), *n.* **1.** an idiom peculiar to Irish English. **2.** an Irish characteristic. Also, **Hi·ber·ni·an·ism** (hī bûr/nĭ ə nĭz/əm).

hi·bis·cus (hī bĭs/kəs, hĭ-), *n.* any of the herbs, shrubs, or trees of the malvaceous genus *Hibiscus,* many of which, as the shrub althea, *H. syriacus,* have large showy flowers. [t. L, t. Gk.: m. *ibĭskos* mallow]

hic·cup (hĭk/ŭp, -əp), *n.* **1.** a quick, involuntary inspiration suddenly checked by closure of the glottis, producing a characteristic sound. **2.** (*usually pl.*) the condition of having such spasms: *to have the hiccups.* —*v.i.* **3.** to make the sound of a hiccup. **4.** to have the hiccups. Also, **hic·cough** (hĭk/ŭp, -əp). [earlier *hickock,* f. *hick* (imit.) + -OCK. Cf. LG *hick* hiccup]

hic ja·cet (hĭk jā/sĕt), *Latin.* here lies (often used to begin epitaphs on tombstones).

hick (hĭk), *Slang.* —*n.* **1.** an unsophisticated person. **2.** a farmer. —*adj.* **3.** pertaining to or characteristic of hicks. [familiar form of *Richard,* man's name]

hick·ey (hĭk/ĭ), *n., pl.* **-eys. 1.** any device. **2.** *Elect.* a fitting used to mount a lighting fixture in an outlet box or on a pipe or stud.

Hick·ok (hĭk/ŏk), *n.* **James Butler,** ("*Wild Bill*") 1837–76, U.S. frontiersman.

hick·o·ry (hĭk/ə rĭ), *n., pl.* **-ries. 1.** any of the North American trees constituting the juglandaceous genus *Carya,* certain of which, as the pecan, *C. illinoensis* (*C. Pecan*), bear sweet, edible nuts (**hickory nuts**), and others, as the shagbark, *C. ovata,* yield valuable hard wood and edible nuts. **2.** the wood of such a tree. **3.** a switch, stick, etc., of this wood. [t. Amer. Ind. (Va.). Cf. Algonquian *pawcohiccora* walnut kernel mush]

hick·wall (hĭk/wôl/), *n.* any of certain European woodpeckers, esp. the green woodpecker, *Gecinus viridis.*

hid (hĭd), *v.* pt. and pp. of **hide.**

hi·dal·go (hī dăl/gō; *Sp.* ē däl/gô), *n., pl.* **-gos** (-gōz; *Sp.* -gôs). (in Spain) a man of the lower nobility. [t. Sp., contr. of *hijo de algo* son of (man of) property]

Hi·dal·go (hī dăl/gō; *Sp.* ē däl/gô), *n.* state in central Mexico. 867,142 pop. (est. 1952); 8057 sq. mi. *Cap.:* Pachuca.

Hi·dat·sa (hē dät/sä), *n.* **1.** a Siouan tribe dwelling on the Missouri river. **2.** their language.

hid·den (hĭd/ən), *adj.* **1.** concealed; obscure; latent. —*v.* **2.** pp. of **hide.** —**Syn.** secret, covert; occult.

hid·den·ite (hĭd/ən īt/), *n.* a rare, transparent emerald-green or yellowish-green variety of spodumene, a valuable gem. [named after W. E. *Hidden,* who discovered it (1879). See -ITE[1]]

hide[1] (hīd), *v.,* **hid, hidden** or **hid, hiding.** —*v.t.* **1.** to conceal from sight; prevent from being seen or discovered. **2.** to obstruct the view of; cover up: *the sun was hidden by clouds.* **3.** to conceal from knowledge; keep secret: *to hide one's feelings.* —*v.i.* **4.** to conceal oneself; lie concealed. —*n.* **5.** *Brit.* a covered place to hide in while shooting. Cf. *U.S.* **blind** (def. 19). [ME *hide*(n), OE *hȳdan,* c. MLG *hüden*] —**hid/er,** *n.* —**Syn.** **1.** screen, mask, cloak, veil, shroud, disguise. HIDE, CONCEAL, SECRETE mean to put out of sight or in a secret place. HIDE is the general word: *to hide or conceal one's money or purpose, a dog hides a bone.* CONCEAL, somewhat more formal, is to cover from sight: *a rock hid or concealed them from view.* SECRETE means to hide carefully, in order to keep secret: *the banker secretes important papers.* **3.** dissemble, suppress. —**Ant. 1.** reveal, display.

hide[2] (hīd), *n., v.,* **hided, hiding.** —*n.* **1.** the skin of an animal, esp. one of the larger animals, raw or dressed: *the hide of a calf.* **2.** *Slang.* the human skin. —*v.t.* **3.** *Colloq.* to flog or thrash. [ME; OE *hȳd,* c. G *haut*] —**Syn. 1.** See **skin.**

hide[3] (hīd), *n.* an old English measure of land, usually 120 acres, considered adequate for one free family and its dependents. [ME; OE *hīd*(*e*), *hīg*(*i*)*d,* f. *hīg*(*an*) family, household + -*id,* suffix of appurtenance]

hide-and-seek (hīd/ən sēk/), *n.* a children's game in which some hide and others seek them.

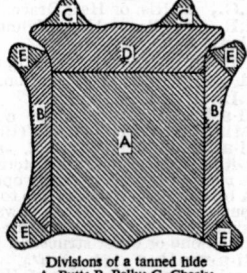

Divisions of a tanned hide
A. Butt; B. Belly; C. Cheek;
D. Shoulder; E. Shank

hide·bound (hīd/bound/), *adj.* **1.** narrow and rigid in opinion: *a hidebound pedant.* **2.** (of a horse, etc.) having the back and ribs bound tightly by the hide. [f. HIDE[2] + BOUND]

hid·e·ous (hĭd/ĭ əs), *adj.* **1.** horrible or frightful to the senses; very ugly: *a hideous monster.* **2.** shocking or revolting to the moral sense: *a hideous crime.* [ME *hidous,* t. AF, der. *hi*(*s*)*de* horror, fear; orig. uncert.] —**hid/e·ous·ly,** *adv.* —**hid/e·ous·ness,** *n.* —**Syn. 1, 2.** grisly, grim; repulsive, detestable, odious. —**Ant. 1.** attractive, pleasing.

hide-out (hīd/out/), *n.* a safe place for hiding (usually from the law).

hid·ing[1] (hī/dĭng), *n.* **1.** act of concealing; concealment: *to remain in hiding.* **2.** a place or means of concealment. [f. HIDE[1] + -ING[1]]

hid·ing[2] (hī/dĭng), *n.* *Colloq.* a flogging or thrashing. [f. HIDE[2] + -ING[1]]

hi·dro·sis (hī drō/sĭs), *n.* *Pathol.* **1.** excessive perspiration due to drugs, disease, or the like. **2.** any of certain diseases characterized by sweating. [NL, special use of Gk. *hidrōsis* perspiration] —**hi·drot·ic** (hī drŏt/ĭk), *adj.*

hie (hī), *v.i.,* **hied, hieing** or **hying.** to hasten; speed; go in haste. [ME; OE *hīgian* strive. Cf. D *hijgen* pant]

hi·er·arch (hī/ə rärk/), *n.* **1.** one who rules or has authority in sacred things. **2.** a chief priest. **3.** one of a body of officials or minor priests in some ancient Greek temples. [t. ML: s. *hierarcha,* t. Gk.: m. *hierárchēs* steward of sacred rites] —**hi/er·ar/chal,** *adj.*

hi·er·ar·chi·cal (hī/ə rär/kə kəl), *adj.* of or belonging to a hierarchy. Also, **hi·er·ar/chic.** —**hi·er·ar/chi·cal·ly,** *adv.*

hi·er·ar·chism (hī/ə rär/kĭz əm), *n.* hierarchical principles, rule, or influence.

hi·er·ar·chy (hī/ə rär/kĭ), *n., pl.* **-chies. 1.** any system of persons or things in a graded order, etc. **2.** *Science.* a series of successive terms of different rank. The terms *phylum, class, order, family, genus,* and *species* constitute a hierarchy in zoology. **3.** government by ecclesiastical rulers. **4.** the power or dominion of a hierarch. **5.** an organized body of ecclesiastical officials in successive ranks or orders: *the Roman Catholic hierarchy.* **6.** one of the three divisions of the angels, each made up of three orders, conceived as constituting a graded body. **7.** the collective body of angels (**celestial hierarchy**).

hi·er·at·ic (hī/ə răt/ĭk), *adj.* **1.** pertaining to priests or to the priesthood; priestly. **2.** noting or pertaining to a form of ancient Egyptian writing consisting of abridged forms of hieroglyphics, used by the priests in their records. **3.** noting or pertaining to certain styles in art whose types or methods are fixed by or as by religious tradition. [t. L: s. *hieraticus,* t. Gk.: m. *hierātikós* priestly, sacerdotal] —**hi/er·at/i·cal·ly,** *adv.*

hiero-, a word element meaning "sacred," as in *hierocracy.* [t. Gk., comb. form of *hierós* holy]

hi·er·oc·ra·cy (hī/ə rŏk/rə sĭ), *n., pl.* **-cies.** rule or government by priests or ecclesiastics. —**hi·er·o·crat·ic** (hī/ər ə krăt/ĭk), *adj.*

hi·er·o·dule (hī/ə ə dūl/, -dōōl/), *n.* a slave in an ancient Greek temple, dedicated to the service of a deity. [t. Gk.: m.s. *hieródoulos* temple slave]

hi·er·o·glyph·ic (hī/ə rə glĭf/ĭk, hī/rə-), *adj.* Also, **hi·er·o·glyph/i·cal. 1.** designating or pertaining to a writing system, particularly that of the ancient Egyptians, in which many of the symbols are conventionalized pictures of the thing named by the words for which the symbols stand. **2.** inscribed with hieroglyphic symbols. **3.** hard to decipher; hard to read. —*n.* **4.** Also, **hi/er·o·glyph/.** a hieroglyphic symbol. **5.** (*usually pl.*) hieroglyphic writing. **6.** a figure or symbol with a hidden meaning. **7.** (*pl.*) writing difficult to decipher. [t. LL: s. *hieroglyphicus,* t. Gk: m. *hieroglyphikós*] —**hi·er·o·glyph/i·cal·ly,** *adv.*

hi·er·ol·o·gy (hī/ə rŏl/ə jĭ), *n.* literature or learning regarding sacred things.

Hi·er·on·y·mite (hī/ə rŏn/ə mīt/), *n.* a member of the "Congregation of Hermits of St. Jerome."

Hi·er·on·y·mus (hī/ə rŏn/ə məs), *n.* Jerome (Saint).

hi·er·o·phant (hī/ə rə fănt/, hī ĕr/ə-), *n.* **1.** (in ancient Greece, etc.) an official expounder of rites of worship and sacrifice. **2.** any interpreter of sacred mysteries or esoteric principles. [t. LL: s. *hierophantēs,* t. Gk.] —**hi·er·o·phan·tic** (hī/ə rə făn/tĭk, hī ĕr/ə-), *adj.*

hi·fa·lu·tin (hī/fə lōō/tən), *adj. Colloq.* highfalutin.

hi-fi (hī/fī/), *adj.* high fidelity, as in radio or phonograph equipment.

Hig·gin·son (hĭg/ĭn sən), *n.* **Thomas Wentworth,** 1823–1911, U.S. author, soldier, and social reformer.

hig·gle (hĭg/əl), *v.i.,* **-gled, -gling.** to bargain, esp. in a petty way; haggle. [appar. var. of HAGGLE]

hig·gle·dy-pig·gle·dy (hĭg/əl dĭ pĭg/əl dĭ), *Colloq.* —*adv.* **1.** in a jumbled confusion. —*adj.* **2.** confused; jumbled. —*n.* **3.** confusion; a disorderly jumble.

hig·gler (hĭg/lər), *n.* a huckster or peddler.

high (hī), *adj.* **1.** having a great or considerable reach or extent upward; lofty; tall. **2.** having a specified extent upward. **3.** situated above the ground or some base; elevated. **4.** intensified; exceeding the common

Hiero-glyph-ics

degree or measure; strong; intense, energetic: *high speed.* **5.** expensive, costly, or dear. **6.** exalted in rank, station, estimation, etc.; of exalted character or quality: *a high official.* **7.** *Music.* **a.** acute in pitch. **b.** a little sharp, or above the desired pitch. **8.** produced by relatively rapid vibrations; shrill: *high sounds.* **9.** extending to or from an elevation: *a high dive.* **10.** of great amount, degree, force, etc.: *a high temperature.* **11.** chief; principal; main: *the high altar of a church.* **12.** of great consequence; important; grave; serious: *high treason.* **13.** lofty; haughty; arrogant: *he spoke in a high and mighty manner.* **14.** advanced to the utmost extent, or to the culmination: *high noon.* **15.** elated; merry or hilarious: *high spirits.* **16.** *Colloq.* excited with drink. **17.** remote: *high latitude, high antiquity.* **18.** extreme in opinion or doctrine, esp. religious or political. **19.** designating or pertaining to highland or inland regions: *the High Germans.* **20.** *Biol.* having a relatively complex structure: *the higher mammals.* **21.** *Auto.* operating at or pertaining to the highest transmission gear ratio. **22.** *Phonet.* pronounced with the tongue relatively close to the roof of the mouth: *"feed" and "food" have high vowels.* **23.** (of meat, esp. game) tending toward a desirable amount of decomposition; slightly tainted. **24. high relief.** See **relief** (defs. 9, 10) and **alto-relievo.** **25. on high, a.** at or to a height; above. **b.** in heaven. —*adv.* **26.** at or to a high point, place, or level, or a high rank or estimate, a high amount or price, or a high degree. **27.** *Naut.* close to the wind (said of a ship when sailing by the wind, with reference to the smallest angle with the wind at which the sails will remain full and the ship make headway). **28. high and low,** everywhere. —*n.* **29.** *Auto.* a transmission gear providing the highest forward speed ratio, usually turning the drive shaft at the same rate as the engine crankshaft. **30.** *U.S. Colloq.* high school. **31.** *Meteorol.* a pressure system characterized by relatively high pressure at its center; an anticyclone. **32.** *Cards.* the ace or highest trump out, esp. in games of the seven-up family. [ME *heigh,* etc., OE *hēah,* c. G *hoch*] —**Syn. 1.** HIGH, LOFTY, TALL, TOWERING refer to that which has considerable height. HIGH is a general term, and denotes either extension upward or position at a considerable height: *six feet high, a high shelf.* LOFTY denotes imposing or even inspiring height: *lofty crags.* TALL is applied either to that which is high in proportion to its breadth, or to anything higher than the average of its kind: *a tall tree, building.* TOWERING is applied to that which rises to a great or conspicuous height as compared with something else: *a towering mountain, cliff.* **6.** elevated, eminent. —**Ant. 1.** low.

high·ball (hī′bôl′), *n.* *U.S.* a drink of whiskey or other liquor diluted with water, seltzer, or ginger ale, and served with ice in a tall glass.

high·bin·der (hī′bĭn′dər), *n.* *U.S. Slang.* **1.** a member of a secret Chinese band or society employed for blackmail, assassination, etc. **2.** a ruffian or rowdy.

high·born (hī′bôrn′), *adj.* of high rank by birth.

high·boy (hī′boi′), *n.* a tall chest of drawers supported on legs. Cf. **lowboy.**

high·bred (hī′brĕd′), *adj.* **1.** of superior breed. **2.** characteristic of superior breeding: *highbred manners.*

high·brow (hī′brou′), *n.* *Colloq.* **1.** a person of intellectual tastes. Cf. **lowbrow.** —*adj.* **2.** of or pertaining to highbrows. **3.** being a highbrow.

High Church, a party in the Anglican Church which lays great stress on church authority and jurisdiction, ritual, etc. (opposed to *Low Church* and *Broad Church*). —**High′-Church′,** *adj.* —**High Churchman.**

high·col·ored (hī′kŭl′ərd), *adj.* **1.** deep in color. **2.** florid or red: *a high-colored complexion.*

high comedy, comedy dealing with polite society, depending largely on witty dialogue. Cf. **low comedy.**

high day, 1. a holy or festal day. **2.** heyday.

higher criticism, the study of literature, esp. the Bible, by scientific and historical techniques.

higher education, education beyond secondary education.

higher mathematics, the more scientifically treated and advanced portions of mathematics customarily embracing all beyond ordinary arithmetic, geometry, algebra, and trigonometry.

high·er-up (hī′ər ŭp′), *n.* *U.S. Colloq.* one occupying a superior position.

high explosive, a class of explosive, as TNT, in which the reaction is so rapid as to be practically instantaneous, used for bursting charges in shells and bombs.

high·fa·lu·tin (hī′fə lōō′tən), *adj.* *Colloq.* pompous; haughty; pretentious. Also, **hifalutin, high′fa·lu′ting.**

high·fi·del·i·ty (hī′fĭ dĕl′ə tĭ), *adj.* *Electronics.* (of an amplifier, radio receiver, etc.) reproducing the full audio range of the original signal of sounds with relatively little distortion. Also, **hi-fi.**

high·fil·er (hī′fīl′ər), *n.* **1.** one who or that which flies high. **2.** one who is extravagant or goes to extremes in aims, pretensions, opinions, etc. Also, **high′fly′er.**

high-flown (hī′flōn′), *adj.* **1.** extravagant in aims, pretensions, etc. **2.** pretentiously lofty; bombastic.

high·fly·ing (hī′flī′ĭng), *adj.* **1.** that flies high, as a bird. **2.** extravagant or extreme in aims, opinions, etc.

high-fre·quen·cy (hī′frē′kwən sĭ), *adj.* noting or pertaining to frequencies above the upper limit of the audible range, esp. as used in radio.

High German, 1. any form of the German of

central and southern Germany, Switzerland, and Austria, including Old High German and Middle High German. **2.** standard German.

high-grade (hī′grād′), *adj.* **1.** of superior quality. **2.** (of ore) with a relatively high yield of the metal for which it is mined.

high-hand·ed (hī′hăn′dĭd), *adj.* overbearing; arbitrary: *high-handed oppression.* —**high′-hand′ed·ly,** *adv.* —**high′-hand′ed·ness,** *n.*

high hat, a top hat.

high-hat (*v.* hī′hăt′; *adj.* hī′hăt′), *v.,* **-hatted, -hatting,** *adj.* *U.S. Slang.* —*v.t.* **1.** to snub or treat condescendingly. —*adj.* **2.** snobbish. **3.** fashionable.

high·hole (hī′hōl′), *n.* *U.S. Dial.* flicker². Also, **high-hold·er** (hī′hōl′dər).

high·jack (hī′jăk′), *v.t., v.i.* *U.S. Slang.* hijack.

high jump, *Athletics.* **1.** a vertical jump in which one attempts to go as high as possible. **2.** a contest for the highest such jump.

high·land (hī′lənd), *n.* **1.** an elevated region; a plateau: *a jutting highland.* **2.** (*pl.*) a mountainous region or elevated part of a country. —*adj.* **3.** of, pertaining to, or characteristic of highlands.

High·land·er (hī′lən dər), *n.* **1.** a member of the Gaelic race of the Highlands. **2.** a soldier of a Highland regiment. **3.** (*l.c.*) an inhabitant of high land.

Highland fling, a vigorous Scotch country dance, a form of the reel.

High·land Park (hī′lənd), *n.* a city in SE Michigan, within the city limits of Detroit. 38,063 (1960).

High·lands (hī′ləndz), *n.pl.* a mountainous region in Scotland, N of the Grampians.

high·light (hī′līt′), *v.,* **-lighted, -lighting,** *n.* —*v.t.* **1.** to emphasize or make prominent. **2.** *Art.* to emphasize (the areas of greatest brightness) with paint or by exposing lighter areas. —*n.* **3.** Also, **high light. a.** conspicuous or striking part: *the highlight of his talk.* **4.** an important event, scene, etc. **5.** *Art.* the point of most intense light in a picture or form.

high·ly (hī′lĭ), *adv.* **1.** in or to a high degree: *highly amusing.* **2.** with high appreciation or praise: *to speak highly of a person.* **3.** at or to a high price.

High Mass, *Rom. Cath. Ch.* a Mass celebrated according to the complete rite by a priest or prelate attended by a deacon and subdeacon, parts of the Mass being chanted or sung by the ministers and parts by the choir. During a High Mass incense is burned before the oblations, the altar, the ministers, and the people.

high-mind·ed (hī′mīn′dĭd), *adj.* **1.** having or showing high, exalted principles or feelings: *a high-minded ruler.* **2.** proud or arrogant. —**high′-mind′ed·ly,** *adv.* —**high′-mind′ed·ness,** *n.* —**Syn. 1.** See **noble.**

high-necked (hī′nĕkt′), *adj.* (of a garment) high at the neck.

high·ness (hī′nĭs), *n.* **1.** state of being high; loftiness; dignity. **2.** (*cap.*) a title of honor given to royal or princely personages (prec. by *His, Your,* etc.).

high-oc·tane gasoline (hī′ŏk′tān), gasoline with a relatively high octane number, used when efficiency and antiknock qualities are desirable. See **octane number.**

high place, (in Semitic religions) a place of worship, usually on a hilltop.

High Point, a city in central North Carolina. 62,063 (1960).

high-pres·sure (hī′prĕsh′ər), *adj.* **1.** having or involving a pressure above the normal: *high-pressure steam.* **2.** vigorous; persistent: *high-pressure salesmanship.*

high-priced (hī′prīst′), *adj.* expensive.

high priest, chief priest.

high-proof (hī′prōōf′), *adj.* containing a high percentage of alcohol: *high-proof spirits.*

high rise, a building, as an apartment or office building, having a comparatively large number of stories.

high·road (hī′rōd′), *n.* **1.** a main road; a highway. **2.** an easy or certain course: *the highroad to success.*

high school, 1. a school following the ordinary grammar school and corresponding to grades 9 through 12. **2.** either of two schools, one (**junior high school**) corresponding to the upper grades or grade of the ordinary grammar school together with one or more years of the ordinary high school, and another (**senior high school**) corresponding to the remainder.

high sea, 1. sea or ocean beyond the three-mile limit. **2.** (*usually pl.*) the open, unenclosed waters of any sea or ocean; common highway. **3.** (*usually pl.*) the area within which transactions are subject to court of admiralty jurisdiction.

high-sound·ing (hī′soun′dĭng), *adj.* having an imposing or pretentious sound: *high-sounding titles.*

high-spir·it·ed (hī′spĭr′ə tĭd), *adj.* having a high, proud, or bold spirit; mettlesome.

high-strung (hī′strŭng′), *adj.* at great tension; highly nervous: *high-strung nerves, high-strung persons.*

hight (hīt), *adj. Archaic.* called or named: *Childe Harold was he hight.* [ME; OE *heht,* reduplicated preterit of *hātan* name, call, promise, command, c. G *heissen*; current meaning taken from OE *hātte,* passive of *hātan*]

high tea, *Brit.* an evening meal, commonly supper.

high-ten·sion (hī′tĕn′shən), *adj. Elect.* (of a device, circuit, circuit component, etc.) subjected to, or capable of operating under, a relatively high voltage, usually 1000 volts or more.

high-test (hī′tĕst′), *adj.* (of gasoline) boiling at a comparatively low temperature.

high tide, 1. the tide at high water. 2. the time of high water. 3. the culminating point.

high time, 1. the right time; the time just before it is too late: *it's high time that was done.* 2. *Slang.* an enjoyable and gay time: *a high old time at the party.*

high-toned (hī′tōnd′), *adj.* 1. high in tone or pitch. 2. having high principles; dignified. 3. *U.S. Colloq.* fashionable or stylish.

high treason, treason against the sovereign or state.

high-ty-tigh-ty (hī′tĭ tī′tĭ), *interj., adj.* hoity-toity.

high water, 1. high tide. 2. water at its greatest elevation, as in a river.

high-wa-ter mark (hī′wô′tər, -wŏt′ər), 1. a mark showing the highest level reached by a body of water. 2. the highest point of anything.

high-way (hī′wā′), *n.* 1. a main road, as one between towns. 2. any public passage, either a road or waterway. 3. any main or ordinary route, track, or course.

high-way-man (hī′wā′mən), *n., pl.* **-men.** a robber on the highway, esp. one on horseback.

high-wrought (hī′rôt′), *adj.* 1. wrought with a high degree of skill; ornate. 2. highly agitated.

H.I.H., His, or Her, Imperial Highness.

Hii-u-maa (hē′ōō mä′), *n.* an island in the Baltic, E of and belonging to the Estonian Republic of the Soviet Union. 373 sq. mi. Danish, **Dagö.**

hi-jack (hī′jăk′), *U.S. Slang.* —*v.t.* 1. to steal (liquor or other goods) from bootleggers or smugglers while it is in transit. —*v.i.* 2. to engage in such stealing. Also, **highjack.** [back formation from HIJACKER]

hi-jack-er (hī′jăk′ər), *n.* one who hijacks. [f. HIGH-(WAYMAN) + *jacker,* appar. der. *jack,* v., hunt by night with aid of a jack light]

hike (hīk), *v.,* **hiked, hiking,** *n.* —*v.i.* 1. to march or tramp, as soldiers or pleasure seekers. —*v.t.* 2. to move, draw, or raise with a jerk. —*n.* 3. a march or tramp. [? akin to HITCH] —**hik′er,** *n.*

hi-lar-i-ous (hĭ lâr′ĭ əs, hī-), *adj.* 1. boisterously gay. 2. cheerful. [f. HILARI(TY) + -OUS] —**hi-lar′i-ous-ly,** *adv.* —**hi-lar′i-ous-ness,** *n.*

hi-lar-i-ty (hĭ lăr′ə tĭ, hī-), *n.* 1. boisterous gaiety. 2. cheerfulness. [t. L: m.s. *hilaritas*] —**Syn.** 1. See **mirth.**

Hil-a-ry of Poitiers (hĭl′ə rĭ), **Saint,** A.D. c300–368, French bishop and theologian. French, **Hi-laire** (ē lĕr′).

Hil-de-brand (hĭl′də brănd′), *n.* See **Gregory VII.**

Hil-des-heim (hĭl′dĕs hīm′), *n.* a city in N West Germany. 81,200 (est. 1953).

hill (hĭl), *n.* 1. a conspicuous natural elevation of the earth's surface, smaller than a mountain. 2. an artificial heap or pile: *anthill.* 3. a little heap of earth raised about a cultivated plant or a cluster of such plants. 4. the plant or plants so surrounded. —*v.t.* 5. to surround with hills: *to hill potatoes.* 6. to form into a hill or heap. [ME; OE *hyll,* c. MD *hille;* akin to L *collis* hill, *columen* top, *columna* COLUMN] —**hill′er,** *n.* —**Syn.** 1. eminence; mound, knoll, hillock; foothill.

Hill (hĭl), *n.* 1. **Ambrose Powell,** 1825–65, Confederate general in the U.S. Civil War. 2. **James Jerome,** 1838–1916, U.S. railroad builder and financier, born in Canada.

hill-bil-ly (hĭl′bĭl′ĭ), *n., pl.* **-lies.** *U.S. Colloq.* a person, usually uncouth or ignorant, living in the backwoods or mountains of the South. [f. HILL- + BILLY]

Hill-man (hĭl′mən), *n.* **Sidney,** 1887–1946, U.S. labor leader, born in Lithuania.

hill myna, any of the Asiatic birds constituting the genus *Eulabes* (of the starling family, *Sturnidae*), esp. *E. religiosa,* easily tamed and taught to speak.

hill-ock (hĭl′ək), *n.* a little hill. —**hill′ock-y,** *adj.*

hill-side (hĭl′sīd′), *n.* the side or slope of a hill.

hill-site (hĭl′sīt′), *n.* situation on a hill; an elevated site.

hill station, any resort city in S Asia at a high altitude where relief may be found from the tropical heat.

hill-top (hĭl′tŏp′), *n.* the top or summit of a hill.

hill-y (hĭl′ĭ), *adj.,* **hillier, hilliest.** 1. abounding in hills: *hilly country.* 2. elevated; steep. —**hill′i-ness,** *n.*

Hi-lo (hē′lō), *n.* a seaport in the Hawaiian Islands, on the island of Hawaii. 25,966 (1960).

hilt (hĭlt), *n.* 1. the handle of a sword or dagger. 2. the handle of any weapon or tool. **to the hilt,** fully; completely: *armed to the hilt.* —*v.t.* 4. to furnish with a hilt. [ME *hylt,* OE *hilt, hilte,* c. MD *hilt, hilte;* of obscure orig.] —**hilt′ed,** *adj.*

Hil-ton (hĭl′tən), *n.* **James,** 1900–54, British novelist.

hi-lum (hī′ləm), *n., pl.* **-la** (-lə). 1. *Bot.* **a.** the mark or scar on a seed produced by separation from its funicle or placenta. See diag. under **seed.** **b.** the nucleus of a granule of starch. 2. *Anat.* the region at which the vessels, nerves, etc., enter or emerge from a part. [t. L: little thing, trifle]

him (hĭm), *pron.* objective case of *he.* [ME and OE; dat. of *hē* HE]

H.I.M., His, or Her, Imperial Majesty.

Hi-ma-chal Pra-desh (hĭ mä′chəl prə dāsh′), a centrally administered territory in N India. 1,117,003 pop.; 10,904 sq. mi.; *Cap.:* Simla.

Hi-ma-la-yas (hĭ mäl′yəz, hĭm′ə lā′əz), *n.pl.* **The,** a lofty mountain system extending ab. 1500 mi. along the border between India and Tibet. Highest peak (in the world), Mt. Everest, 29,028 ft. Also, **The Himalaya** or

Himalaya Mountains. [t. Skt.: lit., snow dwelling] —**Hi-ma-la-yan** (hĭ mäl′yən, hĭm′ə lā′ən), *adj.*

hi-mat-i-on (hĭ măt′ĭ ŏn′), *n., pl.* **-matia** (-măt′ĭ ə). *Gk. Antiq.* a garment consisting of a rectangular piece of cloth thrown over the left shoulder and wrapped about the body. [t. Gk.]

Hi-me-ji (hē′mĕ jē′), *n.* a city in S Japan, on Honshu island, W of Kobe. 212,100 (1950).

Himm-ler (hĭm′lər), *n.* **Heinrich** (hīn′rĭkH), 1900–45, high Nazi party leader in Germany; head of Gestapo.

him-self (hĭm sĕlf′; *medially often* ĭm-), *pron.* 1. a reflexive form of *him: he cut himself.* 2. an emphatic form of *him* or *he* used: **a.** as object: *he used it for himself.* **b.** in apposition to a subject or object: *he himself did it.* 3. his proper or normal self; his usual state of mind (used after *be, become* or *came*): *he is himself again.*

Him-yar-ite (hĭm′yə rīt′), *n.* 1. one of an ancient people of southern Arabia, of an advanced civilization, speaking an Arabic dialect closely akin to Ethiopic. 2. a descendant of these people. —*adj.* 3. Himyaritic. [f. Ar. *Himyar* (name of a tribe and an old dynasty of Yemen) + -ITE[1]]

Him-yar-it-ic (hĭm′yə rĭt′ĭk), *adj.* 1. pertaining to the Himyarites and to the remains of their civilization. —*n.* 2. a Semitic language anciently spoken in southern Arabia, surviving in a small area of the southern coast.

hind[1] (hīnd), *adj.,* **hinder, hindmost** or **hindermost.** situated in the rear or at the back; posterior: *the hind legs of an animal.* [? short for BEHIND, but cf. OE *hindan,* adv., from behind, G *hinten,* adv.] —**Syn.** See **back**[1].

hind[2] (hīnd), *n. Zool.* the female of the deer, chiefly the red deer, esp. in and after the third year. [ME and OE; c. Icel. *hind.* Cf. D and G *hinde*]

hind[3] (hīnd), *n. Archaic.* 1. a peasant or rustic. 2. a farm laborer. [ME *hine,* sing., earlier ME and OE *hīne,* pl., der. *hī*(*g*)*na,* gen. pl. of *hīgan* members of a household, domestics. See HIDE[3]]

Hind., 1. Hindustan. 2. Hindustani.

hind-brain (hīnd′brān′), *n. Anat.* 1. the cerebellum, pons, and medulla oblongata or the embryonic nervous tissue from which they develop; the entire rhombencephalon or some part of it. 2. the metencephalon.

Hin-de-mith (hĭn′də mĭt),*n.* **Paul** (poul,) 1895–1963, German composer.

Hin-den-burg (hĭn′dən bûrg′; *Ger.* -bŏŏrkH′), *n.* 1. **Paul von** (poul fən), (*Paul von Beneckendorff und von Hindenburg*) 1847–1934, German field marshal; 2nd president of Germany, 1925–34. 2. German name of Zabrze.

Hindenburg line, a line of elaborate fortification established by the German army in World War I, near the French-Belgian border, from Lille SE to Metz.

hin-der[1] (hĭn′dər), *v.t.* 1. to interrupt; check; retard: *to be hindered by storms.* 2. to prevent from acting or taking place; stop: *to hinder a man from committing a crime.* —*v.i.* 3. to be an obstacle or impediment. [ME *hindre*(*n*), OE *hindrian* (c. G. *hindern,* etc.), der. *hinder* behind, back] —**hin′der-er,** *n.* —**hin′der-ing-ly,** *adv.* —**Syn.** 1. impede, encumber, delay, hamper, obstruct, trammel. 2. block, thwart. See **prevent.** —**Ant.** 1. expedite. 2. aid.

hind-er[2] (hĭn′dər), *adj.* situated at the rear or back; posterior: *the hinder part of the ship.* [ME, appar. repr. OE *hinder,* adv., behind, c. G *hinter,* prep.]

hind-gut (hīnd′gŭt′), *n. Embryol., Zool.* the lower portion of the embryonic digestive canal from which the colon and rectum develop.

Hin-di (hĭn′dē), *n.* 1. one of the modern Indic languages of northern India, usually divided into Eastern and Western Hindi. 2. a literary language derived from Hindustani, used by Hindus. [t. Hind., der. *Hind* India]

hind-most (hīnd′mōst′), *adj.* furthest behind; nearest the rear; last. Also, **hind-er-most** (hīn′dər mōst′).

Hin-doo (hĭn′dōō), *n., pl.* **-doos,** *adj.* Hindu.

Hin-doo-ism (hĭn′dōō ĭz′əm), *n.* Hinduism.

Hin-doo-sta-ni (hĭn′dōō stä′nĭ, -stăn′ĭ), *adj., n.* Hindustani. Also, **Hin-do-sta-ni** (hĭn′dō stä′nĭ, -stăn′ĭ).

hind-quar-ter (hīnd′kwôr′tər), *n.* 1. the posterior end of a halved carcass of beef, lamb, etc., sectioned usually between the twelfth and thirteenth ribs. 2. rear part.

hin-drance (hĭn′drəns), *n.* 1. an impeding, stopping, or preventing. 2. a means or cause of hindering. —**Syn.** 2. impediment, encumbrance, obstruction, check; restraint. See **obstacle.** —**Ant.** 2. aid.

hind-sight (hīnd′sīt′), *n.* perception of the nature and exigencies of a case after the event: *hindsight is easier than foresight.*

Hin-du (hĭn′dōō), *n.* 1. one of the Hindu or Indian race. 2. (in Anglo-Indian usage) any native of India who adheres to a form of the ancient national religion, which recognizes the primacy of the Brahman caste, and therefore excludes Mohammedans, Sikhs, Parsees, Buddhists, etc. 3. any native of Hindustan or India. —*adj.* 4. of or pertaining to the people of Hindustan generally. 5. of or pertaining to natives of India accepting the Brahmanic religion. Also, **Hindoo.** [t. Hind., Pers., der. *Hind* India]

Hin-du-ism (hĭn′dōō ĭz′əm), *n.* the religious and social doctrines and rites of the Hindus, characterized by faith in one supreme deity and by its system of divinely ordained caste. Also, **Hindooism.**

---

b., blend of, blended; c., cognate with; d., dialect, dialectal; der., derived from; f., formed from; g., going back to; m., modification of; r., replacing; s., stem of; t., taken from; ?, perhaps.   See the full key on inside cover.

Hin·du Kush (hĭn/dōō kŏosh/), a lofty mountain system largely in NE Afghanistan, extending W from the Himalayas. Highest peak, Tirach Mir, 25,420 ft. Also, **Hindu Kush Mountains.**

Hin·du·stan (hĭn/dōō stän/, -stän/), n. 1. Persian name of India, esp. the part N of the Deccan. 2. the predominantly Hindu areas of the peninsula of India as contrasted to Pakistan, the predominantly Moslem areas. See **India.**

Hin·du·sta·ni (hĭn/dōō stä/nĭ, -stän/ĭ), n. 1. a standard language or lingua franca of northern India based on a dialect of Western Hindi spoken about Delhi. —*adj.* 2. of or pertaining to Hindustan, its people, or their languages. Also, **Hindoostani, Hindostani.** [t. Hind., Pers., der. *Hindustan* (f. *hindu* Hindu + *stan* country)]

hind·ward (hīnd/wərd), *adv.*, *adj.*, backward.

hinge (hĭnj), n., v., **hinged, hinging.** —*n.* 1. the movable joint or device on which a door, gate, shutter, lid, or the like, turns or moves. 2. a natural anatomic joint at which motion occurs about a transverse axis, as that of the knee or a bivalve shell. 3. that on which something turns or depends; principle; central rule. —*v.i.* 4. to depend or turn on, or as if on, a hinge: *everything hinges on his decision.* —*v.t.* 5. to furnish with or attach by a hinge or hinges. 6. to attach as by a hinge. 7. to cause to depend: *to hinge action upon future sales.* [ME *heng, hing,* OE *hencg.* See HANG, V.] —**hinged,** *adj.*

hin·ny (hĭn/ĭ), n., *pl.* -**nies.** the offspring of a stallion and she-donkey. See **mule**[1] (defs. 1, 2). [t. L: m.s. *hinnus*]

hint (hĭnt), n. 1. an indirect or covert suggestion or implication; an intimation. 2. *Obs.* an occasion or opportunity. —*v.t.* 3. to give a hint of. —*v.i.* 4. to make indirect suggestion or allusion (usually fol. by *at*). [var. of *hent,* n., der. HENT, V., seize] —**hint/er,** *n.*

—**Syn.** 1. allusion, insinuation, innuendo; memorandum, reminder; inkling. 3. imply. HINT, INTIMATE, INSINUATE, SUGGEST denote the conveying of an idea to the mind indirectly or without full or explicit statement. To HINT is to convey an idea covertly or indirectly, but intelligibly: *to hint that one would like a certain present, to hint that bits of gossip might be true.* To INTIMATE is to give a barely perceptible hint, often with the purpose of influencing action: *to intimate that something may be possible.* To IN-SINUATE is to hint artfully, often at what one would not dare to say directly: *to insinuate something against someone's reputation.* SUGGEST denotes particularly recalling something to the mind or starting a new train of thought by means of association of ideas: *the name doesn't suggest anything to me.* —**Ant.** 3. express, declare.

hin·ter·land (hĭn/tər länd/; *Ger.* -länt/), n. 1. the area on the landward side of a port that it serves in the export and import of commodities. 2. the land lying behind a coast district. 3. an area or sphere of influence in the unoccupied interior claimed by the state possessing the coast. 4. the remote or less developed parts of a country. [G: lit., hinder land, i.e. land behind]

hip[1] (hĭp), n., v., **hipped, hipping.** —*n.* 1. the projecting part of each side of the body formed by the side of the pelvis and the upper part of the femur, with the flesh covering them; the haunch. 2. the hip joint. 3. **have someone on** or **upon the hip,** to have someone at a disadvantage. 4. *Archit.* the inclined projecting angle formed by the junction of a sloping side and a sloping end, or of two adjacent sloping sides, of a roof. See illus. under **hip roof.** —*v.t.* 5. to injure or dislocate the hip of. 6. *Archit.* to form (a roof) with a hip or hips. [ME; OE *hype,* c. G *hüfte*] —**hip/less,** *adj.* —**hip/like/,** *adj.*

hip[2] (hĭp), n. the ripe fruit of a rose, esp. of a wild rose. [ME *hepe,* OE *hēope* hip, briar, c. OHG *hiufo* bramble]

hip[3] (hĭp), *interj.* an exclamation used in cheers or in signaling for cheers: *hip, hip, hurrah!* [orig. unknown]

hip·bone (hĭp/bōn/), n. 1. the innominate bone. 2. the ilium. 3. the neck of the femur.

hip joint, the joint between the hip and the thigh.

hip·parch (hĭp/ärk), n. *Gk. Antiq.* a commander of cavalry. [t. Gk.: s. *hipparchos*]

Hip·par·chus (hĭ pär/kəs), n. 1. died 514 B.C., tyrant of Athens. 2. fl. 146–126 B.C., Greek astronomer, mathematician, and geographer.

hipped[1] (hĭpt), *adj.* 1. having hips. 2. having the hip injured or dislocated. 3. *Archit.* formed with a hip or hips, as a roof. [f. HIP[1] + -ED[3]]

hipped[2] (hĭpt), *adj.* 1. *U.S. Slang.* having an obsession: *he's hipped on playing a tuba.* 2. Also, **hip/pish.** *Chiefly Brit.* melancholy. 3. vexed. [earlier *hypped,* der. *hyp,* n., short for HYPOCHONDRIA]

hip·po (hĭp/ō), n., *pl.* -**pos.** *Colloq.* hippopotamus.

Hip·po (hĭp/ō), n. Hippo Regius.

hip·po·cam·pus (hĭp/ə kăm/pəs), n., *pl.* -**pos, -pi** (-pī). 1. *Class. Myth.* a sea horse with two forefeet, and a body ending in the tail of a dolphin or fish. 2. *Anat.* an enfolding of cerebral cortex into the cavity of a cerebral hemisphere having the shape in cross section of a sea horse. [t. L: sea monster, t. Gk.: m. *hippokámpos*]

hip·po·cras (hĭp/ə krăs/), n. an old medicinal cordial made of wine mixed with spices, etc. [ME *ypocras,* t. OF; from the name of *Hippocrates*]

Hip·poc·ra·tes (hĭ pŏk/rə tēz/), n. 460?-357 B.C., Greek physician, known as the father of medicine. —**Hip·po·crat·ic** (hĭp/ə krăt/ĭk), *adj.*

Hippocratic oath, an oath embodying the duties and obligations of physicians, usually taken by those about to enter upon the practice of medicine.

Hip·po·crene (hĭp/ə krēn/, hĭp/ə krē/nĭ), n. a spring on Mount Helicon, sacred to the Muses and regarded as a source of poetic inspiration. [t. L, t. Gk.: m. *Hippokrēnē,* for *Hippou krēnē* horse's fountain]

hip·po·drome (hĭp/ə drōm/), n. 1. an arena or structure for equestrian and other spectacles. 2. (in ancient Greece and Rome) a course or circus for horse races and chariot races. [t. L: m.s. *hippodromos* a race course, t. Gk.]

hip·po·griff (hĭp/ə grĭf/), n. a fabulous creature resembling a griffin but having the body and hind parts of a horse. Also, **hip/po·gryph/.** [t. F: m. *hippogriffe,* t. It.: m. *ippogrifo,* f. *ippo-* (t. Gk.: m. *híppos* horse) + *grifo* GRIFFIN[1]]

Hip·pol·y·te (hĭ pŏl/ə tē/), n. *Gk. Legend.* a queen of the Amazons, slain by Hercules.

Hip·pol·y·tus (hĭ pŏl/ə təs), n. *Gk. Legend.* the son of Theseus by Hippolyte, who was falsely accused by his stepmother Phaedra of ravishing her. Theseus called upon Poseidon for vengeance, and the god sent a sea monster which so terrified Hippolytus' horses that they dragged him to death.

Hip·pom·e·nes (hĭ pŏm/ə nēz/), n. (in some stories) the successful suitor of Atalanta.

hip·po·pot·a·mus (hĭp/ə pŏt/ə məs), n., *pl.* -**muses, -mi** (-mī/). a large herbivorous mammal, *Hippopotamus amphibius,* having a thick hairless body, short legs, and large head and muzzle, found in and near the rivers, lakes, etc., of Africa, and able to remain under water for a considerable time. [t. L, t. Gk.: lit., river horse; r. ME *ypotame,* t. OF, t. ML: m. *ypotamus*]

Hippopotamus. *Hippopotamus amphiblus* (13 ft. long, 4½ ft. or more high at the shoulder)

Hip·po Re·gi·us (hĭp/ō rē/jĭ əs), a seaport of ancient Numidia: St. Augustine was bishop here; the site of modern Bône, Algeria. Also, **Hippo.**

Hip·po Za·ry·tus (hĭp/ō zə rī/təs), an ancient city in N Africa: the site of modern Bizerte, Tunisia.

hip roof, *Archit.* a roof with sloping ends and sides; a hipped roof.

hip·shot (hĭp/shŏt/), *adj.* 1. having the hip dislocated. 2. lame; awkward. [f. HIP[1], n. + SHOT[2], pp.]

Hi·ram (hī/rəm), n. tenth century B.C., king of Tyre. I Kings 5.

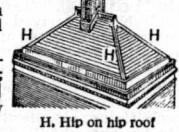

H. Hip on hip roof

hir·cine (hûr/sīn, -sĭn), *adj.* 1. of, pertaining to, or resembling a goat. 2. having a goatish odor. 3. lustful. [t. L: m.s. *hircīnus* of a goat]

hire (hīr), v., **hired, hiring,** n. —*v.t.* 1. to engage the services of for hire: *to hire a clerk.* 2. to engage the temporary use of for hire: *to hire a car.* 3. to grant the temporary use of, or the services of, for a compensation (often fol. by *out*). 4. to pay for the desired action or conduct of; bribe; reward. —*v.i.* 5. *U.S.* to engage oneself for a compensation (usually fol. by *out*). [ME; OE *hȳr(i)an,* c. G *heuern*] —*n.* 6. the price or compensation paid, or contracted to be paid, for the temporary use of something or for personal services or labor; pay. 7. act of hiring. 8. the fact of being hired. [ME; OE *hȳr,* c. G *heuer*] —**hir/a·ble,** *adj.* —**hir/er,** *n.*

—**Syn.** 1, 2. let, lease. HIRE, CHARTER, RENT refer to paying money for the use of something. HIRE is a general word, most commonly applied to paying money for labor or services, but is also used in reference to paying for the temporary use of teams, trucks, halls, etc.; in New England, it is used in speaking of borrowing money on which interest is to be paid (to distinguish from borrowing from a friend, who would not accept any interest): *to hire a gardener, a delivery truck, a hall for a convention.* CHARTER formerly meant to pay for the use of a vessel, but is now applied with increasing frequency to hiring any conveyance for the use of a group: *to charter a boat, a bus.* RENT is used in the latter sense, also, but is usually applied to paying a set sum once or at regular intervals for the use of a dwelling, room, personal effects, etc: *to rent a business building.*

hire·ling (hīr/lĭng), n. 1. one serving for hire (now usually in contempt). 2. a mercenary. —*adj.* 3. serving for hire (now usually in contempt). 4. venal; mercenary.

Hir·o·hi·to (hĭr/ō hē/tō; *Jap.* hē/rō hē/tō), n. born 1901, emperor of Japan since 1926.

Hir·o·shi·ma (hĭr/ə shē/mə; *Jap.* hē/rō shē/mä), n. a seaport in SW Japan, on Honshu island: the first military use of the atomic bomb, Aug. 6, 1945. 343,968 (1940); 171,902 (1946); 285,712 (1950).

hir·sute (hûr/sōot, hûr/sōot/), *adj.* 1. hairy. 2. *Bot., Zool.* covered with long, rather stiff hairs. 3. of, pertaining to, or of the nature of hair. [t. L: m.s. *hirsūtus* rough, hairy] —**hir/sute·ness,** n.

Hir·u·din·e·a (hĭr/ōō dĭn/ĭ ə), n.pl. a class of annelid worms comprising the leeches. [NL, der. L *hirūdō* leech]

ăct, āble, dâre, ärt; ĕbb, ēqual; ĭf, īce; hŏt, ōver, ôrder, oil, bŏŏk, ōōze, out; ŭp, ūse, ûrge; ə = a in alone; ch, chief; g, give; ng, ring; sh, shoe; th, thin; ᵺ, that; zh, vision. See the full key on inside cover.

hi·run·dine (hĭrŭn′dĭn, -dīn), *adj.* of, pertaining to, or resembling the swallow. [t. LL: s. *hirundineus*]

his (hĭz), *pron.* **1.** the possessive form of *he: this book is his.* **2.** the person(s) or thing(s) belonging to him: *himself and his, a friend of his.* —*adj.* **3.** belonging to, pertaining to, or owned by him; made, done, experienced, etc., by him. [ME and OE; gen. of masc. *hē* HE, also of neut. *hit* IT]

His·pa·ni·a (hĭspā′nĭə, -nyə), *n. Poetic.* Spain, [t. L the Spanish peninsula (with Portugal)]

His·pan·ic (hĭspăn′ĭk), *adj.* Spanish.

His·pan·i·cism (hĭspăn′əsĭz′əm), *n.* a Spanish idiom.

His·pan·io·la (hĭs′pənyō′lə; *Sp.* ēs′pänyō′lä). *n.* an island in the West Indies, including the republic of Haiti and the Dominican Republic. 5,796,805 pop. (est. 1953); 29,843 sq. mi. Formerly, Haiti.

his·pid (hĭs′pĭd), *adj. Bot., Zool.* rough with stiff hairs, bristles, or minute spines. [t. L: s. *hispidus*] —**his·pid′·i·ty**, *n.*

hiss (hĭs), *v.i.* **1.** to make or emit a sharp sound like that of the letter *s* prolonged, as a goose or a serpent does, or as steam does rushing through a small opening. **2.** to express disapproval or contempt by making this sound. —*v.t.* **3.** to express disapproval of by hissing. **4.** to force or drive by hissing (fol. by *away, down,* etc.). **5.** to utter with a hiss. —*n.* **6.** a hissing sound, esp. in disapproval. [unexplained var. of d. E *hish,* ME *hisshe(n)* hiss, OE *hyscan* jeer at, rail] —**hiss′er,** *n.*

hiss·ing (hĭs′ĭng), *n.* **1.** act of hissing. **2.** the sound of a hiss. **3.** *Archaic.* an occasion or object of scorn.

hist (hĭst), *interj.* **1.** a sibilant exclamation used to attract attention, command silence, etc. —*v.t.* **2.** to use the exclamation "hist" to.

hist., **1.** histology. **2.** historical. **3.** history.

his·tam·i·nase (hĭs′tăm′ənās′), *n.* an enzyme capable of making histamine inactive, used in treating allergies.

his·ta·mine (hĭs′təmēn′, -mĭn), *n.* an amine, $C_5H_9N_3$, obtained from histidine and found in ergot. It is released by the tissues in allergic reactions, is a powerful uterine stimulant, and lowers the blood pressure. —**his·ta·min·ic** (hĭs′təmĭn′ĭk), *adj.*

his·ti·dine (hĭs′tədēn′, -dĭn), *n.* an amino acid, $C_6H_9N_3O_2$, derived from fish protamines or from ptomaines when acted upon by sulfuric acid, converted by putrefactive organisms into histamine. [f. HIST- + -ID³ + -INE². Cf. G *histidin*]

histo-, a word element meaning "tissue," as in *histogen.* Also, before vowels, **hist-.** [t. Gk., comb form of *histós* web, tissue; also used as comb. form of Gk. *histán* check]

his·to·gen (hĭs′təjĕn), *n. Bot.* the regions in a plant in which tissues undergo differentiation.

his·to·gen·e·sis (hĭs′təjĕn′əsĭs), *n. Biol.* the formation and differentiation of a tissue.

his·to·gram (hĭs′təgrăm′), *n. Statistics.* a graph of a frequency distribution in which equal intervals of values are marked on a horizontal axis and the frequency corresponding to each interval is indicated by the height of a rectangle having the interval as its base.

his·toid (hĭs′toid), *adj. Pathol.* denoting a tumor composed of connective tissue or its equivalent.

his·tol·o·gy (hĭstŏl′əjĭ), *n.* **1.** the science that treats of organic tissues. **2.** the study of the structure, esp. the microscopic structure, of organic tissues. —**his·to·log·i·cal** (hĭs′təlŏj′ə kəl), **his′to·log′ic,** *adj.* —**his·tol′o·gist,** *n.*

his·tol·y·sis (hĭstŏl′əsĭs), *n. Biol.* disintegration or dissolution of organic tissues.

his·tone (hĭs′tōn), *n. Biochem.* any of a class of protein substances, as globin, having marked basic properties. Also, **his·ton** (hĭs′tŏn). [f. HIST- + -ONE. Cf. G *histon*]

his·to·ri·an (hĭstôr′ĭən), *n.* **1.** a writer of history. **2.** an expert in history; an authority on history.

his·tor·ic (hĭstôr′ĭk, -tŏr′-), *adj.* **1.** well-known or important in history: *historic scenes.* **2.** historical.

his·tor·i·cal (hĭstôr′əkəl, -tŏr′-), *adj.* **1.** relating to or concerned with history or historical events. **2.** dealing with or treating of history or historical events. **3.** pertaining to or of the nature of history: *historical evidence.* **4.** pertaining to or of the nature of history as opposed to legend or fiction: *the historical King Arthur.* **5.** narrated or mentioned in history; belonging to the past. **6.** historic. **7.** *Gram.* used in the statement of past facts or the narration of past events. [f. s. L *historicus* (t. Gk.: m. *historikós*) + -AL¹] —**his·tor′i·cal·ly,** *adv.* —**his·tor′i·cal·ness,** *n.*

historical geography, **1.** the study of the geography of a past period or periods. **2.** geographic history.

historical method, the development of general principles by the study of the historical facts.

historical present, *Gram.* the present tense used in narrating a past event as if it were happening at the time of narration. Also, **historic present.**

historical school, **1.** a group of economists who adhere to the so-called historical method, as compared with the method of theoretical analysis. **2.** *Law.* the school of jurists who maintain that law is not to be regarded as made by commands of the sovereign, but is the result of its historical and social circumstances.

his·to·ric·i·ty (hĭs′tərĭs′ətĭ), *n.* historical authenticity.

his·to·ri·og·ra·pher (hĭs′tôr′ĭŏg′rəfər), *n.* **1.** a historian. **2.** an official historian, as of a court, an institution, etc. [f. s. LL *historiographus* (t. Gk.: m. *historiográphos*) + -ER¹] —**his·to′ri·og′ra·phy,** *n.*

his·to·ry (hĭs′tərĭ), *n., pl.* **-ries.** **1.** the branch of knowledge dealing with past events. **2.** the record of past events, esp. in connection with the human race. **3.** a continuous, systematic written narrative, in order of time, of past events as relating to a particular people, country, period, person, etc. **4.** the aggregate of past events. **5.** a past worthy of record or out of the ordinary: *a ship with a history.* **6.** a systematic account of any set of natural phenomena, without reference to time. **7.** a drama representing historical events. [ME, t. L: m.s. *historia,* t. Gk.: a learning or knowing by inquiry, information, narrative, history] —**Syn.** **2.** account, record, chronicle, annals. See **narrative.**

his·tri·on·ic (hĭs′trĭŏn′ĭk), *adj.* **1.** of or pertaining to actors or acting. **2.** artificial; affected. Also, **his′tri·on′i·cal.** [t. LL: s. *histriōnicus*] —**his′tri·on′i·cal·ly,** *adv.*

his·tri·on·ics (hĭs′trĭŏn′ĭks), *n.pl.* **1.** dramatic representation; theatricals; acting. **2.** artificial behavior, speech, etc., for effect.

hit¹ (hĭt), *v.,* **hit, hitting,** *n.* —*v.t.* **1.** to deal a blow or stroke; bring forcibly into collision: *to hit a child.* **2.** to come against with an impact or collision, as a missile, a flying fragment, a falling body, or the like does. **3.** to reach with a missile, a weapon, a blow, or the like (intentionally or otherwise), as one throwing, shooting, or striking. **4.** to succeed in striking: *to hit the mark.* **5.** to drive or propel by a stroke. **6.** to touch effectively; affect severely. **7.** to assail effectively and sharply: *to be hit by satire.* —*v.i.* **8.** to strike with a missile, a weapon, or the like; deal a blow or blows. **9.** to drive the piston in the cylinder of an internal-combustion engine by the combustion of fuel. **10. hit or miss,** whether one hits or misses; at haphazard. —*n.* **11.** an impact or collision, as of one thing against another. **12.** a stroke that reaches an object; a blow. **13.** a stroke of satire, censure, etc. **14.** *Baseball.* a ball so hit that even when fielded without error it enables the batter to reach base safely and without forcing out another baserunner. **15.** *Backgammon.* **a.** a game won by a player after his opponent has thrown off one or more men from the board. **b.** any winning game. [ME *hitte, hutte, hete,* of unknown orig.] —**hit′ter,** *n.* —**Syn.** **1.** See **strike, beat.**

hit² (hĭt), *v.,* **hit, hitting,** *n.* —*v.t.* **1.** to come or light upon; meet with; find: *to hit the right road.* **2.** to agree with; suit exactly: *this hits my fancy.* **3.** to guess correctly. **4.** to succeed in representing or producing exactly: *to hit a likeness in a portrait.* **5.** *U.S. Colloq.* to arrive at: *to hit town.* **6.** *U.S. Colloq.* to go to or upon: *to hit the trail.* **7. hit it off,** *Colloq.* to agree; get on, as with a person, or with each other. **8. hit off, a.** to represent, reproduce, or describe aptly. **b.** to produce readily or offhand. —*v.i.* **9.** to come into collision (often fol. by *against, on,* or *upon*). **10.** to come or light (fol. by *upon* or *on*): *to hit on a new way.* —*n.* **11.** a successful stroke, performance, or production; success: *the play is a hit.* **12.** an effective or telling expression or saying. [ME *hitte(n),* OE *hittan,* t. Scand.; cf. Icel. *hitta* come upon (by chance), meet]

hitch (hĭch), *v.t.* **1.** to make fast, esp. temporarily, by means of a hook, rope, strap, etc.; tether. **2.** to harness (an animal) to a vehicle (often fol. by *up*): *to hitch up one's trousers.* **4.** to move or draw (something) with a jerk. —*v.i.* **5.** to harness an animal to a vehicle (fol. by *up*). **6.** to become fastened or caught, as on something. **7.** to stick, as when caught. **8.** to fasten oneself or itself to something (often fol. by *on*). **9.** to move jerkily: *to hitch along.* **10.** *Colloq.* to get on together; agree. **11.** to hobble or limp. —*n.* **12.** a making fast, as to something, esp. temporarily. **13.** *Naut., etc.* any of various forms of knot or fastening made with rope or the like. **14.** a halt; an obstruction: *a hitch in the proceedings.* **15.** a hitching movement; a jerk or pull. **16.** a hitching gait; a hobble or limp. **17.** a fastening that joins a movable tool to the mechanism that pulls it. **18.** *U.S. Colloq.* period of military service or the like. [ME *hytche(n)* orig. uncert.] —**hitch′er,** *n.* —**Syn.** **1.** fasten, attach, tie, tether. **2.** yoke. —**Ant.** **1.** loosen.

hitch-hike (hĭch′hīk′), *v.i.,* **-hiked, -hiking.** *Colloq.* to travel by walking, with occasional rides in passing automobiles. —**hitch′hik′er,** *n.*

hitching post, a post to which horses, etc., are tied.

hith·er (hĭth′ər), *adv.* **1.** to or toward this place: *to come hither.* —*adj.* **2.** on or toward this side; nearer: *the hither side of the hill.* **3.** earlier; more remote. [ME and OE *hider,* c. Icel. *hedhra;* der. demonstrative stem represented by HE]

hith·er·most (hĭth′ərmōst′), *adj.* nearest in this direction.

hith·er·to (hĭth′ərtōō′), *adv.* **1.** up to this time; until now: *a fact hitherto unknown.* **2.** *Archaic.* to here.

hith·er·ward (hĭth′ərwərd), *adv.* hither. Also, **hith′er·wards.**

Hit·ler (hĭt′lər), *n.* Adolf (ăd′ŏlf, ä′dŏlf: *Ger.* ä′dôlf), ("*der Führer*") 1889–1945, Nazi dictator of Germany, born in Austria: Chancellor, 1933–45; Führer, 1934–45.

Hit·tite (hĭt′īt), *n.* **1.** one of a powerful, civilized, ancient people who flourished in Asia Minor and adjoining regions (1900–1200 B.C.). **2.** records in cuneiform inscriptions of an ancient language of Asia Minor, derived from the same stock as the primitive Indo-European. **3.** records, in hieroglyphics, of a language ascribed to the Hittites, perhaps unrelated to the preceding. —*adj.* **4.** having to do with the Hittites or their language. [f. Heb. *Hitt(im)*, (cf. Hittite *Khatti*) + -ITE¹, r. earlier *Hethite* (cf. Vulgate *Hethaei*)]

hive (hīv), *n.*, *v.*, **hived**, **hiving.** —*n.* **1.** an artificial shelter for honeybees; a beehive. **2.** the bees inhabiting a hive. **3.** something resembling a beehive in structure or use. **4.** a place swarming with busy occupants: *a hive of industry.* **5.** a swarming or teeming multitude. —*v.t.* **6.** to gather into or cause to enter a hive. **7.** to shelter as in a hive. **8.** to store up in a hive. **9.** to lay up for future use or enjoyment. —*v.i.* **10.** to enter a hive. **11.** to live together in a hive. [ME; OE *hȳf.* Cf. Icel. *húfr* ship's hull] —**hive′less,** *adj.* —**hive′like′,** *adj.*

hives (hīvz), *n.* any of various eruptive diseases of the skin, as the wheals of urticaria. [orig. Scot.]

H.J., (L *hic jacet*) here lies.

H.J.S., (L *hic jacet sepultus*) here lies buried.

hl., hectoliter.

hm., hectometer.

H.M., His (or Her) Majesty.

H.M.S., **1.** His, or Her, Majesty's Service. **2.** His, or Her, Majesty's Ship.

H.M.S. Pinafore, an operetta (1878) by Gilbert and Sullivan.

ho (hō), *interj.* **1.** an exclamation of surprise, exultation, etc., or, when repeated, derisive laughter. **2.** a call to attract attention (sometimes specially used after a word denoting a destination): *westward ho!* [ME; c. Icel. *hō*]

Ho, *Chem.* holmium.

ho·ac·tzin (hō ăk′tsĭn), *n.* hoatzin.

Hoang·ho (hwäng′hō′; *Chin.* -hü′), *n.* Hwang Ho.

hoar (hōr), *adj.* **1.** gray or white with age. **2.** grayhaired with age; old. **3.** gray or white, as with frost. —*n.* **4.** hoariness. **5.** a hoary coating or appearance. **6.** hoarfrost. [ME *hor,* OE *hār,* c. G *hehr* august, sublime]

hoard (hōrd), *n.* **1.** an accumulation of something for preservation or future use: *a hoard of money.* —*v.t.* **2.** to accumulate for preservation or future use. —*v.i.* **3.** to accumulate money, food, or the like. [ME *hord(e),* OE *hord,* c. OHG *hort* treasure] —**hoard′er,** *n.*

hoard·ing¹ (hōr′dĭng), *n.* **1.** act of one who hoards. **2.** (*pl.*) that which is hoarded. [f. HOARD + -ING¹]

hoard·ing² (hōr′dĭng), *n.* *Brit.* **1.** a temporary fence enclosing a building during erection. **2.** a billboard. [der. obs. *hoard,* n., appar. t. MD: m. *horde* hurdle. Cf. obs. F *hourd* scaffolding]

Hoare (hōr), *n.* **Sir Samuel John Gurney** (gûr′nĭ), born 1880, British statesman.

hoar·frost (hōr′frôst′, -frŏst′), *n.* frost (def. 3).

hoar·hound (hōr′hound′), *n.* horehound.

hoarse (hōrs), *adj.,* **hoarser, hoarsest.** **1.** having a vocal tone characterized by weakness of intensity and excessive breathiness; husky. **2.** having a raucous voice. **3.** making a harsh, low sound. [ME *hoors,* appar. t. Scand.; cf. Icel. *hāss;* r. ME *hoos,* OE *hās,* c. LG *hēs*] —**hoarse′ly,** *adv.* —**hoarse′ness,** *n.* —**Syn. 1.** gruff, harsh, grating.

hoar·y (hōr′ĭ), *adj.,* **hoarier, hoariest.** **1.** gray or white with age. **2.** ancient or venerable. **3.** gray or white. —**hoar′i·ness,** *n.*

ho·at·zin (hō ăt′sĭn), *n.* a South American crested bird, *Opisthocomus hoazin,* remarkable for claws on its wings. Also, **hoactzin.** [native name]

hoax (hōks), *n.* **1.** a humorous or mischievous deception, esp. a practical joke. —*v.t.* **2.** to deceive by a hoax. [appar. contr. of *hocus*] —**hoax′er,** *n.*

hob¹ (hŏb), *n.* **1.** a projection or shelf at the back or side of a fireplace. **2.** a rounded peg or pin used as a target in certain games, as quoits. **3.** any of these games. [var. of obs. *hub* hob (in a fireplace); ? same as HUB]

hob² (hŏb), *n.* **1.** a hobgoblin or elf. **2.** *Colloq.* mischief: *to play hob.* [ME *Hob,* for *Robert,* or *Robin,* man's name]

Ho·bart (hō′bärt, -bərt), *n.* a seaport in and the capital of Tasmania, in the S part. 95,223 (1954).

Hob·be·ma (hŏb′ə mä), *n.* **Meindert** (mīn′dərt), c1638–1709, Dutch landscape painter.

Hobbes (hŏbz), *n.* **Thomas,** 1588–1679, English philosopher.

Hob·bism (hŏb′ĭz əm), *n.* the doctrines of Hobbes, who advocated unreserved submission on the part of the subject to the will of the sovereign in all things.

hob·ble (hŏb′əl), *v.,* **-bled, -bling,** *n.* —*v.i.* **1.** to walk lamely; limp. **2.** to proceed irregularly and haltingly: *hobbling verse.* —*v.t.* **3.** to cause to limp. **4.** to fasten together the legs of (a horse, etc.) so as to prevent free motion. **5.** to embarrass; impede; perplex. —*n.* **6.** act of hobbling; an uneven, halting gait; a limp. **7.** a rope, strap, etc., used to hobble an animal. **8.** *Dial.* or *Colloq.* an awkward or difficult situation. [ME *hobelen;* appar. akin to *hob* protuberance, uneven ground. Cf. G HG *hoppeln* jolt] —**hob′bler,** *n.* —**hob′bling,** *adj.* —**hob′bling·ly,** *adv.*

hob·ble·bush (hŏb′əl bŏosh′), *n.* a caprifoliaceous shrub, *Viburnum alnifolium,* with white flowers and berrylike fruit.

hob·ble·de·hoy (hŏb′əl dĭ hoi′), *n.* **1.** an adolescent boy. **2.** an awkward, clumsy boy. [orig. uncert.]

hobble skirt, a woman's skirt which is so narrow at the bottom that it restricts her ability to walk naturally.

hob·by¹ (hŏb′ĭ), *n., pl.* **-bies. 1.** a favorite occupation, topic, etc., pursued for amusement. **2.** *Dial.* a small horse. **3.** a child's hobbyhorse. [ME *hoby, hobyn,* prob. for *Robin,* or *Robert,* man's name. Cf. DOBBIN, HOB². Def. 2 was original meaning, whence def. 3 and *hobbyhorse.* Def. 1 is short for *hobbyhorse*] —**hob′by·ist′,** *n.*

hob·by² (hŏb′ĭ), *n., pl.* **-bies.** a small Old World falcon, *Falco subbuteo,* formerly flown at such small game as larks. [ME, t. OF: m. *hobet,* dim. of *hobe* hobby (falcon), prob. ult. der. L *albus* white (as applied to a special kind of falcon), ? also b. with OF *hober* hop]

hob·by·horse (hŏb′ĭ hôrs), *n.* **1.** a stick with a horse's head, or a rocking horse, ridden by children. **2.** a figure of a horse, attached at the waist of a performer in a morris dance, pantomime, etc.

hob·gob·lin (hŏb′gŏb′lĭn), *n.* **1.** anything causing superstitious fear; a bogy. **2.** a mischievous goblin. **3.** (*cap.*) Puck; Robin Goodfellow. [f. HOB² + GOBLIN]

hob·nail (hŏb′nāl′), *n.* a large-headed nail for protecting the soles of heavy boots and shoes. [f. HOB¹ + NAIL]

hob·nailed (hŏb′nāld′), *adj.* **1.** furnished with hobnails. **2.** rustic or clownish.

hob·nob (hŏb′nŏb′), *v.i.,* **-nobbed, -nobbing. 1.** to associate on very friendly terms. **2.** to drink together. [earlier *hab* or *nab* alternately, lit., have or have not]

ho·bo (hō′bō), *n., pl.* **-bos, -boes.** *U.S.* **1.** a tramp or vagrant. **2.** a wandering worker. [rhyming formation, ? based on *beau* fop, used as (sarcastic) word of greeting, e.g. in *hey, bo!*] —**ho′bo·ism,** *n.*

Ho·bo·ken (hō′bō kən), *n.* a seaport in NE New Jersey, opposite New York City. 48,441 (1960).

Hob·son's choice (hŏb′sənz), the choice of taking either the thing offered or nothing. [after Thomas *Hobson,* about 1544–1631, of Cambridge, England, who rented horses, and obliged each customer to take in his turn the horse nearest the stable door or none at all]

Hoch·hei·mer (hŏk′hī′mər; *Ger.* hŏKH′-), *n.* a Rhine wine produced at Hochheim, near Mainz, Germany.

Ho Chi Minh (hō′chē′mĭn′), *n.* born 1892, Indochinese leader; president (1945) of Republic of Viet Nam.

hock¹ (hŏk), *n.* **1.** the joint in the hind leg of the horse, etc., above the fetlock joint, corresponding to the ankle in man but raised from the ground and protruding backward when bent. See illus. under HORSE. **2.** a corresponding joint in a fowl. —*v.t.* **3.** to hamstring. [ME *hoch, hogh, howh,* OE *hōh* hock, heel. Cf. HEEL¹]

hock² (hŏk), *n. Chiefly Brit.* any white Rhine wine. [short for *Hockamore* HOCHHEIMER]

hock³ (hŏk), *v.t., n. U.S. Slang.* pawn. [t. D: m. *hok* hovel, prison, debt]

hock·ey (hŏk′ĭ), *n.* **1.** a game in which opposing sides seek with clubs curved at one end to drive a ball (in **field hockey**) or disk (in **ice hockey**) into their opponent's goal. **2.** the club so used (**hockey stick**). [der. *hock* stick with hook at end, var. of HOOK]

hock·shop (hŏk′shŏp), *n. U.S. Slang.* pawn shop.

ho·cus (hō′kəs), *v.t.,* **-cused, -cusing,** or (*esp. Brit.*) **-cussed, -cussing. 1.** to play a trick on; hoax; cheat. **2.** to stupefy with drugged liquor. **3.** to drug (liquor).

ho·cus-po·cus (hō′kəs pō′kəs), *n., v.,* **-cused, -cusing,** or (*esp. Brit.*) **-cussed, -cussing.** —*n.* **1.** a formula used in conjuring or incantation. **2.** a juggler's trick; sleight of hand. **3.** trickery or deception. —*v.t.* **4.** to play tricks on or with. —*v.i.* **5.** to perform tricks. [orig. jugglers' jargon, simulating Latin]

hod (hŏd), *n.* **1.** a portable trough for carrying mortar, bricks, etc., fixed crosswise on top of a pole and carried on the shoulder. **2.** a coal scuttle. [cf. MD *hodde* basket, c. HG *hotte,* OF *hotte* (t. G), d. E *hot* (t. OF) pannier]

Ho·dei·da (hō dā′ĭ dä), *n.* the chief seaport of Yemen, in SW Arabia, on the Red Sea. ab. 50,000.

Hodg·en·ville (hŏj′ən vĭl), *n.* a town in central Kentucky: birthplace of Abraham Lincoln. 1695 (1950).

hodge·podge (hŏj′pŏj′), *n.* a heterogenous mixture; a jumble. [var. of HOTCHPOTCH]

hod·man (hŏd′mən), *n., pl.* **-men.** hod carrier.

hoe (hō), *n., v.,* **hoed, hoeing.** —*n.* **1.** a long-handled implement with a thin, flat blade usually set transversely, used to break up the surface of the ground, destroy weeds, etc. —*v.t.* **2.** to dig, scrape, weed, cultivate, etc., with a hoe. —*v.i.* **3.** to use a hoe. [ME *howe,* t. OF: m. *houe,* t. Gmc.; cf. G *haue*] —**ho′er,** *n.* —**hoe′like′,** *adj.*

hoe·cake (hō′kāk′), *n. Southern U.S.* a cake made with corn meal, originally baked on a hoe.

Hoek van Hol·land (hōōk vän hŏl′änt), Dutch name of Hook of Holland.

Hoes

A, B, Dutch hoes; C, Warren hoe; D, Hoe and rake combination; E, Common garden hoe; F, Weeding hoe

Ho·fer (hō′fər), *n.* **Andreas** (än drā′äs), 1767–1810, Tyrolese patriot.

Hoff·mann (hôf′män), *n.* **Ernst Theodor Wilhelm** (ĕrnst tā′ō dōr′ vĭl′hĕlm), 1776–1822, German writer, musician, painter, and jurist.

Hof·mann (hôf′mən; *Pol.* hôf′män), *n.* **Jose** (jō′zəf), 1876–1957, U.S. pianist and composer, born in Poland.

hog (hŏg, hôg), *n.*, *v.*, **hogged, hogging.** —*n.* **1.** an omnivorous nonruminant mammal of the family *Suidae*, suborder *Artiodactyla*, and order *Ungulata*; a pig, sow, or boar: a swine. **2.** a domesticated swine weighing more than 120 pounds, raised for market. **3.** *Colloq.* a selfish, gluttonous, or filthy person. —*v.t.* **4.** *Slang.* to appropriate selfishly; take more than one's share of. **5.** to arch (the back) upward like that of a hog. **6.** to cut (a horse's mane) short. —*v.i.* **7.** to droop at both ends, as a ship. [ME; OE *hogg*, t. OBritish; cf. Welsh *hwch* sow] —**hog′like′,** *adj.*

ho·gan (hō′gŏn), *n.* a Navaho Indian dwelling, a structure of posts and branches covered with earth.

Ho·garth (hō′gärth), *n.* **William,** 1697–1764, British painter and engraver. —**Ho·garth′i·an,** *adj.*

hog·back (hŏg′băk′, hôg′-), *n.* *Geol.* a long, sharply crested ridge, generally formed of steeply inclined strata that are especially resistant to erosion.

hog cholera, a specific, acute, usually fatal, highly contagious disease of swine caused by a filterable virus.

hog·fish (hŏg′fĭsh′, hôg′-), *n.*, *pl.* **-fishes,** (*esp.* collectively) **-fish.** any of various fishes, as *Lachnolaemus maximus,* a labroid food fish of the Florida coast and the West Indies, or *Percina caprodes,* a darter of American lakes and streams, or *Orthopristis chrysopterus,* one of the grunts of the southern coasts of the U.S.

Hogg (hŏg), *n.* **James,** ("the Ettrick Shepherd") 1770–1835, Scottish poet.

hog·gish (hŏg′ĭsh, hôg′ĭsh), *adj.* **1.** like or befitting a hog. **2.** selfish; gluttonous; filthy. —**hog′gish·ly,** *adv.* —**hog′gish·ness,** *n.*

hog-nose snake (hŏg′nōz′, hôg′-), any of the harmless American snakes constituting the genus *Heterodon,* notable for their hoglike snouts and their curious actions and contortions when disturbed.

hog·nut (hŏg′nŭt′, hôg′-), *n.* **1.** the nut of the brown hickory, *Carya glabra.* **2.** the tree itself. **3.** the pignut. **4.** the earthnut of Europe, *Conopodium denudatum.*

hog peanut, a twining fabaceous plant, *Amphicarpa bracteata,* with pods which ripen in or on the ground.

hogs·head (hŏgz′hĕd′, hôgz′-), *n.* **1.** a large cask of varying capacities depending on locality or purpose, esp. one containing from 63 to 140 gallons. **2.** a varying unit of liquid measure, esp. one containing 63 wine gallons. [ME *hoggeshed,* lit., hog's head; unexplained]

hog·tie (hŏg′tī′, hôg′-), *v.t.*, **-tied, -tying. 1.** to tie as a hog is tied, with all four feet together. **2.** to hamper.

Hogue (ōg), *n.* **La** (lä). See **La Hogue.**

hog·wash (hŏg′wŏsh′, -wôsh′, hôg′-), *n.* **1.** refuse given to hogs; swill. **2.** any worthless stuff. **3.** meaningless or insincere talk, etc.

Hoh·en·lin·den (hō′ən lĭn′dən), *n.* a village in S West Germany, in Bavaria, near Munich: French victory over the Austrians, 1800.

Hoh·en·lo·he (hō′ən lō′ə), *n.* a German princely family, fl. 12–19th centuries.

Hoh·en·stau·fen (hō′ən shtou′fən), *n.* a German princely family, founded in the 11th century, which ruled Germany 1138–1208 and 1215–54, and Sicily 1194–1266.

Hoh·en·zol·lern (hō′ən zŏl′ərn; *Ger.* hō′ən tsôl′ərn), *n.* a German princely family which attained prominence after 1415 as rulers of Brandenburg, Prussia, which became the kingdom of Prussia in 1701: rulers of the German Empire, 1871–1918, and of Rumania, 1866–1947.

hoicks (hoiks), *interj.* a cry used to incite hounds in hunting. Also, **hoick** (hoik).

hoi·den (hoi′dən), *n.*, *adj.* hoyden.

hoi pol·loi (hoi′ pə loi′), the common people; the masses (sometimes preceded pleonastically by *the*).

hoist (hoist), *v.t.* **1.** to raise or lift, esp. by some mechanical appliance: *to hoist sail.* —*n.* **2.** an apparatus for hoisting, as an elevator. **3.** (esp. in England) a freight elevator. **4.** act of hoisting; a lift. **5.** *Naut.* a. the vertical length of any sail other than a course. b. the perpendicular height of a sail or flag. [later form of *hoise;* cf. G *hissen*] —**hoist′er,** *n.* —**Syn. 1.** See **raise.**

hoi·ty-toi·ty (hoi′tĭ toi′tĭ), *interj.* **1.** an exclamation denoting somewhat contemptuous surprise. —*adj.* **2.** giddy; flighty. **3.** assuming; haughty. —*n.* **4.** giddy behavior. **5.** haughtiness. Also, **highty-tighty** for 1–3. [redupl. deriv. of obs. *hoit,* v., to romp, riot]

ho·key-po·key (hō′kĭ pō′kĭ), *n.* **1.** hocus-pocus; trickery. **2.** ice cream sold by street vendors.

Ho·kiang (hŭ′jyäng′), *n.* a former province in NE China, in Manchuria.

Hok·kai·do (hôk′kī dō′), *n.* a large island in N Japan. 4,584,000 pop. (est. 1954); 30,303 sq. mi. Formerly, Yezo.

ho·kum (hō′kəm), *n.* *Slang.* **1.** nonsense; bunk. **2.** elements of low comedy introduced into a play or the like for the laughs they may bring. **3.** sentimental or pathetic matter of an elementary or stereotyped kind introduced into a play or the like. [b. HOCUS-POCUS and BUNKUM]

Ho·ku·sai (hō′kōō sī′), *n.* **Katsushika** (kä′tsōō shē′kä), 1760–1849, Japanese painter and illustrator.

Hol·bein (hôl′bīn; *Ger.* hôl′-), *n.* **1. Hans** (häns), ("the elder") c1460–1524, German painter. **2.** his son, **Hans,** ("the younger") 1497?–1543, German painter.

HOLC, Home Owners' Loan Corporation.

hold¹ (hōld), *v.*, **held; held** or (*Archaic*) **holden; holding;** *n.* —*v.t.* **1.** to have or keep in the hand; keep fast; retain: *to be held until called for.* **2.** to bear, sustain, or support with the hand, arms, etc., or by any means. **3.** to keep in a specified state, relation, etc.: *to hold the enemy in check.* **4.** to engage in; preside over; carry on; pursue; observe or celebrate: *to hold a meeting.* **5.** to keep back from action; hinder or restrain. **6.** to have the ownership or use of; keep as one's own; occupy: *to hold office.* **7.** to contain or be capable of containing: *this basket holds two bushels.* **8.** to have or keep in the mind; think or believe; entertain: *to hold a belief.* **9.** to regard or consider: *to hold a person responsible.* **10.** to decide legally. **11.** to regard with affection: *to hold one dear.* **12.** to keep forcibly, as against an adversary. —*v.i.* **13.** to remain or continue in a specified state, relation, etc.: *to hold still.* **14.** to remain fast; adhere; cling: *the anchor holds.* **15.** to keep or maintain a grasp on something. **16.** to maintain one's position against opposition; continue in resistance. **17.** to hold property by some tenure; derive title (foll. by *from* or *of*). **18.** to remain attached, faithful, or steadfast: *to hold to one's purpose.* **19.** to remain valid; be in force: *the rule does not hold.* **20.** to keep going on; proceed. **21.** to refrain or forbear (usually in the imperative). **22.** Some special verb phrases are:
hold or **keep back, 1.** to restrain or check. **2.** to cancel.
hold forth, 1. to put forward to view; propose. **2.** to harangue.
hold in, 1. to restrain, check, or curb. **2.** to restrain or contain oneself.
hold off, 1. to keep aloof or at a distance. **2.** to refrain from action.
hold on, 1. to keep fast hold on something. **2.** to continue; keep going. **3.** *Colloq.* to stop or halt (chiefly in the imperative).
hold one's own, to maintain one's position or condition.
hold one's tongue or **one's peace,** to keep silent; cease or refrain from speaking.
hold out, 1. to offer or present. **2.** to extend or stretch forth. **3.** to keep out; keep back. **4.** to continue to endure or resist; last. **5.** to refuse to yield or submit. **6.** *U.S. Slang.* to keep back something expected or due.
hold over, 1. to keep for future consideration or action; postpone. **2.** *Music.* to prolong (a tone) from one measure to the next. **3.** to remain in possession or in office beyond the regular term.
hold up, 1. to keep in an erect position. **2.** to present to notice; exhibit; display. **3.** to stop. **4.** to stop by force in order to rob. **5.** to support or uphold: *gold holds up its price.* **6.** to keep up; maintain one's position, condition, etc.; endure. **7.** to stop; cease.
hold water, 1. to retain water; not let water run through. **2.** to prove sound, tenable, or valid: *Mr. Black's claims will not hold water.*
—*n.* **23.** act of holding fast by a grasp of the hand or by some other physical means; grasp; grip: *take hold.* **24.** something to hold a thing by, as a handle; something to grasp for support. **25.** a thing that holds fast or supports something else. **26.** a controlling force, or dominating influence: *to have a hold on a person.* **27.** *Music.* a pause (symbol). **28.** a prison or prison cell. **29.** a receptacle for something. **30.** *Archaic.* a fortified place, or stronghold. [ME *holden,* OE *h(e)aldan,* c. G *halten*] —**Syn. 6.** possess, own. See **have. 7.** See **contain. 9.** deem, esteem.

hold² (hōld), *n.* *Naut.* the interior of a ship below the deck, esp. where the cargo is stowed. [var. of HOLE, c. D *hol* hole, hold]

hold·all (hōld′ôl′), *n.* **1.** *Chiefly Brit.* a portable case or bag for miscellaneous articles, used by soldiers, travelers, etc. **2.** a container of odds and ends.

hold·back (hōld′băk′), *n.* **1.** the iron or strap on the shaft of a vehicle to which the breeching of the harness is attached, enabling the horse to hold back or to back the vehicle. **2.** a restraint; check.

hold·er (hōl′dər), *n.* **1.** something to hold a thing with. **2.** one who has the ownership, possession, or use of something; an owner; a tenant. **3.** *Law.* one who has the legal right to enforce a negotiable instrument.

hold·fast (hōld′făst′, -fäst′), *n.* something used to hold or secure a thing in place; a catch, hook, or clamp.

hold·ing (hōl′dĭng), *n.* **1.** act of one who or that which holds. **2.** land, or a piece of land, held, esp. of a superior. **3.** (*often pl.*) property owned, esp. stocks, bonds, and real estate.

holding company, *Finance.* **1.** a company controlling, or able to control, other companies by virtue of stock ownership in these companies. **2.** a company which owns stocks or securities of other companies, deriving income from them.

hold·o·ver (hōld′ō′vər), *n.* *U.S. Colloq.* something which remains behind from a former period.

hold·up (hōld′ŭp′), *n.* *U.S. Colloq.* **1.** a forcible stopping and robbing of a person. **2.** anything like this.

hole (hōl), *n.*, *v.*, **holed, holing.** —*n.* **1.** an opening through anything; an aperture. **2.** a hollow place in a solid body or mass; a cavity: *a hole in the ground.* **3.** the excavated habitation of an animal; a burrow. **4.** a small, dingy, or mean abode. **5.** a dungeon. **6.** *Colloq.* an embarrassing position or predicament: *to find oneself in a hole.* **7.** *U.S.* a cove or small harbor. **8.** *Colloq.* a fault or flaw: *to pick holes in a plan.* **9.** a deep, still place in a stream: *a swimming hole.* **10.** *Sports.*

a. a small cavity, into which a marble, ball, or the like is to be played. **b.** a score made by so playing. —*v.t.* **11.** to make a hole or holes in. **12.** to put or drive into a hole. **13.** *Golf.* to drive the ball into (a hole). **14.** to bore (a tunnel, etc.). —*v.i.* **15.** to make a hole or holes. **16.** *Golf.* to drive the ball into a hole (often fol. by *out*). **17.** to go into a hole; retire for the winter, as a hibernating animal (usually fol. by *up*). [ME; OE *hol* hole, cave, den, orig. neut. of *hol,* adj., c. G *hohl* hollow] —**hole/less,** adj. —**hole/y,** adj.
—**Syn. 1, 2.** HOLE, CAVITY, EXCAVATION refer to a hollow place in anything. HOLE is the common word for this idea: *a hole in turf.* CAVITY is a more formal or scientific term for a hollow within the body or in a substance, whether with or without a passage outward: *a cavity in a tooth, the cranial cavity.* An EXCAVATION is an extended hole made by digging out or removing material: *an excavation before the construction of a building.*

hol·i·but (hŏl′ə bət), *n., pl.* **-buts,** (*esp. collectively*) **-but.** halibut.

hol·i·day (hŏl′ə dā′), *n.* **1.** a day fixed by law or custom on which ordinary business is suspended in commemoration of some event or in honor of some person, etc. **2.** any day of exemption from labor. **3.** (*often pl.*) *Chiefly Brit.* a period of cessation from work, or of recreation; a vacation. **4.** *Archaic.* holy day. —*adj.* **5.** pertaining to a festival; joyous: *a holiday mood.* **6.** suited only to a holiday. —*v.i.* **7.** *Brit.* to vacation: to *holiday at the seaside.* [ME; OE *hāligdæg* holy day]

ho·li·ly (hō′lə lǐ), *adv.* **1.** piously or devoutly. **2.** sacredly. [ME; OE *hāliglīce,* f. *hālig* HOLY + *-līce* -LY]

ho·li·ness (hō′lǐ nǐs), *n.* **1.** state or character of being holy; sanctity. **2.** (*cap.*) a title of the Pope, and formerly also of other high ecclesiastical dignitaries, etc. (prec. by *his* or *your*). [ME *holynesse,* OE *hālignes*]

Hol·ins·hed (hŏl′ǐnz hĕd′, hŏl′ǐn shĕd′), *n.* **Raphael,** died c1580, English chronicler.

ho·lism (hō′lǐz əm), *n.* *Philos.* the theory that "wholes" (which are more than the mere sums of their parts) are fundamental aspects of the real. [f. HOL(O)- + -ISM] —**ho/list,** n. —**ho·lis/tic,** adj.

Hol·land (hŏl′ənd), *n.* **1.** the Netherlands. **2.** a medieval county and province on the North Sea, now in North and South Holland provinces of Netherlands.

hol·lan·daise sauce (hŏl′ən dāz′), a yellow sauce of eggs, lemon juice or vinegar, butter, and seasonings.

Hol·land·er (hŏl′ən dər), *n.* a native of the Netherlands; a Dutchman.

Hol·lands gin (hŏl′əndz), gin originally made in Holland, distinguished from other gins by the juniper being mixed in the mash.

hol·ler (hŏl′ər), *Dial.* —*v.i.* **1.** to cry aloud; shout. —*v.t.* **2.** to shout (something). —*n.* **3.** a loud cry of pain, surprise, to attract attention, etc. [var. of HOLLO]

hol·lo (hŏl′ō, hə lō′), *interj., n., pl.* **-los,** *v.,* **-loed, -loing.** —*interj.* **1.** an exclamation to call attention or in answer to one who hails. —*n.* **2.** a cry of "hollo"; a shout. **3.** a shout of exultation. —*v.i.* **4.** to cry "hollo"; shout. —*v.t.* **5.** to shout (something). **6.** to cry "hollo" to. Also, **hallo, halloa, hol/la, hoo/loa, hullo.**

hol·low (hŏl′ō), *adj.* **1.** having a hole or cavity within; not solid; empty: *a hollow ball.* **2.** having a depression or concavity: *a hollow surface.* **3.** sunken, as the cheeks or eyes. **4.** (of sound) not resonant; dull, muffled, or deep: *a hollow voice.* **5.** without substantial or real worth; vain: *a hollow victory.* **6.** insincere or false: *hollow compliments.* **7.** hungry. —*n.* **8.** an empty space within anything; a hole; a depression or cavity. **9.** a valley: *Sleepy Hollow.* —*v.t.* **10.** to make hollow. **11.** form by making hollow (often fol. by *out*). —*v.i.* **12.** to become hollow. —*adv.* **13.** in a hollow manner. **14.** *Colloq.* utterly (often prec. by *all* for emphasis): *to beat someone all hollow.* [ME *hol(o)u, holw(e),* n., adj., OE *holh* hollow (place)] —**hol/low·ly,** adv. —**hol/low·ness,** n.

hol·low-eyed (hŏl′ō īd′), *adj.* having sunken eyes.

hol·low·ware (hŏl′ō wâr′), *n.* silver dishes, as serving dishes, etc., having some depth. Cf. **flatware.**

hol·ly (hŏl′ǐ), *n., pl.* **-lies. 1.** any of the trees or shrubs of the genus *Ilex,* esp. those species having glossy, spiny-edged leaves and small, whitish flowers succeeded by bright-red berries. **2.** the foliage and berries, much used for decoration, esp. during the Christmas season. [ME *holig, holi,* OE *holegn* (with loss of -*n*); akin to D and G *hulst,* F *houx,* Welsh *celyn*]

hol·ly·hock (hŏl′ǐ hŏk′, -hôk′), *n.* **1.** a tall malvaceous plant, *Althea rosea,* common in cultivation, having showy flowers of various colors. **2.** the flower itself. [ME *holihoc,* f. *holi* HOLY + *hoc* mallow, OE *hocc*]

holly oak, the holm oak.

Hol·ly·wood (hŏl′ǐ wŏod′), *n.* the NW part of Los Angeles, California: center of American motion-picture industry.

holm¹ (hōm), *n. Chiefly Brit. Dial and Scot.* **1.** a low, flat tract of land beside a river or stream. **2.** a small island, esp. one in a river or lake. [ME and OE, t. Scand.; cf. Icel. *holmr* islet]

holm² (hōm), *n.* **1.** the holm oak. **2.** *Brit. Dial.* the holly. [ME; dissimilated var. of *holn,* OE *holen* holly (dental + dental became dental + labial)]

Hol·man-Hunt (hōl′mən hŭnt′), *n.* **William,** 1827-1910, British painter.

Holmes (hōmz), *n.* **1. Oliver Wendell,** 1809-94, U.S. author and physician. **2.** his son, **Oliver Wendell,**

1841-1935, associate justice of the U.S. Supreme Court, 1902-32. **3. Sherlock,** a detective in many mystery stories by Sir Arthur Conan Doyle.

hol·mic (hōl′mǐk), *adj. Chem.* of or containing holmium (Ho⁺³).

hol·mi·um (hōl′mǐ əm), *n. Chem.* a rare-earth element found in gadolinite. Symbol: Ho; *at. wt.:* 164.94; *at. no.:* 67. [NL; named after *Stockholm,* in Sweden]

holm oak, an evergreen oak, *Quercus ilex,* of southern Europe, with foliage resembling that of the holly.

holo-, a word element meaning "whole" or "entire," as in *holocaust.* [t. Gk., comb. form of *holos*]

hol·o·blas·tic (hŏl′ə blăs′tǐk), *adj. Embryol.* (of eggs which undergo total cleavage) wholly germinal (opposed to *meroblastic*).

hol·o·caine (hŏl′ə kān′), *n.* **1.** *Chem.* a colorless crystalline basic compound, $C_{18}H_{22}N_2O_2$, used as a local anesthetic. **2.** *Pharm.* a local anesthetic resembling cocaine in its action, used chiefly for the eye.

hol·o·caust (hŏl′ə kôst′), *n.* **1.** great or wholesale destruction of life, esp. by fire. **2.** an offering devoted wholly to burning; a burnt offering. [t. LL: s. *holocaustum,* t. Gk.: m. *holókauston* a burnt offering, prop. neut. of *holókaustos* burnt whole] —**hol/o·caus/tic,** adj.

hol·o·cene (hŏl′ə sēn′), *adj. Geol.* designating or pertaining to the Human or Recent era. [f. HOLO- + -CENE]

Hol·o·fer·nes (hŏl′ə fûr′nēz), *n. Bible.* a general of Nebuchadnezzar killed by Judith in the apocryphal Book of Judith.

hol·o·graph (hŏl′ə grăf′, -gräf′), *adj.* **1.** wholly written by the person in whose name it appears: *a holograph letter.* —*n.* **2.** a holograph writing. [t. LL: s. *holographus,* t. Gk.: m. *hológraphos*]

hol·o·graph·ic (hŏl′ə grăf′ǐk), *adj. Law.* (of wills) totally in the handwriting of the testator and therefore not requiring attestation of witnesses.

hol·o·he·dral (hŏl′ə hē′drəl), *adj.* (of a crystal) having all the planes or faces required by the maximum symmetry of the system to which it belongs. [f. HOLO- + s. Gk. *hédra* seat, base + -AL¹]

hol·o·phote (hŏl′ə fōt′), *n.* an apparatus by which practically all the light from a lighthouse lamp, etc., is thrown in the desired direction. [f. HOLO- + m.s. Gk. *phōs* light] —**hol/o·pho/tal,** adj.

hol·o·phras·tic (hŏl′ə frăs′tǐk), *adj.* expressing a whole phrase or sentence in a single word. [f. HOLO- + m.s. Gk. *phrastikós* suited for expressing]

hol·o·thu·ri·an (hŏl′ə thŏor′ǐ ən), *n.* any of the *Holothuroidea.* [f. s. NL *Holothūria* genus name (t. L, t. Gk.: m. *holothoúria*) + -AN]

Hol·o·thu·roi·de·a (hŏl′ə thŏo roi′dǐ ə), *n.pl.* a class of echinoderms known as sea cucumbers, having a long leathery body and tentacles around the anterior end.

holp (hōlp), *v. Archaic.* pt. of **help.**

hol·pen (hōl′pən), *v. Archaic.* pp. of **help.**

Hol·stein (hōl′stīn, -stēn *for 1;* hōl′stīn; *Ger.* hōl′shtīn *for 2*), *n.* **1.** one of a breed of large, black-and-white dairy cattle, originating in North Holland and Friesland. Also, **Hol·stein-Frie·sian** (hōl′stīn frē′zhən, -stēn-). **2.** a district in N Germany at the base of the peninsula of Jutland: a former duchy. See **Schleswig-Holstein.**

hol·ster (hōl′stər), *n.* a leather case for a pistol, attached to a belt or a saddle. [var. of *hulster,* t. Sw.: m. *hölster,* whence also D *holster;* akin to OE *heolstor* cover] —**hol/stered,** adj.

Holstein. *Bos taurus*
(4 ft. high at the shoulder)

holt (hōlt), *n. Chiefly Poetic.* **1.** a wood or grove. **2.** a wooded hill. [ME *holte,* OE *holt,* c. G *holz* wood]

ho·lus-bo·lus (hō′ləs bō′ləs), *adv. Colloq.* all at once.

ho·ly (hō′lǐ), *adj.,* **-lier, -liest,** *n., pl.* **-lies.** —*adj.* **1.** specially recognized as or declared sacred by religious use or authority; consecrated: *a holy day.* **2.** dedicated or devoted to the service of God, the church, or religion: *a holy man.* **3.** saintly or godly; pious or devout. **4.** of religious purity, exaltation, solemnity, etc.: *a holy love.* **5.** entitled to worship or profound religious reverence because of divine character or origin, or connection with God or divinity: *holy Bible.* **6.** religious: *holy rites.* —*n.* **7.** a place of worship; a sacred place. **8.** that which is holy. [ME *holi,* OE *hālig, hāleg,* c. D and G *heilig,* akin to HALE² and HEAL]
—**Syn. 1.** blessed, HOLY, SACRED, CONSECRATED, HALLOWED imply possession of a sanctity which is the object of religious veneration. HOLY refers to the divine, that which has its sanctity directly from God or is connected with Him: *Remember the Sabbath day to keep it holy.* That which is SACRED, while sometimes accepted as entitled to religious veneration, may have its sanctity from human authority: *a sacred oath.* That which is CONSECRATED is specially or formally dedicated to some religious use: *a life consecrated to service.* That which is HALLOWED has been made holy by being worshiped: *a hallowed shrine.*

Holy Alliance, a league formed by the principal sovereigns of Europe (without the Pope and Sultan) in 1815 after the fall of Napoleon, with the professed object of Christian brotherhood, but the practical object of repressing revolution.

Holy Bible, Bible (def. 1).

Holy City, a city regarded as particularly sacred by the adherents of a religious faith, as Jerusalem by Jews and Christians, Mecca and Medina by Mohammedans, Benares by Hindus, Rome by Roman Catholics, etc.

Holy Communion. See communion (def. 5b).

Holy Cross, Mountain of the, a peak in central Colorado, in the Sawatch Range: snow-filled cross-shaped crevasses; a national monument (2 sq. mi.). 13,996 ft.

holy day, a consecrated day or religious festival, esp. one other than Sunday.

Holy Father, a title of the Pope.

Holy Ghost, the third person of the Trinity.

Holy Grail, grail.

Holy Innocents' Day, Dec. 28, a day of religious observance commemorating the slaughter of the children of Bethlehem by Herod's order; Childermas. Matt. 2:16.

Holy Land, Palestine; now divided between Israel and Jordan.

Holy Office, a congregation of the Roman Catholic Church entrusted with matters pertaining to the faith and doctrine of the Church. Cf. **inquisition** (def. 6).

holy of holies, 1. a place of special sacredness. 2. the inner and smaller chamber of the Jewish tabernacle and temple entered only by the high priest only once a year.

Hol·yoke (hōl′yōk), n. a city in S Massachusetts, on the Connecticut river. 52,689 (1960).

holy orders, 1. the rite or sacrament of ordination. 2. the rank or status of an ordained Christian minister. 3. the major degrees or grades of the Christian ministry.

Holy Roman Empire, the empire in western and central Europe which began with the coronation of Otto the Great, king of Germany, as Roman emperor A.D. 962, and ended with the renunciation of the Roman imperial title by Francis II in 1806, regarded theoretically as the continuation of the Western Empire and as the temporal form of a universal dominion whose spiritual head was the Pope. It is sometimes regarded as originating with Charlemagne, who was crowned Roman emperor A.D. 800.

Holy Rood, 1. the cross on which Jesus died. 2. (l.c.) a crucifix, esp. one above a rood screen.

Holy Roman Empire, A.D. 1200

Holy Saturday, the Saturday in Holy Week.

Holy Scripture, scripture (def. 1).

Holy See, Rom. Cath. Ch. 1. the see of Rome; the office or jurisdiction of the Pope. 2. the papal court.

Holy Sepulcher, the sepulcher in which the body of Jesus lay between His burial and His resurrection.

Holy Spirit, the Holy Ghost.

ho·ly·stone (hō′lĭ stōn′), n., v., **-stoned, -stoning.** —n. 1. a soft sandstone used for scrubbing the decks of a ship. —v.t. 2. to scrub with a holystone.

Holy Thursday, 1. Ascension Day. 2. Rom. Cath. Ch. the Thursday in Holy Week; Maundy Thursday.

ho·ly·tide (hō′lĭ tīd′), n. Archaic. a holy season.

holy water, water blessed by a priest.

Holy Week, the week preceding Easter Sunday.

Holy Writ, the Scriptures.

hom·age (hŏm′ĭj, ŏm′-), n. 1. respect or reverence paid or rendered. 2. the formal acknowledgment by which a feudal tenant or vassal declared himself to be the man of his lord, owing him faith and service. 3. the relation thus established of a vassal to his lord. 4. something done or given in acknowledgment or consideration of vassalage. [ME, t. OF, ult. der. LL homo vassal, L man] —Syn. 1. deference, obeisance; honor, tribute.

hom·bre (ŏm′brĕ), n. Spanish. man.

hom·burg (hŏm′bûrg), n. a felt hat with a soft crown dented lengthwise and a partially rolled brim.

home (hōm), n., adj., adv., v., **homed, homing.** —n. 1. a house, apartment, or other shelter that is the fixed residence of a person, a family, or a household. 2. a place of one's domestic affections. 3. an institution for the homeless, sick, etc. 4. the dwelling place or retreat of an animal. 5. the place or region where something is native or most common. 6. any place of existence or refuge: a heavenly home. 7. one's native place or own country. 8. the goal. 9. Baseball. the plate at which the batter stands and which he must return to and touch after running around the bases, in order to score a run. 10. at home, a. in one's own house or country. b. in a situation familiar to one; at ease. c. prepared to receive social visits. —adj. 11. of, pertaining to, or connected with one's home or country; domestic. 12. that strikes home, or to the mark aimed at; to the point: a home thrust. —adv. 13. to, toward, or at home: to go home. 14. deep; to the heart; effectively and completely. 15. to the mark or point aimed at: to strike home. 16. Naut. all the way; as far as possible: to heave the hawser home. —v.i. 17. to go or return home. 18. (of guided missiles, aircraft, etc.) to proceed, esp. under control of an automatic aiming mechanism toward an airport, fixed or moving target, etc. 19. to have the

home where specified.' —v.t. 20. to bring or send home. 21. to provide with a home. 22. to direct, esp. under control of an automatic aiming device, toward an airport, target, etc. [ME; OE hām home, dwelling, c. G heim] —Syn. 1. abode, dwelling, habitation; domicile, residence. See **house.**

Home, Douglas- Sir Alec. See **Douglas-Home, Sir Alec.**

home·bred (hōm′brĕd′), adj. 1. bred at home; native; indigenous; domestic. 2. unpolished; unsophisticated.

home·brew (hōm′brōō′), n. beer or other beverage brewed at home, as for home consumption.

home economics, the art and science of homemaking, including the purchase, preparation, and service of food, the selection and making of clothing, the choice of furnishings, the care of children, etc.

home·land (hōm′lănd′), n. one's native land.

home·less (hōm′lĭs), adj. 1. having no home. 2. affording no home: the homeless sea. —**home′less·ly,** adv. —**home′less·ness,** n.

home·like (hōm′līk′), adj. like or suggestive of home; familiar; comfortable. —**home′like′ness,** n.

home·ly (hōm′lĭ), adj., **-lier, -liest.** 1. proper or suited to the home or to ordinary domestic life; plain; unpretentious: homely fare. 2. U.S. not good-looking; ugly. 3. not having elegance, refinement, or cultivation. [ME] —**home′li·ness,** n. —Syn. 1. See **simple.**

home·made (hōm′mād′), adj. made at home.

homeo-, a word element meaning "similar" or "like," as in homeomorphism. Also, **homoeo-, homoio-.** [t. Gk.: m. homoio-, comb. form of hómoios like]

Home Office, the department of the English government corresponding to the U.S. Dept. of the Interior.

ho·me·o·mor·phism (hō′mĭ ə môr′fĭz əm), n. similarity in crystalline form, but not necessarily in chemical composition. Also, **homoeomorphism.** [f. ,m.s. Gk. homoiómorphos (of like form + -ism)] —**ho′me·o·mor′phous,** adj.

ho·me·o·path·ic (hō′mĭ ə păth′ĭk), adj. 1. of, pertaining to, or according to the principles of homeopathy. 2. practicing or advocating homeopathy. Also, **homoeopathic.** —**ho′me·o·path′i·cal·ly,** adv.

ho·me·op·a·thist (hō′mĭ ŏp′ə thĭst), n. one who practices or favors homeopathy. Also, **homoeopathist, ho·me·o·path** (hō′mĭ ə păth′).

ho·me·op·a·thy (hō′mĭ ŏp′ə thĭ), n. a method of treating disease by drugs, given in minute doses, which produce in a healthy person symptoms similar to those of the disease (opposed to allopathy). Also, **homoeopathy.**

ho·me·o·stat·ic (hō′mĭ ō stăt′ĭk), adj. describing an organism in physiological equilibrium maintained by coördinated functioning of the brain, heart, liver, etc. [f. HOMEO- + STATIC] —**ho′me·o·sta′sis** (-stā′sĭs), n.

Ho·mer (hō′mər), n. 1. c10th cent. B.C., Greek epic poet, reputed author of the Iliad and Odyssey. 2. Winslow, 1836-1910, U.S. painter.

hom·er[1] (hō′mər), n. Colloq. 1. Baseball. a home run. 2. a homing pigeon. [f. HOME + -ER[1]]

ho·mer[2] (hō′mər), n. a Hebrew unit of capacity equal to 10 baths in liquid measure or 10 ephahs in dry measure; kor. [t. Heb.: m. khomer, lit., heap]

Ho·mer·ic (hō mĕr′ĭk), adj. of, pertaining to, or suggestive of Homer or his poetry. —**Ho·mer′i·cal·ly,** adv.

Homeric laughter, loud, hearty laughter.

home rule, self-government in local matters by a city, province, state, or other component part of a country.

home ruler, an advocate of home rule.

home run, Baseball. a run made on a hit which enables the batter, without aid from fielding errors of the opponents, to make a nonstop circuit of the bases.

home·sick (hōm′sĭk′), adj. ill or depressed from a longing for home. —**home′sick′ness,** n.

home·spun (hōm′spŭn′), adj. 1. spun or made at home: homespun cloth. 2. made of such cloth. 3. plain; unpolished; simple. —n. 4. cloth made at home, or of homespun yarn. 5. cloth of similar appearance to that hand-spun and hand-woven. 6. Obs. a rustic person.

home·stead (hōm′stĕd, -stĭd), n. 1. U.S. a dwelling with its land and buildings, occupied by the owner as a home, and exempted by law (**homestead law**) from seizure or sale for debt. 2. any dwelling with its land and buildings. [OE hāmstede, f. hām HOME + stede place]

Home·stead (hōm′stĕd, -stĭd), n. a borough in SW Pennsylvania, near Pittsburgh. 10,046 (1950).

Homestead Act, a special act (1862) of Congress which made homesteads available to the people.

home·stead·er (hōm′stĕd′ər), n. 1. one who holds a homestead. 2. U.S. a settler under the Homestead Act.

home stretch, the straight part of a race track leading to the finish line, after the last turn.

home·ward (hōm′wərd), adv. 1. Also, **home′wards,** toward home. —adj. 2. directed toward home.

home·work (hōm′wûrk′), n. 1. the part of a lesson or lessons prepared at home. 2. any work done at home, esp. work on contract for manufacturers or middlemen.

home·y (hō′mĭ), adj., **homier, homiest.** Colloq. homelike. Also, **homy.** —Syn. See **simple.**

hom·i·cid·al (hŏm′ə sī′dəl), adj. 1. pertaining to homicide. 2. having a tendency to homicide. —**hom′i·cid′al·ly,** adv.

hom·i·cide[1] (hŏm′ə sīd′), n. the killing of one human

---

b., blend of, blended; c., cognate with; d., dialect, dialectal; der., derived from; f., formed from; g., going back to; m., modification of; r., replacing; s., stem of; t., taken from; ?, perhaps. See the full key on inside cover.

being by another. [ME, t. OF, t. L: m.s. *homicīdium*]

hom·i·cide[2] (hŏm′ə sīd′), *n.* a murderer. [ME, t. OF, t. L: m. *homicīda* manslayer]

hom·i·let·ic (hŏm′ə lĕt′ĭk), *adj.* **1.** pertaining to preaching or to homilies. **2.** of the nature of a homily. **3.** of homiletics. Also, **hom·i·let·i·cal**. [t. Gk.: m.s. *homilētikós* affable] **—hom′i·let′i·cal·ly,** *adv.*

hom·i·let·ics (hŏm′ə lĕt′ĭks), *n.* the art of preaching; the branch of practical theology that treats of homilies or sermons. [pl. of HOMILETIC. See -ICS]

hom·i·list (hŏm′ə lĭst), *n.* one who writes or delivers homilies.

hom·i·ly (hŏm′ə lĭ), *n., pl.* **-lies. 1.** a religious discourse addressed to a congregation; a sermon. **2.** an admonitory or moralizing discourse. [t. ML: m.s. *homīlia*, t. Gk.: discourse; r. ME *omelie*, t. OF]

homing device, a mechanism incorporated into a guided missile, airplane, etc., which aims it toward its objective.

homing pigeon, a pigeon trained to fly home from a distance, employed to carry messages.

hom·i·ny (hŏm′ə nĭ), *n.* white corn hulled and crushed or coarsely ground: prepared for use as food by boiling in water or milk. [t. Algonquian (New England or Va.); cf. *tackhummin* grind corn (der. *ahäm* he beats, he pounds + *min* berry, fruit)]

Ho·mo (hō′mō), *n., pl.* **Homines** (hŏm′ə nēz′), the primate genus that includes modern man, *Homo sapiens,* and a number of closely related extinct species, as the Neanderthal man. [L: man]

homo-, a combining form meaning "the same" (opposed to *hetero-*), as in *homocercal.* [t. Gk., comb. form of *homós* same]

ho·mo·cer·cal (hō′mə sûr′kəl, hŏm′ə-), *adj. Ichthyol.* **1.** having the tail or the caudal fin symmetrical as to its upper and under halves. **2.** denoting such an equal or caudal fin. [f. HOMO- + m.s. Gk. *kérkos* tail + -AL[1]]

Homocercal tail

ho·mo·chro·mat·ic (hō′mə krō-măt′ĭk, hŏm′ə-), *adj.* pertaining to or of one hue; monochromatic. **—ho·mo·chro·ma·tism** (hō′mə krō′mə tĭz′əm, hŏm′ə-), *n.*

ho·mo·chro·mous (hō′mə krō′məs, hŏm′ə-), *adj. Bot., Zool.* being all of one color, as a composite flower or flower head. [t. Gk.: m. *homóchrōmos*]

homoeo-, var. of homeo-.

ho·moe·o·mor·phism (hō′mĭ ə môr′fĭz əm), *n.* homeomorphism. **—ho′moe·o·mor′phous,** *adj.*

ho·moe·op·a·thy (hō′mĭ ŏp′ə thĭ), *n.* homeopathy. **—ho·moe·o·path·ic** (hō′mĭ ə păth′ĭk), *adj.* **—ho′moe·op′a·thist** (hō′mĭ ŏp′ə thist), **ho·moe·o·path** (hō′mĭ ə păth′), *n.*

ho·mog·a·mous (hō mŏg′ə məs), *adj. Bot.* **1.** having flowers or florets which do not differ sexually (opposed to *heterogamous*). **2.** having the stamens and pistils maturing simultaneously (opposed to *dichogamous*). [t. Gk.: m. *homógamos* married to the same wife]

ho·mog·a·my (hō mŏg′ə mĭ), *n.* **1.** *Bot.* state of being homogamous. **2.** *Biol.* interbreeding of individuals of like characteristics.

ho·mo·ge·ne·i·ty (hō′mə jə nē′ə tĭ, hŏm′ə-), *n.* composition from like parts; congruity of constitution.

ho·mo·ge·ne·ous (hō′mə jē′nĭ əs, hŏm′ə-), *adj.* **1.** composed of parts all of the same kind; not heterogeneous. **2.** of the same kind or nature; essentially alike. **3.** *Math.* **a.** having a common property. **b.** denoting a sum of terms all of the same degree. [t. ML: m. *homogeneus,* t. Gk.: m. *homogenēs* of the same kind] **—ho′mo·ge′ne·ous·ly,** *adv.* **—ho′mo·ge′ne·ous·ness,** *n.*

ho·mog·e·nize (hō mŏj′ə nīz′, hō′mə jə-), *v.t.,* **-nized, -nizing.** to make homogeneous; form by mixing and emulsifying: *homogenized milk.* **—ho·mog·e·ni·za·tion** (hō mŏj′ə nə zā′shən, hō′mə jē′nə-), *n.* **—ho·mog·e·niz·er** (hō mŏj′ə nī′zər, hō′mə jə-), *n.*

ho·mog·e·nous (hō mŏj′ə nəs), *adj. Biol.* corresponding in structure because of a common origin.

ho·mog·e·ny (hō mŏj′ə nĭ), *n. Biol.* correspondence of structure and embryological development. [t. Gk.: m. *homogéneia* community of origin]

ho·mog·o·nous (hō mŏg′ə nəs), *adj. Bot.* pertaining to monoclinous flowers which do not differ in the relative length of stamens and pistils. **—ho·mog′o·nous·ly,** *adv.*

ho·mog·o·ny (hō mŏg′ə nĭ), *n. Bot.* state of being homogonous. [f. HOMO- + s. Gk. *gónos* offspring + -y[3]]

hom·o·graph (hŏm′ə grăf′, -gräf′), *n.* a word of the same written form as another, but of different origin and signification, as *homer*[1] (a home run) and *homer*[2] (a unit of measure). **—hom′o·graph′ic,** *adj.*

homoio-, var. of homeo-.

Ho·moi·ou·si·an (hō′moi ōō′sĭ ən, -ou′sĭ ən), *n.* **1.** one of a 4th century church party which maintained that the essence of the Son is similar to, but not the same with, that of the Father. **—***adj.* **2.** relating to the Homoiousians or their belief. [f. s. LGk. *homoioúsios* of like substance + -AN]

ho·mol·o·gate (hō mŏl′ə gāt′), *v.t.,* **-gated, -gating.** to approve; ratify. [t. ML: m.s. *homologātus,* pp. of *homologáre,* t. Gk.: m. *homologein* agree to, allow] **—ho·mol′o·ga′tion,** *n.*

ho·mo·log·i·cal (hō′mə lŏj′ə kəl), *adj.* homologous. Also, **ho′mo·log′ic. —ho′mo·log′i·cal·ly,** *adv.*

ho·mol·o·gize (hō mŏl′ə jīz′), *v.,* **-gized, -gizing.** **—v.t. 1.** to make or show to be homologous. **—v.i. 2.** to be homologous; correspond.

ho·mol·o·gous (hō mŏl′ə gəs), *adj.* **1.** having the same or a similar relation; corresponding, as in relative position, structure, etc. **2.** *Biol.* corresponding in type of structure and in origin, but not necessarily in function: *the wing of a bird and the foreleg of a horse are homologous.* **3.** *Chem.* of the same chemical type, but differing by a fixed increment in certain constituents. **4.** *Immunol., Med., etc.* pertaining to the relation between bacteria and the immune serum prepared from them. [t. ML: m. *homologus,* t. Gk.: m *homólogos.* agreeing, of one mind]

homologous chromosomes, *Biol.* pairs of similar chromosomes, one of maternal, the other of paternal origin, which synapse or pair at the reduction divisions. They carry the Mendelian pairs of alleles or genes.

hom·o·logue (hŏm′ə lŏg′, -lôg′), *n.* **1.** something homologous. **2.** *Biol.,* a homologous organ or part.

ho·mol·o·gy (hō mŏl′ə jĭ), *n., pl.* **-gies. 1.** state of being homologous; homologous relation or correspondence. **2.** *Biol.* **a.** a fundamental similarity due to community of descent. **b.** a structural similarity of two segments of one animal based on a common developmental origin. **3.** *Chem.* the similarity of organic compounds of a series in which each member differs from its adjacent compounds by a single group. [t. LL: m.s. *homologia,* t. Gk.: agreement, assent, conformity]

ho·mo·mor·phism (hō′mə môr′fĭz əm, hŏm′ə-), *n.* **1.** *Biol.* correspondence in form or external appearance but not in type of structure and in origin. **2.** *Bot.* possession of perfect flowers of only one kind. **3.** *Zool.* resemblance between the young and the adult. Also, **ho′mo·mor′phy. —ho′mo·mor′phic,** **ho′mo·mor′phous,** *adj.*

hom·o·nym (hŏm′ə nĭm), *n.* **1.** a word like another in sound and perhaps in spelling, but different in meaning, as *meat* and *meet.* **2.** a homophone. **3.** a homograph. **4.** a namesake. **5.** *Biol.* a name given to a species or genus, which has been used at an earlier date for a different species or genus, and which is therefore rejected. [t. L: s. *homōnymus* having the same name, t. Gk.: m. *homōnymos*] **—hom′o·nym′ic,** *adj.*

ho·mon·y·mous (hō mŏn′ə məs), *adj.* **1.** of the nature of homonyms; having the same name. **2.** *Optics.* denoting or pertaining to the images formed in a kind of double vision in which the image seen by the right eye is on the right side and vice versa.

ho·mon·y·my (hō mŏn′ə mĭ), *n.* homonymous state.

Ho·mo·ou·si·an (hō′mō ōō′sĭ ən, -ou′sĭ ən, hŏm′ō-), *n.* **1.** one of a 4th century church party which maintained that the essence or substance of the Father and the Son is the same. **—***adj.* **2.** *(l.c.)* pertaining to the Homoöusians or their doctrines. [f. s. LGk. *homoousios* of the same substance + -AN]

hom·o·phone (hŏm′ə fōn′), *n.* **1.** *Phonet.* a word pronounced the same as another, whether spelled the same or not: *heir* and *air* are homophones. **2.** (in writing) an element which represents the same spoken unit as another, as (usually) English *ks* and *x.*

hom·o·phon·ic (hŏm′ə fŏn′ĭk), *adj.* **1.** having the same sound. **2.** having one part or melody predominating (opposed to *polyphonic*). [f. s. Gk. *homóphōnos* of the same sound + -IC]

ho·moph·o·nous (hō mŏf′ə nəs), *adj.* identical in pronunciation.

ho·moph·o·ny (hō mŏf′ə nĭ), *n.* **1.** the quality of being homophonic. **2.** homophonic music.

ho·mop·ter·ous (hō mŏp′tər əs), *adj.* pertaining or belonging to the *Homoptera,* a suborder of hemipterous insects having wings of the same texture throughout, comprising the aphids, cicadas, etc. [t. Gk.: m. *homópteros* with the same plumage]

Ho·mo sa·pi·ens (hō′mō sā′pĭ ĕnz′), modern man, the single surviving species of the genus *Homo* and of the primate family, *Hominidae,* to which it belongs. [L]

ho·mo·sex·u·al (hō′mə sĕk′shŏŏ əl, hŏm′ə-), *adj.* **1.** pertaining to or exhibiting homosexuality. **—***n.* **2.** a homosexual person.

ho·mo·sex·u·al·i·ty (hō′mə sĕk′shŏŏ ăl′ə tĭ, hŏm′ə-), *n.* sexual feeling for a person of the same sex, with an impulse towards genital expression.

ho·mos·po·rous (hō mŏs′pə rəs, hō′mə spôr′əs), *adj. Bot.* having spores of one kind only.

ho·mos·po·ry (hō mŏs′pə rĭ), *n.* the production of a single kind of spore, neither microspore nor megaspore.

ho·mo·tax·is (hō′mə tăk′sĭs, hŏm′ə-), *n.* similarity of arrangement, as of geological strata, which, though not necessarily contemporaneous, have the same relative position. **—ho′mo·tax′ic,** *adj.*

ho·mo·thal·lic (hō′mə thăl′ĭk, hŏm′ə-), *adj. Bot.* having all mycelia alike, the opposite sexual functions being performed by different cells of a single mycelium. [f. HOMO- + s. Gk. *thallós* sprout + -IC]

ho·mo·zy·go·sis (hō′mə zĭ gō′sĭs, -zī-, hŏm′ə-), *n. Biol.* the union of like gametes, resulting in a homozygote. [f. HOMO- + Gk. *zýgōsis* joining]

ho·mo·zy·gote (hō′mə zī′gōt, -zĭg′ōt, hŏm′ə-), *n. Biol.* an organism with identical pairs of genes with respect to any given pair of hereditary characters, and hence breeding true for those characteristics. **—ho·mo·zy·gous** (hō′mə zī′gəs, hŏm′ə-), *adj.*

Homs (hŏms), *n.* a city in W Syria. 127,273 (est. 1953).

ho·mun·cu·lus (hō mŭng′kyə ləs), *n., pl.* **-li** (-lī′). **1.** a dwarf. **2.** a spermatozoön [t. L, dim. of *homo* man]
hom·y (hō mĭ′), *adj.,* **-mier, -miest.** homey.
Hon., Honorable.
hon., **1.** honorably. **2.** *Chiefly Brit.* honorary.
Ho·nan (hō′nän′; *Chin.* hŭ′nän′), *n.* a province in E China. 44,214,594 pop. (1953); 59,459 sq. mi. *Cap.:* Kaifeng.
Hond., Honduras.
Hon·do (hŏn′dō), *n.* Honshu.
Hon·du·ras (hŏn dŏŏr′əs, -dyŏŏr′-), *n.* **1.** a republic in Central America. 1,711,000 pop. (est. 1956); 59,161 sq. mi. *Cap.:* Tegucigalpa. **2.** See **British Honduras.** —**Hon·du′ran,** *adj., n.*
hone (hōn), *n., v.,* **honed, honing.** —*n.* **1.** a whetstone of fine, compact texture, esp. one for sharpening razors. —*v.t.* **2.** to sharpen on or as on a hone: *to hone a razor.* [ME; OE *hān* stone, rock, c. Icel. *hein* hone]
hon·est (ŏn′ĭst), *adj.* **1.** honorable in principles, intentions, and actions; upright: *an honest person.* **2.** showing uprightness and fairness; gained fairly: *honest methods.* **3.** open; sincere: *an honest face.* **4.** genuine or unadulterated: *honest commodities.* **5.** chaste or virtuous. [ME *honeste,* t. OF, t. L: m. *honestus* honorable, worthy, virtuous] —**hon′est·ly,** *adv.* —**Syn. 1.** fair, just, incorruptible, trusty, trustworthy; truthful. **3.** straightforward, frank, candid. —**Ant. 1.** corrupt.
hon·es·ty (ŏn′ĭs tĭ), *n.* **1.** the quality or fact of being honest; uprightness, probity, or integrity. **2.** truthfulness, sincerity, or frankness. **3.** freedom from deceit or fraud. **4.** *Bot.* a cruciferous herb, *Lunaria annua,* with purple flowers and semitransparent satiny pods. **5.** *Archaic.* chastity. —**Syn. 1.** fairness, justice; rectitude. **2.** candor. See **honor.** —**Ant. 1.** crookedness.
hone·wort (hōn′wûrt′), *n.* any of several umbelliferous plants, esp. a kind of parsley.
hon·ey (hŭn′ĭ), *n., pl.* **honeys,** *adj., v.,* **honeyed** or **honied, honeying.** —*n.* **1.** a sweet, viscid fluid produced by bees from the nectar collected from flowers, and stored in their nests or hives as food. **2.** the nectar of flowers. **3.** any of various similar products produced by insects or in other ways. **4.** something sweet, delicious, or delightful: *the honey of flattery.* **5.** sweet one; darling (a term of endearment). —*adj.* **6.** of or like honey; sweet; dear. —*v.i.* **7.** *Archaic or U.S.* to talk sweetly; use endearments. [ME *huny,* OE *hunig,* c. D and G *honig*] —**hon′ey·like′,** *adj.*
hon·ey·bee (hŭn′ĭ bē′), *n.* a bee that collects and stores honey, specif. *Apis mellifera.*
hon·ey·comb (hŭn′ĭ kōm′), *n.* **1.** a structure of wax containing rows of hexagonal cells, formed by bees for the reception of honey and pollen and of their eggs. **2.** any substance, as a casting of iron, etc., having cells like those of a honeycomb. **3.** the reticulum of a ruminant. —*adj.* **4.** having the structure or appearance of a honeycomb: *honeycomb weave.* —*v.t.* **5.** to reduce to a honeycomb; pierce with many holes or cavities: *a rock honeycombed with passages.* **6.** to penetrate in all parts: *a city honeycombed with vice.* [ME *hunycomb,* OE *hunigcamb*]
honey creeper, any of the small, usually brightly colored, somewhat scansorial, tropical or semitropical American birds of the family *Coerebidae.*
hon·ey·dew (hŭn′ĭ dū′, -dōō′), *n.* **1.** the sweet material which exudes from the leaves of certain plants in hot weather. **2.** a sugary material secreted by plant lice, leaf hoppers, etc.
honeydew melon, a sweet-flavored, white-fleshed muskmelon with a smooth, pale-green rind.
honey eater, any of the numerous oscine birds constituting the family *Meliphagidae,* chiefly of Australasia, with a bill and tongue adapted for extracting the nectar from flowers.
hon·eyed (hŭn′ĭd), *adj.* **1.** dulcet or mellifluous; ingratiating: *honeyed words.* **2.** containing, consisting of, or resembling honey: *honeyed drinks.* Also, **honied.**
honey guide, any of various small, dull-colored nonpasserine birds (genus *Indicator, Prodotiscus, Melichneutes,* etc.), of Africa, Asia, and the East Indies, some of which are said to guide men or animals to places where honey may be found.
honey locust, a thorny North American tree, *Gleditsia triacanthos,* bearing small compound leaves and pods with a sweet pulp.
hon·ey·moon (hŭn′ĭ mōōn′), *n.* **1.** a holiday spent by a newly married couple in traveling or visiting. **2.** the first month immediately after marriage. —*v.i.* **3.** to spend one's honeymoon (usually fol. by *in* or *at*). —**hon′ey·moon′er,** *n.*
honey plant, any plant especially useful in furnishing nectar to bees, as the cleome or figwort.
hon·ey·suck·er (hŭn′ĭ sŭk′ər), *n.* **1.** a bird that eats the nectar of flowers. **2.** a honey eater.
hon·ey·suck·le (hŭn′ĭ sŭk′əl), *n.* **1.** any of the upright or climbing shrubs constituting the caprifoliaceous genus *Lonicera,* some species of which are cultivated for their fragrant white, yellow, or red tubular flowers. **2.** any of various other fragrant or ornamental plants. [ME *honiesoukel,* f. *honisouke* (OE *hunisūce*) lit., honey-suck + *-el,* dim. suffix] —**hon′ey·suck′led,** *adj.*
hon·ey·sweet (hŭn′ĭ swēt′), *adj.* sweet as honey.
hong (hŏng), *n.* **1.** (in China) a group of rooms or buildings forming a warehouse, factory, etc. **2.** one of

the foreign factories formerly maintained at Canton. [t. Chinese (Cantonese): row, rank (Mandarin *hang*)]
Hong Kong (hŏng′ kŏng′), **1.** a British crown colony in SE China, comprising the island of Hong Kong (32 sq. mi.) and the adjacent mainland. 2,277,000 pop. (est. 1954); 390 sq. mi. *Cap.:* Victoria. **2.** Victoria. Also, **Hongkong.**
hon·ied (hŭn′ĭd), *adj.* honeyed.
ho·ni soit qui mal y pense (ô nē′ swả′ kē′ mȧl ē pãns′), *French.* shamed be the one who thinks evil of it (motto of the Order of the Garter).
honk (hŏngk, hôngk), *n.* **1.** the cry of the wild goose. **2.** any similar sound, as of an automobile horn. —*v.i.* **3.** to emit a honk. [imit.] —**honk′er,** *n.*
honk·y-tonk (hŏng′kĭ tŏngk′, hông′kĭ tôngk′), *n.* *U.S. Slang.* a cheap, sordid cabaret, etc. [orig. uncert.]
Hon·o·lu·lu (hŏn′ə lōō′lōō), *n.* a seaport in the Hawaiian Islands, on the island of Oahu: capital of Hawaii. 294,179 (1960).
hon·or (ŏn′ər), *n.* **1.** high public esteem; fame; glory: *a roll of honor.* **2.** credit or reputation for behavior that is becoming or worthy. **3.** a source of credit or distinction: *to be an honor to one's family.* **4.** high respect, as for worth, merit, or rank: *to be held in honor.* **5.** such respect manifested: *to be received with honor.* **6.** a special privilege or favor: *I have the honor to acknowledge your letter.* **7.** (*usually pl.*) high rank, dignity, or distinction: *political honors.* **8.** a deferential title, esp. of judges and mayors (prec. by *his, your,* etc.). **9.** highminded character or principles; fine sense of one's obligations: *a man of honor.* **10.** (*usually pl.*) special rank or distinction conferred by a university, college, or school upon a student for eminence in scholarship or success in some particular subject. **11.** chastity or purity in a woman. **12.** *Bridge, etc.* any one of the five highest trump cards. **13.** *Golf.* the preference of teeing off before the other players or side, given after the first hole to the player or players who won the previous hole. **14. do honor to,** a. to show respect to. b. to be a credit to. —*v.t.* **15.** to hold in honor or high respect; revere. **16.** to treat with honor. **17.** to confer honor or distinction upon. **18.** to worship (the Supreme Being). **19.** to show a courteous regard for: *to honor an invitation.* **20.** *Com.* to accept and pay (a draft, etc.) when due. Also, *Brit.,* **honour.** [ME *onur, honour, honor,* t. OF: (m.) *onur,* g. L *honor* honor, repute] —**hon′or·er,** *n.* —**hon′or·less,** *adj.*
—**Syn. 4.** respect, deference, homage; reverence, veneration. HONOR, CONSIDERATION, DISTINCTION refer to the regard in which one is held by his fellows. HONOR suggests a combination of liking and respect: *his townsmen held him in great honor.* CONSIDERATION suggests honor because of proved worth: *a man worthy of the highest consideration.* DISTINCTION suggests particular honor because of qualities or accomplishments: *he achieved distinction at an early age as a violinist.* **9.** probity, uprightness. HONOR, HONESTY, INTEGRITY, SINCERITY refer to one who is characterized by possession of the highest moral principles and the absence of deceit or fraud. HONOR denotes a fine sense of, and a strict conformity to, what is considered morally right or due: *a high sense of honor, on one's honor.* HONESTY denotes the presence of probity and particularly the absence of deceit or fraud, esp. in business dealings: *uncompromising honesty and trustworthiness.* INTEGRITY indicates a soundness of moral principle which no power or influence can impair: *a man of unquestioned integrity and dependability.* SINCERITY implies absence of dissimulation or deceit, and a strong adherence to truth: *his sincerity was evident in every word.* **15.** esteem, venerate. —**Ant. 9.** dishonesty.
hon·or·a·ble (ŏn′ər ə bəl), *adj.* **1.** in accordance with principles of honor; upright: *an honorable man.* **2.** of high rank, dignity, or distinction; noble, illustrious, or distinguished. **3.** entitling to honor or distinction: prefixed to the names of certain officials and others, esp. in England as a title of the younger children of peers, from earls to barons. *Abbr.:* Hon. **4.** (of persons or things) worthy of honor and high respect. **5.** bringing honor or credit; consistent with honor: *an honorable peace.* Also, *Brit.,* **honourable.** —**hon′or·a·ble·ness,** *n.* —**hon′or·a·bly,** *adv.* —**Syn. 1.** honest, noble, highminded. **4.** estimable. —**Ant. 1.** untrustworthy.
hon·o·rar·i·um (ŏn′ə râr′ĭ əm), *n., pl.* **-rariums, -raria** (-râr′ĭ ə). **1.** an honorary reward, as in recognition of professional services on which no price may be set. **2.** a fee for services rendered by a professional person. [t. L, prop. neut. of *honōrārius* HONORARY]
hon·or·ar·y (ŏn′ə rĕr′ĭ), *adj.* **1.** given for honor only, without the usual duties, privileges, emoluments, etc.: *an honorary title.* **2.** holding a title or position conferred for honor only: *an honorary president.* **3.** (of an obligation) depending on one's honor for fulfillment. **4.** given, made, or serving as a token of honor: *an honorary gift.* [t. L: m.s. *honōrārius* relating to honor]
hon·or·if·ic (ŏn′ə rĭf′ĭk), *adj.* Also, **hon′or·if′i·cal.** **1.** doing or conferring honor. **2.** having the quality of an honorific. —*n.* **3.** (in certain languages, as Chinese and Japanese) a class of forms used to show respect, especially in direct address. **4.** a title or term of respect. *Examples:* Doctor, Professor, Rt. Hon. [t. L: s. *honōrificus.* See HONOR, n., -(I)FIC] —**hon′or·if′i·cal·ly,** *adv.*
Ho·no·ri·us (hō nōr′ĭ əs), *n.* **1.** **Flavius** (flā′vĭ əs), A.D. 384-423, Roman emperor of the Western Empire, A.D. 395-423. **2.** the name of four popes.
honor man, one who takes honors on graduation from a college or university.

honor point, *Her.* a point midway between the heart point and top of an escutcheon. See diag. under **escutcheon.**

honors of war, *Mil.* privileges granted to a capitulating force, as of marching out of their camp or entrenchments with all their arms and with colors flying.

honor system, a system of management, as in schools, penal institutions, etc., whereby obedience to rules is sought by putting persons upon their honor, rather than by using special guards and constraints.

hon·our (ŏn′ər), *n.*, *v.t. Brit.* honor. —**hon′our·a·ble,** *adj.*

Hon·shu (hŏn′shōō), *n.* the chief island of Japan. 65,696,000 (est. 1953); 88,851 sq. mi. Also, **Hondo.**

hooch (hōōch), *n. U.S. Slang.* **1.** alcoholic beverages. **2.** liquor illicitly distilled and distributed. [short for *hoochinoo,* alter. of *Hutanuwu,* name of Alaskan Indian tribe which made liquor]

hood (hŏŏd), *n.* **1.** a soft or flexible covering for the head and neck, either separate or attached to a cloak or the like. **2.** something resembling or suggesting this, as a hood-shaped petal or sepal, etc. **3.** the cover over an automobile engine. **4.** *Brit.* the top of an automobile. **5.** *Falconry.* a cover for the entire head of a hawk, used when it is not in pursuit of game. **6.** *Slang.* a hoodlum. —*v.t.* **7.** to furnish with a hood. **8.** to cover with, or as with, a hood. [ME *hode,* OE *hōd,* c. G *hut* hat] —**hood′less,** *adj.* —**hood′like′,** *adj.*

Hood (hŏŏd), *n.* **1.** Mount, a volcanic peak in N Oregon, in the Cascade Range. 11,253 ft. **2. John Bell,** 1831–79, Confederate general in the U.S. Civil War. **3. Thomas,** 1799–1845, British poet and humorist. **4. Robin.** See **Robin Hood.**

-hood, a suffix denoting state, condition, character, nature, etc., or a body of persons of a particular character or class: *childhood, likelihood, priesthood, sisterhood.* [ME *-hode, -hod,* OE *-hād,* c. G *-heit;* orig. separate word, OE *hād* condition, state, etc.]

hood·ed (hŏŏd′ĭd), *adj.* **1.** having or covered with, a hood. **2.** hood-shaped. **3.** *Zool.* having on the head a hoodlike formation, crest, arrangement of colors, or the like. **4.** *Bot.* cucullate.

hooded seal, *Zool.* bladdernose.

hood·ie (hŏŏd′ĭ; *Scot.* hōō′dĭ), *n. Scot.* the hooded crow, *Corvus cornix.* Also, **hoodie crow.**

hood·lum (hŏŏd′ləm), *n. U.S.* a petty gangster; ruffian. [orig. uncert.] —**hood′lum·ism,** *n.*

hood·man-blind (hŏŏd′mən blīnd′), *n. Archaic* blindman's buff.

hoo·doo (hōō′dōō), *n., pl.* **-doos,** *v.,* **-dooed, -dooing.** —*n.* **1.** voodoo. **2.** *Colloq.* a person or thing that brings bad luck. **3.** *Colloq.* bad luck. —*v.t.* **4.** *Colloq.* to bring or cause bad luck to. [appar. var. of **VOODOO**]

hood·wink (hŏŏd′wĭngk′), *v.t.* **1.** to deceive; humbug. **2.** to blindfold. **3.** to cover or hide. —**hood′wink′er,** *n*

hoo·ey (hōō′ĭ), *U.S. Slang.* —*interj.* **1.** an exclamation of disapproval. —*n.* **2.** silly or worthless stuff; nonsense.

hoof (hŏŏf, hōōf), *n., pl.* **hoofs,** (*Rare*) **hooves;** *v.* —*n.* **1.** the horny covering protecting the ends of the digits or incasing the foot in certain animals, as the ox, horse, etc. **2.** the entire foot of a horse, donkey, etc. **3.** a hoofed animal; one of a herd. **4.** (in humorous use) the human foot. **5. on the hoof,** (of livestock) alive; not butchered. —*v.i.* **6.** *Colloq.* to walk. **7.** *Colloq.* to dance. [ME; OE *hōf,* c. G *huf*] —**hoof′like′,** *adj.*

hoof·bound (hŏŏf′bound′, hōōf′-), *adj.* (of horses) having the heels of the hoofs dry and contracted, causing lameness.

hoofed (hŏŏft, hōōft), *adj.* having hoofs; ungulate.

hoof·er (hŏŏf′ər, hōōf′ər), *n. Slang.* one who makes dancing an occupation, as a chorus girl.

Hoogh·ly (hōōg′lĭ), *n.* a river in NE India, in W Bengal: the westernmost channel by which the Ganges enters the Bay of Bengal. ab. 120 mi. Also, **Hugli.**

hook (hŏŏk), *n.* **1.** a curved or angular piece of metal or other firm substance catching, pulling, or sustaining something. **2.** a fishhook. **3.** that which catches; a snare; a trap. **4.** something curved or bent like a hook, as a mark or symbol, etc. **5.** a sharp curve or angle in the length or course of anything. **6.** a curved spit of land: *Sandy Hook.* **7.** a recurved and pointed organ or appendage of an animal or plant. **8.** *Golf.* a drive or other stroke which curves to the left of the player striking the ball. **9.** *Baseball.* a curve. **10.** *Cricket.* act of pulling. **11.** *Boxing.* a swinging stroke or blow. **12.** *Music.* a stroke or line attached to the stem of eighth notes, sixteenth notes, etc. **13.** by hook or by crook, by any means, fair or foul. **14. on one's own hook,** *Slang.* on one's own responsibility. —*v.t.* **15.** to seize, fasten, or catch hold of and draw with or as with a hook. **16.** to catch (fish) with a fishhook. **17.** *Slang.* to seize by stealth, pilfer, or steal. **18.** to catch by artifice. **19.** to catch on the horns, or attack with the horns. **20.** to catch hold of and draw (loops of yarn) through cloth with or as with a hook. **21.** *Sports.* to strike with a hook or so as to result in a hook. **22.** to make hook-shaped; crook. **23. hook up, a.** to fasten with a hook or hooks. **b.** to put together (mechanical apparatus) and connect it to the source of power. **24. hook it,** *Slang.* to depart. —*v.i.* **25.** to become attached or fastened by or as by a hook; join on. **26.** to curve or bend like a hook. **27.**

Slang. to depart. [ME *hoke,* OE *hōc,* c. D *hoek* hook angle, corner, point of land] —**hook′less,** *adj.* —**hook′like′,** *adj.*

hook·ah (hŏŏk′ə), *n.* a tobacco pipe with a long, flexible tube by which the smoke is drawn through a vase of water and thus cooled. Also, **hook′a.** [t. Ar.: m. *ḥuqqa* box, vase, pipe for smoking]

hook-and-lad·der truck (hŏŏk′-ən lăd′ər), a fire engine with ladders, axes, etc., whose crew is used in making rescues.

hooked (hŏŏkt), *adj.* **1.** bent like a hook; hook-shaped. **2.** having a hook or hooks. **3.** made with a hook. —**hook·ed·ness** (hŏŏk′ĭd nĭs), *n.*

Hookah

hooked rug, *U.S.* a rug made by drawing loops of yarn or cloth through a foundation of burlap, or the like, to form a pattern.

hook·er (hŏŏk′ər), *n.* **1.** *Colloq.* a kind of small fishing smack. **2.** any old-fashioned or clumsy vessel. [t. D: m. *hoeker,* der. *hoek* **HOOK**]

Hook·er (hŏŏk′ər), *n.* **1.** Joseph, 1814–79, Union general in the U.S. Civil War. **2. Richard,** 1554?–1600, English author and clergyman. **3. Thomas,** 1586?–1647, English Puritan clergyman: one of the founders of the colony of Connecticut.

Hook of Holland (hŏŏk), a cape and harbor in SW Netherlands. Dutch, **Hoek van Holland.**

hook·up (hŏŏk′ŭp′), *n.* **1.** *Radio.* **a.** a diagram of radio apparatus, showing the connection of the different elements. **b.** the elements as set up for operation. **2.** combination; connection.

hook·worm (hŏŏk′wûrm′), *n.* **1.** any of certain bloodsucking nematode worms, as *Ancylostoma duodenale* and *Necator americanus,* parasitic in the intestine of man and other animals. **2.** hookworm disease.

hookworm disease, a disease characterized by severe anemia, caused by hookworms.

hook·y¹ (hŏŏk′ĭ), *adj.* **1.** full of hooks. **2.** hook-shaped. [f. **HOOK** + **-Y¹**]

hook·y² (hŏŏk′ĭ), *n.* in phrase **play hooky,** to be unjustifiably absent from school. [f. **HOOK** (def. 27) + **-Y³**]

hoo·li·gan (hōō′lə gən), *Slang.* —*n.* **1.** a hoodlum. —*adj.* **2.** of or like hooligans. [var. of *Houlihan,* Irish surname which came to be assoc. with rowdies] —**hoo′li·gan·ism,** *n.*

hoop (hŏŏp, hōōp), *n.* **1.** a circular band or ring of metal, wood, or other stiff material. **2.** such a band to hold together the staves of a cask, tub, etc. **3.** a large ring of iron or wood for a child to roll along the ground. **4.** something resembling a hoop. **5.** that part of a finger ring which surrounds the finger. **6.** *Chiefly Brit.* one of the iron arches used in croquet. **7.** a circular band of stiff material used to expand a woman's skirt. **8.** a hoop skirt. —*v.t.* **9.** to bind or fasten with a hoop or hoops. **10.** to encircle; embrace. [ME *hop*(*e*), late OE *hōp,* c. D *hoep*] —**hooped,** *adj.* —**hoop′like′,** *adj.*

hoo·poe (hōō′pōō), *n.* any of the Old World nonpasserine birds constituting the family *Upupidae,* esp. *Upupa epops,* a European species with an erectile fanlike crest. [var. of obs. *hoopoop,* c. LG *huppup* (imit. of its cry); cf. L *upupa*]

hoop skirt, **1.** a woman's skirt, made to stand out from the waist by an undergarment of flexible hoops connected by tapes. **2.** the framework for such a skirt.

hoop snake, a harmless snake, *Abastor erythrogrammus,* believed to take its tail in its mouth and roll along like a hoop.

hoo·ray (hŏŏ rā′), *interj., v.i., n. Chiefly Brit.* hurrah.

hoose·gow (hōōs′gou), *n. U.S. Slang.* a jail. Also **hoos′gow.** [t. Sp.: m. *juzga*(*d*)*o,* court of justice (in Mex. Sp.) jail]

Hoo·sier (hōō′zhər), *n. U.S.* an inhabitant of Indiana. [orig. uncert.]

hoot (hōōt), *v.i.* **1.** to cry out or shout, esp. in disapproval or derision. **2.** (of an owl) to utter its cry. **3.** to utter a similar sound. **4.** *Brit.* to blow a horn or whistle; honk. —*v.t.* **5.** to assail with shouts of disapproval or derision. **6.** to drive (*out, away, off,* etc.) by hooting. **7.** to express in hoots. —*n.* **8.** the cry of an owl. **9.** any similar sound, as an inarticulate shout. **10.** a cry or shout, esp. of disapproval or derision. **11.** *Brit.* a honk or factory whistle. **12.** a thing of no value: *I don't give a hoot.* [ME *huten;* prob. imit.] —**hoot′er,** *n.*

Hoo·ton (hōō′tən), *n.* **Earnest Albert** (ûr′nĭst), 1887–1954, U.S. anthropologist and writer.

hoot owl, an owl that hoots (distinguished from *screech owl*).

Hoo·ver (hōō′vər), *n.* **Herbert Clark,** 1874–1964, 31st president of the U.S., 1929–33.

Hoover Dam, official name of **Boulder Dam.**

Hoo·ver·ville (hōō′vər vĭl), *n.* a collection of huts and shacks, as at the edge of a city, housing the unemployed during the 1930's. [named after Herbert **HOOVER**]

hooves (hŏŏvz, hōōvz), *n. Rare.* pl. of **hoof.**

hop¹ (hŏp), *v.,* **hopped, hopping,** *n.* —*v.i.* **1.** to leap; move by leaping with all feet off the ground. **2.** to spring or leap on one foot. **3.** to make a flight or trip.

4. *Colloq.* (of an airplane, etc.) to leave the ground in beginning a flight (often fol. by *off*). **5.** *Colloq.* to dance. **6.** to limp. —*v.t.* **7.** *Colloq.* to hop about (a place), off (something elevated), or over (a fence, ditch, etc.). **8.** *Colloq.* to jump onto: *to hop a train.* **9.** *Colloq.* (of an airplane, etc.) to cross by a flight. —*n.* **10.** an act of hopping; short leap. **11.** a leap on one foot. **12.** *Colloq.* a flight of an airplane. **13.** *Colloq.* a dance, or dancing party. **14.** *Slang.* opium. [ME *hoppen*, OE *hoppian*, c. G *hopfen*]

hop² (hŏp). *n. v.*, **hopped, hopping.** —*n.* **1.** one of the twining plants of three species of the genus *Humulus*, the male flowers of which grow in panicled racemes and the female in conelike forms. **2.** (*pl.*) the dried ripe cones of the female flowers of the hop plant, used in brewing, medicine, etc. —*v.t.* **3.** to treat or flavor with hops. [ME *hoppe*, t. MD, c. G *hopfen*]

hop clover, a trefoil, *Trifolium procumbens*, whose withered yellow flowers resemble the strobiles of hop.

hope (hōp). *n. v.*, **hoped, hoping.** —*n.* **1.** expectation of something desired; desire accompanied by expectation. **2.** a particular instance of such expectation or desire: *a hope of success.* **3.** confidence in a future event; ground for expecting something: *there is no hope of his recovery.* **4.** a person or thing that expectations are centered in: *the hope of the family.* —*v.t.* **5.** to look forward with desire and more or less confidence. **6.** to trust in the truth of a matter (with a clause): *I hope that you are satisfied.* —*v.i.* **7.** to have an expectation of something desired: *we hope to see you, to hope for his pardon.* **8.** *Archaic.* to trust or rely. [ME; OE *hopa*, c. G *hoffe*] —Syn. **7.** See **expect.**

Hope (hōp). *n.* **Anthony,** (*Sir Anthony Hope Hawkins*) 1863–1933, British novelist.

hope chest, a chest or the like in which a young unmarried woman collects articles toward furnishing a home of her own in the event of her future marriage.

hope·ful (hōp′fəl), *adj.* **1.** full of hope; expressing hope: *hopeful words.* **2.** exciting hope; promising advantage or success: *a hopeful prospect.* —*n.* **3.** a promising young person. —**hope′ful·ly,** *adv.* —**hope′ful·ness,** *n.* —Syn. **1.** expectant, sanguine; optimistic, confident.

Ho·peh (hō′pā′; *Chin.* hŭ′bā′), *n.* a province in NE China. 35,984,644 pop. (1953). 54,154 sq. mi. *Cap.* Peiping. Also, **Ho′pei′.** Formerly, **Chihli.**

hope·less (hōp′lĭs). *adj.* **1.** affording no hope; desperate: *a hopeless case.* **2.** without hope; despairing: *hopeless grief.* —**hope′less·ly,** *adv.* —**hope′less·ness,** *n.* —Syn. **1, 2.** HOPELESS, DESPAIRING, DESPONDENT, DESPERATE all describe an absence of hope. HOPELESS is used of a feeling of futility and passive abandonment of oneself to fate: *hopeless and grim, he still clung to the cliff.* DESPAIRING refers to the loss of hope in regard to a particular situation whether important or trivial; it suggests an intellectual judgment concerning probabilities: *despairing of victory, despairing of finding his gloves.* DESPONDENT always suggests melancholy and depression; it refers to an emotional state rather than to an intellectual judgment: *despondent over ill health; she became more and more despondent and suspicious.* DESPERATE conveys a suggestion of recklessness resulting from loss of hope: *as the time grew shorter, he became desperate.* DESPERATE may apply either to feelings or to situations: *the case seems hopeless but is not yet desperate; a desperate remedy.* DESPAIRING and DESPONDENT may apply only to feelings.

Ho·pi (hō′pĭ), *n.*, *pl.* **-pis. 1.** a Pueblo tribe of Shoshonean speech affiliation inhabiting (now) nine stone-built towns in northern Arizona. **2.** their language.

Hop·kins (hŏp′kĭnz), *n.* **1. Sir Frederick Gowland,** 1861–1947, British biochemist. **2. Gerard Manley,** 1844–89, British poet. **3. Harry Lloyd,** 1890–1946, U.S. political official: special assistant to President Roosevelt, 1942. **4. Johns,** 1795–1873, U.S. financier and philanthropist. **5. Mark,** 1802–87, U.S. clergyman and educator.

Hop·kin·son (hŏp′kĭn sən), *n.* **Francis,** 1731–91, American patriot and writer.

hop·lite (hŏp′līt), *n.* a heavy-armed foot soldier of ancient Greece. [t. Gk.: m.s. *hoplĭtēs*]

hop-o′-my-thumb (hŏp′ə mĭ thŭm′), *n.* a tiny person.

hopped up, *U.S. Slang.* very aroused; excited.

hop·per (hŏp′ər), *n.* **1.** one who or that which hops. **2.** any one of various jumping insects, as grasshoppers, leaf hoppers, cheese maggots, etc. **3.** a funnel-shaped chamber in which materials are stored temporarily and later discharged through the bottom.

hopper car, *Railroads.* a car for coal, sand, etc., with devices by which the contents can be speedily dumped.

hop·ple (hŏp′əl), *v.t.*, **-pled, -pling.** to hobble; tether.

hop·scotch (hŏp′skŏch′), *n.* a children's game in which the player hops from one compartment to another of an oblong figure traced on the ground, without touching a line. [f. HOP¹ + SCOTCH (def. 2)]

hor., 1. horizon. **2.** horizontal. **3.** horology.

Hor·ace (hŏr′ĭs, hŏr′-), *n.* (*Quintus Horatius Flaccus*) 65–8 B.C., Roman lyric poet and satirist.

Ho·rae (hōr′ē), *n.pl. Gk. Myth.* goddesses of the seasons and of the hours, and hence of regularity and orderliness.

ho·ral (hōr′əl), *adj.* pertaining to an hour or hours; hourly. [t. LL: s. *hōrālis*, der. L *hōra* HOUR]

ho·ra·ry (hōr′ə rĭ), *adj.* **1.** pertaining to an hour; indicating the hours: *the horary circle.* **2.** occurring every hour; hourly. **3.** lasting an hour. [t. ML: m.s. *hōrārius*, der. L *hōra* HOUR]

Ho·ra·tian (hə rā′shən, hō-), *adj.* **1.** of or pertaining to Horace. **2.** resembling the poetry or style of Horace.

Horatian ode. See ode (def. 5).

Ho·ra·tius (hə rā′shəs, hō-), *n. Rom. Legend.* a hero celebrated for his defense of the bridge over the Tiber against the Etruscans.

horde (hôrd). *n., v.*, **horded, hording.** —*n.* **1.** a great company or multitude (often in disparagement). **2.** a tribe or troop of Asiatic nomads. **3.** any nomadic group. —*v.i.* **4.** to gather in a horde. [t. F, ult. t. Turk.: m. *urdū* camp. See URDU]

Ho·reb (hōr′ĕb), *n. Bible.* (apparently) Mount Sinai.

hore·hound (hōr′hound′), *n.* **1.** a perennial herb, *Marrubium vulgare*, a native in the Old World, with downy leaves and small whitish flowers and containing a bitter medicinal juice. **2.** any of various plants of the mint family. **3.** a brittle candy flavored with the extract of the herb. Also, **hoarhound.** [ME *horehune*, OE *hārhūne*, f. *hār* grey + *hūne* horehound]

ho·ri·zon (hə rī′zən), *n.* **1.** the line or circle which forms the apparent boundary between earth and sky (**apparent** or **visible horizon**). **2.** *Astron.* **a.** the plane which is tangent to the earth at the place of the observer and extends to the celestial sphere (**sensible horizon**). **b.** the great circle of the celestial sphere whose plane is parallel to the sensible horizon of a particular place and passes through the center of the earth, or the plane itself (**astronomical** or **celestial horizon**). **3.** the limit or range of perception, knowledge, or the like. **4.** *Geol.* a plane in rock strata characterized by particular features, as occurrence of distinctive fossil species. **5.** one of the series of distinctive layers found in a vertical cross section of any well-developed soil. [t. L, t. Gk.: bounding circle, horizon, prop. ppr., bounding; r. ME *orizonte*, t. OF] —**ho·ri′zon·less,** *adj.*

hor·i·zon·tal (hôr′ə zŏn′təl, hŏr′-), *adj.* **1.** at right angles to the vertical: *a horizontal position.* **2.** near, on, or parallel to the horizon. **3.** of or pertaining to the horizon. **4.** measured or contained in a plane parallel to the horizon: *a horizontal distance.* —*n.* **5.** a horizontal line, plane, position, etc. —**hor′i·zon·tal′i·ty, hor′i·zon′tal·ness,** *n.* —**hor′i·zon′tal·ly,** *adv.*

horizontal bar, *Gymnastics.* a bar for swinging, chinning, and other gymnastic exercises.

horizontal union, a labor union organized by skills or trades of its members rather than by industries.

hor·mone (hôr′mōn), *n. Physiol.* any of various substances which are formed in endocrine organs and which activate specifically receptive organs when transported to them by the body fluids. The internal secretions of the thyroid gland, insulin, etc., are hormones. [t. Gk.: m. *hormōn*, ppr., setting in motion]

Hor·muz (hôr′mŭz), *n.* **Strait of,** a strait between Iran and Trucial Oman, connecting the Persian Gulf and the Gulf of Oman. Also, **Ormuz.**

horn (hôrn), *n.* **1.** a hard, projected, often curved and pointed, hollow and permanent growth (usually one of a pair, a right and a left) on the head of certain mammals, as cattle, sheep, goats, antelopes, etc. (**true horn**). **2.** each of the pair of solid, deciduous, usually branched, bony growths, or antlers, on the head of a deer. **3.** some similar growth, as the tusk of a narwhal. **4.** a process projecting from the head of an animal and suggestive of a horn, as a feeler, tentacle, crest, etc. **5.** the substance of which true horns are composed. **6.** any similar substance, as that of hoofs, nails, corns, etc. **7.** an article made of horn, as a thimble, a spoon, or a shoehorn. **8.** any hornlike projection or extremity. **9.** something formed from or resembling the hollow horn of an animal: *a drinking horn.* **10.** a part like a horn of an animal attributed to deities, demons, etc.: *the devil's horn.* **11.** *Obs.* the imaginary projection on a cuckold's brow. **12.** *Music.* a wind instrument, orig. formed from the hollow horn of an animal but now usually made of brass or other metal or material. **13.** *Slang.* a trumpet. **14.** an instrument for sounding a warning signal: *automobile horn.* **5.** *Aeron.* any of certain short, armlike levers on an airplane. **16.** *Radio.* a tube of varying cross section used in some loud-speakers to couple the diaphragm to the sound transmitting space. **17.** the high protuberant part at the front and top of a saddle; the pommel. **18.** one of the extremities of the crescent moon. **19.** a symbol of power, as in the Bible: *an horn of salvation.* **20.** *Logic.* each of the alternatives of a dilemma. —*v.t.* **21.** to butt or gore with the horns. **22.** to furnish with horns. **23.** to give the shape of a horn to. —*v.i.* **24. horn in,** *U.S. Slang.* to thrust oneself forward obtrusively. —*adj.* **25.** made of horn.

Horns
A. French or orchestral horn;
B. C. Military bugles, with and without keys; D. Hunting horn;
E. Coaching horn

---

b., blend of, blended; c., cognate with; d., dialect, dialectal; der., derived from; f., formed from; g., going back to; m., modification of; r., replacing; s., stem of; t., taken from; ?, perhaps. See the full key on inside cover.

[ME horn(e), OE *horn*, c. G *horn*; akin to L *cornu*, Gk. *kēras* horn] —**horned**, *adj.* —**horn'less**, *adj.* —**horn'-like'**, *adj.*

Horn (hôrn), *n.* **Cape**, a headland on a small island at the S extremity of South America.

horn·beam (hôrn'bēm'), *n.* any of the shrubs or small trees constituting the betulaceous genus *Carpinus*, with a heavy, hard wood, as the American species *C. caroliniana* (**American hornbeam**).'

horn·bill (hôrn'bĭl'), *n.* any of the large nonpasserine, tropical Old World birds constituting the family *Bucerotidae*, characterized by a very large bill surmounted by a horny protuberance, sometimes of enormous size.

horn·blende (hôrn'blĕnd'), *n.* any of the common black and dark-colored aluminous varieties of amphibole. [t. G] —**horn·blen'dic**, *adj.*

hornblende schist, *Petrog.* a variety of schist containing needles of hornblende which lie in parallel planes in the rock.

horn·book (hôrn'bŏŏk'), *n.* **1.** a leaf or page containing the alphabet, religious materials, etc., covered with a sheet of transparen horn and fixed in a frame with a handle, formerly used in teaching children to read. **2.** a primer, or book of rudiments.

horned pout, a large-headed fresh-water catfish, *Ameiurus nebulosus*, one of the bullheads, with conspicuous barbels.

horned toad, any of various small, harmless lizards, genus *Phrynosoma*, of western North America, with flattened body and hornlike spines on the head and body.

horned viper. See **viper** (def. 4).

hor·net (hôr'nĭt), *n.* any large, strong, social wasp of the family *Vespidae* having an exceptionally severe sting, as the **giant hornet** of Europe, *Vespa crabo*, introduced in the U.S., and the **bald-faced hornet**, *Dolichovespula maculata*, of North America. [ME *harnete*, OE *hyrnet*(u), c. G *hornisse*]

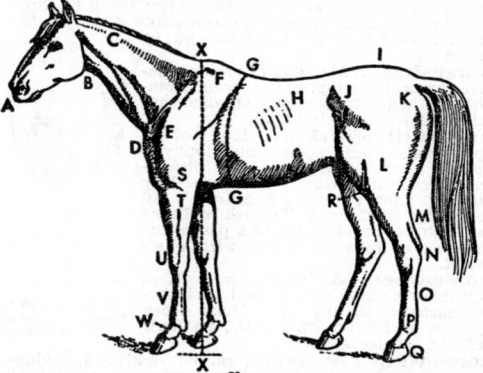
American hornet.
Vespa maculata
(Ab. 1 in. long)

hor·ni·to (hôr nē'tō; *Sp.* ôr nē'tô), *n.*, *pl.* **-tos** (-tōz; *Sp.* -tôs). *Geol.* a low oven-shaped mound, common in the volcanic districts of South America, etc., usually emitting hot smoke and vapors from its sides and summit. [t. Sp., dim. of *horno*, g. L *furnus* oven]

horn-mad (hôrn'măd'), *adj.* **1.** enraged enough to gore with the horns, as a bull. **2.** raging mad; furious.

horn of plenty, the cornucopia.

horn·pipe (hôrn'pīp'), *n.* **1.** an English folk clarinet with an oxhorn to conceal the reed and another one to form the bell. **2.** a lively dance (orig. to hornpipe music) usually by a single person, popular among sailors. **3.** a piece of music for or in the style of such a dance.

horn silver, cerargyrite.

horn·stone (hôrn'stōn'), *n.* **1.** a variety of quartz resembling flint. **2.** an argillaceous rock baked and partly recrystallized by the heat of an igneous intrustion.

horn·swog·gle (hôrn'swŏg'əl), *v.t.*, **-gled**, **-gling**. *Slang.* to swindle, cheat, or hoax.

horn·tail (hôrn'tāl'), *n.* any of various wasplike insects of the family *Siricidae*, the females of which have a hornlike spine at the end of the abdomen.

horn·worm (hôrn'wûrm'), *n.* any of various caterpillars of sphinx moths and hawk moths, as the tobacco worm, characterized by a hornlike caudal projection.

horn·wort (hôrn'wûrt'), *n.* any plant of the genus *Ceratophyllum*, comprising aquatic herbs common in ponds and slow streams.

horn·y (hôr'nĭ), *adj.*, **hornier**, **horniest**. **1.** hornlike through hardening; callous: *horny hands*. **2.** consisting of a horn or a hornlike substance; corneous. **3.** more or less translucent, like horn. **4.** having a horn or horns or hornlike projections. —**horn'i·ness**, *n.*

horol., horology.

hor·o·loge (hôr'ə lōj', -lŏj', hôr'-), *n.* any instrument for indicating the time. [t. L: m.s. *hōrologium*, t. Gk.: m. *hōrológion* an instrument for telling the hour; r. ME *orloge*, t. OF]

hor·o·log·ic (hôr'ə lŏj'ĭk, hôr'-), *adj.* pertaining to a horologe or to horology. Also, **hor'o·log'i·cal**.

ho·rol·o·gist (hō rŏl'ə jĭst), *n.* an expert in horology. Also, **ho·rol'o·ger**.

ho·rol·o·gy (hō rŏl'ə jĭ), *n* the art or science of making timepieces or of measuring time.

hor·o·scope (hôr'ə skōp', hôr'-), *n.* **1.** a diagram of the heavens for use in calculating nativities, etc. **2.** the art or practice of foretelling future events by observation of the stars and planets. [ME and OE *horoscopus*, t. L, t. Gk.: m. *hōroskópos* nativity, horoscope]

ho·ros·co·py (hō rŏs'kə pĭ), *n.* **1.** the casting or taking of horoscopes. **2.** the aspects of the heavens at a given moment, esp. that of a person's birth.

Hor·o·witz (hôr'ə wĭts, hôr'-; *Russ.* hô'rŏ vĭts), *n.* **Vladimir** (vlăd'ə mĭr'; *Russ.* vlä dē'mĭr'), born 1904, Russian pianist, now in U.S.

hor·ren·dous (hô rĕn'dəs, hŏ-), *adj.* dreadful; horrible. [t. L: m. *horrendus*, ger. of *horrēre* bristle, shudder] —**hor·ren'dous·ly**, *adv.*

hor·rent (hôr'ənt, hŏr'-), *adj.* bristling; standing erect like bristles. [t. L: s. *horrens*, ppr., standing on end. Cf. HORRID]

hor·ri·ble (hôr'ə bəl, hŏr'-), *adj.* **1.** causing or tending to cause horror; dreadful: *a horrible sight.* **2** extremely unpleasant; deplorable; excessive: *horrible conditions.* [ME, t. OF, t. L: m. *horribilis* terrible, fearful] —**hor'ri·ble·ness**, *n.* —**hor'ri·bly**, *adv.* —**Syn. 1.** terrible, awful, appalling, frightful; hideous, grim, ghastly, shocking, revolting, repulsive, horrid. —**Ant. 1.** attractive.

hor·rid (hôr'ĭd, hŏr'-), *adj.* **1.** such as to cause horror; dreadful; abominable. **2.** *Colloq.* extremely unpleasant or disagreeable: *horrid weather.* [t. L: s. *horridus* bristling, rough] —**hor'rid·ly**, *adv.* —**hor'rid·ness**, *n.*

hor·rif·ic (hô rĭf'ĭk, hŏ-), *adj.* causing horror. [t. L: s. *horrificus*]

hor·ri·fy (hôr'ə fī', hŏr'-), *v.t.*, **-fied**, **-fying**. to cause to feel horror; strike with horror; shock intensely. [t. L: m. *horrificāre* cause horror] —**hor'ri·fi·ca'tion**, *n.*

hor·rip·i·la·tion (hô rĭp'ə lā'shən, hŏ-), *n.* a bristling of the hair on the skin from cold, fear, etc.; goose flesh. [t. LL: s. *horripilātio*, der. L *horripilāre* bristle with hairs]

hor·ror (hôr'ər, hŏr'-), *n.* **1.** a shuddering fear or abhorrence; a painful emotion excited by something frightful or shocking: *to shrink back in horror.* **2.** anything that excites such a feeling: *the horrors of war.* **3.** a character, look, appearance, etc., such as to excite a shuddering fear: *a scene of horror.* **4.** *Colloq.* something considered atrocious or bad: *that hat is a horror.* **5.** a painful or intense aversion or repugnance: *a horror of publicity.* **6.** *Obs.* a bristling. [t. L; r. ME *orrour*, t. OF] —**Syn. 1.** See **terror**.

Hor·sa (hôr'sə), *n.* died A.D. 455, chief of the Jutes; brother of Hengist. Cf. **Hengist**.

hors de com·bat (ôr də kôN bä'), *French.* out of the fight; disabled; no longer able to fight.

hors d'oeu·vre (ôr dœ'vr), *pl.* **d'oeuvres** (dœ'vr). a relish such as olives or radishes, served before or between the regular courses of a meal. [t. F: aside from (the main body of the) work]

horse (hôrs), *n.*, *pl.* **horses**, (*esp. collectively*) **horse**, *v.*, **horsed**, **horsing**, *adj.* —*n.* **1.** a large, solid-hoofed quadruped, *Equus caballus*, domesticated since prehistoric times, and employed as a beast of draft and burden and for carrying a rider. **2.** the male horse, in distinction from the female or mare; a stallion or gelding. **3.** any animal of the family *Equidae* (**horse family**), which includes the ass, zebra, etc. **4.** soldiers serving on horseback; cavalry: *a thousand horse.* **5.** something on which a person rides, sits, or exercises, as if on a horse's back: *rocking horse.* **6.** a leather-covered block having two pommels, used for vaulting and other gymnastic exercises. **7.** a frame, block, etc. with legs on which something is mounted or supported. **8.** (in opprobrious or playful use) a man; fellow. **9.** *U.S. School Slang.* a crib, translation, or other illicit aid to study. **10.** *Mining.* a mass of rock enclosed within a lode or vein. **11.** *Chess. Colloq.* a knight. —*v.t.* **12.** to provide with a horse or horses. **13.** to set on horseback. **14.** to set or carry on a person's back or on one's own back. **15.** to place on a person's back or on a wooden horse or the like to be flogged. **16.** to flog. **17.** *Colloq.* to drive or urge (a person) at work, esp. unfairly or tyrannically. **18.** *Slang.* to make (a person) the target of boisterous jokes. **19.** *Slang.* to perform boisterously, as a part or a scene in a play. —*v.i.* **20.** to mount or go on a horse. —*adj.* **21.** unusually large for one of its kind. [ME and OE *hors*, c. OS and OHG *hros*, G *ross*, Icel. *hross*]

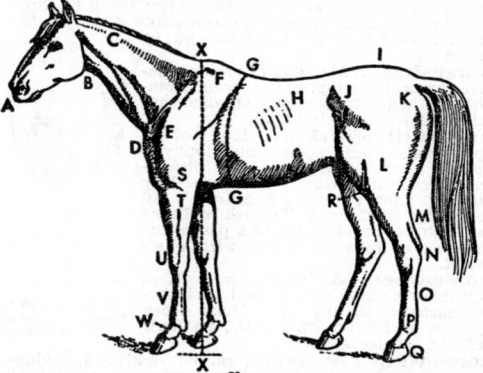

Horse
A. Muzzle; B. Gullet; C. Crest; D. Chest; E. Shoulder; F. Withers; GG. Girth; H. Loin; I. Croup; J. Hip; K. Haunch; L. Thigh; M. Hamstring; N. Hock; O. Cannon; P. Fetlock; Q. Hoof; R. Stifle; S. Elbow; T. Arm; U. Knee; V. Shank; W. Pastern. XX. Height

horse·back (hôrs'băk'), *n.* **1.** the back of a horse: *on horseback.* **2.** *U.S.* a low ridge of sand, gravel, or rock. Cf. **hogback**. —*adv.* **3.** on horseback: *to ride horseback.*

horse·car (hôrs'kär'), *n.* **1.** *U.S.* a streetcar drawn by a horse or horses. **2.** a car fitted for the transportation of horses, either by railroad or by autotruck.

horse chestnut, **1.** the shiny, brown nutlike seed of several species of *Aesculus*, ornamental trees bearing large digitate leaves and upright clusters of showy white, red, or yellow flowers, principally *A. Hippocastanum* (common **horse chestnut**) and *A. glabra* (Ohio buckeye). **2.** the tree itself.

horse·cloth (hôrs/klôth′, -klŏth′), *n.* a cloth used to cover a horse, or as part of its trappings.

horse·flesh (hôrs/flĕsh′), *n.* **1.** the flesh of a horse. **2.** horses collectively, esp. for riding, racing, etc.

horse·fly (hôrs/flī′), *n.*, *pl.* **-flies.** any of certain flies of the family *Tabanidae* that bite horses; gadfly.

Horse Guards, 1. a body of cavalry serving as a guard. **2.** the guard, a brigade of cavalry, of the British royal family.

horse·hair (hôrs/hâr′), *n.* **1.** a hair, or the hair, of a horse, esp. from the mane or tail. **2.** a sturdy, glossy fabric woven of horsehair.

horse·hide (hôrs/hīd′), *n.* **1.** the hide of a horse. **2.** leather made from the hide of a horse.

horse latitudes, *Naut.* belts of northern and southern latitudes lying between the region of westerly winds and the region of the trade winds, marked by light baffling winds and occasional calms.

horse·laugh (hôrs/lăf′, -läf′), *n.* a loud, coarse laugh.

horse·leech (hôrs/lēch′), *n.* a large leech, as *Haemopsis sanguisorba*, said to attack the mouths of horses while they are drinking.

horse·less (hôrs/lĭs), *adj.* **1.** without a horse. **2.** self-propelled: *a horseless carriage.*

horse mackerel, 1. the common tunny, *Thunnus thynnus.* **2.** a carangoid fish, *Trachurus symmetricus,* of the Pacific coast of the U.S.

horse·man (hôrs/mən), *n.*, *pl.* **-men. 1.** a rider on horseback. **2.** one who attends to horses or is skilled in managing them.

horse·man·ship (hôrs/mən ship′), *n.* **1.** the management of horses. **2.** equestrian skill.

horse marine, 1. a member of an imaginary corps of mounted marine soldiers. **2.** (formerly) a marine mounted on horseback, or a cavalryman doing duty on shipboard. **3.** a person out of his element.

horse·mint (hôrs/mĭnt′), *n.* **1.** a wild mint, *Mentha longifolia,* orig. a native of Europe but now found in America. **2.** any of various other menthaceous plants, as *Monarda punctata,* an erect odorous herb of America.

horse nettle, a prickly North American solanaceous weed, *Solanum carolinense.*

horse pistol, a kind of large pistol formerly carried by horsemen.

horse·play (hôrs/plā′), *n.* rough or boisterous play.

horse·pow·er (hôrs/pou′ər), *n.* a unit for measuring power, or rate of work, equivalent to 550 foot-pounds per second.

horse·rad·ish (hôrs/răd′ĭsh), *n.* **1.** a cultivated cruciferous plant, *Armoracia rusticana.* **2.** its pungent root, ground and used as a condiment and in medicine.

horse rake, a large, wheeled rake drawn by a horse.

horse sense, *Colloq.* plain, practical, common sense.

horse·shoe (hôrs/shoo′), *n.*, *v.*, **-shoed, -shoeing. —n. 1.** a U-shaped iron plate nailed to a horse's hoof to protect it. **2.** something shaped like a horseshoe. **3.** (*pl. construed as sing.*) a game using horseshoes or similar pieces, the object being to throw the piece so as to encircle an iron stake 30 or 40 feet away. **—v.t. 4.** to put horseshoes on; to shoe.

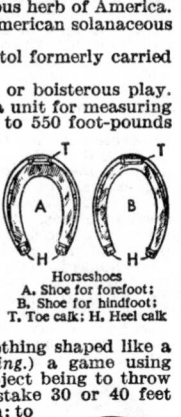

Horseshoes
A. Shoe for forefoot;
B. Shoe for hindfoot;
T. Toe calk; H. Heel calk

horseshoe crab, any of various marine arthropods, esp. of the genus *Limulus,* with a carapace shaped somewhat like a horseshoe; king crab.

horse·tail (hôrs/tāl′), *n.* **1.** any of the perennial, herbaceous, pteridophytic plants constituting the widely distributed genus *Equisetum,* characterized by hollow, jointed stems. **2.** a horse's tail formerly used as a Turkish military standard or as an ensign of a pasha, the number of tails increasing with one's rank.

horse·weed (hôrs/wēd′), *n.* **1.** a troublesome asteraceous weed, *Erigeron canadense.* **2.** any of various other plants, as *Lactuca canadensis,* an herb of the lettuce genus.

Horseshoe crab
Limulus polyphemus
(Ab. 2 ft. long)

horse·whip (hôrs/hwĭp′), *n.*, *v.*, **-whipped, -whipping. —n. 1.** a whip for controlling horses. **—v.t. 2.** to beat with a horsewhip.

horse·wom·an (hôrs/woom′ən), *n.*, *pl.* **-women. 1.** a woman who rides on horseback. **2.** a woman who is skillful in managing or riding horses.

hors·y (hôr/sĭ), *adj.*, **horsier, horsiest. 1.** pertaining to, characteristic of, or of the nature of a horse or horses: *horsy talk.* **2.** dealing with, interested in, or devoted to horses, horse racing, etc. **3.** *Slang.* gross in size, appearance, etc. **—hors/i·ness,** *n.*

hort., 1. horticultural. **2.** horticulture.

hor·ta·tive (hôr/tə tĭv), *adj.* hortatory. [t. L: m.s. *hortātīvus*] **—hor/ta·tive·ly,** *adv.*

hor·ta·to·ry (hôr/tə tôr′ĭ), *adj.* encouraging; inciting;

exhorting; urging to some course of conduct or action: *a hortatory address.* [t. LL: m.s. *hortātōrius* encouraging]

Hor·tense (ôr tăns′), *n.* (*Eugénie Hortense de Beauharnais*) 1783–1837, queen of Holland (mother of Louis Napoleon).

Hor·thy (hôr/tĭ), *n.* **Miklos von** (mĭk′lōsh fôn), 1868–1957, Hungarian admiral; regent of Hungary, 1920–45.

hor·ti·cul·ture (hôr/tə kŭl′chər), *n.* **1.** the cultivation of a garden. **2.** the art of cultivating garden plants. [f. *horti-* (comb. form of L *hortus* garden) + CULTURE] **—hor/ti·cul/tur·al,** *adj.* **—hor/ti·cul/tur·ist,** *n.*

hor·tus sic·cus (hôr/təs sĭk′əs), a collection of dried plants; a herbarium. [t. L: dry garden]

Ho·rus (hôr/əs), *n. Egyptian Myth.* a solar deity, the son of Osiris and Isis. [t. LL, t. Gk.: m. *Hōros,* t. Egyptian: m. *Hur,* lit., hawk]

Hos., Hosea.

ho·san·na (hō zăn′ə), *interj.* **1.** an exclamation, orig. an appeal to God for deliverance, used in praise of God or Christ. **—n. 2.** a cry of "hosanna." **3.** a shout of praise or adoration; an acclamation. [t. LL, t. Gk., t. Heb.: m. *hosh*(i)*′āhnnā* save, pray !]

hose (hōz), *n.*, *pl.* **hose,** (*Archaic*) **hosen,** *v.*, **hosed, hosing. —n. 1.** an article of clothing for the foot and lower part of the leg; a stocking. **2.** a garment for the legs and thighs, as tights or breeches, formerly worn by men. **3.** a flexible tube for conveying water, etc., to a desired point: *a garden hose.* **4.** a sheath, or sheathing part, as that enclosing the kernel of grain. **—v.t. 5.** to water, wash, or drench by means of a hose. [ME and OE, c. D *hoos,* G *hose,* Icel. *hosa*]

Ho·se·a (hō zē′ə, -zā′ə), *n.* **1.** a Hebrew prophet of the 8th century B.C. **2.** the first of the books of the minor prophets in the Old Testament. [t. Heb.: m. *Hōshēa′,* with *s* from *Osēe* (Vulgate and Septuagint)]

ho·sier (hō/zhər), *n.* one who makes or deals in hose or stockings, or goods knitted or woven like hose.

ho·sier·y (hō/zhə rĭ), *n.* **1.** hose or stockings of any kind. **2.** the business of a hosier.

hosp., hospital.

hos·pice (hŏs/pĭs), *n.* a house of shelter or rest for pilgrims, strangers, etc., esp. one kept by a religious order. [t. F, t. L: m.s. *hospitium* hospitality]

hos·pi·ta·ble (hŏs/pĭ tə bəl *or*, esp. Brit., hŏs pĭt′ə bəl), *adj.* **1.** affording a generous welcome to guests or strangers: *a hospitable city.* **2.** inclined to or characterized by hospitality: *a hospitable reception.* **3.** favorably receptive or open (fol. by *to*): *hospitable to new ideas.* [t. F (obs.). f. s. LL *hospitāre* receive as a guest + -*able* -ABLE] **—hos/pi·ta·ble·ness,** *n.* **—hos/pi·ta·bly,** *adv.*

hos·pi·tal (hŏs/pĭ təl), *n.* **1.** an institution in which sick or injured persons are given medical or surgical treatment. **2.** a similar establishment for the care of animals. **3.** *Brit.* an old people's home. [ME, t. OF, t. LL: s. *hospitāle* inn, prop. neut. of L *hospitālis* pertaining to guests, hospitable]

—Syn. 1. retreat. HOSPITAL, ASYLUM, SANATORIUM, SANITARIUM are names of institutions for persons needing some sort of care. A HOSPITAL is an institution in which sick or injured persons are given medical or surgical treatment, ray therapy, etc.: *the woman was in the hospital awaiting an operation.* An ASYLUM is an institution (usually owned by the state) for the care of particularly afflicted or dependent persons; though it originally meant a place of refuge, the word has acquired unpleasant connotations, so that HOSPITAL is now the preferred term for that type of institution also: *an asylum for the deaf (insane, blind); an orphan asylum.* The terms SANATORIUM and SANITARIUM are sometimes used interchangeably. However, the former, stressing curative and healing measures, often means a health resort for persons needing mainly rest and recuperation in pleasant surroundings: *nature therapy and raw foods are specialties of this sanatorium.* SANITARIUM stresses hygienic conditions, and usually has patients needing special treatment: *the sanitarium for tubercular patients.*

Hos·pi·tal·er (hŏs/pĭ tal ər), *n.* **1.** a member of a religious and military order (**Knights Hospitalers**) taking its origin about the time of the first Crusade (1096–99) from a hospital at Jerusalem. **2.** (*l.c.*) a person, esp. a member of a religious order, devoted to the care of the sick or needy in hospitals. Also, **Hos/pi·tal·ler.** [ME, t. OF: m. *hospitalier,* der. *hospital* HOSPITAL]

hos·pi·tal·i·ty (hŏs/pə tăl′ə tĭ), *n.*, *pl.* **-ties.** the reception and entertainment of guests or strangers with liberality and kindness.

hos·pi·tal·ize (hŏs/pĭ tə līz′), *v.t.*, **-ized, -izing.** to place for care in a hospital. **—hos/pi·tal·i·za/tion,** *n.*

hos·pi·tal·man (hŏs/pĭ tal mən), *n. U.S. Navy.* an enlisted man working as a hospital assistant; corpsman.

hos·po·dar (hŏs/pə där′), *n.* a former title of governors or princes of Walachia and Moldavia. [Rumanian]

host¹ (hōst), *n.* **1.** one who entertains guests in his own home or elsewhere: *the host at a theater party.* **2.** the landlord of an inn. **3.** an animal or plant from which a parasite obtains nutrition. [ME (*h*)*oste,* t. OF, g. L *hospes* host, guest, stranger. Cf. GUEST, HOST²]

host² (hōst), *n.* **1.** a multitude or great number of persons or things: *a host of details.* **2.** *Archaic.* an army. [ME, t. OF, g. L *hostis* stranger, enemy, ML army. Cf. GUEST, HOST¹]

Host (hōst), *n. Eccles.* the bread consecrated in the celebration of the Eucharist; a consecrated wafer. [ME *hoste,* t. ML: m.s. *hostia,* in L animal sacrificed]

---

b., blend of, blended; c., cognate with; d., dialect, dialectal; der., derived from; f., formed from; g., going back to; m., modification of; r., replacing; s., stem of; t., taken from; ?, perhaps. See the full key on inside cover.

hos·tage (hŏs′tĭj), *n.* **1.** a person given or held as a security for the performance of certain actions. **2.** the condition of a hostage. **3.** a security or pledge. [ME (h)ostage, t. OF, der. oste guest, g. s. L hospes and ? b. with s. L obses hostage] **—hos′tage·ship′,** *n.*

hos·tel (hŏs′təl), *n.* **1.** a supervised lodging place for young people traveling by bicycle or walking. **2.** Brit. a residence hall at a university. **3.** Archaic. an inn. [ME (h)ostel, t. OF, der. oste guest]

hos·tel·ry (hŏs′təl rĭ), *n., pl.* **-ries.** Archaic. a hostel or inn. [ME (h)ostelerie, t. OF, der. hostel. See HOSTEL]

host·ess (hōs′tĭs), *n.* **1.** a female host; a woman who entertains guests. **2.** a woman employed in a restaurant or place of amusement to seat the guests, etc. **3.** a paid dancing partner. **4.** a female innkeeper.

hos·tile (hŏs′təl; Brit. -tīl), *adj.* **1.** opposed in feeling, action, or character; unfriendly; antagonistic: hostile criticism. **2.** of or characteristic of an enemy: hostile ground. [late ME, t. L: m.s. hostīlis, der. hostis enemy. See HOST²] **—hos′tile·ly,** *adv.*
—Syn. **1.** warlike; adverse, averse, opposed. HOSTILE, INIMICAL indicate that which characterizes an enemy or something injurious to one's interests. HOSTILE applies to the spirit, attitude, or action of an enemy: they showed a hostile and menacing attitude. INIMICAL applies to an antagonistic or injurious tendency or influence: their remarks were inimical to his reputation. —Ant. **2.** amicable.

hos·til·i·ty (hŏs tĭl′ə tĭ), *n., pl.* **-ties. 1.** hostile state; enmity; antagonism. **2.** a hostile act. **3.** (pl.) acts of warfare. —Syn. **1.** animosity, ill will, unfriendliness; opposition. **3.** war, warfare, fighting.

hos·tler (hŏs′lər, ŏs′lər), *n.* Archaic. one who takes care of horses, esp. at an inn. [var. of OSTLER]

hot (hŏt), *adj.* **hotter, hottest,** *adv., v.,* **hotted, hotting.** —adj. **1.** having or communicating heat; having a high temperature: a hot stove. **2.** actively conducting current: a hot wire. **3.** having a sensation of great bodily heat; attended with or producing such a sensation. **4.** having an effect as of burning on the tongue, skin, etc., as pepper, mustard, a blister, etc. **5.** having or showing intense feeling; ardent or fervent; vehement; excited: hot temper. **6.** lustful. **7.** violent, furious, or intense: the hottest battle. **8.** strong or fresh, as a scent or trail. **9.** new: hot from the press. **10.** following very closely; close: to be hot on one's heels. **11.** Games. close to the sought-for object or answer. **12.** Slang. fashionable and exciting. **13.** Jazz. **a.** (of a musician) performing in an enthusiastic manner, with improvisatory or decorative additions to the original melody. **b.** (of music) marked by such improvisation. **c.** arousing, or capable of arousing, enthusiasm and admiration. **14.** Slang. recently stolen or otherwise illegally obtained. **15.** radioactive, esp. to a degree injurious to health. **16.** in hot water, Colloq. in trouble. **17.** make (it, etc.) hot for, Colloq. to make (a place or a situation) unpleasant for. —adv. **18.** in a hot manner; hotly. —v.t. **19.** Brit. to heat. [ME ho(o)t, OE hāt, c. G heiss] **—hot′ly,** *adv.* **—hot′ness,** *n.* —Syn. **1.** heated; torrid, sultry. **4.** pungent, biting, peppery. **5.** angry. —Ant. **1.** cold.

hot air, Slang. empty, pretentious talk or writing.

hot·bed (hŏt′bĕd′), *n.* **1.** a bed of earth, heated by fermenting manure, etc., and usually covered with glass, for growing plants out of season. **2.** a place favoring rapid growth, esp. of something bad: a hotbed of vice.

hot-blood·ed (hŏt′blŭd′ĭd), *adj.* having hot blood; excitable; impetuous.

hot·box (hŏt′bŏks′), *n.* an overheated journal box, in a railroad car or locomotive, caused by the friction of a rapidly revolving axle.

hotch·pot (hŏch′pŏt′), *n.* Law. the bringing together of shares or properties in order to divide them equally, esp. when they are to be divided among the children of a parent dying intestate. [ME hochepot, t. OF: ragout, f. hocher shake + pot pot]

hotch·potch (hŏch′pŏch′), *n.* Brit. **1.** hodgepodge. **2.** Law. hotchpot. [riming var. of HOTCHPOT]

hot cockles, a children's game in which someone covers his eyes and attempts to guess who has hit him.

hot cross bun, a bun with a cross of frosting on it, eaten chiefly during Lent.

hot dog, Colloq. a hot frankfurter or wiener (sausage), esp. as served in a split roll.

ho·tel (hō tĕl′; Brit. also ō tĕl′), *n.* a public house offering lodging, food, etc. for travelers, etc. (commonly preceded in England by an rather than a). [t. F: (earlier hostel) HOSTEL]
—Syn. HOTEL, HOUSE, INN, TAVERN refer to establishments for the lodging or entertainment of travelers and others. HOTEL is the common word, suggesting a more or less commodious establishment with up-to-date appointments though this is not necessarily true: Grand Hotel, the best hotel in the city. The word HOUSE is often used in the name of a particular hotel, the connotation being wealth and luxury: the Parker House, the Palmer House. INN suggests a place of homelike comfort and old-time appearance or ways; it is used for quaint or archaic effect in the names of some public houses and hotels in the U.S.: The Pickwick Inn, The Wayside Inn. A TAVERN, like the English PUBLIC HOUSE, is a house where liquors are sold for drinking on the premises; until recently it was archaic or dialectal in the U.S., but has been revived to substitute for saloon, which had unfavorable connotations: taverns are required to close by two o'clock in the morning. The word has also been used in the sense of INN, esp. in New England, ever since Colonial days.

Hô·tel des In·va·lides (ō tĕl′ dĕ zăn vá lēd′), the

site in Paris of Napoleon's tomb: orig. a hospital for invalided veterans.

hô·tel de ville (ō tĕl′ də vĕl′), French. a city hall.

hô·tel Dieu (ō tĕl dyœ′), French. a hospital.

hot·foot (hŏt′fŏŏt′), *n., pl.* **-foots,** *v., adv.* —n. **1.** a practical joke in which a match, inserted surreptitiously between the sole and upper of the victim's shoe, is lit and allowed to burn down. —v.i. **2.** to go in great haste: to hotfoot it. —adv. **3.** with great speed in going; in hot haste.

hot·head (hŏt′hĕd′), *n.* a hot-headed person.

hot·head·ed (hŏt′hĕd′ĭd), *adj.* hot or fiery in spirit or temper; impetuous; rash. **—hot′-head′ed·ly,** *adv.* **—hot′-head′ed·ness,** *n.*

hot·house (hŏt′hous′), *n.* an artificially heated greenhouse for the cultivation of tender plants.

hothouse lamb, a lamb born in the fall or early winter, usually reared indoors, specially fed, and marketed when from 9 to 16 weeks of age.

hot plate, 1. a portable appliance for cooking, heated formerly by a gas burner beneath, now chiefly by an electrical unit in the appliance. **2.** a dish of warm food.

hot pot, Chiefly Brit. mutton or beef cooked with potatoes, etc., in a covered pot.

hot-press (hŏt′prĕs′), *n.* **1.** a machine applying heat in conjunction with mechanical pressure, as for producing a smooth surface on paper, for expressing oil, etc. —v.t. **2.** to subject to treatment in a hot-press.

hot rod, U.S. Slang. a car (usually an old one) whose engine has been altered for increased speed.

Hot Springs, a city 28,337 (1960) in central Arkansas, adjoining **Hot Springs National Park,** a tourist area having many therma mineral springs.

hot·spur (hŏt′spûr′), *n.* an impetuous person; a hothead. [first applied to Sir Henry PERCY]

Hot·ten·tot (hŏt′ən tŏt′), *n.* **1.** a member of a native South African yellowish-brown race of low stature, probably of mixed Bushman and Bantu (Negro) origin. **2.** the language of the Hottentots, having no certain affinity. [t. D, orig. phrase hot en tot "hot and tot" (words supposedly frequent in Hottentot speech)]

Hou·dan (hŏŏ′dăn), *n.* a breed of the domestic fowl of French origin, having a heavy, globular crest and evenly mottled black-and-white plumage. [named after Houdan, town in France, near Paris]

Hou·di·ni (hŏŏ dē′nĭ), *n.* Harry, (Ehrich Weiss) 1874–1926, U.S. magician and writer.

Hou·don (ŏŏ dôn′), *n.* Jean Antoine (zhän än twän′), 1741–1828, French sculptor.

Hou·ma·yun (hŏŏ mä′yŏŏn), *n.* Humayun.

hound¹ (hound), *n.* **1.** a dog of any of various breeds used in the chase and commonly hunting by scent. **2.** any dog. **3.** Slang. a mean, despicable fellow. **4.** Slang. an addict: a movie hound. **5.** a player in hare and hounds. —v.t. **6.** to hunt or track with hounds, or as a hound does; pursue. **7.** to incite (a hound, etc.) to pursuit or attack; urge on. [ME; OE hund, c. G hund. Cf. L canis, Gk. kýon dog]

hound² (hound), *n.* **1.** Naut. a projection at a masthead, serving to support rigging or trestletrees. **2.** a bar usually used in pairs to strengthen various portions of the running gear of a vehicle. [ME hūn, t. Scand.; cf. Icel. hūnn knob at the masthead]

hound's-tongue (houndz′tŭng′), *n.* **1.** a troublesome boraginaceous weed, Cynoglossum officinale, with prickly nutlets and tonguelike leaves. **2.** any other plant of the genus Cynoglossum. [ME hundestunge, trans. of L cynoglóssum, t. Gk.: m. kynóglōsson dog-tongued]

hour (our), *n.* **1.** a space of time equal to one 24th part of a mean solar day or civil day; 60 minutes. **2.** a short or limited period of time. **3.** a particular or appointed time: the hour of death. **4.** the present time: the man of the hour. **5.** any definite time of day, or the time indicated by a timepiece: what is the hour? **6.** (pl.) time spent for work, study, etc.: after hours. **7.** (pl.) customary time of going to bed and getting up: to keep late hours. **8.** distance normally covered in an hour's traveling. **9.** Astron. **a.** a unit of measure of right ascension, etc., representing 15 degrees, or the 24th part of a great circle. **b.** See sidereal hour. **10.** Educ. **a.** a single period of class instruction. **b.** one unit of academic credit, usually representing attendance at one scheduled period of instruction per week throughout a semester, quarter, or term. **11.** (pl.) Eccles. **a.** the seven stated times of the day for prayer and devotion. **b.** the offices or services prescribed for these times. **c.** a book containing them. **12.** the Hours, Class. Myth. the Horae. [ME ure, ore, hore, t. OF, g. L hōra time, season, hour, t. Gk.; akin to YEAR]

hour circle, Astron. any great circle in the celestial sphere passing through the celestial poles.

hour·glass (our′glăs′, -gläs′), *n.* an instrument for measuring time, consisting of two bulbs of glass joined by a narrow passage through which a quantity of sand (or mercury) runs in just an hour.

hour hand, the hand that indicates the hours on a clock or watch.

Hourglass

hou·ri (hŏŏr′ĭ, hour′ĭ), *n., pl.* **-ris.** one of the beautiful virgins provided in Paradise to all faithful Mohammedans. [t. F, t. Pers.: m. hūrī, der. Ar. hūr, pl. of ahwar black-eyed, orig. applied to gazelles]

hour·ly (our'lĭ), *adj.* **1.** of, pertaining to, occurring, or done each successive hour. **2.** frequent; continual. *—adv.* **3.** every hour; hour by hour. **4.** frequently.

house (*n.* hous; *v.* houz), *n., pl.* **houses** (hou'zĭz), *v.*, **housed, housing.** *—n.* **1.** a building for human habitation. **2.** a place of lodgment, rest, etc., as of an animal. **3.** a household. **4.** a building for any purpose: *a house of worship.* **5.** a place of entertainment; a theater. **6.** the audience of a theater, etc. **7.** a family regarded as consisting of ancestors and descendants: *the house of Hapsburg.* **8.** the building in which a legislative or deliberative body meets. **9.** the body itself: *the House of Representatives.* **10.** a quorum of such a body. **11.** a firm or commercial establishment: *the house of Rothschild.* **12.** an advisory or deliberative group, esp. in church or college affairs. **13.** a college in English-style universities. **14.** a residential hall for students, esp. in colleges. **15.** the members or residents of any such house. **16. put** or **set one's house in order,** to put one's affairs into good condition. **17. bring down the house,** to be well received or applauded. **18. on the house,** free; as a gift from the management. *—v.t.* **19.** to put or receive into a house; provide with a house. **20.** to give shelter to; harbor; lodge. **21.** to remove from exposure; put in a safe place. **22.** *Naut.* to place in a secure or protected position. **23.** *Carp.* to fix in a socket or the like. *—v.i.* **24.** to take shelter; dwell. [ME *hous*, OE *hūs*, c. D *huis*, G *haus*, Icel. and Goth. *hūs*] **—house'less,** *adj.*
—Syn. 1. domicile. HOUSE, DWELLING, RESIDENCE, HOME are terms applied to a place to live in. DWELLING is now chiefly poetic, or in legal use, as in a lease. RESIDENCE implies size and elegance of structure and surroundings. These two terms and HOUSE have always had reference to the structure to be lived in. HOME has recently taken on this meaning and become practically equivalent to HOUSE, the new meaning tending to crowd out the older connotations of family ties and domestic comfort. See **hotel.**

House (hous), *n.* **Col. Edward Mandell** (măn'dəl), 1858–1938, U.S. diplomatic agent and political adviser.

house agent, *Brit.* real-estate agent.

house·boat (hous'bōt'), *n.* a boat fitted up for use as a floating dwelling but not suited to rough water.

house·break·er (hous'brā'kər), *n.* **1.** one who breaks into and enters a house with a felonious intent. **2.** *Brit.* one who dismantles houses. **—house'break'ing,** *n.*

house·bro·ken (hous'brō'kən), *adj.* trained to live indoors, as a dog.

house·carl (hous'kärl'), *n.* a member of the household troops or bodyguard of a Danish or early English king or noble. [modernization of OE *hūscarl,* t. Scand.; cf. Icel. *hūskarl* houseman]

house coat, a long, tailored, dresslike garment of one piece, worn about the house.

house·dress (hous'drĕs'), *n.* a dress worn in the house, esp. while doing housework.

Housefly.
Musca domestica
(¼ in. long)

house·fly (hous'flī'), *n., pl.* **-flies.** a common dipterous insect, *Musca domestica,* found in nearly all parts of the world.

house·hold (hous'hōld', -ōld'), *n.* **1.** the people of a house collectively; a family, including servants, etc.; a domestic establishment. *—adj.* **2.** of or pertaining to a household; domestic: *household furniture.*

household arts, *Educ.* instruction concerned with homemaking, family living, and allied skills.

house·hold·er (hous'hōl'dər), *n.* **1.** one who holds or occupies a house. **2.** the head of a family.

house·keep·er (hous'kē'pər), *n.* a woman who does or directs the work of a household.

house·keep·ing (hous'kē'pĭng), *n.* **1.** the maintaining of a house or domestic establishment. **2.** the management of household affairs.

hou·sel (hou'zəl), *n.* *Archaic.* the Eucharist. [ME; OE *hūsl,* c. Goth. *hūnsl* sacrifice]

house·leek (hous'lēk'), *n.* **1.** a crassulaceous Old World herb, *Sempervivum tectorum,* with pink flowers and thick, succulent leaves, found growing on the roofs and walls of houses. **2.** any plant of the genus *Sempervivum.*

house·line (hous'lĭn'), *n.* *Naut.* a small line of three strands, used for seizings, etc.

house·maid (hous'mād'), *n.* a female servant employed in general work in a household.

housemaid's knee, *Pathol.* inflammation of the bursa over the anterior region of the kneepan.

house·mas·ter (hous'măs'tər, -mäs'tər), *n.* (in English boys' schools) a teacher who is in charge of a residence.

house·moth·er (hous'mŭŧh'ər), *n.* a woman who is head of a group, esp. of students, living together.

House of Burgesses, the assembly of representatives in colonial Virginia.

House of Commons, the elective house of the British parliament.

house of correction, a place for the confinement and reform of persons convicted of minor offenses and not regarded as confirmed criminals.

House of Delegates, the lower house of the General Assembly in Virginia, West Virginia, and Maryland.

House of Lords, the nonelective house of the Parliament of Great Britain and Northern Ireland.

House of Peers, the upper house of the Imperial Diet, the Japanese legislature.

House of Representatives, the lower legislative branch in national and state governing bodies, as in the United States, Australia, Mexico, etc.

house organ, a periodical issued by a business house, etc., presenting news of its activities, etc.

house party, **1.** an entertainment of guests for some days at a host's house, esp. in the country. **2.** the guests.

house physician, a resident physician in a hospital, hotel, or other public institution.

house·top (hous'tŏp'), *n.* the top or roof of a house.

house·warm·ing (hous'wôr'mĭng), *n.* a party to celebrate beginning one's occupancy of a new home.

house·wife (hous'wĭf' *or usually* hŭz'ĭf *for 2*), *n., pl.* **-wives** (-wīvz'). **1.** the woman in charge of a household. **2.** *Chiefly Brit.* a small case for needles, thread, etc.

house·wife·ly (hous'wīf'lĭ), *adj.* of, like, or befitting a housewife. **—house'wife'li·ness,** *n.*

house·wif·er·y (hous'wī'fərĭ, -wĭf'rĭ, hŭz'ĭf'rĭ), *n.* the function or work of a housewife; housekeeping.

house·work (hous'wûrk'), *n.* the work of cleaning, cooking, etc., to be done in housekeeping.

hous·ing[1] (hou'zĭng), *n.* **1.** something serving as a shelter, covering, or the like; a shelter; lodging. **2.** houses collectively. **3.** act of one who houses or puts under shelter. **4.** the providing of houses for the community: *the housing of veterans.* **5.** *Mach.* a frame, plate, or the like, that supports a part of a machine, etc. **6.** *Carp.* the space made in one piece of wood, or the like, for the insertion of another. **7.** *Naut.* **a.** the inboard end of a bowsprit. **b.** the part of a mast which is below deck. **8.** a niche for a statue. [f. HOUSE, v. + -ING[1]]

hous·ing[2] (hou'zĭng), *n.* **1.** a covering of cloth for the back and flanks of a horse or other animal, for protection or ornament. **2.** a covering of cloth or the like. **3.** (*often pl.*) a caparison or trapping. [f. *house* (ME, t. OF: m. *houce*) covering of cloth + -ING[1]]

Hous·man (hous'mən), *n.* **Alfred Edward,** 1859–1936, British poet and classical scholar.

Hous·ton (hū'stən), *n.* **1. Sam,** 1793–1863, U.S. frontier hero and soldier: president of Texas, 1836–38. **2.** a city in SE Texas: a port on a ship canal, ab. 50 mi. from the Gulf of Mexico. 938,219 (1960).

hous·to·ni·a (hōō stō'nĭ ə), *n.* any herb of the North American rubiaceous genus *Houstonia,* as *H. caerulea,* the common bluet or innocence. [NL; named after Dr. W. *Houston* (d. 1733), British botanist. See -IA]

Hou·yhn·hnm (hōō ĭn'əm, hwĭn'əm), *n.* (in Swift's *Gulliver's Travels*) one of a race of horses endowed with reason, who rule the Yahoos, a race of degraded, brutish creatures having the form of man.

hove (hōv), *v.* pt. and pp. of **heave.**

hov·el (hŭv'əl, hŏv'-), *n., v.,* **-eled, -eling,** or (*esp. Brit.*) **-elled, -elling.** *—n.* **1.** a small, mean dwelling house; a wretched hut. **2.** an open shed, as for sheltering cattle, tools, etc. *—v.t.* **3.** to shelter or lodge as in a hovel. [ME *hovel, hovyl;* orig. uncert.]

hov·er (hŭv'ər, hŏv'-), *v.i.* **1.** to hang fluttering or suspended in the air: *a hovering bird.* **2.** to keep lingering about; wait near at hand. **3.** to remain in an uncertain or irresolute state; waver: *hovering between life and death.* *—n.* **4.** act of hovering. **5.** state of hovering. [ME *hoveren,* freq. of *hoven* hover; orig. uncert.] **—hov'er·er,** *n.* **—hov'er·ing·ly,** *adv.* **—Syn. 1.** See **fly**[1].

Hov·ey (hŭv'ĭ), *n.* **Richard,** 1864–1900, U.S. poet.

how (hou), *adv.* **1.** in what way or manner; by what means: *how did it happen?* **2.** to what extent, degree, etc.: *how much?* **3.** at what price: *how do you sell these apples?* **4.** in what state or condition: *how are you?* **5.** for what reason; why. **6.** to what effect or with what meaning: *how do you mean?* **7.** what? *—n.* **8.** a question beginning with "how." **9.** way or manner of doing: *to consider all the hows and wherefores.* [ME *hou, how,* OE *hū,* c. D *hoe;* akin to WHO]

How·ard (hou'ərd), *n.* **1. Catherine,** died 1542, fifth wife of Henry VIII. **2. Henry.** See **Surrey,** Earl of.

how·be·it (hou bē'ĭt), *adv.* **1.** nevertheless. *—conj.* **2.** *Obs.* although. [ME *how be* it however it may be. Cf. ALBEIT]

how·dah (hou'də), *n.* (in the East Indies) a seat, commonly with a railing and a canopy, placed on the back of an elephant. [t. Hind.: m. *haudah,* t. Ar.: m. *haudaj*]

Howe (hou), *n.* **1. Elias,** 1819–67, U.S. inventor (of the sewing machine). **2. Julia Ward,** 1819–1910, U.S. author. **3. Richard,** 1725–99, British admiral. **4. William,** (*5th Viscount Howe*) 1729–1814, British general: commander in chief of the British forces, 1775–78, in the American Revolutionary War.

how·e'er (hou âr'), *conj., adv.* however.

How·ells (hou'əlz), *n.* **William Dean,** 1837–1920, U.S. novelist and editor.

how·ev·er (hou ĕv'ər), *conj.* **1.** nevertheless; yet; in spite of that. *—adv.* **2.** to whatever extent or degree; no matter how (far, much, etc.). **3.** in whatever manner. **4.** *Brit.* (interrogatively) how under any circumstances: *however did you manage?* [ME] **—Syn. 1.** See **but**[1].

how·itz·er (hou'ĭt sər), *n.* a comparatively short-barreled cannon, used esp. for curved fire, as in reaching troops behind cover. [earlier *hauwitzer,* appar. t. D: m. *houwitser,* t. earlier *houwits(e)* catapult. Cf. G *haubitze,* earlier *haufnitz,* t. Czech: m. *houfnice* catapult]

howl (houl) *v.i.* **1.** to utter a loud, prolonged, mournful cry, as that of a dog or wolf. **2.** to utter a similar cry in distress, pain, rage, etc.; wail. **3.** to make a sound like an animal howling: *the wind is howling.* —*v.t.* **4.** to utter with howls. **5.** to drive or force by howls. —*n.* **6.** the cry of a dog. wolf, etc. **7.** a cry or wail, as of pain or rage. **8.** a sound like wailing: *the howl of the wind.* **9.** a loud scornful laugh or yell. [ME *houle.* Cf. G *heulen;* imit.]

How·land Island (hou′lənd), a small island in the central Pacific, near the equator: U.S. aerological station and airfield. 1 sq. mi.

howl·er (hou′lər). *n.* **1.** one who or that which howls. **2.** Also, **howling monkey.** any of the large, prehensile-tailed tropical American monkeys of the genus *Alouatta,* the males of which make a howling noise. **3.** *Colloq.* an especially ludicrous blunder, as in a school recitation.

How·rah (hou′rä). *n.* a city in NE India, on the Hooghly river opposite Calcutta. 433,630 (1951).

how·so·ev·er (hou′sō·ĕv′ər), *adv.* **1.** to whatsoever extent or degree. **2.** in whatsoever manner.

hoy·den (hoi′dən), *n.* **1.** a rude or ill-bred girl; tomboy. —*adj.* **2.** hoydenish; boisterous. Also, **hoiden.** [orig. uncert.] —**hoy′den·ish,** *adj.* —**hoy′den·ish·ness,** *n.*

Hoyle (hoil), *n.* **Edmund** or **Edmond,** 1672–1769, British writer on card games.

HP, **1.** Also. **H.P.** *Elect.* high power. **2.** Also, **H.P., h.p.** high pressure. **3.** Also. **hp, H.P., h.p.** horsepower.

H.Q., headquarters. Also. **h.q.**

Hr., (Ger. *Herr*) equivalent of **Mr.**

hr., *pl.* **hrs.** hour; hours.

H.R., House of Representatives.

H.R.H., His, or Her, Royal Highness.

H.R.I.P., (L *hic requiescit in pace*) here rests in peace.

Hrolf (hrôlf), *n.* See **Rollo.**

H.S., **1.** High School. **2.** *Brit.* Home Secretary.

h.s., (L *hoc sensu*) in this sense.

H.S.H., His, or Her, Serene Highness.

ht., height.

Hsing·an (shǐng′än′), *n.* a former province in NE China, in Manchuria.

Hsin·king (shǐn′jǐng′). *n.* Changchun.

H.S.M., His, or Her, Serene Majesty.

hua·ra·che (hwä rä′chě), *n.* a Mexican sandal, woven of leather strips. Also, **hua·ra·cho** (hwä rä′chô).

Huás·car (wäs′kär), *n.* c1495–1533, Inca ruler of Peru.

Huas·ca·rán (wäs′kä rän′), *n.* a mountain in W Peru, in the Andes. 22,205 ft.

hub (hŭb), *n.* **1.** the central part of a wheel, as that part into which the spokes are inserted. **2.** the part in central position around which all else revolves: *the hub of the universe.* **3. the Hub,** Boston, Mass. **4.** the peg or hob used as a target in quoits, etc. **5.** *Coining.* a design of hardened steel in relief used as a punch in making a die. [cf. HOB¹]

hub·ba hub·ba (hŭb′ə hŭb′ə), *U.S. Slang.* an exclamation of liking or approval. Also, **hub′a hub′a.**

Hub·bard (hŭb′ərd), *n.* **Elbert,** 1856–1915, U.S. author.

hub·bub (hŭb′ŭb), *n.* **1.** a loud, confused noise, as of many voices. **2.** tumult; uproar. —**Syn. 1.** See **noise.**

hu·bris (hū′brĭs), *n.* insolence or wanton violence stemming from excessive pride. Also, **hybris.** [Gk.]

huck·a·back (hŭk′ə băk′), *n.* toweling of linen or cotton, of a distinctive weave. Also, **huck.**

huck·le·ber·ry (hŭk′əl bĕr′Y), *n., pl.* **-ries. 1.** the dark-blue or black edible berry of any of various shrubs of the ericaceous genus *Gaylussacia.* **2.** a shrub yielding such a berry. **3.** blueberry (def. 1). [var. of *hurtleberry* WHORTLEBERRY]

Huckleberry Finn (fǐn), **The Adventures of,** a novel (1884) by Mark Twain.

huck·le·bone (hŭk′əl bōn′), *n. Anat.* **1.** the hipbone. **2.** the anklebone, astragalus, or talus.

huck·ster (hŭk′stər), *n.* Also, **huck′ster·er. 1.** a retailer of small articles; a hawker. **2.** a street peddler in fruits and vegetables. **3.** a cheaply mercenary person. **4.** *U.S. Slang.* an advertising man. —*v.i.* **5.** to deal in small articles or make petty bargains. [ME *huccster, hokester.* Cf. LG *höken* to retail goods]

Hud·ders·field (hŭd′ərz fēld′), *n.* a city in central England, in SW Yorkshire. 127,600 (est. 1956).

hud·dle (hŭd′əl), *v.,* **-dled, -dling,** *n.* —*v.t.* **1.** to heap or crowd together confusedly. **2.** to draw (oneself) closely together; nestle (often fol. by *up*). **3.** to do hastily and carelessly (often fol. by *up, over,* or *together*). **4.** to put on (clothes) with careless haste (often fol. by *on*). —*v.i.* **5.** to gather or crowd together in a confused mass. **6.** *Football.* to get together in a huddle to determine the next play. —*n.* **7.** a confused heap, mass, or crowd; a jumble. **8.** confusion or disorder. **9.** *Colloq.* a conference held in secret. **10.** *Football.* a gathering of the team behind the scrimmage line for instructions, signals, etc. [cf. ME *hodre,* c. LG *hudren*] —**hud′dler,** *n.*

Hu·di·bras·tic (hū′də brās′tYk), *adj.* **1.** of or pertaining to, or resembling the style of, Samuel Butler's **Hudibras** (published 1663–78), a mock-heroic satirical poem written in tetrameter couplets. **2.** of a playful burlesque style.

Hud·son (hŭd′sən), *n.* **1. Henry,** died 1611?, English navigator and explorer in North America. **2. William Henry,** 1841–1922, British naturalist and author. **3.** a river in E New York, flowing S to New York Bay. 306 mi.

Hudson Bay, a large inland sea in N Canada. ab. 850 mi. long; ab. 600 mi. wide; ab. 400,000 sq. mi.

Hudson seal, muskrat fur which has been plucked and dyed to give the appearance of seal.

Hudson Strait, a strait connecting Hudson Bay and the Atlantic. ab. 450 mi. long; ab. 100 mi. wide.

hue¹ (hū), *n.* **1.** that property of color by which the various regions of the spectrum are distinguished, as red, blue, etc. **2.** variety of a color; a tint: *pale hues.* **3.** color: *all the hues of the rainbow.* **4.** *Obs.* form or appearance. **5.** *Obs.* complexion. [ME *hewe,* OE *hīw* form, appearance, color]

hue² (hū), *n.* outcry. as of pursuers; clamor. [ME *hu,* t. OF. der. *heur* cry out, shout; prob. imit.]

Hué (hwĕ), *n.* a seaport in E Indochina, in Vietnam: the former capital of Annam. 96,388 (est. 1953).

hue and cry, 1. *Law.* the pursuit of a felon or an offender with loud outcries or clamor to give an alarm. **2.** any public clamor against or over something.

hued (hūd), *adj.* having a hue or color: *golden-hued.*

Huel·va (wĕl′vä), *n.* a seaport in SW Spain, near the Gulf of Cádiz. 65,490 (1950).

Huer·ta (wĕr′tä). *n.* **Victoriano** (vĕk′tō ryä′nō), 1854–1916, Mexican general: president of Mexico, 1913–14.

huff (hŭf), *n.* **1.** a sudden swell of anger; a fit of resentment: *to leave in a huff.* —*v.t.* **2.** to give offense to; make angry. **3.** to treat with arrogance or contempt; bluster at; hector or bully. **4.** *Checkers.* to remove (a piece) from the board as penalty for failing to make a compulsory capture. —*v.i.* **5.** to take offense. **6.** *Archaic.* to swell with pride or arrogance; swagger or bluster. **7.** *Brit. Dial.* to puff or blow. [imit.]

huff·ish (hŭf′Ysh), *adj.* **1.** petulant. **2.** swaggering; hectoring. —**huff′ish·ly,** *adv.* —**huff′ish·ness,** *n.*

huff·y (hŭf′Y), *adj.,* **huffier, huffiest. 1.** easily offended or touchy. **2.** offended; sulky: *a huffy mood.* —**huff′i·ly,** *adv.* —**huff′i·ness,** *n.*

hug (hŭg), *v.,* **hugged, hugging,** *n.* —*v.t.* **1.** to clasp tightly in the arms, esp. with affection; embrace. **2.** to cling firmly or fondly to: *to hug an opinion.* **3.** to keep close to, as in sailing or going along: *to hug the shore.* —*v.i.* **4.** to cling together; lie close. —*n.* **5.** a tight clasp with the arms; a warm embrace. [cf. Icel. *hugga* console]

huge (hūj), *adj.,* **huger, hugest.** extraordinarily large in bulk, quantity, or extent: *a huge mountain.* [ME *huge, hoge;* ? aphetic var. of OF *ahuge* great, large, high; orig. uncert.] —**huge′ly,** *adv.* —**huge′ness,** *n.*
—**Syn.** mammoth, gigantic, colossal; vast; stupendous; bulky. HUGE, ENORMOUS, IMMENSE, TREMENDOUS imply great magnitude. HUGE, when used of concrete objects, usually adds the idea of massiveness, bulkiness, or even shapelessness: *a huge mass of rock, a huge collection of antiques.* ENORMOUS, lit. out of the norm, applies to what exceeds in extent, magnitude, or degree, a norm or standard: *an enormous iceberg, enormous curiosity.* TREMENDOUS applies to anything so huge as to be astonishing or to inspire awe: *a tremendous amount of equipment.* IMMENSE, lit. not measurable, is particularly applicable to what is exceedingly great, without reference to a standard: *immense buildings.* All are used figuratively: *a huge success, enormous curiosity, tremendous effort, immense joy.* —**Ant.** small, tiny, diminutive.

hug·ger-mug·ger (hŭg′ər mŭg′ər). *n.* **1.** disorder or confusion; a muddle. **2.** *Archaic.* secrecy or concealment: *in hugger-mugger.* —*adj.* **3.** secret or clandestine. **4.** disorderly or confused. —*v.t.* **5.** to keep secret or concealed. —*v.i.* **6.** to act secretly; take secret counsel.

Hugh Ca·pet (hū kā′pYt, kăp′Yt; *Fr.* kà pĕ′). See **Capet.**

Hughes (hūz), *n.* **1. Charles Evans,** 1862–1948, U.S. statesman: chief justice of the United States Supreme Court, 1930–41. **2. Langston** (lăng′stən), born 1902, U.S. writer. **3. Thomas,** 1822–96, British author.

Hug·li (hōōg′lē), *n.* Hooghly.

hug-me-tight (hŭg′mē tīt′), *n.* *U.S.* a tight, sometimes sleeveless, knitted jacket.

Hu·go (hū′gō; *Fr.* ygō′), *n.* **Victor Marie** (vYk′tər mə rē′; *Fr.* vēk tôr′ mà rē′), **Viscount,** 1802–85, French poet, novelist, and dramatist.

Hu·gue·not (hū′gə nŏt′), *n.* a member of the Reformed or Calvinistic communion of France in the 16th and 17th centuries; a French Protestant. [t. F, earlier *eiguenot,* t. Swiss G: m. *eidgenosse* confederate, f. *eid* oath + *genoss* companion, associate, influenced by name *Hugues* Hugh]

hu·la-hu·la (hōō′lə hōō′lə), *n.* a kind of native Hawaiian dance with intricate arm movements which tell a story in pantomime. Also, **hu′la.** [t. Hawaiian]

hulk (hŭlk), *n.* **1.** the body of an old or dismantled ship. **2.** a dismasted wreck. **3.** a vessel specially built to serve as a storehouse, prison, etc., and not for sea service. **4.** a bulky or unwieldy person or mass of anything. **5.** *Archaic.* a heavy, unwieldy vessel. —*v.i.* **6.** to loom in bulky form; be bulky (often fol. by *up*). **7.** *Dial.* to lounge or slouch in a heavy, loutish manner. [ME *hulke,* OE *hulc,* prob. t. ML: s. *hulcus,* t. Gk.: m. *holkás* trading vessel]

hulk·ing (hŭl′kYng), *adj.* bulky; heavy and clumsy. Also, **hulk′y.**

hull¹ (hŭl), *n.* **1.** the husk, shell, or outer covering of a seed or fruit. **2.** the calyx of certain fruits, as the strawberry and raspberry. **3.** any covering or envelope. —*v.t.* **4.** to remove the hull of. [ME; OE *hulu* husk; pod; akin to *helan* cover, hide. Cf. HALL, HELL, HOLE] —**hull′er,** *n.*

---

hull² (hŭl), *n*. **1.** the frame or body of a ship, exclusive of masts, yards, sails, and rigging. **2.** *Aeron*. **a.** the boatlike fuselage of a flying boat on which the plane lands or takes off. **b.** the cigar-shaped arrangement of girders enclosing the gasbag of a rigid dirigible. —*v.t.* **3.** to strike or pierce the hull of (a ship), as with a torpedo. [orig. uncert. Cf. HULL¹, HOLD², HOLE]

Hull (hŭl), *n*. **1.** Cordell, 1871–1955, U.S. statesman: Secretary of State, 1933–44. **2.** William, 1753–1825, American general. **3.** Official name, Kingston-upon-Hull. a seaport in E England, on the Humber estuary. 299,068 (1951). **4.** a city in SE Canada, on the Ottawa river opposite Ottawa. 43,403 (1951).

hul·la·ba·loo (hŭl′ə bə loo′), *n*. a clamorous noise or disturbance; an uproar.

hul·lo (hə lō′), *interj., n., v.* **1.** hollo. **2.** hello.

hum (hŭm), *v*., **hummed, humming**, *n., interj*. —*v.i.* **1.** to make a low, continuous, droning sound. **2.** to give forth an indistinct sound of mingled voices or noises. **3.** to utter an indistinct sound in hesitation, embarrassment, dissatisfaction, etc.; hem. **4.** to sing with closed lips, without articulating words. **5.** *Colloq*. to be in a state of busy activity: *to make things hum*. —*v.t.* **6.** to sound, sing, or utter by humming. **7.** to bring, put, etc., by humming: *to hum a child to sleep*. —*n*. **8.** act or sound of humming; an inarticulate or indistinct murmur; a hem. —*interj*. **9.** an inarticulate sound uttered in hesitation, dissatisfaction, etc. [ME *humme*, c. G *hummen* hum; imit. Cf. HUMBLEBEE] —**hum′mer,** *n*.

hu·man (hū′mən), *adj*. **1.** of, pertaining to, or characteristic of man: *human nature*. **2.** having the nature of man; being a man: *the human race*. **3.** of or pertaining to mankind generally: *human affairs*. —*n*. **4.** *Colloq. or Humorous*. a human being. [t. L: s. *hūmānus* of a man; r. ME *humain*, t. OF] —**hu′man·ness,** *n*.

—**Syn. 1.** HUMAN, HUMANE may refer to that which is, or should be, characteristic of human beings. In thus describing characteristics, HUMAN may refer to good and bad traits of mankind alike (*human kindness, human weakness*), with, perhaps, more emphasis upon the latter, HUMAN being seen then in contrast to DIVINE: *to err is human, to forgive divine; he was only human*. HUMANE (the original spelling of HUMAN, and since 1700 restricted in meaning) takes into account only the nobler aspects of man: a HUMANE person is, specifically, one actuated by benevolence in his treatment of his fellows, or of helpless animals; the word once had also connotations of courtesy and refinement (hence, the application of HUMANE to those branches of learning intended to refine the mind).

hu·mane (hū mān′), *adj*. **1.** characterized by tenderness and compassion for the suffering or distressed: *humane feelings*. **2.** (of branches of learning or literature) tending to refine; polite: *humane studies*. [var. of HUMAN. Cf. GERMANE, GERMAN] —**hu·mane′ly,** *adv*. —**hu·mane′ness,** *n*. —**Syn. 1.** merciful, kind, kindhearted, tender. See **human**. —**Ant. 1.** brutal.

hu·man·ism (hū′mən ĭz′əm), *n*. **1.** any system or mode of thought or action in which human interests predominate. **2.** devotion to or study of the humanities; polite learning; literary culture. **3.** (*sometimes cap*.) the studies, principles, or culture of the Humanists (def. 4).

hu·man·ist (hū′mən ĭst), *n*. **1.** a student of human nature or affairs. **2.** one devoted to or versed in the humanities. **3.** a classical scholar. **4.** (*sometimes cap*.) one of the scholars of the Renaissance who pursued and disseminated the study and understanding of the cultures of ancient Rome and Greece. —**hu′man·is′tic,** *adj*.

hu·man·i·tar·i·an (hū măn′ə târ′ĭ ən), *adj*. **1.** having regard to the interests of all mankind; broadly philanthropic. **2.** pertaining to ethical or theological humanitarianism. —*n*. **3.** one who professes ethical or theological humanitarianism. **4.** a philanthropist.

hu·man·i·tar·i·an·ism (hū măn′ə târ′ĭ ə nĭz′əm), *n*. **1.** humanitarian principles or practices; comprehensive philanthropy. **2.** *Ethics*. **a.** the doctrine that man's obligations are concerned wholly with the welfare of the human race. **b.** the doctrine that mankind may become perfect without divine aid. **3.** *Theol*. the doctrine that Jesus Christ possessed a human nature only.

hu·man·i·ty (hū măn′ə tĭ), *n., pl*. **-ties. 1.** the human race; mankind. **2.** the condition or quality of being human; human nature. **3.** the quality of being humane; kindness; benevolence. **4.** polite learning in its various branches, as grammar, rhetoric, poetry, etc. **5. the humanities, a.** the study of the Latin and Greek classics. **b.** the study of literature, philosophy, art, etc., as distinguished from the social and physical sciences. [ME *humanitee*, t. F: m. *humanité*, t. L: m.s. *hūmānitas*]

hu·man·ize (hū′mən īz′), *v*., **-ized, -izing.** —*v.t.* **1.** to make humane, kind, or gentle. **2.** to make human. —*v.i.* **3.** to become human or humane. —**hu′man·i·za′-tion,** *n*. —**hu′man·iz′er,** *n*.

hu·man·kind (hū′mən kīnd′), *n*. the human race.

hu·man·ly (hū′mən lĭ), *adv*. **1.** in a human manner; by human means. **2.** according to human knowledge.

human nature, 1. the quality inherent in all persons by virtue of their common humanity. **2.** *Sociol*. the make-up of conduct of human beings that distinguishes them from other animal forms, generally regarded as produced by living in primary groups.

hu·ma·num est er·ra·re (hū mā′nəm ĕst ĕr âr′ĭ), *Latin*. to err is human.

Hu·ma·yun (hoo mä′yoon), *n*. 1508–56, Mogul emperor of Hindustan. Also, **Houmayun.**

Hum·ber (hŭm′bər), *n*. the estuary of the Ouse and Trent rivers in E England. 37 mi. long.

Hum·bert I (hŭm′bərt), (*Umberto I*) 1844–1900, king of Italy, 1878–1900.

hum·ble (hŭm′bəl, ŭm′-), *adj*., **-bler, -blest,** *v*., **-bled, -bling.** —*adj*. **1.** low in station, grade of importance, etc.; lowly: *humble origin*. **2.** modest; meek; without pride. **3.** courteously respectful: *in my humble opinion*. **4.** low in height. level, etc. —*v.t.* **5.** to lower in condition, importance, or dignity; abase. **6.** to make meek: *to humble one's heart*. [ME, t. OF, g. L *humilis* low, humble] —**hum′ble·ness,** *n*. —**hum′bler,** *n*. —**hum′-bling,** *adj*. —**hum′bling·ly,** *adv*. —**hum′bly,** *adv*. —**Syn. 1.** unassuming, plain, common, poor. **2.** submissive. **5.** HUMBLE, DEGRADE, HUMILIATE suggest lowering or causing to seem lower. To HUMBLE is to bring down the pride of another (often righteous) or to reduce him to a state of abasement: *to humble an arrogant enemy*. To DEGRADE is to demote in rank or standing, or to reduce to a low level in condition, manners, or morals: *to degrade an officer, one's dependents*. To HUMILIATE is to make others feel or appear inadequate or unworthy, esp. in some public setting: *to humiliate a sensitive person*. —**Ant. 1.** noble, illustrious. **2.** self-assertive. **3.** insolent; proud. **5.** elevate. **6.** exalt.

hum·ble·bee (hŭm′bəl bē′), *n. Chiefly Brit*. bumblebee.

humble pie, 1. *Obs*. a pie made of the umbles (inward, less delectable parts) of deer, etc. **2. eat humble pie,** to be humiliated; be forced to apologize humbly.

Hum·boldt (hŭm′bōlt; *Ger*. hoom′bōlt), *n*. **1.** Fried-rich Heinrich Alexander (frē′drĭKH hīn′rĭKH ä′lĕk-sän′dər), Baron von, 1769–1859, German scientist and writer. **2. Karl Wilhelm** (kärl vĭl′hĕlm), Baron von, 1767–1835, German philologist and statesman.

hum·bug (hŭm′bŭg), *n., v*., **-bugged, -bugging.** —*n*. **1.** a deluding trick; a hoax; a fraud. **2.** quality of falseness or deception. **3.** one who seeks to impose deceitfully upon others; a cheat; an impostor. —*v.t.* **4.** to impose upon by humbug or false pretense; delude. —*v.i.* **5.** to practice humbug. [orig. unknown] —**hum′bug′-ger,** *n*. —**Syn. 1.** imposture, deception. **2.** pretense, sham. **3.** pretender, deceiver, charlatan.

hum·bug·ger·y (hŭm′bŭg′ər ĭ), *n*. pretense; sham.

hum·ding·er (hŭm′dĭng′ər), *n. Slang*. a person or thing remarkable of its kind.

hum·drum (hŭm′drŭm′), *adj*. **1.** lacking variety; dull: *a humdrum existence*. —*n*. **2.** humdrum character or routine; monotony. **3.** monotonous or tedious talk. **4.** a dull boring fellow. [varied redupl. of HUM]

Hume (hūm), *n*. **David,** 1711–76, Scottish philosopher and historian.

hu·mer·al (hū′mər əl), *adj*. **1.** of the shoulder. **2.** *Anat., Zool*. of or related to the humerus or brachium. [f. s. L *humerus* shoulder + -AL¹]

hu·mer·us (hū′mər əs), *n., pl*. **-meri** (-mə rī′). *Anat., Zool*. **1.** (in man) the single long bone in the arm which extends from the shoulder to the elbow. See diag. under **shoulder. 2.** the brachium. **3.** a corresponding bone in the forelimb of other animals or in the wings of birds. [t. L, prop. *umerus* shoulder]

hu·mic (hū′mĭk), *adj. Chem*. of or denoting something (as an acid) derived from humus. [f. s. L *humus* ground, mould + -IC]

hu·mid (hū′mĭd), *adj*. moist or damp, with liquid or vapor: *humid air*. [t. L: s. (*h*)*ūmidus* moist] —**hu′-mid·ly,** *adv*. —**hu′mid·ness,** *n*. —**Syn.** See **damp.**

hu·mid·i·fy (hū mĭd′ə fī′), *v.t*., **-fied, -fying.** to make humid. —**hu·mid′i·fi·ca′tion,** *n*. —**hu·mid′i·fi′er,** *n*.

hu·mid·i·ty (hū mĭd′ə tĭ), *n*. **1.** humid condition; dampness. **2.** *Meteorol*. the ratio (percentage) of the water vapor in the atmosphere to the amount required to saturate it at the same temperature (called specifically **relative humidity**).

hu·mi·dor (hū′mə dôr′), *n*. a container or storage room for cigars or other preparations of tobacco, fitted with means for keeping the tobacco suitably moist.

hu·mil·i·ate (hū mĭl′ĭ āt′), *v.t*., **-ated, -ating.** to lower the pride or self-respect of; cause a painful loss of dignity to; mortify. [t. LL: m.s. *humiliātus*, pp., humbled] —**Syn.** degrade, abase, debase; dishonor, disgrace, shame. See **humble.** See also **ashamed.** —**hu·mil′i-at′ing,** *adj*. —**hu·mil′i·at′ing·ly,** *adv*. —**Ant.** exalt, honor.

hu·mil·i·a·tion (hū mĭl′ĭ ā′shən), *n*. **1.** act of humiliating. **2.** state or feeling of being humiliated; mortification. —**Syn. 2.** See **shame.**

hu·mil·i·ty (hū mĭl′ə tĭ), *n., pl*. **-ties.** quality of being humble; modest sense of one's own significance. [ME *humilite*, t. F, t. L: m.s. *humilitas*] —**Syn.** lowliness, meekness. —**Ant.** pride.

hum·ming (hŭm′ĭng), *adj*. **1.** that hums; buzzing. **2.** *Colloq*. extraordinarily active, intense, great, or big. **3.** *Colloq*. foaming, strong, or heady: *humming ale*.

hum·ming·bird (hŭm′ĭng-bûrd′), *n*. any of numerous very small American birds constituting the family *Trochilidae*, characterized by narrow wings whose rapid vibration produces a hum, by slender bill, and usually by brilliant plumage.

hummingbird moth, any of the hawk moths.

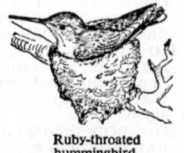

Ruby-throated
hummingbird.
Archilochus colubris
(Ab. 3 in. long)

hum·mock (hŭm′ək), *n.* **1.** an elevated tract rising above the general level of a marshy region. **2.** a knoll or hillock. **3.** a ridge in an ice field.

hum·mock·y (hŭm′ək ĭ), *adj.* **1.** abounding in hummocks. **2.** like a hummock.

hu·mor (hū′mər, ū′-), *n.* **1.** the quality of being funny: *the humor of a situation.* **2.** the faculty of perceiving what is amusing or comical: *sense of humor.* **3.** the faculty of expressing the amusing or comical. **4.** speech or writing showing this faculty. **5.** (*pl.*) amusing or comical features: *humors of the occasion.* **6.** mental disposition or tendency; frame of mind. **7.** capricious or freakish inclination; whim or caprice; odd traits. **8.** *Old Physiol.* one of the four chief bodily fluids, blood, choler or yellow bile, phlegm, and melancholy or black bile (**cardinal humors**), regarded as determining, by their relative proportions in the system, a person's physical and mental constitution. **9.** *Biol.* any animal or plant fluid, whether natural or morbid, such as the blood or lymph. **10. out of humor,** displeased or dissatisfied; cross. —*v.t.* **11.** to comply with the humor of; indulge: *to humor a child.* **12.** to accommodate oneself to. Also, *Brit.,* **humour.** [ME *humour,* t. AF, g. L (*h*)*ūmor* moisture, liquid] —**hu′mor·less,** *adj.*

—**Syn. 3.** HUMOR, WIT are contrasting terms which agree in referring to an ability to express a sense of the clever or amusing. HUMOR consists in the bringing together of certain incongruities which arise naturally from situation or character, frequently so as to illustrate some fundamental absurdity in human nature or conduct; it is a more kindly trait than wit: *a genial and mellow type of humor.* WIT is a purely intellectual, often spontaneous, manifestation of cleverness and quickness of apprehension in discovering analogies between things really unlike, and expressing them in brief, diverting, and sometimes sharp observations or remarks: *humor produces a smile, but wit produces sudden laughter.* **6.** temperament, mood. **11.** HUMOR, GRATIFY, INDULGE imply attempting to satisfy the wishes or whims of (oneself or) others. To HUMOR is to comply with the mood, fancy, or caprice of another, as in order to satisfy, soothe, or manage: *to humor an invalid, a child.* To GRATIFY is to please by satisfying the likings or desires: *to gratify someone by praising him.* INDULGE suggests a yielding to wishes by way of favor or complaisance, and may imply a habitual or excessive yielding to whims: *to indulge an unreasonable demand.*

hu·mor·esque (hū′mə rĕsk′), *n.* a musical composition of humorous or capricious character. [t. G: m. *humoreske,* f. L *hūmor* HUMOR + *-eske* -ESQUE]

hu·mor·ist (hū′mər ĭst, ū′-), *n.* **1.** one who exercises the faculty of humor. **2.** a professional writer, actor, etc., whose work is humorous. —**hu′mor·is′tic,** *adj.*

hu·mor·ous (hū′mər əs, ū′-), *adj.* **1.** characterized by humor; amusing; funny: *the humorous side of things.* **2.** having or showing the faculty of humor; droll; facetious: *a humorous person.* **3.** *Obs.* pertaining or due to the bodily humors. **4.** *Obs.* moist. —**hu′mor·ous·ly,** *adv.* —**hu′mor·ous·ness,** *n.*

—**Syn. 1.** jocose, jocular, comic, comical. HUMOROUS, WITTY, FACETIOUS, WAGGISH imply that which arises from cleverness or a sense of fun. HUMOROUS implies a genuine sense of fun and the comic, impersonal or gently personal: *a humorous account, a humorous view of life.* WITTY implies quickness to perceive the amusing, striking, or unusual and to express it cleverly and entertainingly; it sometimes becomes rather sharp and unkind, particularly in quick repartee of a personal nature: *a witty and interesting companion, witty at someone else's expense.* FACETIOUS suggests a desire or attempt to be jocular or witty, often unsuccessful or inappropriate or trifling: *a facetious treatment of a serious subject.* WAGGISH suggests the spirit of sly mischief and roguery of the constant joker (making jokes, not playing them), with no harm intended: *a waggish good humor.* —**Ant. 1.** solemn, sober, serious.

hu·mour (hū′mər, ū′-), *n., v.t.* *Brit.* humor.

hump (hŭmp), *n.* **1.** a rounded protuberance, esp. on the back, as that due to abnormal curvature of the spine in man, or that normally present in certain animals such as the camel and bison. **2.** a low, rounded rise of ground; hummock. **3. the hump, a.** *Brit. Slang.* a fit of bad humor: *to get the hump.* **b.** (*cap.*) (in World War II) the Himalayas. —*v.t.* **4.** to raise (the back, etc.) in a hump. **5.** *U.S. Slang.* to exert (oneself) in a great effort. **6.** *Australian Slang.* **a.** to place or bear on the back or shoulder. **b.** to carry. —*v.i.* **7.** to rise in a hump. **8.** *U.S. Slang.* to exert oneself. [back formation from HUMPBACKED] —**humped,** *adj.* —**hump′less,** *adj.*

hump·back (hŭmp′băk′), *n.* **1.** a back with a hump. **2.** one who has such a back. **3.** a whale of the genus *Megaptera,* with a humplike back.

hump·backed (hŭmp′băkt′), *adj.* having a hump on the back. [b. *crumpbacked* and *huckbacked* (or *hunchbacked*)]

Hum·per·dinck (hōŏm′pər dĭngk′), *n.* **Engelbert** (ĕng′əl bĕrt′), 1854–1921, German composer.

humph (hŭmf), *interj.* an expression indicating disbelief, dissatisfaction, contempt, etc.

Hum·phrey (hŭm′frĭ), *n.* **1.** (*Duke of Gloucester*) 1391–1447, English soldier and statesman (youngest son of Henry IV). **2.** **Hubert Horatio** (hū′bərt hə rā′shē ō), born 1911, vice-president of the U.S. since 1965.

Hump·ty Dump·ty (hŭmp′tĭ dŭmp′tĭ), the subject of a nursery riddle; he (an egg) fell from a wall and could not be put together again.

hump·y (hŭmp′ĭ), *adj.* **humpier, humpiest. 1.** full of humps. **2.** humplike.

hu·mus (hū′məs), *n.* the dark organic material in soils, produced by the decomposition of vegetable or animal matter, essential to fertility and favorable moisture supply. [t. L: earth, ground]

Hun (hŭn), *n.* **1.** a member of a warlike Asiatic people who devastated Europe in the 4th and 5th centuries. **2.** a barbarous, destructive person. [sing. of *Huns,* OE *Hūnas,* Icel. *Hunar.* Cf. LL *Hunnī,* Chinese *Han;* all from native name of people]

Hu·nan (hōō′nän′), *n.* a province in S China. ab. 33,226,954 pop. (1953). 78,378 sq. mi. *Cap.:* Changsha.

hunch (hŭnch), *v.t.* **1.** to thrust out or up in a hump: *to hunch one's back.* —*v.i.* **2.** to thrust oneself forward jerkily; lunge forward. —*n.* **3.** a hump. **4.** *U.S. Colloq.* a premonition or suspicion. **5.** a lump or thick piece. [appar. back formation from HUNCHBACKED]

hunch·back (hŭnch′băk′), *n.* humpback (def. 2).

hunch·backed (hŭnch′băkt′), *adj.* humpbacked. [b. *huckbacked* and *bunchbacked*]

hun·dred (hŭn′drəd), *n., pl.* **-dreds,** (*as after a numeral*) **-dred. 1.** a cardinal number, ten times ten. **2.** a symbol for this number, as 100 or C. **3.** a set of a hundred persons or things: *a hundred of the men.* **4.** a historical administrative division of an English county. **5.** a similar division in colonial Pennsylvania, Delaware, and Virginia, and still surviving in Delaware. —*adj.* **6.** amounting to one hundred in number. [ME *hondred,* OE *hundred,* c. G *hundert*]

hun·dred·fold (hŭn′drəd fōld′), *adj.* **1.** comprising a hundred parts or members. **2.** a hundred times as great or as much. —*adv.* **3.** in a hundredfold measure.

hun·dred-per·cent·er (hŭn′drəd pər sĕn′tər), *n.* a patriotic, or sometimes jingoistic, person.

hun·dredth (hŭn′drədth), *adj.* **1.** next after the ninety-ninth. **2.** being one of a hundred equal parts. —*n.* **3.** a hundredth part, esp. of one ($^{1}/_{100}$). **4.** the hundredth member of a series.

hun·dred·weight (hŭn′drəd wāt′), *n., pl.* **-weights,** (*as after a numeral*) **-weight.** a unit of avoirdupois weight commonly equivalent to 100 pounds in the U.S. and 112 pounds in England.

Hun·e·ker (hŭn′ə kər), *n.* **James Gibbons,** 1860–1921, U.S. author.

hung (hŭng), *v.* pt. and pp. of **hang.**

Hung., **1.** Hungarian. **2.** Hungary.

Hun·gar·i·an (hŭng gâr′ĭ ən), *adj.* **1.** of or pertaining to Hungary or its people. —*n.* **2.** a native or inhabitant of Hungary; a Magyar. **3.** the language of Hungary, of the Ugric group; Magyar. [f. HUNGARY + -AN]

Hun·ga·ry (hŭng′gə rĭ), *n.* a republic in central Europe. (as of 1947 boundaries) 9,805,623 pop. (est. 1955). 35,926 sq. mi. *Cap.:* Budapest. Hungarian, **Magyar-ország.**

hun·ger (hŭng′gər), *n.* **1.** the painful sensation or state of exhaustion caused by need of food: *to collapse from hunger.* **2.** a craving appetite; need for food. **3.** strong or eager desire: *hunger for praise.* —*v.i.* **4.** to feel hunger; be hungry. **5.** to have a strong desire. —*v.t.* **6.** to subject to hunger; starve. [ME; OE *hungor,* c. G *hunger*]

hunger strike, a persistent refusal to eat, as a protest against imprisonment, restraint, compulsion, etc.

hun·gry (hŭng′grĭ), *adj.,* **-grier, -griest. 1.** craving food; having a keen appetite. **2.** indicating, characteristic of, or characterized by hunger: *a lean and hungry look.* **3.** strongly or eagerly desirous. **4.** lacking needful or desirable elements; not fertile; poor: *hungry land.* **5.** *Rare.* marked by scarcity of food. [ME; OE *hungrig.* See -Y[1]] —**hun′gri·ly,** *adv.* —**hung′ri·ness,** *n.*

—**Syn. 1.** ravenous, famishing. HUNGRY, FAMISHED, STARVED describe a condition resulting from a lack of food. HUNGRY is a general word, expressing various degrees of eagerness or craving for food: *hungry between meals, desperately hungry after a long fast, hungry as a bear.* FAMISHED denotes the condition of one reduced to actual suffering from want of food but sometimes is used lightly or in an exaggerated statement: *famished after being lost in a wilderness, simply famished* (hungry). STARVED denotes a condition resulting from long-continued lack or insufficiency of food, and implies enfeeblement, emaciation, or death (originally death from any cause, but now death from lack of food): *to look thin and starved; by the end of the terrible winter, thousands had starved* (to death). It is also used humorously: *I'm simply starved* (hungry). —**Ant. 1.** satiated, surfeited.

hunk (hŭngk), *n.* *Colloq.* a large piece or lump; a chunk.

hunks (hŭngks), *n. sing. and pl.* **1.** a crabbed, disagreeable person. **2.** a covetous, sordid man; a miser.

hunk·y[1] (hŭngk′ĭ), *adj.* *U.S. Slang.* **1.** Also, **hunk·y-do·ry** (hŭngk′ĭ dôr′ĭ). satisfactory; well; right. **2.** even; leaving no balance. [orig. unknown]

hunk·y[2] (hŭngk′ĭ), *n., pl.* **hunkies.** *U.S. Slang and Derogatory.* an unskilled or semiskilled workman of foreign birth, esp. a Hungarian. [? der. HUNGARIAN]

hunt (hŭnt), *v.t.* **1.** to chase (game or other wild animals) for the purpose of catching or killing. **2.** to scour (a region) in pursuit of game. **3.** to use or manage (a horse, etc.) in the chase. **4.** to pursue with force, hostility, etc.: *he was hunted from the village.* **5.** to search for; seek; endeavor to obtain or find. **6.** to search (a place) thoroughly. **7.** *Bell Ringing.* to alter the place of (a bell) in a hunt. —*v.i.* **8.** to engage in the chase. **9.** to make a search or quest (often fol. by *for* or *after*). **10.** *Bell Ringing.* to alter the place of a bell in its set according to certain rules. —*n.* **11.** act of hunting game or other wild animals; the chase. **12.** a body of persons associated for the purpose of hunting; an association of huntsmen. **13.** a pack of hounds engaged in the chase. **14.** a district hunted with hounds. **15.** pursuit. **16.** a search. **17.** *Bell Ringing.* a regularly varying order of permutations in the ringing of a group of from five to twelve bells. [ME *hunte(n)*, OE *huntian*, der. *hunta* hunter. Cf. OE *hentan* pursue] —**Syn.** 1. pursue, track.

Hunt (hŭnt), *n.* **1. (James Henry) Leigh** (lē), 1784– 1859, British essayist and poet. **2. William Holman,** 1827–1910, British painter.

hunt·er (hŭn′tər), *n.* **1.** one who hunts game or other wild animals; a huntsman. **2.** one who searches or seeks for something: *a fortune hunter.* **3.** an animal that hunts game or prey, esp. a dog or horse used in hunting.

hunt·ing (hŭn′tĭng), *n.* **1.** act of one who or that which hunts. **2.** *Elect.* the periodic oscillating of a rotating electromechanical system about a mean space position, as in a synchronous motor. —*adj.* **3.** of, for, or engaged in hunting: *a hunting cap.*

hunting case, a watchcase with a hinged cover to protect the crystal, orig. against accidents in hunting.

Hunt·ing·don·shire (hŭn′tĭng dən shĭr′, -shər), *n.* a county in E England. 69,302 (1951); 366 sq. mi. *Co. seat:* Huntingdon. Also, **Hun′ting·don, Hunts** (hŭnts).

hunting knife, a knife sometimes used to kill the game, but more commonly to skin and cut it up.

Hun·ting·ton (hŭn′tĭng tən), *n.* a city in W West Virginia, on the Ohio river. 83,627 (1960).

Huntington Park, a city in SW California, near Los Angeles. 29,920 (1960).

hunt·ress (hŭn′trĭs), *n.* **1.** a woman who hunts. **2.** a mare employed in hunting.

hunts·man (hŭnts′mən), *n., pl.* **-men.** *Chiefly Brit.* **1.** a hunter. **2.** the manager of a hunt.

hunts·man's-cup (hŭnts′manz kŭp′), *n.* a plant of the genus *Sarracenia,* particularly *S. purpurea,* the pitcher plant of bogs.

Hunts·ville (hŭnts′vĭl), *n.* a city in Alabama. 72,365 (1960).

Hu·nya·di (hŏŏ′nyŏ dĭ′), *n.* **János** (yä′nōsh), (*Johannes Corvinus Huniades*) c1387–1456, Hungarian patriot.

Hu·on pine (hū′ŏn), a large taxaceous tree, *Dacrydium Franklinii,* of Tasmania. [named after the river *Huon,* in Tasmania]

Hu·pa (hōō′pə), *n.* an Athabascan language of north-western California.

Hu·peh (hōō′pā′; *Chin.* hōō′bē′), *n.* a province in central China. 27,789,693 pop. (1953); 71,955 sq. mi. *Cap.:* Wuchang.

hur·dle (hûr′dəl), *n., v.,* **-dled, -dling.** —*n.* **1.** a barrier in a race track, to be leaped by the contestants. **2. the hurdles,** a race in which such barriers are leaped. **3.** a difficult problem to be overcome; obstacle. **4.** *Chiefly Brit.* a movable rectangular frame of interlaced twigs, crossed bars, or the like, as for a temporary fence. **5.** a frame or sledge on which criminals were formerly drawn to the place of execution. —*v.t.* **6.** to leap over (a hurdle, etc.) as in a race. **7.** to master (a difficulty, problem etc.). **8.** to construct with hurdles; enclose with hurdles —*v.i.* **9.** to leap over a hurdle or other barrier. [ME *hirdel, hurdel,* OE *hyrdel,* f. *hyrd-* (c. G *hürde* hurdle) + *-l* suffix; akin to L *crātis* wickerwork, Gk. *kýrtos* basket, cage] —**hur′dler,** *n.*

hurds (hûrdz), *n.pl.* hards.

hur·dy-gur·dy (hûr′dĭ gûr′dĭ), *n., pl.* **-dies. 1.** a barrel organ or similar instrument played by turning a crank. **2.** a lute or guitar-shaped stringed musical instrument sounded by the revolution, against the strings, of a rosined wheel turned by a crank. [appar. imit.]

hurl (hûrl), *v.t.* **1.** to drive or throw with great force. **2.** to throw down; overthrow. **3.** to utter with vehemence. —*v.i.* **4.** to throw a missile. **5.** *Baseball.* to pitch a ball. —*n.* **6.** a forcible or violent throw; a fling. [ME *hurlen;* early assoc. with HURTLE, but prop. freq. of obs. *hurr* (imit.) make a vibrating sound. Cf. obs. *hurling,* n., roll of thunder, a G *hurlen* roll, rumble (said of thunder)] —**hurl′er,** *n.*

hurl·y (hûr′lĭ), *n., pl.* **hurlies.** commotion; hurly-burly.

hurl·y-burl·y (hûr′lĭ bûr′lĭ), *n., pl.* **-burlies,** *adj.* —*n.* **1.** commotion; tumult. —*adj.* **2.** full of commotion; tumultuous. [m. *hurling and burling*]

Hu·ron (hyŏŏr′ən), *n.* **1. Lake,** a lake between Lakes Michigan and Erie: second in area of the Great Lakes. ab. 23,000 sq. mi. **2.** one of an Indian tribe, the north-western member of the Iroquoian family, living west to Lake Huron. [t. F: unkempt person, bristly savage; applied to Indians about 1600]

hur·rah (hə rä′, -rô′), *interj.* **1.** an exclamation of joy, exultation, applause, or the like. —*v.i.* **2.** to shout "hurrah." —*n.* **3.** the exclamation "hurrah." Also, **hur·ray** (hə rā′); *esp. Brit.,* **hooray.**

hur·ri·cane (hûr′ĭ kān′), *n.* **1.** a violent tropical cyclonic storm. **2.** a storm of the most intense severity. **3.** anything suggesting a violent storm. [t. Sp.: m. *huracán,* t. Carib]

hurricane deck, a light upper deck on passenger steamers, etc.

hurricane lamp, 1. a candlestick with a chimney. **2.** *Chiefly Brit.* a kerosene lantern.

hur·ried (hûr′ĭd), *adj.* **1.** driven or impelled to hurry, as a person. **2.** characterized by or done with hurry;

hasty. —**hur′ried·ly,** *adj.* —**hur′ried·ness,** *n.*

hur·ry (hûr′ĭ), *v.,* **-ried, -rying,** *n., pl.* **-ries.** —*v.i.* **1.** to move, proceed, or act with haste, often undue haste. —*v.t.* **2.** to drive or move (someone or something) with speed, often with confused haste. **3.** to hasten; urge forward (often fol. by *up*). **4.** to impel with undue haste to thoughtless action: *to be hurried into a decision.* —*n.* **5.** need or desire for haste: *to be in a hurry to begin.* **6.** hurried movement or action; haste. [orig. obscure; ? imit.] —**hur′ry·ing·ly,** *adv.* —**Syn. 1.** See haste. **3.** accelerate, quicken; expedite; hustle. **6.** bustle; celerity; expedition, dispatch. —**Ant. 3.** delay.

hur·ry-scur·ry (hûr′ĭ skûr′ĭ), *n., pl.* **-ries,** *adv., adj., v.,* **-ried, -rying.** —*n.* **1.** headlong, disorderly haste; hurry and confusion. —*adv.* **2.** with hurrying and scurrying. **3.** confusedly; in a bustle. —*adj.* **4.** characterized by headlong, disorderly flight or haste. —*v.i.* **5.** to rush or go hurry-scurry. Also, **hur′ry-skur′ry.** [var. reduplication of HURRY]

hurt (hûrt), *v.,* **hurt, hurting,** *n.* —*v.t.* **1.** to cause bodily injury to (with or without consequent pain). **2.** to cause bodily pain to or in: *the wound still hurts him.* **3.** to damage (a material object, etc.) by striking, rough use, or otherwise: *to hurt furniture.* **4.** to affect adversely; harm: *to hurt one's reputation.* **5.** to cause mental pain to; grieve: *to hurt one's feelings.* —*v.i.* **6.** to cause pain (bodily or mental): *my finger still hurts.* **7.** to cause injury, damage, or harm. —*n.* **8.** a blow that inflicts a wound; bodily injury. **9.** injury; damage or harm. **10.** an injury that gives mental pain, as an insult. [ME *hurte(n),* prob. t. OF: m. *hurter* strike against, der. *hurt* a blow] —**Syn. 8.** See **injury.**

hurt·er (hûr′tər), *n.* **1.** a supporting or strengthening part. **2.** (in a vehicle) a butting piece on the shoulder of an axle against which the hub strikes. [ME *hurtour,* f. HURT, v. + *-our* -OR². Cf. F *hurtoir* a knocker]

hurt·ful (hûrt′fəl), *adj.* such as to cause hurt or injury; injurious; harmful. —**hurt′ful·ly,** *adv.* —**hurt′ful·ness,** *n.* —**Syn.** destructive, pernicious; noxious.

hur·tle (hûr′təl), *v.,* **-tled, -tling,** *n.* —*v.i.* **1.** to strike together or against something. **2.** to rush violently and noisily. **3.** to resound, as in collision or rapid motion. —*v.t.* **4.** to drive violently; fling; dash. **5.** to dash against; collide with. —*n.* **6.** clash; collision; shock; clatter. [ME; freq. of HURT]

Hus (hŭs; *Ger., Czech.* hŏŏs), *n.* Huss.

hus·band (hŭz′bənd), *n.* **1.** the man of a married pair (correlative of *wife*). —*v.t.* **2.** to manage, esp. with prudent economy; economize: *to husband one's resources.* **3.** to provide with a husband. **4.** *Rare.* to act as a husband to; marry. **5.** *Obs.* to till; cultivate. [ME *husbond(e),* OE *hūsbōnda,* f. *hūs* house + *bōnda* householder (t. Scand.; cf. Icel. *bōndi*)] —**hus′band·less,** *adj.*

hus·band·man (hŭz′bənd mən), *n., pl.* **-men.** a farmer.

hus·band·ry (hŭz′bən drĭ), *n.* **1.** the business of a farmer; agriculture; farming. **2.** careful or thrifty management; frugality; thrift. **3.** the management of domestic affairs, or of resources generally.

Hu·sein ibn-A·li (hŏŏ sīn′ Yb′ən ä lē′, -ä′lē; hŏŏ-sān′), 1856–1931, king of Hejaz, 1916–24.

hush (hŭsh), *interj.* **1.** a command to be silent or quiet. —*v.i.* **2.** to become or be silent or quiet. —*v.t.* **3.** to make silent; silence. **4.** to suppress mention of; keep concealed. **5.** to calm or allay: *to hush someone's fears.* —*n.* **6.** silence or quiet, esp. after noise. —*adj.* **7.** *Archaic.* silent; quiet. [appar. back formation from ME *hussht,* also *hust, huyst,* adj. (orig. interj.), taken as pp. Cf. WHIST¹]

hush money, a bribe to keep silent about something.

husk (hŭsk), *n.* **1.** the dry external covering of certain fruits or seeds, esp. (*U.S.*) of an ear of corn. **2.** the enveloping or outer part of anything, esp. when dry or worthless. —*v.t.* **3.** to remove the husk from. [ME *huske;* f. *hus-* (cf. OE *hosu* pod, husk) + *-k* suffix. See -OCK] —**husk′er,** *n.* —**husk′like′,** *adj.*

husk·ing (hŭs′kĭng), *n.* **1.** act of removing husks, esp. (*U.S.*) those of corn. **2.** a husking bee.

husking bee, *U.S.* a gathering of persons to assist in husking corn, usually a kind of merrymaking.

husk·y¹ (hŭs′kĭ), *adj.,* **huskier, huskiest,** *n., pl.* **huskies.** —*adj.* **1.** *U.S. Colloq.* burly; big and strong. **2.** having a semiwhispered vocal tone; somewhat hoarse. **3.** abounding in husks. **4.** like husks. —*n.* **5.** *U.S. Colloq.* a big and strong person. [f. HUSK, n. + -Y¹] —**husk′i·ly,** *adv.* —**husk′i·ness,** *n.*

husk·y² (hŭs′kĭ), *n., pl.* **huskies.** (*also cap.*) an Eskimo dog. [? a shortened var. of ESKIMO]

Huss (hŭs; *Ger., Czech.* hŏŏs), *n.* **John,** 1369?–1415, Bohemian religious reformer and martyr. Also, **Hus.**

hus·sar (hŏŏ zär′), *n.* **1.** (orig.) one of a body of light Hungarian cavalry formed during the 15th century. **2.** one of a class of similar troops, usually with striking or showy uniforms, in European armies. [t. Hung.: m. *huszár,* orig. freebooter, t. OSerbian: m. *husar,* var. of *kursar,* t. It.: m. *corsaro* CORSAIR]

Hus·serl (hŏŏs′ĕrl), *n.* **Edmund** (ĕt′mŏŏnt), 1859– 1938, German philosopher.

Huss·ite (hŭs′īt), *n.* a follower of John Huss.

hus·sy (hŭs′ĭ, hŭz′ĭ), *n., pl.* **-sies. 1.** an ill-behaved girl. **2.** a worthless woman. [familiar var. of HOUSE-WIFE (ME *huswif*)]

---

b., blend of, blended; c., cognate with; d., dialect, dialectal; der., derived from; f., formed from; g., going back to; m., modification of; r., replacing; s., stem of; t., taken from; ?, perhaps. See the full key on inside cover.

hus·tings (hŭs′tĭngz), *n. pl. or sing. Brit.* **1.** the temporary platform from which candidates for Parliament were (before 1872) nominated and addressed the electors. **2.** any electioneering platform. **3.** election proceedings. [ME *husting*, t. Scand.; cf. Icel. *hūsthing* house assembly, council summoned by king or leader]

hus·tle (hŭs′əl), *v.*, **-tled, -tling,** *n.* —*v.i.* **1.** *Colloq.* to proceed or work rapidly or energetically. **2.** to push or force one's way. —*v.t.* **3.** to force roughly or hurriedly: *they hustled him out of the city.* **4.** to shake, push, or shove roughly. —*n.* **5.** *Colloq.* energetic activity, as in work. **6.** discourteous shoving, pushing, or jostling. [var. sp. of *hussell, hus(s)le*, t. D: s. *husselen*, assimilated var. of *hutselen*, freq. of *hutsen* shake, jog] —**hus′tler,** *n.*

hut (hŭt), *n., v.,* **hutted, hutting.** —*n.* **1.** a small, rude, or humble dwelling. **2.** *Mil.* a wooden or metal structure for the temporary housing of troops. —*v.t.* **3.** to place in or furnish with a hut. —*v.i.* **4.** to lodge or take shelter in a hut. [t. F: m. *hutte*, t. G: m. *hütte*; prob. akin to HIDE¹] —**hut′like′,** *adj.* —**Syn. 1.** See **cottage.**

hutch (hŭch), *n.* **1.** a pen for confining small animals: *rabbit hutch.* **2.** a hut or cabin. **3.** *U.S. Dial.* a fisherman's shanty. **4.** a chest, box, or trough: a *grain hutch.* **5.** a baker's kneading trough. —*v.t.* **6.** to put away in or as in a hutch; hoard. [ME *huche*, t. OF, t. ML: m.s. *hūtica* chest; ? of Gmc. orig.]

Hutch·ins (hŭch′ĭnz), *n.* **Robert Maynard** (mā′nərd), born 1899, U.S. educator.

Hutch·in·son (hŭch′ĭn sən), *n.* **1.** a city in central Kansas, on the Arkansas river. 11,222 (1960). **2. Mrs. Anne Marbury,** 1590?–1643, British religious enthusiast in New England. **3. Thomas,** 1711–80, British colonial governor of Massachusetts, 1769–74.

hut·ment (hŭt′mənt), *n.* an encampment of huts.

Hux·ley (hŭks′lĭ), *n.* **1. Aldous Leonard** (ôl′dəs), 1894–1963, British novelist and essayist. **2.** his brother, **Julian Sorrell,** born 1887, British biologist and writer. **3.** their grandfather, **Thomas Henry,** 1825–95, British biologist and writer.

Huy·ghens (hī′gənz; *Du.* hoi′gĕns), *n.* **Christian** (krĭs′tĭ än′), 1629–95, Dutch mathematician, physicist, and astronomer.

Huys·mans (*Du.* hois′mäns; *Fr.* wēs mäNs′), *n.* **Joris Karl** (yō′rĭs kärl), 1848–1907, French novelist.

huz·za (hə zä′), *interj., n., pl.* **-zas,** *v.* **-zaed, -zaing.** —*interj.* **1.** an exclamation of exultation, applause, or the like. —*n.* **2.** the exclamation "huzza." —*v.i.* **3.** to shout "huzza." —*v.t.* **4.** to salute with huzzas: *crowds huzzaed the triumphant hero.*

Hwang Hai (hwäng′ hī′), Chinese name of the **Yellow Sea.**

Hwang Ho (hwäng′ hō′; *Chin.* hü′), a river flowing from W China into the Gulf of Pohai. ab. 2700 mi. Also, **Hoangho, Yellow River.** See map under **Yangtze.**

hy·a·cinth (hī′ə sĭnth), *n.* **1.** any of the bulbous liliaceous plants constituting the genus *Hyacinthus,* esp. *H. orientalis,* widely cultivated for its spikes of fragrant, white or colored, bell-shaped flowers. **2.** a hyacinth bulb or flower. **3.** (among the ancients) a plant supposed to spring from the blood of Hyacinthus and variously identified as iris, gladiolus, larkspur, etc. **4.** a reddish-orange zircon; the jacinth. **5.** (among the ancients) an uncertain gem, possibly our amethyst or sapphire. [t. L: s. *hyacinthus*, t. Gk.: m. *hyákinthos* kind of flower, also a gem. Cf. JACINTH.]

hy·a·cin·thine (hī′ə sĭn′thĭn, -thīn), *adj.* **1.** of or like the hyacinth. **2.** adorned with hyacinths.

Hy·a·cin·thus (hī′ə sĭn′thəs), *n. Gk. Myth.* a beautiful youth (loved by Apollo but killed out of jealousy by Zephyrus) from whose blood sprang a flower marked with the letters of an exclamation of grief, "AI AI."

Hy·a·des (hī′ə dēz′), *n.pl.* **1.** *Astron.* a group of stars comprising a moving cluster in the constellation Taurus, supposed by the ancients to indicate the approach of rain when they rose with the sun. **2.** *Gk. Myth.* a group of nymphs, sisters of the Pleiades.

hy·ae·na (hī ē′nə), *n.* hyena.

hy·a·line (hī′ə lĕn′, -lĭn *for 1, 2;* hī′ə lĭn, -lĭn′ *for 3, 4*), *n.* **1.** Also, **hy·a·lin** (hī′ə lĭn). *Biochem.* a horny substance found in hydatid cysts, closely resembling chitin. **2.** *Anat.* the hyaloid membrane. **3.** something glassy or transparent. —*adj.* **4.** glassy; crystalline; transparent. [t. LL: m.s. *hyalinus*, t. Gk.: m. *hyálinos* of glass]

hyaline cartilage, *Anat.* the typical translucent form of cartilage, containing little fibrous tissue.

hy·a·lite (hī′ə līt′), *n.* a colorless variety of opal, sometimes transparent like glass, and sometimes whitish and translucent. [f. HYAL(O)- + -ITE¹]

hyalo-, a word element meaning "glass." Also, before vowels, **hyal-.** [t. Gk., comb. form of *hýalos*]

hy·a·loid (hī′ə loid′), *n.* **1.** *Anat.* the hyaloid membrane of the eye. —*adj.* **2.** glassy; hyaline. [t. Gk.: m.s. *hyaloeidēs* like glass. See HYALO-, -OID]

hyaloid membrane, *Anat.* the capsule of the vitreous humor of the eye, a delicate, pellucid, and nearly structureless membrane.

hy·a·lo·plasm (hī′ə lō plăz′əm), *n. Biol.* the pellucid portion of the protoplasm of a cell, as distinguished from the granular and reticular portions.

hy·brid (hī′brĭd), *n.* **1.** the offspring of two animals or plants of different races, breeds, varieties, species, or genera. **2.** a half-breed; a mongrel. **3.** anything derived from heterogeneous sources, or composed of elements of different or incongruous kinds. —*adj.* **4.** bred from two distinct races, breeds, varieties, species, or genera. **5.** composed of elements originally drawn from different languages, as a word. [t. L: s. *hybrida,* var. of *hibrida* offspring of a tame sow and wild boar, a mongrel] —**Syn. 4.** HYBRID, MONGREL refer to animals or plants of mixed origin. HYBRID is the scientific term: *hybrid corn, a hybrid variety of sheep.* MONGREL, used originally of dogs to denote especially the offspring of repeated crossings of different breeds, is now extended to other animals and to plants; it is usually depreciatory, as denoting mixed, nondescript, or degenerate breed or character: *a mongrel pup.* —**Ant. 4.** purebred, thoroughbred.

hy·brid·ism (hī′brə dĭz′əm), *n.* **1.** Also, **hy·brid·i·ty** (hī brĭd′ə tĭ). hybrid character. **2.** the production of hybrids.

hy·brid·ize (hī′brə dīz′), *v.,* **-ized, -izing.** —*v.t.* **1.** to cause to produce hybrids; cross. **2.** to form in a hybrid manner: *to hybridize plants.* —*v.i.* **3.** to cause the production of hybrids by crossing different species, etc. Also, *esp. Brit.,* **hy·brid·ise′.** —**hy′brid·iz′er,** *n.*

hy·bris (hī′brĭs), *n.* hubris.

hy·dan·to·in (hī dăn′tō ĭn), *n.* a colorless, needlelike, crystalline compound, $C_3H_4N_2O_2$, used in the synthesis of pharmaceutical substances and resins. [irreg. f. Gk. *hýd(ōr)* water + (*all*)*antoin* (f. ALLANTO(IS) + -IN²)]

hy·da·tid (hī′də tĭd), *n.* **1.** a cyst with watery contents, produced in man and animals by a tapeworm in the larval state. **2.** the encysted larva of a tapeworm; a cysticercus. [t. Gk.: s. *hydatis* watery vesicle]

Hyde (hīd), *n.* **1. Douglas,** 1860?–1949, Irish author and statesman: president of Eire, 1938–45. **2. Edward.** See **Clarendon,** 1st Earl of. **3. Mr.,** the criminal side of the leading character in Stevenson's *Dr. Jekyll and Mr. Hyde.* See **Jekyll.**

Hyde Park, 1. a park in London, England. **2.** a village in SE New York, on the Hudson: site of the estate and burial place of Franklin D. Roosevelt.

Hy·der·a·bad (hī′dər ə băd′, -băd′, hī′drə-), *n.* **1.** a former state in S India: now a part of Andhra Pradesh. **2.** the capital of Andra Pradesh, in the western part. 803,048 (1951). **3.** a city in Pakistan, in Sind province, on the Indus river. 241,801 (1951).

Hy·der A·li (hī′dər ä′lē, ä lē′), died 1782, a Mohammedan ruler of Mysore and military leader against the British in India. Also, **Haidar Ali.**

hyd·no·car·pate (hĭd′nō kär′pāt), *n. Chem.* a salt or ester of hydnocarpic acid. [f. s. NL *Hydnocarpus* (f. Gk.: *hýdno(n)* truffle + m. *karpós* fruit) + -ATE²]

hyd·no·car·pic acid (hĭd′nō kär′pĭk), *Chem.* a white crystalline acid, $C_5H_7-(CH_2)_{10}-COOH$, obtained from chaulmoogra oil, used to treat leprosy.

hydr-¹, var. of **hydro-¹,** before vowels, as in *hydrangea.*

hydr-², var. of **hydro-²,** before vowels, as in *hydrazine.*

hy·dra (hī′drə), *n., pl.* **-dras, -drae** (-drē). **1.** (*cap. or l.c.*) *Gk. Myth.* a monstrous serpent, slain by Hercules, represented as having nine heads, each of which was replaced by two after being cut off, unless the wound was cauterized. **2.** *Zool.* any of the fresh-water polyps constituting the genus *Hydra.* **3.** any persistent evil arising from many sources or difficult to overcome. **4.** (*cap.*) *Astron.* a southern constellation, representing a sea serpent. [t. L, t. Gk.: water serpent; r. ME *ydre*, t. OF]

hy·drac·id (hī drăs′ĭd), *n. Chem.* an acid which contains no oxygen.

hy·dran·gea (hī drăn′jə, -drăn′jĭ ə), *n.* any shrub of the genus *Hydrangea,* species of which are cultivated for their large showy white, pink, or blue flower clusters. [t. NL, f. *hydr-* HYDR-¹ + m. Gk. *ange(on)* vessel + -*a* (ending); so called from cup-shaped seed capsule]

hy·drant (hī′drənt), *n.* an upright pipe with a spout, nozzle, or other outlet, usually in the street, for drawing water from a main or service pipe.

hy·dranth (hī′drănth), *n.* the terminal part of a hydroid polyp that bears the mouth and tentacles and contains the stomach region. [f. HYDR(A) (def. 2) + s. Gk. *ánthos* flower]

hy·drar·gyr·i·a·sis (hī′drär jĭ rī′ə sĭs), *n. Pathol.* mercurial poisoning; mercurialism.

hy·drar·gy·rum (hī drär′jĭ rəm), *n. Chem.* mercury. [NL, der. L *hydrargyrus,* t. Gk.: m. *hydrárgyros*]

hy·dras·tine (hī drăs′tēn, -tĭn), *n.* **1.** a yellow medicine from goldenseal, formerly used as a stomachic. **2.** an alkaloid found in the root of goldenseal. [f. HYDRAST(IS) + -INE²]

hy·dras·tis (hī drăs′tĭs), *n.* goldenseal (def. 2).

hy·drate (hī′drāt), *n., v.,* **-drated, -drating.** *Chem.* —*n.* **1.** any of a class of compounds containing chemically combined water. In some hydrates the bonds may be weak covalence linkages, as in washing soda, $Na_2CO_3 \cdot 10H_2O$, which loses its water of hydration on standing in the air; in others, they may be primary valence bonds, as in sulfuric acid, H_2SO_4, a monohydrate of SO_3. —*v.t.* **2.** to combine chemically with water. —**hy·dra′tion,** *n.* —**hy′dra·tor,** *n.*

hy·drat·ed (hī′drā′tĭd), *adj.* chemically combined with water in its molecular form.

ăct, āble, dâre, ärt; ĕbb, ēqual; Ĭf, īce; hŏt, ōver, ôrder, oil, bŏŏk, ōōze, out; ŭp, ūse, ûrge; ə = a in alone; ᴄh, chief; g, give; ng, ring; sh, shoe; th, thin; ᴛh, that; zh, vision. See the full key on inside cover.

hydraul., hydraulics.

hy·drau·lic (hĭ drô′lĭk), *adj.* **1.** operated by or employing water or other liquid. **2.** pertaining to water or other liquid, or to hydraulics. **3.** hardening under water, as a cement. [t. L: s. *hydraulicus*, t. Gk.: m. *hydraulikós* pertaining to the water organ] —**hy·drau′li·cal·ly,** *adv.*

hydraulic brake, a brake operated by fluid pressures in cylinders and connecting tubular lines.

hydraulic machinery, mechanical devices such as pumps, turbines, couplings, etc., in which the flow of a liquid either produces or is produced by their operation.

hydraulic press, a machine permitting a small force applied to a small piston to produce through fluid pressure a large force on a large piston.

hydraulic ram, a device by which the energy of descending water is utilized to raise a part of the water to a height greater than that of the source.

hy·drau·lics (hĭ drô′lĭks), *n.* the science treating of the laws governing water or other liquids in motion and their applications in engineering; practical or applied hydrodynamics. [pl. of HYDRAULIC. See -ICS]

hy·dra·zine (hī′drə zēn′, -zĭn), *n. Chem.* **1.** a compound, N_2H_4, which is a weak base in solution and forms a large number of salts resembling ammonium salts, used as a reducing agent and as a jet-propulsion fuel. **2.** a class of substances derived by replacing one or more hydrogen atoms in hydrazine by an organic radical. [f. HYDR-² + AZ(O)- + -INE²]

hy·dra·zo·ic (hī′drə zō′ĭk), *adj.* denoting or pertaining to hydrazoic acid; triazoic.

hy·dra·zo·ic acid (hī′drə zō′ĭk), *Chem.* an acid composed of hydrogen alnd nitrogen, HN_3, occurring as a very explosive, colorless liquid with a penetrating odor.

hy·dride (hī′drīd, -drĭd), *n. Chem.* **1.** a compound of hydrogen with another element or a radical. **2.** (formerly) a hydroxide. Also, **hy·drid** (hī′drĭd).

hy·dri·od·ic (hī′drī ŏd′ĭk), *adj.* **1.** a colorless gas, HI, with a suffocating odor. **2.** an aqueous solution of this gas. [f. HYDR-² + IOD(INE) + -IC]

hydro-¹, a word element meaning "water," as in *hydrogen.* Also, **hydr-.** [t. Gk., comb. form of *hýdōr* water]

hydro-², *Chem.* a word element often indicating combination of hydrogen with a negative element or radical: *hydrobromic.* Also, **hydr-.** [comb. form of HYDROGEN]

hy·dro·air·plane (hī′drō âr′plān′), *n.* a hydroplane.

hy·dro·bro·mic acid (hī′drə brō′mĭk), *Chem.* **1.** a colorless gas, HBr, with a pungent odor. **2.** an aqueous solution of this gas.

hy·dro·car·bon (hī′drə kär′bən), *n. Chem.* any of a class of compounds containing only hydrogen and carbon, such as methane, CH_4, ethylene, C_2H_4, acetylene, C_2H_2, and benzene, C_6H_6. [f. HYDRO-² + CARBON]

hy·dro·cele (hī′drə sēl′), *n. Pathol.* an accumulation of serous fluid, usually about the testis. [t. L, t. Gk.]

hy·dro·ceph·a·lus (hī′drə sĕf′ə ləs), *n. Pathol.* an accumulation of serous fluid within the cranium, esp. in infancy, often causing great enlargement of the head. [NL, der. Gk. *hydroképhalon* water in the head] —**hy′·dro·ceph′a·lous,** *adj.*

hy·dro·chlo·ric acid (hī′drə klôr′ĭk), a colorless gas, HCl, or an aqueous solution of it, which is extensively used in chemical and industrial processes; muriatic acid. [f. HYDRO-¹ + CHLORIC]

hy·dro·chlo·ride (hī′drə klôr′īd, -ĭd), *n. Chem.* a salt formed by the direct union of hydrochloric acid with an organic base, rendering the latter more soluble.

hy·dro·cy·an·ic acid (hī′drō sī an′ĭk), a colorless, poisonous liquid, HCN, with an odor like that of bitter almonds; prussic acid. [f. HYDRO-² + CYANIC]

hy·dro·dy·nam·ic (hī′drō dī năm′ĭk, -dĭ-), *adj.* **1.** pertaining to forces in or motions of fluids. **2.** pertaining to hydrodynamics.

hy·dro·dy·nam·ics (hī′drō dī năm′ĭks, -dĭ-), *n.* the science of the mechanics of fluids, generally liquids, including hydrostatics and hydrokinetics.

hy·dro·e·lec·tric (hī′drō ĭ lĕk′trĭk), *adj.* pertaining to the generation and distribution of electric energy derived from the energy of falling water or other hydraulic source. —**hy·dro·e·lec·tric·i·ty** (hī′drō ĭ lĕk′tris′ə tĭ), *n.*

hy·dro·flu·or·ic acid (hī′drō flōō ôr′ĭk, -ŏr′-), a colorless, corrosive, volatile liquid, HF, used for etching glass and as a condensing agent in chemical syntheses, such as alkylation. [f. HYDRO-² + FLUORIC]

hy·dro·foil (hī′drə foil′), *n.* **1.** one of two or more skilike members, mounted at the ends of struts beneath a boat, supporting the hull above the surface of the water when a certain speed has been attained. **2.** a boat equipped with such members.

hy·dro·gen (hī′drə jən), *n. Chem.* a colorless, odorless, inflammable gas, which combines chemically with oxygen to form water: the lightest of the known elements. *Symbol:* H; *at. wt.:* 1.008; *at. no.:* 1; *weight of one liter at 760 mm. pressure and 0° C.:* .08987 g. [t. F: m. *hydrogène,* t. hydro- HYDRO-¹ + -gène -GEN]

hy·dro·gen·ate (hī′drə jə nāt′), *v.t.,* -ated, -ating. to combine or treat with hydrogen. —**hy′/dro·gen·a′/tion,** *n.*

hydrogen bomb, a bomb whose potency is based on the release of nuclear energy resulting from the fusion of hydrogen isotopes in the formation of helium. It is many times more powerful than the atom bomb.

hydrogen ion, *Chem.* ionized hydrogen of the form H+.

hy·dro·gen·ize (hī′drə jə nīz′, hī drŏj′ə-), *v.t.,* -ized -izing. hydrogenate.

hy·drog·e·nous (hī drŏj′ə nəs), *adj.* **1.** of or containing hydrogen. **2.** formed or produced by water.

hydrogen peroxide, a colorless, unstable, oily liquid, H_2O_2, the aqueous solution of which is used as an antiseptic and a bleaching agent.

hydrogen sulfide, a colorless, inflammable, cumulatively poisonous gas, H_2S, smelling like rotten eggs.

hy·drog·ra·phy (hī drŏg′rə fī), *n.* **1.** the science of the measurement, description, and mapping of the surface waters of the earth, with special reference to their use for navigation. **2.** those parts of a map, collectively, that represent surface waters. —**hy·drog′ra·pher,** *n.* —**hy·dro·graph·ic** (hī′drə grăf′ĭk), **hy′dro·graph′i·cal,** *adj.* —**hy′dro·graph′i·cal·ly,** *adv.*

hy·droid (hī′droid), *adj.* **1.** denoting or pertaining to that form of hydrozoan which is asexual and grows into branching colonies by budding. —*n.* **2.** that phase of a hydrozoan coelenterate that consists of polyp forms usually growing as an attached colony. [f. HYDR(A) (def. 2) + -OID]

hy·dro·ki·net·ic (hī′drō kī nĕt′ĭk, -kĭ-), *adj.* **1.** pertaining to the motion of fluids. **2.** pertaining to hydrokinetics. Also, **hy′dro·ki·net′i·cal.**

hy·dro·ki·net·ics (hī′drō kī nĕt′ĭks, -kĭ-), *n.* the branch of hydromechanics that treats of the laws governing liquids or gases in motion.

hy·drol·o·gy (hī drŏl′ə jī), *n.* the science dealing with water on the land, its properties, laws, geographical distribution, etc. —**hy·dro·log·ic** (hī′drə lŏj′ĭk), **hy′dro·log′i·cal,** *adj.* —**hy·drol′o·gist,** *n.*

hy·drol·y·sis (hī drŏl′ə sĭs), *n., pl.* -ses (-sēz′). chemical decomposition by which a compound is resolved into other compounds by taking up the elements of water.

hy·dro·lyt·ic (hī′drə lĭt′ĭk), *adj.* producing hydrolysis, or related to the process or results of hydrolysis.

hy·dro·lyze (hī′drə līz′), *v.t., v.i.,* -lyzed, -lyzing. to subject or be subjected to hydrolysis. Also, *esp. Brit.,* **hy′dro·lyse′.** —**hy′dro·lyz′a·ble,** *adj.*

hy·dro·man·cy (hī′drə măn′sĭ), *n.* divination by means of water. [t. F: m. *hydromancie,* t. LL: m.s. *hydromantîa,* f. Gk.: *hydro-* HYDRO-¹ + m. *manteîa* divination] —**hy′dro·man′tic,** *adj.*

hy·dro·me·chan·ics (hī′drō mə kăn′ĭks), *n.* hydrodynamics (def. 1). —**hy′dro·me·chan′i·cal,** *adj.*

hy·dro·me·du·sa (hī′drō mĭ dū′sə, -dōō′-), *n., pl.* -sae (-sē). the medusa form of a hydrozoan coelenterate. [NL. See HYDRO-¹, MEDUSA] —**hy′dro·me·du′san,** *adj.*

hy·dro·mel (hī′drə mĕl′), *n.* a liquor consisting of honey and water: when fermented, known also as mead. [t. L: m. *hydromeli,* t. Gk.: honey water]

hy·dro·met·al·lur·gy (hī′drə mĕt′ə lûr′jĭ), *n.* the practice of extracting metals from ores by leaching with solutions such as mercury, cyanides, acids, brines, etc. —**hy′dro·met′al·lur′gi·cal,** *adj.*

hy·dro·me·te·or (hī′drə mē′tĭ ər), *n. Meterol.* state or effect of water, water vapor, or ice in the atmosphere, as rain, ice crystals, hail, fog, and clouds.

hy·drom·e·ter (hī drŏm′ə tər), *n.* a sealed cylinder with weighted bulb and graduated stem for determining the specific gravity of liquids by reading the level of the liquid on the emerging stem. —**hy·dro·met·ric** (hī′drə mĕt′rĭk), **hy·dro·met′ri·cal,** *adj.* —**hy·drom′e·try,** *n.*

hy·drop·a·thy (hī drŏp′ə thĭ), *n.* the treatment of disease by the use of water; hydrotherapy. [f. HYDRO-¹ +-PATHY] —**hy·dro·path·ic** (hī′drə păth′ĭk), **hy′dro·path′i·cal,** *adj.* —**hy′dro·path′a·thist, hy′dro·path′i·cal,** *adj.*

hy·dro·phane (hī′drə fān′), *n.* a partly translucent variety of opal, which becomes more translucent or transparent when immersed in water. —**hy′droph·a·nous** (hī drŏf′ə nəs), *adj.*

hy·dro·pho·bi·a (hī′drə fō′bĭ ə), *n. Pathol.* **1.** rabies. **2.** a morbid dread of water, as in rabies; any morbid or unnatural dread of water. [t. LL, t. Gk.: horror of water] —**hy·dro·pho·bic** (hī′drə fō′bĭk, -fŏb′ĭk), *adj.*

hy·dro·phone (hī′drə fōn′), *n.* **1.** an instrument employing the principles of the microphone, used to detect the flow of water through a pipe. **2.** a device for locating sources of sound under water, as for detecting submarines by the noise of their engines, etc. **3.** *Med.* an instrument used in auscultation, whereby sounds are intensified through a column of water.

hy·dro·phyl·la·ceous (hī′drō fĭ lā′shəs), *adj.* of or belonging to the widespread family *Hydrophyllaceae,* mostly consisting of herbaceous plants.

hy·dro·phyte (hī′drə fīt′), *n.* a plant growing in water or very moist ground. —**hy·dro·phyt·ic** (hī′drə fĭt′ĭk), *adj.*

hy·drop·ic (hī drŏp′ĭk), *adj.* dropsical. Also, **hy·drop′i·cal.** [t. L: s. *hydrōpicus,* t. Gk.: m. *hydrōpikós;* r. ME *ydropik,* t. OF]

hy·dro·plane (hī′drə plān′), *n., v.,* -planed, -planing. —*n.* **1.** an airplane provided with floats, or with a boatlike underpart, enabling it to light upon or ascend from water. **2.** an attachment to an airplane enabling it to glide on the water. **3.** a light, high-powered boat, usually with one or more steps in the bottom, designed to plane along the surface of the water at very high speeds. **4.** a horizontal rudder for submerging or elevating a submarine boat. —*v.i.* **5.** to skim over water in the manner of a hydroplane. **6.** to travel in a hydroplane (boat).

hy·dro·pon·ics (hī'drə pŏn'ĭks), *n.* the cultivation of plants by placing the roots in liquid nutrient solutions rather than in soil; soilless growth of plants. [f. HYDRO¹- + s. L. *ponere* place + -ICS] —**hy'dro·pon'ic,** *adj.*

hy·dro·qui·none (hī'drə kwĭ'nōn', -kwĭn'ōn), *n. Chem.* a white, crystalline compound, C₆H₄(OH)₂, formed by the reduction of quinone, used to inhibit autoxidation reactions. Also, **hy·dro·quin·ol** (hī'drə kwĭn'ōl, -ŏl)

hydros., hydrostatics.

hy·dro·scope (hī'drə skōp'), *n.* an optical apparatus which enables the observer to view objects below the surface of the sea. —**hy·dro·scop·ic** (hī'drə skŏp'ĭk), *adj.*

hy·dro·sol (hī'drə sŏl', -sōl'), *n. Phys. Chem.* a colloidal suspension in water. Also, **hy·dro·sole** (hī'drə sōl'). [f. HYDRO- + SOL(UTION)]

hy·dro·some (hī'drə sōm'), *n. Zool.* the entire body of a compound hydrozoan. Also, **hy·dro·so·ma** (hī'drə sō'mə).

hy·dro·sphere (hī'drə sfĭr'), *n.* the water on the surface of the globe; the water of the oceans.

hy·dro·stat (hī'drə stăt'), *n.* **1.** an electrical device for detecting the presence of water, as from overflow or leakage. **2.** any of various devices for preventing injury to a steam boiler from low water.

hy·dro·stat·ic (hī'drə stăt'ĭk), *adj.* of or pertaining to hydrostatics. Also, **hy·dro·stat·i·cal.** —**hy·dro·stat·i·cal·ly,** *adv.*

hy·dro·stat·ics (hī'drə stăt'ĭks), *n.* the statics of fluids, a branch of science usually confined to the equilibrium and pressure of liquids.

hy·dro·sul·fate (hī'drə sŭl'fāt), *n. Chem.* a compound between sulfuric acid and an organic base, esp. with alkaloids. Also, **hy·dro·sul·phate.**

hy·dro·sul·fide (hī'drə sŭl'fīd, -fĭd), *n. Chem.* **1.** a compound containing the HS⁻¹ radical. **2.** (loosely) a sulfide. Also, **hy·dro·sul·fid** (hī'drə sŭl'fĭd), **hy·dro·sul·phide.**

hy·dro·sul·fite (hī'drə sŭl'fīt), *n.* sodium hyposulfite, Na₂S₂O₄, used as a bleach. Also, **hy·dro·sul·phite.**

hy·dro·sul·fu·rous (hī'drō sŭl fyoor'əs, -sŭl'fə rəs), *adj.* hyposulfurous. Also, **hy·dro·sul·phur·ous.**

hy·dro·tax·is (hī'drō tăk'sĭs), *n.* a movement of organisms toward or away from water.

hy·dro·ther·a·peu·tics (hī'drō thěr'ə pū'tĭks), *n.* that branch of therapeutics which deals with the curative use of water. —**hy·dro·ther'a·peu'tic,** *adj.*

hy·dro·ther·a·py (hī'drə thěr'ə pĭ'), *n.* treatment of disease by means of water. —**hy·dro·the·rap·ic** (hī'drō thə răp'ĭk), *adj.*

hy·dro·ther·mal (hī'drə thŭr'məl), *adj. Geol.* **1.** denoting or pertaining to the action of hot, aqueous solutions or gases within or on the surface of the earth. **2.** designating the results of such action.

hy·dro·tho·rax (hī'drə thō'răks), *n. Pathol.* the presence of serous fluid in one or both pleural cavities. —**hy·dro·tho·rac·ic** (hī'drō thō răs'ĭk), *adj.*

hy·dro·trop·ic (hī'drə trŏp'ĭk), *adj. Bot.* **1.** turning or tending toward moisture, as growing organs. **2.** taking a particular direction with reference to moisture.

hy·drot·ro·pism (hī drŏt'rə pĭz'əm), *n. Bot., Zool.* **1.** a tropism in response to water. **2.** hydrotropic tendency or growth.

hy·drous (hī'drəs), *adj.* **1.** containing water. **2.** *Chem.* containing water or its elements in some kind of union, as in hydrates or in hydroxides.

hy·drox·ide (hī drŏk'sīd, -sĭd), *n. Chem.* a compound containing the hydroxyl (OH) group. Also, **hy·drox·id** (hī drŏk'sĭd).

hy·drox·y acid (hī drŏk'sĭ'), **1.** organic acid containing both a carboxyl and a hydroxyl group. **2.** one of a class of organic acids containing a hydroxyl group and showing properties of both an alcohol and acid.

hy·drox·yl radical or **group** (hī drŏk'sĭl), *Chem.* a univalent radical or group, OH, containing hydrogen and oxygen. Also, **hy·drox·yl.**

hy·drox·yl·a·mine (hī drŏk'sĭl ə mēn', -ăm'ĭn), *n. Chem.* an unstable, weakly basic, crystalline compound, NH₂OH, used as a reducing agent, analytical reagent, and chemical intermediate.

Hy·dro·zo·a (hī'drə zō'ə), *n.pl.* a class of coelenterates that comprises solitary or colonial polyps and free-swimming medusae.

hy·dro·zo·an (hī'drə zō'ən), *adj.* **1.** pertaining to the *Hydrozoa.* —*n.* **2.** a member of the *Hydrozoa.* [t. NL *Hydrozōön* (f. hydro-, comb. form of hydra (def. 2) + m. Gk. *zōion* animal) + -AN]

hy·e·na (hī ē'nə), *n.* any of the nocturnal carnivores of the family *Hyaenidae,* feeding chiefly on carrion, as *Hyaena hyaena,* the **striped laughing hyena,** an African and Asiatic species about the size of a large dog, *H. brunnea,* the **brown hyena** of South Africa, and *Crocuta crocuta,* the **spotted hyena** of Africa south of the Sahara. Also, **hyaena.** [t. L: m. *hyaena,* t. Gk.: m. *hýaina,* der. *hýs* hog; r. ME *hiene,* t. OF]

Striped laughing hyena,
Hyaena hyaena (Total length
4½ ft., tail 1¼ ft.)

Hy·ge·ia (hī jē'ə), *n. Class. Myth.* the goddess of health,

daughter of Aesculapius. [t. Gk., late var. of *Hygīeia,* personification of *hygīeia* health]

hy·giene (hī'jēn, -jī'ēn'), *n.* the science which deals with the preservation of health. Also, **hy·gi·en·ics** (hī'jĭ'ĕn'ĭks, -jē'nĭks). [t. F, t. Gk.: m.s. *hygieinós* healthful, sanitary]

hy·gi·en·ic (hī'jĭ'ĕn'ĭk, -jē'nĭk), *adj.* **1.** sanitary. **2.** pertaining to hygiene. —**hy·gi·en·i·cal·ly,** *adv.* —Syn. **1.** See **sanitary.**

hy·gi·en·ist (hī'jī'ən ĭst), *n.* an expert in hygiene. Also, **hy·ge·ist** (hī'jē ĭst), **hy'gie·ist.**

hygro-, a word element meaning "wet," "moist." Also, before vowels, **hygr-.** [t. Gk., comb. form of *hygrós*]

hy·gro·graph (hī'grə grăf', -gräf'), *n.* a self-recording hygrometer.

hy·grom·e·ter (hī grŏm'ə tər), *n.* an instrument for determining the humidity of the atmosphere.

hy·gro·met·ric (hī'grə mĕt'rĭk), *adj.* pertaining to the hygrometer or hygrometry.

hy·grom·e·try (hī grŏm'ə trĭ), *n.* the branch of physics that treats of the determination of the humidity of air and gases.

hy·gro·scope (hī'grə skōp'), *n.* an instrument which indicates the approximate humidity of the air.

hy·gro·scop·ic (hī'grə skŏp'ĭk), *adj.* absorbing or attracting moisture from the air.

hy·ing (hī'ĭng), *v.* pres. part. of **hie.**

Hyk·sos (hĭk'sōs, -sŏs), *n.pl.* a succession of foreign rulers of Egypt between the 13th and 18th dynasties, c2000 B.C.

hy·la (hī'lə), *n.* a tree toad. [NL, t. Gk.: m. *hýlē* wood]

hylo-, a word element meaning "wood," "matter." [t. Gk., comb. form of *hýlē*]

hy·lo·zo·ism (hī'lə zō'ĭz əm), *n.* the doctrine that matter is inseparable from life, which is a property of matter. [f. HYLO- + s. Gk. *zōē̄* life + -ISM] —**hy'lo·zo'ist,** *n.* —**hy'lo·zo·is'tic,** *adj.* —**hy'lo·zo·is'ti·cal·ly,** *adv.*

hy·men (hī'mən), *n. Anat.* a fold of mucous membrane partially closing the external orifice of the vagina in a virgin. [t. Gk.: thin skin, membrane]

Hy·men (hī'mən), *n. Gk. Myth.* the god of marriage, represented as a young man bearing a bridal torch.

hy·me·ne·al (hī'mə nē'əl), *adj.* **1.** pertaining to marriage. —*n.* **2.** marriage song.

hy·me·nop·ter (hī'mə nŏp'tər), *n.* hymenopteron. —**hy'me·nop'ter·an,** *adj.,* *n.*

hy·me·nop·ter·on (hī'mə nŏp'tər ən), *n.,* *pl.* **-tera** (-tər ə). a hymenopterous insect.

hy·me·nop·ter·ous (hī'mə nŏp'tər əs), *adj.* belonging or pertaining to the *Hymenoptera,* an order of insects having (when winged) four membranous wings, and including the wasps, bees, ants, ichneumon flies, sawflies, etc. [t. Gk.: m. *hymenópteros* membrane-winged]

Hy·met·tus (hī mĕt'əs), *n.* a mountain in SE Greece, near Athens: famous for honey produced there. 3370 ft.

hymn (hĭm), *n.* **1.** a song or ode in praise or honor of God, a deity, a nation, etc. —*v.t.* **2.** to praise or celebrate in a hymn; express in a hymn. —*v.i.* **3.** to sing hymns. [t. LL: s. *hymnus,* t. Gk.: m. *hýmnos;* r. ME *ymne* (t. OF) and ME *ymyn,* OE *ym(e)n,* t. LL (Eccl.): (m.) s. *ymnus*] —**hymn'like',** *adj.*

hym·nal (hĭm'nəl), *n.* **1.** Also, **hymn'book'.** a book of hymns for use in divine worship. —*adj.* **2.** of or pertaining to hymns.

hym·nist (hĭm'nĭst), *n.* a composer of hymns.

hym·no·dy (hĭm'nə dĭ'), *n.* **1.** the singing or the composition of hymns or sacred songs. **2.** hymns collectively. [t. ML: m.s. *hymnōdia,* t. Gk.: m. *hymnōidía* the singing of a hymn] —**hym'no·dist,** *n.*

hym·nol·o·gy (hĭm nŏl'ə jĭ), *n.* **1.** the study of hymns, their history, classification, etc. **2.** the composition of hymns. **3.** hymns collectively. —**hym·no·log·ic** (hĭm'nə lŏj'ĭk), **hym'no·log'i·cal,** *adj.* —**hym·nol'o·gist,** *n.*

hy·oid (hī'oid), *Anat.* —*adj.* **1.** denoting or pertaining to a U-shaped bone at the root of the tongue in man, or a corresponding bone or collection of bones in animals. See diag. under **mouth.** —*n.* **2.** the hyoid bone, cartilage, arch, ligament, etc. [t. NL: m.s. *hyoïdēs,* t. Gk.: m. *hyoeidēs* shaped like the letter upsilon]

hy·os·cine (hī'ə sēn', -sĭn), *n.* **1.** *Chem.* an alkaloid chemically identical with scopolamine, used as a mydriatic, etc. **2.** (*cap.*) a trademark for this substance. [syncopated var. of HYOSCYAMINE]

hy·os·cy·a·mine (hī'ə sī'ə mēn', -mĭn), *n. Chem.* a poisonous alkaloid, C₁₇H₂₃NO₃, obtained from henbane and other solanaceous plants, used as a sedative, mydriatic, etc. [f. s. L *hyoscyamus* (t. Gk.: m. *hyoskýamos* henbane, lit., hog's bean) + -INE²]

hyp., 1. hypotenuse. **2.** hypothesis. **3.** hypothetical.

hyp-, var. of hypo-, before most vowels, as in *hypethial.*

hyp·a·byss·al (hĭp'ə bĭs'əl), *adj. Geol.* intermediate in texture, as some igneous rocks, between coarse-grained forms and extrusive lava.

hyp·aes·the·sia (hĭp'əs thē'zhə ən), *n.* hypesthesia. —**hyp·aes·the·sic** (hĭp'əs thē'sĭk), *adj.*

hy·pae·thral (hī pē'thrəl, hī-), *adj.* hypethral.

Hy·pa·tia (hī pā'shə), *n.* died A.D. 415, a wise and beautiful woman of Alexandria, Egypt.

hyper-, **1.** a prefix meaning "over," and usually implying excess or exaggeration. **2.** *Chem.* the same as **super-**, indicating the highest of a series of compounds: *hyperchloric acid.* The prefix *per-* is now generally used for *hyper-*: *perchloric, permanganic, etc.* [t. Gk., repr. *hypér,* prep., over, above, beyond, as adv. overmuch, beyond measure; akin to SUPER, OVER]

hy·per·a·cid·i·ty (hī'pər ə sĭd'ə tĭ'), *n.* excessive acidity as of the gastric juice. **—hy·per·ac·id** (hī'pər-ăs'ĭd), *adj.*

hy·per·a·cu·sis (hī'pər ə kū'sĭs), *n. Pathol.* excessive acuteness of the sense of hearing. [NL, f. Gk.: *hyper-* HYPER- + m. *ákousis* hearing]

hy·per·ae·mi·a (hī'pər ē'mĭ ə), *n.* hyperemia. **—hy'-per·ae'mic**, *adj.*

hy·per·aes·the·sia (hī'pər əs thē'zhə, -zhĭ'ə), *n.* hyperesthesia. **—hy·per·aes·thet·ic** (hī'pər əs thĕt'ĭk), *adj.*

hy·per·al·ge·si·a (hī'pər ăl jē'zĭ ə, -sĭ'ə), *n. Pathol.* an exaggerated feeling or sense of pain. [NL, f. Gk.: *hyper-* HYPER- + s. *álgēsis* sense of pain + *-ia* -IA] **—hy'per·al·ge'sic,** *adj.*

hy·per·bo·la (hī pûr'bə lə), *n., pl.* **-las.** *Geom.* a curve consisting of two distinct and similar branches, formed by the intersection of a plane with a right circular cone when the plane makes a greater angle with the base than does the generator of the cone. [NL, t. Gk.: m. *hyperbolḗ,* lit., a throwing beyond. See HYPERBOLE]

Hyperbola
DBE, GAH. Opposite branches of a hyperbola; F, F', Foci; C, Center; AB, Transverse axis; A'B', Conjugate axis; NCP, A diameter

hy·per·bo·le (hī pûr'bə lē', -lĭ'), *n. Rhet.* obvious exaggeration, for effect; an extravagant statement not intended to be understood literally. [t. L, t. Gk.: a throwing beyond, excess, hyperbole, also a hyperbola]

hy·per·bol·ic (hī'pər bŏl'ĭk), *adj.* **1.** having the nature of hyperbole; exaggerated. **2.** using hyperbole, or exaggerating. **3.** of or pertaining to the hyperbola. Also, **hy'per·bol'i·cal.** **—hy'per·bol'i·cal·ly,** *adv.*

hy·per·bo·lism (hī pûr'bə lĭz'əm), *n.* the use of hyperbole.

hy·per·bo·lize (hī pûr'bə līz'), *v.,* **-lized, -lizing.** **—v.i. 1.** to use hyperbole; exaggerate. **—v.t. 2.** to represent or express with hyperbole or exaggeration.

hy·per·bo·loid (hī pûr'bə loid'), *n. Math.* a quadric surface having a finite center and some of its plane sections hyperbolas.

Hy·per·bo·re·an (hī'pər bôr'ĭ ən), *n.* **1.** *Gk. Legend.* one of a people supposed to live in a land of perpetual sunshine and plenty beyond the north wind. **2.** of the Hyperboreans. **3.** arctic; frigid. [t. LL: s. *Hyperboreānus,* in L *Hyperboreus,* t. Gk.: m. *Hyperbóreos* beyond the north wind. See BOREAS]

hy·per·crit·ic (hī'pər krĭt'ĭk), *n.* one who is excessively or captiously critical.

hy·per·crit·i·cal (hī'pər krĭt'ə kəl), *adj.* excessively critical; overcritical. **—hy'per·crit'i·cal·ly,** *adv.*

hy·per·du·li·a (hī'pər dyŏō lī'ə, -dŏō-), *n. Rom. Cath. Theol.* the veneration offered to the Virgin Mary as the most exalted of mere creatures. [t. ML. See HYPER-, DULIA]

hy·per·e·mi·a (hī'pər ē'mĭ ə), *n. Pathol.* an increase in the blood in any part of the body. Also, **hyperaemia.** [NL. See HYPER-, -EMIA] **—hy'per·e'mic,** *adj.*

hy·per·es·the·sia (hī'pər əs thē'zhə, -zhĭ'ə), *n. Pathol.* increased sense of pain, heat, cold, or touch. Also, **hyperaesthesia. —hy·per·es·thet·ic** (hī'pər əs thĕt'-ĭk), *adj.*

hy·per·eu·tec·tic (hī'pər yŏō tĕk'tĭk), *adj.* noting or pertaining to steel containing over 0.85% carbon in a eutectic alloy.

hy·per·ex·ten·sion (hī'pər ĭk stĕn'shən), *n. Physiol.* **1.** the extension of a part beyond the plane of the body, as when the arm is drawn back to its maximum extent. **2.** the state of being so drawn.

Hy·pe·ri·on (hī pĭr'ĭ ən), *n. Gk. Myth.* **1.** a Titan, a son of Uranus and Gaea: the father of Helios, Selene, and Eos. **2.** (later) Apollo. [t. L, t. Gk.]

hy·per·ir·ri·ta·bil·i·ty (hī'pər ĭr'ə tə bĭl'ə tĭ'), *n. Med.* increased irritability.

hy·per·ki·ne·sia (hī'pər kĭ nē'zhə, -zhĭ'ə, -kī-), *n. Pathol.* abnormal amount of muscular action; spasm. [NL, f. Gk.: *hyper-* HYPER- + s. *kínēsis* movement + *-ia* -IA] **—hy·per·ki·net·ic** (hī'pər kĭ nĕt'ĭk, -kī-), *adj.*

hy·per·me·ter (hī pûr'mə tər), *n. Pros.* a verse or line having one or more syllables at the end in addition to those proper to the meter. **—hy·per·met·ric** (hī'-pər mĕt'rĭk), **hy'per·met'ri·cal,** *adj.*

hy·per·me·tro·pi·a (hī'pər mə trō'pĭ ə), *n. Pathol.* a condition of the eye in which parallel rays are focused behind the retina, distant objects being seen more distinctly than near ones; far-sightedness. [NL, f. Gk.: s. *hypérmetros* beyond measure + *-opia* -OPIA] **—hy·per·me·tro·pic** (hī'pər mə trŏp'ĭk), *adj.*

hy·per·me·trop·ic (hī'pər mə trŏp'ĭk), *adj.* pertaining to or affected with hypermetropia; far-sighted.

Hy·perm·nes·tra (hī'pərm nĕs'trə), *n. Gk. Legend.*

the one daughter of Danaüs who refused to kill her husband as commanded by her father.

hy·per·o·pi·a (hī'pər ō'pĭ ə), *n.* hypermetropia. **—hy·per·op·ic** (hī'pər ŏp'ĭk), *adj.*

hy·per·os·to·sis (hī'pər ŏs tō'sĭs), *n., pl.* **-ses** (-sēz). *Anat., Pathol.* **1.** an increase or outgrowth of bony tissue. **2.** an overgrowth of bone.

hy·per·phys·i·cal (hī'pər fĭz'ə kəl), *adj.* above or beyond the physical; immaterial; supernatural.

hy·per·pi·e·sia (hī'pər pī ē'zhə, -zhĭ'ə), *n. Pathol.* unusually high blood pressure. [NL, f. Gk.: *hyper-* HYPER- + s. *píesis* pressure + *-ia* -IA]

hy·per·pi·tu·i·ta·rism (hī'pər pĭ tū'ə tə rĭz'əm, -tŏō'-), *n. Pathol.* **1.** overactivity of the pituitary gland. **2.** the resultant condition, i.e., giantism or acromegaly.

hy·per·pla·sia (hī'pər plā'zhə, -zhĭ'ə), *n.* **1.** *Pathol., Bot.* abnormal multiplication of cells. **2.** *Pathol.* enlargement of a part due to numerical increase of its cells. **—hy·per·plas·ic** (hī'pər plăs'ĭk), **hy'per·plas'tic,** *adj.*

hy·per·ploid (hī'pər ploid'), *adj. Biol.* pertaining to a chromosome number in excess of the diploid but not a multiple of it. [f. HYPER- + (DI)PLOID]

hy·perp·ne·a (hī'pərp nē'ə, hī'pər nē'ə), *n. Pathol.* energetic or labored respiration. Also, **hy'perp·noe'a.** [NL, f. Gk.: *hyper-* HYPER- + m. *pnoiē* breathing]

hy·per·py·rex·i·a (hī'pər pī rĕk'sĭ'ə), *n. Pathol.* an abnormally high fever. **—hy'per·py·rex'i·al,** *adj.*

hy·per·sen·si·tive (hī'pər sĕn'sə tĭv), *adj.* **1.** excessively sensitive. **2.** *Pathol.* allergic to a substance to which a normal individual does not react. **—hy'per·sen'si·tive·ness, hy·per·sen'si·tiv'i·ty,** *n.*

hy·per·son·ic (hī'pər sŏn'ĭk), *adj.* describing velocities much greater than the velocity of sound in the medium.

hy·per·sthene (hī'pər sthēn'), *n.* a common mineral of the pyroxene group, iron magnesium silicate, occurring in green to black masses as an important constituent of basic igneous rocks. [f. HYPER- + m.s. Gk. *sthénos* strength (with reference to frangibility)] **—hy·per·sthen·ic** (hī'pər sthĕn'ĭk), *adj.*

hy·per·ten·sion (hī'pər tĕn'shən), *n. Pathol.* **1.** elevation of the blood pressure, especially the diastolic pressure. **2.** an arterial disease of which this is the outstanding sign.

hy·per·thy·roid·ism (hī'pər thī'roi dĭz'əm), *n. Pathol.* **1.** overactivity of the thyroid gland. **2.** a pathological condition, consisting of a complex of symptoms, produced by this. **—hy'per·thy'roid,** *n.*

hy·per·ton·ic (hī'pər tŏn'ĭk), *adj.* **1.** *Physiol.* possessing too much tone. **2.** *Chem.* denoting a solution of higher osmotic pressure than another solution with which it is compared.

hy·per·tro·phy (hī pûr'trə fĭ), *n., pl.* **-phies,** *v.,* **-phied, -phying. —n. 1.** *Pathol., Bot.* enlargement of a part or organ; excessive growth. **2.** excessive growth or accumulation of any kind. **—v.t., v.i. 3.** to affect with or undergo hypertrophy. **—hy·per·troph·ic** (hī'pər trŏf'-ĭk), *adj.*

hyp·es·the·sia (hĭp'əs thē'zhə, -zhĭ'ə), *n. Pathol.* diminished sense of pain, heat, cold, or touch. Also, **hyp·aesthesia. —hyp·es·the·sic** (hĭp'əs thē'sĭk), *adj.*

hy·pe·thral (hī pē'thrəl, hĭ-), *adj.* open to the sky or having no roof, as a building (used esp. of classical architecture). Also, **hypaethral.** [f. s. L *hypaethrus* (t. Gk.: m. *hýpaithros* under the sky) + -AL¹]

hy·pha (hī'fə), *n., pl.* **-phae** (-fē). *Bot.* (in fungi) one of the threadlike elements of the mycelium. [NL, t. Gk.: m. *hyphḗ* web] **—hy'phal,** *adj.*

hy·phen (hī'fən), *n.* **1.** a short line (-) used to connect the parts of a compound word or the parts of a word divided for any purpose. **—v.t. 2.** hyphenate. [t. LL, t. Gk.: name of sign, special use of *hyphén,* adv., prop. phrase *hyph'hén* under one, together]

hy·phen·ate (hī'fə nāt'), *v.,* **-ated, -ating,** *adj.* **—v.t. 1.** to join by a hyphen. **2.** to write with a hyphen. **—adj. 3.** hyphenated. **—hy'phen·a'tion,** *n.*

hy·phen·ize (hī'fə nīz'), *v.t.,* **-ized, -izing.** hyphenate.

hypno-, a word element meaning "sleep" or "hypnosis," as in *hypnology.* Also, before vowels (usually), **hypn-.** [t, G.k. comb. form of *hýpnos* sleep]

hyp·no·a·nal·y·sis (hĭp'nō ə năl'ə sĭs), *n. Psychoanal.* a method employed by some psychoanalysts who attempt to secure analytic data, free associations and early emotional reactions while the patient is under hypnosis.

hyp·noi·dal (hĭp noi'dəl), *adj. Psychol.* in a state which resembles that of mild hypnosis but is (usually) not induced hypnotically. Also, **hyp'noid.**

hyp·nol·o·gy (hĭp nŏl'ə jĭ), *n.* the science dealing with the phenomena of sleep. **—hyp·no·log·ic** (hĭp'nə lŏj'-ĭk), **hyp'no·log'i·cal,** *adj.* **—hyp·nol'o·gist,** *n.*

hyp·no·sis (hĭp nō'sĭs), *n., pl.* **-ses** (-sēz). **1.** *Psychol.* a condition or state, allied to normal sleep, which can be artificially produced and is characterized by marked susceptibility to suggestion, loss of will power, more or less loss of sensation, etc. **2.** the production of sleep. **3.** a sleepy condition. **4.** hypnotism. [NL, der. Gk. *hypnoûn* put to sleep]

hyp·no·ther·a·py (hĭp'nō thĕr'ə pĭ), *n.* treatment of disease by means of hypnotism.

hyp·not·ic (hĭp nŏt'ĭk), *adj.* **1.** pertaining to hypnosis or hypnotism. **2.** susceptible to hypnotism, as a person. **3.** hypnotized. **4.** inducing sleep. **—n. 5.** an agent or drug that produces sleep; a sedative. **6.** one subject to hypnotic influence. **7.** a person under the influence of hypnotism. [t. LL: s. *hypnōticus*, t. Gk.: m. *hypnōtikós* inclined to sleep] **—hyp·not/i·cal·ly**, *adv.*

hyp·no·tism (hĭp/nə tĭz/əm), *n.* **1.** the science dealing with the induction of hypnosis. **2.** the induction of hypnosis. **3.** hypnosis.

hyp·no·tist (hĭp/nə tĭst), *n.* one who hypnotizes.

hyp·no·tize (hĭp/nə tīz/), *v.t.*, **-tized, -tizing.** to put in the hypnotic state. Also, *esp. Brit.*, **hyp/no·tise/. —hyp/no·tiz/a·ble**, *adj.* **—hyp/no·ti·za/tion**, *n.* **—hyp/no·tiz/er**, *n.*

hy·po¹ (hī/pō), *n. Chem.* sodium thiosulfate, Na2S2O3·· 5H2O, a photographic fixing agent. [short for HYPOSULFITE]

hy·po² (hī/pō), *n. Slang.* a hypodermic needle or injection. [short for HYPODERMIC]

hypo-, **1.** a prefix meaning "under," either in place or in degree ("less," "less than"). **2.** *Chem.* a prefix applied to the inorganic acids (as *hypochlorous acid*) and to their salts (as *potassium hypochlorite*) to indicate a low valence state for the designated element. Also, **hyp-.** [t. Gk. repr. *hypó*, prep. and adv., under; akin to SUB-]

hy·po·a·cid·i·ty (hī/pō ə sĭd/ə tĭ), *n.* acidity in a lesser degree than is usual or normal, as of the gastric juice.

hy·po·blast (hī/pə blăst/, hĭp/ə-), *n. Embryol.* the inner layer of a gastrula, consisting of endoblast, or endoblast and mesoblast. **—hy/po·blas/tic,** *adj.*

hyp·o·caust (hĭp/ə kôst/, hī/pə-), *n.* a hollow space or system of flues in the floor or walls of a Roman building or room, which received and distributed the heat from a furnace. [t. L: s. *hypocaustum*, t. Gk.: m. *hypó kauston* room heated from below]

hy·po·chlo·rous acid (hī/pə klōr/əs, hĭp/ə-), *Chem.* an acid, HClO, whose solutions have strong bleaching properties.

hy·po·chon·dri·a (hī/pə kŏn/drĭ ə, hĭp/ə-), *n.* **1.** *Psychiatry.* a morbid condition characterized by depressed spirits and fancies of ill health, referable to the physical condition of the body or one of its parts. **2.** (*orig. as pl.*) the parts of the body under the cartilage of the breastbone and above the navel. [t. LL: pl., the abdomen, t. Gk.: m. *hypochóndria* (neut. pl.) def. 2; orig. thought to be the seat of melancholy]

hy·po·chon·dri·ac (hī/pə kŏn/drĭ ăk/, hĭp/ə-), *adj.* Also, **hy·po·chon·dri·a·cal** (hī/pō kŏn drī/ə kəl, hĭp/ō-). **1.** pertaining to or suffering from hypochondria or morbid depression. **2.** of or pertaining to the hypochondria (def. 2): *the hypochondriac regions.* **—n. 3.** a person suffering from or subject to hypochondria. **—hy/po·chon·dri/a·cal·ly,** *adv.*

hy·po·chon·dri·um (hī/pə kŏn/drĭ əm, hĭp/ə-), *n., pl.* **-dria** (-drĭ ə). *Anat., Zool.* **1.** either of two regions of the human abdomen, situated on opposite sides (left and right) of the epigastrium, above the lumbar regions. **2.** a corresponding region in lower animals. [NL]

hyp·o·co·ris·tic (hĭp/ə kô rĭs/tĭk, hī/pə-), *adj.* endearing, as a pet name; diminutive; euphemistic. [t. Gk.: m.s. *hypokoristikós*]

hy·po·cot·yl (hī/pə kŏt/əl, hĭp/ə-), *n. Bot.* (in the embryo of a plant) that part of the stem below cotyledons. [HYPO- + COTYL- (EDON)] **—hy/po·cot/y·lous,** *adj.*

hy·poc·ri·sy (hĭ pŏk/rə sĭ), *n., pl.* **-sies. 1.** act of pretending to have a character or beliefs, principles, etc., that one does not possess. **2.** pretense of virtue or piety; false goodness. [ME *ypocrisie*, t. OF, t. LL: m.s. *hypocrisis*, t. Gk.: m. *hypókrisis* acting of a part, pretense] **—Syn. 1.** See deceit.

hyp·o·crite (hĭp/ə krĭt), *n.* one given to hypocrisy; one who feigns virtue or piety; a pretender. [ME *ypocrite*, t. OF, t. LL: m.s. *hypocrita*, t. Gk.: m. *hypokritḗs* actor, pretender, hypocrite] **—hyp/o·crit/i·cal,** *adj.* **—hyp/o·crit/i·cal·ly,** *adv.*

hy·po·cy·cloid (hī/pə sī/kloid, hĭp/ə-), *n. Geom.* a curve generated by the motion of a point on the circumference of a circle which rolls internally, without slipping, on a given circle. **—hy/po·cy·cloi/dal,** *adj.*

hy·po·derm (hī/pə dûrm/), *n.* **1.** the epidermis of an arthropod. **2.** *Bot.* hypodermis. **—hy/po·der/mal,** *adj.*

hy·po·der·mic (hī/pə dûr/mĭk), *adj.* **1.** characterized by the introduction of medical remedies under the skin: *hypodermic injection.* **2.** introduced under the skin: *a hypodermic needle.* **3.** pertaining to parts under the skin. **4.** lying under the skin, as tissue. **—n. 5.** a hypodermic remedy. **6.** a hypodermic injection. **7.** the administration of drugs into subcutaneous body tissues. **8.** a hypodermic syringe. **—hy/po·der/mi·cal·ly,** *adv.*

hypodermic needle, a hollow needle used to inject solutions subcutaneously.

hypodermic syringe, a small glass piston or barrel syringe having a detachable hollow needle used to inject solutions subcutaneously.

hy·po·der·mis (hī/pə dûr/mĭs, hĭp/ə-), *n.* **1.** *Zool.* the surface epithelium of an invertebrate when covered over

P
C
H
R

Seedling of a bean
H. Hypocotyl;
C. Cotyledons;
P. Plumule;
R. Roots

H
P
C
H

C.
H. Hypocycloid
traced by point P; C' Center
of moving circle; C Center
of fixed circle

by the noncellular secretion that it produces. **2.** *Bot.* a tissue or layer of cells beneath the epidermis. [NL]

hy·po·eu·tec·tic (hī/pō yōō tĕk/tĭk, hĭp/ō-), *adj. Metall.* noting or pertaining to steel containing less than 0.85% carbon in a eutectic alloy.

hy·po·gas·tric (hī/pə găs/trĭk, hĭp/ə-), *adj. Anat.* **1.** situated below the stomach. **2.** of or pertaining to the hypogastrium.

hy·po·gas·tri·um (hī/pə găs/trĭ əm, hĭp/ə-), *n., pl.* **-tria** (-trĭ ə). *Anat.* **1.** the lower part of the abdomen. **2.** the region between the right and left iliac regions. [NL, t. Gk.: m. *hypogástrion*, prop. neut. of *hypogástrios* abdominal]

hy·po·ge·al (hī/pə jē/əl, hĭp/ə-), *adj.* underground; subterranean. [f. s. L *hypogēus* (t. Gk.: m. *hypógeios* underground) + -AL¹]

hyp·o·gene (hī/pə jēn/, hĭp/ə-), *adj. Geol.* formed beneath the earth's surface, as granite (opposed to *epigene*). [f. HYPO- + -*gene* (var. of -GEN)]

hy·pog·e·nous (hī pŏj/ə nəs, hī-), *adj. Bot.* growing beneath, or on the under surface, as fungi on leaves.

hy·po·ge·ous (hī/pə jē/əs, hĭp/ə-), *adj.* **1.** underground; subterranean. **2.** *Bot.* growing or remaining underground. [t. L: m. *hypogēus*, t. Gk.: m. *hypógeios*]

hyp·o·ge·um (hī/pə jē/əm, hĭp/pə-), *n., pl.* **-gea** (-jē/ə). *Anc. Archit.* **1.** the underground part of a building. **2.** an underground structure; an artificial cave. [t. L, t. Gk.: m. *hypógeion*, neut. of *hypógeios* underground]

hy·po·glos·sal (hī/pə glŏs/əl, hĭp/ə-), *Anat., Zool.* **—adj. 1.** situated under the tongue wholly or in part. **—n. 2.** a hypoglossal nerve. [f. HYPO- + s. Gk. *glōssa* tongue + -AL¹]

hypoglossal nerve, either of the last pair of cranial nerves which gives rise to the movements of the tongue.

hy·pog·y·nous (hī pŏj/ə nəs, hī-), *adj. Bot.* **1.** situated on the receptacle beneath the pistil, as stamens, etc. **2.** having stamens, etc., so arranged. **—hy·pog/y·ny,** *n.*

hy·po·nas·ty (hī/pə năs/tĭ, hĭp/ə-), *n. Bot.* increased growth along the lower surface of an organ or part, causing it to bend upward. [f. HYPO- + s. Gk. *nastós* pressed close, compact + -Y³] **—hy/po·nas/tic,** *adj.*

hy·po·ni·trous acid (hī/pə nī/trəs), *Chem.* an unstable crystalline acid, H2N2O2.

hy·po·phos·phite (hī/pə fŏs/fīt), *n. Chem.* a salt of hypophosphorus acid, containing the radical H2PO2⁻¹.

hy·po·phos·phor·ic acid (hī/pō fŏs fôr/ĭk, -fôr/-), *Chem.* a tetrabasic acid, H4P2O6, produced by the slow oxidation of phosphorus in moist air.

hy·po·phos·pho·rous acid (hī/pə fŏs/fə rəs), *Chem.* a monobasic acid of phosphorus, H3PO2, having salts which are used in medicine.

hy·poph·y·sis (hī pŏf/ə sĭs, hī-), *n., pl.* **-ses** (-sēz/). *Anat.* the pituitary gland of the brain. [NL, t. Gk.: undergrowth, process]

hy·po·pi·tu·i·ta·rism (hī/pō pī tū/ə tə rĭz/əm, -tōō/-, hĭp/ō-), *n. Pathol.* **1.** abnormally diminished activity of the pituitary gland. **2.** the pathological condition produced by this, resulting in obesity, retention of adolescent traits, and, in extreme cases, dwarfism.

hy·po·pla·sia (hī/pə plā/zhə, -zhĭ ə, hĭp/ə-), *n.* **1.** *Pathol., Bot.* abnormal deficiency of cells or structural elements. **2.** *Pathol.* an underdeveloped condition in which an organ or structure remains immature or subnormal in size. [f. HYPO- + -PLASIA]

hy·po·py·on (hī pō/pī ŏn/, hī-), *n. Pathol.* an effusion of pus into the anterior chamber of the eye, or that cavity which contains the aqueous humor. [NL, t. Gk.: ulcer, prop. neut. of *hypópyos* tending to suppuration]

hy·pos·ta·sis (hī pŏs/tə sĭs, hī-), *n., pl.* **-ses** (-sēz/). **1.** *Metaphys.* **a.** that which stands under and supports; foundation. **b.** the underlying or essential part of anything as distinguished from attributes; substance, essence, or essential principle. **2.** *Theol.* **a.** one of the three real and distinct subsistences in the one undivided substance or essence of God. **b.** a person of the Trinity. **c.** the one personality of Christ in which His two natures, human and divine, are united. **3.** *Med.* the accumulation of blood or solids of a fluid by gravity due to poor circulation or standing. [t. LL, t. Gk.: substance, nature, essence, also sediment]

hy·po·stat·ic (hī/pə stăt/ĭk, hĭp/ə-), *adj.* **1.** of or pertaining to a hypostasis; elementary. **2.** *Theol.* pertaining to or constituting a distinct personal being or subsistence. **3.** *Med.* arising from downward pressure. **4.** *Genetics.* (of nonallelic genes) recessive. Also, **hy/po·stat/i·cal.** [t. Gk.: m.s. *hypostatikós* pertaining to substance] **—hy/po·stat/i·cal·ly,** *adv.*

hy·pos·ta·tize (hī pŏs/tə tīz/, hī-), *v.t.*, **-tized, -tizing.** to treat or regard as a distinct substance or reality. Also, *esp. Brit.*, **hy·pos/ta·tise/. —hy·pos/ta·ti·za/-tion,** *n.*

hyp·o·style (hĭp/ə stīl/, hī/pə-), *Archit.* **—adj. 1.** having many columns carrying the roof or ceiling: *a hypostyle hall.* **—n. 2.** a hypostyle structure. [t. Gk.: m.s. *hypóstȳlos* resting on pillars]

hy·po·sul·fite (hī/pə sŭl/fīt), *n. Chem.* **1.** a salt of hyposulfurous acid. **2.** sodium thiosulfate, antichlor, or hypo (Na2S2O3·5H2O), a bleach and photographic fixing agent. Also, **hy/po·sul/phite.**

hy·po·sul·fu·rous acid (hī/pō sŭl fyŏŏr/əs, -sŭl/fər əs), an acid, H2S2O4, next in a series below sulfurous acid.

ăct, āble, dâre, ärt; ĕbb, ēqual; ĭf, īce; hŏt, ōver, ôrder, oil, bŏŏk, ōōze, out; ŭp, ūse, ûrge; ə = a in alone; ch, chief; g, give; ng, ring; sh, shoe; th, thin; ŧh, that; zh, vision. See the full key on inside cover.

hy·po·tax·is (hī′pə tăk′sĭs, hĭp′ə-), *n. Gram.* dependent relation or construction, as of clauses. [NL, t. Gk.: subjection] —**hy′po·tac′tic,** *adj.*

hy·pot·e·nuse (hī pŏt′ə nūs′, -nōōs′), *n. Geom.* the side of a right triangle opposite the right angle. Also, **hypothenuse.** [t. LL: m.s. *hypotēnūsa,* t. Gk.: m. *hypoteīnousa,* ppr. fem., subtending]

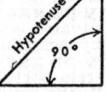

Hypotenuse of a right triangle

hy·po·thal·a·mus (hī′pə thăl′ə məs, hĭp′ə-), *n. Anat.* the portion of the diencephalon concerned with emotional expression and visceral responses.

hy·poth·ec (hī pŏth′ĭk, hī′-), *n. Rom. and Civil Law.* a lien held by a creditor on the property of his debtor without possession of it. It may be created either by agreement or by operation of law. [t. LL: s. *hypothēca,* t. Gk.: m. *hypothēkē* deposit, pledge]

hy·poth·e·car·y (hī pŏth′ə kĕr′ĭ, hī-), *adj.* **1.** of or pertaining to a hypothec. **2.** created or secured by a hypothec.

hy·poth·e·cate (hī pŏth′ə kāt′, hī-), *v.t.,* **-cated, -cating. 1.** to pledge to a creditor as security without delivering over; mortgage. **2.** to put in pledge by delivery, as stocks given as security for a loan. [t. ML: m.s. *hypothēcātus,* pp., of *hypothēcāre,* der. LL *hypothēca* HYPOTHEC] —**hy·poth′e·ca·tion,** *n.* —**hy·poth′e·ca′tor,** *n.*

hy·poth·e·nuse (hī pŏth′ə nūs′, -nōōs′, hī′-), *n.* hypotenuse.

hy·po·ther·mia (hī′pō thûr′mĭə), *n.* **1.** subnormal body temperature. **2.** the artificial reduction of body temperature to slow metabolic processes: usually to facilitate heart surgery. [f. HYPO- + Gk. *thérm(ē)* heat + -IA] —**hy′po·ther′mal,** *adj.*

hy·poth·e·sis (hī pŏth′ə sĭs, hī′-), *n., pl.* **-ses** (-sēz′). **1.** a proposition (or set of propositions) proposed as an explanation for the occurrence of some specified group of phenomena, either asserted merely as a provisional conjecture to guide investigation (**a working hypothesis**), or accepted as highly probable in the light of established facts. **2.** a proposition assumed as a premise in an argument. **3.** the antecedent of a conditional proposition. **4.** a mere assumption or guess. [NL, t. Gk.: supposition, postulate] —**Syn. 1.** See **theory.**

hy·poth·e·size (hī pŏth′ə sīz′, hī′-), *v.,* **-sized, -sizing.** —*v.i.* **1.** to form a hypothesis. —*v.t.* **2.** to assume by hypothesis. Also, *esp. Brit.,* **hy·poth′e·sise′.**

hy·po·thet·i·cal (hī′pə thĕt′ə kəl), *adj.* **1.** assumed by hypothesis; supposed: *a hypothetical case.* **2.** pertaining to, involving, or of the nature of hypothesis: *hypothetical reasoning.* **3.** given to making hypotheses: *a hypothetical person.* **4.** *Logic.* **a.** conditional; characterizing propositions having the form *if A, then B.* **b.** (of a syllogism) having a premise which is a hypothetical proposition. **c.** (of a proposition) not well supported by evidence, whose status is therefore highly conjectural. Also, **hy′po·thet′ic.** [f. *hypothetic* (t. Gk.: m.s. *hypothetikós* supposed) + -AL¹] —**hy′po·thet′i·cal·ly,** *adv.*

hy·po·thy·roid·ism (hī′pō thī′roid ĭz′əm, hĭp′ō-), *n. Pathol.* **1.** abnormally diminished activity of the thyroid gland. **2.** the condition produced by a deficiency of thyroid secretion, resulting in goiter, myxedema, and, in children, cretinism.

hy·po·ton·ic (hī′pə tŏn′ĭk, hĭp′ə-), *adj. Physiol.* under the normal tone.

hy·po·xan·thine (hī′pə zăn′thēn, -thĭn), *n. Chem.* a crystalline alkaloid, $C_5H_4N_4O$, related to xanthine and found in animal and vegetable tissues. —**hy′po·xan′thic,** *adj.*

hyp·som·e·ter (hĭp sŏm′ə tər), *n.* **1.** an instrument for measuring altitude by determining the boiling point of a liquid at the given height. **2.** (sometimes) the boiler of a hypsometer. [f. Gk. *hýpso(s)* height + -METER]

hyp·som·e·try (hĭp sŏm′ə trĭ), *n.* vertical control in mapping; the establishment of elevations or altitudes. —**hyp·so·met′ric** (hĭp′sə mĕt′rĭk), **hyp′so·met′ri·cal,** *adj.* —**hyp′so·met′ri·cal·ly,** *adv.*

hy·ra·coid (hī′rə koid′), *adj.* belonging or pertaining to the order *Hyracoidea,* that comprises the hyraxes. [f. s. NL *hyrax* HYRAX + -OID] —**hy·ra·coi·de·an** (hī′rə koi′dĭ ən), *adj., n.*

hy·rax (hī′răks), *n., pl.* **hyraxes, hyraces** (hī′rə sēz′). any of a number of small, timid mammals of Asia and Africa, superficially resembling the ground hog but having tiny hoofs and other distinctive characteristics. They constitute a separate order, the *Hyracoidae,* the **rock hyrax,** genus *Procavia* (or *Hyrax*), living mostly in rocky places, the closely similar **tree hyrax** of Africa, genus *Dendrohyrax,* being arboreal. [NL, t. Gk.: shrewmouse]

Hyr·ca·ni·a (hər kā′nĭ ə), *n.* an ancient province of the Persian empire, SE of the Caspian Sea. —**Hyr·ca′ni·an,** *adj.*

hy·son (hī′sən), *n.* a Chinese green tea, the early crop and the inferior leaves being called **young hyson** and **hyson skin** respectively. [t. Chinese (Cantonese): m. *hei-ch′un,* lit., blooming spring (Mandarin *hsi-ch′un*)]

hys·sop (hĭs′əp), *n.* **1.** an aromatic labiate herb, *Hyssopus officinalis,* with blue flowers. **2.** (in the Bible and derived use) a plant, perhaps the caper, whose twigs were used in ceremonial sprinkling. [t. L: s. *hyssōpus,* t. Gk.: m. *hýssōpos* kind of plant; r. OE *ysope*]

hyster-, var. of **hystero-,** before vowels, as in *hysterectomy.*

hys·ter·ec·to·my (hĭs′tə rĕk′tə mĭ), *n., pl.* **-mies.** *Surg.* the excision of the uterus.

hys·ter·e·sis (hĭs′tə rē′sĭs), *n. Physics.* any of several effects resembling a sort of internal friction suffered by a body subjected to a varying stress or intensity, as of magnetism, electricity, or physical strain. They are accompanied by heat losses. [NL, t. Gk.: deficiency] —**hys·ter·et·ic** (hĭs′tə rĕt′ĭk), *adj.*

hysteresis loop, loop¹ (def. 6b).

hys·te·ri·a (hĭs tĭr′ĭə, -tĕr′-), *n.* **1.** morbid or senseless emotionalism; emotional frenzy. **2.** a psychoneurotic disorder characterized by violent emotional outbreaks, perversion of sensory and motor functions, and various morbid effects due to autosuggestion. [f. HYSTER- + -IA]

hys·ter·ic (hĭs tĕr′ĭk), *n.* **1.** (*usually pl.*) a fit of hysteria; hysteria. **2.** a person subject to hysteria. —*adj.* **3.** hysterical.

hys·ter·i·cal (hĭs tĕr′ə kəl), *adj.* **1.** resembling or suggesting hysteria; emotionally disordered. **2.** of, pertaining to, or characteristic of hysteria: *Her hysterical behavior at the funeral revealed how much she really loved him.* **3.** suffering from or subject to hysteria. [f. s. L *hystericus* (t. Gk.: m. *hysterikós* suffering in the uterus) + -AL¹] —**hys·ter′i·cal·ly,** *adv.*

hysterical fever, an increase in temperature without obvious cause other than hysteria.

hystero-, a word element meaning "uterus," as in *hysterotomy.* Also, **hyster-.** [t. Gk., comb. form of *hystéra*]

hys·ter·oid (hĭs′tə roid′), *adj.* resembling hysteria. Also, **hys′ter·oi·dal.** [f. HYSTER- + -OID]

hys·ter·on prot·er·on (hĭs′tə rŏn′ prŏt′ə rŏn′), **1.** *Logic.* an attempted proof of a proposition which is based on premises that can be established only with the help of that proposition. This involves a fallacy, since it inverts the true order of logical dependence. **2.** *Rhet.* a figure of speech in which the logical order of two elements in discourse is reversed. [t. LL, t. Gk.: *hýsteron* (neut. of *hýsteros* latter), *próteron* (neut. of *próteros* being before, sooner)]

hys·ter·ot·o·my (hĭs′tə rŏt′ə mĭ), *n., pl.* **-mies.** *Surg.* the operation of cutting into the uterus, as used in Caesarean section.

hys·tri·co·mor·phic (hĭs′trə kō môr′fĭk), *adj.* belonging or pertaining to the *Hystricomorpha,* the suborder of rodents that includes the porcupines, chinchilla, agouti, coypu, guinea pig, etc. [f. *hystrico-* (comb. form of L *hystrix* porcupine, t. Gk.) + -MORPHIC]

hy·zone (hī′zōn), *n. Chem.* triatomic hydrogen, H_3.

I

I¹, i (ī), *n., pl.* **I's** or **Is, i's** or **is. 1.** the 9th letter of the English alphabet. **2.** any sound represented by the letter I. **3.** an I-shaped object. **4.** Roman numeral for 1. See **Roman numerals.**

I² (ī), *pron., nom.* **I,** *poss.* **my** or **mine,** *obj.* **me;** *pl. nom.* **we,** *poss.* **ours** or **our,** *obj.* **us;** *n., pl.* **I's.** —*pron.* **1.** the subject form of the singular pronoun of the first person, used by a speaker of himself. —*n.* **2.** the pronoun *I* used as a noun: *the "I" in this novel is John.* **3.** *Metaphys.* the ego. [ME *ik, ich, i,* OE *ic, ih, c,* G *ich,*; akin to L *ego,* Gk. *egṓ*]

I, *Chem.* iodine.

I., 1. Independent. **2.** Island; Islands. **3.** Isle; Isles.

i., 1. intransitive. **2.** island.

-i-, an ending for the first element of many compounds, originally found in the combining form of many Latin and Greek words, but often used in English as a connective irrespective of etymology, as in *cuneiform, Frenchify,* etc.

-ia, a suffix of nouns, esp. having restricted application in various fields, thus, in medicine (disease: *malaria*), in geography (countries: *Rumania*), in botany (genera: *Wistaria*), in names of Roman feasts (*Lupercalia*), in Latin or Latinizing plurals (*Reptilia, bacteria*), and in collectives (*insignia, militia*). [t. L or Gk., both f. *-i-* orig. or connective vowel + *-a* (fem. sing. nom. ending) or *-a* (neut. pl. nom. ending)]

Ia., Iowa.

b., blend of, blended; c., cognate with; d., dialect, dialectal; f., formed from; g., going back to; m., modification of; r., replacing; s., stem of; t., taken from; ?, perhaps. See the full key on inside cover.

I·a·go (Yä′gō), *n.* the villain in Shakespeare's *Othello*.

-ial, var. of **-al**[1], as in *judicial, imperial.* [t. L: s. *-iālis, -iāle,* adj. suffix, f. *-i-,* orig. or connective vowel + *-ālis,-āle* -AL[1]]

i·amb (Y′ămb), *n.* Pros. a metrical foot of two syllables, a short followed by a long, or an unaccented by an accented (˘ —), as in *Come live | with me | and be | my love.* [t. L: s. *iambus* an iambic verse or poem, t. Gk.: m. *iambos*]

i·am·bic (Yăm′bYk), *adj.* 1. Pros. **a.** pertaining to the iamb. **b.** consisting of or employing an iamb or iambs. **2.** Gk. Lit. of a kind of satirical poetry written in iambs. —*n.* 3. Pros. a. an iamb. **b.** (usually pl.) a verse or poem consisting of iambs. **4.** a satirical poem in this meter.

i·am·bus (Yăm′bəs), *n., pl.* **-bi** (-bī), **-buses.** iamb.

-ian, var. of **-an,** as in *amphibian, Grecian.* [t. L: s. *-iānus,* f. *-i-* orig. or connective vowel + *-ānus* -AN]

-iana. See **-ana, -ana.**

Ia·şi (yäsh), *n.* Rumanian name of **Jassy.**

-iasis, a suffix of nouns denoting state or condition, esp. a morbid condition or a form of disease, as in *psoriasis.* [NL, t. Gk.: f. *-i-* orig. or connective vowel (see -I-) + *-āsis* -ASIS]

i·at·ric (iăt′rYk), *adj.* pertaining to a physician or to medicine. Also, **i·at·ri·cal.** [t. Gk.: s. *iātrikós*]

-iatry, a combining form meaning "medical care," as in *psychiatry.* [t. Gk.: m.s. *iātreia* healing]

ib., ibidem.

I·ba·dan (ē bä′dän), *n.* a city in SW Nigeria, in British West Africa. 459,196 (1953).

I·bá·ñez (ē bän′yĕth), *n.* See **Blasco Ibáñez.**

I-beam (Y′bēm′), *n.* a beam in the shape of the capital I.

I·be·ri·a (Y bYr′Y ə), *n.* 1. Also, **Iberian Peninsula.** a peninsula in SW Europe, comprising Spain and Portugal. **2.** an ancient region S of the Caucasus: modern Georgia. [t. L, t. Gk., ancient Greek name of Spain]

I·be·ri·an (Y bYr′Y ən), *adj.* 1. of or pertaining to Iberia in Europe or its inhabitants. **2.** Ethnol. denoting or pertaining to a dark dolichocephalic race inhabiting parts of southern Europe and northern Africa, comprising the ancient Iberians, some of the ancient Britons, and other peoples, and their descendants. **3.** of or pertaining to ancient Iberia in Asia or its inhabitants. —*n.* 4. one of the ancient inhabitants of Iberia in Europe, from whom the Basques are supposed to be descended. **5.** the language of the ancient Iberians of Europe, from which Basque developed. **6.** one of the ancient inhabitants of Iberia in Asia.

I·ber·ville (ē bĕr vēl′), *n.* Pierre le Moyne (pyĕr lə mwän′), Sieur d', 1661–1706, French naval officer, born in Canada: founder of first Louisiana settlement (1699).

i·bex (Y′bĕks), *n., pl.* **ibexes, ibices** (Yb′ə sēz′, Y′bə-), (*esp. collectively*) **ibex.** any of various Old World wild goats with large recurved horns, esp. *Capra ibex,* of the Alps and Apennines. [t. L]

Asiatic ibex, *Capra sibirica* (Ab. 3½ ft. high at the shoulder)

ibid., ibidem.

i·bi·dem (Y bī′dĕm), *adv.* Latin. in the same book, chapter, page, etc.

i·bis (Y′bYs), *n., pl.* **ibises** (Y′bYs Yz), (*esp. collectively*) **ibis.** 1. any of various large wading birds of warm regions, allied to the herons and storks, forming the family Threskiornithidae. **2.** the **sacred ibis,** *Threskiornis aethiopica* of Egypt and other parts of Africa, with white-and-black plumage, venerated by the ancient Egyptians. [t L, t. Gk.; of Egyptian orig.]

Wood ibis, *Mycteria americana* (4 ft. long; bill 8½ in. long)

-ible, var. of **-able,** occurring in words taken from the Latin, as in *credible, horrible, legible, visible,* or modeled on the Latin type as *addible* (for *addable*), *reducible.* [ME *-ible,* t. OF, t. L: m.s. *-ibilis,* var. of *-bilis* after consonant stems. See -BLE]

ibn-Rushd (Yb′ən rōōsht′), *n.* Arabic name of Averroës.

ibn-Sa·ud (Yb′ən sä ōōd′), *n.* 1. Abdul-Aziz (äb dōōl′ä zēz′), 1880–1953, ruler of Nejd, 1901–32, king of Saudi Arabia 1932–1953. **2.** his son, Abdul-Aziz al Faisal (äl fī′səl), born 1901, king since 1953.

ibn-Si·na (Yb′ən sē′nä), *n.* Arabic name of Avicenna.

Ib·ra·him Pa·sha (Yb′rä hēm′ pä′shä), 1789–1848, Egyptian general, governor of Syria.

Ib·sen (Yb′sən; *Nor.* Yp′sən), *n.* Henrik (hĕn′rYk), 1828–1906, Norwegian dramatist and poet.

-ic, 1. a suffix forming adjectives from nouns or stems not used as words themselves, meaning "pertaining to or belonging to" (*poetic, metallic, Homeric*), found extensively in adjective nouns of a similar type (*public, magic*), and in nouns the adjectives of which end in *-ical* (*music, critic*). **2.** Chem. a suffix showing that an element is present in a compound at a high valence, at least higher than when the suffix *-ous* is used. [repr. in part s. Gk. *-ikos;* often s. L *-icus;* sometimes F *-ique*]

I·ça (ē′sä), *n.* Brazilian name of **Putumayo.**

-ical, a compound suffix forming adjectives from nouns (*rhetorical*), providing synonyms to words ending

in *-ic* (*poetical*), and providing an adjective with additional meanings to those in the *-ic* form (*economical*). [f. -IC + -AL[1]; in some cases repr. LL *-icālis,* f. adj. endings *-ic(us)* -IC + *-ālis* -AL[1]]

I·car·i·an (Y kâr′Y ən, Y-), *adj.* of or like Icarus.

Ic·a·rus (Yk′ə rəs, Y′kə-), *n.* Gk. Legend. the son of Daedalus. Together they escaped from Crete using wings made of wax and feathers, but Icarus, flying so high that the sun melted his wings, drowned in the Aegean.

I.C.B.M., intercontinental ballistic missile. Also, **ICBM.**

I.C.C., Interstate Commerce Commission. Also, **ICC**

ice (Ys), *n., v.,* **iced, icing,** *adj.* —*n.* 1. the solid form of water, produced by freezing; frozen water. **2.** the frozen surface of a body of water. **3.** any substance resembling this: *camphor ice.* **4.** U.S. a frozen dessert made of sweetened water and fruit juice. **5.** Brit. ice cream. **6.** icing. **7.** reserve; formality: *to break the ice.* **8.** Slang. a diamond or diamonds. **9.** on thin ice, in a risky or delicate situation. **10.** cut no ice, U.S. Colloq. to have no importance. —*v.t.* 11. to cover with ice. **12.** to change into ice; freeze. **13.** to cool with ice, as a drink. **14.** to refrigerate with ice, as a fish. **15.** to make cold as if with ice. **16.** to cover (cakes, etc.) with icing; frost. —*v.i.* 17. to freeze. —*adj.* 18. of ice. [ME *is(e),* OE *īs,* c. G *eis*] —*iced′ness* —*ice′like,* *adj.*

-ice, a suffix used in many nouns to indicate state or quality, as in *service, justice.* [ME *-ice,* *-ys(e),* etc., t. OF: m. *-ice, -ise,* g. L *-itius, -itia, -itium*]

ice age, Geol. the glacial epoch.

ice bag, a bag containing ice, applied to the head.

ice·berg (Ys′bûrg′), *n.* a large floating mass of ice, detached from a glacier and carried out to sea. [half Anglicization, half adoption of D *ijsberg* ice mountain, c. G *eisberg,* Sw. *isberg*]

ice·blink (Ys′blYngk′), *n.* a luminous appearance near the horizon, due to the reflection of light from ice.

ice·boat (Ys′bōt′), *n.* 1. a triangular frame with runners, sails, etc., for sailing on ice. **2.** icebreaker (def. 1).

ice·bound (Ys′bound′), *adj.* 1. held fast or hemmed in by ice; frozen in: *an icebound ship.* **2.** obstructed or shut off by ice: *an icebound harbor.*

ice·box (Ys′bŏks′), *n.* a box or chest to hold ice for keeping food, etc., cool.

ice·break·er (Ys′brā′kər), *n.* 1. a strong ship for breaking channels through ice. **2.** a tool or machine for chopping ice into small pieces. **3.** a structure of masonry or timber for protection against moving ice.

ice·cap (Ys′kăp′), *n.* a cap of ice over an area (sometimes vast), sloping in all directions from the center.

ice-cold (Ys′kōld′), *adj.* cold as ice.

ice cream, 1. a frozen food made of cream, sweetened and variously flavored. **2.** (in commercial use) a food made in imitation of this, and containing milk, egg whites, custard, cornstarch, etc.

iced (Yst), *adj.* 1. covered with ice. **2.** cooled by means of ice. **3.** Cooking. covered with icing.

ice field, a large ice floe.

ice floe, a large sheet of floating ice.

ice foot, a belt of ice along the shore in polar regions, formed where snow on the shore meets the sea water.

ice·house (Ys′hous′), *n.* a building for storing ice.

Icel., 1. Iceland. 2. Icelandic.

Ice·land (Ys′lənd), *n.* a large island in the N Atlantic between Greenland and Denmark: formerly Danish, it has been an independent republic since 1944. 158,000 pop. (est. 1955); 39,698 sq. mi. Cap.: Reykjavik. —Ice·land·er (Ys′lăn′dər, -lən dər), *n.*

Ice·lan·dic (Ys lăn′dYk), *adj.* 1. pertaining to Iceland, its inhabitants, or their language. —*n.* 2. the language of Iceland, a Scandinavian language.

Iceland moss, an edible lichen, *Cetraria islandica,* of arctic regions, used to some extent in medicine.

Iceland spar, a transparent variety of calcite that is double-refracting and is used for polarizing light.

ice·man (Ys′măn′), *n., pl.* **-men** (-mĕn′). U.S. a man engaged in gathering, storing, selling, or delivering ice.

ice needles, Meteorol. a form of precipitation consisting of very small ice crystals that seem to float in the air.

I·ce·ni (Y sē′nī), *n.pl.* an ancient Celtic tribe of eastern England, whose queen, Boudicca, headed the insurrection of A.D. 61 against the Romans. [t. L]

ice pack, a large area of floating ice, as in arctic seas.

ice pick, a pick or other tool for breaking ice.

ice plant, one of the figworts, *Mesembryanthemum crystallinum,* a succulent, low shrub, orig. of the Old World, with leaves covered by glistening vesicles.

ice-scoured area (Ys′skourd′), Phys. Geog. an area having surface features resulting from scouring by an advancing ice sheet during glaciation.

ice sheet, 1. a broad, thick sheet of ice covering an extensive area for a long period of time. **2.** a glacier covering a large fraction of a continent.

ice skate, (usually pl.) 1. a thin metal runner attached to the shoe, for skating on ice. **2.** a shoe fitted with such a runner.

ice-skate (Ys′skāt′), *v.i.* **-skated, -skating.** to skate on ice.

I·chang (ē′chäng′), *n.* a city in central China, in Hupeh province: a port on the Yangtze river. 81,000 (est. 1950).

ich dien (Ɣкн dēn′), *German.* I serve (motto of the Prince of Wales).

ich·neu·mon (Ɣk nū′mən, -nōō′-), *n.* **1.** a slender carnivorous mammal, *Herpestes ichneumon,* of Egypt, resembling the weasel in form and habits, but the size of a cat: said to devour crocodiles' eggs. **2.** an ichneumon fly. [t. L, t. Gk.: lit., tracker]

ichneumon fly, any insect belonging to the large hymenopterous family *Ichneumonidae,* whose larvae are parasites and destroy caterpillars and other larvae.

ich·nite (Ɣk′nīt), *n. Paleontol.* a fossil footprint. [f. s. Gk. *íchnos* track + -ɪᴛᴇ¹]

ich·nog·ra·phy (Ɣk nŏg′rə fĭ), *n., pl.* **-phies. 1.** the drawing of ground plans. **2.** a ground plan. [t. L: m.s. *ichnographia,* t. Gk.: a tracing out. See -ɢʀᴀᴘʜʏ] —**ich·no·graph·ic** (Ɣk′nə grăf′Ɣk), **ich′no·graph/i·cal,** *adj.*

i-chor¹ (Ī′kôr, Ī′kər), *n. Class. Myth.* an ethereal fluid supposed to flow in the veins of the gods. [t. Gk.]

i-chor² (Ī′kôr, Ī′kər), *n. Pathol.* an acrid watery discharge, as from an ulcer or wound. [NL, t. Gk.] —**i-chor·ous** (Ī′kər əs), *adj.*

ichth., ichthyology. Also, **ichthyol.**

ich·thy·ic (Ɣk′thĭ′Ɣk), *adj.* piscine. [t. Gk.: m. s. *ichthyïkós* fishy]

ichthyo-, a word element meaning "fish," as in *ichthyology.* Also, before vowels, **ichthy-.** [t. Gk., comb. form of *ichthýs*]

ich·thy·oid (Ɣk′thĭ oid′), *adj.* **1.** Also, **ich′thy·oi/dal.** fishlike. **—***n.* **2.** any fishlike vertebrate. [t. Gk.: m.s. *ichthyoeidḗs* fishlike. See -ᴏɪᴅ]

ich·thy·ol (Ɣk′thĭ ŏl′, -ôl′), *n. Pharm.* **1.** a dark-brown to black syrupy compound, $C_{28}H_{36}O_8S_3(NH_3)_2.2H_2O$, used as an astringent, antiseptic, and alterative, esp. for skin diseases. **2.** (*cap.*) a trademark for this drug. [f. ɪᴄʜᴛʜʏ- + -ᴏʟ²; so called because obtained from rocks containing fossilized fishes]

ich·thy·ol·o·gy (Ɣk′thĭ ŏl′ə jĭ), *n.* the branch of zoölogy that treats of fishes. —**ich·thy·o·log·ic** (Ɣk′thĭ ə lŏj′Ɣk), **ich·thy·o·log′i·cal,** *adj.* —**ich′thy·ol′o·gist,** *n.*

ich·thy·or·nis (Ɣk′thĭ ôr′nĭs), *n.* any of an extinct genus of toothed birds, *Ichthyornis,* with vertebrae resembling those of fishes. [NL, f. Gk.: *ichthy-* ɪᴄʜᴛʜʏ- + *órnis* bird]

ich·thy·o·saur (Ɣk′thĭ ə sôr′), *n.* any of an extinct order, *Ichthyosauria,* of marine reptiles, fishlike in form, ranging from 4 to 40 feet in length, with a round tapering body, a large head, four paddle-like flippers, and a vertical caudal fin. [t. NL: s. *ichthyosaurus,* f. Gk.: *ichthyo-* ɪᴄʜᴛʜʏᴏ- + m. *saûros* lizard]

Ichthyosaur,
Stenopterygius quadriscissus
(4 ft. long)

ich·thy·o·sau·rus (Ɣk′thĭ ə sôr′əs), *n., pl.* **-sauri** (-sôr′ī). ichthyosaur.

ich·thy·o·sis (Ɣk′thĭ ō′sĭs), *n. Pathol.* a congenital disease in which the epidermis continually flakes off in large scales or plates. —**ich·thy·ot·ic** (Ɣk′thĭ ŏt′Ɣk), *adj.*

-ician, a compound suffix especially applied to an expert in a field, as in *geometrician.* [f. -ɪᴄ + -ɪᴀɴ; r. ME *-icien,* t. OF]

i-ci-cle (Ī′sĭ kəl), *n.* a pendent tapering mass of ice formed by the freezing of dripping water. [ME *isykle,* OE *īsgicel,* f. *īs* ice + *gicel* icicle. Cf. Icel. *jökull* mass of ice, glacier] —**i′ci-cled,** *adj.*

i-ci-ly (Ī′sə lĭ), *adv.* in an icy manner.

i-ci-ness (Ī′sĭ nĭs), *n.* the state of being icy or very cold.

ic-ing (Ī′sĭng), *n.* a preparation of sugar, often made with egg whites, for covering cakes, etc.; frosting.

icing sugar, *Brit.* powdered sugar.

i·ci on parle fran·çais (ē sē′ ôn pàrl frän sĕ′), *French.* French spoken here.

ick·er (Ɣk′ər), *n. Scot.* the fruit-bearing spike of any cereal plant. [d. var. of ᴇᴀʀ², O Northumbrian *eher,* *æhher*]

Ick·es (Ɣk′ēz), *n.* **Harold LeClair,** 1874–1952, U.S. political official.

i-con (Ī′kŏn), *n., pl.* **icons, icones** (Ī′kə nēz′). **1.** a picture, image, or other representation. **2.** *Eastern Ch.* a representation in painting, enamel, etc., of some sacred personage, as Christ or a saint or angel, itself venerated as sacred. **3.** *Logic.* a sign or representation which stands for its object by virtue of a resemblance or analogy to it. Also, **eikon, ikon.** [t. L, t. Gk.: m. *eikṓn* likeness, image] —**Syn. 2.** See **image.**

i-con-ic (ī kŏn′Ɣk), *adj.* **1.** pertaining to or of the nature of an icon, portrait, or image. **2.** *Art.* (of statues, portraits, etc.) executed according to a convention or tradition. Also, **i·con/i·cal.** [t. L: s. *īconicus,* t. Gk.: m. *eikonikós* representing a figure, copied]

icono-, a word element meaning "likeness" or "image," as in *iconography.* [t. Gk., comb. form of *eikṓn*]

i-con-o-clasm (ī kŏn′ə klăz′əm), *n.* the action or spirit of iconoclasts.

i-con-o-clast (ī kŏn′ə klăst′), *n.* **1.** a breaker or destroyer of images, esp. those set up for religious veneration. **2.** one who attacks cherished beliefs as based on error or superstition. [t. LL: s. *īconoclastēs,* t. LGk.: m. *eikonoklástēs,* f. *eikono-* ɪᴄᴏɴᴏ- + *klástēs* breaker] —**i·con′o·clas′tic,** *adj.* —**i·con′o·clas′ti·cal·ly,** *adv.*

i·con·o·graph·ic (ī kŏn′ə grăf′Ɣk), *adj.* of or pertaining to icons. Also, **i·con·o·graph/i·cal.**

i·co·nog·ra·phy (ī′kə nŏg′rə fĭ), *n., pl.* **-phies. 1.** the making of an icon; representation by means of drawing, painting, or carving figures, etc. **2.** the subject matter of an icon, image, or representation, or of groups of them. **3.** the description or analysis of icons. [t. ML: m.s. *iconographia,* t. Gk.: m. *eikonographía.* See ɪᴄᴏɴᴏ-, -ɢʀᴀᴘʜʏ]

i·co·nol·a·try (ī′kə nŏl′ə trĭ), *n.* the worship or adoration of icons. —**i·co·nol·a·ter,** *n.*

i·co·nol·o·gy (ī′kə nŏl′ə jĭ), *n.* **1.** the branch of knowledge concerned with pictorial or sculptural representations. **2.** such representations collectively. **3.** symbolical representation. **4.** a description or interpretation of statues, pictures, etc. —**i·con·o·log·i·cal** (ī kŏn′ə lŏj′ə kəl), *adj.* —**i′co·nol′o·gist,** *n.*

i·con·o·scope (ī kŏn′ə skōp′), *n. Television.* **1.** the cathode-ray tube which focuses the optical image which the cathode-ray beam scans. **2.** (*cap.*) a trademark for this tube.

i·con·o·sta·sis (ī′kə nŏs′tə sĭs), *n., pl.* **-ses** (-sēz′). *Eastern Ch.* a partition or screen on which icons are placed, separating the sanctuary from the main part of the church. Also, **i·con·o·stas** (ī kŏn′ə stăs′). [NL, t. NGk.: m. *eikonóstasis,* f. Gk.: *eikono-* ɪᴄᴏɴᴏ- + *stásis* a standing, station]

i·co·sa·he·dron (ī′kō sə hē′drən), *n., pl.* **-drons, -dra** (-drə). a solid figure having twenty faces. [t. Gk.: m. *eikosáedron*] —**i′co·sa·he′dral,** *adj.*

Regular icosahedron

-ics, a suffix of nouns, originally plural as denoting things pertaining to a particular subject, but now mostly used as singular as denoting the body of matters, facts, knowledge, principles, etc., pertaining to a subject, and hence a science or art, as in *ethics, physics, politics, tactics.* [pl. of -ɪᴄ; orig. repr. Gk. *-iká* (in L *-ica*), prop. neut. pl. adj. suffix meaning (things) pertaining to]

ic·ter·ic (Ɣk tĕr′Ɣk), *adj. Pathol.* pertaining to or affected with icterus; jaundiced. Also, **ic·ter/i·cal.** [t. L: s. *ictericus,* t. Gk.: m. *ikterikós*]

ic·ter·us (Ɣk′tər əs), *n. Pathol.* jaundice. [NL, t. Gk.: m. *íkteros*]

ic·tus (Ɣk′təs), *n., pl.* **-tuses, -tus. 1.** *Pros.* rhythmical or metrical stress. **2.** *Pathol.* **a.** a fit. **b.** a stroke, as sunstroke. [t. L: blow, stroke]

i-cy (Ī′sĭ), *adj.,* **icier, iciest. 1.** made of or covered with ice. **2.** resembling ice. **3.** cold: *icy wind.* **4.** slippery: *icy road.* **5.** without warmth of feeling; frigid: *an icy stare.* [late ME *isy,* OE *īsig.* See ɪᴄᴇ, -ʏ¹]

id (Ɣd), *n. Psychoanal.* the part of the psyche residing in the unconscious which is the source of instinctive energy. Its impulses, which seek satisfaction in accordance with the pleasure principle, are modified by the ego and the superego before they are given overt expression. [special use of L *id* it, as trans. of G *es*]

I'd (īd), contraction of *I would, I should,* or *I had.*

-id¹, **1.** a noun suffix meaning "daughter of," as in *Nereid,* and used also (*Astron.*) to form names of meteors appearing to radiate in showers from particular constellations, etc., as in *Andromedid.* **2.** a suffix used in naming epics, as in *Aeneid.* [t. L: *-id-* (nom. *-is*), fem. patronymic suffix, t. Gk.]

-id², a suffix of nouns and adjectives indicating members of a zoölogical family, as in *cichlid,* or of some other group or division, as in *acarid, arachnid,* as in *NL: s. *-idae,* in zoölogical family names pl. of L *-idēs* (masc. patronymic suffix), t. Gk.; sometimes, t. NL: s. *-ida,* in group names, taken as neut. pl. of L *-idēs.* Cf. F *-ide*]

-id³, var. of **-ide,** as in *parotid.*

-id⁴, a quasi suffix common in adjectives, esp. of states which appeal to the senses, as in *torrid, acid.* [t. L: s. *-idus*]

id., idem.

I-da (Ī′də), *n.* **Mount. 1.** a peak in NW Asia Minor, overlooking the site of ancient Troy and the Aegean. 5810 ft. **2.** Modern name, **Mount Psiloriti:** the highest mountain of Crete.

Ida., Idaho. Also, **Id.**

-idae, *Zool.* a suffix of the names of families, as in *Canidae.* [(N)L, t. Gk.: m. *-idai,* pl. of *-idēs,* patronymic suffix]

I-da-ho (Ī′də hō′), *n.* a State in the NW United States. 667,191 pop. (1960); 83,557 sq. mi. *Cap.:* Boise. *Abbr.:* Id., Ida. —**I′da-ho′an,** *n., adj.*

-ide, a noun suffix in names of chemical compounds, as in *bromide.* Also, **-id.** [abstracted from ᴏxɪᴅᴇ]

i-de·a (ī dē′ə), *n.* **1.** any conception existing in the mind as the result of mental apprehension or activity. **2.** a thought, conception, or notion: *what an ideal* **3.** an impression: *a general idea of what it's like.* **4.** an opinion, view, or belief. **5.** a plan of action; an intention: *the idea of becoming an engineer.* **6.** a fantasy. **7.** *Philos.* **a.** a concept developed by the mind (if empirical, in close connection with sense perception). **b.** a conception of what is desirable, or what ought to be; a governing conception or principle; ideal. **c.** (in Platonic philosophy) an archetype or pattern of which the individual objects in any natural class are imperfect copies and from which

b., blend of, blended; **c.,** cognate with; **d.,** dialect, dialectal; **der.,** derived from; **f.,** formed from; **g.,** going back to; **m.,** modification of; **r.,** replacing; **s.,** stem of; **t.,** taken from; **?,** perhaps. See the full key on inside cover.

they derive their being. **8.** *Music.* a theme, phrase, or figure. **9.** *Obs.* a likeness. **10.** *Obs.* a mental image. [t. L, t. Gk., der. *ideīn* see; orig. in def. **7c.**] —**i·de′a·less,** *adj.*

i·de·al (Idē′əl, idēl′), *n.* **1.** a conception of something in its highest perfection. **2.** a standard of perfection or excellence. **3.** a person or thing regarded as realizing such a conception or conforming to such a standard, and taken as a model for imitation. **4.** an ultimate object or aim of endeavor, esp. one of high or noble character. **5.** that which exists only in idea. —*adj.* **6.** conceived as constituting a standard of perfection or excellence: *ideal beauty.* **7.** regarded as perfect in its kind: *an ideal spot for a home.* **8.** existing only in idea. **9.** not real or practical; visionary. **10.** based upon an ideal or ideals: *the ideal school in art.* **11.** *Philos.* **a.** existing as an archetype or Platonic idea. **b.** pertaining to a possible state of affairs considered as highly desirable. **c.** pertaining to or of the nature of idealism. [t. LL: s. *ideālis.* der. L *idea* IDEA] —**i·de′al·ness,** *n.*
—**Syn. 1, 2.** IDEAL, EXAMPLE, MODEL refer to something considered as a standard to strive toward or something considered worthy of imitation. An IDEAL is a concept or standard of perfection, existing merely as an image in the mind, or based upon a person or upon conduct: *the high ideals of a religious person; Sir Philip Sidney was considered the ideal in gentlemanly conduct.* An EXAMPLE is a person or his conduct or achievements regarded as worthy of being followed or imitated in a general way; or sometimes, as properly to be avoided: *an example of courage; a bad example to one's children.* A MODEL is primarily a physical shape to be closely copied, but is also a pattern for exact imitation in conduct or character: *they took their leader as a model.*

i·de·al·ise (Idē′əlīz′), *v.t., v.i.,* -**ised,** -**ising.** *Chiefly Brit.* idealize.

i·de·al·ism (Idē′əlĭz′əm), *n.* **1.** the cherishing or pursuing of ideals, as for attainment. **2.** the practice of idealizing. **3.** something idealized; an ideal representation. **4.** the imaginative treatment of subjects in art or literature, usually on a high ethical plane and devoid of accidental details (opposed to *realism*). **5.** *Philos.* **a.** any system or theory which maintains that the real is of the nature of thought, or that the object of external perception consists of ideas. **b.** the tendency to represent things in an ideal form, or as they might be rather than as they are, with emphasis on values.

i·de·al·ist (Idē′əlĭst), *n.* **1.** one who cherishes or pursues ideals, as for attainment. **2.** a visionary or unpractical person. **3.** one who represents things as they might be rather than as they are. **4.** a writer or artist who treats subjects imaginatively. **5.** one who accepts the doctrines of idealism. —*adj.* **6.** idealistic.

i·de·al·is·tic (Idē′əlĭs′tĭk), *adj.* pertaining to idealism or to idealists. —**i·de′al·is′ti·cal·ly,** *adv.*

i·de·al·i·ty (Ī′dĭăl′ətĭ), *n., pl.* -**ties.** **1.** ideal quality or character. **2.** capacity to idealize. **3.** *Philos.* state of existing only in idea and not in actuality.

i·de·al·ize (Idē′əlīz′), *v.,* -**ized,** -**izing.** —*v.t.* **1.** to make ideal; represent in an ideal form or character; exalt to an ideal perfection or excellence. —*v.i.* **2.** to represent something in an ideal form; imagine or form an ideal or ideals. Also, *esp. Brit.,* **idealise.** —**i·de′al·i·za·tion,** *n.* —**i·de′al·iz′er,** *n.*

i·de·al·ly (Idē′əlĭ), *adv.* **1.** in accordance with an ideal; perfectly. **2.** in idea, thought, or imagination.

ideal type, *Sociol.* an imaginary construction of what an object would be if it were allowed to develop without any interference from accidental or irrelevant factors.

i·de·ate (*v.* Idē′āt; *n.* Idē′ĭt, -āt), *v.,* -**ated,** -**ating,** *n.* —*v.t.* **1.** to form in idea, thought, or imagination. —*v.i.* **2.** to form ideas; think. —*n.* **3.** *Philos.* the external object of which an idea is formed. —**i′de·a′tion,** *n.* —**i′de·a′tion·al,** *adj.* —**i′de·a′tion·al·ly,** *adv.*

i·dée fixe (ēdē fēks′), *French.* a fixed idea; obsession.

i·dem (Ī′dĕm, Ĭd′ĕm), *pron., adj. Latin.* the same as previously given or mentioned.

i·den·tic (Idĕn′tĭk), *adj.* **1.** identical. **2.** *Diplomacy.* (of action, notes, etc.) identical in form, as when two or more governments deal simultaneously with another government. [t. ML: s. *identicus*]

i·den·ti·cal (Idĕn′təkəl), *adj.* **1.** agreeing exactly. **2.** same, or being the same one. [f. IDENTIC + -AL¹. See IDENTITY] —**i·den′ti·cal·ly,** *adv.* —**i·den′ti·cal·ness,** *n.*

identical classes, *Logic.* classes denoted by two terms whose extensions contain the same individuals as members.

identical proposition, a proposition expressed by two sentences having the same meaning.

identical twin, one of a pair of twins of the same sex which develop from one fertilized ovum.

i·den·ti·fi·ca·tion (Idĕn′təfəkā′shən), *n.* **1.** act of identifying. **2.** state of being identified. **3.** something that identifies one: *have you any identification?*

i·den·ti·fy (Idĕn′təfī′), *v.,* -**fied,** -**fying.** —*v.t.* **1.** to recognize or establish as being a particular person or thing; attest or prove to be as purported or asserted: *to identify handwriting, identify the bearer of a check.* **2.** *Biol.* to determine to what group (a given specimen) belongs. **3.** to make, represent to be, or regard or treat as the same or identical. **4.** to associate in feeling, interest, action, etc. (fol. by *with*). **5.** *Psychol.* to make (oneself) one with another person by putting oneself in his place. **6.** to serve as a means of identification for. —*v.i.* **7.** to make oneself one with another or others. —**i·den′ti·fi′a·ble,** *adj.* —**i·den′ti·fi′er,** *n.*

i·den·ti·ty (Idĕn′tətĭ), *n., pl.* -**ties.** **1.** state or fact of remaining the same one, as under varying aspects or conditions. **2.** the condition of being oneself or itself, and not another: *he doubted his own identity.* **3.** condition or character as to who a person or what a thing is: *a case of mistaken identity.* **4.** state or fact of being the same one. **5.** exact likeness in nature or qualities. **6.** an instance or point of sameness or likeness. [t. LL: m.s. *identitas,* appar. f. L *identi-* (as in *identidem* repeatedly), for *īdem* the same + *-tas* -TY²]

ideo-, a word element meaning "idea," as in *ideograph.* [t. Gk., comb. form of *idéa* idea]

id·e·o·graph (Ĭd′Ĭəgrăf′, -gräf′, Ī′dĬ-), *n.* a written symbol which represents something in the nonsymbolic world directly instead of standing for a sound of a word in the language of its users. Also, **id·e·o·gram** (Ĭd′Ĭəgrăm′, Ī′dĬ-). —**id′e·o·graph′ic, id′e·o·graph′i·cal,** *adj.* —**id′e·o·graph′i·cal·ly,** *adv.*

id·e·og·ra·phy (Ĭd′Ĭŏg′rəfĬ, Ī′dĬ-), *n.* the use of ideographs.

i·de·o·log·ic (Ī′dĬəlŏj′Ĭk, Ĭd′Ĭ-), *adj.* **1.** pertaining to ideology. **2.** speculative; visionary. Also, **i′de·o·log′i·cal.** —**i′de·o·log′i·cal·ly,** *adv.*

i·de·ol·o·gist (Ī′dĬŏl′əjĬst, Ĭd′Ĭ-), *n.* **1.** an expert in ideology. **2.** one who deals with systems of ideas. **3.** a visionary.

i·de·ol·o·gy (Ī′dĬŏl′əjĬ, Ĭd′Ĭ-), *n., pl.* -**gies.** **1.** the body of doctrine, myth, and symbols of a social movement, institution, class, or large group. **2.** such a body of doctrine, etc., with reference to some political and cultural plan, as that of fascism, along with the devices for putting it into operation. **3.** *Philos.* **a.** the science of ideas. **b.** a system which derives ideas exclusively from sensation. **4.** theorizing of a visionary or unpractical nature.

ides (īdz), *n.pl.* (in the ancient Roman calendar) the 15th day of March, May, July, or October, and the 13th day of the other months. [t. F, t. L: m. *īdūs,* pl.]

id est (Ĭd ĕst′), *Latin.* that is.

idio-, a word element meaning "peculiar" or "proper to one," as in *idiosyncrasy.* [t. Gk., comb. form of *ídios* own, private, peculiar]

id·i·o·blast (Ĭd′Ĭəblăst′), *n. Bot.* a cell which differs greatly from the surrounding cells or tissue.

id·i·o·cy (Ĭd′ĬəsĬ), *n., pl.* -**cies.** **1.** the condition of being an idiot; extreme degree of mental deficiency. **2.** senseless folly. [? t. Gk.: m.s. *idiōteia* uncouthness, defenseless condition; or der. IDIOT, on model of *prophecy* from *prophet*]

id·i·o·graph·ic (Ĭd′Ĭəgrăf′Ĭk), *adj. Psychol.* pertaining to the intensive study of an individual case, as a personality or social situation (opposed to *nomothetic*).

id·i·om (Ĭd′Ĭəm), *n.* **1.** a form of expression peculiar to a language. **2.** a variety or form of a language; a dialect. **3.** the language peculiar to a people. **4.** the peculiar character or genius of a language. **5.** a distinct style or character, as in music, art, etc.: *the idiom of Bach.* [t. LL: m.s. *idiōma,* t. Gk.: a peculiarity]

id·i·o·mat·ic (Ĭd′Ĭəmăt′Ĭk), *adj.* **1.** peculiar to or characteristic of a particular language. **2.** exhibiting the characteristic modes of expression of a language. Also, **id′i·o·mat′i·cal.** [t. Gk.: m.s. *idiōmatikós*] —**id′i·o·mat′i·cal·ness,** *n.*

id·i·o·mor·phic (Ĭd′Ĭəmôr′fĬk), *adj.* **1.** noting or pertaining to a mineral constituent of a rock, which has its own characteristic outward crystalline form, and not one forced upon it by the other constituents of the rock. **2.** having its own form. —**id′i·o·mor′phi·cal·ly,** *adv.*

id·i·o·path·ic (Ĭd′Ĭəpăth′Ĭk), *adj. Pathol.* of unknown cause, as a disease.

id·i·op·a·thy (Ĭd′Ĭŏp′əthĬ), *n., pl.* -**thies.** *Pathol.* a disease not preceded or occasioned by any other. [t. Gk.: m.s. *idiopátheia.* See IDIO-, -PATHY]

id·i·o·phone (Ĭd′Ĭəfōn′), *n. Music.* an instrument made of some solid, naturally sonorous material, as cymbals, xylophones, glass harmonicas, etc.

id·i·o·plasm (Ĭd′Ĭəplăz′əm), *n. Biol.* germ plasm. —**id′i·o·plas′mic, id·i·o·plas·mat·ic** (Ĭd′Ĭəplăz măt′Ĭk), *adj.*

id·i·o·syn·cra·sy (Ĭd′ĬəsĬng′krəsĬ, -sĬn′-), *n., pl.* -**sies.** **1.** any tendency, characteristic, mode of expression, or the like, peculiar to an individual. **2.** the physical constitution peculiar to an individual. **3.** a peculiarity of the physical or the mental constitution, esp. susceptibility toward drugs, food, etc. See **allergy** (def. 1). [t. Gk.: m.s. *idiosynkrāsia*] —**id·i·o·syn·crat·ic** (Ĭd′ĬəsĬn krăt′Ĭk), *adj.* —**id′i·o·syn·crat′i·cal·ly,** *adv.*

id·i·ot (Ĭd′Ĭət), *n.* **1.** an utterly foolish or senseless person. **2.** one hopelessly deficient, esp. from birth, in the ordinary mental powers; one lacking the capacity to develop beyond the mental level of three or four years. [ME, t. L: s. *idiōta,* t. Gk.: m. *idiōtēs* a private, nonprofessional, or ignorant person]

id·i·ot·ic (Ĭd′Ĭŏt′Ĭk), *adj.* of or like an idiot; senselessly foolish. Also, **id′i·ot′i·cal.** [t. LL: s. *idioticus,* t. Gk.: m. *idiōtikós* private, unskillful] —**id′i·ot′i·cal·ly,** *adv.* —**Syn.** half-witted, stupid. —**Ant.** intelligent.

id·i·ot·ism (Ĭd′ĬətĬz′əm), *n.* **1.** idiotic conduct or action. **2.** idiocy. **3.** *Obs.* an idiom. [f. IDIOT + ISM; in def. 3. t. F: m. *idiotisme,* t. LL: m.s. *idiōtismus* a common way of speaking, t. Gk.: m.s. *idiōtismós* common manners]

-idium, a diminutive suffix (Latinization of Greek *-idion*) used in zoölogical, biological, botanical, anatomical, and chemical terms.

i·dle (ī′dəl), *adj.,* idler, idlest, *v.,* idled, idling. —*adj.* **1.** unemployed, or doing nothing: *idle workmen.* **2.** unoccupied, as time: *idle hours.* **3.** not kept busy or in use or operation: *idle machinery.* **4.** habitually doing nothing or avoiding work. **5.** of no real worth, importance, or significance: *idle talk.* **6.** baseless or groundless: *idle fears.* **7.** frivolous or vain: *idle pleasures.* **8.** futile or ineffective: *idle threats.* **9.** useless: *idle rage.* —*v.i.* **10.** to pass time in idleness. **11.** to move, loiter, or saunter idly. **12.** *Mach.* to operate, usually at minimum speed, while the transmission is disengaged. —*v.t.* **13.** to pass (time) in idleness. **14.** to cause (a person) to be idle. [ME and OE ĭdel, c. G *eitel*] —**i′dle·ness,** *n.* —**i′dly,** *adv.*
—**Syn. 1.** IDLE, INDOLENT, LAZY, SLOTHFUL apply to one who is not active. To be IDLE is to be inactive or not working at a job. The word may be derogatory, but not necessarily so, since one may be relaxing temporarily or may be idle through necessity: *pleasantly idle on a vacation, to be idle because one is unemployed or because supplies are lacking.* The INDOLENT person is naturally disposed to avoid exertion: *indolent and slow in movement, an indolent and contented fisherman.* The LAZY person is averse to exertion or work, and esp. to continued application; the word is usually derogatory: *too lazy to earn a living; incurably lazy.* SLOTHFUL denotes a reprehensible unwillingness to do such work as is demanded of man: *so slothful as to be a burden on others.*

idle pulley, *Mach.* a loose pulley made to press or rest on a belt in order to tighten or guide it.

i·dler (ī′dlər), *n.* **1.** one who idles. **2.** *Mach.* an idle pulley or wheel. **3.** *Railroads.* an empty car.

i·dlesse (ī′dlĕs), *n.* *Poetic.* idleness.

idle wheel, *Mach.* **1.** a cogwheel placed between two other cogwheels in order to transfer the motion of one to the other without changing the direction of rotation. **2.** an idle pulley.

I·dle·wild (ī′dəl wīld′), *n.* former name of John F. Kennedy International Airport.

I. Idle wheel; C, Cogwheel

I·do (ē′dō), *n.* a revised and simplified form of Esperanto, put forth in 1907.

i·do·crase (ī′də krās′, ĭd′ə-), *n.* the mineral vesuvianite. [t. F, f. Gk.: m. *eidos* form + m. *krasis* mixture]

i·dol (ī′dəl), *n.* **1.** an image or other material object representing a deity to which religious worship is addressed. **2.** *Bible.* a false god, as of a heathen people. **3.** any person or thing blindly adored or revered: *a matinee idol.* **4.** a mere image or semblance of something, visible but without substance, as a phantom. **5.** a figment of the mind. **6.** a false conception or notion; fallacy. [ME, t. OF: m. *idole*, t. L: m. *īdōlum*, t. Gk.: m. *eidōlon* image, phantom, idol] —**Syn. 1.** See image.

i·dol·a·ter (ī dŏl′ə tər), *n.* **1.** a worshiper of idols. **2.** an adorer or devotee. Also, **i·dol·ist** (ī′dəl ĭst). [ME *idolatrer*, t. OF: m. *idolatre*, g. LL *īdōlolatrēs*, t. Gk.: m. *eidōlolátrēs* idol worshiper] —**i·dol·a·tress** (ī dŏl′ə trĭs), *n. fem.*

i·dol·a·trize (ī dŏl′ə trīz′), *v.,* **-trized, -trizing.** —*v.t.* **1.** to idolize. —*v.i.* **2.** to worship idols.

i·dol·a·trous (ī dŏl′ə trəs), *adj.* **1.** pertaining to or of the nature of idolatry. **2.** worshiping idols. **3.** used in or designed for idolatry. **4.** blindly adoring. —**i·dol′a·trous·ly,** *adv.* —**i·dol′a·trous·ness,** *n.*

i·dol·a·try (ī dŏl′ə trĭ), *n., pl.* **-tries.** **1.** the worship of idols. **2.** blind adoration, reverence, or devotion. [ME *idolatrie*, t. OF, g. LL *īdōlolatria*, t. Gk.: m. *eidōlolatreía*]

i·dol·ism (ī′də lĭz′əm), *n.* **1.** idolatry. **2.** idolizing.

i·dol·ize (ī′də līz′), *v.t.,* **-ized, -izing.** to regard with blind adoration or devotion. Also, *esp. Brit.,* **i′dol·ise′.** —**i′dol·i·za′tion,** *n.* —**i′dol·iz′er,** *n.*

I·dom·e·neus (ī dŏm′ə nūs′, -nōōs′), *n. Gk. Legend.* a Cretan king and important chief of the Greek army in the Trojan War.

i·do·ne·ous (ī dō′nĭ əs), *adj.* fit. [t. L: m. *idōneus*]

I·du·mae·a (ĭd′yŏŏ mē′ə, ī′dyŏŏ-), *n.* Greek name of Edom. Also, **Id′u·me′a.** —**Id′u·mae′an,** *adj., n.*

I·dun (ē′dŏŏn), *n. Scand. Myth.* Ithunn.

i·dyl (ī′dəl), *n.* **1.** a poem or prose composition consisting of a "little picture," usually describing pastoral scenes or events or any charmingly simple episode, appealing incident, or the like. **2.** a simple descriptive or narrative piece in verse or prose. **3.** material suitable for an idyl. **4.** an episode or scene of idyllic charm. **5.** *Music.* a composition, usually instrumental, of a pastoral or sentimental character. Also, **i′dyll.** [t. L: m.s. *īdyllium*, t. Gk.: m. *eidýllion,* dim. of *eidos* form]

i·dyl·ist (ī′dəl ĭst), *n.* a writer of idyls. Also, *esp. Brit.,* **i′dyll·ist.**

i·dyl·lic (ī dĭl′ĭk), *adj.* **1.** suitable for or suggestive of an idyl; charmingly simple or poetic. **2.** of, pertaining to, or of the nature of an idyl. —**i·dyl′li·cal·ly,** *adv.*

-ie, a hypocoristic suffix of nouns, same as **-y²,** as in *dearie, laddie, Willie.*

IE, Indo-European. Also, **I.E.**

i.e., id est.

Ie·per (ē′pər), *n.* Flemish name of Ypres.

-ier, var. of **-eer,** as in *brigadier, halberdier,* etc. [t. F g. L *-ārius*]

if (ĭf), *conj.* **1.** in case that; granting or supposing that on condition that. **2.** even though. **3.** whether. —*n.* **4.** a condition; a supposition. [ME; OE *gif,* c. Icel. *if* later *ef* (also used as n., *ef* doubt)]
—**Syn. 1, 2.** IF, PROVIDED, PROVIDING imply a condition on which something depends. IF is general. It may be used to indicate suppositions or hypothetical condition (often involving doubt or uncertainty): *if you like, we can go straight home; if I had known, I wouldn't have gone.* IF may mean "even though": *if I am wrong, you are not right.* I may mean "whenever": *if I do not understand, I ask questions.* PROVIDED always indicates some stipulation: *I will subscribe ten dollars provided that you do, too; provided he goes, we can go along.* PROVIDING means "just in case some certain thing should happen": *providing he should come we must have extra supplies ready.*

if·fy (ĭf′ĭ), *adj. Colloq.* indefinite; doubtful.

If·ni (ēf′nē), *n.* a Spanish colony on the NW coast o Africa. 34,115 pop. (est. 1951); 741 sq. mi.

I.F.S., Irish Free State.

-ify, var. of **-fy,** used when preceding stem or word element ends in a consonant, as in *intensify.* [f. -I- + -FY]

I.G., **1.** Indo-Germanic. **2.** Inspector General.

Ig·dra·sil (ĭg′drə sĭl), *n. Scand. Myth.* Ygdrasil.

ig·loo (ĭg′lōō), *n., pl.* **-loos. 1.** an Eskimo hut, dome shaped, built of blocks of hard snow. **2.** an excavation made by a seal in the snow over its breathing hole in the ice. Also, **ig′lu.** [t. Eskimo: house]

Ig·na·tius (ĭg nā′shəs), *n.* **Saint,** (*Ignatius Theophorus* died A.D. c107?, bishop of Antioch; Christian martyr

Ignatius of Loy·o·la (loi ō′lə), **Saint,** (*Iñigo Lōpe de Recalde*) 1491–1556, Spanish soldier and priest founder of the Jesuit order.

ig·ne·ous (ĭg′nĭ əs), *adj.* **1.** *Geol.* produced under con ditions involving intense heat, as rocks of volcanic origi or rocks crystallized from molten magma. **2.** pertaining to or of the nature of fire. [t. L: m. *igneus* of fire]

igneous rock, See rock¹ (def. 2a).

ig·nes·cent (ĭg nĕs′ənt), *adj.* **1.** emitting sparks o fire, as certain stones when struck with steel. **2.** burst ing into flame. —*n.* **3.** an ignescent substance. [t. L s. *ignescens,* ppr., taking fire]

ig·nis fat·u·us (ĭg′nĭs făch′ōō əs), *pl.* **ignes fatu** (ĭg′nēz făch′ōō ī′). **1.** a flitting phosphorescent ligh seen at night, chiefly over marshy ground, and supposed to be due to spontaneous combustion of gas from de composed organic matter; a will-o′-the-wisp. **2.** some thing deluding or misleading. [NL: foolish fire]

ig·nite (ĭg nīt′), *v.,* **-nited, -niting.** —*v.t.* **1.** to set on fire; kindle. **2.** *Chem.* to heat intensely; roast. —*v.i.* **3** to take fire; begin to burn. [t. L: m.s. *ignītus,* pp. —**ig·nit′a·ble, ig·nit′i·ble,** *adj.* —**ig·nit′a·bil′i·ty ig·nit′i·bil′i·ty,** *n.* —**Syn. 1.** See kindle.

ig·nit·er (ĭg nī′tər), *n.* **1.** one who or that which ignites. **2.** *Electronics.* the carborundum rod used to initiate the discharge in an ignitron tube.

ig·ni·tion (ĭg nĭsh′ən), *n.* **1.** act of igniting. **2.** state of being ignited. **3.** (in an internal-combustion engine) the process which ignites the fuel in the cylinder. **4.** means or device for igniting.

ig·ni·tron (ĭg nī′trŏn, ĭg′nə trŏn), *n. Electronics.* a mer cury-pool cathode-arc rectifier with a carborundum roc projecting into the mercury pool. The tube conducts current when the anode is positive.

ig·no·ble (ĭg nō′bəl), *adj.* **1.** of low character, aims etc.; mean; base. **2.** of low grade or quality; inferior **3.** not noble; of humble birth or station. **4.** *Falconry* denoting short-winged hawks which chase or rake afte the quarry (opposite to *noble*). [t. L: m.s. *ignōbilis* unknown, low-born] —**ig′no·bil′i·ty, ig·no′ble·ness** *n.* —**ig·no′bly,** *adv.* —**Syn. 1.** degraded, dishonor able, contemptible, vulgar. **3.** lowly, obscure, plebeian

ig·no·min·i·ous (ĭg′nə mĭn′ĭ əs), *adj.* **1.** marked by or attended with ignominy; discreditable; humiliating *an ignominious retreat.* **2.** covered with or deserving ignominy; contemptible. [t. L: m.s. *ignōminiōsus]* —**ig′no·min′i·ous·ly,** *adv.* —**ig′no·min′i·ous·ness,** *n.*

ig·no·min·y (ĭg′nə mĭn′ĭ), *n., pl.* **-minies. 1.** dis grace; dishonor; public contempt. **2.** base quality or conduct; a cause of disgrace. [t. L: m.s. *ignōminia* disgrace, dishonor] —**Syn. 1.** See disgrace.

ig·no·ra·mus (ĭg′nə rā′məs), *n., pl.* **-muses.** an igno rant person. [t. L: we do not know, we disregard]

ig·no·rance (ĭg′nə rəns), *n.* state or fact of being ignorant; lack of knowledge, learning, or information

ig·no·rant (ĭg′nə rənt), *adj.* **1.** destitute of knowledge unlearned. **2.** lacking knowledge or information as to a particular subject or fact. **3.** uninformed; unaware. **4.** due to or showing lack of knowledge: *an ignoran statement.* [ME, t. L: s. *ignōrans,* ppr., not knowing —**ig′no·rant·ly,** *adv.*
—**Syn. 1, 2.** IGNORANT, ILLITERATE, UNLETTERED, UNEDU CATED mean lacking in knowledge or in training. IGNORANT may mean knowing little or nothing, or it may mean un informed about a particular subject: *an ignorant person can be dangerous; to be ignorant of mathematics.* ILLITERATE originally meant lacking a knowledge of literature or simila learning, but is specifically applied to one unable to read or write: *the illiterate voter; necessary training for illiterate soldiers.* UNLETTERED is a translation of the word ILLITER ATE, but emphasizes the idea of being without knowledge of or love of literature: *unlettered though highly trained i*

science. Uneducated refers especially to lack of schooling or to lack of access to a body of knowledge equivalent to that learned in schools: *uneducated but highly intelligent.*

ig·nore (ig nōr′), *v.t.*, **-nored, -noring. 1.** to refrain from noticing or recognizing: *ignore his remarks.* **2.** *Law.* (of the grand jury) to reject (a bill of indictment) as without sufficient evidence. [t. L: m.s. *ignōrāre* not to know, disregard] —**ig·nor′er,** *n.* —**Syn. 1.** overlook; slight, disregard.

Ig·o·rot (ig′ə rōt′, ē′gə-), *n., pl.* **-rot, -rots.** a member of a people of the Malay stock in northern Luzon, Philippine Islands, comprising various tribes, some noted as head-hunters. Also **Ig·or·ro·te** (ē′gôr rō′tē). [t. Sp.: m. *igorrote,* from native name]

I·graine (ī grān′), *n. Arthurian Romance.* the mother of King Arthur. Also, **Ygerne.**

i·gua·na (i gwä′nə), *n.* **1.** any lizard of the genus *Iguana* of tropical America, esp. *I. iguana,* a large, arboreal, herbivorous species 5 feet or more in length, esteemed as food. **2.** a lizard of a related genus. [t. Sp.: from Carib name] —**i·gua·ni·an** (i gwä′nĭ ən), *adj., n.*

i·guan·o·don (i gwän′ə dŏn′), *n.* any member of the extinct bipedal dinosaurian genus *Iguanodon,* found fossil in Europe, comprising reptiles from 15 to 30 feet long, with denticulate teeth like those of the iguana. [f. iguan(a) + m.s. Gk. *odoús* tooth]

I·guas·sú (ē′gwä sōō′), *n.* a river in S Brazil, flowing W to the Paraná river. 380 mi.

Iguassú Falls, falls of great volume on the Iguassú river, on the boundary between Brazil and Argentina. 210 ft. high. Also, **Victoria Falls.**

I.G.Y., International Geophysical Year.

ih·ram (ē räm′), *n.* the dress worn by Mohammedan pilgrims to Mecca, consisting of two white cotton cloths, one round the waist, the other over the left shoulder. [t. Ar., der. *ḥarama* forbid]

IHS, shortening of Greek ΙΗΣΟΤΣ Jesus, sometimes taken as representing: **1.** (L *Iesus Hominum Salvator*) Jesus, Saviour of Men. **2.** (L *In Hoc Signo Vinces*) In this sign (the cross) shalt thou conquer. **3.** (L *In Hoc Salus*) in this (cross) is salvation.

IJs·sel (ī′səl), *n.* a branch of the Rhine in central Netherlands, flowing N to Ijssel Lake. 70 mi.

IJssel Lake, a lake in NW Netherlands: created by diking of the Zuider Zee. 465 sq. mi. Dutch, **IJsselmeer.**

Ikh·na·ton (ĭk nä′tən), *n.* See **Amenhotep IV.**

i·kon (ī′kŏn), *n.* icon.

il-¹, var. of **in-²,** (by assimilation) before *l,* as in *illation.*

il-², var. of **in-³,** (by assimilation) before *l,* as in *illogical.*

-il, var. of **-ile,** as in *civil.*

Il, *Chem.* illinium.

i·lang-i·lang (ē′läng ē′läng), *n.* ylang-ylang.

-ile, a suffix of adjectives expressing capability, susceptibility, liability, aptitude, etc., as in *agile, docile, ductile, fragile, prehensile, tensile, volatile.* Also, **-il.** [t. L: m.s. *-ilis;* also used to repr. L *-īlis*]

il·e·ac (ĭl′ĭ ăk′), *adj.* of or pertaining to the ileum. [t. LL: s. *iliacus* pertaining to the flank, der. L *īlium*]

Ile de France (ēl də fräns′), **1.** a former province in N France, including Paris and the region around it. **2.** former name of **Mauritius.**

Ile du Dia·ble (ēl dy dyä′bl), French name of **Devil's Island.**

il·e·i·tis (ĭl′ĭ ī′tĭs), *n.* inflammation of the ileum, of uncertain origin.

ileo-, a word element meaning "ileum," as in *ileostomy.* [t. L, comb. form of *ileum* groin, flank]

il·e·os·to·my (ĭl′ĭ ŏs′tə mĭ), *n., pl.* **-mies.** *Surg.* the formation of an artificial opening into the ileum.

il·e·um (ĭl′ĭ əm), *n.* **1.** *Anat.* the third and lowest division of the small intestine, continuous with the jejunum and ending at the caecum. See diag. under **intestine. 2.** *Entomol.* a narrower part of the intestine of an insect, following the stomach. [NL, in LL groin, flank, in L (usually pl.) *ilia* flanks, entrails]

il·e·us (ĭl′ĭ əs), *n. Pathol.* severe colic attended with vomiting, etc., due to intestinal obstruction. [t. L, t. Gk.: m. *ileós,* var. of *eileós* colic]

i·lex (ī′lĕks), *n.* **1.** the holm oak. **2.** any tree or shrub of the genus *Ilex.* **3.** holly. [NL: the holly genus, L the holm oak]

il·ford (ĭl′fərd), *n.* a city in SE England, in Essex, near London. 180,600 (est. 1956).

il·i·ac (ĭl′ĭ ăk′), *adj.* of or pertaining to the ilium. [t. LL: s. *iliacus* pertaining to the flank, der. L *īlium*]

Il·i·ad (ĭl′ĭ əd), *n.* **1.** Greek epic poem describing the siege of Troy, ascribed to Homer. **2.** any similar poem; a long narrative. **3.** a long series of woes, etc. [t. L: s *Ilias,* t. Gk., der. *Ilion* Ilium, Troy] —**Il′i·ad′ic,** *adj.*

Il·i·on (ĭl′ĭ ən), *n.* Greek name of ancient **Troy.**

-ility, a compound suffix making abstract nouns from adjectives by replacing the adj. suffixes: *-il(e), -le,* as in *civility, sterility, ability.* [t. F: m. *-ilité,* t. L: m. *-ilitas*]

Il·i·um (ĭl′ĭ əm), *n.* Latin name of ancient **Troy.**

il·i·um (ĭl′ĭ əm), *n., pl.* **ilia** (ĭl′ĭ ə). *Anat.* the broad upper portion of either innominate bone. See diag. under **pelvis.** [NL, special use of L *īlium* flank]

ilk (ĭlk), *adj.* **1.** same. **2.** *Scot.* and *N. Eng.* each; every. —*n.* **3.** family, class, or kind: *he and all his ilk.* [ME *ilk,* OE *elc, ylc,* var. of *ǣlc* each]

ilk·a (ĭl′kə), *adj. Scot.* and *N. Eng.* ilk. [f. ilk + a¹ (indef. art.)]

ill (ĭl), *adj.,* **worse, worst,** *n., adv.* —*adj.* **1.** physically disordered, as the health; unwell, sick, or indisposed. **2.** evil, wicked, or bad: *ill repute.* **3.** objectionable, unsatisfactory, poor, or faulty: *ill manners.* **4.** hostile or unkindly: *ill feeling.* **5.** unfavorable or adverse: *ill luck.* **6.** unskillful; inexpert. —*n.* **7.** evil. **8.** harm or injury. **9.** a disease or ailment. **10.** trouble or misfortune. **11.** *Archaic.* wickedness or sin. —*adv.* **12.** in an ill manner; wickedly. **13.** unsatisfactorily or poorly: *ill at ease.* **14.** in a hostile or unfriendly manner. **15.** unfavorably or unfortunately. **16.** with displeasure or offense. **17.** faultily or improperly. **18.** with trouble, difficulty, or inconvenience: *Buying a new car is an expense we can ill afford.* [ME *ill,* t. Scand.; cf. Icel. *illr* ill, bad]
—**Syn. 1.** ill, sick mean being in bad health, not being well. ill is the more formal word. In the U.S. the two words are used practically interchangeably except that sick is always used when the word modifies the following noun or is used as a collective noun: *he is very sick (ill) of a fever; he looks sick (ill); a sick person; a home for the sick.* There are certain phrases, also, in which sick is used: *sick at heart; sick for home; it makes me sick.* In England, sick is not interchangeable with ill, but usually has the connotation of nausea; sick is however used before nouns, in the collective, and in set phrases, just as in the U.S.: *he is ill, she felt ill, he looks ill; a sick man, to care for the sick,* and the like. **2.** See **bad¹.** —**Ant. 1.** well, healthy.

I'll (īl), contraction of *I will* or *I shall.*

Ill., Illinois.

ill., 1. illustrated. **2.** illustration.

ill-ad·vised (ĭl′əd vīzd′), *adj.* acting or done without due consideration; imprudent. —**ill-ad·vis·ed·ly** (ĭl′əd vī′zĭd lĭ), *adv.*

Il·lam·pu (ē yäm′pōō), *n.* See **Sorata, Mount.**

ill-at-ease (ĭl′ət ēz′), *adj.* uncomfortable; uneasy.

il·la·tion (ĭ lā′shən), *n.* **1.** act of inferring. **2.** an inference or conclusion. [t. LL: s. *illātio* a carrying in]

il·la·tive (ĭl′ə tĭv, ĭ lā′tĭv), *adj.* pertaining to or expressing illation; inferential: *an illative word such as "therefore."* [t. L: m.s. *illātivus*] —**il′la·tive·ly,** *adv.*

il·laud·a·ble (ĭ lô′də bəl), *adj.* not laudable. —**il·laud′a·bly,** *adv.*

ill-bod·ing (ĭl′bō′dĭng), *adj.* foreboding evil; inauspicious; unlucky: *ill-boding stars.*

ill-bred (ĭl′brĕd′), *adj.* showing or due to lack of proper breeding; unmannerly; rude: *he remained serene in a houseful of ill-bred children.*

il·le·gal (ĭ lē′gəl), *adj.* not legal; unauthorized. [t. ML: s. *illēgālis,* f. L: *il-* il- + *lēgālis* legal] —**il·le′gal·ly,** *adv.* —**il·le′gal·ness,** *n.* —**Syn.** unlawful; illegitimate; illicit; unlicensed.

il·le·gal·i·ty (ĭl′ē găl′ə tĭ), *n., pl.* **-ties. 1.** illegal condition or quality; unlawfulness. **2.** an illegal act.

il·le·gal·ize (ĭ lē′gə līz′), *v.t.* to make illegal: *they even wanted to illegalize smoking.*

il·leg·i·ble (ĭ lĕj′ə bəl), *adj.* not legible; impossible or hard to read or decipher: *This letter is completely illegible.* —**il·leg′i·bil′i·ty, il·leg′i·ble·ness,** *n.* —**il·leg′i·bly,** *adv.*

il·le·git·i·ma·cy (ĭl′ĭ jĭt′ə mə sĭ), *n., pl.* **-cies.** state or quality of being illegitimate.

il·le·git·i·mate (ĭl′ĭ jĭt′ə mĭt), *adj.* **1.** not legitimate; unlawful: *an illegitimate act.* **2.** born out of wedlock: *an illegitimate child.* **3.** irregular; not in good usage. **4.** *Logic.* not in accordance with the principle of inference. —**il′le·git′i·mate·ly,** *adv.*

ill fame, bad repute or name.

ill-fat·ed (ĭl′fā′tĭd), *adj.* **1.** destined to an unhappy fate: *an ill-fated person.* **2.** bringing bad fortune.

ill-fa·vored (ĭl′fā′vərd), *adj.* **1.** not pleasant in appearance; ugly: *an ill-favored child.* **2.** offensive; unpleasant; objectionable. —**ill′-fa′vored·ly,** *adv.* —**ill′-fa′vored·ness,** *n.*

ill-found·ed (ĭl′foun′dĭd), *adj.* on a weak or illogical basis: *an ill-founded plea for mercy.*

ill-got·ten (ĭl′gŏt′ən), *adj.* acquired by evil means: *ill-gotten gains.*

ill humor, a disagreeable mood. —**ill′-hu′mored,** *adj.* —**ill′-hu′mored·ly,** *adv.*

il·lib·er·al (ĭ lĭb′ər əl), *adj.* **1.** not generous in giving; niggardly. **2.** narrow-minded; bigoted. **3.** without culture; unscholarly; vulgar. [t. L: s. *illiberālis* mean, sordid] —**il·lib′er·al·i·ty, il·lib′er·al·ness,** *n.* —**il·lib′er·al·ly,** *adv.*

il·lic·it (ĭ lĭs′ĭt), *adj.* not permitted or authorized; unlicensed; unlawful. [t. L: s. *illicitus* forbidden] —**il·lic′it·ly,** *adv.* —**il·lic′it·ness,** *n.*

Il·li·ma·ni (ē′yē mä′nē), *n.* a mountain in W Bolivia, in the Andes, near La Paz. 21,188 ft.

il·lim·it·a·ble (ĭ lĭm′ĭt ə bəl), *adj.* not limitable; limitless; boundless. —**il·lim′it·a·bil′i·ty, il·lim′it·a·ble·ness,** *n.* —**il·lim′it·a·bly,** *adv.*

il·lin·i·um (ĭ lĭn′ĭ əm), *n. Chem.* a former name for promethium. [f. illin(ois) + -ium]

Il·li·nois (ĭl′ə noi′, -noiz′), *n.* **1.** a State in the central United States: a part of the Midwest. 10,081,158 pop. (1960); 56,400 sq. mi. *Cap.:* Springfield. *Abbr.:* Ill. **2.** a river flowing from NE Illinois SW to the Mississippi, connected by a canal with Lake Michigan. 273 mi. [t.F., t. Illinois Indian, c. Shawnee *hileni,* Fox *ineniwa* man g., Proto-Algonquian *elenyiwa*] —**Il′li·nois′an,** *n., adj.*

Il·li·nois (ĭl'ə noi', -noiz'), n., pl. **-nois** (-noi', -noiz'). **1.** (pl.) a confederacy of North American Indians of Algonquian stock, formerly occupying Illinois and adjoining regions westward. **2.** an Indian of this confederacy.

il·lit·er·a·cy (ĭ lĭt'ər ə sĭ), n., pl. **-cies. 1.** lack of ability to read and write. **2.** state of being illiterate; lack of education. **3.** Rare. a literal or a literary error.

il·lit·er·ate (ĭ lĭt'ər ĭt), adj. **1.** unable to read and write: an illiterate tribe. **2.** lacking education. **3.** showing lack of culture. —n. **4.** an illiterate person. [t. L: m.s. illiterātus unlettered] —**il·lit'er·ate·ly,** adv. —**il·lit'er·ate·ness,** n. —Syn. **1.** See **ignorant.**

ill-judged (ĭl'jŭjd'), adj. injudicious; unwise.

ill-look·ing (ĭl'loŏk'ĭng), adj. **1.** ugly. **2.** sinister.

ill-man·nered (ĭl'măn'ərd), adj. having bad manners; impolite; rude. —**ill'-man'nered·ly,** adv.

ill nature, unkindly or unpleasant disposition.

ill-na·tured (ĭl'nā'chərd), adj. having or showing an unkindly or unpleasant disposition. —**ill'-na'tured·ly,** adv. —**ill'-na'tured·ness,** n. —Syn. See **cross.**

ill·ness (ĭl'nĭs), n. **1.** a state of bad health; sickness. **2.** an attack of sickness. **3.** Obs. wickedness.

il·log·i·cal (ĭ lŏj'ə kəl), adj. not logical; contrary to or disregardful of the rules of logic; unreasonable. —**il·log'i·cal'i·ty, il·log'i·cal·ness,** n. —**il·log'i·cal·ly,** adv.

ill-o·mened (ĭl'ō'mənd), adj. having or attended by bad omens; ill-starred.

ill-starred (ĭl'stärd'), adj. **1.** under the influence of an evil star; ill-fated; unlucky. **2.** disastrous.

ill temper, bad disposition. —**ill'-tem'pered,** adj. —**ill'-tem'pered·ly,** adv. —**ill'-tem'pered·ness,** n.

ill-timed (ĭl'tīmd'), adj. badly timed; inopportune.

ill-treat (ĭl'trēt'), v.t. to treat badly; maltreat. —**ill'-treat'ment,** n.

il·lume (ĭ loŏm'), v.t., **-lumed, -luming.** Poetic. to illuminate.

il·lu·mi·nant (ĭ loŏ'mə nənt), n. an illuminating agent or material.

il·lu·mi·nate (v. ĭ loŏ'mə nāt'; adj., n. ĭ loŏ'mə nĭt, -nāt'), v., **-nated, -nating,** adj., n. —v.t. **1.** to supply with light; light up. **2.** to throw light on (a subject); make lucid or clear. **3.** Chiefly Brit. to decorate with lights, as in celebration. **4.** to enlighten, as with knowledge. **5.** to make resplendent or illustrious. **6.** to decorate (a letter, a page, a manuscript, etc.) with color, gold, or the like. —v.i. **7.** to display lights, as in celebration. **8.** to become illuminated. —adj. **9.** Archaic. illuminated. **10.** Obs. enlightened. —n. **11.** Archaic. one who is or affects to be specially enlightened. [t. L: m.s. illūmĭnātus, pp.] —**il·lu'mi·nat'ing,** adj. —**il·lu'mi·nat'ing·ly,** adv.

il·lu·mi·na·ti (ĭ loŏ'mə nä'tī, -nä'tē), n.pl., sing. **-to** (-tō). **1.** persons possessing or claiming to possess superior enlightenment. **2.** (cap.) a name given to different religious societies or sects because of their claim to enlightenment. [t. L, pl. of illūmĭnātus enlightened]

il·lu·mi·na·tion (ĭ loŏ'mə nā'shən), n. **1.** act of illuminating. **2.** fact or condition of being illuminated. **3.** Chiefly Brit. a decoration consisting of lights. **4.** intellectual or spiritual enlightenment. **5.** the intensity of light falling at a given place on a lighted surface; the luminus flux per unit area at a given point on an intercepting surface. **6.** a supply of light. **7.** decoration, as of a letter, page, or manuscript, with a painted design in color, gold, etc.

il·lu·mi·na·tive (ĭ loŏ'mə nā'tĭv), adj. illuminating.

il·lu·mi·na·tor (ĭ loŏ'mə nā'tər), n. **1.** one who or that which illuminates. **2.** a device for illuminating, such as a light source with lens or a mirror for concentrating light. **3.** one who paints manuscripts, books, etc., with designs in color, gold, or the like.

il·lu·mine (ĭ loŏ'mĭn), v.t., v.i., **-mined, -mining.** to illuminate or be illuminated. [ME illumyne(n), t. F: m. illuminer, t. L: m. illūmĭnāre light up] —**il·lu'mi·na·ble,** adj.

il·lu·mi·nism (ĭ loŏ'mə nĭz'əm), n. **1.** the doctrines or claims of Illuminati. **2.** a doctrine advocating enlightenment. —**il·lu'mi·nist,** n.

illus., 1. illustrated. **2.** illustration.

ill-use (v. ĭl'ūz'; n. ĭl'ūs'), v., **-used, -using,** n. —v.t. **1.** to treat badly, unjustly, or cruelly. —n. **2.** Also, **ill-us·age** (ĭl'ū'sĭj, -zĭj). bad, unjust, or cruel treatment.

il·lu·sion (ĭ loŏ'zhən), n. **1.** something that deceives by producing a false impression. **2.** act of deceiving; deception; delusion; mockery. **3.** state of being deceived, or an instance of this; a false impression or belief. **4.** Psychol. a perception of a thing which misrepresents it, or gives it qualities not present in reality. **5.** a very thin, delicate kind of tulle. [ME, t. L: s. illūsio mocking, illusion]

—Syn. **1.** ILLUSION, DELUSION, HALLUCINATION refer to mental deceptions which arise from various causes. An ILLUSION is a false mental image or conception which may

Optical illusion.
The parallel verticals
seem to diverge under
the influence of the
oblique crosspiece.

be a misinterpretation of a real appearance or may be something imagined. It may be pleasing, harmless, or even useful: a mirage is an illusion, he had an illusion that the doorman was a general. A DELUSION is a fixed mistaken conception of something which really exists, and is not capable of correction or removal by examination or reasoning. DELUSIONS are often mischievous or harmful, as those of a fanatic or a lunatic: the delusion that all food is poisoned. A HALLUCINATION is a completely groundless false conception, belief, or opinion, caused by a disordered imagination; it is particularly frequent today in the pathological sense, according to which it denotes hearing or seeing something that does not exist: hallucinations caused by nervous disorders. —Ant. **1.** reality.

il·lu·sion·al (ĭ loŏ'zhən əl), adj. pertaining to or characterized by illusions.

il·lu·sion·ism (ĭ loŏ'zhə nĭz'əm), n. a theory or doctrine that the material world is an illusion.

il·lu·sion·ist (ĭ loŏ'zhən ĭst), n. **1.** one subject to illusions. **2.** a conjurer. **3.** an adherent of illusionism.

il·lu·sive (ĭ loŏ'sĭv), adj. illusory. —**il·lu'sive·ly,** adv. —**il·lu'sive·ness,** n.

il·lu·so·ry (ĭ loŏ'sə rĭ), adj. **1.** causing illusion; deceptive. **2.** of the nature of an illusion; unreal. —**il·lu'so·ri·ly,** adv. —**il·lu'so·ri·ness,** n.

illust., 1. illustrated. **2.** illustration.

il·lus·trate (ĭl'ə strāt', ĭ lŭs'trāt), v.t., **-trated, -trating. 1.** to make clear or intelligible, as by examples; exemplify. **2.** to furnish (a book, etc.) with drawings or pictorial representations intended for elucidation or adornment. **3.** Archaic. to enlighten. [t. L: m.s. illustrātus, pp., illuminated]

il·lus·tra·tion (ĭl'ə strā'shən), n. **1.** that which illustrates, as a picture in a book, etc. **2.** a comparison or an example intended for explanation or corroboration. **3.** act of rendering clear; explanation; elucidation. **4.** illustriousness; distinction. —Syn. **2.** See **case**[1].

il·lus·tra·tive (ĭ lŭs'trə tĭv, ĭl'ə strā'tĭv), adj. serving to illustrate. —**il·lus'tra·tive·ly,** adv.

il·lus·tra·tor (ĭl'ə strā'tər, ĭ lŭs'trā tər), n. **1.** an artist who makes illustrations. **2.** one who or that which illustrates.

il·lus·tri·ous (ĭ lŭs'trĭ əs), adj. **1.** highly distinguished; renowned; famous. **2.** glorious, as deeds, etc. **3.** Obs. luminous; bright. [f. L illustri(s) lighted up, bright + -ous] —**il·lus'tri·ous·ly,** adv. —**il·lus'tri·ous·ness,** n.

ill will, hostile or unfriendly feeling. —**ill-willed** (ĭl'wĭld'), adj.

il·ly (ĭl'ĭ, ĭl'lĭ), adv. ill.

Il·lyr·i·a (ĭ lĭr'ĭ ə), n. an ancient country along the E coast of the Adriatic.

Il·lyr·i·an (ĭ lĭr'ĭ ən), adj. **1.** pertaining to Illyria. —n. **2.** a native or inhabitant of Illyria. **3.** an extinct Indo-European language probably allied with Albanian. **4.** a group of Indo-European languages including Albanian.

il·men·ite (ĭl'mə nīt'), n. a very common black mineral, iron titanate, FeTiO₃, occurring in crystals but more commonly massive. [f. Ilmen (name of mountain range in the Urals) + -ITE[1]]

I.L.O., International Labor Organization.

I·lo·i·lo (ē'lō ē'lō), n. a seaport in the Philippine Islands, on Panay. 121,000 (est. 1954).

I·lo·ka·no (ē'lō kä'nō), n., pl. **-nos** (-nōz). **1.** an Indonesian language of Luzon. **2.** (in the Philippines) a Christian Malay. [t. Sp.: m. Ilocano, der Ilocos the name of two provinces, lit. river run, from Tagalog ilog river]

Il Tro·va·to·re (ēl trō'vä tō'rĕ), an opera (1853) by Verdi.

I'm (īm), contraction of I am.

im-[1], var. of in-[2] used before b, m, and p, as in imbrute, immingle.

im-[2], var. of in-[3] used before b, m, and p, as in immoral, imparity, imperishable.

im-[3], var. of in-[1], before b, m, and p, as in imbed, impearl.

I.M., Isle of Man.

im·age (ĭm'ĭj), n., v., **-aged, -aging.** —n. **1.** a likeness or similitude of a person, animal, or thing. **2.** an optical counterpart or appearance of an object, such as is produced by reflection from a mirror, refraction by a lens, or the passage of luminous rays through a small aperture. **3.** a mental picture or representation; an idea or conception. **4.** Psychol. the reliving of a sensation in the absence of the original stimulus. **5.** form, appearance, or semblance. **6.** a counterpart or copy: the child is the image of its mother. **7.** a symbol or emblem. **8.** a type or embodiment. **9.** a description of something in speech or writing. **10.** Rhet. a figure of speech, esp. a metaphor or a simile. **11.** Archaic. an illusion or apparition. —v.t. **12.** to picture or represent in the mind; imagine; conceive. **13.** to make an image of. **14.** to set forth in speech or writing; describe. **15.** to reflect the likeness of; mirror. **16.** to symbolize or typify. **17.** Rare. to resemble. [ME, t. F, t. L: m. imāgo copy, image]

—Syn. **1.** IMAGE, ICON, IDOL refer to material representations of persons or things. An IMAGE is a representation as in a statue or effigy, and is sometimes regarded as an object of worship: to set up an image of Apollo, an image of a saint, graven images. An ICON, in the Greek or Orthodox Eastern Church, is a representation of Christ, an angel, or a saint, in dainting, relief, mosaic, or the like: at least two icons are *found in each church.* Small icons are also carried by the peasants; these are folded tablets of wood or metal, with representations of sacred subjects in enamel or in designs of black and white or silver: *an icon is honored by offerings of incense and lights.* An IDOL is an image, statue, or the like, representing a deity and worshiped as such: *a wooden idol, the heathen worship idols;* fig., *to make an idol of wealth.*

im·age·ry (ĭm′ĭj rĭ, ĭm′ĭj ə rĭ), *n., pl.* **-ries. 1.** the formation of images, figures, or likenesses of things, or such images collectively: *a dream's dim imagery.* **2.** *Psychol.* a person's tendencies to form images. **3.** images or statues. **4.** the use of rhetorical images. **5.** figurative description or illustration; rhetorical images collectively. **—im·a·ge·ri·al** (ĭm′ə jĭr′ĭ əl), *adj.*

im·ag·i·na·ble (ĭ măj′ə nə bəl), *adj.* capable of being imagined or conceived. **—im·ag′i·na·ble·ness,** *n.* **—im·ag′i·na·bly,** *adv.*

im·ag·i·nal (ĭ măj′ə nəl), *adj. Entomol.* **1.** of or pertaining to an imago. **2.** in the form of an imago.

im·ag·i·nar·y (ĭ măj′ə nĕr′ĭ), *adj., n., pl.* **-naries. —adj. 1.** existing only in the imagination or fancy; not real; fancied: *an imaginary illness.* **2.** *Math.* noting or pertaining to a quantity or expression involving the square root of a negative quantity. **—n. 3.** *Math.* an imaginary expression or quantity. **—im·ag′i·nar′i·ly,** *adv.* **—i·mag′i·nar′i·ness,** *n.* **—Syn. 1.** visionary, shadowy, chimerical; baseless, unreal.

im·ag·i·na·tion (ĭ măj′ə nā′shən), *n.* **1.** the action of imagining, or of forming mental images or concepts of what is not actually present to the senses. **2.** the faculty of forming such images or concepts. **3.** the power of reproducing images stored in the memory under the suggestion of associated images (**reproductive imagination**), or of recombining former experiences in the creation of new images different from any known by experience (**productive or creative imagination**). **4.** the faculty of producing ideal creations consistent with reality, as in literature (distinguished from *fancy*). **5.** the product of imagining; a conception or mental creation, often a baseless or fanciful one. **6.** *Archaic.* a plan, scheme, or plot. [ME, t. L: s. *imāginātio*] **—im·ag′i·na′tion·al,** *adj.* **—Syn. 4.** See **fancy.**

im·ag·i·na·tive (ĭ măj′ə nā′tĭv, -nə tĭv), *adj.* **1.** characterized by or bearing evidence of imagination: *an imaginative tale.* **2.** pertaining to or concerned with imagination: *the imaginative faculty.* **3.** given to imagining, as persons. **4.** having exceptional powers of imagination. **5.** fanciful. **—im·ag′i·na′tive·ly,** *adv.* **—im·ag′i·na′tive·ness,** *n.*

im·ag·ine (ĭ măj′ĭn), *v.,* **-ined, -ining. —v.t. 1.** to form a mental image of (something not actually present to the senses). **2.** to think, believe, or fancy. **3.** to assume or suppose. **4.** to conjecture or guess: *I cannot imagine whom you mean.* **5.** *Archaic.* to plan, scheme, or plot. **—v.i. 6.** to form mental images of things not present to the senses; use the imagination. **7.** to suppose; think; conjecture. [ME *imagine*(*n*), t. F: m. *imaginer,* t. L: m. *imāginārī* picture to oneself, fancy] **—im·ag′in·er,** *n.* **—Syn. 1.** IMAGINE, CONCEIVE, CONCEIVE OF, REALIZE refer to bringing something before the mind. To IMAGINE is, literally, to form a mental image of something: *imagine yourself in London.* To CONCEIVE is to relate ideas or feelings to one another in a pattern: *how has the author conceived the first act of his play?* To CONCEIVE OF is to comprehend through the intellect something not perceived through the senses: *Wilson conceived of a world free from war.* To REALIZE is to make an imagined thing real or concrete to oneself, to grasp fully its implications: *to realize the extent of one's folly.*

im·ag·ism (ĭm′ə jĭz′əm), *n.* a method or movement in poetic composition, originating about 1912, which aimed particularly at "images" or clear pictures of what the poet has in mind without vagueness or symbolism, and used rhythm or cadence rather than the conventional metrical forms. See **free verse. —im′ag·ist,** *n., adj.* **—im′ag·is′tic,** *adj.*

i·ma·go (ĭ mā′gō), *n., pl.* **imagoes, imagines** (ĭ măj′ə nēz′). **1.** *Entomol.* an adult insect. **2.** *Psychoanal.* an idealized concept of a loved one, formed in childhood and retained uncorrected in adult life. [NL, special use of L *imāgo* image]

i·mam (ĭ mäm′), *n.* **1.** the officiating priest of a mosque. **2.** the title for a Mohammedan religious leader or chief. **3.** one of a succession of seven or twelve religious leaders, believed to be divinely inspired, of the Shiites. Also, **i·maum** (ĭ mäm′, ĭ mŏm′). [t. Ar.: m. *imām* leader, guide]

i·mam·ate (ĭ mä′māt), *n.* **1.** the office of an imam. **2.** the region or territory governed by an imam.

i·ma·ret (ĭ mä′rĕt), *n.* (among the Turks) a hospice for pilgrims, etc. [Turk., t. Ar.: m. *'imāra*(*t*) building, dwelling place]

im·bal·ance (ĭm băl′əns), *n.* **1.** the state or condition of lacking balance. **2.** faulty muscular or glandular coördination.

im·balm (ĭm bäm′), *v.t. Obs.* embalm.

im·be·cile (ĭm′bə sĭl), *n.* **1.** a person of defective mentality above the grade of idiocy. **—adj. 2.** mentally feeble. **3.** showing mental feebleness or incapacity. **4.** silly; absurd. **5.** *Rare.* weak or feeble. [F, t. L: m.s. *imbēcillus* weak, feeble] **—im′be·cile·ly,** *adv.*

im·be·cil·i·ty (ĭm′bə sĭl′ə tĭ), *n., pl.* **-ties. 1.** feebleness of mind; mental weakness that falls short of absolute idiocy. **2.** an instance or point of weakness or feebleness. **3.** silliness or absurdity. **4.** an instance of it.

im·bed (ĭm bĕd′), *v.t.,* **-bedded, -bedding.** embed.

im·bibe (ĭm bīb′), *v.,* **-bibed, -bibing. —v.t. 1.** to drink in, or drink. **2.** to absorb or take in as if by drinking. **3.** to take or receive into the mind, as knowledge, ideas, etc. **—v.i. 4.** to drink; absorb liquid or moisture. **5.** *Obs.* to soak or saturate; imbue. [ME, t. L: m. *imbibere* drink in] **—im·bib′er,** *n.* **—Syn. 1.** See **drink.**

im·bi·bi·tion (ĭm′bĭ bĭsh′ən), *n.* act of imbibing.

im·bri·cate (*adj.* ĭm′brə kĭt, -kāt′; *v.* ĭm′brə kāt′), *adj., v.,* **-cated, -cating. —adj.** Also, **im′bri·cat′ed. 1.** bent and hollowed like a roof tile. **2.** like, or decorated with lines or curves resembling overlapping tiles. **3.** *Biol.* overlapping like tiles, as scales, leaves, etc. **4.** characterized by, or as by, overlapping scales. **—v.t., v.i. 5.** to overlap like tiles or shingles. [t. L: m.s. *imbricātus,* pp., covered with tiles] **—im′bri·cate·ly,** *adv.* **—im′bri·ca′tive,** *adj.*

A, Imbricate flowerbud; B, Imbricate scale of cone

im·bri·ca·tion (ĭm′brə kā′shən), *n.* **1.** an overlapping, as of tiles or shingles. **2.** a decorative pattern imitating this.

im·bro·glio (ĭm brōl′yō), *n., pl.* **-glios. 1.** an intricate and perplexing state of affairs; a complicated or difficult situation. **2.** a misunderstanding or disagreement of a complicated nature, as between persons or nations. **3.** a confused heap. [t. It.: confusion, der. *imbrogliare* confuse, embroil]

Imbrication on roof and column

im·brue (ĭm brōō′), *v.t.,* **-brued, -bruing. 1.** to wet in or with something that stains, now esp. blood. **2.** (of blood, etc.) to wet or stain. [ME *enbrewe*(*n*), t. OF: m. *embreuver* give to drink, ult der. L *bibere* drink] **—im·brue′ment,** *n.*

im·brute (ĭm brōōt′), *v.t., v.i.,* **-bruted, -bruting.** to degrade or sink to the level of a brute. Also, **embrute.** [f. IM-¹ + BRUTE, *n.*] **—im·brute′ment,** *n.*

im·bue (ĭm bū′), *v.t.,* **-bued, -buing. 1.** to impregnate or inspire, as with feelings, opinions, etc. **2.** to saturate with moisture, impregnate with color, etc. **3.** to imbrue. [t. L: m.s. *imbuere*] **—im·bue′ment,** *n.*

im·id·az·ole (ĭm′ə dăz′ōl, -ĭd ə zōl′), *n. Chem.* an organic heterocyclic compound, $C_3H_4N_2$; glyoxalin. [f. IMID(E) + AZ(O)- + -OLE]

im·ide (ĭm′īd, ĭm′ĭd), *n. Chem.* a compound derived from ammonia by replacement of two hydrogen atoms by acidic radicals, characterized by the NH group. Also, **im·id** (ĭm′ĭd). [arbitrary alter. of AMIDE]

imido-, *Chem.* a combining form indicating an imide.

i·mine (ĭ mēn′, ĭm′ĭn), *n. Chem.* a compound containing the NH group united with a nonacid radical. [alter. of AMINE modeled on IMIDE]

imino-, a combining form indicating an imine.

imit., 1. imitation. **2.** imitative.

im·i·ta·ble (ĭm′ə tə bəl), *adj.* that may be imitated. **—im′i·ta·bil′i·ty,** *n.*

im·i·tate (ĭm′ə tāt′), *v.t.,* **-tated, -tating. 1.** to follow or endeavor to follow in action or manner. **2.** to mimic or counterfeit. **3.** to make a copy of; reproduce closely. **4.** to have or assume the appearance of; simulate. [t. L: m.s. *imitātus,* pp., having copied] **—im′i·ta′tor,** *n.* **—Syn. 3.** IMITATE, COPY, DUPLICATE, REPRODUCE all mean to follow or try to follow an example or pattern. IMITATE is the general word for the idea: *to imitate someone's handwriting, behavior.* To COPY is to make a fairly exact imitation of an original creation: *to copy a sentence, a dress, a picture.* To DUPLICATE is to produce something which exactly resembles or corresponds to something else; both may be originals: *to duplicate the terms of two contracts.* To REPRODUCE is to make a likeness or reconstruction of an original: *to reproduce a 16th century theater.*

im·i·ta·tion (ĭm′ə tā′shən), *n.* **1.** a result or product of imitating. **2.** act of imitating. **3.** *Sociol.* the copying of patterns of activity and thought of other groups or individuals. **4.** *Biol.* close external resemblance of an organism to some other organism or to objects in its environment. **5.** *Psychol.* a response or state of mind which in some respects resembles the activating stimulus-situation. **6.** a counterfeit. **7.** a literary composition that imitates the manner or subject of another author or work. **8.** (in the arts) the imaginative representation of the actions, motives, or natures of men or of their environments; mimesis. **9.** *Music.* the repetition of a melodic phrase at a different pitch or key from the original, or in a different voice part. **—adj. 10.** made to imitate a genuine or superior article or thing: *imitation pearls.* [t. L: s. *imitātio*] **—im′i·ta′tion·al,** *adj.*

im·i·ta·tive (ĭm′ə tā′tĭv), *adj.* **1.** imitating or copying, or given to imitating. **2.** characterized by or involving imitation or copying. **3.** *Biol.* mimetic. **4.** made in imitation of something. **5.** onomatopoeic. **—im′i·ta′tive·ly,** *adv.* **—im′i·ta′tive·ness,** *n.*

im·mac·u·late (ĭ măk′yə lĭt), *adj.* **1.** free from spot or stain; spotlessly clean, as linen. **2.** free from moral blemish or impurity; pure, or undefiled. **3.** free from fault or flaw; free from errors, as a text. **4.** *Zoöl., Bot.*

ăct, āble, dâre, ärt; ĕbb, ēqual; Ỹf, īce; hŏt, ōver, ôrder, oil, bŏŏk, ōōze, out; ŭp, ūse, ûrge; ə = a in alone; ch, chief; g, give; ng, ring; sh, shoe; th, thin; ŧħ, that; zh, vision. See the full key on inside cover.

without spots or colored marks; unicolor. [late ME, t. L: m.s. *immaculātus* unspotted] —**im·mac′u·la·cy, im·mac′u·late·ness,** *n.* —**im·mac′u·late·ly,** *adv.*

Im·mac·u·late Con·cep·tion, *Rom. Cath. Ch.* the unique privilege by which the Virgin Mary was conceived in her mother's womb without the stain of original sin, through the anticipated merits of Jesus Christ.

im·ma·nent (Ĭm′ə nənt), *adj.* 1. remaining within; indwelling; inherent. 2. (of a mental act) taking place within the mind of the subject, and having no effect outside of it. [t. LL: s. *immanens,* ppr., remaining in] —**im′ma·nence, im′ma·nen·cy,** *n.* —**im′ma·nent·ly,** *adv.*

Im·man·u·el (Ĭ măn′yōŏ əl), *n.* a name to be given to Christ (Matt. 1:23) as the son of a virgin (Isa. 7:14). Also, **Emmanuel.** [t. Heb.: m. '*Immānū'ēl,* lit., God with us]

im·ma·te·ri·al (Ĭm′ə tĬr′Ĭ əl), *adj.* 1. of no essential consequence; unimportant. 2. not material; incorporeal; spiritual. [t. ML: s. *immāteriālis,* f. LL: *im-* IM-² + *māteriālis* MATERIAL; r. ME *immaterielle,* t. F] —**im′ma·te′ri·al·ly,** *adv.* —**im·ma′te·ri·al·ness,** *n.*

im·ma·te·ri·al·ism (Ĭm′ə tĬr′Ĭ ə lĬz′əm), *n.* 1. the doctrine that there is no material world, but that all things exist only in and for minds. Cf. **idealism** (def. 5). 2. the doctrine that only immaterial substances or spiritual beings exist (opposed to *materialism*). —**im′ma·te′ri·al·ist,** *n.*

im·ma·te·ri·al·i·ty (Ĭm′ə tĬr′Ĭ ăl′ə tĬ), *n., pl.* **-ties.** 1. state or character of being immaterial. 2. something immaterial.

im·ma·te·ri·al·ize (Ĭm′ə tĬr′Ĭ ə līz′), *v.t.,* **-ized, -izing.** to make immaterial.

im·ma·ture (Ĭm′ə tyŏŏr′, -tōŏr′), *adj.* 1. not mature, ripe, developed, or perfected. 2. *Phys. Geog.* youthful. 3. *Archaic.* premature. [t. L: m.s. *immātūrus* unripe] —**im′ma·ture′ly,** *adv.* —**im·ma·tu′ri·ty, im′ma·ture′ness,** *n.*

im·meas·ur·a·ble (Ĭ mĕzh′ər ə bəl), *adj.* incapable of being measured; limitless. —**im·meas′ur·a·bil′i·ty, im·meas′ur·a·ble·ness,** *n.* —**im·meas′ur·a·bly,** *adv.*

im·me·di·a·cy (Ĭ mē′dĬ ə sĬ), *n.* 1. the character of being immediate. 2. *Philos.* **a.** direct presence; spontaneous existence, not mediated by anything; not represented and not inferred. **b.** the direct content of the mind as distinguished from representation or cognition.

im·me·di·ate (Ĭ mē′dĬ Ĭt), *adj.* 1. occurring or accomplished without delay; instant: *an immediate reply.* 2. pertaining to the present time or moment: *our immediate plans.* 3. having no time intervening; present or next adjacent: *the immediate future.* 4. having no object or space intervening; nearest or next: *in the immediate vicinity.* 5. without intervening medium or agent; direct: *an immediate cause.* 6. having a direct bearing: *immediate consideration.* 7. *Metaphys.* indemonstrable; intuitive. [t. ML: m.s. *immediātus* not mediate] —**im·me′di·ate·ness,** *n.* —**Syn.** 5. See **direct.**

im·me·di·ate·ly (Ĭ mē′dĬ Ĭt lĬ), *adv.* 1. without lapse of time, or without delay; instantly; at once. 2. without intervening medium or agent; concerning or affecting directly. 3. with no object or space intervening. 4. closely: *immediately in the vicinity.* —*conj.* 5. *Chiefly Brit.* immediately that; the moment that; as soon as. —**Syn.** 1. IMMEDIATELY, DIRECTLY, INSTANTLY, PRESENTLY, were originally close synonyms denoting complete absence of delay or of any lapse of time. INSTANTLY is the only one retaining the meaning of action or occurrence on the instant: *he replied instantly to the accusation;* it is never used with the future tense (which must suggest a slight delay). IMMEDIATELY may have the same force: *he immediately got up;* more often, a slight delay: *the game will begin immediately.* DIRECTLY and PRESENTLY, now archaic or dialectal have weakened greatly in meaning and at present imply an appreciable lapse of time, so that they are equivalent to *soon,* or *in a little while: You go ahead; we'll be there presently* (*directly*). The expressions which have supplanted them are *right away* (which, in its turn, is also weakening) and *at once* (which is still equivalent to immediately): *he will come right away, I want to see him at once.*

im·med·i·ca·ble (Ĭ mĕd′ə kə bəl), *adj.* incurable.

Im·mel·mann turn (Ĭm′əl măn′, -mən), a maneuver in which an airplane makes a half loop, then resumes its normal level position by making a half-roll: used to gain altitude while changing to the opposite direction.

im·me·mo·ri·al (Ĭm′ə mōr′Ĭ əl), *adj.* extending back beyond memory, record, or knowledge: *from time immemorial.* [t. ML: s. *immemoriālis,* f. L: *im-* IM-² + *memoriālis* MEMORIAL] —**im′me·mo′ri·al·ly,** *adv.*

im·mense (Ĭ mĕns′), *adj.* 1. vast; huge; very great: *an immense territory.* 2. immeasurable; boundless. 3. *Slang.* very good or fine. [t. L: m.s. *immensus* boundless, unmeasured] —**im·mense′ly,** *adv.* —**im·mense′ness,** *n.* —**Syn.** 1. See **huge.**

im·men·si·ty (Ĭ mĕn′sə tĬ), *n., pl.* **-ties.** 1. vastness; hugeness; enormous extent: *the immensity of the Roman empire.* 2. state of being immense; boundless extent; infinity. 3. a vast expanse; an immense quantity.

im·men·su·ra·ble (Ĭ mĕn′shŏŏ rə bəl, -sə rə-), *adj.* immeasurable. [t. LL: m.s. *immensurābilis*]

im·merge (Ĭ mûrj′), *v.,* **-merged, -merging.** —*v.t.* 1. to immerse. —*v.i.* 2. to plunge, as into a fluid. 3. to disappear as by plunging. [t. L: m.s. *immergere*] —**im·mer′gence,** *n.*

im·merse (Ĭ mûrs′), *v.t.,* **-mersed, -mersing.** 1. to plunge into or place under a liquid; dip; sink. 2. to bap-

tize by immersion. 3. to embed; bury. 4. to involve deeply; absorb. [t. L: m.s. *immersus,* pp., dipped] —**Syn.** 1. See **dip.**

im·mersed (Ĭ mûrst′), *adj.* 1. plunged or sunk in or as in a liquid. 2. *Biol.* somewhat or wholly sunk in the surrounding parts, as an organ. 3. baptized.

im·mer·sion (Ĭ mûr′shən), *n.* 1. act of immersing. 2. state of being immersed. 3. baptism by plunging the whole person into water. 4. state of being deeply engaged; absorption. 5. *Astron.* the disappearance of a celestial body by passing either behind another or into its shadow. Cf. **emersion.**

im·mer·sion·ism (Ĭ mûr′shə nĬz′əm), *n.* 1. the doctrine that immersion is essential to Christian baptism. 2. the practice of baptism by immersion. —**im·mer′·sion·ist,** *n.*

im·mesh (Ĭm mĕsh′), *v.t.* enmesh.

im·me·thod·i·cal (Ĭm′mə thŏd′ə kəl), *adj.* not methodical; without method. —**im′me·thod′i·cal·ly,** *adv.*

im·mi·grant (Ĭm′ə grənt), *n.* 1. one who or that which immigrates. 2. a person who migrates into a country for permanent residence. —*adj.* 3. immigrating.

im·mi·grate (Ĭm′ə grāt′), *v.,* **-grated, -grating.** —*v.i.* 1. to pass or come into a new habitat or place of residence. 2. to come into a country of which one is not a native for the purpose of permanent residence. —*v.t.* 3. to introduce as settlers. [t. L: m.s. *immigrātus,* pp.] —**im′mi·gra′tor,** *n.* —**Syn.** 1. See **migrate.**

im·mi·gra·tion (Ĭm′ə grā′shən), *n.* 1. act of immigrating. 2. immigrants.

im·mi·nence (Ĭm′ə nəns), *n.* 1. state or fact of being imminent or impending: *imminence of war.* 2. that which is imminent; impending evil or danger.

im·mi·nent (Ĭm′ə nənt), *adj.* 1. likely to occur at any moment; impending: *war is imminent.* 2. projecting or leaning forward; overhanging. [t. L: s. *imminens,* ppr., projecting over] —**im′mi·nent·ly,** *adv.* —**Syn.** 1. IMMINENT, IMPENDING, THREATENING apply to that which menaces or portends misfortune or disaster. IMMINENT is applied usually to danger or evil that hangs, as it were, over one's head, ready to fall at any moment: *because of recent heavy rains, a flood was imminent.* IMPENDING is similarly used, but with less suggestion of immediateness: *a reform has been impending for some time.* THREATENING is applied loosely to that which indicates coming evil, or conveys some ominous or unfavorable suggestion: *threatening weather, sky, a threatening frown.* —**Ant.** 1. distant, remote.

im·min·gle (Ĭm mĬng′gəl), *v.t., v.i.,* **-gled, -gling.** to mingle in; intermingle.

im·mis·ci·ble (Ĭ mĬs′ə bəl), *adj.* not miscible; incapable of being mixed. —**im·mis′ci·bil′i·ty,** *n.* —**im·mis′ci·bly,** *adv.*

im·mit·i·ga·ble (Ĭ mĬt′ə gə bəl), *adj.* not mitigable; not to be mitigated. [t. LL: m.s. *immītigābilis*] —**im·mit′i·ga·bil′i·ty,** *n.* —**im·mit′i·ga·bly,** *adv.*

im·mix (Ĭm mĬks′), *v.t.* to mix in; mingle. [back formation from ME *immixt,* pp. (t. L: s. *immixtus,* pp., intermingled), appar. taken as pp. of E formation]

im·mix·ture (Ĭm mĬks′chər), *n.* 1. act of inmixing. 2. state of being inmixed; involvement.

im·mo·bile (Ĭ mō′bĬl, -bēl), *adj.* 1. not mobile; immovable. 2. that does not move; motionless. [t. L: m.s. *immōbilis;* r. ME *inmobill,* f. IN-³ + MOBIL(E)]

im·mo·bil·i·ty (Ĭm′ō bĬl′ə tĬ), *n.* the character or condition of being immobile or irremovable.

im·mo·bi·lize (Ĭ mō′bə līz′), *v.t.,* **-lized, -lizing.** 1. to make immobile; fix so as to be or become immovable. 2. *Finance.* to establish a monetary reserve by withdrawing (specie) from circulation; create fixed capital in place of (circulating capital). 3. to deprive of the capacity for mobilization. Also, *esp. Brit.,* **im·mo′bi·lise′.** —**im·mo′bi·li·za′tion,** *n.*

im·mod·er·ate (Ĭ mŏd′ər Ĭt), *adj.* 1. not moderate; exceeding just or reasonable limits; excessive; extreme. 2. *Obs.* intemperate. 3. *Obs.* without bounds. [t. L: m.s. *immoderātus* without measure] —**im·mod′er·ate·ly,** *adv.* —**im·mod′er·ate·ness,** *n.* —**Syn.** 1. exorbitant, unreasonable; inordinate; extravagant.

im·mod·er·a·tion (Ĭ mŏd′ə rā′shən), *n.* lack of moderation.

im·mod·est (Ĭ mŏd′Ĭst), *adj.* 1. not modest in conduct, utterance, etc.; indecent; shameless. 2. not modest in assertion or pretension; forward; impudent. —**im·mod′est·ly,** *adv.* —**im·mod′es·ty,** *n.*

im·mo·late (Ĭm′ə lāt′), *v.t.,* **-lated, -lating.** 1. to sacrifice. 2. to kill as a sacrificial victim; offer in sacrifice. [t. L: m.s. *immolātus,* pp., sacrificed, orig. sprinkled with sacrificial meal] —**im′mo·la′tor,** *n.*

im·mo·la·tion (Ĭm′ə lā′shən), *n.* 1. act of immolating. 2. state of being immolated. 3. a sacrifice.

im·mor·al (Ĭ mŏr′əl, Ĭ môr′-), *adj.* not moral; not conforming to the moral law. —**im·mor′al·ly,** *adv.* —**Syn.** IMMORAL, ABANDONED, DEPRAVED describe one who makes no attempt to curb self-indulgence. IMMORAL (the weakest of these words), referring to conduct, applies to one who does not obey or conform to standards of morality, but is licentious and perhaps dissipated. ABANDONED, referring to condition, applies to one hopelessly and usually passively, sunk in wickedness and unrestrained appetites. DEPRAVED, referring to character, applies to one who voluntarily seeks evil and viciousness.

im·mo·ral·i·ty (Ĭm′ə răl′ə tĬ), *n., pl.* **-ties.** 1. immoral quality, character, or conduct; wickedness; vice. 2. sexual impurity; unchastity. 3. an immoral act.

im·mor·tal (ĭ môr'təl), *adj.* **1.** not mortal; not liable or subject to death; undying. **2.** remembered or celebrated through all time. **3.** not liable to perish or decay; imperishable; everlasting. **4.** perpetual, lasting, or constant: *an immortal enemy.* **5.** pertaining to immortal beings or immortality. —*n.* **6.** an immortal being. **7.** a person, esp. an author, of enduring fame. **8.** (*usually pl.*) one of the gods of classical mythology. [ME, t. L: s. *immortālis* undying] —**im·mor'tal·ly,** *adv.*

im·mor·tal·i·ty (ĭm'ôr tăl'ə tĭ), *n.* **1.** immortal condition or quality; unending life. **2.** enduring fame.

im·mor·tal·ize (ĭ môr'tə līz'), *v.t.,* **-ized, -izing. 1.** to make immortal; endow with immortality. **2.** to bestow unending fame upon; perpetuate. Also, *esp. Brit.,* **im·mor'tal·ise'.** —**im·mor'tal·i·za'tion,** *n.* —**im·mor'tal·iz'er,** *n.*

im·mor·telle (ĭm'ôr tĕl'), *n.* an everlasting (plant or flower) esp. *Xeranthemum annuum.* [t. F, prop. fem. of *immortel,* t. L: m.s. *immortālis* IMMORTAL]

im·mo·tile (ĭ mō'tɪl), *adj.* not motile.

im·mov·a·ble (ĭ mōō'və bəl), *adj.* **1.** incapable of being moved; fixed; stationary. **2.** not moving; motionless. **3.** not subject to change; unalterable. **4.** incapable of being affected with feeling; emotionless: *an immovable heart or face.* **5.** incapable of being moved from one's purpose, opinion, etc.; steadfast; unyielding. **6.** not changing from one date to another in different years: *an immovable feast.* **7.** *Law.* **a.** not liable to be removed, or permanent in place. **b.** (of property) real, as distinguished from personal. —*n.* **8.** something immovable. **9.** (*pl.*) *Law.* lands and the appurtenances thereof, as trees, buildings, etc. —**im·mov'a·bil'i·ty, im·mov'a·ble·ness,** *n.* —**im·mov'a·bly,** *adv.*

im·mune (ĭ myōōn'), *adj.* **1.** protected from a disease or the like, as by inoculation. **2.** exempt. —*n.* **3.** one who is immune. [ME, t. L: m.s. *immūnis* exempt]

im·mu·ni·ty (ĭ mū'nə tĭ), *n., pl.* **-ties. 1.** state of being immune from or insusceptible to a particular disease or the like. **2.** exemption from any natural or usual liability. **3.** exemption from obligation, service, duty, or liability to taxation, jurisdiction, etc. **4.** special privilege. **5.** *Eccles.* **a.** the exemption of ecclesiastical persons and things from secular or civil liabilities, duties, and burdens. **b.** a particular exemption of this kind. [ME, t. L: m.s. *immūnitas* exemption, ML sanctuary] —Syn. **1.** See **exemption.**

im·mu·nize (ĭm'yə nīz', ĭ mū'nīz), *v.t.,* **-nized, -nizing.** to make immune. —**im'mu·ni·za'tion,** *n.*

mmunol., immunology.

im·mu·nol·o·gy (ĭm'yōō nŏl'ə jĭ), *n.* that branch of medical science which deals with immunity from disease and the production of such immunity. —**im·mu·no·log·ic** (ĭ mū'nə lŏj'ĭk), **im·mu·no·log'i·cal,** *adj.* —**im'mu·nol'o·gist,** *n.*

im·mu·no·re·ac·tion (ĭ mū'nō rĭ ăk'shən), *n. Immunol.* an antigen-antibody reaction.

im·mure (ĭ myŏŏr'), *v.t.,* **-mured, -muring. 1.** to enclose within walls. **2.** to shut in; confine. **3.** to imprison. **4.** to build into or entomb in a wall. **5.** *Obs.* to surround with walls; fortify. [t. ML: m.s. *immūrāre,* der. L *im-* IM-[1] + *murus* wall] —**im·mure'ment,** *n.*

im·mu·si·cal (ĭ mū'zə kəl), *adj.* unmusical.

im·mu·ta·ble (ĭ mū'tə bəl), *adj.* not mutable; unchangeable; unalterable; changeless. —**im·mu'ta·bil'i·ty, im·mu'ta·ble·ness,** *n.* —**im·mu'ta·bly,** *adv.*

imp (ĭmp), *n.* **1.** a little devil or demon; an evil spirit. **2.** a mischievous child. **3.** *Archaic.* a scion or offshoot. **4.** *Archaic.* an offspring. —*v.t.* **5.** *Falconry.* **a.** to graft (feathers) into a wing. **b.** to furnish (a wing, etc.) with feathers as to make good losses or deficiencies and improve powers of flight. **6.** to add a piece to; mend or repair. [ME and OE *impe* a shoot, a graft]

Imp., **1.** (L *Imperator*) Emperor. **2.** (L *Imperatrix*) Empress.

imp., **1.** imperative. **2.** imperfect. **3.** imperial. **4.** impersonal. **5.** import. **6.** importer. **7.** imprimatur.

im·pact (*n.* ĭm'păkt; *v.* ĭm päkt'), *n.* **1.** the striking of one body against another. **2.** an impinging: *the impact of light on the eye.* **3.** an impacting; forcible impinging: *the tremendous impact of the shot.* [n. use of v.] —*v.t.* **4.** to drive or press closely or firmly into something; pack in. [t. L: s. *impactus,* pp., driven in]

im·pact·ed (ĭm păk'tĭd), *adj.* **1.** wedged in. **2.** *Dentistry.* denoting a tooth incapable of growing out or erupting and remaining within the jawbone. **3.** driven together; tightly packed.

im·pac·tion (ĭm păk'shən), *n.* **1.** act of impacting. **2.** state of being impacted; close fixation. **3.** *Dentistry.* a tooth which has not erupted that is embedded in the jawbone.

im·pair (ĭm pâr'), *v.t., v.i.* **1.** to make or become worse; diminish in value, excellence, etc.; weaken. —*n.* **2.** *Archaic.* impairment. [ME *empeire(n),* t. OF: m. *empeirer,* ult. der. L *in-* IN-[1] + *pējor* worse] —**im·pair'er,** *n.* —**im·pair'ment,** *n.* —Syn. **1.** See **injure.**

im·pale (ĭm pāl'), *v.t.,* **-paled, -paling. 1.** to fix upon a sharpened stake or the like. **2.** to pierce with a sharpened stake thrust up through the body, as for torture or punishment. **3.** to fix upon, or pierce through with, anything pointed. **4.** to make helpless as if pierced through. **5.** to enclose with or as with pales or stakes; fence in; hem in. Also, **empale.** [t. ML: m.s. *impālāre,* der. L *im-* IM-[1] + *pālus* stake] —**im·pale'ment,** *n.*

im·pal·pa·ble (ĭm păl'pə bəl), *adj.* **1.** not palpable; incapable of being perceived by the sense of touch; intangible. **2.** incapable of being readily grasped by the mind: *impalpable distinctions.* **3.** (of powder) so fine that when rubbed between the fingers no grit is felt. —**im·pal'pa·bil'i·ty,** *n.* —**im·pal'pa·bly,** *adv.*

im·pa·na·tion (im'pə nā'shən), *n. Theol.* the doctrine that the body and blood of Christ are in the bread and wine after consecration. [t. ML: s. *impānāre* embody in bread, der. L *im-* IM-[1] + *pānis* bread]

im·pan·el (ĭm păn'əl), *v.t.,* **-eled, -eling** or (*esp. Brit.*) **-elled, -elling. 1.** to enter on a panel or list for jury duty. **2.** to select (a jury) from the panel. **3.** to make a list of. Also, **empanel.** —**im·pan'el·ment,** *n.*

im·par·a·dise (ĭm păr'ə dīs'), *v.t.,* **-dised, -dising.** to put in or as in paradise; make supremely happy.

im·par·i·ty (ĭm păr'ə tĭ), *n., pl.* **-ties.** lack of parity or equality; disparity; an inequality.

im·park (ĭm pärk'), *v.t.* **1.** to shut up as in a park. **2.** to enclose as a park. [t. AF: m.s. *enparker.* See IM-[1], PARK] —**im'par·ka'tion,** *n.*

im·part (ĭm pärt'), *v.t.* **1.** to make known, tell, or relate: *to impart a secret.* **2.** to give, bestow, or communicate. **3.** to grant a part or share of. —*v.i.* **4.** *Archaic.* to grant a part or share; give. [ME, t. L: m. *impartire* share] —**im'par·ta'tion, im·part'ment,** *n.* —**im·part'er,** *n.* —Syn. **1.** See **communicate.**

im·par·tial (ĭm pär'shəl), *adj.* not partial; unbiased; just. —**im·par·ti·al·i·ty** (ĭm'pär shĭ ăl'ə tĭ), **im·par'tial·ness,** *n.* —**im·par'tial·ly,** *adv.* —Syn. See **fair**[1].

im·part·i·ble (ĭm pär'tə bəl), *adj.* not partible; indivisible. [t. LL: m.s. *impartibilis*] —**im·part'i·bil'i·ty,** *n.* —**im·part'i·bly,** *adv.*

im·pass·a·ble (ĭm păs'ə bəl, -päs'-), *adj.* not passable; that cannot be passed over, through, or along: *muddy, impassable roads.* —**im·pass'a·bil'i·ty, im·pass'a·ble·ness,** *n.* —**im·pass'a·bly,** *adv.*

im·passe (ĭm păs', ĭm'păs; *Fr.* ăN päs'), *n.* **1.** a position from which there is no escape. **2.** a road or way that has no outlet. [t. F]

im·pas·si·ble (ĭm păs'ə bəl), *adj.* **1.** incapable of suffering pain. **2.** incapable of suffering harm. **3.** incapable of emotion; impassive. [t. LL: m.s. *impassibilis.* See IM-[2], PASSIBLE] —**im·pas'si·bil'i·ty, im·pas'si·ble·ness,** *n.* —**im·pas'si·bly,** *adv.*

im·pas·sion (ĭm păsh'ən), *v.t.* to fill, or affect strongly, with passion. [t. It.: s. *impassionare,* der. *im-* IM-[1] + *passione* PASSION]

im·pas·sion·ate (ĭm păsh'ən ĭt), *adj. Now Rare.* free from passion; dispassionate. [t. It.: m. *impassionato,* pp., der. *im-* IM-[2] + *passione* PASSION]

im·pas·sioned (ĭm păsh'ənd), *adj.* filled with passion; passionate; ardent. —**im·pas'sioned·ly,** *adv.* —**im·pas'sioned·ness,** *n.*

im·pas·sive (ĭm păs'ĭv), *adj.* **1.** without emotion; apathetic; unmoved. **2.** calm; serene. **3.** unconscious. **4.** not subject to suffering. —**im·pas'sive·ly,** *adv.* —**im·pas'sive·ness, im·pas·siv·i·ty** (ĭm'păs ĭv'ə tĭ), *n.*

im·paste (ĭm pāst'), *v.t.,* **-pasted, -pasting. 1.** to cover with or enclose in a paste. **2.** to form into a paste. **3.** to lay on thickly, as paint. [t. It.: m.s. *impastare,* der. *im-* IM-[1] + *pasta* (g. LL *pasta* PASTE)] —**im·pas·ta·tion** (ĭm'păs tā'shən), *n.*

im·pas·to (ĭm päs'tō, -päs'-), *n. Painting.* **1.** the laying on of colors thickly. **2.** color so laid on. [t. It., der. *impastare.* See IMPASTE]

im·pa·tience (ĭm pā'shəns), *n.* **1.** lack of patience. **2.** eager desire for relief or change; restlessness. **3.** intolerance of anything that thwarts or hinders.

im·pa·ti·ens (ĭm pā'shĭ ĕnz'), *n.* any of a genus, *Impatiens,* of annual balsaminaceous plants having irregular flowers, in which the calyx and corolla are not clearly distinguishable. [NL, n. use of L ppr. See IMPATIENT]

im·pa·tient (ĭm pā'shənt), *adj.* **1.** not patient; not bearing pain, opposition, etc., with composure. **2.** indicating lack of patience: *an impatient answer.* **3.** intolerant (fol. by *of*): *impatient of any interruptions.* **4.** restless in desire or expectation; eagerly desirous (to do something). [ME *impacient,* t. L: m.s. *impatiens* not bearing or enduring] —**im·pa'tient·ly,** *adv.*

im·pav·id (ĭm păv'ĭd), *adj.* fearless. [t. L: s. *impavidus*] —**im·pav'id·ly,** *adv.*

im·pawn (ĭm pôn'), *v.t.* to put in pawn; pledge.

im·peach (ĭm pēch'), *v.t.* **1.** to accuse (a public official) before a competent tribunal of misconduct in office. **2.** to challenge the credibility of: *to impeach a witness.* **3.** to bring an accusation against. **4.** to call in question; cast an imputation upon: *to impeach one's motives.* **5.** to call to account. —*n.* **6.** *Obs.* impeachment. [ME *empech-e(n),* t. OF: m. *empechier* hinder, g. LL *impedicāre* catch, entangle, der. L *in-* IN-[2] + *pedica* fetter] —**im·peach'er,** *n.*

im·peach·a·ble (ĭm pē'chə bəl), *adj.* **1.** liable to be impeached. **2.** making one liable to impeachment, as an offense. —**im·peach'a·bil'i·ty,** *n.*

im·peach·ment (ĭm pēch'mənt), *n.* **1.** the impeaching of a public official before a competent tribunal. **2.** (in Congress or a State legislature) the presentation of formal charges against a public official by the lower house, trial to be before the upper house. **3.** the demonstration that a witness is less worthy of belief. **4.** act of impeaching. **5.** state of being impeached.

im·pearl (ĭm pûrl′), v.t. **1.** to form into pearllike drops. **2.** to make pearllike or pearly. **3.** Poetic. to adorn with pearls or pearllike drops.

im·pec·ca·ble (ĭm pĕk′ə bəl), adj. **1.** faultless or irreproachable: impeccable manners. **2.** not liable to sin; exempt from the possibility of doing wrong. —n. **3.** an impeccable person. [t. LL: m.s. impeccābilis, Cf. PECCABLE] —im·pec′ca·bil′i·ty, n. —im·pec′ca·bly, adv.

im·pec·cant (ĭm pĕk′ənt), adj. not sinning; sinless. —im·pec′can·cy, n.

im·pe·cu·ni·ous (ĭm′pə kū̄′nĭ′əs), adj. having no money; penniless; poor. —im·pe·cu′ni·ous·ly, adv. —im′pe·cu′ni·ous·ness, im·pe·cu·ni·os·i·ty (ĭm′pə kū̄′nĭ ŏs′ə tĭ), n. —Syn. See poor.

im·ped·ance (ĭm pē′dəns), n. **1.** Elect. the apparent resistance, or total opposition to current of an alternating-current circuit, consisting of two components, reactance and true or ohmic resistance. **2.** Physics. the ratio of pressure to particle velocity at a given point in a sound wave. [f. IMPEDE + -ANCE]

im·pede (ĭm pēd′), v.t., -ped·ed, -ped·ing. to retard in movement or progress by means of obstacles or hindrances; obstruct; hinder. [t. L: m.s. impedīre entangle, hamper (orig., as to the feet)] —im·ped′er, n. —im·ped′ing·ly, adv. —Syn. See prevent.

im·pe·di·ent (ĭm pē′dĭ ənt), adj. **1.** impeding. —n. **2.** that which impedes. [t. L: s. impediens, ppr.]

im·ped·i·ment (ĭm pĕd′ə mənt), n. **1.** some physical defect, esp. a speech disorder: an impediment in speech. **2.** obstruction or hindrance; obstacle. **3.** (usually pl.) impedimenta. **4.** Law. (esp. Eccles.) a. a bar, usually of blood or affinity, to marriage: a diriment impediment. b. a restraint on marriage, preventing a completely lawful union: a minor impediment. [ME, t. L: s. impedimentum hindrance] —im·ped′i·men′tal, im·ped·i·men·ta·ry (ĭm pĕd′ə mĕn′tər ĭ), adj. —Syn. 2. See obstacle.

im·ped·i·men·ta (ĭm pĕd′ə mĕn′tə), n.pl. **1.** supplies carried with an army. **2.** Law. impediments. [t. L]

im·ped·i·tive (ĭm pĕd′ə tĭv), adj. tending to impede.

im·pel (ĭm pĕl′), v.t., -pelled, -pel·ling. **1.** to drive or urge forward; press on; incite or constrain to action in any way. **2.** to drive, or cause to move, onward; propel; impart motion to. [t. L: m.s. impellere] —im·pel′ler, n. —Syn. 1. See compel.

im·pel·lent (ĭm pĕl′ənt), adj. **1.** impelling. —n. **2.** an impelling agency or force.

im·pend (ĭm pĕnd′), v.i. **1.** to be imminent; be near at hand. **2.** to hang or be suspended; overhang (fol. by over). [t. L: s. impendēre hang over]

im·pend·ent (ĭm pĕn′dənt), adj. impending. —im·pend′ence, im·pend′en·cy, n.

im·pend·ing (ĭm pĕn′dĭng), adj. **1.** about to happen; imminent. **2.** overhanging. —Syn. 1. See imminent.

im·pen·e·tra·bil·i·ty (ĭm pĕn′ə trə bĭl′ə tĭ, ĭm′pĕn-), n. **1.** impenetrable quality. **2.** Physics. that property of matter in virtue of which two bodies cannot occupy the same space simultaneously.

im·pen·e·tra·ble (ĭm pĕn′ə trə bəl), adj. **1.** not penetrable; that cannot be penetrated, pierced, or entered. **2.** inaccessible to ideas, influences, etc. **3.** incapable of being comprehended; unfathomable: an impenetrable mystery. **4.** Physics. excluding all other bodies from the space occupied. —im·pen′e·tra·ble·ness, n. —im·pen′e·tra·bly, adv.

im·pen·i·tent (ĭm pĕn′ə tənt), adj. not penitent; obdurate. —im·pen′i·tence, im·pen′i·ten·cy, im·pen′i·tent·ness, n. —im·pen′i·tent·ly, adv.

im·pen·nate (ĭm pĕn′āt), adj. featherless or wingless.

imper., imperative.

im·per·a·tive (ĭm pĕr′ə tĭv), adj. **1.** not to be avoided or evaded: an imperative duty. **2.** of the nature of or expressing a command; commanding. **3.** Gram. designating or pertaining to the verb mode specialized for use in command, requests, and the like, or a verb inflected for this mode, as listen! go! run! etc. —n. **4.** a command. **5.** Gram. a. the imperative mode. b. a verb therein. [t. L: m.s. imperātīvus of a command] —im·per·a·ti·val (ĭm pĕr′ə tī′vəl), adj. —im·per′a·tive·ly, adv. —im·per′a·tive·ness, n.

im·pe·ra·tor (ĭm′pə rā′tər), n. **1.** an absolute or supreme ruler. **2.** a title of the Roman emperors. **3.** a temporary title accorded a victorious Roman general. [t. L. Cf. EMPEROR] —im·per·a·to·ri·al (ĭm pĕr′ə tōr′ĭ əl), adj. —im·per′a·to′ri·al·ly, adv.

im·per·cep·ti·ble (ĭm′pər sĕp′tə bəl), adj. **1.** very slight, gradual, or subtle: imperceptible gradations. **2.** not perceptible; not affecting the perceptive faculties. —im′per·cep′ti·bil′i·ty, im′per·cep′ti·ble·ness, n. —im′per·cep′ti·bly, adv.

im·per·cep·tion (ĭm′pər sĕp′shən), n. lack of perception.

im·per·cep·tive (ĭm′pər sĕp′tĭv), adj. not perceptive; lacking perception. —im·per·cep·tiv·i·ty (ĭm′pər sĕp tĭv′ə tĭ), im′per·cep′tive·ness, n.

imperf., imperfect.

im·per·fect (ĭm pûr′fĭkt), adj. **1.** characterized by or subject to defects. **2.** not perfect; lacking completeness: imperfect vision. **3.** Bot. (of a flower) lacking certain parts; esp., diclinous. **4.** Gram. denoting action or state still in process at some temporal point of reference, particularly in the past. b. In English, action in process is expressed in six tense forms of the verb called

the progressive tenses: present progressive, he is carrying; past progressive, he was carrying; past perfect progressive, he had been carrying. **5.** Law. without legal effect or support; unenforceable. **6.** Music. noting the consonances of third and sixth. Cf. perfect (def. 12 a). —n. **7.** Gram. a. the imperfect tense. b. another verb formation or construction with imperfect meaning. c. a form therein. For example: Latin portabam, "I was carrying" or English was doing in he was doing it when I came. [t. L: s. imperfectus unfinished; r. ME imparfit, t. F: m. imparfait] —im·per′fect·ly, adv. —im·per′fect·ness, n.
—Syn. 2. IMPERFECT, RUDIMENTARY, UNDEVELOPED mean not complete or fully developed. That which is IMPERFECT is not complete or is defective in some respect; it may have met with some mishap while it was still developing: an imperfect specimen of butterfly, knowledge of a subject. That which is RUDIMENTARY is still in an early stage of development or in an embryonic stage; or it may be a vestige of something the development of which has been arrested: rudimentary buds, the rudimentary facts, rudimentary organs. That which is UNDEVELOPED has not fully grown, or not grown to normal size or extent: an undeveloped adolescent, an undeveloped talent. —Ant. 1. complete, perfect, developed.

im·per·fec·tion (ĭm′pər fĕk′shən), n. **1.** an imperfect detail: a law full of imperfections. **2.** the character or condition of being imperfect.

im·per·fec·tive (ĭm′pər fĕk′tĭv), adj. **1.** Gram. denoting an aspect of the verb, as in Russian, which indicates incompleteness of the action or state at a temporal point of reference. —n. **2.** Gram. a. the imperfective aspect. b. a verb therein.

im·per·fo·rate (ĭm pûr′fə rĭt, -rāt′), adj. **1.** Also, im·per′fo·rat′ed. not perforate; having no perforation. **2.** Philately. having no perforations or cuts to separate the individual stamps roughly. —n. **3.** an imperforate stamp. —im·per′fo·ra′tion, n.

im·pe·ri·al (ĭm pĭr′ĭ əl), adj. **1.** of or pertaining to an empire. **2.** of or pertaining to an emperor or empress. **3.** characterizing the rule or authority of a sovereign state over its dependencies. **4.** of the nature or rank of an emperor or supreme ruler. **5.** of a commanding quality, manner, or aspect. **6.** domineering; imperious. **7.** befitting an emperor or empress; very fine or grand; magnificent. **8.** of special size or quality, as various products, commodities, etc. **9.** (of weights and measures) conforming to the standards legally established in Great Britain. —n. **10.** Chiefly Brit. a small part of the beard left growing beneath the under lip. **11.** a size of paper, 23 x 31 inches in America, 22 x 30 inches in England. **12.** a Russian gold coin originally worth 10 rubles, and from 1897–1917 worth 15 rubles. **13.** the top of a carriage, esp. of a diligence. **14.** a case for luggage carried there. **15.** a member of an imperial party; or of imperial troops. **16.** an emperor or empress. **17.** any of various articles of special size or quality. [ME, t. L: s. imperiālis of the empire or emperor] —im·pe′ri·al·ly, adv. —im·pe′ri·al·ness, n.

im·pe·ri·al·ism (ĭm pĭr′ĭ əl ĭz′əm), n. **1.** the policy of extending the rule or authority of an empire or nation over foreign countries, or of acquiring and holding colonies and dependencies. **2.** advocacy of imperial interests. **3.** (in British use) the policy of so uniting the separate parts of an empire with separate governments as to secure for certain purposes a single state. **4.** imperial government. **5.** an imperial system of government. —im·pe′ri·al·ist, n., adj. —im·pe′ri·al·is′tic adj. —im·pe′ri·al·is′ti·cal·ly, adv.

Imperial Valley, an irrigated agricultural region in SE California and adjacent Mexico: formerly a part of the Colorado Desert, it is largely below sea level and contains the Salton Sink.

im·per·il (ĭm pĕr′əl), v.t., -iled, -iling or (esp. Brit.) -illed, -illing. to put in peril; endanger. —im·per′il·ment, n.

im·pe·ri·ous (ĭm pĭr′ĭ əs), adj. **1.** domineering, dictatorial, or overbearing: an imperious tyrant, imperious temper. **2.** urgent; imperative: imperious need. [t. L: m.s. imperiōsus commanding] —im·pe′ri·ous·ly, adv. —im·pe′ri·ous·ness, n.

im·per·ish·a·ble (ĭm pĕr′ĭsh ə bəl), adj. not perishable; indestructible; enduring. —im·per′ish·a·bil′i·ty, im·per′ish·a·ble·ness, n. —im·per′ish·a·bly, adv.

im·pe·ri·um (ĭm pĭr′ĭ əm), n., pl. -peria (-pĭr′ĭ ə). **1.** command; supreme power. **2.** Law. the right to command the force of the state in order to enforce the law. [t. L. Cf. EMPIRE]

im·per·ma·nent (ĭm pûr′mə nənt), adj. not permanent. —im·per′ma·nence, im·per′ma·nen·cy, n.

im·per·me·a·ble (ĭm pûr′mĭ ə bəl), adj. **1.** not permeable; impassable. **2.** (of substances) not permitting the passage of a fluid through the pores, interstices, etc. —im·per′me·a·bil′i·ty, im·per′me·a·ble·ness, n. —im·per′me·a·bly, adv.

impers., impersonal.

im·per·son·al (ĭm pûr′sən əl), adj. **1.** not personal; without personal reference or connection: an impersonal remark. **2.** having no personality: an impersonal deity. **3.** Gram. a. (of a verb) having only third person singular forms, rarely if ever accompanied by an expressed subject, as Latin pluit (it's raining), or accompanied regularly by an empty subject word, as English it's raining. b. (of a pronoun) indefinite, as French on (one). —n. **4.** Gram. an impersonal verb or pronoun. —im·per′son·al′i·ty, n. —im·per′son·al·ly, adv.

im·per·son·ate (Ĭm pûr'sə nāt'), v., -ated, -ating, adj. —v.t. 1. to assume the character of; pretend to be. 2. to represent in personal or bodily form; personify; typify. 3. to personate, esp. on the stage. —adj. 4. embodied in a person; invested with personality. —im·per'son·a'tion, n. —im·per'son·a'tor, n.

im·per·ti·nence (Ĭm pûr'tə nəns), n. 1. unmannerly intrusion or presumption; insolence. 2. impertinent quality or action; irrelevance. 3. inappropriateness or incongruity. 4. triviality or absurdity. 5. something impertinent.

im·per·ti·nen·cy (Ĭm pûr'tə nən sĭ), n., pl. -cies. impertinence.

im·per·ti·nent (Ĭm pûr'tə nənt), adj. 1. intrusive or presumptuous, as persons or their actions: an impertinent boy. 2. not pertinent or relevant; irrelevant: any impertinent detail. 3. inappropriate or incongruous. 4. trivial, silly, or absurd. [ME, t. LL: s. impertinens not belonging] —im·per'ti·nent·ly, adv.
—Syn. 1. IMPERTINENT, IMPUDENT, INSOLENT refer to bold, rude, and arrogant behavior. IMPERTINENT, from its primary meaning of not pertinent and hence inappropriate or out of place, has come to imply often an unseemly intrusion into what does not concern one, or a presumptuous rudeness toward one entitled to deference or respect: an impertinent interruption, question, manner toward a teacher. IMPUDENT suggests a bold and shameless impertinence: an impudent speech, young rascal. INSOLENT suggests insulting or arrogantly contemptuous behavior: unbearably insolent toward those in authority. —Ant. 1. polite, civil, deferential.

im·per·turb·a·ble (Ĭm'pər tûr'bə bəl), adj. incapable of being perturbed or agitated; not easily excited; calm: imperturbable composure. —im'per·turb'a·bil'i·ty, im'per·turb'a·ble·ness, n. —im'per·turb'a·bly, adv.

im·per·tur·ba·tion (Ĭm'pər tər bā'shən), n. freedom from perturbation; tranquillity; calmness.

im·per·vi·ous (Ĭm pûr'vĭ əs), adj. 1. not pervious; impermeable: impervious to water. 2. impenetrable: impervious to reason. Also, im·per'vi·a·ble. —im·per'vi·ous·ly, adv. —im·per'vi·ous·ness, n.

im·pe·ti·go (Ĭm'pə tī'gō), n. Pathol. a contagious skin disease, esp. of children, marked by a superficial pustular eruption, particularly on the face. [t. L, der. impetere attack] —im·pe·tig·i·nous (Ĭm'pə tĭj'ə nəs), adj.

im·pe·trate (Ĭm'pə trāt'), v.t., -trated, -trating. 1. to obtain by entreaty. 2. to entreat, or ask urgently for. [t. L: m.s. impetrātus, pp., obtained by request] —im'pe·tra'tion, n. —im'pe·tra'tive, adj. —im'pe·tra'tor, n.

im·pet·u·os·i·ty (Ĭm pĕch'ŏŏ ŏs'ə tĭ, Ĭm'pĕch-), n., pl. -ties. 1. impetuous quality. 2. an impetuous action.

im·pet·u·ous (Ĭm pĕch'ŏŏ əs), adj. 1. acting with or characterized by sudden or rash energy: an impetuous girl. 2. having great impetus; moving with great force; violent: the impetuous winds. [ME, t. LL: m.s. impetuōsus, der. L impetus an attack] —im·pet'u·ous·ly, adv. —im·pet'u·ous·ness, n.
—Syn. 1. IMPETUOUS, IMPULSIVE both refer to persons who are hasty and precipitate in action, or to actions not preceded by thought. IMPETUOUS suggests eagerness, violence, rashness: impetuous vivacity, impetuous desire, impetuous words. IMPULSIVE emphasizes spontaneity and lack of reflection: an impulsive act of generosity. —Ant. 1. cautious, deliberate.

im·pe·tus (Ĭm'pə təs), n. 1. moving force; impulse; stimulus: a fresh impetus. 2. the force with which a moving body tends to maintain its velocity and overcome resistance; energy of motion. [t. L: onset, attack]

impf., imperfect.

im·pi (Ĭm'pĭ), n., pl. -pies. a band of Kaffir warriors. [Zulu]

im·pi·e·ty (Ĭm pī'ə tĭ), n., pl. -ties. 1. lack of piety; lack of reverence for God; ungodliness. 2. lack of dutifulness or respect. 3. an impious act, practice, etc.

im·pinge (Ĭm pĭnj'), v.i., -pinged, -pinging. 1. to strike or dash; collide (fol. by on, upon, or against): rays of light impinging on the eye. 2. to encroach or infringe (fol. by on or upon). 3. Obs. to come into violent contact with. [t. L: m.s. impingere drive in or at, strike against] —im·pinge'ment, n.

im·pi·ous (Ĭm'pĭ əs), adj. 1. not pious; lacking reverence for God; ungodly. 2. Rare. not reverent toward parents. [t. L: m. impius] —im'pi·ous·ly, adv. —im'·pi·ous·ness, n.

imp·ish (Ĭm'pĭsh), adj. of or like an imp; mischievous. —imp'ish·ly, adv. —imp'ish·ness, n.

im·pla·ca·ble (Ĭm plā'kə bəl, -plăk'ə-), adj. not placable; not to be appeased or placated; inexorable: an implacable enemy. —im·pla'ca·bil'i·ty, im·pla'ca·ble·ness, n. —im·pla'ca·bly, adv. —Syn. See inflexible.

im·pla·cen·tal (Ĭm'plə sĕn'təl), adj. Zool. having no placenta, as a monotreme or marsupial.

im·plant (v. Ĭm plănt', -plänt'; n. Ĭm'plănt', -plänt'), v.t. 1. to instill or inculcate: implant sound principles. 2. to plant in something; infix: implant living tissue. 3. to plant: implant the seeds. —n. 4. Med. a. tissue implanted into the body by grafting. b. a small tube containing a radioactive substance, as radium, surgically implanted in tissue for the treatment of tumors, cancer, etc. [f. IM-¹ + PLANT, v.] —im·plant'er, n.

im·plan·ta·tion (Ĭm'plăn tā'shən), n. 1. act of implanting. 2. state of being implanted. 3. Pathol. a. the movement of cells to a new region. b. metastasis, when spontaneous. 4. Med. the application of solid medicine underneath the skin.

im·plau·si·ble (Ĭm plô'zə bəl), adj. not plausible; not having the appearance of truth or credibility. —im·plau'si·bly, adv.

im·plead (Ĭm plēd'), v.t. 1. to sue in a court of justice. 2. to accuse; impeach. 3. Rare. to plead (a suit, etc.). [ME emplede(n), t. AF: m. empleder, var. of OF emplaidier, f. em- IM-¹ + plaidier PLEAD]

im·ple·ment (n. Ĭm'plə mənt; v. -mĕnt'), n. 1. an instrument, tool, or utensil: agricultural implements. 2. an article of equipment or outfit, as household furniture or utensils, ecclesiastical vessels or vestments, etc. 3. a means; agent. —v.t. 4. to provide with implements. 5. to execute, as a piece of work. 6. to satisfy, as requirements or conditions. 7. to fill out or supplement. [late ME, t. LL: s. implementum a filling up (hence, prob., a thing that completes a want), der. L implēre fill up] —im·ple·men'tal, adj. —Syn. 1. See tool.

im·ple·tion (Ĭm plē'shən), n. 1. act of filling. 2. state of being filled. 3. that which fills up; a filling. [t. LL: s. implētio, der. L implēre fill up]

im·pli·cate (Ĭm'plə kāt'), v.t., -cated, -cating. 1. to involve as being concerned in a matter, affair, condition, etc.: to be implicated in a crime. 2. to imply as a necessary circumstance, or as something to be inferred or understood. 3. to fold or twist together; intertwine; interlace: implicated leaves. [t. L: m.s. implicātus, pp., entangled, involved] —Syn. 1. See involve.

im·pli·ca·tion (Ĭm'plə kā'shən), n. 1. act of implying. 2. state of being implied. 3. something implied or suggested as naturally to be inferred without being expressly stated. 4. Logic. the relation which holds between two propositions (or classes of propositions) in virtue of which one is logically deducible from the other. 5. act of involving. 6. state of being involved in some matter: implication in a conspiracy. 7. act of intertwining or entangling. 8. the resulting condition.

im·pli·ca·tive (Ĭm'plə kā'tĭv), adj. tending to implicate or imply; characterized by or involving implication. —im'pli·ca·tive·ly, adv.

im·plic·it (Ĭm plĭs'ĭt), adj. 1. (of belief, confidence, obedience, etc.) unquestioning, unreserved, or absolute. 2. implied, rather than expressly stated: an implicit consent. 3. virtually contained (fol. by in). 4. Obs. entangled. [t. L: s. implicitus, var. of implicātus, pp., entangled, involved] —im·plic'it·ly, adv. —im·plic'it·ness, n.

im·plied (Ĭm plīd'), adj. involved, indicated, or suggested by implying; tacitly understood: an implied rebuke.

im·pli·ed·ly (Ĭm plī'ĭd lĭ), adv. by implication.

im·plode (Ĭm plōd'), v., -ploded, -ploding. —v.i. 1. to burst inward (opposed to explode). —v.t. 2. Phonet. to pronounce by implosion. [f. IM-¹ + -plode, modeled on EXPLODE]

im·plore (Ĭm plōr'), v., -plored, -ploring. —v.t. 1. to call upon in urgent or piteous supplication, as for aid or mercy; beseech; entreat: they implored him to go. 2. to make urgent supplication for (aid, mercy, pardon, etc.): implore forgiveness. —v.i. 3. to make urgent or piteous supplication. [t. L: m.s. implōrāre invoke with tears] —im·plo·ra·tion, n. —im·plor·a·to·ry (Ĭm plōr'ə tōr'ĭ), adj. —im·plor'er, n. —im·plor'ing·ly, adv. —im·plor'ing·ness, n. —Syn. 2. crave, beg. —Ant. 2. spurn, reject.

im·plo·sion (Ĭm plō'zhən), n. 1. a bursting inward (opposed to explosion). 2. Phonet. (of stops) a. a beginning marked by abrupt interruption of the breath stream, as for p, t, k. b. an ending marked by abrupt intake of air. [f. IM-¹ + -plosion, modeled on EXPLOSION]

im·plo·sive (Ĭm plō'sĭv), Phonet. —adj. 1. characterized by a partial vacuum behind the point of closure. —n. 2. an implosive stop.

im·ply (Ĭm plī'), v.t., -plied, -plying. 1. to involve as a necessary circumstance: speech implies a speaker. 2. (of words) to signify or mean. 3. to indicate or suggest, as something naturally to be inferred, without express statement. 4. Obs. to enfold. [ME implie(n), t. OF: m. emplier, g. L implicāre enfold, entangle, involve]

im·pol·i·cy (Ĭm pŏl'ə sĭ), n. bad policy; inexpediency.

im·po·lite (Ĭm'pə līt'), adj. not polite or courteous; uncivil; rude. —im'po·lite'ly, adv. —im'po·lite'ness, n. —Syn. discourteous, disrespectful; insolent.

im·pol·i·tic (Ĭm pŏl'ə tĭk), adj. inexpedient; injudicious. —im·pol'i·tic·ly, adv. —im·pol'i·tic·ness, n.

im·pon·der·a·ble (Ĭm pŏn'dər ə bəl), adj. 1. not ponderable; that cannot be weighed. —n. 2. an imponderable thing, force, or agency. —im·pon'der·a·bil'i·ty, im·pon'der·a·ble·ness, n. —im·pon'der·a·bly, adv.

im·port (v. Ĭm pōrt', Ĭm'pōrt; n. Ĭm'pōrt), v.t. 1. to bring in from a foreign country, as merchandise or commodities, for sale, use, processing, or reëxport. 2. to bring or introduce from one use, connection, or relation into another. 3. to convey as a meaning or implication, as words, statements, actions, etc., do; to make known or express. 4. to be of consequence or importance to; concern. 5. to be incumbent on; be the duty of. —v.i. 6. to be of consequence or importance; matter. —n. 7. that which is imported from abroad; an imported commodity or article. 8. act of importing or bringing in; importation, as of goods from abroad. 9. meaning; implication; purport. 10. consequence or importance: matters of great import. [ME, t. L: s. importāre bring in, bring about] —im·port′a·ble, *adj.* —im·port′a·bil′i·ty, *n.* —im·port′er, *n.*

im·por·tance (ĭm pôr′təns), *n.* **1.** the quality or fact of being important. **2.** important position or standing; personal or social consequence. **3.** consequential air or manner. **4.** *Obs.* an important matter. **5.** *Obs.* importunity. **6.** *Obs.* import or meaning. —**Syn. 1.** IMPORTANCE, CONSEQUENCE refer to a quality, character, or standing such as to entitle to attention or consideration. IMPORTANCE, referring originally to the bringing or involving of noteworthy results, is the general term. CONSEQUENCE, though of the same general sense, is a weaker word, less suggestive of seriousness, dignity, or extensiveness: *fair weather is a matter of consequence to the tourist, but of real importance to the farmer.*

im·por·tant (ĭm pôr′tənt), *adj.* **1.** of much significance or consequence: *an important event.* **2.** mattering much (fol. by *to*): *details important to a fair decision.* **3.** of more than ordinary title to consideration or notice: *an important example.* **4.** prominent: *an important part.* **5.** of considerable influence or authority, as a person, position, etc. **6.** of social consequence or distinction, as a person, family, etc. **7.** pompous. **8.** *Obs.* importunate. [t. F, t. ML: s. *importans,* ppr., of *importāre* be of consequence, L bring in, cause] —im·por′tant·ly, *adv.*

im·por·ta·tion (ĭm′pôr tā′shən), *n.* **1.** the bringing in of merchandise from foreign countries, for sale, use, processing, or reëxport. **2.** something imported.

im·por·tu·na·cy (ĭm pôr′chə nə sĭ), *n.* quality of being importunate.

im·por·tu·nate (ĭm pôr′chə nĭt), *adj.* **1.** urgent or persistent in solicitation. **2.** pertinacious, as solicitations or demands. **3.** troublesome. —im·por′tu·nate·ly, *adv.* —im·por′tu·nate·ness, *n.*

im·por·tune (ĭm′pôr tūn′, -tōōn′, ĭm pôr′chən), *v.,* -tuned, -tuning, *adj.* —*v.t.* **1.** to beset with solicitations; beg urgently or persistently. **2.** to beg for (something) urgently or persistently. **3.** *Obs.* to annoy. **4.** *Obs.* to press; impel. —*v.i.* **5.** to make urgent or persistent solicitations. —*adj.* **6.** *Rare.* importunate. [ME, t. MF: m. *importun,* t. L: s. *importūnus* unfit, inconvenient, troublesome] —im′por·tune′ly, *adv.* —im′por·tun′er, *n.*

im·por·tu·ni·ty (ĭm′pôr tū′nə tĭ, -tōō′-), *n., pl.* -ties. **1.** state of being importunate; persistence in solicitation. **2.** (*pl.*) importunate solicitations or demands.

im·pose (ĭm pōz′), *v.,* -posed, -posing. —*v.t.* **1.** to lay on or set as something to be borne, endured, obeyed, fulfilled, etc.: *to impose taxes.* **2.** to put or set by, or as by, authority: *to impose an arbitrary meaning upon words.* **3.** to obtrude or thrust (oneself, one's company, etc.) upon others. **4.** to pass or palm off fraudulently or deceptively. **5.** to lay on (the hands) ceremonially, as in confirmation or ordination. **6.** *Print.* to lay (type pages, etc.) in proper order on an imposing stone or the like and secure in a chase for printing. **7.** to subject to some penalty, etc. **8.** *Archaic.* to put or place on something, or in a particular place. —*v.i.* **9.** to make an impression on the mind; to impose one's or its authority or influence. **10.** to obtrude oneself or one's requirements, as upon others. **11.** to presume, as upon patience, good nature, etc. **12.** (of something fraudulent) to produce a false impression or act with a delusive effect (fol. by *upon* or *on*). [t. F: m.s. *imposer,* f. im-IM-¹ + *poser* put (see POSE²)] —im·pos′a·ble, *adj.* —im·pos′er, *n.*

im·pos·ing (ĭm pō′zĭng), *adj.* making an impression on the mind, as by great size, stately appearance, etc. —im·pos′ing·ly, *adv.* —im·pos′ing·ness, *n.*

imposing stone, *Print.* a slab resting upon a frame, on which pages of type or plates are imposed and on which type correcting in the page is done. Also, **imposing table.**

im·po·si·tion (ĭm′pə zĭsh′ən), *n.* **1.** the laying on of something as a burden, obligation, etc. **2.** something imposed, as a burden, etc; an unusual or extraordinarily burdensome requirement or task. **3.** act of imposing by or as by authority. **4.** an imposing upon a person as by taking undue advantage of his good nature, or something that has the effect of doing this. **5.** act of imposing fraudulently or deceptively on others; imposture. **6.** the ceremonial laying on of hands, as in confirmation. **7.** *Print.* the arrangement of pages in proper order in a chase for printing. **8.** *Rare.* act of putting, placing, or laying on.

im·pos·si·bil·i·ty (ĭm pŏs′ə bĭl′ə tĭ, ĭm′pŏs-), *n., pl.* -ties. **1.** the quality of being impossible. **2.** something impossible.

im·pos·si·ble (ĭm pŏs′ə bəl), *adj.* **1.** not possible; that cannot be, exist, or happen. **2.** that cannot be done or effected. **3.** that cannot be true, as a rumor. **4.** not to be done, endured, etc., with any degree of reason or propriety: *an impossible situation.* **5.** utterly impracticable. **6.** hopelessly unsuitable, undesirable, or objectionable: *an impossible person.* [ME, t. L: m.s. *impossibilis*] —im·pos′si·bly, *adv.*

im·post¹ (ĭm′pōst), *n.* **1.** a tax, tribute, or duty. **2.** a customs duty. **3.** *Racing.* the weight (including that of the jockey) assigned to a horse in a race. —*v.t.* **4.** to determine customs duties on, according to the kind of imports. [t. ML: s. *impostus* a tax, L *impositus* laid on]

im·post² (ĭm′pōst), *n.* *Archit.* **1.** the point where an arch rests on a wall or column. See diag. under **arch.** **2.** the condition of such resting or meeting. [t. F: m.

im·poste, t. It.: m. *imposta* architectural impost, der. *impostare* set upon, der. L. *positus,* pp., placed]

im·pos·tor (ĭm pŏs′tər), *n.* **1.** one who imposes fraudulently upon others. **2.** one who practices deception under an assumed character or name. [t. LL, der. L *impōnere* impose] —**Syn. 1.** pretender, deceiver, cheat.

im·pos·tume (ĭm pŏs′chōōm, -tūm), *n. Now Rare.* an abscess. Also, **im·pos·thume.** [ME *empostume,* t. OF, var. of *apostume,* t. LL: m. *apostūma,* var. of *apostēma,* t. Gk.: lit., separation (of pus)]

im·pos·ture (ĭm pŏs′chər), *n.* **1.** the action or practice of imposing fraudulently upon others. **2.** deception practiced under an assumed character or name, as by an impostor. **3.** an instance or piece of fraudulent imposition. [t. LL: m.s. *impostūra,* der. L *impōnere* impose]
—im·pos′tur·ous, *adj.*

im·po·sure (ĭm pō′zhər), *n.* imposition.

im·po·tence (ĭm′pə təns), *n.* **1.** the condition or quality of being impotent; weakness. **2.** complete failure of sexual power, esp. in the male. **3.** *Obs.* lack of self-restraint. Also, **im′po·ten·cy.**

im·po·tent (ĭm′pə tənt), *adj.* **1.** not potent; lacking power or ability. **2.** utterly unable (to do something). **3.** without force or effectiveness. **4.** lacking bodily strength, or physically helpless, as an aged person or a cripple. **5.** wholly lacking in sexual power. **6.** *Obs.* without restraint. —im′po·tent·ly, *adv.*

im·pound (ĭm pound′), *v.t.* **1.** to shut up in a pound, as a stray animal. **2.** to confine within an enclosure or within limits: *water impounded in a reservoir.* **3.** to seize, take, or appropriate summarily. **4.** to seize and retain in custody of the law, as a document for evidence. —im·pound·age (ĭm poun′dĭj), *n.* —im·pound′er, *n.*

im·pov·er·ish (ĭm pŏv′ər ĭsh, -pŏv′rĭsh), *v.t.* **1.** to reduce to poverty: *a country impoverished by war.* **2.** to make poor in quality, productiveness, etc.; exhaust the strength or richness of: *to impoverish the soil.* Also, **empoverish.** [ME *empoveris(en),* t. OF: m. *empoveriss-,* s. *empoverir,* der. *em-* EM-¹ + *povre* POOR] —im·pov′er·ish·er, *n.* —im·pov′er·ish·ment, *n.*

im·pov·er·ished (ĭm pŏv′ər ĭsht, -pŏv′rĭsht), *adj.* susceptible to poverty. —**Syn.** See **poor.**

im·prac·ti·ca·ble (ĭm prăk′tə kə bəl), *adj.* **1.** not practicable; that cannot be put into practice with the available means: *an impracticable plan.* **2.** unsuitable for practical use or purposes, as a device, material, etc. **3.** (of ground, places, etc.) impassable. **4.** (of persons, etc.) hard to deal with because of stubbornness, stupidity, etc. —im·prac′ti·ca·bil′i·ty, im·prac′ti·ca·ble·ness, *n.* —im·prac′ti·ca·bly, *adv.*

im·prac·ti·cal (ĭm prăk′tə kəl), *adj.* not practical.

im·pre·cate (ĭm′prə kāt′), *v.t.,* -cated, -cating. to call down or invoke (esp. evil or curses, as upon a person. [t. L: m.s. *imprecātus,* pp., having invoked] —im′pre·ca′tor, *n.* —im·pre·ca·to·ry (ĭm′prə kə tōr′ĭ), *adj.*

im·pre·ca·tion (ĭm′prə kā′shən), *n.* **1.** the act of imprecating; cursing. **2.** a curse or malediction.

im·preg·na·ble¹ (ĭm prĕg′nə bəl), *adj.* **1.** strong enough to resist attack; not to be taken by force: *an impregnable fort.* **2.** not to be overcome or overthrown: *an impregnable argument.* [ME *imprenable,* t. F: *im-* IM-¹ + *prenable* PREGNABLE] —im·preg′na·bil′i·ty, *n.* —im·preg′na·bly, *adv.* —**Syn. 1.** See **invincible.**

im·preg·na·ble² (ĭm prĕg′nə bəl), *adj.* capable of impregnation, as an egg. [f. IMPREGN(ATE) + -ABLE]

im·preg·nate (*v.* ĭm prĕg′nāt; *adj.* ĭm prĕg′nĭt, -nāt), *v.,* -nated, -nating, *adj.* —*v.t.* Also, *Obs.* or *Poetic,* im·pregn (ĭm prēn′). **1.** to make pregnant; get with child or young. **2.** to fertilize. **3.** to charge with something infused or permeating throughout; saturate. **4.** to fill interstices with a substance. **5.** to furnish with some actuating or modifying element infused or introduced; imbue, infect, or tincture. —*adj.* **6.** impregnated. [t. LL: m.s. *impraegnātus,* pp., made pregnant] —im′preg·na′tion, *n.* —im·preg′na·tor, *n.*

im·pre·sa (ĭm prā′zə; *It.* ĕm prĕ′zä), *n. Obs. except Hist.* **1.** a device or emblem. **2.** a motto. Also, **im·prese** (ĭm prēz′). [t. It.: enterprise]

im·pre·sa·ri·o (ĭm′prə sär′ĭ ō′; *It.* ĕm′prĕ sä′ryō), *n., pl.* -sarios, *It.* -sari (-sä′rē). **1.** the organizer or manager of an opera or concert company. **2.** a personal manager, teacher, or trainer of concert artists. [t. It., der. *impresa* enterprise] —im′pre·sa′ri·o·ship′, *n.*

im·pre·scrip·ti·ble (ĭm′prĭ skrĭp′tə bəl), *adj. Law.* not subject to prescription. —im′pre·scrip′ti·bly, *adv.*

im·press¹ (*v.* ĭm prĕs′; *n.* ĭm′prĕs), *v.,* -pressed or (*Archaic*) -prest; -pressing; *n.* —*v.t.* **1.** to affect deeply or strongly in mind or feelings; influence in opinion. **2.** to fix deeply or firmly on the mind or memory, as ideas, facts, etc. **3.** to urge, as something to be remembered or done. **4.** to press (a thing) into or on something. **5.** to produce (a mark, figure, etc.) by pressure; stamp; imprint. **6.** to apply with pressure, so as to leave a mark. **7.** to subject to, or mark by, pressure with something. **8.** to furnish with a mark, figure, etc., by or as by stamping. **9.** *Elect.* to produce (a voltage), or cause (a voltage) to appear or be produced on a conductor, circuit, etc. —*n.* **10.** act of impressing. **11.** a mark made by or as by pressure; stamp; imprint. **12.** a distinctive character or effect imparted. [ME *impresse(n),* t. L: m.s. *impressus,* pp., pressed upon] —im·press′er, *n.*

im·press² (ĭm prĕs′), *v.t.,*

im·press² (v. Ym prĕs′; n. Ym′prĕs), v., **-pressed** or (Archaic) **-prest; -pressing;** n. —v.t. **1.** to press or force into public service, as seamen. **2.** to seize or take for public use. —n. **3.** impressment. [f. IM-¹ + PRESS²]

im·press·i·ble (Ym prĕs′ə bəl), adj. capable of being impressed; impressionable. —**im·press′i·bil′i·ty,** n.

im·pres·sion (Ym prĕsh′ən), n. **1.** a strong effect produced on the intellect, feelings, or conscience. **2.** the first and immediate effect upon the mind in outward or inward perception; sensation. **3.** the effect produced by an agency or influence. **4.** a notion, remembrance, or belief, often one that is vague or indistinct. **5.** a mark, indentation, figure, etc., produced by pressure. **6.** Print., etc. **a.** the process or result of printing from type, plates, etc. **b.** a printed copy from type, a plate, an engraved block, etc. **c.** one of a number of printings made at different times from the same set of type, without alteration (as distinguished from an edition). **d.** the total number of copies of a book, etc., printed at one time from the one setting of type. **7.** Dentistry. a mold taken in plastic materials or plaster of Paris of teeth and the surrounding tissues. **8.** an image in the mind caused by something external to it. **9.** act of impressing. **10.** state of being impressed. [ME, t. L: s. impressio. See IMPRESS¹]

im·pres·sion·a·ble (Ym prĕsh′ən ə bəl, -prĕsh′nə-), adj. **1.** easily impressed or influenced; susceptible. **2.** capable of being impressed. —**im·pres′sion·a·bil′i·ty, im·pres′sion·a·ble·ness,** n.

im·pres·sion·ism (Ym prĕsh′ə nYz′əm), n. **1.** a way of painting (developed 1865–75) with informal subject matter and effects of light noted directly as they impress the artist, and developed as a method of expressing luminosity with juxtaposed touches of pure color. **2.** a theory and practice in literature which emphasizes immediate aspects of objects or actions without attention to details. **3.** a late 19th century and early 20th century method of musical composition, marked by the use of unorthodox means to express impressions or emotions (as in the work of Debussy). —**im·pres′sion·ist,** n., adj. —**im·pres′sion·is′tic,** adj.

im·pres·sive (Ym prĕs′Yv), adj. such as to impress the mind; arousing solemn feelings: an impressive ceremony. —**im·pres′sive·ly,** adv. —**im·pres′sive·ness,** n.

im·press·ment (Ym prĕs′mənt), n. the impressing of men, property, etc., as for public service or use. [f. IMPRESS² + -MENT]

im·pres·sure (Ym prĕsh′ər), n. Archaic. impression.

im·prest¹ (Ym′prĕst), n. **1.** an advance of money, esp. for some public business. **2.** Brit. (formerly) an advance payment made to a soldier or sailor at enlistment. [f. IM-¹ + prest (t. OF: s. prester lend, g. L. praestāre stand for). Cf. It. imprestare lend]

im·prest² (Ym prĕst′), v. Archaic. pt. and pp. of **impress.**

im·pri·ma·tur (Ym′prY mā′tər, -prī-), n. **1.** an official license to print or publish a book, etc. **2.** license; sanction; approval. [NL: let it be printed]

im·pri·mis (Ym prī′mYs), adv. Latin. in the first place.

im·print (n. Ym′prYnt; v. Ym prYnt′), n. **1.** a mark made by pressure; a figure impressed or printed on something. **2.** any impression or impressed effect. **3.** Bibliog. information printed at the foot of the title page of a book indicating the name of the publisher, usually supplemented with the place and date of publication. **4.** the printer's name and address as indicated on any printed matter. —v.t. **5.** to impress (a quality, character, or distinguishing mark). **6.** to produce (a mark, etc.) on something by pressure. **7.** to bestow (a kiss). **8.** to fix firmly on the mind, memory, etc. **9.** to make an imprint upon. [ME empreynte(n), t. OF: m. empreinter, der. empreinte a stamp, ult. der. L imprimere impress, imprint] —**im·print′er,** n.

im·pris·on (Ym prYz′ən), v.t. **1.** to put into or confine in a prison; detain in custody. **2.** to shut up as if in a prison; hold in restraint. —**im·pris′on·ment,** n.

im·prob·a·bil·i·ty (Ym prŏb′ə bYl′ə tY, Ym′prŏb-), n., pl. **-ties. 1.** the quality or fact of being improbable; unlikelihood. **2.** something improbable or unlikely.

im·prob·a·ble (Ym prŏb′ə bəl), adj. not probable; unlikely to be true or to happen. —**im·prob′a·bly,** adv.

im·pro·bi·ty (Ym prō′bə tY, -prŏb′ə tY), n. the reverse of probity; dishonesty; wickedness. [ME improbite, t. L: m.s. improbitas wickedness]

im·promp·tu (Ym prŏmp′tū, -tōo), adj. **1.** made or done without previous preparation: an impromptu address. **2.** suddenly or hastily prepared, made, etc.: an impromptu dinner. **3.** improvised, or having the character of an improvisation, as music. —adv. **4.** without preparation: verses written impromptu. —n. **5.** something impromptu; an impromptu speech, musical composition, performance, etc. [t. L: m. in promptū in readiness] —Syn. **1.** See extemporaneous.

im·prop·er (Ym prŏp′ər), adj. **1.** not proper; not strictly belonging, applicable, or right: an improper use for a thing. **2.** not in accordance with propriety of behavior, manners, etc.: improper conduct. **3.** unsuitable or inappropriate, as for the purpose or occasion: improper tools. **4.** abnormal or irregular. —**im·prop′er·ly,** adv. —**im·prop′er·ness,** n.

—Syn. **1-3.** IMPROPER, INDECENT, UNBECOMING, UNSEEMLY are applied to that which is unfitting or not in accordance with propriety. IMPROPER has a wide range, being applied to whatever is not suitable or fitting, and often specifically to what does not conform to the standards of conventional morality: improper diet, improper behavior in church, improper language. INDECENT, a strong word, is applied to what is offensively contrary to standards of propriety and esp. of modesty: indecent behavior, literature. UNBECOMING is applied to what is especially unfitting in the person concerned: conduct unbecoming a minister. UNSEEMLY is applied to whatever is unfitting or improper under the circumstances: unseemly mirth. —Ant. **1.** fitting. **2.** modest. **3.** suitable.

improper fraction, a fraction having the numerator greater than the denominator.

im·pro·pri·ate (adj. Ym prō′prY Yt, -āt′; v. Ym prō′prY āt′), adj., v., **-ated, -ating.** —adj. **1.** Brit. Eccles. Law. devolved into the hands of a layman. **2.** Obs. appropriated to private use. —v.t. **3.** Brit. Eccles. Law. to place (ecclesiastical property) in lay hands. **4.** Obs. to appropriate. [t. ML: m.s. impropriātus, pp. of impropriāre, der. L im- IM-¹ + proprius one's own, PROPER] —**im·pro′pri·a′tion,** n.

im·pro·pri·a·tor (Ym prō′prY ā′tər), n. a layman in possession of church property or revenues.

im·pro·pri·e·ty (Ym′prə prī′ə tY), n., pl. **-ties. 1.** quality of being improper; incorrectness. **2.** inappropriateness. **3.** unseemliness. **4.** an erroneous or unsuitable expression, act, etc. **5.** an improper use of a word.

im·prove (Ym prōov′), v., **-proved, -proving.** —v.t. **1.** to bring into a more desirable or excellent condition: to improve one's health. **2.** to make (land) more profitable or valuable by enclosure, cultivation, etc.; increase the value of (real property) by betterments, as buildings. **3.** to turn to account; make good use of: to improve an opportunity. —v.i. **4.** to increase in value, excellence, etc.; become better: the situation is improving. **5.** to make improvements (fol. by on or upon): to improve on one's earlier rank. [t. AF: m. emprower, der. OF em- IM-¹ + prou profit] —**im·prov′a·ble,** adj. —**im·prov′a·bil′i·ty, im·prov′a·ble·ness,** n. —**im·prov′a·bly,** adv. —**im·prov′er,** n. —**im·prov′ing·ly,** adv.

—Syn. **1.** IMPROVE, AMELIORATE, BETTER imply bringing to a more desirable state. IMPROVE usually implies remedying a lack or a felt need: to improve a process, oneself (gain additional knowledge, etc.). AMELIORATE, a formal word, implies improving oppressive, unjust, or difficult conditions: to ameliorate working conditions. To BETTER is to improve conditions which, though not bad, are unsatisfying: to better an attempt, oneself (gain a higher salary). —Ant. **1.** worsen.

im·prove·ment (Ym prōov′mənt), n. **1.** the act of improving. **2.** the state of being improved. **3.** a change or addition whereby a thing is improved. **4.** some thing or person that represents an advance on another in excellence or achievement. **5.** a bringing into a more valuable or desirable condition, as of land or real property; a making or becoming better; a betterment. **6.** something done or added to real property which increases its value. **7.** profitable use: the improvement of one's time.

im·prov·i·dent (Ym prŏv′ə dənt), adj. **1.** not provident; lacking foresight; incautious or unwary. **2.** neglecting to provide for future needs. —**im·prov′i·dence,** n. —**im·prov′i·dent·ly,** adv. —Syn. **1.** thoughtless, careless, heedless. **2.** shiftless, thriftless, unthrifty; wasteful, prodigal. —Ant. **1.** prudent. **2.** economical.

im·pro·vi·sa·tion (Ym′prə vī zā′shən, Ym′prŏv ə-), n. **1.** act of improvising. **2.** something improvised.

im·prov·i·sa·tor (Ym prŏv′ə zā′tər, Ym′prə vī-), n. one who improvises.

im·prov·i·sa·to·ry (Ym′prə vī′zə tōr′Y, -vYz′ə-), adj. of or pertaining to an improvisator or improvisation. —**im·prov·i·sa·to·ri·al** (Ym prŏv′Y zə tōr′Y əl), adj. —**im·prov′i·sa·to′ri·al·ly,** adv.

im·pro·vise (Ym′prə vīz′), v., **-vised, -vising.** —v.t. **1.** to prepare or provide offhand or hastily; extemporize. **2.** to compose (verse, music, etc.) on the spur of the moment. **3.** to recite, sing, etc., extemporaneously. —v.i. **4.** to compose, utter, or execute anything extemporaneously: he improvised in rhyme. [t. F: m.s. improviser, t. It.: m. improvvisare, der. improvviso extempore, g. L improvīsus unforeseen, unexpected] —**im·pro·vis′er,** n.

im·pro·vised (Ym′prə vīzd′), adj. made or said without previous preparation. —Syn. See extemporaneous.

im·prov·vi·sa·to·re (ēm′prŏv vē′zä tô′rĕ), n., pl. **-ri** (-rē). Italian. an improvisator.

im·pru·dent (Ym prōod′ənt), adj. not prudent; lacking prudence or discretion. [t. L: s. imprūdens] —**im·pru′dence,** n. —**im·pru′dent·ly,** adv.

im·pu·dence (Ym′pyə dəns), n. **1.** the quality or fact of being impudent; effrontery; insolence. **2.** impudent conduct or language. **3.** Obs. lack of modesty; shamelessness. Also, **im′pu·den·cy.** —Syn. **1.** impertinence, rudeness; brazenness, face. —Ant. **1.** courtesy.

im·pu·dent (Ym′pyə dənt), adj. **1.** characterized by a shameless boldness, assurance, or effrontery: impudent behavior. **2.** Obs. shameless or brazenly immodest. [t. L: s. impudens shameless] —**im′pu·dent·ly,** adv. —Syn. **1.** insolent, rude, saucy, pert; brazen. See impertinent. —Ant. **1.** polite.

im·pu·dic·i·ty (Ym′pyōo dYs′ə tY), n. immodesty.

im·pugn (Ym pūn′), v.t. **1.** to assail by words or arguments, as statements, motives, veracity, etc.; call in question; challenge as false. **2.** Rare. to assail a person for his statements or actions. [ME impugne(n), t. OF: m. impugner, t. L. impugnāre attack] —**im·pugn′a·ble,** adj. —**im·pug·na·tion** (Ym′pəg nā′shən), n. —**im·pugn·ment** (Ym pūn′mənt), n. —**im·pugn′er,** n.

im·pu·is·sant (ĭmpū′əsənt), *adj.* impotent; feeble; weak. [t. F. See IM-², PUISSANT] —**im·pu′is·sance,** *n.*

im·pulse (ĭm′pŭls), *n.* **1.** the inciting influence of a particular feeling, mental state, etc.: *to act under the impulse of pity.* **2.** sudden, involuntary inclination prompting to action, or a particular instance of it: *to be swayed by impulse.* **3.** an impelling action or force, driving onward or inducing motion. **4.** the effect of an impelling force; motion induced; impetus given. **5.** *Physiol.* a stimulus conveyed by the nervous system, muscle fibers, etc., either exciting or limiting organic functioning. **6.** *Mech.* the product of a force and the time during which it acts (sometimes restricted to cases in which the force is great and the time short, as in the blows of a hammer). **7.** *Elect.* a single, usually sudden, flow of current in one direction. [t. L: *m.s impulsus* a push against]

im·pul·sion (ĭm pŭl′shən), *n.* **1.** the act of impelling, driving onward, or pushing. **2.** the resulting state or effect; impulse; impetus. **3.** the inciting influence of some feeling or motive; mental impulse. **4.** constraining or inciting action on the mind or conduct: *divine impulsion.* [ME, t. L: s. *impulsio* influence, instigation]

im·pul·sive (ĭm pŭl′sĭv), *adj.* **1.** actuated or swayed by emotional or involuntary impulses: *an impulsive child.* **2.** having the power or effect of impelling; characterized by impulsion: *impulsive forces.* **3.** inciting to action: *an impulsive influence on humanity.* **4.** *Mech.* (of forces) acting momentarily; not continuous. —**im·pul′sive·ly,** *adv.* —**im·pul′sive·ness,** *n.* —**Syn. 1.** See **impetuous.**

im·pu·ni·ty (ĭm pū′nə tĭ), *n.* exemption from punishment. [t. L: m.s *impūnitas* omission of punishment] —**Syn.** See **exemption.**

im·pure (ĭm pyŏŏr′), *adj.* **1.** not pure; mixed with extraneous matter, esp. of an inferior or contaminating kind: *impure water.* **2.** modified by admixture, as color. **3.** mixed or combined with something else: *an impure style of architecture.* **4.** ceremonially unclean, as things, animals, etc. **5.** not morally pure; unchaste: *impure language.* **6.** marked by foreign and unsuitable elements or characteristics, as a style of art or of literary expression. [t. L: m.s *impūrus* not pure] —**im·pure′ly,** *adv.* —**im·pure′ness,** *n.*

im·pu·ri·ty (ĭm pyŏŏr′ə tĭ), *n., pl.* **-ties. 1.** the quality or state of being impure. **2.** (*often pl.*) that which is or makes impure: *impurities in drinking water.*

im·put·a·ble (ĭm pū′tə bəl), *adj.* that may be imputed; attributable. —**im·put′a·bil′i·ty, im·put′a·ble·ness,** *n.* —**im·put′a·bly,** *adv.*

im·pu·ta·tion (ĭm′pyŏŏ tā′shən), *n.* **1.** the act of imputing. **2.** an attribution, esp. of fault, crime, etc.

im·pute (ĭm pūt′), *v.t.,* **-puted, -puting. 1.** to attribute something discreditable to a person. **2.** to attribute or ascribe. **3.** *Law.* to charge. **4.** *Theol.* to attribute (righteousness, guilt, etc.) vicariously; ascribe as derived from another. **5.** *Obs.* to charge (a person) with fault. [ME, t. L: m.s *imputāre* bring into the reckoning] —**im·put·a·tive** (ĭm pū′tə tĭv), *adj.* —**im·put′a·tive·ly,** *adv.* —**im·put′a·tive·ness,** *n.* —**im·put′er,** *n.* —**Syn. 2.** See **attribute.**

impv., imperative.

in (ĭn), *prep.* **1.** a particle expressing inclusion, situation, presence, existence, action, etc., within limits, as of place, time, circumstances, etc., used to express: **a.** inclusion within space or limits, a whole, material or immaterial surroundings, etc.: *in the city, in the army, dressed in white, in politics.* **b.** inclusion within, or occurrence during the course of or at the expiration of, a period or limit of time: *in ancient times, to do a task in an hour, return in ten minutes.* **c.** situation, condition, occupation, action, manner, relation, means, etc.: *in darkness, in sickness, in service, in crossing the street, in confidence, in French.* **d.** object or purpose: *in honor of the event.* **e.** motion or direction from without to a point within (now usually into), or transition from one state to another: *to put in operation, break in two.* —*adv.* **2.** in or into some place, position, state, relation, etc. **3.** on the inside, or within. **4.** in one's house or office. **5.** in office or power. **6.** in possession or occupancy. **7.** having the turn to play, in a game. —*adj.* **8.** that is or gets in; internal; inward; incoming; inbound. —*n.* **9.** (*pl.*) those who are in, as the political party in power. **10. ins and outs, a.** nooks or recesses; windings and turnings. **b.** intricacies: *to know the ins and outs of a business.* [ME and OE, c. D and G *in,* Icel. *ī,* Goth. *in;* akin to L *in,* Gk. *en*]

in-¹, a prefix representing English IN, as in *income, indwelling, inland,* but used also as a verb-formative with transitive, intensive, or sometimes little apparent force, as in *intrust, inweave,* etc. It often assumes the same phases as **in-²,** as **en-, em-,** and **im-³.** [ME and OE; repr. IN, adv.]

in-², a prefix of Latin origin meaning primarily "in," but used also as a verb-formative with the same force as **in-¹,** as in *incarcerate, incantation.* Also, **-il¹, im-¹, ir-².** Cf. **em-, en-.** [t. L, repr. *in,* prep. (in F *en*), c. IN, prep.]

in-³, a prefix of Latin origin corresponding to English *un-,* having a negative or privative force, freely used as an English formative, esp. of adjectives and their derivatives and of nouns, as in *inattention, indefensible, inexpensive, inorganic, invariable.* This prefix assumes the

same phonetic phases as **in-²,** as in *impartial, immeasurable, illiterate, irregular,* etc. In French it became *en-* and thus occurs unfelt in such words as enemy (French *ennemi,* Latin *inimicus,* lit., not friendly). Also, **il-², im-², ir-².** [t. L; akin to Gk. *an-, a-,* ᴀ-⁶, and UN-²] —**Syn.** The prefixes IN- and UN- may both have, among other uses, a negative force. IN- is the form from the classical languages (Greek and Latin) and is therefore used in learned words or in words derived from those languages: *inaccessible, inaccuracy, inadequate,* etc. UN- is the native form going back to Old English, used in words of native origin, and sometimes used in combination with words of other origins, if these words are in common use: *unloving, unmanly, unfeeling, unnecessary, unsafe.* Occasionally the prefix UN- is used with a frequently used word in a common meaning, as in *unsanitary* (not clean), and IN- with the same word in a more technical sense, as *insanitary* (likely to cause disease). In England the prefix IN- is more commonly used than in the United States.

-in¹, a suffix used in adjectives of Greek or Latin origin meaning "pertaining to," and (in nouns thence derived) also imitated in English, as in *coffin, cousin, lupin* (*lupine*), etc.; and occurring unfelt in abstract nouns formed as nouns in Latin, as *ruin.* [ME *-in, -ine,* t. OF, t. L: m. *-inus, -ina, -inum,* t. Gk.: m. *-inos, -inē, -inon*]

-in², a noun suffix used in a special manner in chemical and mineralogical nomenclature, as in *glycerin, acetin,* etc. In spelling usage wavers between *-in* and *-ine.* In chemistry a certain distinction of use is attempted, basic substances having the termination *-ine* rather than *-in,* as *aconitine, aniline,* etc., and *-in* being restricted to certain neutral compounds, glycerides, glucosides, and proteids, as *albumin, palmitin,* etc., but this distinction is not always observed. [t. NL: s. *-ina.* See *-INE²*]

In, *Chem.* indium.

in., inch; inches.

in·a·bil·i·ty (ĭn′ə bĭl′ə tĭ), *n.* lack of ability; lack of power, capacity, or means. —**Syn.** See **disability.**

in ab·sen·ti·a (ĭn ăb sĕn′shĭ ə), *Latin.* in or during (one's) absence.

in·ac·ces·si·ble (ĭn′ăk sĕs′ə bəl), *adj.* not accessible; inapproachable. —**in′ac·ces′si·bil′i·ty, in′ac·ces′si·ble·ness,** *n.* —**in′ac·ces′si·bly,** *adv.*

in·ac·cu·ra·cy (ĭn ăk′yər ə sĭ), *n., pl.* **-cies. 1.** the quality of being inaccurate. **2.** that which is inaccurate. —**Syn. 2.** error, mistake, blunder, slip.

in·ac·cu·rate (ĭn ăk′yər ĭt), *adj.* not accurate. —**in·ac′cu·rate·ly,** *adv.* —**in·ac′cu·rate·ness,** *n.* —**Syn.** inexact, loose; incorrect, erroneous, wrong, faulty.

In·a·chus (ĭn′ə kəs), *n.* Gk. *Myth.* a river god who became the first king of Argos; father of Io.

in·ac·tion (ĭn ăk′shən), *n.* absence of action; idleness.

in·ac·ti·vate (ĭn ăk′tə vāt′), *v.t.,* **-vated, -vating. 1.** to make inactive. **2.** *Immunol.* to stop the activity of (certain biological substances).

in·ac·tive (ĭn ăk′tĭv), *adj.* **1.** not active; inert. **2.** indolent; sluggish; passive. **3.** *Mil.* not on active duty or status. **4.** *Phys. Chem.* denoting a compound which does not rotate the plane of vibration of polarized light. —**in·ac·ti·va·tion** (ĭn′ăk tə vā′shən, ĭn ăk′/-), *n.* —**in·ac′tive·ly,** *adv.* —**in·ac′tiv·i·ty, in·ac′tive·ness,** *n.* —**Syn. 1, 2.** INACTIVE, DORMANT, INERT, SLUGGISH, TORPID suggest lack of activity. INACTIVE indicates absence of action, indisposition to activity, or cessation of activity: *an inactive compound, life, file of papers.* DORMANT suggests the quiescence or inactivity of that which sleeps but may be roused to action: *a dormant volcano.* INERT suggests the condition of dead matter, with no inherent power of motion or action; it may also mean unable to move, or heavy and hard to move: *an inert mass, inert from hunger.* SLUGGISH expresses slowness of natural activity or of that which does not move readily or vigorously: *a sluggish stream, brain.* TORPID suggests a state of suspended physical powers, a condition particularly of animals which hibernate: *snakes are torpid in cold weather.* —**Ant. 1.** lively.

in·a·dapt·a·ble (ĭn′ə dăp′tə bəl), *adj.* not adaptable; incapable of being adapted. —**in′a·dapt′a·bil′i·ty,** *n.*

in·ad·e·quate (ĭn ăd′ə kwĭt), *adj.* not adequate. —**in·ad′e·qua·cy, in·ad′e·quate·ness,** *n.* —**in·ad′e·quate·ly,** *adv.* —**Syn.** inapt, incompetent; insufficient, incommensurate; defective, imperfect, incomplete.

in·ad·mis·si·ble (ĭn′əd mĭs′ə bəl), *adj.* not admissible; *inadmissible evidence.* —**in′ad·mis′si·bil′i·ty,** *n.* —**in′ad·mis′si·bly,** *adv.*

in·ad·vert·ence (ĭn′əd vûr′təns), *n.* **1.** quality of being inadvertent; heedlessness. **2.** an act or effect of inattention; an oversight. [t. ML: m.s *inadvertentia*]

in·ad·vert·en·cy (ĭn′əd vûr′tən sĭ), *n., pl.* **-cies.** = inadvertence.

in·ad·vert·ent (ĭn′əd vûr′tənt), *adj.* **1.** not attentive; heedless. **2.** characterized by lack of attention, as actions, etc. **3.** unintentional: *an inadvertent insult.* —**in′ad·vert′ent·ly,** *adv.*

in·ad·vis·a·ble (ĭn′əd vī′zə bəl), *adj.* not advisable; inexpedient. —**in′ad·vis′a·bil′i·ty,** *n.* —**in′ad·vis′a·bly,** *adv.*

-inae, *Zool.* a suffix of the names of subfamilies. [t. L, fem. pl. of adjectives ending in *-inus.* See **-INE¹**]

in ae·ter·num (ĭn ē tûr′nəm), *Latin.* forever.

in·al·ien·a·ble (ĭn āl′yən ə bəl), *adj.* not alienable; that cannot be transferred to another: *inalienable rights.* —**in·al′ien·a·bil′i·ty,** *n.* —**in·al′ien·a·bly,** *adv.*

in·al·ter·a·ble (ĭn ôl′tər ə bəl), *adj.* not alterable. —**in·al′ter·a·bil′i·ty,** *n.* —**in·al′ter·a·bly,** *adv.*

---

b., blend of, blended; **c.,** cognate with; **d.,** dialect, dialectal; **der.,** derived from; **f.,** formed from; **g.,** going back to; **m.,** modification of; **r.,** replacing; **s.,** stem of; **t.,** taken from; **?,** perhaps. See the full key on inside cover.

in·am·o·ra·ta (ĭn·ăm′ə·rä′tə, ĭn·ăm′-), *n.*, *pl.* **-tas.** a female lover: a woman who loves or is loved. [t. It.: m. *inamorata* sweetheart (fem.), der. *amore* love, g. L *amor*]

in·am·o·ra·to (ĭn·ăm′ə·rä′tō, ĭn·ăm′-), *n.* a male lover. [see INAMORATA]

in-and-in (ĭn′ənd·ĭn′), *adv.* repeatedly within the same family, strain, etc.: *to breed stock in-and-in.*

in·ane (ĭn·ān′), *adj.* **1.** lacking sense or ideas; silly: *inane questions.* **2.** empty; void. —*n.* **3.** that which is inane or void; the void of infinite space. [t. L: m. s. *inānis* empty, vain] —**in·ane′ly,** *adv.*

in·an·i·mate (ĭn·ăn′ə·mĭt), *adj.* **1.** not animate; lifeless. **2.** spiritless; sluggish; dull. —**in·an′i·mate·ly,** *adv.* —**in·an′i·mate·ness,** *n.*

in·a·ni·tion (ĭn′ə·nĭsh′ən), *n.* **1.** exhaustion from lack of nourishment; starvation. **2.** emptiness. [ME, t. LL: s. *inānitio,* der. L *inānire* make empty]

in·an·i·ty (ĭn·ăn′ə·tĭ), *n.*, *pl.* **-ties.** **1.** lack of sense or ideas; silliness. **2.** an inane remark, etc. **3.** emptiness.

in·ap·peas·a·ble (ĭn′ə·pēz′ə·bəl), *adj.* not appeasable; not to be appeased: *inappeasable anger.*

in·ap·pe·tence (ĭn·ăp′ə·təns), *n.* lack of appetence or appetite. Also, **in·ap′pe·ten·cy.**

in·ap·pli·ca·ble (ĭn·ăp′lə·kə·bəl), *adj.* not applicable; unsuitable. —**in·ap′pli·ca·bil′i·ty, in·ap′pli·ca·ble·ness,** *n.* —**in·ap′pli·ca·bly,** *adv.*

in·ap·po·site (ĭn·ăp′ə·zĭt), *adj.* not pertinent. —**in·ap′po·site·ly,** *adv.*

in·ap·pre·ci·a·ble (ĭn′ə·prē′shĭ·ə·bəl), *adj.* imperceptible; insignificant: *an inappreciable difference.* —**in′ap·pre′ci·a·bly,** *adv.*

in·ap·pre·ci·a·tive (ĭn′ə·prē′shĭ·ā′tĭv), *adj.* not appreciative; lacking in appreciation. —**in′ap·pre′ci·a′tive·ly,** *adv.* —**in′ap·pre′ci·a′tive·ness,** *n.*

in·ap·pre·hen·si·ble (ĭn′ăp·rĭ·hĕn′sə·bəl), *adj.* not to be grasped by the senses or intellect.

in·ap·pre·hen·sion (ĭn′ăp·rĭ·hĕn′shən), *n.* lack of apprehension.

in·ap·pre·hen·sive (ĭn′ăp·rĭ·hĕn′sĭv), *adj.* **1.** not apprehensive (often fol. by *of*). **2.** without apprehension.

in·ap·proach·a·ble (ĭn′ə·prō′chə·bəl), *adj.* **1.** not approachable. **2.** without rival. —**in′ap·proach′a·bil′i·ty,** *n.* —**in′ap·proach′a·bly,** *adv.*

in·ap·pro·pri·ate (ĭn′ə·prō′prĭ·ĭt), *adj.* not appropriate. —**in′ap·pro′pri·ate·ly,** *adv.* —**in′ap·pro′pri·ate·ness,** *n.*

in·apt (ĭn·ăpt′), *adj.* **1.** not apt or fitted. **2.** without aptitude or capacity. —**in·apt′ly,** *adv.* —**in·apt′ness,** *n.* —**Syn. 1.** unsuited, unsuitable, inappropriate.

in·apt·i·tude (ĭn·ăp′tə·tūd′, -tood′), *n.* **1.** lack of aptitude; unfitness. **2.** unskillfulness.

in·arch (ĭn·ärch′), *v.t.* *Bot.* to graft by uniting a growing branch to a stock without separating the branch from its parent stock. [f. IN-² + ARCH¹]

in·arm (ĭn·ärm′), *v.t.* to hold in, or as in the arms.

in·ar·tic·u·late (ĭn′är·tĭk′yə·lĭt), *adj.* **1.** not articulate; not uttered or emitted with expressive or intelligible modulations: *inarticulate sounds.* **2.** unable to use articulate speech: *inarticulate with rage.* **3.** *Anat., Zool.* not jointed; having no articulation or joint. [t. LL: m.s. *inarticulātus* not distinct. See IN-³, ARTICULATE] —**in′ar·tic′u·late·ly,** *adv.* —**in′ar·tic′u·late·ness,** *n.*

Inarching

in·ar·ti·fi·cial (ĭn·är′tə·fĭsh′əl), *adj.* **1.** not artificial; natural; artless; plain or simple. **2.** inartistic. —**in·ar′ti·fi′ci·al′i·ty,** *n.* —**in·ar·ti·fi′cial·ly,** *adv.*

in·ar·tis·tic (ĭn′är·tĭs′tĭk), *adj.* **1.** not artistic; aesthetically poor. **2.** lacking in artistic sense. Also, **in′ar·tis′ti·cal.** —**in′ar·tis′ti·cal·ly,** *adv.*

in·as·much as (ĭn′əz·mŭch′), **1.** in view of the fact that; seeing that; since. **2.** in so far as; to such a degree as. —**Syn. 1.** See **because.**

in·at·ten·tion (ĭn′ə·tĕn′shən), *n.* **1.** lack of attention; negligence. **2.** an act of neglect.

in·at·ten·tive (ĭn′ə·tĕn′tĭv), *adj.* not attentive. —**in′at·ten′tive·ly,** *adv.* —**in′at·ten′tive·ness,** *n.*

in·au·di·ble (ĭn·ô′də·bəl), *adj.* incapable of being heard. —**in·au′di·bil′i·ty,** *n.* —**in·au′di·bly,** *adv.*

in·au·gu·ral (ĭn·ô′gyə·rəl, -gə·rəl), *adj.* **1.** of or pertaining to an inauguration. —*n.* **2.** an address, as of a president, at the beginning of a term of office. [t. F, der. *inaugurer,* t. L: m. *inaugurāre* INAUGURATE]

in·au·gu·rate (ĭn·ô′gyə·rāt′, -gə-), *v.t.,* **-rated, -rating. 1.** to make a formal beginning of; initiate; commence; begin. **2.** to induct into office with formal ceremonies; install. **3.** to introduce into public use by some formal ceremony. [t. L: m.s. *inaugurātus,* pp., consecrated or installed with augural ceremonies] —**in·au′gu·ra′tion,** *n.* —**in·au′gu·ra′tor,** *n.*

Inauguration Day, *U.S.* the day on which the president is inaugurated, being Jan. 20 of every year next after a year whose number is divisible by four. Prior to the Twentieth Amendment to the Constitution (ratified Feb. 6, 1933), it was March 4.

in·aus·pi·cious (ĭn′ô·spĭsh′əs), *adj.* not auspicious. —**in′aus·pi′cious·ly,** *adv.* —**in′aus·pi′cious·ness,** *n.*

in·be·ing (ĭn′bē′ĭng), *n.* **1.** the condition of existing in something else; immanence. **2.** inward nature.

in·board (ĭn′bôrd′), *adv., adj. Naut.* within the hull or interior, or toward the center, of a ship.

in·born (ĭn′bôrn′), *adj.* implanted by nature; innate. —**Syn.** inbred, inherent, natural, native. —**Ant.** acquired.

in·bound (ĭn′bound′), *adj.* inward bound: *inbound ships.*

in·breathe (ĭn·brēth′), *v.t.,* **-breathed, -breathing. 1.** to breathe in; infuse. **2.** to inspire.

in·bred (ĭn′brĕd′), *adj.* **1.** bred within; innate; native. **2.** resulting from or involved in inbreeding.

in·breed (ĭn·brēd′), *v.t.,* **-bred, -breeding. 1.** to breed (animals) in-and-in. **2.** to breed within; engender.

in·breed·ing (ĭn′brē′dĭng), *n. Biol.* the mating of related individuals such as cousins, sire-daughter, brother-sister, or self-fertilized plants. Inbreeding automatically fixes the genes, making them homozygous.

in·burst (ĭn′bûrst′), *n.* a bursting in; irruption.

inc., **1.** inclosure. **2.** included. **3.** including. **4.** inclusive. **5.** (*also cap.*) incorporated. **6.** increase.

In·ca (ĭng′kə), *n.* **1.** one of the dominant groups of South American Indians who occupied Peru prior to the Spanish conquest. **2.** the chief ruler of the race. [t. Sp., Pg., t. Peruvian] —**In′can,** *n., adj.*

in·cage (ĭn·kāj′), *v.t.,* **-caged, -caging.** encage.

in·cal·cu·la·ble (ĭn·kăl′kyə·lə·bəl), *adj.* **1.** that cannot be calculated; beyond calculation. **2.** that cannot be forecast. **3.** uncertain. —**in·cal′cu·la·bil′i·ty, in·cal′cu·la·ble·ness,** *n.* —**in·cal′cu·la·bly,** *adv.*

in·ca·les·cent (ĭn′kə·lĕs′ənt), *adj.* increasing in heat. [t. L: s. *incalescens,* ppr.] —**in′ca·les′cence,** *n.*

in·can·desce (ĭn′kən·dĕs′), *v.i., v.t.,* **-desced, -descing.** to glow or cause to glow with heat. [t. L: m.s. *incandescere* grow hot, glow]

in·can·des·cence (ĭn′kən·dĕs′əns), *n.* the state of a body caused by approximately white heat, when it may be used as a source of artificial light. Also, **in′can·des′cen·cy.**

in·can·des·cent (ĭn′kən·dĕs′ənt), *adj.* **1.** (of light, etc.) produced by incandescence. **2.** glowing or white with heat. **3.** intensely bright; brilliant. [t. L: s. *incandescens,* ppr., growing hot] —**in′can·des′cent·ly,** *adv.*

incandescent lamp, a lamp whose light is due to the glowing of some material, as the common electric lamp which contains a filament rendered luminous by the passage of current through it.

in·can·ta·tion (ĭn′kăn·tā′shən), *n.* **1.** the chanting or uttering of words purporting to have magical power. **2.** the formula employed; a spell or charm. **3.** magical ceremonies. **4.** magic; sorcery. [ME *incantacion,* t. LL: m.s. *incantātio* enchantment]

in·ca·pa·ble (ĭn·kā′pə·bəl), *adj.* **1.** not capable. **2.** not having the capacity or power for a specified act or function (fol. by *of*). **3.** not open to the influence; not susceptible or admitting (fol. by *of*): *incapable of exact measurement.* **4.** without ordinary capability or ability; incompetent: *incapable workers.* **5.** without qualification, esp. legal qualification (often fol. by *of*): *incapable of holding public office.* —*n.* **6.** a thoroughly incompetent person. [t. LL: m.s. *incapābilis.* See IN-³, CAPABLE] —**in·ca′pa·bil′i·ty, in·ca′pa·ble·ness,** *n.* —**in·ca′pa·bly,** *adv.*

—**Syn. 1.** INCAPABLE, INCOMPETENT, INEFFICIENT, UNABLE are applied to one who or that which is lacking in ability, preparation, or power for whatever is to be done. INCAPABLE usually means inherently lacking in ability or power: *incapable of appreciating music; a bridge incapable of carrying heavy loads.* INCOMPETENT, generally used only of persons, means unfit or unqualified for a particular task: *incompetent as an administrator.* INEFFICIENT means wasteful in the use of effort or power: *an inefficient manager, inefficient methods.* UNABLE usually refers to a temporary condition of inability to do some specific thing: *unable to relax, to go to a concert.*

in·ca·pa·cious (ĭn′kə·pā′shəs), *adj.* **1.** not capacious; lacking capacity; narrow; limited. **2.** mentally incapable. [f. INCAPACI(TY) + -OUS] —**in′ca·pa′cious·ness,** *n.*

in·ca·pac·i·tate (ĭn′kə·păs′ə·tāt′), *v.t.,* **-tated, -tating. 1.** to deprive of capacity; make incapable or unfit; disqualify. **2.** *Law.* to deprive of power to perform acts with legal consequences. —**in′ca·pac′i·ta′tion,** *n.*

in·ca·pac·i·ty (ĭn′kə·păs′ə·tĭ), *n., pl.* **-ties. 1.** lack of capacity; incapability. **2.** legal disqualification. [t. ML: m. *incapācitas*]

in·car·cer·ate (*v.* ĭn·kär′sə·rāt′; *adj.* ĭn·kär′sər·ĭt, -sə·rāt′), *v.,* **-ated, -ating,** *adj.* —*v.t.* **1.** to imprison; confine. **2.** to enclose; constrict closely. —*adj.* **3.** imprisoned. [t. ML: m.s. *incarcerātus,* pp. of *incarcerāre,* der. L *in-* IN-² + *carcer* prison] —**in·car′cer·a′tion,** *n.* —**in·car′cer·a′tor,** *n.*

in·car·di·nate (ĭn·kär′də·nāt′), *v.t.,* **-nated, -nating. 1.** to institute as a cardinal. **2.** to institute as chief presbyter, priest, etc., in a particular church or place. [t. ML: m.s. *incardinātus,* pp. See CARDINAL] —**in·car′di·na′tion,** *n.*

in·car·na·dine (ĭn·kär′nə·dīn′, -dĭn), *adj., n., v.,* **-dined, -dining.** —*adj.* **1.** flesh-colored; pale red. **2.** crimson. —*n.* **3.** an incarnadine color. —*v.t.* **4.** to make incarnadine. [t. F: m. *incarnadin,* t. d. It.: m. *incarnadino,* ult. der. LL *incarnātus.* See INCARNATE]

in·car·nate (*adj.* Ynkär′nYt, -nāt; *v.* Ynkär′nāt), *adj.*, *v.*, -nated, -nating. —*adj.* 1. embodied in flesh; invested with a bodily, esp. a human, form: *a devil incarnate.* 2. personified or typified, as a quality or idea: *chivalry incarnate.* 3. flesh-colored or crimson. —*v.t.* 4. to put into or represent in a concrete form, as an idea. 5. to be the embodiment or type of. 6. to embody in flesh; invest with a bodily, esp. a human, form. [ME, t. LL: m.s. *incarnātus*, pp., made flesh]

in·car·na·tion (Yn′kärnā′shən), *n.* 1. an incarnate being or form. 2. a living being embodying a deity or spirit. 3. assumption of human form or nature, as by a divine being: *the incarnation of God in Christ.* 4. a person or thing representing or exhibiting some quality, idea, etc., in typical form. 5. act of incarnating. 6. state of being incarnated. [ME, t. LL: s. *incarnātio*]

in·case (Ynkās′), *v.t.*, -cased, -casing. to enclose in or as in a case. Also, **encase.** [f. IN-² + CASE²] —**in·case′ment,** *n.*

in·cau·tion (Ynkô′shən), *n.* lack of caution; heedlessness; carelessness. [f. IN-³ + CAUTION]

in·cau·tious (Ynkô′shəs), *adj.* not cautious. —**in·cau′tious·ly,** *adv.* —**in·cau′tious·ness,** *n.*

in·cen·di·a·rism (Ynsĕn′dYərYz′əm), *n.* act or practice of an incendiary; malicious burning.

in·cen·di·ar·y (Ynsĕn′dYĕr′Y), *adj.*, *n.*, *pl.* -aries. —*adj.* 1. used or adapted for setting property on fire: *incendiary bombs.* 2. of or pertaining to the criminal setting on fire of property. 3. tending to arouse strife, sedition, etc.; inflammatory: *incendiary speeches.* —*n.* 4. one who maliciously sets fire to buildings or other property. 5. *Mil.* a shell containing phosphorus or similar material producing great heat. 6. one who stirs up strife, sedition, etc.; an agitator. [t. L: m.s. *incendiārius* causing fire]

in·cense¹ (Yn′sĕns), *n.*, *v.*, -censed, -censing. —*n.* 1. an aromatic gum or other substance producing a sweet odor when burned, used esp. in religious ceremonies. 2. the perfume or smoke arising from such a substance when burned. 3. any pleasant perfume or fragrance. 4. homage or adulation. —*v.t.* 5. to perfume with incense. 6. to burn incense for. —*v.i.* 7. to burn or offer incense. [t. LL: m.s. *incensum* incense, prop. pp. neut. of L *incendere* set on fire; r. ME *encens,* t. OF]

in·cense² (Ynsĕns′), *v.t.*, -censed, -censing. to inflame with wrath; make angry; enrage. [ME *incence*(*n*), t. L: m.s. *incensus,* pp., set on fire, kindled] —**in·cense′ment,** *n.* —**Syn.** See enrage.

in·cen·tive (Ynsĕn′tYv), *n.* 1. that which incites to action, etc. —*adj.* 2. inciting, as to action; stimulating; provocative. [ME, t. L: m.s. *incentīvus* inciting, setting the tune] —**in·cen′tive·ly,** *adv.* —**Syn.** 1. See motive.

in·cept (Ynsĕpt′), *v.i.* 1. *Brit.* to complete the taking of a degree of master or doctor in a university, esp. Cambridge. —*v.t.* 2. to take in; intussuscept. [t. L: s. *inceptus,* pp. begun, commenced] —**in·cep′tor,** *n.*

in·cep·tion (Ynsĕp′shən), *n.* 1. beginning; start. 2. *Brit.* act of incepting in a university.

in·cep·tive (Ynsĕp′tYv), *adj.* 1. *Gram.* (of a derived verb, or of an aspect in verb inflection) expressing the beginning of the action indicated by the underlying verb. For example: Latin verbs in *-sco* generally have inceptive force, as *calescō* "become or begin to be hot" from *caleō* "be hot." 2. beginning; initial. —*n.* 3. *Gram.* **a.** the inceptive aspect. **b.** a verb therein. —**in·cep′tive·ly,** *adv.*

in·cer·ti·tude (Ynsûr′tətūd′,-tōōd′), *n.* 1. uncertainty; doubtfulness. 2. insecurity. [f. IN-³ + CERTITUDE]

in·ces·sant (Ynsĕs′ənt), *adj.* continuing without interruption: *an incessant noise.* [t. LL: s. *incessans* unceasing] —**in·ces′san·cy, in·ces′sant·ness,** *n.* —**in·ces′sant·ly,** *adv.* —**Syn.** ceaseless, unceasing, continual, continuous, constant. —**Ant.** intermittent.

in·cest (Yn′sĕst), *n.* 1. the crime of sexual intercourse between persons related by blood or marriage within the degrees in which marriage is prohibited. 2. **spiritual incest,** *Eccles.* sexual intercourse between persons who have been baptized or confirmed together. [ME, t. L: s. *incestus,* or *incestum* (neut.) unchaste]

in·ces·tu·ous (Ynsĕs′chōōəs), *adj.* 1. guilty of incest. 2. involving incest. —**in·ces′tu·ous·ly,** *adv.* —**in·ces′tu·ous·ness,** *n.*

inch¹ (Ynch), *n.* 1. a unit of length, ¹/₁₂ foot, equivalent to 2.54 centimeters. In the U.S., it is defined by law in terms of the meter, 39.37 in. being exactly equal to one meter. 2. a very small amount of anything: *flogged within an inch of his life.* 3. **by inches,** or **inch by inch,** very gradually. 4. **every inch,** in every respect: *every inch a king.* —*v.i.*, *v.t.* 5. to move by inches or small degrees. [ME; OE *ynce,* t. L: m.s. *uncia* twelfth part, inch, ounce. Cf. OUNCE¹]

inch² (Ynch), *n.* *Scot.* an island. [ME, t. Gaelic: m. *innse,* gen. of *innis* island]

inch·meal (Ynch′mēl′), *adv.* by inches; inch by inch; little by little (often prec. by *by*).

in·cho·ate (Ynkō′Yt), *adj.* 1. just begun; incipient. 2. rudimentary. [t. L: m.s. *inchoātus, incohātus,* pp., begun] —**in·cho′ate·ly,** *adv.* —**in·cho′ate·ness,** *n.*

in·cho·a·tion (Yn′kō ā′shən), *n.* beginning; origin.

in·cho·a·tive (Ynkō′ətYv), *adj.* 1. *Gram.* inceptive. 2. *Rare.* inchoate. —*n.* 3. *Gram.* an inceptive.

In·chon (Yn′chŏn′), *n.* a seaport in W South Korea. 265,767 (1949). Also, **Chemulpo.** Japanese, **Jinsen.**

inch·worm (Ynch′wûrm′), *n.* measuring worm.

in·ci·dence (Yn′sədəns), *n.* 1. the range of occurrence or influence of a thing, or the extent of its effects: *the incidence of a disease.* 2. the falling, or direction or manner of falling, of a ray of light, etc., on a surface. 3. a falling upon, affecting, or befalling. 4. the fact or the manner of being incident. 5. *Geom.* partial coincidence of two figures, as of a line and a plane containing it.

in·ci·dent (Yn′sədənt), *n.* 1. an occurrence or event. 2. a distinct piece of action, or an episode, as in a story, play, etc. 3. something that occurs casually in connection with something else. 4. something appertaining or attaching to something else. 5. (in England as a euphemism in World War II) a case of bombing. —*adj.* 6. likely or apt to happen (fol. by *to*). 7. naturally appertaining: *hardships incident to the life of an explorer.* 8. conjoined or attaching, esp. as subordinate to a principal thing. 9. falling or striking on something. [ME, t. L: s. *incidens,* ppr., befalling] —**Syn.** 1. See event.

in·ci·den·tal (Yn′sədĕn′təl), *adj.* 1. happening or likely to happen in fortuitous or subordinate conjunction with something else. 2. liable to happen or naturally appertaining (fol. by *to*). 3. incurred casually and in addition to the regular or main amount: *incidental expenses.* —*n.* 4. something incidental, as a circumstance. 5. (*pl.*) minor expenses. —**Syn.** 1. casual, chance, fortuitous; contingent. —**Ant.** 1. fundamental.

in·ci·den·tal·ly (Yn′sədĕn′təlY), *adv.* 1. in an incidental manner. 2. by the way.

in·cin·er·ate (YnsYn′ərāt′), *v.t.*, *v.i.*, -ated, -ating. to burn or reduce to ashes; cremate. [t. ML: m.s. *incinerātus,* pp., of *incinerāre,* der. L *in-* IN-² + *cinis* ashes] —**in·cin′er·a′tion,** *n.*

in·cin·er·a·tor (YnsYn′ərā′tər), *n.* a furnace or apparatus for incinerating.

in·cip·i·ent (YnsYp′Yənt), *adj.* beginning to exist or appear; in an initial stage. [t. L: s. *incipiens,* ppr.] —**in·cip′i·ence, in·cip′i·en·cy,** *n.* —**in·cip′i·ent·ly,** *adv.*

in·ci·pit (Yn′sY pYt), *Latin.* (here) begins.

in·cise (Ynsīz′), *v.t.*, -cised, -cising. 1. to cut into; cut marks, etc. upon. 2. to make (marks, etc.) by cutting; engrave; carve. [t. F: m.s. *inciser,* ult. der. L *incisus,* pp., cut into]

in·cised (Ynsīzd′), *adj.* 1. cut into: *the incised gums.* 2. made by cutting: *an incised wound.*

in·ci·sion (YnsYzh′ən), *n.* 1. a cut, gash, or notch. 2. act of incising. 3. a cutting into, esp. for surgical purposes. 4. incisiveness; keenness. [ME, t. L: s. *incīsio*]

in·ci·sive (Ynsī′sYv), *adj.* 1. penetrating, trenchant, or biting: *an incisive tone of voice.* 2. sharp; keen; acute. 3. adapted for cutting: *the incisive teeth.* —**in·ci′sive·ly,** *adv.* —**in·ci′sive·ness,** *n.*

in·ci·sor (Ynsī′zər), *n.* a tooth in the anterior part of the jaw adapted for cutting. [t. NL]

in·ci·so·ry (Ynsī′sərY), *adj.* adapted for cutting, as the incisor teeth.

in·cis·ure (YnsYzh′ər), *n.* *Anat.* a notch, as in a bone or other structure. —**in·cis′ur·al,** *adj.*

in·cite (Ynsīt′), *v.t.*, -cited, -citing. to urge on; stimulate or prompt to action. [late ME, t. L: m.s. *incitāre* set in motion] —**in·ci·ta·tion** (Yn′sī tā′shən, -sY′-), *n.* —**in·cit′er,** *n.* —**in·cit′ing·ly,** *adv.* —**Syn.** encourage; instigate, provoke, goad, spur, arouse, fire; induce.

in·cite·ment (Ynsīt′mənt), *n.* 1. act of inciting. 2. that which incites; motive; incentive.

in·ci·vil·i·ty (Yn′səvYl′ətY), *n.*, *pl.* -ties. 1. the quality or fact of being uncivil; uncivil behavior or treatment. 2. an uncivil act.

incl., 1. inclosure. 2. including. 3. inclusive.

in·clasp (Ynkläsp′, -kläsp′), *v.t.* enclasp.

in·clem·ent (Ynklĕm′ənt), *adj.* (of the weather, etc.) not clement; severe or harsh. [t. L: s. *inclēmens* harsh] —**in·clem′en·cy,** *n.* —**in·clem′ent·ly,** *adv.*

in·clin·a·ble (YnklI′nəbəl), *adj.* 1. having a mental bent or tendency in a certain direction; inclined. 2. favorable. 3. capable of being inclined.

in·cli·na·tion (Yn′klənā′shən), *n.* 1. a set or bent (esp. of the mind or will); a liking or preference: *much against his inclination.* 2. that to which one is inclined. 3. act of inclining. 4. state of being inclined. 5. deviation or amount of deviation from a normal, esp. horizontal or vertical, direction or position. 6. an inclined surface. 7. *Math.* the difference in direction of two lines or two planes as measured by the angle. 8. *Astron.* **a.** one of the elements of an orbit of a planet, etc. **b.** the angle between the orbital plane and the ecliptic or other suitably chosen plane. [late ME, t. L: s. *inclīnātio* a leaning] —**in·cli·na′tion·al,** *adj.* —**Syn.** 1. tendency; propensity. —**Ant.** 1. distaste.

in·cli·na·to·ry (YnklI′nətōr′Y), *adj.* related to or characterized by inclination.

in·cline (*v.* YnklĪn′; *n.* Yn′klĪn, YnklĪn′), *v.*, -clined, -clining, *n.* —*v.i.* 1. to have a mental tendency; be disposed. 2. to deviate from the vertical or horizontal; slant. 3. to tend in a physical sense; approximate: *the leaves incline to a blue.* 4. to tend in course or character 5. to lean; bend. —*v.t.* 6. to dispose (a person) in mind, habit, etc. (fol. by *to*). 7. to bow (the head, etc.). 8. to cause to lean or bend in a particular direction. 9. to turn toward (to listen favorably): *incline one's ear.* —*n.* 10. an inclined surface; a slope. [t. L: m. s. *inclīnāre* incline; r. ME *enclyne,* t. OF: m. *encliner*] —**in·clin′er,** *n.*

·clined (ĭn·klīnd′), *adj.* **1.** disposed, esp. favorably (fol. by *to*): *inclined to stay.* **2.** having a (physical) tendency. **3.** deviating in direction from the horizontal r vertical; sloping. **4.** in a irection making an angle ith anything else.

·clined plane, a plane urface inclined to the horison, or forming with a horizontal plane any angle but a ight angle.

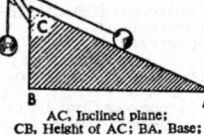

AC, Inclined plane;
CB, Height of AC; BA, Base;
BAC, Angle of inclination

·cli·nom·e·ter (ĭn′klə-ŏm′ə·tər), *n.* **1.** *Aeron.* an nstrument for measuring the ngle an aircraft makes with the horizontal. **2.** an inrument for determining the inclination or dip of the arth's magnetic force by the dip of a magnetic needle. [. INCLINE + -O- + -METER]

·close (ĭn·klōz′), *v.t.*, **-closed, -closing.** enclose. -in·clos′er, *n.*

·clo·sure (ĭn·klō′zhər), *n.* enclosure.

·clude (ĭn·klōōd′), *v.t.*, **-cluded, -cluding.** **1.** to conain, embrace, or comprise, as a whole does parts or ny part or element. **2.** to place in an aggregate, class, ategory, or the like. **3.** to contain as a subordinate lement; involve as a factor. [ME *include(n)*, t. L: m. *nclūdere* shut in] —in·clud′i·ble, in·clud′a·ble, *adj.* —**Syn.** 1. INCLUDE, COMPREHEND, COMPRISE, EMBRACE imly containing parts of a whole. To INCLUDE is to contain as part or member, or among the parts and members, of a whole: *the list includes many new names.* To COMPREHEND is o have within the limits, scope, or range of references, as ither a part or the whole number of items concerned: *the lan comprehends several projects.* To COMPRISE is to consist f, as the various parts serving to make up the whole: *this enus comprises fifty species.* EMBRACE emphasizes the extent r assortment of that which is included: *the report embraces a great variety of subjects.* —**Ant.** 1. exclude.

·clud·ed (ĭn·klōō′dĭd), *adj.* **1.** enclosed; embraced; omprised. **2.** *Bot.* not projecting beyond the mouth of he corolla, as stamens or a style.

·clu·sion (ĭn·klōō′zhən), *n.* **1.** the act of including. . the state of being included. **3.** that which is included. **4.** *Biol.* a body suspended in the cytoplasm, as granule, etc. **5.** *Mineral.* a solid body or a body of gas r liquid enclosed within the mass of a mineral. [t. L: s. *nclūsio*]

·clusion body, *Pathol.* a particle which takes a haracteristic stain, found in a virus-infected cell.

·clu·sive (ĭn·klōō′sĭv), *adj.* **1.** including in consideration or account, as the stated limit or extremes: *from ix to ten inclusive.* **2.** including a great deal, or including everything concerned; comprehensive. **3.** that ncludes; enclosing; embracing. **4. inclusive of,** including. —in·clu′sive·ly, *adv.* —in·clu′sive·ness, *n.*

·co·er·ci·ble (ĭn′kō·ûr′sə·bəl), *adj.* **1.** not coercible. . *Physics.* incapable of being reduced to a liquid form y any amount of pressure.

·cog (ĭn·kŏg′), *adj., adv., n.* *Colloq.* incognita or incognito.

·cog·i·ta·ble (ĭn·kŏj′ə·tə·bəl), *adj.* unthinkable. [t LL: m.s. *incogitābilis*] —in·cog′i·ta·bil′i·ty, *n.*

·cog·i·tant (ĭn·kŏj′ə·tənt), *adj.* **1.** thoughtless; inonsiderate. **2.** not having the faculty of thinking.

·cog·ni·ta (ĭn·kŏg′nə·tə), *adj.* **1.** (of a woman or girl) aving the real name or identity concealed. —*n.* **2.** a woman or girl who is incognita. [fem. of INCOGNITO]

·cog·ni·to (ĭn·kŏg′nə·tō′), *adj., adv., n., pl.* **-tos.** —*adj.* **1.** having one's identity concealed, as under an ssumed name (esp. to avoid notice or formal attenions). —*adv.* **2.** with the real identity concealed: *to ravel incognito.* —*n.* **3.** one who is incognito. **4.** the tate of being incognito. [t. It., t. L: m. *incognitus* nknown]

·cog·ni·zant (ĭn·kŏg′nə·zənt), *adj.* not cognizant; without knowledge; unaware (fol. by *of*). —in·cog′·i·zance, *n.*

·co·her·ence (ĭn′kō·hĭr′əns), *n.* **1.** the state of eing incoherent. **2.** something incoherent; an incoerent statement, etc.

·co·her·en·cy (ĭn′kō·hĭr′ən·sĭ), *n., pl.* **-cies.** incoerence.

·co·her·ent (ĭn′kō·hĭr′ənt), *adj.* **1.** without logical onnection; disjointed; rambling: *an incoherent sentence.* . characterized by such thought or language, as a person: *incoherent with rage.* **3.** not coherent or cohering: n *incoherent mixture.* **4.** without physical cohesion; oose: *incoherent dust.* **5.** without unity or harmony of lements: *an incoherent public.* **6.** without congruity of parts; uncoördinated. **7.** naturally different, or inompatible, as things. —in·co·her′ent·ly, *adv.*

·com·bus·ti·ble (ĭn′kəm·bŭs′tə·bəl), *adj.* **1.** not ombustible; incapable of being burned. —*n.* **2.** an inombustible substance. —in′com·bus·ti·bil′i·ty, in′com·bus′ti·ble·ness, *n.* —in′com·bus′ti·bly, *adv.*

·come (ĭn′kŭm), *n.* **1.** the returns that come in periodically, esp. annually, from property, business, labor, tc.; revenue; receipts. **2.** something that comes in. . *Rare.* a coming in. —**Syn.** 1. interest, salary, wages, annuity, gain, return, earnings. —**Ant.** 1. outgo, expenditure.

·com·er (ĭn′kŭm′ər), *n.* **1.** one who comes in. **2.** an mmigrant. **3.** an intruder. **4.** a successor.

income tax, a tax levied on incomes; an annual government tax on personal incomes, usually graduated and with certain deductions and exemptions.

in·com·ing (ĭn′kŭm′ĭng), *adj.* **1.** coming in: *the incoming tide.* **2.** succeeding: *the incoming mayor.* **3.** immigrant. **4.** accruing, as profit. **5.** entering, as a tenant or an officeholder. **6.** *Scot.* ensuing. —*n.* **7.** a coming in: *the incoming of spring.* **8.** (*usually pl.*) that which comes in, esp. revenue.

in·com·men·su·ra·ble (ĭn′kə·mĕn′shə·rə·bəl, -sə·rə-), *adj.* **1.** not commensurable; having no common measure or standard of comparison. **2.** utterly disproportionate. **3.** *Math.* (of two or more quantities) having no common measure. —*n.* **4.** that which is incommensurable. **5.** *Math.* one of two or more incommensurable quantities. —in′com·men′su·ra·bil′i·ty, in′com·men′su·ra·ble·ness, *n.* —in′com·men′su·ra·bly, *adv.*

in·com·men·su·rate (ĭn′kə·mĕn′shə·rĭt, -sə·rĭt), *adj.* **1.** not commensurate; disproportionate; inadequate: *means incommensurate to our wants.* **2.** incommensurable. —in′com·men′su·rate·ly, *adv.* —in′com·men′su·rate·ness, *n.*

in·com·mode (ĭn′kə·mōd′), *v.t.*, **-moded, -moding.** **1.** to inconvenience or discomfort. **2.** to impede; hinder. [t. L: m.s. *incommodāre*]

in·com·mo·di·ous (ĭn′kə·mō′dĭ·əs), *adj.* **1.** not affording sufficient room. **2.** inconvenient. —in′com·mo′di·ous·ly, *adv.* —in′com·mo′di·ous·ness, *n.*

in·com·mod·i·ty (ĭn′kə·mŏd′ə·tĭ), *n., pl.* **-ties. 1.** inconvenience. **2.** something inconvenient.

in·com·mu·ni·ca·ble (ĭn′kə·mū′nə·kə·bəl), *adj.* **1.** incapable of being communicated, imparted, or told to others. **2.** incommunicative. —in′com·mu′ni·ca·bil′i·ty, in′com·mu′ni·ca·ble·ness, *n.* —in′com·mu′ni·ca·bly, *adv.*

in·com·mu·ni·ca·do (ĭn′kə·mū′nə·kä′dō), *adj.* (esp. of a prisoner) deprived of communication with others. [t. Sp.: m. *incomunicado*, der. *comunicar* COMMUNICATE]

in·com·mu·ni·ca·tive (ĭn′kə·mū′nə·kā′tĭv), *adj.* not communicative; reserved. —in′com·mu′ni·ca′tive·ly, *adv.* —in′com·mu′ni·ca′tive·ness, *n.*

in·com·mut·a·ble (ĭn′kə·mū′tə·bəl), *adj.* **1.** not exchangeable. **2.** unchangeable. —in′com·mut′a·bil′i·ty, in′com·mut′a·ble·ness, *n.* —in′com·mut′a·bly, *adv.*

in·com·pact (ĭn′kəm·pakt′), *adj.* not compact; loose. —in′com·pact′ly, *adv.* —in′com·pact′ness, *n.*

in·com·pa·ra·ble (ĭn·kŏm′pə·rə·bəl, -prə·bəl), *adj.* **1.** matchless or unequaled: *incomparable beauty.* **2.** not comparable. —in·com′pa·ra·bil′i·ty, in·com′pa·ra·ble·ness, *n.* —in·com′pa·ra·bly, *adv.*

in·com·pat·i·ble (ĭn′kəm·păt′ə·bəl), *adj.* **1.** not compatible; incapable of existing together in harmony. **2.** contrary or opposed in character; discordant. **3.** that cannot coexist or be conjoined. **4.** *Logic.* (of two or more propositions) that cannot be true simultaneously. **5.** (of positions, ranks, etc.) unable to be held simultaneously by one person. **6.** *Pharm., Med.* pertaining to drugs or the like which interfere with one another chemically or physiologically and therefore can not be prescribed together. —*n.* **7.** (*usually pl.*) an incompatible person or thing. **8.** an incompatible drug or the like. **9.** (*pl.*) *Logic.* two or more attributes which cannot simultaneously belong to the same object. —in′com·pat′i·bil′i·ty, in′com·pat′i·ble·ness, *n.* —in′com·pat′i·bly, *adv.* —**Syn.** 1. See **inconsistent.**

in·com·pe·tence (ĭn·kŏm′pə·təns), *n.* **1.** the character or condition of being incompetent; inability. **2.** *Law.* the condition of lacking the power to act with legal effectiveness. Also, **in·com′pe·ten·cy.**

in·com·pe·tent (ĭn·kŏm′pə·tənt), *adj.* **1.** not competent; lacking qualification or ability: *an incompetent candidate.* **2.** characterized by or showing incompetence. **3.** *Law.* not legally qualified; inadmissible, as evidence. —*n.* **4.** an incompetent person. **5.** *Law.* a person lacking power to act with legal effectiveness. [t. LL: s. *incompetens* insufficient] —in·com′pe·tent·ly, *adv.* —**Syn.** 1. See **incapable.**

in·com·plete (ĭn′kəm·plēt′), *adj.* not complete; lacking some part. [ME, t. LL: m.s. *incomplētus*] —in′com·plete′ly, *adv.* —in′com·plete′ness, in′com·ple′tion, *n.*

in·com·pli·ant (ĭn′kəm·plī′ənt), *adj.* **1.** not compliant; unyielding. **2.** not pliant. —in′com·pli′ance, in′com·pli′an·cy, *n.* —in′com·pli′ant·ly, *adv.*

in·com·pre·hen·si·ble (ĭn′kŏm·prĭ·hĕn′sə·bəl, ĭn·kŏm′-), *adj.* not comprehensible; not understandable; unintelligible. —in′com·pre·hen·si·bil′i·ty, in′com·pre·hen′si·ble·ness, *n.* —in′com·pre·hen′si·bly, *adv.*

in·com·pre·hen·sive (ĭn′kŏm·prĭ·hĕn′sĭv, ĭn·kŏm′-), *adj.* not comprehensive. —in′com·pre·hen′sive·ly, *adv.* —in′com·pre·hen′sive·ness, *n.*

in·com·press·i·ble (ĭn′kəm·prĕs′ə·bəl), *adj.* not compressible. —in′com·press′i·bil′i·ty, *n.*

in·com·put·a·ble (ĭn′kəm·pū′tə·bəl), *adj.* incalculable.

in·con·ceiv·a·ble (ĭn′kən·sē′və·bəl), *adj.* not conceivable; unimaginable; unthinkable; incredible. —in′con·ceiv′a·bil′i·ty, in′con·ceiv′a·ble·ness, *n.* —in′con·ceiv′a·bly, *adv.*

in·con·clu·sive (ĭn′kən·klōō′sĭv), *adj.* **1.** not conclusive; not such as to settle a question: *inconclusive evidence.* **2.** without final results: *inconclusive experiments.* —in′con·clu′sive·ly, *adv.* —in′con·clu′sive·ness, *n.*

in·con·den·sa·ble (ĭn/kən děn/sə bəl), *adj.* not condensable; incapable of being condensed. Also, **in/-con·den/si·ble.** —**in/con·den/sa·bil/i·ty,** *n.*

in·con·dite (ĭn kŏn/dĭt), *adj.* **1.** ill-constructed. **2.** crude. [t. L: m.s. *inconditus* disordered]

in·con·form·i·ty (ĭn/kən fôr/mə tĭ), *n.* lack of conformity; failure or refusal to conform.

in·con·gru·ent (ĭn kŏng/grōō ənt), *adj.* not congruent; incongruous. —**in·con/gru·ence,** *n.* —**in·con/-gru·ent·ly,** *adv.*

in·con·gru·i·ty (ĭn/kŏng grōō/ə tĭ), *n., pl.* **-ties. 1.** the quality of being incongruous. **2.** something incongruous.

in·con·gru·ous (ĭn kŏng/grōō əs), *adj.* **1.** out of keeping or place; inappropriate; unbecoming: *an incongruous effect.* **2.** not harmonious in character; inconsonant; lacking harmony of parts: *incongruous mixtures.* **3.** inconsistent: *acts incongruous with their principles.* [t. L: m. *incongruus*] —**in·con/gru·ous·ly,** *adv.* —**in·con/gru·ous·ness,** *n.* —**Syn. 3.** See **inconsistent.**

in·con·sec·u·tive (ĭn/kən sĕk/yə tĭv), *adj.* not consecutive. —**in/con·sec/u·tive·ly,** *adj.* —**in/con·sec/u·tive·ness,** *n.*

in·con·se·quent (ĭn kŏn/sə kwĕnt/, -kwənt), *adj.* **1.** characterized by lack of sequence in thought, speech, or action. **2.** not following from the premises: *an inconsequent deduction.* **3.** characterized by lack of logical sequence: *inconsequent reasoning.* **4.** irrelevant: *an inconsequent remark.* **5.** not in keeping with the general character or design: *inconsequent ornamentation.* [t. L: s. *inconsequens* without connection] —**in·con/se·quence/,** *n.* —**in·con/se·quent·ly,** *adv.*

in·con·se·quen·tial (ĭn/kŏn sə kwĕn/shəl, ĭn kŏn/-), *adj.* **1.** of no consequence; trivial. **2.** inconsequent; illogical; irrelevant. —**in·con·se·quen/ti·al/i·ty,** *n.* —**in/con·se·quen/tial·ly,** *adv.*

in·con·sid·er·a·ble (ĭn/kən sĭd/ər ə bəl), *adj.* **1.** small, as in value, amount, size, etc. **2.** not worthy of consideration or notice; trivial. —**in/con·sid/er·a·ble·ness,** *n.* —**in/con·sid/er·a·bly,** *adv.*

in·con·sid·er·ate (ĭn/kən sĭd/ər ĭt), *adj.* **1.** without due regard for the rights or feelings of others: *it was inconsiderate of him to forget.* **2.** done or acting without consideration; thoughtless. —**in/con·sid/er·ate·ly,** *adv.* —**in/con·sid/er·ate·ness, in/con·sid/er·a/tion,** *n.*

in·con·sist·en·cy (ĭn/kən sĭs/tən sĭ), *n., pl.* **-cies. 1.** the quality of being inconsistent. **2.** something inconsistent. Also, **in/con·sist/ence.**

in·con·sist·ent (ĭn/kən sĭs/tənt), *adj.* **1.** lacking in harmony between the different parts or elements; self-contradictory. **2.** lacking agreement, as one thing with another, or two or more things in relation to each other; at variance. **3.** not consistent in principles, conduct, etc. **4.** acting at variance with professed principles. **5.** *Logic.* incompatible. —**in/con·sist/ent·ly,** *adv.*
—**Syn. 2.** INCONSISTENT, INCOMPATIBLE, INCONGRUOUS refer to things which are out of keeping with each other. That which is INCONSISTENT involves variance, discrepancy, or even contradiction, esp. from the point of view of truth, reason, or logic: *his actions are inconsistent with his statements.* INCOMPATIBLE implies incapability of close association or harmonious relationship, as from differences of nature, character, temperament, and the like: *actions incompatible with honesty of purpose, qualities which make two people incompatible.* That which is INCONGRUOUS is inappropriate or out of keeping, often to the point of being ridiculous or absurd: *incongruous characters or situations frequently provide a basis for comedy.* —**Ant. 1.** harmonious.

in·con·sol·a·ble (ĭn/kən sō/lə bəl), *adj.* not consolable: *inconsolable grief.* —**in/con·sol/a·bil/i·ty, in/-con·sol/a·ble·ness,** *n.* —**in/con·sol/a·bly,** *adv.*

in·con·so·nant (ĭn kŏn/sə nənt), *adj.* not consonant or in accord. —**in·con/so·nance,** *n.* —**in·con/so·nant·ly,** *adv.*

in·con·spic·u·ous (ĭn/kən spĭk/yōō əs), *adj.* not conspicuous, noticeable, or prominent. —**in/con·spic/u·ous·ly,** *adv.* —**in/con·spic/u·ous·ness,** *n.*

in·con·stant (ĭn kŏn/stənt), *adj.* not constant; changeable; fickle; variable: *inconstant winds.* —**in·con/stan·cy,** *n.* —**in·con/stant·ly,** *adv.*

in·con·sum·a·ble (ĭn/kən sōō/mə bəl), *adj.* not consumable; incapable of being consumed.

in·con·test·a·ble (ĭn/kən tĕs/tə bəl), *adj.* not contestable; not admitting of dispute; incontrovertible: *incontestable proof.* —**in/con·test/a·bil/i·ty, in/con·test/a·ble·ness,** *n.* —**in/con·test/a·bly,** *adv.*

in·con·ti·nent¹ (ĭn kŏn/tə nənt), *adj.* **1.** not continent; not holding or held in; unceasing or unrestrained: *an incontinent flow of talk.* **2.** lacking in restraint, esp. over the sexual appetite. **3.** unable to contain or retain (usually fol. by *of*). **4.** *Pathol.* unable to restrain natural discharges or evacuations. [ME, t. L: s. *incontinens* not holding back] —**in·con/ti·nence, in·con/ti·nen·cy,** *n.* —**in·con/ti·nent·ly,** *adv.*

in·con·ti·nent² (ĭn kŏn/tə nənt), *adv. Archaic.* immediately; at once; straightway. Also, **in·con/ti·nent·ly.** [ME, t. F, t. LL: m. *in continentī (tempore)* in continuous (time), without pause]

in·con·trol·la·ble (ĭn/kən trō/lə bəl), *adj.* not controllable; uncontrollable: *an incontrollable desire.*

in·con·tro·vert·i·ble (ĭn/kŏn trə vûr/tə bəl, ĭn kŏn/-), *adj.* not controvertible; indisputable: *absolute and incontrovertible truth.* —**in/con·tro·vert/i·bil/i·ty, in/con·tro·vert/i·ble·ness,** *n.* —**in/con·tro·vert/i·bly,** *adv.*

in·con·ven·ience (ĭn/kən vēn/yəns), *n., v.,* **-ienced, -iencing.** —*n.* **1.** the quality or state of being inconvenient. **2.** an inconvenient circumstance or thing; something that causes discomfort, trouble, etc. —*v.* **3.** to put to inconvenience; incommode.

in·con·ven·ien·cy (ĭn/kən vēn/yən sĭ), *n., pl.* **-cies.** inconvenience.

in·con·ven·ient (ĭn/kən vēn/yənt), *adj.* arranged or happening in such a way as to be awkward, inopportune, disadvantageous, or troublesome: *an inconvenient time for a visit.* [ME, t. L: s. *inconveniens* not consonant] —**in/con·ven/ient·ly,** *adv.* —**Syn.** untimely; annoying.

in·con·vert·i·ble (ĭn/kən vûr/tə bəl), *adj.* **1.** (of paper money) not capable of being converted into specie. **2.** not interchangeable. —**in/con·vert/i·bil/i·ty, in/-con·vert/i·ble·ness,** *n.* —**in/con·vert/i·bly,** *adv.*

in·con·vin·ci·ble (ĭn/kən vĭn/sə bəl), *adj.* not convincible; incapable of being convinced. —**in/con·vin/ci·bil/i·ty,** *n.* —**in/con·vin/ci·bly,** *adv.*

in·co·ör·di·nate (ĭn/kō ôr/də nĭt), *adj.* not coördinate; not coördinated.

in·co·ör·di·na·tion (ĭn/kō ôr/də nā/shən), *n.* lack of coördination.

incor., 1. Also, **incorp.** incorporated. **2.** incorrect.

in·cor·po·rate¹ (*v.* ĭn kôr/pə rāt/; *adj.* ĭn kôr/pə rĭt/ -prĭt/), *v.,* **-rated, -rating,** *adj.* —*v.t.* **1.** to create or form a corporation. **2.** to form into a society or organization. **3.** to put or introduce into a body or mass as an integral part or parts. **4.** to take in or include as part or parts, as the body or mass does. **5.** to form or combine into one body or uniform substance, as ingredients. **6.** *Rare.* to embody. —*v.i.* **7.** to unite or combine so as to form one body. **8.** to form a corporation. —*adj.* **9.** incorporated, as a company. **10.** *Rare.* combined into one body, mass, or substance. **11.** *Obs.* embodied. [ME, t. LL: m.s. *incorporātus* pp., embodied. See IN-²] —**in·cor/po·ra/tion,** *n.* —**in·cor/po·ra/tive,** *adj.*

in·cor·po·rate² (ĭn kôr/pə rĭt, -prĭt), *adj.* not embodied; incorporeal. [t. LL: m.s. *incorporātus.* See IN-³]

in·cor·po·rat·ed (ĭn kôr/pə rā/tĭd), *adj.* **1.** formed or constituted as a corporation. **2.** combined in one body; made part of.

in·cor·po·ra·tor (ĭn kôr/pə rā/tər), *n.* **1.** one of the signers of the articles or certificate of incorporation. **2.** one of the persons to whom the charter is granted in a corporation created by special act of the legislature. **3.** one who incorporates.

in·cor·po·re·al (ĭn/kôr pōr/ĭ əl), *adj.* **1.** not corporeal; immaterial. **2.** pertaining to immaterial beings. **3.** *Law.* without material existence, but existing in contemplation of law, as a franchise. —**in/cor·po/re·al·ly,** *adv.*

in·cor·po·re·i·ty (ĭn kôr/pə rē/ə tĭ, ĭn/kôr-), *n., pl.* **-ties.** the quality of being incorporeal; disembodied existence or entity. Also, **in/cor·po/re·al/i·ty.**

in·cor·rect (ĭn/kə rĕkt/), *adj.* **1.** not correct as to fact: *an incorrect statement.* **2.** improper: *incorrect behavior.* **3.** not correct in form or manner: *an incorrect copy.* —**in/cor·rect/ly,** *adv.* —**in/cor·rect/ness,** *n.* —**Syn. 1.** erroneous, inaccurate, inexact; untrue, wrong. **2.** faulty, improper.

in·cor·ri·gi·ble (ĭn kôr/ĭ jə bəl, -kŏr/-), *adj.* **1.** not corrigible; bad beyond correction or reform: *an incorrigible liar.* **2.** impervious to punishment; willful; uncontrollable: *an incorrigible child.* **3.** firmly fixed: *an incorrigible habit.* —*n.* **4.** one who is incorrigible. —**in·cor/ri·gi·bil/i·ty, in·cor/ri·gi·ble·ness,** *n.* —**in·cor/ri·gi·bly,** *adv.*

in·cor·rupt (ĭn/kə rŭpt/), *adj.* **1.** not corrupt; not debased or perverted; morally upright. **2.** not to be bribed. **3.** free from decomposition or putrefaction. **4.** not vitiated by errors or alterations. Also, **in/cor·rupt/ed.** —**in/cor·rupt/ly,** *adv.* —**in/cor·rupt/ness,** *n.*

in·cor·rupt·i·ble (ĭn/kə rŭp/tə bəl), *adj.* **1.** not corruptible; incapable of corruption: *a man of incorruptible integrity.* **2.** that cannot be perverted or bribed: *incorruptible by money.* —**in/cor·rupt/i·bil/i·ty, in/-cor·rupt/i·ble·ness,** *n.* —**in/cor·rupt/i·bly,** *adv.*

in·cor·rup·tion (ĭn/kə rŭp/shən), *n. Archaic.* incorrupt condition.

incr., 1. increased. **2.** increasing.

in·cras·sate (*v.* ĭn krăs/āt; *adj.* ĭn krăs/ĭt, -āt), *v.,* **-sated, -sating,** *adj.* —*v.t.* **1.** to thicken. **2.** *Pharm.* to make (a liquid) thicker by addition of another substance or by evaporation. —*v.i.* **3.** to become thick or thicker. —*adj.* **4.** Also, **in·cras/sat·ed.** *Bot., Entomol.* thickened or swollen. [t. LL: m.s. *incrassātus,* pp.] —**in/cras·sa/tion,** *n.*

in·crease (*v.* ĭn krēs/; *n.* ĭn/krēs), *v.,* **-creased, -creasing,** *n.* —*v.t.* **1.** to make greater in any respect; augment; add to. **2.** to make more numerous. —*v.i.* **3.** to become greater or more numerous: *sales increased.* **4.** to multiply by propagation. **5.** *Poetic.* to wax, as the moon. —*n.* **6.** growth or augmentation in numbers: *the increase of crime.* **7.** multiplication by propagation; production of offspring. **8.** offspring or progeny. **9.** act or process of increasing. **10.** that by which something is increased. **11.** the result of increasing. **12.** produce of the earth. **13.** product; profit; interest. [ME *encrese(n),* t. AF: m. *encres(s)-,* var. of OF *encrei(s)-,* s. *encreistre,* g. L *increscere*] —**in·creas/a·ble,** *adj.* —**in·creas/er,** *n.* —**in·creas/ing·ly,** *adv.* —**Syn. 1.** INCREASE, AUGMENT, ENLARGE may all mean to make larger. To INCREASE means to make greater, as in quantity, extent, degree: *to increase someone's salary, to increase the velocity, increase the (degree of) concentration.* ENLARGE means to increase in size, extent, or range: *to enlarge a building, a business, one's conceptions.* AUGMENT, a more formal word, means to increase or enlarge especially by addition from the outside: *to augment one's income (by doing extra work).*

in·cre·ate (ĭn/krĭ āt/, ĭn/krĭ āt/), *adj.* 1. not created; uncreated. 2. existing without having been created.

in·cred·i·ble (ĭn krĕd/ə bəl), *adj.* 1. seeming too extraordinary to be possible: *an incredible story.* 2. not credible; that cannot be believed. —**in·cred/i·bil/i·ty, in·cred/i·ble·ness,** *n.* —**in·cred/i·bly,** *adv.*

in·cre·du·li·ty (ĭn/krə dū/lə tĭ, -dōō/-), *n.* the quality of being incredulous; a refusal of belief.

in·cred·u·lous (ĭn krĕj/ə ləs), *adj.* 1. not credulous; indisposed to believe; skeptical. 2. indicating unbelief: *an incredulous smile.* —**in·cred/u·lous·ly,** *adv.* —**in·cred/u·lous·ness,** *n.* —Syn. 1. See doubtful.

in·cre·ment (ĭn/krə mənt, ĭng/-), *n.* 1. something added or gained; an addition or increase. 2. profit. 3. act or process of increasing; growth. 4. *Math.* **a.** the difference between two values of a variable; an increase (positive, negative, or zero) in an independent variable. **b.** the increase of a function due to this. [ME, t. L: s. *incrēmentum* an increase] —**in/cre·men/tal,** *adj.*

in·cres·cent (ĭn krĕs/ənt), *adj.* increasing or waxing, as the moon. [t. L: s. *increscens,* ppr.]

in·cre·tion (ĭn krē/shən), *n.* 1. a substance, as an autacoid, secreted internally. 2. the process of such secretion. [back formation from *incretionary,* f. IN-² + *-cretionary,* modeled on *concretionary*]

in·crim·i·nate (ĭn krĭm/ə nāt/), *v.t.,* -nated, -nating. 1. to charge with a crime or fault. 2. to involve in an accusation. [t. ML: m.s. *incrīminātus,* pp., accused of a crime. See IN-², CRIMINATE] —**in·crim/i·na/tion,** *n.* —**in·crim/i·na/tor,** *n.* —**in·crim·i·na·to·ry** (ĭn krĭm/- ə nə tōr/ĭ), *adj.*

in·crust (ĭn krŭst/), *v.t.* 1. to cover or line with a crust or hard coating. 2. to form into a crust. 3. to deposit as a crust. Also, **encrust.** [t. L: s. *incrustāre*]

in·crus·ta·tion (ĭn/krŭs tā/shən), *n.* 1. an incrusting or being incrusted. 2. a crust or coat of anything on the surface of a body; a covering, coating, or scale. 3. the inlaying or addition of enriching materials on a surface. 4. the inlaid or added enriching materials to a surface or an object. Also, **encrustation.**

in·cu·bate (ĭn/kyə bāt/, ĭng/-), *v.,* -bated, -bating. —*v.t.* 1. to sit upon (eggs) for the purpose of hatching. 2. to hatch (eggs), as by sitting upon them or by artificial heat. 3. to maintain (bacterial cultures, etc.) at the most favorable temperature for development. 4. to keep at even temperature, as immature infants. 5. to produce as if by hatching. —*v.i.* 6. to sit upon eggs. 7. to undergo incubation. 8. to brood upon. [t. L: m.s. *incubātus,* pp., hatched, sat on] —**in/cu·ba/tive,** *adj.*

in·cu·ba·tion (ĭn/kyə bā/shən, ĭng/-), *n.* 1. the act or process of incubating. 2. the condition or quality of being incubated. —**in/cu·ba/tion·al,** *adj.*

incubation period, *Pathol.* the period between infection and the appearance of signs of a disease.

in·cu·ba·tor (ĭn/kyə bā/tər, ĭng/-), *n.* 1. an apparatus for hatching eggs artificially, consisting essentially of a case heated by a lamp or the like. 2. a boxlike apparatus in which prematurely born infants are kept at a constant and suitable temperature. 3. a device in which bacterial cultures, etc. are developed at a constant suitable temperature. 4. one who or that which incubates. [t. L]

in·cu·bus (ĭn/kyə bəs, ĭng/-), *n., pl.* -bi (-bī/), -buses. 1. an imaginary demon or evil spirit supposed to descend upon sleeping persons. 2. something that weighs upon or oppresses one like a nightmare. 3. a nightmare. [ME, t. LL: nightmare, ML a demon, der. L *incubāre* lie on]

in·cu·des (ĭn kū/dēz), *n.* pl. of incus.

in·cul·cate (ĭn kŭl/kāt, ĭn/kŭl kāt/), *v.t.,* -cated, -cating. to impress by repeated statement or admonition; teach persistently and earnestly (usually fol. by *upon* or *in*). [t. L: m.s. *inculcātus,* pp., stamped in, impressed upon] —**in/cul·ca/tion,** *n.* —**in/cul·ca/tor,** *n.*

in·cul·pa·ble (ĭn kŭl/pə bəl), *adj.* not culpable; blameless. —**in·cul/pa·bly,** *adv.*

in·cul·pate (ĭn kŭl/pāt, ĭn/kŭl pāt/), *v.t.,* -pated, -pating. 1. to charge with fault; blame; accuse. 2. to involve in a charge; incriminate. [t. ML: m.s. *inculpātus,* pp. of *inculpāre,* f. in- IN-² + *culpāre* blame] —**in/cul·pa/tion,** *n.*

in·cul·pa·to·ry (ĭn kŭl/pə tōr/ĭ), *adj.* tending to inculpate; imputing blame; incriminating.

in·cult (ĭn kŭlt/), *adj. Archaic.* 1. uncultivated; untilled. 2. wild; rude; unrefined. [t. L: s. *incultus*]

in·cum·ben·cy (ĭn kŭm/bən sĭ), *n., pl.* -cies. 1. the state of being incumbent. 2. that which is incumbent. 3. an incumbent weight or mass. 4. the position or term of an incumbent. 5. *Now Rare.* a duty or obligation.

in·cum·bent (ĭn kŭm/bənt), *adj.* 1. resting on one; obligatory: *a duty incumbent upon me.* 2. lying, leaning, or pressing on something: *incumbent posture.* —*n.* 3. the holder of an office. 4. *Brit.* one who holds an ecclesiastical benefice. [ME, t. L: s. *incumbens,* ppr., leaning upon] —**in·cum/bent·ly,** *adv.*

in·cum·ber (ĭn kŭm/bər), *v.t.* encumber.

in·cum·brance (ĭn kŭm/brəns), *n.* encumbrance.

in·cu·nab·u·la (ĭn/kyōō năb/yə lə), *n.pl., sing.* -lum (-ləm). 1. books produced in the infancy of printing (before 1500) from movable type. 2. the earliest stages or first traces of anything. [t. L: cradle, beginning, swaddling clothes] —**in/cu·nab/u·lar,** *adj.*

in·cur (ĭn kûr/), *v.t.,* -curred, -curring. 1. to run or fall into (some consequence, usually undesirable or injurious). 2. to become liable or subject to through one's own action; bring upon oneself: *to incur his displeasure.* [ME, t. L: m.s. *incurrere* run into, or against]

in·cur·a·ble (ĭn kyōōr/ə bəl), *adj.* 1. not curable. —*n.* 2. one suffering from an incurable disease. —**in·cur/a·bil/i·ty, in·cur/a·ble·ness,** *n.* —**in·cur/a·bly,** *adv.*

in·cu·ri·ous (ĭn kyōōr/ĭ əs), *adj.* 1. not curious; inattentive or unobservant. 2. indifferent. 3. deficient in interest or novelty. —**in·cu·ri·os·i·ty** (ĭn/kyōōr ĭ ŏs/ə tĭ), **in·cu/ri·ous·ness,** *n.* —**in·cu/ri·ous·ly,** *adv.*

in·cur·rence (ĭn kûr/əns), *n.* the act of incurring, bringing on, or subjecting oneself to something.

in·cur·rent (ĭn kûr/ənt), *adj.* carrying, or relating to, an inward current. [t. L: s. *incurrens,* ppr., running into]

in·cur·sion (ĭn kûr/zhən, -shən), *n.* 1. a hostile entrance into or invasion of a place or territory, esp. one of sudden character. 2. a harmful inroad. 3. a running in: *the incursion of sea water.* [ME, t. L: s. *incursio* onset]

in·cur·sive (ĭn kûr/sĭv), *adj.* making incursions.

in·cur·vate (*adj.* ĭn kûr/vĭt, -vāt; *v.* ĭn kûr/vāt), *adj., v.,* -vated, -vating. —*adj.* 1. curved, esp. inward. —*v.t.* 2. to make curved; turn from a straight line or course; curve, esp. inward. [t. L: m.s. *incurvātus,* pp., bent in] —**in/cur·va/tion,** *n.*

in·curve (*v.* ĭn kûrv/; *n.* ĭn/kûrv/), *v.,* -curved, -curving, *n. Baseball.* —*v.t.* 1. to curve inward. —*n.* 2. an inward-curving ball, i.e. toward the batter. [t. L: m.s. *incurvāre* bend in]

in·cus (ĭng/kəs), *n., pl.* **incudes** (ĭn kū/dēz). *Anat.* the middle one of a chain of three small bones in the middle ear of man and other mammals. See diag. under **ear.** [t. L: anvil] See diag. under **ear.**

in·cuse (ĭn kūz/), *adj.* 1. hammered or stamped in, as a figure on a coin. —*n.* 2. an incuse figure or impression. [t. L: m.s. *incūsus,* pp., forged with a hammer]

Ind (ĭnd), *n.* 1. *Now Poetic.* India. 2. *Obs.* the Indies.

ind-, var. of **indo-** before vowels, as in *indene.*

Ind., 1. India. 2. Indian. 3. Indiana. 4. Indies.

ind., 1. independent. 2. index. 3. indicative.

in·da·ba (ĭn dä/bä), *n.* a conference or consultation between or with South African natives. [Zulu]

in·da·mine (ĭn/də mēn/, -mĭn), *n. Chem.* any of a certain series of basic organic compounds which form bluish and greenish salts: used in the manufacture of dyes. Also, **in·da·min** (ĭn/də mĭn). [f. IND(IGO) + AMINE]

in·debt (ĭn dĕt/), *v.t.* to place under obligation for benefits, favors, assistance, etc., received (used chiefly in *indebted,* pp.). [first used in pp., ME *endetted,* after OF *endetter,* der. en- EN-¹ + *dette* DEBT] —**in·debt/ed,** *adj.*

in·debt·ed·ness (ĭn dĕt/ĭd nĭs), *n.* 1. state of being indebted. 2. an amount owed. 3. debts collectively.

in·de·cen·cy (ĭn dē/sən sĭ), *n., pl.* -cies. 1. the quality of being indecent. 2. impropriety; indelicacy or immodesty. 3. obscenity. 4. an indecent act, remark, etc.

in·de·cent (ĭn dē/sənt), *adj.* 1. offending against recognized standards of propriety or good taste; vulgar: *indecent language.* 2. not decent; unbecoming or unseemly: *indecent conduct.* —**in·de/cent·ly,** *adv.* —Syn. 2. See improper.

in·de·cid·u·ate (ĭn/dĭ sĭj/ōō ĭt, -āt/), *adj.* 1. *Zool.* not deciduate. 2. *Bot.* having permanent leaves.

in·de·cid·u·ous (ĭn/dĭ sĭj/ōō əs), *adj. Bot.* 1. not deciduous, as leaves. 2. (of trees) evergreen.

in·de·ci·pher·a·ble (ĭn/dĭ sī/fər ə bəl), *adj.* not decipherable. —**in/de·ci/pher·a·bil/i·ty,** *n.*

in·de·ci·sion (ĭn/dĭ sĭzh/ən), *n.* inability to decide.

in·de·ci·sive (ĭn/dĭ sī/sĭv), *adj.* 1. not decisive or conclusive: *a severe but indecisive battle.* 2. characterized by indecision, as persons; irresolute; undecided. —**in/de·ci/sive·ly,** *adv.* —**in/de·ci/sive·ness,** *n.*

indecl., indeclinable.

in·de·clin·a·ble (ĭn/dĭ klī/nə bəl), *adj. Gram.* not declined, especially of a word belonging to a form class most of whose members are declined, as the Latin adjective *decem* (ten). —**in/de·clin/a·bly,** *adv.*

in·de·com·pos·a·ble (ĭn/dē kəm pō/zə bəl), *adj.* not decomposable.

in·dec·o·rous (ĭn dĕk/ə rəs, ĭn/dĭ kōr/əs), *adj.* not decorous; violating propriety; unseemly. [t. L: m. *indecōrus*] —**in·dec/o·rous·ly,** *adv.* —**in·dec/o·rous·ness,** *n.*

in·de·co·rum (ĭn/dĭ kōr/əm), *n.* 1. indecorous behavior or character. 2. something indecorous. [t. L, prop. neut. of *indecōrus* indecorous]

in·deed (ĭn dēd/), *adv.* 1. in fact; in reality; in truth; truly (used for emphasis, to confirm and amplify a previous statement, to indicate a concession or admission, or, interrogatively, to obtain confirmation). —*interj.* 2. an expression of surprise, incredulity, irony, etc. [ME *in dede.* See IN, prep., DEED, n.]

indef., indefinite.

in·de·fat·i·ga·ble (ĭn/dĭ făt/ə gə bəl), *adj.* incapable of being tired out; not yielding to fatigue. [t. L: m.s. *indēfatigābilis*] —**in/de·fat/i·ga·bil/i·ty, in/de·fat/i·ga·ble·ness,** *n.* —**in/de·fat/i·ga·bly,** *adv.*

in·de·fea·si·ble (ĭn/dĭ fē/zə bəl), *adj.* not defeasible; not to be annulled or made void; not forfeitable. —**in/-de·fea/si·bil/i·ty,** *n.* —**in/de·fea/si·bly,** *adv.*

in·de·fect·i·ble (ĭn/dĭ fĕk/tə bəl), *adj.* 1. not defectible; not liable to defect or failure; unfailing.· 2. not liable to fault or imperfection; faultless. —**in/de·fect/-i·bil/i·ty,** *n.* —**in/de·fect/i·bly,** *adv.*

in·de·fec·tive (ĭn/dĭ fĕk/tĭv), *adj.* not defective.

in·de·fen·si·ble (ĭn/dĭ fĕn/sə bəl), *adj.* 1. that cannot be justified; inexcusable: *an indefensible remark.* 2. that cannot be defended by force of arms: *an indefensible frontier.* —**in/de·fen/si·bil/i·ty, in·de·fen/si·ble·ness,** *n.* —**in/de·fen/si·bly,** *adv.*

in·de·fin·a·ble (ĭn/dĭ fī/nə bəl), *adj.* not definable. —**in/de·fin/a·ble·ness,** *n.* —**in/de·fin/a·bly,** *adv.*

in·def·i·nite (ĭn dĕf/ə nĭt), *adj.* 1. not definite; without fixed or specified limit; unlimited: *an indefinite number.* 2. not clearly defined or determined; not precise. 3. *Gram.* not specifying precisely, as the indefinite pronoun *some.* 4. *Bot.* a. very numerous or not easily counted, as stamens. b. (of an inflorescence) indeterminate. [t. L: m.s. *indēfīnītus*] —**in·def/i·nite·ly,** *adv.* —**in·def/i·nite·ness,** *n.* —**Syn.** 2. vague, obscure.

indefinite article, the article (as *a, an*) which classes as "single and unidentified" the noun it modifies.

in·de·his·cent (ĭn/dĭ hĭs/ənt), *adj. Bot.* not dehiscent; not opening at maturity. —**in·de·his/cence,** *n.*

in·del·i·ble (ĭn dĕl/ə bəl), *adj.* 1. incapable of being deleted or obliterated: *an indelible impression.* 2. making indelible marks: *an indelible pencil.* [t. L: m.s. *in-dēlēbilis* that cannot be destroyed] —**in·del/i·bil/i·ty, in·del/i·ble·ness,** *n.* —**in·del/i·bly,** *adv.*

in·del·i·ca·cy (ĭn dĕl/ə kə sĭ), *n., pl.* -**cies.** 1. the quality of being indelicate. 2. something indelicate.

in·del·i·cate (ĭn dĕl/ə kĭt), *adj.* 1. not delicate; lacking delicacy. 2. offensive to a sense of propriety, or modesty; unrefined. —**in·del/i·cate·ly,** *adv.*

in·dem·ni·fi·ca·tion (ĭn dĕm/nə fə kā/shən), *n.* 1. the act of indemnifying. 2. the state of being indemnified. 3. that which serves to indemnify; compensation.

in·dem·ni·fy (ĭn dĕm/nə fī/), *v.t.,* -**fied,** -**fying.** 1. to compensate for damage or loss sustained, expense incurred, etc. 2. to engage to make good or secure against anticipated loss; give security against (future damage or liability). —**in·dem/ni·fi/er,** *n.*

in·dem·ni·tee (ĭn dĕm/nə tē/), *n.* one who receives indemnity.

in·dem·ni·tor (ĭn dĕm/nə tər), *n.* one who gives indemnity.

in·dem·ni·ty (ĭn dĕm/nə tĭ), *n., pl.* -**ties.** 1. protection or security against damage or loss. 2. compensation for damage or loss sustained. 3. something paid by way of such compensation. 4. legal exemption from liabilities or penalties incurred by one's actions. 5. legal exemption from penalties attaching to unconstitutional or illegal actions, granted to public officers and other persons. [late ME, t. LL: m.s. *indemnitas,* der. L *indemnis* unharmed]

in·de·mon·stra·ble (ĭn/dĭ mŏn/strə bəl, ĭn dĕm/ən-), *adj.* not demonstrable; incapable of being demonstrated or proved. —**in/de·mon/stra·bil/i·ty,** *n.* —**in/de·mon/stra·bly,** *adv.*

in·dene (ĭn/dēn), *n. Chem.* a colorless liquid hydrocarbon, C₉H₈, obtained from coal tar by fractional distillation. [f. IND- + -ENE]

in·dent¹ (*v.* ĭn dĕnt/; *n.* ĭn/dĕnt, ĭn dĕnt/), *v.t.* 1. to form deep recesses in: *the sea indents the coast.* 2. to set in or back from the margin, as the first line of a paragraph. 3. to sever (a document drawn up in duplicate) along an irregular line as a means of identification. 4. to cut or tear the edge of (copies of a document) in an irregular way. 5. to make toothlike notches in; notch. 6. to indenture, as an apprentice. 7. to draw an order upon. 8. to order, as commodities. —*v.i.* 9. to form a recess. 10. to enter into an agreement by indenture; make a compact. 11. to make out an order or requisition in duplicate. 12. *Brit. Mil.* to make a requisition. 13. *Obs.* to draw upon a person or thing for something. —*n.* 14. a toothlike notch or deep recess; an indentation. 15. an indention. 16. *Brit.* an official requisition for stores. 17. an order for goods. 18. an indenture. 19. a certificate issued by the U.S. government at the close of the Revolutionary War, for the principal or interest due on the public debt. [ME *endente(n),* t. OF: m. *endenter,* der. *en-* EN-¹ + *dent* tooth] —**in·dent/er,** *n.*

in·dent² (*v.* ĭn dĕnt/; *n.* ĭn/dĕnt, ĭn dĕnt/), *v.t.* 1. to dent or press in so as to form a dent. 2. to make a dent in. —*n.* 3. a dent. [ME, f. IN-² + DENT¹]

in·den·ta·tion (ĭn/dĕn tā/shən), *n.* 1. a cut, notch, or deep recess: *various bays and indentations.* 2. a series of incisions or notches. 3. a notching or being notched. 4. an indention. [f. INDENT¹ + -ATION]

in·den·tion (ĭn dĕn/shən), *n.* 1. an indenting. 2. an indentation. 3. an indenting of a line or lines, and leaving of blank space. 4. the blank space so left.

in·den·ture (ĭn dĕn/chər), *n., v.,* -**tured,** -**turing.** —*n.* 1. a deed or agreement executed in two or more copies with edges correspondingly indented as a means of identification. 2. any deed or sealed agreement. 3. a contract by which a person, as an apprentice, is bound

Indented molding

to service. 4. any official or formal list, certificate, etc., authenticated for use as a voucher or the like. 5. the formal agreement between a group of bondholders and the debtor as to the terms of the debt. 6. indentation. —*v.t.* 7. to bind by indenture, as an apprentice. 8. *Obs.* to indent; wrinkle; furrow. [ME *endenture,* t. OF: m. *endenteure* indentation]

in·de·pend·ence (ĭn/dĭ pĕn/dəns), *n.* 1. the state or quality of being independent. 2. freedom from subjection, or from the influence of others. 3. exemption from external control or support. 4. a competency. —**Syn.** 1. See **freedom.**

In·de·pend·ence (ĭn/dĭ pĕn/dəns), *n.* a city in W Missouri: starting point of the Santa Fe and Oregon trails. 62,328 (1960).

Independence Day, *U.S.* July 4, a holiday commemorating the adoption of the Declaration of Independence on July 4, 1776.

in·de·pend·en·cy (ĭn/dĭ pĕn/dən sĭ), *n., pl.* -**cies.** 1. independence. 2. a territory not under the control of any other power. 3. (*cap.*) *Eccles.* a. the principle that the individual congregation or church is an autonomous and equalitarian society free from any external ecclesiastical control. b. the polity based on this principle.

in·de·pend·ent (ĭn/dĭ pĕn/dənt), *adj.* 1. not influenced by others in matters of opinion, conduct, etc.; thinking or acting for oneself: *an independent person.* 2. not subject to another's authority or jurisdiction; autonomous; free. 3. not influenced by the thought or action of others: *independent research.* 4. not dependent; not depending or contingent on something else for existence, operation, etc. 5. (adverbially) independently. 6. not relying on another or others for aid or support. 7. declining others' aid or support; refusing to be under obligations to others. 8. possessing a competency. 9. sufficient for a competency. 10. expressive of a spirit of independence; self-confident; unconstrained. 11. free from party commitments in voting. 12. *Math.* (of a quantity or function) not depending upon another for value. 13. (*cap.*) *Eccles.* of or pertaining to the Independents. —*n.* 14. an independent person or thing. 15. *Pol.* one who votes without blind loyalty to any organized party. 16. (*cap.*) *Eccles.* an adherent of an Independency. 17. *Brit.* a Congregationalist. —**in/de·pend/ent·ly,** *adv.*

independent clause, *Gram.* main clause.

in·de·scrib·a·ble (ĭn/dĭ skrī/bə bəl), *adj.* not describable. —**in/de·scrib/a·bil/i·ty, in/de·scrib/a·ble·ness,** *n.* —**in/de·scrib/a·bly,** *adv.*

in·de·struct·i·ble (ĭn/dĭ strŭk/tə bəl), *adj.* not destructible. —**in/de·struct/i·bil/i·ty, in/de·struct/i·ble·ness,** *n.* —**in/de·struct/i·bly,** *adv.*

in·de·ter·mi·na·ble (ĭn/dĭ tûr/mə nə bəl), *adj.* 1. not determinable; incapable of being ascertained. 2. incapable of being decided or settled. 3. *Rare.* interminable. —*n.* 4. that which is indeterminable. —**in/-de·ter/mi·na·bly,** *adv.*

in·de·ter·mi·nate (ĭn/dĭ tûr/mə nĭt), *adj.* 1. not determinate; not fixed in extent; indefinite; uncertain. 2. not clear; vague: *a cloudy and indeterminate meaning.* 3. not established. 4. not settled or decided. 5. *Bot.* (of an inflorescence) having the axis or axes not ending in a flower or bud, thus allowing further elongation. —**in/-de·ter/mi·nate·ly,** *adv.* —**in/de·ter/mi·nate·ness,** *n.*

indeterminate sentence, *Penol.* a penalty imposed by a court which has relatively wide limits or no limits, as imprisonment for one to ten years.

in·de·ter·mi·na·tion (ĭn/dĭ tûr/mə nā/shən), *n.* 1. condition or quality of being indeterminate. 2. an unsettled state, as of the mind.

in·de·ter·min·ism (ĭn/dĭ tûr/mə nĭz/əm), *n. Philos.* 1. the doctrine that human actions, though somewhat influenced by preëxisting psychological and other conditions, are not entirely governed by them, but contain a certain freedom and spontaneity. 2. the theory that the will is to some extent independent of the strength of motives, or may itself modify their strength in choice. —**in/de·ter/min·ist,** *n., adj.*

in·dex (ĭn/dĕks), *n., pl.* -**dexes,** -**dices** (-də sēz/), *v.* —*n.* 1. a detailed alphabetical key to names, places, and topics in a book with reference to their page location in the book. 2. something used or serving to point out; a sign, token, or indication: *a true index of his character.* 3. something that serves to direct attention to some fact, condition, etc.; a guiding principle. 4. a pointer or indicator in a scientific instrument. 5. a piece of wood, metal, or the like, serving as a pointer or indicator. 6. *Print., etc.* a sign (☞) used to point out a particular note, paragraph, etc. 7. the index finger; the forefinger. 8. *Science.* a number or formula expressing some property, ratio, etc., of a thing indicated. 9. *Alg.* a. an exponent. b. the integer n in a radical $\sqrt[n]{\ }$ defining the n-th root: $\sqrt[5]{7}$ *is a radical having index three.* 10. (*cap.*) a list of books which Roman Catholics are forbidden by Church authority to read without special permission, or which are not to be read unless expurgated or corrected (L *Index Librorum Prohibitorum,* **Index of Prohibited Books**), or a list of books of the latter class only, with specification of objectionable passages (L *Index Expurgatorius,* **Expurgatory Index**). 11. *Obs.* a table of contents. 12. *Obs.* a preface. —*v.t.* 13. to provide with an index, as a book. 14. to enter in an index, as a word. 15. to serve to indicate. [ME, t. L:

index, forefinger, sign] **—in′dex·er**, *n.* **—in·dex·i·cal** (ĭn dĕk′sə kəl), *adj.* **—in′dex·less**, *adj.*

index finger, the forefinger.

index number, *Statistics.* a series of numbers which shows relative changes in prices, immigration, etc.

In·di·a (ĭn′dĬə), *n.* a large peninsula in southern Asia, S of the Himalayas and projecting into the Indian Ocean. Politically, India is divided into the two states of India (318,690,-000 pop., est. 1955; 1,246,-880 sq. mi. *Cap.*: New Delhi) and **Pakistan** (83,-603,000 pop., est. 1956; 360,780 sq. mi. *Cap.*: Karachi), and the smaller areas of Portuguese India. The state of India became an independent republic on Jan. 26, 1950. Both India and Pakistan are in the British Commonwealth of Nations. [OE, t. L, t. Gk., der. *Indós* river Indus (t. Pers.: m. *Hind*, c. Skt. *Sindhu* river Indus, orig. river)]

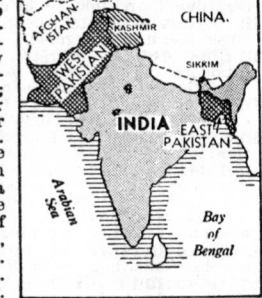

India, February, 1950

India ink, 1. a black pigment, made chiefly in China and Japan, consisting of lampblack mixed with a binding material and molded into sticks or cakes. 2. a liquid ink from this.

In·di·a·man (ĭn′dĬə mən), *n., pl.* **-men.** a ship in the India trade, esp. a large one of the East India Company.

In·di·an (ĭn′dĬən), *n.* 1. a member of the aboriginal race of America or of any of the aboriginal North and South American stocks, often excepting the Eskimos (**American Indian**). 2. *Colloq.* any of the American Indian languages. 3. a member of any of the native races of India or the East Indies (**East Indian**). 4. a European, esp. an Englishman, who resides or has resided in India or the East Indies. **—adj.** 5. denoting, belonging to, or pertaining to the race embracing the aborigines of America. 6. of or pertaining to India or the East Indies (often **East Indian**). 7. made of Indian corn: *Indian meal*, **Cf. f. INDIA + -AN**]

In·di·an·a (ĭn′dĬ ăn′ə), *n.* a State in the central United States: a part of the Midwest, 4,662,498 pop. (1960); 36,291 sq. mi. *Cap.*: Indianapolis. *Abbr.*: Ind. **—In·di·an·i·an** (ĭn′dĬ ăn′Ĭ ən), *adj., n.*

Indian agency, headquarters of an Indian agent.

Indian agent, 1. one serving as an agent among the Indians. 2. (in later use) an official representing the United States in dealing with an Indian tribe or tribes.

In·di·an·ap·o·lis (ĭn′dĬə năp′ə lĬs), *n.* the capital of Indiana, in the central part. 476,258 (1960).

Indian club, a gymnasium hand apparatus made of wood or metal, bottle-shaped, usually used in pairs.

Indian corn, *Chiefly Brit.* maize.

Indian Empire, (prior to political developments in India in 1947) British India, and the Indian states ruled by native princes but under indirect British control.

Indian file, single file, as of persons walking.

Indian giver, *U.S. Colloq.* one who takes back a gift.

Indian hemp, 1. a plant, genus *Apocynum*, native to America, whose root has laxative and emetic properties. 2. an East Indian variety of hemp, *Cannabis sativa* or *indica.* Cf. **cannabis.**

Indian licorice, a fabaceous woody shrub, *Abrus precatorius*, of India, etc., whose seeds are used for beads, and whose root is employed as a substitute for licorice.

Indian mallow, 1. a malvaceous plant, *Abutilon Theophrasti*, with yellow flowers and velvety leaves, introduced into America, etc., from southern Asia. 2. any of certain related species.

Indian meal, *Chiefly Brit.* corn meal.

Indian millet, durra.

Indian Ocean, an ocean S of Asia, E of Africa, and W of Australia. ab. 28,350,000 sq. mi.

Indian paintbrush, any of several showy species of the scrophulariaceous genus *Castilleja*, as *C. linariaefolia* of southwestern U.S. (the State flower of Wyoming).

Indian pipe, a leafless saprophytic plant, *Monotropa uniflora*, of North America and Asia, having a solitary flower, and resembling a tobacco pipe.

Indian pudding, a sweet pudding made of corn meal.

Indian red, 1. earth of a yellowish-red color, found esp. in the Persian Gulf, which serves as a pigment and as a polish for gold and silver objects. 2. a pigment of that color prepared by oxidizing the salts of iron.

Indian rice, a gramineous plant of marshes of the central and southeastern U.S., *Zizania aquatica.*

Indian summer, a period of mild, dry weather, usually accompanied by a hazy atmosphere, occurring in the U.S. and Canada in late autumn or early winter.

Indian Territory, a former territory of the United States: now in E Oklahoma. ab. 31,000 sq. mi.

Indian tobacco, a common American herb, *Lobelia inflata*, with small blue flowers and inflated capsules.

Indian turnip, 1. the jack-in-the-pulpit. 2. its root.

India paper, 1. a fine, thin but opaque paper made in the Orient, used chiefly in the production of thin-paper editions and for impressions of engravings. 2. a thin, tough, rag paper used in printing Bibles, prayerbooks, large reference works, etc.

India print, a cotton fabric block-printed in India.

India rubber, 1. a highly elastic substance obtained from the milky juice of numerous tropical plants, used for rubbing out pencil marks, and variously in the arts and manufactures; caoutchouc; gum elastic; rubber. 2. *U.S. Obs.* a rubber overshoe. Also, **india rubber.**

In·dic (ĭn′dĬk), *adj.* 1. of or pertaining to India; Indian. 2. of or pertaining to a subgroup of the Indo-Iranian languages, associated with India ancient and modern. [t. L: s. *Indicus*, t. Gk.: m. *Indikós*]

indic., 1. indicating. 2. Also, **ind.** indicative.

in·di·can (ĭn′də kən), *n.* 1. *Chem.* a glucoside, $C_{14}H_{17}NO_6$, which occurs in plants yielding indigo, and from which indigo is obtained. 2. *Biochem.* a component of urine, indoxyl potassium sulfate, $C_8H_6O_4SK$. [f. s. L *indicum* indigo + -AN]

in·di·cant (ĭn′də kənt), *adj.* 1. indicating. 2. indicative. **—n.** 3. that which indicates.

in·di·cate (ĭn′də kāt′), *v.t.* **-cated, -cating.** 1. to be a sign of; betoken; imply: *his hesitation indicates unwillingness.* 2. to point out or point to; direct attention to: *to indicate a place on a map.* 3. to show, or make known: *the thermometer indicates temperature.* 4. to state or express, esp. briefly or in a general way: *to indicate one's intentions.* 5. *Med.* **a.** (of symptoms, etc.) to point out (a particular remedy, treatment, etc.) as suitable or necessary. **b.** to show the presence of (a disease, etc.). [t. L: m.s. *indicātus*, pp.]

in·di·ca·tion (ĭn′də kā′shən), *n.* 1. anything serving to indicate or point out, as a sign, token, etc. 2. *Med.* a special symptom or the like which points out a suitable remedy or treatment or shows the presence of a disease. 3. the act of indicating. 4. the degree marked by an instrument.

in·dic·a·tive (ĭn dĬk′ə tĬv), *adj.* 1. that indicates; pointing out; suggestive (fol. by *of*). 2. *Gram.* designating or pertaining to the verb mode of ordinary statements, questions, etc., in contrast to hypothetical statements or those made without reference to a specific actor or time of action. For example: in the sentence *John plays football*, the verb *plays* is in the indicative mode. **—n.** 3. *Gram.* **a.** the indicative mode. **b.** a verb therein. [late ME t. L: m.s. *indicātīvus*] **—in·dic′a·tive·ly**, *adv.*

in·di·ca·tor (ĭn′də kā′tər), *n.* 1. one who or that which indicates. 2. a pointing or directing device, as a pointer on an instrument. 3. an instrument which indicates the condition of a machine, etc. 4. a pressure gauge; an apparatus for recording the variations of pressure or vacuum in the cylinder of an engine. 5. *Chem.* a substance used (esp. in volumetric analysis) to indicate (as by a change in color) the condition of a solution, the point at which a certain reaction ends and another begins, etc.

in·di·ca·to·ry (ĭn də kə tōr′Ĭ), *adj.* serving to indicate.

in·di·ces (ĭn′də sēz′), *n.* pl. of **index.**

in·di·ci·a (ĭn dĬsh′Ĭ ə), *n.pl., sing.* **-dicium** (-dĬsh′Ĭ əm). 1. envelope markings substituted for stamps or other regular cancellations in a large shipment of mail. 2. *Rare.* indications. [t. L, pl. of *indicium* sign, mark] **—in·di·cial** (ĭn dĬsh′əl), *adj.*

in·dict (ĭn dĬt′), *v.t.* 1. to charge with an offense or crime; accuse. 2. (of a grand jury) to bring a formal accusation against, as a means of bringing to trial. [ME *endite(n)*, t. AF: m. *enditer* accuse, indict. Cf. OF *enditer* INDITE] **—in·dict′er, in·dict′or,** *n.*

in·dict·a·ble (ĭn dĬ′tə bəl), *adj.* 1. liable to be indicted, as a person. 2. making one liable to be indicted, as an offense.

in·dic·tion (ĭn dĬk′shən), *n.* 1. a proclamation made every 15 years in the later Roman Empire, fixing the valuation of property to be used as a basis for taxation. 2. a tax based on such valuation. 3. the recurring fiscal period of 15 years in the Roman Empire, long used for dating ordinary events. 4. a specified year in this period. 5. the number indicating it. 6. *Rare.* authoritative proclamation. [ME, t. L: s. *indictio*]

in·dict·ment (ĭn dĬt′mənt), *n.* 1. the act of indicting. 2. *Law.* a formal accusation presented by a grand jury, usually required for felonies and other serious crimes. 3. an accusation. 4. the state of being indicted.

In·dies (ĭn′dēz), *n.pl.* 1. the West Indies. 2. a region in and near S and SE Asia: India, Indochina, and the East Indies. 3. the East Indies.

in·dif·fer·ence (ĭn dĬf′ər əns), *n.* 1. lack of interest or concern. 2. unimportance. 3. the quality or fact of being indifferent. 4. mediocre quality. Also, **in·dif′fer·en·cy.**

—Syn. 1. INDIFFERENCE, UNCONCERN, LISTLESSNESS, APATHY, INSENSIBILITY all imply lack of feeling. INDIFFERENCE denotes an absence of feeling or interest; UNCONCERN, an absence of concern or solicitude, a calm or cool indifference in the face of what might be expected to cause uneasiness or apprehension; LISTLESSNESS, an absence of inclination or interest, a languid indifference to what is going on about one; APATHY, profound indifference suggestive of mental faculties either naturally sluggish or dulled by sickness and grief. INSENSIBILITY denotes an absence of capacity for feeling, or of susceptibility to emotional influences. **—Ant.** 1. eagerness, responsiveness.

in·dif·fer·ent (ĭn dĬf′ər ənt), *adj.* 1. without interest or concern; not caring; apathetic. 2. having no feeling favorable or unfavorable to some thing or person;

impartial. **3.** neutral in character or quality; neither good nor bad: *an indifferent specimen.* **4.** falling short of any standard of excellence; not very good: *indifferent success.* **5.** of only moderate amount, extent, etc. **6.** not making a difference, or mattering, either way, as to a person. **7.** immaterial or unimportant. **8.** not essential or obligatory, as an observance. **9.** making no difference or distinction, as between persons or things: *indifferent justice.* **10.** neutral in chemical, electrical, or magnetic quality. **11.** *Biol.* not differentiated or specialized, as cells or tissues. [ME, t. L: s. *indifferens* (def. 3)] —**in·dif'fer·ent·ly,** *adv.*

in·dif·fer·ent·ism (ĭn dĭf'ər ən tĭz'əm), *n.* **1.** systematic indifference. **2.** adiaphorism. **3.** the principle that differences of religious belief are essentially unimportant. —**in·dif'fer·ent·ist,** *n.*

in·di·gence (ĭn'də jəns), *n.* indigent state; poverty.

in·di·gene (ĭn'də jēn'), *n.* one who or that which is indigenous or native; a native; an autochthon. Also, **in·di·gen** (ĭn'də jən). [t. F, t. L: m. *indigena*]

in·dig·e·nous (ĭn dĭj'ə nəs), *adj.* **1.** originating in and characterizing a particular region or country; native (fol. by *to*): *the plants indigenous to Canada.* **2.** innate; inherent; natural (fol. by *to*). [t. LL: m. *indigenus,* der. L *indigena* native] —**in·dig'e·nous·ly,** *adv.* —**in·dig'e·nous·ness, in·di·gen·i·ty** (ĭn'də jĕn'ə tĭ), *n.*

in·di·gent (ĭn'də jənt), *adj.* **1.** lacking the necessaries of life; needy; poor. **2.** destitute (fol. by *of*). **3.** *Archaic.* deficient in what is requisite. [ME, t. L: s. *indigens,* ppr.] —**in·di·gent·ly,** *adv.*

in·di·gest·ed (ĭn'də jĕs'tĭd, -dĭ-), *adj.* **1.** without arrangement or order. **2.** unformed or shapeless. **3.** not digested; undigested. **4.** not duly considered.

in·di·gest·i·ble (ĭn'də jĕs'tə bəl, -dĭ-), *adj.* not digestible; not easily digested. —**in·di·gest·i·bil'i·ty, in'di·gest'i·ble·ness,** *n.* —**in'di·gest'i·bly,** *adv.*

in·di·ges·tion (ĭn'də jĕs'chən, -dĭ-), *n.* incapability of, or difficulty in, digesting food; dyspepsia.

in·di·ges·tive (ĭn'də jĕs'tĭv, -dĭ-), *adj.* attended with or suffering from indigestion; dyspeptic.

in·dign (ĭn dīn'), *adj.* **1.** *Archaic.* unworthy. **2.** *Archaic.* unbecoming or disgraceful. **3.** *Now Poetic.* undeserved. [ME *indigne,* t. F, t. L: m.s. *indignus*]

in·dig·nant (ĭn dĭg'nənt), *adj.* affected with or characterized by indignation. [t. L: s. *indignans,* ppr., deeming unworthy] —**in·dig'nant·ly,** *adv.*

in·dig·na·tion (ĭn'dĭg nā'shən), *n.* displeasure at something deemed unworthy, unjust, or base; righteous anger. —**Syn.** See **anger.**

in·dig·ni·ty (ĭn dĭg'nə tĭ), *n., pl.* **-ties. 1.** injury to dignity; slighting or contemptuous treatment; a humiliating affront, insult, or injury. **2.** *Obs.* unworthiness. **3.** *Obs.* disgrace or disgraceful action. [t. L: m.s. *indignitas* unworthiness] —**Syn. 1.** See **insult.**

in·di·go (ĭn'də gō'), *n., pl.* **-gos, -goes. 1.** a blue dye obtained from various plants, esp. of the genus *Indigofera.* **2.** indigo blue or indigotin, the coloring principle of this dye. **3.** a plant of the leguminous genus *Indigofera.* **4.** deep violet blue, between violet and blue in the spectrum. [t. Sp. or Pg., t. L: m.s. *indicum* indigo, lit., Indian (dye); t. Gk.: m. *indikón*] —**in·di·got·ic** (ĭn'də gŏt'ĭk), *adj.*

indigo blue, 1. the color indigo. **2.** the essential coloring principle (a chemical compound, $C_{16}H_{10}N_2O_2$), which is contained, along with other substances, in the dye indigo, and which can also be prepared artificially. —**in'di·go-blue',** *adj.*

indigo bunting, a North American fringilline songbird, *Passerina cyanea,* the male of which is indigo blue. Also, **indigo bird, indigo finch.**

in·di·goid (ĭn'də goid'), *adj.* **1.** of or pertaining to that group of vat dyes which have a molecular structure like that of indigo. —*n.* **2.** an indigoid substance. [f. INDIG(O) + -OID]

in·dig·o·tin (ĭn dĭg'ə tĭn, ĭn'də gō'tĭn), *n.* indigo blue.

in·di·rect (ĭn'də rĕkt', -dĭ-), *adj.* **1.** not direct in space; deviating from a straight line: *an indirect course in sailing.* **2.** coming or resulting otherwise than directly or immediately, as effects, consequences, etc.: *an indirect advantage.* **3.** not direct in action or procedure; not straightforward; crooked: *indirect methods.* **4.** not descending in a direct line of succession, as a title or inheritance. **5.** not direct in bearing, application, force, etc.: *indirect evidence.* **6.** *Gram.* not consisting exactly of the words originally used, as in *He said he was hungry* instead of the direct *He said, 'I am hungry.'* —**in'di·rect'ly,** *adv.* —**in'di·rect'ness,** *n.*

indirect initiative, a procedure in which a statute or amendment, proposed by popular petition, must receive legislative consideration before submission to the voters.

in·di·rec·tion (ĭn'də rĕk'shən, -dĭ-), *n.* **1.** indirect action or procedure. **2.** a roundabout course or method. **3.** deceitful or crooked dealing.

indirect lighting, reflected or diffused light, used in interiors to avoid glare, shadows, etc.

indirect object, (in English and some other languages) the object with reference to which (for whose benefit, etc.) the action of a verb is performed, in English distinguished from the direct object by its position in the sentence or by the use of a preposition (*to* or *for*), e.g. *the boy* in *he gave the boy a book* or *he gave a book to the boy.*

indirect tax, a tax demanded from persons who reimburse themselves at the expense of others, the tax being levied on commodities before they reach the consumer and paid ultimately as part of their market price.

in·dis·cern·i·ble (ĭn'dĭ zûr'nə bəl, -sûr'-), *adj.* not discernible; imperceptible. —**in'dis·cern'i·ble·ness,** *n.* —**in'dis·cern'i·bly,** *adv.*

in·dis·cerp·ti·ble (ĭn'dĭ sûrp'tə bəl), *adj.* not disceptible; indivisible. —**in'dis·cerp'ti·bil'i·ty,** *n.*

in·dis·cov·er·a·ble (ĭn'dĭs kŭv'ər ə bəl), *adj.* not discoverable; undiscoverable.

in·dis·creet (ĭn'dĭs krēt'), *adj.* not discreet; lacking prudence; lacking sound judgment: *indiscreet praise.* —**in'dis·creet'ly,** *adv.* —**in'dis·creet'ness,** *n.*

in·dis·crete (ĭn'dĭs krēt', ĭn dĭs'krēt), *adj.* not discrete. [t. L: m.s. *indiscrētus* not separated]

in·dis·cre·tion (ĭn'dĭs krĕsh'ən), *n.* **1.** lack of discretion; imprudence. **2.** an indiscreet act or step.

in·dis·crim·i·nate (ĭn'dĭs krĭm'ə nĭt), *adj.* **1.** not discriminating: *indiscriminate in one's friendships.* **2.** not discriminate; confused: *indiscriminate slaughter.* —**in'dis·crim'i·nate·ly,** *adv.* —**in'dis·crim'i·nate·ness,** *n.* —**Syn. 1.** See **miscellaneous.**

in·dis·crim·i·nat·ing (ĭn'dĭs krĭm'ə nā'tĭng), *adj.* not discriminating. —**in'dis·crim'i·nat'ing·ly,** *adv.*

in·dis·crim·i·na·tion (ĭn'dĭs krĭm'ə nā'shən), *n.* **1.** the fact of not discriminating. **2.** the condition of not being discriminated. **3.** lack of discrimination. —**in'dis·crim'i·na'tive,** *adj.*

in·dis·pen·sa·ble (ĭn'dĭs pĕn'sə bəl), *adj.* **1.** not dispensable; absolutely necessary or requisite: *an indispensable man.* **2.** that cannot be disregarded or neglected: *an indispensable obligation.* —*n.* **3.** one who or that which is indispensable. —**in'dis·pen'sa·bil'i·ty, in'dis·pen'sa·ble·ness,** *n.* —**in'dis·pen'sa·bly,** *adv.* —**Syn. 1.** See **necessary.**

in·dis·pose (ĭn'dĭs pōz'), *v.t.,* **-posed, -posing. 1.** to put out of the proper condition (for something); make unfit; disqualify. **2.** to make ill, esp. slightly. **3.** to disincline; render averse or unwilling.

in·dis·posed (ĭn'dĭs pōzd'), *adj.* **1.** sick or ill, esp. slightly: *indisposed with a cold.* **2.** disinclined or unwilling. —**Syn. 1.** See **sick.**

in·dis·po·si·tion (ĭn'dĭs pə zĭsh'ən), *n.* **1.** state of being indisposed; a slight illness. **2.** disinclination.

in·dis·put·a·ble (ĭn'dĭs pū'tə bəl, ĭn dĭs'pyə-), *adj.* not disputable. —**in'dis·put·a·bil'i·ty, in'dis·put'a·ble·ness,** *n.* —**in'dis·put'a·bly,** *adv.*

in·dis·sol·u·ble (ĭn'dĭ sŏl'yə bəl, ĭn dĭs'əl yə bəl), *adj.* **1.** not dissoluble; incapable of being dissolved, decomposed, undone, or destroyed. **2.** firm or stable. **3.** perpetually binding or obligatory. —**in'dis·sol'u·bil'i·ty, in'dis·sol'u·ble·ness,** *n.* —**in'dis·sol'u·bly,** *adv.*

in·dis·tinct (ĭn'dĭs tĭngkt'), *adj.* **1.** not distinct; not clearly marked off or defined. **2.** not clearly distinguishable or perceptible, as to the eye, ear, or mind. **3.** not distinguishing clearly. [t. L: s. *indistinctus*] —**in'dis·tinct'ly,** *adv.* —**in'dis·tinct'ness,** *n.*

in·dis·tinc·tive (ĭn'dĭs tĭngk'tĭv), *adj.* **1.** without distinctive characteristics. **2.** not capable of making distinction. —**in'dis·tinc'tive·ly,** *adv.* —**in'dis·tinc'tive·ness,** *n.*

in·dis·tin·guish·a·ble (ĭn'dĭs tĭng'gwĭsh ə bəl), *adj.* **1.** not distinguishable. **2.** indiscernible. —**in'dis·tin'guish·a·ble·ness,** *n.* —**in'dis·tin'guish·a·bly,** *adv.*

in·dite (ĭn dīt'), *v.t.,* **-dited, -diting. 1.** to compose or write, as a speech, poem, etc. **2.** *Archaic.* to treat in a literary composition. **3.** *Obs.* to dictate. **4.** *Obs.* to prescribe. [ME *endite(n),* t. OF: m. *enditer* dictate, write, g. L *in-* IN-² + *dictāre* pronounce. Cf. INDICT] —**in·dite'ment,** *n.* —**in·dit'er,** *n.*

in·di·um (ĭn'dĭ əm), *n. Chem.* a rare metallic element, soft, white, malleable and easily fusible, found combined in various ores, esp. sphalerite: so called from the two indigo-blue lines in its spectrum. *Symbol:* In; *at. wt.:* 114.76; *at. no.:* 49; *sp. gr.:* 7.3 at 20°C. [f. IND(O)- + -IUM]

in·di·vert·i·ble (ĭn'də vûr'tə bəl), *adj.* not divertible; not to be turned aside. —**in'di·vert'i·bly,** *adv.*

individ., individual.

in·di·vid·u·al (ĭn'də vĭj'ōō əl), *adj.* **1.** single; particular; separate. **2.** existing as a distinct, indivisible entity, or considered as such: *individual members.* **3.** pertaining or peculiar to a single person or thing: *individual tastes.* **4.** intended for the use of one person only: *individual portions.* **5.** distinguished by peculiar and marked characteristics; exhibiting individuality: *a highly individual style.* **6.** of which each is different or of a different design from the others: *a set of individual coffee cups.* —*n.* **7.** a single human being, as distinguished from a group. **8.** a person: *a strange individual.* **9.** a distinct, indivisible entity; a single thing, being, instance, or item. **10.** a group considered as a unit. **11.** *Biol.* **a.** a single or simple organism capable of independent existence. **b.** a member of a compound organism or colony, as one of the distinct elements or zoöids which make up a compound hydrozoan, or sometimes (when a whole plant or tree is regarded as a colony or compound organism) a single shoot or bud. [ME, t. ML: m.s. *individuālis,* der. L *indīviduus* indivisible] —**Syn.** See **person.**

in·di·vid·u·al·ism (ĭn'də vĭj'ōō əl ĭz'əm), *n.* **1.** a social theory advocating the liberty, rights, or independent action of the individual. **2.** the principle or habit of independent thought or action. 3. the pursuit of individual rather than common or collective interests; egoism. 4. individual character; individuality. 5. an individual peculiarity. 6. *Philos.* a. the doctrine of pure egoism, or that nothing exists but the individual self. b. the doctrine that nothing is real but individual things. c. the principle that all actions are determined by, or at least exist for, the benefit of the individual and not the mass of men.

in·di·vid·u·al·ist (ĭn'də vĭj'ōō əl ĭst), n. 1. one characterized by individualism in thought or action. 2. an advocate of individualism. —**in·di·vid'u·al·is'tic**, adj.

in·di·vid·u·al·i·ty (ĭn'də vĭj'ōō ăl'ə tĭ), n., pl. -**ties.** 1. the particular character, or aggregate of qualities, which distinguishes one person or thing from others: *a person of marked individuality*. 2. (pl.) individual characteristics. 3. a person or thing of individual or distinctive character. 4. the state or quality of being individual; existence as a distinct individual. 5. the interests of the individual as distinguished from the interests of the community. 6. *Archaic.* state or quality of being indivisible or inseparable. —**Syn. 1.** See **character.**

in·di·vid·u·al·ize (ĭn'də vĭj'ōō ə līz'), v.t., -ized, -izing. 1. to make individual; give an individual or distinctive character to. 2. to mention, indicate, or consider individually; specify; particularize. —v.i. 3. to become individual; specialize. 4. to mention or consider individuals; particularize. —**in·di·vid'u·al·i·za'tion**, n. —**in·di·vid'u·al·iz'er**, n.

in·di·vid·u·al·ly (ĭn'də vĭj'ōō ə lĭ), adv. 1. in an individual manner. 2. separately. 3. personally.

in·di·vid·u·ate (ĭn'də vĭj'ōō āt'), v.t., -ated, -ating. 1. to form into an individual or distinct entity. 2. to give an individual or distinctive character to; individualize. [t. ML: m.s. *individuātus*, pp. of *indīvīduāre*, der. L *indīviduus*. See INDIVIDUAL]

in·di·vid·u·a·tion (ĭn'də vĭj'ōō ā'shən), n. 1. act of individuating. 2. state of being individuated; individual existence; individuality. 3. *Philos.* the determination or contraction of a general nature to an individual mode of existence; development of the individual from the general.

in·di·vis·i·ble (ĭn'də vĭz'ə bəl), adj. 1. not divisible; incapable of being divided: *one nation indivisible*. —n. 2. something indivisible. —**in'di·vis'i·bil'i·ty, in'di·vis'i·ble·ness**, n. —**in'di·vis'i·bly**, adv.

Indo-, a word element meaning "of or in India" as in *Indo-African* (of India and Africa), or "Indian" as in *Indo-British* (British in India). [t. L, t. Gk., comb. form of L *Indus*, Gk. *Indós*]

indo-, a combining form of indigo. Also, **ind-**.

In·do·chi·na (ĭn'dō chī'na), n. 1. Also, **Farther India**, a peninsula in SE Asia between the Bay of Bengal and the South China Sea, comprising South Vietnam, North Vietnam, Cambodia, Laos, Thailand, Malaya, and Burma. 2. French Indochina.

In·do·chi·nese (ĭn'dō chī nēz', -nēs'), adj., n., pl. -**nese.** —adj. 1. of or pertaining to Indochina. 2. of or pertaining to the Mongoloid peoples of Indochina or their languages. —n. 3. Sino-Tibetan.

in·doc·ile (ĭn dŏs'ĭl), adj. not docile; not amenable to teaching. —**in·do·cil·i·ty** (ĭn'dō sĭl'ə tĭ) n.

in·doc·tri·nate (ĭn dŏk'trĭ nāt'), v.t., -nated, -nating. 1. to instruct (in a doctrine, etc.). 2. to teach or inculcate. 3. to imbue (a person, etc.) with learning. [f. IN-² + s. L *doctrīna* teaching, DOCTRINE + -ATE¹] —**in·doc'tri·na'tion**, n. —**in·doc'tri·na'tor**, n.

In·do-Eu·ro·pe·an (ĭn'dō yōōr'ə pē'ən), adj. 1. of or pertaining to a major family of languages that includes most of the languages of Europe (now spread to other parts of the world), of Asia, and a few scattered others. —n. 2. this family of languages. 3. a member of one of the races speaking the Indo-European languages. Also, **In·do-Ger·man·ic** (ĭn'dō jər măn'ĭk) for 1, 2.

In·do-Hit·tite (ĭn'dō hĭt'īt), n. a linguistic stock comprising Indo-European and the Anatolian languages.

In·do-I·ra·ni·an (ĭn'dō ĭ rā'nĭ ən, -ĭ rā'nĭ ən), n. one of the principal groups within the Indo-European family of languages, including Persian and the Indo-European languages of India.

in·dole (ĭn'dōl), n. a colorless, low-melting solid, C₈H₇N, with a fecal odor, found in the oil of jasmine and clove and as a putrefaction product from animals' intestines, used in perfumery and as a reagent. Also, **in·dol** (ĭn'dōl, -dŏl). [f. IND- + -OLE]

in·do·lence (ĭn'də ləns), n. the state of being indolent. [t. L: m.s. *indolentia* freedom from pain]

in·do·lent (ĭn'də lənt), adj. 1. having or showing a disposition to avoid exertion: *an indolent person*. 2. *Pathol.* causing little or no pain. [t. LL: s. *indolens* not suffering] —**in'do·lent·ly**, adv. —**Syn. 1.** See **idle.**

in·dom·i·ta·ble (ĭn dŏm'ə tə bəl), adj. that cannot be subdued or overcome; as persons, pride, courage, etc. [t. LL: m.s. *indomitābilis*, der. L *in-* IN-³ + s. *domitāre* (freq. of *domāre* tame)] —**in·dom'i·ta·ble·ness**, n. —**in·dom'i·ta·bly**, adv. —**Syn.** See **invincible.**

In·do·ne·sia (ĭn'dō nē'sha, -zha), n. 1. the East Indies. 2. Republic of, a republic, proclaimed Aug. 1945,

of former areas in the Malay Archipelago, including Sumatra, Java, Celebes, parts of Borneo and Timor, the Moluccas, and associated islands. 81,900,000 pop. (est. 1955); ab. 580,000 sq. mi. *Cap.:* Djakarta. Formerly, **Dutch East Indies.**

In·do·ne·sian (ĭn'dō nē'shən, -zhən), n. 1. a member of the ethnic group consisting of the natives of Indonesia, the Filipinos, and the Malays of Malaya; Malaysian. 2. a member of a light-colored race supposed to have been dominant in the Malay Archipelago before the Malays, and believed to constitute one element of the present mixed population of Malaysia and perhaps Polynesia. 3. a group of Austronesian languages, including those of Formosa, the Philippines, Madagascar, and Indonesia, as well as Malay; Malayan. —adj. 4. of or pertaining to the Malay Archipelago. 5. pertaining to the Indonesians or their languages. 6. of Indonesia. [f. INDO- + s. Gk. *nêsos* island + -IAN]

in·door (ĭn'dōr'), adj. occurring, used, etc., in a house or building, rather than out of doors: *indoor games*.

in·doors (ĭn'dōrz'), adv. in or into a house or building.

in·do·phe·nol (ĭn'dō fē'nōl, -nŏl), n. 1. a coal-tar dye resembling indigo and giving indigo-blue shades. 2. any of various related dyes. [f. INDO- + PHENOL]

In·dore (ĭn dōr'), n. 1. a former state in central India; now part of Madhya Pradesh. 2. a city in central India, in W Madhya Pradesh. 310,859 (1951).

in·dorse (ĭn dôrs'), v.t., -dorsed, -dorsing. endorse. [var. of *endorse*, conformed to ML *indorsāre* put on the back. See IN-², DORSUM] —**in·dors'a·ble**, adj. —**in·dor·see** (ĭn'dôr sē', ĭn dôr'sē), n. —**in·dorse'ment**, n. —**in·dors'er, in·dor'sor**, n.

in·dox·yl (ĭn dŏk'sĭl), n. *Chem.* a crystalline compound, C₈H₇NO, which is formed by the hydrolysis of indican and is readily oxidized to furnish indigo.

In·dra (ĭn'dra), n. *Hinduism.* the Vedic god who presides over the deities of the middle realm (the air).

in·draft (ĭn'drăft', -dräft'), n. 1. a draft or drawing inward. 2. an inward flow or current. Also, *esp. Brit.*, **in'draught'.**

in·drawn (ĭn'drôn'), adj. drawn in; introspective.

in·dri (ĭn'drĭ), n., pl. -**dris.** a short-tailed lemur, *Indri indri*, of Madagascar, about two feet in length. [t. Malagasy, said to be an exclamation, "lo! see!", erroneously taken as the name of the animal]

in·du·bi·ta·ble (ĭn dū'bə tə bəl, -dōō'-), adj. that cannot be doubted; unquestionable; certain. —**in·du'bi·ta·ble·ness**, n. —**in·du'bi·ta·bly**, adv.

in·duce (ĭn dūs', -dōōs'), v.t., -duced, -ducing. 1. to lead or move by persuasion or influence, as to some action, state of mind, etc.: *to induce a person to go*. 2. to bring about, produce, or cause: *opium induces sleep*. 3. *Physics.* to produce (an electric current, etc.) by induction. 4. *Logic.* to assert or establish (a proposition about a class of phenomena) on the basis of observations on a number of particular facts. [ME *induce(n)*, t. L: m. *indūcere* lead in, bring in, persuade] —**in·duc'er**, n. —**in·duc'i·ble**, adj. —**Syn. 1.** See **persuade.**

in·duce·ment (ĭn dūs'mənt, -dōōs'-), n. 1. the act of inducing. 2. something that induces or persuades; an incentive. —**Syn. 2.** See **motive.**

in·duct (ĭn dŭkt'), v.t. 1. to lead or bring in; introduce, esp. formally, as into a place, office, etc. 2. to introduce in knowledge or experience (fol. by *to*). 3. *U.S.* to bring into military service. [ME, t. L: s. *inductus*, pp.]

in·duct·ance (ĭn dŭk'təns), n. *Elect.* 1. that property of a circuit by virtue of which electromagnetic induction takes place. 2. a piece of equipment providing inductance in a circuit or other system; inductor.

in·duc·tee (ĭn'dŭk tē'), n. a person inducted into military service.

in·duc·tile (ĭn dŭk'tĭl), adj. not ductile; not pliable. —**in'duc·til'i·ty**, n.

in·duc·tion (ĭn dŭk'shən), n. 1. *Elect., Magnetism.* a. the process by which a body having electrical or magnetic properties calls forth similar properties in a neighboring body without direct contact, as (1) the process by which the relative motion of a wire and magnetic field produces an e.m.f. in the wire; (2) the process by which a changing current in a circuit produces an e.m.f. in the same or a neighboring circuit. b. a tendency of electric currents to resist change. 2. *Logic.* a. the process of discovering explanations for a set of particular facts, by estimating the weight of observational evidence in favor of a proposition which (usually) asserts something about that entire class of facts. b. a conclusion reached by this process. 3. a bringing forward or adducing, as of facts, evidence, etc. 4. the act of inducing, bringing about, or causing: *induction of the hypnotic state*. 5. *Physiol.* the process whereby a tissue stimulates or alters other adjacent tissues. 6. the act of inducting; introduction or initiation. 7. formal introduction into an office or benefice; installation. 8. an introductory unit in a literary work; a prelude or scene, independent of the main performance but related to it. 9. *Archaic.* a preface. [ME, t. L: s. *inductio*]

induction coil, *Elect.* a transformer designed as two concentric coils with a common soft iron core, with the inner coil (primary) of few turns and the outer coil (secondary) of a great number of turns. When the primary is excited by rapidly interrupted or variable current, high voltage is induced in the secondary.

ăct, āble, dâre, ärt; ĕbb, ēqual; ĭf, īce; hŏt, ōver, ôrder, oil, bŏŏk, ōōze, out; ŭp, ūse, ûrge; ə = a in alone; ch, chief; g, give; ng, ring; sh, shoe; th, thin; ᵺ, that; zh, vision. See the full key on inside cover.

in·duc·tive (Ĭn dŭk′tĬv), *adj.* **1.** pertaining to or involving electrical or magnetic induction. **2.** operating by induction: *an inductive machine.* **3.** pertaining to or employing logical induction. **4.** *Physiol.* eliciting some reaction within an organism. **5.** serving to induce; leading or influencing (fol. by *to*). **6.** introductory. **—in·duc′tive·ly,** *adv.* **—in·duc′tive·ness,** *n.* —Syn. 3. See **deductive.**

in·duc·tiv·i·ty (Ĭn′dŭk tĬv′ə tĬ), *n., pl.* **-ties. 1.** an inductive property. **2.** capacity of producing induction. **3.** inductance.

in·duc·tor (Ĭn dŭk′tər), *n.* **1.** *Elect.* a device, the primary purpose of which is to introduce inductance into an electric circuit. **2.** one who inducts, as into office.

in·due (Ĭn dū′, -dōō′), *v.t.,* **-dued, -duing.** endue.

in·dulge (Ĭn dŭlj′), *v.,* **-dulged, -dulging.** **—v.i. 1.** to indulge oneself; yield to an inclination (fol. by *in*): *to indulge in apple pie.* **—v.t. 2.** to yield to, satisfy, or gratify (desires, feelings, etc.). **3.** to yield to the wishes or whims of: *to indulge a child.* **4.** to allow (oneself) to follow one's will (fol. by *in*). **5.** *Com.* to grant an extension of time, for payment or performance, to (a person, etc.) or on (a bill, etc.). **6.** *Now Rare.* to grant (something) by favor. [t. L: m.s. *indulgēre* be kind, yield, grant] **—in·dulg′er,** *n.* **—in·dulg′ing·ly,** *adv.* —Syn. 3. See **humor.**

in·dul·gence (Ĭn dŭl′jəns), *n., v.,* **-genced, -gencing.** **—n. 1.** the act or practice of indulging; gratification of desire. **2.** indulgent allowance or tolerance. **3.** humoring. **4.** something granted or taken in gratification of desire. **5.** *Rom. Cath. Ch.* a remission of the temporal punishment still due to sin after it has been forgiven. **6.** *Eng. and Scot. Hist.* (in the reigns of Charles II and James II) a grant by the king to Protestant Dissenters and Roman Catholics to be free from certain penalties imposed upon them by legislation on account of their religion. **7.** *Com.* an extension, through favor, of time for payment or performance. **—v.t. 8.** *Rom. Cath. Ch.* to furnish with an indulgence.

in·dul·gen·cy (Ĭn dŭl′jən sĬ), *n., pl.* **-cies.** indulgence.

in·dul·gent (Ĭn dŭl′jənt), *adj.* characterized by or showing indulgence: *an indulgent parent.* [t. L: s. *indulgens,* ppr.] **—in·dul′gent·ly,** *adv.*

in·du·line (Ĭn′dyə lēn′, -lĬn), *n.* any of a large class of dyes yielding colors similar to indigo. [f. IND- + *ul-* (t. L: s. *-ulum,* dim. suffix) + -INE²]

in·dult (Ĭn dŭlt′), *n.* *Rom. Cath. Ch.* a general faculty granted for a specific time or a specific number of cases by the Holy See to bishops and others, of doing something not permitted; a grant, privilege, favor. [t. LL: s. *indultum* indulgence, prop. pp. neut.]

in·du·pli·cate (Ĭn dū′plə kĬt, -kāt′, -dōō′-), *adj. Bot.* folded or rolled inward (said of the parts of the calyx or corolla in estivation when the edges are bent abruptly toward the axis, or of leaves in vernation when the edges are rolled inward and then arranged about the axis without overlapping. Also, **in·du′pli·ca′tive.** [f. IN-² + DUPLICATE (def. 2)] **—in·du′pli·ca′tion,** *n.*

in·du·rate (*v.* Ĭn′dyōō rāt′, -dōō-; *adj.* Ĭn′dyōō rĬt, -dōō-), *v.,* **-rated, -rating,** *adj.* **—v.t., v.i. 1.** to make or become hard; harden; inure. **—adj. 2.** hardened; callous; inured. [ME, t. L: m.s. *indūrātus,* pp.] **—in·du·ra′tion,** *n.* **—in·du·ra′tive,** *adj.*

In·dus (Ĭn′dəs), *n.* a river flowing from W Tibet through Kashmir and SW through Pakistan to the Arabian Sea. ab. 2000 mi.

in·du·si·um (Ĭn dū′zĬ əm, -zhĬ əm, -dōō′-), *n., pl.* **-sia** (-zĬ ə, -zhĬ ə). **1.** *Bot.* a membranous outgrowth covering the sori in ferns. **2.** *Anat., Zool.* an enveloping layer or membrane. [t. L: tunic] **—in·du′si·al,** *adj.*

in·dus·tri·al (Ĭn dŭs′trĬ əl), *adj.* **1.** of or pertaining to, of the nature of, or resulting from industry or productive labor: *the industrial arts.* **2.** having highly developed industries: *an industrial nation.* **3.** engaged in an industry or industries: *industrial workers.* **4.** pertaining to the workers in industries: *industrial training.* **5.** noting or pertaining to a form of life insurance for the working classes, with policies for comparatively low sums and with premiums payable weekly. **—n. 6.** a worker in some industry, esp. a manufacturing industry. **7.** one who conducts or owns an industrial enterprise. **8.** (*pl.*) stocks or bonds of industrial enterprises. [f. m. INDUSTRY + -AL¹. Cf. F *industriel*] **—in·dus′tri·al·ly,** *adv.*

in·dus·tri·al·ism (Ĭn dŭs′trĬ ə lĬz′əm), *n.* **1.** an economic organization of society built largely on mechanized industry rather than agriculture, craftsmanship, or commerce. **2.** the industrial branch of work or labor.

in·dus·tri·al·ist (Ĭn dŭs′trĬ ə lĬst), *n.* **1.** one who conducts or owns an industrial enterprise. **2.** a person employed in or concerned with some branch of industry.

in·dus·tri·al·ize (Ĭn dŭs′trĬ ə līz′), *v.t.,* **-ized, -izing. 1.** to introduce industry into (an area) on a large scale. **2.** to imbue with the spirit of industrialism. Also, *esp. Brit.,* **in·dus′tri·al·ise′.** **—in·dus′tri·al·i·za′tion,** *n.*

industrial revolution, the term applied to the social and economic changes in England from the mid 18th to the mid 19th centuries during the beginnings and growth of modern industrialism.

industrial school, 1. a school for teaching one or more branches of industry. **2.** a school for educating neglected children committed to its care and training them to some form of industry.

Industrial Workers of the World, an international industrial union, organized in Chicago in 1905. It disintegrated after World War I.

in·dus·tri·ous (Ĭn dŭs′trĬ əs), *adj.* **1.** hard-working; diligent: *an industrious person.* **2.** *Obs.* skillful. [t. L: m.s. *industriōsus* diligent] **—in·dus′tri·ous·ly,** *adv.* **—in·dus′tri·ous·ness,** *n.* —Syn. 1. See **busy.**

in·dus·try (Ĭn′dəs trĬ), *n., pl.* **-tries. 1.** a trade or manufacture: *the steel industry.* **2.** the ownership and management of companies, factories, etc.: *friction between labor and industry.* **3.** systematic work or labor. **4.** assiduous activity at any work or task. [ME *industrie,* t. L: m. *industria* diligence]

in·dwell (Ĭn′dwĕl′), *v.,* **-dwelt, -dwelling.** **—v.t. 1.** to inhabit. **—v.i. 2.** to dwell (fol. by *in*). **—in′dwell′er,** *n.*

In·dy (dăɴ dē′), *n.* **Vincent d'** (văɴ săɴ′), 1851–1931, French composer.

-ine¹, an adjective suffix meaning "of or pertaining to," "of the nature of," "made of," "like," as in *asinine, crystalline, equine, marine.* [t. L: m. *-īnus;* also m. *-inus,* t. Gk.: m. *-inos*]

-ine², 1. a noun suffix denoting some action, procedure, art, place, etc., as in *discipline, doctrine, medicine, latrine.* **2.** a suffix occurring in many nouns of later formation and various meanings, as in *famine, routine, grenadine, vaseline.* **3.** a noun suffix used particularly in chemical terms, as *bromine, chlorine,* and esp. names of basic substances, as *amine, aniline, caffeine, quinine, quinoline.* Cf. -in². [t. F, g, L *-ina,* orig. fem. of *-inus;* also used to repr. Gk. *-inē,* fem. n. suffix, as in *heroine*]

in·earth (Ĭn ûrth′), *v.t. Chiefly Poetic.* to bury; inter.

in·e·bri·ant (Ĭn ē′brĬ ənt), *adj.* **1.** inebriating; intoxicating. **—n. 2.** an intoxicant. [t. L: s. *inēbrians,* ppr.]

in·e·bri·ate (*v.* Ĭn ē′brĬ āt′; *n., adj.* Ĭn ē′brĬ Ĭt), *v.,* **-ated, -ating,** *n., adj.* **—v.t. 1.** to make drunk; intoxicate. **2.** to intoxicate mentally or emotionally; exhilarate. **—n. 3.** an intoxicated person. **4.** a habitual drunkard. **—adj. 5.** Also, **in·e′bri·at′ed.** drunk; intoxicated. [t. L: m.s. *inēbriātus,* pp.] **—in·e′bri·a′tion,** *n.* —Syn. 4. See **drunkard.**

in·e·bri·e·ty (Ĭn′Ĭ brī′ə tĬ), *n.* drunkenness.

in·ed·i·ble (Ĭn ĕd′ə bəl), *adj.* not edible; unfit to be eaten. **—in·ed′i·bil′i·ty,** *n.*

in·ed·it·ed (Ĭn ĕd′Ĭt Ĭd), *adj.* **1.** unpublished. **2.** not edited.

in·ef·fa·ble (Ĭn ĕf′ə bəl), *adj.* **1.** that cannot be uttered or expressed; inexpressible; unspeakable: *ineffable joy.* **2.** that must not be uttered: *the ineffable name.* [ME, t. L: m.s. *ineffābilis*] **—in·ef′fa·bil′i·ty, in·ef′fa·ble·ness,** *n.* **—in·ef′fa·bly,** *adv.*

in·ef·face·a·ble (Ĭn′Ĭ fā′sə bəl), *adj.* not effaceable; indelible: *an ineffaceable impression.* **—in·ef·face′a·bil′i·ty,** *n.* **—in·ef·face′a·bly,** *adv.*

in·ef·fec·tive (Ĭn′Ĭ fĕk′tĬv), *adj.* **1.** not effective; ineffectual, as efforts. **2.** inefficient, as a person. **3.** lacking in artistic effect, as a design or work. **—in·ef·fec′tive·ly,** *adv.* **—in·ef·fec′tive·ness,** *n.*

in·ef·fec·tu·al (Ĭn′Ĭ fĕk′chōō əl), *adj.* **1.** not effectual; without satisfactory or decisive effect: *an ineffectual remedy.* **2.** unavailing; futile: *his efforts were ineffectual.* **3.** powerless or impotent. **—in·ef·fec′tu·al′i·ty, in·ef·fec′tu·al·ness,** *n.* **—in·ef·fec′tu·al·ly,** *adv.* —Syn. 2. See **useless.**

in·ef·fi·ca·cious (Ĭn′ĕf ə kā′shəs), *adj.* not able to produce the desired effect. **—in·ef·fi·ca′cious·ly,** *adv.* **—in·ef·fi·ca′cious·ness, in·ef·fi·cac′i·ty** (Ĭn′ĕf ə kăs′ə tĬ), *n.*

in·ef·fi·ca·cy (Ĭn ĕf′ə kə sĬ), *n.* lack of efficacy or power to produce the desired effect.

in·ef·fi·cien·cy (Ĭn′Ĭ fĬsh′ən sĬ), *n.* the condition or quality of being inefficient; lack of efficiency.

in·ef·fi·cient (Ĭn′Ĭ fĬsh′ənt), *adj.* not efficient; unable to effect or accomplish in a capable, economical way. **—in·ef·fi′cient·ly,** *adv.* —Syn. See **incapable.**

in·e·las·tic (Ĭn′Ĭ lăs′tĬk), *adj.* not elastic; lacking elasticity; unyielding. **—in·e·las·tic·i·ty** (Ĭn′Ĭ lăs tĬs′ə tĬ), *n.*

in·el·e·gance (Ĭn ĕl′ə gəns), *n.* **1.** the state or character of being inelegant; lack of elegance. **2.** that which is inelegant or ungraceful.

in·el·e·gan·cy (Ĭn ĕl′ə gən sĬ), *n., pl.* **-cies.** inelegance.

in·el·e·gant (Ĭn ĕl′ə gənt), *adj.* not elegant; not nice or refined; vulgar. **—in·el′e·gant·ly,** *adv.*

in·el·i·gi·ble (Ĭn ĕl′Ĭ jə bəl), *adj.* **1.** not eligible; not proper or suitable for choice. **2.** legally disqualified to hold an office. **3.** legally disqualified to function as a juror, voter, witness, or to become the recipient of a privilege. **—n. 4.** one who is ineligible, esp. as a suitor, husband, or member of an athletic team. **—in·el′i·gi·bil′i·ty,** *n.* **—in·el′i·gi·bly,** *adv.*

in·el·o·quent (Ĭn ĕl′ə kwənt), *adj.* not eloquent. **—in·el′o·quence,** *n.* **—in·el′o·quent·ly,** *adv.*

in·e·luc·ta·ble (Ĭn′Ĭ lŭk′tə bəl), *adj.* that cannot be escaped from, as a fate. [t. L: m.s. *inēluctābilis*] **—in′e·luc′ta·bil′i·ty,** *n.* **—in·e·luc′ta·bly,** *adv.*

in·e·lud·i·ble (Ĭn′Ĭ lōō′də bəl), *adj.* not eludible; inescapable. **—in′e·lud′i·bly,** *adv.*

in·ept (Ĭn ĕpt′), *adj.* **1.** not apt, fitted, or suitable; unsuitable. **2.** inappropriate; out of place. **3.** absurd or foolish, as a proceeding, remark, etc. [t. L: s. *ineptus*] **—in·ept′ly,** *adv.* **—in·ept′ness,** *n.*

in·ept·i·tude (Ĭn ĕp′tə tūd′, -tōōd′), *n.* **1.** the quality of being inept. **2.** an inept act or remark.

---

b., blend of, blended; c., cognate with; d., dialect, dialectal; der., derived from; f., formed from; g., going back to; m., modification of; r., replacing; s., stem of; t., taken from; ?, perhaps.   See the full key on inside cover.

in·e·qual·i·ty (ĭn′Ĭ kwŏl′ə tĬ), n., pl. **-ties. 1.** the condition of being unequal; lack of equality; disparity: *inequality of treatment.* **2.** social disparity: *the inequality between the rich and the poor.* **3.** inadequacy. **4.** injustice; partiality. **5.** unevenness, as of surface. **6.** an instance of unevenness. **7.** variableness, as of climate. **8.** *Astron.* **a.** any component part of the departure from uniformity in astronomical phenomena, esp. in orbital motion. **b.** the amount of such a departure. **9.** *Math.* an expression of two unequal quantities connected by the sign > or <, as, *a > b*, "*a* is greater than *b*"; *a < b*, "*a* is less than *b*." [late ME, t. ML: m.s. *inaequālitas* unevenness]

inequi-, a word element meaning "unequal" or "unequally," as in *inequidistant.* [f. IN-³ + EQUI-]

in·e·qui·lat·er·al (ĭn′ē kwə lăt′ər əl), adj. not equilateral. **—in′e·qui·lat′er·al·ly,** adv.

in·eq·ui·ta·ble (ĭn ĕk′wə tə bəl), adj. not equitable; unfair. **—in·eq′ui·ta·bly,** adv.

in·eq·ui·ty (ĭn ĕk′wə tĬ), n., pl. **-ties. 1.** lack of equity; unfairness. **2.** an unfair circumstance or proceeding.

in·e·rad·i·ca·ble (ĭn′Ĭ răd′ə kə bəl), adj. not eradicable; that cannot be eradicated, rooted out, or removed utterly. **—in′e·rad′i·ca·bly,** adv.

in·e·ras·a·ble (ĭn′Ĭ rā′sə bəl), adj. not erasable; not to be erased or effaced. **—in′e·ras′a·bly,** adv.

in·er·ra·ble (ĭn ĕr′ə bəl, -ûr′-), adj. incapable of erring; infallible. [t. LL: m.s. *inerrābilis*] **—in·er′ra·bil′i·ty, in·er′ra·ble·ness,** n. **—in·er′ra·bly,** adv.

in·er·rant (ĭn ĕr′ənt, -ûr′-), adj. free from error. [t. L: s. *inerrans,* ppr., not wandering] **—in·er′ran·cy,** n.

in·er·rat·ic (ĭn′Ĭ răt′Ĭk), adj. not erratic or wandering; fixed, as a so-called "fixed" star.

in·ert (ĭn ûrt′), adj. **1.** having no inherent power of action, motion, or resistance: *inert matter.* **2.** without active properties, as a drug. **3.** of an inactive or sluggish habit or nature. [t. L: s. *iners* unskilled, idle] **—in·ert′ly,** adv. **—in·ert′ness,** n. **—Syn. 3.** See inactive.

in·er·tia (in ûr′shə), n. **1.** inert condition; inactivity; sluggishness. **2.** *Physics.* **a.** that property of matter by which it retains its state of rest or of uniform rectilinear motion so long as it is not acted upon by an external force. **b.** an analogous property of a force: *electric inertia.* [t. L: lack of skill, inactivity] **—in·er′tial,** adj.

in·es·cap·a·ble (ĭn′ĕs kā′pə bəl), adj. that cannot be escaped.

in es·se (ĭn ĕs′Ĭ), *Latin.* in being; in actuality; actually existing (contrasted with *in posse*).

in·es·sen·tial (ĭn′Ĭ sĕn′shəl), adj. **1.** not essential; not necessary; nonessential. **2.** *Rare.* without essence; insubstantial. **—n. 3.** that which is not essential. **—in′es·sen′ti·al′i·ty,** n.

in·es·ti·ma·ble (ĭn ĕs′tə mə bəl), adj. **1.** that cannot be estimated, or too great to be estimated. **2.** of incalculable value. [ME, t. F, t. L: m.s. *inaestimābilis.* See IN-³, ESTIMABLE] **—in·es′ti·ma·bly,** adv.

in·ev·i·ta·ble (ĭn ĕv′ə tə bəl), adj. **1.** that cannot be avoided, or escaped; certain or necessary: *an inevitable conclusion.* **2.** sure to befall, happen, or come, by the very nature of things: *one's inevitable fate.* **—n. 3.** that which is unavoidable. [ME, t. L: m.s. *inēvitābilis.* See IN-³, EVITABLE] **—in·ev′i·ta·bil′i·ty, in·ev′i·ta·ble·ness,** n. **—in·ev′i·ta·bly,** adv.

in·ex·act (ĭn′Ĭg zăkt′), adj. not exact; not strictly accurate. **—in·ex·act′ly,** adv. **—in·ex·act′ness,** n.

in·ex·act·i·tude (ĭn′Ĭg zăk′tə tūd′, -tōōd′), n. state or character of being inexact or inaccurate; inexactness. [f. IN-³ + EXACTITUDE]

in·ex·cus·a·ble (ĭn′Ĭk skū′zə bəl), adj. not excusable; incapable of being justified. **—in′ex·cus′a·bil′i·ty, in′ex·cus′a·ble·ness,** n. **—in′ex·cus′a·bly,** adv.

in·ex·e·cu·tion (ĭn ĕk′sə kū′shən), n. lack or neglect of execution.

in·ex·er·tion (ĭn′Ĭg zûr′shən), n. lack of exertion.

in·ex·haust·i·ble (ĭn′Ĭg zôs′tə bəl), adj. **1.** not exhaustible; incapable of being exhausted: *an inexhaustible supply.* **2.** unfailing; tireless. **—in′ex·haust′i·bil′i·ty, in′ex·haust′i·ble·ness,** n. **—in′ex·haust′i·bly,** adv.

in·ex·ist·ent (ĭn′Ĭg zĬs′tənt), adj. **1.** not existent; having no existence. **2.** existing within; inherent. **—in′ex·ist′ence, in·ex·ist′en·cy,** n.

in·ex·o·ra·ble (ĭn ĕk′sə rə bəl), adj. **1.** unyielding or unalterable: *inexorable facts.* **2.** not to be persuaded, moved, or affected by prayers or entreaties. [t. L: m. s. *inexōrābilis.* See IN-³, EXORABLE] **—in·ex′o·ra·bil′i·ty, in·ex′o·ra·ble·ness,** n. **—in·ex′o·ra·bly,** adv. **—Syn. 2.** relentless, unrelenting, implacable. See inflexible.

in·ex·pe·di·ent (ĭn′Ĭk spē′dĬ ənt), adj. not expedient; not suitable, judicious, or advisable. **—in′ex·pe′di·ence, in′ex·pe′di·en·cy,** n. **—in′ex·pe′di·ent·ly,** adv.

in·ex·pen·sive (ĭn′Ĭk spĕn′sĬv), adj. not expensive; costing little. **—in′ex·pen′sive·ly,** adv. **—in′ex·pen′sive·ness,** n. **—Syn.** See cheap.

in·ex·pe·ri·ence (ĭn′Ĭk spĬr′Ĭ əns), n. lack of experience, or of knowledge or skill gained from experience.

in·ex·pe·ri·enced (ĭn′Ĭk spĬr′Ĭ ənst), adj. not experienced; without knowledge or skill gained from experience. **—Syn.** untrained, unskilled, inexpert; raw, green.

in·ex·pert (ĭn′Ĭk spûrt′), adj. not expert; unskilled. **—in′ex·pert′ly,** adv. **—in′ex·pert′ness,** n.

in·ex·pi·a·ble (ĭn ĕk′spĬ ə bəl), adj. **1.** not to be expiated; admitting of no expiation or atonement: *an inexpiable crime.* **2.** not to be appeased by expiation; im-

placable: *inexpiable hate.* [t. L: m.s. *inexpiābilis*] **—in·ex′pi·a·ble·ness,** n. **—in·ex′pi·a·bly,** adv.

in·ex·plain·a·ble (ĭn′Ĭk splā′nə bəl), adj. not explainable; incapable of being explained; inexplicable.

in·ex·pli·ca·ble (ĭn ĕks′plə kə bəl or, esp. Brit., ĭn′Ĭk splĬk′ə bəl), adj. not explicable; incapable of being explained. [late ME, t. L: m.s. *inexplicābilis* that cannot be unfolded] **—in·ex′pli·ca·bil′i·ty, in·ex′pli·ca·ble·ness,** n. **—in·ex′pli·ca·bly,** adv.

in·ex·plic·it (ĭn′Ĭk splĬs′Ĭt), adj. not explicit or clear; not clearly stated. [t. L: s. *inexplicitus*] **—in′ex·plic′it·ly,** adv. **—in′ex·plic′it·ness,** n.

in·ex·press·i·ble (ĭn′Ĭk sprĕs′ə bəl), adj. **1.** not expressible; that cannot be uttered or represented in words: *inexpressible grief.* **—n. 2.** (pl.) *Humorous and Archaic.* breeches or trousers. **—in′ex·press′i·bil′i·ty, in′ex·press′i·ble·ness,** n. **—in′ex·press′i·bly,** adv.

in·ex·pres·sive (ĭn′Ĭk sprĕs′Ĭv), adj. **1.** not expressive; lacking in expression. **2.** *Archaic.* inexpressible. **—in′ex·pres′sive·ly,** adv. **—in′ex·pres′sive·ness,** n.

in·ex·pug·na·ble (ĭn′Ĭk spŭg′nə bəl), adj. that cannot be taken by force; impregnable; unconquerable: *an inexpugnable fort.* [t. L: m.s. *inexpugnābilis*] **—in′ex·pug′na·bil′i·ty, in′ex·pug′na·ble·ness,** n. **—in′ex·pug′na·bly,** adv.

in·ex·ten·si·ble (ĭn′Ĭk stĕn′sə bəl), adj. not extensible. **—in·ex·ten′si·bil′i·ty,** n.

in ex·ten·so (ĭn Ĭk stĕn′sō), *Latin.* at full length.

in·ex·tin·guish·a·ble (ĭn′Ĭk stĬng′gwĬsh ə bəl), adj. not extinguishable; not to be extinguished, quenched, suppressed, or brought to an end: *inextinguishable fire, inextinguishable rage.* **—in′ex·tin′guish·a·bly,** adv.

in·ex·tir·pa·ble (ĭn′Ĭk stûr′pə bəl), adj. incapable of being extirpated: *an inextirpable disease.*

in ex·tre·mis (ĭn Ĭk strē′mĬs), *Latin.* **1.** in extremity. **2.** near death.

in·ex·tri·ca·ble (ĭn ĕks′trə kə bəl), adj. **1.** from which one cannot extricate oneself: *an inextricable maze.* **2.** that cannot be disentangled, undone, or loosed, as a tangle, knot, grasp, etc. **3.** hopelessly intricate, involved, or perplexing: *inextricable confusion.* [late ME, t. L: m.s. *inextrīcābilis*] **—in·ex′tri·ca·bil′i·ty, in·ex′tri·ca·ble·ness,** n. **—in·ex′tri·ca·bly,** adv.

inf., 1. (*also cap.*) infantry. **2.** infinitive. **3.** information. **4.** (L *infra*) below; after.

in·fal·li·ble (ĭn făl′ə bəl), adj. **1.** not fallible; exempt from liability to error, as persons, their judgment, pronouncements, etc. **2.** absolutely trustworthy or sure: *an infallible rule.* **3.** unfailing in operation; certain: *an infallible remedy.* **4.** *Rom. Cath. Ch.* immune from fallacy or liability to error in expounding matters of faith or morals in virtue of the promise made by Christ to the Church. **—n. 5.** an infallible person or thing. [late ME, t. ML: m.s. *infallibilis.* See IN-³, FALLIBLE] **—in·fal′li·bil′i·ty, in·fal′li·ble·ness,** n. **—in·fal′li·bly,** adv. **—Syn. 2, 3.** See reliable.

in·fa·mous (ĭn′fə məs), adj. **1.** of evil fame or repute: *an infamous city.* **2.** such as to deserve or to cause evil repute; detestable; shamefully bad: *infamous conduct.* **3.** *Law.* **a.** deprived of credit and of certain rights as a citizen, in consequence of conviction of certain offenses. **b.** (of offenses, etc.) involving such deprivation. [ME, t. ML: m.s. *infāmōsus* (in L *infāmis*)] **—in′fa·mous·ly,** adv. **—in′fa·mous·ness,** n. **—Syn. 1.** disreputable, notorious. **2.** disgraceful, scandalous; nefarious, odious, wicked. **—Ant. 1.** honored. **2.** praiseworthy.

in·fa·my (ĭn′fə mĬ), n., pl. **-mies. 1.** evil fame, shameful notoriety, or public reproach. **2.** infamous character or conduct. **3.** an infamous act or circumstance. **4.** *Law.* the loss of credit and rights incurred by conviction of an infamous offense. [late ME, t. L: m.s. *infāmia*] **—Syn. 1.** See disgrace.

in·fan·cy (ĭn′fən sĬ), n., pl. **-cies. 1.** the state or period of being an infant; babyhood; early childhood. **2.** the corresponding period in the existence of anything: *the infancy of the world.* **3.** infants collectively. **4.** *Law.* the period of life to the age of majority (in the common law, to the end of the twenty-first year); minority; nonage. [t. L: m.s. *infantia,* lit., inability to speak]

in·fant (ĭn′fənt), n. **1.** a child during the earliest period of its life, or a baby. **2.** *Law.* a person who is not of full age, esp. one who has not attained the age of twenty-one years. **3.** a beginner, as in learning. **4.** anything in the first period of existence or the first stage of progress. **—adj. 5.** of or pertaining to infants or infancy: *infant years.* **6.** being in infancy: *an infant child.* **7.** being in the earliest stage: *an infant industry.* **8.** of or pertaining to the legal state of infancy; minor. [t. L: s. *infans* young child, prop. adj., not speaking; r. ME *enfaunt,* t. OF] **—in′fant·hood′,** n.

in·fan·ta (ĭn făn′tə), n. **1.** a daughter of the king of Spain or of Portugal. **2.** an infante's wife. [t. Sp. and Pg. See INFANTE]

in·fan·te (ĭn făn′tā), n. a son of the king of Spain or of Portugal, not heir to the throne. [t. Sp. and Pg., g. L *infans* INFANT]

in·fan·ti·cide¹ (ĭn făn′tə sĬd′), n. the killing of an infant. [t. LL: m.s. *infanticidium*] **—in·fan′ti·cid′al,** adj.

in·fan·ti·cide² (ĭn făn′tə sĬd′), n. one who kills an infant. [t. LL: m.s. *infanticida*]

in·fan·tile (ĭn′fən tĬl′, -tĬl), adj. **1.** characteristic of or befitting an infant; babyish; childish: *infantile behavior.* **2.** of or pertaining to infants: *infantile diseases.* **3.** being

in the earliest stage. [t. LL: m.s. *infantīlis*] —**Syn.**
1. See **childish.**

infantile spinal paralysis, *Pathol.* an acute disease, most common in infants but often attacking older children and even adults, characterized by inflammation of the nerve cells, mainly of the anterior horns of the spinal cord, resulting in a motor paralysis, followed by muscular atrophy, etc., and often by permanent deformities if not treated. Also, **infantile paralysis.**

in·fan·ti·lism (ĭn·făn′tə·lĭz′əm), *n.* 1. a pattern of speech characterized by those deviations from normal articulation or voice that are typical of very young children. 2. *Psychol.* the persistence in an adult of markedly childish anatomical, physiological, or psychological characteristics.

in·fan·tine (ĭn′fən·tīn′, -tĭn), *adj.* infantile.

in·fan·try (ĭn′fən·trĭ), *n.* soldiers or military units that fight on foot, with bayonets, rifles, machine guns, grenades, mortars, etc. [t. F: m. *infanterie* i. It.: m. *infanteria*, der. *infante* youth, foot soldier. See INFANT]

in·fan·try·man (ĭn′fən·trĭ·mən), *n., pl.* **-men.** a soldier of the infantry.

infants' school, *Brit.* a primary school for children from about five to seven years of age. Also, **infant school.**

in·farct (ĭn·färkt′), *n. Pathol.* a circumscribed portion of tissue which has been suddenly deprived of its blood supply by embolism or thrombosis and which, as a result, is undergoing death (necrosis), to be replaced by scar tissue. [t. L: s. *infar(c)tus*, pp., stuffed in]

in·farc·tion (ĭn·färk′shən), *n. Pathol.* 1. the formation of an infarct. 2. an infarct.

in·fat·u·ate (*v.* ĭn·făch′ōō·āt′; *adj.* ĭn·făch′ōō·ĭt, -āt′), *v.,* **-ated, -ating,** *adj.* —*v.t.* 1. to affect with folly; make fatuous. 2. to inspire or possess with a foolish or unreasoning passion, as of love. —*adj.* 3. infatuated. —*n.* 4. a person who is infatuated. [t. L: m.s. *infatuātus,* pp., made foolish]

in·fat·u·at·ed (ĭn·făch′ōō·ā′tĭd), *adj.* made foolish by love; blindly in love. —**in·fat′u·at′ed·ly,** *adv.*

in·fat·u·a·tion (ĭn·făch′ōō·ā′shən), *n.* 1. the act of infatuating. 2. the state of being infatuated. 3. foolish or all-absorbing passion.

in·fea·si·ble (ĭn·fē′zə·bəl), *adj.* not feasible; impracticable. —**in·fea′si·bil′i·ty,** *n.*

in·fect (ĭn·fĕkt′), *v.t.* 1. to impregnate (a person, organ, wound, etc.) with disease-producing germs. 2. to affect with disease. 3. to impregnate with something that affects quality, character, or condition, esp. unfavorably: *to infect the air with poison gas.* 4. to taint, contaminate, or affect morally: *infected with greediness.* 5. to imbue with some pernicious belief, opinion, etc. 6. to affect so as to influence feeling or action: *his courage infected the others.* 7. *Law.* to taint with illegality, or expose to penalty, forfeiture, etc. —*adj.* 8. *Archaic.* infected. [ME *infect(en),* t. L: (m.) s. *infectus,* pp., put in, dyed, imbued, infected] —**in·fec′tor,** *n.*

in·fec·tion (ĭn·fĕk′shən), *n.* 1. the action of infecting. 2. an infecting with germs of disease, as through the medium of infected insects, air, water, clothing, etc. 3. an infecting agency or influence. 4. state of being infected. 5. an infectious disease. 6. the condition of suffering an infection. 7. an influence or impulse passing from one to another and affecting feeling or action. 8. *Gram.* (in Celtic languages) assimilation in which a vowel is influenced by a following vowel. 9. *Rare.* (in humorous use) affection.

in·fec·tious (ĭn·fĕk′shəs), *adj.* 1. communicable by infection, as diseases. 2. causing or communicating infection. 3. tending to spread from one to another: *laughter is infectious.* 4. *Law.* capable of contaminating with illegality; exposing to seizure or forfeiture. 5. *Obs.* diseased. —**in·fec′tious·ly,** *adv.* —**in·fec′tious·ness,** *n.* —**Syn.** 3. See **contagious.**

infectious disease, 1. a disease caused by germs, as bacteria or filterable viruses. 2. any disease, produced by the action of a microörganism in the body, which may or may not be contagious.

infectious mon·o·nu·cle·o·sis (mŏn′ō·nū′klĭ·ō′sĭs, -nŏŏ′-), glandular fever.

infectious myx·o·ma (mĭk·sō′mə), a highly fatal, rapidly spreading virus disease of rabbits.

in·fec·tive (ĭn·fĕk′tĭv), *adj.* infectious. —**in·fec′tive·ness, in/fec·tiv′i·ty,** *n.*

in·fe·cund (ĭn·fē′kənd, -fĕk′ənd), *adj.* not fecund; unfruitful; barren. —**in·fe·cun·di·ty** (ĭn′fĭ·kŭn′də·tĭ), *n.*

in·fe·lic·i·tous (ĭn′fə·lĭs′ə·təs), *adj.* 1. not felicitous, happy, or fortunate; unhappy. 2. inapt or inappropriate: *an infelicitous remark.* —**in·fe·lic′i·tous·ly,** *adv.*

in·fe·lic·i·ty (ĭn′fə·lĭs′ə·tĭ), *n., pl.* **-ties.** 1. the state of being unhappy; unhappiness. 2. ill fortune. 3. an unfortunate circumstance; a misfortune. 4. inaptness or inappropriateness as of action or expression. 5. something inapt or infelicitous: *infelicities of style.*

in·felt (ĭn′fĕlt′), *adj.* felt within; heartfelt.

in·fer (ĭn·fûr′), *v.,* **-ferred, -ferring.** —*v.t.* 1. to derive by reasoning; conclude or judge from premises or evidence. 2. (of facts, circumstances, statements, etc.) to indicate or involve as a conclusion; imply. 3. to imply or hint. —*v.i.* 4. to draw a conclusion, as by reasoning. [t. L: s. *inferre* bring in or on, infer] —**in·fer·a·ble** (ĭn·fûr′ə·bəl, ĭn′fər-), *adj.* —**in·fer′a·bly,** *adv.*

in·fer·ence (ĭn′fər·əns), *n.* 1. the act or process of inferring. 2. that which is inferred: *to make rash inferences.*

3. *Logic.* **a.** the process of deriving the strict logical consequences of assumed premises. **b.** the process of arriving at some conclusion which, though it is not logically derivable from the assumed premises, possesses some degree of probability relative to the premises. **c.** a proposition reached by a process of inference.

in·fer·en·tial (ĭn′fə·rĕn′shəl), *adj.* pertaining to or depending on inference. —**in·fer·en′tial·ly,** *adv.*

in·fe·ri·or (ĭn·fĭr′ĭ·ər), *adj.* 1. lower in station, rank, degree, or grade (fol. by *to*). 2. of comparatively low grade; poor in quality: *an inferior brand.* 3. less important, valuable, or excellent: *an inferior workman.* 4. lower in place or position (now chiefly in scientific or technical use): *the inferior maxillary bone.* 5. *Bot.* a. situated below some other organ. **b.** (of a calyx) inserted below the ovary. **c.** (of an ovary) having a superior calyx. 6. *Astron.* **a.** (of a planet) having an orbit within that of the earth: applied to the planets Mercury and Venus. **b.** (of a conjunction of an inferior planet) taking place between the sun and the earth. **c.** lying below the horizon: *the inferior part of a meridian.* 7. *Print.* lower than the main line of type, as the figures in chemical formulas. —*n.* 8. one inferior to another or others, as in rank or merit. 9. *Print.* an inferior letter or figure. [ME, t. L, compar. of *inferus* being below, under, nether. Cf. UNDER] —**in·fe·ri·or·i·ty** (ĭn·fĭr′ĭ·ôr′ə·tĭ, -ŏr′-), *n.* —**in·fe′ri·or·ly,** *adv.*

inferiority complex, feelings arising from one's real or imagined inferiorities. Also, **inferiority feelings.**

in·fer·nal (ĭn·fûr′nəl), *adj.* 1. of or pertaining to the lower world of classical mythology: *the infernal regions.* 2. of, inhabiting, or befitting hell. 3. hellish; fiendish; diabolical: *an infernal plot.* 4. *Colloq.* outrageous: *an infernal nuisance.* [ME, t. L: s. *infernālis* of the lower regions] —**in·fer′nal·i·ty,** *n.* —**in·fer′nal·ly,** *adv.*

infernal machine, an explosive mechanical apparatus intended to destroy life or property.

in·fer·no (ĭn·fûr′nō), *n., pl.* **-nos.** 1. hell; the infernal regions. 2. an infernal or hell-like region. 3. **The Inferno,** the title of a part of Dante's *Divine Comedy.* [t. It.: hell, g. L *infernus* underground]

in·fer·tile (ĭn·fûr′tĭl), *adj.* not fertile; unfruitful; unproductive; barren: *infertile soil.* —**in′fer·til′i·ty,** *n.*

in·fest (ĭn·fĕst′), *v.t.* 1. to haunt or overrun in a troublesome manner, as predatory bands, destructive animals, vermin, etc., do. 2. to be numerous in, as anything troublesome: *the cares that infest the day.* 3. *Now Rare.* to harass. —*v.i.* 4. to become confirmed in evil; become habitually vicious. [late ME, t. L: s. *infestāre* assail, molest] —**in·fest′er,** *n.*

in·fes·ta·tion (ĭn′fĕs·tā′shən), *n.* 1. the act of infesting. 2. the state of being infested. 3. a harassing or troublesome invasion.

in·feu·da·tion (ĭn′fyōō·dā′shən), *n. Eng. Law.* 1. the grant of an estate in fee. 2. the relation of lord and vassal established by the grant and acceptance of such an estate. [t. ML: s. *infeudātio,* der. *infeudāre* enfeoff]

in·fi·del (ĭn′fə·dəl), *n.* 1. an unbeliever. 2. one who does not accept a particular faith, esp. Christianity (formerly applied by Christians esp. to a Mohammedan). 3. (in Mohammedan use) one who does not accept the Mohammedan faith. —*adj.* 4. without religious faith. 5. due to or manifesting unbelief. 6. not accepting a particular faith, esp. Christianity or Mohammedanism; heathen. 7. rejecting the Christian religion while accepting no other; not believing in the Bible or any divine revelation: used especially of persons belonging to Christian communities. 8. of or pertaining to unbelievers or infidels. [late ME, t. L: s. *infidēlis* unfaithful, L unbelieving] —**Syn.** 2, 3. See **atheist.**

in·fi·del·i·ty (ĭn′fə·dĕl′ə·tĭ), *n., pl.* **-ties.** 1. unfaithfulness. 2. adultery. 3. lack of religious faith, esp. Christian. 4. a breach of trust.

in·field (ĭn′fēld′), *n.* 1. *Baseball.* **a.** the diamond. **b.** the three basemen and the shortstop. 2. that part of farmlands nearest to the buildings.

in·field·er (ĭn′fēl′dər), *n. Baseball.* an infield player.

in·fil·trate (ĭn·fĭl′trāt), *v.,* **-trated, -trating,** *n.* —*v.t.* 1. to filter into or through; permeate. 2. to cause to pass in by, or as by, filtering: *the troops infiltrated the enemy lines.* —*v.i.* 3. to pass in or through a substance, etc., by or as by filtering. —*n.* 4. that which infiltrates. 5. *Pathol.* cells or a substance which pass into the tissues and form a morbid accumulation. —**in·fil′tra·tive,** *adj.*

in·fil·tra·tion (ĭn′fĭl·trā′shən), *n.* 1. the act or process of infiltrating. 2. the state of being infiltrated. 3. that which infiltrates; an infiltrate. 4. *Mil.* a method of attack in which small bodies of soldiers or individual soldiers penetrate into the enemy's line at weak or unguarded points, in order to bring fire eventually upon the enemy's flanks or rear.

infin., infinitive.

in·fi·nite (ĭn′fə·nĭt), *adj.* 1. immeasurably great: *a truth of infinite importance.* 2. indefinitely or exceedingly great: *infinite sums of money.* 3. unbounded or unlimited; perfect: *the infinite wisdom of God.* 4. endless or innumerable; inexhaustible. 5. *Math.* **a.** not finite. **b.** (of an assemblage) having the same number of elements as some proper part of itself. 6. *n.* that which is infinite. 7. **the Infinite** or **the Infinite Being,** God. 8. *Math.* an infinite quantity or magnitude. 9. the boundless regions of space. [ME, t. L: m.s. *infinītus*] —**in·fi·nite·ly,** *adv.* —**in·fi·nite·ness,** *n.*

in·fin·i·tes·i·mal (ĭn′fĭn ə tĕs′ə məl), *adj.* **1.** indefinitely or exceedingly small; minute: *the infinitesimal vessels of the nervous system.* **2.** immeasurably small; less than an assignable quantity: *to an infinitesimal degree.* **3.** pertaining to or involving infinitesimals. **—*n.* 4.** an infinitesimal quantity. **5.** *Math.* a variable having zero as a limit. **—in′fin·i·tes′i·mal·ly,** *adv.*

infinitesimal calculus, the differential calculus and the integral calculus, considered together.

in·fin·i·ti·val (ĭn′fĭn ə tī′vəl), *adj. Gram.* of or pertaining to the infinitive mode.

in·fin·i·tive (ĭn fĭn′ə tĭv), *Gram. n.* **1.** (in many languages) a noun form derived from verbs, which names the action or state without specifying the subject, as Latin *esse* to be, *fuisse* to have been. **2.** (in English) the simple form of the verb (*come, take, eat*) used after certain other verbs (I didn't *come*), or this simple form preceded by *to* (the **marked infinitive,** I wanted *to come*). *—adj.* **3.** of or pertaining to the infinitive or its meaning. [late ME, t. LL: m.s. *infīnītīvus* unlimited, indefinite] **—in·fin′i·tive·ly,** *adv.*

in·fin·i·tude (ĭn fĭn′ə tūd′, -to͞od′), *n.* **1.** infinity: *divine infinitude.* **2.** an infinite extent, amount, or number.

in·fin·i·ty (ĭn fĭn′ə tĭ), *n., pl.* **-ties. 1.** the state of being infinite: *the infinity of God.* **2.** that which is infinite. **3.** infinite space, time, or quantity: *any time short of infinity.* **4.** an infinite extent, amount, or number. **5.** an indefinitely great amount or number. **6.** *Math.* **a.** the concept of increasing without bound. **b.** infinite distance, or an infinitely distant part of space. [ME *infinite,* t. L: m.s. *infīnitas*]

in·firm (ĭn fûrm′), *adj.* **1.** feeble in body or health. **2.** not steadfast, unfaltering, or resolute, as persons, the mind, etc.: *infirm of purpose.* **3.** not firm, solid, or strong: *an infirm support.* **4.** unsound or invalid, as an argument, a title, etc. *—v.t.* **5.** *Rare.* to invalidate. [ME, t. L: s. *infirmus*] **—in·firm′ly,** *adv.* **—in·firm′ness,** *n.*

in·fir·ma·ry (ĭn fûr′mə rĭ), *n., pl.* **-ries. 1.** a place for the care of the infirm, sick, or injured; a hospital. **2.** a dispensary. [t. ML: m.s. *infirmāria,* der. L *infirmus* infirm]

in·fir·mi·ty (ĭn fûr′mə tĭ), *n., pl.* **-ties. 1.** a physical weakness or ailment: *the infirmities of age.* **2.** the state of being infirm; lack of strength. **3.** a moral weakness or failing. [ME *infirmyte,* t. L: m.s. *infirmitas*]

in·fix (*v.* ĭn fĭks′; *n.* ĭn′fĭks′), *v.t.* **1.** to fix, fasten, or drive in: *he infixed the fatal spear.* **2.** to implant: *the habits they infixed.* **3.** to fix in the mind or memory, as a fact or idea; impress. **4.** *Gram.* to add as an infix. *—v.i.* **5.** *Gram.* (of a linguistic form) to admit an infix. *—n.* **6.** *Gram.* an affix which is inserted within the body of the element to which it is added, as Latin *m* in *accumbō* I lie down, as compared with *accubuī* I lay down. [t. L: s. *infixus,* pp., fastened in] **—in·fix′ion,** *n.*

in fla·gran·te de·lic·to (ĭn flə grăn′tĭ dĭ lĭk′tō), *Latin.* in the very act of committing the offense.

in·flame (ĭn flām′), *v.,* **-flamed, -flaming.** *—v.t.* **1.** to set aflame or afire. **2.** to light or redden with or as with flames: *the setting sun inflames the sky.* **3.** to kindle or excite (passions, desires, etc.). **4.** to arouse to a high degree of passion or feeling. **5.** to affect in appearance by passion, etc. **6.** to make more violent. **7.** to excite inflammation in: *her eyes were inflamed with crying.* **8.** to raise (the blood, bodily tissue, etc.) to a morbid or feverish heat. *—v.i.* **9.** to burst into flame; take fire. **10.** to be kindled, as passion. **11.** to become hot with passion, as the heart. **12.** to become morbidly affected with inflammation. [ME *enflame(n),* t. OF: m. *enflamer,* g. L *inflammāre* set on fire] **—in·flam′er,** *n.* **—in·flam′ing·ly,** *adv.* **—Syn. 1.** See **kindle.**

in·flam·ma·ble (ĭn flăm′ə bəl), *adj.* **1.** capable of being set on fire; combustible. **2.** easily roused to passion; excitable. *—n.* **3.** something inflammable. **—in·flam′ma·bil′i·ty, in·flam′ma·ble·ness,** *n.* **—in·flam′ma·bly,** *adv.*

in·flam·ma·tion (ĭn′flə mā′shən), *n.* **1.** the act of inflaming. **2.** the state of being inflamed. **3.** *Pathol.* a reaction of the body to injurious agents, commonly characterized by heat, redness, swelling, pain, etc., and disturbed function.

in·flam·ma·to·ry (ĭn flăm′ə tōr′ĭ), *adj.* **1.** tending to inflame; kindling passion, anger, etc.: *inflammatory speeches.* **2.** *Pathol.* pertaining to or attended with inflammation. **—in·flam′ma·to′ri·ly,** *adv.*

in·flate (ĭn flāt′), *v.,* **-flated, -flating.** *—v.t.* **1.** to distend; swell or puff out; dilate. **2.** to distend with gas: *inflate a balloon.* **3.** to puff up with pride, satisfaction, etc. **4.** to elate. **5.** to expand (currency, prices, etc.) unduly; raise above the previous or proper amount or value. *—v.i.* **6.** to cause inflation. **7.** to become inflated. [t. L: m.s. *inflātus,* pp., puffed up] **—in·flat′a·ble,** *adj.* **—in·flat′er, in·fla′tor,** *n.* **—Syn. 1.** See **expand.**

in·flat·ed (ĭn flā′tĭd), *adj.* **1.** distended with air or gas; swollen. **2.** puffed up, as with pride. **3.** turgid or bombastic, as language. **4.** resulting from inflation: *inflated values of land.* **5.** unduly expanded, as currency. **6.** *Bot.* hollow or swelled out with air: *inflated perianth.* **—in·flat′ed·ness,** *d.*

in·fla·tion (ĭn flā′shən), *n.* **1.** undue expansion or increase of the currency of a country, esp. by the issuing of paper money not redeemable in specie. **2.** a substantial rise of prices caused by an undue expansion in paper money or bank credit. **3.** the act of inflating. **4.** the state of being inflated.

in·fla·tion·ar·y (ĭn flā′shə nĕr′ĭ), *adj.* of or causing inflation: *inflationary legislation.*

in·fla·tion·ism (ĭn flā′shə nĭz′əm), *n.* the policy or practice of inflation through expansion of currency or bank deposits.

in·fla·tion·ist (ĭn flā′shən ĭst), *n.* an advocate of inflation through expansion of currency or bank deposits.

in·flect (ĭn flĕkt′), *v.t.* **1.** to bend; turn from a direct line or course. **2.** to modulate (the voice). **3.** *Gram.* **a.** to apply inflection to (a word). **b.** to recite or display all, or a distinct set of, the inflections of (a word), in a fixed order: *to inflect Latin "amō" as "amō, amās, amat," etc. or "nauta" as "nauta, nautae, nautae, nautam, nautā,"* etc. **4.** *Bot.* to bend in. *—v.i.* **5.** *Gram.* to be characterized by inflection. [ME *inflecte(n),* t. L: m. *inflectere* bend] **—in·flec′tive,** *adj.* **—in·flec′tor,** *n.*

in·flec·tion (ĭn flĕk′shən), *n.* **1.** modulation of the voice; change in pitch or tone of voice. **2.** *Gram.* **a.** the existence in a language of sets of forms built normally on a single stem, having different syntactic functions and meanings, but all those of a single stem being members of the same fundamental part of speech and constituting forms of the same "word." **b.** the set of forms of a single word, or a recital or display thereof in a fixed order. **c.** a single pattern of formation of such sets, as *noun inflection, verb inflection.* **d.** a change in the form of a word, generally by affixation by means of which a change of meaning or relationship to some other word or group of words is indicated. **e.** the affix added to the stem to produce this change. For example: the *-s* in *dogs* and *-ed* in *played* are inflections. **3.** a bend or angle. **4.** *Math.* a change of curvature from convex to concave or vice versa. Also, *esp. Brit.,* **inflexion. —in·flec′tion·al,** *adj.* **—in·flec′tion·al·ly,** *adv.* **—in·flec′tion·less,** *adj.*

inflection point, *Math.* a point of inflection on a curve.

in·flexed (ĭn flĕkst′), *adj. Bot., Zool.* inflected; bent or folded downward or inward: *an inflexed leaf.*

in·flex·i·ble (ĭn flĕk′sə bəl), *adj.* **1.** not flexible; rigid: *an inflexible rod.* **2.** unyielding in temper or purpose: *inflexible to threats.* **3.** unalterable; not permitting variation: *the law is inflexible.* [ME, t. L: m.s. *inflexibilis.* See IN-[3], FLEXIBLE] **—in·flex′i·bil′i·ty, in·flex′i·ble·ness,** *n.* **—in·flex′i·bly,** *adv.*

—Syn. 2. INFLEXIBLE, RELENTLESS, IMPLACABLE, INEXORABLE imply having the quality of not being turned from a purpose. INFLEXIBLE means unbending, adhering undeviatingly to a set plan, purpose, or the like: *inflexible in interpretation of rules, an inflexible will.* RELENTLESS suggests such a pitiless and unremitting following of purpose as to convey a sense of inevitableness: *as relentless as the passing of time.* IMPLACABLE means incapable of being placated or appeased: *implacable in wrath.* INEXORABLE means stern, rigorous, and unmoved by prayer or entreaty: *inexorable in demanding payment.* **—Ant. 2.** pliant.

in·flex·ion (ĭn flĕk′shən), *n. Chiefly Brit.* inflection. **—in·flex′ion·al,** *adj.* **—in·flex′ion·al·ly,** *adv.*

in·flict (ĭn flĭkt′), *v.t.* **1.** to lay on: *to inflict a dozen lashes.* **2.** to impose as something that must be borne or suffered: *to inflict punishment.* **3.** to impose (anything unwelcome). [t. L: s. *inflictus,* pp., struck against] **—in·flict′er, in·flic′tor,** *n.* **—in·flic′tive,** *adj.*

in·flic·tion (ĭn flĭk′shən), *n.* **1.** the act of inflicting. **2.** something inflicted, as punishment, suffering, etc.

in·flo·res·cence (ĭn′flō rĕs′əns,), *n.* **1.** a flowering or blossoming. **2.** *Bot.* **a.** the arrangement of flowers on the axis. See the illus. on the next page. **b.** the flowering part of a plant. **c.** a flower cluster. **d.** flowers collectively. **e.** a single flower. [t. NL: m.s. *inflōrescentia,* der. LL *inflōrescens,* ppr., coming into flower] **—in′flo·res′cent,** *adj.*

in·flow (ĭn′flō′), *n.* that which flows in; influx.

in·flu·ence (ĭn′flo͝o əns), *n., v.,* **-enced, -encing.** *—n.* **1.** invisible or insensible action exerted by one thing or person on another. **2.** power of producing effects by invisible or insensible means: *spheres of influence.* **3.** a thing or person that exerts action by invisible or insensible means: *beneficial influences.* **4.** electrostatic induction. **5.** *Astrol.* **a.** the supposed radiation of an ethereal fluid from the stars, regarded in astrology as affecting human actions and destinies, etc. **b.** the exercise of occult power by the stars, or such power as exercised. **6.** *Poetic.* the exercise of similar power by human beings. **7.** *Obs.* influx. *—v.t.* **8.** to exercise influence on; modify, affect, or sway: *to influence a person by bribery.* **9.** to move or impel to, or to do, something. [ME, t. ML: m.s. *influentia,* lit., a flowing in, der. L *influens* influent] **—in′flu·enc·er,** *n.* **—Syn. 2.** sway, rule. See **authority.**

in·flu·ent (ĭn′flo͝o ənt), *adj.* **1.** flowing in. *—n.* **2.** a tributary. [ME, t. L: s. *influens,* ppr., flowing in]

in·flu·en·tial (ĭn′flo͝o ĕn′shəl), *adj.* having or exerting influence, esp. great influence. [f. s. ML *influentia* INFLUENCE + -AL[1]] **—in′flu·en′tial·ly,** *adv.*

in·flu·en·za (ĭn′flo͝o ĕn′zə), *n.* **1.** *Pathol.* an acute, extremely contagious, commonly epidemic disease characterized by general prostration, and occurring in several forms with varying symptoms, usually with nasal catarrh and bronchial inflammation, and due to a specific microörganism; grippe. **2.** *Vet. Sci.* an acute, contagious disease occurring in horses and swine, manifested by fever, depression, and catarrhal inflammations of the eyes, nasal passages, and bronchi. [t. It.: influx of disease, epidemic, influenza. See INFLUENCE] **—in′flu·en′zal,** *adj.* **—in′flu·en′za·like′,** *adj.*

in·flux (ĭn′flŭks′), *n.* **1.** the act of flowing in; an inflow. **2.** the place or point at which one stream flows into another or into the sea. **3.** the mouth of a stream. [t. LL: s. *influxus*, der. L *influere* flow in]

in·fold (ĭn fōld′), *v.t.* **1.** to wrap up; envelop: *infolded in a magic mantle.* **2.** to clasp; embrace. **3.** to imply or involve. **4.** to form into a fold or folds: *a cambium layer deeply infolded where it extends downwards.* **5.** to fold in or inward. Also, **enfold.** —**in·fold′er,** *n.* —**in·fold′ment,** *n.*

in·form[1] (ĭn fôrm′), *v.t.* **1.** to impart knowledge of a fact or circumstance to: *he informed him of his arrival.* **2.** to supply (oneself) with knowledge of a matter or subject: *he informed himself of all the pertinent facts.* **3.** to give character to; pervade with determining effect on the character. **4.** to animate or inspire. **5.** *Now Rare.* to train or instruct. **6.** *Obs.* to make known; disclose. **7.** *Obs.* to impart form to. —*v.i.* **8.** to give information, esp. to furnish incriminating evidence to a prosecuting officer. [t. L: s. *informāre*; r. ME *enforme,* t. OF] —**in·form′er,** *n.* —**in·form′ing·ly,** *adv.* —**Syn. 1.** apprise; notify, advise, tell. **2.** acquaint.

in·form[2] (ĭn fôrm′), *adj.* without form; formless. [t. L: s. *informis* shapeless. See IN-[3]]

Forms of Inflorescence
A. Spike of plantain, *Plantago major;* B. Simple umbel of milkweed, *Asclepias syriaca;* C. Corymb of red chokeberry, *Aronia arbutifolia;* D. Raceme of lily of the valley, *Convallaria majalis;* E. Spadix within the spathe of calla, *Calla palustris;* F. Flower head of buttonbush, *Cephalanthus occidentalis;* G. Anthodium of goldenrod, genus *Solidago;* H. Female catkin of willow, genus *Salix;* I. Compound umbel of water parsnip, *Sium cicutaefolium;* J. Panicle of blue cohosh, *Caulophyllum thalictroides;* K. Cyme of chickweed, genus *Cerastium*

in·for·mal (ĭn fôr′məl), *adj.* **1.** not according to prescribed or customary forms; irregular: *informal proceedings.* **2.** without formality; unceremonious: *an informal visit.* **3.** denoting speech characterized by colloquial usage, having the flexibility of grammar, syntax, and pronunciation allowable in conversation. **4.** characterizing the second singular pronominal or verbal form, or its use, in certain languages: *the informal "tu" in French.* —**in·for′mal·ly,** *adv.* —**Syn. 3.** See **colloquial.**

in·for·mal·i·ty (ĭn′fôr măl′ə tĭ), *n., pl.* **-ties. 1.** state of being informal; absence of formality. **2.** an informal act.

in·form·ant (ĭn fôr′mənt), *n.* **1.** one who gives information. **2.** one who supplies linguistic forms for analysis.

in·for·ma·tion (ĭn′fər mā′shən), *n.* **1.** knowledge communicated or received concerning some fact or circumstance; news. **2.** knowledge on various subjects, however acquired. **3.** the act of informing. **4.** the state of being informed. **5.** *Law.* **a.** an official criminal charge presented, usually by the prosecuting officers of the state, without the interposition of a grand jury. **b.** a criminal charge made under oath, before a justice of the peace, of an offense punishable summarily. **6.** in communication theory, the successive selection of signs without regard to meaning. [t. L: s. *informātio;* r. ME *enformacion,* t. OF] —**in·for·ma′tion·al,** *adj.*

—**Syn.** **2.** INFORMATION, KNOWLEDGE, WISDOM are terms for human acquirements through reading, study, and practical

experience. INFORMATION applies to facts told, read, communicated, which may be unorganized and even unrelated: *to pick up useful information.* KNOWLEDGE is an organized body of information, or the comprehension and understanding consequent on having acquired and organized a body of facts: *a knowledge of chemistry.* WISDOM is a knowledge of people, life, and conduct, with the facts so thoroughly assimilated as to have produced sagacity, judgment, and insight: *to use wisdom in handling people.* —**Ant. 2.** ignorance.

in·form·a·tive (ĭn fôr′mə tĭv), *adj.* affording information; instructive: *an informative book.*

in·for·tune (ĭn fôr′chən), *n.* **1.** *Astrol.* a planet or aspect of evil influence, esp. Saturn or Mars. **2.** *Obs.* misfortune. [ME, t. F. See IN-[3], FORTUNE]

in·fra (ĭn′frə), *adv. Latin.* below (in a text). Cf. **supra.**

infra-, a prefix meaning "below" or "beneath," as in *infra-axillary* (below the axilla). [t. L, repr. *infrā,* adv. and prep., below, beneath]

in·fra·cos·tal (ĭn′frə kŏs′təl, -kôs′-), *adj.* below the ribs.

in·fract (ĭn frăkt′), *v.t.* to break; violate or infringe. [t. L: s. *infractus,* pp., broken off] —**in·frac′tor,** *n.*

in·frac·tion (ĭn frăk′shən), *n.* breach; violation; infringement: *an infraction of a treaty or law.*

in·fra dig (ĭn′frə dĭg′), *Chiefly Brit. Colloq.* infra dignitatem.

in·fra dig·ni·ta·tem (ĭn′frə dĭg′nə tā′təm), *Latin.* beneath (one's) dignity.

in·fra·lap·sar·i·an (ĭn′frə lăp sâr′ĭ ən), *n.* **1.** one who believes in infralapsarianism. —*adj.* **2.** pertaining to infralapsarianism or those who hold it. [f. INFRA- + s. L *lapsus* a fall + -ARIAN]

in·fra·lap·sar·i·an·ism (ĭn′frə lăp sâr′ĭ ə nĭz′əm), *n. Theol.* the doctrine, held by Augustinians and by many Calvinists, that God planned the creation, permitted the fall, elected a chosen number, planned their redemption, and suffered the remainder to be eternally punished.

in·fran·gi·ble (ĭn frăn′jə bəl), *adj.* **1.** unbreakable. **2.** inviolable. —**in·fran′gi·bil′i·ty, in·fran′gi·ble·ness,** *n.* —**in·fran′gi·bly,** *adv.*

in·fra·red (ĭn′frə rĕd′), *adj.* **1.** the part of the invisible spectrum contiguous to the red end of the visible spectrum, comprising radiation of greater wave length than that of red light. —*adj.* **2.** denoting or pertaining to the infrared or its component rays.

in·fra·son·ic (ĭn′frə sŏn′ĭk), *adj.* of velocities approximately equal to the velocity of sound in the medium.

in·fre·quen·cy (ĭn frē′kwən sĭ), *n.* the state of being infrequent. Also, **in·fre′quence.**

in·fre·quent (ĭn frē′kwənt), *adj.* **1.** happening or occurring at long intervals or not often: *infrequent visits.* **2.** not constant, habitual, or regular: *an infrequent visitor.* **3.** not plentiful. —**in·fre′quent·ly,** *adv.*

in·fringe (ĭn frĭnj′), *v.,* **-fringed, -fringing.** —*v.t.* **1.** to commit a breach or infraction of; violate or transgress. —*v.i.* **2.** to encroach or trespass (fol. by *on* or *upon*): *don't infringe on his privacy.* [t. L: m.s. *infringere* break off] —**in·fring′er,** *n.* —**Syn. 2.** See **trespass.**

in·fringe·ment (ĭn frĭnj′mənt), *n.* **1.** a breach or infraction, as of a law, right, or obligation; violation; transgression. **2.** act of infringing.

in·fun·dib·u·li·form (ĭn′fŭn dĭb′yə lə fôrm′), *adj. Bot.* funnel-shaped.

in·fun·dib·u·lum (ĭn′fŭn dĭb′yə ləm), *n., pl.* **-la (-lə). 1.** a funnel-shaped organ or part. **2.** *Anat.* **a.** a funnel-shaped extension of the cerebrum connecting the pituitary body to the base of the brain. **b.** a space in the right auricle at the root of the pulmonary artery. [t. L: funnel] —**in·fun·dib·u·lar** (ĭn′fŭn dĭb′yə lər), **in·fun·dib·u·late** (ĭn′fŭn dĭb′yə lāt′), *adj.*

Infundibuliform corolla

in·fu·ri·ate (*v.* ĭn fyŏŏr′ĭ āt′; *adj.* ĭn fyŏŏr′ĭ ĭt), *v.,* **-ated, -ating,** *adj.* —*v.t.* **1.** to make furious; enrage. —*adj.* **2.** infuriated. [t. ML: m.s. *infuriātus,* pp., enraged] —**in·fu′ri·ate·ly,** *adv.* —**in·fu′ri·at′ing·ly,** *adv.* —**in·fu′ri·a′tion,** *n.* —**Syn. 1.** See **enrage.**

in·fus·cate (ĭn fŭs′kāt), *adj. Entomol.* darkened with a fuscous or brownish shade. Also, **in·fus′cat·ed.** [t. L: m.s. *infuscātus,* pp., darkened]

in·fuse (ĭn fūz′), *v.t.,* **-fused, -fusing. 1.** to introduce as by pouring; cause to penetrate; instil (fol. by *into*). **2.** to imbue or inspire (*with*). **3.** to pour in. **4.** to steep or soak (a plant, etc.) in a liquid so as to extract its soluble properties or ingredients. [ME, t. L: m.s. *infūsus,* pp., poured in or on] —**in·fus′er,** *n.*

in·fu·si·ble[1] (ĭn fū′zə bəl), *adj.* not fusible; incapable of being fused or melted. [f. IN-[3] + FUSIBLE] —**in·fu′si·bil′i·ty, in·fu′si·ble·ness,** *n.*

in·fu·si·ble[2] (ĭn fū′zə bəl), *adj.* capable of being infused. [f. INFUSE, v. + -IBLE]

in·fu·sion (ĭn fū′zhən), *n.* **1.** act of infusing. **2.** that which is infused. **3.** a liquid extract obtained from a substance by steeping or soaking it in water. **4.** *Med.* the introduction of a saline or other solution into a vein.

in·fu·sion·ism (ĭn fū′zhə nĭz′əm), *n. Theol.* the doctrine that the soul existed in a previous state and is infused into the body at conception or birth. —**in·fu′sion·ist,** *n.*

in·fu·sive (ĭn fū′sĭv), *adj.* infusing.

In·fu·so·ri·a (ĭn′fū sôr′ĭ ə), *n.pl.* **1.** *Zool.* protozoans of the class *Infusoria,* mostly microscopic and aquatic,

b., blend of, blended; **c.,** cognate with; **d.,** dialect, dialectal; **der.,** derived from; **f.,** formed from; **g.,** going back to; **m.,** modification of; **r.,** replacing; **s.,** stem of; **t.,** taken from; **?,** perhaps.   See the full key on inside cover.

having vibratile cilia. 2. *Obs.* any of a miscellaneous variety of minute or microscopic animal and vegetable organisms (constituting the old group *Infusoria*) frequently developed in infusions of decaying organic matter. [t. NL, der. L *infūsus*, pp., poured in. See -ORY]

in·fu·so·ri·al (Yn/fyŏŏ sōr/Y əl), *adj.* containing or consisting of infusorians: *infusorial earth.*

in·fu·so·ri·an (Yn/fyŏŏ sōr/Y ən), *n.* any of the *Infusoria.*

in fu·tu·ro (Yn fyŏŏ tyŏŏr/ō, -tŏŏr/ō), *Latin.* in the future.

-ing¹, a suffix of nouns formed from verbs, expressing the action of the verb or its result, product, material, etc., as in *the art of building, a new building, cotton wadding.* It is also used to form nouns from other words than verbs, as in *offing, shirting.* Verbal nouns ending in *-ing* are often used attributively, as in *the printing trade,* and in composition, as in *drinking song.* In some compounds, as *sewing machine,* the first element might reasonably be regarded as the participial adjective (see **-ing²**), the compound thus meaning "a machine that sews"; but it is commonly taken as a verbal noun, the compound being explained as "a machine for sewing." [ME *-ing,* OE *-ing, -ung*]

-ing², a suffix forming the present participle of verbs, such participles being often used as adjectives (participial adjectives), as in *warring factions.* Cf. **-ing¹**. [ME *-ing, -inge*; r. ME *-inde, -ende,* OE *-ende*]

in·gath·er (Yn găth/ər), *v.t.* to gather in; collect; bring in, as a harvest. —**in·gath/er·er,** *n.*

Inge (Yng), *n.* **William,** 1860–1954, British clergyman and author; ex-dean of St. Paul's Cathedral, London.

In·ge·low (Yn/jə lō/), *n.* **Jean,** 1820–97, British author.

in·gem·i·nate (Yn jĕm/ə nāt/), *v.t.,* **-nated, -nating.** to repeat; reiterate. [t. LL: m.s. *ingemĭnātus,* pp., redoubled] —**in·gem/i·na/tion,** *n.*

in·gen·er·ate¹ (Yn jĕn/ər Yt), *adj.* not generated; self-existent. [t. LL: m.s. *ingenerātus.* See IN-³]

in·gen·er·ate² (*v.* Yn jĕn/ə rāt/; *adj.* Yn jĕn/ər Yt), *v.,* **-ated, -ating,** *adj.* *Now Rare.* —*v.t.* **1.** to engender. —*adj.* **2.** inborn; innate. [t. L: m.s. *ingenerātus,* pp., generated within. See IN-²] —**in·gen/er·a/tion,** *n.*

in·gen·ious (Yn jēn/yəs), *adj.* **1.** (of things, actions, etc.) showing cleverness of invention or construction: *an ingenious machine.* **2.** having inventive faculty; skillful in contriving or constructing: *an ingenious mechanic.* [ME, t. L: m.s. *ingeniōsus* of good natural talents] —**in·gen/ious·ly,** *adv.* —**in·gen/ious·ness,** *n.* —**Syn. 2.** INGENIOUS, INGENUOUS are now distinct from each other and should not be confused or thought of as synonyms. INGENIOUS means clever, inventive, resourceful in contriving new explanations or methods, and the like: *an ingenious executive.* INGENUOUS means frank, candid, free from guile or deceit: *an ingenuous and sincere statement.*

in·gé·nue (ăN zhě nY/), *n., pl.* **-nues** (-nYz/; *Fr.* -nY/). **1.** the part of an ingenuous girl, esp. as represented on the stage. **2.** the actress who plays such a part. [t. F, fem. of *ingénu* ingenuous, t. L: s. *ingenuus*]

in·ge·nu·i·ty (Yn/jə nŭ/ə tY, -nōō/-), *n., pl.* **-ties. 1.** the quality of being ingenious; inventive talent. **2.** skillfulness of contrivance or design, as of things, actions, etc. **3.** an ingenious contrivance. **4.** *Obs.* ingenuousness. [t. L: m.s. *ingenuitas* frankness. Cf. INGENUOUS]

in·gen·u·ous (Yn jĕn/yŏŏ əs), *adj.* **1.** free from reserve, restraint, or dissimulation. **2.** artless; innocent. [t. L: m. *ingenuus* native, innate, freeborn, noble, frank] —**in·gen/u·ous·ly,** *adv.* —**in·gen/u·ous·ness,** *n.* —**Syn. 1.** frank, candid. See **ingenious. 2.** naïve, guileless.

In·ger·soll (Yng/gər sōl/, -sŏl/, -səl), *n.* **Robert Green,** 1833–99, U.S. lawyer, agnostic, and writer.

in·gest (Yn jĕst/), *v.t.* *Physiol.* to put or take (food, etc.) into the body. [t. L: s. *ingestus,* pp., carried, or poured in] —**in·ges/tion,** *n.* —**in·ges/tive,** *adj.*

in·ges·ta (Yn jĕs/tə), *n.pl.* substances ingested. [t. L]

in·gle (Yng/gəl), *n.* *Scot.* a household fire or fireplace.

in·gle·nook (Yng/gəl nŏŏk/), *n.* *Chiefly Brit.* a corner by the fire.

in·gle·side (Yng/gəl sīd/), *n.* *Scot.* a fireside.

In·gle·wood (Yng/gəl wŏŏd/), *n.* a city in SW California, near Los Angeles. 63,390 (1960).

in·glo·ri·ous (Yn glōr/Y əs), *adj.* **1.** shameful; disgraceful: *inglorious flight.* **2.** *Now Rare.* not famous. —**in·glo/ri·ous·ly,** *adv.* —**in·glo/ri·ous·ness,** *n.*

in·go·ing (Yn/gō/Yng), *adj.* going in; entering.

in·got (Yng/gət), *n.* **1.** the casting obtained when melted metal is poured into a mold (**ingot mold**) with the expectation that it be further processed. **2.** a cast metal mass, formed by rolling, etc., or by smelting and casting to shape. —*v.t.* **3.** to make ingots of; shape into ingots. [ME: mold for metal. Cf. OE *ingyte* pouring in]

in·graft (Yn grăft/, -gräft/), *v.t.* engraft. —**in·graft/ment,** *n.*

in·grain (*v.* Yn grān/; *adj., n.* Yn/grān/), *v.t.* **1.** to fix deeply and firmly, as in the nature or mind. —*adj.* **2.** ingrained; firmly fixed. **3.** (of carpets) made of yarn dyed before weaving, and so woven as to show the pattern on both sides. **4.** dyed in grain, or through the fiber. **5.** dyed in the yarn, or in a raw state, before manufacture. —*n.* **6.** yarn, wool, etc., dyed before manufacture. **7.** an ingrain carpet. Also, **engrain** for 1, 2.

in·grained (Yn grānd/, Yn/grānd/), *adj.* **1.** fixed firmly; deep-rooted: *ingrained habits.* **2.** inveterate; thorough.

in·grate (Yn/grāt), *n.* **1.** an ungrateful person. —*adj.* **2.** *Archaic.* ungrateful. [ME, t. L: m.s. *ingrātus* unpleasing, not grateful]

in·gra·ti·ate (Yn grā/shY āt/), *v.t.,* **-ated, -ating.** to establish (oneself) in the favor or good graces of others. [f. IN-² + s. L *grātia* favor, grace + -ATE¹] —**in·gra/ti·at/ing·ly,** *adv.* —**in·gra/ti·a/tion,** *n.*

in·gra·ti·a·to·ry (Yn grā/shY ə tōr/Y), *adj.* serving or intended to ingratiate.

in·grat·i·tude (Yn grăt/ə tūd/, -tōŏd/), *n.* the state of being ungrateful; unthankfulness.

in·gra·ves·cent (Yn/grə vĕs/ənt), *adj.* *Pathol.* increasing in severity, as a disease. [t. L: s. *ingravescens,* ppr., growing heavier] —**in/gra·ves/cence,** *n.*

in·gre·di·ent (Yn grē/dY ənt), *n.* **1.** something that enters as an element into a mixture: *the ingredients of a cake.* **2.** a constituent element of anything. [late ME. t. L: s. *ingrediens,* ppr., entering] —**Syn. 1.** See **element.**

In·gres (ăN/gr), *n.* **Jean Auguste Dominique** (zhäN ō gyst/ dō mē nēk/), 1780–1867, French painter.

in·gress (Yn/grĕs), *n.* **1.** act of going in or entering. **2.** the right of going in. **3.** a means or place of going in; an entrance. [ME, t. L: s. *ingressus* entrance] —**in·gres/sion,** *n.* —**in·gres/sive,** *adj.* —**in·gres/sive·ness,** *n.*

in·group (Yn/grŏŏp/), *n.* *Sociol.* a group reserving favorable treatment and acceptance to its own members and denying them to members of other groups.

in·grow·ing (Yn/grō/Yng), *adj.* **1.** growing into the flesh: *an ingrowing nail.* **2.** growing within or inward.

in·grown (Yn/grōn/), *adj.* **1.** having grown into the flesh: *an ingrown toenail.* **2.** grown within or inward.

in·growth (Yn/grōth/), *n.* **1.** growth inward. **2.** something formed by growth inward.

in·gui·nal (Yng/gwə nəl), *adj.* of, pertaining to, or situated in the groin. [t. L: s. *inguinālis*]

in·gulf (Yn gŭlf/), *v.t.* engulf.

in·gur·gi·tate (Yn gûr/jə tāt/), *v.,* **-tated, -tating.** —*v.t.* **1.** to swallow greedily or in great quantity, as food. **2.** to engulf. —*v.i.* **3.** to drink largely; swill. [t. L: m.s. *ingurgitātus,* pp., poured in] —**in·gur/gi·ta/tion,** *n.*

in·hab·it (Yn hăb/Yt), *v.t.* **1.** to live or dwell in (a place), as persons or animals. **2.** to have its seat, or exist, in. —*v.i.* **3.** to live or dwell, as in a place. [t. L: s. *inhabitāre*; r. ME *enhabite,* t. F] —**in·hab/it·a·ble,** *adj.* —**in·hab/it·a·bil/i·ty,** *n.* —**in·hab/i·ta/tion,** *n.*

in·hab·it·an·cy (Yn hăb/ə tən sY), *n., pl.* **-cies.** residence as an inhabitant. Also, **in·hab/it·ance.**

in·hab·it·ant (Yn hăb/ə tənt), *n.* a person or an animal that inhabits a place; a permanent resident. Also, **in·hab/it·er.** [late ME, t. L: s. *inhabitans,* ppr., dwelling in]

in·hal·ant (Yn hā/lənt), *adj.* **1.** serving for inhalation. —*n.* **2.** an apparatus or medicine used for inhaling.

in·ha·la·tion (Yn/hə lā/shən), *n.* **1.** act of inhaling. **2.** a medicinal preparation to be inhaled.

in·ha·la·tor (Yn/hə lā/tər), *n.* an apparatus to help one inhale air, anesthetic, medicinal vapors, etc.

in·hale (Yn hāl/), *v.,* **-haled, -haling.** —*v.t.* **1.** to breathe in; draw in by, or as by, breathing: *to inhale air.* —*v.i.* **2.** to inhale, esp. smoke of cigarettes, cigars, etc.: *do you inhale?* [t. L: m.s. *inhālāre*]

in·hal·er (Yn hā/lər), *n.* **1.** an apparatus used in inhaling medicinal vapors, anesthetics, etc. **2.** a respirator. **3.** one who inhales.

In·ham·ba·ne (Yn/yəm bä/nə), *n.* a seaport in SE Mozambique. Municipal district. 64,536 (1950).

in·har·mon·ic (Yn/här mŏn/Yk), *adj.* not harmonic.

in·har·mo·ni·ous (Yn/här mō/nY əs), *adj.* not harmonious; discordant. [f. IN-³ + HARMONIOUS] —**in/har·mo/ni·ous·ly,** *adv.* —**in/har·mo/ni·ous·ness,** *n.*

in·haul (Yn/hôl/), *n.* *Naut.* a rope for hauling in a sail or spar. Also, **in/haul/er.**

in·here (Yn hYr/), *v.i.,* **-hered, -hering.** to exist permanently and inseparably (in), as a quality, attribute, or element; belong intrinsically; be inherent. [t. L: m.s. *inhaerēre* stick in or to]

in·her·ence (Yn hYr/əns), *n.* **1.** the state or fact of inhering or being inherent. **2.** *Philos.* the relation of an attribute to its subject.

in·her·en·cy (Yn hYr/ən sY), *n., pl.* **-cies. 1.** inherence. **2.** something inherent.

in·her·ent (Yn hYr/ənt), *adj.* **1.** existing in something as a permanent and inseparable element, quality, or attribute. **2.** *Gram.* standing before a noun. **3.** *Rare.* inhering; infixed. [t. L: m.s. *inhaerens,* ppr., sticking in or to] —**in·her/ent·ly,** *adv.* —**Syn. 1.** See **essential.**

in·her·it (Yn hĕr/Yt), *v.t.* **1.** to take or receive (property, a right, a title, etc.) as the heir of the former owner. **2.** to succeed (a person) as heir. **3.** to receive (anything) as by succession from predecessors. **4.** to receive as one's portion. **5.** *Obs.* to make (one) heir (fol. by *of*). —*v.i.* **6.** to take or receive property, etc., as being heir to it. **7.** to have succession as heir. **8.** to receive qualities, powers, duties, etc., as by inheritance (fol. by *from*). [ME *enherite(n),* t. OF: m. *enheriter,* f. en- EN-¹ + *heriter* (g. L *hērēditāre* inherit)]

in·her·it·a·ble (Yn hĕr/ə bəl), *adj.* **1.** capable of being inherited. **2.** capable of inheriting; qualified to inherit. —**in·her/it·a·bil/i·ty, in·her/it·a·ble·ness,** *n.*

in·her·it·ance (Yn hĕr/ə təns), *n.* **1.** that which is or may be inherited; any property passing at the owner's death to the heir or those entitled to succeed. **2.** any-

thing received from progenitors or predecessors as if by succession: *an inheritance of family pride.* **3.** portion, peculiar possession, or heritage: *the inheritance of the saints.* **4.** act or fact of inheriting: *to receive property by inheritance.* **5.** the right of inheriting.
—**Syn. 1.** INHERITANCE, HERITAGE denote something inherited. INHERITANCE is the common term for property or any possession that comes to an heir: *an inheritance from one's parents, a farm came to him by inheritance.* HERITAGE, a dignified or literary word, indicates whatever is bequeathed to a subsequent generation by an individual or by society: *our heritage from Greece and Rome.*
in·her·i·tance tax, a tax on those acquiring property by inheritance or bequest.
in·her·it·ed (ĭn hĕr′ə tĭd), *adj.* **1.** received by inheritance. **2.** *Gram.* found also in an earlier stage of the same language, esp. in the earliest reconstructed stage.
in·her·i·tor (ĭn hĕr′ə tər), *n.* one who inherits; heir. —**in·her·i·tress** (ĭn hĕr′ə trĭs), *n.fem.*
in·her·i·trix (ĭn hĕr′ə trĭks), *n.*, *pl.* **inheritrices** (ĭn-hĕr′ə trī′sēz). a female inheritor.
in·he·sion (ĭn hē′zhən), *n.* state or fact of inhering; inherence. [t. LL: m.s. *inhaesio*]
in·hib·it (ĭn hĭb′ĭt), *v.t.* **1.** to restrain, hinder, arrest, or check (an action, impulse, etc.). **2.** to prohibit; forbid. [late ME, t. L: s. *inhibitus*, pp., held back, restrained] —**in·hib′it·er,** *n.* —**Syn. 2.** See forbid.
in·hi·bi·tion (ĭn′ə bĭsh′ən, ĭn′hĭ-), *n.* **1.** act of inhibiting. **2.** state of being inhibited. **3.** *Psychol.* the blocking of any psychological process by another psychological process. **4.** *Physiol.* a restraining, arresting, or checking, as of action: **a.** the reduction of a reflex or other activity as the result of an antagonistic stimulation. **b.** a state created at synapses making them less excitable to other sources of stimulation.
in·hib·i·tor (ĭn hĭb′ĭt ər), *n.* **1.** *Chem.* a substance that decreases the rate of or stops completely a chemical reaction. **2.** an inhibiter.
in·hib·i·to·ry (ĭn hĭb′ə tôr′ē), *adj.* serving or tending to inhibit. Also, **in·hib′i·tive.**
in hoc sig·no vin·ces (ĭn hŏk sĭg′nō vĭn′sēz), *Latin.* in this sign shalt thou conquer (motto used by Constantine the Great, from his vision of a cross with these words before battle).
in·hos·pi·ta·ble (ĭn hŏs′pĭ tə bəl; *less often* ĭn′hŏs pĭt′-ə bəl), *adj.* **1.** not inclined to or characterized by hospitality, as persons, actions, etc. **2.** (of a region, climate, etc.) not offering shelter, favorable conditions, etc. —**in·hos′pi·ta·ble·ness,** *n.* —**in·hos′pi·ta·bly,** *adv.*
in·hos·pi·tal·i·ty (ĭn′hŏs pə tăl′ə tē, ĭn hŏs′-), *n.* lack of hospitality; inhospitable attitude toward visitors, etc.
in·hu·man (ĭn hū′mən), *adj.* **1.** lacking natural human feeling or sympathy for others; brutal. **2.** not human. [late ME unhumayn, t. L: m.s. *inhūmānus.* See IN-³] —**in·hu′man·ly,** *adv.* —**in·hu′man·ness,** *n.*
in·hu·mane (ĭn′hū mān′), *adj.* not humane; lacking humanity or kindness. —**in′hu·mane′ly,** *adv.*
in·hu·man·i·ty (ĭn′hū măn′ə tē), *n.*, *pl.* **-ties. 1.** state or quality of being inhuman or inhumane; cruelty: *man's inhumanity to man.* **2.** an inhuman or inhumane act.
in·hu·ma·tion (ĭn′hū mā′shən), *n.* act of inhuming, especially as opposed to cremation; interment.
in·hume (ĭn hūm′), *v.t.,* **-humed, -huming.** to bury; inter. [t. L: m.s. *inhūmāre* bury in the ground]
in·im·i·cal (ĭn ĭm′ə kəl), *adj.* **1.** adverse in tendency or effect: *a climate inimical to health.* **2.** unfriendly or hostile: *inimical opinions.* [t. LL: s. *inimīcālis,* der. L *inimīcus* unfriendly, an enemy] —**in·im′i·cal′i·ty,** *n.* —**in·im′i·cal·ly,** *adv.* —**Syn. 1.** See hostile.
in·im·i·ta·ble (ĭn ĭm′ə tə bəl), *adj.* incapable of being imitated; surpassing imitation. —**in·im′i·ta·bil′i·ty, in·im′i·ta·ble·ness,** *n.* —**in·im′i·ta·bly,** *adv.*
in·i·on (ĭn′ē ən), *n. Craniol.* a point at the external occipital protuberance of the skull. [t. NL, t. Gk.: back of the head]
in·iq·ui·tous (ĭ nĭk′wə təs), *adj.* characterized by iniquity. —**in·iq′ui·tous·ly,** *adv.* —**in·iq′ui·tous·ness,** *n.*
in·iq·ui·ty (ĭ nĭk′wə tē), *n.*, *pl.* **-ties. 1.** gross injustice; wickedness. **2.** a violation of right or duty; wicked action; sin. [ME *iniquite,* t. L: m.s. *inīquitas* injustice]
init., initial.
in·i·tial (ĭ nĭsh′əl), *adj., n., v.,* **-tialed, -tialing** or (*esp. Brit.*) **-tialled, -tialling.** —*adj.* **1.** of or pertaining to the beginning; incipient: *the initial step in a process.* **2.** at the beginning of a word or syllable. —*n.* **3.** an initial letter, as of a word. **4.** the first letter of a proper name. **5.** a letter of extra size or ornamental character used at the beginning of a chapter or other division of a book, etc. —*v.t.* **6.** to mark or sign with an initial or initials. [t. L: s. *initiālis* of the beginning] —**in·i′tial·ly,** *adv.*
in·i·ti·ate (*v.* ĭ nĭsh′ē āt′; *adj., n.* ĭ nĭsh′ē ĭt, -āt′), *v.,* **-ated, -ating,** *adj., n.* —*v.t.* **1.** to begin, set going, or originate: *to initiate reforms.* **2.** to introduce into the knowledge of some art or subject. **3.** to admit with formal rites into secret knowledge, a society, etc. **4.** to propose (a measure) by initiative procedure: *to initiate a constitutional amendment.* —*adj.* **5.** initiated; begun. **6.** admitted into a society, etc., or into the knowledge of a subject. —*n.* **7.** one who has been initiated. [t. L: m.s. *initiātus,* pp., begun, initiated] —**in·i′ti·a′tor,** *n.* —**in·i·ti·a·tress** (ĭ nĭsh′ē ā′trĭs), **in·i·ti·a·trix** (ĭ nĭsh′ē-ā′trĭks), *n. fem.* —**Syn. 1.** commence; introduce, inaugurate. See begin. —**Ant. 1.** discontinue.

in·i·ti·a·tion (ĭ nĭsh′ē ā′shən), *n.* **1.** formal admission into a society, etc. **2.** the ceremonies of admission. **3.** act of initiating. **4.** fact of being initiated.
in·i·ti·a·tive (ĭ nĭsh′ē ə tĭv, -ĭ ā′tĭv), *n.* **1.** an introductory act or step; leading action: *to take the initiative.* **2.** readiness and ability in initiating action; enterprise: *to lack initiative.* **3.** *Govt.* **a.** procedure by which a specified number of voters may propose a statute, constitutional amendment, or ordinance, and compel a popular vote on its adoption. **b.** the general right or ability to present a new bill or measure, as in a legislature. —*adj.* **4.** serving to initiate; pertaining to initiation. —**in·i′ti·a·tive·ly,** *adv.*
in·i·ti·a·to·ry (ĭ nĭsh′ē ə tôr′ē), *adj.* **1.** introductory; initial: *an initiatory step.* **2.** serving to initiate or admit into a society, etc. —**in·i′ti·a·to′ri·ly,** *adv.*
in·ject (ĭn jĕkt′), *v.t.* **1.** to force (a fluid, etc.) into a passage, cavity, or tissue. **2.** to introduce (something new or different) into a thing: *to inject comedy into a situation.* **3.** to introduce arbitrarily or inappropriately. **4.** to interject (a remark, suggestion, etc.), as into conversation. [t. L: s. *injectus,* pp., thrown or put in]
in·jec·tion (ĭn jĕk′shən), *n.* **1.** act of injecting. **2.** that which is injected. **3.** a liquid injected into the body, esp. for medicinal purposes, as a hypodermic or an enema. **4.** state of being hyperemic or bloodshot.
in·jec·tor (ĭn jĕk′tər), *n.* **1.** one who or that which injects. **2.** a device for forcing water into a steam boiler.
in·ju·di·cious (ĭn′jōō dĭsh′əs), *adj.* not judicious; showing lack of judgment; unwise; imprudent. —**in′ju·di′cious·ly,** *adv.* —**in′ju·di′cious·ness,** *n.*
in·junc·tion (ĭn jŭngk′shən), *n.* **1.** *Law.* a judicial process or order requiring the person or persons to whom it is directed to do or (more commonly) not to do a particular thing. **2.** act of enjoining. **3.** that which is enjoined; a command, order or admonition. [t. LL: s. *injunctio* command] —**in·junc′tive,** *adj.*
in·jure (ĭn′jər), *v.t.,* **-jured, -juring. 1.** to do or cause harm of any kind to; damage; hurt; impair: *to injure the hand.* **2.** to do wrong or injustice to. [back formation from INJURY, n., r. earlier *injury,* v.] —**in′jur·er,** *n.* —**Syn. 1.** INJURE, IMPAIR mean to harm or damage something. INJURE is a general term referring to any kind or degree of damage: *to injure one's spine, to injure one's reputation.* To IMPAIR is to make imperfect in any way, often with a suggestion of progressive deterioration and of permanency in the result: *one's health is impaired by overwork.* —**Ant. 1.** benefit.
in·jured (ĭn′jərd), *adj.* **1.** harmed, damaged, or hurt. **2.** offended; wronged: *an injured look.*
in·ju·ri·ous (ĭn jŏor′ē əs), *adj.* **1.** harmful, hurtful, or detrimental, as in effect: *injurious habits.* **2.** doing or involving injury or wrong, as to another. **3.** insulting or abusive. [late ME, t. L: m.s. *injuriōsus,* wrongful] —**in·ju′ri·ous·ly,** *adv.* —**in·ju′ri·ous·ness,** *n.* —**Syn. 1.** deleterious, pernicious; baneful, destructive, ruinous. **2.** unjust, wrongful, prejudicial. **3.** offensive; derogatory, defamatory, slanderous. —**Ant. 1.** beneficial.
in·ju·ry (ĭn′jər ē), *n.*, *pl.* **-juries. 1.** harm of any kind done or sustained: *to escape without injury.* **2.** a particular form or instance of harm: *severe bodily injuries.* **3.** wrong or injustice done or suffered. **4.** *Law.* a wrong or detriment caused by the deliberate or negligent act of another and actionable in a court of law. **5.** *Obs.* injurious speech; calumny. [ME *injurie,* t. L: m. *injūria* wrong, harm, insult]
—**Syn. 1-3.** INJURY, HURT, WOUND refer to material or moral impairments or wrongs. INJURY, originally denoting a wrong done or suffered, is hence used for any kind of evil, impairment, or loss, caused or sustained: *physical injury, injury to one's reputation.* HURT suggests esp. physical injury, often bodily injury attended with pain: *a bad hurt from a fall.* A WOUND is usually a physical hurt caused by cutting, shooting, etc., or an emotional hurt: *a serious wound in the shoulder, to inflict a wound by betraying someone's trust.* —**Ant. 1.** benefit.
in·jus·tice (ĭn jŭs′tĭs), *n.* **1.** quality or fact of being unjust. **2.** unjust action or treatment; violation of another's rights. **3.** an unjust act or circumstance. [ME, t. F, t. L: m.s. *injustitia*]
ink (ĭngk), *n.* **1.** a fluid or viscous substance used for writing or printing. **2.** a dark protective fluid ejected by the cuttlefish and other cephalopods. —*v.t.* **3.** to mark, stain, cover, or smear with ink. [ME *inke, enke,* t. OF: m. *enque,* g. LL *encaustum,* t. Gk.: m. *énkauston* kind of ink] —**ink′er,** *n.* —**ink′less,** *adj.* —**ink′-like′,** *adj.*
ink·ber·ry (ĭngk′bĕr′ē), *n.*, *pl.* **-ries. 1.** a shrub, *Ilex glabra,* with leathery evergreen leaves and black berries. **2.** the pokeweed. **3.** the berry of either plant.
Ink·er·man (ĭng′kər män′), *n.* a locality in the SW Soviet Union, in the Crimea: Russian defeat, 1854.
ink·horn (ĭngk′hôrn′), *n.* a small container of horn or other material, formerly used to hold writing ink.
in·kle (ĭng′kəl), *n.* **1.** a kind of linen tape. **2.** the linen thread or yarn from which this tape is made.
ink·ling (ĭngk′lĭng), *n.* **1.** a hint, intimation, or slight suggestion. **2.** a vague idea or notion. [f. *inkle,* v., hint (ME *incle*) + -ING¹. Cf. OE *inca* suspicion]
ink·stand (ĭngk′stănd′), *n.* **1.** a stand for holding ink, pens, etc. **2.** a cuplike container for ink.
ink·well (ĭngk′wĕl′), *n.* a container for ink. Also, *Brit.,* **ink·pot** (ĭngk′pŏt′).
ink·wood (ĭngk′wŏŏd′), *n.* a sapindaceous tree,

Exothea paniculata, of the West Indies and Florida, with hard reddish-brown wood.

ink·y (Ÿngk′Ÿ), *adj.* **inkier, inkiest.** **1.** black as ink: *inky shadows.* **2.** resembling ink. **3.** stained with ink: *inky fingers.* **4.** of or pertaining to ink. **5.** consisting of or containing ink. **6.** written with ink. —**ink′i·ness,** *n.*

inky cap, any species of mushroom (genus *Coprinus*) whose gills disintegrate into blackish liquid after the spores mature, esp. *C. atramentarius.*

in·laid (Ÿn′lād′, Ÿn lād′), *adj.* **1.** set in the surface of a thing: *an inlaid design in wood.* **2.** decorated or made with a design set in the surface: *an inlaid table.*

in·land (*adj.* Ÿn′lend; *adv., n.* Ÿn′lānd′, -lend), *adj.* **1.** pertaining to or situated in the interior part of a country or region: *inland cities.* **2.** carried on within a country; domestic; not foreign: *inland trade;* (*Brit.*) *inland revenue* (U.S. "internal revenue"); (*Brit.*) *inland mails* (U.S. "domestic mails"). **3.** confined to a country; drawn and payable in the same country. —*adv.* **4.** in or toward the interior of a country. —*n.* **5.** the interior part of a country, away from the border. [ME and OE; f. IN-¹ + LAND]

in·land·er (Ÿn′len der), *n.* a person living inland.

Inland Sea, a sea in SW Japan, enclosed by the islands of Honshu, Shikoku, and Kyushu. ab. 240 mi. long.

in-law (Ÿn′lô′), *n. Colloq.* a relative by marriage.

in·lay (*v.* Ÿn lā′; *n.* Ÿn′lā′), *v.,* **-laid, -laying,** *n.* —*v.t.* **1.** to decorate (an object) with veneers of fine materials set in its surface. **2.** to insert, or apply (layers of fine materials) in a surface of an object. **3.** *Hort.* to place (a fitted scion) into a prepared stock, as in an inlay graft. —*n.* **4.** inlaid work. **5.** veneer of fine material inserted in something else, esp. for ornament. **6.** a design or decoration made by inlaying. **7.** *Dentistry.* a filling of metal, porcelain, or plastic which is fitted and fastened into a tooth as a solid mass. **8.** *Hort.* an inlay graft. **9.** the act or process of inlaying. —**in′lay′er,** *n.*

inlay graft, *Hort.* a graft in which the scion is matched into a place in the stock from which a piece of corresponding bark has been removed.

in·let (*n.* Ÿn′lĕt; *v.* Ÿn lĕt′), *n., v.,* **-let, -letting.** —*n.* **1.** an indentation of a shore line, usually long and narrow, or a narrow passage between islands. **2.** a place of admission; an entrance. **3.** something put in or inserted. —*v.t.* **4.** to put in; insert.

in·li·er (Ÿn′lī′er), *n. Geol.* outcrop of a formation completely surrounded by another of later date.

in loc. cit., (L *in loci citato*) in the place cited.

in lo·co (Ÿn lō′kō), *Latin.* in place; in the proper place.

in lo·co pa·ren·tis (Ÿn lō′kō pe rĕn′tÿs), *Latin.* in the place of a parent; replacing a parent.

in·ly (Ÿn′lÿ), *adv. Now Poetic.* **1.** inwardly. **2.** intimately; deeply. —*adj.* **3.** *Obs.* inward. [ME *inliche,* OE *inlice,* der. *inlic* inward]

in·mate (Ÿn′māt′), *n.* **1.** one who dwells with another or others in the same house. **2.** one of those confined in a hospital, prison, etc. [f. IN-¹ + MATE¹]

in me·di·as res (Ÿn mē′dÿ ăs′ rēz′), *Latin.* in the middle of things: *Homer began his story in medias res.*

in mem., in memoriam.

in me·mo·ri·am (Ÿn me mōr′Ÿ ăm′), in memory (of); to the memory (of); as a memorial (to). [t. L]

In Memoriam A.H.H., a long elegiac poem (1850) by Tennyson, on his friend Arthur Henry Hallam.

in·mesh (Ÿn mĕsh′), *v.t.* enmesh.

in·most (Ÿn′mōst′, -mest), *adj.* **1.** situated furthest within: *the inmost recesses of the forest.* **2.** most intimate: *one's inmost thoughts.* [ME; OE *innemest,* a double superl., f. *inne* within + -*m*- + -*est* (superl. suffix). See IN-¹, -MOST]

inn (Ÿn), *n.* **1.** a public house that provides lodging, food, etc., for travelers and others; a small hotel: *a wayside inn.* **2.** a tavern. **3.** *Brit.* **a.** a house or place of residence for students (now only in names of buildings derived from such use): *the Inns of Court.* **b.** a legal society occupying such a house. [ME *inne,* OE *inn* house] —**inn′less,** *adj.* —**Syn. 1.** See **hotel.**

in·nate (Ÿ nāt′, Ÿn′āt), *adj.* **1.** inborn; existing or as if existing in one from birth: *innate modesty.* **2.** arising from the constitution of the mind, rather than acquired from experience: *innate ideas.* [late ME *innat,* t. L: s. *in-nātus,* pp., inborn] —**in·nate′ly,** *adv.* —**in·nate′ness,** *n.*

in·ner (Ÿn′er), *adj.* **1.** situated farther within; interior: *an inner door.* **2.** more intimate, private, or secret: *the inner circle of his friends.* **3.** mental or spiritual: *the inner life.* **4.** not obvious; esoteric: *an inner meaning.* [ME; OE *innera,* compar. of *inne* within. Cf. INMOST] —**in′ner·ness,** *n.*

in·ner-di·rect·ed (Ÿn′er dÿ rĕk′tÿd), *adj.* guided by one's own set of values rather than external pressures. —**inner direction.**

Inner Light, (as used by the Society of Friends) the light of Christ in the soul.

Inner Mongolia. See **Mongolia** (def. 2).

in·ner·most (Ÿn′er mōst′, -mest), *adj.* **1.** farthest inward; inmost. —*n.* **2.** innermost part. [ME, f. INNER + -MOST]

Inner Temple. See **Inns of Court.**

in·ner·vate (Ÿ nûr′vāt, Ÿn′er vāt′), *v.t.,* **-vated, -vating. 1.** to communicate nervous energy to; stimulate through nerves. **2.** to grow nerves into. [f. IN-² + NERVE + -ATE¹]

in·ner·va·tion (Ÿn′er vā′shen), *n.* **1.** act of innervating. **2.** state of being innervated. **3.** *Anat.* the disposition of nerves in a body or some part of it.

in·nerve (Ÿ nûrv′), *v.t.,* **-nerved, -nerving.** to supply with nervous energy; invigorate; animate.

In·ness (Ÿn′Ÿs), *n.* **1. George,** 1825–94, U.S. painter. **2.** his son **George,** 1854–1926, U.S. painter.

in·ning (Ÿn′Ÿng), *n.* **1.** *Baseball.* a round in which both teams bat, with each side getting three outs. **2.** (in other games) a similar opportunity to score. **3.** an opportunity for activity; a turn: *now the opposition will have its inning.* **4.** reclaiming, as of marsh or flooded land. **5.** land reclaimed from the sea, etc. **6.** enclosure, as of waste land. **7.** harvesting, as of crops. [ME *inninge,* OE *innung* a putting in]

in·nings (Ÿn′Ÿngz), *n.pl.* (construed as sing.) *Chiefly Brit.* inning (defs. 1, 2, 3).

inn·keep·er (Ÿn′kē′per), *n.* the keeper of an inn.

in·no·cence (Ÿn′e sens), *n.* **1.** state or fact of being innocent; freedom from sin or moral wrong. **2.** freedom from legal or specific wrong; guiltlessness: *the prisoner proved his innocence.* **3.** simplicity or guilelessness. **4.** lack of knowledge or sense. **5.** harmlessness or innocuousness. **6.** an innocent person or thing. **7.** the common North American bluet. **8.** a scrophulariaceous herb, *Collinsia verna,* with a blue-and-white flower. **9.** an allied and widely distributed California herb, *C. bicolor.*

in·no·cen·cy (Ÿn′e sen sÿ), *n.* innocence (defs. 1–6).

in·no·cent (Ÿn′e sent), *adj.* **1.** free from any moral wrong; not tainted with sin; pure: *innocent children.* **2.** free from legal or specific wrong; guiltless: *to be innocent of crime.* **3.** not involving evil intent or motive: *an innocent misrepresentation.* **4.** free from any quality that can cause physical or moral injury; harmless: *innocent fun.* **5.** devoid (fol. by *of*): *a law innocent of merit.* **6.** having or showing the simplicity or naïveté of an unworldly person: *she looks so innocent.* —*n.* **7.** an innocent person. **8.** a young child. **9.** a guileless person. **10.** a simpleton or idiot. **11.** (*pl.*) *U.S.* the common bluet. [ME, t. L: s. *innocens* harmless] —**in′no·cent·ly,** *adv.*
—**Syn. 1.** sinless, virtuous; faultless, impeccable. **2.** INNOCENT, BLAMELESS, GUILTLESS imply freedom from the responsibility of having done wrong. INNOCENT may imply having done no wrong at any time, and having not even a knowledge of evil: *an innocent victim.* BLAMELESS denotes freedom from blame, esp. moral blame: *a blameless life.* GUILTLESS denotes freedom from guilt or responsibility for wrongdoing, usually in a particular instance: *guiltless of a crime.* **6.** simple, naïve, unsophisticated, artless, guileless, ingenuous.

In·no·cent (Ÿn′e sent), *n.* the name of 13 popes.

Innocent II, (*Gregorio Papareschi*) died 1143, Italian ecclesiastic; pope, 1130–43.

Innocent III, (*Giovanni Lotario de' Conti*) 1161?–1216, Italian ecclesiastic; pope, 1198–1216.

Innocent IV, (*Sinibaldo de Fieschi*) died 1254, Italian ecclesiastic; pope, 1243–54.

Innocent XI, (*Bendetto Odescalchi*) 1611–89, Italian ecclesiastic; pope, 1676–89.

in·noc·u·ous (Ÿ nŏk′yōō es), *adj.* not harmful or injurious; harmless. [t. L: m. *innocuus*] —**in·noc′u·ous·ly,** *adv.* —**in·noc′u·ous·ness,** *n.*

in·nom·i·nate (Ÿ nŏm′e nÿt), *adj.* having no name; anonymous. [t. LL: m.s. *innominātus* unnamed]

innominate bone, *Anat.* either of the two bones forming the sides of the pelvis, each consisting of three consolidated bones, known as ilium, ischium, and pubis.

in·no·vate (Ÿn′e vāt′), *v.,* **-vated, -vating.** —*v.i.* **1.** to bring in something new; make changes in anything established (fol. by *on* or *in*). —*v.t.* **2.** to bring in (something new) for the first time. **3.** *Obs.* to alter. [t. L: m.s. *innovātus,* pp., renewed, altered] —**in′no·va′tive,** *adj.* —**in′no·va′tor,** *n.*

in·no·va·tion (Ÿn′e vā′shen), *n.* **1.** something new or different introduced. **2.** act of innovating; introduction of new things or methods. —**in′no·va′tion·ist,** *n.*

in·nox·ious (Ÿ nŏk′shes), *adj.* harmless; innocuous. —**in·nox′ious·ly,** *adv.* —**in·nox′ious·ness,** *n.*

Inn River (Ÿn), a river flowing from E Switzerland through Austria and Germany into the Danube. 320 mi.

Inns·bruck (Ÿnz′brŏŏk; *Ger.* Ÿns′brŏŏk), *n.* a city in W Austria, on the Inn river. 95,055 (1955).

Inns of Court, the four voluntary legal societies in England (**Lincoln's Inn, the Inner Temple, the Middle Temple,** and **Gray's Inn**), which have the exclusive privilege of calling candidates to the English bar, after they have received such instruction and taken such examinations as the Inns provide. **2.** the buildings owned and used by the Inns.

in·nu·en·do (Ÿn′yōō ĕn′dō), *n., pl.* **-does. 1.** an indirect intimation about a person or thing, esp. of a derogatory nature. **2.** *Law.* **a.** a parenthetic explanation or specification in a pleading. **b.** (in an action for slander or libel) the explanation and elucidation of the words alleged to be defamatory. **c.** the word or expression thus explained. [t. L: intimation, abl. gerund of *innuere* give a nod, intimate]

in·nu·mer·a·ble (Ÿ nū′mer e bel, -nōō′-), *adj.* **1.** very numerous. **2.** incapable of being numbered or counted. Also, **in·nu′mer·ous.** —**in·nu′mer·a·ble·ness,** *n.* —**in·nu′mer·a·bly,** *adv.* —**Syn. 1.** See **many.**

in·nu·tri·tion (Ÿn′yōō trÿsh′en, -nōō′-), *n.* lack of nutrition. —**in′nu·tri′tious,** *adj.*

---

in·ob·serv·ance (ĭn′əb zûr′vəns), *n.* **1.** lack of observance or noticing; inattention: *drowsy inobservance.* **2.** nonobservance —**in′ob·serv′ant,** *adj.*

in·oc·u·la·ble (ĭ nŏk′yə lə bəl), *adj.* capable of being inoculated. —**in·oc′u·la·bil′i·ty,** *n.*

in·oc·u·lant (ĭ nŏk′yə lənt), *n.* an inoculating substance.

in·oc·u·late (ĭ nŏk′yə lāt′), *v.,* **-lated, -lating,** *n.* —*v.t.* **1.** to implant (a disease) in a person or animal by the introduction of germs or virus, as through a puncture, in order to produce a mild form of the disease and thus secure immunity. **2.** to impregnate (a person or animal) thus. **3.** to introduce (microörganisms) into surroundings suited to their growth, esp. into the body. **4.** to imbue (a person, etc.), as with ideas. —*v.i.* **5.** to perform inoculation —*n.* **6.** a substance to be inoculated. [late ME, t. L: m.s. *inoculātus,* pp., grafted, implanted] —**in·oc′u·la′tive,** *adj.* —**in·oc′u·la′tor,** *n.*

in·oc·u·la·tion (ĭ nŏk′yə lā′shən), *n.* act of inoculating.

in·oc·u·lum (ĭ nŏk′yə ləm), *n.* the substance used to make an inoculation. [NL]

in·o·dor·ous (ĭn ō′dər əs), *adj.* not odorous; odorless. —**in·o′dor·ous·ness,** *n.*

in·of·fen·sive (ĭn′ə fĕn′sĭv), *adj.* **1.** doing no harm; harmless; unoffending: *a mild, inoffensive man.* **2.** not objectionable, or not being a cause of offense. —**in′of·fen′sive·ly,** *adv.* —**in′of·fen′sive·ness,** *n.*

in·of·fi·cious (ĭn′ə fĭsh′əs), *adj.* **1.** *Law.* not in accordance with moral duty: *an inofficious testament or will* (one disposing of property contrary to the dictates of natural affection or to just expectations). **2.** disobliging. [t. L: m.s. *inofficiōsus.* See IN-³, OFFICIOUS]

I·nö·nü (ĭ nœ nY′), *n.* Ismet (ĭs mĕt′), born 1884, president of Turkey, 1938–1950.

in·op·er·a·ble (ĭn ŏp′ər ə bəl), *adj.* **1.** not operable. **2.** not admitting of a surgical operation without undue risk.

in·op·er·a·tive (ĭn ŏp′ə rā′tĭv, -ŏp′ə rə-), *adj.* **1.** not operative; not in operation. **2.** without effect: *inoperative remedies.* —**in·op′er·a·tive·ness,** *n.*

in·op·por·tune (ĭn ŏp′ər tūn′, -tōōn′), *adj.* not opportune; inappropriate; (with regard to time) unseasonable: *an inopportune visit.* —**in·op′por·tune′ly,** *adv.* —**in·op′por·tune′ness,** *n.*

in·or·di·nate (ĭn ôr′də nĭt), *adj.* **1.** not within proper limits; excessive: *inordinate demands.* **2.** disorderly. **3.** unrestrained in conduct, etc. **4.** irregular: *inordinate hours.* [ME *inordinat,* t. L: s. *inordinātus* disordered] —**in·or·di·na·cy** (ĭn ôr′də nə sĭ), **in·or′di·nate·ness,** *n.* —**in·or′di·nate·ly,** *adv.*

inorg., inorganic.

in·or·gan·ic (ĭn′ôr găn′ĭk), *adj.* **1.** not having the organization which characterizes living bodies. **2.** not characterized by vital processes. **3.** *Chem.* noting or pertaining to compounds not containing carbon, excepting cyanides and carbonates. Cf. **organic** (def. 1). **4.** not fundamental; extraneous. —**in·or·gan′i·cal·ly,** *adv.*

inorganic chemistry, the branch of chemistry which treats of inorganic substances.

in·os·cu·late (ĭn ŏs′kyə lāt′), *v.i., v.t.,* **-lated, -lating. 1.** to unite by openings, as arteries in anastomosis. **2.** to connect or join so as to become or make continuous, as fibers. **3.** to unite intimately. [f. IN-² + m.s. LL *osculātus,* pp., supplied with a mouth or outlet] —**in·os′cu·la′tion,** *n.*

in·o·si·tol (ĭ nō′sə tōl′, -tŏl′), *n. Chem.* a sweet crystalline substance, C₆H₆(OH)₆, first found in heart muscle, but widely distributed in plants and seeds as phytin, and also occurring in animal tissue and in urine. Also, **in·o·site** (ĭn′ə sīt′). [f. *inosit(e)* (f. in-, comb. form repr. Gk. *ís* fiber, + -OS(E)² + -ITE¹) + -OL²]

in·pa·tient (ĭn′pā′shənt), *n.* a patient who is lodged and fed as well as treated in a hospital.

in per·pe·tu·um (ĭn pər pĕt′yōŏ əm), *Latin.* forever.

in per·so·nam (ĭn pər sō′năm), *Latin.* against a person, as a legal proceeding.

in pet·to (ĭn pĕt′ō; *It.* ēn pĕt′tō), *Italian.* not disclosed (of cardinals whom the Pope appoints but does not name in consistory).

in·phase (ĭn′fāz′), *adj. Elect.* in synchronism.

in pos·se (ĭn pŏs′Y), *Latin.* in possibility, rather than in actual existence (distinguished from *in esse*).

in·put (ĭn′pŏŏt′), *n.* **1.** that which is put in. **2.** the power supplied to a machine. **3.** *Scot.* a contribution.

in·quest (ĭn′kwĕst), *n.* **1.** a legal or judicial inquiry, esp. before a jury. **2.** one made by a coroner (**coroner's inquest**). **3.** the body of men appointed to hold such an inquiry, esp. a coroner's jury. **4.** their decision or finding. [ME *enqueste,* t. OF, g. L *inquīsīta* (*rēs*) (a thing) inquired into, prop. pp. fem.]

in·qui·e·tude (ĭn kwī′ə tūd′, -tōōd′), *n.* **1.** restlessness; uneasiness. **2.** (*pl.*) disquieting thoughts.

in·qui·line (ĭn′kwə līn′, -lĭn), *n. Zool.* an animal that lives in an abode properly belonging to another; a guest. [t. L: m.s. *inquilīnus*] —**in·qui·lin·i·ty** (ĭn′kwə lĭn′ə tY), *n.* —**in·qui·li·nous** (ĭn′kwə lī′nəs), *adj.*

in·quire (ĭn kwīr′), *v.,* **-quired, -quiring.** —*v.t.* **1.** to seek to learn by asking: *to inquire a person's name.* **2.** *Obs.* to seek. **3.** *Obs.* to question (a person). —*v.i.* **4.** to seek information by questioning; ask: *to inquire*

after a person. **5.** to make investigation (fol. by *into*). Also, **enquire.** [t. L: m.s. *inquīrere;* r. ME *enquere,* t. OF] —**in·quir′er,** *n.* —**in·quir′ing·ly,** *adv.* —**Syn. 1.** INQUIRE, ASK, QUESTION imply that a person (or persons) addresses another (or others) to obtain information. ASK is the general word: *ask what time it is.* INQUIRE is more formal and always implies asking about something specific: *inquire about a rumor.* To QUESTION implies repetition and persistence in asking; it often applies to legal examination or investigation: *question the survivor of an accident.* —**Ant. 1.** tell.

in·quir·y (ĭn kwīr′Y, ĭn′kwə rY), *n., pl.* **-quiries. 1.** a seeking for truth, information, or knowledge. **2.** an investigation, as into a matter. **3.** act of inquiring, or seeking information by questioning; interrogation. **4.** a question or query. Also, **enquiry.** —**Syn. 2.** See **investigation.**

in·qui·si·tion (ĭn′kwə zĭsh′ən), *n.* **1.** act of inquiring; inquiry; research. **2.** an investigation, or process of inquiry. **3.** an inquiry conducted by judicial officers or such nonjudicial officers as coroners. **4.** the finding of such an inquiry. **5.** the document embodying the result of such inquiry. **6.** (*cap.*) *Rom. Cath. Ch.* a special tribunal (officially, the **Holy Office**) for the defense of Catholic teaching in faith and morals, the judgment of heresy, the application of canonical punishment, and the judgment of mixed marriages and the Pauline privileges. [ME *inquisicion,* t. L: m.s. *inquīsītio* a searching into] —**in·qui·si′tion·al,** *adj.*

in·qui·si·tion·ist (ĭn′kwə zĭsh′ən Yst), *n.* an inquisitor.

in·quis·i·tive (ĭn kwĭz′ə tĭv), *adj.* **1.** given to inquiry or research; desirous of or eager for knowledge; curious: *inquisitive attention.* **2.** unduly curious; prying. —*n.* **3.** an inquisitive person. —**in·quis′i·tive·ly,** *adv.* —**in·quis′i·tive·ness,** *n.* —**Syn. 2.** See **curious.**

in·quis·i·tor (ĭn kwĭz′ə tər), *n.* **1.** one who makes inquisition. **2.** a questioner, esp. an inquisitive one. **3.** one who investigates by virtue of his office. **4.** a member of the Inquisition. —**in·quis·i·tress** (ĭn kwĭz′ə trĭs), *n. fem.*

in·quis·i·to·ri·al (ĭn kwĭz′ə tōr′Y əl), *adj.* **1.** pertaining to an inquisitor or inquisitors, or to inquisition. **2.** exercising the office of an inquisitor. **3.** *Law.* pertaining to a trial with one person or group acting as prosecutor and judge, or to secret criminal prosecutions. **4.** resembling an inquisitor. **5.** inquisitive. —**in·quis′-i·to′ri·al·ly,** *adv.* —**in·quis′i·to′ri·al·ness,** *n.*

in re (ĭn rē′), *Latin.* in the matter of.

in rem (ĭn rĕm′), *Latin.* against a thing, as a legal proceeding for its recovery.

in re·rum na·tu·ra (ĭn rĭr′əm nə tyŏŏr′ə, -tōŏr′ə), *Latin.* in the nature of things.

I.N.R.I., (L *Iesus Nazarenus, Rex Iudaeorum*) Jesus of Nazareth, King of the Jews.

in·road (ĭn′rōd′), *n.* **1.** forcible or serious encroachment: *inroads on our savings.* **2.** a hostile or predatory incursion; a raid; a foray.

in·rush (ĭn′rŭsh′), *n.* a rushing in; an influx. —**in′-rush′ing,** *n., adj.*

ins., **1.** inches. **2.** inspector. **3.** insulated. **4.** insurance.

I.N.S., International News Service, a news-gathering agency.

in·sal·i·vate (ĭn săl′ə vāt′), *v.t.,* **-vated, -vating.** to mix with saliva, as food. —**in·sal′i·va′tion,** *n.*

in·sa·lu·bri·ous (ĭn′sə lōō′brĭ əs), *adj.* unfavorable to health. —**in′sa·lu′bri·ous·ly,** *adv.* —**in·sa·lu·bri·ty** (ĭn′sə lōō′brə tY), *n.*

in·sane (ĭn sān′), *adj.* **1.** not sane; not of sound mind; mentally deranged. **2.** characteristic of one mentally deranged. **3.** set apart for the use of mentally deranged persons: *an insane asylum.* **4.** utterly senseless: *an almost insane attempt.* —**in·sane′ly,** *adv.* —**in·sane′-ness,** *n.* —**Syn. 1.** demented; lunatic, crazed, crazy; maniacal. See **mad.** **2.** foolish, senseless.

in·san·i·tar·y (ĭn săn′ə tĕr′Y), *adj.* not sanitary; unhealthful: *insanitary houses.* —**in·san′i·tar′i·ness,** *n.*

in·san·i·ta·tion (ĭn săn′ə tā′shən), *n.* lack of sanitation or sanitary regulation; insanitary condition.

in·san·i·ty (ĭn săn′ə tY), *n., pl.* **-ties. 1.** condition of being insane; more or less permanent derangement of one or more psychical functions, due to disease of the mind. **2.** *Law.* such unsoundness of mind as affects legal responsibility or capacity. **3.** extreme folly. —**Syn. 1.** derangement, dementia; lunacy, craziness, madness.

in·sa·tia·ble (ĭn sā′shə bəl, -shĭ ə-), *adj.* not satiable; incapable of being satisfied: *insatiable desire.* —**in·sa′-tia·bil′i·ty, in·sa′tia·ble·ness,** *n.* —**in·sa′tia·bly,** *adv.*

in·sa·ti·ate (ĭn sā′shĭ Yt), *adj.* insatiable: *insatiate greed.* —**in·sa′ti·ate·ly,** *adv.* —**in·sa′ti·ate·ness,** *n.*

in·scribe (ĭn skrĭb′), *v.t.,* **-scribed, -scribing. 1.** to write or engrave (words, characters, etc.). **2.** to mark (a surface) with words, characters, etc., esp. in a durable or conspicuous way. **3.** to address or dedicate (a book, photograph, etc.) informally, esp. by a handwritten note. **4.** to enroll, as on an official list. **5.** *Brit.* to record or register the names of purchasers of (stocks, etc.). **6.** *Geom.* to draw or delineate (one figure) within another figure so that the inner lies in the boundary of the outer at as many points as possible. [t. L: m.s. *inscrībere* write in or upon] —**in·scrib′a·ble,** *adj.* —**in·scrib′er,** *n.*

in·scrip·tion (ĭn skrĭp′shən), *n.* **1.** something inscribed. **2.** a brief, more or less informal dedication, as of a book or a work of art. 3. *Bibliog.* a note inscribed in a book, usually signed. 4. *Archaeol.* a historical, religious, or other record cut, impressed, painted, or written on stone, brick, metal, or other hard surface. 5. act of inscribing. 6. *Brit.* a. an inscribing of issued securities. b. such inscribed securities. [ME, t. L: s. *inscriptio*] —in·scrip′tion·al, *adj.* —in·scrip′tion·less, *adj.*

in·scrip·tive (ĭn·skrĭp′tĭv), *adj.* pertaining to or of the nature of an inscription. —in·scrip′tive·ly, *adv.*

in·scroll (ĭn·skrōl′), *v.t.* to write on a scroll.

in·scru·ta·ble (ĭn·skrōō′tə bəl),*adj.* 1. incapable of being searched into or scrutinized; impenetrable to investigation. 2. impenetrable or unfathomable physically. [late ME, t. LL: m.s. *inscrūtābilis*] —in·scru′ta·bil′i·ty, in·scru′ta·ble·ness, *n.* —in·scru′ta·bly, *adv.* —Syn. 1. See mysterious.

in·sculp (ĭn·skŭlp′), *v.t. Now Rare.* to carve in or on something; engrave. [t. L: s. *insculpere*]

in·sect (ĭn′sĕkt), *n.* 1. *Zool.* any animal of the subphylum or class *Insecta*, a group of small, air-breathing arthropods characterized by a body clearly divided into three parts: head, thorax, and abdomen, and by having only three pairs of legs, and usually having two pairs of wings. 2. any small, air-breathing arthropod, such as a spider, tick, or centipede, having superficial, general similarity to the *Insecta*. 3. a contemptible person. —*adj.* 4. like an insect. 5. contemptible. [t. L: s. *insectum* (so called from the segmented form), prop. neut. of *insectus*, pp., cut in or up] —in·sect′like′, *adj.*

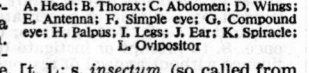

Diagram of a typical insect, the grasshopper: A. Head; B. Thorax; C. Abdomen; D. Wings; E. Antenna; F. Simple eye; G. Compound eye; H. Palpus; I. Legs; J. Ear; K. Spiracle; L. Ovipositor

in·sec·tar·i·um (ĭn′sĕk târ′ĭ əm), *n., pl.* -tariums, -taria (-târ′ĭ ə). a place in which a collection of living insects is kept, as in a zoo. [NL]

in·sec·tar·y (ĭn′sĕk tĕr′ĭ), *n., pl.* -taries. a laboratory for the study of live insects, their life histories, effects on plants, reaction to insecticides, etc.

in·sec·ti·cide[1] (ĭn sĕk′tə sīd′), *n.* a substance or preparation used for killing insects. [f. s. L *insectum* an insect + -(I)CIDE[1]] —in·sec′ti·cid′al, *adj.*

in·sec·ti·cide[2] (ĭn sĕk′tə sīd′), *n.* the killing of insects. [f. s. L *insectum* insect + -(I)CIDE[2]]

in·sec·ti·vore (ĭn sĕk′tə vōr′), *n.* 1. an insectivorous animal or plant. 2. any of the *Insectivora*, the mammalian order that includes the moles, the shrews, and the Old World hedgehogs. [t. NL: m.s. *insectivorus*, f. L: s. *insectum* insect + -i- + -*vorus* devouring]

in·sec·tiv·o·rous (ĭn′sĕk tĭv′ə rəs), *adj.* adapted to feeding on insects, as shrews, moles, hedgehogs, etc.

in·se·cure (ĭn′sĭ kyŏor′), *adj.* 1. exposed to danger; unsafe. 2. not firm or safe: *insecure foundations.* 3. not free from fear, doubt, etc. —in′se·cure′ly, *adv.* —Syn. 2. See uncertain.

in·se·cu·ri·ty (ĭn′sĭ kyŏor′ə tĭ), *n., pl.* -ties. 1. unsafe condition; lack of assurance or sureness; uncertainty; instability. 2. something insecure.

in·sem·i·nate (ĭn sĕm′ə nāt′), *v.t.,* -nated, -nating. 1. to sow; inject seed into. 2. to impregnate. 3. to sow as seed in something; implant. [t. L: m.s. *insēminātus,* pp., sowed, planted in] —in·sem′i·na′tion, *n.*

in·sen·sate (ĭn sĕn′sāt, -sĭt), *adj.* 1. not endowed with sensation: *insensate stone.* 2. without feeling; unfeeling. 3. without sense, understanding, or judgment. —in·sen′sate·ly, *adv.* —in·sen′sate·ness, *n.*

in·sen·si·ble (ĭn sĕn′sə bəl), *adj.* 1. incapable of feeling or perceiving; deprived of sensation; unconscious, as a person after a violent blow. 2. without, or not subject to, a particular feeling: *insensible to shame.* 3. unconscious, unaware, or inappreciative: *we are not insensible of your kindness.* 4. not perceptible by the senses: *insensible transitions.* 5. unresponsive in feeling. 6. not susceptible of emotion or passion; void of any feeling. 7. *Now Rare.* not endowed with feeling or sensation, as matter. —in·sen′si·bly, *adv.*

in·sen·si·bil·i·ty (ĭn sĕn′sə bĭl′ə tĭ), *n., pl.* -ties. 1. lack of physical sensibility; absence of feeling or sensation. 2. lack of moral sensibility or susceptibility of emotion. —Syn. 2. See indifference.

in·sen·si·tive (ĭn sĕn′sə tĭv), *adj.* 1. not sensitive: *an insensitive skin.* 2. not susceptible to agencies or influences: *insensitive to light.* 3. deficient in sensibility or acuteness of feeling: *an insensitive nature.* —in·sen′si·tive·ness, in·sen′si·tiv′i·ty, *n.*

in·sen·ti·ent (ĭn sĕn′shĭ ənt, -shənt), *adj.* without sensation or feeling; inanimate. —in·sen′ti·ence, *n.*

in·sep·a·ra·ble (ĭn sĕp′ər ə bəl), *adj.* 1. incapable of being separated, parted, or disjoined: *inseparable companions.* —*n.* (*usually pl.*) 2. something inseparable. 3. an inseparable companion or friend. —in·sep′a·ra·bil′i·ty, in·sep′a·ra·ble·ness, *n.* —in·sep′a·ra·bly, *adv.*

in·sert (*v.* ĭn sûrt′; *n.* ĭn′sûrt), *v.t.* 1. to put or set in: *to insert a key in a lock.* 2. to introduce into the body of a paper: *to insert an ad in a newspaper.* —*n.* 3. something inserted, or to be inserted. 4. an extra leaf printed independently of the sheets comprising the book but included when the book is bound. 5. (in the postal service)

a paper, circular, etc., placed within the folds of a newspaper or the leaves of a book, periodical, etc. [t. L: s. *insertus,* pp., put in] —in·sert′er, *n.*

in·sert·ed (ĭn sûr′tĭd), *adj.* 1. *Bot.* (esp. of the parts of a flower) attached to or growing out of some part. 2. *Anat.* having an insertion, as a muscle, tendon, or ligament; attached, as the more movable end of a muscle.

in·ser·tion (ĭn sûr′shən), *n.* 1. act of inserting: *each insertion of an ad.* 2. something inserted: *an insertion into a text.* 3. *Bot., Zool., etc.* a. the manner or place of attachment, as of an organ. b. attachment of a part or organ, with special reference to the site or manner of such attachment. 4. lace, embroidery, or the like, to be sewed at each edge between parts of other material.

in·ses·so·ri·al (ĭn′sĕ sōr′ĭəl), *adj.* 1. adapted for perching, as a bird's foot. 2. habitually perching, as a bird. 3. of or pertaining to birds that perch. [f. s. NL *Inessorēs* the perching birds (considered as an order), pl. of *inessor* (f. *in* on + *sessor* sitter) + -IAL]

in·set (*n.* ĭn′sĕt′; *v.* ĭn sĕt′), *n., v.,* -set, -setting. —*n.* 1. something inserted; an insert. 2. a smaller picture, map, etc., inserted within the border of a larger one. 3. influx. 4. act of setting in. —*v.t.* 5. to set in; insert. 6. to insert as an inset. 7. to insert an inset in.

in·sheathe (ĭn shēth′), *v.t.,* -sheathed, -sheathing. to enclose in or as in a sheath; sheathe.

in·shore (ĭn′shōr′), *adj.* 1. close to the shore: *the ship lay inshore.* 2. lying near the shore; operating close to the shore: *inshore fishing.* —*adv.* 3. toward the shore: *they went closer inshore.* 4. inshore of, closer to the shore than: *inshore of the reef is a lagoon.*

in·shrine (ĭn shrīn′), *v.t.,* -shrined, -shrining. enshrine.

in·side (*prep., adv.* ĭn′sīd′; *n., adj.* ĭn′sīd′), *prep.* 1. inside of; within: *inside the circle.* —*adv.* 2. in or into the inner part: *to be inside.* 3. within the space or period (fol. by *of*): *to break down inside of a mile.* 4. on the inside: *he walks inside.* —*n.* 5. the inner part; interior: *the inside of the house.* 6. the inner side or surface: *the inside of the hand.* 7. (*often pl.*) *Colloq.* the inward parts of the body, esp. the stomach and intestines. 8. the inward nature. 9. an inside passenger or place in a coach, etc. 10. (*pl.*) internal thoughts or feelings, etc. —*adj.* 11. situated or being on or in the inside; interior; internal: *an inside seat.* 12. acting, employed, done, or originating within a building or place: *the robbery was an inside job.* 13. derived from the inner circle of those concerned in and having private knowledge of a case: *inside information.* 14. inside track, *Colloq.* advantage. —Syn. 5. INSIDE, INTERIOR both refer to the inner part or space within something. INSIDE is a common word, and is used with reference to things of any size, small or large: *the inside of a pocket.* INTERIOR, somewhat more formal, denotes the inner part or the space or the regions within; it usually suggests considerable size or extent, and sometimes a richness of decoration: *the interior of a country, of the earth; interior of a cathedral.* —Ant. 5. outside, exterior.

in·sid·er (ĭn·sī′dər), *n.* 1. one who is inside some place, society, etc. 2. *Colloq.* one who is within a limited circle of persons who understand the actual facts in a case. 3. *Colloq.* one who has some special advantage.

in·sid·i·ous (ĭn sĭd′ĭ əs), *adj.* 1. intended to entrap or beguile: *an insidious design.* 2. stealthily treacherous or deceitful: *an insidious enemy.* 3. operating or proceeding inconspicuously but with grave effect: *an insidious disease.* [t. L: s. *insidiōsus* cunning, artful] —in·sid′i·ous·ly, *adv.* —in·sid′i·ous·ness, *n.*

in·sight (ĭn′sīt′), *n.* 1. a sight had or given into something: *this little insight into the life of the village.* 2. penetrating mental vision or discernment; faculty of seeing into inner character or underlying truth: *a man of great insight.* 3. *Psychol.* a. the sudden grasping of a solution; configurational learning. b. the ability to see oneself as others see one; self-knowledge. c. (in psychiatry) the capacity of a mental patient to know that he is suffering from mental disorder. [ME; f. IN-[1] + SIGHT]

in·sig·ni·a (ĭn sĭg′nĭ ə), *n. pl., sing.* insigne (-nē). 1. badges or distinguishing marks of office of honor: *military insignia.* 2. distinguishing marks or signs of anything: *insignia of mourning.* [t. L, pl. of *insigne* mark, badge, prop. neut. of *insignis* distinguished by a mark]

in·sig·nif·i·cance (ĭn′sĭg nĭf′ə kəns), *n.* quality or condition of being insignificant; lack of significance.

in·sig·nif·i·can·cy (ĭn′sĭg nĭf′ə kən sĭ), *n., pl.* -cies. 1. insignificance. 2. an insignificant person or thing.

in·sig·nif·i·cant (ĭn′sĭg nĭf′ə kənt), *adj.* 1. unimportant, trifling, or petty, as things, matters, details, etc. 2. too small to be important: *an insignificant sum.* 3. of no consequence, influence, or distinction, as persons. 4. without weight of character; contemptible: *an insignificant fellow.* 5. without meaning; meaningless, as terms. —*n.* 6. a word, thing, or person without significance. —in·sig·nif′i·cant·ly, *adv.*

in·sin·cere (ĭn′sĭn sîr′), *adj.* not sincere; not honest in the expression of actual feeling. —in′sin·cere′ly, *adv.*

in·sin·cer·i·ty (ĭn′sĭn sĕr′ə tĭ), *n. pl.* -ties. quality of being insincere; lack of sincerity; deceitfulness.

in·sin·u·ate (ĭn sĭn′yŏŏ āt′), *v.,* -ated, -ating. —*v.t.* 1. to suggest or hint slyly. 2. to instill or infuse subtly or artfully into the mind: *to insinuate doubt.* 3. to bring or introduce into a position or relation by indirect or artful methods: *to insinuate oneself into the favor of another.* —*v.i.* 4. to make insinuations. [t. L: m.s. *in-*

sinuātus, pp., brought in by windings or turnings]
—**in·sin'u·at'ing·ly**, *adv.* —**in·sin'u·a'tive**, *adj.*
—**in·sin'u·a'tor**, *n.* —Syn. 1. See hint.

in·sin·u·a·tion (ĭn sĭn'yŏŏ ā'shən), *n.* 1. covert or artful suggestion or hinting, as of something not plainly stated. 2. a suggestion or hint of this kind. 3. subtle or artful instillment into the mind. 4. act of insinuating; a winding, worming, or stealing in. 5. ingratiation: *he made his way by flattery and insinuation.* 6. the art or power of stealing into the affections and pleasing. 7. an ingratiating act or speech.

in·sip·id (ĭn sĭp'ĭd), *adj.* 1. without distinctive, interesting, or attractive qualities: *an insipid tale.* 2. without sufficient taste to be pleasing, as food or drink: *a rather insipid fruit.* [t. LL: s. *insipidus* tasteless] —**in'si·pid'i·ty, in·sip'id·ness,** *n.* —**in·sip'id·ly,** *adv.*

in·sip·i·ence (ĭn sĭp'ĭ əns), *n.* lack of wisdom; folly. [late ME, t. L: m.s. *insipientia*] —**in·sip'i·ent,** *adj.*

in·sist (ĭn sĭst'), *v.i.* 1. to be emphatic, firm, or pertinacious on some matter of desire, demand, intention, etc.: *he insisted on that privilege.* 2. to lay emphasis in assertion: *to insist on the justice of a claim.* 3. to assert or maintain positively. 4. to dwell with earnestness or emphasis (fol. by *on* or *upon*): *to insist on a point in a discourse.* [t. L: s. *insistere* insist, stand or press upon] —**in·sist'er,** *n.*

in·sist·ence (ĭn sĭs'təns), *n.* 1. act or fact of insisting. 2. quality of being insistent.

in·sist·en·cy (ĭn sĭs'tən sĭ), *n., pl.* **-cies.** 1. quality of being insistent; insistence. 2. that which is insistent.

in·sist·ent (ĭn sĭs'tənt), *adj.* 1. insisting; earnest or emphatic in dwelling upon, maintaining, or demanding something; persistent. 2. compelling attention or notice: *an insistent tone.* —**in·sist'ent·ly,** *adv.*

in si·tu (ĭn sī'tū), *Latin.* in its original place.

in·snare (ĭn snâr'), *v.t.,* **-snared, -snaring.** ensnare.

in·so·bri·e·ty (ĭn'sə brī'ə tĭ), *n.* lack of sobriety.

in·so·cia·ble (ĭn sō'shə bəl), *adj. Rare.* unsociable. —**in·so'cia·bil'i·ty,** *n.* —**in·so'cia·bly,** *adv.*

in·so·far (ĭn'sə fär'), *adv.* to such an extent (usually fol. by *as*). Also, **in so far.**

in·so·late (ĭn'sō lāt'), *v.t.,* **-lated, -lating.** to expose to the sun's rays; treat by exposure to the sun's rays. [t. L: m.s. *insōlātus,* pp., placed in the sun]

in·so·la·tion (ĭn'sō lā'shən), *n.* 1. exposure to the sun's rays, specif. as a process of treatment. 2. sunstroke. 3. *Meteorol.* solar radiation received on a given body or over a given area. [t. LL: s. *insōlātiō*]

in·sole (ĭn'sōl'), *n.* 1. the inner sole of a shoe or boot. 2. a thickness of warm or waterproof material laid as an inner sole within a shoe.

in·so·lence (ĭn'sə ləns), *n.* 1. insolent behavior or speech. 2. the quality of being insolent.

in·so·lent (ĭn'sə lənt), *adj.* 1. boldly rude or disrespectful; contemptuously impertinent; insulting: *an insolent reply.* —*n.* 2. an insolent person. [ME, t. L: s. *insolens* unaccustomed, unusual, excessive, arrogant] —**in'so·lent·ly,** *adv.* —Syn. 1. See **impertinent.**

in·sol·u·ble (ĭn sŏl'yə bəl), *adj.* 1. incapable of being dissolved: *insoluble salts.* 2. that cannot be solved: *an insoluble problem.* [ME, t. L: s. *insolūbilis*] —**in·sol'u·bil'i·ty, in·sol'u·ble·ness,** *n.* —**in·sol'u·bly,** *adv.*

in·solv·a·ble (ĭn sŏl'və bəl), *adj.* incapable of being solved or explained: *an insolvable problem.*

in·sol·ven·cy (ĭn sŏl'vən sĭ), *n.* 1. the condition of being insolvent; bankruptcy.

in·sol·vent (ĭn sŏl'vənt), *Law.* —*adj.* 1. not solvent; unable to satisfy creditors or discharge liabilities, either because liabilities exceed assets or because of inability to pay debts as they mature. 2. pertaining to bankrupt persons or bankruptcy. —*n.* 3. one who is insolvent.

in·som·ni·a (ĭn sŏm'nĭ ə), *n.* inability to sleep, esp. when chronic; sleeplessness. [t. L] —**in·som'ni·ous,** *adj.*

in·som·ni·ac (ĭn sŏm'nĭ ăk'), *n.* one who suffers from insomnia.

in·so·much (ĭn'sō mŭch'), *adv.* 1. to such an extent or degree (*that*); so (*that*). 2. inasmuch (*as*).

in·sou·ci·ance (ĭn sōō'sĭ əns; *Fr.* ăN sōō syäNs'), *n.* the quality of being insouciant. [t. F, der. *insouciant* INSOUCIANT]

in·sou·ci·ant (ĭn sōō'sĭ ənt; *Fr.* ăN sōō syäN'), *adj.* free from concern; without anxiety; carefree. [t. F, der. *soucier* care, g. L *sollicitāre*] —**in·sou'ci·ant·ly,** *adv.*

in·soul (ĭn sōl'), *v.t.* ensoul.

in·span (ĭn spăn'), *v.t.,* **-spanned, -spanning.** *South Africa.* to yoke or harness. [t. D: m.s. *inspannen*]

in·spect (ĭn spĕkt'), *v.t.* 1. to look carefully at or over; view closely and critically: *to inspect every part.* 2. to view or examine formally or officially: *to inspect troops.* [t. L: s. *inspectus,* pp.]

in·spec·tion (ĭn spĕk'shən), *n.* 1. inspecting, esp. careful or critical inspecting or viewing. 2. formal or official viewing or examination: *an inspection of the troops.* 3. a district under an inspector. [ME, t. L: s. *inspectiō*] —**in·spec'tion·al,** *adj.* —Syn. 2. See **examination.**

in·spec·tive (ĭn spĕk'tĭv), *adj.* 1. given to making inspection. 2. pertaining to inspection.

in·spec·tor (ĭn spĕk'tər), *n.* 1. one who inspects. 2. an officer appointed to inspect. 3. an officer of police, usually ranking next below a superintendent. [t. L] —**in·spec'to·ral, in·spec·to·ri·al** (ĭn'spĕk tōr'ĭ əl), *adj.* —**in·spec'tor·ship',** *n.*

in·spec·tor·ate (ĭn spĕk'tər ĭt), *n.* 1. the office or function of an inspector. 2. a body of inspectors. 3. a district under an inspector.

in·sphere (ĭn sfîr'), *v.t.,* **-sphered, -sphering.** ensphere.

in·spir·a·ble (ĭn spîr'ə bəl), *adj.* capable of being inspired.

in·spi·ra·tion (ĭn'spə rā'shən), *n.* 1. an inspiring or animating action or influence: *I cannot write without inspiration.* 2. something inspired, as a thought. 3. a result of inspired activity. 4. a thing or person that inspires. 5. *Theol.* a. a divine influence directly and immediately exerted upon the mind or soul of a man. b. the divine quality of the writings or words of men so influenced. 6. the drawing of air into the lungs; inhalation. 7. act of inspiring. 8. state of being inspired.

in·spi·ra·tion·al (ĭn'spə rā'shən əl), *adj.* 1. imparting inspiration. 2. under the influence of inspiration; inspired. 3. of or pertaining to inspiration. —**in'spi·ra'tion·al·ly,** *adv.*

in·spi·ra·to·ry (ĭn spîr'ə tōr'ĭ), *adj.* pertaining to inspiration or inhalation.

in·spire (ĭn spīr'), *v.,* **-spired, -spiring.** —*v.t.* 1. to infuse an animating, quickening, or exalting influence into: *his courage inspired his followers.* 2. to produce or arouse (a feeling, thought, etc.): *to inspire confidence in others.* 3. to affect with a specified feeling, thought, etc.: *inspire a person with distrust.* 4. to influence or impel: *opposition inspired him to a greater effort.* 5. to animate, as an influence, feeling, thought, or the like does: *inspired by a belief in a better future.* 6. to communicate or suggest by a divine or supernatural influence: *writings inspired by God.* 7. to guide or control by divine influence. 8. to prompt or instigate (utterances, etc.) by influence without avowal of responsibility. 9. to give rise to, occasion, or cause. 10. to take (air, gases, etc.) into the lungs in breathing; inhale. 11. *Archaic.* to infuse (breath, life, etc. *into*) by breathing. 12. *Archaic.* to breathe into or upon. —*v.i.* 13. to give inspiration. 14. to inhale. [ME *inspire*(n), t. L: m. *inspīrāre* breathe into] —**in·spir'er,** *n.* —**in·spir'ing·ly,** *adv.*

in·spir·it (ĭn spîr'ĭt), *v.t.* to infuse (new) spirit or life into. —**in·spir'it·ing·ly,** *adv.*

in·spis·sate (ĭn spĭs'āt), *v.t., v.i.,* **-sated, -sating.** to thicken, as by evaporation; make or become dense. [t. LL: m.s. *inspissātus,* pp.] —**in'spis·sa'tion,** *n.*

inst., 1. instant. See **instant** (def. 5). 2. (*also cap.*) institute. 3. (*also cap.*) institution. 4. instrumental.

in·sta·bil·i·ty (ĭn'stə bĭl'ə tĭ), *n.* state of being instable; lack of stability or firmness.

in·sta·ble (ĭn stā'bəl), *adj.* not stable; unstable.

in·stall (ĭn stôl'), *v.t.* 1. to place in position for service or use, as a system of electric lighting, etc. 2. to establish in any office, position, or place. 3. to induct into an office, etc., with ceremonies or formalities, as by seating in a stall or official seat. [t. ML: s. *installāre.* See-[2], IN-STALL[1]] —**in·stall'er,** *n.*

in·stal·la·tion (ĭn'stə lā'shən), *n.* 1. something installed. 2. a system of machinery or apparatus placed in position for use. 3. act of installing. 4. fact of being installed. 5. *Mil.* any large supporting unit requiring much equipment, buildings, etc. [t. ML: s. *installātiō*]

in·stall·ment[1] (ĭn stôl'mənt), *n.* 1. any of several parts into which a debt or other sum payable is divided for payment at successive fixed times: *to pay for furniture by installments.* 2. a single portion of something furnished or issued by parts at successive times: *a serial in six installments.* Also, **in·stal'ment.** [f. IN-[2] + obs. *stalment* installment (der. STALL[1], v., arrange payment)]

in·stall·ment[2] (ĭn stôl'mənt), *n.* 1. act of installing. 2. fact of being installed; installation. Also, **in·stal'ment.** [f. INSTALL, v. + -MENT]

installment plan, *Chiefly U.S.* a system for paying a debt in fixed amounts at specified intervals.

in·stance (ĭn'stəns), *n., v.,* **-stanced, -stancing.** —*n.* 1. a case of anything: *fresh instances of oppression.* 2. an example put forth in proof or illustration: *an instance of carelessness.* 3. for instance, for example; as an example. 4. *Archaic.* urgency in speech or action. 5. at the instance of, at the urgency, solicitation, instigation, or suggestion of. 6. legal process (now chiefly in certain expressions): *a court of last instance.* 7. *Archaic.* urgency. 8. *Obs.* an impelling motive. —*v.t.* 9. to cite as an instance or example. 10. *Now Rare.* to exemplify by an instance. —*v.i.* 11. *Now Rare.* to cite an instance. [ME *instaunce,* t. AF, t. L: m.s. *instantia* presence, urgency] —Syn. 2. See **case**[1].

in·stan·cy (ĭn'stən sĭ), *n.* 1. quality of being instant; urgency; pressing nature. 2. *Rare.* immediateness.

in·stant (ĭn'stənt), *n.* 1. an infinitesimal or very short space of time; a moment: *not an instant too soon.* 2. the point of time now present, or present with reference to some action or event. 3. a particular moment: *at the instant of contact.* —*adj.* 4. succeeding without any interval of time; immediate: *instant relief.* 5. present; current (now used elliptically): *the 10th instant* (the tenth day of the present month). 6. pressing or urgent: *instant need.* —*adv.* 7. *Poetic.* instantly. [late ME, t. L: s. *instans,* ppr., standing upon, insisting, being at hand] —Syn. 1. See **minute**[1].

in·stan·ta·ne·ous (ĭn'stən tā'nĭ əs), *adj.* 1. occurring, done, or completed in an instant: *an instantaneous explosion.* 2. existing at or pertaining to a particular

---

b., blend of, blended; c., cognate with; d., dialect, dialectal; der., derived from; f., formed from; g., going back to; m., modification of; r., replacing; s., stem of; t., taken from; ?, perhaps. See the full key on inside cover.

instant: *the instantaneous position of something.* **—in/-stan·ta·ne·ous·ly,** *adv.* **—in/stan·ta/ne·ous·ness,** *n.*

in·stan·ter (ĭn stăn/tər), *adv.* instantly. [t. L: urgently]

in·stant·ly (ĭn/stənt lĭ), *adv.* **1.** immediately; at once. **2.** *Archaic.* urgently. **—Syn. 1.** See **immediately.**

in·star[1] (ĭn/stär), *n.* an insect in any one of its periods of postembryonic growth between molts. [t. L: form, likeness]

in·star[2] (ĭn stär/), *v.t.,* **-starred, -starring. 1.** to place as a star. **2.** to make a star of. **3.** to set with or as with stars. [f. IN-[1] + STAR]

in·state (ĭn stāt/), *v.t.,* **-stated, -stating. 1.** to put into a certain state, condition, or position; install. **2.** *Obs.* to endow with something. **—in·state/ment,** *n.*

in sta·tu quo (ĭn stā/tū kwō/, stăch/ōō), *Latin.* in the state in which (anything was or is).

in·stau·ra·tion (ĭn/stô rā/shən), *n.* renewal; restoration; renovation; repair. [t. L: s. *instaurātio*]

in·stead (ĭn stĕd/), *adv.* **1.** in the stead or place; in lieu (fol. by *of*): *come by plane instead of by train.* **2.** in one's (its, their, etc.) stead: *she sent the boy instead.* [orig. two words, *in stead* in place]

in·step (ĭn/stĕp/), *n.* **1.** the arched upper surface of the human foot between the toes and the ankle. **2.** the part of a shoe, stocking, etc., over the instep. **3.** the front of the hind leg of a horse, etc., between the hock and the pastern joint; cannon. [appar. f. IN-[1] + STEP, but with orig. notion uncert.]

in·sti·gate (ĭn/stə gāt/), *v.t.,* **-gated, -gating. 1.** to spur on, set on, or incite to some action or course: *to instigate someone to commit a crime.* **2.** to bring about by incitement; foment: *to instigate a quarrel.* [t. L: m.s. *instīgātus,* pp.] **—in/sti·ga/tive,** *adj.* **—in/sti·ga/tor,** *n.*

in·sti·ga·tion (ĭn/stə gā/shən), *n.* **1.** act of instigating. **2.** an incentive. [late ME, t. L: s. *instīgātio*]

in·stil (ĭn stĭl/), *v.t.,* **-stilled, -stilling.** instill. **—in·stil/ment,** *n.*

in·still (ĭn stĭl/), *v.t.* **1.** to infuse slowly or by degrees into the mind or feelings; insinuate; inject: *courtesy must be instilled in childhood.* **2.** to put in drop by drop. [t. L: s. *instīllāre* pour in by drops] **—in·still/er,** *n.* **—in·still/ment,** *n.*

in·stil·la·tion (ĭn/stə lā/shən), *n.* **1.** act of instilling. **2.** something instilled.

in·stinct[1] (ĭn/stĭngkt), *n.* **1.** *Sociol., Psychol., etc.* an inborn pattern of activity and re ponse common to a given biological stock. **2.** innate impulse or natural inclination, or a particular natural inclination or tendency. **3.** a natural aptitude or gift for something: *an instinct for art.* **4.** natural intuitive power. [late ME, t. L: s. *instinctus,* n., instigation, impulse]

in·stinct[2] (ĭn stĭngkt/), *adj.* urged or animated from within; infused or filled with some active principle (fol. by *with*). [t. L: s. *instinctus,* pp., instigated, impelled]

in·stinc·tive (ĭn stĭngk/tĭv), *adj.* **1.** pertaining to or of the nature of instinct. **2.** prompted by or resulting from instinct. Also, **in·stinc·tu·al** (ĭn stĭngk/chŏō əl), *adj.* **—in·stinc/tive·ly,** *adv.*

in·sti·tute (ĭn/stə tūt/, -tōōt/), *v.,* **-tuted, -tuting,** *n.* **—v.t. 1.** to set up or establish: *institute a government.* **2.** to set on foot; inaugurate; initiate: *institute a new course.* **3.** to set in operation: *institute a suit.* **4.** to bring into use or practice: *to institute laws.* **5.** to establish in an office or position. **6.** *Eccles.* to assign to or invest with a spiritual charge. **—n. 7.** a society or organization for carrying on a particular work, as of literary, scientific, or educational character. **8.** the building occupied by such a society. **9.** *Educ.* an institution, generally beyond the secondary school level, devoted to instruction in technical subjects, usually separate but sometimes organized as a part of a university. **b.** a unit within a university organized for advanced instruction and research in a relatively narrow field of subject matter. **c.** a short instructional program set up for a special group interested in some specialized type of activity. **10.** an established principle, law, custom, or organization. **11.** (*pl.*) an elementary textbook of law designed for beginners. **12.** something instituted. [ME *institut,* pp., set up, established, t. L: s. *institūtus*]

in·sti·tut·er (ĭn/stə tū/tər, -tōō/-), *n.* institutor.

in·sti·tu·tion (ĭn/stə tū/shən, -tōō/-), *n.* **1.** an organization or establishment for the promotion of a particular object, usually one for some public, educational, charitable, or similar purpose. **2.** the building devoted to such work. **3.** a concern engaged in some activity, as a retail store, broker, or insurance company. **4.** *Sociol.* an organized pattern of group behavior, well-established and accepted as a fundamental part of a culture, such as slavery. **5.** any established law, custom, etc. **6.** *Colloq.* any familiar practice or object. **7.** act of instituting or setting up; establishment: *the institution of laws.* **8.** *Eccles.* **a.** the origination of the Eucharist, and enactment of its observance, by Christ. **b.** the investment of a clergyman with a spiritual charge.

in·sti·tu·tion·al (ĭn/stə tū/shən əl, -tōō/-), *adj.* **1.** of, pertaining to, or established by institution. **2.** pertaining to organized societies or to the buildings devoted to their work. **3.** of the nature of an institution. **4.** *Advertising.* having good will and a wider reputation as the primary object rather than the securing of present purchasers. **5.** pertaining to institutes or principles, esp. of jurisprudence. **—in/sti·tu/tion·al·ly,** *adv.*

in·sti·tu·tion·al·ism (ĭn/stə tū/shən ə lĭz/əm, -tōō/-), *n.* **1.** the system of institutions or organized societies for public, charitable, or similar purposes. **2.** strong attachment to established institutions, as of religion.

in·sti·tu·tion·al·ize (ĭn/stə tū/shən ə līz/, -tōō/-), *v.t.,* **-ized, -izing. 1.** to make institutional. **2.** to make into or treat as an institution.

in·sti·tu·tion·ar·y (ĭn/stə tū/shə nĕr/ĭ, -tōō/-), *adj.* **1.** of or relating to an institution or to institutions; institutional. **2.** of or pertaining to institution, esp. ecclesiastical institution.

in·sti·tu·tive (ĭn/stə tū/tĭv, -tōō/-), *adj.* tending or intended to institute or establish. **—in/sti·tu/tive·ly,** *adv.*

in·sti·tu·tor (ĭn/stə tū/tər, -tōō/-), *n.* **1.** one who institutes or founds. **2.** *Prot. Episc. Ch.* one who institutes a minister into a parish or church. Also, **instituter.**

instr., 1. instructor. **2.** instrument. **3.** instrumental.

in·struct (ĭn strŭkt/), *v.t.* **1.** to direct or command; furnish with orders or directions: *the doctor instructed me to diet.* **2.** to furnish with knowledge, esp. by a systematic method; teach; train; educate. **3.** to furnish with information; inform or apprise. **4.** *Law.* (of a judge) tc outline or explain the legal principles involved in a case, for the guidance of (the jury). [late ME *instructe,* t. L: m.s. *instructus,* pp., built, prepared, furnished, instructed] **—Syn. 2.** tutor, coach; drill, discipline; indoctrinate; school.

in·struc·tion (ĭn strŭk/shən), *n.* **1.** act or practice of instructing or teaching; education. **2.** knowledge or information imparted. **3.** an item of such knowledge or information. **4.** (*usually pl.*) an order or direction. **5.** act of furnishing with authoritative directions. [late ME, *instruccion,* t. L: m.s. *instructio*] **—in·struc/tion·al,** *adj.* **—Syn. 1.** tutoring, coaching; training, drill; indoctrination; schooling. **5.** command, mandate.

in·struc·tive (ĭn strŭk/tĭv), *adj.* serving to instruct or inform; conveying instruction, knowledge, or information. **—in·struc/tive·ly,** *adv.* **—in·struc/tive·ness,** *n.*

in·struc·tor (ĭn strŭk/tər), *n.* **1.** one who instructs; a teacher. **2.** the academic rank given in American colleges to a teacher inferior in grade to the lowest grade of professor. [late ME, t. ML: teacher, L preparer] **—instruc/tor·less,** *adj.* **—in·struc/tor·ship/,** *n.* **—in·struc·tress** (ĭn strŭk/trĭs), *n. fem.* **—Syn. 1.** tutor, schoolmaster, preceptor, pedagogue.

in·stru·ment (ĭn/strə mənt), *n.* **1.** a mechanical device or contrivance; a tool; an implement: *a surgeon's instruments.* **2.** a contrivance for producing musical sounds: *a stringed instrument.* **3.** a thing with or by which something is effected; a means; an agency: *an instrument of government.* **4.** a formal legal document, as a contract, promissory note, deed, grant, etc. **5.** one who is used by another. **6.** a device for measuring the present value of the quantity under observation. [ME, t. L: m.s. *instrūmentum*] **—Syn. 1.** See **tool.**

in·stru·men·tal (ĭn/strə mĕn/təl), *adj.* **1.** serving as an instrument or means. **2.** of or pertaining to an instrument. **3.** helpful; useful. **4.** performed on or written for a musical instrument or musical instruments: *instrumental music.* **5.** *Gram.* **a.** (in some inflected languages) denoting a case having as its chief function the indication of means or agency. For example: Old English *beseah blīthe andweitan* "looked with a happy countenance." **b.** denoting the affix or other element characteristic of this case, or a word containing such an element. **c.** similar to such a case form in function or meaning, as the Latin *instrumental ablative, gladiō* "by means of a sword." **—n. 6.** *Gram.* **a.** the instrumental case. **b.** a word in that case. **c.** a construction of similar meaning. [ME, t. ML: s. *instrūmentālis*]

in·stru·men·tal·ism (ĭn/strə mĕn/tə lĭz/əm), *n. Philos.* the theory that the function of thought is to be instrumental to control of the environment, or that ideas have value according to their function in human experience or progress.

in·stru·men·tal·ist (ĭn/strə mĕn/tə lĭst), *n.* **1.** one who performs on a musical instrument. **2.** an advocate of instrumentalism. **—in·stru·men/tal·is/tic,** *adj.*

in·stru·men·tal·i·ty (ĭn/strə mĕn/tăl/ə tĭ), *n., pl.* **-ties. 1.** the quality of being instrumental. **2.** the fact or function of serving some purpose. **3.** a means or agency. **4.** helpfulness; usefulness.

in·stru·men·tal·ly (ĭn/strə mĕn/tə lĭ), *adv.* **1.** by the use of an instrument. **2.** with or on an instrument.

in·stru·men·ta·tion (ĭn/strə mĕn tā/shən), *n.* **1.** the arranging of music for instruments, esp. for an orchestra. **2.** the use of, or work done by, instruments. **3.** instrumental agency; instrumentality.

in·sub·or·di·nate (ĭn/sə bôr/də nĭt), *adj.* **1.** not submitting to authority; disobedient: *insubordinate crew.* **2.** not lower. **—n. 3.** one who is insubordinate. **—in/sub·or/di·nate·ly,** *adv.* **—in/sub·or/di·na/tion,** *n.*

in·sub·stan·tial (ĭn/səb stăn/shəl), *adj.* **1.** not substantial; slight. **2.** without reality; unreal: *this insubstantial pageant.* **—in/sub·stan/ti·al/i·ty,** *n.*

in·suf·fer·a·ble (ĭn sŭf/ər ə bəl), *adj.* not to be endured; intolerable; unbearable: *insufferable insolence.* **—in·suf/fer·a·ble·ness,** *n.* **—in·suf/fer·a·bly,** *adv.*

in·suf·fi·cien·cy (ĭn/sə fĭsh/ən sĭ), *n.* deficiency in amount, force, or fitness; inadequateness: *insufficiency of supplies.* Also, **in/suf·fi/cience.**

in·suf·fi·cient (ĭn/sə fĭsh/ənt), *adj.* **1.** not sufficient; lacking in what is necessary or required: *an insufficient* *answer.* **2.** deficient in force, quality, or amount; inadequate: *insufficient protection.* **—in'suf·fi'cient·ly,** *adv.*

in·suf·flate (ĭn·sŭf'lāt, ĭn'sə flāt'), *v.t.,* **-flated, -flating. 1.** to blow or breathe (something) in. **2.** *Med.* to blow (air or a medicinal substance) into some opening or upon some part of the body. **3.** *Eccles.* to breathe upon, especially upon one being baptized or the water of baptism. [t. LL: m.s. *insufflātus,* pp., breathed into] **—in'·suf·fla'tion,** *n.* **—in·suf·fla·tor** (ĭn'sə flā'tər), *n.*

in·su·lar (ĭn'sə lər), *adj.* **1.** of or pertaining to an island or islands: *insular possessions.* **2.** dwelling or situated on an island. **3.** forming an island: *insular rocks.* **4.** detached; standing alone. **5.** characteristic or suggestive of inhabitants of an island. **6.** narrow or illiberal: *insular prejudices.* **7.** *Pathol.* occurring in or characterized by one or more isolated spots, patches, or the like. **8.** *Anat.* pertaining to existing tissue, as an island (def. 6), esp. to Langerhans Islets. **—n. 9.** an inhabitant of an island. [t. LL: s. *insulāris* an island] **—in·su·lar·i·ty** (ĭn'sə lăr'ə tĭ), *n.* **—in'su·lar·ism,** *n.* **—in'su·lar·ly,** *adv.*

in·su·late (ĭn'sə lāt'), *v.t.,* **-lated, -lating. 1.** to cover or surround (an electric wire, etc.) with nonconducting material. **2.** *Physics, etc.* to separate by the interposition of a nonconductor, in order to prevent or reduce the transfer of electricity, heat, or sound. **3.** to place in an isolated situation or condition; segregate. [t. L: m.s. *insulātus* made into an island]

in·su·la·tion (ĭn'sə lā'shən), *n.* **1.** material used for insulating. **2.** act of insulating. **3.** resulting state.

in·su·la·tor (ĭn'sə lā'tər), *n.* **1.** *Elect.* **a.** a material of such low conductivity that the flow of current through it can usually be neglected. **b.** insulating material, often glass or porcelain, in a unit form so designed as to support a charged conductor and electrically isolate it. **2.** one who or that which insulates.

in·su·lin (ĭn'sə lĭn), *n.* **1.** *Med.* an extract obtained from the pancreas of animals (which apparently contains the hormone of this organ, furnished by its islands), used in the treatment of diabetes, and causing a reduction of sugar in the blood and urine. **2.** (*cap.*) a trademark for this extract. [f. s. L *insula* island (with reference to the islands of the pancreas) + -IN²]

in·sult (*v.* ĭn sŭlt'; *n.* ĭn'sŭlt), *v.t.* **1.** to treat insolently or with contemptuous rudeness; affront. **2.** *Rare.* to attack; assault. **—v.i. 3.** *Archaic.* to behave with insolent triumph; exult contemptuously (fol. by *on, upon,* or *over*). **—n. 4.** an insolent or contemptuously rude action or speech; affront. **5.** something having the effect of an affront. **6.** *Archaic.* an attack or assault. [t. L: s. *insultāre* leap on or at, insult] **—in·sult'er,** *n.* **—in·sult'ing,** *adj.* **—in·sult'ing·ly,** *adv.*

—Syn. 4. INSULT, INDIGNITY, AFFRONT, SLIGHT imply an act which injures another's honor, self-respect, etc. INSULT implies such insolence of speech or manner as deeply humiliates or wounds one's feelings and arouses to anger. INDIGNITY is especially used of inconsiderate, contemptuous treatment towards one entitled to respect. AFFRONT implies open disrespect or offense shown, as it were, to the face; SLIGHT, perhaps only inadvertent, indifference or disregard, but may indicate ill-concealed contempt.

in·su·per·a·ble (ĭn sōō'pər ə bəl), *adj.* incapable of being passed over, overcome, or surmounted: *an insuperable barrier.* **—in·su'per·a·bil'i·ty, in·su'per·a·ble·ness,** *n.* **—in·su'per·a·bly,** *adv.*

in·sup·port·a·ble (ĭn'sə pôr'tə bəl), *adj.* not endurable; insufferable. **—in'sup·port'a·ble·ness,** *n.* **—in'·sup·port'a·bly,** *adv.*

in·sup·press·i·ble (ĭn'sə prĕs'ə bəl), *adj.* that cannot be suppressed. **—in'sup·press'i·bly,** *adv.*

in·sur·a·ble (ĭn shŏŏr'ə bəl), *adj.* **1.** capable of being insured, as against risk of loss or harm. **2.** proper to be insured. **—in·sur'a·bil'i·ty,** *n.*

in·sur·ance (ĭn shŏŏr'əns), *n.* **1.** the act, system, or business of insuring property, life, the person, etc., against loss or harm arising in specified contingencies, as fire, accident, death, disablement, or the like, in consideration of a payment proportioned to the risk involved. **2.** the contract thus made, set forth in a written or printed agreement (policy). **3.** the amount for which anything is insured. **4.** the premium paid for insuring a thing.

in·sur·ant (ĭn shŏŏr'ənt), *n.* the person who takes out an insurance policy.

in·sure (ĭn shŏŏr'), *v.,* **-sured, -suring. —v.t. 1.** to make sure, secure, or certain: *to insure one's safety.* **2.** to guarantee against risk of loss or harm. **3.** to secure indemnity to or on, in case of loss, damage, or death. **4.** to issue or procure an insurance policy on. **—v.i. 5.** to issue or procure an insurance policy. [var. of ENSURE]

in·sured (ĭn shŏŏrd'), *n.* a person covered by an insurance policy.

in·sur·er (ĭn shŏŏr'ər), *n.* **1.** one who contracts to indemnify against losses, etc. **2.** one who insures.

in·sur·gence (ĭn sûr'jəns), *n.* an act of insurgency.

in·sur·gen·cy (ĭn sûr'jən sĭ), *n.* **1.** state of being insurgent. **2.** a condition of insurrection against an existing government by a group not recognized as a belligerent.

in·sur·gent (ĭn sûr'jənt), *n.* **1.** one who rises in forcible opposition to lawful authority; one who engages in armed resistance to a government or to the execution of laws. **2.** *U.S. Pol.* a member of a section of a political party that revolts against the methods or policies of the party. **—adj. 3.** rising in revolt; rebellious. [t. L: s. *insurgens,* ppr., rising on or up]

in·sur·mount·a·ble (ĭn'sər moun'tə bəl), *adj.* incapable of being surmounted, passed over, or overcome: *an insurmountable obstacle.* **—in'sur·mount'a·bly,** *adv.*

in·sur·rec·tion (ĭn'sə rĕk'shən), *n.* **1.** act of rising in arms or open resistance against civil or established authority. **2.** a revolt. [late ME, t. LL: s. *insurrectio,* der. L *insurgere* rise up] **—in'sur·rec'tion·al,** *adj.* **—in'·sur·rec'tion·al·ly,** *adv.* **—in'sur·rec'tion·ism,** *n.* **—in'sur·rec'tion·ist,** *n.* **—Syn. 2.** See revolt.

in·sur·rec·tion·ar·y (ĭn'sə rĕk'shə nĕr'ĭ), *adj., n., pl.* **-aries. —adj. 1.** pertaining to or of the nature of insurrection. **2.** given to insurrection. **—n. 3.** one who engages in insurrection; an insurgent.

in·sus·cep·ti·ble (ĭn'sə sĕp'tə bəl), *adj.* **1.** not admitting (fol. by *of*): *insusceptible of flattery.* **2.** not accessible or sensitive (fol. by *to*): *insusceptible to infection.* **—in'sus·cep'ti·bil'i·ty,** *n.*

in·swathe (ĭn swāth'), *v.t.,* **-swathed, -swathing.** to enswathe.

in·swept (ĭn'swĕpt'), *adj.* tapering at the front or tip, as an airplane wing.

int., 1. interest. **2.** interior. **3.** interjection. **4.** internal. **5.** international. **6.** interpreter. **7.** intransitive.

in·tact (ĭn tăkt'), *adj.* remaining uninjured, unaltered, sound, or whole; unimpaired. [late ME, t. L: s. *intactus*] **—in·tact'ness,** *n.* **—Syn.** See complete.

in·tagl·io (ĭn tăl'yō, -tāl'-; *It.* ēn tä'lyō), *n., pl.* **intaglios, intagli** (ĕn tä'lyē). **1.** a gem, seal, piece of jewelry, or the like, cut with an incised or sunken design. **2.** incised carving, as opposed to carving in relief. **3.** ornamentation with a figure or design sunk below the surface. **4.** an incised or countersunk die. **5.** a figure or design so produced. **6.** a printmaking process by which the printing ink is transferred to paper, etc., from areas sunk below the surface. [t. It., der. *intagliare* cut in, engrave]

in·take (ĭn'tāk'), *n.* **1.** the point at which a fluid is taken into a channel, pipe, etc. **2.** act of taking in. **3.** that which is taken in. **4.** quantity taken in: *the intake of oxygen.* **5.** a narrowing or contraction.

in·tan·gi·ble (ĭn tăn'jə bəl), *adj.* **1.** incapable of being perceived by the sense of touch, as incorporeal or immaterial things. **2.** not definite or clear to the mind: *intangible arguments.* **3.** (of an asset) existing only in connection with something else, as the good will of a business. **—n. 4.** something intangible. **—in·tan'gi·bil'i·ty, in·tan'gi·ble·ness,** *n.* **—in·tan'gi·bly,** *adv.*

in·tar·si·a (ĭn tär'sĭ ə), *n.* a highly developed form of inlay or marquetry in wood produced in Italy during the Renaissance period. [t. It., der. *intarsiare* inlay]

in·te·ger (ĭn'tə jər), *n.* **1.** one of the numbers 0, 1, 2, 3, 4, etc.; a whole number, as distinguished from a fraction or a mixed number. **2.** a complete entity. [t. L: untouched, whole, entire]

in·te·ger vi·tae (ĭn'tə jər vī'tē), *Latin.* blameless in life; innocent. (Horace, *Odes,* I.)

in·te·gra·ble (ĭn'tə grə bəl), *adj. Math.* capable of being integrated, as a mathematical function or differential equation.

in·te·gral (ĭn'tə grəl), *adj.* **1.** of or pertaining to a whole; belonging as a part of the whole; constituent or component: *the integral parts of the human body.* **2.** necessary to the completeness of the whole. **3.** made up of parts which together constitute a whole. **4.** entire or complete: *his integral love.* **5.** *Arith.* pertaining to or being an integer; not fractional. **6.** *Math.* pertaining to or involving integrals. **—n. 7.** an integral whole. **8.** *Math.* the result of the operation inverse to differentiation (see **integration,** def. 4); an expression from which a given function, equation, or system of equations is derived by differentiation. [t. LL: s. *integrālis*] **—in·te·gral·i·ty** (ĭn'tə grăl'ə tĭ), *n.* **—in'te·gral·ly,** *adv.*

integral calculus, the branch of mathematics dealing with the finding and properties of integrals.

in·te·grand (ĭn'tə grănd'), *n. Math.* the expression to be integrated. [t. L: s. *integrandus,* ger. of *integrāre* make whole]

in·te·grant (ĭn'tə grənt), *adj.* **1.** making up, or belonging as a part to, a whole; constituent. **—n. 2.** an integrant part. [t. L: s. *integrans,* ppr., making whole]

in·te·grate (ĭn'tə grāt'), *v.,* **-grated, -grating. —v.t. 1.** to bring together (parts) into a whole. **2.** to make up or complete as a whole, as parts do. **3.** to indicate the total amount or the mean value of. **4.** *Math.* to find the integral of. **5.** *U.S.* to combine educational facilities and student bodies, previously segregated by race, into one unified system. **—v.i. 6.** *U.S.* (of school systems, etc.) to become unified. [t. L: m.s. *integrātus,* pp., made whole] **—in'te·gra'tive,** *adj.*

in·te·gra·tion (ĭn'tə grā'shən), *n.* **1.** act of integrating; combination into an integral whole. **2.** behavior, as of the individual, in harmony with the environment. **3.** *Psychol.* the organization of personality traits into a hierarchy of functions. **4.** *Math.* the operation of finding the integral of a function or equation (the inverse of *differentiation*). **5.** *U.S.* the combination of educational and other public facilities, previously segregated by race, into one unified system. [t. L: s. *integratio* renewal, restoration]

in·te·gra·tion·ist (ĭn'tə grā'shən ĭst), *n. U.S.* one who favors integration (def. 5.).

in·te·gra·tor (ĭn'tə grā'tər), *n.* **1.** one who or that which integrates. **2.** an instrument for performing numerical integrations.

in·teg·ri·ty (ĭn tĕg′rə tĭ), *n.* **1.** soundness of moral principle and character; uprightness; honesty. **2.** state of being whole, entire, or undiminished: *to preserve the integrity of the empire.* **3.** sound, unimpaired, or perfect condition: *the integrity of the text.* [late ME, t. L: m.s. *integritas*] **—Syn. 1.** See **honor.**

in·teg·u·ment (ĭn tĕg′yə mənt), *n.* **1.** a skin, shell, rind, or the like. **2.** a covering. [t. L: s. *integumentum*]

in·teg·u·men·ta·ry (ĭn tĕg′yə mĕn′tə rĭ), *adj.* of, pertaining to, or like an integument.

in·tel·lect (ĭn′tə lĕkt′), *n.* **1.** the power or faculty of the mind by which one knows or understands, in distinction from that by which one feels and that by which one wills; the understanding. **2.** understanding or mental capacity, esp. of a high order. **3.** a particular mind or intelligence, esp. of a high order. **4.** the person possessing it. **5.** minds collectively, as of a number of persons, or the persons themselves. [ME, t. L: s. *intellectus* a discerning, perceiving] **—Syn. 1.** See **mind.**

in·tel·lec·tion (ĭn′tə lĕk′shən), *n.* **1.** the action or process of understanding; the exercise of the intellect. **2.** a particular act of the intellect. **3.** a conception or idea as the result of such an act.

in·tel·lec·tive (ĭn′tə lĕk′tĭv), *adj.* **1.** having power to understand; intelligent. **2.** of or pertaining to the intellect. **—in′tel·lec′tive·ly,** *adv.*

in·tel·lec·tu·al (ĭn′tə lĕk′chŏŏ əl), *adj.* **1.** appealing to or engaging the intellect: *intellectual pursuits.* **2.** of or pertaining to the intellect: *intellectual powers.* **3.** directed or inclined toward things that involve the intellect: *intellectual tastes.* **4.** possessing or showing intellect or mental capacity, esp. to a high degree: *an intellectual writer.* **5.** characterized by or suggesting a predominance of intellect: *an intellectual face.* **—n. 6.** an intellectual being or person. **7.** (*often pl.*) a member of a class or group professing, or supposed to possess, enlightened judgment and opinions with respect to public or political questions. **8.** (*pl.*) *Rare.* things pertaining to the intellect. **9.** (*pl.*) *Archaic.* the mental faculties. [ME, t. L: s. *intellectuālis*] **—in′tel·lec′tu·al·ly,** *adv.* **—in′tel·lec′tu·al·ness,** *n.* **—Syn. 4.** See **intelligent.**

in·tel·lec·tu·al·ism (ĭn′tə lĕk′chŏŏ ə lĭz′əm), *n.* **1.** the exercise of the intellect; devotion to intellectual pursuits. **2.** *Philos.* **a.** the doctrine that knowledge is wholly or chiefly derived from pure reason. **b.** the belief that reason is the final principle of reality. **—in′tel·lec′tu·al·ist,** *n.* **—in′tel·lec′tu·al·is′tic,** *adj.*

in·tel·lec·tu·al·i·ty (ĭn′tə lĕk′chŏŏ ăl′ə tĭ), *n., pl.* **-ties. 1.** quality of being intellectual. **2.** intellectual character or power.

in·tel·lec·tu·al·ize (ĭn′tə lĕk′chŏŏ ə līz′), *v.t., v.i.,* **-ized, -izing.** to make or become intellectual. **—in′tel·lec′tu·al·i·za′tion,** *n.*

in·tel·li·gence (ĭn tĕl′ə jəns), *n.* **1.** capacity for understanding and for other forms of adaptive behavior; aptitude in grasping truths, facts, meaning. **2.** good mental capacity: *a task requiring intelligence.* **3.** the faculty of understanding. **4.** (*often cap.*) an intelligent being, esp. an incorporeal one. **5.** knowledge of an event, circumstance, etc., received or imparted; news; information. **6.** the gathering or distribution of information, esp. secret information. **7.** a staff of persons engaged in obtaining such information; secret service. **8.** *Rare.* interchange of information, thoughts, etc., or communication. **—Syn. 1.** See **mind.**

intelligence bureau, a governmental department charged with obtaining information, esp. for the use of the army or navy. Also, **intelligence department.**

intelligence office, 1. an intelligence bureau. **2.** *U.S. Obs.* an employment office, esp. for servants.

intelligence quotient, the mental age divided by the actual age. A child with a mental age of 12 years and an actual age of 10 years has an intelligence quotient, or IQ, of 1.2 (usually expressed as 120). In the computation of the IQ, age above 15 or 16 is commonly ignored.

in·tel·li·genc·er (ĭn tĕl′ə jən sər), *n.* **1.** one who or that which conveys information. **2.** an informer; a spy.

intelligence test, any of several psychological tests, either verbal or nonverbal, which attempt to measure the mental development of an individual.

in·tel·li·gent (ĭn tĕl′ə jənt), *adj.* **1.** having a good understanding or mental capacity; quick to understand, as persons or animals: *intelligent statesmen.* **2.** showing quickness of understanding, as actions, utterances, etc.: *an intelligent answer.* **3.** having the faculty of understanding: *an intelligent being.* **4.** *Rare.* having understanding or knowledge (fol. by *of*). [t. L: s. *intelligens,* var. of *intellegens,* ppr.] **—in·tel′li·gent·ly,** *adv.*
—Syn. 1. INTELLIGENT, INTELLECTUAL describe distinctive mental capacity. INTELLIGENT often suggests a natural quickness of understanding: *an intelligent reader.* INTELLECTUAL implies not only having a high degree of understanding, but also a capacity and taste for the higher forms of knowledge: *intellectual interests.* **2.** See **sharp.**

in·tel·li·gen·tial (ĭn tĕl′ə jĕn′shəl), *adj.* **1.** of or pertaining to the intelligence or understanding. **2.** endowed with intelligence. **3.** conveying information.

in·tel·li·gent·si·a (ĭn tĕl′ə jĕnt′sĭ ə, -gĕnt′sĭ ə), *n.pl.* a class or group of persons having or claiming special enlightenment in views or principles; the intellectuals. [t. Russ., t. L: m. *intelligentia* intelligence]

in·tel·li·gi·bil·i·ty (ĭn tĕl′ə jə bĭl′ə tĭ), *n., pl.* **-ties. 1.** quality or character of being intelligible; capability of being understood. **2.** something intelligible.

in·tel·li·gi·ble (ĭn tĕl′ə jə bəl), *adj.* **1.** capable of being understood; comprehensible: *an intelligible reason.* **2.** *Philos.* apprehensible by the mind. [ME, t. L: m.s. *intelligibilis,* var. of *intellegibilis*] **—in·tel′li·gi·ble·ness,** *n.* **—in·tel′li·gi·bly,** *adv.*

in·tem·er·ate (ĭn tĕm′ər ĭt), *adj.* *Now Rare.* inviolate; undefiled; unsullied; pure. [t. L: m.s. *intemerātus*]

in·tem·per·ance (ĭn tĕm′pər əns, -prəns), *n.* **1.** immoderate indulgence in alcoholic liquors. **2.** excessive indulgence of a natural appetite or passion. **3.** lack of moderation or due restraint, as in action or speech.

in·tem·per·ate (ĭn tĕm′pər ĭt, -prĭt), *adj.* **1.** given to or characterized by immoderate indulgence in intoxicating drink. **2.** immoderate as regards indulgence of appetite or passion. **3.** not temperate; unrestrained or unbridled. **4.** extreme in temperature, as climate, etc. **—in·tem′per·ate·ly,** *adv.* **—in·tem′per·ate·ness,** *n.*

in·tend (ĭn tĕnd′), *v.t.* **1.** to have in mind as something to be done or brought about: *he intends to enlist.* **2.** to design or mean for a particular purpose, use, recipient, etc.: *a book intended for reference.* **3.** to design to express or indicate. **4.** *Obs.* (of words, etc.) to signify. **5.** *Archaic.* to direct (the eyes, mind, etc.). **—v.i. 6.** to have a purpose or design: *he may intend otherwise.* **7.** *Obs.* to set out on one's course. [ME *intende(n),* t. L: m. *intendere* extend, intend; r. ME *entenden,* t. OF: m. *entendre*] **—in·tend′er,** *n.*
—Syn. 1. INTEND, MEAN, DESIGN, PROPOSE imply knowing what one wishes to do and setting this as a goal. TO INTEND is to have in mind something willed to be done or brought about: *no offense was intended.* MEAN is a simpler word for the same idea as INTEND, but suggests perhaps less definite thought or conscious choice: *he means to go away.* DESIGN implies planning to effect a particular result; the things to be done have a definite relationship to one another: *to design a plan for Christmas decorations.* PROPOSE suggests setting up a program before oneself for accomplishment, or offering it for consideration: *we propose to beautify our city.*

in·tend·ance (ĭn tĕn′dəns), *n.* **1.** a department of the public service, as in France, or the officials in charge of it. **2.** the official quarters of an intendant. **3.** the function of an intendant; superintendence; intendancy.

in·tend·an·cy (ĭn tĕn′dən sĭ), *n., pl.* **-cies. 1.** the office or function of an intendant. **2.** a body of intendants. **3.** a district under the charge of an intendant. [t. Sp.: m. *intendencia*]

in·tend·ant (ĭn tĕn′dənt), *n.* **1.** one who has the direction or management of some public business, the affairs of an establishment, etc.; a superintendent. **2.** the title of various public officials in France and elsewhere. [t. F, t. L: m.s. *intendens,* ppr., extending, attending]

in·tend·ed (ĭn tĕn′dĭd), *adj.* **1.** purposed or designed: *to produce the intended effect.* **2.** prospective: *one's intended wife.* **—n. 3.** *Colloq.* an intended husband or wife.

in·tend·ment (ĭn tĕnd′mənt), *n.* **1.** *Law.* the manner of understanding, construing, or viewing something. **2.** *Obs.* intention; design; purpose.

in·ten·er·ate (ĭn tĕn′ə rāt′), *v.t.,* **-ated, -ating.** *Now Rare.* to make soft or tender; soften. [f. IN-[2] + L *tener* TENDER[1] + -ATE[1]] **—in·ten′er·a′tion,** *n.*

intens., intensive.

in·tense (ĭn tĕns′), *adj.* **1.** existing or occurring in a high or extreme degree: *intense heat.* **2.** acute, strong, or vehement, as sensations, feelings, or emotions: *intense anxiety.* **3.** of an extreme kind; very great, strong, keen, severe, etc.: *an intense gale.* **4.** *Photog.* strong: *intense light.* **5.** having the characteristic qualities in a high degree: *the intense vault of heaven.* **6.** strenuous or earnest, as activity, exertion, diligence, thought, etc.: *an intense life.* **7.** exhibiting a high degree of some quality or action. **8.** having or showing great strength or vehemence of feeling, as a person, the face, language, etc. **9.** susceptible to strong emotion; emotional: *an intense person.* [ME, t. L: m.s. *intensus,* pp., stretched tight, intense] **—in·tense′ly,** *adv.* **—in·tense′ness,** *n.*

in·ten·si·fy (ĭn tĕn′sə fī′), *v.,* **-fied, -fying. —v.t. 1.** to make intense or more intense. **2.** *Photog.* to make more dense or opaque, as a negative or print. **—v.i. 3.** to become intense or more intense. **—in·ten′si·fi·ca′tion,** *n.* **—in·ten′si·fi′er,** *n.* **—Syn. 1.** See **aggravate.**

in·ten·sion (ĭn tĕn′shən), *n.* **1.** intensification; increase in degree. **2.** intensity; high degree. **3.** relative intensity; degree. **4.** exertion of the mind; determination. **5.** *Logic.* the sum of the attributes contained in a concept or connoted by a term. Cf. **extension** (def. 10). [t. L: s. *intensio*]

in·ten·si·ty (ĭn tĕn′sə tĭ), *n., pl.* **-ties. 1.** quality or condition of being intense. **2.** great energy, strength, vehemence, etc., as of activity, thought, or feeling. **3.** high or extreme degree, as of cold. **4.** the degree or extent to which something is intense. **5.** *Speech.* **a.** loudness or softness of vocal tone. **b.** carrying power of voice. **6.** the strength or sharpness of a color due especially to its degree of freedom from admixture with its complementary color. **7.** *Photog.* strength, as of light. **8.** *Physics.* **a.** the strength of an electric current in amperes. **b.** potential difference; voltage. **c.** the strength of an electrical or magnetic field. **d.** the magnitude, as of a force, per unit of area, volume, etc.

in·ten·sive (ĭn tĕn′sĭv), *adj.* **1.** of, pertaining to, or characterized by intensity: *intensive fire from machine guns.* **2.** intensifying. **3.** *Med.* **a.** increasing in intensity or degree. **b.** instituting treatment to the limit of safety. **4.** *Econ.* of or denoting methods designed to increase effectiveness, as (in *Agric.*) a more thorough tillage, the application of fertilizers, etc., to secure the most from each acre (opposed to *extensive*). **5.** *Gram.* indicating increased emphasis or force. For example: *certainly, tremendously* are intensive adverbs. —*n.* **6.** something that intensifies. **7.** *Gram.* an intensive element or formation, as -*self* in *himself*, or Latin -*tō* in *iac-tō*, 'I hurl' compared with *iacō*, 'I throw.' [t. ML: m.s. *intensīvus*] —**in·ten'sive·ly,** *adv.* —**in·ten'sive·ness,** *n.*

in·tent[1] (ĭn·tĕnt'), *n.* **1.** an intending or purposing, as to commit some act: *criminal intent.* **2.** that which is intended; purpose; aim; design; intention: *my intent was to buy.* **3.** *Law.* the state of a person's mind which directs his actions toward a specific object. **4. to all intents and purposes, a.** for all practical purposes; practically. **b.** for all the ends and purposes in view. **5.** the end or object intended. **6.** *Obs.* meaning. [partly ME *intent,* var. of *entent,* t. OF: intention, g. L *intentus* a stretching out; partly ME *intente,* var. of *entente,* t. OF: purpose, ult. der. L *intendere* stretch out] —**Syn. 2.** See **intention.**

in·tent[2] (ĭn·tĕnt'), *adj.* **1.** firmly or steadfastly fixed or directed (upon something): *an intent gaze.* **2.** having the gaze or thoughts earnestly fixed on something: *intent on one's job.* **3.** bent, as on some purpose: *intent on revenge.* **5.** earnest: *an intent person.* [t. L: s. *intentus,* pp., stretched, intent] —**in·tent'ly,** *adv.* —**in·tent'ness,** *n.*

in·ten·tion (ĭn·tĕn'shən), *n.* **1.** act of determining mentally upon some action or result; a purpose or design. **2.** the end or object intended. **3.** *Colloq.* (*pl.*) purposes with respect to a proposal of marriage. **4.** act or fact of intending or purposing. **5.** *Logic.* **a.** a general concept. **b. first intention,** a general conception obtained by abstraction from the ideas or images of sensible objects. **c. second intention,** a general conception obtained by reflection and abstraction applied to first intentions as objects. **6.** *Surg., Med.* a manner or process of healing, as in the healing of a lesion or fracture without granulation (**healing by first intention**) or the healing of a wound by granulation after suppuration (**healing by second intention**). **7.** *Rare.* intentness. **8.** meaning. [t. L: s. *intentio;* r. ME *entencion,* t. OF] —**Syn. 2.** INTENTION, INTENT, PURPOSE all refer to a wish which one means to carry out. INTENTION is the general word: *his intentions are good.* INTENT is chiefly legal or poetical: *intent to kill.* PURPOSE implies having a goal or a settled determination to achieve something: *there was no purpose in his actions.*

in·ten·tion·al (ĭn·tĕn'shən·əl), *adj.* **1.** done with intention or on purpose: *an intentional insult.* **2.** of or pertaining to intention or purpose. **3.** *Metaphys.* **a.** pertaining to an appearance, phenomenon, or representation in the mind; phenomenal; representational. **b.** pertaining to the capacity of mind to refer to objects of all sorts. —**in·ten'tion·al·ly,** *adv.* —**Syn. 1.** See **deliberate.**

in·ter (ĭn·tûr'), *v.t.,* -**terred,** -**terring. 1.** to deposit (a dead body, etc.) in a grave or tomb; bury, esp. with ceremonies. **2.** *Obs.* to put into the earth. [ME *enter(n),* t. OF: m. *enterrer,* der. en- EN-[1] + *terre* earth (g. L *terra*)]

inter-, a prefix meaning "between," "among," "mutually," "reciprocally," "together," as in *intercellular,* in *tercity, intermarry, interweave.* [t. L, comb. form of *inter,* adv. and prep., between, among, during]

in·ter·act (ĭn'tər·ăkt'), *v.i.* to act on each other. —**in'ter·ac'tive,** *adj.*

in·ter·ac·tion (ĭn'tər·ăk'shən), *n.* action on each other; reciprocal action.

in·ter a·li·a (ĭn'tər ā'lĭ·ə), *Latin.* among other things.

in·ter a·li·os (ĭn'tər ā'lĭ·ōs'), *Latin.* among others.

in·ter·Al·lied (ĭn'tər·ə·līd', -ăl'īd), *adj.* between or among allied nations, esp. the Allies of World War I.

in·ter·blend (ĭn'tər·blĕnd'), *v.t., v.i.,* -**blended** or -**blent,** -**blending.** to blend, one with another.

in·ter·bor·ough (ĭn'tər·bûr'ō), *adj.* between boroughs.

in·ter·brain (ĭn'tər·brān'), *n. Anat.* the diencephalon.

in·ter·breed (ĭn'tər·brēd'), *v.t., v.i.,* -**bred,** -**breeding.** to breed by the crossing of different animal or plant species, breeds, varieties, or individuals.

in·ter·ca·lar·y (ĭn·tûr'kə·lĕr'ĭ), *adj.* **1.** interpolated; interposed; intervening. **2.** inserted or interpolated in the calendar, as an extra day, month, etc. **3.** having such an inserted day, month, etc., as a particular year. [t. L: m.s. *intercalārius.*]

in·ter·ca·late (ĭn·tûr'kə·lāt'), *v.t.,* -**lated,** -**lating. 1.** to interpolate; interpose. **2.** to insert (an extra day, month, etc.) in the calendar. [t. L: m.s. *intercalātus,* pp.] —**in·ter'ca·la'tive,** *adj.*

in·ter·ca·la·tion (ĭn·tûr'kə·lā'shən), *n.* **1.** act of intercalating; insertion or interpolation, as in a series. **2.** that which is intercalated; an interpolation.

in·ter·cede (ĭn'tər·sēd'), *v.i.,* -**ceded,** -**ceding. 1.** to interpose in behalf of one in difficulty or trouble, as by pleading or petition: *to intercede with the governor for a condemned man.* **2.** *Rom. Hist.* (of a tribune or other magistrate) to interpose a veto. [t. L: m.s. *intercēdere* intervene] —**in'ter·ced'er,** *n.*

in·ter·cel·lu·lar (ĭn'tər·sĕl'yə·lər), *adj.* situated between or among cells or cellules.

in·ter·cept (*v.* ĭn'tər·sĕpt'; *n.* ĭn'tər·sĕpt'), *v.t.* **1.** to take or seize on the way from one place to another; cut off from the intended destination: *to intercept a*

messenger. **2.** to stop the natural course of (light, water, etc.). **3.** to stop or check (passage, etc.). **4.** to prevent or cut off the operation or effect of: *to intercept the view.* **5.** to cut off from access, sight, etc. **6.** *Chiefly Math.* to mark off or include, as between two points or lines. —*n.* **7.** an interception. **8.** *Math.* an intercepted part of a line. [t. L: s. *interceptus,* pp.] —**in'ter·cep'tive,** *adj.*

in·ter·cep·tion (ĭn'tər·sĕp'shən), *n.* **1.** act of intercepting. **2.** state or fact of being intercepted. **3.** *Mil.* engaging an enemy force in an attempt to hinder or prevent it from carrying out its mission.

Arc of circle intercepted by line between points X and Y

in·ter·cep·tor (ĭn'tər·sĕp'tər), *n.* **1.** one who or that which intercepts. **2.** *Mil.* a type of fighter airplane with a high rate of climb and speed, used chiefly for the interception of enemy aircraft. Also, **in'ter·cept'er.**

in·ter·ces·sion (ĭn'tər·sĕsh'ən), *n.* **1.** act of interceding. **2.** an interposing or pleading in behalf of one in difficulty or trouble. **3.** *Relig.* **a.** an interposing or pleading with God in behalf of another or others, as that of Christ (see Heb. 7:25) or that of the saints in behalf of men. **b.** a pleading against others (See Rom. 11:2). **4.** *Rom. Hist.* the interposing of a veto, as by a tribune. [t. L: s. *intercessio*] —**in'ter·ces'sion·al,** *adj.*

in·ter·ces·sor (ĭn'tər·sĕs'ər, ĭn'tər·sĕs'ər), *n.* one who intercedes.

in·ter·ces·so·ry (ĭn'tər·sĕs'ər·ĭ), *adj.* making intercession: *the Lord's Prayer has an intercessory petition.*

in·ter·change (*v.* ĭn'tər·chānj'; *n.* ĭn'tər·chānj'), *v.* -**changed,** -**changing,** *n.* —*v.t.* **1.** to put each of (two things) in the place of the other. **2.** to cause (one thing) to change places with another; transpose. **3.** to give and receive (things) reciprocally; exchange: *they interchanged gifts.* **4.** to cause to follow one another alternately: *to interchange cares with pleasures.* —*v.i.* **5.** to occur by turns or in succession; alternate. **6.** to change places, as two persons or things, or as one with another. —*n.* **7.** act of interchanging; reciprocal exchange: *the interchange of commodities.* **8.** a changing of places, as between two persons or things, or of one with another. **9.** alternation; alternate succession. **10.** a system for routing traffic on and off superhighways and for linking them. [f. INTER- + CHANGE; r. ME *enterchaunge,* t. OF: m. *entrechangier* (v.), *entrechange*(n.)] —**in'ter·chang'er,** *n.*

in·ter·change·a·ble (ĭn'tər·chān'jə·bəl), *adj.* **1.** capable of being put or used in the place of each other, as two things: *interchangeable words.* **2.** (of one thing) that may be put in the place of, or may change places with, something else. —**in'ter·change'a·bil'i·ty,** *n.*/ **ter·change'a·ble·ness,** *n.* —**in'ter·change'a·bly,** *adv.* —**Syn. 2.** See **exchangeable.**

in·ter·clav·i·cle (ĭn'tər·klăv'ə·kəl), *n. Zool., Anat.* a median membrane bone developed between the collarbones, or in front of the breastbone, in many vertebrates. —**in·ter·cla·vic·u·lar** (ĭn'tər·klə·vĭk'yə·lər), *adj.*

in·ter·col·le·gi·ate (ĭn'tər·kə·lē'jĭ·ĭt, -jĭt), *adj.* between colleges, or representative of different colleges.

in·ter·co·lo·ni·al (ĭn'tər·kə·lō'nĭ·əl), *adj.* between colonies, as of one country. —**in·ter·co·lo'ni·al·ly,** *adv.*

in·ter·co·lum·ni·a·tion (ĭn'tər·kə·lŭm'nĭ·ā'shən), *n. Archit.* **1.** the space between two adjacent columns, usually the clear space between the lower parts of the shafts. **2.** the system of spacing between columns. [f. s. L *intercolumnium* space between columns + -ATION]

in·ter·com (ĭn'tər·kŏm'), *n. Slang.* an intercommunication system, as of an airplane or a tank.

in·ter·com·mon (ĭn'tər·kŏm'ən), *v.i. Eng. Law.* to share in the use of a common. [ME *entercomen,* t. AF: m. *entrecomuner,* f. *entre-* INTER- + *comuner* share]

in·ter·com·mu·ni·cate (ĭn'tər·kə·mū'nə·kāt'), *v.t., v.i.,* -**cated,** -**cating.** to communicate mutually, as people or rooms. —**in'ter·com·mu'ni·ca'tion,** *n.* —**in'ter·com·mu'ni·ca'tive,** *adj.*

in·ter·com·mun·ion (ĭn'tər·kə·mūn'yən), *n.* mutual communion, association, or relations.

in·ter·com·mu·ni·ty (ĭn'tər·kə·mū'nə·tĭ), *n., pl.* -**ties.** common ownership, use, participation, etc.

in·ter·con·nect (ĭn'tər·kə·nĕkt'), *v.t.* to connect, one with another. —**in'ter·con·nec'tion,** *n.*

in·ter·con·ti·nen·tal (ĭn'tər·kŏn'tə·nĕn'təl), *adj.* between continents: *intercontinental trade.*

in·ter·cos·tal (ĭn'tər·kŏs'təl, -kôs'təl), *adj.* **1.** pertaining to muscles, parts, or intervals between the ribs. **2.** situated between the ribs. —*n.* **3.** an intercostal muscle, part, or space. [t. NL: s. *intercostālis.* See INTER-, COSTA, -AL[1]] —**in'ter·cos'tal·ly,** *adv.*

in·ter·course (ĭn'tər·kōrs'), *n.* **1.** dealings or communication between individuals. **2.** interchange of thoughts, feelings, etc. **3.** sexual relations. [f. INTER- + COURSE; r. late ME *entercourse,* t. OF: m. *entrecors,* g. L *intercursus* a running between]

in·ter·crop (ĭn'tər·krŏp'), *v.t., v.i.,* -**cropped,** -**cropping.** *Agric.* to use (the space) between the rows of an orchard, vineyard, or field for the simultaneous production of a different cultivated crop.

in·ter·cross (ĭn'tər·krôs', -krŏs'), *v.t.* **1.** to cross (things), one with another. **2.** to cross (each other), as streets do. **3.** to cross in interbreeding. —*v.i.* **4.** to cross each other. **5.** to interbreed. —*n.* **6.** an instance of cross-fertilization.

---

b., blend of, blended; c., cognate with; d., dialect, dialectal; der., derived from; f., formed from; g., going back to; m., modification of; r., replacing; s., stem of; t., taken from; ?., perhaps. See the full key on inside cover.

in·ter·cur·rent (ĭn/tər kûr/ənt), *adj.* **1.** intervening, as of time or events. **2.** *Pathol.* (of a disease) occurring while another disease is in progress. [t. L: s. *intercurrens*, ppr., running between] —**in/ter·cur/rence,** *n.*

in·ter·de·nom·i·na·tion·al (ĭn/tər dĭ nŏm/ə nā/shən-əl), *adj.* between (religious) denominations.

in·ter·den·tal (ĭn/tər dĕn/tal), *adj.* **1.** between teeth. **2.** *Phonet.* with the tip of the tongue between the upper and lower front teeth.

in·ter·de·pend·ent (ĭn/tər dĭ pĕn/dənt), *adj.* mutually dependent; dependent on each other. —**in/ter·de·pend/ence, in/ter·de·pend/en·cy,** *n.* —**in/ter·de·pend/ent·ly,** *adv.*

in·ter·dict (*n.* ĭn/tər dīkt/; *v.* ĭn/tər dīkt/), *n.* **1.** *Rom. Law.* a general or special order of the Roman praetor forbidding or commanding an act; the procedure by which an interdict was sought. **2.** *Civil Law.* any prohibitory act or decree of a court or an administrative officer. **3.** *Rom. Cath. Ch.* a punishment by which the faithful, remaining in communion with the Church, are prohibited from participation in certain sacred acts. —*v.t.* **4.** *Eccles.* to cut off authoritatively from certain ecclesiastical functions and privileges. **5.** to forbid; prohibit. [t. L: s. *interdictus*, pp.; r. ME *entredite*(n), t. OF: m. *eniredit*, pp. of *entredire*] —**in/ter·dic/tive,** *adj.* —**in/ter·dic/tor,** *n.*

in·ter·dic·tion (ĭn/tər dĭk/shən), *n.* **1.** act of interdicting. **2.** state of being interdicted. **3.** an interdict.

in·ter·dic·to·ry (ĭn/tər dĭk/tə rĭ), *adj.* interdicting.

in·ter·est (ĭn/tər ĭst, -trĭst), *n.* **1.** the feeling of one whose attention or curiosity is particularly engaged by something: *to have little interest in a subject.* **2.** a particular feeling of this kind: *a man of varied intellectual interests.* **3.** the power of exciting such feeling; interesting quality: *questions of great interest.* **4.** concernment, importance, or moment: *a matter of primary interest.* **5.** a business, cause, or the like, in which a number of persons are interested. **6.** a share in the ownership of property, in a commercial or financial undertaking, or the like. **7.** any right of ownership in property, commercial undertakings, etc. **8.** a number or group of persons, or a party, having a common interest: *the banking interest.* **9.** (*pl.*) the group of persons or organizations having extensive financial or business interests. **10.** something in which one has an interest, as of ownership, advantage, attention, etc. **11.** the relation of being affected by something in respect of advantage or detriment: *an arbitrator having no interest in the outcome.* **12.** benefit or advantage: *to have one's own interest in mind.* **13.** regard for one's own advantage or profit; self-interest: *rival interests.* **14.** influence from personal importance or capability; power of influencing the action of others. **15. in the interest** (or **interests**) **of,** on the side of what is advantageous to; in behalf of: *in the interest of good government.* **16.** *Com.* **a.** payment, or a sum paid, for the use of money borrowed (the principal), or for the forbearance of a debt. **b.** the rate percent per unit of time represented by such payment. **17.** something added or thrown in above an exact equivalent. —*v.t.* **18.** to engage or excite the attention or curiosity of: *a story which interested him greatly.* **19.** to concern (a person, etc.) in something; involve: *every citizen is interested in this law.* **20.** to cause to have a personal concern or share; induce to participate: *to interest a person in an enterprise.* **21.** *Rare.* to concern, relate to, or affect. [late ME, n. use of L *interest* it concerns; r. ME *interesse,* t. ML: compensation for loss, n. use of L inf.]

in·ter·est·ed (ĭn/tər ĭs tĭd, -trĭs tĭd, -tə rĕs/tĭd), *adj.* **1.** having an interest in something; concerned: *those interested should apply in person.* **2.** participating; having an interest or share; having money involved: *one interested in the funds.* **3.** having the attention or curiosity engaged: *an interested spectator.* **4.** characterized by a feeling of interest. **5.** influenced by personal or selfish motives: *an interested witness.* —**in/ter·est·ed·ly,** *adv.* —**in/ter·est·ed·ness,** *n.*

in·ter·est·ing (ĭn/tər ĭs tĭng, -trĭs tĭng, -tə rĕs/tĭng), *adj.* **1.** arousing a feeling of interest: *an interesting face.* **2.** engaging or exciting and holding the attention or curiosity: *an interesting book.* —**in/ter·est·ing·ly,** *adv.* —**in/ter·est·ing·ness,** *n.*

—**Syn. 2.** INTERESTING, PLEASING, GRATIFYING mean satisfying to the mind. That which is INTERESTING occupies the mind with no connotation of pleasure or displeasure: *an interesting account of a battle.* That which is PLEASING engages the mind favorably: *a pleasing account of the wedding.* That which is GRATIFYING fulfils expectations, requirements, etc.: *a gratifying account of his whereabouts.*

in·ter·face (ĭn/tər fās/), *n.* a surface regarded as the common boundary of two bodies or spaces.

in·ter·fa·cial (ĭn/tər fā/shal), *adj.* **1.** included between two faces. **2.** pertaining to an interface.

in·ter·fere (ĭn/tər fĭr/), *v.i.,* **-fered, -fering. 1.** to clash; come in collision; be in opposition: *the claims of two nations may interfere.* **2.** to come into opposition, as one thing with another, esp. with the effect of hampering action or procedure: *these interruptions interfere with the work.* **3.** to interpose or intervene for a particular purpose. **4.** to take a part in the affairs of others; meddle: *to interfere with others' disputes.* **5.** (of things) to strike against each other, or one against another, so as to hamper or hinder action; come into physical collision. **6.** to strike one foot or leg against the opposite foot or leg in going, as a horse. **7.** *Football, etc.* to obstruct the

action of an opposing player in a way barred by the rules. **8.** *Physics.* to cause interference. [t. OF: m. *entreferir* strike each other, f. *entre-* INTER- + *ferir* (g. L *ferīre* strike)] —**in/ter·fer/er,** *n.* —**in/ter·fer/ing·ly,** *adv.*

in·ter·fer·ence (ĭn/tər fĭr/əns), *n.* **1.** act or fact of interfering. **2.** *Physics.* the reciprocal action of waves (as of light, sound, etc.), when meeting, by which they reinforce or cancel each other. **3.** *Radio.* **a.** the jumbling of radio signals because signals other than the desired ones are being received. **b.** the signals which produce the incoherence.

interference drag, the additional drag due to interaction of two aerodynamic bodies.

in·ter·fe·ren·tial (ĭn/tər fə rĕn/shal), *adj.* of or pertaining to interference.

in·ter·fer·om·e·ter (ĭn/tər fə rŏm/ə tər), *n. Physics.* an instrument for measuring small lengths or distances by means of the interference of two rays of light.

in·ter·file (ĭn/tər fīl/), *v.t.,* **-filed, -filing.** to combine into a single arrangement two or more similarly arranged sets of items, as cards, documents, etc.

in·ter·flow (*v.* ĭn/tər flō/; *n.* ĭn/tər flō/), *v.i.* **1.** to flow into each other; intermingle. —*n.* **2.** interflowing.

in·ter·flu·ent (ĭn/tər flōō/ənt), *adj.* interflowing.

in·ter·fluve (ĭn/tər flōōv/), *n.* the higher land separating adjacent stream valleys.

in·ter·fold (ĭn/tər fōld/), *v.t.* to fold, one within another; fold together.

in·ter·fuse (ĭn/tər fūz/), *v.,* **-fused, -fusing.** —*v.t.* **1.** to pour (something) between or through; diffuse throughout. **2.** to intersperse, intermingle, or permeate with something. **3.** to blend or fuse, one with another. —*v.i.* **4.** to become blended or fused, one with another. [t. L: m. s. *interfūsus,* pp.] —**in/ter·fu/sion,** *n.*

in·ter·gla·cial (ĭn/tər glā/shal), *adj. Geol.* occurring or formed between times of glacial action.

in·ter·grade (*n.* ĭn/tər grād/; *v.* ĭn/tər grād/), *n., v.,* **-graded, -grading.** —*n.* **1.** an intermediate grade. —*v.i.* **2.** to pass gradually, one into another, as different species. —**in/ter·gra·da/tion,** *n.* —**in·ter·gra·di·ent** (ĭn/tər grā/dĭ ənt), *adj.*

in·ter·growth (ĭn/tər grōth/), *n.* growth or growing together, as of one thing with another.

in·ter·im (ĭn/tər ĭm), *n.* **1.** an intervening time; the meantime: *in the interim.* **2.** a temporary or provisional arrangement. **3.** (*cap.*) *Eccles. Hist.* any of three provisional arrangements for the settlement of religious differences between German Protestants and Roman Catholics during the Reformation. —*adj.* **4.** belonging to or connected with an intervening period of time; temporary: *an interim order.* —*adv.* **5.** *Now Rare.* meantime. [t. L: in the meantime]

in·te·ri·or (ĭn tĭr/ĭ ər), *adj.* **1.** being within; inside of anything; internal; further toward a center: *the interior parts of a house.* **2.** of or pertaining to that which is within; inside: *an interior view.* **3.** situated inside of and at a distance from the coast or border: *the interior parts of a country.* **4.** pertaining to the inland. **5.** domestic: *the interior trade.* **6.** inner, private, or secret: *an interior cabinet.* **7.** mental or spiritual. **8.** *Geom.* (of an angle) inner, as an angle formed between two parallel lines when cut by a third line, or an angle formed by two adjacent sides of a closed polygon. —*n.* **9.** the internal part; the inside. **10.** *Art.* **a.** the inside part of a building, considered as a whole from the point of view of artistic design or general effect, convenience, etc., or a single room or apartment so considered. **b.** a pictorial representation of the inside of a building, room, etc.

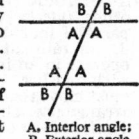

A. Interior angle; B. Exterior angle

11. the inland parts of a region, country, etc.: *the interior of Africa.* **12.** the domestic affairs of a country as distinguished from its foreign affairs: *the Department of the Interior.* **13.** the inner or inward nature or character of anything. [t. L: inner] —**in·te·ri·or·i·ty** (ĭn tĭr/ĭ ŏr/ə tĭ, -ŏr/-), *n.* —**in·te/ri·or·ly,** *adv.*

interior decorator, a person whose occupation is planning the decoration, furnishings, draperies, etc., of homes, rooms, or offices.

interior drainage, a drainage system whose waters do not continue to the ocean either on the surface or underground, but evaporate within the land area.

interj., interjection.

in·ter·ject (ĭn/tər jĕkt/), *v.t.* **1.** to throw in abruptly between other things. **2.** to interpolate; interpose: *to interject a careless remark.* **3.** *Rare.* to come between. [t. L: s. *interjectus,* pp.] —**in/ter·jec/tor,** *n.*

in·ter·jec·tion (ĭn/tər jĕk/shən), *n.* **1.** act of throwing between; an interjecting. **2.** the utterance of ejaculations expressive of emotion; an ejaculation or exclamation. **3.** something, as a remark interjected. **4.** *Gram.* **a.** (in many languages) a form class, or "part of speech," comprising words which constitute utterances or clauses in themselves, without grammatical connection. **b.** such a word as English *tut-tut!* Such words often include speech sounds not otherwise found in the language. **c.** any word or construction similarly used, as English *goodness me!* —**in/ter·jec/tion·al,** *adj.* —**in/ter·jec/-tion·al·ly,** *adv.*

in·ter·jec·to·ry (ĭn/tər jĕk/tə rĭ), *adj.* **1.** interjectional. **2.** interjected. —**in/ter·jec/to·ri·ly,** *adv.*

in·ter·knit (ĭn'tər nĭt'), v.t., **-knitted** or **-knit**, **-knit-ting**. to knit together, one with another; intertwine.

in·ter·lace (ĭn'tər lās'), v., **-laced**, **-lacing**. —r.i. 1. to cross one another as if woven together; intertwine; blend intricately: interlacing boughs. 2. Rare. to become intermingled. —v.t. 3. to dispose (threads, strips, parts, branches, etc.) so as to intercross one another, passing alternately over and under. 4. to mingle; blend. 5. to diversify as with threads woven in. 6. to intersperse or intermingle. —in'ter·lace'ment, n.

In·ter·la·ken (ĭn'tər lä'kən, ĭn'tər lä'kən), a town in central Switzerland between the lakes of Brienz and Thun: a famous tourist center. 4,368 (1950).

in·ter·lam·i·nate (ĭn'tər lăm'ə nāt'), v.t., **-nated**, **-nating**. to interlay or lay between laminae; interstratify. —in'ter·lam'i·na'tion, n.

in·ter·lard (ĭn'tər lärd'), v.t. 1. to diversify with something intermixed or interjected; intersperse (fol. by with): to interlard one's speech with oaths. 2. (of things) to be intermixed in. 3. Obs. to mix, as fat with lean. [t. F: m.s. entrelarder, f. entre- INTER- + larder LARD, v.]

in·ter·lay (ĭn'tər lā'), v.t., **-laid**, **-laying**. 1. to lay between; interpose. 2. to diversify with something laid between or inserted: silver interlaid with gold.

in·ter·leaf (ĭn'tər lēf'), n., pl. **-leaves** (-lēvz'). an additional leaf, usually blank, inserted between or bound with the regular printed leaves of a book.

in·ter·leave (ĭn'tər lēv'), v.t., **-leaved**, **-leaving**. 1. to provide blank leaves in (a book) for notes or written comments. 2. to insert blank leaves between (the regular printed leaves).

in·ter·li·brar·y loan (ĭn'tər lī'brĕr'Y, -brərY', -brY), 1. a system by which one library borrows a publication from another library. 2. a loan made in this way.

in·ter·line¹ (ĭn'tər līn'), v.t., **-lined**, **-lining**. 1. to write or insert (words, etc.) between the lines of writing or print. 2. to mark or inscribe (a document, book, etc.) between the lines. [late ME, t. ML: s. interlineāre]

in·ter·line² (ĭn'tər līn'), v.t., **-lined**, **-lining**. to provide (a garment) with an inner lining, between the ordinary lining and the outer fabric. [f. INTER- + LINE²]

in·ter·lin·e·al (ĭn'tər lĭn'Y əl), adj. 1. interlinear. 2. Rare. alternating in lines. —in'ter·lin'e·al·ly, adv.

in·ter·lin·e·ar (ĭn'tər lĭn'Y ər), adj. 1. situated between the lines; inserted between lines. 2. having interpolated lines; interlined: an interlinear translation. 3. having the same text in various languages set in alternate lines: the interlinear Bible.

in·ter·lin·e·ate (ĭn'tər lĭn'Y āt'), v.t., **-ated**, **-ating**. to interline¹. —in'ter·lin'e·a'tion, n.

In·ter·lin·gua (ĭn'tər lĭng'gwə), n. an auxiliary international language developed between 1924 and 1951, based primarily upon the principal languages of the Western world. It was devised mainly to facilitate scientific communication. [INTER- + LINGUA]

in·ter·lin·ing¹ (ĭn'tər lī'nĭng), n. 1. an inner lining placed between the ordinary lining and the outer fabric of a garment. 2. material used for this purpose. [f. INTERLINE² + -ING¹]

in·ter·lin·ing² (ĭn'tər lī'nĭng), n. interlineation.

in·ter·link (v. ĭn'tər lĭngk'; n. ĭn'tər lĭngk'), v.t. 1. to link, one with another. —n. 2. a connecting link.

in·ter·lock (ĭn'tər lŏk'), v.i. 1. to engage with each other: interlocking branches. 2. to fit into each other, as parts of machinery, so that all action is simultaneous. 3. (of railroad switches, signals, etc.) to arrange and operate in an interlocking system. —v.t. 4. to lock one with another. 5. to fit the parts of together so that all must move together, or in the same way. 6. Railroads. to arrange (switches, etc.) so that their positions are not independent of one another and their movements succeed each other in prearranged order. —in'ter·lock'er, n.

in·ter·lo·cu·tion (ĭn'tər lə kū'shən), n. conversation; dialogue. [t. L: s. interlocūtio a speaking between]

in·ter·loc·u·tor (ĭn'tər lŏk'yə tər), n. 1. the man in the middle of the line of performers of a minstrel troupe, who carries on a conversation with the end men. 2. one who takes parts in a conversation or dialogue. 3. one who enters into conversation with another. —in·ter·loc·u·tress (ĭn'tər lŏk'yə trĭs), in·ter·loc·u·trice, in·ter·loc·u·trix (ĭn'tər lŏk'yə trĭks), n. fem.

in·ter·loc·u·to·ry (ĭn'tər lŏk'yə tōr'Y), adj. 1. of the nature of, pertaining to, or occurring in conversation: interlocutory instruction. 2. interjected into the main course of speech. 3. Law. a. pronounced during the course of an action, as a decision; not finally decisive of a case. b. pertaining to a provisional decision.

in·ter·lope (ĭn'tər lōp'), v.i., **-loped**, **-loping**. 1. to intrude into some region or field of trade without a proper license. 2. to thrust oneself into the affairs of others. [f. INTER- + LOPE, v.] —in'ter·lop'er, n.

in·ter·lude (ĭn'tər lōōd'), n. 1. an intervening episode, period, space, etc. 2. a form of short dramatic piece, esp. of a light or farcical character, formerly introduced between the parts of miracle plays and moralities or given as part of other entertainments. 3. one of the early English farces or comedies (such as those by John Heywood) which grew out of such pieces. 4. an intermediate performance or entertainment, as between the acts of a play. 5. an instrumental passage or a piece of music rendered between the parts of a song, church service, drama, etc. [ME, t. ML: m.s. interlūdium, f. inter- INTER- + -lūdium, der. L lūdus play]

in·ter·lu·nar (ĭn'tər lōō'nər), adj. pertaining to the moon's monthly period of invisibility between the old moon and the new.

in·ter·lu·na·tion (ĭn'tər lōō nā'shən), n. the interlunar period.

in·ter·mar·ry (ĭn'tər mâr'Y), v.i., **-ried**, **-rying**. 1. to become connected by marriage, as two families, tribes, or castes. 2. to marry within the limits of the family or of near relationship. 3. to marry, one with another. —in'ter·mar'riage, n.

in·ter·max·il·lar·y (ĭn'tər măk'sə lĕr'Y), adj. 1. situated between the maxillary or upper jawbones. 2. of or pertaining to the back and middle of the upper jaw: intermaxillary teeth. 3. (in Crustacea) situated between those somites of the head which bear the maxillae.

in·ter·med·dle (ĭn'tər mĕd'əl), v.i., **-dled**, **-dling**. to take part in a matter, esp. officiously; interfere; meddle. —in'ter·med'dler, n.

in·ter·me·di·a·cy (ĭn'tər mē'dY ə sY), n. state of being intermediate, or of acting intermediately.

in·ter·me·di·ar·y (ĭn'tər mē'dY ĕr'Y), adj., n., pl. **-aries**. —adj. 1. being between; intermediate. 2. acting between persons, parties, etc.; serving as an intermediate agent or agency: an intermediary power. —n. 3. an intermediate agent or agency; a go-between. 4. a medium or means. 5. an intermediate form or stage.

in·ter·me·di·ate¹ (ĭn'tər mē'dY ĭt), adj. 1. being, situated, or acting between two points, stages, things, persons, etc.: the intermediate links. —n. 2. something intermediate. 3. Chem. a derivative of the initial material formed before the desired product of a chemical process. 4. Rare. an intermediary. [t. ML: m. s. intermediātus, der. L intermedius between] —in'ter·me'di·ate·ly, adv. —in'ter·me'di·ate·ness, n.

in·ter·me·di·ate² (ĭn'tər mē'dY āt'), v.i., **-ated**, **-ating**. to act as an intermediary; intervene; mediate. [f INTER- + MEDIATE, v.] —in'ter·me'di·a'tion, n. —in'ter·me'di·a·tor, n.

intermediate frequency, Radio. the middle frequency in a superheterodyne receiver, at which most of the amplification takes place.

in·ter·ment (ĭn tûr'mənt), n. act of interring; burial.

in·ter·mez·zo (ĭn'tər mĕt'sō, -mĕd'zō; It. ēn'tĕr mĕd'dzō), n., pl. **-zos**, **-zi** (-sē, -zē; It. -dzē). 1. a short dramatic, musical, or other entertainment of light character introduced between the acts of a drama or opera. 2. a short musical composition between main divisions of an extended musical work. 3. an independent musical composition of similar character. [t. It., g. L intermedius between]

in·ter·mi·gra·tion (ĭn'tər mī grā'shən), n. reciprocal migration; interchange of habitat by migrating bodies.

in·ter·mi·na·ble (ĭn tûr'mə nə bəl), adj. 1. that cannot be terminated; unending: interminable talk. 2. endless; having no limits: interminable sufferings. [ME, t. LL: m.s. interminābilis] —in'ter·mi·na·bly, adv.

in·ter·min·gle (ĭn'tər mĭng'gəl), v.t., v.i., **-gled**, **-gling**. to mingle, one with another. —in'ter·min'gle·ment, n.

in·ter·mis·sion (ĭn'tər mĭsh'ən), n. 1. a period during which action temporarily ceases; an interval between periods of action or activity: we smoked in the lobby during the intermission. 2. act of intermitting. 3. state of being intermitted. [t. L: s. intermissio]

in·ter·mis·sive (ĭn'tər mĭs'Yv), adj. 1. characterized by intermission. 2. intermittent.

in·ter·mit (ĭn'tər mĭt'), v., **-mitted**, **-mitting**. —v.t. 1. to discontinue temporarily; suspend. —v.i. 2. to stop or pause at intervals, or be intermittent. 3. to cease, stop, or break off operations for a time. [t. L: m.s. intermittere leave off, omit, leave an interval] —in'ter·mit'ting·ly, adv.

in·ter·mit·tent (ĭn'tər mĭt'ənt), adj. 1. that intermits, or ceases for a time: an intermittent process. 2. alternately ceasing and beginning again: an intermittent fever. 3. (of streams, lakes, or springs) recurrent; showing water only part of the time. —in'ter·mit'tence, in'ter·mit'ten·cy, n. —in'ter·mit'tent·ly, adv.

intermittent fever, a malarial fever in which feverish periods lasting a few hours alternate with periods in which the temperature is normal.

in·ter·mix (ĭn'tər mĭks'), v.t., v.i. to intermingle.

in·ter·mix·ture (ĭn'tər mĭks'chər), n. 1. act of intermixing. 2. a mass of ingredients mixed together. 3. something added by intermixing.

in·ter·mo·lec·u·lar (ĭn'tər mə lĕk'yə lər, -mō-), adj. between molecules.

in·ter·mun·dane (ĭn'tər mŭn'dān), adj. 1. between worlds. 2. between heavenly bodies.

in·tern¹ (v. ĭn tûrn'; n. ĭn'tûrn), v.t. 1. to oblige to reside within prescribed limits under prohibition to leave them, as prisoners of war or enemy aliens, or as combatant troops who take refuge in a neutral country. 2. to hold within a country until the termination of a war, as a vessel of a belligerent which has put into a neutral port and remained beyond a limited period allowed. —v.i. 3. someone interned. [t. F: s. interner, ult. der. L internus internal]

in·tern² (ĭn'tûrn), n. Also, **interne**. 1. a resident member of the medical staff of a hospital, commonly a recent medical graduate acting as assistant. 2. an inmate. —v.i. 3. to be or perform the duties of an intern. [t. F: m. interne, t. L: m. internus internal] —in'tern·ship', n.

in·tern[3] (ĭn tûrn′), adj., n. Arch. internal. [L internus]

in·ter·nal (ĭn tûr′nəl), adj. 1. situated or existing in the interior of something; interior: internal organs. 2. of or pertaining to the inside or inner part. 3. to be taken inwardly: internal stimulants. 4. existing, occurring, or found within the limits or scope of something. 5. existing or occurring within a country; domestic: internal affair. 6. pertaining to the domestic affairs of a country. 7. of the mind or soul; mental or spiritual; subjective. 8. Anat., Zool. inner; not superficial; away from the surface or next to the axis of the body or of a part: the internal carotid artery. —n. 9. (pl.) entrails. 10. inner or intrinsic attribute. [t. ML: s. internālis, der. L internus inward] —in′ter·nal′i·ty, n. —in·ter′nal·ly, adv.

in·ter·nal-com·bus·tion (ĭn tûr′nəl kəm bŭs′chən), adj. of or pertaining to an internal-combustion engine.

internal-combustion engine, an engine of one or more working cylinders in which the process of combustion takes place within the cylinder.

internal medicine, the branch of medicine concerned with the diagnosis and cure of internal disorders.

internat., international.

in·ter·na·tion·al (ĭn′tər năsh′ən əl), adj. 1. between or among nations: an international armament race. 2. of or pertaining to different nations or their citizens: a matter of international concern. 3. pertaining to the relations between nations: international law. 4. (cap.) of or pertaining to any association known as an International. —n. 5. (cap.) a socialistic association (in full, **International Workingmen's Association**) intended to unite the working classes of all countries in promoting their own interests and social and industrial reforms, by political means, formed in London in 1864, and dissolved in Philadelphia in 1876 (**First International**). 6. (cap.) an international socialistic association formed in 1889, uniting socialistic groups or political parties of various countries, and holding international congresses from time to time (**Second International**). 7. (cap.) an ultraradical and communistic association formed in Moscow, under Bolshevist auspices, in 1919 (dissolved, 1943), uniting communist groups of various countries and advocating the attainment of its ends by revolutionary or violent measures (**Third or Communist International**). 8. (cap.) the Socialist organization formed in 1921 (**Vienna International**, often called the **Two-and-a-half International**). 9. (cap.) the socialistic association formed in 1923 by the uniting of the Second International and the Vienna International at Hamburg and called in full the **Labor and Socialist International**. 10. a loose federation of small ultraradical groups formed in 1936 (orig. under the leadership of Leon Trotsky), and hostile to the Soviet Union (sometimes called the **Fourth or Trotskyist International**). —in′ter·na′tion·al′i·ty, n. —in·ter·na′tion·al·ly, adv.

international candle. See candle (def. 3c).

international date line, date line (def. 2).

In·ter·na·tio·nale (ăn těr nä syô näl′), n. a revolutionary song, first sung in France in 1871 and since popular as a song of workers and Communists.

International Geophysical Year, the 18-month period from July 1, 1957 to Dec. 31, 1958, designated as a time of intensive geophysical exploration and sharing of knowledge by scientists of all countries.

in·ter·na·tion·al·ism (ĭn′tər năsh′ən ə lĭz′əm), n. 1. the principle of coöperation among nations, to promote their common good, sometimes as contrasted with nationalism, or devotion to the interests of a particular nation. 2. international character, relations, coöperation, or control. 3. (cap.) the principles or methods advocated by any association known as an International.

in·ter·na·tion·al·ist (ĭn′tər năsh′ən əl ĭst), n. 1. an advocate of internationalism. 2. one versed in international law and relations. 3. (cap.) a member or adherent of an International.

in·ter·na·tion·al·ize (ĭn′tər năsh′ən ə līz′), v.t., -ized, -izing. to make international; bring under international control. —in′ter·na′tion·al·i·za′tion, n.

International Labor Office, an organization formed in 1919, devoted to standardizing international labor practices and including representatives of government, management, and labor.

international law, the body of rules which civilized nations recognize as binding them in their conduct towards one another.

international nautical mile. See mile (def. 1c). Also, **international air mile.**

International News Service, See **United Press International.**

International Phonetic Alphabet, an alphabet designed to provide a consistent and universally understood system of letters and other symbols for writing the speech sounds of all languages.

in·terne (ĭn′tûrn), n. intern[2].

in·ter·ne·cine (ĭn′tər nē′sīn, -sĭn), adj. 1. mutually destructive. 2. characterized by great slaughter. [t. L: m. s. internecīnus, der. internecium slaughter]

in·tern·ee (ĭn′tûr nē′), n. one who is or has been interned, as a prisoner of war.

in·tern·ist (ĭn′tûr nĭst, ĭn tûr′nĭst), n. a physician specializing in the diagnosis and non-surgical treatment of adult diseases. [f. INTERN(AL MEDICINE) + -IST]

in·tern·ment (ĭn tûrn′mənt), n. 1. act of interning. 2. state or condition of being interned; confinement.

internment camp, (during wartime) a military camp for the confinement of enemy aliens, prisoners of war, etc.

in·ter·node (ĭn′tər nōd′), n. a part or space between two nodes, knots, or joints, as the portion of a plant stem between two nodes. —in′ter·nod′al, adj.

in·ter nos (ĭn′tər nōs′), Latin. between or among us.

in·ter·nun·cial (ĭn′tər nŭn′shal), adj. Anat. (of a nerve cell or a chain of nerve cells) linking the incoming and outgoing nerve fibers of the nervous system.

in·ter·nun·ci·o (ĭn′tər nŭn′shĭ ō′), n., pl. -cios. a papal ambassador ranking next below a nuncio. [t. It., t. L: m. internuntius]

in·ter·o·ce·an·ic (ĭn′tər ō′shĭ ăn′ĭk), adj. between oceans: an interoceanic canal.

in·ter·o·cep·tive (ĭn′tər ō sěp′tĭv), adj. Physiol. pertaining to interoceptors, the stimuli impinging upon them, and the nerve impulses initiated by them.

in·ter·o·cep·tor (ĭn′tər ō sěp′tər), n. a nerve ending or sense organ responding to stimuli originating from within the body. [f. intero- inside (NL comb. form modeled on extero- outside) + -ceptor. See RECEPTOR]

in·ter·os·cu·late (ĭn′tər ŏs′kyə lāt′), v.i., -lated, -lating. 1. to interpenetrate; inosculate. 2. to form a connecting link. —in′ter·os′cu·la′tion, n.

in·ter·pel·lant (ĭn′tər pĕl′ənt), n. one who interpellates. [t. F, ppr. of interpeller, t. L: m. interpellāre interrupt in speaking]

in·ter·pel·late (ĭn′tər pĕl′āt, ĭn tûr′pə lāt′), v.t., -lated, -lating. to call formally upon (a minister or member of the government) in interpellation. [t. L: m. s. interpellātus, pp., interrupted in speaking] —in·ter·pel·la·tor (ĭn′tər pə lā′tər, ĭn tûr′pə lā′tər), n.

in·ter·pel·la·tion (ĭn′tər pə lā′shən, ĭn tûr′pə-), n. a procedure in some legislative bodies of asking a government official to explain an act or policy, usually leading in parliamentary government to a vote of confidence. [t. L: s. interpellātiō interruption]

in·ter·pen·e·trate (ĭn′tər pĕn′ə trāt′), v., -trated, -trating. —v.t. 1. to penetrate thoroughly; permeate. 2. to penetrate reciprocally. —v.i. 3. to penetrate between things or parts. 4. to penetrate each other. —in′ter·pen′e·tra′tion, n. —in′ter·pen′e·tra′tive, adj.

in·ter·phone (ĭn′tər fōn′), n. a telephone connecting offices, stations, etc., as in a building or ship.

in·ter·plan·e·tar·y (ĭn′tər plăn′ə těr′ē), adj. Astron. situated within the solar system, but not within the atmosphere of the sun or any planet.

in·ter·play (n. ĭn′tər plā′; v. ĭn′tər plā′), n. 1. reciprocal play, action, or influence: the interplay of plot and character. —v.i. 2. to exert influence on each other.

in·ter·plead (ĭn′tər plēd′), v.i. Law. to litigate with each other in order to determine which is the rightful claimant against a third party.

in·ter·plead·er (ĭn′tər plē′dər), n. Law. 1. a proceeding by which two parties making the same claim against a third party determine judicially which is the rightful claimant. 2. a party who interpleads.

in·ter·po·late (ĭn tûr′pə lāt′), v., -lated, -lating. —v.t. 1. to alter (a text, etc.) by the insertion of new matter, esp. deceptively or without authorization. 2. to insert (new or spurious matter) thus. 3. to introduce (something additional or extraneous) between other things or parts; interject; interpose; intercalate. 4. Math. to insert or find intermediate terms in (a sequence). —v.i. 5. to make interpolations. [t. L: m.s. interpolātus, pp. furbished, altered, falsified] —in·ter′po·lat′er, in·ter′po·la′tor, n. —in·ter′po·la′tive, adj.

in·ter·po·la·tion (ĭn tûr′pə lā′shən), n. 1. act of interpolating. 2. the fact of being interpolated. 3. something interpolated, as a passage introduced into a text.

in·ter·pose (ĭn′tər pōz′), v., -posed, -posing. —v.t. 1. to place between; cause to intervene: to interpose an opaque body between a light and the eye. 2. to put (a barrier, obstacle, etc.) between, or in the way. 3. to bring (influence, action, etc.) to bear between parties, or in behalf of a party or person. 4. to put in (a remark, etc.) in the midst of a conversation, discourse, or the like. —v.i. 5. to come between other things; assume an intervening position or relation. 6. to step in between parties at variance; mediate. 7. to put in or make a remark by way of interruption. [t. F: m.s. interposer. See INTER-, POSE[1]] —in′ter·pos′er, n. —in′ter·pos′ing·ly, adv. in′ter·pos′al, n.

in·ter·po·si·tion (ĭn′tər pə zĭsh′ən), n. 1. act or fact of being interposed. 2. something interposed. 3. U.S. the doctrine that an individual State may oppose any Federal action it believes encroaches on its sovereignty.

in·ter·pret (ĭn tûr′prĭt), v.t. 1. to set forth the meaning of; explain or elucidate: to interpret omens. 2. to explain, construe, or understand in a particular way: to interpret a reply as favorable. 3. to bring out the meaning of (a dramatic work, music, etc.) by performance or execution. 4. to translate. —v.i. 5. to translate what is said in a foreign language. 6. to give an explanation. [ME interprete(n), t. L: m. interpretārī explain] —in·ter′pret·a·ble, adj. —in·ter′pret·a·bil′i·ty, n. —in·ter′pret·er, n. —in·ter′pre·tive, adj. —in·ter′pre·tive·ly, adv. —Syn. 1. See explain.

in·ter·pre·ta·tion (ĭn tûr′prə tā′shən), n. 1. act of interpreting; elucidation: the interpretation of nature. 2. an explanation given: to put a wrong interpretation on a passage. 3. a construction placed upon something: a charitable interpretation. 4. a way of interpreting. 5. the rendering of a dramatic part, music, etc., so as to bring out the meaning, or to indicate one's particular conception of it. **6.** translation. [ME, t. L: s. *interpretātio*] —in·ter'pre·ta'tion·al, *adj.*

in·ter·pre·ta·tive (ĭn tûr'prə tā'tĭv), *adj.* **1.** serving to interpret; explanatory. **2.** deduced by interpretation. —in·ter'pre·ta'tive·ly, *adv.*

in·ter·ra·cial (ĭn'tər rā'shəl), *adj.* **1.** existing between races, or members of different races. **2.** of or for persons of different races: *interracial camps for children.*

in·ter·ra·di·al (ĭn'tər rā'dĭ əl), *adj.* situated between the radii or rays: *the interradial petals in an echinoderm.*

in·ter·reg·num (ĭn'tər rĕg'nəm), *n., pl.* **-nums, -na** (-nə). **1.** an interval of time between the close of a sovereign's reign and the accession of his normal or legitimate successor. **2.** any period during which a state has no ruler or only a temporary executive. **3.** any pause or interruption in continuity. [t. L, f. *inter-* INTER- + *regnum* REIGN] —in'ter·reg'nal, *adj.*

in·ter·re·late (ĭn'tər rĭ lāt'), *v.t.,* **-lated, -lating.** to bring into reciprocal relation.

in·ter·re·lat·ed (ĭn'tər rĭ lā'tĭd), *adj.* reciprocally related: *the interrelated sets of wires.* —in'ter·re·la'tion·ship', *n.*

in·ter·re·la·tion (ĭn'tər rĭ lā'shən), *n.* reciprocal relation. —in'ter·re·la'tion·ship', *n.*

in·ter·rex (ĭn'tər rĕks'), *n., pl.* **interreges** (ĭn'tər-rē'jēz). a person holding supreme authority in a state during an interregnum. [t. L, f. *inter-* INTER- + *rex* king]

interrog., **1.** interrogation. **2.** interrogative.

in·ter·ro·gate (ĭn tĕr'ə gāt'), *v.,* **-gated, -gating.** —*v.t.* **1.** to ask a question or a series of questions of (a person). **2.** to examine by questions; question: *they were interrogated by the police.* —*v.i.* **3.** to ask questions. [late ME, t. L: m. s. *interrogātus*, pp.] —in·ter'ro·gat'·ing·ly, *adv.* —in·ter'ro·ga'tor, *n.*

in·ter·ro·ga·tion (ĭn tĕr'ə gā'shən), *n.* **1.** act of interrogating; questioning. **2.** a question. **3.** an interrogation point. —in·ter'ro·ga'tion·al, *adj.*

interrogation point, question mark. Also, **interrogation mark.**

in·ter·rog·a·tive (ĭn'tə rŏg'ə tĭv), *adj.* **1.** pertaining to or conveying a question. **2.** *Gram.* (of an element or construction) forming or constituting a question: *an interrogative pronoun, an interrogative sentence.* —*n.* **3.** *Gram.* an interrogative word, element, or construction, as "who?" and "what?" —in·ter'rog'a·tive·ly, *adv.*

in·ter·rog·a·to·ry (ĭn'tə rŏg'ə tôr'ĭ), *adj., n., pl.* **-tories.** —*adj.* **1.** interrogative; questioning. —*n.* **2.** a question or inquiry. **3.** *Law.* a formal or written question. —in'ter·rog'a·to'ri·ly, *adv.*

in ter·ro·rem clause (ĭn tĕr rôr'ĕm), *Law.* a clause in a will stating that a beneficiary who starts a will contest shall lose his legacy.

in·ter·rupt (ĭn'tə rŭpt'), *v.t.* **1.** to make a break in (an otherwise continuous extent, course, process, condition, etc.). **2.** to break off or cause to cease, as in the midst or course: *he interrupted his work to answer the bell.* **3.** to stop (a person) in the midst of doing or saying something, esp. as by an interjected remark: *I don't want to be interrupted.* —*v.i.* **4.** to cause a break or discontinuance; interrupt action or speech: *please don't interrupt.* [ME *interrupte*(*n*), t. L: m. s. *interruptus*, pp., broken apart] —in'ter·rup'tive, *adj.*
—**Syn. 1, 3.** INTERRUPT, DISCONTINUE, SUSPEND imply breaking off something temporarily or permanently. INTERRUPT may have either meaning: *to interrupt a meeting.* To DISCONTINUE is to stop or leave off, often permanently: *to discontinue a building program.* To SUSPEND is to break off relations, operations, proceedings, privileges, etc. for a longer or shorter period, usually intending to resume at a stated time: *to suspend operations during a strike.*

interrupted screw, a screw with a discontinuous helix, as in a cannon breech, formed by cutting away part or parts of the thread, sometimes with part of the shaft beneath, used with a lock nut having corresponding male sections.

in·ter·rupt·er (ĭn'tə rŭp'tər), *n.* **1.** one who or that which interrupts. **2.** *Elect.* a device for interrupting or periodically making and breaking a circuit. Also, **in'ter·rup'tor.**

in·ter·rup·tion (ĭn'tə rŭp'shən), *n.* **1.** act of interrupting. **2.** state of being interrupted. **3.** something that interrupts. **4.** cessation; intermission.

in·ter·scap·u·lar (ĭn'tər skăp'yə lər), *adj. Anat., Zool.* between the scapulae or shoulder blades.

in·ter·scho·las·tic (ĭn'tər skə lăs'tĭk), *adj.* between elementary or secondary schools: *interscholastic football.*

in·ter se (ĭn'tər sē'), *Latin.* **1.** among or between themselves. **2.** (in livestock breeding) mating animals similarly bred to each other.

in·ter·sect (ĭn'tər sĕkt'), *v.t.* **1.** to cut or divide by passing through or lying across: *one road intersects another.* —*v.i.* **2.** to cross, as lines. **3.** *Geom.* to have, as two geometrical loci, one or more points in common: *intersecting lines.* [t. L: s. *intersectus*, pp., cut off]

in·ter·sec·tion (ĭn'tər sĕk'shən), *n.* act, fact, or place of intersecting. —in'ter·sec'tion·al, *adj.*

in·ter·sep·tal (ĭn'tər sĕp'təl), *adj.* between septa.

in·ter·sex (ĭn'tər sĕks'), *n. Biol.* an individual displaying characteristics of both the male and female sexes of the species.

in·ter·si·de·re·al (ĭn'tər sĭ dĭr'ĭ əl), *adj.* interstellar.

in·ter·space (*n.* ĭn'tər spās'; *v.* ĭn'tər spās'), *n., v.,* **-spaced, -spacing.** —*n.* **1.** a space between things. **2.** an intervening interval of time. —*v.t.* **3.** to put a

space between. **4.** to occupy or fill the space between. —in'ter·spa'tial, *adj.*

in·ter·sperse (ĭn'tər spûrs'), *v.t.,* **-spersed, -spersing. 1.** to scatter here and there among other things: *to intersperse flowers among shrubs.* **2.** to diversify with something scattered or introduced here and there: *his speech was interspersed with long and boring quotations from the poets.* [t. L: m.s. *interspersus* strewn] —in·ter·sper·sion (ĭn'tər spûr'shən, -zhən), *n.*

in·ter·state (ĭn'tər stāt'), *adj.* between or jointly involving states: *interstate commerce.* Cf. **intrastate.**

in·ter·stel·lar (ĭn'tər stĕl'ər), *adj.* among the stars; intersidereal: *interstellar space.*

in·ter·stice (ĭn tûr'stĭs), *n.* **1.** an intervening space. **2.** a small or narrow space between things or parts; small chink, crevice, or opening. **3.** *Rare.* an interval of time. [t. L: m. s. *interstitium* space between]

in·ter·sti·tial (ĭn'tər stĭsh'əl), *adj.* **1.** pertaining to, situated in, or forming interstices. **2.** *Anat.* situated between the cellular elements of a structure or part: *interstitial tissue.* —in'ter·sti'tial·ly, *adv.*

in·ter·strat·i·fy (ĭn'tər străt'ə fī'), *v.,* **-fied, -fying.** —*v.i.* **1.** to lie in interposed or alternate strata. —*v.t.* **2.** to interlay with or interpose between other strata. **3.** to arrange in alternate strata. —in'ter·strat'i·fi·ca'tion, *n.*

in·ter·tex·ture (ĭn'tər tĕks'chər), *n.* **1.** act of interweaving. **2.** the condition of being interwoven. **3.** something formed by interweaving.

in·ter·trib·al (ĭn'tər trī'bəl), *adj.* between tribes: *intertribal warfare.*

in·ter·trop·i·cal (ĭn'tər trŏp'ə kəl), *adj. Geog.* between the tropics (of Cancer and Capricorn).

in·ter·twine (ĭn'tər twīn'), *v.t., v.i.,* **-twined, -twining.** to twine together. —in'ter·twine'ment, *n.* —in'ter·twin'ing·ly, *adv.*

in·ter·twist (ĭn'tər twĭst'), *v.t., v.i.* to twist together. —in'ter·twist'ing·ly, *adv.*

in·ter·ur·ban (ĭn'tər ûr'bən), *adj.* **1.** between cities. —*n.* **2.** an interurban train or car.

in·ter·val (ĭn'tər vəl), *n.* **1.** an intervening period of time: *an interval of fifty years.* **2.** a period of cessation; a pause: *intervals between attacks.* **3.** *Brit. Theat.* an intermission. **4.** a space intervening between things, points, limits, qualities, etc.: *an interval of ten feet between columns.* **5. at intervals,** at particular times or places with gaps in between. **6.** the space between soldiers or units in military formation. **7.** *Music.* the difference in pitch between two tones, as, **a. harmonic interval,** an interval between two tones sounded simultaneously. **b. melodic interval,** an interval between two tones sounded successively. **8.** *U.S. and Canada.* intervale. [ME *intervall*, t. L: s. *intervallum*]

in·ter·vale (ĭn'tər vāl'), *n. U.S. and Canada.* a low-lying tract of land, as along a river, between hills, etc. [var. of INTERVAL, assoc. with VALE[1]]

in·ter·vene (ĭn'tər vēn'), *v.i.,* **-vened, -vening. 1.** to come between in action; intercede: *to intervene in a dispute.* **2.** to come or be between, as in place, time, or a series. **3.** to fall or happen between other events or periods: *nothing interesting has intervened.* **4.** (of things) to occur incidentally so as to modify a result. **5.** to come in, as something not belonging. **6.** *Law.* to interpose and become a party to a suit pending between other parties. [t. L: m. s. *intervenire* come between] —in'ter·ven'er, *n.*

in·ter·ven·ient (ĭn'tər vĕn'yənt), *adj.* **1.** intervening, as in place, time, order, or action. **2.** incidental.

in·ter·ven·tion (ĭn'tər vĕn'shən), *n.* **1.** act or fact of intervening. **2.** the interposition or interference of one state in the affairs of another: *intervention in the domestic policies of smaller nations.* —in'ter·ven'tion·al, *adj.*

in·ter·ven·tion·ist (ĭn'tər vĕn'shən ĭst), *n.* one who favors intervention, as in the affairs of another state.

in·ter·view (ĭn'tər vū'), *n.* **1.** the conversation of a writer or reporter with a person or persons from whom material for a news or feature story or other writing is sought. **2.** the report of such conversation. **3.** a meeting of persons face to face, esp. for formal conference. —*v.t.* **4.** to have an interview with: *to interview the president.* [t. F: m. *entervue*, der. *entrevoir*, refl., see (each other), f. *entre-* INTER- + *voir* (g. L *vidēre*) see] —in'ter·view'er, *n.*

in·ter·volve (ĭn'tər vŏlv'), *v.t., v.i.,* **-volved, -volving.** to roll, wind, or involve, one within another. [f. INTER- + m.s. L *volvere* roll]

in·ter·weave (ĭn'tər wēv'), *v.,* **-wove or -weaved; -woven or -wove or -weaved; -weaving.** —*v.t.* **1.** to weave together, one with another, as threads, strands, branches, roots, etc. **2.** to intermingle or combine as if by weaving: *to interweave truth with fiction.* —*v.i.* **3.** to become woven together, interlaced, or intermingled. —in'ter·weave'ment, *n.* —in'ter·weav'er, *n.*

in·tes·ta·cy (ĭn tĕs'tə sĭ), *n.* state or fact of being intestate at death.

in·tes·tate (ĭn tĕs'tāt, -tĭt), *adj.* **1.** dying without having made a will. **2.** not disposed of by will; not legally devised or bequeathed. —*n.* **3.** one who dies intestate. [ME, t. L: m. s. *intestātus* having made no will]

in·tes·ti·nal (ĭn tĕs'tə nəl; *Brit.* ĭn'tĕs tī'nəl), *adj.* **1.** of or pertaining to the intestine. **2.** occurring or found in the intestine. [t. ML: s. *intestīnālis*] —in·tes'ti·nal·ly, *adv.*

---

b., blend of, blended; c., cognate with; d., dialect, dialectal; der., derived from; f., formed from; g., going back to; m., modification of; r., replacing; s., stem of; t., taken from; ?, perhaps. See the full key on inside cover.

in·tes·tine (ĭntĕs′tĭn), *n.* *Anat.* **1.** the lower part of the alimentary canal, extending from the pylorus to the anus. **2.** a definite portion of this part. The **small intestine** comprises the duodenum, jejunum, and ileum; the **large intestine** comprises the caecum, colon, and rectum. —*adj.* **3.** internal; domestic; civil: *intestine strife.* [t. L: m. s. *intestina,* pl., entrails]

in·thral (ĭnthrôl′), *v.t.*, **-thralled, -thralling.** inthrall.

in·thrall (ĭnthrôl′), *v.t.* enthrall.

in·throne (ĭnthrōn′), *v.t.* **-throned, -throning.** enthrone.

in·ti·ma (ĭn′tə mə), *n.*, *pl.* **-mae** (-mē′). *Anat.* the innermost membrane or lining of some organ or part, esp. that of an artery, vein, or lymphatic. [t. NL, prop. fem. of L *intimus* inmost]

in·ti·ma·cy (ĭn′tə mə sĭ), *n.*, *pl.* **-cies. 1.** state of being intimate; intimate association or friendship. **2.** an instance of this. **3.** illicit sexual relations.

in·ti·mate[1] (ĭn′tə mĭt), *adj.* **1.** associated in close personal relations: *an intimate friend.* **2.** characterized by or involving personally close or familiar association: *an intimate gathering.* **3.** private; closely personal: *one's intimate affairs.* **4.** maintaining illicit sexual relations. **5.** (of acquaintance, knowledge, etc.) arising from close personal connection or familiar experience. **6.** detailed; deep: *a more intimate analysis.* **7.** close union or combination of particles or elements: *an intimate mixture.* **8.** inmost; deep within. **9.** pertaining to the inmost or essential nature; intrinsic: *the intimate structure of an organism.* **10.** pertaining to or existing in the inmost mind: *intimate beliefs.* —*n.* **11.** an intimate friend or associate. [in form t. LL: m. s. *intimātus,* pp., put or pressed into, but with sense of L *intimus* inmost] —**in′ti·mate·ly,** *adv.* —**in′ti·mate·ness,** *n.* —Syn. 1. See familiar.

in·ti·mate[2] (ĭn′tə māt′), *v.t.*, **-mated, -mating. 1.** to make known indirectly; hint; suggest. **2.** *Rare.* to make known, esp. formally; announce. [t. LL: m.s. *intimātus,* pp., put or pressed into, announced] —**in′ti·ma′tion,** *n.* —Syn. 1. See hint.

in·tim·i·date (ĭntĭm′ə dāt′), *v.t.*, **-dated, -dating. 1.** to make timid, or inspire with fear; overawe; cow. **2.** to force into or deter from some action by inducing fear: *to intimidate a voter.* [t. ML: m.s. *intimidātus,* pp., made afraid. See TIMID] —**in·tim′i·da′tion,** *n.* —**in·tim′i·da′tor,** *n.* —Syn. 2. See discourage.

in·tinc·tion (ĭntĭngk′shən), *n.* (in the Eucharistic service) act of steeping the bread in the wine, to enable the communicants to receive the two conjointly. [t. LL: s. *intinctio,* der. L *intingere* dip in]

in·ti·tle (ĭntī′təl), *v.t.*, **-tled, -tling.** entitle.

in·tit·ule (ĭntĭt′ūl), *v.t.*, **-uled, -uling.** *Archaic.* to give a title to; entitle. [t. LL: m.s. *intitulāre.* der. L *in-* IN-² + *titulus* TITLE] —**in·tit′u·la′tion,** *n.*

in·to (ĭn′tōō; *unstressed* ĭn′tŏŏ, -tə), *prep.* **1.** in to; in and to (expressing motion or direction toward the inner part of a place or thing, and hence entrance or inclusion within limits, or change to new circumstances, relations, condition, form, etc.). **2.** *Math.* by: with *divide* (formerly, sometimes, *multiply*) implied. [ME *in to*]

in·toed (ĭn′tōd′), *adj.* having inwardly turned toes.

in·tol·er·a·ble (ĭntŏl′ər ə bəl), *adj.* **1.** not tolerable; unendurable; insufferable: *intolerable agony.* —*adv.* **2.** *Obs.* exceedingly. —**in·tol′er·a·bil′i·ty, in·tol′er·a·ble·ness,** *n.* —**in·tol′er·a·bly,** *adv.* —Syn. 1. unbearable.

in·tol·er·ance (ĭntŏl′ər əns), *n.* **1.** lack of toleration; indisposition to tolerate contrary opinions or beliefs. **2.** incapacity or indisposition to bear or endure: *intolerance of heat.* **3.** an intolerant act.

in·tol·er·ant (ĭntŏl′ər ənt), *adj.* **1.** not tolerating contrary opinions, esp. in religious matters; bigoted: *an intolerant zealot.* **2.** unable or indisposed to tolerate or endure (fol. by *of*): *intolerant of excesses.* —*n.* **3.** one who does not favor toleration. —**in·tol′er·ant·ly,** *adv.* —Syn. 1. INTOLERANT, FANATICAL, BIGOTED refer to strongly illiberal attitudes. INTOLERANT implies active (often violent) refusal to allow others to have or put into practice beliefs different from one's own: *intolerant in politics.* To be BIGOTED is to be so strongly attached to one's own belief as to be hostile to all others: *a bigoted person.* FANATICAL applies to unreasonable, often violent, action in maintaining one's beliefs and (often religious) practices: *a fanatical religious sect.* —Ant. liberal.

in·tomb (ĭntōōm′), *v.t.* entomb. —**in·tomb′ment,** *n.*

in·to·nate (ĭn′tō nāt′), *v.t.*, **-nated, -nating. 1.** to utter with a particular tone or modulation of voice. **2.** to intone or chant. [t. ML: m.s. *intonātus,* pp.]

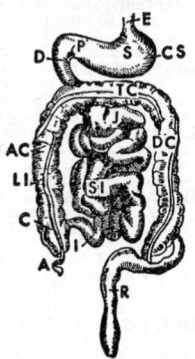

+E
P
D
S
CS
TC
AC
DC
LI
SI
C
I
A
R

Human intestines
E. End of esophagus; CS.
Cardiac end of stomach; S.
Stomach; P. Pylorus; D.
Duodenum; J. Jejunum; SI.
Small intestine; I. Ileum;
LI. Large intestine; C. Cae-
cum; A. Vermiform appen-
dix; AC. Ascending colon;
TC. Transverse colon; DC.
Descending colon, R;
Rectum

in·to·na·tion (ĭn′tō nā′shən), *n.* **1.** the pattern or melody of pitch changes revealed in connected speech; esp., the pitch pattern of a sentence, which distinguishes kinds of sentences and speakers of different nationalities. **2.** act of intonating. **3.** the manner of producing musical tones, specifically the relation in pitch of tones to their key or harmony. **4.** the opening phrase in a Gregorian chant, usually sung by but one or two voices.

in·tone (ĭntōn′), *v.*, **-toned, -toning.** —*v.t.* **1.** to utter with a particular tone; intonate. **2.** to give tone or variety of tone to; vocalize. **3.** to utter in a singing voice (the first tones of a section in a liturgical service). **4.** to recite in monotone. —*v.i.* **5.** to speak or recite in a singing voice, esp. in monotone. **6.** *Music.* to produce a tone, or a particular series of tones, like a scale, esp. with the voice; sing or chant. [late ME, t. ML: m.s. *intonāre.* Cf. INTONATE] —**in·ton′er,** *n.*

in·tor·sion (ĭntôr′shən), *n.* a twisting or winding, as of the stem of a plant.

in·tort (ĭntôrt′), *v.t.* to twist inward, curl, or wind: *intorted horns.* [t. L: s. *intortus,* pp.]

in to·to (ĭn tō′tō), *Latin.* in all; in the whole; wholly.

in·tox·i·cant (ĭntŏk′sə kənt), *adj.* **1.** intoxicating. —*n.* **2.** an intoxicating agent, as liquor or certain drugs.

in·tox·i·cate (*v.* ĭntŏk′sə kāt′; *adj.* ĭntŏk′sə kĭt, -kāt′), *v.*, **-cated, -cating,** *adj.* —*v.t.* **1.** to affect temporarily with loss of control over the physical and mental powers, by means of alcoholic liquor, a drug, or other substance. **2.** to excite mentally beyond self-control or reason. **3.** *Obs.* to poison. —*v.i.* **4.** to cause or produce intoxication: *an intoxicating liquor.* —*adj.* **5.** *Archaic.* intoxicated. [ME, t. ML: m. s. *intoxicātus,* pp., poisoned. See TOXIC] —**in·tox′i·cat′ing·ly,** *adv.* —**in·tox′i·ca′tive,** *adj.*

in·tox·i·cat·ed (ĭntŏk′sə kā′tĭd), *adj.* **1.** drunk. **2.** excited mentally beyond reason or self-control.

in·tox·i·ca·tion (ĭntŏk′sə kā′shən), *n.* **1.** inebriation; drunkenness. **2.** *Pathol.* poisoning. **3.** act of intoxicating. **4.** overpowering action or effect upon the mind.

intr., intransitive.

intra-, a prefix meaning "within," freely used as an English formative, esp. in scientific terms, sometimes in opposition to *extra-.* Cf. **intro-.** [t. L, repr. *intrā,* adv. and prep., within, akin to *interior* inner, and *inter* between]

in·tra·car·di·ac (ĭn′trə kär′dĭ ăk′), *adj.* endocardial.

in·tra·cel·lu·lar (ĭn′trə sĕl′yə lər), *adj.* within a cell or cells.

in·tra·cra·ni·al (ĭn′trə krā′nĭ əl), *adj.* within the cranium or skull.

in·trac·ta·ble (ĭntrăk′tə bəl), *adj.* **1.** not docile; stubborn: *an intractable disposition.* **2.** (of things) hard to deal with; unmanageable. —**in·trac′ta·bil′i·ty, in·trac′ta·ble·ness,** *n.* —**in·trac′ta·bly,** *adv.*

in·tra·dos (ĭntrā′dŏs), *n.* *Archit.* the interior curve or surface of an arch or vault. Cf. **extrados.** See diag. under **arch.** [t. F, f. L *intra-* INTRA- + F *dos* (g. L *dorsum* back)]

in·tra·mo·lec·u·lar (ĭn′trə mə lĕk′yə lər, -mō-), *adj.* within the molecule or molecules.

in·tra·mu·ral (ĭn′trə myŏŏr′əl), *adj.* **1.** engaged in or pertaining to a single college, or its students *intramural athletics.* **2.** within the walls or enclosing limits, as of a city or a building. **3.** *Anat.* within the substance of a wall, as of an organ.

in·tra mu·ros (ĭn′trə myŏŏr′ōs), *Latin.* within the walls, as of a city.

in·tra·mus·cu·lar (ĭn′trə mŭs′kyə lər), *adj.* located or occurring within a muscle.

intrans., intransitive.

in·tran·si·gent (ĭntrăn′sə jənt), *adj.* **1.** uncompromising, esp. in politics; irreconcilable. —*n.* **2.** one who is irreconcilable, esp. in politics. Also, *French,* **in·tran·si·geant** (ăn trăn zē zhän′). [t. F: m. *intransigeant,* t. Sp., der. (*los*) *intransigentes* revolutionary party refusing compromise, f. L: *in-* IN-³ + *transigentēs,* ppr. pl. coming to an agreement] —**in·tran′si·gence, in·tran′si·gen·cy,** *n.* —**in·tran′si·gent·ly,** *adv.*

in·tran·si·tive (ĭntrăn′sə tĭv), *adj.* **1.** having the quality of an intransitive verb. —*n.* **2.** an intransitive verb. —**in·tran′si·tive·ly,** *adv.*

intransitive verb, a verb that is never accompanied by a direct object, as *come, sit, lie,* etc.

in tran·si·tu (ĭn trăn′sə tū′, -tōō′), *Latin.* in transit; on the way.

in·trant (ĭn′trənt), *n.* one who enters (esp. a college, association, etc.); entrant. [t. L: s. *intrans,* ppr., entering]

in·tra·state (ĭn′trə stāt′), *adj.* within a state, esp. one of the United States: *intrastate commerce.*

in·tra·tel·lu·ric (ĭn′trə tə lŏŏr′ĭk), *adj.* **1.** *Geol.* located in, taking place in, or resulting from action, beneath the lithosphere. **2.** *Petrog.* designating the period of crystallization of an eruptive rock which precedes its extrusion on the surface or the crystals in a porphyritic lava formed prior to its extrusion.

in·tra·ve·nous (ĭn′trə vē′nəs), *adj.* **1.** within a vein or the veins. **2.** noting or pertaining to an injection into a vein. —**in′tra·ve′nous·ly,** *adv.*

in·treat (ĭntrēt′), *v.t.*, *v.i.* entreat.

in·trench (ĭntrĕnch′), *v.t.*, *v.i.* entrench. —**in·trench′er,** *n.* —**in·trench′ment,** *n.*

in·trep·id (ĭn trĕp'ĭd), *adj.* fearless; dauntless: *intrepid courage*. [t. L: s. *intrepidus* not alarmed] —**in'·tre·pid'i·ty,** *n.* —**in·trep'id·ly,** *adv.*

in·tri·ca·cy (ĭn'trə kə sĭ), *n., pl.* -**cies.** **1.** intricate character or state. **2.** an intricate part, action, etc.

in·tri·cate (ĭn'trə kĭt), *adj.* **1.** perplexingly entangled or involved: *a maze of intricate paths.* **2.** confusingly complex; complicated; hard to understand: *an intricate machine.* [late ME, t. L: m. s. *intricātus,* pp., entangled] —**in'tri·cate·ly,** *adv.* —**in'tri·cate·ness,** *n.*

in·tri·gant (ĭn'trə gənt; *Fr.* ăn trē gäN'), *n., pl.* -**gants** (-gənts; *Fr.* -gäN'). one who carries on intrigue. Also, **in'tri·guant.** [t. F, t. It.: m. *intrigante,* ppr. of *intrigare.* See INTRIGUE, v.]

in·tri·gante (ĭn'trə gänt', -gänt'; *Fr.* ăn trē gäNt'), *n., pl.* -**gantes** (-gänts', -gänts'; *Fr.* gäNt'). a woman intrigant.

in·trigue (*v.* ĭn trēg'; *n.* ĭn trēg', ĭn'trēg), *v.,* -**trigued,** -**triguing,** —*v.t.* **1.** to excite the curiosity or interest of by puzzling, novel, or otherwise arresting qualities. **2.** to take the fancy of: *her hat intrigued me.* **3.** to beguile by appeal to the curiosity, interest, or fancy (fol. by *into*). **4.** to puzzle: *I am intrigued by this event.* **5.** to bring or force by underhand machinations. **6.** *Now Rare.* to entangle. **7.** *Obs.* to trick or cheat. **8.** *Obs.* to plot for. —*v.i.* **9.** to use underhand machinations; plot craftily. **10.** to carry on a clandestine or illicit love affair. —*n.* **11.** the use of underhand machinations to accomplish designs. **12.** a plot or crafty dealing: *political intrigues.* **13.** a clandestine or illicit love affair. **14.** the series of complications forming the plot of a play. [t. F: s. *intriguer,* t. It.: m. *intrigare,* g. L *intrīcāre* entangle, perplex] —**in·tri'guer,** *n.* —**in·tri'·guing·ly,** *adv.*

in·trin·sic (ĭn trĭn'sĭk), *adj.* **1.** belonging to a thing by its very nature: *intrinsic merit.* **2.** *Anat.* (of certain muscles, nerves, etc.) belonging to or lying within a given part. Also, **in·trin'si·cal.** [t. ML: m.s. *intrinsecus* inward (L inwardly)] —**in·trin'si·cal·ly,** *adv.* —**Syn. 1.** See **essential.** —**Ant. 1.** accidental.

intro-, a prefix meaning "inwardly," "within," occasionally used as an English formative. Cf. **intra-.** [t. L, repr. *intro,* adv., inwardly, within]

intro., **1.** introduction. **2.** introductory. Also, **introd.**

in·tro·duce (ĭn'trə dūs', -dōōs'), *v.t.,* -**duced,** -**ducing.** **1.** to bring into notice, knowledge, use, vogue, etc.: *to introduce a fashion.* **2.** to bring forward for consideration, as a proposed legislative bill, etc. **3.** to bring forward with preliminary or preparatory matter: *to introduce a subject with a long preface.* **4.** to bring (a person) to the knowledge or experience of something (fol. by *to*): *to introduce a person to chess.* **5.** to lead, bring, or put into a place, position, surroundings, relations, etc.: *to introduce a figure into a design.* **6.** to bring (a person) into the acquaintance of another: *he introduced his sister to us.* **7.** to present formally, as to a person, an audience, or society: *she was introduced at court.* [late ME, t. L: m.s. *intrōdūcere* lead in] —**in'tro·duc'er,** *n.* —**in'tro·duc'i·ble,** *adj.*

—**Syn. 6, 7.** INTRODUCE, PRESENT mean to bring persons into personal acquaintance with each other, as by announcement of names, and the like. INTRODUCE is the ordinary term, referring to making persons acquainted who are ostensibly equals: *to introduce a friend to one's sister.* PRESENT, a more formal term, suggests a degree of ceremony in the process, and implies (if only as a matter of compliment) superior dignity, rank, or importance in the person to whom another is presented: *to present a visitor to the president.*

in·tro·duc·tion (ĭn'trə dŭk'shən), *n.* **1.** act of introducing. **2.** a formal presentation of one person to another or others. **3.** something introduced. **4.** a preliminary part, as of a book, musical composition or the like, leading up to the main part. **5.** an elementary treatise: *an introduction to botany.* [ME, t. L: s. *intrōductio*]

—**Syn. 4.** INTRODUCTION, FOREWORD, PREFACE refer to material given at the front of a book to explain or introduce it to the reader. An INTRODUCTION is a formal preliminary statement or guide to the book: *his purpose is stated in the introduction.* A FOREWORD is often an informal statement made to the reader. It is the same as PREFACE, but FOREWORD was substituted for it during the vogue for restoring native terms: *an unusual foreword, a short preface.*

in·tro·duc·to·ry (ĭn'trə dŭk'tə rĭ), *adj.* serving to introduce; preliminary; prefatory. Also, **in'tro·duc'tive.** —**in'tro·duc'to·ri·ly,** *adv.* —**Syn.** See **preliminary.**

in·tro·it (ĭn trō'ĭt), *n.* **1.** *Rom. Cath. Ch.* part of a psalm with an antiphon recited by the celebrant of Mass at the foot of the altar and, at High Mass, sung by the choir when the priest begins the Mass. **2.** *Anglican Ch.* psalm or anthem sung as the celebrant of the holy communion is entering the sanctuary. **3.** (esp. in the Anglican Ch.) a musical composition at the beginning of the service. [late ME, t. L: s. *introitus* entrance]

in·tro·jec·tion (ĭn'trə jĕk'shən), *n.* *Psychoanal.* a primitive and early unconscious psychic process by which an external object or individual is represented by an image which in turn is incorporated into the psychic apparatus of someone else. [f. INTRO- + s. L *-jectio* a throwing]

in·tro·mit (ĭn'trə mĭt'), *v.t.,* -**mitted,** -**mitting.** *Now Rare.* to send, put, or let in; introduce; admit. [ME *intromitten*), t. L: m. *intrōmittere* send in] —**in·tro·mis·sion** (ĭn'trə mĭsh'ən), *n.* —**in'tro·mit'tent,** *adj.*

in·trorse (ĭn trôrs'), *adj.* *Bot.* turned or facing inward, as anthers which open toward the gynoecium. [t. L: m. s. *introrsus*] —**in·trorse'ly,** *adv.*

in·tro·spect (ĭn'trə spĕkt'), *v.i.* **1.** to practice introspection; consider one's own internal state or feelings. —*v.t.* **2.** to look into; examine [t. L: s. *intrōspectus,* pp., looked into] —**in'tro·spec'tive,** *adj.* —**in'tro·spec'tive·ly,** *adv.* —**in'tro·spec'tive·ness,** *n.*

in·tro·spec·tion (ĭn'trə spĕk'shən), *n.* **1.** observation or examination of one's own mental states or processes. **2.** sympathetic introspection, *Sociol.* a study of human conduct by imagining oneself as engaged in that conduct.

in·tro·ver·sion (ĭn'trə vûr'shən, -zhən), *n.* **1.** act of introverting. **2.** introverted state. **3.** *Psychol.* interest directed inward or upon the self. Cf. **extroversion.** —**in·tro·ver·sive** (ĭn'trə vûr'sĭv), *adj.*

in·tro·vert (*n., adj.* ĭn'trə vûrt'; *v.* ĭn'trə vûrt'), *n.* **1.** *Psychol.* one characterized by introversion; a person concerned chiefly with his own thoughts. Cf. **extrovert.** **2.** *Zool., etc.* a part that is or can be introverted. —*adj.* **3.** marked by introversion. —*v.t.* **4.** to turn inward. **5.** to direct (the mind, etc.) inward or upon the self. **6.** *Zool., etc.* to insheathe a part of, within another part; invaginate. [f. INTRO- + s. L *vertere* turn]

in·trude (ĭn trōōd'), *v.,* -**truded,** -**truding.** —*v.t.* **1.** to thrust or bring in without reason, permission, or welcome. **2.** *Geol.* to thrust or force in. —*v.i.* **3.** to thrust oneself in; come uninvited: *to intrude upon his privacy.* [t. L: m.s. *intrūdere* thrust in] —**in·trud'er,** *n.* —**in·trud'ing·ly,** *adv.* —**Syn. 3.** See **trespass.**

in·tru·sion (ĭn trōō'zhən), *n.* **1.** act of intruding: *an unwarranted intrusion.* **2.** *Law.* a wrongful entry after the determination of a particular estate, made before the remainderman or reversioner has entered. **3.** *Geol.* **a.** the forcing of extraneous matter, as molten rock, into some other formation. **b.** the matter forced in.

in·tru·sive (ĭn trōō'sĭv), *adj.* **1.** intruding. **2.** characterized by or involving intrusion. **3.** apt to intrude; coming unbidden or without welcome. **4.** *Geol.* **a.** (of rocks) having been forced, while molten or plastic, into fissures or other openings or between layers of other rocks. **b.** noting or pertaining to plutonic rocks. **5.** *Phonet.* inserted without grammatical or historical justification. —**in·tru'sive·ly,** *adv.* —**in·tru'sive·ness,** *n.*

in·trust (ĭn trŭst'), *v.t.* entrust.

in·tu·bate (ĭn'tyōō bāt'), *v.t.,* -**bated,** -**bating.** *Med.* **1.** to insert a tube into. **2.** to treat by inserting a tube, as into the larynx. —**in'tu·ba'tion,** *n.*

in·tu·it (ĭn'tyōō ĭt, -tōō-; ĭn tū'ĭt, -tōō'-), *v.t., v.i.,* -**ited,** -**iting.** to know, or receive knowledge, by intuition. [t. L: s. *intuitus,* pp.]

in·tu·i·tion (ĭn'tyōō ĭsh'ən, -tōō-), *n.* **1.** direct perception of truths, facts, etc., independently of any reasoning process. **2.** *Philos.* **a.** an immediate cognition of an object not inferred or determined by a previous cognition of the same object. **b.** any object or truth so discerned. **c.** pure, untaught, noninferential knowledge. [t. ML: s. *intuitio,* der. L *intuēri* look at, consider]

in·tu·i·tion·al (ĭn'tyōō ĭsh'ən əl, -tōō-), *adj.* **1.** pertaining to or of the nature of intuition. **2.** characterized by intuition; having intuition. **3.** based on intuition as a principle. —**in·tu·i'tion·al·ly,** *adv.*

in·tu·i·tion·al·ism (ĭn'tyōō ĭsh'ən ə lĭz'əm, -tōō-), *n.* intuitionism. —**in·tu·i'tion·al·ist,** *n.*

in·tu·i·tion·ism (ĭn'tyōō ĭsh'ə nĭz'əm, -tōō-), *n.* **1.** *Ethics.* the doctrine that moral values and duties can be discerned directly. **2.** *Metaphys.* **a.** the doctrine that in perception external objects are given immediately, without the intervention of a representative idea. **b.** the doctrine that knowledge rests upon axiomatic truths discerned directly. —**in·tu·i'tion·ist,** *n., adj.*

in·tu·i·tive (ĭn tū'ə tĭv, -tōō'-), *adj.* **1.** perceiving by intuition, as a person, the mind, etc. **2.** perceived by, resulting from, or involving intuition: *intuitive knowledge.* **3.** of the nature of intuition. —**in·tu'i·tive·ly,** *adv.* —**in·tu'i·tive·ness,** *n.*

in·tu·i·tiv·ism (ĭn tū'ə tĭ vĭz'əm, -tōō'-), *n.* **1.** ethical intuitionism. **2.** intuitive perception; insight. —**in·tu'i·tiv·ist,** *n.*

in·tu·mesce (ĭn'tyōō mĕs', -tōō-), *v.i.,* -**mesced,** -**mescing.** **1.** to swell up, as with heat; become tumid. **2.** to bubble up. [t. L: s. *intumescere* swell up]

in·tu·mes·cence (ĭn'tyōō mĕs'əns, -tōō-), *n.* **1.** a swelling up as with congestion. **2.** swollen state. **3.** a swollen mass. —**in'tu·mes'cent,** *adj.*

in·turn (ĭn'tûrn'), *n.* an inward turn, as of the toes.

in·tus·sus·cept (ĭn'təs sə sĕpt'), *v.t.* to take within, as one part of the intestine into an adjacent part; invaginate. [back formation from INTUSSUSCEPTION] —**in'tus·sus·cep'tive,** *adj.*

in·tus·sus·cep·tion (ĭn'təs sə sĕp'shən), *n.* **1.** a taking within. **2.** *Physiol.* the conversion into protoplasm of foreign matter taken in by a living organism. **3.** *Pathol.* the slipping of one part within another; invagination. [f. L: *intus* within + s. *susceptio* a taking up]

in·twine (ĭn twīn'), *v.t., v.i.,* -**twined,** -**twining.** entwine.

in·twist (ĭn twĭst'), *v.t.* entwist.

in·u·lase (ĭn'yə lās'), *n.* *Biochem.* an enzyme which converts inulin into levulose. [f. INUL(IN) + -ASE]

in·u·lin (ĭn'yə lĭn), *n.* *Chem.* a polysaccharide obtained from the roots of certain plants, esp. elecampane, dahlia, and Jerusalem artichoke, which undergoes hydrolysis to the dextrorotatory form of fructose. [f. s. L *inula* elecampane + -IN²]

in·unc·tion (ĭn ŭngk′shən), *n.* **1.** act of anointing. **2.** *Med.* the rubbing in of an oil or ointment. **3.** an unguent. [late ME, t. L: s. *inunctio* an anointing]

in·un·dant (ĭn ŭn′dənt), *adj. Poetic.* inundating.

in·un·date (ĭn′ən dāt′, -ŭn-, ĭn ŭn′dāt), *v.t.*, **-dated, -dating. 1.** to overspread with a flood; overflow; flood; deluge. **2.** to overspread as with or in a flood; overwhelm. [t. L: m. s. *inundātus*, pp., overflowed] —**in′un·da′tion,** *n.* —**in′un·da′tor,** *n.* —**Syn. 1.** See **flood.**

in·ur·bane (ĭn′ûr bān′), *adj.* not urbane; lacking in courtesy or suavity. —**in·ur·ban·i·ty** (ĭn′ûr băn′ə tĭ), *n.*

in·ure (ĭn yŏŏr′), *v.*, **-ured, -uring.** —*v.t.* **1.** to toughen or harden by exercise; accustom; habituate (fol. by *to*): *to inure a person to danger.* —*v.i.* **2.** to come into use; take or have effect. Also, **enure.** [late ME, v. use of obs. phrase *in ure* in use, f. IN, prep., + obs. *ure* use, work (t. AF, g. L *opera*)] —**in·ure′ment,** *n.*

in·urn (ĭn ûrn′), *v.t.* **1.** to put into an urn, esp. a funeral urn. **2.** to bury; inter. —**in·urn′ment,** *n.*

in·u·tile (ĭn ū′tĭl), *adj.* useless; of no use or service; unprofitable. [late ME, t. L: m. s. *inūtilis*]

in·u·til·i·ty (ĭn′yŏŏ tĭl′ə tĭ), *n., pl.* **-ties. 1.** uselessness. **2.** a useless thing or person.

inv., 1. invented. **2.** inventor. **3.** invoice.

in va·cu·o (ĭn văk′yŏŏ ō′), *Latin.* in a vacuum.

in·vade (ĭn vād′), *v.*, **-vaded, -vading.** —*v.t.* **1.** to enter as an enemy; go into with hostile intent: *Caesar invaded Britain.* **2.** to enter like an enemy: *locusts invaded the fields.* **3.** to enter as if to take possession: *to invade a friend's quarters.* **4.** to intrude upon: *to invade the privacy of a family.* **5.** to encroach or infringe upon: *to invade the rights of citizens.* —*v.i.* **6.** to make an invasion. [late ME, t. L: m.s. *invādere* go into, attack] —**in·vad′er,** *n.*

in·vag·i·na·ble (ĭn văj′ə nə bəl), *adj.* capable of being invaginated; susceptible of invagination.

in·vag·i·nate (*v.* ĭn văj′ə nāt′; *adj.* ĭn văj′ə nĭt, -nāt′), *v.*, **-nated, -nating,** *adj.* —*v.t.* **1.** to insert or receive as into a sheath; sheathe. **2.** to fold or draw (a tubular organ, etc.) back within itself; introvert; intussuscept. —*v.i.* **3.** to become invaginated; undergo invagination. **4.** to form a pocket by turning in. —*adj.* **5.** invaginated. [f. IN-² + s. L *vāgīna* sheath + -ATE¹]

in·vag·i·na·tion (ĭn văj′ə nā′shən), *n.* **1.** act or process of invaginating. **2.** *Embryol.* the inward movement of a portion of the wall of a blastula in the formation of a gastrula. **3.** *Pathol.* intussusception.

in·va·lid¹ (ĭn′və lĭd; *Brit.* -lēd′), *n.* **1.** an infirm or sickly person: *a hopeless invalid.* **2.** a soldier or sailor disabled for active service. —*adj.* **3.** deficient in health; weak; sick: *his invalid sister.* **4.** of or for invalids: *invalid diets.* —*v.t.* **5.** to affect with disease; make an invalid: *invalided for life.* **6.** to class, or remove from active service, as an invalid. —*v.i.* **7.** to become an invalid. **8.** (of a soldier or a sailor) to retire from active service because of illness or injury. [t. L: s. *invalidus* infirm, not strong]

in·val·id² (ĭn văl′ĭd), *adj.* **1.** not valid; of no force, weight, or cogency; weak: *invalid arguments.* **2.** without legal force, or void, as a contract. [f. IN-³ + VALID] —**in·val′id·ly,** *adv.*

in·val·i·date (ĭn văl′ə dāt′), *v.t.*, **-dated, -dating. 1.** to render invalid. **2.** to deprive of legal force or efficacy. —**in·val′i·da′tion,** *n.* —**in·val′i·da′tor,** *n.*

in·va·lid·ism (ĭn′və lĭd ĭz′əm), *n.* prolonged ill health.

in·va·lid·i·ty (ĭn′və lĭd′ə tĭ), *n.* lack of validity.

in·val·u·a·ble (ĭn văl′yŏŏ ə bəl), *adj.* that cannot be valued or appraised; of inestimable value. —**in·val′u·a·ble·ness,** *n.* —**in·val′u·a·bly,** *adv.* —**Syn.** priceless, precious. —**Ant.** worthless.

in·var (ĭn vär′), *n.* **1.** an iron alloy, containing 35.5% nickel, having a very low coefficient of expansion at atmospheric temperatures. **2.** (*cap.*) a trademark for this alloy. [short for INVARIABLE]

in·var·i·a·ble (ĭn vâr′ĭ ə bəl), *adj.* not variable or not capable of being varied; not changing or not capable of being changed; always the same. —**in·var′i·a·bil′i·ty, in·var′i·a·ble·ness,** *n.* —**in·var′i·a·bly,** *adv.* —**Syn.** unalterable, unchanging, uniform, constant.

in·var·i·ant (ĭn vâr′ĭ ənt), *adj.* **1.** unvarying; invariable; constant. —*n.* **2.** *Math.* an invariable quantity.

in·va·sion (ĭn vā′zhən), *n.* **1.** act of invading or entering as an enemy. **2.** the entrance or advent of anything troublesome or harmful, as disease. **3.** entrance as if to take possession or overrun. **4.** infringement by intrusion. [t. LL: s. *invāsio* an attack]

in·va·sive (ĭn vā′sĭv), *adj.* **1.** characterized by or involving invasion; offensive: *invasive war.* **2.** invading, or tending to invade; intrusive.

in·vec·tive (ĭn vĕk′tĭv), *n.* **1.** vehement denunciation; an utterance of violent censure or reproach. **2.** a railing accusation; vituperation. —*adj.* **3.** censoriously abusive; vituperative; denunciatory. [ME, t. LL: m.s. *invectīvus* abusive] —**in·vec′tive·ly,** *adv.* —**in·vec′tive·ness,** *n.* —**Syn. 1.** See **abuse.**

in·veigh (ĭn vā′), *v.i.* to attack vehemently in words; rail: *to inveigh against democracy.* [ME *inveh*, t. L: s. *invehere* carry or bear into, assail] —**in·veigh′er,** *n.*

in·vei·gle (ĭn vē′gəl, -vā′gəl), *v.t.*, **-gled, -gling. 1.** to draw by beguiling or artful inducements (fol. by *into*, sometimes *from, away,* etc.): *to inveigle a person into playing bridge.* **2.** to allure, win, or seduce by beguiling. [late ME *enve(u)gle*, t. F: m.s. *aveugler* blind, delude] —**in·vei′gle·ment,** *n.* —**in·vei′gler,** *n.*

in·vent (ĭn vĕnt′), *v.t.* **1.** to originate as a product of one's own contrivance: *to invent a machine.* **2.** to produce or create with the imagination: *to invent a story.* **3.** to make up or fabricate as something merely fictitious or false: *to invent excuses.* **4.** *Obs.* to come upon; find. —*v.i.* **5.** to devise something new, as by ingenuity. [late ME t. L.: s. *inventus*, pp. discovered, found out] —**in·vent′i·ble,** *adj.* —**Syn. 1.** See **discover.**

in·vent·er (ĭn vĕn′tər), *n.* inventor.

in·ven·tion (ĭn vĕn′shən), *n.* **1.** act of inventing. **2.** *Patent Law.* the conception of an idea and the means or apparatus by which the result is obtained. **3.** anything invented or devised. **4.** the exercise of imaginative or creative power in literature or art. **5.** act of producing or creating by exercise of the imagination. **6.** the power or faculty of inventing, devising, or originating. **7.** something fabricated, as a false statement. **8.** *Sociol.* the creation of a new culture trait, pattern, etc. **9.** *Music.* a short piece, contrapuntal in nature, generally based on one subject. **10.** *Speech.* (classically) one of the five steps in speech preparation, the process of choosing ideas appropriate to the subject, audience, and occasion. **11.** *Archaic.* act of finding. [ME, t. L: s. *inventio*]

in·ven·tive (ĭn vĕn′tĭv), *adj.* **1.** apt at inventing, devising, or contriving. **2.** having the function of inventing. **3.** pertaining to, involving, or showing invention. —**in·ven′tive·ly,** *adv.* —**in·ven′tive·ness,** *n.*

in·ven·tor (ĭn vĕn′tər), *n.* one who invents, esp. one who devises some new process, appliance, machine, or article; one who makes inventions. Also, **inventer.**

in·ven·to·ry (ĭn′vən tōr′ĭ), *n., pl.* **-tories,** *v.*, **-toried, -torying.** —*n.* **1.** a detailed descriptive list of articles, with number, quantity, and value of each. **2.** a formal list of movables, as of a merchant's stock of goods. **3.** a complete listing of work in progress, raw materials, finished goods on hand, etc., made each year by a business concern. **4.** items in such a list. **5.** the value of a stock of goods. —*v.t.* **6.** to make an inventory of; enter in an inventory. [late ME, t. ML: m. s. *inventōrium*, L *inventārium* list] —**in′ven·to′ri·al,** *adj.* —**in′ven·to′ri·al·ly,** *adv.* —**Syn. 1.** See **list¹.**

in·ve·rac·i·ty (ĭn′və răs′ə tĭ), *n., pl.* **-ties. 1.** untruthfulness. **2.** an untruth.

In·ver·ness (ĭn′vər nĕs′), *n.* **1.** Also, **In·ver·ness-shire** (ĭn′vər nĕs′shĭr, -shər), a county in NW Scotland. 85,200 pop. (est. 1956); 4211 sq. mi. **2.** its county seat: a seaport. 28,115 (1951). **3.** an overcoat with a long, removable cape (**Inverness cape**).

in·verse (*adj., n.* ĭn vûrs′, ĭn′vûrs; *v.* ĭn vûrs′), *adj., n., v.*, **-versed, -versing.** —*adj.* **1.** reversed in position, direction, or tendency: *inverse order.* **2.** opposite to in nature or effect, as a mathematical relation or operation: *subtraction is the inverse operation to addition.* **3.** inverted, or turned upside down. —*n.* **4.** an inverted state or condition. **5.** that which is inverse; the direct opposite. —*v.t.* **6.** *Now Rare.* to invert. [t. L: m.s. *inversus*, pp., turned about] —**in·verse′ly,** *adv.*

in·ver·sion (ĭn vûr′zhən, -shən), *n.* **1.** act of inverting. **2.** an inverted state. **3.** *Rhet.* reversal of the usual or natural order of words; anastrophe. **4.** *Anat.* the turning inward of a part, as the foot (opposed to *eversion*). **5.** *Chem.* a hydrolysis of certain carbohydrates, as cane sugar, which results in a reversal of direction of the rotatory power of the carbohydrate solution, the plane of polarized light being bent from right to left or vice versa. **6.** *Music.* **a.** the process, or result, of transposing the tones of an interval or chord so that the original bass becomes an upper voice. **b.** (in counterpoint) the transposition of the upper voice part below the lower, and vice versa. **c.** presentation of a melody in contrary motion to its original form. **7.** *Psychiatry.* assumption of the sexual role of the opposite sex; homosexuality. **8.** *Phonet.* retroflexion. **9.** *Meteorol.* a reversal in the normal temperature lapse rate, in which the temperature rises with increased elevation, instead of falling. **10.** something inverted. [t. L: s. *inversio*]

in·ver·sive (ĭn vûr′sĭv), *adj.* characterized by inversion.

in·vert (*v.* ĭn vûrt′; *adj., n.* ĭn′vûrt), *v.t.* **1.** to turn upside down. **2.** to reverse in position, direction, or order. **3.** to turn or change to the opposite or contrary, as in nature, bearing, or effect: *to invert a process.* **4.** *Chem.* to subject to inversion. See **inversion** (def. 5). **5.** *Phonet.* to articulate, as a retroflex vowel. —*adj.* **6.** *Chem.* inverted. —*n.* **7.** one who or that which is inverted. **8.** a homosexual. [t. L: s. *invertere* turn about, upset] —**in·vert′er,** *n.* —**in·vert′i·ble,** *adj.* —**Syn. 2.** See **reverse.**

in·vert·ase (ĭn vûr′tās), *n. Biochem.* an enzyme which causes the inversion of cane sugar, thus changing it into invert sugar. It is found in yeast and in the digestive juices of animals. [INVERT + -ASE]

in·ver·te·brate (ĭn vûr′tə brĭt, -brāt′), *adj.* **1.** *Zool.* not vertebrate; without a backbone. **2.** without strength of character. —*n.* **3.** an invertebrate animal. **4.** one who lacks strength of character. —**in·ver·te·bra·cy** (ĭn vûr′tə brə sĭ), **in·ver′te·brate·ness,** *n.*

inverted commas, *Brit.* quotation marks.

inverted mordent, *Music.* a pralltriller.

ăct, āble, dâre, ärt; ĕbb, ēqual; ĭf, īce; hŏt, ōver, ôrder, oil, bŏŏk, ōōze, out; ŭp, ūse, ûrge; ə = a in alone; ch, chief; g, give; ng, ring; sh, shoe; th, thin; ᵺ, that; zh, vision. See the full key on inside cover.

in·ver·tor (ĭn vûr′tər), *n.* *Elect.* a converter.

invert soap, an emulsifiable salt whose action is responsible for soapy qualities.

invert sugar, a mixture of the dextrorotatory forms of glucose and fructose formed naturally in fruits and produced artificially in syrups or fondants by treating cane sugar with acids.

in·vest (ĭn věst′), *v.t.* **1.** to put (money) to use, by purchase or expenditure, in something offering profitable returns, esp. interest or income. **2.** to spend: *to invest large sums in books.* **3.** to clothe. **4.** to cover or adorn as an article of attire does. **5.** *Rare.* to put on (a garment, etc.). **6.** to cover or surround as if with a garment, or like a garment: *spring invests the trees with leaves.* **7.** to surround (a place) with military forces or works so as to prevent approach or escape; besiege. **8.** to endue or endow: *to invest a friend with every virtue.* **9.** to belong to, as a quality or character does. **10.** to settle or vest (a power, right, etc.), as in a person. **11.** to clothe in or with the insignia of office. **12.** to install in an office or position; furnish with power, authority, rank, etc. *—v.i.* **13.** to invest money; make an investment. [late ME, t. L: s. *investīre* clothe] **—in·ves′tor,** *n.*

in·ves·ti·ga·ble (ĭn věs′tə gə bəl), *adj.* capable of being investigated.

in·ves·ti·gate (ĭn věs′tə gāt′), *v.,* **-gated, -gating.** *—v.t.* **1.** to search or inquire into; search or examine into the particulars of; examine in detail: *to investigate a murder.* *—v.i.* **2.** to make inquiry, examination, or investigation. [t. L: m.s. *investīgātus,* pp., tracked, traced out] **—in·ves′ti·ga·tive, in·ves·ti·ga·to·ry** (ĭn věs′tə gə tōr′ĭ), *adj.* **—in·ves′ti·ga·tor,** *n.*

in·ves·ti·ga·tion (ĭn věs′tə gā′shən), *n.* act or process of investigating; a searching inquiry in order to ascertain facts; a detailed or careful examination.

—Syn. INVESTIGATION, EXAMINATION, INQUIRY, RESEARCH express the idea of an active effort to find out something. An INVESTIGATION is a systematic, minute, and thorough attempt to learn the facts about something complex or hidden; it is often formal and official: *an investigation of a bank failure.* An EXAMINATION is an orderly attempt to obtain information about or to make a test of something, often something open to observation: *a physical examination.* An INQUIRY is an investigation made by asking questions rather than by inspection, or fig., by study of available evidence: *an inquiry into a proposed bond issue.* RESEARCH is careful and sustained investigation usually into a subject covering a wide range, or into remote recesses of knowledge: *chemical research.*

in·ves·ti·tive (ĭn věs′tə tĭv), *adj.* **1.** serving to invest: *an investitive act.* **2.** pertaining to investiture.

in·ves·ti·ture (ĭn věs′tə chər), *n.* **1.** act of investing. **2.** *Brit.* formal bestowal or presentation of a possessory or prescriptive right, as to a fief, usually involving the giving of insignia. **3.** state of being invested, as with a garment, quality, etc. **4.** *Archaic.* that which invests. [ME, t. ML: m. *investītūra*]

in·vest·ment (ĭn věst′mənt), *n.* **1.** the investing of money or capital in order to secure profitable returns, esp. interest or income. **2.** a particular instance or mode of investing. **3.** a thing invested in. **4.** that which is invested. **5.** act of investing or state of being invested, as with a garment. **6.** *Biol.* any covering, coating, outer layer, or integument, as of an animal or vegetable body. **7.** *Archaic.* a garment or vestment. **8.** an investing with a quality, attribute, etc. **9.** investiture with an office, dignity, or right. **10.** the surrounding of a place with military forces or works, as in besieging.

in·vet·er·a·cy (ĭn vět′ər ə sĭ), *n.* state of being inveterate: *the inveteracy of people's prejudices.*

in·vet·er·ate (ĭn vět′ər ĭt), *adj.* **1.** confirmed in a habit, practice, feeling, or the like: *an inveterate gambler.* **2.** firmly established by long continuance, as a disease or sore, a habit or practice (often bad), or a feeling (often hostile); chronic. [ME *inveterat,* t. L: s. *inveterātus,* pp., rendered old] **—in·vet′er·ate·ly,** *adv.* **—in·vet′er·ate·ness,** *n.*

in·vid·i·ous (ĭn vĭd′ĭ əs), *adj.* **1.** such as to bring odium, unpopularity, or envious dislike: *an invidious honor.* **2.** calculated to excite ill will or resentment or give offense: *invidious remarks.* **3.** offensively or unfairly discriminating: *invidious comparisons.* **4.** *Obs.* envious. [t. L: m.s. *invidiōsus* envious] **—in·vid′i·ous·ly,** *adv.* **—in·vid′i·ous·ness,** *n.*

in·vig·i·late (ĭn vĭj′ə lāt′), *v.i.,* **-lated, -lating.** **1.** *Brit.* to keep watch over students at an examination. **2.** *Obs.* to keep watch. [t. L: m.s. *invigilātus,* pp., watched over] **—in·vig′i·la′tion,** *n.* **—in·vig′i·la′tor,** *n.*

in·vig·or·ant (ĭn vĭg′ər ənt), *n.* a tonic.

in·vig·or·ate (ĭn vĭg′ə rāt′), *v.t.,* **-ated, -ating.** to give vigor to; fill with life and energy: *to invigorate the body.* [f. IN-² + VIGOR + -ATE¹] **—in·vig′or·at′ing·ly,** *adv.* **—in·vig′or·a′tion,** *n.* **—in·vig′or·a′tive,** *adj.* **—in·vig′or·a′tive·ly,** *adv.* **—in·vig′or·a′tor,** *n.* **—Syn.** See animate.

in·vin·ci·ble (ĭn vĭn′sə bəl), *adj.* **1.** that cannot be conquered or vanquished: *the Invincible Armada.* **2.** insuperable; insurmountable: *invincible difficulties.* [ME, t. L: m.s. *invincibilis.* See IN-³, VINCIBLE] **—in·vin′ci·bil′i·ty, in·vin′ci·ble·ness,** *n.* **—in·vin′ci·bly,** *adv.* **—Syn.** **1.** INVINCIBLE, IMPREGNABLE, INDOMITABLE suggest that which cannot be overcome or mastered. INVINCIBLE is applied to that which cannot be conquered in combat or war, or overcome or subdued in any manner: *an invincible army, invincible courage.* IMPREGNABLE is applied to a place

or position that cannot be taken by assault or siege, and hence to whatever is proof against attack: *an impregnable fortress, impregnable virtue.* INDOMITABLE implies having an unyielding spirit, or stubborn persistence in the face of opposition or difficulty: *indomitable will.* **—Ant.** **1.** conquerable.

Invincible Armada, Armada (def. 1).

in·vi·o·la·ble (ĭn vī′ə lə bəl), *adj.* **1.** that must not be violated; that is to be kept free from violence or violation of any kind, or treated as if sacred: *an inviolable sanctuary.* **2.** that cannot be violated, subjected to violence, or injured. **—in·vi′o·la·bil′i·ty, in·vi′o·la·ble·ness,** *n.* **—in·vi′o·la·bly,** *adv.*

in·vi·o·late (ĭn vī′ə lĭt, -lāt′), *adj.* **1.** free from violation, injury, desecration, or outrage. **2.** undisturbed. **3.** unbroken. **4.** not infringed. **—in·vi·o·la·cy** (ĭn vī′ə lə sĭ), **in·vi′o·late·ness,** *n.* **—in·vi′o·late·ly,** *adv.*

in·vis·i·ble (ĭn vĭz′ə bəl), *adj.* **1.** not visible; not perceptible by the eye: *invisible ink.* **2.** withdrawn from or out of sight. **3.** not perceptible or discernible by the mind: *invisible differences.* **4.** (of colors) of a very deep shade, or a scarcely distinguishable hue: *invisible green.* **5.** not ordinarily found in financial statements: *good will is an invisible asset.* **6.** concealed from public knowledge. *—n.* **7.** an invisible thing or being. **8.** (prec. by *the*) **a.** the unseen or spiritual world. **b.** (*cap.*) God. **—in·vis′i·bil′i·ty, in·vis′i·ble·ness,** *n.* **—in·vis′i·bly,** *adv.*

in·vi·ta·tion (ĭn′və tā′shən), *n.* **1.** act of inviting. **2.** the written or spoken form with which a person is invited. **3.** attraction or allurement. [t. L: s. *invītātiō*]

in·vi·ta·to·ry (ĭn vī′tə tōr′ĭ), *adj.* serving to invite; conveying an invitation.

in·vite (*v.* ĭn vīt′; *n.* ĭn′vīt), *v.,* **-vited, -viting,** *n.* *—v.t.* **1.** to ask in a kindly, courteous, or complimentary way, to come or go to some place, gathering, entertainment, etc., or to do something: *to invite friends to dinner.* **2.** to request politely or formally: *to invite donations.* **3.** to act so as to bring on or render probable: *to invite danger.* **4.** to give occasion for. **5.** to attract, allure, or tempt. *—v.i.* **6.** to give invitation; offer attractions or allurements. *—n.* **7.** *Slang.* an invitation. [t. L: m.s. *invītāre*] **—in·vit′er,** *n.* **—Syn.** **1.** See call.

in·vit·ing (ĭn vī′tĭng), *adj.* that invites; esp., attractive, alluring, or tempting: *an inviting offer.* **—in·vit′ing·ly,** *adv.* **—in·vit′ing·ness,** *n.*

in·vo·cate (ĭn′və kāt′), *v.t.,* **-cated, -cating.** *Now Rare.* invoke. [t. L: m.s. *invocātus,* pp.] **—in·vo·ca·tive** (ĭn vŏk′ə tĭv, ĭn′və kā′tĭv), *adj.* **—in′vo·ca′tor,** *n.*

in·vo·ca·tion (ĭn′və kā′shən), *n.* **1.** act of invoking; calling upon a deity, etc., for aid, protection, inspiration, etc. **2.** a form of words used in invoking, esp. as part of a public religious service. **3.** an entreaty for aid and guidance from a Muse, deity, etc., at the beginning of an epic or epiclike poem. **4.** a calling upon a spirit by incantation, or the incantation or magical formula used.

in·vo·ca·to·ry (ĭn vŏk′ə tōr′ĭ), *adj.* pertaining to or of the nature of invocation.

in·voice (ĭn′vois), *n., v.,* **-voiced, -voicing.** *—n.* **1.** a written list of merchandise, with prices, delivered or sent to a buyer. **2.** an itemized bill containing the prices which comprise the total charge. **3.** the merchandise or shipment itself. *—v.t.* **4.** to make an invoice of. **5.** to enter in an invoice. [m. *invoyes,* pl. of (obs.) *invoy* invoice, t. F: m. *envoy* sending, thing sent. See ENVOY]

in·voke (ĭn vōk′), *v.t.,* **-voked, -voking.** **1.** to call for with earnest desire; make supplication or prayer for: *to invoke God's mercy.* **2.** to call on (a divine being, etc.), as in prayer. **3.** to appeal to, as for confirmation. **4.** to call on to come or to do something. **5.** to call forth or upon (a spirit) by incantation; conjure. [late ME, t. L: m. *invocāre*] **—in·vok′er,** *n.*

in·vol·u·cel (ĭn vŏl′yə sĕl′), *n.* *Bot.* a secondary involucre, as in a compound cluster of flowers. [t. NL: m.s. *involucellum,* dim. of L *involūcrum* cover]

in·vo·lu·crate (ĭn′və loo′krĭt, -krāt), *adj.* having an involucre.

A. Involucel; B. Involucre

in·vo·lu·cre (ĭn′və loo′kər), *n.* **1.** *Bot.* a collection or rosette of bracts subtending a flower cluster, umbel, or the like. **2.** a covering, esp. a membranous one. [t. F, t. L: m. *involūcrum* wrapper, covering] **—in′vo·lu′cral,** *adj.*

in·vo·lu·crum (ĭn′və loo′krəm), *n., pl.* **-cra** (-krə). involucre.

in·vol·un·tar·y (ĭn vŏl′ən tĕr′ĭ), *adj.* **1.** not voluntary; acting, or done or made, without one's own volition, or otherwise than by one's own will or choice: *an involuntary listener.* **2.** unintentional. **3.** *Physiol.* acting independently of, or done or occurring without, conscious control: *involuntary muscles.* **—in·vol′un·tar′i·ly,** *adv.* **—in·vol′un·tar′i·ness,** *n.* **—Syn.** **1, 3.** See automatic.

in·vo·lute (ĭn′və loot′), *adj.* **1.** involved or intricate. **2.** *Bot.*

A. Involute leaves of branch of poplar; B. Transverse section rolled inward from the edge, as a leaf. 3. *Zool.* (of shells) having the whorls closely wound. —*n.* 4. *Geom.* any curve of which a given curve is the evolute. [t. L: m.s. *involūtus*, pp., rolled up] —**in'vo·lut'ed·ly,** *adv.*

in·vo·lu·tion (ĭn'və lōō'shən), *n.* 1. act of involving. 2. state of being involved. 3. something complicated. 4. *Bot., etc.* a. a rolling up or folding in upon itself. b. a part so formed. *Involute of a circle* 5. *Biol.* retrograde development; degeneration. 6. *Physiol.* bodily changes involving a lessening of activity, esp. of the sex organs, occurring in late middle age. 7. *Gram.* complicated construction; the separation of the subject from its predicate by the interjection of matter that should follow the verb or be placed in another sentence. 8. *Math.* the raising of a quantity or expression to any given power. [t. LL: s. *involūtio* a rolling up]

in·volve (ĭn vŏlv'), *v.t.,* **-volved, -volving.** 1. to include as a necessary circumstance, condition, or consequence; imply; entail. 2. to affect, as something within the scope of operation. 3. to include, contain, or comprehend within itself or its scope. 4. to bring into an intricate or complicated form or condition. 5. to bring into difficulties (fol. by *with*): *a plot to involve one government with another.* 6. to cause to be inextricably associated or concerned, as in something embarrassing or unfavorable. 7. to combine inextricably (fol. by *with*). 8. to implicate, as in guilt or crime, or in any matter or affair. 9. to be highly or excessively interested in. 10. to roll, wrap, or shroud, as in something that surrounds. 11. to envelop or infold, as the surrounding thing does. 12. to swallow up, engulf, or overwhelm. 13. to roll up on itself; wind spirally, coil, or wreathe. 14. *Math.* to raise to a given power. [ME, t. L: m.s. *involvere* roll in or on, enwrap, involve] —**in·volve'ment,** *n.* —**in·volv'er,** *n.*
—**Syn.** 6. INVOLVE, ENTANGLE, IMPLICATE imply getting a person connected or bound up with something from which it is difficult for him to extricate himself. To INVOLVE is to bring more or less deeply into something, esp. of a complicated, embarrassing, or troublesome nature: *to involve someone in debt.* To ENTANGLE (usually pass. or reflex.) is to involve so deeply in a tangle as to confuse and make helpless: *to entangle oneself in a mass of contradictory statements.* To IMPLICATE is to connect a person with something discreditable or wrong: *implicated in a plot.* —**Ant.** 6. extricate.

in·vul·ner·a·ble (ĭn vŭl'nər ə bəl), *adj.* 1. incapable of being wounded, hurt, or damaged. 2. proof against attack: *invulnerable arguments.* —**in·vul'ner·a·bil'i·ty, in·vul'ner·a·ble·ness,** *n.* —**in·vul'ner·a·bly,** *adv.*

in·wall (ĭn wôl'), *v.t.* to enclose with a wall.

in·ward (ĭn'wərd), *adv.* Also, **inwards.** 1. toward the inside or interior, as of a place, a space, or a body. 2. into the mind or soul. 3. in the mind or soul, or mentally or spiritually; inwardly. 4. *Rare.* in the inside or interior. —*adj.* 5. proceeding or directed toward the inside or interior. 6. situated within; interior; internal: *an inward room.* 7. pertaining to the inside or inner part. 8. located within the body: *the inward parts.* 9. pertaining to the inside of the body: *inward convulsions.* 10. inland: *inward passage.* 11. intrinsic; inherent; essential: *the inward nature of a thing.* 12. inner, mental, or spiritual: *inward peace.* 13. muffled or indistinct, as the voice. 14. *Archaic.* domestic. 15. *Obs.* closely personal; intimate; familiar. 16. *Obs.* private or secret. —*n.* 17. the inward or internal part; the inside. 18. (*pl.*) the inward parts of the body.[ME *in(ne)ward,* OE *in(ne)weard,* f. *in(ne)* IN, adv. + *-weard* -WARD]

in·ward·ly (ĭn'wərd lĭ'), *adv.* 1. in or on, or with reference to, the inside or inner part. 2. privately; secretly: *laughing inwardly.* 3. in low tones; not aloud. 4. *Now Rare.* toward the inside, interior, or center.

in·ward·ness (ĭn'wərd nĭs), *n.* 1. the state of being inward or internal. 2. depth of thought or feeling; earnestness. 3. occupation with what concerns man's inner nature; spirituality. 4. the inward or intrinsic character of a thing. 5. inward meaning. 6. *Obs.* intimacy.

in·wards (ĭn'wərdz), *adv.* 1. inward. —*n.pl.* 2. inward (def. 18).

in·weave (ĭn wēv'), *v.t.,* **-wove** or **-weaved; -woven** or **-wove** or **-weaved; -weaving.** 1. to weave in or together. 2. to introduce into or as into a fabric in weaving. 3. to combine or diversify with something woven in. Also, **enweave.**

in·wind (ĭn wīnd'), *v.t.,* **-wound, -winding.** enwind.

in·wrap (ĭn răp'), *v.t.,* **-wrapped, -wrapping.** enwrap.

in·wreathe (ĭn rēth'), *v.t.,* **-wreathed, -wreathing.** enwreathe.

in·wrought (ĭn rôt'), *adj.* 1. wrought or worked with something by way of decoration. 2. wrought or worked in, as a decorative pattern. 3. worked in or closely combined with something.

I·o (ī'ō), *n.* *Gk. Legend.* the daughter of Inachus of Argos, loved by Zeus and changed by jealous Hera into a white heifer. See Argus (def. 1).

I·o (ī'ō), *n., pl.* **Ios.** Io moth.

Io, *Chem.* ionium.

Io·an·ni·na (yô ä'nē nä', yä'nē nä'), *n.* a city in NW Greece. 32,315 (1951). Serbian, **Janina** or **Yanina.**

iod-, var. of **iodo-,** usually before vowels, as in *iodic.*

i·o·date (ī'ə dāt'), *n., v.,* **-dated, -dating.** —*n.* 1. *Chem.* a salt of iodic acid, as *sodium iodate,* NaIO₃. —*v.t.* 2. to iodize. —**i'o·da'tion,** *n.*

i·od·ic (ī ŏd'ĭk), *adj.* *Chem.* containing iodine, esp. in the pentavalent state (I⁺⁵). [f. IOD- + -IC]

i·o·dide (ī'ə dīd', -dĭd), *n.* *Chem.* a compound, usually of two elements only, one of which is iodine; a salt of hydriodic acid. Also, **i·o·did** (ī'ə dĭd).

i·o·dim·e·try (ī'ə dĭm'ə trĭ), *n.* *Chem.* iodometry.

i·o·dine (ī'ə dīn', -dĭn; in *Chem.* -dēn'), *n.* *Chem.* a nonmetallic element occurring, at ordinary temperatures, as a grayish-black crystalline solid, which sublimes to a dense violet vapor when heated: used in medicine as an antiseptic, and in the arts. *Symbol:* I; *at.wt.:* 126.92; *at.no.:* 53; *sp. gr.:* (solid) 4.93 at 20°C. Also, **i·o·din** (ī'ə dĭn). [f. F *iode* iodine (t. Gk.: m. *iōdēs,* prop., rust-colored, but taken to mean violetlike) +-INE²]

iodine-131, *Chem.* a radioactive isotope of iodine, of atomic weight 131, used in the diagnosis and treatment of disorders of the thyroid gland.

i·o·dism (ī'ə dĭz'əm), *n.* *Pathol.* a morbid condition due to the use of iodine or its compounds.

i·o·dize (ī'ə dīz'), *v.t.,* **-dized, -dizing.** to treat, impregnate, or affect with iodine. —**i'o·diz'er,** *n.*

iodo-, a word element meaning "iodine," as in *iodometry.* Also, **iod-.** [comb. form repr. NL *iōdum*]

i·o·do·form (ī ō'də fôrm', ī ŏd'ə-), *n.* *Chem.* a yellowish crystalline compound, CHI₃, analogous to chloroform: used as an antiseptic. [f. IODO- + FORM(YL)]

i·o·dol (ī'ə dōl', -dŏl'), *n.* *Chem.* a crystalline compound, C₄HI₄N: used as a substitute for iodoform.

i·o·dom·e·try (ī'ə dŏm'ə trĭ), *n.* *Chem.* a volumetric analytical procedure for determining iodine, or materials which will liberate iodine or react with iodine. Also, **iodimetry.** —**i·o·do·met·ric** (ī'ə dō mĕt'rĭk), *adj.*

i·o·dous (ī ō'dəs, ī ŏd'əs), *adj.* 1. *Chem.* containing iodine, esp. in the divalent state (I⁺²). 2. like iodine.

I·o·lan·the (ī'ə lăn'thĭ), *n.* an operetta (1882) by Gilbert and Sullivan.

i·o·lite (ī'ə līt'), *n.* cordierite. [f. Gk. *ío(n)* violet + -LITE]

I·o moth (ī'ō), a showy and beautiful moth of North America, *Automeris io,* of yellow coloration, with prominent pink and bluish eyespots on the hinder wings.

i·on (ī'ən, ī'ŏn), *n.* *Physics, Chem.* 1. an electrically charged atom, radical, or molecule, formed by the loss or gain of one or more electrons. **Positive ions,** created by electron loss, are called *cations* and are attracted to the cathode in electrolysis. **Negative ions,** created by electron gain, are called *anions* and are attracted to the anode. The valence of an ion is equal to the number of electrons lost or gained and is indicated by a plus sign for cations and minus for anions, thus: Na⁺, Cl⁻, Ca⁺⁺, S⁼. 2. one of the electrically charged particles formed in a gas by the action of an electric discharge, etc. [t. Gk., ppr. neut. of *ienai* go] —**i·on·ic** (ī ŏn'ĭk), *adj.*

-ion, a suffix of nouns denoting action or process, state or condition, or sometimes things or persons, as in *allusion, communion, flexion, fusion, legion, opinion, suspicion, union.* Also, **-tion** and **-ation.** Cf. **-cion, -xion.** [t. L: s. *-io;* suffix forming nouns, esp. from verbs]

I·o·na (ī ō'nə), *n.* a small island in the Hebrides, off W coast of Scotland: center of early Celtic Christianity.

ion exchange, the process of reciprocal transfer of ions between a solution and a resin.

I·o·ni·a (ī ō'nĭ ə), *n.* an ancient region on the W coast of Asia Minor and adjacent islands.

I·o·ni·an (ī ō'nĭ ən), *adj.* 1. pertaining to Ionia. 2. pertaining to a branch of the Greek race named from Ion, the legendary founder. —*n.* 3. an Ionian Greek.

Ionian Islands, the islands along the W coast of Greece, including Corfu, Levkas, Ithaca, Cephalonia, and Zante, and Corfu off the S coast.

Ionian Sea, an arm of the Mediterranean between S Italy, E Sicily, and Greece.

I·on·ic (ī ŏn'ĭk), *adj.* 1. *Archit.* noting or pertaining to one of the three Greek orders, distinguished by its slender proportions, the volutes on the capitals, and the continuous (often figured) frieze. See illus. under **order.** 2. *Pros.* noting or employing one of two feet consisting of two long and two short syllables: **the greater Ionic,** two long and two short syllables, – – ˘ ˘; **the lesser Ionic,** two short and two long syllables, ˘ ˘ – –. 3. pertaining to the Ionians. —*n.* 4. *Pros.* an Ionic foot, verse, or meter. 5. (*also l.c.*) *Print.* a style of type. 6. a dialect of ancient Greek, including Attic and the language of Homer. [t. L: s. *Ionicus,* t. Gk.: m. *Iōnikós*]

i·o·ni·um (ī ō'nĭ əm), *n.* *Chem.* a naturally occurring radioactive isotope of thorium. *Symbol:* Io; *at. wt.:* 230; *at. no.:* 90.

i·on·ize (ī'ə nīz'), *v.,* **-ized, -izing.** —*v.t.* 1. to separate or change into ions. 2. to produce ions in. —*v.i.* 3. to become changed into the form of ions, as by dissolving. Also, *esp. Brit.,* **i·on·ise'.** —**i·on·i·za·tion** (ī'ə nə zā'shən), *n.* —**i'on·iz'er,** *n.*

i·o·none (ī'ə nōn'), *n.* either one or a mixture of two unsaturated ketones, C₁₃H₂₀O, used in perfumery.

i·on·o·sphere (ī ŏn'ə sfîr'), *n.* 1. the succession of ionized layers that constitute the outer regions of the earth's atmosphere beyond the stratosphere, considered as beginning with the Heaviside layer at about 60 miles, and extending several hundred miles up. 2. *Obsolesc.* the Heaviside layer.

i·o·ta (ī ō'tə), *n.* 1. the ninth letter (I, ι = English I, i) of the Greek alphabet (the smallest letter). 2. a very small quantity; a tittle; a jot.

ăct, āble, dâre, ärt; ĕbb, ēqual; ĭf, īce; hŏt, ōver, ôrder, oil, bŏŏk, ōōze, out; ŭp, ūse, ûrge; ə = a in alone; ch, chief; g, give; ng, ring; sh, shoe; th, thin; th̲, that; zh, vision. See the full key on inside cover.

i·o·ta·cism (ī'ō'tə sĭz'əm), *n.* conversion of other vowel sounds into that of iota (English ē). [t. L: s. *iōtacismus*, t. Gk. m. *iōtakismós*]

I O U (ī'ō'ū'), a written acknowledgment of a debt containing the expression *I O U* (I owe you). Also, **I.O.U.**

-ious, a termination consisting of the suffix -ous with a preceding original or euphonic vowel i. Cf. **-eous.**

I·o·wa (ī'ə wə; *locally* ī'ə wā'), *n.* 1. a State in the central United States: a part of the Midwest. 2,757,537 (1960). 56,280 sq. mi. *Cap.:* Des Moines. *Abbr.:* Ia. 2. a river flowing from N Iowa SE to the Mississippi. 291 mi. 3. a Siouan language. **—I·o·wan** (ī'ə wən), *adj., n.*

Iowa City, a city in SE Iowa. 33,443 (1960).

IPA, International Phonetic Alphabet.

ip·e·cac (ĭp'ə kăk'), *n.* 1. the dried root of two small, shrubby South American rubiaceous plants *Cephaelis Ipecacuanha,* and *C. acuminata,* used as an emetic, purgative, etc. 2. a drug consisting of the roots of these plants. 3. the plants themselves. Also, **ip·e·cac·u·an·ha** (ĭp'ə kăk'yōō ăn'ə). [t. Pg., t. Tupi: m. *ipe-kaaguêne,* f. *ipeh* low + *kaá* leaves + *guêne* vomit]

Iph·i·ge·ni·a (ĭf'ə jĭ nī'ə), *n.* Gk. *Legend.* the daughter of Agamemnon and Clytemnestra. She became a priestess of Artemis after the goddess saved her from sacrifice by Agamemnon. She saved her brother Orestes' life. According to one version she was sacrificed by her father.

ip·o·moe·a (ĭp'ə mē'ə, ī'pə-), *n.* 1. any plant of the genus *Ipomoea,* of the morning-glory family, containing many species with ornamental flowers. 2. the dried root of the convolvulaceous plant, *Ipomoea orizabensis,* yielding a resin which is a cathartic. [t. NL, f. Gk.: s. *ĩps* kind of worm + m. *hómoios* like]

ip·se dix·it (ĭp'sĭ dĭk'sĭt), *Latin.* 1. he himself said it. 2. an assertion without proof.

ip·so fac·to (ĭp'sō făk'tō), *Latin.* by the fact itself; by that very fact: *it is condemned ipso facto.*

Ip·sus (ĭp'səs), *n.* an ancient village in central Asia Minor, in Phrygia: the scene of a battle between the successors of Alexander the Great, 301 B.C.

Ips·wich (ĭps'wĭch), *n.* a seaport in E England, in Suffolk. 110,300 (est. 1956).

IQ, intelligence quotient. Also, **I.Q.**

i.q., (L *idem quod*) the same as.

I·qui·que (ē kē'kě), *n.* a seaport in N Chile. 48,000 (est. 1954).

ir-¹, var. of in-², before r, as in *irradiate.*

ir-², var. of in-³, before r, as in *irreducible.*

Ir, *Chem.* iridium.

Ir., 1. Ireland. 2. Irish.

i·ra·cund (ī'rə kŭnd'), *adj.* prone to anger; irascible. [t. L: s. *īrācundus* angry] **—i'ra·cun'di·ty,** *n.*

i·ra·de (ĭ rä'dě), *n.* a decree of the Sultan of Turkey. [Turk., t. Ar.: m. *irāda* will, desire]

I·rak (ĭ räk'; *Pers.* ē räk'), *n.* Iraq.

I·ran (ĭ rän', ĭ-; *Pers.* ē rän'), *n.* a kingdom in SW Asia; former official name (until 1935), **Persia.** 21,794,000 pop. (est. 1955); ab. 635,000 sq. mi. *Cap.:* Teheran.

I·ra·ni·an (ĭ rā'nĭ ən), *adj.* 1. pertaining to Iran (or Persia). 2. pertaining to Iranian (def. 3). *—n.* 3. a subgroup of Indo-European languages including Persian and Pushtu. 4. Persian (the language). 5. an inhabitant of Iran; a Persian.

I·raq (ĭ räk'; *Pers.* ē räk'),*n.* a republic in SW Asia, N of Saudi Arabia and W of Iran, centering in the Tigris-Euphrates basin of Mesopotamia. 6,590,000 pop. (est. 1958); 172,000 sq. mi. *Cap.:* Baghdad. Also, **Irak.**

I·ra·qi (ē rä'kě), *n., pl.* -qis, *adj. —n.* 1. a native of Iraq. 2. Also, **Iraqi Arabic.** the dialect of Arabic spoken in Iraq. *—adj.* 3. of Iraq or its inhabitants.

i·ras·ci·ble (ĭ răs'ə bəl, ī răs'-), *adj.* 1. easily provoked to anger: *an irascible old man.* 2. characterized by, excited by, or arising from anger: *an irascible nature.* [ME, t. LL: m.s. *irascibilis*] **—i·ras'ci·bil'i·ty, i·ras'ci·ble·ness,** *n.* **—i·ras'ci·bly,** *adv.*

i·rate (ī'rāt, ī rāt'), *adj.* angry; enraged: *the irate colonel.* [t. L: m.s. *īrātus,* pp.] **—i'rate·ly,** *adv.*

I.R.B.M., intermediate range ballistic missile. Also, **IRBM.**

ire (īr), *n.* anger; wrath. [ME, t. OF, t. L: m. *īra*] **—ire'less,** *adj.*

Ire., Ireland.

ire·ful (īr'fəl), *adj.* 1. full of ire; wrathful: *an ireful look.* 2. irascible. **—ire'ful·ly,** *adv.* **—ire'ful·ness,** *n.*

Ire·land (īr'lənd), *n.* 1. a large western island of the British Isles, comprising Northern Ireland and the Republic of Ireland. 4,333,514 pop. (1950); 32,375 sq. mi. Latin, Hibernia. 2. **Republic of,** a republic occupying most of the island of Ireland; formerly associated with the British Commonwealth of Nations. 2,895,000 pop. (est. 1955); 27,137 sq. mi. *Cap.:* Dublin. Formerly (1922-37), **Irish Free State;** (1937-49) **Eire.**

I·re·ne (ī rē'ně), *n.* Gk. *Myth.* the daughter of Themis by Zeus. She became the goddess of peace.

i·ren·ic (ī rĕn'ĭk, ī rē'nĭk), *adj.* peaceful; tending to promote peace. Also, **i·ren·i·cal.** [t. Gk.: m.s. *eirēnikós*] **—i·ren'ics** (ī rĕn'ĭks, ī rē'nĭks), *n.* irenic theology.

ir·i·da·ceous (ĭr'ə dā'shəs, ī'rə-), *adj.* 1. belonging to the *Iridaceae,* or iris family of plants, which includes, besides various flags, the crocus, gladiolus, and freesia. 2. resembling or pertaining to plants of the genus *Iris.* [f. s. NL *Iris* the iris genus (see IRIS) + -ACEOUS]

ir·i·des·cence (ĭr'ə dĕs'əns), *n.* iridescent quality; a play of lustrous, changing colors.

ir·i·des·cent (ĭr'ə dĕs'ənt), *adj.* displaying colors like those of the rainbow. [f. s. L *iris* rainbow + -ESCENT] **—ir'i·des'cent·ly,** *adv.*

i·rid·ic (ĭ rĭd'ĭk, ī rĭd'-), *adj. Chem.* of or containing iridium, esp. in the tetravalent state (Ir+4).

i·rid·i·um (ĭ rĭd'ĭ əm, ī rĭd'-), *n. Chem.* a precious metallic element resembling platinum: used in platinum alloys and for the points of gold pens. *Symbol:* Ir; *at.wt.:* 193.1; *at.no.:* 77; *sp.gr.:* 22.4 at 20°C. [t. NL, der. L *iris* rainbow; named from its iridescence in solution]

ir·i·dize (ĭr'ə dīz', ī'rə-), *v.t.* **-dized, -dizing.** to cover with iridium. **—ir'i·di·za'tion,** *n.*

ir·i·dos·mine (ĭr'ə dŏz'mĭn, -dŏs'-, ī'rə-), *n.* a native alloy of iridium and osmium, usually containing some rhodium, ruthenium, platinum, etc., used esp. for the points of gold pens. Also, **ir·i·dos·mi·um** (ĭr'ə dŏz'mĭ əm, -dŏs'-, ī'rə-). [f. IRID(IUM) + OSM(IUM) + -INE³]

ir·i·dous (ĭr'ə dəs, ī'rə-), *adj. Chem.* containing trivalent iridium (Ir+3).

i·ris (ī'rĭs), *n., pl.* **irises, irides** (ĭr'ə dēz', ī'rə-). 1. *Anat.* the contractile circular diaphragm forming the colored portion of the eye and containing a circular opening (the pupil) in its center. See diag. under **eye.** 2. *Bot.* a. a family of plants, *Iridaceae.* b. any plant of the genus *Iris,* including various perennial herbs with handsome flowers and sword-shaped leaves; the fleur-de-lis or flag. c. the flower of any such plant. d. orrisroot. 3. (*cap.*) Gk. *Myth.* a messenger of the gods, regarded as the goddess of the rainbow. 4. a rainbow. 5. any appearance resembling a rainbow. [ME, t. L, t. Gk.]

iris diaphragm, *Optics, Photog.* a composite diaphragm with a central aperture readily adjustable for size, used to regulate the amount of light admitted to a lens or optical system.

I·rish (ī'rĭsh), *adj., n., pl.* **Irish.** *—adj.* 1. of or characteristic of Ireland or its people. *—n.* 2. the inhabitants of Ireland and their descendants elsewhere. 3. the aboriginal Celtic-speaking people of Ireland. 4. the Celtic language of Ireland in its historical (Old Irish, Middle Irish) or modern form. 5. Irish English. [ME *Irisc, Iris(c)h,* der. OE *Iras,* pl., people of Ireland (c. Icel. *Irar*)]

Irish English, 1. the English dialects spoken in Ireland. 2. the standard English of Ireland.

Irish Free State, former name of the **Republic of Ireland** (1922-37).

I·rish·ism (ī'rĭsh ĭz'əm), *n.* Irish idiom, custom, etc.

I·rish·man (ī'rĭsh mən), *n., pl.* **-men.** a man born in Ireland or of Irish ancestry. **—I'rish·wom'an,** *n. fem.*

Irish moss, 1. a purplish-brown, cartilaginous seaweed, *Chondrus crispus,* of the Atlantic coasts of Europe and North America; carrageen. 2. this seaweed, dried and bleached, used to keep solids in suspension, as in hand lotions, and for making soup and blancmange.

Irish Pale. See **pale²** (def. 6).

Irish potato, the common white potato.

Irish Sea, a part of the Atlantic between Ireland and England.

Irish setter
(24 in. high at the shoulder)

Irish setter, a dark mahogany-red variety of setter.

Irish stew, a stew usually made of mutton, lamb, or beef, with potatoes, onions, etc.

Irish terrier, one of a breed of small, active, intelligent dogs with wiry hair, usually of a reddish tinge.

Irish wolfhound, a shaggy-coated breed of wolfhound, the tallest known dog, developed in Ireland as early as the third century A.D. See illus. below.

Irish terrier
(18 in. high at the shoulder)

i·ri·tis (ī rī'tĭs), *n. Pathol.* inflammation of the iris of the eye. [t. NL; f. IR(IS) + -ITIS] **—i·rit·ic** (ī rĭt'ĭk), *adj.*

irk (ûrk), *v.t.* to weary, annoy, or trouble: *it irked him to wait.* [ME *irke, yrk(e).* Cf. MHG *erken* disgust]

irk·some (ûrk'səm), *adj.* 1. causing weariness, disgust, or annoyance: *irksome restrictions.* 2. *Obs.* distressing. **—irk'some·ly,** *adv.* **—irk'some·ness,** *n.* **—Syn.** 1. See **tedious.**

Ir·kutsk (ĭr kōōtsk'), *n.* a city in the S Soviet Union in Asia, W of Lake Baikal. 314,000 (est. 1956).

i·ron (ī'ərn), *n.* 1. *Chem.* a ductile, malleable, silver-white metallic element, scarcely known in a pure condition, but abundantly used in its crude or impure forms con-

Irish wolfhound
(31 in. high at the shoulder)

taining carbon (**pig iron, cast iron, steel,** and **wrought iron**: see these entries) for making tools, implements machinery, etc. *Symbol:* Fe (Lat. *ferrum*); *at. wt.:* 55.85; *at. no.:* 26; *sp. gr.:* 7.86 at 20°C. **2.** something hard, strong, rigid, unyielding, or the like: *hearts of iron.* **3.** an instrument, utensil, weapon, etc., made of iron. **4.** an iron implement used heated for smoothing or pressing cloth, etc. **5.** an iron-headed golf club intermediate between a cleek and a mashie: *a driving iron.* **6.** a branding iron. **7.** *Slang.* a pistol. **8.** *Archaic.* a sword. **9.** a harpoon. **10.** *Med.* a preparation of iron, or containing iron, used as a tonic, etc. **11.** (*pl.*) an iron shackle or fetter. **12. in irons,** *Naut.* lying head to the wind and lacking steerageway to cast off on either tack. **13. too many irons in the fire,** too many undertakings. —*adj.* **14.** made of iron. **15.** resembling iron in color, firmness, etc.: *an iron will.* **16.** stern, harsh, or cruel. **17.** not to be broken. **18.** degenerate, debased, or wicked. **19.** pertaining to the iron age. —*v.t.* **20.** to smooth or press with a heated iron, as clothes, etc. —*v.i.* **21.** to press clothes, etc., with a heated iron. **22.** to furnish, mount, or arm with iron. **23.** to shackle or fetter with irons. [ME *iren, ysen,* OE *īren, īsen, īsern,* c. G *eisen*] —**i′ron·less,** *adj.* —**i′ron·like′,** *adj.*

Iron Age, 1. *Archaeol.* the age of the history of Old World mankind (subsequent to the stone and bronze ages) marked by the use of iron implements. **2.** (*l.c.*) *Class. Myth.* the last and worst age of the world. **3.** (*l.c.*) any age or period of degeneracy or wickedness.

i·ron·bark (ī′ərn bärk′), *n.* any of the various Australian eucalyptuses with a hard, solid bark, as *Eucalyptus resinifera,* a tall tree yielding a valuable timber, and a gum.

i·ron·bound (ī′ərn bound′), *adj.* **1.** bound with iron. **2.** rock-bound; rugged. **3.** hard, rigid, or unyielding.

i·ron·clad (ī′ərn klăd′), *adj.* **1.** covered or cased with iron plates, as a vessel for naval warfare; armor-plated. **2.** very rigid or strict: *an ironclad agreement.* —*n.* **3.** one of the first naval ships fitted with armor.

iron curtain, a state of rigid censorship and secrecy. [coined by Winston Churchill in 1946 to describe the line of demarcation between western Europe and the Russian zone of influence]

Iron Duke, The, nickname of the first Duke of Wellington.

i·rone (īrōn′, ī′rōn), *n.* a colorless liquid, C₁₄H₂₂O, obtained from the orrisroot, and used in perfumery.

i·ron·er (ī′ər nər), *n.* one who or that which irons.

Iron Gate, a gorge cut by the Danube through the Carpathian Mountains, between Yugoslavia and SW Rumania. 2 mi. long. Also, **Iron Gates.**

i·ron·gray (ī′ərn grā′), *adj.* of a gray like that of freshly broken iron.

Iron Guard, a Rumanian anti-Semitic fascist party, eliminated after World War II.

iron horse, 1. a locomotive. **2.** a bicycle or tricycle.

i·ron·i·cal (ī rŏn′ə kəl), *adj.* **1.** pertaining to, of the nature of, or characterized by irony: *an ironical compliment.* **2.** using, or addicted to irony: *an ironical speaker.* Also, **i·ron·ic.** [f. s. L *ironicus* (t. Gk.: m. *eirōnikós* dissembling, feigning ignorance) + -ᴀʟ¹] —**i·ron′i·cal·ly,** *adv.* —**i·ron′i·cal·ness,** *n.*

iron lung, a chamber in which alternate pulsations of high and low pressure can be used to force normal lung movements, used esp. in some cases of infantile paralysis.

i·ron·mas·ter (ī′ərn măs′tər, -mäs′tər), *n. Chiefly Brit.* a manufacturer of iron; the master of ironworks.

i·ron·mon·ger (ī′ərn mŭng′gər), *n. Chiefly Brit.* a dealer in hardware.

i·ron·mon·ger·y (ī′ərn mŭng′gə rĭ), *n., pl.* -geries. *Chiefly Brit.* the goods, shop, or business of an ironmonger.

iron pyrites, 1. pyrite, or ordinary pyrites; fool's gold. **2.** marcasite. **3.** pyrrhotite.

i·ron·side (ī′ərn sīd′), *n.* **1.** a person with great power of endurance or resistance. **2.** (*cap., usually pl.*) **a.** Edmund II of England. **b.** Oliver Cromwell. **c.** one of Cromwell's troopers. **3.** (*pl.*) an ironclad.

i·ron·smith (ī′ərn smĭth′), *n.* a worker in iron; a blacksmith.

i·ron·stone (ī′ərn stōn′), *n.* any ore of iron (commonly a carbonate of iron) with clayey or siliceous impurities.

i·ron·ware (ī′ərn wâr′), *n.* articles of iron, as pots, kettles, tools, etc.; hardware.

i·ron·weed (ī′ərn wēd′), *n.* any of certain North American plants of the composite genus *Vernonia,* bearing tubular flowers, chiefly purple or red.

i·ron·wood (ī′ərn wŏŏd′), *n.* **1.** any of various trees with hard, heavy wood, as *Carpinus caroliniana,* an American species of hornbeam, or *Lyonothamnus floribundus,* found on the islands off the coast of southern California. **2.** the wood.

i·ron·work (ī′ərn wûrk′), *n.* **1.** work in iron. **2.** parts or articles made of iron: *ornamental ironwork.*

i·ron·work·er (ī′ərn wûrk′kər), *n.* **1.** a worker in iron. **2.** one employed in the erection of steel bridges, etc.

i·ron·works (ī′ərn wûrks′), *n. pl. or sing.* an establishment where iron is smelted or where it is cast or wrought.

i·ro·ny¹ (ī′rə nĭ), *n., pl.* **-nies.** **1.** a figure of speech in which the literal meaning of a locution is the opposite of that intended, esp., as in the Greek sense, when the locution understates the effect intended: employed in ridicule or merely playfully. **2.** an ironical utterance or expression. **3.** simulated ignorance in discussion (**Socratic irony**). **4.** (in tragedy) the quality or effect of speeches understood by the audience but not grasped by the speakers on the stage (**tragic irony**). **5.** an outcome of events contrary to what was, or might have been, expected. **6.** an ironical quality. [t. L: m. s. *īrōnīa,* t. Gk.: m. *eirōneía* dissimulation, understatement]
—**Syn. 1.** IRONY, SARCASM, SATIRE agree in indicating derision of something or someone. In IRONY the essential feature is the contradiction between the literal and the intended meaning, since one thing is said and another is implied; it attacks or derides, or, often, is merely playful: *"Beautiful weather, isn't it?"* (the weather is perfectly detestable). *"If you try hard, you may be able to do worse"* (what you have done is quite bad enough). In SARCASM the characteristic feature is the harsh or cutting quality; it may be ironical or may state directly what is meant: *"A fine musician you've turned out to be! You couldn't play one piece correctly if you had two assistants."* SATIRE, originally applied to a literary composition which attacks by means of irony or sarcasm, denotes also the use of such means formally in writing or speaking, for some serious purpose (as the exposing or denouncing of abuses) or in a malicious or merely playful spirit: *Swift's satires; a speech of satire against the wasteful city administration.*

i·ron·y² (ī′ər nĭ), *adj.* consisting of, containing, or resembling iron. [ME *yrony;* f. IRON + -ʏ¹]

Ir·o·quoi·an (ĭr′ə kwoi′ən), *adj.* belonging to or constituting a linguistic family of the Iroquoian-Caddoan stock of North American Indians, of Canada and the eastern U.S., including the Iroquois confederacy, the Cherokees, Wyandots or Hurons, Erie, and others.

Ir·o·quoi·an-Cad·do·an (ĭr′ə kwoi′ən kăd′ō ən), *n.* an American Indian linguistic stock combining the Iroquoian and Caddoan families and perhaps related to the Siouan-Muskogean stock.

Ir·o·quois (ĭr′ə kwoi′, -kwoiz′), *n.sing. and pl.* **1.** a member of the Indian confederacy, the Five Nations, comprising the Mohawks, Oneidas, Onondagas, Cayugas, and Senecas, with, later, the Tuscaroras. —*adj.* **2.** belonging or relating to the Iroquois or their tribes. [t. F, f. m. Algonquian *irinakhoiw* real adders + F suffix -*ois*]

ir·ra·di·ant (ĭ rā′dĭ ənt), *adj.* irradiating; radiant; shining. —**ir·ra′di·ance, ir·ra′di·an·cy,** *n.*

ir·ra·di·ate (*v.* ĭ rā′dĭ āt′; *adj.* ĭ rā′dĭ ĭt, -āt′), *v.,* **-ated, -ating,** *adj.* —*v.t.* **1.** to shed rays of light upon; illuminate. **2.** to illumine intellectually or spiritually. **3.** to brighten as if with light. **4.** to radiate (light, etc.). **5.** to heat with radiant energy. **6.** to cure by being exposed to radiation, as of ultraviolet light. **7.** to expose to radiation. —*v.i.* **8.** to emit rays; shine. **9.** to become radiant. —*adj.* **10.** irradiated; bright. [t. L: m.s. *irradiātus,* pp., illumined] —**ir·ra′di·a·tive,** *adj.* —**ir·ra′di·a′tor,** *n.*

ir·ra·di·a·tion (ĭ rā′dĭ ā′shən), *n.* **1.** act of irradiating. **2.** state of being irradiated. **3.** intellectual or spiritual enlightenment. **4.** a ray of light; a beam. **5.** *Optics.* the apparent enlargement of a bright object when seen against a dark ground. **6.** the use of x-rays or other radiations for the treatment of disease, etc. **7.** the process of exposure to radiation. **8.** the intensity of radiation falling on a given point; radiant energy received per unit of time per unit area of irradiated surface.

ir·ra·tion·al (ĭ răsh′ə nəl), *adj.* **1.** without the faculty of, or not endowed with, reason: *irrational animals.* **2.** without, or deprived of, sound judgment. **3.** not in accordance with reason; utterly illogical: *irrational fear.* **4.** *Arith.* not capable of being exactly expressed by a ratio of two integers. **5.** *Math.* (of functions) not expressible as the ratio of two polynomials. **6.** *Gk. and Lat. Pros.* **a.** of or pertaining to a substitution in the normal metrical pattern, esp. a long syllable for a short syllable. **b.** noting a foot containing such a substitution. [late ME, t. L: s. *irrationālis*] —**ir·ra′tion·al·ly,** *adv.* —**ir·ra′tion·al·ness,** *n.*

ir·ra·tion·al·ism (ĭ răsh′ən ə lĭz′əm), *n.* irrationality in thought or action.

ir·ra·tion·al·i·ty (ĭ răsh′ə năl′ə tĭ), *n., pl.* **-ties. 1.** the quality of being irrational. **2.** an irrational, illogical, or absurd action, thought, etc.

Ir·ra·wad·dy (ĭr′ə wŏd′ĭ), *n.* a river flowing S through Burma to the Bay of Bengal. ab. 1250 mi.

ir·re·claim·a·ble (ĭr′ĭ klā′mə bəl), *adj.* not reclaimable; incapable of being reclaimed. —**ir·re·claim′a·bil′i·ty, ir·re·claim′a·ble·ness,** *n.* —**ir·re·claim′a·bly,** *adv.*

ir·rec·on·cil·a·ble (ĭ rĕk′ən sī′lə bəl, *for emphasis often* ĭ rĕk′ən sī′-), *adj.* **1.** that cannot be harmonized or adjusted; incompatible: *two irreconcilable statements.* **2.** that cannot be brought to acquiescence or content; implacably opposed: *irreconcilable enemies.* —*n.* **3.** one who or that which is irreconcilable. **4.** one who remains opposed to agreement or compromise. —**ir·rec′on·cil′a·bil′i·ty, ir·rec′on·cil′a·ble·ness,** *n.* —**ir·rec′on·cil·a·bly,** *adv.*

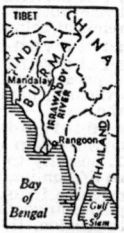

Irrawaddy River

ir·re·cov·er·a·ble (Ir/Ĭ kŭv/ər ə bəl), *adj.* **1.** that cannot be regained: *an irrecoverable debt.* **2.** that cannot be remedied or rectified: *irrecoverable sorrow.* —**ir/re·cov/er·a·ble·ness,** *n.* —**ir/re·cov/er·a·bly,** *adv.*

ir·re·cu·sa·ble (Ir/Ĭ kū/zə bəl), *adj.* not to be objected to or rejected. [t. LL: m. s. *irrecūsābilis* not to be refused] —**ir/re·cu/sa·bly,** *adv.*

ir·re·deem·a·ble (Ir/Ĭ dē/mə bəl), *adj.* **1.** not redeemable; incapable of being bought back or paid off. **2.** not convertible into specie, as paper money. **3.** beyond redemption; irreclaimable. **4.** irremediable, irreparable, or hopeless. —**ir/re·deem/a·bly,** *adv.*

ir·re·den·tist (Ir/Ĭ dĕn/tĬst), *n.* **1.** (*usually cap.*) a member of an Italian association which became prominent in 1878, advocating the redemption, or the incorporation into Italy, of certain neighboring regions (**Italia irredenta**) having a primarily Italian population. **2.** a member of a party in any country advocating the acquiring of some region, actually included in another country, but claimed as properly belonging to the former country by reason of racial or other ties. —*adj.* **3.** pertaining to or advocating irredentism. [t. It.: s. *irredentista,* der. (*Italia*) *irredenta* (Italy) unredeemed, fem. of *irredento,* f. L: *in-* IN-³ + m. *redemptus,* pp., redeemed] —**ir/re·den/tism,** *n.*

ir·re·duc·i·ble (Ir/Ĭ dū/sə bəl, -dōō/-), *adj.* **1.** not reducible; incapable of being reduced or diminished: *the irreducible minimum.* **2.** incapable of being brought into a different condition or form. —**ir/re·duc/i·bil/i·ty,** **ir/re·duc/i·ble·ness,** *n.* —**ir/re·duc/i·bly,** *adv.*

ir·re·fra·ga·ble (Ir/ĕf/rə gə bəl), *adj.* not to be refuted; undeniable. [t. LL: m.s. *irrefragābilis*] —**ir·ref/ra·ga·bil/i·ty,** *n.* —**ir·ref/ra·ga·bly,** *adv.*

ir·re·fran·gi·ble (Ir/Ĭ frăn/jə bəl), *adj.* **1.** not to be broken or violated; inviolable: *an irrefrangible rule of etiquette.* **2.** incapable of being refracted: *x-rays are irrefrangible.* —**ir/re·fran/gi·bly,** *adv.*

ir·ref·u·ta·ble (Ir/ĕf/yə tə bəl, Ir/Ĭ fū/tə bəl), *adj.* not refutable; incontrovertible: *irrefutable logic.* —**ir·ref/u·ta·bil/i·ty,** *n.* —**ir·ref/u·ta·bly,** *adv.*

irreg., **1.** irregular. **2.** irregularly.

ir·re·gard·less (Ir/Ĭ gärd/lĬs), *adj. Colloq.* regardless (not generally regarded as good usage).

ir·reg·u·lar (Ir rĕg/yə lər), *adj.* **1.** without symmetry, even shape, formal arrangement, etc.: *an irregular pattern.* **2.** not characterized by any fixed principle, method, or rate: *irregular intervals.* **3.** not according to rule, or to the accepted principle, method, course, order, etc. **4.** not conformed or conforming to rules of justice or morality, as conduct, transactions, mode of life, etc., or persons. **5.** *Bot.* not uniform, (of a flower) having the members of some or all of its floral circles or whorls differing from one another in size or shape, or extent of union. **6.** *Gram.* not conforming to the most prevalent pattern of formation, inflection, construction, etc.: *the verbs "keep" and "see" are irregular in their inflection.* **7.** *Mil.* (formerly, of troops) not belonging to the established forces. —*n.* **8.** one who or that which is irregular. **9.** *Mil.* a soldier not of a regular military force. [t. ML: s. *irregulāris;* r. ME *irreguler,* t. OF. See IR-², REGULAR] —**ir·reg/u·lar·ly,** *adv.*
—**Syn.** **1.** unsymmetrical, uneven. **2.** unmethodical, unsystematic; disorderly, capricious, erratic, eccentric, lawless. **3.** anomalous, unusual. IRREGULAR, ABNORMAL, EXCEPTIONAL imply a deviation from the regular, the normal, the ordinary, or the usual. IRREGULAR, not according to rule, refers to any deviation, as in form, arrangement, action, and the like; it may imply such deviation as a mere fact, or as regrettable, or even censurable. ABNORMAL implies a deviation from the common rule, resulting in a nontypical form or nature of a thing: *a two-headed calf is abnormal, abnormal lack of emotion.* EXCEPTIONAL means out of the ordinary or unusual; it may refer merely to the rarity of occurrence, or to the superiority of quality: *an exceptional case, an exceptional mind.*

ir·reg·u·lar·i·ty (Ir rĕg/yə lăr/ə tĬ), *n., pl.* **-ties.** **1.** state or fact of being irregular. **2.** something irregular.

ir·rel·a·tive (Ir rĕl/ə tĬv), *adj.* **1.** not relative; without relation (fol. by *to*). **2.** irrelevant. —**ir·rel/a·tive·ly,** *adv.* —**ir·rel/a·tive·ness,** *n.*

ir·rel·e·vance (Ir rĕl/ə vəns), *n.* **1.** the quality of being irrelevant: *the irrelevance of his arguments.* **2.** an irrelevant thing, act, etc.

ir·rel·e·van·cy (Ir rĕl/ə vən sĬ), *n., pl.* **-cies.** irrelevance.

ir·rel·e·vant (Ir rĕl/ə vənt), *adj.* **1.** not relevant; not applicable or pertinent: *irrelevant remarks.* **2.** *Law.* (of evidence) having no probative value upon any issue in the case. —**ir·rel/e·vant·ly,** *adv.*

ir·re·liev·a·ble (Ir/Ĭ lē/və bəl), *adj.* not relievable.

ir·re·li·gion (Ir/Ĭ lĬj/ən), *n.* **1.** lack of religion. **2.** hostility to or disregard of religion; impiety. —**ir/re·li/gion·ist,** *n.*

ir·re·li·gious (Ir/Ĭ lĬj/əs), *adj.* **1.** not religious; impious; ungodly. **2.** showing disregard for or hostility to religion. [t. LL: m.s. *irreligiōsus*] —**ir/re·li/gious·ly,** *adv.* —**ir/re·li/gious·ness,** *n.*

ir·re·mem·e·a·ble (Ir rĕm/ĭ ə bəl, Ir ē/mĬ-), *adj. Now Poetic.* from which one cannot return. [t. L: m.s. *irremeābilis*] —**ir·rem/e·a·bly,** *adv.*

ir·re·me·di·a·ble (Ir/Ĭ mē/dĬ ə bəl), *adj.* not remediable; irreparable: *irremediable disease.* —**ir/re·me/di·a·ble·ness,** *n.* —**ir/re·me/di·a·bly,** *adv.*

ir·re·mis·si·ble (Ir/Ĭ mĬs/ə bəl), *adj.* **1.** not remissible; unpardonable, as a sin. **2.** that cannot be remitted, as a

duty. —**ir/re·mis/si·bil/i·ty,** **ir/re·mis/si·ble·ness,** *n.* —**ir/re·mis/si·bly,** *adv.*

ir·re·mov·a·ble (Ir/Ĭ mōō/və bəl), *adj.* not removable. —**ir/re·mov/a·bil/i·ty,** *n.* —**ir/re·mov/a·bly,** *adv.*

ir·rep·a·ra·ble (Ir rĕp/ə rə bəl), *adj.* not reparable; incapable of being rectified, remedied, or made good: *an irreparable loss.* —**ir·rep/a·ra·bil/i·ty,** **ir·rep/a·ra·ble·ness,** *n.* —**ir·rep/a·ra·bly,** *adv.*

ir·re·peal·a·ble (Ir/Ĭ pē/lə bəl), *adj.* not repealable. —**ir/re·peal/a·bly,** *adv.*

ir·re·place·a·ble (Ir/Ĭ plā/sə bəl), *adj.* that cannot be replaced: *an irreplaceable souvenir.*

ir·re·plev·i·sa·ble (Ir/Ĭ plĕv/ə sə bəl), *adj. Law.* not replevisable or repleviable: that cannot be replevied. Also, **ir·re·plev·i·a·ble** (Ir/Ĭ plĕv/Ĭ ə bəl).

ir·re·press·i·ble (Ir/Ĭ prĕs/ə bəl), *adj.* not repressible. —**ir/re·press/i·bil/i·ty,** **ir/re·press/i·ble·ness,** *n.* —**ir/re·press/i·bly,** *adv.*

ir·re·proach·a·ble (Ir/Ĭ prō/chə bəl), *adj.* not reproachable; free from blame. —**ir/re·proach/a·ble·ness,** *n.* —**ir/re·proach/a·bly,** *adv.*

ir·re·sist·i·ble (Ir/Ĭ zĬs/tə bəl), *adj.* not resistible; that cannot be resisted or withstood: *an irresistible impulse.* —**ir/re·sist/i·bil/i·ty,** **ir/re·sist/i·ble·ness,** *n.* —**ir/re·sist/i·bly,** *adv.*

ir·res·o·lute (Ir rĕz/ə lōōt/), *adj.* not resolute; doubtful or undecided; infirm of purpose; vacillating. —**ir·res/o·lute/ly,** *adv.* —**ir·res/o·lute/ness,** *n.*

ir·res·o·lu·tion (Ir rĕz/ə lōō/shən), *n.* lack of resolution; lack of decision or purpose; vacillation.

ir·re·solv·a·ble (Ir/Ĭ zŏl/və bəl), *adj.* not resolvable; incapable of being resolved; not analyzable; not solvable.

ir·re·spec·tive (Ir/Ĭ spĕk/tĬv), *adj.* without regard to something else, esp. something specified; independent (fol. by *of*): *irrespective of all rights.* —**ir/re·spec/tive·ly,** *adv.*

ir·re·spir·a·ble (Ir/Ĭ spir/ə bəl, Ir rĕs/pĬ rə bəl), *adj.* not respirable; unfit for respiration.

ir·re·spon·si·ble (Ir/Ĭ spŏn/sə bəl), *adj.* **1.** not responsible; not answerable or accountable: *an irresponsible ruler.* **2.** not capable of responsibility; done without a sense of responsibility: *mentally irresponsible.* —*n.* **3.** an irresponsible person. —**ir/re·spon/si·bil/i·ty,** **ir/re·spon/si·ble·ness,** *n.* —**ir/re·spon/si·bly,** *adv.*

ir·re·spon·sive (Ir/Ĭ spŏn/sĬv), *adj.* not responsive; not responding, or not responding readily, as in speech, action, or feeling. —**ir/re·spon/sive·ness,** *n.*

ir·re·ten·tive (Ir/Ĭ tĕn/tĬv), *adj.* not retentive; lacking power to retain, esp. mentally. —**ir/re·ten/tive·ness,** *n.*

ir·re·trace·a·ble (Ir/Ĭ trā/sə bəl), *adj.* not retraceable; that cannot be retraced: *an irretraceable step.*

ir·re·triev·a·ble (Ir/Ĭ trē/və bəl), *adj.* not retrievable; irrecoverable; irreparable. —**ir/re·triev/a·bil/i·ty,** **ir/re·triev/a·ble·ness,** *n.* —**ir/re·triev/a·bly,** *adv.*

ir·rev·er·ence (Ir rĕv/ər əns), *n.* **1.** the quality of being irreverent; lack of reverence or respect. **2.** the condition of not being reverenced: *to be held in irreverence.*

ir·rev·er·ent (Ir rĕv/ər ənt), *adj.* not reverent; manifesting or characterized by irreverence; deficient in veneration or respect: *an irreverent reply.* [t. L: s. *irreverens*] —**ir·rev/er·ent·ly,** *adv.*

ir·re·vers·i·ble (Ir/Ĭ vûr/sə bəl), *adj.* not reversible; that cannot be reversed. —**ir/re·vers/i·bil/i·ty,** **ir/re·vers/i·ble·ness,** *n.* —**ir/re·vers/i·bly,** *adv.*

ir·rev·o·ca·ble (Ir rĕv/ə kə bəl), *adj.* not to be revoked or recalled; that cannot be repealed or annulled: *an irrevocable decree.* —**ir·rev/o·ca·bil/i·ty,** **ir·rev/o·ca·ble·ness,** *n.* —**ir·rev/o·ca·bly,** *adv.*

ir·ri·ga·ble (Ir/Ĭ gə bəl), *adj.* that may be irrigated.

ir·ri·gate (Ir/ə gāt/), *v.t.,* **-gated, -gating.** **1.** to supply (land) with water by means of streams passing through it, esp. artificial streams provided to promote vegetation. **2.** *Med.* to supply (a wound, etc.) with a constant flow of some liquid. **3.** *Now Rare.* to moisten; wet. [t. L: m.s. *irrigātus,* pp.] —**ir/ri·ga/tor,** *n.*

ir·ri·ga·tion (Ir/ə gā/shən), *n.* **1.** the supplying of land with water from artificial channels to promote vegetation. **2.** *Med.* the covering or washing out of anything with water or other liquid for the purpose of making or keeping it moist, as in local medical treatment. **3.** state of being irrigated. —**ir/ri·ga/tion·al,** *adj.*

ir·ri·ga·tive (Ir/ə gā/tĬv), *adj.* serving for or pertaining to irrigation.

ir·rig·u·ous (Ir rĬg/yōō əs), *adj. Now Rare.* well-watered, as land. [t. L: m. *irriguus*]

ir·ri·ta·bil·i·ty (Ir/ə tə bĬl/ə tĬ), *n., pl.* **-ties.** **1.** the quality of being irritable. **2.** an irritable state or condition. **3.** *Physiol., Biol.* the ability to be excited to a characteristic action or function by the application of some stimulus: *protoplasm displays irritability by responding to heat, etc.* [t. L: m.s. *irritābilitas*]

ir·ri·ta·ble (Ir/ə tə bəl), *adj.* **1.** easily irritated; readily excited to impatience or anger. **2.** *Physiol., Biol.* displaying irritability (def. 3). **3.** *Pathol.* susceptible to physical irritation; liable to shrink, become inflamed, etc., when stimulated: *an irritable wound.* [t. L: m.s. *irritābilis*] —**ir/ri·ta·ble·ness,** *n.* —**ir/ri·ta·bly,** *adv.*

ir·ri·tant (Ir/ə tənt), *adj.* **1.** irritating. —*n.* **2.** anything that irritates. **3.** *Pathol., Med.* something, as a poison or a therapeutic agent, producing irritation. [t. L: s. *irritans,* ppr.] —**ir/ri·tan·cy,** *n.*

ir·ri·tate (ĭr′ə tāt′), v.t., -tated, -tating. 1. to excite to impatience or anger. 2. Physiol., Biol. to excite (a living system) to some characteristic action or function. 3. Pathol. to bring (a bodily part, etc.) to an abnormally excited or sensitive condition. [t. L: m.s. irritātus, pp.] —ir′ri·ta′tor, n.
—Syn. 1. vex, chafe, fret, gall; nettle, ruffle, pique; incense, anger, enrage, infuriate. IRRITATE, EXASPERATE, PROVOKE mean to annoy or stir to anger. To IRRITATE is to excite to impatience or angry feeling, often of no great depth or duration: to irritate by refusing to explain an action. To EXASPERATE is to irritate to a point where self-control is threatened or lost: to exasperate by continual delays and excuses. To PROVOKE is to stir to a sudden, strong feeling of resentful anger as by unwarrantable acts or wanton annoyance: to tease and provoke an animal until it attacks one.

ir·ri·tat·ing (ĭr′ə tā′tĭng), adj. causing irritation; provoking: an irritating reply. —ir′ri·tat′ing·ly, adv.

ir·ri·ta·tion (ĭr′ə tā′shən), n. 1. act of irritating. 2. state of being irritated. 3. Physiol., Pathol. a. the bringing of a bodily part or organ to an abnormally excited or sensitive condition. b. the condition itself.

ir·ri·ta·tive (ĭr′ə tā′tĭv), adj. 1. serving or tending to irritate. 2. Pathol. characterized or produced by irritation of some bodily part, etc.: an irritative fever.

ir·rup·tion (ĭ rŭp′shən), n. a breaking or bursting in; a violent incursion or invasion. [t. L: s. irruptio]

ir·rup·tive (ĭ rŭp′tĭv), adj. 1. characterized by or pertaining to irruption. 2. Petrol. intrusive.

Ir·tish (ĭr tĭsh′), n. a river flowing from the Altai Mountains NW through the W Soviet Union in Asia to the Ob river. ab. 2300 mi. Also, **Ir·tysh′**.

Ir·ving (ûr′vĭng), n. 1. Sir Henry, (John Henry Brodribb) 1838–1905, British actor. 2. Washington, 1783–1859, U.S. essayist, story writer, and historian.

Ir·ving·ton (ûr′vĭng tən), n. a town in NE New Jersey, near Newark. 59,379 (1960).

is (ĭz), v. 3rd pers. sing. pres. indic. of be. [OE is, c. Icel. es, er; akin to G ist, Goth. ist, L est, Gk. estí, Skt. ástí. See BE]

is-, var. of iso-, before some vowels, as in isallobar.

Is., 1. Also, **Isa.** Isaiah. 2. Also, is. Island. 3. Isle.

I·saac (ī′zək), n. a patriarch, son of Abraham and Sarah, and father of Jacob. Gen. 17:19. [t. L (Vulgate), t. Gk. (Septuagint), t. Heb.: m. Yitshāq, lit., laughs]

I·saacs (ī′zəks), n. Sir Isaac Alfred, 1855–1948, Australian jurist: governor general of Australia, 1931–36.

Is·a·bel·la I (ĭz′ə bĕl′ə), (the Catholic) 1451–1504, joint ruler, 1474–1504, of Castile and León, with her husband Ferdinand V, and patron of Columbus. Also, Spanish, **I·sa·bel** (ē′sä bĕl′).

i·sa·gog·ic (ī′sə gŏj′ĭk), adj. 1. introductory, esp. to the interpretation of the Bible. —n. 2. (usually pl.) a. introductory studies. b. the department of theology which is introductory to exegesis and the literary history of the Bible. [t. L: s. īsagōgicus introductory, t. Gk.: m. eisagōgikós, lit., leading into]

I·sa·iah (ī zā′ə, ī zī′ə), n. 1. a great Hebrew prophet of the eighth century B.C. 2. a long book of the Old Testament, belonging to the second division of the Hebrew canon and the first book of the major prophets. [ult. t. Heb.: m. Yeshaʿyāh, lit., Jehovah's salvation]

i·sal·lo·bar (ī săl′ə bär′), n. Meteorol. a line on a weather map connecting places having equal pressure changes. [t. IS- + ALLO- + -BAR. See ISOBAR]

I·sar (ē′zär), n. a river flowing from W Austria NE through S West Germany to the Danube. 215 mi.

i·sa·rithm (ī′sə rĭth′əm), n. isopleth.

Is·car·i·ot (ĭs kăr′ī ət), n. 1. the surname of Judas, the betrayer of Jesus. Mark 3:19, 14:10–11. 2. one who betrays another; a traitor. [t. L: s. Iscariōta, t. Gk.: m. Iskariōtēs, t. Heb.: m. ish-qerīyōth man of Kerioth (a place in Palestine)]

is·che·mi·a (ĭs kē′mī ə), n. Pathol. local anemia produced by local obstacles to the arterial flow. Also, ischae′mi·a. [t. NL, f. s. Gk. íschein check + -(a)emia -EMIA] —is·che·mic (ĭs kē′mĭk, -kĕm′ĭk), adj.

Is·chia (ē′skyä), n. 1. an island off the SW coast of Italy, near Naples: earthquake, 1883. 10,385 pop. (1951); 18 sq. mi. 2. a seaport on this island. 3188 (1951).

is·chi·ad·ic (ĭs kĭ ăd′ĭk), adj. pertaining to the schium; sciatic. Also, **is·chi·at·ic** (ĭs kĭ ăt′ĭk).

is·chi·um (ĭs kĭ əm), n., pl. -chia (-kĭ ə). Anat. 1. the lowermost of the three parts composing either innominate bone. See diag. under pelvis. 2. either of the bones on which the body rests when sitting. [t. NL, t. Gk.: m. ischíon hip joint, haunch, ischium] —is′chi·al, adj.

-ise¹, var. of -ize, as in exercise.

-ise², a noun suffix indicating quality, condition, or function, as in merchandise, franchise.

I·sère (ē zĕr′), n. a river in SE France, flowing from the Alps to the Rhone river. ab. 150 mi.

I·seult (ĭ sōōlt′), n. Arthurian Romance. 1. the daughter of Angus, king of Ireland, and wife of Mark, king of Cornwall, loved by Tristram. 2. daughter of the king of Brittany, and wife of Tristram. Also, Isolde, Isolt.

Is·fa·han (ĭs′fə hän′), n. a city in central Iran: the capital of Persia from the 16th into the 18th centuries. 196,134 (est. 1950). Also, Ispahan.

-ish¹, 1. a suffix used to form adjectives from nouns, with the sense of: a. "belonging to" (a people, country, etc.), as in British, Danish, English, Spanish. b. "after the manner of," "having the characteristics of," "like,"

as in babyish, girlish, mulish (such words being now often depreciatory). c. "addicted to," "inclined or tending to," as in bookish, freakish. 2. a suffix used to form adjectives from other adjectives, with the sense of "somewhat," "rather," as in oldish, reddish, sweetish. [ME; OE -isc, c. G -isch, Gk. -iskos; akin to -ESQUE]
—Syn. 1. b. The suffixes -ISH, -LIKE, -LY agree in indicating that something resembles something else. One of the common meanings of -ISH is derogatory; that is, it indicates that something has the bad qualities of something else, or that it has qualities similar which are not suitable to it: childish, mannish (of a woman). The suffix -LIKE, in the formation of adjectives, is usually complimentary: childlike innocence, godlike serenity. In an adverbial function, it may be slightly disparaging: manlike, he wanted to run the show. The suffix -LY, when it means having the nature or character of, is distinctly complimentary: kingly, manly, motherly.

-ish², a suffix forming simple verbs. [t. F: m. -iss-, extended stem of verbs in -ir, g. L -isc-, in inceptive verbs]

Ish·er·wood (ĭsh′ər wŏŏd), n. Christopher, born 1904, British novelist and playwright.

Ish·ma·el (ĭsh′mĭ əl), n. 1. the outcast son of Abraham and Hagar. See Gen. 16:11, 12. 2. any outcast. [t. Heb.: m. Yishmāʿēl, lit., God will hear]

Ish·ma·el·ite (ĭsh′mĭ ə līt′), n. 1. a descendant of Ishmael (from whom the Arabs claim descent). 2. a wanderer; an outcast. —**Ish·ma·el·it′ish**, adj.

Ish·tar (ĭsh′tär), n. the chief goddess of the Babylonians and Assyrians. Cf. Astarte. [t. Akkadian]

Is·i·dore of Seville (ĭz′ə dōr′), (Isidorus Hispalensis) A.D. c560–636, Spanish archbishop and Latin encyclopedist.

i·sin·glass (ī′zĭng glăs′, -gläs′), n. 1. a pure, transparent or translucent form of gelatin, esp. that derived from the air bladders of certain fishes. 2. mica. [t. MD: pop. m. (by assoc. with GLASS) of hysenblas, c. G hausenblase isinglass, lit., sturgeon bladder.]

I·sis (ī′sĭs), n. an Egyptian goddess, sister and wife of Osiris, usually distinguished by the solar disk and cow's horns on her head. [t. L, t. Gk., t. Egyptian: m. Ese]

Is·ken·de·run (ĭs kĕn′də rōōn′), n. a seaport in S Turkey, on the Gulf of Iskenderun, an inlet of the Mediterranean. 22,946 (1950). Also, Alexandretta.

isl., 1. (pl. isls.) island. 2. isle.

Is·lam (ĭs′ləm, ĭs läm′), n. 1. the religious system of the Almighty Potentate Allah according to Mohammed; Mohammedanism. 2. the whole body of Mohammedan believers, their civilization, and their lands. [t. Ar.: submission to the will of God)] —**Is·lam·ic** (ĭs lăm′ĭk, -lä′mĭk), **Is·lam·it·ic** (ĭs′lə mĭt′ĭk), adj.

Islamic Republic of Mauritania, Official name of Mauritania (def. 1).

Is·lam·ism (ĭs′lə mĭz′əm), n. Mohammedanism.

Is·lam·ite (ĭs′lə mīt′), n. a Mohammedan.

is·land (ī′lənd), n. 1. a tract of land completely surrounded by water, and not large enough to be called a continent. 2. a clump of woodland in a prairie. 3. an isolated hill. 4. something resembling an island. 5. a platform in the middle of a street, at a crossing, for the safety of pedestrians. 6. Physiol., Anat. an isolated portion of tissue or aggregation of cells. —v.t. 7. to make into an island. 8. to dot with islands. 9. to place on an island; isolate. [ME iland, yland, OE iland, igland, f. ig, ieg island + land land; -s inserted through erroneous assoc. with ISLE] —**is′land·like′**, adj.

is·land·er (ī′lən dər), n. a native or inhabitant of an island.

Islands of the Blessed, Gk. Myth. imaginary is lands said to lie in the remote western part of the ocean whither after death the souls of heroes and good men were supposed to be transported.

island universe, Astron. a galaxy.

isle (īl), n., v., isled, isling. —n. 1. a small island: the British Isles. 2. Now Chiefly Poetic. an island. —v.t. 3. to make into or as into an isle. 4. to place on or as on an isle. —v.i. 5. to dwell or remain on an isle. [ME isle, ile, t. OF, g. L insula]

Isle of Man. See Man, Isle of.

Isle of Pines. See Pines, Isle of.

Isle of Wight. See Wight, Isle of.

Isle Roy·ale (īl′ roi′əl), a large island in Lake Superior: a part of Michigan; now a national park. 208 sq. mi.

is·let (ī′lĭt), n. a small island. [t. F: m. islette (now ilette), dim. of isle ISLE]

Is·ling·ton (ĭz′lĭng tən), n. a N borough of London, England. 235,645 (1951).

isls., islands.

ism (ĭz′əm), n. a distinctive doctrine, theory, system, or practice: this is the age of isms. [n. use of -ISM]

-ism, a suffix of nouns denoting action or practice, state or condition, principles, doctrines, a usage or characteristic, etc., as in baptism, barbarism, criticism, Darwinism, plagiarism, realism. Cf. -ist and -ize. [ult. (often directly) t. Gk.: s. -ismos, -isma, noun suffix. See -IZE]

Is·ma·il·i·an (ĭs′mä ĭl′ĭ ən), n. a member of a sect of Shiite Mohammedans whose doctrines vary widely from those of orthodox Mohammedans.

Is·ma·il Pa·sha (ĭs′mä ēl′ pä shä′), 1830–95, viceroy and khedive of Egypt, 1863–79.

is·n't (ĭz′ənt), contraction of is not.

iso-, 1. a prefix meaning "equal." 2. Chem. a prefix added to the name of one compound to denote another isomeric with it. Also, **is-**. [t. Gk., comb. form of ísos equal]

ăct, āble, dâre, ärt; ĕbb, ēqual; ĭf, īce; hŏt, ōver, ôrder, oil, bŏŏk, ōōze, out; ŭp, ūse, ûrge; ə = a in alone; ch, chief; g, give; ng, ring; sh, shoe; th, thin; th, that; zh, vision. See the full key on inside cover.

i·so·ag·glu·ti·na·tion (ī′sō·ə glōō′tə nā′shən), *n. Med.* the clumping of the red blood cells of an animal by a tranfusion from another animal of the same species.

i·so·ag·glu·ti·nin (ī′sō·ə glōō′tə nĭn), *n.* an agglutinin which can effect isoagglutination.

i·so·bar (ī′sə bär′), *n.* **1.** *Meteorol., etc.* a line drawn on a weather map, etc., connecting all points having the same barometric pres-
sure (reduced to sea level) at a specified time or over a certain period. **2.** *Physics, Chem.* Also, **i·so·bare** (ī′sə bâr′). one of the two atoms of different atomic number, but having the same atomic weight. [t.Gk.: s. *isobarēs* of equal weight]

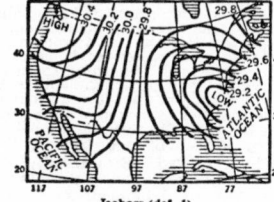

Isobars (def. 1)

i·so·bar·ic (ī′sə bär′-ĭk), *adj.* **1.** having or showing equal barometric pressure. **2.** of or pertaining to isobars.

i·so·car·pic (ī′sə kär′pĭk), *adj. Bot.* having carpels equal in number to the other floral parts.

i·so·cheim (ī′sə kīm′), *n. Climatology.* a line on a map connecting places which have the same mean winter temperature. Also, **i′so·chime′**. [f. ISO- + m.s. Gk. *cheîma* winter] —**i′so·chei′mal,** *adj.*

i·so·chor (ī′sə kôr′), *n. Physics.* a line representing the variation in pressure with temperature, under a constant volume. Also, **i′so·chore′**. [f. ISO- + s. Gk. *chôra* place] —**i·so·chor·ic** (ī′sə kôr′ĭk, -kōr′-), *adj.*

i·so·chro·mat·ic (ī′sō krō măt′ĭk), *adj.* **1.** *Optics.* having the same color or tint. **2.** *Physics.* involving radiation of constant wave length or frequency. **3.** *Photog.* orthochromatic.

i·so·chron (ī′sə krŏn′), *n.* a mathematical function representing one percent of maturation time and used in the sciences of development. Also, **i·so·chrone** (ī′sə krōn′).

i·soch·ro·nal (ī sŏk′rə nəl), *adj.* **1.** equal or uniform in time. **2.** performed in equal intervals of time. **3.** characterized by motions or vibrations of equal duration. [f. s. Gk. *isóchronos* equal in age or time + -AL[1]] —**i·soch′-
ro·nal·ly,** *adv.*

i·soch·ro·nism (ī sŏk′rə nĭz′əm), *n.* isochronal character or action.

i·soch·ro·nize (ī sŏk′rə nīz′), *v.t.,* **-nized, -nizing.** to make isochronal.

i·soch·ro·nous (ī sŏk′rə nəs), *adj.* isochronal. —**i·soch′-
ro·nous·ly,** *adv.*

i·soch·ro·öus (ī sŏk′rō əs), *adj.* having the same color throughout.

i·so·cli·nal (ī′sə klī′nəl), *adj.* **1.** of or pertaining to equal inclination; inclining or dipping in the same direction. **2.** denoting or pertaining to a line on the earth's surface connecting points of equal dip or inclina-
tion of the earth's magnetic field. **3.** *Geol.* noting or pertaining to a fold of strata which is of the nature of an isocline. —*n.* **4.** an isoclinal line. Also, **i·so·clin·ic** (ī′sə klĭn′ĭk). [f. s. Gk. *isoklīnēs* equally balanced + -AL[1]]

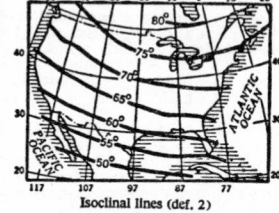

Isoclinal lines (def. 2)

i·so·cline (ī′sə klīn′), *n. Geol.* a fold of strata so tightly compressed that the parts on each side dip in the same direction. [t. Gk.: m.s. *isoklīnēs* equally balanced]

i·soc·ra·cy (ī sŏk′rə sĭ), *n., pl.* **-cies.** a government in which all have equal political power. [t. Gk.: m.s. *isokratía.* See ISO-, -CRACY] —**i·so·crat·ic** (ī′sə krăt′ĭk), *adj.*

I·soc·ra·tes (ī sŏk′rə tēz′), *n.* 436–338 B.C., an Athenian orator and teacher of oratory.

i·so·cy·a·nine (ī′sə sī′ə nēn′, -nĭn), *n. Chem.* a member of the cyanines. See **cyanine.**

i·so·di·a·met·ric (ī′sə dī′ə mět′rĭk), *adj.* **1.** having equal diameters or axes. **2.** *Bot.* having the diameter similar throughout, as a cell. **3.** (of crystals) having two, or three, equal horizontal axes and a third, or fourth, unequal axis at right angles thereto.

i·so·di·mor·phism (ī′sō dī môr′fĭz əm), *n. Crystall.* isomorphism between the forms of two dimorphous substances. —**i′so·di·mor′phous,** *adj.*

i·so·dy·nam·ic (ī′sō dī năm′ĭk, -dī′-), *adj.* **1.** pertain-
ing to or characterized by equality of force, intensity, or the like. **2.** denoting or pertaining to a line on the earth's surface connecting points of equal horizontal intensity of the earth's magnetic field. Also, **i′so·dy·nam′i·cal.**

i·so·e·lec·tric point (ī′sō ĭ lĕk′trĭk), *Chem.* the pH at which a substance is electrically neutral or at which it is at its minimum ionization.

i·so·ga·mete (ī′sō gə mēt′), *n. Biol.* one of a pair of conjugating gametes, exhibiting no sexual or morphological differentiation.

i·sog·a·mous (ī sŏg′ə məs), *adj. Biol.* having two similar gametes in which no differentiation can be dis-
tinguished, or reproducing by the union of such gametes (opposed to *heterogamous*).

i·sog·a·my (ī sŏg′ə mĭ), *n. Biol.* the fusion of two gametes of similar form, as in certain algae.

i·sog·e·nous (ī sŏj′ə nəs), *adj. Biol.* of the same or similar origin, as parts derived from the same or corresponding tissues of the embryo. [f. ISO- + -GENOUS] —**i·sog′e·ny,** *n.*

i·so·ge·o·therm (ī′sə jē′ə thûrm′), *n. Phys. Geog.* an imaginary line or surface passing through points in the interior of the earth which have the same mean temperature. [f. ISO- + GEO- + s. Gk. *thérmē* heat] —**i′so·ge′-
o·ther′mal, i′so·ge′o·ther′mic,** *adj.*

i·so·gloss (ī′sə glŏs′, -glôs′), *n.* an imaginary line sep-
arating two localities which differ in some feature of their speech. [f. ISO- + s. Gk. *glôssa* word, speech, tongue]

i·sog·o·nal (ī sŏg′ə nəl), *adj.* **1.** equiangular; isogonic. —*n.* **2.** an isogonal line.

isogonal line, a line on the earth's surface connecting points of equal declination of the earth's magnetic field.

i·so·gon·ic (ī′sə gŏn′ĭk), *adj.* **1.** having or pertaining to equal angles. **2.** denoting or pertaining to an isogonal line. —*n.* **3.** an isogonal line. [f. m.s. Gk. *isogónios* having equal angles + -IC]

i·so·gram (ī′sə grăm′), *n. Meteorol., Geog.* a line repre-
senting equality with respect to a given variable, used to relate places on maps, charts, etc.

i·so·graph (ī′sə grăf′, -gräf′), *n.* a line drawn on a map to indicate areas having common linguistic characteristics. —**i·so·graph·ic** (ī′sə grăf′ĭk), *adj.*

i·so·hel (ī′sə hĕl′), *n.* a line on a map, etc., connecting places which receive equal amounts of sunshine.

i·so·hy·et (ī′sə hī′ət), *n.* a line drawn on a map con-
necting points having equal rainfall at a certain time or for a stated period. [f. ISO- + s. Gk. *hyetós* rain]

i·so·la·ble (ī′sə lə bəl, ĭs′ə-), *adj.* that can be isolated.

i·so·late (ī′sə lāt′, ĭs′ə-), *v.t.,* **-lated, -lating. 1.** to set or place apart; detach or separate so as to be alone. **2.** *Med.* to keep (an infected person) from contact with noninfected ones. **3.** *Chem.* to obtain (a substance) in an uncombined or pure state. **4.** *Elect.* to insulate. [back formation from *isolated,* ppl. adj., f. s. It. *isolato* (g. L *insulātus*; see INSULATE) + -ED[2]] —**i′so·la′tor,** *n.*

isolating language, a language which uses few or no bound forms.

i·so·la·tion (ī′sə lā′shən, ĭs′ə-), *n.* **1.** act of isolating. **2.** state of being isolated. **3.** the complete separation from others of a person suffering from contagious or infectious disease. **4.** the separation of a nation from other nations by a policy of nonparticipation in inter-
national affairs. **5.** *Sociol.* See **social isolation.** —**Syn. 2.** see solitude.

i·so·la·tion·ist (ī′sə lā′shən ĭst, ĭs′ə-), *n.* one who fa-
vors a policy of nonparticipation in international affairs. —**i′so·la′tion·ism,** *n.*

I·solde (ī sōld′, ī sōl′də; *Ger.* ē zōl′də), *n.* Iseult. Also, **I·solt** (ī sōlt′).

i·so·leu·cine (ī′sə lōō′sēn, -sĭn), *n.* an amino acid, $C_2H_5CH(CH_3)$ $CH(NH_2)COOH$, occurring in casein.

i·so·mag·net·ic (ī′sō măg nĕt′ĭk), *adj.* **1.** denoting or pertaining to an imaginary line on the earth's surface, or a corresponding line on a map or the like, connecting places which have the same magnetic elements. —*n.* **2.** an isomagnetic line.

i·so·mer (ī′sə mər), *n. Chem.* a compound which is isomeric with one or more other compounds.

i·so·mer·ic (ī′sə mĕr′ĭk), *adj. Chem.* (of compounds) composed of the same kinds and numbers of atoms which differ from each other in the arrangement of the atoms and, therefore, in one or more properties. [f. s. Gk. *isomerēs* having equal parts + -IC]

i·som·er·ism (ī sŏm′ə rĭz′əm), *n.* state or condition of being isomeric.

i·som·er·ous (ī sŏm′ər əs), *adj.* **1.** having an equal number of parts, markings, etc. **2.** *Bot.* (of a flower) having the same number of members in each whorl.

i·so·met·ric (ī′sə mĕt′rĭk), *adj.* **1.** pertaining to or having equality of measure. **2.** *Crystall.* noting or pertaining to that system of crystallization which is char-
acterized by three equal axes at right angles to one an-
other. **3.** *Pros.* of equal measure; made up of regular feet. Also, **i′so·met′ri·cal.** [f. s. Gk. *isómetros* of equal measure + -IC] —**i′so·met′ri·cal·ly,** *adv.*

i·so·me·tro·pi·a (ī′sō mə trō′pĭ ə), *n.* a condition in which the refraction is the same in the two eyes. [f. ISO- + s. Gk. *métron* measure + -OPIA]

i·som·e·try (ī sŏm′ə trĭ), *n.* **1.** equality of measure. **2.** *Geog.* equality with respect to height above sea level.

i·so·morph (ī′sə môrf′), *n.* **1.** an organism which is isomorphic with another or others. **2.** an isomorphous substance.

i·so·mor·phic (ī′sə môr′fĭk), *adj.* **1.** *Biol.* being of the same or of like form; different in ancestry, but alike in appearance. **2.** *Crystall.* isomorphous.

i·so·mor·phism (ī′sə môr′fĭz əm), *n.* state or property of being isomorphous or isomorphic.

i·so·mor·phous (ī′sə môr′fəs), *adj. Chem., Crystall.* (of a substance) undergoing a more or less extended continuous variation in chemical composition, with accompanying variations in physical and chemical properties, but maintaining the same crystal structure.

i·so·ni·a·zid (ī/sə nī/ə zĭd), *n.* *Chem.* isonicotinic acid hydrazide, $C_6H_7N_3O$, used in the treatment of tuberculosis.

i·son·o·my (ī sŏn/ə mī), *n.* equality of political rights. [t. Gk.: m.s. *isonomía*] —**i·so·nom·ic** (ī/sə nŏm/ĭk), *adj.*

I·son·zo (ē zŏn/tsō), *n.* a river forming a part of the boundary between Italy and Yugoslavia, flowing from the Julian Alps S to the Gulf of Trieste. 75 mi.

i·so·oc·tane (ī/sō ŏk/tān), *n.* an isomer of octane used to determine the knocking qualities of a gasoline.

i·so·pi·es·tic (ī/sō pī ĕs/tĭk), *adj.* 1. isobaric; denoting equal pressure. —*n.* 2. an isobar (def. 1). [f. ISO- + s. Gk. *piestós*, vbl. adj. of *piézein* press + -IC]

i·so·pleth (ī/sə plĕth/), *n.* a line drawn on a map through all points having the same numerical value of any element, or of the ratio of values of two elements. [t. Gk.: s. *isoplēthēs* equal in number]

i·so·pod (ī/sə pŏd/), *n.* 1. any of the *Isopoda*, an order or suborder of crustaceans (fresh-water, marine, and terrestrial) with seven pairs of legs, and body flattened dorsoventrally. —*adj.* 2. pertaining to the *Isopoda*. 3. having the feet all alike, or similar in character. [t. NL: s. *Isopoda*, pl., genus type. See ISO-, -POD] —**i·sop·o·dan** (ī sŏp/ə dən), *adj.*, *n.* —**i·sop/o·dous**, *adj.*

i·so·prene (ī/sə prēn/), *n.* *Chem.* a colorless liquid hydrocarbon, C_5H_8, of the terpene class, produced from rubber or from oil of turpentine by pyrolysis and convertible into rubber by polymerization. [? f. ISO- + PR(OPYL) + -ENE]

i·so·pro·pyl (ī/sə prō/pĭl), *n.* *Chem.* the univalent radical, $(CH_3)_2CH$.

isopropyl ether, a colorless liquid, $(C_3H_7)_2O$, used as a solvent for waxes, fats, etc.

i·sos·ce·les (ī sŏs/ə lēz/), *adj.* (of a triangle) having two sides equal. See illus. under **triangle.** [t. LL, t. Gk.: m. *isoskelēs* with equal legs]

i·so·seis·mic (ī/sə sīz/mĭk, -sĭs/-), *adj.* 1. pertaining to equal intensity of earthquake shock. 2. noting or pertaining to an imaginary line on the earth's surface connecting points characterized by such intensity. —*n.* 3. an isoseismic line. Also, **i/so·seis/mal.**

i·sos·ta·sy (ī sŏs/tə sī), *n.* 1. *Geol.* the equilibrium of the earth's crust, a condition in which the forces tending to elevate balance those tending to depress. 2. equilibrium when there is pressure from all sides; hydrostatic equilibrium. [f. ISO- + m. Gk. *stásis* a standing]

i·so·stat·ic (ī/sə stăt/ĭk), *adj.* pertaining to or characterized by isostasy.

i·so·there (ī/sə thīr/), *n.* *Climatology.* a line connecting places on the earth's surface which have the same mean summer temperature. [f. ISO- + m.s. Gk. *théros* summer] —**i·soth·er·al** (ī sŏth/ər əl), *adj.*

i·so·therm (ī/sə thûrm/), *n.* 1. *Climatology.* a line connecting points on the earth's surface having the same (mean) temperature. 2. *Physics, Chem.* an isothermal line. [f. ISO- + s. Gk. *thérmē* heat]

i·so·ther·mal (ī/sə thûr/məl), *adj.* 1. *Physics, Chem.* pertaining to or indicating equality of temperature. 2. *Climatology.* pertaining to an isotherm. —*n.* 3. *Climatology.* an isotherm. —**i/so·ther/mal·ly,** *adv.*

isothermal line, *Physics, Chem.* a line or graph showing relations of variables under conditions of uniform temperature.

isothermal process, *Meteorol.* a process which takes place without change in temperature.

i·so·ton·ic (ī/sə tŏn/ĭk), *adj.* 1. pertaining to solutions characterized by equal osmotic pressure. 2. *Physiol.* a. noting or pertaining to a solution containing just enough salt to prevent the destruction of the red blood corpuscles when added to the blood. b. noting or pertaining to a contraction of a muscle when under a constant tension. 3. *Music.* of or characterized by equal tones. [f. s. Gk. *isótonos* having equal accent or tone + -IC]

i·so·tope (ī/sə tōp/), *n.* *Chem.* any of two or more forms of a chemical element, having the same number of protons in the nucleus and, hence, the same atomic number, but having different numbers of neutrons in the nucleus and, hence, different atomic weights. There are 275 isotopes of the 81 stable elements in addition to over 800 radioactive isotopes, so that isotopic forms of every element are known. Isotopes of a single element possess almost identical properties. [f. ISO- + m.s. Gk. *tópos* place] —**i·so·top·ic** (ī/sə tŏp/ĭk), *adj.*

i·sot·o·py (ī sŏt/ə pī), *n.* isotopic character.

i·so·trop·ic (ī/sə trŏp/ĭk, -trō/pĭk), *adj.* 1. *Physics.* having one or more properties that are the same in all directions. 2. *Zool.* lacking axes which are predetermined, as in some eggs. Also, **i·sot·ro·pous** (ī sŏt/rə pəs). [f. ISO- + s. Gk. *trópos* turn, way + -IC]

i·sot·ro·py (ī sŏt/rə pī), *n.* state or property of being isotropic.

Is·pa·han (ĭs/pə hän/), *n.* Isfahan.

Is·ra·el (ĭz/rī əl), *n.* 1. a name given to Jacob after he had wrestled with the angel. Gen. 32:28. 2. the people traditionally descended from Israel or Jacob; the Hebrew or Jewish people. 3. God's chosen people; the elect. 4. a republic in SW Asia, on the Mediterranean: formed as a Jewish state May, 1948. 1,813,000 pop. (est. 1956); 7984 sq. mi. *Cap.:* Jerusalem. 5. the northern kingdom of the Hebrews, including the ten tribes, sometimes called by the name of the chief tribe, Ephraim. *Cap.:*

Samaria. 6. the northern and southern kingdoms of the Hebrews. 7. the Christian church. Gal. 6:16. [ult. t. Heb.: m. Yisrā/ēl (appar.) he who striveth with God]

Is·rae·li (ĭz rā/lī), *n.*, *pl.* -lis, *adj.* —*n.* 1. a native or inhabitant of Israel (def. 4). —*adj.* 2. of Israel (def. 4).

Is·ra·el·ite (ĭz/rī ə līt/), *n.* 1. a descendant of Israel or Jacob; a Hebrew; a Jew. 2. one of God's chosen people. —*adj.* 3. pertaining to Israel; Jewish.

Is·ra·el·it·ish (ĭz/rī ə lī/tĭsh), *adj.* of the Israelites; Hebrew. Also, **Is·ra·el·it·ic** (ĭz/rī ə lĭt/ĭk).

Is·ra·fil (ĭz/rə fēl/), *n.* (in Koran) the angel of music.

Is·sei (ēs/sā/), *n.*, *pl.* -sei. a person of Japanese ancestry, born in Japan, who has come to the United States to live, but retains his allegiance to Japan. [t. Jap: first born, first generation]

is·su·a·ble (ĭsh/ōō ə bəl), *adj.* 1. that may be issued or may issue. 2. forthcoming. 3. *Law.* that admits of issue being taken. [f. ISSU(E) + -ABLE] —**is/su·a·bly,** *adv.*

is·su·ance (ĭsh/ōō əns), *n.* 1. act of issuing. 2. issue.

is·su·ant (ĭsh/ōō ənt), *adj.* 1. emerging. 2. *Her.* (of a beast) having only the upper half seen.

is·sue (ĭsh/ōō or, esp. Brit., ĭs/ū), *n.*, *v.*, -sued, -suing. —*n.* 1. act of sending, or promulgation; delivery; emission. 2. that which is issued. 3. a quantity issued at one time: *the daily issues of a newspaper.* 4. *Bibliog.* the printing of copies of a work from the original setting of type, but with some slight changes in the preliminary or appended matter. 5. a point in question or dispute, as between contending parties in an action at law. 6. a point or matter the decision of which is of special or public importance: *the political issues.* 7. a point the decision of which determines a matter: *the real issue.* 8. a point at which a matter is ready for decision: *to bring a case to an issue.* 9. something proceeding from any source, as a product, effect, result, or consequence. 10. the ultimate result, event, or outcome of a proceeding, affair, etc.: *the issue of a contest.* 11. a distribution of food (rations), clothing, equipment, or ammunition to a number of officers or enlisted men, or to a military unit. 12. offspring or progeny: *to die without issue.* 13. a going, coming, passing, or flowing out: *free issue and entry.* 14. a place or means of egress; an outlet or vent. 15. that which comes out, as an outflowing stream. 16. *Pathol.* a. a discharge of blood, pus, or the like. b. an incision, ulcer, or the like emitting such a discharge. 17. *Now Law.* the yield or profit from land or other property. 18. *Obs.* a proceeding or action. 19. **at issue, a.** in controversy: *a point at issue.* **b.** in disagreement. **c.** inconsistent; inharmonious (fol. by *with*). 20. **join issue, a.** to join in controversy. **b.** to submit an issue jointly for legal decision. 21. **take issue,** to disagree. —*v.t.* 22. to put out; deliver for use, sale, etc.; put into circulation. 23. to print (a publication) for sale or distribution. 24. to distribute (food, clothing, etc.) to one or more officers or enlisted men or to a military unit. 25. to send out; discharge; emit. —*v.i.* 26. to go, pass, or flow out; come forth; emerge: *to issue forth to battle.* 27. to be sent or put forth authoritatively or publicly, as a writ, money, etc. 28. to be published, as a book. 29. to come or proceed from any source. 30. to arise as a result or consequence; result. 31. *Now Chiefly Law.* to proceed as offspring, or be born or descended. 32. *Chiefly Law.* to come as a yield or profit, as from land. 33. to have the specified outcome. 34. to result (often fol. by *in*). 35. to end. [ME, t. OF, der. pp. of *issir, eissir,* g. L *exīre* go out] —**is/sue·less,** *adj.* —**is/su·er,** *n.* —Syn. 26. See **emerge.**

Is·sus (ĭs/əs), *n.* an ancient town of Cilicia, in Asia Minor, near modern Alexandretta: victory of Alexander over Darius III, 333 B.C.

Is·syk-Kul (ĭs/ĭk kōōl/), *n.* a large mountain lake in the SW Soviet Union in Asia. ab.2240 sq. mi.

-ist, a suffix of nouns, often accompanying verbs ending in -ize or nouns ending in -ism, denoting one who does, practices, or is concerned with something, or holds certain principles, doctrines, etc., as in *apologist, dramatist, machinist, plagiarist, realist, socialist, theorist.* [ult. (often directly) t. Gk.: s. *-istēs* noun suffix. See -IZE, -ISM]

Is·tan·bul (ĭs/tän bōōl/, -tän-; *Turk.* ĭs täm/bōōl), *n.* a city in European Turkey, on the Bosporus. 1,214,616 (1955). Formerly, **Constantinople.** Ancient, **Byzantium.** [Turk. alter. of MGk. *eis tēn pólin* in(to) the city]

Isth., isthmus. Also, **isth.**

isth·mi·an (ĭs/mī ən), *adj.* 1. of or pertaining to an isthmus. 2. (*cap.*) of the Isthmus of Corinth or of Panama. —*n.* 3. a native or inhabitant of an isthmus.

Isthmian games, one of the great national festivals of ancient Greece, held every two years on the Isthmus of Corinth.

isth·mus (ĭs/məs), *n.*, *pl.* -muses, -mi (-mī). 1. a narrow strip of land, bordered on both sides by water, connecting two larger bodies of land. 2. (*cap.*) the Isthmus of Suez. 3. (*cap.*) the Isthmus of Panama. 4. *Anat.* etc. a connecting part, organ, or passage, esp. when narrow or joining structures or cavities larger than itself. [t. L, t. Gk.: m. *isthmós* narrow passage, neck, isthmus]

ăct, āble, dâre, ärt; ĕbb, ēqual; ĭf, īce; hŏt, ōver, ôrder, oil, bŏŏk, ōōze, out; ŭp, ūse, ûrge; ə = a in alone; ch, chief; g, give; ng, ring; sh, shoe; th, thin; ŧħ, that; zh, vision.   See the full key on inside cover.

-istic, a suffix of adjectives (and in the plural of nouns from adjectives) formed from nouns in -*ist*, and having reference to such nouns, or to associated nouns in -*ism*, as in *deistic, euphuistic, puristic,* etc. In nouns it has usually a plural form, as in *linguistics.* [f. -IST + -IC]

-istical. See -istic, -al[1].

-istics. See -istic, -ics.

is·tle (Ĭst′lĕ, -lɪ̄), *n.* a fiber from various tropical American trees of the species *Agave* or *Yucca,* used in making bagging, carpets, etc. Also, **ixtle.** [t. Mex.: m. *ixtli*]

Is·tri·a (Ĭs′trĭ ə; *It.* ēs′tryä), *n.* a peninsula at the N end of the Adriatic, in NE Italy and NW Yugoslavia. —**Is′tri·an,** *adj., n.*

it (Ĭt), *pron., nom. it, poss.* **its** or (*Obs.* or *Dial.*) **it,** *obj.* **it;** *pl. nom.* **they,** *poss.* **their** or **theirs,** *obj.* **them;** *n.* —*pron.* **1.** a personal pronoun of the third person and neuter gender, corresponding to *he* and *she,* used (**a**) as a substitute for a neuter noun or a noun representing something possessing sex when sex is not particularized or considered: *the baby lost its rattle;* (**b**) to refer to some matter expressed or understood, or some thing or notion not definitely conceived: *how goes it?* (**c**) to refer to the subject of inquiry or attention, whether impersonal or personal, in sentences asking or stating what or who this is: *who is it? it is I;* (**d**) as the grammatical subject of a clause of which the logical subject is a phrase or clause, generally following, regarded as in apposition with it: *it is hard to believe that;* (**e**) in impersonal constructions: *it snows;* and (**f**) without definite force after an intransitive verb: *to foot it* (go on foot). —*n.* **2.** (in children's games) the player called upon to perform some task, as in tag the one who must catch the other players. [ME and OE *hit* (gen. *his,* dat. *him,* acc. *hit),* neut. of *hē* HE]

it·a·col·u·mite (Ĭt′ə kŏl′yə mīt′), *n.* a sandstone consisting of interlocking quartz grains and mica scales, found in Brazil, North Carolina, etc., and remarkable for its flexibility when in thin slabs. [f. *Itacolumi,* mountain in Brazil + -ITE[1]]

Ital., **1.** Italian. **2.** Italy. Also, **It.**

ital., italic (type).

I·ta·lia (ē tä′lyä), *n.* Italian name of **Italy.**

Italia ir·re·den·ta (ēr′rē dĕn′tä). See **irredentist.**

I·tal·ian (Ĭ tăl′yən), *adj.* **1.** of or pertaining to Italy, its people, or their language. —*n.* **2.** a native or inhabitant of Italy. **3.** a Romance language, the language of Italy, official also in Switzerland. [ME, t. L: s. *Italiānūs*]

I·tal·ian·ate (*adj.* Ĭ tăl′yə nāt′, -yən Ĭt; *v.* Ĭ tăl′yə nāt′), *adj., v.,* -ated, -ating. —*adj.* **1.** Italianized; conforming to the Italian type or style. —*v.t.* **2.** to Italianize.

Italian East Africa, a former Italian territory in E Africa, formed in 1936 by the merging of Eritrea and Italian Somaliland with newly conquered Ethiopia: taken by British Imperial forces, 1941.

I·tal·ian·ism (Ĭ tăl′yə nĭz′əm), *n.* **1.** an Italian practice, trait, or idiom. **2.** Italian quality or spirit.

I·tal·ian·ize (Ĭ tăl′yə nīz′), *v.,* -ized, -izing. —*v.i.* **1.** to become Italian in manner, etc.; speak Italian. —*v.t.* **2.** to make Italian. —**I·tal′ian·i·za′tion,** *n.*

Italian Somaliland, Trust Territory of, Somalia.

Italian sonnet, a form of sonnet, popularized by Petrarch. It is divided into two definite parts: the first 8 lines rhyme *abbaabba;* the last six lines rhyme by twos or threes in various combinations (*cdecde, cdcdcd,* etc.).

i·tal·ic (Ĭ tăl′Ĭk), *adj.* **1.** designating or pertaining to a style of printing types in which the letters usually slope to the right (thus, *italic*), patterned upon a compact manuscript hand, and used for emphasis, etc. **2.** (*cap.*) of or pertaining to Italy, esp. ancient Italy or its tribes. —*n.* **3.** (*often pl.*) italic type. **4.** (*cap.*) a principal group of Indo-European languages, including Latin and other languages of ancient Italy, notably Oscan and Umbrian, and closely related to Celtic. [t. L: s. *Italicus*]

I·tal·i·cism (Ĭ tăl′ə sĭz′əm), *n.* Italianism.

i·tal·i·cize (Ĭ tăl′ə sīz′), *v.,* -cized, -cizing. —*v.t.* **1.** to print in italic type. **2.** to underscore with a single line, as in indicating italics. —*v.i.* **3.** to use italics.

It·a·ly (Ĭt′ə lɪ̄), *n.* a republic in S Europe, comprising a peninsula S of the Alps, and the islands of Sicily, Sardinia, Elba, etc.: a kingdom, 1870–1946. 48,178,000 pop. (est. 1956); 119,772 sq. mi. (1945). *Cap.:* Rome. **Italia.**

I·tas·ca (Ī tăs′kə), *n.* **Lake,** a small lake in N Minnesota: one of the sources of the Mississippi river.

itch (Ĭch), *v.i.* **1.** to have or feel a peculiar irritation of the skin which causes a desire to scratch the part affected. **2.** to have a desire to do or to get something: *itch after honor.* **3.** an itching palm, a grasping disposition; greed. —*n.* **4.** the sensation of itching. **5.** the **itch,** a contagious disease caused by the itch mite which burrows into the skin; scabies. **6.** an uneasy or restless desire or longing: *an itch for authorship.* [ME (y)*icchen,* OE *gicc(e)an,* c. D *jeuken,* G *jucken*]

itch mite, a parasitic mite, *Sarcoptes scabiei,* causing itch or scabies in man and a form of mange in animals.

itch·y (Ĭch′ɪ̄), *adj.,* **itchier, itchiest. 1.** having an itching sensation. **2.** of the nature of itching. —**itch′i·ness,** *n.*

-ite[1], a suffix of nouns denoting esp. (**a**) persons associated with a place, tribe, leader, doctrine, system, etc., as in *Campbellite, Israelite, laborite;* (**b**) minerals and

fossils, as in *ammonite, anthracite;* (**c**) explosives, as in *cordite, dynamite;* (**d**) chemical compounds, esp. salts of acids whose names end in -*ous,* as in *phosphite, sulfites;* (**e**) pharmaceutical and commercial products, as in *vulcanite;* (**f**) a member or component of a part of the body, as in *somite.* [ult. (often directly) t. Gk.: m. -*ītēs* (fem. -*ītis*), noun and adj. suffix. Cf. -ITIS]

-ite[2], a suffix forming adjectives and nouns from adjectives, and some verbs, as in *composite, opposite, requisite, erudite,* etc. [t. L: m. -*itus,* -*ītus,* pp. ending]

i·tem (ī′təm), *n., v.* ī′təm; *adv.* ī′tĕm), *n.* **1.** a separate article or particular: *fifty items on the list.* **2.** a separate piece of information or news, as in a newspaper. **3.** *Obs.* an admonition or warning. **4.** *Obs.* an intimation or hint. —*v.t.* **5.** to set down or enter as an item, or by or in items. **6.** to make a note or memorandum of. —*adv.* **7.** *Obs.* or *Archaic.* likewise. [ME, t. L: (adv.) just so, likewise]

i·tem·ize (ī′tə mīz′), *v.t.,* -ized, -izing. to state by items; give the particulars of: *to itemize an account.* —**i′tem·i·za′tion,** *n.* —**i′tem·iz′er,** *n.*

it·er·ance (Ĭt′ər əns), *n. Rare.* iteration.

it·er·ant (Ĭt′ər ənt), *adj.* repeating. [t. L: s. *iterans,* ppr.]

it·er·ate (Ĭt′ə rāt′), *v.t.,* -ated, -ating. **1.** to utter again or repeatedly. **2.** to do (something) over again or repeatedly. [t. L: m. s. *iterātus,* pp.] —**it′er·a′tion,** *n.*

it·er·a·tive (Ĭt′ə rā′tĭv), *adj.* **1.** repeating; making repetition; repetitious. **2.** *Gram.* frequentative.

Ith·a·ca (Ĭth′ə kə), *n.* **1.** one of the Ionian Islands, off the W coast of Greece: the legendary home of Ulysses. 5803 pop. (1951); 37 sq. mi. **2.** a city in S New York at the S end of Cayuga Lake. 28,799 (1960).

I·thunn (ē′thŏŏn), *n. Scand. Myth.* the goddess, wife of Bragi, who guarded in Asgard the apples eaten by the gods to preserve their youth. Also, **I′thun,** Idun.

ith·y·phal·lic (Ĭth′ə făl′Ĭk), *adj.* **1.** pertaining to the phallus, as carried in ancient festivals of Bacchus. **2.** grossly indecent; obscene. **3.** *Anc. Pros.* noting or pertaining to any of several meters employed in hymns sung in Bacchic processions. —*n.* **4.** a poem in ithyphallic meter. **5.** an indecent poem. [t. L: s. *ithyphallicus,* t. Gk.: m. *ithyphallikós,* der. *ithýphallos* erect phallus]

i·tin·er·an·cy (ī tĭn′ər ən sɪ̄, Ĭ tĭn′-), *n.* **1.** act of traveling from place to place. **2.** a going about from place to place in the discharge of duty or the prosecution of business. **3.** a body of itinerants. **4.** state of being itinerant. **5.** the system of rotation governing the ministry of the Methodist Church. Also, **i·tin′er·a·cy.**

i·tin·er·ant (ī tĭn′ər ənt, Ĭ tĭn′-), *adj.* **1.** itinerating; journeying; traveling from place to place, or on a circuit, as a preacher, judge, or peddler. —*n.* **2.** one who travels from place to place, esp. for duty or business. [t. LL: s. *itinerans,* ppr.] —**i·tin′er·ant·ly,** *adv.*

i·tin·er·ar·y (ī tĭn′ə rĕr′ɪ̄, Ĭ tĭn′-), *n., pl.* -aries, *adj.* —*n.* **1.** a line or route of travel; a route. **2.** an account of a journey; a record of travel. **3.** a book describing a route or routes of travel, with information for travelers. **4.** a plan of travel. —*adj.* **5.** pertaining to traveling or travel routes. **6.** itinerant.

i·tin·er·ate (ī tĭn′ə rāt′, Ĭ tĭn′-), *v.i.,* -ated, -ating. to go from place to place, esp. in a regular circuit, as to preach. [t. LL: m. s. *itinerātus,* pp.] —**i·tin′er·a′tion,** *n.*

-ition, a noun suffix, as in *expedition, extradition,* etc., being -*tion* with a preceding original or formative vowel, or, in other words, -*ite*[1] + -*ion.* [t. L: s. -*itio,* -*ītio.* Cf. F -*ition,* G -*ition*]

-itious, an adjective suffix occurring in adjectives associated with nouns in -*tion,* as *expeditious,* etc. [t. L: m. -*icius,* -* īcius*]

-itis, a noun suffix used in pathological terms denoting inflammation of some part or organ, as in *bronchitis, gastritis, neuritis.* [t. Gk. See -ITE[1]]

-itive, a suffix of adjectives and nouns of adjectival origin, as in *definitive, fugitive.* [t. L: m.s. -*itivus,* -*ītivus*]

I·to (ē′tō′), *n.* **Prince Ito Hirobumi** (hē′rō bōō′mĕ), 1841–1909, Japanese statesman.

-itol, *Chem.* a suffix used in names of alcohols containing more than one hydroxyl group. [f. -ITE[1] + -OL[1]]

its (Ĭts), *adj.* possessive form of **it.** [poss. case of IT, formerly written *it's*]

it's (Ĭts), contraction of *it is.*

it·self (Ĭt sĕlf′), *pron.* emphatic or reflexive form of **it.**

-ity, a suffix forming abstract nouns of condition, characteristics, etc., as in *jollity, civility, Latinity.* [ME -*ite,* t. F: m. -*ité,* g. L -*itāt-,* s. -*itas*]

-ium, a suffix representing Latin neuter suffix, used esp. to form names of metallic elements.

I·van III (ī′vən; *Russ.* Ỹ vän′), (*the Great*) 1440–1505, grand duke of Muscovy. 1462–1505.

Ivan IV, (*the Terrible*) 1530–84, grand duke of Muscovy, 1533–47, and first czar of Russia, 1547–84.

I·van·hoe (ī′vən hō′), *n.* a novel (1819) by Sir Walter Scott about England in the twelfth century.

I·va·no·vo (Ỹ vä′nŏ′vŏ), *n.* a city in the central Soviet Union, NE of Moscow. 319,000 (est. 1956). Formerly, **I·va·no·vo-Voz·ne·sensk** (Ỹ vä′nŏ vŏ vŏz nĕ sĕnsk′).

-ive, a suffix of adjectives (and nouns of adjectival origin) expressing tendency, disposition, function, connection, etc., as in *active, corrective, destructive, detective, passive, sportive.* Cf. -ATIVE. [t. L: m.s. -*īvus;* also repr. F -*if* (masc.), -*ive* (fem.), g. L]

I've (īv), contraction of *I have*.

Ives (īvz), *n.* **1. Charles**, 1874–1954, U.S. composer. **2. Frederick Eugene**, 1856–1937, U.S. inventor. **3. James Merritt**, 1824–95, U.S. lithographer. See **Currier**.

i·vied (ī'vĭd), *adj.* covered or overgrown with ivy: *ivied walls.*

i·vo·ry (ī'və rĭ, ī'vrĭ), *n., pl.* **-ries**, *adj.* —*n.* **1.** the hard white substance, a variety of dentine, composing the main part of the tusks of the elephant, walrus, etc., used for carvings, billiard balls, etc. **2.** a tusk, as of an elephant. **3.** dentine of any kind. **4.** some substance resembling ivory. **5.** *Slang.* a tooth, or the teeth. **6.** an article made of ivory, as a carving or a billiard ball. **7.** (*pl.*) *Slang.* **a.** the keys of a piano, accordion, etc. **b.** dice. **8.** the hard endosperm (**vegetable ivory**) of the ivory nut, used for ornamental purposes, buttons, etc. **9.** creamy or yellowish white. —*adj.* **10.** consisting or made of ivory. **11.** of the color ivory. [ME *yvory*, etc., t. OF: m. *yvoire*, g. L *eboreus* made of ivory] —**i'vo·ry·like'**, *adj.*

ivory black, a fine black pigment made by calcining ivory.

Ivory Coast, a republic in W Africa: independent member of the French Community; formerly part of French West Africa. 2,482,000 pop.; 127,520 sq. mi. *Cap.*: Abidjan.

ivory gull, a white arctic gull, *Pagophila eburnea.*

ivory nut, **1.** the seed of a low-growing South American palm, *Phytelephas macrocarpa*, forming the source of vegetable ivory. **2.** a similar seed from other palms.

ivory palm, the palm yielding the common ivory nut.

ivory tower, **1.** a place withdrawn from the world and worldly acts and attitudes. **2.** an attitude of aloofness. [trans. of F *tour d'ivoire*, first used by Sainte-Beuve]

i·vy (ī'vĭ), *n., pl.* **ivies**. **1.** a climbing vine, *Hedera helix*, with smooth, shiny, evergreen leaves, yellowish inconspicuous flowers, and black berries, widely grown as an ornamental (**English ivy**). **2.** any of various other climbing or trailing plants, as *Parthenocissus tricuspidata* (**Japanese ivy**), *Glecoma hederacea* (**ground ivy**), etc. [ME; OE *ĭfig*; akin to G *efeu*] —**i'vy·like'**, *adj.*

English ivy, Hedera helix

ivy vine, a vinelike plant, *Ampelopsis cordata*, of the U.S., differing from the grape vine esp. in having a corolla of wholly separate petals.

I.W., Isle of Wight.

i·wis (ĭ wĭs'), *adv. Obs.* certainly. Also, **ywis**. [ME adv. use of neut. of OE adj. *gewis* certain, c. D *gewis*, G *gewiss* certain, certainly; akin to **wit**, v., know]

I·wo Ji·ma (ē'wo jē'mȧ; *Jap.* ē'wô jē'mä), one of the Volcano Islands, in the N Pacific, S of Japan: taken by U.S. forces in a costly campaign, Feb.-Mar., 1945.

I.W.W., Industrial Workers of the World.

Ix·elles (ēk sĕl'), *n.* a city in central Belgium, near Brussels. 92,298 (est. 1952).

ix·i·a (ĭk'sĭ ȧ), *n.* any plant of the iridaceous genus *Ixia*, comprising South African plants with sword-shaped leaves and showy ornamental flowers. [t. NL (named with ref. to the juice), t. Gk.: birdlime]

Ix·i·on (ĭk sī'ən), *n. Gk. Legend.* a king of the Lapithae, who was punished by Zeus for his love for Hera by being bound on an eternally revolving wheel in Tartarus.

Ix·tac·ci·huatl (ēs'tä sē'wä təl), *n.* an extinct volcano in S central Mexico, SE of Mexico City. 17,342 ft. Also, **Iztaccihuatl**.

ix·tle (ĭks'tlē, -tlĭ, ĭs'-), *n.* istle.

I·ye·ya·su (ē'yĕ'yä'sōō), *n.* **Tokugawa** (tō'kōō gä'wä), 1542–1616, Japanese general and statesman.

Iy·yar (ē'yär), *n.* (in the Jewish calendar) the eighth month of the year. Also, **I'yar**. [t. Heb., ult. from Akkadian]

iz·ard (ĭz'ərd), *n.* the chamois which inhabits the Pyrenees. [t. F: m. *isard*]

-ization, a suffix combination of -ize with -ation.

-ize, a suffix of verbs having the sense (**a**) intransitively, of following some line of action, practice, policy, etc., as in *Atticize, apologize, economize, theorize, tyrannize*, or of becoming (as indicated), as *crystallize* and *oxidize* (intr.), and (**b**) transitively, of acting toward or upon, treating, or affecting in a particular way, as in *baptize, colonize, patronize, stigmatize*, or of making or rendering (as indicated), as in *civilize, legalize, mobilize, realize*. Also, **-ise**[1]. Cf. **-ism** and **-ist**. [ult. (often directly) t. Gk.: m. s. *-izein*. Cf. F *-iser*, G *-isieren*, etc.]

I·zhevsk (ĭ zhĕfsk'), *n.* a city in the E Soviet Union in Europe. 252,000 (est. 1956).

Iz·mir (ĭz'mĭr), *n.* a seaport in W Turkey on the **Gulf of Izmir**, an arm of the Aegean: important city of Asia Minor. 268,310 (1955). Also, **Smyrna**.

Iz·tac·ci·huatl (ēs'täk sē'wä təl), *n.* Ixtaccihuatl.

iz·zard (ĭz'ərd), *n. Colloq.* **1.** the letter Z. **2. from A to izzard**, from beginning to end; completely. [unexplained var. of **zed**]

J

J, j (jā), *n., pl.* **J's** or **Js**, **j's** or **js**. **1.** a consonant, the 10th letter of the English alphabet. **2.** Roman numeral for 1.

J, *Physics.* joule.

J., **1.** Journal. **2.** Judge. **3.** Justice.

Ja., January.

J.A., Judge Advocate.

jab (jăb), *v.*, **jabbed, jabbing**, *n.* —*v.t., v.i.* **1.** to poke, or thrust smartly or sharply, as with the end or point of something. —*n.* **2.** a poke with the end or point of something; a smart or sharp thrust. Also, **job**. [var. (orig. Scot.) of JOB[2]]

Jab·al·pur (jŭb'əl pŏr'), *n.* a city in central India, in Madhya Pradesh. 203,659 (1951). Also, **Jubbulpore**.

jab·ber (jăb'ər), *v.i., v.t.* **1.** to talk or utter rapidly, indistinctly, imperfectly, or nonsensically; chatter. —*n.* **2.** jabbering talk or utterance; gibberish. [appar. imit.] —**jab'ber·er**, *n.* —**jab'ber·ing·ly**, *adv.*

jab·i·ru (jăb'ə rōō'), *n.* a large wading bird, *Jabiru mycteria*, of the stork family, inhabiting the warmer parts of America. [t. Tupi-Guarani]

jab·o·ran·di (jăb'ə răn'dĭ), *n., pl.* **-dis**. **1.** any of certain South American shrubs of the rutaceous genus *Pilocarpus*. **2.** the dried leaflets of *Pilocarpus jaborandi* and other species containing the alkaloid, pilocarpine, used as a sudorific and sialagogue. [t. Tupi-Guarani]

ja·bot (zhă bō' or, esp. *Brit.*, zhăb'ō), *n.* a falling ruffle, cascade, or other arrangement of lace, embroidery, or the like, worn at the neck or the front of the waist by women and formerly by men. [t. F: lit., bird's crop]

J.A.C., Junior Association of Commerce.

jac·a·mar (jăk'ə mär'), *n.* any bird of the tropical American family *Galbulidae*, usually bright-green above, with long bills. [t. Tupi: m. *jacamá-ciri*]

ja·ca·na (zhä'sə nä'), *n.* any of several tropical, plover-like, aquatic birds of the family *Jacanidae*, most of them having extremely long toes and claws for walking on floating water plants. [t. Pg., t. Tupi: m. *jasanã*]

jac·a·ran·da (jăk'ə răn'də), *n.* **1.** any of the tall tropical American trees constituting the bignoniaceous genus *Jacaranda*. **2.** their fragrant ornamental wood. **3.** any of various related or similar trees. **4.** their wood.

Ja·car·ta (jə kär'tə), *n.* Djakarta.

ja·cinth (jā'sĭnth, jăs'ĭnth), *n.* hyacinth (def. 4). [ME *iacynt*, t. OF: m. *jacinte*, g. L *hyacinthus* HYACINTH]

jack[1] (jăk), *n.* **1.** (*cap.*) a nickname for the name John. **2.** a man or fellow. **3.** (*cap.* or *l.c.*) a sailor. **4.** any of various mechanical contrivances or devices, as a contrivance for raising great weights small distances. **5.** a device for turning a spit, etc. **6.** *U.S.* any of the four knaves in playing cards. **7.** jackstone. **8.** *Brit.* a small bowl used as a mark for the players to aim at, in the game of bowls. **9.** a small union or ensign used by a ship or vessel as a signal, etc., and flown from the jack staff as an indication of nationality. **10.** jackass. **11.** jack rabbit. **12.** *Elect.* a connecting device to which the wires of a circuit may be attached and which is arranged for the insertion of a plug. **13.** *Naut.* a horizontal bar or crosstree of iron at the topgallant masthead, to spread the royal shrouds. **14. every man jack**, every one without exception. —*v.t.* **15.** to lift or move with or as with a jack, or contrivance for raising (usually fol. by *up*). **16.** *Colloq.* to raise (prices, wages, etc.) (usually fol. by *up*). **17.** *U.S.* to seek (game or fish) with a jack light. [orig. proper name *Jack*, earlier *Jacken*, dissimilated var. of *Jankin*, f. *Jan* John + -KIN]

Ratchet type jack (def. 4)
A. Lifting foot;
B. Handle

jack[2] (jăk), *n.* **1.** a Polynesian moraceous tree, *Artocarpus Leterophyllus*, with a fruit resembling breadfruit. **2.** the fruit itself, one of the largest known (up to 60 lbs.). [t. Pg.: m. *jaca*, t. Malayalam: m. *chakka*]

jack[3] (jăk), *n.* **1.** a defensive coat, usually of leather, formerly worn by foot soldiers and others. **2.** *Archaic.* a container for liquor, orig. of waxed leather coated with tar. [ME *iacke*, t. OF: m. *jaque, jaques*, t. Sp.: m. *jaco*, ? t. Ar.: m. *shakk*]

ăct, āble, dâre, ärt; ĕbb, ēqual; ĭf, īce; hŏt, ōver, ôrder, oil, bŏŏk, ōōze, out; ŭp, ūse, ûrge; ə = a in alone; ch, chief; g, give; ng, ring; sh, shoe; th, thin; th, that; zh, vision. See the full key on inside cover.

jack-a-dan·dy (jăk′ə dăn′dĭ), n., pl. **-dies.** dandy¹ (def. 1).

jack·al (jăk′ôl, -əl), n. **1.** any of several races of wild dog of the genus *Canis*, esp. *Canis aureus*, of Asia and Africa, which hunt in packs at night and which were formerly supposed to hunt prey for the lion. **2.** one who does drudgery for another, or who meanly serves the purpose of another. [t. Turk.: m. *chakăl*, t. Pers.: m. *shag(h)ăl*]

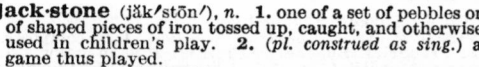

Black-backed jackal,
Canis mesomelas
(Total length 43 in., tail 11 in.)

jack·a·napes (jăk′ə nāps′), n. **1.** a pert, presuming man; whippersnapper. **2.** Archaic. an ape or monkey. [var. of ME *Jack Napes*, nickname of William, Duke of Suffolk, whose badge was an ape's clog and chain; prob. orig. used as name for tame ape or monkey]

jack·ass (jăk′ăs′), n. **1.** a male donkey. **2.** a very stupid or foolish person. [f. JACK¹ + ASS]

jack·boot (jăk′boot′), n. a large leather boot reaching up over the knee, orig. one serving as armor.

jack crosstree, jack (def. 13).

jack·daw (jăk′dô′), n. **1.** a glossy black European bird, *Coloeus monedula*, of the crow family, frequenting steeples, ruins, etc. **2.** the great-tailed grackle, *Cassidix Mexicanus*, a large glossy blackbird of the southern U.S. and Mexico. [f. JACK¹ + DAW, n.]

jack·et (jăk′ĭt), n. **1.** a short coat, in various forms, worn by both men and women. **2.** something designed to be fastened about the body for other purpose than clothing: *a strait jacket.* **3.** an outer covering: *a book jacket.* **4.** a metal casing, as the steel covering of a cannon, the steel cover around the core of a bullet, or the water jacket on certain types of machine guns. **5.** U.S. a folded paper or open envelope containing an official document. —*v.t.* **6.** to cover with a jacket. [ME *iaquet*, t. OF: m. *jaquete*, dim. of *jaque* JACK³] —**jack′·et·ed,** adj. —**jack′et·less,** adj. —**jack′et·like′,** adj.

Jack Frost, frost or freezing cold personified.

jack-in-the-box (jăk′ĭn *t̲h̲ə* bŏks′), n. a toy consisting of a figure, enclosed in a box, which springs out when the lid is unfastened. Also, **jack′-in-a-box′.**

jack-in-the-pul·pit (jăk′ĭn *t̲h̲ə* pŏŏl′pĭt), n. an araceous herb, *Arisaema atrorubens* (*A. triphyllum*), of North America, having an upright spadix arched over by a spathe; Indian turnip.

Jack Ketch (kĕch), Brit. a public executioner or hangman. [from a British executioner, *Jack* (or John) *Ketch* (d. 1686)]

jack·knife (jăk′nīf′), n., pl. **-knives.** U.S. **1.** a large pocketknife. **2.** a type of dive in which the diver assumes a folded position of the body while moving through the air, and straightens out before entering the water.

jack ladder, Jacob's ladder (def. 2).

jack light, U.S. a portable cresset, oil-burning lantern, or electric light used in hunting or fishing at night.

jack-of-all-trades (jăk′əv ôl′trādz′), n. one who can do any kind of work or business.

jack-o'-lan·tern (jăk′ə lăn′tərn), n. a lantern made of a rind, as a pumpkin shell, with holes cut to represent human eyes, nose, mouth, etc.

jack pine, a slender pine, *Pinus Banksiana*, covering tracts of barren land in Canada and the northern U.S.

jack pot, Poker. a pot that accumulates until a player opens the betting with a pair of jacks or better.

jack rabbit, any of various large hares of western North America, having very long limbs and ears.

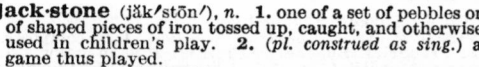

Black-tailed jack rabbit,
Lepus alleni (2 ft. long)

jack·screw (jăk′skroo′), n. a jack for raising weights, operated by a screw.

jack·snipe (jăk′snīp′), n. **1.** a small, relatively short-billed snipe, *Limnocryptes minima*, of Europe and Asia. **2.** any of several related snipes. **3.** the pectoral sandpiper. [f. JACK¹ + SNIPE]

Jack·son (jăk′sən), n. **1.** Andrew, 1767–1845, U.S. general, 7th president of the U.S., 1829–37. **2.** Helen Hunt, (*Helen Maria Fiske*) 1831–85, U.S. novelist and poet. **3.** Robert Houghwout (hou′ət), 1892–1954, U.S. jurist: associate justice of U.S. Supreme Court, 1941–54. **4.** Thomas Jonathan, ("*Stonewall Jackson*") 1824–63, Confederate general in the U.S. Civil War. **5.** the capital of Mississippi, in the central part. 144,422 (1960). **6.** a city in S Michigan. 50,720 (1960). **7.** a city in W Tennessee. 33,849 (1960).

Jackson Day, U.S. Jan. 8, celebrated by Democratic party dinners in commemoration of Jackson's victory at New Orleans, 1815.

Jack·so·ni·an (jăk sō′nĭ ən), adj. **1.** of or pertaining to Andrew Jackson. —n. **2.** a follower of Jackson.

Jack·son·ville (jăk′sən vĭl′), n. a seaport in NE Florida, on the St. Johns river. 201,030 (1960).

jack·stay (jăk′stā′), n. Naut. **1.** a rope, rod, or the like, on a yard or gaff, for bending a sail to. **2.** a rod or rope running up and down on the forward side of a mast, for a yard to travel on; a traveler (def. 5b).

jack·stone (jăk′stōn′), n. **1.** one of a set of pebbles or of shaped pieces of iron tossed up, caught, and otherwise used in children's play. **2.** (pl. construed as sing.) a game thus played.

jack·straw (jăk′strô′), n. **1.** a straw-stuffed figure of a man. **2.** an insignificant person. **3.** one of a number of straws, or strips of wood, bone, etc., used in a game in which they are thrown on a table in confusion and are to be picked up singly without disturbing the others. **4.** (pl. construed as sing.) the game itself.

Jack Tar, a sailor. Also, **jack tar.**

jack towel, a long towel with the ends sewed together, for hanging on a roller.

Jack·y (jăk′ĭ), n. **1.** (often l.c.) a sailor. **2.** (l.c.) Slang or Brit. Dial. gin.

Ja·cob (jā′kəb), n. the second son of Isaac, the twin brother of Esau, and father of the 12 patriarchs. Gen. 25:24–34. [t. LL: s. *Jacobus*, t. Gk.: m. *Iákōbos* Jacob, James, t. Heb.: m. *Ya'aqōb* Jacob, explained as one who takes by the heel, a supplanter. See Gen. 25:26, 27:36]

Jac·o·be·an (jăk′ə bē′ən), adj. **1.** of or pertaining to James I of England or his times. —n. **2.** a Jacobean writer, personage, etc. [f. m.s. NL *Jacobaeus*, der. LL *Jacōbus* James (see JACOB) + -AN]

Jacobean architecture, late English Gothic architecture, showing Italian influence.

Jac·o·bin (jăk′ə bĭn), n. **1.** a member of a famous club or society of French revolutionists organized in 1789, so called from the convent in Paris in which they met. They developed clubs throughout France and worked for the success of the Mountain (def. 4) and the Reign of Terror. **2.** an extreme radical, esp. in politics. **3.** a Dominican friar. **4.** (l.c.) an artificial variety of the domestic pigeon, whose neck feathers form a hood. [ME, t. ML: s. *Jacōbinus*, der. LL *Jacōbus* James (see JACOB)] —**Jac′o·bin′ic, Jac′o·bin′i·cal,** adj. —**Jac·o·bin·i·cal·ly,** adv.

Jac·o·bin·ism (jăk′ə bĭ nĭz′əm), n. **1.** the principles of the Jacobins. **2.** extreme radicalism, esp. in politics. **3.** a concept or characteristic like that of the Jacobins.

Jac·o·bin·ize (jăk′ə bĭ nīz′), v.t., **-ized, -izing.** to imbue with Jacobinism.

Jac·o·bite (jăk′ə bīt′), n. a partisan or adherent of James II of England after his overthrow (1688), or of his descendants. [t. ML: m. *Jacōbīta*, der. LL *Jacōbus* James (see JACOB)] —**Jac·o·bit·ic** (jăk′ə bĭt′ĭk), **Jac′o·bit′i·cal,** adj.

Jac·o·bit·ism (jăk′ə bĭt′ĭz əm), n. the principles of the Jacobites.

Jacob's ladder, 1. a ladder leading up to heaven which Jacob saw in his dream. Gen. 28:12. **2.** Naut. a rope ladder with wooden steps.

Ja·cob's-lad·der (jā′kəbz lăd′ər), n. **1.** a garden plant, *Polemonium caeruleum*, whose leaves have a ladderlike arrangement. **2.** any of certain related species.

ja·co·bus (jə kō′bəs), n. an English gold coin struck in the reign of James I. [t. LL. See JACOB]

Jac·quard loom (jə kärd′; *Fr.* zhă kär′), a pattern loom for weaving elaborate designs. [named after J. M. *Jacquard* (1752–1834), French inventor]

Jacque·mi·not (jăk′mĭ nō′; *Fr.* zhăk mē nō′), n. a deep-red variety of the rose. [named after J. F. *Jacqueminot* (1787–1865), French general]

Jac·que·rie (zhăk rē′), n. **1.** the revolt of the peasants of northern France against the nobles in 1358. **2.** (l.c.) any revolt of peasants. [F: (in OF *Jaquerie*) peasants; der. *Jaques* (see JACK¹) taken as a name for a peasant]

jac·ta·tion (jăk tā′shən), n. **1.** boasting. **2.** Pathol. a restless tossing of the body. [t. L: s. *jactātio* a throwing]

jac·ti·ta·tion (jăk′tə tā′shən), n. **1.** Law. the assertion of a false claim, to the injury of another. **2.** Pathol. jactation (def. 2). [t. ML: s. *jactitātio*, der. L *jactitāre* bring forward in public, utter]

jade¹ (jād), n. **1.** either of two minerals, jadeite or nephrite, sometimes green, highly esteemed as an ornamental stone for carvings, jewelry, etc. **2.** Also, **jade green,** green, varying from bluish green to yellowish green. [t. F, t. Sp.: m. (*piedra de*) *ijada*, lit., (stone of) colic (Sp. *ijada* pain in the side, colic, der. L *īlia* flanks. See ILEUM] —**jade′like′,** adj.

jade² (jād), n., v., **jaded, jading.** —n. **1.** a horse, esp. one of inferior breed, or worn-out, or vicious. **2.** (in opprobrious use) a woman. —v.t., v.i. **3.** to make or become exhausted by working hard; to weary or fatigue; tire. [ME, orig. uncert. Cf. Icel. *jalda* mare] —**jad′ish,** adj. —**jad′ish·ly,** adv. —**jad′ish·ness,** n.

jad·ed (jā′dĭd), adj. **1.** worn out. **2.** sated: *a jaded appetite.* —**jad′ed·ly,** adv. —**jad′ed·ness,** n.

jade-green (jād′grēn′), adj. of the color of jade.

jade·ite (jād′īt), n. a mineral, essentially sodium aluminum silicate, NaAlSi₂O₆, occurring in tough masses, whitish to dark green. See jade¹ (def. 1).

jae·ger (yā′gər; *for 1 also* jā′-), n. **1.** any of the rapacious sea birds constituting the family *Stercorariidae* which pursue weaker birds in order to make them disgorge their prey; a skua. **2.** a hunter. **3.** a member of any of certain groups of sharpshooters in the German or Austrian army. Also, **jäger, yager.** [t. G: hunter. der. *jagen* hunt]

Ja·én (hä ĕn′), n. a city in S Spain. 67,134 (1950).

Jaf·fa (jăf′ə; *locally* yä′fä), n. a seaport in W Israel. 101,580 (est. 1946). See **Tel-Aviv.** Ancient, **Joppa.**

---

b., blend of, blended; c., cognate with; d., dialect, dialectal; der., derived from; f., formed from; g., going back to; m., modification of; r., replacing; s., stem of; t., taken from; ?, perhaps. See the full key on inside cover.

Jaff·na (jăf′nə), *n.* a seaport in N Ceylon. 77,218 (1953).

jag[1] (jăg), *n., v.,* **jagged, jagging.** —*n.* 1. a sharp projection on an edge or surface. —*v.t.* 2. to cut or slash, esp. in points or pendants along the edge; form notches, teeth, or ragged points in. [ME *jaggen;* ? imit.]

jag[2] (jăg), *n.* 1. *Dial.* a load, as of hay or wood. 2. *U.S. Slang.* as much liquor as one can carry. 3. *U.S. Slang.* a fit of intoxication: *to have a jag on.* [? orig. a load of broom or furze. Cf. OE *ceacga* broom, furze]

Jag·an·nath (jŭg′ə nät′, -nôt′), *n.* Juggernaut. Also, **Jag·an·na·tha** (jŭg′ə nät′hə).

jä·ger (yā′gər), *n.* jaeger.

jag·ged (jăg′ĭd), *adj.* having notches, teeth, or ragged edges. —**jag′ged·ly,** *adv.* —**jag′ged·ness,** *n.*

jag·gy (jăg′ĭ), *adj.,* **-gier, -giest.** jagged; notched.

jag·uar (jăg′wär), *n.* a large, ferocious, spotted feline, *Panthera onca,* of tropical America. [t. Tupi-Guarani: m. *jaguara*]

ja·gua·run·di (jä′gwə rŭn′dĭ), *n., pl.* **-dis.** a short-legged, long-bodied South American cat, *Felis eyra.*

Jah·veh (yä′vĕ), *n.* Yahweh. Also, **Jah′ve, Jah** (yä).

Jaguar, Panthera onca (Total length ab. 7 ft., tail 2 ft.)

jai a·lai (hī ä lī′), a game resembling handball, esp. popular in Cuba, played on an indoor court with basketlike racquets.

jail (jāl), *n.* 1. a prison, esp. one for the detention of persons awaiting trial or convicted of minor offenses. —*v.t.* 2. to take into or hold in custody. Also, *Brit.,* **gaol.** [ME *jaiole,* t. OF: prison, cage; ult. der. L *cavea* cavity, enclosure, cage. See **GAOL**] —**jail′less,** *adj.* —**jail′like′,** *adj.*

jail·bird (jāl′bûrd′), *n.* one who is or has been confined in jail; a criminal.

jail delivery, 1. a deliverance of imprisoned persons, esp. by force. 2. act of clearing a jail of prisoners by bringing them to trial, as at the assizes in England.

jail·er (jā′lər), *n.* the keeper of a jail. Also, **jail′or.**

Jain (jīn), *n.* 1. an adherent of Jainism. —*adj.* 2. of or pertaining to the Jains or their religion. [t. Hind.: m. *jaina.* g. Skt. *jaina,* der. *jina,* lit., conqueror]

Jain·ism (jī′nĭz əm), *n.* a dualistic, ascetic religion founded in the 6th century B.C. by a Hindu reformer as a revolt against the caste system and the vague world spirit of Hinduism. —**Jain′ist,** *n.*

Jai·pur (jī′pŏŏr), *n.* 1. a former state in N India, now part of Rajasthan. 2. the capital of Rajasthan; known as the "pink city" because of its buildings of that color. 291,130 (1951).

Ja·kar·ta (jə kär′tə), *n.* Djakarta.

jal·ap (jăl′əp), *n.* 1. a purgative drug from the tuberous root of a plant, *Ipomoeapurga Exogonium Jalapa,* of Mexico, or of some other convolvulaceous plants. 2. any of these plants. [t. Sp.: m. *jalapa;* named after the city. See **JALAPA**] —**ja·lap·ic** (jä lăp′ĭk), *adj.*

Ja·la·pa (hä lä′pä), *n.* a city in E Mexico: the capital of Vera Cruz state. 51,166 (1950).

jal·a·pin (jăl′ə pĭn), *n.* a resin which is one of the purgative principles of jalap. [ME **JALAP** + **-IN**[2]]

Ja·lis·co (hä lēs′kō), *n.* a state in W Mexico. 1,821,612 pop. (est. 1952); 31,152 sq. mi. *Cap.:* Guadalajara.

ja·lop·y (jə lŏp′ĭ), *n., pl.* **-lopies.** *Colloq.* an old, decrepit, or unpretentious automobile.

jal·ou·sie (zhăl′ŏŏ zē′ or, esp. Brit., zhăl′ŏŏ zē′), *n.* a kind of blind or shutter made with slats fixed at an angle. [t. F: lit., jealousy]

jam[1] (jăm), *v.,* **jammed, jamming,** *n.* —*v.t.* 1. to press or squeeze tightly between bodies or surfaces, so that motion or extrication is made difficult or impossible. 2. to bruise or crush by squeezing. 3. to press, push, or thrust violently, as into a confined space or against some object. 4. to fill or block up by crowding: *crowds jam the doors.* 5. to cause to become wedged, caught, or displaced, so that it cannot work, as a machine, part, etc. 6. *Radio.* **a.** to interfere with (signals, etc.) by sending out others of approximately the same frequency. **b.** (of signals, etc.) to interfere with (other signals, etc.). —*v.i.* 7. to become wedged or fixed; stick fast. 8. to press or push violently, as into a confined space or against one another. 9. (of a machine, etc.) to become unworkable as through the wedging or displacement of a part. 10. *Jazz Slang.* to enliven a composition by impromptu variations and improvisations. —*n.* 11. act of jamming. 12. state of being jammed. 13. mass of objects jammed together; esp. in logging, the accumulation of timber blocking a river. 14. *U.S. Colloq.* a fix; pickle. (est. 1952); 31,152 sq. mi. [appar. imit. Cf. **CHAMP**[1]] —**Syn.** 1. wedge, pack, crowd; ram, force.

jam[2] (jăm), *n.* a preserve of whole fruit, slightly crushed, boiled with sugar. [? same as **JAM**[1]] —**jam′like′,** *adj.*

Jam., Jamaica.

Ja·mai·ca (jə mā′kə), *n.* an island in the West Indies, S of Cuba: formerly a British colony; became independent on Aug. 6, 1962. 1,606,546 pop. (1960); 4413 sq. mi. *Cap.:* Kingston.

Ja·mai·can (jə mā′kən), *adj.* 1. of, pertaining to, or obtained from the island of Jamaica. —*n.* 2. a native or an inhabitant of Jamaica.

jamb[1] (jăm), *n.* 1. the side of an opening; a vertical piece forming the side of a doorway, window, or the like. 2. jambeau. Also, **jambe.** [ME *jambe,* t. F: leg, jamb, g. LL *gamba* hoof]

jamb[2] (jăm), *v.t., v.i., n.* jam[1] (defs. 1–9, 11–13).

jam·beau (jăm′bō), *n., pl.* **-beaux** (-bōz). armor for the leg; a greave.

jam·bo·ree (jăm′bə rē′), *n.* 1. *U.S. Slang.* a carousal; any noisy merrymaking. 2. a large gathering or rally of boy scouts, usually international or interregional. [appar. b. **JABBER** and F *soirée,* with *-m-* from **JAM**[1] crowd]

J. Jamb

James (jāmz), *n.* 1. an apostle, son of Zebedee and brother of the apostle John. (Matt. 4:21). 2. ("*James the Lord's brother*") the reputed author of the Epistle of James. Gal. 1:19, Mark, 6:3. 3. Also, **James the Less.** ("*James the son of Alphaeus*") an apostle. Matt. 10:3. 4. the General Epistle of James, in the New Testament. 5. the name of six kings of Scotland. 6. **Henry,** 1811–82, U.S. writer on religious and social problems (father of Henry and William James). 7. **Henry,** 1843–1916, U.S. novelist in England (brother of William James). 8. **Jesse,** 1847–82, U.S. outlaw and bandit. 9. **William,** 1842–1910, U.S. psychologist and philosopher (brother of Henry James).

James I, 1566–1625, king of England, 1603–25; as **James VI,** king of Scotland, 1567–1625.

James II, 1633–1701, king of England, 1685–88.

James Bay, a S arm of Hudson Bay, in E Canada between Ontario and Quebec provinces. ab. 300 mi. long.

Jame·son (jām′sən), *n.* **Sir Leander Starr,** 1853–1917, British physician and colonial administrator.

James River, 1. a river flowing from the W part of Virginia E to Chesapeake Bay. 340 mi. 2. a river flowing from central North Dakota S through South Dakota to the Missouri river. 710 mi.

James·town (jāmz′toun′), *n.* 1. a ruined village in E Virginia: the first permanent English settlement in North America, 1607. 2. a city in SW New York. 41,818 (1960).

Jam·mu and Kash·mir (jŭm′ŏŏ; kăsh mĭr′), official name of **Kashmir** (including feudatories).

jam session, a meeting of musicians for a spontaneous and improvisatory performance of swing music without scores, for their own enjoyment.

Jam·shed·pur (jăm shĕd pŏŏr′), *n.* a city in NE India, in Bihar state. 193,775 (1951).

Jam·shid (jăm shēd′), *n.* *Persian Myth.* the king of the Peris who, given a human form as punishment for his boast of immortality, became a powerful and wonderworking Persian king. Also, **Jam·shyd′.**

Jan., January.

Ja·ná·ček (yä′nä chĕk′), *n.* Leoš (lĕ′ôsh), 1854–1928, Czech composer.

Jane Eyre (jān âr′), novel (1847) by Charlotte Brontë.

Janes·ville (jānz′vĭl), *n.* a city in S Wisconsin. 35,164 (1960).

Ja·net (zhà nĕ′), **Pierre Marie Félix** (pyĕr mà rē′ fĕ lēks′), 1859–1947, French psychologist and neurologist.

jan·gle (jăng′gəl), *v.,* **-gled, -gling,** *n.* —*v.i.* 1. to sound harshly or discordantly: *a jangling noise.* 2. to speak angrily; wrangle. —*v.t.* 3. to cause to sound harshly or discordantly. —*n.* 4. a harsh or discordant sound. 5. an altercation; quarrel. [ME *jangle(n),* t. OF: m. *jangler* chatter, tattle; of Gmc. orig.] —**jan′gler,** *n.*

Ja·nic·u·lum (jə nĭk′yə ləm), *n.* a ridge near the Tiber in Rome.

Ja·ni·na (yä′nē nä′), *n.* Serbian name of **Ioannina.**

jan·i·tor (jăn′ə tər), *n.* 1. a person employed to take care of a building, offices, etc. 2. a doorkeeper or porter. [t. L: doorkeeper. See **JANUS**] —**jan·i·to·ri·al** (jăn ə tōr′ĭ əl), *adj.* —**jan·i·tress** (jăn′ə trĭs), *n. fem.*

Jan·i·zar·y (jăn′ə zĕr′ĭ), *n., pl.* **-zaries.** 1. an infantryman in the Turkish sovereign's personal standing army existing from the 14th century until 1826. 2. any Turkish soldier. Also, **jan′i·zar′y, Jan·is·sar·y** (jăn′ə sĕr′ĭ). [t. F: m. *janissaire,* t. Turk.: m. *yeñicheri* new soldiery]

Jan May·en (yän mī′ĕn), a volcanic island in the Arctic Ocean between Greenland and Norway: a possession of Norway. 144 sq. mi.

Jan·sen (jăn′sən; Du. yän′sən), *n.* **Cornelis** (kôr nā′lĭs), (*Cornelius Jansenius*) 1585–1638, Dutch theologian.

Jan·sen·ism (jăn′sə nĭz′əm), *n.* the doctrinal system of Cornelis Jansen, Roman Catholic bishop of Ypres, and his followers, which maintained the radical corruption of human nature and the inability of the will to do good, and that Christ died for the predestined and not for all men. —**Jan′sen·ist,** *n.* —**Jan′sen·is′tic,** *adj.*

Jan·u·ar·y (jăn′yŏŏ ĕr′ĭ, -ə rĭ), *n., pl.* **-aries.** the first month of the year, containing 31 days. [t. L: m.s.

Jānuārius the month of *Janus* (see JANUS); r. ME *Jenever,* t. ONF, and OE *Ianuarius,* t. L]

Ja·nus (jā′nəs), *n.* an ancient Italian (perhaps solar) deity, regarded by the Romans as presiding over doors and gates and over beginnings and endings, commonly represented with two faces in opposite directions. [L]

Ja·nus-faced (jā′nəs fāst′), *adj.* deceitful.

Jap (jăp), *adj., n. Colloq. and Derogatory.* Japanese.

Jap., Japanese.

Ja·pan (jə păn′), *n.* **1.** Japanese, **Nippon.** a constitutional monarchy on a chain of islands off the E coast of Asia: main islands, Hokkaido, Honshu, Kyushu, and Shikoku. 90,000,000 (est. 1956); 141,529 sq. mi. (1950). *Cap.:* Tokyo. **2. Sea of,** an arm of the Pacific between Honshu and Hokkaido islands and the mainland of Asia. ab. 405,000 sq. mi.

ja·pan (jə păn′), *n., adj., v.,* **-panned, -panning.** —*n.* **1.** any of various hard, durable, black varnishes (orig. from Japan) for coating wood, metal, etc. **2.** work varnished and figured in the Japanese manner. —*adj.* **3.** of or pertaining to japan. —*v.t.* **4.** to varnish with japan; lacquer. **5.** to coat with any material which gives a hard, black gloss.

Japan clover, a drought-resistant perennial leguminous plant, *Lespedeza striata,* introduced to the southern Atlantic states from Asia, having numerous tiny trifoliate leaves valued for pasturage and hay.

Japan current, a warm current of the western North Pacific, starting off southeastern China, flowing past Japan, and continuing into the open Pacific.

Jap·a·nese (jăp′ə nēz′, -nēs′), *adj., n., pl.* **-nese.** —*adj.* **1.** of or pertaining to Japan, its people, or their language. —*n.* **2.** a native of Japan, or a descendant of one. **3.** the language of Japan (no known congeners).

Japanese beetle, a scarabaeid beetle, *Popillia japonica,* introduced into the eastern U.S. from Japan about 1916. It is very injurious to the foliage of fruit and other trees, and its larvae destroy lawns.

Japanese ivy, a woody, Oriental, climbing shrub, *Parthenocissus tricuspidata.*

Japanese persimmon, 1. the soft edible fruit of *Diospyrus Kaki,* orange or reddish in color, often 3 inches in diameter. **2.** the tree.

Japanese river fever, a group of infectious diseases occurring in Japan, the East Indies, and probably elsewhere, transmitted by the bites of mites.

jape (jāp), *v.,* **japed, japing,** —*v.i.* **1.** *Archaic.* to jest; joke; gibe. —*n.* **2.** a joke; jest; gibe. [ME; orig. uncert.] —**jap′er,** *n.*

Ja·pheth (jā′fĭth), *n. Bible.* the third son of Noah. [ult. t. Heb.: m. *Yepheth*]

Ja·phet·ic (jə fĕt′ĭk), *adj.* **1.** of or pertaining to Japheth. **2.** *Obs.* Indo-European.

ja·pon·i·ca (jə pŏn′ə kə), *n.* **1.** the camellia, *Camellia japonica.* **2.** the Japanese quince, *Chaenomeles lagenaria,* an Asiatic shrub with clusters of scarlet flowers and yellowish fruit. [t. NL, fem. of *Japonicus* of Japan]

Ja·pu·rá (zhä′pŏō rä′), *n.* a river flowing from the Andes in SW Colombia E through NW Brazil to the Amazon. ab. 1750 mi. Also, **Yapurá.**

Ja·ques (jā′kwĕz, -kwĭz, jāks), *n.* a disillusioned and satiric observer of life, in Shakespeare's *As You Like It.*

jar¹ (jär), *n.* **1.** a broad-mouthed earthen or glass vessel, commonly cylindrical in form. **2.** the quantity contained in it. [t. F: m. *jarre,* t. Pr.: m. *jarro,* or Sp.: m. *jarra,* t. Ar.: m. *jarrah* earthen vessel]

jar² (jär), *v.,* **jarred, jarring.** —*v.i.* **1.** to produce a harsh, grating sound; sound discordantly. **2.** to have a harshly unpleasant effect upon the nerves, feelings, etc., or upon the person. **3.** to vibrate audibly; rattle. **4.** to vibrate or shake (without reference to sound). **5.** to be at variance; conflict; clash. —*v.t.* **6.** to cause to sound harshly or discordantly. **7.** to cause to rattle or shake. **8.** to have a harshly unpleasant effect upon (the feelings, nerves, etc., or the person). —*n.* **9.** a harsh, grating sound. **10.** a discordant sound or combination of sounds. **11.** a vibrating movement, as from concussion. **12.** a harshly unpleasant effect upon the mind or feelings due to physical or other shock. **13.** a quarrel; conflict, as of opinions, etc. [OE *ceorran* creak]

jar³ (jär), *n.* **1.** a turn or turning. **2. on the jar,** ajar. [var. of CHAR³, CHARE. Cf. AJAR]

jar·di·niere (jär′də nĭr′; *Fr.* zhȧr dē nyĕr′), *n.* an ornamental receptacle or stand for holding plants, flowers, etc. [t. F, fem. of *jardinier* gardener, der. *jardin* GARDEN]

jar·gon¹ (jär′gən, -gŏn), *n.* **1.** unintelligible or meaningless talk or writing; gibberish. **2.** (in contempt) any talk or writing which one does not understand. **3.** the language peculiar to a trade, profession, or other group: *medical jargon.* **4.** a conventionalized form of a language which has been greatly simplified by its speakers to make it more intelligible to foreigners, especially servants or employees, as pidgin English. **5.** a kind of speech abounding in uncommon or unfamiliar words. **6.** a lingua franca. —*v.i.* **7.** to utter or talk jargon or a jargon. [ME, t. OF, ult. der. *garg-* throat] —Syn. **3.** See **language.**

jar·gon² (jär′gŏn), *n.* a colorless-to-smoky variety of the mineral zircon. [t. F, t. It.: m. *giargone,* ? ult. t. Pers.: m. *zargūn* gold-colored. Cf. ZIRCON]

jar·gon·ize (jär′gə nīz′), *v.,* **-ized, -izing.** —*v.i.* **1.** to talk jargon or a jargon. —*v.t.* **2.** to translate into jargon.

jarl (yärl), *n. Scand. Hist.* a chieftain; an earl. [t. Scand.; cf. Icel. *jarl.* See EARL]

jar·o·site (jăr′ə sīt′, jə rō′sīt), *n.* a yellowish or brownish mineral, $K_2Fe_6(SO_4)_4(OH)_{12}$, occurring in crystals or massive. [named after Barrano *Jaroso,* in Almeria, southeastern Spain. See -ITE¹]

Jar·row (jăr′ō), *n.* a seaport in NE England at the mouth of the Tyne river. 28,541 (1951).

Jas., James.

jas·mine (jăs′mĭn, jăz′-), *n.* **1.** any of the fragrant-flowered shrubs constituting the oleaceous genus *Jasminum.* **2.** any of various plants of other genera, as *Gelsemium sempervirens* (**yellow jasmine**), *Gardenia jasminoides* (**Cape jasmine**) and *Plumeria rubra* (**red jasmine,** the frangipani). Also, **jessamine.** [t. F: m. *jasmin,* t. Ar.: m. *yâsmîn,* t. Pers.] —**jas′mine-like′,** *adj.*

Ja·son (jā′sən), *n. Gk. Legend.* the leader of the Argonautic expedition in quest of the Golden Fleece. He was the husband of Medea. See **Golden Fleece** and **Medea.**

jas·per (jăs′pər), *n.* a compact, opaque, often highly colored, cryptocrystalline variety of quartz, commonly used in decorative carvings. [ME *jaspre,* t. OF, var. of *jaspe,* t. L: m.s. *iaspis,* t. Gk.; of Eastern orig.]

Jas·per Park (jăs′pər), a national park in the Canadian Rockies in Canada, in western Alberta. 4400 sq. mi.

Jas·sy (yäs′ē), *n.* a city in NE Rumania. 94,075 (1948). Rumanian, **Iasi.**

Jat (jät, jŏt), *n.* a member of an important Indo-Aryan people living mainly in northwestern India. In early times they offered vigorous resistance to the Moslem invaders of India. [t. Hind.]

ja·to (jā′tō), *n. Aeron.* a jet-assisted takeoff.

jaun·dice (jŏn′dĭs, jän′-), *n., v.,* **-diced, -dicing.** —*n.* **1.** *Pathol.* a morbid bodily condition due to the presence of bile pigments in the blood, characterized by yellowness of the skin, the whites of the eyes, etc., by lassitude, and by loss of appetite. **2.** state of feeling in which views are colored or judgment is distorted. —*v.t.* **3.** to affect with jaundice. **4.** to affect with envy, jealousy, etc. [ME *jaunes, jaundis,* t. OF: m. *jaunisse,* der. *jaune* yellow, g. L *galbinus* greenish-yellow]

jaunt (jŏnt, jänt), *v.i.* **1.** to make a short journey, esp. for pleasure. —*n.* **2.** such a journey. [? nasalized var. of *jot* jog, jolt] —**Syn. 2.** See **excursion.**

jaunting car, a light two-wheeled vehicle, popular in Ireland, having seats on each side set back to back and a perch in front for the driver.

Jaunting car

jaun·ty (jŏn′tĭ, jän′-), *adj.,* **-tier, -tiest. 1.** easy and sprightly in manner or bearing. **2.** smartly trim or effective, as dress. [earlier *janty,* t. F: m. *gentil.* See GENTLE, GENTEEL] —**jaun′ti·ly,** *adv.* —**jaun′ti·ness,** *n.*

Jau·rès (zhō rĕs′), *n.* **Jean Léon** (zhän lĕ ôN′), 1859-1914, French socialist and author.

Jav., Javanese.

Ja·va (jā′və), *n.* **1.** an island in Indonesia. 51,637,072 pop. (with Madura; est. 1955); 48,920 sq. mi. **2.** a kind of coffee obtained from Indonesia. **3.** *U.S. Slang.* any coffee.

Java man, Pithecanthropus.

Jav·a·nese (jăv′ə nēz′, -nēs′), *adj., n., pl.* **-nese.** —*adj.* **1.** of or pertaining to the island of Java, its people, or their language. —*n.* **2.** a member of the native Malayan race of Java, esp. of that branch of it in the central part of the island. **3.** the language of central Java, of the Austronesian family.

Ja·va·ry (zhä′vä rē′), *n.* a river forming part of the boundary between Peru and Brazil, flowing NE to the upper Amazon. ab. 450 mi. Also, **Ja′va·ri′.**

Java Sea, a sea between Java and Borneo: naval engagement, 1942.

Java sparrow, a finchlike bird, *Munia oryzivora,* of the East Indies and Malaya: a common cage bird.

jave·lin (jăv′lĭn, jăv′ə lĭn), *n.* **1.** a spear to be thrown by hand. **2.** *Sports.* a wooden spear about 8½ feet long, hurled for distance. —*v.t.* **3.** to strike or pierce with or as with a javelin. [t. F: m. *javeline;* prob. from Celtic]

Ja·vel water (zhə vĕl′), sodium hypochlorite, NaOCl, dissolved in water, used as a bleach, antiseptic, etc. Also, **Javelle water.**

jaw (jô), *n.* **1.** one of the two bones or structures (upper and lower) which form the framework of the mouth. **2.** *Dentistry.* either jawbone containing its complement of teeth and covered by the soft tissues. **3.** the mouth parts collectively, or the mouth. **4.** anything likened to this: *the jaws of a gorge, of death, etc.* **5.** one of two or more parts, as of a machine, which grasp or hold something: *the jaws of a vise.* **6.** *Slang.* offensive talk. —*v.i.* **7.** *Slang.* to talk; gossip. **8.** *Slang.* to scold or use abusive language. —*v.t.* **9.** *Slang.* to scold. [ME *jawe, jowe,* t. OF: m. *jo(u)e* cheek, jaw] —**jaw′less,** *adj.*

---

b., blend of, blended; c., cognate with; d., dialect, dialectal; der., derived from; f., formed from; g., going back to; m., modification of; r., replacing; s., stem of; t., taken from; ?, perhaps. See the full key on inside cover.

jaw·bone (jô/bōn/), n. 1. any bone of the jaws; a maxilla or mandible. 2. the bone of the lower jaw.

jaw·break·er (jô/brā/kər), n. 1. Colloq. a word hard to pronounce. 2. Also, **jaw crusher.** a machine to break up ore, consisting of a fixed plate and a hinged jaw moved by a toggle joint. —**jaw/break/ing,** adj.

Jax·ar·tes (jăk sär/tēz), n. ancient name of Syr Darya.

jay (jā), n. 1. any of several crested or uncrested birds of the corvine subfamily Garrulinae, all of them robust, noisy, and mischievous, as the **common jay**, Garrulus glandarius, of Europe, the **bluejay**, Cyanocitta cristata, of America, and the plain gray **Canada jay**, Perisoreus canadensis. 2. Slang. a simple-minded or gullible person; a simpleton. [ME, t. OF. Cf. ML gaius; ? t. Gmc.]

Jay (jā), n. **John,** 1745–1829, American statesman and jurist; first chief justice of the U.S. Supreme Court, 1789–95.

Jay·hawk·er (jā/hô/kər), n. 1. a native of Kansas. 2. (l.c.) U.S. Slang. a plundering marauder; esp., one of the freebooting guerrillas in Kansas, Missouri, and other States before and during the Civil War.

jay·walk (jā/wôk/), v.i. Colloq. to cross a street otherwise than by a regular crossing or in a heedless manner, as against traffic lights. [f. JAY (see def. 2) + WALK] —**jay/walk/er,** n. —**jay/walk/ing,** n.

jazz (jăz), n. 1. dance music, usually of a "hot" improvisatory nature, with syncopated rhythms, such as is played by a jazz band. 2. a piece of such music. 3. dancing or a dance performed to such music, as with violent bodily motions and gestures. 4. lively comedy elements introduced into a play, poem, etc. 5. Slang. liveliness; spirit. —adj. 6. of the nature of or pertaining to jazz. —v.t. 7. to play (music) in the manner of jazz. 8. Slang. to put vigor or liveliness into (often fol. by up). —v.i. 9. to dance to such music. 10. Slang. to act or proceed with great energy or liveliness. [orig. obscure; said to have been long used by Negroes of the southern U.S., esp. those of Louisiana]

jazz band, a band adapted for or devoted to the playing of jazz, which uses melodic instruments such as the trumpet, trombone, clarinet, and saxophone, and rhythmic instruments such as drums, piano, and guitar, producing novel tonal effects often adopted from vocal style, such as vibrato and sliding from tone to tone.

jazz·y (jăz/ĭ), adj., jazzier, jazziest. Slang. pertaining to or suggestive of jazz music; wildly active or lively.

J. C., 1. Jesus Christ. 2. Julius Caesar. 3. jurisconsult.

J. C. B., (L Juris Civilis Baccalaureus) Bachelor of Civil Law.

J. C. D., (L Juris Civilis Doctor) Doctor of Civil Law.

jct., junction. Also, jctn.

J. D., 1. (L Juris Doctor) Doctor of Law. 2. (L Jurum Doctor) Doctor of Laws. 3. (L Juris Doctor) Doctor of Jurisprudence.

Je., June.

jeal·ous (jĕl/əs), adj. 1. feeling envious resentment against a successful rival or at success, advantages, etc., (fol. by of): to be jealous of a victor. 2. characterized by or proceeding from suspicious fears or envious resentment: jealous intrigues. 3. inclined to or troubled by suspicions or fears of rivalry, as in love or aims: a jealous husband. 4. solicitous or vigilant in maintaining or guarding something. 5. (in Biblical use) intolerant of unfaithfulness or rivalry: the Lord is a jealous God. 6. Obs. zealous. [ME gelos, jalous, t. OF, g. LL zēlōsus, der. L zēlus, t. Gk.: m. zēlos zeal] —**jeal/ous·ly,** adv. —**jeal/ous·ness,** n.

jeal·ous·y (jĕl/ə sĭ), n., pl. -ousies. 1. envious resentment against a successful rival or the possessor of any coveted advantage. 2. mental uneasiness from suspicion or fear of rivalry, as in love or aims. 3. state or feeling of being jealous. 4. an instance of jealous feeling.

jean (jēn, jān), n. 1. a stout twilled cotton fabric. 2. (pl.) clothes of this material; trousers; overalls. [prob. t. F: m. Gênes Genoa]

Jeanne d'Arc (zhän därk/), French name of **Joan of Arc.**

Jeans (jēnz), n. **Sir James Hopwood,** 1877–1946, British mathematician, physicist, and astronomer.

Jebb (jĕb), n. **Sir Richard Claverhouse** (klăv/ər hous/), 1841–1905, British classical scholar.

jeb·el (jĕb/əl), n. Arabic. mountain.

Jeb·el Mu·sa (jĕb/əl mōō/sä), a mountain in NW Morocco, opposite Gibraltar: one of the Pillars of Hercules. ab. 2750 ft.

Jed·burgh (jĕd/bûr/ō, -bə rə), n. a border town in SE Scotland; ruins of a famous abbey. 4083 (1951).

Jed·da (jĕd/də), n. Jidda.

jeep (jēp), n. a small (usually ¼ ton capacity) military motor vehicle. [? special use of jeep name of fabulous animal in comic strip "Popeye," or alter. of G.P. (for General Purpose Vehicle)]

jeer¹ (jĭr), v.i. 1. to speak or shout derisively; gibe or scoff rudely. —v.t. 2. to treat with scoffs or derision; make a mock of. 3. to drive (out, off, etc.) by jeers. —n. 4. a jeering utterance; a derisive or rude gibe. [? OE cēir clamor, der. cēgan call out] —**jeer/er,** n. —**jeer/ing·ly,** adv. —**Syn.** 1. See **scoff.**

jeer² (jĭr), n. (usually pl.) Naut. tackle for hoisting or lowering heavy yards. [? lit., mover, der. GEE, interj.]

je·fe (hĕ/fĕ), n. Spanish. leader; commanding officer. [Sp, t. OF: m. chief. g. L caput head]

Jef·fers (jĕf/ərz), n. **Robinson,** 1887–1962, U.S. poet.

Jef·fer·son (jĕf/ər sən), n. 1. **Joseph,** 1829–1905, U.S. actor. 2. **Thomas,** 1743–1826, American statesman, writer, and 3rd president of the U.S., 1801–09; important in framing the Declaration of Independence. 3. **Mount,** a peak in NW Oregon, in the Cascade Range. 10,495 ft.

Jefferson City, the capital of Missouri, in the central part, on the Missouri river. 28,228 (1960).

Jefferson Day, April 13, Jefferson's birthday, sometimes celebrated with Democratic Party dinners.

Jef·fer·so·ni·an (jĕf/ər sō/nĭ ən), adj. 1. of or pertaining to Thomas Jefferson or his political theories. —n. 2. an adherent of Jefferson.

Jef·frey (jĕf/rĭ), n. **Francis,** (Lord Jeffrey) 1773–1850, Scottish jurist, editor, and critic.

Jef·freys (jĕf/rĭz), n. **George,** (1st baron Jeffreys) 1648–1689, British judge, notorious for his unjudicial conduct.

je·had (jĭ häd/), n. jihad.

Je·hol (jə hŏl/, rĕ/hō/; native rŭ/hŭ/), n. 1. a province in NE China: incorporated into Manchukuo by the Japanese. 1935. 5,160,822 (1953); 74,297 sq. mi. Cap.: Chengteh. 2. Chengteh.

Je·hosh·a·phat (jĭ hŏsh/ə făt/, -hŏs/-), n. a king of Judah, son of Asa, who reigned in the 9th century B.C. 1 Kings 22:41–50.

Je·ho·vah (jĭ hō/və), n. 1. a name of God in the Old Testament, an erroneous rendering of the ineffable name, JHVH, in the Hebrew Scriptures. 2. (in modern Christian use) God.

Jehovah's Witnesses, a sect of Christians who are pacifists and do not recognize the authority of the state when it conflicts with religious principles.

Je·ho·vist (jĭ hō/vĭst), n. 1. the author of the earliest major source of the Pentateuch in which God is characteristically referred to as Yahweh (erroneously Jehovah). See **Yahweh.** 2. one who maintains that the vowel points annexed to the word Jehovah in Hebrew are the proper vowels of the word, and express the true pronunciation. —adj. 3. characterized by the use of the name Jehovah for God (applied to part of the Pentateuch). —**Je·ho/vism,** n.

Je·ho·vis·tic (jē/hō vĭs/tĭk), adj. pertaining to or written by a Jehovist. Also, **Yahwiatic.**

Je·hu (jē/hū), n. 1. son of Hanani, a prophet of Judah under Jehoshaphat in the 9th century B.C. 1 Kings 16. 2. (l.c.) a fast driver. 3. (l.c.) Slang. any driver.

je·june (jĭ jōōn/), adj. 1. deficient in nourishing or substantial qualities. 2. unsatisfying to the mind. [t. L: m.s. jējūnus fasting, empty, dry, poor] —**je·june/ly,** adv. —**je·june/ness,** je·ju·ni·ty (jĭ jōō/nə tĭ), n.

je·ju·num (jĭ jōō/nəm), n. Anat. the middle portion of the small intestine, between the duodenum and the ileum. See diag. under **intestine.** [t. NL, prop. neut. of L jējūnus empty]

Je·kyll (jē/kəl, jĕk/əl), n. **Dr.,** the central figure, who at times becomes a vicious being, in Stevenson's Dr. Jekyll and Mr. Hyde (1886).

jell (jĕl), v.i. Colloq. to form a jelly.

Jel·li·coe (jĕl/ĭ kō/), n. **John Rushworth,** (1st Earl Jellicoe) 1859–1935, British admiral.

jel·lied (jĕl/ĭd), adj. 1. brought to the consistency of jelly. 2. containing or spread over with jelly.

jel·li·fy (jĕl/ə fī/), v., -fied, -fying. —v.t. 1. to make into a jelly; reduce to a gelatinous state. —v.i. 2. to become gelatinous; turn into jelly. —**jel/li·fi·ca/tion,** n.

jel·ly (jĕl/ĭ), n., pl. -lies, v., -lied, -lying. —n. 1. a food preparation of a soft, elastic consistency due to the presence of gelatin, pectin, etc., as fruit juice boiled down with sugar. 2. anything of the consistency of jelly. —v.t., v.i. 3. to bring or come to the consistency of jelly. [ME gele, t. OF: m. gelee frost, jelly, g. L gelāta, prop. pp. fem., frozen] —**jel/ly·like/,** adj.

jel·ly·fish (jĕl/ĭ fĭsh/), n., pl. -fishes, (esp. collectively) -fish. any of various marine coelenterates of a soft, gelatinous structure, esp. one with an umbrellalike body and long, trailing tentacles; a medusa.

jem·a·dar (jĕm/ə där/), n. India. 1. any of various government officials. 2. the chief of a body of servants. 3. a native officer in a sepoy regiment, corresponding in rank to a lieutenant. [t. Hind., s. Pers.: m. jama'dār, lit., holder or leader of an aggregation (of men)]

Je·mappes (zhə mȧp/), n. a town in SW Belgium, near Mons: French victory over the Austrians, 1792. 12,812 (est. 1948).

jem·my (jĕm/ĭ), n., pl. -mies, v.t., -mied, -mying. Brit. jimmy.

Je·na (yā/nä), n. a city in East Germany, in Thuringia: Napoleon decisively defeated the Prussians there, 1806. 83,073 (est. 1955).

je ne sais quoi (zhən sĕ kwä/), French. I know not what; an indefinable something.

Jen·ghis Khan (jĕn/gĭz kän/, jĕng/-), Genghis Khan. Also, **Jen/ghiz Khan/.**

Jellyfish, genus Cephea
A. Disk or umbrella; B. Ramifications of brachia; C. Tentacles; D. Pillar supporting disk; E. Short tentacles

Jen·ner (jĕn′ər), *n.* **1. Edward,** 1749–1823, British physician, discoverer of smallpox vaccine. **2. Sir William,** 1815–98, British physician.

jen·net (jĕn′ĭt), *n.* **1.** a small Spanish horse. **2.** a female donkey; jenny ass. Also, **genet.** [ME *genett*, t. OF: m. *genet*, t. Sp.: m. *jinete* mounted soldier, horse, t. Ar.: m. *Zenāta*, name of a Berber tribe noted for its cavalry]

jen·ny (jĕn′ĭ), *n.*, *pl.* **-nies. 1.** a spinning jenny. **2.** female of some animals: *jenny wren.* [prop. woman's name]

jeop·ard·ize (jĕp′ər dīz′), *v.t.*, **-ized, -izing.** to put in jeopardy; hazard; risk; imperil. Also, **jeop′ard.**

jeop·ard·y (jĕp′ər dĭ), *n.* **1.** hazard or risk of loss or harm. **2.** peril or danger: *for a moment his life was in jeopardy.* **3.** *Law.* the hazard of being found guilty, and of consequent punishment, undergone by criminal defendants on trial. [ME *iuparti*, etc., t OF: m. *jeu parti*, lit., divided game, even game or chance]

Jeph·thah (jĕf′thə), *n.* judge of Israel. Judg. 11–14.

je·quir·i·ty (jə kwĭr′ə tĭ), *n.*, *pl.* **-ties. 1.** the Indian licorice plant, *Abrus precatorius*, of India and Brazil, whose seed (**jequirity bean**) is used as a bead and in medicine. **2.** the seeds collectively. [t. F: m. *jéquirity*, t. Tupi-Guarani: m. *jekiritī*]

Jer., 1. Jeremiah. **2.** Jersey.

jer·bo·a (jər bō′ə), *n.* any of various mouselike rodents of North Africa and Asia, as of the genera *Jaculus, Dipus*, etc., with long hind legs used for jumping. [t. NL, t. Ar.: m. *yarbū*]

Jerboa. *Jaculus laculus*
(Body 5½ in. long, tall 8 in.)

je·reed (jə rēd′), *n.* a blunt wooden javelin used in games by horsemen in Arabia, Persia, etc. Also, **jerid, jerreed, jer·rid.** [t. Ar.: m. *jarīd* rod, shaft]

jer·e·mi·ad (jĕr′ə mī′ăd), *n.* a lamentation; a lugubrious complaint. [t. F: m. *jérémiade*, der. *Jérémie* Jeremiah; with ref. to the Biblical "Lamentations of Jeremiah"]

Jer·e·mi·ah (jĕr′ə mī′ə), *n.* **1.** one of the greatest of the Hebrew prophets, whose career extended from about 650 to 585 B.C. **2.** a book of the Old Testament. [ult. t. Heb.: m. *Yirmeyāh*]

Je·rez (hĕ rĕth′, -rĕs′), *n.* a city in SW Spain: noted for its sherry wine. 120,021 (est. 1955). Also **Jerez de la Fron·te·ra** (dĕ lä frŏnt ĕ′rä). Formerly, **Xeres.**

Jer·i·cho (jĕr′ə kō′), *n.* an ancient city of Palestine, N of the Dead Sea.

je·rid (jə rēd′), *n.* jereed.

Je·ri·tza (yĕ′rē tsä′), *n.* **Ma·ria** (mä rē′ä), born 1887, Austrian operatic soprano.

jerk¹ (jûrk), *n.* **1.** a quick, sharp thrust, pull, throw, or the like; a sudden start. **2.** *Physiol.* a sudden movement of an organ or a part. **3. the jerks, Western and Southern U.S.** the paroxysms or violent spasmodic muscular movements sometimes resulting from excitement in connection with religious services. **4.** (*pl.*) *Brit.* physical exercises. **5.** *Slang.* an unknowing, unsophisticated, or unconventional person. —*v.t.* **6.** to give a sudden thrust, pull, or twist to. **7.** to move or throw with a quick, suddenly arrested motion. **8.** to utter in a broken, spasmodic way. —*v.i.* **9.** to give a jerk or jerks. **10.** to move with a quick, sharp motion; move spasmodically.

jerk² (jûrk), *v.t.* **1.** to preserve meat, esp. beef (**jerked beef**) by cutting in strips and curing by drying in the sun. —*n.* **2.** jerked meat, esp. beef. [t. Amer. Sp.: m. *charquear*, der. *charque, charqui* jerked meat, charqui, t. Peruvian Ind.]

jer·kin (jûr′kĭn), *n.* a close-fitting jacket or short coat, as one of leather worn in the 16th and 17th centuries.

jerk·wa·ter (jûrk′wô′tər, -wŏt′ər), *n. U.S. Colloq.* **1.** a train not running on the main line. —*adj.* **2.** off the main line. **3.** of minor importance. [appar. f. JERK¹, v. + WATER]

jerk·y (jûr′kĭ), *adj.*, **jerkier, jerkiest.** characterized by jerks or sudden starts; spasmodic. —**jerk′i·ly,** *adv.* —**jerk′i·ness,** *n.*

Jerkin

Jer·o·bo·am (jĕr′ə bō′əm), *n.* **1.** the first king of the northern kingdom of Israel (def. 5). **2.** (*l.c.*) an oversized bottle for champagne, containing 104 ounces.

Je·rome (jə rōm′, jĕr′əm), *n.* **Saint,** (*Eusebius Sophronius Hieronymus*) A.D. c340–420, monk and scholar of the Latin Church, maker of the Latin version of the Bible known as the Vulgate.

Jer·ry (jĕr′ĭ), *n.*, *pl.* **-ries.** *Chiefly Brit. Colloq.* **1.** nickname for a German. **2.** (collectively) Germans.

jer·ry-build (jĕr′ĭ bĭld′), *v.t.*, **-built, -building.** to build cheaply and flimsily. —**jer′ry-build′er,** *n.*

Jer·sey (jûr′zĭ), *n.* **1.** a British island in the English Channel: the largest of the Channel Islands. 55,248 (est. 1954); 45 sq. mi. *Cap.:* St. Helier. **2.** New Jersey.

Jer·sey (jûr′zĭ), *n.*, *pl.* **-seys.** one of a breed of dairy cattle smaller than the Guernsey, originating on the island of Jersey. Their milk contains the highest percentage of butterfat of the milk of any dairy breed.

jer·sey (jûr′zĭ), *n.*, *pl.* **-seys. 1.** a close-fitting knitted woolen jacket or shirt worn by seamen, athletes, and others. **2.** a similar garment of knitted material of wool, silk, etc. worn by women. **3.** jersey cloth.

Jersey City, a seaport in NE New Jersey, opposite New York City. 276,101 (1960).

jersey cloth, a machine-knitted fabric of wool, silk, or rayon, used for making garments, etc.

Je·ru·sa·lem (jĭ rōō′sə ləm), *n.* an ancient holy city, the principal city of Palestine and place of pilgrimage for Jews, Christians, and Moslems; now divided between Israel and Jordan (the Israeli part has been the capital of Israel since 1950). 190,213 (est. 1954). [ult. t. Heb.]

Jerusalem artichoke, 1. a species of sunflower, *Helianthus tuberosus*, having edible tuberous underground stems or rootstocks. **2.** the tuber itself. [t. It.: alter. (by pop. etymology) of *girasole* sunflower, f. s. of *girare* turn + *sole* sun]

Jerusalem cross, a cross whose four arms are each capped with a crossbar.

Jes·per·sen (yĕs′pər sən), *n.* **Jens Otto Harry** (yĕns ŏt′ō här′ē), 1860–1943, Danish linguist.

jess (jĕs), *Falconry.* —*n.* **1.** a short strap fastened round the leg of a hawk and attached to the leash. —*v.t.* **2.** to put jesses on (a hawk). [ME *ges*, t. OF, der. *jeter* throw, g. LL *jectāre*, r. L *jactāre*] —**jessed** (jĕst), *adj.*

jes·sa·mine (jĕs′ə mĭn), *n.* jasmine.

jes·sant (jĕs′ənt), *adj. Her.* **1.** shooting up, as a plant. **2.** coming forth; issuant. **3.** lying across.

Jes·se (jĕs′ĭ), *n.* father of David. I Sam. 16.

jest (jĕst), *n.* **1.** a witticism, joke, or pleasantry. **2.** a piece of raillery or banter. **3.** sport or fun: *to speak half in jest, half in earnest.* **4.** the object of laughter, sport, or mockery; a laughingstock. **5.** *Obs.* an exploit. See **gest.** —*v.i.* **6.** to speak in a playful, humorous, or facetious way; joke. **7.** to speak or act in mere sport, rather than in earnest; trifle (*with*). **8.** to utter derisive speeches; gibe or scoff. —*v.t.* **9.** to jest at; deride; banter. [var. of GEST¹] —**Syn. 1.** See joke.

jest·er (jĕs′tər), *n.* **1.** one who is given to witticisms, jokes, and pranks. **2.** a professional fool or clown, kept by a prince or noble, esp. during the Middle Ages.

jest·ing (jĕs′tĭng), *adj.* **1.** given to jesting; playful. **2.** fit for joking; unimportant; trivial: *no jesting matter.* —*n.* **3.** pleasantry; triviality. —**jest′ing·ly,** *adv.*

Je·su (jē′zōō, -sōō), *n. Poetic.* Jesus. [t. L, oblique (usually voc.) case form of *Jesus* JESUS]

Jes·u·it (jĕzh′ōō ĭt, jĕz′yōō-), *n.* **1.** a member of a Roman Catholic religious order (**Society of Jesus**) founded by Ignatius Loyola in 1534. **2.** a crafty, intriguing, or equivocating person (in allusion to the methods ascribed to the order by its opponents). [t. NL: s. *Jesuita*, f. L. See JESU, -IT(E)¹] —**Jes′u·it′ic, Jes′u·it′i·cal,** *adj.* —**Jes′u·it′i·cal·ly,** *adv.*

Jes·u·it·ism (jĕzh′ōō ĭ tĭz′əm, jĕz′yōō-), *n.* **1.** the system, principles, or practices of the Jesuits. **2.** (*usually l.c.*) a principle or practice such as casuistry ascribed to the Jesuits by their opponents. Also, **Jes′u·it·ry.**

Jes·u·it·ize (jĕzh′ōō ĭ tīz′, jĕz′yōō-), *v.t.*, *v.i.*, **-ized, -izing.** to make or be Jesuitical.

Je·sus (jē′zəs), *n.* born c6 B.C., crucified c A.D. 29, the founder of the Christian religion. Also, **Jesus Christ.** [ME and OE, t. LL, t. Gk.: m. *Iēsoûs*, t. Heb.: m. *Yeshūa*, earlier *Yehōshūa*, lit., Jehovah is salvation]

jet¹ (jĕt), *n.*, *v.*, **jetted, jetting.** —*n.* **1.** a free or submerged stream of fluid produced by efflux from a nozzle, orifice, etc. **2.** that which so issues, as water or gas. **3.** the spout used: *gas jet.* **4.** a jet plane. —*v.i.*, *v.t.* **5.** to shoot forth in a stream; spout. [t. F, der. *jeter*, v.]

jet² (jĕt), *n.* **1.** a compact black coal, susceptible of a high polish, used for making beads, jewelry, buttons, etc. **2.** a deep, glossy black. **3.** *Obs.* black marble. —*adj.* **4.** consisting or made of jet. **5.** of the color jet; black as jet. [ME *gete, iete*, t. OF: m. *jaiet*, g. L *gagātēs*, t. Gk, der. *Gāgai*, town in Lycia, Asia Minor]

jet-black (jĕt′blăk′), *adj.* deep-black: *jet-black hair.*

jet-lin·er (jĕt′lī′nər), *n.* a commercial jet plane.

jet plane, a plane operated by jet propulsion.

jet propulsion, a method of producing a propelling force upon an air or water craft through the reaction of a high-velocity jet, usually of heated gases, discharged toward the rear. —**jet′pro·pelled′,** *adj.*

jet·sam (jĕt′səm), *n.* **1.** goods thrown overboard to lighten a vessel in distress. **2.** such goods when washed ashore. See **flotsam.** [var. of *jetson*, syncopated form of *jettison*; final -m as in FLOTSAM, etc.]

jet set, *Often Disparaging.* those men and women who make frequent international jet trips between resorts, compliant hosts, etc., in order to find amusement, sustenance, or the like.

jet stream, a substratospheric wind, generally westerly, moving at a velocity as high as 200 m.p.h.

jet·ti·son (jĕt′ə sən, -zən), *n.* **1.** act of casting overboard. **2.** jetsam. —*v.t.* **3.** to throw (cargo, etc.) overboard, esp. to lighten a vessel in distress. **4.** to throw off, as an obstacle or burden. [t. AF: m. *getteson*, var. of OF *getaison*, der. *geter* throw]

jet·ton (jĕt′ən), *n.* an inscribed counter or token. [t., m. *jeton,* der. *jeter* throw, cast, cast up (accounts, etc.)]

jet·ty¹ (jĕt′ĭ), *n., pl.* **-ties.** 1. a pier or structure of stones, piles, or the like, projecting into the sea or other body of water so as to protect a harbor, deflect the current, etc. 2. a wharf or landing pier. 3. the piles or wooden structure protecting a pier. [ME *gette,* t. OF: m. *jetee,* n. use of fem. pp. of *jeter* throw]

jet·ty² (jĕt′ĭ), *adj.* 1. made of jet. 2. resembling jet; black as jet, or of the color jet. [f. JET² + -Y¹]

jeu de mots (zhœ də mō′), *French.* a pun.

jeu d es·prit (zhœ dĕs prē′), *French.* a witticism.

Jev·ons (jĕv′ənz), *n.* **William Stanley,** 1835–82, British economist and logician.

Jew (jōō), *n.* 1. one of the Hebrew or Jewish people; a Hebrew; an Israelite. —*adj.* 2. of Jews; Jewish. —*v.t.* 3. *(l.c.) U.S. Colloq. and Offensive.* to bargain sharply with; beat (*down*) in price. [ME *Jeu, Giu,* t. OF: m. *Juieu,* g. L *Jūdaeus,* t. Gk.: m. *Ioudaîos,* prop. one of the tribe of Judah, ult. der. Heb. *Yehūdāh* Judah]

Jew-bait·ing (jōō′bā′tĭng), *n.* active anti-Semitism. —**Jew′-bait′er,** *n.*

jew·el (jōō′əl), *n., v.,* **-eled, -eling** or (*esp. Brit.*) **-elled, -elling.** —*n.* 1. a cut and polished stone; a gem. 2. a fashioned ornament for personal adornment, usually set with gems. 3. a precious possession. 4. a thing or person of great worth or rare excellence. 5. a precious stone (or some substitute) used as a bearing of great durability in a watch or delicate instrument. 6. an ornamental boss of glass, sometimes cut with facets, in stained-glass work. 7. something resembling a gem in appearance, ornamental effect, etc., as a star, a berry, etc. —*v.t.* 8. to set or adorn with jewels. [ME *iuel,* t. AF, ult. der. L *jocus* jest, sport] —**jew′el·like′,** *adj.*

jew·el·er (jōō′ələr), *n.* one who makes, or deals in, jewels or jewelry. Also, *esp. Brit.,* **jew′el·ler.**

jew·el·fish (jōō′əl fĭsh′), *n., pl.* **-fishes,** (*esp. collectively*) **-fish.** a brilliantly colored aquarium fish, *Hemichromis binaculatus.*

jew·el·ry (jōō′əl rĭ), *n.* jewels; articles made of gold, silver, precious stones, etc., for personal adornment. Also, *esp. Brit.,* **jew′el·ler·y.**

jew·el·weed (jōō′əl wēd′), *n.* an American touch-me-not, as *Impatiens biflora,* with orange-yellow flowers spotted with brown, or *I. pallida.*

Jew·ess (jōō′ĭs), *n.* a Jewish girl or woman.

Jew·ett (jōō′ĭt), *n.* **Sarah Orne** (ôrn), 1849–1909, U.S. short-story writer and novelist.

jew·fish (jōō′fĭsh′), *n., pl.* **-fishes,** (*esp. collectively*) **-fish.** any of several large marine fishes, *family Serranidae,* frequenting southern waters, such as the **spotted jewfish** (*Promicropsi taiara*) and the **black jewfish** (*Epinephelus nigritus*) of the south coast of the U.S., West Indies, etc., and the **California jewfish** (*Stereolepsi gigas*), all reaching a weight of several hundred pounds. [appar. f. JEW + FISH]

Jew·ish (jōō′ĭsh), *adj.* 1. of, pertaining to, or characteristic of the Jews; Hebrew. —*n.* 2. Yiddish.

Jewish calendar, the lunisolar calendar in use among the Jews, reckoning from the Creation (dated traditionally during the year 3761 B.C.), the year containing 12 or (in intercalary years) 13 months, of 29 or 30 days each, which, beginning during September or October, are as follows: Tishri, Heshvan, Kislev, Tebet, Shebat, Adar, Veadar (occurring only on intercalary years), Nisan, Iyyar, Sivan, Tammuz, Ab, and Elul.

Jew·ry (jōō′rĭ), *n., pl.* **-ries.** 1. the Jewish people. 2. a district inhabited by Jews; a ghetto. 3. *Archaic.* Judea. [ME *Jewerie,* t. AF: m. *juerie,* var. of OF *juierie*]

Jew's-harp (jōōz′härp′), *n.* a steel tongue within an iron frame, held between the jaws and plucked while the varying position of the mouth changes the tone. Also, **Jews′-harp′.** [appar. jocular in orig., as it is not a harp and has no connection with the Jews]

Jew's pitch, asphalt or maltha. Also, **Jews′ pitch.**

Jez·e·bel (jĕz′ə bəl), *n.* 1. the wife of Ahab, king of Israel, notorious for her conduct. I Kings 16:31, 21:25, II Kings 9:30–37. 2. a shameless, abandoned woman.

Jew's-harp

Jez·re·el (jĕz′rĭ′əl, jĕz rēl′), **Plain of,** Esdraelon.

jg, junior grade. Also, **j.g.**

Jhan·si (jän′sē), *n.* a city in central India, in Uttar Pradesh. 127,365 (est. 1956).

Jhe·lum (jā′ləm), *n.* a river flowing from S Kashmir into the Chenab river in Pakistan. ab. 450 mi.

jib¹ (jĭb), *n. Naut.* 1. a triangular sail (or either of two triangular sails, **inner jib** and **outer jib**) set in front of the forward (or single) mast. See illus. under **sail.** 2. any of certain similar sails set beyond the jib proper, as a **flying jib.** [? akin to GIBBET]

jib² (jĭb), *v.i., v.t.,* **jibbed, jibbing.** jibe¹.

jib³ (jĭb), *v.,* **jibbed, jibbing,** *n.* —*v.i.* 1. *Chiefly Brit.* to move restively sidewise or backward instead of forward, as an animal in harness; balk. 2. *Brit.* to hold back or balk at doing something. —*n.* 3. a horse or other animal that jibs. [orig. uncert.] —**jib′ber,** *n.*

jib⁴ (jĭb), *n.* the projecting arm of a crane; the boom of a derrick. [appar. short for GIBBET]

jib boom, *Naut.* a spar forming a continuation of a bowsprit. See illus. under **bowsprit.**

jibe¹ (jĭb), *v.,* **jibed, jibing,** *n. Naut.* —*v.i.* 1. to shift from one side to the other when running before the wind, as a fore-and-aft sail or its boom. 2. to alter the course so that the sail shifts in this manner. —*v.t.* 3. to cause (a sail, etc.) to jibe. —*n.* 4. act of jibing. Also, **gybe.** [var. of *gybe,* t. D: m. *gijben*]

jibe² (jĭb), *v.t., v.i.,* **jibed, jibing,** *n.* gibe. —**jib′er,** *n.*

jibe³ (jĭb), *v.i.,* **jibed, jibing.** *U.S. Colloq.* to agree; be in harmony or accord. [orig. uncert.]

Ji·bu·ti (jē bōō′tē), *n.* Djibouti.

Jid·da (jĭd′də), *n.* the seaport of Mecca in Saudi Arabia, on the Red Sea. 100,000 (est. 1954). Also, **Jedda.**

jif·fy (jĭf′ĭ), *n., pl.* **-fies.** *Colloq.* a very short time: *to do something in a jiffy.* Also, **jiff.** [orig. unknown]

jig¹ (jĭg), *n., v.,* **jigged, jigging.** —*n.* 1. a device for holding the work in a machine tool, esp. one for accurately guiding a drill or group of drills so as to insure uniformity in successive pieces machined. 2. a device used in fishing, esp. a hook or collection of hooks loaded with metal or having a spoon-shaped piece of bone or other material attached, for drawing through the water. 3. an apparatus for separating ore from gangue, etc., by shaking in or treating with water. —*v.t.* 4. to treat, cut, or produce by using any of the mechanical contrivances called jigs. —*v.i.* 5. to use a jig (mechanical contrivance). [var. of GAUGE. Cf. E *jeg* kind of gauge]

jig² (jĭg), *n., v.,* **jigged, jigging.** —*n.* 1. a rapid, lively, springy, irregular dance for one or more persons, usually in triple rhythm. 2. a piece of music for, or in the rhythm of, such a dance. 3. *Dial. and Slang.* a piece of sport, a prank, or a trick. 4. **the jig is up,** the game is up; there is no further chance. —*v.t.* 5. to dance (a jig or any lively dance). 6. to sing or play in the time or rhythm of a jig. 7. to move with a jerky or bobbing motion; jerk up and down or to and fro. —*v.i.* 8. to dance or play a jig. 9. to move with a quick, jerky motion; hop; bob. [appar. var. of JOG, v.] —**jig′like′,** *adj.*

jig·ger¹ (jĭg′ər), *n.* 1. one who or that which jigs. 2. *Naut.* **a.** a small sail set in the stern of a canoe, yawl, etc. **b.** the mast or sail nearest the stern of a vessel with five masts, or the fifth, from forward, if she has more than five. **c.** a light tackle used about the deck of a ship. 3. any of various mechanical devices, many of which have a jerky or jolting motion. 4. *Colloq.* some contrivance, article, or part that one cannot name more precisely: *What is that little jigger on the pistol?* 5. a jig for separating ore or for fishing. 6. *Golf.* an ironheaded club, a cross between a mashie and a mid-iron, used in making an approach. 7. *Billiards.* a bridge. 8. *U.S.* a 1½ oz. measure used in cocktail recipes. [f. JIG¹ + -ER¹]

jig·ger² (jĭg′ər), *n.* a chigoe.

jig·gered (jĭg′ərd), *adj.* a word used as a vague substitute for a profane word: *I'm jiggered if I know.*

jig·gle (jĭg′əl), *v.,* **-gled, -gling.** —*v.t., v.i.* 1. to move up and down or to and fro with short, quick jerks. —*n.* 2. a jiggling movement. [freq. of JIG²]

jig saw, a narrow saw mounted vertically in a frame, used for cutting curves.

jig-saw puzzle (jĭg′sô′), a picture sawed or cut up into small irregular pieces to form a puzzle.

ji·had (jĭ häd′), *n.* 1. a war of Mohammedans upon others, with a religious object. 2. any crusade, as against some belief. Also, **jehad.** [t. Ar.: effort, strife]

Ji·lo·lo (jĭ lō′lō), *n.* Halmahera.

jilt (jĭlt), *v.t.* 1. to cast off (a lover or sweetheart) after encouragement or engagement. —*n.* 2. a woman who jilts a lover. [orig. uncert.] —**jilt′er,** *n.*

Jim Crow (jĭm krō′), *U.S.* 1. (in contemptuous use) Negro. 2. a practice or policy of segregating Negroes, as in public places, public vehicles, etc. —**Jim-Crow,** **jim-crow,** *adj.*

Ji·mé·nez (hē mě′něs), *n.* **Juan Ramón** (hwän rä-mōn′), 1881–1958, Spanish poet.

Ji·mé·nez de Cis·ne·ros (hē mě′něth dě sēs ně′rōs), **Francisco** (frän thēs′kō), 1436–1517, Spanish cardinal and statesman. Also, **Ximenes, Ximenez.**

jim·my (jĭm′ĭ), *n., pl.* **-mies,** *v.,* **-mied, -mying.** —*n.* 1. a short crowbar used by burglars. —*v.t.* 2. to force open by a jimmy, as a door. Also, *Brit.,* **jemmy.** [appar. a special use of *Jimmy,* familiar form of *James*]

jim·son weed (jĭm′sən), a datura, *Datura stramonium,* a coarse, ill-smelling weed with white flowers and poisonous leaves. Also, **Jimson weed.** [alter. of *Jamestown weed;* named after *Jamestown,* Va.]

jin·gal (jĭn′gəl), *n.* a large musket fired from a rest, often mounted on a carriage: formerly used by natives in India, China, etc. Also, **gingal, gingall.**

jin·gle (jĭng′gəl), *v.,* **-gled, -gling,** *n.* —*v.i.* 1. to make clinking or tinkling sounds, as coins, keys, etc., when struck together. 2. to move or proceed with such sounds. 3. to sound in a manner suggestive of this, as verse or any sequence of words: *a jingling ballad.* 4. to make rhymes. —*v.t.* 5. to cause to jingle. —*n.* 6. a clinking or tinkling sound, as of small bells or of small pieces of metal struck together. 7. something that makes such a sound, as a small bell or a metal pendant. 8. a musical succession of like sounds, as in rhyme or alliteration, without particular regard for sense; jingling verse. 9. a piece of such verse. 10. *Ireland and Au-*

stralia. a covered two-wheeled car. [ME *gynglen*, appar. imit.; but cf. D *jengelen*] —**jin′gling·ly**, *adv.* —**jin′-gly**, *adj.*

Jingling Johnny, *Music.* a crescent (def. 6).

jin·go (jĭng′gō), *n., pl.* **-goes**, *adj.* —*n.* 1. one who boasts of his country's preparedness for war, or who favors a bellicose or blustering foreign policy; a chauvin-ist. 2. (*orig.*) a Conservative supporter of Disraeli's Near Eastern policy (1877–78). 3. *Colloq.* a word used in vehement asseveration in the phrase "by jingo!" —*adj.* 4. of jingoes. 5. characterized by jingoism. [orig. uncert.; first used in conjurer's jargon]

jin·go·ism (jĭng′gō·ĭz′əm), *n.* the spirit, policy, or practices of jingoes. —**jin′go·ist**, *n., adj.* —**jin′go·is′-tic**, *adj.*

jinks (jĭngks), *n.pl.* *Colloq.* romping games or play; boisterous, unrestrained merrymaking, esp. in the phrase *high jinks.*

jinn (jĭn), *n.pl., sing.* **jinni.** 1. *Mohammedan Myth.* a class of spirits lower than the angels, capable of appear-ing in human and animal forms, and influencing mankind for good and evil. 2. (*construed as sing. with pl.* **jinns**) a spirit of this class. [t. Ar., pl. of *jinnī* a demon. Cf. GENIE.]

Jin·nah (jĭn′ə), *n.* **Mo-hammed Ali** (mō·hăm′ĭd ä′lē), 1876–1948, Moslem leader in India: gover-nor general of Pakistan, 1947–1948.

jin·rik·i·sha (jĭn·rĭk′shô, -shä), *n.* a small two-wheeled hooded vehicle drawn by one or more men, used in Japan and elsewhere. Also, **jin·rick′sha.** [t. Jap.: lit. manpower carriage]

Jinrikisha

Jin·sen (jĭn′sĕn′), *n.* Japanese name of **Inchon.**

jinx (jĭngks), *n.* *Colloq.* a person, thing, or influence supposed to bring bad luck. [var. of *jynx*, t. L: m. *iynx*, t. Gk.: bird (wryneck) used in witchcraft, hence, a spell]

ji·pi·ja·pa (hē′pē·hä′pä), *n.* 1. a tropical American palmlike plant (*Carludovica palmata,* family *Cyclan-thaceae*). 2. a Panama hat made from the young leaves of this plant. [named after a town in Ecuador]

jit·ney (jĭt′nĭ), *n., pl.* **-neys,** *v.,* **-neyed, -neying.** —*n.* 1. *U.S. Colloq.* an automobile which carries passengers, orig. each for a fare of five cents. 2. *U.S. Slang.* a five-cent piece. —*v.t., v.i.* 3. to carry or ride in a jitney.

jit·ter (jĭt′ər), *U.S. Slang.* —*n.* 1. (*pl.*) nervousness; nerves. —*v.i.* 2. to behave nervously. [var. of *chitter* shiver. Cf. CHATTER.]

jit·ter·bug (jĭt′ər·bŭg′), *n., v.,* **-bugged, -bugging.** —*n.* 1. one whose enthusiastic responses to the rhythms of swing music take the form of violent and unpredictable dance motions. —*v.i.* 2. to dance in such a manner.

jit·ter·y (jĭt′ər·ĭ), *adj.* *U.S. Slang.* nervous; jumpy.

jiu·jit·su (jōō·jĭt′sōō), *n.* jujitsu. Also, **jiu·jut′su.**

jive (jīv), *n.* *Slang.* 1. the talk of swing enthusiasts. 2. swing music.

JJ., 1. Judges. 2. Justices.

Jno., John.

jo (jō), *n., pl.* **joes.** *Scot.* sweetheart. Also, **joe.** [var. of JOY]

Jo·a·chim (yō′ä·КНĭm, yō·ä′-), *n.* **Joseph** (yō′zĕf), 1831–1907, German violinist and composer.

Joan (jōn), *n.* 1. mythical female pope about A.D. 855–858. 2. ("Fair Maid of Kent") 1328–85, wife of Edward, the Black Prince, and mother of Richard II.

jo·an·nes (jō·ăn′ēz), *n., pl.* **-nes.** johannes.

Joan of Arc, 1412–31, French heroine, called "the Maid of Orléans," who aroused the spirit of nationality in France against the English and was burned by them as a witch. In 1920 she was canonized. Also, *French,* **Jeanne d'Arc.**

job[1] (jŏb), *n., v.,* **jobbed, jobbing,** *adj.* —*n.* 1. a piece of work; an individual piece of work done in the routine of one's occupation or trade. 2. a piece of work of defined character undertaken for a fixed price. 3. anything one has to do. 4. *U.S.* a situation, or post of employment. 5. *Colloq.* an affair, matter, occurrence, or state of affairs: *to make the best of a bad job.* 6. the unit or material being worked upon. 7. the product or result. 8. a piece of public or official business carried through with a view to improper private gain. 9. *Slang.* a theft or robbery, or any criminal deed. —*v.i.* 10. to work at jobs or odd pieces of work; work by the piece. 11. to do business as a jobber. 12. to turn public business, etc., improperly to private gain. —*v.t.* 13. to buy in large quantities and sell to dealers in smaller lots. 14. to let out (work) in separate portions, as among dif-ferent contractors or workmen. —*adj.* 15. of or for a particular job or transaction. 16. bought or sold to-gether; lumped together: used chiefly in the phrase *job lot.* [orig. uncert.] —**job′less,** *adj.* —**job′less·ness,** *n.* —Syn. 4. See **position.**

job[2] (jŏb), *v.t., v.i.,* **jobbed, jobbing,** *n.* jab. [ME *jobbe(n);* ? imit. Cf. JAB]

Job (jōb), *n.* 1. the much-afflicted hero of a dramatic Old Testament book of wisdom. 2. the book itself. [ult. t. Heb.: m. *Iyyōbh*]

job·ber (jŏb′ər), *n.* 1. a wholesale merchant, esp. one selling to retailers. 2. (formerly) a merchant who dealt

in special, odd, or job lots. 3. one who perpetrate corrupt public or official jobs. 4. a pieceworker.

job·ber·y (jŏb′ər·ĭ), *n.* 1. the practice of making im proper private gains from a public business or trus 2. the perpetration of corrupt public or official jobs.

job lot, 1. any large lot of goods handled by a jobbe 2. a sundry amount, usually of poor quality.

job printer, a printer who does miscellaneous work as the printing of cards, posters, etc. —**job printing**

Job's comforter, one who depresses and discourage under the appearance or with the purpose of consolin

Job's-tears (jōbz′tĭrz′), *n.pl.* 1. the hard, nearl globular involucres which surround the female flowers i a species of grass, *Coix Lacryma-Jobi,* and which whe ripe are used as beads. 2. (*construed as sing., l.c.*) th grass itself, native in Asia but cultivated elsewhere.

job work, 1. miscellaneous printing work, as card circulars, posters, etc. 2. work done by the job.

Jo·cas·ta (jō·kăs′tə), *n.* Gk. Legend. the wife of Laiu and the mother, and later the wife, of Oedipus.

Jock (jŏk), *n.* nickname for a Scot.

jock·ey (jŏk′ĭ), *n., pl.* **-eys,** *v.,* **-eyed, -eying.** —*n* 1. one who professionally rides horses in races. —*v* 2. to ride (a horse) as a jockey. 3. to bring, put, etc by skillful maneuvering. 4. to trick or cheat. 5. t manipulate trickily. —*v.i.* 6. to aim at an advantag by skillful maneuvering. 7. to act trickily; seek a advantage by trickery. [dim. of *Jock,* Scot. var. c *Jack*] —**jock′ey·ship′,** *n.*

jock·o (jŏk′ō), *n., pl.* **jockos.** 1. the chimpanze 2. (*cap.*) a familiar name for any monkey. [t. F, from V Afr. name of the chimpanzee, recorded as *engeco, ncheko*

jock·strap (jŏk′străp′), *n.* an athletic supporter wor by men.

jo·cose (jō·kōs′), *adj.* given to or characterized b joking; jesting; humorous; playful. [t. L: m.s. *jocōsus*] —**jo·cose′ly,** *adv.* —**jo·cose′ness,** *n.* —Syn. See **jovia**

jo·cos·i·ty (jō·kŏs′ə·tĭ), *n., pl.* **-ties.** 1. state o of being jocose. 2. joking or jesting. 3. a joke or jes

joc·u·lar (jŏk′yə·lər), *adj.* given to, characterized by intended for, or suited to joking or jesting; waggish facetious. [t. L: s. *joculāris*] —**joc′u·lar·ly,** *adv.* —Syn See **jovial.**

joc·u·lar·i·ty (jŏk′yə·lăr′ə·tĭ), *n., pl.* **-ties.** 1. state o quality of being jocular. 2. jocular speech or behavio 3. a jocular remark or act.

joc·und (jŏk′ənd, jō′kənd), *adj.* cheerful; merry; ga blithe; glad. [ME, t. LL: s. *jocundus* pleasant] —**joc′ und·ly,** *adv.* —Syn. See **jovial.**

jo·cun·di·ty (jō·kŭn′də·tĭ), *n., pl.* **-ties.** 1. state o being jocund; gaiety. 2. a jocund remark or act.

Jodh·pur (jōd′pŏŏr), *n.* 1. Also, Marwar. a forme state in NW India, now in Rajasthan. 2. a city i Rajasthan. 180,717 (1951).

jodh·purs (jōd′pərz, jōd′-), *n.pl.* riding breeche reaching to the ankle, and fitting closely from the kne down, worn also in sports, etc. [named after JODHPUR

Joe (jō), *n.* *U.S. Colloq.* G. I. Joe.

joe (jō), *n.* jo.

Jo·el (jō′əl), *n.* a Hebrew prophet of the postexilia period, second among the "minor prophets" in the pro phetic canon. [ult. t. Heb.: m. *Yō′ēl*]

joe-pye weed (jō′pī′), 1. a tall composite weed *Eupatorium purpureum,* of North America, with cluster of pinkish or purple flowers. 2. a related species, E *maculatum,* with similar flowers, and stems that are ofte spotted with purple (**spotted joe-pye weed**).

jo·ey (jō′ĭ), *n., pl.* **-eys.** *Australia.* 1. any youn animal, esp. a kangaroo. 2. a young child. [t. nativ Australian: m. *joě*]

Jof·fre (zhôf′r), *n.* **Joseph Jacques Césaire** (zhō·zĕf zhäk sě·zĕr′), 1852–1931, French general in World War I

jog[1] (jŏg), *v.,* **jogged, jogging,** *n.* —*v.t.* 1. to move o shake with a push or jerk. 2. to give a slight push to, a to arouse the attention; nudge. 3. to stir up by hint o reminder: *to jog a person's memory.* 4. *Print.* to straight en (sheets of paper) by jolting them into alignment —*v.i.* 5. to move with a jolt or jerk. 6. to go or trave with a jolting pace or motion. 7. to go in a steady o humdrum fashion (fol. by *on* or *along*). —*n.* 8. a shake a slight push; a nudge. 9. a slow, steady walk, trot, etc 10. act of jogging. [b. *jot* jolt and *shog* shake (bot now d.)] —**jog′ger,** *n.*

jog[2] (jŏg), *n.* *Chiefly U.S.* an irregularity of line or sur face; a projection; a notch. [var. of JAG[1]]

jog·gle (jŏg′əl), *v.,* **-gled, -gling,** *n.* —*v.t.* 1. to shak slightly; move to and fro as by repeated jerks. 2. t join or fasten by a joggle or joggles. 3. to fit or faste with dowels. —*v.i.* 4. to move irregularly; have a jo ging or jolting motion; shake. —*n.* 5. act of joggling 6. a slight shake; a jolt. 7. a moving with jolts or jerk 8. a projection on one of two joining surfaces, or a notcl on the other, to prevent slipping. 9. a key or dowel be tween two surfaces, as for joining two blocks of masonry 10. a joint formed in either way. [freq. of JOG[1]]

joggle post, *Bldg. Trades.* a post having shoulders o notches for receiving the lower ends or feet of struts.

Jog·ja·kar·ta (jŏg′yä·kär′tä), *n.* a city in Indonesia in S Java. 244,379 (est. 1952). Also, **Jokyakarta.** Dutch **Djokjakarta.**

jog trot, 1. a slow, regular, jolting pace, as of horse. 2. a routine or humdrum mode of procedure.

o·han·nes (jō hăn′ēz), *n., pl.* **-nes.** a Portuguese gold coin formerly current, worth about $9, and named from King John (João) V (who reigned 1706–50), by whom it was first issued. Also, **joannes.** [t. NL and ML, var. of LL *Jōannes.* See JOHN]

o·han·nes·burg (jō hän′Ỹs bûrg′, yō hän′əs bœrkн′), *n.* a city in the N part of the Republic of South Africa, in Transvaal: gold mines. 629,847 (1951); with suburbs, 1,189,443 (1951).

John (jŏn), *n.* **1.** the Apostle John, to whom is attributed the authorship of the fourth Gospel, three Epistles, and the Book of Revelation. **2.** the fourth Gospel, in the New Testament. **3.** one of the three Epistles of John, referred to as 1, 2, and 3 John. **4.** John the Baptist. Mark 1:4, etc. **5.** any of several characters with this name in the Bible. **6.** name of twenty-three popes. **7.** (*John Lackland*) 1167?–1216, king of England, 1199–1216, who signed the Magna Charta in 1215. **8.** **Augustus Edwyn,** 1879–1961, British painter and etcher. [ME *Iohan, John,* OE *Iohannis,* t. ML: m. *Jōhannes,* LL *Jōannes.* t. Gk.: m. *Iōánnēs,* t. Heb.: m. *Yōḥānān,* lit., Jehovah hath been gracious]

John I, (*"the Great"*) 1357–1433, king of Portugal, 1385–1433.

John III, (*John Sobieski*) 1624–96, king of Poland, 1674–96.

John XXIII, (*Angelo Giuseppe Roncalli*), 1881–1963, Italian ecclesiastic: pope 1958–63.

John Bull, **1.** the English people. **2.** the typical Englishman.

John Doe, a fictitious personage in legal proceedings.

John Do·ry (dōr′Ỹ). a thin, deep-bodied marine fish, *Zeus faber,* with spiny plates along the base of the dorsal and anal fins. Also, **John Do′ree.** [f. JOHN + DORY² (*doree*), the name of the fish]

Joh·ne's disease (yō′nəz), *Vet. Sci.* a chronic diarrheal disease of cattle and sheep caused by infection with an organism related to the tubercle bacillus.

John F. Kennedy International Airport, *n.* formerly Idlewild, principal airport for New York City.

John Hancock, *U.S. Colloq.* one's signature. [from the first signer of the Declaration of Independence]

John·ny·cake (jŏn′Ỹ kāk′), *n. U.S.* a kind of cake or bread made of corn meal, water or milk, and often eggs, etc.; corn bread. [orig. obscure. The first element may be from obs. *jonakin, jonikin* (appar. of Indian origin) a form of thin griddlecake]

John·ny-jump-up (jŏn′Ỹ jŭmp′ŭp′), *n. U.S.* **1.** any of certain violets, esp. *Viola Kitaibeliana* var. *Rafinesqii.* **2.** a small form of the pansy, *Viola tricolor.*

Johnny on the spot, *Colloq.* one who is on hand to perform a duty, seize an opportunity, etc.

John of Austria, Don, 1547?–1578, Spanish naval commander and general.

John of Gaunt (gônt, gänt). See **Gaunt.**

John of Ley·den (lī′dən), 1509?–36, Dutch Anabaptist.

John o'Groat's House (ə grōts′, ə grōts′), a place at the northern tip of Scotland, often appearing in the phrase *from Land's End to John O'Groats.*

John·son (jŏn′sən), *n.* **1.** **Andrew,** 1808–75, 17th president of the U. S., 1865–69. **2.** **Charles Spurgeon** (spûr′jən), 1893–1956, U.S. educator and sociologist. **3.** **James Weldon,** 1871–1938, U.S. author. **4.** **Lyndon Baines** (lin′dən bānz), born 1908, 36th president of the U. S., since 1963. **5.** **Samuel,** 1709–84, British author and lexicographer. **6.** **Sir William,** 1715–74, American colonial administrator and soldier, born in Ireland.

Johnson City, a city in NE Tennessee. 29,892 (1960).

John·son·ese (jŏn′sə nēz′, -nēs′), *n.* a literary style characterized by pompous phraseology and many words of Latin origin (so called from that of Samuel Johnson).

John·so·ni·an (jŏn sō′nỸ ən), *adj.* having the quality of Johnsonese.

John·ston (jŏn′stən, -sən), *n.* **1.** **Albert Sidney,** 1803–62, Confederate general in the U. S. Civil War. **2.** **Joseph Eggleston** (ĕg′əl stən), 1807–91, Confederate general in the U. S. Civil War.

Johns·town (jŏnz′toun′), *n.* a city in SW Pennsylvania: disastrous flood, 1889. 53,949 (1960).

John the Baptist, forerunner of Jesus. Mat. 3.

Jo·hore (jə hōr′), *n.* a state in the former Federation of Malaya: now part of the Federation of Malaysia. 505,522 pop. (1957); 7330 sq. mi. *Cap.:* Johore.

joie de vi·vre (zhwȧ də vē′vr), *French.* joy of living.

join (join), *v.t.* **1.** to bring or put together, in contact or connection. **2.** to come into contact, connection, or union with: *the brook joins the river.* **3.** to bring together in relation, purpose, action, coexistence, etc.: *to join forces.* **4.** to become a member of (a society, regiment, party, etc.). **5.** to come into the company of: *I'll join you later.* **6.** to unite in marriage. **7.** to meet or engage in (battle, conflict, etc.). **8.** to adjoin: *his land joins mine.* **9.** *Geom.* to draw a curve or straight line between. —*v.i.* **10.** to come into or be in contact or connection, or form a junction. **11.** to become united, associated, or combined; associate or ally oneself (fol. by *with*). **12.** to take part with others (often fol. by *in*). **13.** to be contiguous or close; lie or come together; form a junction. **14.** to enlist in a branch of the armed forces. **15.** *Obs.* to meet in battle or conflict. —*n.* **16.** joining. **17.** a place or line of joining; a seam. [ME *join(en),* t. OF: m. *joindre,* g. L *jungere* join, yoke]

—**Syn. 1.** link, couple, fasten, attach; conjoin, combine; associate; consolidate, amalgamate. JOIN, CONNECT, UNITE all imply bringing two or more things together more or less closely. JOIN may refer to a connection or association of any degree of closeness, but often implies direct contact: *one joins the corners of a mortise together.* CONNECT implies a joining as by a tie, link, wire, etc.: *one connects two batteries.* UNITE implies a close joining of two or more things so as to form one: *one unites layers of veneer sheets to form plywood.*

join·der (join′dər), *n.* **1.** act of joining. **2.** *Law.* **a.** the joining of causes of action in a suit. **b.** the joining of parties in a suit. **c.** the acceptance by a party to an action of an issue tendered. [t. F: m. *joindre* JOIN]

join·er (joi′nər), *n.* **1.** one who or that which joins. **2.** a carpenter, esp. one who constructs doors, windows, and other fittings of houses, ships, etc. *Joiner* is used in England where Americans say *carpenter.*

join·er·y (joi′nə rỸ), *n.* **1.** the art or trade of a joiner. **2.** a joiner's work or his product.

joint (joint), *n.* **1.** the place or part in which two things, or parts of one thing, are joined or united, either rigidly or so as to admit of motion; an articulation. **2.** (in an animal body) **a.** the movable place or part where two bones or two segments join. **b.** the hingelike or other arrangement of such a part. **3.** out of joint, **a.** dislocated. **b.** out of order; in a bad state. **4.** *Biol.* **a.** a portion, esp. of an animal or plant body, connected with another portion by an articulation, node, or the like. **b.** a portion between two articulations, nodes, or the like. **5.** *Bot.* the part of a stem from which a branch or a leaf grows; a node. **6.** one of the portions into which a carcass is divided by a butcher. **7.** *Geol.* a fracture plane in rocks, generally at right angles to the bedding of sedimentary rocks and variously oriented in igneous and metamorphic rocks, commonly arranged in two or more sets of parallel intersecting systems. **8.** *U.S. Slang.* **a.** a cheap, sordid place, as for opium smoking or the illicit sale of liquor. **b.** any resort or abode. [ME *iointe,* t. OF: m. *joint, jointe* (n. use of pp. of *joindre* JOIN) g. L *junctus, juncta,* prop. pp. of *jungere*] —*adj.* **9.** shared by or common to two or more. **10.** sharing or acting in common. **11.** joined or associated, as in relation, interest, or action: *joint owners.* **12.** held, done, etc., by two or more in conjunction or in common: *joint ownership.* **13.** *Law.* joined together in obligation or ownership. **14.** *Parl. Proc.* of or pertaining to both legislative branches. **15.** (of diplomatic action) in which two or more governments are formally united. —*v.t.* **16.** to unite by a joint or joints. **17.** to form or provide with a joint or joints. **18.** to divide at a joint, or separate into pieces. **19.** to prepare (a board, etc.) for fitting into a joint. [ME, t. OF, pp. of *joindre* JOIN]

joint account, a bank account in the names of two or more persons or parties.

Joint Chiefs of Staff, *U.S.* the Chiefs of Staff of the Army, of Naval Operations, and of the Air Force, serving, with a Chairman, as the principal military advisory board to the President and Secretary of Defense.

joint·ed (join′tĬd), *adj.* provided with joints; formed with knots or nodes.

joint·er (join′tər), *n.* **1.** one who or that which joins. **2.** an implement or machine used in making joints. **3.** *Agric.* an instrument with a triangular head, used with a plow to bury trash.

joint ill, *Vet. Sci.* a disease of young foals (horses) characterized by swollen inflamed joints, high fever, and, usually, by death a few days after birth.

joint·ly (joint′lỸ), *adv.* together; in common.

joint resolution, a resolution adopted by both branches of a legislative assembly and requiring the signature of the chief executive to become law.

joint stock, **1.** stock or capital divided into a number of shares. **2.** a pool of stock held in common.

joint-stock company (joint′stŏk′), **1.** *U.S. Law.* an unincorporated business partnership or association of individuals, of which the capital is represented by transferable shares of stock. **2.** *Brit. Law.* any incorporated business with transferable shares of stock.

joint-stock corporation, a corporation whose ownership is divided into transferable shares, the object usually being the division of profits among the members in proportion to the number of shares held by each.

join·ture (join′chər), *n. Law.* an estate or property settled on a woman in consideration of marriage, and to be enjoyed by her after her husband's decease. [ME, t. F, g. L *junctūra* a joining]

joint·weed (joint′wēd′), *n.* an American polygonaceous herb, *Polygonella articulata,* with many-jointed spikelike racemes of small white or rose-colored flowers.

joint·worm (joint′wûrm′), *n.* the larva of certain hymenopterous insects of the family *Eurytomidae,* very injurious to grain, esp. at the joints of the stalk.

Join·ville (zhwăṅ vēl′), *n.* **Jean de** (zhäṅ də), c1224–c1319, French chronicler.

joist (joist), *n.* **1.** one of the pieces of timber to which are fastened the boards of a floor, the laths of a ceiling, or the like. —*v.t.* **2.** to furnish with or fix on joists. [ME *giste,* t. OF, der. *gesir* lie, rest, g. L *jacēre* lie; akin to GIST] —**joist′less,** *adj.*

A. Joist; B. Floor boards

Jo·kai (yō′koi), *n.* **Maurus** (mou′rŏŏs) or **Mór** (mōr′), 1825–1904, Hungarian author.

joke (jōk), *n.*, *v.*, **joked, joking.** —*n.* **1.** something said or done to excite laughter or amusement; a playful or mischievous trick or remark. **2.** an amusing or ridiculous circumstance. **3.** an object of joking or jesting; a thing or person laughed at rather than taken seriously. **4.** a matter for joking about; trifling matter: *the loss was no joke.* **5.** joking or jesting. —*v.i.* **6.** to speak or act in a playful or merry way. **7.** to say something in mere sport, rather than in earnest. —*v.t.* **8.** to subject to jokes; banter, rally, or chaff. [t. L: m.s. *jocus* jest, sport] —joke′less, *adj.* —jok′ing·ly *adv.*
—**Syn.** . witticism, jape; quip quirk, sally. JOKE, JEST refer to something said (or done) in sport, or to cause amusement A JOKE is something said or done for the sake of exciting laughter; it may be raillery, a witty remark, or a prank or trick: *to tell a joke.* JEST, today a more formal word, nearly always refers to joking language and is more suggestive of scoffing or ridicule than is JOKE: *to speak in jest.*

jok·er (jō′kər), *n.* **1.** one who jokes. **2.** an extra playing card in a pack, used in some games, often counting as the highest card or to represent a card of any denomination or suit the holder wishes. **3.** *U.S.* a clause or expression inserted in a legislative bill with the unavowed object of defeating the ostensible purpose of the bill if passed. **4.** a hidden clause in any paper, document, etc., which largely changes its apparent nature. **5.** any device or expedient for getting the better of another.

Jok·ya·kar·ta (jōk′yä·kär′tä), *n.* Jogjakarta.

Jo·li·et (jō′lĭ·ĕt′, jō′lĭ·ĕt′; *Fr.* zhô lyĕ′ *for 1 also*), *n.* **1.** Also, Jol′li·et′. **Louis** (lwē), 1645–1700, French explorer of the Mississippi. **2.** a city in NE Illinois. 66,780 (1960).

jol·li·fi·ca·tion (jŏl′ə·fə·kā′shən), *n.* jolly merrymaking; a jolly festivity. [f. JOLLY, adj. + -FICATION]

jol·li·fy (jŏl′ə·fī′), *v.t.*, *v.i.*, **-fied, -fying.** *Colloq.* to make or be jolly or merry.

jol·li·ty (jŏl′ə·tĭ), *n.*, *pl.* **-ties.** **1.** jolly state, mood, or proceedings. **2.** (*pl.*) jolly festivities.

jol·ly (jŏl′ĭ), *adj.*, **-lier, -liest,** *v.*, **-lied, -lying,** *n.*, *pl.* **-lies,** *adv.* —*adj.* **1.** in good spirits, gay: *in a moment he was as jolly as ever.* **2.** cheerfully festive or convivial. **3.** *Chiefly Brit. Colloq.* fine; pleasing. **4.** *Brit. Colloq.* big or great: *a jolly fool.* **5.** joyous, glad, or gay. —*v.t.* **6.** *Colloq.* to talk or act agreeably to (a person) in order to keep him in good humor; banter pleasantly. **7.** *Colloq.* to make fun of. —*v.i.* **8.** *Colloq.* to jolly a person. —*n.* **9.** *Colloq.* a bit of agreeable talk or action intended to put or keep a person in good humor, often in order to secure some end. —*adv.* **10.** *Brit. Colloq.* extremely; very: *jolly well.* [ME *joli*(*f*), t. OF, ? ult. of Gmc. orig.; cf. Icel. *jōl* YULE] —jol′li·ly, *adv.* —jol′li·ness, *n.* —**Syn. 1, 2.** merry, sportive, playful. See **gay.**

jolly boat, a ship's work boat, smaller than a cutter, hoisted at the stern of a sailing vessel for handy use.

Jolly Rog·er (rŏj′ər), the pirates' flag.

Jo·lo (hô lō′), *n.* **1.** one of the Philippine Islands, in the SW part: the main island of the Sulu Archipelago. 116,000 pop. (est. 1948); 345 sq. mi. **2.** a seaport on this island. 18,282 (1948).

jolt (jōlt), *v.t.*, *v.i.* **1.** to jar or shake as by a sudden rough thrust; shake up roughly, as in passing over an uneven road. —*n.* **2.** a jolting shock or movement. [b. *jot* jolt and obs. *joll* knock about] —jolt′er, *n.*

jolt·y (jōl′tĭ), *adj.* jolting.

Jo·nah (jō′nə), *n.* **1.** a Hebrew prophet who for his impiety was thrown overboard from his ship to allay a tempest. He was swallowed by a large fish and lived in its belly three days before he was vomited up. **2.** a book of the Old Testament bearing his name. **3.** any person regarded as bringing bad luck. Also, **Jo·nas** (jō′nəs).

Jon·a·than (jŏn′ə·thən), *n.* **1.** son of Saul, and friend of David. 1 Sam. 13, etc. **2.** *Hort.* a variety of red apple that matures in early fall. **3.** *Obsolesc.* a generic nickname for Americans, or, esp., New Englanders (often prefaced by *Brother*). [ult. t. Heb.: m. *Yonāthān*]

Jones (jōnz), *n.* **1. Casey** (kā′sĭ), (*John Luther Jones*), ?–1900, U.S. railroad engineer whose heroic death in train wreck inspired popular song about him. **2. Daniel,** born 1881, British phonetician. **3. Henry Arthur,** 1851–1929, British dramatist. **4. Inigo** (ĭn′ĭ gō′), 1572–1652, British architect. **5. John Paul,** 1747–92, American naval commander in the Revolutionary War, born in Scotland.

jon·gleur (jŏng′glər; *Fr.* zhôN glœr′), *n.* (in medieval France and Norman England) an itinerant minstrel or entertainer who sang songs (sometimes of his own composition), told stories, and otherwise entertained people. [t. F, b. OF *jogleor* and *jangler* JANGLE. See JUGGLER]

jon·quil (jŏng′kwĭl, jŏn′-), *n.* a species of narcissus, *Narcissus Jonquilla,* with long, narrow, rushlike leaves and fragrant yellow or white flowers. [t. F: m. *jonquille,* t. Sp.: m. *junquillo,* dim. of *junco,* g. L *juncus* a rush]

Jon·son (jŏn′sən), *n.* **Ben,** 1573?–1637, English dramatist and poet.

Jop·lin (jŏp′lĭn), *n.* city in SW Missouri. 38,958 (1960).

Jop·pa (jŏp′ə), *n.* ancient name of Jaffa.

Jor·dan (jôr′dən), *n.* **1.** a country in SW Asia, consisting of what was formerly Trans-Jordan plus a part of Palestine. 1,403,000 pop. (est. 1954); 37,264 sq.mi. *Cap.*: Amman. Official name, **Hashemite Kingdom of Jordan. 2.** a river flowing from S Lebanon through the Sea of Galilee and S between Israel and Jordan, then through W Jordan into the Dead Sea. ab. 200 mi. **3. David Starr,** 1851–1931, U. S. biologist and educator.

Jordan almond, a large, hard-shelled, high-quali[ty] type of Spanish almond. [ME *jardyne* (t. F: m. *jard*[in] garden) *almaunde,* i.e. garden almond. See ALMOND]

jo·rum (jōr′əm), *n.* a large bowl or vessel for holdi[ng] drink, or its contents: *a jorum of punch.* [said to [be] named after *Joram,* who brought to David vessels [of] silver, gold, and brass. See 2 Sam. 8:10]

Jo·seph (jō′zəf), *n.* **1.** a Hebrew patriarch, the fir[st] son of Jacob by Rachel. His brothers sold him into sla[v]ery in Egypt. Gen. 30:22–24, Gen. 37. **2.** the husba[nd] of Mary, the mother of Jesus. Matt. 1:16–25. **3.** (*l.c.*) a long cloak with a cape, worn chiefly in the 18t[h] century, esp. by women. [ult. t. Heb.: m. *Yōsēph*]

Joseph II, 1741–90, emperor of the Holy Roma[n] Empire, 1765–90.

Jo·se·phine (jō′zə fēn′), *n.* 1763–1814, first wife [of] Napoleon Bonaparte.

Joseph of Ar·i·ma·the·a (ăr′ə mə thē′ə), a ri[ch] Israelite who believed in Christ and who laid the bo[dy] of Jesus in the tomb. Matt. 27:57–60.

Jo·se·phus (jō sē′fəs), *n.* **Flavius** (flā′vĭ əs), A.D. 37[?]–95. Jewish historian, writing in Aramaic and Greek.

josh (jŏsh), *U.S. Slang.* —*v.t.*, *v.i.* **1.** to chaff; banter [in] a teasing way. —*n.* **2.** a chaffing remark; a piece [of] bant[er]. [? var. of d. *joss* jostle] —josh′er, *n.*

Josh., Joshua.

Josh·u·a (jŏsh′ōō ə), *n.* **1.** the successor of Moses [as] leader of the Israelites. Exodus 17:9–14. **2.** a book [of] the Old Testament. [ult. t. Heb.: m. *Yehōshūa*′]

Joshua tree, a tree, *Yucca brevifolia,* growing in ari[d] or desert regions of the southwestern U. S. See **yucca.**

joss (jŏs), *n.* a Chinese deity or idol. [pidgin Englis[h] t. Pg.: m. *deos,* g. L *deus* god]

joss house, a Chinese temple for idol worship.

joss stick, a slender stick of a dried fragrant past[e] burned by the Chinese as incense, etc.

jos·tle (jŏs′əl), *v.*, **-tled, -tling,** *n.* —*v.t.* **1.** to strike [or] push roughly or rudely against; elbow roughly; hustl[e] **2.** to drive or force by or as by pushing or shovin[g] —*v.i.* **3.** to collide (fol. by *with*) or strike or push (fol. b[y] *against*) as in passing or in a crowd; push or elbow one['s] way rudely. **4.** to strive as with collisions, rough pus[h]ing, etc., for room, place, or any advantage. —*n.* **5.** collision, shock, or push. Also, **justle.** [ME *justil,* freq. [of] *just* JOUST] —jos′tle·ment, *n.* —jos′tler, *n.*

jot (jŏt), *n.*, *v.*, **jotted, jotting.** —*n.* **1.** the least part [of] something; a little bit: *I don't care a jot.* —*v.t.* **2.** [to] write or mark down briefly (usually fol. by *down*). [t. L[.] m. *iōta* IOTA] —jot′ter, *n.*

jot·ting (jŏt′ĭng), *n.* **1.** act of one who jots. **2.** som[e]thing jotted down; a brief note or memorandum.

Jo·tun (yô′tŏon), *n. Scand. Myth.* one of a supe[r] natural race of giants. Also, **Jo′tunn, Jö·tunn** (yœ′[ ] tŏon). [Icel., prop. *Jötunn,* c. OE *eoten* giant]

Jo·tun·heim (yô′tŏon hām′), *n. Scand. Myth.* th[e] outer world, or realm of giants; Utgard. Als[o] **Jo′tunn·heim′, Jö·tunn·heim** (yœ′tŏon hām′). [Icel.]

Jou·bert (zhōō bĕr′), *n.* **Joseph** (zhô zĕf′), 1754–182[4] French moralist and essayist.

joule (joul, jōōl), *n. Physics.* a unit of work or energ[y] equal to 10[7] ergs; one watt-second (approximately 0.7[ ] foot-pounds). [named after J. P. JOULE]

Joule (joul), *n.* **James Prescott,** 1818–89, Britis[h] physicist.

jounce (jouns), *v.*, **jounced, jouncing,** *n.* —*v.i.*, *v.t.* [1.] to move violently up and down; bounce. —*n.* **2.** a jounc[e]ing movement. [? b. obs. *joll* knock about and BOUNCE]

jour., journal.

Jour·dan (zhōōr dän′), *n.* **Jean Baptiste** (zhän bä[ ] tēst′), **Count,** 1762–1833, French marshal.

jour·nal (jûr′nəl), *n.* **1.** a daily record, as of occur[ ] rences, experiences, or observations. **2.** a register of th[e] daily transactions of a public or legislative body. **3.** [a] periodical, as the weekly newspapers of the 17th centur[y,] esp. the serials devoted to learned societies and pro[ ] fessions. **4.** a newspaper, magazine, or the like. **5.** *Book[ ] keeping.* **a.** a daybook. **b.** (in double entry) a book i[n] which all transactions are entered (from the daybook or blotter) in systematic form, to facilitate postin[g] into the ledger. **6.** *Naut.* a log or logbook. **7.** *Mach.* that part of a shaft or axle in actual contact with [a] bearing. [ME, t. OF, g. LL *diurnālis* DIURNAL]

journal box, *Mach.* a bearing or box which contain[s] a journal (def. 7).

jour·nal·ese (jûr′nə lēz′, -lēs′), *n.* the style of writin[g] or expression (less considered than that of convention[al] literary work) supposed to characterize newspapers.

jour·nal·ism (jûr′nə lĭz′əm), *n.* **1.** the occupation [of] writing for, editing, and conducting newspapers an[d] other periodicals. **2.** newspapers collectively.

jour·nal·ist (jûr′nəl ĭst), *n.* one engaged in jour[ ] nalism (used more widely in England than U.S.).

jour·nal·is·tic (jûr′nə lĭs′tĭk), *adj.* of, pertaining to or characteristic of journalists or journalism. —jour[ ] nal·is′ti·cal·ly, *adv.*

jour·nal·ize (jûr′nə līz′), *v.*, **-ized, -izing.** —*v.t.* **1.** [to] enter or record in a journal. **2.** to tell or relate, as don[e] in a journal. **3.** (in double-entry bookkeeping) to sys[ ] tematize and enter in a journal, preparatory to postin[g] to the ledger. —*v.i.* **4.** to keep or make entries in [a] journal. **5.** to engage in journalism. Also, *esp. Brit.* **jour·nal·ise′.**

jour·ney (jûr′nĭ), *n.*, *pl.* **-neys**, *v.*, **-neyed**, **-neying.** —*n.* **1.** a course of travel from one place to another, esp. by land. **2.** a distance traveled, or suitable for traveling, in a specified time: *a day's journey.* —*v.i.* **3.** to make a journey; travel. [ME *jorney*, t. OF: m. *jornee* a day's time, ult. der. L *diurnus* of the day, daily] —**jour′ney·er**, *n.* —**Syn. 1.** excursion, jaunt; tour; expedition; pilgrimage. See **trip.**

jour·ney·man (jûr′nĭmən), *n.*, *pl.* **-men.** **1.** one who has served his apprenticeship at a trade or handicraft, and who works at it for another. **2.** *Obs.* one hired to do work for another usually for a day. [f. *journey* a day's work (obs.) + MAN]

jour·ney·work (jûr′nĭwûrk′), *n.* the work of a journeyman.

joust (jŭst, joust), *n.* **1.** a combat in which two armored knights or men-at-arms on horseback opposed each other with lances. **2.** (*pl.*) a tournament. —*v.i.* **3.** to contend in a joust or tournament. Also, **just.** [ME *j(o)uste(n)*, t. OF: m. *j(o)uster*, ult. der. L *juxtā* near] —**joust′er**, *n.*

Jove (jōv), *n.* **1.** Jupiter. **2.** *Poetic.* the planet Jupiter. **3. by Jove,** a mild oath, esp. common in England. [t. L: n.s. *Jovis.* See JUPITER]

jo·vi·al (jō′vĭəl), *adj.* **1.** endowed with or characterized by a hearty, joyous humor or a spirit of good-fellowship. **2.** (*cap.*) of or pertaining to the god Jove or Jupiter. [t. L: s. *Joviālis* of Jupiter (in astrology the planet is regarded as exerting a happy influence)] —**jo′vi·al·ly**, *adv.* —**jo′vi·al·ness**, *n.* —**Syn. 1.** merry, jolly, convivial, gay. JOVIAL, JOCOSE, JOCULAR, JOCUND agree in referring to someone who is in a good humor. JOVIAL suggests a hearty, joyous humor: *a jovial person.* JOCOSE refers to that which causes laughter; it suggests someone who is playful and given to jesting: *with jocose and comical airs.* JOCULAR means humorous, facetious, mirthful, and waggish: *jocular enough to keep up the spirits of all around him.* JOCUND, now a literary word, suggests a cheerful, light-hearted, and sprightly gaiety: *glad and jocund company.* —**Ant. 1.** saturnine, morose, gloomy, staid.

jo·vi·al·i·ty (jō′vĭăl′ə tĭ), *n.* state or quality of being jovial; merriment; jollity.

Jo·vi·an (jō′vĭən), *adj.* **1.** of the god Jupiter. **2.** of the planet Jupiter. **3.** (*Flavius Claudius Jovianus*) A.D. c332-364, Roman emperor, A.D. 363-364.

Jow·ett (joul′ĭt), *n.* **Benjamin,** 1817–93, British educator, Greek scholar, translator, and theologian.

jowl¹ (joul, jōl), *n.* **1.** a jaw, esp. the under jaw. **2.** the cheek. [ME *chawl, chavel*, OE *ceafl* jaw; akin to D *kevel* gum, d. G *kiefel* jaw, chap, Icel. *kjaptr* mouth, jaw]

jowl² (joul, jōl), *n.* **1.** a fold of flesh hanging from the jaw, as of a fat person. **2.** the dewlap of cattle. **3.** the wattle of fowls. [ME *cholle*, appar. der. OE *ceole* throat]

joy (joi), *n.* **1.** an emotion of keen or lively pleasure arising from present or expected good; exultant satisfaction; great gladness; delight. **2.** a source or cause of gladness or delight: *a thing of beauty is a joy forever.* **3.** a state of happiness or felicity. **4.** the manifestation of glad feeling; outward rejoicing; festive gaiety. —*v.i.* **5.** to feel joy; be glad; rejoice. —*v.t.* **6.** *Obs.* to gladden. [ME *joie*, t. OF, g. L *gaudia*, pl. of *gaudium* joy, gladness] —**Syn. 1.** rapture. **3.** bliss. See **pleasure.**

joy·ance (joi′əns), *n.* *Archaic.* joyous feeling; gladness.

Joyce (jois), *n.* **James,** 1882–1941, Irish author.

joy·ful (joi′fəl), *adj.* **1.** full of joy, as a person, the heart, etc.; glad; delighted. **2.** showing or expressing joy, as looks, actions, speech, etc. **3.** causing or bringing joy, as an event, a sight, news, etc.; delightful. —**joy′ful·ly**, *adv.* —**joy′ful·ness**, *n.* —**Syn. 1.** joyous, happy, blithe; buoyant, elated, jubilant. See **gay.**

joy·less (joi′lĭs), *adj.* **1.** destitute of joy or gladness. **2.** causing no joy or pleasure. —**joy′less·ly**, *adv.* —**joy′less·ness**, *n.* —**Syn. 1.** sad, cheerless; gloomy, dismal.

joy·ous (joi′əs), *adj.* joyful. —**joy′ous·ly**, *adv.* —**joy′ous·ness**, *n.*

joy ride, *Colloq.* a pleasure ride in an automobile, esp. when the car is driven recklessly or used without the owner's permission. —**joy rider.** —**joy riding.**

joy stick, the control stick of an airplane.

J.P., jet propulsion.

J.P., Justice of the Peace.

Jr., Junior. Also, **jr.**

Juan de Fu·ca (jōō′ən dĭ fū′kə; *Sp.* hwän′dĕ fōō′kä) a strait between Vancouver island and NW Washington. ab. 100 mi. long; 15–20 mi. wide.

Juan Fer·nán·dez (jōō′ən fər nän′dĕz; *Sp.* hwän′ fĕr nän′dĕth), a group of three islands in the S Pacific, ab. 400 miles W of and belonging to Chile: Alexander Selkirk, the supposed prototype of "Robinson Crusoe," was marooned here, 1704.

Juá·rez (hwä′rĕs), *n.* **1. Benito Pablo** (bĕ nē′tô pä′blô), 1806–72, president of Mexico, 1853–63, and 1867–72. **2.** Ciudad. See Ciudad Juárez.

Ju·ba (jōō′bä), *n.* a river flowing from S Ethiopia S through Somalia to the Indian Ocean. ab. 1000 mi. Italian, Giuba.

ju·ba (jōō′bə), *n.* a lively dance developed by plantation Negroes of the U.S.

Ju·bal (jōō′bəl), *n.* son of Lamech by Adah, and purported inventor of musical instruments. Gen. 4:21.

jub·bah (jŏŏb′bə), *n.* a kind of long outer garment with sleeves, worn in Mohammedan countries. [t. Ar.]

Jub·bul·pore (jŭb′əl pôr′), *n.* Jabalpur.

ju·be (jōō′bē), *n.* *Archit.* **1.** a screen with an upper platform, separating the choir of a church from the nave and often supporting a rood. **2.** a rood loft. [t. L: bid thou, the first word of a formula spoken from the gallery above the rood screen]

ju·bi·lant (jōō′bə lənt), *adj.* **1.** jubilating; rejoicing; exultant. **2.** expressing or exciting joy; manifesting or denoting exultation or gladness. [t. L: s. *jūbilans*, ppr.] —**ju′bi·lance, ju′bi·lan·cy**, *n.* —**ju′bi·lant·ly**, *adv.*

ju·bi·late (jōō′bə lāt′), *v.i.*, **-lated, -lating. 1.** to manifest or feel great joy; rejoice; exult. **2.** to celebrate a jubilee or joyful occasion. [t. L: m.s. *jūbilātus*, pp. of *jūbilāre* shout for joy] —**ju·bi·la·to·ry** (jōō′bə lə tôr′ĭ), *adj.*

Ju·bi·la·te (jōō′bə lä′tĭ, -lä′tĭ), *n.* **1.** the 100th Psalm (99th in the Vulgate), used as a canticle in the Anglican liturgy. **2.** the third Sunday (**Jubilate Sunday**) after Easter (when the 66th psalm, 65th in the Vulgate, is used as the introit). **3.** a musical setting of this psalm. [t. L: shout ye, the first word of both psalms in the Vulgate]

ju·bi·la·tion (jōō′bə lä′shən), *n.* **1.** act of jubilating; rejoicing; exultation. **2.** a joyful or festive celebration.

ju·bi·lee (jōō′bə lē′), *n.* **1.** the celebration of any of certain anniversaries, as the 25th (**silver jubilee**), 50th (**golden jubilee**), or 60th or 75th (**diamond jubilee**). **2.** the completion of the 50th year of any continuous course or period, as of existence or activity, or its celebration. **3.** *Rom. Cath. Ch.* an appointed year (or other period) now ordinarily every 25th year, in which remission from the penal consequences of sin is granted upon repentance and the performance of certain religious acts. **4.** (among the ancient Hebrews) a year to be observed every 50th year (see Lev. 25), and to be announced by the blowing of trumpets, during which the fields were to be left untilled, alienated lands to be restored, and Hebrew bondmen to be set free. **5.** any season or occasion of rejoicing or festivity. **6.** rejoicing or jubilation. [ME *jubile*, t. F, t. LL: m.s. *jūbilaeus*, t. Gk.: m. *iōbēlaios*, der. Heb. *yōbēl* ram, ram's horn (used as a trumpet; cf. Lev. 25:9)]

Jud., 1. Judges. **2.** Judith (Apocrypha).

Ju·dae·a (jōō dē′ə), *n.* Judea. —**Ju·dae′an**, *adj.*, *n.*

Ju·dah (jōō′də), *n.* **1.** the fourth son of Jacob and Leah. Gen. 29:35, etc. **2.** the powerful tribe of his descendants. **3.** an ancient kingdom in S Palestine, including the tribes of Judah and Benjamin. *Cap.:* Jerusalem. See **Israel.** [ult. t. Heb.: m. *Yehūdāh*]

Ju·da·ic (jōō dā′ĭk), *adj.* of or pertaining to the Jews; Jewish.

Ju·da·ism (jōō′dĭ ĭz′əm), *n.* the religious system and polity of the Jews.

Ju·da·ist (jōō′dĭ ĭst), *n.* **1.** an adherent of Judaism. **2.** a Jewish Christian in the early church who followed or advocated Jewish rites or practices. —**Ju′da·is′tic**, *adj.*

Ju·da·ize (jōō′dĭ īz′), *v.*, **-ized, -izing.** —*v.i.* **1.** to conform to Judaism in any respect; adopt or affect the manners or customs of the Jews. —*v.t.* **2.** to bring into conformity with Judaism. —**Ju′da·i·za′tion**, *n.* —**Ju′da·iz′er**, *n.*

Ju·das (jōō′dəs), *n.* **1.** Judas Iscariot, the disciple who betrayed Jesus. Mark 3:19. **2.** one treacherous enough to betray a friend. **3.** one of the twelve apostles (not Judas Iscariot). Luke 6:16; Acts 1:13; John 14:22. —**Ju′das·like′**, *adj.*

Judas Maccabaeus. See **Maccabaeus.**

Judas tree, 1. a purple-flowered leguminous European and Asiatic tree, *Cercis Siliquastrum*, supposed to be the kind upon which Judas hanged himself. **2.** any of various other trees of the same genus, as the redbud.

Jude (jōōd), *n.* a short book of the New Testament, written by a "brother of James" (and possibly of Jesus).

Ju·de·a (jōō dē′ə), *n.* the S part of Palestine under the Romans. Also, **Judaea.**

Ju·de·an (jōō dē′ən), *adj.* **1.** relating to Judea. **2.** of or pertaining to the Jews. —*n.* **3.** a native or inhabitant of Judea. **4.** a Jew. Also, **Judaean.** [f. m.s. L *Jūdaeus* (see JEW) + -AN]

Jude the Obscure, a novel (1895) by Thomas Hardy.

Judg., Judges.

judge (jŭj), *n.*, *v.*, **judged, judging.** —*n.* **1.** a public officer authorized to hear and determine causes in a court of law; a magistrate charged with the administering of justice. **2.** a person appointed to decide in any competition or contest; an authorized arbiter. **3.** one qualified to pass a critical judgment: *a judge of horses.* **4.** an administrative head of the Hebrew nation in the period between Joshua's death and Saul's accession. —*v.t.* **5.** to try (a person or a case) as a judge does; pass sentence on or in. **6.** to form a judgment or opinion of or upon; decide upon critically; estimate. **7.** to decide or decree judicially or authoritatively. **8.** to infer, think, or hold as an opinion. **9.** (of the Hebrew judges) to govern. —*v.i.* **10.** to act as a judge; pass judgment. **11.** to form an opinion or estimate. **12.** to make a mental judgment. [ME *juge*, t. OF, g. L *judex*] —**judg′er**, *n.* —**judge′less**, *adj.* —**judge′like′**, *adj.* —**judge′ship**, *n.* —**Syn. 1.** justice. **2.** arbitrator. JUDGE, REFEREE, UMPIRE refer to one who is entrusted with decisions affecting others. JUDGE, in its legal and other uses, implies particularly that

judge advocate one has qualifications and authority for giving decisions in matters at issue: *a judge appointed to the Supreme Court.* A REFEREE usually examines and reports on the merits of a case as an aid to a court. An UMPIRE gives the final ruling when arbitrators of a case disagree. 3. connoisseur, critic. 8. conclude; consider, deem, regard. See **think**[1]. **10.** adjudge, adjudicate.

judge advocate, *Mil., Naval.* the officer appointed to present the army or navy case before a court-martial, and assist in seeing that justice is done.

Judg·es (jŭj′Yz), *n.* a book of the Old Testament, containing the history of Israel under the leaders (judges) from Deborah to Samuel.

judg·ment (jŭj′mənt), *n.* **1.** act of judging. **2.** *Law.* **a.** the judicial decision of a cause in court. **b.** the obligation, esp. a debt, arising from a judicial decision. **c.** the certificate embodying such a decision. **3.** ability to judge justly or wisely, esp. in matters affecting action; good sense; discretion. **4.** the forming of an opinion, estimate, notion, or conclusion, as from circumstances presented to the mind. **5.** the opinion formed. **6.** a misfortune regarded as inflicted by divine sentence, as for sin. **7.** the final trial of all mankind, both the living and the dead, at the end of the world (often, **Last Judgment**). Also, *esp. Brit.,* **judge′ment.** —Syn. **2.** a verdict, decree. **3.** understanding; discrimination, discernment, perspicacity; sagacity.

judgment day, the day of God's final judgment of mankind at the end of the world; doomsday.

ju·di·ca·ble (jōō′də kə bəl), *adj.* **1.** capable of being judged or tried. **2.** liable to be judged or tried.

ju·di·ca·tive (jōō′də kā′tĭv), *adj.* having ability to judge; judging: *the judicative faculty.*

ju·di·ca·tor (jōō′dəkā′tər), *n.* one who acts as judge or sits in judgment. [t. LL]

ju·di·ca·to·ry (jōō′də kə tôr′Y), *adj., n., pl.* **-tories.** —*adj.* **1.** of or pertaining to judgment or the administration of justice: *judicatory power.* [t. LL: m.s. *jūdicātōrius*] —*n.* **2.** a court of justice; a tribunal. **3.** the administration of justice. [t. LL: m.s. *jūdicātōrium,* prop. neut. of *jūdicātōrius* of a judge]

ju·di·ca·ture (jōō′də kə chər), *n.* **1.** the administration of justice, as by judges or courts. **2.** the office, function, or authority of a judge. **3.** the extent of jurisdiction of a judge or court. **4.** a body of judges. **5.** the power of administering justice by legal trial and determination. [t. ML: m.s. *jūdicātūra,* der. *jūdicātus,* pp., judged]

ju·di·ci·a·ble (jōō dYsh′Yə bəl), *adj.* capable of being judged or tried.

ju·di·cial (jōō dYsh′əl), *adj.* **1.** pertaining to judgment in courts of justice or to the administration of justice: *judicial proceedings.* **2.** pertaining to courts of law or to judges: *judicial functions.* **3.** of or pertaining to a judge; proper to the character of a judge; judgelike. **4.** inclined to make or give judgments; critical; discriminating. **5.** decreed, sanctioned, or enforced by a court: *a judicial separation.* **6.** pertaining to judgment or decision in a dispute or contest: *a judicial duel.* **7.** inflicted by God as a judgment or punishment. [ME, t. L: s. *jūdiciālis* of a court of justice] —**ju·di′cial·ly,** *adv.* —Syn. **4.** See **judicious.**

ju·di·ci·a·ry (jōō dYsh′Y ĕr′Y, -dYsh′ərY), *adj., n., pl.* **-aries.** —*adj.* **1.** pertaining to judgment in courts of justice, or to courts or judges; judicial. —*n.* **2.** the judicial branch of government. **3.** the system of courts of justice in a country. **4.** the judges collectively.

ju·di·cious (jōō dYsh′əs), *adj.* **1.** using or showing judgment as to action or practical expediency; discreet, prudent, or politic. **2.** having, exercising, or showing good judgment; wise, sensible, or well-advised: *a judicious selection.* [t. F: m. *judicieux,* der. L *jūdicium* judgment] —**ju·di′cious·ly,** *adv.* —**ju·di′cious·ness,** *n.* —Syn. **1.** See **practical. 2.** JUDICIOUS, JUDICIAL both refer to a balanced and wise judgment. JUDICIOUS implies the possession and use of discerning and discriminating judgment: *a judicious use of one's time.* JUDICIAL has connotations of judgments made in a courtroom, and refers to a fair and impartial kind of judgment: *cool and judicial in examining the facts.* —**Ant. 1.** unwise.

Ju·dith (jōō′dYth), *n.* **1.** an apocryphal book of the Old Testament. **2.** its heroine, who delivered her people by entering the camp of Holofernes and slaying him in his sleep. [ult. t. Heb.: m. *yehūdhīth* the Jewess]

ju·do (jōō′dō), *n.* jujitsu.

Ju·dy (jōō′dY), *n.* the wife of Punch in the puppet show called *Punch and Judy.* [a familiar var. of *Judith,* woman's name]

jug (jŭg), *n., v.,* **jugged, jugging.** —*n.* **1.** a vessel in various forms for holding liquids, commonly having a handle, often a spout or lip, and sometimes a lid. **2.** the contents of any such vessel. **3.** *U.S.* a deep vessel, usually of earthenware, with a handle and a narrow neck stopped by a cork. **4.** *Slang.* a prison or jail. —*v.t.* **5.** to put into a jug. **6.** *Slang.* to commit to jail, or imprison. [? special use of *Jug,* hypocoristic var. of *Joan* or *Joanna,* woman's name]

ju·gal (jōō′gəl), *adj.* of or pertaining to the cheek or the cheekbone. [t. L: s. *jugālis,* der. *jugum* a yoke]

jugal bone, 1. (in man) the cheekbone, or principal bone of the cheek. **2.** a corresponding bone in animals.

ju·gate (jōō′gāt, -gYt), *adj. Bot.* having the leaflets in pairs, as a pinnate leaf. [t. L: m.s. *jugātus,* pp., joined]

jugged hare (jŭgd), *Chiefly Brit.* hare prepared by seething in a jar.

Jug·ger·naut (jŭg′ər nôt′), *n.* **1.** the Hindu divinity Krishna, the eighth incarnation of Vishnu. **2.** an idol of this deity, at Puri in Orissa, India, annually drawn on an enormous car under whose wheels devotees are said to have thrown themselves to be crushed. **3.** anything to which a person blindly devotes himself or is cruelly sacrificed. Also, **Jagannath, Jagannatha.** [t. Hind.: m. *Jagannāth,* g. Skt. *Jagannātha* lord of the world]

jug·gle (jŭg′əl), *v.,* **-gled, -gling,** *n.* —*v.t.* **1.** to perform conjuring tricks with (balls, knives, etc.). **2.** to manipulate by artifice or trickery: *to juggle accounts.* —*v.i.* **3.** to perform feats of manual or bodily dexterity, such as tossing up and keeping in continuous motion a number of balls, plates, knives, etc. **4.** to use artifice or trickery. —*n.* **5.** act of juggling; a trick; a deception. [ME *jogel(en),* t. OF: m. *jogler,* g. L *joculārī* jest]

jug·gler (jŭg′lər), *n.* **1.** one who performs juggling feats, as with balls, knives, etc. **2.** one who deceives by trickery; a trickster. [ME *jugelour, jogeler,* t. OF: m. *jogleor,* g. L *joculātor* jester]

jug·gler·y (jŭg′lə rY), *n., pl.* **-gleries. 1.** the art or practice of a juggler. **2.** the performance of juggling feats. **3.** any trickery or deception.

ju·glan·da·ceous (jōō′glăn dā′shəs), *adj.* belonging to the *Juglandaceae,* or walnut family of trees. [f. s. L *jūglans* walnut + -ACEOUS]

Ju·go·slav (ū′gō släv′, -släv′), *n., adj.* Yugoslav. Also, **Ju′go-Slav′.** —**Ju·go·slav′ic,** *adj.*

Ju·go·sla·vi·a (ū′gō slä′vY ə), *n.* Yugoslavia. —**Ju′go·sla′vi·an,** *adj., n.*

jug·u·lar (jŭg′yə lər, jōō′gyə-), *adj.* **1.** *Anat.* **a.** of or pertaining to the throat or neck. **b.** noting or pertaining to any of certain large veins of the neck, esp. one (**external jugular vein**) collecting blood from the superficial parts of the head, or one (**internal jugular vein**) receiving blood from within the skull. **2.** (of a fish) having the ventral fins at the throat, in advance of the pectoral fins. —*n.* **3.** *Anat.* a jugular vein. [t. NL: m. *jugulāris,* der. L *jugulum* collarbone, throat, dim. of *jugum* a yoke]

ju·gu·late (jōō′gyə lāt′), *v.t.,* **-lated, -lating. 1.** to check or suppress (disease, etc.) by extreme measures. **2.** *Rare.* to cut the throat of; kill. [t. L: m.s. *jugulātus,* pp., slain] —**ju′gu·la′tion,** *n.*

Ju·gur·tha (jōō gûr′thə), *n.* died 104 B.C., king of Numidia, 112?–104 B.C.

juice (jōōs), *n.* **1.** the liquid part of plant or animal substance. **2.** any extracted liquid. **3.** *U.S. Slang.* **a.** electric power. **b.** gasoline, fuel oil, etc. used to run an engine. [ME *jus,* t. OF, g. L: broth] —**juice′less,** *adj.*

juic·y (jōō′sY), *adj.,* **juicier, juiciest. 1.** full of juice; succulent. **2.** interesting; vivacious; colorful. —**juic′i·ly,** *adv.* —**juic′i·ness,** *n.*

ju·jit·su (jōō jYt′sōō), *n.* a Japanese method of offense and defense without weapons in personal encounter which employs the strength and weight of the opponent to his disadvantage or undoing. Also, **jiujitsu, jiujutsu, ju·jut′su.** [t. Jap.: soft (or pliant) art]

ju·ju (jōō′jōō), *n.* (among native tribes of western Africa) **1.** some object venerated superstitiously and used as a fetish or amulet. **2.** the magical power attributed to such an object. **3.** a ban or interdiction effected by it. [t. West Afr.]

ju·jube (jōō′jōōb), *n.* **1.** the edible plumlike fruit of any of certain Old World trees of the genus *Zizyphus.* **2.** any tree producing this fruit. [t. F, t. ML: m. *jujuba,* t.LL: m. *zizyphum,* t. Gk.: m. *zizyphon*]

juke box (jōōk), *U.S. Slang.* a coin-operated phonograph permitting selection of the record to be played.

Jukes (jōōks), *n.* the fictitious name of an actual New York family whose history over several generations showed a high incidence of disease, delinquency, and poverty.

Jul., July.

ju·lep (jōō′lYp), *n.* **1.** a sweet drink, variously prepared and sometimes medicated. **2.** mint julep. [ME, t. OF, t. Ar.: m. *julāb,* t. Pers.: m. *gulāb* rose water, julep]

Ju·lian (jōōl′yən), *n.* ("the Apostate," *Flavius Claudius Julianus*), A.D. 331–363, Roman emperor, A.D. 361–363, who opposed Christianity.

Ju·li·an·a Lou·i·se Em·ma Ma·rie Wil·hel·mi·na (jōō′lY ăn′ə; *Du.* yr′lY ä′nä; lōō ē′sə ĕm′ä mä rē′ vYl hĕl mē′nä), born 1909, Queen of the Netherlands since 1948.

Julian Alps, a mountain range in NW Yugoslavia. Highest peak, Mt. Triglav, 9394 ft.

Julian calendar, the calendar established by Julius Caesar in 46 B.C. which fixed the length of the year at 365 days, with 366 days in every fourth year (leap year), and months similar to the present day calendar.

ju·li·enne (jōō′lY ĕn′; *Fr.* zhY lyĕn′), *adj.* **1.** (of vegetables) cut into thin strips or small pieces. —*n.* **2.** a clear soup containing vegetables cut into thin strips or small pieces. [t. F, special use of *Julienne,* woman's name]

Ju·li·et (jōō′lY ət, jōō′lY ĕt′), *n.* the heroine of Shakespeare's *Romeo and Juliet.*

Ju·li·us Cae·sar (jōō′lY əs sē′zər), **1.** See **Caesar** (def. 1). **2.** historical tragedy (ab. 1600) by Shakespeare.

Jul·lun·dur (jŭl′ən dər), *n.* a city in NW India, in central Punjab. 168,816 (1951).

u·ly (jōō lī′), n., pl. **-lies.** the seventh month of the year, containing 31 days. [ME *Julie*, OE *Julius*, t. L; named after *Julius* Caesar, who was born in this month]

um·ble (jŭm′bəl), v., **-bled, -bling,** n. —v.t. **1.** to mix in a confused mass; put or throw together without order. **2.** to muddle or confuse mentally. —v.i. **3.** to mix or come together confusedly; be mixed up. —n. **4.** a confused mixture; a medley. **5.** a state of confusion or disorder. **6.** a small, flat, sweet cake, now commonly round, with a small hole in the middle. [? b. JOIN and TUMBLE] —**jum′bler,** n. —**Syn. 5.** muddle, hodgepodge; farrago; mess; chaos. —**Ant. 5.** order.

umble sale, *Brit.* a rummage sale.

um·bo (jŭm′bō), n., pl. **-bos,** adj. *Colloq.* —n. **1.** a big, clumsy person, animal, or thing. —adj. **2.** very large.

um·na (jŭm′nə), n. a river in N India, flowing from the Himalayas SE to the Ganges at Allahabad. 860 mi.

ump (jŭmp), v.i. **1.** to spring clear of the ground or other support by a sudden muscular effort; leap. **2.** to move or go suddenly or abruptly, as with a leap. **3.** *Checkers.* to jump, and thus capture, an opponent's piece. **4.** to rise suddenly in amount, price, etc. **5.** to pass abruptly as if by a leap: *to jump to a conclusion.* **6.** *Motion Pictures.* to fail to line up properly with the preceding or following shots, due to mechanical fault in camera or projector. **7.** *Contract Bridge.* to bid exceptionally and unnecessarily high in order to indicate additional strength.
—v.t. **8.** to pass over by a leap: *to jump a stream.* **9.** to cause to jump or leap. **10.** to skip or pass over. **11.** *Checkers.* to capture (an opponent's man) by leaping over it to an unoccupied square. **12.** *Bridge.* to raise (the bid) by more than the necessary overcall. **13.** to abscond from, or evade by absconding: *to jump one's bail.* **14.** to seize (a mining claim, etc.), as on the ground of some flaw in the holder's title. **15.** to spring off or leave (the track), as trains do. **16.** *U.S.* to get on or off (a train, etc.) by jumping.
—n. **17.** act of jumping; a leap. **18.** a space or obstacle or apparatus cleared in a leap. **19.** a sudden rise in amount, price, etc. **20.** a sudden upward or other movement of an inanimate object. **21.** an abrupt transition from one point or thing to another, with omission of what intervenes. **22.** *U.S. Colloq.* a head start in time or space; advantageous beginning. **23.** *Sports.* any of several athletic games which feature a leap or jump. **24.** *Motion Pictures.* a break in the continuity of action due to a failure to match action between a long shot and a closer shot of the same scene. **25.** a sudden start, as from nervous excitement. **26.** *(pl.)* a physical condition characterized by such starts. [appar. imit.]
—**Syn. 1.** spring, bound; skip, hop. JUMP, LEAP, VAULT imply propelling oneself by a muscular effort of the legs, either into the air or from one position or place to another. JUMP and LEAP are often used interchangeably, but JUMP indicates more particularly the springing movement of the feet in leaving the ground or support: *to jump up and down.* LEAP (which formerly also meant to run) indicates the passage, by a springing movement, from one point or position to another: *to leap across a brook.* VAULT implies leaping over or upon something: *to vault (over) a fence.*

ump ball, *Basketball.* a ball tossed between two opposing players by the referee.

ump bid, *Bridge.* any bid which is higher than that needed to increase the bid made previously.

ump·er[1] (jŭmp′ər), n. **1.** one who or that which jumps. **2.** a boring tool or device worked with a jumping motion. **3.** *Elect.* a short length of conductor used to make a connection, usually temporary, between terminals, around a break in a circuit, or around an instrument. **4.** a kind of sled. [f. JUMP, v. + -ER[1]]

ump·er[2] (jŭmp′ər), n. **1.** a one-piece, sleeveless dress worn with blouse or guimpe by women and children. **2.** *Chiefly Brit.* a loose jacket worn by women over a blouse. **3.** a loose outer jacket worn esp. by workmen and sailors. **4.** *(pl.)* rompers. [der. *jump,* nasalized var. of *jup* short coat (t. F: m. *juppe*). See -ER[2]]

umping bean, the seed of any of certain Mexican euphorbiaceous plants (genus *Sebastiania,* etc.), which is inhabited by the larva of a small moth whose movements cause the seed to move about or jump.

umping jack, a toy consisting of a jointed figure of a man which is made to jump, or go through various contortions, as by pulling a string attached to its limbs.

ump·ing-off place (jŭmp′ĭng ôf′, -ŏf′), *U.S.* an out-of-the-way place; the farthest limit of anything settled or civilized.

ump·y (jŭmp′ĭ), adj., **jumpier, jumpiest. 1.** characterized by or inclined to sudden, involuntary starts, esp. from nervousness, fear, excitement, etc. **2.** causing to jump or start. —**jump′i·ness,** n.

Jun., 1. June. **2.** Junior.

Junc., Junction.

un·ca·ceous (jŭng kā′shəs), adj. pertaining or belonging to, or resembling, the *Juncaceae,* or rush family of plants. [f. s. L *juncus* a rush + -ACEOUS]

un·co (jŭng′kō), n., pl. **-cos.** any of several small finches of the North American genus *Junco,* all with white on the outer tail feathers; snowbird. [t. Sp., t. L: m. *juncus* a rush]

unc·tion (jŭngk′shən), n. **1.** act of joining; combination. **2.** state of being joined; union. **3.** a place or sta-

tion where railroad lines meet or cross. **4.** a place of joining or meeting. [t. L: s. *junctio* a joining]
—**Syn. 4.** JUNCTION, JUNCTURE refer to a place, line, or point at which two or more things join. A JUNCTION is a place where things come together: *the junction of two rivers.* A JUNCTURE is a line or point at which two bodies are joined, or a point of exigency or crisis in time: *the juncture of head and neck, a critical juncture in a struggle.*

junc·ture (jŭngk′chər), n. **1.** a point of time, esp. one made critical or important by a concurrence of circumstances. **2.** a critical state of affairs; a crisis; a critical moment. **3.** the line or point at which two bodies are joined; a joint or articulation; a seam. **4.** act of joining. **5.** state of being joined; junction. **6.** something by which two things are joined. [ME, t. L: m. *junctūra* joining, joint] —**Syn. 3.** See **junction.**

June (jōōn), n. the sixth month of year, containing 30 days. [ME; OE *Iuni,* t. L: s. *Jūnius;* named after the *Jūnius* gens of Rome]

Ju·neau (jōō′nō), n. a seaport in and the capital of Alaska, in the SE part. 6,797 (1960).

June·ber·ry (jōōn′bĕr′ĭ), n., pl. **-ries.** the American serviceberry, *Amelanchier canadensis.*

June bug, 1. (in the northern U.S.) any of the large, brown scarabaeid beetles of the genus *Phyllophaga* (*Lachnosterna*), which appear about June. **2.** (in the southern U.S.) a large, greenish scarabaeid beetle, *Cotinis nitida;* the figeater. Also, **June beetle.**

Jung (yŏŏng), n. **Carl Gustav** (kärl gŏŏs′-täf), 1875–1961, Swiss psychiatrist and psychologist.

Northern June bug. *Phyllophaga fusca* (1 in. long)

Jung·frau (yŏŏng′frou′), n. a peak in the Bernese Alps, in S Switzerland. 13,668 ft.

jun·gle (jŭng′gəl), n. **1.** wild land overgrown with dense, rank vegetation, often nearly impenetrable, as in parts of India. **2.** a tract of such land. **3.** a wilderness of dense overgrowth; a piece of swampy thick-set forest land. **4.** *U.S. Slang.* a camp for hoboes or tramps. [t. Hind.: m. *jangal* desert, forest, g. Skt. *jangala* dry, desert]

jungle fever, a severe variety of malarial fever occurring in the East Indies and other tropical regions.

jungle fowl, any of various East Indian gallinaceous birds of the genus *Gallus,* certain species of which are supposed to have given rise to the domestic fowl.

jun·ior (jōōn′yər), adj. **1.** younger (often used, esp. as abbreviated *Jr.* or *Jun.,* after the name of a person who is the younger of two persons bearing the name, as a son having the same name as his father). **2.** of more recent appointment or admission, as to an office or status; of lower rank or standing. **3.** (in American universities, colleges, and schools) noting or pertaining to the class or year next below that of the senior. **4.** *Law.* subordinate to preferred creditors, mortgagees, and the like. **5.** of later date; subsequent to. —n. **6.** a person who is younger than another. **7.** one who is of more recent entrance into, or of lower standing in, an office, class, profession, etc.; one employed as the subordinate of another. **8.** a student who is in the next to the final year of a course of study. [t. L, contr. of *juvenior,* compar. of *juvenis* young]

junior college, a collegiate institution extending through the first one or two years of college instruction, and granting a certificate of title instead of a degree.

junior high school. See **high school** (def. 2).

jun·ior·i·ty (jōōn yôr′ə tĭ, -yŏr′-), n. state or fact of being junior in age, standing, etc.

ju·ni·per (jōō′nə pər), n. **1.** any of the coniferous evergreen shrubs or trees constituting the genus *Juniperus,* esp. *J. communis,* whose cones form purple berries used in making gin and in medicine as a diuretic, or *J. virginiana,* a North American species. **2.** a tree mentioned in the Bible. 1 Kings, 19:4. [ME *junipere,* t. L: m. *jūniperus.* See GENEVA and GIN[1]]

Jun·ius (jōōn′yəs), n. the pen name of the unknown author of public political letters (1768–72) against the British ministry.

junk[1] (jŭngk), n. **1.** any old or discarded material, as metal, paper, rags, etc. **2.** *Colloq.* anything that is regarded as worthless or mere trash. **3.** old cable or cordage used when untwisted for making gaskets, swabs, oakum, etc. **4.** hard salt meat used for food on shipboard. —v.t. **5.** *Colloq.* to cast aside as junk; discard as no longer of use. [orig. uncert.]

junk[2] (jŭngk), n. a kind of seagoing ship used in Chinese and other waters, having square sails spread by battens, a high stern, and usually a flat bottom. [t. Pg.: m. *junco,* t. Malay: m. *jong, ajong,* appar. t. Javanese: (m.) *jong*]

Canton trading junk

Jun·ker (yŏŏng′kər), n. **1.** a member of a class of aristocratic landholders, esp. in East Prussia, strongly devoted to maintaining the social and political privileges of their group. **2.** a narrow-minded, haughty, overbearing member of the aristocracy of Prussia, etc. [t. G, in MHG *junc herre* young gentleman]

Jun·ker·dom (yŏŏng′kər dəm), *n.* 1. the body of Junkers. 2. (*sometimes l.c.*) a. the condition or character of a Junker. b. the spirit or policy of the Junkers.
Jun·ker·ism (yŏŏng′kə rĭz′əm), *n.* (*sometimes l.c.*) the spirit or policy of the Junkers.
jun·ket (jŭng′kĭt), *n.* 1. a sweet custardlike food of flavored milk curded with rennet. 2. (*cap.*) a trademark for this food. 3. a trip by a legislative committee ostensibly to obtain information. 4. a feast or merrymaking; a picnic; a pleasure excursion. —*v.i.* 5. to feast; picnic; go on a junket or pleasure excursion, esp. at public expense. —*v.t.* 6. to entertain; feast; regale: *to junket her neighbors.* [ME *jonket* basket made of rushes, *joncate* curded food made in a vessel of rushes, t. OF: m. *jonquette*, der. *jonc* a rush, g. L *juncus*] —**jun′ket·er,** *n.* —**Syn.** 3. See excursion.
junk·man (jŭngk′măn′), *n., pl.* **-men.** a dealer in junk, or old metal, paper, rags, etc.
Ju·no (jōō′nō), *n.* 1. *Rom. Myth.* an ancient Roman goddess, the wife of Jupiter, presiding over marriage and women. Cf. **Hera.** 2. a woman of imposing figure or appearance.
Ju·no·esque (jōō′nō ĕsk′), *adj.* (of a woman) stately.
Ju·not (zhy nō′), *n.* Andoche (än dôsh′), (*Duc d'Abrantès*) 1771–1813, French marshal.
jun·ta (jŭn′tə), *n.* 1. a meeting; a council. 2. a deliberative or administrative council, esp. in Spain. 3. a junto. [t. Sp., g. L *juncta*, fem. pp., joined]
jun·to (jŭn′tō), *n., pl.* **-tos.** a self-appointed committee, esp. with political aims; cabal. [erron. var. of JUNTA]
Ju·pi·ter (jōō′pə tər), *n.* 1. the supreme deity of the ancient Romans, the god of the heavens, manifesting himself esp. in atmospheric phenomena; Jove (Cf. **Zeus**). 2. the largest planet, fifth in order from the sun. Its period of revolution is 11.86 years, its mean distance from the sun about 483,000,000 miles. Its diameter is about one tenth that of the sun (11 times that of the earth). It has 12 satellites. Symbol: ♃. [t. L, var. of *Jūppiter*, contr. of *Jovis pater* father Jove]
Jupiter Symphony, forty-first symphony (1788) by Mozart.
ju·pon (jōō′pŏn, jōō pŏn′; *Fr.* zhy pôn′), *n.* a closefitting tunic, usually padded and bearing heraldic arms, worn over armor. [ME *jupone*, t. F: m. *jupon*, der. *jupe* jacket, t. Ar.: m. *jubbah*]
ju·ral (jŏŏr′əl), *adj.* 1. pertaining to law; legal. 2. pertaining to rights and obligations. [f. s. L *jūs* right, law + -AL¹] —**ju′ral·ly,** *adv.*
Ju·ra Mountains (jŏŏr′ə; *Fr.* zhy rä′), a mountain range between France and Switzerland, extending from the Rhine to the Rhone. Highest peak, Crêt de la Niege, 5654 ft.
Ju·ras·sic (jŏŏ răs′ĭk), *Stratig.* —*adj.* 1. pertaining to a mid-Mesozoic geological period or system of rocks named from the Jura Mountains. —*n.* 2. a period or system following the Triassic and preceding the Cretaceous. [t. F: m. *jurassique*]
ju·rat (jŏŏr′ăt), *n.* 1. *Law.* a certificate on an affidavit, by the officer, showing by whom, when, and before whom it was sworn to. 2. a sworn officer; a magistrate; a member of a permanent jury. [t. ML: s. *jūrātus*, lit., one sworn, *jūrātum*, neut., that which is sworn, prop. pp. of L *jūrāre* swear]
Jur. D., (L *Juris Doctor*) Doctor of Law.
ju·rel (hŏŏ rĕl′), *n.* any of certain carangoid food fishes of the genus *Caranx* as *C. latus*, a species of the West Indies, etc. [t. Sp., ult. der. Gk. *saûros* a sea fish]
ju·rid·i·cal (jŏŏ rĭd′ə kəl), *adj.* 1. of or pertaining to the administration of justice. 2. of or pertaining to law or jurisprudence; legal. Also, **ju·rid′ic.** [f. s. L *jūridicus* relating to justice + -AL¹] —**ju·rid′i·cal·ly,** *adv.*
juridical days, days in court on which law is administered; days on which the court can lawfully sit.
ju·ris·con·sult (jŏŏr′ĭs kən sŭlt′, -kŏn′sŭlt), *n.* 1. *Rom. and Civil Law.* one authorized to give legal advice. 2. *Civil Law.* a master of the civil law. *Abbr.:* J. C. [t. L: s. *jūrisconsultus* one skilled in the law]
ju·ris·dic·tion (jŏŏr′ĭs dĭk′shən), *n.* 1. the right, power, or authority to administer justice by hearing and determining controversies. 2. power; authority; control. 3. the extent or range of judicial or other authority. 4. the territory over which authority is exercised. [ME, t. L: s. *jūrisdictio* administration of the law, authority] —**ju′ris·dic′tion·al,** *adj.* —**ju′ris·dic′tion·al·ly,** *adv.*
ju·ris·pru·dence (jŏŏr′ĭs prōō′dəns), *n.* 1. the science or philosophy of law. 2. a body or system of laws. 3. a department of law: *medical jurisprudence.* 4. *Civil Law.* decisions of courts of appeal or other higher tribunals. [t. L: m.s. *jūrisprūdentia* the science of the law] —**ju·ris·pru·den·tial** (jŏŏr′ĭs prōō dĕn′shəl), *adj.*
ju·ris·pru·dent (jŏŏr′ĭs prōō′dənt), *adj.* 1. versed in jurisprudence. —*n.* 2. one versed in jurisprudence.
ju·rist (jŏŏr′ĭst), *n.* 1. one who professes the science of law. 2. one versed in the law. 3. one who writes on the subject of law. [t. ML: s. *jūrista*, der. L *jūs* right, law]
ju·ris·tic (jŏŏ rĭs′tĭk), *adj.* of or pertaining to a jurist or to jurisprudence; relating to law; juridical; legal. Also, **ju·ris′ti·cal.** —**ju·ris′ti·cal·ly,** *adv.*
juristic act, an act not involving the exercise of legal authority which changes, ends, or affects the basis of a legal right.

ju·ror (jŏŏr′ər), *n.* 1. one of a body of persons sworn to deliver a verdict in a case submitted to them; a member of any jury. 2. one of the panel from which a jury is selected. 3. one who has taken an oath or sworn allegiance. [ME *jurour*, t. AF, g. L *jūrātor* swearer]
Ju·ru·á (zhōō′rōō ä′), *n.* a river flowing from E Peru NE through W Brazil to the Amazon. ab. 1200 mi.
ju·ry¹ (jŏŏr′ĭ), *n., pl.* **juries.** 1. a body of persons sworn to render a verdict or true answer on a question or questions officially submitted to them. 2. such a body selected according to law and sworn to inquire into or determine the facts concerning a cause or an accusation submitted to them and to render a verdict. See **grand jury** and **petty jury.** 3. a body of persons chosen to adjudge prizes, etc., as in a competition. [ME *juree* t. AF, der. *jure* one sworn, ult. der. L *jūrāre* swear] —**ju′ry·less,** *adj.*
ju·ry² (jŏŏr′ĭ), *adj. Naut.* makeshift, temporary, as for an emergency. [first found in *jury mast,* prob. t. OF: m. *ajurie* relief, help, der. L *adjūtāre* help]
ju·ry·man (jŏŏr′ĭ mən), *n., pl.* **-men.** a juror.
jury mast, *Naut.* a temporary mast replacing one that has been broken or carried away. [see JURY²]
jur·y·rigged (jŏŏr′ĭ rĭgd′), *adj. Naut.* temporarily rigged. [see JURY²]
jus¹ (zhy), *n. French.* juice; gravy. [F, t. L]
jus² (jŭs), *n., pl.* **jura** (jŏŏr′ə). *Law.* 1. a right. 2. law as a system or in the abstract. [t. L: law, right]
jus ca·no·ni·cum (jŭs kə nŏn′ĭ kəm), canon law.
jus ci·vi·le (jŭs sĭ vī′lĭ), *Rom. Law.* the rules and principles of law derived from the customs and legislation of Rome, as opposed to those derived from the customs of all nations (**jus gentium**) or from fundamental ideas of right and wrong implicit in the human mind (**jus naturale**).
jus di·vi·num (jŭs dĭ vī′nəm), *Latin.* divine law.
jus gen·ti·um (jŭs jĕn′shĭ əm). See **jus civile.**
jus na·tu·ra·le (jŭs năt′yŏŏ rā′lĭ). See **jus civile.**
Jus·se·rand (zhys rän′), *n.* Jean Jules (zhäN zhyl) 1855–1932, French diplomat and author.
jus·sive (jŭs′ĭv), *adj. Gram.* 1. expressing a mild command. The jussive mood occurs in the Semitic languages. —*n.* 2. a jussive form or construction. [f. s. L *jussus,* pp., commanded + -IVE]
just¹ (jŭst), *adj.* 1. actuated by truth, justice, and lack of bias: *to be just in one's dealings.* 2. in accordance with true principles; equitable; evenhanded: *a just award.* 3. based on right; rightful; lawful: *a just claim.* 4. agreeable to truth or fact; true; correct: *a just statement.* 5. given or awarded rightly, or deserved, as a sentence, punishment, reward, etc. 6. in accordance with standards, or requirements; proper, or right: *just proportions.* 7. righteous (esp. in Biblical use). 8. actual, real, or true. —*adv.* 9. within a brief preceding time, or but a moment before: *they have just gone.* 10. exactly or precisely: *that is just the point.* 11. by a narrow margin; barely: *it just missed the mark.* 12. only or merely: *he is just an ordinary man.* 13. *Colloq.* actually; truly; positively: *the weather is just glorious.* [ME, t. L: s. *justus* righteous] —**Syn.** 1. upright; equitable, fair, impartial. 4. accurate, exact; honest. 5. rightful, legitimate, deserved, merited, condign. —**Ant.** 1. biased. 4. untrue. 5. unjustified.
just² (jŭst), *n., v.i.* joust. —**just′er,** *n.*
jus·tice (jŭs′tĭs), *n.* 1. the quality of being just; righteousness, equitableness, or moral rightness: *to uphold the justice of a cause.* 2. rightfulness or lawfulness, as of a claim or title; justness of ground or reason: *to complain with justice.* 3. the moral principle determining just conduct. 4. conformity to this principle as manifested in conduct; just conduct, dealing, or treatment. 5. the requital of desert as by punishment or reward. 6. the maintenance or administration of law, as by judicial or other proceedings: *a court of justice.* 7. judgment of persons or causes by judicial process: *to administer justice in a community.* 8. a judicial officer; a judge or magistrate. 9. **do justice to,** a. to render or concede what is due to (a person or thing, merits, good intentions, etc.); treat or judge fairly. b. to exhibit (oneself) in a just light, as in doing something: *the speaker hardly did justice to himself this evening.* c. to show just appreciation of (something) by action: *to do justice to a good dinner by eating heartily.* [ME *justise,* t. OF, t. L: m.s. *justitia*]
justice of the peace, a local officer having jurisdiction to try and determine minor civil and criminal cases and to hold preliminary examinations of persons accused of more serious crimes, and having authority to administer oaths, solemnize marriages, etc.
jus·tice·ship (jŭs′tĭs shĭp′), *n.* the office of a justice.
jus·ti·ci·ar·y (jŭs tĭsh′ĭ ĕr′ĭ), *adj., n., pl.* **-aries.** —*adj.* 1. of or pertaining to the administration of justice. —*n.* 2. Also, **jus·ti·ci·ar** (jŭs tĭsh′ĭ ər), *Brit. Hist.* the chief administrator of justice and government from the time of William I to that of Henry III. [t. ML: m.s. *justitiārius* judge, der. L *justitia* justice]
jus·ti·fi·a·ble (jŭs′tə fī′ə bəl), *adj.* capable of being justified; that can be shown to be, or can be defended as being, just or right; defensible. —**jus′ti·fi′a·bil′i·ty, jus′ti·fi′a·ble·ness,** *n.* —**jus′ti·fi′a·bly,** *adv.*
jus·ti·fi·ca·tion (jŭs′tə fə kā′shən), *n.* 1. something that justifies; a defensive plea; an excuse; a justifying

fact or circumstance. **2.** act of justifying. **3.** state of being justified. **4.** *Theol.* the act of God whereby man is made or accounted just, or freed from the guilt or penalty of sin. **5.** *Print.* arrangement, as of type, by adjusting the spaces so that it fills a line precisely, or holds a cut in place.

us·ti·fi·ca·to·ry (jŭs'tĭf'∂k∂tōr'Y, jŭs't∂f∂kā't∂rY), *adj.* serving to justify; affording justification. Also, **jus·ti·fi·ca·tive** (jŭs't∂f∂kā'tYv).

us·ti·fi·er (jŭs't∂fī'∂r), *n.* one who or that which justifies.

us·ti·fy (jŭs't∂fī'), *v.*, **-fied, -fying.** —*v.t.* **1.** to show (an act, claim, statement, etc.) to be just, right, or warranted: *the end justifies the means.* **2.** to defend or uphold as blameless, just, or right. **3.** declare guiltless; absolve; acquit. **4.** *Print.* to adjust exactly; make (lines) of the proper length by spacing. —*v.i.* **5.** *Law.* **a.** to show a satisfactory reason or excuse for something done. **b.** to qualify as bail or surety. **6.** *Print.* to conform or fit exactly, as lines of type. [ME *justifie(n)*, t. OF: m. *justifier*, t. LL: m. *justificāre* act justly towards] —**Syn.** **2.** vindicate; exonerate, exculpate. —**Ant.** **2.** accuse, condemn.

Jus·tin·i·an I (jŭs tĭn'Y ∂n), ("*the Great,*" *Flavius Anicius Justinianus*) A.D. 483-565, Byzantine emperor, A.D. 527-565, whose leading jurists formulated a code of laws called the **Justinian Code.**

Jus·tin Mar·tyr (jŭs'tYn mär't∂r), **Saint,** A.D. c100-c165, Christian saint, philosopher, and martyr, born in Syria.

us·ti·ti·a om·ni·bus (jŭs tYsh'Y∂ ŏm'n∂b∂s), *Latin.* justice to all (motto of the District of Columbia).

us·tle (jŭs'∂l), *v.t., v.i.*, **-tled, -tling,** *n.* jostle.

ust·ly (jŭst'lY), *adv.* **1.** in a just manner; honestly; fairly. **2.** in conformity to fact or rule; accurately.

ust·ness (jŭst'nYs), *n.* **1.** quality or state of being just, equitable, or right; lawfulness. **2.** conformity to fact or rule; correctness; exactness; accuracy.

ut (jŭt), *v.*, **jutted, jutting,** *n.* —*v.i.* **1.** to extend beyond the main body or line; project; protrude (often fol. by *out*). —*n.* **2.** something that juts out; a projection or protruding point. [var. of JET, v.]

Jute (jōot), *n.* **1.** a strong fiber used for making fabrics, cordage, etc., obtained from two tiliaceous East Indian plants, *Corchorus capsularis* and *C. olitorius.* **2.** either

of these plants. **3.** any plant of the same genus. **4.** a coarse fabric obtained from jute plant and woven into burlap or gunny. [t. Bengali: m. *jhŏto*, g. Skt. *jūta* braid of hair] —**jute'like',** *adj.*

Jute (jōot), *n.* a member of a continental Germanic tribe which invaded Britain and settled there in the 5th century. [t. ML: m.s. *Iutī, pl.,* t. OE] —**Jut'ish,** *adj.*

Jut·land (jŭt'l∂nd), *n.* a peninsula comprising the continental portion of Denmark: a major naval engagement between the British and German fleets was fought W of this peninsula, 1916. 1,956,836 pop. (est. 1954); 11,411 sq. mi. Danish, **Jylland.**

Ju·tur·na (jōo tûr'n∂), *n. Gk. Myth.* a fountain nymph said to have been beloved by Zeus.

Ju·ve·nal (jōo'v∂ n∂l), *n.* (*Decimus Junius Juvenalis*) A.D. c60-c140, Roman satirical poet.

ju·ve·nal (jōo'v∂ n∂l), *n. Ornithol.* the plumage stage of an altricial bird when it leaves the nest. [t. L: s. *juvenālis*, var. of *juvenīlis* young, pertaining to youth]

ju·ve·nes·cent (jōo'v∂ nĕs'∂nt), *adj.* becoming youthful; growing young again; youthful. [t. L: s. *juvenescens*, ppr., reaching the age of youth] —**ju've·nes'cence,** *n.*

ju·ve·nile (jōo'v∂ n∂l, -nYl, -nīl'), *adj.* **1.** pertaining to, suitable for, or intended for young persons: *juvenile behavior, juvenile books, a juvenile court.* **2.** young. —*n.* **3.** a young person; a youth. **4.** *Theat.* **a.** a youthful male role. **b.** an actor who plays such parts. **5.** *Ornithol.* a young bird in the stage when it has fledged, if altricial, or has replaced down of hatching, if precocial. **6.** a book for young people. [t. L: m.s. *juvenīlis* of youth] —**ju've·nile·ly,** *adv.* —**ju've·nile·ness,** *n.*

ju·ve·nil·i·a (jōo'v∂ nYl'Y∂), *n.pl.* works, esp. writings, produced in youth.

ju·ve·nil·i·ty (jōo'v∂ nYl'∂ tY), *n., pl.* **-ties. 1.** juvenile state, character, or manner. **2.** (*pl.*)youthful qualities or performances. **3.** young persons collectively.

juxta-, a word element meaning "near," "close to," "beside." [comb. form repr. L *juxtā*, prep., adv.]

jux·ta·pose (jŭks't∂pōz'), *v.t.*, **-posed, -posing.** to place in close proximity or side by side.

jux·ta·po·si·tion (jŭks't∂p∂zYsh'∂n), *n.* **1.** a placing close together. **2.** position side by side. [t. F, f. L: *juxtā* JUXTA- + s. *positio* a placing, position]

Jy., July.

Jyl·land (yYl'län), *n.* Danish name of **Jutland.**

K

K, k (kā), *n., pl.* **K's** or **Ks, k's** or **ks.** a consonant, the 11th letter of the English alphabet.

K, *Chem.* potassium.

K., 1. *Chess.* King. **2.** Knight.

k., 1. *Elect.* capacity. **2.** karat or carat. **3.** kilogram. **4.** *Chess.* king. **5.** knight. **6.** knot. **7.** kopeck.

K2, *n.* a mountain peak in N W India, in the Karakoram range in N Kashmir: second loftiest peak in the world. 28,250 ft. Also, **Godwin Austen.**

ka (kä), *n. Egypt. Relig.* a presiding or second spirit supposed to be present in a man or statue. [t. Egyptian]

Kaa·ba (kä'b∂, kä'∂b∂), *n.* a small cube-shaped building in the Great Mosque at Mecca, containing a sacred stone said to have been turned black by the tears of repentant pilgrims or, according to another tradition, by the sins of those who have touched it: the most sacred shrine of the Mohammedans. Also, **Caaba.** [t. Ar.: m. *ka'ba* a square building, der. *ka'b* cube]

kab (kăb), *n.* cab².

kab·a·la (kăb'∂l∂, k∂bä'l∂), *n.* cabala. Also, **kab'ba·la.**

ka·bob (k∂bŏb'), *n.* **1.** (*pl.*) an Oriental dish consisting of small pieces of meat seasoned and roasted on a skewer. **2.** *Anglo-Indian.* roast meat in general. Also, **cabob.** [t. Ar.: m. *kabab*]

ka·bu·ki (kä bōo'kY), *n.* a form of Japanese popular theater, with stylized acting, music, and dancing, in which male actors play all dramatic roles.

Ka·bul (kä'bōol), *n.* **1.** the capital of Afghanistan, in the NE part. 310,000 (est. 1953). **2.** a river flowing from NE Afghanistan E to the Indus in Pakistan. ab. 360 mi.

Ka·byle (k∂bīl'), *n.* **1.** one of a branch of the Berber race dwelling in Algeria and Tunisia. **2.** their language, a Berber dialect. [t. Ar.: m. *qabīla* tribe]

ka·di (kä'dY, kä'dY), *n., pl.* **-dis.** cadi.

Kaf·fir (kăf'∂r, kä'f∂r), *n.* **1.** a member of a South African Negroid race inhabiting parts of the Cape of Good Hope, Natal, etc. **2.** a Bantu language. **3.** (*l.c.*) any of certain grain sorghums, varieties of *Sorghum vulgare*, with stout, short-jointed, leafy stalks, cultivated in South Africa and introduced into the U.S. [t. Ar.: m. *kāfir* unbeliever]

Kaf·frar·i·a (k∂frâr'Y∂), *n.* a region in the S part of the Union of South Africa: inhabited mostly by Kaffirs.

Kaf·ir (kăf'∂r, kä'f∂r), *n.* **1.** a member of a nationality of Indo-European speech, in Kafiristan. **2.** Kaffir.

Ka·fi·ri·stan (kä'fĭ rĭ stän'), *n.* a mountainous region in NE Afghanistan. ab. 5000 sq. mi.

Kaf·ka (käf'kä), *n.* **Franz** (fränts), Bohemian novelist, 1883-1924.

kaf·tan (käf't∂n, käf tän'), *n.* caftan.

Ka·ga·no·vich (kä'gä nô'vYch), *n.* **Lazar Moiseevich** (lä'zär moi sĕ'∂ vYch), born 1893, Soviet statesman.

Ka·ga·wa (kä'gä wä'), *n.* **Toyohiko** (tô'yô hē'kô), 1888-1960, Japanese reformer and social worker.

Ka·ge·ra (kä gĕ'rä), *n.* a river in equatorial Africa, flowing into Lake Victoria from the west: the most remote headstream of the Nile. ab. 430 mi.

Ka·go·shi·ma (kä'gô shē'mä), *n.* a seaport in SW Japan, on Kyushu island. 229,462 (1951).

kai·ak (kī'ăk), *n.* kayak.

Kai·e·teur (kī'ĕ tōōr'), *n.* a waterfall in central British Guiana, on a tributary of the Essequibo river. ab. 760 ft. high.

kaif (kīf), *n.* kef.

Kai·feng (kī'fŭng'), *n.* a city in E China: the capital of Honan province. 281,000 (est. 1950).

kail (kāl), *n.* kale.

Kair·ouan (kĕr wän'), *n.* a city in NE Tunisia: a holy city of Islam. 33,968 (1956). Also, **Kair·wan** (kīr wän').

Kai·ser (kī'z∂r), *n.* **1.** a German emperor. **2.** an Austrian emperor. **3.** *Hist.* a ruler of the Holy Roman Empire. **4.** (*l.c.*) an emperor; a Caesar. [t. G, r. ME *caiser(e), keiser(e)*, t. Scand. (cf. Icel *keisari*); t. ME and OE *cāsere*, ult. t. L: m. *Caesar*] —**kai'ser·ship',** *n.*

Kai·sers·lau·tern (kī'z∂rs lou't∂rn), *n.* a city in SW West Germany, in the Palatinate. 79,900 (est. 1953).

Ka·jar (kä jär'), *n.* Persian or Iranian dynasty which ruled 1794-1925.

ka·ka (kä'k∂), *n.* any of certain New Zealand parrots of the genus *Nestor*, esp. *N. meridionalis*, a species about the size of a crow with a mostly greenish, olive-brown coloration. [t. Maori]

ka·ka·po (kä'kä pō'), *n., pl.* **-pos** (-pōz'), a large, almost flightless, nocturnal parrot, *Strigops habroptilus*, of New Zealand. [t. Maori: f. *kaka* parrot + *po* night]

ka·ke·mo·no (kä'kĕ mô'nô), *n., pl.* **-nos.** an upright Japanese wall picture, usually long and narrow, painted on silk, paper or other material, and mounted on a roller. [t. Jap.: f. *kake* hang + *mono* thing]

ka·ki (kä′kē), *n., pl.* **-kis.** 1. the Japanese persimmon tree. 2. its fruit. [t. Jap.]

kal., kalends.

Ka·la·ha·ri (kä′lähä′rē), *n.* a desert region in SW Africa, largely in Bechuanaland. ab. 350,000 sq. mi.

Kal·a·ma·zoo (kăl′əməzōō′), *n.* a city in SW Michigan. 82,089 (1960).

Ka·lat (kəlät′), *n.* a state in W Pakistan, in the province of Baluchistan. Also, **Khelat.**

kale (kāl), *n.* 1. a plant of the mustard family, *Brassica oleracea,* var. *acephala,* with leaves not forming a head, used as a potherb. 2. *Scot.* cabbage or greens. 3. *U.S. Slang.* money. Also, **kail.** [ME *cale,* var. of COLE]

ka·lei·do·scope (kəlī′dəskōp′), *n.* an optical instrument in which bits of colored glass, etc., in a rotating tube are shown by reflection in continually changing symmetrical forms. [f. s. Gk. *kalós* beautiful + Gk. *eído(s)* form + -SCOPE] —**ka·lei·do·scop·ic** (kəlī′dəskōp′ĭk), **ka·lei·do·scop·i·cal,** *adj.* —**ka·lei·do·scop′·i·cal·ly,** *adv.*

kal·ends (kăl′əndz), *n.pl.* calends.

Ka·le·va·la (kä′lĭ vä′lə), *n.* the national epic of Finland. [t. Finnish: lit., house of a hero]

kale·yard (kāl′yärd′), *n. Scot.* a kitchen garden.

kaleyard school, school of writers describing homely life in Scotland, with much use of Scottish dialect: in vogue toward the close of the 19th century, when books by J. M. Barrie and others were appearing.

Kal·gan (käl′gän′), *n.* former name of **Wanchuan.**

kal·i (kăl′ī, kā′lī), *n., pl.* **kalis.** glasswort. [t. Ar.: m. *qali* (*qilā*). See ALKALI]

kal·ian (käl yän′), *n.* an Eastern tobacco pipe in which the smoke is drawn through water. [t. Pers.]

Ka·li·da·sa (kä′lĭdä′sä), *n.* Hindu dramatist and poet of the 6th century or earlier.

Ka·li·nin (kä lē′nĭn), *n.* 1. Mikhail Ivanovich (mĭhä ēl′ ĭ vä′nŏ vĭch), 1875–1946, president of the Praesidium of the Supreme Council of the Soviet Union, 1938–1946. 2. Formerly, **Tver.** a city in the central Soviet Union in Europe, on the Volga. 240,000 (est. 1956).

Ka·li·nin·grad (kä lē′nĭn gräd′), *n.* a seaport in the W Soviet Union; formerly the capital of East Prussia. 188,000 (est. 1956). German, **Königsberg.**

ka·liph (kā′lĭf, kăl′ĭf), *n.* caliph.

Ka·lisz (kä′lĭsh), *n.* a city in central Poland. 53,809 (1950). German, **Kalisch** (kä′lĭsh).

Kal·li·kaks (kăl′əkăks′), *n.pl.* **The,** the fictitious name of an actual New Jersey family whose history over several generations showed a high incidence of disease, delinquency, and poverty.

Kal·mar (käl′mär), *n.* a seaport in SE Sweden, on **Kalmar Sound,** a strait between Öland and the mainland. 28,312 (est. 1953).

kal·mi·a (käl′mĭ ə), *n.* any plant of the North American ericaceous genus *Kalmia,* comprising evergreen shrubs with showy flowers, as *K. latifolia,* the mountain laurel. [t. NL, after P. *Kalm* (1715–79), Swedish botanist]

Kal·muck (käl′mŭk), *n.* 1. a member of any of a group of Buddhistic Mongol tribes of a region extending from western China to the valley of the lower Volga river. 2. their language, a member of the Mongolian family. Also, **Kal′muk.** [ult. t. Tatar: lit., deserter]

ka·long (kä′lŏng), *n.* any of the large fruit bats or flying foxes, belonging to the genus *Pteropus.* [t. Malay]

kal·so·mine (kăl′səmīn′, -mĭn), *n., v.t.,* **-mined, -mining.** calcimine. [orig. obscure]

Ka·lu·ga (kä lōō′gä), *n.* a city in the central Soviet Union in Europe, SW of Moscow. 80,000 (est. 1948).

Ka·ma (kä′mä), *n.* a river flowing from the Ural area in the Soviet Union into the Volga S of Kazan. ab. 1100 mi.

Ka·ma·ku·ra (kä′mäkōō′rä), *n.* a town in central Japan, on Honshu island: great statue of Buddha.

ka·ma·la (kə mä′lə, kăm′ə lə), *n.* a powder from the capsules of an East Indian euphorbiaceous tree, *Mallotus philippinensis,* used as a yellow dye and in medicine as an anthelmintic. [t. Skt.]

Kam·chat·ka (kăm chăt′kə; *Russ.* käm chät′kä), *n.* a peninsula in the E Soviet Union in Asia, extending S between the Bering Sea and the Sea of Okhotsk. ab. 750 mi. long; ab. 104,000 sq. mi.

kame (kām), *n.* 1. *Phys. Geog.* a ridge or mound of detrital material, esp. of stratified sand and gravel left by a retreating ice sheet. 2. *Scot.* comb. [var. of COMB¹]

Ka·me·rad (kä′mə rät′), *n. German.* comrade (used as a shout of surrender).

Ka·me·run (kä′mə rōōn′), *n.* German name of **Cameroons** (def. 1).

Ka·mi·ka·ze (kä′mĭ kä′zĕ), *n.pl. Japanese.* suicide pilots. [Jap.: divine wind]

Kam·pa·la (käm pä′lä), *n.* the capital of Uganda. 46,735 (1959).

kam·seen (kăm sēn′), *n.* khamsin. Also, **kam·sin** (kăm′sĭn).

Kan., Kansas.

Ka·nak·a (kə năk′ə, kăn′ə kə), *n.* 1. a native Hawaiian. 2. a South Sea islander. [t. Hawaiian: lit., man]

Ka·na·rese (kä′nə rĕz′, -rēs′), *adj., n., pl.* **-rese** —*adj.* 1. of or pertaining to Kanara, a part of the Bombay province of India. —*n.* 2. one of a Dravidian people of the districts of North and South Kanara, in south western India. 3. a Dravidian language of southern India in any of its historical, standard, or dialect forms

Ka·na·za·wa (kä′nä zä′wä), *n.* a seaport in central Japan, on Honshu island. 252,017 (1950).

Kan·chen·jun·ga (kän′chən jŏong′gə), *n.* a peak of the E Himalayas, on the boundary between Nepal and Sikkim: third loftiest peak in the world. 28,146 ft. Also **Kan·chan·jan·ga** (kän′chən jäng′gə), or Kinchinjunga

Kan·da·har (kŭn′də här′), *n.* a city in S Afghanistan. 80,000 (est. 1953).

Kan·din·ski (kän dĭn′skĭ, *Russ.* kän dēn′skĭ), *n.* **Vasili** (vä sē′lĭ), 1866–1944, Russian painter and author.

Kan·dy (kăn′dĭ; *native* kăn′dē), *n.* a city in central Ceylon: famous Buddhist temples. 57,539 (1953).

Kangaroo. *Macropus rufus*
(Total length 8½ ft., tail 3½ ft.)

kan·ga·roo (kăng′gə rōō′), *n., pl.* **-roos,** (*esp. collectively*) **-roo.** any of a family, *Macropodidae,* of herbivorous marsupials of the Australian region with powerful hind legs developed for leaping, a sturdy tail serving as a support and balance, a small head, and very short fore limbs. [? t. native Australian] —**kan′ga·roo′like′,** *adj*

kangaroo court, *Colloq.* an unauthorized or irregular court conducted with disregard for or perversion of legal procedure, as a mock court by prisoners in a jail or an irregularly conducted court in a frontier district

kangaroo rat, 1. any of various small jumping rodents of the family *Heteromyidae,* of Mexico and the western U.S., such as those of the genus *Dipodomys.* 2. an Australian rodent of the genus *Notomys,* found in arid areas.

Kang Te (käng′ tĕ′). See **Pu-Yi.**

Kan·ka·kee (kăng′kə kē′), *n.* a city in NE Illinois. 27,666 (1960).

Kan·nap·o·lis (kə năp′ə lĭs), *n.* a city in W North Carolina. 34,647 (1960).

Ka·no (kä′nō), *n.* a city in N Nigeria. 130,173 (1953).

Kan·pur (kän′pŏŏr), *n.* Indian name for Cawnpore.

Kans., Kansas.

Kan·sas (kăn′zəs), *n.* 1. a State in the central United States: a part of the Midwest. 2,178,611 pop. (1960). 82,276 sq. mi. *Cap.:* Topeka. *Abbr.:* Kans. or Kan. 2. a river in NE Kansas, flowing E to the Missouri river. 169 mi. —**Kan′san,** *adj., n.*

Kansas City, 1. a city in W Missouri at the confluence of the Kansas and the Missouri rivers. 475,539 (1960). 2. a city in NE Kansas, adjacent to Kansas City, Missouri. 121,901 (1960).

Kan·su (kăn′sōō′; *Chin.* gän′sōō′), *n.* a province in NW China. 12,928,102 pop. (1953); 151,160 sq. mi. *Cap.:* Lanchow.

Kant (känt; *Ger.* känt), *n.* **Immanuel** (ĭ män′yŏŏ əl; *Ger.* ĭ mä′nŏō ĕl′), 1724–1804, German philosopher.

kan·tar (kän tär′), *n.* (in Mohammedan countries) a unit of weight corresponding to the hundredweight, but varying in different localities. [t. Ar.: m. *qinṭar,* ult. t. L: m. *centenārium* one hundred (lbs.) weight. See QUINTAL]

Kant·i·an (kăn′tĭ ən), *adj.* 1. of or pertaining to Immanuel Kant. —*n.* 2. a follower of Kant.

Kant·i·an·ism (kăn′tĭ ən ĭz′əm), *n.* the doctrine of Immanuel Kant that every attribute is merely a mode in which the mind is affected, and has no application to a thing in itself. A thing in itself is unthinkable, and ideas are of two kinds only: those presented in sensation, and those introduced in the process of thinking. Religious and strict moral ideas are, however, admitted as regulative principles.

Kao·hsiung (gou′shyŏŏng′), *n.* a seaport in SW Formosa. 118,435. (1953). Also, **Takao.**

ka·o·li·ang (kä′ō lĭ′äng′), *n.* one of the varieties of grain sorghums, *Sorghum vulgare.* [t. Chinese (Mandarin): f. *kao* tall + *liang* millet]

ka·o·lin (kä′ə lĭn), *n.* a fine white clay used in the manufacture of porcelain. Also, **ka′o·line.** [t. F, t. Chinese: m. *Kao-ling* high hill, name of a mountain in China which yielded the first kaolin sent to Europe]

ka·o·lin·ite (kä′ə lĭn nīt′), *n.* hydrated aluminum disilicate, $Al_2Si_2O_5(OH)_4$, a very common mineral, the commonest constituent of kaolin.

Ka·pell·meis·ter (kä pĕl′mīs′tər), *n., pl.* **-ter.** 1. choir leader. 2. a conductor of an orchestra. 3. bandmaster. [G: f. *kapelle* chapel (choir) + *meister* master]

ka·pok (kā′pŏk, kăp′ək), *n.* the silky down which invests the seeds of a silk-cotton tree (kapok tree), *Ceiba pentandra,* of the East Indies, Africa, and tropical America: used for stuffing pillows, etc. and for sound insulation. [t. Malay: m. *kāpoq*]

kap·pa (kăp′ə), *n.* the tenth letter of the Greek alphabet (K, k).

ka·put (kä pŏŏt′), *adj.* smashed; ruined; done for. [G]

a·ra·chi (kə rä/chĭ), *n.* a seaport in and the former apital of Pakistan. 1,126,417 (1951).

a·ra·fu·to (kä/räfōō/tō), *n.* Japanese name of the S art of Sakhalin.

a·ra·gan·da (kä/rägän/dä), *n.* a city in the SW oviet Union in Asia. 350,000 (est. 1956).

ar·a·ite (kär/əīt/), *n.* one of a Jewish sect which rose in the 8th century in opposition to the Talmud.

a·ra·ko·ram (kä/räkŏr/əm), *n.* 1. a lofty mountain ange in NW India, in N Kashmir. Highest peak, K2, 8,250 ft. 2. a pass traversing this range, on the route rom India to Sinkiang province, China. 18,317 ft.

a·ra·ko·rum (kä/räkŏr/əm), *n.* See **Mongol Empire.**

a·ra·kul (kär/əkəl), *n.* 1. an Asiatic breed of sheep ised primarily for the production of lambskin fur. Black s the prevailing color of the lambs, but the fleeces of the ld sheep turn to various shades of brown and gray. ?. caracul (the fur). [orig. place name, widely used in ?urkestan, esp. in naming lakes]

a·ra Kum (kä rä/ kōōm/), a desert in the SW Soviet Jnion in Asia, S of the Aral Sea and largely in the ?urkmen Republic. ab. 110,000 sq. mi.

a·ra Sea (kä/rä), an arm of the Arctic Ocean be-ween Novaya Zemlya and the N Soviet Union.

ar·at (kär/ət), *n.* a twenty-fourth part (used in ex-ressing the fineness of gold, pure gold being 24 karats ine). [t. F, t. It.: m. *carato*, t. Ar.: m. *qīrāṭ* a light weight, . Gk.: m. *kerátion* carob bean, carat, dim. of *kéras* horn]

a·ra·te (kə rä/tē), *n.* a method developed in Japan of lefending oneself without the use of weapons by striking ensitive areas on an attacker's body with the hands, lbows, knees, or feet.

a·re·lia (kə rēl/yə; *Rus.* kä rě/lYä/), *n.* a former au-onomous republic in the NW Soviet Union.

a·re·lo-Fin·nish Soviet Socialist Republic (kə rē/lō fĭn/ĭsh), formerly, a constituent republic of the ioviet Union, in the NW part; reduced in 1957 to an utonomous Soviet Socialist Republic in the Russian ioviet Federated Socialist Republic.

arl-Marx-Stadt (kärl/märks/shtät/), *n.* a city in East Germany, in former state of Saxony. 290,153 (est. 1955). Formerly, **Chemnitz.**

ar·lo·vy Va·ry (kär/lō vĭ vä/rĭ), Czech name of Carlsbad.

arls·bad (kärlz/băd; *Ger.* kärls/bät), *n.* German name of Carlsbad.

arls·ruh·e (kärls/rōō/ə), *n.* a city in SW West Ger-many: former capital of former state of Baden. 222,556 (est. 1955).

ar·ma (kär/mə), *n.* 1. *Hinduism and Buddhism.* the cosmic operation of retributive justice, according to which one's status in life is determined by his deeds in a previous incarnation. 2. *Theos.* the doctrine of inevitable consequence. 3. fate; destiny. [t. Skt.: deed, action]

ar·nak (kär/näk), *n.* a village in Upper Egypt, on the Nile: the N part of the ruins of ancient Thebes.

ar·roo (kə rōō/), *n., pl.* (for def. 2) **-roos.** 1. a vast plateau in the S part of the Union of South Africa, in Cape of Good Hope province. ab. 100,000 sq. mi.; 3000–4000 ft. high. 2. (*l.c.*) one of the arid tablelands, with red clay soil, n South Africa. Also, **ka·roo/.** [later var. of *Karoo*, appar. mishearing of Hottentot *torố* karroo or *garo* desert]

aryo-, a word element meaning "nucleus of a cell." t. Gk., comb. form of *kár̆yon* nut, kernel]

ar·y·o·ki·ne·sis (kär/ĭ ōkĭ nē/sĭs, -kĭ-), *n. Biol.* 1. mitosis. 2. the series of active changes which take place in the nucleus of a living cell in the process of division. [f. KARYO- + Gk. *kínēsis* movement] —**kar·y·o·ki·net·ic** (kär/ĭ ōkĭ nět/Yk, -kĭ-), *adj.*

ar·y·o·lymph (kär/ĭ ōlĭmf/), *n. Bot.* the trans-parent or translucent fluid in a nucleus.

ar·y·om·i·tome (kär/ĭ ŏm/ə tōm/), *n. Biol.* the net-work or reticulum in the nucleus of a cell. [f. KARYO-+ s. Gk. *mítos* thread + *-ome*, var. of -OMA]

ar·y·o·plasm (kär/ĭ ə plăz/əm), *n. Biol.* the sub-stance of the nucleus of a cell. —**kar·y·o·plas/mic**, *adj.*

ar·y·o·some (kär/ĭ ə sōm/), *n. Biol.* 1. any of certain irregular or spherical bodies observed in and supposed to be in a portion of the netlike structure in the nucleus of a cell. See diag. under **cell.** 2. the nucleus of a cell. 3. a chromosome. [f. KARYO- + -SOME[3]]

ar·y·o·tin (kär/ĭ ō/tYn), *n. Biol.* nuclear material; chromatin. [f. s. Gk. *karyôtós* nutlike + -IN[2]]

Kas·bah (käs/bä), *n.* the older, native quarter of Algiers. Also, **Casbah.**

ka·sher (kä/shər), *adj., n.* kosher.

Kash·gar (käsh/gär/), *n.* a city in extreme W China, in Sinkiang. 50,000 (est. 1950). Also, **Shufu.**

Kash·mir (käsh mĭr/), *n.* a state adjacent to the repub-lic of India, Pakistan, Sinkiang, and Tibet. Sovereignty in dispute between India and Pakistan since 1947. 4,410,-000 pop. (est. 1953); 82,258 sq. mi. *Cap.*: Srinagar. Also, **Cashmere.** Official name, **Jammu and Kashmir.** —**Kash·mir·i·an** (käsh mĭr/ĭ ən), *adj., n.*

ash·mir (käsh/mĭr), *n.* cashmere.

Kashmir rug, an Oriental handmade rug, woven flat without pile, and having the patterns which entirely cover its surface embroidered of colored yarns.

Kas·sa (kŏsh/shŏ), *n.* Hungarian name of Košice.

Kas·sa·la (kä/sä lä/), *n.* a city in the E Sudan, near Eritrea: taken by the Italians, 1894. 30,026 (est. 1940).

Kas·sel (käs/əl), *n.* a city in West Germany, 192,515 (est. 1955). Also, **Cassel.**

Kas·tro (käs/trō), *n.* Mytilene (def. 2).

ka·tab·o·lism (kə täb/əlĭz/əm), *n.* catabolism.

Ka·tah·din (kə tä/dĭn), *n.* **Mount,** the highest peak in Maine, in the central part. 5273 ft.

Ka·thi·a·war (kä/tē äwär/), *n.* a peninsula on the W coast of India.

kath·ode (käth/ōd), *n.* cathode.

kat·i·on (kăt/ī/ən), *n.* cation.

Kat·mai (kăt/mī), *n.* 1. **Mount,** an active volcano in SW Alaska: eruption, 1912. ab. 7500 ft. 2. a national monument including Mt. Katmai and the Valley of Ten Thousand Smokes. ab. 1700 sq. mi.

Kat·man·du (kăt/mändōō/), *n.* the capital of Nepal. 108,805 (est. 1941).

Ka·to·wi·ce (kä/tō vě/tsě), *n.* a city in S Poland. 191,-000 (est. 1954). German, **Kat·to·witz** (kä/tō vĭts).

Kat·rine (kăt/rĭn), *n.* **Loch,** a beautiful lake in central Scotland: scene of Scott's *Lady of the Lake.* 8 mi. long.

Kat·te·gat (kăt/əgăt/), *n.* the strait between Jutland and Sweden. 40–70 mi. wide. Also, **Cattegat.**

Katydid.
Platyphyllum concavum
(About 1¾ in. long)

ka·ty·did (kā/tY dYd), *n.* any of the large, usually green, long-horned Amer-ican grasshoppers of the family *Tettigo-niidae*, known for the loud note of the males of some species, notably *Platy-phyllum concavum*. [imit. of the sound made]

Ka·u·a·i (kä/ōō ä/ē), *n.* one of the Hawaiian Islands, in the NW part of the group. 29,905 pop. (1950); 511 sq. mi.

Kauf·man (kôf/mən), *n.* **George S.,** 1889–1961, U.S. dramatist.

Kau·nas (kou/näs), *n.* a city in the W Soviet Union, in the Lithuanian Republic. 195,000 (est. 1956). Russian, **Kovno.**

kau·ri (kour/ĭ), *n., pl.* **-ris.** 1. a tall coniferous tree, *Agathis australis*, of New Zealand, yielding a valuable timber and a resin. 2. its wood. 3. kauri resin. 4. any of various other trees of the genus *Agathis*. [t. Maori]

kauri resin, the resin, used in making varnish, which exudes from the thick bark of the kauri. Also, **kauri gum, kauri copal.**

kau·ry (kour/ĭ), *n., pl.* **-ries.** kauri.

ka·va (kä/və), *n.* 1. a Polynesian shrub, *Piper methys-ticum*, of the pepper family. Its root has aromatic and pungent qualities. 2. a fermented, intoxicating bever-age made from the roots of the kava. [t. Polynesian]

Ka·ver·i (kô/vərĭ), *n.* Cauvery.

Ka·wa·gu·chi (kä/wägōō/chě), *n.* a city in central Japan, on Honshu island near Tokyo. 124,783 (1950).

Ka·wa·sa·ki (kä/wä sä/kē), *n.* a seaport in central Japan, on Honshu island, near Tokyo. 319,226 (1950).

Kay (kā), *n.* Sir, *Arthurian Romance.* the rude, boastful foster brother and seneschal of Arthur.

kay·ak (kī/ăk), *n.* an Eskimo hunting craft with a skin cover on a light framework, made watertight by flexible closure around the waist of the occu-pant. Also, **kaiak.** [t. Eskimo]

Kayak

Kay·se·ri (kī/sě rē/), *n.* a city in central Turkey. 81,127 (1955). Ancient, **Caesarea.**

Ka·zak Soviet Socialist Republic (kä zäk/), a constituent republic of the Soviet Union, E and N of the Caspian Sea. 8,500,000 (est. 1956); 1,055,900 sq. mi. *Cap.*: Alma-Ata. Also, **Ka·zakh,** **Ka·zak·stan** (kä/zäk stän/).

Ka·zan (kä zän/y), *n.* a city in the E Soviet Union in Europe, near the Volga. 565,000 (est. 1956).

K.B., 1. *Chess.* king's bishop. 2. King's Bench. 3. Knight Bachelor.

kc., kilocycle; kilocycles.

K.C., 1. King's Counsel. 2. Knight Commander. 3. Knights of Columbus.

K.C.B., Knight Commander of the Bath.

ke·a (kā/ə, kē/ə), *n.* a large, greenish New Zealand parrot, *Nestor notabilis*. [t. Maori]

Ke·a (kē/ä), *n.* Keos.

Kean (kēn), *n.* Edmund, 1787–1833, British tragedian.

Kear·ny (kär/nĭ), *n.* 1. a city in NE New Jersey, near Newark. 37,472 (1960). 2. Philip, 1815–62, U.S. general.

keat (kēt), *n.* the young of the guinea fowl.

Keats (kēts), *n.* John, 1795–1821, British poet.

Ke·ble (kē/bəl), *n.* John, 1792–1866, British clergyman and poet.

Kech·ua (kěch/wə), *n.* 1. a Kechua-speaking Indian of Peru, Bolivia, or Ecuador. 2. the language spoken orig-inally by the Indians of Cuzco, Peru, spread widely by the conquests of the Incas. Also, **Quechua.** [native name] —**Kech/uan,** *adj., n.*

keck (kěk), *v.i.* 1. to retch; be nauseated. 2. to feel or show disgust or strong dislike. [cf. OE *cecil* choking]

Kecs·ke·mét (kěch/kě māt/), *n.* a city in central Hungary. 64,170 (est. 1954).

ked (kěd), *n.* the sheep tick.

Ke·dah (kā/dä), *n.* a state in the former Federation of Malaya: now part of the federation of Malaysia. 701,964 pop. (1957); 3660 sq. mi. *Cap.*: Alor Star.

ked·dah (kĕd/ə), *n.* kheda.

kedge (kĕj), *v.,* **kedged, kedging,** *n.* —*v.t.* **1.** to warp or pull (a ship, etc.) along by means of a rope attached to an anchor. —*v.i.* **2.** to move by being pulled along with the aid of an anchor. —*n.* **3.** Also, **kedge anchor. a** small anchor used in kedging and otherwise.

Ke·dron (kē/drən), *n.* a ravine in Jordan, E of Jerusalem: in ancient times a brook, Also, **Kidron.**

ke·ef (kĭ′ĕf′), *n.* kef (def. 2).

keel[1] (kēl), *n.* **1.** a longitudinal timber, or combination of timbers, iron plates, or the like, extending along the middle of the bottom of a vessel from stem to stern and supporting the whole frame. See diag. under **gunwale. 2. a** ship. **3.** a part corresponding to a ship's keel in some other structure, as in a dirigible balloon. **4.** *Bot., Zool.* a longitudinal ridge, as on a leaf or bone; a carina. —*v.t., v.i.* **5.** to turn or upset so as to bring the wrong side or part uppermost. [ME *kele,* t. Scand.; cf. Icel. *kjölr*]

keel[2] (kēl), *n.* a fatal disease of domestic ducks. [special use of **KEEL**[1]]

keel·boat (kēl/bōt/), *n.* a shallow freight boat or barge, built with a keel and decked over, used on rivers of the western U.S.

keel·haul (kēl/hôl/), *v.t. Naut.* to haul (a person) under the keel of a vessel, as for punishment. [t. D: m.s. *kielhalen,* f. *kiel* keel + *halen* haul]

Kee·ling Islands (kē/lĭng), Cocos Islands.

keel·son (kĕl/sən, kēl/-), *n. Naut.* a strengthening line of timbers or iron plates in a ship, above and parallel with the keel. Also, **kelson.** [der. **KEEL**[1]; orig. obscure]

Kee·lung (kē/lŏŏng/), *n.* a seaport on the N coast of Formosa. 174,254 (1953).

keen[1] (kēn), *adj.* **1.** sharp, or so shaped as to cut or pierce substances readily: *a keen blade.* **2.** sharp, piercing, or biting: *a keen wind, keen satire.* **3.** characterized by strength and distinctness of perception, as the ear or hearing, the eye, sight, etc. **4.** having or showing great mental penetration or acumen: *keen reasoning.* **5.** animated by or showing strong feeling or desire: *keen competition.* **6.** intense, as feeling, desire, etc. **7.** ardent; eager (often fol. by *about, for,* etc., or an infinitive). [ME *kene,* OE *cēne,* c. G *kühn* bold] —**keen/ly,** *adv.* —**keen/ness,** *n.* —Syn. 1, 4. See **sharp.**

keen[2] (kēn), *Irish.* —*n.* **1.** a wailing lament for the dead. —*v.t.* **2.** to wail in lamentation for the dead. [t. Irish: m *caoine,* der. *caoinim* I lament] —**keen/er,** *n.*

keep (kēp), *v.,* **kept, keeping,** *n.* —*v.t.* **1.** to maintain in one's action or conduct: *to keep watch, step, or silence.* **2.** to cause to continue in some place, position, state, course, or action specified: *to keep a light burning.* **3.** to maintain in condition or order, as by care and labor. **4.** to hold in custody or under guard, as a prisoner; detain; prevent from coming or going. **5.** to have habitually in stock or for sale. **6.** to maintain in one's service or for one's use or enjoyment. **7.** to have the charge or custody of. **8.** to withhold from the knowledge of others: *to keep a secret.* **9.** to withhold from use; reserve. **10.** to maintain by writing, entries, etc.: *to keep a diary.* **11.** to record (business transactions, etc.) regularly: *to keep records.* **12.** to observe; pay obedient regard to (a law, rule, promise, etc.). **13.** to conform to; follow; fulfill: *to keep one's word.* **14.** to observe (a season, festival, etc.) with formalities or rites: *to keep Christmas.* **15.** to maintain or carry on, as an establishment, business, etc.; manage: *to keep house.* **16.** to guard; protect. **17.** to maintain or support (a person, etc.). **18.** to take care of; tend: *to keep sheep.* **19.** to maintain in active existence, or hold, as an assembly, court, fair, etc. **20.** to remain in (a place, etc.). **21.** to maintain one's position in or on. **22.** to continue to follow (a path, track, course, etc.). **23.** to continue to hold or have: *to keep a thing in mind.* **24.** to save, hold, or retain. —*v.i.* **25.** to continue in an action, course, position, state, etc.: *to keep in sight.* **26.** to remain, or continue to be, as specified: *to keep cool.* **27.** to remain or stay in a place: *to keep indoors.* **28.** to continue unimpaired or without spoiling: *the milk will keep on ice.* **29.** to admit of being reserved for a future occasion. **30.** to keep oneself or itself (fol. by *away, back, off, out,* etc.): *keep off the grass.* **31.** to restrain oneself: *try to keep from smiling.* **32.** Some special verb phrases are: **keep in with,** *Colloq.* to keep oneself in favor with. **keep time, 1.** to record time, as a watch or clock does. **2.** to beat, mark, or observe the rhythmic accents. **3.** to perform rhythmic movements in unison. **keep to, 1.** to adhere to (an agreement, plan, facts, etc.). **2.** to confine oneself to: *to keep to one's bed.* **keep to oneself,** to hold aloof from the society of others. **keep track of, tabs on,** to keep account (of). **keep up, 1.** to maintain an equal rate of speed, activity, or progress, as with another. **2.** to bear up; continue without breaking down, as under strain. —*n.* **33.** subsistence; board and lodging: *to work for one's keep.* **34.** the innermost and strongest structure or central tower of a medieval castle. **35.** (*pl.*) a game in which the winner has the right to keep his winnings. **36. for keeps,** *Colloq.* **a.** for keeping as one's own permanently: *to play for keeps.* **b.** permanently; altogether. [ME *kepen,* OE *cēpan* observe, heed, regard, await, take; akin to Icel. *kōpa* stare] —Syn. 2. KEEP, RESERVE, RETAIN, WITHHOLD refer to having and holding in possession. KEEP (a common word) and RETAIN (a more formal one) agree in meaning to continue to have or hold, as opposed to losing, parting with, or giving up: *to keep a book for a week.* To RESERVE is to keep for some

future use, occasion, or recipient, or to hold back for a time *to reserve judgment.* To WITHHOLD is generally to hold back altogether: *to withhold help.* **4.** detain, hold, confine.

keep·er (kē/pər), *n.* **1.** one who keeps, guards, or watches. **2.** something that keeps, or serves to guard, hold in place, retain, etc. **3.** something that keeps or lasts well, as a fruit. **4.** a guard ring. —**keep/er·less,** *adj.* —Syn. 1. guard, warden; custodian, guardian.

keep·ing (kē/pĭng), *n.* **1.** just conformity in things or elements associated together: *his deeds are not in keeping with his words.* **2.** act of one who or that which keeps; observance, custody, or care. **3.** maintenance or keep. **4.** holding, reserving, or retaining. —Syn. 2. See **custody.**

keep·sake (kēp/sāk/), *n.* anything kept, or given to be kept, for the sake of the giver.

Kee·wa·tin (kē wā/tĭn), *n.* a district in N Canada, in the Northwest Territories. 228,160 sq. mi.

kef (kāf), *n.* (among the Arabs) **1.** a state of drowsy contentment, as from the use of a narcotic. **2.** Also, **keef.** a substance, esp. a smoking preparation of hemp leaves, used to produce this state. Also, **kief, kaif.**

keg (kĕg), *n.* **1.** a small cask or barrel, usually holding from 5 to 10 gallons. **2.** a unit of weight, equal to 100 lbs., used for nails. [late ME *cag,* t. Scand.; cf. Icel. *kaggi*]

Kei·jo (kā/jō/, -rō/), *n.* Japanese name of Seoul.

keir (kĭr), *n.* kier.

Kei·tel (kī/təl), *n.* **Wilhelm** (vĭl/hĕlm), 1882–1946, German marshal: chief of Nazi High Command.

Keith (kēth), *n.* **Sir Arthur,** 1866–1955, British anthropologist.

Ke·lan·tan (kə län/tän/), *n.* a state in the former Federation of Malaya: now part of the federation of Malaysia. 505,522 pop. (1957); 5750 sq. mi. *Cap.:* Kota Bahru.

Kel·ler (kĕl/ər), *n.* **Helen Adams,** born 1880, U.S. author, blind and deaf, who learned to speak.

Kel·logg (kĕl/ôg, -ŏg, -əg), *n.* **Frank Billings,** 1856–1937, U.S. statesman.

ke·loid (kē/loid), *n. Pathol.* a kind of fibrous tumor forming hard, irregular, clawlike excrescences upon the skin. Also, **cheloid.** [*k*- var., f. Gk. *kēl*(is) stain + -OID; *ch*- var., f. Gk. *chēl*(ē) claw + -OID]

kelp (kĕlp), *n.* **1.** any of the large brown seaweeds belonging to the family *Laminariaceae.* **2.** the ash of such seaweeds. [ME *culp;* ult. orig. unknown]

kel·pie (kĕl/pĭ), *n.* **1.** *Scot.* a fabled water spirit, usually in the form of a horse, reputed to give warning of or to cause drowning. **2.** *Australian.* a breed of sheep dogs. [orig. uncert.]

kel·py (kĕl/pĭ), *n., pl.* **-pies.** kelpie.

kel·son (kĕl/sən), *n.* keelson.

Kelt (kĕlt), *n.* Celt. —**Kelt/ic,** *n., adj.*

kelt (kĕlt), *n.* a salmon that has spawned.

kel·ter (kĕl/tər), *n. Brit. Dial.* kilter.

Kel·vin (kĕl/vĭn), *n.* **William Thomson, 1st Baron,** 1824–1907, British physicist and mathematician.

Kelvin scale, *Physics.* a scale of temperature (**Kelvin temperature**), based on thermodynamic principles, in which zero is equivalent to −459.4°F. or −273°C.

Ke·mal A·ta·türk (kĕ mäl/ ä/tä tÿrk/), (*Mustafa Kemal Pasha*) 1880–1938, president of Turkey, 1923–38.

Kem·ble (kĕm/bəl), *n.* **1. Frances Anne,** or **Fanny,** (*Mrs. Butler*) 1809–93, British actress and author. **2. John Philip,** 1757–1823, British tragedian.

Ke·me·ro·vo (kĕ/mĕ rō vō), *n.* a city in the S Soviet Union in Asia. 240,000 (est. 1956).

Kem·pis (kĕm/pĭs), *n.* **Thomas à** (ə), 1380?–1471, German churchman and reputed author.

ken (kĕn), *n., v.,* **kenned** or **kent, kenning.** —*n.* **1.** range of sight or vision. **2.** knowledge or cognizance; mental perception. —*v.t.* **3.** *Archaic.* to see; descry; recognize. **4.** *Scot.* to have acquaintance with. **5.** *Scot. Law.* to acknowledge as heir; recognize by a judicial act. —*v.i.* **6.** *Archaic., Scot.,* or *Brit. Dial.* to have knowledge of something. [ME *kennen,* OE *cennan,* c. Icel. *kenna* make known, know (cf. later E senses), G *kennen* know; orig. a causative of the verb represented by CAN[1]]

Ken., Kentucky.

Ken·dal green (kĕn/dəl), **1.** a green woolen cloth formerly in use. **2.** green produced by a dye extracted from the woadwaxen plant.

Ken·il·worth (kĕn/əl wûrth/), *n.* a town in central England, in Warwickshire: ruined castle. 10,738 (1951).

Ken·ne·bec (kĕn/ə bĕk/), *n.* a river flowing through W Maine S to the Atlantic. 164 mi.

Ken·ne·dy (kĕn/ə dĭ), *n.* **1. John Fitzgerald,** 1917–63, 35th president of the United States, 1961–63. **2. Cape,** formerly Cape Canaveral, on the E. coast of Florida: site of U.S. missile test center. **3. John F., International Airport.** See John F. Kennedy International Airport.

ken·nel (kĕn/əl), *n., v.,* **-neled, -neling** or (*esp. Brit.*) **-nelled, -nelling.** —*n.* **1.** a house for a dog or dogs. **2.** (*often pl.*) an establishment where dogs are bred. **3.** (*in contemptuous use*) a wretched abode. —*v.t.* **4.** to put into or keep in a kennel. —*v.i.* **5.** to take shelter or lodge in a kennel. [ME *kenel,* t. ONF, g. VL *canīle,* der. L *canīs* dog]

Ken·nel·ly-Heav·i·side layer (kĕn/ə lĭ hĕv/ĭ sīd/), Heaviside layer.

ken·ning (kĕn/ĭng), *n.* a descriptive poetical name used for, or in addition to, the usual name of a person or thing. *Example:* "a wave traveler" for "a boat." [t. Icel.]

---

b., blend of, blended; c., cognate with; d., dialect, dialectal; der., derived from; f., formed from; g., going back to; m., modification of; r., replacing; s., stem of; t., taken from; ?, perhaps. See the full key on inside cover.

Ken·ny (kĕn'ĭ), *n.* **Elizabeth,** (*Sister Kenny*) 1884?–1952, Australian nurse: developed a method of treating infantile paralysis.

ke·no (kē'nō), *n.* a game of chance, adapted from lotto for gambling purposes.

ke·no·gen·e·sis (kē'nō jĕn'ə sĭs, kĕn'ō-), *n.* cenogenesis.

Ke·no·sha (kĭ nō'shə), *n.* a city in SE Wisconsin: a port on Lake Michigan. 67,899 (1960).

ke·no·sis (kĭ nō'sĭs), *n.* **1.** *Theol.* the renunciation of the divine nature or dignity in the incarnation (used of Christ, "who, being in the form of God . . . took upon himself the form of a servant, and was made in the likeness of men." Phil. 2:6, 7, R.V.). **2.** one of several doctrines or concepts about this. [t. NL, t. Gk.: an emptying] **—ke·not·ic** (kĭ nŏt'ĭk), *adj.*

Ken·sing·ton (kĕn'zĭng tən), *n.* a W borough of London, England. 168,054 (1951).

Kent (kĕnt), *n.* **1.** a county in SE England. 1,564,324 pop. (1951); 1525 sq. mi. *Cap.:* Maidstone. **2.** an ancient English kingdom in SE Britain. See map under **Mercia. 3.** James, 1763–1847, U.S. jurist. **4.** Rockwell, born 1882, U.S. painter and writer.

Kent·ish (kĕn'tĭsh), *adj.* of or pertaining to Kent.

kent·ledge (kĕnt'lĭj), *n. Naut.* pig iron used as permanent ballast. [orig. obscure]

Ken·tuck·y (kən tŭk'ĭ), *n.* **1.** a State in the E central United States. 3,038,156 pop. (1960); 40,395 sq. mi. *Cap.:* Frankfort. *Abbr.:* Ky. or Ken. **2.** a river flowing from E Kentucky NW to the Ohio river. 259 mi. **—Ken·tuck'i·an,** *adj., n.*

Kentucky bluegrass, a common grass, *Poa pratensis,* esp. of the Mississippi valley, highly valued for pasturage and hay.

Kentucky coffee tree, a tall tree of North America, *Gymnocladus dioica,* whose seeds (**Kentucky coffee beans**) were formerly used as a substitute for coffee.

Ken·ya (kĕn'yə, kēn'-), *n.* **1.** an independent state in E Africa: member of the Brit. Commonwealth; formerly a British crown colony and protectorate. 7,290,000 pop. (est. 1961); 219,730 sq. mi. *Cap.:* Nairobi. **2. Mount,** volcanic mountain in Kenya. 17,040 ft.

Ke·o·kuk (kē'ə kŭk'), *n.* a city in SE Iowa, on the Mississippi: large power dam. 16,316 (1960).

Ke·os (kē'ŏs), *n.* an island of the Cyclades, off the SE coast of Greece. 3108 pop. (1951); 56 sq. mi. Also, **Zea.**

Ke·phal·le·ni·a (kĕ'fä lē nē'ä), *n.* Greek name of **Cephalonia.**

kep·i (kĕp'ĭ), *n., pl.* **kep·is.** a French military cap with a flat circular top and a horizontal visor. [t. F, t. d. G: m. *käppi,* dim. of G *kappe* cap]

Kep·ler (kĕp'lər), *n.* **Johann** (yō'hän), 1571–1630, German astronomer.

kept (kĕpt), *v.* pt. and pp. of **keep.**

Ke·ra·la (kā'rŭ lŭ), *n.* a state in SW India. 13,550,000 pop. (est. 1956); 15,035 sq. mi. *Cap.:* Trivandrum. Formerly, **Travancore.**

ke·ram·ic (kĭ răm'ĭk), *adj.* ceramic.

ker·a·tin (kĕr'ə tĭn), *n. Zool.* an albuminous substance, consisting of the dead outer corneal skin layer, and variously modified into horn, feathers, hair, hoofs. Also, **ceratin.** [f. s. Gk. *kéras* horn + -IN²]

ker·a·tog·e·nous (kĕr'ə tŏj'ə nəs), *adj.* producing horn or a horny substance. [f. *kerato-* (comb. form repr. Gk. *kéras* horn) + -GENOUS]

ker·a·toid (kĕr'ə toid'), *adj.* resembling horn; horny. [t. Gk.: m.s. *keratoeidḗs*]

Ker·a·tol (kĕr'ə tōl, -tŏl'), *n. Trademark.* a leatherlike water-proofed synthetic cloth.

ker·a·to·plas·ty (kĕr'ə tō plăs'tĭ), *n., pl.* **-ties.** a plastic surgical operation upon the cornea; specif., a corneal transplantation.

kerb (kûrb), *n., v.t. Brit.* curb (defs. 4, 10).

kerb·stone (kûrb'stōn'), *n. Brit.* curbstone.

Kerch (kĕrch), *n.* a seaport in the SW Soviet Union, on **Kerch Strait,** a strait connecting the Sea of Azov and the Black Sea. 120,000 (est. 1948).

ker·chief (kûr'chĭf), *n.* **1.** a cloth worn as a head covering, esp. by women. **2.** a cloth worn or carried on the person. [ME *curchef,* contr. of *coverchef* t. OF: m. *couverchief,* f. *covrir* COVER + *chief* head. Cf. CHIEF]

Ke·ren·ski (kĕ rĕn'skĭ), *n.* **Aleksandr Feodorovich** (ä'lĕksän'dər fē ŏ'dō rō'vĭch), born 1881, Russian revolutionist; premier, 1917. Also, **Ke·ren'sky.**

Ker·e·san (kĕr'ə sən), *n.* a linguistic stock of Pueblo tribes of the Rio Grande valley and neighboring areas.

kerf (kûrf), *n.* **1.** the cut or incision made by a saw or other instrument. **2.** that which is cut. [ME *kerf, kyrf,* OE *cyrf* a cutting, akin to *ceorfan,* v., cut, CARVE]

Ker·gue·len (kûr'gə lən'; Fr. kĕr gälän'), *n.* a desolate island in the S Indian Ocean: a possession of France. ab. 1400 sq. mi.

Ker·ky·ra (kĕr'kə rä'), *n.* Greek name of **Corfu.**

Ker·man (kĕr män'), *n.* a city in SE Iran. 50,000 (est. 1949).

ker·mes (kûr'mēz), *n.* **1.** a red dye formerly prepared from the dried bodies of the females of a scale insect, *Kermes ilices,* which lives on certain oaks of the Mediterranean region. **2.** the small evergreen oak, *Puercus*

coccifera, on which it is found. [t. Ar., Pers.: m. *qirmiz.* Cf. CARMINE, CRIMSON]

ker·mis (kûr'mĭs), *n.* **1.** (in the Low Countries) an annual fair or festival attended with sports and merrymaking. **2.** *U.S.* a similar entertainment, usually for charitable purposes. Also, **ker'mess, kirmess.** [t. D, var. of *kermisse, kerkmisse* church mass (on the anniversary of the dedication of a church)]

kern[1] (kûrn), *n. Archaic.* **1.** a band of light-armed foot soldiers of ancient Ireland. **2.** (in Ireland or sometimes in the Scottish Highlands) a soldier. **3.** an Irish peasant. Also, **kerne.** [ME *kerne,* t. Irish: m. *ceithern* band of foot soldiers. See CATERAN]

kern[2] (kûrn), *Print.* **—n. 1.** a part of the face of a type projecting beyond the body or shank, as in certain italic letters. **—v.t. 2.** to form or furnish with a kern, as a type or letter. [t. F: m. *carne* point, g. s. L *cardo* hinge]

Kern (kûrn), *n.* **Jerome David,** 1885–1945, U.S. composer.

ker·nel (kûr'nəl), *n., v.,* **-neled, -neling** or (*esp. Brit.*) **-nelled, -nelling. —n. 1.** the softer, usually edible, part contained in the shell of a nut or the stone of a fruit. **2.** the body of a seed within its husk or integuments. **3.** a grain, as of wheat. **4.** the central part of anything; the nucleus; the core. **—v.t. 5.** to enclose as a kernel. [ME *kirnel, curnel,* OE *cyrnel,* dim. of *corn* seed, grain. See CORN¹] **—ker'nel·less,** *adj.*

kern·ite (kûr'nīt), *n.* a mineral, hydrated sodium borate, ($Na_2B_4O_7 \cdot 4H_2O$), occurring in transparent colorless crystals: the principal source of boron compounds in the U.S.

ker·o·sene (kĕr'ə sēn', kĕr'ə sēn'), *n.* an oil for lamps and heating, a mixture of hydrocarbons, distilled from petroleum, bituminous shale, coal, etc.; illuminating or burning oil. [f. Gk. *kērós* wax + -ENE]

Ker·ry (kĕr'ĭ), *n.* a county in SW Ireland, in Munster. 1815 sq. mi. 121,823 (prelim. 1956); *Co. seat:* Tralee.

ker·ry (kĕr'ĭ), *n., pl.* **-ries.** one of a breed of small dairy cattle originating in Kerry.

ker·sey (kûr'zĭ), *n., pl.* **-seys. 1.** a compact, wellfulled woolen cloth with a fine nap and smooth face. **2.** a coarse twilled woolen cloth with a cotton warp. [ME; ? named after *Kersey,* in Suffolk, England]

kes·trel (kĕs'trəl), *n.* a common small falcon, *Falco tinnunculus,* of northern parts of the Eastern Hemisphere, notable for hovering in the air with its head to the wind. [var. of earlier *castrel.* Cf. F *cresselle*]

ketch (kĕch), *n.* a fore-and-aft rigged vessel with a large mainmast and a smaller mast aft, but forward of the rudder post. [earlier *catch,* appar. der. CATCH, v.]

Ketch·i·kan (kĕch'ə kän'), *n.* a seaport in SE Alaska. 6,483 (1960).

ketch·up (kĕch'əp), *n.* catchup. [appar. t. Chinese (Amoy d.): m. *kê-tsiap* brine of pickled fish. Cf. Malay *Kechop* sauce (? t. Chinese)]

ke·tene (kē'tēn), *n. Chem.* **1.** a gas, $H_2C = C = O$, with a penetrating odor, obtained from acetic anhydride or acetone. **2.** a class of compounds having the type formulas, $RHC = C = O$ and $R_2C = C = O$. [f. KET(ONE) + -ENE]

ke·to-e·nol tautomerism (kē'tō ē'nōl, -nōl), *Chem.* a type of tautomerism in which the individual tautomers may be isolated as a keto form and an enol.

ke·to form (kē'tō), *Chem.* (in a keto-enol tautomeric substance) the form with the characteristics of a ketone.

ke·tone (kē'tōn), *n. Chem.* any of a class of organic compounds, having the general formula, RCOR, containing the carbonyl group, CO, attached to two organic radicals, as acetone, CH_3COCH_3. [t. G: m. *keton,* with -*e* from *acetone,* of the G equivalent of which *keton* is a form aphetically der.] **—ke·ton·ic** (kĭ tŏn'ĭk), *adj.*

ke·tose (kē'tōs), *n. Chem.* any of the sugars which have a ketone group or its equivalent.

ke·to·sis (kĭ tō'sĭs), *n. Pathol.* condition of having too much of a ketone in the body, as in diabetes, acidosis, etc. [f. KET(ONE) + -OSIS]

Ket·ter·ing (kĕt'ər ĭng), *n.* a city in SW Ohio. 54,462 (1960).

ket·tle (kĕt'əl), *n.* **1.** a container for boiling liquids, cooking foods, etc.; a pot. **2.** teakettle. **3.** kettledrum. **4. kettle of fish,** a mess, muddle, or awkward state of things (often preceded ironically by *pretty, fine,* etc.). **5.** a kettle hole. [ME *ketel,* OE *cetel* (t. G *kessel*), t. L: m.s. *catillus,* dim. of *catīnus* bowl, pot]

ket·tle·drum (kĕt'əl drŭm'), *n.* a drum consisting of a hollow hemisphere of brass or copper with a skin stretched over it, which can be accurately tuned.

kettle hole, a kettle-shaped cavity in rock or detrital material, esp. in glacial drift.

Kettledrum

kev·el (kĕv'əl), *n. Naut.* a sturdy bit, bollard, etc., on which the heavier hawsers of a ship may be secured. [ME *kevile,* t. ONF: m. *keville* pin, g. L *clāvicula* little key]

Kew (kū), *n.* a part of Richmond, in SE England, near London: famous botanical gardens. 4362 (1951).

Kew·pie (kū'pĭ), *n. Trademark.* a small, very plump doll, usually made of plaster or celluloid.

key[1] (kē), *n., pl.* **keys,** *adj., v.,* **keyed, keying. —n. 1.** an instrument for fastening or opening a lock by mov-

ing its bolt. **2.** a means of attaining, understanding‘ solving, etc.: *the key to a problem.* **3.** a book or the like containing the solutions or translations of material given elsewhere as exercises. **4.** a systematic explanation of abbreviations, symbols, etc., used in a dictionary, map, etc. **5.** something that secures or controls entrance to a place. **6.** a pin, bolt, wedge, or other piece inserted in a hole or space to lock or hold parts of a mechanism or structure together; a cotter. **7.** a contrivance for grasping and turning a bolt, nut, etc. **8.** one of a set of levers or parts pressed in operating a telegraph, typewriter, etc. **9.** *Music.* **a.** that part of the lever mechanism of piano, organ, or wood wind, which a finger operates. **b.** the keynote or tonic of a scale. **c.** the relationship perceived between all tones in a given unit of music to a single tone or a keynote; tonality. **d.** the principal tonality of a composition: *symphony in the key of C minor.* **10.** tone or pitch, as of voice: *to speak in a high key.* **11.** strain, or characteristic style, as of expression or thought. **12.** *Elect.* **a.** a device for opening and closing electrical contacts. **b.** a hand-operated switching device ordinarily formed of concealed spring contacts with an exposed handle or push button, capable of switching one or more parts of a circuit. **13.** *Bot., Zool.* a systematic tabular classification of the significant characteristics of the members of a group of organisms to facilitate identification and comparison. **14.** *Masonry.* a keystone. **15.** degree of intensity, as of feeling or action. **16.** *Bot.* a samara.
—*adj.* **17.** chief; major; fundamental: *the key industries of a nation.*
—*v.t.* **18.** to bring to a particular degree of intensity of feeling, excitement, energy, etc. (often fol. by *up*). **19.** to adjust (speech, etc.) as if to a particular key. **20.** *Music.* to regulate the key or pitch of. **21.** to fasten, secure, or adjust with a key, wedge, or the like, as parts of a mechanism. **22.** to provide with a key or keys. **23.** to lock with, or as with, a key. **24.** *Masonry.* to provide (a key) at a juncture of members. [ME *key(e)*, OE *cǽg*, c. OFris. *kei, kai*]

key² (kē), *n., pl.* **keys.** a reef or low island; cay. [t. Sp.: m. *cayo*, t. F: m. *quai*, older *cai*; of Celtic orig.]

Key (kē), *n.* **Francis Scott,** 1780–1843, U.S. lawyer: author of *The Star-Spangled Banner.*

key·board (kē′bôrd′), *n.* **1.** the row or set of keys in a piano, typewriter, etc. **2.** any of two or more sets of keys, as in large organs or harpsichords.

key fruit, *Bot.* a samara.

key·hole (kē′hōl′), *n.* a hole for a key to a lock.

Keynes (kānz), *n.* **John Maynard** (mā′nərd, -närd), **1st Baron,** 1883–1946, British economist and writer.

key·note (kē′nōt′), *n., v., -noted, -noting.* —*n.* **1.** *Music.* the note or tone on which a key (system of tones) is founded; the tonic. **2.** the determining principle governing the spirit of thought, action, etc. **3.** the line of policy to be followed by a party in a political (or other) campaign, as set forth authoritatively in advance in a public speech or other formal announcement. —*v.t.* **4.** to announce the policy of (a political party, etc.). **5.** *Music.* to give the keynote of.

key·not·er (kē′nō′tər), *n.* one who gives the keynote, as of a political campaign or convention.

Key·ser·ling (kī′zər lǐng), *n.* **Hermann Alexander** (her′mänˈä′lě ksän′dər), **Count,** 1880–1946, German writer and traveler.

key signature, *Music.* (in notation) the group of sharps or flats placed after the clef to indicate the tonality of the music following.

key·stone (kē′stōn′), *n.* **1.** the wedge-shaped piece at the summit of an arch, regarded as holding the other pieces in place. See diag. under **arch.** **2.** something on which associated things depend.

Key West, 1. an island in S Florida, in the Gulf of Mexico. **2.** a seaport on this island: the southernmost city in the U.S.; naval base. 33,956 (1960).

kg., 1. keg; kegs. **2.** kilogram; kilograms.

K.G., Knight of the Garter.

Kha·ba·rovsk (hä bä′rôfsk), *n.* **1.** Formerly, **Far Eastern Region.** a maritime territory in the E Soviet Union in Asia. **2.** the capital of this territory, in the SE part: a port on the Amur river. 280,000 (est. 1956).

Khai·bar Pass (kī′bər), Khyber Pass.

khak·i (kăk′ǐ, kä′kǐ), *n., pl.* **khakis. 1.** dull yellowish brown. **2.** stout twilled cotton uniform cloth of this color. **3.** a similar fabric of wool. —*adj.* **4.** of the color of khaki. **5.** made of khaki. [t. Hind.: dusty, der. *khāk* dust]

kha·lif (kā′lǐf, kăl′ǐf), *n.* caliph. Also, **kha·li·fa** (kə lē′fə).

Khal·ki·di·ke (hälˈkē dē′kē), *n.* Greek name of **Chalcidice.**

kham·sin (kăm′sǐn, kăm sēn′), *n.* a hot southerly wind (varying from SE to SW) that blows regularly in Egypt for about 50 days, commencing about the middle of March. Also, **kamseen, kamsin.** [t. Ar.: lit., fifty]

khan¹ (kän, kăn), *n.* **1.** (in the Manchu-Mongol-Turkish-Tatar group of languages) the title borne by hereditary rulers, as **a.** hereditary chief of a tribal following. **b.** hereditary lord of a territorial domain. **c.** the supreme ruler of the Tatar tribes, as well as emperor of China, during the middle ages: a descendant of Genghis Khan. **3.** a title of respect in Iran, Afghanistan, India, etc. [ME, t. Turk. (whence Pers. and Ar.): lord, prince]

khan² (kän, kăn), *n.* an inn or caravansary. [t. Pers.]

khan·ate (kän′āt, kăn′āt), *n.* the dominion of a khan.

Kha·ni·a (kä nē′ə; *Gk.* hän yä′), *n.* Greek name of **Canea.**

Khar·kov (kär′kôf, -kôv; *Rus.* här′kôf), *n.* a city in the S Soviet Union in Europe: former capital of the Ukrainian Republic. 877,000 (est. 1956).

Khar·toum (кнär tōōm′), *n.* the capital of the Sudan, at the junction of the White and Blue Nile rivers: besieged, 1895; retaken by the British, 1898. 82,673 pop. (est. 1953). Also, **Khar·tum′.**

khed·a (kĕd′ə), *n.* (in India) an enclosure constructed to ensnare wild elephants. Also, **khed′ah, keddah.**

khe·dive (kə dēv′), *n.* title of the Turkish viceroys in Egypt, 1867–1914. [t. Turk.: m. *khediv*, t. Pers.: m. *khidīv* lord, sovereign] —**khe·di′val, khe·di·vi·al** (kə dē′vǐ əl), *adj.*

Khe·lat (kə lät′), *n.* Kalat.

Kher·son (hĕr sôn′), *n.* a city in the SW Soviet Union: a port on the Dnieper near the Black Sea. 134,000 (est. 1956).

Khi·os (kǐ′ôs; *Gk.* hē′ôs), *n.* Greek name of **Chios.**

Khi·va (hē′vä), *n.* a former Asiatic khanate along the Amu Darya river, S of the Aral Sea: now divided between the Uzbek and Turkman republics of the U.S.S.R.

Khmer (kmĕr), *n.* **1.** a member of the Cambodian nation, of Mon-Khmer affiliation, which during the Middle Ages produced an important civilization in Indo-China. **2.** a language of Cambodia, of the Mon-Khmer family.

Kho·tan (кнō′tän′), *n.* **1.** an oasis in W China, in SW Sinkiang. **2.** the chief city in this oasis. 50,000 (est. 1950).

Khrush·chev (krōōsh′chôf; *Russ.* кнrōō shchôf′) *n.* **Nikita,** b. 1894, Soviet official: First Secretary of Communist Party, 1953–64. Premier 1958–64.

Khu·fu (kōō′fōō), *n.* Cheops.

Khy·ber Pass (kī′bər), the chief mountain pass between Pakistan and Afghanistan, W of Peshawar 33 mi. long; 6825 ft. high. Also, **Khaibar Pass.**

ki·a·boo·ca wood (kī′ə bōō′kə), Padouk wood.

ki·ang (kǐ′äng′), *n.* onager (def. 1).

Kiang·ling (kyäng′lǐng′; *Chin.* jyäng′-), *n.* a city in central China, in Hupeh province, on the Yangtze. 15,000. Also, **Kingchow.**

Kiang·si (kyäng′sē′; *Chin.* jyäng′sē′), *n.* a province in SE China. 16,772,865 pop. (1953); 66,600 sq. mi. *Cap.:* Nanchang.

Kiang·su (kyäng′sōō′; *Chin.* jyäng′sōō′), *n.* a maritime province in E China. 41,252,192 pop. (1953); 42,056 sq. mi. *Cap.:* Nanking.

Kiao·chow (kyou′chou′; *Chin.* jyou′jō′), *n.* a territory (ab. 200 sq. mi.) in E China, in the Shantung peninsula around Kiachow Bay, an inlet of the Yellow Sea: leased to Germany, 1898–1914. Chief city, Tsingtao.

kibe (kīb), *n.* a chapped or ulcerated chilblain, esp. on the heel. [ME; cf. Welsh *cibi*]

Ki·bei (kē′bā′), *n., pl.* **-bei.** a person of Japanese descent, born in the U.S., who goes to Japan for an education. [t. Jap. t. Chinese: returned to America]

kib·itz (kǐb′ǐts), *v.i. Colloq.* to act as a kibitzer.

kib·itz·er (kǐb′ǐtsər), *n. Colloq.* **1.** a spectator at a card game who looks at the players' cards over their shoulders. **2.** a giver of unwanted advice. [t. Yiddish, f. colloq. G *kiebitz* kibitzer (prop. lapwing) + -*er* -ER¹]

kib·lah (kǐb′lä), *n.* **1.** the point (the Kaaba at Mecca) toward which Mohammedans turn at prayer. **2.** the "facing" towards Mecca, wherever orthodox Mohammedans pray. [t. Ar.: m. *qibla*]

ki·bosh (kī′bŏsh, kǐ bŏsh′), *n. Slang.* **1.** nonsense. **2. put the kibosh on,** to render definitely impossible or out of the question. [cf. Yiddish *kibosh* 18 pence]

kick (kǐk), *v.t.* **1.** to give a blow or thrust to with the foot. **2.** to drive, force, make, etc., by or as by kicks. **3.** *Football.* to win (a goal) by a kick. **4.** to strike in recoiling. —*v.i.* **5.** to strike out with the foot. **6.** to have the habit of thus striking out, as a horse. **7.** *Colloq.* to resist, object, or complain. **8.** to recoil, as a firearm when fired. **9. kick off, a.** *Football.* to give the ball the first kick, which starts the play. **b.** *Slang.* to die. —*n.* **10.** act of kicking; a blow or thrust with the foot. **11.** power or disposition to kick. **12.** a recoil, as of a gun. **13.** *Slang.* an objection or complaint. **14.** *Slang.* any thrill or excitement that gives pleasure; any act that gives satisfaction. **15.** *Slang.* a stimulating or intoxicating quality in alcoholic drink. **16.** *Slang.* vigor, energy. or vim. **17.** *Football.* the right of or a turn at kicking the ball. [ME *kike.* Cf. Icel. *kikna* sink at the knees] —**kick′er,** *n.*

Kick·a·poo (kǐk′ə pōō′), *n.* an Algonquian language.

kick·back (kǐk′băk′), *n. Colloq.* **1.** a response, usually vigorous. **2.** the practice of an employer, foreman, or person in a supervisory position of taking back a portion of the wages due to workers.

---

b., blend of, blended; **c.,** cognate with; **d.,** dialect, dialectal; **der.,** derived from; **f.,** formed from; **g.,** going back to; **m.,** modification of; **r.,** replacing; **s.,** stem of; **t.,** taken from; **?,** perhaps. See the full key on inside cover.

kick·off (kĭk′ôf′, -ŏf′), n. *Football*. a place kick down the field from the 40-yard line of the side kicking, as at the beginning of the first and third periods.

kick·shaw (kĭk′shô′), n. 1. any fancy dish in cookery. 2. any dainty, unsubstantial, or paltry trifle. [t. F: alter. of *quelque chose* something]

kid¹ (kĭd), n., v., kidded, kidding. —n. 1. a young goat. 2. leather made from the skin of a kid or goat, used in making shoes and gloves. 3. (*pl.*) *Colloq.* gloves of this leather. 4. *Slang.* a child or young person. —v.i., v.t. 5. (of a goat) to give birth to (young). [ME, appar. t. Scand.; cf. Icel. *kidh*, Sw. and Dan. *kid*]

kid² (kĭd), v., kidded, kidding. n. *Slang.* —v.t. 1.to tease; banter; jest with. 2. to humbug or fool. —v.i. 3. to speak or act deceptively, in jest; jest. —n. 4. kidding; humbug; chaffing. [? special use of KID¹ (def. 4)] —**kid′der**, n.

kid³ (kĭd), n. a tublike wooden vessel in which food is served to sailors. [? var. of KIT¹]

Kidd (kĭd), n. **William**, ("*Captain Kidd*") c1645–1701, British navigator and privateer, hanged for piracy.

Kid·der·min·ster (kĭd′ər mĭn′stər), n. a kind of ingrain carpet.

kid·nap (kĭd′năp), v.t., -naped, -naping or (*esp. Brit.*) -napped, -napping. to steal or abduct (a child or other person); carry off (a person) against his will by unlawful force or by fraud, often with a demand for ransom. [f. KID¹ (def. 4) + *nap*, v., seize] —**kid′nap·er;** *esp. Brit.*, **kid′nap·per,** n.

kid·ney (kĭd′nĭ), n., pl. -neys. 1. (in man) either of a pair of bean-shaped glandular organs, about 4 inches in length, in the back part of the abdominal cavity, which excrete urine. 2. a corresponding organ in other vertebrate animals, or an organ of like function in invertebrates. 3. the meat of an animal's kidney used as a food. 4. constitution or temperament. 5. kind, sort, or class. [ME *kidenei*, f. *kiden*- (orig. and meaning uncert.) + *ey* egg] —**kid′ney·like′,** adj.

kidney bean, 1. the common bean, *Phaseolus vulgaris*. 2. its kidney-shaped seed.

kid·ney-shaped (kĭd′nĭ shāpt′), adj. having the general shape of a long oval indented at one side.

Section of human kidney
A. Suprarenal gland;
B. Cortex; C. Tubular portion, consisting of cones; D, Papilla;
E. Pelvis; F. Ureter

kidney vetch, an Old World leguminous herb, *Anthyllis vulneraria*, formerly used as a remedy for kidney diseases.

kidney worm, a nematode worm of the family *Strongylidae*, *Stephanurus dentatus*, parasitic in the kidneys of pigs.

Ki·dron (kē′drən), n. Kedron.

kief (kēf), n. kef.

Kief·fer (kē′fər), n. *Hort.* a hybrid variety of pear, grown in eastern U.S.

Kiel (kēl), n. a seaport in N West Germany at the Baltic end of the **Kiel Canal**, a ship canal (61 mi. long) connecting the North and Baltic Seas. 257,294 (est. 1955).

Kiel·ce (kyĕl′tsĕ), n. a city in S Poland. 58,253 (1950).

kier (kĭr), n. a large boiler or vat used in bleaching, etc. Also, **keir**. [t. Scand.; cf. Icel. *ker* tub]

Kier·ke·gaard (kĭr′kə gôr′), n. **Soren Aabye** (sœ′rən ô′by), 1813–55, Danish religious philosopher.

kie·sel·guhr (kē′zəl gŏŏr′), n. diatomaceous earth. [t. G: f. *kiesel* flint + *guhr* earthy deposit]

Ki·ev (kē′ĕf), n. a city in the SW Soviet Union, on the Dnieper. 991,000 (est. 1956).

kil., kilometer; kilometers.

Ki·lau·e·a (kē′lou ä′ä), n. a crater on active Mauna Loa volcano in Hawaii. 2 mi. wide; 4040 ft. high.

Kil·dare (kĭl dâr′), n. a county in E Ireland, in Leinster. 65,927 (prelim. 1956); 654 sq. mi. *Co. seat:* Kildare.

kil·der·kin (kĭl′dər kĭn), n. 1. a unit of capacity, usually equal to half a barrel or two firkins. 2. *Obs.* an English unit of capacity, equal to 18 U.S. gallons. [ME, t. MD: m. (by dissimilation) *kyn(d)erkyn*, var. of *kinnekyn*, f. *kinne* (orig. and meaning uncert.) + *-kyn* -KIN]

Kil·i·man·ja·ro (kĭl′ĭ män jä′rō), n. a volcanic mountain in N Tanganyika: highest peak in Africa. 19,321 ft.

Kil·ken·ny (kĭl kĕn′ĭ), n. 1. a county in SE Ireland, in Leinster. 64,148 pop. (prelim. 1956); 796 sq. mi. 2. its county seat. 10,572 (1951).

kill¹ (kĭl), v.t. 1. to deprive (any living creature or thing) of life in any manner; cause the death of; slay. 2. to destroy; do away with; extinguish: *kill hope*. 3. to destroy or neutralize the active qualities of. 4. to spoil the effect of. 5. to get rid of (time) by some method (usually easy) of spending it. 6. to overcome completely or with irresistible effect. 7. to cancel (a word, paragraph, item, etc.). 8. to defeat or veto (a legislative bill, etc.). 9. *Elect.* to render (a circuit) dead. 10. *Lawn Tennis.* to hit (a ball) with such force that its return is impossible. —v.i. 11. to inflict or cause death. 12. to commit murder. —n. 13. act of killing (game, etc.). 14. an animal killed. [ME *cullen*, *kyllen*; appar. der. OE *-colla* in *morgen-colla* morning slaughter)]
—**Syn. 1.** slaughter, massacre, butcher; hang, electrocute, behead, guillotine, strangle, garrote. KILL, EXECUTE, MURDER all mean to deprive of life. KILL is the general word, with no implication of the manner of killing, the agent or cause or the nature of what is killed (whether human being, animal, or plant): *to kill a person.* EXECUTE is used of (any means of) putting to death in accordance with a legal sentence: *to execute a criminal.* MURDER is used of killing a human being unlawfully, esp. after premeditation: *he murdered him for his money.*

kill² (kĭl), n. *U.S. Dial.* a channel; a creek; a stream; a river. [t. D: m. *kil*]

Kil·lar·ney (kĭl lär′nĭ), n. 1. a town in SW Ireland. 6298 (1951). 2. **Lakes of,** three beautiful lakes nearby.

kill·deer (kĭl′dĭr), n. the largest and commonest of the ring plovers of America, *Charadrius vociferus*. Also, **kill·dee** (kĭl′dē′). [imit. of its note]

killdeer plover. See plover (def. 1).

kill·er (kĭl′ər), n. 1. one who or that which kills. 2. any of various ravenous, gregarious cetaceans of the dolphin family, esp. of the genus *Orca*, as *O. gladiator*, the common species of the northern Atlantic.

kil·lick (kĭl′ĭk), n. 1. a small anchor or weight for mooring a boat, sometimes consisting of a stone secured by pieces of wood. 2. any anchor. Also, **kil·lock** (kĭl′ək).

Kil·lie·cran·kie (kĭl′ĭ krăng′kĭ), n. a pass in the Grampians in central Scotland: battle, 1689.

kil·li·fish (kĭl′ĭ fĭsh′), n., pl. -fishes, (*esp. collectively*) -fish. any of various small fishes, esp. of the genus *Fundulus* (family *Cyprinodontidae*), which abound in shallow bays, channels, rivers, etc. of eastern North America and other regions.

kill·ing (kĭl′ĭng), n. 1. act of one who or that which kills. 2. the total game killed on a hunt. 3. *Colloq.* a stroke of extraordinary execution, as in a successful speculation in stocks. —adj. 4. that kills. 5. exhausting. 6. *Colloq.* irresistibly funny. —**kill′ing·ly,** adv.

kill·joy (kĭl′joi′), n. a person or thing that spoils the joy or enjoyment of others.

Kil·mar·nock (kĭl mär′nək), n. a city in SW Scotland, SW of Glasgow. 43,400 (est. 1956).

Kil·mer (kĭl′mər), n. **Joyce**, 1886–1918, U.S. poet.

kiln (kĭl, kĭln), n. 1. a furnace or oven for burning, baking, or drying something, esp. one for calcining limestone or one for baking bricks. —v.t. 2. to burn, bake, or treat in a kiln. [ME *kylne*, OE *cyl(e)n*, ult. t. L: m. *culīna* kitchen]

kiln-dry (kĭl′drī′, kĭln′-), v.t., -dried, -drying. to dry in a kiln.

kil·o (kĭl′ō, kē′lō), n., pl. -los. 1. kilogram. 2. kilometer.

kilo-, a prefix meaning "thousand," used in the nomenclature of the metric system and of other scientific systems of measurement. [t. F, repr. Gk. *chilioi*]

kil·o·am·pere (kĭl′ō ăm′pĭr), n. *Elect.* a unit of current equal to 1000 amperes.

kil·o·cal·o·rie (kĭl′ə kăl′ə rĭ), n. *Physics.* a large calorie. See calorie (def. 1b). Also, kilogram calorie.

kil·o·cy·cle (kĭl′ə sī′kəl), n. a unit equal to 1000 cycles: used esp. in radio as 1000 cycles per second for expressing the frequency of electromagnetic waves.

kil·o·gram (kĭl′ə grăm′), n. *Metric System.* a unit of mass and weight, equal to 1000 grams, and equivalent to 2.2046 pounds avoirdupois. Also, *esp. Brit.*, **kil′o·gramme′.** [t. F: m. *kilogramme*. See KILO-, -GRAM]

kil·o·gram-me·ter (kĭl′ə grăm′mē′tər), n. *Metric System.* a unit of work, being the work done by one kilogram of force when its point of appreciation moves a distance of one meter in the direction of the force. It is equivalent to about 7.2 foot-pounds. Also, *esp. Brit.*, **kil′o·gram′-me′tre.**

kil·o·li·ter (kĭl′ə lē′tər), n. *Metric System.* 1000 liters; a cubic meter. Also, *esp. Brit.*, **kil′o·li′tre.** [t. F: m. *kilolitre*. See KILO-, LITER]

kilom., kilometer.

kil·o·me·ter (kĭl′ə mē′tər; *occas.* kĭ lŏm′ə tər), n. *Metric System.* a unit of length, the common measure of distances equal to 1000 meters, and equivalent to 3280.8 feet or 0.621 mile. Also, *esp. Brit.*, **kil′o·me′tre.** [t. F: m. *kilomètre*. See KILO-, -METER] —**kil·o·met·ric** (kĭl′ə mĕt′rĭk), **kil′o·met′ri·cal,** adj.

kil·o·ton (kĭl′ə tŭn′), n. 1. 1000 tons. 2. an explosive force equal to that of 1000 tons of TNT.

kil·o·volt (kĭl′ə vōlt′), n. *Elect.* a unit of electromotive force equal to 1000 volts.

kil·o·watt (kĭl′ə wŏt′), n. *Elect.* a unit of power, equal to 1000 watts. [f. KILO- + WATT]

kil·o·watt-hour (kĭl′ə wŏt′our′), n. *Elect.* a unit of energy equivalent to that transferred or expended in one hour by one kilowatt of power, approx. 1.34 hp hour.

Kil·pat·rick (kĭl păt′rĭk), n. **Hugh Judson** (jŭd′sən), 1836–81, Union general in the U.S. Civil War.

kilt (kĭlt), n. 1. any short, pleated skirt, esp. one worn by men in the Scottish highlands. [n. use of *kilt*, v.t.] —v.t. 2. to draw or tuck up (the skirt, etc.) about one. 3. to pleat (cloth, a skirt, etc.) in deep vertical folds. [ME *kylte*, prob. t. Scand.; cf. Dan. *kilte* tuck up] —**kilt′like′,** adj.

kilt·ed (kĭl′tĭd), adj. 1. wearing a kilt. 2. pleated.

kil·ter (kĭl′tər), n. *U.S. Dial.* good condition; order: *the engine was out of kilter.* Also, *Brit. Dial.*, kelter.

kilt·ing (kĭl′tĭng), n. an arrangement of flat pleats set close together, each hiding half of the last.

Kim·ber·ley (kĭm′bər lĭ), n. a city in the central part of the Republic of South Africa, in Cape of Good Hope province: diamond mines. With suburbs, 58,777 (1951).

ki·mo·no (kə mō′nə, -nō), *n., pl.* **-nos.** 1. a wide-sleeved robe characteristic of Japanese costume. 2. a woman's loose dressing gown. [t. Jap.]

kin (kĭn), *n.* 1. one's relatives collectively, or kinsfolk. 2. family relationship or kinship. 3. **of kin,** of the same family; related; akin. 4. *Archaic.* a group of persons descended from a common ancestor, or constituting a family, clan, tribe, or race. 5. *Archaic.* a relative or kinsman. —*adj.* 6. of kin; related; akin. 7. of the same kind or nature; having affinity. [ME; OE *cynn,* c. OHG *chunni,* Icel. *kyn,* Goth. *kuni;* from Gmc. root equivalent to L *gen-,* Gk. *gen-,* Skt. *jan-* beget, produce] —**kin′-less,** *adj.*

-kin, a diminutive suffix, attached to nouns to signify a little object of the kind mentioned: *lambkin, catkin.* [ME; akin to D and LG *-ken,* G *-chen*]

kin·aes·the·sia (kĭn′əs thē′zhə), *n.* kinesthesia. Also, **kin′aes·the′sis.**

Kin·car·dine (kĭn kär′dĭn), *n.* a county in E Scotland. 47,403 pop. (1951); 379 sq. mi. *Co. seat:* Stonehaven. Also, **Kin·car·dine·shire** (kĭn kär′dĭn shĭr′, -shər).

Kin·chin·jun·ga (kĭn′chĭn jŏŏn′gä), *n.* Kanchenjunga.

kind[1] (kīnd), *adj.* 1. of a good or benevolent nature or disposition, as a person. 2. having, showing, or proceeding from benevolence: *kind words.* 3. indulgent, considerate, or helpful (often fol. by *to*): *to be kind to animals.* 4. *Archaic.* loving. 5. adaptable; tractable. [ME *kinde,* OE *gecynde,* der. *gecynd* nature. See KIND[2]] —**Syn.** 1. KIND, GRACIOUS, KINDHEARTED, KINDLY imply a sympathetic attitude toward others, and a willingness to do good or give pleasure. KIND implies a deep-seated characteristic shown either habitually or on occasion by considerate behavior: *a kind father.* GRACIOUS applies to kindness from a superior or older person to a subordinate, an inferior, a child, etc.: *a gracious old lady.* KINDHEARTED implies an emotionally sympathetic nature, sometimes easily imposed upon: *a kindhearted old woman.* KINDLY, a mild word, refers usually to general disposition, appearance, manner, etc.: *a kindly face.* —**Ant.** 1. cruel.

kind[2] (kīnd), *n.* 1. a class or group of individuals of the same nature or character, esp. a natural group of animals or plants. 2. nature or character as determining likeness or difference between things: *things differing in degree rather than in kind.* 3. a person or thing as being of a particular character or class: *he is a strange kind of hero.* 4. a more or less adequate or inadequate example, or a sort, of something: *the vines formed a kind of roof.* 5. **in kind, a.** in something of the same kind in the same way: *to retaliate in kind.* **b.** in the particular kind of thing, or in goods or natural produce, instead of money. 6. **kind of** (used adverbially), *Colloq.* after a fashion; to some extent; somewhat; rather: *the room was kind of dark.* 7. *Archaic.* the nature, or natural disposition or character: *after one's kind.* 8. *Obs.* gender; sex. [ME *kinde,* OE *gecynd.* See KIN]

kin·der·gar·ten (kĭn′dər gär′tən), *n.* a school for furthering the mental, moral, and physical development of young children by means of games, occupations, etc., that make use of their natural tendency to express themselves in action. [t. G: children's garden]

kin·der·gart·ner (kĭn′dər gärt′nər), *n.* 1. a child who attends a kindergarten. 2. a kindergarten teacher. Also, **kin′der·gar′ten·er.**

kind·heart·ed (kīnd′här′tĭd), *adj.* having or showing a kind heart; kindly. —**kind′heart′ed·ly,** *adv.* —**kind′heart′ed·ness,** *n.* —**Syn.** See kind[1].

kin·dle (kĭn′dəl), *v.,* **-dled, -dling.** —*v.t.* 1. to set (a fire, flame, etc.) to burning or blazing. 2. to set fire to, or ignite (fuel or any combustible matter). 3. to excite; stir up or set going; to animate, rouse, or inflame. 4. to light up, illuminate, or make bright. —*v.i.* 5. to begin to burn, as combustible matter, a light, or a fire or flame. 6. to become roused, ardent, or inflamed. 7. to become lighted up, bright, or glowing, as the sky at dawn or the eyes with ardor. [ME *kindlen,* prob. t. Scand.; cf. Icel. *kynda* kindle, *kyndill* candle, torch] —**kin′dler,** *n.* —**Syn.** 1-3. KINDLE, IGNITE, INFLAME imply setting something on fire. TO KINDLE is especially to cause something gradually to begin burning; it is often used figuratively: *to kindle someone's interest.* TO IGNITE is to set something on fire with a sudden burst of flame: *to ignite dangerous hatreds.* INFLAME, a literary word meaning to set aflame, is now found chiefly in figurative uses, as referring to unnaturally hot, sore, or swollen conditions in the body, or to exciting the mind by strong emotion: *the wound was greatly inflamed.* —**Ant.** 1. quench, smother, extinguish.

kind·li·ness (kīnd′lĭ nĭs), *n.* 1. state or quality of being kindly; benevolence. 2. a kindly deed.

kin·dling (kĭn′dlĭng), *n.* 1. material for starting a fire. 2. act of one who kindles.

kind·ly (kīnd′lĭ), *adj.,* **-lier, -liest,** *adv.* —*adj.* 1. having, showing, or proceeding from a benevolent disposition or spirit; kindhearted; good-natured; sympathetic: *kindly people.* 2. gentle or mild, as rule or laws. 3. pleasant, genial, or benign. 4. favorable, as soil for crops. [ME *kyndly,* OE *gecyndelīc,* f. *gecynde* KIND[1] + *-līc* -LY] —*adv.* 5. in a kind manner; with sympathetic or helpful kindness. 6. cordially or heartily: *we thank you kindly.* 7. with liking; favorably: *to take kindly to an idea.* [ME; OE *gecyndelīce.* See -LY] —**Syn.** 1. See kind[1].

kind·ness (kīnd′nĭs), *n.* 1. state or quality of being kind. 2. a kind act: *his many kindnesses to me.* 3. kind behavior: *I will never forget your kindness.* 4. friendly feeling, or liking. —**Syn.** 2. service, favor.

kin·dred (kĭn′drĭd), *n.* 1. a body of persons related to another, or a family, tribe, or race. 2. one's relatives collectively; kinsfolk, or kin. 3. relationship by birth or descent, or sometimes by marriage; kinship. 4. natural relationship, or affinity. —*adj.* 5. associated by origin, nature, qualities, etc.: *kindred languages.* 6. related by birth or descent, or having kinship: *kindred tribes.* 7. belonging to kin or relatives: *kindred blood.* [ME *kinrede(n).* See KIN, -RED]

kine (kīn), *n.pl. Archaic.* pl. of **cow.**

kin·e·mat·ics (kĭn′ə măt′ĭks), *n.* 1. that branch of mechanics which treats of pure motion, without reference to mass or cause. 2. the theory of mechanical contrivance for converting one kind of motion into another (**applied kinematics**). [f. s. Gk. *kīnēma* motion + -ICS] —**kin′e·mat′ic,** **kin·e·mat′i·cal,** *adj.*

kin·e·mat·o·graph (kĭn′ə măt′ə grăf′, -gräf′), *n., v.t., v.i.* cinematograph.

kin·e·scope (kĭn′ə skōp′), *n., v.,* **-scoped, -scoping.** *Television.* —*n.* 1. a cathode-ray tube with a fluorescent screen on which the image is reproduced. 2. the recording of a television program on motion picture film for later broadcasting. 3. (*cap.*) a trademark for this tube. —*v.t.* 4. to record (a program) on motion picture film for later broadcasting.

kin·es·the·sia (kĭn′əs thē′zhə), *n.* the sensation of movement or strain in muscles, tendons, joints. Also, **kinaesthesia, kin·es·the·sis** (kĭn′əs thē′sĭs). [NL, f. Gk.: s. *kīnein* move + *-aisthesia* perception] —**kin·es·thet·ic** (kĭn′əs thĕt′ĭk), *adj.*

ki·net·ic (kĭ nĕt′ĭk, kī-), *adj.* 1. pertaining to motion. 2. caused by motion. [t. Gk.: m.s. *kīnētikós*]

ki·net·ics (kĭ nĕt′ĭks, kī-), *n.* the branch of mechanics which treats of the action of forces in producing or changing the motion of masses.

kinetic theory of gases, a theory that the particles in a gas move freely and rapidly along straight lines but often collide, resulting in variations in their velocity and direction. Pressure is thus interpreted as the force due to the impacts of these particles, and other macroscopic variables are similarly treated.

kinetic theory of heat, a theory that a body's temperature is determined by the average kinetic energy of its particles and that an inflow of motion into increases this energy.

kinetic theory of matter, the theory that matter is composed of small particles, all in random motion.

kin·folks (kĭn′fōks′), *n.pl. Colloq.* kinsfolk. Also, **kin′folk′.**

king (kĭng), *n.* 1. a male sovereign or monarch; a man who holds by life tenure (and usually by hereditary right) the chief authority over a country and people. 2. (*cap.*) God or Christ: *King of Kings, King of heaven.* 3. a person or thing preëminent in its class: *the lion is the king of beasts, an oil king.* 4. a playing card bearing a picture of a king. 5. the chief piece in a game of chess, moving one square at a time in any direction. 6. a piece that has moved entirely across the board in the game of checkers or draughts and has been crowned. [ME; OE *cyng, cynig, cyning,* c. D *koning,* G *könig,* Icel. *konungr,* Sw. *konung,* Dan. *konge*] —**king′less,** *adj.*

King (kĭng), *n.* 1. Rufus (rōō′fəs), 1755-1827, American statesman. 2. William Lyon Mackenzie (mə-kĕn′zĭ), 1874-1950, Canadian statesman; prime minister, 1921-1926, 1926-1930, and 1935-1948.

king·bird (kĭng′bûrd′), *n.* any of various flycatchers of the New World family *Tyrannidae,* esp. *Tyrannus tyrannus,* a pugnacious bird of the eastern U.S.

king·bolt (kĭng′bōlt′), *n.* a vertical bolt connecting the body of a horse-drawn vehicle with the fore axle, the body of a railroad car with a truck, etc.

King Charles spaniel, a small black-and-tan toy spaniel with a rounded head, short muzzle, full eyes, and well-fringed ears and feet.

King·chow (jĭng′jō′), *n.* Kiangling.

king cobra, a large cobra, *Naja hannah,* of southeastern Asia.

king crab, a horseshoe crab.

king·craft (kĭng′kräft′, -kräft′), *n.* the art of ruling as king; royal statesmanship.

king·cup (kĭng′kŭp′), *n.* 1. any of various common buttercups, as *Ranunculus bulbosus.* 2. *Chiefly Brit.* the marsh marigold.

king·dom (kĭng′dəm), *n.* 1. a state or government having a king or queen as its head. 2. anything conceived as constituting a realm or sphere of independent action or control: *the kingdom of thought.* 3. a realm or province of nature, esp., one of the three great divisions of natural objects: *the animal, vegetable, and mineral kingdoms.* 4. the spiritual sovereignty of God or Christ. 5. the domain over which this extends, whether in heaven or on earth. [ME; OE *cyningdōm*] —**Syn.** 1. KINGDOM, MONARCHY, REALM refer to the state or domain ruled by a king or queen. A KINGDOM is a governmental unit ruled by a king or queen: *the kingdom of Norway.* A MONARCHY is primarily a form of government in which a single person is sovereign; it is also the type of powers exercised by the monarch: *this kingdom is not an absolute monarchy.* A REALM is the domain (including the subjects) over which the king has jurisdiction; fig., a sphere of power or influence: *the laws of the realm.*

king·fish (kĭng′fĭsh′), *n., pl.* **-fishes,** (esp. *collectively*) **-fish.** 1. any of various fishes conspicuous for size or some other quality. **2.** a marine food fish, *Menticirrus nebulosus,* of the drumfish family, much esteemed for food in the northeastern U.S. **3.** a marine food fish, *Genyonemus lineatus,* of the California coast. **4.** the opah. **5.** the Spanish mackerel.

king·fish·er (kĭng′fĭsh′ər), *n.* any of numerous fish- or insect-eating birds of the almost cosmopolitan family *Alcedinidae,* all of which are stout-billed and small-footed, and many of which are crested or brilliantly colored. Those which eat fish capture them by diving.

king·hood (kĭng′hŏŏd), *n.* kingship.

King James Version. See **Authorized Version.**

King·lake (kĭng′lāk′), *n.* **Alexander William,** 1809–1891, British historian and traveler.

King Lear (lîr), a tragedy (1605) by Shakespeare.

king·let (kĭng′lĭt), *n.* **1.** a king ruling over a small country or territory. **2.** any of the diminutive greenish birds constituting the genus *Regulus,* esp. the **ruby-crowned kinglet** (*R. calendula*) of America, the **fire-crest** (*R. ignicapillus*) of Europe, and the **goldcrest** or **golden-covered kinglet** (*R. regulus*) of both Europe and North America.

king·ly (kĭng′lĭ), *adj.,* **-lier, -liest,** *adv.* —*adj.* **1.** being a king. **2.** consisting of kings or of royal rank. **3.** resembling, suggesting, or befitting a king; kinglike: *he strode into the room with a kingly air.* **4.** pertaining or proper to a king or kings. —*adv.* **5.** in a kingly manner. —**king′li·ness,** *n.*
—**Syn. 3, 4.** princely, sovereign, majestic, august, magnificent, exalted, grand. KINGLY, REGAL, ROYAL refer to that which is closely associated with a king, or is suitable for one. What is KINGLY may either belong to a king, or be befitting, worthy of, or like a king: *a kingly presence, appearance, graciousness.* REGAL is especially applied to the office of kingship or the outward manifestations of grandeur and majesty: *regal authority, bearing, splendor, munificence.* ROYAL is applied especially to what pertains to or is associated with the person of a monarch: *the royal family, word, robes, salute; a royal residence.*

king·pin (kĭng′pĭn′), *n.* **1.** (in bowling games) **a.** the pin in the center when the pins are in place. **b.** the pin at the front apex. **2.** *Colloq.* the principal person in a company, etc. **3.** *Colloq.* the chief element of any system or the like. **4.** kingbolt.

king post, a vertical post between the apex of a triangular roof truss and the tie beam.

Kings (kĭngz), *n.pl.* certain books of the Bible which contain the history of the reigns of the kings of Israel and Judah (usually the 11th and 12th books of the Old Testament, called I Kings and II Kings).

A. King post; B. Tie beam; C. Strut or brace

king salmon, chinook salmon.

King's Bench, *Brit. Law.* (formerly) the most important trial court, having primary jurisdiction over criminal matters affecting the king's peace and an acquired civil jurisdiction concurrent with the Court of Common Pleas, with appellate jurisdiction over the Court of Common Pleas. Also, **Queen's Bench.**

king's English, correct English usage.

king's evidence, *Brit. Law.* state's evidence. Also, **queen's evidence.**

king's evil, scrofula: orig. so called because it was supposed to be curable by the touch of the sovereign.

king·ship (kĭng′shĭp), *n.* **1.** kingly state, office, or dignity. **2.** kingly rule. **3.** aptitude for kingly duties. **4.** a title used in referring to a king (prec. by *his, your,* etc.).

king-size (kĭng′sīz′), *adj. Colloq.* larger than the usual size. Also, **king′-sized′.**

Kings·ley (kĭngz′lĭ), *n.* **1. Charles,** 1819–75, British clergyman, novelist, and poet. **2. Sidney,** born 1906, U.S. dramatist.

Kings Mountain (kĭngz), a ridge in N South Carolina: American victory over the British, 1780.

king snake, any of certain large harmless American snakes, esp. *Lampropeltis getulus,* which feed on other snakes, including rattlesnakes.

King's speech, (in the English parliament) a speech reviewing domestic conditions and foreign relations, prepared by the ministry in the name of the sovereign, and read at the opening of the Parliament either by the sovereign in person or by commission.

Kings·ton (kĭngz′tən, kĭng′stən), *n.* **1.** a seaport in and the capital of Jamaica. 142,464 (est. 1953). **2.** a city in SE Canada: a port at the E end of Lake Ontario. 33,459 (1951). **3.** a city in SE New York, on the Hudson. 29,260 (1960). **4.** a borough in E Pennsylvania, on the Susquehanna river opposite Wilkes-Barre. 61,055 (1960).

Kings·ton-up·on-Hull (kĭngz′tən ə pŏn′hŭl′), *n.* official name of **Hull** (def. 3).

King-teh-chen (jĭng′dŭ′jĕn′), *n.* a city in E China, in Kiangsi province: fine porcelain. 87,000 (1948).

king truss, a truss framed with a king post.

king·wood (kĭng′wŏŏd′), *n.* **1.** a Brazilian wood streaked with violet tints, used esp. in cabinetwork. **2.** the tree, *Dalbergia cearensis,* which yields it.

kink (kĭngk), *n.* **1.** a twist or curl, as in a thread, rope, or hair, caused by its doubling or bending upon itself. **2.** a crick, as in the neck or back. **3.** a mental twist, as an odd notion, or a whim or crotchet. —*v.i.,* *v.t.* **4.** to form

or cause to form a kink or kinks. as a rope. [orig. nautical term, prob. t. D: twist, twirl. Cf. Icel. *kinka* nod archly]

kin·ka·jou (kĭng′ka jōō′), *n.* a pale-brown, soft-furred, arboreal, prehensile-tailed mammal, *Potos flavus,* of Central and South America, related to the raccoon. [t. Canadian F; orig. the same word as CARCAJOU]

kink·y (kĭngk′ĭ), *adj.,* kinkier, kinkiest. full of kinks. —**kink′i·ness,** *n.*

Kinkajou, *Potos flavus* (Total length 33 in., tail 17 in.)

ki·no gum (kē′nō), the reddish or black catechulike inspissated juice or gum of certain tropical trees, esp. that from *Pterocarpus marsupium,* a tall fabaceous tree of India and Ceylon: used in medicine, tanning, etc. [appar. t. W Afr. (Gambia)]

Kin·ross (kĭn rôs′, -rŏs′), *n.* a county in E Scotland. 7200 pop. (est. 1956); 82 sq. mi. *Co. seat:* Kinross. Also, **Kin·ross·shire** (kĭn rôs′shĭr, -shər, -rŏs′-).

Kin·sey (kĭn′zĭ) *n.* **Alfred Charles,** 1894–1956, U.S. zoölogist: director of a survey of human sex behavior.

kins·folk (kĭnz′fōk′), *n.pl.* relatives or kindred. Also, *Colloq.,* kinfolks, kinfolk.

Kin·sha·sa (kin shä′sə), *n.* the capital of the Republic of the Congo, in the W part: a port on the Congo river, 370,490 (est. 1959).

kin·ship (kĭn′shĭp), *n.* **1.** state or fact of being of kin; family relationship. **2.** relationship by nature, qualities, etc.; affinity. —**Syn. 1.** See **relationship.**

kins·man (kĭnz′mən), *n., pl.* **-men. 1.** a male blood relative. **2.** (sometimes) a relative by marriage. **3.** a person of the same race. —**kins′wom′an,** *n. fem.*

ki·osk (kĭ′ŏsk′, kĭ′ŏsk), *n.* **1.** a kind of open pavilion or summerhouse common in Turkey and Iran. **2.** a similar structure used as a bandstand, as a newsstand, etc. [t. Turk.: m. *kiūshk* pavilion]

Kio·to (kyō′tō′), *n.* Kyoto.

Ki·o·wa (kĭ′ə wə), *n.* a linguistic stock of western Kansas and eastern Colorado, related to Uto-Aztecan.

kip (kĭp), *n.* **1.** the hide of a young or small beast. **2.** a bundle or set of such hides, containing a definite number. [ME *kipp,* t. MLG: m. *kip* pack (of hides), akin to Icel. *kippi* bundle]

Kip·ling (kĭp′lĭng), *n.* **Rudyard** (rŭd′yərd), 1865–1936, British writer and poet.

kip·per (kĭp′ər), *n.* **1.** a kippered fish, esp. a herring. **2.** a method of curing fish by splitting, salting, drying, and smoking. —*v.t.* **3.** to cure (herring, salmon, etc.) by cleaning, salting, etc., and drying in the air or in smoke. [? special use of *kipper,* OE *cypera* spawning salmon]

Kirch·hoff (kĭrKH′hôf), *n.* **Gustav Robert** (gŏŏs′täf rō′bĕrt), 1824–87, German physicist.

Kir·ghiz (kĭr gēz′), *n., pl.* **-ghiz, -ghizes. 1.** a member of a widespread people of Mongolian physical type and Turkic speech, dwelling chiefly in west central Asia. **2.** their language.

Kirghiz Soviet Socialist Republic, a constituent republic of the Soviet Union, in the Asiatic part adjoining Sinkiang, China. 1,900,000 pop. (est. 1956); ab. 77,800 sq. mi. *Cap.:* Frunze.

Kirghiz Steppe, a vast steppe in the SW Soviet Union in Asia, in Kazak Republic. Also, **The Steppes.**

Ki·rin (kē′rĭn′), *n.* **1.** a province in NE China, in Manchuria. 11,290,073 pop. (1953); 45,000 sq. mi. **2.** the capital of this province. 247,000 (est. 1950).

kirk (kûrk), *n.* **1.** *Scot. and N. Eng.* a church. **2. the Kirk,** *Eng.* the Established Church of Scotland, as distinguished from the Scottish Episcopal Church. [ME, t. Scand.; cf. Icel. *kirkja,* c. CHURCH]

Kirk·cud·bright (kər kōō′brĭ), *n.* a county in SW Scotland. 30,200 pop. (est. 1956); 896 sq. mi. *Co. seat:* Kircudbright. Also, **Kirk·cud·bright·shire** (kər kōō′brĭ shĭr, -shər).

kirk·man (kûrk′mən), *n., pl.* **-men. 1.** *Scot. and N. Eng.* a member or follower of the Kirk. **2.** *Scot.* a churchman.

Kir·man (kĭr män′), *n.* a Persian rug marked by ornate flowing designs and light, muted colors. [var. of *Kerman,* name of a town and province in Iran]

kir·mess (kûr′mĭs), *n.* kermis.

Ki·rov (kē′rôf), *n.* a city in the E Soviet Union in Europe. 211,000 (est. 1956). Formerly, **Vyatka.**

Ki·ro·va·bad (kē′rō vä bät′), *n.* a city in the SW Soviet Union, in Azerbaijan Republic. 111,000 (est. 1956). Formerly, **Elisavetpol** or **Gandzha.**

Ki·ro·vo·grad (kē′rō vō grät′), *n.* a city in the SW Soviet Union, in the Ukrainian Republic. 115,000 (est. 1956). Formerly, **Elisavetgrad** or **Zinovievsk.**

kirsch·was·ser (kĭrsh′väs′ər), *n.* a colorless brandy distilled in Germany, Alsace, and Switzerland from wild black cherries. Also, **kirsch.** [t. G: cherry water]

kir·tle (kûr′təl), *n.* **1.** a woman's gown or skirt. **2.** *Archaic* or *Dial.* a man's tunic or coat. [ME *kurtel,* OE *cyrtel,* c. Icel. *kyrtill* tunic, ult. der. L *curtus* cut short]

Ki·shi·nev (kĭ′shĭ nyôf′), *n.* a city in the SW Soviet Union: capital of the Moldavian Republic. 190,000 (est. 1956). Rumanian, **Chisinău.**

Kis·lev (kĭs′lĕf), *n.* (in the Jewish calendar) the third month of the year. [t. Heb.]

kis·met (kĭz′mĕt, kĭs′-), *n.* fate; destiny. [t. Turk.. t. Pers.: m. *qismat,* t. Ar., der. *qasama* divide]

kiss (kĭs), *v.t.* **1.** to touch or press with the lips, while compressing and then separating them, in token of greeting, affection, etc. **2.** to touch gently or lightly. **3.** to put, bring, take, etc., by, or as if by, kissing. —*v.i.* **4.** to kiss someone, something, or each other. —*n.* **5.** act of kissing. **6.** a slight touch or contact. **7.** a baked confection of egg whites and confectioners' sugar, served as a cooky. **8.** a piece of toffeelike confectionery, sometimes containing nuts, coconut, or the like. [ME *kysse(n)*, OE *cyssan* (c. G *küssen*), der. *coss* a kiss, c. G *kuss*] —**kiss′a·ble,** *adj.* —**kiss′er,** *n.*

kissing bug, any of certain assassin bugs which have been known to pierce a person's lip.

Kist·na (kĭst′nə), *n.* a river in S India, flowing from the Western Ghats E to the Bay of Bengal. ab. 800 mi.

kit[1] (kĭt), *n.* **1.** a set or collection of tools, supplies, etc., for a special purpose. **2.** the case containing these, or this with its contents. **3.** *Colloq.* a set, lot, or collection of things or persons. **4.** a wooden tub, pail, etc., usually circular. [ME *kyt, kitt,* appar. t. MD: m. *kitte* kind of tub. Cf. Norw. *kitte* bin]

kit[2] (kĭt), *n.* a kind of small violin, used by the dancing masters from the 16th to the 18th century. [orig. uncert.]

kit[3] (kĭt), *n.* shortened form of *kitten.*

kitch·en (kĭch′ən), *n.* **1.** a room or place equipped for or appropriated to cooking. **2.** the culinary department; cuisine. [ME *kitchene,* OE *cycene,* ult. t. L: m. *coquina*]

kitchen cabinet, *U.S. Colloq.* a group of unofficial advisers to a president or governor.

kitch·en·er (kĭch′ən ər), *n.* **1.** one employed in, or in charge of, a kitchen. **2.** an elaborate kitchen stove.

Kitch·en·er (kĭch′ən ər), *n.* a city in SE Canada, in S Ontario. with suburbs, 63,009 (1951).

Kitchener of Khartoum, Horatio Herbert Kitchener, 1st Earl, 1850–1916, British field marshal.

kitch·en·ette (kĭch′ə nĕt′), *n.* a small kitchen.

kitchen garden, a garden in which vegetables and fruit for the table are grown. —**kitchen gardener.**

kitchen midden, *Anthropol.* a mound consisting of shells of edible mollusks and other refuse, marking the site of a prehistoric human habitation. [translation of Dan. *kökkenmödding*]

kitchen police, *Mil.* **1.** duty as assistant to the cooks. *Abbr.:* K.P. **2.** soldiers on kitchen duty.

kitch·en·ware (kĭch′ən wâr′), *n.* cooking equipment or utensils.

kite (kīt), *n., v.,* **kited, kiting.** —*n.* **1.** a light frame covered with some thin material, to be flown in the wind at the end of a long string. **2.** any of various falconiform birds of the genera *Milvus, Elanus, Elanoides,* etc., with long, pointed wings, which prey on small quarry, as *Elanus leucurus,* the **white-tailed kite** of North and South America. **3.** a person who preys on others; a sharper. **4.** *Naut.* any light sail that is usually spread in light winds, and furled in a strong breeze. **5.** *Com.* a fictitious negotiable instrument, not representing any actual transaction, used for raising money or sustaining credit. —*v.i.* **6.** *Colloq.* to fly or move with a rapid or easy motion like that of a kite. **7.** *Com.* to obtain money or credit through kites. —*v.t.* **8.** *Com.* to employ as a kite. [ME *kyte,* OE *cȳta;* akin to G *kauz* kind of owl]

kith (kĭth), *n.* one's acquaintances or friends (now chiefly Scot. and N Eng. except in *kith and kin* and often confused in meaning with *kin*). [ME *kitthe,* OE *cȳth, cȳththu* knowledge, acquaintance, native land, der. *cūth* known, pp. of *cunnan* CAN[1]]

kith and kin, acquaintances and kindred, or friends and relatives.

kith·a·ra (kĭth′ə rə), *n.* a musical instrument of ancient Greece; cithara. [t. Gk.]

kit·ten (kĭt′ən), *n.* **1.** a young cat. —*v.t., v.i.* **2.** to bring forth (kittens). [ME *kitoun, kyton,* t. d. OF; cf. OF *chitoun, chaton,* dim. of *chat* cat] —**kit′ten·like′,** *adj.*

kit·ten·ish (kĭt′ən ĭsh), *adj.* kittenlike; artlessly playful. —**kit′ten·ish·ly,** *adv.* —**kit′ten·ish·ness,** *n.*

kit·ti·wake (kĭt′ĭ wāk′), *n.* either of two gulls of the genus *Rissa,* having the hind toe very short or rudimentary. [imit. of its cry]

Kit·tredge (kĭt′rĭj), *n.* George Lyman (lī′mən), 1860–1941, U.S. philologist and educator.

kit·ty[1] (kĭt′ĭ), *n., pl.* **-ties. 1.** a kitten. **2.** a pet name for a cat. [f. KIT[3] + -Y[2]]

kit·ty[2] (kĭt′ĭ), *n., pl.* **-ties. 1.** a pool into which each player in a card game puts a certain amount of his winnings, for some special purpose, as to pay for refreshments, etc. **2.** any similar pool. **3.** the cards left over after a deal which may be used by the highest bidder. [appar. familiar der. of *kitcot,* phonetic var. of *kidcot* prison, f. KID[1] (in sense of slave or criminal) + COT[2]]

Kit·ty·hawk (kĭt′ĭ hôk′), *n.* a village in NE North Carolina: Wright brothers' airplane flight, 1903.

Kiung·chow (kyōŏng′chō′, -chou′; *Chin.* jyōŏng′jō′), *n.* a seaport in S China, on Hainan island. ab. 59,000. Also, **Kiungshan** (kyōŏng′shän′; *Chin.* jyōŏng′-).

Kiu·shu (kū′shōō′), *n.* Kyushu.

ki·va (kē′və), *n.* a large chamber, often wholly or partly underground, in a Pueblo Indian village, used for religious ceremonies and other purposes. [t. N Amer. Ind. (Hopi)]

Ki·wa·nis (kĭ wä′nĭs), *n.* an organization, founded in 1915, comprising many clubs throughout the U.S. and Canada, aiming to provide leadership for the realization of higher ideals in business, industrial, and professional life. [coined word] —**Ki·wa·ni·an** (kĭ wä′nĭ ən), *n., adj.*

ki·wi (kē′wĭ), *n., pl.* **-wis** (-wĭz). **1.** an apteryx (flightless ratite bird of New Zealand). **2.** *Colloq.* a man in an aviation service who does not make flights. **3.** *Australian Colloq.* a New Zealander. [t. Maori]

Kiz·il Ir·mak (kĭz′ĭl ĭr mäk′), a river flowing through central Turkey N to the Black Sea. ab. 600 mi.

Kjö·len (chœ′lən), *n.* a mountain range between Norway and Sweden. Highest peak, Mt. Kebnekaise, 7005 ft.

K.K.K., Ku Klux Klan. Also, **KKK.**

K Kt, *Chess.* king's knight.

kl., kiloliter.

Kla·gen·furt (klä′gən fōŏrt′), *n.* a city in S Austria. 62,782 (1951).

Klai·pe·da (klī′pĕ dä′), *n.* Lithuanian name of **Memel.**

Klam·ath (klăm′əth), *n.* a river flowing from SW Oregon through NW California into the Pacific. ab. 250 mi.

Klamath Falls, a city in SW Oregon. 16,949 (1960).

Klamath Lakes, two lakes draining into the Klamath river: **Upper Klamath Lake** in SW Oregon, **Lower Klamath Lake** in N California.

Klan (klăn), *n.* Ku Klux Klan.

Klans·man (klănz′mən), *n., pl.* **-men.** a member of the Ku Klux Klan.

Klau·sen·burg (klou′zən bōŏrкн′), *n.* German name of Cluj.

Klebs-Löf·fler bacillus (klăps/lœf′lər), the bacillus *Corynebacterium diphtheriae,* which causes diphtheria.

Klee (klā), *n.* Paul (poul), 1879–1940, Swiss artist.

Kleen·ex (klē′nĕks), *n. Trademark.* a soft clothlike tissue, used esp. as a handkerchief.

Klein (klīn), *n.* Felix (fē′lĭks; *Ger.* fā′-), 1849–1925, German mathematician.

klepht (klĕft), *n.* a Greek or Albanian brigand, exalted in the war of Greek independence as a patriotic robber; guerilla. [t. mod. Gk.: s. *klĕphtēs,* Gk. *klĕptēs* thief]

klep·to·ma·ni·a (klĕp′tə mā′nĭ ə), *n.* an irresistible desire to steal, without regard to personal needs. Also, **cleptomania.** [t. NL, f. Gk.: m.s. *klĕptēs* thief + *-mania* -MANIA]

klep·to·ma·ni·ac (klĕp′tə mā′nĭ ăk′), *n.* one affected with kleptomania. Also, **cleptomaniac.**

klieg eyes (klēg), inflammation and edema of the eyes as a result of prolonged exposure to arc lights, as the klieg lights of the motion-picture industry.

klieg light, a floodlight with an arc-light source used in motion-picture studios to project a beam of high actinic power. [named after *Kliegl* brothers, the inventors]

Kling·sor (klĭng′zōr), *n.* an enchanter in Wagner's opera *Parsifal.*

klip·spring·er (klĭp′sprĭng′ər), *n.* a small, active African antelope, *Oreotragus oreotragus,* of mountainous regions from the Cape of Good Hope to Ethiopia. [t. S Afr. D: cliff springer]

Klon·dike (klŏn′dīk), *n.* **1.** a region of the Yukon territory in NW Canada: gold rush, 1897–98. **2.** a river in this region, flowing into the Yukon. **3.** (*l.c.*) a card game of solitaire.

Klop·stock (klŏp′shtôk), *n.* **Friedrich Gottlieb** (frē′drĭкн gôt′lēp), 1724–1803, German poet.

Kluck (klōŏk), *n.* **Alexander H. R. von** (ä′lĕ ksän′dər fän), 1846–1934, German general.

klys·tron (klĭs′trŏn, klī′strən), *n.* **1.** a vacuum tube containing an electron gun, a **buncher resonator** which changes the velocity of the electron beam in accordance with a signal, a **drift tube** in which the electron velocity does not change, a **catcher resonator** which abstracts energy from the electron beam, and a **collector electrode** for the electrons. It has several ultra-high-frequency applications. **2.** (*cap.*) a trademark for this tube. Cf. **resonator** (def. 4). [appar. der. Gk. *klystēr* syringe]

km., **1.** kilometer; kilometers. **2.** kingdom.

km/sec, kilometers per second.

kn., kronen.

knack (năk), *n.* **1.** a faculty or power of doing something with ease as from special skill; aptitude. **2.** a habit or practice. [ME *knak;* ? akin to *knack,* v., strike (imit.)] —**Syn. 1.** aptness, facility, dexterity.

knag·gy (năg′ĭ), *adj.* knotty; rough with knots. [f. *knag* (ME, c. G *knagge* knot, peg) + -Y[1]]

knap·sack (năp′săk′), *n.* a leather or canvas case for clothes and the like, carried on the back, esp. by soldiers. [t. LG: f. s. *knappen* bite, eat + *sack* SACK[1]]

knap·weed (năp′wēd′), *n.* a plant of the composite genus *Centaurea,* esp. *C. nigra,* a perennial weed with rose-purple flowers set on a dark-colored knoblike involucre. [ME *knopweed.* See KNOP, WEED[1]]

knar (när), *n.* a knot on a tree or in wood. [ME *knarre,* c. D *knar*] —**knarred,** *adj.*

knave (nāv), *n.* **1.** an unprincipled or dishonest fellow. **2.** *Cards.* a jack. **3.** *Archaic.* a male servant or man of humble position. [ME; OE *cnafa,* c. G *knabe* boy] —**Syn. 1.** KNAVE, RASCAL, ROGUE, SCOUNDREL are disparaging terms applied to persons considered base, dishonest, or worthless. KNAVE, formerly merely a boy or servant, in modern use emphasizes baseness of nature and intention: *a dishonest and swindling knave.* RASCAL suggests shrewdness and trickery in dishonesty: *a plausible rascal.* A ROGUE is a worthless fellow who sometimes preys extensively upon the community by fraud: *photographs of criminals in a rogues' gallery.* A SCOUNDREL is a blackguard and rogue of the worst sort: *a thorough scoundrel.* RASCAL and ROGUE are often used humorously (*an entertaining rascal, a saucy rogue*) but KNAVE and SCOUNDREL are not.

knav·er·y (nā′vər ĭ), *n., pl.* **-eries.** 1. action or practice characteristic of a knave. 2. unprincipled or dishonest dealing; trickery. 3. a knavish act or practice.

knav·ish (nā′vĭsh), *adj.* 1. like or befitting a knave; dishonest. 2. waggish; mischievous. —**knav′ish·ly,** *adv.* —**knav′ish·ness,** *n.*

knead (nēd), *v.t.* 1. to work (dough, etc.) into a uniform mixture by pressing, folding and stretching. 2. to manipulate by similar movements, as the body in massage. 3. to make by kneading. [ME *kneden,* OE *cnedan,* c. G *kneten*] —**knead′er,** *n.*

knee (nē), *n., v.,* **kneed, kneeing.** —*n.* 1. the joint or region in man between the thigh and the lower part of the leg. 2. the joint or region of other vertebrates corresponding or homologous to the human knee, as in the leg of a bird, the hind limb or a horse, etc. 3. a joint or region likened to this but not homologous with it, as the tarsal joint of a bird, or the carpal joint in the fore limb of the horse, cow, etc. 4. the part of a garment covering the knee. 5. something resembling a knee joint, esp. when bent, as a fabricated support or brace with a leg running at an angle to the main member. —*v.t.* 6. to strike or touch with the knee. —*v.i.* 7. *Obs. or Poetic.* to go down on the knees; kneel. [ME *know(e), kne(w),* OE *cnēo(w),* c. D and G *knie.* Cf. KNEEL]

knee action, *Auto.* a method of suspending the front wheels of a motor vehicle to the chassis by individual spindle and coil-spring mountings for each wheel.

knee breeches, breeches reaching to or just below the knee.

knee·cap (nē′kăp′), *n.* 1. the patella, the flat, movable bone at the front of the knee. 2. a protective covering, usually knitted, for the knee.

knee-deep (nē′dēp′), *adj.* 1. so deep as to reach the knees: *the snow lay knee-deep.* 2. submerged or covered by something having such depth.

knee-high (nē′hī′), *adj.* as high as the knees.

knee jerk, a brisk reflex lifting of the leg induced by tapping the tendon below the kneecap; patellar reflex.

kneel (nēl), *v.,* **knelt** or **kneeled, kneeling,** *n.* —*v.i.* 1. to fall or rest on the knees or a knee, as in supplication or homage. —*n.* 2. the action or position of kneeling. [ME *knele(n), knewlen,* OE *cnēowlian* (c. D *knielen,* LG *knelen*), der. *cnēow* KNEE] —**kneel′er,** *n.*

knee·pad (nē′păd′), *n.* a pad to protect the knee section of stockings, etc., or to protect the knee.

knee·pan (nē′păn′), *n.* the kneecap or patella.

knee·piece (nē′pēs′), *n.* armor for the knee, of hardened leather or of steel.

knee-sprung (nē′sprŭng′), *adj. Vet. Sci.* (of a horse, mule, etc.) having a forward bowing of the knee caused by inflammatory shortening of the flexor tendons.

knell (nĕl), *n.* 1. the sound made by a bell rung slowly for a death or a funeral. 2. any sound announcing the death of a person or the extinction, failure, etc.. of something. 3. any mournful sound. —*v.i.* 4. to sound, as a bell, esp. as a funeral bell. 5. to give forth a mournful, ominous, or warning sound. —*v.t.* 6. to proclaim or summon by, or as by, a bell. [ME *knelle, knylle,* OE *cnyllan* strike, ring (a bell), c. Icel. *knylla* beat, strike]

knelt (nĕlt), *v.* pt. and pp. of **kneel.**

knew (nū, nōō), *v.* pt. of **know.**

Knick·er·bock·er (nĭk′ər bŏk′ər), *n.* 1. a descendant of the Dutch settlers of New York. 2. any New Yorker.

knick·ers (nĭk′ərz), *n.pl.* 1. loosely fitting short breeches gathered in at the knee. 2. a bloomerlike undergarment worn by women. Also, **knick·er·bock·ers** (nĭk′ər bŏk′ərz). [der. KNICKERBOCKER]

knick·knack (nĭk′năk′), *n.* 1. a pleasing trifle; a trinket or gimcrack. 2. a bit of bric-à-brac. Also, **nicknack.** [distinctive redupl. of KNACK]

knife (nīf), *n., pl.* **knives,** *v.,* **knifed, knifing.** —*n.* 1. a cutting instrument consisting essentially of a thin blade (usually of steel and with a sharp edge) attached to a handle. 2. a knifelike weapon; a dagger; a short sword. 3. any blade for cutting, as in a tool or machine. —*v.t.* 4. to apply a knife to; cut, stab, etc., with a knife. 5. *U.S. Slang.* to endeavor to defeat in a secret or underhand way. [ME *knif,* OE *cnif,* c. Icel. *knīfr*] —**knife′less,** *adj.* —**knife′like′,** *adj.*

knife edge, 1. the edge of a knife. 2. anything very sharp. 3. a wedge, on the fine edge of which a scale beam, pendulum, or the like, oscillates.

knife-edged (nīf′ĕjd′), *adj.* having a thin, sharp edge.

knife switch, *Elect.* a form of air switch in which the moving element, usually a hinged blade, enters or embraces the contact clips.

knight (nīt), *n.* 1. *Medieval Hist.* **a.** a mounted soldier serving under a feudal superior. **b.** a man, usually of noble birth, who after an apprenticeship as page and squire was raised to honorable military rank and bound to chivalrous conduct. 2. any person of a rank similar to that of the medieval knight. 3. a man upon whom a certain dignity, corresponding to that of the medieval knight, is conferred by a sovereign because of personal merit or for services rendered to the country. In the British Empire he holds the rank next below that of a baronet, and the title *Sir* is prefixed to the Christian name, as in *Sir John Smith.* Neither the dignity nor the title is hereditary. 4. *Chess.* a piece shaped like a horse's head, moving one square horizontally or vertically, and then one square obliquely. It captures only on the terminal square. 5. a member of any order or association of men bearing the name of *Knights: Knights of Pythias.* —*v.t.* 6. *Hist.* to dub or create (one) a knight. [ME; OE *cniht* boy, manservant, c. D and G *knecht*] —**knight′less,** *adj.*

knight banneret, banneret[1] (def. 2).

knight-er·rant (nīt′ĕr′ənt), *n., pl.* **knights-errant.** *Hist.* a wandering knight; a knight who traveled in search of adventures, to exhibit military skill, etc.

knight-er·rant·ry (nīt′ĕr′ən trĭ), *n., pl.* **knight-errantries.** 1. conduct or a performance like that of a knight-errant. 2. quixotic conduct or action.

knight·head (nīt′hĕd′), *n. Naut.* either of the two timbers rising from the keel or stem of a ship, one on each side, and supporting the inner end of the bowsprit.

knight·hood (nīt′hŏŏd), *n.* 1. the rank or dignity of a knight. 2. the profession or vocation of a knight. 3. knightly character or qualities. 4. the body of knights.

knight·ly (nīt′lĭ), *adj.* 1. of or belonging to a knight: *knightly deeds.* 2. characteristic of a knight. 3. being or resembling a knight. 4. composed of knights. —*adv.* 5. in a manner befitting a knight. —**knight′li·ness,** *n.*

Knights Hospitalers. See Hospitaler (def. 1).

Knights of Columbus, a Roman Catholic fraternal organization, founded in 1882, aiming to associate men of the church for religious and civic usefulness.

Knights of Pythias, a secret fraternal order founded at Washington, D.C., in 1864.

Knights of St. John of Jerusalem, Knights Hospitaler. See Hospitaler (def. 1).

Knight Templar. See Templar (def. 2).

knit (nĭt), *v.,* **knitted** or **knit, knitting,** *n.* —*v.t.* 1. to form fabric, such as jersey cloth or hose, by interlacing loops of yarn with hand needles or a power machine. 2. to join closely and firmly together, as members or parts. 3. to contract into folds or wrinkles: *to knit the brow.* —*v.i.* 4. to become closely and firmly joined together; grow together, as broken bones do. 5. to contract, as the brow does. 6. to become closely or intimately united. —*n.* 7. fabric produced by interlooping of a yarn or yarns. [ME *knitte,* OE *cynttan* tie, der. *cnotta* KNOT[1]] —**knit′ter,** *n.*

knit·ting (nĭt′ĭng), *n.* 1. act of a person or thing that knits. 2. act of forming a fabric by looping a continuous yarn. 3. knitted work.

knitting needle, an instrument for knitting; a straight, slender rod, usually steel, with rounded ends.

knives (nīvz), *n.* pl. of **knife.**

knob (nŏb), *n.* 1. a rounded (or otherwise shaped) projecting part forming the handle of a door, drawer, or the like. 2. a rounded lump or protuberance on the surface or at the end of something, as a knot on a tree trunk, a pimple on the skin, etc. 3. *Archit.* an ornamental boss, as of carved work. 4. a rounded hill or mountain, esp. an isolated one. [ME. Cf. G *knobbe*] —**knobbed,** *adj.* —**knob′like′,** *adj.*

knob·by (nŏb′ĭ), *adj.,* **-bier, -biest.** 1. abounding in knobs. 2. knoblike. —**knob′bi·ness,** *n.*

knob·ker·rie (nŏb′kĕr′ĭ), *n.* a short, heavy stick or club with a knob on one end, used for both striking and throwing by South African natives. [t. S Afr. D: m. *knopkiri,* f. *knop* knob + Hottentot *kiri* stick, club]

knock (nŏk), *v.i.* 1. to strike a sounding blow with the fist, knuckles, or anything hard, esp. on a door, window, or the like, as in seeking admittance, calling attention, giving a signal, etc. 2. to make a noise as of striking or pounding, as machinery. 3. *U.S. Slang.* to make harsh or ill-natured criticisms. 4. to strike in collision. 5. *Colloq.* to wander in an aimless way (fol. by *about*). —*v.t.* 6. to give a sounding or forcible blow to; hit; strike; beat. 7. to drive, force, or render by a blow or blows: *to knock a man senseless.* 8. to strike (a thing) against something else. 9. *U.S. Slang.* to criticize illnaturedly or harshly. 10. Some special verb phrases are: **knock off,** *Colloq.* 1. to dispose of, or get rid of. 2. to stop doing something, esp. work. 3. to disable, overcome, or defeat completely. **knock down,** 1. (in auctions) to signify the sale of (the thing bid for) by a blow with a hammer or mallet; assign as sold to the highest bidder. 2. to take apart (an automobile, machine, etc.) in order to facilitate handling. 3. *U.S. Colloq.* (of a car conductor or other employee) to embezzle (money) from passengers' fares or other sums passing through his hands. **knock out,** to defeat (an opponent) in a pugilistic contest by striking him down with a blow after which he does not rise within a prescribed time. **knock out** or **knock out of the box,** *Baseball.* to cause (a pitcher) to be removed by making too many hits. —*n.* 11. act or the sound of knocking. 12. a rap, as at a door. 13. a blow or thump. 14. *U.S. Slang.* an ill-natured criticism or comment. 15. the noise resulting from faulty combustion or from incorrect functioning of some part of an internal-combustion engine. [ME *knokke,* unexpl. var. of *knoke,* OE *cnocian,* c. Icel. *knoka;* ? imit. in orig.] —**Syn.** 1. See **strike.**

knock·a·bout (nŏk′ə bout′), n. 1. Naut. a small handy yacht with a jib and mainsail but no bowsprit. —adj. 2. suitable for rough use, as a garment. 3. characterized by knocking about; rough; boisterous.

knock·down (nŏk′doun′), adj. 1. such as to knock something down; overwhelming; irresistible: a knockdown blow. 2. constructed in separate parts, so as to be readily knocked down or taken apart, as a boat, a piece of furniture, etc. —n. 3. such an object. 4. act of knocking down, esp. by a blow. 5. that which fells or overwhelms.

knock·er (nŏk′ər), n. 1. one who or that which knocks. 2. a hinged knob, bar, etc., on a door, for use in knocking.

knock-knee (nŏk′nē′), n. 1. inward curvature of the legs, causing the knees to knock together in walking. 2. (pl.) such knees. —**knock′-kneed′**, adj.

knock·out (nŏk′out′), n. 1. act of knocking out. 2. state or fact of being knocked out. 3. a knockout blow. 4. U.S. Slang. a person or thing of overwhelming success or attractiveness. —adj. 5. that knocks out.

knoll¹ (nōl), n. a small, rounded hill or eminence; a hillock. [ME knol, OE cnol(l) c. Norw. knoll hillock]

knoll² (nōl), v.t. 1. to ring a knell for; announce by strokes of a bell or the like. 2. Archaic or Dial. to ring or toll (a bell). —v.i. 3. to sound, as a bell; ring. 4. to sound a knell. —n. 5. a stroke of a bell in ringing or tolling. [ME; akin to KNELL]

knop (nŏp), n. a small, rounded protuberance; a knob; a boss, stud, or the like, as for ornament. [ME and OE; c. G knopf]

Knos·sos (nŏs′əs), n. a ruined city in Crete: capital of the ancient Minoan civilization. Also, **Cnossus.**

knot¹ (nŏt), n., v., **knotted, knotting.** —n. 1. an interlacement of a cord, rope, or the like, drawn tight into a lump or knob, as for fastening to something. 2. a piece of ribbon or similar material tied or folded upon itself and used or worn as an ornament. 3. a cluster of persons or things. 4. a protuberance in the tissue of a plant; an excrescence on a stem, branch, or root; a node or joint in a stem, esp. when of swollen form. 5. the hard, cross-grained mass of wood at the place where a branch joins the trunk of a tree. 6. a part of this mass showing in a piece of lumber, etc. 7. any of various diseases of trees characterized by the formation of an excrescence, knob, or gnarl. 8. Naut. a. one of a series of equal divisions on a log line, marked off by strings knotted through the strands, and made of such a length that the number running out in a certain time will indicate the ship's speed in nautical miles per hour. b. a unit of speed of one nautical mile an hour. c. nautical mile. 9. something involved or intricate; a difficulty; a knotty problem. 10. a bond or tie. —v.t. 11. to tie in a knot or knots; form a knot or knots in. 12. to secure by a knot. 13. to form protuberances, bosses, or knobs in; make knotty. —v.i. 14. to become tied or tangled in a knot or knots. 15. to form knots or joints. [ME knot(te), OE cnotta, c. D knot] —**knot′-less,** adj. —Syn. 3. group, company. 4. lump, knob, gnarl. 9. perplexity, puzzle.

Knots
A. Overhand; B. Figure of eight; C. Slipknot; D. Bowknot; E. Bowline; F. Square knot; G. Granny's knot; H. Single carrick bend; I. Matthew Walker; J. Half hitch; K. Clove hitch; L. Blackwall hitch

knot² (nŏt), n. a wading bird, Calidris canutus, of the snipe family. [orig. unknown]

knot·grass (nŏt′gras′, -gräs′), n. 1. a common polygonaceous weed, Polygonum aviculare, with nodes in its stems. 2. any of certain other species of this genus.

knot·hole (nŏt′hōl′), n. a hole in a board or plank formed by the falling out of a knot or a portion of a knot.

knot·ted (nŏt′ĭd), adj. 1. knotty. 2. Bot. having many nodes or nodelike swellings; gnarled. 3. Zool. having one or more swellings; nodose.

knot·ty (nŏt′ĭ), adj., **-tier, -tiest.** 1. characterized by knots; full of knots. 2. involved, intricate, or difficult: a knotty problem. —**knot′ti·ness,** n.

knot·weed (nŏt′wēd′), n. any of various knotty-stemmed plants of the polygonaceous genus Polygonum, as P. maritimum (**seaside knotweed**), a glaucous herb of sandy soils.

knout (nout), n. 1. a kind of whip or scourge formerly used in Russia for flogging criminals. —v.t. 2. to flog with the knout. [t. F, t. Russ.: m. knut]

know (nō), v., **knew, known, knowing,** n. —v.t. 1. to perceive or understand as fact or truth, or apprehend with clearness and certainty. 2. to have fixed in the mind or memory: to know a poem by heart. 3. to be cognizant or aware of; to be acquainted with (a thing, place, person, etc.), as by sight, experience, or report. 4. to understand from experience or attainment (fol. by how before an infinitive): to know how to make something. 5. to be able to distinguish, as one from another. 6. **know the ropes,** to know the various ropes about a vessel, as a sailor does. b. Colloq. to understand the details or methods of any business or the like. —v.i. 7. to have knowledge, or clear and certain perception, as of fact or truth. 8. to be cognizant or aware as of some fact, circumstance, or occurrences; have information, as about something. —n. 9. the fact of knowing; knowledge: now chiefly in the colloquial phrase **in the know** (in the circle of those who have inside knowledge). [ME knowe(n), knawe(n), OE (ge)cnāwan, c. OHG -cnāan know, Icel. knā (pres. ind.) know how, can; akin to L (g)noscere, Gk. gignōskein] —**know′er,** n. —Syn. 1. KNOW, COMPREHEND, UNDERSTAND imply being aware of meanings. To KNOW is to be aware of something as a fact or truth: he knows the basic facts of the subject; I know that he agrees with me. To COMPREHEND is to know something thoroughly and to perceive its relationships to certain other ideas, facts, etc. To UNDERSTAND is to be fully aware not only of the meaning of something but also its implications: I could comprehend all he said, but did not understand that he was joking.

know·a·ble (nō′ə bəl), adj. that may be known. —**know′a·ble·ness,** n.

know-how (nō′hou′), n. knowledge of how to do something; faculty or skill for a particular thing.

know·ing (nō′ĭng), adj. 1. shrewd, sharp, or astute; often, affecting or suggesting shrewd or secret understanding of matters: a knowing glance. 2. that knows; having knowledge or information; intelligent; wise. 3. conscious; intentional; deliberate. —**know′ing·ly,** adv. —**know′ing·ness,** n.

knowl·edge (nŏl′ĭj), n. 1. acquaintance with facts, truths, or principles, as from study or investigation; general erudition. 2. familiarity or conversance, as with a particular subject, branch of learning, etc. 3. acquaintance; familiarity gained by sight, experience, or report: a knowledge of human nature. 4. fact or state of knowing; perception of fact or truth; clear and certain mental apprehension. 5. state of being cognizant or aware, as of a fact or circumstance. 6. **to one's knowledge, a.** according to one's certain knowledge. **b.** (with a negative) so far as one knows: I never saw him, to my knowledge. 7. that which is known, or may be known. 8. the body of truths or facts accumulated by mankind in the course of time. 9. the sum of what is known. 10. cognizance of facts, or range cognizance: this has happened twice within my knowledge. [ME knowleche, der. KNOW] —Syn. 1. See **information.** 4. understanding. 8. learning, lore, erudition, scholarship; wisdom, science.

knowl·edge·a·ble (nŏl′ĭjəbəl), adj. Colloq. possessing knowledge or understanding; intelligent.

known (nōn), v. pp. of **know.**

know-noth·ing (nō′nŭth′ĭng), n. 1. an ignoramus. 2. an agnostic. 3. (cap.) a member of a political party (the **American party,** orig. a secret society whose members professed ignorance concerning it), prominent from 1853 to 1856, whose aim was to keep the control of the government in the hands of native citizens. —adj. 4. grossly ignorant. 5. agnostic. 6. (cap.) of or pertaining to the Know-Nothings.

known quantity, Math. a quantity whose value is given: in algebra, etc., frequently represented by a letter from the first part of the alphabet, as a, b, or c.

Knox (nŏks), n. 1. **Henry,** 1750–1806, American general: first Secretary of War, 1789–94. 2. **John,** 1505?–1572, leader of the Protestant Reformation in Scotland, preacher, statesman, and historian.

Knox·ville (nŏks′vĭl), n. a city in E Tennessee, on the Tennessee river. 111,827 (1960).

Knt., Knight.

knuck·le (nŭk′əl), n., v., **-led, -ling.** —n. 1. a joint of a finger, esp. one of the joints at the roots of the fingers. 2. the rounded prominence of such a joint when the finger is bent. 3. a joint of meat, consisting of the parts about the carpal or tarsal joint of a quadruped. 4. an angle between two members or surfaces of a vessel. 5. See **brass knuckles.** 6. a cylindrical projecting part on a hinge, through which an axis or pin passes; the joint of a hinge. —v.i. 7. to hold the knuckles close to the ground in playing marbles. 8. to apply oneself vigorously or earnestly, as to a task (fol. by down). 9. to yield or submit (often fol. by down or under). [ME knokel; akin to D kneukel, G knöchel, dim. of a word repr. by D knok, G knochen bone]

knuckle ball, Baseball. a slow pitched ball which curves in different directions before reaching the plate.

knuck·le·bone (nŭk′əl bōn′), n. 1. (in man) a bone forming a knuckle of a finger. 2. (in quadrupeds) a bone homologous with a wrist, ankle, or finger bone of man, or its knobbed end.

knuck·le-dust·er (nŭk′əl dŭs′tər), n. brass knuckles.

knuckle joint, 1. a joint forming a knuckle. 2. Mach. a flexible hinged joint formed by two abutting links.

knurl (nûrl), n. 1. a small ridge or the like, esp. one of a series, as on the edge of a thumbscrew to assist in obtaining a firm grip. —v.t. 2. to make knurls or ridges on. [appar. der. knur lump, knot, ME knurre]

knurled (nûrld), adj. 1. having small ridges on the edge or surface; milled. 2. having knurls or knots; gnarled.

knurl·y (nûr′lĭ), adj., **knurlier, knurliest.** having knurls or knots; gnarled.

Knut (kə nōōt′, -nŭt′), n. Canute.

K.O., knockout. Also, **k.o.**

ko·a·la (kō·ä′lə), *n.* a sluggish, tailless, gray, furry, arboreal marsupial, *Phascolarctos cinereus*, of Australia, about 2 feet long. [t. native Australian]

Ko·be (kō′bě′), *n.* a seaport in S Japan, on S Honshu island. 765,435 (1950).

Kö·ben·havn (kœ′pən houn′), *n.* Danish name of **Copenhagen.**

Ko·blenz (kō′blěnts), *n.* Coblenz.

ko·bold (kō′bōld, -bŏld), *n.* (in German folklore) **1.** a kind of spirit or goblin, often mischievous, that haunts houses. **2.** a spirit that haunts mines or other underground places. [t. G]

Koch (kōkн), *n.* **Robert** (rō′běrt), 1843–1910, German bacteriologist and physician.

Koala, *Phascolarctos cinereus* (28 to 32 in. long)

Ko·chi (kō′chē′), *n.* a seaport in SW Japan, on Shikoku island. 161,640 (1950).

Ko·da·chrome (kō′də krōm′), *n.* a trademark for a photographic film which is sensitive to and reproduces color.

Ko·dak (kō′dǎk), *n., v.,* **-daked, -daking.** —*n. Trademark.* **1.** a portable photographic camera, esp. adapted for instantaneous work, employing a continuous roll of sensitized film upon which successive negatives are made. —*v.t., v.i.* **2.** to photograph with a Kodak. [arbitrary word coined by George Eastman] —**ko′dak·er,** *n.*

Ko·di·ak (kō′dǐ·ǎk′), *n.* an island in the N Pacific, near the base of the Alaska Peninsula. ab. 100 mi. long.

Ko·dok (kō′dŏk), *n.* See **Fashoda.**

ko·el (kō′əl), *n.* a cuckoo of the genus *Eudynamys,* as the **Indian koel,** *E. orientalis.* [t. Hind.: m. *kōil,* der. Skt. *kokila*]

Koest·ler (kěst′lər), *n.* **Arthur,** born 1905, Hungarian novelist.

K. of C., Knights of Columbus.

Koff·ka (kôf′kä), *n.* **Kurt** (kŏŏrt), 1886–1941, German psychologist in U.S.

K. of P., Knights of Pythias.

Koh·i·noor (kō′ə nŏŏ r′), *n.* one of the world's large diamonds, 109 carats, first discovered in India and now part of the British crown jewels. [t. Pers.: m. *kōh-i-nūr* mountain of light]

kohl (kōl), *n.* a powder, as finely powdered sulfide of antimony, used in the East to darken the eyelids, make eyebrows, etc. [t. Ar.: m. *kohl.* Cf. ALCOHOL]

Köh·ler (kœ′lər), *n.* **Wolfgang** (vôlf′gäng), born 1887, German psychologist.

kohl·ra·bi (kōl′rä′bǐ), *n., pl.* **-bies.** a cultivated variety of *Brassica oleracea,* var. *gongylodes,* whose stem above ground swells into an edible bulblike formation. [t. G, b. G *kohl* cabbage and It. *cauli* (or *cavoli*) *rape,* pl. of *cavolo rapa* cabbage turnip. Cf. COLE, RAPE²]

Koi·ne (koi nā′), *n.* the standard Greek of Attic type which replaced other dialects and flourished under the Roman Empire. [Gk., short for *koinē diálektos* common dialect]

Ko·kand (kō känt′), *n.* a city in the SW Soviet Union in Asia, in Uzbek Republic: formerly the center of a powerful khanate. 85,000 (est. 1948).

Ko·ko·mo (kō′kə mō′), *n.* a city in central Indiana 47,197 (1960).

Ko·ko Nor (kō′kō′ nôr′), **1.** a lake in W China, in Chinghai province. ab. 2300 sq. mi. **2.** Chinghai.

Ko·ku·ra (kō′kō·ŏŏ rä′), *n.* a seaport in SW Japan, on Kyushu island. 194,453 (1950).

ko·la (kō′lə), *n.* **1.** the kola nut. **2.** an extract prepared from it. **3.** the tree producing it. Also, **cola.** [t. W Afr.]

Ko·la (kō′lä), *n.* a peninsula in the NW Soviet Union in Europe between the White and Barents seas.

ko·la nut (kō′lə), a brownish seed, about the size of a chestnut, produced by a sterculiaceous tree of western tropical Africa, the West Indies, and Brazil, *Cola nitida,* and containing both caffein and theobromine: used as a stimulant in soft drinks. Also, **cola nut.**

Ko·lar Gold Fields (kō′lär′), a city in S India, in Mysore state: rich mining district. 159,084 (1951).

ko·lin·sky (kə lǐn′skǐ), *n., pl.* **-skies. 1.** the red sable, or Siberian mink, *Putorius sibiricus,* about 15 inches long, with a bushy tail 8 or 10 inches long, the fur uniformly buff or tawny, somewhat paler below, varied with black and white on the head. **2.** the fur of such an animal. [t. Russ.: m. *Kolinski,* adj., pertaining to KOLA]

kol·khoz (kōl hôz′), *n.* U.S.S.R. a collective farm, the holding being common property of all.

Koll·witz (kôl′vǐts), *n.* **Käthe** (kě′tə), 1867–1945, German artist.

Köln (kœln), *n.* German name of **Cologne.**

Ko·lozs·vár (kō′lŏzh vär′), *n.* Hungarian name of **Cluj.**

Ko·ly·ma (kō′lǐ mä′), *n.* a river in the NE Soviet Union in Asia, flowing NE to the Arctic Ocean. ab. 1000 mi. Also, **Ko·li·ma′.**

Kom·in·tern (kŏm′ǐn tûrn′), *n.* Comintern.

Ko·mu·ra (kō′mŏŏ rä′), *n.* **Marquis Jutaro** (jŏŏ′tä·rō′), 1855–1911, Japanese statesman and diplomat.

Ko·na·kri (kō′nä krē′), *n.* Conakry.

Kö·nig·grätz (kœ′nǐкн grěts′), *n.* a town in NW Czechoslovakia, on the Elbe in Bohemia: the Prussians defeated the Austrians near here in the Battle of Sadowa, 1866. ab. 18,000.

Kö·nigs·berg (kœ′nǐgz bûrg′; *Ger.* kœ′nǐкнs běrкн′), *n.* German name of **Kaliningrad**

Kö·nigs·hüt·te (kœ′nǐкнs hy′tə), *n.* German name of **Chorzów.**

Kon·stanz (kōn′shtänts), *n.* German name of **Constance.**

Ko·nya (kôn′yä), *n.* a city in S Turkey. 93,125 (1955). Also, **Ko′nia.**

Koo (kŏŏ), *n.* **Wellington** (*Vi Kyuin Wellington Koo*), born 1888, Chinese statesman and diplomat.

koo·doo (kŏŏ′dŏŏ), *n., pl.* **-doos.** a large handsome African antelope, *Strepsiceros strepsiceros,* the males of which have large corkscrewlike horns. Also, **kudu.** [t. S Afr. (Hottentot)]

kook·a·bur·ra (kŏŏk′ə bûr′ə), *n. Australia.* the laughing jackass. [t. native Australian]

Greater koodoo, *Strepsiceros strepsiceros* (5 ft. high at the shoulder, total length 9 ft., horns 3 to 4 ft. long)

Koo·te·nay (kŏŏ′tə nā′), *n.* a river flowing from SE British Columbia, through NW Montana and N Idaho, swinging back into Canada where it enters **Kootenay Lake** (75 mi. long) and empties into the Columbia river. ab. 400 mi. Spelled **Koo′te·nai′** in the U.S.

kop (kŏp), *n.* (in South Africa) a hill. [t. D: head]

ko·peck (kō′pěk), *n.* a Russian monetary unit and copper coin, 1/100 of a ruble, equivalent to about 1/2 of a U.S. cent. Also, **ko/pek, copeck.** [t. Russ.: m. *kopeika*]

kop·je (kŏp′ǐ), *n. South African.* a small hill. [D, dim. of *kop* KOP]

kor (kôr), *n.* homer². [t. Heb.]

Ko·ran (kō rän′, -rän′), *n.* the sacred scripture of Islam, believed by orthodox Mohammedans to contain revelations made in Arabic by Allah directly to Mohammed. [t. Ar.: m *qur'ān* reading, recitation, der. *qara'a* read] —**Ko·ran·ic** (kō rän′ǐk), *adj.*

Kor·do·fan (kôr′dō fän′), *n.* a province in the central Sudan. 1,945,965 pop. (est. 1953); ab. 147,100 sq. mi. *Cap.:* El Obeid.

Ko·re·a (kō rē′ə), *n.* a country in E Asia, on a peninsula SE of Manchuria and between the Sea of Japan and the Yellow Sea: under Japanese rule, 1910–45; currently divided in the vicinity of 38° N into **South Korea** (21,687,000, est. 1954; 36,600 sq. mi.; *Cap.:* Seoul) and **North Korea** (8,800,000, est. 1951; 50,000 sq. mi.; *Cap.:* Pyongyang). Outbreak of war (June 25, 1950) led to United Nations aid in defense of South Korea. Japanese, **Chosen.**

Korea

Ko·re·an (kō rē′ən), *adj.* **1.** of Korea, its people, or language. —*n.* **2.** a native or inhabitant of Korea. **3.** the language of Korea, of no known linguistic affinity.

Korea Strait, the strait between Korea and Japan, connecting the Sea of Japan and the East China Sea.

Kor·o·seal (kôr′ə sēl′, kōr′-), *n.* a trademark for a plastic derived from vinyl chloride by polymerization.

ko·ru·na (kô rŏŏ′nä), *n., pl.* **koruny** (kô rŏŏ′nǐ), **korun** (kô rŏŏn′). the monetary unit of Czechoslovakia, stabilized in 1929 to equal $0.03 in the U.S., now worth about 2 cents. *Symbol:* Kcs. [t. Czech, t. L: m. *corōna* crown]

Kos (kŏs, kôs), *n.* Cos.

Kos·ci·us·ko (kŏs′ǐ ŭs′kō), *n.* **1. Thaddeus** (thǎd′Ǐ·əs), (*Tadeusz Kościuszko*) 1746–1817, Polish patriot and general who served as an officer in the American Revolutionary army. **2. Mount,** the highest mountain in Australia, in SE New South Wales. 7328 ft.

ko·sher (kō′shər), *adj.* **1.** fit, lawful, or ritually permitted, according to the Jewish law: used of food and vessels for food ritually proper for use, esp. of meat slaughtered in accordance with the law of Moses. **2.** *U.S. Slang.* genuine. —*n.* **3.** *Colloq.* kosher food. Also, **kasher.** [t. Heb.: m. *kāshēr* fit, proper, lawful]

Ko·ši·ce (kō′shǐ tsě), *n.* a city in SE Czechoslovakia, in Slovakia. 51,689 (1947). Hungarian, **Kassa.**

Kos·suth (kŏs′ŏŏth; *Hung.* kô′shŏŏt), *n.* **1. Francis** or **Ferencz** (fěr′ěnts), 1841–1914, Hungarian patriot, statesman, and writer. **2.** his father, **Louis** or **Lajos** (lŏ′yôsh), 1802–94, Hungarian patriot and orator.

Ko·stro·ma (kôs′trō mä′), *n.* a city in the central Soviet Union in Europe, on the Volga. 156,000 (est. 1956).

Ko·sy·gin (kō sē′gǐn), *n.* **A·lek·sei Ni·ko·la·ye·vich** (ä lěk sā′nǐ kō lä′yə vich), born 1904, Russian politician: Premier since 1964.

ko·to (kō′tō; *Jap.* kô′tô′), *n., pl.* **-tos.** a Japanese musical instrument having numerous strings, stretched over a vaulted, wooden sounding board: plucked with the fingers. [t. Jap.]

ko·tow (kō′tou′), *n., v.i., n.* kowtow. —**ko′tow·er,** *n.*

Kot·ze·bue (kôt′sə bŏŏ′), *n.* **August Friedrich Ferdinand von** (ou′gŏŏst frē′drǐкн fěr′dǐ nänt fən), 1761–1819, German dramatist.

kou·mis (kŏŏ′mǐs), *n.* kumiss. Also, **kou′miss.**

Kous·se·vitz·ky (kŏŏ sə vǐts′kǐ), *n.* **Serge** or **Sergei Alexandrovich** (sěrzh *or* sěr gā′ ä′lě ksän drô′vǐch), 1874–1951, Russian-born orchestra conductor in U.S.

Kov·no (kôv′nŏ), *n.* Russian name of **Kaunas.**

Ko·weit (kō wāt′), *n.* Kuwait.

Kow·loon (kou′lōōn′), *n.* **1.** a peninsula in SE China, opposite Hong Kong island: a part of Hong Kong Colony leased from China. ab. 1,000,000 (est. 1954); 3 sq. mi. **2.** a seaport on this peninsula.

kow·tow (kou′tou′, kō′-), *v.i.* **1.** to knock the forehead on the ground while kneeling, as an act of reverence, worship, apology, etc. **2.** to act in an obsequious manner; show servile deference. —*n.* **3.** act of kowtowing. Also, **kotow.** [t. Chinese (Mandarin): m. *k'o-t'ou,* lit., knock-head] —**kow′tow′er,** *n.*

Ko·zhi·ko·da (kō′zhĭ kō′dä), *n.* Indian name for Calicut.

KP, *Chess.* king's pawn.

K.P., **1.** Kitchen Police. **2.** Knight of the Order of St. Patrick. **3.** Knights of Pythias.

KR, *Chess.* king's rook.

Kr, *Chem.* krypton.

kr., **1.** kreutzer. **2.** krona; kronor. **3.** krone²; kronen. **4.** krone¹; kroner.

Kra (krä), *n.* Isthmus of, the narrowest part of the Malay peninsula, between the Bay of Bengal and the Gulf of Siam. ab. 35 mi. wide.

kraal (kräl), *n.* **1.** a village of South African natives, usually surrounded by a stockade or the like and often having a central space for cattle, etc. **2.** the kraal as a social unit. **3.** *South African.* an enclosure for cattle, etc. —*v.t.* **4.** to shut up in a kraal, as cattle. [t. S Afr. D. t. Pg.: m. *curral* enclosure. Cf. CORRAL]

Krafft-E·bing (kräft′ā′bĭng), *n.* **Richard** (rĭKH′ärt), **Baron von,** 1840–1902, German psychiatrist.

kraft (kräft, kräft), *n.* a strong paper, usually brown, processed from wood pulp: used in bags and as wrapping paper. [G *Kraft* strength]

krait (krīt), *n.* any of the extremely venomous snakes of the genus *Bungarus* of India and southeastern Asia. [t. Hind.: m. *karait*]

Kra·ka·tau (krä′kä tou′), *n.* a small volcanic island in the U.S. of Indonesia between Java and Sumatra: violent eruption, 1883. Also, **Kra·ka·to·a** (krä′kä tō′ä).

kra·ken (krä′kən, krä′-), *n.* a mythical sea monster said to appear at times off Norway. [t. Norw.]

Kra·ków (krä′kōōf), *n.* Polish name of Cracow.

kran (krän), *n.* a Persian monetary unit and silver coin, equal to about 8 U.S. cents.

Kras·no·dar (kräs′nō där′), *n.* a city in the S Soviet Union in Europe: a port near the Sea of Azov. 271,000 (est. 1952). Formerly, **Ekaterinodar.**

Kras·no·yarsk (kräs′nō yärsk′), *n.* a city in the S Soviet Union in Asia, on the Yenisei. 328,000 (est. 1956).

K-ra·tion (kā′răsh′ən, -rā′shən), *n.* *U.S. Army.* one of the emergency field rations used when other rations are not available.

Kre·feld (krā′fĕld; *Ger.* -fĕlt), *n.* a city in W West Germany, in the Rhineland. 198,083 (est. 1955). Also, **Crefeld.**

Kreis·ler (krīs′lər), *n.* **Fritz** (frĭts), 1875–1962, Austrian violinist, in the U.S.

Krem·en·chug (krĕm′ĕn chŏŏk′), *n.* a city in the SW Soviet Union, on the Dnieper river. 110,000 (est. 1948).

krem·lin (krĕm′lĭn), *n.* **1.** the citadel of a Russian town or city. **2.** (*cap.*) the citadel of Moscow, including within its walls the chief office of the Soviet government. [t. Russ.: m. *kreml* citadel]

kreut·zer (kroit′sər), *n.* **1.** a former German coin equivalent to about half a U. S. cent. **2.** an Austrian copper coin (no longer coined) and monetary unit, equal to one hundredth of a florin. [t. G: m. *kreuzer,* der. *kreuz* cross (orig. the device on the coin)]

Kreutzer Sonata, a sonata for violin and pianoforte (1803, Op. 47) by Beethoven.

Kreym·borg (krām′bôrg), *n.* **Alfred,** born 1883, U.S. poet and author.

krieg·spiel (krēg′spēl′), *n.* a game designed to teach military science by means of blocks or the like, representing guns, etc., moved on maps or other surfaces.

Kriem·hild (krēm′hĭlt), *n.* the legendary heroine of the *Nibelungenlied,* wife of Siegfried and avenger of his death: the counterpart of the Scandinavian Gudrun.

krim·mer (krĭm′ər), *n.* a lambskin from the Crimean region, dressed as a fur, with wool in loose soft curls and usually whitish or pale gray. Also, **crimmer.** [t. G., der. *Krim* Crimea]

kris (krēs), *n.* creese.

Krish·na (krĭsh′nə), *n.* the most popular Hindu deity, as an incarnation of Vishnu: the famous teacher in the Bhagavad Gita. [t. Skt., special use of *krishna* black]

Kriss Krin·gle (krĭs′ krĭng′gəl), Santa Claus. [t. G: m. *Christkindl, -del* Christ child, Christmas gift]

Kri·voi Rog (krĭ voi′ rôg′), a city in the SW Soviet Union, in the Ukrainian Republic. 322,000 (est. 1956).

Kró·lew·ska Hu·ta (krōō lĕf′skä hŏŏ′tä), Chorzów.

kro·na (krō′nə; *Sw.* krōō′nä), *n., pl.* **-nor** (-nôr). a silver coin and monetary unit of Sweden, worth about 19½ U.S. cts. [t. Sw. See KRONE¹]

kro·ne¹ (krō′nŏ), *n., pl.* **-ner** (-nêr). the monetary unit and a silver coin of Denmark and of Norway, equal to about 14 U.S. cents. [t. Dan. and Norw., c. Icel. and Sw. *krona* crown]

kro·ne² (krō′nə), *n., pl.* **-nen** (-nən). **1.** a former German gold coin equal to 10 marks, or about $2.38. **2.** for-

mer monetary unit and a silver coin of Austria, equal to 100 heller, or about 20.3 U.S. cents. [t. G. See KRONE¹]

Kro·nos (krō′nŏs), *n.* Cronus.

Kron·stadt (krŏn shtät′ *for 1;* krŏn′shtät *for 2*), *n.* **1.** a seaport in the NW Soviet Union, on an island in the Gulf of Finland, W of Leningrad: naval base. 50,000 (est. 1948). **2.** German name of **Brasov.**

kroon (krōōn), *n., pl.* **kroons, krooni** (krōō′nĭ). the coin and monetary unit of Estonia equivalent to the Swedish krona. [t. Estonian: crown]

Kro·pot·kin (krō pŏt′kĭn; *Russ.* krō pôt′-), *n.* **Peter** (*Prince Pëtr Alekseevich*), 1842–1921, Russian anarchist, writer, and geographer, in England.

Kru·ger (krōō′gər; *Du.* krY′gər), *n.* **Stephanus Johannes Paulus** (stĕ fä′nŏŏs yō hän′əs pou′lŏŏs), ("*Oom Paul*") 1825–1904, Boer statesman and president of the South African Republic, 1883–1900.

Kru·gers·dorp (krōō′gərz dôrp′; *Du.* krY′gərs-), *n.* a city in the NE Republic of South Africa, in Transvaal, near Johannesburg. With suburbs, 75,647 (1951).

krul·ler (krŭl′ər), *n.* cruller.

Krupp (krŭp; *Ger.* krŏŏp), *n.* **Alfred** (äl′frät), 1812–87, German manufacturer of armaments.

Krup·ska·ya (krōōp′skä yä), *n.* **Nadezhda Konstantinovna** (nä dĕzh′dä kŏn′stän tē′nŏv nä), 1869–1939, Russian social worker and wife of Nikolai Lenin.

kryp·ton (krĭp′tŏn), *n.* *Chem.* an inert monatomic gaseous element present in very small amounts in the atmosphere, of some use in high-power, tungsten-filament light bulbs. *Symbol:* Kr; *at. wt.:* 83.7; *at. no.:* 36; *weight of one liter at 0°C., and 760 mm. pressure:* 3.708. [t. NL. t. Gk., neut. of *kryptós* hidden. See CRYPT]

Kshat·ri·ya (kshät′rĭ yə), *n.* a member of the military caste among the Hindus. [t. Skt., der. *kshatra* rule, n.]

Kt, *Chess.* knight.

Kt., Knight.

kt., **1.** karat; carat. **2.** knot.

K.T., Knights Templars.

Kua·la Lum·pur (kwä′lə lŏŏm′pŏŏr′), a city in the SW Malay Peninsula, capital of Selangor and of the federation of Malaysia. 316,230 (1957).

Ku·blai Khan (kōō′blī kän′), 1216?–94, Mongol emperor, 1259–94, founder of the Mongol dynasty in China.

Ku·bla Khan (kōō′blə kän′), a poetic fragment (1816) by Coleridge.

ku·chen (kōō′KHən), *n.* a yeast-raised coffee cake, usually including fruit. [G]

ku·dos (kū′dŏs), *n.* glory; renown. [t. Gk.: m. *kŷdos*]

Kud·run (kŏŏd′rŏōn, kŏŏ′l′/-), *n.* Gudrun.

ku·du (kōō′dōō), *n.* koodoo.

Kuen·lun (kŏŏn′lŏŏn′), *n.* Kunlun.

Kui·by·shev (kwē′bə shĕf′; *Russ.* kŏō′Y bwē shĕf′), *n.* a city in the E Soviet Union in Europe: a port on the Volga. 760,000 (est. 1956). Formerly, **Samara.**

Ku Klux Klan (kū′ klŭks′ klän′), **1.** a secret organization in the southern U.S., active for several years after the Civil War, which aimed to suppress the newly acquired powers of the Negroes and to oppose carpetbaggers from the North, and was responsible for many lawless and violent proceedings. **2.** a secret organization (**Knights of the Klu Klux Klan**) inspired by the former, founded in 1915 and active in the southern and other parts of the U. S., admitting to membership none but native-born, white, Gentile, Protestant Americans, and professing Americanism as its object. Also, **Ku Klux.** [? f. m. Gk. *kŷklos* circle + m. CLAN]

ku·lak (kōō läk′), *n.* *Russia.* **1.** (before the revolution) a hard-fisted merchant or a village usurer. **2.** (more recently) any peasant who employed hired labor or possessed any machinery. [t. Russ.: fist, tight-fisted person]

Kul·tur (kŏŏl tōōr′), *n.* **1.** culture as a social force causing evolutionary development to higher forms of civilization. **2.** a civilization characteristic of a time or a people. [G, t. L: m.s. *cultūra* CULTURE]

Kul·tur·kampf (kŏŏl tōōr′kämpf′), *n.* the conflict between the German imperial government and the Roman Catholic Church from 1872 or 1873 until 1886, chiefly over the control of educational and ecclesiastical appointments. [G: civilization struggle]

Ku·ma·mo·to (kōō′mä mō′tō), *n.* a city in SW Japan, on Kyushu island. 267,506 (1950).

Ku·mas·i (kōō mäs′Y), *n.* the capital of Ashanti, in Ashanti in Ghana. 59,420 (1948).

ku·miss (kōō′mYs), *n.* **1.** a slightly alcoholic beverage made from fermented mare's or camel's milk, drunk by Asiatic nomads, etc. **2.** a similar drink prepared from other milk, esp. that of the cow, and used for dietetic and medicinal purposes. Also, **koumis, koumiss, koumyss.** [t. Russ.: m. *kumys,* t. Tatar: m. *kumiz.* Cf. F *koumis,* G *kumys*]

küm·mel (kYm′əl; *Ger.* kYm′əl), *n.* a colorless cordial or liqueur flavored with cumin, caraway seeds, etc., made esp. in the Baltic area. [t. G: cumin, kümmel]

kum·mer·bund (kŭm′ər bŭnd′), *n.* cummerbund.

kum·quat (kŭm′kwŏt), *n.* **1.** a small, round or oblong citrus fruit with a sweet rind and acid pulp, used chiefly for preserves, being the fruit of *Fortunella japonica* and related species, rutaceous shrubs native in China and cultivated in Japan, Florida, California, etc. **2.** the plant itself. Also, **cumquat.** [t. Chinese, Cantonese pronunciation of Mandarin *kin ku,* lit., gold orange]

---

b., blend of, blended; c., cognate with; d., dialect, dialectal; der., derived from; f., formed from; g., going back to; m., modification of; r., replacing; s., stem of; t., taken from; ?, perhaps. See the full key on inside cover.

Kun (kŏŏn), *n.* **Béla** (bā′lŏ). 1885–1937, Hungarian Communist leader.

Kung-fu-tse (kŏŏng′fŏŏ′dzŭ′), *n.* Chinese name of Confucius.

Kun·lun (kŏŏn′lŏŏn′), *n.* a lofty mountain system bordering to the N the Tibetan plateau and extending W across central China. Highest peak, ab. 25,000 ft. Also, **Kuenlun.**

Kun·ming (kŏŏn′mǐng′), *n.* a city in SW China: the capital of Yünnan province; an important transshipment point on the Burma Road in World War II. 500,000 (est. 1950). Also, **Yünnan.**

kunz·ite (kŏŏnts′īt), *n.* a transparent lilac variety of spodumene, used as a gem. [named after G. F. *Kunz,* American expert in precious stones. See -ITE¹]

Kuo·min·tang (kwō′mǐn′tăng′; *Chin.* gwō′mǐn′- däng′), *n.* a Chinese political party, deriving historically from earlier parties and political societies organized or led by Sun Yat-sen, formerly controlling a large part of China. [t. Chinese (Mandarin): f. *kuo* nation + *min* people + *tang* party]

Ku·ra (kŏŏ rä′), *n.* a river flowing from NE Turkey through the Georgian and Azerbaijan Republics of the Soviet Union SE to the Caspian Sea. ab. 810 mi.

Kurd (kûrd; *Pers.* kŏŏrd), *n.* a member of a pastoral and warlike people speaking an Iranian language and dwelling chiefly in Kurdistan. —**Kurd′ish,** *adj.,* *n.*

Kur·di·stan (kûr′dĭ stän′; *Pers.* kŏŏr′dĭ stän′), *n.* **1.** a mountain and plateau region in SE Turkey, NW Iran, and N Iraq, peopled largely by Kurds. ab. 74,000 sq. mi. **2.** any of several rugs woven by the Kurds of Turkey or Iran.

Ku·re (kŏŏ′rĕ′), *n.* a seaport in SW Japan, on Honshu island. 187,775 (1950).

Kurg (kŏŏrg), *n.* Coorg.

Ku·rile Islands (kŏŏr′ĭl, kŏŏ rēl′), a chain of small islands off the NE coast of Asia, extending from N Japan to the S tip of Kamchatka: renounced by Japan in 1945; under Soviet Administration. Also, **Kur′il Islands.** Japanese, **Chishima.**

Kur·land (kŏŏr′land), *n.* Courland.

Ku·ro·ki (kŏŏ′rŏ kē′), *n.* **Count Tamemoto** (tä′mĕ- mō′tŏ), 1844–1923, Japanese general.

Ku·ro·pat·kin (kŏŏ′rŏ păt′kĭn), *n.* **Aleksei Niko-laevich** (ä′lĕ ksĕ′ĭ nĭ′kŏ lä′yə vĭch), 1848–1925, Russian general.

Kursk (kŏŏrsk), *n.* a city in the central Soviet Union in Europe. N of Kharkov. 179,000 (est. 1956).

Kutch (kŭch), *n.* Cutch.

Ku·tu·zov (kŏŏ tŏŏ′zŏf), *n.* **Mikhail Ilarionovich** (mĭ′hä ēl′ ˈ Ĭ lä′rĭ ŏ nŏ′vĭch), 1745–1813, Russian general.

Ku·wait (kŏŏ wīt′), *n.* **1.** a sheikdom in NE Arabia, on the NW coast of the Persian Gulf: a British protectorate. 150,000 (est. 1952); ab. 8000 sq. mi. **2.** a seaport in and the capital of this sheikdom. 25,000 (est. 1952). Also, **Koweit.**

Kuyp (koip), *n.* Cuyp.

Kuz·netsk Basin (kŏŏz nĕtsk′), an industrial region in the S Soviet Union in Asia: coal fields.

Kv-a., Kilovolt ampere.

kvass (kväs), *n.* quass.

kw., kilowatt.

Kwa·ki·u·tl (kwä′kĭ ōō′təl), *n.* a group of American Indians of Wakashan linguistic stock in SW and British Columbia (including Vancouver Island), Canada, the two great divisions of which are Nootka and Kwakiutl, the latter meaning "beach at north side of river," or, in native folk etymology, "smoke of the world."

Kwang·chow (gwäng′jō′), *n.* Canton.

Kwang·cho·wan (gwäng′jō′wän′), *n.* a territory in S China on the SW coast of Kwangtung province: leased to France, 1898–1945. ab. 250,000; ab. 190 sq. mi.

Kwang·si (kwäng′sē′; *Chin.* gwäng′-), *n.* a province in S China. 19,560,822 pop. (1953); 85,452 sq. mi. *Cap.:* Yungning.

Kwang·tung (kwäng′tŏŏng′; *Chin.* gwäng′dŏŏng′), *n.* a province in SE China. 34,770,059 pop. (1953); 85,447 sq. mi. *Cap.:* Canton.

Kwan·tung (kwän′tŏŏng′; *Chin.* gwän′dŏŏng′), *n.* a territory in NE China at the tip of Liaotang Peninsula, Manchuria: leased to Japan, 1905–45; part of Shantung province. Also, **Kwangtung.**

kwa·shi·or·kor (kwä′shǐ ôr′kər, -ôr kôr′; kwä′shǐ- ôr′kər), *n.* *Pathol.* a nutritional disease, chiefly of children in Africa, associated with a heavy corn diet and the resultant lack of protein, and characterized by edema, potbelly, and changes in skin pigmentation.

Kwei·chow (kwā′chou′; *Chin.* gwā′jō′), *n.* a province in S China. 15,037,310 pop. (1953); 68,139 sq. mi. *Cap.:* Kweiyang.

Kwei·lin (gwā′lĭn′), *n.* a city in S China: the former capital of Kwangsi province. 131,000 (est. 1950).

Kwei·sui (gwā′swā′), *n.* a city in N China, in Inner Mongolia: the capital of Suiyüan province. 110,000 (est. 1950). Formerly, **Kwei·hwa·ting** (gwā′hwä′tǐng′).

Kwei·yang (gwā′yäng′), *n.* a city in S China: the capital of Kweichow province. 260,000 (est. 1951).

K.W.H., kilowatt-hour. Also, **kw-h, kw-hr, kw.-hr.**

Ky., Kentucky.

ky·ack (kī′ăk), *n.* *Western U.S.* a type of knapsack which can hang from either side of a pack animal.

ky·a·nite (kī′ə nīt′), *n.* cyanite.

Kyd (kĭd), *n.* **Thomas,** 1558–94, English dramatist.

ky·lix (kī′lĭks, kĭl′ĭks), *n.,* *pl.* **kylikes** (kĭl′ə kēz′). cylix.

ky·mo·graph (kī′mə grăf′, -gräf′), *n.* **1.** an instrument by which variations of fluid pressure, as the waves of the pulse, can be measured and graphically recorded. **2.** an instrument measuring the angular oscillations of an airplane in flight with respect to axes fixed in space. Also, **cymograph.** [f. *kymo-* (comb. form of Gk. *kŷma* wave) + -GRAPH] —**ky′mo·graph′ic,** *adj.*

Kym·ric (kĭm′rĭk), *adj.,* *n.* Cymric.

Kym·ry (kĭm′rĭ), *n.pl.* Cymry.

Kyo·to (kyō′tō′), *n.* a city in central Japan, on S Honshu island: the capital of Japan, A.D. 784–1868. 1,101,854 (1950). Also, **Kioto.**

ky·pho·sis (kī fō′sĭs), *n.* *Pathol.* a curvature of the spine, convex backward. [t. NL, t. Gk.: hunched state]

Kyr·i·e e·le·i·son (kĭr′ĭ ē′ ə lā′ə sŏn′), **1.** "Lord, have mercy," a brief petition used in various offices of the Eastern and Roman churches. **2.** a response or petition in the Anglican service, beginning with the words, "Lord, have mercy upon us." **3.** a musical setting of either of these. [t. Gk.: m. *Kŷrie eléēson*]

Ky·the·ra (kē′thē rä′), *n.* Greek name of Cerigo.

Kyu·shu (kū′shōō′), *n.* a large island in SW Japan. 12,529,000 (est. 1953); 15,750 sq. mi. Also, **Kiushu.**

L

L¹, l (ĕl), *n.,* *pl.* **L's** or **Ls, l's** or **ls. 1.** a consonant, the 12th letter of the English alphabet. **2.** the Roman numeral for 50. See **Roman numerals.**

L², *pl.* **L's. 1.** something having a shape like that of the letter L. **2.** ell. **3.** Also, **l.** *Elect.* coefficient of inductance. **4.** elevated railroad. **5.** Latin. **6.** *Physics.* length. **7.** (L *libra*) pound. **8.** *Geog.* (terrestrial) longitude.

L., 1. Lake. **2.** Latin. **3.** latitude. **4.** law. **5.** left. **6.** (L *liber*) book. **7.** Liberal. **8.** Low.

l., 1. latitude. **2.** law. **3.** leaf. **4.** league. **5.** left. **6.** length. **7.** (pl. **ll.**) line. **8.** link. **9.** lira; liras. **10.** liter.

l-, *Chem.* levo-. Also, **l**

la¹ (lä), *n.* *Music.* the syllable used for the sixth tone of a scale, and sometimes for the tone A. See **sol-fa.** (def. 1). [See GAMUT]

la² (lô, lä), *interj.* an exclamation of wonder, surprise, etc. [ME and OE; weak var. of OE *lā* LO]

La, *Chem.* lanthanum.

La., Louisiana.

laa·ger (lä′gər), *South African.* —*n.* **1.** a camp or encampment, esp. within a circle of wagons. —*v.t.,* *v.i.* **2.** to arrange or encamp in a laager. Also, **lager.** [t. S Afr. D, var. of *lager,* c. G *lager* camp. Cf. LAIR]

Laa·land (lô′län), *n.* an island of SE Denmark, S of Zealand. 87,150 pop. (1945); 479 sq. mi. Also, **Lolland.**

lab (lăb), *n.* *U.S. Colloq.* laboratory.

Lab., 1. Labrador. **2.** Laborite.

La·ban (lā′bən), *n.* *Bible.* the Syrian father-in-law of Jacob. Gen. 24:29–60.

lab·a·rum (lăb′ə rəm), *n.,* *pl.* **-ra** (-rə). **1.** an ecclesiastical standard or banner, as for carrying in procession. **2.** the military standard of Constantine the Great and later Christian emperors of Rome, bearing Christian symbols. [t. L, corresp. to Gk. *lábaron;* ult. orig. unknown]

lab·da·num (lăb′də nəm), *n.* a resinous juice that exudes from various rockroses of the genus *Cistus:* used in perfumery, fumigating substances, medicinal plasters, etc. Also, **ladanum.** [t. ML, m. L *lādanum,* t. Gk.: m. *lādanon* mastic. Cf. Pers. *lādan* shrub]

ăct, āble, dâre, ärt; ĕbb, ēqual; ĭf, īce; hŏt, ōver, ôrder, oil, bŏŏk, ōōze, out; ŭp, ūse, ûrge; ə = a in alone; ch, chief; g, give; ng, ring; sh, shoe; th, thin; ŧh, that; zh, vision. See the full key on inside cover.

lab·e·fac·tion (lăb/ə făk/shən), *n.* a shaking or weakening; overthrow; downfall. Also, *esp. Brit.*, **lab·e·fac·ta·tion** (lăb/ə făk tā/shən). [f. s. L *labefactus*, pp., weakened + -ION]

la·bel (lā/bəl), *n.*, *v.*, **-beled**, **-beling** or (*esp. Brit.*) **-belled**, **-belling.** —*n.* **1.** a slip of paper or other material, marked or inscribed, for affixing to something to indicate its nature, ownership, destination, etc. **2.** a short word or phrase of description for a person, group, movement, etc. **3.** a strip or narrow piece of anything. **4.** *Archit.* a molding or dripstone over a door or window, esp. one which extends horizontally across the top of the opening and vertically downward for a certain distance at the sides. —*v.t.* **5.** to affix a label to; mark with a label. **6.** to designate or describe by or on a label: *the bottle was labeled poison.* **7.** to put in a certain class; to describe by a verbal label. [ME, t. OF, ult. der. L root *lamb-* lick] —**la·bel·er**; *esp. Brit.*, **la·bel·ler**, *n.*

La Belle Dame Sans Mer·ci (là běl dàm säN měr sē/), a ballad (1819) by Keats.

la·bel·lum (lə běl/əm), *n.*, *pl.* **-bella** (-běl/ə). *Bot.* that division of the corolla of an orchidaceous plant which differs more or less markedly from the other divisions, often forming the most conspicuous part. [t. L, dim. of *labrum* lip]

la·bi·a (lā/bǐ ə), *n.* pl. of labium.

la·bi·al (lā/bǐ əl), *adj.* **1.** pertaining to or of the nature of a labium. **2.** *Music.* giving forth tones produced by the impact of a stream of air upon the sharp edge of a lip, as a flute or the flue pipes of an organ. **3.** of or pertaining to the lips. **4.** *Phonet.* involving lip articulation, as *p, v, m, w,* or a rounded vowel. [t. ML: s. *labiālis,* der. L *labium* lip] —**la/bi·al·ly**, *adv.*

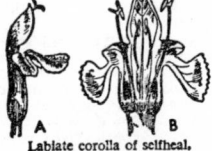

L. Labellum, lady's-slipper. *Cypripedium hirsutum*

la·bi·al·ize (lā/bǐ ə līz/), *v.t.*, **-ized**, **-izing.** *Phonet.* to give a labial character to (a sound), e.g., to round (a vowel). —**la·bi·al·i·za/tion**, *n.*

la·bi·ate (lā/bǐ āt/, -ǐt), *adj.* **1.** lipped; having parts which are shaped or arranged like lips. **2.** *Bot.* **a.** belonging to the Labiatae (or *Menthaceae,* formerly *Lamiaceae*), the mint family of plants, most of which have bilabiate corollas. **b.** (usually) two-lipped; bilabiate: said of a gamopetalous corolla or gamosepalous calyx. —*n.* **3.** a labiate plant.

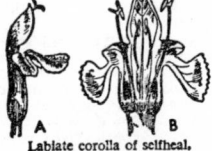

Labiate corolla of selfheal, *Prunella vulgaris*
A. Seen from the side;
B. Laid open, front view

La·biche (là bēsh/), *n.* **Eugène Marin** (œ zhěn/ mà-räN/), 1815–88, French dramatist.

la·bile (lā/bǐl), *adj.* **1.** apt to lapse or change; unstable; lapsable. **2.** *Med.* noting or pertaining to a mode of application of electricity in which the active electrode is moved over the part to be acted upon. [late ME *labyl,* t. LL: m.s. *lābilis,* der. L *lābī* fall, slide. Cf. LAPSE] —**la·bil·i·ty** (lə bĭl/ə tǐ), *n.*

la·bi·o·den·tal (lā/bǐ ō děn/təl), *Phonet.* —*adj.* **1.** with the lower lip close to the upper front teeth, as in *f* or *v.* —*n.* **2.** a labiodental sound.

la·bi·o·ve·lar (lā/bǐ ō vē/lər), *Phonet.* —*adj.* **1.** with simultaneous bilabial and velar articulations. —*n.* **2.** a labiovelar sound.

la·bi·um (lā/bǐ əm), *n.*, *pl.* **-bia** (-bǐ ə). **1.** a lip or liplike part. **2.** *Anat.* **a.** either lip, upper or under, of the mouth, respectively called **labium superiore** and **labium inferiore.** **b.** one of the four "lips" guarding the orifice of the vulva, including the two outer cutaneous folds (**labia majora**) and the two inner membranous folds (**labia minora**). **3.** *Bot.* the lower lip of a bilabiate corolla. **4.** *Entomol.* the posterior unpaired member of the mouth parts of an insect, formed by the united second maxillae. [t. L: lip]

La Bo·hème (là bō ěm/), an opera (1896) by Puccini.

la·bor (lā/bər), *n.* **1.** bodily toil for the sake of gain or economic production. **2.** those engaged in such toil considered as a class: *the rights of labor.* **3.** work, esp. of a hard or fatiguing kind. **4.** a work or task done or to be done: *the twelve labors of Hercules.* **5.** the pangs and efforts of childbirth; travail. —*v.i.* **6.** to perform labor; exert one's powers of body or mind; work; toil. **7.** to work (*for*); strive, as toward a goal. **8.** to be burdened, troubled, or distressed: *you are laboring under a misapprehension.* **9.** to be in travail or childbirth. **10.** to roll or pitch heavily, as a ship. —*v.t.* **11.** to work hard and long at; elaborate: *don't labor the point.* **12.** *Archaic or Poetic.* to work or till (soil, etc.). Also, *Brit.*, **labour.** [ME *labour,* t. OF, t. L: m. *labor* toil, distress] —**la/bor·ing·ly**, *adv.* —**Syn. 3.** toil, exertion. See **work.** —**Ant. 3.** leisure. **6.** rest.

lab·o·ra·to·ry (lăb/rə tōr/ǐ, lăb/ə rə-; *Brit.* lə bŏr/ə tə-rǐ), *n.*, *pl.* **-ries**, *adj.* —*n.* **1.** a building or part of a building fitted with apparatus for conducting scientific investigations, experiments, tests, etc., or for manufacturing chemicals, medicines, etc. **2.** any place where or in which similar processes are carried on by natural forces. —*adj.* **3.** serving a function in a laboratory. **4.** relating to techniques of work in a laboratory. [ML: m.s. *labōrātōrium* workshop] —**lab/o·ra·to/ri·al**, *adj.*

Labor Day, (in most States of the U.S. and in Canada) a legal holiday, commonly the first Monday in September, in honor of labor.

la·bored (lā/bərd), *adj.* **1.** laboriously formed; made or done with laborious pains or care. **2.** not easy, natural, or spontaneous: *a labored style.* Also, *Brit.* **la/boured.** —**Syn. 1.** See **elaborate.**

la·bor·er (lā/bər ər), *n.* **1.** one engaged in work which requires bodily strength rather than skill or training: *a day laborer.* **2.** one who labors. Also, *Brit.* **la/bour·er.**

la·bo·ri·ous (lə bōr/ǐ əs), *adj.* **1.** requiring much labor, exertion, or perseverance: *a laborious undertaking.* **2.** requiring labor in construction or execution. **3.** given to or diligent in labor. [ME, t. L: m.s. *labōriōsus*] —**la·bo/ri·ous·ly**, *adv.* —**la·bo/ri·ous·ness**, *n.* —**Syn. 1.** toilsome, arduous, onerous. **3.** hard-working, industrious, assiduous. —**Ant. 1.** easy. **3.** lazy.

La·bor·ite (lā/bə rīt/), *n.* a member of a party advocating labor interests, as in British politics.

labor market, the available supply of labor considered with reference to the demand for it.

la·bor om·ni·a vin·cit (lā/bôr ŏm/nǐ ə vǐn/sǐt), *Latin.* toil conquers all things (motto of Oklahoma).

la·bor-sav·ing (lā/bər sā/vǐng), *adj.* saving, or effecting economy in, labor: *a labor-saving device.*

labor union, an organization of wage earners or salaried employees for mutual aid and protection, and for dealing collectively with employers; a trade union.

la·bour (lā/bər), *n.*, *v.i.*, *v.t. Brit.* labor.

Labour Party, the British political party representing socialist groups, trade unions, and labor in general. It was formed in the latter part of the 19th century, but did not exert much political influence until the 1920's.

Lab·ra·dor (lăb/rə dôr/), *n.* **1.** a peninsula in NE North America between Hudson Bay, the Atlantic, and the Gulf of St. Lawrence, containing the Canadian provinces of Newfoundland and Quebec. ab. 500,000 sq. mi. **2.** the portion of Newfoundland in the E part of this peninsula. 7890 (1951); ab. 120,000 sq. mi.

lab·ra·dor·ite (lā/rə dôr īt/, lăb/rə dôr/ǐt), *n.* a mineral of the plagioclase feldspar group, often characterized by a brilliant change of colors with blue and green most common. [f. *Labrador,* where it was discovered + -ITE[1]]

la·bret (lā/brět), *n.* a lip ornament worn by primitive tribes, in a pierced hole. [f. s. L *labrum* lip + -ET]

la·broid (lăb/roid), *adj.* **1.** belonging to or resembling the *Labridae,* a family of thick-lipped marine fishes including the tautog, cunners, etc. —*n.* **2.** a labroid fish. [f. s. L *lābrus* kind of fish + -OID]

la·brum (lā/brəm, lăb/rəm), *n.*, *pl.* labra (lā/brə, lăb/rə). **1.** a lip or liplike part. **2.** *Zool.* **a.** the anterior unpaired member of the mouth parts of an arthropod, projecting in front of the mouth. **b.** the outer margin of the aperture of a gastropod's shell. **3.** *Anat.* a ring of cartilage about the edge of a joint surface of a bone. [t. L: lip]

La Bru·yère (là brv yěr/), **Jean de** (zhäN də), 1645–1696, French moralist and author.

La·bu·an (lā/bōō än/), *n.* an island off the coast of Sabah, now part of the federation of Malaysia: formerly one of the Straits Settlements. 9253 pop. (est. 1947); 35 sq. mi. *Cap.:* Victoria.

la·bur·num (lə bûr/nəm), *n.* any of several small leguminous trees, having pendulous racemes of yellow flowers, somewhat similar to those of wisteria. *Laburnum anagyroides* of Europe is most common. [t. L]

lab·y·rinth (lăb/ə rǐnth), *n.* **1.** an intricate combination of passages in which it is difficult to find one's way or to reach the exit. **2.** a maze of paths bordered by high hedges, as in a park or garden. **3.** a complicated or tortuous arrangement, as of streets, buildings, etc. **4.** any confusingly intricate state of things or events; an entanglement. **5.** (*cap.*) *Gk. Myth.* the Cretan maze constructed by Daedalus, and inhabited by the fabled Minotaur. **6.** *Anat.* **a.** the internal ear, a complex structure including a bony portion (**osseous labyrinth**) and a membranous portion (**membranous labyrinth**) contained in it. **b.** the aggregate of air chambers in the ethmoid bone, between the eye and the upper part of the nose. [t. L: s. *labyrinthus,* t. Gk.: m. *labýrinthos*]

lab·y·rin·thine (lăb/ə rǐn/thǐn, -thēn), *adj.* **1.** pertaining to or forming a labyrinth. **2.** mazy; intricate. Also, **lab·y·rin·thi·an** (lăb/ə rǐn/thǐ ən), **lab/y·rin/thic.**

lac[1] (lăk), *n.* a resinous substance deposited on the twigs of various trees in southern Asia by the lac insect, and used in the manufacture of varnishes, sealing wax, etc., and in the production of a red coloring matter. See **shellac.** [t. Hind.: m. *lākh,* g. Skt. *lākshā*]

lac[2] (lăk), *n. India.* **1.** the sum of 100,000, esp. of rupees. The usual pointing for sums of Indian money above a lac is with a comma after the number of lacs: Rs. 30,52,000 (i.e., thirty lacs and fifty-two thousand) instead of 3,052,000. **2.** an indefinitely large number. Also, **lakh.** [t. Hind.: m. *lākh,* g. Skt. *laksha* mark, hundred thousand]

Lac·ca·dive Islands (lăk/ə dǐv/), a group of small islands and coral reefs in the Arabian Sea, off the SW coast of India: a part of Madras province. 18,393 pop. (1941); ab. 80 sq. mi.

lac·co·lith (lăk/ə lǐth), *n. Geol.* a mass of igneous rock formed from lava which when rising from below did not find its way to the surface, but spread out laterally into

laccolithic a lenticular body, thereby causing the overlying strata to bulge upward. Also, **lac·co·lite** (lăk'ə līt'). [f. m. Gk. *lákko(s)* pond + -LITH] —**lac'co·lith'ic, lac·co·lit·ic** (lăk'ə lĭt'ĭk), *adj.*

lace (lās), *n., v.,* **laced, lacing.** —*n.* **1.** a netlike ornamental fabric made of threads by hand or machine. **2.** a cord or string for holding or drawing together, as when passed through holes in opposite edges: *shoe laces.* **3.** ornamental cord or braid, as on uniforms. **4.** spirits added to coffee or other beverage. —*v.t.* **5.** to fasten, draw together, or compress by means of a lace. **6.** to pass (a cord, etc.) as a lace, as through holes. **7.** to adorn or trim with lace. **8.** to compress the waist of (a person) by drawing tight the laces of a corset, etc. **9.** to interlace or intertwine. **10.** *Colloq.* to lash, beat, or thrash. **11.** to mark or streak, as with color. **12.** to intermix, as coffee with spirits. —*v.i.* **13.** to be fastened with a lace. [ME *las,* t. OF: m. *laz* noose, string, g. L *laqueus* noose, snare. Cf. LASSO] —**lace'-like',** *adj.*

Lac·e·dae·mon (lăs'ə dē'mən), *n.* ancient Sparta. —**Lac·e·dae·mo·ni·an** (lăs'ə dĭ mō'nĭ ən), *adj., n.*

lace·mak·ing (lās'mā'kĭng), *n.* the art, act, or process of making lace.

lac·er·ate (*v.* lăs'ə rāt'; *adj.* lăs'ə rāt', -ər ĭt), *v.,* **-ated, -ating,** *adj.* —*v.t.* **1.** to tear roughly; mangle: *to lacerate the flesh.* **2.** to hurt: *to lacerate a person's feelings.* —*adj.* **3.** lacerated. [t. L: m.s. *lacerātus,* pp.] —**Syn. 1.** See **maim.**

lac·er·at·ed (lăs'ə rā'tĭd), *adj.* **1.** mangled; jagged. **2.** *Bot., Zool.* having the edge variously cut as if torn into irregular segments, as a leaf.

lac·er·a·tion (lăs'ə rā'shən), *n.* **1.** act of lacerating. **2.** the result of lacerating; rough, jagged tear.

lac·er·til·i·an (lăs'ər tĭl'ĭ ən), *adj.* **1.** of or pertaining to the *Lacertilia,* an order (or suborder) of reptiles comprising the common lizards and their allies. See **saurian** (def. 1). —*n.* **2.** a lacertilian reptile. [f. s. NL *Lacertilia,* pl. (der. L *lacerta* lizard) + -AN]

lace·wing (lās'wĭng'), *n.* any of various neuropterous insects of the family *chrysopidae,* with delicate lacelike wings, whose larvae prey chiefly on aphids.

La Chaise (là shĕz'), Père François d'Aix de (pĕr frän swä' dĕks də), 1624–1709, French Roman Catholic priest, confessor to Louis XIV.

lach·es (lăch'ĭz), *n.* *Law.* neglect to do a thing at the proper time, esp. such delay as will bar a party from bringing a legal proceeding. [ME *lachesse,* t. AF, var. of *Laschesse,* der. *lasche* loose, g. L *laxus* lax]

Lach·e·sis (lăk'ə sĭs), *n.* *Class. Myth.* that one of the three Fates whose duty it was to determine the length of each individual's life, or, sometimes, to decide his fate during life. [t. L, t. Gk.: lit., lot, destiny]

lach·ry·mal (lăk'rə məl), *adj.* **1.** of or pertaining to tears; producing tears. **2.** characterized by tears; indicative of weeping. **3.** *Anat., etc.* denoting, pertaining to, or situated near the glands, ducts, or the like, concerned in the secretion or conveyance of tears. —*n.* **4.** (*pl.*) *Anat.* tear-secreting glands. **5.** a lachrymatory. Also, **lacrimal, lacrymal.** [t. ML: s. *lachrymālis, lacrimālis,* der. L *lacrima* tear]

Section of human eye showing
A. lachrymal duct, and
B. lachrymal gland

lach·ry·ma·to·ry (lăk'rə mə tōr'ĭ), *adj., n., pl.* **-ries.** —*adj.* **1.** of, pertaining to, or causing the shedding of tears. —*n.* **2.** a small, narrow-necked vase found in ancient Roman tombs, formerly thought to have been used for containing the tears of bereaved friends.

lach·ry·mose (lăk'rə mōs'), *adj.* **1.** given to shedding tears; tearful. **2.** suggestive of or tending to cause tears; mournful. [t. L: m.s. *lac(h)rimōsus,* der *lac(h)rima* tear] —**lach'ry·mose'ly,** *adv.*

lac·ing (lā'sĭng), *n.* **1.** act of one who or that which laces. **2.** a laced fastening, or a lace for such use. **3.** a trimming of lace or braid. **4.** a thrashing.

la·cin·i·ate (lə sĭn'ĭ āt', -ĭt), *adj. Bot., Zool.* cut into narrow, irregular lobes; slashed; jagged. [f. s. L *lacinia* lappet + -ATE¹]

Laciniate leaf

lac insect (lăk), a homopterous insect, *Laccifer lacca* of India the females of which produce lac.

lack (lăk), *n.* **1.** deficiency or absence of something requisite, desirable, or customary: *lack of money or skill.* **2.** something lacking or wanting: *skilled labor was the chief lack.* —*v.t.* **3.** to be deficient in, destitute of, or without: *to lack strength.* **4.** to fall short in respect of: *the vote lacks three of being a majority.* —*v.i.* **5.** to be absent, wanting, or requisite or desirable. [ME *lak,* t. MLG or MD: deficiency. Cf. Icel. *lakr* deficient] —**Syn. 1.** want, need, dearth, scarcity, paucity. —**Ant. 1.** surplus.

lack·a·dai·si·cal (lăk'ə dā'zə kəl), *adj.* sentimentally or affectedly languishing; weakly sentimental; listless. [f. *lackadaisy,* var. of LACKADAY (see ALACK) + -ICAL] —**lack'a·dai'si·cal·ly,** *adv.* —**lack'a·dai'si·cal·ness,** *n.*

lack·a·day (lăk'ə dā'), *interj.* *Archaic.* alack.

Lack·a·wan·na (lăk'ə wŏn'ə), *n.* a city in W New York, on Lake Erie, near Buffalo. 29,564 (1960).

lack·er (lăk'ər), *n., v.t.* lacquer. —**lack'er·er,** *n.*

lack·ey (lăk'ĭ), *n., pl.* **-eys,** *v.,* **-eyed, -eying.** —*n.* **1.** a footman or liveried manservant. **2.** a servile follower. —*v.t.* **3.** to attend as a lackey does. Also, **lacquey.** [t. F: m. *laquais,* t. Sp.: m. *lacayo* foot soldier]

lack·lus·ter (lăk'lŭs'tər), *adj.* **1.** lacking luster or brightness; dull. —*n.* **2.** a lack of luster; that which lacks brightness. Also, *esp. Brit.,* **lack'lus'tre.**

La·co·ni·a (lə kō'nĭ ə), *n.* an ancient country in the S part of Greece. *Cap.:* Sparta. —**La·co'ni·an,** *adj., n.*

la·con·ic (lə kŏn'ĭk), *adj.* using few words; concise. Also, **la·con'i·cal.** [t. L: s. *lacōnicus,* t. Gk.: m. *lakōnikós* Laconian] —**la·con'i·cal·ly,** *adv.*

lac·o·nism (lăk'ə nĭz'əm), *n.* **1.** laconic brevity. **2.** a laconic utterance or sentence. Also, **la·con·i·cism** (lə kŏn'ə sĭz'əm). [t. Gk.: m.s. *lakōnismós* imitation of Lacedaemonians, who were noted for brief, pithy speech]

La Co·ru·ña (lä kō rōō'nyä), a seaport in NW Spain. 141,049 (est. 1955). Also, **Coruña.**

lac·quer (lăk'ər), *n.* **1.** a protective coating consisting of a resin and/or a cellulose ester dissolved in a volatile solvent, sometimes with pigment added. **2.** any of various resinous varnishes, esp. a natural varnish obtained from a Japanese tree, *Rhus verniciflua,* used to produce a highly polished, lustrous surface on wood, etc. **3.** ware coated with such a varnish, and often inlaid. —*v.t.* **4.** to coat with or as with lacquer. Also, **lacker.** [t. F (obs.): m. *lacre* sealing wax, ult. t. Ar.: m. *lakk,* t. Pers.: m. *lāk*] —**lac'quer·er,** *n.*

lac·quey (lăk'ĭ), *n., pl.* **-queys,** *v.t.,* **-queyed, -queying.** lackey.

lac·ri·mal (lăk'rə məl), *adj., n.* lachrymal. Also, **lac'ry·mal.**

la·crosse (lə krôs', -krŏs'), *n.* a game of ball, of American Indian origin, played by two teams of 10 players each, who strive to send a ball through a goal by means of long-handled racquets. [t. F: m. *la crosse* the crook (the racquet used in the game). See CROSSE]

La Crosse (lə krôs', krŏs'), a city in W Wisconsin, on the Mississippi. 47,575 (1960).

lact-, a word element meaning "milk." Also, **lacto-.** [t. L: m. *lacti-,* comb. form of *lac*]

lac·tam (lăk'tăm), *n.* *Biochem.* an organic compound formed from an amino acid by elimination of water from the amino and carboxyl groups. [f. LACT- + AM(MONIA)]

lac·tase (lăk'tās), *n.* *Chem.* an enzyme capable of hydrolyzing lactose into glucose and galactose.

lac·tate (lăk'tāt), *n., v.,* **-tated, -tating.** —*n.* **1.** *Chem.* an ester or salt of lactic acid. —*v.i.* **2.** to produce milk.

lac·ta·tion (lăk tā'shən), *n.* **1.** the secretion or formation of milk. **2.** the period of milk production.

lac·te·al (lăk'tĭ əl), *adj.* **1.** pertaining to, consisting of, or resembling milk; milky. **2.** *Anat.* conveying or containing chyle. —*n.* **3.** *Anat.* any of the minute lymphatic vessels which convey chyle from the small intestine to the thoracic duct. [f. s. L *lacteus* milky + -AL¹] —**lac'te·al·ly,** *adv.*

lac·te·ous (lăk'tĭ əs), *adj.* milky; of the color of milk.

lac·tes·cent (lăk tĕs'ənt), *adj.* **1.** becoming or being milky. **2.** *Bot.* forming a milky juice. **3.** *Entomol.* secreting a milky fluid. [t. L: s. *lactescens,* ppr.] —**lac·tes'cence,** *n.*

lac·tic (lăk'tĭk), *adj.* pertaining to or obtained from milk.

lactic acid, *Chem.* an acid, $CH_3CHOHCOOH$, found in sour milk.

lac·tif·er·ous (lăk tĭf'ə rəs), *adj.* **1.** producing milk; concerned with the secretion of milk. **2.** conveying milk or a milky fluid. [f. LL *lactifer* milk-bearing + -OUS]

lacto-, var. of lact-, before consonants.

lac·to·ba·cil·lus (lăk'tō bə sĭl'əs), *n., pl.* **-cilli** (-sĭl'ī). any bacterium of the genus *Lactobacillus,* a group of aerobic, long, slender rods which produce large amounts of lactic acid in the fermentation of carbohydrates, esp. in milk. The species most important to man is *Lactobacillus acidophilus.* See **acidophilus milk.**

lac·to·fla·vin (lăk'tō flā'vĭn), *n.* riboflavin.

lac·tom·e·ter (lăk tŏm'ə tər), *n.* an instrument for determining the specific gravity of milk.

lac·tone (lăk'tōn), *n.* *Chem.* one of a class of internal esters derived from hydroxy acids. —**lac·ton·ic** (lăk-tŏn'ĭk), *adj.*

lac·to·pro·te·in (lăk'tō prō'tē ĭn, -prō'tēn), *n.* any protein existing in milk.

lac·tose (lăk'tōs), *n.* *Chem.* a crystalline disaccharide, $C_{12}H_{22}O_{11}$, present in milk, used as a food and in medicine; milk sugar. [f. LACT- + -OSE²]

la·cu·na (lə kū'nə), *n., pl.* **-nae** (-nē), **-nas. 1.** a pit or cavity; an interstitial or intercellular space as in plant or animal tissue. **2.** *Anat.* one of the numerous minute cavities in the substance of bone, supposed to contain nucleate cells. **3.** *Bot.* an air space lying in the midst of the cellular tissue of plants. **4.** a gap or hiatus, as in a manuscript. [t. L: gap]

la·cu·nal (lə kū'nəl), *adj.* **1.** of or pertaining to a lacuna. **2.** having lacunae. Also, **lac·u·nar·y** (lăk'yōō-nĕr'ĭ, lə kū'nə rĭ).

la·cu·nar (lə kū'nər), *adj., n., pl.* **lacunars, lacunaria** (lăk'yōō nâr'ĭ ə). —*adj.* **1.** lacunal. [f. LACUN(A) + -AR] —*n.* **2.** *Archit.* **a.** a ceiling, or an undersurface, as of a cornice, formed of sunken compartments. **b.** one of the compartments. [t. L, der. *lacūna* pit, hollow]

la·cu·nose (lǝkū/nōs), *adj.* full of or having lacunae.

la·cus·trine (lǝkŭs/trĭn), *adj.* **1.** of or pertaining to a lake. **2.** living or occurring on or in lakes, as various animals and plants. **3.** formed at the bottom or along the shore of lakes, as geological strata. [f. s. L **lacustris* (der. *lacus* lake, modeled on *palustris* of a swamp) +-INE¹]

lac·y (lā/sǐ), *adj.*, **lacier, laciest.** resembling lace; lacelike. —**lac/i·ly,** *adv.* —**lac/i·ness,** *n.*

lad (lăd), *n.* **1.** a boy or youth (in common use in England but literary in U.S.). **2.** *Colloq.* (in familiar use) any male. [ME *ladde* attendant, OE *Ladda* (nickname), of obscure orig. Cf. Norw. *askeladd* male Cinderella]

lad·a·num (lăd/ǝnǝm), *n.* labdanum.

lad·der (lăd/ǝr), *n.* **1.** a structure of wood, metal, or rope, commonly consisting of two sidepieces between which a series of bars or rungs are set at suitable distances, forming a means of ascent or descent. **2.** something like a ladder. **3.** a means of rising, as to eminence: *ladder of success.* [ME; OE *hlǣder,* c. G *leiter*]

ladder stitch, an embroidery stitch in which crossbars at equal distances are produced between two solid ridges of raised work.

lad·die (lăd/ǐ), *n. Chiefly Scot.* a young lad; a boy.

lade (lād), *v.*, **laded, laden** or **laded, lading.** —*v.t.* **1.** to put (something) on or in as a burden, load, or cargo; load. **2.** to load oppressively; burden: *laden with responsibilities.* **3.** to fill abundantly: *trees laden with fruit.* **4.** to lift or throw in or out, as a fluid, with a ladle or other utensil. —*v.i.* **5.** to take on a load. **6.** to lade a liquid. [ME *lade(n),* OE *hladan* load, draw (water), c. D *laden,* akin to G *laden* load. Cf. LADLE.]

La·din (lǝdēn/), *n.* **1.** a Rhaeto-Romanic language of the southern Tyrol. **2.** Romansh. **3.** a person who speaks Ladin. [t. Romansh, g. L *Latīnus* Latin]

lad·ing (lā/dǐng), *n.* **1.** act of lading. **2.** that with which something's laden; load; freight; cargo.

La·di·no (lǝdē/nō), *n.* **1.** a mixed Spanish and Hebrew dialect spoken by Jews of Spanish extraction now living in Turkey and elsewhere. **2.** (in Spanish America) a mestizo. [t. Sp., g. L *Latīnus* Latin]

Lad·is·laus (lăd/ǐslôs/), *n.* **Saint,** 1040–95, king of Hungary, 1077–95. Also, **Lad·is·las** (lăd/ǐs las, -lâs/).

la·dle (lā/dǝl), *n., v.,* **-dled, -dling.** —*n.* **1.** a long-handled utensil with a dish-shaped or cup-shaped bowl for dipping or conveying liquids. —*v.t.* **2.** to dip or convey with or as with a ladle. [ME *ladel,* OE *hlǣdel,* der. *hladan* LADE] —**la/dle·ful/,** *n.* —**la/dler,** *n.*

La·do·ga (lä/dō gä), *n.* a lake in the NW Soviet Union, NE of Leningrad: largest lake in Europe. ab. 7000 sq. mi.

La·drone Islands (lǝdrōn/), former name of **Marianas Islands.** Also, **La·drones** (lǝdrōnz/; *Sp.* lä drō/nĕs).

la·dy (lā/dǐ), *n., pl.* **-dies,** *adj.* —*n.* **1.** a woman of good family or social position, or of good breeding, refinement, etc. (correlative of *gentleman*). **2.** a polite term for any woman. **3.** (*cap.*) in Great Britain, the proper title of any woman whose husband is higher in rank than baronet or knight, or who is the daughter of a nobleman not lower than an earl, though the title is given by courtesy also to the wives of baronets and knights. **4.** a woman who has proprietary rights or authority, as over a manor (correlative of *lord*). **5.** (*cap.*) the Virgin Mary (usually, **Our Lady**). **6.** the mistress of a household: *the lady of the house.* **7.** a woman who is the object of chivalrous devotion. —*adj.* **8.** being a lady: *a lady reporter.* **9.** of a lady; ladylike. [ME *lavedi, levedi,* OE *hlǣfdige,* ? orig. meaning loaf-kneader, f. *hlāf* LOAF¹ + *-dige,* akin to *dāh* DOUGH. Cf. LORD] —**Syn. 1.** See **woman.**

la·dy·bird (lā/dǐ bûrd/), *n.* ladybug. [f. LADY (uninflected poss. case) Virgin Mary + BIRD; i.e., (our) Lady's bird]

la·dy·bug (lā/dǐ bŭg/), *n.* a beetle of the family *Coccinellidae,* of graceful form and delicate coloration. The larvae feed upon plant lice and small insects. Also, **lady beetle.**

Ladybug.
Epilachna borealis

Lady Chapel, a chapel dedicated to the Virgin Mary, attached to a church, and generally behind the high altar at the extremity of the apse.

Lady Day, 1. the feast of the Annunciation, March 25. **2.** one of various days celebrated in honor of the Virgin Mary. **3.** *Brit.* the spring quarter day, when quarterly rents and accounts are due.

la·dy·fin·ger (lā/dǐ fǐng/gǝr), *n.* a small, finger-shaped sponge cake.

la·dy·fish (lā/dǐ fǐsh/), *n., pl.* **-fishes,** (*esp. collectively*) **-fish.** a small game fish, *Albula vulpes,* of tropical waters.

lady in waiting, a lady who is in attendance upon a queen or princess.

la·dy·kill·er (lā/dǐ kǐl/ǝr), *n. Slang.* a man supposed to be dangerously fascinating to ladies. —**la/dy·kill/·ing,** *n., adj.*

la·dy·like (lā/dǐ līk/), *adj.* **1.** like a lady. **2.** befitting a lady: *ladylike manners.* —**la/dy·like/ness,** *n.*

la·dy·love (lā/dǐ lŭv/), *n.* a beloved lady; sweetheart.

la·dy·ship (lā/dǐ shǐp/), *n.* **1.** (*often cap.*) the form used in speaking of or to a woman having the title of *Lady* (prec. by *her, your,* etc.). **2.** the rank of a lady.

lady's maid, a maid who is a lady's personal attendant in dressing, etc.

La·dy·smith (lā/dǐ smǐth/), *n.* a city in the E part of the Union of South Africa, in Natal: besieged by Boers, 1899–1900. 16,317 (1951).

la·dy's-slip·per (lā/dǐz slǐp/ǝr), *n.* **1.** any plant of the genus *Cypripedium,* comprising orchids whose flowers have a protruding labellum somewhat resembling a slipper. **2.** any plant of several other genera of the orchid family whose flowers resemble *Cypripedium,* as *Paphi opedilum, Phragmipedium,* and *Selenipedium.* Also, **la/dy-slip/per.**

la·dy's-smock (lā/dǐz smǒk/), *n.* a cruciferous plant, *Cardamine pratensis,* with white or purple flowers.

la·dy's-tress·es (lā/dǐz trĕs/ǐz), *n.* any orchid of the genus *Spiranthes.*

La·er·tes (lā ûr/tēz), *n. Gk. Leg.* father of Odysseus.

Lae·tar·e Sunday (lē târ/ǐ), *Rom. Cath. Ch.* the fourth Sunday of Lent when the Introit begins with "Laetare Jerusalem." Isaiah 66:10.

laevo-, var. of **levo-.**

lae·vo·ro·ta·tion (lē/vō rō tā/shǝn), *n.* levorotation.

lae·vo·ro·ta·to·ry (lē/vō rō/tǝ tōr/ǐ), *adj.* levorotatory.

La Farge (lǝ färzh/, färj/), **John,** 1835–1910, U.S. painter, artist in stained glass, and author.

La·fa·yette (lăf/ǐ yĕt/, lä/fǐ-; *Fr.* lả få yĕt/ *for 1;* läf/ǐ yĕt/ *for 2*), *n.* **1. Marie Joseph Paul Yves Roch Gilbert du Motier** (mả rē/ zhō zĕf/ pōl ēv rŏk zhĕl bĕr/ dY mō tyĕ/), **Marquis de,** 1757–1834, French soldier, statesman, and liberal leader, who served in the American Revolutionary Army and took a leading part in the French Revolutions of 1789 and 1830. **2.** a city in N Indiana, on the Wabash. 42,330 (1960). **3.** a city in S Louisiana. 40,400 (1960).

La·fitte (lä fēt/), *n.* **Jean** (zhän), c1780–1844, French privateer.

La Fol·lette (lǝ fǒl/ǐt), **Robert Marion,** 1855–1925, U.S. political leader; U.S. senator, 1906–25.

La Fon·taine (lä fôn tĕn/), **Jean** de (zhän dǝ), 1621–1695, French poet and writer of fables.

lag¹ (lăg), *v.,* **lagged, lagging,** *n.* —*v.i.* **1.** to move slowly; fall behind; hang back (often fol. by *behind*). **2.** *Marbles.* to throw one's shooting marble toward a line on the ground in order to decide on the order of play. **3.** *Billiards.* (in deciding the order of play) to drive the cue ball to the end cushion and return, the winner being the one who comes nearest to the head rail. —*n.* **4.** a lagging or falling behind; retardation. **5.** *Mech.* the amount of retardation of some movement. **6.** *Marbles, Billiards.* act of lagging. [t. Scand.; cf. Norw. *lagga* go slowly] —**Syn. 1.** loiter, linger. —**Ant. 1.** hasten.

lag² (lăg), *v.,* **lagged, lagging,** *n. Slang.* —*v.t.* **1.** to send to penal servitude. —*n.* **2.** a convict. **3.** a term of penal servitude. [orig. unknown]

lag³ (lăg), *n., v.,* **lagged, lagging.** —*n.* **1.** one of the staves or strips which form the periphery of a wooden drum, the casing of a steam cylinder, or the like. —*v.t.* **2.** to cover, as a steam boiler, to prevent radiation of heat. [t. Scand.; cf. Sw. *lagg* stave]

lag·an (lăg/ǝn), *n. Law.* anything sunk in the sea, but attached to a buoy, etc., so that it may be recovered. Also, **ligan.** [t. OF; of Scand. orig. and akin to LIE², LAY¹]

Lag b'O·mer (läg bō/mǝr), a Jewish holiday, thirty-third day from the second day of Passover. [t. Heb.: *lag* thirty-third (day) in the '*omer* count of forty-nine days from Passover to the Feast of the Pentecost]

la·ger¹ (lä/gǝr, lô/-), *n.* a beer stored from 6 weeks to 6 months before use. Also, **lager beer.** [short for *lager beer,* half adoption, half trans. of G *lagerbier*]

la·ger² (lä/gǝr), *n., v.t., v.i. South African.* laager.

La·ger·kvist (lä/gǝr kvǐst/), *n.* **Pär** (pär), b. 1891, Swedish novelist; Nobel Prize for Literature, 1951.

La·ger·löf (lä/gǝr lœf/), *n.* **Selma** (sĕl/mä), 1858–1940, Swedish author.

lag·gard (lăg/ǝrd), *adj.* **1.** lagging; backward; slow. —*n.* **2.** one who lags; lingerer. —**lag/gard·ly,** *adv.* —**lag/gard·ness,** *n.*

lag·ger (lăg/ǝr), *n.* one who lags; a laggard.

lag·ging¹ (lăg/ǐng), *n.* act of lagging behind. [f. LAG¹ + -ING¹]

lag·ging² (lăg/ǐng), *n.* **1.** act of covering a boiler, etc., with heat-insulating material. **2.** the covering formed. **3.** the material used. [f. LAG³ + -ING¹]

La Gio·con·da (lä jōkōn/dä). See **Mona Lisa.**

la·gniappe (lăn yăp/, lăn/yăp), *n.* something given with a purchase to a customer, by way of compliment or for good measure. Also, **la·gnappe/.** [t. Louisiana F, f. Amer. Sp.: m. *la ñapa* the gift]

lag·o·morph (lăg/ǝ môrf/), *n.* any of the *Lagomorpha,* an order of mammals resembling the rodents but having two pairs of upper incisors, and including the hares, rabbits, and pikas, formerly classified as a suborder of rodents. [f. Gk. *lagō(s)* hare + -MORPH]

la·goon (lǝgōōn/), *n.* **1.** an area of shallow water separated from the sea by low banks. **2.** any small, pondlike body of water, esp. one communicating with a larger body of water. Also, **la·gune/.** [t. It., Sp.: m. *laguna,* g. L *lacūna* pool, pond]

Lagoon Islands, Ellice Islands.

La·gos (lä/gōs, lā/gǒs), *n.* a seaport in and the capital of Nigeria, in the SW part. Municipal area, 267,407 pop. (1953); 24 sq. mi.

La Grange (lả gränzh/ *for 1;* lǝ gränj/ *for 2*), **1. Joseph Louis** (zhō zĕf/ lwē), **Count,** 1736–1813, French mathematician and astronomer, born in Italy. **2.** a city in W Georgia. 25,025 (1950).

Lag·thing (läg′tǐng′), *n.* See **Storthing**.

La Guai·ra (lä gwī′rä), a seaport in N Venezuela: the port of Caracas. 16,279 (1951).

La Guar·di·a (lə gwär′dǐ̵ə), **Fiorello Henry** (fē′ə-rĕl′ō), 1882–1947, U.S. political leader.

La Hogue (lä ôg′), a roadstead off the NW coast of France: naval battle, 1692. Also, **La Hougue** (lä ōōg′).

La·hore (lə hōr′), *n.* a city in Pakistan, in W Punjab; capital of West Pakistan. 849,476 (1951).

Lai·bach (lī′bäкн), *n.* German name of **Ljubljana**.

la·ic (lā′ǐk), *adj.* **1.** Also, **la′i·cal.** lay; secular. —*n.* **2.** layman. [t. LL: s. *lāicus*, t. Gk.: m. *lāïkós*, der. *lāós* people] —**la′i·cal·ly**, *adv.*

la·i·cize (lā′ə sīz′), *v.t.*, **-cized, -cizing.** to deprive of clerical character. —**la′i·ci·za′tion**, *n.*

laid (lād), *v.* pt. and pp. of **lay¹**.

laid paper, paper with fine parallel and cross lines produced in manufacturing. Cf. **wove paper**.

lain (lān), *v.* pp. of **lie²**.

lair (lâr), *n.* **1.** the den or resting place of a wild beast. **2.** a place in which to lie or rest; a bed. —*v.t.* **3.** to place in a lair. **4.** to serve as a lair for. —*v.i.* **5.** to go to, lie in, or have a lair. [ME *leir*, OE *leger*, c. D and OHG *leger* bed, camp; akin to LIE²]

laird (lârd), *n.* Scot. a landed proprietor. [var. of LORD] —**laird′ship**, *n.*

lais·ser-al·ler (lĕ sĕ̵ä lĕ̵′), *n.* French. unrestraint.

lais·sez faire (lĕs′ā fâr′; *Fr.* lĕ sĕ fĕr′), the theory or system of government that upholds the autonomous character of the economic order, believing that government should intervene as little as possible in the direction of economic affairs. Also, **lais′ser faire′**. [t. F: lit., allow to act]

la·i·ty (lā′ə tǐ), *n.* **1.** laymen, as distinguished from clergymen. **2.** the people outside of a particular profession, as distinguished from those belonging to it. [f. LAY³+ -TY²]

La·ius (lā′əs, lā′ȳəs), *n.* Gk. Legend. a king of Thebes, killed unwittingly by his son, Oedipus.

lake¹ (lāk), *n.* **1.** a body of water (fresh or salt) of considerable size, surrounded by land. **2.** some similar body of water or other liquid. [ME; OE *lacu* stream, pool, pond; r. ME *lac*, t. OF, t. L: s. *lacus* lake, tank]

lake² (lāk), *n.* **1.** any of various pigments prepared from animal, vegetable, or coal-tar coloring matters by union (chemical or other) with metallic compounds. **2.** a red pigment prepared from lac or cochineal by combination with a metallic compound. [t. F: m. *laque*, t. Pers.: m. *lāk*. See LAC¹]

Lake (lāk), *n.* **Simon**, 1866–1945, U.S. engineer and naval architect.

Lake Charles, a city in SW Louisiana. 63,392 (1960).

Lake District, a picturesque mountainous region abounding in lakes, in NW England.

lake dweller, an inhabitant of a lake dwelling.

lake dwelling, a dwelling, esp. of prehistoric times, built on piles or other support over the surface of a lake.

lake herring, a cisco (whitefish), *Leucichthys artedi*, of the Great Lakes and small glacial lakes of eastern North America.

Lake·hurst (lāk′hûrst), *n.* a borough in central New Jersey: naval air station; dirigible hangar. 1518 (1950).

Lake·land (lāk′lənd), *n.* a city in central Florida. 41,350 (1960).

Lake of the Woods, a lake between N Minnesota and Ontario and Manitoba provinces, Canada: summer resort region. ab. 90 mi. long; 1851 sq. mi.

lake poets, the poets Wordsworth, Coleridge, and Southey (from their residence in the Lake District).

lake trout, a large, fork-tailed char, *Cristivomer namaycush*, common in the Great Lakes and to the northward, a fish of commercial importance. Cf. **brook trout**.

Lake·wood (lāk′wŏŏd′), *n.* a city in NE Ohio, on Lake Erie, near Cleveland. 66,154 (1960).

lakh (läk), *n.* **lac²**.

lak·y¹ (lā′kǐ), *adj.* of or like a lake. [f. LAKE¹ + -Y¹]

lak·y² (lā′kǐ), *adj.* of the color of a lake pigment. [f. LAKE² + -Y¹]

lall (läl), *v.i.* Phonet. to make imperfect *l* or *r* sounds, or both, often by substituting *w* for *r* and *y* for *l*. [imit. See LALLATION]

Lal·lan (läl′ən), Scot. —*adj.* **1.** belonging to the Lowlands of Scotland. —*n.* **2.** the Lowland Scottish dialect.

lal·la·tion (lä lā′shən), *n.* Phonet. a speech defect consisting in pronouncing an *l* sound instead of *r*. [f. s. L *lallāre* sing lullaby + -ATION]

Lam., Lamentations.

lam¹ (läm), *v.t.*, **lammed, lamming.** Slang. to beat; thrash. [t. Scand.; cf. Icel. *lamda*, past tense of *lemja* beat; akin to LAME¹]

lam² (läm), *n.*, *v.*, **lammed, lamming.** Slang. —*n.* **1.** precipitate escape. **2. on the lam**, escaping or fleeing. **3. take it on the lam**, to flee or escape in great haste. —*v.i.* **4.** to run quickly; run off or away. [special use of LAM¹. Cf. *beat it* be off]

la·ma (lä′mə), *n.* a priest or monk of the form of Buddhism prevailing in Tibet, Mongolia, etc. [t. Tibetan: m. *blama* (*b-* is silent)]

La·ma·ism (lä′mə ĭz′əm), *n.* the form of Buddhism in Tibet and Mongolia which has developed an organized hierarchy and a host of deities and saints. —**La′ma·ist**, *n.*

La Man·cha (lä män′chä), a barren plateau region in central Spain: the home of Cervantes' Don Quixote.

La·marck (lə märk′; *Fr.* lȧ mȧrk′), *n.* **Jean Baptiste Pierre Antoine de Monet de** (zhän bȧ tēst′ pyĕr än-twán′ də mô nĕ′ də), 1744–1829, French biologist.

La·marck·i·an (lə mär′kǐ ən), *adj.* **1.** of or pertaining to Jean de Lamarck or his theory of organic evolution. —*n.* **2.** one who holds this theory.

La·marck·ism (lə mär′kǐz əm), *n.* Biol. the theory that characters acquired by habits, use, disuse, or adaptations to changes in environment may be inherited.

La·mar·tine (lä mȧr tēn′), *n.* **Alphonse Marie Louis de** (ȧl fôns′ mȧ rē′ lwē də), 1790–1869, French poet, historian, and statesman.

la·ma·ser·y (lä′mə sĕr′ĭ), *n.*, *pl.* **-series.** (in Tibet, Mongolia, etc.) a monastery of lamas.

lamb (läm), *n.* **1.** a young sheep. **2.** the meat of a young sheep. **3.** one who is young, gentle, meek, innocent, etc. **4. the Lamb**, Christ. **5.** one who is easily cheated, esp. an inexperienced speculator. —*v.i.* **6.** to give birth to a lamb. [ME and OE, c. G *lamm*]

Lamb (läm), *n.* **Charles**, ("*Elia*"), 1775–1834, British essayist and critic.

lam·baste (läm bāst′), *v.t.*, **-basted, -basting.** Slang. **1.** to beat severely. **2.** (in sailors' use) to beat with a rope's end. [appar. f. LAM³ + BASTE³]

lamb·da (läm′də), *n.* the eleventh letter of the Greek alphabet (Λ, λ).

lamb·doid (läm′doid), *adj.* having the shape of the Greek capital lambda (Λ). Also, **lamb·doi′dal**. [t. NL: s. *lambdoīdēs*, t. Gk.: m. *lambdoeidēs*. See LAMBDA, -OID]

lambdoidal suture, Anat. the suture between the occipital and the two parietal bones of the skull, continued forward between the parietal bones. See diag. under **cranium**.

lam·ben·cy (läm′bən sǐ), *n.*, *pl.* **-cies. 1.** the quality of being lambent. **2.** that which is lambent.

lam·bent (läm′bənt), *adj.* **1.** running or moving lightly over a surface: *lambent tongues of flame.* **2.** playing lightly and brilliantly over a subject: *lambent wit.* **3.** softly bright: *a steady, lambent light.* [t. L: s. *lambens*, ppr., licking] —**lam′bent·ly**, *adv.*

lam·bert (läm′bərt), *n.* the brightness of a perfectly diffusing surface emitting or reflecting one lumen per square centimeter: the cgs unit of brightness. [named after J. H. *Lambert*, German physicist, (d. 1777)]

Lam·beth (läm′bǐth), *n.* a S borough of London, England. 230,105 (1951).

Lambeth Palace, the London residence of the Archbishop of Canterbury, near the Thames in S London.

Lambeth walk, Brit. a type of dance popular in the late 1930's.

lamb·kin (läm′kǐn), *n.* **1.** a little lamb. **2.** any young and tender creature. [ME *lambkyn*. See LAMB, -KIN]

lamb·like (läm′līk′), *adj.* like a lamb; gentle; meek.

Lamb of God, Christ.

lam·bre·quin (läm′brə kǐn, läm′bər-), *n.* **1.** a textile fabric worn over a helmet in medieval times to protect it from heat, rust, and sword blows. **2.** a hanging or drapery covering the upper part of an opening, as a door or window, or suspended from a shelf. [t. F, t. Flemish: m. *lamperkin*, dim of *lamper* veil]

lamb·skin (läm′skǐn′), *n.* **1.** the skin of a lamb, esp. when dressed with the wool on. **2.** leather made from such skin. **3.** parchment made from such skin.

lame¹ (läm), *adj.*, **lamer, lamest**, *v.*, **lamed, laming.** —*adj.* **1.** crippled or physically disabled, as a person or animal, esp. in the foot or leg so as to limp or walk with difficulty. **2.** impaired or disabled through defect or injury, as a limb. **3.** defective in quality or quantity; insufficient: *a lame excuse.* —*v.t.* **4.** to make lame or defective. [ME; OE *lama*, c. G *lahm*] —**lame′ly**, *adv.* —**lame′ness**, *n.*

lame² (läm; *Fr.* lȧm), *n.* one of numerous overlapping plates used in building elements of flexible armor. [t. F, g. L *lāmina* thin piece or plate]

la·mé (lä mā′; *Fr.* lȧ mā′), *n.* an ornamental fabric in which metallic threads are woven with silk, wool, rayon, or cotton. [t. F: lit., laminated, der. *lame* gold or silver thread or wire]

lame duck (läm), **1.** U.S. Colloq. a Congressman who has failed of reëlection and is serving at the last session of his term. **2.** Colloq. a person or thing that is disabled, helpless, ineffective, or inefficient.

la·mel·la (lə mĕl′ə), *n.*, *pl.* **-mellae** (-mĕl′ē), **-mellas. 1.** a thin plate, scale, membrane, or layer, as of bone, tissue, cell walls, etc. **2.** Bot. **a.** an erect scale or blade inserted at the junction of the claw and limb in some corollas, and forming a part of their corona or crown. **b.** a gill, one of the radiating vertical plates on the under side of the pileus of an agaric. **c.** (in mosses) a thin sheet of cells standing up along the midrib of a leaf. [t. L, dim. of *lāmina* LAMINA]

la·mel·lar (lə mĕl′ər, läm′ə lər), *adj.* **1.** referring to a lamella or lamellae. **2.** lamellate.

lam·el·late (läm′ə lāt′, -lǐt; lə mĕl′āt, -ǐt), *adj.* **1.** composed of or having lamellae. **2.** flat; platelike. Also, **lam′el·lat′ed**.

la·mel·li·branch (lə mĕl′ə brăngk′), *n.* Zool. any of the Lamellibranchiata. [t. NL: m. *Lāmellibranchia*, pl., f. L *lāmelli-* thin plate + Gk. *bránchia* gills] —**la·mel·li·bran·chi·ate** (lə mĕl′ə brăng′kǐ āt′, -ǐt), *adj.*, *n.*

ăct, āble, dâre, ärt; ĕbb, ēqual; ĭf, īce; hŏt, ōver, ôrder, oil, bŏŏk, ōōze, out; ŭp, ūse, ûrge; ə = a in alone; ch, chief; g, give; ng, ring; sh, shoe; th, thin; ᴅ, that; zh, vision. See the full key on inside cover.

La·mel·li·bran·chi·a·ta (lə mĕl/ə brăng/kĭ ā/tə), n.pl. a class of mollusks comprising the oysters, clams, mussels, scallops, etc., characterized by a bivalve shell enclosing the headless body and lamellate gills.

la·mel·li·corn (lə mĕl/ə kôrn/), adj. Entomol. 1. having antennae with lamellate and leaflike terminal segments, as beetles of the group Lamellicornia, which includes the scarabaeids and stag beetles. 2. (of antennae) having leaflike terminal segments. —n. 3. a lamellicorn beetle. [t. NL: s. lāmellicornis, f. L: lāmelli- thin plate + -cornis horned]

la·mel·li·ros·tral (lə mĕl/ə rŏs/trəl), adj. Ornith. having a beak equipped with thin plates or lamellae for straining water and mud from food, as the ducks, geese, swans, and flamingoes. Also, **la·mel·li·ros·trate** (lə mĕl/ə rŏs/trāt). [f. L lāmelli- thin plate + ROSTRAL]

la·mel·lose (lə mĕl/ōs, lăm/ə lōs/), adj. lamellate.

la·ment (lə mĕnt/), v.t. 1. to feel or express sorrow or regret for; mourn for or over: lament his absence, one's folly. —v.i. 2. to feel, show, or express grief, sorrow, or sad regret. —n. 3. an expression of grief or sorrow. 4. a formal expression of sorrow or mourning, esp. in verse or song; an elegy or dirge. [t. L: s. lāmentāri wail, weep] —la·ment/er, n. —la·ment/ing, adj. —la·ment/ing·ly, adv. —Ant. 2. rejoice.

lam·en·ta·ble (lăm/ən tə bəl), adj. 1. that is to be lamented: a lamentable occurrence. 2. Now Rare. mournful. —lam/en·ta·ble·ness, n. —lam/en·ta·bly, adv.

lam·en·ta·tion (lăm/ən tā/shən), n. 1. act of lamenting. 2. a lament. 3. Lamentations, book of the Old Testament, ascribed by tradition to Jeremiah.

la·ment·ed (lə mĕn/tĭd), adj. 1. mourned for, as one who is dead: the late lamented Grady. 2. regretted.

la·mi·a (lā/mĭ ə), n., pl. -mias, -miae (-mĭ ē/). 1. Class. Myth. one of a class of fabulous monsters, commonly represented with the head and breast of a woman and the body of a serpent, said to allure youths and children in order to suck their blood. 2. a vampire; a female demon. [ME, t. L, t. Gk]

la·mi·a·ceous (lā/mĭ ā/shəs), adj. Bot. belonging or pertaining to the mint family (Lamiaceae, Menthaceae, or, more commonly, Labiatae) including species valued as aromatic and in medicine. See labiate (def. 2a). [f. s. NL Lamiāceae (der. L lāmium dead nettle) + -ous]

lam·i·na (lăm/ə nə), n., pl. -nae (-nē/), -nas. 1. a thin plate, scale, or layer. 2. a layer or coat lying over another: applied to the plates of minerals, bones, etc. 3. Bot. the blade or expanded portion of a leaf. [t. L: thin plate, leaf, layer. Cf. LAMELLA]

lam·i·na·ble (lăm/ə nə bəl), adj. capable of being laminated.

lam·i·nar (lăm/ə nər), adj. composed of, or arranged in, laminae.

laminar flow, Hydraulics. a flow of a viscous fluid in which neighboring "layers" are not mixed.

lam·i·nate (v. lăm/ə nāt/; adj. lăm/ə nāt/, -nĭt), v., -nated, -nating, adj. —v.t. 1. to separate or split into thin layers. 2. to form (metal) into a lamina, as by beating or rolling. 3. to construct by placing layer upon layer. 4. to cover or overlay with laminae. —v.i. 5. to split into thin layers. —adj. 6. composed of, or having, a lamina or laminae.

lam·i·nat·ed (lăm/ə nā/tĭd), adj. formed of, or set in, thin layers or laminae.

lam·i·na·tion (lăm/ə nā/shən), n. 1. act or process of laminating. 2. state of being laminated. 3. laminated structure; arrangement in thin layers. 4. a lamina.

lam·i·ni·tis (lăm/ə nī/tĭs), n. Vet. Science. inflammation of sensitive laminae in the hoof of a horse, caused by overwork, overfeeding, etc. [t. NL]

lam·i·nose (lăm/ə nōs/), adj. laminate; laminar.

Lam·mas (lăm/əs), n. 1. Rom. Cath. Ch. a church festival observed on August 1 in memory of St. Peter's imprisonment and miraculous deliverance. 2. (orig.) a harvest festival formerly held in England on August 1 (**Lammas Day**). [ME Lammasse, OE hlāfmæsse loaf mass. See -MAS]

Lam·mas·tide (lăm/əs tīd/), n. the season of Lammas.

lam·mer·gei·er (lăm/ər gī/ər), n. the bearded vulture, Gypaëtus barbatus, the largest European bird of prey, ranging in the mountains from southern Europe to China. Also, **lam/mer·geir/, lam/mer·gey·er.** [t. G: m. lämmergeier, lit., lambs' vulture (from its preying on lambs)]

lamp (lămp), n. 1. any of various devices for using an illuminant, as gas or electricity, or for heating, as by burning alcohol. 2. a vessel for containing an inflammable liquid, as oil, which is burned at a wick as a means of illumination. 3. Poetic. a torch. 4. Poetic. a celestial body, as the moon. 5. a source of intellectual or spiritual light. 6. (pl.) Slang. the eyes. [ME lampe, t. OF, g. L lampas, t. Gk.: torch, light, lamp]

lamp·black (lămp/blăk/), n. a fine black pigment consisting of almost pure carbon collected as soot from the smoke of burning oil, gas, etc.

Lam·pe·du·sa (lăm/pĕ dōō/zä), n. a small Italian island in the Mediterranean between Tunisia and Malta.

lam·per eel (lăm/pər), lamprey.

lam·pi·on (lăm/pĭ ən), n. a kind of lamp, often of colored glass. [t. F, t. It.: m. lampione carriage or street lamp, der. lampa LAMP]

lamp·light (lămp/lĭt/), n. the light shed by a lamp.

lamp·light·er (lămp/lī/tər), n. 1. one who lights street lamps. 2. a contrivance for lighting lamps.

lam·poon (lăm pōōn/), n. 1. a malicious or virulent satire upon a person, in either prose or verse. —v.t. 2. to assail in a lampoon. [t. F: m. lampon, said to be m. lampons let us drink (used in songs or verses), impv. of lamper] —lam·poon/er, lam·poon/ist, n.

lamp·post (lămp/pōst/), n. a post, usually iron, used to support a lamp which lights a street, park, etc.

lam·prey (lăm/prĭ), n., pl. -preys. any of the eellike cyclostome fishes constituting the group Hypercoartia. Some species attach themselves to fishes and rasp a hole in the flesh with their horny teeth so that they can suck the blood of the victim. [ME, t. OF: m. *lampreie, g. LL lamprēda]

lamp shell, a brachiopod.

Spotted sea lamprey, Petromyzon marinus (Ab. 1 ft. long)

la·na·i (lä nä/ē), n., pl. -nais. Hawaiian. a veranda.

La·na·i (lä nä/ē), n. one of the Hawaiian Islands, in the central part of the group. 3136 pop. (1950); 141 sq. mi.

Lan·ark (lăn/ərk), n. a county in S Scotland. 1,621,600 pop. (est. 1956); 898 sq. mi. Co. seat: Lanark. Also, **Lan·ark·shire** (lăn/ərk shĭr/, -shər).

la·nate (lā/nāt), adj. woolly; covered with something resembling wool. [t. L: m.s. lānātus]

Lan·ca·shire (lăng/kə shĭr/, -shər), n. a county in NW England. 5,117,853 pop. (1951); 1878 sq. mi. Co. seat: Lancaster. Also, **Lancaster.**

Lan·cas·ter (lăng/kə stər; for 1 also lăng/kăs/tər), n. 1. a city in SE Pennsylvania. 61,055 (1960). 2. a city in NW England. 49,530 (est. 1956). 3. Lancashire. 4. English royal house, 1399–1461.

Lan·cas·tri·an (lăng kăs/trĭ ən), adj. 1. of or pertaining to the English royal house of Lancaster, descended from John of Gaunt (Duke of Lancaster), and including Henry IV, Henry V, and Henry VI. —n. 2. an adherent or member of the house of Lancaster, esp. in the Wars of the Roses. 3. a native or resident of Lancashire. Also, **Lancaster.**

lance (lăns, läns), n., v., lanced, lancing. —n. 1. a long, shafted weapon with a metal head, used by mounted soldiers in charging. 2. a soldier armed with this weapon. 3. an implement resembling the weapon, as a spear for killing a harpooned whale. 4. a lancet. —v.t. 5. to open with, or as if with, a lancet: to lance an abscess. [ME, t. F, g. L lancea]

lance corporal, Brit. Mil. a private appointed to act as corporal, without increase in pay; an acting corporal.

lance·let (lăns/lĭt, läns/-), n. a small fish-like animal, of the genus Branchiostoma (Amphioxus), found in sand in shallow waters, related to the vertebrates. [f. LANCE, n. + -LET]

Lancelet, Branchiostoma pulchellum (Ab. 2½ in. long)

Lan·ce·lot (lăn/sə lət, -lŏt/, län/-), n. Arthurian Romance. the greatest of Arthur's knights, and the lover of Queen Guinevere.

lan·ce·o·late (lăn/sĭ ə lāt/, -lĭt). adj. 1. shaped like the head of a lance. 2. (of leaves, etc.) narrow, and tapering toward the apex or (sometimes) each end. [t. L: m.s. lanceolātus, der. lanceola, dim. of lancea LANCE]

lanc·er (lăn/sər, län/-), n. a mounted soldier armed with a lance.

lance rest, (in medieval armor) a support, bolted to the breastplate, upon which the lance rested when couched for use.

lanc·ers (lăn/sərz, län/-), n.pl. 1. a form of quadrille (dance). 2. music for such a set of dances.

lance sergeant, Brit. Mil. a corporal appointed to act as sergeant, without increase in pay; an acting sergeant.

Lanceolate leaf

lan·cet (lăn/sĭt, län/-), n. 1. a small surgical instrument, usually sharp-pointed and two-edged, for letting blood, opening abscesses, etc. 2. Archit. a. a lancet arch. b. a lancet window. [late ME lawnset, t. OF: m. lancette, dim. of lance LANCE]

lancet arch, Archit. an arch the head of which is acutely pointed.

lan·cet·ed (lăn/sə tĭd, län/-), adj. having a lancet arch or lancet windows.

lancet fish, a large marine fish of the genus Alepisaurus, with enormous daggerlike teeth.

lancet window, Archit. a high, narrow window terminating in a lancet arch.

lance·wood (lăns/wŏŏd/, läns/-), n. 1. the tough, elastic wood of any of various trees, as Oxandra lanceolata, of tropical America, used for carriage shafts, cabinetwork, etc. 2. a tree which yields it.

Lan·chow (län/jō/), n. a city in N China, on the Hwang Ho: capital of Kansu. 156,000 (est. 1950).

lan·ci·nate (lăn/sə nāt/), v.t., -nated, -nating. to tear or rend; stab or pierce. [t. L: m.s. lancinātus, pp.] —lan/ci·na/tion, n.

land (lănd), n. 1. the solid substance of the earth's surface. 2. the exposed part of the earth's surface, as distinguished from the submerged part: to travel by land.

b., blend of, blended; **c.,** cognate with; **d.,** dialect, dialcetal; der., derived from; **f.,** formed from; **g.,** going back to; **m.,** modification of; **r.,** replacing; **s.,** stem of; **t.,** taken from; ?, perhaps. See the full key on inside cover.

3. ground, esp. with reference to quality, character, or use: *forest land.* **4.** *Law.* **a.** any part of the earth's surface which can be owned as property, and everything annexed to it, whether by nature or by the hand of man. **b.** any hereditament, tenement, or other interest held in land. **5.** *Econ.* natural resources as a factor of production. **6.** a part of the earth's surface marked off by natural or political boundaries or the like; a region or country. **7.** the people of a country; a nation. **8.** a realm or domain: *the land of the living.* **9.** a surface between furrows, as on a millstone or on the interior of a rifle barrel. —*v.t.* **10.** to bring to or put on land or shore: *to land passengers or goods from a vessel.* **11.** to bring into, or cause to arrive in, any place, position, or condition. **12.** *Colloq.* to catch or capture; gain. **13.** *Angling.* to bring (a fish) to land, or into a boat, etc., as with a hook or a net. —*v.i.* **14.** to come to land or shore: *the boat lands at Cherbourg.* **15.** to go or come ashore from a ship or boat. **16.** to alight upon the ground, as from an airplane, a train, or after a jump or the like. **17.** to come to rest or arrive in any place, position, or condition. [ME and OE, c. G *land*]

lan·dau (lăn′dô, -dou), *n.* **1.** a four-wheeled, two-seated vehicle with a top made in two parts, which may be let down or folded back. **2.** a sedan-type automobile with a short convertible back. [named after *Landau*, town in Germany]

Landau

lan·dau·let (lăn′dō lĕt′), *n.* an automobile having a convertible top for the back seat, with the front seat either roofed or open. Also, **lan/dau·lette/.**

land bank, a banking association which issues its notes in exchange for mortgages on land or other real property transactions.

land·ed (lăn′dĭd), *adj.* **1.** owning land: *a landed proprietor.* **2.** consisting of land: *landed property.*

land·fall (lănd′fôl′), *n.* **1.** an approach to or sighting of land. **2.** the land sighted or reached.

land grant, a tract of land given by the government, as for colleges, railroads, etc.

land-grant college or **university,** *U.S.* a college or university entitled to support from the Federal government under the Morrill Acts (1862, 1890).

land·grave (lănd′grāv′), *n.* **1.** the title of certain princes. **2.** (orig.) a German count having jurisdiction over a considerable territory. [t. G: m. *landgraf*]

land·gra·vi·ate (lănd grā′vĭ ĭt, -āt′), *n.* the office, jurisdiction, or territory of a landgrave.

land·gra·vine (lănd′grə vēn′), *n.* **1.** the wife of a landgrave. **2.** a woman of the rank of a landgrave. [t. G: m. *landgräfin*]

land·hold·er (lănd′hōl′dər), *n.* a holder, owner, or occupant of land. —**land·hold/ing,** *adj.*

land·ing (lăn′dĭng), *n.* **1.** act of one who or that which lands. **2.** a place where persons or goods are landed, as from a ship. **3.** *Archit.* **a.** the floor at the head or foot of a flight of stairs. **b.** a platform between flights of stairs.

landing gear, the wheels, floats, etc., of an aircraft, upon which it moves on ground or water.

land·la·dy (lănd′lā′dĭ), *n.*, *pl.* **-dies. 1.** a woman who owns and leases land, buildings, etc. **2.** a woman who owns or runs an inn, lodging house, or boarding house.

land·less (lănd′lĭs), *adj.* without land; owning no land.

land·locked (lănd′lŏkt′), *adj.* **1.** shut in more or less completely by land. **2.** living in waters shut off from the sea, as some fish: *a landlocked salmon.*

landlocked salmon. See **salmon** (def. 2).

land·lord (lănd′lôrd′), *n.* **1.** one who owns and leases land, buildings, etc., to another. **2.** the master of an inn, lodging house, etc. **3.** a landowner.

land·lord·ism (lănd′lôr dĭz′əm), *n.* the practice under which ownership is had by one and land is occupied by such owner's tenants.

land·lub·ber (lănd′lŭb′ər), *n. Naut.* a landsman or raw seaman. [f. LAND + LUBBER]

land·mark (lănd′märk′), *n.* **1.** a conspicuous object on land that serves as a guide, as to vessels at sea. **2.** a prominent or distinguishing feature, part, event, etc. **3.** something used to mark the boundary of land.

land mine, a large ground-concealed explosive bomb.

land office, a government office for the transaction of business relating to public lands.

land-office business, *U.S. Colloq.* a rushing business.

Land of Promise, Canaan, the land promised by God to Abraham. Gen. 12.

Lan·dor (lăn′dər, -dôr), *n.* **Walter Savage,** 1775–1864, British author.

land·own·er (lănd′ō′nər), *n.* an owner or proprietor of land. —**land/own′er·ship/,** *n.* —**land/own′ing,** *n., adj.*

Lan·dow·ska (lăn dou′skə, län dôf′skä), *n.,* **Wanda** (Pol. vän′dä), 1879–1959, American harpsichordist born in Poland.

land-poor (lănd′pŏŏr′), *adj.* in need of ready money while owning much unremunerative land.

land power, 1. a nation having an important and powerful army. **2.** military power on land.

land·scape (lănd′skāp′), *n., v.,* **-scaped, -scaping.** —*n.* **1.** a view or prospect of rural scenery, more or less extensive, such as is comprehended within the scope or range of vision from a single point of view. **2.** a piece of such scenery. **3.** a picture representing natural inland or coastal scenery. **4.** such pictures as a class. —*v.t.* **5.** to improve the landscape. —*v.i.* **6.** to do landscape gardening as a profession. [earlier *landskip, landscap,* t. D: m. *landschap,* c. OE *landsceap, landscipe,* G *landschaft* region. See LAND, -SHIP]

landscape architecture, the art of arranging or modifying the features of a landscape, the streets, buildings, etc., to secure beautiful or advantageous effects. —**landscape architect.**

landscape gardening, the art of arranging trees, shrubbery, paths, fountains, etc., to produce picturesque effects. —**landscape gardener.**

Land·seer (lănd′sĭr, -sȳər), *n.* **Sir Edwin Henry,** 1802–73, British painter, esp. of animals.

Land's End, the SW tip of England.

lands·knecht (länts′knĕкнt), *n.* lansquenet.

land·slide (lănd′slīd′), *n.* **1.** the sliding down of a mass of soil, detritus, or rock on a steep slope. **2.** the mass itself. **3.** an election in which a particular candidate or party receives an overwhelming mass or majority of votes. **4.** any overwhelming victory. Also, *esp. Brit.,* **land·slip** (lănd′slĭp′) for 1, 2.

lands·man (lăndz′mən), *n., pl.* **-men. 1.** one who lives, or engages in an occupation, on land (opposed to *seaman*). **2.** *Naut.* **a.** a sailor on his first voyage. **b.** an inexperienced seaman, rated below an ordinary seaman.

Lands·ting (läns′tǐng′), *n.* the upper house of the Danish Rigsdag or parliament. Also, **Lands·thing** (läns′tǐng′). [Dan., f. *lands,* poss. of *land* land + *t(h)ing* parliament]

Land·sturm (länt′shtŏŏrm′), *n.* (in Germany, Switzerland, etc.) **1.** a general levy of the people in time of war. **2.** the force so called out or subject to such call, consisting of all men capable of bearing arms and not in the army, navy, or Landwehr. [G: land storm]

land·ward (lănd′wərd), *adv.* **1.** Also, **land/wards.** toward the land or interior. —*adj.* **2.** lying, facing, or tending toward the land or away from the coast: *a landward breeze.* **3.** being in the direction of the land.

Land·wehr (länt′vär′), *n.* (in Germany, Austria, etc.) that part of the organized military forces of the nation which has completed a certain amount of compulsory training and of which continuous service is required only in time of war. [G: land defense]

lane (lān), *n.* **1.** a narrow way or passage between hedges, fences, walls, or houses. **2.** any narrow or well-defined passage, track, channel, or course. **3.** a fixed route pursued by ocean steamers or airplanes. **4.** a part of a highway for traffic moving in one line. **5.** (in sprint races) each of the spaces between the cords or chalked lines which mark the courses of the competitors. [ME and OE, c. D *laan*] —**Syn. 1.** See **path.**

Lang (lăng), *n.* **1. Andrew,** 1844–1912, British writer. **2. Cosmo Gordon** (kŏz′mō), 1864–1945, British clergyman: archbishop of Canterbury, 1928–1942.

lang., language.

Lang·er·hans (läng′ər häns′), *n.* See **pancreas.**

Lang·land (lăng′lənd), *n.* **William,** c1330–c1400, English poet.

Lang·ley (lăng′lĭ), *n.* **1. Edmund of.** See **York, 1st Duke of. 2. Samuel Pierpont,** 1834–1906, U.S. astronomer, physicist, and pioneer in aeronautics. **3. William.** See **Langland.**

Lang·muir (lăng′myŏŏr), *n.* **Irving,** 1881–1957, U.S. chemist.

Lan·go·bard (läng′gə bärd′), *n.* a member of an ancient Germanic tribe which finally settled in N Italy. [t. LL: s. *Langobardī,* pl., of Gmc. orig.]

Lan·go·bar·dic (läng′gə bär′dĭk), *adj.* **1.** pertaining to the Langobards. —*n.* **2.** the language of the Langobards, a dialect of High German.

lan·grage (lăng′grĭj), *n.* a kind of shot consisting of bolts, nails, etc., fastened together or enclosed in a case, formerly used for damaging sails and rigging in battles at sea. Also, **lan·grel.** [orig. unknown]

lang·syne (lăng′sīn′, -zīn′; *Scot.* läing′sin′). *Scot.* —*adv.* **1.** long since; long ago. — *n.* **2.** time long past. [f. *lang* long + *syne,* contr. of ME *sithen,* OE *siththan* since]

Lang·ton (lăng′tən), *n.* **Stephen,** died 1228, English cardinal and archbishop of Canterbury.

lan·guage (lăng′gwĭj), *n.* **1.** communication by voice in the distinctively human manner, using arbitrary, auditory symbols in conventional ways with conventional meanings. **2.** any set or system of such symbols as used in a more or less uniform fashion by a number of people, who are thus enabled to communicate intelligibly with one another. **3.** the nonlinguistic means of communication of animals: *the language of birds.* **4.** communication of meaning in any way: *the language of flowers.* **5.** linguistics. **6.** instruction in one or more languages: *language study.* **7.** the speech or phraseology peculiar to a class, profession, etc. **8.** form or manner of expression: *in his own language.* **9.** speech or expression of a particular character: *flowery language.* **10.** diction or style of writing. [ME, t. OF: m. *langage,* der. *langue* tongue, g. L *lingua*]

—**Syn. 1.** See **speech. 2.** LANGUAGE, DIALECT, JARGON, VERNACULAR refer to patterns of vocabulary, syntax, and usage characteristic of communities of various sizes and types. **Language** is applied to the general pattern of a people or race: *the English language.* **Dialect** is applied to certain forms or varieties of a language, often those which provincial communities or special groups retain (or develop) even after a standard has been established: *Scottish dialect.* A **jargon** is an artificial pattern used by a particular (usually occupational) group within a community; or a special pattern created for communication in business or trade between members of the groups speaking different languages: *the jargon of the theater, the Chinook jargon.* A **vernacular** is the authentic natural pattern of speech, now usually on the colloquial level, used by persons indigenous to a certain community, large or small.

Langue·doc (läng dŏk'), *n.* a former province in S France. *Cap.:* Toulouse.

langue d'oc (läng dôk'), **1.** the Romance language of medieval southern France. **2.** Provençal. [OF: "*oc*" language, i.e. the language in which *oc* yes was used. See **langue d'oïl**]

langue d'o·ïl (läng dô ēl', dô'l), the French of medieval northern France. [OF: "*oïl*" language (OF *oïl* yes). See **langue d'oc**]

lan·guet (läng'gwĕt), *n.* any of various small tongue-shaped parts, processes, or projections. [ME, t. F: m. *languette,* dim. of *langue,* g. L *lingua* tongue]

lan·guette (läng'gwĕt), *n. Music.* a thin plate fastened to the mouth of certain organ pipes. [t. F']

lan·guid (läng'gwĭd), *adj.* **1.** drooping or flagging from weakness or fatigue; faint. **2.** lacking in spirit or interest; indifferent. **3.** lacking in vigor or activity; slack; dull: *a languid market.* [t. L: s. *languidus*] —**lan'guid·ly,** *adv.* —**lan'guid·ness,** *n.* —Syn. **1.** weak, feeble, weary, exhausted. —Ant. **1.** vigorous. **3.** energetic.

lan·guish (läng'gwĭsh), *v.i.* **1.** to become or be weak or feeble; droop or fade. **2.** to lose activity and vigor. **3.** to pine or suffer under any unfavorable conditions: *to languish ten years in a dungeon.* **4.** to pine with desire or longing for. **5.** to assume an expression of tender, sentimental melancholy. —*n.* **6.** act of languishing. **7.** a languishing expression. [ME *languish(en),* t. F: m. *languiss-,* s *languir,* der. L *languēre*] —**lan'guish·er,** *n.*

lan·guish·ing (läng'gwĭsh ĭng), *adj.* **1.** becoming languid, in any way. **2.** lingering: *a languishing death.* **3.** expressive of languor; indicating tender, sentimental melancholy: *a languishing sigh.* —**lan'guish·ing·ly,** *adv.*

lan·guish·ment (läng'gwĭsh mənt), *n.* **1.** act of languishing. **2.** languishing condition. **3.** a languishing expression.

lan·guor (läng'gər), *n.* **1.** physical weakness or faintness. **2.** lack of energy; indolence. **3.** emotional softness or tenderness. **4.** lack of spirit. **5.** soothing or oppressive stillness. [t. L; r. ME *langur,* t. OF]

lan·guor·ous (läng'gər əs), *adj.* **1.** characterized by languor; languid. **2.** inducing languor: *languorous fragrance.* —**lan'guor·ous·ly,** *adv.*

lan·gur (lŭng gŏŏr'), *n.* any of certain large, slender, long-limbed, long-tailed Asiatic monkeys of the subfamily *Colobinae,* as the entellus (the sacred monkey of India). [t. Hind. Cf. Skt. *längülin* having a tail]

lan·iard (län'yərd), *n.* lanyard.

La·nier (lə nîr'), *n.* **Sidney,** 1842–81, U.S. poet and musician.

lan·i·tal (län'ə tăl'), *n.* a casein derivative which is chemically and functionally similar to wool. [f. s. L *lāna* wool + -ITE¹ + -AL³]

lank (längk), *adj.* **1.** meagerly slim; lean; gaunt: *a tall, lank man.* **2.** (of plants, etc.) unduly long and slender. **3.** (of a purse, etc.) only partially filled. **4.** (of hair) straight and flat. [OE *hlanc,* akin to OHG *hlanca* loin, side. Cf. **flank**] —**lank'ly,** *adv.* —**lank'ness,** *n.*

Lan·kes·ter (läng'kəstər, -kĕs'tər), *n.* **Sir Edwin Ray,** 1847–1929, British zoölogist.

lank·y (längk'ĭ), *adj.,* **lankier, lankiest.** somewhat lank; ungracefully tall and thin. —**lank'i·ly,** *adv.* —**lank'i·ness,** *n.*

lan·ner (län'ər), *n.* **1.** a falcon, *Falco biarmicus,* of southern Europe, northern Africa, and southern Asia. **2.** Falconry. the female of this bird. Cf. **lanneret.** [ME *lanere,* t. OF: m. *lanier* cowardly (bird)]

lan·ner·et (län'ə rĕt'), *n.* Falconry. the male lanner, which is smaller than the female. [ME *lanret,* t. OF, F: m. *laneret,* der. *lanier* **lanner**]

lan·o·lin (län'ə lĭn), *n.* a fatty substance, extracted from wool, used in ointments. Also, **lan·o·line** (län'ə lĭn, -lēn'). [f. s. L *lāna* wool + -OL² + -IN²]

Lan·sing (län'sĭng), *n.* **1.** the capital of Michigan, in the S part. 107,807 (1960). **2. Robert,** 1864–1928, U.S. lawyer and statesman; secretary of state, 1915–20.

lans·que·net (läns'kə nĕt'), *n.* mercenary foot soldier, commonly armed with a pike or lance, formerly used in the German and other Continental armies. Also, **landsknecht.** [t. F, t. G: m. *landsknecht,* f. *lands* land's + *knecht* manservant. See **knight**]

lan·ta·na (län tā'nə, -tä'/-), *n.* any plant of the verbenaceous, mostly tropical genus *Lantana,* including species much cultivated for their aromatic yellow or orange flowers, as *L. camara.* [NL]

lan·tern (län'tərn), *n.* **1.** a transparent or translucent case for enclosing a light and protecting it from the wind, rain, etc. **2.** a magic lantern. **3.** a street lamp on which the French Revolutionaries hanged aristocrats. **4.** the chamber at the top of a lighthouse, surrounding the

---

light. **5.** *Archit.* **a.** a more or less open construction on the top of a tower or crowning a dome. **b.** any light decorative structure of relatively small size crowning a roof. **c.** a raised construction on the roof of a building, designed to admit light. **d.** an open-sided structure on a roof to let out smoke or to assist ventilation. [ME *lanterne,* t. F, t. L: m. *lanterna,* t. Gk.: m.s. *lamptēr* a light, torch, b. with L *lucerna* a lamp]

lantern fish, any small marine fish of the family *Myctophidae,* with rows of luminescent spots, living in the open sea and coming to the surface at night.

lantern fly, any of certain tropical homopterous insects (of the family *Fulgoridae*), formerly supposed to emit light.

lantern jaws, long, thin jaws (with sunken cheeks). —**lan'tern-jawed',** *adj.*

lantern slide, slide (def. 12).

lantern wheel, a wheel used like a pinion consisting essentially of two parallel disks or heads whose peripheries are connected by a series of bars which engage with the teeth of another wheel. Also, **lantern pinion.**

Lantern wheel (at left)

lan·tha·nide (län'thə nīd', -nĭd), *n. Chem.* one of the rare-earth elements of atomic number 58–71, inclusive.

lan·tha·num (län'thə nəm), *n. Chem.* a rare-earth, trivalent, metallic element, allied to aluminum, found in certain rare minerals, as monazite. *Symbol:* La; *at. wt.:* 138.92; *at. no.:* 57; *sp. gr.:* 6.15 at 20°C. [t. NL, der. Gk. *lanthánein* escape notice]

lant·horn (länt'hôrn', län'tərn), *n. Obs.* lantern.

Lan·tsang (län'tsäng'), *n.* Chinese name of **Mekong.**

la·nu·gi·nose (lə nū'jə nōs', -nōō'-), *adj.* **1.** covered with lanugo, or soft, downy hairs. **2.** of the nature of down; downy. Also, **la·nu·gi·nous** (lə nū'jə nəs, -nōō'-). [t. L: m.s. *lānūginōsus* woolly]

la·nu·go (lə nū'gō, -nōō'-), *n. Biol.* a coat of delicate, downy hairs, esp. that with which the human fetus or a newborn infant is covered. [t. L: woolly substance]

lan·yard (län'yərd), *n.* **1.** *Naut.* **a.** a short rope or cord for securing or holding something, esp. a rope rove through deadeyes to secure and tighten rigging. **b. knife lanyard,** a cord to which a knife is attached, worn by seamen around the neck. **2.** *Mil.* a cord with a small hook at one end, used in firing certain kinds of cannon. Also, **laniard.** [b. ME *lanyer* (t. F: m. *lanière* rope) and **yard¹**]

La·oag (lä wäg'), *n.* a seaport in the Philippine Islands, on NW Luzon. 22,218 (1948).

La·oc·o·ön (lā ŏk'ə wän', -ōŏn'), *n. Gk. Legend.* a priest of Apollo at Troy who warned the Trojans against the Trojan Horse and, with his two sons, was killed by serpents sent by Athena or Apollo.

La·od·i·ce·a (lā ŏd'ə sē'ə, lā'ə də sē'ə), *n.* an ancient seaport of Syria, on the site of modern Latakia.

La·od·i·ce·an (lā ŏd'ə sē'ən, lā'ə də sē'ən), *adj.* **1.** lukewarm; indifferent, esp. in religion (like the early Christians of Laodicea). —*n.* **2.** one who is lukewarm or indifferent, esp. in religion.

La·om·e·don (lā ŏm'ə dŏn'), *n. Gk. Legend.* father of Priam, and founder and king of Troy.

La·os (lā'ŏs; *Fr.* lä ôs'), *n.* a country in southeast Asia; formerly a part of French Indochina. 1,260,000 pop. (est. 1953); 91,500 sq. mi. *Cap.:* Vientiane. —**La·o·tian** (lā'ō'shən), *adj., n.*

Lao-tse (lou'dzŭ'), *n.* born c604 B.C., Chinese philosopher, the supposed founder of Taoism. Also, **Lao'tsze, Lao'-tzu'.**

lap¹ (läp), *n.* **1.** the part of the clothing that lies on the front portion of the body from the waist to the knees when one sits. **2.** this portion of the body, esp. as the place in or on which something is held or a child is nursed, cherished, etc. **3.** that in which anything rests or reposes, or is nurtured or fostered. **4.** a laplike or hollow place, as a hollow among hills. **5.** the front part of a skirt, esp. as held up to contain something. **6.** a loose border or fold. **7.** a part of a garment which projects or extends over another: *the front lap of a coat.* [ME *lappe,* OE *læppa,* c. D *lap*; akin to G *lappen* lap]

lap² (läp), *v.,* **lapped, lapping,** *n.* —*v.t.* **1.** to fold over or about something; wrap or wind round something. **2.** to enwrap in something; wrap up; clothe. **3.** to enfold or hold in or as in the lap; nurse, fondle, or cherish. **4.** to lay (something) partly over something underneath; lay (things) together, one partly over another. **5.** to lie partly over (something underneath). **6.** to get a lap or more ahead of (a competitor) in racing. **7.** to cut or polish (a gem, etc.) with a lap. **8.** to join, as by scarfing, to form a single piece with the same dimensions throughout. —*v.i.* **9.** to be folded over; fold or wind round something. **10.** to lie partly over or alongside of something else; lie together, one partly over or beside another. **11.** to lie upon and extend beyond a thing. **12.** to extend beyond a limit. —*n.* **13.** act of lapping. **14.** the amount of a material required to go round a thing once. **15.** a single round or circuit of the course in racing. **16.** act of overlapping. **17.** state of overlapping. **18.** the point or place of overlapping. **19.** an overlapping part. **20.** the extent or amount of overlapping. **21.** a rotating wheel or disk holding an abrasive or polishing powder on its surface, used for gems, cutlery, etc. [ME *lappe(n)*; appar. der. **lap¹**] —**lap'per,** *n.*

lap³ (lăp), v., **lapped, lapping,** n. —v.t. **1.** (of water) to wash against or beat upon (something) with a lapping sound. **2.** to take up (liquid) with the tongue; lick up. —v.i. **3.** (of water) to wash with a sound as of licking up a liquid. **4.** to take up liquid with the tongue; lick up a liquid. —n. **5.** act of lapping liquid. **6.** the lapping of water against something. **7.** the sound of this. **8.** something lapped up, as liquid food for dogs. [ME *lappe,* unexplained var. of *lape,* OE *lapian,* c. MLG *lapen;* akin to L *lambere,* Gk. *láptein* lick, lap] —lap/-per, n.

La Paz (lä päs/), a city in W Bolivia: seat of the government (Sucre is the nominal capital). 266,763 pop. (1950); ab. 12,000 ft. high.

lap-board (lăp/bôrd/), n. a thin, flat board to be held on the lap for use as a table.

lap dog, a small pet dog.

la-pel (ləpĕl/), n. a part of a garment folded back on the breast, esp. a continuation of a coat collar. [dim. of LAP¹]

La Pé-rouse (lä pĕ rōōz/), Jean François de Galaup (zhän frän swä/ də gả lō/), **Count de,** 1741–88?, French naval officer and explorer.

lap-ful (lăp/fŏŏl/), n., pl. **-fuls.** as much as the lap can hold.

lap-i-dar-y (lăp/ə dĕr/Y), n., pl. **-daries,** adj. —n. **1.** a workman who cuts, polishes, and engraves precious stones. **2.** an old book on the lore of gems. —adj. **3.** pertaining to the cutting or engraving of precious stones. **4.** of or pertaining to inscriptions cut in stone, or to any formal inscriptions. **5.** characteristic of or suitable for monumental inscriptions. [ME *lapidarie,* t. L: m. *lapidārius* of stones or stone (as n., a stonecutter)]

lap-i-date (lăp/ə dāt/), v.t., **-dated, -dating. 1.** to pelt with stones. **2.** to stone to death. [t. L: m.s. *lapidātus,* pp.] —lap/i-da/tion, n.

la-pid-i-fy (ləpĭd/ə fī/), v.t., v.i., **-fied, -fying.** to turn to stone; petrify. —la-pid/i-fi-ca/tion, n.

la-pil-li (ləpĭl/ī), n.pl., sing. **-pillus** (-pĭl/əs). stony particles or fragments ejected from volcanoes, technically those of rounded shape and less than an inch in diameter. [t. L, dim. of *lapis* a stone]

lap-in (lăp/ĭn; Fr. là păn/), n. **1.** a rabbit. **2.** its fur. [t. F]

la-pis (lā/pĭs, lăp/Ys), n., pl. **lapides** (lăp/ə dēz/). Latin. a stone (used in Latin phrases).

lap-is laz-u-li (lăp/Ys lăz/yŏŏ lĪ/, -lY), **1.** a deep-blue stone containing sodium, aluminum, calcium, sulfur, and silicon, and consisting of a mixture of several minerals, used chiefly for ornamental purposes. **2.** sky-blue; azure. [t. ML: f. L *lapis* stone + ML *lazulī,* gen. of *lazulum* lapis lazuli (see AZURE)]

Lap-i-thae (lăp/ə thē/), n.pl. Gk. Legend. a mythical people of Thessaly, who defeated the centaurs in a war which arose at the wedding of Pirithoüs.

lap joint, a joint used where two boards intersect and one or both are cut out to allow for the intersection.

La-place (lä plas/), n **Pierre Simon** (pyĕr sē môn/), **Marquis de,** 1749–1827, French astronomer and mathematician.

Lap-land (lăp/lănd/), n. a region inhabited by Lapps in N Norway, N Sweden, N Finland, and the Kola peninsula of the NW Soviet Union.

La Pla-ta (lä plä/tä), **1.** a seaport in E Argentina. 325,165 (est. 1953). **2.** See **Plata, Río de la.**

Lapp (lăp), n. **1.** Also, **Lap-land-er** (lăp/lăn/dər). one of a Finnic people of northern Norway, Sweden, and Finland, and adjacent regions, characterized by dwarfish stature and short, broad heads. **2.** Also, **Lap/pish.** any of the languages of the Lapps, closely related to Finnish. [t. Sw.]

lap-pet (lăp/Yt), n. **1.** a small lap, flap, or loosely hanging part, esp. of a garment or headdress. **2.** a loose fold of flesh or the like. **3.** a lobe of the ear, etc. **4.** Ornith. a wattle or other fleshy process on a bird's head. [dim. of LAP¹]

lap robe, a fur robe, blanket, etc., to cover the lap and legs when riding in an automobile, etc.

laps-a-ble (lăp/sə bəl), adj. liable to lapse.

lapse (lăps), n., v., **lapsed, lapsing.** —n. **1.** a slip or slight error: a lapse of memory. **2.** a failure or miscarriage through some fault, slip, or negligence: a lapse of justice. **3.** a gliding or passing away, as of time. **4.** act of falling, slipping, sliding, etc., slowly or as by degrees. **5.** Law. the termination of a right or privilege through neglect to exercise it or through failure of some contingency. **6.** a falling, or sinking to a lower grade, condition, or degree: a lapse into savagery. **7.** a moral fall, as from rectitude. **8.** a falling into disuse. —v.i. **9.** to pass slowly, silently, or by degrees. **10.** Law. **a.** to pass from one to another by lapse. **b.** to become void, as a legacy to one who predeceases the testator. **11.** to fail or sink to a lower grade or condition. **12.** to fall, slip, or glide, esp. downward. **13.** to deviate from principles, accuracy, etc.; make a slip or error. **14.** to

pass away, as time. [late ME, t. L: m.s. *lapsus,* n., a fall, slip] —laps/er, n.

lapse rate, Meteorol. the rate of decrease of atmospheric temperature with increase of elevation vertically above a given location.

lap-streak (lăp/strēk/), adj. **1.** (of a boat) built with each plank overlapping the one below it; clinker-built. —n. **2.** a lapstreak boat. [f. LAP², n. + STREAK]

lap-sus ca-la-mi (lăp/səs kăl/ə mī/), Latin. a slip of the pen.

lap-sus lin-guae (lăp/səs lĭng/gwē), Latin. a slip of the tongue.

Lap-tev Sea (lăp/tĕf), an arm of the Arctic Ocean N of the Soviet Union in Asia, between Taimyr Peninsula and the New Siberian Islands. Also, **Nordenskjöld Sea.**

La-pu-ta (ləpū/tə), n. an imaginary flying island described in Swift's Gulliver's Travels, whose inhabitants were engaged in all sorts of ridiculous projects.

lap-wing (lăp/wYng/), n. a large Old World plover, Vanellus vanellus, with strikingly upcurved slender crest, erratic courtship flight, and shrill cries; pewit; green plover. [ME *lapwinge,* OE *hlēapewince,* f. *hlēapan* leap + -wince (akin to OHG *winkan* waver, totter, and OE *wincian* wink)]

lar (lär), n., pl. **lares** (lâr/ēz, lā/rēz), **lars** (lärz). See **lares.**

Lar-a-mie (lăr/ə mĪ), n. **1.** a city in SE Wyoming. 17,520 (1960). **2. Fort,** a former U.S. fort in SE Wyoming: an important post on the Oregon Trail.

lar-board (lär/bôrd/; Naut. -bərd), Naut. —n. **1.** the side of a ship to the left of a person looking from the stern toward the bow; port (opposed to *starboard*). —adj. **2.** on, or pertaining to, the larboard. [early mod. E *larborde* (assimilated to STARBOARD); r. ME *laddeborde,* f. *ladde* (orig. unknown) + *borde,* OE *bord* ship's side]

lar-ce-nous (lär/sə nəs), adj. **1.** of, like, or of the nature of larceny. **2.** guilty of larceny. —lar/ce-nous-ly, adv.

lar-ce-ny (lär/sə nY), n., pl. **-nies.** Law. the wrongful taking and carrying away of the personal goods of another from his possession with intent to convert them to the taker's own use: distinguished as **grand larceny** and **petty** (or **petit**) **larceny,** depending on the value of the property taken. [late ME, appar. f. m. AF *larcin* (g. L *latrōcinium* robbery) + -Y³]

larch (lärch), n. **1.** any of the coniferous trees constituting the pinaceous genus Larix, characterized by a tough, durable wood. **2.** the wood of such a tree. [t. G: m. *lärche,* ult. t. L: m.s. *larix*]

lard (lärd), n. **1.** the rendered fat of hogs, esp. the internal fat of the abdomen. —v.t. **2.** to apply lard or grease to. **3.** to prepare or enrich (lean meat, etc.) with pork or bacon, esp. with lardons. **4.** to intersperse with something for improvement or ornamentation. [ME, t. OF: fat of pork, bacon, g. L *lār(i)dum* fat of pork] —lard/like/, adj. —lard/y, adj.

lar-da-ceous (lär dā/shəs), adj. lardlike; fatty.

lard-er (lär/dər), n. a room or place where food is kept; a pantry. [ME, t. OF: m. *lardier,* der. *lard* LARD]

Lard-ner (lärd/nər), n. **Ring,** (Ringgold Wilmer Lardner) 1885–1933, U.S. writer of short stories.

lar-don (lär/dən), n. a piece of pork or bacon used in larding, esp. as drawn through the substance of meat, etc., with a kind of needle or pin. Also, **lar-doon** (lär-dōōn/). [late ME, t. F, der. *lard* LARD, n.]

La-re-do (lərā/dō), n. a city in S Texas, on the Rio Grande. 60,678 (1960).

lar-es (lâr/ēz, lā/rēz), n., pl. of **lar.** Roman Myth. household or other tutelary gods or spirits. [L]

lares and pe-na-tes (pənā/tēz), **1.** household gods. See **lares, penates. 2.** the cherished possessions of a family or household.

large (lärj), adj., **larger, largest,** n., adv. —adj. **1.** being of more than common size, amount, or number. **2.** of great scope or range; extensive or broad: large powers. **3.** on a great scale: a large producer. **4.** grand or pompous. **5.** Obs. generous. **6.** Obs. unrestrained by decorum. **7.** Obs. (of the wind) free; fair. —n. **8.** freedom; unrestraint: Obs. except in **at large,** a. at liberty; free from restraint or confinement: the murderer is at large. **b.** at length; to a considerable length: to discourse at large on a subject. **c.** as a whole; in general: the country at large. **d.** representing the whole of a state, district, or body, not one division or part of it: a Congressman at large. **9. in large,** or **in the large,** on a large scale: viewed in the large. —adv. **10.** Naut. before the wind; with the wind free or on the quarter, or in such a direction that studdingsails will draw. [ME, t. OF, g. L *larga,* fem. of *largus* abundant, liberal] —large/ness, n. —Syn. **1.** big, huge, enormous, immense, gigantic, colossal; massive; vast. See **great.** —Ant. **1.** small.

large calorie. See **calorie** (def. 1b).

large-heart-ed (lärj/här/tYd), adj. having or showing generosity. —large/-heart/ed-ness, n.

large-ly (lärj/lY), adv. **1.** to a great extent; in great part. **2.** in great quantity; much.

large-mind-ed (lärj/mĭn/dYd), adj. having or showing tolerant views or liberal ideas. —large/-mind/ed-ness, n.

large-scale (lärj/skāl/), adj. **1.** very extensive; of great scope. **2.** made to a large scale: a large-scale map.

lar·gess (lär′jĭs), *n.* **1.** generous bestowal of gifts. **2.** the gifts or a gift (as of money) so bestowed. **3.** *Archaic.* generosity. Also, **lar′gesse**, t. OF: m. *largesse*, der. *large* LARGE]

lar·ghet·to (lärgĕt′ō), *adj.*, *n.*, *pl.* **-ghettos.** *Music.* —*adj.* **1.** somewhat slow; not so slow as largo, but usually slower than andante. —*n.* **2.** a larghetto movement. [t. It., dim. of *largo* LARGO]

larg·ish (lär′jĭsh), *adj.* rather large.

lar·go (lär′gō), *adj.*, *n.*, *pl.* **-gos.** *Music.* —*adj.* **1.** slow; in a broad, dignified style. —*n.* **2.** a largo movement. [t. It., g. L *largus* large]

lar·i·at (lăr′Yət), *n.* *U.S.* **1.** a long, noosed rope for catching horses, cattle, etc.; a lasso. **2.** a rope or cord for picketing horses or mules while grazing. [t. Sp.: m. *la reata* the rope]

lar·ine (lăr′Yn), *adj.* **1.** of the nature of or resembling a gull. **2.** of or pertaining to the suborder *Lari*, family *Laridae*, or subfamily *Larinae*, containing the gulls. [t. NL: m.s. *Larinae*, der. LL *larus*, t. Gk.: m. *láros* kind of sea bird]

La·ris·sa (lərĭs′ə; *Gk.* lä′rē·sä′), *n.* a city in E Greece, in Thessaly. 41,016 (1951). Also, **La′ri·sa′**.

lark¹ (lärk), *n.* **1.** any of numerous oscine singing birds, mostly of the Old World, of the family *Alaudidae*, characterized by an unusually long, straight hind claw, esp. the skylark, *Alauda arvensis*. **2.** any of various similar birds of other families, as the meadow lark (*Icteridae*) of America, and the titlark (*Motacillidae*) of America and Europe. [ME *larke*, OE *lāwerce*, c. G *lerche*]

lark² (lärk), *Colloq.* —*n.* **1.** a merry or hilarious adventure; prank. —*v.i.* **2.** to play pranks; have fun. [orig. uncert.] —**lark′er**, *n.* —**lark·some** (lärk′səm), *adj.*

lark·spur (lärk′spûr′), *n.* *Bot.* any plant of the genus *Delphinium*, so called from the spur-shaped formation of the calyx and petals. [f. LARK¹ + SPUR]

La Roche·fou·cauld (lå rôsh foō·kō′), **François de** (frän swä′ də), (*Prince de Marcillac*) 1613–80, French writer.

La Ro·chelle (lå rô·shĕl′), a seaport in W France: besieged as a Huguenot stronghold, 1627–28. 58,799 (1954).

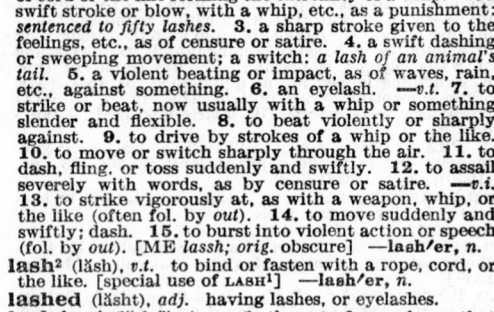
Flower of field larkspur, *Delphinium consolida*, cut longitudinally

La·rousse (lå·roōs′), *n.* **Pierre Athanase** (pyĕr å tå näz′), 1817–75, French grammarian, lexicographer, and encyclopedist.

lar·ri·kin (lăr′ə kĭn), *n.* *Chiefly Australian Slang.* —*n.* **1.** a street rowdy; a hoodlum. —*adj.* **2.** disorderly; rowdy. [? f. *Larry* (hypocoristic var. of *Lawrence*) + -KIN]

lar·rup (lăr′əp), *v.t.*, **-ruped**, **-ruping**. *Colloq.* to beat; thrash. [cf. D *larpen* thrash] —**lar′rup·er**, *n.*

lar·va (lär′və), *n.*, *pl.* **-vae** (-vē). **1.** *Entomol.* the young of any insect which undergoes metamorphosis. **2.** any animal in an analogous immature form. **3.** the young of any invertebrate animal. [t. NL, special use of L *larva* ghost, specter, skeleton, mask]

lar·val (lär′vəl), *adj.* **1.** of or in the form of a larva. **2.** *Pathol.* (of disease) masked; not clearly defined.

lar·vi·cide (lär′və sīd′), *n.* an agent for killing larvae.

la·ryn·ge·al (lərĭn′jĭəl), *adj.* of or pertaining to the larynx. Also, **la·ryn·gal** (lərĭng′gəl). [f. s. NL *laryngeus* (der. *larynges*, pl. of *larynx* LARYNX) + -AL¹]

lar·yn·gi·tis (lär′ən jī′tĭs), *n.* *Pathol.* inflammation of the larynx. [t. NL; f. LARYNG(O)- + -ITIS] —**lar·yn·git·ic** (lär′ən jĭt′ĭk), *adj.*

laryngo-, a combining form of **larynx**. Also, before vowels, **laryng-**.

la·ryn·go·scope (lərĭng′gə skōp′), *n.* *Med.* an apparatus for examining the larynx. —**la·ryn·go·scop·ic** (lərĭng′gə skŏp′Yk), *adj.*

lar·ynx (lăr′Yngks), *n.*, *pl.* **larynges** (lərĭn′jēz), **lar·ynxes.** **1.** *Anat.* the cavity at the upper end of the human trachea or windpipe, containing the vocal cords and acting as the organ of voice. **2.** *Zool.* **a.** a similar vocal organ in other mammals, etc. **b.** a corresponding structure in other animals. [t. NL, t. Gk.]

La Salle (lə säl′; *Fr.* lå sål′), **René Robert** (rə nĕ′ rô bĕr′), **Cavelier de**, 1643–87, French explorer of the Mississippi.

Section of human larynx
A. Larynx; B. Epiglottis; C. Trachea; D. Esophagus

las·car (lăs′kər), *n.* an East Indian sailor. [t. Pg.: m. *laschar*, short for *lasquarin* soldier, t. Hind. (Pers.): m. *lashkarī*, adj., military (as n., soldier), der. *lashkar* army, camp]

Las Ca·sas (läs kä′säs), **Bartolomé de** (bär tō·lō mĕ′ dĕ), 1474–1566, Spanish missionary in the Americas.

las·civ·i·ous (lə sĭv′Yəs), *adj.* **1.** inclined to lust; wanton or lewd. **2.** inciting to lust or wantonness. [t. LL: m.s. *lascīviōsus*, der. L *lascīvia* wantonness] —**las·civ′i·ous·ly**, *adv.* —**las·civ′i·ous·ness**, *n.*

la·ser (lā′zər), *n.* a maser that amplifies radiation of frequencies within or near the range of visible light. [short for *l(ight) a(mplification by) s(timulated) e(mission of) r(adiation)*]

lash¹ (lăsh), *n.* **1.** the flexible part of a whip; the piece of cord or the like forming the extremity of a whip. **2.** a swift stroke or blow, with a whip, etc., as a punishment: *sentenced to fifty lashes.* **3.** a sharp stroke given to the feelings, etc., as of censure or satire. **4.** a swift dashing or sweeping movement; a switch: *a lash of an animal's tail.* **5.** a violent beating or impact, as of waves, rain, etc., against something. **6.** an eyelash. —*v.t.* **7.** to strike or beat, now usually with a whip or something slender and flexible. **8.** to beat violently or sharply against. **9.** to drive by strokes of a whip or the like. **10.** to move or switch sharply through the air. **11.** to dash, fling, or toss suddenly and swiftly. **12.** to assail severely with words, as by censure or satire. —*v.i.* **13.** to strike vigorously at, as with a weapon, whip, or the like (often fol. by *out*). **14.** to move suddenly and swiftly; dash. **15.** to burst into violent action or speech (fol. by *out*). [ME *lassh*; orig. obscure] —**lash′er**, *n.*

lash² (lăsh), *v.t.* to bind or fasten with a rope, cord, or the like. [special use of LASH¹] —**lash′er**, *n.*

lashed (lăsht), *adj.* having lashes, or eyelashes.

lash·ing¹ (lăsh′Yng), *n.* **1.** the act of one who or that which lashes. **2.** a whipping. **3.** a severe scolding. [f. LASH¹ + -ING¹]

lash·ing² (lăsh′Yng), *n.* **1.** a binding or fastening with a rope or the like. **2.** the rope or the like used. [f. LASH² + -ING¹]

Lash·io (lăsh′yō), *n.* a town in Upper Burma, in the Northern Shan States. 4638 (1931).

Lash·kar (lŭsh′kər), *n.* a part of Gwalior city in N India. Total pop. of urban community 241,577 (1951).

Las·ki (lăs′kĭ), *n.* **Harold Joseph**, 1893–1950, British Socialist leader and author.

Las Pal·mas (läs päl′mäs), a seaport in the Canary Islands, on Gran Canaria. 166,644 (est. 1955).

La Spe·zia (lä spĕ′tsyä), a seaport in NW Italy, on the Ligurian Sea: naval base. 109,000 (est. 1954).

lass (lăs), *n.* **1.** a girl or young woman. **2.** any woman. **3.** a female sweetheart. [ME *lasse*; orig. uncert.]

Las·sa (lä′sə, -sä), *n.* Lhasa.

Las·salle (lə säl′; *Ger.* lä säl′), *n.* **Ferdinand** (fĕr′dY nänt′), 1825–64, German socialist and writer.

Las·sen Volcanic National Park (lăs′ən). a national park in the Sierra Nevada Mountains, including **Lassen Peak** (10,465 ft.), an active volcano. 163 sq. mi.

las·sie (lăs′Y), *n.* a little lass.

las·si·tude (lăs′ə tūd′, -toōd′), *n.* weariness of body or mind from strain, oppressive climate, etc.; languor. [t. L: m. *lassitūdo* weariness]

las·so (lăs′ō; *older* lă soō′), *n.*, *pl.* **-sos, -soes**, *v.*, **-soed, -soing.** —*n.* **1.** a long rope or line of hide or other material, with a running noose at one end, used for catching horses, cattle, etc. —*v.t.* **2.** to catch with a lasso. [t. Sp.: m. *lazo*, g. L *laqueus* noose, snare. Cf. LACE]

last¹ (lăst, läst), *adj.* **1.** occurring or coming latest, or after all others, as in time, order, or place: *the last line on the page.* **2.** latest; next before the present; most recent: *last week.* **3.** being the only remaining: *one's last dollar.* **4.** final: *in his last hours.* **5.** conclusive; the *last word in an argument.* **6.** utmost; extreme. **7.** coming after all others in importance. **8.** coming after all others in suitability or likelihood. **9.** *Eccles.* extreme or final, as to a dying person (applied to the sacraments of penance, viaticum, and extreme unction collectively). —*adv.* **10.** after all others. **11.** on the most recent occasion. **12.** in the end; finally; in conclusion. —*n.* **13.** that which is last. **14.** *Colloq.* the final mention or appearance: *to see the last of that woman.* **15.** the end or conclusion. **16.** at long last, after much has intervened. [ME *last, latst,* syncopated var. of *latest,* OE *latost, lætest,* superl. of *læt* late]

—**Syn.** **1.** LAST, FINAL, ULTIMATE refer to what comes as an ending. That which is LAST comes or stands after all others in a stated series or succession; LAST may refer to objects or activities: *a seat in the last row.* That which is FINAL comes at the end, or serves to end or terminate, admitting of nothing further; FINAL is rarely used of objects: *to make a final attempt.* That which is ULTIMATE (literally, most remote) is the last that can be reached, as in progression or regression, experience, or a course of investigation: *ultimate truths.*

last² (lăst, läst), *v.i.* **1.** to go on, or continue in progress, existence or life; endure: *so long as the world lasts.* **2.** to continue unexpended or unexhausted; be enough (*for*): *while our money lasts.* **3.** to continue in force, vigor, effectiveness, etc.: *to last in a race.* [ME *lasten,* OE *lǣstan* follow, perform, continue, last (der. *lāst* track), c. OHG *leisten* follow. See LAST³] —**last′er,** *n.*

last³ (lăst, läst), *n.* **1.** a model of the human foot, of wood or other material, on which boots or shoes are shaped, as in the making. —*v.t.* **2.** to shape on or fit to a last. [ME; OE *lǣste* (der. *lāst* sole of foot, track), c. G *leisten* last] —**last′er,** *n.*

last⁴ (lăst, läst), *n.* any of various large units of weight or capacity, varying in amount in different localities and for different commodities, often equivalent to 4000 pounds. [ME; OE *hlæst,* c. G *last* load; akin to LADE]

Las·tex (lăs′tĕks), *n.* a trademark for a yarn made from a core of latex rubber covered with fabric strands.

last·ing (lăs′tYng, läs′-), *adj.* **1.** that lasts; enduring; permanent; durable. —*n.* **2.** a strong, durable, closely woven fabric, used for the uppers of shoes, for covering buttons, etc. —**last′ing·ly,** *adv.* —**last′ing·ness,** *n.*

Last Judgment. See **judgment** (def. 7).

last·ly (lăst/lĭ, läst/-), *adv.* finally, in conclusion, or in the last place.

Last Supper, the supper of Jesus and His apostles on the eve of His crucifixion, at which He instituted the sacrament of the Lord's Supper.

Las Ve·gas (läs vā/gəs), a city in SE Nevada. 64,405 (1960).

lat (lăt), *n., pl.* **lats** (lăts), **latu** (lä/tŏŏ). **1.** the Latvian monetary unit, equal to 0.29+ gram of gold. **2.** a Latvian coin equal to $0.1930 in U.S. [abstracted from *Lat(vija)* Latvia]

Lat., Latin.

lat., latitude.

Lat·a·ki·a (lăt/ə kē/ə *or, esp. for 1,* lä/tä kē/ä), *n.* **1.** a seaport in NW Syria. 48,984 (est. 1953). Ancient, Laodicea. **2.** a variety of Turkish tobacco.

latch (lăch), *n.* **1.** a device for holding a door, gate, or the like closed, consisting basically of a bar falling or sliding into a catch, groove, hole, etc. —*v.t.* **2.** to close or fasten with a latch. **3. latch on to,** *Slang.* to fasten or attach (oneself) to [ME. *lacche,* OE *læccan* take hold of, catch, take]

latch·et (lăch/ĭt), *n. Archaic.* a strap or lace for fastening a shoe. [ME *lachet,* t. OF, d. var. of *lacet,* dim. of *laz* LACE]

latch·key (lăch/kē/), *n.* a key for drawing back or releasing a latch, esp. on an outer door.

latch·string (lăch/strĭng/), *n.* a string passed through a hole in a door, for raising the latch from the outside: *their latchstring was always out to strangers.*

late (lāt), *adj.,* **later** or **latter,** **latest** or **last,** *adv.,* **later, latest.** —*adj.* **1.** occurring, coming, or being after the usual or proper time: *late frosts.* **2.** continued until after the usual time or hour; protracted: *a late session.* **3.** far advanced in time: *a late hour.* **4.** belonging to time just before the present: *the latest fashions.* **5.** immediately preceding that which now exists: *his late residence.* **6.** recently deceased: *the late president.* **7.** occurring at an advanced stage in life: *a late marriage.* **8.** belonging to an advanced period or stage in the history or development of something: *Late Latin.* **9. of late,** recently. —*adv.* **10.** after the usual or proper time, or after delay: *to come late.* **11.** until after the usual time or hour; until a late hour at night: *to work late.* **12.** at or to an advanced time, period, or stage. **13.** recently but no longer. [ME; OE *læt* slow, late, c. G *lass* slothful] —**late/ness,** *n.* —**Syn. 1.** tardy, slow, dilatory; delayed, belated. **4.** See **modern.** —**Ant. 1.** early.

lat·ed (lā/tĭd), *adj. Poetic.* belated.

la·teen (lă tēn/, lə-), *adj.* pertaining to or having a lateen sail or sails. [t. F: m. *(voile) latine* Latin (sail)]

la·teen-rigged (lă tēn/rĭgd/, lə-), *adj.* having lateen sails.

lateen sail, a triangular sail extended by a long tapering yard, slung at about one quarter the distance from the lower end, which is brought down at the tack: used in xebecs, feluccas, etc., on the Mediterranean.

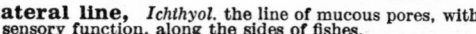

Lateen sail

Late Greek, the Greek of the early Byzantine Empire and of the patristic literature, from about A.D. 300 to 700.

Late Latin, the Latin of the late Western Roman Empire and of patristic literature, from about A.D. 300 to 700.

late·ly (lāt/lĭ), *adv.* of late; recently; not long since: *he had lately gone into the country.*

la·ten·cy (lā/tən sĭ), *n.* state of being latent.

latency period, *Psychoanal.* the stage of personality development, extending from about 4 or 5 years of age to the beginning of puberty, during which sexual urges often appear to lie dormant.

la·tent (lā/tənt), *adj.* **1.** hidden; concealed; present, but not visible or apparent: *latent ability.* **2.** *Pathol.* (of an infectious agent) remaining in a resting or hidden phase; dormant. **3.** *Psychol.* below the surface, but potentially able to achieve expression. **4.** *Bot.* (of buds which are not externally manifest) dormant or undeveloped. [t. L: s. *latens,* ppr., lying hid] —**la/tent·ly,** *adv.* —**Syn. 1.** LATENT, POTENTIAL refer to powers or possibilities existing but hidden or not yet actualized. LATENT emphasizes the hidden character or the dormancy of what is named: *latent qualities, defects, diseases.* That which is POTENTIAL exists in an as yet undeveloped state, but is thought of as capable of coming into full being or activity at some future time: *potential genius, tragedy.* POTENTIAL may be applied also to tangibles: *high-tension wires are a potential source of danger.* —**Ant. 1.** actual, active, effectual.

latent period, 1. *Pathol.* the period that elapses before the presence of a disease is manifested by symptoms. **2.** *Physiol.* the lag between stimulus and reaction.

lat·er·al (lăt/ər əl), *adj.* **1.** of or pertaining to the side; situated at, proceeding from, or directed to a side: *a lateral view.* **2.** *Phonet.* with the voice or breath passing beside the tongue: *"l" is a lateral sound.* —*n.* **3.** a lateral part or extension, as a branch or shoot. **4.** *Mining.* a small drift off to the side of a principal one. **5.** *Phonet.* a lateral sound. **6.** *Football.* a lateral pass. [t. L: s. *laterālis,* der. *latus* side] —**lat/er·al·ly,** *adv.*

lateral line, *Ichthyol.* the line of mucous pores, with sensory function, along the sides of fishes.

lateral pass, *Football.* a pass in which the ball is thrown in a direction almost parallel with the goal line.

Lat·er·an (lăt/ər ən), *n.* **1.** a complex of papal buildings in Rome, the residence of the popes throughout the Middle Ages. It contains the Church of St. John in the Lateran (ranking highest of all Roman Catholic churches), a papal palace, rebuilt 1586, and several other buildings. —*adj.* **2.** pertaining to the general church councils held there. [t. L: s. *Laterānus,* Roman family name]

lat·er·ite (lăt/ə rīt/), *n. Geol.* **1.** a reddish ferruginous soil formed in tropical regions by the decomposition of the underlying rocks. **2.** a similar soil formed of materials transported by water. **3.** any soil produced by the decomposition of the rocks beneath it. [f. L *later* brick + -ITE[1]] —**lat·er·it·ic** (lăt/ə rĭt/ĭk), *adj.*

la·tes·cent (lə tĕs/ənt), *adj.* becoming latent. [t. L: s. *latescens,* ppr., hiding oneself] —**la·tes/cence,** *n.*

la·tex (lā/tĕks), *n., pl.* **latices** (lăt/ə sēz/), **latexes** (lā/těk sĭz). *Bot.* a milky liquid in certain plants, as milkweeds, euphorbias, poppies, the plants yielding India rubber, etc., which coagulates on exposure to the air. [t. L: liquid]

lath (lăth, läth), *n., pl.* **laths** (lăthz, läths, läthz, läths), *v.* —*n.* **1.** a thin, narrow strip of wood used with others like it to form a groundwork for supporting the slates or other covering of a roof or the plastering of a wall or ceiling, to construct latticework, and for other purposes. **2.** such strips collectively. **3.** work consisting of such strips. **4.** wire cloth or the like used in place of laths, as in plastering. **5.** a thin, narrow, flat piece of wood used for any purpose. —*v.t.* **6.** to cover or line with laths. [ME *la(th)the,* r. ME *latt,* OE *lætt,* c. D *lat*] —**lath/like/,** *adj.*

lathe (lāth), *n., v.,* **lathed, lathing.** —*n.* **1.** a machine for use in working metal, wood, etc., which holds the material and rotates it about a horizontal axis against a tool that shapes it. —*v.t.* **2.** to cut, shape, or otherwise treat on a lathe. [ME *lath* stand, t. Scand.; cf. Dan. *-lad* stand, lathe, c. OE *hlæd* heap, mound]

lath·er[1] (lăth/ər), *n.* **1.** foam or froth made from soap moistened with water, as by a brush for shaving. **2.** foam or froth formed in profuse sweating, as of a horse. —*v.i.* **3.** to form a lather, as soap. **4.** to become covered with lather, as a horse. —*v.t.* **5.** to apply lather to; cover with lather. **6.** *Colloq.* to beat or flog. [ME, OE *lēathor,* c. Icel. *lauthr* washing soda, foam] —**lath/er·er,** *n.*

lath·er[2] (lăth/ər, läth/ər), *n.* a workman who puts up laths. [f. LATH, v. + -ER[1]]

lath·er·y (lăth/ə rĭ), *adj.* consisting of, covered with, or capable of producing lather.

lath·ing (lăth/ĭng, läth/ĭng), *n.* **1.** act or process of applying laths to a wall or the like. **2.** work consisting of laths; laths collectively. Also, **lath·work** (lăth/wûrk/, läth/-).

lath·y (lăth/ĭ, läth/ĭ), *adj.* lathlike; long and thin.

lat·i·ces (lăt/ə sēz/), *n.* a pl. of **latex.**

lat·i·cif·er·ous (lăt/ə sĭf/ər əs), *adj. Bot.* bearing or containing latex. [f. s. L *latex* a liquid + -(I)FEROUS]

lat·i·fun·di·um (lăt/ə fŭn/dĭ əm), *n., pl.* **-dia** (-dĭ/ə). *Rom. Hist.* a great estate. [t. L: f. *lāti-* (comb. form of *lātus* broad) + s. *fundus* estate + -*ium* -IUM]

Lat·i·mer (lăt/ə mər), *n.* **Hugh,** c1490–1555, English Protestant Reformation bishop, reformer, and martyr.

Lat·in (lăt/ən, -ĭn), *n.* **1.** the Italic language spoken in ancient Rome, fixed in 2d-1st century B.C., becoming the official language of the Empire. **2.** one of the forms of literary Latin, as Medieval Latin, Late Latin, Biblical Latin, Liturgical Latin, or of nonclassical Latin, as Vulgar Latin. **3.** a native or inhabitant of Latium; an ancient Roman. **4.** a member of any Latin race. **5.** a Roman Catholic. —*adj.* **6.** denoting or pertaining to those peoples (the Italians, French, Spanish, Portuguese, Rumanians, etc.) using languages derived from that of ancient Rome. **7.** noting or pertaining to the Western Church (which from early times down to the Reformation everywhere used Latin as its official language) or the Roman Catholic Church. **8.** of or pertaining to Latium or its inhabitants. [ME and OE, t. L: s. *Latīnus*]

Latin America, part of the American continents south of the United States, in which Romance languages are officially spoken. —**Lat/in-A·mer/i·can,** *adj., n.*

Latin Church, the Roman Catholic Church.

Latin cross, an upright bar crossed near the top by a shorter transverse piece. See illus. under **cross.**

Lat·in·ism (lăt/ə nĭz/əm), *n.* a mode of expression imitating Latin.

La·tin·ist (lăt/ə nĭst), *n.* a specialist in Latin.

La·tin·i·ty (lə tĭn/ə tĭ), *n.* **1.** use of the Latin language. **2.** Latin style or idiom.

La·tin·ize (lăt/ə nīz/), *v.,* **-ized, -izing.** —*v.t.* **1.** to cause to conform to the customs, etc., of the Latins or Latin Church. **2.** to intermix with Latin elements. **3.** to translate into Latin. —*v.i.* **4.** to use words and phrases from Latin: *he Latinizes frequently in his poetry.* —**Lat/in·i·za/tion,** *n.*

Latin Quarter, the quarter of Paris on the south side of the Seine, frequented for centuries by students and artists. [t. F: trans. of *Quartier Latin*]

Latin school, U.S. (esp. formerly) a preparatory school in which Latin is taught.

lat·ish (lā'tĭsh), *adj.* somewhat late.

lat·i·tude (lăt'ə tūd', -tōod'), *n.* **1.** *Geog.* **a.** the angular distance north or south from the equator of a point on the earth's surface, measured on the meridian of the point. **b.** a place or region as marked by this distance. **2.** freedom from narrow restrictions; permitted freedom of action, opinion, etc. **3.** *Astron.* the angular distance of a heavenly body from the ecliptic (**celestial latitude**), or from the galactic plane (**galactic latitude**). **4.** *Photog.* the range of exposures over which proportional representation of subject brightness is obtained. [ME, t. L: m. *lātitūdo* breadth] —**Syn. 2.** See **range**.

LATITUDE AND PARALLEL

LONGITUDE AND MERIDIAN

lat·i·tu·di·nal (lăt'ə tū'də nəl, -tōō'-), *adj.* pertaining to latitude. —**lat'i·tu'di·nal·ly**, *adv.*

lat·i·tu·di·nar·i·an (lăt'ə tū'də när'ĭ ən, -tōō'-), *adj.* **1.** allowing, or characterized by, latitude in opinion or conduct, esp. in religious views. —*n.* **2.** one who is latitudinarian in opinion or conduct. **3.** *Anglican Ch.* one of those divines in the 17th century who maintained the wisdom of the episcopal form of government and ritual, but denied that they possess divine origin and authority. —**lat'i·tu'di·nar'i·an·ism**, *n.*

La·ti·um (lā'shĭ əm), *n.* an ancient country in Italy, SE of Rome.

La·to·na (lə tō'nə), *n. Class. Myth.* the Roman name of the Greek goddess Leto, mother of Apollo and Diana.

La Trappe (lä trăp'), an abbey in Normandy, France, at which the Trappist order was founded.

la·tri·a (lə trī'ə), *n. Rom. Cath. Theol.* that supreme worship which may be offered to God only. Cf. **dulia**, **hyperdulia**. [t. LL, t. Gk.: m. *latreía* service, worship]

la·trine (lə trēn'), *n.* a privy, esp. in a camp, barracks, a factory, and the like. [t. F, t. L: m. *lātrīna*]

lat·ten (lăt'ən), *n.* **1.** a brasslike alloy, commonly made in thin sheets, formerly much used for church utensils. **2.** tin plate. **3.** any metal in thin sheets. [ME *latoun*, t. OF: m. *laton*, der. *latte*. See **LATTICE**]

lat·ter (lăt'ər), *adj.* **1.** being the second mentioned of two (opposed to *former*): *I prefer the latter proposition to the former.* **2.** more advanced in time; later: *in these latter days of human progress.* **3.** nearer, or comparatively near, to the end or close: *the latter years of one's life.* **4.** *Poetic.* being the concluding part of. [ME *latt(e)re*, OE *lætra*, compar. of *læt* late]

lat·ter-day (lăt'ər dā'), *adj.* **1.** of a latter or more advanced day or period, or modern: *latter-day problems.* **2.** of the concluding or final days of the world.

Latter-day Saint, a Mormon.

lat·ter·ly (lăt'ər lĭ), *adv.* **1.** of late; lately. **2.** in the latter or concluding part of a period.

lat·ter·most (lăt'ər mōst', -məst), *adj.* latest; last.

lat·tice (lăt'ĭs), *n., v.,* **-ticed, -ticing.** —*n.* **1.** a structure of crossed wooden or metal strips with open spaces between, used as a screen, etc. **2.** a window, gate, or the like, so constructed. —*v.t.* **3.** to furnish with a lattice or latticework. **4.** to form into or arrange like latticework. [ME *latis*, t. OF: m. *lattis*, der. *latte* lath, t. Gmc.; cf. OE *lætt* lath]

lat·tice·work (lăt'ĭs wûrk'), *n.* **1.** work consisting of crossed strips with openings between. **2.** a lattice.

lat·tic·ing (lăt'ĭs ĭng), *n.* **1.** act or process of furnishing with or making latticework. **2.** latticework.

Lat·vi·a (lăt'vĭ ə), *n.* a de facto constituent republic of the Soviet Union, in the W part, on the Baltic: an independent state, 1918–40. 2,000,000 (est. 1956); 25,395 sq. mi. *Cap.:* Riga. Lettish, **Lat·vi·ja** (lăt'vɪ yä'). Official name, **Latvian Soviet Socialist Republic.**

Lat·vi·an (lăt'vĭ ən), *adj.* **1.** of or pertaining to Latvia. —*n.* **2.** a native or inhabitant of Latvia. **3.** Lettish.

laud (lôd), *v.t.* **1.** to praise; extol. —*n.* **2.** music or a song in praise or honor of anyone. **3.** (*pl.*) *Eccles.* a canonical hour, characterized esp. by psalms of praise (**laudes**), which follows, and is usually recited with, matins. [ME *laude*, back formation from *laudes*, pl., t. L: praises] —**laud'er**, *n.*

Laud (lôd), *n.* **William,** 1573–1645, archbishop of Canterbury and opponent of Puritanism, executed for treason.

laud·a·ble (lô'də bəl), *adj.* **1.** praiseworthy or commendable: *a laudable idea.* **2.** *Med. Obs.* healthy, wholesome, or not noxious. —**laud'a·bil'i·ty, laud'a·ble·ness,** *n.* —**laud'a·bly,** *adv.*

lau·da·num (lô'də nəm, lôd'nəm), *n.* **1.** the tincture of opium. **2.** (formerly) any preparation in which opium was the chief ingredient. [orig. ML var. of **LADANUM**; arbitrarily used by Paracelsus to name a remedy based on opium]

lau·da·tion (lô dā'shən), *n.* act of lauding; praise.

laud·a·to·ry (lô'də tôr'ĭ), *adj.* containing or expressing praise: *overwhelmed by the speaker's laudatory remarks.* Also, **laud'a·tive.**

Lau·der (lô'dər), *n.* **Sir Harry MacLennan** (mə klĕn'ən), 1870–1950, Scottish ballad singer and comedian.

laugh (lăf, läf), *v.i.* **1.** to express mirth, amusement, derision, etc., by an explosive, inarticulate sound of the voice, facial expressions, etc. **2.** to experience the emotion so expressed. **3.** to utter a cry or sound resembling the laughing of human beings, as some animals do. **4.** laugh **at**, to make fun of; deride; ridicule. **5.** laugh **in** or **up one's sleeve**, to laugh inwardly at something. **6.** to drive, put, bring, etc., by or with laughter. **7.** to utter with laughter: *he laughed his consent.* —*n.* **8.** act or sound of laughing, or laughter. **9.** an expression of mirth, derision, etc., by laughing. [ME *laugh(en)*, d. OE *hlæhhan*, OE *hliehhan*, c. Icel. *hlæja*, Goth *hlahjan*; akin to G *lachen*] —**laugh'er**, *n.*

—**Syn. 1.** chortle, cackle, cachinnate, hawhaw, guffaw, roar; giggle, snicker, snigger, titter. **8.** LAUGH, CHUCKLE, GRIN, SMILE, refer to methods of expressing mirth, appreciation of humor, etc. A LAUGH may be a sudden, voiceless exhalation, but is usually an audible sound, either soft or loud: *a hearty laugh.* CHUCKLE suggests a barely audible series of sounds expressing private amusement or satisfaction: *a delighted chuckle.* A SMILE is a (usually pleasant) lighting up of the face and an upward curving of the corners of the lips (which may or may not be open); it may express amusement or mere recognition, friendliness, etc.: *a courteous smile.* A GRIN, in which the teeth are usually visible, is like an exaggerated smile, less controlled in expressing the feelings: *a friendly grin.*

laugh·a·ble (lăf'ə bəl, läf'ə-), *adj.* such as to excite laughter; funny; amusing; ludicrous. —**laugh'a·ble·ness,** *n.* —**laugh'a·bly,** *adv.* —**Syn.** See **funny.**

laugh·ing (lăf'ĭng, läf'ĭng), *n.* **1.** laughter. —*adj.* **2.** that laughs; giving vent to laughter, as persons. **3.** no laughing matter, a serious matter. **4.** uttering sounds like human laughter, as some birds. **5.** suggesting laughter by brightness, etc. —**laugh'ing·ly,** *adv.*

laughing gas, nitrous oxide, N_2O, which when inhaled sometimes produces exhilarating effects: used as an anesthetic in dentistry, etc.

laughing jackass, a harsh-voiced Australian bird, *Dacelo gigas* (a kind of kingfisher).

laugh·ing·stock (lăf'ĭng stŏk', läf'ĭng-), *n.* a butt for laughter; an object of ridicule.

laugh·ter (lăf'tər, läf'-), *n.* **1.** the action or sound of laughing. **2.** an experiencing of the emotion expressed by laughing: *inward laughter.* **3.** an expression or appearance of merriment or amusement. **4.** a subject or matter for laughing. [ME; OE *hleahtor*]

launce (läns, läns), *n.* sand launce.

Laun·ces·ton (lôn'sĕs'tən, län'-), *n.* a city in N Tasmania. With suburbs, 37,634 (1954).

launch[1] (lônch, länch), *n.* **1.** a heavy open boat. **2.** the largest boat carried by a warship. [t. Sp., Pg.: m. *lancha*]

launch[2] (lônch, länch), *v.t.* **1.** to set (a boat) afloat; lower into the water. **2.** to cause (a newly built ship) to move or slide from the stocks into the water. **3.** to start on a course, career, etc. **4.** to set going: *to launch a scheme.* **5.** to send forth; start off (forcefully): *the plane was launched from the deck of the carrier.* **6.** to throw or hurl: *to launch a spear.* —*v.i.* **7.** to burst out or plunge boldly into action, speech, etc. **8.** to start out or forth; push out or put forth on the water. —*n.* **9.** the sliding or movement of a boat or vessel from the land or dock into the water. [ME *launche(n)*, t. ONF: m. *lancher*, var. of central OF *lancier* LANCE, v.] —**launch'er**, *n.*

launching pad, a concrete slab from which rockets are launched.

laun·der (lôn'dər, län'-), *v.t.* **1.** to wash and iron (clothes, etc.). —*v.i.* **2.** to do or wash laundry. —*n.* **3.** (in ore dressing) a passage carrying products of intermediate grade, and residue, which are in water suspension. [ME *lander* one who washes, contr. of *lavender*, t. OF: m. *lavandier* a washer, t. LL: m.s. *lavandārius*, der. L *lavandus*, ger. of *lavāre* to wash] —**laun'der·er**, *n.*

laun·dress (lôn'drĭs, län'-), *n.* a woman whose occupation is the washing and ironing of clothes, etc.

laun·dry (lôn'drĭ, län'-), *n., pl.* **-dries. 1.** articles of clothes, etc., to be washed. **2.** a place or establishment where clothes, etc. are laundered. **3.** act of laundering.

laun·dry·man (lôn'drĭ mən, län'-), *n., pl.* **-men. 1.** a man who works in or conducts a laundry. **2.** a man who collects and delivers laundry.

laun·dry·wom·an (lôn'drĭ wŏŏm'ən, län'-), *n., pl.* **-women.** a laundress.

lau·ra·ceous (lô rā'shəs), *adj.* belonging to the *Lauraceae*, or laurel family of plants. [f. s. L *laurus* laurel + -ACEOUS]

lau·re·ate (lôr'ĭ ĭt), *adj.* **1.** crowned or decked with laurel as a mark of honor. **2.** specially recognized or distinguished, or deserving of distinction, esp. for poetic merit: *poet laureate.* **3.** consisting of laurel. —*n.* **4.** one crowned with laurel. **5.** a poet laureate. [ME *laureat*, t. L: s. *laureātus* (def. 1)] —**lau're·ate·ship'**, *n.*

lau·rel (lôr'əl, lŏr'-), *n., v.t.,* **-reled, -reling** or (*esp. Brit.*) **-relled, -relling.** —*n.* **1.** a small lauraceous evergreen tree, *Laurus nobilis,* of Europe (the **true laurel**). **2.** any tree of the same genus (*Laurus*). **3.** any of various trees or shrubs similar to the true laurel, as *Kalmia latifolia,* a large ericaceous shrub with glossy leaves and showy flowers (the American, or **mountain laurel**) or *Rhododendron maximum,* the great rhododendron (or **great laurel**). **4.** the foliage of the true laurel as an emblem of victory or distinction. **5.** a branch or wreath of it. **6.** (*usually pl.*) honor won, as by achievement. —*v.t.* **7.** to adorn or wreathe with laurel. **8.** to honor with marks of distinction. [ME *laurer*, *laureal*, t. F. m. *laurier*, *lorier*, der. OF *lor*, g. L *laurus* laurel]

Lau·rel (lôr/əl, lŏr/əl), *n.* a city in SE Mississippi. 27,889 (1960).

Lau·ren·tian (lô rĕn/shən), *adj.* **1.** of or pertaining to the St. Lawrence river. **2.** *Geol.* noting or pertaining to a series of rocks of the Archean system, occurring in Canada near the St. Lawrence river and the Great Lakes.

Laurentian Mountains, a range of low mountains in E Canada between the St. Lawrence and Hudson Bay.

Lau·ren·tides Park (lôr/ən tīdz/; *Fr.* lō rän tēd/), a national park in SE Canada, in Quebec province between the St. Lawrence and Lake St. John.

Lau·ri·er (lôr/ĭ ā/; *Fr.* lō ryĕ/), *n.* Sir Wilfrid, 1841–1919, prime minister of Canada, 1896–1911.

lau·rus·ti·nus (lôr/ə stī/nəs), *n.* a caprifoliaceous evergreen garden shrub, *Viburnum tinus,* native in southern Europe, with white or pinkish flowers. [t. NL: f. L *laurus* laurel + *tinus* kind of plant]

Lau·sanne (lō zän/; *Fr.* lō zàn/), *n.* a city in W Switzerland, on the Lake of Geneva. 109,000 (est. 1952).

laus De·o (lôs dē/ō, lous dā/ō), *Latin.* praise (be) to God.

Lau·trec (lō trĕk/), *n.* See **Toulouse-Lautrec.**

lau·wine (lô/wĭn; *Ger.* lou vē/nə), *n.* lawine.

la·va (lä/və, lăv/ə), *n.* **1.** the molten or fluid rock which issues from a volcano or volcanic vent. **2.** the substance formed when this solidifies, occurring in many varieties differing greatly in structure and constitution. [t. It. (Neapolitan): orig., stream, der. *lavare* wash, g. L]

la·va·bo (lə vä/bō), *n., pl.* **-boes.** *Eccles.* **1.** the ritual washing of the celebrant's hands after the offertory in the Mass, accompanied in the Roman rite by the recitation of Psalms 26:6–12, or, in the Douay Version, Psalms 25:6–12 (so called from the first word of this passage in the Latin version). **2.** the passage recited. **3.** the small towel or the basin used. **4.** (in many medieval monasteries) a large stone basin from which the water issued by a number of small orifices around the edge, for the performance of ablutions. [t. L: I will wash]

lav·age (lăv/ĭj; *Fr.* là vàzh/), *n.* **1.** a washing. **2.** *Med.* **a.** cleansing by injection or the like. **b.** the washing out of the stomach. [t. F, der. *laver* LAVE]

La·val (là vàl/), *n.* Pierre (pyĕr), 1883–1945, premier of France, 1931–32, 1935–36; premier of Vichy France, 1942–44; convicted of treason and executed.

lav·a·liere (lăv/ə lĭr/), *n.* an ornamental, usually jeweled, pendant on a small chain, worn by women about the neck. Also, **lav/a·lier/;** *French,* **la·val·lière** (là và lyĕr/). [named after the Duchesse de *La Vallière* (1644–1710), mistress of Louis XIV of France]

la·va·tion (lä vā/shən), *n.* the process of washing. —**la·va/tion·al,** *adj.*

lav·a·to·ry (lăv/ə tôr/ĭ), *n., pl.* **-ries.** **1.** a room fitted up with means for washing the hands and face, and often with other toilet conveniences. **2.** a bowl or basin for washing or bathing purposes. **3.** any place where washing is done. [ME *lavatorie,* t. LL: m. *lavātōrium*]

lave (lāv), *v.,* **laved, laving.** —*v.t.* **1.** *Poetic.* to wash; bathe. **2.** *Poetic.* (of a river, the sea, etc.) to wash or flow against. —*v.i.* **3.** to bathe. **4.** to wash or flow as against something. [ME; OE *lafian* pour water on, wash. Cf. F *laver,* L *lavāre*]

lav·en·der (lăv/ən dər), *n.* **1.** pale, bluish purple. **2.** a plant of the menthaceous genus *Lavandula,* esp. *L officinalis,* a small Old World shrub with spikes of fragrant pale-purple flowers, yielding an oil (**oil of lavender**) used in medicine and perfumery. **3.** the dried flowers or other parts of this plant placed among linen, etc., for scent or as a preservative. [ME *lavendre,* t. AF, t. ML: m.s. *lavendula, livendula;* ? der. L *lavāre* wash or L *livēre* be livid or bluish]

la·ver (lā/vər), *n.* **1.** *Poetic.* a basin, bowl, or cistern to wash in. **2.** *Poetic.* any bowl or pan for water. **3.** *Old Testament.* a large basin upon a foot or pedestal in the court of the Jewish tabernacle, and subsequently in the temple, containing water for the ablutions of the priests, and for the washing of the sacrifices in the temple service. **4.** *Eccles.* the font or the water of baptism. **5.** any spiritually cleansing agency. [ME, t. OF: m. *laveoir,* g. LL *lavātōrium* lavatory]

la·ver (lā/vər), *n.* any of several edible seaweeds, esp. of the genus *Porphyra.* [t. L: kind of water plant]

La Vé·ren·drye (là vě rän drē/), Pierre Gaultier de Varennes (pyĕr gō tyĕ/ də và rĕn/), Sieur de, 1685–1749, French-Canadian explorer of North America.

lav·ish (lăv/ĭsh), *adj.* **1.** using or bestowing in great abundance or without stint (often fol. by *of*): *lavish of time.* **2.** expended, bestowed, or occurring in profusion: *lavish gifts, lavish spending.* [late ME, adj. use of obs. *lavish* profusion, t. OF: m. *lavache* deluge] —*v.t.* **3.** to expend or bestow in great abundance or without stint: *to lavish favors on a person.* [v. use of adj.] —**lav/ish·er,** *n.* —**lav/ish·ly,** *adv.* —**lav/ish·ness,** *n.* —**Syn. 1, 2.** unstinted, extravagant, excessive. LAVISH, PRODIGAL, PROFUSE refer to that which exists in abundance and is poured out copiously. LAVISH suggests (sometimes excessive) generosity and openhandedness: *lavish hospitality, much too lavish.* PRODIGAL suggests wastefulness, improvidence, and reckless impatience of restraint: *a prodigal extravagance.* PROFUSE emphasizes abundance, but may suggest overemotionalism, exaggeration, and the like: *profuse thanks, compliments, apologies.* —**Ant. 2.** limited.

La·voi·sier (là vwà zyĕ/), *n.* Antoine Laurent (än twàn/ lō rän/), 1743–94, French chemist.

law (lô), *n.* **1.** the principles and regulations emanating from a government and applicable to a people, whether in the form of legislation or of custom and policies recognized and enforced by judicial decision. **2.** any written or positive rule, or collection of rules, prescribed under the authority of the state or nation, whether by the people in its constitution, as the **organic law,** or by the legislature in its **statute law,** or by the treaty-making power, or by municipalities in their ordinances or **bylaws. 3.** the controlling influence of such rules; the condition of society brought about by their observance: *to maintain law and order.* **4.** a system or collection of such rules. **5.** the department of knowledge concerned with these rules; jurisprudence: *to study law.* **6.** the body of such rules concerned with a particular subject or derived from a particular source: *commercial law.* **7.** an act of the supreme legislative body of a state or nation, as distinguished from the constitution. **8.** the principles applied in the courts of common law, as distinguished from equity. **9.** the profession which deals with law and legal procedure: *to practice law.* **10.** legal action; litigation: *to go to law.* **11.** any rules or injunctions that must be obeyed: *to lay down the law.* **12.** (in philosophical and scientific use) **a.** a statement of a relation or sequence of phenomena invariable under the same conditions. **b.** a mathematical rule. **13.** a commandment or a revelation from God. **14.** (*often cap.*) a divinely appointed order or system. **15. the Law,** the Mosaic law (often in contrast to *the gospel*). **16.** the five books of Moses (the Pentateuch) containing this system and forming the first of the three Jewish divisions of the Old Testament. **17.** the preceptive part of the Bible, esp. of the New Testament, in contradistinction to its promises: *the law of Christ.* **18.** *Chiefly Brit. Sports.* an allowance given a weaker competitor. [ME *law, lagh,* OE *lagu,* t. Scand.; cf. Icel. *lag* layer, pl. *lög* law, lit. that which is laid down; akin to LAY[1], LIE[2]]

Law (lô), *n.* John, 1671–1729, Scottish financier.

law-a·bid·ing (lô/ə bī/dĭng), *adj.* abiding by or keeping the law; obedient to law: *law-abiding citizens.*

law·break·er (lô/brā/kər), *n.* one who breaks or violates the law. —**law/break/ing,** *n., adj.*

Lawes (lôz), *n.* Harry, 1596–1662, English song writer.

law·ful (lô/fəl), *adj.* **1.** allowed or permitted by law; not contrary to law. **2.** legally qualified or entitled: *lawful king.* **3.** recognized or sanctioned by law. **4.** valid; legitimate: *a lawful marriage.* —**law/ful·ly,** *adv.* —**law/ful·ness,** *n.* —**Syn. 1.** legal. **3.** licit.

law·giv·er (lô/gĭv/ər), *n.* one who gives or promulgates a law or a code of laws. —**law/giv/ing,** *n., adj.*

la·wine (lô/wĭn; *Ger.* lä vē/nə), *n.* an avalanche. Also, **lauwine.** [t. G. Cf. L *lābī* fall down, slip, slide]

law·less (lô/lĭs), *adj.* **1.** regardless of or contrary to law: *lawless violence.* **2.** uncontrolled by law; unbridled: *lawless passions.* **3.** without law; not regulated by law. —**law/less·ly,** *adv.* —**law/less·ness,** *n.*

law·mak·er (lô/mā/kər), *n.* one who makes or enacts law; a legislator. —**law/mak/ing,** *n., adj.*

law merchant, the principles and rules, drawn chiefly from custom, determining the rights and obligations of commercial transactions; commercial law.

lawn[1] (lôn), *n.* **1.** a stretch of grass-covered land, esp. one closely mowed, as near a house, etc. **2.** *Archaic or Dial.* a glade. [earlier *laund,* t. OF: m. *la(u)nde* wooded ground; of Celtic orig.] —**lawn/y,** *adj.*

lawn[2] (lôn), *n.* a thin or sheer linen or cotton fabric, either plain or printed. [ME *laun(e), laund(e);* prob. named after *Laon,* city in northern France, where much linen was made] —**lawn/y,** *adj.*

lawn mower, a machine for cutting grass.

lawn sleeves, **1.** the sleeves of lawn of an Anglican bishop. **2.** the office of an Anglican bishop. **3.** an Anglican bishop or bishops.

lawn tennis, a form of tennis, played on an unenclosed rectangular plot on a lawn or other level surface.

law of contradiction, *Logic.* the law which asserts that a proposition cannot be both true and false, or alternatively that a thing cannot both have and not have a given property.

Law of Moses, the Pentateuch or Torah.

law of nations, **1.** international law. **2.** (in Roman use) the body of rules common to the law of all nations.

Law·rence (lôr/əns, lŏr/-), *n.* **1.** D(avid) H(erbert), 1885–1930, British novelist and poet. **2.** Ernest Orlando, 1901–1958, U.S. physicist: inventor of cyclotron. **3.** James, 1781–1813, U.S. naval officer in the War of 1812. **4.** Sir Thomas, 1769–1830, British portrait painter. **5.** Thomas Edward, (after 1927, *Thomas Edward Shaw,* "*Lawrence of Arabia*") 1888–1935, British soldier, archaeologist, and writer. **6.** a city in NE Massachusetts, on the Merrimack river. 70,933 (1960).

law·suit (lô/sōōt/), *n.* a suit at law; a prosecution of a claim in a law court.

Law·ton (lô/tən), *n.* a city in SW Oklahoma. 61,697 (1960).

law·yer (lô/yər), *n.* **1.** one whose profession it is to conduct suits in court or to give legal advice and aid. **2.** *New Testament.* an interpreter of the Mosaic law. **3.** a burbot (so called from the beardlike barbel).

lax (lăks), *adj.* **1.** lacking in strictness or severity; careless or negligent: *lax morals.* **2.** not rigidly exact or precise; vague: *lax ideas of a subject.* **3.** loose or slack; not tense, rigid, or firm: *a lax cord.* **4.** open or not retentive, as the bowels. **5.** having the bowels unduly open, as a person. **6.** loosely cohering; open or not compact, as a panicle of a plant. **7.** *Phonet.* pronounced with relatively relaxed muscles. [ME, t. L: s. *laxus* loose, slack] —**lax′ly,** *adv.* —**lax′ness,** *n.*

lax·a·tion (lăk sā′shən), *n.* **1.** a loosening or relaxing. **2.** state of being loosened or relaxed. **3.** a laxative. [ME *laxacion,* t. L: m. s. *laxātio* a widening]

lax·a·tive (lăk′sə tĭv), *n.* **1.** *Med.* a laxative medicine or agent. —*adj.* **2.** *Med.* mildly purgative. **3.** *Pathol.* **a.** (of the bowels) subject to looseness. **b.** (of a disease) characterized by looseness of the bowels. [t. L: m.s. *laxātivus* loosening; r. ME *laxatif,* t. F]

lax·i·ty (lăk′sə tĭ), *n.* state or quality of being lax or loose. [t. L: m.s. *laxitas*]

lay¹ (lā), *v.,* **laid, laying,** *n.* —*v.t.* **1.** to put or place in a position of rest or recumbency: *to lay a book on a desk.* **2.** to bring, throw, or beat down, as from an erect position: *to lay a person low.* **3.** to cause to subside: *to lay the dust.* **4.** to allay, appease, or suppress: *to lay a person's doubts.* **5.** to smooth down or make even: *to lay the nap of cloth.* **6.** to bury. **7.** to bring forth and deposit (an egg or eggs). **8.** to deposit as a wager; stake; bet: *I'll lay you ten to one.* **9.** to put away for future use (fol. by *by*). **10.** to place, set, or cause to be in a particular situation, state, or condition: *to lay hands on a thing.* **11.** to place before a person, or bring to a person's notice or consideration: *he laid his case before the commission.* **12.** to put to; place in contiguity; apply: *to lay a hand on a child.* **13.** to set (a trap, etc.). **14.** to place or locate (a scene): *the scene is laid in France.* **15.** to present, bring forward, or prefer, as a claim, charge, etc. **16.** to impute, attribute, or ascribe. **17.** to impose as a burden, duty, penalty, or the like: *to lay an embargo on shipments of oil.* **18.** to bring down (a stick, etc.), as on a person, in inflicting punishment. **19.** to dispose or place in proper position or in an orderly fashion: *to lay bricks.* **20.** to set (a table). **21.** to form by twisting strands together, as a rope. **22.** to place on or over a surface, as paint; cover or spread with something else. **23.** to devise or arrange, as a plan. **24.** *Naut.* to head a ship toward (an object or compass point), esp. on the closest course she will make to the wind. **25.** to move a cannon in vertical plane for elevation. **26.** to put (dogs) on a scent. **27.** Some special phrases are: **lay hold of** or **on,** to grasp; seize; catch. **lay off, 1.** to put aside. **2.** to dismiss, esp. temporarily, as a workman. **3.** to mark or plot off. **lay on the table,** (in parliamentary use) to table (def. 18). **lay out, 1.** to extend at length. **2.** to spread out to the sight, air, etc.; spread out in order. **3.** to stretch out and prepare (a body) for burial. **4.** *Slang.* to expend (money) for a particular purpose. **5.** to exert (oneself) for some purpose, effect, etc. **6.** to plot or plan out. **lay siege to,** to besiege. **lay to,** *Naut.* **1.** to check the motion of (a ship). **2.** to put (a ship, etc.) in a dock or other place of safety. **lay up, 1.** to put away, as for future use; store up. **2.** to cause to remain in bed or indoors through illness. —*v.i.* **28.** to lay eggs. **29.** to wager or bet. **30.** to deal or aim blows (fol. by *on, at, about,* etc.). **31.** to apply oneself vigorously. **32.** *Colloq.* to lie in wait (fol. by *for*). **33.** *Colloq.* or *Dial.* to plan or scheme (often fol. by *out*). **34.** *Naut.* to take a specified position. **35.** (in substandard use) to lie. —*n.* **36.** the way or position in which a thing is laid or lies. **37.** *Ropemaking.* the quality of a fiber rope characterized by the degree of twist, the angles formed by the strands, and by the fibers in the strands. **38.** a share of the profits or the catch of a whaling or fishing voyage, distributed to officers and crew. [ME *lay(en), legge(n),* OE *lecgan* (causative of *licgan* LIE²), c. D *leggen,* G *legen,* Icel. *leggja,* Goth. *lagjan*] —**Syn. 1.** place; deposit, set. See **put, lie².**

lay² (lā), *v.* pt. of **lie².**

lay³ (lā), *adj.* **1.** belonging to, pertaining to, or performed by the people or laity, as distinguished from the clergy: *a lay sermon.* **2.** not belonging to, connected with, or proceeding from a profession, esp. the law or medicine. [ME *laye,* t. OF: m. *lai,* g. LL *lāicus* LAIC]

lay⁴ (lā), *n.* a short narrative or other poem, esp. one to be sung. **2.** a song. [ME *lai,* t. OF, ? t. Gmc. cf. OHG *leich* song]

Lay·a·mon (lā′ə mən, lā′yə-), *n.* fl. c1200, English chronicler in verse. [modern misspelling of early ME *Laghamon,* ME *Lawman.* See LAW, MAN]

Lay·ard (lârd, lā′ərd), *n.* Sir Austen Henry, 1817–94, British archaeologist, writer, and diplomat.

lay brother, a man who has taken religious vows and habit, but is employed chiefly in manual labor.

lay day, 1. *Com.* one of a certain number of days allowed by a charter party for loading or unloading a vessel without demurrage. **2.** *Naut.* a day in which a vessel is delayed in port.

lay·er (lā′ər), *n.* **1.** a thickness of some material laid on or spread over a surface; a stratum. **2.** something which is laid. **3.** one who or that which lays. **4.** *Hort.* **a.** a shoot or twig placed partly under ground while still attached to the living stock, for the purpose of propagation. **b.** a plant which has been propagated by layerage. —*v.t.* **5.** to make a layer of. **6.** *Hort.* to propagate by layers. [ME, f. LAY¹ + -ER¹]

lay·er·age (lā′ər ĭj), *n.* *Hort.* a method of propagating plants by causing their shoots to take root while still attached to the mother plant.

layer cake, a cake made in layers with a cream, jelly, or other filling between layers.

lay·ette (lā ĕt′), *n.* an outfit of clothing, toilet articles, etc., for a newborn child. [t. F: box, drawer, layette, dim. of *laie* chest, trough, t. Flemish: m. *laeye*]

lay figure, 1. a jointed model of the human body, usually of wood, from which artists work in the absence of a living model. **2.** a similar figure used in shops to display costumes. **3.** a mere puppet or nonentity; a person of no importance. [r. obs. *layman* (t. D: m. *leeman,* f. *lee* joint, limb (c. E *lith,* now d.) + *man* MAN), with *figure* substituted for *man,* to avoid confusion with eccl. term]

lay·man (lā′mən), *n., pl.* **-men.** one of the laity; one not a clergyman or not a member of some particular profession. [f. LAY³ + MAN]

lay·off (lā′ôf′, -ŏf′), *n.* **1.** act of laying off. **2.** an interval of enforced unemployment.

lay·out (lā′out′), *n.* **1.** a laying or spreading out. **2.** an arrangement or plan. **3.** the plan or sketch of a page or advertisement indicating the arrangement of materials. **4.** *Slang.* a display; a spread. **5.** a collection or set of tools, implements, or the like.

lay·o·ver (lā′ō′vər), *n.* stopover.

lay·wom·an (lā′wŏm′ən), *n., pl.* **-women.** a female member of the laity.

laz·ar (lăz′ər; *more formally* lā′zər), *n.* *Archaic.* **1.** a person, esp. a beggar or poor person, infected with a loathsome disease. **2.** a leper. [ME, t.ML: s. *lazarus,* special use of LAZARUS] —**laz′ar·like′,** *adj.*

laz·a·ret·to (lăz′ə rĕt′ō), *n., pl.* **-tos.** **1.** a hospital for those affected with contagious or loathsome diseases. **2.** a building or a ship set apart for quarantine purposes. **3.** *Naut.* a place in some merchant ships, usually near the stern, in which provisions and stores are kept. Also, **laz·a·ret** (lăz′ə rĕt′), **laz·a·rette′.** [t. It.: m. *lazzaretto,* var. of Venetian *lazareto,* b. *nazareto* (abbr. from name of leper hospital *Santa Maria di Nazaret*) and *lazaro* lazar, leper]

Laz·a·rus (lăz′ə rəs), *n.* **1.** the beggar, "full of sores," of the parable in Luke 16:19–31. **2.** the brother of Mary and Martha, and friend of Jesus, who raised him from the dead. John 11:1–44; 12:1–18. **3.** Emma, 1849–87, U.S. poet. [t. LL, t. Gk.: m. *Lázaros,* t. Heb.: m. *El'āzār* Eleazar]

laze (lāz), *v.,* **lazed, lazing.** —*v.i.* **1.** to be lazy; idle or lounge lazily. —*v.t.* **2.** to pass (time, etc.) lazily (fol. by *away*). [back formation from LAZY]

laz·u·lite (lăz′yə līt′), *n.* an azure-blue mineral, hydrous magnesium iron aluminum phosphate, (FeMg)Al₂P₂O₈(OH)₂. [f. s. ML *lāzulum* lapis lazuli + -ITE¹]

laz·u·rite (lăz′yə rīt′), *n.* a mineral, sodium aluminum silicate and sulfide, Na₅Al₃Si₃O₁₂S₃, occurring in deep-blue crystals and used for ornamental purposes. [f. ML *lāzur* AZURE + -ITE¹]

la·zy (lā′zĭ), *adj.,* **lazier, laziest. 1.** disinclined to exertion or work; idle. **2.** slow-moving; sluggish; *a lazy stream.* **3.** noting a kind of livestock brand which is placed on its side instead of upright. [orig. uncert.] —**la′zi·ly,** *adv.* —**la′zi·ness,** *n.* —**Syn. 1.** indolent, slothful. See **idle.** —**Ant. 1.** industrious; active.

la·zy·bones (lā′zĭ bōnz′), *n.* *Colloq.* a lazy person.

lazy Su·san (sōō′zən), a large revolving tray for food, placed at the center of the table.

lazy tongs, a kind of extensible tongs for grasping objects at a distance, consisting of a series of pairs of crossing pieces, each pair pivoted together in the middle and connected with the next pair at the extremities.

Lazy tongs

lb., *pl.* **lbs., lb.** (L *libra,* pl. *librae*) pound (weight).

L.C., Library of Congress.

l.c., 1. left center. **2.** letter of credit. **3.** (L *loco citato*) in the place cited. **4.** *Print.* lower case.

L/C, letter of credit. Also, l/c.

l.c.d., lowest common denominator.

L.C.L., *Com.* less than carload lot. Also, l.c.l.

L.C.M., least common multiple. Also, l.c.m.

LD, Low Dutch. Also, **L.D.**

Ld., 1. Limited. **2.** Lord.

l.e., *Football.* left end.

lea¹ (lē), *n.* *Poetic.* a tract of open ground, esp. grassland; a meadow. [ME *ley,* OE *lēa(h),* c. OHG *lōh,* L *lūcus* grove]

lea² (lē), *n.* a measure of yarn of varying quantity, for wool usually 80 yards, cotton and silk 120 yards, linen 300 yards. [ME, ? akin to F *lier* tie]

lea., **1.** league. **2.** leather.

leach (lēch), *v.t.* **1.** to cause (water, etc.) to percolate through something. **2.** to remove soluble constituents from (ashes, etc.) by percolation. —*v.i.* **3.** (of ashes, etc.) to undergo the action of percolating water. **4.** to percolate, as water. —*n.* **5.** a leaching. **6.** the material leached. **7.** a vessel for use in leaching. [unexplained var. of *letch,* v. (whence d. *letch,* n., bog, etc.), OE *leccan* moisten, wet, causative of LEAK]

lay·er (lā′ər), *n.* **1.** a thickness of some material laid on or spread over a surface; a stratum. **2.** something which is laid. **3.** one who or that which lays. **4.** *Hort.* **a.** a shoot or twig placed partly under ground while still attached to the living stock, for the purpose of propagation. **b.** a plant which has been

Layer (def. 4)

leach·y (lē′chĭ), *adj.* porous.

Lea·cock (lē′kŏk), *n.* **Stephen Butler,** 1869–1944, Canadian humorist and economist.

lead[1] (lēd), *v.,* **led, leading,** *n.* —*v.t.* **1.** to take or conduct on the way; go before or with to show the way. **2.** to conduct by holding and guiding: *to lead a horse by a rope.* **3. lead the way,** to go in advance of others, esp. as a guide. **4.** to guide in direction, course, action, opinion, etc.; to influence or induce: *too easily led.* **5.** to conduct or bring (water, wire, etc.) in a particular course. **6.** (of a road, passage, etc.) to serve to bring (a person, etc.) to a place through a region, etc. **7.** to take or bring: *the prisoners were led in.* **8.** to be at the head of, command, or direct (an army, organization, etc.). **9.** to go at the head of or in advance of (a procession, list, body, etc.); to be first in or go before. **10.** to have the directing or principal part in (a movement, proceedings, etc.). **11.** to begin or open, as a dance, discussion, etc. **12.** to act as leader of (an orchestra, etc.). **13.** to go through or pass (life, etc.): *to lead a dreary existence.* **14.** *Cards.* to begin a round, etc., with (a card or suit specified). **15.** to aim and fire a firearm or cannon ahead of (a moving target) in order to allow for the travel of the target while the bullet or shell is reaching it.
—*v.i.* **16.** to act as a guide; show the way. **17.** to be led, or submit to being led, as an animal. **18.** to afford passage to a place, etc., as a road, stairway, or the like does. **19.** to go first; be in advance. **20.** to take the directing or principal part. **21.** to take the initiative (often fol. by *off*). **22.** *Boxing.* to take the offensive by jabbing an opponent. **23.** *Cards.* to make the first play. —*n.* **24.** the first or foremost place; position in advance of others. **25.** the extent of advance. **26.** something that leads. **27.** a guiding indication. **28.** precedence. **29.** *Theat.* **a.** the principal part in a play. **b.** the person who plays it. **30.** *Cards.* **a.** the act or right of playing first, as in a round. **b.** the card, suit, etc., so played. **31.** *Journalism.* a short summary serving as an introduction to a news story or article. **32.** *Elect.* **a.** a single conductor, often flexible and insulated, used in connections between pieces of electrical apparatus. **b.** an antenna lead-in wire. **33.** *Boxing.* act of taking the offensive by jabbing an opponent. **34.** *Naut.* the course of a rope. **35.** an open channel through a field of ice. **36.** *Mining.* **a.** a lode. **b.** an auriferous deposit in an old river bed. **37.** act of aiming a gun ahead of a target moving across the line of fire. [ME *leden,* OE *lǣdan* (causative of *līthan* go, travel), c. D *leiden,* G *leiten,* Icel. *leidha*] —**Syn. 1.** See **guide.**

lead[2] (lĕd), *n.* **1.** *Chem.* a heavy, comparatively soft, malleable bluish-gray metal, sometimes found native, but usually combined as sulfide, in galena. *Symbol:* Pb; *at. wt.:* 207.21; *at. no.:* 82; *sp. gr.:* 11.34 at 20°C. **2.** something made of this metal or one of its alloys. **3.** a plummet or mass of lead suspended by a line, as for taking soundings. **4.** bullets; shot. **5.** black lead or graphite. **6.** a small stick of it as used in pencils. **7.** *Print.* Also, **leading.** a thin strip of type metal or brass, less than type high, for increasing the space between lines of type. **8.** frames of lead in which panes are fixed, as in windows of stained glass. **9.** (*pl.*) sheets or strips of lead used for covering roofs. **10.** white lead. —*v.t.* **11.** to cover, line, weight, treat, or impregnate with lead or one of its compounds. **12.** *Print.* to insert leads between the lines of. **13.** to fix (window glass) in position with leads. [ME *lede,* OE *lēad,* c. D *lood,* G *lot* plummet]

lead arsenate, *Chem.* plumbous arsenate, Pb₃(AsO₄)₂, a very poisonous crystalline compound, used as an insecticide.

lead·en (lĕd′ən), *adj.* **1.** consisting or made of lead. **2.** inertly heavy, or hard to lift or move, as weight, the limbs, etc. **3.** oppressive, as the air. **4.** sluggish, as the pace. **5.** dull, spiritless, or gloomy, as the mood, thoughts, etc. **6.** of a dull gray: *leaden skies.* —**lead′en·ly,** *adv.* —**lead′en·ness,** *n.*

lead·er (lē′dər), *n.* **1.** one who or that which leads. **2.** a guiding or directing head, as of an army, movement, etc. **3.** *Music.* **a.** a conductor or director, as of an orchestra, band, or chorus. **b.** the player at the head of the first violins in an orchestra, the principal cornetist in a band, or the principal soprano in a chorus, to whom any incidental solos are usually assigned. **4.** a horse harnessed at the front of a team. **5.** a principal or important editorial article, as in a newspaper. **6.** a featured article of trade, esp. one offered at a low price to attract customers. **7.** a pipe for conveying rainwater. etc. **8.** *Naut.* a piece of metal or wood having apertures for lines to lead them to their proper places. **9.** (*pl.*) *Print.* a row of dots or short lines to lead the eye across a space. **10.** *Fishing.* **a.** a length of silkworm gut or the like, to which the fly or baited hook is attached. **b.** the net used to direct fish into a weir, pound, etc. —**lead′er·less,** *adj.*

lead·er·ship (lē′dər·shĭp′), *n.* **1.** the position, function, or guidance of a leader. **2.** ability to lead.

lead·ing[1] (lē′dĭng), *n.* **1.** act of one who or that which leads; guidance, direction; lead. —*adj.* **2.** directing; guiding. **3.** chief; principal; most important; foremost. [f. LEAD[1] + -ING[1]]

lead·ing[2] (lĕd′ĭng), *n.* **1.** a covering or framing of lead. **2.** *Print.* lead[2] (def. 7). [f. LEAD[2] + -ING]

lead·ing article (lē′dĭng), a principal editorial article in a newspaper; a leader.

lead·ing edge (lē′dĭng), *Aeron.* the edge of an airfoil or propeller blade facing the direction of motion.

lead·ing question (lē′dĭng), a question so worded as to suggest the proper or desired answer.

lead·ing string (lē′dĭng), **1.** a string for leading and supporting a child when learning to walk. **2.** excessively restraining guidance.

lead·ing tone (lē′dĭng), *Music.* the seventh degree of the scale.

lead-in wire (lĕd′ĭn′), *Radio.* that portion of the antenna connected to the receiving set.

lead line (lĕd), *Naut.* a line used in taking soundings.

lead·off (lĕd′ôf′, -ŏf′), *n.* **1.** an act which starts something; start; beginning. —*adj.* **2.** *Baseball.* the player who is first in the batting order.

lead pencil (lĕd), an implement for writing or drawing made of graphite in a wooden or metal holder.

lead·plant (lĕd′plănt′, -plänt′), *n.* a North American shrub of the family *Leguminosae, Amorpha canescens,* so called on account of the gray cast of its twigs and leaves.

lead poisoning (lĕd), *Pathol.* a diseased condition due to the introduction of lead into the system, common among workers in lead or its compounds; plumbism.

leads·man (lĕdz′mən), *n., pl.* **-men.** *Naut.* a man who heaves the lead in taking soundings.

lead·y (lĕd′ĭ), *adj.* like lead; leaden.

Leaf of pansy. *Viola tricolor* B. Blade; P. Petiole; S. Stipule

leaf (lēf), *n., pl.* **leaves** (lēvz), *v.* —*n.* **1.** one of the expanded, usually green, organs, borne by the stem of a plant. **2.** any similar or corresponding lateral outgrowth of a stem. **3.** a petal: *a rose leaf.* **4.** foliage or leafage. **5. in leaf,** covered with foliage or leaves. **6.** *Bibliog.* a unit generally comprising two printed pages of a book, one on each side, but also applied to blank or illustrated pages. **7.** a thin sheet of metal, etc. **8.** a lamina or layer. **9.** a sliding, hinged, or detachable flat part, as of a door, table top, etc. **10.** a single strip of metal in a composite, or leaf, spring. **11.** a layer of fat, esp. that about the kidneys of a hog. —*v.i.* **12.** to put forth leaves. —*v.t.* **13.** *U.S.* to thumb (*through*) the pages of; turn leaves. [ME *leef,* OE *lēaf,* c. G *laub*] —**leaf′like′,** *adj.*

leaf·age (lē′fĭj), *n.* foliage.

leaf hopper, any of the leaping homopterous insects of the family *Cicadellidae,* including many crop pests.

leaf lard, lard prepared from the leaf of the hog.

leaf·less (lēf′lĭs), *adj.* without leaves. —**leaf′less·ness,** *n.*

leaf·let (lēf′lĭt), *n.* **1.** one of the separate blades or divisions of a compound leaf. **2.** a small leaflike part or structure. **3.** a small or young leaf. **4.** a small flat or folded sheet of printed matter, as for distribution.

leaf spring, a long, narrow, multiple spring composed of several layers of spring metal bracketed together. See illus. under **spring.**

leaf·stalk (lēf′stôk′), *n.* petiole (def. 1).

leaf·y (lē′fĭ), *adj.* **leafier, leafiest. 1.** abounding in, covered with, or consisting of leaves or foliage: *the leafy woods.* **2.** leaflike; foliaceous. —**leaf′i·ness,** *n.*

league[1] (lēg), *n., v.,* **leagued, leaguing.** —*n.* **1.** a covenant or compact made between persons, parties, states, etc., for the maintenance or promotion of common interests or for mutual assistance or service. **2.** the aggregation of persons, parties, states, etc., associated in such a covenant; a confederacy. **3. in league,** united by or having a compact or agreement; allied (often fol. by *with*). —*v.t.* **4.** to unite in a league; combine. [ME *ligg,* t. OF: m. *ligue,* t. It.: m. *liga, lega,* der. *legare,* g. L *ligare* bind] —**Syn. 1.** See **alliance.**

league[2] (lēg), *n.* **1.** a unit of distance, varying at different periods and in different countries, in English-speaking countries usually estimated roughly at 3 miles. **2.** a square league, as a unit of land measure. [ME *le(u)ge,* t. LL: m. *leuga, leuca,* said to be of Gallic orig.]

League of Nations, the organization of nations of the world to promote world peace and coöperation which was created by the Treaty of Versailles (1919) and dissolved, April, 1946, by action of its 21st Assembly.

lea·guer[1] (lē′gər), *n., v.t.* *Archaic.* —*v.t.* **1.** to besiege. —*n.* **2.** a siege. **3.** a military camp, esp. of a besieging army. [t. D: m. *leger* bed, camp. See LAIR, LAAGER]

lea·guer[2] (lē′gər), *n.* a member of a league. [f. LEAGUE[1] + -ER[1]]

Le·ah (lē′ə), *n.* the first wife of Jacob.

Lea·hy (lā′hĭ), *n.* **William David,** 1875–1959, U.S. admiral and diplomat.

leak (lēk), *n.* **1.** an unintended hole, crack, or the like by which water, etc., enters or escapes. **2.** any avenue or means of unintended entrance or escape, or the entrance or escape itself. **3.** *Elect.* a point where current escapes from a conductor, as because of poor insulation. **4.** act of leaking. —*v.i.* **5.** to let water, etc., enter or escape, as through an unintended hole, crack, permeable material, or the like: *the roof is leaking.* **6.** to pass in or out in this manner, as water, etc.: *gas leaking from a pipe.* **7.** to transpire or become known undesignedly (fol. by *out*). —*v.t.* **8.** to let (water, etc.) leak in or out. [ME *leke,* t. Scand.; cf. Icel. *leka* drip, leak, c. M D *leken*]

leak·age (lē/kǐj), n. **1.** act of leaking; leak. **2.** that which leaks in or out. **3.** the amount that leaks in or out. **4.** *Com.* an allowance for loss by leaking.

leakage current, *Elect.* a relatively small current flowing through or across the surface of an insulator when a voltage is impressed upon it.

leak·y (lē/kǐ), *adj.,* **leakier, leakiest. 1.** allowing water, etc., to leak in or out. **2.** apt to disclose secrets, as a person. —**leak/i·ness,** n.

leal (lēl), *adj. Archaic or Scot.* loyal. [ME *lele,* t. OF: m. *leial.* See LOYAL] —**leal/ly,** *adv.*

lean¹ (lēn), *v.,* **leaned** or (*esp. Brit.*) **leant, leaning,** n. —*v.i.* **1.** to incline or bend from a vertical position or in a particular direction. **2.** to incline in feeling, opinion, action, etc.: *to lean toward socialism.* **3.** to rest against or on something for support: *lean against a wall.* **4.** to depend or rely: *to lean on empty promises.* —*v.t.* **5.** to incline or bend: *he leaned his head forward.* **6.** to cause to lean or rest (fol. by *against, on, upon,* etc.): *lean your arm against the railing.* —*n.* **7.** act of leaning; inclination. [ME *lene(n),* OE *hleonian,* c. G *lehnen;* akin to L *-clīnāre* incline]

lean² (lēn), *adj.* **1.** (of persons or animals) scant of flesh; not plump or fat: *lean cattle.* **2.** (of meat) containing little or no fat. **3.** lacking in richness, fullness, quantity, etc.: *a lean diet, lean years.* —*n.* **4.** that part of flesh which consists of muscle rather than fat. **5.** the lean part of anything. [ME *lene,* OE *hlǣne*] —**lean/ly,** *adv.* —**lean/ness,** n. —**Syn. 1.** skinny. See **thin.**

Le·an·der (lǐ ǎn/dər), n. See **Hero and Leander.**

lean·ing (lē/nǐng), n. inclination; tendency: *strong literary leanings.*

leant (lěnt), *v. Chiefly Brit.* pt. and pp. of **lean¹.**

lean-to (lēn/tōō/), *n., pl.* **-tos. 1.** a shack or shed supported at one side by trees or posts and with an inclined roof. **2.** a roof of single pitch, the higher end abutting a wall or larger building. **3.** a structure with such a roof.

leap (lēp), *v.,* **leaped** or **leapt, leaping,** n. —*v.i.* **1.** to spring through the air from one point or position to another: *to leap over a ditch.* **2.** to move quickly and lightly: *to leap aside.* **3.** to pass, come, rise, etc., as if with a bound: *to leap to a conclusion.* —*v.t.* **4.** to jump over: *to leap a wall.* **5.** to pass over as if by a leap. **6.** to cause to leap. —*n.* **7.** a spring, jump, or bound; a light springing movement. **8.** the space cleared in a leap. **9.** a place leaped, or to be leaped, over or from. **10.** an abrupt transition. [ME *lepe(n),* OE *hlēapan* leap, run, c. G *laufen* run. Cf. LOPE] —**leap/er,** n. —**Syn. 1.** See **jump.**

leap·frog (lēp/frôg/,-frŏg/), *n., v.* **-frogged, frogging.** —*n.* **1.** a game in which one player leaps over another who is in a stooping posture. —*v.t., v.i.* **2.** to jump over (a person or thing) in, or as in, leapfrog; to move or advance (something) by leaping in this manner over intervening obstacles.

leapt (lěpt, lēpt), *v.* a pt. and pp. of **leap.**

leap year, a year containing 366 days, or one day (Feb. 29) more than the ordinary year, to offset the difference in length between the ordinary year and the astronomical year (being, in practice, every year whose number is exactly divisible by 4, as 1948, except centenary years not exactly divisible by 400, as 1900).

Lear (lǐr), n. **1.** See **King Lear. 2. Edward,** 1812–88, British humorist and painter.

learn (lûrn), *v.,* **learned** (lûrnd) or **learnt, learning.** —*v.i.* **1.** to acquire knowledge of or skill in by study, instruction, or experience: *to learn French.* **2.** to memorize. **3.** to become informed of or acquainted with; ascertain: *to learn the truth.* —*v.i.* **4.** to acquire knowledge or skill: *to learn rapidly.* **5.** to become informed (fol. by *of*): *to learn of an accident.* [ME *lernen,* OE *leornian,* c. G *lernen;* akin to OE *gelǣran* teach] —**learn/er,** n. —**Syn. 1.** LEARN, ASCERTAIN, DETECT, DISCOVER imply adding to one's store of facts. To LEARN is to add to one's knowledge or information: *to learn a language.* To ASCERTAIN is to verify facts by inquiry or analysis: *to ascertain the truth about an event.* To DETECT implies becoming aware of something which had been obscure, secret, or concealed: *to detect a flaw in reasoning.* To DISCOVER is also used with obj. clauses as a synonym of LEARN in order to suggest that the new information acquired is surprising to the learner: *I discovered that she had been married before.*

learn·ed (lûr/nǐd), *adj.* **1.** having much knowledge; scholarly: *a group of learned men.* **2.** of or showing learning. —**learn/ed·ly,** *adv.* —**learn/ed·ness,** n.

learn·ing (lûr/nǐng), n. **1.** knowledge acquired by systematic study in any field or fields of scholarly application. **2.** the act or process of acquiring knowledge or skill. **3.** *Psychol.* the modification of behavior through interaction with the environment. —**Syn. 1.** LEARNING, ERUDITION, LORE, SCHOLARSHIP refer to knowledge existing or acquired. LEARNING is knowledge acquired by systematic study, as of literature, history, or science: *a body of learning; fond of literary learning.* ERUDITION suggests a thorough, formal, and profound sort of knowledge obtained by extensive research; it is esp. applied to knowledge in fields other than those of mathematics and physical sciences: *a man of vast erudition in languages.* LORE is accumulated knowledge in a particular field, esp. of a curious, anecdotal, or traditional nature; the word is now somewhat poetic: *gypsy lore.* SCHOLARSHIP is the formalized learning which is taught in schools, esp. as actively employed by one trying to master some field of knowledge or extend its bounds: *high standards of scholarship in history.*

lease (lēs), *n., v.,* **leased, leasing.** —*n.* **1.** an instrument conveying property to another for a definite period, or at will, usually in consideration of rent or other periodical compensation. **2.** the property leased. **3.** the period of time for which it is made. **4.** an allotted period or term. [ME *lese,* t. AF: m. *les* a letting, der. OF *laissier* let] —*v.t.* **5.** to grant the temporary possession or use of (lands, tenements, etc.) to another, usually for compensation at a fixed rate; let. **6.** to take or to hold by a lease, as lands. [ME *lese(n),* t. AF: m. *lesser* let go, let, g. L *laxāre* loosen] —**leas/er,** n.

lease·hold (lēs/hōld/), n. **1.** a land interest acquired under a lease. —*adj.* **2.** held by lease.

lease·hold·er (lēs/hōl/dər), n. a tenant under a lease.

leash (lēsh), n. **1.** a thong or line for holding a dog or other animal in check. **2.** *Sports.* a brace and a half, as of hounds. **3.** a set of three. —*v.t.* **4.** to secure or hold in or as in a leash. [ME *lees, lese,* t. OF: m. *laisse,* g. L *laxa,* fem. of L *laxus* loose, lax.]

least (lēst), *adj.* **1.** little beyond all others in size, amount, degree, etc.; smallest; slightest: *the least distance.* **2.** lowest in consideration or dignity. —*n.* **3.** that which is least; the least amount, quantity, degree, etc. **4. at least,** a. at the least or lowest estimate. b. at any rate; in any case. **5. in the least,** in the smallest degree, as a thing not in the least likely. —*adv.* **6.** to the least extent, amount, or degree. [ME *leest(e),* OE *lǣst,* superl. of *lǣs(sa)* LESS]

least common multiple. See **common multiple.**

least flycatcher, a small flycatcher, *Empidona minimus,* of eastern North America; the chebec.

least sandpiper, a small American shore bird or peep, *Erolia minutilla,* related to the several stints of Europe, and known in England as the American stint.

least squares, *Statistics.* a method of determining constants from observations, by minimizing squares of residuals between observations and their theoretical expected values.

least·wise (lēst/wīz/), *adv. Colloq.* at least; at any rate. Also, **least·ways** (lēst/wāz/).

leath·er (lĕth/ər), n. **1.** the skin of animals prepared for use by tanning or a similar process. **2.** some article or appliance made of this material. —*v.t.* **3.** to cover or furnish with leather. **4.** *Colloq.* to beat with a leather strap. [ME *lether,* OE *lether* (in compounds), c. D and G *leder,* Icel. *ledhr*]

leath·er·back (lĕth/ər bǎk/), n. a large marine turtle, *Dermochelys coriacea,* with a longitudinally ridged flexible carapace formed of a mosaic of small bony plates embedded in a leathery skin.

leath·ern (lĕth/ərn), *adj.* **1.** made of leather. **2.** resembling leather. [ME and OE *lether(e)n.* See -EN²]

leath·er·neck (lĕth/ər nĕk/), n. *Slang.* a U.S. marine.

leath·er·oid (lĕth/ər oid/), n. a substitute for leather, used in making bags, suitcases, etc., consisting mostly of vegetable fiber, as paper stock, variously treated.

leath·er·wood (lĕth/ər wŏŏd/), n. an American shrub, *Dirca palustris,* with a tough bark.

leath·er·y (lĕth/ər ǐ), *adj.* like leather; tough and flexible.

leave¹ (lēv), *v.,* **left, leaving.** —*v.t.* **1.** to go away from, depart from, or quit, as a place, a person, or a thing. **2.** to let stay or be as specified: *to leave a door unlocked.* **3.** to desist from, stop, or abandon (fol. by *off*). **4.** to let (a person, etc.) remain in a position to do something without interference: *leave him alone.* **5.** to let (a thing) remain for action or decision. **6.** to omit (fol. by *out*). **7.** to allow to remain in the same place, condition, state, etc.: *there is plenty of work left.* **8.** to let remain, or have remaining behind, after going, disappearing, ceasing, etc.: *the wound left a scar.* **9.** to have remaining after death: *he leaves a widow.* **10.** to give in charge; give for use after one's death or departure. **11.** to have as a remainder after subtraction: *2 from 4 leaves 2.* —*v.i.* **12.** to go away, depart, or set out: *we leave for Europe tomorrow.* [ME *leve(n),* OE *lǣfan* (der. *lāf* remainder). c. OHG *leiben,* Icel. *leifa,* Goth. *-laibjan*] —**leav/er,** n. —**Syn. 1.** vacate; abandon, forsake, desert. **4.** See **let¹. 10.** bequeath, will; devise, transmit.

leave² (lēv), n. **1.** permission to do something. **2.** permission to be absent, as from duty: *to be on leave.* **3.** the time this permission lasts: *30 days' leave.* **4.** a farewell: *to take leave of someone.* [ME *leve,* OE *lēaf.* Cf. D (*oor*)*lof,* G (*ur*)*laub,* (*ver*)*laub* FURLOUGH]

leave³ (lēv), *v.i.,* **leaved, leaving.** to put forth leaves; leaf. [var. of LEAF, v.i.]

leaved (lēvd), *adj.* having leaves; leafed.

leav·en (lĕv/ən), n. **1.** a mass of fermenting dough reserved for producing fermentation in a new batch of dough. **2.** an agency which works in a thing to produce a gradual change or modification. —*v.t.* **3.** to produce bubbles of gas in (dough or batter) by means of any of a variety of leavening agents. **4.** to permeate with an altering or transforming influence. [ME *levain,* t. OF, g. L *levāmen* that which raises] —**leav/en·ing,** n.

Leav·en·worth (lĕv/ən wûrth/, -wərth), n. **1.** a city in NE Kansas. 22,052 (1960). **2.** a federal prison there.

leaves (lēvz), n. pl. of **leaf.**

Leaves of Grass, a book of poems (first version, 1855; final (9th) edition, 1891–92) by Whitman.

leave-tak·ing (lēv/tā/kǐng), n. the saying of farewell.

b., blend of, blended; c., cognate with; d., dialect, dialectal; der., derived from; f., formed from; g., going back to; m., modification of; r., replacing; s., stem of; t., taken from; ?, perhaps. See the full key on inside cover.

leav·ing (lē'vĭng), n. 1. that which is left; residue. 2. (pl.) remains; refuse.

leav·y (lē'vĭ), adj., **leavier, leaviest.** Poetic. leafy.

Leb·a·nese (lĕb'ə nēz', -nēs'), adj. 1. of or pertaining to Lebanon. —n. 2. a native of Lebanon.

Leb·a·non ((lĕb'ə nən), n. 1. a republic at the E end of the Mediterranean, N of Israel. 1,383,000 pop. (est. 1954); 3927 sq. mi. Cap.: Beirut. 2. a city in SE Pennsylvania. 30,045 (1960).

Lebanon Mountains, a mountain range extending the length of Lebanon, in the central part. Highest peak, 10,049 ft.

Le·bens·raum (lā'bəns roum'), n. additional territory desired by a nation for expansion of trade, etc. [G: room for living]

Le Bour·get (lə bŏŏr zhě'), one of two international airports for Paris. See Orly.

Le·brun (lə brœn'), n. 1. Albert (ȧl bĕr', 1871–1950, president of France, 1932–40. 2. Also, **Le Brun. Charles** (shȧrl), 1619–90, French painter. 3. **Marie Anne Elisabeth Vigée** (má rē' ȧn ē lē zá bĕt' vē zhě'), (Madame Vigée-Lebrun) 1755–1842, French painter.

lech·er (lĕch'ər), n. a man immoderately given to sexual indulgence; a lewd man. [ME lechur, t. OF: m. lecheor gourmand, sensualist, der. lechier lick, live in sensuality, t. Gmc.; cf. LICK]

lech·er·ous (lĕch'ər əs), adj. 1. given to or characterized by lechery. 2. inciting to lechery. —**lech'er·ous·ly,** adv. —**lech'er·ous·ness,** n.

lecher wires, Electronics. parallel wires of such length and terminations that the system will resonate (i.e., standing waves will appear) if the frequency of the excitation is correct.

lech·er·y (lĕch'ər ĭ), n. free indulgence of lust.

lec·i·thin (lĕs'ə thĭn), n. Biochem. one of a group of yellow-brown fatty substances, found in animal and plant tissues and egg yolk, composed of units of choline, phosphoric acid, fatty acids, and glycerol. [f. m.s. Gk. lēkithos egg yolk + -IN²]

Leck·y (lĕk'ĭ), n. **William Edward Hartpole,** 1838–1903, British historian and writer, born in Ireland.

Le·conte de Lisle (lə kônt' də lēl'), **Charles Marie** (shȧrl má rē'), 1818–94, French poet.

Le Cor·bu·sier (lə kôr by zyě'), (Charles Édouard Jeanneret) 1887–1965, Swiss modern architect in France.

Le Creu·sot (lə krœ zō'), a city in E France. 28,663 (1954).

lect., 1. lecture. 2. lecturer.

lec·tern (lĕk'tərn), n. a reading desk in a church, esp. that from which the lessons are read. [earlier lecturn, Latinized and metathetic var. of ME lettrun, t. OF, t. ML: m. lectrum, der. L legere read]

lec·tion (lĕk'shən), n. 1. a reading or version of a passage in a particular copy of a text. 2. a lesson, or portion of sacred writing, read in divine service. [ME, t. L: s. lectio a reading]

lec·tion·ar·y (lĕk'shə nĕr'ĭ), n., pl. **-aries.** a book, or a list, of lections for reading in divine service.

lec·tor (lĕk'tər), n. a reader, as of lectures in a college or university or of scriptural lessons. [late ME, t. L]

lec·ture (lĕk'chər), n., v., **-tured, -turing.** —n. 1. a discourse read or delivered before an audience, esp. for instruction or to set forth some subject: a lecture on Picasso. 2. a speech of warning or reproof as to conduct; a long, tedious reprimand. —v.i. 3. to give a lecture. —v.t. 4. to deliver a lecture to or before; instruct by lectures. 5. to rebuke or reprimand at some length. [ME, t. LL: m. lectura, der. L legere read]

lec·tur·er (lĕk'chər ər), n. 1. one who lectures. 2. a temporary appointee who performs instructional duties in a college or university, usually on a part-time basis.

lec·ture·ship (lĕk'chər shĭp'), n. the office of lecturer.

led (lĕd), v. pt. and pp. of lead¹.

Le·da (lē'də), n. Gk. Myth. the mother by Zeus or by her husband Tyndareus of Helen, Clytemnestra, Castor, and Pollux.

ledge (lĕj), n. 1. any relatively narrow, horizontal projecting part, or any part affording a horizontal shelflike surface. 2. a more or less flat shelf of rock protruding from a cliff or slope. 3. a reef, ridge, or line of rocks in the sea or other water bodies. 4. Mining. a. a layer or mass of rock underground. b. a lode or vein. [ME legge transverse bar, OE lecg (exact meaning not clear), der. lecgan LAY¹] —**ledged,** adj.

ledg·er (lĕj'ər), n. 1. Bookkeeping. an account book of final entry, containing all the accounts. 2. a horizontal timber fastened to the vertical uprights of a scaffold, to support the putlogs. 3. a flat slab of stone laid over a grave or tomb. [ME legger (book), der. leggen LAY¹ (see LEDGE)]

ledger board, the horizontal part of a fence, rail, etc.

ledger line, Music. leger line.

ledger tackle, Angling. fishing apparatus set up so that the lead lies on the bottom.

lee¹ (lē), n. 1. shelter. 2. the side or part that is sheltered or turned away from the wind. 3. Chiefly Naut. the quarter or region toward which the wind blows.

—adj. 4. Chiefly Naut. pertaining to, situated in, or moving toward the quarter or region toward which the wind blows (opposed to weather). [ME; OE hlēo shelter]

lee² (lē), n. (usually pl.) that which settles from a liquid, esp. from wine; sediment; dregs. [ME lie, t. OF, g. LL lia, of Gallic orig.]

Lee (lē), n. 1. **Charles,** 1731–82, American Revolutionary general, born in England. 2. **Fitzhugh** (fĭts'hū'), 1835–1905, U.S. general. 3. **Francis Lightfoot,** 1734–97, American patriot. 4. **Henry,** ("Light-Horse Harry") 1756–1818, American Revolutionary general (father of Robert E. Lee). 5. **Richard Henry,** 1732–94, American patriot and statesman. 6. **Robert E.,** 1807–1870, Confederate general in the U.S. Civil War. 7. **Sir Sidney,** 1859–1926, British biographer and critic.

lee·board (lē'bōrd'), n. a flat board let down vertically into the water on the lee side of a ship or boat to prevent leeward motion.

leech¹ (lēch), n. 1. any of the blood-sucking or carnivorous, usually aquatic, worms constituting the class Hirudinea, certain fresh-water species of which were formerly much used by physicians for bloodletting. 2. an instrument used for drawing blood. 3. a person who clings to another with a view to gain. 4. Archaic. a physician. —v.t. 5. to apply leeches to so as to bleed. 6. Archaic. to cure; heal. [ME leche, OE lǣce (by confusion with lǣce physician); r. ME liche, OE lȳce, der. lūcan draw out, burst out] —**leech'like,** adj.

leech² (lēch), n. Naut. 1. either of the perpendicular or sloping edges of a square sail. 2. the after edge of a fore-and-aft sail. [ME lek, leche, appar. c. G liek bolt rope, leech rope; akin to G leik leech line]

Leeds (lēdz), n. a city in N England, in Yorkshire. 508,600 (est. 1956).

leek (lēk), n. 1. a plant of the lily family, Allium Porrum, allied to the onion but having a cylindrical bulb, and used in cookery. 2. any of various allied species. [ME; OE lēac, c. G lauch]

leek-green (lēk'grēn'), adj. dull bluish-green.

leer (lĭr), n. 1. a side glance, esp. of sly or insulting suggestion or malicious significance. —v.i. 2. to look with a leer. [? v. use of obs. leer cheek, OE hlēor] —**leer'ing·ly,** adv.

leer·y (lĭr'ĭ), adj. Slang. 1. wary. 2. knowing.

lees (lēz), n. pl. of lee².

lee shore, a shore toward which the wind blows.

leet (lēt), n. Brit., Archaic. 1. a special type of manorial court or its jurisdiction. 2. its meeting day. [ME lete, t. AF, ? t. OE: m. lǣth landed property]

lee tide, a tidal current running in the direction toward which the wind is blowing. Also, **leeward tide.**

Leeu·wen·hoek (lā'vən hŏŏk'), n. **Anton van** (än'tŏn vän), 1632–1723, Dutch naturalist and maker of microscopes.

lee·ward (lē'wərd; Naut. lŏŏ'ərd), adj. 1. pertaining to, situated in, or moving toward the quarter toward which the wind blows (opposed to windward). —n. 2. the lee side; the point or quarter toward which the wind blows. —adv. 3. toward the lee.

Lee·ward Islands (lē'wərd), 1. a group of islands in the N Lesser Antilles of the West Indies, extending from Puerto Rico SE to Martinique. 2. a former British colony now divided into the four colonies of Antigua, St. Kitts, and Montserrat (in the Federation of the West Indies) and the British Virgin Islands.

lee·way (lē'wā'), n. 1. the lateral movement of a ship to leeward, or the resulting deviation from her true course. 2. Aeron. the amount a plane is blown off its normal course by cross winds. 3. Colloq. extra space, time, money, etc.

left¹ (lĕft), adj. 1. belonging or pertaining to the side of a person or thing which is turned toward the west when facing north (opposed to right). —n. 2. the left side, or what is on the left side. 3. (in continental Europe) that part of a legislative assembly which sits on the left side of the chamber as viewed by the president, a position customarily assigned to representatives holding socialistic or radical views. 4. (often cap.) a party holding such views. [ME; special use of d. OE left (OE lyft) weak, infirm. Cf. MD and MLG lucht]

left² (lĕft), v. pt. and pp. of leave¹.

left-hand (lĕft'hănd'), adj. 1. on or to the left. 2. of, for, or with the left hand.

left-hand·ed (lĕft'hăn'dĭd), adj. 1. having the left hand more serviceable than the right; preferably using the left hand. 2. adapted to or performed by the left hand. 3. situated on the side of the left hand. 4. moving or rotating from right to left. 5. ambiguous or doubtful: a left-handed compliment. 6. clumsy or awkward. 7. morganatic (from the bridegroom's giving the bride his left hand instead of his right as was customary at morganatic weddings). —**left'-hand'ed·ly,** adv. —**left'-hand'ed·ness,** n.

left·ist (lĕf'tĭst), n. 1. a member of a socialistic or radical party or a person sympathizing with their views. —adj. 2. having socialistic or radical political ideas. [f. LEFT¹ (def. 3) + -IST]

left·o·ver (lĕft'ō'vər), n. 1. something left over or remaining. 2. a remnant of food, as from a meal.

left·ward (lĕft'wərd), adv. 1. Also, **left'wards.** toward or on the left. —adj. 2. situated on the left. 3. directed toward the left.

---

left wing, 1. members of a socialistic or radical political party, or those favoring extensive political reform. **2.** such a group, party, or a group of such parties. —left′wing′, adj. —left′-wing′er, n.

leg (lĕg), n., v., **legged, legging.** —n. **1.** one of the members or limbs which support and move the human or animal body. **2.** that part of the limb between the knee and the ankle. **3.** something resembling or suggesting a leg in use, position, or appearance. **4.** that part of a garment, such as a stocking, trousers, or the like, which covers the leg. **5.** one of the supports of a piece of furniture. **6.** one of the sides of a pair of dividers or compasses. **7.** one of the sides of a triangle other than the base or hypotenuse. **8.** a timber, bar, etc., serving to prop or shore up a structure. **9.** one of the distinct portions of any course: *the last leg of a trip.* **10.** *Naut.* **a.** one of the series of straight runs which make up the zigzag course of a sailing ship. **b.** one straight or nearly straight part of a multiple-sided course in a sailing race. **11.** *Sports.* the first part of a contest successfully completed, when a second or third part is required to determine the winner. **12.** *Cricket.* **a.** the part of the field to the left of and behind the batsman as he faces the bowler (or to the right of and behind him if he is left-handed). **b.** the fielder occupying this part of the field. **13. have not a leg to stand on,** not to have any good reason at all. **14. pull (one's) leg,** to make fun of (one); to tease. **15. shake a leg,** *Slang.* to hurry up. —v. **16. leg it,** *Colloq.* to walk or run. [ME, t. Scand.; cf. Icel. *leggr*] —leg′less, adj.

leg., 1. legal. **2.** legate. **3.** legato. **4.** legislative. **5.** legislature.

leg·a·cy (lĕg′ə sĭ), n., pl. **-cies. 1.** *Law.* a gift of property, esp. personal property, as money, by will; a bequest. **2.** anything handed down by an ancestor or predecessor. [ME *legacie*, t. OF: legateship, t. ML: m.s. *lēgātia*, der. L *lēgātus* LEGATE]

le·gal (lē′gəl), adj. **1.** appointed, established, or authorized by law; deriving authority from law. **2.** of or pertaining to law; connected with the law or its administration: *the legal profession.* **3.** permitted by law, or lawful: *such acts are not legal.* **4.** recognized by law rather than by equity. **5.** characteristic of the profession of the law: *a legal mind.* **6.** *Theol.* **a.** of or pertaining to the Mosaic law. **b.** of or pertaining to the doctrine of salvation by good works rather than through free grace. —n. **7.** (pl.) legally authorized investments which may be made by fiduciaries as savings banks, trustees, etc. [t. L: s. *lēgālis* pertaining to law] —le′gal·ly, adv.

legal cap, *U.S.* ruled writing paper made in long sheets, with the fold at the top, for lawyers' use.

le·gal·ism (lē′gə lĭz′əm), n. **1.** strict adherence, or the principle of strict adherence, to law or prescription. **2.** *Theol.* the doctrine of salvation by good works. —le′gal·ist, n. —le′gal·is′tic, adj.

le·gal·i·ty (lĭ găl′ə tĭ), n., pl. **-ties. 1.** state or quality of being in conformity with the law; lawfulness. **2.** attachment to or observance of law. **3.** *Theol.* reliance on good works for salvation, rather than on free grace.

le·gal·ize (lē′gə lĭz′), v.t., **-ized, -izing.** to make legal; authorize; sanction. —le′gal·i·za′tion, n.

Le Gal·lienne (lə găl yĕn′, găl′yən), **1.** Eva, born 1899, U.S. actress and director. **2.** her father, Richard, 1866-1947, British poet and writer.

legal reserve, *Banking.* cash assets of Federal Reserve banks, member banks, savings banks, etc., held in accordance with provisions established in law.

legal separation, *Law.* a judicial act effecting a limited divorce.

legal tender, *Law.* currency which may be lawfully tendered or offered in payment of money debts and which may not be refused by creditors.

Le·gas·pi (lĕ gäs′pĭ), n. a seaport in the Philippine Islands, on SE Luzon. 78,828 (1948). Formerly, **Albay.**

leg·ate (lĕg′ĭt), n. **1.** an ecclesiastic delegated by the Pope as his representative. **2.** *Rom. Hist.* **a.** an assistant to a general or to a consul or magistrate, in the government of any army or a province; a commander of a legion. **b.** a provincial governor of senatorial rank appointed by the emperor. **3.** an envoy. [ME *legat*, t. L: s. *lēgātus* deputy, prop. pp., deputed] —leg′ate·ship′, n.

leg·a·tee (lĕg′ə tē′), n. one to whom a legacy is bequeathed.

le·ga·tion (lĭ gā′shən), n. **1.** a diplomatic minister and his staff when the minister is not of the highest (or ambassadorial) rank. **2.** the official residence or place of business of a minister. **3.** the office or position of a legate. [late ME, t. L: s. *lēgātio* embassy] —le·ga·tion·ar·y (lĭ gā′shə nĕr′ĭ), adj.

le·ga·to (lĭ gä′tō; *It.* lĕ gä′tō), adj. *Music.* smooth and connected, without breaks between the successive tones (opposed to *staccato*). [t. It., pp. of *legare*, g. L *ligāre* bind]

leg·a·tor (lĭ gā′tər, lĕg′ə tōr′), n. one who bequeaths; a testator. —leg·a·to·ri·al (lĕg′ə tōr′ĭ əl), adj.

leg·end (lĕj′ənd), n. **1.** a nonhistorical or unverifiable story handed down by tradition from earlier times and popularly accepted as historical. **2.** matter of this kind. **3.** an inscription, esp. on a coin, a coat of arms, a monument, or under a picture, or the like. **4.** a story of the life of a saint. **5.** *Obs. except Hist.* a collection of such stories. **6.** a collection of stories of any admirable person. [ME *legende*, t. OF, t. ML: m. *legenda*, lit., things to be read, orig. neut. pl. gerundive of L *legere* read]

—**Syn. 1.** LEGEND, FABLE, MYTH refer to fictitious stories, usually handed down by tradition (though some fables are modern). LEGEND, originally denoting a story concerning the life of a saint, is applied to any fictitious story, sometimes involving the supernatural, and usually concerned with a real person, place, or other subject: *the legend of St. Andrew.* A FABLE is specifically a fictitious story (often with animals or inanimate things as speakers or actors) designed to teach a moral: *a fable about industrious bees.* A MYTH is one of a class of stories, usually concerning gods, heroes, imaginary animals, etc., current since primitive times, the purpose of which is to attempt to explain some belief or natural phenomenon: *the Greek myth about Demeter.* —Ant. **1.** fact.

leg·end·ar·y (lĕj′ən dĕr′ĭ), adj., n., pl. **-aries.** —adj. **1.** pertaining to or of the nature of a legend or legends. **2.** celebrated or described in legend. —n. **3.** a collection of legends.

Le·gen·dre (lə zhäN′dr), n. **Adrien Marie** (á drĕăN′ mȧrē′), 1752-1833, French mathematician.

leg·end·ry (lĕj′ən drĭ), n. legends collectively.

Lé·ger (lĕ zhĕ′), n. **Fernand** (fĕr näN′), 1881-1955, French artist.

leg·er·de·main (lĕj′ər də mān′), n. **1.** sleight of hand. **2.** trickery; deception. **3.** any artful trick. [ME, t. F: m. *léger de main* light(ness) of hand]

leg·er line (lĕj′ər), *Music.* a short line added when necessary above or below the lines of a staff to increase the range of the staff. Also, **ledger line.** [var. of *ledger line*, f. LEDGER (special use) + LINE[1]]

le·ges (lē′jēz), n. pl. of **lex.**

leg·ged (lĕg′ĭd, lĕgd), adj. having a specified number or kind of legs: *one-legged, long-legged.*

leg·ging (lĕg′ĭng), n. (*usually pl.*) an extra outer covering for the leg, usually extending from the ankle to the knee, but sometimes higher.

leg·gy (lĕg′ĭ), adj. having awkwardly long legs.

Leg·horn (lĕg′hôrn′ for 1–3; lĕg′ərn, -hôrn′ for 4), n. **1.** Livorno. **2.** a fine, smooth, plaited straw. **3.** (*l.c.*) a hat, etc., made of it. **4.** one of a Mediterranean breed of the domestic fowl, characterized by prolific laying of white-shelled eggs.

leg·i·ble (lĕj′ə bəl), adj. **1.** that may be read or deciphered, esp. with ease, as writing or printing. **2.** that may be discerned or distinguished. [ME, t. LL: m.s. *legibilis*, der. L *legere* read] —leg′i·bil′i·ty, leg′i·ble·ness, n. —leg′i·bly, adv.

le·gion (lē′jən), n. **1.** an infantry brigade in the army of ancient Rome, numbering from 3000 to 6000 men, and usually combined with from 300 to 700 cavalry. **2.** a military or semimilitary unit. **3. the Legion, a.** the American Legion. **b.** the French Foreign Legion. **4.** any large body of armed men. **5.** any great host or multitude, whether of persons or of things. [ME, t. OF, t. L: s. *legio*]

le·gion·ar·y (lē′jə nĕr′ĭ), adj., n., pl. **-aries.** —adj. **1.** pertaining or belonging to a legion. **2.** constituting a legion or legions. —n. **3.** *Hist.* a soldier of a legion. **4.** *Brit.* a member of the British Legion (corresponding to the U.S. *legionnaire*).

legionary ant, 1. an army ant. **2.** any driver ant.

le·gion·naire (lē′jə nâr′), n. **1.** (*often cap.*) a member of the American Legion. **2.** legionary. [t. F]

Legion of Honor, a French order of distinction, instituted in 1802 by Napoleon, membership being granted for meritorious civil or military services.

Legis., Legislature.

leg·is·late (lĕj′ĭs lāt′), v., **-lated, -lating.** —v.i. **1.** to exercise the function of legislation; make or enact laws. —v.t. **2.** to effect, bring (*into*), put (*out*), etc., by legislation. [back formation from LEGISLATION or LEGISLATOR]

leg·is·la·tion (lĕj′ĭs lā′shən), n. **1.** act of making or enacting laws. **2.** a law or a body of laws enacted. [t. LL: s. *lēgislātio*, L *lēgis lātio* the proposing of a law]

leg·is·la·tive (lĕj′ĭs lā′tĭv), adj. **1.** having the function of making laws: *a legislative body.* **2.** of or pertaining to legislation: *legislative proceedings.* **3.** ordained by legislation: *a legislative penalty.* **4.** pertaining to a legislature: *a legislative recess.* —n. **5.** the legislature. —leg′is·la′tive·ly, adv.

leg·is·la·tor (lĕj′ĭs lā′tər), n. **1.** one who gives or makes laws. **2.** a member of a legislative body. [t. L: *legis lātor* bringer of a law] —leg·is·la·tress (lĕg′ĭs·lā′trĭs), n. fem.

leg·is·la·to·ri·al (lĕj′ĭs lə tōr′ĭ əl), adj. of or pertaining to legislators or legislations.

leg·is·la·ture (lĕj′ĭs lā′chər), n. the legislative body of a country or state, esp. (in the U.S.) of a State.

le·gist (lē′jĭst), n. one versed in law.

le·git (lə jĭt′), *Slang.* —adj. **1.** legitimate; truthful. —n. **2.** the legitimate theater or stage employing actors in person, as opposed to motion pictures.

le·git·im (lĕj′ə tĭm), n. *Civil Law.* that part of a decedent's estate which must be left to his wife, children, or other relative(s). [t. L: s. *lēgitima (pars)* lawful (part)]

le·git·i·ma·cy (lĭ jĭt′ə mə sĭ), n. state or fact of being legitimate.

le·git·i·mate (adj. lĭ jĭt′ə mĭt; v. lĭ jĭt′ə māt′), adj., v., **-mated, -mating.** —adj. **1.** according to law; lawful.

2. in accordance with established rules, principles, or standards. **3.** of the normal or regular type or kind. **4.** in accordance with the laws of reasoning; logically inferable; logical: *a legitimate conclusion.* **5.** born in wedlock, or of parents legally married. **6.** resting on or ruling by the principle of hereditary right: *a legitimate sovereign.* **7.** genuine; not spurious. —*v.t.* **8.** to make or pronounce lawful. **9.** to establish as lawfully born. **10.** to show or declare to be legitimate or proper. **11.** to authorize; justify. [late ME, t. ML: m. s. *lēgitimātus,* pp. of *lēgitimāre* make lawful, der. L *lēgitimus* lawful] —le·git′i·mate·ly, *adv.* —le·git′i·mate·ness, *n.* —le·git′i·ma′tion, *n.*

legitimate drama, **1.** drama for production on the stage (as opposed to motion pictures). **2.** drama as literature (as distinct from farce and melodrama).

le·git·i·ma·tize (lǐ jǐt′ə mə tīz′), *v.t.,* -tized, -tizing. to legitimate.

le·git·i·mist (lǐ jǐt′ə mǐst), *n.* a supporter of legitimate authority, esp. of a claim to a throne based on direct descent. —le·git′i·mism, *n.* —le·git′i·mis′tic, *adj.*

le·git·i·mize (lǐ jǐt′ə mīz′), *v.t.,* -mized, -mizing. to legitimate. —le·git′i·mi·za′tion, *n.*

leg-of-mut·ton (lĕg′ə mŭt′ən, -əv-), *adj.* having the triangular shape of a leg of mutton, as a sail, sleeve, etc.

Le·gree (lǐ grē′), *n.* **Simon, 1.** the brutal slave dealer in *Uncle Tom's Cabin* by Harriet Beecher Stowe. **2.** a harsh and brutal master.

leg·ume (lĕg′ūm, lǐ gūm′), *n.* **1.** any plant of the family *Leguminosae,* esp. those used for feed, food, or soil-improving crop. **2.** the pod or seed vessel of such a plant, which is usually dehiscent by both sutures, thus dividing into two parts or valves. **3.** any table vegetable of the family *Leguminosae.* [t. F, t. L: m. *legūmen* legume, pulse, lit., something gathered (or picked)]

le·gu·min (lǐ gū′mən), *n.* Biochem. a protein resembling casein, obtained from the seeds of leguminous and other plants. [f. LEGUME + -IN²]

le·gu·mi·nous (lǐ gū′mə nəs), *adj.* **1.** pertaining to, of the nature of, or bearing legumes. **2.** belonging or pertaining to the *Leguminosae,* an order or family regarded as comprising the legume-bearing plants, and sometimes subdivided into the bean, senna, and mimosa families. [f. s. L *legūmen* LEGUME + -OUS]

Le·hár (lā′här), *n.* **Franz** (fränts), 1870–1948, Hungarian composer of operettas.

Le Ha·vre (lə hä′vrə; Fr. lə à′vr), a seaport in N France at the mouth of the Seine. 139,810 (1954). Also, **Havre.**

Le·high (lē′hī), *n.* a river in E Pennsylvania, flowing into the Delaware river. ab. 120 mi.

Leh·man (lē′mən, lā′-), *n.* **Herbert Henry,** 1878–1963, U.S. banker and statesman.

le·hu·a (lā hōō′ä), *n.* **1.** a red-flowered tree, *Metrosideros polymorpha,* common in the Pacific islands and having a hard wood. **2.** the bright-red corymbose flower of this tree, the territorial flower of Hawaii. [t. Hawaiian]

lei¹ (lā′ē, lā), *n., pl.* **leis.** (in the Hawaiian Islands) a wreath of flowers, leaves, etc., for the neck or head. [t. Hawaiian]

lei² (lā), *n.* pl. of **leu.**

Leib·nitz (līb′nǐts; Ger. līp′nǐts), *n.* **Gottfried Wilhelm von** (gôt′frēt vǐl′hělm fən), 1646–1716, German philosopher, writer, and mathematician. Also, **Leib′niz.** —Leib·nitz·i·an (līb nǐt′sǐ ən), *adj., n.*

Leices·ter (lĕs′tər), *n.* **1. Robert Dudley, Earl of,** 1532?–88, English statesman: favorite of Queen Elizabeth. **2.** a city in central England: county seat of Leicestershire. 284,000 (est. 1956). **3.** Leicestershire. **4.** one of a large English variety of early-maturing sheep with coarse, long wool and a heavy mutton yield.

Leices·ter·shire (lĕs′tər shǐr′, -shər), *n.* a county in central England. 631,077 pop. (1951); 832 sq. mi. **Co.** *seat:* Leicester. Also, **Leicester.**

Lei·den (lī′dən), *n.* a city in W Netherlands. 92,734 (est. 1954). Also, **Leyden.**

Leigh·ton (lā′tən), *n.* **Frederic, Baron,** 1830–96, British painter and sculptor.

Lein·ster (lĕn′stər), *n.* a province in E Ireland. 1,336,- 397 (prelim. 1956); 7643 sq. mi.

lei·o·my·o·ma (lī′ō mī ō′mə), *n., pl.* -omata (-ō′mə tə), -omas. a tumor made up of nonstriated muscular tissue. Cf. **rhabdomyoma.** [f. *leio-* t. Gk., comb. form of *leios* smooth) + MYOMA]

Leip·zig (līp′sǐg, -sǐk; Ger. līp′tsıкн), *n.* a city in East Germany, in Saxony. 613,707 (est. 1955). Also, **Leip·sic** (līp′sǐk).

leis·ter (lē′stər), *n.* **1.** a spear having three or more prongs, used to strike a fish. —*v.t.* **2.** to strike (a fish) with a leister. [t. Scand.; cf. Icel. *liōstr,* der. *liōsta* strike]

lei·sure (lē′zhər, lĕzh′ər), *n.* **1.** the condition of having one's time free from the demands of work or duty; ease: *enjoying a life of leisure.* **2.** free or unoccupied time. **3. at leisure, a.** with free or unrestricted time. **b.** without haste. **c.** unengaged; disengaged. **4.** at one's leisure, when one has leisure. —*adj.* **5.** free or unoccupied: *leisure hours.* **6.** having leisure: *the leisure class.* [ME *leiser,* t. OF: m. *leisir* (inf.), g. L *licēre* be permitted]

lei·sure·ly (lē′zhər lǐ, lĕzh′ər-), *adj.* Also, **lei·sured** (lē′zhərd, lĕzh′ərd). **1.** acting, proceeding, or done without haste; deliberate: *a leisurely speech.* **2.** showing

or suggesting ample leisure; unhurried: *a leisurely manner.* —*adv.* **3.** in a leisurely manner; without haste. —lei′sure·li·ness, *n.* —Syn. **1.** See **slow.**

Leith (lēth), *n.* a seaport in SE Scotland, on the Firth of Forth: now a part of Edinburgh.

leit·mo·tif (līt′mō tēf′), *n.* (in a music drama) a motif or theme associated throughout the work with a particular person, situation, or idea. Also, **leit′mo·tiv′.** [t. G: (m.) *leitmotiv* leading motive]

Lek (lĕk), *n.* See **Rhine.**

Le·ly (lē′lǐ; Du. lā′lǐ), *n.* **Sir Peter** (pē′tər; Du. pā′-), (*Pieter van der Faes*) 1618–80, Dutch portrait painter in England.

Le·mai·tre (lə mě′tr), *n.* **François Élie Jules** (fränswà′ ělē′ zhYl′), 1853–1915, French critic and writer.

lem·an (lĕm′ən, lē′mən), *n.* Archaic. **1.** a sweetheart. **2.** a mistress. [ME *lemman,* earlier *leofmon,* f. *leof* dear (see LIEF) + *mon* MAN]

Le·man (lē′mən), *n.* **Lake.** See **Geneva, Lake of.**

Le Mans (lə män′), a city in NW France. 111,891 (1954).

Lem·berg (lĕm′bûrg; Ger. lĕm′běrкн), *n.* German name of **Lwów.**

lem·ma¹ (lĕm′ə), *n., pl.* **lemmas, lemmata** (lĕm′ə tə). **1.** a subsidiary proposition introduced in proving some other proposition; a helping theorem. **2.** an argument, theme, or subject. **3.** the heading of a gloss, annotation, etc. [t. L, t. Gk.: m. *lĕmma* premise]

lem·ma² (lĕm′ə), *n., pl.* **lemmas, lemmata** (lĕm′ə tə). Bot. a bract in a grass spikelet just below the pistil and stamens. [t. Gk.: m. *lĕmma* shell, husk]

Lemming. Lemmus lemmus (6 in. long)

lem·ming (lĕm′ǐng), *n.* any of various small, mouselike rodents of the genera *Lemmus, Myopus,* and *Dicrostonyx,* of far northern regions, as L. *lemmus,* of Norway, Sweden, etc. [t. Norw.]

Lem·nos (lĕm′nŏs; Gk. lĕm′nŏs), *n.* a Greek island in the NE Aegean. 24,016 pop. (1951); 186 sq. mi. *Cap.:* Kastro. —Lem·ni·an (lĕm′nǐ on), *adj., n.*

lem·on (lĕm′ən), *n.* **1.** the yellowish acid fruit of the subtropical rutaceous tree, *Citrus Limon.* **2.** the tree itself. **3.** clear, light yellow color. **4.** *Slang.* something distasteful, disappointing, or unpleasant. —*adj.* **5.** having a clear, light yellow color. [ME *lymon,* t. OF: m. *limon,* t. Ar., Pers.: m. *līmūn*]

lem·on·ade (lĕm′ə nād′), *n.* **1.** a beverage consisting of lemon juice mixed with water and sweetened. **2.** *Brit.* lemon soda, usually in bottles. Also, *Brit.,* **lemon squash.** [t. F: m. *limonade,* der. *limon* LEMON]

lemon geranium, Bot. a hybrid plant, *Pelargonium Limoneum,* whose leaves give off a lemon fragrance.

lemon verbena, a verbenaceous garden shrub, *Lippia citriodora,* with long, slender leaves that have a lemonlike fragrance.

Lem·pert operation (lĕm′pərt), Surg. fenestration. [named after *Julius Lempert,* born 1890, American otologist who devised it]

lem·pi·ra (lĕm pē′rä), *n.* the monetary unit and gold coin of Honduras, stabilized in 1926 as equal to 50 cents in the U.S. [t. Amer. Sp.; named after a native chief]

le·mur (lē′mər), *n.* any of various small, arboreal, chiefly nocturnal mammals, esp. of the genus *Lemur,* allied to the monkeys, usually having a foxlike face and woolly fur, and found chiefly in Madagascar. [t. NL, der. L *lemures, pl.,* ghosts, specters; so called because of nocturnal habits. Cf. LEMURES] —le′mur·like′, *adj.*

lem·u·res (lĕm′yə rēz′), *n.pl.* (among the ancient Romans) the spirits of the departed. [t. L. Cf. LEMUR]

lem·u·roid (lĕm′yə roid′), *adj.* **1.** lemurlike; of the lemur kind. —*n.* **2.** a lemur.

Lemur. Lemur catta (Ab. 3¼ ft. long)

Le·na (lē′nə; Russ. lǐ′nä), *n.* a river flowing from near Lake Baikal, in the S Soviet Union in Asia, through the Yakutsk Republic into the Arctic Ocean. ab. 2800 mi.

lend (lĕnd), *v.,* lent, lending. —*v.t.* **1.** to give the temporary use of (money, etc.) for a consideration. **2.** to grant the use of (something) with the understanding that it (or its equivalent in kind) shall be returned. **3.** to furnish or impart: *distance lends enchantment to the view.* **4.** to give or contribute obligingly or helpfully: *to lend one's aid to a cause.* **5.** to adapt (oneself or itself) to something. —*v.i.* **6.** to make a loan or loans. [ME *lende;* r. ME *lene(n),* OE *lænan,* der. *læn* loan] —lend′er, *n.*

Lend-Lease Act (lĕnd′lēs′), an act of Congress (Mar. 11, 1941) enabling the U.S. government to furnish material aid to nations at war with Germany and Italy.

L'En·fant (län fän′), *n.* **Pierre Charles** (pyěr shärl), 1754–1825, French engineer: planned Washington, D.C.

length (lĕngkth, lĕngth), *n.* **1.** the linear magnitude of anything as measured from end to end: *the length of a river.* **2.** extent from beginning to end of a series, enumeration, account, book, etc. **3.** extent in time; duration: *the length of a battle.* **4.** a distance determined by the length of something specified: *to hold a thing at arm's length.* **5.** a piece or portion of a certain or a known length: *a length of rope.* **6.** a stretch or extent of something, esp. a long stretch. **7.** the extent, or an extent, of going, proceeding, etc. **8.** the quality or fact of being long rather than short: *a journey remarkable for its length.* **9.** the measure from end to end of a horse, boat, etc., as a unit of distance in racing: *a horse wins by two lengths.* **10.** *Pros. and Phonet.* **a.** (of a vowel or syllable) quantity (whether long or short). **b.** the quality of vowels. **11. at length, a.** to or in the full extent. **b.** after a time; in the end. [ME and OE, der. *lang* LONG[1]. See -TH[1]]

length·en (lĕngk′thən, lĕng′-), *v.t.* **1.** to make greater in length. —*v.i.* **2.** to become greater in length. —**Syn. 1.** LENGTHEN, EXTEND, STRETCH, PROLONG, PROTRACT agree in the idea of making longer. To LENGTHEN is to make longer, either in a material or an immaterial sense: *to lengthen a dress.* To EXTEND is to lengthen beyond some original point or so as to reach a certain point: *to extend a railway line by a hundred miles.* To STRETCH is primarily to lengthen by drawing or tension: *to stretch a rubber band.* Both PROLONG and PROTRACT mean esp. to lengthen in time, and therefore apply to intangibles. To PROLONG is to continue beyond the desired, estimated, or allotted time: *to prolong an interview.* To PROTRACT is to draw out to undue length or to be slow in coming to a conclusion: *to protract a discussion.* —**Ant. 1.** shorten.

length·ways (lĕngkth′wāz′, lĕngth′-), *adv.* lengthwise.

length·wise (lĕngkth′wīz′, lĕngth′-), *adv., adj.* in the direction of the length.

length·y (lĕngk′thĭ, lĕng′-), *adj.,* **length·i·er, length·i·est.** having or being of great length, esp. speeches, writings, etc. —**length′i·ly,** *adv.* —**length′i·ness,** *n.*

le·ni·en·cy (lē′nĭ ən sĭ, lēn′yən-), *n.* the quality of being lenient. Also, **le′ni·ence.**

le·ni·ent (lē′nĭ ənt, lēn′yənt), *adj.* **1.** mild, clement, or merciful, as in treatment, spirit, or tendency; gentle. **2.** *Archaic.* softening, soothing, or alleviative. [t. L: s. *lēniens,* ppr., softening] —**le′ni·ent·ly,** *adv.*

Len·in (lĕn′ĭn), *n.* **Nikolai** (nĭ kŏ′lĭ), (*Vladimir Ilich Ulyanov*) 1870–1924, Russian revolutionary leader and writer. He was the chief leader of the 1917 Revolution, and head of the Soviet government from 1917 to 1924.

Le·ni·na·kan (lĕ′nĭ nä kän′), *n.* a city in the SW Soviet Union, in the Armenian Republic. 103,000 (est. 1956). Formerly, **Aleksandropol.**

Len·in·grad (lĕn′ĭn grād′; *Rus.* lĕ′nĭn grät′), *n.* a seaport in the NW Soviet Union: capital of the Russian Empire, 1703–1917. 3,176,000 (est. 1956). Formerly, **St. Petersburg** or **Petrograd.**

Len·in·ism (lĕn′ĭ nĭz′əm), *n.* Russian communism as taught by Nikolai Lenin, with emphasis on the "dictatorship of the proletariat."

le·nis (lē′nĭs), *adj., n., pl.* **lenes** (lē′nēz). *Phonet.* —*adj.* **1.** pronounced with relatively weak muscular tension and breath pressure, resulting in weak sound effect: thus, in *potato* the second *t* is lenis; the first, fortis. —*n.* **2.** a lenis consonant. [t. L: gentle]

le·ni·tion (lĭ nĭsh′ən), *n.* *Phonet.* a weakening of the articulation of a consonant, often leading to radical sound changes and even to loss of the sound. [f. LENI(S) + -TION]

len·i·tive (lĕn′ə tĭv), *adj.* **1.** softening, soothing, or mitigating, as medicines or applications. **2.** mildly laxative. —*n.* **3.** a lenitive medicine or application; a mild laxative. **4.** *Rare.* anything that softens or soothes.

len·i·ty (lĕn′ə tĭ), *n., pl.* **-ties. 1.** the quality or fact of being mild or gentle, as toward others. **2.** a lenient act. [t. L: m.s. *lēnitas*]

le·no (lē′nō), *adj.* (of a weave) having the warp yarns woven in twisted pairs between the filling yarns, usually in a light, gauzy fabric.

lens (lĕnz), *n., pl.* **lenses. 1.** a piece of transparent substance, usually glass, having two (or two main) opposite surfaces, either both curved or one curved and one plane, used for changing the convergence of light rays, as in magnifying, or in correcting errors of vision. **2.** a combination of such pieces. **3.** some analogous device, as for affecting sound waves, electromagnetic radiation, or streams of electrons. **4.** *Anat.* a part of the eye, a crystalline lens (which is shaped like a convexo-convex lens)]

Lenses (def. 1)

A, Plano-concave; B, Biconcave (concavo-concave); C, Plano-convex; D, Biconvex (convexo-convex); E, The meniscus (converging convexo-concave, or converging meniscus); F, Concavo-convex

lent (lĕnt), *v.* pt. and pp. of **lend.**

Lent (lĕnt), *n.* **1.** an annual season of fasting and penitence in preparation for Easter, beginning on Ash Wednesday and including the forty weekdays next before Easter, observed by the Roman Catholic, Anglican, and other churches. **2.** (in the Middle Ages) a period from Martinmas (Nov. 11) to Christmas, known as St. Martin's Lent. [ME *lente(n)*, OE *len(c)ten* spring, Lent; akin to D *lente* spring, G *lenz*]

len·ta·men·te (lĕn′tä mĕn′tĕ), *adv.* *Music.* slowly. [It., der. *lento* LENTO]

len·tan·do (lĕn tän′dō), *adj.* *Music.* becoming slower. [It. ger. of *lentare* slacken, der. L *lentus* slow]

Lent·en (lĕn′tən), *adj.* (*often l.c.*) of, pertaining to, or suitable for Lent. [f. LENT + -EN[2]]

len·ti·cel (lĕn′tə sĕl′), *n.* *Bot.* a body of cells formed in the periderm of a stem, appearing on the surface of the plant as a lens-shaped spot, and serving as a pore. [t. NL: m.s. *lenticella,* var. of L *lenticula* LENTIL]

len·tic·u·lar (lĕn tĭk′yə lər), *adj.* **1.** of or pertaining to a lens. **2.** convexo-convex. **3.** resembling a lentil (seed) in form. [t. L: s. *lenticulāris* lentil-shaped]

len·ti·go (lĕn tī′gō), *n., pl.* **-tigines** (-tĭj′ə nēz′). *Med.* a freckle. [t. L, der. *lens* a lentil]

len·til (lĕn′tĭl), *n.* **1.** an annual plant, *Lens culinaris,* having flattened, convexo-convex seeds which constitute a food similar to peas and beans. **2.** the seed. [ME *lentille,* t. F, g. L *lenticula,* dim. of *lens* a lentil]

len·tis·si·mo (lĕn tĭs′ə mō′; *It.* lĕn tēs′sē mō′). *Music.* —*adj.* **1.** very slow. —*adv.* **2.** very slowly. [It., der. *lento* LENTO]

len·to (lĕn′tō). *Music.* —*adj.* **1.** slow. —*adv.* **2.** slowl [It., g. L *lentus*]

l'en·voi (lĕn′voi, lĕn voi′; *Fr.* län vwå′), *n.* the envoy of a poetical or prose composition. Also, **l'en′voy.** [t. OF: (m.) *l'envoy,* lit., the sending. See ENVOY[1]]

Le·o (lē′ō), *n., gen.* **Leonis** (lĭ ō′nĭs). **1.** a zodiacal constellation; the Lion. **2.** the fifth sign of the zodiac. See diag. under **zodiac.** [t. L. See LION]

Le·o I (lē′ō; *It.* lā′ō). **Saint,** ("*Leo the Great*") died A.D. 461, Italian cleric; pope, A.D. 440–461.

Leo III. Saint, died A.D. 816, Italian ecclesiastic; pope, A.D. 795–816.

Leo X, (*Giovanni de'Medici*) 1475–1521, Italian ecclesiastic; pope, 1513–21.

Leo XIII, (*Gioacchino Pecci*) 1810–1903, Italian ecclesiastic; pope, 1878–1903.

Leom·in·ster (lĕm′ĭn stər), *n.* a city in N Massachusetts. 27,929 (1960).

Le·ón (lĕ ôn′), *n.* **1.** a province in NW Spain: formerly a kingdom. 574,262 (est. 1955); 5936 sq. mi. **2.** the capital of this province. 64,178 (est. 1955). **3.** a city in central Mexico, in Guanajuato state. 121,663 (1951). **4.** a city in W Nicaragua: the former capital. 30,544 (1950).

Le·o·nar·desque (lē′ə när dĕsk′), *adj.* resembling the manner of Leonardo da Vinci.

Le·o·nar·do (lē′ə när′dō, lā′ō när′dō), *n.* See **Vinci.**

Le·on·ca·val·lo (lĕ ōn′kä väl′lō), *n.* **Ruggiero** (rōōd-jĕ′rō), 1858–1919, Italian operatic composer.

Le·o·nid (lē′ə nĭd), *n., pl.* **Leonids, Leonides** (lĭ ŏn′ə dēz′). *Astron.* any of a shower of meteors occurring about Nov. 15 and appearing to radiate from Leo. [back formation from *Leonides,* pl., t. L. See LEO, -ID[1]]

Le·on·i·das (lĭ ŏn′ə dəs), *n.* died 480 B.C., Spartan king, 491?–480 B.C., slain in the battle of Thermopylae.

le·o·nine (lē′ə nīn′), *adj.* **1.** of or pertaining to the lion. **2.** lionlike. [ME *leonyne,* t. L: m.s. *leōninus*]

leop·ard (lĕp′ərd), *n.* **1.** a large, ferocious, spotted Asiatic or African carnivore, *Panthera pardus,* of the cat family, usually tawny, with black markings; the Old World panther. **2.** any of various related animals, as the jaguar (**American leopard**), the cheetah (**hunting leopard**), and the ounce (**snow leopard**). **3.** *Her.* a lion pictured as walking with his head turned toward the spectator, one front paw usually raised. [ME, t. OF, t. LL: s. *leopardus,* t. LGk.: m. *leópardos.* See LION, PARD[1]] —**leop·ard·ess** (lĕp′ər dĭs), *n. fem.*

Leopard and leopardess, *Panthera pardus*
(Total length 7 ft., tail 1½ ft.)

Le·o·par·di (lē′ō pär′dē), *n.* **Count Giacomo** (jä′kō-mō′), 1798–1837, Italian poet.

Le·o·pold I (lē′ə pōld′), **1.** 1640–1705, emperor of the Holy Roman Empire, 1658–1705. **2.** 1790–1865, king of Belgium, 1831–65.

Leopold II, 1. 1747–92, emperor of the Holy Roman Empire, 1790–92. **2.** 1835–1909, king of Belgium, 1865–1909.

Leopold III, born 1901, king of Belgium, 1934–1951.

Le·o·pold·ville (lē′ə pōld vĭl′; *Fr.* lĕ ō pōld vēl′), *n.* former name of **Kinshasa.**

le·o·tard (lē′ə tärd′), *n.* a close-fitting, sleeveless garment with a low neck and tight fits, worn by acrobats, dancers, etc.

Le·pan·to (lĭ păn′tō; *It.* lĕ′pän tō′), *n.* **1.** a seaport in W Greece, on the **Strait of Lepanto,** a strait opening into the Gulf of Corinth: Turkish seapower here destroyed here in a famous naval battle, 1571. **2. Gulf of.** See **Corinth, Gulf of.**

lep·er (lĕp′ər), *n.* a person affected with leprosy. [ME *lepre,* t. OF: leprosy, t. L: m. *lepra,* t. Gk., prop. fem. of *leprós* scaly]

leper house, a hospital or asylum for lepers.

lepido-, a word element meaning "scale," used esp. in scientific terms. [t. Gk., comb. form of *lepis* scale]

le·pid·o·lite (lĭ pĭd′ə lĭt′, lĕp′ə də lĭt′), *n.* a mineral of the mica group, potassium lithium aluminum silicate, commonly occurring in lilac, rose-colored, or grayish-white scaly masses. [f. LEPIDO- + -LITE]

lep·i·dop·ter·on (lĕp'ə dŏp'tər ən), n., pl. **-tera** (-tər ə). any lepidopterous insect.

lep·i·dop·ter·ous (lĕp'ə dŏp'tər əs), adj. belonging or pertaining to the *Lepidoptera*, an order of insects comprising the butterflies, moths, and skippers, which in the adult state have four membranous wings more or less covered with small scales. Also, **lep'i·dop'ter·al**. [f. s. NL *Lepidoptera*, pl., having wings + -OUS. See LEPIDO-, -PTEROUS] —**lep'i·dop'ter·an**, adj., n.

lep·i·do·si·ren (lĕp'ə dō sī'rən), n. a lungfish, *Lepidosiren paradoxa*, of the Amazon River, South America, having an eel-shaped body. [t. NL, f. Gk.: *lepidosiren* siren]

lep·i·dote (lĕp'ə dōt'), adj. *Bot.* covered with scurfy scales or scaly spots. [t. Gk.: m.s. *lepidōtós* scaly]

Lep·i·dus (lĕp'ə dəs), n. **Marcus Aemilius** (mär'kəs ē mĭl'Ĭ əs), died 13 B.C., Roman politician. Octavian, Antony, and Lepidus formed the second triumvirate.

Le·pon·tine Alps (lĭ pŏn'tīn), a central range of the Alps in S Switzerland and N Italy. Highest peak, Mt. Leone, 11,684.

lep·o·rine (lĕp'ə rīn', -rĭn), adj. *Zool.* of, pertaining to, or resembling the hare. [t. L: m.s. *leporīnus*]

lep·re·chaun (lĕp'rə kôn'), n. *Irish Folklore.* a pygmy, sprite, or goblin. [earlier *lubrican*, t. Irish: m. *lupracān*, metathetic var. of *luchorpán* a pigmy sprite, f. *lu* little + *corpán*, dim. of *corp* body (t. L: m. *corpus*)]

lep·ro·sar·i·um (lĕp'rə sâr'Ĭ əm), n., pl. **-saria** (-sâr'Ĭ ə). a hospital for the treatment of leprosy.

lep·ro·sy (lĕp'rə sĭ), n. a mildly infectious disease due to a microörganism, *Bacillus leprae*, and variously characterized by ulcerations, tubercular nodules, spots of pigmentary excess or deficit, loss of fingers and toes, anesthesia in certain nerve regions, etc. Also, **Hansen's disease**. [f. s. L *leprōsus* leprous + -Y³]

lep·rous (lĕp'rəs), adj. **1.** affected with leprosy. **2.** of or like leprosy. [ME, t. LL: m.s. *leprōsus*, der. L *lepra* leprosy. See LEPER] —**lep'rous·ly**, adv.

lepto-, a combining form meaning "fine," "small," "thin," often occurring in terms of zoölogy and botany. [t. Gk., comb. form of *leptós*]

lep·ton (lĕp'tŏn), n., pl. **-ta** (-tə). a minor modern Greek coin equal to one hundredth of a drachma. [t. Gk., prop. neut. of *leptós* small]

lep·to·phyl·lous (lĕp'tō fĭl'əs), adj. having long, slender leaves. [f. LEPTO- + -PHYLLOUS]

lep·tor·rhine (lĕp'tər rĭn), adj. *Anthropol.* having a narrow and a high-bridged nose. [f. LEPTO- + m.s. Gk. *rhís* nose]

Ler·mon·tov (lĕr'mən tôf'), n. **Mikhail Yurievich** (mĭ hä ēl' yōōr'yə vĭch), 1814–41, Russian author.

Ler·ner (lûr'nər), n. **Max**, born 1902, U.S. author.

le roi est mort, vive le roi! (lə rwä ĕ môr', vēv lə rwä'), *French.* the king is dead, long live the king!

Le Sage (lə säzh'), **Alain René** (á lăn' rə nā'), 1668–1747, French novelist and dramatist.

Les·bi·an (lĕz'bĬ ən), adj. **1.** of or pertaining to Lesbos. **2.** erotic (from the reputed character of the ancient inhabitants of Lesbos and the tone of their poetry). —n. **3.** an inhabitant of Lesbos. **4.** (l.c.) one addicted to Lesbianism.

Les·bi·an·ism (lĕz'bĬ ə nĭz'əm), n. homosexual relations between women.

Les·bos (lĕz'bŏs; Gk. lĕz'vôs), n. ancient and modern name of Mytilene (def. 1).

Les Cayes (lĕ kĕ'), a seaport on the SW coast of Haiti. 11,608 (1950). Formerly, **Aux Cayes**.

lese maj·es·ty (lēz' măj'Ĭs tĭ), *Law.* any crime or offense against the sovereign power in a state. [t. F: m. *lèse-majesté*, t. L: m. *laesa mājestas* injured sovereignty]

le·sion (lē'zhən), n. **1.** an injury; a hurt; a wound. **2.** *Pathol.* any localized, morbid structural change in the body. [late ME, t. ML: s. *lēsio*, L *laesio* an injury]

Les Mi·sé·ra·bles (lĕ mē zē rà'bl), a novel (1862) by Victor Hugo.

less (lĕs), adv. **1.** to a smaller extent, amount, or degree: *less exact.* —adj. **2.** smaller in size, amount, degree, etc.; not so large, great, or much: *less speed.* **3.** lower in consideration, dignity, or importance: *no less a person than the manager.* —n. **4.** a smaller amount or quantity. —prep. **5.** minus; without: *a year less two days.* [ME; OE *lǣs(sa)*, c. OFris. *lēs(sa)* less; a compar. form (positive lacking, superl. *least*)] —**Syn. 2.** See **less, fewer.**

-less, a suffix of adjectives meaning "without," as in *childless, peerless.* In adjectives derived from verbs, it indicates failure or inability to perform or be performed, e.g., *resistless, countless.* [ME *-les*, OE *-lēas*, repr. *lēas*, adj., free from, without, c. Icel. *lauss* free, LOOSE]

les·see (lĕ sē'), n. one to whom a lease is granted. —**les·see'ship,** n.

less·en (lĕs'ən), v.i. **1.** to become less. —v.t. **2.** to make less. **3.** to represent as less; depreciate; disparage. —**Syn. 1.** decrease, diminish. **3.** reduce.

Les·seps (lĕs'əps; Fr. lĕ sĕps'), n. **Viscount Ferdinand de** (fĕr dē nän' də), 1805–94, French diplomat, promoter of the construction of the Suez Canal.

less·er (lĕs'ər), adj. **1.** less; smaller, as in size, amount, importance, etc.: *a lesser evil.* **2.** being the smaller of less important of two. [late ME, f. LESS + -ER⁴]

Lesser Antilles. See Antilles.

Lesser Bear, *Astron.* Ursa Minor.

Lesser Dog, *Astron.* Canis Minor.

Les·sing (lĕs'Ĭng), n. **Gotthold Ephraim** (gôt'hôlt ā'frä Ĭm), 1729–81, German critic and dramatist.

les·son (lĕs'ən), n. **1.** something to be learned or studied: *a music lesson.* **2.** a part of a book or the like assigned to a pupil for study: *the lesson for today is on page 22.* **3.** a useful or salutary piece of practical wisdom imparted or learned: *this experience taught me a lesson.* **4.** something from which one learns or should learn, as an instructive or warning example: *this experience was a lesson to me.* **5.** a reproof or punishment intended to teach one better ways. **6.** a portion of Scripture or other sacred writing read, or appointed to be read, at divine service. —v.t. **7.** to admonish or reprove. [ME, t. OF: m. *leçon*, g. L *lectio* a reading]

les·sor (lĕs'ôr, lĕ sôr'), n. one who grants a lease.

lest (lĕst), conj. **1.** for fear that; that . . . not; so that . . . not. **2.** (after words expressing fear, danger, etc.) that: *there was danger lest the plan become known.* [ME *leste*, late OE *the lǣste*, earlier *thȳ lǣs the* lest (lit., whereby less that; *the* is the relative particle)]

let¹ (lĕt), v., **let, letting,** n. —v.t. **1.** to allow or permit. **2.** to allow to pass, go, or come. **3.** to cause or allow to escape. **4.** to grant the occupancy or use of (land, buildings, rooms, space, etc., or movable property) for rent or hire (occasionally fol. by *out*). **5.** to contract for performance: *to let work to a carpenter.* **6.** to cause or make: *to let one know.* **7.** (as an auxiliary used to propose or order): *let me see.* **8.** to disappoint; fail (fol. by *down*). **9. let on, a.** to allow to be known. **b.** *Colloq.* to pretend. —v.i. **10.** to be rented or leased. **11.** *Colloq.* to be dismissed or ended, as school (fol. by *out*). **12.** *Colloq.* to cease; stop (fol. by *up*). —n. **13.** *Brit.* a lease. [ME *leten*, OE *lǣtan*, c. D *laten*, G *lassen*; akin to LATE] —**Syn. 1.** LET, LEAVE, though not synonyms, are often confused, LEAVE being the one used more frequently in both meanings. A further confusion of the verb LEAVE with the noun LEAVE may have helped to perpetuate the misuse. (The noun LEAVE, meaning "permission," might readily be associated with LET, whose most common meaning is "permit" or "allow." The verb LEAVE, however, does not have a meaning of "permit" or "allow"; its most common meaning is "to go away from.") In the constructions in which the confusion arises, it should be noted that, although either verb can take a noun object, only LET can take the infinitive (with *to* not expressed). In certain idiomatic expressions, the two verbs are used in parallel constructions, but the meanings differ widely: LET it out means "allow it to escape" (as the breath), but LEAVE it out means "omit it" (as a sentence). LET him alone means "allow him to be without interference" (don't bother him), but LEAVE him alone means "go away, so that he will be alone." See **allow.**

let² (lĕt), n., v., **letted** or **let, letting.** —n. **1.** *Archaic.* hindrance or obstruction; an impediment or obstacle: *without let or hindrance.* **2.** *Tennis.* an interference with the course of the ball (of some kind specified in the rules) on account of which the stroke or point must be played over again. —v.t. **3.** *Archaic.* to hinder; stand in the way of. [ME *letten*, OE *lettan*, (der. *lǣt* slow, tardy, LATE), c. Icel. *letja* hinder]

-let, a diminutive suffix, e.g., *kinglet*, used often for little objects, e.g., *frontlet, bracelet.* [t. OF: m. *-elet*, f. *-el* (sometimes g. L *-ellus*, dim. suffix, sometimes g. L *-āle*, neut. See -AL¹) + -ET]

l'é·tat, c'est moi (lĕ tá', sĕ mwá'), *French.* I am the state (supposed to have been said by Louis XIV).

let·down (lĕt'doun'), n. **1.** a decrease in some exertion of force or energy: *a letdown in sales.* **2.** disillusion or disappointment. **3.** a humbling or deflating.

le·thal (lē'thəl), adj. of, pertaining to, or such as to cause death; deadly. [t. L: s. *lēt(h)ālis*]

le·thar·gic (lĭ thär'jĭk), adj. **1.** pertaining to or affected with lethargy; drowsy; sluggish. **2.** producing lethargy. Also, **le·thar'gi·cal.** —**le·thar'gi·cal·ly**, adv.

leth·ar·gy (lĕth'ər jĭ), n., pl. **-gies. 1.** a state of drowsy dullness or suspension of the faculties and energies; apathetic or sluggish inactivity. **2.** *Pathol.* a morbid state or a disorder characterized by overpowering drowsiness or sleep. [t. L: m.s. *lēthargia*, t. Gk.: forgetfulness; r. ME *litargie*, t. ML: m. *litargia*]

Le·the (lē'thĭ), n. **1.** *Gk. Myth.* a river in Hades, whose water caused forgetfulness of the past in those who drank of it. **2.** forgetfulness; oblivion. [t. L, t. Gk.: lit., forgetfulness] —**Le·the·an** (lĭ the'ən), adj.

Le·to (lē'tō), n. *Gk. Myth.* the mother by Zeus of Apollo and Artemis.

l'é·toile du nord (lĕ twäl' dy nôr'), *French.* the star of the north (motto of Minnesota).

Lett (lĕt), n. **1.** one of a people living on and near the eastern coast of the Baltic Sea, closely related to the Lithuanians. **2.** the Lettish language.

let·ter (lĕt'ər), n. **1.** a communication in writing or printing addressed to a person or a number of persons. **2.** one of the marks or signs conventionally used in writing and printing to represent speech sounds; an alphabetic character. **3.** a printing type bearing such a mark or character. **4.** a particular style of type. **5.** such types collectively. **6.** actual terms or wording, as distinct from general meaning or intent. **7.** (pl.) literature in general; belles-lettres. **8.** (pl.) the profession of literature, or authorship: *a man of letters.* **9. to the letter, a.** with close adherence to the actual wording

ăct, āble, dâre, ärt; ĕbb, ēqual; Ĭf, īce; hŏt, ōver, ôrder, oil, bŏŏk, ōoze, out; ŭp, ūse, ûrge; ə = a in alone; ch, chief; g, give; ng, ring; sh, shoe; th, thin; t̵h, that; zh, vision. See the full key on inside cover.

or the literal meaning. **b.** to the fullest extent. *—v.t.* **10.** to mark or write with letters. [ME, t. OF: m. *lettre,* g. L *littera, lītera,* alphabetic character, pl. epistle, literature] *—let'ter·er, n.* **—Syn. 7.** See **literature.**

letter box, *Chiefly Brit.* mailbox.

letter carrier, *U.S.* postman.

let·tered (lĕt'ərd), *adj.* **1.** educated or learned. **2.** pertaining to or characterized by polite learning or literary culture. **3.** marked with or as with letters.

let·ter·gram (lĕt'ər grăm'), *n.* night letter.

let·ter·head (lĕt'ər hĕd'), *n.* **1.** a printed heading on letter paper, esp. one giving the name and address of a business concern, an institution, etc. **2.** a sheet of paper with such a heading.

let·ter·ing (lĕt'ər ĭng), *n.* **1.** act or process of inscribing with or making letters. **2.** the letters themselves.

letter of advice, 1. a document, esp. in commercial shipments, giving specific information as to the consignor's agent in the consignee's territory, his bank, warehouse, etc. **2.** *Com.* a drawer's document, usually forwarded ahead of the bill of lading and other papers giving title to goods shipped by the drawer, that a bill has been issued against the drawee.

letter of credit, 1. an order issued by a banker, allowing a person named to draw money to a specified amount from correspondents of the issuer. **2.** an instrument issued by a banker, authorizing a person named to make drafts upon the issuer up to an amount specified.

letter of marque, license or commission granted by a state to a private citizen to capture and confiscate the merchant ships of another nation. Also, **letter of marque and reprisal.**

let·ter·per·fect (lĕt'ər pûr'fĭkt),*adj.* **1.** knowing one's part, lesson, or the like, perfectly. **2.** accurate; exact.

let·ter·press (lĕt'ər prĕs'), *n.* **1.** matter printed from letters or type, rather than from engraved plates. **2.** printed text or reading matter, as distinguished from illustrations, etc.

letters of administration, *Law.* an instrument issued by a court or public official authorizing an administrator to take control of and dispose of the estate of a decedent.

letters of credence, papers formally authorizing a nation's diplomatic agents, issued by the appointing state.

letters patent, *Law.* a written or printed instrument issued by the sovereign power, conferring upon a patentee for a limited time the exclusive right to make, use, and sell his invention.

letters testamentary, *Law.* an instrument issued by a court or public official authorizing an executor to take control of and dispose of the estate of a decedent.

Let·tic (lĕt'ĭk), *adj.* **1.** pertaining or related to the Letts. *—n.* **2.** Lettish. **3.** *Obs.* the Baltic group of languages.

Let·tish (lĕt'ĭsh), *adj.* **1.** pertaining to the Letts or their language. *—n.* **2.** the language of Latvia.

let·tre de ca·chet (lĕt'r də kä shě'), *French Hist.* a letter under the seal of the sovereign, esp. one ordering imprisonment, frequently without trial.

let·tre de change (lĕt'r də shäNzh'), *French.* a letter or bill of exchange.

let·tuce (lĕt'ĭs), *n.* **1.** an important salad plant, *Lactuca sativa,* in many varieties, having large, succulent leaves which are much used for salad. **2.** any species of *Lactuca.* [ME *letuse,* t. OF: m. *laitues,* pl., g. L *lactūca*]

let·up (lĕt'ŭp'), *n.* *Colloq.* cessation; pause.

le·u (lě'ōō), *n., pl.* **lei** (lā). the Rumanian monetary unit equal to 100 bani and worth about one U.S. cent.

Leu·cas (lōō'kəs), *n.* Levkas. Also, **Leu'kas.**

leu·ce·mi·a (lōō sē'mĭ ə), *n.* leukemia.

leu·cine (lōō'sēn, -sĭn), *n.* *Biochem.* a white crystalline amino acid, $C_6H_{13}NO_2$, a constituent of proteins and also synthesized. Also, **leu·cin** (lōō'sĭn). [f. LEUC(O)- + -INE[2]]

leu·cite (lōō'sīt), *n.* a whitish or grayish mineral, potassium aluminum silicate, $KAlSi_2O_6$, found in certain volcanic rocks. [t. G: m. *leucit,* f. *leuc-* LEUC(O)- + *-it* -ITE[1]] *—leu·cit·ic* (lōō sĭt'ĭk), *adj.*

leuco-, a word element meaning "white." Also, before vowels, **leuc-.** [t. Gk.: m. *leuko-,* comb. form of *leukós*]

leu·co base (lōō'kō), *Chem.* a noncolored or slightly colored compound made by reducing a dye and which is readily oxidized to regenerate the dye.

leu·co·crat·ic (lōō kə krăt'ĭk), *adj.* *Geol.* composed predominantly of light-colored minerals. [f. LEUCO- + -CRAT + -IC]

leu·co·cyte (lōō'kə sīt'), *n.* *Physiol.* one of the white or colorless corpuscles of the blood, concerned in the destruction of disease-producing microörganisms, etc.

leu·co·cy·the·mi·a (lōō'kō sī thē'mĭ ə), *n.* *Pathol.* leukemia. Also, **leu'co·cy·thae'mi·a.** [NL. See LEUCO-, -CYTE, -HEMIA]

leu·co·cyt·ic (lōō'kə sĭt'ĭk), *adj.* **1.** pertaining to leucocytes. **2.** characterized by an excess of leucocytes.

leu·co·cy·to·sis (lōō'kō sī tō'sĭs), *n.* *Physiol., Pathol.* the presence of an increased number of leucocytes in the blood, esp. when temporary, as in infection, and not due to leukemia. [NL. See LEUCOCYTE, -OSIS] *—leu·co·cy·tot·ic* (lōō'kō sī tŏt'ĭk), *adj.*

leu·co·ma·ine (lōō kō'mə ēn', -ĭn), *n.* *Biochem.* any of a class of poisonous nitrogenous substances normally produced in a living animal body through metabolism. [f. LEUCO- + (PTO)MAINE]

leu·co·pe·ni·a (lōō'kə pē'nĭ ə), *n.* *Physiol.* a decrease in the number of white cells in the blood.

leu·co·plast (lōō'kə plăst'), *n.* *Bot.* one of the colorless bodies found within the protoplasm of vegetable cells, and serving as points around which starch forms.

leu·co·poi·e·sis (lōō'kō poi ē'sĭs), *n.* *Physiol.* the formation and development of the white blood cells.

leu·cor·rhe·a (lōō'kə rē'ə), *n.* *Pathol.* a whitish discharge from the female genital organs. Also, **leu'cor·rhoe'a.** [NL. See LEUCO-, -RRHEA]

leu·co·stic·te (lōō'kō stĭk'tĭ), *n.* any of several montane finches of the genus *Leucosticte,* commonly called rosy finches, as the Aleutian rosy finch (*L. tephrocotis griseonucha*).

Leuc·tra (lōōk'trə), *n.* a town in ancient Greece, in Boeotia: Thebans defeated Spartans here, 371 B.C.

leu·ke·mi·a (lōō kē'mĭ ə), *n.* *Pathol.* a somewhat rare, almost uniformly fatal disease, characterized by excessive production of white blood cells, which are usually found in greatly increased numbers in the blood. There is an accompanying anemia, often severe, and the spleen and lymphatic glands are usually enlarged and in a state of great activity. Also, **leu·kae'mi·a, leucemia.** [t. NL, f. s. Gk. *leukós* white + -emia -EMIA]

lev (lĕf), *n., pl.* **leva** (lĕ'və). the monetary unit and a gold coin of Bulgaria equal to 100 stotinki and stabilized in 1928 to equal approx. one cent in the U.S.

Lev., Leviticus.

Le Val·lois-Per·ret (lə văl wä' pĕ rĕ'), a suburb of Paris in N France, on the Seine. 62,871 (1954).

Le·vant (lĭ vănt'), *n.* **1.** lands bordering the E shore of the Mediterranean and the Aegean, esp. Syria, Lebanon, and Israel. **2.** (*l.c.*) a superior grade of morocco having a large and prominent grain, orig. made in the Levant; Levant morocco. [t. F, prop. ppr. of (*se*) *lever* rise (with reference to the rising sun). See LEVANT]

Levant dollar, a silver coin used for trade purposes, originally minted in Austria, and circulating in Ethiopia, Eritrea, Aden, etc.; Maria Theresa thaler. Its value changes with the price of silver and economic conditions of countries where it is used.

Le·van·tine (lĭ văn'tĭn, lĕv'ən t n', -tēn'), *adj.* **1.** of or pertaining to the Levant. *—n.* **2.** a native or a vessel of the Levant. [f. LEVANT + -INE[1]. Cf. F *levantin*]

Levant morocco, levant (def. 2).

le·va·tor (lĭ vā'tər, -tôr), *n., pl.* **levatores** (lĕv'ə tōr'ēz). **1.** that which raises or elevates. **2.** *Anat.* a muscle that raises some part of the body. **3.** *Surg.* an instrument used to raise a depressed part of the skull. [t. L: a lifter]

lev·ee[1] (lĕv'ĭ), *n.* **1.** *Southern U.S.* an embankment for preventing the overflowing of a river. **2.** *Agric.* one of the small continuous ridges surrounding fields that are to be irrigated. **3.** *Hist.* a landing place for vessels; a quay. [t. F: m. *levée,* der. *lever* raise. See LEVER]

lev·ee[2] (lĕv'ĭ, lĕ vē'), *n.* **1.** (in Great Britain) a public court assembly, held in the early afternoon, at which men only are received. **2.** a reception: *a presidential levee at the White House.* **3.** *Hist.* a reception of visitors held on rising from bed, as formerly by a royal or other personage. [t. F: m. *levé, lever* a rising. See LEVER]

lev·el (lĕv'əl), *adj., n., v.,* **-eled, -eling** or (*esp. Brit.*) **-elled, -elling,** *adv.* *—adj.* **1.** having no part higher than another; having an even surface. **2.** being in a plane parallel to the plane of the horizon; horizontal. **3.** on an equality, as one thing with another, or two or more things with one another. **4.** even, equable, or uniform. **5.** mentally well-balanced: *a level head.* **6. one's level best,** *Colloq.* one's very best; one's utmost. *—n.* **7.** a device used for determining, or adjusting something to, a horizontal surface. **8.** such a device consisting of a glass tube containing alcohol or ether with a movable bubble which when in the center indicates horizontalness. **9.** a surveying instrument combining such a device with a mounted telescope. **10.** a measuring of differences in elevation with such an instrument. **11.** an imaginary line or surface everywhere perpendicular to the plumb line. **12.** the horizontal line or plane in which anything is situated, with regard to its elevation. **13.** level position or condition. **14.** a level tract of land, or an extent of country approximately horizontal and unbroken by irregularities. **15.** a level or flat surface. **16.** one of various positions with respect to height; a height (*of*): *the water rose to a level of thirty feet.* **17.** a position or plane, high or low: *acting on the level of amateurs.* *—v.t.* **18.** to make (a surface) level or even: *to level ground before building.* **19.** to raise or lower to a particular level, or position. **20.** to bring (something) to the level of the ground; knock down, as a person: *the city was leveled by one atomic bomb.* **21.** to bring (two or more things) to an equality of status, condition, etc. **22.** to make even or uniform, as coloring. **23.** to aim or point at a mark, as a weapon, etc. **24.** to turn (looks, etc.) in a particular direction. **25.** *Survey.* to find the relative elevation of different points in (land) as with a level. *—v.i.* **26.** to bring things or persons to a common level. **27.** to aim a weapon, etc. **28.** to direct the mind,

---

b., blend of, blended; c., cognate with; d., dialect, dialectal; der., derived from; f., formed from; g., going back to; m., modification of; r., replacing; s., stem of; t., taken from; ?, perhaps. See the full key on inside cover.

purpose, etc., at something. **29.** *Survey.* to take levels; use a level. **30.** *Aeron.* to fly parallel to the ground, usually just before landing (fol. by *off*).
—*adv.* **31.** in a level, direct or even way or line. [ME *livel*, t. OF, ult. g. L *lībella*, dim. of *lībra* a balance, level] —**lev′el·er**; esp. *Brit.*, **lev′el·ler**, *n.* —**lev′-el·ly**, *adv.* —**lev′el·ness**, *n.*
—**Syn. 1, 2.** LEVEL, EVEN, FLAT, SMOOTH suggest a uniform surface without marked unevenness. That which is LEVEL is parallel to the horizon: *a level surface; a billiard table must be level.* FLAT is applied to any plane surface free from marked irregularities: *a flat roof.* With reference to land or country, FLAT connotes lowness or unattractiveness; LEVEL does not suggest anything derogatory. That which is EVEN is free from irregularities, though not necessarily level or plane: *an even land surface with no hills.* SMOOTH suggests a high degree of evenness in any surface, esp. to the touch and sometimes to the sight: *as smooth as silk.*

lev·el-head·ed (lĕv′əl·hĕd′ĭd), *adj.* having common sense and sound judgment.

leveling rod, *Survey.* a graduated rod used for measuring heights in connection with a surveyor's level.

Le·ven (lē′vən), *n.* Loch, a lake in E Scotland: ruins of a castle in which Mary Queen of Scots was imprisoned.

lev·er (lĕv′ər, lē′vər), *n.* **1.** a bar or rigid piece acted upon at different points by two forces, as a voluntarily applied force (the *power*) and a resisting force (the *weight*), which generally tend to rotate it in opposite directions about a fixed axis or support (the *fulcrum*). **2.** any of various mechanical devices operating on this principle, as a crowbar. —*v.t.*, *v.i.* **3.** to move with or apply a lever. [ME *levere*, t. OF: *leveor*, lit., raiser, der. *lever* raise, (refl.) rise, g. L *levāre* lighten, lift, raise] —**lev′er·like′**, *adj.*

Le·ver (lē′vər), *n.* **Charles James,** 1806–72, Irish novelist.

lev·er·age (lĕv′ər·ĭj, lē′vər·ĭj), *n.* **1.** the action of a lever. **2.** the mechanical advantage or power gained by using a lever. **3.** increased power of action.

lev·er·et (lĕv′ər·ĭt), *n.* a young hare. [ME, t. OF: m. *levrete*, dim. of *levre*, g. L *lepus* hare]

Le·ver·rier (lə·vĕ·ryĕ′), *n.* **Urbain** (yr·băn′), 1811–77, French astronomer.

Le·vi (lē′vī), *n.* *Bible.* a son of Jacob and Leah: ancestor of the Levites. Gen. 29:34, etc. [t. Heb.: m. *Lēwī*]

lev·i·a·ble (lĕv′ī·ə·bəl), *adj.* **1.** that may be levied. **2.** liable or subject to a levy.

le·vi·a·than (lĭ·vī′ə·thən), *n.* **1.** a sea monster mentioned in the Old Testament. Job 41. **2.** any huge marine animal, as the whale. **3.** anything, esp. a ship, of huge size. [ME, t. LL, t. Heb.: m. *liwyāthān*, prob. meaning the coiling up (snake)]

lev·i·gate (lĕv′ə·gāt), *v.t.*, **-gated, -gating.** **1.** to rub, grind, or reduce to a fine powder, as in a mortar, with or without the addition of a liquid. **2.** *Chem.* to make a homogeneous mixture of, as gels. [t. L: m.s. *lēvigātus*, pp., made smooth] —**lev′i·ga′tion**, *n.*

lev·in (lĕv′ĭn), *n.* *Archaic.* lightning. [ME *leven(e)*, presumably repr. OE **lēamne* or the like, c. Goth. *lauhmuni* lightning]

lev·i·rate (lĕv′ə·rĭt, -rāt′, lē′və-), *n.* a custom, as among the ancient Hebrews, requiring a man under certain circumstances to marry the widow of his brother or nearest kinsman. [f. L *lēvir* husband's brother + -ATE[1]] —**lev·i·rat·ic** (lĕv′ə·răt′ĭk, lē′vĭ-), **lev′i·rat′-i·cal**, *adj.*

Le·vis (lē′vīz), *n.pl.* *Trademark.* heavy blue denim trousers reinforced with copper rivets at the strain points. [pl. of *Levi* (*Strauss*), name of manufacturer]

Lev·it, Leviticus.

lev·i·tate (lĕv′ə·tāt′), *v.*, **-tated, -tating.** —*v.i.* **1.** to rise or float in the air by reason of lightness, or, now usually, through some alleged supernatural power that overcomes gravity. —*v.t.* **2.** to cause to rise or float in the air. [f. LEVIT(Y) + -ATE[1]; modeled on GRAVITATE] —**lev′i·ta′tor**, *n.*

lev·i·ta·tion (lĕv′ə·tā′shən), *n.* **1.** act or phenomenon of levitating. **2.** (among spiritualists) the alleged phenomenon of bodies heavier than air being by spiritual means rendered buoyant in the atmosphere. **3.** an illusory object floating about in the air, esp. in dreams.

Le·vite (lē′vīt), *n.* **1.** a descendant of Levi; one of the tribe of Levi. **2.** one of those who assisted the priests in the tabernacle and temple. [ME, t. LL: m.s. *levita, levites*, t. Gk.: (m.) *levītēs*, der. *Leuí* Levite, t. Heb.]

Le·vit·i·cal (lĭ·vĭt′ə·kəl), *adj.* of or pertaining to the Levites, the book of Leviticus, or the law (**Levitical law**) contained in the book of Leviticus.

Le·vit·i·cus (lĭ·vĭt′ə·kəs), *n.* the third book of the Old Testament, containing laws relating to the priests and Levites and to the forms of Jewish ceremonial observance. [t. LL, t. Gk.: m. *Leuïtikos*, der. *Leuïtēs* LEVITE]

lev·i·ty (lĕv′ə·tĭ), *n.*, *pl.* **-ties. 1.** lightness of mind, character, or behavior; lack of proper seriousness or earnestness. **2.** an instance or exhibition of this. **3.** fickleness. **4.** lightness in weight. [t. L: m.s. *levitas*]

Lev·kas (lĕf′käs), *n.* an island in the Ionian group, off the W coast of Greece. 37,752 pop. (1951); 114 sq. mi. Also, **Leucas.** Italian, **Santa Maura.**

levo-, *Chem.* denoting a substance which rotates the plane of polarized light to the left. *Abbr.:* **l-, l.** [comb. form repr. L *laevus* left]

le·vo·glu·cose (lē′vō·glōō′kōs), *n.* *Chem.* the levorotatory form of glucose.

le·vo·ro·ta·tion (lē′vō·rō·tā′shən), *n.* *Optics, Chem., etc.* the rotation of the plane of polarization of light to the left. Also, **laevorotation.**

le·vo·ro·ta·to·ry (lē′vō·rō′tə·tōr′ĭ), *adj.* *Optics, Chem., etc.* turning the plane of polarization of light to the left, as certain crystals, etc. Also **laevorotatory.**

lev·u·lin (lĕv′yə·lĭn), *n.* *Chem.* an amorphous substance from which levulose can be formed, occurring in the tubers of certain species of helianthus, etc.

lev·u·lin·ic acid (lĕv′yə·lĭn′ĭk), a hygroscopic acid, $CH_3COCH_2CH_2COOH$, derived from the nucleic acid of the thymus. It is industrially obtained from sugar by reaction with hydrochloric acid, and used to clean metals, such as milk cans, to guard against bacterial infection.

lev·u·lose (lĕv′yə·lōs′), *n.* *Chem.* fructose; fruit sugar. [f. m.s. L *laevus* left + -ULE + -OSE[2]]

lev·y (lĕv′ĭ), *n.*, *pl.* **levies,** *v.*, **levied, levying.** —*n.* **1.** a raising or collecting, as of money or troops, by authority or force. **2.** that which is raised, as a tax assessment or a body of troops. —*v.t.* **3.** to make a levy of; collect (taxes, contributions, etc.). **4.** to impose as an assessment (*on*). **5.** to raise or enlist (troops, etc.) for service. **6.** to set going, start, or make (war, etc.). —*v.i.* **7.** to make a levy. **8.** *Law.* to seize or attach property by judicial order. [ME, t. F: m. *levée*, der. *lever* raise. See LEVER] —**lev·i·er** (lĕv′ĭ·ər), *n.*

lev·y en masse (lĕv′ĭ ĕn mäs′, än mäs′), a preparation for defense by a country threatened with invasion, by organized groups of civilians. [t. F: m. *levée en masse*]

lewd (lōōd), *adj.* **1.** inclined to, characterized by, or inciting to lust or lechery. **2.** obscene or indecent, as language, songs, etc. **3.** *Obs.* base or vile. [ME *leud, lewede*, OE *lǣw(e)de* lay, adj.; orig. uncert.] —**lewd′ly**, *adv.* —**lewd′ness**, *n.*

Lew·es (lōō′ĭs), *n.* **1. George Henry,** 1817–78, British philosophical writer and critic. **2.** a city in SE England, in Sussex: battle, 1264. 13,104 (1951).

Lew·is (lōō′ĭs), *n.* **1. John Llewellyn** (lōō ĕl′ĭn), born 1880, U.S. labor leader. **2. Matthew Gregory,** (*Monk Lewis*) 1775–1818, British novelist and dramatist. **3. Meriwether** (mĕr′ĭ·wĕth′ər), 1774–1809, U.S. explorer: leader of the Lewis and Clark expedition. **4. Sinclair,** 1885–1951, U.S. novelist.

lew·is·ite (lōō′ə·sīt′), *n.* a chemical warfare agent, $C_2H_2AsCl_3$, characterized by its vesicant action. [named after W. Lee *Lewis*, Am. chemist. See -ITE[1]]

Lew·is·ton (lōō′ĭs·tən), *n.* a city in SW Maine, on the Androscoggin river. 40,804 (1960).

Lewis with Har·ris (hăr′ĭs), the northernmost island of the Hebrides, in NW Scotland. 26,466 pop. (1951); 825 sq. mi.

lex (lĕks), *n.*, *pl.* **leges** (lē′jēz). *law.* [L: the law]

lex·i·cal (lĕk′sə·kəl), *adj.* **1.** pertaining to words or to a vocabulary, as that of an author or a language. **2.** pertaining to or of the nature of a lexicon. [f. LEXIC(ON) + -AL[1]]

lexical meaning, *Gram.* that part of the meaning of a linguistic form which does not depend on its membership in a particular form class, esp. (of inflected words) the meaning common to all the members of an inflectional paradigm, e.g., the meaning common to *eat, eats, ate, eaten*, despite their differences in form.

lexicog., **1.** lexicographical. **2.** lexicography.

lex·i·cog·ra·pher (lĕk′sə·kŏg′rə·fər), *n.* a writer or compiler of a dictionary. [f. m.s. LGk. *lexikográphos* (f. *lexikó(n)* wordbook + -*gráphos* writer) + -ER[1]]

lex·i·cog·ra·phy (lĕk′sə·kŏg′rə·fĭ), *n.* the writing or compiling of dictionaries. —**lex·i·co·graph·ic** (lĕk′sə·kō·grăf′ĭk), **lex′i·co·graph′i·cal**, *adj.* —**lex′i·co·graph′i·cal·ly**, *adv.*

lex·i·con (lĕk′sə·kən), *n.* **1.** a wordbook or dictionary, esp. of Greek, Latin, or Hebrew. **2.** the list or vocabulary of words belonging to a particular subject, field, or class. [? t. NL (much used in Latin titles of dictionaries), t. Gk.: m. *lexikón*, neut. of *lexikós* of or for words]

Lex·ing·ton (lĕk′sĭng·tən), *n.* **1.** a town in E Massachusetts, NW of Boston: the first battle of the American Revolution was fought here, April 19, 1775. 27,691 (1960). **2.** a city in N Kentucky. 62,810 (1960).

lex lo·ci (lĕks lō′sī), *Latin.* the law of a place.

lex non scrip·ta (lĕks nŏn skrĭp′tə), *Latin.* unwritten law; common law.

lex scrip·ta (lĕks skrĭp′tə), *Latin.* written law; statute law.

lex ta·li·o·nis (lĕks tăl′ĭ·ō′nĭs), *Latin.* the law of retaliation.

Ley·den (lī′dən), *n.* Leiden.

Leyden Jar, *Elect.* a device for storing electric charge, consisting essentially of a glass jar lined inside and outside, for about two thirds of its height, with tinfoil. [named after *Leyden* (*Leiden*), city in Holland]

Ley·te (lā′tā; *Sp.* -tĕ), *n.* one of the Philippine Islands, in central part of group: focal point of the U.S. invasion of the Philippines, 1944. 1,006,- 891 pop. (1948); 3085 sq. mi.

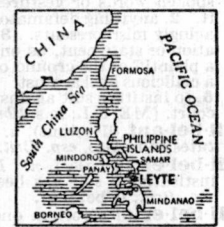

Ley·ton (lā′tən), *n.* a city in SE England, in Essex, near London. 105,978 (1951).

lf., *Baseball.* left fielder.

L.F., low-frequency.

LG, Low German. Also, **L.G.**

l.g., *Football.* left guard.

LGk., Late Greek. Also, **L.Gk.**

l.h., *Music.* left hand.

Lha·sa (lä′sə, -sä), *n.* the capital of Tibet, in the SE part: sacred city of Lamaism. 25,000 (est. 1950); ab. 12,000 ft. high. Also, **Lassa.**

l.h.b., *Football.* left halfback.

L.H.D., (L *Litterarum Humaniorum Doctor*) Doctor of the More Humane Letters; Doctor of the Humanities.

L-head engine (ĕl′hĕd′), an internal-combustion engine in which both valves are located in a pocket at one side of the piston.

li (lē), *n., pl.* **li** (lē). a Chinese unit of distance, equivalent to about one third of a mile.

Li, *Chem.* lithium.

li·a·bil·i·ty (lī′ə bĭl′ə tĭ′), *n., pl.* **-ties.** 1. an obligation, esp. for payment; debt or pecuniary obligations (opposed to *asset*). 2. something disadvantageous. 3. state or fact of being liable: *liability to jury duty, liability to disease.*

liability insurance, employers' liability insurance.

li·a·ble (lī′ə bəl), *adj.* 1. subject, exposed, or open to something possible or likely, esp. something undesirable. 2. under legal obligation; responsible or answerable. [late ME, f. s. F *lier* bind (g. L *ligăre*) + -ABLE] —**li′a·ble·ness,** *n.* —Syn. 1. See likely.

li·ai·son (lē′ä zōn′, lē′ə zŏn′, -zən; lī ā′zən; *Fr.* lyĕ zōn′), *n.* 1. *Mil., etc.* the contact maintained between units, in order to ensure concerted action. 2. a similar connection or relation to be maintained between non-military units, bodies, etc. 3. an illicit intimacy between a man and a woman. 4. *Cookery.* a thickening, as of beaten eggs and cream, for sauces, soups, etc. 5. *Phonet.* a type of sandhi in which the final written consonant of one word is pronounced in syllable with a following init al vowel (used especially of French, as where the preconsonantal form of the word shows no consonant corresponding to the consonant joined by liaison). [f. F, g. L *ligătio* a binding]

Li·a·kou·ra (lyä′kōō rä′), *n.* See **Parnassus, Mount.**

li·a·na (lĭ ä′nə, lĭ än′ə), *n.* a climbing plant or vine. Also, **li·ane** (lĭ än′). [t. F: m. *liane,* earlier *liorne,* b. with *viorne* (g. L *viburnum* viburnum) and *lier* bind (g. L *ligăre*)]

liang (lyäng), *n., pl.* **liang.** a Chinese unit of weight, equal to ¹⁄₁₆ catty, and equivalent to about 1¹⁄₃ ounce; a haikwan tael.

Liao (lyou), *n.* a river in NE China, flowing through S Manchuria into the Gulf of Liaotung. ab. 600 mi.

Liao·ning (lyou′nĭng′), *n.* a province in NE China, in Manchuria. 18,545,147 pop. (1953); 25,969 sq. mi. Formerly, **Fengtien.**

Liao·peh (lyou′bŭ′), *n.* a former province in NE China, in Manchuria. 4,634,700 pop. (1946); 47,612 sq. mi.

Liao·tung (lyou′dŏŏng′), *n.* 1. a peninsula in NE China, in Manchuria, extending S into the Yellow Sea. 2. Gulf of, a gulf W of this peninsula.

Liao·yang (lyou′yäng′), *n.* a city in NE China, in Manchuria, S of Mukden. 105,000 (est. 1950).

li·ar (lī′ər), *n.* one who lies, or tells lies.

Li·ard (lī′ər′, -ärd′), *n.* a river in W Canada, flowing from S Yukon through N British Columbia and the Northwest Territories into the Mackenzie river. 550 mi.

Li·as (lī′əs), *n. Stratig.* the lowermost main part of the European Jurassic. [ME, t. OF: m. *liois* kind of limestone, of Gmc. orig.] —**Li·as·sic** (lī ăs′ĭk), *adj.*

Lib., Liberal.

lib., 1. (L *liber*) book. 2. librarian. 3. library.

li·ba·tion (lī bā′shən), *n.* 1. a pouring out of wine or other liquid in honor of a deity. 2. the liquid poured out. [ME, t. L: s. *lībātio*]

Li·bau (lē′bou), *n.* German name of **Liepāja.**

Li·ba·va (lĭ bä′vä), *n.* Russian name of **Liepāja.**

li·bel (lī′bəl), *n., v.,* **-beled, -beling,** (*esp. Brit.*) **-belled, -belling.** —*n.* 1. *Law.* a defamation by written or printed words, pictures, or in any form other than by spoken words or gestures. b. the crime of publishing it. 2. anything defamatory, or that maliciously or damagingly misrepresents. 3. *Law.* a formal written declaration or statement, as one containing the allegations of a plaintiff or the ground of a charge. —*v.t.* 4. to publish a malicious libel against. 5. to misrepresent damagingly. 6. to institute suit against by a libel, as in an admiralty court. [ME, t. L: m.s. *libellus,* dim. of *liber* book]

li·bel·ant (lī′bəl ənt), *n. Law.* one who libels, or institutes suit. Also, *esp. Brit.,* **li′bel·lant.**

li·bel·ee (lī′bə lē′), *n. Law.* one against whom a libel instituting a suit has been filed; the respondent. Also, *esp. Brit.,* **li′bel·lee′.**

li·bel·er (lī′bəl ər), *n.* one who libels; one who publishes a libel assailing another. Also, *esp. Brit.,* **li′bel·ler.**

li·bel·ous (lī′bəl əs), *adj.* containing, constituting, or involving a libel; maliciously defamatory. Also, *esp. Brit.,* **li′bel·lous.** —**li′bel·ous·ly,** *adv.*

li·ber (lī′bər), *n. Bot.* phloem. [t. L]

lib·er·al (lĭb′ər əl, lĭb′rəl), *adj.* 1. favorable to progress or reform, as in religious or political affairs. 2. (*often cap.*) noting or pertaining to a political party advocating measures of progressive political reform: *the Liberal party.* 3. favorable to or in accord with the policy of leaving the individual as unrestricted as possible in the opportunities for self-expression or self-fulfillment. 4. of representational forms of government rather than aristocracies and monarchies. 5. free from prejudice or bigotry; tolerant. 6. giving freely or in ample measure: *a liberal donor.* 7. given freely or abundantly: *a liberal donation.* 8. not strict or rigorous: *a liberal interpretation of a rule.* 9. befitting a freeman, a gentleman, or a nonprofessional person. —*n.* 10. a person of liberal principles or views, esp. in religion or politics. 11. (*often cap.*) a member of a liberal party in politics, esp. of the Liberal Party in Great Britain. [ME, t. L: s. *liberālis* pertaining to a free man] —**lib′er·al·ly,** *adv.* —**lib′er·al·ness,** *n.* —Syn. 7. See ample.

liberal arts, the course of instruction at a modern college granting an academic (as distinguished from an engineering or other technical) degree, comprising the arts, natural sciences, social sciences, and humanities. [Anglicization of L *artēs liberālēs* arts of freemen]

lib·er·al·ism (lĭb′ər ə lĭz′əm, lĭb′rə-), *n.* 1. liberal principles, as in religion or politics. 2. (*sometimes cap.*) the principles and practices of a liberal party in politics. 3. a movement in modern Protestantism which emphasizes freedom from tradition and authority, the adjustment of religious beliefs to scientific conceptions, and the spiritual capacities of men. —**lib′er·al·ist,** *n., adj.* —**lib′er·al·is′tic,** *adj.*

lib·er·al·i·ty (lĭb′ə răl′ə tĭ′), *n., pl.* **-ties.** 1. the quality of being liberal in giving; generosity; bounty. 2. a liberal gift. 3. breadth of mind. 4. liberalism.

lib·er·al·ize (lĭb′ər ə līz′, lĭb′rə-), *v.t., v.i.,* **-ized, -izing.** to make or become liberal. —**lib′er·al·i·za′tion,** *n.* —**lib′er·al·iz′er,** *n.*

Liberal Party, a British political party, a fusion of Whigs and Radicals, formed in the 1830's, and one of the dominant political parties in Great Britain until World War I.

lib·er·ate (lĭb′ə rāt′), *v.t.,* **-ated, -ating.** 1. to set free, as from bondage; release. 2. to disengage; set free from combination, as a gas. [t. L: m.s. *liberātus,* pp.] —**lib′er·a′tion,** *n.* —**lib′er·a′tor,** *n.* —**lib·er·a·tress** (lĭb′ə rā′trĭs), *n. fem.*

Li·be·ri·a (lī bĭr′ĭ ə), *n.* a republic in W Africa: founded by freed American slaves, 1822. 1,250,000 pop. (est. 1954); ab. 43,000 sq. mi. *Cap.:* Monrovia. —**Li·be′ri·an,** *adj., n.*

lib·er·tar·i·an (lĭb′ər târ′ĭ ən), *n.* 1. one who advocates liberty, esp. with regard to thought or conduct. 2. one who maintains the doctrine of the freedom of the will. [f. LIBERT(Y) + -ARIAN] —**lib′er·tar′i·an·ism,** *n.*

li·ber·ti·cide¹ (lĭ bûr′tə sīd′), *n.* a destroyer of liberty. [f. LIBERTY + -CIDE¹]

li·ber·ti·cide² (lĭ bûr′tə sīd′), *n.* destruction of liberty. [f. LIBERTY + -CIDE²] —**li·ber′ti·cid′al,** *adj.*

lib·er·tine (lĭb′ər tēn′), *n.* 1. one free from restraint or control. 2. one free from moral restraints. 3. a dissolute man. —*adj.* 4. characteristic of a libertine. 5. free from moral restraints; dissolute; licentious. [ME, t. L: m.s. *libertīnus* freedman]

lib·er·tin·ism (lĭb′ər tēn ĭz′əm, -tĭn-), *n.* libertine practices or habits of life; licentiousness.

lib·er·ty (lĭb′ər tĭ′), *n., pl.* **-ties.** 1. freedom from arbitrary or despotic government, or, often, from other rule or law than that of a self-governing community. 2. freedom from external or foreign rule, or independence. 3. freedom from control, interference, obligation, restriction, hampering conditions, etc.; power or right of doing, thinking, speaking, etc., according to choice. 4. freedom from captivity, confinement, or physical restraint: *the prisoner soon regained his liberty.* 5. leave granted to a sailor, esp. in the navy, to go ashore. 6. the freedom of, or right of frequenting or using a place, etc. 7. unwarranted or impertinent freedom in action or speech, or a form or instance of it. 8. at liberty, a. free from bondage, captivity, confinement, or restraint. b. unoccupied or disengaged. c. free, permitted, or privileged to do or be as specified. [ME *libertie,* t. OF: m. *liberte,* t. L: m.s. *libertas*] —Syn. 4. See freedom.

liberty cap, a kind of cap used as a symbol of liberty (from the cap of this kind given to a freedman in ancient Rome at his manumission).

Liberty Ship, a U. S. merchant ship built in large numbers during World War II, carrying about 10,000 gross tons.

Li·bia (lē′byä), *n.* Italian name of Libya (def. 2).

li·bid·i·nous (lĭ bĭd′ə nəs), *adj.* full of lust; lustful; lewd. [ME *lybydynous,* t. L: m.s. *libidinōsus*] —**li·bid′i·nous·ly,** *adv.* —**li·bid′i·nous·ness,** *n.*

li·bi·do (lĭ bī′dō, -bē′dō), *n.* 1. *Psychoanal.* all of the instinctual energies and desires which are derived from the id. 2. the innate actuating or impelling force in living beings; the vital impulse or "urge." [t. L: pleasure, longing] —**li·bid·i·nal** (lĭ bĭd′ə nəl), *adj.*

---

b., blend of, blended; c., cognate with; d., dialect, dialectal; der., derived from; f., formed from; g., going back to; m., modification of; r., replacing; s., stem of; t., taken from; ?, perhaps. See the full key on inside cover.

li·bra (lī′brə *for 1*; lē′brä *for 2*), *n.*, *pl.* **-brae** (-brē) for 1, **-bras** (-bräs) for 2. 1. the ancient Roman pound (containing 5053 grains). 2. sol³ (def. 1). [(def. 1) t. L; (def. 2) t. Sp., g. L]

Li·bra (lī′brə), *n.*, *gen.* **-brae** (-brē). 1. *Astron.* the Balance, a zodiacal constellation. 2. the seventh sign of the zodiac. See diag. under **zodiac**. [t. L: pound, balance, level]

li·brar·i·an (lī brâr′Y ən), *n.* 1. a person trained in library science and engaged in library service. 2. an officer in charge of a library.

li·brar·i·an·ship (lī brâr′Y ən shĬp′), *n.* 1. a profession concerned with organizing collections of books and related materials in libraries and servicing these resources to readers and others. 2. the office or work of a librarian.

li·brar·y (lī′brĕr′Y, -brə rY, -brY), *n.*, *pl.* **-braries.** 1. a place set apart to contain books and other literary material for reading, study, or reference, as a room, set of rooms, or building where books may be read or borrowed. 2. a public body organizing and maintaining such an establishment: *the Library of Congress.* 3. a commercial establishment lending books for a fixed charge. 4. a collection of manuscripts, publications, and other materials for reading, study, or reference. 5. a series of books of similar character, or alike in size, binding, etc., issued by a single publishing house. 6. *Brit.* a ticket agency for theaters, etc. [ME *librarie*, t. L: m. *librārium* place to keep books]

library science, the body of knowledge and techniques utilized for well-organized library service.

li·bra·tion (lī brā′shən), *n. Astron.* a real or apparent oscillatory motion, esp. of the moon. [t. L: s. *librātio* balance, a moving from side to side]

li·bra·to·ry (lī′brə tôr′Y), *adj.* oscillatory.

li·bret·tist (lī brĕt′Yst), *n.* the writer of a libretto.

li·bret·to (lī brĕt′ō; *It.* lē brĕt′tô), *n.*, *pl.* **-tos, -ti** (-tē). 1. the text or words of an opera or other extended musical composition. 2. a book or booklet containing such a text. [t. It., dim. of *libro* book, g. L *liber*]

li·bri·form (lī′brə fôrm′), *adj. Bot.* having the form of or resembling liber. [f. LIB(E)R + -(I)FORM]

Lib·y·a (lĬb′Y ə), *n.* 1. *Anc. Geog.* the part of N Africa W of Egypt. 2. a constitutional monarchy in N Africa between Tunisia and Egypt. 1,153,000 (est. 1958); 679,400 sq. mi. *Capitals:* Tripoli *and* Benghazi.

Lib·y·an (lĬb′Y ən), *adj.* 1. of or pertaining to Libya. —*n.* 2. a native or inhabitant of Libya. 3. Berber (def. 2), esp. in its ancient form.

Libyan Desert, a part of the Sahara W of the Nile, in E Libya, W Egypt, and NW Sudan.

lice (līs), *n.* pl. of **louse.**

li·cence (lī′səns), *n.*, *v.*, **-cenced, -cencing.** license. —li′cenc·er, *n.*

li·cense (lī′səns), *n.*, *v.*, **-censed, -censing.** —*n.* 1. formal permission or leave to do or not to do something. 2. formal permission from a constituted authority to do something, as to carry on some business or profession, etc. 3. a certificate of such permission; an official permit. 4. freedom of action, speech, thought, etc., permitted or conceded. 5. intentional deviation from rule, convention, or fact, as for the sake of literary or artistic effect: *poetic license.* 6. excessive or undue freedom or liberty. 7. licentiousness. —*v.t.* 8. to grant authoritative permission or license to. [ME *licence,* t. OF, t. L: m.s. *licentia*] —li′cens·a·ble, *adj.* —li′cens·er, (*in Law*) li′cen·sor, *n.*

li·cen·see (lī′sən sē′), *n.* one to whom a license is granted. Also, li′cen·cee′.

li·cen·ti·ate (lī sĕn′shĬ Yt, -āt′), *n.* 1. one who has received a license, as from a university, to practice an art or profession. 2. the holder of a certain university degree intermediate between that of bachelor and that of doctor, now confined chiefly to certain continental European universities. —li·cen′ti·ate·ship′, *n.*

li·cen·tious (lī sĕn′shəs), *adj.* 1. sensually unbridled; libertine; lewd. 2. unrestrained by law or morality; lawless; immoral. 3. going beyond customary or proper bounds or limits. [t. ML: m.s. *licentiōsus*] —li·cen′tious·ly, *adv.* —li·cen′tious·ness, *n.*

li·chee (lē′chē′), *n.* litchi.

li·chen (lī′kən), *n.* 1. any one of the group, *Lichenes,* of the *Thallophyta,* compound plants (fungi in symbiotic union with algae) having a vegetative body (thallus) growing in greenish, gray, yellow, brown, or blackish crustlike patches or bushlike forms on rocks, trees, etc. 2. *Pathol.* any of various eruptive skin diseases. [t. L, Gk.: m. *leichén*] —li′chen·like′, *adj.* —li′chen·ous, *adj.*

li·chen·in (lī′kən Yn), *n. Chem.* a polysaccharide starch, $C_6H_{10}O_5$, a white gelatinous substance derived from certain mosses. [f. LICHEN + -IN²]

li·chen·oid (lī′kə noid′), *adj.* lichenlike.

li·chen·ol·o·gy (lī′kə nŏl′ə jY), *n.* the branch of botany that treats of lichens.

Lich·field (lĬch′fēld′), *n.* a town in central England, in Staffordshire: birthplace of Samuel Johnson. 10,624 (1951).

lich gate (lĬch), (in England and elsewhere) a roofed gate to a churchyard, under which a bier is set down to await the coming of the clergyman. Also, **lych gate.** [f. *lich* (OE *lic,* c. D *lijk*) body, corpse + GATE]

li·chi (lē′chē′), *n.*, *pl.* **-chis.** litchi.

lic·it (lĬs′Yt), *adj.* permitted; lawful. [late ME, t. L:s. *licitus,* pp.] —**lic′it·ly,** *adv.*

lick (lĭk), *v.t.* 1. to pass the tongue over the surface of (often fol. by *up, off, from,* etc.). 2. to make by strokes of the tongue: *to lick the plate clean.* 3. to pass or play lightly over, as waves or flames do. 4. *Colloq.* to beat, thrash, or whip, as for punishment. 5. *Colloq.* to overcome in a fight, war, etc.; defeat. 6. *Colloq.* to outdo; surpass. —*n.* 7. a stroke of the tongue over something. 8. a small quantity. 9. a place to which wild animals resort to lick salt occurring naturally there. 10. *Colloq.* a blow. 11. *Colloq.* a brief or brisk stroke of activity or endeavor. 12. *Colloq.* speed. [ME *licke(n),* OE *liccian,* c. D *likken,* G *lecken;* akin to L *lingere*] —**lick′er,** *n.*

lick·er·ish (lĭk′ər Ysh), *adj. Archaic.* 1. eager for choice food. 2. greedy. 3. lustful. Also, **liquorish.** [earlier *lickerous* (influenced by *lick* and *liquor,* with substitution of suffix -ISH¹ for -OUS), ME *likerous,* repr. an AF var. of OF *lecheros,* der. *lecheor* gourmand, sensualist. See LECHER]

lick·ing (lĭk′Yng), *n.* 1. *Colloq.* a beating or thrashing. 2. act of one who or that which licks.

lick·spit·tle (lĭk′spĬt′əl), *n.* an abject toady.

lic·o·rice (lĭk′ər Ys, lĭk′rYsh), *n.* 1. a leguminous plant, *Glycyrrhiza glabra,* of Europe and Asia. 2. the sweet-tasting dried root of this plant, or an extract made from it, used in medicine, confectionery, etc. 3. any of various related or similar plants. Also, **liquorice, liquorish.** [ME *lycorys,* t. AF, t. LL: m.s. *liquiritia,* L *glycyrrhīza,* t. Gk.: m. *glýkyrrhīza;* influenced by L *liquor* liquor]

lic·tor (lĭk′tər), *n.* (in ancient Rome) one of a body of attendants on certain magistrates, who preceded them carrying the fasces. [ME, t. L]

lid (lĭd), *n.* 1. a movable piece, whether separate or hinged, for closing the opening of a vessel, box, etc.; a movable cover. 2. an eyelid. 3. (in mosses) **a.** the cover of the capsule; operculum. **b.** the upper section of a pyxidium. 4. *Slang.* a hat. [ME; OE *hlid,* c. D and G *lid*] —**lid′ded,** *adj.*

Lid·dell Hart (lĭd′əl härt′), **Basil Henry,** born 1895, British writer on military science and affairs.

lid·less (lĭd′lĭs), *adj.* 1. having no lid. 2. (of eyes) having no lids. 3. *Poetic.* vigilant.

Li·do (lē′dō; *It.* -dô), *n.* a chain of sandy islands in NE Italy, lying between the Lagoon of Venice and the Adriatic: fashionable beach resort.

lie¹ (lī), *n.*, *v.*, **lied, lying.** —*n.* 1. a false statement made with intent to deceive; an intentional untruth; a falsehood. 2. something intended or serving to convey a false impression. 3. the charge or accusation of lying; a flat contradiction. 4. **give the** (**to**), **a.** to charge with lying; contradict flatly. **b.** to imply or show to be false; belie. [ME; OE *lyge,* c. Icel. *lygi*] —*v.i.* 5. to speak falsely or utter untruth knowingly, as with intent to deceive. 6. to express what is false, or convey a false impression. 7. to get (*out*), as of a difficulty, by lies. —*v.t.* 8. to bring, put, etc., by lying: *to lie oneself out of a difficulty.* [ME *lien,* OE *lēogan,* c. Goth. *liugan*] —**Syn. 1.** See **falsehood.**

lie² (lī), *v.*, **lay, lain, lying,** *n.* —*v.i.* 1. to be in a recumbent or prostrate position, as on a bed or the ground; recline. 2. to assume such a position (fol. by *down*): *to lie down on the ground.* 3. to be buried (in a particular spot). 4. to rest in a horizontal position; be stretched out or extended: *a book lying on the table.* 5. to be or remain in a position or state of inactivity, subjection, restraint, concealment, etc.: *to lie in ambush.* 6. to rest, press, or weigh (fol. by *on* or *upon*): *these things lie upon my mind.* 7. to depend (fol. by *on* or *upon*). 8. to be found, occur, or be (where specified): *the fault lies here.* 9. to be placed or situated: *land lying along the coast.* 10. to consist or be grounded (fol. by *in*): *the real remedy lies in education.* 11. to be in or have a specified direction: *the trail from here lies to the west.* 12. *Law.* to be sustainable or admissible, as an action or appeal. 13. *Archaic.* to lodge; sojourn. 14. lie in, to be confined in childbed. 15. **lie to,** *Naut.* (of a ship) to lie comparatively stationary, usually with the head as near the wind as possible. —*n.* 16. manner of lying; the relative position or direction in which something lies (the English say *lie of the land* where Americans say *lay of the land*). 17. the place where a bird, beast, or fish is accustomed to lie or lurk. 18. *Golf.* the ground position of the golf ball. [ME *lie(n), liggen,* OE *licgan,* c. D *liggen,* G *liegen,* Icel. *liggja,* Goth. *ligan*] —**Syn. 1.** LIE, LAY, often confused, are not synonyms. LIE, meaning "to recline or rest," does not require an object. Its principal parts, too, are irregular, and are therefore distinctive. LAY (originally *to cause to lie*), with its forms *laid, have laid, laying,* etc., means "to put or place." If "put" or "place" can be substituted in a contemplated sentence, the verb to use is LAY. Moreover, since one must always "put" or "place" *something,* the verb LAY is used only when there is a grammatical object to complete the sense. (It should be noticed, however, that the past tense of LIE is also spelled LAY.)

Lie (lē), *n.* 1. **Jonas,** 1880–1940, U.S. painter, born in Norway. 2. **Trygve Halvdan** (trĭg′və hälv′dän; *Nor.* trȳg′va), born 1896, Norwegian statesman: secretary general of United Nations, 1946–1953.

Lie·big (lē′bYкн), *n.* **Justus** (yŏos′tŏos), **Baron von** (fən), 1803–73, German chemist.

Lieb·knecht (lēp′knĕкнt), *n.* **Wilhelm** (vĭl′hĕlm), 1826–1900, German journalist and political leader.

Liech·ten·stein (lĭk′tən stīn′; *Ger.* lĬKH′tən shtīn′), *n.* a small principality in central Europe between Austria and Switzerland. 14,000 pop. (est. 1953); 65 sq. mi. *Cap.:* Vaduz.

lied (lēd; *Ger.* lēt), *n., pl.* **lieder** (lē′dər). *German.* a German song, lyric, or ballad.

lie·der·kranz (lē′dər kränts′), *n.* **1. a.** a cheese mellower than Camembert but not as strong as Limburger. **b.** (*cap.*) a trademark for this cheese. **2.** a German choral society or singing club, esp. of men. [G: garland of songs]

lief (lēf), *adv.* **1.** Also, **lieve.** gladly; willingly. —*adj. Archaic.* **2.** willing. **3.** dear. [ME *leef*, OE *lēof*, c. G *lieb*]

liege (lēj), *n.* **1.** a lord entitled to allegiance and service. **2.** a vassal or subject, as of a ruler. —*adj.* **3.** entitled to, or owing, allegiance and service. **4.** pertaining to the relation between vassal and lord. **5.** loyal; faithful. [ME *lige*, t. OF: liege, free, exempt, g. LL *leticus*, der. *letus* free man, g. Gmc. orig.]

Li·ège (lĬ āzh′; *Fr.* lyĕzh), *n.* a city in E Belgium, on the Meuse river: one of the first cities attacked in World War I. 156,728 (est. 1952).

liege·man (lēj′mən), *n., pl.* **-men. 1.** a vassal; a subject. **2.** a faithful follower.

Lieg·nitz (lēg′nĭts), *n.* a city in SW Poland: formerly in Germany. 34,000 (est. 1955). Polish, **Lignica.**

lien (lēn, lē′ən), *n.* a legal right to hold property or to have it sold or applied for payment of a claim. [t. F, g. L *ligāmen* band, tie]

li·en·ter·y (lī′ən tĕr′ĭ), *n. Pathol.* a form of diarrhea in which the food is discharged undigested or only partly digested. [t. ML: m.s. *lienteria*, t. Gk.: m. *leienteria*] —**li′en·ter′ic,** *adj.*

Li·e·pā·ja (lē′ĕ̇′pä yä), *n.* a seaport in the W Soviet Union, in the Latvian Republic, on the Baltic. 80,000 (est. 1948). Russian, **Libava.** German, **Libau.**

li·er (lī′ər), *n.* one who lies (down, etc.).

li·erne (lĬ ûrn′), *n. Archit.* a short connecting rib in vaulting. [late ME, t. F, var. of *lierne*. See LIANA]

Lie·tu·va (lĬ′ĕ̇ tōō′vä), *n.* Lithuanian name of **Lithuania.**

lieu (lōō), *n.* **1.** place; stead. **2. in lieu of,** instead of. [ME *liue*, t. F: m. *lieu*, g. L *locus* place]

Lieut., lieutenant.

lieu·ten·an·cy (lōō tĕn′ən sĭ), *n., pl.* **-cies. 1.** the office, authority, incumbency, or jurisdiction of a lieutenant. **2.** lieutenants collectively.

lieu·ten·ant (lōō tĕn′ənt; *in Brit. use, except in the navy,* lĕf tĕn′ənt), *n.* **1.** *Mil.* a commissioned officer ranking next below a captain. **a. first lieutenant,** an officer ranking between a second lieutenant and a captain. **b. second lieutenant,** the commissioned officer of the lowest rank, ranking below a first lieutenant. **2.** *Nav.* a commissioned officer ranking next below a lieutenant commander. **a. lieutenant junior grade,** a commissioned officer ranking between an ensign and a lieutenant senior grade. **b. lieutenant senior grade,** an officer ranking between lieutenant junior grade and lieutenant commander. **3.** one who holds an office, civil or military, in subordination to a superior, for whom he acts. [ME *levetenant*, t. F: m. *lieutenant*, f. *lieu* (g. L *locus*) place + *tenant*, ppr. of *tenir* (g. L *tenēre*) hold]

lieutenant colonel, *Mil.* a commissioned officer ranking next below a colonel and next above a major.

lieutenant commander, *Nav.* an officer next in rank below a commander and next above a lieutenant, senior grade.

lieutenant general, *Mil.* an officer ranking next below a general and next above a major general.

lieutenant governor, **1.** *U.S.* a State officer next in rank to the governor, whose place he takes in case of the latter's absence, disability, or death. **2.** *Brit.* a deputy governor.

lieve (lēv), *adv.* lief.

life (līf), *n., pl.* **lives. 1.** the condition which distinguishes animals and plants from inorganic objects and dead organisms. The distinguishing manifestations of life are: growth through metabolism, reproduction, and the power of adaptation to environment through changes originating internally. **2.** (collectively) the distinguishing phenomena (esp. metabolism, growth, reproduction, and spontaneous adaptation to environment) of plants and animals, arising out of the energy relationships with protoplasm. **3.** the animate existence, or the term of animate existence, of an individual: *to risk one's life.* **4.** a corresponding state, existence, or principle of existence conceived as belonging to the soul: *eternal life.* **5.** the term of existence, activity, or effectiveness of something inanimate, as a machine or a lease. **6.** a living being: *several lives were lost.* **7.** living things collectively, whether animals or plants: *insect life.* **8.** course or mode of existence: *married life.* **9.** a biography: *a life of Churchill.* **10.** animation, liveliness: *a speech full of life.* **11.** that which makes or keeps alive; the vivifying or quickening principle. **12.** existence in the world of affairs, society, etc. **13.** one who or that which enlivens: *the life of the party.* **14.** effervescence or sparkle, as of wines. **15.** pungency or strong, sharp flavor, as of substances when fresh or in good condition. **16.** the living form or model as the subject or representation in art. [ME; OE *līf*, c. D *lijf* body, G *leib*, Icel. *līf* life, body] —**Syn. 10.** vivacity, sprightliness; spirit. —**Ant. 10.** inertness, dullness.

life assurance, life insurance.

life belt, a beltlike life preserver.

life-blood (līf′blŭd′), *n.* **1.** the blood necessary to life. **2.** the element that vivifies or animates anything.

life-boat (līf′bōt′), *n.* a boat, provisioned and equipped for abandoning ship, carried in davits so it may be lowered quickly.

life buoy, a buoyant device (in various forms) for throwing, as from a vessel, to persons in the water, to enable them to keep afloat until rescued.

life cycle, the course of development from the fertilization of the egg to the production of a new generation of germ cells.

life expectancy, the probable life span of an individual or class of persons, determined statistically, and affected by such factors as heredity, physical condition, nutrition, occupation, etc.

life-guard (līf′gärd′), *n.* *U.S.* a man employed on a bathing beach to aid in case of accident to bathers.

life history, *Biol.* **1.** the series of living phenomena exhibited by an organism in the course of its development from the egg to its adult state. **2.** a life cycle.

life insurance, a contract insuring payment of a specific sum of money to a named beneficiary, or to the insured's estate, upon the death of the assured, or which provides for payment to the policyholder should he survive a specified period of time. Also, **life assurance.**

life-less (līf′lĭs), *adj.* **1.** not endowed with life: *lifeless matter.* **2.** destitute of living things: *a lifeless planet.* **3.** deprived of life, or dead: *lifeless bodies.* **4.** without animation, liveliness, or spirit: *lifeless performance.* **5.** insensible, as one in a faint. —**life′less·ly,** *adv.* —**life′less·ness,** *n.* —**Syn. 1.** inanimate, inorganic. **3.** See dead. **4.** dull; inactive, inert, passive; sluggish, torpid; spiritless. —**Ant. 1, 3.** living. **4.** lively.

life-like (līf′līk′), *adj.* resembling or simulating real life: *a lifelike picture.* —**life′like′ness,** *n.*

life line, 1. a line fired across a vessel by which a hawser for a breeches buoy may be hauled aboard. **2.** a line or rope for saving life, as one attached to a life boat. **3.** the line by which a diver is lowered and raised. **4.** any of several lines, which are anchored and used by bathers for support. **5.** a route over which supplies can be sent to an area otherwise isolated.

life-long (līf′lông′, -lŏng′), *adj.* lasting or continuing through life: *lifelong regret.*

life net, a strong net or the like held by firemen or others to catch persons jumping from a burning building.

life preserver, 1. a buoyant jacket, belt, or other like device for saving persons in the water from sinking and drowning. **2.** *Brit.* a weapon, esp. a short stick with a loaded head, used for self-defense; a blackjack.

lif·er (līf′ər), *n. Slang.* one sentenced to jail for life.

life-sav·er (līf′sā′vər), *n.* **1.** a person who rescues another from danger of death, esp. from drowning. **2.** a life guard. **3.** *Slang.* someone or something which saves one from trouble, embarrassment, etc. —**life′sav′ing,** *adj., n.*

life-size (līf′sīz′), *adj.* of the size of life or the living original: *life-size picture or statue.*

life span, the longest period over which the life of any plant or animal organism or species may extend, according to the available biological knowledge concerning it. Cf. **life expectancy.**

life-time (līf′tīm′), *n.* the time that one's life continues; one's term of life: *peace within our lifetime.*

life-work (līf′wûrk′), *n.* the work, labor, or task of a lifetime.

lift (lĭft), *v.t.* **1.** to move or bring (something) upward from the ground or other support to some higher position; hoist. **2.** to raise or direct upward: *to lift the hand, head, or eyes.* **3.** to hold up or display on high. **4.** to raise in rank, condition, estimation, etc.; elevate or exalt. **5.** to send up audibly or loudly by utterance: *to lift the voice.* **6.** *Colloq.* to steal; plagiarize. **7.** *U.S.* to pay off a mortgage, etc. **8.** *Golf.* to pick or take up. —*v.i.* **9.** to go up; give to upward pressure: *the lid won't lift.* **10.** to pull or strain in the effort to lift something: *to lift at a heavy weight.* **11.** to move upward or rise; rise and disperse, as clouds, fog, etc. **12.** to rise to view above the horizon when approached, as land seen from the sea. —*n.* **13.** act of lifting, raising, or rising: *the lift of a hand.* **14.** extent of rise, or distance through which anything is raised. **15.** lifting or raising force. **16.** the weight or load lifted. **17.** a helping upward or onward. **18.** a ride in a vehicle, given to help along a traveler on foot. **19.** exaltation or uplift, as in feeling. **20.** a device or apparatus for lifting. **21.** *Chiefly Brit.* an elevator, a dumbwaiter, or the like, in a building. **22.** a rise or elevation of ground. **23.** *Aeron.* the component of the force exerted by the air on an airfoil having a direction opposite to the force of gravity, and causing an aircraft to stay aloft. **24.** one of the layers of leather forming the heel of a boot or shoe. **25.** *Mining.* a slice or thickness (of ore) mined in one operation. [ME *lifte(n)*, t. Scand.; cf. Icel. *lypta* lift, der. *lopt* air, sky] —**lift′er,** *n.* —**Syn. 1.** See **raise.**

lift pump, any pump which merely lifts or raises a liquid (distinguished from *force pump*).

lig·a·ment (lĭg′əmənt), *n., pl.* **ligaments, ligamenta** (lĭg′ə mĕn′tə). **1.** *Anat.* a band of tissue, usually white and fibrous, serving to connect bones, hold organs in lace, etc. **2.** a connecting tie; bond. [ME, t. L: s. *ligamentum* a tie, band]

g·a·men·tous (lĭg′ə·mĕn′təs), *adj.* pertaining to, of he nature of, or forming a ligament. Also, **lig·a·men·a·ry** (lĭg′ə·mĕn′ə·rĭ).

gan (lĭ′gən), *n. Law.* lagan.

gate (lĭ′gāt), *v.t.*, **-gated, -gating.** to bind, as with ligature; tie up, as a bleeding artery. [t. L: m.s. *ligātus*, p.] **—li·ga′tion,** *n.*

g·a·ture (lĭg′ə·chŏŏr′, -chər), *n., v.,* **-tured, -turing.** **—n. 1.** act of binding or tying up. **2.** anything that erves for binding or tying up, as a band, bandage, or ord. **3.** a tie or bond. **4.** *Print. and Writing.* a stroke r bar connecting two letters. **5.** *Print.* a character or ype combining two or more letters, as *fi, ffl*. **6.** *Music.* a slur. **b.** a group of notes connected by a slur. **7.** *Surg.* thread or wire for constriction of blood vessels, etc., r for removing tumors by strangulation. **—v.t. 8.** to ind with a ligature; tie up; ligate. [ME, t. LL: m.s. *igātūra*, der. L *ligāre* bind]

ght¹ (lĭt), *n., adj., v.,* **lighted** or **lit, lighting. —n. . .** that which makes things visible, or affords illuminaion: *all colors depend on light.* **2.** *Physics.* **a.** electro-nagnetic radiation to which the organs of sight react, anging in wave length from about 4000 to 7700 ang-trom units and propagated at a speed of about 186,300 niles per second. It is considered variously as a wave, orpuscular, or quantum phenomenon. Also called *uminous* or *radiant energy.* **b.** the sensation produced y it on the organs of sight. **c.** a similar form of radiant nergy which does not affect the retina, as ultraviolet or nfrared rays. **3.** an illuminating agent or source, as the un, a lamp, or a beacon. **4.** the light, radiance, or illu-nination from a particular source: *the light of a candle.* **5.** the illumination from the sun, or daylight. **6.** day-reak or dawn. **7.** daytime. **8.** measure or supply of ight; illumination: *the wall cuts off our light.* **9.** a par-icular light or illumination in which an object seen takes n a certain appearance: *viewing the portrait in various ights.* **10.** *Art.* **a.** the effect of light falling on an object r scene as represented in a picture. **b.** one of the bright-st parts of a picture. **11.** the aspect in which a thing ppears or is regarded: *this shows up in a favorable light.* **12.** a gleam or sparkle, as in the eyes. **13.** a means of gniting, as a spark, flame, match, or the like: *could you ive me a light?* **14.** state of being visible, exposed to view, or revealed to public notice or knowledge: *to come o light.* **15.** a window, or a pane or compartment of a vindow. **16.** mental or spiritual illumination or en-ightenment: *to throw light on a mystery.* **17.** (*pl.*) in-ormation, ideas, or mental capacities possessed: *to act ccording to one's lights.* **18.** a person who is an illu-ninating or shining example; a luminary. **19.** a light-ouse. **20.** *Archaic.* the eyesight. **21. see the light,** **.** to come into existence. **b.** to be made public, or ublished, as a book. **c.** to accept or understand an idea. **—adj. 22.** having light or illumination, rather than dark: *he lightest room in the entire house.* **23.** pale, whitish, r not deep or dark in color: *a light red.* **—v.t. 24.** to set burning (a candle, lamp, pipe for smok-ng, etc.); kindle (a fire); ignite (fuel, a match, etc.). **25.** to give light to; illuminate. **26.** to furnish with ight or illumination. **27.** to make bright as with ight or color (usually with *up*): *a huge room lighted p with candles.* **28.** to brighten (the face, etc.): *smile lighted up her face.* **29.** to conduct with a light: *candle to light you to bed.* **—v.i. 30.** to take fire or become kindled. **31.** to become right as with light or color: *the sky lights up at sunset.* **32.** to brighten with animation or joy, as the face, eyes, tc. (often fol. by *up*). ME; OE *lēoht*, c. D and G *licht*; akin to Icel. *ljōs*, Goth. *iuhath*, also to L *lux* light, Gk. *leukós* light, bright]

ght² (lĭt), *adj.* **1.** of little weight; not heavy: *a light oad.* **2.** of little weight in proportion to bulk; of low pecific gravity: *a light metal.* **3.** of less than the usual r average weight: *light clothing.* **4.** weighing less than he proper or standard amount: *to use light weights in rade.* **5.** of small amount, force, intensity, etc.: *a light ote, a light rain, light sleep.* **6.** easy to endure, deal with, r perform: *light taxes.* **7.** not profound, serious, or eavy: *light reading.* **8.** of little moment or importance: *rivial: the loss was no light matter.* **9.** easily digested, as ood. **10.** not heavy or strong, as wine, etc. **11.** spongy r well leavened, as bread. **12.** porous or friable, as soil. **13.** slender or delicate in form or appearance: *a light, raceful figure.* **14.** airy or buoyant in movement: *light s air.* **15.** nimble or agile: *light fingers.* **16.** free from ny burden of sorrow or care: *a light heart.* **17.** cheerful; ay: *a light laugh.* **18.** characterized by lack of proper eriousness; frivolous: *light conduct.* **19.** wanton. **20.** easily swayed or changing; volatile: *to be light of ove.* **21.** dizzy; slightly delirious: *his head is light.* **22.** *Mil.* lightly armed or equipped: *light infantry.* **23.** laden or encumbered but slightly or not at all: *a hip sailing light.* **24.** adapted by small weight or slight uild for small loads or swift movement: *light vessels.* **25.** (of wind) having a velocity up to 7 mi. per hour; aving a Beaufort scale number of 1 (**light air**: 1–3 mi. er hour) or 2 (**light breeze**: 4–7 mi. per hour). **26.** *Pho-et.* **a.** having a less than normally strong pronunciation, s of a vowel or syllable. **b.** (of *l* sounds) resembling a ront vowel in quality: *French l is lighter than English l.* **—adv. 27.** lightly. [ME; OE *lēoht, līht*, c. D *licht*, G *leicht*]

light³ (lĭt), *v.i.*, **lighted** or **lit, lighting. 1.** to get down or descend, as from a horse or a vehicle. **2.** to come to rest, as on a spot or thing; land. **3.** to come by chance, happen, or hit (fol. by *on* or *upon*): *to light on a clue.* **4.** to fall, as a stroke, weapon, vengeance, choice, etc., on a place or person. **5.** *Slang.* to jump on or attack (fol. by *into*). [ME *liht(en)*, OE *līhtan* alight, orig. make light, relieve of a weight, der. *līht* LIGHT², adj.]

light·en¹ (lī′tən), *v.i.* **1.** to become lighter or less dark; brighten. **2.** to shine, gleam, or be bright. **3.** to flash as or like lightning. **4.** to reveal by light. **5.** to brighten (the face, eyes, etc.). **6.** to give light to; illuminate. **—v.t. 7.** to flash (something) like lightning. [ME, f. LIGHT¹, adj. + -EN¹] **—light′en·er,** *n.*

light·en² (lī′tən), *v.t.* **1.** to make lighter; lessen the weight of (a load, etc.); reduce the load of (a ship, etc.). **2.** to make less burdensome; mitigate: *to lighten taxes.* **3.** to cheer or gladden. [ME, f. LIGHT², adj. + -EN¹]

light·er¹ (lī′tər), *n.* one who or that which lights. [ME; f. LIGHT¹, v. + -ER¹]

light·er² (lī′tər), *n.* **1.** a vessel, commonly a flat-bottomed unpowered barge, used in lightening or un-loading and also in loading ships, or in transporting goods for short distances. **—v.t. 2.** to convey in or as in a lighter. [ME, f. LIGHT², v. + -ER¹]

light·er·age (lī′tər·ĭj), *n.* **1.** the use of lighters. **2.** a fee paid for lighter service.

light·er-than-air (lī′tər·than·âr′), *adj.* **1.** *Aeron.* of less specific gravity than the air. **2.** of or pertaining to such aircraft.

light·face (lĭt′fās′), *n. Print.* a type characterized by thin lines.

light-fin·gered (lĭt′fĭng′gərd), *adj.* having nimble fingers, esp. in picking pockets; thievish.

light-foot·ed (lĭt′fŏŏt′ĭd), *adj.* stepping lightly or nimbly. Also, *Poetic,* **light′-foot′.** **—light′-foot′ed·ly,** *adv.* **—light′-foot′ed·ness,** *n.*

light-head·ed (lĭt′hĕd′ĭd), *adj.* **1.** having or showing a frivolous or volatile disposition: *light-headed persons.* **2.** giddy, dizzy, or delirious. **—light′-head′ed·ly,** *adv.* **—light′-head′ed·ness,** *n.*

light-heart·ed (lĭt′här′tĭd), *adj.* carefree; cheerful; gay: *a light-hearted laugh.* **—light′-heart′ed·ly,** *adv.* **—light′-heart′ed·ness,** *n.*

light heavyweight, *Boxing.* a fighter whose weight is between 160 and 175 pounds.

light-horse·man (lĭt′hôrs′mən), *n., pl.* **-men.** a light-armed cavalry soldier.

light·house (lĭt′hous′), *n.* a tower or other structure displaying a light or lights for the guidance of mariners.

light·ing (lī′tĭng), *n.* **1.** act of igniting or illuminating. **2.** arrangement or method of lights. **3.** the way light falls upon a face, object, etc., esp. in a picture.

light·ish (lī′tĭsh), *adj.* rather light, as in color.

light·less (lĭt′lĭs), *adj.* **1.** without light; receiving no light; dark. **2.** giving no light.

light·ly (lĭt′lĭ), *adv.* **1.** with little weight, force, in-tensity, etc.: *to press lightly on a bell.* **2.** to but a small amount or degree. **3.** easily; without trouble or effort: *lightly come, lightly go.* **4.** cheerfully: *to take bad news lightly.* **5.** frivolously: *to behave lightly.* **6.** without due consideration or reason (often with a negative): *an offer not lightly to be refused.* **7.** nimbly: *to leap lightly aside.* **8.** indifferently or slightingly: *to think lightly of one's achievements.* **9.** airily; buoyantly: *flags floating lightly.*

light-mind·ed (lĭt′mīn′dĭd), *adj.* having or showing a light mind; characterized by levity; frivolous. **—light′-mind′ed·ly,** *adv.* **—light′-mind′ed·ness,** *n.*

light·ness¹ (lĭt′nĭs), *n.* **1.** state of being light, illu-minated, or whitish. **2.** thin or pale coloration. [ME *lightnesse*, OE *līhtnes*, f. *līht* light, bright + *-nes* -NESS]

light·ness² (lĭt′nĭs), *n.* **1.** state or quality of being light in weight. **2.** light as to specific gravity: *the light-ness of cork.* **3.** the quality of being agile, nimble, or graceful. **4.** lack of pressure or burdensomeness. **5.** gay-ness; cheerfulness. **6.** levity in actions, thought, or speech. [f. LIGHT², adj. + -NESS]

light·ning (lĭt′nĭng), *n.* a flashing of light, or a sud-den illumination of the heavens, caused by the discharge of atmospheric electricity. [var. of *lightening*, f. LIGHT-EN¹, v. + -ING¹]

lightning arrester, a device preventing damage to radio, telephonic, or other electrical equipment from lightning or other high-voltage currents, reducing the voltage of a surge applied to its terminals, interrupting follow current if present, and restoring itself to its orig-inal operating condition.

lightning bug, *U.S.* a firefly.

lightning rod, a rodlike conductor installed to divert atmospheric electricity away from a structure and pro-tect the structure from lightning by providing a path to earth.

light-o'-love (lĭt′ə·lŭv′), *n.* a wanton coquette.

light quantum, *Physics.* a photon.

lights (lĭts), *n.pl.* the lungs, esp. of sheep, pigs, etc.

light·ship (lĭt′shĭp′), *n.* a ship anchored in a specific location and displaying a light or lights for the guidance of mariners.

light·some¹ (lĭt′səm), *adj.* **1.** light, esp. in form, ap-pearance, or movement; airy; buoyant; agile; nimble. **2.** cheerful; gay. **3.** frivolous. [f. LIGHT³ + -SOME¹] **—light′some·ly,** *adv.* **—light′some·ness,** *n.*

light·some² (līt/səm), *adj.* **1.** luminous. **2.** well-lighted or illuminated. [f. LIGHT¹ + -SOME¹] —**light/-some·ness,** *n.*

lights out, *Chiefly Mil.* a signal that all or certain lights are to be extinguished.

light-struck (līt/strŭk/), *adj. Photog.* (of film, etc.) injured or fogged by accidental exposure to light.

light·weight (līt/wāt/), *adj.* **1.** light in weight. —*n.* **2.** one of less than average weight. **3.** *Colloq.* a person of little mental force or of slight influence or importance. **4.** a boxer or other contestant who weighs between 127 and 135 pounds.

light·wood (līt/wŏŏd/), *n.* **1.** wood used in lighting a fire. **2.** (in the southern U.S.) resinous pine wood.

light-year (līt/yĭr/), *n. Astron.* the distance traversed by light in one year (about 5,880,000,000,000 miles): used as a unit in measuring stellar distances.

lig·ne·ous (lĭg/nĭ əs), *adj.* of the nature of or resembling wood; woody. [t. L: m. *ligneus* wooden]

ligni-, var. of ligno-.

Lig·ni·ca (lĕg nĭ/tsä), *n.* Polish name of **Liegnitz.**

lig·ni·form (lĭg/nə fôrm/), *adj.* having the form of wood; resembling wood, as a variety of asbestos.

lig·ni·fy (lĭg/nə fī/), *v.,* **-fied, -fying.** —*v.t.* **1.** to convert into wood. —*v.i.* **2.** to become wood. —**lig/ni·fi·ca/tion,** *n.*

lig·nin (lĭg/nĭn), *n. Bot.* an organic substance which, with cellulose, forms the chief part of woody tissue.

lig·nite (lĭg/nīt), *n.* an imperfectly formed coal, usually dark-brown, and often having a distinct woody texture; brown coal. [t. F, der. L *lignum* wood. See -ITE¹] —**lig·nit·ic** (lĭg nĭt/ĭk), *adj.*

ligno-, a word element meaning "wood." [comb. form repr. L *lignum*]

lig·no·cel·lu·lose (lĭg/nō sĕl/yə lōs/), *n.* any of various compounds of lignin and cellulose found in wood and other fibers.

lig·nose (lĭg/nōs), *n.* one of the constituents of lignin. [t. L: m.s. *lignōsus* woody]

lig·num vi·tae (lĭg/nəm vī/tē), **1.** the hard, extremely heavy wood of either of two species of guaiacum, *Guaiacum officinale* and *G. sanctum,* used for making pulleys, rulers, etc., and formerly thought to have great medicinal powers. **2.** either tree. **3.** any of various other trees with a similar hard wood. [NL: wood of life]

lig·ro·in (lĭg/rō ĭn), *n. Chem.* a petroleum ether. Also, **lig/ro·ine.**

lig·u·la (lĭg/yə lə), *n., pl.* **-lae** (-lē/), **-las. 1.** *Bot., Zool.* a tonguelike or strap-shaped part or organ. **2.** *Bot.* **a.** the membranous appendage projecting from the summit of the leaf sheath in many grasses. **b.** the blade formed by the gamopetalous corolla in the ray flowers of numerous composite plants. Also, **lig·ule** (lĭg/ūl). [t. L: strap, var. of *lingula,* dim. of *lingua* tongue] —**lig/-u·lar,** *adj.*

A. Ligula; B. Leaf blade; C. Leaf sheath; D. Stem

lig·u·late (lĭg/yə lĭt, -lāt/), *adj.* **1.** having or forming a ligula. **2.** strap-shaped.

lig·ure (lĭg/yŏŏr), *n.* an unidentified precious stone mentioned in the Bible. See Ex. 28:19. [ME *ligury,* t. LL: m.s. *ligūrius,* t. Gk.: m. *ligýrion* (used to render Heb. *leshem*)]

Li·gu·ri·a (lĭ gyŏŏr/ĭ ə), *n.* a department in NW Italy. 1,562,877 pop. (est. 1952); 2099 sq. mi. —**Li·gu/ri·an,** *adj., n.*

Ligurian Sea, a part of the Mediterranean between Corsica and the NW coast of Italy.

Li Hung-chang (lē/ hŏŏng/jäng/), 1823-1901, Chinese statesman.

lik·a·ble (lī/kə bəl), *adj.* such as to be liked; pleasing. Also, **likeable.** —**lik/a·ble·ness,** *adj.*

like¹ (līk), *adj.* (Poetic. **liker, likest**) *prep., adv., conj., n.* —*adj.* **1.** resembling (followed by a noun or pronoun): *he is just like his father.* **2.** characteristic of: *it would be like him to come without notice.* **3.** of the same form, appearance, kind, character, amount, etc.: *a like instance.* **4.** corresponding or agreeing in general or in some noticeable respect; similar; analogous: *drawing, painting, and other like arts.* **5.** bearing resemblance. **6.** giving promise or indication of: *it looks like rain.* **7.** disposed or inclined to (after *feel*): *to feel like going to bed.* **8.** *Archaic* or *Dial.* probable or likely. **9.** *Archaic, Dial.* or *Colloq.* likely to (do, be, etc.). **10.** *Now Dial.* or *Colloq.* about (to do, etc.). —*prep.* **11.** in like manner with; similarly to; in the manner characteristic of: *to work like a beaver.* —*adv.* **12.** *Colloq.* likely or probably: *like enough.* **13.** *Dial.* or *Slang.* as it were: *of a sudden like.* **14. in like manner,** *Archaic.* to a like extent or degree; equally, or alike. —*conj.* **15.** *Colloq.* like as, just as, or as. **16.** *Colloq.* as if: *he acted like he was afraid.* —*n.* **17.** something of a similar nature (prec. by *the*): *oranges, lemons, and the like.* **18.** a like person or thing, or like persons or things; a counterpart, match, or equal: *no one has seen his like in a long time.* [ME; OE *gelic,* c. D *gelijk,* G *gleich,* Icel. *glíkr,* Goth. *galeiks* like, lit. of the same body, or form]

like² (līk), *v.,* **liked, liking,** *n.* —*v.t.* **1.** to take pleasure in; find agreeable to one's taste. **2.** to regard with favor, or have a kindly or friendly feeling for (a person, etc.). —*v.i.* **3.** to feel inclined, or wish: *come whenever you like.*

4. *Dial.* or *Colloq.* to come near (doing something). **5.** *Obs.* or *Archaic.* to suit the tastes or wishes. **6.** (*usually pl.*) a favorable feeling; preference: *likes and dislikes.* [ME *like(n),* OE *lician,* c. D *lijken,* Icel. *líka*]

-like, suffixal use of like¹, *adj.,* e.g., *childlike, lifelike, horselike,* sometimes hyphenated. —Syn. See -ish¹.

like·a·ble (lī/kə bəl), *adj.* likable. —**like/a·ble·ness,** *n.*

like·li·hood (līk/lĭ hŏŏd/), *n.* **1.** state of being likely or probable; probability. **2.** a probability or chance of something: *there is a strong likelihood of his succeeding.* **3.** *Obs.* or *Archaic.* promising character, or promise. Also, **like/li·ness.**

like·ly (līk/lĭ), *adj.,* **-lier, -liest,** *adv.* —*adj.* **1.** probably or apparently going or destined (to do, be, etc.): *not likely to happen.* **2.** seeming like truth, fact, or certainty, or reasonably to be believed or expected; probable; *a likely story.* **3.** apparently suitable: *a likely spot to build on.* **4.** promising: *a fine likely boy.* —*adv.* **5.** probably. [ME: t. Scand.; cf. Icel. *líkligr,* f. *líkr* LIKE¹ adj. + -*ligr* -LY]
—Syn. **1.** LIKELY, APT, LIABLE are not alike in indicating probability; though APT is used colloquially, and LIABLE mistakenly, in this sense. LIKELY is the only one of these words which means "probable" or "to be expected": *it is likely to rain today.* APT refers to a natural bent or inclination; if something is natural and easy, it is often probable; hence APT comes to be associated with LIKELY and to be used informally as a substitute for it: *he is apt at drawing he is apt to do well at drawing.* LIABLE should not be used to mean "probable." When used with an infinitive, it may remind one of LIKELY: *he is liable to be arrested.* But the true meaning, susceptibility to something unpleasant, or exposure to risk, becomes evident when it is used with a prepositional phrase: *he is liable to arrest, liable to error.*

like-mind·ed (līk/mīn/dĭd), *adj.* having a like opinion or purpose. —**like/-mind/ed·ness,** *n.*

lik·en (lī/kən), *v.t.* to represent as like; compare.

like·ness (līk/nĭs), *n.* **1.** a representation, picture, or image, esp. a portrait. **2.** the semblance or appearance of something: *to assume the likeness of a swan.* **3.** state or fact of being like.

like·wise (līk/wīz/), *adv.* **1.** moreover; also; too. **2.** in like manner. [abbr. of *in like wise.* See LIKE¹, -WISE, *n.*]

li·kin (lē/kēn/), *n.* a Chinese provincial duty imposed on articles of trade in transit. [t. Chinese: f. *li* 1/1000 of an ounce + *kin* money]

lik·ing (lī/kĭng), *n.* **1.** preference, inclination, or favor. **2.** pleasure or taste: *much to his liking.* **3.** the state or feeling of one who likes. [ME; OE *lícung,* der. *lícian* please]

li·lac (lī/lək), *n.* **1.** any of the oleaceous shrubs constituting the genus *Syringa,* as *S. vulgaris,* the common garden lilac, with large clusters of fragrant purple or white flowers. **2.** pale reddish purple. [t. F (Obs.), or t. Sp.: t. Ar.: m. *līlak,* t. Pers. var. of *nīlak* bluish, der. *nīl* blue, indigo (c. Skt. *nīla* dark-blue); cf. ANIL]

li·la·ceous (lī lā/shəs), *adj.* of or approaching the color lilac.

lil·i·a·ceous (lĭl/ĭ ā/shəs), *adj.* **1.** of or like the lily. **2.** belonging to the *Liliaceae,* or lily family of plants, sometimes subdivided in smaller units such as the *Melanthiaceae, Alliaceae, Convallariaceae, Smilacaceae, Trilliaceae,* etc. [t. LL: m. *līliāceus,* der. L *līlium* LILY]

lil·ied (lĭl/ĭd), *adj.* **1.** lilylike; white. **2.** abounding in lilies.

Lil·i·en·thal (lĭl/ĭ ən thôl/ *for 1*; lē/lē ən täl/ *for 2*), *n.* **1. David Ely,** born 1899, U.S. public administrator: chairman, U.S. Atomic Energy Commission 1947-1950. **2. Otto** (ôt/ō), 1848-96, German aeronautical engineer and inventor.

Lil·ith (lĭl/ĭth), *n.* **1.** *Bible* and *Talmudic Lit.* a female demon that dwells in deserted places and assaults children. **2.** *Jewish Legend.* Adam's first wife. [t. Heb., ult. t. Akkadian]

Li·li·u·o·ka·la·ni (lē lē/ŏŏ ō kä lä/nē), *n.* **Lydia Kamekeha** (kä/mě kē/hä), 1838-1917, last queen of the Hawaiian Islands, 1891-93.

Lille (lēl), *n.* a city in N France. 194,616 (1954). Formerly, **Lisle.**

lil·li·bul·le·ro (lĭl/ĭ bə lĭr/ō), *n.* a part of the refrain to a song deriding the Irish Roman Catholics, popular in England during and after the Revolution of 1688. **2.** the song, or the tune to which it was sung.

Lil·li·put (lĭl/ĭ pŭt/, -pət), *n.* an imaginary country inhabited by tiny people, described in Swift's *Gulliver's Travels.*

Lil·li·pu·tian (lĭl/ĭ pū/shən), *adj.* **1.** tiny; diminutive. —*n.* **2.** an inhabitant of Lilliput. **3.** a tiny being. **4.** a person of small intellect or importance.

lilt (lĭlt), *n.* **1.** rhythmic swing or cadence. **2.** a lilting song or tune. —*v.t., v.i.* **3.** to sing or play in a light, tripping, or rhythmic manner. [ME *lulte;* D *lui* pipe]

lil·y (lĭl/ĭ), *n., pl.* **lilies,** *adj.* —*n.* **1.** any plant of the genus *Lilium,* comprising scaly-bulbed herbs with showy funnel-shaped or bell-shaped flowers of various colors, as *L. candidum* (**Madonna lily**), *L. longiflorum eximium* or *L. Harrisii* (once the common **Easter lily**), or *L. philadelphicum* (**Orangecup lily**). **2.** the flower or the bulb of such a plant. **3.** any of various related or similar plants or their flowers, as the Mariposa lily or the calla lily. **4.** fleur-de-lis. —*adj.* **5.** white as a lily. **6.** delicately fair. **7.** pure; unsullied. **8.** pale. [ME and OE *lilie,* t. L: m. *līlium,* t. Gk.: m. *leírion*] —**lil/y·like/,** *adj.*

lily iron, a harpoon whose head may be detached.

li·y-liv·ered (lĭl′ĭ lĭv′ərd), *adj.* cowardly.

lily of the valley, *pl.* **lilies of the valley.** a stemless convallariaceous herb, *Convallaria majalis,* with a raceme of drooping, bell-shaped, fragrant white flowers.

lily pad, the large, floating leaf of a water lily.

Li·ma (lē′mə *for 1;* lī′mə *for 2) n.* **1.** the capital of Peru, in the W part, near the Pacific coast. 926,400 (est. 1952). **2.** a city in NW Ohio. 51,037 (1960).

li·ma bean (lī′mə), **1.** a kind of bean, including several varieties of *Phaseolus limensis,* with a broad, flat, edible seed. **2.** the seed, much used for food.

li·ma·cine (lī′mə sīn′, -sĭn, lĭ′mə-), *adj.* pertaining to, or having the characteristics of, the slugs. [f. s. L *limax* slug, snail + -INE[1]]

limb[1] (lĭm), *n.* **1.** a part or member of an animal body distinct from the head and trunk, as a leg, arm, or wing. **2.** a large or main branch of a tree. **3.** a projecting part or member: *the four limbs of a cross.* **4.** a person or thing regarded as a part, member, branch, offshoot, or scion of something. **5.** *Colloq.* an imp, young scamp, or mischievous child. **6. out on a limb,** *U.S. Colloq.* at a great disadvantage. [ME and OE *lim,* c. Icel. *limr*] **—limbed** (lĭmd), *adj.* **—limb′less,** *adj.* **—Syn. 1.** See **member. 2.** See **branch.**

limb[2] (lĭm), *n.* **1.** the edge of the disk of the sun, moon, or planet. **2.** the graduated edge of a quadrant or similar instrument. **3.** *Bot.* the upper spreading part of a gamopetalous corolla; the expanded portion of a petal, sepal, or leaf. **4.** *Archery.* the upper or lower portion of a bow. [t. L: s. *limbus* border. Cf. LIMBUS and LIMBO]

lim·bate (lĭm′bāt), *adj. Bot., Zool.* bordered, as a flower in which one color is surrounded by an edging of another. [t. LL: m.s. *limbātus,* der. L *limbus* LIMB[2]]

lim·ber[1] (lĭm′bər), *adj.* **1.** bending readily; flexible; pliant. **2.** characterized by ease in bending the body; supple; lithe. **—v.i. 3.** to make oneself limber (fol. by *up*). **—v.t. 4.** to make limber. [see LIMP[2]] **—lim′-ber·ly,** *adv.* **—lim′ber·ness,** *n.* **—Syn. 1.** See **flexible.**

lim·ber[2] (lĭm′bər), *Mil.* **—n. 1.** the detachable forepart of the carriage of a field gun, consisting of two wheels, an axle, a pole, etc. **—v.t., v.i. 2.** to attach the limber to (a gun), in preparation for moving away (usually fol. by *up*). [late ME, ? t. F: m. *limonière*]

lim·ber[3] (lĭm′bər), *n.* (*usually pl.*) *Naut.* one of a series of holes or channels for the passage of water to the pumpwell. [? t. F: alter. of *lumiere* hole, lit. light]

lim·bic (lĭm′bĭk), *adj.* pertaining to or of the nature of a limbus or border; marginal.

lim·bo (lĭm′bō), *n.* **1.** (*often cap.*) a supposed region on the border of hell or heaven, the abode after death of unbaptized infants (**limbo of infants**), or one serving as the temporary abode of the righteous who died before the coming of Christ (**limbo of the fathers or patriarchs**). **2.** a place to which persons or things are regarded as being relegated when cast aside, forgotten, past, or out of date. **3.** prison, jail, or confinement. [ME, t. L, abl. of *limbus* border, edge, ML limbo]

Lim·bourg (lăn boōr′), *n.* See **Limburg.**

Lim·burg (lĭm′bûrg; *Du.* lĭm′bœrkн), *n.* medieval duchy in W Europe: now divided into provinces of **Limburg** in SE Netherlands and **Limbourg** in NE Belgium.

Lim·burg·er (lĭm′bûr′gər), *n.* a variety of soft cheese of strong odor and flavor. Also, **Limburg cheese.**

lim·bus (lĭm′bəs), *n., pl.* **-bi** (-bī). **1.** limbo. **2.** (in scientific or technical use) a border, edge, or limb. [t.L]

lime[1] (līm), *n., v.,* **limed, liming. —n. 1.** the oxide of calcium, CaO, a white caustic solid (**quicklime** or **unslaked lime**) prepared by calcining limestone, etc., used in making mortar and cement. When treated with water it produces calcium hydroxide, $Ca(OH)_2$, or **slaked lime. 2.** any calcium compounds for improving crops on lime-deficient soils. **3.** birdlime. **—v.t. 4.** to treat (soil, etc.) with lime or compounds of calcium. **5.** to smear (twigs, etc.) with birdlime. **6.** to catch with, or as with, birdlime. [ME; OE *līm,* c. D *lijm,* G *leim,* L *limus* slime; akin to LOAM]

lime[2] (līm), *n.* **1.** the small, greenish-yellow, acid fruit of a tropical tree, *Citrus aurantifolia,* allied to the lemon. **2.** the tree. [t. F, t. Sp.: m. *lima;* akin to LEMON]

lime[3] (līm), *n.* linden. [unexplained var. of obs. *line, lind,* ME and OE *lind.* See LINDEN]

lime burner, one who makes lime by burning or calcining limestone, etc.

lime·house (līm′hous′), *n.* a district in the East End of London, noted for its squalor.

lime·kiln (līm′kĭl′, -kĭln′), *n.* a kiln or furnace for making lime by calcining limestone or shells.

lime·light (līm′līt′), *n.* **1.** a strong light thrown upon the stage to illuminate particular persons or objects. **2.** the glare of public observation or notoriety.

li·men (lī′měn), *n., pl.* **limens, limina** (lĭm′ə nə). *Psychol.* threshold (def. 4). [t. L]

lim·er·ick (lĭm′ər ĭk), *n.* a kind of humorous verse of five lines, in which the first and second lines rhyme with the fifth line, and the shorter third line rhymes with the shorter fourth. [named after *Limerick,* Ireland; orig., a song with refrain, "Will you come up to Limerick?"]

Lim·er·ick (lĭm′ər ĭk), *n.* **1.** a county in SW Ireland, in Munster. 137,770 pop. (prelim. 1956); 1037 sq. mi. **2.** its county seat: a seaport at the head of the Shannon estuary. 56,869 (prelim. 1956).

Li·mes (lī′mēz), *n.* **1.** a boundary. **2.** the Siegfried Line. [t. L]

lime·stone (līm′stōn′), *n.* a rock consisting wholly or chiefly of calcium carbonate, originating principally from the calcareous remains of organisms, and when heated yielding quicklime.

lime tree, (in the Old World) the linden or basswood.

lime twig, 1. a twig smeared with birdlime to catch birds. **2.** a snare.

lime·wa·ter (līm′wô′tər, -wŏt′ər), *n.* **1.** an aqueous solution of slaked lime, used medicinally and otherwise. **2.** water containing naturally an unusual amount of calcium carbonate or calcium sulfate.

lim·ey (lī′mĭ), *n., pl.* **-eys.** *Colloq.* a British sailor or ship (from the prescribed use of lime juice against scurvy).

li·mic·o·line (lī mĭk′ə lĭn′, -lĭn), *adj.* shore-inhabiting; of or pertaining to numerous birds of the families *Charadriidae* (plovers) and *Scolopacidae* (sandpipers). [f. s. LL *limicola* dweller in mud + -INE[1]]

lim·i·nal (lĭm′ə nal, lī′mə-), *adj. Psychol.* of or pertaining to the limen. [f. s. L *līmen* threshold + -AL[1]]

lim·it (lĭm′ĭt), *n.* **1.** the final or furthest bound or point as to extent, amount, continuance, procedure, etc.: *the limit of vision.* **2.** a boundary or bound, as of a country, tract, district, etc. **3.** *Obs.* an area or region within boundaries. **4.** *Math.* (of a function) a number such that the value of the function can be made arbitrarily close to this number by restricting its argument to be sufficiently near the point at which the limit is to be taken. **5.** *Games.* the maximum sum by which a bet may be raised at any one time. **—v.t. 6.** to restrict by or as by fixing limits (fol. by *to*): *to limit questions to 25 words.* **7.** to confine or keep within limits: *to limit expenditures.* **8.** *Obs. Eccl. Law.* to fix or assign definitely or specifically. [ME *lymyte,* t. OF: m. *limite,* t. L: m.s. *līmes* boundary] **—lim′it·a·ble,** *adj.* **—lim′it·er,** *n.*

lim·i·tar·y (lĭm′ə tĕr′ĭ), *adj.* **1.** of, pertaining to, or serving as a limit. **2.** subject to limits; limited.

lim·i·ta·tion (lĭm′ə tā′shən), *n.* **1.** that which limits; a limit or bound; a limiting condition or circumstance; restriction. **2.** act of limiting. **3.** state of being limited. **4.** *Law.* the assignment, as by statute, of a period of time within which an action must be brought, or the period of time assigned: *a statute of limitations.*

lim·i·ta·tive (lĭm′ə tā′tĭv), *adj.* limiting; restrictive.

lim·it·ed (lĭm′ĭt ĭd), *adj.* **1.** confined within limits; restricted, circumscribed, or narrow: *a limited space.* **2.** restricted with reference to governing powers by limitations prescribed in a constitution: *a limited monarchy.* **3.** *Chiefly Brit.* restricted as to amount of liability: *a limited company.* **4.** (of railroad trains, buses, etc.) restricted as to number or class of passengers, time occupied in transit, etc. **—n. 5.** *U.S.* a limited train, bus, etc. **—lim′it·ed·ly,** *adv.* **—lim′it·ed·ness,** *n.*

limited edition, an edition of a book of which there is an announced limited number of copies available.

limited payment insurance, life insurance where increased premiums for a stipulated period of years cause the insurance to become full paid at an age short of the maturity date of the policy.

limited policy, *Insurance.* a policy which covers only certain types of losses within an area of risks.

lim·it·ing (lĭm′ĭt ĭng), *adj. Gram.* of the nature of a limiting adjective or a restrictive clause.

limiting adjective, *Gram.* (in English and some other languages) one of a small group of adjectives, which modify the nouns to which they are applied by restricting rather than describing or qualifying. *This, some,* and *certain* are limiting adjectives.

lim·it·less (lĭm′ĭt lĭs), *adj.* without limit; boundless.

limn (lĭm), *v.t.* **1.** to represent in drawing or painting. **2.** *Archaic.* to portray in words. [ME *lymne(n),* var. of *lumine* illuminate, t. OF: m. *luminer,* ult. der. L *lūmen* light]

lim·nol·o·gy (lĭm nŏl′ə jĭ), *n.* the scientific study of bodies of fresh water, as lakes and ponds, with reference to their physical, geographical, biological, and other features. [f. s. Gk. *límnē* lake + -(o)LOGY]

Li·moges (lĭ mōzh′; *Fr.* lē môzh′), *n.* **1.** a city in central France. 105,990 (1954). **2.** Also, **Limoges ware.** a type of porcelain manufactured at Limoges.

lim·o·nene (lĭm′ə nēn′), *n. Chem.* a liquid terpene, $C_{10}H_{16}$, occurring in two optically different forms, the dextrorotatory form being present in the essential oils of lemon, orange, etc., and the levorotatory in Douglas fir needle oil. [f. s. NL *limonum* lemon + -ENE]

li·mo·nite (lī′mə nīt′), *n.* an important iron ore, a hydrated ferric oxide, $2Fe_2O_3 \cdot 3H_2O$, varying in color from dark brown to yellow. [f. m. Gk. *leimōn* meadow + -ITE[1]] **—li·mo·nit·ic** (lī′mə nĭt′ĭk), *adj.*

Li·mou·sin (lē moō zăn′), *n.* a former province in central France. *Cap.* Limoges.

lim·ou·sine (lĭm′ə zēn′, lĭm′ə zēn′), *n.* an automobile having a permanently enclosed compartment for from three to five persons, the roof of which projects forward over the driver's seat in front. [t. F, der. *Limousin*]

limp[1] (lĭmp), *v.i.* **1.** to walk with a labored, jerky movement, as when lame. **2.** to proceed in a lame or faulty manner: *his verse limps.* **—n. 3.** a lame movement or gait. [ME; cf. MHG *limphin* limp and OE *lemphealt* lame] **—limp′er,** *n.*

limp² (lĭmp), *adj.* **1.** lacking stiffness or firmness, as of substance, fiber, structure, or bodily frame: *a limp body.* **2.** without proper firmness, force, energy, etc., as of character. [akin to Icel. *limpa* indisposition] **—limp′ly,** *adv.* **—limp′ness,** *n.*

lim·pet (lĭm′pĭt), *n. Zool.* any of various marine gastropods with a low conical shell open beneath, found adhering to rocks, used for bait and sometimes for food. [ME *lempet,* OE *lempedu,* t. LL: m. *lamprēda* limpet, LAMPREY]

lim·pid (lĭm′pĭd), *adj.* **1.** clear, transparent, or pellucid, as water, crystal, air, etc. **2.** free from obscurity; lucid: *a limpid style.* [t. L: s. *limpidus*] **—lim·pid′i·ty, lim′pid·ness,** *n.* **—lim′pid·ly,** *adv.*

limp·kin (lĭmp′kĭn), *n.* a large, loud-voiced, wading bird, *Aramus guarauna,* intermediate in size and character between the cranes and the rails, which inhabits Florida, Central America, and the West Indies.

Lim·po·po (lĭm·pō′pō), *n.* a river flowing from the Union of South Africa through S Mozambique into the Indian Ocean. ab. 1000 mi. Also, **Crocodile River.**

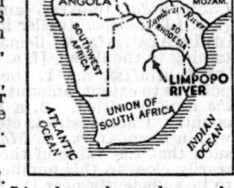

im·u·loid (ĭm′yə loid′), *Zool.* **—adj. 1.** resembling or pertaining to the horseshoe crabs, esp. to *Limulus.* **—n. 2.** a horseshoe crab. [f. LIM-UL(US) + -OID]

lim·u·lus (lĭm′yə ləs), *n., pl.* **-li** (-lī′). a crab of the genus *Limulus;* a horseshoe crab. [t. NL, t. L: somewhat askew, dim. of *līmus* sidelong]

lim·y (lī′mĭ), *adj.,* **limier, limiest. 1.** consisting of, containing, or like lime. **2.** smeared with bird lime.

lin., **1.** lineal. **2.** linear.

lin·age (lī′nĭj), *n.* **1.** alignment. **2.** number of lines of written or printed matter covered. Also, **lineage.**

lin·al·o·öl (lĭ nål′ō ōl′, -ōl′, lĭn′ə lō ōl′), *n. Chem.* a colorless, liquid, unsaturated alcohol, $C_{10}H_{17}OH$, related to the terpenes, found in several essential oils. [f. Sp. *linalo(e)* fragrant Mexican wood + -OL¹]

inch·pin (ĭnch′pĭn′), *n.* a pin inserted through the end of an axletree to keep the wheel on. [f. *linch-,* OE *lynis* linchpin (c. G *lünse*) + PIN]

Lin·coln (lĭng′kən), *n.* **1.** Abraham, 1809–65, 16th president of the U.S., 1861–65. **2.** Benjamin, 1733–1810, American Revolutionary general. **3.** the capital of Nebraska, in the SE part. 128,521 (1960). **4.** a city in E England. 70,500 (est. 1956). **5.** Lincolnshire. **6.** one of a large English variety of mutton sheep, with a heavy fleece of coarse, long wool.

Lincoln Park, a city in SE Michigan. 53,933 (1960).

Lin·coln·shire (lĭng′kən shĭr′, -shər), *n.* a county in E. England. 705,822 pop. (1951); 2663 sq. mi. *Co. seat:* Lincoln. Also, **Lincoln.**

Lincoln's Inn. See Inns of Court.

Lind (lĭnd), *n.* Jenny (jĕn′ĭ), (Mrs. Otto Goldschmidt) 1820–87, Swedish soprano.

Lind·bergh (lĭnd′bûrg, lĭn′-), *n.* Charles Augustus, born 1902, U.S. aviator who made the first nonstop solo flight from New York to Paris in 1927.

lin·den (lĭn′dən), *n.* any of the trees of the genus *Tilia,* which have yellowish or cream-colored flowers and more or less heart-shaped leaves, as *T. europaea,* a common European species, and *T. americana,* a large American species often cultivated as a shade tree. [n. use of obs. ME and OE adj. *linden* pertaining to a lime tree, f. *lind* lime tree (c. G *linde*) + -EN²]

Lin·den (lĭn′dən), *n.* a city in NE New Jersey, near Newark. 39,931 (1960).

Lind·es·nes (lĭn′dəs nĕs′), *n.* a cape at the S tip of Norway, on the North Sea. Also, **The Naze.**

Lind·say (lĭnd′zĭ, lĭn′-), *n.* **1.** Howard, born 1889, U.S. dramatist and actor. **2.** (Nicholas) Vachel (vā′chəl), 1879–1931, U.S. poet.

Lind·sey (lĭnd′sĭ), *n.* Benjamin Barr, 1869–1943, U.S. jurist and authority on juvenile delinquency.

line¹ (lĭn), *n., v.,* **lined, lining. —n. 1.** a mark or stroke long in proportion to its breadth, made with a pen, pencil, tool, etc., on a surface. **2.** something resembling a traced line, as a band of color, a seam, a furrow, etc.: *lines of stratification in rock.* **3.** a furrow or wrinkle on the face, etc. **4.** something arranged along a line, esp. a straight line; a row or series: *a line of trees.* **5.** a row of written or printed letters, words, etc.: *a page of thirty lines.* **6.** a verse of poetry. **7.** (*pl.*) the spoken words of a drama, etc., or of an actor's part: *the hero forgot his lines.* **8.** a short written message: *a line from a friend.* **9.** an indication of demarcation; boundary; limit: *to draw a line between right and wrong.* **10.** a course of action, procedure, thought, etc.: *the Communist party line.* **11.** a course of direction; route: *the line of march.* **12.** a continuous series of persons in chronological succession, esp. in family descent: *a line of great kings.* **13.** (*pl.*) outline or contour: *a ship of fine lines.* **14.** (*pl.*) plan of construction, action, or procedure: *two books written on the same lines.* **15.** (*pl.*) *Colloq.* a certificate of marriage. **16.** (*pl.*) one's lot or portion. **17.** a department of activity; a kind of occupation or business. **18.** any transportation company or system. **19.** a system of public conveyances, as buses, steamers, etc.,

plying regularly between places. **20.** a strip of railroad track, a railroad, or a railroad system. **21.** *Elect.* a wire circuit connecting two or more pieces of electrical apparatus, esp. **a.** the wire or wires connecting points or stations in a telegraph or telephone system. **b.** the system itself. **22.** *Television.* one scanning line. **23.** *Fine Arts.* a mark from a crayon, pencil, brush, etc., in a work of graphic art, which defines the limits of the forms employed and is used either independently or in combination with modeling by means of shading. **24.** *Math.* a continuous extent of length, straight or curved, without breadth or thickness; the trace of a moving point. **25.** a straight line drawn from an observed object to the fovea of the eye. **26.** a circle of the terrestrial or of the celestial sphere: *the equinoctial line.* **27.** *Geog.* the equator (prec. by *the*). **28.** a supply of commercial goods of the same general class. **29.** *Law.* a limit defining one estate from another; the outline or boundary of a piece of real estate. **30.** *Bridge.* the line drawn between points counting towards game (**below the line**) and bonus, sometimes known as honor points (**above the line**). **31.** *Music.* one of the straight, horizontal, parallel strokes of the staff, or placed above or below it. **32.** *Mil.* **a.** a trench or rampart. **b.** a series of military fieldworks: *the Maginot line.* **33.** (*pl.*) a distribution of troops, sentries, etc., for the defense of a position or for an attack: *within the enemy's lines.* **34.** the line of arrangement of an army or the ships of a fleet as drawn up ready for battle: *line of battle.* **35.** a body or formation of troops or ships drawn up abreast. **36.** the combatant forces of an army, as distinguished from the supply services, etc. **37.** the class of officers in charge of the fighting operations and the operating of warships. **38.** (formerly) the regular forces of an army or navy. **39.** a thread, string, cord, rope, or the like. **40.** a strong cord or slender rope. **41.** a cord, wire, or the like used for measuring or as a guide. **42.** *Naut.* **a.** a length of rope for any purpose. **b.** a pipe or hose: *a steam line.* **43.** a cord bearing a hook or hooks, used in fishing. **44.** *Football.* the players lined up even with the ball before a down begins, as distinguished from the backs. **—v.i. 45.** to take a position in a line; range. **—v.t. 46.** to bring into a line, or into line with others. **47.** to trace by or as by a line or lines; delineate: *to line streets.* **48.** to mark with a line or lines: *to line paper for writing.* **49.** to sketch verbally or in writing; outline. **50.** to arrange a line along: *to line a coast with colonies.* **51.** to form a line along: *people lined the streets.* **52.** to measure or test with a line. [ME *lyne, line,* OE *līne* line, row, rule (c. G *leine* cord, Icel. *līna* line, rope), t. L: m. *līnea* thread, string, der. *līnum* flax] **—line′like′,** *adj.*

line² (lĭn), *v.t.,* **lined, lining. 1.** to cover or fit on the inner side with something: *walls lined with bookcases.* **2.** to provide with a layer of material applied to the inner side: *to line a coat with silk.* **3.** to furnish or fill: *to line one's pocket with money.* **4.** to reinforce the back of a book with glued fabric, paper, vellum, etc. [ME *lyne(n),* der. *line, n.,* flax, linen, OE *līn,* t. L: s. *līnum*]

lin·e·age¹ (lĭn′ĭ ĭj), *n.* **1.** lineal descent from an ancestor; ancestry or extraction. **2.** the line of descendants of a particular ancestor; family; race. [f. LINE(AGE) + -AGE; r. ME *linage,* t. OF: m. *lignage,* der. *ligne* LINE¹]

lin·e·age² (lī′nĭj), *n.* linage.

lin·e·al (lĭn′ĭ əl), *adj.* **1.** being in the direct line, as a descendant, ancestor, etc., or descent, etc. **2.** of or transmitted by lineal descent. [ME, t. LL: s. *līneālis,* der. L *līnea* LINE¹] **—lin′e·al·ly,** *adv.*

lin·e·a·ment (lĭn′ĭ ə mənt), *n.* **1.** a feature or detail of a face, body or figure, considered with respect to its outline or contour. **2.** a distinctive characteristic. [ME, t. L: s. *līneāmentum*]

lin·e·ar (lĭn′ĭ ər), *adj.* **1.** extended in a line: *a linear series.* **2.** involving measurement in one dimension only; pertaining to length: *linear measure.* **3.** of or pertaining to a line or lines: *linear perspective.* **4.** consisting of or involving lines: *linear design.* **5.** looking like a line: *linear nebulae.* **6.** *Math.* of the first degree, as an equation. **7.** resembling a thread; narrow and elongated: *a linear leaf.* [t. L: s. *līneāris,* der. *līnea* LINE¹] **—lin′e·ar·ly,** *adv.*

linear perspective, that branch of perspective which regards only the apparent positions, magnitudes, and forms of objects delineated.

lin·e·ate (lĭn′ĭ ĭt, -āt′), *adj.* marked with lines, esp. longitudinal and more or less parallel lines. Also, **lin′e·at′ed.** [t. L: m.s. *līneātus,* pp. lined]

Linear leaf

lin·e·a·tion (lĭn′ĭ ā′shən), *n.* **1.** a marking with or tracing by lines. **2.** a division into lines. **3.** a line; an outline. **4.** an arrangement or group of lines.

line breeding, *Genetics.* a form of mild inbreeding directed toward keeping the offspring closely related to a highly admired ancestor.

line engraving, **1.** style of engraving that flourished about 1600–1850 in which the burin makes curved regular furrows that markedly swell and taper. **2.** a plate so engraved. **3.** a print or picture made from it.

line·man (lĭn′mən), *n., pl.* **-men. 1.** one who sets up or keeps in repair telegraph, telephone, or other wires. **2.** one who gives sights on line in surveying, etc. **3.** *Football.* a player who plays on the forward line.

lin·en (lĭn′ən), *n.* **1.** fabric woven from flax yarns. **2.** clothes or other articles made of linen cloth or some substitute, as cotton. **3.** yarn made of flax fiber. **4.** thread made of flax yarns. —*adj.* **5.** made of linen. [ME *lin(n)en*, n. and adj., OE *linnen*, *linen*, adj., f. *lin* linen + -EN²]

nen draper, *Brit.* a drygoods merchant.

nen paper, paper made from pure linen or from substitutes which produce a similar paper finish.

ne of credit, the amount of credit a customer is authorized to utilize.

ne officer, *Mil.* a captain or a lieutenant.

ne of force, *Physics.* a line in a field of force whose direction at any point is that of the force in the field at that point.

n·e·o·late (lĭn′ĭəlāt′), *adj. Zool., Bot.* marked with minute lines; finely lineate. Also, **lin′e·o·lat′ed**. [f. s. L lineola, dim. of linea LINE¹ + -ATE¹]

n·er¹ (lī′nər), *n.* **1.** one of a commercial line of steamships or airplanes. **2.** one who or that which traces by or marks with lines. **3.** *Baseball.* a ball batted with much force nearly parallel to the ground. [f. LINE¹ + -ER¹]

n·er² (lī′nər), *n.* **1.** one who fits or provides linings. **2.** something serving as a lining. [f. LINE² + -ER¹]

nes·man (līnz′mən), *n., pl.* **-men.** **1.** a lineman, as on a telegraph line, etc. **2.** (in certain games) an official employed to watch the lines which mark out the field, etc. **3.** *Football.* **a.** an official who marks the distances gained and lost in the progress of the play and otherwise assists the referee and field judge. **b.** a forward.

ne squall, *Meteorol.* (on a map) a more or less continuous line of thunderstorms or clouds of severe turbulence marking the position of an advancing cold front.

ne-up (lĭn′ŭp′), *n.* **1.** a particular order or disposition of persons or things as lined up or drawn up for action: *the line-up of players in a football game.* **2.** the persons or things themselves: *the police line-up.* **3.** *Games.* the arrangement of the players. **4.** an organization of people, companies, etc., for some common purpose. Also, **line′up′**.

ne·y (lī′nĭ), *adj.,* **linier, liniest.** liny.

ing¹ (lĭng), *n., pl.* **ling, lings.** **1.** an elongated marine ganoid food fish, *Molva molva,* of Greenland and northern Europe. **2.** either of the two species of burbot, freshwater food fishes of northeastern North America, *Lota maculosa,* and northern Eurasia, *Lota lota.* **3.** any of various other fishes. [ME *ling, lenge;* akin to LONG¹]

ing² (lĭng), *n.* the common heather, *Calluna vulgaris.* [ME *lyng,* t. Scand.; cf. Icel. *lyng,* Dan. *lyng,* Sw. *ljung*]

ling¹, suffix found in some nouns, often pejorative, denoting one concerned with (*hireling, underling*); also diminutive (*princeling, duckling*). [ME and OE]

ling², an adverbial suffix expressing direction, position, state, etc., as in *darkling, sideling.* [ME and OE]

ing., linguistics.

in·ga (lĭng′gə), *n.* **1.** *Sanskrit Gram.* the masculine gender. **2.** (in popular Hindu mythology) a phallus, symbol of Siva. Also, **lin·gam** (lĭng′gəm). [t. Skt.: *linga* (stem), neut. nom. *lingam*]

in·ga·yén Gulf (lĭng′gä-yĕn′), a gulf on the NW coast of Luzon, in the Philippine Islands: focal point of the Japanese invasion of Luzon, Dec., 1941; reinvaded by U.S. forces, Jan., 1945.

in·ger (lĭng′gər), *v.i.* **1.** to remain or stay on in a place longer than is usual or expected, as if from reluctance to leave it. **2.** to remain alive; continue or persist, although tending to cease or disappear: *hope lingers.* **3.** to dwell in contemplation, thought, or enjoyment. **4.** to be tardy in action; delay; dawdle. **5.** to walk slowly; to saunter along. —*v.t.* **6.** to drag out or protract. **7.** to pass (time, life, etc.) in a leisurely or a tedious manner (fol. by *away* or *out*). [ME *lenger,* freq. of *lenge,* OE *lengan* delay, der. *lang* LONG¹] —**lin′ger·er**, *n.*

in·ge·rie (län′zhə-rē′, lăn′zhə-rē′, -jə-; *Fr.* lănzh-rē′), *n.* **1.** underwear or other garments of linen, cotton, silk, rayon, lace, etc., worn by women. **2.** linen goods in general. [t. F, der. *linger* linen draper, der. *linge* linen, g. L *linum* flax]

in·go (lĭng′gō), *n., pl.* **-goes.** (in contemptuous or humorous use) **1.** language. **2.** peculiar or unintelligible language. **3.** language or terminology peculiar to a particular field, group, etc. [t. Lingua Franca, t. Pr.: m. *lengo,* b. with It. *lingua,* both g. L *lingua* tongue]

in·gua (lĭng′gwə), *n., pl.* **-guae** (-gwē). the tongue or a part like a tongue. [t. L]

in·gua fran·ca (lĭng′gwə frăng′kə), **1.** a jargon which is widely used as an international auxiliary language. **2.** (*cap.*) the Italian-Provençal jargon formerly widely used in eastern Mediterranean ports. [t. It.: Frankish tongue]

in·gual (lĭng′gwəl), *adj.* **1.** of or pertaining to the tongue or some tonguelike part. **2.** pertaining to languages. **3.** *Phonet.* articulated with the tongue, esp. with the tip of the tongue. [t. ML: s. *lingualis,* der. L *lingua* tongue, language] —**lin′gual·ly**, *adv.*

in·gui·form (lĭng′gwəfôrm′), *adj.* tongue-shaped. [f. s. L *lingua* tongue + -(I)FORM]

lin·guist (lĭng′gwĭst), *n.* **1.** a person who is skilled in foreign languages; polyglot. **2.** a person who investigates linguistic phenomena. [f. s. L *lingua* language + -IST]

lin·guis·tic (lĭng-gwĭs′tĭk), *adj.* **1.** of or belonging to language: *linguistic change.* **2.** of or pertaining to linguistics. Also, **lin·guis′ti·cal.** —**lin·guis′ti·cal·ly**, *adv.*

linguistic form, any meaningful unit of speech, as a sentence, phrase, word, suffix, etc.

lin·guis·tics (lĭng-gwĭs′tĭks), *n.* the science of language, including among its fields phonetics, phonemics, morphology, and syntax, and having as principal divisions **descriptive linguistics,** which treats the classification and arrangement of the features of language, and **comparative** (or **historical**) **linguistics,** which treats linguistic change, especially by the study of data taken from various languages.

linguistic stock, 1. a parent language and all its derived dialects and languages. **2.** the people speaking any of these dialects or languages.

lin·gu·late (lĭng′gyəlāt′), *adj.* formed like a tongue; ligulate. [t. L: m.s. *lingulātus*]

lin·i·ment (lĭn′əmənt), *n.* a liquid preparation, usually oily, for rubbing on or applying to the skin, as for sprains, bruises, etc. [ME, t. LL: s. *linimentum*]

li·nin (lī′nĭn), *n. Biol.* the substance forming the netlike structure which connects the chromatin granules in the nucleus of a cell. [f. s. L *linum* flax + -IN²]

lin·ing (lī′nĭng), *n.* **1.** that with which something is lined; a layer of material on the inner side of something. **2.** *Bookbinding.* the material used to strengthen the back of a book after the sheets have been folded, backed, and sewed. **3.** act of one who or that which lines something. [ME, f. LINE² + -ING¹]

link¹ (lĭngk), *n.* **1.** one of the rings or separate pieces of which a chain is composed. **2.** anything serving to connect one part or thing with another; a bond or tie. **3.** a ring, loop, or the like: *a link of hair.* **4.** one of a number of sausages in a chain. **5.** one of the 100 wire rods forming the divisions of a surveyor's chain of 66 feet. **6.** the set or effective length of one of these rods used as a measuring unit, equal to 7.92 in. **7.** *Chem.* bond. **8.** *Elect.* fuse link. **9.** *Mach.* a rigid movable piece or rod connected with other parts by means of pivots or the like, for the purpose of transmitting motion. —*v.t., v.i.* **10.** to join by or as by a link or links; unite. [ME *link(e),* t. Scand.; cf. Sw. *länk,* c. OE *hlence* corselet] —**Syn. 2.** See bond.

link² (lĭngk), *n. Obs.* a torch of tow and pitch or the like. [? special use of LINK¹]

link·age (lĭngk′ĭj), *n.* **1.** act of linking. **2.** state or manner of being linked. **3.** a system of links. **4.** *Biol.* the association or correlation of two or more hereditary characters because their genes are located on the same pair of chromosomes. This results in the parental combinations occurring more frequently in the progeny than the nonparental. A group of such linked genes is termed a **linkage group. 5.** *Mech.* any of various mathematical or drawing devices consisting of a combination of bars or pieces pivoted together so as to turn about one another, usually in parallel planes. **6.** *Elect.* the product of the magnetic flux passing through an electric circuit by the number of turns in the circuit.

link·boy (lĭngk′boi′), *n.* a boy hired to carry a torch for a pedestrian on dark streets. Also, **link′man.**

linked (lĭngkt), *n. Biol.* exhibiting linkage.

link motion, a mechanism for operating a valve in a steam engine, one feature of which is a slotted bar (the **link**) in which slides a block (the **link block**) which terminates the rod working the valve.

links (lĭngks), *n.pl.* a golf course. [ME *lynkys* slopes, OE *hlincas,* pl. of *hlinc* rising ground, der. *hlin* (cf. *klinian* lean, recline)]

Link trainer (lĭngk), *Aeron.* a ground training device used in instrument-flight training.

link·work (lĭngk′wûrk′), *n.* **1.** a thing composed of links, as a chain. **2.** a linkage. **3.** *Mach.* a mechanism or device in which motion is transmitted by links.

Lin·lith·gow (lĭn-lĭth′gō), *n.* former name of West Lothian.

Lin·nae·us (lĭ-nē′əs), *n.* **Carolus** (kär′ələs), (*Carl von Linné*) 1707-78, Swedish botanist.

Lin·ne·an (lĭ-nē′ən), *adj.* **1.** of or pertaining to Linnaeus, who established the binomial system of scientific nomenclature. **2.** noting or pertaining to, a system of botanical classification introduced by him and formerly used (based mainly on the number or characteristics of the stamens and pistils). Also, **Lin·nae′an.**

lin·net (lĭn′ĭt), *n.* **1.** a small Old World fringilline song bird, *Carduelis cannabina.* **2.** any of various related birds, as the house finch, *Carpodacus mexicanus,* of North America (**California linnet**). [ME *linet,* OE *linete,* short for *linetwige,* lit., flax-plucker]

lin·o·le·ic acid (lĭn′ə-lē′ĭk, lī-nō′lĭ′ĭk), *Chem.* an unsaturated fatty acid, $C_{17}H_{31}COOH$, occurring as a glyceride in drying oils such as linseed oil.

li·no·le·um (lĭ-nō′lĭ′əm), *n.* a floor covering formed by coating burlap or canvas with linseed oil, powdered cork, and rosin. Pigments are added to create the desired colors and patterns. [f. L: s. *linum* flax + *oleum* oil]

Lin·o·type (lī′nətīp), *n. Trademark.* a kind of typesetting machine, with keyboard, which casts solid lines of type. [orig. phrase, "*line o' type*" line of type]

lin·sang (lĭn′săng), n. a catlike, viverrine carnivore with retractile claws and a long tail, of the genus *Prionodon* (or *Linsang*) of the East Indies, or *Poina* of Africa. [t. Javanese]

lin·seed (lĭn′sēd′), n. flaxseed. [ME *linsed*, OE *līnsǣd*, f. *līn* flax + *sǣd* seed]

linseed oil, a drying oil obtained by pressing linseed, used in making paints, printing inks, linoleum, etc.

lin·sey-wool·sey (lĭn′zĭ wŏŏl′zĭ), n., pl. **-seys. 1.** a coarse fabric woven from linen warp and coarse wool filling. **2.** any poor or incongruous mixture. [ME *lynsy wolsye*, f. *lynsy* (f. OE *līn* flax + ME *-sey*, meaningless suffix) + *wolsye* (f. OE *wull* wool + ME *-sey*)]

lin·stock (lĭn′stŏk′), n. a staff with one end forked to hold a match, formerly used in firing cannon. [earlier *lyntstock*, t. D: m. *lontstok*, f. *lont* match + *stok* stick]

lint (lĭnt), n. **1.** a soft material for dressing wounds, etc., procured by scraping or otherwise treating linen cloth. **2.** bits of thread. [ME *lyn(e)t* flax, ? OE *līnwyrt*, f. *līn* flax + *wyrt* WORT]

lin·tel (lĭn′təl), n. a horizontal supporting member above an opening such as a window or a door. [ME *lyntel*, t. OF: m. *lintel, lintel, linter*, g. VL *līmitāle*, dim. of L *līmes* boundary, LIMIT]

lint·er (lĭn′tər), n. **1.** (pl.) short cotton fibers which stick to seeds after a first ginning. **2.** a machine which removes lint from cloth.

lint·y (lĭn′tĭ), adj., **lintier, lintiest. 1.** full of or covered with lint. **2.** like lint: *linty bits on his coat.*

lin·y (lī′nĭ), adj., **linier, liniest. 1.** full of or marked with lines. **2.** linelike. Also, **liney.**

Lin-yu (lĭn′ū′), n. a city in NE China, in Hopeh province, on the Gulf of Liaotung; strategically located at the E end of the Great Wall. 25,000 (1950). Formerly, Shanhaikwan.

Lin Yu·tang (lĭn′ ū′täng′), born 1895, Chinese author.

Linz (lĭnts), n. a city in N Austria: a port on the Danube. 184,685 (1951).

li·on (lī′ən), n. **1.** a large, grayish-tan cat, *Panthera leo,* native in Africa and southern Asia, the male of which usually has a mane. **2.** this animal as the national emblem of Great Britain. **3.** a man of great strength, courage, etc. **4.** a person of note or celebrity who is much sought after. **5.** an object of interest or note. **6.** (*cap.*) *Astron.* Leo. [ME, t. OF, g. s. L *leo,* t. Gk.: m. *leōn.* Cf. LEO]

li·on·ess (lī′ən ĭs), n. a female lion.

Lion and lioness. *Panthera leo*
(3 ft. high at the shoulder, total length 8 to 9 ft.)

li·on-heart·ed (lī′ən-här′tĭd), adj. courageous; brave.

li·on·ize (lī′ə nīz′), v., **-ized, -izing. —v.t. 1.** to treat (a person) as a celebrity. **2.** to visit or exhibit the objects of interest of (a place). **—v.i. 3.** to visit the objects of interest of a place. **—li′on·i·za′tion,** n.

Li·ons (lī′ənz), n. Gulf of, a wide bay of the Mediterranean off the S coast of France. Also, **Gulf of the Lion.** French, **Golfe du Li·on** (gôlf dγ lē ôN′).

lip (lĭp), n., adj., v., **lipped, lipping. —n. 1.** either of the two fleshy parts or folds forming the margins of the mouth and performing an important function in speech. **2.** (*pl.*) these parts as organs of speech. **3.** speech as passing between them: *to hang on a person's lips.* **4.** *Slang.* impudent talk. **5.** a liplike part or structure. **6.** *Bot.* either of the two parts (**upper** and **lower**) into which the corolla or calyx of certain plants (esp. the mint family) is divided. **7.** *Zool.* a. labium. b. the outer or the inner margin of the aperture of a gastropod's shell. **8.** *Music.* the position and arrangement of lips and tongue in playing a wind instrument. **9.** any edge or rim. **10.** the margin or edge of a container. **11.** a projecting edge, as of a pitcher. **12.** the edge of an opening or cavity, as of a canyon or a wound. **13.** the rim of the lateral hole in a flue pipe. **14.** the blade at the end of an auger which cuts the chip after it has been circumscribed by the spur. **—adj. 15.** of or pertaining to the lips or a lip. **16.** pertaining to, characterized by, or made with the lips. **17.** superficial or insincere: *pay lip service.* **—v.t. 18.** to touch with the lips. **19.** *Golf.* to hit the ball over the rim of (the hole). **20.** to utter, esp. softly. **21.** *Obs.* to kiss. **—v.i. 22.** to use the lips in playing a musical wind instrument. [ME *lip(pe),* c. D *lip,* G *lippe;* akin to L *labium, labrum*]

lip-, var. of lipo-, before vowels, as in *lipectomy.*

Lip·a·ri Islands (lĭp′ə rē′; *It.* lē′pä rē′), a group of volcanic islands N of Sicily, belonging to Italy. 11,799 pop. (1951); 44 sq. mi.

li·pase (lī′pās, lĭp′ās), n. *Biochem.* one of the ferments produced by the liver, pancreas, and other organs of the digestive system which convert oils or fats into fatty acids and glycerol. [f. LIP(O)- + -ASE]

lip·ec·to·my (lĭ pĕk′tə mĭ), n., pl. **-mies.** *Surg.* an operation for removal of superficial fat, usually a pendulous abdominal apron of fat, in obese persons.

li·pid (lī′pĭd, lĭp′ĭd), n. *Biochem.* any of a group of organic compounds which make up the fats and other

esters which have analogous properties. They have a greasy feeling and are insoluble in water, but soluble in alcohols, ethers, and other fat solvents. Also, **li·pide** (lī′pĭd, lĭp′īd). [f. LIP- + -ID³]

Li Po (lē′ pō′; *Chin.* lē′ bō′), A.D. c700–762, Chinese poet. Also, **Li Tai Po.**

lipo-, *Chem.* a word element connoting fat as in *lipochrome,* a fat-soluble pigment. Also, **lip-.** [t. Gk., comb. form of *lipos* fat]

lip·oid (lĭp′oid, lī′poid), adj. **1.** fatty; resembling fat. **—n. 2.** one of a group of fats or fatlike substances such as lecithins, waxes, etc. [f. LIP- + -OID]

li·pol·y·sis (lĭ pŏl′ə sĭs), n. *Chem.* the resolution of fats into fatty acids and glycerol, as by lipase. [f. LIPO- + -LYSIS] **—lip·o·lyt·ic** (lĭp′ə lĭt′ĭk), adj.

li·po·ma (lĭ pō′mə), n., pl. **-mata** (-mə tə), **-mas.** *Pathol.* a tumor made up of fat tissue; a fatty tumor [f. LIP- + -OMA]

Lip·pe (lĭp′ə), n. a former state in NW Germany; now part of North Rhine-Westphalia.

lipped (lĭpt), adj. **1.** having lips or a lip. **2.** *Bot.* labiate.

Lip·pi (lēp′pē), n. **1.** Filippino (fē/lēp pē′nō), 1457?–c1505, Italian painter. **2.** his father, **Fra Filippo** (frä fē lēp′pō) or **Fra Lippo** (frä lēp′pō), c1406–69, Italian painter.

Lipp·mann (lĭp′mən), n. **Walter,** born 1889, U.S. journalist and author.

lip reading, the reading or understanding, as by a deaf person, of the movements of another's lips when forming words. **—lip reader.**

lip service, service with words only; insincere profession of devotion or good will.

lip·stick (lĭp′stĭk′), n. a stick or elongated piece of cosmetic preparation for heightening the color of the lips.

liq., **1.** liquid. **2.** liquor.

li·quate (lī′kwāt), v.t., **-quated, -quating.** *Metall.* **1.** to heat (a metal, etc.) sufficiently to melt the more fusible portion and so separate a metal from impurities or other metals. **2.** to separate by such a fusion (often fol. by *out*). [t. L: m.s. *liquātus,* pp., made liquid, melted] **—li·qua·tion** (lī kwā′shən), n.

liq·ue·fac·tion (lĭk′wə făk′shən), n. the process of liquefying or making liquid.

liq·ue·fy (lĭk′wə fī′), v.t., v.i., **-fied, -fying.** to make or become liquid. [late ME, t. L: m.s. *liquefacere* make liquid] **—liq′ue·fi′a·ble,** adj. **—liq′ue·fi′er,** n.

li·ques·cent (lĭ kwĕs′ənt), adj. **1.** becoming liquid; melting. **2.** tending toward a liquid state. [t. L: s. *liquescens,* ppr.] **—li·ques′cence, li·ques′cen·cy,** n.

li·queur (lĭ kûr′ *or, esp. Brit.,* -kyŏŏr′; *Fr.* lē kœr′), n. any of a class of alcoholic liquors, usually strong, sweet, and highly flavored, as chartreuse, curaçao, etc.; a cordial. [t. F. See LIQUOR]

liq·uid (lĭk′wĭd), adj. **1.** composed of molecules which move freely among themselves but do not tend to separate like those of gases; neither gaseous nor solid. **2.** of or pertaining to liquids: *liquid measure.* **3.** such as to flow like water. **4.** clear, transparent, or bright: *liquid eyes.* **5.** sounding smoothly or agreeably: *liquid tones.* **6.** in cash or easily convertible into cash: *liquid assets.* **7.** *Phonet.* palatal or palatalized, esp. referring to Spanish palatal *ll* and *ñ* as compared to *l, n.* **8.** a liquid substance. **9.** *Phonet.* either *r* or *l.* [ME, t. L: s. *liquidus*] **—liq′uid·ly,** adv. **—liq′uid·ness,** n. **—Syn. 8.** LIQUID, FLUID agree in referring to that which is not solid. LIQUID commonly refers to substances such as water, oil, alcohol, and the like, which are neither solids nor gaseous: *water ceases to be a liquid when it is frozen or turned to steam.* FLUID is applied to anything that flows, whether liquid or gaseous: *pipes can carry fluids from place to place.*

liquid air, air in its liquid state; an intensely cold, transparent liquid.

liq·uid·am·bar (lĭk′wĭd ăm′bər; *for genus* -bär), n. **1.** any tree of the genus *Liquidambar,* as *L. Styraciflua,* a large American tree having star-shaped leaves and, in warm regions, exuding a fragrant yellowish balsamic liquid used in medicine. **2.** this liquid. See **storax** (def. 2). [t. NL, f. s. L *liquidus* LIQUID + ML *ambar* AMBER]

liq·ui·date (lĭk′wə dāt′), v., **-dated, -dating. —v.t. 1.** to settle or pay (a debt, etc.): *to liquidate a claim.* **2.** to reduce (accounts) to order; determine the amount of (indebtedness or damages). **3.** to convert into cash. **4.** *Slang.* to murder (a person). **5.** to break up, abolish, or do away with. **—v.i. 6.** to liquidate debts or accounts; go into liquidation. [t. ML: m.s. *liquidātus,* pp., der. L *liquidus* LIQUID]

liq·ui·da·tion (lĭk′wə dā′shən), n. **1.** the process of realizing upon assets and of discharging liabilities in winding up the affairs of a business, estate, etc. **2.** the process of converting securities or commodities into cash for the purpose of taking profits or preventing losses. **3.** liquidated state.

liq·ui·da·tor (lĭk′wə dā′tər), n. a court-appointed receiver who directs the liquidation of a business.

liquid crystal, a liquid having different optical properties in different directions and other crystalline characteristics.

liquid fire, flaming petroleum or the like as employed against the enemy in warfare.

liquid glass, water glass (def. 5).

---

b., blend of, blended; c., cognate with; d., dialect, dialectal; der., derived from; f., formed from; g., going back to; m., modification of; r., replacing; s., stem of; t., taken from; ?, perhaps. See the full key on inside cover.

l·quid·i·ty (lĭkwĭd'ə tĭ), *n.* liquid state or quality.

liquid measure, the system of units of capacity ordinarily used in measuring liquid commodities, such as milk, oil, etc.: 4 gills = 1 pint; 2 pints = 1 quart; 4 quarts = 1 gallon.

liq·uor (lĭk'ər), *n.* **1.** a distilled or spirituous beverage (as brandy or whiskey) as distinguished from a fermented beverage (as wine or beer). **2.** any liquid substance. **3.** *Pharm.* a solution of a medicinal substance in water. **4.** a solution of a substance, esp. a concentrated one used in the industrial arts. —*v.t., v.i.* **5.** *Slang.* to furnish with or imbibe liquor or drink (often fol. by *up*). [t. L: liquid (state), liquid; r. ME *licur, licour,* t. OF]

liq·uo·rice[1] (lĭk'ər ĭs, lĭk'rĭsh), *n.* licorice. Also, **liq·uor·ish** (lĭk'ər ĭsh).

liq·uo·rice[2] (lĭk'ər ĭs), *adj. Archaic.* lickerish.

li·ra (lē'rä), *n., pl.* **lire** (lē'rĕ), **liras.** **1.** the monetary unit and a coin of Italy, equal to 100 centesimi, present value .16 cent. **2.** a monetary unit and a gold coin of Turkey, equal to 100 piasters, and equivalent to about 8 cents; formerly called the Turkish pound. [t. It., d. var. of *lib(b)ra,* g. L *lībra* pound]

ir·i·o·den·dron (lĭr'ĭ ō dĕn'drən), *n., pl.* **-drons, -dra** (-drə). a tree of the magnoliaceous genus *Liriodendron,* of which the tulip tree, *L. Tulipifera,* native in eastern North America, is the chief representative (see **tulip tree**). [t. NL, f. m.s. Gk. *leírion* lily + -*dendron* -DENDRON]

ir·i·pipe (lĭr'ĭ pīp'), *n.* **1.** *Hist.* the tail or pendent part at the back of a hood, as in 14th and 15th century French costume. **2.** a scarf or tippet; a hood. [t. ML: m.s. *liripipium;* orig. unknown]

is·bon (lĭz'bən), *n.* a seaport in and the capital of Portugal, on the Tagus estuary. 783,226 (1950). Portuguese, **Lis·bo·a** (lēzh bô'ə).

isle (līl), *n.* knit goods, as gloves or hose, made of lisle thread. —*adj.* **2.** made of lisle thread.

isle (līl; *Fr.* lēl), *n.* former name of Lille.

isle (lēl), *n.* **de. 1.** See **Leconte de Lisle. 2.** See **Rouget de Lisle.** Also, **l'Isle.**

isle thread (līl), a smooth, hard-twisted linen or cotton thread. [orig., LISLE thread]

isp (lĭsp), *n.* **1.** a speech defect consisting in pronouncing *s* and *z* like or nearly like the *th* sounds of *thin* and *this,* respectively. **2.** the act, habit, or sound of lisping. —*v.i., v.i.* **3.** to pronounce or speak with a lisp. [ME *wlispe, lipse,* OE *-wlispian* (in *āwlyspian*), der. *wlisp* lisping. Cf. D *lispen,* G *lispeln*] —**lisp'er,** *n.* —**lisp'ing·ly,** *adv.*

is pen·dens (lĭs pĕn'dĕnz), *Latin.* **1.** a pending suit listed on the court docket. **2.** the rule placing property involved in litigation under the court's jurisdiction.

is·some (lĭs'əm), *adj.* **1.** lithesome or lithe, esp. of body; limber or supple. **2.** agile or active. Also, **lis'som.** [var. of LITHESOME] —**lis'some·ness,** *n.*

is·sot·ri·chous (lĭ sŏt'rə kəs), *adj. Anthropol.* having straight hair. [f. Gk. *lissó(s)* smooth + s. Gk. *thríx* hair + -OUS]

ist[1] (lĭst), *n.* **1.** a record consisting of a series of names, words, or the like; a number of names of persons or things set down one after another. —*v.t.* **2.** to set down together in a list; to make a list of. **3.** to enter in a list with others. **4.** to enlist. **5.** to register a security on a stock exchange so that it may be traded there. —*v.i.* **6.** to enlist. [special use of LIST[2]. Cf. F *liste* (t. G) in same sense]
—**Syn. 1.** LIST, CATALOGUE, INVENTORY, ROLL, SCHEDULE imply a definite arrangement of items. LIST denotes a series of names, items, or figures arranged in a row or rows: *a list of groceries.* CATALOGUE adds the idea of alphabetical or other orderly arrangement, and, often, descriptive particulars and details: *a library catalogue.* An INVENTORY is a detailed descriptive list of property, stock, goods, or the like made for legal or business purposes: *a store inventory.* A ROLL is a list of names of members of some defined group often used to ascertain their presence or absence: *a class roll.* A SCHEDULE is a methodical (esp. official) list, often indicating the time or sequence of certain events: *a train schedule.*

ist[2] (lĭst), *n.* **1.** a border or bordering strip of anything (now chiefly or only of cloth). **2.** a selvage. **3.** selvages collectively. **4.** a strip of cloth or other material. **5.** a strip or band of any kind. **6.** a stripe of color. **7.** a division of the hair or beard. **8.** one of the ridges or furrows of earth thrown up by a lister. —*adj.* **9.** made of selvages or strips of cloth. —*v.t.* **10.** to border or edge. **11.** to arrange in strips, bands, or stripes. **12.** to apply list or strips of cloth to. **13.** to produce furrows and ridges in (land) by means of a lister. **14.** (in cotton culture) to prepare (land) for the crop by making alternating ridges and furrows. **15.** to shape (a block, stave, etc.) roughly by chopping. [ME *lyst(e),* OE *līste,* c. D *lijst,* G *leiste*]

ist[3] (lĭst), *n.* **1.** a careening, or leaning to one side, as of a ship. —*v.i.* **2.** (of a ship) to careen; incline to one side: *the ship listed to starboard.* —*v.t.* **3.** to cause (a ship) to lean to one side: *the weight of the misplaced cargo listed the ship to starboard.* [orig. obscure]

ist[4] (lĭst), *Archaic.* —*v.t.* **1.** to be pleasing to; please. **2.** to like or desire. —*v.i.* **3.** to like; wish; choose. [ME *luste(n),* OE *lystan,* c. G *lüsten,* Icel. *lysta*]

ist[5] (lĭst), *Archaic or Poetic.* —*v.i.* **1.** to listen. —*v.t.* **2.** to listen to. [ME *list(e),* OE *hlystan,* der. *hlyst* hearing (c. Icel. *hlust* ear); akin to LISTEN]

lis·tel (lĭs'təl), *n. Archit.* a narrow list or fillet. [t. F, t. It.: m. *listello,* dim. of *lista,* t. OHG]

lis·ten (lĭs'ən), *v.t., v.i.* **1.** to give attention with the ear; attend closely for the purpose of hearing; give ear. **2.** to give heed; yield to advice. [ME *lis(t)ne(n),* OE *hlysnan,* c. MHG *lüsenen;* akin to LIST[5]] —**lis'ten·er,** *n.* —**Syn. 1.** See **hear.**

listening post, 1. *Mil.* a post or position, as in advance of a defensive line, established for the purpose of listening to detect the enemy's movements. **2.** any position maintained to obtain information.

Lis·ter (lĭs'tər), *n.* **Joseph, 1st Baron,** 1827–1912, British surgeon: the first to use antiseptics in surgery.

list·er (lĭs'tər), *n.* a plow with a double moldboard used to prepare the soil for planting by producing furrows and ridges, and often fitted with attachments for dropping and covering the seeds. Also, **lister plow.** [see LIST[2] (def. 8)]

Lis·ter·ism (lĭs'tə rĭz'əm), *n.* an antiseptic method introduced by Lister, involving the spraying of the parts under operation with a carbolic acid solution.

list·less (lĭst'lĭs), *adj.* **1.** feeling no inclination toward or interest in anything. **2.** characterized by or indicating such feeling: *a listless mood.* [late ME, f. LIST[4] + -LESS] —**list'less·ly,** *adv.*

list·less·ness (lĭst'lĭs nĭs), *n.* **1.** state of being listless. **2.** languid inattention. —**Syn. 2.** See **indifference.**

list price, *Com.* price given in a catalogue.

lists (lĭsts), *n.pl.* **1.** the barriers enclosing the field of combat at a tournament. **2.** the enclosed field. **3.** any place or scene of combat. **4. enter the lists,** to take part in a contest or competition. [ME *liste* boundary, limit (same word as LIST[2])]

Liszt (lĭst), *n.* **Franz** (fränts), 1811–86, Hungarian composer and pianist.

lit[1] (lĭt), *v.* pt. and pp. of **light**[1] and **light**[3].

lit[2] (lĭt), *n.* litas.

lit., 1. liter. **2.** literal. **3.** literally. **4.** literary. **5.** literature.

Li Tai Po (lē' tī' bô'), Li Po.

lit·a·ny (lĭt'ə nĭ), *n., pl.* **-nies. 1.** a ceremonial or liturgical form of prayer consisting of a series of invocations or supplications with responses which are the same for a number in succession. **2.** Also, **The Litany.** the "general supplication" of this form in the Book of Common Prayer. [t. LL: m.s. *litanīa,* t. Gk.: m. *litaneía* litany, an entreating; r. ME *letanie,* t. OF]

li·tas (lē'täs), *n., pl.* **-tai** (-tä), **-tu** (-tōō). the monetary unit and a coin of Lithuania equal to 10 cents in the U.S.

Lit. B., (L *Lit(t)erarum Baccalaureus*) Bachelor of Letters; Bachelor of Literature.

li·tchi (lē'chē'; *Chin.* lē'dzū'), *n., pl.* **-tchis. 1.** the fruit of a Chinese sapindaceous tree, *Litchi chinensis,* consisting of a thin, brittle shell, enclosing a sweet, jellylike pulp and a single seed. **2.** the tree. Also, **lichee, lichi.**

litchi nut, the brownish, dried litchi fruit. [t. Chinese]

Lit. D., (L *Lit(t)erarum Doctor*) Doctor of Letters; Doctor of Literature.

lit de jus·tice (lē də zhys tēs'), *French.* **1.** the sofa upon which the king of France sat when holding formal sessions of the parliament. **2.** such a session.

-lite, a word element used in names of minerals, or fossils: *chrysolite, aerolite.* [t. F, t. Gk.: m. *lithos* stone. Cf. G -*lit(h)*]

li·ter (lē'tər), *n. Metric System.* a unit of capacity equal to the volume of one kilogram of water at its maximum density, or very nearly one cubic decimeter, and equivalent to 1.0567 U.S. liquid quarts. Also, *esp. Brit.,* **litre.** [t. F: m. *litre,* der. *litron* old measure of capacity, der. LL *lītra* measure for liquids, t. Gk.: pound]

lit·er·a·cy (lĭt'ər ə sĭ), *n.* state of being literate; possession of education.

literacy test, an examination to determine whether a person meets the literacy requirement for voting, etc.

lit·er·al (lĭt'ər əl), *adj.* **1.** following the letter, or exact words, of the original, as a translation. **2.** (of persons) tending to construe words in the strict sense or in an unimaginative way; matter-of-fact; prosaic. **3.** in accordance with, involving, or being the natural or strict meaning of the words or word; not figurative or metaphorical: *the literal meaning of a word.* **4.** true to fact; not exaggerated: *a literal statement of conditions.* **5.** being actually such, without exaggeration or inaccuracy: *the literal extermination of a city.* **6.** of or pertaining to the letters of the alphabet. **7.** of the nature of letters. **8.** expressed by letters. **9.** affecting a letter or letters: *a literal error.* [ME, t. LL: m.s. *litterālis,* der. *littera* LETTER] —**lit'er·al·ness,** *n.*

lit·er·al·ism (lĭt'ər əl ĭz'əm), *n.* **1.** adherence to the exact letter or the literal sense, as in translation or interpretation. **2.** a peculiarity of expression resulting from this. **3.** exact representation or portrayal, without idealization, as in art or literature. —**lit'er·al·ist,** *n., adj.* —**lit'er·al·is'tic,** *adj.*

lit·er·al·i·ty (lĭt'ər ăl'ĭ tĭ), *n., pl.* **-ties. 1.** the quality of being literal. **2.** a literal interpretation.

lit·er·al·ize (lĭt'ər ə līz'), *v.t.* **-ized, -izing.** to make literal; interpret literally. —**lit'er·al·iz'er,** *n.*

lit·er·al·ly (lĭt'ər ə lĭ), *adv.* **1.** in a literal manner; word for word: *to translate literally.* **2.** in the literal sense. **3.** actually; without exaggeration or inaccuracy: *the city was literally destroyed.*

lit·er·ar·y (lĭt'ə rĕr'ĭ), *adj.* **1.** pertaining to or of the nature of books and writings, esp. those classed as literature: *literary history.* **2.** versed in or acquainted with literature. **3.** engaged in writing books, etc. or in literature as a profession: *a literary man.* —**lit'er·ar'i·ly,** *adv.* —**lit'er·ar'i·ness,** *n.*

lit·er·ate (lĭt'ər ĭt), *adj.* **1.** able to read and write. **2.** having an education; educated. **3.** literary. —*n.* **4.** one who can read and write. **5.** a learned person. [ME *litterate,* t. L: m. *litterātus, līterātus* lettered]

lit·e·ra·ti (lĭt'ə rä'tĭ, -rä'tĭ), *n.pl.* men of learning; men of letters; scholarly or literary people. [t. L]

lit·e·ra·tim (lĭt'ə rā'tĭm), *adv.* letter for letter; literally. [t. ML, der. L *littera* LETTER²]

lit·e·ra·ture (lĭt'ər ə chər, -chŏŏr', lĭt'rə-), *n.* **1.** writings in which expression and form, in connection with ideas of permanent and universal interest, are characteristic or essential features, as poetry, romance, history, biography, essays, etc.; belles-lettres. **2.** the entire body of writings of a specific language, period, people, subject, etc.: *the literature of England.* **3.** the writings dealing with a particular subject. **4.** the profession of a writer or author. **5.** literary work or production. **6.** *Colloq.* printed matter of any kind, as circulars or advertising matter. **7.** *Rare.* polite learning or literary culture. [ME *litterature,* t. F, t. L: m. *litterātūra* learning] —**Syn. 1.** LITERATURE, BELLES-LETTRES, LETTERS refer to artistic writings worthy of being remembered. In the broadest sense, LITERATURE includes any type of writings on any subject: *the literature of medicine;* usually, however, it means the body of artistic writings of a country or period which are characterized by beauty of expression and form and by universality or intellectual and emotional appeal: *English literature of the sixteenth century.* BELLES-LETTRES is a more specific term for such writings: *his talent is not for scholarship but for belles-lettres.* LETTERS (rare today outside of certain fixed phrases) refers to literature as a domain of study or creation: *a man of letters.*

lith-, a combining form meaning "stone." Also, **litho-.** [t. Gk., comb. form of *líthos*]

-lith, a noun termination meaning "stone," as in *acrolith, coccolith, megalith, nephrolith, paleolith:* sometimes occurring in words as *batholith, laccolith,* that are variants of forms in *-lite.* Cf. **-lite.** [see LITH-]

Lith., 1. Lithuania. **2.** Lithuanian.

lith., 1. lithograph. **2.** lithography.

lith·arge (lĭth'ärj, lĭ thärj'), *n.* lead monoxide, a yellow earthy substance used in compounding glazes and glasses. [ME *litarge,* t. OF, t. L: m.s. *lithargyrus,* t. Gk.: m. *lithárgyros* spume of silver]

lithe (lĭth), *adj.* bending readily; pliant; limber; supple. Also, **lithe·some** (lĭth'səm). [ME *lith(e),* OE *lithe,* c. G *lind* mild] —**lithe'ly,** *adv.* —**lithe'ness,** *n.*

lith·i·a (lĭth'ĭ ə, -yə), *n.* a white oxide of lithium, Li₂O. [t. NL, der. Gk. *líthos* stone]

lithia water, a mineral water, natural or artificial, containing lithium salts.

lith·ic (lĭth'ĭk), *adj.* **1.** pertaining to or consisting of stone. **2.** *Pathol.* pertaining to stony concretions, or calculi, formed within the body, esp. in the bladder. **3.** *Chem.* of, pertaining to, or containing lithium. [t. Gk.: m.s. *lithikós* of stones]

-lithic, an adjective suffix identical with **lithic,** used especially in archaeology, e.g., *paleolithic.*

lith·i·um (lĭth'ĭ əm), *n. Chem.* a soft silver-white metallic element (the lightest of all metals) occurring combined in certain minerals. Symbol: Li; *at. wt.:* 6.94; *at. no.:* 3; *sp. gr.:* 0.53 at 20°C. [t. NL, f. s. Gk. *líthos* stone + *-ium* -IUM; so named because found in minerals]

litho-, var. of lith-, before consonants, as in *lithography.*

litho., 1. lithograph. **2.** lithography.

lithog., 1. lithograph. **2.** lithography.

lith·o·graph (lĭth'ə grăf', -gräf'), *n.* **1.** a print produced by lithography. —*v.t.* **2.** to produce or copy by lithography.

li·thog·ra·pher (lĭ thŏg'rə fər), *n.* a person who works at lithography.

li·thog·ra·phy (lĭ thŏg'rə fĭ), *n.* **1.** the art or process of producing a picture, writing, or the like, on a flat, specially prepared stone, with some greasy or oily substance, and of taking ink impressions from this as in ordinary printing. **2.** a similar process in which a substance other than stone, as aluminum or zinc, is used. —**lith·o·graph·ic** (lĭth'ə grăf'ĭk), **lith·o·graph·i·cal,** *adj.* —**lith·o·graph'i·cal·ly,** *adv.*

lith·oid (lĭth'oid), *adj.* stonelike; stony. Also, **li·thoi'dal.** [t. Gk.: m.s. *lithoeidēs.* See LITH-, -OID]

lithol., lithology.

li·thol·o·gy (lĭ thŏl'ə jĭ), *n.* **1.** the science dealing with the minute mineral characters of rock specimens. **2.** *Med.* the science treating of calculi in the human body. —**lith·o·log·ic** (lĭth'ə lŏj'ĭk), **lith·o·log'i·cal,** *adj.*

lith·o·marge (lĭth'ə märj'), *n.* kaolin (clay) in compact, massive, usually impure form. [t. NL: m. *lithomarga,* f. *litho-* LITHO- + L *marga* marl]

lith·o·phyte (lĭth'ə fīt'), *n.* **1.** *Zool.* a polyp with a hard or stony structure, as a coral. **2.** *Bot.* any plant growing on the surface of rocks. —**lith·o·phyt·ic** (lĭth'ə fĭt'ĭk), *adj.*

lith·o·pone (lĭth'ə pōn'), *n.* a white pigment consisting of zinc sulfide and barium sulfate, used in the manufacture of linoleum and rubber articles. [f. LITHO- + -pone (orig. uncert.)]

lith·o·sphere (lĭth'ə sfĭr'), *n.* the crust of the earth.

li·thot·o·my (lĭ thŏt'ə mĭ), *n., pl.* **-mies.** *Surg.* the operation or art of cutting for stone in the urinary bladder. [t. LL: m.s. *lithotomia,* t. Gk. See LITHO-, -TOMY] —**lith·o·tom·ic** (lĭth'ə tŏm'ĭk), *adj.* —**li·thot'o·mist,** *n.*

lith·o·trite (lĭth'ə trīt'), *n. Surg.* an instrument for performing lithotrity.

li·thot·ri·ty (lĭ thŏt'rə tĭ), *n., pl.* **-ties.** *Surg.* the operation of crushing stone in the urinary bladder into particles that may be voided. [f. LITHO- + s. L *trītus,* pp., rubbed + -Y³]

Lith·u·a·ni·a (lĭth'ŏŏ ā'nĭ ə), *n.* a de facto constituent republic of the Soviet Union in the W part, on the Baltic: an independent state, 1918–40. 2,700,000 pop. (est. 1956); 24,100 sq. mi. *Cap.:* Vilna. Official name, Lithuanian Soviet Socialist Republic. Lithuanian, Lietuva. —**Lith·u·a'ni·an,** *adj., n.*

lith·y (lĭth'ĭ), *adj. Archaic.* lithe.

lit·i·ga·ble (lĭt'ə gə bəl), *adj.* subject to litigation.

lit·i·gant (lĭt'ə gənt), *n.* **1.** one engaged in a lawsuit. —*adj.* **2.** litigating; engaged in a lawsuit. [t. L: s. *litigans,* ppr.]

lit·i·gate (lĭt'ə gāt'), *v.,* **-gated, -gating.** —*v.t.* **1.** to make the subject of a lawsuit; to contest at law. **2.** to dispute (a point, etc.). —*v.i.* **3.** to carry on a lawsuit. [t. L: m.s. *litigātus,* pp.] —**lit'i·ga'tor,** *n.*

lit·i·ga·tion (lĭt'ə gā'shən), *n.* **1.** the process of litigating. **2.** a lawsuit.

li·ti·gious (lĭ tĭj'əs), *adj.* **1.** of or pertaining to litigation. **2.** overly inclined to litigate: *a litigious person.* [ME, t. L: m.s. *litigiōsus* disputatious] —**li·ti'gious·ly,** *adv.* —**li·ti'gious·ness,** *n.*

lit·mus (lĭt'məs), *n.* a blue coloring matter obtained from certain lichens, esp. *Roccella tinctoria.* In alkaline solution litmus turns blue, in acid solution red; hence it is widely used as an indicator, esp. in the form of strips of paper impregnated with a solution of the coloring matter (**litmus paper**). [ME *litmose,* t. Scand.; cf. Icel *litmosi* dyeing-moss]

lit·o·ral (lĭt'ə rəl), *adj.* littoral.

li·to·tes (lī'tə tēz', -tō-, lĭt'ə-), *n. Rhet.* a figure in which an affirmative is expressed by the negative of its contrary, as in *not bad at all.* [t. NL, t. Gk.: diminution]

li·tre (lē'tər), *n. Chiefly Brit.* liter.

Litt. B., (L *Lit(t)erarum Baccalaureus*) Bachelor of Letters; Bachelor of Literature.

Litt. D., (L *Lit(t)erarum Doctor*) Doctor of Letters; Doctor of Literature.

lit·ter (lĭt'ər), *n.* **1.** things scattered about; scattered rubbish. **2.** a condition of disorder or untidiness. **3.** a number of young brought forth at one birth. **4.** a framework of canvas stretched between two parallel bars, for the transportation of the sick and the wounded. **5.** a vehicle carried by men or animals, consisting of a bed or couch, often covered and curtained, suspended between shafts. **6.** straw, hay, etc., used as bedding for animals, or as a protection for plants. **7.** the rubbish of dead leaves and twigs scattered upon the floor of the forest. —*v.t.* **8.** to strew (a place) with scattered objects. **9.** to scatter (objects) in disorder. **10.** to be strewed about (a place) in disorder (fol. by *up*). **11.** to give birth to (young): said chiefly of animals. **12.** to supply (an animal) with litter for a bed. **13.** to use (straw, hay, etc.) for litter. **14.** to cover (a floor, etc.) with litter, or straw, hay, etc. —*v.i.* **15.** to give birth to a litter. [ME *litere,* t. AF, der. *lit* bed, g. L *lectus*] —**Syn. 3.** See brood.

lit·ter·y (lĭt'ər ĭ), *adj.* of or covered with litter; untidy.

lit·te·rae hu·ma·ni·o·res (lĭt'ə rē' hū măn'ĭ ōr'ēz) (at Oxford and Cambridge universities) the faculty and school of classical languages and culture.

lit·té·ra·teur (lĭt'ə rə tûr'; *Fr.* lē tā rä tœr'), *n.* a writer of literary works. Also, **lit'te·ra·teur'.** [t. F, t. L: m. *litterator*]

lit·tle (lĭt'əl), *adj.,* **less** or **lesser, least;** or **littler, littlest;** *adv.,* **less, least;** *n.* —*adj.* **1.** small in size; not big or large: *a little child.* **2.** small in extent or duration; short; brief: *a little while.* **3.** small in number: *a little army.* **4.** small in amount or degree; not much: *little hope.* **5.** being such on a small scale: *little farmers.* **6.** small in force; weak: *a little voice.* **7.** small in consideration, dignity, consequence, etc.: *little discomforts.* **8.** mean, narrow, or illiberal: *a little mind.* **9.** endearingly small or considered as such: *Bless your little heart.* **10.** amusingly small or so considered: *I understand his little ways.* —*adv.* **11.** not at all (before a verb): *he little knows what awaits him.* **12.** in only a small amount or degree; not much: *a zeal little tempered by humanity.* —*n.* **13.** that which is little; a small amount, quantity, or degree. **14.** a short distance: *please step back a little.* **15.** a short time: *stay here a little.* [ME and OE *lytel,* c. D *luttel,* d. G *lützel*] —**lit'tle·ness,** *n.*

—**Syn. 1-4.** LITTLE, DIMINUTIVE, MINUTE, SMALL refer to that which is not large or significant. LITTLE (the opposite of *big*) is very general, covering size, extent, number, quantity, amount, duration, or degree: *a little boy, a little time.* SMALL (the opposite of *large* and of *great*) can many times be used interchangeably with LITTLE, but is especially applied to what is limited or below the average in size: *small oranges.* DIMINUTIVE denotes (usually physical) size that is much less than the average or ordinary; it may suggest delicacy: *the baby's diminutive fingers, diminutive in size but autocratic in manner.* MINUTE suggests that which is so tiny that it is difficult to discern, or that which implies attentiveness to the smallest details: *a minute quantity, examination.*

Little America, the base of the Antarctic expeditions of Adm. Richard E. Byrd, on the Bay of Whales, S of the Ross Sea.

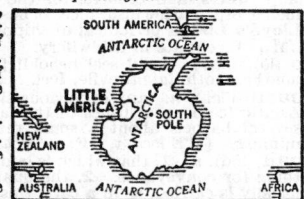

Little Bear, *Astron.* Ursa Minor.

Little Dipper, the Dipper (def. 3b).

Little Dog, See dog (def. 7).

Little Englander, *Brit.* one who believes that the best interests of England are served by attention to England itself rather than the Empire.

Little Fox, *Astron.* Vulpecula.

little hours, *Rom. Cath. Ch.* the hours of prime, tierce, sext, and nones, and sometimes also vespers and complin.

lit·tle·neck (lĭt′əl nĕk′), *n.* the hard or round clam, *Venus mercenaria,* when young and small, but of a size suitable for eating raw on the half shell.

little office, *Rom. Cath. Ch.* a service, resembling the Breviary but shorter, in honor of the Virgin Mary.

Little Rock, the capital of Arkansas. in the central part, on the Arkansas river. 107,813 (1960).

Little Russia, an indefinite region in the SW Soviet Union, consisting mainly of the Ukraine, but sometimes including adjacent areas.

Little Russian, a member of a division of the Russian people dwelling in southern and southwestern Soviet Union in Europe and in adjoining regions. Cf. Ruthenian.

little theater, 1. a small theater, producing plays whose effectiveness would be lost in larger houses. 2. plays that would not draw audiences sufficient to fill the ordinary theater, esp. as produced by a movement in the early 20th century, identified with various theatrical experiments and innovations. 3. amateur theatricals.

lit·to·ral (lĭt′ərəl), *adj.* 1. pertaining to the shore of a lake, sea, or ocean. [t. L: s. *littorālis*] —*n.* 2. a littoral region. [t. It.: m. *littorale,* t. L: m. *littorālis*]

li·tu (lē′tōō), *n.* pl. of litas.

li·tur·gi·cal (lĭ tûr′jə kəl), *adj.* 1. of or pertaining to public worship. 2. having to do with liturgies or forms of public worship. 3. of or pertaining to the liturgy or Eucharistic service. 4. of or pertaining to liturgics. Also, li·tur′gic. [f. m.s. Gk. *leitourgikós* ministering + -AL¹] —li·tur′gi·cal·ly, *adv.*

liturgical Latin, the Latin characteristic of the liturgies of the Western Church.

li·tur·gics (lĭ tûr′jĭks), *n.* 1. the science or art of conducting public worship. 2. the study of liturgies.

li·tur·gist (lĭt′ər jĭst), *n.* 1. an authority on liturgies. 2. a compiler of a liturgy or liturgies. 3. one who uses, or favors the use of, a liturgy.

li·tur·gy (lĭt′ər jĭ), *n., pl.* -gies. 1. a form of public worship; a ritual. 2. a collection of formularies for public worship. 3. a particular arrangement of services. 4. a particular form or type of the Eucharistic service. 5. the service of the Eucharist, esp. in the Eastern Church. [t. ML: m.s. *liturgia,* t. Gk.: m. *leitourgía* public duty, public worship]

Lit·vi·nov (lĭt vē′nôf), *n.* **Maksim Maksimovich** (mäk sēm′ mäk′sĭ mō′vĭch), 1876–1951, Soviet statesman.

liv·a·ble (lĭv′ə bəl), *adj.* 1. suitable for living in; habitable. 2. that can be lived with; companionable. 3. worth living; endurable. Also, **liveable.** —**liv′a·ble·ness,** *n.*

live¹ (lĭv), *v.,* lived (lĭvd), living. —*v.i.* 1. to have life, as an animal or plant; be alive; be capable of vital functions. 2. to continue to live; remain alive: *to live long.* 3. to continue in existence, operation, memory, etc.; last: *looks which lived in my memory.* 4. to escape destruction or remain afloat, as at sea. 5. to maintain life; rely for maintenance: *to live on one's income.* 6. to feed or subsist (fol. by *on* or *upon*): *to live on rice.* 7. to dwell or reside: *to live in a cottage.* 8. to pass life (as specified): *they lived happily ever after.* 9. to direct or regulate one's life: *to live by the golden rule.* 10. to experience or enjoy life to the full. 11. live in (or out), to reside at (or away from) the place of one's work. —*v.t.* 12. to pass (life): *to live a life of ease.* 13. to carry out or exhibit in one's life. 14. live down, to live so as to cause (something) to lose force or be forgotten: *to live down a mistake.* [ME *liv(i)en,* OE *lifian, libban,* c. D *leven,* G *leben*]

live² (līv), *adj.* 1. being in life, living, or alive: *live animals.* 2. of or pertaining to life of living beings: *live weight* (the weight of an animal while living). 3. characterized by or indicating the presence of living creatures. 4. full of life, energy, or activity. 5. *Colloq.* alert; wide-awake; up-to-date. 6. *Chiefly U.S. Colloq.* of present interest, as a question or issue. 7. burning or glowing, as a coal. 8. vivid or bright, as color. 9. flowing freely, as water. 10. fresh, as air. 11. loaded or unexploded, as a cartridge or shell. 12. *Elect.* electrically connected to a source of potential difference, or electrically charged so as to have a potential different from

that of earth: *a live wire.* 13. moving, or imparting motion or power: *the live center on a lathe.* 14. still in use, or to be used, as type set up or copy for printing. 15. (of a radio or TV program) broadcast or televised at the moment it is being presented at the studio. [aphetic var. of ALIVE, used attributively]

live·a·ble (lĭv′ə bəl), *adj.* livable.

live-bear·er (līv′bâr′ər), *n.* any fish of the viviparous family *Poeciliidae,* esp. those kept in home aquariums.

live center (līv). See center (def. 10a).

lived (līvd), *adj.* having life or a life (as specified): *long-lived.*

live-for·ev·er (līv′fər ĕv′ər), *n.* the garden variety of orpine, *Sedum purpureum,* an Old World succulent.

live·li·hood (līv′lĭ hŏŏd′), *n.* means of maintaining life; maintenance: *to gain a livelihood.* [earlier *liveliod,* metathetic var. of ME *livilod,* OE *līf(ge)lād* life-support (cf. LIFE, LODE, LOAD); current form influenced by obs. *livelihood* liveliness] —**Syn.** See living.

live load (līv), a load that is applied temporarily, as the weight of a train passing over a bridge.

live·long (lĭv′lông′, -lŏng′), *adj.* 1. long to the full extent (used of time): *the livelong day.* 2. whole or entire. [alter. (by assoc. with LIVE¹) of *leeve long,* ME *leve longe* dear long. Cf. LIEF, LONG¹]

live·ly (līv′lĭ), *adj.,* -lier, -liest, *adv.* —*adj.* 1. full or suggestive of life or vital energy; active, vigorous, or brisk: *a lively discussion.* 2. animated, spirited, vivacious, or sprightly: *a lively tune.* 3. eventful, stirring, or exciting: *a lively time.* 4. strong, keen, or distinct: *a lively recollection.* 5. striking, telling, or effective, as an expression or instance. 6. vivid or bright, as color or light. 7. sparkling, as wines. 8. fresh, as air. 9. rebounding quickly, as a baseball. 10. riding the sea buoyantly, as a ship. —*adv.* 11. with activity, vigor, or animation; briskly. [ME; OE *līflic*] —**live′li·ly,** *adv.* —**live′li·ness,** *n.*

liv·en (lī′vən), *v.t.* 1. to put life into; rouse; cheer (often fol. by *up*). —*v.i.* 2. to become more lively; brighten (usually fol. by *up*). —**liv′en·er,** *n.*

live oak (līv), 1. an evergreen species of oak, *Quercus virginiana,* of the southern U.S., with a hard wood used in shipbuilding, etc. 2. any of various related trees.

liv·er¹ (lĭv′ər), *n.* 1. (in man) a large, reddish-brown glandular organ (divided by fissures into five lobes) in the upper right-hand side of the abdominal cavity, secreting bile and performing various metabolic functions, and formerly supposed to be the seat of love, desire, courage, etc. 2. an organ in other animals similar to the human liver, often used as food. [ME; OE *lifer,* c. D *lever,* G *leber,* Icel. *lifr*]

liv·er² (lĭv′ər), *n.* 1. one who lives. 2. one who leads a life (as specified): *an evil liver.* 3. a dweller. [f. LIVE¹ + -ER¹]

liver extract, an extract of mammalian liver, used to treat anemia.

liv·er·ied (lĭv′ər ĭd, lĭv′rĭd), *adj.* clad in livery, as servants.

liv·er·ish (lĭv′ər ĭsh), *adj.* 1. having one's liver out of order. 2. disagreeable as to disposition.

Liv·er·pool (lĭv′ər pōōl′), *n.* a seaport in W England, on the Mersey estuary. 773,700 (est. 1956).

liv·er·wort (lĭv′ər wûrt′), *n.* any of the cryptogamic plants which belong to the class *Hepaticae,* comprising mosslike or thalloid plants which grow mostly on damp ground, in water, or on tree trunks.

liv·er·wurst (lĭv′ər wûrst′, -wōōrst′), *n.* a sausage made with a large percentage of liver. [half trans., half adoption of G *leberwurst*]

liv·er·y (lĭv′ər ĭ, lĭv′rĭ), *n., pl.* -eries. 1. a distinctive dress, badge, or device provided for retainers, as of a feudal lord. 2. a kind of uniform worn by servants, now only menservants, of a person or household. 3. a distinctive dress worn by an official, a member of a company or guild, etc. 4. Also, **livery company,** the entire guild company entitled to wear such livery. 5. characteristic dress, garb, or outward appearance: *the green livery of summer.* 6. the keep, or feeding, stabling, etc., of horses for pay. 7. *U.S.* a livery stable. 8. *Law.* an ancient method of conveying a freehold by formal delivery of possession. [ME *livere, levere,* t. AF: m. *liverē,* pp. of *liver* deliver, g. L *līberāre* liberate]

liv·er·y·man (lĭv′ər ĭ mən, lĭv′rĭ-), *n., pl.* -men. 1. a keeper of or an employee in a livery stable. 2. *Brit.* a member of a livery company. 3. *Obs.* a person in livery.

livery stable, a stable where horses and vehicles are cared for or let out for pay.

lives (līvz), *n.* pl. of life.

live steam (līv), 1. steam fresh from the boiler and at full pressure. 2. steam which has performed no work or only part of its work.

live·stock (līv′stŏk′), *n.* the horses, cattle, sheep, and other useful animals kept or raised on a farm or ranch.

live wire (līv), *Slang.* an energetic, alert person.

liv·id (lĭv′ĭd), *adj.* 1. having the discolored bluish appearance due to a bruise, to congestion of blood vessels, etc., as the flesh, face, hands, or nails. 2. dull blue; dark grayish blue. [t. L: s. *lividus*] —**liv′id·ly,** *adv.* —**liv′id·ness,** or **liv·id′i·ty,** *n.*

liv·ing (lĭv′ĭng), *adj.* 1. that lives; alive, or not dead. 2. in actual existence or use: *living languages.* 3. active; strong: *a living faith.* 4. burning or glowing, as a coal.

5. flowing freely, as water. **6.** lifelike, as a picture. **7.** of or pertaining to living beings: *within living memory.* **8.** pertaining to or sufficient for living: *living conditions.* —**n. 9.** the act or condition of one who or that which lives: *living is very expensive these days.* **10.** manner or course of life: *holy living.* **11.** means of maintaining life; livelihood: *to earn one's living.* **12.** *Brit.* an ecclesiastical office or cure, as a rectory, with revenues attached. —**liv'ing·ly,** *adv.* —**liv'ing·ness,** *n.*
—**Syn. 1.** live, quick. **3.** lively, vigorous. **11.** LIVING, LIVELIHOOD, MAINTENANCE, SUPPORT refer, directly or indirectly, to what is earned or spent for subsistence. LIVING and LIVELIHOOD (a somewhat more formal word), both refer to what one earns to keep (oneself) alive, but are seldom interchangeable within the same phrase: *to earn one's living, to seek one's livelihood.* "To make a living" suggests making just enough to keep alive, and is particularly frequent in the negative: *you cannot make a living out of that.* "To make a livelihood out of something" suggests rather making a business of it: *to make a livelihood out of trapping foxes.* MAINTENANCE and SUPPORT refer usually to what is spent for the living of another: *to provide for the maintenance or support of someone.* MAINTENANCE occasionally refers to the allowance itself provided for livelihood: *they are entitled to a maintenance from this estate.*

living room, *U.S.* a room for general use; parlor.
Liv·ing·ston (lĭv'ĭng stən), *n.* **Robert R.,** 1746–1813, U.S. statesman and jurist.
Liv·ing·stone (lĭv'ĭng stən), *n.* **1. David,** 1813–73, Scottish missionary and explorer in Africa. **2.** a town in Northern Rhodesia, on the Zambesi river, near Victoria Falls: the former capital. 7899 (est. 1946).
living wage, a wage on which it is possible for a wage earner to live according to minimum customary standards.
Li·vo·ni·a (lĭ vō'nĭ ə), *n.* a former Russian province on the Baltic: now part of the Latvian and Estonian republics of the Soviet Union.
Li·vor·no (lē vôr'nō), *n.* a seaport in W Italy, on the Ligurian sea. 148,000 (est. 1954). Also, **Leghorn.**
li·vre (lē'vər; *Fr.* lē'vr), *n.* an old French money of account and coin, with gradual reductions in value. [t. F, g. L *libra* pound]
Liv·y (lĭv'ĭ), *n.* (*Titus Livius*) 59 B.C.–A.D. 17, Roman historian.
lix·iv·i·ate (lĭk sĭv'ĭ āt'), *v.t.,* **-ated, -ating.** to treat with a solvent; leach. [f. LIXIVI(UM) + -ATE¹] —**lix·iv'i·a'tion,** *n.*
lix·iv·i·um (lĭk sĭv'ĭ əm), *n., pl.* **lixiviums, lixivia** (lĭk sĭv'ĭ ə). **1.** the solution, containing alkaline salts, obtained by leaching wood ashes with water; lye. **2.** any solution obtained by leaching. [t. L, prop. neut. of *lixivius* made into lye]
liz·ard (lĭz'ərd), *n.* **1.** any of the typical lizards of the Old World family *Lacertidae,* esp. of the genus *Lacerta.* **2.** any reptile of the order *Sauria,* including also larger forms, the monitors, geckos, chameleons, and various limbless forms. **3.** *Slang.* an idler or lounger in places of social enjoyment, public resort, etc. **4. The Lizard,** Lizard Head. [ME *lesard,* t. OF (masc.), also *lesarde,* fem., t. L: m. *lacertus,* masc., *lacerta,* fem.]

Common lizard, Lacerta vivipara (Total length 5 or 6 in.)

lizard fish, any of various large-mouthed fishes (family *Synodontidae*) with lizardlike heads, esp. *Synodus foetens* of the Atlantic coast of the United States and *Synodus lucioceps* of California.
Lizard Head, a promontory in SW England, in Cornwall: the southernmost point in England. Also, **The Lizard.**
Lju·blja·na (lū'blyä'nä), *n.* a city in NW Yugoslavia: capital of Slovenia. 138,211 (1953). German, **Laibach.**
ll., **1.** lines. **2.** (L *loco laudato*) in the place cited.
LL, **1.** Late Latin. **2.** Low Latin. Also, **L.L.**
lla·ma (lä'mə), *n.* **1.** a woolly-haired South American ruminant of the genus *Lama* (or *Auchenia*), probably a domesticated variety of the guanaco, used as a beast of burden. **2.** the fine, soft fleece of the llama, combined with the wool for coating. [t. Sp., t. Kechua]
Llan·el·ly (lăn ĕ'lĭ), *n.* a seaport in S Wales. 34,329 (1951).
lla·no (lä'nō; *Sp.* lyä'nō, yä'-), *n., pl.* **-nos** (-nōz; *Sp.* -nōs). (in Spanish America) an extensive grassy plain with few trees. [t. Sp.: a plain, as adj., flat, level, g. L *plānus* PLAIN²]

Llama, Lama glama (Ab. 3½ ft. high at the shoulder)

Lla·no Es·ta·ca·do (lä'nō ĕs'tə kä'dō), a large plateau in W Texas and SE New Mexico: cattle-grazing region. 1000–5000 ft. high. Also, **Staked Plain.**
LL.B., (L *Legum Baccalaureus*) Bachelor of Laws.
LL.D., (L *Legum Doctor*) Doctor of Laws.
LL.M., (L *Legum Magister*) Master of Laws.
Lloyd George (loid jôrj'), **David,** 1863–1945, British statesman; prime minister, 1916–22.
Lloyd's (loidz), *n.* an association at the Royal Ex-

change, London, comprising underwriters, merchants, ship-owners, and brokers, for the furtherance of commerce, esp. marine insurance. It has published since 1716 **Lloyd's List,** a periodical of shipping intelligence.
L.M., Licentiate in Midwifery.
lo (lō), *interj.* look! see! behold! [ME; OE *lā!* lo! behold! c. Goth. *laían* revile, Icel. *lā* scold]
loach (lōch), *n.* any of various slender European and Asiatic fresh-water fishes of the family *Cobitidae,* with several barbels about a small mouth: related to the minnows. [ME *loch,* t. OF: m. *loche;* ? of Celtic orig.]
load (lōd), *n.* **1.** that which is laid on or placed in anything for conveyance. **2.** the quantity that can be or usually is carried, as in a cart; this quantity taken as a unit of measure or weight. **3.** anything upborne or sustained: *the load of fruit on a tree.* **4.** something that weighs down or oppresses like a burden. **5.** the charge of a firearm. **6.** (*pl.*) *Colloq.* a great quantity or number: *loads of people.* **7.** the weight supported by a structure or part. **8.** *Elect.* the power delivered by a generator, motor, power station, or transformer (often fol. by *on*). **9.** *Mech.* the external resistance overcome by an engine, dynamo, or the like, under a given condition, measured by the power required. **10.** *Slang.* a sufficient quantity of liquor drunk to intoxicate. —*v.t.* **11.** to put a load on or in: *to load a cart.* **12.** to supply abundantly or excessively with something: *to load a person with gifts.* **13.** to weigh down, burden, or oppress. **14.** to add to the weight of, often fraudulently. **15.** lo ad dice, to make dice heavier on one side than on the others by fraudulent means so as to cause them to fall with a particular face upward. **16.** *Insurance.* to add to the net premium. See **loading** (def. 5). **17.** to take on as a load: *a vessel loading coal.* **18.** to charge a firearm. —*v.i.* **19.** to put on or take on a load. **20.** to load a firearm. **21.** to become loaded. [ME *lode;* orig. the same word as LODE (OE *lād* way, course, carrying), but now differentiated in spelling and sense and assoc. with LADE] —**load'er,** *n.*
—**Syn. 4.** LOAD, BURDEN referred originally to something placed on a person or animal or put into a vehicle for conveyance; LOAD has still retained this concrete meaning, BURDEN has lost it, except in such fixed phrases as: *beast of burden,* and *a ship of 1500 tons burden* (carrying capacity). Both words have come to be used figuratively to refer to duties, cares, etc., that are oppressively heavy and this is now the main meaning of BURDEN: *you have taken a load off my mind; some children are a burden.*
load displacement, *Naut.* the amount of water displaced by a ship when it is fully loaded.
load factor, *Elect.* the ratio of the average load over a designated period of time to the peak load occurring in that period.
load·ing (lō'dĭng), *n.* **1.** act of one who or that which loads. **2.** that with which something is loaded, a load; a burden; a charge. **3.** *Elect.* the process of adding inductances to a telephone circuit, radio antenna, etc. **4.** the ratio of the gross weight of an airplane to engine power (**power loading**), wing span (**span loading**), or wing area (**wing loading**). **5.** *Insurance.* an addition to the net mathematical premium, to cover expenses and contingencies and to allow for a margin of safety.
loading coil, *Elect.* an inductance coil used to improve the characteristics of a transmission line.
load line, *Naut.* one of several lines on the side of a ship established by statue and indicating the maximum legal draft for a certain set of conditions.
load·star (lōd'stär'), *n.* lodestar.
load·stone (lōd'stōn'), *n.* **1.** a variety of magnetite which possesses magnetic polarity and attracts iron. **2.** a piece of this serving as a magnet. **3.** something that attracts. Also, **lodestone.** [f. LOAD + STONE]
loaf¹ (lōf), *n., pl.* **loaves** (lōvz). **1.** a portion of bread or cake baked in a mass of definite form. **2.** a shaped or molded mass of food, as of sugar, chopped meat, etc.: *a veal loaf.* [ME *lo(o)f,* OE *hlāf* loaf, bread, c. G *laib*]
loaf² (lōf), *v.i.* **1.** to lounge or saunter lazily and idly. **2.** to idle away time. —*v.t.* **3.** to idle (*away*): *to loaf one's life away.* [orig. obscure] —**loaf'er,** *n.*
loaf·er (lō'fər), *n.* a casual, moccasinlike shoe.
loam (lōm), *n.* **1.** a loose soil composed of clay and sand, esp. a kind containing organic matter and of great fertility. **2.** a mixture of clay, sand, straw, etc., used in making molds for founding, and in plastering walls, stopping holes, etc. **3.** *Archaic.* earth. **4.** *Obs.* clay. —*v.t.* **5.** to cover or stop with loam. [ME *loam, lam(e),* OE *lām,* c. D *leem,* G *lehm* loam, clay] —**loam'y,** *adj.*
loan (lōn), *n.* **1.** act of lending; a grant of the use of something temporarily: *the loan of a book.* **2.** something lent or furnished on condition of being returned, esp. a sum of money lent at interest. —*v.t.* **3.** to make a loan of; lend. **4.** *Chiefly U.S.* to lend (money) at interest. —*v.i.* **5.** *Chiefly U.S.* to make a loan or loans. [ME *lon(e), lan(e),* OE *lān,* appar. t. Scand.; cf. Icel. *lān,* c. OE *loan,* grant] —**loan'er,** *n.*
Lo·an·da (lō än'də), *n.* Luanda.
loan office, **1.** an office for making loans. **2.** a pawnbroker's shop. **3.** a public office for receiving subscriptions to a government loan.
loan shark, *U.S. Colloq.* one who loans money at an excessive rate of interest.
loan word, a word of one language adopted into another at any period in history. Examples: *wine* (into Old English from Latin), *blitz* (into Modern English from German). [trans. of G *lehnwort*]

b., blend of, blended; c., cognate with; d., dialect, dialectal; der., derived from; f., formed from; g., going back to; m., modification of; r., replacing; s., stem of; t., taken from; ?, perhaps. See the full key on inside cover.

loath (lōth), *adj.* reluctant, averse, or unwilling. Also, **loth.** [ME *lothe*, OE *lāth* hostile, hateful, c. Icel. *leidhr* loathed, D *leed*, G *leid* sorrow] **—Syn.** See **reluctant.**

loathe (lōth), *v.t.* 1. to feel hatred, disgust, or intense aversion for. 2. to feel a physical disgust for (food, etc.). [ME *lothien*, OE *lāthian* be hateful, der. *lāth* LOATH] **—loath′er,** *n.* **—Syn.** 1. abominate, detest.

loath·ing (lō′thĬng), *n.* 1. strong dislike mingled with disgust; intense aversion. 2. physical disgust, as for food. **—loath′ing·ly,** *adv.* **—Syn.** 1. See **aversion.**

loath·ly[1] (lōth′lĬ; *older* lōth′lĬ), *adv.* reluctantly; unwillingly. [f. LOATH + -LY]

loath·ly[2] (lōth′lĬ), *adj. Literary.* loathsome. [f. LOATHE + -LY]

loath·some (lōth′səm), *adj.* 1. such as to excite loathing; hateful; disgusting. 2. physically disgusting; sickening. **—loath′some·ly,** *adv.* **—loath′some·ness,** *n.*

loaves (lōvz), *n.* pl. of **loaf**[1].

lob[1] (lŏb), *n., v.,* **lobbed, lobbing.** *—n.* 1. *Tennis.* a ball struck high to the back of the opponent's court. 2. *Cricket.* a slow underhand ball. *—v.t.* 3. *Tennis.* to strike (a ball) high into the air to the back of the opponent's court. 4. *Cricket.* to bowl with a slow movement. *—v.i.* 5. *Tennis.* to lob a ball. [ME *pollack*; later, bumpkin; as v., move clumsily. See LUBBER]

lob[2] (lŏb), *n.* lobworm.

lo·bar (lō′bər), *adj.* of or pertaining to a lobe, as of the lungs: *lobar pneumonia.*

lo·bate (lō′bāt), *adj.* 1. having a lobe or lobes; lobed. 2. having the form of a lobe. 3. *Ornithol.* noting or pertaining to a foot in which the individual toes have membranous flaps along the sides. Also, **lo′bat·ed.** [t. NL: m.s. *lobātus*, der. LL *lobus* LOBE] **—lo′bate·ly,** *adv.*

lo·ba·tion (lō bā′shən), *n.* 1. lobate formation. 2. a lobe.

lob·by (lŏb′Ĭ), *n., pl.* **-bies,** *v.,* **-bied, -bying.** *—n.* 1. a corridor, vestibule, or entrance hall, as in a public building, often serving as an anteroom. 2. *Chiefly U.S.* the persons who frequent a legislative lobby or chamber, esp. to influence the members. *—v.i.* 3. to frequent the lobby of a legislative chamber to influence the members. 4. to solicit the votes of members of a legislative body in the lobby or elsewhere. *—v.t.* 5. *Chiefly U.S.* to influence (legislators), or urge or procure the passage of (a bill), by lobbying. [t. ML: m.s. *lobia, lobium* covered walk; of Gmc. origin (cf. G *laube* an arbor). See LODGE]

lob·by·ism (lŏb′Ĭz əm), *n.* U.S. 1. the system of lobbying. 2. the practices of those who lobby. **—lob′by·ist,** *n.*

lobe (lōb), *n.* 1. a roundish projection or division, as of an organ, a leaf, etc. 2. *Anat.* the soft pendulous lower part of the external ear. See diag. under **ear.** [t. F, t. LL: m.s. *lobus,* t. Gk.: m. *lobós*]

lobed (lōbd), *adj.* 1. having a lobe or lobes; lobate. 2. *Bot.* (of a leaf) having lobes or divisions extending less than halfway to the middle of the base.

lo·bel·ia (lō bēl′yə), *n.* any of the herbaceous plants constituting the genus *Lobelia,* comprising many species, both wild and cultivated, with blue, red, yellow, or white flowers. [t. NL, named after M. de *Lobel* (1538–1616), Flemish botanist, physician to James I of England]

lob·lol·ly (lŏb′lŏl′Ĭ), *n., pl.* **-lies.** 1. a pine, *Pinus Taeda,* of the southern U.S. 2. the wood of this tree. Also, **loblolly pine.**

loblolly boy, *Obs.* the attendant of a ship's surgeon.

lo·bo (lō′bō), *n., pl.* **-bos.** *Zool.* a large gray wolf of the western U.S. [t. Sp., g. L *lupus* wolf]

lo·bot·o·my (lō bŏt′ə mĬ), *n. Surgery.* the cutting into or across a lobe of the brain, usually of the cerebrum, to alter brain function, especially in the treatment of mental disorders.

lob·scouse (lŏb′skous), *n. Prov. Eng. and Naut.* a stew of meat, potatoes, onions, shipbiscuit, etc.

lob·ster (lŏb′stər), *n.* 1. any of various large, edible, marine, stalk-eyed, decapod crustaceans of the family *Homaridae,* esp. of the genus *Homarus.* 2. the spiny lobster (which see). 3. any of various similar crustaceans, as certain crawfishes. [ME *lobster, lop(i)ster,* OE *loppestre,* der. *loppe* spider (both creatures having many projecting parts). See LOP[1], -STER]

Lobster. *Homarus americanus*

lobster pot, a trap in which lobsters are caught.

lob·ule (lŏb′ūl), *n.* 1. a small lobe. 2. a subdivision of a lobe. [t. NL: m.s. *lobulus,* dim. of LL *lobus* LOBE] **—lob′u·lar,** *adj.*

lob·worm (lŏb′wûrm′), *n.* the lugworm. Also, **lob.**

lo·cal (lō′kəl), *adj.* 1. pertaining to or characterized by place, or position in space: *local situation.* 2. pertaining to, characteristic of, or restricted to a particular place or particular places: *a local custom.* 3. pertaining to a town or a small district rather than the entire state or country. 4. pertaining to or affecting a particular part or particular parts, as of a system or object: *a local disease.* 5. stopping at all stations: *a local train.* *—n.* 6. a local train, bus, etc. 7. a newspaper item of local interest. 8. a local branch of a union, fraternity, etc. [ME, t. LL: s. *locālis,* der. L *locus* place]

local color, 1. distinctive characteristics or peculiarities of a place or period as represented in literature, drama, etc., or observed in reality. 2. the natural color of any particular object or part in a picture.

lo·cale (lō kăl′, -käl′), *n.* a place or locality, esp. with reference to events or circumstances connected with it. [t. F: m. *local,* n. use of adj. See LOCAL, adj.]

local government, the administration of the local affairs of a town or district by its inhabitants, rather than by the state or country at large.

lo·cal·ism (lō′kə lĬz′əm), *n.* 1. a manner of speaking, pronunciation, usage, or inflection that is peculiar to one locality. 2. a local custom. 3. attachment to a particular locality. 4. provincialism.

lo·cal·i·ty (lō kăl′ə tĬ), *n., pl.* **-ties.** 1. a place, spot, or district, with or without reference to things or persons in it. 2. the place in which a thing is or occurs. 3. state or condition of being local or having place.

lo·cal·ize (lō′kə līz′), *v.t.,* **-ized, -izing.** to make local; fix in, or assign or restrict to, a particular place or locality. **—lo′cal·iz′a·ble,** *adj.* **—lo′cal·i·za′tion,** *n.*

lo·cal·ly (lō′kə lĬ), *adv.* 1. in a particular place, or places. 2. with regard to place. 3. in a local respect.

local option, a right of choice exercised by a minor political division, esp. as to allowing the sale of liquor.

Lo·car·no (lō kär′nō), *n.* a town in S Switzerland, on Lake Maggiore: Locarno Pact, 1925. 7767 (1950).

lo·cate (lō′kāt), *v.,* **-cated, -cating.** *—v.t.* 1. to discover the place or location of: *to locate a leak in a pipe.* 2. *Chiefly U.S.* to set, fix, or establish in a place, situation, or locality; place; settle: *to locate one's headquarters in Dallas.* 3. *U.S.* to enter a claim to (a tract of land); to take up (land). 4. to refer (something), as by opinion or statement, to a particular place: *locate the garden of Eden in Babylonia.* *—v.i.* 5. *U.S.* to establish oneself in a place; settle. [t. L: m.s. *locātus,* pp., placed]

lo·ca·tion (lō kā′shən), *n.* 1. a place of settlement or residence: *a good location for a doctor.* 2. a place or situation occupied: *a house in a fine location.* 3. a tract of land located, or of designated situation or limits: *a mining location.* 4. *Motion Pictures.* a place, outside of the studio, affording suitable environment for photographing particular plays, incidents, etc. 5. act of locating. 6. state of being located. 7. *Civil Law.* a letting or lease (from the point of view of the lessor).

loc·a·tive (lŏk′ə tĬv), *Gram.* *—adj.* 1. (in some inflected languages) denoting a case, having as chief function indication of place in or at which, as Latin *domī* "at home." *—n.* 2. the locative case. 3. a word in that case. [t. ML: m.s. *locātīvus.* See LOCATE, -IVE]

lo·ca·tor (lō′kā tər, lō kā′tər), *n.* U.S. one who fixes the boundaries of a land or mining claim. [t. L]

loc. cit., loco citato.

loch (lŏk, lŏkH), *n. Scot.* 1. a lake. 2. an arm of the sea, esp. when partially landlocked. [t. Gaelic. Cf. LOUGH]

lo·chi·a (lō′kĬ ə, lŏk′Ĭ ə), *n.pl. Med.* the liquid discharge from the uterus after childbirth. [t. NL, t. Gk.: neut. pl. of *lóchios* pertaining to childbirth] **—lo·chi·al** (lō′kĬ əl), *adj.*

lo·ci (lō′sī), *n.* pl. of **locus.**

lock[1] (lŏk), *n.* 1. a device for securing a door, gate, lid, drawer, or the like, in position when closed, consisting of a bolt or system of bolts propelled and withdrawn by a mechanism operated by a key, dial, etc. 2. a device to keep a wheel from rotating, as in descending a hill. 3. a contrivance for fastening or securing something. 4. the mechanism in a firearm by means of which it can be kept from operating. 5. an enclosed portion of a canal, river, etc., with gates at each end, for raising or lowering vessels from one level to another. 6. any of various grapples or holds in wrestling, esp. any hold in which an arm or leg of one wrestler is intertwined about the body of his opponent. *—v.t.* 7. to fasten or secure (a door, building, etc.) by the operation of a lock. 8. to shut in a place fastened by a lock or locks, as for security or restraining (fol. by *up, in,* etc.): *to lock a prisoner in a cell.* 9. to exclude by or as by a lock (usually fol. by *out*). 10. to make fast or immovable by or as by a lock: *to lock a wheel.* 11. to fasten or fix firmly, as by engaging parts (often fol. by *up*). 12. *Print.* to make (type, etc.) immovable in a chase by securing the quoins (fol. by *up*). 13. to join or unite firmly by interlinking or intertwining: *to lock arms.* 14. to move (a ship) by means of a lock or locks, as in a canal. 15. to furnish with locks, as a canal. 16. to enclose (a waterway) with a lock (fol. by *off*). *—v.i.* 17. to become locked: *this door locks with a key.* 18. to become fastened, fixed, or interlocked. 19. to go or pass by means of a lock or locks, as a vessel. 20. to construct locks in waterways. [ME; OE *loc* fastening; akin to OE *lūcan,* D *luiken,* Icel. *lūka,* Goth. *galūkan* shut, close]

lock[2] (lŏk), *n.* 1. a tress or portion of hair. 2. (*pl.*) the hair of the head. 3. a flock or small portion of wool, cotton, flax, etc. [ME *locke,* OE *locc* lock of hair, c. Icel. *lokkr,* D lok curl, G *locke*]

lock·age (lŏk′Ĭj), *n.* 1. the construction, use, or operation of locks, as in a canal or stream. 2. passage through a lock or locks. 3. toll paid for such passage.

Locke (lŏk), *n.* John, 1632–1704, British philosopher.

lock·er (lŏk′ər), *n.* 1. a chest, drawer, compartment, closet, or the like, that may be locked. 2. *Naut.* a chest or compartment in which to stow things. 3. one who or that which locks.

Lock·er-Lamp·son (lŏk'ər lăm'sən), *n.* **Frederick,** 1821–95, British poet and author.

lock·et (lŏk'ĭt), *n.* a small case for a miniature portrait, a lock of hair, or other keepsake, usually worn on a necklace. [ME, t. F: m. *loquet* latch, catch, dim. of OF *loc* lock, t. Gmc.; cf. LOCK¹]

lock·jaw (lŏk'jô'), *n.* *Pathol.* tetanus in which the jaws become firmly locked together.

lock nut, **1.** a supplementary nut screwed down upon another to prevent it from shaking loose. **2.** a nut in which spontaneous motion is prevented by springs fitting between the threads, or by interlocking parts. Also, **lock'nut/**.

lock·out (lŏk'out'), *n.* **1.** the closing of a business or wholesale dismissal of employees by the employer because the employees refuse to accept his terms or because the employer refuses to operate on terms set by a union. —*v.t.* **2.** to conduct a lockout against (employees).

Lock·port (lŏk'pôrt'), *n.* a city in W New York, on the New York State Barge Canal. 26,443 (1960).

lock·smith (lŏk'smĭth'), *n.* one who makes or mends locks.

lock step, a mode of marching in very close file, in which the leg of each person moves with and closely behind the corresponding leg of the person ahead.

lock stitch, a sewing-machine stitch in which two threads are locked together at small intervals.

lock·up (lŏk'ŭp'), *n.* **1.** a jail. **2.** act of locking up.

Lock·yer (lŏk'yər), *n.* **Sir Joseph Norman,** 1836–1920, British astronomer.

lo·co (lō'kō), *n., pl.* **-cos,** *v.* **-coed, -coing,** *adj.* *U.S.* —*n.* **1.** locoweed. **2.** loco disease. —*v.t.* **3.** to poison with locoweed. **4.** to make crazy. —*adj.* **5.** *U.S. Slang.* insane; crazy. [t. Sp.: insane, g. L *glaucus* sparkling]

lo·co ci·ta·to (lō'kō sĭ tā'tō), *Latin.* in the place, or passage, already mentioned. *Abbr.:* loc. cit.

loco disease, a disease affecting the brain of animals, caused by eating locoweed.

Lo·co·fo·co (lō'kō fō'kō), *n.* the equal-rights or radical section of the Democratic party in the United States about 1835.

lo·co·mo·tion (lō'kə mō'shən), *n.* act or power of moving from place to place. [f. L *locō*, abl. of *locus* place + MOTION]

lo·co·mo·tive (lō'kə mō'tĭv), *n.* **1.** a self-propelled vehicle running on a railroad track, designed to pull railroad cars. **2.** any self-propelled vehicle. —*adj.* **3.** moving or traveling by means of its own mechanism or powers. **4.** serving to produce such movement, or adapted for or used in locomotion: *locomotive organs.* **5.** of or pertaining to movement from place to place. **6.** having the power of locomotion. [f. L *locō*, abl. of *locus* place + MOTIVE, *adj.*]

lo·co·mo·tor (lō'kə mō'tər), *adj.* **1.** of or pertaining to locomotion. —*n.* **2.** one who or that which has locomotive power.

locomotor a·tax·i·a (ə tăk'sĭ ə), *Pathol.* a degenerative disease of the spinal cord, marked by loss of control over the muscular movements, mainly in walking.

lo·co·weed (lō'kō wēd'), *n.* any of various fabaceous plants of the genera *Astragalus* and *Oxytropis* of the southwestern U.S., producing loco disease in sheep, horses, etc. [f. LOCO + WEED¹]

Lo·cris (lō'krĭs), *n.* either of two districts in the central part of ancient Greece. —**Lo·cri·an** (lō'krĭ ən), *n.*

loc·u·lar (lŏk'yə lər), *adj.* having one or more loculi, chambers, or cells. [t. LL: s. *locularis* kept in boxes, der. L *locus* box, cell]

loc·u·late (lŏk'yə lāt', -lĭt), *adj.* *Bot.* having one or more loculi. Also, **loc'u·lat/ed.** [t. L: m.s. *loculātus* furnished with compartments]

loc·u·lus (lŏk'yə ləs), *n., pl.* **-li** (-lī'). **1.** *Bot., Zool., Anat.* a small compartment or chamber; a cell. **2.** *Bot.* **a.** the cell of a carpel in which the seed is located. **b.** the cell of an anther in which the pollen is located. [t. L: m.s. *locuius* little place, box, dim. of *locus* place]

lo·cum te·nens (lō'kəm tē'nĕnz), *Chiefly Brit.* a temporary substitute, esp. for a clergyman or doctor. [ML]

lo·cus (lō'kəs), *n., pl.* **loci** (lō'sī). **1.** a place; a locality. **2.** *Math.* a curve or other figure considered as generated by a point, line, or surface, which moves or is placed according to a definite law. **3.** *Genetics.* the chromosomal position of a gene as determined by its linear order relative to the other genes on that chromosome. [t. L: place]

lo·cus clas·si·cus (lō'kəs klăs'ə kəs), *Latin.* a passage commonly cited to illustrate or explain a subject.

lo·cus si·gil·li (lō'kəs sĭ jĭl'ī), *Latin.* the place of the seal (on a document, etc.). *Abbr.:* L.S.

lo·cust (lō'kəst), *n.* **1.** any of the grasshoppers with short antennae which constitute the family *Locustidae,* including the notorious migratory species, such as *Locusta migratoria* of the Old World, and the Rocky Mountain locust, *Melanoplus spretus,* which swarm in immense numbers and strip the vegetation from large areas. **2.** any of various cicadas, as *Magicicada septendecim* (the seventeen-year locust). **3.** a thorny-branched, white-flowered American fabaceous

Migratory locust, *Locusta migratoria* (2 in. long)

tree, *Robinia pseudoacacia.* **4.** its durable wood. **5.** any of various other trees, as the carob and the honey locust. [ME, t. L: s. *locusta* locust, lobster]

lo·cus·ta (lō kŭs'tə), *n., pl.* **-tae** (-tē). *Bot.* the spikelet of grasses. [t. NL, special use of L *locusta* LOCUST]

lo·cu·tion (lō kū'shən), *n.* **1.** a particular form of expression; a phrase or expression. **2.** style of speech or verbal expression; phraseology. [ME, t. L: s. *locūtio*]

lode (lōd), *n.* **1.** a veinlike deposit, usually metalliferous. **2.** any body of ore set off from adjacent rock formations. [ME; OE *lād* way, course, carrying (see LOAD), c. OHG *leita* procession, Icel. *leidh* way, course]

lode·star (lōd'stär'), *n.* **1.** a star that shows the way. **2.** Polaris. **3.** something that serves as a guide or on which the attention is fixed. Also, **loadstar.** [ME *loode sterre.* See LOAD, LODE, STAR, n.]

lode·stone (lōd'stōn'), *n.* loadstone.

lodge (lŏj), *n., v.,* **lodged, lodging.** —*n.* **1.** a small, slight or rude shelter or habitation, as of boughs, poles, skins, earth, rough boards, or the like; cabin or hut. **2.** a house used as a temporary abode, as in the hunting season. **3.** a summer cottage. **4.** a house or cottage, as in a park or on an estate, occupied by a gatekeeper, caretaker, gardener, or the like. **5.** a place of abode or sojourn. **6.** the meeting place of a branch of a secret society. **7.** the members composing the branch. **8.** the home of a college head or master at Cambridge University, England. **9.** *U.S.* an Indian habitation. **10.** den or habitation of an animal or animals, esp. beavers. —*v.i.* **11.** to have a habitation or quarters, esp. temporarily, as in a place or house. **12.** to live in hired quarters in another's house. **13.** to be fixed or implanted, or be caught in a place or position. —*v.t.* **14.** to furnish with a habitation or quarters, esp. temporarily. **15.** to furnish with a room or rooms in one's house for payment, or have as a lodger. **16.** to serve as a habitation or shelter for, as a house does; shelter; harbor. **17.** to put or deposit, as in a place, for storage or keeping. **18.** to bring or send into a particular place or position: *to lodge a bullet in one's heart.* **19.** to vest (power, etc.). **20.** to lay (information, a complaint, etc.) before a court or the like. **21.** to beat down or lay flat, as vegetation in a storm. **22.** to track (a deer) to its lair. [ME *loge,* t. OF: hut, orig. leafy shelter, t. Gmc. (cf. OHG *laube* arbor)] —*Syn.* **1.** See **cottage.**

Lodge (lŏj), *n.* **1. Henry Cabot** (kăb'ət), 1850–1924, U.S. political leader; senator, 1893–1924. **2. Sir Oliver Joseph,** 1851–1940, British physicist and writer. **3. Thomas,** c1558–1625, English dramatist and writer.

lodg·er (lŏj'ər), *n.* one who lives in hired quarters in another's house.

lodg·ing (lŏj'ĭng), *n.* **1.** accommodation in a house, esp. in rooms for hire: *to furnish board and lodging.* **2.** a place of abode, esp. a temporary one. **3.** (*pl.*) a room or rooms hired for residence in another's house.

lodging house, a house in which lodgings are let, esp. a house other than an inn or hotel.

lodg·ment (lŏj'mənt), *n.* **1.** act of lodging. **2.** state of being lodged. **3.** something lodged or deposited. **4.** *Mil.* a position or foothold gained from an enemy, or an intrenchment made upon it. **5.** a lodging place; lodgings. Also, *esp. Brit.,* **lodge/ment.**

Lo·di (lō'dē), *n.* a town in N Italy, in Lombardy: Napoleon defeated the Austrians near here, 1796. 35,194 (1951).

Łódz (lŏŏj), *n.* a city in central Poland. 655,000 (est. 1954). Russian, **Lodz** (lŏdz).

Loeb (lōb; *Ger.* lœb), *n.* **Jacques** (zhäk), 1859–1924, German physiologist and experimental biologist in U.S.

lo·ess (lō'ĭs; *Ger.* lœs), *n.* a loamy deposit formed by wind, usually yellowish and calcareous, common in the Mississippi valley and in Europe and Asia. [t. G]

Lo·fo·ten Islands (lō'fōōt'ən), a group of islands NW of and belonging to Norway: rich fishing grounds. 30,000 pop. (est. 1945); 474 sq. mi.

loft (lôft, lŏft), *n.* **1.** the space between the underside of a roof and the ceiling of a room beneath it. **2.** a gallery or upper level in a church, hall, etc., designed for a special purpose: *a choir loft.* **3.** a hayloft. **4.** *U.S.* any upper story of a warehouse, mercantile building, or factory, esp. of buildings designed for small, light industries. **5.** *U.S.* a building consisting of such lofts. **6.** *Golf.* **a.** the slope of the face of a club backward from the vertical, tending to drive the ball upward. **b.** act of lofting. **c.** a lofting stroke. —*v.t.* **7.** *Golf.* **a.** to slant the face of (a club). **b.** to hit (a ball) into the air or over an obstacle. **c.** to clear (an obstacle) thus. **8.** to provide (a house, etc.) with a loft. —*v.i.* **9.** *Golf.* to loft the ball. [ME *lofte,* late OE *loft,* t. Scand.; cf. Icel. *lopt* the air, sky, an upper room; akin to LIFT¹, LIFT²]

loft·ing iron (lôf'tĭng, lŏf'-), *Golf.* an iron-headed club used in lofting the ball. Also, **loft/er.**

loft·y (lôf'tĭ, lŏf'-), *adj.,* **loftier, loftiest. 1.** extending high in the air; of imposing height: *lofty mountains.* **2.** exalted in rank, dignity, or character. **3.** elevated in style or sentiment, as writings, etc. **4.** haughty; proud. —**loft/i·ly,** *adv.* —**loft/i·ness,** *n.* —*Syn.* **1.** See **high.**

log (lôg, lŏg), *n., v.,* **logged, logging.** —*n.* **1.** an unhewn portion or length of the trunk or a large limb of a felled tree. **2.** something inert or heavy. **3.** *Naut.* **a.** a device for determining the speed of and distance covered by a ship. **b.** chip log, a chip (**log chip**) attached to the end of a line (**log line**) thrown over the stern to measure the speed of a ship. **c. patent log,** a screw-shaped implement on the end of a line trailing astern which indicates speed and distance. **4.** the official record of a ship's voyage; logbook. **5.** a listing of navigational, meteorological, and other significant data concerning an air journey. **6.** the register of the operation of a machine. **7.** a record kept of development during the drilling of a well, esp. of the geological formations penetrated. —*v.t.* **8.** to cut (trees) into logs. **9.** to cut down the trees or timber on (land). **10.** *Naut.* **a.** to enter in a ship's log. **b.** to travel (a distance) according to the indication of a log. —*v.i.* **11.** to cut down trees and get out logs from the forest for timber. [ME *logge*; appar. var. of LUG², n.]

log., logarithm.

Lo·gan (lō′gən), *n.* Mount, a mountain in W Canada, in SW Yukon Territory: the second highest peak in North America. 19,850 ft.

lo·gan·ber·ry (lō′gən bĕr′ĭ), *n., pl.* **-ries.** the large, dark-red acid fruit of the plant *Rubus loganobaccus*, with long prostrate canes, of California origin. [named after J. H. *Logan*, of Calif., by whom first grown]

lo·ga·ni·a·ceous (lō gā′nĭ ā′shəs), *adj.* belonging to the *Loganiaceae*, a family of herbs, shrubs, and trees of tropical and subtropical regions, including the nux vomica tree and other plants with poisonous properties. [f. s. NL *Logania*, the typical genus (named after James *Logan* 1674–1751, of Philadelphia) + -ACEOUS]

Lo·gans·port (lō′gənz pōrt′). *n.* a city in N Indiana, on the Wabash. 21,106 (1960).

log·a·oe·dic (lŏg′ə ē′dĭk, lōg′ə-). *Pros.* —*adj.* **1.** composed of dactyls and trochees or of anapests and iambs, producing a movement somewhat suggestive of prose. —*n.* **2.** a logaoedic verse. [t. LL: s. *logaoedicus*, t. Gk.: m. *logaoidikós*, f. s. *lógos* prose + s. *aoidé* song + -*ikos*-IC]

log·a·rithm (lŏg′ə rĭth′əm, -rĭth′əm, lōg′ə-), *n. Math.* the exponent of that power to which a fixed number (called the base) must be raised in order to produce a given number (called the *antilogarithm*) : 3 is the *logarithm of 8 to the base 2.* [t. NL: s. *logarithmus*, f. Gk.: s. *lógos* proportion + m. *arithmós* number]

log·a·rith·mic (lŏg′ə rĭth′mĭk, -rĭth′mĭk, lōg′ə-), *adj.* pertaining to a logarithm or logarithms. Also, **log′a·rith′mi·cal.** —**log′a·rith′mi·cal·ly,** *adv.*

log·book (lŏg′bŏok′, lōg′-), *n. Naut.* **1.** a book in which are officially recorded the indications of the log, as well as the weather and other important particulars of a ship's voyage. **2.** the record itself.

loge (lōzh; *Fr.* lōzh), *n.* a box in a theater or opera house. [t. F. See LODGE.]

log·ger (lŏg′ər, lōg′ər), *n.* **1.** the person who cuts trees into suitable lengths after the trees have been felled. **2.** a tractor used in logging. **3.** a machine for loading logs.

log·ger·head (lŏg′ər hĕd′, lōg′ər-), *n.* **1.** a thickheaded or stupid person; a blockhead. **2.** Also, **logger-head turtle.** a large-headed marine turtle, *Caretta caretta,* of all oceans. **3.** Also, **loggerhead shrike.** a common North American butcherbird, *Lanius ludovicianus,* gray above, white below, with black and white wings and tail and black facial mask. **4.** a ball or bulb of iron with a long handle, used, after being heated, to melt tar, heat liquids, etc. **5.** a rounded post in the stern of a whaleboat, around which the harpoon line is passed. **6. at loggerheads,** engaged in dispute. [back formation from *loggerheaded,* var. of obs. *log-headed* stupid]

log·gia (lŏj′ə, lōj′ĭ ə; *It.* lōd′jä), *n., pl.* **-gias; It. -gie** (-jĕ). **1.** a gallery or arcade open to the air on at least one side. **2.** a space within the body of a building but open to the air on one side, serving as an open-air room or as an entrance porch. [t. It. See LODGE, n.]

log·ging (lŏg′ĭng, lōg′ĭng), *n.* the process, work, or business of cutting down trees and getting out logs from the forest for timber.

log·i·a (lŏg′ĭ ə), *n.* pl. of logion.

log·ic (lŏj′ĭk), *n.* **1.** the science which investigates the principles governing correct or reliable inference. **2.** reasoning or argumentation, or an instance of it. **3.** the system or principles of reasoning applicable to any branch of knowledge or study. **4.** reasons or sound sense, as in utterances or actions. **5.** convincing force: *the irresistible logic of facts.* [ME *logik,* t. ML: m.s. *logica,* t. Gk.: m. *logikē,* prop. fem. of *logikós* pertaining to reason]

log·i·cal (lŏj′ə kəl), *adj.* **1.** according to the principles of logic: *a logical inference.* **2.** reasoning in accordance with the principles of logic, as a person, the mind, etc. **3.** reasonable; reasonably to be expected: *war was the logical consequence of such threats.* **4.** of or pertaining to logic. —**log′i·cal·i·ty, log′i·cal·ness,** *n.* —**log′i·cal·ly,** *adv.*

logical positivism, a philosophy stressing the logical and linguistic analysis of science.

lo·gi·cian (lō jĭsh′ən), *n.* one skilled in logic.

lo·gi·on (lŏg′ĭ ŏn′), *n., pl.* logia (lŏg′ĭ ə). **1.** a traditional saying or maxim, as of a religious teacher. **2.** (*often cap.*) a saying of Jesus (used esp. with reference to sayings of Jesus contained in collections supposed to have been among the sources of the present Gospels, or to sayings ascribed to Jesus but not recorded in the Gospels). [t. Gk.: announcement, oracle]

lo·gis·tic (lō jĭs′tĭk), *adj.* pertaining to military logistics. Also, **lo·gis′ti·cal.** [see LOGISTICS]

lo·gis·tics (lō jĭs′tĭks), *n.* the branch of military science concerned with the mathematics of transportation

and supply, and the movement of bodies of troops. [t. F: m. *logistique,* der. *loger* lodge, or *logis* lodging. See -ICS]

logo-, a word element denoting speech. [t. Gk., comb. form of *lógos* word, speech]

log·o·gram (lŏg′ə grăm′, lōg′ə-), *n.* a conventional abbreviated symbol for a frequently recurring word or phrase. Also, **log·o·graph** (lŏg′ə grăf′, -grăf′, lōg′ə-). —**log·o·gram·mat·ic** (lŏg′ə grə măt′ĭk, lōg′ə-), *adj.*

log·o·graph·ic (lŏg′ə grăf′ĭk, lōg′ə-), *adj.* **1.** consisting of logograms: *logographic writing.* **2.** of or pertaining to logography. Also, **log′o·graph′i·cal.**

lo·gog·ra·phy (lō gŏg′rə fĭ), *n.* **1.** printing with logotypes. **2.** a method of longhand reporting, each of several reporters in succession taking down a few words. [t. Gk.: m.s. *logographia* a writing of speeches]

log·o·griph (lŏg′ə grĭf, lōg′ə-), *n.* **1.** an anagram, or a puzzle involving anagrams. **2.** a puzzle in which a certain word, and other words formed from any or all of its letters, must be guessed from indications given in a set of verse. [t. F: m. *logogriphe,* f. Gk.: *logo-* LOGO- + m. *griphos* fishing basket, riddle] —**log′o·griph′ic,** *adj.*

lo·gom·a·chy (lō gŏm′ə kĭ), *n., pl.* **-chies. 1.** contention about words, or in words merely. **2.** a game played with cards, each bearing one letter, with which words are formed. [t. Gk.: m.s. *logomachia.* See LOGO-, -MACHY] —**lo·gom′a·chist,** *n.*

log·os (lŏg′ŏs), *n.* **1.** (*often cap.*) *Philos.* the rational principle that governs and develops the universe. **2.** (*cap.*) *Theol.* Jesus Christ, the Divine Word (see John, 1 : 1, 14), the second person of the Trinity. [t. Gk.: word, speech, reason, account, reckoning, proportion]

log·o·type (lŏg′ə tĭp′, lōg′ə-), *n. Print.* a single type bearing two or more distinct (not combined) letters, or a syllable or word. Cf. **ligature.** —**log′o·typ′y,** *n.*

log·roll (lŏg′rōl′, lōg′-), *Chiefly U.S.* —*v.t.* **1.** to procure the passage of (a bill) by logrolling. —*v.i.* **2.** to engage in political logrolling. —**log′roll′er,** *n.*

log·roll·ing (lŏg′rō′lĭng, lōg′-), *n.* **1.** *Chiefly U.S.* (used esp. with reference to legislators) the combining of two or more persons to assist one of them, in consideration of like combined assistance in the interest of each of the others in return. **2.** the action of rolling logs to a particular place. **3.** birling.

log·wood (lŏg′wŏod′, lōg′-), *n.* **1.** the heavy brownish-red heartwood of a West Indian and Central American caesalpiniaceous tree, *Haematoxylon campechianum,* much used in dyeing. **2.** the tree itself.

lo·gy (lō′gĭ), *adj.,* **-gier, -giest.** *U.S.* heavy; sluggish; dull. [orig. uncert. Cf. D *log* heavy, dull]

-logy, 1. a combining form naming sciences or bodies of knowledge, e.g., *paleontology, theology.* **2.** a termination of many nouns referring to writing, collections, e.g., *trilogy, martyrology.* [t. Gk.: m.s. *-logia,* der. *log-* speak, *lógos* discourse; r. earlier *-logie,* t. F. Cf. G *-logie*]

Lo·hen·grin (lō′ən grĭn, -grēn′), *n.* **1.** *German Legend.* the son of Parzival, and a knight of the Holy Grail. **2.** a romantic opera (composed, 1846–48; premiere, 1850) by Wagner.

loin (loin), *n.* **1.** (*usually pl.*) the part or parts of the body of man or of a quadruped animal on either side of the vertebral column, between the false ribs and hipbone. **2.** a cut of meat from this region of an animal, esp. a portion including the vertebrae of such parts. **3.** *Biblical and Poetic.* the part of the body which should be clothed or girded, or which is regarded as the seat of physical strength and generative power. [ME *loyne,* t. OF: m. *loigne,* ult. der. L *lumbus*]

loin·cloth (loin′klôth′, -klŏth′), *n.* a piece of cloth worn about the loins or hips.

Loire (lwär), *n.* a river flowing from S France into the Atlantic: the longest river in France. ab. 625 mi.

loi·ter (loi′tər), *v.i.* **1.** to linger idly or aimlessly in or about a place. **2.** to move or go in a slow or lagging manner: *to loiter along.* **3.** to waste time or dawdle over work, etc. —*v.t.* **4.** to pass (time, etc.) in an idle or aimless manner (fol. by *away*). [ME *lotere,* appar. freq. of obs. *lote* lurk, ME *lotie(n), lutie(n), loyt.* Cf. OE *lūtian* lurk] —**loi′ter·er,** *n.* —**loi′ter·ing·ly,** *adv.*

—**Syn. 1.** LOITER, DALLY, DAWDLE, IDLE imply moving or acting slowly, stopping for unimportant reasons, and in general wasting time. To LOITER is to linger aimlessly: *to loiter until late.* To DALLY is to loiter indecisively or to delay sportively as if free from care or responsibility: *to dally on the way home.* To DAWDLE is to saunter, stopping often, and taking a great deal of time, or to fritter away time working in a half-hearted way: *to dawdle over a task.* To IDLE is to move slowly and aimlessly, or to spend a great deal of time doing nothing: *to idle away the hours.*

Lo·ki (lō′kĭ), *n. Scand. Myth.* the god of destruction, and father of Hel and the serpent of Midgard. [t. Icel.]

loll (lŏl), *v.i.* **1.** to recline or lean in a relaxed or indolent manner; lounge: *to loll on a sofa.* **2.** to hang loosely or droopingly. —*v.t.* **3.** to allow to hang or droop. —*n.* **4.** act of lolling. **5.** one who or that which lolls. [ME *lolle, lulle.* Cf. MD *lollen* sleep] —**loll′er,** *n.*

Lol·land (lō′län), *n.* Laaland.

Lol·lard (lŏl′ərd), *n.* an English or Scottish follower of the religious teaching of John Wycliffe from the 14th century to the 16th. [ME, t. MD: m. *lollaerd* mumbler, der. *lollen* mumble, hum]

lol·li·pop (lŏl′ĭ pŏp′), *n.* a kind of taffy or other candy, often a piece on the end of a stick.

Lom·bard (lŏm′bərd, -bärd, lŭm′-), *n.* **1.** a native or inhabitant of Lombardy. **2.** a Langobard. —*adj.* **3.** Also, **Lom·bar′dic.** pertaining to the Lombards or Lombardy. [ME, t. OF, t. It.: m. *lombardo*, g. LL *Longobardus*, L *Langobardus*, t. Gmc. See LANGOBARD]

Lom·bard (lŏm′bərd, -bärd, lŭm′-; Fr. lôn bȧr′), *n.* **Pe·ter,** (*Petrus Lombardus*) c1100–1160 or 1164, Italian theologian; bishop of Paris.

Lombard Street, a street in London, England, famous as a financial center.

Lom·bard·y (lŏm′bərdǐ, lŭm′-), *n.* a department in N Italy: a former kingdom. 6,722,000 pop. (est. 1954); 9190 sq. mi.

Lombardy poplar. See **poplar** (def. 1).

Lom·bok (lŏm bŏk′), *n.* an island in Indonesia, E of Java. 701,290 pop. (1930); 1826 sq. mi.

Lom·bro·si·an school (lŏm brō′zǐ ən), a school of criminology, holding the theories and employing the methods developed by Lombroso.

Lom·bro·so (lŏm brō′sō), *n.* **Cesare** (chĕ′zä rĕ′), 1836–1909, Italian physician and criminologist.

lo·ment (lō′mĕnt), *n. Bot.* a legume which is contracted in the spaces between the seeds, and breaks at maturity into one-seeded indehiscent joints. [ME *lomente*, t. L: m. *lōmentum* bean meal] —**lo′ment·like′,** *adj.*

lo·men·ta·ceous (lō′mən tā′shəs), *adj. Bot.* of the nature of a loment; lomentlike.

lo·men·tum (lō mĕn′təm), *n., pl.* **-ta** (-tə) *Bot.* loment. [t. L]

Lo·mond (lō′mənd), *n.* **Loch,** a lake in W Scotland. 23 mi. long; 27 sq. mi.

Lon·don (lŭn′dən), *n.* **1.** a metropolis in SE England, on the Thames: capital of the United Kingdom and the British commonwealth. **2. City of,** an old city in the central part of London county: the ancient nucleus of the metropolis. 5268 (1951); 1 sq. mi. **3. County of,** an administrative county comprising the City of London and the 28 metropolitan boroughs. 3,347,982 (1951); 117 sq. mi. **4. Greater,** an urban area comprising the City of London, London and Middlesex counties, and parts of Essex, Kent, Surrey, and Hertfordshire. 8,346,137 (1951); 693 sq. mi. **5.** a city in SE Canada, in S Ontario. 95,343 (1951). **6. Jack,** 1876–1916, U.S. short-story writer and novelist.

Lon·don·der·ry (lŭn′dən dĕr′ĭ), *n.* **1.** a county in Northern Ireland. 105,448 pop. (1951); 804 sq. mi. **2.** its county seat: a seaport. 50,092 pop. (1951). Also, **Derry.**

Lon·don·er (lŭn′dən ər), *n.* a native or inhabitant of London.

lone (lōn), *adj.* **1.** being alone; unaccompanied; solitary: *a lone traveler.* **2.** standing apart, or isolated, as a house. **3.** *Poetic.* lonely. **4.** lonesome. **5.** unmarried or widowed. [aphetic var. of ALONE, used attributively] **Syn. 1.** See **alone.**

lone·ly (lōn′lǐ), *adj.,* **-li·er, -li·est. 1.** lone; solitary; without company. **2.** destitute of sympathetic or friendly companionship or relationships: *a lonely exile.* **3.** remote from men or from places of human habitation or resort: *a lonely road.* **4.** standing apart; isolated: *a lonely tower.* **5.** affected with, characterized by, or causing a depressing feeling of being alone; lonesome: *a lonely heart.* —**lone′li·ly,** *adv.* —**lone′li·ness,** *n.* —**Syn. 1.** See **alone.**

lone·some (lōn′səm), *adj.* **1.** lonely in feeling; depressed by solitude or by a sense of being alone: *to feel lonesome.* **2.** attended with or causing such a state of feeling: *a lonesome journey.* **3.** depressingly lonely in situation: *a lonesome road.* —**lone′some·ly,** *adv.* —**lone′some·ness,** *n.* —**Syn. 1.** See **alone.**

Lone Star State, Texas (a nickname).

long¹ (lông, lŏng), *adj.,* **longer** (lông′gər, lŏng′-), **longest** (lông′gist, lŏng′-), *n., adv.* —*adj.* **1.** having considerable or great extent from end to end; not short: *a long distance.* **2.** having considerable or great extent in duration: *a nice long visit.* **3.** having considerable or great extension from beginning to end, as a series, enumeration, account, book, etc.; not brief. **4.** having a specified extension in space, duration, etc.: *ten feet long.* **5.** continuing too long: *a long speech.* **6.** beyond the normal extension in space, duration, quantity, etc.: *a long dozen* (thirteen). **7.** extending to a great distance in space or time: *a long memory.* **8.** having a long time to run, as a promissory note. **9.** *Chiefly Law.* distant or remote in time: *a long date.* **10.** relatively much extended: *a long arm.* **11.** tall. **12.** (of the head or skull) of more than ordinary length from front to back. **13.** *Phonet.* **a.** lasting a relatively long time: "*feed*" has a longer vowel than "*feet*" or "*fit.*" **b.** belonging to a class of sounds considered as usually longer in duration than another class, such as the vowel of *bought* as compared to *hot*: conventionally, the vowels of *mate, meet, mite, mote, moot* and *mute.* **14. Com. a.** owning some commodity or stock. **b.** depending for profit on a rise in prices. **15.** (in gambling) **a.** of an exceptionally large difference

in proportional amounts on an event: *long odds.* **b.** of or pertaining to the larger number in the odds in betting. **16. in the long run,** after a long course of experience; in the final result. —*n.* **17.** a long time: *before long.* **18.** something that is long. —*adv.* **19.** for or through a great extent of space or, esp., time: *a reform long advocated.* **20.** for or throughout a specified extent, esp. of time: *how long did he stay?* **21.** (in elliptical expressions) gone, occupying, delaying, etc., a long or a specified time: *don't be long.* **22.** (for emphasis, after nouns denoting a period of time) throughout the whole length: *all summer long.* **23.** at a point of time far distant from the time indicated: *long before.* **24. so** (or **as) long as,** provided that. [ME *longe,* OE *lang, long,* c. D and G *lang*]

long² (lông, lŏng), *v.i.* **1.** to have a prolonged or unceasing desire, as for something not immediately (if ever) attainable. **2.** to have an earnest or strong desire. [ME *longen,* OE *langian* lengthen (impersonal), yearn, der. *lang* LONG¹]

long., longitude.

lon·gan (lŏng′gən), *n.* **1.** the small, one-seeded, greenish-brown, pleasant-tasting fruit of the large evergreen, sapindaceous tree, *Euphoria Longan,* native in China and allied to the litchi. **2.** the tree. Also, **lungan.** [t. NL: s. *longanum,* t. Chinese: m. *lung-yen* dragon's eye]

Long Beach, a city in SW California, S of Los Angeles: a seaside resort. 344,168 (1960).

long·boat (lông′bōt′, lŏng′-), *n. Naut.* the largest and strongest boat belonging to a sailing ship.

long·bow (lông′bō′, lŏng′-), *n.* **1.** the bow drawn by hand and discharging a long feathered arrow. **2. draw the longbow,** to tell exaggerated stories.

long·cloth (lông′klôth′, lŏng′klŏth′), *n.* a kind of muslin, light and soft in texture.

long distance, *U.S.* telephone service between distant points. —**long′-dis′tance,** *adj.*

long-drawn (lông′drôn′, lŏng′-), *adj.* **1.** drawn out; prolonged: *a long-drawn narrative.* **2.** long.

lon·ge·ron (lŏn′jə ron; Fr. lônzh rôn′), *n. Aeron.* a main longitudinal brace or support on an airplane. [t. F, der. *long* LONG¹]

lon·gev·i·ty (lŏn jĕv′ə tǐ), *n.* **1.** length or duration of life. **2.** long life; great duration of life.

lon·ge·vous (lŏn jē′vəs), *adj.* long-lived; living to a great age. [t. L: m. *longaevus* aged]

Long·fel·low (lông′fĕl′ō, lŏng′-), *n.* **Henry Wadsworth** (wŏdz′wərth), 1807–82, U.S. poet.

long green, *U.S. Slang.* paper currency.

long·hand (lông′hănd′, lŏng′-), *n.* writing of the ordinary kind, in which the words are written out in full (distinguished from *shorthand*).

long·head (lông′hĕd′, lŏng′-), *n.* **1.** a dolichocephalic person. **2.** a head with a cephalic index of 76 and under.

long·head·ed (lông′hĕd′ĭd, lŏng′-), *adj.* **1.** dolichocephalic. **2.** of great discernment or foresight; far-seeing or shrewd. —**long′-head′ed·ness,** *n.*

long·horn (lông′hôrn′, lŏng′-), *n.* one of a kind of cattle predominating on the ranges of northern Mexico and the Great Plains of the U.S. in the early 19th century, developed from Spanish cattle introduced at Vera Cruz about 1521, characterized by long horns and rangy conformation.

long house, 1. a house of great length, particularly a communal dwelling of the Iroquois and of other North American tribes. **2.** (*caps.*) the league of the Iroquois.

lon·gi·corn (lŏn′jə kôrn), *adj.* **1.** having long antennae, as beetles of the group *Longicornia* (family *Cerambycidae*). **2.** belonging to this group. —*n.* **3.** a longicorn or long-horned beetle. [t. NL: s. *longicornis,* f. L: *longi-* long + *-cornis* horned]

long·ing (lông′ĭng, lŏng′-), *n.* **1.** prolonged, unceasing, or earnest desire. **2.** an instance of it. —*adj.* **3.** having a prolonged or earnest desire. **4.** characterized by or showing such desire: *a longing look.* —**long′ing·ly,** *adv.* —**Syn. 1.** See **desire.**

Lon·gi·nus (lŏn jī′nəs), *n.* **Dionysius Cassius** (dī′ə nĭsh′əs kăsh′əs), A.D. c213–273, Greek rhetorician and philosophical critic.

long·ish (lông′ĭsh, lŏng′-), *adj.* somewhat long.

Long Island, an island in SE New York: the boroughs of Brooklyn and Queens of New York City are located at its W end. 118 mi. long; 12–20 mi. wide; 1682 sq. mi.

Long Island Sound, an arm of the Atlantic between Connecticut and Long Island. ab. 110 mi. long.

lon·gi·tude (lŏn′jə tūd′, -tōōd′), *n.* **1.** *Geog.* angular distance east or west on the earth's surface, measured by the angle contained between the meridian of a particular place and some prime meridian, as that of Greenwich, England, or by the corresponding difference in time. **2.** *Astron.* the arc of the ecliptic measured eastward from the vernal equinox to the foot of the great circle passing through the poles of the ecliptic and the point on the celestial sphere in question (**celestial longitude**). [ME, t. L: m. *longitūdo* length]

lon·gi·tu·di·nal (lŏn′jə tū′də nəl, -tōō′-), *adj.* **1.** of or pertaining to longitude or length: *longitudinal distance.* **2.** *Zool.* pertaining to or extending along the long axis of the body, or the direction from front to back, or head to

tail. 3. extending in the direction of the length of a thing; running lengthwise. See diag. under **section.** —lon′gi·tu′di·nal·ly, *adv.*

long jump, *Athletics.* broad jump.

long-leaf pine (lông′lēf′, lŏng′-), **1.** an important American pine, *Pinus palustris,* valued as a source of turpentine and for its timber. **2.** the wood of this tree.

long measure, linear measure.

long moss, Florida moss.

Lon·go·bard (lŏng′gō bärd′), *n.* Langobard.

Long Parliament, *Eng. Hist.* the Parliament which assembled Nov. 3, 1640, was expelled by Cromwell in 1653, reconvened in 1659, and was dissolved in 1660.

long pig, *Maori and Polynesian.* human meat eaten by cannibals.

long-shore (lông′shŏr′, lŏng′-). *adj.* existing, found, or employed along the shore: *longshore fisheries.*

long-shore-man (lông′shŏr′man, lŏng′-), *n., pl.* **-men.** a man employed on the wharves of a port, as in loading and unloading vessels. [f. *longshore,* aphetic var. of *alongshore* + -MAN]

long-sight-ed (lông′sī′tĭd, lŏng′-), *adj.* **1.** far-sighted; hypermetropic. **2.** having great foresight; foreseeing remote results. —**long′-sight′ed·ness,** *n.*

Longs Peak (lôngz, lŏngz), a peak in the Rocky Mountain National Park, in N Colorado. 14,255 ft.

long-spur (lông′spûr′, lŏng′-), *n.* any of various fringilline birds of the genera *Calcarius* and *Rhynchophanes* inhabiting treeless northern regions and characterized by a long, spurlike hind claw.

long-stand-ing (lông′stăn′dĭng, lŏng′-), *adj.* existing or occurring for a long time: *a longstanding feud.*

Long-street (lông′strēt′, lŏng′-), *n.* **James,** 1821–1904, Confederate general in the U.S. Civil War.

long-suf-fer-ing (lông′sŭf′ər ĭng, lŏng′-), *adj.* **1.** enduring injury or provocation long and patiently. —*n.* **2.** long and patient endurance of injury or provocation.

long-term bond, (lông′tûrm′, lŏng′-), a bond not maturing for several years or more.

long tom (tŏm), **1.** *Army Slang.* cannon. **2.** long heavy cannon formerly carried by small naval vessels.

long ton, a ton of 2,240 pounds.

long-wind-ed (lông′wĭn′dĭd, lŏng′-), *adj.* **1.** talking or writing at tedious length, as persons. **2.** continued to a tedious length in speech or writing: *another of his long-winded election speeches.* —**long′-wind′ed·ly,** *adv.* —**long′-wind′ed·ness,** *n.*

long-wise (lông′wīz′, lŏng′-), *adv.* lengthwise. Also, **long-ways** (lông′wāz′, lŏng′-).

loo (loo), *n., pl.* **loos, v.,** **looed, looing.** —*n.* **1.** a game at cards in which forfeits are paid into a pool. **2.** the forfeit or sum paid into the pool. **3.** the fact of being looed. —*v.t.* **4.** to subject to a forfeit at loo.

look (look), *v.i.* **1.** to fix the eyes upon something or in some direction in order to see. **2.** to glance or gaze, in a manner specified: *to look questioningly at a person.* **3.** to use the sight in seeking, searching, examining, watching, etc.: *to look through the papers.* **4.** to tend, as in bearing or significance: *conditions look toward war.* **5.** to appear or seem (as specified) to the eye: *to look pale.* **6.** to seem to the mind: *the case looks promising.* **7.** to direct the mental regard or attention: *to look at the facts.* **8.** to direct the expectations or hopes (esp. fol by *for* or *to*). **9.** to have an outlook or afford a view: *the window looks upon the street.* **10.** to face or front: *the house looks to the east.* **11.** Some special phrases are: **look after, 1.** to follow with the eye, as a person or thing moving away. **2.** to seek, as something desired. **3.** to take care of: *to look after a child.*
look for, 1. to seek, as a person or thing. **2.** to anticipate; expect.
look in, 1. to take a look into a place. **2.** to come in for a brief visit.
look on, to be a mere spectator.
look out, 1. to look forth, as from a window or a place of observation. **2.** to be on guard: *look out for trouble.* **3.** to take watchful care (fol. by *for*): *to look out for oneself.*
look to, 1. to direct the glance or gaze to. **2.** to give attention to. **3.** to direct the expectations or hopes to, as for something desired. **4.** to look forward expectantly to.
look up, 1. to direct the eyes upward. **2.** *Colloq.* to rise in amount or value; improve. **3.** *U.S.* to search for: *to look up the date.*
—*v.t.* **12.** to try to find; seek: *to look a name up in a directory.* **13.** to express or suggest by looks: *to look daggers at a person.* **14.** to bring, put, etc., by looks. **15.** *Obs.* to view, inspect, or examine.
—*n.* **16.** act of looking: *a look of inquiry.* **17.** a visual search or examination. **18.** way of looking or appearing to the eye or to the mind; aspect: *the look of an honest man.* **19.** (*pl.*) general aspect; appearance: *to like the looks of a place, good looks.*
[ME *lōke*(*n*), OE *lōcian.* Cf. d. G *lugen* look out, spy]
—**Syn. 1.** See **seem.**

look-er (look′ər), *n.* **1.** one who looks. **2.** *U.S. Slang.* an unusually handsome person.

look-er-on (look′ər ŏn′), *n., pl.* **lookers-on.** one who looks on; a spectator.

looking glass, 1. a mirror made of glass with a metallic or amalgam backing. **2.** such glass as a material.

look-out (look′out′), *n.* **1.** act of looking out. **2.** a watch kept, as for something that may come or happen. **3.** a person or group stationed or employed to keep such a watch. **4.** a station or place from which a watch is kept. **5.** view; prospect; outlook. **6.** *Colloq.* the proper object of one's watchful care or concern.

Lookout Mountain, a mountain ridge in Georgia, Tennessee, and Alabama: a battle of the Civil War was fought on this ridge near Chattanooga, Tennessee, 1863. Highest point, 2126 ft.

loom[1] (loom), *n.* **1.** a machine or apparatus for weaving yarn or thread into a fabric. **2.** the art or the process of weaving. **3.** the part of an oar between the blade and the handle. —*v.t.* **4.** to weave on a loom. [ME *lome,* OE *gelōma* tool, implement. Cf. HEIRLOOM]

loom[2] (loom), *v.i.* **1.** to appear indistinctly, or come into view in indistinct and enlarged form. **2.** to rise before the vision with an appearance of great or portentous size. —*n.* **3.** a looming appearance, as of something seen indistinctly at a distance or through a fog. [cf. d. Sw. *loma* move slowly]

loom[3] (loom), *n.* **1.** loon[1]. **2.** a guillemot or murre. [t. Scand.; cf. Icel. *lōmr,* Sw. *lom.* See LOON[1]]

L.O.O.M., Loyal Order of Moose.

loon[1] (loon), *n.* any of several large, short-tailed web-footed, fish-eating diving birds of the northern hemisphere, constituting the genus *Gavia,* as the common loon or great northern diver, *Gavia immer,* of the New and Old Worlds. [var. of LOOM[3]]

loon[2] (loon), *n.* a worthless, sorry, lazy, or stupid fellow. [ME *lowen, loun.* Cf. Icel. *lūinn* exhausted]

loon-y (loo′nĭ), *adj.,* **loonier, looniest,** *n., pl.* **loonies.** —*adj.* **1.** lunatic; crazy. **2.** *Slang.* extremely or senselessly foolish. —*n.* **3.** *Slang.* a lunatic. Also, **luny.** [var. of *luny,* familiar shortening of LUNATIC] —**loon′i·ness,** *n.*

loop[1] (loop), *n.* **1.** a folding or doubling of a portion of a cord, lace, ribbon, etc. upon itself, so as to leave an opening between the parts. **2.** anything shaped more or less like a loop, as a line drawn on paper, a part of a letter, a part of a path, a line of motion, etc. **3.** a curved piece or a ring of metal, wood, etc., used for the insertion of something, or as a handle, or otherwise. **4.** *Aeron.* a maneuver executed in such a manner that the airplane performs a closed curve in a vertical plane. **5.** *Physics.* the part of a vibrating string, column of air, or the like, between two adjacent nodes; antinode. **6.** *Elect.* **a.** a closed electric or magnetic circuit. **b.** a closed curve showing the relation between the magnetizing force and the induction in a ferromagnetic substance when the magnetizing field is carried through a complete cycle. —*v.t.* **7.** to form into a loop or loops. **8.** to make a loop or loops in. **9.** to enfold or encircle in or with something arranged in a loop. **10.** to fasten by forming into a loop, or by means of something formed into a loop. **11.** to fly (an airplane) in a loop or series of loops. **12.** to construct a closed electric or magnetic circuit. —*v.i.* **13.** to make or form a loop or loops. **14.** to move by forming loops, as a measuring worm. [ME *loupe.* Cf. Gaelic and Irish *lub* loop, bend]

loop[2] (loop), *n.* *Archaic.* a small or narrow opening, as in a wall; a loophole. [ME *loupe.* Cf. MD *lūpen* peer]

loop-er (loo′pər), *n.* **1.** one who or that which loops something or forms loops. **2.** a measuring worm. **3.** the thread holder in a sewing machine using two threads.

loop-hole (loop′hōl′), *n., v.,* **-holed, -holing.** —*n.* **1.** a small or narrow opening, as in a wall, for looking through, or for admitting light and air, or particularly, in a fortification, for the discharge of missiles against an enemy outside. **2.** an opening or aperture. **3.** an outlet, or means of escape or evasion. —*v.t.* **4.** to furnish with loopholes. [f. LOOP[2] + HOLE, n.]

loop-y (loo′pĭ), *adj.* full of loops.

loose (loos), *adj.,* **looser, loosest,** *adv., v.,* **loosed, loosing.** —*adj.* **1.** free from bonds, fetters, or restraint: *to get one's hand loose.* **2.** free or released from fastening or attachment: *a loose end.* **3.** uncombined, as a chemical element. **4.** not bound together, as papers or flowers. **5.** not put up in a package or other container: *loose mushrooms.* **6.** *Colloq.* unemployed or unappropriated: *loose funds.* **7.** wanting in retentiveness or power of restraint: *a loose tongue.* **8.** lax, as the bowels. **9.** free from moral restraint, or lax in principle or conduct. **10.** wanton or unchaste: *a loose woman.* **11.** not firm or rigid: *a loose tooth, a loose rein.* **12.** not fitting closely, as garments. **13.** not close or compact in structure or arrangement; having spaces between the parts, or open: *a loose weave.* **14.** (of earth, soil, etc.) not cohering: *loose sand.* **15.** not strict, exact, or precise: *loose thinking.* **16.** **at loose ends,** in an unsettled or disorderly condition. —*adv.* **17.** in a loose manner; loosely. —*v.t.* **18.** to let loose, or free from bonds or restraint. **19.** to release, as from constraint, obligation, penalty, etc. **20.** *Chiefly Naut.* to set free from fastening or attachment: *loose a boat from its moorings.* **21.** to unfasten, undo, or untie, as a bond, fetter, or knot. **22.** to shoot, or let fly. **23.** to make less tight; slacken or relax. **24.** *Archaic.* to render less firmly fixed, or loosen. —*v.i.* **25.** to loose something. **26.** to let go a hold. **27.** to weigh anchor. **28.** to shoot or let fly an arrow, etc. **29.** to become loose. [ME *los, loos,* t. Scand.; cf. Icel. *lauss* loose, free, empty. c. D and G *los* loose, free] —**loose′ly,** *adv.* —**loose′ness,** *n.*

loose-joint·ed (lōōs′join′tĭd), *adj.* **1.** having loose joints. **2.** loosely built or framed.

loos·en (lōō′sən), *v.t.* **1.** to unfasten or undo, as a bond or fetter. **2.** to make less tight; slacken or relax: *to loosen one's grasp.* **3.** to make less firmly fixed in place: *to loosen a clamp.* **4.** to let loose or set free from bonds, restraint, or constraint. **5.** to make less close or compact in structure or arrangement. **6.** to make less dense or coherent: *to loosen the soil.* **7.** to open, or relieve the costiveness of, (the bowels). **8.** to relax in strictness or severity, as restraint or discipline. —*v.i.* **9.** to become loose or looser. —**loos′en·er,** *n.*

loose sentence, a sentence containing subordinate elements not necessary to its completeness.

loose·strife (lōōs′strīf′), *n.* **1.** any of various leafy-stemmed herbs of the primulaceous genus *Lysimachia,* as *L. vulgaris,* a common yellow-flowered species (**yellow loosestrife**), and *L. quadrifolia,* a species with leaves in whorls of four or five (**whorled loosestrife**). **2.** any of various herbaceous plants of the lythraceous genus *Lythrum,* as *L. Salicaria,* a purple-flowered species (**purple loosestrife**). [f. LOOSE, v., + STRIFE, erroneous trans. of L *lysimachia* (actually der. Gk. proper name *Lysimachos,* lit., the one loosing (i.e. ending) strife)]

loot (lōōt), *n.* **1.** spoils or plunder taken by pillaging, as in war. **2.** anything dishonestly and ruthlessly appropriated: *a burglar's loot.* **3.** act of looting or plundering: *the loot of a conquered city.* —*v.t.* **4.** to take or carry off, as loot. **5.** to despoil by taking loot; plunder or pillage (a city, house, etc.), as in war. **6.** to rob, as by burglary, corrupt practice in public office, etc. —*v.i.* **7.** to take loot; plunder. [t. Hind.: m. *lūt*] —**loot′er,** *n.* —**Syn.** 5. sack, rifle.

lop[1] (lŏp), *v.,* **lopped, lopping,** *n.* —*v.t.* **1.** to cut off the branches, twigs, etc., of (a tree or other plant). **2.** to cut off the head, limbs, etc., of (a person) or parts of (a thing). **3.** to cut off (branches, twigs, etc.) from a tree or other plant. **4.** to cut off (the head, limbs, etc.) from a person. —*v.i.* **5.** to cut off branches, twigs, etc., as of a tree. **6.** to remove parts by or as by cutting. —*n.* **7.** parts or a part lopped off. **8.** the smaller branches and twigs of trees. [ME (def. 8), etymologically identical with obs. *lop* spider, both objects being marked by many projecting parts] —**lop′per,** *n.*

lop[2] (lŏp), *v.,* **lopped, lopping.** —*v.i.* **1.** to hang loosely or limply; droop. **2.** to sway, move, or go in a drooping or heavy, awkward way. —*v.t.* **3.** to let hang or droop. [der. obs. *lop,* n., lobe (var. of LAP[1] lobe); lit., to behave like a *lop,* i.e., to dangle, hang loosely]

lope (lōp), *v.,* **loped, loping,** *n.* —*v.i.* **1.** to move or run with bounding steps, as a quadruped, or with a long, easy stride, as a person. **2.** to canter leisurely with a rather long, easy stride, as a horse. —*v.t.* **3.** to cause to lope, as a horse. —*n.* **4.** the act or the gait of loping. **5.** a long, easy stride. [late ME, var. of obs. *loup* leap, t. Scand.; cf. Icel. *hlaupa*] —**lop′er,** *n.*

lop-eared (lŏp′ĭrd′), *adj.* having ears that lop or hang down.

lo·pho·branch (lō′fə brăngk′, lŏf′ə-), *n.* **1.** any of the *Lophobranchii,* an order or group of teleostean fishes having gills in tufts, as the sea horses, pipefishes, etc. —*adj.* **2.** belonging or pertaining to the *Lophobranchii.* [f. Gk.: *lopho(s)* crest + m.s. *branchia* gills] —**lo·pho·bran·chi·ate** (lō′fə brăng′kĭ ĭt, -āt′, lŏf′ə-), *adj., n.*

lop·py (lŏp′ĭ), *adj.* lopping; limp. [f. LOP[2] + -Y[1]]

lop·sid·ed (lŏp′sīd′ĭd), *adj.* **1.** lopping or inclining to one side. **2.** heavier, larger, or more developed on one side than on the other; unsymmetrical. —**lop′sid′ed·ly,** *adv.* —**lop′sid′ed·ness,** *n.*

loq., loquitur.

lo·qua·cious (lō kwā′shəs), *adj.* **1.** talking or disposed to talk much or freely; talkative. **2.** characterized by or showing a disposition to talk much: *a loquacious mood.* [f. LOQUACI(TY) + -OUS] —**lo·qua′cious·ly,** *adv.* —**Syn.** 1. See **talkative.**

lo·quac·i·ty (lō kwăs′ə tĭ), *n.* **1.** state of being loquacious. **2.** loquacious flow of talk. [t. L: m.s. *loquācitas*]

lo·quat (lō′kwŏt, -kwät), *n.* **1.** a small, evergreen, malaceous tree, *Eriobotrya japonica,* native in China and Japan, but cultivated elsewhere for ornament and for its yellow, plumlike fruit. **2.** the fruit. [t. Chinese (Canton): m. *luh kwat* rush orange]

lo·qui·tur (lō′kwə tər), *v.* *Latin.* he (or she) speaks.

Lo·rain (lō rān′), *n.* a city in N Ohio: a port on Lake Erie. 68,932 (1950).

lo·ran (lō′rən), *n.* a device by which a navigator can locate his position by determining the time displacement between radio signals from two known stations. [short for *lo(ng) ra(nge) n(avigation)*]

Lor·ca (lôr′kä), *n.* a city in SE Spain. 70,998 (1950).

lord (lôrd), *n.* **1.** one who has dominion over others; a master, chief, or ruler. **2.** one who exercises authority from property rights; an owner or possessor of land, houses, etc. **3.** a feudal superior; the proprietor of a manor. **4.** a titled nobleman, or peer, or one whose ordinary appellation contains by courtesy the title *Lord* or some higher title. **5. Lords,** the temporal and spiritual members of the House of Lords. **6.** (*cap.*) *Brit.* **a.** the title (in collocation with some other word or words) of certain high officials: *Lord Mayor of London.* **b.** (in ceremonious use) the title of a bishop: *Lord Bishop of Durham.* **c.** the title substituted in less formal use for marquis, earl, viscount, etc.: *Lord Kitchener for*

Earl Kitchener. **7.** (*cap.*) the Supreme Being, Jehovah, or God. **8.** (*cap.*) the Savior, Jesus Christ. **9.** *Astrol.* a planet having dominating influence. —*interj.* **10.** (*often cap.*) the noun Lord (God) used as an exclamation of surprise, etc. —*v.i.* **11.** to play the lord; behave in a lordly manner; domineer (often with indefinite *it*): *to lord it over someone.* [ME *lord, loverd,* OE *hlāford,* f. *hlāf* LOAF[1] + *weard* keeper. Cf. LADY, WARD]

Lord Chancellor, the highest judicial officer of the British crown, law adviser of the ministry, keeper of the great seal, presiding officer in the House of Lords, etc.

lord·less (lôrd′lĭs), *adj.* having no lord.

Lord Lieutenant, *Brit.* **1.** the title of various high officials holding authority deputed from a sovereign. **2.** (formerly) the viceroy in Ireland.

lord·ling (lôrd′lĭng), *n.* a little or petty lord.

lord·ly (lôrd′lĭ), *adj.,* **-lier, -liest,** *adv.* —*adj.* **1.** suitable for a lord, as things; grand or magnificent. **2.** insolently imperious: *lordly contempt.* **3.** of or pertaining to a lord or lords. **4.** having the character or attributes of a lord, as a person. **5.** befitting a lord, as actions. —*adv.* **6.** in the manner of a lord. —**lord′li·ness,** *n.* —**Syn.** 2. haughty, arrogant. —**Ant.** 2. meek.

Lord of hosts, Jehovah, the Supreme Ruler.

Lord of Misrule, a person formerly chosen to direct revels and sports.

lor·do·sis (lôr dō′sĭs), *n.* *Pathol.* anterior curvature of the spine; i.e., convexity anterior or to the front. [t. NL, t. Gk.: a bending back] —**lor·dot·ic** (lôr dŏt′ĭk), *adj.*

Lord Protector, protector (def. 2b).

Lord Provost, provost (def. 1a).

Lord's day, the, Sunday.

lord·ship (lôrd′shĭp), *n.* **1.** (*often cap.*) the form used in speaking of or to a man having the title of Lord, or of or to a judge, as in British use (prec. by *his, your,* etc.). **2.** the state or dignity of a lord. **3.** *Hist.* **a.** the authority or power of a lord. **b.** the domain of a lord.

Lord's Prayer, the, the prayer given by Jesus to His disciples. Matt. 6:9–13; Luke, 11:2–4.

Lord's Supper, the, **1.** the last supper of Jesus and His disciples. **2.** the sacrament in commemoration of this; the Eucharist; the communion; the Mass.

Lord's table, the, the communion table or the altar.

lore[1] (lōr), *n.* **1.** the body of knowledge, esp. of a traditional, anecdotal, or popular nature, on a particular subject: *the lore of herbs.* **2.** learning, knowledge, or erudition. **3.** *Archaic.* **a.** teaching or instruction. **b.** that which is taught. [ME; OE *lār,* c. D *leer,* G *lehre* teaching. Cf. LEARN] —**Syn.** 1. See **learning.**

lore[2] (lōr), *n.* *Zool.* the space between the eye and the bill of a bird, or a corresponding space in other animals, as serpents. [t. L: m.s. *lōrum* thong]

Lor·e·lei (lôr′ə lī′; *Ger.* lō′rə-), *n.* *German Legend.* an enchantress who, by her singing, caused sailors to wreck their boats on her rock in the Rhine. [t. G]

Lo·rentz (lō′rĕnts), *n.* **Hendrik Antoon** (hĕn′drĭk än′tōn), 1853–1928, Dutch physicist.

lor·gnette (lôr nyĕt′), *n.* **1.** a pair of eyeglasses mounted on a long handle. **2.** opera glasses. [t. F, der. *lorgner* look sidelong at, eye, der. OF *lorgne* squinting]

lor·gnon (lôr nyôn′), *n.* **1.** an eyeglass, or a pair of eyeglasses. **2.** opera glasses. [F, der. *lorgner.* See LORGNETTE]

lo·ri·ca (lō rī′kə), *n., pl.* **-cae** (-sē). **1.** *Zool.* a hard protective case or sheath, as the protective coverings secreted by certain infusorians. **2.** a cuirass or corselet, orig. of leather. [t. L: a corselet, a defense]

lor·i·cate (lôr′ə kāt′, lôr′-), *adj.* covered with a lorica. Also, **lor′i·cat′ed.**

Lo·ri·ent (lô ryän′), *n.* a seaport in NW France, in Brittany: shipbuilding; held by the Germans during World War II. 47,095 (1954).

lor·i·keet (lôr′ə kēt′, lôr′-, lôr′ə kĕt′, lôr′-), *n.* any of various small lories. [f. LORY + (PARRA)KEET]

lo·ris (lôr′ĭs), *n., pl.* **-ris.** **1.** a small, slender, tailless, large-eyed, nocturnal lemur, *Loris gracilis,* of Ceylon (**slender loris**). **2.** any lemur of the related genus *Nycticebus* (**slow loris**). [t. NL, t. D: m. *loeris* booby]

lorn (lôrn), *adj.* **1.** *Archaic.* forsaken, desolate, wretched, or forlorn. **2.** *Obs.* lost, ruined, or undone. [ME *lorn,* OE *loren,* pp. of *-lēosan* LOSE (recorded in compounds)]

Lor·rain (lō rān′; *Fr.* lô rän′), *n.* **Claude** (klôd; *Fr.* klōd), (**Claude Gelée**) 1600–82, French landscape painter.

Lor·raine (lō rān′; *Fr.* lô rĕn′), *n.* **1.** a medieval kingdom in W Europe along the Moselle, Meuse, and Rhine rivers. **2.** a region in NE France, once included in this kingdom: a former province. See **Alsace-Lorraine.** **3. Cross of,** a cross having two horizontal arms, the upper one shorter than the other.

lor·ry (lôr′ĭ, lŏr′ĭ), *n., pl.* **-ries.** **1.** *Brit.* a motor truck, esp. for heavy work. **2.** any of various vehicles or cars running on rails, as for transporting material in a mine or factory. **3.** a long, low, horse-drawn wagon without sides, common in England. [cf. d. E *lurry* pull, drag, lug]

lo·ry (lôr′ĭ), *n., pl.* **-ries.** any of various parrots (subfamily *Loriinae*) of the Malay Archipelago, Australia, etc., mostly bright-colored, brush-tongued, and of small size. [t. Malay: m. *lūrī*]

los·a·ble (lōō′zə bəl), *adj.* that may be lost.

Los An·ge·les (lŏs ăng′gə ləs, ăn′jə ləs, -lēz′), a seaport in SW California. 2,479,015 (1960): with suburbs 5,923,644 (1960); 452 sq. mi.

---

b., blend of, blended; c., cognate with; d., dialect, dialectal; der., derived from; f., formed from; g., going back to; m., modification of; r., replacing; s., stem of; t., taken from; ?, perhaps. See the full key on inside cover.

lose (lo͞oz), *v.*, **lost, losing.** —*v.t.* **1.** to come to be without, by some chance, and not know the whereabouts of: *to lose a ring.* **2.** to suffer the loss or deprivation of: *to lose one's life.* **3.** to be bereaved of by death: *to lose a child.* **4.** to fail to keep, preserve, or maintain: *to lose one's balance.* **5.** to cease to have: *to lose all fear.* **6.** to bring to destruction or ruin (now chiefly in the pass ve): *ship and crew were lost.* **7.** to have slip from sight, hearing, attention, etc.: *to lose a face in a crowd.* **8.** to come separated from and ignorant of (the way, etc.). **9.** to leave far behind in a pursuit, race, etc. **10.** to use to no purpose, or waste: *to lose time in waiting.* **11.** to fail to have, get, catch, etc.; miss: *to lose a bargain.* **12.** to fail to win (a prize, stake, etc.). **13.** to be defeated in (a game, lawsuit, battle, etc.). **14.** to cause the loss of: *the delay lost the battle for them.* **15.** to let (oneself) go astray; become bewildered: *to be lost in a wood.* **16.** to absorb or engross in something to the exclusion of knowledge or consciousness of all else (usually used reflexively or in the passive): *to be lost in thought.* —*v.i.* **17.** to suffer loss: *to lose on a contract.* **18.** to lose ground, fall behind, or fail to hold one's own, as in a race or other contest. **19.** to fail to win, as in a contest; be defeated. [ME *lose(n)*, OE *-lēōsan;* r. ME *lese(n)*, OE *-lēosan* (cf. *choose,* r. *chese*), c. G. *(ver)lieren.* See LOSS] —**los′er,** *n.*

los·ing (lo͞o′zing), *adj.* **1.** that loses. —*n.* **2.** (*pl.*) losses. —**los′ing·ly,** *adv.*

loss (lôs, lŏs), *n.* **1.** detriment or disadvantage from failure to keep, have, or get: *to bear the loss of a robbery.* **2.** that which is lost. **3.** amount or number lost. **4.** a being deprived of or coming to be without something that one has had: *loss of friends.* **5.** the accidental or inadvertent losing of something dropped, misplaced, or of unknown whereabouts: *to discover the loss of a document.* **6.** a losing by defeat, or failure to win: *the loss of a bet.* **7.** failure to make good use of something, as time; waste. **8.** failure to preserve or maintain: *loss of speed.* **9.** destruction or ruin. **10.** *Mil.* **a.** the losing of soldiers by death, capture, etc. **b.** (*often pl.*) the number of soldiers so lost. **11.** *Insurance.* **a.** occurrence of a risk, as death or damage to property, covered by a contract of insurance so as to result in insurer liability. **b.** that which causes such a loss. **c.** an example of such a loss. **12.** *Elect.* the difference between power input and power output of an electric circuit, device, machine, or system incident to the process of electric transmission or energy conversion. **13.** **at a loss, a.** in a state of bewilderment or uncertainty. **b.** in a state of embarrassment for lack of something: *to be at a loss for words.* [ME; OE *los* destruction, c. Icel. *los* breaking up; akin to LOSE]

loss leader, a popular article which is sold at a loss for the purpose of attracting trade to a retail store.

loss ratio, *Insurance.* the ratio of paid-in premiums to losses sustained during a certain period.

lost (lôst, lŏst), *adj.* **1.** no longer possessed or retained: *lost friends.* **2.** no longer to be found: *lost articles.* **3.** having gone astray or lost the way; bewildered as to place, direction, etc. **4.** not used to good purpose, as opportunities, time, labor, etc.; wasted. **5.** that one has failed to win: *a lost prize.* **6.** attended with defeat: *a lost battle.* **7.** destroyed or ruined: *lost ships.* **8. lost to, a.** no longer belonging to. **b.** no longer possible or open to: *the opportunity was lost to him.* **c.** insensible to: *to be lost to all sense of duty.* —*v.* **9.** pt. of **lose.**

lost cause, a cause for which defeat has occurred or is inevitable.

Lost Pleiad. See **Pleiades** (def. 1).

lot (lŏt), *n.*, *v.*, **lotted, lotting.** —*n.* **1.** one of a set of objects drawn from a receptacle, etc., to decide a question or choice by chance. **2.** the casting or drawing of such objects as a method of deciding something: *to choose a person by lot.* **3.** the decision or choice so made. **4.** allotted share or portion. **5.** the portion in life assigned by fate or Providence, or one's fate, fortune, or destiny. **6.** a distinct portion or piece of land. **7.** a piece of land forming a part of a district, city, or other community. **8.** *Motion Pictures.* the site of a motion picture being filmed, esp. a studio. **9.** a distinct portion or parcel of anything, as of merchandise. **10.** a number of things or persons collectively. **11.** *Colloq.* a person of a specified sort. **12.** (*often pl.*) *Colloq.* a great many or a great deal: *a lot of books.* **13.** *Chiefly Brit.* a tax or duty. —*v.t.* **14.** to cast or draw lots for. **15.** to divide or distribute by lot. **16.** to assign to one as his lot; allot. **17.** to divide into lots, as land. —*v.i.* **18.** to draw lots. [ME; OE *hlot,* akin to G *loos,* Icel. *hlutr,* Goth. *hlauts*]

Lot (lŏt), *n. Bible.* the nephew of Abraham. His wife was changed into a pillar of salt for looking back during their flight from Sodom. Gen. 13:1–12, 19. [t. Heb]

Lot (lôt), *n.* a river in S France, flowing W to the Garonne. ab. 300 mi.

loth (lōth), *adj.* loath.

Lo·thair I (lō thâr′, -târ′), c795–855, emperor of the Holy Roman Empire, 843–855.

Lothair II, (*"the Saxon"*) c1070–1137, emperor of the Holy Roman Empire, 1125–37.

Lo·thaire (lō tĕr′), *n.* French name for **Lothair.**

Lo·thar (lō′tär, lō tär′), *n.* German name for **Lothair.**

Lo·thar·i·o (lō thâr′i ō′), *n., pl.* **-tharios.** a jaunty libertine; a rake.

Lo·thi·ans (lō′thĭ ənz, -thĭ-), *n.pl.* **The,** three counties in Scotland: East Lothian, Midlothian, West Lothian.

Lo·ti (lô tē′), *n.* **Pierre** (pyĕr), (*Louis Marie Julien Viaud*) 1850–1923, French novelist.

lo·tion (lō′shən), *n. Pharm., etc.* a watery liquid containing insoluble medicinal matter applied externally to the skin without rubbing. [ME, t. L: s. *lōtio* a washing]

lot·ter·y (lŏt′ərĭ), *n., pl.* **-teries. 1.** a scheme or arrangement for raising money, as for some public, charitable, or private purpose, by the sale of a large number of tickets, certain among which, as determined by chance after the sale, entitle the holders to prizes. **2.** any scheme for the distribution of prizes by chance. **3.** any affair of chance. [t. It.: m. *lotteria,* der. *lotto* lot, t. F: m. *lot,* t. Gmc.; cf. LOT]

lot·to (lŏt′ō), *n.* a game played by drawing numbered disks from a bag or the like and cover ng corresponding numbers on cards. [t. It. See LOTTERY]

lo·tus (lō′təs), *n.* **1.** a plant, commonly identified with a species of jujube or of elm tree, referred to in Greek legend as yielding a fruit which induced a state of dreamy and contented forgetfulness in those who ate it. **2.** the fruit itself. **3.** either of the two species of water lilies, *Nelumbium Nelumbo* (**sacred lotus of India**) or *N. pentapetalum* (**water chinquapin**). **4.** any of various nymphaeaceous plants, as either of two Egyptian water lilies, *Nymphaea Lotus* or *N. caerulea.* **5.** a representation of such a plant, common in Egyptian and Hindu decorative art. **6.** any of the shrubbery herbs, with red, pink, or white flowers, constituting the leguminous genus *Lotus,* certain of which are valued as pasture plants. Also, **lo′tos.** [t. L, t. Gk.: m. *lōtós*]

lo·tus-eat·er (lō′təs ē′tər), *n.* **1.** an eater of the fruit which induced languor and forgetfulness of home. Homer's *Odyssey,* ix. **2.** one who leads a life of dreamy, indolent ease, indifferent to the busy world.

loud (loud), *adj.* **1.** striking strongly upon the organs of hearing, as sound, noise, the voice, etc.; strongly audible. **2.** making, emitting, or uttering strongly audible sounds: *loud knocking.* **3.** full of sound or noise, or resounding. **4.** clamorous, vociferous, or blatant. **5.** emphatic or insistent: *to be loud in one s praises.* **6.** *Colloq.* strong or offensive in smell. **7.** excessively striking to the eye, or offensively showy, as colors, dress or the wearer, etc. **8.** obtrusively vulgar, as manners, persons, etc. —*adv.* **9.** loudly. [ME; OE *hlūd,* c. G *laut*] —**loud′ly,** *adv.* —**loud′ness,** *n.*
—**Syn. 1.** resounding; deafening; stentorian. LOUD, NOISY describe a strongly audible sound or sounds. LOUD means characterized by a full, powerful sound or sounds, which make a strong impression on the organs of hearing: *a loud voice, laugh, report.* NOISY refers to a series of sounds, and suggests clamor and discordance, or persistence in making loud sounds which are disturbing and annoying: *a noisy crowd.* **7.** gaudy, flashy, showy. —**Ant. 1.** quiet.

loud·ish (lou′dĭsh), *adj.* somewhat loud.

loud-mouthed (loud′mouthd′, -moutht′), *adj.* loud of voice or utterance; vociferous; blatant.

loudspeak·er (loud′spē′kər), *n.* any of various devices by which speech, music, etc., can be made audible throughout a room, hall, or the like.

lough (lŏk, lŏKH), *n. Irish.* **1.** a lake. **2.** an arm of the sea. [ME, t. Irish: m. *loch.* Cf. LOCH]

lou·is (lo͞o′ĭ), *n., pl.* **louis** (lo͞o′ĭz). louis d'or.

Lou·is (lo͞o′ĭs), *n.* **Joe,** (*Joseph Louis Barrow*) born 1914, U.S. heavyweight boxing champion, 1937–1949.

Lou·is (lo͞o′ĭ, lo͞o′ĭs; Fr. lwē), *n.* name of 18 kings of France.

Louis I, (*"le Débonnaire," "the Pious"*) A.D. 778–840, king of France and emperor of the Holy Roman Empire, A.D. 814–840 (son of Charlemagne).

Louis II, (*"the German"*) A.D. 804?–876, king of all Germany E of Rhine by Treaty of Verdun (A.D. 843). German, **Ludwig II.**

Louis II de Bourbon. See **Condé.**

Louis IV, (*"the Bavarian"*) 1287?–1347, emperor of the Holy Roman Empire, 1314–47.

Louis V, (*"le Fainéant"*) A.D. 967?–987, king of France, A.D. 986–987; the last of the Carolingian family of rulers in France.

Louis IX, (*Saint Louis*) 1215–70, king of France, 1226–1270; canonized in 1297.

Louis XI, 1423–83, king of France, 1461–83.

Louis XII, (*"the Father of the People"*) 1462–1515, king of France, 1498–1515.

Louis XIII, 1601–43, king of France, 1610–43.

Louis XIV, (*"the Great"*) 1638–1715, king of France, 1643–1715.

Louis XV, 1710–74, king of France, 1715–74.

Louis XVI, 1754–93, king of France from 1774, deposed in 1792, guillotined in 1793.

Louis XVII, 1785–95, son of Louis XVI. He never reigned, but was called king of France, 1793–95, by the monarchists.

Louis XVIII, 1755–1824, king of France, 1814–24.

Lou·is·burg (lo͞o′ĭs bûrg′), *n.* a seaport in SE Canada, on Cape Breton Island, Nova Scotia: the important French fortress here was captured by the British, 1745, 1758. 1120 (1951).

lou·is d'or (lo͞o′ĭ dôr′; Fr. lwē), a French gold coin, issued 1640–1795, worth from about $4 to about $4.60. Also, **louis.** [F: gold louis]

Lou·ise (lo͞o ēz′), *n.* **Lake,** a glacial lake in the Canadian Rockies, in SW Alberta, Canada: resort. 5670 ft. high.

ăct, āble, dâre, ärt; ĕbb, ēqual; ĭf, īce; hŏt, ōver, ôrder, oil, bŏŏk, o͞oze, out; ŭp, ūse, ûrge; ə = a in alone; ch, chief; g, give; ng, ring; sh, shoe; th, thin; th, that; zh, vision. See the full key on inside cover.

Lou·i·si·an·a (lŏŏ ē′zĬ ăn′ə, lŏŏ′Ĭ zĬ′-), _n._ a State in the S United States. 3,257,022 pop. (1960); 48,522 sq. mi. _Cap._: Baton Rouge. _Abbrev._: La. —**Lou·i′si·an′an, Lou·i·si·an·i·an** (lŏŏ ē′zĬ ăn′Ĭ ən, lŏŏ′Ĭ zĬ′-), _adj., n._

Louisiana Purchase, The, a huge territory which the United States purchased from France in 1803, extending from the Mississippi to the Rocky Mountains and from the Gulf of Mexico to British America.

Louis Napoleon, Napoleon III.

Louis Phi·lippe (fē lēp′), 1773–1850, king of France, 1830–48.

Louis Qua·torze (kə tôrz′; _Fr._ kȧ tôrz′), of the period of Louis XIV of France or the styles of architecture, decoration, etc., prevailing about that time (1650–1700), relying more upon classical models than those of the Louis Treize period, and richly ornamented.

Louis Quinze (kăNz), of the period of Louis XV of France or the styles of architecture, decoration, etc., (known as _rococo_) prevailing about that time (1700–1750), smaller in scale and more delicate in ornament than those of the Louis Quatorze period.

Louis Seize (sěz), of the period of Louis XVI of France or the styles of architecture, decoration, etc. prevailing about that time (1750–1790), characterized by a recurrence of classical models.

Louis Treize (trěz), of the period of Louis XIII of France or the styles of architecture, decoration, etc., prevailing about that time (1600–1650), less light and elegant than those of the earlier Renaissance, and employing forms and features based on the classical.

Lou·is·ville (lŏŏ′Ĭ vĬl′), _n._ a city in N Kentucky: a port on the Ohio river; Kentucky Derby. 390,639 (1960).

lounge (lounj), _v._, **lounged, loung·ing,** _n._ —_v.i._ **1.** to pass time idly and indolently. **2.** to recline indolently; loll. **3.** to move or go (_about, along, off,_ etc.) in a leisurely, indolent manner. —_v.t._ **4.** to pass (time, etc.) in lounging (fol. by _away_ or _out_). —_n._ **5.** a kind of sofa for reclining on, with or without a back, and with a headrest at one end. **6.** a place for lounging, esp. a large room, as in a hotel, or esp. in England, a high-class part of a public house. **7.** the act or a spell of lounging. **8.** a lounging gait. [? akin to obs. _lungis_ laggard, t. OF: m. _longis_ one who is long (i.e. slow)] —**loung′er,** _n._

loup (lŏŏ), _n._ a cloth mask, often of silk, which covers only half the face. [F: lit., wolf, g. L _lupus_]

loupe (lŏŏp), _n._ **1.** a magnifying glass used by jewelers, esp. one which fits over the eye. **2.** a jewel of perfect luster or brilliance. [F]

loup-ga·rou (lŏŏ gȧ rŏŏ′), _n., pl._ **loups-garous** (lŏŏ-gȧ rŏŏ′). _French._ a werewolf; a lycanthrope. [F: f. _loup_ wolf (g. L _lupus_) + _garou_ werewolf, of Gmc. orig.]

loup·ing ill (lou′pĭng, lō′-), an acute, virus-induced infectious disease of sheep, affecting the nervous system, and transmitted by a tick, which also attacks man.

lour (lour), _v.i., n._ lower².

Lourdes (lŏŏrd), _n._ a city in SW France: famous shrine. 15,829 (1954).

Lou·ren·ço Mar·ques (lō rěn′sō̇ mär′kĕs; _Port._ lō-rěn′sŏŏ mär′kĕzh), a seaport in and the capital of Mozambique, on Delagoa Bay. 93,303 (1950).

louse (lous), _n., pl._ **lice** (līs). **1.** any of the small, wingless, blood-sucking insects of the order _Anoplura,_ including several species associated with man, as the **human louse,** _Pediculus humanus_ (including the races known as **head louse,** _P. capitis,_ and **body louse,** _P. corporis_), and the **crab louse,** _Phthirus pubis._ **2.** any of various other insects parasitic on animals or plants, as those of the order _Mallophaga_ (**biting bird lice**) or the homopterous family _Aphididae_ (**plant lice**). [ME _lows(e),_ _lous(e),_ OE _lūs_ (pl. _lȳs_), c. G _laus_]

louse·wort (lous′wûrt′), _n._ any of the scrophulariaceous herbs constituting the large genus _Pedicularis,_ as _P. sylvatica_ (**pasture lousewort**), an English species formerly supposed to breed lice in sheep, and _P. canadensis_ (**wood betony**).

Head louse. _Pediculus capitis_

lous·y (lou′zĬ), _adj.,_ **lousier, lousiest. 1.** infested with lice. **2.** _Slang._ mean, or contemptible. **3.** _Slang._ well supplied. —**lous′i·ly,** _adv._ —**lous′i·ness,** _n._

lout (lout), _n._ an awkward, stupid person; a boor. [akin to archaic _lout_ bow or obs. _lout_ lurk]

lout·ish (lou′tĬsh), _adj._ like or characteristic of a lout; boorish. —**lout′ish·ly,** _adv._ —**lout′ish·ness,** _n._

Lou·vain (lŏŏ văn′), _n._ a city in central Belgium. 35,272 (1947).

lou·ver (lŏŏ′vər), _n._ **1.** a turret or lantern on the roof of a medieval building, to supply ventilation or light. **2.** an arrangement of louver boards or the like closing a window or other opening, or a single louver board. **3.** one of a number of slitlike openings in the hood or body of an automobile for the escape of heated air from within. [ME _lover,_ t. OF; orig. obscure]

louver board, one of a series of overlapping, sloping boards, slats, or the like, in an opening, so arranged as to admit air but exclude rain.

Lou·vre (lŏŏ′vr), _n._ a royal palace (begun 1541) in Paris, largely occupied since 1793 by a famous museum.

Louys (lwē), _n._ Pierre (pyěr), 1870–1925, French author.

lov·a·ble (lŭv′ə bəl), _adj._ of such a nature as to attract love; amiable. Also, **loveable.** —**lov′a·bil′i·ty, lov′a·ble·ness,** _n._ —**lov′a·bly,** _adv._

lov·age (lŭv′Ĭj), _n._ a European apiaceous herb, _Levisticum officinale,_ cultivated in old gardens. [ME _loveache,_ t. OF: alter. of _levesche,_ g. LL _levisticum,_ appar. alter. of L _ligusticum,_ prop. neut. of _Ligusticus_ Ligurian]

love (lŭv), _n., v.,_ **loved, loving.** —_n._ **1.** a strong or passionate affection for a person of the opposite sex. **2.** sexual passion or desire, or its gratification. **3.** an object of love or affection; a sweetheart. **4.** (_cap._) a personification of sexual affection, as Eros or Cupid. **5.** a feeling of warm personal attachment or deep affection, as for a friend (or between friends), parent, child, etc. **6.** strong predilection or liking for anything: _love of books._ **7.** the benevolent affection of God for His creatures, or the reverent affection due from them to God. **8.** _Tennis, etc._ nothing; no score. **9. for love, a.** out of affection. **b.** for nothing; without compensation. **10. in love,** feeling deep affection or passion (often fol. by _with_). [ME; OE _lufu,_ c. OHG _luba_] —_v.t._ **11.** to have love or affection for. **12.** to have a strong or passionate affection for (one of the opposite sex). **13.** to have a strong liking for; take great pleasure in: _to love music._ —_v.i._ **14.** to have love or affection, esp., to be or fall in love with one of the opposite sex. [ME; OE _lufian,_ der. _lufu_ LOVE, n.]
—**Syn. 1, 5.** LOVE, AFFECTION, DEVOTION all mean a deep and enduring emotional regard, usually for another person. LOVE may apply to various kinds of regard: the charity of the Creator, reverent adoration toward God or toward a person, the relation of parent and child, the regard of friends for each other, romantic feelings for one of the opposite sex, etc. AFFECTION is a fondness for persons of either sex, that is enduring and tender, but calm. DEVOTION is an intense love and steadfast, enduring loyalty to a person; it may also imply consecration to a cause. —**Ant. 5.** hate.

love·a·ble (lŭv′ə bəl), _adj._ lovable.

love affair, a particular experience of being in love.

love apple, the tomato.

love·bird (lŭv′bûrd′), _n._ any of various small parrots, esp. of the genera _Agapornis,_ of Africa, and _Psittacula,_ of South America, remarkable for the fact that the members of each pair keep close together when perching.

love feast, 1. (among the early Christians) a meal eaten in token of brotherly love and charity. **2.** a rite practiced by a few denominations such as Mennonites and Dunkers; a fellowship meal. **3.** a banquet or gathering of persons to promote good feeling.

love-in-a-mist (lŭv′Ĭn ə mĬst′), _n. Bot._ a ranunculaceous plant, _Nigella damascena,_ with feathery dissected leaves and whitish or blue flowers.

love-in-i-dle·ness (lŭv′Ĭn Ĭ′dəl nĬs), _n._ the wild pansy, _Viola tricolor._

love knot, a knot of ribbon as a token of love.

Love·lace (lŭv′lās), _n._ Richard, 1618–58, British poet.

love·less (lŭv′lĬs), _adj._ **1.** devoid of or unattended with love. **2.** feeling no love. **3.** receiving no love. —**love′less·ly,** _adv._ —**love′less·ness,** _n._

love-lies-bleed·ing (lŭv′lĬz blē′dĬng), _n._ any of several species of amaranth, esp. _Amaranthus caudatus,_ with spikes of crimson flowers.

love·lock (lŭv′lŏk′), _n._ **1.** any conspicuous lock of hair. **2.** (formerly) a long, flowing lock or curl, dressed separately from the rest of the hair, worn by courtiers.

love·lorn (lŭv′lôrn′), _adj._ forsaken by one's love; forlorn or pining from love. —**love′lorn′ness,** _n._

love·ly (lŭv′lĬ), _adj.,_ **-lier, -liest. 1.** charmingly or exquisitely beautiful: _a lovely flower._ **2.** having a beauty that appeals to the heart as well as to the eye, as a person, a face, etc. **3.** _Colloq._ delightful, or highly pleasing: _to have a lovely time._ **4.** of a great moral or spiritual beauty: _lovely character._ [ME _lovelich,_ OE _luflic_ amiable] —**love′li·ness,** _n._ —**Syn. 2.** See **beautiful.**

lov·er (lŭv′ər), _n._ **1.** one who is in love with a person of the opposite sex (now used almost exclusively of the man). **2.** (_pl._) a man and woman in love with each other. **3.** one who has a strong predilection or liking for something: _a lover of music._ **4.** one who loves.

Lov·er (lŭv′ər), _n._ Samuel, 1797–1868, Irish novelist, artist, and composer.

love seat, a seat for two persons.

love·sick (lŭv′sĬk′), _adj._ **1.** languishing with love. **2.** expressive of such languishing. —**love′sick′ness,** _n._

lov·ing (lŭv′Ĭng), _adj._ feeling or showing love; affectionate; fond: _loving glances._ —**lov′ing·ly,** _adv._ —**lov′ing·ness,** _n._

loving cup, a large cup, as of silver, commonly with several handles, given as a prize, award, etc.

lov·ing-kind·ness (lŭv′Ĭng kīnd′nĬs), _n._ kindness arising from love (used primarily of the Deity).

low¹ (lō), _adj._ **1.** situated or occurring not far above the ground, floor, or base: _a low shelf._ **2.** not far above the horizon, as a heavenly body. **3.** lying or being below the general level: _low ground._ **4.** (of a garment) low-necked. **5.** designating or pertaining to regions near the sea level or sea as opposed to highland or inland regions: _low Countries._ **6.** prostrate or dead: _to lay one low._ **7.** profound or deep, as a bow. **8.** of small

---

extent upward, or not high or tall: *low walls.* **9.** rising but slightly from a surface: *low relief.* **10.** of less than average or normal height or depth, as a liquid, stream, etc. **11.** lacking in strength or vigor; feeble; weak. **12.** affording little strength or nourishment, as diet. **13.** small in amount, degree, force, etc.: *a low number.* **14.** denoted by a low number: *a low latitude* (one near the equator). **15.** assigning or attributing no great amount, value, or excellence: *a low estimate of something.* **16.** depressed or dejected: *low spirits.* **17.** far down in the scale of rank or estimation; humble: *low birth.* **18.** of inferior quality or character: *a low type of intellect.* **19.** lacking in dignity or elevation, as of thought or expression. **20.** groveling or abject; mean or base: *a low trick.* **21.** coarse or vulgar: *low company.* **22.** *Biol.* having a relatively simple structure; not complex in organization. **23.** *Music.* produced by relatively slow vibrations, as sounds; grave in pitch. **24.** not loud: *a low murmur.* **25.** relatively late or recent, as a date. **26.** *Chiefly Brit.* holding to Low Church principles and practices. **27.** *Phonet.* pronounced with the tongue held relatively low in the mouth: *"hot"* has a low vowel. **28.** *Auto.* of or pertaining to low-transmission gear ratio. —*adv.* **29.** in or to a low position, point, degree, etc. **30.** near the ground, floor, or base; not aloft. **31.** humbly. **32.** cheaply. **33.** at or to a low pitch. **34.** in a low tone; softly; quietly. **35.** far down in time, or late. —*n.* **36.** that which is low. **37.** *Auto.* a transmission gear ratio providing the least forward speed, usually used to start a motor vehicle, or for extra power; first. **38.** *Meteorol.* a pressure system characterized by relatively low pressure at the center. **39.** *Cards.* the lowest trump card, esp. in games of the seven-up family. [ME *lowe, lohe,* earlier *lah,* t. Scand.; cf. Icel. *lāgr,* akin to LIE²] —**low′ness,** *n.* —**Syn. 17.** lowly, meek, obscure. **20.** ignoble, degraded, sordid. **21.** See **mean².** **23.** deep. **24.** subdued. —**Ant. 17.** lofty.

low² (lō), *v.i.* **1.** to utter the sound characteristic of cattle; moo. —*v.t.* **2.** to utter by or as by lowing. —*n.* **3.** the act or the sound of lowing. [ME *low(en),* OE *hlōwan,* c. D *loeien*]

Low (lō), *n.* **David,** 1891–1963, British cartoonist.

Low Archipelago (lō), Tuamoto Archipelago.

low area, *Meteorol.* a region where the atmospheric or barometric pressure is lower than that of the surrounding regions: *the low area in the central part of a cyclone.*

low·born (lō′bôrn′), *adj.* of humble birth.

low·boy (lō′boi′), *n.* a low chest of drawers supported on short legs.

low·bred (lō′brĕd′), *adj.* characterized by or characteristic of low or vulgar breeding.

low·brow (lō′brou′), *Colloq.* —*n.* **1.** a person of low intellectual caliber or culture. —*adj.* **2.** being a lowbrow. **3.** pertaining or proper to lowbrows.

Low Church, a Low-Church party in the Anglican Church.

Low-Church (lō′chûrch′), *adj.* laying stress on sacraments and church authority, etc.; holding evangelical views (used of a party in the Anglican Church and opposed to *High-Church*). —**Low′-Church′man,** *n.*

low comedy, comedy which depends on physical action and situation rather than on wit and dialogue.

Low Countries, the lowland region near the North Sea, forming the lower basin of the Rhine, Meuse, and Scheldt rivers, divided in the Middle Ages into numerous small states: corresponding to modern Netherlands, Belgium, and Luxemburg.

low-down (lō′doun′), *n.* **1.** *Slang.* the actual, unadorned facts or truth on some subject (prec. by *the*). —*adj.* **2.** *Chiefly U.S. Colloq.* low, esp. in the social or moral scale; degraded.

Low·ell (lō′əl), *n.* **1.** **Abbott Lawrence,** 1856–1943, U.S. educator; president of Harvard, 1909–33. **2.** his sister, **Amy Lawrence,** 1874–1925, U.S. poet and critic. **3.** **James Russell,** 1819–91, U.S. poet, essayist, and diplomat. **4.** **Percival,** 1855–1916, U.S. astronomer (brother of A. L. Lowell). **5.** a city in NE Massachusetts, on the Merrimack river. 92,107 (1960).

low·er¹ (lō′ər), *v.t.* **1.** to reduce in amount, price, degree, force, etc. **2.** to make less loud, as the voice. **3.** to bring down in rank or estimation, degrade, or humble; abase (oneself), as by some sacrifice of dignity. **4.** to cause to descend, or let down: *to lower a flag.* **5.** to make lower in height or level: *to lower the water in a canal.* **6.** *Music.* to make lower in pitch; flatten. —*v.i.* **7.** to become lower or less. **8.** to descend; sink. [v. use of *lower,* compar. of LOW¹, adj.] —**Syn. 1.** decrease, diminish. **3.** humiliate. —**Ant. 1.** raise, increase.

low·er² (lou′ər), *v.i.* **1.** to be dark and threatening, as the sky or the weather. **2.** to frown, scowl, or look sullen. —*n.* **3.** a dark, threatening appearance, as of the sky, weather, etc. **4.** a frown or scowl. Also, **lour.** [ME *loure(n)* frown, lurk; cf. G *lauern* lurk]

Low·er Austria (lō′ər), a province in NE Austria. 1,254,150 pop. (est. 1953); 7092 sq. mi.

Lower California, a narrow peninsula in NW Mexico between the Gulf of California and the Pacific, forming two territories of Mexico. 343,743 pop. (est. 1952); 55,634 sq. mi. *Capitals:* Mexicali (Northern Territory) and La Paz (Southern Territory). Spanish, **Baja California.**

Lower Canada, the name of Quebec province, 1791–1841.

lower case, *Print.* the lower half of a pair of cases, which contains the small letters of the alphabet.

low·er-case (lō′ər kās′), *adj.,* *v.,* **-cased, -casing.** —*adj.* **1.** (of a letter) small (as opposed to *capital*). **2.** *Print.* pertaining to or belonging in the lower case. See **case²** (def. 7). —*v.t.* **3.** to print or write with a lower-case letter or letters.

Lower Egypt. See **Egypt.**

Lower House, (*often l.c.*) one of two branches of a legislature, generally more representative and with more members than the upper branch.

low·er·ing (lou′ər ĭng), *adj.* **1.** dark and threatening, as the sky, clouds, weather, etc. **2.** frowning or sullen, as the face, gaze, etc. —**low′er·ing·ly,** *adv.*

low·er·most (lō′ər mōst′), *adj.* lowest.

Lower Saxony, a state in N West Germany. 6,541,-200 pop. (est. 1956); 18,266 sq. mi. *Cap.:* Hanover. German, **Niedersachsen.**

lower world, 1. the regions of the dead, conceived by the ancients as lying beneath the earth's surface; Hades. **2.** the earth as distinguished from the heavenly bodies or from heaven.

lowest common multiple. See **common multiple.**

Lowes·toft (lōs′tôft; *locally* -təf), *n.* a seaport in E England, in Suffolk: famous for a type of china. 43,720 (est. 1956).

low explosive, a relatively slow-burning explosive, usually set off by heat or friction, and used for propelling charges in guns or for ordinary blasting.

Low German, 1. the Germanic speech of northern Germany and the Low Countries. **2.** Plattdeutsch.

low·land (lō′lənd), *n.* **1.** land low with respect to neighboring country. **2. the Lowlands,** a low, level region in S, central, and E Scotland. —*adj.* **3.** of, pertaining to, or characteristic of lowland or lowlands.

Low·land·er (lō′lən dər), *n.* **1.** a native of the Lowlands. **2.** (*l.c.*) an inhabitant of lowland or lowlands.

Low Latin, any form of nonclassical Latin, as Late Latin, Vulgar Latin, or Medieval Latin.

low·ly (lō′lĭ), *adj.,* **-lier, -liest,** *adv.* —*adj.* **1.** humble in station, condition, or nature: *a lowly cottage.* **2.** low in growth or position. **3.** humble in spirit; meek. —*adv.* **4.** in a low position, manner, or degree. **5.** in a lowly manner; humbly. —**low′li·ness,** *n.* —**Syn. 3.** modest.

Low Mass, a Mass said, and not sung, by a priest, assisted by a server only.

low-mind·ed (lō′mīn′dĭd), *adj.* having or showing a low, coarse, or vulgar mind; mean. —**low′-mind′-ed·ly,** *adv.* —**low′-mind′ed·ness,** *n.*

low-necked (lō′nĕkt′), *adj.* (of a garment) cut low so as to leave the neck and shoulders exposed; décolleté.

low-pitched (lō′pĭcht′), *adj.* **1.** pitched in a low register or key. **2.** produced by slow vibrations; relatively grave in pitch or soft in sound. **3.** (of a roof) having a low proportion of vertical to lateral dimension.

low-pres·sure (lō′prĕsh′ər), *adj.* having or involving a low or below-normal pressure (as of steam, etc.).

low-spir·it·ed (lō′spĭr′ĭt ĭd), *adj.* depressed; dejected. —**low′-spir′it·ed·ly,** *adv.* —**low′-spir′it·ed·ness,** *n.*

Low Sunday, the Sunday next after Easter.

low-ten·sion (lō′tĕn′shən), *adj.* *Elect.* **1.** having or designed for use at low voltage, usually less than 750 volts. **2.** the winding of a transformer designed to operate at the lower voltage. Cf. **high-tension.**

low-test (lō′tĕst′), *adj.* (of gasoline) boiling at a comparatively high temperature.

low tide, 1. the tide at low water. **2.** the time of low water. **3.** the lowest point of decline of anything.

low-volt·age (lō′vōl′tĭj), *adj.* denoting an electric system with an operating voltage under 750 volts.

low water, water at its lowest level, as in a river.

lox¹ (lŏks), *n.* a kind of smoked salmon, often eaten with cream cheese, bagels, etc.

lox² (lŏks), *n.* *Colloq.* liquid oxygen. [short for L(IQUID) OX(YGEN)]

lox·o·drom·ic (lŏk′sə drŏm′ĭk), *adj.* pertaining to oblique sailing or sailing on rhumbs (**loxodromic lines**). Also, **lox′o·drom′i·cal.** [f. Gk. *loxó(s)* oblique + s. Gk. *drómos* a running, course + -IC]

lox·o·drom·ics (lŏk′sə drŏm′ĭks), *n.* the art of oblique sailing. Also, **lox·od·ro·my** (lŏk sŏd′rə mĭ).

loy·al (loi′əl), *adj.* **1.** faithful to one's allegiance, as to the sovereign, government, or state: *a loyal subject.* **2.** faithful to one's oath, engagements or obligations: *to be loyal to a vow.* **3.** faithful to any leader, party, or cause, or to any person or thing conceived as imposing obligations: *a loyal friend.* **4.** characterized by or showing faithfulness to engagements, allegiance, obligations, etc.: *loyal conduct.* [t. F, g. L *lēgālis* LEGAL] —**loy′-al·ly,** *adv.* —**Syn. 2.** See **faithful.**

loy·al·ist (loi′əl ĭst), *n.* **1.** one who is loyal; a supporter of the sovereign or the existing government, esp. in time of revolt. **2.** (*sometimes cap.*) one who remained loyal to the British government during the American Revolution. **3.** (*cap.*) an adherent of the Republic during the Spanish Civil War. —**loy′al·ism,** *n.*

loy·al·ty (loi′əl tĭ), *n.,* *pl.* **-ties. 1.** state or quality of being loyal; faithfulness to engagements or obligations. **2.** faithful adherence to a sovereign or government, or to a leader, cause, or the like. —**Syn. 2.** LOYALTY, ALLEGIANCE, FIDELITY all imply a sense of duty or of devoted attachment to something or

---

someone. LOYALTY connotes sentiment and the feeling of devotion which one holds for one's country, creed, family, friends, etc. ALLEGIANCE applies particularly to a citizen's duty to his country, or, by extension, one's obligation to support a party, cause, leader, etc. FIDELITY implies unwavering devotion and allegiance to a person, principle, etc.

Loy·o·la (loi ō′lə), *n.* **Ignatius** (ĭg nā′shəs), (*Iñigo López de Recalde*) 1491–1556, Spanish soldier, priest, and saint, founder of the Jesuit order.

loz·enge (lŏz′ĭnj), *n.* **1.** a small flavored cake or confection of sugar, often medicated, orig. diamond-shaped. **2.** *Math.* diamond. [ME *losenge*, t. OF, appar. der. Pr. *lausa* stone slab]

LP (ĕl′pē′), *adj.* **1.** denoting a phonograph record impressed with microgrooves that revolves at 33⅓ revolutions per minute. **—n. 2.** such a record. **3.** a trademark for such a record. [initials of *long-playing*]

LSD *Pharm.* lysergic acid diethylamide, a crystalline solid, $C_{15}H_{15}N_2CON(C_2H_5)_2$, that produces temporary hallucinations and a schizophrenialike psychotic state, used in medical research of mental disorders. Also called **LSD-25.**

L.S.S., Lifesaving Service.

l.s.t., local standard time.

Lt., Lieutenant.

l.t., 1. *Football.* left tackle. **2.** local time. **3.** long ton.

Ltd., *Chiefly Brit.* limited. See **limited** (def. 3). Also, **ltd.**

Lu, *Chem.* lutecium.

Lu·a·la·ba (lōō′ə lä′bä), *n.* a river in the SE Republic of the Congo: a headstream of the Congo river.

Lu·an·da (lōō än′də), *n.* a seaport in and the capital of Angola, in SW Africa. 168,500 (est. 1953). Also, **Loanda, Sao Paulo de Loanda.**

lub·ber (lŭb′ər), *n.* **1.** a big, clumsy, stupid person. **2.** (among sailors) an awkward or unskilled seaman; landlubber. [ME *lober*, akin to Norw. *lubb(a)* short, stout person. See LOB]

lub·ber·ly (lŭb′ər lĭ), *adj.* **1.** like or of a lubber. **—adv. 2.** in a lubberly manner. **—lub′ber·li·ness,** *n.*

lubber's hole, *Naut.* an open space in the platform at the head of a lower mast, through which a sailor may mount and descend without going outside the rim.

Lub·bock (lŭb′ək), *n.* **1.** a city in NW Texas. 128,691 (1960). **2. Sir John,** (*Baron Avebury*) 1834–1913, British statesman, scientist, and writer.

Lü·beck (ly′bĕk), *n.* a seaport in N West Germany: important Baltic port in the medieval Hanseatic League. 228,766 (est. 1955). See map under **Hanseatic Cities.**

Lu·blin (lyōō′blĭn), *n.* a city in E Poland. 129,000 (est. 1954). Russian, **Lyublin.**

lu·bri·cant (lōō′brə kənt), *n.* **1.** a lubricating material. **—adj. 2.** lubricating.

lu·bri·cate (lōō′brə kāt′), *v.t.,* **-cated, -cating. 1.** to apply some oily, greasy, or other substance to, in order to diminish friction; oil or grease, as parts of a mechanism. **2.** to make slippery or smooth. [t. L: m.s *lūbricātus,* pp., made slippery] **—lu′bri·ca′tion,** *n.* **—lu′bri·cat·ing, adj.**

lu·bri·ca·tor (lōō′brə kā′tər), *n.* a person or a device that lubricates or furnishes lubricant.

lu·bri·cious (lōō brĭsh′əs), *adj.* wanton; lewd.

lu·bric·i·ty (lōō brĭs′ə tĭ), *n., pl.* **-ties. 1.** slipperiness or oily smoothness of surface. **2.** capacity for lubrication. **3.** shiftiness. **4.** lewdness. [t. LL: m.s. *lūbricitas,* der. L *lūbricus* lubricous]

lu·bri·cous (lōō′brə kəs), *adj.* **1.** slippery, as of surface; of an oily smoothness. **2.** unstable; uncertain; shifty. **3.** lewd. [t. L: m. *lūbricus*]

Lu·can (lōō′kən), *n.* (*Marcus Annaeus Lucanus*) A.D. 39–65, Roman poet, born in Spain.

Lu·ca·ni·a (lōō kā′nĭ ə), *n.* **1.** an ancient region in S Italy, NW of the Gulf of Taranto. **2.** a modern department in S Italy, comprising most of the ancient region. 647,000 (est. 1954); 3856 sq. mi.

Lu·ca (lōō′kä), *n.* a city in NW Italy. 87,000 (est.).

lu·cent (lōō′sənt), *adj.* *Archaic.* **1.** shining. **2.** transparent. [t. L: s. *lūcens,* ppr., shining] **—lu′cence, lu′cen·cy,** *n.*

lu·cerne (lōō sûrn′), *n.* *Chiefly Brit.* alfalfa. [t. F: m. *luzerne,* t. Pr.: m. *luzerno,* ult. der. L *lux* light]

Lu·cerne (lōō sûrn′; *Fr.* ly sĕrn′), *n.* **1.** a canton in central Switzerland. 229,200 pop. (est. 1952); 576 sq. mi. **2.** the capital of this canton; 61,600 (est. 1952) on **Lake of Lucerne** (24 mi. long; 44 sq. mi.). German, **Luzern.**

lu·ces (lōō′sēz), *n.* pl. of **lux.**

Lu·cian (lōō′shən), *n.* A.D. c120–c180, Greek humorist and satirist.

lu·cid (lōō′sĭd), *adj.* **1.** shining or bright. **2.** clear or transparent. **3.** easily understood: *a lucid explanation.* **4.** characterized by clear perception or understanding; rational or sane: *a lucid interval.* [t. L: s. *lūcidus*] **—lu·cid′i·ty, lu′cid·ness,** *n.* **—lu′cid·ly, adv.**

Lu·ci·fer (lōō′sə fər), *n.* **1.** a proud rebellious archangel, identified with Satan, who fell from heaven. **2.** the planet Venus when appearing as the morning star. **3.** (*l.c.*) a friction match. [t. L: the morning star, prop. adj., light-bringing]

lu·cif·er·ase (lōō sĭf′ə rās′), *n.* *Biochem.* an enzyme which is present in the luminous organs of fireflies, etc., and which, acting upon luciferin, produces luminosity. [f. L *lūcifer* light-bringing + -ASE]

lu·cif·er·in (lōō sĭf′ər ĭn), *n.* *Biochem.* a protein occurring in fireflies, etc., luminous when acted upon by

luciferase. [f. L *lūcifer* light-bringing + -IN²]

lucifer match, lucifer (def. 3.)

lu·cif·er·ous (lōō sĭf′ər əs), *adj.* bringing or giving light. [f. L *lūcifer* light-bringing + -OUS]

Lu·ci·na (lōō sī′nə), *n.* Roman goddess of child birth.

Lu·cite (lōō′sīt), *n.* *Trademark.* a plastic compound, (thermoplastic methyl methacrylate resin), with unusual optical properties, used for reflectors, ornaments, airplane windows, etc. [f. s. L *lux* light + -ITE¹]

luck (lŭk), *n.* **1.** that which happens to a person, as if by chance, in the course of events: *to have good luck.* **2.** good fortune; advantage or success considered as the result of chance: *to wish one luck.* **3.** some object on which good fortune is supposed to depend. [ME *lucke,* t. LG or D: m. *luk,* also *geluk,* c. G *glück*]

luck·i·ly (lŭk′ə lĭ), *adv.* by good luck; fortunately: *Luckily he had enough money to pay the bill.*

luck·less (lŭk′lĭs), *adj.* having no luck. **—luck′-less·ly,** *adv.* **—luck′less·ness,** *n.*

Luck·now (lŭk′nou), *n.* a city in N India, in Uttar Pradesh: the British besieged here several months (1857–58) during the Sepoy Rebellion. 444,711 (1951).

luck·y (lŭk′ĭ), *adj.* **luckier, luckiest. 1.** having or attended with good luck; fortunate. **2.** happening fortunately: *a lucky accident.* **3.** bringing or presaging good luck, or supposed to do so: *a lucky penny.*

lu·cra·tive (lōō′krə tĭv), *adj.* profitable; remunerative: *a lucrative business.* [ME, t. L: m.s. *lucrātivus*] **—lu′cra·tive·ly, adv.** **—lu′cra·tive·ness,** *n.*

lu·cre (lōō′kər), *n.* gain or money as the object of sordid desire. [ME, t. L: m.s. *lucrum* gain]

Lu·cre·tius (lōō krē′shəs), *n.* (*Titus Lucretius Carus*) c96–c55 B.C., Roman poet. **—Lu·cre′tian, adj.**

lu·cu·brate (lōō′kyōō brāt′), *v.i.,* **-brated, -brating. 1.** to work, write, study, etc., laboriously, esp. at night. **2.** to write learnedly. [t. L: m.s. *lūcubrātus,* pp.] **—lu′cu·bra′tor,** *n.*

lu·cu·bra·tion (lōō′kyōō brā′shən), *n.* **1.** laborious work, study, etc., esp. at night. **2.** a learned or carefully written production. **3.** (*often pl.*) any literary effort.

lu·cu·lent (lōō′kyōō lənt), *adj.* **1.** clear or lucid, as explanations, etc. **2.** convincing. [ME, t. L: s. *lūculentus*] **—lu′cu·lent·ly, adv.**

Lu·cul·lus (lōō kŭl′əs), *n.* **Lucius Licinius** (lōō′shəs lĭ sĭn′ĭ əs), c110–57 ? B.C., Roman consul and general, famous for his great wealth and luxury. **—Lu·cul′lan, Lu·cul·le·an** (lōō klē′ən), **Lu·cul′li·an, adj.**

lu·cus a non lu·cen·do (lōō′kəs ā nŏn lōō sĕn′dō), *Latin.* a grove (so called) from not being light (used as a type of illogical or absurd derivation or reasoning).

Lud·dite (lŭd′īt), *n.* a member of any of various bands of workmen in England (1811–16) organized to destroy manufacturing machinery, under the belief that its use diminished employment.

Lu·den·dorff (lōō′dən dôrf′), *n.* **Erich Friedrich Wilhelm von** (ā′rĭкн frē′drĭкн vĭl′hĕlm fən), 1865–1937, German general.

Lü·der·itz (ly′dər ĭts), *n.* a seaport in South-West Africa: diamond-mining center. 3925 (1951).

Lu·dhi·a·na (lōō′dĭ ä′nä), *n.* a city in NW India, in East part of Punjab state. 153,795 (1951).

lu·di·crous (lōō′də krəs), *adj.* such as to cause laughter or derision; ridiculous; amusingly absurd: *a ludicrous incident.* [t. L: m. *lūdicrus* sportive] **—lu′di·crous·ly, adv.** **—lu′di·crous·ness,** *n.* **—Syn.** laughable, comical.

Lud·wig (lōōt′vĭкн, lōōd′-), *n.* **Emil** (ā′mēl), 1881–1948, German biographer.

Lud·wig II (lōōt′vĭкн, lōōd′-), *n.* See **Louis II.**

Lud·wigs·ha·fen (lōōt′vĭкнs hä′fən, lōōd′-), *n.* a city in W West Germany, on the Rhine opposite Mannheim. 150,200 (est. 1955).

lu·es (lōō′ēz), *n.* syphilis. [t. L: plague]

luff (lŭf), *Naut.* **—n. 1.** the forward edge of a fore-and-aft sail. **—v.i. 2.** to bring the head of a sailing vessel closer to or directly into the wind, with sails shaking. [early ME *lof, loof,* appar. t. OF: m. *lof* a contrivance for altering a ship's course (later, as also D *loef,* the weather side), of Gmc. orig.]

Luft·waf·fe (lōōft′väf′ə), *n.* *German.* (under the Nazis) the German Air Force.

lug¹ (lŭg), *v.,* **lugged, lugging,** *n.* **—v.t. 1.** to pull along or carry with force or effort. **2.** *Colloq.* to bring (*in* or *into*) unnaturally or irrelevantly: *to lug personal habits into a discussion.* **3.** (of a ship) to carry more sail in a strong breeze than is safe or desirable. **—v.i. 4.** to pull; tug. **—n. 5.** an act of lugging; a forcible pull; a haul. [ME *lugg(e),* t. Scand.; cf. Sw. *lugga* pull by the hair]

lug² (lŭg), *n.* **1.** a projecting piece by which anything is held or supported. **2.** a leather loop dependent from a saddle, through which a shaft is passed for support. [? special use of LUG¹; but cf. d. *lug* limb]

lug³ (lŭg), *n.* lugsail. [see LUGSAIL]

lug⁴ (lŭg), *n.* lugworm. [cf. D *log* heavy, unwieldy]

Lu·gansk (lōō gänsk′), *n.* former name of **Voroshilovgrad.**

lug·gage (lŭg′ĭj), *n.* *Chiefly Brit.* baggage. [f. LUG¹ + -AGE]

lug·ger (lŭg′ər), *n.* a vessel with lugsails. [der. LUGSAIL]

lug·sail (lŭg′sāl′; *Naut.* -səl), *n.* *Naut.* a quadrilateral sail bent upon a yard that crosses the mast obliquely. Also, **lug.** [f. *lug* pole (now d.) + SAIL]

---

b., blend of, blended; c., cognate with; d., dialect, dialectal; der., derived from; f., formed from; g., going back to; m., modification of; r., replacing; s., stem of; t., taken from; ?, perhaps. See the full key on inside cover.

lu·gu·bri·ous (lōō gū′brĭ əs, -gōō′-), *adj.* mournful; doleful; dismal: *lugubrious tones.* [f. L *lūgubri(s)* mournful + -ous] —**lu·gu′bri·ous·ly,** *adv.* —**lu·gu′bri·ous·ness,** *n.*

lug·worm (lŭg′wûrm′), *n.* any annelid of the genus *Arenicola,* comprising marine worms with tufted gills, which burrow in the sand of the seashore and are much used for bait. Also, **lug.** [f. LUG⁴ + WORM]

Luke (lōōk), *n.* 1. the Evangelist; an early Christian disciple, probably a gentile, a physician, and companion of St. Paul; traditionally, the author of the third Gospel. 2. the third Gospel, in the New Testament. [t. L: m. *Lūcas,* t. Gk.: m. *Loukâs*]

luke·warm (lōōk′wôrm′), *adj.* 1. moderately warm, tepid. 2. having or showing little ardor or zeal; indifferent: *lukewarm applause.* [ME *lukewarme,* f. *luke* tepid (appar. der. *lew* tepid, OE *-hlēow*) + *warme* WARM] —**luke′warm′ly,** *adv.* —**luke′warm′ness,** *n.*

lull (lŭl), *v.t.* 1. to put to sleep or rest by soothing means: *to lull a child by singing.* 2. to soothe or quiet. —*v.i.* 3. to become lulled, quieted, or stilled. —*n.* 4. a lulled condition; a temporary quiet or stillness: *a lull in a storm.* 5. a soothing sound: *the lull of falling waters.* [ME *lulle(n).* Cf. Sw. *lulla,* G *lullen,* also L *lallāre* sing lullaby]

lull·a·by (lŭl′ə bī′), *n., pl.* **-bies,** *v.,* **-bied, -bying.** —*n.* 1. the utterance "lullaby" or a song containing it; a cradlesong. 2. any lulling song. —*v.t.* 3. to lull with or as with a lullaby. [orig. interj., *lulla!* + *by!*]

Lul·ly (lŭl′ĭ; *for 1 also* Fr. lȳ lē′), *n.* 1. **Jean Baptiste** (zhän bä tēst′), 1632–87, Italian composer in France. 2. **Raymond,** c1235–1315, Spanish philosopher and missionary.

lum·ba·go (lŭm bā′gō), *n. Pathol.* myalgia in the lumbar region; rheumatic pain in the muscles of the small of the back. [t. LL, der. L *lumbus* loin]

lum·bar (lŭm′bər), *adj.* 1. of or pertaining to the loin or loins. —*n.* 2. a lumbar vertebra, artery, or the like. [t. NL: s. *lumbāris,* der. L *lumbus* loin]

lum·ber¹ (lŭm′bər), *n.* 1. *U.S. and Canada.* timber sawed or split into planks, boards, etc. 2. miscellaneous useless articles that are stored away. —*v.i.* 3. *U.S. and Canada.* to cut timber and prepare it for market. —*v.t.* 4. to heap together in disorder. 5. to fill up or obstruct with miscellaneous useless articles; encumber. [orig. uncert.] —**lum′ber·er,** *n.*

lum·ber² (lŭm′bər), *v.i.* 1. to move clumsily or heavily, esp. from great or ponderous bulk. 2. to make a rumbling noise. [ME *lomere(n).* Cf. d. Sw. *lomra* resound, *loma* walk heavily]

lum·ber·ing¹ (lŭm′bər ĭng), *n. U.S. and Canada.* the trade or business of cutting and preparing timber. [f. LUMBER¹ + -ING¹]

lum·ber·ing² (lŭm′bər ĭng), *adj.* 1. moving clumsily or heavily; awkward. 2. that rumbles. [f. LUMBER² + -ING²] —**lum′ber·ing·ly,** *adv.*

lum·ber·jack (lŭm′bər jăk′), *n. U.S. and Canada.* one who works at lumbering.

lum·ber·man (lŭm′bər mən), *n., pl.* **-men.** *U.S. and Canada.* 1. one who cuts and prepares timber. 2. one who deals in lumber.

lum·ber·yard (lŭm′bər yärd′), *n. U.S. and Canada.* a yard where lumber is stored for sale.

lum·bri·cal (lŭm′brə kəl), *Anat.* one of four wormlike muscles in the palm of the hand and in the sole of the foot. Also, **lum·bri·ca·lis** (lŭm′brə kā′lĭs). [t. NL: s. *lumbricālis,* der. L *lumbricus* earthworm]

lum·bri·coid (lŭm′brə koid′), *adj.* resembling an earthworm. [f. s. L *lumbricus* earthworm + -OID]

lu·men (lōō′mən), *n., pl.* **-mina** (-mə nə). 1. the unit of luminous flux; the light emitted by a source of one international candle in a unit solid angle. 2. *Anat.* the canal, duct, or cavity of a tubular organ. 3. *Bot.* (of a cell) the cavity which the cell walls enclose. [t. L: light, window]

Lu·mi·nal (lōō′mə nəl), *n.* a trademark for phenobarbital.

lu·mi·nar·y (lōō′mə nĕr′ĭ), *n., pl.* **-naries.** 1. a celestial body, as the sun or moon. 2. a body or thing that gives light. 3. a person who enlightens mankind or makes some subject clear. [late ME, t. ML: m.s. *lūminārium* a light, lamp, heavenly body]

lu·mi·nesce (lōō′mə nĕs′), *v.i.,* **-nesced, -nescing.** to exhibit luminescence.

lu·mi·nes·cence (lōō′mə nĕs′əns), *n.* an emission of light not due directly to incandescence and occurring at a temperature below that of incandescent bodies: a term including phosphorescence, fluorescence, etc.

lu·mi·nes·cent (lōō′mə nĕs′ənt), *adj.* characterized by or pertaining to luminescence. [f. s. L *lūmen* light + -ESCENT]

lu·mi·nif·er·ous (lōō′mə nĭf′ər əs), *adj.* producing light. [f. s. L *lūmen* light + -(I)FEROUS]

lu·mi·nos·i·ty (lōō′mə nŏs′ə tĭ), *n., pl.* **-ties.** 1. the quality of being luminous. 2. something luminous.

lu·mi·nous (lōō′mə nəs), *adj.* 1. radiating or reflecting light; shining. 2. lighted up or illuminated; well lighted. 3. brilliant intellectually; enlightening, as a writer or his writings. 4. clear; readily intelligible. [ME *luminose,* t. L: m. *lūminōsus*] —**lu·mi·nous·ly,** *adv.* —**lu′mi·nous·ness,** *n.*

luminous energy, light.

luminous flux, rate of transmission of luminous energy; luminous power. Its unit is the lumen.

luminous intensity, *Photom.* (of a light source) the luminous flux emitted per unit solid angle. A source of 1 candle emits 4 lumens.

lum·mox (lŭm′əks), *n. U.S. Colloq.* a clumsy, stupid person.

lump¹ (lŭmp), *n.* 1. a piece or mass of solid matter without regular shape, or of no particular shape. 2. a protuberance or swelling: *a lump on the head.* 3. an aggregation, collection, or mass: *in the lump.* 4. *Colloq.* a stupid, clumsy person. —*adj.* 5. in the form of a lump or lumps: *lump sugar.* 6. including a number of items taken together or in the lump: *a lump sum.* —*v.t.* 7. to unite into one aggregation, collection, or mass. 8. to deal with in the lump or mass. 9. to make into a lump or lumps. 10. to raise into or cover with lumps. —*v.i.* 11. to form or raise a lump or lumps. 12. to move heavily. [ME *lumpe, lomp(e).* Cf. Dan. *lump(e)* lump, d. Norw. *lump* block]

lump² (lŭmp), *v.t. Colloq.* to endure or put up with (a disagreeable necessity): *if you don't like it, you can lump it.* [orig. uncert.]

lump·er (lŭmp′ər), *n.* a laborer employed to load and unload vessels in port.

lump·fish (lŭmp′fĭsh′), *n., pl.* **-fishes,** (*esp. collectively*) **-fish,** a clumsy-looking fish, *Cyclopterus lumpus,* with a high, ridged back, of the Northern Atlantic Ocean.

lump·ish (lŭmp′ĭsh), *adj.* 1. like a lump. 2. clumsy or stupid: *she called him a lumpish boor.* —**lump′ish·ly,** *adv.* —**lump′ish·ness,** *n.*

lump·suck·er (lŭmp′sŭk′ər), *n.* a lumpfish.

lump·y (lŭmp′ĭ), *adj.,* **lumpier, lumpiest.** 1. full of lumps: *lumpy gravy.* 2. covered with lumps, as a surface. 3. like a lump, as in being heavy or clumsy. 4. (of water) rough or choppy. —**lump′i·ly,** *adv.* —**lump′i·ness,** *n.*

lumpy jaw, *Pathol.* actinomycosis of the jaw.

Lu·na (lōō′nə), *n.* 1. the moon, personified by the Romans as a goddess. 2. *Alchemy.* silver. [t. L: moon]

lu·na·cy (lōō′nə sĭ), *n., pl.* **-cies.** 1. intermittent insanity. 2. any form of insanity (usually, except idiocy). 3. extreme foolishness or an instance of it: *her decision to resign was sheer lunacy.* 4. *Law.* unsoundness of mind sufficient to incapacitate one for civil transactions. [f. LUN(ATIC) + -ACY]

luna moth, a large American moth, *Tropaea luna,* with light-green coloration, purple-brown markings, lunate spots, and long tails. Also, **Luna moth.**

lu·nar (lōō′nər), *adj.* 1. of or pertaining to the moon: *the lunar orbit.* 2. measured by the moon's revolutions: *a lunar month.* 3. resembling the moon; round or crescent-shaped. 4. of or pertaining to silver. [t. L: s. *lūnāris* of the moon, crescent]

lunar caustic, *Med., Chem.* silver nitrate, AgNO₃, esp. in a sticklike mold, used to cauterize tissues.

lu·nar·i·an (lōō nâr′ĭ ən), *n.* 1. a supposed inhabitant of the moon. 2. a selenographer.

lunar month. See month (def. 5).

lunar year. See year (def. 4).

lu·nate (lōō′nāt), *adj.* crescent-shaped. Also, **lu′nat·ed.** [t. L: m.s. *lūnātus*]

lu·na·tic (lōō′nə tĭk), *n.* 1. an insane person. —*adj.* Also, **lu·nat·i·cal** (lōō nāt′ə kəl). 2. insane or mad; crazy. 3. indicating lunacy; characteristic of a lunatic. 4. designated for or used by the insane: *a lunatic asylum.* [ME *lunatik,* t. L: m.s. *lūnāticus* mad, der. L *lūna* moon] —**lu·nat′i·cal·ly,** *adv.*

lu·na·tion (lōō nā′shən), *n.* the time from one new moon to the next (about 29½ days); a lunar month.

lunch (lŭnch), *n.* 1. a light meal between breakfast and dinner; luncheon. 2. a light meal. —*v.i.* 3. to eat lunch: *we lunched quite late today.* —*v.t.* 4. to provide lunch for: *they lunched us in regal fashion.* [short for LUNCHEON] —**lunch′er,** *n.*

lunch·eon (lŭn′chən), *n.* lunch. [b. LUMP¹ and d. *nuncheon* (ME *nonshench,* f. *non* noon + *shench* (OE *scenc*) a drink)]

lunch·eon·ette (lŭn′chə nĕt′), *n.* a lunchroom or restaurant where lunches are served.

lunch·room (lŭnch′rōōm′, -rŏŏm′), *n.* a restaurant that specializes in serving light meals. Also, **lunch room.**

Lun·dy's Lane (lŭn′dĭz), a road near Niagara Falls, in Ontario, Canada: battle between the British and Americans, 1814.

lune¹ (lōōn), *n.* 1. anything shaped like a crescent or a half moon. 2. a crescent-shaped plane figure bounded by two arcs of circles, either on a plane or a spherical surface. [t. F, g. L *lūna* moon]

lune² (lōōn), *n.* the line for holding a hawk. [ME; var. of *loigne,* t. OF; g. LL *longia,* der. L *longus* long]

lu·nette (lōō nĕt′), *n.* 1. any of various objects or spaces of crescentlike or semicircular outline or section. 2. an arched or rounded aperture or window, as in a vault. 3. a painting, etc., filling an arched space, usually a semicircle or a flatter chord of a circle. 4. *Fort.* a work consisting of a salient angle with two flanks and an open gorge. 5. *Ordn.* a towing ring in the trail plate of a towed vehicle, as a gun carriage. Also, **lu·net** (lōō′nĭt). [t. F, dim. of *lune* moon. See LUNE¹]

Lu·né·ville (lȳ nĕ vēl′), *n.* a city in NE France: treaty between France and Austria, 1801. 22,690 (1954).

ăct, āble, dâre, ärt; ĕbb, ēqual; ĭf, īce; hŏt, ōver, ôrder, oil, bŏŏk, ōōze, out; ŭp, ūse, ûrge; ə = a in alone; ch, chief; g, give; ng, ring; sh, shoe; th, thin; ŧh, that; zh, vision. See the full key on inside cover.

lung (lŭng), *n.* **1.** either of the two saclike respiratory organs in the thorax of man and the higher vertebrates. **2.** an analogous organ in certain invertebrates, as arachnids, terrestrial gastropods, etc. [ME *lunge(n)*, OE *lungen*, c. G *lunge*; akin to LIGHT². Cf. LIGHTS lungs]

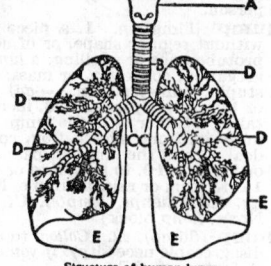

Structure of human lungs
A, Larynx; B, Trachea; C, Bronchi; D, Ramifications of bronchial tubes; E, Uncut smooth surface

lun·gan (lŭng′gən), *n.* longan.

lunge¹ (lŭnj), *n.*, *v.*, **lunged, lunging.** —*n.* **1.** a thrust, as in fencing. **2.** any sudden forward movement; plunge. —*v.i.* **3.** to make a lunge or thrust; move with a lunge. —*v.t.* **4.** to thrust; cause to move with a lunge. [apheptic var. of *allonge* (obs.), t. F, der. *allonger* lengthen, extend, *lunge*, der. *à* to (g. L *ad*) + *long* long (g. L *longus*)]

lunge² (lŭnj), *n.*, *v.*, **lunged, lunging.** —*n.* **1.** a long rope used to guide a horse during training or exercise. **2.** a ring or circular track for such training or exercise. —*v.t.* **3.** to train or exercise (a horse) by the use of a lunge or rope, or on a lunge or track. [t. F: m. *longe* halter, lunge, var. of OF *loigne*. See LUNE²]

lung·fish (lŭng′fĭsh′), *n.*, *pl.* **-fishes,** (*esp. collectively*) **-fish.** a dipnoan.

Lung·ki (loong′kē′), *n.* Changchowfu.

lung·worm (lŭng′wûrm′), *n.* **1.** any nematode worm of the superfamily *Metastrongylidae*, parasitic in lungs of various mammals. **2.** a nematode worm of the genus *Rhabdias*, parasitic in the lungs of reptiles and amphibians.

lung·wort (lŭng′wûrt′), *n.* **1.** a European blue-flowered boraginaceous plant, *Pulmonaria officinalis.* **2.** an American blue-flowered plant, *Mertensia virginica*, of the same family.

luni-, a word element meaning "moon." [comb. form repr. L *lūna*]

lu·ni·so·lar (loo′nə sō′lər), *adj.* pertaining to or based upon the relations or joint action of the moon and sun: *the lunisolar cycle.*

lu·ni·tid·al (loo′nə tī′dəl), *adj.* pertaining to that part of the tidal movement dependent on the moon.

lunitidal interval, the period of time between the moon's transit and the next high lunar tide.

lunk·head (lŭngk′hĕd′), *n.* *U.S. Colloq.* a thick-headed or stupid person; a blockhead.

Lunt (lŭnt), *n.* Alfred, born 1893, U.S. actor.

lu·nu·la (loo′nyə lə), *n.*, *pl.* **-lae** (-lē′). something shaped like a narrow crescent, as the small white area at the base of the human fingernail. Also, **lu·nule** (loo′-nūl). [t. L, dim. of *lūna* moon]

lu·nu·lar (loo′nyə lər), *adj.* crescent-shaped: *lunular markings.*

lu·nu·late (loo′nyə lāt′), *adj.* **1.** having lunular markings. **2.** crescent-shaped. Also, **lu′nu·lat′ed.**

lun·y (loo′nĭ), *adj.*, **lunier, luniest,** *n.*, *pl.* **lunies.** loony.

Lu·per·ca·li·a (loo′pər kā′lĭ ə), *n.pl.* an ancient Roman festival celebrated annually on Feb. 15 in honor of Lupercus, a rustic deity identified with the Roman Faunus and the Greek Pan. [t. L.]

lu·pine¹ (loo′pĭn), *n.* any plant of the leguminous genus *Lupinus*, as *L. albus* (**white lupine**), a European herb with edible seeds cultivated from ancient times, or *L. perennis*, a wild species with blue, pink, or white flowers common in sandy soil in the eastern U. S. [ME, t. L: m.s. *lupīnus, lupīnum.* See LUPINE²]

lu·pine² (loo′pĭn), *adj.* **1.** pertaining to or resembling the wolf. **2.** allied to the wolf. **3.** savage; ravenous. [t. L: m.s. *lupīnus* of a wolf]

lu·pu·lin (loo′pyə lĭn), *n.* the glandular hairs of the hop, *Humulus lupulus*, used in medicine. [f. s. NL *lupulus* (dim. of L *lupus* hop) + -IN²]

lu·pus (loo′pəs), *n.* *Pathol.* a cutaneous disease due to the tubercle bacillus. [t. L: wolf]

lurch¹ (lûrch), *n.* **1.** sudden leaning or roll to one side, as of a ship or a staggering person. **2.** a sudden swaying or staggering movement. —*v.i.* **3.** to make a lurch; move with lurches; stagger: *the wounded man lurched across the room at his assailant.* [orig. obscure; first in nautical use]

lurch² (lûrch), *n.* **1.** the position of one discomfited or in a helpless plight: *to leave someone in the lurch.* **2.** a situation at the close of various games in which the loser scores nothing or is far behind his opponent. [t. F: m. *lourche* a game so called, as adj. discomfited; ? orig.]

lurch·er (lûr′chər), *n.* **1.** one who lurks or prowls; a petty thief; a poacher. **2.** a crossbred hunting dog.

lure (loor), *n.*, *v.*, **lured, luring.** —*n.* **1.** anything that attracts, entices, or allures. **2.** a decoy; a bait, esp. an artificial one, used in angling. **3.** a feathered decoy, sometimes baited, on a long thong, used in falconry to recall the hawk. **4.** a flap or tassel dangling from the

dorsal fin of pediculate fish. —*v.t.* **5.** to decoy; entice; allure. **6.** to draw as by a lure. [ME, t. OF: m. *leurre*, t. Gmc.; cf. G *luder* bait] —**lur′er,** *n.*

lu·rid (loor′ĭd), *adj.* **1.** lighted up or shining with an unnatural or wild (esp. red or fiery) glare: *a lurid sky.* **2.** glaringly vivid or sensational: *lurid tales.* **3.** terrible in fiery intensity, fierce passion, or wild unrestraint: *lurid crimes.* **4.** wan, pallid, or ghastly in hue. [t. L: s. *lūridus* pale-yellow, wan] —**lu′rid·ly,** *adv.* —**lu′rid-ness,** *n.*

lurk (lûrk), *v.i.* **1.** to lie in concealment, as men in ambush; remain in or about a place secretly or furtively. **2.** to go furtively; slink; steal. **3.** to exist unperceived or unsuspected. [ME, freq. of LOWER². Cf. Norw. *lurka* sneak away] —**lurk′er,** *n.* —**lurk′ing·ly,** *adv.* —Syn. **1.** LURK, SKULK, SNEAK, PROWL suggest avoiding observation, often because of a sinister purpose. To LURK is to lie in wait for someone, or to hide about a place, often without motion for periods of time. SKULK suggests cowardliness and stealth of movement. SNEAK emphasizes the attempt to avoid being seen. It has connotations of slinking and of an abject meanness of manner, whether the object is to avoid punishment for some misdeed or whether there is a sinister intent. PROWL implies the definite purpose of seeking for prey; it suggests continuous action in roaming or wandering, slowly and quietly but watchfully, as a cat that is hunting mice.

Lu·sa·ka (loo sä′kə), *n.* a city in and the capital of Zambia.

Lu·sa·ti·a (loo sä′shǐ ə, -shə), *n.* a region between the Oder and Elbe rivers, in East Germany and SW Poland.

Lu·sa·tian (loo sä′shən), *n.* Sorbian.

lus·cious (lŭsh′əs), *adj.* **1.** highly pleasing to the taste or smell: *luscious peaches.* **2.** sweet to the senses or the mind. **3.** sweet to excess, or cloying. [late ME; ? aphetic var. of DELICIOUS] —**lus′cious·ly,** *adv.* —**lus′cious-ness,** *n.* —Syn. **2.** See **delicious.**

lush¹ (lŭsh), *adj.* **1.** tender and juicy, as plants or vegetation; succulent; luxuriant. **2.** characterized by luxuriant vegetation. [ME *lusch*, prob. var. of *lasch*, t. OF: m. *lasche* loose, slack] —**lush′ly,** *adv.* —**lush′ness,** *n.*

lush² (lŭsh), *Slang.* —*n.* **1.** intoxicating liquor. **2.** a drunken person. —*v.i.* **3.** to drink liquor. —*v.t.* **4.** to drink (liquor). [orig. uncert.]

lush·y (lŭsh′ĭ), *adj.* *Slang.* drunk; tipsy.

Lu·si·ta·ni·a (loo′sə tā′nĭ ə), *n.* **1.** an ancient region and Roman province in the Iberian Peninsula, corresponding largely to modern Portugal. **2.** a British steamship sunk by a German submarine in the North Atlantic on May 7, 1915: one of the events leading up to U.S. entry into World War I.

lust (lŭst), *n.* **1.** passionate or overmastering desire (fol. by *for* or *of*): *lust for power.* **2.** sexual desire or appetite. **3.** unbridled or lawless sexual desire or appetite. **4.** sensuous desire or appetite considered as sinful. **5.** *Obs.* pleasure or delight. —*v.i.* **6.** to have strong sexual desire. **7.** to have a strong or inordinate desire (often fol. by *for* or *after*). [ME *luste*, OE *lust*, c. D and G *lust* pleasure, desire]

lus·ter¹ (lŭs′tər), *n.* **1.** state or quality of shining by reflecting light; glitter, glisten, sheen, or gloss: *the luster of satin.* **2.** some substance used to impart sheen or gloss. **3.** radiant or luminous brightness; radiance. **4.** radiance of beauty, excellence, merit, distinction, or glory: *achievements that add luster to one's name.* **5.** a shining object. **6.** a chandelier, or candleholder, usually ornamented with cut-glass pendants. **7.** a fabric of wool and cotton with a lustrous surface. **8.** *Ceramics.* a shiny, metallic, sometimes iridescent film produced on the surface of pottery or porcelain. **9.** *Mineral.* the nature of the surface of a mineral with respect to its reflecting qualities: *greasy luster.* —*v.t.* **10.** to finish with a luster or gloss. —*v.i.* **11.** *Rare.* to shine with luster. Also, *esp. Brit.*, **lustre.** [t. F: m. *lustre*, t. It.: m. *lustro*, der. *lustrare* to shine, g. L: illuminate]

lus·ter² (lŭs′tər), *n.* lustrum. Also, *esp. Brit.*, **lus′tre.**

lus·tered (lŭs′tərd), *adj.* having a luster.

lust·ful (lŭst′fəl), *adj.* **1.** full of or imbued with lust; libidinous. **2.** *Archaic.* lusty. —**lust′ful·ly,** *adv.* —**lust′ful-ness,** *n.*

lust·i·hood (lŭst′ĭ hŏŏd′), *n.* *Archaic.* lustiness.

lus·tral (lŭs′trəl), *adj.* **1.** of, pertaining to, or employed in the lustrum or rite of purification. **2.** occurring every five years. [t. L: s. *lustrālis*]

lus·trate (lŭs′trāt), *v.t.*, **-trated, -trating.** to purify by a propitiatory offering or other ceremonial method. [t. L: m.s. *lustrātus*, pp.] —**lus·tra′tion,** *n.*

lus·tre (lŭs′tər), *n.*, *v.t.*, *v.i.*, **-tred, -tring.** *Chiefly Brit.* luster.

lus·trous (lŭs′trəs), *adj.* **1.** having luster; shining; glossy, as silk; bright, as eyes. **2.** brilliant or splendid. —**lus′trous·ly,** *adv.* —**lus′trous-ness,** *n.*

lus·trum (lŭs′trəm), *n.*, *pl.* **-trums, -tra** (-trə). **1.** a period of five years. **2.** a lustration or ceremonial purification of the ancient Roman people performed every five years, after the taking of the census. [t. L]

lust·y (lŭs′tĭ), *adj.*, **lustier, lustiest. 1.** full of or characterized by healthy vigor. **2.** hearty, as a meal or the like. [ME; f. LUST, n. + -Y¹] —**lust′i·ly,** *adv.* —**lust′i-ness,** *n.* —Syn. **1.** robust, strong, sturdy. —Ant. **1.** feeble.

lu·sus na·tu·rae (loo′səs nə tyŏŏr′ē, -tōōr′ē), *Latin.* a deformed person or thing; a freak. [L: a jest of nature]

lu·ta·nist (lōō/tənĭst), *n.* a player on the lute. Also, **lu/te·nist.** [t. ML: s. *lūtānista,* der. *lūtāna* lute]

lute (lōōt), *n., v.,* **luted, luting.** —*n.* 1. a stringed musical instrument formerly much used, having a long, fretted neck and a hollow, typically pear-shaped body with a vaulted back, the strings being plucked with the fingers of one hand (or struck with a plectrum) and stopped on the frets with those of the other. —*v.i.* 2. to play on a lute. [ME, t. OF: m. *lut,* t. Pr.: m. *laüt,* t. Ar.: m. *al-'ūd* the lute]

Lute

lu·te·ci·um (lōō tē/shǐ əm), *n. Chem.* a rare-earth, trivalent, metallic element. *Symbol:* Lu; *at. wt.:* 174.99; *at. no.:* 71. Also, **lu·te/ti·um.** [NL, der. L *Lutetia* Paris]

lu·te·o·lin (lōō/tǐ ə lĭn), *n. Chem.* a yellow coloring matter obtained from the weed, *Reseda Luteola;* used in dyeing silk, etc., and formerly in medicine. [t. F: m. *lutéoline,* der. L *lūteolus* yellowish]

lu·te·ous (lōō/tǐ əs), *adj.* yellow, generally orangish or reddish. [t. L: m. *lūteus* golden-yellow]

Luth., Lutheran.

Lu·ther (lōō/thər; *Ger.* lŏŏt/ər), *n.* **Martin** (mär/tēn), 1483–1546, German leader of the Protestant Reformation; a theological writer, and translator of the Bible.

Lu·ther·an (lōō/thər ən), *adj.* 1. of or pertaining to Luther, adhering to his doctrines, or belonging to one of the Protestant churches which bears his name. —*n.* 2. a follower of Luther, or an adherent of his doctrines; a member of the Lutheran Church. —**Lu/ther·an·ism,** *n.*

lu·thern (lōō/thərn), *n.* a dormer window.

lut·ist (lōō/tĭst), *n.* 1. a lute player. 2. a maker of lutes.

Lüt·zen (lŭt/sən), *n.* a town in East Germany, near Leipzig: noted for two battles, 1632, 1813. 5739 (1946).

Lüt·zow-Holm Bay (lŭ/tsöf hōlm/), an inlet of the Indian Ocean on the coast of Antarctica between Queen Maud Land and Enderby Land.

lux (lŭks), *n., pl.* **luces** (lōō/sēz). the international unit of illumination, being the illumination received by a surface at a distance of one meter from a light source whose intensity is taken as unity. It equals 0.0929 footcandle, or 1 lumen per square meter. [t. L: light]

Lux., Luxembourg.

lux·ate (lŭk/sāt), *v.t.,* **-ated, -ating.** to put out of joint; dislocate. [t. L: m.s. *luxātus,* pp.] —**lux·a/tion,** *n.*

luxe (lŏŏks, lŭks; *Fr.* lyks), *n.* luxury; elegance: *articles de luxe.* See **de luxe.** [t. F, t. L: m. *luxus*]

Lux·em·bourg (lŭk/səm bûrg/; *Fr.* lyk sän bōōr/), *n.* 1. a grand duchy between Germany, France, and Belgium. 309,000 pop. (est. 1953); 999 sq. mi. 2. the capital of this duchy. 66,382 (est. 1953). 3. a province in SE Belgium: formerly a part of the grand duchy of Luxembourg. 215,129 (est. 1952); 1706 sq. mi. *Cap.:* Arlon. Also, **Lux·em·burg** (lŭk/səm bûrg/; *Ger.* lŏŏk/səm bōōrкн/).

Lux·or (lŭk/sôr), *n.* a town in Upper Egypt, on the Nile: ruins of ancient Thebes. ab. 15,000.

lux·u·ri·ance (lŭg zhŏŏr/ǐ əns, lŭk shŏŏr/-), *n.* the condition of being luxuriant; luxuriant growth or productiveness; rich abundance. Also, **lux·u/ri·an·cy.**

lux·u·ri·ant (lŭg zhŏŏr/ǐ ənt, lŭk shŏŏr/-), *adj.* 1. abundant or exuberant in growth, as vegetation. 2. producing abundantly, as soil. 3. richly abundant, profuse, or superabundant. 4. florid, as imagery or ornamentation. [t. L: s. *luxurians,* ppr., growing rank] —**lux·u/ri·ant·ly,** *adv.*

lux·u·ri·ate (lŭg zhŏŏr/ǐ āt/, lŭk shŏŏr/-), *v.i.,* **-ated, -ating.** 1. to indulge in luxury; revel; enjoy oneself without stint. 2. to take great delight. [t. L: m.s. *luxuriātus,* pp., grown exuberantly, indulged to excess] —**lux·u/ri·a/tion,** *n.*

lux·u·ri·ous (lŭg zhŏŏr/ǐ əs, lŭk shŏŏr/-), *adj.* 1. characterized by luxury; ministering or conducing to luxury: *a luxurious hotel.* 2. given or inclined to luxury. —**lux·u/ri·ous·ly,** *adv.* —**lux·u/ri·ous·ness,** *n.*

lux·u·ry (lŭk/shə rǐ), *n., pl.* **-ries.** 1. anything conducive to sumptuous living, usually a delicacy, elegance, or refinement of living rather than a necessity. 2. any form or means of enjoyment. 3. free indulgence in sumptuous living, costly food, clothing, comforts, etc. 4. the means of luxurious enjoyment or sumptuous living. [ME *luxurie* lust, t. L: m. *luxuria*]

Lu·zern (lōō tsĕrn/), *n.* German name of **Lucerne.**

Lu·zon (lōō zŏn/; *Sp.* lōō sôn/), *n.* the chief island of the Philippine Islands, in the N part of the group. 9,073,655 pop. (1948); 40,420 sq. mi. *Cap.:* Manila.

lv., leave; leaves. 2. livre; livres.

Lwów (lvōōf), *n.* a city in the SW Soviet Union: formerly in Poland. 387,000 (est. 1956). German, **Lemberg.** Russian, **Lvov** (lvôf).

LXX, Septuagint.

-ly, 1. the normal adverbial suffix, added to almost any descriptive adjective, e.g., *gladly, gradually.* 2. the adverbial suffix applied to units of time meaning "per," e.g., *hourly.* [ME *-li, -lich(e),* OE *-līce,* der. *-lic.* See def. 3] 3. adjective suffix meaning "like," e.g., *saintly, manly.* [ME *-li, -ly, lich(e),* OE *-līc,* c. G *-lich,* repr. a Gmc. noun (OE *līc,* etc.) meaning body. See **LIKE**[1]] —**Syn.** 3. See **-ish**[1].

ly·ard (lǐ/ərd), *adj. Brit. Dial.* of a streaked gray. Also, **ly·art** (lǐ/ərt). [ME, t. OF: m. *liart;* of obscure orig.]

Lyau·tey (lyō tě/), *n.* **Louis Hubert Gonzalve** (lwē y bĕr/ gôN zalv/), 1854–1934, marshal of France, administrator in Morocco.

ly·can·thrope (lǐ/kən thrōp/, lǐ kăn/thrōp), *n.* 1. a person affected with lycanthropy. 2. a werewolf or alien spirit in the physical form of a bloodthirsty wolf. [t. Gk.: m.s. *lykánthrōpos,* lit., wolf-man]

ly·can·thro·py (lǐ kǎn/thrə pǐ), *n.* 1. a kind of insanity in which the patient imagines himself to be a wolf or other wild beast. 2. the supposed or fabled assumption of the form of a wolf by a human being. —**ly·can·throp·ic** (lǐ/kən thrŏp/ǐk), *adj.*

Ly·ca·on (lǐ kā/ŏn), *n. Gk. Myth.* an Arcadian king who tested the divinity of the disguised Zeus by offering him a plate of human flesh. As punishment, Zeus turned him into a wolf.

Lyc·a·o·ni·a (lǐk/ǐ ō/nǐ ə), *n.* an ancient country in S Asia Minor: later a Roman province.

ly·cée (lē sě/), *n.* (in France) a secondary school maintained by the state. [F, t. L: m.s. *Lycēum* **LYCEUM**]

ly·ce·um (lǐ sē/əm), *n.* 1. *U.S.* an association for discussion and popular instruction by lectures and other means. 2. a building, hall, or the like, devoted to instruction by lectures; a library, etc. 3. (*cap.*) a public place with covered walks outside of ancient Athens, where Aristotle taught. 4. (*cap.*) the Aristotelian or Peripatetic school of philosophy. 5. lycée. [t. L, t. Gk.: m. *Lýkeion* the Lyceum at Athens (so named from the neighboring temple of Apollo), prop. neut. of *Lý́keios* an epithet of Apollo]

lych gate (lǐch), lich gate.

lych·nis (lǐk/nǐs), *n.* any of the showy-flowered plants constituting the caryophyllaceous genus *Lychnis,* as *L. chalcedonica* (**scarlet lychnis**), cultivated for its flowers, and *L. coronaria,* the rose campion. [t. L, t. Gk.]

Ly·ci·a (lǐsh/ǐ ə), *n.* an ancient country in SW Asia Minor: later a Roman province.

Ly·ci·an (lǐsh/ǐ ən), *adj.* 1. of or pertaining to Lycia. —*n.* 2. an inhabitant of Lycia. 3. the language of Lycia, probably related to the cuneiform Hittite.

Lyc·i·das (lǐs/ə dəs), *n.* an elegy (1637) by Milton in memory of his college mate, Edward King.

ly·co·po·di·um (lǐ/kə pō/dǐ əm), *n.* any plant of the genus *Lycopodium,* which comprises erect or creeping, usually mosslike, evergreen-leaved pteridophytic plants, as *L. clavatum,* the common club moss, and *L. obscurum,* the ground pine, both much used in Christmas decorations. Also, **ly·co·pod** (lǐ/kə pŏd/). [t. NL: f. m. Gk. *lýko(s)* wolf + *-podium* -**PODIUM**]

Ly·cur·gus (lǐ kûr/gəs), *n.* fl. 9th? century B.C., political reformer of Sparta, reputed founder of Spartan constitution.

lydd·ite (lǐd/īt), *n.* a high explosive consisting chiefly of picric acid. [named after *Lydd,* in Kent, England. See -**ITE**[1]]

Lyd·i·a (lǐd/ǐ ə), *n.* an ancient kingdom in W Asia Minor: under Croesus, a wealthy empire including most of Asia Minor.

Lyd·i·an (lǐd/ǐ ən), *adj.* 1. of or pertaining to Lydia. 2. (of music) softly or sensuously sweet; voluptuous. —*n.* 3. an inhabitant of Lydia. 4. the language of Lydia, probably Anatolian.

lye (lǐ), *n.* any solution resulting from leaching, percolation, or the like. [ME *lie, ley,* OE *lēag,* c. G *lauge*]

Ly·ell (lǐ/əl), *n.* **Sir Charles,** 1797–1875, British geologist.

ly·ing[1] (lǐ/ǐng), *n.* 1. the telling of lies; untruthfulness. —*adj.* 2. that lies; untruthful; false. [der. **LIE**[1]. See -**ING**[1], -**ING**[2]]

ly·ing[2] (lǐ/ǐng), *v.* pres. part. of **lie.**

ly·ing-in (lǐ/ǐng ǐn/), *n.* 1. confinement in childbed. —*adj.* 2. pertaining to childbirth: *a lying-in hospital.*

Ly·ly (lǐl/ǐ), *n.* **John,** 1554?–1606, English writer of romances and plays. See **euphuism.**

lymph (lǐmf), *n. Anat., Physiol.* a clear yellowish, slightly alkaline fluid (which may be regarded as dilute blood minus the red corpuscles) derived from the tissues of the body and conveyed to the blood stream by the lymphatic vessels. [t. L: s. *lympha* water]

lymph-, a combining form of **lymph,** as in *lymphoid.*

lym·phad (lǐm/făd), *n.* a galley with one mast and usually a yard upon it.

lym·phad·e·ni·tis (lǐm făd/ə nǐ/tǐs, lǐm/fə də-), *n. Pathol.* inflammation of a lymphatic gland. [f. **LYMPH-** + **ADEN-** + -**ITIS**]

lym·phan·gi·al (lǐm făn/jǐ əl), *adj.* relating to the lymphatic vessels.

lym·phan·gi·i·tis (lǐm făn/jǐ ǐ/tǐs), *n. Pathol.* inflammation of the lymphatic vessels. [t. NL, f. *lymph-* **LYMPH-** + m. Gk. *angei(on)* vessel + -*itis* -**ITIS**]

lym·phat·ic (lǐm făt/ǐk), *adj.* 1. pertaining to, containing, or conveying lymph: *a lymphatic vessel.* 2. noting, pertaining to, or having a temperament characterized by sluggishness of thought and action, formerly supposed to be due to an excess of lymph in the system. —*n.* 3. a lymphatic vessel. [t. NL: s. *lymphāticus* pertaining to lymph. Cf. L *lymphāticus* mad]

lymph cell, lymphocyte.

lymph gland, any of the glandlike bodies occurring in the lymphatic vessels and supposed to be a source of leucocytes. Also, **lymph node, lymphatic gland.**

lympho-, var. of **lymph-,** before consonants.

lym·pho·cyte (lĭm′fə sīt′), *n. Anat.* a leucocyte formed in lymphoid tissues, with little cytoplasm and no cytoplasmic granules. Their numbers are increased in certain diseases such as tuberculosis and typhoid fever. Also, **lymph cell.**

lymph·oid (lĭm′foid), *adj.* **1.** resembling, of the nature of, or pertaining to, lymph. **2.** noting or pertaining to a tissue (**lymphoid tissue**) forming the greater part of the lymphatic glands. **3.** pertaining to a lymphocyte.

Lyrate leaf

lyn·ce·an (lĭn sē′ən), *adj.* **1.** lynxlike. **2.** sharp-sighted.

lynch (lĭnch), *v.t.* to put (a person) to death (by hanging, burning, or otherwise) by some concerted action without authority or process of law, for some offense known or imputed. [see LYNCH LAW] —**lynch′er,** *n.* —**lynch′ing,** *n.* —**Syn.** See **hang.**

Lynch·burg (lĭnch′bûrg), *n.* a city in central Virginia. 54,790 (1960).

lynch law, the administration of summary punishment, esp. death, upon an offender (actual or reputed) by private persons acting in concert without authority of law. [orig. *Lynch's law;* named after the author, Captain William *Lynch,* 1742–1820, of Virginia]

Lynn (lĭn), *n.* a seaport in E Massachusetts, on Massachusetts Bay. 94,478 (1960).

Lyn·wood (lĭn′wŏŏd), *n.* a city in SW California. 31,614 (1960).

lynx (lĭngks), *n., pl.* **lynxes,** (*esp. collectively*) **lynx.** any of various wildcats of the genus *Lynx,* having long limbs and short tail, and usually with tufted ears, as *L. rufus,* the **bay lynx,** a common North American species, and *L. canadensis,* a large, densely furred species of Canada and the northern U.S. [ME, t. L, t. Gk.] —**lynx′like′,** *adj.*

Bay lynx, *Lynx rufus*
(3 ft. long)

lynx-eyed (lĭngks′īd′), *adj.* sharp-sighted.

Ly·on (lī′ən), *n.* **Mary,** 1797–1849, U.S. leader in education for women: founder of Mount Holyoke College.

Ly·on·nais (lē ô nĕ′), *n.* a former province in E France.

ly·on·naise (lī′ə nāz′; *Fr.* lē ô nĕz′), *adj.* (of food, esp. fried potatoes) cooked with pieces of onion. [t. F]

Ly·on·nesse (lī′ə nĕs′), *n. Arthurian Romance.* the mythical region where Sir Tristram was born, located near Cornwall in SW England, and supposed to have been submerged by the sea. [t. OF: m. *Leonois*]

Ly·ons (lī′ənz), *n.* a city in E France at the confluence of the Rhone and Saône rivers. 471,270 (1954). French, **Lyon** (lyôṉ).

ly·oph·il·ize (lī ŏf′ə līz), *v.t.,* **-ized, -izing.** to freeze-dry.

Ly·ra (lī′rə), *n. Astron.* a northern constellation, containing Vega, one of the brightest stars in the sky. [t. L, t. Gk.: lyre]

ly·rate (lī′rāt, -rĭt), *adj.* **1.** *Bot.* (of a pinnate leaf) divided transversely into several lobes, the smallest at the base. See the illus. above. **2.** *Zool.* lyre-shaped, as the tail of certain birds. Also, **ly′rat·ed.**

lyre (līr), *n.* **1.** a musical instrument of ancient Greece, consisting of a sound box (usually a turtle shell), with two curving arms carrying a cross bar (yoke) from which strings are stretched to the body, used to accompany the voice in singing and recitation. **2.** (*cap.*) *Astron.* Lyra. [ME *lire,* t. OF, t. L: m. *lyra,* t. Gk.]

Woman playing an ancient Greek lyre

lyre-bird (līr′bûrd′), *n.* an Australian passerine bird of the genus *Menura,* the male of which has a long tail which is lyrate when spread. See illus. in next column.

lyr·ic (lĭr′ĭk), *adj.* Also, **lyr′i·cal. 1.** (of poetry) having the form and musical quality of a song, and esp. the character of a songlike outpouring of the poet's own thoughts and feelings (as distinguished from *epic* and *dramatic* poetry, with their more extended and set forms and their presentation of external subjects). **2.** pertaining to or writing such poetry: *a lyric poet.* **3.** characterized by or indulging in a spontaneous, ardent expression of feeling. **4.** pertaining to, rendered by, or employing singing. **5.** pertaining, adapted, or sung to the lyre, or composing poems to be sung to the lyre: *ancient Greek lyric odes.* **6.** (of a voice) relatively light of volume and modest in range (most suited for graceful, cantabile melody). —*n.* **7.** a lyric poem. **8.** *Colloq.* the words of a song. [t. L: s. *lyricus,* t. Gk.: m. *lyrikós* of a lyre] —**lyr′i·cal·ly,** *adv.* —**lyr′i·cal·ness,** *n.*

Lyrebird.
Menura superba
(Total length ab. 3 ft.,
tail ab. 1½ ft.)

lyr·i·cism (lĭr′ə sĭz′əm), *n.* **1.** lyric character or style, as in poetry. **2.** lyric outpouring of feeling; emotionally expressed enthusiasm.

lyr·i·cist (lĭr′ə sĭst′), *n.* **1.** a lyric poet. **2.** one who writes the words for songs.

lyr·ism (lĭr′ĭzəm), *n.* **1.** lyricism. **2.** lyric enthusiasm.

lyr·ist (lir′ĭst *for 1;* lĭr′ĭst *for 2*), *n.* **1.** one who plays on the lyre. **2.** a lyric poet.

Lys (lēs), *n.* a river flowing from N France through W Belgium into the Scheldt river at Ghent. ab. 100 mi.

Ly·san·der (lī săn′dər), *n.* died 395 B.C., Spartan naval commander and statesman.

lyse (līs), *v.,* **lysed, lysing.** *Immunol., Biochem.* —*v.t.* **1.** to cause dissolution or destruction of cells in by lysing. —*v.i.* **2.** to undergo lysis. [back formation from LYSIN]

Lys·i·as (lĭs′ĭ əs), *n.* c450–c380 B.C., Athenian orator.

Ly·sim·a·chus (lī sĭm′ə kəs), *n.* c360–281 B.C., Macedonian general and king of Thrace, 306–281 B.C.

ly·sin[1] (lī′sĭn), *n. Immunol., Biochem.* an antibody which disintegrates the bacterial cell (bacteriolysis) or the red blood cell (hemolysis). [special use of LYSIN(E)]

ly·sin[2] (lī′sĭn), *n.* lysine.

ly·sine (lī′sēn, -sĭn), *n. Biochem.* an amino acid essential for animal growth, $C_6H_{14}N_2O_2$, formed by hydrolyzing many of the proteins. Also, **lysin.** [f. s. Gk. *lýsis* a loosening + -IN[2]]

Ly·sip·pus (lī sĭp′əs), *n.* fl. c360–c316 B.C., Greek sculptor.

ly·sis (lī′sĭs), *n.* **1.** *Immunol., Biochem.* the dissolution or destruction of cells by lysins. **2.** *Med.* the gradual recession of a disease, as distinguished from the crisis, in which the change is abrupt. [NL, t. Gk.: a loosing]

-lysis, a word element, especially scientific, meaning breaking down, decomposition, as in *analysis, electrolysis.* [t. Gk. See LYSIS]

Ly·sol (lī′sôl, -sŏl), *n. Trademark.* a clear, brown, oily liquid, a solution of cresols in soap: used as a disinfectant and antiseptic. [f. s. Gk. *lýsis* solution + -OL[2]]

lys·so·pho·bi·a (lĭs′ə fō′bĭ ə), *n. Psychiatry.* an obsessive fear of losing the mind; dread of insanity. [f. s. Gk. *lýssa* rage, rabies + -(o)PHOBIA]

-lyte, a word element denoting something subjected to a certain process (indicated by a noun ending in *-lysis*), as in *electrolyte.* [t. Gk.: m. *-lytos* that may be or is loosed]

lyth·ra·ceous (lĭth rā′shəs, lĭ thrā′-), *adj.* belonging to the *Lythraceae,* or loosestrife family of plants.

lyt·ic (lĭt′ĭk), *adj.* pertaining to *lyte* or *-lysis,* especially adapted in biochemistry to hydrolytic enzyme action. [independent use of -LYTIC]

-lytic, a termination of adjectives corresponding to nouns in *-lysis,* as in *analytic (analysis), paralytic (paralysis).* [t. Gk.: m.s. *-lytikós*]

lyt·ta (lĭt′ə), *n., pl.* **lyttas, lyttae** (lĭt′ē). a long, wormlike cartilage in the tongue of the dog and other carnivorous animals.

Lyt·ton (lĭt′ən), *n.* **1. Edward George Earle Lytton Bulwer-Lytton,** 1st Baron, 1803–73, British novelist, dramatist, and politician. **2.** his son, **Edward Robert Bulwer-Lytton,** 1st Earl of, (*Owen Meredith*) 1831–91, British diplomatist and poet.

Lyu·blin (lyŏŏ′blĭn), *n.* Russian name of Lublin.

-lyze, a word element making verbs of processes represented by nouns in *-lysis,* e.g., *catalyze.* [b. -LY(SIS) and -(I)ZE]

M

M (ĕm), *n., pl.* **M's** or **Ms, m's** or **ms. 1.** a consonant, the 13th letter of the English alphabet. **2.** the Roman numeral for 1000. **3.** *Print.* em.

M, 1. Medieval. **2.** Middle. Also **m**

M., 1. Majesty. **2.** Manitoba. **3.** (L *meridies*) noon.

4. Monday. **5.** (*pl.* **MM.**) Monsieur. **6.** mountain.

m., 1. male. **2.** mark (German money). **3.** married. **4.** masculine. **5.** *Mech.* mass. **6.** medium. **7.** (L *meridies*) noon. **8.** meter. **9.** mile. **10.** minim. **11.** minute. **12.** modification of. **13.** month. **14.** morning.

---

b., blend of, blended; c., cognate with; d., dialect, dialectal; der., derived from; f., formed from; g., going back to; m., modification of; r., replacing; s., stem of; t., taken from; ?, perhaps.   See the full key on inside cover.

M'-, Mac.

m-, *Chem.* abridgment of **meta-** (def. 2).

ma (mä), *n. Colloq.* mamma; mother.

Ma, *Chem.* masurium.

M.A., 1. (L *Magister Artium*) Master of Arts. 2. Military Academy.

ma'am (măm, mäm; *unstressed* məm), *n.* 1. *Colloq.* madam. 2. *Brit.* the term of address used to the Queen or to a royal princess.

Maas (mäs), *n.* Dutch name for the part of the **Meuse** river in the Netherlands.

Maas·tricht (mäs'trĭkнt), *n.* a city in SE Netherlands, on the Maas river. 83,644 (est. 1954). Also, **Maestricht.**

Mab·i·no·gi·on (măb'ə nō'gĭ ən), *n.* The, a collection of medieval Welsh romances which were translated (1838–1849) by Lady Charlotte Guest.

Mac, a prefix found in many family names of Irish or Scottish Gaelic origin. Also written **Mc-, Mc-,** and **M'-.** [t. Irish and Gaelic: son]

ma·ca·bre (mə kä'bər, -brə), *adj.* 1. gruesome; horrible; grim; ghastly. 2. of or suggestive of the allegorical dance of death (**danse macabre**) in which a skeleton Death leads people to the grave. Also, **ma·ca'ber.** [ME, t. F. ? ult. t. Ar.: m. *maqbara* graveyard]

mac·ad·am (mə kăd'əm), *n.* 1. a macadamized road or pavement. 2. the broken stone used in making such a road. [named after J. L. *McAdam* (1756–1836), Scottish inventor]

mac·ad·am·ize (mə kăd'ə mīz'), *v.t.,* **-ized, -izing.** to construct (a road) by laying and rolling successive layers of broken stone. —**mac·ad'am·i·za'tion,** *n.*

Ma·cao (mə kou'), *n.* 1. a Portuguese overseas territory in S China, on a peninsula of **Macao island** and two small adjacent islands at the mouth of the Chu-Kiang. 187,772 pop. (1950); 6 sq. mi. 2. the seaport and capital of this territory. 166,544 (1950). Portuguese, **Ma·cá·u** (mekä'ŏŏ).

ma·caque (mə kăk'), *n.* any monkey of the genus *Macaca,* chiefly found in Asia, characterized by cheek pouches and, generally, a short tail. [t. F, t. Pg.: m. *macaco,* t. Afr. (Congo)]

mac·a·ro·ni (măk'ə rō'nĭ), *n., pl.* **-nis, -nies.** 1. a kind of paste of Italian origin, prepared from wheat flour, in the form of dried, hollow tubes, to be cooked for food. 2. an English dandy of the 18th century who affected foreign ways. Also, **maccaroni.** [t. It.: m. *maccaroni,* now *maccheroni,* pl. of *maccarone,* now *maccherone,* ult. der. LGk. *makaría* food of broth and pearl barley, orig. happiness]

Pig-tailed macaque. *Macaca nemestrina* (Total length 2½ ft., tail 7 to 9 in.)

mac·a·ron·ic (măk'ə rŏn'ĭk), *adj.* Also, **mac'a·ron'·i·cal.** 1. characterized by a mixture of Latin words with words from another language, or with non-Latin words provided with Latin terminations, as a kind of burlesque verse. 2. involving a mixture of languages. 3. mixed; jumbled. —*n.* 4. (*pl.*) macaronic verses. [t. ML: s. *macarōnicus,* der. It. *maccaroni* MACARONI] —**mac'a·ron'i·cal·ly,** *adv.*

mac·a·roon (măk'ə rōōn'), *n.* a sweet drop cooky made of egg whites, sugar, little or no flour, and frequently almond paste, coconut, etc. [t. F: m. *macaron,* t. It.: m. *maccarone,* sing., MACARONI]

Mac·Ar·thur (mək är'thər), *n.* Douglas, 1880–1964, U.S. general.

Ma·cas·sar (mə kăs'ər), *n.* 1. a seaport in Indonesia, on SW Celebes island. 100,000 (est. 1951). 2. Strait of, a strait between Borneo and Celebes: naval engagement between the Allies and the Japanese, Jan., 1942. Dutch, **Makassar.**

Macassar oil, 1. (originally) an oil for the hair stated to be made from materials obtained from Macassar. 2. a similar oil or preparation for the hair.

Ma·cau·lay (mə kô'lĭ), *n.* 1. Rose, 1889?–1958, British novelist and poet. 2. Thomas Babington Macaulay, Baron, 1800–59, British essayist, historian, poet, and statesman.

ma·caw (mə kô'), *n.* any of various large, long-tailed parrots, chiefly of the genus *Ara,* of tropical and subtropical America, noted for their brilliant plumage and harsh voice. [t. Pg.: m. *macao;* of Brazilian orig.]

Mac·beth (măk bĕth', măk-), *n.* a tragedy (first played in 1606) by Shakespeare.

Mac·ca·bae·us (măk'ə bē'əs), *n.* Judas (jōō'dəs), a Jewish patriot, a leader of the Maccabees.

Mac·ca·be·an (măk'ə bē'ən), *adj.* of or pertaining to the Maccabees or to Judas Maccabaeus.

Mac·ca·bees (măk'ə bēz'), *n. pl.* 1. a family of heroes, deliverers of Judea during the Syrian persecutions of 175–164 B.C. 2. the last two books of the Apocrypha, recording the struggle of the Maccabees.

mac·ca·boy (măk'ə boi'), *n.* a kind of snuff, usually rose-scented. Also, **mac'co·boy'.** [m. *Macouba,* name of district in Martinique]

mac·ca·ro·ni (măk'ə rō'nĭ), *n., pl.* **-nis, -nies.** macaroni.

Mac·don·ald (mək dŏn'əld), *n.* 1. George, 1824–

1905, Scottish novelist and poet. 2. Sir John Alexander, 1815–91, Canadian statesman; prime minister, 1867–73 and 1878–91.

Mac·Don·ald (mək dŏn'əld), *n.* James Ramsay, 1866–1937, British labor leader and statesman; prime minister in 1924 and 1929–35.

Mac·Don·ough (mək dŏn'ə), *n.* Thomas, 1783–1825, U.S. naval officer: defeated British on Lake Champlain, 1814.

Mac·Dow·ell (mək dou'əl), *n.* Edward Alexander, 1861–1908, U.S. composer and pianist.

mace[1] (mās), *n.* 1. *Hist.* a clublike weapon of war often with a flanged or spiked metal head. 2. a staff borne before or by certain officials as a symbol of office. 3. the bearer of such a staff. 4. *Billiards.* a light stick with a flat head, formerly used at times instead of a cue. [ME, t. OF. Cf. L *mateola* mallet]

mace[2] (mās), *n.* a spice ground from the layer between a nutmeg shell and its outer husk, resembling nutmeg in flavor. [ME *macis,* t. OF, t. L: m. *mac(c)is* a spice]

mace·bear·er (mās'bâr'ər), *n.* macer.

Maced., Macedonia.

mac·é·doine (măs'ĭ dwän'; *Fr.* mȧ sĕ dwän'), *n.* 1. a mixture of vegetables, served as a salad or otherwise. 2. a jellied mixture of fruits. 3. a medley. [t. F: lit., Macedonian]

Mac·e·don (măs'ə dŏn'), *n.* Macedonia (def. 1).

Mac·e·do·ni·a (măs'ə dō'nĭ ə), *n.* 1. an ancient country in the Balkan Peninsula, N of ancient Greece. 2. a region in S Europe, including parts of Greece, Bulgaria, and Yugoslavia. —**Mac'e·do'ni·an,** *adj., n.*

Ma·cei·ó (mä'sā ô'). *n.* a seaport in E Brazil. 102,300 (est. 1952).

Macedonia (def. 2)

mac·er (mā'sər), *n.* one who bears a mace[1] (def. 2). [ME *masere,* t. OF: m. *maissier,* der. *masse* MACE[1]]

mac·er·ate (măs'ə rāt'), *v.,* **-ated, -ating.** —*v.t.* 1. to soften, or separate the parts of (a substance) by steeping in a liquid, with or without heat. 2. to soften or break up (food) by action of a solvent. 3. to cause to grow thin. —*v.i.* 4. to undergo maceration. 5. to become thin; waste away. [t. L: m.s. *mācerātus,* pp.] —**mac'er·at'er, mac'er·a'tor,** *n.* —**mac'er·a'-tion,** *n.*

mach., 1. machine. 2. machinery. 3. machinist.

mach (mŏk), *n.* a unit of velocity equal to the velocity of sound in the medium, usually air; mach 1 in air is about 730 miles per hour at sea level. [named after Ernst *Mach* (1838–1916), Austrian physicist]

Ma·cha·do (mä chä'dô), *n.* Gerardo (hĕ rär'dô), (*Gerardo Machado y Morales*) 1871–1939, president of Cuba, 1925–33.

Mach·en (măk'ən), *n.* Arthur, 1863–1947, British novelist and essayist.

ma chère (mȧ shĕr'), *French.* my dear (fem.).

ma·che·te (mä chā'tā, mə shĕt'; *Sp.* mä chĕ'tĕ), *n.* a large, heavy knife used esp. in Spanish-American countries as both a tool and a weapon. [t. Sp., ult. der. L *mactāre* slaughter]

Mach·i·a·vel·li (măk'ĭ ə vĕl'ĭ; *It.* mä'kyä vĕl'lē), *n.* Niccolò di Bernardo (nĕk'kô lô' dē bĕr när'dô), 1469–1527, Italian statesman and writer on government.

Mach·i·a·vel·li·an (măk'ĭ ə vĕl'ĭ ən), *adj.* 1. of, like, or befitting Machiavelli. 2. being or acting in accordance with Machiavelli's political doctrines, which placed expediency above political morality, and countenanced the use of craft and deceit in order to maintain the authority and effect the purposes of the ruler. 3. characterized by subtle or unscrupulous cunning; wily; astute. —*n.* 4. a follower of Machiavelli or his doctrines. Also, **Mach'i·a·vel'i·an.** —**Mach'i·a·vel'li·an·ism, Mach'i·a·vel'lism,** *n.*

ma·chic·o·lat·ed (mə chĭk'ə lā'tĭd), *adj.* furnished with machicolations. [f. s. ML *machicolātus,* pp., + -ED[2]]

ma·chic·o·la·tion (mə chĭk'ə lā'shən), *n. Archit.* 1. an opening in the floor between the corbels of a projecting gallery or parapet, as on a wall or in the vault of a passage, through which missiles, molten lead, etc., might be cast upon an enemy beneath. 2. a projecting gallery or parapet with such openings.

mach·i·nate (măk'ə nāt'), *v.,* **-nated, -nating.** to contrive or devise, esp. artfully or with evil purpose. [t. L: m.s. *māchinātus,* pp.] —**mach'i·na'tor,** *n.*

mach·i·na·tion (măk'ə nā'shən), *n.* 1. the act or process of machinating. 2. (*usually pl.*) a crafty scheme; evil design; plot.

ma·chine (mə shēn'), *n., v.,* **-chined, -chining.** —*n.* 1. an apparatus consisting of interrelated parts with separate functions, which is used in the performance of some kind of work: *a sewing*

A. Machicolation; B. Parapet; C. Corbels

machine. **2.** a mechanical apparatus or contrivance; a mechanism. **3.** something operated by a mechanical apparatus, as an automobile, a bicycle, or an airplane. **4.** *Mech.* **a.** a device which transmits and modifies force or motion. **b. simple machines,** the six (sometimes more) elementary mechanisms: the lever, wheel and axle, pulley, screw, wedge, and inclined plane. **5.** a contrivance, esp. in the ancient theater, for producing stage effects. **6. some agency, personage, incident, or other** feature introduced for effect into a literary composition. **7.** any complex agency or operating system: *the machine of government.* **8.** the body of persons conducting and controlling the activities of a political party or other organization. **9.** a person or agency acting like a mere mechanical apparatus. —*v.t.* **10.** to make, prepare, or finish with a machine. [t. F, t. L: m. *māchĭna,* t. d. Gk.: m. *māchĭnē,* Attic Gk. *mēchanē*]

machine gun, a small arm operated by a mechanism, able to deliver a rapid and continuous fire of bullets as long as the firer keeps pressure on the trigger.

ma·chine-gun (mə·shēn′gŭn′), *v.t.,* -gunned, -gunning. to shoot at, using a machine gun.

ma·chin·er·y (mə·shē′nə·rĭ), *n., pl.* -eries. **1.** machines or mechanical apparatus. **2.** the parts of a machine, collectively: *the machinery of a watch.* **3.** contrivances for producing stage effects. **4.** personages, incidents, etc., introduced into a literary composition, as in developing a story or plot. **5.** any system by which action is maintained: *the machinery of government.*

machine shop, a workshop in which metal and other substances are cut, shaped, etc., by machine tools.

machine tool, a power-operated machine, as a lathe, etc., used for general cutting and shaping operations.

ma·chin·ist (mə·shē′nĭst), *n.* **1.** a person who operates machinery, esp. a highly trained and skilled operator of machine tools. **2.** one who makes and repairs machines. **3.** *U.S. Navy.* a warrant officer whose duty is to assist the engineer officer in the engine room. **4.** a person who builds or operates machinery in a theater.

Mach number (mŏk), a number indicating the ratio between the air speed of an object and the speed of sound at a given altitude, etc.

-machy, a combining form meaning combat, as in *logomachy.* [t. Gk.: m. s. *-machia,* der. *-machos* fighting]

mac·in·tosh (măk′ĭn·tŏsh′), *n.* mackintosh.

Mack·en·sen (măk′ən·zən), *n.* **August von** (ou′gōost fən), 1849–1945, German field marshal.

Mac·ken·zie (mə·kĕn′zĭ), *n.* **1. Sir Alexander,** 1755?–1820, Scottish explorer in Canada. **2. William Lyon,** 1795–1861, Canadian political leader and journalist, born in Scotland. **3.** a river in NW Canada, flowing from the Great Slave Lake NW to the Arctic Ocean. ab. 900 mi.; with tributaries, ab. 2525 mi. **4.** a district in NW Canada, in the SW part of the Northwest Territories. 527,490 sq. mi.

mack·er·el (măk′ər·əl), *n., pl.* **-el,** (*occasionally, esp. with reference to different species*) **-els. 1.** an abundant food fish of the North Atlantic, *Scomber scombrus,* with wavy cross markings on the back and streamlined for swift swimming. **2.** Spanish mackerel. **3.** any of various other streamlined fishes, as the Atka mackerel, *Pleuropterygius monopterygius,* of the Aleutian Islands. [ME *makerel,* t. OF: m. *maquerel;* orig. unknown]

mackerel sky, 1. a sky spotted with small white fleecy clouds. **2.** an extensive group of cirro-cumulus or alto-cumulus clouds, esp. when well-marked in their arrangement.

Mack·i·nac (măk′ə·nô′), *n.* **1. Strait of,** a strait joining Lakes Michigan and Huron. Least width, 4 mi. **2.** an island in Lake Huron at the entrance of this strait: Michigan state park; summer resort. 3 mi. long. **3.** a town on this island.

mack·i·naw (măk′ə·nô′), *n.* a Mackinaw coat. [shortened form of *Michilli-mackinaw,* name of an island near the strait connecting Lakes Michigan and Huron; said to mean turtle in Ojibwa; cf. *mícimakinak* big turtle]

Mackinaw blanket, a kind of thick blanket, often woven with bars of color, formerly much used in the northern and western U.S. by Indians, lumbermen, etc.

Mackinaw boat, a flat-bottomed boat with sharp prow and square stern, propelled by oars and sometimes sails, as used on the upper Great Lakes.

Mackinaw coat, a short coat of a thick, blanket-like, commonly plaid, woolen material.

Mackinaw trout, the lake trout.

mack·in·tosh (măk′ĭn·tŏsh′), *n.* **1.** a raincoat made of cloth rendered waterproof by India rubber. **2.** such cloth. **3.** any raincoat. Also, **macintosh.** [named after Charles *Mackintosh* (1766–1843), the inventor]

mack·le (măk′əl), *n., v.,* -led, -ling. —*n.* **1.** a blur in printing, as from a double impression. —*v.t., v.i.* **2.** to blur, as from a double impression in printing. Also, **macule.** [t. F: m. *macule,* t. L: m. *macula* spot]

Mac·i·ar·en (mə·klär′ən), *n.* **Ian** (ē′ən, ī′ən), pen name of John Watson.

ma·cle (măk′əl), *n. Crystall.* a twin. [t. F, t. L: m. s. *macula* spot]

Mac·Leish (mək·lēsh′), *n.* **Archibald,** b. 1892, U.S. poet.

Mac·leod (mə·kloud′), *n.* **Fiona** (fĭ·ō′nə), pen name of William Sharp.

Mac·Ma·hon (măk·mä·ŏn′), *n.* **Marie Edme Patrice Maurice,** (mȧ·rē′ ĕd′mə pȧ·trēs′ mō·rēs′), **Count de,** (*Duke of Magenta*) 1808–93, president of France, 1873–79.

Mac·Mil·lan (mək·mĭl′ən), *n.* **Donald Baxter,** born 1874, U.S. arctic explorer.

Mac·mil·lan (mək·mĭl′ən), *n.* (*Maurice*) **Harold,** born 1894, British prime minister and first lord of the treasury 1957–63.

Mac·Mon·nies (mək·mŭn′ĭz), *n.* **Frederick William,** 1863–1937, U.S. sculptor and painter.

Ma·con (mā′kən), *n.* a city in central Georgia. 69,764 (1960).

Mac·pher·son (mək·fûr′sən), *n.* **James,** 1736–96, Scottish author or translator of the poems of "Ossian."

Mac·quar·ie (mə·kwôr′ĭ, -kwŏr′ĭ), *n.* a river in SE Australia, in New South Wales, flowing NW to the Darling river. ab. 750 mi.

mac·ra·mé (măk′rə·mā′), *n.* a kind of lace or ornamental work made by knotting thread or cord in patterns. [cf. Turk. *maqrama* towel, handkerchief, etc.]

Mac·rea·dy (mə·krē′dĭ), *n.* **William Charles,** 1793–1873, British tragedian.

macro-, a word element meaning "long," "large," "great," "excessive," used esp. in biology and botany, contrasting with *micro-.* Also, before vowels, **macr-.** [t. Gk.: m. *makro-,* comb. form of *makrós*]

mac·ro·cosm (măk′rə·kŏz′əm), *n.* the great world, or universe (opposed to *microcosm*). [t. F: m. *macrocosme.* t. ML: m.s. *macrocosmus,* f. *macro-* MACRO- + m. Gk. *kósmos* world] —**mac′ro·cos′mic,** *adj.*

mac·ro·cyst (măk′rə·sĭst′), *n.* **1.** a cyst of large size, esp. the archicarp of certain *Discomycetes.* **2.** a multinuclear mass of protoplasm enclosed in a cyst.

mac·ro·cyte (măk′rə·sīt′), *n. Pathol.* an abnormally large red blood cell. —**mac·ro·cyt·ic** (măk′rə·sĭt′ĭk), *adj.*

macrocytic anemia (măk′rə·sĭt′ĭk), *Pathol.* an anemia characterized by predominance of macrocytes.

mac·ro·ga·mete (măk′rō·ɡə·mēt′), *n. Biol.* the female (and larger) of two conjugating gametes.

mac·ro·graph (măk′rə·grăf′, -gräf′), *n.* a photograph or other image equal to or larger than the original.

ma·cron (mā′krŏn, măk′rŏn), *n.* a short horizontal line used as a diacritic over a vowel to indicate that it is a "long" sound, as in *fāte.* [t. Gk.: m. *makrón,* neut., long]

mac·ro·phys·ics (măk′rə·fĭz′ĭks), *n.* the part of physics that deals with physical objects large enough to be observed and treated directly.

mac·ro·scop·ic (măk′rə·skŏp′ĭk), *adj.* visible to the naked eye (opposed to *microscopic*).

mac·ro·spore (măk′rə·spōr′), *n. Bot.* megaspore.

ma·cru·ran (mə·krŏor′ən), *adj.* **1.** belonging or pertaining to the *Macrura,* a group of stalk-eyed decapod crustaceans with long tails, including lobsters, shrimps, etc. —*n.* **2.** a macruran crustacean. [f. s. NL *macrūra,* pl. (f. Gk.: s. *makrós* long + m. *ourá* tail) + -AN]

ma·cru·rous (mə·krŏor′əs), *adj.* long-tailed, as the lobster (opposed to *brachyurous*).

mac·u·la (măk′yə·lə), *n., pl.* **-lae** (-lē′). a spot on the sun, in the skin, or the like. [ME, t. L] —**mac′u·lar,** *adj.*

mac·u·late (*v.* măk′yə·lāt′; *adj.* măk′yə·lĭt), *v.,* -lated, -lating, *adj.* —*v.t.* **1.** to mark with a spot or spots; stain. **2.** to sully or pollute. —*adj.* **3.** spotted; stained. **4.** defiled or impure. [late ME, t. L: m.s. *maculātus,* pp.]

mac·u·la·tion (măk′yə·lā′shən), *n.* **1.** act of spotting. **2.** a spotted condition. **3.** a marking of spots, as on an animal. **4.** a disfiguring spot or stain. **5.** defilement.

mac·ule (măk′ūl), *n., v.t., v.i.,* -uled, -uling. mackle.

mad (măd), *adj.,* **madder, maddest,** *v.,* **madded, madding.** —*adj.* **1.** disordered in intellect; insane. **2.** *Colloq.* moved by anger. **3.** (of wind, etc.) furious in violence. **4.** (of animals) **a.** abnormally furious: *a mad bull.* **b.** affected with rabies; rabid: *a mad dog.* **5.** wildly excited; frantic: *mad haste.* **6.** senselessly foolish or imprudent: *a mad scheme.* **7.** wild with eagerness or desire; infatuated: *to be mad about someone.* **8.** wildly gay or merry: *to have a mad time.* **9. like mad, a.** in the manner of a madman. **b.** with great haste, impetuosity, or enthusiasm. —*v.t.* **10.** *Archaic.* to make mad. —*v.i.* **11.** *Archaic.* to be, become, or act mad. [ME *mad, madd(e),* OE *gemǣd(d), gemǣded,* pp. of a verb der. from OE *gemād* mad, c. OHG *gameit* foolish]

—**Syn. 1.** demented, lunatic, deranged, maniacal. **2.** furious, exasperated, angry. **6.** MAD, CRAZY, INSANE are used to characterize wildly impractical or foolish ideas, actions, etc. MAD suggests senselessness and rashness: *the scheme of selling the bridge was absolutely mad.* CRAZY suggests recklessness and impracticality: *a crazy young couple.* INSANE is used with some opprobrium to express unsoundness and possible harmfulness: *the new traffic system is simply insane.*

Madag., Madagascar.

Mad·a·gas·car (măd′ə·găs′kər), *n.* a former French island colony in the Indian Ocean, ab. 240 mi. off the S E coast of Africa; an independent republic since 1958. See **Malagasy Republic.** —**Mad′a·gas′can,** *n., adj.*

mad·am (măd′əm), *n., pl.* **madams, mesdames** (mā·däm′). **1.** a polite term of address used orig. to a woman of rank or authority, but now used to any woman. **2.** the woman in charge of a brothel. [ME *madame,* t. OF, orig. *ma dame* my lady. See DAME]

mad·ame (măd'əm; *Fr.* mȧ dȧm'), *n.*, *pl.* **mesdames** (mē dȧm'). a conventional French title of respect, orig. for a woman of rank, used distinctively to or of a married woman, either separately or prefixed to the name. *Abbr.*: Mme., *pl.* Mmes. [t. F. See MADAM]

Madame Butterfly, an opera (1904) by Puccini.

Ma·da·ri·a·ga (mä'dä ryä'gä), *n.* Salvador de (säl'-vä dôr' dě), born 1886, Spanish author and diplomat.

mad·cap (măd'kăp'), *adj.* 1. wildly impulsive; lively: *a madcap girl.* —*n.* 2. a madcap person, esp. a girl.

mad·den (măd'ən), *v.t.* 1. to make mad or insane. 2. to infuriate. —*v.i.* 3. to become mad; act as if mad; rage.

mad·den·ing (măd'ən ĭng), *adj.* 1. driving to madness or frenzy. 2. infuriating; exasperating. 3. raging; furious. —**mad'den·ing·ly,** *adv.*

mad·der (măd'ər), *n.* 1. a plant of the rubiaceous genus *Rubia,* esp. *R. tinctorum,* a European herbaceous climbing plant with panicles of small yellowish flowers. 2. the root of this plant, used to some extent (esp. formerly) in medicine, and particularly for making dyes which give red and other colors. 3. the dye or coloring matter itself. 4. a color produced by such a dye. [ME *mad(d)er,* OE *mæd(e)re,* c. Icel. *madhra*]

Mad·dern (măd'ərn), *n.* Minnie. See **Fiske, Mrs.**

mad·ding (măd'ĭng), *adj.* 1. mad; acting as if mad: *the madding crowd.* 2. making mad.

made (mād), *v.* 1. pt. and pp. of **make.** —*adj.* 2. produced by making, preparing, etc. 3. artificially produced. 4. invented or made-up. 5. assured of success or fortune: *a made man.*

Ma·dei·ra (mə dĭr'ə; *Port.* mä dě'rə), *n.* 1. a group of five islands of the NW coast of Africa, belonging to Portugal. 269,769 pop. (1950); 308 sq. mi. *Cap.:* Funchal. 2. the chief island of this group. 266,990 pop. (1950); 286 sq. mi. 3. (*often l.c.*) a rich strong white wine resembling sherry made there. 4. a river flowing from W Brazil NE to the Amazon: the chief tributary of the Amazon. ab. 2100 mi. [t. Pg.: lit., wood, timber, g. L *māteria;* so called because island was once a thick forest]

mad·e·moi·selle (măd'mwȧ zĕl'; *Fr.* mȧd mwȧ zĕl'), *n.*, *pl.* **mesdemoiselles** (*Fr.* mĕd mwȧ zĕl'). the conventional French title of respect for a girl or unmarried woman, either used separately or prefixed to the name. *Abbr.*: Mlle., Mlle. [F., orig. *ma demoiselle* my demoiselle. See DEMOISELLE, DAMSEL]

Ma·de·ro (mä dĕ'rō), *n.* Francisco Indalecio (frän-sēs/kō ēn'dä lě'syō), 1873–1913, president of Mexico, 1911–13.

made-up (mād'ŭp'), *adj.* 1. concocted; invented: *a made-up story.* 2. artificial, as of the complexion. 3. put together; finished.

mad·house (măd'hous'), *n.* 1. an asylum for the insane. 2. a place of commotion and confusion.

Madh·ya Pra·desh (mŭd'yə prə dāsh'), a state in central India. 26,000,000 (est. 1956); 171,201 sq. mi. *Cap.:* Bhopal.

Mad·i·son (măd'ə sən), *n.* 1. James, 1751–1836, 4th president of the U.S., 1809–17. 2. Mrs., (*Dolly Madison,* née *Dorothy Payne*) 1768–1849, wife of James. 3. the capital of Wisconsin, in the S part. 126,706 (1960).

Madison Avenue, a street in New York City on which are concentrated the offices of many advertising and public relations firms and which has, therefore, become a symbol of their attitudes, methods, etc.

mad·ly (măd'lĭ), *adv.* 1. insanely. 2. wildly; furiously: *they worked madly to fix the bridge.* 3. foolishly.

mad·man (măd'măn', -mən), *n.*, *pl.* **-men.** an insane person.

mad·ness (măd'nĭs), *n.* 1. state of being mad; insanity. 2. rabies. 3. senseless folly. 4. frenzy; rage.

Ma·doe·ra (mä dōō'rä), *n.* Dutch name of Madura.

Ma·don·na (mə dŏn'ə), *n.* 1. the Virgin Mary (usually prec. by *the*). 2. a picture or statue representing the Virgin Mary. 3. (*l.c.*) an Italian title of respect for a woman. [t. It.: my lady. See DONNA]

mad·ras (măd'rəs, mə drăs', -dräs'), *n.* 1. a light cotton fabric with cords set at intervals or with woven stripes or figures, often of another color, used for shirts, etc. 2. a thin curtain fabric of a light, gauzelike weave with figures of heavier yarns. 3. a large brightly colored kerchief, of either silk or cotton, often used for turbans. [named after MADRAS]

Ma·dras (mə drăs', -dräs'), *n.* 1. a large state in S India: formerly a presidency; boundaries readjusted in 1956 on a linguistic basis. 30,000,000 (est. 1956); 50,110 sq. mi. 2. a seaport in and the capital of this state, on the Bay of Bengal. 1,416,056 (1951).

ma·dre (mä'drě), *n. Spanish.* mother. [Sp., g. L *māter*]

mad·re·pore (măd'rə pōr'), *n.* any of various corals (**madreporarians**) of the genus *Madrepora,* noted for reef-building in tropical seas. [t. F, t. It.: m. *madrepora,* appar. f. *madre* mother (g. L *māter*) + m. *poro* t. Gk.: m. *pôros* kind of stone)] —**mad·re·por·ic** (măd'rə pōr'ĭk, -pŏr'-), *adj.*

Ma·drid (mə drĭd'; *Sp.* mä drēd'), *n.* the capital of Spain, in the central part. 1,767,698 (est. 1956).

mad·ri·gal (măd'rĭ gəl), *n.* 1. a lyric poem suitable for musical setting, usually short and often of amatory character (esp. in vogue in the 16th century and later in

Madrepore

Italy, France, England, and elsewhere). 2. a part song without instrumental accompaniment, usually for five or six voices, and making abundant use of contrapuntal imitation. 3. any part song. 4. any song. [t. It.: m. *madrigale,* g. L *mātricāle* simple, naïve, der. *mātrix* womb]

mad·ri·gal·ist (măd'rĭ gəl ĭst), *n.* a composer or a singer of madrigals.

ma·dro·ña (mə drō'nyə), *n.* an ericaceous evergreen tree or shrub, *Arbutus Menziesii,* of western North America, having a hard wood and a smooth bark, and bearing a yellow, scarcely edible berry. [t. Sp.: the arbutus or strawberry tree, ult. der. L *mātūrus* ripe]

ma·dro·ño (mə drō'nyō), *n.*, *pl.* **-ños.** madroña.

Ma·du·ra (mä dōōr'ä *for 1,* mäj'ōō rə *for 2*), *n.* 1. Dutch, **Madoera.** an island in Indonesia, off the NE coast of Java. pop. (with Java) 51,637,072 (est. 1955); 2112 sq. mi. 2. a city in S India, in Madras. 361,781 (1951).

ma·du·ro (mə dōōr'ō), *adj.* (of cigars) strong and darkly colored. [t. Sp.: mature, g. L *mātūrus*]

mad·wom·an (măd'wŏom'ən), *n.*, *pl.* **-women.** a mad or insane woman.

mad·wort (măd'wûrt'), *n.* 1. any of several plants, as an alyssum, gold-of-pleasure. 2. a boraginaceous plant, *Asperugo procumbens.*

Mae·an·der (mē ăn'dər), *n.* ancient name of Menderes (def. 1).

Ma·e·ba·shi (mä'ě bä'shě), *n.* a city in central Japan, on Honshu island. 156,898 (1950).

Mae·ce·nas (mē sē'nəs), *n.* 1. Gaius Cilnius (gā'əs sĭl'nĭ əs), between 73 and 63 b.c.–8 b.c., Roman statesman, friend and patron of Vergil and Horace. 2. a generous patron, esp. of the arts.

Mael·strom (māl'strəm), *n.* 1. a famous whirlpool off the NW coast of Norway. 2. (*l.c.*) any great or violent whirlpool. 3. (*l.c.*) a restless confusion of affairs, influence, etc. [t. early mod. D: now spelled *maalstroom,* f. *malen* grind, whirl + *stroom* stream]

mae·nad (mē'năd), *n.*, 1. a female attendant of Bacchus; a bacchante. 2. any frenzied or raging woman. Also, **menad.** [t. L: s. *Maenas,* t. Gk.: m. *mainás* a mad woman] —**mae·nad'ic,** *adj.*

ma·es·to·so (mä'ĕs tô'sō), *adj., adv. Music.* with majesty; stately. [It., der. *maestà* majesty, t. L: m. *mājestas*]

Maes·tricht (mäs'trĭкнt), *n.* Maastricht.

maes·tro (mīs'trō; *It.* mä ĕs'trō), *n.*, *pl.* **-tri** (-trē). 1. an eminent musical composer, teacher, or conductor. 2. a master of any art. [It.: master]

Mae·ter·linck (mā'tər lĭngk'; *Fr.* mȧ tĕr lănk'; *Du.* mä'tər lĭngk'), *n.* Maurice (mō rēs'), 1862–1949, Belgian dramatist, essayist, and poet.

Mae West, an inflatable life-preserver vest for aviators who fall in the sea. [f. *Mae West,* U.S. actress]

Maf·e·king (măf'ə kĭng'), *n.* a town in the N part of the Union of South Africa: administrative seat of the Bechuanaland protectorate; besieged for 217 days by the Boers, 1899–1900. 6870 (1946).

maf·fick (măf'ĭk), *v.i. Brit.* to celebrate with extravagant public demonstrations. [back formation from MAFEKING; the relief of the city was celebrated in London with extravagant joy] —**maf'fick·er,** *n.*

Ma·fi·a (mä'fĭ ä'), *n.* 1. (in Sicily) a. (*l.c.*) a popular spirit of hostility to legal restraint and to the law, often manifesting itself in criminal acts. b. a 19th century secret society (similar to the Camorra in Naples) acting in this spirit. 2. a criminal secret society of Sicilians or other Italians, at home or in foreign countries. Also, **Maf'fi·a.** [t. Sicilian: boldness, bravery, der. *Màffio,* var. of *Maffèo,* t. L: m. *Matthaeus* Matthew]

ma foi (mȧ fwȧ'), *French.* my faith! really!

mag., 1. magazine. 2. magnetism. 3. magnitude.

Ma·gal·la·nes (mä'gä yä'něs), *n.* Punta Arenas.

mag·a·zine (măg'ə zēn', măg'ə zēn'), *n.* 1. a periodical publication, usually bound and with a paper cover, containing miscellaneous articles or pieces, in prose or verse, often with illustrations. 2. a room or place for keeping gunpowder and other explosives, as in a fort or on a warship. 3. a building or place for keeping military stores, as arms, ammunition, provisions, etc. 4. a collection of war munitions. 5. a metal receptacle for a number of cartridges which is inserted into certain types of automatic weapons and which must be removed when empty and replaced by a full receptacle in order to continue firing. 6. a supply chamber in a stove, a camera, etc. 7. a storehouse; warehouse. [t. F: m. *magasin,* t. It.: m. *magazzino* storehouse, t. Ar.: m. *makhāzin,* pl. of *makhzan* storehouse]

mag·a·zin·ist (măg'ə zē'nĭst), *n.* one engaged in magazine work, esp. writing for magazines.

Mag·da·le·na (măg'dä lě'nä), *n.* a river flowing from SW Colombia N to the Caribbean. ab. 1060 mi.

Magdalena Bay, a bay on the SW coast of Lower California, Mexico. ab. 40 mi. long.

Mag·da·lene (măg'də lēn', măg'də lē'ně), *n.* 1. the, Mary Magdalene. Mark 15:40, 16:9; John 20:1–18. 2. (*l.c.*) a reformed prostitute. Also, **Mag·da·len** (măg'də lən).

Mag·da·le·ni·an (măg'də lē'nĭ ən), *adj.* denoting the period or culture stage in the Old World Stone Age (upper Paleolithic) in which Cro-Magnon man reached his highest level of industry and art. [from (La) *Madeleine*, France, where implements and art of this period were found]

Magdalenian period, the most advanced culture of the European paleolithic period, named from discoveries in La Madeleine, France.

Mag·de·burg (măg′də bûrg′; *Ger.* mäg′də bŏŏrкн′), *n.* a city in East Germany. 261,392 (est. 1955).

mage (māj), *n.* *Archaic.* a magician. [ME, t. F, t. L: m.s. *magus*]

Ma·gel·lan (mə jĕl′ən), *n.* **1.** Ferdinand, c1480–1521, Portuguese navigator, discoverer of the Strait of Magellan and the Philippine Islands. **2. Strait of,** a strait near the S tip of South America between the mainland of Chile and Tierra del Fuego and other islands, connecting the Atlantic and Pacific Oceans. ab. 360 mi. long; 2½–17 mi. wide.

Mag·el·lan·ic (măj′ə lăn′ĭk), *adj.* pertaining to or named after Ferdinand Magellan.

Magellanic cloud, *Astron.* either of two bright cloudlike patches of stars in the southern heavens.

ma·gen·ta (mə jĕn′tə), *n.* **1.** fuchsin. **2.** reddish purple. [named after MAGENTA; discovered year of battle.]

Ma·gen·ta (mə jĕn′tə), *n.* a town in N Italy, W of Milan: the French and Sardinians defeated the Austrians here, 1859. 15,294 (1951).

Mag·gio·re (mə jôr′ĭ; *It.* mäd jô′rĕ), *n.* Lago (lä′gô), a lake in N Italy and S Switzerland. 83 sq. mi.

mag·got (măg′ət), *n.* **1.** the legless larva of a fly, as of the housefly. **2.** a fly larva living in decaying matter. **3.** an odd fancy; whim. [ME *magot*; orig. uncert.]

mag·got·y (măg′ətĭ), *adj.* **1.** infested with maggots, as food. **2.** having queer notions; full of whims.

Ma·gi (mā′jī), *n.pl.,* *sing.* **-gus** (-gəs). **1.** (*also l.c.*) the three "wise men" who "came from the east" to Jerusalem to do homage to the infant Jesus. Matt. 2:1–12. **2.** the "Wise Men" or Zoroastrian priests of ancient Media and Persia, reputed to possess supernatural powers. [See MAGUS] —**Ma·gi·an** (mā′jĭ ən), *adj.* —**Ma′gi·an·ism,** *n.*

mag·ic (măj′ĭk), *n.* **1.** the pretended art of producing effects beyond the natural human power by means of supernatural agencies or through command of occult forces in nature. **2.** the exercise of this art. **3.** the effects produced. **4.** power or influence exerted through this art. **5.** any extraordinary or irresistible influence: *the magic in a great name.* **6.** legerdemain; conjuring. —*adj.* Also, **mag′i·cal.** (Note: *magic* is generally not used predicatively, and *magical* is used both predicatively and attributively.) **7.** employed in magic: *magic spells.* **8.** mysteriously enchanting: *magic beauty.* **9.** of, pertaining to, or due to magic: *magic rites.* **10.** producing the effects of magic; like magic. [ME *magike,* t. LL: m. *magica,* in L *magicē,* t. Gk.: m. *magikē,* prop. fem. of *magikós* Magian, magic] —**mag′i·cal·ly,** *adv.* —**Syn. 1.** enchantment. MAGIC, NECROMANCY, SORCERY, WITCHCRAFT imply producing results through mysterious influences or unexplained powers. MAGIC may have glamorous and attractive connotations; the other terms suggest the harmful and sinister. MAGIC is an art of using some occult force of nature: *fifty years ago television would have seemed to be magic.* NECROMANCY is an art of prediction, supposedly because of communicating with the dead (it is called "the black art," because Greek *nekro,* dead, was confused with Latin *niger,* black): *necromancy led to violating graves.* SORCERY, originally divination by casting lots, came to mean supernatural knowledge gained through the aid of evil spirits, and often used for evil ends: *spells and charms used in sorcery.* WITCHCRAFT esp. suggests a malign kind of magic, often used by aged and half-crazed women against innocent victims: *those accused of witchcraft were executed.*

Magic Flute, The, an opera (1791) by Mozart.

ma·gi·cian (mə jĭsh′ən), *n.* **1.** one skilled in magic arts. **2.** a juggler; conjurer. [ME *magicien,* t. OF, der. L *magicus* MAGIC] —**Syn. 1.** sorcerer, necromancer.

magic lantern, a lantern-slide projector.

Magic Mountain, The, a novel (1924, Eng. trans. 1926) by Thomas Mann.

Ma·gi·not line (măzh′ə nō′; *Fr.* má zhē nō′), a zone of French fortifications erected along the French-German border in the years preceding World War II.

mag·is·te·ri·al (măj′ĭs tĭr′ĭ əl), *adj.* **1.** of, pertaining to, or befitting a master; authoritative: *a magisterial pronouncement.* **2.** imperious; domineering. **3.** of or befitting a magistrate or his office. **4.** of the rank of a magistrate. [t. ML: s. *magisteriālis,* der. LL *magisterius,* der. L *magister* MASTER] —**mag·is·te′ri·al·ly,** *adv.*

mag·is·tra·cy (măj′ĭs trə sĭ), *n.,* *pl.* **-cies.** **1.** the office or function of a magistrate. **2.** a body of magistrates. **3.** the district under a magistrate. Also, **mag·is·tra·ture** (măj′ĭs trā′chər).

mag·is·tral (măj′ĭs trəl), *adj.* **1.** *Pharm.* prescribed or prepared for a particular occasion, as a remedy (opposed to *officinal*). **2.** *Fort.* principal. **3.** *Rare.* magisterial. —*n.* **4.** magistral line. [t. L: s. *magistrālis* of a master]

magistral line, *Fort.* the line from which the position of the other lines of fieldworks is determined.

mag·is·trate (măj′ĭs trāt′, -trĭt), *n.* **1.** a civil officer charged with the administration of the law. **2.** a minor judicial officer, as a justice of the peace or a police justice, having jurisdiction to try minor criminal cases

and to conduct preliminary examinations of persons charged with serious crimes. [ME *magistrat,* t. L: s. *magistrātus* the office of a chief, a magistrate]

mag·ma (măg′mə), *n.,* *pl.* **-mata** (-mə tə). **1.** any crude mixture of finely divided mineral or organic matters. **2.** *Geol.* molten material beneath the solid crust of the earth, from which igneous rock is formed. **3.** *Chem., Pharm.* a paste composed of solid and liquid matter. [t. L, t. Gk.: a salve] —**mag·mat·ic** (măg măt′ĭk), *adj.*

Mag·na Char·ta (măg′nə kär′tə). **1.** the "great charter" of English liberties, forced from King John by the English barons at Runnymede, June 15, 1215. **2.** any fundamental constitution or law guaranteeing rights. Also, **Mag′na Car′ta.** [t. ML: great charter]

mag·na cum lau·de (măg′nə kŭm lô′dĭ, măg′nə kŏŏm lou′dĕ), *Latin.* with great praise (the second highest of the honors granted at graduation).

Mag·na Grae·ci·a (măg′nə grē′shĭ ə), ancient name of the colonial cities of Greece in S Italy.

mag·na·nim·i·ty (măg′nə nĭm′ə tĭ), *n.,* *pl.* **-ties. 1.** quality of being magnanimous. **2.** a magnanimous act.

mag·nan·i·mous (măg năn′ə məs), *adj.* **1.** generous in forgiving an insult or injury; free from petty resentfulness or vindictiveness. **2.** high-minded; noble. **3.** proceeding from or revealing nobility of mind, etc. [t. L: m. *magnanimus* great-souled] —**mag·nan′i·mous·ly,** *adv.* —**mag·nan′i·mous·ness,** *n.* —**Syn. 2.** See **noble.**

mag·nate (măg′nāt), *n.* **1.** a great or dominant person in a district or, esp. in some field of business: *a railroad magnate.* **2.** a person of eminence or distinction in any field. **3.** a member of the upper house of certain European parliaments, as formerly in Hungary and Poland. [late ME, t. LL: m.s. *magnas,* der. L *magnus* great]

mag·ne·sia (măg nē′shə, -zhə), *n.* magnesium oxide, a white tasteless substance used in medicine as an antacid and laxative. [ME, t. ML (in alchemy), t. Gk.: (*hē*) *Magnēsia* (*lithos*), (the) Magnesian (stone); t. stone from Magnesia in Thessaly] —**mag·ne′sian,** **mag·ne·sic** (măg nē′sĭk), *adj.*

Mag·ne·si·a (măg nē′shĭ ə, -zhĭ ə), *n.* ancient name of Manisa.

mag·ne·site (măg′nĭ sīt′), *n.* a mineral, magnesium carbonate, MgCO₃, usually occurring in white masses.

mag·ne·si·um (măg nē′shĭ əm, -zhəm), *n.* *Chem.* a light, ductile, silver-white metallic element which burns with a dazzling white light, used in lightweight alloys. *Symbol:* Mg; *at. wt.:* 24.32; *at no.:* 12; *sp. gr.:* 1.74 at 20°C. [NL, der. *magnesia* MAGNESIA]

magnesium light, the strongly actinic white light produced when magnesium is burned, used in photography, signaling, pyrotechnics, etc.

mag·net (măg′nĭt), *n.* **1.** a body (as a piece of iron or steel) which, like loadstone, possesses the property of attracting certain substances, esp. iron. **2.** loadstone. **3.** a thing or person that attracts, as by some inherent power or charm. [late ME *magnete,* t. L: m.s. *magnes* loadstone, magnet, t. Gk.: *Magnēs* (*lithos*) (stone) of Magnesia (in Thessaly), loadstone. Cf. MAGNESIA]

mag·net·ic (măg nĕt′ĭk), *adj.* **1.** of or pertaining to a magnet or magnetism. **2.** having the properties of a magnet. **3.** capable of being magnetized or attracted by a magnet. **4.** pertaining to the earth's magnetism: *the magnetic equator.* **5.** exerting a strong attractive power or charm: *a magnetic personality.* Also, **mag·net′i·cal.** —**mag·net′i·cal·ly,** *adv.*

magnetic equator, the aclinic line.

magnetic field, a condition of space in the vicinity of a magnet or electric current which manifests itself as a force on magnetic objects within that space.

magnetic flux, 1. the total magnetic induction through a given cross section. **2.** magnetomotive force divided by reluctance.

magnetic induction, a measure of the magnetic effect at a given point.

magnetic needle, a slender magnetized steel rod which, when adjusted to swing in a horizontal plane, as in a compass, indicates the direction of the earth's magnetic fields or the approximate north and south.

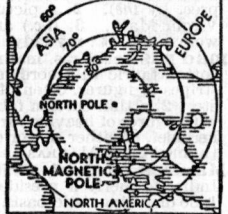

magnetic north, the direction in which the needle of a compass points, differing in most places from true north.

magnetic pole, 1. a pole of a magnet. **2.** either of the two points on the earth's surface where the dipping needle of a compass stands vertical, one in the arctic, the other in the antarctic.

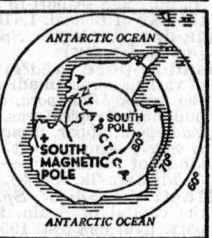

mag·net·ism (măg′nə tĭz′əm), *n.* **1.** the characteristic properties possessed by magnets; the molecular properties common to magnets. **2.** the agency producing magnetic phenomena. **3.** the science dealing with magnetic phenomena. **4.** magnetic or attractive power or charm.

Magnetic Poles

mag·net·ite (măg′nə tīt′), *n.* a very common black iron oxide, Fe₃O₄, that is strongly attracted by a magnet; an important iron ore.

mag·net·ize (măg′nə tīz), *v.t.,* **-ized, -izing. 1.** to communicate magnetic properties to. **2.** to exert an attracting or compelling influence upon. **3.** *Obs.* to mesmerize. —**mag′net·i·za′tion,** *n.* —**mag′net·iz′er,** *n.*

mag·ne·to (măg nē′tō), *n., pl.* **-tos.** a small electric generator, the poles of which are permanent magnets, as a hand-operated generator for telephone signaling, or the generator producing sparks in an internal-combustion engine. [short for MAGNETO-ELECTRIC (machine)]

magneto-, a combining form of **magnet** or **magnetic.**

mag·ne·to·chem·is·try (măg nē′tō kĕm′ĭs trĭ), *n.* the study of magnetic and chemical phenomena in their relation to one another. —**mag·ne′to·chem′i·cal,** *adj.*

mag·ne·to·e·lec·tric (măg nē′tō ĭ lĕk′trĭk), *adj.* pertaining to the induction of electric currents by means of magnets. Also, **mag·ne′to·e·lec′tri·cal.**

mag·ne·to·e·lec·tric·i·ty (măg nē′tō ĭ lĕk′trĭs′ə tĭ), *n.* electricity developed by the action of magnets.

mag·ne·to·gen·er·a·tor (măg nē′tō jĕn′ər ā′tər), *n.* a magnetoelectric generator.

mag·ne·tom·e·ter (măg′nə tŏm′ə tər), *n.* an instrument for measuring magnetic forces. —**mag′ne·tom′e·try,** *n.*

mag·ne·to·mo·tive (măg nē′tō mō′tĭv), *adj.* producing magnetic effects, or pertaining to such production.

magnetomotive force, magnetic flux multiplied by reluctance, the force which gives rise to magnetic effects or magnetic flux.

mag·ne·ton (măg′nə tŏn′), *n. Physics.* a hypothetical ultimate magnetic particle.

mag·ne·tron (măg′nə trŏn′), *n. Electronics.* a two-element vacuum tube in which the flow of electrons is under the influence of an external magnetic field, used to generate extremely short radio waves. [f. MAGNE(T) + (ELEC)TRON]

magni-, **1.** a word element meaning "large," "great," as in *magnify.* **2.** *Zool.* a word element denoting length. [t. L, comb. form of *magnus* great]

mag·nif·ic (măg nĭf′ĭk), *adj. Archaic.* **1.** magnificent; imposing. **2.** grandiose; pompous. Also, **mag·nif′i·cal.** [t. L: s. *magnificus*] —**mag·nif′i·cal·ly,** *adv.*

Mag·nif·i·cat (măg nĭf′ə kăt′), *n.* **1.** the hymn of the Virgin Mary in Luke, 1:46-55, beginning "My soul doth magnify the Lord," used as a canticle at evensong or vespers. **2.** a musical setting of it. [Mag, familiar nify, the first word of the hymn in the Vulgate]

mag·ni·fi·ca·tion (măg′nə fə kā′shən), *n.* **1.** act of magnifying. **2.** state of being magnified. **3.** the power to magnify. **4.** a magnified copy or reproduction.

mag·nif·i·cence (măg nĭf′ə səns), *n.* **1.** the quality or state of being magnificent; splendor; grandeur; impressiveness; sublimity. **2.** impressiveness of surroundings. [ME, t. OF, t. L: m.s. *magnificentia*] —**Syn. 1.** sumptuousness, pomp, state, majesty.

mag·nif·i·cent (măg nĭf′ə sənt), *adj.* **1.** making a splendid appearance or show: *a magnificent cathedral.* **2.** extraordinarily fine; superb: *a magnificent opportunity.* **3.** noble; sublime: *a magnificent poem.* **4.** great in deeds (now only as a title): *Lorenzo the Magnificent.* **5.** *Rare.* lavish. [t. OF, t. L: *magnificent-* (recorded in compar., superl., and other forms), for *magnificus.* See MAGNIFIC] —**mag·nif′i·cent·ly,** *adv.*

—**Syn. 1.** august, stately, majestic, imposing; sumptuous, grand. MAGNIFICENT, GORGEOUS, SPLENDID, SUPERB are terms of high admiration and all are used colloquially in weak hyperbole. That which is MAGNIFICENT is beautiful, princely, grand, or ostentatious: *a magnificent display of paintings.* That which is GORGEOUS moves one to admiration by the richness and (often colorful) variety of its effects: *a gorgeous array of handsome gifts.* That which is SPLENDID is dazzling or impressive in its brilliance, radiance, or excellence: *splendid jewels, a splendid body of scholars.* That which is SUPERB is above others in, or is of the highest degree of, excellence or elegance (less often, today, of grandeur): *a superb rendition of a song, superb wines.* —**Ant. 1.** modest.

mag·nif·i·co (măg nĭf′ə kō′), *n., pl.* **-coes.** **1.** a Venetian grandee. **2.** any grandee or great personage. [t. It., t. L: m. *magnificus* MAGNIFIC]

mag·ni·fy (măg′nə fī′), *v.,* **-fied, -fying.** —*v.t.* **1.** to increase the apparent size of, as a lens does. **2.** to make greater in size; enlarge. **3.** to cause to seem greater or more important. **4.** *Archaic.* to extol; praise. —*v.i.* **5.** to increase or be able to increase the apparent size of an object, as a lens does. [ME *magnifie(n),* t. L: m. *magnificāre* make much of] —**mag′ni·fi′er,** *n.* —**Syn. 2.** augment, increase, amplify. **3.** exaggerate, overstate. —**Ant. 1, 2.** reduce. **3.** minimize.

mag·nil·o·quent (măg nĭl′ə kwənt), *adj.* speaking or expressed in a lofty or grandiose style. [L *magniloquus* + -ENT] —**mag·nil′o·quence,** *n.* —**mag·nil′o·quent·ly,** *adv.*

Mag·ni·to·gorsk (măg nĭ′tə gôrsk′), *n.* a city in the Soviet Union, on the Ural river near the boundary between Europe and Asia. 284,000 (est. 1956).

mag·ni·tude (măg′nə tūd′, -tōōd′), *n.* **1.** size; extent: *to determine the magnitude of an angle.* **2.** great amount, importance, etc.: *affairs of magnitude.* **3.** greatness; great size: *the magnitude of the loss.* **4.** moral greatness: *magnitude of mind.* **5.** *Astron.* the brightness of a star expressed according to an arbitrary numerical system (the brightest degree being the **first magnitude,** and

those less bright the **second, third,** or other **magnitude**). Stars brighter than the sixth magnitude are visible to the unaided eye. **6.** *Math.* a number characteristic of a quantity and forming a basis for comparison with similar quantities. [ME, t. L: m. *magnitūdo* greatness]

mag·no·li·a (măg nō′lĭ ə), *n.* **1.** any plant of the genus *Magnolia,* comprising shrubs and trees with large, usually fragrant flowers and an aromatic bark, much cultivated for ornament. **2.** the magnolia blossom. [NL; named from P. *Magnol* (1638–1715), a French botanist]

mag·no·li·a·ceous (măg nō′lĭ ā′shəs), *adj.* belonging to the *Magnoliaceae,* or magnolia family of plants, including the magnolias generally, the tulip trees, etc.

mag·num (măg′nəm), *n., pl.* **-nums** *for 1,* **-na** (-nə) *for 2.* **1.** a large bottle for wine or spirits, containing about 50 ounces. **2.** *Anat.* a bone of the carpus, at the base of the metacarpal bone of the middle finger. [t. L, neut. of *magnus* great]

magnum o·pus (ō′pəs), **1.** a great work. **2.** one's chief work, esp. a literary or artistic work. [L]

mag·nus hitch (măg′nəs), a knot like a clove hitch but with one more turn, used to bend a line onto a spar, etc.

mag·pie (măg′pī′), *n.* **1.** any of various noisy, mischievous, corvine birds of the genus *Pica,* having a long, graduated tail and black-and-white plumage, as the **black-billed magpie,** *P. pica,* of Europe and North America, and the **yellow-billed magpie,** *P. nuttalli,* of California. **2.** a chattering person. [f. *Mag,* familiar var. of *Margaret,* woman's name + PIE²]

M.Agr., Master of Agriculture.

mag·uey (măg′wā; *Sp.* mä gĕ′ĕ), *n.* **1.** any of several species of the amaryllidaceous genus *Agave,* esp. *A. Cantala,* or the allied genus *Eurcraea.* **2.** the fiber from these plants. [t. Sp., prob. from Haitian]

Ma·gus (mā′gəs), *n.* **1.** (*also l.c.*) See **Magi** (def. 1). **2.** (*l.c.*) an ancient astrologer or charlatan, esp. Simon Magus. Acts 8:9–24. [ME, t. L, t. Gk.: m. *Mágos,* t. OPers.: m. *magus*]

Mag·yar (măg′yär; *Hung.* mŏ′dyŏr), *n.* **1.** a member of the ethnic group, of the Finno-Ugric stock, which forms the predominant element of the population of Hungary. **2.** the Hungarian language. —*adj.* **3.** of or pertaining to the Magyars or their language; Hungarian. [t. Hung.]

Ma·gyar·or·szág (mŏ′dyŏr ôr′säg), *n.* Hungarian name of **Hungary.**

Ma·ha·bha·ra·ta (mə hä′bä′rə tə), *n.* one of the two chief epics of ancient India. Its central subject is the war between the Kauravas and the Pandavas. Also, **Ma·ha·bha·ra·tam** (mə hä′bä′rə təm). [t. Skt.: f. *mahā-* great + *Bhārata* descendant of a king or a tribe named *Bharata*]

Ma·han (mə hän′), *n.* **Alfred Thayer** (thā′ər), 1840–1914, U.S. naval officer and writer on naval history.

ma·ha·ra·jah (mä′hə rä′jə; *Hind.* mə hä′rä′jə), *n.* the title of certain great ruling princes in India. Also, **ma′ha·ra′ja.** [t. Skt.: great raja]

ma·ha·ra·nee (mä′hə rä′nē; *Hind.* mə hä′rä′nē), *n.* India. **1.** the wife of a maharajah. **2.** a female sovereign in her own right. Also, **ma′ha·ra′ni.** [t. Hind.: great queen]

ma·hat·ma (mə hät′mə, -hät′-), *n.* **1.** an adept in Brahmanism. **2.** *Theosophy.* one of a class of reputed beings with preternatural powers. [t. Skt.: m. *mahātman* great-souled] —**ma·hat′ma·ism,** *n.*

Mah·di (mä′dē), *n., pl.* **-dis.** **1.** (in Mohammedan usage) the title of an expected spiritual and temporal ruler destined to establish a reign of righteousness throughout the world. **2.** any of various claimants of this title, esp. Mohammed Ahmed (died 1885), who set up in the Egyptian Sudan an independent government which lasted until 1898. [t. Ar.: m. *mahdīy,* lit., the guided or directed one] —**Mah·dism** (mä′dĭz əm), *n.* —**Mah′dist,** *n.*

Ma·hi·can (mə hē′kən), *n.* **1.** a tribe or confederacy of North American Indians of Algonquian speech, centralized formerly in the upper Hudson valley. **2.** an Indian of this confederacy. **3.** a member of the Mohegan Indian tribe formerly in Connecticut. Also, **Mohican.** [t. Amer. Ind. (Algonquian): wolf]

mah-jongg (mä′jông′, -jŏng′), *n.* a game of Chinese origin, for four persons (or, sometimes, 3, 2, or 5), with 136 (or sometimes 144) dominolike pieces or tiles marked in suits, counters, and dice. Also, **mah′-jong′.** [t. Chinese (Mandarin): m. *ma-ch′iao* sparrow (lit., hemp-bird), pictured on the first tiles of one of the suits]

Mah·ler (mä′lər), *n.* **Gustav** (gŏŏs′täf), 1860–1911, Bohemian composer and conductor.

mahl·stick (mäl′stĭk′, môl′-), *n.* a painter's stick, held in one hand as a support for the hand which holds the brush. Also, **maulstick.** [t. D: m. *maalstok*]

Mah·mud II (mä mōōd′), 1785–1839, sultan of Turkey, 1809–39. Also, **Mah′moud.**

ma·hog·a·ny (mə hŏg′ə nĭ), *n., pl.* **-nies,** *adj.* —*n.* **1.** any of certain tropical American meliaceous trees, esp. *Swietenia Mahagoni* and *S. macrophylla,* yielding a hard, reddish-brown wood highly esteemed for making fine furniture, etc. **2.** the wood itself. **3.** any of various related or similar trees, or their wood. **4.** a reddish-brown color. —*adj.* **5.** pertaining to or made of mahogany. **6.** of the color mahogany. [? t. some non-Carib W. Indian tongue]

Ma·hom·et (məhŏm′ĭt), n. Mohammed. —**Ma·hom′-et·an,** adj., n.

Ma·hound (məhound′, -hōōnd′), n. **1.** the prophet Mohammed. **2.** Scot. the devil. [early ME Mahun, Mahum, t. OF, shortened form of Mahomet, b. with HOUND]

ma·hout (məhout′), n. (in the East Indies) the keeper and driver of an elephant. [t. Hind.: m. mahāut]

Mah·rat·ta (mərăt′ə), n. a member of a Hindu people inhabiting central and western India. Also, **Maratha.** [t. Hind.: m. Marhatā]

Mahratta Confederacy, a loose league of states in central and western India, broken up in 1818.

Mah·rat·ti (mərăt′ĭ), n. the language of the Mahrattas; an Indic language of western India. Also, **Marathi.**

Mäh·ren (mĕ′rən), n. German name of Moravia.

Mäh·risch-Os·trau (mĕ′rĭsh ôs′trou), n. German name of Moravská Ostrava.

mah·zor (mäкнzôr′), n. a Hebrew prayer book containing the ritual for festivals. See **siddur.**

Ma·ia (mā′yə, mī′ə), n. Gk. Myth. the eldest of the Pleiades, mother by Zeus of Hermes.

maid (mād), n. **1.** a girl; young unmarried woman. **2.** a spinster (usually in the expression old maid). **3.** a female servant. **4. the Maid,** Joan of Arc. [apocopated var. of MAIDEN]

maid·en (mā′dən), n. **1.** a maid; girl; young unmarried woman. **2.** Also, **the Maiden,** an instrument resembling the guillotine, formerly used in Edinburgh for beheading criminals. **3.** Cricket. a maiden over. **4.** a maiden horse. **5.** a maiden race. —adj. **6.** of, pertaining to, or befitting a girl or unmarried woman. **7.** unmarried: a maiden lady. **8.** made, tried, appearing, etc., for the first time: maiden voyage. **9.** (of a horse, etc.) that never has won a race or a prize. **10.** (of a prize or a race) offered for or open only to maiden horses, etc. **11.** untried, as a knight, soldier, or weapon. [ME; OE mægden, f. mægd- + -en -EN⁵]

maid·en·hair (mā′dənhâr′), n. any of the ferns constituting the genus Adiantum. The cultivated species have fine, glossy stalks and delicate, finely divided fronds.

maid·en·head (mā′dənhĕd′), n. **1.** maidenhood; virginity. **2.** the hymen.

maid·en·hood (mā′dənhŏŏd′), n. the state or time of being a maiden; virginity.

maid·en·ly (mā′dənlĭ), adj. **1.** pertaining to a maiden: maidenly years. **2.** characteristic of or befitting a maiden: maidenly behavior. —**maid′en·li·ness,** n.

maiden name, a woman's surname before marriage.

maiden over, Cricket. an over in which no runs are made.

Maid Marian, 1. (orig.) Queen of the May, one of the characters in the old morris dance. **2.** a morris dance. **3.** Robin Hood's sweetheart.

maid of honor, 1. the chief unmarried attendant of a bride. **2.** an unmarried woman, usually of noble birth, attendant on a queen or princess.

Maid of Orleans, Joan of Arc.

maid·serv·ant (mād′sûr′vənt), n. a female servant.

Maid·stone (mād′stōn′, -stən), n. a city in SE England: the county seat of Kent. 55,500 (est. 1956).

ma·ieu·tic (mā ū′tĭk), adj. (of the Socratic mode of inquiry) bringing out ideas latent in the mind. Also, **ma·ieu′ti·ca.** [t. Gk.: m.s. maieutikós of midwifery]

mai·gre (mā′gər), adj. containing neither flesh nor its juices, as food permissible on days of religious abstinence. [t. F. See MEAGER]

mai·hem (mā′hĕm), n. mayhem.

mail¹ (māl), n. **1.** letters, packages, etc., arriving or sent by post. **2.** the system of transmission of letters, etc., by post. **3.** a train, boat, person, etc., by which postal matter is carried. —adj. **4.** of or pertaining to mail: a mail bag. —v.t. **5.** to send by mail; place in a postoffice or mailbox for transmission. [ME male bag, t. OF, t. Gmc.; cf. OHG malha wallet]

mail² (māl), n. **1.** flexible armor of interlinked rings, the ends riveted, butted, or soldered. **2.** defensive armor. —v.t. **3.** to clothe or arm with mail. [ME maille, t. F, g. L macula spot, mesh of a net]

mail·box (māl′bŏks′), n. **1.** a public box for the mailing of letters. **2.** a private box for the delivery of mail.

Coat of mail and detail of same

mailed (māld), adj. clad or armed with mail: the mailed fist. [f. MAIL² + -ED²]

mailing machine, a machine which addresses, stamps, or otherwise handles letters, or the like.

Mail·lol (mä yŏl′), n. Aristide (á rĕs tēd′), 1861–1944, French sculptor and artist.

mail·man (māl′măn′), n., pl. -men. one who delivers mail; postman.

mail-or·der house (māl′ôr′dər), a business house conducting a business by receiving orders (**mail orders**) and payment by mail and shipping goods to the buyers.

maim (mām), v.t. **1.** to deprive of the use of some bodily member; mutilate; cripple. **2.** to impair; make essentially defective. —n. **3.** Rare. an injury or defect. [var. of MAYHEM] —**maim′er,** n.

—**Syn. 1.** MAIM, LACERATE, MANGLE, MUTILATE indicate the infliction of painful and severe injuries on the body. To MAIM is to injure by giving a disabling wound, or by depriving a person of one or more members or their use: maimed in an accident. To LACERATE is to inflict severe cuts and tears on the flesh or skin: to wound and lacerate an arm. To MANGLE is to chop undiscriminatingly or to crush or rend by blows or pressure as if caught in machinery: bodies mangled in a train wreck. To MUTILATE is to injure the completeness or beauty of a body, esp. by cutting off an important member: to mutilate a statue, a tree, a person.

Mai·mon·i·des (mī mŏn′ə dēz′), n. (Moses ben Maimon) 1135–1204, Spanish-Jewish scholar and philosopher.

main¹ (mān), adj. **1.** chief; principal; leading: the main office. **2.** sheer; utmost, as strength, force, etc.: by main force. **3.** of or pertaining to a broad expanse: main sea. **4.** Gram. See **main clause. 5.** Obs. strong or mighty. **6.** Obs. high-ranking; essential. **7.** Naut. pertaining to the mainmast or mainsail. —n. **8.** a principal pipe or duct in a system used to distribute water, gas, etc. **9.** strength; force; violent effort: with might and main. **10.** the chief or principal part or point. **11.** Poetic. the open ocean; high sea. **12.** the mainland. **13. in the main,** for the most part. [ME meyn, OE mægen strength, power, c. Icel. megin strength, main part] —**Syn. 1.** cardinal, prime, paramount.

main² (mān), n. a cockfighting match. [orig. obscure]

Main (mān; Ger. mīn), n. a river flowing from the Bohemian Forest in East Germany W to the Rhine at Mainz in West Germany. 305 mi.

main clause, Gram. (in a complex sentence) the clause which may stand syntactically as a sentence by itself; independent clause. For example: in I was out when he came in, the main clause is I was out.

Maine (mān), n. **1.** a State in the NE United States, on the Atlantic coast. 969,265 pop. (1960); 33,215 sq. mi. Cap.: Augusta. Abbr.: Me. **2.** a former province in NW France. Cap.: Le Mans. **3.** a U.S. battleship blown up in Havana harbor, Cuba, Feb. 15, 1898: one of the events precipitating the Spanish-American War.

main·land (mān′lănd, -lənd), n. the principal land, as distinguished from islands or peninsulas. —**main·land′er,** n.

Main·land (mān′lănd, -lənd), n. **1.** the largest of the Shetland Islands, NE of Scotland. 15,172 pop. (1951); ab. 200 sq. mi. **2.** Pomona (def. 3).

main line, a through railroad route; a principal line of a railroad as contrasted with a branch or secondary line.

main·ly (mān′lĭ), adv. **1.** chiefly; principally; for the most part. **2.** Obs. greatly.

main·mast (mān′măst′, -mäst′; Naut. -məst), n. Naut. **1.** the principal mast in a ship or other vessel. **2.** (in a schooner, brig, bark, etc.), the second mast from the bow. **3.** (in a yawl or ketch) the mast nearer the bow.

main·sail (mān′sāl′; Naut. -səl), n. Naut. **1.** (in a square-rigged vessel) the sail bent to the main yard. See illus. under **sail. 2.** (in a fore-and-aft rigged vessel) the large sail set abaft the mainmast.

main·sheet (mān′shēt′), n. Naut. a sheet of a mainsail.

main·spring (mān′sprĭng′), n. **1.** the principal spring in a mechanism, as in a watch. **2.** the chief motive power; the impelling cause.

main·stay (mān′stā′), n. **1.** Naut. the stay which secures the mainmast forward. **2.** a chief support.

Main Street, a novel (1920) by Sinclair Lewis.

main·tain (mān tān′), v.t. **1.** to keep in existence or continuance; preserve; retain: to maintain good relations with Canada. **2.** to keep in due condition, operation, or force; keep unimpaired: to maintain order, maintain public highways. **3.** to keep in a specified state, position, etc. **4.** to affirm; assert (with a clause, or with an object and infinitive). **5.** to assert to be true. **6.** to support in speech or argument, as a statement, etc. **7.** to keep or hold against attack: to maintain one's ground. **8.** to provide with the means of existence. [ME mainten(en), t. F: m. maintenir, g. L manū tenēre hold in the hand] —**main·tain′er,** n. —**Syn. 1.** keep up, continue. **5.** contend, claim. **6.** uphold, defend, vindicate. **8.** provide for. See **support.** —**Ant. 1.** break (off). **5.** deny. **6.** contradict.

main·te·nance (mān′tə nəns), n. **1.** act of maintaining. **2.** state of being maintained. **3.** means of provision for maintaining; means of subsistence. **4.** Law. an officious intermeddling in a suit in which the meddler has no interest, by assisting either party with means to prosecute or defend it. —**Syn. 3.** support, livelihood. See **living.**

maintenance of membership, an arrangement or agreement between an employer and a labor union by which employees who are members of the union at the time the agreement is made, or who subsequently join, must either remain members until the agreement expires, or be discharged.

Main·te·non (măNt nôN′), n. Marquise de, (Françoise d' Aubigné) 1635–1719, second wife of Louis XIV.

main·top (mān′tŏp′), n. Naut. a platform at the head of the lower mainmast.

---

b., blend of, blended; c., cognate with; d., dialect, dialectal; der., derived from; f., formed from; g., going back to; m., modification of; r., replacing; s., stem of; t., taken from; ?, perhaps. See the full key on inside cover.

main-top·gal·lant (mān'tə găl'ənt, -tŏp-), n. the main-topgallantmast, its sail, or yard. See illus. under **sail**.
main-top·gal·lant·mast (mān'tə găl'ənt măst', -măst', -məst; -tŏp-), n. Naut. the mast next above the main-topmast.
main-top·mast (mān'tŏp'məst), n. Naut. the mast next above the lower mainmast.
main-top·sail (mān'tŏp'səl), n. Naut. the sail set on the main-topmast. See illus. under **sail**.
main yard, Naut. the lower yard on the mainmast.
Mainz (mīnts), n. a city in W West Germany: a port at the confluence of the Rhine and Main rivers. 117,015 (est. 1955). French, **Mayence.**
mai·son·ette (mā'zə nĕt'), n. Brit. a small apartment.
Mait·land (māt'lənd), n. Frederic William, 1850–1906, British legal historian and lawyer.
maî·tre d'hô·tel (mĕ'tr dō tĕl'), 1. steward; butler. 2. a headwaiter. 3. the owner or manager of a hotel. 4. (of foods) with a sauce of melted butter, minced parsley, and lemon juice or vinegar. [t. F: house master]
maize (māz), n. Technical and Brit. 1. a widely cultivated cereal plant, Zea Mays, occurring in many varieties, bearing grain in large ears or spikes; corn; Indian corn. 2. its grain. 3. corn color; a pale yellow. [t. Sp.: m. maíz, t. Antillean: m. maysi, mahiz, t. Arawak: m. marise]
Maj., Major.
ma·jes·tic (mə jĕs'tĭk), adj. characterized by or possessing majesty; of lofty dignity; regal; stately; grand. Also, **ma·jes·ti·cal. —ma·jes·ti·cal·ly,** adv.
maj·es·ty (măj'ĭs tĭ), n., pl. -ties. 1. regal, lofty, or stately dignity; imposing character; grandeur. 2. supreme greatness or authority; sovereignty. 3. a royal personage, or royal personages collectively. 4. (usually cap.) a title used when speaking of or to a sovereign (prec. by his, your, etc.). [ME maieste, t. F: m. majesté, t. L: m.s. mājestas greatness, grandeur, majesty]
ma·jol·i·ca (mə jŏl'ə kə, mə yŏl'-), n. 1. a kind of Italian pottery coated with enamel and decorated, often in rich colors. 2. a more or less similar pottery made elsewhere. [t. It.: m. maiolica MAJORCA]
ma·jor (mā'jər), n. 1. Mil. a commissioned officer ranking next below a lieutenant colonel and next above a captain. 2. one of superior rank in a specified class. 3. U.S. a subject or field of study chosen by a student to represent his principal interest and upon which he concentrates a large share of his efforts. 4. a person of full legal age. 5. Music. a major interval, chord, scale, etc. —adj. 6. greater, as in size, amount, extent, importance, rank, etc.: the major part of the town. 7. greater, as in rank or importance: a major question. 8. of or pertaining to the majority. 9. Logic. broader or more extensive. The **major term** of a syllogism is the term that enters into the predicate of the conclusion; the **major premise** is that premise of a syllogism which contains the major term. 10. of full legal age. 11. Music. a. (of an interval) being between the tonic and the second, third, sixth, and seventh degrees of a major scale: the major third, sixth, etc. b. (of a chord) having a major third between the root and the note next above it. 12. elder; senior: used after a name: Cato Major. In English public schools, used after a boy's name to distinguish him from a younger boy of the same name. 13. U.S. noting or pertaining to educational majors: a major field of study. —v.i. 14. U.S. to pursue a major or principal subject or course of study (fol. by in). [ME, t. L: greater, superior, compar. of magnus great] —Syn. 6. See **capital¹.**
Ma·jor·ca (mə jôr'kə), n. a Spanish island in the W Mediterranean: the largest of the Balearic Islands. 328,000 pop. (est. 1954); 1405 sq. mi. Cap.: Palma. Spanish, **Mallorca.**
ma·jor·do·mo (mā'jər dō'mō), n., pl. -mos. 1. a man in charge of a great household, as that of a sovereign; a chief steward. 2. a steward or butler. [t. Sp.: m. mayordomo, or t. It.: m. maggiordomo, t. ML: m. mājor domūs chief officer of the house]
major general, Mil. an officer ranking next below a lieutenant general and next above a brigadier general. **—ma·jor-gen'er·al·cy, ma·jor-gen'er·al·ship',** n.
ma·jor·i·ty (mə jôr'ə tĭ, -jŏr'-), n., pl. -ties. 1. the greater part or number: the majority of mankind. 2. a number of voters or votes, jurors, or others in agreement, constituting more than half of the total number. 3. the excess whereby the greater number, as of votes, surpasses the remainder. 4. the party or faction with the majority vote. 5. the state or time of being of full legal age: to attain one's majority. 6. the military rank or office of a major. [t. F: m. majorité, t. ML: m.s. mājōritas, der. L mājor MAJOR]
major league, either of the two main professional baseball leagues (American or National) in the U.S.
major orders. See orders (def. 15).
Major Prophets. See prophet (def. 4b).
major scale, mode, or **key,** a scale, mode, or key whose third tone forms a major third with the fundamental tone. See illus. under **scale.**
major suit, Bridge. hearts or spades (because they have higher point values).
ma·jus·cule (mə jŭs'kūl), adj. 1. large, as letters (whether capital or uncial). 2. written in such letters (opposed to minuscule). —n. 3. a majuscule letter. [t. F, t. L: m. mājusculus somewhat greater or larger] **—ma·jus'cu·lar,** adj.
Ma·kas·sar (mə kăs'ər), n. Dutch name of **Macassar.**

make (māk), v., made, making, n. —v.t. 1. to bring into existence by shaping material, combining parts, etc.: to make a dress. 2. to produce by any action or causative agency: to make trouble. 3. to cause to be or become; render: to make an old man young. 4. to constitute; appoint: to make someone a judge. 5. to put into proper condition for use: to make a bed. 6. to bring into a certain form or condition: to make clay into bricks. 7. to cause, induce, or compel (to do something): to make a horse go. 8. to give rise to; occasion. 9. to produce, earn, or win for oneself: to make a fortune. 10. to compose, as a poem. 11. to draw up, as a legal document. 12. to do; effect: to make a bargain. 13. to fix; establish; enact: to make laws. 14. to become by development; prove to be: he will make a good lawyer. 15. to form in the mind, as a judgment, estimate, or plan. 16. to entertain mentally, as doubt, scruple, etc. 17. to judge or infer as to the truth, nature, meaning, etc.: what do you make of it? 18. to estimate; reckon: to make the distance ten miles. 19. (of material or parts) to compose; form: two and two make four. 20. to bring to; bring up the total to: to make an even dozen. 21. to serve for or as: to make good reading. 22. to be sufficient to constitute; be essential to. 23. to assure the success or fortune of. 24. to put forth; deliver: to make a speech. 25. to accomplish by traveling, etc.: to make sixty miles an hour. 26. to arrive at or reach: to make a port. 27. Colloq. to secure a place on, as a team. 28. Cards. a. to name (the trump). b. to achieve a trick with (a card). c. Bridge. to achieve (a bid). d. to mix up or shuffle (the cards). 29. Sports and Games. to earn as a score. 30. to close (an electric circuit). —v.i. 31. to act or start (to do, or as if to do, something). 32. to cause oneself, or something understood, to be as specified: to make sure. 33. to show oneself in action or behavior: to make merry. 34. to direct or pursue the course; go: to make for home. 35. to rise, as the tide, or as water in a ship, etc. 36. to be of effect; operate (usually fol. by for or against). 37. to go toward; approach, esp. hostilely (fol. by for). 38. to go off or depart suddenly or hastily; run off (fol. by off). 39. Some special verb phrases are:
make away with, 1. to get rid of. 2. to kill or destroy.
make believe, 1. to pretend. 2. to cause to believe.
make heavy weather, Naut. to roll and pitch in heavy seas.
make out, 1. to write out (a bill, a check, etc.). 2. to prove; establish. 3. to discern; decipher. 4. to finish or complete. 5. U.S. Colloq. to manage; succeed.
make over, 1. to make anew; alter: to make over a dress. 2. to hand over into the possession or charge of another. 3. to transfer the title of (property); convey.
make sternway, to move backwards; go astern.
make time, Colloq. to go fast.
make up, 1. (of parts) to constitute; form. 2. to put together; construct; compile. 3. to concoct; invent. 4. to compensate for; make good. 5. to complete. 6. to prepare; put in order. 7. to bring to a definite conclusion, as one's mind. 8. to settle amicably, as differences. 9. to become reconciled after a quarrel. 10. Print. to arrange set type, etc., into columns or pages. 11. to prepare for a part, as on the stage, by appropriate dress, cosmetics, etc. 12. to adjust or balance, as accounts; to prepare, as statements. 13. Educ. to repeat a course (or examination in which one has failed) or to take an (examination) from which one has been absent. 14. to beautify artificially, as the face. 15. to make (oneself) up by appropriate dress, etc., as for a part.
make up to, 1. Colloq. to try to be on friendly terms with; fawn on. 2. to make advances; pay court to. —n. 40. style or manner of being made; form; build. 41. production with reference to the maker: our own make. 42. disposition; character; nature. 43. act or process of making. 44. on the make, Slang. intent on gain or one's own advantage. 45. quantity made; output. 46. Cards. act of naming the trump, or the suit named as trump. 47. Elect. the closing of an electric circuit (opp. to break). [ME make(n), OE macian, c. LG and D maken, G machen] —Syn. 1. form; build; produce; fabricate, create. MAKE, CONSTRUCT, MANUFACTURE mean to put into definite form, to produce, or to put parts together to make a whole. MAKE is the general term: bees make wax. CONSTRUCT, more formal, means to put parts together, usually according to a plan or design: to construct a building. MANUFACTURE refers to producing from raw materials, now almost entirely by means of machinery: to manufacture automobiles. The term is used contemptuously of producing imitations of works of art, etc. and is also used abstractly with the same idea of denying genuineness: to manufacture an excuse. 6. convert; transform, change, turn. 9. get, gain, acquire, obtain. 12. perform, execute, accomplish. —Ant. 1. destroy. 9. lose.
make and break, Elect. a device for alternately making and breaking an electric circuit.
make-be·lieve (māk'bə lēv'), n. 1. pretense; sham. 2. a pretender. —adj. 3. pretended; sham.
make·fast (māk'făst', -fäst'), n. Naut. any structure to which a vessel is tied up, as a bollard, buoy, etc.
make-peace (māk'pēs'), n. Rare. a peacemaker.
mak·er (mā'kər), n. 1. one who makes. 2. (cap.) God. 3. Law. the party executing a legal instrument, esp. a promissory note. 4. Bridge, Pinochle, etc. the one who first designates the successful bid. 5. Archaic. a poet.

make-read·y (māk/rĕd/ĭ), *n.* the process of preparing a form for printing by overlays or underlays to equalize the impression.

make·shift (māk/shĭft/), *n.* **1.** a temporary expedient; substitute. —*adj.* **2.** serving as or a makeshift.

make-up (māk/ŭp/), *n.* **1.** the way in which an actor or other person dresses himself, paints his face, etc., for a part. **2.** the articles used for this purpose, esp., cosmetics, etc. **3.** the manner of being made up or put together; composition. **4.** physical or mental constitution. **5.** *Print.* the arrangement of set type, cuts, etc.. into columns or pages. **6.** *Colloq.* (in education) a course or examination taken to make up a deficiency.

make·weight (māk/wāt/), *n.* **1.** something put in a scale to complete a required weight. **2.** anything added to supply a lack.

Ma·ke·yev·ka (mä kĕ/yĕf kä), *n.* a city in the SW Soviet Union. 311,000 (est. 1956). Also, **Ma·ke/ev·ka.**

Ma·khach Ka·la (mä häch/ kä lä/), a seaport in the Soviet Union, on the Caspian Sea. 106,000 (est. 1956).

mak·ing (mā/kǐng), *n.* **1.** act of one who or that which makes. **2. in the making,** being made; not yet finished. **3.** structure; constitution; make-up. **4.** means or cause of success or advancement: *to be the making of someone.* **5.** (*often pl.*) material of which something may be made. **6.** something made. **7.** the quantity made.

mal-, a prefix having attributive relation to the second element, meaning "bad," "wrongful," "ill," as in *maladjustment, malpractice.* [t. F, repr. *mal,* adv. (g. L *male* badly, ill), or *mal,* adj. (g. L *malus*) bad]

Mal., **1.** Malachi. **2.** Malayan.

Mal·a·bar Coast (măl/ə bär/), a region along the entire SW coast of India, extending from the Arabian Sea inland to the Western Ghats.

Ma·lac·ca (mə lăk/ə), *n.* **1.** a settlement in the SW Malay Peninsula: now part of the federation of Malaysia, formerly a part of the British Straits Settlement and the former Federation of Malaya. 69,848 (1957); 640 sq. mi. **2.** a seaport in and the capital of this state. 54,507 (1947). **3. Strait of,** a strait between Sumatra and the Malay Peninsula. 35–185 mi. wide.

Malacca cane, a cane or walking stick made of the brown, often mottled or clouded stem of an East Indian rattan palm, *Calamus scipionum.* [named after *Malacca*]

ma·la·ceous (mə lā/shəs), *adj.* belonging to the *Malaceae,* or apple family of plants, which includes the apple, pear, quince, medlar, loquat, hawthorn, etc. [f. s. L *mālus* apple tree + -ACEOUS]

Mal·a·chi (măl/ə kī/), *n.* Hebrew prophet of the 5th century B.C. and author of the last book of the "minor prophets" which bears his name.

mal·a·chite (măl/ə kīt/), *n.* a green mineral basic copper carbonate, $Cu_2CO_3(OH)_2$, an ore of copper, also used for making ornamental articles. [t. F, f. s. Gk. *maláchē* mallow + -*ite* -ITE¹]

mal·a·col·o·gy (măl/ə kŏl/ə jĭ), *n.* the science that treats of mollusks. [f. m. Gk. *malakó(s)* soft (with ref. to the soft body of the mollusks) + -LOGY]

mal·a·cos·tra·can (măl/ə kŏs/trə kən), *adj.* **1.** Also, **mal/a·cos/tra·cous.** belonging to the *Malacostraca,* a subclass of crustaceans, a comparatively complex organization, including lobsters, shrimps, crabs, etc. —*n.* **2.** a malacostracan crustacean. [f. s. NL *Malacostraca* (t. Gk.: m. *malakóstraka* (neut. pl.) soft-shelled) + -AN]

mal·ad·just·ed (măl/ə jŭs/tĭd), *adj.* badly adjusted.

mal·ad·just·ment (măl/ə jŭst/mənt), *n.* a faulty adjustment.

mal·ad·min·is·ter (măl/əd mĭn/əs tər), *v.t.* to manage (esp. public affairs) badly or inefficiently. —**mal/·ad·min/is·tra/tion,** *n.* —**mal/ad·min/is·tra/tor,** *n.*

mal·a·droit (măl/ə droit/), *adj.* lacking in adroitness; unskilful; awkward. [t. F. See MAL-, ADROIT] —**mal/·a·droit/ly,** *adv.* —**mal/a·droit/ness,** *n.*

mal·a·dy (măl/ə dĭ), *n., pl.* **-dies.** **1.** any bodily disorder or disease, esp. one that is chronic or deep-seated. **2.** any form of disorder: *social maladies.* [ME *maladie,* t. OF, der. *malade* sick, g. LL *male habitus,* lit., ill-conditioned] —**Syn. 1.** See *disease.*

ma·la fi·de (mā/lə fī/dĭ), *Latin.* in bad faith; not genuine (opposed to *bona fide*).

Mál·a·ga (măl/ə gə; *Sp.* mä/lä gä/), *n.* a seaport in S Spain, on the Mediterranean. 288,096 (est. 1955).

Mal·a·ga (măl/ə gə), *n.* **1.** a sweet strong white wine with a pronounced muscat grape flavor, produced in the province of Málaga, Spain. **2.** any of the grapes grown in or exported from Málaga.

Mal·a·gas·y (măl/ə gäs/ĭ), *n., pl.* **-gasy, -gasies.** **1.** a native of the Malagasy Republic. **2.** an Austronesian language, the language of the Malagasy Republic.

Malagasy Republic, an island republic in the Indian ocean, about 240 mi. off the SE coast of Africa: independent member of the French Community. 5,071,000 pop.; 227,800 sq. mi. *Cap.:* Tananarive. Formerly, **Madagascar.**

ma·la·gue·na (măl/ə gān/yə *or, often,* -gwän/-; *Sp.* mä/lä gĕ/nyä), *n., pl.* **-gue·nas** (-gān/yəz *or, often,* -gwän/-; *Sp.* -gĕ/nyäs). *n.* a Spanish dance similar to the fandango, originating in Málaga.

ma·laise (mä lāz/; *Fr.* mȧ lĕz/), *n.* a condition of indefinite bodily weakness or discomfort, often marking the onset of a disease. [t. F: f. *mal* ill + *aise* EASE]

Ma·lan (mä län/), *n.* **Daniel,** 1874–1959, South African leader; prime minister, 1948–1954.

mal·an·ders (măl/ən dərz), *n. pl.* a dry, scabby or scurfy eruption or scratch behind the knee in horses. [late ME, t. F: m. *malandres,* t. L: m. *malandria* blisters on the neck]

mal·a·pert (măl/ə pûrt/), *Archaic.* —*adj.* **1.** bold; saucy. —*n.* **2.** a malapert person. [ME, t. OF: f. *mal* badly + *appert,* for *espert,* g. L *expertus* EXPERT] —**mal/a·pert/ly,** *adv.* —**mal/a·pert/ness,** *n.*

Mal·a·prop (măl/ə prŏp/), *n.* **Mrs.,** the "old weather-beaten she-dragon" of Sheridan's *Rivals* (1775), noted for her misapplication of words.

mal·a·prop·ism (măl/ə prŏp ĭz/əm), *n.* **1.** act or habit of ridiculously misusing words. **2.** a word so misused. [named after Mrs. MALAPROP. Cf. MALAPROPOS]

mal·a·pro·pos (măl/ăp rə pō/), *adj.* **1.** inappropriate. —*adv.* **2.** inappropriately. [t. F: *mal à propos* not to the point. See MAL-, APROPOS]

ma·lar (mā/lər), *Anat.* —*adj.* **1.** of or pertaining to the cheekbone or cheek. —*n.* **2.** Also, **malar bone.** the cheekbone. [t. NL: s. *mālāris,* der. L *māla* cheekbone]

Mä·lar·en (mĕ/lär ən), *n.* a lake in S Sweden, extending ab. 80 mi. W from Stockholm; ab. 440 sq. mi.

ma·lar·i·a (mə lâr/ĭ ə), *n.* **1.** any of a group of diseases, usually intermittent or remittent, and characterized by attacks of chills, fever, and sweating: formerly supposed to be due to swamp exhalations, but now known to be caused by five or more species of parasitic protozoans which are transferred to the human blood by mosquitoes (genus *Anopheles*) and which occupy and destroy the red blood corpuscles. **2.** unwholesome or poisonous air. [t. It.: contr. of *mala aria* bad air] —**ma·lar/i·al, ma·lar/i·an, ma·lar/i·ous,** *adj.*

mal·as·sim·i·la·tion (măl/ə sĭm/ə lā/shən), *n. Pathol.* imperfect assimilation or nutrition.

mal·ate (măl/āt, mā/lāt), *n. Chem.* a salt or ester of malic acid. [f. MAL(IC) + -ATE²]

Ma·la·wi (mä lä/wē), *n.* an independent state in SE Africa on the W and S shores of Lake Nyasa: member of the Brit. Commonwealth; formerly a British protectorate and part of the Federation of Rhodesia and Nyasaland. 2,600,000 pop. (est. 1956); 49,177 sq. mi. *Cap.:* Zomba.

Ma·lay (mā/lā, mə lā/), *adj.* **1.** of or pertaining to the Malays or their country or language. **2.** noting or pertaining to the so-called "brown" race, characterized by short stature, roundish skull, moderate prognathism, and straight black hair. —*n.* **3.** a member of the dominant people of the Malay Peninsula and adjacent islands. **4.** an Austronesian language, widespread in the East Indies as a language of commerce.

Ma·lay·a (mə lā/ə), *n.* **1.** the Malay Peninsula. **2. Federation of,** a former federation (1957–62) in the S Malay Peninsula, comprising eleven states: Johore, Kedah, Kelantan, Malacca, Negri Sembilan, Pahang, Penang, Perak, Perlis, Selangor, and Trengganu. See **Malaysia** (def. 2).

Mal·a·ya·lam (măl/ə yä/ləm), *n.* a Dravidian language spoken in extreme southwestern India.

Ma·lay·an (mə lā/ən), *adj.* **1.** Malay. —*n.* **2.** a Malay. **3.** Indonesian (def. 3).

Malay Archipelago, an extensive archipelago in the Indian and Pacific Oceans, SE of Asia: the islands of the East Indies, including the Sunda and Philippine Islands, the Moluccas, and Borneo. Also **Malaysia.**

Ma·lay·o-Pol·y·ne·sian (mə lā/ō pŏl/ə nē/shən, -zhən), *adj.* Austronesian.

Malay Peninsula, a peninsula in SE Asia, consisting of Malaya and the S part of Thailand. Also, **Malaya.**

Ma·lay·sia (mə lā/zhə, -shə), *n.* **1.** Malay Archipelago. **2.** an independent federation in SE Asia comprising the former British territories of Malaya, Sabah, and Sarawak; member of the British Commonwealth of Nations. 8,487,000 pop. (est. 1961); ab. 126,530 sq. mi. *Cap.:* Kuala Lumpur.

Ma·lay·sian (mə lā/zhən, -shən), *n.* **1.** a native of Malaysia. **2.** Indonesian (def. 1). **3.** Malay (def. 3). —**Ma·lay/sian,** *adj.*

Malay States, a former group of states in the Malay Peninsula, under British protection. See **Malaya** (def. 2).

mal·con·tent (măl/kən tĕnt/), *adj.* **1.** discontented; dissatisfied. **2.** dissatisfied with the existing administration; inclined to rebellion. —*n.* **3.** a malcontent person. [t. OF. See MAL-, CONTENT²]

mal de mer (mȧl də mĕr/), *French.* seasickness.

Mal·den (môl/dən), *n.* a city in E Massachusetts, near Boston. 57,676 (1960).

Mal·dive Islands (măl/dĭv), a group of atolls in the Indian Ocean, SW of India: a dependency of Ceylon; briefly a republic in 1953. 81,950 (1956); 115 sq. mi.

mal du pa·ys (mȧl dy pĕ ē/), *French.* homesickness.

male (māl), *adj.* **1.** belonging to the sex which begets young, or any division or group corresponding to it. **2.** pertaining to or characteristic of this sex; masculine. **3.** composed of males: *a male choir.* **4.** *Bot.* **a.** designating or pertaining to any reproductive structure which produces or contains elements that bring about the fertilization of the female element. **b.** (of seed plants)

---

b., blend of, blended; c., cognate with; d., dialect, dialectal; der., derived from; f., formed from; g., going back to; m., modification of; r., replacing; s., stem of; t., taken from; ?, perhaps.   See the full key on inside cover.

staminate. **5.** *Mach.* designating some part, etc., whic h fits into a corresponding part. —*n.* **6.** a male human being; a man or boy. **7.** any animal of male sex. **8.** *Bot.* a staminate plant. [ME, t. OF, g. L *masculus*] —**Syn. 1.** MALE, MASCULINE, VIRILE are descriptive of one belonging to the paternal sex. MALE always refers to sex, whether of human beings, animals, or plants: *male animals are often larger than the females.* MASCULINE applies to the qualities that properly characterize the male sex: *a masculine love of sports.* The term may be applied to women, also, in either of two ways. It usually suggests some incongruity (as, *a masculine appearance*), but it may be used with complimentary implications: *she has a masculine mind.* VIRILE is a strong and comprehensive term, which formerly emphasized obvious maleness, but now usually implies the vigor, health, and force of mature manhood: *a virile opponent.*

Male·branche (mål bränsh/), *n.* **Nicolas de** (nē-kô lä/ də), 1638–1715, French philosopher.

mal·e·dic·tion (mål/ə dǐk/shən), *n.* **1.** a curse; the utterance of a curse. **2.** slander. [late ME, t. L: s. *maledictio* abuse] —**mal·e·dic·to·ry** (mål/ə dǐk/tə rǐ/), *adj.*

mal·e·fac·tion (mål/ə fåk/shən), *n.* an evil deed.

mal·e·fac·tor (mål/ə fåk/tər), *n.* **1.** an offender against the law; a criminal. **2.** one who does evil. [late ME, t. L] —**mal·e·fac·tress** (mål/ə fåk/trǐs), *n. fem.*

ma·lef·ic (mə lěf/ǐk), *adj.* productive of evil; malign. [t. L: s. *maleficus* evil-doing]

ma·lef·i·cence (mə lěf/ə səns), *n.* **1.** the doing of evil or harm. **2.** maleficent or harmful character.

ma·lef·i·cent (mə lěf/ə sənt), *adj.* doing evil or harm; harmful. [f. L: back formation from *maleficientia* MALEFICENCE. Cf. BENEFICENT]

ma·le·ic acid (mə lē/ǐk), *Chem.* crystalline dibasic acid, $C_2H_2(COOH)_2$, an isomer of fumaric acid.

Ma·len·kov (mål/ən kôf; *Russ.* mä lěn kôf/), *n.* **Georgi** (gä ôr/gē) **Maximilianovich**, b. 1902, Soviet leader; Premier from 1953 until resignation in 1955.

ma·lev·o·lence (mə lěv/ə ləns), *n.* state or feeling of being malevolent; ill will. —**Syn.** MALEVOLENCE, MALIGNITY, RANCOR suggest the wishing of harm to others. MALEVOLENCE is a smoldering ill will: *a vindictive malevolence in his expression.* MALIGNITY is a deep-seated and virulent disposition to injure; it is more dangerous than MALEVOLENCE, because it is not only more completely concealed but it often instigates harmful acts: *the malignity of his nature was shocking.* RANCOR is a lasting, corrosive, and implacable hatred and resentment.

ma·lev·o·lent (mə lěv/ə lənt), *adj.* **1.** wishing evil to another or others; showing ill will. **2.** *Astrol.* evil or malign in influence. [t. L: s. *malevolens* wishing ill] —**ma·lev·o·lent·ly,** *adv.*

mal·fea·sance (mål fē/zəns), *n.* *Law.* the wrongful performance of an act which the actor has no right to perform. [t. F: m. *malfaisance* evil-doing, der. *malfaisant,* f. *mal* evil + *faisant,* ppr. of *faire* do, g. L *facere*] —**mal·fea/sant,** *adj., n.*

mal·for·ma·tion (mål/fôr mā/shən), *n.* faulty or anomalous formation or structure, esp. in a living body.

mal·formed (mål fôrmd/), *adj.* faultily formed.

mal·func·tion (mål/fŭngk/shən), *n.* **1.** failure to function properly. —*v.i.* **2.** to fail to function properly. [f. MAL- + FUNCTION]

mal·gré (mål grē/), *prep.* French. despite.

Mal·herbe (mål ěrb/), *n.* **François de** (frän swä/ də), 1555–1628, French poet and critic.

Ma·li (mä/lǐ), **Republic of,** an independent republic in W Africa: member of the French Community. 3,700,000 pop. (est. 1958); 463,500 sq. mi. *Cap.:* Bamako. Formerly, French Sudan.

mal·ic (mål/ǐk, mā/lǐk), *adj.* pertaining to or derived from apples. [t. F: m. *malique,* der. L *mālum* apple]

malic acid, *Chem.* a crystalline, dibasic hydroxy acid, $C_2H_3OH(COOH)_2$, occurring in apples and other fruits.

mal·ice (mål/ǐs), *n.* **1.** desire to inflict injury or suffering on another. **2.** *Law.* evil intent on the part of one who commits a wrongful act injurious to others. [ME, t. OF, g. L *malitia* badness, spite, malice] —**Syn. 1.** ill will, spite, spitefulness; animosity, enmity; malevolence. See grudge. —**Ant. 1.** benevolence; good will.

malice aforethought, *Law.* (in homicide) the distinguishing characteristic between common-law murder and manslaughter, such as an intent to kill, or to do serious bodily harm, except when a killing is committed in the heat of passion from a reasonable provocation.

ma·li·cious (mə lǐsh/əs), *adj.* **1.** full of, characterized by, or showing malice; malevolent. **2.** *Law.* motivated by vicious, wanton, or mischievous purposes. —**ma·li/cious·ly,** *adv.* —**ma·li/cious·ness,** *n.*

ma·lign (mə līn/), *v.t.* **1.** to speak ill of; slander. —*adj.* **2.** evil in effect; pernicious; baleful. **3.** having or showing an evil disposition; malevolent. [ME *maligne,* t. OF, t. L: m. *malignus* ill-disposed] —**ma·lign/er,** *n.* —**ma·lign/ly,** *adv.*

ma·lig·nant (mə lǐg/nənt), *adj.* **1.** disposed to cause suffering or distress; malicious. **2.** very dangerous; harmful in influence or effect. **3.** *Pathol.* deadly; tending to produce death, as a disease, tumor, etc. [t. LL: s. *malignans, -antis,* injuring maliciously] —**ma·lig/nance, ma·lig/nan·cy,** *n.* —**ma·lig/nant·ly,** *adv.*

ma·lig·ni·ty (mə lǐg/nə tǐ), *n., pl.* **-ties. 1.** state or character of being malign; malevolence. **2.** (*pl.*) malignant feelings, actions, etc. [late ME, t. L: m.s. *malignitas*]

Ma·lines (mə lēnz/; *Fr.* må lēn/), *n.* French Mechlin.

ma·lines (mə lēn/; *Fr.* må lēn/), *n.* **1.** Also, **ma·line/.** a delicate net resembling tulle, originally made by hand

in the town of Mechlin, Belgium. **2.** Mechlin lace.

ma·lin·ger (mə lǐng/gər), *v.i.* to feign sickness or injury, esp. in order to avoid duty, work, etc. [t. F: m. *malingre* sickly, ailing. f. *mal* bad(ly) + OF *heingre* haggard, of Gmc. orig.] —**ma·lin/ger·er,** *n.*

Ma·li·now·ski (mä/lǐ nôf/skǐ), *n.* **Bronislaw Kasper** (brô nē/slåf kås/pěr), 1884–1942, Polish anthropologist, in the U.S.

mal·i·son (mål/ə zən, -sən), *n.* *Archaic or Dial.* a curse. [ME, t. OF: m. *maleiçon,* g. L *maledictio* MALEDICTION]

mall (môl, mål), *n.* **1.** a shaded walk, usually public. **2.** the mallet used in the game of pall-mall. **3.** the game. **4.** the place or alley where it was played. [ME *malle,* t. OF: m. *ma(i)l,* g. L *malleus* hammer]

mal·lard (mål/ərd), *n., pl.* **-lards,** (*esp. collectively*) **-lard. 1.** a common, almost cosmopolitan, wild duck, *Anas platyrhynchos,* from which the domestic ducks descended. **2.** a male of this species. [ME, t. OF: m. *malart,* prob. t. Gmc.: m. proper name *Madalhart,* given to animal in beast epic]

Mal·lar·mé (må lär mě/), *n.* **Stéphane** (stě fån/), 1842–1898, French poet.

mal·le·a·ble (mål/ǐ ə bəl), *adj.* **1.** capable of being extended or shaped by hammering or by pressure with rollers. **2.** adaptable or tractable. [ME *malliable,* t. OF: m. *malleable,* der. L *malleäre* beat with a hammer. See -ABLE] —**mal·le·a·bil/i·ty, mal/le·a·ble·ness,** *n.*

malleable cast iron, white cast-iron castings given a special heat treatment to make them tough.

malleable iron, 1. malleable cast iron. **2.** the purest form of commercial iron, easily welded or forged.

mal·lee (mål/ē), *n.* **1.** any of various dwarf Australian species of *Eucalyptus,* as *Eucalyptus dumosa* and *E. oleosa,* which sometimes form large tracts of brushwood. **2.** such brushwood. [t. Australian]

mal·le·muck (mål/ə mŭk/), *n.* any of various oceanic birds, as the fulmar or albatross. [t. D: m. *mallemok,* f. m. *mal* foolish + *mok* gull]

mal·le·o·lar (mə lē/ə lər), *adj. Anat.* pertaining to a malleolus. [f. MALLEOL(US) + -AR¹]

mal·le·o·lus (mə lē/ə ləs), *n., pl.* **-li** (-lī/). *Anat.* either of two bony protuberances, one on each side of the ankle, situated in man at the lower end of the fibula and tibia respectively. [t. L, dim. of *malleus* hammer]

mal·let (mål/ǐt), *n.* **1.** a hammerlike tool with a head commonly of wood but occasionally of rawhide, plastic, etc., used for driving any tool with a wooden handle, as a chisel. **2.** the wooden implement used to strike the balls in croquet. **3.** the stick used to drive the ball in polo. [ME *maylet,* t. OF: m. *maillet,* dim. of *mail* MALL]

mal·le·us (mål/ǐ əs), *n., pl.* **-lei** (-lī/). *Anat.* the outermost of three small bones in the middle ear of man and other mammals. See diag. under **ear.** [t. L: hammer]

Mal·lor·ca (mä lyôr/kä), *n.* Spanish name of **Majorca.**

mal·low (mål/ō), *n.* **1.** any plant of the genus *Malva,* comprising herbs with leaves usually angularly lobed or dissected, and purple, pink, or white flowers, as *M. sylvestris,* common in Europe, and *M. neglecta* (*M. rotundifolia*), the dwarf mallow. **2.** any malvaceous plant, as the marsh mallow. [ME *malue,* OE *mealwe,* t. L: m. *malva*]

malm (mäm), *n.* **1.** a kind of soft, friable limestone. **2.** a chalk-bearing soil of the southeastern part of England. [ME *malme,* OE *mealm,* c. Icel. *mâlmr* ore]

Mal·mé·dy (mål mě dē/), *n.* See **Eupen and Malmédy.**

Malm·ö (mål/mō; *Sw.* mälm/œ/), *n.* a seaport in S Sweden, on the Sound opposite Copenhagen, Denmark. 209,473 (est. 1956).

malm·sey (mäm/zǐ), *n.* a strong, sweet wine of a high flavor, orig. made in Greece, but now in Madeira. [ME *malmesey,* t. ML: m.s. *malmasia,* t. NGk.: alter. of *Monemvasia* a seaport in southern Greece]

mal·nu·tri·tion (mål/nū trǐsh/ən, -noo-), *n.* imperfect nutrition; lack of proper nutrition.

mal·oc·clu·sion (mål/ə klōo/zhən), *n.* faulty occlusion, closing, or meeting, as of opposing teeth in the upper and lower jaws.

mal·o·dor (mål ō/dər), *n.* a bad odor; a stench.

mal·o·dor·ous (mål ō/dər əs), *adj.* having a bad odor. —**mal·o/dor·ous·ly,** *adv.* —**mal·o/dor·ous·ness,** *n.*

Ma·lone (mə lōn/), *n.* **Edmond,** 1741–1812, Irish scholar and editor of Shakespeare.

ma·lo·nic acid (mə lō/nǐk, -lŏn/ǐk), a dibasic acid, $CH_2(COOH)_2$, easily decomposed by heat. [t. F: m. *malonique,* alter. of *malique* MALIC]

malonic ester, *Chem.* a colorless fluid, $CH_2(COOC_2H_5)_2$, used in organic syntheses.

Mal·o·ry (mål/ə rǐ), *n.* **Sir Thomas,** fl. 1470, English translator and compiler of *Morte d'Arthur.*

Mal·pi·ghi (mål pē/gē), *n.* **Marcello** (mär chěl/lō), 1628–94, Italian anatomist. —**Mal·pigh·i·an** (mål pǐg/ǐ ən), *adj.*

mal·pigh·i·a·ceous (mål pǐg/ǐ ā/shəs), *adj.* belonging or pertaining to the *Malpighiaceae,* a large family of tropical plants, certain of which are cultivated for ornamental purposes. [f. s. NL *Malpighia* the typical genus (named after MALPIGHI) + -ACEOUS]

Malpighian bodies, *Anat.* certain small round bodies occurring in the cortical substance of the kidney. Also, **Malpighian corpuscles.**

Malpighian layer, *Anat.* the layer of nonhorny cells in the epidermis.

ăct, āble, dâre, ärt; ěbb, ēqual; ǐf, īce; hŏt, ōver, ôrder, oil, bŏŏk, ōoze, out; ŭp, ūse, ûrge; ə = a in alone; ch, chief; g, give; ng, ring; sh, shoe; th, thin; t͟h, that; zh, vision. See the full key on inside cover.

Malpighian tubes, the excretory organs of insects, tubular outgrowths of the alimentary canal near the junction of the ventriculus and intestine. Also, **Malpighian vessels.**

mal·po·si·tion (măl'pə zĭsh'ən), n. Pathol. faulty or wrong position, esp. of a part or organ of the body or of a fetus in the uterus.

mal·prac·tice (măl prăk'tĭs), n. 1. improper professional action or treatment by a physician, as from reprehensible ignorance or neglect or with criminal intent. 2. any improper conduct. —mal·prac·ti·tion·er (măl'prăk tĭsh'ən ər), n.

Mal·raux (mȧlrō'), n. André (äɴ drě'), born 1901, French novelist.

malt (môlt), n. 1. germinated grain (usually barley), used in brewing and distilling. 2. liquor produced from malt by fermentation, as beer or ale. —v.t. 3. to convert (grain) into malt. 4. to treat or mix with malt or malt product. 5. to make (liquor) with malt. —v.i. 6. to become malt. 7. to produce malt from grain. [ME; OE mealt, c. G malz; akin to MELT]

Mal·ta (môl'ta), n. 1. a British island in the Mediterranean between Sicily and Africa: naval station. 288,082 (est. 1954); 95 sq. mi. 2. a British colony consisting of this island and two small adjacent islands. 315,952 (est. 1954); 122 sq. mi. Cap.: Valletta.

Malta fever, undulant fever.

malt·ase (môl'tās), n. Biochem. an enzyme which converts maltose into dextrose and causes similar cleavage of many other glucosides. [f. MALT + -ASE]

malted milk, 1. a soluble powder made of dehydrated milk and malted cereals. 2. a beverage made from this powder dissolved, usually, in milk.

Mal·tese (môl tēz', -tēs'), adj., n., pl. -tese. —adj. 1. of or pertaining to Malta, its people, or their language. —n. 2. a native or inhabitant of Malta. 3. the Arabic dialect spoken in Malta.

Maltese cat, a bluish-gray variety of domestic cat.

Maltese cross, a cross having four equal arms that expand in width outward. See illus. under **cross.**

malt extract, a sweet gummy substance derived from an infusion of malt.

mal·tha (măl'thə), n. 1. any of various cements or mortars, bituminous or otherwise. 2. any of various natural mixtures of hydrocarbons, as ozocerite. 3. a viscous mineral liquid or semiliquid bitumen; a mineral tar. [late ME, t. L, t. Gk.: mixture of wax and pitch]

Mal·thus (măl'thəs), n. Thomas Robert, 1766–1834, British political economist.

Mal·thu·si·an (măl thōō'zĭ ən), adj. 1. of or pertaining to T. R. Malthus, who contended that population, tending to increase faster than the means of subsistence, should be checked by social and moral restraints. —n. 2. a follower of Malthus. —Mal·thu'si·an·ism, n.

malt liquor, an alcoholic beverage, as beer, fermented from malt.

malt·ose (môl'tōs), n. Chem. a white crystalline sugar, $C_{12}H_{22}O_{11}H_2O$, formed by the action of diastase (as in malt) on starch. Also, **malt sugar.** [f. MALT + -OSE[2]]

mal·treat (măl trēt'), v.t. to treat ill; handle roughly or cruelly; abuse. [t. F: m. maltraiter. See MAL-, TREAT, v.] —mal·treat'ment, n.

malt·ster (môlt'stər), n. a maker of or dealer in malt.

malt·y ((môl'tĭ), adj. of, like, or containing malt.

mal·va·ceous (măl vā'shəs), adj. belonging to the Malvaceae, or mallow family of plants, which includes the abutilon, althea, hollyhock, okra, cotton plant, etc. [t. L: m. malvāceus of mallows]

mal·va·si·a (măl'və sē'ə), n. a sweet grape from which malmsey wine is made. [t. It. See MALMSEY]

Mal·vern (môl'vərn), n. an urban area in W England, in Worcestershire, comprising several small towns and villages on the E slope of the **Malvern Hills:** mineral springs; resort. 21,681 (1951).

Malvern Hill (môl'vərn), a plateau in E Virginia, SE of Richmond: battle, 1862.

mal·ver·sa·tion (măl'vər sā'shən), n. improper or corrupt behavior in office. [t. F, der. malverser, t. L: m. male versārī behave wrongly]

mal·voi·sie (măl'voi zĭ', -və-), n. 1. malmsey wine. 2. malvasia grape. [t. F; r. ME malvesie MALMSEY, t. OF]

ma·ma (mä'mə, mə mä'), n. mother; mamma.

mam·ba (mäm'bä), n. any of the long, slender, arboreal African snakes of the genus Dendroaspis, whose bite is almost certain death, and which are said to attack without provocation. [t. S Afr. (Kaffir): m. m'namba]

mam·bo (mäm'bō), n. a ballroom dance of Latin-American origin, somewhat resembling the rumba.

Mam·e·luke (măm'ə lōōk'), n. 1. a member of an Egyptian military class, originally slaves, in power from 1250 to 1517, and influential under Turkish rule until destroyed by Mohammed Ali in 1811. 2. (l.c.) (in Mohammedan countries) a slave. [t. Ar.: m. mamlūk slave]

ma·mey (mä mä', -mě'), n. mammee.

mam·ma[1] (mä'mə, mə mä'), n. (esp. in childish use) mother. [redupl. of a syllable common in natural infantile utterance. Cf. F maman, L mamma, Gk. mámmē, Russ. and Lith. mama]

mam·ma[2] (măm'ə), n., pl. mammae (măm'ē). Comp. Anat. the organ, characteristic of mammals, which in the female secretes milk; a breast or udder. [OE, t. L: breast, pap]

mam·mal (măm'əl), n. a member of the Mammalia. —mam'mal·like', adj.

Mam·ma·li·a (mă mā'lĭə), n.pl. a class of vertebrates whose young feed upon milk from the mother's breast. Most species (except cetaceans) are more or less hairy, all have a diaphragm, and all (except the monotremes) are viviparous. [NL, neut. pl. of LL mammālis of the breast] —mam·ma'li·an, n., adj.

mam·mal·o·gy (mă măl'ə jĭ), n. the science that treats of mammals. [f. MAMMA(LIA) + -LOGY]

mam·ma·ry (măm'ə rĭ), adj. Anat., etc. of or pertaining to the mamma or breast; mammalike.

mam·ma·to·cu·mu·lus (mă mā'tō kū'myə ləs), n., pl. -li (-lī'). Meteorol. a cloud formation whose lower surface forms pockets or festoons.

mam·mee (mä mä', -mě'), n. 1. a tall, tropical American resin-yielding tree, Mammea americana. 2. Also, **mammee apple.** its large, edible fruit. 3. sapodilla. 4. marmalade tree. Also, **mamey.** [t. Sp.: m. mamey; from Haitian]

mam·mif·er·ous (mă mĭf'ərəs), adj. having mammae; mammalian. [f. s. L mamma breast + -(I)FEROUS]

mam·mil·la (mă mĭl'ə), n., pl. -millae (-mĭl'ē). 1. Anat. the nipple of the mamma or breast. 2. any nipplelike process or protuberance. [t. L, dim. of mamma MAMMA[2]]

mam·mil·lar·y (măm'ə lěr'ĭ), adj. of, pertaining to, or resembling a mammilla.

mam·mil·late (măm'ə lāt'), adj. having a mammilla or mammillae. Also, **mam'mil·lat'ed.**

mam·mon (măm'ən), n. 1. New Testament. riches or material wealth. Mat. 6:24; Luke 16:9, 11, 13. 2. (cap.) a personification of riches as an evil spirit or deity. [t. LL: s. mammōna, t. Gk.: m. mamōnās, t. Aram.: m. māmōn(ā) riches] —mam'mon·ish, adj.

Mammillary structure of malachite

mam·mon·ism (măm'ə nĭz'əm), n. the greedy pursuit of riches. —mam'mon·ist, mam'mon·ite', n. —mam'mon·is'tic, adj.

mam·moth (măm'əth), n. 1. a large, extinct species of elephant, Mammuthus primigenius, the northern woolly mammoth, which resembled the present Indian elephant but had a hairy coat and long, curved tusks. 2. any of various related extinct species of elephant, as the **imperial mammoth,** Mammuthus imperator, the largest mammoth. —adj. 3. huge; gigantic: a mammoth enterprise. [t. Russ.: m. mammot', now mamant'] —Syn. 3. See **gigantic.**

Columbian mammoth. Mammuthus columbi (9 ft. high, 16 ft. long, tusks ab. 9 ft.)

Mammoth Cave, a large limestone cavern in central Kentucky: a national park.

mam·my (măm'ĭ), n., pl. -mies. 1. (in childish use) mother. 2. Southern U.S. a colored female nurse or old family servant.

Ma·mo·ré (mä'mō rě'), n. a river flowing generally N through Bolivia and joining the Beni on the Brazilian border to form the Madeira river. ab. 700 mi.

man (măn), n., pl. men, v., manned, manning. —n. 1. Anthropol. an individual (genus Homo, family Hominidae, class Mammalia) at the highest level of animal development, mainly characterized by his exceptional mentality. 2. the human creature or being as representing the species or as distinguished from other beings, animals, or things; the human race; mankind. 3. a human being; a person: to elect a new man. 4. the male human being, as distinguished from woman. 5. a husband: man and wife. 6. one; anyone (prec. by a): to give a man a chance. 7. a male follower, subordinate, or employee: officers and men of the army. 8. one having manly qualities or virtues. 9. Obs. manly character or courage. 10. a male servant; a valet. 11. a word of familiar address implying disparagement, impatience, etc. 12. one of the pieces used in playing certain games, as chess or checkers. 13. Hist. a liegeman; vassal. 14. to a man, all; to the last man. [ME and OE mann, man (pl. menn, men), c. Icel. madhr, D man, G mann] —v.t. 15. to furnish with men, as for service or defense. 16. to take one's place for service, as at a gun, post, etc. 17. to make manly; brace. 18. to accustom (a hawk) to the presence of men. [ME manne(n), OE mannian]

Man (măn), n. Isle of, an island in the Irish Sea: one of the British Isles. 55,253 pop. (1951); 227 sq. mi. Cap.: Douglas.

Man., 1. Manila. 2. Manitoba.

ma·na (mä'nä), n. Anthropol. impersonal, supernatural force which may be concentrated in objects or persons.

man about town, a frequenter of theaters, clubs, etc.

---

b., blend of, blended; c., cognate with; d., dialect, dialectal; der., derived from; f., formed from; g., going back to; m., modification of; r., replacing; s., stem of; t., taken from; ?, perhaps. See the full key on inside cover.

Man·a·bo·zho (măn′ə bō′zhō), *n.*, *pl.* **-zhos.** the trickster–culture hero of the Ottawa, Chippewa, Potawatomi, and other Central Algonquian tribes; referred to under a variety of names (Manabozho, Michabo, Nanabush, Nenabozho, etc.).

man·a·cle (măn′ə kəl), *n.*, *v.*, **-cled, -cling.** —*n.* (*usually pl.*) **1.** a shackle for the hand; handcuff. **2.** a restraint. —*v.t.* **3.** to handcuff; fetter. **4.** to hamper; restrain. [ME *manicle*, t. OF: handcuff, t. L: m. *manicula*, dim. of *manus* hand]

man·age (măn′ĭj), *v.*, **-aged, -aging.** —*v.t.* **1.** to bring about; succeed in accomplishing: *he managed to see the governor.* **2.** to take charge or care of: *to manage an estate.* **3.** to dominate or influence (a person) by tact, address, or artifice. **4.** to handle, direct, govern, or control in action or use. **5.** to wield (a weapon, tool, etc.). **6.** to succeed in accomplishing a task, purpose, etc. **7.** to contrive to get along. **8.** to handle or train (a horse) in the exercises of the manège. **9.** *Obs.* or *Archaic.* to use sparingly. —*v.i.* **10.** to conduct affairs. [t. It.: m. *maneggiare* handle, train (horses), der. *mano* hand, g. L *manus*; sense influenced by F *manège* act of managing and *ménage* household] —**Syn. 1.** arrange, contrive. **4.** guide, conduct, regulate, engineer. See **rule. 5.** handle, manipulate.

man·age·a·ble (măn′ĭj ə bəl), *adj.* that may be managed; governable; contrivable; tractable. —**man′age·a·bil′i·ty, man′age·a·ble·ness,** *n.* —**man′age·a·bly,** *adv.*

managed currency, a monetary system governed by an administrative organization or according to some specially contrived set of rules (contrasted with the automatic gold standard).

man·age·ment (măn′ĭj mənt), *n.* **1.** act or manner of managing; handling, direction, or control. **2.** skill in managing; executive ability. **3.** the person or persons managing an institution, business, etc.: *conflicts between labor and management.* —**Syn. 1.** regulation, administration; superintendence, care, charge.

man·ag·er (măn′ĭj ər), *n.* **1.** one who manages. **2.** one charged with the management or direction of an institution, a business, or the like. **3.** one who manages resources and expenditures, as of a household. —**man′ag·er·ship′,** *n.* —**Syn. 1.** administrator, executive, superintendent, supervisor; boss.

man·ag·er·ess (măn′ĭj ər ĭs; *Brit.* măn′ə jə rĕs′), *n. Chiefly Brit.* a female manager.

man·a·ge·ri·al (măn′ə jĭr′ĭ əl), *adj.* pertaining to management or a manager: *managerial functions.* —**man′a·ge′ri·al·ly,** *adv.*

Ma·na·gua (mä nä′gwä), *n.* the capital of Nicaragua, in the W part, on **Lake Managua** (38 mi. long): almost totally destroyed by an earthquake, 1931. 109,352 (1950).

man·a·kin (măn′ə kĭn), *n.* **1.** any of various songless passerine birds, family *Pipridae*, of the warmer parts of America, mostly small and brilliantly colored. **2.** manikin. [var. of MANIKIN]

ma·ña·na (mä nyä′nä), *n.*, *adv.* Spanish. tomorrow; the indefinite future.

Ma·ná·os (mä nous′), *n.* a city in N Brazil, on the Río Negro near its confluence with the Amazon: a seaport ab. 900 mi. from the Atlantic. 110,678 (est. 1952). Also, **Ma·naus′.**

Ma·nas·sas (mə năs′əs), *n.* a town in NE Virginia: battles of Bull Run, 1861, 1862. 1804 (1950).

Ma·nas·seh (mə năs′ə), *n.* **1.** son of the patriarch Joseph. Gen. 41:51. **2.** one of the ten tribes of Israel. **3.** king of Judah, of the 7th century B.C. II Kings 21.

man-at-arms (măn′ət ärmz′), *n.*, *pl.* **men-at-arms. 1.** a soldier. **2.** a heavy-armed soldier on horseback.

man·a·tee (măn′ə tē′), *n.* any of various herbivorous, gregarious sirenians constituting the genus *Trichechus*, having two flippers in front and a spoon-shaped tail, of West Indian, Floridan, and Gulf coast waters. [t. Sp.: m. *manatí*, t. Carib.: m. *manatoui*] —**man·a·toid** (măn′ə toid′), *adj.*

Florida manatee.
Trichechus manatus latirostris
(11 to 13 ft. long)

ma·nav·el·ins (mə năv′əl ĭnz), *n.pl. Naut. Slang.* miscellaneous pieces of gear and material. Also, **ma·nav′il·ins.**

Man·ches·ter (măn′chĕs′tər, -chĭs tər), *n.* **1.** a city in W England, in Lancashire: connected with the Mersey estuary by a ship canal (35½ mi. long). 686,200 (est. 1956). **2.** a city in S New Hampshire. 88,282 (1960).

man·chi·neel (măn′chə nēl′), *n.* a tropical American euphorbiaceous tree or shrub, *Hippomane Mancinella*, with a milky, highly caustic, poisonous sap. [t. F: m. *mancenille*, t. Sp.: m. *manzanilla*, dim. of *manzana* apple, g. L (*māla*) *Matiāna* (apples) of Matius (author of a cooking manual)]

Man·chu (măn chōō′), *n.* **1.** one of a Mongolian people inhabiting Manchuria, who conquered China in the 17th century. **2.** a Tungusic language, spoken by the Manchus. —*adj.* **3.** of or pertaining to the Manchus, their country, or their language.

Man·chu·kuo (măn′chōō′kwō′; *Chin.* măn′jō′kwō′), *n.* a former country (1932–45) in E Asia, N of China, under Japanese control. It included Manchuria and parts of Inner Mongolia. Now a part of China. Also, **Man′chou′kuo′.**

Man·chu·ri·a (măn chŏŏr′ĭ ə), *n.* a region in NE China, formerly comprising nine provinces of that country; ancestral home of the Manchus. ab. 413,000 sq. mi. —**Man·chu′ri·an,** *adj.*, *n.*

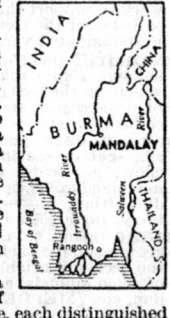

man·ci·ple (măn′sə pəl), *n.* a steward or purveyor, esp. of an English college or Inn of Court, or other institution. [ME, t. OF: slave, servant, t. L: m.s. *mancipium* purchase, possession, a slave]

-mancy, a word element meaning "divination," as in *necromancy.* [ME *-manci*(*e*), *-mancy*(*e*), t. OF: (m.) *mancie*, g. LL *mantía*, t. Gk.: m. *manteía* divination]

Man·dae·an (măn dē′ən), *n.* **1.** a member of an ancient Gnostic sect still surviving in southern Mesopotamia. **2.** the Aramaic language of the Mandaean sacred books. —*adj.* **3.** of the Mandaeans. [f. m.s. Mandaean *mandayyā* (der. *mandā* knowledge) + -AN]

Man·da·lay (măn′də lā′, măn′də lā′), *n.* a city in central Burma, on the Irrawaddy river: the former capital of Upper Burma. 182,367 (1953).

man·da·mus (măn dā′məs), *n.* **1.** *Law.* a writ from a superior court to an inferior court, or to an officer, a corporation, etc., commanding a specified thing to be done. **2.** (in early English law) any prerogative writ directing affirmative action. —*v.t.* **3.** *Colloq.* to intimidate or serve with such writ. [t. L: we command]

Man·dan (măn′dăn), *n.* a Siouan language.

man·da·rin (măn′də rĭn), *n.* **1.** a member of any of the nine ranks of public officials in the Chinese Empire, each distinguished by a particular kind of button worn on the cap. **2.** (*cap.*) standard Chinese. **3.** (*cap.*) the north China language, esp. that of Peking. **4.** a small, flattish citrus fruit of which the tangerine is one variety, native in southwestern Asia, of a characteristic sweet and spicy flavor. **5.** the tree producing it, *Citrus reticulata*, and related species. [t. Chinese pidgin E, t. Pg.: m. *mandarim*, der. *mandar* to command, b. with Malay and Hind. *mantrī*, g. Skt. *mantrin* counselor, der. *mantra* thought, counsel]

mandarin duck, a crested duck, *Aix galericulata*, with variegated plumage of purple, green, chestnut and white, native in China.

man·da·tar·y (măn′də tĕr′ĭ), *n.*, *pl.* **-taries.** a person or nation holding a mandate. [t. LL: m.s. *mandātārius*, der. L *mandātum* MANDATE]

man·date (*n.* măn′dāt, -dĭt; *v.* măn′dāt), *n.*, *v.*, **-dated, -dating.** —*n.* **1.** a commission given to one nation (the mandatary) by an associated group of nations (such as the League of Nations) to administer the government and affairs of a people in a backward territory. **2.** a mandated territory. **3.** *Pol.* the instruction as to policy given or supposed to be given by the electors to a legislative body or to one or more of its members. **4.** a command from a superior court or official to an inferior one. **5.** a command; order. **6.** an order issued by the pope, esp. one commanding the preferment of a certain person to a benefice. **7.** *Roman and Civil Law.* a contract by which one engages gratuitously to perform services for another. **8.** *Roman Law.* an order or decree by the emperor, esp. to governors of provinces. —*v.t.* **9.** to consign (a territory, etc.) to the charge of a particular nation under a mandate. [t. L: m.s. *mandātum*, prop. pp. neut. of *mandāre* commit, enjoin, command]

man·da·tor (măn dā′tər), *n.* one who gives a mandate.

man·da·to·ry (măn′də tōr′ĭ), *adj.*, *n.*, *pl.* **-ries.** —*adj.* **1.** pertaining to, of the nature of, or containing a mandate. **2.** obligatory. **3.** *Law.* permitting no option: *a mandatory clause.* **4.** having received a mandate, as a nation. —*n.* **5.** mandatary.

Man·de·ville (măn′də vĭl), *n.* **1.** Bernard, 1670?–1733, British philosopher and writer of satires, born in Holland. **2.** Sir John, the ostensible (British) author of a 14th century book of travels.

man·di·ble (măn′də bəl), *n.* **1.** the bone of the lower jaw. **2.** (in birds) a. the lower part of the beak: the lower jaw. b. (*pl.*) the upper and lower parts of the beak; the jaws. **3.** (in arthropods) one of the first pair of mouth-part appendages, typically a jawlike biting organ, but styliform or setiform in piercing and sucking species. [t. LL: m.s. *mandibula, mandibulum* jaw]

Head of bee
M. Mandible (def. 3)
A. Antenna

man·dib·u·lar (măn dĭb′yə lər), *adj.* pertaining to or of the nature of a mandible.

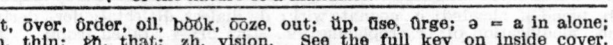

man·dib·u·late (măndĭb'yəlĭt, -lāt'), *adj.* having mandibles.

Man·din·go (măndĭng'gō), *n.*, *pl.* **-gos, -goes,** *adj.* —*n.* **1.** a member of any of a number of Negro peoples forming an extensive linguistic group in western Africa. **2.** a principal language of West Africa. —*adj.* **3.** of the Mandingos or their language.

man·do·lin (măn'dəlĭn', măn/dəlĭn'), *n.* a musical instrument with a pear-shaped wooden body (smaller than that of the lute) and a fretted neck, usually having metal strings plucked with a plectrum. [t. F: m. *mandoline,* t. It.: m. *mandolino,* dim. of *mandola, mandora,* var. of *pandora.* See PANDORA, BANDORE] —**man·do·lin'ist,** *n.*

Mandolin

man·drag·o·ra (măndrăg'ərə), *n.* **1.** mandrake. **2.** a mandrake root. [OE, t. LL, in L *mandragoras,* t. Gk.]

man·drake (măn'drāk, -drĭk), *n.* **1.** a narcotic, short-stemmed European solanaceous herb, *Mandragora officinarum,* with a fleshy, often forked root fancied to resemble a human form. **2.** *U.S.* the May apple. [ME; popular etymological alter. of MANDRAGORA which was interpreted as MAN + DRAKE²]

Mandrake

man·drel (măn'drəl), *n.* *Mach.* a spindle, axle, bar or arbor, usually tapered, pressed into a hole in a piece of work to support the work during the machining process, as between the centers of a lathe. Also, **man'dril.** [t. F, dissimilated var. of *mandrin*]

man·drill (măn'drĭl), *n.* a large, ferocious-looking baboon, *Papio sphinx,* of western Africa, the male of which has the face marked with blue and scarlet and the muzzle ribbed. [f. MAN + DRILL⁴]

man·du·cate (măn'jōōkāt', man'dyōō-), *v.t.*, **-cated, -cating.** *Rare.* to chew; masticate; eat. [t. L: m.s. *manducātus,* pp.] —**man·du·ca'tion,** *n.* —**man·du·ca·to·ry** (măn'jōō kə tōr'ĭ), *adj.*

mane (mān), *n.* the long hair growing on the back of or about the neck and neighboring parts of some animals, as the horse, lion, etc. [ME; OE *manu,* c. G *mähne*] —**maned** (mānd), *adj.*

Mandrill. *Papio sphinx* (Ab. 3½ ft. long)

man-eat·er (măn'ē'tər), *n.* **1.** a cannibal. **2.** an animal, esp. a tiger, lion, or shark, that eats or is said to eat men. **3.** the great white shark, *Carcharodon carcharias,* reputedly the most dangerous shark to man.

maned wolf, the largest wild South American canid, *Chrysocyon jubatus,* a red-coated, large-eared, long-legged fox, found in Paraguay and Matto Grosso.

ma·nège (mănĕzh', -nāzh'), *n.* **1.** the art of training and riding horses. **2.** the action or movements of a trained horse. **3.** a school for training horses and teaching horsemanship. Also, **ma·nege'.** [t. F. See MANAGE]

ma·nes (mā'nēz), *n.pl.* **1.** (among the ancient Romans) the deified souls of the dead. **2.** the spirit or shade of a particular dead person. Also, **Ma'nes.** [L]

Ma·net (mä nĕ'), *n.* Édouard (ĕ dwär'), 1832–83, French impressionist painter.

ma·neu·ver (mənōō'vər), *n.*, *v.*, **-vered, -vering.** —*n.* **1.** a planned and regulated movement or evolution of troops, war vessels, etc. **2.** (*pl.*) a series of tactical exercises usually carried out in the field by large bodies of troops in imitation of war. **3.** an adroit move; artful proceeding, measure, etc. **4.** maneuvering; artful management. —*v.t.* **5.** to change the position of (troops, vessels, etc.) by a maneuver. **6.** to bring, put, drive, or make by maneuvers. **7.** to manipulate with skill or adroitness. —*v.i.* **8.** to perform a maneuver or maneuvers. **9.** to scheme. Also, **manoeuvre.** [t. F: m. *manœuvre* manipulation, der. *manœuvrer* work, g. LL *manū operāre* work by hand] —**ma·neu'ver·a·ble,** *adj.* —**ma·neu'ver·a·bil'i·ty,** *n.* —**ma·neu'ver·er,** *n.*

man·ful (măn'fəl), *adj.* having or showing manly spirit; resolute. —**man'ful·ly,** *adv.* —**man'ful·ness,** *n.* —Syn. See manly.

man·ga·nate (măng'gə nāt'), *n.* *Chem.* a salt of manganic acid: *potassium manganate* K₂MnO₄.

man·ga·nese (măng'gə nēs', -nēz'), *n.* *Chem.* a hard, brittle, grayish-white metallic element, whose oxide (**manganese oxide,** MnO₂) is a valuable oxidizing agent, used as alloying agent in steel to give it toughness. *Symbol:* Mn; *at. wt.:* 54.93; *at. no.:* 25; *sp. gr.:* 7.2 at 20°C. [t. F, t. It., t. ML: m. *magnēsia* MAGNESIA]

manganese steel, a steel alloy containing 10 to 14 per cent of manganese, used for railway switches and other devices involving heavy wear and strain.

man·gan·ic (măn găn'ĭk), *adj.* *Chem.* of or containing manganese, esp. in the trivalent state (Mn +³).

manganic acid, *Chem.* an acid, H₂MnO₄, not known in the free state.

man·ga·nite (măng'gə nīt'), *n.* **1.** a gray to black mineral, hydrous manganese oxide, MnO(OH), a minor ore of manganese. **2.** *Chem.* any of a series of salts containing tetravalent manganese, and derived from the acids H₄MnO₄ or H₂MnO₃. [f. MANGAN(ESE) + -ITE¹]

man·ga·nous (măng'gə nəs, măn găn'əs), *adj.* *Chem.* containing divalent manganese (Mn +²).

mange (mānj), *n.* any of various skin diseases due to parasitic mites affecting animals and sometimes man, characterized by loss of hair and scabby eruptions. [late ME *manjewe,* t. OF: m. *manjue* itch, der. *mangier* eat, g. L *mandūcāre* chew]

man·gel-wur·zel (măng'gəl wûr'zəl), *n.* *Chiefly Brit.* a coarse variety of the common beet, *Beta vulgaris,* extensively cultivated as food for cattle, etc. Also, **man'gel.** [t. G, var. of *mangoldwurzel* beet root]

man·ger (mān'jər), *n.* a box or trough, as in a stable, from which horses or cattle eat. [ME, t. OF: m. *mangeoire,* der. L *mandūcāre* chew]

man·gle¹ (măng'gəl), *v.t.*, **-gled, -gling. 1.** to cut, slash, or crush so as to disfigure: *a corpse mangled in battle.* **2.** to mar; spoil: *to mangle a text by poor typesetting.* [ME *mangel(en),* t. AF: m. *mangler,* ? freq. of OF *mahaignier* MAIM] —**man'gler,** *n.* —Syn. **1.** See maim.

man·gle² (măng'gəl), *n.*, *v.*, **-gled, -gling.** —*n.* **1.** a machine for smoothing or pressing cloth, household linen, etc., by means of rollers. —*v.t.* **2.** to smooth with a mangle. [t. D: m. *mangel,* t. ult. akin to MANGONEL]

man·go (măng'gō), *n.*, *pl.* **-goes, -gos. 1.** the oblong, slightly acid fruit of a tropical anacardiaceous tree, *Mangifera indica,* which is eaten ripe, or preserved or pickled. **2.** the tree itself. [t. Pg.: m. *manga,* t. Malay: m. *manggā,* t. Tamil: m. *mānkāy*]

man·go·nel (măng'gə nĕl'), *n.* a large ancient military engine, or powerful crossbow, for throwing arrows, darts, or stones. [ME, t. OF, dim. der. LL *manganum,* t. Gk.: m. *mánganon* engine of war]

man·go·steen (măng'gə stēn'), *n.* **1.** the juicy edible fruit of an East Indian resin-yielding tree, *Garcinia Mangostana.* **2.** the tree itself. [t. Malay: m. *mangustan*]

man·grove (măng'grōv, măn'-), *n.* **1.** any tree or shrub of the tropical genus *Rhizophora,* the species of which are mostly low trees remarkable for a copious development of interlacing adventitious roots above the ground. **2.** any of various similar plants, as the **white mangrove,** *Avicennia marina,* a valued source of tannin. [f. m. Sp. *mangle* (t. Malay: alter. of *manggi-manggi* mangrove) + GROVE]

man·gy (mān'jĭ), *adj.*, **-gier, -giest. 1.** having, caused by, or like the mange. **2.** contemptible; mean. **3.** squalid; shabby. —**man'gi·ly,** *adv.* —**man'gi·ness,** *n.*

man·han·dle (măn'hăn'dəl, măn hăn'dəl), *v.t.*, **-dled, -dling. 1.** to handle roughly. **2.** to move by force of men, without mechanical appliances.

Man·hat·tan (măn hăt'ən), *n.* **1.** an island in New York City between the Hudson, East, and Harlem rivers. 13½ mi. long; 2½ mi. greatest width; 22¼ sq. mi. **2.** a borough of New York City approximately coextensive with Manhattan Island: chief business district. 1,698,281 (1960). **3.** a cocktail of whiskey and sweet vermouth, often with a dash of bitters and a cherry.

Manhattan Beach, a city in SW California, SW of Los Angeles. 33,934 (1960).

Manhattan District, the large-scale project which developed the atomic bomb.

man·hole (măn'hōl'), *n.* a hole, usually with a cover, through which a man may enter a sewer, drain, steam boiler, etc., as to make repairs.

man·hood (măn'hŏŏd), *n.* **1.** state of being a man or adult male person. **2.** manly qualities. **3.** men collectively. **4.** state of being human.

man-hour (măn'our'), *n.* an hour of work by one man, used as an industrial time unit.

ma·ni·a (mā'nĭə), *n.* **1.** great excitement or enthusiasm; craze. **2.** *Psychiatry.* a form of insanity characterized by great excitement, with or without delusions, and in its acute stage by great violence. [late ME, t. L, t. Gk.: madness]

-mania, a combining form of mania (as in *megalomania*), extended to mean exaggerated desire or love for, as *Anglomania.*

ma·ni·ac (mā'nĭ ăk'), *n.* **1.** a raving lunatic; a madman. —*adj.* **2.** raving with madness; mad.

ma·ni·a·cal (mə nī'ə kəl), *adj.* of or pertaining to mania or a maniac. —**ma·ni·a·cal·ly,** *adv.*

ma·nic (mā'nĭk, măn'ĭk), *adj.* *Med.* pertaining to mania. [t. Gk.: m.s. *manikós* insane]

man·ic-de·pres·sive (măn'ĭk dĭ'prĕs'ĭv), *Psychiatry.* —*adj.* **1.** having a mental disorder marked by cyclothymic manifestations of excitation and depression. —*n.* **2.** one who is suffering from this disorder.

Man·i·che·an (măn'ə kē'ən), *n.* **1.** an adherent of the religious system of the Persian teacher Mani or Manichaeus (A.D. 216?–276?), composed of Gnostic Christian, Buddhistic, Zoroastrian, and various other elements, the principal feature being a dualistic theology which represented a conflict between light and darkness and included belief in the inherent evil of matter. —*adj.* **2.** of or pertaining to Mani or the Manicheans. Also, Man'i·chae'an. [f. LL: (m.) s. *Manichaeus* (t. L Gk.: m. *Manichaios;* from the name of the founder of the sect) + -AN] —**Man'i·chae·an·ism,** **Man'i·che·ism,** *n.*

man·i·cure (măn'ə kyŏŏr'), *n.*, *v.*, **-cured, -curing.** —*n.* **1.** professional care of the hands and fingernails. **2.** a manicurist. —*v.t.*, *v.i.* **3.** to care for (the hands and fingernails). [t. F, f. L: m.s. *manus* hand + m. *cura* care]

man·i·cur·ist (măn'ə kyŏŏr'ĭst), *n.* a person who does manicuring.

---

b., blend of, blended; c., cognate with; d., dialect, dialectal; der., derived from; f., formed from; g., going back to; m., modification of; r., replacing; s., stem of; t., taken from; ?, perhaps. See the full key on inside cover.

man·i·fest (măn'ə·fĕst'), *adj.* **1.** readily perceived by the eye or the understanding; evident; obvious; apparent; plain: *a manifest error.* **2.** *Psychoanal.* apparent or disguising (used of conscious feelings and ideas which conceal and yet incorporate unconscious ideas and impulses): *the manifest content of a dream as opposed to the latent content which it conceals.* —*v.t.* **3.** to make manifest to the eye or the understanding; show plainly. **4.** to prove; put beyond doubt or question. **5.** to record in a ship's manifest. —*n.* **6.** a list of a ship's cargo, signed by the master, for the information and use of custom-house officers. **7.** a list of goods transported by land. [ME, t. L: *as. manifestus* palpable, evident] —**man'i·fest'ly,** *adv.* —**man'i·fest'ness,** *n.* —**Syn.** 1. clear, distinct. 3. reveal. See **display.**

man·i·fes·ta·tion (măn'ə·fĕs·tā'shən), *n.* **1.** act of manifesting. **2.** state of being manifested. **3.** a means of manifesting; indication. **4.** a public demonstration, as for political effect. **5.** *Spiritualism.* a materialization.

man·i·fes·to (măn'ə·fĕs'tō), *n., pl.* **-toes.** a public declaration, as of a sovereign or government, or of any person or body of persons taking important action, making known intentions, objects, motives, etc.; a proclamation. [t. It.: manifest, n.]

man·i·fold (măn'ə·fōld'), *adj.* **1.** of many kinds, numerous and varied: *manifold duties.* **2.** having many different parts, elements, features, forms, etc. **3.** doing or operating several things at once. —*n.* **4.** something having many different parts or features. **5.** a copy or facsimile, as of writing, such as is made by manifolding. **6.** a pipe with a number of inlets or outlets. —*v.t.* **7.** to make copies of, as with carbon paper. [ME *monifald,* OE *manigfeald.* See **MANY, -FOLD**] —**man'i·fold'ly,** *adv.* —**man'i·fold'ness,** *n.* —**Syn.** 1. See **many.**

man·i·fold·er (măn'ə·fōl'dər), *n.* a contrivance for making manifolds or copies, as of writing.

man·i·kin (măn'ə·kĭn), *n.* **1.** a little man; a dwarf; pygmy. **2.** mannequin. **3.** a model of the human body for teaching anatomy, demonstrating surgical operations, etc. Also, **manakin, mannikin.** [t. D: m. *manneken,* dim. of *man* man. Cf. **MANNEQUIN**]

Ma·nil·a (mə·nĭl'ə), *n.* **1.** a seaport in and the capital of the Republic of the Philippines, on W Luzon island. 1,400,000 (est. 1954). See **Quezon City.** **2.** Manila hemp. **3.** Manila paper.

Manila Bay, a large bay in the Philippine Islands, in W Luzon island; the American fleet under Admiral Dewey defeated the Spanish fleet here, 1898.

Manila hemp, a fibrous material obtained from the leaves of the abacá, *Musa textilis,* used for making ropes, fabrics, etc.

Manila paper, strong light-brown paper derived orig. from Manila hemp, but now also from wood-pulp substitutes not of equal strength.

Manila rope, rope manufactured from Manila hemp.

ma·nil·la (mə·nĭl'ə), *n.* **1.** Manila hemp. **2.** Manila paper.

man in the street, the average citizen.

man·i·oc (măn'ī·ŏk', mā'nī·ŏk'), *n.* cassava. [repr. Sp., Pg. *mandioca,* Tupi *manioca,* Guarani *mandio*]

man·i·ple (măn'ə·pəl), *n.* **1.** a subdivision of the Roman legion, consisting of 120 or 60 men. **2.** *Eccles.* one of the Eucharistic vestments, consisting of an ornamental band or strip worn on the left arm near the wrist. See illus. under **chasuble.** [ME, t. OF, t. L: m.s. *manipulus* handful, company]

ma·nip·u·late (mə·nĭp'yə·lāt'), *v.t.,* **-lated, -lating.** **1.** to handle, manage, or use, esp. with skill, in some process of treatment or performance. **2.** to manage or influence by artful skill: *to manipulate prices.* **3.** to adapt or change (accounts, figures, etc.) to suit one's purpose or advantage. [back formation from **MANIPU-LATION**] —**ma·nip'u·la'tive, ma·nip'u·la·to'ry,** *adj.* —**ma·nip'u·la'tor,** *n.*

ma·nip·u·la·tion (mə·nĭp'yə·lā'shən), *n.* **1.** skillful or artful management. **2.** act of manipulating. **3.** state or fact of being manipulated. [t. F, der. L *manipulus* handful]

Ma·ni·pur (mŭn'ī·pŏor'), *n.* a centrally-administered territory in NE India between Assam and Burma. 579,058 pop. (1951); 8620 sq. mi. *Cap.:* Imphal.

Ma·ni·sa (mä'nĭ·sä'), *n.* a city in W Turkey, near the Aegean; the Romans defeated Antiochus the Great here, 190 B.C. 48,484 (1955). Ancient, **Magnesia.**

man·i·to (măn'ə·tō), *n., pl.* **-tos.** (among the Algonquian Indians) a good or evil spirit; a being or object of supernatural power. Also, **man·i·tou** (măn'ə·tōō'). [t. Algonquian (Mass. d.): m. *manitto* he is a god]

Man·i·to·ba (măn'ə·tō'bə), *n.* **1.** a province in central Canada. 809,000 (est. 1953); 246,512 sq. mi. *Cap.:* Winnipeg. **2.** a lake in the S part of this province. 1817 sq. mi.; ab. 120 mi. long. —**Man'i·to'ban,** *adj., n.*

Man·i·tou·lin (măn'ə·tōō'lĭn), *n.* a Canadian island in N Lake Huron. ab. 80 mi. long.

Man·i·to·woc (măn'ə·tə·wŏk'), *n.* a city in E Wisconsin; a port on Lake Michigan. 32,275 (1960).

Ma·ni·za·les (mä'nē·sä'lĕs), *n.* a city in W Colombia. 138,680 (est. 1954).

man·kind (măn'kīnd' *for 1;* măn'kīnd' *for 2*), *n.* **1.** the human race; human beings collectively. **2.** men, as distinguished from women.

man·like (măn'līk'), *adj.* **1.** resembling a man. **2.** belonging or proper to a man; manly: *manlike fortitude.*

man·ly (măn'lĭ), *adj.,* **-lier, -liest,** *adv.* —*adj.* **1.** possessing qualities proper to a man; strong; brave; honorable. **2.** pertaining to or befitting a man: *manly sports.* —*adv.* **3.** *Archaic.* in a manly manner. —**man'li·ly,** *adv.* —**man'li·ness,** *n.*
—**Syn.** 1. MANLY, MANFUL, MANNISH mean possessing the qualities of a man. MANLY implies possession of the noblest and most worthy qualities a man can have (as opposed to servility, insincerity, underhandedness, etc.): *a manly man is the noblest work of God.* MANFUL has particular reference to courage, strength, and industry: *manful resistance.* MANNISH applies to that which resembles man: *a boy with a mannish voice.* Applied to a woman, the term is derogatory, suggesting ostentatious imitation of man: *a mannish stride.*

Mann (män *for 1, 3;* män *for 2*), *n.* **1.** Heinrich (hīn'rĭKH), 1871–1950, German writer in U.S. (brother of Thomas). **2.** Horace, 1796–1859, U.S. educational reformer: established first training school for teachers in the U.S. **3.** Thomas (tō'mäs), 1875–1955, German novelist, in U.S. after 1938.

man·na (măn'ə), *n.* **1.** the food miraculously supplied the children of Israel in the wilderness. Ex. 16:14–36. **2.** divine or spiritual food. **3.** anything likened to the manna of the Israelites. **4.** an exudate of the flowering ash, *Fraxinus Ornus,* of southern Europe, used in pharmacy. [OE, t. LL, t. Gk., t. Heb.: m. *măn*]

man·ne·quin (măn'ə·kĭn), *n.* **1.** a person employed to wear clothing to exhibit to customers. **2.** a figure or model used by artists, tailors, etc. Also, **manikin.** [t. F, t. D: m. *manneken.* See **MANIKIN**]

man·ner (măn'ər), *n.* **1.** way of doing, being done, or happening; mode of action, occurrence, etc. **2.** characteristic or customary way of doing: *houses built in the Mexican manner.* **3.** (*pl.*) the prevailing customs, modes of living, etc., of a people, class, period, etc. **4.** a person's outward bearing; way of addressing and treating others. **5.** (*pl.*) ways of behaving, esp. with reference to polite standards: *bad manners.* **6.** good or polite ways of behaving: *have you no manners?* **7.** air of distinction: *he had quite a manner.* **8.** kind; sort: *all manner of things.* **9.** characteristic style in art, literature, or the like: *verses in the manner of Spenser.* **10.** mannered style; mannerism. **11.** *Obs. or Archaic.* nature; character; guise. **12.** by all manner of means, by all means; certainly. **13. in a manner,** after a fashion. [ME *manere,* t. AF: orig., way of handling, g. L *manuāria,* fem. of *manuārius* of or for the hand]
—**Syn.** 2. mode, fashion, style; habit, custom. 4. demeanor; deportment. MANNER, AIR, BEARING all refer to one's outward aspect or behavior. MANNER applies to a distinctive mode of behavior, or social attitude toward others, etc.: *a gracious manner.* AIR applies to outward appearance insofar as this is distinctive or indicative: *an air of martyrdom.* AIRS imply affectation: *airs and graces.* BEARING applies especially to carriage: *a noble bearing.*

man·nered (măn'ərd), *adj.* **1.** having (specified) manners: *ill-mannered.* **2.** having mannerisms; affected.

Man·ner·heim (măn'ər·hām'), *n.* Baron Carl Gustaf Emil (kärl gŏos'tăf ā'mēl), 1867–1951, Finnish soldier and statesman.

man·ner·ism (măn'ə·rĭz'əm), *n.* **1.** marked or excessive adherence to an unusual manner, esp. in literary work. **2.** a habitual peculiarity of manner. —**man'·ner·ist,** *n.* —**man'ner·is'tic,** *adj.*

man·ner·less (măn'ər·lĭs), *adj.* without (good) manners.

man·ner·ly (măn'ər·lĭ), *adj.* **1.** having or showing (good) manners; courteous; polite. —*adv.* **2.** with (good) manners; courteously; politely. —**man'ner·li·ness,** *n.*

Mann·heim (măn'hīm; *Ger.* män'hīm), *n.* a city in SW West Germany, in Baden-Württemberg, on the Rhine. 290,670 (est. 1955.)

man·ni·kin (măn'ə·kĭn), *n.* manikin.

Man·ning (măn'ĭng), *n.* Henry Edward, 1808–92. British Roman Catholic cardinal and writer.

man·nish (măn'ĭsh), *adj.* **1.** characteristic of or natural to a man. **2.** resembling a man. **3.** imitating a man. —**man'nish·ly,** *adv.* —**man'nish·ness,** *n.* —**Syn.** 2. See **manly.**

man·ni·tol (măn'ə·tōl', -tŏl'), *n.* *Chem.* a white, sweetish, crystalline, carbohydrate alcohol, HOCH₂(CHOH)₄-CH₂OH, occurring in three optically different forms, the common one being found in the manna of the ash *Fraxinus Ornus,* and in other plants.

man·nose (măn'ōs), *n.* a hexose, $C_6H_{12}O_6$, obtained from the hydrolysis of the ivory nut, and yielding mannitol on reduction. [f. MANN(A) + -OSE²]

ma·noeu·vre (mə·nōō'vər), *n., v.t., v.i.,* **-vred, -vring.** maneuver.

man of God, **1.** a saint, prophet, etc. **2.** a clergyman.

Man of Sorrows, Jesus Christ. Cf. Isa. 53:3.

man of the world, a sophisticated man.

man-of-war (măn'əv·wôr'), *n., pl.* **men-of-war.** **1.** a warship. **2.** See **Portuguese man-of-war.**

ma·nom·e·ter (mə·nŏm'ə·tər), *n.* an instrument for determining the pressure of gases, vapors, or liquids. [t. F: m. *manomètre,* f. Gk. *manó*(s) thin, rare + F *-mètre* METER] —**man·o·met·ric** (măn'ə·mĕt'rĭk), *adj.*

Ma·non (må·nôn'), *n.* an opera (1884) by Massenet.

man on horseback, a military leader who acquires such influence over the people as to threaten the existence of the government.

man·or (măn'ər), *n.* **1.** (in England) a landed estate or territorial unit, orig. of the nature of a feudal lordship, consisting of a lord's demesne and of lands within which he has the right to exercise certain privileges and exact certain fees, etc. 2. *Obs.* the mansion of a lord with the land pertaining to it. [ME *manere*, t. OF: m. *manoir*, n. use of *manoir*, inf., dwell, g. L *manēre* remain] —**ma·no·ri·al** (mə nōr′Y əl), *adj.*

manor house, the house or mansion of the lord of a manor.

man-o'-war bird, the frigate bird.

man power, 1. the power supplied by the physical exertions of a man or men. 2. a unit assumed to be equal to the rate at which a man can do mechanical work, commonly taken as $^1/_{10}$ horsepower. 3. rate or work in terms of this unit. 4. power in terms of men available or required: *the man power of an army.*

man·rope (măn′rōp′), *n. Naut.* a rope placed at the side of a gangway, ladder, or the like, to serve as a rail.

man·sard (măn′särd), *n.* 1. Also, **mansard roof.** a form of curb roof the lower slope of which approaches the vertical and usually contains dormer windows, while the upper slope is nearly flat. 2. the story under such a roof. [named after F. *Mansarde,* French architect (1598–1666)]

Mansard roof

manse (măns), *n.* 1. the house and land occupied by a minister or parson. 2. (orig.) the dwelling of a landholder, with the land attached. [late ME, t. ML: m.s. *mansa* dwelling, orig. pp. fem. of L *manēre* remain]

man·serv·ant (măn′sûr′vənt), *n., pl.* **menservants.** a male servant.

Mans·field (mănz′fēld), *n.* 1. **Katherine,** (*Kathleen Beauchamp, Mrs. John Middleton Murry*) 1888–1923, British short-story writer. 2. **Richard,** 1857–1907, U.S. actor, born in England. 3. a city in central England, in Nottinghamshire. 51,870 (est. 1956). 4. a city in N Ohio. 47,325 (1960). 5. **Mount,** a mountain in N Vermont: highest peak of the Green Mountains. 4393 ft.

man·sion (măn′shən), *n.* 1. an imposing or stately residence. 2. a manor house. 3. (*often pl.*) *Brit.* an apartment house. 4. *Archaic.* a place of abode. 5. *Oriental and Medieval Astron.* each of twenty-eight divisions of the ecliptic occupied by the moon on successive days. [ME, t. OF, t. L: s. *mansio* a remaining, dwelling]

man·slaugh·ter (măn′slô′tər), *n.* 1. the killing of a human being by a human being; homicide. 2. *Law.* the killing of a human being unlawfully but without malice aforethought. See **malice aforethought.**

man·slay·er (măn′slā′ər), *n.* one who kills a human being; a homicide. —**man′slay′ing,** *n., adj.*

Man·sur (män sōōr′), *n.* See **al-Mansur.**

man·ta (măn′tə; *Sp.* män′tä), *n.* 1. (in Spain and Spanish America) a cloak or wrap. 2. (in South America) a kind of wrap worn by women. 3. the type of blanket or cloth used on a horse or mule. 4. *Mil.* a movable shelter formerly used to protect besiegers; a mantelet. 5. a manta ray. [t. Sp., t. Pr.: blanket]

manta ray, a huge tropical ray, reaching a width of twenty feet, with earlike flaps on either side of the head.

man·teau (măn′tō; *Fr.* män tō′), *n., pl.* **-teaus** (-tōz), *Fr.* **-teaux** (-tō′). *Obs.* a mantle or cloak, esp. one worn by women. [t. F. See **MANTLE**]

Man·te·gna (män tě′nyä), *n.* **Andrea** (än drě′ä), 1431–1506, Italian painter and engraver.

man·tel (măn′təl), *n.* 1. the more or less ornamental structure above and about a fireplace, usually having a shelf or projecting ledge. 2. Also, **man′tel·piece′.** the shelf. [var. of **MANTLE**]

man·tel·et (măn′təl ĕt′, mănt′lY̌t), *n.* 1. a short mantle. 2. Also, **mantlet.** *Mil.* **a.** a manta (def. 4). **b.** any of various bulletproof shelters or screens. [ME, t. OF, dim. of *mantel* **MANTLE**]

Man·tell (măn tĕl′, măn′tĕl), *n.* **Robert Bruce,** 1854–1928, British actor in America and England.

man·tel·let·ta (măn′tə lĕt′ə), *n. Rom. Cath. Ch.* a sleeveless vestment of silk or woolen stuff reaching to the knees, worn by cardinals, bishops, abbots, etc. [t. It., dim. of *mantello,* der. L *mantellum* **MANTLE**]

man·tel·tree (măn′təl trē′), *n.* a wooden beam or arch forming the lintel of a fireplace; mantelpiece.

man·tic (măn′tY̌k), *adj.* 1. of or pertaining to divination. 2. having the power of divination. [t. Gk.: m.s. *mantikós* prophetic, of a prophet] —**man′ti·cal·ly,** *adv.*

man·til·la (măn tY̌l′ə), *n.* 1. a silk or lace head scarf arranged over a high comb and falling over the back and shoulders, worn in Spain, Mexico, etc. 2. a short mantle or light cape. [t. Sp., dim. of *manta.* See **MANTA**]

Man·ti·ne·a (măn′tY̌ nē′ə), *n.* an ancient city of Arcadia, in S Greece: battles, 362 B.C., 207 B.C.

man·tis (măn′tY̌s), *n., pl.* **-tis·es, -tes** (-tēz). any of the carnivorous orthopterous insects constituting the family *Mantidae,* which have a long prothorax and which are remarkable for their manner of holding the forelegs doubled up as if in prayer. [NL, t. Gk.: prophet, kind of insect]

Praying mantis, *Mantis religiosa* (Ab. 2½ in. long)

mantis crab, *Zool.* any of the stomatopod crustaceans with appendages resembling those of the mantis. Also, **mantis shrimp.**

man·tis·sa (măn tY̌s′ə), *n. Math.* the decimal part of a logarithm. Cf. **characteristic** (def. 3). [t. L: an addition]

man·tle (măn′təl), *n., v.,* **-tled, -tling.** —*n.* 1. a loose, sleeveless cloak. 2. something that covers, envelops, or conceals. 3. a single or paired outgrowth of the body wall that lines the inner surface of the valves of the shell in mollusks and brachiopods. 4. a chemically prepared, incombustible network hood for a gas jet, which, when the jet is lighted, becomes incandescent and gives a brilliant light. 5. *Ornith.* the back, scapular, and inner wing feathers taken together, esp. when these are all of the same color. 6. the outer enveloping masonry of a blast furnace over the hearth. —*v.t.* 7. to cover with or as with a mantle; envelop; conceal. —*v.i.* 8. to spread like a mantle, as a blush over the face. 9. to flush; blush. 10. to spread out first one wing and then the other over the corresponding outstretched leg, as a hawk does by way of relief. 11. (of a liquid) to be or become covered with a coating; foam. [ME *mantel,* OE *mæntel,* t. L: m.s. *mantellum, mantēlum* cloak]

mantle rock, *Phys. Geog.* the layer of disintegrated and decomposed rock fragments, including soil, just above the solid rock of the earth's crust; regolith.

mant·let (mănt′lY̌t), *n. Mil.* mantelet (defs. 2a, 2b).

Man·tu·a (măn′chōō ə), *n.* a city in N Italy, in Lombardy: birthplace of Vergil. 55,000 (est. 1954). Italian, **Man·to·va** (män′tō vä′). —**Man′tu·an,** *adj., n.*

man·tu·a (măn′chōō ə), *n.* 1. a kind of loose gown formerly worn by women. 2. a mantle. [m. *MANTUA,* due to assoc. with *Mantua,* in Italy]

Ma·nu·a Islands (mä nōō′ä), a group of three small islands in the E part of American Samoa. 2537 pop. (1950).

man·u·al (măn′yōō əl), *adj.* 1. of or pertaining to the hand or hands; done by the hand or hands. 2. of the nature of a manual or handy book. —*n.* 3. a small book, esp. one giving information or instructions. 4. *Mil.* prescribed exercises in the handling of the rifle: *the manual of the rifle.* 5. *Music.* a keyboard played with the hands. [t. L: s. *manuālis* (as n., ML *manuāle*) of the hand; r. ME *manuel,* t. OF] —**man′u·al·ly,** *adv.*

manual training, the training of pupils in the various manual crafts and arts by actual practice (used esp. in U.S. schools to mean training in woodworking).

ma·nu·bri·um (mə nū′brY̌əm, -nōō′-), *n., pl.* **-bria** (-brY̌ə), **-briums.** 1. *Anat., Zool.* a segment, bone, cell, etc., resembling a handle. 2. *Anat.* **a.** the uppermost of the three portions of the sternum. **b.** the long process of the malleus. [t. L: a handle]

manuf., 1. manufacture. 2. manufacturer. 3. manufacturing.

man·u·fac·to·ry (măn′yə făk′tə rY̌), *n., pl.* **-ries.** a factory.

man·u·fac·ture (măn′yə făk′chər), *n., v.,* **-tured, -turing.** —*n.* 1. the making of goods or wares by manual labor or by machinery, esp. on a large scale. 2. the making of anything. 3. the thing or material manufactured. —*v.t.* 4. to make or produce by hand or machinery, esp. on a large scale. 5. to work up (material) into form for use. 6. to produce artificially; invent fictitiously. 7. to produce by mere mechanical industry. [t. F, f. L: *manū,* abl. of *manus* hand + m. *factūra* a making] —**man′u·fac′tur·ing,** *n.*

—Syn. 4. MANUFACTURE, ASSEMBLE, FABRICATE apply to processes in industry. MANUFACTURE, originally to make by hand, now means to make by machine or by industrial process: *to manufacture rubber tires* To ASSEMBLE is to fit together the manufactured parts of something mechanical: *to assemble an automobile.* To FABRICATE is to construct or build by fitting standardized parts together: *to fabricate houses.* See **make.**

man·u·fac·tur·er (măn′yə făk′chər ər), *n.* 1. one who owns or runs a manufacturing plant. 2. one who manufactures.

man·u·mis·sion (măn′yə mY̌sh′ən), *n.* 1. act of manumitting. 2. state of being manumitted.

man·u·mit (măn′yə mY̌t′), *v.t.,* **-mitted, -mitting.** to release from slavery or servitude. [t. L: m.s. *manūmittere*] —**man′u·mit′ter,** *n.*

ma·nure (mə nyōōr′, -nōōr′), *n., v.,* **-nured, -nuring.** —*n.* 1. any natural or artificial substance for fertilizing the soil. 2. dung or refuse of the stable, etc. —*v.t.* 3. to treat (land) with fertilizing matter; apply manure to. [ME *maynour(en),* v., t. AF: m. *maynoverer* work by hand, der. OF *manuevre.* See **MANEUVER,** n.] —**ma·nur′er,** *n.*

ma·nus (mā′nəs), *n., pl.* **-nus.** 1. *Anat.* the distal segment of the forelimb of a vertebrate, including the carpus and the forefoot or hand. 2. *Rom. Law.* power over persons, as that of the husband over the wife. [t. L: hand]

man·u·script (măn′yə skrY̌pt′), *n.* 1. a book, document, letter, etc., written by hand. 2. an author's copy of his work, written by hand or typewriter, which is used as the basis for typesetting. 3. writing, as distinguished from print. —*adj.* 4. written or typed by hand (not printed). [t. ML: s. *manūscriptus,* lit., handwritten] —**man′u·script′al,** *adj.*

Ma·nu·ti·us (mə nū′shY̌ əs, -nōō′-), *n.* **Aldus** (ōl′dəs, ăl′-), (*Aldo Manuzio*) 1450–1515, Italian printer.

---

b., blend of, blended; c., cognate with; d., dialect, dialectal; der., derived from; f., formed from; g., going back to; m., modification of; r., replacing; s., stem of; t., taken from; ?, perhaps. See the full key on inside cover.

man·ward (măn/wərd), *adv.* 1. Also, **man/wards.** toward man. —*adj.* 2. directed toward man.

Manx (măngks), *adj.* 1. of or pertaining to the Isle of Man, its inhabitants, or their language. —*n.* 2. (*construed as pl.*) the inhabitants of the Isle of Man. 3. the Gaelic of the Isle of Man, virtually extinct. [metathetic and syncopated form of earlier *Maniske*]

manx cat, a tailless variety of the domestic cat.

Manx·man (măngks/man), *n., pl.* **-men.** a native or inhabitant of the Isle of Man.

man·y (mĕn/ĭ), *adj.*, **more, most.** 1. constituting or forming a large number: *many people.* 2. relatively numerous (after *as, so, too,* or *how*): *six may be too many.* 3. being one of a large number (fol. by *a* or *an*): *many a day.* —*n.* 4. a great or considerable number (often followed by a noun with *of* expressed or understood): *a great many people.* 5. (as a collective plural) many persons or things. [ME *mani, manye,* etc., OE *manig,* c. G *manch*]
—**Syn.** 1. multifarious, multitudinous, myriad. MANY, INNUMERABLE, MANIFOLD, NUMEROUS imply the presence or succession of a large number of units. MANY is a popular and common word for this idea: *many times.* NUMEROUS, a more formal word, refers to a great number, or to containing very many units: *letters too numerous to mention.* INNUMERABLE denotes number that is beyond count, or, more loosely, what is extremely difficult to count: *the innumerable stars in the sky.* MANIFOLD implies not only that the number is large but also that there is variety or complexity. —**Ant.** 1. few, single.

man·y·plies (mĕn/ĭ plīz/), *n.* *Zool.* the omasum (so called from the many plies or folds of its membrane). [f. MANY + *plies,* pl. of PLY[2]]

man·y-sid·ed (mĕn/ĭ sī/dĭd), *adj.* 1. having many sides. 2. having many aspects, capabilities, etc.: *a many-sided man.* —**man/y-sid/ed·ness,** *n.*

Man·za·nil·lo (măn/sä nē/yô), *n.* a seaport in SE Cuba. 36,295 (1953).

man·za·ni·ta (măn/zə nē/tə), *n.* 1. any of various shrubs of the ericaceous genus *Arctostaphylos,* of the western U.S. 2. the fruit of one of these shrubs. [t. Sp., dim. of *manzana* apple. See MANCHINEEL]

Man·zo·ni (măn dzô/nē), *n.* Alessandro (ä/lĕs sän/drô), 1785–1873, Italian novelist and poet.

Ma·o·ri (mä/ô rĭ, mou/rĭ, mä/rĭ), *n., pl.* **-ris.** 1. a member of the native "brown" race or Polynesians of New Zealand. 2. their language, of the Polynesian group of Austronesian.

Mao Tse-tung (mou/ dzŭ/dŏŏng/), born 1893, Chinese communist leader.

map (măp), *n., v.*, **mapped, mapping.** —*n.* 1. a representation, on a flat surface, of a part or the whole of the earth's surface, the heavens, or a heavenly body. 2. a maplike representation of anything. 3. *off the map,* out of existence, into oblivion: *whole cities were wiped off the map.* —*v.t.* 4. to represent or delineate in or as in a map. 5. to sketch or plan (often fol. by *out*): *to map out a new career.* [t. ML: m.s. *mappa* (*mundī*) map (of the world), in L *mappa* napkin]
—**Syn.** 1. MAP, CHART, GRAPH refer to representations of surfaces, areas, or facts. MAP most commonly refers to a representation of the surface of the earth or a section of it, or an area of the sky: *a map of England.* A CHART may be an outline map with symbols conveying information superimposed on it, a map designed esp. for navigators on water or in the air, a diagram, or a table giving information in an orderly form: *a chart of the shoals off a coast.* A GRAPH may be a diagram representing a set of interrelated facts by means of dots or lines on a coördinate background; or it may use small figures (people, animals, machines, etc.) appropriate to the facts being represented, each figure standing for a specific number in statistics being given: *a graph of the rise in population from 1900–1940.*

Map (măp), *n.* Walter, died c1209, Welsh author and churchman. Also, **Mapes** (māps, mä/pĕz).

ma·ple (mā/pəl), *n.* 1. any tree of the genus *Acer,* of the north temperate zone, species of which are valued for shade and ornament, for their wood, or for their sap, from which a syrup (**maple syrup**) and a sugar (**maple sugar**) are obtained. 2. the wood of any such tree. [ME *mapel,* OE *mapel* in *mapeltrēow* maple tree]

Ma·quis (mȧ·kē/), *n. sing. and pl. French.* a member of one of the French underground groups resisting the Germans in World War II. [F, special use of *maquis, makis* wild, bushy land (Corsican d.)]

mar (mär), *v.t.*, **marred, marring.** 1. to damage; impair; ruin. 2. to disfigure; deface. [ME *marre,* OE *merran* hinder, waste, c. OHG *merrien* hinder]
—**Syn.** 1, 2. spoil, injure; blot. MAR, DEFACE, DISFIGURE, DEFORM agree in applying to some form of injury. MAR is general, but usually refers to an external or surface injury, if it is a physical one: *the table top was marred by dents and scratches.* DEFACE refers to a surface injury which may be temporary or easily repaired: *a table cloth defaced by penciled notations.* DISFIGURE applies to external injury of a more permanent and serious kind: *a birthmark disfigured one side of his face.* DEFORM suggests that something has been distorted or internally injured so severely as to change its normal form or qualities, or else that some fault has interfered with its proper development: *deformed by an accident which had crippled him, to deform feet by binding them.* —**Ant.** 2. enhance, adorn.

Mar., March.

mar., 1. maritime. 2. married.

mar·a·bou (măr/ə bŏŏ/), *n.* 1. any of three large storks,

Leptoptilus crumeniferus of Africa, and *L. dubius,* adjutant bird, and *L. javanicus* of the East Indies, having under the wings and tail soft, downy feathers that are used in millinery and for making a furlike trimming or material. 2. one of the feathers. 3. the trimming or material made of them. [t. F: m. *marabout,* orig. a Mohammedan hermit]

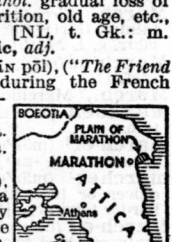

Marabou.
Leptoptilus crumeniferus
(Total length ab. 3½ ft.)

Mar·a·cai·bo (măr/ə kī/bō; *Sp.* mä/rä kī/bô), *n.* 1. a seaport in NW Venezuela. 304,313 (est. 1953). 2. Gulf of, a gulf on the NW coast of Venezuela. 3. Lake, a lake in NW Venezuela, connected with the gulf. ab. 100 mi. long; ab. 75 mi wide.

Ma·ra·jó (mä/rä zhô/), *n.* an island at the mouth of the Amazon in N Brazil. ab. 20,000 sq. mi.

Ma·ra·ñón (mä/rä nyôn/), *n.* a river flowing from W Peru N and then E, joining the Ucayali to form the Amazon. ab. 1000 mi.

ma·ras·ca (mə răs/kə), *n.* a wild cherry, *Prunus Cerasus* var. *Marasca,* with small, acid, bitter fruit, from which maraschino is made.

mar·a·schi·no (măr/ə skē/nô), *n.* a cordial or liqueur distilled from marascas. [t. It., der. (*a*)*marasca* kind of cherry, der. *amaro* bitter, g. L *amārus*]

maraschino cherry, a cherry cooked in colored syrup and flavored with imitation maraschino.

ma·ras·mus (mə răz/məs), *n.* *Pathol.* gradual loss of flesh and strength, as from malnutrition, old age, etc., rather than from actual disease. [NL, t. Gk.: m. *marasmós* a wasting] —**ma·ras/mic,** *adj.*

Ma·rat (mȧ rȧ/), *n.* Jean Paul (zhän pôl), ("*The Friend of the People*") 1743–93, leader during the French Revolution, assassinated by Charlotte Corday.

Ma·ra·tha (mə rä/tə), *n.* Mahratta.

Ma·ra·thi (mə rä/tē, -rät/ē), *n.* Mahratti.

mar·a·thon (măr/ə thŏn/, -thən), *n.* 1. any long-distance race. 2. a foot race of about 26 miles. 3. any long contest with endurance as the primary factor: *a dance marathon.* 4. (*cap.*) a plain in Attica, ab. 20 mi. NE of Athens, Greece: the Athenians defeated the Persians there, 490 B.C. 5. (*cap.*) an ancient village near this plain. [defs. 1–3 from the messenger's running to Athens to carry news of the Greek victory over the Persians (see def. 4)] —**mar/a·thon/er,** *n.*

BOEOTIA
PLAIN OF MARATHON
MARATHON
ATTICA
Athens
Marathon, 450 B.C.

Mar·a·tho·ni·an (măr/ə thō/nĭ ən), *adj.* 1. of or pertaining to Marathon. —*n.* 2. a native or inhabitant of Marathon.

ma·raud (mə rôd/), *v.i.* 1. to rove in quest of plunder; make a raid for booty. —*v.t.* 2. to raid for plunder. —*n.* 3. act of marauding. [t. F: s. *marauder,* der. *maraud* rogue, vagabond] —**ma·raud/er,** *n.* —**ma·raud/ing,** *adj.*

mar·a·ve·di (măr/ə vā/dĭ), *n., pl.* **-dis.** 1. a gold coin struck by the Moors in Spain. 2. an obsolete Spanish copper coin unit of low value. [t. Sp., t. Ar.: m. *Murābiṭin* name of the Moorish dynasty of the Almoravides (11th and 12th centuries), pl. of *murābiṭ* member of a religious order]

mar·ble (mär/bəl), *n., adj., v.*, **-bled, -bling.** —*n.* 1. limestone in a more or less crystalline state and capable of taking a polish, occurring in a wide range of colors and variegations, and much used in sculpture and architecture. 2. a variety of this stone. 3. a piece of this stone. 4. a work of art carved in marble. 5. a marbled appearance or pattern; marbling. 6. something resembling marble in hardness, coldness, smoothness, etc. 7. *Games.* **a.** a little ball of stone, baked clay, glass, etc., used in a children's game. **b.** (*pl.* construed *as sing.*) the game itself. —*adj.* 8. consisting of marble. 9. like marble, as being hard, cold, unfeeling, etc. 10. of variegated or mottled color. —*v.t.* 11. to color or stain like variegated marble. [ME *marbre,* t. OF, g. L *marmor*]

marble cake, a loaf cake given a marblelike appearance by the use of masses of dark and light batter.

Mar·ble·head (mär/bəl hĕd/, mär/bəl hĕd/), *n.* a resort in NE Massachusetts: yachting. 18,521 (1960).

mar·bling (mär/blĭng), *n.* 1. act, process, or art of coloring or staining in imitation of variegated marble. 2. an appearance like that of variegated marble. 3. *Bookbinding.* marblelike decoration on the paper edges, lining, or binding boards of a book.

mar·bly (mär/blĭ), *adj.* rigid, cold, etc., like marble.

Mar·burg (mär/bûrg; *Ger.* mär/bŏŏrĸʜ), *n.* a city in central West Germany. 42,700 (est. 1953).

marc (märk; *Fr.* mȧr), *n.* 1. the grapes contained in the wine press, and the residue (skins and pips) remaining after the juice is expressed. 2. the brandy distilled from grape pomace. [t. F, der. *marcher* treat, press]

mar·ca·site (mär/kə sīt/), *n.* 1. a common mineral (white iron pyrites), iron disulfide (FeS₂), of the same composition as pyrite, but differing in crystal system. 2. (formerly) any of the crystallized forms of iron pyrites, much used in the 18th century for ornaments. **3.** a specimen or ornament of this substance. [t. ML: m.s. *marcasíta*, t. Ar.: m. *marqashīṭā*, from Aram.]

mar·cel (mär sĕl′), *v.*, **-celled, -celling,** *n.* —*v.t.* **1.** to wave (the hair) by means of special irons, producing the effect of regular, continuous waves (**marcel waves**). —*n.* **2.** a marcelling. **3.** a marcelled condition. [from *Marcel*, a French hairdresser, the originator]

Mar·cel·lus (mär sĕl′əs), *n.* **Marcus Claudius** (mär′kəs klô′dĭ′əs), 268?–208 B.C., Roman general in the second Punic war.

mar·ces·cent (mär sĕs′ənt), *adj. Bot.* withering but not falling off, as a part of a plant. [t. L: s. *marcescens*, ppr., withering] —**mar·ces′cence,** *n.*

march[1] (märch), *v.i.* **1.** to walk with regular and measured tread, as soldiers; advance in step in an organized body. **2.** to walk in a stately or deliberate manner. **3.** to proceed; advance. —*v.t.* **4.** to cause to march. —*n.* **5.** act or course of marching. **6.** the distance traversed in a single course of marching. **7.** advance; forward movement: *the march of progress.* **8.** a piece of music with a rhythm suited to accompany marching. **9.** steal **a march,** to gain an advantage secretly or slyly (often fol. by *on* or *upon*). [t. F: s. *marcher* walk, march, go, earlier *trample*, der. L *marcus* hammer]

march[2] (märch), *n.* **1.** a tract of land along a border of a country; frontier. **2.** (*pl.*) the border districts between England and Scotland, or England and Wales. —*v.i.* **3.** to touch at the border; border (fol. by *upon, with,* etc.). [ME *marche,* t. OF, t. Gmc.; cf. OHG *marka*]

March (märch), *n.* the third month of the year, containing thirty-one days. [ME, t. AF: m. *marche,* c. OF *marz,* g. L *Martius,* lit., month of Mars]

March (märkʜ), *n.* German name of the **Morava** (def. 1).

March., Marchioness.

Mär·chen (mĕr′ḵʜən), *n. German.* fairy story; folk tale.

march·er[1] (mär′chər), *n.* one who marches (on foot). [f. MARCH[1] + -ER[1]]

march·er[2] (mär′chər), *n. Hist.* an inhabitant of, or an officer or lord having jurisdiction over, marches or border territory. [f. MARCH[2] + -ER[1]]

March·es (mär′chĭz), *n.* **The,** a department in central Italy, on the Adriatic. 1,370,000 (est. 1954); 3743 sq. mi.

mar·che·sa (mär kě′zä), *n., pl.* **-se** (-zě). *Italian.* marchioness. [It., fem. of *marchese*]

mar·che·se (mär kě′zě), *n.,pl.* **-si** (-zē). *Italian.* marquis.

mar·chion·ess (mär′shən ĭs, mär′shə nĕs′), *n.* **1.** the wife or widow of a marquis. **2.** a lady holding in her own right the rank equal to that of a marquis. [t. ML: m.s. *marchiōnissa,* fem. of *marchio* MARQUIS]

march·pane (märch′pān′), *n.* marzipan. [t. F, d. var. of *massepain, marcepain,* t. It.: m. *marzapane,* orig. sugar-candy box, t. Ar.: m. *martabān* glazed vessel]

Mar·co·ni (mär kō′nĭ; *It.* -kô′nē), *n.* **Gugliemo** (gōō-lyĕl′mô),1874–1937, Italian inventor of the first successful wireless telegraph.

Mar·co Po·lo (mär′kō pō′lō). See **Polo, Marco.**

Mar·cus Au·re·li·us (mär′kəs ô rē′lĭ əs, ô rēl′yəs), (*Marcus Aurelius Antoninus*) A.D. 121–180, emperor of Rome, A.D. 161–180: Stoic philosopher and writer.

Mar·cy (mär′sĭ), *n.* **Mount,** a mountain in NE New York: the highest peak of the Adirondack Mountains. 5344 ft.

Mar·di gras (mär′dĭ grä′), Shrove Tuesday; the last day of carnival: celebrated in Paris, New Orleans, etc., with special festivities. [t. F: meat-eating Tuesday]

Mar·duk (mär′dŏŏk), *n. Babylonian. Relig.* the chief of the Babylonian deities. [t. Babylonian.]

mare[1] (mâr), *n.* the female of the horse kind. [ME *mare, mere,* OE *mere, myre* (c. Icel. *merr*), fem. of *mearh* horse (c. OHG *marah,* Icel. *marr*). Cf. MARSHAL]

mare[2] (mâr), *n. Obs.* the evil spirit supposed to cause bad dreams. [ME and OE, c. Icel. *mara*]

ma·re clau·sum (mâr′ĭ klô′səm), *Latin.* a closed sea (within the jurisdiction of a particular nation).

Mare Island (mâr), an island in the N part of San Francisco Bay, California: U.S. navy yard.

ma·re li·be·rum (mâr′ĭ lĭb′ə rəm), *Latin.* an open sea (to which all countries have unrestricted access).

ma·rem·ma (mə rěm′ə), *n., pl.* **-remme** (-rěm′ē). **1.** a marshy, unhealthy region near the seashore, as in Italy. **2.** the miasma associated with such a region. [t. It., g. L *maritima,* fem. of *maritimus* maritime]

Ma·ren·go (mə rěng′gō), *n.* a village in NW Italy, in Piedmont: Napoleon defeated the Austrians here, 1800.

ma·re nos·trum (mâr′ĭ nŏs′trəm), *Latin.* our sea (esp. the Mediterranean, to the Romans and Italians).

mare's-nest (mârz′nĕst′), *n.* something imagined to be an extraordinary discovery but proving to be a delusion or a hoax.

mare's-tail (mârz′tāl′), *n.* **1.** an erect aquatic Old World plant, *Hippuris vulgaris,* with crowded whorls of narrow, hairlike leaves. **2.** a cirrus cloud resembling a horse's tail.

Mar·ga·ret of Anjou (mär′gə rĭt, -grĭt), 1430–82, queen of England, wife of Henry VI.

Margaret of Navarre, 1492–1549, queen of Navarre, noted for her poems, short stories, and letters.

Margaret of Valois, 1553–1615, first queen of Henry IV of France.

mar·gar·ic acid (mär gär′ĭk, -gär′ĭk), *Chem.* a white, fatty acid, $C_{17}H_{34}O_2$, resembling stearic acid and obtained from lichens or synthetically. [f. s. Gk. *márgaron* pearl + -ic]

mar·ga·rine (mär′jə rěn′; *less often* -gə-), *n.* **1.** a butterlike product made by emulsifying refined vegetable oils in cultured skim milk. **2.** oleomargarine. Also, **mar·ga·rin** (mär′jə rĭn, -gə-). [t. F: f. s. Gk. *márgaron* white of pearl + -ine -INE[2]]

Mar·gate (mär′gāt), *n.* a seaside resort in SE England, in Kent. 42,487 (1951).

mar·gay (mär′gā), *n.* a small tiger cat, *Gelis tigrina,* of tropical America.

marge[1] (märj), *n. Poetic.* margin.

marge[2] (märj), *n. Chiefly Brit. Colloq.* margarine.

mar·gin (mär′jĭn), *n.* Also, *Archaic,* **mar·gent** (mär′jənt). **1.** a border or edge. **2.** (*pl.*) the space bordering the printed or written matter on a page. **3.** a limit, or a condition, etc., beyond which something ceases to exist or be possible: *the margin of consciousness.* **4.** an amount allowed or available beyond what is actually necessary. **5.** *Finance.* **a.** security, as a percentage in money, deposited with a broker as a provision against loss on transactions on behalf of his principal. **b.** the amount representing the customer's investment or equity in such an account. **6.** *Com.* the difference between the cost and the selling price. **7.** *Econ.* the point at which the return from economic activity barely covers the cost of production, and below which production is unprofitable. —*v.t.* **8.** to provide with a margin or border. **9.** to furnish with marginal notes, as a document. **10.** to enter in the margin, as of a book. **11.** *Finance.* to deposit a margin upon. [ME *margyn,* t. L: m.s. *margo* border, edge] —Syn. **1.** See **edge.**

mar·gin·al (mär′jə nəl), *adj.* **1.** pertaining to a margin. **2.** situated on the border or edge. **3.** written or printed in the margin of a page: *a marginal note.* **4.** *Econ.* **a.** supplying goods at a rate merely covering the cost of production. **b.** of or pertaining to goods produced and marketed at margin: *marginal profits.* [t. NL: s. *marginālis,* der. L *margo* MARGIN] —**mar′gin·al·ly,** *adv.*

mar·gi·na·li·a (mär′jə nā′lĭ ə, -nāl′yə), *n.pl.* marginal notes. [NL]

marginal man, *Sociol.* a person who lives on the margins of two cultural groups without feeling identified with either group.

mar·gin·ate (mär′jə nāt′), *adj., v.,* **-nated, -nating.** —*adj.* Also, **mar′gin·at·ed. 1.** having a margin. **2.** *Entomol.* having the margin of a distinct color: *marginate with purple.* —*v.t.* **3.** to furnish with a margin; border. [t. L: m.s. *marginātus,* pp.] —**mar′gin·a′tion,** *n.*

mar·grave (mär′grāv), *n.* **1.** the hereditary title of the rulers of certain states. **2.** *Hist.* a hereditary German title, equivalent to *marquis.* **3.** (orig.) a German military governor of a mark, or border province. [t. MD: m. *markgrave* mark or border count]

mar·gra·vi·ate (mär grā′vĭ āt′, -ĭt), *n.* the province of a margrave.

mar·gra·vine (mär′grə vēn′), *n.* the wife of a margrave.

mar·gue·rite (mär′gə rēt′), *n.* **1.** the common European daisy, *Bellis perennis.* **2.** any of several flowers of the daisy kind, esp. *Chrysanthemum frutescens,* cultivated for its numerous white-rayed, yellow-centered flowers. [t. F: daisy, pearl, t. L: m. *margarita* pearl]

ma·ri·age de con·ve·nance (mä ryäzh′ də kôn və-näns′), *French.* a marriage of convenience or expediency, usually for money or position.

Mar·i·an (mär′ĭ ən), *adj.* **1.** of or pertaining to the Virgin Mary. **2.** of or pertaining to some other Mary, as Mary, queen of England, or Mary, queen of Scotland. —*n.* **3.** one who has a particular devotion to the Virgin Mary. **4.** an adherent or defender of Mary, Queen of Scots.

Ma·ri·a·na·o (mä′rē ä nä′ō), *n.* a city in NW Cuba, near Havana. 226,252 (1953).

Ma·ri·a·nas Islands (mä′rē ä′näs), group of 15 small islands in the Pacific, E of the Philippine Islands: formerly mandated to Japan (except Guam); now under U.S. trusteeship. 43,105 pop. (est. 1955); 453 sq. mi. Also, **Ladrone Islands** or **Ladrones.**

Mar·i·anne (mär′ĭ än′), *n.* a popular name for the French Republic personified.

Ma·ri·a The·re·sa (mə rē′ə tə rē′sə, -zə, mə rī′ə), 1717–80, archduchess of Austria, queen of Hungary and Bohemia, 1740–80. German, **Ma·ri·a The·re·si·a** (mä rē′ä tě rä′zĭ ä′).

Maria Theresa thaler, Levant dollar.

Ma·rie An·toi·nette (mə rē′ än′twə nĕt′; *Fr.* mȧ rē′ än twȧ nĕt′), 1755–93, queen of France, 1774–93, and wife of Louis XVI, executed in the French Revolution.

Ma·rie Byrd Land (mə rē′ bûrd′), a part of Antarctica, SE of the Ross Sea: discovered and explored by Adm. Richard E. Byrd; claimed by the U.S.

Ma·rie Lou·ise (mə rē′ lōō ēz′; *Fr.* mȧ rē′ lwēz′), 1791–1847, empress of France, second wife of Napoleon I.

Ma·ri·en·bad (mä rē′ən bäd′), *n.* a spa and resort town in W Czechoslovakia, in Bohemia. 8417 (1947).

mar·i·gold (măr′ə gōld′), *n.* **1.** any of various chiefly golden-flowered plants esp. of the composite genus *Tagetes,* as *T. erecta,* with strong-scented foliage. See also **marsh marigold. 2.** any of various other plants, esp. of the asteraceous genus *Calendula,* as *C. officinalis,* a common garden plant of some use in dyeing and medicine. [ME, f. MARY (the Virgin) + GOLD]

ma·ri·jua·na (mä′rə hwä′nə), *n.* **1.** the Indian hemp, *Cannabis sativa.* **2.** its dried leaves and flowers, used in cigarettes as a narcotic. Also, **ma·ri·hua′na.** [t. Amer. Sp.; ? native word, b. with name *Maria Juana* Mary Jane]

ma·rim·ba (mə rĭm′bə), *n.* a musical instrument, originating in Africa but popularized and perfected in Central America, formed of strips of wood of various sizes (often having resonators beneath to reinforce the sound), struck by hammers or sticks. [t. West Afr.]

ma·ri·na (mə rē′nə), *n.* a boat basin offering dockage and other service for small craft. [It. and Sp.: of the sea]

Modern marimba

mar·i·nade (*n.* măr′ə nād′; *v.* măr′ə nād′), *n., v.,* **-naded, -nading.** —*n.* **1.** a pickling liquid, usually of vinegar or wine with oil, herbs, spices, etc., to steep meat, fish, vegetables, etc., in before cooking. **2.** meat or fish steeped in it. —*v.t.* **3.** to marinate. [t. F, der. *mariner* pickle in brine, der. *marin* MARINE]

mar·i·nate (măr′ə nāt′), *v.t.,* **-nated, -nating. 1.** to let stand in a seasoned vinegar-oil mixture; marinade. **2.** to apply French dressing to (a food) which will be used later in a salad with mayonnaise. [f. s. F *mariner* (see MARINADE) + -ATE¹] —**mar′i·na′tion,** *n.*

Ma·rin·du·que (mä′rĭn dōō′kĕ), *n.* one of the Philippine Islands, between Luzon and Mindora islands. 85,828 pop. (1948); 347 sq. mi.

ma·rine (mə rēn′), *adj.* **1.** of or pertaining to the sea; existing in or produced by the sea. **2.** pertaining to navigation or shipping; nautical; naval; maritime. **3.** serving on shipboard, as soldiers. **4.** of or belonging to the marines. **5.** adapted for use at sea: *a marine barometer.* —*n.* **6.** seagoing vessels collectively, esp. with reference to nationality or class; shipping in general. **7.** one of a class of naval troops serving both on shipboard and on land. **8.** a member of the U. S. Marine Corps. **9.** a picture with a marine subject. **10.** naval affairs, or the department of a government (as in France) having to do with such affairs. [ME *maryne,* t. F: m. *marin* (fem. *marine*), g. L *marīnus* of the sea]

Marine Corps, a branch of the U.S. Navy, trained, organized, and equipped very much as land soldiers are, and usually employed as a landing force.

marine insurance, insurance covering loss or damage to maritime property occasioned by any of the numerous perils on and of the sea.

mar·i·ner (măr′ə nər), *n.* one who directs or assists in the navigation of a ship; seaman; sailor. [ME, t. AF, der. F *marin* MARINE] —**Syn.** See **sailor.**

Mar·i·ol·a·try (mâr′ĭ ŏl′ə trĭ), *n.* (in opprobrious use) the religious veneration of the Virgin Mary. [f. MARY + (ID)OLATRY] —**Mar′i·ol·a·ter,** *n.* —**Mar′i·ol·a·trous,** *adj.*

Mar·i·on (măr′ĭ ən, mâr′-), *n.* **1.** Francis, 1732?–95, American Revolutionary general. **2.** a city in central Ohio. 37,079 (1960). **3.** a city in central Indiana. 37,854 (1960).

mar·i·o·nette (măr′ĭ ə nĕt′), *n.* a puppet moved by strings or the hands, as on a mimic stage. [t. F, der. *Marion,* dim. of *Marie* Mary]

Mar·i·po·sa lily (măr′ə pō′sə, -zə), any of the plants constituting the liliaceous genus *Calochortus,* of the western U. S. and Mexico, having tuliplike flowers of various colors. Also, **Mariposa tulip.** [t. Sp.: *mariposa* butterfly, ult. der. *posar* to rest, g. L *pausāre*]

mar·ish (măr′ĭsh), *Archaic or Poetic.* —*n.* **1.** a marsh. —*adj.* **2.** marshy. [ME, t. OF. See MORASS]

Mar·ist (mâr′ĭst), *n. Rom. Cath. Ch.* a member of the "Society of Mary," founded in 1816 for missionary and educational work in the name of the Virgin Mary.

Ma·ri·tain (må rē tăn′), *n.* Jacques (zhåk), born 1882, French philosopher and diplomat.

mar·i·tal (măr′ə tal), *adj.* **1.** of or pertaining to marriage. **2.** of or pertaining to a husband. [t. L: s. *maritālis* pertaining to married people] —**mar′i·tal·ly,** *adv.*

mar·i·time (măr′ə tīm′), *adj.* **1.** connected with the sea in relation to navigation, shipping, etc.: *maritime law.* **2.** of or pertaining to the sea. **3.** bordering on the sea. **4.** living near the sea. **5.** characteristic of a seaman; nautical. [t. L: m.s. *maritimus* of the sea]

Maritime Alps, a range of the Alps in SE France and NW Italy.

Maritime Provinces, the Canadian provinces of Nova Scotia, New Brunswick, and Prince Edward Island.

Ma·rit·sa (mä′rēt sä′), *n.* a river flowing from S Bulgaria along the boundary between Greece and European Turkey into the Aegean. ab. 300 mi.

mar·i·um (măr′ĭ əm), *n.* one of the large, dark, fairly

level plains on the moon, probably lava beds, which look like "seas." [t. NL, der. L *mare* sea]

Ma·ri·u·pol (mä′rĭ ōō′pŏl′y), *n.* Zhdanov.

Mar·i·us (mâr′ĭ əs), *n.* **Gaius** (gā′əs), c155–86 B.C., Roman general and consul: opponent of Sulla.

Ma·ri·vaux (må rē vō′), *n.* **Pierre Carlet de Chamblain de** (pyĕr kår lĕ′ də shăn blăn′ də), 1688–1763, French novelist and dramatist.

mar·jo·ram (mär′jə rəm), *n.* any plant of the mint family of the genus *Origanum,* esp. the species *Marjorana hortensis* (**sweet marjoram**) which is used in cookery, or *O. vulgare,* a wild species native in Europe and naturalized in North America. [ME *majorane,* t. OF, ult. der. L *amāracus*]

mark¹ (märk), *n.* **1.** a visible trace or impression upon anything, as a line, cut, dent, stain, bruise, etc.: *a birthmark.* **2.** a badge, brand, or other visible sign assumed or imposed. **3.** a symbol used in writing or printing: *a punctuation mark.* **4.** a sign, usually a cross, made by an illiterate person by way of signature. **5.** an affixed or impressed device, symbol, inscription, etc., serving to give information, identify, indicate origin or ownership, attest to character or comparative merit, or the like. **6.** a sign, token, or indication. **7.** a symbol used in rating conduct, proficiency, attainment, etc., as of pupils in a school. **8.** something serving as an indication of position: *bookmark.* **9.** a recognized standard: *to be below the mark.* **10.** note, importance, or distinction: *a man of mark.* **11.** a distinctive trait. **12.** an object aimed at, as a target. **13.** an object or end desired or striven for, as a goal. **14.** an object of derision, scorn, hostile schemes, swindling, or the like: *an easy mark.* **15.** *Track.* the starting point allotted to a contestant. **16.** *Boxing.* the middle of the stomach. **17.** *Bowls.* See **jack¹** (def. 8). **18.** (on a nautical leadline) one of the measured indications of depth, consisting of a white, blue, or red rag, a bit of leather, or a knot of small line. **19.** *Brit.* model. **20.** a tract of land held in common by a medieval community of freemen. **21.** *Obs. except Hist. and Archaic.* a boundary; frontier. **22.** **beside the mark,** irrelevant. —*v.t.* **23.** to be a distinguishing feature of: *a day marked by rain.* **24.** to put a mark or marks on. **25.** to attach or affix to (something) figures or signs indicating price, identification, etc., as a trademark: *to mark a book down to 49 cents.* **26.** to trace or form by or as by marks (often fol. by *out*). **27.** to indicate or designate by or as by marks. **28.** to single out; destine. **29.** to record, as a score. **30.** to make manifest. **31.** to give heed or attention to. **32.** to separate (fol. by *off*). **33.** to notice or observe. **34.** **mark time,** to suspend advance or progress temporarily, as while awaiting development. **b.** *Mil.* to move the feet alternately as in marching, but without advancing. —*v.i.* **35.** to take notice; give attention; consider. [ME; OE *mearc* boundary, land mark, c. G *mark;* akin to L *margo* border] —**Syn. 11.** characteristic, feature.

mark² (märk), *n.* **1.** a silver coin, and, until 1924, the monetary unit of Germany. See **reichsmark. 2.** the monetary unit and a coin of Finland; markka. **3.** an obsolete silver coin of Scotland originally worth 13s.-4d. **4.** a former European unit of weight, esp. for gold and silver, generally equal to 8 ounces. [ME; OE *m(e)arc,* c. G *mark*]

Mark (märk), *n.* **1.** one of the four Evangelists, traditionally considered the author of the second Gospel. **2.** the second Gospel, in the New Testament. **3.** King, *Arthurian Romance.* ruler of Cornwall, husband of Iseult and uncle to Sir Tristram. [t. L: m. s. *Marcus*]

Mark An·to·ny (märk ăn′tə nĭ). See **Antony.**

mark·down (märk′doun′), *n.* a reduction in price.

marked (märkt), *adj.* **1.** strikingly noticeable; conspicuous: *with marked success.* **2.** watched as an object for suspicion or vengeance: *a marked man.* **3.** having a mark or marks. —**mark·ed·ly** (mär′kĭd lĭ), *adv.* —**mark′ed·ness,** *n.*

mark·er (mär′kər), *n.* **1.** one who or that which marks. **2.** something used as a mark or indication, as a bookmark, tombstone, etc. **3.** one who records a score, etc. **4.** a counter used in card playing.

mar·ket (mär′kĭt), *n.* **1.** a meeting of people for selling and buying. **2.** the assemblage of people at such a meeting. **3.** an open space or a covered building where such meetings are held, esp. for the sale of food, etc. **4.** a store for the sale of food: *a meat market.* **5.** trade or traffic, esp. as regards a particular commodity. **6.** a body of persons carrying on extensive transactions in a specified commodity: *the cotton market.* **7.** the field of trade or business: *the best shoes in the market.* **8.** demand for a commodity: *an unprecedented market for leather.* **9.** a region where anything is or may be sold: *the foreign market.* **10.** current price or value: *a rising market.* **11.** **at the market,** at the best obtainable price in the open market. —*v.i.* **12.** to deal (buy or sell) in a market. —*v.t.* **13.** to carry or send to market for disposal. **14.** to dispose of in a market; sell. [ME and late OE, t. VL: m.s. *marcātus,* L *mercātus* trading, traffic, market]

mar·ket·a·ble (mär′kĭt ə bəl), *adj.* **1.** readily salable. **2.** pertaining to selling or buying. —**mar′ket·a·bil′i·ty,** *n.*

market order, an order to purchase or sell at the current market price.

åct, āble, dåre, ärt; ĕbb, ēqual; Yf, īce; hŏt, ōver, ôrder, oil, bŏŏk, ōōze, out; ŭp, ūse, ûrge; ə = a in alone; ch, chief; g, give; ng, ring; sh, shoe; th, thin; ŧħ, that; zh, vision. See the full key on inside cover.

market place, a place, esp. an open space in a town, where a market is held.

market price, the price at which a commodity, security, or service is selling in the open market. Also, **market value.**

market town, a town where a market is held.

Mark·ham (märʹkəm), n. **1. Edwin,** 1852–1940, U. S. poet. **2. Mount,** a mountain in Antarctica, SW of the Ross Sea. ab. 15,100 ft.

mark·ing (märʹkĭng), n. **1.** a mark, or a number or pattern of marks. **2.** act of one who or that which marks.

mark·ka (märkʹkä), n., pl. **-kaa** (-kä). mark² (def. 2). [t. Finn., t. Sw.: m. *mark*]

marks·man (märksʹmən), n., pl. **-men. 1.** one skilled in shooting at a mark; one who shoots well. **2.** *U.S. Army.* the lowest qualification at target practice. **—marksʹman·shipʹ,** n.

mark·up (märkʹŭpʹ), n. the amount or percentage added to the cost of the article in fixing the selling price: *a 50% markup on cameras.*

marl¹ (märl), n. **1.** a soil or earthy deposit consisting of clay and calcium carbonate, used esp. as a fertilizer. **2.** *Poetic.* earth. —*v.t.* **3.** to fertilize with marl. [ME, t. OF, g. LL *margila*, dim. of L *marga*] **—mar·la·ceous** (märläʹshəs), adj.]

marl² (märl), v.t. *Naut.* to wind (a rope, etc.) with marline, every turn being secured by a hitch. [t. D: s. *marlen*, appar. freq. of *marren* tie. Cf. MARLINESPIKE]

Marl·bor·ough (märlʹbərə, -brə, môlʹ-), n. **John Churchill, 1st Duke of,** 1650–1722, British general who defeated the French at Blenheim in 1704.

mar·lin (märʹlĭn), n. any of a genus (*Makaira*) of large, powerful fishes with a spearlike snout, as *M. ampla*, of the warm waters of the Atlantic, a favorite big game fish. [short for MARLINESPIKE]

mar·line (märʹlĭn), n. *Naut.* small cord of two loosely twisted strands, used for seizing. [half adoption, half trans. of D *marlijn*, f. *marr(en)* tie + *lijn* LINE¹]

mar·line·spike (märʹlĭn spīkʹ), n. *Naut.* a pointed iron implement used in marling, separating the strands of rope in splicing, etc. Also, **mar·lin·spikeʹ.** [orig. *marling spike.* See MARL², SPIKE]

A. Marlinespike; B. Marlinespike separating strands of rope

Mar·lowe (märʹlō), n. **1. Christopher,** 1564–93, English dramatist and poet. **2. Julia,** (*Sarah Frances Frost, Mrs. E. H. Sothern*) 1866–1950, U. S. actress, born in England.

mar·ma·lade (märʹməlādʹ, märʹməlädʹ), n. a clear, jellylike preserve with fruit (usually citrus) suspended in small pieces. [late ME, t. F: m. *marmelade*, t. Pg.: m. *marmelada*, der. *marmelo* quince, g. L *melimelum*, t. Gk.: m. *melimēlon*, lit. honey apple]

marmalade tree, a sapotaceous tree, *Calocarpum Sapota*, of tropical America, with a durable wood resembling mahogany and a fruit used in preserving.

Mar·ma·ra (märʹmərə), n. **Sea of,** a sea between European and Asiatic Turkey, connected with the Black Sea by the Bosporus, and with the Aegean by the Dardanelles. ab. 170 mi. long; ab. 50 mi. wide; about 4800 sq. mi. Also, **Mar·mo·ra** (märʹmərə, mär môrʹə).

Mar·mo·la·da (märʹmōläʹdä), n. a mountain in N Italy: highest peak in the Dolomite Alps. 11,020 ft.

mar·mo·re·al (märmôrʹⁱəl), adj. of or like marble. Also, **mar·mo·re·an.** [f. s. L *marmoreus* of marble + -AL¹]

mar·mo·set (märʹməzĕtʹ), n. any of various small, squirrellike South and Central American monkeys, genera *Callithrix* and *Leontocebus*, and allied genera, with soft fur and a long, slightly furry, nonprehensile tail. [ME *marmusette*, t. OF: m. *marmouset* grotesque little figure, der. OF *merme* under age, g. L *minimus* least, b. with Gk. *mormōtōs* frightful]

Ring-tailed marmoset, *Callithrix lacchus* (Total length 22 in., tail 12 in.)

mar·mot (märʹmət), n. **1.** any of the bushy-tailed, thick-set rodents constituting the genus *Marmota*, as the common woodchuck. **2.** any of certain related animals, as the prairie dogs. [t. F: m. *marmotte*, back formation from *marmottaine*, g. L *mūsmontānus*, f. *mūs* mouse + *montānus* of the mountains]

Marne (märn; Fr. màrn), n. a river in NE France, flowing W to the Seine near Paris; battles, 1914, 1918, 1944. 325 mi.

ma·roon¹ (mərōōnʹ), n., adj. dark brownish-red. [t. F: m. *marron*, t. It.: m. *marrone* chestnut]

ma·roon² (mərōōnʹ), v.t. **1.** to put ashore and leave on a desolate island or coast by way of punishment, as was done by buccaneers, etc. **2.** to isolate as if on a desolate island.

Hoary marmot, *Marmota caligata* (Total length 27 to 28 in.)

—*n.* **3.** one of a class of Negroes, orig. fugitive slaves, living in the wilder parts of the West Indies and Dutch Guiana. [t. F: m. *marron*. Cf. Sp. *cimarrón* wild, der. *cimarra* bushes]

Ma·ros (mŏʹrōsh), n. Hungarian name of **Mures.**

mar·plot (märʹplŏtʹ), n. one who mars or defeats a plot, design, or project by officious interference.

Marq., **1.** Marquess. **2.** Marquis.

Mar·quand (märkwŏndʹ), n. **J(ohn) P(hillips),** 1893–1960, U.S. novelist.

marque (märk), n. seizure by way of reprisal. [t. F, t. Pr.: m. *marca*, der. *marcar* seize in reprisal, der. *marc* token of pledge, t. Gmc. See MARK¹]

mar·quee (märkēʹ), n. **1.** a rooflike shelter, as of glass, projecting above an outer door and over a sidewalk or a terrace. **2.** *Chiefly Brit.* a large tent or tentlike shelter with open sides, esp. one for temporary use in entertainments, receptions, etc. [assumed sing. of MARQUISE (def. 4) taken as pl.]

Marquee (def. 1)

Mar·que·sas Islands (märkäʹsəs), a group of French islands in the S Pacific. 2988 pop. (1951); 480 sq. mi.

mar·que·try (märʹkətrĭ), n. inlaid work of variously colored woods or other materials, esp. in furniture. Also, **mar·que·te·rie** (märʹkətrĭ). [t. F: m. *marqueterie*, der. *marqueter* mark, checker, inlay, ult. der. *marque* MARK¹]

Mar·quette (märkĕtʹ), n. **Jacques** (zhàk), (*Père Marquette*) 1637–1675, French Jesuit missionary and explorer.

mar·quis (märʹkwĭs; Fr. màrkēʹ), n. a nobleman ranking next below a duke and above an earl or count. Also, *Brit.*, **mar·quess** (märʹkwĭs). [t. F; r. ME *markis*, t. OF: m. *marchis*, der. *marche* MARK¹]

Mar·quis (märʹkwĭs), n. **Donald Robert Perry,** 1878–1937, U.S. humorist and writer.

mar·quis·ate (märʹkwĭzĭt), n. **1.** the rank of a marquis. **2.** the territory ruled by a marquis or a margrave.

mar·quise (märkēzʹ; Fr. màrkēzʹ), n. **1.** the wife or widow of a marquis. **2.** a lady holding the rank equal to that of a marquis. **3.** a common diamond shape, pointed oval, usually with normal brilliant facets. **4.** marquee. [t. F, fem. of *marquis*]

mar·qui·sette (märʹkĭzĕtʹ, -kwĭ-), n. a lightweight open fabric of leno weave in cotton, rayon, silk, or nylon. [t. F, dim. of *marquise*]

Mar·ra·kech (märräʹkĕsh), n. a city in W Morocco, former capital of Southern Sultanate. 215,312 (1952). Also, **Mar·ra·kesh, Morocco.**

mar·riage (märʹĭj), n. **1.** the legal union of a man with a woman for life; state or condition of being married; the legal relation of spouses to each other; wedlock. **2.** the formal declaration or contract by which act a man and a woman join in wedlock. **3.** any intimate union. [ME *mariage*, t. OF, der. *marier* MARRY¹] —Syn. 1. MARRIAGE, WEDDING, NUPTIALS are terms for the ceremony uniting couples in wedlock. MARRIAGE is the simple and usual term, without implications as to circumstances and without emotional connotations: *to announce the marriage of a daughter.* WEDDING has strong emotional, even sentimental, connotations, and suggests the accompanying festivities, whether elaborate or simple: *a beautiful wedding, a reception after the wedding.* NUPTIALS is a formal and lofty word applied to the ceremony and attendant social events; it does not have emotional connotations but strongly implies surroundings characteristic of wealth, rank, pomp, and grandeur: *royal nuptials.*

mar·riage·a·ble (märʹĭjəbəl), adj. fit, esp. old enough, for marriage. **—marʹriage·a·bilʹi·ty, marʹriage·a·ble·ness,** n.

Marriage of Fig·a·ro (fĭgʹərō; Fr. fēgàrōʹ), an opera (1786) by Mozart.

marriage portion, dowry.

mar·ried (märʹĭd), adj. **1.** united in wedlock; wedded. **2.** pertaining to marriage or married persons.

mar·ron (märʹən), n. a chestnut; esp. as used in cookery, or candied or preserved in syrup. [t. F. See MAROON¹]

mar·rons gla·cés (màrôⁿʹ glàsēʹ), *French.* chestnuts glazed or coated with sugar.

mar·row (märʹō), n. **1.** a soft fatty, vascular tissue in the interior cavities of bones. **2.** the inmost or essential part. **3.** strength or vitality. **4.** rich and nutritious food. [ME *marowe, marw*(*e*), OE *mearg*, c. G *mark*]

mar·row·bone (märʹōbōnʹ), n. **1.** a bone containing edible marrow. **2.** (*pl.*) (in humorous use) the knees. **3.** (*pl.*) crossbones.

mar·row·fat (märʹōfătʹ), n. **1.** a tall variety of the pea, with a large seed. **2.** the seed.

marrow squash, *U.S.* any variety of *Cucurbita Pepo* with a smooth surface, oblong shape, and hard rind.

mar·ry¹ (märʹĭ), v., **-ried, -rying.** —*v.t.* **1.** to take in marriage. **2.** to unite in wedlock. **3.** to give in marriage. **4.** to unite intimately. **5.** *Naut.* to join together, as two ropes, end to end without increasing the diameter. —*v.i.* **6.** to take a husband or wife; wed. [ME *marie*(*n*), t. F: m. *marier*, g. L *marītāre* wed] **—marʹri·er,** n.

mar·ry² (märʹĭ), interj. *Archaic.* an exclamation of surprise, etc. [euphemistic var. of MARY (the Virgin)]

Mar·ry·at (märʹĭət), n. **Frederick,** 1792–1848, British novelist and naval officer.

Mars (märz), n. **1.** the ancient Roman god of war.

2. *Astron.* the planet next outside the earth, fourth in order from the sun. Its period of revolution is 686.9 days, its mean distance from the sun about 142,000,000 miles, and its diameter 4230 miles. It has two satellites.

Mar·sa·la (mär sä′lä), *n.* a seaport in W Sicily. 74,371 (1951).

Mar·seil·laise (mär′sə läz′; *Fr.* mȧr sě′yěz′), *n.* the French national song, written in 1792 by Rouget de Lisle.

Mar·seilles (mär sā′; *older* -sālz′; *Fr.* -sě′y), *n.* a seaport in SE France. 661,492 (1954). Also, French, **Mar·seille′.**

mar·seilles (mär sālz′), *n.* a thick cotton fabric woven in figures or stripes, with an embossed effect.

marsh (märsh), *n.* a tract of low, wet land; a swamp. [ME *mershe,* OE *mersc,* syncopated var. of *merisc* (c. G. *marsch*), f. *mere* pool + *-isc* -ISH¹. See MERE²]

Marsh (märsh), *n.* Reginald, 1898–1954, U.S. painter.

mar·shal (mär′shəl), *n., v.,* **-shaled, -shaling** or (*esp. Brit.*) **-shalled, -shalling.** —*n.* **1.** a military officer of high rank. In many other countries the title is commonly modified by some other term: thus, in England, it has the form *field marshal* and in France, *marshal of France.* **2.** an administrative officer of a U. S. judicial district who performs duties similar to those of a sheriff. **3.** a court officer serving processes, attending court, giving personal attention to the judges, etc. **4.** the police officer in some communities. **5.** a high officer of a royal household or court. **6.** a person charged with the arrangement or regulation of ceremonies, etc. —*v.t.* **7.** to arrange in due or proper order. **8.** to array for battle, etc. **9.** to usher or lead. [ME *mareschal,* t. OF, g. VL *mariscalcus* groom, t. Gmc.; cf. OE *mearh* horse, *scealc* servant] —**mar′shal·cy, mar′shal·ship′,** *n.* —**mar′shal·er;** *esp. Brit.,* **mar′shal·ler,** *n.* —**Syn. 7.** See **gather.**

Mar·shall (mär′shəl), *n.* **1.** George Catlett (kăt′lỸt), 1880–1959, U.S. general and statesman: secretary of state 1947–1949; secretary of defense 1950–1951. **2.** John, 1755–1835, U. S. jurist and statesman: chief justice of the Supreme Court, 1801–35.

Marshall Islands, a group of 24 atolls in the N Pacific: formerly mandated to Japan; now under U.S. trusteeship. 14,260 pop. (est. 1955); 74 sq. mi.

Marshall Plan, former name of **European Recovery Program.**

Mar·shal·sea (mär′shəl sē′), *n. Brit. Hist.* **1.** the court of the marshal of the royal household. **2.** a prison in London, latterly a debtors' prison (abolished in 1849).

marsh elder, 1. *U.S.* any of various composite plants of the genus *Iva,* as *I. frutescens,* which grows in saltmarshes. **2.** the cranberry tree.

marsh gas, a gaseous decomposition product of organic matter, consisting largely of methane.

marsh harrier, a well-known hawk, *Circus aeruginosus,* of the Old World, having a cream-colored head.

marsh hawk, a slender American hawk, *Circus cyaneus hudsonius,* which frequents marshes and meadows, feeding on frogs, snakes, etc.

marsh hen, any of various rails or raillike birds.

marsh·mal·low (märsh′măl′ō; *incorrectly often* -měl′ō), *n.* **1.** a sweetened paste or confection made from the mucilaginous root of the marsh mallow. **2.** a similar confection containing gum arabic or gelatin, sugar, corn syrup, and flavoring. [ME *marshmalue,* OE *merscmealwe.* See MARSH, MALLOW]

marsh mallow, an Old World mallow, *Althaea officinalis,* with pink flowers, found in marshy places.

marsh marigold, a yellow-flowered ranunculaceous plant, *Caltha palustris,* growing in marshes and meadows; cowslip.

marsh wren, either of two American species of marsh-inhabiting wrens, the long-billed (*Telmatodytes palustris*), or the short-billed (*Cistothorus platensis*).

marsh·y (mär′shY), *adj.,* **marshier, marshiest. 1.** like a marsh; soft and wet. **2.** pertaining to a marsh. **3.** consisting of or containing marsh. —**marsh′i·ness,** *n.*

mar·si·po·branch (mär′sĭ pō brăngk′), *adj.* **1.** belonging to the *Marsipobrachii* or *Cyclostomata,* a group or class of vertebrates comprising the cyclostomes (the lampreys and hagfishes), characterized by pouchlike gills. —*n.* **2.** a marsipobranch fish.

Mars·ton (mär′stən), *n.* John, c1575–1634, English dramatist and satirical poet.

Marston Moor, a former moor in NE England, W of York: Cromwell victory over the Royalists, 1644.

mar·su·pi·al (mär sōō′pĭ əl), *adj.* **1.** pertaining to, resembling, or having a marsupium. **2.** of or pertaining to the marsupials. —*n.* **3.** any of the *Marsupialia,* the order which includes all of the viviparous, but nonplacental, mammals, such as the opossums, kangaroos, wombats, bandicoots, etc. Most members have a marsupium containing the mammary glands and serving as a receptacle for the young. [t. NL: s. *marsūpiālis,* der. L. *marsūpium.* See MARSUPIUM]

mar·su·pi·um (mär sōō′pĭ əm), *n., pl.* **-pia** (-pĭ ə). the pouch or fold of skin on the abdomen of a female marsupial. [t. L: pouch, t. Gk.: m. *marsȳpion, marsippion,* dim. of *mársipos* bag, pouch]

mart (märt), *n.* **1.** market; trading center. **2.** *Archaic.* a fair. [t. D, spoken var. of *markt* MARKET]

Mar·tel. See **Charles Martel.**

Mar·tel·lo tower (mär těl′ō), *Fort.* a circular, towerlike fort with guns on the top. Also, **mar·tel′lo.**

mar·ten (mär′tən, -tỸn), *n., pl.* **-tens,** (*esp. collectively*) **-ten. 1.** any of various slender, fur-bearing carnivores of the genus *Martes,* as the American **pine marten,** *M. americana,* of the northern U.S. and Canada. **2.** the fur of such an animal, generally a dark brown. [ME *martren,* t. OF: m. *martrine,* prop. the fur, n. use of *martrin,* adj., der. *martre* marten; from Gmc.]

Marten, *Martes americana*
(Total length 2 ft., tail 7⅓ in.)

Mar·tha (mär′thə), *n. Bible.* the sister of Lazarus, whose house in Bethany Jesus often visited. Luke 10: 38–42; John 11:1–44.

Martha's Vineyard, an island off SE Massachusetts: summer resort. 5577 pop. (1950); 108¾ sq. mi.

mar·tial (mär′shəl), *adj.* **1.** inclined or disposed to war; warlike; brave. **2.** pertaining to or connected with the army and navy. **3.** pertaining to or appropriate for war: *martial music.* **4.** characteristic of or befitting a warrior: *a martial stride.* [ME, t. L: s. *martiālis* of Mars] —**mar′tial·ly,** *adv.* —**mar′tial·ness,** *n.*

Mar·tial (mär′shəl), *n.* (*Marcus Valerius Martialis*) A.D. c40–c102, Roman writer of epigrams, born in Spain.

martial law, the law imposed upon an area by state or national military forces when civil authority has broken down.

Mar·tian (mär′shən, -shỸən), *adj.* **1.** pertaining to the planet Mars. —*n.* **2.** a supposed inhabitant of the planet Mars. [f. s. L *Martius* of Mars + -AN]

mar·tin (mär′tən, -tỸn), *n.* any of various swallows, as *Chelidon urbica,* the common European **house martin,** which builds its nest about houses, or *Progne subis,* the American **purple martin,** one of the largest birds of the swallow family. [late ME, from *Martin,* man's name]

Mar·tin (mär′tən, -tỸn), *n.* **1.** Homer Dodge, 1836–97, U.S. landscape painter. **2.** Joseph William, born 1884, U.S. political leader. **3.** Saint, A.D. c316–397 or 400, French bishop.

Mar·ti·neau (mär′tĭ nō′), *n.* Harriet, 1802–76, British writer.

mar·ti·net (mär′tə nět′, mär′tə nět′), *n.* a rigid disciplinarian, esp. military or naval. [from General *Martinet,* French drillmaster of the reign of Louis XIV] —**mar′ti·net′ish,** *adj.* —**mar′ti·net′ism,** *n.*

mar·tin·gale (mär′tən gāl′), *n.* **1.** a strap of a horse's harness passing from the bit or headgear, between the forelegs, to the girth, for holding the head down. See illus. under **harness. 2.** *Naut.* a short, perpendicular spar under the bowsprit end, used for guying down the jib boom. **3.** a gambling system in which the stakes are doubled after each loss. [t. F, t. Pr.: m. *marte(n)galo,* fem. of *marte(n)gan,* inhabitant of Martigue (supposedly noted for stinginess)]

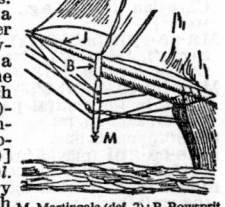
M. Martingale (def. 2); B. Bowsprit cap; J. Jib boom

mar·ti·ni (mär tē′nē), *n., pl.* **-nis.** a cocktail of gin and dry vermouth, usually served with an olive or twist of lemon peel.

Mar·ti·nique (mär′tə nēk′), *n.* an island in the West Indies, in the Lesser Antilles, forming a department of France. 239,130 pop. (1954); 425 sq. mi. *Cap.:* Fort-de-France.

Mar·tin·mas (mär′tỸn məs), *n.* a church festival, November 11, in honor of St. Martin. [f. *Martin* + -MAS]

mart·let (märt′lỸt), *n.* a European martin. [t. F: m. *martelet,* var. of *martinet,* dim. of *martin* MARTIN]

mar·tyr (mär′tər), *n.* **1.** one who willingly suffers death rather than renounce his religion. **2.** one who is put to death or endures great suffering on behalf of any belief, principle, or cause. **3.** one undergoing severe or constant suffering. —*v.t.* **4.** to put to death as a martyr. **5.** to make a martyr of. **6.** to torment or torture. [ME *marter,* OE *martyr,* t. L, t. Gk.: s. *mártys,* orig., witness]

mar·tyr·dom (mär′tər dəm), *n.* **1.** the condition, sufferings, or death of a martyr. **2.** extreme suffering.

mar·tyr·ize (mär′tə rīz′), *v.t.,* **-ized, -izing. 1.** to make a martyr of. **2.** to torment. —**mar′tyr·i·za′tion,** *n.*

mar·tyr·ol·o·gy (mär′tə rŏl′ə jỸ), *n., pl.* **-gies. 1.** the branch of knowledge dealing with the lives of martyrs. **2.** an account or history of martyrs. **3.** such histories collectively. **4.** a list of martyrs. —**mar′tyr·o·log·i·cal** (mär′tər ə lŏj′ə kəl), *adj.* —**mar′tyr·ol·o·gist,** *n.*

mar·tyr·y (mär′tə rỸ), *n., pl.* **-tyries.** a shrine, chapel, or the like, erected in honor of a martyr. [t. LL: m.s. *martyrium,* t. LGk.: m. *martýrion*]

mar·vel (mär′vəl), *n., v.,* **-veled, -veling** or (*esp. Brit.*) **-velled, -velling.** —*n.* **1.** a wonderful thing; a wonder or prodigy. **2.** *Archaic.* the feeling of wonder. —*v.t.* **3.** to wonder at (now fol. only by a clause as object). **4.** to wonder or be curious about (fol. by a clause). —*v.i.* **5.** to be affected with wonder, as at something surprising or extraordinary. [ME *merveille,* t. F, g. L *mīrābilia* wonderful things, prop. neut. pl. of *mīrābilis* wonderful]

Mar·vell (mär′vəl), *n.* **Andrew,** 1621–78, British poet.

mar·vel-of-Pe·ru (mär′vəl əv pə rōō′), *n.* the four-o'clock (plant).

mar·vel·ous (mär′vəl əs), *adj.* **1.** such as to excite wonder; surprising; extraordinary. **2.** improbable or incredible (often used absolutely in the phrase *the marvelous*). Also, *esp. Brit.,* **mar′vel·lous.** —**mar′vel·ous·ly,** *adv.* —**mar′vel·ous·ness,** *n.*

Mar·war (mär′wär), *n.* Jodhpur (def. 1).

Marx (märks), *n.* **Karl** (kärl), 1818–83, German founder of modern socialism and communism.

Marx·i·an (märk′sĭ ən), *adj.* of or pertaining to Karl Marx or his theories. —**Marx′i·an·ism,** *n.*

Marx·ism (märk′sĭzəm), *n.* the system of thought developed by Karl Marx, along with Engels, esp. the doctrine that the state throughout history has been a device for the exploitation of the masses by a dominant class, that class struggle has been the main agency of historical change, and that the capitalist state contained from the first the "seeds of its own decay" and will inevitably, after a transitional period known as "the dictatorship of the proletariat," be superseded by a socialist order and a classless society.

Marx·ist (märk′sĭst), *n.* **1.** an adherent of Karl Marx or his theories. —*adj.* **2.** of Karl Marx or his theories.

Mar·y (mâr′ĭ), *n.* **1.** *New Testament.* **a.** the mother of Jesus. Matt. 1:18–25. Often called the **Virgin Mary** or **Saint Mary. b.** the sister of Lazarus and Martha. Luke 10:38–42; John 11:1–2. **2.** 1867–1953, queen of England, 1910–36, wife of George V. [ME *Marie,* OE *Maria,* t. L, t. Gk., t. Heb.: m. *Miryām*]

Mary I, ("Bloody Mary") 1516–58, queen of England, 1553–58, and wife of Philip II of Spain. Also, **Mary Tudor.**

Mary II, 1662–94, queen of England, 1689–94, joint ruler with her husband, William III.

Mar·y·land (mĕr′ə lənd), *n.* a State in the E United States, on the Atlantic coast. 3,100,689 pop. (1960); 10,577 sq. mi. *Cap.:* Annapolis. *Abbr.:* Md.

Mary Magdalene, Mary of Magdala, mentioned in Luke 8:2, and traditionally identified with the repentant woman in Luke 7:37–50.

Mary Stu·art (stū′ərt, stŏŏ′-), 1542–87, queen of Scotland, 1542–67, beheaded for plotting to assassinate her cousin, Queen Elizabeth of England. Also, **Mary, Queen of Scots.**

mar·zi·pan (mär′zə păn′), *n.* a confection made of almonds reduced to a paste with sugar, etc., and molded into various forms, usually diminutive fruits and vegetables. Also, **marchpane.** [t. G. See MARCHPANE]

-mas, a final element in certain names of holidays and Christian feasts, e.g., *Michaelmas.* [comb. form of MASS²]

Ma·sa·ryk (mä′sä rĭk), *n.* **Tomáš Garrigue** (tô′mäsh gə rēg′), 1850–1937, Czech statesman; first president of Czechoslovakia, 1918–35.

Mas·ba·te (mäs bä′tě), *n.* one of the Philippine Islands, in the central part of the group. 211,113 pop. (1948); 1262 sq. mi.

masc., masculine.

Mas·ca·gni (mäs kä′nyě), *n.* **Pietro** (pyě′trô), 1863–1945, Italian operatic composer.

mas·ca·ra (mäs kâr′ə), *n.* a substance used to color the eyelashes. [t. Sp.: a mask]

mas·cle (mäs′kəl), *n.* *Her.* a bearing in the form of a voided lozenge. [ME, prob. for OF *macle,* g. L *macula* spot, mesh of a net. Cf. MAIL²]

mas·cot (mäs′kət, -kŏt), *n.* a person, animal, or thing supposed to bring good luck. [t. F: m. *mascotte,* dim. of Pr. *masco* witch; of Gmc. orig.]

mas·cu·line (mäs′kyə lĭn), *adj.* **1.** having manlike qualities; strong; manly: *a masculine voice.* **2.** pertaining to or characteristic of a man or men: *masculine attire.* **3.** *Gram.* denoting or pertaining to one of the three genders of Latin, German, Greek, etc., or one of the two of French, Spanish, etc., so termed because most or all nouns denoting males belong to it. Not all masculine nouns, however, denote persons or things having to do with the male sex. Spanish *hombre* "man," *dedo* "finger," *sol* "sun" are all masculine. **4.** (of a woman) mannish. —*n.* **5.** *Gram.* the masculine gender. **6.** a noun of that gender. **7.** another element marking that gender. [ME *masculin,* t. L: as. *masculinus* male] —**mas′cu·line·ly,** *adv.* —**mas′cu·lin′i·ty, mas′cu·line·ness,** *n.* —*Syn.* 1. See **male.**

masculine rhyme, *Pros.* a rhyme of but a single stressed syllable; single rhyme: *disdain, complain.*

Mase·field (mās′fēld, māz′-), *n.* **John,** born 1878, British author; poet laureate since 1930.

ma·ser (mā′zər), *n.* a device for amplifying electrical impulses by stimulated emission of radiation. [short for *m*(*icrowave*) *a*(*mplification by*) *s*(*timulated*) *e*(*mission of*) *r*(*adiation*)]

mash (mäsh), *n.* **1.** a soft, pulpy mass. **2.** pulpy condition. **3.** a mess of boiled grain, bran, meal, etc., fed warm to horses and cattle. **4.** crushed malt or meal of grain mixed with hot water to form wort. —*v.t.* **5.** to crush. **6.** to reduce to a soft, pulpy mass, as by heating or pressure. **7.** to mix (crushed malt, etc.) with hot water to form wort. **8.** *Obsolesc. Slang.* to flirt with. [ME *masche,* OE *māsc-* (in compounds), c. G *maisch*] —**mash′er,** *n.*

Ma·shar·brum (mŭsh′ər brōōm′), *n.* a mountain in N India, in the Himalayas. ab. 25,700 ft.

mash·ie (mäsh′ĭ), *n.* *Golf.* a club having a short iron head with a sloping face for making lofting shots. [alter. of F *massue* club]

mash·y (mäsh′ĭ), *n., pl.* **mashies.** mashie.

Mas·i·nis·sa (mäs′ə nĭs′ə), *n.* c238–149 B.C., king of Numidia who aided Scipio against Hannibal. Also, **Massinissa.**

mas·jid (mŭs′jĭd), *n.* mosque. Also, **musjid.** [t. Ar. See MOSQUE]

mask (mäsk, mäsk), *n.* **1.** a covering for the face, esp. one worn for disguise; a false face. **2.** a piece of cloth, silk, or plastic material, covering the face of an actor, to symbolize the character he represents: used in Greek and Roman drama and in some modern plays. **3.** anything that disguises or conceals; a disguise; a pretense. **4.** a person wearing a mask. **5.** a masquerade or revel. **6.** a masque (defs. 1, 2). **7.** a likeness of a face, as one molded in plaster after death. **8.** the face or head, as of a fox. **9.** *Archit., etc.* a representation of a face or head, generally grotesque, used as an ornament. **10.** a covering of wire, gauze, etc., to protect the face, as from splinters, dust, a hard pitched ball, etc. **11.** a gas mask. **12.** *Fort.* a screen, as of earth or brush, for concealing or protecting a battery or any military operation. —*v.t.* **13.** to disguise or conceal. **14.** to cover with a mask. **15.** *Fort.* to conceal (a battery or any military operation) from the enemy. **16.** to hinder (an army, etc.) from conducting an operation. —*v.i.* **17.** to put on a mask; disguise oneself. [t. F: m. *masque,* t. It.: m. *maschera,* der. LL *masca*]

mas·ka·longe (mäs′kə lŏnj′), *n.* muskellunge.

masked ball, a ball at which masks are worn.

mask·er (mäs′kər, mäs′-), *n.* one who masks; one who takes part in a masque. Also, **masquer.**

mas·och·ism (mäz′ə kĭz′əm), *n.* *Psychiatry.* the condition in which sexual gratification depends on suffering, physical pain, and humiliation. [named after Leopold von Sacher *Masoch* (1836–95), Austrian novelist, who described it] —**mas′och·ist,** *n.* —**mas′och·is′tic,** *adj.*

ma·son (mā′sən), *n.* **1.** one who builds with brick, stone, or the like. **2.** one who molds cement, concrete, etc., in imitation of stonework. **3.** (*often cap.*) a Freemason. —*v.t.* **4.** to construct of or strengthen with masonry. [ME, t. OF: m. *maçon,* der. LL *maccāre* beat; of Gmc. orig.]

mason bee, any of certain bees of the family *Megachilidae,* which construct their nests of clay.

Ma·son City (mā′sən), a city in N Iowa. 30,642 (1960).

Ma·son-Dix·on line (mā′sən dĭk′sən), the boundary between Pennsylvania and Maryland, partly surveyed by Charles Mason and Jeremiah Dixon between 1763 and 1767, popularly considered before the extinction of slavery as a line of demarcation between free and slave States. Also, **Mason and Dixon's line.**

ma·son·ic (mə sŏn′ĭk), *adj.* (*often cap.*) pertaining to or characteristic of Freemasons or Freemasonry.

ma·son·ite (mā′sə nīt′), *n.* **1.** a kind of wood-fiber material, pressed in sheets and used for partitions, insulation, etc. **2.** (*cap.*) a trademark for this substance.

Mason jar, a glass jar with an airtight screw top, much used in home canning. [named after American patentee, John L. *Mason*]

ma·son·ry (mā′sən rĭ), *n., pl.* **-ries. 1.** the art or occupation of a mason. **2.** work constructed by a mason, esp. stonework. **3.** (*often cap.*) freemasonry.

Ma·so·ra (mə sôr′ə), *n.* **1.** the Hebrew tradition, formed gradually through a succession of centuries, as to the correct form of the text of the Scriptures. **2.** the collection of critical notes in which it is embodied. Also, **Ma·so′rah, Massora.** [t. Heb.: (m.) *māsorāh* tradition]

Mas·o·rete (mäs′ə rēt′), *n.* **1.** a Hebrew scholar versed in the Masora. **2.** one of the body of Jewish scholars who reduced the Masora to writing. Also, **Mas·o·rite** (mäs′ə rīt′), **Massorete.**

Mas·o·ret·ic (mäs′ə rĕt′ĭk), *adj.* of or pertaining to the Masora, the Masoretes, or their system. Also, **Mas′o·ret′i·cal.**

Mas·pe·ro (mäs pə rō′), *n.* **Sir Gaston Camille Charles** (gäs tôn′ kȧ mē′y shȧrl), 1846–1916, a French Egyptologist.

Mas·qat (mŭs kät′), *n.* Arabic name of Muscat.

masque (mäsk, mäsk), *n.* **1.** a form of aristocratic entertainment in 16th and 17th century England, orig. consisting of pantomime and dancing but later with dialogue and song, in elaborate productions given by amateur and professional actors. **2.** a dramatic composition for such entertainment. **3.** a masquerade; a revel. Also, **mask.** [see MASK]

mas·quer (mäs′kər, mäs′-), *n.* masker.

mas·quer·ade (mäs′kə rād′), *n., v.,* **-aded, -ading.** —*n.* **1.** an assembly of persons wearing masks and other disguises, and often rich or fantastic dress, for dancing, etc. **2.** disguise such as is worn at such an assembly. **3.** disguise, or false outward show. **4.** a going about under false pretenses. —*v.i.* **5.** to go about under false pretenses or a false character. **6.** to disguise oneself. **7.** to take part in a masquerade. [t. F: m. *mascarade,* t. It.: m. *mascherata,* der. *maschera* MASK] —**mas′quer·ad′er,** *n.*

---

b., blend of, blended; c., cognate with; d., dialect, dialectal; der., derived from; f., formed from; g., going back to; m., modification of; r., replacing; s., stem of; t., taken from; ?, perhaps.   See the full key on inside cover.

mass (măs), *n.* **1.** a body of coherent matter, usually of indefinite shape and often of considerable size: *a mass of dough.* **2.** an aggregation of incoherent particles, parts, or objects regarded as forming one body: *a mass of troops.* **3.** a considerable assemblage, number, or quantity: *a mass of errors.* **4.** an expanse, as of color, light, or shade in a painting. **5.** the main body, bulk, or greater part of anything: *the great mass of American products.* **6.** bulk, size, or massiveness. **7.** *Physics.* that property of a body, commonly but inadequately defined as the measure of the quantity of matter in it, to which its inertia is ascribed: the quotient of the weight of the body and the acceleration due to gravity. **8.** *Pharm.* a preparation of thick, pasty consistency, from which pills are made. **9. the masses,** the great body of the common people; the working classes or lower social orders. —*v.i.* **10.** to come together in or form a mass or masses: *the clouds are massing in the west.* —*v.t.* **11.** to gather into or dispose in a mass or masses; assemble: *the houses are massed in blocks, to mass troops.* [ME *masse,* t. L: m. *massa* mass, lump] —**Syn. 2.** aggregate, aggregation, assemblage. **3.** collection, accumulation, pile, conglomeration. **6.** See **size¹**. **11.** assemble; collect, gather. —**Ant. 11.** disperse.

Mass (măs), *n.* **1.** the celebration of the Eucharist. See **High Mass, Low Mass. 2.** a musical setting of certain parts of this service (now chiefly as celebrated in the Roman Catholic Church), as the Kyrie Eleison, Gloria, Credo, Sanctus and Benedictus, Agnus Dei. Also, **mass.** [ME *masse,* OE *mæsse,* t. VL: m. *messa,* L *missa;* orig. application of L term uncert.]

Mass., Massachusetts.

Mas·sa·chu·setts (măs′ə chōō′sĭts), *n.* **1.** a State in the NE United States, on the Atlantic coast. 5,148,578 pop. (1960); 8257 sq. mi. *Cap.:* Boston. *Abbr.:* Mass. **2.** an Algonquian language.

Massachusetts Bay, a large, open bay off the E coast of Massachusetts.

mas·sa·cre (măs′ə kər), *n., v.,* **-cred, -cring.** —*n.* **1.** the unnecessary, indiscriminate killing of a number of human beings, as in barbarous warfare or persecution, or for revenge or plunder. **2.** a general slaughter of human beings. —*v.t.* **3.** to kill indiscriminately or in a massacre. [t. F, der. OF *macecler* to butcher, der. *mache-col* butcher, f. s. *macher* smash (g. *maccāre* to strike; of Gmc. orig.) + *col* neck (g. L *collum*); ? also influenced by *masseller* butcher, g. L *macellārius*] —**mas·sa·crer** (-krər), *n.* —**Syn. 3.** See **slaughter.**

mas·sage (mə săzh′; *esp. Brit.* măs′äzh), *n., v.,* **-saged, -saging.** —*n.* **1.** act or art of treating the body by rubbing, kneading, or the like, to stimulate circulation, increase suppleness, etc. —*v.t.* **2.** to treat by massage. [t. F, der. *masser* knead, der. *masse* mass] —**mas·sag′er, mas·sag′ist,** *n.* —**mas·sa·geuse** (măs′ə zhœz′), *n. fem.*

mas·sa·sau·ga (măs′ə sô′gə), *n.* a small rattlesnake, *Sistrurus miliarius,* of the southern U.S.

Mas·sa·soit (măs′ə soit′), *n.* c1580–1661, American Indian chief who was friendly with the Plymouth colony (father of King Philip).

Mas·sa·ua (măs sä′wä), *n.* a seaport in Eritrea, on the Red Sea. 17,169 (1939). Also, **Mas·sa′wa.**

mass defect, *Physics.* the difference between the mass of a nucleus and the total mass of its constituent particles, due to the equality of mass and energy.

mas·sé (må sā′; *esp. Brit.* măs′ĭ), *n. Billiards.* a stroke made by hitting the cue ball with the cue held almost or quite perpendicular to the table. Also, **massé shot.** [t. F, pp. of *masser* strike by a massé, der. *masse* kind of cue, **MACE¹**]

Mas·sé·na (må sě nä′), *n.* **André** (äɴ drě′), (*Prince d'Essling*) 1758–1817, French marshal under Napoleon I.

mass-en·er·gy equivalence (măs′ĕn′ər jĭ), *Physics.* the theory that mass and energy are connected and equivalent. Equivalent to a given mass is an energy equal to the mass times the square of the velocity of light.

Mas·se·net (măs ně′), *n.* **Jules Émile Frédéric** (zhyl ě měl′ frě dě rěk′), 1842–1912, French composer.

mas·se·ter (må sē′tər), *n. Anat.* an important masticatory muscle which serves to close the jaws by raising the mandible. [t. NL, t. Gk.: m. *masētēr* a chewer] —**mas·se·ter·ic** (măs′ə tĕr′ĭk), *adj.*

mas·seur (mă sœr′), *n.* a man who practices massage. [t. F, der. *masser* to massage] —**mas·seuse** (mă sœz′), *n. fem.*

Mas·sey (măs′ĭ), *n.* **Vincent,** born 1887, governor general of Canada 1952–59.

mas·si·cot (măs′ĭ kŏt′), *n.* monoxide of lead, PbO, in the form of a yellow powder, used as a pigment and drier. [t. F, t. Sp.: m. *mazacote* soda, t. Ar.: m. *shabb qubţī* Egyptian alum]

mas·sif (măs′ĭf; *Fr.* må sēf′), *n.* **1.** a compact portion of a mountain range, containing one or more summits. **2.** a band or zone of the earth's crust raised or depressed as a unit and bounded by faults. [t. F, n. use of *massif* **MASSIVE**]

Mas·sil·lon (măs′ə lən), *n.* a city in NE Ohio. 31,236 (1960).

Mas·sine (må sēn′), *n.* **Léonide** (lě ô nēd′), born 1896, U.S. dancer and choreographer, born in Russia.

Mas·sin·ger (măs′ən jər), *n.* **Philip,** 1583–1640, English dramatist.

Mas·si·nis·sa (măs′ə nĭs′ə), *n.* Masinissa.

mas·sive (măs′ĭv), *adj.* **1.** consisting of or forming a large mass; bulky and heavy. **2.** large, as the head or forehead. **3.** solid or substantial; great or imposing. **4.** *Mineral.* without outward crystal form, although perhaps crystalline in internal structure. **5.** *Geol.* homogeneous. **6.** *Med.* affecting a large continuous mass of bodily tissue, as a disease. [ME *massife,* t. F: m. *massif,* der. *masse* **MASS¹**] —**mas′sive·ly,** *adv.* —**mas′siveness,** *n.*

mass meeting, a large or general assembly to discuss or hear discussed some matter of common interest.

Mass Observation, *Brit. Trademark.* research or poll on public opinion *Abbr.:* M.O.

Mas·so·ra (mə sôr′ə), *n.* Masora.

Mas·so·rete (măs′ə rēt′), *n.* Masorete.

mas·so·ther·a·py (măs′ō thĕr′ə pĭ), *n. Med.* treatment by massage. [f. F *mass*(er), v., massage + -o- + **THERAPY**]

mass spectrograph, *Physics.* a device for separating atoms or molecules of different masses by utilizing the fact that the ions of such entities are deflected in a magnetic field by an amount which depends on the mass.

mass·y (măs′ĭ), *adj., massier, massiest.* massive. —**mass′i·ness,** *n.*

mast¹ (măst, mäst), *n.* **1.** a tall spar rising more or less vertically from the keel or deck of a vessel, which supports the yards, sails, etc. **2. before the mast.** *Naut.* as an unlicensed seaman (from the quarters of seamen forward of the foremast in the forecastle). **3.** any upright pole. —*v.t.* **4.** to provide with a mast or masts. [ME; OE *mæst,* c. G *mast;* akin to L *mālus*] —**mast′like,** *adj.*

mast² (măst, mäst), *n.* the fruit (acorns, chestnuts, beechnuts, etc.) of certain forest trees, esp. as food for swine. [ME; OE *mæst,* c. G *mast;* akin to **MEAT**]

mast-, var. of **masto-,** before vowels, as in *mastectomy.*

mas·ta·ba (măs′tə bə), *n.* an ancient Egyptian tomb, rectangular in plan, with sloping sides and a flat roof. Also, **mas′ta·bah.** [t. Ar. (Egypt. d.): bench]

mas·tec·to·my (măs tĕk′tə mĭ), *n., pl.* **-mies.** *Surg.* the operation of removing the breast or mamma. [f. **MAST-** + **-ECTOMY**]

mas·ter (măs′tər, mäs′-), *n.* **1.** one who has the power of controlling, using, or disposing of something at pleasure: *a master of several languages.* **2.** an employer of workmen or servants. **3.** the commander of a merchant vessel. **4.** the male head of a household. **5.** an owner of a slave, horse, dog, etc. **6.** a presiding officer. **7.** *Chiefly Brit.* a male teacher, tutor, or schoolmaster. **8.** a person whose teachings one accepts or follows. **9.** (*cap.*) Christ (prec. by *the, our,* etc.). **10.** a victor. **11.** a workman qualified to teach apprentices and to carry on his trade independently. **12.** a man eminently skilled in something, as an occupation, art, or science. **13.** a painting or other work of art by such a man. **14. the old masters,** a title given collectively to the eminent painters of earlier periods. **15.** an officer of the court to whom some or all of the issues in a case may be referred for the purpose of taking testimony and making a report to the court. **16.** *Educ.* **a.** a person who has taken a certain advanced degree at a college or university, orig. conveying qualification to teach: *master of arts.* **b.** such a degree. **17.** a title of respect for a man or a boy (now *mister* in ordinary speech except when applied to boys). **18.** a youth or boy; young gentleman. —*adj.* **19.** being master, or exercising mastery. **20.** chief or principal; *the master bedroom.* **21.** directing or controlling. **22.** dominating or predominant. **23.** being a master carrying on his trade independently, rather than a workman employed by another. **24.** being a master of some occupation, art, etc.; eminently skilled. **25.** characteristic of a master; showing mastery. —*v.t.* **26.** to conquer or subdue; reduce to subjection. **27.** to rule or direct as master. **28.** to make oneself master of; to become an adept in. [ME *maister,* OE *magister,* t. L] —**mas′ter·dom,** *n.* —**mas′ter·less,** *adj.*

mas·ter-at-arms (măs′tər ət ärmz′, mäs′-), *n., pl.* **masters-at-arms.** *Naval.* a petty officer who has various duties, such as keeping order on the ship, taking charge of prisoners, etc.

master builder, 1. a building contractor. **2.** an architect.

mas·ter·ful (măs′tər fəl, mäs′-), *adj.* **1.** having or showing the qualities of a master; authoritative; domineering. **2.** showing great skill; masterly. —**mas′ter·ful·ly,** *adv.* —**mas′ter·ful·ness,** *n.*

master hand, 1. an expert. **2.** great expertness.

master key, a key that will open a number of locks whose proper keys are not interchangeable.

mas·ter·ly (măs′tər lĭ, mäs′-), *adj.* **1.** like or befitting a master, as in skill or art. —*adv.* **2.** in a masterly manner. —**mas′ter·li·ness,** *n.*

master mason, 1. a Freemason who has reached the third degree. **2.** an expert mason.

master mechanic, a mechanic in charge of other mechanics.

mas·ter·mind (măs′tər mĭnd′), *v.t.* to plan and direct activities skillfully: *the revolt was masterminded by two colonels.*

Master of Arts, 1. a master's degree, esp. in the liberal arts, granted by a college or other authorized body, usually based on at least one year of study beyond the bachelor's degree. **2.** one holding this degree.

ăct, āble, dâre, ärt; ĕbb, ēqual; ĭf, īce; hŏt, ōver, ôrder, oil, bŏŏk, ōoze, out; ŭp, ūse, ûrge; ə = a in alone; ch, chief; g, give; ng, ring; sh, shoe; th, thin; ŧħ, that; zh, vision. See the full key on inside cover.

master of ceremonies, a person who directs the entertainment at a party, dinner, etc.

Master of Science, 1. an academic degree similar to the Master of Arts, but taken in the field of natural sciences or mathematics. **2.** one holding this degree.

mas·ter·piece (măs'tər pēs', mäs'-), n. **1.** one's most excellent production, as in an art: *the masterpiece of a painter.* **2.** any production of masterly skill. **3.** a consummate example of skill or excellence of any kind.

Mas·ters (măs'tərz, mäs'-), n. Edgar Lee, 1869–1950, U.S. poet and novelist.

master sergeant, *U.S.* a noncommissioned officer of the highest rank.

mas·ter·ship (măs'tər shĭp', mäs'-) n. **1.** the office, function, or authority of a master. **2.** control. **3.** mastery, as of a subject. **4.** masterly skill or knowledge.

mas·ter·sing·er (măs'tər sĭng'ər, mäs'-), n. Meistersinger (def. 1).

master stroke, a masterly action or achievement.

mas·ter·work (măs'tər wûrk', mäs'-), n. a masterpiece.

master workman, 1. a workman in charge. **2.** one who is master of his craft.

mas·ter·y (măs'tə rĭ, mäs'-), n., pl. **-ter·ies. 1.** state of being master; power of command or control. **2.** command or grasp, as of a subject. **3.** victory. **4.** the action of mastering, as a subject, etc. **5.** expert skill or knowledge. [f. MASTER + -Y³; r. ME *maistrie,* t. OF, der. *maistre* MASTER]

mast·head (măst'hĕd', mäst'-), n. **1.** the top or head of the mast of a ship or vessel; technically, the top or head of the lower mast, but by extension the highest point of the mast. **2.** a statement printed (usually on the editorial page) in all issues of a newspaper, magazine, etc., giving the name, owner, staff, etc. —*v.t. Naut.* **3.** to hoist to the top or head of a mast. **4.** to send to the masthead as a punishment.

mas·tic (măs'tĭk), n. **1.** an aromatic, astringent resin obtained from a small anacardiaceous evergreen tree, *Pistacia lentiscus,* native in the Mediterranean region: used in making varnish. **2.** a similar resin yielded by other trees of the same genus, or a resin likened to it. **3.** a tree yielding a mastic, esp. *Pistacia lentiscus.* **4.** a pasty form of cement used for filling holes in masonry or plastered walls. [ME *mastyk,* t. OF: m. *mastic,* t. L: m.s. *mastichum,* t. Gk.: m. *mastíchē*]

mas·ti·cate (măs'tə kāt'), v.t., v.i., **-cat·ed, -cat·ing 1.** to chew. **2.** to reduce to a pulp by crushing or kneading, as rubber. [t. LL: m.s. *masticātus,* pp., chewed] —**mas'ti·ca'tion,** n. —**mas'ti·ca'tor,** n.

mas·ti·ca·to·ry (măs'tə kə tōr'ĭ), *adj., n., pl.* **-tories.** —*adj.* **1.** of, pertaining to, or used in or for mastication. —*n.* **2.** a medicinal substance to be chewed, as to promote the secretion of saliva.

mas·tiff (măs'tĭf, mäs'-), n. one of a breed of powerful, stoutly built dogs with large head, drooping ears, and pendulous lips. [ME, t. OF, b. *mastin* mastiff and *mestif* mongrel]

Mastiff
(30 in. or more high at the shoulder)

mas·ti·tis (măs tī'tĭs), n. **1.** *Pathol.* inflammation of the breast. **2.** *Vet. Sci.* garget. [t. NL; see MAST-, -ITIS]

masto-, a word element meaning the breast, mastoid. Also, **mast-.** [t. Gk., comb. form of *mastós* breast]

mas·to·don (măs'tə dŏn'), n. any of various species of large, extinct mammals (genus *Mammut,* etc.) of the elephant kind, characterized by nipplelike elevations on the molar teeth. [t. NL, f. Gk.: *mast-* MAST- + m.s. *odoús* tooth]

Mastodon. *Mammut americanum*
(Ab. 9 ft. high at the shoulder, 15 ft. long)

mas·toid (măs'toid), *adj.* **1.** resembling a breast or nipple. **2.** denoting the nipplelike process of the temporal bone behind the ear. **3.** of or pertaining to the mastoid process. —*n.* **4.** the mastoid process. [t. Gk.: m.s. *mastoeidḗs* like the breast]

mas·toid·ec·to·my (măs'toi dĕk'tə mĭ), n., pl. **-mies.** *Surg.* the removal of part of a mastoid bone.

mas·toid·i·tis (măs'toi dī'tĭs), n. *Pathol.* inflammation of the mastoid process of the temporal bone of the skull. [f. MASTOID + -ITIS]

mas·tur·bate (măs'tər bāt'), v.i., **-bat·ed, -bat·ing.** to practice masturbation. —**mas'tur·ba'tor,** n.

mas·tur·ba·tion (măs'tər bā'shən), n. sexual self-gratification; onanism (def. 2). [t. L: s. *masturbātio*]

Ma·su·ri·a (mə zŏor'ĭə), n. a region in NE Poland, formerly in East Prussia, containing the **Masurian Lakes,** near which the Germans defeated the Russians, 1914–15. German, **Ma·su·ren** (mä zŏo'rən).

ma·su·ri·um (mə sŏor'ĭ əm), n. *Chem.* former name of **technetium.** [f. MASUR(IA) + -IUM]

mat¹ (măt), n., v., **matted, matting.** —n. **1.** a piece of fabric made of plaited or woven rushes, straw, hemp, or other fiber, or a similar article made of some other material, used to cover a floor, to wipe the shoes on, etc. **2.** a smaller piece of material, often ornamental, set under a dish of food, a lamp, vase, etc. **3.** a thick covering, as of padded canvas, laid on a floor on which wrestlers contend, in order to protect them. **4.** a thickly growing or thick and tangled mass, as of hair or weeds. **5.** a sack made of matting, as for coffee or sugar. **6.** *Print.* **a.** the intaglio (usually of papier-mâché), impressed from type or cut, from which a stereotype plate is cast. **b.** the brass die used in a linotype, each carrying a letter in intaglio. —*v.t.* **7.** to cover with or as with mats or matting. **8.** to form into a mat, as by interweaving. —*v.i.* **9.** to become entangled; form tangled masses. [ME *matte,* OE *meatt(e),* t. LL: m. *matta*]

mat² (măt), n. a more or less wide, framelike piece of pasteboard or other material placed in front of a picture. [t. F. See MAT¹, MAT³, adj.]

mat³ (măt), *adj., n., v.,* **matted, matting.** —*adj.* **1.** lusterless and dull in surface. —*n.* **2.** a dull or dead surface, without luster, produced on metals, as gold or silver, by some special operation. **3.** a tool for producing it. —*v.t.* **4.** to finish with a mat surface. [t. F, der. *matir* make dull or weak, der. *mat* mated (in chess), t. Ar.: m. *māt,* t. Pers.: (the king) died]

Mat·a·be·les (măt'ə bē'lĭz), n.pl. a Zulu people whom the Boers forced out of the Transvaal in 1837, now living in Matabeleland, a region in Southern Rhodesia.

mat·a·dor (măt'ə dôr'), n. **1.** the man who kills the bull in bullfights. **2.** one of the principal cards in skat and certain other games. [t. Sp., g. L *mactātor* slayer]

Mat·a·mo·ros (măt'ə mōr'əs; *Sp.* mä'tä mō'rōs), n. a seaport in NE Mexico, on the Rio Grande opposite Brownsville, Texas. 45.737 (1950).

Mat·a·nus·ka (măt'ə nŏos'kə), n. a valley in S Alaska, NE of Anchorage: recently developed as an agricultural region by homesteaders.

Ma·tan·zas (mə tän'zəs; *Sp.* mä tän'säs), n. a seaport on the NW coast of Cuba. 67,558 (1953).

Mat·a·pan (măt'ə păn'), n. **Cape,** a cape in S Greece: the S tip of the Peloponnesus.

match¹ (măch), n. **1.** a short, slender piece of wood or other material tipped with a chemical substance which produces fire when rubbed on a rough or chemically prepared surface. **2.** a wick, cord or the like, prepared to burn at an even rate, used to fire cannon, etc. [ME *matche,* t. OF: m. *meiche;* orig. uncert.]

match² (măch), n. **1.** a person or thing that equals or resembles another in some respect. **2.** a person or thing that is an exact counterpart of another. **3.** one able to cope with another as an equal: *to meet one's match.* **4.** a corresponding or suitably associated pair. **5.** *Chiefly Brit.* a contest or game. **6.** an engagement for a contest or game. **7.** a person considered with regard to suitability as a partner in marriage. **8.** a matrimonial compact or alliance. —*v.t.* **9.** to equal, or be equal to. **10.** to be the match or counterpart of: *the color of the skirt does not match that of the coat.* **11.** to adapt; make to correspond. **12.** to fit together, as two things. **13.** to procure or produce an equal to. **14.** to place in opposition or conflict. **15.** to provide with an adversary or competitor of equal power: *the teams were well matched.* **16.** to encounter as an adversary with equal power. **17.** to prove a match for. **18.** to unite in marriage; procure a matrimonial alliance for. —*v.i.* **19.** to be equal or suitable. **20.** to correspond; be of corresponding size, shape, color, pattern, etc. **21.** to ally oneself in marriage. [ME *macche,* OE *gemæcca* mate, fellow] —**match'a·ble,** *adj.* —**match'er,** n.

match·board (măch'bōrd'), n. a board which has a tongue cut along one edge and a groove in the opposite edge: used in making floors, etc., the tongue of one such board fitting into the groove of the next.

match·less (măch'lĭs), *adj.* having no equal; peerless: *matchless courage.* —**match'less·ly,** *adv.* —**match'less·ness,** n. —**Syn.** unrivaled, inimitable.

match·lock (măch'lŏk'), n. **1.** an old form of gunlock in which the priming was ignited by a slow match. **2.** a hand gun, usually a musket, with such a lock.

match·mak·er¹ (măch'mā'kər), n. **1.** one who makes, or seeks to bring about, matrimonial matches. **2.** one who makes or arranges matches for contests, etc. [f. MATCH² + MAKER] —**match'mak'ing,** n., adj.

match·mak·er² (măch'mā'kər), n. one who makes matches for burning. [f. MATCH¹ + MAKER] —**match'mak'ing,** n., adj.

match play, *Golf.* play in which the score is reckoned by counting the holes won by each side.

match point, the final point needed to win a contest.

match·wood (măch'wŏod'), n. **1.** wood suitable for matches. **2.** splinters.

mate¹ (māt), n., v., **mated, mating.** —n. **1.** one joined with another in any pair. **2.** a counterpart. **3.** husband or wife. **4.** one of a pair of mated animals. **5.** a habitual associate; comrade; partner. **6.** an officer of a merchant vessel who ranks below the captain or master (called first mate, second mate, etc., when there are more than one on a ship). 7. an assistant to a warrant officer or other functionary on a ship. 8. *Archaic.* a suitable associate. —*v.t.* 9. to join as a mate or as mates. 10. to match or marry. 11. to pair, as animals. 12. to join suitably, as two things. 13. to treat as comparable, as one thing with another. —*v.i.* 14. to associate as a mate or as mates. 15. to marry. 16. to pair. 17. to consort; keep company. [ME, t. MLG, var. of *gemate*; akin to OE *gemetta* sharer of food, guest. See MEAT]

mate² (māt), *n.*, *v.t.*, **mated, mating.** *Chess.* checkmate. [ME *mate(n)*, t. OF: m. *mater*, der. *mat* checkmated, overcome, t. Ar. See MAT³, CHECKMATE]

ma·te³ (mä'tā, māt'ā), *n.* maté.

ma·té (mä'tā, māt'ā), *n.* 1. a tealike South American beverage made from the leaves of a species of holly, *Ilex paraguariensis*, native to Paraguay and Brazil. 2. the plant itself. Also, **mate.** [t. Sp.: prop., a vessel, t. Peruvian: m. *mati* calabash]

ma·ter (mā'tər), *n. Brit. Colloq.* mother. [L]

ma·ter do·lo·ro·sa (mā'tər dō'lō rō'sə), *Latin.* 1. the sorrowful mother. 2. (*cap.*) the mother of Christ sorrowing for her son, esp. as represented in art.

ma·ter·fa·mil·i·as (mā'tər fə mĭl'ĭ ăs'), *n. Latin.* the mother of a family.

ma·te·ri·al (mə tĭr'ĭ əl), *n.* 1. the substance or substances of which a thing is made or composed. 2. any constituent element of a thing. 3. anything serving as crude or raw matter for working upon or developing. 4. a textile fabric. 5. (*pl.*) articles of any kind requisite for making or doing something: *writing materials.* —*adj.* 6. formed or consisting of matter; physical; corporeal: *the material world.* 7. relating to, concerned with, or involving matter: *material force.* 8. concerned or occupied unduly with corporeal things or interest. 9. pertaining to the physical rather than the spiritual or intellectual aspect of things: *material civilization.* 10. of substantial import, of much consequence, or important. 11. pertinent or essential (fol. by *to*). 12. *Law.* (of evidence, etc.) likely to influence the determination of a cause. 13. *Philos.* of or pertaining to matter as distinguished from form. [ME, t. LL: s. *māteriālis*, der. *māteria* matter] —**ma·te'ri·al·ness,** *n.* —**Syn.** 1. See **matter.**

ma·te·ri·al·ism (mə tĭr'ĭ ə lĭz'əm), *n.* 1. the philosophical theory which regards matter and its motions as constituting the universe, and all phenomena, including those of mind, as due to material agencies. 2. *Ethics.* the doctrine that self-interest is and ought to be the first law of life. 3. devotion to material rather than spiritual objects, needs, and considerations.

ma·te·ri·al·ist (mə tĭr'ĭ ə lĭst), *n.* 1. an adherent of philosophical materialism. 2. one absorbed in material interests; one who takes a material view of life. —**ma·te'ri·al·is'tic,** *adj.* —**ma·te'ri·al·is'ti·cal·ly,** *adv.*

ma·te·ri·al·i·ty (mə tĭr'ĭ ăl'ə tĭ), *n., pl.* **-ties.** 1. material nature or quality. 2. something material.

ma·te·ri·al·ize (mə tĭr'ĭ ə līz'), *v.,* **-ized, -izing.** —*v.t.* 1. to give material form to. 2. to invest with material attributes. 3. to make physically perceptible. 4. to render materialistic. —*v.i.* 5. to assume material or bodily form. 6. to come into perceptible existence; appear. —**ma·te'ri·al·i·za'tion,** *n.* —**ma·te'ri·al·iz'er,** *n.*

ma·te·ri·al·ly (mə tĭr'ĭ ə lĭ), *adv.* 1. to an important degree; considerably. 2. with reference to matter or material things; physically. 3. *Philos.* with regard to matter or substance as distinguished from form.

ma·te·ri·a med·i·ca (mə tĭr'ĭ ə mĕd'ĭ kə), 1. the remedial substances employed in medicine. 2. the branch of medicine treating of these. [t. ML: medical material]

ma·té·ri·el (mə tĭr'ĭ ĕl'), *n.* 1. the aggregate of things used or needed in any business, undertaking, or operation (distinguished from *personnel*). 2. *Mil.* arms, ammunition, and equipment in general. [t. F. See MATERIAL]

ma·ter·nal (mə tûr'nəl), *adj.* 1. of or pertaining to, befitting, having the qualities of, or being a mother. 2. derived from a mother. 3. related through a mother: *his maternal aunt.* [late ME, f. s. L *māternus* of a mother + -AL¹] —**ma·ter'nal·ly,** *adv.*

ma·ter·ni·ty (mə tûr'nə tĭ), *n.* 1. state of being a mother; motherhood. 2. motherliness.

maternity hospital, a hospital for the care of women during confinement in childbirth.

mat·e·y (mā'tĭ), *Brit. Colloq.* —*adj.* 1. comradely; cozy. —*n.* 2. comrade; chum.

math., 1. mathematical. 2. mathematics.

math·e·mat·i·cal (măth'ə măt'ĭ kəl), *adj.* 1. of, pertaining to, or of the nature of mathematics. 2. employed in the operations of mathematics. 3. having the exactness or precision of mathematics. Also, **math'e·mat'ic.** [f. *mathematic* MATHEMATICS + -AL¹] —**math'e·mat'i·cal·ly,** *adv.*

mathematical expectation, *Statistics.* the average of a set of possible values of a variable, the values weighted by the probabilities associated with these values.

mathematical logic, a modern development of formal logic employing a special notation or symbolism capable of manipulation in accordance with precise rules; symbolic logic.

math·e·ma·ti·cian (măth'ə mə tĭsh'ən), *n.* an expert in mathematics.

math·e·mat·ics (măth'ə măt'ĭks), *n.* the science that treats of the measurement, properties, and relations of quantities, including arithmetic, geometry, algebra, etc.

[pl. of *mathematic,* t. L: s. *mathēmaticus,* t. Gk.: m. *mathēmatikós* pertaining to science. See -ICS]

Math·er (măth'ər, măth'-), *n.* 1. **Cotton,** 1663-1728, American clergyman and author. 2. his father, **Increase,** 1639-1723, American clergyman and author.

Ma·thu·ra (mŭ thoō'rŭ), *n.* a city in N India, in Uttar Pradesh: Hindu shrine and holy city: reputed birthplace of Krishna. 98,552 (1951). Formerly, **Muttra.**

mat·in (măt'ĭn), *n.* 1. (*pl.*) *Eccles.* **a.** the first of the seven canonical hours, or the service for it, properly beginning at midnight, sometimes at daybreak. **b.** the order for public morning prayer in the Anglican Church. 2. *Poetic.* a morning song, esp. of a bird. —*adj.* 3. Also, **mat'in·al.** pertaining to the morning or to matins. Also, **mattin.** [ME *matyn,* (pl. *matines*), t. OF: m. *matin* morning, g. L *mātūtīnus* of or in the morning]

mat·i·née (măt'ə nā'; *esp.* Brit. măt'ə nā'), *n.* an entertainment, esp. a dramatic or musical performance, held in the daytime, usually in the afternoon. Also, **mat'i·nee'.** [t. F, der. *matin* morning. See MATIN]

Ma·tisse (má tēs'), *n.* **Henri** (än rē'), 1869-1954, French painter.

mat·rass (măt'rəs), *n. Chem.* 1. a rounded, long-necked, glass vessel, used for distilling, etc. 2. a small glass closed at one end. Also, **matrass.**

matri-, a word element meaning "mother." [t. L, comb. form of *māter*]

ma·tri·arch (mā'trĭ ärk'), *n.* a woman holding a position analogous to that of a patriarch, as in a family or tribe. [f. MATRI- + -ARCH; modeled on PATRIARCH] —**ma'tri·ar'chal, ma'tri·ar'chic,** *adj.*

ma·tri·ar·chate (mā'trĭ är'kĭt, -kāt), *n.* 1. a matriarchal system or community. 2. *Sociol.* a social order believed to have preceded patriarchal tribal society in the early period of human communal life, embodying rule by the mothers, or by all adult women.

ma·tri·ar·chy (mā'trĭ är'kĭ), *n., pl.* **-chies.** the matriarchal system; a form of social organization, as in certain primitive tribes, in which the mother is head of the family, and in which descent is reckoned in the female line, the children belonging to the mother's clan.

ma·tri·ces (mā'trĭ sēz', măt'rĭ-), *n.* pl. of **matrix.**

ma·tri·cide¹ (mā'trə sīd', măt'rə-), *n.* one who kills his mother. [t. L: m. s. *mātrīcīda.* See MATRI-, -CIDE¹] —**ma'tri·cid'al,** *adj.*

ma·tri·cide² (mā'trə sīd', măt'rə-), *n.* act of killing one's mother. [t. L: m.s. *mātrīcīdium.* See MATRI-, -CIDE²]

ma·tric·u·lant (mə trĭk'yə lənt), *n.* one who matriculates; a candidate for matriculation.

ma·tric·u·late (*v.* mə trĭk'yə lāt'; *n.* mə trĭk'yə lĭt), *v.,* **-lated, -lating.** —*v.t.* 1. to enroll or admit to membership and privileges by enrolling, esp. in a college or university. —*v.i.* 2. to be matriculated. —*n.* 3. one who has been matriculated. [f. s. LL *mātrīcula,* dim. of *mātrix* public register, roll + -ATE¹] —**ma·tric'u·la'tion,** *n.* —**ma·tric'u·la'tor,** *n.*

mat·ri·mo·ni·al (măt'rə mō'nĭ əl), *adj.* of or pertaining to matrimony; nuptial. —**mat'ri·mo'ni·al·ly,** *adv.*

mat·ri·mo·ny (măt'rə mō'nĭ), *n., pl.* **-nies.** the rite, ceremony, or sacrament of marriage. [ME *matrimonye,* t. L: m. *mātrimōnium* marriage]

matrimony vine, any of the plants constituting the solanaceous genus *Lycium,* species of which are cultivated for their foliage, flowers, and berries; boxthorn.

ma·trix (mā'trĭks, măt'rĭks), *n., pl.* **matrices** (mā'-trĭ sēz', măt'rĭ-), **matrixes.** 1. that which gives origin or form to a thing, or which serves to enclose it. 2. *Anat.* a formative part, as the corium beneath a nail. 3. *Biol.* the intercellular substance of a tissue. 4. the womb. 5. the rock in which a crystallized mineral is embedded. 6. *Mining.* gangue. 7. *Print.* **a.** a mold for casting type faces. **b.** mat¹ (def. 6). 8. (in a punching machine) a perforated block upon which the object to be punched is rested. [t. L: breeding animal, LL womb, source]

ma·tron (mā'trən), *n.* 1. a married woman, esp. one of ripe years and staid character or established position. 2. a woman in charge of the feminine or domestic affairs of an institution or the like. [ME *matrone,* t. OF, t. L: m. *mātrōna* married woman] —**ma·tron·al** (mā'-trən əl, măt'rən-), *adj.*

ma·tron·age (mā'trən ĭj, măt'rən-), *n.* 1. state of being a matron. 2. guardianship by a matron. 3. matrons collectively.

ma·tron·ly (mā'trən lĭ), *adj.* 1. like a matron, or having the characteristics of a matron. 2. characteristic of or suitable for a matron. —**ma'tron·li·ness,** *n.*

matron of honor, a married woman acting as the principal attendant of the bride at a wedding.

Ma·tsu (mä'tsoō'), a Chinese island off the SE coast of China. See **Quemoy.**

Ma·tsu·ya·ma (mä'tsoō yä'mä), *n.* a seaport in SW Japan, on Shikoku island. 163,859 (1950).

Matt., Matthew.

matte (măt), *n. Metall.* an unfinished metallic product of the smelting of certain sulfide ores, esp. those of copper. [t. F. See MAT¹]

mat·ted¹ (măt'ĭd), *adj.* 1. covered with a dense growth or a tangled mass. 2. covered with mats or matting. 3. formed into a mat; entangled in a thick mass: *matted hair.* 4. formed of mats, or of plaited or woven material. [f. MAT¹ + -ED²]

mat·ted² (măt′ĭd), *adj.* having a dull finish. [f. MAT³ + -ED²]

Mat·te·ot·ti (mät′tĕ ôt′tē), *n.* **Giacomo** (jä′kō mô′), 1885–1924, Italian socialist leader.

mat·ter (măt′ər), *n.* **1.** the substance or substances of which physical objects consist or are composed. **2.** physical or corporeal substance in general (whether solid, liquid, or gaseous), esp. as distinguished from incorporeal substance (as spirit or mind), or from qualities, actions, etc. **3.** whatever occupies space. **4.** a particular kind of substance: *coloring matter*. **5.** some substance excreted by a living body, esp. pus. **6.** the material or substance of a discourse, book, etc., often as distinguished from the form. **7.** things written or printed: *printed matter*. **8.** a thing, affair, or business: *a matter of life and death*. **9.** an amount or extent reckoned approximately: *a matter of ten miles*. **10.** something of consequence: *it is no matter*. **11.** importance or significance: *what matter?* **12.** the trouble or difficulty (prec. by *the*): *there is nothing the matter*. **13.** ground, reason, or cause. **14.** *Philos.* that stuff which by integrative organization forms chemical substances and living things. In Aristotelian tradition *matter* is to *form* as *potentiality* to *actuality*. **15.** *Law.* statement or allegation. **16.** *Print.* **a.** material for work; copy. **b.** type set up. —*v.i.* **17.** to be of importance; signify: *it matters little*. **18.** to suppurate. [ME *matere*, t. OF, t. L: m.s. *māteria* stuff, material]
—**Syn. 1.** MATTER, MATERIAL, STUFF, SUBSTANCE refer to that of which physical objects are composed (though all these terms are also used abstractly). MATTER, as distinct from mind and spirit, is a broad word which applies to anything perceived, or known to be occupying space: *solid matter, gaseous matter*. MATERIAL usually means some definite kind, quality, or quantity of matter, esp. as intended for use: *woolen material, a house built of good materials*. STUFF, a less technical word, with approximately the same meanings as MATERIAL, is characterized by being of colloquial level when it refers to physical objects (*dynamite is queer stuff*), and of literary or poetic application when it is used abstractly (*the stuff that dreams are made of*). SUBSTANCE is the matter that composes a thing, thought of in relation to its essential properties: *a sticky substance*.

Mat·ter·horn (măt′ər hôrn′), *n.* a peak in the Pennine Alps on the Swiss-Italian border. 14,780 ft. French, **Mont Cervin.**

mat·ter-of-course (măt′ər əv kôrs′), *adj.* occurring or proceeding as if in the natural course of things.

mat·ter-of-fact (măt′ər əv făkt′), *adj.* adhering to actual facts; not imaginative; prosaic; commonplace.

Mat·thew (măth′ū), *n.* **1.** a customs collector at Capernaum summoned to be one of the twelve apostles. Matt. 9:9–13. **2.** the first Gospel in the New Testament. [t. F: m. *Mathieu*, t. LL: m. *Matthaeus*, t. Gk.: m. *Matthatos*, t. Heb: m. *Mattĭthyāh*]

Matthew of Paris, c1200–59, English chronicler.

Matthew Walker, a kind of knot. See **knot.**

Mat·thi·as (mə thī′əs), *n.* a disciple chosen to take the place of Judas Iscariot as one of the apostles. Acts 1:23–26. [see MATTHEW]

mat·tin (măt′ĭn), *n., adj.* matin.

mat·ting¹ (măt′ĭng), *n.* **1.** a coarse fabric of rushes, grass, straw, hemp, or the like, used for covering floors, wrapping, etc. **2.** material for mats. [f. MAT¹ + -ING¹]

mat·ting² (măt′ĭng), *n.* a dull, slightly roughened surface, free from polish, produced by the use of the mat. [f. MAT³ + -ING¹]

mat·tock (măt′ək), *n.* an instrument for loosening the soil in digging, shaped like a pickax, but having one end broad instead of pointed. [ME *mattok*, OE *mattuc*]

mat·toid (măt′oid), *n.* a person of abnormal mentality bordering on insanity. [t. It.: m. *mattoide*, der. *matto* mad, g. L *mattus* intoxicated]

mat·trass (măt′rəs), *n.* *Chem.* matrass.

mat·tress (măt′rĭs), *n.* **1.** a case filled with hair, straw, cotton, etc., usually quilted or fastened together at intervals, used as or on a bed. **2.** a mat woven of brush, poles, or similar material used to prevent erosion of the surface of dikes, jetties, embankments, dams, etc. [ME *materas*, t. OF, t. It.: m. *materasso*, t. Ar.: m. (*al-*)*matrah* (the) mat, cushion]

mat·u·rate (măch′ŏŏ rāt′, măt′yŏŏ-), *v.i.* -rated, -rating. **1.** to suppurate. **2.** to mature. [t. L: m.s. *māturātus*, pp., ripened] —**ma·tur·a·tive** (mə chŏŏr′ə tĭv, măch′ŏŏ rā′tĭv, măt′yŏŏ-), *adj.*

mat·u·ra·tion (măch′ŏŏ rā′shən, măt′yŏŏ-), *n.* **1.** act or process of maturating. **2.** *Biol.* the second phase of gametogenesis resulting in the production of mature eggs and sperms from oögonia and spermatogonia.

ma·ture (mə tyŏŏr′, -tŏŏr′), *adj., v.,* -tured, -turing. —*adj.* **1.** complete in natural growth or development, as plant and animal forms, cheese, wine, etc. **2.** ripe, as fruit. **3.** fully developed in body or mind, as a person. **4.** pertaining to or characteristic of full development: *a mature appearance*. **5.** completed, perfected, or elaborated in full by the mind: *mature plans*. **6.** *Com.* having reached the limit of its time; having become payable or due, as a note. **7.** *Med.* in a state of perfect suppuration. **8.** *Phys. Geog.* (of topographical features) exhibiting the stage of maximum stream development, as in the process of erosion of a land surface. —*v.t.* **9.** to make mature; esp., to ripen. **10.** to bring to full development. **11.** to complete or perfect. —*v.i.* **12.** to become mature, esp. to ripen. **13.** to come to full development. **14.** *Com.* to become due, as a note. [late ME, t. L: m.s.

mātūrus ripe, timely, early] —**ma·ture′ly,** *adv.* —**ma·ture′ness,** *n.* —Syn. **1.** See **ripe.**

ma·tu·ri·ty (mə tyŏŏr′ə tĭ, -tŏŏr′-), *n.* **1.** state of being mature; ripeness. **2.** full development; perfected condition. **3.** *Physiol.* period following attainment of full development of bodily structure and reproductive faculty. **4.** *Com.* **a.** state of being due. **b.** the time when a note or bill of exchange becomes due.

ma·tu·ti·nal (mə tū′tə nəl, -tōō′-), *adj.* pertaining to or occurring in the morning; early in the day. [t. L: s. *mātūtīnālis* of the morning] —**ma·tu′ti·nal·ly,** *adv.*

matz·o (mät′sō), *n., pl.* **matzoth** (mät′sōth), **matzos** (mät′sōs). a cake of unleavened bread, eaten by Jews during the Feast of Passover. [t. Heb.: m. *matstsāh* cake of unleavened bread]

Mau·beuge (mō bœzh′), *n.* a city in N France, on the Sambre river, near the Belgian border. 24,215 (1954).

maud (môd), *n.* **1.** a gray woolen plaid worn by shepherds and others in S Scotland. **2.** a rug or wrap of like material, used as a traveling robe, etc. [orig. uncert.]

maud·lin (môd′lĭn), *adj.* **1.** tearfully or weakly emotional or sentimental. **2.** tearfully or emotionally silly from drink. [from *Maudlin*, familiar var. of *Magdalen* (Mary Magdalene), often represented in art as weeping] —**maud′lin·ly,** *adv.* —**maud′lin·ness,** *n.*

Maugham (môm), *n.* **William Somerset**, born 1874, British novelist, dramatist, and short-story writer.

mau·gre (mô′gər), *prep. Archaic.* in spite of; notwithstanding. Also, **mau′ger.** [ME *maugre*, t. OF: prop., illwill, spite. See MAL-, GREE²]

Ma·u·i (mä′ōō ē′, mou′ē), *n.* one of the Hawaiian Islands, in the central part of the group. 40,103 pop. (1950); 728 sq. mi.

maul (môl), *n.* **1.** a heavy hammer, as for driving piles. **2.** *Obs.* a heavy club or mace. —*v.t.* **3.** to handle or use roughly. **4.** *U.S.* to split with a maul and a wedge, as a rail. [var. of MALL] —**maul′er,** *n.*

Maul·main (môl mān′, môl-), *n.* Moulmein.

maul·stick (môl′stĭk′), *n.* mahlstick.

Mau·na Ke·a (mou′nə kā′ə, mō′nə kē′ə), an extinct volcano on the island of Hawaii. 13,784 ft.

Mau·na Lo·a (mou′nə lō′ə, mō′nə lō′ə), an active volcano on the island of Hawaii. 13,680 ft.

maund (mônd), *n.* a unit of weight in India and other parts of Asia, varying greatly according to locality: in India, from about 25 to 82.286 pounds (the latter being the government maund). [t. Hind., Pers.: m. *mān*]

maun·der (môn′dər), *v.i.* **1.** to talk in a rambling, foolish, or imbecile way. **2.** to move, go, or act in an aimless, confused manner. —**maun′der·er,** *n.*

maun·dy (môn′dĭ), *n.* **1.** the ceremony of washing the feet of the poor, esp. commemorating Jesus' washing of His disciples' feet on Maundy Thursday. **2.** Also, **maundy money.** money distributed as alms in conjunction with the ceremony of maundy or on Maundy Thursday. [ME *maunde*, t. OF: m. *mande*, t. L: m.s. *mandātum* a command, mandate]

Maun·dy Thursday (môn′dĭ), the Thursday of Holy Week, commemorating Jesus' last supper and His washing of the disciples' feet upon that day. See John 13:5, 14, 34.

Mau·pas·sant (mō på säN′), *n.* **(Henri René Albert) Guy de** (äN rē′ rə nē′ àl bĕr′ gē də), 1850–93, French short-story writer and novelist.

Mau·re·ta·ni·a (môr′ə tā′nĭ ə), *n.* an ancient kingdom in NW Africa: it included the territory that is modern Morocco and part of Algeria. Also, **Mauritania.**

Mau·ri·ac (mō ryàk′), *n.* **François** (fräN swä′), b. 1885, French novelist; Nobel Prize for Literature, 1952.

Mau·rice (môr′ĭs, mŏr′ĭs), *n.* **1.** 1521–53, elector of Saxony. **2.** of Nassau, 1567–1625, Dutch statesman.

Mau·ri·ta·ni·a (môr′ə tā′nĭ ə), *n.* **1.** a republic in W Africa: independent member of the French Community; largely in the Sahara Desert. 730,000 (est. 1959); 418,120 sq. mi. *Cap.:* Nouakchott. Official name, **Islamic Republic of Mauritania. 2.** Mauretania.

Mau·ri·tius (mō rĭsh′əs, -rĭsh′ĭ əs), *n.* **1.** an island in the Indian Ocean, E of Madagascar. 538,918 pop. (1954); 720 sq. mi. **2.** a British colony consisting of this island and dependencies. 555,536 pop. (1954); 809 sq. mi. *Cap.:* Port Louis.

Mau·rois (mō rwà′), *n.* **André** (äN drē′), **(Emile Herzog)** born 1885, French biographer and novelist.

mau·so·le·um (mô′sō lē′əm), *n., pl.* -leums, -lea (-lē′ə). **1.** a stately and magnificent tomb. **2.** (*cap.*) a magnificent tomb erected at Halicarnassus in Asia Minor in 350 B.C. See **Seven Wonders of the World.** [t. L, t. Gk.: m. *mausoleion* the tomb of Mausolus (king of Caria)]

mauve (mōv), *n.* **1.** pale bluish purple. **2.** a purple dye obtained from aniline, the first of the coal-tar dyes (discovered in 1856). —*adj.* **3.** of the color of mauve: *a mauve dress.* [t. F: orig., mallow, g. L *malva* MALLOW]

mav·er·ick (măv′ər ĭk), *n. U.S.* **1.** (in cattle-raising regions) **a.** an animal found without an owner's brand. **b.** a calf separated from its dam. **2.** a dissenter. [prob. named after Samuel *Maverick*, a Texas cattle raiser who neglected to brand his cattle]

ma·vis (mā′vĭs), *n.* the European throstle or song thrush, *Turdus philomelus*. [ME *mavys*, t. OF: m.] *mauvis;* of Celtic orig.]

ma·vour·neen (mə vŏŏr′nēn, -vôr′-), *n. Irish.* my darling. Also, **ma·vour′nin.** [t. Irish: m. *mo mhuirnĭn*]

---

b., blend of, blended; c., cognate with; d., dialect, dialectal; der., derived from; f., formed from; g., going back to; m., modification of; r., replacing; s., stem of; t., taken from; ?, perhaps. See the full key on inside cover.

maw (mô), *n.* 1. the mouth, throat, or gullet as concerned in devouring (now chiefly of animals or in figurative use). 2. the crop or craw of a fowl. 3. the stomach. [ME *mawe*, OE *maga*, c. G *magen*]

mawk·ish (mô′kĭsh), *adj.* 1. sickish or slightly nauseating. 2. characterized by sickly sentimentality. [f. *mawk* maggot (t. Scand.; cf. Icel. *madhkr*) + -ISH¹] —**mawk′ish·ly**, *adv.* —**mawk′ish·ness**, *n.*

Maw·son (mô′sən), *n.* Sir Douglas, 1882–1958, Australian antarctic explorer, born in England.

nax., maximum.

nax·il·la (măk sĭl′ə), *n., pl.* maxil-lae (măk sĭl′ē). 1. a jaw or jawbone, esp. the upper. 2. one of the paired appendages immediately behind the mandibles of arthropods. [t. L: jaw]

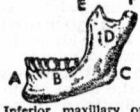

max·il·lar·y (măk′sə lĕr′ĭ, măk sĭl′-ər ĭ), *adj., n., pl.* -laries. —*adj.* 1. of or pertaining to a jaw, jawbone, or maxilla. —*n.* 2. a maxilla or maxillary bone.

Inferior maxillary or lower jaw bone of man A. Symphisis; B. Ramus; C, Angle of jaw; D. Ascending ramus; E. Coronold process; F. Condyle.

max·im (măk′sĭm), *n.* 1. an expression, esp. an aphoristic or sententious one, of a general truth, esp. as to conduct. 2. a principle of conduct. [ME *maxime*, t. OF, t. L: m. *maxima* (*prōpositio*), lit., greatest (proposition)] —**Syn.** 1. See proverb.

Max·im (măk′sĭm), *n.* 1. Sir Hiram Stevens, 1840–1916, British inventor of a machine gun. 2. his brother, Hudson, 1853–1927, U.S. inventor.

max·i·ma (măk′sə mə), *n.* a pl. of maximum.

max·i·mal (măk′sə məl), *adj.* of or being a maximum; greatest possible; highest. —**max′i·mal·ly**, *adv.*

Max·i·mal·ist (măk′sə məl ĭst), *n.* a member of an extremist group or faction of socialists, as of a faction of the Russian Social Revolutionary party.

Max·i·mil·ian (măk′sə mĭl′yən), *n.* 1832–67, archduke of Austria and emperor of Mexico, 1864–67.

Maximilian I, 1459–1519, emperor of the Holy Roman Empire, 1493–1519.

Maximilian II, 1527–76, emperor of the Holy Roman Empire, 1564–76.

max·im·ite (măk′sə mīt′), *n.* a powerful explosive consisting largely of picric acid. [named after Hudson MAXIM (1853–1927), U.S. inventor. See -ITE¹]

max·i·mize (măk′sə mīz′), *v.t.* -mized, -mizing. to increase to the greatest possible amount or degree. [f. s. L *maximus* greatest + -IZE] —**max′i·mi·za′tion**, *n.* —**max′i·miz′er**, *n.*

max·i·mum (măk′sə məm), *n., pl.* -ma (-mə), -mums, *adj.* —*n.* 1. the greatest quantity or amount possible, assignable, allowable, etc.; the highest amount, value, or degree attained or recorded (opposed to *minimum*). 2. *Math.* a value of a function at a certain point which is not exceeded in the immediate vicinity of that point. —*adj.* 3. that is a maximum; greatest possible; highest. 4. pertaining to a maximum or maximums. [t. L, neut. of *maximus* greatest]

maximum likelihood estimation, *Statistics.* a method of estimating population characteristics from a sample by choosing the values of the parameters which will maximize the probability of getting the particular sample actually obtained from the population.

Max Mul·ler (măks mŭl′ər; *Ger.* măks mY′lər), **Frie′-drich.** See Müller, Friedrich Max.

Max·well (măks′wĕl), *n.* See Clerk-Maxwell.

max·well (măks′wĕl), *n.* *Elect.* a unit of magnetic flux, being the flux through a square centimeter in a field in air whose intensity is one gauss. [named after James Clerk *Maxwell*, 1831–1879, British physicist]

may (mā), *v., pres.* 1 **may,** 2 (*Archaic*) **mayest** or **mayst,** 3 **may,** *pl.* **may;** *pret.* **might.** 1. used as an auxiliary to express: **a.** possibility, opportunity, or permission: *you may enter.* **b.** wish or prayer: *may you live long.* **c.** contingency, esp. in clauses expressing condition, concession, purpose, result, etc. **d.** *Archaic.* ability or power (more commonly *can*). 2. *Law.* (in a statute) must (when used not to confer a favor, but to impose a duty). [OE *mæg,* 1st and 3rd pers. sing. pres. ind. of *magan,* c. G *mögen*] —**Syn.** 1. See can¹.

May (mā), *n.* 1. the fifth month of the year, containing 31 days. 2. the early part of springtime, as of life. 3. the festivities of May Day. 4. (*l.c.*) *Brit.* the hawthorn. 5. Cape, a cape at the SE tip of New Jersey, on Delaware Bay. —*v.i.* 6. to gather flowers in the spring: *to go a maying.* [ME; OE *Maius,* t. L]

Ma·ya (mä′yə), *n.* 1. a member of an aboriginal people of Yucatan which had attained a relatively high civilization before the discovery of America. 2. the historical and modern language of the Mayas, of Mayan stock.

Ma·ya·güez (mä′yägwĕs′), *n.* a seaport in W Puerto Rico. 58,944 (1950).

Ma·yan (mä′yən), *adj.* 1. of or pertaining to the Mayas. —*n.* 2. a member of the Mayan tribe. 3. a linguistic stock of southern Mexico, Guatemala, and British Honduras, including Maya and Quiche, and probably related to Penutian.

May apple, 1. an American perennial herb, *Podophyllum peltatum,* bearing an edible, yellowish, egg-shaped fruit. 2. the fruit.

may·be (mā′bĭ, -bē), *adv.* perhaps. [short for *it may be*]

May Day, the first day of May, long celebrated with various festivities, as the crowning of the May queen, dancing round the Maypole, etc., and, in recent years, often marked by labor parades, etc.

May·day (mā′dā′), *n.* (according to international radio regulations) the radio telephonic distress signal used by ships or aircraft. [t. F: alter. of *m'aidez* help me]

Ma·yence (má yäNs′), *n.* French name of Mainz.

May·fair (mā′fâr′), *n.* a fashionable locality in London, England, E of Hyde Park.

May·flow·er (mā′flou′ər), *n.* 1. the ship in which the Pilgrim Fathers sailed from Southampton to the New World in 1620. 2. any of various plants whose flowers blossom in May: **a.** (in the U.S.) chiefly the trailing arbutus, hepatica, and anemone. **b.** (in England) the hawthorn, cowslip, etc.

Mayflower compact, an agreement to establish a government, entered into by the Pilgrims in the cabin of the Mayflower, November 12, 1620.

May fly, 1. any of the *Ephemerida,* an order of delicate-winged insects having the forewings much larger than the hind wings, the larvae being aquatic, and the winged adults being very short-lived; an ephemerid. 2. an artificial fly made in imitation of this fly.

may·hap (mā′hăp′, mā′hăp), *adv.* *Archaic.* perhaps. [short for *it may hap*]

may·hem (mā′hĕm, mā′əm), *n.* *Law.* the crime of violently inflicting a bodily injury rendering a man less able to defend himself or to annoy his adversary (now often extended by statute to include any willful mutilation of another's body). Also, **maihem.** [ME *maheym,* t. AF, var. of OF *mahaigne* injury. See MAIM]

May·ing (mā′Ying), *n.* the celebration of May Day.

May·o (mā′ō), *n.* 1. Charles Horace, 1865–1939, U.S. surgeon. 2. his brother, William James, 1861–1939, U.S. surgeon. 3. a county in NW Ireland, in Connaught province. 133,036 (prelim. 1956); 2084 sq. mi. *Co. seat:* Castlebar.

Ma·yon (mä yōn′), *n.* an active volcano in the Philippine Islands, on SE Luzon island. ab. 8000 ft.

may·on·naise (mā′ə nāz′), *n.* a thick dressing of egg yolks, vinegar or lemon juice, seasonings, and oil, used for salads or vegetables. [t. F: earlier *magnonaise, mahonnaise,* ult. der. *Mahon,* a port of the Balearic Islands]

may·or (mā′ər, mâr), *n.* the principal officer of a municipality; the chief magistrate of a city or borough. [ME *maire,* t. F, g. L *mājor* greater. Cf. MAJOR] —**may′-or·ship′,** *n.*

may·or·al·ty (mā′ər əl tĭ, mâr′əl-), *n., pl.* -ties. 1. the office of a mayor. 2. his period of service.

may·or·ess (mā′ər Ys, mâr′Ys), *n.* 1. *U.S.* a woman mayor. 2. *Brit.* the wife of a mayor.

Ma·yotte (má yōt′), *n.* one of the Comoro Islands, in the Indian Ocean, NW of Madagascar. 19,241 (est. 1953); 143 sq. mi.

May·pole (mā′pōl′), *n.* a high pole, decorated with flowers or ribbons, for the merrymakers to dance round at May Day (or May) festivities. Also, **may′pole′.**

may·pop (mā′pŏp′), *n.* 1. the edible fruit of a passion flower, *Passiflora incarnata,* of the southern U.S. 2. the plant itself. [? repr. a Virginia var. of Algonquian *maracock*]

May queen, a girl or young woman crowned with flowers and honored as queen in the sports of May Day.

mayst (māst), *v.* *Archaic.* 2nd pers. sing. pres. indic. of may.

May·time (mā′tīm′), *n.* the month of May. Also, **May·tide** (mā′tīd′).

may tree, *Brit.* the hawthorn.

may·weed (mā′wēd′), *n.* a composite herb, *Anthemis Cotula,* native in Europe and Asia, and naturalized in America, having pungent, ill-scented foliage, and flower heads with a yellow disk and white rays. [f. obs. *mayth* mayweed (OE *mægtha*) + WEED¹, with loss of *-th*]

May·wood (mā′wŏod), *n.* a city in NE Illinois, near Chicago. 27,330 (1960).

Maz·a·rin (măz′ə rĭn, măz′ə rēn′; *Fr.* má zà răn′), *n.* Jules (zhYl) (*Giulio Mazarini*) 1602–61, French cardinal and statesman, born in Italy; chief minister of Louis XIV, 1642–61.

Ma·zat·lán (mä′sät län′), *n.* a seaport in W Mexico, in Sinaloa state. 41,459 (1950).

Maz·da·ism (măz′də Yz′əm), *n.* Zoroastrianism. Also, **Maz′de·ism.**

maze (māz), *n., v.,* mazed, mazing. —*n.* 1. a confusing network of intercommunicating paths or passages; a labyrinth. 2. a state of bewilderment or confusion. 3. a winding movement, as in dancing. [ME; n. use of MAZE, v.] —*v.t.* 4. *Archaic* or *Dial.* to stupefy or daze. [ME *mase*(*n*); aphetic var. of AMAZE] —**maze′ment,** *n.* —**maze′like′,** *adj.*

ma·zur·ka (mə zûr′kə, -zŏór′-), *n.* 1. a lively Polish dance in moderately quick triple rhythm. 2. music for, or in the rhythm of, this dance. Also, **ma·zour′ka.** [t. Pol.: woman of Mazovia (district in Poland)]

ma·zy (mā′zĭ), *adj.,* -zier, -ziest. mazelike; full of intricate windings. —**ma′zi·ly,** *adv.* —**ma′zi·ness,** *n.*

maz·zard (măz′ərd), *n.* a wild sweet cherry, *Prunus Avium,* used as a rootstock for cultivated varieties of cherries. [earlier *mazer.* Cf. obs. *mazers* spots, MEASLES]

Maz·zi·ni (mät tsē′nē, mäd dzē′-), *n.* **Giuseppe** (jŏō zĕp′pĕ), 1805–72, Italian patriot and revolutionist.

M.B., *Chiefly Brit.* (L *Medicinae Baccalaureus*) Bachelor of Medicine.

M.B.A., Master of Business Administration.

Mc-, Mac.

M.C., 1. Master Commandant. 2. Master of Ceremonies. 3. Member of Congress.

Mc·Car·thy·ism (mə kär′thĭ ĭz′əm), *n.* 1. public accusation of disloyalty, esp. of pro-Communist activity, in many instances unsupported by proof or based on slight, doubtful or irrelevant evidence. 2. unfairness in investigative technique. 3. persistent search for and exposure of disloyalty, esp. in government offices. [from Joseph R. *McCarthy*, 1909–1957, U.S. Senator, + -ism]

Mc·Clel·lan (mə klĕl′ən), *n.* **George Brinton**, 1826–85, Union general in the U.S. Civil War.

Mc·Cor·mack (mə kôr′mĭk), *n.* **John**, 1884–1945, Irish-American tenor singer.

Mc·Cor·mick (mə kôr′mĭk), *n.* 1. **Cyrus Hall**, 1809–1884, U.S. inventor (of harvesting machinery). 2. **Robert Rutherford**, 1880–1955, U.S. newspaper publisher.

Mc·Coy (mə koi′), *n.* **the real**, the best of its kind.

Mc·Dow·ell (mək dou′əl), *n.* **Irvin**, 1818–85, Union general in the U.S. Civil War.

Mc·Guf·fey (mə gŭf′ĭ), *n.* **William Holmes**, 1800–73, U.S. educator: editor of *McGuffey's Readers.*

Mc·Hen·ry (mək hĕn′rĭ), *n.* **Fort**, a former U.S. fort in N Maryland at the entrance to Baltimore harbor: unsuccessfully bombarded by the British, 1814, during which Key wrote *The Star Spangled Banner.*

Mc·In·tosh (măk′ĭn tŏsh′), *n. Hort.* a high quality, red eating apple that ripens in early autumn.

Mc·Kees·port (mə kēz′pōrt), *n.* a city in SW Pennsylvania, near Pittsburgh. 45,489 (1960).

Mc·Kin·ley (mə kĭn′lĭ), *n.* 1. **William**, 1843–1901, 25th president of U.S., 1897–1901. 2. **Mount**, a mountain in central Alaska: highest peak of N America. 20,300 ft.

Mc·Mur·do Sound (mək mûr′dō), an i.let of Ross Sea, in Antarctica, N of Victoria Land.

Md., Maryland.

M.D., (L *Medicinae Doctor*) Doctor of Medicine.

M-day (ĕm′dā′), *n. Mil.* mobilization day: a day assumed by the Defense Department as the first day of mobilization, used by the military for planning purposes.

Mdme., *pl.* **Mdmes.** *Brit.* Madame.

M.D.S., Master of Dental Surgery.

mdse., merchandise.

me (mē; *unstressed* mĭ), *pers.pron.* objective case of the pronoun *I*. [ME *mē*, OE *me*, dat. sing. (c. D *mij*, G *mir*); akin to L *mē* (acc.), etc.]

ME, Middle English. Also, **M.E.**

Me, *Chem.* methyl.

Me., Maine.

M.E., 1. Mechanical Engineer. 2. Methodist Episcopal. 3. Middle English. 4. Mining Engineer.

mead¹ (mēd), *n. Poetic.* a meadow. [ME *mede*, OE *mǣd*. See MEADOW]

mead² (mēd), *n.* 1. an alcoholic liquor made by fermenting honey and water. 2. any of various nonalcoholic beverages. [ME *mede*, OE *medu*, c. G *met*]

Mead (mēd), *n.* **Lake**, a lake made by Hoover Dam in the Colorado river, in NW Arizona and SE Nevada: largest artificial lake in world. 115 mi. long; 227 sq. mi.

Meade (mēd), *n.* **George Gordon**, 1815–72, Union general in the U.S. Civil War.

mead·ow (mĕd′ō), *n.* 1. a piece of grassland, whether used for the raising of hay or for pasture. 2. a low, level tract of uncultivated ground, as along a river, producing coarse grass. [ME *medwe*, OE *mǣdw-*, in inflectional forms of *mǣd* (cf. MEAD¹); akin to G *matte*]

meadow grass, any grass of the genus *Poa*, esp. *P. pratensis*, the Kentucky bluegrass.

meadow lark, a common American songbird of the genus *Sturnella* (family *Icteridae*), esp. the **eastern meadow lark**, *S. magna*, and **western meadow lark**, *S. neglecta*, both of which are robust, yellow-breasted birds about the size of the American robin.

meadow rue, any plant of the ranunculaceous genus *Thalictrum*, having leaves resembling those of rue, esp. (in North America) *T. dioicum* (**early meadow rue**).

mead·ow·sweet (mĕd′ō swēt′), *n. Brit.* 1. any plant of the rosaceous genus *Spiraea*, esp. *S. latifolia*, a low shrub with white or pink flowers. 2. any plant of the closely related genus *Filipendula* (or *Ulmaria*).

mead·ow·y (mĕd′ō ĭ), *adj.* pertaining to, resembling, or consisting of meadow.

mea·ger (mē′gər), *adj.* 1. deficient in quantity or quality, or without fullness or richness. 2. having little flesh, lean, or thin. 3. maigre. Also, **mea′gre.** [ME *megre*, t. OF: m. *maigre*, g. L *macer* lean] —**mea′ger·ly**, *adv.* —**mea′ger·ness**, *n.* —Syn. 1. See scanty.

meal¹ (mēl), *n.* 1. one of the regular repasts of the day, as breakfast, lunch, or supper. 2. the food eaten or served for a repast. [ME; OE *mǣl* measure, fixed time, occasion, meal, c. G *mal* time, *mahl* meal]

meal² (mēl), *n.* 1. the edible part of any grain (now usually excluding wheat) or pulse ground to a (coarse) powder and unbolted. 2. *U.S.* coarse, unbolted grain, corn meal, or Indian meal. 3. any ground or powdery

substance, as of nuts or seeds, resembling this. [ME *mele*, OE *melu*, c. G *mehl*]

meal·time (mēl′tīm′), *n.* the usual time for a meal.

meal worm, the larva of the beetle, *Tenebrio molitor*, which infests granaries. It is raised in great numbers as food for birds and animals.

meal·y (mē′lĭ), *adj.*, **mealier, mealiest.** 1. having the qualities of meal; powdery; soft, dry, and crumbly: *mealy potatoes.* 2. of the nature of, or containing, meal; farinaceous. 3. covered with or as with meal or powder. 4. flecked as if with meal, or spotty. 5. pale, as the complexion. 6. mealy-mouthed. —**meal′i·ness**, *n.*

meal·y-mouthed (mē′lĭ mouthd′, -moutht′), *adj.* 1. avoiding the use of plain terms, as from timidity, excessive delicacy, or hypocrisy. 2. using soft words.

mean¹ (mēn), *v.*, **meant, meaning.** —*v.t.* 1. to have in the mind as in intention or purpose (often with an infinitive as object): *I mean to talk to him.* 2. to intend for a particular purpose, destination, etc.: *they were meant for each other.* 3. to intend to express or indicate: *By "liberal" I mean ....* 4. (of words, things, etc.) to have as the signification; signify. —*v.i.* 5. to be minded or disposed; have intentions: *he means well.* [ME *mene(n)*, OE *mǣnan*, c. G *meinen*] —Syn. 1. purpose, contemplate. See intend. 4. import; denote, indicate.

mean² (mēn), *adj.* 1. inferior in grade, quality, or character. 2. low in station, rank, or dignity. 3. of little importance or consequence. 4. unimposing or shabby: *a mean abode.* 5. without moral dignity; small-minded or ignoble: *mean motives.* 6. penurious, stingy, or miserly: *a man who is mean about money.* 7. *U.S. Colloq.* pettily offensive or unaccommodating; nasty. 8. *U.S. Colloq.* small, humiliated, or ashamed: *to feel mean over some ungenerous action.* 9. *U.S. Colloq.* in poor physical condition. 10. *U.S. Colloq.* troublesome or vicious, as a horse. [ME *mene*, aphetic var. of *imene*, OE *gemǣne*, c. G *gemein* common] —Syn. 2. common, humble. 3. insignificant, petty, paltry. 5. contemptible, despicable. MEAN, LOW, BASE, SORDID, and VILE all refer to ignoble characteristics worthy of dislike, contempt, or disgust. MEAN suggests pettiness and small-mindedness: *to take a mean advantage.* Low suggests coarseness and vulgarity: *low company.* BASE suggests selfish cowardice or moral depravity: *base motives.* SORDID suggests a wretched uncleanness, or sometimes an avariciousness without dignity or moral scruples: *a sordid slum, sordid gain.* VILE suggests disgusting foulness or repulsiveness: g. *vile insinuation, a vile creature.* —Ant. 1. noble, admirable.

mean³ (mēn), *n.* 1. (*usually pl.*) an agency, instrumentality, method, etc., used to attain an end: *there are no means that he will not resort to;* (often with sense and construction of *sing.*) *a means of communication.* 2. (*pl.*) disposable resources, esp. pecuniary resources: *to live beyond one's means.* 3. (*pl.*) considerable pecuniary resources: *a man of means.* 4. something intermediate; that which is midway between two extremes. 5. *Math.* **a.** a quantity having a value intermediate between the values of other quantities; an average, esp. the arithmetic mean. **b.** either the second or third term in a proportion of four terms. 6. *Logic.* the middle term in a syllogism. 7. **by all means, a.** at any cost; without fail. **b.** (in emphasis) certainly: *go, by all means.* 8. **by any means**, in any way; at all. 9. **by no means, a.** in no way; not at all: *a thing by no means certain.* **b.** on no account; certainly not: *a practice by no means to be recommended.* —*adj.* 10. occupying a middle position or an intermediate place. 11. intermediate in kind, quality, degree, time, etc. [ME *mene*, t. OF: m. *meien*, g. LL *mediānus* in the middle] —Syn. 10. moderate.

me·an·der (mĭ ăn′dər), *v.i.* 1. to proceed by a winding course. 2. to wander aimlessly. —*n.* 3. (*usually pl.*) a turning or winding; a winding path or course. 4. a circuitous movement or journey. 5. an intricate variety of fret or fretwork. [t. L, t. Gk.: m. *maíandros* a winding, orig. the name of a winding river (now Mendere) in western Asia Minor] —**me·an′der·ing·ly**, *adv.* —Syn. 2. See stroll.

mean distance, the arithmetic mean of the greatest and least distances of a planet from the sun, called the semimajor axis, and used in stating the size of an orbit.

mean·ing (mē′nĭng), *n.* 1. that which is intended to be, or actually is, expressed or indicated; signification; import. —*adj.* 2. intending. 3. expressive or significant: *a meaning look.* —**mean′ing·ly**, *adv.* —Syn. 1. tenor, gist, drift, trend. MEANING, PURPORT, SENSE, SIGNIFICANCE denote that which is expressed or indicated by something. MEANING is the general word denoting that which is intended to be or actually is expressed or indicated: *the meaning of a word or glance.* SENSE may be used to denote a particular meaning (among others) of a word or phrase: *the word has become obsolete in this sense.* SENSE may also be used loosely to refer to "intelligible meaning": *there's no sense in what he says.* SIGNIFICANCE refers particularly to a meaning that is implied rather than expressed (*the significance of her glance*); or to a meaning the importance of which may not be easy to perceive immediately: *the real significance of his words was not grasped at the time.* PURPORT is mainly limited to the meaning of a formal document, speech, important conversation, etc., and refers to the gist of something fairly complicated: *the purport of his letter to the editor.* 3. See expressive.

mean·ing·ful (mē′nĭng fəl), *adj.* full of meaning; significant.

mean·ing·less (mē′nĭng lĭs), *adj.* without meaning or significance. —**mean′ing·less·ly**, *adv.* —**mean′ing·less·ness**, *n.*

---

b., blend of, blended; c., cognate with; d., dialect, dialectal; der., derived from; f., formed from; g., going back to; m., modification of; r., replacing; s., stem of; t., taken from; ?, perhaps. See the full key on inside cover.

mean·ly (mēn′lĭ), *adv.* in a mean manner; poorly; basely; stingily. [f. MEAN² + -LY]

mean·ness (mēn′nĭs), *n.* **1.** state or quality of being mean. **2.** a mean act.

mean noon, *Astron.* the moment when the mean sun's center crosses the meridian.

mean solar time, *Astron.* time measured by the hour angle of the mean sun. Also, **mean time.**

means test, *Brit.* an inquiry into the income of a person who receives unemployment relief.

mean sun, *Astron.* an imaginary and fictitious sun moving uniformly in the celestial equator and taking the same time to make its annual circuit as the true sun does in the ecliptic.

meant (mĕnt), *v.* pt. and pp. of **mean¹**.

mean·time (mēn′tīm′), *n.* **1.** the intervening time. —*adv.* **2.** in the intervening time; during the interval; at the same time. Also, **mean·while** (mēn′hwīl′).

mea·sled (mē′zəld), *adj.* affected with measles (def. 3).

mea·sles (mē′zəlz), *n.* **1.** an acute infectious disease occurring mostly in children, characterized by catarrhal and febrile symptoms and an eruption of small red spots; rubeola. **2.** any of certain other eruptive diseases, as rubella (German measles). **3.** a disease in swine and other animals caused by the larvae of certain tapeworms of the genus *Taenia.* **4.** (*pl.*) the larvae which cause measles. [partly ME *maseles,* c. D *mazelen,* akin to G *masern* measles, pl. of *maser* spot; partly ME *mesels,* akin to OHG *māsa* spot]

mea·sly (mē′zlĭ), *adj.*, **-sli·er, -sli·est. 1.** infected with measles, as an animal or its flesh. **2.** pertaining to or resembling measles. **3.** *Slang.* wretchedly poor or unsatisfactory.

meas·ur·a·ble (mĕzh′ər ə bəl), *adj.* that may be measured. —**meas′ur·a·bil′i·ty, meas′ur·a·ble·ness,** *n.* —**meas′ur·a·bly,** *adv.*

meas·ure (mĕzh′ər). *n., v.,* **-ured, -ur·ing.** —*n.* **1.** act or process of ascertaining the extent, dimensions, quantity, etc., of something, esp. by comparison with a standard. **2.** size, dimensions, quantity, etc., as thus ascertained. **3.** an instrument, as a graduated rod or a vessel of standard capacity, for measuring. **4.** a unit or standard of measurement. **5.** a definite or known quantity measured out. **6.** a system of measurement. **7.** any standard of comparison, estimation, or judgment. **8.** a quantity, degree, or proportion. **9.** a limit, or an extent or degree not to be exceeded: *to know no measure.* **10.** reasonable bounds or limits: *beyond measure.* **11.** a legislative bill or enactment. **12.** an action or procedure intended as a means to an end: *to take measures to avert suspicion.* **13.** a short rhythmical movement or arrangement, as in poetry or music. **14.** a particular kind of such arrangement. **15.** a metrical unit. **16.** *Poetic.* an air or melody. **17.** *Archaic.* a slow, stately dance or dance movement. **18.** *Music, etc.* the music contained between two bar lines; bar. **19.** (*pl.*) *Geol.* beds; strata. —*v.t.* **20.** to ascertain the extent, dimensions, quantity, capacity, etc., of, esp. by comparison with a standard. **21.** to mark or lay off or out, or deal out, with reference to measure (often fol. by *off* or *out*). **22.** to estimate the relative amount, value, etc., of, by comparison with some standard. **23.** to judge of or appraise by comparison with something else. **24.** to serve as the measure of. **25.** to adjust or proportion. **26.** to bring into comparison or competition. **27.** to travel over or traverse. —*v.i.* **28.** to take measurements. **29.** to admit of measurement. **30.** to be of a specified measure. [ME *mesure(n),* t. OF: m. *mesurer,* g. L *mensūrāre*] —**meas′ur·er,** *n.*

M, Measure (def. 18)

meas·ured (mĕzh′ərd), *adj.* **1.** ascertained or apportioned by measure. **2.** accurately regulated or proportioned. **3.** regular or uniform, as in movement; rhythmical. **4.** deliberate and restrained: *measured speech.* **5.** in the form of meter or verse; metrical. —**meas′·ured·ly,** *adv.*

Measure for Measure, a comedy (1604) by Shakespeare.

meas·ure·less (mĕzh′ər lĭs), *adj.* without bounds; unlimited; immeasurable: *caverns measureless to man.* —**meas′ure·less·ly,** *adv.* —**meas′ure·less·ness,** *n.*

meas·ure·ment (mĕzh′ər mənt), *n.* **1.** act of measuring. **2.** an ascertained dimension. **3.** extent, size, etc., ascertained by measuring. **4.** a system of measuring or of measures.

measuring worm, the larva of any geometrid moth, which progresses by bringing the rear end of the body forward and then advancing the front end.

meat (mēt), *n.* **1.** the flesh of animals as used for food. **2.** food in general: *meat and drink.* **3.** the edible part of anything, as a fruit, nut, etc. **4.** the principal meal: *to say grace before meat.* [ME and OE *mete,* c. OHG *maz*] —**meat′less,** *adj.*

me·a·tus (mĭ ā′təs), *n., pl.* **-tus·es, -tus.** *Anat.* an opening or foramen, esp. in a bone or bony structure, as the opening of the ear, nose, etc. See diag. under **ear.** [t. L: passage]

meat·y (mē′tĭ), *adj.,* **meat·i·er, meat·i·est. 1.** of or like meat. **2.** abounding in meat. **3.** full of substance; pithy.

Mec·ca (mĕk′ə), *n.* **1.** a city in W Saudi Arabia: capital of Hejaz; one of two federal capitals; birthplace of Mohammed; spiritual center of Islam. 150,000 (est. 1954). **2.** any center or goal for many people. —**Mec′can,** *adj., n.*

mech., 1. mechanical. **2.** mechanics. **3.** mechanism.

me·chan·ic (mə kăn′ĭk), *n.* **1.** a skilled worker with tools or machines. **2.** one who repairs machinery. [ME, t. L: s. *mĕchanicus,* t. Gk.: m. *mĕchanikós* of machines]

me·chan·i·cal (mə kăn′ə kəl), *adj.* **1.** having to do with machinery. **2.** of the nature of a device or contrivance for controlling or utilizing material forces, or of a mechanism or machine. **3.** acting or operated by means of such a contrivance, or of a mechanism or machine. **4.** produced by such means. **5.** acting or performed without spontaneity, spirit, individuality, etc. **6.** belonging or pertaining to the subject matter of mechanics. **7.** pertaining to, or controlled or effected by, physical forces. **8.** explaining phenomena as due to mechanical action or the material forces of the universe, as philosophical theories or their advocates. **9.** subordinating the spiritual to the material; materialistic. **10.** involving the material objects or physical conditions: *hindered by mechanical difficulties.* **11.** pertaining to or concerned with the use of tools and the like, or the contrivance and construction of machines or mechanisms. **12.** pertaining to or concerned with manual labor or skill. **13.** exhibiting skill in the use of tools and the like, in the contrivance of machines, etc.: *a mechanical genius.* —**me·chan′i·cal·ly,** *adv.* —**me·chan′i·cal·ness,** *n.*

mechanical drawing, drawing, as of machinery, done with the aid of rulers, scales, compasses, etc.

mech·a·ni·cian (mĕk′ə nĭsh′ən), *n.* one skilled in constructing, working, or repairing machines.

me·chan·ics (mə kăn′ĭks), *n.* **1.** the branch of knowledge concerned (both theoretically and practically) with machinery or mechanical appliances. **2.** the science dealing with the action of forces on bodies and with motion, and comprising kinetics, statics, and kinematics. **3.** (*construed as pl.*) the mechanical or technical part or aspect.

Me·chan·ics·ville (mə kăn′ĭks vĭl), *n.* a village in E Virginia, near Richmond: battle, 1862.

mech·an·ism (mĕk′ə nĭz′əm), *n.* **1.** a piece of machinery. **2.** the machinery, or the agencies or means, by which a particular effect is produced or a purpose is accomplished. **3.** machinery or mechanical appliances in general. **4.** the structure, or arrangement of parts, of a machine or similar device, or of anything analogous. **5.** such parts collectively. **6.** mechanical execution, as in painting or music; technique. **7.** the theory that everything in the universe is produced by matter in motion. **8.** *Philos., Biol.* a natural process interpreted as machinelike or as explicable in terms of Newtonian physics. **9.** *Psychoanal.* (used as an analogy drawn from mechanics) the operation and interaction of psychological forces. [t. NL: s. *mĕchanismus,* f. Gk.: s. *mĕchanē* machine + m. *-ismos* -ISM]

mech·a·nist (mĕk′ə nĭst), *n.* **1.** one who believes in mechanism. **2.** *Rare.* a mechanician.

mech·a·nis·tic (mĕk′ə nĭs′tĭk), *adj.* pertaining to mechanists or mechanism, or to mechanics (def. 1), or to mechanical theories in philosophy, etc.

mech·a·nize (mĕk′ə nīz′), *v.t.,* **-nized, -nizing. 1.** to make mechanical. **2.** to operate or perform by or as if by machinery. **3.** to introduce machinery into (an industry, etc.). **4.** *Mil.* to equip with tanks and other armored motor vehicles. —**mech′a·ni·za′tion,** *n.*

mech·a·no·ther·a·py (mĕk′ə nō thĕr′ə pĭ), *n.* curative treatment by mechanical means. [f. s. Gk. *mĕchanē* machine + -o- + THERAPY]

Mech·lin (mĕk′lĭn), *n.* a city in N Belgium. 62,714 (1947). French, **Malines.** Flemish, **Mech·e·len** (mĕkH′-ə lən).

Mechlin lace, 1. (orig.) handmade bobbin lace with raised cord, made in Flanders. **2.** (now) a similar lace copied by machine.

Meck·len·burg (mĕk′lən bûrg′; *Ger.* -bŏŏrʀH′), *n.* a former state in NE Germany, formed in 1934 from the two states **Meck·len·burg-Schwe·rin** (mek′lən bŏŏrʀH′ shvä rēn′) and **Meck·len·burg-Stre·litz** (mĕk′lən-bŏŏrʀH′ shtrā′lĭts).

med., 1. medical. **2.** medicine. **3.** medieval. **4.** medium.

M.Ed., Master of Education.

med·al (mĕd′əl), *n., v.,* **-aled, -aling** or (*esp. Brit.*) **-alled, -alling.** —*n.* **1.** a flat piece of metal, circular in form, bearing an inscription, device, etc., issued to commemorate a person, action, or event, or given to serve as a reward for bravery, merit, or the like. —*v.t.* **2.** to decorate or honor with a medal. [t. F: m. *médaille,* t. It.: m. *medaglia,* ult. der. L *metallum* metal]

med·al·ist (mĕd′əl ĭst), *n.* **1.** a designer, engraver, or maker of medals. **2.** one to whom a medal has been awarded. Also, *esp. Brit.,* **med′al·list.**

me·dal·lic (mə dǎl´ĭk), *adj.* pertaining to medals.
me·dal·lion (mə dǎl´yən), *n.* 1. a large medal. 2. *Archit.* **a.** a tablet, usually rounded, often bearing objects represented in relief. **b.** a member in a decorative design resembling a panel. [t. F: m. *médaillon*, t. It.: m. *medaglione*, aug of *medaglia* MEDAL]
Medal of Honor, *U.S.* a medal awarded by Congress to soldiers, sailors, and marines who, in action involving actual conflict with an enemy, distinguish themselves conspicuously by gallantry and intrepidity at the risk of life above and beyond the call of duty.
medal play, *Golf.* play in which the score is reckoned by counting the strokes taken to complete the round.
Me·dan (mě dän´), *n.* a city in Indonesia, in NE Sumatra. 190,831 (est. 1952).
med·dle (měd´əl), *v.i.*, -dled, -dling. to concern or busy oneself with or in something without warrant or necessity; interfere. [ME *medle(n)*, t. OF: m. *medler*, ult. der. L *miscēre* mix] —**med´dler,** *n.*
med·dle·some (měd´əl səm), *adj.* given to meddling. —**med´dle·some·ly,** *adv.* —**med´dle·some·ness,** *n.*
Mede (měd), *n.* a native or inhabitant of Media, an ancient kingdom of Asia, south of the Caspian Sea.
Me·de·a (mĭ dē´ə), *n.* 1. *Gk. Legend.* a sorceress, daughter of Aeëtes, king of Colchis, and wife of Jason, whom she assisted in obtaining the Golden Fleece. 2. a play (431 B.C.) by Euripides.
Me·del·lín (mě´dě yēn´), *n.* a city in W Colombia. 431,380 (est. 1954).
Med·ford (měd´fərd). *n.* a city in E Massachusetts, near Boston. 64,971 (1960).
me·di·a¹ (mē´dĭ ə), *n.* a pl. of medium.
me·di·a² (mē´dĭ ə), *n.*, *pl.* -diae (-dĭ ē´). 1. *Phonet., Gram.* a voiced stop: b, d, g. 2. *Anat.* the middle layer of an artery or lymphatic vessel. [t. L: middle (fem. adj.)]
Me·di·a (mē´dĭ ə), *n.* an ancient country in W Asia, S of the Caspian Sea, corresponding generally to NW Iran. *Cap.:* Ecbatana.

Media, 500 B.C.

me·di·a·cy (mē´dĭ ə sĭ), *n.* state of being mediate.
me·di·ae·val (mē´dĭ ē´vəl, měd´ĭ-), *adj.* medieval. —**me´di·ae´val·ism,** *n.* —**me´di·ae´val·ist,** *n.*
me·di·al (mē´dĭ əl), *adj.* 1. situated in or pertaining to the middle; median; intermediate. 2. pertaining to a mean or average; average. 3. ordinary. 4. within a word or syllable; neither initial nor final. —*n.* 5. a medial linguistic element. 6. *Phonet.* media² (def. 1). [t. LL: s. *mediālis*, der. L *medius* middle] —**me´di·al·ly,** *adv.*
me·di·an (mē´dĭ ən), *adj.* 1. noting or pertaining to a plane dividing something into two equal parts, esp. one dividing an animal into right and left halves. 2. situated in or pertaining to the middle; medial. —*n.* 3. the middle number in a given sequence of numbers: *4 is the median of 1, 3, 4, 8, 9.* 4. a line through a vertex of a triangle bisecting the opposite side. [t. L: s. *mediānus* in the middle] —**me´di·an·ly,** *adv.*
Me·di·an (mē´dĭ ən), *adj.* 1. of or pertaining to Media or the Medes. —*n.* 2. a Mede.
me·di·as·ti·num (mē´dĭ ǎs tī´nəm), *n.*, *pl.* -tina (-tī´nə). *Anat.* 1. a median septum or partition between two parts of an organ, or paired cavities of the body. 2. the partition separating the right and left thoracic cavities, formed of the two inner pleural walls, and, in man, containing all the viscera of the thorax except the lungs. [t. ML, prop. neut. of ML *mediastinus* in the middle, der. L *medius* middle] —**me´di·as·ti´nal,** *adj.*
me·di·ate (*v.* mē´dĭ āt´; *adj.* mē´dĭ ĭt), *v.*, -ated, -ating, *adj.* —*v.t.* 1. to bring about (an agreement, peace, etc.) between parties by acting as mediator. 2. to settle (disputes, etc.) by mediation; reconcile. 3. to effect (a result), convey (a gift), etc., as or by an intermediary or medium. —*v.i.* 4. to act between parties to effect an agreement, compromise, or reconciliation. 5. to occupy an intermediate place or position. —*adj.* 6. acting through, dependent on, or involving an intermediate agency; not direct or immediate. [ME. t. LL: m.s. *mediātus*, pp., divided, situated in the middle] —**me´di·ate·ly,** *adv.*
me·di·a·tion (mē´dĭ ā´shən), *n.* 1. action in mediating between parties, as to effect an agreement or reconciliation. 2. *Internat. Law.* an attempt to effect a peaceful settlement between disputing nations through the friendly good offices of another power.
me·di·a·tive (mē´dĭ ā´tĭv), *adj.* mediating; mediatory.
me·di·a·tize (mē´dĭ ə tīz´), *v.t.*, -tized, -tizing. to annex (a principality) to another state (while allowing certain rights to its former sovereign). [t. F: m. *médiatiser*, or t. G: m. *mediatisieren*, der. LL *mediātus*, pp., divided] —**me´di·a·ti·za´tion,** *n.*
me·di·a·tor (mē´dĭ ā´tər), *n.* 1. one who mediates. 2. one who mediates between parties at variance.
me·di·a·to·ry (mē´dĭ ə tōr´ĭ), *adj.* 1. pertaining to mediation. 2. having the function of mediating. Also, **me´di·a·to´ri·al.**

med·ic¹ (měd´ĭk), *n.* *Colloq.* a doctor, medical student, or medical corpsman.
med·ic² (měd´ĭk), *n.* any plant of the fabaceous genus *Medicago,* as *M. sativa* (alfalfa), and *M. lupulina* (black medic), an herb with black pods. [t. L: s. *mēdica,* t. Gk.: m. (*pōa*) *Mēdikē* Median (grass)]
med·i·ca·ble (měd´ə kə bəl), *adj.* susceptible of medical treatment; curable. [t. L: m.s. *medicābilis*]
med·i·cal (měd´ə kəl), *adj.* 1. of or pertaining to the science or practice of medicine. 2. curative; medicinal; therapeutic: *medical properties.* [t. LL: s. *medicālis,* der. L *medicus* of healing] —**med´i·cal·ly,** *adv.*
medical jurisprudence, the science which treats of the application of medical knowledge to questions of civil and criminal law; forensic (or legal) medicine.
me·dic·a·ment (mə dĭk´ə mənt, měd´ə kə-), *n.* a curative or healing substance. [t. L: s. *medicāmentum*] —**med·i·ca·men·tal** (měd´ə kə měn´təl), **med´i·ca·men´ta·ry,** *adj.*
med·i·care (měd´ĭ kâr), *n.* (in the U.S. and Canada) comprehensive medical or health insurance sponsored by the national government. [b. *medi(cal) care*]
med·i·cate (měd´ə kāt´), *v.t.*, -cated, -cating. 1. to treat with medicine or medicaments. 2. to impregnate with a medicine. [t. L: m.s. *medicātus,* pp., cured]
med·i·ca·tion (měd´ə kā´shən), *n.* 1. the use or application of medicine. 2. a medicament; a medicinal agent.
med·i·ca·tive (měd´ə kā´tĭv), *adj.* medicinal.
Med·i·ci (měd´ə chĭ; *It.* mě´dē chē´), *n.* 1. an Italian family of the city of Florence, rich and powerful in the 15th and 16th centuries. 2. **Catherine de'** (dĭ), (Fr. *Catherine de Médicis*) 1519–89, queen of Henry II of France, and mother of Francis II, Charles IX, and Henry III. 3. **Cosmo** (kǒz´mō), or **Cosimo, de'** (kō´zě mō´ dě), (*"the Elder"*) 1389–1464, Italian banker, statesman, and patron of art and literature. 4. **Cosmo,** or **Cosimo, de',** (*"the Great"*) 1519–74, duke of Florence and first grand duke of Tuscany. 5. **Giovanni de'** (jō vän´ně dě). See **Leo X.** 6. **Giulio de'** (jōō´lyō dě), Clement VII. 7. **Lorenzo de'** (lō rěn´tsō dě), (*"Lorenzo the Magnificent"; Lorenzo I*) 1449–1492, ruler of Florence, patron of art and literature, and poet. 8. **Marie de'** (mə rē´; *Fr.* mà rē´ də), (*Maria de'*) 1573–1642, queen of Henry IV of France, and regent of France, 1610–17. Also, *French,* **Médicis.**
me·dic·i·nal (mə dĭs´ə nəl), *adj.* pertaining to, or having the properties of, a medicine; curative; remedial: *medicinal properties, medicinal substances.* [ME, t. L: s. *medicīnālis* of medicine] —**me·dic´i·nal·ly,** *adv.*
med·i·cine (měd´ə sən; *Brit.* měd´sĭn), *n.*, *v.*, -cined, -cining. —*n.* 1. any substance or substances used in treating disease; a medicament; a remedy. 2. the art or science of restoring or preserving health or due physical condition, as by means of drugs, surgical operations or appliances, manipulations, etc. (often divided into medicine proper, surgery, and obstetrics). 3. the art or science of treating disease with drugs or curative substances (distinguished from *surgery* and *obstetrics*). 4. the medical profession. 5. any object or practice regarded by savages as of magical efficacy. —*v.t.* 6. to administer medicine to. [ME. t. L: m. *medicīna*]
medicine ball, a large, solid, leather-covered ball, thrown from one person to another for exercise.
medicine lodge, 1. a structure used for various ceremonials of the North American Indians. 2. (*caps.*) the most important religious society among the Central Algonquian tribes of North America.
medicine man, (among American Indians and other primitive peoples) a man supposed to possess mysterious or supernatural powers.
Mé·di·cis (mě´dē sēs´), *n.* French name for **Medici.**
med·i·co (měd´ə kō´), *n.*, *pl.* -cos. *Slang.* a doctor. [t. It. and Sp., t. L: m. *medicus* a physician]
me·di·e·val (mē´dĭ ē´vəl, měd´Y-), *adj.* of or pertaining to, characteristic of, or in the style of the Middle Ages: *medieval architecture.* See **Middle Ages.** Also, **me·diaeval.** [f. m. NL *medi(um) aev(um)* middle age + -AL¹] —**me´di·e´val·ly,** *adv.*
Medieval Greek, the Greek language of the Middle Ages, usually dated A.D. 700–1500. Also, **Middle Greek.**
me·di·e·val·ism (mē´dĭ ē´vəl ĭz´əm, měd´Y-), *n.* 1. the spirit, practices, or methods of the Middle Ages. 2. devotion to or adoption of medieval ideals or practices. 3. a medieval belief, practice, or the like. Also, **mediaevalism.**
me·di·e·val·ist (mē´dĭ ē´vəl ĭst, měd´Y-), *n.* 1. an expert in medieval history and affairs. 2. one in sympathy with the spirit and methods of the Middle Ages.
Medieval Latin, the Latin language of the literature of the Middle Ages (usually dated A.D. 700 to 1500), including many Latinized words from other languages.
Me·di·na (mě dē´nä), *n.* a city in W Saudi Arabia, where Mohammed was first accepted as the supreme Prophet from Allah, and where his tomb is located. 45,000 (est. 1954).
me·di·o·cre (mē´dĭ ō´kər, mē´dĭ ō´kər), *adj.* of middling quality; of only moderate excellence; neither good nor bad; indifferent; ordinary: *a person of mediocre abilities.* [t. F, t. L: m. *mediocris* in a middle state] —**Syn.** medium, average, commonplace.
me·di·oc·ri·ty (mē´dĭ ŏk´rə tĭ), *n.*, *pl.* -ties. 1. state or quality of being mediocre. 2. mediocre ability or accomplishment. 3. a person of but moderate ability.

edit., Mediterranean.

med·i·tate (mĕd′ə tāt′), v., **-tated, -tating.** —v.t. 1. to consider in the mind as something to be done or effected; to intend or purpose. —v.i. 2. to engage in thought or contemplation; reflect. [t. L: m.s. *meditātus*, pp.] —med′i·ta′tor, n. —Syn. 1. contemplate, plan. 2. ponder, muse, ruminate; cogitate, think.

med·i·ta·tion (mĕd′ə tā′shən), n. 1. act of meditating. 2. continued thought; reflection; contemplation.

med·i·ta·tive (mĕd′ə tā′tĭv), adj. given to, characterized by, or indicative of meditation. —med′i·ta′tive·ly, adv. —med′i·ta′tive·ness, n. —Syn. See pensive.

Med·i·ter·ra·ne·an (mĕd′ə tə rā′nĭ ən), n. 1. the Mediterranean Sea. —adj. 2. pertaining to, situated on or near, or dwelling about the Mediterranean Sea. [f. s. L *mediterrāneus* midland, inland + -AN]

Mediterranean fever, undulant fever.

Mediterranean race, a Caucasian race division inhabiting the area bordering the Mediterranean Sea, including the ancient Iberians, Ligurians, Minoans, and some Hamites, and most modern Mediterranean peoples except those in the Balkan and Anatolian peninsulas.

Mediterranean Sea, the sea between Africa, Europe, and Asia. ab. 1,145,000 sq. mi.; greatest known depth, 14,436 ft.

me·di·um (mē′dĭ əm), n., pl. **-diums, -dia** (-dĭ ə), adj. —n. 1. a middle state or condition; a mean. 2. something intermediate in nature or degree. 3. an intervening substance, as air, etc., through which a force acts or an effect is produced. 4. the element in which an organism has its natural habitat. 5. one's environment; surrounding things, conditions, or influences. 6. an agency, means, or instrument: *newspapers as an advertising medium.* 7. Biol. the substance by which specimens are displayed or preserved. 8. *Bacteriol.* a nutritive substance containing protein, carbohydrates, salts, water, etc., either liquid or solidified through the addition of gelatin or agar-agar, in or upon which microörganisms are grown for study. 9. *Painting.* a liquid with which pigments are mixed for application. 10. a person serving or conceived as serving, as an instrument for the manifestation of another personality or of some alleged supernatural agency: *a spiritualistic medium.* —adj. 11. intermediate in degree, quality, etc.: *a man of medium size.* [t. L: (neut. adj.) middle, intermediate]

me·di·um·is·tic (mē′dĭ ə mĭs′tĭk), adj. pertaining to a spiritualistic medium.

med·lar (mĕd′lər), n. 1. a small malaceous tree, *Mespilus germanica*, the fruit of which resembles an open-topped crab apple and is not edible until in the early stages of decay. 2. its fruit. 3. any of certain other malaceous trees. 4. the fruit of such a tree. [ME *medler*, t. OF, var. of *meslier* the medlar tree, der. *mesle*, the fruit, g. L *mespilum*, t. Gk.: m. *mĕspilon*]

med·ley (mĕd′lĭ), n., pl. **-leys**, adj. —n. 1. a mixture, esp. of heterogeneous elements; a jumble. 2. a piece of music combining airs or passages from various sources. —adj. 3. mixed; mingled; motley. [ME *medlee*, t. OF, var. of *meslee* a mixing, orig. pp. fem. of *mesler* mix]

Mé·doc (mā dôk′), n. 1. a district in SW France, NW of Bordeaux. 2. a claret wine produced there.

me·dul·la (mĭ dŭl′ə), n., pl. **-dullae** (-dŭl′ē). 1. *Anat.* a. the marrow of bones. b. the soft marrowlike center of an organ, such as the kidney, suprarenal, etc. c. the medulla oblongata. 2. *Bot.* the pith of plants. See diag. under *exogen*. [t. L: marrow, pith]

medulla oblongata (ŏb′lŏng gā′tə), *Anat.* the lowest or hindmost part of the brain, continuous with the spinal cord. [t. NL: prolonged medulla]

med·ul·lar·y (mĕd′ə lĕr′ĭ, mĭ dŭl′ər ĭ), adj. pertaining to, consisting of, or resembling the medulla of an organ or the medulla oblongata.

medullary ray, *Bot.* (in the stems of exogenous plants) one of the vertical bands or plates of parenchymatous tissue which radiate between the pith and the bark. See diag. under *exogen*.

medullary sheath, 1. *Bot.* a narrow zone made up of the innermost layer of woody tissue immediately surrounding the pith in plants. See diag. under *exogen*. 2. myelin.

med·ul·lat·ed (mĕd′ə lā′tĭd, mĭ dŭl′ā tĭd), adj. *Anat.* covered by a medullary substance; having myelin sheaths.

Me·du·sa (mĭ dū′sə, -zə, -dōō′-), n., pl. **-sas**. *Gk. Legend.* that one of the three Gorgons slain by Perseus and whose head was afterward borne on the shield of Athena.

me·du·sa (mĭ dū′sə, -zə, -dōō′-), n., pl. **-sas, -sae** (-sē, -zē). *Zool.* a jellyfish. —**me·du·soid** (mĭ dū′soid, -dōō′-), adj.

me·du·san (mĭ dū′sən, -dōō′-), adj. 1. pertaining to a medusa or jellyfish. —n. 2. a medusa or jellyfish.

meed (mēd), n. *Archaic.* a reward or recompense for service or desert. [ME *mede*, OE *mēd*, c. G *miete* hire]

meek (mēk), adj. 1. humbly patient or submissive, as under provocation from others. 2. unduly patient or submissive; spiritless; tame. 3. *Obs.* gentle; kind. [ME *meke, meoc*, t. Scand.; cf. Icel. *mjūkr* soft, mild, meek] —**meek′ly**, adv. —**meek′ness**, n. —Syn. 1. forbearing; yielding, docile; humble. See gentle.

Meer (mĭr; Du. mār), n. **Jan van der** (yän vän dər). ("Vermeer of Delft") 1632–1675, Dutch painter.

meer·schaum (mĭr′shəm, -shôm), n. a mineral, hydrous magnesium silicate, H₄Mg₂Si₃O₁₀, occurring in

white, claylike masses, used for ornamental carvings, for pipe bowls, etc.; sepiolite. 2. a tobacco pipe the bowl of which is made of this substance. [t. G: sea foam]

Mee·rut (mē′rət), n. a city in N India, in Uttar Pradesh. 158,407 (1951).

meet¹ (mēt), v., **met, meeting**, n. —v.t. 1. to come into contact, junction, or connection with. 2. to come before or to (the eye, gaze, ear, etc.). 3. to come upon or encounter; come face to face with or into the presence of. 4. to go to the place of arrival of, as to welcome, speak with, accompany, etc.: *to meet one's guests at the door.* 5. to come into the company of (a person, etc.) in intercourse, dealings, conference, etc. 6. to come into personal acquaintance with, as by formal presentation: *to meet the governor.* 7. to face, eye, etc., directly or without avoidance. 8. to encounter in opposition or conflict. 9. to oppose: *to meet charges with countercharges.* 10. to cope or deal effectively with (an objection, difficulty, etc.). 11. to satisfy (needs, obligations, demands, etc.). 12. to come into conformity with (wishes, expectations, views, etc.). 13. to encounter in experience: *to meet hostility.* —v.i. 14. to come together, face to face, or into company: *we met on the street.* 15. to assemble, as for action or conference as a committee, a legislature, a society, etc. 16. to become personally acquainted. 17. to come into contact or form a junction, as lines, planes, areas, etc. 18. to be conjoined or united. 19. to concur or agree. 20. to come together in opposition or conflict, as adversaries, hostile forces, etc. 21. **meet with**, a. to encounter; come across. b. to experience; undergo; receive (praise, blame, etc.). —n. 22. a meeting, as of huntsmen for a hunt, or cyclists for a ride, etc. 23. those assembled at such a meeting. 24. the place of meeting. [ME *mete(n)*, OE *mētan, gemētan*, der. *mōt, gemōt* meeting. See MOOT] —Syn. 1. intersect, converge. 7. confront, face. 11. settle; discharge, fulfill. 15. gather, congregate, convene. 22. suffer. —Ant. 1. diverge.

meet² (mēt), adj. suitable; fit; proper. [ME *mete*, repr. d. OE form, r. OE *gemǣte* suitable, c. G *gemäss* conformable]

meet·ing (mē′tĭng), n. 1. a coming together. 2. an assembling, as of persons for some purpose. 3. an assembly or gathering held. 4. the persons present. 5. a hostile encounter; a duel. 6. an assembly for religious worship, esp. of Quakers. 7. junction or union.

meeting house, 1. a house or building for religious worship. 2. a house of worship of Quakers.

meet·ly (mēt′lĭ), adv. suitably; fittingly; properly.

mega-, a word element meaning "great," and, in physics, 1,000,000 times a given unit, as in *megohm, megacycle*. Also, before vowels, **meg-**. [t. Gk., comb. form of *mĕgas*]

meg·a·ce·phal·ic (mĕg′ə sə făl′ĭk), adj. 1. *Craniom.* having a skull with a large cranial capacity or one exceeding the mean. Cf. **microcephalic**. 2. large-headed. Also, **meg·a·ceph·a·lous** (mĕg′ə sĕf′ə ləs). [f. MEGA- + m.s. Gk. *kephalē* head + -IC]

meg·a·cy·cle (mĕg′ə sī′kəl), n. *Physics.* a million cycles, esp. a million cycles per second. See **kilocycle**.

Me·gae·ra (mĭ jē′rə), n. *Gk. Myth.* one of the Furies.

meg·a·ga·mete (mĕg′ə gə mēt′), n. a macrogamete.

meg·a·lith (mĕg′ə lĭth), n. *Archaeol.* a stone of great size, esp. in ancient constructive work (as the Cyclopean masonry) or in primitive monumental remains (as menhirs, dolmens, cromlechs, etc.). —**meg′a·lith′ic**, adj.

megalo-, a word element denoting bigness or exaggeration. [t. Gk., comb. form of *mĕgas* great]

meg·a·lo·ce·phal·ic (mĕg′ə lō sə făl′ĭk), adj. megacephalic. Also, **meg·a·lo·ceph·a·lous** (mĕg′ə lō sĕf′ə ləs). —**meg′a·lo·ceph′a·ly**, n.

meg·a·lo·ma·ni·a (mĕg′ə lə mā′nĭ ə), n. 1. *Psychiatry.* a form of mental alienation marked by delusions of greatness, wealth, etc. 2. a mania for big or great things. [t. NL. See MEGALO-, -MANIA]

meg·a·lo·ma·ni·ac (mĕg′ə lə mā′nĭ ăk′), n. one who is afflicted with megalomania. —**meg·a·lo·ma·ni·a·cal** (mĕg′ə lō mə nī′ə kəl), adj.

meg·a·lop·o·lis (mĕg′ə lŏp′ə lĭs), n. a metropolitan region, esp. a combination of several large cities having separate centers but with suburbs that touch one another. Also, **meg·a·po·lis** (mĭ găp′ə lĭs).

meg·a·lo·pol·i·tan (mĕg′ə lō pŏl′ə tən), adj. 1. pertaining to or characteristic of a megalopolis. —n. 2. an inhabitant of a megalopolis.

meg·a·lo·saur (mĕg′ə lə sôr′), n. any of the gigantic carnivorous dinosaurs that constitute the extinct genus *Megalosaurus*. [t. NL: s. *megalosaurus*] —**meg′a·lo·sau′ri·an**, adj., n.

meg·a·phone (mĕg′ə fōn′), n. a device for magnifying sound, or for directing it in increased volume, as a large funnel-shaped instrument used in addressing a large audience out of doors or in calling to a distance. —**meg·a·phon·ic** (mĕg′ə fŏn′ĭk), adj.

meg·a·pod (mĕg′ə pŏd′), adj. having large feet.

meg·a·pode (mĕg′ə pōd′), n. any of the *Megapodiidae*, a family of large-footed Australian gallinaceous birds.

Meg·a·ra (mĕg′ə rə; Gk. mĕ′gä rä′), n. a city of ancient Greece: the capital of **Meg·a·ris** (mĕg′ə rĭs), a district between the gulfs of Corinth and Aegina.

meg·a·spo·ran·gi·um (mĕg′ə spō răn′jĭ əm), n., pl. **-gia** (-jĭ ə). *Bot.* a sporangium containing megaspores.

meg·a·spore (mĕg′ə spōr′), n. *Bot.* 1. the larger of the two kinds of spores produced by some pteridophytes. 2. the embryo sac of a flowering plant.

meg·a·spo·ro·phyll (měg/ə spōr/ə fǐl), n. Bot. a sporophyll producing megasporangia only.

meg·a·there (měg/ə thǐr/), n. any of the huge sloth-like animals constituting the extinct genus Megatherium. [t. NL: m.s. megathērium, f. Gk.: mega- MEGA- + m. thērion beast]

meg·a·ton (měg/ə tŭn/), n. 1. 1,000,000 tons. 2. an explosive force equal to that of 1,000,000 tons of TNT.

Me·gid·do (mə gǐd/ō), n. an ancient city in N Israel, on the plain of Esdraelon: scene of many battles; probably the same as Armageddon in the Bible.

meg·ohm (měg/ōm/), n. Elect. a large unit of resistance, equal to a million ohms.

me·grim (mē/grǐm), n. 1. (pl.) morbid low spirits. 2. Archaic. a whim or caprice. 3. Obs. migraine. [ME migraine, t. F, t. LL: m. hemicrānia HEMICRANIA]

Me·hem·et A·li (mǐ hěm/ět ä lē/, ä/lē), 1769–1849, pasha and viceroy of Egypt. Also, **Mohammed Ali.**

Meigs (měgz), n. Fort, a former U.S. fort in NW Ohio: unsuccessfully attacked by the British, 1813.

Mei·ji (mā/jē/), n. Jap. Hist. the reign style of the Japanese Emperor Mutsuhito, 1867–1912. [Jap.: lit., enlightened peace]

Mei·lhac (mě yàk/), n. Henri (än rē/), 1831–97, French dramatist, collaborator with Ludovic Halévy.

Mein Kampf (mīn kämpf/), the autobiography of Adolf Hitler, setting forth his political philosophy and his plan for the German conquest of Europe.

mei·o·sis (mī ō/sǐs), n. Biol. the maturation process of gametes, consisting of chromosome conjugation and two cell divisions, in the course of which the diploid chromosome number becomes reduced to the haploid. [t. Gk.: a lessening] —**mei·ot·ic** (mī ŏt/ǐk), adj.

Meis·sen (mī/sən), n. a city in East Germany, on the Elbe river: fine porcelain made there. 48,348 (1946).

Meis·so·nier (mě sô nyě/), n. Jean Louis Ernest (zhän lwē ĕr nĕst/), 1815–91, French painter.

Meis·ter·sing·er (mīs/tər sǐng/ər, -zǐng/ər), n., pl. **-singer.** 1. Also, **mastersinger.** a member of one of the guilds, chiefly of workingmen, established during the 14th, 15th, and 16th centuries in the principal cities of Germany, for the cultivation of poetry and music. 2. Die (dē), an opera (1867) by Wagner.

Meit·ner (mīt/nər), n. Lise (lē/zə), born 1878, Austrian nuclear physicist.

Me·kong (mā/kŏng/; Thai. mä kŏng/), n. a river flowing from W China SE along most of the boundary between Thailand and Laos to the South China Sea. ab. 2600 mi. Chinese, **Lantsang.**

melan-, var. of melano-, as in melancholy.

mel·an·cho·li·a (měl/ən kō/lǐ ə), n. Psychiatry. mental disease characterized by great depression of spirits and gloomy forebodings. [t. LL. See MELANCHOLY]

mel·an·cho·li·ac (měl/ən kō/lǐ ǎk/), adj. 1. affected with melancholia. —n. 2. one affected with melancholia.

mel·an·chol·ic (měl/ən kŏl/ǐk), adj. 1. disposed to or affected with melancholy; gloomy; melancholy. 2. pertaining to melancholia. —**mel/an·chol/i·cal·ly,** adv.

mel·an·chol·y (měl/ən kŏl/ǐ), n., pl. **-cholies,** adj. —n. 1. a gloomy state of mind, esp. when habitual or prolonged; depression. 2. sober thoughtfulness; pensiveness. 3. Archaic. a. condition of having too much black bile. b. the bile itself. —adj. 4. affected with, characterized by, or showing melancholy: a melancholy mood. 5. attended with or inducing melancholy or sadness: a melancholy occasion. 6. soberly thoughtful; pensive. [ME melancholie, t. LL: m. melancholia, t. Gk.: black bile] —**Syn.** 1. dejection, despondency; gloominess; hypochondria. 4. See sad. —**Ant.** 5. happy.

Me·lanch·thon (mə lǎngk/thən; Ger. mä länкн/tōn), n. Philipp (fē/lǐp), 1497–1560, German Protestant reformer.

Mel·a·ne·sia (měl/ə nē/shə, -zhə), n. one of the three principal divisions of Oceania, comprising the island groups in the S Pacific, NE of Australia. [f. Gk. mēla(s) black + s. Gk. nêsos island + -IA; ? so named from black appearance of islands seen from sea]

Mel·a·ne·sian (měl/ə nē/shən, -zhən), adj. 1. of or pertaining to Melanesia, its inhabitants, or their languages. —n. 2. a member of any of the dark-skinned, frizzy-haired peoples inhabiting Melanesia. 3. any of the Austronesian languages of Melanesia.

mé·lange (mā länzh/), n. a mixture; medley. [t. F, der. mêler mix. See MEDDLE]

mel·a·nin (měl/ə nǐn), n. Biochem. the dark pigment in the body of man and certain animals, as that occurring in the hair, epidermis, etc., of colored races, or one produced in certain diseases. [f. MELAN- + -IN²]

mel·a·nism (měl/ə nǐz/əm), n. Ethnol. the condition of having a high amount of dark or black pigment granules in the skin, hair, and eyes of a human being.

mel·a·nite (měl/ə nīt/), n. Mineral. a deep-black variety of garnet. [f. MELAN- + -ITE¹]

melano-, a word element meaning "black." [t. Gk., comb. form of mélas black]

Mel·a·noch·ro·i (měl/ə nŏk/rō ī/), n.pl. light-complexioned Caucasians with dark hair. [t. NL, repr. coined Gk. melánōchroi (nom. pl.) black-pale] —**Mel·a·noch·roid** (měl/ə nŏk/roid), adj.

mel·a·noid (měl/ə noid/), adj. 1. of or characterized by melanosis. 2. resembling the color of melanin.

mel·a·no·ma (měl/ə nō/mə), n., pl. **-mata** (-mə tə) Med. a dark-colored tumor. [t. NL. See MELAN-, -OMA]

mel·a·no·sis (měl/ə nō/sǐs), n. Pathol. 1. morbid deposition or development of black or dark pigment in the tissues, sometimes leading to the production of malignant pigmented tumors. 2. a discoloration caused by this. [t. NL, t. Gk.: a blackening] —**mel·a·not·ic** (měl/ə nŏt/ǐk), adj.

mel·an·tha·ceous (měl/ən thā/shəs), adj. belonging to the Melanthaceae, a family of monocotyledonous bulbless plants related to and sometimes classified in the lily family, including the bellwort, white hellebore, etc. [f. s. NL Melanthāceae the typical family (f. Gk. mēl(as) black + s. Gk. ánthos flower + L -āceae, suffix) + -OUS]

mel·a·phyre (měl/ə fīr/), n. any of various dark-colored igneous rocks of porphyritic texture. [t. F: f. Gk. mēla(s) black + F (por)phyre porphyry]

Mel·ba (měl/bə), n. Madame, (Mrs. Nellie Mitchell Armstrong) 1861–1931, Australian operatic soprano.

Melba toast, narrow slices of thin toast.

Mel·bourne (měl/bərn), n. 1. a seaport in SE Australia, in Victoria. With suburbs, 1,524,062 (1953). 2. William Lamp, 2nd Viscount, 1779–1848. British statesman.

Mel·chers (měl/chərz), n. Gari (gär/ī), 1860–1932, U.S. painter.

Mel·chiz·e·dek (měl kǐz/ə děk/), n. 1. Old Testament. a priest-king of Salem. Gen. 14:18. 2. the higher order of priesthood in the Mormon church. [t. LL (Vulgate): m. Melchisedek, t. Gk. (Septuagint), t. Heb.: m. Malkīṣedeq]

meld (měld), Pinochle, etc. —v.t., v.i. 1. to announce and display (a counting combination of cards in the hand) for a score. —n. 2. act of melding. 3. any combination of cards to be melded. [t. G: s. melden announce]

Mel·e·a·ger (měl/ī ā/jər), n. Gk. Legend. the heroic son of Althea. He was an Argonaut, and the slayer of the Calydonian boar. It had been prophesied to his mother that as long as a certain brand remained unburnt Meleager would live; after he killed his uncles in argument over the boar, Althea threw the brand into the fire and so killed her son.

me·lee (mā/lā, měl/ā; Fr. mě lě/), n. a confused general hand-to-hand fight. Also, **mê·lée.** [t. F. See MEDLEY]

me·li·a·ceous (mē/lǐ ā/shəs), adj. belonging to the Meliaceae, a family of trees and shrubs including the azedarach, mahogany, Spanish cedar, etc. [f. s. NL Melia the typical genus (t. Gk.: ash tree) + -ACEOUS]

mel·ic (měl/ǐk), adj. 1. intended to be sung. 2. noting or pertaining to the more elaborate form of Greek lyric poetry, as distinguished from iambic and elegiac poetry. [t. Gk.: s. melikós, der. mélos song]

mel·i·lot (měl/ə lŏt/), n. any of the cloverlike fabaceous herbs constituting the genus Melilotus. [ME mellilot, t. OF, t. L: m.s. melilōtos, t. Gk.: a kind of clover]

mel·i·nite (měl/ə nīt/), n. a high explosive containing picric acid. [f. s. Gk. mēlinos quince-yellow + -ITE¹]

mel·io·rate (měl/yə rāt/), v.t., v.i., **-rated, -rating.** to make or become better; improve; ameliorate. [t. LL: m.s. meliōrātus, pp.] —**mel/io·ra/tion,** n. —**mel/io·ra/tive,** adj. —**mel/io·ra/tor,** n.

mel·io·rism (měl/yə rǐz/əm), n. the doctrine that the world tends to become better, or may be made better by human effort. [f. L melior better + -ISM] —**mel/io·rist,** n., adj. —**mel/io·ris/tic,** adj.

mel·ior·i·ty (měl yŏr/ə tǐ, -yŏr/-), n. superiority.

mel·lif·er·ous (mə lǐf/ər əs), adj. yielding or producing honey. [f. L mellifer honey-bearing + -OUS]

mel·lif·lu·ent (mə lǐf/lŏŏ ənt), adj. mellifluous. [t. LL: s. mellifluens flowing with honey] —**mel·lif/lu·ence,** n. —**mel·lif/lu·ent·ly,** adv.

mel·lif·lu·ous (mə lǐf/lŏŏ əs), adj. 1. sweetly or smoothly flowing: mellifluous tones. 2. flowing with honey; sweetened with or as with honey. [ME, t. LL: m. mellifluus flowing with honey] —**mel·lif/lu·ous·ly,** adv. —**mel·lif/lu·ous·ness,** n.

Mel·lon (měl/ən), n. Andrew William, 1855–1937, U.S. financier; secretary of the treasury, 1921–32.

mel·low (měl/ō), adj. 1. soft and full-flavored from ripeness, as fruit. 2. well-matured, as wines. 3. softened, toned down, or improved as if by ripening. 4. soft and rich, as sound, tones, color, light, etc. 5. genial; jovial. 6. friable or loamy, as soil. —v.t., v.i. 7. to make or become mellow; soften by or as by ripening. [ME mel(o)we, OE meru tender, soft, with change of r to l, presumably by dissimilation in sequence melowe fruit] —**mel/low·ly,** adv. —**mel/low·ness,** n. —**Syn.** 1. See ripe.

me·lo·de·on (mə lō/dǐ ən), n. 1. a small reed organ. 2. a kind of accordion. [pseudo-Gk. var. of melodium (der. MELODY). Cf. ACCORDION]

me·lo·di·a (mə lō/dǐ ə), n. an 8-foot wooden flue-pipe stop organ resembling the clarabella in tone. [t. NL, special use of LL melōdia MELODY]

me·lod·ic (mə lŏd/ǐk), adj. 1. melodious. 2. pertaining to melody as distinguished from harmony and rhythm. —**me·lod/i·cal·ly,** adv.

me·lod·ics (mə lŏd/ǐks), n. that branch of musical science concerned with the pitch and succession of tones.

me·lo·di·ous (mə lō/dǐ əs), adj. 1. of the nature of or characterized by melody; tuneful. 2. producing

b., blend of, blended; c., cognate with; d., dialect, dialectal; der., derived from; f., formed from; g., going back to; m., modification of; r., replacing; s., stem of; t., taken from; ?, perhaps. See the full key on inside cover.

melody or sweet sound. **—me·lo′di·ous·ly,** adv. **—me·lo′di·ous·ness,** n.

mel·o·dist (mĕl′ə dĭst), n. a composer or a singer of melodies.

mel·o·dize (mĕl′ə dīz′), v., **-dized, -dizing. —v.t. 1.** to make melodious. **—v.i. 2.** to make melody. **3.** to blend melodiously. **—mel′o·diz′er,** n.

mel·o·dra·ma (mĕl′ə drä′mə, -drăm′ə), n. **1.** a play which does not observe the dramatic laws of cause and effect and which intensifies sentiment and exaggerates passion. **2.** (in the 17th, 18th and early 19th centuries) a romantic dramatic composition with music interspersed. [t. F: m. *mélodrame,* t. It.: m. *melodramma* musical drama, f. Gk.: *mēlo*(s) song, music + m. *dráma* DRAMA] **—mel·o·dram·a·tist** (mĕl′ə drăm′ə tĭst), n.

mel·o·dra·mat·ic (mĕl′ə drə măt′ĭk), adj. **1.** of, like, or befitting melodrama; sentimental and exaggerated. **—**n. **2.** (pl.) melodramatic behavior. **—mel·o·dra·mat′i·cal·ly,** adv.

mel·o·dy (mĕl′ə dĭ), n., pl. **-dies. 1.** musical sounds in agreeable succession or arrangement. **2.** Music. **a.** the succession of single tones in musical compositions, as distinguished from harmony and rhythm. **b.** the principal part in a harmonic composition; the air. **c.** a rhythmical succession of single tones producing a distinct musical phrase or idea. **3.** a poem suitable for singing. [ME *melodie,* t. OF, t. LL: m. *melōdia,* t. Gk.: m. *melōdía* singing, choral song] **—Syn. 1.** See harmony.

mel·oid (mĕl′oid), n. a blister beetle. [t. NL: s. *Meloïdae* the typical genus, der. *meloē* beetle]

mel·on (mĕl′ən), n. **1.** the fruit of any of various cucurbitaceous plants, as the muskmelon or watermelon. **2.** deep pink; medium crimson. **3. cut a melon,** U.S. Slang. to declare a large extra dividend to shareholders. [ME, t. OF, t. LL: s. *mĕlo,* t. Gk.: short for *mēlopépōn* applelike gourd]

Me·los (mē′lŏs), n. an island of the Cyclades group, in the Aegean, S of Greece: statue of Venus of Milo found here, 1920. 5586 (1951); 61 sq. mi. Also, **Milo, Milos.**

Mel·pom·e·ne (mĕl pŏm′ə nĭ), n. the Muse of tragedy. [t. L, t. Gk., prop. ppr. fem. of *mĕlpesthai* sing]

Mel·rose (mĕl′rōz), n. **1.** a city in E Massachusetts, near Boston. 29,619 (1960). **2.** a village in SE Scotland, on the Tweed river: ruins of a famous abbey.

melt (mĕlt), v., **melted, melted** or **molten, melting,** n. **—v.i. 1.** to become liquefied by heat, as ice, snow, butter, metal, etc. **2.** to become liquid; dissolve. **3.** to pass, dwindle, or fade gradually. **4.** to pass, change, or blend gradually (often fol. by *into*). **5.** to become softened in feeling by pity, sympathy, love, or the like. **6.** Archaic. to fail or faint, as the heart or soul, from fear, grief, etc. **—v.t. 7.** to reduce to a liquid state by heat; fuse. **8.** to cause to pass or fade (*away*). **9.** to cause to pass or blend gradually. **10.** to soften in feeling, as a person, the heart, etc. **—n. 11.** act or process of melting. **12.** the state of being melted. **13.** that which is melted. **14.** a quantity melted at one time. [ME *melte*(n), OE *meltan,* v.i., *m*(i)*eltan,* v.t.; akin to Icel. *melta* digest, Gk. *mĕldein* melt] **—melt′er,** n. **—Syn. 1.** MELT, DISSOLVE, FUSE, THAW imply reducing a solid substance to a liquid state. To MELT is to bring a solid to a liquid condition by the agency of heat: *to melt butter.* DISSOLVE, though sometimes used interchangeably with melt, applies to a different process, depending upon the fact that certain solids, placed in certain liquids, distribute their particles throughout the liquids: *a greater number of solids can be dissolved in water and in alcohol than in any other liquids.* To FUSE is to subject the solid (usually a metal) to a very high temperature; it applies esp. to melting or blending metals together: *bell metal is made by fusing copper and tin.* To THAW is to reduce a frozen substance (whose ordinary condition is liquid) to a liquid or semiliquid form by raising its temperature above the freezing point: *sunshine will thaw ice in a lake.* **—Ant. 2.** solidify.

melt·age (mĕl′tĭj), n. the amount melted or the result of melting.

melting point, the temperature at which a solid substance melts or fuses.

melting pot, 1. a pot in which metals or other substances are melted or fused. **2.** a country in which immigrants of various races are united in citizenship.

mel·ton (mĕl′tən), n. a smooth heavy woolen cloth. used for overcoats, hunting jackets, etc. [from *Melton Mowbray,* town in Leicestershire, England]

Mel·ville (mĕl′vĭl), n. **Herman,** 1819–91, U.S. author.

Melville Island, a Canadian island in the Arctic Ocean, N of Canada. ab. 200 mi. long; ab. 130 mi. wide.

Melville Peninsula, a peninsula in N Canada, SE of the Gulf of Boothia. ab. 250 mi. long.

mem., 1. member. **2.** memoir. **3.** memorandum.

mem·ber (mĕm′bər), n. **1.** each of the persons composing a society, party, community, or other body. **2.** each of the persons included in the membership of a legislative body, as the U.S. Congress (chiefly the House of Representatives) or the British Parliament (chiefly the House of Commons). **3.** a part or organ of an animal body; a limb, as a leg, arm, or wing. **4.** a constituent part of any structural or composite whole, as a subordinate architectural feature of a building or the like. **5.** either side of an algebraic equation. [ME *membre,* t. OF, g. L *membrum* limb, part] **—Syn. 3, 4.** MEMBER. LIMB refer to an integral part of a larger body. MEMBER is the general term applied to any integral part or vital organ of an organized animal body, or,

more widely, to any integral or distinguishable constituent part of a whole which is considered as organic: *the nose, tongue, and arms are members of the body; a member of a facade.* LIMB, which once, like MEMBER, referred to any organ of the body, is now restricted to the legs and arms (particularly of human beings); secondarily applied to the branches of a tree. It has such figurative uses as a *limb of Satan,* or a *limb of the law.* The Victorian "limb" as a prudish euphemism for "leg" stimulated further humorous use of the word.

mem·ber·ship (mĕm′bər shĭp′), n. **1.** state of being a member, as of a society. **2.** the status of a member. **3.** the total number of members belonging to a body.

mem·brane (mĕm′brān), n. a thin, pliable sheet or layer of animal or vegetable tissue, serving to line an organ, connect parts, etc. [t. L: m.s. *membrāna* the skin that covers the several members of the body, parchment]

membrane bone, a bone which originates in membranous tissue (opposed to *cartilage bone*).

mem·bra·nous (mĕm′brə nəs), adj. **1.** consisting of, of the nature of, or resembling membrane. **2.** characterized by the formation of a membrane. Also, **mem·bra·na·ceous** (mĕm′brə nā′shəs).

Me·mel (mā′məl), n. **1.** a seaport in the W Soviet Union, in the Lithuanian Republic. 60,000 (est. 1948). **2.** a territory including this seaport: ceded to Germany by Lithuania, 1939; incorporated into the Soviet Union, 1945. 154,694 pop. (1939); 933 sq. mi. **3.** name of the lower course of the Nieman river. Lithuanian (for defs. 1 and 2), **Klaipeda.**

Memel (def. 1)

me·men·to (mĭ mĕn′tō), n., pl. **-tos, -toes. 1.** something that serves as a reminder of what is past or gone. **2.** anything serving as a reminder or warning. **3.** (cap.) Rom. Cath. Ch. (in the canon of the Mass) either of two prayers beginning with the word "Memento" (remember), the first for persons living, and the second for persons deceased. [t. L, impv. of *meminisse* remember]

me·men·to mo·ri (mĭ mĕn′tō mōr′ī), **1.** Latin. remember that thou must die (lit., to die). **2.** an object, as a skull or the like, serving as a reminder of death.

Mem·ling (mĕm′lĭng), n. **Hans** (häns), c1430–c94, Flemish painter. Also, **Mem·linc** (mĕm′lĭngk).

Mem·non (mĕm′nŏn), n. **1.** a colossal statue near Egyptian Thebes which was said to produce musical sounds when struck by the rays of the morning sun. **2.** Gk. Legend. an Oriental or Ethiopian hero slain by Achilles in the Trojan War. [t. L, t. Gk.]

mem·o (mĕm′ō), n., pl. **memos.** Colloq. memorandum.

mem·oir (mĕm′wär, -wôr), n. **1.** (pl.) records of facts or events in connection with a particular subject, historical period, etc., as known to the writer or gathered from special sources. **2.** (pl.) records of one's own life and experiences. **3.** a biography. **4.** (pl.) a collection of reports made to a scientific or other learned society. [t. F: m. *mémoire,* masc., memorandum, memorial, *mémoire,* fem., MEMORY]

mem·o·ra·bil·i·a (mĕm′ə rə bĭl′ĭ ə), n.pl., sing. **-rabile** (-răb′ə lĭ). matters or events worthy to be remembered. [t. L, neut. pl. of *memorābilis* memorable]

mem·o·ra·ble (mĕm′ə rə bəl), adj. **1.** worthy to be remembered; notable: *a memorable speech.* **2.** easy to be remembered. [t. L: m.s. *memorābilis*] **—mem′o·ra·bil′i·ty, mem′o·ra·ble·ness,** n. **—mem′o·ra·bly,** adv.

mem·o·ran·dum (mĕm′ə răn′dəm), n., pl. **-dums, -da**(-də). **1.** a note made of something to be remembered, as in future action. **2.** a record or written statement of something. **3.** Law. a writing, usually informal, containing the terms of a transaction. **4.** Diplomacy. a summary of the state of a question, the reasons for a decision agreed on, etc. **5.** a document which includes the terms of a shipment of unsold goods and authorizes their return within a specified time. [t. L, neut. of *memorandus* (ger.) that is to be remembered]

me·mo·ri·al (mə mōr′ĭ əl), n. **1.** something designed to preserve the memory of a person, event, etc., as a monument, a periodic observance, etc. **2.** a written statement of facts presented to a sovereign, a legislative body, etc., as the ground of, or expressed in the form of, a petition or remonstrance. **—**adj. **3.** preserving the memory of a person or thing; commemorative: *memorial services.* **4.** of or pertaining to the memory. [ME, t. L: s. *memoriālis* of memory] **—me·mo′ri·al·ly,** adv.

Memorial Day, U.S. **1.** a day, May 30, set apart in most States for observances in memory of dead soldiers and sailors; Decoration Day. **2.** any of several days (April 26, May 10, or June 3) similarly observed in various Southern States.

me·mo·ri·al·ize (mə mōr′ĭ ə līz′), v.t., **-ized, -izing. 1.** to commemorate. **2.** to present a memorial to. **—me·mo′ri·al·i·za′tion,** n. **—me·mo′ri·al·iz′er,** n.

mem·o·rize (mĕm′ə rīz′), v.t., **-rized, -rizing.** to commit to memory, or learn by heart: *Davy finally memorized the poem.* **—mem′o·riz′a·ble,** adj. **—mem′o·ri·za′tion,** n. **—mem′o·riz′er,** n.

mem·o·ry (mĕm′ə rĭ), n., pl. **-ries. 1.** the mental capacity or faculty of retaining and reviving impressions, or of recalling or recognizing previous experiences. **2.** this faculty as possessed by a particular individual: *to*

ăct, āble, dâre, ärt; ĕbb, ēqual; ĭf, īce; hŏt, ōver, ôrder, oil, bŏŏk, ōōze, out; ŭp, ūse, ûrge; ə = a in alone; ch, chief; g, give; ng, ring; sh, shoe; th, thin; ŧħ, that; zh, vision. See the full key on inside cover.

have a good memory. **3.** the act or fact of retaining mental impressions; remembrance; recollection: *to draw from memory*. **4.** the length of time over which recollection extends: *a time within the memory of living men*. **5.** a mental impression retained; a recollection: *one's earliest memories*. **6.** the reputation of a person or thing, esp. after death. **7.** the state or fact of being remembered. **8.** a person or thing remembered. **9.** commemorative remembrance; commemoration: *a monument in memory of Columbus*. **10.** *Speech.* the step in the classical preparation of a speech in which the wording is memorized. [ME *memorie*, t. L: m. *memoria*]

Mem·phis (měm′fĭs), *n.* **1.** a city in SW Tennessee: a port on the Mississippi. 497,524 (1960). **2.** a ruined city in Upper Egypt, on the Nile, S of Cairo: the ancient capital of Egypt. See map under Media.

Mem·phre·ma·gog (měm′frĭ mā′gŏg), *n.* **Lake,** a lake in N Vermont and S Quebec. ab. 30 mi. long.

mem-sa·hib (měm′sä′ĭb, -sä′hĭb), *n.* (in India) a native's term of respect for a European lady. [t. Hind.: f. *mem* (t. E: m. *ma'am*) + *sāhib* master]

men (měn), *n.* pl. of **man.**

men·ace (měn′ĭs), *n., v.,* **-aced, -acing.** —*n.* **1.** something that threatens to cause evil, harm, injury, etc.; a threat. —*v.t.* **2.** to utter or direct a threat against; threaten. **3.** to serve as a probable cause of evil, etc., to. [ME, t. OF, g. L *minācia* a threat] —**men′ac·er,** *n.* —**men′ac·ing·ly,** *adv.*

me·nad (mē′năd), *n.* **maenad.**

mé·nage (mā nàzh′; *Fr.* mě nàzh′), *n.* **1.** a household; a domestic establishment. **2.** housekeeping. Also, **menage′.** [t. F, ult. der. L *mansio* MANSION]

me·nag·er·ie (mə năj′ər ĭ, -năzh′-), *n.* **1.** a collection of wild or strange animals, esp. for exhibition. **2.** a place where they are kept or exhibited. [t. F: management of a household, menagerie, der. *ménage* MENAGE]

Men·ai Strait (měn′ī,-ỹ), a strait between Anglesey island and the mainland of NW Wales. 14 mi. long.

Me·nam (mā năm′), *n.* a river flowing from N Thailand S to the Gulf of Siam. ab. 750 mi. Also, **Chao Phraya.**

Me·nan·der (mĭ năn′dər), *n.* 342?–291 B.C., Greek writer of comedies.

Men·ci·us (měn′shĭ əs), *n.* (Meng-tse) 385 or 372–289 B.C., Chinese philosopher.

Menck·en (měngk′ən), *n.* **Henry Louis,** 1880–1956, U.S. author, editor, and critic.

mend (měnd), *v.t.* **1.** to make whole or sound by repairing, as something broken, worn, or otherwise damaged; repair: *to mend clothes,* (or in England) *to mend a road.* **2.** to remove or correct defects or errors in. **3.** to remove or correct (a defect, etc.). **4.** to set right; make better; improve: *to mend matters.* —*v.i.* **5.** to progress toward recovery, as a sick person. **6.** (of conditions) to improve. —*n.* **7.** act of mending; repair or improvement. **8.** a mended place. **9. on the mend, a.** recovering from sickness. **b.** improving in state of affairs. [aphetic var. of AMEND] —**mend′a·ble,** *adj.* —**mend′er,** *n.* —**Syn. 1.** MEND, DARN, PATCH mean to repair something and thus renew its usefulness. MEND is an informal and general expression which emphasizes the idea of making whole something damaged: *to mend a broken dish, a tear in an apron.* DARN and PATCH are more specific, referring particularly to repairing holes or rents. To DARN is to repair by means of stitches interwoven with one another: *to darn stockings.* To PATCH is to cover a hole or rent (usually) with a piece or pieces of similar material and to secure the edges of these; it implies a more temporary or makeshift repair than the others: *to patch the knees of trousers, a rubber tire.*

men·da·cious (měn dā′shəs), *adj.* **1.** false or untrue: *a mendacious report.* **2.** lying or untruthful. [f. MENDACI(TY) + -OUS] —**men·da′cious·ly,** *adv.* —**men·da′cious·ness,** *n.*

men·dac·i·ty (měn dăs′ə tĭ), *n., pl.* **-ties. 1.** quality of being mendacious. **2.** a falsehood; a lie. [t. LL: m.s. *mendācitas*]

Men·del (měn′dəl), *n.* **Gregor Johann** (grā′gŏr yō′hän), 1822–84, Austrian biologist. —**Men·de·li·an** (měn dē′lĭ ən), *adj.*

men·de·le·vi·um (měn′də lē′vĭ əm), *n.* **Chem.** a synthetic, radioactive element. *Symbol:* Md; *at. no.:* 101. [f. MENDEL(YE)EV + -IUM]

Men·del·ism (měn′də līz′əm), *n.* the theories of heredity advanced by G. J. Mendel. Also, **Men·de·li·an·ism** (měn dē′lĭ ə nĭz′əm).

Mendel's laws, *Genetics.* the basic principles of heredity discovered by Gregor Mendel, showing that alternative hereditary factors of hybrids exhibit a clean-cut separation or segregation from one another, and that different pairs of hereditary traits are independently assorted from each other.

Men·dels·sohn (měn′dəl sən; *Ger.* měn′dəls zōn′), *n.* **1. Felix** (fā′lĭks), (*Jacob Ludwig Felix Mendelssohn-Bartholdy*) 1809–47, German composer of music. **2.** his grandfather, **Moses** (mō′zĕs), 1729–86, German philosopher.

Men·de·lye·ev (měn′də lyā′əf; *Russ.* měn′dĕ lyĕ′ĕf), *n.* **Dmitri Ivanovich** (dmē′trĭ ĭ vä′nŏ vĭch), 1834–1907, Russian chemist: helped develop the periodic law. Also, **Men′de·le′ev, Men′de·lye′ev.**

Men·de·res (měn′dĕ rĕs′), *n.* **1.** Ancient, **Maeander.** a river in W Asia Minor, flowing into the Aegean near Samos. ab. 240 mi. **2.** Ancient, **Scamander.** a river in NW Asia Minor, flowing across the Trojan plain into the Dardanelles. ab. 65 mi.

Men·dès-France (mäN děs fräns′), *n.* **Pierre,** born 1907, French statesman and economist; premier, 1954–1955.

men·di·cant (měn′də kənt), *adj.* **1.** begging, practicing begging, or living on alms. **2.** pertaining to or characteristic of a beggar. —*n.* **3.** one who lives by begging; a beggar. **4.** a mendicant friar. [t. L: s. *mendīcans,* ppr., begging] —**men′di·can·cy,** *n.*

men·dic·i·ty (měn dĭs′ə tĭ), *n.* **1.** the practice of begging. **2.** the condition of life of a beggar. [ME *mendicite,* t. L: m.s. *mendīcitas* beggary]

Men·do·ci·no (měn′də sē′nō), *n.* **Cape,** a cape in NW California: the westernmost point in California.

Men·do·za (měn dō′sä), *n.* a city in W Argentina. 110,180 (est. 1952).

Men·do·za (měn dō′thä, -sä), *n.* **Pedro de** (pě′drō dě), 1487?–1537, Spanish soldier and explorer: founder of Buenos Aires (?1536).

Men·e·la·us (měn′ə lā′əs), *n.* **Gk. Legend.** a king of Sparta, brother of Agamemnon and husband of Helen; one of the leaders of the Greeks before Troy.

Men·e·lik II (měn′ə lĭk), 1844–1913, emperor of Ethiopia, 1889–1913.

Me·nén·dez de A·vi·lés (mĕ nĕn′dĕth dĕ ä′vĕ lĕs′), **Pedro** (pĕ′drō), 1519–74, Spanish admiral and colonizer; founder of St. Augustine, Florida, in 1565.

Me·nes (mē′nĕz), *n.* fl. c4750? B.C., traditional first king of Egypt, founder of 1st dynasty.

Meng-tse (mŭng′dzŭ′), *n.* Chinese name of **Mencius.**

men·ha·den (měn hā′dən), *n., pl.* **-den.** any marine clupeoid fish of the genus *Brevoortia,* esp. *B. tyrannus,* having the appearance of a shad but with a more compressed body, common along the eastern coast of the U.S., and used for making oil and fertilizer. [t. N Amer. (Narragansett) Ind: they manure]

men·hir (měn′hĭr), *n.* **Archaeol.** an upright monumental stone, standing either alone or with others, as in a cromlech, found chiefly in Cornwall. [t. Breton: *men hir* long stone]

me·ni·al (mē′nĭ əl), *adj.* **1.** pertaining or proper to domestic servants. **2.** servile. —*n.* **3.** a domestic servant. **4.** a servile person. [ME, t. AF, der. *meinie,* ult. der. L *mansio* household, MANSION] —**me′ni·al·ly,** *adv.* —**Syn. 2.** See **servile.**

me·nin·ges (mĭ nĭn′jēz), *n.pl., sing.* **meninx** (mē′nĭngks). **Anat.** the three membranes (dura mater, arachnoid, and pia mater) investing the brain and spinal cord. [t. NL, pl. of *mēninx,* t. Gk.: membrane, esp. of the brain] —**me·nin·ge·al** (mĭ nĭn′jĭ əl), *adj.*

men·in·gi·tis (měn′ĭn jī′tĭs), *n.* **Pathol.** inflammation of the meninges, esp. of the pia mater and arachnoid. [t. NL, f. Gk.: s. *mēninx* membrane + *-itis*-ITIS] —**men·in·git·ic** (měn′ĭn jĭt′ĭk), *adj.*

me·nis·cus (mĭ nĭs′kəs), *n., pl.* **-nisci** (-nĭs′ī), **-niscuses. 1.** a crescent or crescent-shaped body. **2.** a lens with a crescent-shaped section. See illus. under lens. **3.** the convex or concave upper surface of a column of liquid, the curvature of which is caused by capillarity. **4.** a disc of cartilage between the articulating ends of the bones in a joint. [t. NL, t. Gk.: m. *mēnīskos* crescent, dim. of *mēnē* moon] —**me·nis·coid** (mĭ nĭs′koid), *adj.*

Menisci (def. 3)
A. Concave, containing water; B. Convex, containing mercury

men·i·sper·ma·ceous (měn′ĭ spər mā′shəs), *adj.* belonging to the *Menispermaceae,* a family of dicotyledonous plants, mostly woody climbers, having small, usually three-parted, dioecious flowers, some possessing medicinal properties. See **moonseed.** [f. s. NL *Menispermum* the typical genus, moonseed (f. Gk.: m. *mēnē* moon + m. *sperma* seed) + -ACEOUS]

Men·non·ite (měn′ə nīt′), *n.* a member of a Christian denomination opposed to infant baptism, the taking of oaths, the holding of public office, and military service.

me·no (mě′nō), *adv.* **Music.** less. [t. It., g. L *minus*]

meno-, a word element meaning "month." [t. Gk., comb. form of *mēn*]

me·nol·o·gy (mĭ nŏl′ə jĭ), *n., pl.* **-gies. 1.** a calendar of the months. **2.** a record or account, as of saints, arranged in the order of a calendar. [t. NL: m.s. *mēnologium,* t. LGk.: m. *mēnológion,* f. *mēno-* MENO- + *lógion* saying]

men·o·pause (měn′ə pôz′), *n.* **Physiol.** the period of irregular menstrual cycles prior to the final cessation of the menses, occurring normally between the ages of 45 and 50. [f. MENO- + PAUSE] —**men′o·pau′sic,** *adj.*

Me·nor·ca (mĕ nôr′kä), *n.* Spanish name of **Minorca.**

men·or·rha·gi·a (měn′ə rā′jĭ ə), *n.* **Pathol.** excessive menstrual discharge. [t. NL. See MENO-, -RRHAGIA]

men·sal[1] (měn′səl), *adj.* monthly. [f. s. L. *mēnsis* month + -AL[1]]

men·sal[2] (měn′səl), *adj.* of, pertaining to, or used at the table. [ME, t. LL: s. *mensālis* of a table]

men·ses (měn′sēz), *n.pl.* **Physiol.** the (approximately) monthly discharge of blood and mucosal tissue from the uterus. [t. L, pl. of *mensis* month]

Men·she·vik (měn′shə vĭk), *n., pl.* **-viki** (-vĭ kē′), **-viks.** *Russia.* **1.** (orig.) a member of the less radical faction (the *Mensheviki*) of the Social Democratic party. **2.** (after the revolution of Nov. 7, 1917) a member of a

Menshevism

less radical socialistic party or group succeeding the earlier Menshevik faction and opposing the Bolshevik government. [t. Russ.: one of smaller (group), der. *menshe* less] —**Men·she·vism** (měn′shə vĭz′əm), *n*. —**Men′she·vist**, *adj*.

mens sa·na in cor·po·re sa·no (měnz sā′nə ĭn kôr′pə rē′ sā′nō), *Latin*. a sound mind in a sound body.

men·stru·al (měn′strŏŏ əl), *adj*. **1.** *Physiol*. of or pertaining to the menses. **2.** monthly. [t. L: s. *menstruālis* monthly]

men·stru·ate (měn′strŏŏ āt′), *v.i.*, **-ated, -ating.** to discharge the menses. —**men′stru·a′tion**, *n*.

men·stru·ous (měn′strŏŏ əs), *adj*. pertaining to menstruation. [t. L: m. *menstruus* monthly]

men·stru·um (měn′strŏŏ əm), *n., pl.* **-struums, -strua** (-strŏŏ ə). a solvent. [t. ML, prop. neut. of L *menstruus* monthly]

men·sur·a·ble (měn′shər ə bəl), *adj*. measurable. [t. LL: m.s. *mensūrābilis*] —**men′sur·a·bil′i·ty**, *n*.

men·su·ral (měn′shə rəl), *adj*. pertaining to measure.

men·su·ra·tion (měn′shə rā′shən), *n*. **1.** that branch of mathematics which deals with the determination of length, area, and volume. **2.** the act, art, or process of measuring. [t. LL: s. *mensūrātio*]

men·su·ra·tive (měn′shə rā′tĭv), *adj*. adapted for or concerned with measuring.

-ment, a suffix of nouns, often concrete, denoting an action or state resulting (*abridgment, refreshment*), a product (*fragment*), or means (*ornament*). [t. F, t. L: s. *-mentum,* suffix forming nouns, usually from verbs]

men·tal¹ (měn′təl), *adj*. **1.** of or pertaining to the mind. **2.** performed by or existing in the mind: *mental arithmetic.* **3.** pertaining to the intellect; intellectual. [ME, t. LL: s. *mentālis*]

men·tal² (měn′təl), *adj*. of or pertaining to the chin. [f. s. L *mentum* chin + -AL¹]

mental age, *Psychol*. the degree of mental development or intelligence of an individual in comparison with the average intelligence of normal children at different ages. It is determined by a graded series of tests, in the form of tasks or questions, designed to measure native ability rather than the result of education: *a child 10 years old with a mental age of 12.*

mental deficiency, *Psychol*. a condition characterized by subnormal intelligence so as to handicap the individual in his school or adult life; feeble-mindedness. It embraces all types of idiocy, imbecility, and moronity.

mental healing, the healing of any ailment or disorder by mental concentration and suggestion.

men·tal·i·ty (měn tăl′ə tĭ), *n., pl.* **-ties.** mental capacity or endowment; intellectuality; mind: *she was of average mentality.*

men·tal·ly (měn′tə lĭ), *adv*. **1.** in or with the mind or intellect; intellectually. **2.** with regard to the mind.

men·tha·ceous (měn thā′shəs), *adj*. belonging to the *Menthaceae* (usually included in the *Labiatae*) or mint family of plants, including the horsemint, peppermint, pennyroyal, savory, etc. [f. s. L *mentha* MINT¹ + -ACEOUS]

men·thene (měn′thēn), *n*. *Chem*. a colorless liquid, C₁₀H₁₈, synthetically obtainable from menthol. [t. G: m. *menthen,* f. s. L *mentha* MINT¹ + *-en* -ENE]

men·thol (měn′thōl, -thŏl), *n*. a colorless, crystalline alcohol, C₁₀H₂₀O, present in peppermint oil, used in perfume and confectionery, and for colds and nasal disorders because of its cooling effect on mucous membranes. [t. G: f. s. L *mentha* MINT¹ + *-ol* -OL¹]

men·tho·lat·ed (měn′thə lā′tĭd), *adj*. **1.** covered or treated with menthol. **2.** saturated with or containing menthol.

men·tion (měn′shən), *v.t.* **1.** to refer briefly to; refer to by name incidentally; name, specify, or speak of. **2.** to say incidentally (with a clause). —*n.* **3.** a speaking of or mentioning; a reference, direct or incidental. [t. L: s. *mentio* a calling to mind, mention; r. ME *mencioun,* t. OF] —**men′tion·a·ble,** *adj*. —**men′tion·er,** *n*.

Men·ton (měn tōn′; *Fr.* män tôn′), *n*. a city in SE France, on the Mediterranean: winter resort. 17,109 (1954). Italian, **Men·to·ne** (měn tō′ně).

Men·tor (měn′tər), *n*. **1.** the friend to whom Odysseus, when departing for Troy, gave the charge of his household. **2.** (*l.c.*) a wise and trusted counselor.

men·u (měn′ū, mā′nū; *Fr.* mə ny′), *n*. **1.** a list of the dishes served at a meal; a bill of fare. **2.** the dishes served. [t. F: detailed list, orig. adj., small, g. L *minūtus* MINUTE²]

Men·u·hin (měn′yŏŏ ĭn), *n*. **Yehudi** (yə hŏŏ′dĭ), born 1917, U.S. violinist.

me·ow (mĭ ou′, myou), *n*. **1.** the sound a cat makes. —*v.i.* **2.** to make such a sound. Also, **miaow, miaou, miaul.**

Meph·i·stoph·e·les (měf′ə stŏf′ə lēz′), *n*. *Medieval Demonology.* one of the seven chief devils. He is represented in Goethe's *Faust* as a crafty, sardonic, and scoffing fiend. —**Meph·is·to·phe·li·an** (měf′ĭs tō fē′lĭ ən), *adj*.

me·phit·ic (mĭ fĭt′ĭk), *adj*. **1.** offensive to the smell. **2.** noxious; pestilential; poisonous. —**me·phit′i·cal·ly,** *adv*.

me·phi·tis (mĭ fī′tĭs), *n*. **1.** a noxious or pestilential exhalation, esp. from the earth. **2.** a noisome or poisonous stench. [t. L]

---

mer·can·tile (mûr′kən tĭl, -tĭl′), *adj*. **1.** of or pertaining to merchants or to trade; commercial. **2.** engaged in trade or commerce. **3.** *Econ*. of or pertaining to the mercantile system. [t. F, t. It., der. *mercante,* g. L *mercans,* ppr., trading] —**Syn. 1.** See **commercial.**

mercantile agency, a concern which obtains information concerning the financial standing, business reputation, and credit ratings of individuals, firms, and corporations for the benefit of its subscribers.

mercantile paper, negotiable commercial paper, as promissory notes given by merchants for goods purchased, drafts drawn against purchasers, etc.

mercantile system, *Econ*. a system of political and economic policy, evolving with the modern national state, which sought to secure the political supremacy of a state in its rivalry with other states. According to this system, money was regarded as a store of wealth, and the great object of a state was the importation of the precious metals, by exporting the utmost possible quantity of its products and importing as little as possible, thus establishing a favorable balance of trade.

mer·can·til·ism (mûr′kən tĭl ĭz′əm, -tĭl ĭz′əm), *n*. **1.** the mercantile spirit. **2.** the mercantile system. —**mer′can·til·ist,** *n*.

mer·cap·tan (mər kăp′tăn), *n*. *Chem*. any of a class of sulfur-containing compounds, with the type formula RSH, the low-boiling members of which have an extremely offensive odor, esp. **ethyl mercaptan,** C₂H₅SH, a colorless liquid, with an offensive, garliclike odor. [t. G: arbitrary abbr. of L expression (*corpus*) *mer*(*curium*) *captan*(*s*) body catching mercury]

Mer·ca·tor (mər kā′tər; *Flem.* měr kä′tôr), *n*. **Gerhard** (gěr′härt), (*Gerhard Kremer*) 1512–94, Flemish cartographer and geographer.

Mercator's projection, a map projection with rectangular grid which is conformable and on which any rhumb line is represented as a straight line: particularly useful for navigation, though the scale varies notably with latitude and areal size, and the shapes of large areas are greatly distorted.

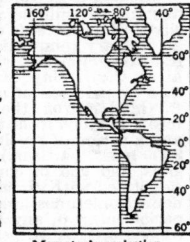

Mercator's projection

mer·ce·nar·y (mûr′sə něr′ĭ), *adj., n., pl.* **-naries.** —*adj.* **1.** working or acting merely for gain. **2.** hired (now only of soldiers serving in a foreign army). —*n.* **3.** a professional soldier serving in a foreign army. **4.** any hireling. [t. L: m.s. *mercēnārius* hired for pay] —**mer′ce·nar′i·ly,** *adv*. —**mer′ce·nar′i·ness,** *n*. —**Syn. 1.** venal, grasping, sordid; acquisitive, avaricious. —**Ant. 1.** unworldly.

mer·cer (mûr′sər), *n*. *Brit*. a dealer in textile fabrics, esp. silks, etc. [ME, t. OF: m. *mercier,* der. OF *merz* goods, wares, g. L *merx*]

mer·cer·ize (mûr′sə rīz′), *v.t.,* **-ized, -izing.** to treat (cotton yarns or fabric) with caustic alkali under tension, increasing strength, luster, and affinity for dye. [from J. Mercer, English calico printer, the patentee (1850) of the process. See -IZE] —**mer′cer·i·za·tion,** *n*.

mer·cer·y (mûr′sə rĭ), *n., pl.* **-ceries.** *Brit*. **1.** a mercer's shop. **2.** mercers' wares. [ME *mercerie,* t. OF, der. *mercier* MERCER]

mer·chan·dise (*n.* mûr′chən dīz′, -dīs′; *v.* mûr′chən dīz′), *n., v.* **-dised, -dising.** —*n.* **1.** goods; commodities; esp. manufactured goods. —*v.i., v.t.* **2.** to trade; buy and sell. Also, **mer′chan·dize′.** [ME *marchandise,* t. OF, der. *marchand* MERCHANT] —**mer′chan·dis′er,** *n*.

mer·chant (mûr′chənt), *n*. **1.** one who buys and sells commodities for profit; (in England chiefly) a wholesaler. **2.** a storekeeper. —*adj.* **3.** pertaining to trade or commerce: *a merchant ship.* **4.** pertaining to the merchant marine. [ME, t. OF: m. *marcheant,* ult. der. L *mercārī* trade]

mer·chant·a·ble (mûr′chən tə bəl), *adj*. marketable: *merchantable war-surplus goods.*

mer·chant·man (mûr′chənt mən), *n., pl.* **-men.** a trading vessel.

merchant marine, **1.** the vessels of a nation engaged in commerce. **2.** the officers and crews of merchant vessels.

Merchant of Venice, The, a comedy (about 1598) by Shakespeare.

mer·ci (měr sē′), *interj*. *French*. thank (you).

Mer·ci·a (mûr′shĭ ə, -shə), *n*. an early English kingdom in central Britain. —**Mer′ci·an,** *adj., n*.

mer·ci beau·coup (měr sē′ bō kŏŏ′), *French*. thank (you) very much.

Mer·cier (měr syě′), *n*. **Dé·siré Joseph** (dě zē rě′ zhō zěf′), 1851–1926, Belgian cardinal and patriot.

Mercia, A.D. 800

mer·ci·ful (mûr′sĭ fəl), *adj*. full of mercy; exercising or characterized by mercy; compassionate. —**mer′ci·ful·ly,** *adv*. —**mer′ci·ful·ness,** *n*. —**Syn.** kind, clement, lenient. —**Ant.** hard-hearted.

ăct, āble, dâre, ärt; ĕbb, ēqual; ĭf, īce; hŏt, ōver, ôrder, oil, bŏŏk, ōoze, out; ŭp, ūse, ûrge; ə = a in alone; ch, chief; g, give; ng, ring; sh, shoe; th, thin; t͡h, that; zh, vision. See the full key on inside cover.

mer·ci·less (mûr′sĭ lĭs), *adj.* without any mercy, pitiless. —**mer′ci·less·ly**, *adv.* —**mer′ci·less·ness**, *n.*

mer·cu·rate (mûr′kyə rāt′), *v.t.*, -rated, -rating. 1. to add mercury to (a compound). 2. *Obsolesc.* to expose to the action of mercury.

mer·cu·ri·al (mər kyŏŏr′ĭ əl), *adj.* 1. pertaining to, consisting of or containing, or caused by the metal mercury. 2. (*cap.*) of or pertaining to the god Mercury or the planet Mercury. 3. sprightly; volatile. 4. flighty; fickle; changeable. —*n.* 5. a preparation of mercury used as a drug. [t. L: s. *mercuriālis* of Mercury] —**mer·cu′ri·al·ly**, *adv.* —**mer·cu′ri·al·ness**, *n.*

mer·cu·ri·al·ism (mər kyŏŏr′ĭ ə lĭz′əm), *n. Pathol.* a morbid condition caused by mercury.

mer·cu·ri·al·ize (mər kyŏŏr′ĭ ə līz′), *v.t.*, -ized, -izing. 1. to make mercurial. 2. to treat or impregnate with mercury or one of its compounds. —**mer·cu′ri·al·i·za′tion**, *n.*

mer·cu·ric (mər kyŏŏr′ĭk), *adj. Chem.* of or containing mercury, esp. in the divalent state (Hg+²).

mercuric chloride, corrosive sublimate. Also, **mercury chloride.**

mer·cu·ro·chrome (mər kyŏŏr′ə krōm′), *n.* 1. an iridescent green powder which dissolves in water to furnish a red solution, used as an antiseptic and germicide. 2. a solution of this compound. 3. (*cap.*) a trademark for this substance or its solution. [f. *mercuro-* (comb. form of MERCURY) + CHROME]

mer·cu·rous (mər kyŏŏr′əs, mûr′kyə rəs), *adj. Chem.* containing monovalent mercury (Hg+¹ or Hg₂+²).

mer·cu·ry (mûr′kyə rĭ), *n., pl.* -ries. 1. *Chem.* a heavy, silver-white metallic element, remarkable for its fluidity at ordinary temperatures; quicksilver. *Symbol:* Hg (for **hydrargyrum**; *at. wt.:* 200.6; *at. no.:* 80; *sp. gr.:* 13.546 at 20° C.; *freezing point:* −38.9° C.; *boiling point:* 357° C. 2. a preparation of mercury (metal) used in medicine. 3. (*cap.*) *Astron.* the planet nearest the sun, having a mean distance from the sun of about 36,000,000 miles, and a period of revolution of 88.0 days. Its diameter is 3000 miles. 4. (*cap.*) a Roman deity, messenger of the gods, and god of commerce, dexterity, and eloquence (identified with *Hermes*). 5. a messenger, or carrier of news (sometimes used as the name of a newspaper or periodical). 6. any herb of the euphorbiaceous genus *Mercurialis*, as *M. perennis* (dog's-mercury), a poisonous weed. [ME, t. L: m.s. *Mercurius* (def. 3, 4; in ML def. 1)]

mercury chloride, mercuric chloride.

mercury fulminate, the mercury salt of fulminic acid, Hg(ONC)₂, which explodes as a result of very slight friction or shock when dry, used as a detonator.

mer·cu·ry-va·por lamp (mûr′kyə rĭ vā′pər), a lamp producing a light with a high actinic and ultraviolet content by means of an electric arc in mercury vapor.

mer·cy (mûr′sĭ), *n., pl.* -cies. 1. compassionate or kindly forbearance shown toward an offender, an enemy, or other person in one's power; compassion, pity, or benevolence. 2. disposition to be merciful: *an adversary wholly without mercy.* 3. discretionary power as to clemency or severity, pardon or punishment, or the like: *to be at the mercy of a conqueror.* 4. an act of forbearance, compassion, or favor, esp. of God toward his creatures. [ME, t. OF: m. *merci*, fem., favor, mercy; masc., thanks, g. L *merces* pay, ML mercy] —Syn. 1. forgiveness, indulgence; clemency, leniency. —Ant. 1. cruelty.

mercy killing, euthanasia.

mercy seat, 1. the gold covering on the ark of the covenant, regarded as the resting place of God (see Ex. 25:17–22). 2. the throne of God.

mere¹ (mĭr), *adj., superl.* **merest**. 1. being nothing more nor better than what is specified; pure and simple. 2. *Chiefly Law.* belonging or pertaining to a single individual or group, or sole. 3. *Obs.* pure or unmixed. 4. *Obs.* absolute or unqualified. [ME, t. L: m. *merus* pure, unmixed, mere] —Syn. 1. MERE, BARE imply a scant sufficiency. They are often interchangeable, but MERE frequently means "no more than (enough)." BARE suggests "scarcely as much as (enough)." Thus *a mere livelihood* means enough to live on but no more; *a bare livelihood* means scarcely enough to live on. —Ant. 1. abundant.

mere² (mĭr), *n. Poetic or Brit. Dial.* a lake; a pond. [ME and OE, c. G *meer*; akin to L *mare* sea]

-mere, a word element meaning "part," as in *blastomere.* [comb. form repr. Gk. *méros*]

Mer·e·dith (mĕr′ə dĭth), *n.* 1. **George**, 1828–1909, British novelist and poet. 2. **Owen**, pen name of Edward Robert Bulwer-Lytton. See Lytton (def. 2).

mere·ly (mĭr′lĭ), *adv.* 1. only as specified, and nothing more; simply: *merely as a matter of form.* 2. *Obs.* purely. 3. *Obs.* absolutely or entirely.

mer·e·tri·cious (mĕr′ə trĭsh′əs), *adj.* 1. alluring by a show of false attractions; showily attractive; tawdry. 2. *Archaic.* of, pertaining to, or characteristic of a prostitute. [t. L: m. *meretricius* of prostitutes] —**mer′e·tri′cious·ly**, *adv.* —**mer′e·tri′cious·ness**, *n.*

mer·gan·ser (mər găn′sər), *n., pl.* -sers, (*esp. collectively*) -ser. any of several saw-billed, fish-eating, diving ducks of the subfamily *Merginae*, as the American **hooded merganser**, *Lophodytes cucullatus*, the male of which has a black-and-white, fanlike crest. [t. NL, f. s. L *mergus* diver (bird) + *anser* goose]

merge (mûrj), *v.*, **merged, merging**. —*v.t.* 1. to cause to be swallowed up or absorbed; to sink the identity of by combination (often fol. by *in* or *into*). —*v.i.* 2. to become swallowed up or absorbed; lose identity by absorption (often fol. by *in* or *into*). [t. L: m.s. *mergere* dip, plunge, sink] —**mer·gence** (mûr′jəns), *n.*

merg·er (mûr′jər), *n.* 1. a statutory combination of two or more corporations by the transfer of the properties to one surviving corporation. 2. any combination of two or more business enterprises into a single enterprise. 3. act of merging.

Mé·ri·da (mĕ′rē dä′), *n.* a city in SE Mexico: the capital of Yucatán state. 159,405 (est. 1951).

Mer·i·den (mĕr′ə dən), *n.* a city in central Connecticut. 51,850 (1960).

me·rid·i·an (mə rĭd′ĭ ən), *n.* 1. *Geog.* **a.** a great circle of the earth passing through the poles and any given point on the earth's surface. **b.** the half of such a circle included between the poles. 2. *Astron.* the great circle of the celestial sphere which passes through its poles and the observer's zenith. 3. a point or period of highest development, greatest prosperity, or the like. —*adj.* 4. of or pertaining to a meridian. 5. of or pertaining to midday or noon: *the meridian hour.* 6. pertaining to a period of greatest maturity, prosperity, splendor, etc.; culminating. [t. L: s. *meridiānus* of midday, of the south; r. ME *meridien*, t. OF]

Me·rid·i·an (mə rĭd′ĭ ən), *n.* a city in E Mississippi. 49,374 (1960).

me·rid·i·o·nal (mə rĭd′ĭ ə nəl), *adj.* 1. of, pertaining to, or resembling a meridian. 2. characteristic of the south or people inhabiting the south, esp. of France. 3. southern; southerly. —*n.* 4. an inhabitant of the south, esp. of France. [ME, t. LL: s. *meridiōnālis* of midday] —**me·rid′i·o·nal·ly**, *adv.*

Mé·ri·mée (mĕ′rē mĕ′), *n.* **Prosper** (prôs pĕr′), 1803–1870, French short-story writer, novelist, and essayist.

me·ringue (mə răng′), *n.* 1. a mixture of sugar and beaten egg whites formed into small cakes and baked, or spread over pastry, etc. 2. a dish made with it. [t. F, t. G: m. *meringe*, lit., cookie of Mehringen]

me·ri·no (mə rē′nō), *n., pl.* -nos, *adj.* —*n.* 1. one of a variety of sheep, originally in Spain, valued for its fine wool. 2. wool from such sheep. 3. a knitted fabric made of wool or wool and cotton. —*adj.* 4. made of merino wool, yarn, or cloth. [t. Sp., g. L (*ariēs*) *mājōrīnus* (male sheep) of the larger sort, der. *mājor* MAJOR]

Merino, *Ovis aries*
(2 ft. high at the shoulder)

Mer·i·on·eth·shire (mĕr′ĭ ŏn′ĭth shĭr′, -shər), *n.* a county in N Wales. 41,465 pop. (1951); 660 sq. mi. *Co. Seat:* Dolgelly. Also, **Mer′i·on′eth.**

mer·i·stem (mĕr′ə stĕm′), *n. Bot.* embryonic tissue; undifferentiated, growing, actively dividing cells. [f. Gk.: s. *meristós* divided + -ēm(a), n. suffix]

mer·it (mĕr′ĭt), *n.* 1. claim to commendation; excellence; worth. 2. something that entitles to reward or commendation; a commendable quality, act, etc.: *the merits of a book or a play.* 3. (*pl.*) the substantial right and wrong of a matter unobscured by technicalities: *the merits of a case.* 4. the state or fact of deserving well; good desert. 5. that which is deserved, whether good or bad. 6. (*sometimes pl.*) state or fact of deserving, or desert: *to treat a person according to his merits.* —*v.t.* 7. to be worthy of; deserve. —*v.i.* 8. *Chiefly Theol.* to acquire merit. [ME *merite*, t. F, t. L: m. *meritum*, prop. pp. neut., deserved, earned] —Syn. 1. MERIT, DESERT, WORTH refer to the quality in a person, action, or thing which entitles to recognition, esp. favorable recognition. MERIT is usually the excellence which entitles to praise: *a man of great merit.* DESERT is the quality which entitles one to a just reward: *according to his deserts.* WORTH is always used in a favorable sense and signifies inherent value or goodness: *the worth of his contribution is incalculable.* —Ant. 1. worthlessness.

mer·it·ed (mĕr′ĭ tĭd), *adj.* deserved. —**mer′it·ed·ly**, *adv.*

mer·i·to·ri·ous (mĕr′ə tōr′ĭ əs), *adj.* deserving of reward or commendation; possessing merit. [ME, t. ML: m. *meritōrius* meritorious, L serving to earn money] —**mer′i·to′ri·ous·ly**, *adv.* —**mer′i·to′ri·ous·ness**, *n.*

merle (mûrl), *n. Chiefly Scot. and Poetic.* the common European blackbird, *Turdus merula.* Also, **merl.** [t. F, g. L *merula, merulus*]

mer·lin (mûr′lĭn), *n.* any of various bold small hawks of the genus *Falco*, esp. the European merlin, *F. columbarius aesalon*, and the closely related North American pigeon hawk, *F. c. columbarius.* [ME *merlion*, t. AF: m. *merlun*, der. OF *esmeril*, t. Gmc.; cf. OHG *smiril*]

Mer·lin (mûr′lĭn), *n. Arthurian Romance.* a venerable magician and seer. [t. Welsh: unexplained m. *Myrddin*]

mer·lon (mûr′lən), *n.* (in a battlement) the solid part between two crenels. See illus. under **battlement**. [t. F, t. It.: m. *merlone*, ult. der. L *mergae* fork]

mer·maid (mûr′mād′), *n.* an imaginary female marine creature, typically having the head and trunk of a woman and the tail of a fish. [ME *mermayde*. See MERE², MAID]

---

mer·man (mûr'măn'), *n., pl.* **-men.** an imaginary man of the sea, corresponding to a mermaid.

mer·o·blas·tic (mĕr'ə blăs'tĭk), *adj. Embryol.* (of large eggs) undergoing partial cleavage (opposed to *holoblastic*). [f. Gk. *mĕro(s)* part + -BLAST + -IC]

Mer·o·ë (mĕr'ō ē), *n.* a ruined city in the Sudan, on the Nile: a capital of ancient Ethiopia.

me·rog·o·ny (mə rŏg'ə nĭ), *Embryol.* the development of egg fragments. [f. Gk. *mĕro(s)* part + -GONY]

Mer·o·vin·gi·an (mĕr'ə vĭn'jĭ ən), *adj.* designating or pertaining to the Frankish dynasty which reigned in Gaul and Germany from about A.D. 500 to A.D. 751.

mer·o·zo·ite (mĕr'ə zō'īt), *n.* one of the products of reproduction in the asexual phase of parasitic protozoans of the class *Sporozoa*, as malaria parasites.

Mer·ri·mac (mĕr'ə măk'), *n.* the first ironclad warship: used by the Confederates in a battle against the *Monitor* (1862).

Mer·ri·mack (mĕr'ə măk'), *n.* a river flowing from central New Hampshire through NE Massachusetts into the Atlantic. 110 mi.

mer·ri·ment (mĕr'ĭ mənt), *n.* 1. merry gaiety; mirth; hilarity; laughter. 2. *Obs.* merrymaking.

mer·ry (mĕr'ĭ), *adj.*, **merrier, merriest.** 1. full of cheer or gaiety; festive; joyous in disposition or spirit. 2. laughingly gay; mirthful; hilarious. 3. *Archaic.* pleasant or delightful: *merry England.* 4. **make merry,** to be gay or festive. [ME *meri(e), myrie, murie,* OE *myr(i)ge, mer(i)ge* pleasant, delightful] —**mer'ri·ly,** *adv.* —**mer'ri·ness,** *n.* —**Syn.** 1. joyous. See **gay.**

mer·ry-an·drew (mĕr'ĭ ăn'drōō), *n.* a clown; buffoon.

mer·ry-go-round (mĕr'ĭ gō round'), *n.* 1. a revolving machine, as a circular platform fitted with hobbyhorses, etc., on which persons, esp. children, ride for amusement. 2. any whirl or rapid round.

mer·ry·mak·er (mĕr'ĭ mā'kər), *n.* one who is making merry.

mer·ry·mak·ing (mĕr'ĭ mā'kĭng), *n.* 1. the act of making merry. 2. a merry festivity; a revel. —*adj.* 3. producing mirth; gay; festive.

mer·ry·thought (mĕr'ĭ thôt'), *n. Chiefly Brit.* the wishbone of a bird. [from the custom of two persons pulling the bone until it breaks; the person holding the longer (sometimes shorter) piece will supposedly marry first or will be granted a wish made at the time]

Mer·sey (mûr'zĭ), *n.* a river in W England, flowing from Derbyshire W to the Irish Sea. ab. 70 mi.

Mer·thyr Tyd·fil (mûr'thər tĭd'vĭl; *Welsh* tŭd'vĭl), a city in SE Wales. 59,500 (est. 1956).

mes-, var. of **meso-,** sometimes used before vowels, as in *mesencephalon.*

me·sa (mā'sə; *Sp.* mĕ'sä), *n.* a land form having a relatively flat top and bounded wholly or in part with steep rock walls, common in arid and semiarid parts of the southwestern U.S. [t. Sp., g. L *mensa* table]

mé·sal·li·ance (mā zăl'ĭ əns; *Fr.* mĕ zăl yäns'), *n.* a marriage with a social inferior; a misalliance. [F: f. *més-* MIS- + *alliance* ALLIANCE[1]]

Me·sa Ver·de (mā'sə vûrd'; *Sp.* mĕ'sä vĕr'dĕ), a national park in SW Colorado. 80 sq. mi.

mes·cal (mĕs kăl'), *n.* 1. either of two species of cactus, *Lophophora Williamsii* or *L. Lewinii*, of Texas and northern Mexico, whose buttonlike tops (**mescal buttons**) are dried and used as a stimulant, esp. by the Indians. 2. an intoxicating spirit distilled from the fermented juice of certain species of agave. 3. any agave yielding this spirit. [t. Sp.: m. *mezcal*, t. Aztec: m. *mexcalli metl* (maguey) liquor]

mes·ca·line (mĕs'kə lēn', -lĭn), *n. Pharm.* a white, water-soluble, crystalline powder, $C_{11}H_{17}NO_3$, obtained from mescal buttons, used in experimental psychology to produce hallucinations. Also, **mezcaline.**

mes·dames (mĕ dàm'), *n.* pl. of **madame.**

mes·de·moi·selles (mĕd mwä zĕl'), *n.* pl. of **mademoiselle.** [t. F]

me·seems (mē sēmz'), *v.impers.; pt.* **meseemed.** *Archaic.* it seems to me.

mes·en·ceph·a·lon (mĕs'ĕn sĕf'ə lŏn'), *n., pl.* **-la** (-lə). *Anat.* the middle segment of the brain; the midbrain. [t. NL. See MES-, ENCEPHALON] —**mes·en·ce·phal·ic** (mĕs'ĕn sə făl'ĭk), *adj.*

mes·en·chyme (mĕs'ĕng kĭm), *n. Embryol.* the nonepithelial mesoderm. Also, **mes·en·chy·ma** (mĕs ĕng'kə mə). [t. NL, f. Gk.: *mes-* MES- + m. *ĕnchyma* infusion] —**mes·en·chy·mal** (mĕs ĕng'kə məl), **mes·en·chym·a·tous** (mĕs'ĕng kĭm'ə təs), *adj.*

mes·en·ter·y (mĕs'ən tĕr'ĭ), *n., pl.* **-teries.** *Anat.* a fold or doubling of the peritoneum, investing and attaching to the posterior wall of the abdomen. [t. NL: m.s. *mesenterium*, t. Gk.: m. *mesentĕrion* the middle intestine] —**mes·en·ter·ic,** *adj.*

mesh (mĕsh), *n.* 1. one of the open spaces of network of a net. 2. *(pl.)* the threads that bound such spaces. 3. *(pl.)* means of catching or holding fast: *caught in the meshes of the law.* 4. a network or net. 5. *Mach.* a. the engagement of gear teeth. b. **in mesh**, with gears engaged. —*v.t.* 6. to catch or entangle in or as in the meshes of a net; enmesh. 7. to form with meshes, as a net. 8. *Mach.* to engage, as gear teeth. —*v.i.* 9. to become enmeshed. 10. *Mach.* to become or be engaged, as the teeth of one wheel with those of another. [cf. OE *mæx* and *mæscre* net]

Me·shach (mē'shăk), *n.* See **Shadrach.**

Mes·hed (mĕsh'hĕd; *Pers.* mäsh häd'), *n.* a city in NE Iran: a Mohammedan shrine. 191,794 (est. 1950).

mesh·work (mĕsh'wûrk'), *n.* meshed work; network.

mesh·y (mĕsh'ĭ), *adj.* formed with meshes; meshed.

me·si·al (mē'zĭ əl, mĕs'ĭ əl), *adj.* medial. [f. MES- -IAL] —**me'si·al·ly,** *adv.*

mes·it·y·lene (mī sĭt'ə lēn', mĕs'ə tə lēn'), *n. Chem.* a colorless, liquid, aromatic hydrocarbon, $C_8H_3(CH_3)_3$, found in coal tar but prepared from acetone. [f. *mesityl* (f. s. Gk. *mesĭtĕs* go-between + -YL) + -ENE]

mes·mer·ic (mĕs mĕr'ĭk, mĕz-), *adj.* hypnotic. —**mes·mer'i·cal·ly,** *adv.*

mes·mer·ism (mĕs'mə rĭz'əm, mĕz'-), *n.* hypnotism. [named after F. A. *Mesmer* (1733–1815), German physician, who propounded the doctrine. See -ISM] —**mes'mer·ist,** *n.*

mes·mer·ize (mĕs'mə rīz', mĕz'-), *v.t.*, **-ized, -izing.** to hypnotize. —**mes'mer·i·za'tion,** *n.* —**mes'mer·iz'er,** *n.*

mesn·al·ty (mē'nəl tĭ), *n. Law.* the estate of a mesne lord. [t. F: m. *mesnalte*, der. OF *mesne* MESNE]

mesne (mēn), *adj. Law.* intermediate or intervening. [t. F, altered sp. of AF *meen* MEAN[3]]

mesne lord, a feudal lord who held land of a superior.

meso-, a word element meaning "middle," used in combination, chiefly in scientific terms. Also, **mes-.** [t. Gk., comb. form of *mĕsos* middle]

mes·o·blast (mĕs'ə blăst', mĕ'sə-), *n. Embryol.* the prospective mesoderm. —**mes'o·blas'tic,** *adj.*

mes·o·carp (mĕs'ə kärp', mĕ'sə-), *n. Bot.* the middle layer of pericarp, as the fleshy part of certain fruits. See diag. under **endocarp.**

mes·o·ce·phal·ic (mĕs'ō sə făl'ĭk, mĕ'sō-), *adj. Cephalom.* having a head with a cephalic index between that of dolichocephaly and brachycephaly.

mes·o·cra·nic (mĕs'ə krā'nĭk, mĕ'sə-), *adj. Craniom.* having a skull with a cranial index between that of dolichocranic and brachycranic skulls.

mes·o·crat·ic (mĕs'ə krăt'ĭk, mē'sə-), *adj. Geol.* composed of light and dark minerals in nearly equal amounts. [f. MESO- + m. s. Gk. *krátos* rule + -IC]

mes·o·derm (mĕs'ə dûrm', mĕ'sə-), *n. Embryol.* the middle germ layer of a metazoan embryo. —**mes'o·der'mal, mes'o·der'mic,** *adj.*

mes·o·gas·tri·um (mĕs'ə găs'trĭ əm, mĕ'sə-), *n. Anat.* the umbilical region of the abdomen, situated above the hypogastrium and below the epigastrium. [t. NL, f. *meso-* MESO- + m. Gk. *gastĕr* belly + -*ium* -IUM] —**mes'o·gas'tric,** *adj.*

me·sog·na·thous (mĭ sŏg'nə thəs), *adj. Anthropol.* 1. having medium, slightly protruding jaws. 2. having a moderate or intermediate gnathic index of from 98 to 103. —**me·sog'na·thism, me·sog'na·thy,** *n.*

Me·so·lon·ghi (mĕ'sō lông'gē), *n.* Missolonghi.

me·son (mē'sŏn, mĕs'ŏn), *n. Physics.* a constituent particle of cosmic rays, having a mass of the order of 200 times that of an electron and a unit negative or positive charge.

mes·o·neph·ros (mĕs'ə nĕf'rŏs, mĕ'sə-), *n. Embryol.* the middle kidney, developing between the pronephros and the metanephros, in proximity with the sex glands. In males of the higher vertebrates, it becomes a part of the epididymis. [t. NL, f. Gk.: *meso-* MESO- + *nephrós* kidney] —**mes'o·neph'ric,** *adj.*

mes·o·phyll (mĕs'ə fĭl', mĕ'sə-), *n. Bot.* the parenchyma which forms the interior parts of a leaf, usually containing chlorophyll.

mes·o·phyte (mĕs'ə fīt', mĕ'sə-), *n. Ecol.* a plant growing under conditions of well balanced moisture supply. Cf. **hydrophyte** and **xerophyte.** —**mes·o·phyt·ic** (mĕs'ə fĭt'ĭk, mĕ'sə-), *adj.*

Mes·o·po·ta·mi·a (mĕs'ə pə tā'mĭ ə), *n.* 1. an ancient country in Asia between the Tigris and Euphrates rivers: the modern kingdom of Iraq includes much of this region. 2. Iraq. —**Mes'o·po·ta'mi·an,** *adj., n.*

mes·or·rhine (mĕs'ə rīn', -rĭn, mĕ'sə-), *n. Anthropol.* having a moderately broad and high-bridged nose. [f. MESO- + m. s. Gk. *rhís* nose]

mes·o·the·li·um (mĕs'ə thē'lĭ əm, mĕ'sə-), *n., pl.* **-lia** (-lĭ ə). *Anat., Embryol.* epithelium of mesodermal origin, which lines the body cavities. [f. MESO- + *-ihelium* as in EPITHELIUM] —**mes'o·the'li·al,** *adj.*

mes·o·tho·rax (mĕs'ə thôr'ăks, mĕ'sə-), *n., pl.* **-thoraxes, -thoraces** (-thôr'ə sēz'). the middle one of the three divisions of an insect's thorax, bearing the second pair of legs and the first pair of wings. —**mes·o·tho·rac·ic** (mĕs'ə thō'răs'ĭk), *adj.*

mes·o·tho·ri·um (mĕs'ə thôr'ĭ əm, mĕz'ə-), *n. Chem.* an isotope of radium (though far more radioactive) formed from thorium minerals, and existing in two forms, **mesothorium I,** *at. no.:* 88; *at. wt.:* 228; *half life:* 6.7 yrs.; **mesothorium II,** *at. no.:* 89; *at. wt.:* 228; *half life:* 6.2 hrs.

mes·o·tron (mĕs'ə trŏn', mĕ'sə-), *n. Physics.* meson.

Mes·o·zo·ic (mĕs'ə zō'ĭk, mĕ'sə-), *n. Stratig.* —*adj.* 1. pertaining to the geological era or rocks intermediate between Paleozoic and Cenozoic; the era of "medieval life" or age of reptiles. —*n.* 2. the era or rocks comprising the Triassic, Jurassic, and Cretaceous periods or systems. [f. MESO- + s. Gk. *zōĕ* life + -IC]

---

act, āble, dâre, ärt; ĕbb, ēqual; ĭf, īce; hŏt, ōver, ôrder, oil, bŏŏk, ōōze, out; ŭp, ūse, ûrge; ə = a in alone; ch, chief; g, give; ng, ring; sh, shoe; th, thin; ŧħ, that; zh, vision. See the full key on inside cover.

mes·quite (mĕs·kēt′, mĕs′kēt), *n*. **1**. a mimosaceous tree or shrub, *Prosopis glandulosa*, of the southwestern U.S., Mexico, etc., whose beanlike pods are rich in sugar and form a valuable fodder. **2**. any species of the genus *Prosopis*. [t. Amer. Sp.: m. *mezquite*, from Aztec name]

mess (mĕs), *n*. **1**. a dirty or untidy condition: *the room was in a mess*. **2**. a state of embarrassing confusion: *his affairs are in a mess*. **3**. an unpleasant or difficult situation: *to get into a mess*. **4**. a dirty or untidy mass, litter, or jumble: *a mess of papers*. **5**. a group regularly taking meals together. **6**. the meal so taken. **7**. a mess hall. **8**. a quantity of food sufficient for a dish or a single occasion. **9**. *Colloq*. or *Dial*. a quantity of food of indefinite amount. **10**. a sloppy or unappetizing preparation of food. **11**. a dish or quantity of soft or liquid food. *—v.t.* **12**. to make dirty or untidy (often fol. by *up*): *to mess up a room*. **13**. to make a mess of, or muddle (affairs, etc.). **14**. to supply with meals, as soldiers, etc. *—v.i.* **15**. to eat in company, esp. as a member of a mess. **16**. to make a dirty or untidy mess. **17**. to busy oneself in an untidy or confused way (often with *around*). **18**. **mess in**, to meddle officiously. [ME *mes*, t. OF: lit., put (on the table), g. L *missum*, pp. neut., sent, put]

mes·sage (mĕs′ĭj), *n*. **1**. a communication, as of information, advice, direction, or the like, transmitted through a messenger or other agency. **2**. an official communication, as from a chief executive to a legislative body: *the President's message to Congress*. **3**. an inspired communication of a prophet. [ME, t. OF, der. *mes* envoy, g. L *missus*, pp., sent]

Mes·sa·li·na (mĕs′ə·lī′nə), *n*. Valeria (və·lĭr′ĭ·ə), died A.D. 48, third wife of the Roman emperor Claudius, notorious for her immorality.

mes·sa·line (mĕs′ə·lēn′, mĕs′ə·lēn′), *n*. a thin, soft, silk fabric with a twilled or a satin weave. [t. F]

Mes·se·ne (mĕ·sē′nē), *n*. a city of ancient Greece: the capital of Mes·se·ni·a (mĕ′sē·nē′ə), a district in the SW Peloponnesus.

mes·sen·ger (mĕs′ən·jər), *n*. **1**. one who bears a message or goes on an errand, esp. as a matter of duty or business. **2**. one employed to convey official despatches or to go on other official or special errands: *a bank messenger*. **3**. a herald or harbinger. **4**. anything regarded as sent on an errand. [ME *messenger*, *messager*, t. OF: (m.) *messager*, der. *message* MESSAGE] **—Syn. 1**. bearer, courier. **3**. forerunner, precursor.

mess hall, a place where a group eats regularly.

Mes·si·ah (mə·sī′ə), *n*. **1**. the title applied to an expected deliverer of the Jewish people, and hence to Jesus (see John 4:25, 26). **2**. any expected deliverer. **3**. an oratorio (1742) by Handel. Also, for defs 1, 2, **Mes·si·as** (mə·sī′əs).[var. of L *Messīas* (Vulgate), t. Gk., Hellenized form of Heb. *māshīah* anointed] **—Mes·si·ah·ship′**, *n*. **—Mes·si·an·ic** (mĕs′ĭ·ăn′ĭk), *adj*.

Mes·si·dor (mĕ·sē·dôr′), *n*. (in the calendar of the first French republic) the tenth month of the year, extending from June 19 to July 18. [F: f. L *messi*(s) harvest + s. Gk. *dōron* gift]

mes·sieurs (mĕs′ərz; *Fr*. mě·syœ′) *n*. pl. of **monsieur**.

Mes·si·na (mĕ·sē′nə), *n*. **1**. a seaport in NE Sicily: totally destroyed by an earthquake, 1908. 232,000 (est. 1954). **2**. **Strait of**, a strait between Sicily and Italy.

Mes·sines (mĕ·sēn′), *n*. a village in W Belgium, near Ypres: battles, 1914, 1917.

mess kit, a portable metal dish with eating utensils, esp. one carried by a soldier in the field.

mess·mate (mĕs′māt′), *n*. an associate in a mess, esp. in a ship's mess.

Messrs., messieurs (used as if a plural of *Mr*.).

mes·suage (mĕs′wĭj), *n*. *Law*. a dwelling house with its adjacent buildings and the lands appropriated to the use of the household. [ME *mesuage*, t. AF: (m.)*me*(*s*)-*suage*, prob. m. *mesnage*. See MENAGE]

mess·y (mĕs′ĭ), *adj*., **messier, messiest**. **1**. of the nature of a mess: *a messy concoction*. **2**. being in a mess: *a messy table*. **3**. attended with or making a mess; dirty; untidy: *messy work*. **—mess′i·ness**, *n*.

mes·tee (mĕs·tē′), *n*. mustee.

mes·ti·zo (mĕs·tē′zō), *n*., *pl*. **-zos, -zoes**. **1**. a person of mixed blood. **2**. (in Spanish America) one who has Spanish and American Indian blood. **3**. one of European and East Indian, Negro, or Malay blood. **4**. a Philippine Island native with Chinese blood. [t. Sp., g. L *mixtīcius* of mixed race] **—mes·ti·za** (mĕs·tē′zə), *n. fem*.

Meš·tro·vić (mĕsh′trə·vĭch; *Yugo*. mĕsh′trô·vĕt′y), *n*. Ivan (ē′vän), 1883–1962, Yugoslav sculptor, in U.S. after 1946.

met (mĕt), *v*. pt. and pp. of **meet**.

met., **1**. metaphor. **2**. metaphysics. **3**. metropolitan.

meta-, a prefix meaning "among," "along with," "after," "behind," and often denoting change, found chiefly in scientific words. **2**. *Chem*. **a**. a prefix meaning "containing least water," used of acids and salts, as in *meta-antimonic*, HSbO₃, *meta-antimonous*, HSbO₂. **b**. a prefix indicating an organic derivative of such an acid. [t. Gk., repr. *metá*, prep., with, after]

me·tab·o·lism (mə·tăb′ə·lĭz′əm), *n*. *Biol*. the sum of the processes or chemical changes in an organism or a single cell by which food is built up (*anabolism*) into living protoplasm and by which protoplasm is broken down (*catabolism*) into simpler compounds with the exchange of energy. [f. META-, + s. Gk. *bolē* change + -ISM] **—met·a·bol·ic** (mĕt′ə·bŏl′ĭk), *adj*.

me·tab·o·lite (mə·tăb′ə·līt′), *n*. a substance acted upon or produced in metabolism.

me·tab·o·lize (mə·tăb′ə·līz′), *v.t*., **-lized, -lizing**. to subject to metabolism; change by metabolism.

met·a·car·pal (mĕt′ə·kär′pəl), *adj*. **1**. of or pertaining to the metacarpus. *—n*. **2**. a metacarpal bone.

met·a·car·pus (mĕt′ə·kär′pəs), *n*., *pl*. **-pi** (-pī). *Anat*. the part of a hand or forelimb (esp. of its bony structure) included between the wrist or carpus and the fingers or phalanges. See diag. under **shoulder**. [t. NL (see META-CARPUS); r. *metacarpium*. t. Gk.: m. *metakárpion*]

met·a·cen·ter (mĕt′ə·sĕn′tər), *n*. the point where the vertical line through the center of buoyancy of a floating body (as a ship) in equilibrium meets the vertical line through the new center of buoyancy when the body is in a slightly inclined position (less than one degree). The equilibrium of the body is stable when this point is above its center of gravity, and unstable when it is below. Also, *esp. Brit*., **met′a·cen′tre**. [t. F: m. *métacentre*, f. Gk.: *meta-* META- + m.s. *kéntron* CENTER¹] **—met′a·cen′tric**, *adj*.

Metacenter of a boat
M, Metacenter; G, Center of gravity; B, Center of buoyancy; B′, Center of buoyancy when boat is displaced

met·a·chro·ma·tism (mĕt′ə·krō′mə·tĭz′əm), *n*. change of color, esp. that due to variation in the temperature of a body. [f. META- + s. Gk. *chrōma* color + -ISM] **—met·a·chro·mat·ic** (mĕt′ə·krō·măt′ĭk), *adj*.

met·a·gal·ax·y (mĕt′ə·găl′ək·sĭ), *n*., *pl*. **-axies**. *Astron*. the complete system of external galaxies, or extragalactic nebulae.

met·age (mē′tĭj), *n*. **1**. the official measurement of contents or weight. **2**. the charge for it. [f. METE, v., + -AGE]

met·a·gen·e·sis (mĕt′ə·jĕn′ə·sĭs), *n*. *Biol*. reproduction characterized by the alternation of a sexual generation and a generation which reproduces asexually by budding. **—met·a·ge·net·ic** (mĕt′ə·jə·nĕt′ĭk), *adj*.

me·tag·na·thous (mə·tăg′nə·thəs), *adj*. *Ornith*. having the tips of the mandibles crossed, as the crossbills. **—me·tag′na·thism**, *n*.

met·al (mĕt′əl), *n*., *v*., **-aled, -aling** or (*esp. Brit*.) **-alled, -alling**. **1**. any of a class of elementary substances, as gold, silver, copper, etc., all of which are crystalline when solid and many of which are characterized by opacity, ductility, conductivity, and a peculiar luster when freshly fractured. **2**. an alloy or mixture composed wholly or partly of such substances. **3**. *Chem*. **a**. a metal (def. 1) in its pure state, as distinguished from alloys. **b**. an element yielding positively charged ions in aqueous solutions of its salts. **4**. formative material; mettle. **5**. *Printing, etc*. **a**. type metal. **b**. the state of being set up in type. **6**. *Brit*. broken stone used for roads or railroad track ballast. **7**. molten glass in the pot or melting tank. **8**. *Her*. either of the tinctures gold (*or*) and silver (*argent*). *—v.t*. **9**. to furnish or cover with metal. [ME, t. OF, L: m.s. *metallum* mine, mineral, metal, t. Gk.: m. *métallon* mine]

metal., **1**. metallurgical. **2**. metallurgy.

met·al·ize (mĕt′ə·līz), *v.t*., **-ized, -izing**, to make metallic; give the characteristics of metal to. Also, **met′al·lize′**. **—met′al·i·za′tion**, *n*.

metall., metallurgy.

me·tal·lic (mə·tăl′ĭk), *adj*. **1**. of, pertaining to, or consisting of metal. **2**. of the nature of metal: *metallic luster, metallic sounds*. **3**. *Chem*. **a**. (of a metal element) being in the free or uncombined state: *metallic iron*. **b**. containing or yielding metal. **—me·tal′li·cal·ly**, *adv*.

met·al·lif·er·ous (mĕt′ə·lĭf′ər·əs), *adj*. containing or yielding metal. [f. L *metallifer* yielding metals + -OUS]

met·al·line (mĕt′ə·lĭn, -līn), *adj*. **1**. metallic. **2**. containing one or more metals or metallic salts.

met·al·log·ra·phy (mĕt′ə·lŏg′rə·fĭ), *n*. **1**. the microscopic study of the structure of metals and alloys. **2**. an art or process allied to lithography, in which metallic plates are substituted for stones. **—me·tal·lo·graph·ic** (mə·tăl′ə·grăf′ĭk), *adj*.

met·al·loid (mĕt′ə·loid′), *n*. **1**. a nonmetal. **2**. an element which is both metallic and nonmetallic, as arsenic, silicon, or bismuth. *—adj*. **3**. of or pertaining to a metalloid. **4**. resembling both a metal and nonmetal.

me·tal·lo·ther·a·py (mə·tăl′ō·thĕr′ə·pī), *n*. *Med*. therapy by the use of metals or their salts.

met·al·lur·gy (mĕt′ə·lûr′jĭ, mĕ·tăl′ər·jĭ), *n*. **1**. the art or science of separating metals from their ores. **2**. the art or science of making and compounding alloys. **3**. the art or science of working or heat-treating metals so as to give them certain desired shapes or properties. [t. NL: m.s. *metallurgia*, f. s. Gk. *metallourgós* mineworker + -*ia* (suffix)] **—met′al·lur′gic, met′al·lur′gi·cal**, *adj*. **—met′al·lur′gi·cal·ly**, *adv*. **—met·al·lur·gist** (mĕt′ə·lûr′jĭst, mĕ·tăl′ər·jĭst), *n*.

met·al·work·ing (mĕt′əl·wûr′kĭng), *n*. act of making metal objects. **—met′al·work′**, *n*. **—met′al·work′er**, *n*.

met·a·mere (mĕt′ə·mĭr′), *n*. a somite. **—met·am·er·al** (mə·tăm′ə·rəl), **met·a·mer·ic** (mĕt′ə·mĕr′ĭk), *adj*.

me·tam·er·ism (mə·tăm′ə·rĭz′əm), *n*. *Zool*. **1**. division into metameres, the developmental process of somite formation. **2**. the condition of consisting of metameres.

met·a·mor·phic (mĕt′ə·môr′fĭk), *adj.* **1.** pertaining to or characterized by change of form, 'or metamorphosis. **2.** *Geol.* pertaining to or exhibiting structural change, or metamorphism.

met·a·mor·phism (mĕt′ə·môr′fĭz·əm), *n.* **1.** metamorphosis. **2.** *Geol.* a change in the structure or constitution of a rock, due to natural agencies, as pressure and heat, esp. when the rock becomes harder and more completely crystalline.

met·a·mor·phose (mĕt′ə·môr′fōz, -fōs), *v.t.,* -phosed, -phosing. **1.** to transform. **2.** to subject to metamorphosis or metamorphism.

met·a·mor·pho·sis (mĕt′ə·môr′fə·sĭs), *n., pl.* -ses (-sēz′). **1.** change of form, structure, or substance, as transformation by magic or witchcraft. **2.** any complete change in appearance, character, circumstances, etc. **3.** a form resulting from any such change. **4.** a change of form during the post-embryonic or embryonic growth of an animal by which it is adapted temporarily to a special environment or way of living usually different from that of the preceding stage: *the metamorphosis of tadpoles into frogs.* **5.** *Pathol.* **a.** a type of alteration or degeneration in which tissues are changed: *fatty metamorphosis of the liver.* **b.** the resultant form. **6.** *Bot.* the structural or functional modification of a plant organ or structure during its development. [t. L, t. Gk.: transformation]

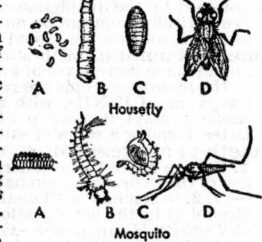

Housefly

Mosquito
Metamorphosis (def. 4)
A, Eggs; B, Larva; C, Pupa; D, Adult

met·a·mor·phous (mĕt′ə·môr′fəs), *adj.* metamorphic.

met·a·neph·ros (mĕt′ə·nĕf′rŏs), *n. Embryol.* the pelvic kidney, developing from the lowest portion of the nephric blastema cords. [t. NL, f. Gk.: *meta-* META- + *nephrós* kidney]

metaph., **1.** metaphysical. **2.** metaphysics.

met·a·phase (mĕt′ə·fāz′), *n. Biol.* the middle stage in mitotic cell division in which the chromosomes in the equatorial plane of the cell split.

met·a·phor (mĕt′ə·fər, -fôr′), *n.* **1.** a figure of speech in which a term or phrase is applied to something to which it is not literally applicable, in order to suggest a resemblance, as *A mighty fortress is our God.* **2.** mixed metaphor, a figurative expression in which two or more metaphors are employed, producing an incongruous assemblage of ideas, as *The king put the ship of state on its feet.* [t. L: s. *metaphora*, t. Gk.: a transfer] —met·a·phor·i·cal (mĕt′ə·fôr′ə·kəl, -fŏr′-), met′·a·phor′ic, *adj.* —met′a·phor′i·cal·ly, *adv.*

met·a·phos·phor·ic acid (mĕt′ə·fŏs·fôr′ĭk, -fŏr′-), *Chem.* an acid, HPO₃, derived from phosphorous pentoxide, and containing the least water of the phosphoric acids. See **phosphoric acid.**

met·a·phrase (mĕt′ə·frāz′), *n., v.,* -phrased, -phrasing. —*n.* **1.** a translation. —*v.t.* **2.** to translate, esp. literally. **3.** to change the phrasing or literary form of. [t. NL: m.s. *metaphrasis,* t. Gk.: a translation]

metaphys., metaphysics.

met·a·phys·i·cal (mĕt′ə·fĭz′ə·kəl), *adj.* **1.** pertaining to or of the nature of metaphysics. **2.** *Philos.* **a.** concerned with abstract thought or subjects, as existence, causality, truth, etc. **b.** concerned with first principles and ultimate grounds, as being, time, substance. **3.** highly abstract or abstruse. **4.** designating or pertaining esp. to that school of early 17th century English poets of whom John Donne was the chief, whose characteristic style is highly intellectual, philosophical, and crowded with ingenious conceits and turns of wit. **5.** *Archaic.* imaginary. —met′a·phys′i·cal·ly, *adv.*

met·a·phy·si·cian (mĕt′ə·fĭ·zĭsh′ən), *n.* one versed in metaphysics. Also, **met·a·phys·i·cist** (mĕt′ə·fĭz′ə·sĭst).

met·a·phys·ics (mĕt′ə·fĭz′ĭks), *n.* **1.** that branch of philosophy which treats of first principles, including the sciences of being (*ontology*) and of the origin and structure of the universe (*cosmology*). It is always intimately connected with a theory of knowledge (*epistemology*). **2.** philosophy, esp. in its more abstruse branches. [t. ML: m. *metaphysica,* t. MGk.: m. *(tà) metaphysikà* (neut. pl.), repr. *tà metà tà physikà* the (works) after the physics; with reference to the arrangement of Aristotle's writings]

met·a·plasm (mĕt′ə·plăz′əm), *n.* **1.** *Biol.* the lifeless matter or inclusions (as starch, pigment, etc.) in the protoplasm of a cell. **2.** *Obsolesc.* a change in the structure of a word by adding, removing, or transposing the sounds of which it is composed or their representation in spelling. **3.** the formation of oblique cases from a stem other than that of the nominative. —met′a·plas′mic, *adj.*

met·a·pro·te·in (mĕt′ə·prō′tē·ĭn, -tēn), *n.* a hydrolytic derivative of protein, insoluble in water, but soluble in dilute acids or alkalies.

met·a·so·ma·tism (mĕt′ə·sō′mə·tĭz·əm), *n. Geol.* **1.** the processes whereby minerals or rocks are replaced by others of different chemical composition as a result of the introduction of material, usually in very hot aqueous solutions, from sources external to the formation undergoing change. **2.** replacement (def. 3). [f. META- + s. Gk. *sôma* body + -ISM]

me·tas·ta·sis (mə·tăs′tə·sĭs), *n., pl.* -ses (-sēz′). **1.** *Physiol., Pathol.* transference of a fluid, disease, or the like, from one part of the body to another. **2.** *Chiefly Pathol.* the translocation of cancerous cells to other parts of the body via the circulation, lymphatics, or membranous surfaces. **3.** a transformation. **4.** *Rhet.* a rapid transition, as from one subject to another. [t. LL, t. Gk.: removal] —met·a·stat·ic (mĕt′ə·stăt′ĭk), *adj.*

me·tas·ta·size (mə·tăs′tə·sīz′), *v.i.,* -sized, -sizing. *Pathol.* (esp. of cells of malignant tumors, or microörganisms) to spread to other regions by dissemination through the circulation or other channels.

met·a·tar·sal (mĕt′ə·tär′səl), *adj.* **1.** of or pertaining to the metatarsus. —*n.* **2.** a metatarsal bone.

met·a·tar·sus (mĕt′ə·tär′səs), *n., pl.* -si (-sī). *Anat., Zool.* **1.** the part of a foot or hind limb (esp. of its bony structure) included between the tarsus and the toes or phalanges. See diag. under **skeleton.** **2.** (in birds) a bone composed of both tarsal and metatarsal elements, extending from the tibia to the phalanges. [NL. See META-, TARSUS]

me·tath·e·sis (mə·tăth′ə·sĭs), *n., pl.* -ses (-sēz′). **1.** the transposition of letters, syllables, or sounds in a word. **2.** *Chem.* a double decomposition, as when two compounds react with each other to form two other compounds. [t. LL, t. Gk.: transposition] —met·a·thet·ic (mĕt′ə·thĕt′ĭk), met′a·thet′i·cal, *adj.*

met·a·tho·rax (mĕt′ə·thōr′ăks), *n., pl.* -thoraxes, -thoraces (-thōr′ə·sēz′). the posterior division of an insect's thorax, bearing the third pair of legs and the second pair of wings. —met·a·tho·rac·ic (mĕt′ə·thō·răs′ĭk), *adj.*

met·a·xy·lem (mĕt′ə·zī′lĕm), *n. Bot.* the part of the primary xylem which is the last to be formed, usually having weblike or pitted surfaces.

Met·a·zo·a (mĕt′ə·zō′ə), *n.pl.* a large zoölogical division comprising all the animals above the protozoans, i.e., those organisms which, although originating from a single cell, are composed of many cells. See **Protozoa.** [t. NL, pl. of *metazōŏn,* f. Gk.: *meta-* META- + *zôion* animal] —met·a·zo′an, *adj., n.* —met′a·zo′ic, *adj.*

Metch·ni·koff (mĕch·nē·kôf′), *n.* Élie (ĕ·lē′), 1845–1916, Russian biologist and bacteriologist, in France.

mete[1] (mēt), *v.t.,* meted, meting. **1.** to distribute or apportion by measure; allot (usually fol. by *out*). **2.** *Archaic.* to measure. [ME; OE *metan,* c. G *messen*]

mete[2] (mēt), *n.* **1.** a limiting mark. **2.** a limit. [ME, t. OF, t. L: m. *mēta* goal-mark, turning post]

met·em·pir·ic (mĕt′ĕm·pĭr′ĭk), *n.* a supporter of the metempirical philosophy. [f. MET(A)- + EMPIRIC]

met·em·pir·i·cal (mĕt′ĕm·pĭr′ə·kəl), *adj.* **1.** beyond, or outside of, the field of experience. **2.** of or pertaining to metempirics.

met·em·pir·ics (mĕt′ĕm·pĭr′ĭks), *n.* the philosophy dealing with things transcending the field of experience, as regards their existence.

me·temp·sy·cho·sis (mə·tĕmp′sə·kō′sĭs, mĕt′əm·sī-), *n., pl.* -ses (-sēz). **1.** the passage of the soul from one body to another. **2.** the rebirth of the soul at death in another body either of human or animal form. [t. L, t. Gk.]

met·en·ceph·a·lon (mĕt′ĕn·sĕf′ə·lŏn), *n., pl.* -la (-lə). *Anat.* the segment of the brain including the cerebellum and pons and the upper portion of the medulla oblongata; the hindbrain. [t. NL. See MET(A)-, ENCEPHALON] —met·en·ce·phal·ic (mĕt′ĕn·sə·făl′ĭk), *adj.*

me·te·or (mē′tē·ər), *n.* **1.** a transient fiery streak in the sky produced by a meteoroid passing through the earth's atmosphere; a bolide or shooting star. **2.** any meteoroid or meteorite. **3.** *Obs.* any atmospheric phenomenon, as hail, a typhoon, etc. [late ME, t. NL: s. *meteŏrum,* t. Gk.: m. *metéŏron* (pl. *metéŏra* phenomena in the heavens), neut. adj., raised, high in air]

meteor., **1.** meteorological. **2.** meteorology.

me·te·or·ic (mē′tĭ·ôr′ĭk, -ŏr′ĭk), *adj.* **1.** pertaining to or like a meteor. **2.** consisting of meteors: *a meteoric shower.* **3.** flashing like a meteor; transiently brilliant: *a meteoric career.* **4.** swift or rapid. **5.** of the atmosphere; meteorological. —me′te·or′i·cal·ly, *adv.*

me·te·or·ite (mē′tĭ·ə·rīt′), *n.* **1.** a mass of stone or metal that has reached the earth from outer space; a fallen meteoroid. **2.** a meteor or a meteoroid. —me·te·or·it·ic (mē′tĭ·ə·rĭt′ĭk), *adj.*

me·te·or·o·graph (mē′tĭ·ər·ə·grăf′, -gräf′; mē′tĭ·ôr′ə-, -ŏr′ə-), *n.* an instrument for automatically recording various meteorological conditions, as of barometric pressure, temperature, etc., at the same time.

me·te·or·oid (mē′tĭ·ə·roid′), *n. Astron.* any of the small bodies, often remnants of comets, traveling through space, which, when encountering the earth's atmosphere, are heated to luminosity, thus becoming meteors.

meteorol., **1.** meteorological. **2.** meteorology.

me·te·or·o·log·i·cal (mē′tĭ·ər·ə·lŏj′ə·kəl), *adj.* pertaining to meteorology, or to phenomena of the atmosphere or weather. Also, **me′te·or·o·log′ic.** —me′te·or·o·log′i·cal·ly, *adv.*

me·te·or·ol·o·gy (mē′tĭ·ə·rŏl′ə·jĭ), *n.* the science dealing with the atmosphere and its phenomena, esp. as relating to weather. [t. Gk.: m.s. *meteŏrologia.* See METEOR, -LOGY] —me′te·or·ol′o·gist, *n.*

me·ter[1] (mē′tər), *n.* the fundamental unit of length in the metric system, equivalent to 39.37 U.S. inches, originally intended to be, and being very nearly, equal to one ten-millionth of the distance from the equator to the pole measured on a meridian, but actually defined as the distance between two lines on a platinum-iridium bar (the "International Prototype Meter") preserved at the International Bureau of Weights and Measures, near Paris. Also, *esp. Brit.*, metre. [t. F.: m. *mètre*, t. Gk.: m. *métron* measure]

me·ter[2] (mē′tər), *n.* **1.** *Pros.* **a.** poetic measure; arrangement of words in regularly measured or patterned or rhythmic lines or verses. **b.** a particular form of such arrangement, depending on the kind and number of feet constituting the verse: *iambic trimeter.* **2.** *Music.* **a.** the rhythmic element as measured by division into parts of equal time value. **b.** the unit of measurement, in terms of number of beats, adopted for a given piece of music. See **measure** (def. 18). Also, *esp. Brit.*, metre. [ME *metir, metur*, OE *mēter*, t. L: m.s. *metrum* poetic meter, verse, t. Gk.: m. *métron* measure; r. ME *metre*, t. F]

me·ter[3] (mē′tər), *n.* **1.** an instrument that measures, esp. one that automatically measures and records the quantity of gas, water, electricity, or the like, passing through it or actuating it. —*v.t.* **2.** to measure by means of a meter. [ME; f. METE[1] + ER[1]]

-meter, a word element used in names of instruments for measuring quantity, extent, degree, etc., e.g., *altimeter, barometer.* [t. NL: m. -*metrum*, t. GK. (see METER[1]). Cf. METER[2]]

me·ter-kil·o·gram-sec·ond system (mē′tər kĭl′ə gram′ sĕk′ənd), a system of units used in science, based on the meter, kilogram, and second as the fundamental units of length, mass, and time.

Meth., Methodist.

meth·ac·ry·late (mĕth·ăk′rə lāt′), *n. Chem.* an ester or salt derived from methacrylic acid.

meth·a·cryl·ic acid (mĕth′ə krĭl′ĭk), a colorless liquid acid, $CH_2C(CH_3)COOH$, produced synthetically, the esters of which are used in making plastics.

meth·ane (mĕth′ān), *n. Chem.* a colorless, odorless, inflammable gas, CH_4, the main constituent of marsh gas and the firedamp of coal mines, and obtained commercially from natural gas; the first member of the methane or paraffin series of hydrocarbons. [f. METH(YL) + -ANE]

methane series, *Chem.* a homologous series of saturated aliphatic hydrocarbons, with the general formula, C_nH_{2n+2}, as *methane* (CH_4), *ethane* (C_2H_6), *etc.*; paraffin series; alkanes.

meth·a·nol (mĕth′ə nōl′, -nŏl′), *n. Chem.* methyl alcohol, or wood alcohol. [f. METHAN(E) + -OL[1]]

met·he·mo·glo·bin (mĕt hē′mə glō′bĭn, -hĕm′ə-, mĕ·thē′mə-), *n. Biochem.* a brownish compound, a combination of oxygen and hemoglobin, formed in the blood, as by the use of certain drugs. [f. MET(A)- + HEMOGLOBIN]

meth·e·na·mine (mĕ thē′nə mēn′, -mĭn), *n. Pharm.* the U.S.P. designation for hexamethylenetetramine, $(CH_2)_6N_4$, a diuretic and urinary antiseptic.

me·thinks (mĭ thĭngks′), *v. impers.; pt.* **methought.** *Archaic* and *Poetic.* it seems to me. [ME *me thinketh*, OE *me thyncth* it seems to me]

me·thi·o·nine (mĕ thī′ə nēn′, -nĭn), *n. Biochem.* an amino acid, $CH_3SCH_2CH_2CH(NH_2)COOH$, found in such proteins as casein, wool, gelatin, etc.

meth·od (mĕth′əd), *n.* **1.** a mode of procedure, esp. an orderly or systematic mode: *a method of instruction.* **2.** a way of doing something, esp. in accordance with a definite plan. **3.** order or system in doing anything: *to work with method.* **4.** orderly or systematic arrangement. [t. L: s. *methodus* mode of procedure, method, t. Gk.: m. *méthodos* a following after, method] —**Syn. 1.** METHOD, MODE, WAY imply a manner in which a thing is done or in which it happens. METHOD refers to a settled kind of procedure, usually according to a definite, established, logical, or systematic plan: *the open-hearth method of making steel, method of solving a problem.* MODE is a more formal word which implies a customary or characteristic fashion of doing something: *kangaroos have a peculiar mode of carrying their young.* WAY, a word in popular use for the general idea, is equivalent to various more specific words: *a child's way* (manner) *of staring at people; the way* (method) *of rapid calculating; the way* (mode) *of holding a pen.*

me·thod·i·cal (mə thŏd′ə kəl), *adj.* performed, disposed, or acting in a systematic way; systematic; orderly: *a methodical man.* Also, **me·thod′ic.** —**me·thod′i·cal·ly,** *adv.* —**me·thod′i·cal·ness,** *n.* —Syn. See orderly.

Meth·od·ism (mĕth′ə dĭz′əm), *n.* the doctrines, polity, and worship of the Methodist Church.

Meth·od·ist (mĕth′ə dĭst), *n.* **1.** a member of one of the Christian denominations which grew out of the revival of religion led by John Wesley. —*adj.* **2.** of or pertaining to the Methodists or Methodism. —**Meth′od·is′tic,** *adj.*

meth·od·ize (mĕth′ə dīz′), *v.t.,* **-ized, -izing. 1.** to reduce to method. **2.** to arrange with method. —**meth′od·iz′er,** *n.*

meth·od·ol·o·gy (mĕth′ə dŏl′ə jĭ), *n., pl.* **-gies.** the science of method, esp.: **a.** a branch of logic dealing with the logical principles underlying the organization of the various special sciences, and the conduct of scientific inquiry. **b.** *Educ.* a branch of pedagogics concerned with analysis and evaluation of subject matter and methods of teaching.

Me·thu·en (mĭ thū′ən), *n.* a town in NE Massachusetts, near Lawrence. 28,114 (1960).

Me·thu·se·lah (mĭ thōō′zə lə), *n.* a Biblical patriarch before the Flood who according to tradition lived 969 years. Gen. 5:27. [t. Heb.: *M'thūshelah*]

meth·yl (mĕth′ĭl), *n. Chem.* a univalent hydrocarbon radical, CH_3, derived from methane. [t. F: m. *méthyle*, back formation from *méthylène* METHYLENE]

methyl acetate, *Chem.* a colorless, combustible, volatile liquid, CH_3COOCH_3, having a fragrant odor, used as a solvent; the methyl ester of acetic acid.

meth·yl·al (mĕth′ə lăl′, mĕth′ə lâl′), *n. Chem.* a liquid compound with a pleasant odor, $CH_2(OCH_3)_2$, used in medicine as a hypnotic. [f. METHYL + AL(COHOL)]

methyl alcohol, *Chem.* a colorless, inflammable, poisonous liquid, CH_3OH, of the alcohol class, formerly obtained by the distillation of wood, but now produced synthetically from carbon monoxide and hydrogen, used as a fuel, solvent, etc.; wood alcohol.

meth·yl·a·mine (mĕth′ə lə mēn′, -äm′ĭn), *n. Chem.* any of three derivatives of ammonia in which one or all of the hydrogen atoms are replaced by methyl radicals; esp., a gas, CH_3NH_2, with an ammonialike odor, the simplest alkyl derivative of ammonia and, like the latter, forming a series of salts.

meth·yl·ate (mĕth′ə lāt′), *n., v.,* **-ated, -ating.** —*n.* **1.** *Chem.* a methyl alcohol derivative in which the hydrogen of the hydroxyl group has been replaced by a metal. —*v.t.* **2.** to combine with methyl. **3.** to mix with methyl alcohol as in the denaturation of ethyl alcohol: *methylated spirits.* [f. METHYL + -ATE[2]]

methylated spirits, denatured or wood alcohol.

meth·yl·a·tion (mĕth′ə lā′shən), *n. Chem.* the process of replacing a hydrogen atom with a methyl radical.

meth·yl·ene (mĕth′ə lēn′), *n. Chem.* a bivalent hydrocarbon radical, CH_2, derived from methane. [t. F: f. s. Gk. *méthy* wine + -*yl* -YL + -*ène* -ENE]

methylene blue, a thiazine dye, $C_{16}H_{18}ClN_3S·3H_2O$ also used as an antidote for cyanide poisoning.

methyl methacrylate, a class of optically clear, transparent thermoplastic resins.

meth·yl·naph·tha·lene (mĕth′əl năf′thə lēn′), *n. Chem.* a compound, $C_{11}H_{10}$, the alpha form of which, a colorless liquid, is used in determining cetane numbers. Cf. **cetane number.**

me·tic·u·lous (mə tĭk′yə ləs), *adj.* solicitous about minute details; minutely or finically careful: *He was meticulous about his personal appearance.* [t. L: m.s. *meticulōsus* fearful] —**me·tic·u·los·i·ty** (mə tĭk′yə lŏs′ə tĭ), *n.* —**me·tic′u·lous·ly,** *adv.*

mé·tier (mĕ tyē′), *n.* trade; profession; line of work or activity. [t. F, g. L *ministerium* MINISTRY]

mé·tis (mē tēs′), *n.* **1.** any person of mixed ancestry. **2.** *U.S.* a person of one-eighth Negro ancestry; an octoroon. **3.** *Canada.* a half-breed of white, esp. French, and Indian parentage. [t. F, g. LL *mizticius* of mixed blood] —**mé·tisse′,** *n. fem.*

me·tol (mē′tŏl, -tōl), *n.* a soluble white powder, $C_{14}H_{18}N_2O_2·H_2SO_4$, used as a developer.

Me·ton·ic cycle (mĭ tŏn′ĭk), a cycle of 19 years, after which the new moon recurs on the same day of the year as at the beginning of the cycle. [named after the discoverer. *Meton*, an Athenian astronomer. See -IC]

met·o·nym (mĕt′ə nĭm), *n.* a word used in metonymy.

met·o·nym·i·cal (mĕt′ə nĭm′ə kəl), *adj.* having the nature of metonymy. Also, **met′o·nym′ic.** —**met′o·nym′i·cal·ly,** *adv.*

me·ton·y·my (mĭ tŏn′ə mĭ), *n. Rhet.* the use of the name of one thing for that of another to which it has some logical relation, as "scepter" for "sovereignty," or "the bottle" for "strong drink." [t. LL: m.s. *metōnymia*, t. Gk.: a change of name]

met·o·pe (mĕt′ə pē′, -ōp), *n. Archit.* one of the square spaces, either decorated or plain, between triglyphs in the Doric frieze. [t. Gk.]

me·tral·gi·a (mĭ trăl′jĭ ə), *n. Pathol.* pain in the uterus. [t. NL, f. Gk.: s. *mētra* uterus + -*algia* -ALGIA]

M. Metope; T. Triglyph

met·ra·zol (mĕt′rə zōl′, -zŏl′), *n.* **1.** a drug, $C_6H_{10}N_4$, which increases the activity of the heart and lungs and is also used to induce a convulsive state for the treatment of certain mental diseases. **2.** (*cap.*) a trademark for this drug.

me·tre (mē′tər), *n. Chiefly Brit.* meter.

met·ric[1] (mĕt′rĭk), *adj.* **1.** pertaining to the meter, or to the system of measures and weights originally based upon it. [t. F: m. *métrique*, der. *mètre* METER[1]]

met·ric[2] (mĕt′rĭk), *adj.* metrical. [t. L: s. *metricus*, t. Gk.: m. *metrikós* pertaining to meter or measure]

met·ri·cal (mĕt′rə kəl), *adj.* **1.** pertaining to meter or poetic measure. **2.** composed in meter or verse. **3.** pertaining to measurement. Also, **metric.** —**met′ri·cal·ly,** *adv.*

me·tri·cian (mĕ trĭsh′ən), *n.* a metrist.

met·rics (mĕt′rĭks), *n.* **1.** the science of meter. **2.** the art of metrical composition.

metric system, a decimal system of weights and measures, adopted first in France, but now widespread over the world, universally used in science, mandatory

---

b., blend of, blended; c., cognate with; d., dialect, dialectal; der., derived from; f., formed from; g., going back to; m., modification of; r., replacing; s., stem of; t., taken from; ?, perhaps. See the full key on inside cover.

for use for all purposes in a large number of countries, and permitted for use in most (as in U.S. and Great Britain). The basic units are the meter (39.37 inches) for length, and the gram (15.432 grains) for mass or weight. Derived units are the liter (0.908 U.S. dry quart, or 1.0567 U.S. liquid quart) for capacity, being the volume of 1000 grams of water under specified conditions; the are (119.6 square yards) for area being the area of a square 10 meters on a side; and the stere (35.315 cubic feet) for volume, being the volume of a cube 1 meter on a side, the term stere being, however, usually restricted to measuring firewood. Names for units larger and smaller than these are formed from the above names by the use of the following prefixes:

| kilo | 1000 | deca | 10 | centi | 0.01 |
| hecto | 100 | deci | 0.1 | milli | 0.001 |

To these are often added mega = 1,000,000, myria = 10,000, and micro = 0.000 001. Not all of the possible units are in common use. In many countries names of old units are applied to roughly similar metric units.

met·ric ton, a unit of 1000 kilograms, equivalent to 2204.62 avoirdupois pounds.

met·ri·fy (mĕt′rə fī′), v.t. **-fied, -fying.** to put into meter; compose in verse. [t. F: m. *métrifier*, t. ML: m.s. *metrificāre* put in meter, f. metri- (comb. form of *metrum* meter) + *-ficāre* -FY] —**met′ri·fi′er,** n.

met·rist (mĕt′rĭst, mē′trĭst), n. one versed in the use of poetic meters. [t. ML: s. *metrista,* der. L *metrum* METER²]

me·tri·tis (mĭ trī′tĭs), n. Pathol. inflammation of the uterus. [t. NL, f. Gk.: s. *mētra* uterus + *-ītis* -ITIS]

me·trol·o·gy (mĭ trŏl′ə jĭ), n., pl. **-gies.** the science of measures and weights. [f. Gk. *métro(n)* measure + -LOGY] —**met·ro·log·i·cal** (mĕt′rə lŏj′ə kəl), adj. —**me·trol′o·gist,** n.

met·ro·nome (mĕt′rə nōm′), n. a mechanical contrivance for marking time, as for music. [f. Gk.: *métro(n)* measure + m.s. *nómos* law] —**met·ro·nom·ic** (mĕt′rə nŏm′ĭk), adj.

me·tro·nym·ic (mē′trə nĭm′-ĭk, mĕt′rə-), adj. **1.** derived from the name of a mother or other female ancestor. —**n. 2.** a metronymic name. [t. Gk.: m. s. *mētrōnymikós* named after one's mother]

me·trop·o·lis (mə trŏp′ə lĭs), n., pl. **-lises** (-lĭs ĭz), **-leis** (-lēs′). **1.** the chief city (not necessarily the capital) of a country, state, or region. **2.** a central or principal point, as of some activity. **3.** the mother city or parent state of an ancient Greek (or other) colony. **4.** the chief see of an ecclesiastical province. [t. LL, t. Gk.: a mother state or city]

met·ro·pol·i·tan (mĕt′rə pŏl′ə tən), adj. **1.** characteristic of a metropolis or chief city, or of its inhabitants. **2.** pertaining to or constituting a mother country. **3.** pertaining to an ecclesiastical metropolis. —**n. 4.** an inhabitant of a metropolis or chief city. **5.** one having metropolitan manners, etc. **6.** the next highest rank to Patriarch in the Russian Orthodox Church. **7.** a citizen of the mother city or parent state of a colony.

me·tror·rha·gi·a (mē′trə rā′jĭ ə, mĕt′rə-), n. Pathol. nonmenstrual discharge of blood from the uterus; uterine hemorrhage. [t. NL, f. Gk.: m.s. *mētra* uterus + -rrhagia -RRHAGIA]

-metry, a word element denoting the process of measuring, abstract for -meter, as in anthropometry, chronometry. [t. Gk.: m.s. -metria, der. -metros measuring]

Met·ter·nich (mĕt′ər nĭKH), n. **Klemens Wenzel Nepomuk Lothar** (klā′mĕns vĕn′tsəl nä′pō mŏŏk lō′tär), **Prince von,** 1773–1859, Austrian statesman.

met·tle (mĕt′əl), n. **1.** the characteristic disposition or temper: to try a man's mettle. **2.** spirit; courage. **3. on one's mettle,** incited to do one's best. [var. of METAL]

met·tle·some (mĕt′əl səm), adj. spirited; courageous. Also, **met·tled** (mĕt′əld).

Metz (mĕts; Fr. mĕs), n. a fortress city in NE France: battles, 1870, 1918, 1940, 1944. 85,701 (1954).

me·um et tu·um (mē′əm ĕt tū′əm, tōō′-), Latin. mine and thine.

Meuse (mūz; Fr. mœz), n. a river flowing from NE France through E Belgium and S Netherlands into the North Sea. 575 mi. Dutch, **Maas.**

mew¹ (mū), n. **1.** the sound a cat makes. —v.i. **2.** to make this sound. [imit.]

mew² (mū), n. a sea gull, esp. the common gull, *Larus canus,* of Europe. [OE, c. G *möwe*]

mew³ (mū), n. **1.** a cage for hawks, esp. while molting. **2.** a place of retirement or concealment. **3.** (usually pl.) Brit. a set of stables about a court or alley. —v.t. **4.** to shut up in or as in a mew; to confine; conceal (often fol. by up). [ME mue, t. OF, der. muer MEW⁴]

mew⁴ (mū), v.t., v.i. to shed (feathers); to molt. [ME mewe(n), t. OF: m. muer molt, change, c. L mūtāre]

mewl (mūl), v.i. to cry as a young child. [imit.]

Mex., **1.** Mexican. **2.** Mexico.

Mex·i·can (mĕk′sə kən), adj. **1.** of or pertaining to Mexico. —n. **2.** a native or inhabitant of Mexico.

Mexican bean beetle, a species of ladybug, *Epilachna varivestris,* which eats the leaves of beans.

Mexican hairless, a very small dog which grows very little hair.

Mex·i·ca·no (mĕk′sə kä′nō), n. any Nahuatl language.

Mexican War, the war between the United States and Mexico, 1846–48.

Mex·i·co (mĕk′sə kō′; Sp. mĕ′hē kō′), n. **1.** a republic in S North America. 30,538,000 pop. (est. 1956); 760,373 sq. mi. Cap.: Mexico City. **2.** a state in central Mexico. 1,448,431 (est. 1952); 8268 sq. mi. Cap.: Toluca. **3. Gulf of,** an arm of the Atlantic between the U.S., Cuba, and Mexico. ab. 716,000 sq. mi.; greatest depth, 12,714 ft.

Mexico City, the capital of the republic of Mexico, in the central part. 2,233,914 pop. (1950). ab. 7400 ft. high. Official name, **México, D. F.**

Mey·er·beer (mī′ər bār′), n. **Giacomo** (jä′kō mô′), (*Jakob Liebmann Beer*) 1791–1864, German composer.

Meyn·ell (mĕn′əl), n. **Alice,** (*Alice Christiana Thompson, Mrs. Wilfred Meynell*) 1850–1922, British poet and essayist.

mez·ca·line (mĕz′kə lēn′, -lĭn), n. mescaline.

me·ze·re·on (mĭ zir′ĭ ŏn′), n. an Old World thymelaeaceous shrub, *Daphne Mezereum,* cultivated for its fragrant purplish-pink flowers, which appear in early spring. [t. ML, t. Ar.: m. *māzariyūn* the camellia]

me·zu·zah (mə zŏŏ′zä), n., pl. **-zoth** (-zōth). Jewish Rel. a piece of parchment inscribed on one side with the passages Deut. 6:4–9 and 11:13–21, and on the other with the word "Shaddai" (a name applied to God), and so placed in a case that the divine name is visible from the outside, the case being attached to the doorpost of a house in fulfillment of the injunction in each of the passages. Also, **me·zu′za.** [t. Heb.: doorpost (see Deut. 6:9, 11:20)]

mez·za·nine (mĕz′ə nēn′, -nĭn), n. a low story between two other stories of greater height, esp. when the low story and the one beneath it form part of one composition; an entresol. [t. F, t. It.: m. *mezzanino,* dim. of *mezzano* middle, g. L *mediānus* MEDIAN]

mez·zo (mĕt′sō, mĕz′ō; It. mĕd′dzō), adj. middle; medium; half. [t. It., g. L *medius* middle]

mez·zo·re·lie·vo (mĕt′sō rĭ lē′vō), n., pl. **-vos** (-vōz). middle relief, between alto-relievo and bas-relief. Also, Italian, **mez·zo·ri·lie·vo** (mĕd′zō rē lyĕ′vō). [t. It.]

mez·zo·so·pran·o (mĕt′sō sə prăn′ō, -prä′nō, mĕz′ō-), n., pl. **-pranos, -prani** (-prä′nē). Music. **1.** a voice or voice part intermediate in compass between soprano and contralto. **2.** a person having such a voice. [t. It.]

mez·zo·tint (mĕt′sō tĭnt′, mĕz′ō-), n. **1.** a method of engraving on copper or steel by burnishing or scraping away a uniformly roughened surface. **2.** a print produced by this method. —v.t. **3.** to engrave in mezzotint. [t. It.: m. *mezzotinto* half-tint]

MF, Middle French. Also, **M.F.**

mf., **1.** Music. (It. *mezzo forte*). moderately loud. **2.** microfarad.

mfg., manufacturing.

mfr., **1.** manufacture. **2.** (pl. **mfrs.**) manufacturer.

Mg, Chem. magnesium.

mg., milligram; milligrams.

mgr., **1.** manager. **2.** Monseigneur. **3.** Monsignor.

MHG, Middle High German.

mho (mō), n. Elect. a unit of electrical conductivity, equal to the conductivity of a body whose resistance is one ohm; a reciprocal ohm. [coined by Lord Kelvin (1824–1907); reversed spelling of OHM]

M.H.R., Member of the House of Representatives.

mi (mē), n. Music. the syllable used for the third tone of a scale, and sometimes for the tone E. See **sol-fa** (def. 1). [See GAMUT]

mi., **1.** mile; miles. **2.** mill; mills.

Mi·am·i (mī ăm′ĭ, -ə), n. **1.** a city in SE Florida: seaside winter resort. 291,688 (1960). **2.** a river flowing S through W Ohio into the Ohio river. ab. 160 mi.

Mi·am·i (mī ăm′ĭ, -ə), n., pl. **Miamis. 1.** (pl.) a North American Indian tribe of the Algonquian family, formerly located in N Indiana, S Michigan, perhaps Illinois; now extinct as a tribe. **2.** a member of this tribe.

Miami Beach, a city in SE Florida. 63,145 (1960).

mi·aow (mĭ ou′, myou), n., v.i. meow. Also **mi·aou′, mi·aul** (mĭ oul′ mĭ ôl′) [imit.]

mi·as·ma (mī ăz′mə, mĭ-), n., pl. **-mata** (-mə tə), **-mas.** noxious exhalations from putrescent organic matter; poisonous effluvia or germs infecting the atmosphere. [t. NL, t. Gk.: pollution] —**mi·as′mal, mi·as·mat·ic** (mī′ăz măt′ĭk), **mi·as·mat′i·cal, mi·as′mic,** adj.

mib (mĭb), n. Dial. **1.** marble (def. 7a). **2.** (pl. construed as sing.) the game of marbles.

Mic., Micah.

mi·ca (mī′kə), n. any member of a group of minerals, hydrous disilicates of aluminum with other bases, chiefly potassium, magnesium, iron, and lithium, that separate readily into thin, tough, often transparent, and usually elastic laminae. [t. NL, special use of L *mica* crumb, grain, little bit]

mi·ca·ceous (mī kā′shəs), adj. **1.** consisting of, containing, or resembling mica. **2.** of or pertaining to mica.

Mi·cah (mī′kə), n. **1.** a Hebrew prophet of the 8th century B.C. **2.** the sixth book of the "Minor Prophets," in the Old Testament, which bears his name.

Mi·caw·ber (mĭ kô′bər), n. **Wilkins,** (in Dickens'

David Copperfield) the improvident, chronically unlucky father of a family, who persists in his optimism.

mice (mīs), *n.* pl. of **mouse**.

mi·celle (mī·sĕl′), *n. Phys. Chem.* a colloidal particle formed by the reversible aggregation of dissolved molecules. Electrically charged micelles form colloidal electrolytes, as soaps and detergents. [t. NL: m. *micella*, dim. of L *mica* crumb]

Mich., 1. Michaelmas. 2. Michigan.

Mi·chael (mī′kəl), *n.* a militant archangel. Dan. 10:13.

Michael I, (*Mihai*) born 1921, king of Rumania, 1927–30 and 1940–47.

Mich·ael·mas (mĭk′əl məs), *n. Chiefly Brit.* 1. a festival celebrated on Sept. 29, in honor of the archangel Michael. 2. Sept. 29 (**Michaelmas day**). [OE (*Sanct*) *Michaeles masse* St. Michael's mass]

Michaelmas daisy, *Brit.* an aster.

Mi·chel·an·ge·lo (mī′kəl ăn′jə lō′, mĭk′əl-; *It.* mē′kĕl än′jĕ lō′), *n.* (*Michelangolo, Michelangelo Buonarroti*) 1475–1564, Italian sculptor, painter, architect, and poet.

Mi·che·let (mēsh lĕ′), *n.* **Jules** (zhyl), 1798–1874, French historian.

Mi·chel·son (mī′kəl sən), *n.* **Albert Abraham,** 1852–1931, U.S. physicist, born in Germany.

Mich·i·gan (mĭsh′ə gən), *n.* 1. a State in the N central United States. 7,823,194 (1960); 58,216 sq. mi. *Cap.:* Lansing. *Abbr.:* Mich. 2. **Lake,** a lake between Wisconsin and Michigan: one of the five Great Lakes. ab. 22,400 sq. mi.

Michigan City, a city in NW Indiana: a port on Lake Michigan. 36,653 (1960).

Mick·ey (mĭk′ĭ), *n., pl.* **-eys.** a drink to which a sleeping drug has been added. Also, **Mickey Finn** (fĭn).

Mic·kie·wicz (mĭts kyĕ′vĭch), *n.* **Adam** (ä′däm), 1798–1855, Polish poet.

mick·le (mĭk′əl), *adj. Archaic or Brit. Dial.* great; large; much. [ME *mikel,* OE *micul,* var. of *micel* MUCH]

Mic·mac (mĭk′măk), *n.* 1. (*pl.*) a tribe of Algonquian Indians inhabiting the southern shores of the Gulf of St. Lawrence. 2. a member of this tribe.

mi·cra (mī′krə), *n.* a pl. of **micron.**

mi·cri·fy (mī′krə fī′), *v.t.,* **-fied, -fying.** to make small or insignificant. [f. MICR(O)- + -IFY; modeled on MAGNIFY]

micro-, a word element meaning "very small," used to mean "enlarging" (*microphone*), as a combining form of **microscopic** (*microörganism*), and to represent the millionth part of a unit (*microgram*). Also, before vowels, **micr-.** [t. Gk.: m. *mikro-,* comb. form of *mikrós* small]

mi·cro·a·nal·y·sis (mī′krō ə năl′ə sĭs), *n., pl.* **-ses** (-sēz′). *Chem.* the analysis of extremely small quantities. —**mi·cro·an·a·lyt·i·cal** (mī′krō ăn′ə lĭt′ə kəl), *adj.*

mi·cro·bar·o·graph (mī′krō băr′ə grăf′, -gräf′), *n. Meteorol.* a barograph for recording minute fluctuations of atmospheric pressure.

mi·crobe (mī′krōb), *n.* 1. a microörganism, usually one of vegetable nature; a germ. 2. a bacterium, esp. one causing disease. [t. F, f. Gk.: m. *mikro-* MICRO- + m.s. *bíos* life] —**mi·cro·bi·al** (mī krō′bĭ əl), **mi·cro′bic,** *adj.*

mi·cro·bi·ol·o·gy (mī′krō bī ŏl′ə jĭ), *n.* the science concerned with the occurrence, activities, and utilization of the extremely small, microscopic and submicroscopic organisms. —**mi′cro·bi·o·log′i·cal,** *adj.* —**mi′cro·bi·ol′o·gist,** *n.*

mi·cro·ce·phal·ic (mī′krō sə făl′ĭk), *adj.* 1. *Craniom.* having a skull with a small cranial capacity. 2. *Pathol.* having an abnormally small skull. Also, **mi·cro·ceph·a·lous** (mī′krō sĕf′ə ləs). —**mi′cro·ceph′a·ly,** *n.*

mi·cro·chem·is·try (mī′krō kĕm′ĭs trĭ), *n.* chemistry as concerned with minute or microscopic objects or quantities. —**mi′cro·chem′i·cal,** *adj.*

mi·cro·cli·ma·tol·o·gy (mī′krō klī′mə tŏl′ə jĭ), *n.* a branch of climatology dealing with studies of small-scale climatic conditions, as local climatic changes induced by planting trees as a windbreak.

mi·cro·cline (mī′krə klīn′), *n.* a mineral of the feldspar group. potassium aluminum silicate, KAlSi₃O₈, identical in composition with orthoclase but differing in crystal system, used in making porcelain. [t. G: m. *mikroklin,* f. Gk.: *mikro-* MICRO- + s. *klīneīn* incline]

mi·cro·coc·cus (mī′krə kŏk′əs), *n., pl.* **-cocci** (-kŏk′sī). any member of the genus *Micrococcus,* comprising globular or oval bacterial organisms, of which certain species cause disease, and others produce fermentation, coloration, etc. [t. NL. See MICRO-, -COCCUS]

mi·cro·cop·y (mī′krə kŏp′ĭ), *n., pl.* **-copies.** a greatly reduced photographic copy of a book page, etc., usually read by enlargement on a ground-glass screen.

mi·cro·cosm (mī′krə kŏz′əm), *n.* 1. a little world (opposed to *macrocosm*). 2. anything regarded as a world in miniature. 3. man viewed as an epitome of the universe. [t. F: m. *microcosme,* t. LL: m.s. *microcosmus,* t. LGk.: m. *mikrós kósmos* little world] —**mi′cro·cos′mic, mi′cro·cos′mi·cal,** *adj.*

microcosmic salt, *Chem.* a phosphate of sodium and ammonium, NaNH₄HPO₄4H₂O, orig. obtained from human urine, much used as a blowpipe flux in testing metallic oxides.

mi·cro·crys·tal·line (mī′krō krĭs′tə lĭn, -līn′), *adj.* minutely crystalline; composed of microscopic crystals.

mi·cro·cyte (mī′krə sīt′), *n.* 1. a minute cell or corpuscle. 2. *Pathol.* an abnormally small-sized red blood cell, usually deficient in hemoglobin.

mi·cro·de·tec·tor (mī′krō dĭ tĕk′tər), *n.* 1. an instrument measuring small quantities or changes. 2. *Elect.* a sensitive galvanometer.

mi·cro·dont (mī′krə dŏnt′), *adj.* 1. having small or short teeth. —*n.* 2. a small or short tooth. —**mi′cro·don′tous,** *adj.*

mi·cro·far·ad (mī′krō făr′əd, -ăd), *n. Elect.* a convenient unit of capacitance in common use, equal to one millionth of a farad.

mi·cro·film (mī′krə fĭlm′), *n.* 1. a narrow film, esp. of motion-picture stock, on which microcopies are made. 2. microphotograph.

mi·cro·ga·mete (mī′krō gə mēt′), *n. Biol.* (in heterogamous reproduction) the smaller of the two gametes, usually the male cell.

mi·cro·gram (mī′krō grăm′), *n.* a small unit of mass or weight used in microchemistry, equal to a millionth part of a gram. *Abbr.:* μg. Also, *esp. Brit.,* **mi′cro·gramme′.**

mi·cro·graph (mī′krō grăf′, -gräf′), *n.* 1. an instrument for executing extremely minute writing or engraving. 2. a photograph or a drawing of an object as seen through a microscope.

mi·crog·ra·phy (mī krŏg′rə fĭ), *n.* 1. the description or delineation of microscopic objects. 2. examination or study with the microscope. 3. the art or practice of writing in very small characters. —**mi·cro·graph·ic** (mī′krō grăf′ĭk), *adj.*

mi·cro·groove (mī′krə grōōv′), *n.* 1. (in a phonograph record) a needle groove about ½ the conventional width, permitting more grooves than is possible on conventional records. 2. a record with such grooves. 3. (*cap.*) a trademark for such a groove or record.

mi·cro·inch (mī′krō ĭnch′), *n.* a unit of length equal to a millionth of an inch.

mi·cro·li·ter (mī′krō lē′tər), *n.* a unit of capacity equal to a millionth of a liter, used esp. in microchemistry. *Abbr.:* μ l or λ. Also, *esp. Brit.,* **mi′cro·li′tre.**

mi·crol·o·gy (mī krŏl′ə jĭ), *n.* excessive attention to petty details or distinctions. [t. Gk.: m.s. *mikrología.* See MICRO-, -LOGY]

mi·crom·e·ter (mī krŏm′ə tər), *n.* 1. any of various devices for measuring minute distances, angles, etc., as in connection with a telescope or microscope. 2. a micrometer caliper. [t. F: m. *micromètre,* f. *micro-* MICRO- + *-mètre* -METER]

micrometer caliper, an instrument for measuring thickness (as of wire or sheet metal) with precision.

micrometer screw, a screw with a very fine thread and a graduated head, used in micrometers, etc.

mi·crom·e·try (mī krŏm′ə trĭ), *n.* the method or art of measuring with a micrometer.

mi·cro·mil·li·me·ter (mī′krō mĭl′ə mē′tər), *n.* the millionth part of a millimeter; a millimicron. Also, *esp. Brit.,* **mi′cro·mil′li·me′tre.**

mi·cro·mo·tion (mī′krō mō′shən), *n.* a motion, esp. a periodic one, of very short duration or length.

mi·cron (mī′krŏn), *n., pl.* **-cra** (-krə), **-cras.** 1. the millionth part of a meter. *Symbol:* μ. 2. *Phys. Chem.* a colloidal particle whose diameter is between .2 and 10 μ. Also, **mikron.** [t. NL, t. Gk.: m. *mikrŏn* (neut. adj.) small]

Mi·cro·ne·sia (mī′krə nē′zhə, -shə), *n.* groups of small Pacific islands, N of the equator, E of the Philippine Islands: the main groups included are the Marianas, the Caroline, and the Marshall islands. [f. MICRO- + s. Gk. *nēsos* island + -IA]

Mi·cro·ne·sian (mī′krə nē′zhən, -shən), *adj.* 1. of Micronesia, its inhabitants, or their languages. —*n.* 2. a native of Micronesia. 3. any of the Austronesian languages or dialects spoken in the Micronesian islands.

mi·cro·ör·gan·ism (mī′krō ôr′gə nĭz′əm), *n.* a microscopic (animal or vegetable) organism.

mi·cro·par·a·site (mī′krō păr′ə sīt′), *n.* a parasitic microörganism. —**mi·cro·par·a·sit·ic** (mī′krō păr′ə sĭt′ĭk), *adj.*

mi·cro·phone (mī′krə fōn′), *n.* an instrument which is capable of transforming the air-pressure waves of sound into changes in electric currents or voltages. Qualifying adjectives, as *condenser, crystal, velocity,* etc., describe the method of developing the electric quantity. —**mi·cro·phon·ic** (mī′krə fŏn′ĭk), *adj.*

mi·cro·pho·to·graph (mī′krō fō′tə grăf′, -gräf′), *n.* 1. a small photograph requiring optical enlargement to render it visible in detail. 2. *Library Science.* a film reproduction of a large or bulky publication, as a file of newspapers, used to conserve space or to copy material which is difficult to obtain. 3. a photomicrograph. —**mi′cro·pho′to·graph′ic,** *adj.* —**mi·cro·pho·tog·ra·phy** (mī′krō fə tŏg′rə fĭ), *n.*

mi·cro·print (mī′krō prĭnt′), *n.* a microphotograph reproduced in print and read by a magnifying device.

mi·cro·pyle (mī′krə pīl′), *n.* 1. *Zool.* any minute opening in the coverings of an ovum, through which spermatozoa may gain access to the interior. 2. *Bot.* the minute orifice or opening in the integuments of an ovule. [t. F, f. Gk.: m. *mikro-* MICRO- + *pyle* gate, orifice] —**mi′cro·py′lar,** *adj.*

mi·cro·py·rom·e·ter (mī′krō pī rŏm′ə tər), *n.* an optical pyrometer for use with small glowing bodies.

micros., microscopy.

mi·cro·scope (mī′krə skōp′), *n.* an optical instrument having a magnifying lens or a combination of lenses for inspecting objects too small to be seen, or to be seen distinctly and in detail, by the naked eye. [t. NL: m.s. *microscopium*, f. *micro-* MICRO- + m. s. Gk. *skopein* view + *-ium* -IUM]

mi·cro·scop·ic (mī′krə skōp′ĭk), *adj.* **1.** so small as to be invisible or indistinct without the use of the microscope. **2.** very small; tiny. **3.** of or pertaining to the microscope or its use. **4.** performing the work of a microscope. **5.** suggestive of the use of the microscope: *microscopic exactness.* Also, **mi′·cro·scop′i·cal.** —**mi′·cro·scop′·i·cal·ly**, *adv.*

mi·cros·co·py (mī krŏs′kə pī, mī′krə skō′pī), *n.* **1.** the use of the microscope. **2.** microscopic investigation. —**mi·cros·co·pist** (mī krŏs′kə pĭst, mī′krə skō′pĭst), *n.*

Monocular microscope A. Eyepiece; B. Adjusting screw; C. Tube; D. Objective; E. Stage; F. Substage; G. Illuminating mirror

mi·cro·seism (mī′krō sī′zəm, -səm), *n. Geol.* a vibration of the ground recorded by seismographs but not believed to be due to an earthquake. [f. MICRO- + s. Gk. *seismós* earthquake] —**mi·cro·seis·mic** (mī′krō sīz′mĭk, -sīs′-), **mi′·cro·seis′mi·cal**, *adj.*

mi·cro·some (mī′krə sōm′), *n. Biol.* one of the minute granules in the protoplasm of animal and plant cells. [t. NL: m.s. *microsōma*. See MICRO-, -SOME[3]]

mi·cro·spo·ran·gi·um (mī′krō spō răn′jī əm), *n., pl.* **-gia** (-jī ə). *Bot.* a sporangium containing microspores. [t. NL. See MICRO-, SPORANGIUM]

mi·cro·spore (mī′krə spōr′), *n. Bot.* **1.** the smaller of two kinds of spores produced by some pteridophytes. **2.** a pollen grain.

mi·cro·spo·ro·phyll (mī′krə spōr′ə fĭl), *n. Bot.* a sporophyll bearing microsporangia.

mi·cro·stom·a·tous (mī′krə stŏm′ə təs, -stō′mə-), *adj.* having or pertaining to a very small mouth. Also, **mi·cros·to·mous** (mī krŏs′tə məs). [f. MICRO- + s. Gk. *stóma* mouth + -OUS]

mi·cro·tome (mī′krə tōm′), *n.* an instrument for cutting very thin sections, as of organic tissue, for microscopic examination.

mi·crot·o·my (mī krŏt′ə mī), *n.* the cutting of very thin sections, as with the microtome. —**mi·cro·tom·ic** (mī′krə tŏm′ĭk), **mi′·cro·tom′i·cal**, *adj.* —**mi·crot′o·mist**, *n.*

mi·cro·waves (mī′krō wāvz′), *n.pl. Electronics.* electromagnetic waves of extremely high frequency, approximately comprising the wave-length range from 50 cm. to 1 mm.

mic·tu·rate (mĭk′chə rāt′), *v.i.*, **-rated, -rating.** to pass urine; urinate. [f. s. L *micturīre* desire to make water + -ATE[1]]

mic·tu·ri·tion (mĭk′chə rĭsh′ən), *n.* act of passing urine. [f. s. L *micturītus*, pp. of *micturīre* desire to urinate + -ION]

mid[1] (mĭd), *adj.* **1.** at or near its middle point: *in mid air.* **2.** occupying a middle place or position: *in the mid nineties of the last century.* **3.** *Phonet.* having a tongue position intermediate between high and low: *beet, bet,* and *hot* have high, mid, and low vowels respectively. —*n.* **4.** *Archaic.* the middle. [ME; OE *midd,* c. OHG *mitti,* Icel. *midhr,* Goth. *midjis* middle; akin to L *medius,* Gk. *mésos,* Skt. *madhya* middle]

mid[2] (mĭd), *prep.* amid. Also, **'mid.**

mid-, a combining form of "middle."

Mid., Midshipman.

mid., middle.

Mi·das (mī′dəs), *n.* **1.** *Gk. Legend.* a Phrygian king, son of Gordius, who was given by Dionysus the power of turning into gold whatever he touched. **2.** a man of great wealth or great moneymaking ability.

mid·brain (mĭd′brān′), *n.* the mesencephalon.

mid·day (mĭd′dā′), *n.* **1.** the middle of the day; noon. —*adj.* **2.** of or pertaining to the middle part of the day. [ME; OE *middæg*]

mid·den (mĭd′ən), *n.* **1.** *Archaic or Dial.* a dunghill or refuse heap. **2.** *Brit.* a kitchen midden. [ME *myd(d)yng,* t. Scand.; cf. Dan. *mödding*]

mid·dle (mĭd′əl), *adj., n., v.,* **-dled, -dling.** —*adj.* **1.** equally distant from extremes or limits: *the middle point of a line.* **2.** intervening or intermediate: *the middle distance.* **3.** medium: *a man of middle size.* **4.** (*cap.*) (in the history of a language) intermediate between periods classified as Old and New or Modern: *Middle English.* **5.** *Gram.* (in some languages) denoting a voice of verb inflection, in which the subject is represented as acting on or for itself, in contrast to the active voice in which the subject acts, and the passive, in which the subject is acted upon, as in Greek *gráphomai* "I write for myself," *gráphō* "I write." **6.** *Rare.* at or near its middle. —*n.* **7.** the point, part, etc., equidistant from extremes or limits. **8.** the waist, or middle part of the human body. **9.** something intermediate; a mean. —*v.t., v.i.* **10.** *Chiefly Naut.* to fold in half. [ME and OE *middel,* c. G *mittel*]

—**Syn. 7.** MIDDLE, CENTER, MIDST indicate something from which two or more other things are (approximately or exactly) equally distant. MIDDLE denotes the point or part equidistant from or intermediate between extremes or limits in space or in time (activity): *the middle of a road.* CENTER, a more precise word, is ordinarily applied to a point within circular, globular, or regular bodies, or wherever a similar exactness appears to exist (*the center of the earth*); it may also be used metaphorically (still suggesting the core of a sphere): *center of interest.* MIDST usually suggests that a person or thing is closely surrounded or encompassed on all sides, esp. by that which is thick or dense: *the midst of a storm.*

middle age, the period between youth and old age.

mid·dle-aged (mĭd′əl ājd′), *adj.* **1.** intermediate in age between youth and old age; commonly, from about 45 to about 60 years old. **2.** characteristic of or suitable for middle-aged people.

Middle Ages, the time in European history between classical antiquity and the Italian Renaissance (from the late 5th century to about A.D. 1350); sometimes restricted to the later part of this period (after 1100); sometimes extended to 1450 or 1500.

Middle Atlantic States, New York, New Jersey, and Pennsylvania.

middle C, *Music.* the note indicated by the first leger line above the bass staff and the first below the treble staff.

middle class, 1. the class of the people intermediate between the classes of higher and lower social rank or standing. **2.** (in Great Britain) the class socially and conventionally intermediate between the aristocratic class and the laboring class. **3.** an intermediate class.

mid·dle-class (mĭd′əl klăs′, -kläs′), *adj.* belonging or pertaining to or characteristic of a middle class, esp., the social middle class; bourgeois.

Middle Congo, a former overseas territory in the SE part of French Equatorial Africa: now an independent republic. See Congo (def. 2b).

middle distance, *Painting, etc.* the space between the foreground and the background or distance.

middle ear, *Anat.* the tympanum.

Middle East, 1. the lands from the E shores of the Mediterranean and Aegean to India: the Near East less the Balkan States. **2.** (formerly) the area including Iran, Afghanistan, India, Tibet, and Burma.

Middle English, the English language of the period 1100–1500.

Middle French, the French language of the period 1400–1600.

Middle Greek, Medieval Greek.

Middle High German, the High German language from 1100 to 1450.

Middle Irish, the Irish language of the later Middle Ages.

Middle Kingdom, 1. Also, **Middle Empire.** the second great period in the history of the ancient Egyptian kingdom, about 2200 B.C. to 1690 B.C., comprising Dynasties XI–XIV. **2.** the Chinese term for China proper (the 18 inner provinces). **3.** the Chinese Empire (from its supposed position in the center of the earth).

mid·dle·man (mĭd′əl măn′), *n., pl.* **-men. 1.** an intermediary who distributes goods or securities from producer to consumer on h s own account and risk. **2.** one who acts as an intermediary between others.

mid·dle·most (mĭd′əl mōst′), *adj.* midmost.

mid·dle-of-the-road·er (mĭd′əl əv thə rōd′ər), *n.* one who advocates or follows a moderate course in politics, religion, etc.

Mid·dles·brough (mĭd′əlz brə), *n.* a seaport in NE England, on the Tees estuary. 149,900 (est. 1956).

Mid·dle·sex (mĭd′əl sĕks′), *n.* a county in SE England, bordering W and N London. 2,269,315 pop. (1951). 232 sq. mi.

Middle Temple. See Inns of Court.

middle term, *Logic.* that term of a syllogism which appears twice in the premises, but is eliminated from the conclusion.

Mid·dle·ton (mĭd′əl tən), *n.* **Thomas,** c1570–1627, English dramatist.

Mid·dle·town (mĭd′əl toun′), *n.* **1.** a city in SW Ohio, on the Miami river. 42,115 (1960). **2.** a city in central Connecticut, on the Connecticut river. 33,250 (1960). **3.** a city in SE New York. 23,475 (1960).

mid·dle·weight (mĭd′əl wāt′), *n.* **1.** one of average weight. **2.** a boxer or other contestant intermediate in weight between a light heavyweight and a welterweight, with a maximum weight of 160 pounds.

Middle West, that region of the United States bounded on the E and W by the Allegheny Mountains and the Rocky Mountains, and on the S by the Ohio river and the S extremities of Missouri and Kansas. —**Middle Western.** —**Middle Westerner.**

mid·dling (mĭd′lĭng), *adj.* **1.** medium in size, quality, grade, rank, etc.; moderately large, good, etc. **2.** *Colloq. or Dial.* in fairly good health. —*adv.* **3.** *Colloq. or Dial.* moderately; fairly. —*n.* **4.** (*pl.*) any of various products or commodities of intermediate quality, grade, etc., as the coarser particles of ground wheat mingled with bran. —**mid′dling·ly**, *adv.*

mid·dy (mĭd′ī), *n., pl.* **-dies. 1.** *Colloq.* a midshipman. **2.** a middy blouse.

middy blouse, a loose blouse with a sailor collar, and often extending below the waistline to terminate in a broad band or fold, worn by children, young girls, etc.

Mid·gard (mĭd′gärd), *n. Scand. Myth.* the abode of humanity, joined to heaven by the rainbow bridge of the gods. Also, **Mid·garth** (mĭd′gärth); *Icelandic,* **Mithgarthr.**

midge (mĭj), *n.* **1.** any of numerous minute flies (order *Diptera*), esp. those of the family *Chironomidae.* See **gnat. 2.** a small or diminutive person. [ME *mydge,* OE *mycg,* c. G *mücke*]

midg·et (mĭj′ĭt), *n.* **1.** a very small person. **2.** something very small of its kind. [f. MIDGE + -ET] —**Syn. 1.** See **dwarf.**

mid·gut (mĭd′gŭt′), *n.* the middle part of the alimentary canal.

Mi·di (mē dē′), *n.* **1.** the south. **2.** the south of France. [F: midday, the south, f. *mi* half (g. L *medius*) + *di* day (g. L *dies*)]

Mid·i·an (mĭd′ĭ ən), *n.* the fourth son of Abraham. Gen. 25:2.

Mid·i·an·ite (mĭd′ĭ ə nīt′), *n.* a member of a desert tribe of northwest Arabia near the Gulf of Aqaba, descended from Midian. Ex. 2:15–22; Judges 6–8.

mid·i·ron (mĭd′ī′ərn), *n. Golf.* an iron club whose face has a medium degree of slope, used for far approaches.

mid·land (mĭd′lənd), *n.* **1.** the middle or interior part of a country. —*adj.* **2.** in or of the midland; inland. **Mid·lands** (mĭd′ləndz), *n. pl.* the central part of England; the midland counties.

mid·leg (*n.* mĭd′lĕg′; *adv.* -lĕg′), *n.* **1.** the middle part of the leg. **2.** one of the second pair of legs of an insect. —*adv.* **3.** at the middle of the leg.

Mid·lo·thi·an (mĭd lō′thĭ ən), *n.* a county in SE Scotland. 572,800 pop.(est. 1956); 366 sq. mi. *Co. seat:* Edinburgh. Formerly, **Edinburgh.**

mid·most (mĭd′mōst′), *adj.* **1.** being in the very middle; middlemost; middle. **2.** at or near its middle point. —*adv.* **3.** in the midmost part; in the midst.

mid·night (mĭd′nīt′), *n.* **1.** the middle of the night; 12 o'clock at night. —*adj.* **2.** of or pertaining to midnight. **3.** resembling midnight, as in darkness. **4. burn the midnight oil,** to study or work far into the night. —**mid′night·ly,** *adj., adv.*

midnight sun, the sun visible at midnight in midsummer in arctic and antarctic regions.

mid·noon (mĭd′nōōn′), *n.* midday; noon.

mid·rash (mĭd′räsh), *n., pl.* **midrashim** (mĭd rä′shĕm), **midrashoth** (mĭd rä′shōth). *Hebrew Literature.* **1.** the traditional Jewish interpretation of Scripture, whether of its legal or its nonlegal portions. **2.** (*cap.*) a series of books, of various titles, containing the traditional Jewish interpretation of Scripture, arranged in the form of commentaries or homilies upon certain books of the Bible or upon selected passages from various books of the Bible. [t. Heb.: commentary]

mid·rib (mĭd′rĭb′), *n. Bot.* the central or middle rib of a leaf.

mid·riff (mĭd′rĭf), *n.* **1.** the diaphragm (in the body). **2.** the middle part of the body, between the chest and the waist. **3.** a dress which exposes this part of the body. —*adj.* **4.** denoting or pertaining to such a dress. [ME *mydryf,* OE *midhrif,* f. *midd* mid + *hrif* belly]

mid·sag·it·tal plane (mĭd′săj′ə təl), *Craniom., Cephalom.* a plane passing through the nasion at right angles to the biparionic or the bitragal plane, when the skull or head is oriented in the Frankfurt Horizontal.

mid·ship (mĭd′shĭp′), *adj.* in or belonging to the middle part of a ship.

mid·ship·man (mĭd′shĭp′mən), *n., pl.* -**men. 1.** *U.S. Navy and Coast Guard.* one of the rank held by young men while attending, and before graduation from, the service academies. **2.** *Brit. Navy.* **a.** an officer of the rank held by young men on leaving the government naval schools. **b.** (formerly) one of a class of boys or young men who had various minor duties and who formed the group from which officers were chosen.

mid·ship·mite (mĭd′shĭp mīt′), *n.* (in humorous use) a midshipman.

mid·ships (mĭd′shĭps′), *adv.* amidships.

midst¹ (mĭdst), *n.* **1.** the position of anything surrounded by other things or parts, or occurring in the middle of a period of time, course of action, etc. **2.** the middle point, part, or stage. **3. in our** (your, their) **midst,** in the midst of us (you, them). [? f. *mids* middle + meaningless -*t,* or f. MID¹ + -EST] —**Syn. 1.** See **middle.**

midst² (mĭdst), *prep. Poetic.* amidst.

mid·stream (mĭd′strēm′), *n.* the middle of the stream.

mid·sum·mer (mĭd′sŭm′ər), *n.* the middle of summer.

Midsummer Night's Dream, a comedy (1595) by Shakespeare.

mid·Vic·to·ri·an (mĭd′vĭk tôr′ĭ ən), *adj.* **1.** of, pertaining to, or characteristic of the middle portion of the reign of Queen Victoria (reigned 1837–1901) in England: *mid-Victorian writers or ideas.* —*n.* **2.** a person, as a writer, belonging to the mid-Victorian time. **3.** a person of mid-Victorian ideas, tastes, etc.

mid·way (mĭd′wā′), *adv., adj.* **1.** in or to the middle of the way or distance; halfway. —*n.* **2.** a place or part situated midway. **3.** a place for side shows and other

amusements at any fair or the like. [ME *mydwaye,* OE *midweg*]

Mid·way (mĭd′wā′), *n.* airport in Chicago.

Midway Islands, several islets in the N Pacific, ab. 1200 mi. NW of Hawaii: the Japanese were defeated in a naval engagement near here, June, 1942. 416 pop. (1950); 2 sq. mi.

mid·week (mĭd′wēk′), *n.* **1.** the middle of the week. **2.** (*cap.*) (among the Quakers) Wednesday. —*adj.* **3.** occurring in the middle of the week.

mid·week·ly (mĭd′wēk′lĭ), *adj.* **1.** midweek. —*adv.* **2.** in the middle of the week.

Mid·west (mĭd′wĕst′), *U.S.* —*n.* **1.** Middle West. —*adj.* **2.** Middle Western. Also, **Mid·west·ern** (mĭd′wĕs′tərn). —**Mid′west′ern·er,** *n.*

mid·wife (mĭd′wīf′), *n., pl.* -**wives** (-wīvz′). a woman who assists women in childbirth. [ME, f. *mid* with, adv. (OE *mid,* c. G *mit*) + WIFE]

mid·wife·ry (mĭd′wĭf′ə rĭ, -wĭf′rĭ), *n.* the art or practice of assisting women in childbirth.

mid·win·ter (mĭd′wĭn′tər), *n.* the middle of winter.

mid·year (mĭd′yĭr′), *n.* **1.** the middle of the year. **2.** (*pl.*) *Colloq.* midyear examinations. —*adj.* **3.** pertaining to or occurring in midyear.

mien (mēn), *n.* air, bearing, or aspect, as showing character, feeling, etc.: *a man of noble mien.* [der. *demean,* v., influenced by F *mine* aspect, t. Breton: m. *min* beak]

miff (mĭf), *Colloq.* —*n.* **1.** petulant displeasure; a petty quarrel. —*v.t.* **2.** to give offense to; offend. —*v.i.* **3.** to take offense. [? imit. of an exclamation of disgust]

might¹ (mīt), *v.* pt. of **may.** [ME; OE *mihte*]

might² (mīt), *n.* **1.** power to do or accomplish; ability; effective power or force of any kind. **2.** superior power: *the doctrine that might makes right.* [ME *myghte,* OE *miht, meaht,* c. G *macht*] —**Syn. 1.** force, puissance. **2.** See **strength.** —**Ant. 1.** powerlessness.

might·i·ly (mī′tə lĭ), *adv.* **1.** in a mighty manner; powerfully; vigorously. **2.** to a great extent or degree; very much.

might·y (mī′tĭ), *adj.,* **mightier, mightiest. 1.** having, characterized by, or showing might or power: *mighty rulers.* **2.** of great size; huge: *a mighty oak.* **3.** *Colloq.* great in amount, extent, degree, or importance. —*adv.* **4.** *Colloq.* very: *to be mighty pleased.* —**might′i·ness,** *n.* —**Syn. 1.** See **powerful.**

mi·gnon (mĭn′yŏn; *Fr.* mē nyôN′), *adj. masc.* small and pretty; delicately pretty. [t. F, der. stem *mign*– Cf. Celt. *mino* tender, soft] —**mi·gnonne** (mĭn′yŏn; *Fr.* mē nyôN′), *adj. fem.*

mi·gnon·ette (mĭn′yə nĕt′), *n.* **1.** a plant, *Reseda odorata,* common in gardens, having racemes of small, fragrant, greenish-white flowers with prominent reddish-yellow or brownish anthers. **2.** light green as of reseda plants. [t. F: m. *mignonnette,* dim. of *mignon* MIGNON]

mi·graine (mī′grān, mĭ grān′), *n.* a paroxysmal headache confined to one side of the head and usually associated with nausea; hemicrania. [t. F. See MEGRIM]

mi·grant (mī′grənt), *adj.* **1.** migrating; migratory. —*n.* **2.** one who or that which migrates, as a migratory bird. [t. L: s. *migrans,* ppr.]

mi·grate (mī′grāt), *v.i.,* -**grated,** -**grating. 1.** to go from one country, region, or place of abode to settle in another. **2.** to pass periodically from one region to another, as certain birds, fishes, and animals. **3.** (at English universities) to change from one college to another. [t. L: m.s. *migrātus,* pp.] —**mi·gra·tor,** *n.* —**Syn. 1.** MIGRATE, EMIGRATE, IMMIGRATE are used of changing one's abode from one country or part of a country to another. To MIGRATE is to make such a move either once or repeatedly: *to migrate from Ireland to the United States.* To EMIGRATE is to leave a country, usually one's own (and take up residence in another): *each year many people emigrate from Europe.* To IMMIGRATE is to enter and settle in a country not one's own: *there are many inducements to immigrate to South America.* MIGRATE is applied both to people or to animals that move from one region to another, esp. periodically; the other terms are generally applied to movements of men.

mi·gra·tion (mī grā′shən), *n.* **1.** the action of migrating: *the right of migration.* **2.** a migratory movement: *preparations for the migration.* **3.** a number or body of persons or animals migrating together. **4.** *Chem.* a movement or change of place of atoms within a molecule. [t. L: s. *migrātiō*] —**mi·gra′tion·al,** *adj.*

migration of ions, *Chem.* the movement of ions toward an electrode, during electrolysis.

mi·gra·to·ry (mī′grə tôr′ĭ), *adj.* **1.** migrating: *migratory species.* **2.** pertaining to a migration: *migratory movements of birds.* **3.** roving or nomad.

mi·ka·do (mĭ kä′dō), *n., pl.* -**dos. 1.** (often *cap.*) a title of the emperor of Japan. **2.** (*cap.*) an operetta (1885) by Gilbert and Sullivan. [t. Jap.: lit., exalted gate]

mike (mīk), *n. Slang.* a microphone.

mi·kron (mī′krŏn), *n., pl.* -**kra, -kras.** micron.

mil (mĭl), *n.* **1.** a unit of length equal to .001 of an inch, used in measuring the diameter of wires. **2.** a military unit of angle equal to the angle subtended by an arc of 1/6400 of a circumference. This is the **artillery mil;** it has practically superseded the nearly equivalent **infantry mil,** defined as the angle subtended by an arc of 1/1000 of the radius. **3.** *Pharm.* a milliliter (.001 of a liter), or cubic centimeter. **4.** *Palestine.* a bronze coin equal to 0.001 of an English pound. [short for L *millēsimus* thousandth]

M

M. Midrib

mil., 1. military. 2. militia.

mi·la·dy (mĭ lā′dĭ), n., pl. -dies. a Continental rendering of English *my lady*, used in speaking to or of an English lady. Also, **mi·la′di.**

mil·age (mī′lĭj), n. mileage.

Mi·lan (mĭ lăn′, mĭl′ən), n. a city in N Italy, in Lombardy: famous cathedral. 1,303,000 (est. 1954). Italian, **Mi·la·no** (mē lä′nô). —**Mil·an·ese** (mĭl′ə nēz′, -nēs′), adj., n.

Mi·laz·zo (mē lät′tsô), n. a seaport in NE Sicily. 22,296 (1951).

milch (mĭlch), adj. denoting a cow, goat, or other milk-giving animal. [ME *milche*; akin to MILK]

mild (mīld), adj. 1. amiably gentle or temperate in feeling or behavior toward others. 2. characterized by or showing such gentleness, as manners, speech, etc. 3. not cold, severe, or extreme, as air, weather, etc. 4. gentle or moderate in force or effect: *mild penalties*. 5. softly shining, as light, etc. 6. not sharp, pungent, or strong: *mild flavor*. 7. not acute, as disease, etc. 8. moderate in intensity, degree, or character: *mild regret*. 9. *Brit. Dial.* easily worked, as soil, stone, wood, etc. 10. *Obs.* kind or gracious. [ME and OE, c. G *mild*] —**mild′ly,** adv. —**mild′ness,** n. —**Syn.** 2. See **gentle.** 3. temperate, moderate, clement. —**Ant.** 1. forceful.

mil·dew (mĭl′dū′, -dōō′), n. 1. a plant disease usually characterized by a whitish coating or a discoloration on the surface, caused by any of various parasitic fungi. 2. any of these fungi. 3. similar coating or discoloration, due to fungi, on cotton and linen fabrics, paper, leather, etc., when exposed to moisture. —v.t., v.i. 4. to affect or become affected with mildew. [ME; OE *mildēaw, meledēaw*, lit., honeydew] —**mil′dew′y,** adj.

mile (mīl), n. 1. a unit of distance: **a.** the statute mile, used as a unit of distances on land in the English-speaking countries, equal to 5280 ft. or 1760 yards. **b.** nautical, or geographical, mile, officially fixed in the U.S. at 6,080.20 feet, and in Great Britain at 6080 feet. **c.** the international nautical or air mile, a unit of distance in sea and air navigation, equal to 1.852 kilometers, (6,076.097 feet), recommended by the International Hydrographic Bureau for international adoption and adopted by a number of countries. 2. other units of varying length at different periods and in different countries, e.g., the old **Roman mile** having been equivalent to about 1620 yds. or the present **Swedish mile** being equal to 10 km. [ME *myle*, OE *mīl*, t. L: m. *mīlia (passuum)* a thousand (paces)]

mile·age (mī′lĭj), n. 1. the aggregate number of miles made or traveled over in a given time. 2. length, extent, or distance in miles. 3. an allowance for traveling expenses at a fixed rate per mile, esp. to a public official. 4. a fixed charge per mile, as for railroad transportation. 5. a mileage ticket. Also, **milage.**

mileage ticket, 1. a book or ticket of coupons good for a certain number of miles of transportation at a fixed rate per mile. 2. one of the coupons.

mile·post (mīl′pōst′), n. a post set up to mark distance by miles, as along a highway.

mil·er (mī′lər), n. one who is trained to race a mile.

mi·les glo·ri·o·sus (mī′lēz glôr′ĭ ō′səs), pl. **milites gloriosi** (mĭl′ĭ tēz′ glôr′ĭ ō′sī). *Latin.* a braggart soldier.

mile·stone (mīl′stōn′), n. 1. a stone set up to mark distance by miles, as along a highway or other line of travel. 2. a birthday or some event regarded as marking a stage in the journey of life.

Mi·le·tus (mī lē′təs), n. an ancient city on the Aegean coast of Asia Minor. —**Mi·le·sian** (mī lē′shən, -zhən), adj., n.

mil·foil (mĭl′foil′), n. the plant yarrow. [ME, t. OF, g. L *mīlifolium, millefolium*, lit., thousand leaves]

Mil·ford Haven (mĭl′fərd), 1. a bay in SW Wales. 2. a seaport on the N side of this bay. 11,717 (1951).

Mi·lhaud (mē yō′), n. **Darius** (dà ryys′), born 1892, French composer, now living in the U.S.

mil·i·ar·i·a (mĭl′ĭ âr′ĭ ə), n. *Pathol.* an inflammatory disease of the skin, located about the sweat glands, marked by the formation of vesicles or papules resembling millet seeds; miliary fever. [t. NL, prop. fem. of L *miliārius* MILIARY]

mil·i·ar·y (mĭl′ĭ ĕr′ĭ, mĭl′yə rĭ), adj. 1. resembling a millet seed or seeds. 2. *Pathol.* accompanied by spots (papules) or vesicles resembling millet seeds: *miliary fever*. [t. L: m.s. *miliārius* of millet]

miliary tuberculosis, *Pathol.* tuberculosis in which the bacilli are spread by the blood from one point of infection, producing small tubercles in other parts of the body.

mi·lieu (mē lyœ′), n. medium or environment. [t. F: f. *mi* (g. L *medius*) middle + *lieu* (g. L *locus*) place]

milit., military.

mil·i·tant (mĭl′ə tənt), adj. 1. combative; aggressive: *a militant reformer*. 2. engaged in warfare; warring. —n. 3. one engaged in warfare or strife; a militant person. [ME, t. L: s. *mīlitans*, prp. serving as a soldier] —**mil′i·tan·cy,** n. —**mil′i·tant·ly,** adv.

mil·i·ta·rism (mĭl′ə tə rĭz′əm), n. 1. military spirit or policy. 2. the principle of maintaining a large military establishment. 3. the tendency to regard military efficiency as the supreme ideal of the state, and to subordinate all other interests to those of the military.

mil·i·ta·rist (mĭl′ə tə rĭst), n. 1. one imbued with militarism. 2. one skilled in the art of war. —**mil′i·ta·ris′tic,** adj. —**mil′i·ta·ris′ti·cal·ly,** adv.

mil·i·ta·rize (mĭl′ə tə rīz′), v.t., -rized, -rizing. 1. to make military. 2. to imbue with militarism. —**mil′i·ta·ri·za′tion,** n.

mil·i·tar·y (mĭl′ə tĕr′ĭ), adj. 1. of or pertaining to the army, armed forces, affairs of war, or a state of war. 2. of or pertaining to soldiers. 3. befitting a soldier. 4. following the life of a soldier. 5. having the characteristics of a soldier; soldierly. —n. 6. soldiers generally; the army. [t. L: m. *mīlitāris*] —**mil′i·tar′i·ly,** adv. —**Ant.** 1. civilian.

military attaché, an army officer on the official staff of an ambassador or minister to a foreign country.

military law, rules and regulations applicable to persons in the military and naval services.

military police, soldiers who perform police duties within the army.

mil·i·tate (mĭl′ə tāt′), v.i., -tated, -tating. to operate (*against* or *in favor of*); have effect or influence: *every fact militated against his argument*. [t. L: m.s. *mīlitātus*, pp. of *mīlitāre* be a soldier] —**mil′i·ta′tion,** n.

mi·li·tia (mĭ lĭsh′ə), n. 1. a body of men enrolled for military service, called out periodically for drill and exercise but for actual service only in emergencies. 2. *U.S.* **a.** all able-bodied males who are or intend to become citizens, and are more than 18 and not more than 45 years of age. **b.** unorganized or reserve militia, that portion of the militia not belonging to the National Guard or the Organized Reserves, or the Naval or Marine Reserves. 3. a body of citizen soldiers as distinguished from professional soldiers. [t. L: military service, soldiery]

mi·li·tia·man (mĭ lĭsh′ə mən), n., pl. -men. one serving in the militia.

mil·i·um (mĭl′ĭ əm), n., pl. **milia** (mĭl′ĭ ə). *Pathol.* a small white or yellowish nodule resembling a millet seed, produced in the skin by the retention of a sebaceous secretion. [t. L: millet]

milk (mĭlk), n. 1. an opaque white or bluish-white liquid secreted by the mammary glands of female mammals, serving for the nourishment of their young, and, in the case of the cow and some other animals, used for food or as a source of dairy products. 2. any liquid resembling this, as the liquid within a coconut, the juice or sap (latex) of certain plants, or various pharmaceutical preparations. —v.t. 3. to press or draw milk by hand or machine from the udder of (a cow or other animal). 4. to extract as if by milking; draw (out). 5. to extract something from as if by milking. 6. to drain strength, information, wealth, etc., from; exploit. —v.i. 7. to yield milk, as a cow. 8. to milk a cow or other animal. [ME; OE *milc, meolc*, c. G *milch*]

milk-and-wa·ter (mĭlk′ən wô′tər, -wŏt′ər), adj. weak or insipid; wishy-washy.

milk bar, a place, often with an open front, where milk drinks, sandwiches, etc., are sold.

milk·er (mĭl′kər), n. 1. one who milks. 2. milking machine. 3. a cow or other animal that gives milk.

milk fever, 1. *Pathol.* fever coinciding with the beginning of lactation, formerly believed to be due to lactation, but really due to infection. 2. *Vet. Sci.* an acute condition often affecting dairy cows immediately after calving, causing somnolence and paralysis.

milk·fish (mĭlk′fĭsh′), n., pl. -fishes, (esp. collectively) -fish. a herringlike fish, *Chanos chanos*, extensively cultivated in southeastern Asia.

milking machine, an apparatus for milking cows.

milk leg, *Pathol.* a painful swelling of the leg, due to thrombosis of the large veins, occurring most frequently in connection with parturition.

milk·maid (mĭlk′mād′), n. a woman who milks cows or is employed in a dairy.

milk·man (mĭlk′măn′), n., pl. -men. a man who sells or delivers milk.

milk of magnesia, *Pharm.* an antacid or laxative composed of a milky form of magnesium hydroxide, Mg(OH)₂, suspension in water.

milk punch, a beverage containing milk and alcoholic liquor with sugar, flavoring, etc.

milk shake, a frothy drink made of ice-cold milk, flavoring, and usually ice cream, shaken together.

milk sickness, a malignant disease of man, formerly common in some parts of middlewestern U.S., caused by consuming milk from cattle which had been poisoned by eating some kinds of snakeroot.

milk snake, a gray and black nonvenomous snake, *Lampropeltis triangulum*, with an arrow-shaped mark over the occiput, found widely in eastern North America.

milk·sop (mĭlk′sŏp′), n. a soft, unmanly fellow; an effeminate man or youth. —**milk′sop′ism,** n.

milk sugar, lactose, the largest solid constituent of milk.

milk tooth, one of the temporary teeth of a mammal which are replaced by the permanent teeth.

milk vetch, 1. a herb, esp. a European species *Astragalus Glycyphyllos*, of the fabaceous genus *Astragalus*, reputed to increase the secretion of milk in goats. 2. any herb of certain allied genera.

milk·weed (mĭlk′wēd′), n. 1. any of various plants (mostly with milky juice) of the family *Asclepiadaceae*, esp. those of the genus *Asclepias*, as *A. syriaca* (the **common milkweed**). **2.** any of various plants with a milky juice, as certain spurges.

milk-white (mĭlk′hwīt′), *adj.* of a white or slightly blue-white color, such as that of milk.

milk·wort (mĭlk′wûrt′), *n.* **1.** any of the herbs and shrubs constituting the genus *Polygala*, having (mostly) spikes or spikelike racemes of variously colored flowers, formerly reputed to increase the secretion of milk. **2.** a primulaceous seaside plant, *Glaux maritima*, having small purplish-white flowers (**sea milkwort**).

milk·y (mĭl′kĭ), *adj.,* **milkier, milkiest. 1.** of or like milk. **2.** of a chalky white. **3.** giving a good supply of milk. **4.** meek, tame, or spiritless. —**milk′i·ness,** *n.*

Milky Way, *Astron.* the faintly luminous band stretching across the heavens, composed of innumerable stars too faint for unassisted vision; the Galaxy. [trans. of L *via lactea*]

mill¹ (mĭl), *n.* **1.** a building or establishment fitted with machinery, in which any of various mechanical operations or forms of manufacture is carried on: *a steel mill.* **2.** a mechanical appliance or a building or establishment equipped with appliances for grinding grain into flour. **3.** a machine for grinding, crushing, or pulverizing any solid substance: *a coffee mill.* **4.** a steel roller for receiving and transferring an impressed design, as to a calico-printing cylinder or a banknote-printing plate. **5.** a machine which does its work by rotary motion, as one used by a lapidary for cutting and polishing precious stones. **6.** any of various other apparatuses for working materials into due form or performing other mechanical operations. **7.** *Slang.* a boxing match or fist fight. —*v.t.* **8.** to grind, work, treat, or shape in or with a mill. **9.** to finish the edge of (a coin, etc.) with a series of fine notches or transverse grooves. **10.** to beat or stir, as to a froth: *to mill chocolate.* **11.** *Slang.* to beat or strike; fight; overcome. —*v.i.* **12.** to move confusedly in a circle, as a herd of cattle. **13.** *Slang.* to fight or box. [ME *mille, myln,* OE *mylen,* t. LL: m.s. *molīnum,* der. L *mola* millstone, mill]

mill² (mĭl), *n.* a U.S. money of account, equal to one thousandth of a dollar or one tenth of a cent. [short for L *millēsimus* thousandth, modeled on CENT]

Mill (mĭl), *n.* **1. James,** 1773–1836, British philosopher, historian, and economist. **2.** his son, **John Stuart,** 1806–73, British philosopher and economist.

Mil·lais (mĭ lā′), *n.* **Sir John Everett,** 1829–96, British painter.

Mil·lay (mĭ lā′), *n.* **Edna St. Vincent,** (*Mrs. Eugen Jan Boissevain*) 1892–1950, U.S. poet.

mill·board (mĭl′bōrd′), *n.* *Bookbinding.* a strong, thick pasteboard used to make book covers.

mill·dam (mĭl′dăm′), *n.* a dam built in a stream to furnish a head of water for turning a mill wheel.

milled (mĭld), *adj.* having undergone the operations of a mill.

mil·le·nar·i·an (mĭl′ə nâr′Ĭ an), *adj.* **1.** of or pertaining to a thousand, esp. the thousand years of the prophesied millennium. —*n.* **2.** a believer in the millennium.

mil·le·nar·y (mĭl′ə nĕr′Ĭ), *adj., n., pl.* **-naries.** —*adj.* **1.** consisting of or pertaining to a thousand, esp. a thousand years. **2.** pertaining to the millennium. —*n.* **3.** an aggregate of a thousand. **4.** millennium. **5.** millenarian. [t. LL: m.s. *millēnārius* (def. 1)]

mil·len·ni·al (mĭ lĕn′Ĭ əl), *adj.* **1.** of or pertaining to a millennium or the millennium. **2.** worthy or suggestive of the millennium. —**mil·len′ni·al·ly,** *adv.*

mil·len·ni·um (mĭ lĕn′Ĭ əm), *n., pl.* **-niums, -nia** (-Ĭə). **1.** a period of a thousand years. **2.** a thousandth anniversary. **3.** the period of "a thousand years" (a phrase variously interpreted) during which Christ is to reign on earth, according to the prophetic statement in Rev. 20:1–7. **4.** a period of general righteousness and happiness, esp. in the indefinite future. [t. NL, f. L *mille* thousand + *-ennium* as in BIENNIUM]

mil·le·pede (mĭl′ə pēd′), *n.* millipede.

mil·le·pore (mĭl′ə pōr′), *n.* a coralline hydrozoan of the genus *Millipora,* having a smooth calcareous surface with many perforations. [t. NL: m.s. *millepora,* f. L *mille* thousand + m. *porus* PORE²]

mill·er (mĭl′ər), *n.* **1.** one who keeps or operates a mill, esp. a grain mill. **2.** a milling machine. **3.** any of various moths that look as if they were powdered with flour. [ME; OE *myle(n)weard.* See MILL¹, WARD]

Mill·er (mĭl′ər), *n.* **Joaquin** (wä kēn′), (*Cincinnatus Heine Miller*) 1841–1913, U.S. poet.

Mil·le·rand (mēl rän′), *n.* **Alexandre** (à lĕk sän′dr), 1859–1943, president of France, 1920–24.

mill·er·ite (mĭl′ə rīt′), *n.* a mineral, nickel sulfide (NiS), occurring in bronze-colored slender crystals, a minor ore of nickel. [named after W. H. Miller (1801–80), British crystallographer. See -ITE²]

Mill·er·ite (mĭl′ə rīt′), *n.* a member of the Adventist church founded by William Miller (1782–1849), a U.S. preacher, who taught that the second advent of Christ and the beginning of the millennium were to occur in the immediate future (at first, about 1843).

mil·les·i·mal (mĭ lĕs′ə məl), *adj.* **1.** thousandth. **2.** consisting of thousandth parts. —*n.* **3.** a thousandth part. [f. s. L *millēsimus* thousandth + -AL¹]

mil·let (mĭl′Ĭt), *n.* **1.** a cereal grass, *Setaria italica,* extensively cultivated in the East and in southern Europe for its small seed or grain (used as a food for man

and fowls), but in the U.S. grown chiefly for fodder. **2.** any of various related or similar grasses cultivated as grain plants or forage plants, as **Indian millet,** and **pearl millet. 3.** the grain of any of these grasses. [ME, t. F, dim. of *mil,* g. L *milium*]

Mil·let (mĭ lā′; *Fr.* mē lĕ′), *n.* **Jean François** (zhän frän swä′), 1814–75, French painter.

milli-, a word element meaning "thousand," used in the metric system for the division of the unit by 1,000. [t. L, comb. form of *mille*]

mil·liard (mĭl′yərd, -yärd), *n.* *Brit.* a thousand millions. [t. F, der. L *mille* thousand]

mil·li·ar·y (mĭl′Ĭ ĕr′Ĭ), *adj.* **1.** pertaining to the ancient Roman mile of a thousand paces. **2.** marking a mile. [t. L: m.s. *milliārius* containing a thousand]

mil·li·bar (mĭl′ə bär′), *n.* *Meteorol.* a widely used unit of atmospheric pressure, equal to 0.001 bar.

mil·lier (mē lyē′), *n.* 1000 kilograms; a metric ton. [F, der. L *mille* thousand]

mil·li·gram (mĭl′ə grăm′), *n.* a unit of one one-thousandth of a gram, equivalent to 0.0154 grain. Also, *esp. Brit.,* **mil′li·gramme/.**

Mil·li·kan (mĭl′ə kən), *n.* **Robert Andrews,** 1868–1953, U.S. physicist.

mil·li·li·ter (mĭl′ə lē′tər), *n.* a unit of capacity in the metric system, equal to one thousandth of a liter, and equivalent to 0.033815 fluid ounces, or 0.061025 cu. in. Also, *esp. Brit.,* **mil′li·li·tre.**

mil·li·me·ter (mĭl′ə mē′tər), *n.* a unit of length in the metric system equal to one thousandth of a meter, and equivalent to 0.03937 inch. Also, *esp. Brit.,* **mil′li·me′tre.** [t. F: m. *millimètre.* See MILLI-, METER¹]

mil·li·mi·cron (mĭl′ə mī′krŏn), *n., pl.* **-cra** (-krə). a unit of length, the 1000th part of a micron. *Symbol:* mμ.

mil·li·ner (mĭl′ə nər), *n.* one who makes or sells hats for women. [var. of obs. *Milaner* an inhabitant of Milan, a dealer in articles from Milan]

mil·li·ner·y (mĭl′ə nĕr′Ĭ, -nə rĬ), *n.* **1.** articles made or sold by milliners. **2.** the business or trade of a milliner.

mill·ing (mĭl′Ĭng), *n.* **1.** act of subjecting something to the operation of a mill. **2.** the process of producing plane and formed surfaces. **3.** the process of finishing the edge of a coin, etc., with fine notches or transverse grooves. **4.** *Slang.* a thrashing.

milling machine, a machine tool used to produce plane and formed surfaces.

mil·lion (mĭl′yən), *n.* **1.** one thousand times one thousand. **2.** the amount of a thousand thousand units of money, as pounds, dollars, or francs. **3.** a very great number. **4.** the multitude, or the mass of the common people (prec. by *the*). —*adj.* **5.** amounting to one million in numbers. [ME *millioun,* t. OF: m. *million,* t. It.: m. *milione,* aug. of *mille* thousand, g. L *mille*]

mil·lion·aire (mĭl′yə nâr′), *n.* **1.** a person worth a million or millions, as of pounds, dollars, or francs. **2.** a very rich person. Also **mil′lion·naire/.** [t. F: m. *millionnaire,* der. *million* MILLION]

mil·lionth (mĭl′yənth), *adj.* **1.** coming last in a series of a million. **2.** being one of a million equal parts. —*n.* **3.** the millionth member of a series; a millionth part, esp. of one (¹/₁,₀₀₀,₀₀₀).

mil·li·pede (mĭl′ə pēd′), *n.* any one of the many arthropods belonging to the class *Diplopoda.* These are slow-moving, mostly herbivorous, myriapods having a cylindrical body of numerous segments, most of which bear two pairs of legs. Also, **millepede.** [t. L: m.s. *millepeda* wood louse, f. *mille* thousand + m.s. *pēs* foot]

Millipede, *Cambala annulata* (1 in. long)

mill·pond (mĭl′pŏnd′), *n.* a pond for supplying water to drive a mill wheel.

mill·race (mĭl′rās′), *n.* **1.** the channel in which the current of water driving a mill wheel flows to the mill. **2.** the current itself.

Mills grenade (mĭlz), *Mil.* a type of high-explosive grenade weighing about 1.5 pounds. [named after the inventor, Sir Wm. *Mills* (1856–1932)]

mill·stone (mĭl′stōn′), *n.* **1.** either of a pair of circular stones between which grain or other substance is ground, as in a mill. **2.** something that grinds or crushes. **3.** a heavy burden (in allusion to Matt. 18:6).

mill·stream (mĭl′strēm′), *n.* the stream in a millrace.

mill wheel, a wheel, esp. a water wheel, to drive a mill.

mill·work (mĭl′wûrk′), *n.* **1.** ready-made carpentry work from a mill. **2.** work done in a mill.

mill·wright (mĭl′rīt′), *n.* one who designs, builds, or sets up mills or mill machinery.

Milne (mĭln), *n.* **Alan Alexander,** 1882–1956, British writer of plays, books for children, and novels.

Mil·ner (mĭl′nər), *n.* **Alfred, 1st Viscount,** 1854–1925, British statesman and colonial administrator.

Mi·lo (mē′lō), *n.* Melos. Also, **Mi·los** (mē′lŏs).

mi·lord (mĭ lôrd′), *n.* a Continental rendering of English *my lord,* used in speaking to or of an English lord or gentleman.

milque·toast (mĭlk′tōst′), *n.* a very timid person [named after Caspar *Milquetoast,* a comic-strip character]

mil·reis (mĭl′rās′; *Port.* mēl rās′), *n., pl.* **-reis. 1.** a former Brazilian silver coin and monetary unit, equal to 1,000 reis, or about 5.3 U.S. cents. **2.** a Portuguese gold coin and former monetary unit (superseded in 1911 by the escudo). [t. Pg.: a thousand reis, f. *mil* a thousand (g. L *mille*) + *reis*, pl. of *real*, lit., REGAL]

milt (mĭlt), *n.* **1.** the secretion of the male generative organs of fishes. **2.** the organs themselves. [ME and OE *milte*, c. G *milz*, etc.; akin to MELT]

milt·er (mĭl′tər), *n.* a male fish in breeding time.

Mil·ti·a·des (mĭl tī′ə dēz′), *n.* died c488 B.C., Athenian general who was victorious over the Persians in the battle of Marathon in 490 B.C.

Mil·ton (mĭl′tən), *n.* **John,** 1608–74, British poet.

Mil·ton·ic (mĭl tŏn′ĭk), *adj.* of or pertaining to the poet Milton or resembling his majestic style. Also, **Mil·to·ni·an** (mĭl tō′nĭ ən).

Mil·town (mĭl′toun), *n.* *Trademark.* a tranquilizer.

Mil·wau·kee (mĭl wô′kĭ), *n.* a city in SE Wisconsin: a port on Lake Michigan. 741,324 (1960).

Mi·lyu·kov (mĭ′lyŏŏ kôf′), *n.* **Pavel Nikolaevich** (pä′vĕl nĭ kō lä′yə vĭch), 1859–1943, Russian statesman and historian.

mime (mīm), *n.*, *v.*, **mimed, miming.** —*n.* **1.** a comedian; jester; clown. **2.** a player in an ancient Greek or Roman kind of farce which depended for effect largely upon ludicrous actions and gestures. **3.** such a farce. **4.** the dialogue for such a player. —*v.t.* **5.** to mimic. —*v.i.* **6.** to play a part by mimicry, esp. without words. [t. L: m.s. *mīmus*, t. Gk.: m. *mīmos*] —**mim′er,** *n.*

Mim·e·o·graph (mĭm′ĭ ə grȧf′, -grȧf′), *n.* *Trademark.* **1.** a stencil device for duplicating letters, drawings, etc. —*v.t.* **2.** to make copies using a Mimeograph. [f. *mimeo-* (repr. Gk. *mīméomai* I imitate; cf. MIME) + -GRAPH]

mi·me·sis (mĭ mē′sĭs, mī-), *n.* **1.** *Rhet.* imitation or reproduction of the supposed words of another, as in order to represent his character. **2.** *Biol.* imitation. **3.** *Zool.* mimicry. [t. NL, t. Gk.: imitation]

mi·met·ic (mĭ mĕt′ĭk, mī-), *adj.* **1.** characterized by, exhibiting, or of the nature of mimicry: *mimetic gestures.* **2.** mimic or make-believe. [t. Gk.: m.s. *mīmētikós*] —**mi·met′i·cal·ly,** *adv.*

mim·e·tite (mĭm′ə tīt′, mī′mə-), *n.* a mineral, lead chloroarsenate, $Pb_5As_3O_{12}Cl$, occurring in yellow to brown prismatic crystals or globular masses: a minor ore of lead. [t. G: m. *mimetit*, f.s. Gk. *mīmētés* imitator + -*it* -ITE[1]]

mim·ic (mĭm′ĭk), *v.*, **-icked, -icking,** *n.*, *adj.* —*v.t.* **1.** to imitate or copy in action, speech, etc., often playfully or derisively. **2.** to imitate unintelligently or servilely; ape. **3.** (of things) to be an imitation of; simulate —*n.* **4.** one apt at imitating or mimicking. **5.** one who or that which imitates or mimics; an imitator or imitation. **6.** *Obs.* a mime. —*adj.* **7.** being merely an imitation or reproduction of the true thing, often on a smaller scale: *a mimic battle.* **8.** apt at or given to imitating; imitative; simulative. [t. L: s. *mīmicus*, t. Gk.: m. *mīmikós* belonging to mimes]

mim·ic·ry (mĭm′ĭk rĭ), *n.*, *pl.* **-ries. 1.** the act, practice, or art of mimicking. **2.** *Zool.* the close external resemblance, as if from imitation or simulation, of an animal to some different animal or to surrounding objects, esp. as serving for protection or concealment. **3.** an instance, performance, or result of mimicking.

Mi·mir (mē′mĭr), *n.* *Scand. Myth.* the custodian of the spring of wisdom; his head, cut off by the Vanir, came into Odin's possession and gave him information and advice thenceforth.

mi·mo·sa (mĭ mō′sə, -zə), *n.* any plant of the genus *Mimosa*, native in tropical or warm regions, and comprising trees, shrubs, and plants having usually bipinnate and often sensitive leaves, and small flowers in globular heads or cylindrical spikes, esp., the sensitive plant, *M. pudica.* [t. NL, der. L *mīmus* MIME; apparently so named from seeming mimicry of animal life]

mim·o·sa·ceous (mĭm′ə sā′shəs, (mĭ′mə-), *adj.* belonging to the *Mimosaceae*, or mimosa family of plants, usually treated as part of the larger family *Leguminosae.*

Mims (mĭmz), *n.* **Fort,** a stockade in SW Alabama, near the junction of the Alabama and Tombigbee rivers: Indian massacre, 1813.

min., **1.** mineralogical. **2.** mineralogy. **3.** minim. **4.** minimum. **5.** mining. **6.** minor. **7.** minute; minutes.

mi·na[1] (mī′nə), *n.*, *pl.* **minae** (mī′nē), **minas.** an ancient unit of weight and value, equal to the sixtieth part of a talent. [t. L, t. Gk.: m. *mnâ*; prob. of Babylonian orig.]

mi·na[2] (mī′nə), *n.* myna.

mi·na·cious (mĭ nā′shəs), *adj.* menacing; threatening. [f. s. L *mināciae* threats + -OUS] —**mi·na′cious·ly,** *adv.* —**mi·na′cious·ness,** **mi·nac·i·ty** (mĭ năs′ə tĭ), *n.*

min·a·ret (mĭn′ə rĕt′, mĭn′ə rĕt′), *n.* a lofty, often slender, tower or turret attached to a Mohammedan mosque, surrounded by or furnished with one or more balconies, from which the muezzin calls the people to prayer. [t. Sp.: m. *minarete,* t. Ar.: m. *manāra(t),* orig., lighthouse]

Minaret

Mi·nas Basin (mī′nəs), the easternmost arm of the Bay of Fundy, in Nova Scotia: noted for high tides.

min·a·to·ry (mĭn′ə tôr′ĭ), *adj.* menacing; threatening. Also, **min′a·to′ri·al.** [t. LL: m.s. *minātōrius,* der. L *minārī* threaten] —**min′a·to′ri·ly,** *adv.*

mince (mĭns), *v.*, **minced, mincing,** *n.* —*v.t.* **1.** to cut or chop into very small pieces. **2.** to subdivide minutely, as land, a subject, etc. **3.** to soften or moderate (one's words, etc.) to a milder form. **4.** to speak of (matters) in polite or euphemistic terms. **5.** to perform or utter with affected elegance. —*v.i.* **6.** to walk or move with short, affectedly dainty steps. **7.** to act, behave, or speak with affected elegance. —*n.* **8.** *Brit.* hash. [ME *mynce(n),* t. OF: m. *mincier* make small, ult. der. L *minūtus* small. Cf. MINISH]

mince-meat (mĭns′mēt′), *n.* **1.** a mixture composed of minced apples, suet (and sometimes meat), candied citron, etc., with raisins, currants, etc., for filling a pie (mince pie). **2.** anything cut up very small.

minc·ing (mĭn′sĭng), *adj.* **1.** affectedly nice or elegant, as the gait, behavior, air, speech, etc. **2.** walking, acting, or speaking in an affectedly nice or elegant manner. —**minc′ing·ly,** *adv.*

mind (mīnd), *n.* **1.** that which thinks, feels, and wills, exercises perception, judgment, reflection, etc., as in a human or other conscious being: *the processes of the mind.* **2.** *Psychol.* the psyche; the totality of conscious and unconscious activities of the organism. **3.** the intellect or understanding, as distinguished from the faculties of feeling and willing; the intelligence. **4.** a particular instance of the intellect or intelligence, as in a person. **5.** a person considered with reference to intellectual power: *the greatest minds of the time.* **6.** intellectual power or ability. **7.** reason, sanity, or sound mental condition: *to lose one's mind.* **8.** way of thinking and feeling, disposition, or temper: *many men, many minds.* **9.** opinion or sentiments: *to read someone's mind.* **10.** inclination or desire. **11.** purpose, intention, or will. **12.** psychical or spiritual being, as opposed to matter. **13.** a conscious or intelligent agency or being: *the doctrine of a mind pervading the universe.* **14.** remembrance or recollection: *to keep in mind.* **15.** put in mind, to remind. **16.** commemoration.
—*v.t.* **17.** to pay attention to, heed, or obey (a person, advice, instructions, etc.). **18.** to apply oneself or attend to: *to mind one's own business.* **19.** to look after; take care of; tend: *to mind the baby.* **20.** to be careful, cautious, or wary concerning: *mind what you say.* **21.** to care about or feel concern at. **22.** (in negative and interrogative expressions) to feel disturbed or inconvenienced by; object to: *would you mind handing me that book?* **23.** to regard as concerning oneself or as mattering: *never mind what he does.* **24.** *Dial.* to perceive or notice. **25.** *Archaic or Dial.* to remember. **26.** *Archaic or Dial.* to remind.
—*v.i.* **27.** to take notice, observe, or understand (chiefly in the imperative). **28.** to obey. **29.** to be careful or wary. **30.** to care, feel concern, or object (often in negative and interrogative expressions): *mind if I go?* **31.** to regard a thing as concerning oneself or as mattering: *never mind about them.*
[ME *mind(e),* OE *gemynd* memory, thought, c. Goth. *gamunds* memory; akin to L *mens* mind]
—Syn. **1.** MIND, INTELLECT, INTELLIGENCE refer to mental equipment or qualities. MIND is that part of man which thinks, feels, and wills, as contrasted with body: *his mind was capable of grasping the significance of the problem.* INTELLECT is reasoning power as distinguished from feeling; it is often used in a general sense to characterize high mental ability: *to appeal to the intellect, rather than the emotions.* INTELLIGENCE is ability to learn and to understand; it is also mental alertness or quickness of understanding: *a dog has more intelligence than many other animals.* **6.** MIND, BRAIN, BRAINS may refer to mental capacity. MIND is the philosophical and general term for the center of mental activity, and is therefore used of intellectual powers: *a brilliant mind.* BRAIN is properly the physiological term for the organic structure which makes mental activity possible (*the brain is the center of the nervous system*), but it is often applied, like MIND, to intellectual capacity: *a fertile brain.* The plural BRAINS is the anatomical word (*the brains of an animal used for food*) but, in popular usage, it is applied to intelligence (particularly of a shrewd, practical nature): *that takes brains.*

Min·da·na·o (mĭn′də nä′ō, -nou′), *n.* the second largest of the Philippine Islands, in the S part of the group. 2,702,498 pop. (1948); 36,537 sq. mi.

mind·ed (mīn′dĭd), *adj.* **1.** having a certain kind of mind: *strong-minded.* **2.** inclined or disposed.

mind·ful (mīnd′fəl), *adj.* attentive; careful (usually fol. by *of*). —**mind′ful·ly,** *adv.* —**mind′ful·ness,** *n.*

mind·less (mīnd′lĭs), *adj.* **1.** without intelligence; senseless. **2.** unmindful, careless, or heedless. —**mind′less·ly,** *adv.* —**mind′less·ness,** *n.*

Min·do·ro (mĭn dôr′ō; *Sp.* mēn dô′rô), *n.* one of the Philippine Islands, in the central part of the group. 167,705 pop. (1948); 3922 sq. mi.

mind reading, reading or discerning of the thoughts in the minds of others, esp. by some apparently supernormal power. —**mind reader.**

mind's eye, the imagination.

mine[1] (mīn), *pron.* **1.** possessive form of *I,* used predicatively or without a noun following. **2.** the person(s) or thing(s) belonging to me: *that book is mine, a friend of mine.* —*adj.* **3.** *Archaic.* my (used before a vowel or *h,* or after a noun): *mine eyes, lady mine.* [ME; OE *mīn,* poss. adj. and pron. of first person]

mine[2] (mīn), *n.*, *v.*, **mined, mining.** —*n.* **1.** an excavation made in the earth for the purpose of getting out ores, precious stones, coal, etc. **2.** a place where such minerals may be obtained, either by excavation or by washing the soil. **3.** a deposit of such minerals, either under the ground or at its surface. **4.** an abounding source or store of anything: *this book is a mine of information.* **5.** a subterranean passage made to extend under the enemy's works or position, as for the purpose of securing access or of depositing explosives for blowing up the position. **6.** a device containing a large charge of explosive in a watertight casing moored beneath the surface of the water for the purpose of blowing up an enemy vessel which passes in close proximity to it. **7.** a similar device used on land. —*v.i.* **8.** to dig in the earth for the purpose of extracting ores, coal, etc.; make a mine. **9.** to extract ores, etc., from mines. **10.** to make subterranean passages. **11.** to dig or lay mines, as in military operations. —*v.t.* **12.** to dig in (earth, etc.) in order to obtain ores, coal, etc. **13.** to extract (ores, coal, etc.) from a mine. **14.** to make subterranean passages in or under; burrow. **15.** to make (passages, etc.) by digging or burrowing. **16.** to dig away or remove the foundations of. **17.** to attack, ruin, or destroy by secret or slow methods. **18.** to dig or lay military mines under. [ME, t. OF, of Celtic orig.]

mine field, *Mil., Naval.* an area on land or water throughout which mines have been laid.

mine layer, naval vessel with special equipment for laying underwater mines.

min·er (mī′nər), *n.* **1.** one who works in a mine. **2.** one who digs or lays military mines.

min·er·al (mǐn′ər əl, mǐn′rəl), *n.* **1.** a substance obtained by mining; ore. **2.** any of a class of substances occurring in nature, usually comprising inorganic substances (as quartz, feldspar, etc.) of definite chemical composition and definite crystal structure, but sometimes taken to include aggregations of these substances (more correctly called rocks) and also certain natural products of organic origin, as asphalt, coal, etc. **3.** any substance neither animal nor vegetable. **4.** (*pl.*) *Brit.* soft drinks. [ME, t. OF, t. ML: s. *minerāle*, prop. adj. neut.] —*adj.* **5.** of the nature of a mineral; pertaining to minerals. **6.** impregnated with a mineral or minerals. **7.** neither animal nor vegetable; inorganic: *the mineral kingdom.* [late ME, t. ML: s. *minerālis*, der. *minera* mine, t. OF: m. *miniere*, der. *mine* MINE²]

mineral, **1.** mineralogical. **2.** mineralogy.

min·er·al·ize (mǐn′ər ə līz′, mǐn′rə-), *v.t.,* -ized, -izing. **1.** to convert into a mineral substance. **2.** to transform (a metal) into an ore. **3.** to impregnate or supply with mineral substances. —**min·er·al·i·za′-tion,** *n.* —**min′er·al·iz′er,** *n.*

mineral jelly, a gelatinous product made from petroleum which is used to stabilize some explosives.

min·er·al·o·gist (mǐn′ər äl′ə jǐst, - rŏl′ə-), *n.* a specialist in mineralogy.

min·er·al·o·gy (mǐn′ər äl′ə jǐ, -rŏl′ə-), *n.* the science of minerals. —**min·er·al·og·i·cal** (mǐn′ər ə lŏj′ə kəl), *adj.* —**min′er·al·og′i·cal·ly,** *adv.*

mineral oil, any of a class of oils of mineral origin, as petroleum, consisting of mixtures of hydrocarbons, and used as illuminants, fuels, etc., and in medicine.

mineral pitch, asphalt (bituminous substance).

mineral tar, bitumen of the consistency of tar; maltha.

mineral water, **1.** water containing dissolved mineral salts or gases, esp. such water for medicinal use. **2.** (*pl.*) *Brit.* soft drinks.

mineral wax, ozocerite.

mineral wool, an insulating material consisting of woolly fibers made from melted slag.

Mi·ner·va (mǐ nûr′və), *n.* **1.** *Rom. Myth.* the goddess of wisdom, the arts, and war, identified with the Greek Athena. **2.** a woman of great wisdom or learning.

min·e·stro·ne (mǐn′ə strō′nǐ; *It.* mĕ′nĕ strō′nĕ), *n. Italian.* a soup containing vegetables, herbs, etc., in a broth of chicken or meat. [It., aug. of *minestra* soup, der. *minestrare,* g. L *ministrāre* MINISTER, v.]

mine sweeper, *Naval.* a vessel or ship used for dragging a body of water in order to remove enemy mines.

Ming (mǐng), *n.* the dynasty which ruled China from 1368 to 1644, historically the last dynasty of true Chinese origin. In the Ming period art flourished and there were important revisions of Confucian philosophy. [t. Chinese (Pekin): lit., luminous]

min·gle (mǐng′gəl), *v.,* -gled, -gling. —*v.i.* **1.** to become mixed, blended, or united. **2.** to associate or mix in company. **3.** to take part with others; participate. —*v.t.* **4.** to mix or combine; put together in a mixture; blend. **5.** to unite, join, or conjoin: *joy mingled with pain.* **6.** to associate in company. **7.** to form by mixing, compound, or concoct. [ME *myngle, mengle,* freq. of *menge(n),* OE *mengan*] —**min′gler,** *n.* —**Syn.** **4.** See mix, mixed.

Mi·nho (mē′nyŏ̄), *n.* a river flowing from NW Spain along part of the N boundary of Portugal into the Atlantic. 171 mi. Spanish, **Miño.**

Min·how (mǐn′hō′), *n.* Foochow.

min·i·a·ture (mǐn′ē ə chər, mǐn′ə chər), *n.* **1.** a representation or image of anything on a very small scale. **2.** greatly reduced or abridged form. **3.** a very small painting, esp. a portrait, on ivory, vellum, or the like. **4.** the art of executing such painting. **5.** illumination, as in manuscripts. —*adj.* **6.** on a very small scale; reduced [t. It.: m. *miniatura,* der. L *miniāre* rubricate]

miniature camera, *Photog.* a small camera using film of 35 mm. width or less.

min·i·a·tur·ize (mǐn′ē ə chə rīz′), *v.t.,* -ized, -izing. to reduce in size; to produce an exact working copy in reduced scale. [f. MINIATUR(E) + -IZE] —**min′i·a·tur′-i·za′tion,** *n.*

Min·ié ball (mǐn′ē, -ǐ ā′; *Fr.* mē nyĕ′), (formerly) a conical bullet with a hollow base, expanding, when fired, to fit the rifling. [named after C. E. *Minié* (1814–79), the (French) inventor]

min·i·fy (mǐn′ə fī′), *v.t.,* -fied, -fying. **1.** to make less. **2.** to minimize. [f. L *min(us)* less + -(I)FY]

min·i·kin (mǐn′ə kǐn), *n.* **1.** a person or object that is delicate or diminutive. —*adj.* **2.** delicate; dainty; mincing. [t. MD: m. *minnekijn,* dim. of *minne* love. See -KIN]

min·im (mǐn′əm), *n.* **1.** the smallest unit of liquid measure, the sixtieth part of a fluid dram, or about a drop. **2.** *Music.* a note, formerly the shortest in use, but now equivalent in time value to one half of a semibreve; half note. See illus. under **note.** **3.** the least quantity, or a jot, of anything. **4.** something very small · n-significant. **5.** (*cap.*) a member of a mendicant religious order founded in the 15th century by St. Francis of Paula. —*adj.* **6.** smallest; very small. [ME, t. L: s. *minimus* least, smallest, superl. of *minor* MINOR]

min·i·mal (mǐn′ə məl), *adj.* **1.** pertaining to or being a minimum. **2.** least possible. **3.** smallest; very small. [f. s. L *minimus* least + -AL¹]

Min·i·mal·ist (mǐn′ə məl ǐst), *n.* a member of a less radical group of socialists, as of a faction of the Russian Social Revolutionary party. [f. MINIMAL + -IST]

min·i·mize (mǐn′ə mīz′), *v.t.,* -mized, -mizing. **1.** to reduce to the smallest possible amount or degree. **2.** to represent at the lowest possible estimate; to belittle. —**min′i·mi·za′tion,** *n.* —**min′i·miz′er,** *n.*

min·i·mum (mǐn′ə məm), *n., pl.* -ma (-mə), -mums, *adj.* —*n.* **1.** the least quantity or amount possible, assignable, allowable, etc. **2.** the lowest amount, value, or degree attained or recorded (opposed to *maximum*). **3.** *Math.* a value of a function at a certain point which is less than or equal to the value attained at nearby points. —*adj.* **4.** that is a minimum. **5.** least possible. **6.** lowest: *a minimum rate.* **7.** pertaining to a minimum or minimums. [t. L, neut. of *minimus.* See MINIM]

minimum wage, the lowest wage, fixed by agreement with a union or by legal authority, payable to employees of a particular group.

min·ing (mī′nǐng), *n.* **1.** the action, process, or industry of extracting ores, etc., from mines. **2.** the action of laying explosive mines.

min·ion (mǐn′yən), *n.* **1.** a servile or base favorite of a prince or any patron. **2.** any favorite. **3.** *Print.* a size of type (7 point). —*adj.* **4.** dainty; elegant; trim; pretty. [t. F: m. *mignon* MIGNON]

min·ish (mǐn′ǐsh), *v.t., v.i. Archaic.* to diminish or lessen. [ME *mynyssh(en),* t. OF: m. *menuisier* make small, g. Rom. *minūtiāre,* der. L *minūtus* MINUTE²]

min·is·ter (mǐn′ǐs tər), *n.* **1.** one authorized to conduct religious worship; a clergyman; a pastor. **2.** one authorized to administer sacraments, as at Mass. **3.** *Brit. and Continental.* one appointed by (or under the authority of) the sovereign or executive head of a government to some high office of state, esp. to that of head of an administrative department: *the Minister of Finance.* **4.** a diplomatic representative accredited by one government to another, esp. an envoy. See **envoy¹. 5.** one acting as the agent or instrument of another. —*v.i.* **6.** to administer or apply. **7.** *Archaic.* to furnish; supply. —*v.i.* **8.** to give service, care, or aid; attend, as to wants, necessities, etc. **9.** to contribute, as to comfort, happiness, etc. [t. L: servant; r. ME *menistre,* t. OF]

min·is·te·ri·al (mǐn′ǐs tǐr′ē əl), *adj.* **1.** pertaining to the ministry of religion, or to a minister or clergyman. **2.** *Brit. and Continental.* pertaining to a ministry or minister of state. **3.** pertaining to or invested with delegated executive authority. **4.** of ministry or service. **5.** instrumental. —**min′is·te′ri·al·ly,** *adv.*

min·is·te·ri·al·ist (mǐn′ǐs tǐr′ē əl ǐst), *n. Brit. Pol.* a supporter of the ministry in office.

minister plenipotentiary, *pl.* ministers plenipotentiary. plenipotentiary.

min·is·trant (mǐn′ə strənt), *adj.* **1.** ministering. —*n.* **2.** one who ministers. [t. L: s. *ministrans,* ppr.]

min·is·tra·tion (mǐn′ə strā′shən), *n.* **1.** act of ministering care, aid, religious service, etc. **2.** an instance of it. —**min′is·tra′tive,** *adj.*

min·is·try (mǐn′ǐs trǐ), *n., pl.* -tries. **1.** the service, functions, or profession of a minister of religion. **2.** the body or class of ministers of religion; the clergy. **3.** the service, function, or office of a minister of state. **4.** the policy-forming executive officials in a country, esp. England, taken collectively. **5.** *Brit.* any of the administrative departments of a country. **6.** *Brit.* the building which houses such a department. **7.** *Brit.* the term of office of a minister. **8.** act of ministering; ministration; service. [ME *ministerie,* t. L: m. *ministerium* office, service]

min·i·track (mǐn′ǐ trăk′), *n.* the procedure of tracing the orbit of an artificial satellite and of recording its signals by telemeter. Also, **Min′i·track′.** —**min′i·track′,** *adj.*

min·i·um (mǐn′ē əm), *n.* red lead, Pb_3O_4. [t. L: native cinnabar, red lead]

min·i·ver (mĭn′ə vər), *n.* (in medieval times) a fur of white or spotted white and gray used for linings or trimmings. [ME *meniver*, t. OF: m. *menu vair* small vair. See MENU, VAIR]

mink (mĭngk), *n.*, *pl.* **minks,** (*esp. collectively*) **mink. 1.** a semiaquatic weasellike animal of the genus *Mustela,* esp. the North American *M. vison.* **2.** the valuable fur of this animal, brownish with lustrous outside hairs and thick, soft undercoat. [appar. t. Sw.: m. *mänk*]

Mink. *Mustela vison*
(Total length 2 ft., tail 8 in.)

Min·kow·ski (mĭn kôf′skē), *n.* **Her·mann** (hûr′mən; *Ger.* hĕr′män), 1864–1909, German mathematician.

Minkowski world, a four-dimensional space in which the fourth coordinate is time and in which a single element is represented as a point. Also called **Minkowski universe.**

Minn., Minnesota.

Min·ne·ap·o·lis (mĭn′ĭ ăp′əlĭs), *n.* a city in SE Minnesota, on the Mississippi. 482,872 (1960).

min·ne·sing·er (mĭn′ĭ sĭng′ər), *n.* one of a class of German lyric poets and singers of the 12th, 13th, and 14th centuries. [t. G: *lieue singer*]

Min·ne·so·ta (mĭn′əsō′tə), *n.* **1.** a State in the N central United States. 3,413,864 pop. (1960); 84,068 sq. mi. *Cap.:* St. Paul. *Abbr.:* Minn. **2.** a river flowing from the W border of Minnesota into the Mississippi near St. Paul. 332 mi. —**Min′ne·so′tan,** *adj., n.*

min·now (mĭn′ō), *n.*, *pl.* **-nows,** (*esp. collectively*) **-now. 1.** a small European cyprinoid fish, *Phoxinus phoxinus.* **2.** any fish of the family *Cyprinidae,* mostly small but including some large species, as the carp. **3.** (esp. in the U.S.) any of various other small silvery fishes. [ME *men(a)we,* late OE *myne* (for *mynu*), c. OHG *munewa* kind of fish]

Mi·ño (mē′nyō), *n.* Spanish name of **Minho.**

Mi·no·an (mĭ nō′an), *adj.* of or pertaining to the ancient advanced civilization of Crete, dating (approximately) from 3000 to 1100 B.C. [f. MINO(S) + -AN]

mi·nor (mī′nər), *adj.* **1.** lesser, as in size, extent, or importance, or being the lesser of two: *a minor share, minor faults.* **2.** under legal age. **3.** in English public schools, designating the younger of two students having the same name. **4.** *Music.* **a.** (of an interval) smaller by a half step than the corresponding major interval. **b.** (of a chord) having a minor third between the root and the note next above it. **5.** *Logic.* less broad or extensive: **a. minor term,** (in a syllogism) the term that is the subject of the conclusion. **b. minor premise,** the premise that contains the minor term. **6.** of or pertaining to the minority. **7.** *U.S. Educ.* noting or pertaining to educational minors: *a minor subject.* —*n.* **8.** a person under legal age. **9.** one of inferior rank or importance in a specified class. **10.** *U.S. Educ.* **a.** a subject or a course of study pursued by a student, esp. a candidate for a degree, subordinately or supplementarily to a major or principal subject or course. **b.** a subject for which less credit than a major is granted in colleges or occasionally in high school. **11.** *Music.* a minor interval, chord, scale, etc. **12.** *U.S. Sports.* a minor league. **13.** (*cap.*) a Minorite. —*v.i.* **14. minor in,** to study as a minor subject. [t. L: less, smaller, inferior, younger, a compar. form; r. ME *menour,* t. OF]

Mi·nor·ca (mĭ nôr′kə), *n.* **1.** Spanish, **Menorca.** one of the Balearic Islands, in the W Mediterranean. 43,025 pop. (1940); 271 sq. mi. **2.** one of a Mediterranean breed of white-skinned domestic fowls of moderate size, notable for prolific laying. —**Mi·nor′can,** *adj., n.*

Mi·nor·ite (mī′nər ĭt′), *n.* a Franciscan friar.

mi·nor·i·ty (mĭ nôr′ə tĭ, -nŏr′-, mī-), *n.*, *pl.* **-ties. 1.** the smaller part or number; a number forming less than half of the whole. **2.** a smaller party or group opposed to a majority, as in voting or other action. **3.** the state or period of being a minor or under legal age.

minor key or **mode,** *Music.* a key or mode based on a minor scale.

minor league, *U.S.* any association of professional sports clubs other than the acknowledged major leagues.

minor orders, *Rom. Cath. Ch.* See **order** (def. 15).

Minor Prophets. See **prophet** (def. 4c).

minor scale, *Music.* a scale whose third tone forms a minor third with the fundamental tone. See illus. under **scale.**

minor suit, *Bridge.* diamonds or clubs.

Mi·nos (mī′nəs, -nŏs), *n.* *Gk. Myth.* son of Zeus, and king and lawgiver of Crete: after death, a judge in the lower world. Cf. **Aeacus, Rhadamanthus.**

Mi·not (mī′nət), *n.* a city in N North Dakota. 30,604 (1960).

Min·o·taur (mĭn′ə tôr′), *n.* **1.** *Gk. Myth.* a fabulous monster, half bull and half man, confined in the Cretan labyrinth and fed with human flesh. It was killed by Theseus, with the help of Ariadne. **2.** any devouring or destroying agency. [t. L: s. *Minōtaurus,* t. Gk.: m. *Mīnōtauros,* f. *Mīnō(s)* MINOS + *taûros* bull]

Minsk (mĕnsk), *n.* a city in the W Soviet Union: capital of the White Russian Republic. 412,000 (est. 1956).

min·strel (mĭn′strəl), *n.* **1.** one of a class of medieval musicians who sang or recited to the accompaniment of

instruments. **2.** *Poetic.* any musician, singer, or poet. **3.** one of a troupe of comedians, usually white men made up as Negroes, presenting songs, jokes, etc. [ME *menestral, minstral* t. OF: m. *menestrel,* orig., servant, g. LL *ministeriālis* ministerial]

min·strel·sy (mĭn′strəl sĭ), *n.*, *pl.* **-sies. 1.** the art or practice of a minstrel. **2.** minstrels' songs, ballads, etc.: *a collection of Scottish minstrelsy.*

mint¹ (mĭnt), *n.* **1.** any plant of the labiate genus *Mentha,* comprising aromatic herbs with opposite leaves and small verticillate flowers, as the spearmint, the peppermint, and the horsemint. **2.** a soft or hard confection flavored with peppermint or other flavoring, often served after dinner. [ME and OE *minte* (c. OHG *minza*), t. L: *menta,* t. Gk.: m. *mínthē*]

mint² (mĭnt), *n.* **1.** a place where money is coined by public authority. **2.** a vast amount, esp. of money. —*adj.* **3.** *Philately,* (of a stamp) as issued by the Post Office. **4.** unused. —*v.t.* **5.** to make (coins) by stamping metal. **6.** to coin (money). **7.** to make or fabricate as if by coining: *mint words.* [ME *mynt,* OE *mynet* coin (c. G *münze*), t. L: *monēta* mint, MONEY] —**mint′er,** *n.*

mint·age (mĭn′tĭj), *n.* **1.** act or process of minting. **2.** the product or result of minting; coinage. **3.** the charge for or cost of minting or coining. **4.** the output of a mint. **5.** a stamp or character impressed.

mint julep, a frosted drink made of bourbon whiskey, sugar, crushed ice, and sprigs of fresh mint.

min·u·end (mĭn′yōōĕnd′), *n.* *Math.* the number from which another (the subtrahend) is to be subtracted. [t. L: s. *minuendus,* ger. of *minuere* make smaller]

min·u·et (mĭn′yōōĕt′), *n.* **1.** a slow stately dance of French origin. **2.** a piece of music for such a dance or in its rhythm. [t. F: m. *menuet,* orig. adj., very small (with reference to the small steps taken in the dance), dim. of *menu* small. See MENU]

Min·u·it (mĭn′yōōĭt), *n.* **Peter,** c1580–1638, first governor of the colony of New Netherland.

mi·nus (mī′nəs), *prep.* **1.** less by the subtraction of; decreased by: *ten minus six.* **2.** lacking or without: *a book minus its title page.* —*adj.* **3.** involving or denoting subtraction: *the minus sign.* **4.** negative: *a minus quantity.* **5.** *Colloq.* lacking: *the profits were minus.* **6.** *Bot.* (in heterothallic fungi) designating, in the absence of morphological differentiation, one of the two strains or mycelia which must unite in the sexual process. —*n.* **7.** the minus sign (−). **8.** a minus quantity. **9.** a deficiency or loss. [t. L, adj., neut. of *minor* MINOR]

mi·nus·cule (mĭ nŭs′kūl), *adj.* **1.** small, as letters not capital or uncial. **2.** written in such letters (opposed to *majuscule*). —*n.* **3.** a minuscule letter. **4.** a small cursive script developed in the 7th century from the uncial, which it afterward superseded. [t. L: m.s. *minusculus* rather small, dim. of *minor* MINOR] —**mi·nus′cu·lar,** *adj.*

minus sign, *Math.* the symbol (−) denoting subtraction or a minus quantity.

min·ute¹ (mĭn′ĭt), *n., v.,* **-uted, -uting,** *adj.* —*n.* **1.** the sixtieth part of an hour; sixty seconds. **2.** an indefinitely short space of time: *wait a minute.* **3.** a point of time, an instant, or moment: *come here this minute!* **4.** a rough draft, as of a document. **5.** *Chiefly Brit.* a written summary, note, or memorandum. **6.** (*pl.*) the official record of the proceedings at a meeting of a society, board, committee, council, or other body. **7.** *Geom., etc.* the sixtieth part of a degree, or sixty seconds (often represented by the sign ′), as 12°10′ (twelve degrees and ten minutes). —*v.t.* **8.** to time exactly, as movements, speed, etc. **9.** to make a draft of (a document, etc.). **10.** to record (something) in a memorandum; note (*down*). **11.** to enter in the minutes of a society or other body. —*adj.* **12.** prepared in a very short time: *minute steak.* [ME, t. OF, t. ML: m.s. *minūta* small part or division, prop. fem. of L *minūtus* MINUTE²]

—**Syn. 2.** MINUTE, INSTANT, MOMENT refer to infinitesimal amounts of time. A MINUTE, properly denoting sixty seconds, is often used loosely for any very short space of time (and may be interchangeable with *second*): *just a minute.* An INSTANT is practically a point in time, with no duration, though it is also used to mean a perceptible amount of time: *not an instant's delay.* MOMENT denotes much the same as INSTANT, though with a somewhat greater sense of duration (but somewhat less than MINUTE): *it will take a moment.*

mi·nute² (mī nūt′, -nōōt′, mī′-), *adj.* **1.** extremely small, as in size, amount, extent, or degree: *minute differences.* **2.** of very small scope or individual importance: *minute particulars of a case.* **3.** attentive to or concerned with even very small details or particulars: *a minute observer or report.* [ME, t. L: m.s. *minūtus,* pp., made smaller] —**mi·nute′ness,** *n.* —**Syn. 1.** See **little.**

min·ute gun (mĭn′ĭt), (formerly) a gun fired at intervals of a minute, as in token of mourning or of distress.

min·ute hand (mĭn′ĭt), the hand that indicates the minutes on a clock or watch.

min·ute·ly¹ (mĭn′ĭt lĭ), *adj.* **1.** occurring every minute. —*adv.* **2.** every minute; minute by minute. [f. MINUTE¹ + -LY]

mi·nute·ly² (mĭ nūt′lĭ, -nōōt′-, mī′-), *adv.* in a minute manner, form, or degree; in minute detail. [f. MINUTE² + -LY]

min·ute·man (mĭn′ĭt măn′), *n.*, *pl.* **-men** (-mĕn′). one of a group of American militiamen just before and during the Revolutionary War who held themselves in readiness for instant military service.

ăct, āble, dâre, ärt; ĕbb, ēqual; ĭf, īce; hŏt, ōver, ôrder, oil, bŏŏk, ōōze, out; ŭp, ūse, ûrge; ə = a in alone; ch, chief; g, give; ng, ring; sh, shoe; th, thin; t̲h̲, that; zh, vision.   See the full key on inside cover.

mi·nu·ti·a (mĭ nū′/shĭ ə, -shə, -nōō′/-), *n.*, *pl.* **-tiae** (-shĭ ē′). (*usually pl.*) a small or trivial detail; a trifling circumstance or matter. [t. L: smallness]

minx (mĭngks), *n.* a pert, impudent, or flirtatious girl. [? alter. of *minikins*, f. MINIKIN + hypocoristic -*s*]

Mi·o·cene (mĭ′ə sēn′), *Stratig.* —*adj.* **1.** pertaining to a series of the Tertiary period or system. —*n.* **2.** a division of the Tertiary following Oligocene and preceding Pliocene. [f. *mio*- (repr. Gk. *meîōn* less) + -CENE]

Miq·ue·lon (mĭk′ə lŏn′; *Fr.* mē klôn′), *n.* See **St. Pierre and Miquelon.**

mir (mĭr), *n. Russian.* a Russian village commune.

Mir·a·beau (mĭr′ə bō′; *Fr.* mē rá bō′), *n.* Honoré Gabriel Victor Riqueti (ô nô rē′ gå brē ĕl′ vēk tôr′ rēk tē′), Count de, 1749–91, French Revolutionary statesman and orator.

mi·ra·bi·le dic·tu (mĭ răb′ə lē′ dĭk′tū, -tōō), *Latin.* strange to say; marvelous to relate.

mi·ra·bi·li·a (mĭr′ə bĭl′Ĭə), *n.pl. Latin.* marvels; miracles.

mi·ra·cid·i·um (mĭ′rə sĭd′Ĭəm), *n.*, *pl.* **-cidia** (-sĭd′Ĭ-ə). the larva that hatches from the egg of a trematode worm or fluke.

mir·a·cle (mĭr′ə kəl), *n.* **1.** an effect in the physical world which surpasses all known human or natural powers and is therefore ascribed to supernatural agency. **2.** a wonderful thing: a marvel. **3.** a wonderful or surpassing example of some quality. **4.** a miracle play. [ME, t. OF, t. L: m.s. *mīrāculum*]

miracle play, a medieval dramatic form dealing with religious subjects such as Biblical stories or saints' lives, usually presented in a series or cycle by the craft guilds.

mi·rac·u·lous (mĭ răk′yə ləs), *adj.* **1.** of the nature of a miracle; marvelous. **2.** performed by or involving a supernatural power: *a miraculous cure.* **3.** having power to work miracles; wonder-working: *miraculous drugs.* [t. ML: m.s. *mīrāculōsus*, der. L *mīrāculum* miracle] —**mi·rac′u·lous·ly**, *adv.* —**mi·rac′u·lous·ness**, *n.*

—**Syn. 2.** MIRACULOUS, PRETERNATURAL, SUPERNATURAL refer to that which seems to transcend the laws of nature. MIRACULOUS usually refers to an individual event which apparently contravenes known laws governing the universe: *a miraculous answer*, or *success.* PRETERNATURAL suggests the possession of supernormal gifts or qualities: *dogs have a preternatural sense of smell, bats have a sense of hearing that is preternatural.* SUPERNATURAL suggests divine or superhuman properties: *supernatural aid in battle.*

Mi·ra·flo·res (mē′rä flô′rĕs), *n.pl.* locks on the Panama Canal, near the Pacific entrance.

mi·rage (mĭ räzh′), *n.* an optical illusion, due to atmospheric conditions, by which reflected images of distant objects are seen, often inverted. [t. F, der. (*se*) *mirer* look at (oneself) in a mirror, see reflected, g. VL *mīrāre*. See MIRROR, ADMIRE]

mire (mĭr), *n.*, *v.*, **mired, miring.** —*n.* **1.** a piece of wet, swampy ground. **2.** ground of this kind; wet, slimy soil of some depth, or deep mud. —*v.t.* **3.** to plunge and fix in mire; cause to stick fast in mire. **4.** to involve in difficulties. **5.** to soil with mire or filth; bespatter with mire. —*v.i.* **6.** to sink in mire; stick in the mud. [ME *myre*, t. Scand.; cf. Icel. *mȳrr*]

mirk (mûrk), *n.*, *adj.* murk.

mirk·y (mûr′kĭ), *adj.*, **mirkier, mirkiest.** murky.

Mi·ró (mē rō′), *n.* Joan (hō än′), born 1893, Spanish surrealist painter.

mir·ror (mĭr′ər), *n.* **1.** a reflecting surface, originally polished metal, now usually glass with a metallic or amalgam backing; a looking glass. **2.** *Optics.* a surface (plane, concave, or convex) for reflecting rays of light; a speculum. **3.** something that gives a faithful reflection or true picture of something else. **4.** a pattern for imitation; exemplar. **5.** *Archaic.* a glass, crystal, or the like used by magicians, etc. —*v.t.* **6.** to reflect in or as in a mirror, or as a mirror does. [ME *mirour*, t. OF, der. ML *mīrāre* wonder at, admire, r. L *mīrārī*]

mirth (mûrth), *n.* **1.** rejoicing; joyous gaiety; festive jollity. **2.** humorous amusement, as at something ludicrous, or laughter excited by it. [ME; OE *myr(g)th, myrigth,* der. *myrige* MERRY. See -TH¹]

—**Syn. 2.** MIRTH, GLEE, HILARITY, MERRIMENT refer to the gaiety characterizing people who are enjoying the companionship of others. MIRTH suggests spontaneous amusement or gaiety, manifested briefly in laughter: *uncontrolled outbursts of mirth.* GLEE suggests an effervescence of high spirits or exultation, often manifested in playful or ecstatic gestures; it may apply also to a malicious rejoicing over mishaps to others: *glee over the failure of a rival.* HILARITY implies noisy and boisterous mirth, often exceeding the limits of reason or propriety: *hilarity aroused by practical jokes.* MERRIMENT suggests fun, good spirits, and good nature rather than the kind of wit and sometimes artificial funmaking which cause hilarity: *the house resounded with music and sounds of merriment.* —**Ant. 1.** gloom.

mirth·ful (mûrth′fəl), *adj.* **1.** full of mirth; joyous; jolly; laughingly gay or amused. **2.** affording mirth; amusing. —**mirth′ful·ly**, *adv.* —**mirth′ful·ness**, *n.*

mirth·less (mûrth′lĭs), *adj.* without mirth; joyless; gloomy. —**mirth′less·ly**, *adv.* —**mirth′less·ness**, *n.*

mir·y (mĭr′ĭ), *adj.*, **mirier, miriest. 1.** of the nature of mire; swampy: *miry ground.* **2.** abounding in mire; muddy. **3.** covered or bespattered with mire. **4.** dirty; filthy. —**mir′i·ness**, *n.*

mir·za (mûr′zə; *Pers.* mĭr′zä), *n.* (in Persia) **1.** a royal prince (as a title, placed after the name). **2.** a title of

honor for men (prefixed to the name). [t. Pers., apocopated var. of *mīrzād*, f. *mīr* prince (t. Ar., m. *amīr* EMIR) + *zād* born]

mis-¹, a prefix applied to various parts of speech, meaning "ill," "mistaken," "wrong," or simply negating, as in *mistrial, misprint, mistrust.* [ME and OE *mis*(s)-, c. G *miss*- (see MISS, **v.**); often r. ME *mes*-, t. OF, g. L *minus* (see MINUS)]

mis-², var. of *miso*-, before some vowels, as in *misanthrope.*

mis·ad·ven·ture (mĭs′ad věn′chər), *n.* **1.** a piece of ill fortune; a mishap. **2.** ill fortune.

mis·ad·vise (mĭs′əd vīz′), *v.t.* **-vised, -vising.** to advise wrongly.

mis·al·li·ance (mĭs′ə lī′əns), *n.* an improper alliance or association, esp. in marriage; a mésalliance. [half adoption, half trans. of F *mésalliance*]

mis·al·ly (mĭs′ə lī′), *v.t.* **-lied, -lying.** to ally improperly or unsuitably.

mis·an·thrope (mĭs′ən thrŏp′, mĭz′-), *n.* a hater of mankind. Also, **mis·an·thro·pist** (mĭs ăn′thrə pĭst). [t. Gk.: m.s. *misánthrōpos* hating mankind]

mis·an·throp·ic (mĭs′ən thrŏp′ĭk), *adj.* **1.** of, pertaining to, or characteristic of a misanthrope. **2.** having the character of, or resembling, a misanthrope. Also, **mis′an·throp′i·cal.** —**mis′an·throp′i·cal·ly**, *adv.*

mis·an·thro·py (mĭs ăn′thrə pĭ), *n.* hatred, dislike, or distrust of mankind.

mis·ap·plied (mĭs′ə plīd′), *adj.* mistakenly applied; used wrongly.

mis·ap·ply (mĭs′ə plī′), *v.t.* **-plied, -plying.** to make a wrong application or use of. —**mis·ap·pli·ca·tion** (mĭs′ăp lə kā′shən), *n.*

mis·ap·pre·hend (mĭs′ăp rĭ hĕnd′), *v.t.* to misunderstand.

mis·ap·pre·hen·sion (mĭs′ăp rĭ hĕn′shən), *n.* misunderstanding.

mis·ap·pro·pri·ate (mĭs′ə prō′prĭ āt′), *v.t.* **-ated, -ating. 1.** to put to a wrong use. **2.** to apply wrongfully or dishonestly to one's own use, as funds entrusted to one. —**mis′ap·pro·pri·a′tion**, *n.*

mis·ar·range (mĭs′ə rānj′), *v.t.* **-ranged, -ranging.** to arrange wrongly. —**mis′ar·range′ment**, *n.*

mis·be·come (mĭs′bĭ kŭm′), *v.t.* **-came, -come, -coming.** to be unsuitable, unbecoming, or unfit for.

mis·be·got·ten (mĭs′bĭ gŏt′ən), *adj.* unlawfully or irregularly begotten; illegitimate. Also, **mis′be·got′.**

mis·be·have (mĭs′bĭ hāv′), *v.t.*, *v.i.* **-haved, -having.** to behave badly. —**mis′be·hav′ior**, *n.*

mis·be·lief (mĭs′bĭ lēf′), *n.* **1.** erroneous belief; false opinion. **2.** erroneous or unorthodox religious belief.

mis·be·lieve (mĭs′bĭ lēv′), *v.i.*, *v.t.* **-lieved, -lieving.** —*v.t.* **1.** to believe wrongly; hold an erroneous belief. —*v.i.* **2.** to disbelieve; doubt. —**mis′be·liev′er**, *n.*

mis·be·stow (mĭs′bĭ stō′), *v.t.* to bestow improperly.

mis·brand (mĭs′brănd′), *v.t.* **1.** to brand or label erroneously. **2.** to brand with a simulated trademark or trade name.

misc., **1.** miscellaneous. **2.** miscellany.

mis·cal·cu·late (mĭs kăl′kyə lāt′), *v.t.*, *v.i.* **-lated, -lating.** to calculate wrongly. —**mis′cal·cu·la′tion**, *n.*

mis·call (mĭs kôl′), *v.t.* to call by a wrong name.

mis·car·riage (mĭs kăr′Ĭj), *n.* **1.** failure to attain the right or desired result: *a miscarriage of justice.* **2.** a transmission of goods not in accordance with the contract of shipment. **3.** failure of a letter, etc., to reach its destination. **4.** premature expulsion of a fetus from the uterus, esp. before it is viable.

mis·car·ry (mĭs kăr′Ĭ), *v.i.* **-ried, -rying. 1.** to fail to attain the right end; be unsuccessful. **2.** to go astray or be lost in transit, as a letter. **3.** to have a miscarriage.

mis·ce·ge·na·tion (mĭs′Ĭ jə nā′shən), *n.* **1.** mixture of races by sexual union. **2.** interbreeding between different races. [f. L *miscē(re)* mix + L *gen(us)* race + -ATION]

mis·cel·la·ne·a (mĭs′ə lā′nĭə), *n.pl.* a miscellaneous collection, esp. of literary compositions. [t. L, neut. pl. of *miscellāneus* MISCELLANEOUS]

mis·cel·la·ne·ous (mĭs′ə lā′nĭəs), *adj.* **1.** consisting of members or elements of different kinds: *miscellaneous volumes.* **2.** of mixed character. **3.** having various qualities or aspects; dealing with various subjects. [t. L: m. *miscellāneus*, der. *miscellus* mixed] —**mis′cel·la·ne·ous·ly**, *adv.* —**mis′cel·la·ne·ous·ness**, *n.*

—**Syn. 1.** MISCELLANEOUS, INDISCRIMINATE, PROMISCUOUS refer to mixture and lack of order, and may imply lack of discernment or taste. MISCELLANEOUS emphasizes the idea of the mixture of things of different kinds or natures: *a miscellaneous assortment of furniture.* INDISCRIMINATE emphasizes lack of discrimination in choice and consequent confusion: *indiscriminate praise.* PROMISCUOUS is even stronger than INDISCRIMINATE in its emphasis on complete absence of discrimination: *promiscuous in his friendships.*

mis·cel·la·ny (mĭs′ə lā′nĭ; *Brit.* mĭ sĕl′ə nĭ), *n.*, *pl.* **-nies. 1.** a miscellaneous collection of literary compositions or pieces by several authors, dealing with various topics, assembled in a volume or book. **2.** (*pl.*) miscellaneous collection of articles or entries, as in a book. [Anglicized var. of MISCELLANEA]

mis·chance (mĭs chăns′, -chäns′), *n.* ill luck; a mishap or misfortune. [ME *meschance*, t. OF: m. *mescheance.* See MIS-¹, CHANCE]

b., blend of, blended; c., cognate with; d., dialect, dialectal; der., derived from; f., formed from; g., going back to; m., modification of; r., replacing; s., stem of; t., taken from; ?, perhaps. See the full key on inside cover.

mis·chief (mĭs′chĭf), *n.* **1.** harm or trouble, esp. as due to an agent or cause. **2.** an injury caused by a person or other agent, or an evil due to some cause. **3.** a cause or source of harm, evil, or annoyance. **4.** vexatious or annoying action. **5.** a tendency or disposition to tease, vex, or annoy. **6.** conduct such as to cause petty annoyance by way of sport. **7.** *Colloq.* the devil. [ME *meschief*, t. OF, der. *meschever* succeed ill, f. *mes-* + *chever* come to an end, der. *chef* head, end (see CHIEF)] —Syn. **1.** See damage.

mis·chief-mak·er (mĭs′chĭf mā′kər), *n.* one who makes mischief; one who stirs up discord, as by talebearing. —**mis′chief-mak′ing**, *adj., n.*

mis·chie·vous (mĭs′chə vəs), *adj.* **1.** harmful or injurious. **2.** maliciously or playfully annoying, as persons, actions, etc. **3.** fond of mischief, as children. **4.** roguishly or archly teasing, as speeches, glances, etc. —**mis′chie·vous·ly**, *adv.* —**mis′chie·vous·ness**, *n.*

mis·ci·ble (mĭs′ə bəl), *adj.* capable of being mixed. [f. s. L *miscēre* mix + -IBLE] —**mis·ci·bil′i·ty**, *n.*

mis·col·or (mĭs kŭl′ər), *v.t.* **1.** to give a wrong color to. **2.** to misrepresent.

mis·con·ceive (mĭs′kən sēv′), *v.t., v.i.,* -ceived, -ceiving. to conceive wrongly; misunderstand. —**mis′con·ceiv′er**, *n.*

mis·con·cep·tion (mĭs′kən sĕp′shən), *n.* erroneous conception; a mistaken notion.

mis·con·duct (*n.* mĭs kŏn′dŭkt; *v.* mĭs′kən dŭkt′), *n.* **1.** improper conduct; wrong behavior. **2.** unlawful conduct by an official in regard to his office, or by a person in the administration of justice, such as a lawyer, witness, or juror. —*v.t.* **3.** to mismanage. **4.** to misbehave (oneself).

mis·con·struc·tion (mĭs′kən strŭk′shən), *n.* **1.** wrong construction; misinterpretation. **2.** act of misconstruing.

mis·con·strue (mĭs′kən strōō′, mĭs kŏn′strōō), *v.t.,* -strued, -struing. to construe wrongly; take in a wrong sense; misinterpret; misunderstand.

mis·count (mĭs kount′), *v.t., v.i.* **1.** to count erroneously; miscalculate. —*n.* **2.** an erroneous counting; a miscalculation.

mis·cre·ance (mĭs′krĭ əns), *n. Archaic.* wrong belief; misbelief; false religious faith.

mis·cre·an·cy (mĭs′krĭ ən sĭ), *n. Archaic.* **1.** miscreance. **2.** state or condition of a miscreant; turpitude.

mis·cre·ant (mĭs′krĭ ənt), *adj.* **1.** depraved, villainous, or base. **2.** *Archaic.* misbelieving; holding a false religious belief. —*n.* **3.** a vile wretch; villain. **4.** *Archaic.* a misbelieving person, as a heretic or an infidel. [ME *miscreaunt*, t. OF: m. *mescreant*, f. *mes-* MIS-¹ + *creant*, ppr. of *creire* believe, g. L *crēdere*]

mis·cre·ate (mĭs′krĭ āt′), *v.,* -ated, -ating, —*v.t., v.i.* **1.** *Rare.* to create amiss. —*adj.* **2.** *Archaic.* miscreated.

mis·cre·at·ed (mĭs′krĭ ā′tĭd), *adj.* wrongly created; misshapen; monstrous.

mis·cue (mĭs kū′), *n., v.,* -cued, -cuing. —*n.* **1.** *Billiards, etc.* a slip of the cue, causing it to strike the ball improperly or not at all. —*v.i.* **2.** to make a miscue. **3.** *Theat.* to fail to answer one's cue or to answer another's cue.

mis·date (mĭs dāt′), *v.,* -dated, -dating, *n.* —*v.t.* **1.** to date wrongly; assign or affix a wrong date to. —*n.* **2.** a wrong date.

mis·deal (mĭs dēl′), *v.,* -dealt, -dealing, *n.* —*v.t., v.i.* **1.** to deal wrongly, esp. at cards. —*n.* **2.** a wrong deal. —**mis·deal′er**, *n.*

mis·deed (mĭs dēd′), *n.* an ill deed; a wicked action.

mis·de·mean (mĭs′dĭ mēn′), *v.t., v.i.* to misbehave.

mis·de·mean·ant (mĭs′dĭ mē′nənt), *n.* **1.** one guilty of misbehavior. **2.** *Law.* one convicted of a misdemeanor.

mis·de·mean·or (mĭs′dĭ mē′nər), *n.* **1.** misbehavior; a misdeed. **2.** *Law.* an offense defined as less serious than a felony. Also, *esp. Brit.,* **mis′de·mean′our**.

mis·de·rive (mĭs′dĭ rīv′), *v.i., v.t.,* -rived, -riving. to derive wrongly; assign a wrong derivation to.

mis·de·scribe (mĭs′dĭ skrīb′), *v.t., v.i.,* -scribed, -scribing. to describe incorrectly or falsely. —**mis·de·scrip·tion** (mĭs′dĭ skrĭp′shən), *n.*

mis·di·rect (mĭs′dĭ rĕkt′), *v.t.* to direct wrongly.

mis·di·rec·tion (mĭs′dĭ rĕk′shən), *n.* **1.** a wrong indication, guidance, or instruction. **2.** *Law.* an erroneous charge to the jury by a judge.

mis·do (mĭs dōō′), *v.t., v.i.,* -did, -done, -doing. to do wrongly. [ME *misdo(n)*, OE *misdōn*. See MIS-¹, DO¹] —**mis·do′er**, *n.* —**mis·do′ing**, *n.*

mis·doubt (mĭs dout′), *Archaic.* —*v.t., v.i.* **1.** to doubt or suspect. —*n.* **2.** doubt or suspicion.

mise (mēz, mīz), *n.* a settlement or agreement. [late ME, t. AF, der. *mettre* put, set, g. L *mittere* send]

mis·ease (mĭs ēz′), *n. Archaic.* **1.** discomfort; distress; suffering. **2.** poverty.

mise en scène (mē zän sĕn′), *French.* **1.** the equipment for a stage setting. **2.** stage setting, as of a play. **3.** the surroundings amid which anything is seen.

mis·em·ploy (mĭs′ĕm ploi′), *v.t., v.i.* to employ wrongly or improperly; misuse. —**mis·em·ploy′ment**, *n.*

Mi·se·no (mē zĕ′nō), *n.* a cape in SW Italy, on the N shore of the Bay of Naples: ruins of ancient **Mi·se·num** (mī sē′nəm), a Roman naval station and resort.

mi·ser (mī′zər), *n.* **1.** one who lives in wretched circumstances in order to save and hoard money. **2.** a niggardly, avaricious person. **3.** a wretched or unhappy person. [t. L: wretched, unhappy, sick, bad]

mis·er·a·ble (mĭz′ər ə bəl, mĭz′rə-), *adj.* **1.** wretchedly unhappy, uneasy, or uncomfortable. **2.** wretchedly poor; needy. **3.** *Colloq.* being in poor health; ailing. **4.** of wretched character or quality; contemptible; wretchedly bad. **5.** attended with or causing misery: *a miserable existence.* **6.** manifesting misery. **7.** worthy of pity; deplorable: *a miserable failure.* [t. L: m.s. *miserābilis* pitiable] —**mis′er·a·ble·ness**, *n.* —**mis′er·a·bly**, *adv.* —Syn. **1.** forlorn, disconsolate, doleful. See wretched. **4.** despicable, mean. **7.** pitiable; lamentable. —Ant. happy.

Mis·e·re·re (mĭz′ə râr′ĭ, -rĭr′ĭ), *n. Latin.* **1.** the 51st psalm (50th in the Vulgate and Douay versions), one of the penitential psalms. **2.** a musical setting for it. **3.** (*l.c.*) a prayer or expression asking for mercy. **4.** (*l.c.*) misericord (def. 3). [L: have pity; the first word of the psalm in the Vulgate]

mis·er·i·cord (mĭz′ər ə kôrd′, mĭ zĕr′ə kôrd′), *n.* **1.** a relaxation of a monastic rule. **2.** a room in a monastery where such relaxations were permitted. **3.** a small projection on the underside of a hinged seat of a church stall, which, when the seat was thrown back, gave support to a person standing in the stall. **4.** a medieval dagger, used for the mercy stroke to a wounded foe. Also, **mis′er·i·corde′**. [ME *misericorde*, t. OF, t. L: m.s. *misericordia* mercy]

mis·er·i·cor·di·a (mĭz′ər ə kôr′dĭ ə), *n. Latin.* compassion; mercy.

mi·ser·ly (mī′zər lĭ), *adj.* of, like, or befitting a miser; penurious; niggardly. —**mi′ser·li·ness**, *n.*

mis·er·y (mĭz′ər ĭ), *n., pl.* -eries. **1.** wretchedness of condition or circumstances. **2.** distress caused by privation or poverty. **3.** great distress of mind; extreme unhappiness. **4.** a cause or source of wretchedness. **5.** *Dial.* bodily pain. [ME *miserie*, t. L: m. *miseria*] —Syn. **3.** grief, anguish, woe. See sorrow.

mis·es·teem (mĭs′ĕs tēm′), *v.t.* to esteem wrongly; fail to esteem or respect properly.

mis·es·ti·mate (*v.* mĭs ĕs′tə māt′; *n.* mĭs ĕs′tə mĭt), *v.,* -mated, -mating, *n.* —*v.t.* **1.** to estimate wrongly or incorrectly. —*n.* **2.** wrong estimate.

mis·fea·sance (mĭs fē′zəns), *n. Law.* **1.** wrong, actual or alleged, arising from or consisting of affirmative action (contrasted with *nonfeasance*). **2.** the wrongful performance of a normally lawful act; the wrongful and injurious exercise of lawful authority. [AF: m. *mesfesance*, der. *mesfaire* misdo. See MIS-, FEASANCE, and cf. MALFEASANCE]

mis·fea·sor (mĭs fē′zər), *n. Law.* one guilty of misfeasance.

mis·fire (mĭs fīr′), *v.,* -fired, -firing, *n.* —*v.i.* **1.** to fail to be fired or exploded. —*n.* **2.** a failure in firing.

mis·fit (mĭs fĭt′; *for 3 also* mĭs′fĭt′), *v.,* -fitted, -fitting, *n.* —*v.t., v.i.* **1.** to fit badly. —*n.* **2.** a bad fit; an ill-fitting garment, etc. **3.** a badly adjusted person.

mis·for·tune (mĭs fôr′chən), *n.* **1.** ill or adverse fortune; ill luck. **2.** an instance of this; a mischance or mishap. —Syn. **2.** accident; disaster, calamity, catastrophe; reverse; blow. See affliction.

mis·give (mĭs gĭv′), *v.,* -gave, -given, -giving. —*v.t.* **1.** (of one's mind, heart, etc.) to give doubt or apprehension to. —*v.i.* **2.** to be apprehensive.

mis·giv·ing (mĭs gĭv′ĭng), *n.* a feeling of doubt, distrust, or apprehension. —Syn. See apprehension.

mis·gov·ern (mĭs gŭv′ərn), *v.t.* to govern or manage badly. —**mis·gov′ern·ment**, *n.* —**mis·gov′er·nor**, *n.*

mis·guide (mĭs gīd′), *v.t.,* -guided, -guiding. to guide wrongly; mislead. —**mis·guid′ance**, *n.* —**mis·guid′er**, *n.*

mis·guid·ed (mĭs gī′dĭd), *adj.* misled. —**mis·guid′ed·ly**, *adv.*

mis·han·dle (mĭs hăn′dəl), *v.t.,* -dled, -dling. to handle badly; maltreat.

mis·hap (mĭs′hăp, mĭs hăp′), *n.* an unfortunate accident.

Mish·a·wa·ka (mĭsh′ə wô′kə), *n.* a city in N Indiana, near South Bend. 33,361 (1960).

mis·hear (mĭs hĭr′), *v.t., v.i.,* -heard, -hearing. to hear incorrectly or imperfectly.

mish·mash (mĭsh′măsh′), *n.* a hodgepodge; a jumble.

Mish·nah (mĭsh′nə), *n., pl.* **Mishnayoth** (mĭsh′nä-yōth′). **1.** the collection of oral laws made by Judah ha-Nasi (A.D. c135–c220), which forms the basis of the Talmud. **2.** a paragraph of the Mishnah. Also, **Mish′na**. [t. Heb.: repetition, study] —**Mish·na·ic** (mĭsh-nā′ĭk), **Mish′nic, Mish′ni·cal**, *adj.*

mis·in·form (mĭs′ĭn fôrm′), *v.t.* to give false or misleading information to. —**mis·in·form′ant**, **mis′-in·form′er**, *n.* —**mis′in·for·ma′tion**, *n.*

mis·in·ter·pret (mĭs′ĭn tûr′prĭt), *v.t.* to interpret, explain, or understand incorrectly. —**mis′in·ter·pre·ta′tion**, *n.*

mis·join·der (mĭs join′dər), *n. Law.* a joining in one suit or action of causes or of parties not permitted to be so joined.

mis·judge (mĭs jŭj′), *v.t., v.i.,* -judged, -judging. to judge wrongly or unjustly. —**mis·judg′ment**; *esp. Brit.,* **mis·judge′ment**, *n.*

mis·lay (mĭs·lā′), *v.t.*, **-laid, -laying. 1.** to put in a place afterward forgotten. **2.** to lay or place wrongly; misplace. —**mis·lay′er,** *n.*

mis·lead (mĭs·lēd′), *v.t.*, **-led, -leading. 1.** to lead or guide wrongly; lead astray. **2.** to lead into error of conduct, thought, or judgment. —**mis·lead′er,** *n.* —**mis·lead′ing,** *adj.* —**mis·lead′ing·ly,** *adv.*

mis·like (mĭs·līk′), **-liked, -liking. 1.** to dislike. **2.** to displease. —**mis·lik′er,** *n.* —**mis·lik′ing,** *n.*

mis·man·age (mĭs·măn′ĭj), *v.t., v.i.*, **-aged, -aging.** to manage badly. —**mis·man′age·ment,** *n.*

mis·mar·riage (mĭs·măr′ĭj), *n.* an unsuitable or unhappy marriage.

mis·match (mĭs·măch′), *v.t.* **1.** to match badly or unsuitably. —*n.* **2.** a bad or unsatisfactory match.

mis·mate (mĭs·māt′), *v.t., v.i.*, **-mated, -mating.** to mate amiss or unsuitably.

mis·move (mĭs·mōōv′), *n.* a wrong move, as in a game or any course of procedure.

mis·name (mĭs·nām′), *v.t.*, **-named, -naming.** to call by a wrong name.

mis·no·mer (mĭs·nō′mər), *n.* **1.** a misapplied name or designation. **2.** an error in naming a person or thing. [ME *misnoumer,* t. OF: m. *mesnommer,* n. use of inf., f. *mes-* MIS-- + *nommer* name, g. L *nōmināre.* See NOMINATE]

miso-, a word element referring to hate. [t. Gk., comb. form of *mīsein* to hate, *mīsos* hatred]

mi·sog·a·my (mĭ·sŏg′ə·mĭ, mī-), *n.* hatred of marriage. —**mi·sog′a·mist,** *n.*

mi·sog·y·ny (mĭ·sŏj′ə·nĭ, mī-), *n.* hatred of women. [t. Gk.: m.s. *mīsogynía*] —**mi·sog′y·nist,** *n.* —**mi·sog′y·nous,** *adj.*

mi·sol·o·gy (mĭ·sŏl′ə·jĭ, mī-), *n.* hatred of reason or reasoning. [t. Gk.: m.s. *mīsología* hatred of argument] —**mi·sol′o·gist,** *n.*

mis·o·ne·ism (mĭs′ō·nē′ĭz·əm, mī′sō-), *n.* hatred or dislike of what is new. [t. It.: m. *misoneismo,* f. *miso-* MISO- + s. Gk. *néos* new + *-ismo* -ISM] —**mis′o·ne′ist,** *n.*

mis·pick·el (mĭs′pĭk′əl), *n.* arsenopyrite. [t. G]

mis·place (mĭs·plās′), *v.t.*, **-placed, -placing. 1.** to put in a wrong place. **2.** to place or bestow improperly, unsuitably, or unwisely. —**mis·place′ment,** *n.* —**Syn. 1.** See displace.

mis·play (mĭs·plā′), *n.* a wrong play.

mis·plead (mĭs·plēd′), *v.t., v.i.* to plead incorrectly.

mis·plead·ing (mĭs·plē′dĭng), *n. Law.* a mistake in pleading, as a misjoinder of parties, a misstatement of a cause of action, etc.

mis·print (*n.* mĭs·prĭnt′, mĭs′prĭnt′; *v.* mĭs·prĭnt′), *n.* **1.** a mistake in printing. —*v.t.* **2.** to print incorrectly.

mis·pri·sion (mĭs·prĭzh′ən), *n.* **1.** a wrongful action or commission, esp. of a public official. **2.** neglect to give notice of an act of treason or felony. [ME, t. OF, der. *mesprendre* mistake, do wrong, f. *mes-* MIS-¹ + *prendre* take, g. L *prehendere*]

mis·prize (mĭs·prīz′), *v.t.*, **-prized, -prizing.** to despise; undervalue; slight; scorn. [t. OF: m. *mesprisier,* f. *mes-* MIS-¹ + *prisier* PRIZE²]

mis·pro·nounce (mĭs′prə·nouns′), *v.t., v.i.*, **-nounced, -nouncing.** to pronounce incorrectly. —**mis·pro·nun·ci·a·tion** (mĭs′prə·nŭn′sĭ·ā′shən), *n.*

mis·quote (mĭs·kwōt′), *v.t., v.i.*, **-quoted, -quoting.** to quote incorrectly. —**mis′quo·ta′tion,** *n.*

mis·read (mĭs·rēd′), *v.t.*, **-read, -reading.** to read wrongly; misinterpret.

mis·reck·on (mĭs·rĕk′ən), *v.t., v.i.* to reckon incorrectly; miscalculate.

mis·re·mem·ber (mĭs′rĭ·mĕm′bər), *v.t., v.i.* **1.** to remember incorrectly. **2.** *Dial.* to fail to remember.

mis·re·port (mĭs′rĭ·pōrt′), *v.t.* **1.** to report incorrectly or falsely. —*n.* **2.** an incorrect or false report. —**mis′re·port′er,** *n.*

mis·rep·re·sent (mĭs′rĕp·rĭ·zĕnt′), *v.t.* to represent incorrectly, improperly, or falsely. —**mis′rep·re·sen·ta′tion,** *n.* —**mis′rep·re·sent′er,** *n.* —**mis′rep·re·sen′ta·tive,** *adj.*

mis·rule (mĭs·rōōl′), *n., v.*, **-ruled, -ruling.** —*n.* **1.** bad or unwise rule; misgovernment. **2.** disorder or lawless tumult. —*v.t.* **3.** to misgovern. —**mis·rul′er,** *n.*

miss¹ (mĭs), *v.t.* **1.** to fail to hit, light upon, meet, catch, receive, obtain, attain, accomplish, see, hear, etc.: *to miss a train.* **2.** to fail to perform, attend to, be present at, etc.: *to miss an appointment.* **3.** to perceive the absence or loss of, often with regret. **4.** to escape or avoid: *he just missed being caught.* **5.** to fail to perceive or understand: *to miss the point of a remark.* **6. miss fire, a.** to fail to go off, as a firearm. **b.** to fail in any action; prove unsuccessful. —*v.i.* **7.** to fail to hit, light upon, receive, or attain something. **8.** to fail of effect or success; be unsuccessful. —*n.* **9.** a failure to hit, meet, obtain, or accomplish something. **10.** an omission. [ME *misse,* OE *missan,* c. D and G *missen*]

miss² (mĭs), *n., pl.* **misses. 1.** (*cap.*) the conventional title of respect for an unmarried woman, prefixed to the name. **2.** (without the name) a term of address to an unmarried woman. **3.** a young unmarried woman; a girl. [short for MISTRESS]

Miss., Mississippi.

mis·sal (mĭs′əl), *n.* the book containing the prayers and rites for celebrating Mass, used by the priest at the altar. [ME, t. ML: s. *missāle,* neut. of *missālis,* der. LL *missa* MASS²]

Mis·sa So·lem·nis (mĭs′ə sō·lĕm′nĭs), Mass in D, Op. 123 (1818–23, published 1827) by Beethoven.

mis·say (mĭs·sā′), *v.,* **-said, -saying.** *Archaic.* —*v.t.* **1.** to say or speak ill of; abuse; slander. **2.** to say wrongly. —*v.i.* **3.** to speak wrongly.

mis·sel thrush (mĭs′əl), a large European thrush, *Turdus viscivorus,* which is fond of the berries of the mistletoe. Also, **mis′sel.** [see MISTLE(TOE), THRUSH¹]

mis·shape (mĭs·shāp′), *v.t.*, **-shaped, -shaped** or **-shapen, -shaping.** to shape ill; deform.

mis·shap·en (mĭs·shā′pən), *adj.* badly shaped; deformed. —**mis·shap′en·ly,** *adv.* —**mis·shap′en·ness,** *n.*

mis·sile (mĭs′əl), *n.* **1.** an object or weapon that can be thrown, hurled, or shot, as a stone, a bullet, a lance, or an arrow. **2.** a guided missile. —*adj.* **3.** capable of being thrown, hurled, or shot, as from the hand, a gun, etc. **4.** that discharges missiles. [t. L: something which can be thrown]

miss·ing (mĭs′ĭng), *adj.* lacking; absent; not found.

missing link, 1. a hypothetical form of animal assumed to have constituted a connecting link between the anthropoid apes and man. **2.** something lacking for the completion of a series or sequence of any kind.

mis·sion (mĭsh′ən), *n.* **1.** a body of persons sent to a foreign country to conduct negotiations, establish relations, or the like. **2.** the business with which an agent, envoy, etc., is charged. **3.** *U.S.* a permanent diplomatic establishment abroad: *chief of mission.* **4.** *Mil.* an operation, by one or more war aircraft, against the enemy. **5.** a body of persons sent into a foreign land for religious work among a heathen people, or into any region for the spiritual betterment of the inhabitants. **6.** an establishment of missionaries in a foreign land; a missionary post or station. **7.** a similar establishment in any region, designed for the spiritual betterment of its people. **8.** the district assigned to a missionary priest. **9.** missionary duty or work. **10.** an organization for carrying on missionary work. **11.** (*pl.*) organized missionary work or activities in any country, region, or field: *foreign missions.* **12.** a church or a region with a minister or priest who lives near by but who is non-resident. **13.** a series of special religious services for quickening piety and converting unbelievers: *to preach a mission.* **14.** a self-imposed duty. **15.** a sending or being sent for some duty or purpose. **16.** those sent. [t. L: s. *missio* a sending] —**mis′sion·er,** *n.*

mis·sion·ar·y (mĭsh′ə·nĕr′ĭ), *n., pl.* **-aries,** *adj.* —*n.* **1.** a person sent to work for the propagation of his religious faith in a heathen land or a newly settled district. **2.** any propagandist. **3.** one sent on a mission. —*adj.* **4.** pertaining to or connected with religious missions. **5.** engaged in such a mission, or devoted to work connected with missions. **6.** pertaining to any propaganda. **7.** characteristic of a propagandist. [f. MISSION + -ARY¹]

Missionary Ridge, a ridge in NW Georgia and SE Tennessee: Union victory near Chattanooga, 1863.

mis·sis (mĭs′ĭz, -ĭs), *n. Colloq.* or *Dial.* **1.** a man's wife. **2.** the mistress of a household. Also, **missus.**

miss·ish (mĭs′ĭsh), *adj.* prim; affected; prudish.

Mis·sis·sip·pi (mĭs′ə·sĭp′ĭ), *n.* **1.** a State in the S United States. 2,178,141 pop. (1960); 47,716 sq. mi. *Cap.:* Jackson. *Abbr.:* Miss. **2.** a river flowing from N Minnesota S to the Gulf of Mexico: the principal river of the U.S. 2470 mi.; from the headwaters of the Missouri to the Gulf of Mexico, 3988 mi.

Mis·sis·sip·pi·an (mĭs′ə·sĭp′ĭ·an), *adj.* **1.** of or pertaining to the State of Mississippi or the Mississippi river. **2.** *Stratig.* pertaining to a late Paleozoic geological period or a system equivalent to the Lower Carboniferous of usage outside of North America. **3.** a native or inhabitant of Mississippi. **4.** *Stratig.* the period or system following Devonian and preceding Pennsylvanian.

mis·sive (mĭs′ĭv), *n.* **1.** a written message; a letter. —*adj.* **2.** sent, esp. from an official source. [late ME, t. ML: m.s. *missivus,* der. L *missus,* pp., sent]

Mis·so·lon·ghi (mĭs′ə·lŏng′gĭ), *n.* a town in W Greece: Byron died here, 1824. 13,837 (1951). Also, **Mesolonghi.**

Mis·sou·la (mĭ·zōō′lə), *n.* a city in W Montana. 27,090 (1960).

Mis·sour·i (mĭ·zŏŏr′ĭ, -zŏŏr′ə), *n.* **1.** a State in the central United States. 4,319,813 (1960); 69,674 sq. mi. *Cap.:* Jefferson City. *Abbr.:* Mo. **2.** from **Missouri,** *Slang.* skeptical; requiring proof. **3.** a river flowing from SW Montana into the Mississippi N of St. Louis, Missouri. 2723 mi. **4.** (*pl.*) a North American Indian tribe belonging to the Siouan linguistic stock, located on the Missouri river in early historic times; now extinct as a tribe. —**Mis·sour′i·an,** *adj., n.*

mis·speak (mĭs·spēk′), *v.t., v.i.*, **-spoke, -spoken, -speaking.** to speak, utter, or pronounce incorrectly.

mis·spell (mĭs·spĕl′), *v.t., v.i.*, **-spelled** or **-spelt, -spelling.** to spell incorrectly. —**mis·spell′ing,** *n.*

mis·spend (mĭs·spĕnd′), *v.t.*, **-spent, -spending.** to spend improperly; squander; waste.

mis·state (mĭs·stāt′), *v.t.*, **-stated, -stating.** to state wrongly or misleadingly; make a wrong statement about. —**mis·state′ment,** *n.*

mis·step (mĭs·stĕp′), *n.* **1.** a wrong step. **2.** an error or slip in conduct.

mis·sus (mĭs′əz, -əs), *n. Colloq.* or *Dial.* missis.

miss·y (mĭs′ĭ), *n., pl.* **missies.** *Colloq.* young miss.

mist (mǐst), *n.* **1.** a cloudlike aggregation of minute globules of water suspended in the atmosphere at or near the earth's surface. **2.** *Meteorol.* (by international agreement) a very thin fog in which the horizontal visibility is greater than 1 kilometer; in the U.S., synonymous with *drizzle.* **3.** a cloud of particles resembling a mist. **4.** something which dims, obscures, or blurs. **5.** a hazy appearance before the eyes, as due to tears or to bodily disorders. **6.** a suspension of a liquid in a gas. —*v.i.* **7.** to become misty. **8.** to rain in very fine drops; drizzle. —*v.t.* **9.** to make misty. [ME and OE, c. D, LG, and Sw. *mist*] —Syn. **5.** See **cloud.**

mis·tak·a·ble (mǐs tāʹkə bəl; *commonly* mə stāʹ-), *adj.* that may be mistaken or misunderstood.

mis·take (mǐs tākʹ; *commonly* mə stākʹ), *n., v.,* **-took, -taken, -taking.** —*n.* **1.** an error in action, opinion, or judgment. **2.** a misconception or misapprehension. —*v.t.* **3.** to take or regard as something or somebody else. **4.** to conceive of or understand wrongly; misapprehend; misunderstand. —*v.i.* **5.** to be in error. [ME *mistake*(n), v., t. Scand.; cf. Icel. *mistaka* take by mistake. See MIS-¹, TAKE]
—Syn. **1.** MISTAKE, BLUNDER, ERROR, SLIP refer to deviations from right, accuracy, correctness, or truth. A MISTAKE, grave or trivial, is caused by bad judgment or a disregard of rule or principle: *it was a mistake to argue.* A BLUNDER is a careless, stupid, or gross mistake in action or speech, suggesting awkwardness, heedlessness, or ignorance: *through his blunder the message was lost.* An ERROR (often interchanged with MISTAKE) is an unintentional wandering or deviation from accuracy, or right conduct: *an error in addition.* A SLIP is usually a minor mistake made through haste or carelessness: *a slip of the tongue.*

mis·tak·en (mǐs tāʹkən; *commonly* mə stāʹ-), *adj.* **1.** wrongly conceived, entertained, or done: *a mistaken notion.* **2.** erroneous; wrong. **3.** having made a mistake; being in error. —**mis·takʹen·ly,** *adv.*

Mis·tas·si·ni (mǐsʹtə sēʹnǐ), *n.* a lake in E Canada, in Quebec province. ab. 100 mi. long; 975 sq. mi.

mis·teach (mǐs tēchʹ), *v.t.,* **-taught, -teaching.** to teach wrongly or badly.

mis·ter (mǐsʹtər), *n.* **1.** (*cap.*) the conventional title of respect for a man, prefixed to the name and to certain official designations (usually written *Mr.*). **2.** *Colloq.* (in address, without the name) sir. **3.** the official title used in addressing: **a.** *Mil.* a warrant officer, or a cadet in the U.S. Military Academy. **b.** *Naval.* anyone of a rank lower than that of a commander. **c.** *Naut.* any officer other than the captain. —*v.t.* **4.** *Colloq.* to address or speak of as "mister" or "Mr." [var. of MASTER]

mist-flow·er (mǐstʹflouʹər), *n.* a North American composite plant, *Eupatorium* (*Conoclinium*) *coelestinum,* with heads of blue flowers.

Mis·ti (mēsʹtē), *n.* El Misti.

mis·time (mǐs tīmʹ), *v.t.,* **-timed, -timing.** to time wrongly; perform, say, etc., at a wrong time.

mis·tle·toe (mǐsʹəl tōʹ), *n.* **1.** a European plant, *Viscum album* (family *Loranthaceae*), with yellowish flowers and white berries, growing parasitically on various trees, much used in Christmas decorations. **2.** any of various other plants of the same family, as *Phoradendron flavescens* of the U.S., also used in Christmas decorations. [ME *mistelto,* OE *misteltān* (c. Icel. *mistilteinn*), f. *mistel* mistletoe + *tān* twig]

mis·took (mǐs tŏŏkʹ), *v.* pt. of **mistake.**

mis·tral (mǐsʹtrəl, mǐs trälʹ), *n.* a cold, dry, northerly wind common in southern France and neighboring regions. [t. F: lit., master wind, t. Pr.: important, g. L *magistrālis* MAGISTRAL]

Mis·tral (mēs trälʹ), *n.* **Frédéric** (frā dā rēkʹ), 1830–1914, French Provençal poet.

mis·trans·late (mǐsʹtrǎns lātʹ, -trǎnz-), *v.t., v.i.,* **-lated, -lating.** to translate incorrectly. —**misʹtrans·laʹtion,** *n.*

mis·treat (mǐs trētʹ), *v.t.* to treat badly or wrongly. —**mis·treatʹment,** *n.*

mis·tress (mǐsʹtrǐs), *n.* **1.** a woman who has authority or control; the female head of a household or some other establishment. **2.** a woman employing, or in authority over, servants or attendants. **3.** a female owner, as of a slave, horse, dog, etc. **4.** a woman who has the power of controlling or disposing of something at pleasure. **5.** something regarded as feminine which has control or supremacy: *Great Britain, the mistress of the seas.* **6.** *Brit.* a female teacher; a schoolmistress. **7.** a woman who illicitly occupies the place of a wife. **8.** *Archaic or Poetic.* sweetheart. **9.** *Archaic or Dial.* a term of address for a woman. Cf. **Mrs.** and **Miss.** [ME *maistresse,* t. OF, fem. of *maistre* MASTER]

mis·tri·al (mǐs trīʹəl), *n. Law.* **1.** a trial terminated without conclusion on the merits because of some error. **2.** an inconclusive trial, as where the jury cannot agree.

mis·trust (mǐs trŭstʹ), *n.* **1.** lack of trust or confidence; distrust. —*v.t.* **2.** to regard with mistrust; distrust. **3.** *Rare.* to suspect or surmise. —*v.i.* **4.** to be distrustful. —**mis·trustʹer,** *n.* —**mis·trustʹing·ly,** *adv.*

mis·trust·ful (mǐs trŭstʹfəl), *adj.* full of mistrust; suspicious. —**mis·trustʹful·ly,** *adv.* —**mis·trustʹful·ness,** *n.*

mist·y (mǐsʹtǐ), *adj.,* **mistier, mistiest. 1.** abounding in or clouded by mist; of the nature of or consisting of mist. **2.** appearing as if seen through mist; indistinct in form or outline. **3.** obscure; vague. [ME; OE *mistig*] —**mistʹi·ly,** *adv.* —**mistʹi·ness,** *n.*

mis·un·der·stand (mǐsʹŭn dər stǎndʹ), *v.t.,v.i.,* **-stood, -standing. 1.** to misinterpret the words or actions of (a person). **2.** to understand wrongly; take (words, statements, etc.) in a wrong sense.

mis·un·der·stand·ing (mǐsʹŭn dər stǎnʹdǐng), *n.* **1.** disagreement or dissension. **2.** failure to understand; mistake as to meaning.

mis·un·der·stood (mǐsʹŭn dər stŏŏdʹ), *adj.* **1.** improperly interpreted. **2.** unappreciated.

mis·us·age (mǐs ūʹsǐj, -zʹǐj), *n.* **1.** wrong or improper usage, as of words. **2.** ill-use; bad treatment.

mis·use (*n.* mǐs ūsʹ; *v.* mǐs ūzʹ), *n., v.,* **-used, -using.** —*n.* **1.** wrong or improper use; misapplication. **2.** *Obs.* ill-usage. —*v.t.* **3.** to use wrongly or improperly; misapply. **4.** to ill-use; maltreat.

mis·us·er (mǐs ūʹzər), *n.* **1.** *Law.* abuse of a liberty or benefit or thing. **2.** one who misuses.

mis·val·ue (mǐs vǎlʹū), *v.t.,* **-ued, -uing.** to value wrongly.

mis·word (mǐs wûrdʹ), *v.t.* to word wrongly.

mis·write (mǐs rītʹ), *v.t.,* **-wrote, -written, -writing.** to write incorrectly.

Mitch·ell (mǐchʹəl), *n.* **1. Mount,** a mountain in W North Carolina: highest peak in the E United States. 6684 ft. **2. Maria,** 1818–89, U.S. astronomer. **3. Silas Weir** (wǐr), 1829–1914, U.S. physician and novelist. **4. William,** 1879–1936, U.S. Army officer in World War I: early advocate of strong air force.

mite¹ (mīt), *n.* any of various small arachnids (order *Acari*) with a saclike body, many being parasitic on plants and animals, others living in cheese, flour, unrefined sugar, etc. [ME *myte,* OE *mīte,* c. MD *mīte* (D *mijt*)]

mite² (mīt), *n.* **1.** a small contribution, but all that one can afford (in allusion to Mark 12:41–44): *to contribute one's mite.* **2.** a very small sum of money. **3.** a coin of very small value. **4.** a very small object. **5.** a very small creature. [ME, t. MD; ult. identical with MITE¹]

mi·ter (mīʹtər), *n.* **1.** the official headdress of a bishop in the Western Church, in its modern form a tall cap with a top deeply cleft crosswise, the outline of the front and back resembling that of a pointed arch. **2.** the office or rank of bishop; bishopric. **3.** the official headdress of the ancient Jewish high priest. **4.** a kind of headdress formerly worn by Asiatics. **5.** the abutting surface or bevel on either of the pieces joined in a miter joint. —*v.t.* **6.** to bestow a miter upon, or raise to a rank entitled to it. **7.** to join with a miter joint. **8.** to make a miter joint in; cut to a miter. Also, *esp. Brit.,* **mitre.** [ME *mitre,* t. L: m. *mitra,* t. Gk.: belt, headband, headdress]

Bishop's miter, 14th century

miter box, a box or apparatus for use in cutting miters (def. 5).

mi·tered (mīʹtərd), *adj.* **1.** shaped like a bishop's miter or having a miter-shaped apex. **2.** wearing, or entitled or privileged to wear, a miter. Also, *esp. Brit.,* **mitred.**

miter joint, a joint formed when two pieces of identical cross section are joined at the ends, and where the joined ends are beveled at equal angles.

Miter joint

mi·ter·wort (mīʹtər wûrtʹ), *n.* **1.** any of the low herbs which constitute the saxifragaceous genus *Mitella* (so called from the capsule, which resembles a bishop's miter). **2.** a low loganiaceous plant, *Cynoctonum Mitreola,* of the southeastern U.S. Also, *esp. Brit.,* **mitrewort.**

Mit·ford (mǐtʹfərd), *n.* **Mary Russell,** 1787–1855, British novelist and dramatist.

mith·er (mǐthʹər), *n. Scot. and N. Eng.* mother.

Mith·gar·thr (mǐthʹgär′thər), *n.* Icelandic name for Midgard.

Mith·ras (mǐthʹrǎs), *n. Persian Myth.* the god of light and truth, later of the sun. Also, **Mith·ra** (mǐthʹrə). [t. L, t. Gk., t. OPers.: m. *Mithra*] —**Mith·ra·ic** (mǐth rāʹǐk), *adj.* —**Mith·ra·i·cism** (mǐth rāʹə sǐzʹəm), **Mith·ra·ism** (mǐthʹrā ǐzʹəm), *n.* —**Mith·ra·ist** (mǐthʹrā ǐst), *n.* —**Mith·ra·is·tic,** *adj.*

Mith·ri·da·tes VI (mǐthʹrə dāʹtēz), ("*the Great*") c132–63 B.C., king of Pontus, 120?–63 B.C., and enemy of Rome.

mith·ri·da·tism (mǐthʹrə dāʹtǐzəm), *n.* the production of immunity against the action of a poison by taking the poison in gradually increased doses. [named after MITHRIDATES VI, said to have so immunized himself] —**mith·ri·datʹic** (mǐthʹrə dǎtʹǐk), *adj.*

mit·i·gate (mǐtʹə gātʹ), *v.,* **-gated, -gating.** —*v.t.* **1.** to lessen in force or intensity (wrath, grief, harshness, pain, etc.). **2.** to moderate the severity of (anything distressing). **3.** *Rare.* to make milder or more gentle; mollify. —*v.i.* **4.** to become milder; moderate in severity. [ME, t. L: m.s. *mītigātus,* pp.] —**mitʹi·gaʹtion,** *n.* —**mitʹi·gaʹtive, mit·i·ga·to·ry** (mǐtʹə gə tōrʹǐ), *adj.* —**mitʹi·gaʹtor,** *n.*

mi·tis (mīʹtǐs, mēʹ-), *n.* **1.** Also, **mitis metal.** a malleable iron produced by fusing wrought iron with a small amount of aluminum rendering the product fluid enough to cast. —*adj.* **2.** designating or pertaining to mitis. [t. L: mild]

mi·to·sis (mī tō′sĭs, mǐ-), *n. Biol.* the usual (indirect) method of cell division, characterized typically by the resolving of the chromatin of the nucleus into a thread-like form, which separates into segments or chromosomes, each of which separates longitudinally into two parts, one part of each chromosome being retained in each of two new cells resulting from the original cell. [t. NL, f. s. Gk. *mītos* a thread + *-osis -OSIS*] —**mi·tot·ic** (mī tŏt′ĭk, mǐ-), *adj.* —**mi·tot·i·cal·ly**, *adv.*

mi·trail·leur (mē trä yœr′), *n. French.* one who operates a mitrailleuse.

mi·trail·leuse (mē trä yœz′), *n. French.* a machine gun. [F, der. *mitraille* scrap iron, der. OF *mitre, mite* small coin, fragment of metal]

mi·tral (mī′trəl), *adj.* of or resembling a miter.

mitral valve, *Anat.* the valve between the left auricle and ventricle of the heart which prevents the blood from flowing back into the auricle.

mi·tre (mī′tər), *n., v.t.,* **-tred, -tring.** *Chiefly Brit.* miter. —**mi′tred,** *adj.*

mi·tre·wort (mī′tər wûrt′), *n. Chiefly Brit.* miterwort.

Mi·tro·pou·los (mī trŏ′pōō lôs′), *n.* Dimitri (dǐ mē′trǐ), 1897–1960, Greek orchestra conductor, in U.S.

mitt (mĭt), *n.* **1.** a kind of long glove extending only to, or slightly over, the fingers, worn by women. **2.** *Baseball.* a kind of glove having the side next to the palm of the hand protected by a large, thick mittenlike pad. **3.** a mitten. [apocopated var. of MITTEN]

mit·ten (mĭt′ən), *n.* **1.** a kind of hand covering enclosing the four fingers together and the thumb separately. **2.** a mitt (def. 1). **3.** (*pl.*) *Slang.* boxing gloves. [ME *myteyne*, t. OF: m. *mitaine*, g. Gallo-Rom. *medietāna* half (glove), der. L *medius* middle] —**mit′ten·like′,** *adj.*

mit·ti·mus (mĭt′ə məs), *n. Law.* **1.** a warrant of commitment to prison. **2.** a writ for removing a suit or a record from one court to another. [t. L: we send]

mitz·vah (mĭts′vä), *n., pl.* **-voth** (-vōth). *Jewish Relig.* **1.** an order or commandment from the Bible or the rabbis. **2.** a religious act; a meritorious deed. Also, **mits′vah.** [t. Heb.: m. *miṣwāh* commandment]

mix (mĭks), *v.,* **mixed** or **mixt, mixing,** *n.* —*v.t.* **1.** to put together (substances or things, or one substance or thing with another) in one mass or assemblage with more or less thorough diffusion of the constituent elements among one another. **2.** to put together indiscriminately or confusedly (often fol. by *up*). **3.** to combine, unite, or join: *to mix business and pleasure.* **4.** to put in as an added element or ingredient: *to mix a little soda into the flour.* **5.** to form by combining ingredients: *to mix bread, to mix mortar.* **6.** to crossbreed. **7.** to confuse completely (fol. by *up*). —*v.i.* **8.** to become mixed: *oil and water will not mix.* **9.** to associate, as in company. **10.** to be crossbred, or of mixed breeding. —*n.* **11.** a mixing, or a mixed condition; a mixture. **12.** *Colloq.* a muddle or mess. [back formation from *mixt* mixed, t. F: m. *mixte,* t. L: m. *mixtus,* pp.].

—**Syn. 1.** MIX, BLEND, COMBINE, MINGLE imply bringing two or more things into more or less intimate association. MIX is the general word for such association: *to mix fruit juices.* BLEND implies such a harmonious joining of two or more types of colors, feelings, etc., that the new product formed displays some of the qualities of each: *to blend fragrances or whiskeys.* COMBINE implies such a close or intimate union that distinction between the parts is lost: *to combine forces.* MINGLE usually suggests retained identity of the parts: *to mingle voices.* **2.** jumble, confuse. **9.** consort, mingle.

mixed (mĭkst), *adj.* **1.** put together or formed by mixing. **2.** composed of different constituents or elements; esp. in England, coeducational: *the children go to a mixed school.* **3.** of different kinds combined: *mixed candies.* **4.** comprising persons of different sexes, or of different classes, status, character, opinions, etc.: *mixed company.* **5.** *Law.* involving more than one issue or aspect: *a mixed question of law and fact.* **6.** *Colloq.* mentally confused. **7.** *Phonet.* (of a vowel) central. —**Syn. 1.** MIXED, MINGLED both refer to intimate association of two or more things. MIXED is generally applied to one noun, MINGLED commonly to two or more: *mixed feelings.*

mixed metaphor. See metaphor (def. 2).

mixed number, a number consisting of a whole number and a fraction, as 4½.

mix·er (mĭk′sər), *n.* **1.** one who or that which mixes. **2.** *Colloq.* a person with reference to his sociability: *a good mixer.*

mix·ture (mĭks′chər), *n.* **1.** a product of mixing. **2.** any combination of differing elements, kinds, qualities, etc.: *a curious mixture of eagerness and terror.* **3.** *Chem., Physics.* an aggregate of two or more substances which are not chemically united, and which exist in no fixed proportion to each other. **4.** a fabric woven of yarns combining various colors: *a heather mixture.* **5.** act of mixing. **6.** state of being mixed. **7.** an added element or ingredient; an admixture. [t. L: m.s. *mixtūra*] —**Syn. 1.** blend, combination; compound. **2.** conglomeration, miscellany, jumble; medley; melange, potpourri, hodgepodge, hotchpotch.

mix-up (mĭks′ŭp′), *n.* **1.** a confused state of things; a muddle; a tangle. **2.** *Colloq.* a fight.

miz·zen (mĭz′ən), *Naut.* —*n.* **1.** the lower sail set on the mizzenmast. **2.** a mizzenmast. —*adj.* **3.** of, relating to, or set on the mizzenmast. Also, **miz′en.** [ME *meseyn,* t. F: m. *misaine,* t. It.: m. *mezzana,* prop. fem. of *mezzano* middle, g. L *mediānus.* See MEDIAN]

miz·zen·mast (mĭz′ən mäst′, -măst′; *Naut.* -məst), *n. Naut.* **1.** the aftermost mast of a three-masted vessel, or the third on a vessel with more than three masts. **2.** the after and shorter of the two masts of a yawl or ketch. Also, **miz′en·mast′.**

MKS system, the meter-kilogram-second system.

mkt., market.

ML, Medieval Latin. Also, **M.L.**

ml., **1.** mail. **2.** milliliter.

M.L.A., Modern Language Association.

Mlle., *pl.* **Mlles.** Mademoiselle.

M.L.S., Master of Library Science.

MM., Messieurs.

mm., **1.** (L *millia*) thousands. **2.** millimeter; millimeters.

Mme., *pl.* **Mmes.** madame.

m.m.f., magnetomotive force.

Mn, *Chem.* manganese.

mne·mon·ic (nē mŏn′ĭk), *adj.* **1.** assisting, or intended to assist, the memory. **2.** pertaining to mnemonics or to memory. [t. Gk.: m. s. *mnēmonikós* of memory]

mne·mon·ics (nē mŏn′ĭks), *n.* the art of improving or developing the memory. Also, **mne·mo·tech·nics** (nē′mō tĕk′nĭks).

Mne·mos·y·ne (nē mŏs′ə nē′, -mŏz′-), *n. Gk. Myth.* the goddess of memory, daughter of Uranus and Gaea, and mother (by Zeus) of the Muses.

Mngr., Monsignor.

-mo, a final member of a series of compounds referring to book sizes by numbering the times the sheets are folded, e.g., 12*mo* or *duodecimo.*

Mo, *Chem.* molybdenum.

Mo., **1.** Missouri. **2.** Monday.

mo., **1.** (*pl.* **mos.**) month. **2.** months.

M.O., money order. Also, **m.o.**

mo·a (mō′ə), *n.* any of various extinct, flightless birds of New Zealand, constituting the family *Dinornithidae,* allied to the apteryx but resembling an ostrich. [t. Maori]

Mo·ab (mō′ăb), *n.* an ancient kingdom E of the Dead Sea, in what is now Jordan. —**Mo·ab·ite** (mō′ə bīt′), *n., adj.*

Moa.
Dinornis maximus
(Ab. 10 ft. high)

moan (mōn), *n.* **1.** a prolonged, low, inarticulate sound uttered from or as if from physical or mental suffering. **2.** any similar sound: *the moan of the wind.* **3.** *Archaic.* complaint or lamentation. —*v.i.* **4.** to utter moans, as of pain or grief. **5.** (of the wind, sea, trees, etc.) to make any sound suggestive of such moans. **6.** to utter in lamentation. —*v.t.* **7.** to lament or bemoan: *to moan one's fate.* [ME *mone,* OE **mān* (inferred from its derivative, OE *mǣnan* complain of, lament)] —**moan′ing·ly,** *adv.* —**Syn. 4.** See groan.

moat (mōt), *Fort.* —*n.* **1.** a deep, wide trench surrounding a fortified place, as a town or a castle, usually filled with water. See **bastion.** —*v.t.* **2.** to surround with, or as with, a moat. [ME *mote* moat, (earlier) mound, t. OF: mound, eminence; prob. from Celtic or Gmc.]

mob (mŏb), *n., v.,* **mobbed, mobbing.** —*n.* **1.** a disorderly or riotous assemblage of persons. **2.** a crowd bent on or engaged in lawless violence. **3.** *Sociol.* a group of persons stimulating one another to excitement and losing ordinary rational control over their activity. **4.** (often disparagingly) any assemblage or aggregation of persons, animals, or things; a crowd. **5.** the common mass of people; the populace or multitude. —*v.t.* **6.** to beset or crowd round tumultuously, as from rude curiosity or with hostile intent. **7.** to attack with riotous violence. [short for L *mōbile vulgus* the movable (i.e., excitable) common people]

mob·cap (mŏb′kăp′), *n.* a large, full cap fitting down over the ears, formerly much worn indoors by women.

mo·bile (mō′bəl, mō′bēl), *adj.* **1.** movable; moving readily. **2.** flowing freely, as a liquid. **3.** changing easily in expression, as features. **4.** quickly responding to impulses, emotions, etc., as the mind; versatile. **5.** of or pertaining to a mobile. —*n.* **6.** a hanging or standing construction or sculpture of delicately balanced movable parts (of metal, wood, etc.) which describe rhythmic patterns through their motion. [t. L: movable (neut.)]

Mo·bile (mō bēl′), *n.* a seaport in SW Alabama at the mouth of the **Mobile River,** a river (38 mi.) formed by the Alabama and Tombigbee rivers. 202,779 (1960).

Mo·bile Bay (mō′bēl), a bay of the Gulf of Mexico in SW Alabama: Civil War naval battle, 1864. 36 mi. long; 8–18 mi. wide.

mo·bil·i·ty (mō bĭl′ə tĭ), *n.* **1.** the quality of being mobile. **2.** *Sociol.* the movement of people in a population, as from place to place, or job to job, or social position to social position.

mo·bi·lize (mō′bə līz′), *v.,* **-lized, -lizing.** —*v.t.* **1.** to put (armed forces) into readiness for active service. **2.** to organize or adapt (industries, etc.) for service to the government in time of war. **3.** to put into motion, circulation, or use: *mobilize the wealth of a country.* **4.** to be assembled, organized, etc., for war. [t. F: m.s. *mobiliser,* der. *mobile* MOBILE] —**mo/bi·li·za/tion,** *n.*

mob·oc·ra·cy (mŏb ŏk′rə sĭ), *n., pl.* **-cies.** **1.** rule by the mob; political control by a mob. **2.** the mob as a ruling class. [f. MOB, L. + -(O)CRACY; modeled on DEMOCRACY, etc.] —**mob·o·crat·ic** (mŏb′ə krăt′ĭk), **mob′o·crat/i·cal,** *adj.*

---

b., blend of, blended; c., cognate with; d., dialect, dialectal; der., derived from; f., formed from; g., going back to; m., modification of; r., replacing; s., stem of; t., taken from; ?, perhaps. See the full key on inside cover.

mob·ster (mŏb′stər), *n. Slang.* a member of a gang of criminals. [f. MOB + -STER]

Mo·by Dick (mō′bĭ dĭk′), a novel (1851) by Herman Melville.

Mo·çam·bi·que (mō′səm bē′kə), *n.* Portuguese name of Mozambique.

moc·ca·sin (mŏk′ə sən, -zən), *n.* **1.** a shoe made entirely of soft leather, as deerskin, worn originally by the American Indians. **2.** a venomous snake, *Ancistrodon piscivorus*, of the southern U.S., found in or near water (**water moccasin**). [t. Eastern Algonquian languages (Powhatan and Massachusetts); ? akin to *makak* small case or box]

moccasin flower, 1. the lady's-slipper. **2.** a common cypripedium, *Cypripedium reginae*, of the U.S.

Mo·cha (mō′kə), *n.* **1.** a seaport in Yemen, SW Arabia. ab. 5000. **2.** (*l.c.*) a choice variety of coffee, originally coming from Mocha, Arabia. **3.** (*l.c.*) a flavoring obtained from coffee infusion or combined chocolate and coffee infusion. **4.** (*l.c.*) a glove leather, finer and thinner than doeskin, the best grades of which are made from Arabian goatskins.

mo·chi·la (mō chē′lä), *n. Spanish.* a flap of leather on the seat of a saddle.

mock (mŏk), *v.t.* **1.** to assail or treat with ridicule or derision. **2.** to ridicule by mimicry of action or speech; mimic derisively. **3.** *Poetic.* to mimic, imitate, or counterfeit. **4.** to defy; set at naught. **5.** to deceive, delude, or disappoint. **6. mock up,** to build a mock-up. —*v.i.* **7.** to use ridicule or derision; scoff; jeer (often fol. by *at*). —*n.* **8.** a mocking or derisive action or speech; mockery or derision. **9.** something mocked or derided; an object of derision. **10.** imitation. —*adj.* **11.** being an imitation or having merely the semblance of something: *a mock battle.* [ME *mokken*, t. OF: m. *mocquer*; orig. uncert.] —**mock′er,** *n.* —**mock′ing·ly,** *adv.* —Syn. 1. deride; taunt, flout, gibe; tease. See ridicule. 10. feigned, pretended, sham, counterfeit.

mock·er·y (mŏk′ər ĭ), *n., pl.* **-eries. 1.** ridicule or derision. **2.** a derisive action or speech. **3.** a subject or occasion of derision. **4.** an imitation, esp. of a ridiculous or unsatisfactory kind. **5.** a mere travesty, or mocking pretense. **6.** something absurdly or offensively inadequate or unfitting.

mock·he·ro·ic (mŏk′hĭ rō′ĭk), *adj.* **1.** imitating or burlesquing what is heroic, as in style, character, or action: *mock-heroic dignity.* —*n.* **2.** an imitation or burlesque of what is heroic. —**mock′-he·ro′i·cal·ly,** *adv.*

mock·ing·bird (mŏk′ĭng bûrd′), *n.* **1.** any of several gray, black, and white songbirds of the genus *Mimus*, remarkable for their imitative powers, esp. the celebrated mocker, *M. polyglottos*, of the southern U.S. and Mexico. **2.** any of various allied or similar birds, as the **blue mockingbird,** *Melanotis caerulescens*, of Mexico.

mock orange, the common syringa, *Philadelphus coronarius.*

mock turtle soup, a green soup prepared from a calf's head, or other meat, with seasonings.

mock-up (mŏk′ŭp′), *n.* a model, built to scale, of a machine, apparatus, or weapon, used in studying the construction and in testing a new development, or in teaching men how to operate the actual machine, apparatus, or weapon.

mod., 1. moderate. **2.** *Music.* moderato. **3.** modern.

mod·al (mō′dəl), *adj.* **1.** of or pertaining to mode, manner, or form. **2.** *Music.* **a.** pertaining to mode, as distinguished from key. **b.** based on a scale other than major or minor. **3.** *Gram.* pertaining to mode, or producing varieties in meaning similar to those of different modes. **4.** *Philos.* pertaining to mode as distinguished from substance, matter, or basic attribute. **5.** *Logic.* exhibiting or expressing some phase of modality. [t. ML: s. *modālis*, der. L *modus* MODE[1]] —**mod′al·ly,** *adv.*

mo·dal·i·ty (mō dăl′ə tĭ), *n., pl.* **-ties. 1.** modal quality or state. **2.** a modal attribute or circumstance. **3.** *Logic.* that classification of propositions on the basis of whether what they assert is *contingently* true or false, *possible, impossible,* or *necessary.* **4.** *Med.* the application of a therapeutic agent, usually a physical therapeutic agent.

mode[1] (mōd), *n.* **1.** manner of acting or doing; a method; a way. **2.** the natural disposition or the manner of existence or action of anything; a form: *heat is a mode of motion.* **3.** *Philos.* appearance, form, or disposition taken by a single reality or by an essential property or attribute of it. **4.** *Logic.* **a.** modality. **b.** any of the various forms of valid syllogism. See **mood**[2] (def. 2). **5.** *Music.* any of various arrangements of the diatonic tones of an octave, differing from one another in the order of the whole steps and half steps; a scale. **6.** *Gram.* Also, **mood. a.** (in many languages) a set of categories of verb inflection, whose selection depends either on the syntactic relation of the verb to other verbs in the sentence, or on difference in the speaker's attitude toward the action expressed by the verb (e.g., certainty vs. uncertainty, question vs. statement, wish vs. command, emphasis vs. hesitancy). Latin has indicative, imperative, and subjunctive; Greek adds optative; other languages have still others. **b.** (in some other languages, including English) a similar set of categories marked by the use of special auxiliary words (Eng. *can, could, may, might,* etc.) instead of by, or in addition to, inflection. **c.** any category of such a set. **7.** *Statistics.* (in a statistical population) the category, value, or interval of the variable having the greatest frequency. **8.** *Petrog.* the actual mineral composition of a rock, expressed in percentages by weight. [ME, t. L: m.s. *modus* measure, due measure, manner] —Syn. 1. See method.

mode[2] (mōd), *n.* **1.** customary or conventional usage in manners, dress, etc., esp. as observed by persons of fashion. **2.** a prevailing style or fashion. **3.** light gray, even drab. [t. F, t. L: m.s. *modus* MODE[1]]

mod·el (mŏd′əl), *n., adj., v.,* **-eled, -eling** or (*esp. Brit.*) **-elled, -elling.** —*n.* **1.** a standard for imitation or comparison; a pattern. **2.** a representation, generally in miniature, to show the construction or serve as a copy of something. **3.** an image in clay, wax, or the like to be reproduced in more durable material. **4.** a person or thing that serves as a subject for an artist, etc. **5.** one employed to put on articles of apparel to display them to customers. **6.** mode of structure or formation. **7.** a typical form or style. —*adj.* **8.** serving as a model. **9.** worthy to serve as a model; exemplary. —*v.t.* **10.** to form or plan according to a model. **11.** to give shape or form to; fashion. **12.** to make a model or representation of. **13.** to fashion in clay, wax, or the like. —*v.i.* **14.** to make models. **15.** to produce designs in some plastic material. **16.** to assume a typical or natural appearance, as the parts of a drawing in progress. [t. F: m. *modèle*, t. It.: m. *modello*, dim. of *modo*, t. L: m. *modus* MODE[1]] —**mod′el·er;** *esp. Brit.,* **mod′el·ler,** *n.* —Syn. 1. paragon; prototype. See **ideal.**

mod·el·ing (mŏd′əl ĭng, mŏd′lĭng), *n.* **1.** act or art of one who models. **2.** the process of producing sculptured form with plastic material, usually clay, as for reproduction in a more durable material. **3.** *Graphic Arts.* the process of rendering the illusion of the third dimension. **4.** the undulations of form in sculpture. Also, *esp. Brit.,* **mod′el·ling.**

Mo·de·na (mō′dĕ nä′), *n.* a city in N Italy, in Emilia department. 116,000 (est. 1954).

mod·er·ate (*adj.,* n. mŏd′ər ĭt, mŏd′rĭt; *v.* mŏd′ə rāt′), *adj., n., v.,* **-ated, -ating.** —*adj.* **1.** kept or keeping within due bounds; not extreme, excessive, or intense: *a moderate request.* **2.** of medium quantity, extent, etc.: *a moderate income.* **3.** mediocre; fair: *moderate ability.* **4.** of or pertaining to moderates, as in politics or religion. —*n.* **5.** one who is moderate in opinion or action, or opposed to extreme views and courses, esp. in politics or religion. **6.** (*usually cap.*) a member of a political party advocating moderate reform. —*v.t.* **7.** to reduce the excessiveness of; make less violent, severe, intense, or rigorous. **8.** to preside over or at, as a public meeting. —*v.i.* **9.** to become less violent, severe, intense, or rigorous. **10.** to act as moderator; preside. [ME, t. L: m.s. *moderātus,* pp.] —**mod′er·ate·ly,** *adv.* —**mod′er·ate·ness,** *n.* —Syn. 7. See **allay.**

moderate breeze, *Meteorol.* a wind of Beaufort scale #4, i.e., one within the range of 13–18 miles per hour.

moderate gale, *Meteorol.* a wind of Beaufort scale #7, i.e., one within the range of 32–38 miles per hour.

mod·er·a·tion (mŏd′ə rā′shən), *n.* **1.** quality of being moderate; restraint; avoidance of extremes; temperance. **2.** (*pl.*) *Brit.* (at Oxford University) the first public examinations for the B.A. degree. **3. in moderation,** without excess; limited. **4.** act of moderating.

mod·e·ra·to (mŏd′ə rä′tō), *adj. Music.* moderate; in moderate time. [It.]

mod·er·a·tor (mŏd′ə rā′tər), *n.* **1.** one who or that which moderates. **2.** a presiding officer, as over a public forum, a legislative body, or an ecclesiastical body in the Presbyterian Church. **3.** a substance, as graphite or heavy water, used to slow down neutrons from the high energies at which they are released in fission to lower energies more efficient in causing fission. —**mod′er·a′tor·ship′,** *n.*

mod·ern (mŏd′ərn), *adj.* **1.** of or pertaining to present and recent time; not ancient or remote. **2.** characteristic of present and recent time; not antiquated or obsolete. —*n.* **3.** a person of modern times. **4.** one whose views and tastes are modern. **5.** *Print.* a type style differentiated from *old style* by heavy vertical strokes and straight serifs. [t. LL: s. *modernus,* der. L *modo* just now (orig. abl. of *modus* MODE[1])] —**mod′ern·ly,** *adv.* —**mod′ern·ness,** *n.*
—Syn. 1. MODERN, RECENT, LATE apply to that which is near to or characteristic of the present as contrasted with any other time. MODERN is applied to those things which exist in the present age, esp. in contrast to those of a former age or an age long past; hence the word sometimes has the connotation of up-to-date and, thus, good: *modern ideas.* That which is RECENT is separated from the present or the time of action by only a short interval; it is new, fresh, and novel: *recent developments.* LATE may mean nearest to the present moment: *the latest news.*

modern dance, a form of contemporary theatrical and concert dancing employing a special technique.

Modern English, the English language since c1500.

modern history, history since the Renaissance.

mod·ern·ism (mŏd′ər nĭz′əm), *n.* **1.** modern character; modern tendencies; sympathy with what is modern. **2.** a modern usage or characteristic. **3.** *Theol.* **a.** (*cap.*) movement in Roman Catholic thought which sought to interpret the teachings of the church in the light of philosophic and scientific conceptions prevalent in the late nineteenth and early twentieth centuries; condemned by Pope Pius in 1907. **b.** the liberal theological tendency in Protestantism (opposed to *fundamentalism*).

ăct, āble, dâre, ärt; ĕbb, ēqual; ĭf, īce; hŏt, ōver, ôrder, oil, bŏŏk, ōōze, out; ŭp, ūse, ûrge; ə = a in alone; ch, chief; g, give; ng, ring; sh, shoe; th, thin; ᵗħ, that; zh, vision. See the full key on inside cover.

mod·ern·ist (mŏd′ər nĭst), *n.* **1.** one who follows or favors modern ways, tendencies, etc. **2.** one who advocates the study of modern subjects in preference to ancient classics. **3.** adherent of modernism in theological questions. —*adj.* **4.** of modernists or modernism.

mod·ern·is·tic (mŏd′ər nĭs′tĭk), *adj.* **1.** modern. **2.** of or pertaining to modernism or modernists: *a modernistic painting.*

mo·der·ni·ty (mŏ dûr′nə tĭ, mō-), *n., pl.* **-ties. 1.** the quality of being modern. **2.** something modern.

mod·ern·ize (mŏd′ər nīz′), *v.,* -ized, -izing. —*v.t.* **1.** to make modern; give a modern character or appearance to. —*v.i.* **2.** to become modern; adopt modern ways, views, etc. —**mod′ern·i·za′tion,** *n.* —**mod′·ern·iz′er,** *n.*

mod·est (mŏd′ĭst), *adj.* **1.** having or showing a moderate or humble estimate of one's merits, importance, etc.; free from vanity, egotism, boastfulness, or great pretensions. **2.** free from ostentation or showy extravagance: *a modest house.* **3.** moderate. **4.** having or showing regard for the decencies of behavior, speech, dress, etc.; decent. [t. L: s. *modestus* keeping due measure] —**mod′est·ly,** *adv.*
—**Syn. 4.** MODEST, DEMURE, PRUDISH imply conformity to propriety and decorum, and a distaste for anything coarse or loud. MODEST implies a becoming shyness, sobriety, and proper behavior: *a modest self-respecting person.* DEMURE implied originally a bashful, quiet simplicity, staidness, and decorum; now a modesty either unconscious or cleverly assumed: *a demure young girl.* PRUDISH suggests an exaggeratedly self-conscious modesty or propriety in behavior or conversation of one who wishes to be thought of as easily shocked, and often is intolerant: *a prudish objection to a harmless remark.* —**Ant. 4.** bold, coarse.

mod·es·ty (mŏd′əs tĭ), *n., pl.,* -ties. **1.** the quality of being modest; freedom from vanity, boastfulness, etc. **2.** regard for decency of behavior, speech, dress, etc. **3.** simplicity; moderation.

mod·i·cum (mŏd′ə kəm), *n.* a moderate or small quantity. [late ME, t. L, neut. of *modicus* moderate]

mod·i·fi·ca·tion (mŏd′ə fə kā′shən), *n.* **1.** act of modifying. **2.** state of being modified; partial alteration. **3.** a modified form; a variety. **4.** *Biol.* a change in a living organism acquired from its own activity or environment and not transmitted to its descendants. **5.** limitation or qualification. **6.** *Gram.* **a.** the use of a modifier in a construction, or of modifiers in a class of constructions or in a language. **b.** the meaning of a modifier, esp. as it affects the meaning of the word or other form modified: *limitation is one kind of modification.* **c.** a change in the phonemic shape of a morpheme, word, or other form when it functions as an element in a construction, e.g., the change of *not* to *-n't* in the phrase *doesn't.* **d.** the feature of a construction resulting from such a change, e.g., the phrases *doesn't* and *does not* differ in modification. **e.** an adjustment in the form of a word as it passes from one language to another.

mod·i·fi·ca·to·ry (mŏd′ə fə kā′tər ĭ), *adj.* modifying. Also, **mod′i·fi·ca′tive.**

mod·i·fi·er (mŏd′ə fī′ər), *n.* **1.** one who or that which modifies. **2.** *Gram.* a word, phrase, or sentence element which limits or qualifies the sense of another word, phrase, or element in the same construction: *adjectives are modifiers.*

mod·i·fy (mŏd′ə fī′), *v.,* -fied, -fying. —*v.t.* **1.** to change somewhat the form or qualities of; alter somewhat. **2.** *Gram.* (of a word or larger linguistic form) to stand in a subordinate relation to (another form called the *head*) usually with descriptive, limiting, or particularizing meaning, as in *a good man, good* modifies the head *man.* **3.** to be the modifier or attribute of. **4.** to change (a vowel) by umlaut. **5.** to reduce in degree; moderate; qualify. —*v.i.* **6.** to change; to become changed. [ME *modifie(n),* t. L: m. *modificāre, modificārī* set limits to] —**mod′i·fi′a·ble,** *adj.*
—**Syn. 1.** MODIFY, QUALIFY, TEMPER suggest altering an original statement, condition, or the like, so as to avoid anything excessive or extreme. To MODIFY is to alter in one or more particulars, generally in the direction of leniency or moderation: *to modify demands, rates.* To QUALIFY is to restrict or limit by exceptions or conditions: *to qualify one's praise, hopes.* To TEMPER is to alter the quality of something, generally so as to diminish its force or harshness: *to temper the wind to the shorn lamb.*

Mo·di·glia·ni (mō′dē lyä′nē), *n.* **Amedeo** (ä′mě dě′ō), 1884–1920, Italian painter and sculptor.

mo·dil·lion (mō dĭl′yən, mə-), *n. Archit.* one of a series of ornamental blocks or brackets placed under the corona of a cornice in the Corinthian and other orders. [t. It.: m. *modiglione,* ult. der. L *mutulus*]

mo·di·o·lus (mō dī′ō ləs, mə-), *n., pl.* -li (-lī′). *Anat.* the central conical axis round which the cochlea of the ear winds. [t. NL, dim. of L *modiolus* measure for grain]

Romanesque modillion

mod·ish (mō′dĭsh), *adj.* in accordance with the prevailing mode; fashionable; stylish. —**mod′ish·ly,** *adv.* —**mod′ish·ness,** *n.*

mo·diste (mō dēst′; *Fr.* mô-), *n.* a maker of or dealer in articles of fashionable attire, esp. women's dresses, millinery, etc. [t. F, der. *mode* MODE[2]]

Mo·djes·ka (mō jĕs′kə), *n.* **Helena** (hə lā′nə), (*Madame Modjeska*) 1840–1909, Polish actress and in America.

Mo·dred (mō′drĭd), *n. Arthurian Romance.* the nephew and treacherous killer of Arthur. Also, **Mordred.**

mod·u·late (mŏj′ə lāt′), *v.,* -lated, -lating. —*v.t.* **1.** to regulate by or adjust to a certain measure or proportion; soften; tone down. **2.** to alter or adapt (the voice) fittingly in utterance. **3.** *Music.* **a.** to attune to a certain pitch or key. **b.** to vary the volume of (tone). **4.** *Radio.* to cause the amplitude, frequency, phase, or intensity of (the carrier wave) to vary in accordance with the sound waves or other signals, the frequency of the signal wave usually being very much lower than that of the carrier: frequently applied to the application of sound-wave signals to a microphone to change the characteristic of a transmitted radio wave. —*v.i.* **5.** *Radio.* to modulate a carrier wave. **6.** *Music.* to pass from one key to another. [t. L: m.s. *modulātus,* pp., having measured] —**mod′u·la′tive,** *adj.*

mod·u·la·tion (mŏj′ə lā′shən), *n.* **1.** act of modulating. **2.** state of being modulated. **3.** *Music.* transition from one key to another. **4.** *Gram.* **a.** the use of a particular distribution of stress or pitch in a construction, e.g., the use of rising pitch on the last word of *John is here?* **b.** the feature of a construction resulting from such a use, e.g., the question *John is here?* differs from the statement *John is here* only in modulation.

mod·u·la·tor (mŏj′ə lā′tər), *n.* **1.** one who or that which modulates. **2.** *Radio.* a device for modulating a carrier wave. Cf. **modulate** (def. 4).

mod·ule (mŏj′ōōl), *n.* **1.** a standard or unit for measuring. **2.** a selected unit of measure, ranging in size from a few inches to several feet, used as a basis for planning and standardization of building materials. **3.** *Archit.* the size of some part, as the semidiameter of a column at the base of the shaft, taken as a unit of measure. [t. L: m.s. *modulus,* dim. of *modus* measure, MODE[1]]

mod·u·lus (mŏj′ə ləs), *n., pl.* -li (-lī′). *Physics.* a coefficient (def. 2), esp. of elasticity. [t. L: a small measure. See MODULE]

mo·dus o·pe·ran·di (mō′dəs ŏp′ə răn′dī), *Latin.* mode of operating or working.

mo·dus vi·ven·di (mō′dəs vĭ vĕn′dī), *Latin.* **1.** mode of living. **2.** a temporary arrangement between persons or parties pending a settlement of matters in debate.

Moe·si·a (mē′shĭ ə), *n.* an ancient country in S Europe, S of the Danube and N of ancient Thrace and Macedonia: later a Roman province.

Moe·so·goth (mē′sō gŏth′, -sə-), *n.* one of the Christianized agricultural Goths who settled in Moesia in the 4th century. —**Moe′so·goth′ic,** *adj.*

mo·fette (mō fĕt′; *Fr.* mô-), *n.* **1.** a noxious emanation, consisting chiefly of carbon dioxide, escaping from the earth in regions of nearly extinct volcanic activity. **2.** one of the openings or fissures from which this emanation issues. Also, **mof·fette′.** [t. F, der. *moufir* rot, mold, der. *muffe* mould, t. G: m. *muff*]

Mo·ga·di·scio (*It.* mō′gä dē′shō), *n.* a seaport in E Africa: the capital of Somalia. 50,000 (est. 1952). Also, **Mo·ga·di·shu** (mō′gä dē′shōō).

Mog·a·dor (mŏg′ə dôr′; *Fr.* mô gä dôr′), *n.* a seaport in W Morocco. 22,291 (1952).

Mo·gi·lëv (mō′gĭ lĕf′; *Russ.* mŏ gĭ lyôf′), *n.* a city in the W Soviet Union, on the Dnieper. 106,000 (est. 1956).

Mo·gul (mō′gŭl, mō gŭl′), *n.* **1.** a Mongol or Mongolian. **2.** one of the Mongol conquerors of India who ruled from 1526 to 1857 (nominal rulers from 1803 on). **3.** (*l.c.*) an important person. **4.** (*l.c.*) a steam locomotive, used for hauling heavy trains. [t. Ar. and Pers.: m. *Mughul* Mongol]

mo·hair (mō′hâr′), *n.* **1.** the coat or fleece of an Angora goat. **2.** a fabric made of yarn from this fleece, in a plain weave for draperies and in a pile weave for upholstery. **3.** a garment made of this fabric. [f. obs. *mo(cayare)* mohair (ult. t. Ar.: m. *mukhayyar*) + HAIR]

Mo·ham., Mohammedan.

Mo·ham·med (mō hăm′ĭd), *n.* A.D. 570?–632, Arabian prophet and founder of the Mohammedan religion. Also, **Mahomet, Muhammad.**

Mohammed II, 1430–81, sultan of Turkey, 1451–81; captured Constantinople in 1453.

Mohammed A·li (ä lē′, ä′lē), **1.** 1878–1931, Indian Moslem leader: advocate of Indian independence and associate of Gandhi. **2.** Mehemet Ali.

Mo·ham·med·an (mō hăm′ə dən), *adj.* **1.** of or pertaining to Mohammed or his religious system. —*n.* **2.** a follower of Mohammed; a believer in his religion. Also, **Mahometan, Muhammadan, Muhammedan.**

Mo·ham·med·an·ism (mō hăm′ə də nĭz′əm), *n.* the Mohammedan religion; Islam.

Mo·ha·ve (mō hä′vĭ), *n.* **1.** (*pl.*) a North American Indian tribe belonging to the Yuman linguistic family, located on both sides of the Colorado river. —*adj.* **2.** of or pertaining to the Mohave tribe. Also, **Mojave.** [t. Amer. Ind., der. *homok* three + *avi* mountain]

Mohave Desert, Mojave Desert.

Mo·hawk (mō′hôk), *n., pl.* **Mohawk, Mohawks. 1.** (*pl.*) a tribe of North American Indians, the most easterly of the Iroquois Five Nations, formerly resident along the Mohawk river, New York. **2.** a member of this tribe. [t. N Amer. Ind. (Narragansett): they eat animate things (hence, man-eaters)]

Mo·hawk (mō′hôk), *n.* a river flowing from central New York E to the Hudson. 148 mi.

Mo·he·gan (mō hē′gən), *n.* **1.** (*pl.*) a tribe of Algon-

b., blend of, blended of; c., cognate with; d., dialect, dialectal; der., derived from; f., formed from; g., going back to; m., modification of; r., replacing; s., stem of; t., taken from; ?, perhaps. See the full key on inside cover.

quian-speaking North American Indians, dwelling chiefly along the Thames river, Connecticut, in the 17th century. **2.** Mahican. [t. Amer. Ind. (Algonquian): m. *maingan* wolf]

Mo·hi·can (mō hē′kən), *n.* Mahican.

Mo·hock (mō′hŏk), *n.* one of a class of ruffians, often aristocrats, who infested the London streets at night in the early 18th century. [var. of MOHAWK. Cf. APACHE²]

Mohs scale (mōz), a scale of hardness used in mineralogy. Its degrees are: talc 1; gypsum 2; calcite 3; fluorite 4; apatite 5; feldspar 6; quartz 7; topaz 8; sapphire 9; diamond 10. Cf. **hardness.** [named after Friedrich *Mohs* (1773–1839), German mineralogist]

mo·hur (mō′hər), *n.* a former gold coin of India, in 1835 worth about $7.00: usually called **gold mohur.** [earlier *muhr*, t. Pers.: seal, gold coin]

moi·dore (moi′dōr), *n.* a former gold coin of Portugal and Brazil. [t. Pg.: m. *moeda d'ouro* coin of gold]

moi·e·ty (moi′ə tĭ), *n., pl.* -ties. **1.** a half. **2.** an indefinite portion. **3.** *Anthropol.* one of two units into which a tribe is divided on the basis of unilateral descent. [ME *moit(i)e*, t. OF., g. LL *medietas* half, L the middle]

moil (moil), *v.i.* **1.** to work hard; toil; drudge. —*n.* **2.** toil or drudgery. **3.** confusion, turmoil, or trouble. [ME *moile(n)*, t. OF: m. *moillier* wet, moisten, ult. der. L *mollis* soft] —**moil′er,** *n.*

moire (mwär, mōr), *n.* a watered fabric, as of silk or wool. [t. F., t. E: m. MOHAIR]

moi·ré (mwä rā′, mōr′ā; *Fr.* mwȧ rĕ′), *adj.* **1.** watered as silk; having a wavelike pattern. —*n.* **2.** a design pressed on silk, rayon, etc., by engraved rollers. **3.** moire.

moist (moist), *adj.* **1.** moderately or slightly wet; damp; humid. **2.** (of the eyes) tearful. **3.** accompanied by or connected with liquid or moisture. [ME *moiste*, t. OF: moist, moldy. Cf. L *mūcidus* moldy, musty] —**moist′ly,** *adv.* —**moist′ness,** *n.* —**Syn. 1.** See **damp.**

mois·ten (mois′ən), *v.t., v.i.* to make or become moist. —**moist′en·er,** *n.*

mois·ture (mois′chər), *n.* water or other liquid rendering anything moist. [ME, t. OF: m. *moistour*]

Mo·ja·ve (mō hä′vĭ), *n., adj.* Mohave.

Mo·ja·ve Desert (mō hä′vĭ), a desert in S California: part of the Great Basin. ab. 15,000 sq. mi. Also, **Mohave Desert.**

Mo·ji (mō′jē), *n.* a seaport in SW Japan, on N Kyushu island. 124,399 (1950).

mol (mōl), *n. Chem.* the molecular weight of a substance expressed in grams; gram molecule. Also, **mole.** [t. G, der. *molekül* MOLECULE]

mo·lal (mō′ləl), *adj. Chem.* **1.** pertaining to grammolecular weight, or containing a mol. **2.** pertaining to a solution containing one mol of solute per 1000 grams of solvent.

mo·lar¹ (mō′lər), *n.* **1.** a tooth adapted for grinding with a broad biting surface as in human dentition. There are twelve molar teeth, three in each quadrant. —*adj.* **2.** adapted for grinding, as teeth, esp. those in man, with a broad biting surface, situated behind the bicuspids. **3.** pertaining to such teeth. [t. L: s. *molāris* grinder]

mo·lar² (mō′lər), *adj.* **1.** *Physics.* pertaining to a body of matter as a whole: contrasted with molecular and atomic. **2.** *Chem.* pertaining to a solution containing one mol of solute per liter of solvent. [f. s. L *mōles* mass + -AR¹]

mo·las·ses (mə lăs′ĭz), *n.* any of various thick, darkcolored syrups, as that produced during the refining of sugar, or that produced from sorghum. Cf. **treacle.** [t. Pg.: m. *melaço*, g. LL *mellāceum* must, der. *mel* honey]

mold¹ (mōld), *n.* **1.** a hollow form or matrix for giving a particular shape to something in a molten or plastic state. **2.** that on or about which something is formed or made. **3.** something formed in or on a mold: *a mold of jelly.* **4.** the shape imparted to a thing by a mold. **5.** shape or form. **6.** distinctive nature, or native character. **7.** *Archit.* **a.** a molding. **b.** a group of moldings. —*v.t.* **8.** to work into a required shape or form; shape. **9.** to shape or form in or on a mold. **10.** *Founding.* to form a mold of or from, in order to make a casting. **11.** to produce by or as if by shaping material; form. **12.** to fashion; model the character of. **13.** to ornament with moldings. Also, *esp. Brit.,* **mould.** [ME, t. OF: m. *modle,* g. L *modulus* MODULE] —**mold′a·ble,** *adj.*

mold² (mōld), *n.* **1.** a growth of minute fungi forming on vegetable or animal matter, commonly as a downy or furry coating, and associated with decay. **2.** any of the fungi that produce such a growth. —*v.t., v.i.* **3.** to make or become mold. Also, *esp. Brit.,* **mould.** [ME *mowlde,* appar. var. of *mowled, mouled,* pp. of *moulen,* earlier ME *muwlen,* c. d. Dan. *mugle* grow moldy]

mold³ (mōld), *n.* **1.** loose, friable earth, esp. such as is rich in organic matter and favorable to the growth of plants. **2.** *Poetic.* the ground or earth. Also, *esp. Brit.,* **mould.** [ME and OE *molde,* c. OHG *molta* mold, dust]

Mol·dau (môl′dou), *n.* a river flowing from the Bohemian Forest N through W Czechoslovakia to the Elbe. ab. 270 mi. Czech, **Vltava.**

Mol·da·vi·a (mōl dā′vĭ ə, -vyə), *n.* **1.** a province in NE Rumania: formerly a principality which united with Walachia to form Rumania. 2,598,258 pop. (1948); 14,562 sq. mi. *Cap.:* Jassy. **2.** Official name, **Moldavian Soviet Socialist Republic,** a constituent republic of the Soviet Union, in the SW part: formed in 1940 of the

former autonomous republic of Moldavia and the ceded Rumanian territory of Bessarabia. 2,700,000 pop. (est. 1956); 13,100 sq. mi. *Cap.:* Kishinev. —**Mol·da′vi·an,** *adj., n.*

mol·da·vite (mōl′də vīt′), *n.* a natural green glass, found in Bohemia and thought to be of possible meteoritic origin. Cf. **tektite.**

mold·board (mōld′bôrd′), *n.* the curved board or metal plate in a plow, which turns over the earth from the furrow. Also, *esp. Brit.,* **mouldboard.**

mold·er¹ (mōl′dər), *v.i.* **1.** to turn to dust by natural decay; crumble; waste away. —*v.t.* **2.** to cause to molder. Also, *esp. Brit.,* **moulder.** [freq. of obs. *mold,* v., molder, crumble away (v. use of MOLD³). See -ER⁶]

mold·er² (mōl′dər), *n.* **1.** one who molds; a maker of molds. **2.** *Print.* one of a set of electrotyped plates used only for making duplicate electrotypes. Also, *esp. Brit.,* **moulder.** [f. MOLD¹, v. + -ER¹]

mold·ing (mōl′dĭng), *n.* **1.** act or process of one who or that which molds. **2.** something molded. **3.** *Archit., etc.* **a.** a decorative variety of contour or outline given to cornices, jambs, strips of woodwork, etc. **b.** a shaped member introduced into a structure to afford such variety or decoration. **4.** shaped material in the form of a strip, used for supporting pictures, covering electric wires, etc. Also, *esp. Brit.,* **moulding.**

molding board, the board upon which bread is kneaded, cookies prepared, etc.

mold·y (mōl′dĭ), *adj.,* **moldier, moldiest. 1.** overgrown or covered with mold. **2.** musty, as from decay or age. Also, *esp. Brit.,* **mouldy.** [f. MOLD² + -Y¹] —**mold′i·ness,** *n.*

mole¹ (mōl), *n.* **1.** a small congenital spot or blemish on the human skin, usually of a dark color and slightly elevated, and often hairy. **2.** a pigmented naevus. [ME; OE *māl,* c. OHG *meil* wrinkle, blemish]

mole² (mōl), *n.* any of various small insectivorous mammals, esp. of the family *Talpidae,* living chiefly underground, and having velvety fur, very small eyes, and strong, fossorial forefeet. [ME *molle,* c. MD and MLG *mol*]

Mole, *Scalopus aquaticus* (Ab 6½ to 7 in. long, tail 1 in.)

mole³ (mōl), *n.* **1.** a massive structure, esp. of stone, set up in the water, as for a breakwater or a pier. **2.** an anchorage or harbor protected by such a structure. [t. L: m. *mōles* mass, dam]

mole⁴ (mōl), *n.* mol.

mole⁵ (mōl), *n. Pathol.* a fleshy mass in the uterus formed by a hemorrhagic dead ovum. [t. L: m.s. *mola* false conception, millstone]

Mo·lech (mō′lĕk), *n.* Moloch (defs. 1, 2).

mo·lec·u·lar (mə lĕk′yə lər), *adj.* pertaining to, caused by, or consisting of molecules. [f. s. NL *mōlēcula* MOLECULE + -AR¹] —**mo·lec′u·lar·ly,** *adv.*

molecular beam, a stream of molecules in a vacuum moving in directions almost parallel, produced experimentally by passing the molecules through a series of narrow openings. Also, **molecular ray.**

molecular film, a film or layer one molecule thick.

molecular weight, *Chem.* **1.** the average weight of a molecule of an element or compound measured in units, sixteen of which correspond to the average weight of the oxygen atom. **2.** the sum of the atomic weights of all the atoms in a molecule.

mol·e·cule (mōl′ə kūl′), *n.* **1.** *Chem., Physics.* the smallest physical unit of an element or compound, consisting of one or more like atoms in the first case, and two or more different atoms in the second case. **2.** a quantity of a substance, the weight of which, measured in any chosen unit, is numerically equal to the molecular weight; gram molecule. **3.** any very small particle. [t. NL: m. *mōlēcula,* dim. of L *mōles* mass. Cf. MOLE³, MOL]

mole·hill (mōl′hĭl′), *n.* **1.** a small mound or ridge of earth raised up by moles burrowing under the ground. **2.** something insignificant, esp. an obstacle or difficulty.

mole·skin (mōl′skĭn′), *n.* **1.** the fur of the mole, soft, deep-gray in color, and very fragile. **2.** a stout, napped, twilled cotton fabric used for sportsmen's and laborers' clothing. **3.** (*pl.*) garments, esp. trousers, of this fabric.

mo·lest (mə lĕst′), *v.t.* to interfere with annoyingly, injuriously, or with hostile intent. [ME *moleste(n),* t. L: m. *molestāre*] —**mo·les·ta·tion** (mō′lĕs tā′shən, mŏl′ĕs-), *n.* —**mo·lest′er,** *n.* —**Syn.** See **attack.**

Mo·lière (mō lyĕr′), *n.* (Jean Baptiste Poquelin) 1622–1673, French writer of comedies.

Mo·li·na (mō lē′nä), *n.* **Tirso de** (tēr′sō dĕ), pen name of Gabriel Téllez.

Mo·line (mō lēn′), *n.* a city in NW Illinois, on the Mississippi. 42,705 (1960).

moll (mŏl), *n. Slang.* **1.** the unmarried female companion of a thief, vagrant, or gangster. **2.** a prostitute. [short for *Molly,* var. of MARY]

mol·les·cent (mə lĕs′ənt), *adj.* producing less hardness or firmness; softening. [t. L: s. *mollescens,* ppr.] —**mol·les′cence,** *n.*

mol·li·fy (mōl′ə fī′), *v.t.,* -fied, -fying. **1.** to soften in feeling or temper, as a person, the heart or mind, etc. **2.** to mitigate or appease, as rage. [ME *mollifie(n),* t.

L: m.s. *mollificāre* soften] **—mol′li·fi·ca′tion,** *n.* **—mol′li·fi′er,** *n.* **—mol′li·fy′ing·ly,** *adv.* **—mol′li·fi′able,** *adj.*

Mol·lus·ca (mə lŭs′kə), *n.* a large phylum of invertebrates including the chitins, snails, bivalves, squids, octopi, etc., characterized by the calcareous shell (sometimes lacking) of one, two, or more pieces that wholly or partly encloses the soft unsegmented body provided with gills, mantle, and foot. [see MOLLUSK]

mol·lus·coid (mə lŭs′koid), *adj., n.* denoting, or pertaining to, an animal group comprising the bryozoans and brachiopods. Also, **mol·lus·coi·dal** (mŏl′əs koi′dəl).

mol·lusk (mŏl′əsk), *n.* any of the *Mollusca.* Also, **mol′lusc.** [t. NL: m.s. *mollusca*, pl., in L neut. pl. of *molluscus* soft (applied to a thin-shelled nut)] **—mollus·can** (mə lŭs′kən), *adj., n.* **—mol′lusk·like′,** *adj.*

mol·ly (mŏl′ĭ), *n., pl.* **mollies.** a live-bearing fish of the genus *Mollienisia*, often kept in home aquariums.

mol·ly·cod·dle (mŏl′ĭ kŏd′əl), *n., v.* **-dled, -dling.** **—n.** 1. a man or boy who is used to being coddled; a milksop. **—v.t., v.i.** 2. to coddle; pamper. [f. *Molly* (var. of MARY) + CODDLE] **—mol′ly·cod′dler,** *n.*

Mol·nár (mŏl′när), *n.* **Ferenc** (fĕ′rĕnts), 1878–1952, Hungarian dramatist and novelist.

Mo·loch (mō′lŏk), *n.* 1. a Semitic deity, mentioned in the Bible, whose worship was marked by the sacrifice by burning of children offered by their own parents. 2. anything conceived as requiring frightful sacrifice: *the Moloch of war.* 3. (*l.c.*) a spiny Australian lizard, *Moloch horridus.* Also, **Molech** for 1, 2. [t. L (Vulgate), t. Gk. (Septuagint), t. Heb.: m. *Mōlek,* orig. *melek* king]

Mo·lo·ka·i (mō′lō kä′ē), *n.* one of the Hawaiian Islands, in the central part of the group: leper colony. 5280 pop. (1950); 259 sq. mi.

Mo·lo·tov (mō′lō tôf), *n.* 1. **Viacheslav Mikhailovich** (vyä′chĕ slät′ mī hī′lō vĭch), born 1890, Soviet statesman: Commissar for Foreign Affairs, 1939–1949 and from 1953 to 1956. 2. Also, **Perm.** a city in the W Soviet Union in Asia, on the Kama river. 538,000 (est. 1956).

molt (mōlt), *v.i.* 1. (of birds, insects, reptiles, etc.) to cast or shed the feathers, skin, or the like, to be succeeded by a new growth. **—v.t.** 2. to cast or shed (feathers, etc.) in the process of renewal. **—n.** 3. act or process of molting. 4. that which is dropped in molting. Also, *esp. Brit.,* **moult.** [ME *mout,* OE *-mūtian* change (in *bemūtian* exchange for), t. L: m. *mūtāre* change. Cf. MEW[1]] **—molt′er,** *n.*

mol·ten (mōl′tən), *v.* 1. a pp. of melt. **—adj.** 2. liquefied by heat; in a state of fusion. 3. produced by melting and casting: *a molten image.*

Molt·ke (mōlt′kə), *n.* 1. **Helmuth Karl Bernhard** (hĕl′mōōt kärl bĕrn′härt), **Count von,** 1800–91, German field marshal. 2. **Helmuth Johannes Ludwig** (yō-hän′əs lōōt′vĭKH), **Count von,** 1848–1916, German general.

mol·to (mōl′tō), *adv.* *Music.* much; very. [It., g. L *multum*]

Mo·luc·cas (mō lŭk′əz, mə-), *n.pl.* a group of islands in Indonesia between Celebes and New Guinea. 685,704 pop. (est. 1955); ab. 30,000 sq. mi. Also, **Spice Islands.**

mol. wt., molecular weight.

mo·ly (mō′lĭ), *n., pl.* **molies.** a fabulous herb with a milk-white flower and a black root, said by Homer to have been given by Hermes to Odysseus to counteract the spells of Circe. [t. L, t. Gk.]

mo·lyb·date (mə lĭb′dāt), *n.* *Chem.* a salt of any molybdic acid.

mo·lyb·de·nite (mə lĭb′də nīt′, mŏl′ĭb dē′nīt), *n.* a soft, graphitelike mineral, molybdenum sulfide, MoS₂, occurring in foliated masses or scales: principal ore of molybdenum. [f. s. obs. *molybdena* MOLYBDENUM + -ITE[1]]

mo·lyb·de·nous (mə lĭb′də nəs, mŏl′ĭb dē′nəs), *adj.* *Chem.* containing divalent molybdenum (Mo⁺²).

mo·lyb·de·num (mə lĭb′də nəm, mŏl′ĭb dē′nəm), *n.* *Chem.* a silver-white high-melting metalloid, alloyed with iron in making hard, high-speed cutting tools. *Symbol.:* Mo; *at. wt.:* 95.95; *at. no.:* 42; *sp. gr.:* 10.2. [t. NL, t. L: m. *molybdaena,* t. Gk.: m. *molybdaina* galena]

mo·lyb·dic (mə lĭb′dĭk), *adj.* *Chem.* of or containing molybdenum, esp. in the Mo⁺³ or Mo⁺⁶ state, as *molybdic acid,* H₂MoO₄.

mom (mŏm), *n. U. S. Colloq.* mother.

Mom·ba·sa (mŏm bä′sä, -bäs′ə), *n.* a seaport on **Mombasa island** in Kenya, British East Africa. 84,746 (1948).

mo·ment (mō′mənt), *n.* 1. an indefinitely short space of time; an instant: *wait a moment.* 2. the present or other particular instant: *to recall his name at the moment.* 3. a definite stage, as in a course of events. 4. importance or consequence: *of great moment.* 5. *Statistics.* the average of a given power of the values of a set of variates. 6. *Philos.* an essential or constituent element or factor; momentum. 7. *Mech.* a. tendency to produce motion, esp. about an axis. b. (of a physical quantity) the product of the quantity and its perpendicular distance from an axis: *moment of area, moment of mass, etc.* [ME, t. L: s. *mōmentum* movement, moment of time, etc.] **—Syn.** 1. See minute[1].

mo·men·tar·i·ly (mō′mən tĕr′ə lĭ; *for emphasis* mō′mən tĕr′ə lĭ), *adv.* 1. for a moment; *to hesitate momen-*

---

tarily. 2. every moment; from moment to moment: *danger momentarily increasing.* 3. at any moment: *momentarily liable to occur.*

mo·men·tar·y (mō′mən tĕr′ĭ), *adj.* 1. lasting but a moment; very brief: *a momentary glimpse.* 2. occurring at any moment: *to live in fear of momentary exposure.* 3. *Rare.* constant. **—mo′men·tar′i·ness,** *n.*

mo·ment·ly (mō′mənt lĭ), *adv.* 1. every moment; from moment to moment. 2. for a moment; momentarily.

mo·men·tous (mō mĕn′təs), *adj.* of great importance or consequence; fraught with serious or far-reaching consequences, as events, decisions, etc. **—mo·men′tous·ly,** *adv.* **—mo·men′tous·ness,** *n.* **—Syn.** See **heavy.**

mo·men·tum (mō mĕn′təm), *n., pl.* **-ta** (-tə), **-tums.** 1. *Mech.* the quantity of motion of a moving body, equal to the product of its mass and velocity. 2. impetus, as of a moving body. 3. *Philos.* a moment (def. 6). [t. L. See MOMENT]

Momm·sen (mŏm′sən; *Ger.* môm′zən), *n.* **Theodor** (tā′ō dōr′), 1817–1903, German historian and philologist.

Mo·mus (mō′məs), *n.* 1. *Gk. Myth.* the god of censure and ridicule. 2. (*sometimes l.c.*) a faultfinder; a carping critic. [t. L, t. Gk.: m. *mōmos,* lit., blame, ridicule]

Mon (mŏn), *n.* one of the Mon-Khmer languages.

mon-, var. of **mono-,** before vowels.

Mon., 1. Monday. 2. Monsignor.

mon., 1. monastery. 2. monetary.

mon·a·chal (mŏn′ə kəl), *adj.* monastic. [t. ML: s. *monachālis,* der. LL *monachus* MONK]

mon·a·chism (mŏn′ə kĭz′əm), *n.* monasticism.

Mon·a·co (mŏn′ə kō′; *It.* mō′nä kō′), *n.* 1. a principality on the Mediterranean coast, bordering SE France. 22,000 (est. 1953); ½ sq. mi. 2. the capital of this principality. 1860 (1951).

mon·ad (mŏn′ăd, mō′năd), *n.* 1. *Biol.* a. any simple, single-celled organism. b. a certain type of small, flagellate, colorless, naked amoeboid with one to three flagella. 2. *Chem.* an element, atom, or radical having a valence of one. 3. *Philos.* an entity, conceived after the fashion of the self, and regarded as the ultimate unit of being or as a microcosm. 4. unity. [t. LL: s. *monas,* t. Gk.: s. *monas*] **—mo·nad·ic** (mə năd′ĭk), **mo·nad′i·cal,** *adj.* **—mo·nad′i·cal·ly,** *adv.*

mon·a·del·phous (mŏn′ə dĕl′fəs), *adj.* *Bot.* 1. (of stamens) united into one bundle or set by their filaments. 2. (of a plant or flower) having the stamens so united. [f. MON- + s. Gk. *adelphós* brother + -OUS]

mon·ad·ism (mŏn′ə dĭz′əm, mō′năd ĭz′əm), *n.* *Philos.* 1. the doctrine of monads as ultimate units of being. 2. the philosophy of Leibnitz. Also, **mon·ad·ol·o·gy** (mŏn′ə dŏl′ə jĭ, mō′năd ŏl′-). **—mon′ad·is′tic,** *adj.*

mo·nad·nock (mə năd′nŏk), *n.* 1. *Phys. Geog.* a residual hill or mountain standing well above the surface of a surrounding peneplain. [from def. 2] 2. (*cap.*) **Mount,** an isolated peak in SW New Hampshire. 3186 ft. [t. Amer. Ind.: (object) standing out: isolated]

Mon·a·ghan (mŏn′ə gən), *n.* a county in NE Ireland. 52,013 (prelim. 1956); 498 sq. mi. *Co. seat:* Monaghan.

Mo·na Li·sa (mō′nə lē′zə), a famous portrait by da Vinci.

mo·nan·drous (mə năn′drəs), *adj.* 1. having but one husband at a time. 2. of or characterized by monandry: *the monandrous system.* 3. *Bot.* a. (of a flower) having but one stamen. b. (of a plant) having such flowers. [t. Gk.: m. *mōnandros* having one husband]

mo·nan·dry (mə năn′drĭ), *n.* the practice or the condition of having but one husband at a time.

mo·nan·thous (mə năn′thəs), *adj.* *Bot.* one-flowered. [f. MON- + s. Gk. *ánthos* flower + -OUS]

Mo·na Passage (mō′nə; *Sp.* mō′nä), a strait between Hispaniola and Puerto Rico. ab. 80 mi. wide.

mon·arch (mŏn′ərk), *n.* 1. a hereditary sovereign with more or less limited powers, as a king, queen, emperor, etc. 2. a sole and absolute ruler of a state. 3. one who or that which holds a dominating or preëminent position. 4. a large black-and-red butterfly, *Danaus menippe,* whose larva feeds on milkweed. [late ME, t. LL: s. *monarcha,* t. Gk.: m. *monárchēs* ruling alone]

mo·nar·chal (mə när′kəl), *adj.* 1. pertaining to, characteristic of, or befitting a monarch. 2. having the status of a monarch. Also, **mo·nar·chi·al** (mə när′kĭ əl). **—mo·nar′chal·ly,** *adv.*

mo·nar·chi·cal (mə när′kə kəl), *adj.* 1. of a monarch, or monarchy. 2. characterized by or favoring monarchy. Also, **mo·nar′chic.** **—mo·nar′chi·cal·ly,** *adv.*

mon·ar·chism (mŏn′ər kĭz′əm), *n.* 1. the principles of monarchy. 2. advocacy of monarchical principles. **—mon′ar·chist,** *n., adj.* **—mon′ar·chis′tic,** *adj.*

mon·ar·chy (mŏn′ər kĭ), *n., pl.* **-chies.** 1. a government or state in which the supreme power is actually or nominally lodged in a monarch (known as an **absolute**

Monadelphous flower

Monandrous flower of mare's tail. Hippuris vulgaris

---

or **despotic monarchy** when the monarch's authority is not limited by laws or a constitution and as a **limited or constitutional monarchy** when the monarch's authority is so limited). **2.** supreme power or sovereignty wielded by a single person. [ME *monarchie*, t. LL: m. *monarchia*, t. Gk.] —**Syn. 1.** See **kingdom.**

mo·nar·da (mə när′də), *n.* any of the labiate genus *Monarda*, of mintlike aromatic erect herbs of North America, including horsemint, Oswego tea, etc. [t. NL; named after N. *Monardēs* (1493–1588), Spanish physician and botanist]

mon·as (mŏn′ăs, mō′năs), *n., pl.* **monades** (mŏn′ə-dēz′). monad. [t. LL]

mon·as·ter·y (mŏn′ə stĕr′Y), *n., pl.* **-teries. 1.** a house or place of residence occupied by a community of persons, esp. monks, living in seclusion from the world under religious vows. **2.** the community of persons living in such a place. [ME, t. LL: m.s. *monastērium*, t. LGk.: m. *monastērion* solitary dwelling] —**mon·as·te·ri·al** (mŏn′ə stYr′Y əl), *adj.*

mo·nas·tic (mə năs′tYk), *adj.* Also, **mo·nas′ti·cal. 1.** of or pertaining to monasteries: *monastic architecture.* **2.** of, pertaining to, or characteristic of monks, or other persons living in seclusion from the world under religious vows: *monastic vows of poverty, chastity, and obedience.* —*n.* **3.** a member of a monastic community or order; a monk. [t. ML: s. *monasticus,* t. LGk.: m. *monastikós* living in solitude] —**mo·nas′ti·cal·ly,** *adv.*

mo·nas·ti·cism (mə năs′tə sYz′əm), *n.* the monastic system, condition, or mode of life.

Mo·na·stir (mō′nä stēr′), *n.* Turkish name of **Bitolj.**

mon·a·tom·ic (mŏn′ə tŏm′Yk), *adj. Chem.* **1.** having one atom in the molecule. **2.** containing one replaceable atom or group. **3.** having a valence of one.

mon·au·ral (mŏ nôr′əl), *adj.* of or pertaining to sound transmitted or reproduced over a single transmission path; monophonic.

mon·ax·i·al (mŏn ăk′sY əl), *adj. Bot.* **1.** uniaxial. **2.** having flowers that grow on the primary axis.

mon·a·zite (mŏn′ə zīt′), *n.* a reddish- or yellowish-brown mineral, a phosphate of cerium and lanthanum, (Ce,La) PO₄, the principal ore of thorium. [t. G: m. *monazit,* f. s. Gk. *monázein* be alone + *-it* -ITE¹]

Mön·chen-Glad·bach (mœn′кнən glät′bäкн), *n.* a city in W West Germany, in the Rhineland. 144,828 (est. 1955). Formerly, **München-Gladbach.**

mon cher (môn shĕr′), *French.* my dear (masc.).

Monck (mŭngk), *n.* **George.** See **Monk.**

Mon·day (mŭn′dY), *n.* the second day of the week, following Sunday. [ME *Mone(n)day,* OE *mōn(an)dæg* moon's day, used to render LL *Lūnae dies*]

monde (môNd), *n. French.* the world; people; society.

Mon·dri·aan (môn′drY än), *n.* **Piet** (pēt), 1872–1944, Dutch painter.

mo·ne·cious (mə nē′shəs, mō-), *adj.* monoecious.

Mo·nel metal (mō nĕl′), *n.* **1.** a nonrusting, silvery-white alloy containing about 67 percent nickel, 28 percent copper, and 5 percent other metals, produced from the nickeliferous ores of the Sudbury district in Canada, and used for a great number of purposes. **2.** (*cap.*) a trademark for this metal. Also, **Mo·nell′.** [named after Ambrose *Monell* (d. 1921), of New York]

Mo·nes·sen (mə nĕs′ən, mō-), *n.* a city in SW Pennsylvania, on the Monongahela river. 17,896 (1950).

Mo·net (mō nĕ′), *n.* **Claude** (klōd), 1840–1926, French painter: a founder and leader of the impressionist school.

mon·e·tar·y (mŭn′ə tĕr′Y, mŏn′ə-), *adj.* **1.** of or pertaining to the coinage or currency of a country. **2.** of or pertaining to money, or pecuniary: *monetary consideration.* [t. L: m.s. *monētārius* pertaining to the mint] —**mon·e·tar′i·ly,** *adv.* —**Syn. 1.** See **financial.**

mon·e·tize (mŭn′ə tīz′, mŏn′ə-), *v.t.* **-tized, -tizing. 1.** to legalize as money. **2.** to coin into money: *to monetize gold.* **3.** to give the character of money to. —**mon′e·ti·za′tion,** *n.*

mon·ey (mŭn′Y), *n., pl.* **moneys, monies. 1.** gold, silver, or other metal in pieces of convenient form stamped by public authority and issued as a medium of exchange and measure of value. **2.** current coin. **3.** coin or certificate (as banknotes, etc.) generally accepted in payment of debts and current transactions. **4.** any article or substance similarly used, as checks on demand deposit, wampum, etc. **5.** a particular form or denomination of currency. **6.** a money of account. **7.** property considered with reference to its pecuniary value. **8.** (*pl.*) *Archaic or Legal.* pecuniary sums. **9.** pecuniary profit. [ME *moneye,* t. OF: m. *moneie,* t. L *monēta* mint, money, der. *Jūno Monēta* Juno the Adviser, in whose temple at Rome money was coined] —**Syn. 1.** coin, cash, currency, specie, change. **7.** funds, capital, assets.

mon·ey·bag (mŭn′Y băg′), *n.* **1.** a bag for money. **2.** (*pl. construed as sing.*) a wealthy person.

mon·ey·chang·er (mŭn′Y chān′jər), *n.* one whose business it is to change money at a fixed or official rate.

mon·eyed (mŭn′Yd), *adj.* **1.** having money; wealthy. **2.** consisting of or representing money: *moneyed interests.*

mon·ey·lend·er (mŭn′Y lĕn′dər), *n.* one whose business it is to lend money at interest.

mon·ey·mak·er (mŭn′Y mā′kər), *n.* **1.** one engaged in or successful in gaining money. **2.** something that yields pecuniary profit. —**mon′ey·mak′ing,** *n., adj.*

money of account, a monetary denomination used in reckoning, esp. one not issued as a coin.

money order, an order for the payment of money, as one issued by one post office and payable at another.

mon·ey·wort (mŭn′Y wûrt′), *n.* a creeping primulaceous herb, *Lysimachia Nummularia,* with roundish leaves and yellow flowers.

mon·ger (mŭng′gər), *n.* (usually in compounds) **1.** *Brit.* a dealer in some commodity: *a fishmonger.* **2.** one who busies himself with something in a sordid or petty way: *a scandalmonger.* [ME *mongere,* OE *mangere* (c. Icel. *mangari*), f. L *mang(o)* trader + *-ere* -ER¹] —**mon′-ger·ing,** *n., adj.*

Mon·gol (mŏng′gəl, -gŏl, -gōl), *n.* **1.** one of an Asiatic race now living chiefly in Mongolia. **2.** a member of the Mongolian race. **3.** any Mongolian language. —*adj.* **4.** Mongolian.

Mongol Empire, an empire that under Genghis Khan, in the 13th century, encompassed the larger part of Asia and extended to the Dnieper river in E Europe: its capital was the vast tent city of Karakorum, in N Mongolia.

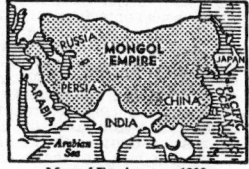

Mongol Empire, A. D. 1200

Mon·go·li·a (mŏng gō′lY ə), *n.* **1.** a vast region in Asia, including Inner Mongolia, the Mongolian People's Republic, and Tannu Tuva. **2. Inner,** the S part of Mongolia, under Chinese control, generally including the provinces of Jehol, Chahar, Suiyüan, and Ningsia; boundaries subjected to frequent change recently. Official name, **Inner Mongolian Autonomous Region. 3. Outer,** former name of **Mongolian People's Republic.**

Mon·go·li·an (mŏng gō′lY-ən), *adj.* **1.** pertaining to Mongolia. **2.** of or pertaining to the Mongol nationality of inner Asia. **3.** denoting or pertaining to the so-called "yellow" race of Asia, characterized chiefly by yellowish complexion, prominent cheekbones, slant eyes, short broad nose, and straight black hair, and embracing the Mongols, Manchus, Chinese, Koreans, Japanese, Annamese, Siamese, Burmans, and Tibetans. **4.** affected with Mongolism. —*n.* **5.** a member of the Mongolian race. **6.** a family of languages, including the languages of the Mongols, perhaps related to the Turkic and Tungusic families.

Mongolian People's Republic, a republic in E central Asia: the N part of Mongolia. 920,000 (est. 1954); ab. 600,000 sq. mi. *Cap.*: Ulan Bator Khoto.

Mon·gol·ic (mŏng gŏl′Yk), *adj.* **1.** Mongolian. —*n.* **2.** Mongolian (def. 6).

Mon·gol·ism (mŏng′gə lYz′əm), *n.* abnormal condition of a child born with a wide, flattened skull, narrow, slanting eyes, and generally a mental deficiency.

Mon·gol·oid (mŏng′gə loid′), *adj.* **1.** resembling the Mongols. **2.** *Anthropol.* **a.** similar or related to the Mongols in physique. **b.** pertaining to the "yellow" race, which embraces Asiatic Mongolians, Indonesian-Malaysians, and American Indians. —*n.* **3.** a person of a Mongoloid race.

mon·goose (mŏng′gōōs), *n., pl.* **-gooses.** a slender ferretlike carnivore, typified by *Herpestes edwardsii,* of India, of the same genus as the common ichneumon, used for destroying rats, etc., and noted for its ability to kill certain venomous snakes without being harmed. Also, **mon′goos.** [t. Mahratti: m. *mangūs*]

Mongoose. *Herpestes Ichneumon* (Total length ab. 3 ft., tail 1½ ft.)

mon·grel (mŭng′grəl, mŏng′-), *n.* **1.** any animal or plant resulting from the crossing of different breeds or varieties. **2.** any cross between different things. —*adj.* **3.** that is a mongrel; being of mixed breed, race, origin, nature, etc. [t. obs. *mong* mixture (OE *gemang*) + -REL]

mongst (mŭngst), *prep. Poetic.* amongst.

mon·i·ker (mŏn′ə kər), *n.* **1.** a symbol or mark used by a tramp to identify himself. **2.** *Slang.* a person's name; a nickname. Also, **mon′ick·er.** [b. MONOGRAM and MARKER]

mo·nil·i·form (mō nYl′ə fôrm′), *adj.* **1.** *Bot. and Zool.* consisting of or characterized by a series of beadlike swellings alternating with contractions, as certain roots, stems, etc. **2.** resembling a string of beads. [f. s. L *monīle* necklace + -(I)FORM]

mon·ism (mŏn′Yz əm, mō′nYz-əm), *n. Philos.* **1.** the doctrine of one ultimate substance or principle, as mind (*idealism*) or matter (*materialism*), or something that is neither mind nor matter but the ground of both. **2.** the position that reality is one (op-

Moniliform fruits of *Sophora japonica*

posed to *pluralism*). [t. NL: s. *monismus*, der. Gk. *mónos* single] —**mon′ist,** *n.* —**mo·nis·tic** (mō-nĭs′tĭk), *adj.* —**mo·nis′ti·cal·ly,** *adv.*

mo·ni·tion (mō nĭsh′ən), *n.* **1.** admonition; warning; caution. **2.** an official or legal notice. **3.** *Law.* a court order summoning a party, either to commence suit by appearance and answer or to answer contempt charges. **4.** a formal notice from a bishop requiring the amendment of an ecclesiastical offense. [ME, t. L: s. *monitio* a reminding]

mon·i·tor (mŏn′ə tər), *n.* **1.** a pupil appointed to assist in the conduct of a class or school, as to help keep order, etc. **2.** one who admonishes, esp. with reference to conduct. **3.** something that serves to remind or give warning. **4.** a device used to govern the operation of a machine; a servomechanism. **5.** an ironclad warship with a low freeboard and one or more revolving turrets, each containing one or more large-caliber guns. The first such vessel, the **Monitor,** was used by Union forces during the Civil War against the Merrimac (1862). **6.** an articulated mounting for a nozzle, usually mechanically operated, which permits a stream of water to be played in any desired direction, as in fire fighting. **7.** any of the large lizards constituting the genus *Varanus* and family *Varanidae* of Africa, southern Asia, and Australia, fabled to give warning of the presence of crocodiles. —*v.t., v.i.* **8.** *Radio.* **a.** to hear (transmitted signals) using a receiving set in order to check the quality of the transmission. **b.** to listen to (broadcasts) for operating compliance, censorship, propaganda analysis, and similar purposes. **9.** to operate by means of a servomechanism. [t. L] —**mon′i·tor·ship′,** *n.*

mon·i·to·ri·al (mŏn′ə tōr′ĭ əl), *adj.* **1.** of or pertaining to a monitor. **2.** monitory.

mon·i·to·ry (mŏn′ə tōr′ĭ), *adj., n., pl.* **-ries.** —*adj.* **1.** serving to admonish or warn; admonitory. **2.** giving monition. —*n.* **3.** Also, **monitory letter.** a letter, as one from a bishop, containing a monition. [late ME, t. L: m.s. *monitōrius,* adj.]

monk (mŭngk), *n.* a man who has withdrawn from the world from religious motives, either as an eremite or, esp., as a member of an order of cenobites living under vows of poverty, chastity, and obedience, according to a rule. [ME; OE *munuc,* ult. t. LL: m.s. *monachus,* t. LGk.: m. *monachōs,* adj., solitary (as n., monk)] —**Syn.** MONK, FRIAR refer to special male groups in the Rom. Cath. Church whose lives are devoted to the service of the church. A MONK is properly a member of a monastery, under a superior; he is bound by a vow of stability, and is a co-owner of the community property of the monastery. Since the Reformation, MONK and FRIAR have been used as if they were the same. A FRIAR is, however, strictly speaking, a member of a mendicant order, whose members are not attached to a monastery and own no community property.

Monk (mŭngk), *n.* **George,** (1st Duke of Albemarle) 1608–70, British general who helped to restore Charles II to the throne of England. Also, **Monck.**

mon·key (mŭng′kĭ), *n., pl.* **-keys,** *v.* **-keyed, -keying.** —*n.* **1.** any member of the mammalian order *Primates,* except man, the anthropoid apes and, usually, the lemurs, e.g. the guenons, macaques, langurs, capuchins, etc. **2.** a person likened to such an animal, as a mischievous child, a mimic, etc. **3.** the fur of certain species of long-haired monkeys. **4.** any of various mechanical devices, as the ram of a pile-driving apparatus. **5.** *Coal Mining.* small passageway or opening. **6.** *Brit. Slang.* five hundred pounds. —*v.i.* **7.** *Colloq.* to play or trifle idly; fool (often fol. by *with*). —*v.t.* **8.** to imitate as a monkey does; ape; mimic. **9.** to mock. [appar. t. LG. Cf. MLG *Moneke* (name of son of Martin the Ape in story of Reynard), f. *mone-* (akin to Sp. and Pg. *mono* ape) + *-ke* (dim. suffix)]

Rhesus monkey,
Macacus rhesus
(Total length 30 in.,
tail 8 to 10 in.)

monkey bread, **1.** the gourdlike fruit of the baobab, eaten by monkeys. **2.** the tree itself.

mon·key-faced owl (mŭng′kĭ fāst′), the barn owl, *Tyto alba.*

monkey flower, any plant of the scrophulariaceous genus *Mimulus,* which includes species cultivated in gardens and greenhouses, as *M. cardinalis,* having a scarlet corolla.

monkey jacket, a short, close-fitting jacket or coat, formerly worn by sailors.

monkey nut, *Brit.* peanut.

mon·key-pot (mŭng′kĭ pŏt′), *n.* the woody, operculate seed vessel of any of certain large South American trees of the genus *Lecythis.*

monkey puzzle, a South American coniferous tree, *Araucaria arauna,* with candelabralike branches, stiff sharp leaves, and edible nuts.

mon·key-shine (mŭng′kĭ shīn′), *n.* *U.S. Slang.* a mischievous or clownish trick or prank.

monkey wrench, a wrench with an adjustable jaw, for turning nuts of different sizes, etc.

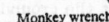

Monkey wrench

Mon-Khmer (mŏn′kmĕr′), *adj.* designating a group of languages spoken chiefly in Indo-China.

monk·hood (mŭngk′hŏŏd), *n.* **1.** the condition or profession of a monk. **2.** monks collectively.

monk·ish (mŭngk′ĭsh), *adj.* (often in depreciatory use) of or pertaining to, characteristic of, or resembling a monk. —**monk′ish·ly,** *adv.* —**monk′ish·ness,** *n.*

monk's cloth, a heavy cotton fabric in a basket weave, used for curtains, bedspreads, etc.

monks·hood (mŭngks′hŏŏd), *n.* a plant of the genus *Aconitum,* esp. *A. Napellus* (so called from the hooded flowers). See **aconite.**

Mon·mouth (mŏn′məth), *n.* **1.** James Scott, Duke of, 1649–85, leader of a rebellion against James II: reputed illegitimate son of Charles II. **2.** Monmouthshire.

Mon·mouth·shire (mŏn′məth shĭr′, -shər), *n.* a county in E Wales. 425,115 pop. (1951); 543 sq. mi. *Co. seat:* Monmouth. Also, **Monmouth.**

mono-, a word element **1.** meaning "alone," "single," "one." **2.** denoting a monomolecular thickness, as in *monofilm, monolayer,* etc. **3.** adapted in chemistry to apply to compounds containing one atom of a particular element. Also, **mon-.** [t. Gk., comb. form of *mónos* alone]

mon·o·bas·ic (mŏn′ə bā′sĭk), *adj.* **1.** *Chem.* (of an acid) containing one replaceable hydrogen atom. **2.** *Biol.* monotypic.

mon·o·carp (mŏn′ə kärp′), *n.* *Bot.* a plant that dies after having once borne fruit.

mon·o·car·pel·lar·y (mŏn′ə kär′pə lĕr′ĭ), *adj.* *Bot.* consisting of a single carpel.

mon·o·car·pic (mŏn′ə kär′pĭk), *adj.* *Bot.* producing fruit but once and then dying.

mon·o·car·pous (mŏn′ə kär′pəs), *adj.* *Bot.* **1.** having a gynoecium which forms only a single ovary. **2.** monocarpic.

mon·o·cha·si·um (mŏn′ə kā′zhĭ əm, -zĭ əm), *n., pl.* **-sia** (-zhĭ ə, -zĭ ə). *Bot.* a form of cymose inflorescence in which the main axis produces only a single branch. [t. NL: f. *mono-* MONO- + s. Gk. *chásis* separation + *-ium* -IUM] —**mon′o·cha′si·al,** *adj.*

mon·o·chord (mŏn′ə kôrd′), *n.* an acoustical instrument consisting of an oblong wooden sounding box, usually with a single string, used for the mathematical determination of musical intervals. [ME *monocorde,* t. OF, t. L: m. *monochordon,* t. Gk.: having a single string]

mon·o·chro·ic (mŏn′ə krō′ĭk), *adj.* of one color. [f. s. Gk. *monóchroos* of one color + -IC]

mon·o·chro·mat·ic (mŏn′ə krō măt′ĭk), *adj.* of, producing, or pertaining to one color or one wave length only. —**mon′o·chro·mat′i·cal·ly,** *adv.*

mon·o·chrome (mŏn′ə krōm′), *n.* **1.** a painting or drawing in different shades of a single color. **2.** the art or method of making these. [t. Gk.: m.s. *monóchrōmos* of one color] —**mon′o·chro′mic, mon′o·chro′mi·cal,** *adj.* —**mon′o·chrom′ist,** *n.*

mon·o·cle (mŏn′ə kəl), *n.* an eyeglass for one eye. [t. F, t. LL: m.s. *monoculus* one-eyed] —**mon′o·cled,** *adj.*

mon·o·cli·nal (mŏn′ə klī′nəl), *Geol.* —*adj.* **1.** dipping in one direction, as strata. **2.** pertaining to strata which dip in the same direction. —*n.* **3.** monocline. —**mon′o·cli′nal·ly,** *adv.*

mon·o·cline (mŏn′ə klīn′), *n.* *Geol.* a monoclinal structure or fold. [f. MONO- + m.s Gk. *klīnein* incline]

mon·o·clin·ic (mŏn′ə klĭn′ĭk), *adj. Crystall.* denoting or pertaining to crystallization in which the crystals have three unequal axes, with one oblique intersection.

mon·o·cli·nous (mŏn′ə klī′nəs, mŏn′ə klī′nəs), *adj. Bot.* (of a plant species, etc.) having both the stamens and pistils in the same flower.

mon·o·cot·y·le·don (mŏn′ə kŏt′ə lē′dən), *n. Bot.* **1.** a plant with only one cotyledon. **2.** a member of the group *Monocotyledonae,* one of the two subclasses of angiospermous plants, characterized in the main by producing seeds with a single cotyledon or seed leaf, and by an endogenous mode of growth. —**mon·o·cot·y·le·don·ous** (mŏn′ə kŏt′ə lē′dən əs, -lĕd′ən-), *adj.*

mo·noc·ra·cy (mō nŏk′rə sĭ), *n., pl.* **-cies.** government by a single person; autocracy. —**mon·o·crat·ic** (mŏn′ə krăt′ĭk), *adj.*

mon·o·crat (mŏn′ə krăt′), *n.* one favoring monocracy.

mo·noc·u·lar (mə nŏk′yə lər), *adj.* **1.** having only one eye. **2.** pertaining to or intended for one eye: *a monocular microscope.* [f. s. LL *monoculus* one-eyed + -AR¹]

mon·o·cul·ture (mŏn′ə kŭl′chər), *n. Agric.* growing some single crop and not using the land in any other way.

mon·o·dac·ty·lous (mŏn′ə dăk′tə ləs), *adj. Zool.* having only one digit or claw. Also, **mon′o·dac′tyl.** [t. Gk.: m. *monodáktylos*]

mo·nod·ic (mə nŏd′ĭk), *adj. Music.* pertaining to monody or homophony. Also, **mo·nod′i·cal.** [t. Gk.: m.s. *monōidikós*] —**mo·nod′i·cal·ly,** *adv.*

mon·o·dra·ma (mŏn′ə drä′mə, -drăm′ə), *n.* a dramatic piece for a single performer. —**mon·o·dra·mat·ic** (mŏn′ə drə măt′ĭk), *adj.*

mon·o·dy (mŏn′ə dĭ), *n., pl.* **-dies.** **1.** a Greek ode sung by a single voice, as in a tragedy; a lament. **2.** a poem in which one person laments another's death. **3.** *Music.* **a.** a style of composition in which one part or melody predominates; homophony, as distinguished from polyphony. **b.** a piece in this style. [t. LL: m.s. *monōdia,* t. Gk.: m. *monōidía* a solo, lament] —**mon′o·dist,** *n.*

mo·noe·cious (mə nē'shəs), *adj.* **1.** *Biol.* having both male and female organs in the same individual; hermaphroditic. **2.** *Bot.* (of a plant species, etc.) having the stamens and the pistils in separate flowers on the same plant. Also, **monecious.** [f. MON- + m.s. Gk. *oikíon* house + -OUS]

mo·nog·a·mist (mə nŏg'ə mĭst), *n.* one who practices or advocates monogamy. —**mo·nog·a·mis'tic,** *adj.*

mo·nog·a·mous (mə nŏg'ə məs), *adj.* **1.** practicing or advocating monogamy. **2.** pertaining to monogamy. [t. LL: m. *monogamus,* t. Gk.: m. *monógamos*]

mo·nog·a·my (mə nŏg'ə mĭ), *n.* **1.** marriage of one woman with one man. **2.** *Zool.* the habit of having only one mate. **3.** the practice of marrying only once during life.

mon·o·gen·e·sis (mŏn'ə jĕn'ə sĭs), *n.* **1.** the theoretical descent of all living things from a single ancestral organism. **2.** the theoretical descent of the whole human race from a single pair. **3.** *Biol.* development of an ovum into an organism similar to its parent, without metamorphosis. Also, **mo·nog·e·ny** (mə nŏj'ə nĭ).

mon·o·ge·net·ic (mŏn'ə jĭ nĕt'ĭk), *adj.* **1.** of or pertaining to monogenesis. **2.** having only one generation in the life cycle; without intermediate nonsexual generations: applied to trematode worms of the subclass *Monogenea.* **3.** *Geol.* resulting from one genetic process.

mon·o·gram (mŏn'ə grăm'), *n.* a character consisting of two or more letters combined or interlaced, commonly one's initials, often printed on stationery, embroidered on clothing, etc. [t. LL: m. *monogramma,* t. LGk.: m. *monógrammon* single-lettered character. See MONO-, GRAM-¹] —**mon·o·gram·mat·ic** (mŏn'ə grə măt'ĭk), *adj.*

mon·o·graph (mŏn'ə grăf', -gräf'), *n.* **1.** a treatise on a particular subject. **2.** an account of a single thing or class of things, as of a species of animals or plants. —**mon'o·graph'ic,** *adj.* —**mon'o·graph'i·cal·ly,** *adv.*

mo·nog·ra·pher (mə nŏg'rə fər), *n.* the writer of a monograph.

mo·nog·y·ny (mə nŏj'ə nĭ), *n.* the practice or the condition of having but one wife at a time. [f. MONO- + m.s. Gk. *-gynía,* der. *gynḗ* woman]

mon·o·hy·dric (mŏn'ə hī'drĭk), *adj.* *Chem.* (of a compound, usually an alcohol) having a single hydroxyl radical.

mo·nol·a·try (mə nŏl'ə trĭ), *n.* the worship of but one god, when other gods are recognized as existing. [f. MONO- + m.s. Gk. *latreía* worship] —**mo·nol·a·ter** (mə nŏl'ə tər), **mo·nol·a·trist** (-trĭst), *n.* —**mo·nol·a·trous,** *adj.*

mon·o·lith (mŏn'ə lĭth), *n.* **1.** a single block or piece of stone of considerable size, esp. when used in architecture or sculpture. **2.** an obelisk, column, statue, etc., formed of a single block of stone. **3.** a stonelike material used for floors. **4.** (*cap.*) a trademark for this material. [t. LL: s. *monolithus,* t. Gk.: m. *monólithos* made of one stone] —**mon'o·lith'ic,** *adj.*

mon·o·logue (mŏn'ə lŏg', -lôg'), *n.* **1.** a prolonged talk or discourse by a single speaker. **2.** any composition, as a poem, in which a single person speaks alone. **3.** a part of a drama in which a single actor speaks alone. **4.** a form of dramatic entertainment by a single speaker. Also, **mon'o·log'.** [f. F, t. Gk.: m.s. *monólogos* speaking alone] —**mon·o·log·ic** (mŏn'ə lŏj'ĭk), **mon·o·log'i·cal,** *adj.* —**mon·o·log·ist** (mŏn'ə lŏg'ĭst, -lôg'-), *n.*

mo·nol·o·gy (mə nŏl'ə jĭ), *n., pl.* **-gies.** **1.** the act or habit of soliloquizing. **2.** *Obs.* a monologue. [t. Gk.: m.s. *monología*]

mon·o·ma·ni·a (mŏn'ə mā'nĭ ə), *n.* **1.** insanity in which the patient is irrational on one subject only. **2.** an exaggerated zeal for, or interest in, some one thing; a craze. —**mon·o·ma·ni·ac** (mŏn'ə mā'nĭ ăk'), *n.* —**mon·o·ma·ni·a·cal** (mŏn'ə mə nī'ə kəl), *adj.*

mon·o·mer (mŏn'ə mər), *n.* *Chem.* a molecule of low molecular weight capable of reacting with identical or different monomers to form a polymer.

mo·nom·er·ous (mə nŏm'ərəs), *adj.* *Bot.* (of flowers) having one member in each whorl. [f. s. Gk. *monomerḗs* consisting of one part + -OUS]

mon·o·me·tal·lic (mŏn'ə mə tăl'ĭk), *adj.* **1.** of or using one metal. **2.** pertaining to monometallism.

mon·o·met·al·lism (mŏn'ə mĕt'ə lĭz'əm), *n.* **1.** the use of one metal only (as gold or silver) as the monetary standard. **2.** the doctrine or actions supporting such a standard. —**mon·o·met'al·list,** *n.*

mo·no·mi·al (mō nō'mĭ əl), *adj.* **1.** *Alg.* consisting of one term only. **2.** *Biol.* denoting or pertaining to a name which consists of a single word or term. —*n.* **3.** *Alg.* a monomial expression or quantity. [irreg. f. MO(NO)- + -*nomial,* after BINOMIAL]

mon·o·mo·lec·u·lar (mŏn'ə mə lĕk'yə lər), *adj.* indicating a thickness of one molecule.

mon·o·mor·phic (mŏn'ə môr'fĭk), *adj.* **1.** *Biol.* having only one form. **2.** of the same or of an essentially similar type of structure. Also, **mon'o·mor'phous.**

Mo·non·ga·he·la (mə nŏng'gə hē'lə), *n.* a river flowing from N West Virginia through SW Pennsylvania into the Ohio river at Pittsburgh. 128 mi.

mon·o·pet·al·ous (mŏn'ə pĕt'ə ləs), *adj.* *Bot.* **1.** gamopetalous. **2.** having but one petal, as a corolla.

mon·o·pho·bi·a (mŏn'ə fō'bĭ ə), *n.* *Psychiatry.* morbid dread of being alone.

mon·o·phon·ic (mŏn'ə fŏn'ĭk), *adj.* monodic.

mon·oph·thong (mŏn'əf thŏng', -thông'), *n.* a single, simple vowel sound; a monophthongal vowel. [t. Gk.: s. *monóphthongos* with one sound]

mon·oph·thon·gal (mŏn'əf thŏng'gəl, -thông'-), *adj.* *Phonet.* (of vowels) of unvarying quality; approximately the same from beginning to end.

mon·o·phy·let·ic (mŏn'ə fī lĕt'ĭk), *adj.* **1.** of or pertaining to a single tribe or stock. **2.** developed from a single ancestral type, as a group of animals. [f. MONO- + m.s. Gk. *phyletikós* belonging to a tribesman]

mon·o·phyl·lous (mŏn'ə fĭl'əs), *adj.* *Bot.* **1.** consisting of one leaf, as a calyx. **2.** having only one leaf. [t. Gk.: m. *monóphyllos*]

Mo·noph·y·site (mə nŏf'ə sīt'), *n.* *Theol.* one holding that there is in Christ but a single nature, or one composite nature, partly divine and partly human, as do members of the Coptic Church of Egypt: used esp. with reference to the controversies of the 5th and 6th centuries. [t. LGk.: m.s. *monophysítēs,* f. mono- MONO- + *phýs(is)* nature + -*ítēs* -ITE¹] —**Mon·o·phy·sit·ic** (mŏn'ə fī sĭt'ĭk), *adj.* —**Mo·noph'y·sit·ism,** *n.*

mon·o·plane (mŏn'ə plān'), *n.* an airplane with a single sustaining plane.

mon·o·ple·gi·a (mŏn'ə plē'jĭ ə), *n. Pathol.* paralysis of only one extremity, upper or lower. [t. NL. See MONO-, -PLEGIA] —**mon·o·pleg·ic** (mŏn'ə plĕj'ĭk, -plē'jĭk), *adj.*

mon·o·pode (mŏn'ə pōd'), *adj.* **1.** having but one foot. —*n.* **2.** a creature having but one foot. **3.** one of a fabled race of men having but one leg. **4.** *Bot.* monopodium. [t. Gk.: m.s. *monópous* one-footed]

mon·o·po·di·um (mŏn'ə pō'dĭ əm), *n., pl.* **-di·a** (-dĭ ə). *Bot.* a single main axis which continues to extend at the apex in the original line of growth, giving off lateral branches beneath in acropetal succession. [NL, f. Gk.: mono- MONO- + m. *pódion* foot] —**mon'o·po'di·al,** *adj.*

mo·nop·o·lism (mə nŏp'ə lĭz'əm), *n.* the existence or prevalence of monopolies.

mo·nop·o·list (mə nŏp'ə lĭst), *n.* **1.** one who has a monopoly. **2.** an advocate of monopoly. —**mo·nop'o·lis'tic,** *adj.*

mo·nop·o·lize (mə nŏp'ə līz'), *v.t.,* **-lized, -lizing.** **1.** to acquire, have, or exercise a monopoly of. **2.** to obtain exclusive possession of; keep entirely to oneself: *she tried to monopolize his time.* —**mo·nop'o·li·za'tion,** *n.* —**mo·nop'o·liz'er,** *n.*

mo·nop·o·ly (mə nŏp'ə lĭ), *n., pl.* **-lies.** **1.** exclusive control of a commodity or service in a particular market, or a control that makes possible the manipulation of prices. **2.** an exclusive privilege to carry on a traffic or service, granted by a sovereign, state, etc. **3.** the exclusive possession or control of something. **4.** something which is the subject of such control; a commodity, service, etc., which is exclusively controlled. **5.** a company or the like having such control. [t. L: m.s. *monopōlium,* t. Gk.: m. *monopṓlion* a right of exclusive sale]

mon·o·sac·cha·ride (mŏn'ə săk'ə rīd', -rĭd), *n. Chem.* a simple sugar, such as glucose, fructose, arabinose, and ribose, occurring in nature or obtained by the hydrolysis of glucosides or polysaccharides.

mon·o·sep·al·ous (mŏn'ə sĕp'ə ləs), *adj. Bot.* **1.** gamosepalous. **2.** having but one sepal, as a calyx.

mon·o·sper·mous (mŏn'ə spûr'məs), *adj. Bot.* one-seeded. Also, **mon'o·sper'mal.**

mon·o·stich (mŏn'ə stĭk'), *n.* **1.** a poem or epigram consisting of a single metrical line. **2.** a single line of poetry. [t. LL: s. *monostichum,* t. Gk.: m. *monóstichon,* adj. neut., consisting of one line]

mon·o·stome (mŏn'ə stōm'), *adj.* having a single mouth, pore, or stoma. Also, **mo·nos·to·mous** (mə nŏs'tə məs). [t. Gk.: m. *monóstomos* with one mouth]

mo·nos·tro·phe (mə nŏs'trə fĭ, mŏn'ə strŏf'), *n.* a poem in which all the strophes or stanzas are of the same metrical form. [t. Gk.: m.s. *monóstrophos.* See MONO-, STROPHE] —**mon·o·stroph·ic** (mŏn'ə strŏf'ĭk), *adj.*

mon·o·sty·lous (mŏn'ə stī'ləs), *adj. Bot.* having but one style.

mon·o·syl·lab·ic (mŏn'ə sĭ lăb'ĭk), *adj.* **1.** having only one syllable, as the word *no.* **2.** having a vocabulary composed exclusively of monosyllables (formerly, erroneously said of Chinese). **3.** using or uttering monosyllables. —**mon'o·syl·lab'i·cal·ly,** *adv.*

mon·o·syl·la·bism (mŏn'ə sĭl'ə bĭz'əm), *n.* **1.** monosyllabic character. **2.** use of monosyllables.

mon·o·syl·la·ble (mŏn'ə sĭl'ə bəl), *n.* a word of one syllable, as *yes* and *no.* [f. MONO- + SYLLABLE. Cf. L *monosyllabon,* t. Gk.]

mon·o·the·ism (mŏn'ə thē'ĭz'əm), *n.* the doctrine or belief that there is but one God. [f. MONO- + s. Gk. *theós* god + -ISM] —**mon'o·the·ist,** *n.* —**mon'o·the·is'tic,** *adj.* —**mon'o·the·is'ti·cal·ly,** *adv.*

mon·o·tone (mŏn'ə tōn'), *n.* **1.** vocal utterance, or series of speech sounds. **2.** a single tone without harmony or variation in pitch. **3.** recitation or singing of words in such a tone. **4.** a person who sings in such manner. **5.** sameness of style, as in composition or writing. —*adj.* **6.** monotonous. [t. NL: m.s. *monotonus,* t. LGk.: m. *monótonos* of one tone]

āct, āble, dâre, ärt; ĕbb, ēqual; ĭf, īce; hŏt, ōver, ôrder, oil, bŏŏk, ōoze, out; ŭp, ūse, ûrge; ə = a in alone; ch, chief; g, give; ng, ring; sh, shoe; th, thin; ŧħ, that; zh, vision. See the full key on inside cover.

Branch of monoecious tree
A. Male catkins;
B. Female catkins;
C. Fruit

mo·not·o·nous (mənŏt′ənəs), *adj.* **1.** unvarying in any respect, lacking in variety, or tiresomely uniform. **2.** characterizing a sound continuing on one note. **3.** having very little inflection; limited to a narrow pitch range. [f. MONOTONE + -OUS] —**mo·not′o·nous·ly**, *adv.* —mo·not/o·nous·ness, *n.* —Syn. 1. tedious, humdrum.

mo·not·o·ny (mənŏt′ənĭ), *n.* **1.** lack of variety, or wearisome uniformity, as in occupation, scenery, etc. **2.** the continuance of an unvarying sound; monotone. **3.** sameness of tone or pitch, as in utterance. [t. LGk.: m.s. *monotonía*]

mon·o·trem·a·tous (mŏn′ə trĕm′ə təs, -trē′mə-), *adj.* of or pertaining to a monotreme.

mon·o·treme (mŏn′ə trēm′), *n.* any of the *Monotremata*, the lowest order of mammals, restricted to the Australian region, and comprising only the duckbill and the echidnas, oviparous mammals in which the genital, urinary, and digestive organs have a common opening. [f. MONO- + m. Gk. *trēma* hole]

mo·not·ri·cha (mənŏt′rə kə), *n.pl.* bacteria having the organs of locomotion at one pole. [f. MONO- + s. Gk. *thríx* hair + -a (repr. L and Gk. neut. pl. suffix -a)] —mon·o·trich·ic (mŏn′ə trĭk′ĭk), mo·not′ri·chous, *adj.*

mon·o·type (mŏn′ə tīp′), *n.* **1.** *Print.* **a.** type composed and cast on separate keyboard and casting machines which produce each character on an individual body. **b.** (*cap.*) a trademark for a machine on which such type is set or cast. **2.** a print from a metal plate on which a picture is painted, as in oil color or printing ink. **3.** the method of producing such a print. **4.** *Biol.* the only or sole type of its group, as a single species constituting a genus. —mon/o·typ′er, *n.*

mon·o·typ·ic (mŏn′ə tĭp′ĭk), *adj.* **1.** having only one type. **2.** of the nature of a monotype. **3.** *Biol.* (of genera) established on the basis of a single species or genus.

mon·o·va·lent (mŏn′ə vā′lənt), *adj.* **1.** *Chem.* having a valence of one, as the cuprous ion (Cu^{+1}). **2.** *Bacteriol.* (of a serum, tissue, etc.) capable of resisting a specific disease organism because of the presence of the proper antibodies or antigens. [f. MONO- + -VALENT] —mon/o·va′lence, mon/o·va/len·cy, *n.*

mon·ox·ide (mŏn ŏk′sīd, mənŏk′-), *n.* *Chem.* an oxide containing one oxygen atom to the molecule.

Mon·roe (mənrō′), *n.* **1.** Harriet, 1861?–1936, U.S. editor and poet. **2.** James, 1758–1831, the 5th president of the United States, 1817–25. **3.** a city in N Louisiana. 52,219 (1960). **4.** Fort, a fort at the entrance to Hampton Roads, in SE Virginia.

Monroe Doctrine, the doctrine, based upon statements contained in the message of President Monroe to Congress (Dec. 2, 1823), that the interposition of any European power to control the destiny of a Spanish-American state should be looked upon as a manifestation of unfriendly disposition toward the U.S., and that the American continents should no longer be subjects for any new European political acquisition.

Mon·ro·vi·a (mŏn rō′vĭ ə), *n.* **1.** a city in SW California. 27,079 (1960). **2.** a seaport in, and the capital of, Liberia, in W Africa. 45,000 (est. 1955).

mons (mŏnz), *n.* *Anat.* a rounded eminence of fatty tissue, covered with hair, over the pubic symphysis of the adult human: called the **mons Veneris** in the female, the **mons pubis** in the male.

Mons (môNs), *n.* a city in SW Belgium. 25,464 (1947).

Mon·sei·gneur (môN sĕ nyœr′), *n., pl.* **Messeigneurs** (mĕ sĕ nyœr′). **1.** a French title of honor given to princes, bishops, and other persons of eminence. **2.** a person bearing this title. Also, **mon·sei·gneur′.** [t. F: my lord. See SEIGNEUR]

mon·sieur (məsyœ′), *n., pl.* **messieurs** (mĕ syœ′). the conventional French title of respect and term of address for a man, corresponding to *Mr.* and to *Sir.* [t. F: my lord (orig. applied to men of high station). See SIRE]

Mon·si·gnor (mŏn sē′nyər; *It.* môn′sē nyôr′), *n., pl.* **Monsignors, Monsignori** (môn′sē nyô′rē). *Rom. Cath. Ch.* **1.** a title conferred upon certain dignitaries. **2.** a person bearing this title. Also, **mon·si′gnor, Mon·si·gno·re** (môn′sē nyô′rē). [t. It.: f. F *mon* my + It. *signor(e)* lord]

mon·soon (mŏn sōōn′), *n.* **1.** the seasonal wind of the Indian Ocean and southern Asia, blowing from the southwest in summer, and from the northeast in winter. **2.** the season during which the southwest monsoon blows, commonly marked by heavy rains. **3.** any wind that reverses with the seasons. **4.** a persistent wind established between water and adjoining land. [t. early mod. D: m. *monssoen*, t. Pg.: m. *monçao*, t. Ar.: m. *mausim* time, season]

mon·ster (mŏn′stər), *n.* **1.** a fabulous animal compounded of brute and human shape or of the shapes of various brutes, as a centaur, a griffin, or a sphinx. **2.** an animal or a plant of abnormal form or structure, as from marked malformation, the absence of certain parts or organs, etc. **3.** something unnatural or monstrous. **4.** a person that excites horror, as by wickedness, cruelty, etc. **5.** any animal or thing of huge size. —*adj.* **6.** huge; enormous; monstrous. [ME *monstre*, t. OF, t. L: m.s. *monstrum* omen, prodigy, monster]

mon·strance (mŏn′strəns), *n.* *Rom. Cath. Ch.* a receptacle in which the consecrated host is exposed for adoration. [ME, t. ML: m.s. *monstrantia*, der. L *monstrāre* show]

mon·stros·i·ty (mŏn strŏs′ə tĭ), *n., pl.* -ties. **1.** state or character of being monstrous. **2.** something monstrous. **3.** a monster. [t. LL: m.s. *monstrōsitas*]

mon·strous (mŏn′strəs), *adj.* **1.** huge; prodigiously great: *a monstrous sum.* **2.** frightful or hideous; revolting; shocking: *a monstrous proposal.* **3.** deviating greatly from the natural or normal form or type. **4.** having the nature or appearance of a fabulous monster. [late ME, t. LL: m.s. *monstrōsus* strange] —**mon′strous·ly,** *adv.* —**mon′strous·ness,** *n.* —Syn. 1. See gigantic. 2. horrible, atrocious.

Mont., Montana.

mon·tage (mŏn tázh′; *Fr.* môN tázh′), *n.* **1.** the art or method of arranging in one composition pictorial elements borrowed from several sources so that the elements are both distinct and blended into a whole, through techniques such as superimposition. **2.** a picture made in this way. **3.** *Motion Pictures.* **a.** a series of scenes, each of extreme brevity, following in rapid succession, used to present a stream of interconnected ideas. **b.** a type of process photography in which objects or other visual images are caused to whirl, flash, or otherwise move into distinctness at one point. **c.** a section of a motion picture using either of these processes. [t. F: mounting, putting together]

Mon·ta·gu (mŏn′tə gū′), *n.* **Lady Mary Wortley** (wûrt′lĭ), (*Mary Pierrepont*) 1689–1762, British author.

Mon·ta·gue (mŏn′tə gū′), *n.* the family name of Romeo in Shakespeare's *Romeo and Juliet.*

Mon·taigne (mŏn tān′; *Fr.* môN tĕn′y), *n.* **Michel Eyquem** (mē shĕl′ ĕ kĕm′), **Seigneur de,** 1533–92, French essayist.

Mon·tan·a (mŏn tăn′ə), *n.* a State in the NW United States. 674,767 pop. (1960); 147,138 sq. mi. *Cap.:* Helena. *Abbr.:* Mont. —**Mon·tan′an,** *adj., n.*

mon·tane (mŏn′tān), *Ecol.* —*adj.* **1.** pertaining to mountain conditions. —*n.* **2.** the lower vegetation belt on mountains. [t. L: m.s. *montānus* of a mountain]

mon·ta·ni sem·per li·be·ri (mŏn tā′nĭ sĕm′pər lĭb′ə rĭ′), Latin. mountaineers (are) always freemen (motto of West Virginia).

mon·tan wax (mŏn′tăn), a dark-brown bituminous wax extracted from lignite and peat and often used for the original disk in phonograph recording. [f. montan (t. L: s. *montānus* of a mountain) + WAX[1]]

Mon·tau·ban (môN tō bäN′), *n.* a city in S France. 38,321 (1954).

Mon·tauk Point (mŏn′tôk), the E end of Long Island, in SE New York.

Mont Blanc (môN bläN′). See **Blanc, Mont.**

Mont·calm (mŏnt kăm′; *Fr.* môN kälm′), *n.* **Louis Joseph** (lwē zhô zĕf′), **Marquis de,** (*Louis Joseph, Marquis de Montcalm de Saint-Véran*) 1712–59, French general: defeated by the British under Wolfe at Quebec in 1759.

Mont·clair (mŏnt klâr′), *n.* a city in NE New Jersey. 43,129 (1960).

mont-de-pié·té (môN′də pyĕ tĕ′), *n., pl.* **monts-de-piété** (môN′-). a public pawnbroking establishment for lending money on reasonable terms, esp. to the poor. [F, t. It.: m. *monte di pietà*, lit., mountain (fund) of pity]

mon·te (mŏn′tĭ, mŏn′tā; *Sp.* môn′tĕ), *n.* a Spanish and Spanish-American gambling game at cards. [t. Sp.: mountain, heap (of cards), g. L *mons* MOUNT[2]]

Mon·te·bel·lo (mŏn′tə bĕl′ō), *n.* a city in SW California, SE of Los Angeles. 32,097.

Mon·te Car·lo (mŏn′tĭ kär′lō; *It.* môn′tĕ kär′lō), a town in Monaco principality, SE France: gambling resort. 9430 (1951). See map under **Monaco.**

Mon·te Cas·si·no (mŏn′tĭ kässē′nō). See **Cassino.**

Mon·te Cor·no (mŏn′tĕ kôr′nō), highest peak in the Apennines, in central Italy. 9585 ft.

mon·teith (mŏn tēth′), *n.* a large bowl commonly of silver, often with a rim for suspending drinking glasses in the cool water within the bowl. It is also used as a punch bowl. [orig. proper name]

Mon·te·ne·gro (mŏn′tə nē′grō; *It.* môn′tĕ nĕ′grō), *n.* a constituent republic of Yugoslavia, in the S part: formerly a kingdom. 458,000 est. (1956); 5345 sq. mi. *Cap.:* Cetinje. —**Mon·te·ne·grin** (mŏn′tə nē′grĭn), *adj., n.*

Mon·te·rey (mŏn′tə rā′), *n.* a city in W California, on Monterey Bay: the capital of California until 1847. 22,618 (1960).

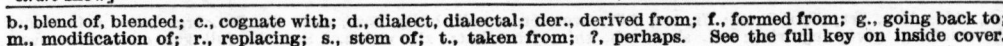

Montenegro, 1871–1914

Monterey Park, a city in SW California, E of Los Angeles. 37,821 (1960).

mon·te·ro (mŏn târ′ō; *Sp.* môn tĕ′rō), *n. pl.* -ros (-rōz; *Sp.* -rôs). a round huntsman's cap with a flap. [t. Sp.: m. *montera* hunting cap, der. *montero* huntsman, der. *monte* MOUNT[2]]

Mon·ter·rey (mŏn′tə rā′; *Sp.* môn′tĕr rĕ′), *n.* a city in NE Mexico: the capital of Nuevo León; battle, 1846. 330,012 (est. 1951).

Mon·tes·pan (mŏn′tĕs păn′; *Fr.* môN tĕs päN′), *n.* **Marquise de,** (*Françoise Athénaïs de Rochechouart*) 1641–1707, mistress of Louis XIV of France.

Mon·tes·quieu (mŏn′tĕskū′; *Fr.* môNˈtĕskyœ′), *n.* (*Charles Louis de Secondat, Baron de la Brède et de Montesquieu*) 1689–1755, French philosophical writer.

Mon·tes·so·ri (mŏn′tə sōr′ĭ; *It.* môn′tĕs sô′rē), *n.* **Maria**, 1870–1952, Italian educator.

Montessori method, a system for training and instructing young children, of which the fundamental aim is self-education by the children themselves, accompanied by special emphasis on the training of the senses. Also, **Montessori system.**

Mon·te·vi·de·o (mŏn′tə vĭ dā′ō, mŏn′tə vĭd′ĭ ō′; *Sp.* môn′tĕ vē dĕ′ō), *n.* a seaport in and the capital of Uruguay. 810,969 (est. 1954).

Mon·te·zu·ma II (mŏn′tə zōō′mə), c1477–1520, Aztec emperor of Mexico, 1503–20, conquered by Cortés and killed in a revolt by his own subjects.

Mont·fort (mŏnt′fərt; *Fr.* môNfôr′), *n.* **1. Simon de** sē môn′də), c1160–1218, French crusader. **2.** his son, **Simon de,** (*Earl of Leicester*) c1208–65, English soldier and statesman.

Mont·gol·fi·er (mŏnt gŏl′fĭ ər; *Fr.* môN gôl fyē′), *n.* **1. Jacques Étienne** (zhàk ĕ tyĕn′), 1745–99, French inventor. **2.** his brother, **Joseph Michel** (zhō zĕf′ mē shĕl′), 1740–1810, French inventor. The Montgolfier brothers invented the balloon and made the first successful flight in 1783. **3.** (*l.c.*) a balloon raised by heated air from a fire in the lower part.

Mont·gom·er·y (mŏnt gŭm′ər ĭ), *n.* **1. Sir Bernard Law,** born 1887, British field marshal. **2. Richard,** 1736–75, American Revolutionary general. **3.** the capital of Alabama, in the central part, on the Alabama river. 134,393 (1960).

Mont·gom·er·y·shire (mŏnt gŭm′ə rĭ shĭr′, –shər), *n.* a county in central Wales. 45,990 pop. (1951); 797 sq. mi. *Co. seat:* Montgomery. Also, **Montgomery.**

month (mŭnth), *n.* **1.** approximately one twelfth of a tropical or solar year (**solar month**). **2.** any of the twelve parts (January, February, etc.) into which the calendar year is divided (**calendar month**). **3.** the time from any day of one calendar month to the corresponding day of the next. **4.** a period of four weeks or 30 days. **5.** the period (**lunar month**) of a complete revolution of the moon with regard to some point, usually the interval (**synodic month**) from one new moon to the next equivalent to 29 days, 12 hours, 44 minutes, and 2.7 seconds. [ME *mon(e)th*, OE *mōnath,* c. G *mond* MOON]

month·ly (mŭnth′lĭ), *adj., n., pl.* **-lies,** *adv.* —*adj.* **1.** pertaining to a month, or to each month. **2.** done, happening, appearing, etc., once a month, or every month. **3.** continuing or lasting for a month. —*n.* **4.** a periodical published once a month. **5.** (*pl.*) menses. —*adv.* **6.** once a month; by the month.

month's mind, *Rom. Cath. Ch.* the remembrance of a deceased person, by a requiem Mass, a month after death.

Mon·ti·cel·lo (mŏn′tə sĕl′ō), *n.* the home of Thomas Jefferson, in central Virginia, near Charlottesville.

mon·ti·cule (mŏn′tĭ kūl′), *n.* **1.** a small mountain, hill, or mound. **2.** a subordinate volcano cone. [t. F, t. LL: m.s. *monticulus,* dim. of L *mons* MOUNT[2]]

Mont·mar·tre (môN mär′tr), *n.* a hilly section in the N part of Paris, France: artists' center; famous cafes.

Mont·mo·ren·cy (mŏnt′mə rĕn′sĭ; *Fr.* môN mô rän sē′), *n.* **Anne** (àn), **Duc de,** 1493–1567, constable of France and French marshal.

Mont·pel·ier (mŏnt pēl′yər), *n.* the capital of Vermont, in the central part. 8599 (1950).

Mont·pel·lier (môN pĕˈlyā′), *n.* a city in S France, near the Mediterranean. 97,501 (1954).

Mont·re·al (mŏnt′rĭ ôl′, mŭnt′–), *n.* a seaport in SE Canada, on an island in the St. Lawrence, in Quebec province. 1,021,520 (1951).

Mon·treuil (môN trœ′y), *n.* a suburb of Paris in N France. 76,252 (1954).

Mont·rose (mŏn trōz′), *n.* **James Graham, Marquis of,** 1612–50, Scottish supporter of Charles I.

Mont-Saint-Michel (môN săN mē shĕl′), *n.* a rocky islet near the coast in NW France, in an inlet of the Gulf of St. Malo: famous abbey and fortress.

Mont·ser·rat (mŏnt′sə răt′), *n.* **1.** an island in the British West Indies: a colony in the Leeward Islands. 14,436 pop. (est. 1955); 32½ sq. mi. *Cap.:* Plymouth. **2.** a mountain (4058 ft.) in NE Spain, NW of Barcelona: the site of **Monserrat Monastery.**

mon·u·ment (mŏn′yə mənt), *n.* **1.** something erected in memory of a person, event, etc., as a pillar, statue, or the like. **2.** a tomb. **3.** any building, megalith, etc., surviving from a past age, and regarded as of historical or archaeological importance. **4.** any work, writing, or the like by a person, regarded as a memorial of him after his death. **5.** any enduring evidence or notable example of something. **6.** an object, as a stone shaft, set in the ground to mark the boundaries of real property. **7.** *Obs.* a statue. [ME, t. L: s. *monumentum*]

mon·u·men·tal (mŏn′yə mĕn′təl), *adj.* **1.** resembling a monument; massive or imposing. **2.** *Fine Arts.* of any size larger than that of life. **3.** historically prominent: *a monumental event.* **4.** *Colloq.* conspicuously great or gross. **5.** of a monument or monuments. **6.** serving as a monument. —**mon′u·men′tal·ly,** *adv.*

mon·u·men·tal·ize (mŏn′yə mĕn′tə lĭz′), *v.t.,* **-ized, -izing.** to establish an enduring memorial or record of.

mon·y (mŏn′ĭ), *adj., n. Scot.* and *N. Eng.* many.

-mony, a noun suffix indicating result or condition, as in *parsimony*; but sometimes having the same function as -ment. [t. L: m.s. *-mōnia, -mōnium*]

Mon·za (mŏn′tsä), *n.* a city in N Italy, in Lombardy. 70,492 (1951).

mon·zo·nite (mŏn′zə nīt′), *n.* any of a group of granular igneous rocks intermediate in composition between syenite and diorite. [t. G: m. *monzonit,* f. *Monzoni* (name of mountain in Tyrol) + *-it* -ITE[1]] —**mon·zo·nit·ic** (mŏn′zə nĭt′ĭk), *adj.*

moo (mōō), *v.,* **mooed, mooing,** *n., pl.* **moos.** —*v.i.* **1.** to utter the characteristic cry of a cow; low. —*n.* **2.** a mooing sound. [imit.]

mooch (mōōch), *Slang.* —*v.i.* **1.** to skulk or sneak. **2.** to hang or rove about. —*v.t.* **3.** to steal. **4.** to get without paying or at another's expense: *to mooch a cigarette.* Also, **mouch.** —**mooch′er,** *n.*

mood[1] (mōōd), *n.* **1.** frame of mind, or state of feeling, as at a particular time. **2.** (*pl.*) fits of uncertainty, gloominess, or sullenness. [ME; OE *mōd* mind, spirit, mood, c. G *mut* courage] —**Syn. 1.** disposition.

mood[2] (mōōd), *n.* **1.** *Gram.* mode. —**2.** *Logic.* any of the various forms of valid syllogisms, depending on the quantity and quality of their constituent propositions. [special use of MOOD[1] by contam. with MODE[1]]

mood·y (mōō′dĭ), *adj.,* **moodier, moodiest. 1.** given to gloomy or sullen moods. **2.** proceeding from or showing such a mood: *a moody silence.* **3.** gloomy; sullen; ill-humored. —**mood′i·ly,** *adv.* —**mood′i·ness,** *n.*

Moo·dy (mōō′dĭ), *n.* **1. Dwight Lyman,** 1837–99, U.S. evangelist. **2. William Vaughn,** 1869–1910, U.S. poet and dramatist.

moon (mōōn), *n.* **1.** the body which revolves around the earth monthly at a mean distance of 238,857 miles, accompanying the earth in its annual revolution about the sun. It is about 2160 miles in diameter. **2.** this heavenly body during a particular lunar month, or during a certain period of time, or at a certain point of time, regarded as a distinct object or entity. **a. new moon,** the moon when in conjunction with the sun and hence invisible, or the phase so represented, or the moon soon afterward when visible as a slender crescent. **b. half moon,** the moon when half its disk is illuminated, occurring when at either quadrature, or quarter. **c. full moon,** the moon when the whole of its disk is illuminated, occurring when in opposition to the sun, or the phase so represented. **d. old moon,** the waning moon. **e. waxing moon,** the moon at any time before it is full, so called because its illuminated area is increasing. **f. waning moon,** the moon at any time after it has been full, so called because its illuminated area is decreasing. **3.** a lunar month, or, in general, a month. **4.** any planetary satellite. **5.** something shaped like an orb or a crescent. —*v.i.* **6.** *Colloq.* to wander about or gaze idly or listlessly. —*v.t.* **7.** to spend (time) idly. [ME *mone,* OE *mōna,* c. OHG *māno;* akin to Gk. *mēnē* moon, *mēn* month, L *mensis* month]

Phases of the moon

The figures on the inner circle show the moon in its orbit round the earth; those on the outer circle represent the moon's corresponding phases as seen from the earth. A. New moon (invisible); B. Waxing crescent; C. First quarter (half moon); D. Gibbous; E. Full moon; F. Gibbous; G. Last quarter (half-moon); H. Waning crescent; L. Earth; J. Sun's rays

moon·beam (mōōn′bēm′), *n.* a ray of moonlight.

moon-blind (mōōn′blīnd′), *adj.* (of horses) afflicted with moon blindness. Also, **moon-eyed** (mōōn′īd′).

moon blindness, *Vet. Sci.* a specific, probably noninfectious disease of horses, of unknown cause, in which the eyes suffer from recurring attacks of inflammation, and which eventually results in opacity and blindness.

moon·calf (mōōn′kăf′, –käf′), *n.* a congenital imbecile. [lit., a person influenced by the moon]

mooned (mōōnd), *adj.* **1.** ornamented with moons or crescents. **2.** shaped like a moon or crescent.

moon-eye (mōōn′ī′), *n. Vet. Sci.* an eye of a horse affected with moon blindness.

moon-fish (mōōn′fĭsh′), *n., pl.* **-fishes,** (*esp. collectively*) **-fish. 1.** any of certain fishes having a deep, sharply compressed, silvery body, as of the carangid genera *Selene* and *Vomer,* as *S. vomer* and *V. setipinnis* of the warmer coastal waters of North and South America. **2.** the opah. **3.** a minnow, *Platypoecilus maculatus.*

moon-flow·er (mōōn′flou′ər), *n.* a night-blooming convolvulaceous plant, *Calonyction aculeatum,* with fragrant white flowers.

moon·light (mōōn′līt′), *n.* **1.** the light of the moon. —*adj.* **2.** pertaining to moonlight. **3.** illuminated by moonlight. **4.** occurring by moonlight, or by night.

moon·light·ing (mōōn′līt′ĭng), *n. Colloq.* working at a job in addition to one's regular, full-time employment.

Moonlight Sonata, the title given to Beethoven's piano sonata, Op. 27 No. 2 (1801) after his death.

moon·lit (mōōn′lĭt′), *adj.* lighted by the moon.

moon·rise (mōōn′rīz′), *n.* **1.** the rising of the moon above the horizon. **2.** the time at which the moon rises above the horizon.

moon-seed (mōōn′sēd′), *n.* any of the climbing herbs

constituting the genus *Menispermum* (family *Menispermaceae*) with greenish-white flowers, so called from the crescent-shaped seeds.

moon·set (mōōn′sĕt′), *n.* **1.** the setting of the moon below the horizon. **2.** the time at which the moon disappears below the horizon.

moon·shine (mōōn′shīn′), *n.* **1.** the light of the moon. **2.** empty or foolish talk, ideas, etc.; nonsense. **3.** *U.S. Colloq.* smuggled or illicitly distilled liquor.

moon·shin·er (mōōn′shī′nər), *n.* *U.S. Colloq.* **1.** an illicit distiller. **2.** one who pursues an illegal trade at night.

moon·shin·y (mōōn′shī′nĭ), *adj.* **1.** like moonlight. **2.** moonlit. **3.** without sense; fictitious; visionary.

moon·stone (mōōn′stōn′), *n.* a white translucent variety of feldspar with a bluish pearly luster, used as a gem.

moon·struck (mōōn′strŭk′), *adj.* injuriously affected in mind (or otherwise), supposedly by the influence of the moon; dazed; crazed. Also, **moon·strick·en** (mōōn′-strĭk′ən).

moon·wort (mōōn′wûrt′), *n.* **1.** any fern of the genus *Botrychium*, esp. *B. Lunaria*, whose fronds have crescent-shaped pinnae. **2.** *Bot.* honesty (def. 4).

moon·y (mōō′nĭ), *adj.*, **moonier, mooniest.** **1.** pertaining to or characteristic of the moon. **2.** resembling the moon in shape. **3.** moonlit. **4.** resembling moonlight. **5.** *Colloq.* mooning, listless, or silly.

moor[1] (mōōr), *n.* *Brit.* **1.** a tract of open, peaty, waste land, often overgrown with heath, common in high latitudes and altitudes where drainage is poor; a heath. **2.** a tract of land preserved for shooting game. [ME *more*, OE *mōr*, c. G *moor* marsh]

moor[2] (mōōr), *v.t.* **1.** to secure (a ship, etc.) in a particular place, as by cables and anchors (esp. two or more) or by lines. **2.** to secure, or fix firmly. —*v.i.* **3.** to moor a ship, etc. **4.** to take up a position or be made secure by anchors or the like; as a ship. [late ME *more*, OE *mār*- (in *mārels* mooring rope), c. MD *māren* moor, tie up]

Moor (mōōr), *n.* **1.** a Mohammedan of the mixed Berber and Arab race inhabiting NW Africa. **2.** one belonging to that group of this race which in the 8th century invaded and conquered Spain. [ME *More*, t. OF. var. of *Maure*, t. L: m. *Maurus*, t. Gk.: m. *Mauros*]

moor·age (mōōr′ĭj), *n.* **1.** act of mooring. **2.** state of being moored. **3.** a place for mooring. **4.** a charge or payment for the use of moorings.

moor cock, *Brit.* the male moorfowl.

Moore (mōōr, mōr), *n.* **1. George,** 1852–1933, Irish novelist, critic, and dramatist. **2. Sir John,** 1761–1809, British general. **3. John Bassett,** 1860–1947, U.S. jurist. **4. Thomas,** 1779–1852, Irish poet.

moor·fowl (mōōr′foul′), *n.*, *Brit.* the red grouse, *Lagopus scoticus.* Also, **moor·bird**.

moor hen, **1.** *Brit.* the female moorfowl. **2.** a common European gallinule, *Gallinula chloropus.*

moor·ing (mōōr′ĭng), *n.* **1.** the act of one who or that which moors. **2.** (*usually pl.*) something by which a ship or the like is moored, as a cable, line, etc. **3.** (*pl.*) the place where a vessel is or may be moored.

mooring mast, the mast or tower to which a dirigible is moored. Also, **mooring tower.**

Moor·ish (mōōr′ĭsh), *adj.* **1.** of or pertaining to the Moors. **2.** in the style of the Moors, as architecture, decoration, etc.

moor·land (mōōr′lănd′), *n.* *Brit.* land consisting of a moor.

moor·wort (mōōr′wûrt′), *n.* a low, ericaceous shrub, *Andromeda Polifolia*, with white flowers, native to swamplands in the Northern Hemisphere.

moose (mōōs), *n.*, *pl.* **moose.** **1.** a large animal, *Alces americanus*, of the deer family, inhabiting Canada and the northern U.S., the male of which has enormous palmate antlers, long legs, and a large, unshapely head. **2.** a similar species, *A. gigas*, found in Alaska. **3.** the European elk, *A. machlis.* [t. N Amer. Ind.; cognate forms in Algonquian, Narragansett, Delaware, etc., meaning "he strips or eats off"]

Moose·head Lake (mōōs′hĕd′), a lake in central Maine. 36 mi. long; 120 sq. mi.

Moose Jaw, a city in SW Canada, in Saskatchewan. 24,335 (1951).

moot (mōōt), *adj.* **1.** subject to argument or discussion; debatable; doubtful: *a moot point.* —*v.t.* **2.** to argue (a case, etc.), esp. in a mock court. **3.** to bring forward (any point, subject, project, etc.) for discussion. —*n.* **4.** an early English assembly of the people, exercising political, administrative, and judicial powers. **5.** an argument or discussion, esp. of a hypothetical legal case. [ME *mote*, OE *mōt*, *gemōt* meeting, assembly, c. Icel. *mōt* D *gemoet*] —**moot′er**, *n.*

moot court, a mock court for the conduct of hypothetical legal cases, as for practice for students of law.

moot hall, (in an English village) a historic building where a moot (def. 4) was once held.

mop (mŏp), *n.*, *v.*, **mopped, mopping.** —*n.* **1.** a bundle of coarse yarn, a piece of cloth, or the like, fastened at the end of a stick or handle, used for washing floors, dishes, etc. **2.** a thick mass, as of hair. —*v.t.* **3.** to rub, wipe, clean, or remove with a mop. **4.** to wipe: *to mop the face with a handkerchief.* **5.** *Mil.* to clear (ground, trenches, towns, etc.) of scattered or remaining enemy

combatants, after attacking forces have gone beyond the place (fol. by *up*). [earlier *map*, ME *mappe*. Cf. L *mappa* napkin, cloth, ? in ML *mop*]

mop·board (mŏp′bōrd′), *n.* a baseboard (def. 1).

mope (mōp), *v.*, **moped, moping,** *n.* —*v.i.* **1.** to be sunk in listless apathy or dull dejection. —*v.t.* **2.** to make listless and dispirited. —*n.* **3.** a person who mopes or is given to moping. **4.** (*pl.*) low spirits. [var. of obs. *mop* make a wry face. Cf. D *moppen* pout] —**mop′er**, *n.* —**mop′ing·ly**, *adv.*

mop·ish (mō′pĭsh), *adj.* given to moping; listless and dejected. —**mop′ish·ly**, *adv.* —**mop′ish·ness**, *n.*

mop·pet (mŏp′ĭt), *n.* **1.** *Obs. or Archaic.* a child or a young girl. **2.** *Colloq.* a doll. [f. (obs.) *mop* baby, rag doll + -ET]

mo·quette (mō·kĕt′), *n.* a kind of carpet with a thick velvety pile. [t. F; orig. uncert.]

mor., morocco.

mo·ra (mōr′ə), *n.*, *pl.* **morae** (mōr′ē), **moras.** *Pros.* the unit of time equivalent to the ordinary or normal short sound or syllable. [t. L: delay]

mo·ra·ceous (mō·rā′shəs), *adj.* belonging to the *Moraceae*, or mulberry family of plants, which includes the mulberry, breadfruit, fig, hemp, hop, Osage orange, etc. [f. s. L *mōrus* mulberry tree + -ACEOUS]

Mo·ra·da·bad (mō′rə·də·bäd′, mō′rä·dä·bäd′), *n.* a city in N India, in Uttar Pradesh. 154,018 (1951).

mo·raine (mə·rān′), *n.* **1.** a ridge, mound, or irregular mass of boulders, gravel, sand, and clay, transported in or on a glacier. **2.** a deposit of such material left on the ground by a glacier. [t. F. Cf. ML *morena* embankment of stakes, It. *mora* cairn] —**mo·rain′al**, **mo·rain′ic**, *adj.*

mor·al (mŏr′əl, mōr′əl), *adj.* **1.** pertaining to or concerned with right conduct or the distinction between right or wrong: *moral considerations.* **2.** concerned with the principles or rules of right conduct; ethical: *moral philosophy.* **3.** expressing or conveying truths or counsel as to right conduct, as a speaker, a literary work, etc.; moralizing. **4.** founded on the fundamental principles of right conduct rather than on enactment or custom: *moral rights.* **5.** capable of conforming to the rules of right conduct. **6.** conforming to the rules of right conduct (opposed to *immoral*): *a moral man.* **7.** sexually virtuous. **8.** being virtually or practically such through the effect on the mind or feelings or on results generally: *a moral victory; moral support.* **9.** depending upon what is observed of human nature and actions or of things generally, rather than upon demonstration: *moral evidence.* **10.** resting upon convincing grounds of probability: *a moral certainty.* —*n.* **11.** the moral teaching or practical lesson contained in a fable, tale, experience, etc. **12.** the embodiment or type of something. **13.** (*pl.*) principles or habits with respect to right or wrong conduct; ethics. [ME, t. L: s. *mōrālis* relating to manners, customs]

—**Syn. 4.** righteous, just. **6.** virtuous, good. **13.** MORALS, ETHICS refer to rules and standards of conduct and practice. MORALS refers to generally accepted customs of conduct and right living in a society, and to the individual's practice in relation to these: *the morals of our civilization.* ETHICS now implies high standards of honest and honorable dealing, of methods used, and of quality of product, esp. in the professions or in business: *ethics of the medical profession.*

mo·rale (mə·răl′, -räl′), *n.* moral or mental condition with respect to cheerfulness, confidence, zeal, etc.: *the morale of troops.* [t. F, fem. of *moral*, adj. See MORAL]

moral hazard, *Insurance.* an insurance company's risk as to the assured's trustworthiness and honesty.

mor·al·ism (mŏr′ə·lĭz′əm, mōr′-), *n.* **1.** the habit of moralizing. **2.** a moral maxim. **3.** the practice of morality, as distinct from religion.

mor·al·ist (mŏr′ə·lĭst, mōr′-), *n.* **1.** one who teaches or inculcates morality. **2.** one who practices morality. —**mor′al·is′tic**, *adj.*

mo·ral·i·ty (mə·răl′ə·tĭ, mō·răl′-), *n.*, *pl.* -ties. **1.** conformity to the rules of right conduct; moral or virtuous conduct. **2.** sexual virtue. **3.** moral quality or character. **4.** the doctrine or system of morals; ethics; duties. **5.** moral instruction; a moral lesson or precept; a moralizing discourse or utterance. **6.** morality play. —**Syn. 1.** See **goodness.**

morality play, a form of allegorical drama in vogue from the 14th to the 16th centuries, employing personifications of virtues and vices.

mor·al·ize (mŏr′ə·līz′, mōr′-), *v.*, **-ized, -izing.** —*v.i.* **1.** to make moral reflections. —*v.t.* **2.** to explain in a moral sense, or draw a moral from. **3.** to improve the morals of. —**mor′al·i·za′tion**, *n.* —**mor′al·iz′er**, *n.* —**mor′al·iz′ing·ly**, *adv.*

mor·al·ly (mŏr′ə·lĭ, mōr′-), *adv.* **1.** in a moral manner. **2.** from a moral point of view. **3.** virtuously. **4.** virtually; practically.

moral philosophy, ethics.

mo·rass (mə·răs′, mō-), *n.* **1.** a tract of low, soft, wet ground. **2.** a marsh or bog. **3.** marshy ground. [t. D: m. *moeras*, in MD *maras*, t. OF: m. *marais*, f. Gmc. orig. See MARSH]

mor·a·to·ri·um (mŏr′ə·tōr′ĭ·əm, mōr′-), *n.*, *pl.* -toria (-tōr′ĭ·ə), -toriums. **1.** a legal authorization to delay payment of money due, as in an emergency. **2.** the period during which such authorization is in effect. [t. NL, prop. neut. of LL *morātōrius* MORATORY]

mor·a·to·ry (môr′ə tôr′Y, mŏr′-), *adj.* authorizing delay of payment: *a moratory law.* [t. LL: m.s. *morātōrius* delaying, der. L *morārī* delay]

Mo·ra·va (mô′rä vä), *n.* **1.** German, **March.** a river flowing from N Czechoslovakia S to the Danube. ab. 210 mi. **2.** a river in E Yugoslavia, flowing N to the Danube. ab. 100 mi.

Mo·ra·vi·a (môrā′vY ə), *n.* a former province in central Czechoslovakia, now (with Silesia and Bohemia) one of the two states (the other being Slovakia) of Czechoslovakia: part of Bohemia-Moravia, 1939–45. Czech, **Morava.** German, **Mähren.**

Mo·ra·vi·an (môrā′vY ən), *adj.* **1.** pertaining to Moravia or its inhabitants. **2.** of or pertaining to the religious body of Moravians. —*n.* **3.** a native or inhabitant of Moravia. **4.** a member of a Christian denomination, Unity of Brethren (also, **Moravian Brethren**), which traces its origin to John Huss. **5.** a dialect of Czech, spoken in Moravia.

Moravian Gate, a corridor between the Sudeten Mountains and the Tatra range of the Carpathians, leading from S Poland into Moravia, Czechoslovakia.

Mo·rav·ská Os·tra·va (mô′räf skä ôs′trä vä), a city in Czechoslovakia, in N Moravia. 183,704 (est. 1948). German, **Mährisch-Ostrau.**

mo·ray (môr′ā, mōrā′), *n., pl.* **-rays.** any of numerous eels of the family *Muraenidae*, esp. those of the genus *Muraena*, as *M. helena*, common in the Mediterranean and valued as a food fish, or *Gymnothorax moringa*, common in West Indian waters (**spotted moray**).

Mor·ay (mŭr′Y), *n.* a county in NE Scotland, on **Moray Firth,** an arm of the North Sea. 49,400 (est. 1956); 476 sq. mi. *Co. seat:* Elgin. Formerly, **Elgin.**

mor·bid (môr′bYd), *adj.* **1.** suggesting an unhealthy mental state; unwholesomely gloomy, sensitive, extreme, etc. **2.** affected by, proceeding from, or characteristic of disease. **3.** pertaining to diseased parts: *morbid anatomy.* [t. L: s. *morbidus* sickly] —**mor′bid·ly,** *adv.* —**mor′bid·ness,** *n.*

mor·bid·i·ty (môr bYd′ə tY), *n.* **1.** morbid state or quality. **2.** the proportion of sickness in a locality.

mor·bif·ic (môr bYf′Yk), *adj.* causing disease. Also, **mor·bif′i·cal.** [t. NL: s. *morbificus*, der. L *morbus* disease] —**mor·bif′i·cal·ly,** *adv.*

mor·bil·li (môr bYl′Y), *n.pl.* measles. [t. ML, pl. of *morbillus*, dim. of L *morbus* disease]

mor·ceau (môrsō′), *n., pl.* **-ceaux** (-sō′). *French.* **1.** morsel. **2.** an excerpt or passage of poetry or music.

mor·da·cious (môr dā′shəs), *adj.* biting; given to biting. [f. *mordaci(ty)* (t. L: m.s. *mordācitas* power of biting) + *-ous*] —**mor·da′cious·ly,** *adv.* —**mor·dac·i·ty** (môr dăs′ə tY), *n.*

mor·dan·cy (môr′dən sY), *n.* mordant quality.

mor·dant (môr′dənt), *adj.* **1.** caustic or sarcastic, as wit, a speaker, etc. **2.** having the property of fixing colors, as in dyeing. —*n.* **3.** a substance used in dyeing to fix the coloring matter, esp. a metallic compound, as an oxide or hydroxide, which combines with the organic dye and forms an insoluble colored compound or lake in the fiber. **4.** an acid or other corrosive substance used in etching to eat out the lines, etc. —*v.t.* **5.** to impregnate or treat with a mordant. [ME, t. OF, ppr. of *mordre,* g. L *mordēre* bite] —**mor′dant·ly,** *adv.*

Mor·de·cai (môr′dY kī′, môr′dY kā′Y), *n.* (in the book of Esther) a cousin of Esther, who delivered Esther and the Jews from Haman. Cf. **Purim.**

mor·dent (môr′dənt), *n. Music.* **1.** a melodic embellishment consisting of a rapid alternation of a principal tone with a supplementary tone a half step below it, called *single* or *short* when the supplementary tone occurs but once, and *double* or *long* when this occurs twice or oftener. **2.** See **inverted mordent.** [t. G, t. It.: m. *mordente*, prop. ppr. of *mordere,* g. L *mordēre* bite]

Written   Played

Mordents
A. Single; B. Double

Mor·dred (môr′drĕd), *n.* Modred.

more (môr), *adj., superl.* **most,** *n., adv.* —*adj.* **1.** in greater quantity, amount, measure, degree, or number (as the comparative of *much* and *many,* with the superlative *most*): *more money.* **2.** additional or further: *do not lose any more time.* —*n.* **3.** an additional quantity, amount, or number. **4.** a greater quantity, amount, or degree. **5.** something of greater importance. **6.** (construed as *pl.*) a greater number of a class specified, or the greater number of persons. —*adv.* **7.** in or to a greater extent or degree: *more rapid.* **8.** in addition; further; again. [ME; OE *māra,* c. OS and OHG *mēro.* See **MOST**]

More (môr), *n.* **1. Hannah,** 1745–1833. British writer on religious subjects. **2. Paul Elmer,** 1864–1937, U.S. essayist, critic, and editor. **3. Sir Thomas,** 1478–1535. English statesman and author: canonized in 1935.

Mo·re·a (mō rē′ə), *n.* modern name sometimes used to designate the Peloponnesus.

Mo·reau (môrō′), *n.* **Jean Victor** (zhäN vēk tôr′), 1763–1813, French general.

mo·reen (mə rēn′), *n.* a heavy fabric of wool, or wool and cotton, commonly watered, used for curtains, petticoats, etc. [? akin to **MOIRE**]

mo·rel (mə rĕl′), *n.* an edible mushroom of the genus *Morchella,* an ascomycetous group in which the fruit body has the aspect of a stalked sponge. [ME *morele,* t. OF, der. L *mōrum* a mulberry]

mo·rel·lo (mə rĕl′ō), *n., pl.* **-los.** a sour cherry, *Prunus Cerasus,* var. *Austera,* with a dark-colored skin and juice. [t. It.: dark-colored (der. L *maurus* moor), ? b. with It. *amarello,* dim. of *amaro* bitter (g. L *amārus*)]

more·o·ver (môr ō′vər), *adv.* beyond what has been said; further; besides. —**Syn.** See **besides.**

mo·res (môr′ēz), *n.pl. Sociol.* folkways of central importance accepted without question and embodying the fundamental moral views of a group. [t. L: customs]

Mo·resque (mə rĕsk′), *adj.* Moorish. [t. F, t. It.: m. *moresco,* der. *Moro* **MOOR**]

Mor·gain le Fay (môr′găn lə fā′, môr′gən), **Morgan le Fay.**

Mor·gan (môr′gən), *n.* one of a breed of light carriage and saddle horses descended from the Morgan horse (see etymology). [named after their sire, a stallion owned by Justin *Morgan* (1747–1798), a New England teacher]

Mor·gan (môr′gən), *n.* **1. Daniel,** 1736–1802, American Revolutionary general. **2. Sir Henry,** c1635–1688, British buccaneer. **3. John Hunt,** 1826–64, Confederate general in the U.S. Civil War. **4. John Pierpont,** 1837–1913, U.S. financier and philanthropist. **5.** his son, **John Pierpont,** 1867–1943, U.S. financier. **6. Thomas Hunt,** 1866–1945, U.S. zoölogist.

mor·ga·nat·ic (môr′gə năt′Yk), *adj.* designating or pertaining to a form of marriage in which a man of high rank takes to wife a woman of lower station with the stipulation that neither she nor the issue (if any) shall have any claim to his rank or property. Also, *Rare,* **mor·gan·ic** (môr găn′Yk). [t. NL: s. *morganaticus,* from ML (*mātrimōnium ad*) *morganāticam* (marriage with) morning gift (in lieu of a share in the husband's possessions), der. OHG *morgan* morning. The morning gift was a gift from a husband to his wife the morning after their marriage] —**mor′ga·nat′i·cal·ly,** *adv.*

mor·gan·ite (môr′gə nīt′), *n.* rose beryl. [named after J. P. **MORGAN.** See **-ITE**[1]]

Mor·gan le Fay (môr′gən lə fā′), *Celtic and Arthurian Legend.* the fairy sister of King Arthur. Also, **Morgain le Fay, Mor·ga·na** (môr gā′nä).

Mor·gan·town (môr′gən toun′), *n.* a city in N West Virginia. 22,487 (1960).

mor·gen (môr′gən), *n.* **1.** a unit of land measure equal to about two acres, formerly in use in Holland and the Dutch colonies and still used in South Africa. **2.** a unit equal to about two thirds of an acre, formerly used in Prussia, Norway, and Denmark. [t. D and G]

Mor·gen·thau (môr′gən thô′), *n.* **Henry, Jr.,** born 1891, U.S. public official: secretary of the treasury, 1934–45.

morgue (môrg), *n.* **1.** a place in which the bodies of persons found dead are exposed for identification. **2.** *Journ.* **a.** the reference library of clippings, mats, books, etc., kept by a newspaper. **b.** the room for it. [t. F; orig. name of building in Paris so used]

mor·i·bund (môr′ə bŭnd′, mŏr′-), *adj.* **1.** in a dying state. **2.** on the verge of extinction or termination: *a moribund political party.* [t. L: s. *moribundus*] —**mor′i·bun′di·ty,** *n.* —**mor′i·bund′ly,** *adv.*

mo·ri·on[1] (môr′Y ŏn′), *n.* an open helmet with a tall comb and a curved brim merging into a peak at front and back. [t. F, t. Sp.: m. *morrión,* der. *morra* crown of the head]

mo·ri·on[2] (môr′Y ŏn′), *n.* a variety of smoky quartz of a dark-brown or nearly black color. [t. L, misreading (in early editions of Pliny's *Nat. Hist.*) of *mormorion*]

Spanish morion, 16th century

Mo·ris·co (mə rYs′kō), *adj., n., pl.* **-cos, -coes.** —*adj.* **1.** Moorish. —*n.* **2.** a Moor. **3.** one of the Moors of Spain. [t. Sp. der. *Moro* **MOOR**]

mo·ri·tu·ri te sa·lu·ta·mus (môr′Y tyŏŏr′Y tē săl′-ŭ tä′məs), *Latin.* we about to die salute thee: said by Roman gladiators as they marched by the Emperor.

Mor·ley (môr′lY), *n.* **1. Christopher Darlington,** 1890–1957, U.S. writer. **2. John,** (*Viscount Morley of Blackburn*) 1838–1923, British writer and statesman.

Mor·mon (môr′mən), *n.* **1.** a member of a religious body in the U.S., founded in 1830 by Joseph Smith and calling itself "The Church of Jesus Christ of Latter-day Saints." **2. The Book of Mormon,** a sacred book of the Mormon Church, supposed to be an abridgment by a prophet (**Mormon**) of a record of certain ancient peoples in America, written on golden plates, and

---

ăct, āble, dâre, ärt; ĕbb, ēqual; Yf, īce; hŏt, ōver, ôrder, oil, bŏŏk, ōōze, out; ŭp, ūse, ûrge; ə = a in alone; ch, chief; g, give; ng, ring; sh, shoe; th, thin; th, that; zh, vision. See the full key on inside cover.

discovered and translated (1827-30) by Joseph Smith. **—adj. 3.** of or pertaining to the Mormons or their religious system: *the Mormon view of Creation.* **—Mor′-mon·ism,** *n.*

morn (môrn), *n. Poetic.* morning. [ME *morn(e),* OE *morne* (dat. of *morgen* morning), c. D and G *morgen*]

Mor·nay (môr nā′), *n.* Philippe de (fē lēp′ də), *(Seigneur du Plessis-Marly)* 1549-1623, French Protestant leader and diplomat.

morn·ing (môr′nĭng), *n.* **1.** the beginning of day; the dawn. **2.** the first part or period of the day, extending from dawn, or from midnight, to noon. **3.** the first or early period of anything. **4.** *(cap.)* the goddess Eos or Aurora. **—adj. 5.** of or pertaining to morning: *the morning hours.* **6.** occurring, appearing, coming, used, etc., in the morning: *the morning sun.* [ME. See MORN, -ING[1], modeled on EVENING] **—Syn. 1.** morn, daybreak, sunrise.

morn·ing-glo·ry (môr′nĭng glôr′ĭ), *n., pl.* **-ries.** any of various convolvulaceous plants, esp. of the genera *Ipomoea* and *Convolvulus,* as *I. purpurea,* a twining plant with cordate leaves and funnel-shaped flowers of various colors, common in cultivation.

morning sickness, nausea occurring in the early part of the day, as a characteristic symptom in the first months of pregnancy.

morning star, 1. a bright planet, seen in the east before sunrise. **2.** an annual plant, *Mentzelia Lindley,* with bright-yellow flowers, native to California.

Mo·ro (môr′ō), *n., pl.* **-ros.** a member of any of the various tribes of Mohammedan Malays in the southern Philippine Islands. [t. Sp.: a Moor]

Mo·roc·co (mə rŏk′ō), *n.* **1.** a kingdom in NW Africa, formerly a sultanate divided into French, Spanish, and International zones. 7,323,000 pop. (est. 1955); 172,104 sq. mi. *Cap.:* Rabat. **2.** Marrakech.—**Mo·roc·can** (mə rŏk′ən), *adj., n.*

mo·roc·co (mə rŏk′ō), *n.* **1.** a fine leather made from goatskins tanned with sumac, orig. in Morocco. **2.** any leather made in imitation of this. Also, **morocco leather.**

mo·ron (môr′ŏn), *n.* a person of arrested intelligence whose mentality is judged incapable of developing beyond that of a normal child of 8 to 12 years of age. [t. Gk., neut. of *mōrós* dull, foolish] **—mo·ron·ic** (mə rŏn′ĭk), *adj.* **—mo′ron·ism, mo·ron·i·ty** (mə rŏn′ə tĭ), *n.*

mo·rose (mə rōs′), *adj.* gloomily or sullenly ill-humored, as a person, mood, etc. [t. L: m.s. *mōrōsus* fretful, morose, particular] **—mo·rose′ly,** *adv.* **—mo·rose′-ness,** *n.* **—Ant.** good-natured.

morph-, var. of morpho- before vowels.

-morph, a word element meaning "form," as in *isomorph.* [t. Gk.: s. *morphē* form]

mor·pheme (môr′fēm), *n. Gram.* any of the minimum meaningful elements in a language, not further divisible into smaller meaningful elements, usually recurring in various contexts with relatively constant meaning: either a word, as *girl, world,* or part of a word, as *-ish* or *-ly* in *girlish* and *worldly.* [f. MORPH(O)- + *-eme,* as in *phoneme*]

Mor·phe·us (môr′fĭ əs, môr′fūs), *n. Gk. Myth.* a minor deity, son of the god of sleep; the god of dreams. [ME, t. L. t. Gk., der. *morphē* form, in allusion to the forms seen in dreams] **—Mor′phe·an,** *adj.*

-morphic, a word element used as adjective termination corresponding to **-morph,** as in *anthropomorphic.* [f. s. Gk. *morphē* form + -IC]

mor·phine (môr′fēn), *n.* a bitter crystalline alkaloid, $C_{17}H_{19}NO_3 \cdot H_2O$, the most important narcotic principle of opium, used in medicine (usually in the form of a sulfate or other salt) to dull pain, induce sleep, etc. Also, **mor·phi·a** (môr′fĭ ə). [t. F; G: m. *morphin,* f. *Morph(eus)* MORPHEUS + *-in* -INE[2]]

mor·phin·ism (môr′fĭ nĭz′əm), *n. Pathol.* **1.** a morbid condition induced by the habitual use of morphine. **2.** the habit inducing it.

morpho-, initial word element answering to **-morph.**

mor·pho·gen·e·sis (môr′fə jĕn′ə sĭs), *n. Embryol.* the structural development of an organism or part. **—mor·pho·ge·net·ic** (môr′fō jə nĕt′ĭk), *adj.*

mor·pho·gen·ic (môr′fə jĕn′ĭk), *adj. Embryol.* **1.** pertaining to morphogenesis. **2.** differentiation-inducing; form-producing: *morphogenic substances.*

mor·phol·o·gy (môr fŏl′ə jĭ), *n.* **1.** that branch of biology which deals with the form and structure of animals and plants, without regard to functions. **2.** the form of an organism considered as a whole. **3.** *Gram.* **a.** the patterns of word formation in a particular language, including inflection, derivation, and composition. **b.** the study and description thereof. See SYNTAX. **4.** *Phys. Geog.* the study of the form of lands. **—mor·pho·log·ic** (môr′fə lŏj′ĭk), **mor′pho·log′i·cal,** *adj.* **—mor′pho·log′i·cal·ly,** *adv.* **—mor·phol′o·gist,** *n.*

-morphous, a word element used as adjective termination corresponding to **-morph,** as in *amorphous.* [t. Gk.: m. *-morphos,* der. Gk. *morphē* form]

Mor·ris (môr′ĭs, mŏr′-), *n.* **1.** Gouverneur (gŭv′ər nĭr′), 1752-1816, American statesman. **2.** Robert, 1734-1806, American patriot and financier. **3.** William, 1834-96, British poet, artist, and reformer.

Morris chair, a kind of large armchair having an adjustable back and loose cushions. [named after William MORRIS]

morris dance, a picturesque dance of English origin, performed by persons in costume, often representing personages of the Robin Hood legend, formerly common in England, esp. in May Day festivities. Also, **mor′ris.** [late ME *moreys daunce* Moorish dance]

Mor·ri·son (môr′ĭ sən, mŏr′-), *n.* **Herbert Stanley,** born 1888, British labor leader and statesman.

Morris Plan bank, a private banking organization in the U.S., originally designed primarily to grant small loans to industrial workers.

mor·ro (môr′rō), *n., pl.* **-ros.** a rounded hill, hillock, or promontory. [Sp.: something round, der. stem *murr-* round, prob. of pre-L orig.]

Morro Castle, an old fort at the entrance to the harbor of Havana, Cuba.

mor·row (môr′ō, mŏr′ō), *n. Archaic.* **1.** morning. **2.** the day next after this or after some other particular day or night. [ME *morwe,* apocopated var. of *morwen,* OE *morgen* morning. See MORN]

Mors (môrz), *n. Rom. Myth.* a deification of death. [t. L]

Morse (môrs), *n.* **1.** Samuel Finley Breese, 1791-1872, U.S. inventor (of the telegraph). **2.** the Morse code. **—adj. 3.** noting or pertaining to the Morse code or the system of communications using it. **4.** pertaining to any code resembling the Morse, as the international.

Morse code, a system of dots, dashes, and spaces, or the corresponding sounds or the like, used in telegraphy and signaling to represent the letters of the alphabet, numerals, etc. Also, **Morse alphabet.**

mor·sel (môr′səl), *n.* **1.** a bite, mouthful, or small portion of food or the like. **2.** a small piece, quantity, or amount of anything; a scrap; a bit. **—v.t. 3.** to distribute in or divide into tiny portions. [ME, t. OF, dim. of *mors* a bite, g. L *morsum,* pp. neut. of *mordēre* bite]

mort (môrt), *n. Obs.* death. [ME, t. OF, g. L *mors*]

mor·tal (môr′təl), *adj.* **1.** liable or subject to death: *all mortal creatures.* **2.** of or pertaining to man as subject to death; human: *this mortal life.* **3.** belonging to this world. **4.** pertaining to death: *mortal throes.* **5.** involving spiritual death (opposed to *venial*): *a mortal sin.* **6.** causing death; fatal: *a mortal wound.* **7.** to the death: *mortal combat.* **8.** deadly or implacable: *a mortal enemy.* **9.** dire, grievous, or bitter: *in mortal fear.* **10.** *Colloq.* long and wearisome. **11.** *Colloq.* extreme; very great: *in a mortal hurry.* **12.** *Colloq.* possible or conceivable: *of no mortal use.* **—n. 13.** a being subject to death; a human being. [ME, t. L: s. *mortālis* subject to death] **—mor′tal·ly,** *adv.* **—Syn. 6.** See fatal.

mor·tal·i·ty (môr tǎl′ə tĭ), *n., pl.* **-ties.** **1.** the condition of being mortal or subject to death; mortal character, nature, or existence. **2.** mortal beings collectively; humanity. **3.** relative frequency of death, or death rate, as in a district or community. **4.** death or destruction on a large scale, as from war, plague, famine, etc. **5.** *Obs.* death.

mortality table, *Insurance.* an actuarial table compiled from statistics on the life spans of an arbitrarily selected population group or of former policyholders.

mor·tar[1] (môr′tər), *n.* **1.** a vessel of hard material, having a bowl-shaped cavity, in which drugs, etc., are reduced to powder with a pestle. **2.** any of various mechanical appliances in which substances are pounded or ground. **3.** a cannon very short in proportion to its bore, for throwing shells at high angles. **4.** some similar contrivance, as for throwing pyrotechnic bombs or a life line. [ME and OE *mortere,* t. L: m.s. *mortārium* vessel in which substances are pounded, or one in which MORTAR is made; in defs. 3 and 4, trans. of F *mortier*]

Mortar and pestle (def. 1)

mor·tar[2] (môr′tər), *n.* **1.** a material which binds stones or the like into a compact mass. **2.** a mixture, as of quicklime, cement, etc., sand, and water which hardens in the air and is used for binding bricks, etc., together. **—v.t. 3.** to plaster or fix with mortar. [ME mortier, t. F: m. *mortier,* g. L *mortārium.* See MORTAR[1]]

mor·tar·board (môr′tər bôrd′), *n.* **1.** a board, commonly square, used by masons to hold mortar. **2.** a kind of academic cap with a close-fitting crown surmounted by a stiff, flat, cloth-covered, square piece.

Morte d'Ar·thur (môrt′ där′thər), a compilation and translation of French Arthurian romances made by Sir Thomas Malory and printed by Caxton in 1485.

Mortarboard (def. 2)

mort·gage (môr′gĭj), *n., v.,* **-gaged, -gaging.** **—n.** *Law.* **1.** a conditional conveyance of property to a creditor as security, as for the repayment of money. **2.** the deed by which such a transaction is effected. **3.** the rights conferred by it, or the state of the property conveyed. **—v.t. 4.** to convey or place (property, esp. houses or land) under a mortgage. **5.** to pledge. [ME *morgage,* t. OF: f. *mort* dead + *gage* pledge, GAGE[1], n.]

mort·ga·gee (môr′gĭ jē′), *n.* one to whom property is mortgaged.

mortgagee clause, a clause attached to a fire-insurance policy, designed to protect the mortgagee against loss or damage.

mort·ga·gor (môr′gĭ jər), *n.* one who mortgages property. Also, **mort′gag·er.**

---

b., blend of, blended; c., cognate with; d., dialect, dialectal; der., derived from; f., formed from; g., going back to; m., modification of; r., replacing; s., stem of; t., taken from; ?, perhaps. See the full key on inside cover.

mor·tice (môr'tĭs), n., v.t. -ticed, -ticing. mortise.

mor·ti·cian (môr tĭsh'ən), n. an undertaker. [f. MOR-T(UARY) + -ICIAN, modeled on PHYSICIAN]

mor·ti·fi·ca·tion (môr'tə fə kā'shən), n. 1. humiliation in feeling, as by some wound to pride. 2. a cause or source of such humiliation. 3. the practice of asceticism by penitential discipline to overcome desire for sin and to strengthen the will. 4. Pathol. the death of one part of the body while the rest is alive; gangrene.

mor·ti·fy (môr'tə fī'), v., -fied, -fying. —v.t. 1. to humiliate in feeling, as by a severe wound to the pride or self-complacency. 2. to bring (the body, passions, etc.) into subjection by abstinence, ascetic discipline, or rigorous austerities. 3. Pathol. to affect with gangrene or necrosis. —v.i. 4. to practice mortification or disciplinary austerities. 5. Pathol. to undergo mortification, or become gangrened or necrosed. [ME mortifie(n), t. OF: m. mortifier, t. LL: m. mortificāre kill, destroy] —mor'ti·fi'er, n. —mor'ti·fy'ing·ly, adv. —Syn. 1. See ashamed.

Mor·ti·mer (môr'tə mər), n. Roger, (1st Earl of March) 1287?–1330, English soldier, the favorite of Queen Isabella, wife of Edward II of England.

mor·tise (môr'tĭs), n., v., -tised, -tising. —n. 1. a rectangular cavity of considerable depth in one piece of wood, etc., for receiving a corresponding projection (tenon) on another piece, so as to form a joint (**mortise and tenon joint**). —v.t. 2. to fasten by, or as by, a mortise. 3. to cut or otherwise form a mortise in, to fit a prescribed tenon. 4. to join securely. Also, **mortice**. [ME mortas, t. OF: m. mortaise, ? t. Ar.: m. murtazz made fast]

A. Mortise: B. Tenon

mort·main (môrt'mān), n. Law. 1. the condition of lands or tenements held without right of alienation, as by an ecclesiastical corporation; inalienable ownership. 2. the holding of land by a corporation or charitable trust beyond the period of time or in violation of the conditions authorized by law. [ME mort(e)mayn(e), t. OF: m. mortemain, trans. of ML mortua manus dead hand]

Mor·ton (môr'tən), n. William Thomas Green, 1819–1868, U.S. dentist: introduced ether as an anesthetic.

mor·tu·ar·y (môr'chŏŏ ĕr'ĭ), n., pl. -aries, adj. —n. 1. a place for the temporary reception of the dead. 2. a customary gift formerly claimed by and due to the incumbent of a parish in England from the estate of a deceased parishioner. —adj. 3. of or pertaining to the burial of the dead. 4. pertaining to or connected with death. [ME, t. ML: m.s. mortuārium, prop. neut. of L mortuārius belonging to the dead]

mor·u·la (môr'yŏŏ lə, -ŏŏ-), n., pl. -lae (-lē'). Embryol. the mass of cells resulting from the cleavage of the ovum before the formation of a blastula. [t. NL, dim. of L mōrum mulberry] —mor'u·lar, adj.

mos., months.

mo·sa·ic (mō zā'ĭk), n. 1. a picture or decoration made of small pieces of stone, glass, etc., of different colors, inlaid to form a design. 2. the process of producing it. 3. something resembling a mosaic in composition. 4. Aerial Surveying. an assembly of aerial photographs taken vertically and matched in such a way as to show a continuous photographic representation of an area (**mosaic map**). 5. Also, **mosaic disease**. Plant Pathol. one of numerous plant diseases, caused by certain viruses, in which varicolored, mottled areas appear on the leaves. —adj. 6. pertaining to or resembling a mosaic or mosaic work. 7. composed of diverse elements combined. [ME, t. ML: s. mosaicus, var. of mūsaicus, lit., of the Muses, artistic]

Mo·sa·ic (mō zā'ĭk), adj. of or pertaining to Moses or the writings and institutions attributed to him. Also, **Mo·sa'i·cal**. [t. NL: s. Mosaicus, ? f. after Hebraicus]

mosaic gold, 1. stannic sulfide. 2. ormolu.

Mosaic Law, 1. the ancient law of the Hebrews, attributed to Moses. 2. the part of the Scripture containing this law; the Pentateuch.

Mos·by (mŏz'bĭ), n. John Singleton, 1833–1916, Confederate cavalry colonel in the U.S. Civil War.

mos·chate (mŏs'kāt, -kĭt), adj. having a musky smell. [t. NL: m.s. moschātus, der. ML moschus musk]

mos·cha·tel (mŏs'kə tĕl', mŏs'kə tĕl'), n. a small, inconspicuous plant, Adoxa moschatellina, having greenish or yellowish flowers with a musky odor. [t. F: m. moscatelle, t. It.: m. moscatella, der. moscato musk]

Mos·cow (mŏs'kou, -kō), n. the capital of the Soviet Union, in the central part of European Soviet Russia. 4,839,000 (est. 1956). Russian, **Mos·kva** (mŏs kvä').

Mo·sel (mō zĕl'), n. Moselle (def. 1).

Mo·selle (mō zĕl'), n. 1. a river flowing from the Vosges mountains in NE France into the Rhine in W West Germany. 320 mi. 2. a light, sprightly white wine made along the Moselle in West Germany.

Mo·ses (mō'zĭz, -zĭs), n. the liberator of the Hebrews from Egypt, leader throughout the years of the desert sojourn, founder of Israel's theocracy, and, according to tradition, its first lawgiver. Ex. 2, Deut. 34. [t. L, t. Gk., t. Heb.: m. Mōsheh]

Moses basket, Brit. a bassinet.

Moses boat, a ship's boat built with a keel. [orig. uncert.; ? named after Moses of Mass., boatbuilder]

mo·sey (mō'zĭ), v.i., -seyed, -seying. U.S. Slang. 1. to move or go along or away; make off. 2. to shuffle along; stroll.

Mos·lem (mŏz'lem, mŏs'-), adj., n., pl., -lems, -lem. —adj. 1. pertaining to the Mohammedan religion, law, or civilization. —n. 2. a Mohammedan. Also, **Muslem, Muslim**. [t. Ar.: m. muslim one submitting (i.e. accepting Islam, lit., submission)] —**Mos·lem·ic** (mŏz lĕm'ĭk, mŏs-), adj.

Mos·lem·ism (mŏz'lə mĭz'əm, mŏs'-), n. Mohammedanism.

mosque (mŏsk, môsk), n. a Mohammedan temple or place of worship. Also, **mosk**. [t. F: m. mosquée, t. It.: m. moschea, t. Ar.: m. masjid, der. sajada prostrate oneself, worship]

Mosque

mos·qui·to (mə skē'tō), n., pl., -toes, -tos. any of various dipterous insects of the family Culicidae (genera Culex, Anopheles, etc.), the females of which have a long proboscis, by means of which they puncture the skin of animals (including man) and draw blood, some species transmitting certain diseases, as malaria and yellow fever. [t. Sp., dim. of mosca, g. L musca a fly]

House mosquito, Culex pipiens (Body ¼ in. long)

mosquito boat, a fast unarmored motorboat armed with torpedoes and small guns.

mosquito fleet, Naut. Slang. a group of small navy boats.

mosquito hawk, a nighthawk.

mosquito net, a screen, curtain, or canopy of net, gauze, or the like (**mosquito netting**), for keeping out mosquitoes.

moss (môs, mŏs), n. 1. any of the cryptogamic plants which belong to the class Musci, of the bryophytes, comprising small leafy-stemmed plants growing in tufts, sods, or mats on moist ground, tree trunks, rocks, etc. 2. a growth of such plants. 3. any of various similar plants, as certain lichens (see **Iceland moss**), the lycopods (see **club moss**), etc. 4. Chiefly Scot. and N. Eng. a swamp or peat bog. —v.t. 5. to cover with a growth of moss. [ME mos(se), OE mos bog, c. D mos moss, G moos bog, moss]

moss agate, a kind of agate or chalcedony containing brown or black mosslike dendritic markings from various impurities.

moss·back (môs'bǎk', mŏs'-), n. U.S. Slang. 1. a person attached to antiquated notions. 2. an extreme conservative.

moss·bunk·er (môs'bŭngk'ər, mŏs'-), n. the menhaden (fish). [t. D: m. marsbanker]

moss-grown (môs'grōn', mŏs'-), adj. 1. overgrown with moss. 2. old-fashioned.

mos·so (môs'sō), adj. Music. moved; fast. [t. It., pp. of muovere move]

moss pink, a species of phlox, Phlox subulata, of the eastern U.S., with showy pink to purple flowers.

moss rose, a cultivated variety of rose with a mosslike growth on the calyx and stem.

moss-troop·er (môs'trōō'pər, mŏs'-), n. 1. one of a class of marauders who infested the mosses or bogs of the border between England and Scotland in the 17th century. 2. any marauder.

moss·y (môs'ĭ, mŏs'ĭ), adj., mossier, mossiest. 1. overgrown with, or abounding in, moss. 2. covered with a mosslike growth. 3. appearing as if covered with moss. 4. resembling moss. —**moss'i·ness**, n.

most (mōst), adj., superl. of more, n., adv. —adj. 1. in the greatest quantity, amount, measure, degree, or number (used as the superlative of much and many, with the comparative more): the most votes. 2. in the majority of instances: most exercise is beneficial. 3. greatest, as in size or extent: the most part. —n. 4. the greatest quantity, amount, or degree; the utmost. 5. the greatest number or the majority of a class specified. 6. the greatest number. 7. the majority of persons (construed as pl.). —adv. 8. in or to the greatest extent or degree (in this sense much used before adjectives and adverbs, and regularly before those of more than two syllables, to form superlative phrases having the same force and effect as the superlative degree formed by the termination -est): most rapid, most wisely. 9. Colloq. almost or nearly. [ME mōst, OE māst (r. ME mest(e), OE mǣst), c. G meist, etc.] —Syn. 9. See almost.

-most, a suffixal use of most found in a series of superlatives, e.g., utmost, foremost. [ME -most, r. ME and OE -mest, a double superl. suffix, f. -ma + -est, both forming superlatives]

most·ly (mōst'lĭ), adv. 1. for the most part; in the main: the work is mostly done. 2. chiefly. —Syn. 2. especially.

Mo·sul (mō sōōl'), n. a city in N Iraq on the Tigris, opposite the ruins of Nineveh. 133,625 (1947).

ăct, āble, dâre, ärt; ĕbb, ēqual; ĭf, īce; hŏt, ōver, ôrder, oil, bŏŏk, ōōze, out; ŭp, ūse, ûrge; ə = a in alone; ch, chief; g, give; ng, ring; sh, shoe; th, thin; ŧh, that; zh, vision.   See the full key on inside cover.

Mosz·kow·ski (môsh kôf'skĭ), *n.* **Moritz** (mō'rĭts), 1854–1925, Polish composer and pianist.

mot (mō), *n.* **1.** a pithy or witty remark. **2.** *Archaic.* a note on a horn, bugle, etc. [t. F: word, saying, note of a horn, etc., g. L *muttum* a mutter, grunt]

mote¹ (mōt), *n.* a particle or speck, esp. of dust. [ME; OE *mot* speck, c. D *mot* grit, sawdust]

mote² (mōt), *v., pt.* **moste** (mōst). *Archaic.* may or might [ME *mot(e)*, OE *mōt*, pres. (c. G *muss*). See MUST, V.]

mo·tel (mō tĕl'), *n.* *U.S.* a roadside hotel providing both lodging, usually in cabins, for travelers and parking space for their motor vehicles. [b. M(OTOR) and (H)OTEL]

mo·tet (mō tĕt'), *n.* *Music.* a vocal composition in polyphonic style, on a Biblical or similar prose text, intended for use in a church service. [ME, t. OF, dim. of *mot* word. See MOT]

moth (môth, mŏth), *n., pl.* **moths** (môthz, mŏthz, môths, mŏths). **1.** any of a very large group of lepidopterous insects, generally distinguished from the butterflies by not having their antennae clubbed and by their (mainly) nocturnal or crepuscular habits. **2.** a clothes moth. [ME *motthe*, OE *moththe*, c. G *motte*]

Clothes moth.
Tinea pellionella
A. Adult; B. Larva

moth ball, a small ball of naphthalene or (sometimes) camphor which repels moths and protects clothing.

moth-eat·en (môth'ē'tən, mŏth'-), *adj.* **1.** eaten or damaged by or as by moths. **2.** decayed. **3.** out of fashion.

moth·er¹ (mŭth'ər), *n.* **1.** a female parent. **2.** (*often cap.*) one's own mother. **3.** *Colloq.* a mother-in-law, stepmother, or adoptive mother. **4.** a term of familiar address for an old or elderly woman. **5.** the head or superior of a female religious community. **6.** a woman looked upon as a mother, or exercising control or authority like that of a mother. **7.** the qualities characteristic of a mother, or maternal affection. **8.** something that gives rise to, or exercises protecting care over, something else. —*adj.* **9.** that is a mother: *a mother bird.* **10.** pertaining to or characteristic of a mother: *mother love.* **11.** derived from one's mother; native: *mother tongue.* **12.** bearing a relation like that of a mother, as in giving origin or rise, or in exercising protective care: *a mother church.* —*v.t.* **13.** to be the mother of; give origin or rise to. **14.** to acknowledge oneself the author of; assume as one's own. **15.** to care for or protect as a mother does. [ME *moder*, OE *mōdor*, c. D *moeder*, G *mutter*, Icel. *mōdhir*; akin to L *māter*, Gk. *mētēr*, Skt. *mātar*-] —**moth'er·less,** *adj.*

moth·er² (mŭth'ər), *n.* a stringy, mucilaginous substance formed on the surface of a liquid undergoing acetous fermentation (as wine changing to vinegar), and consisting of the various bacteria, esp. *Mycoderma aceti*, which cause such fermentation. Also, **mother of vinegar.** [special use of MOTHER¹]

Mother Car·ey's chicken (kâr'ĭz), any of various small petrels, esp. the stormy petrel, *Oceanites oceanicus*.

Mother Goose, the legendary author of the English folk nursery jingles called *Mother Goose's Melodies.*

moth·er·hood (mŭth'ər hŏŏd'), *n.* **1.** the state of being a mother; maternity. **2.** mothers collectively. **3.** the qualities or spirit of a mother.

Mother Hub·bard (hŭb'ərd), **1.** a kind of full, loose gown worn by women. **2.** heroine of a nursery rhyme.

moth·er-in-law (mŭth'ər ĭn lô'), *n., pl.* **mothers-in-law,** the mother of one's husband or wife.

moth·er·land (mŭth'ər lănd'), *n.* **1.** one's native country. **2.** the land of one's ancestors.

mother lode, *Mining.* a rich or principal lode.

moth·er·ly (mŭth'ər lĭ), *adj.* **1.** pertaining to, characteristic of, or befitting a mother: *motherly affection.* **2.** having the character, etc., of a mother. —*adv.* **3.** in the manner of a mother. —**moth'er·li·ness,** *n.*

Mother of God, a designation of the Virgin Mary.

moth·er-of-pearl (mŭth'ər ər pûrl'), *n.* a hard, iridescent substance which forms the inner layer of certain shells, as that of the pearl oyster; nacre.

mother of vinegar, mother².

Mother's Day, *U.S.* a day for acts of grateful affection or remembrance by each person toward his mother, observed annually on the second Sunday in May (in schools, on the Friday preceding).

mother superior, the head of a female religious community.

mother tongue, 1. the language first learned by a person; native language. **2.** a parent language.

Moth·er·well and Wish·aw (mŭth'ər wĕl'; wĭsh'ô), a burgh in S Scotland. 68,154 (1951).

mother wit, common sense.

moth·er·wort (mŭth'ər wûrt'), *n.* a labiate European plant, *Leonorus cardiaca*, with cut leaves having a close whorl of flowers in the axils, a common U.S. weed.

moth·y (môth'ĭ, mŏth'-), *adj.,* **mothier, mothiest. 1.** containing moths. **2.** moth-eaten.

mo·tif (mō tēf'), *n.* **1.** a subject or theme for development or treatment, as in art, literature, or music. **2.** a distinctive figure in a design, as of wallpaper. **3.** a dominant idea or feature. [t. F. See MOTIVE]

mo·tile (mō'təl, -tĭl), *n.* **1.** *Biol.* moving, or capable of moving, spontaneously: *motile cells or spores.* —*n.* **2.**

Psychol. one in whose mind motor images are predominant or especially distinct. [f. s. L *mōtus*, pp., moved, + -ILE] —**mo·til·i·ty** (mō tĭl'ə tĭ), *n.*

mo·tion (mō'shən), *n.* **1.** the process of moving, or changing place or position. **2. in motion,** in active operation; moving. **3.** a movement. **4.** power of movement, as of a living body. **5.** the action or manner of moving the body in walking, etc.; gait. **6.** a bodily movement or change of posture; a gesture. **7.** a proposal formally made to a deliberative assembly: *to make a motion to adjourn.* **8.** *Law.* an application made to a court or judge for an order, ruling, or the like. **9.** a suggestion or proposal. **10.** an inward prompting or impulse; inclination: *of one's own motion.* **11.** *Music.* melodic progression, as the change of a voice part from one pitch to another. **12.** *Mach.* a. a piece of mechanism with a particular action or function. b. the action of such mechanism. —*v.t.* **13.** to direct by a significant motion or gesture, as with the hand: *to motion a person to a seat.* —*v.i.* **14.** to make a significant motion; gesture, as with the hand for the purpose of directing: *to motion to a person.* [ME, t. L: s. *mōtio* a moving] —**Syn. 1.** MOTION, MOVE, MOVEMENT refer to change of position in space. MOTION denotes change of position, either considered apart from, or as a characteristic of, that which moves; usually the former, in which case it is often a somewhat technical or scientific term: *perpetual motion.* The chief uses of MOVE are founded upon the idea of moving a piece, in chess or a similar game, for winning the game; and hence the word denotes any change of position, condition, or circumstances for the accomplishment of some end: *a shrewd move to win votes.* MOVEMENT is always connected with the person or thing moving, and is usually a definite or particular motion: *the movements of a dance.*

mo·tion·less (mō'shən lĭs), *adj.* without, or incapable of, motion. —**mo'tion·less·ly,** *adv.* —**mo'tion·less·ness,** *n.*

motion picture, 1. (*pl.*) consecutive pictures or photographs of objects in motion presented to the eye, esp. by being thrown on a screen by a projector (**motion-picture projector**), so rapidly as to give the illusion that the objects are moving as they did in the original scenes. **2.** a number of such pictures or photographs representing an event, play, or the like; a photoplay.

mo·ti·vate (mō'tə vāt'), *v.t.,* **-vated, -vating.** to provide with a motive or motives.

mo·ti·va·tion (mō'tə vā'shən), *n.* a motivating; a providing of a motive; inducement. —**mo'ti·va'tion·al,** *adj.*

motivation research, the application of the knowledge and techniques of the social sciences (esp. psychology and sociology) to understanding consumer attitudes and behavior: used as a guide in advertising and marketing. Also, **motivational research.**

mo·tive (mō'tĭv), *n., adj., v.,* **-tived, -tiving.** —*n.* **1.** something that prompts a person to act in a certain way or that determines volition; an incentive. **2.** the goal or object of one's actions: *his motive was revenge.* **3.** (in art, literature, and music) a motif. —*adj.* **4.** causing, or tending to cause, motion. **5.** pertaining to motion. **6.** prompting to action. **7.** constituting a motive or motives. —*v.t.* **8.** to provide with a motive. **9.** to motivate. **10.** to relate to a motif or a principal theme or idea in a work of art. [t. ML: m.s. *mōtivum* a moving cause, prop. neut. of *mōtivus* serving to move, der. L *mōtus*, pp., moved; r. ME *motif*, t. OF] —**Syn. 1.** MOTIVE, INCENTIVE, INDUCEMENT apply to whatever moves one to action. MOTIVE is, literally, that which moves a person; an INDUCEMENT, that which leads him on; an INCENTIVE, that which inspires him. MOTIVE is applied mainly to an inner urge that moves or prompts a person to action, though it may also apply to a contemplated result, the desire for which moves the person: *his motive was a desire to be helpful.* INDUCEMENT is never applied to an inner urge, and seldom to a goal (*the pleasure of wielding authority may be an inducement to get ahead*); it is used mainly of opportunities offered by the acceptance of certain conditions, whether these are offered by a second person or by the factors of the situation: *the salary offered me was a great inducement.* INCENTIVE was once used of anything inspiring or stimulating the emotions or imagination (*incentives to piety*); it has retained of this its emotional connotations, but (rather like INDUCEMENT) is today applied only to something offered as a reward, and offered particularly to stimulate competitive activity: *incentives to greater production.* **2.** See **reason.**

motive power, 1. any power used to impart motion. **2.** a source of mechanical energy. **3.** *Railroading.* locomotives, etc., which supply tractive power.

mo·tiv·i·ty (mō tĭv'ə tĭ), *n.* the power of initiating or producing motion.

mot juste (mō zhÿst'), *French.* the exact or appropriate word.

mot·ley (mŏt'lĭ), *adj., n., pl.* **-leys.** —*adj.* **1.** exhibiting great diversity of elements; heterogeneous: *a motley crowd.* **2.** being of different colors combined; parti-colored. **3.** wearing a parti-colored garment: *a motley fool.* —*n.* **4.** a combination of different colors. **5.** a parti-colored effect of color. **6.** the motley or parti-colored garment of the old-time professional fool or jester: *to wear the motley.* **7.** a heterogeneous assemblage. **8.** a medley. [ME, unexplained deriv. of MOTE¹]

Mot·ley (mŏt'lĭ), *n.* **John Lothrop,** 1814–77, U.S. historian and diplomat.

mot·mot (mŏt'mŏt), *n.* any of the tropical and subtropical American birds constituting the family *Momotidae*, related to the kingfishers, and having a serrate bill and chiefly greenish and bluish plumage.

mo·to·cy·cle (mō′tə sī′kəl), *n.* motorcycle.

mo·tor (mō′tər), *n.* **1.** a comparatively small and powerful engine, esp. an internal-combustion engine in an automobile, motorboat, or the like. **2.** any self-powered vehicle. **3.** one who or that which imparts motion, esp. a contrivance (as a steam engine) which receives and modifies energy from some natural source in order to utilize it in driving machinery, etc. **4.** *Elect.* a machine which converts electrical energy into mechanical energy: *an electric motor.* **5.** (*pl.*) *Stock Exchange.* automobile securities. —*adj.* **6.** causing or imparting motion. **7.** pertaining to or operated by a motor. **8.** used in or for, or pertaining to, motor vehicles: *a motor highway.* **9.** *Physiol.* conveying an impulse that results or tends to result in motion, as a nerve. **10.** *Physiol., Psychol.* denoting the effect or phase of any mental process, as the innervation of muscles and glands. **11.** *Psychol.* pertaining to or involving action: *motor images.* —*v.i.* **12.** to ride or travel in an automobile. [t. L: one who moves]

mo·tor·boat (mō′tər bōt′), *n.* a boat propelled by its own mechanical power. —**mo′tor·boat′ing,** *n.*

mo·tor·bus (mō′tər bŭs′), *n.* a passenger bus powered by a motor. Also, **motor coach.**

mo·tor·cade (mō′tər kād′), *n.* a procession or parade of automobiles. [b. MOTOR(CAR) and (CAVAL)CADE]

mo·tor·car (mō′tər kär′), *n.* an automobile.

mo·tor·cy·cle (mō′tər sī′kəl), *n.* a self-propelled bicycle, tricycle, or the like. Also, **motocycle.** —**mo·tor·cy·clist** (mō′tər sī′klĭst), *n.*

motor drive, the mechanical system, including an electric motor, used to operate a machine or machines.

mo·tor·drome (mō′tər drōm′), *n.* a rounded course or track for automobile and motorcycle races.

mo·tored (mō′tərd), *adj.* having a motor or motors, esp. of specified number or type: *a bimotored airplane.*

mo·tor·ist (mō′tər ĭst), *n.* **1.** one who drives an automobile. **2.** the user of a privately owned automobile.

mo·tor·ize (mō′tə rīz′), *v.t.,* **-ized, -izing. 1.** to furnish with a motor or motors, as vehicles. **2.** to supply with motor-driven vehicles in the place of horses and horse-drawn vehicles. —**mo′tor·i·za′tion,** *n.*

motor lorry, *Chiefly Brit.* motor truck.

mo·tor·man (mō′tər mən), *n., pl.* **-men. 1.** one who operates the motor of an electric car or electric locomotive on a railway. **2.** one who operates a motor.

motor mimicry, *Psychol.* empathy.

motor scooter. See **scooter** (def. 2).

motor ship, a ship driven by internal-combustion engines, usually Diesel engines.

motor truck, an automobile truck.

motor van, *Brit.* an automobile truck.

Mott (mŏt), *n.* **Mrs. Lucretia,** (*Lucretia Coffin*) 1793-1880, U.S. social reformer, advocate of women's rights.

motte (mŏt), *n.* *U.S. Dial.* a small patch of woods in prairie land. Also, **mott.** [t. F: mound]

mot·tle (mŏt′əl), *v.,* **-tled, -tling,** *n.* —*v.t.* **1.** to diversify with spots or blotches of a different color or shade. —*n.* **2.** a diversifying spot or blotch of color. **3.** mottled coloring or pattern. [back formation from MOTLEY]

mot·tled (mŏt′əld), *adj.* spotted or blotched in coloring.

mot·to (mŏt′ō), *n., pl.* **-toes, -tos. 1.** a maxim adopted as expressing one's guiding principle. **2.** a sentence, phrase, or word attached to or inscribed on anything as appropriate to it. [t. It. See MOT]

mouch (mōōch), *v.i., v.t.* *Slang.* mooch.

mou·choir (mōō shwär′), *n.* *French.* a handkerchief. [F, der. *moucher* wipe the nose, g. L *muccāre,* der. *muccus* MUCUS]

moue (mōō), *n.* *French.* a pouting grimace. [see MOW³]

mouf·lon (mōōf′lŏn), *n.* a wild sheep, *Ovis musimon,* inhabiting the mountainous regions of Sardinia, Corsica, etc., the male of which has large curving horns. Also, **mouf′flon.** [t. F, t. Corsican, g. LL *mufron*]

mouil·lé (mōō yā′), *adj.* *Phonet.* **1.** palatal or palatalized, esp. referring to sounds spelled *ll* and *ñ* in Spanish, *gl* and *gn* in Italian, etc. **2.** (of French sounds) spelled *l* or *ll* and pronounced as a *y* sound. [t. F, pp. of *mouiller* wet, moisten, der. L *mollis* soft]

mou·jik (mōō zhĭk′, mōō′zhĭk), *n.* muzhik.

Mouk·den (mōōk′dĕn′, mōōk′-), *n.* Mukden.

mou·lage (mōō läzh′), *n.* **1.** the making of a mold in plaster of Paris, etc., of objects, footprints, tire tracks, etc., esp. for identification. **2.** the mold itself. [t. F]

mould (mōld), *n., v.t., v.i.* *Chiefly Brit.* mold. —**mould′er,** *n.* —**mould′ing,** *n.* —**mould′y,** *adj.* —**mould′i·ness,** *n.*

mould·board (mōld′bōrd′), *n.* *Chiefly Brit.* moldboard.

mould·er (mōl′dər), *n., v.i., v.t.* molder.

mou·lin (mōō lăn′), *n.* a nearly vertical shaft or cavity worn in a glacier by surface water falling through a crack in the ice. [t. F, g. LL *molīnum* mill. See MILL¹]

Moul·mein (mōōl′mān′, mōl′-), *n.* a seaport in S Burma at the mouth of the Salween river. 101,720 (1953). Also, **Maulmain.**

moult (mōlt), *v.i., v.t., n.* *Chiefly Brit.* molt.

Moul·trie (mōō′trĭ, mōōl′trĭ), *n.* **Fort,** a fort at the entrance to the harbor of Charleston, South Carolina.

mound (mound), *n.* **1.** an elevation formed of earth or sand, debris, etc., overlying ruins, a grave, etc. **2.** a tumulus or other raised work of earth dating from a pre-historic or long-past period. **3.** a natural elevation of earth; a hillock or knoll. **4.** an artificial elevation of earth, as for a defense work, a dam or barrier, or any other purpose; an embankment. **5.** a heap or raised mass: *a mound of hay.* **6.** *Baseball.* the slightly elevated ground from which the pitcher delivers the ball and which slopes gradually to the base lines. —*v.t.* **7.** to furnish with a mound of earth, as for a defense. **8.** to form into a mound; heap up. [OE *mund* hand, protection]

Mound Builders, the various Indian tribes who, in prehistoric and early historic times, erected the burial mounds and other earthworks of the Mississippi drainage basin and southeastern States.

mount¹ (mount), *v.t.* **1.** to go up or ascend: *to mount stairs.* **2.** to get up on (a platform, a horse, etc.). **3.** to set or place at an elevation: *to be mounted on stilts.* **4.** to furnish with a horse or other mount for riding. **5.** to set on horseback. **6.** to raise or put into position for use, as a gun. **7.** to have or carry (guns) in position for use, as a fortress or a vessel does. **8.** to go or put on (guard), as a sentry or watch. **9.** to fix on or in a support, backing, setting, etc.: *to mount a photograph.* **10.** to provide (a play, etc.) with scenery, costumes, and other appurtenances for production. **11.** to prepare (an animal body or skeleton) as a specimen. **12.** *Micros.* **a.** to prepare (a slide) for microscopic investigation. **b.** to prepare (a sample, etc.) for examination by a microscope, as by placing it on a slide. —*v.i.* **13.** to rise or go to a higher position, level, degree, etc.; ascend. **14.** to rise in amount (often fol. by *up*): *the costs are steadily mounting.* **15.** to get up on the back of a horse, etc., for riding. **16.** to get up on something, as a platform. —*n.* **17.** the act or manner of mounting. **18.** a horse or other animal (or sometimes a bicycle) used, provided, or available for riding. **19.** an act or occasion of riding a horse, esp. in a race. **20.** a support, backing, setting, or the like, on or in which something is, or is to be, mounted or fixed. **21.** *Micros.* the prepared slide. [ME *monte(n),* t. OF: m. *monter,* ult. der. L *mons* mountain] —**Syn. 13.** rise, soar. See **climb.**

mount² (mount), *n.* a mountain or hill (now chiefly poetic, except in proper names, as *Mount Etna*). [ME *mont, munt,* OE *munt,* t. L: m.s. *mons*]

moun·tain (moun′tən, -tĭn), *n.* **1.** a natural elevation of the earth's surface rising more or less abruptly to a summit, and attaining an altitude greater than that of a hill. **2.** something resembling this, as in size: *a mountain of ice.* **3.** a huge amount. **4. the Mountain,** *French Hist.* a popular name for the extreme revolutionary party led by Danton and Robespierre in the legislatures of the French Revolution, whose members occupied the highest seats. It favored the ruthless prosecution of the Revolution and Reign of Terror. —*adj.* **5.** of mountains: *mountain air.* **6.** living, growing, or found on mountains: *mountain people, mountain plants.* **7.** resembling or suggesting a mountain, as in size. [ME t. OF: m. *montaigne,* der. *mont* mountain, g. L *mons*]

mountain ash, 1. any of various small trees of the rosaceous genus *Sorbus,* as the European rowan, *S. Aucuparia,* and the American *S. americana,* both having pinnate leaves and bearing small white corymbose flowers succeeded by bright-red to orange berries. **2.** any of certain other trees, as several Australian species of eucalyptus.

mountain bluebird, a songbird, *Sialia arctica,* of western North America. The male is sky-blue.

mountain cat, 1. cougar. **2.** bobcat.

mountain chain, 1. a connected series of mountains. **2.** two or more mountain ranges of close geographical relation.

mountain cranberry, a vaccinaceous shrub, *Vaccinium Vitis-Idaea,* with evergreen leaves, prostrate stems, and acid red berries edible after cooking.

mountain damson, any of certain tropical American trees of the genus *Simaruba* (family *Simarubaceae*), the bark of whose root is used in medicine as a tonic and astringent, esp. *S. amara,* chiefly of the West Indies.

mountain dew, *Slang.* **1.** Scotch whiskey. **2.** any whiskey, esp. when illicitly distilled.

moun·tain·eer (moun′tə nĭr′), *n.* **1.** an inhabitant of a mountainous district. **2.** a climber of mountains. —*v.i.* **3.** to climb mountains. —**moun′tain·eer′ing,** *n.*

mountain goat, the Rocky Mountain goat, *Oreamnos montanus.*

mountain laurel, the American laurel, *Kalmia latifolia.*

mountain lion, the cougar.

Mountain goat.
Oreamnos montanus
(Ab. 3½ ft. high at the shoulder, total length 5¼ ft.)

moun·tain·ous (moun′tə nəs), *adj.* **1.** abounding in mountains. **2.** of the nature of a mountain. **3.** resembling a mountain or mountains; large and high; huge: *mountainous waves.* —**moun′tain·ous·ly,** *adv.*

mountain range, 1. a series of more or less connected mountains ranged in a line. **2.** a series of mountains, or of more or less parallel lines of mountains, closely related in origin, etc. **3.** an area in which the greater part of the land surface is in considerable degree or slope, upland summits are small or narrow, and there are great differences in elevations within the area (commonly over 2000 feet).

mountain sheep, **1.** the bighorn, *Ovis montana* (or *canadensis*), of the Rocky Mountains, with massive recurving horns. See illus. under **bighorn**. **2.** any of various wild sheep inhabiting mountains.

mountain sickness, *Pathol.* a morbid condition characterized by difficult breathing, headache, nausea, etc., due to the rarefaction of the air at high altitudes.

Mountain time. See **standard time.**

Mountain View, a city in central California, S of San Francisco, 30,889 (1960).

Mount·bat·ten (mountbăt′ən), *n.* **Lord Louis**, born 1900, British admiral; Viceroy of India (1947); Governor General of India 1947–1948.

Mount De·sert Island (dĭ′zûrt′, dĕz′ərt), an island off the central coast of Maine: summer resort; Acadia National Park. 14 mi. long; 8 mi. wide.

moun·te·bank (moun′tə băngk′), *n.* **1.** one who sells quack medicines from a platform in public places, appealing to his audience by tricks, storytelling, etc. **2.** any charlatan or quack. —*v.i.* **3.** to play the mountebank. [t. It.: m. *montambanco*, contr. of *monta in banco* mount-on-(a)-bench] —**moun·te·bank·er·y** (moun′tə băngk′ə rĭ), *n.*

mount·ed (moun′tĭd), *adj.* **1.** seated or riding on a horse or the like. **2.** serving on horseback, or on some special mount, as soldiers, police, etc. **3.** *Mil.* permanently equipped with trucks, tanks, or other vehicles, or horses as means of transportation. **4.** fixed on or in a support, backing, setting, or the like: *mounted gems.* **5.** put into position for use, as guns. —**Ant.** **1.** afoot.

mount·er (moun′tər), *n.* one who or that which mounts.

mount·ing (moun′tĭng), *n.* **1.** the act of one who or that which mounts. **2.** something that serves as a mount, support, setting, or the like.

Mount Mc·Kin·ley National Park (mə kĭn′lĭ), a national park in central Alaska, including Mounts McKinley and Foraker. 3030 sq. mi.

Mount Rai·nier National Park (rā′nĭr′, rā′nĭr), a national park in W Washington, including Mount Rainier. 378 sq. mi.

Mount Rob·son Park (rŏb′sən), a national park in the Rocky Mountains of E British Columbia, Canada.

Mount Ver·non (vûr′nən), **1.** the home and tomb of George Washington in NE Virginia, on the Potomac, 15 mi. below Washington, D.C. **2.** a city in SE New York, near New York City. 76,010 (1960).

mourn (mōrn), *v.i.* **1.** to feel or express sorrow or grief. **2.** to grieve or lament for the dead. **3.** to display the conventional tokens of sorrow after a person's death. —*v.t.* **4.** to feel or express sorrow or grief over (misfortune, loss, or anything regretted); deplore. **5.** to grieve or lament over (the dead). **6.** to utter in a sorrowful manner. [ME *mo(u)rne*, OE *murnan*, c. OHG *mornēn*] —**Syn.** **1.** bewail, bemoan. See **grieve.**

mourn·er (mōr′nər), *n.* **1.** one who mourns. **2.** one who attends a funeral as a mourning friend or relative of the deceased. **3.** (at religious revival meetings) one who professes penitence for sin, with desire for salvation.

mourners' bench, (at religious revival meetings) a bench or seat at the front of the church or room, set apart for mourners or penitent sinners seeking salvation.

mourn·ful (mōrn′fəl), *adj.* **1.** full of, expressing, or showing sorrow or grief, as persons, the tone, etc.; sorrowful; sad. **2.** expressing, or used in, mourning for the dead. **3.** causing, or attended with, sorrow or mourning: *a mournful occasion.* **4.** gloomy, somber, or dreary, as in appearance or character: *mournful shadows.* —**mourn′ful·ly,** *adv.* —**mourn′ful·ness,** *n.*

mourn·ing (mōr′nĭng), *n.* **1.** act of one who mourns; sorrowing or lamentation. **2.** the conventional manifestation of sorrow for a person's death, esp. by the wearing of black, the hanging of flags at halfmast, etc. **3.** the outward tokens of such sorrow, as black garments, etc. —*adj.* **4.** of, pertaining to, or used in mourning. —**mourn′ing·ly,** *adv.* —**Ant.** **1.** rejoicing.

Mourning Becomes Electra, a three-part tragedy (1931) by Eugene O'Neill.

mourning cloak, a European and American butterfly, *Nymphalis antiopa*, having dark wings with a yellow border.

mourning dove, a dove, *Zenaidura macroura*, of North America, so called from its plaintive cooing; regarded as a game bird in parts of the southern U.S.

mouse (*n.* mous; *v.* mouz), *n.*, *pl.* **mice** (mīs), *v.*, **moused,** **mousing.** —*n.* **1.** any of various small rodents of the family *Muridae* and esp. of the introduced Old World genus *Mus*, as *M. musculus*, which infests houses. **2.** any similar animal of some other family, as the *Cricetidae.* **3.** *Slang.* a black eye. —*v.t.* **4.** to hunt out, as a cat hunts out mice. **5.** *Naut.* to secure with a mousing. —*v.i.* **6.** to hunt for or catch mice. **7.** to prowl (about, etc.), as if seeking something. **8.** to seek or search stealthily or watchfully, as if for prey. [ME *mous*, OE *mūs* (pl. *mȳs*), c. G *maus*, L *mūs*]

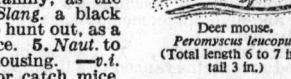

Deer mouse. *Peromyscus leucopus* (Total length 6 to 7 in., tail 3 in.)

mouse-dun (mous′dŭn′), *n.* dark brownish gray.

mouse-ear (mous′ĭr′), *n.* any of various plants with small hairy leaves, as the hawkweed, *Hieracium Pilosella*, the forget-me-not, *Myosotis palustris*, etc.

mous·er (mou′zər), *n.* **1.** an animal that catches mice: commonly used with a qualifying term or with reference to the animal's ability to catch mice. **2.** one who mouses, or seeks or prowls as if for prey.

mouse-tail (mous′tāl′), *n.* any plant of the ranunculaceous genus *Myosurus*, esp. *M. minimus*, the flowers of which have a taillike torus.

mous·ing (mou′zĭng), *n.* *Naut.* several turns of small rope or the like, uniting the shank and point of a hook.

mous·que·taire (mōōs′kə târ′), *n.* musketeer. [F]

mousse (mōōs), *n.* any of various preparations of whipped cream, beaten eggs, gelatine, etc., sweetened and flavored and frozen without stirring. [t. F: moss, froth, of Gmc. orig. See MOSS]

mousse·line (mōōslēn′), *n.* *French.* muslin.

mousse·line de laine (mōōslēn′ də lĕn′), *French.* a thin woolen fabric, often having a printed pattern. [F: lit., woolen muslin]

mousse·line de soie (mōōslēn′ də swä′), *French.* a thin, stiff silk or rayon fabric. [F: lit., silken muslin]

Mous·sorg·sky (mōō sôrg′skĭ), *n.* **Modest Petrovich** (mŏ dĕst′ pĕ trô′vĭch), 1839–81, Russian composer.

mous·tache (məs tăsh′, mŭs′tăsh), *n.* *Chiefly Brit.* mustache.

Mous·te·ri·an (mōōs tĭr′ĭ ən), *adj.* *Anthropol.* pertaining to Paleolithic human relics having the workmanship, finish, and character of the flint scrapers found in the sands of Moustier, France. Also, **Mous·tie′ri·an.**

mous·y (mou′sĭ, mou′zĭ), *adj.*, **mousier, mousiest.** **1.** resembling or suggesting a mouse, as in color, odor, etc. **2.** drab and colorless. **3.** quiet as a mouse. **4.** infested with mice. Also, **mous′ey.**

mouth (*n.* mouth; *v.* mouth), *n.*, *pl.* **mouths** (mouthz), *v.* —*n.* **1.** the opening through which an animal takes in food, or the cavity containing or the parts including the masticating apparatus. **2.** the masticating and tasting apparatus. **3.** a person or other animal as requiring food. **4.** the oral opening or cavity considered as the source of vocal utterance. **5.** utterance or expression: *to give mouth to one's thoughts.* **6.** a grimace made with the lips. **7.** an opening leading out of or into any cavity or hollow place or thing: *the mouth of a cave.* **8.** a part of a river or the like where its waters are discharged into some other body of water: *the mouth of the Nile.* **9.** the opening between the jaws of a vise or the like. **10.** the lateral hole of an organ pipe. **11.** the lateral blowhole of a flute. —*v.t.* **12.** to utter in a sonorous, oratorical, or pompous manner, or with unnecessarily noticeable use of the mouth parts. **15.** to put or take into the mouth. as food. **16.** to press, rub, or mumble with the mouth or lips. **17.** to accustom (a horse) to the use of the bit and bridle. —*v.i.* **18.** to speak or declaim sonorously and oratorically, or with mouthing of the words. **19.** to grimace with the lips. [ME; OE *mūth*, c. G *mund*]

Section of mouth and nose A. Turbinate bones; B. Lachrymal duct; C. Hard palate; D. Tongue; E. Uvula; F. Epiglottis; G. Hyoid bone; H. Larynx; I. Trachea; J. Esophagus; K. Cervical vertebrae

mouth·breed·er (mouth′brē′dər), *n.* any aquarium fish, of the genera *Tilapia* and *Haplochromis*, which care for their young by holding them in the mouth.

mouth·ful (mouth′fōōl′), *n.*, *pl.* **-fuls.** **1.** as much as a mouth can hold. **2.** as much as is taken into the mouth at one time. **3.** a small quantity.

mouth organ, a harmonica (def. 1).

mouth·piece (mouth′pēs′), *n.* **1.** a piece placed at or forming the mouth, as of a receptacle, tube, or the like. **2.** a piece or part, as of an instrument, to which the mouth is applied or which is held in the mouth: *the mouthpiece of a trumpet.* **3.** the part of a bit or bridle, as for a horse, that passes through the animal's mouth. **4.** a person, a newspaper, or the like that voices or communicates the sentiments, decisions, etc., of another or others; a spokesman.

mouth·y (mou′thĭ, mou′thĭ), *adj.*, **mouthier, mouthiest.** loud-mouthed; ranting; bombastic. —**mouth′i·ly,** *adv.* —**mouth′i·ness,** *n.*

mou·ton·née (mōō′tə nā′), *adj.* *Phys. Geog.* designating scattered knobs of rock rounded and smoothed by glacial action. Also, **mou′ton·néed′.** [t. F: lit., rounded like a sheep's back, pp. fem. of *moutonner*, der. *mouton* sheep. See MUTTON]

mov·a·ble (mōō′və bəl), *adj.* **1.** capable of being moved; not fixed in one place, position, or posture. **2.** *Law.* (of property) a. not permanent in place; capable of being moved without injury. b. personal, as distinguished from real. **3.** changing from one date to another in different years. —*n.* **4.** an article of furniture which is not fixed in place. **5.** (*usually pl.*) *Law.* an article of personal property not attached to land. Also, **moveable.** —**mov′a·ble·ness, mov′a·bil′i·ty,** *n.* —**mov′a·bly,** *adv.*

move (mōōv), *v.*, **moved, moving,** *n.* —*v.i.* **1.** to change place or position; pass from one place or situation to another. **2.** to change one's abode; go from one place of residence to another. **3.** to advance, progress, or make progress. **4.** to have a regular motion, as an implement or a machine; turn; revolve. **5.** *Com.* to be disposed of by sale, as goods in stock. **6.** *Colloq.* to start off, or depart: *it's time to be moving.* **7.** (of the bowels) to operate. **8.** to be active in a particular sphere: *to move in society.* **9.** to take action, or act, as in an affair. **10.** to make a formal request, application, or proposal: *to move for a new trial.* —*v.t.* **11.** to change the place or position of; take from one place, posture, or situation to another. **12.** to set or keep in motion; stir or shake. **13.** to prompt, actuate, or impel to some action: *what moved you to do this?* **14.** to cause (the bowels) to act or operate. **15.** to arouse or excite the feelings or passions of; affect with emotion; excite (*to*). **16.** to affect with tender or compassionate emotion; touch. **17.** to propose formally, as to a court or judge, or for consideration by a deliberative assembly. **18.** to submit a formal request or proposal to (a sovereign, a court, etc.). —*n.* **19.** act of moving; a movement. **20.** a change of abode or residence. **21.** an action toward an end; a step. **22.** *Games, etc.* the right or turn to move. [ME *move*(*n*), t. AF: m. *mover*, g. L *movēre*] —**mov'er**, *n.* —**Syn. 1.** See **advance. 11.** remove, transfer, shift. **13.** influence; induce, incite, instigate; lead. **19.** See **motion.** —**Ant. 11.** fix.

move·a·ble (mōō'və bəl), *adj., n.* movable. —**move'a·ble·ness**, **move'a·bil'i·ty**, *n.* —**move'a·bly**, *adv.*

move·ment (mōōv'mənt), *n.* **1.** act or process of moving. **2.** a particular manner of moving. **3.** (*chiefly pl.*) an action or activity, as of a person or a body of persons. **4.** *Mil., Naval.* a change of position or location of troops or ships. **5.** rapid progress of events, or abundance of events or incidents. **6.** the progress of events, as in a narrative or drama. **7.** the suggestion of action, as in a painting or the like. **8.** a series of actions or activities directed or tending toward a particular end: *the antislavery movement.* **9.** the course of tendency, or trend, of affairs in a particular field. **10.** the price change .n the market of some commodity or security. **11.** an evacuation of the bowels. **12.** the material evacuated. **13.** the works, or a distinct portion of the works, of a mechanism, as a watch. **14.** *Music.* **a.** a principal division or section of a sonata, symphony, or the like. **b.** motion; rhythm; time; tempo. **15.** *Pros.* rhythmical structure or character. —**Syn. 1.** See **motion.**

mov·ie (mōō'vĭ), *n. U.S. Colloq.* a motion picture.

mov·ing (mōō'vĭng), *adj.* **1.** that moves. **2.** causing or producing motion. **3.** actuating, instigating, or impelling: *the moving cause of a dispute.* **4.** that excites the feelings or affects with emotion, esp. touching or pathetic. —**mov'ing·ly**, *adv.* —**mov'ing·ness**, *n.*

moving picture, motion picture.

moving staircase, escalator.

mow¹ (mō), *v.,* **mowed, mowed** or **mown, mowing.** —*v.t.* **1.** to cut down (grass, grain, etc.) with a scythe or a machine. **2.** to cut grass, grain, etc., from. **3.** to cut down, destroy, or kill indiscriminately or in great numbers, as men in battle. —*v.i.* **4.** to cut down grass, grain, etc. **5.** to sweep down men in battle. [ME *mowe*(*n*), OE *māwan*, c. G *mähen*] —**mow'er**, *n.*

mow² (mou), *n.* **1.** the place in a barn where hay, sheaves of grain, etc., are stored. **2.** a heap or pile of hay or of sheaves of grain in a barn. [ME *mowe*, OE *mūga, mūha,* c. Icel. *mūgi* swath]

mow³ (mou, mō), *Archaic.* —*n.* **1.** a wry or derisive grimace. —*v.i.* **2.** to make mows, mouths, or grimaces. [ME *mowe,* t. OF: m. *moe* a pouting grimace]

mowe (mou, mō), *n., v.i.,* **mowed, mowing.** *Archaic.* **mow².**

mow·ing (mō'ĭng), *n.* **1.** act of leveling or cutting down grass with a mowing machine or scythe. **2.** as much grass as is cut in any specified period.

mowing machine, a machine for mowing or cutting down standing grass, etc.

mown (mōn), *adj.* mowed; cut as if mowed.

mo·yen âge (mwȧ yě näzh'), *French.* the Middle Ages.

Mozamb., Mozambique.

Mo·zam·bique (mō'zəm bēk'), *n.* **1.** Also, **Portuguese East Africa.** a Portuguese overseas territory in SE Africa. 6,234,000 (est. 1959); 297,731 sq. mi. *Cap.:* Lourenço Marques. **2.** a seaport on an island just off the NE coast of this territory. 12,108 (1950). Portuguese, **Moçambique.**

Mozambique Channel, a channel between Mozambique and Madagascar. ab. 950 mi. long; 250–550 mi. wide.

Mo·zart (mō'zärt; *Ger.* mō'tsärt), *n.* **Wolfgang Amadeus** (vôlf'gäng ä'mä dā'ōōs), 1756–91, Austrian composer.

moz·zet·ta (mō zĕt'ə; *It.* môt sět'tä), *n. Rom. Cath. Ch.* a short cape which covers the shoulders and can be buttoned over the breast, and to which a hood is attached, worn by the pope and by cardinals, bishops, abbots, and other dignitaries. Also, **mo·zet'ta.** [t. It. Cf. AMICE¹, MUTCH]

M.P., 1. melting point. **2.** Member of Parliament. **3.** Metropolitan Police. **4.** Also, **MP, Military Police. 5.** Also, **MP,** Mounted Police.

m.p., melting point.

m.p.h., miles per hour.

MR, M.R., motivation research.

Mr. (mĭs'tər), *pl.* **Messrs.** mister: a title prefixed to a man's name or position, as in *Mr. Lawson, Mr. President.*

Mrs. (mĭs'ĭz, -ĭs, mĭz'-), *pl.* **Mmes.** mistress: a title prefixed to the name of a married woman: *Mrs. Jones.*

MS., *pl.* **MSS.** manuscript. Also, **ms.**

M.S., 1. Master of Science. **2.** Master in Surgery.

m.s., modification of the stem of.

M.Sc., Master of Science.

Msgr., Monsignor.

m'sieur (məsyœ'), *n. French.* contraction of *monsieur.*

m.s.t., mountain standard time.

Ms-Th, *Chem.* mesothorium.

Mt., *pl.* **Mts. 1.** mount: *Mt. Rainier.* **2.** mountain. Also, **mt.**

M.T., metric ton.

m.t., mountain time.

mtn., mountain.

Mt. Rev., Most Reverend.

mu (mū, mōō), *n.* the twelfth letter of the Greek alphabet (M, μ).

much (mŭch), *adj.,* **more, most,** *n., adv.* —*adj.* **1.** in great quantity, amount, measure, or degree: *much work.* —*n.* **2.** a great quantity or amount; a great deal: *much of this is true.* **3.** a great, important, or notable thing or matter: *the house is not much to look at.* **4. to make much of, a.** to treat, represent, or consider as of great importance. **b.** to treat (a person) with great, flattering, or fond consideration. —*adv.* **5.** to a great extent or degree; greatly; far: *much pleased.* **6.** nearly, approximately, or about: *this is much the same as the others.* [ME *muche, moche,* apocopated var. of *muchel, mochel,* OE *mycel*; r. ME *miche*(*l*), OE *micel* great, much, c. Icel. *mikill,* Goth. *mikils,* Gk. *megalo-* great]

Much Ado About Nothing, a comedy (about 1598) by Shakespeare.

much·ness (mŭch'nĭs), *n.* greatness, as in quantity, measure, or degree.

mu·cic acid (mū'sĭk), *Chem.* a dibasic crystalline acid, HOOC(CHOH)₄COOH, obtained by oxidizing certain gums, milk sugar, or galactose.

mu·cid (mū'sĭd), *adj.* moldy; musty. [t. L: s. *mūcidus*] —**mu'cid·ness**, *n.*

mu·ci·lage (mū'sə lĭj), *n.* **1.** any of various preparations of gum, glue, or the like, for causing adhesion. **2.** any of various gummy secretions or gelatinous substances present in plants. [ME, t. F, t. LL: m. *mucilāgo* a musty juice]

mu·ci·lag·i·nous (mū'sə lăj'ə nəs), *adj.* **1.** of, pertaining to, or secreting mucilage. **2.** of the nature of or resembling mucilage; moist, soft, and viscid.

mu·cin (mū'sĭn), *n. Biochem.* any of a group of nitrogenous substances found in mucous secretions, etc., and of varying composition according to their source. [f. s. L *mūcus* MUCUS + -IN²] —**mu/cin·ous**, *adj.*

muck (mŭk), *n.* **1.** farmyard dung, decaying vegetable matter, etc., in a moist state; manure. **2.** a highly organic soil, less than fifty percent combustible, often used as manure. **3.** filth; dirt. **4.** *Brit. Colloq.* something of no value; trash. **5.** *Mining, etc.* earth, rock, or other useless matter to be removed in order to get out the mineral or other substances sought. —*v.t.* **6.** to manure. **7.** to make dirty; soil. **8.** to remove muck from. —*v.i.* **9.** muck about, *Brit.* to idle; putter. [ME *muk,* t. Scand.; cf. Icel. *myki* cow dung]

muck·er (mŭk'ər), *n.* **1.** *Brit. Slang.* a vulgar, ill-bred person. **2.** *Mining, etc.* one who removes muck.

muck·le (mŭk'əl), *n. U.S. Dial.* a wooden cudgel used to kill fish.

muck rake, a rake for use on muck or filth.

muck·rake (mŭk'rāk'), *v.i.,* **-raked, -raking.** *Colloq.* to expose, esp. in print, political or other corruption real or alleged. [f. MUCK + RAKE] —**muck'rak'er**, *n.*

muck·y (mŭk'ĭ), *adj.,* **muckier, muckiest. 1.** of or like muck. **2.** filthy; dirty.

mu·coid (mū'koid), *n. Biochem.* any of a group of substances resembling the mucins, occurring in connective tissue, etc. [f. MUC(IN) + -OID]

mu·co·pro·te·in (mū'kōprō'tē ĭn, -tēn), *n.* a compound containing protein and a carbohydrate group.

mu·co·sa (mūkō'sə), *n., pl.* **-sae** (-sē). *Anat.* a mucous membrane. [t. NL, fem. of L *mūcōsus* MUCOUS] —**mu·co'sal**, *adj.*

mu·cous (mū'kəs), *adj.* **1.** pertaining to, consisting of, or resembling mucus. **2.** containing or secreting mucus: *the mucous membrane.* [t. L: m.s. *mūcōsus* slimy] —**mu·cos·i·ty** (mūkŏs'ə tĭ), *n.*

mucous membrane, a lubricating membrane lining an internal surface or an organ, such as the alimentary, respiratory, and genitourinary canals.

mu·cro (mū'krō), *n., pl.* **mucrones** (mūkrō'nēz). *Bot., Zool.* a short point projecting abruptly, as at the end of a leaf. [t. L: point]

mu·cro·nate (mū'krō nīt, -nāt'), *adj. Bot.* having an abruptly projecting point, as a feather, leaf, etc. Also, **mu'cro·nat'ed.** [t. L: m.s. *mūcrōnātus* pointed]

Mucronate tail feather of chimney swift

mu·cus (mū′kəs), *n.* a viscid secretion of the mucous membranes. [t. L]

mud (mŭd), *n.* wet, soft earth or earthy matter, as on the ground after rain, at the bottom of a pond, or among the discharges from a volcano; mire. [ME *mudde, mode,* c. MLG *mudde*]

mud·cap (mŭd′kăp′), *v.t.,* **-capped, -capping. 1.** to cover with a cap of mud. **2.** (in blasting) to detonate (an explosive capped with mud), as on an exposed rock surface.

mud·cat (mŭd′kăt′), *n.* (in the Mississippi valley) a catfish grown to large size.

mud dauber, any of certain wasps of the family *Sphecidae,* which construct mud cells for their larvae and provision them with insects.

mud·dle (mŭd′əl), *v.,* **-dled, -dling,** *n.* —*v.* **1.** to mix up or jumble together in a confused or bungling way. **2.** to render confused mentally, or unable to think clearly. **3.** to render confused or stupid with drink, or as drink does. **4.** to mix or stir (chocolate, etc.). **5.** to make muddy or turbid, as water. **6. muddle through,** *Brit.* to come to a successful conclusion without planned direction. —*n.* **7.** a muddled condition; a confused mental state. **8.** a confused, disordered, or embarrassing state of affairs, or a mess. [f. MUD + *-le,* freq. and dim. suffix]

mud·dler (mŭd′lər), *n.* **1.** a stick for stirring drinks. **2.** one who muddles or muddles through.

mud·dy (mŭd′Y), *adj.,* **-dier, -diest,** *v.,* **-died, -dying.** —*adj.* **1.** abounding in or covered with mud. **2.** not clear or pure, as color. **3.** dull, as the complexion. **4.** not clear mentally. **5.** obscure or vague, as thought, expression, literary style, etc. —*v.t.* **6.** to make muddy; soil with mud. **7.** to make turbid. **8.** to render confused or obscure. —*v.i.* **9.** to become muddy. —**mud′di·ly,** *adv.* —**mud′di·ness,** *n.*

mud·guard (mŭd′gärd′), *n.* a guard or shield so placed as to protect riders or passengers from mud thrown by the wheel of a bicycle, automobile, or the like.

mud hen, any of various marsh-inhabiting birds, esp. the American coot.

mud puppy, 1. any of the large North American aquatic salamanders of the genus *Necturus,* which have bushy red gills and well-developed limbs. **2.** any of various American salamanders of the genus *Ambystoma.*

mud·sill (mŭd′sYl′), *n.* the lowest sill of a structure, usually placed in or on the ground.

mud·stone (mŭd′stōn′), *n.* a clayey rock of nearly uniform texture throughout, with little or no lamination.

mud·suck·er (mŭd′sŭk′ər), *n.* the long-jawed goby, *Gillichthys mirabilis,* a Californian fish much used as bait.

mud turtle, any of various fresh-water turtles of the U.S., as *Kinosternon subrubrum,* or *Chrysemys picta.*

mu·ez·zin (mū ĕz′Yn, mŏŏ-), *n.* (in Mohammedan communities) the crier who, from a minaret or other part of a mosque, at stated hours five times daily, intones aloud the call summoning the faithful to prayer. [t. Ar.: m. *muazzin,* d. var. of *muadhdhin*]

muff (mŭf), *n.* **1.** a kind of thick tubular case covered with fur or other material, in which the hands are placed for warmth. **2.** a tuft of feathers on the sides of the head of certain fowls. **3.** *Baseball.* a failure to hold a ball that comes into one's hands. **4.** any failure. —*v.t.* **5.** *Colloq.* to perform clumsily, or bungle. **6.** *Baseball.* to fail to hold (a ball that comes into one's hands). —*v.i.* **7.** *Colloq.* to bungle. [t. D: m. *mof,* t. F: m. *moufle;* akin to MUFFLE, n.]

muf·fin (mŭf′Yn), *n.* **1.** a small, round bread made with wheat flour, corn meal, or the like, eaten with butter and usually served hot. **2.** such a bread made from yeast dough. [orig. obscure]

muf·fle (mŭf′əl), *v.,* **-fled, -fling,** *n.* —*v.t.* **1.** to wrap or envelop in a cloak, shawl, scarf, or the like disposed about the person, esp. about the face and neck (often fol. by *up*). **2.** to wrap with something to deaden or prevent sound: *to muffle drums.* **3.** to deaden (sound) by wrappings or other means. —*v.i.* **4.** to muffle oneself (*up*) as in garments or other wrappings. —*n.* **5.** something that muffles. **6.** muffled sound. **7.** an oven or arched chamber in a furnace or kiln, used for heating substances without direct contact with the fire. **8.** the thick, bare part of the upper lip and nose of ruminants and rodents. [ME *mufle(n),* appar. t. OF. Cf. OF *emmoufle* wrapped up]

muf·fler (mŭf′lər), *n.* **1.** a heavy neck scarf. **2.** any of various devices for deadening sound, as the sound of escaping gases of an internal-combustion engine. **3.** anything used for muffling.

muf·ti (mŭf′tY), *n., pl.* **-tis. 1.** civilian dress as opposed to military or other uniform, or as worn by one who usually wears a uniform. **2.** a Mohammedan legal adviser consulted in applying the religious law. **3.** (under the Ottoman Empire) the official head of the state religion, or one of his deputies. **4.** See **Grand Mufti.** [t. Ar.: lit., one who delivers a judgment; orig. Ar. meaning def. 2. Def. 1 from the fact that a mufti is a civil official]

mug (mŭg), *n., v.,* **mugged, mugging.** —*n.* **1.** a drinking cup, usually cylindrical and commonly with a handle. **2.** the quantity it holds. **3.** *Slang.* the face. **4.** *Slang.* the mouth. **5.** *Slang.* a grimace. —*v.t.* **6.** *Slang.* to take a photograph of (a person), esp. in compliance with an official or legal requirement. **7.** *Slang.* (of a thug, etc.)

to assault (a victim, etc.) from the rear by locking the forearm around the neck and throttling. —*v.i.* **8.** *Slang.* to grimace. [ME *mogge,* akin to LG *muck* drinking cup, d. G *muggelig* thick and fat]

mug·ger[1] (mŭg′ər), *n.* one who mugs.

mug·ger[2] (mŭg′ər), *n.* a broad-snouted crocodile, *Crocodilus palustris,* of India, etc., growing to about 12 feet in length. Also, **mug′gar, mug′gur.** [t. Hind.: m. *magar*]

mug·gins (mŭg′Ynz), *n.* **1.** a convention in the card game of cribbage in which a player scores points overlooked by an opponent. **2.** a game of dominoes in which any player, if he can make the sum of the two ends of the line equal five or a multiple of five, adds the number so made to his score. [? orig. surname *Muggins*]

mug·gy (mŭg′Y), *adj.,* **-gier, -giest.** (of the atmosphere, weather, etc.) damp and close; humid and oppressive. [f. d. *mug* mist (t. Scand.; cf. Icel. *mugga*) + -Y1] —**mug′gi·ness,** *n.* —**Ant.** dry.

mug·wump (mŭg′wŭmp′), *n. U.S.* **1.** (in the presidential campaign of 1884) a Republican who refused to support the party nominee (J. G. Blaine). **2.** one who acts as an independent or affects superiority, esp. in politics. [t. Algonquian (Massachusetts): m. *mukquomp* leader, chief, great man, f. m. *moqki* great + *-omp* man] —**mug′wump′er·y,** *n.*

Mu·ham·mad (mŏŏ hăm′əd), *n.* Mohammed. —**Muham′mad·an, Mu·ham′med·an,** *adj., n.*

Mühl·bach (myl′bäKH), *n.* **Luise** (lŏŏ ē′zə), (*Klara Müller Mundt*) 1814–73, German novelist.

Muir (myŏŏr), *n.* **John,** 1838–1914, U.S. naturalist, explorer, and writer.

Muir Glacier, a glacier in SE Alaska, flowing from Mt. Fairweather into the ocean. ab. 350 sq. mi.

mu·jik (mŏŏ zhYk′, mŏŏ′zhYk), *n.* muzhik.

Muk·den (mŏŏk′dĕn′, mŏŏk′-), *n.* a city in NE China, in S Manchuria: the former capital of Manchuria; battle, 1905. 1,790,000 (est. 1954). Also, **Moukden, Fengtien,** or **Shenyang.**

mu·lat·to (mə lăt′ō, mū-), *n., pl.* **-toes,** *adj.* —*n.* **1.** the offspring of parents of whom one is white and the other a Negro. —*adj.* **2.** having a light-brown color (similar to the skin of a mulatto). [t. Sp. and Pg.: m. *mulato,* der. *mulo,* g. L *mūlus* MULE; so called from the hybrid origin]

mul·ber·ry (mŭl′bĕr′Y, -bərY), *n., pl.* **-ries. 1.** the edible, berrylike collective fruit of any tree of the genus *Morus.* **2.** a tree of this genus, as M. *rubra* (**red** or **American mulberry**), with dark-purple fruit, M. *nigra* (**black mulberry**), with dark-colored fruit, and M. *alba* (**white mulberry**), with fruit nearly white and with leaves especially valued as food for silkworms. **3.** a dull, dark, reddish-purple color. [ME *mulberie,* dissimilated var. of *murberie,* OE *mōrberie,* f. s. L *mōrum* mulberry + *berie* BERRY]

mulch (mŭlch), *Hort.* —*n.* **1.** straw, leaves, loose earth, etc., spread on the ground or produced by tillage to protect the roots of newly planted trees, crops, etc. —*v.t.* **2.** to cover with mulch. [n. use of (obs.) *mulch,* adj., ME *molsh* soft, OE *myl(i)sc* mellow; akin to d. G *molsch* soft, overripe]

mulct (mŭlkt), *n.* **1.** a fine; a penalty. —*v.t.* **2.** to punish (a person, or formerly, an offense) by fine or forfeiture. **3.** to deprive of something as a penalty. **4.** to deprive of something by trickery. [t. L: s. *mulcta* fine]

mule[1] (mūl), *n.* **1.** the offspring of a male donkey and a mare, used esp. as a beast of burden because of its patience, sure-footedness, and hardiness. **2.** any hybrid between the donkey and the horse. **3.** *Colloq.* a stupid or stubborn person. **4.** *Biol.* a hybrid, esp. a hybrid between the canary and some other finch. **5.** a machine which spins cotton, etc., into yarn and winds it on spindles. [ME *mule,* t. OF, g. L *mūla;* r. OE *mūl,* t. L: s. *mūlus*]

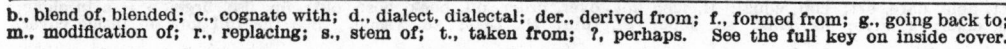

Mule. *Equus caballus x asinus* (Ab. 5 ft. high at the shoulder)

mule[2] (mūl), *n.* a kind of slipper which leaves the heel exposed. [ME, t. F.]

mule deer, a deer, *Odocoileus hemionus,* with large ears, common in western North America.

mule skinner, *U.S. Colloq.* a driver of mules.

mu·le·teer (mū′lə tēr′), *n.* a driver of mules. [t. F: m. *muletier,* der. *mulet,* dim. of OF *mul* MULE1]

mul·ey (mū′lY, mŏŏl′Y), *adj., n., pl.* **-leys.** —*adj.* **1.** (of cattle) hornless; polled. —*n.* **2.** any cow. Also, **mulley.** [var. of d. *motley,* t. Irish: m. *maol,* or t. Welsh: m. *moel,* lit., bald]

Mule deer. *Odocoileus hemionus* (3½ ft. high at the shoulder total length 5½ ft.)

muley saw, *U.S. Colloq.* a saw having a long, stiff blade which is not stretched in a gate but whose motion is directed by clamps at each end mounted on guide rails.

Mul·ha·cén (mŏŏl′ä thĕn′), *n.* a mountain in S Spain: the highest peak in Spain. ab. 11,420 ft.

Mül·heim an der Ruhr (myl/hĭm än dĕr rōōr/), a city in W West Germany, near Essen. 168,280 (est. 1955).

Mul·house (my lōōz/), *n.* a city in E France, near the Rhine. 99,079 (1954). German, **Mül·hau·sen** (myl/-vən/).

mu·li·eb·ri·ty (mū/lĭ ĕb/rə tĭ), *n.* **1.** womanly nature or qualities. **2.** womanhood. [t. LL: m.s. *muliebritas,* der. L *muliebris* womanly]

mul·ish (mū/lĭsh), *adj.* like a mule; characteristic of a mule; stubborn, obstinate, or intractable. —**mul/ish·ly,** *adv.* —**mul/ish·ness,** *n.*

mull[1], *U.S. Colloq.* —*v.i.* **1.** to study or ruminate (*over*), esp. in an ineffective way. —*v.t.* **2.** to make a mess or failure of. [orig. obscure]

mull[2], *v.t.* to heat, sweeten, and spice for drinking, as ale, wine, etc.: *mulled cider.* [orig. uncert.]

mull[3] (mŭl), *n.* a soft, thin kind of muslin. [earlier *mulmul,* t. Hind.: m. *malmal*]

Mull (mŭl), *n.* an island in the Hebrides, in W Scotland. 2419 pop. (1951); ab. 351 sq. mi.

mul·lah (mŭl/ə, mōōl/ə), *n.* **1.** (in Mohammedan countries) a title of respect for one who is learned in, teaches, or expounds the sacred law. **2.** (in Turkey) a provincial judge. Also, **mul/la.** [t. Turk., Pers., and Hind.: m. *mullā,* t. Ar.: m. *mawlā* patron, lord]

mul·lein (mŭl/ən), *n.* **1.** a stout Old World weed, *Verbascum Thapsus,* with coarse woolly leaves and dense spikes of yellow flowers, locally common as a weed in North America. **2.** any plant of the same genus, or any of various similar plants. Also, **mul/len.** [ME *moleyn,* t. AF: m. *moleine,* t der. OF *mol,* g. L *mollis* soft]

mull·er (mŭl/ər), *n.* **1.** an implement of stone or other substance with a flat base for grinding paints, powders, etc., on a slab of stone or the like. **2.** any of various mechanical devices for grinding. [? orig. meaning powderer (der. ME *mul* powder, OE *myl* dust, g .G *müll*)]

Mül·ler (mŭl/ər; *Ger.* my/lər), *n.* **Friedrich Max** (frē/drĭкн mäks), 1823–1900, German Sanskrit scholar and philologist, in England.

mul·let (mŭl/ĭt), *n., pl.* **-lets,** (*esp. collectively*) **-let. 1.** any fish of the family *Mugilidae,* which includes various marine and fresh-water species with a nearly cylindrical body and generally gray coloration, as the wide-ranging **striped mullet,** *Mugil cephalus.* **2.** a goatfish. **3.** a sucker, particularly of the genus *Moxostoma.* **4.** any of various other fishes. [ME *mulet,* t. OF, der. L *mullus* red mullet]

mul·ley (mōōl/ĭ), *adj., n., pl.* **-leys.** muley.

mul·li·gan (mŭl/ĭ gən), *n. U.S. Slang.* a kind of stew containing meat, vegetables, etc.

mul·li·ga·taw·ny (mŭl/ĭ gə tô/nĭ), *n.* a soup of East Indian origin, flavored with curry. [t. Tamil: m. *milagutannīr* pepper water]

mul·lion (mŭl/yən), *Archit.* —*n.* **1.** a vertical member, as of stone or wood, between the lights of a window, the panels in wainscoting, or the like. **2.** one of the radiating bars of a rose window or the like. —*v.t.* **3.** to furnish with, or to form into divisions by the use of, mullions. [metathetic var. of *monial,* t. OF; orig. uncert.]

mul·lock (mŭl/ək), *n. Australasia.* mining refuse; muck. [f. d. *mull* rubbish (see MULLER) + -OCK]

Mu·lock (mū/lŏk), *n.* **Dinah Maria,** (*Mrs. Craik*) 1826–87, British novelist.

Mul·tan (mōōl/tän/), *n.* a city in Pakistan, in W Punjab. 190,122 (1951).

multi-, a word element meaning "many." [t. L, comb. form of *multus* much, many]

mul·ti·cel·lu·lar (mŭl/tĭ sĕl/yə lər), *adj.* composed of several or many cells.

mul·ti·coil (mŭl/tĭ koil/), *adj.* having more than one coil, as an electrical device.

mul·ti·col·ored (mŭl/tĭ kŭl/ərd), *adj.* of many colors.

mul·ti·cyl·in·der (mŭl/tĭ sĭl/ĭn dər), *adj.* having more than one cylinder, as an internal-combustion or steam engine. Also, **mul/ti·cyl/in·dered.**

mul·ti·den·tate (mŭl/tĭ dĕn/tāt), *adj.* having many teeth or toothlike processes.

mul·ti·far·i·ous (mŭl/tə fâr/ĭ əs), *adj.* **1.** having many different parts, elements, forms, etc. **2.** of many kinds, or numerous and varied; manifold (modifying a pl. n.): *multifarious activities.* [t. L: m. *multifārius* manifold] —**mul/ti·far/i·ous·ly,** *adv.* —**mul/ti·far/i·ous·ness,** *n.*

mul·ti·fid (mŭl/tə fĭd), *adj.* cleft into many parts, divisions, or lobes. Also, **mul·tif·i·dous** (mŭl tĭf/ə dəs). [t. L: s. *multifidus*]

mul·ti·flo·rous (mŭl/tĭ flōr/əs), *adj. Bot.* bearing many flowers, as a peduncle.

mul·ti·fold (mŭl/tə fōld/), *adj.* manifold.

mul·ti·fo·li·ate (mŭl/tə fō/lĭ ĭt, -āt/), *adj. Bot.* having many leaves or leaflets.

mul·ti·form (mŭl/tə fôrm/), *adj.* having many forms; of many different forms or kinds. [t. L: s. *multiformis*] —**mul·ti·for·mi·ty** (mŭl/tə fôr/mĭ tĭ), *n.*

Mul·ti·graph (mŭl/tə grăf/, -gräf/), *n.* **1.** *Trademark.* a rotary typesetting and printing machine, commonly used to reproduce typewritten matter. —*v.t., v.i.* **2.** to reproduce with such a machine.

mul·ti·lam·i·nate (mŭl/tĭ lăm/ə nĭt, -nāt/), *adj.* having many laminae or layers.

mul·ti·lat·er·al (mŭl/tĭ lăt/ər əl), *adj.* **1.** having many sides; many-sided. **2.** *Govt.* multipartite. —**mul/ti·lat/er·al·ly,** *adv.*

mul·ti·lob·u·lar (mŭl/tĭ lŏb/yə lər), *adj.* having many lobules.

mul·ti·mil·lion·aire (mŭl/tə mĭl/yən âr/), *n.* one with property worth several millions, as of dollars.

mul·ti·mo·lec·u·lar (mŭl/tĭ mə lĕk/yə lər), *adj.* having many loculi, chambers, or cells.

mul·ti·mo·tored (mŭl/tĭ mō/tərd), *adj.* with a number of motors or engines.

mul·ti·nom·i·nal (mŭl/tĭ nŏm/ə nəl), *adj.* having many names.

mul·ti·nu·cle·ar (mŭl/tĭ nū/klĭ ər, -nōō/-), *adj.* having many or several nuclei, as a cell.

mul·tip·a·ra (mŭl tĭp/ərə), *n., pl.* **-rae** (-rē/). *Obstet.* a woman who has borne two or more children, or who is parturient the second time. [t. NL, fem. of *multiparus* MULTIPAROUS]

mul·tip·a·rous (mŭl tĭp/ərəs), *adj.* **1.** producing many, or more than one, at a birth. **2.** *Bot.* (of a cyme) having many lateral axes. [t. NL: m. *multiparus.* See MULTI-, -PAROUS]

mul·ti·par·tite (mŭl/tĭ pär/tīt), *adj.* **1.** divided into many parts; having many divisions. **2.** *Govt.* denoting an agreement or other instrument in which three or more states participate; multilateral. [t. L: m.s. *multipartītus* much-divided]

mul·ti·ped (mŭl/tə pĕd/), *adj.* having many feet. Also, **mul·ti·pede** (mŭl/tə pēd/). [t. L: s. *multipēs,* adj. and n., many-footed]

mul·ti·phase (mŭl/tə fāz/), *adj. Elect.* having many phases.

mul·ti·ple (mŭl/tə pəl), *adj.* **1.** consisting of, having, or involving many individuals, parts, elements, relations, etc.; manifold. **2.** *Elect.* denoting two or more circuits connected in parallel. **3.** *Bot.* (of a fruit) collective. —*n.* **4.** *Math.* a number which contains another number some number of times without a remainder: *12 is a multiple of 3.* **5.** *Elect.* **a.** a group of terminals arranged to make a circuit or group of circuits accessible at a number of points at any one of which connection can be made. **b.** in **multiple,** in parallel. See **parallel** (def. 11). [t. F, t. LL: m. *multiplus* manifold]

multiple alleles, *Genetics.* a series of three or more alternative or allelic forms of a gene, only two of which can exist in any normal, diploid individual.

multiple cropping, *Agric.* the use of the same field for two or more separate crops, whether of the same or of different kinds, successively during a single year.

multiple factors, *Genetics.* a series of two or more pairs of genes responsible for the development of complex, quantitative characters such as size, yield, etc.

multiple neuritis, *Pathol.* inflammation of several nerves at the same time.

multiple star, *Astron.* three or more stars lying close together in the celestial sphere and usually united in a single gravitational system.

multiple voting, casting ballots in more than one constituency in one election, as in England before, and to some extent after, the franchise reform of 1918.

mul·ti·plex (mŭl/tə plĕks/), *adj.* **1.** manifold; multiple: *multiplex telegraphy.* —*v.t.* **2.** *Elect.* to arrange a circuit for use by multiplex telegraphy. [t. L: manifold]

multiplex telegraphy, a system for sending many messages in each direction, simultaneously, over the same wire or communications channel.

mul·ti·pli·a·ble (mŭl/tə plī/ə bəl), *adj.* that may be multiplied. Also, **mul·ti·pli·ca·ble** (mŭl/tə plĭ/kə bəl).

mul·ti·pli·cand (mŭl/tə plĭ/kănd/), *n. Math.* the number to be multiplied by another. [t. L: s. *multiplicandus,* gerundive of *multiplicāre* MULTIPLY]

mul·ti·pli·cate (mŭl/tə plĭ/kāt/), *adj.* multiple; manifold. [ME, t. L: m.s. *multiplicātus,* pp., multiplied]

mul·ti·pli·ca·tion (mŭl/tə plə kā/shən), *n.* **1.** act or process of multiplying. **2.** the state of being multiplied. **3.** *Arith.* the process of finding the number (the product) resulting from the addition of a given number (the multiplicand) taken as many times as there are units in another given number (the multiplier). **4.** *Math.* any generalization of this operation applicable to numbers other than integers, such as fractions, irrationals, vectors, etc. —**mul/ti·pli·ca/tion·al,** *adj.*

mul·ti·pli·ca·tive (mŭl/tə plə kā/tĭv), *adj.* **1.** tending to multiply or increase. **2.** having the power of multiplying. —**mul/ti·pli·ca/tive·ly,** *adv.*

mul·ti·plic·i·ty (mŭl/tə plĭs/ə tĭ), *n., pl.* **-ties. 1.** a multitude or great number. **2.** state of being multiplex or manifold; manifold variety. [t. LL: m.s. *multiplicitas*]

mul·ti·pli·er (mŭl/tə plī/ər), *n.* **1.** one who or that which multiplies. **2.** *Math.* the number by which another is to be multiplied. **3.** *Physics.* a device for intensifying some phenomenon.

mul·ti·ply (mŭl/tə plī/), *v.,* **-plied, -plying.** —*v.t.* **1.** to make many or manifold; increase the number, quantity, etc., of. **2.** *Math.* to take by addition a given number of times; find the product of by multiplication. **3.** to produce (animals or plants) by propagation. **4.** to increase by procreation. —*v.i.* **5.** to grow in number, quantity, etc.; increase. **6.** *Math.* to perform the process of multiplication. **7.** to increase in number by procreation or natural generation. [ME *multiplie(n),* t. OF: m. *multiplier,* t. L: m. *multiplicāre*]

mul·ti·po·lar (mŭl'tĭ pō'lər), *adj.* having many poles.

mul·ti·tude (mŭl'tə tūd', -tōōd'), *n.* **1.** a great number; host: *a multitude of friends.* **2.** a great number of persons gathered together; a crowd or throng. **3.** the **multitude,** the common people. **4.** the state or character of being many, or numerousness. [ME, t. L: m. *multitūdo*] —Syn. 2. See **crowd.**

mul·ti·tu·di·nous (mŭl'tə tū'də nəs, -tōō'-), *adj.* **1.** forming a multitude or great number, or existing, occurring, or present in great numbers; very numerous. **2.** comprising many items, parts, or elements. **3.** *Poetic.* crowded or thronged. —**mul'ti·tu'di·nous·ly,** *adv.* —**mul'ti·tu'di·nous·ness,** *n.*

mul·ti·va·lent (mŭl'tə vā'lənt, mŭl tĭv'ə lənt), *adj. Chem.* having a valence of three or higher. Cf. **polyvalent.** —**mul·ti·va·lence** (mŭl'tə vā'ləns, mŭl tĭv'ə ləns), *n.*

mul·tum in par·vo (mŭl'təm ĭn pär'vō), *Latin.* much in little; a great deal in a small space or in brief.

mul·ture (mŭl'chər), *n.* a toll or fee given to the proprietor of a mill for the grinding of grain, usually consisting of a fixed proportion of the grain brought or of the flour made. [ME, t. OF: m. *molture,* g. L *molitūra* a grinding]

mum[1] (mŭm), *adj.* **1.** silent; not saying a word: *to keep mum.* —*interj.* **2.** Say nothing! Be silent! [ME; imit. Cf. G *mumm*]

mum[2] (mŭm), *v.i.,* **mummed, mumming. 1.** to say "mum" (with closed lips); call for silence. **2.** to act as a mummer. Also, **mumm.** [v. use of MUM[1]. Cf. OF *momer* mask oneself]

mum[3] (mŭm), *n. Colloq.* chrysanthemum.

mum[4] (mŭm), *n. Colloq.* mother.

mum·ble (mŭm'bəl), *v.,* **-bled, -bling,** *n.* —*v.i.* **1.** to speak indistinctly or unintelligibly, as with partly closed lips; mutter low, indistinct words. **2.** to chew ineffectively, as from loss of teeth: *to mumble on a crust.* —*v.t.* **3.** to utter indistinctly, as with partly closed lips. **4.** to chew, or try to eat, with difficulty, as from loss of teeth. —*n.* **5.** a low, indistinct utterance or sound. [ME *momele,* freq. of (obs.) *mum,* v., make inarticulate sound. Cf. G *mummeln*] —**mum'bler,** *n.* —**mum'bling·ly,** *adv.* —Syn. 3. See **murmur.**

mum·bo jum·bo (mŭm'bō jŭm'bō), **1.** meaningless incantation or ritual. **2.** an object of superstitious awe or reverence. **3.** (*caps.*) the guardian of western Sudan Negro villages symbolized by a masked man who combats evil and punishes women for breaches of tribal laws. **4.** *Slang.* superstition; witchcraft.

mumm (mŭm), *v.i.* mum[2].

mum·mer (mŭm'ər), *n.* **1.** one who wears a mask or fantastic disguise, esp. as formerly and still locally at Christmas, New Year's, and other festive seasons. **2.** (in humorous use) an actor. [late ME, t. OF: m. *momeur,* der. *momer* MUM[2]]

mum·mer·y (mŭm'ə rĭ), *n., pl.* **-mer·ies. 1.** performance of mummers. **2.** any mere theatrical performance or ceremony or empty spectacular pretense, or what is regarded as such. [t. F: m. *momerie*]

mum·mi·fy (mŭm'ə fī), *v.,* **-fied, -fying.** —*v.t.* **1.** to make (a dead body) into a mummy, as by embalming and drying. **2.** to make like a mummy. —*v.i.* **3.** to dry or shrivel up. —**mum'mi·fi·ca'tion,** *n.*

mum·my (mŭm'ĭ), *n., pl.* **-mies,** *v.,* **-mied, -mying.** —*n.* **1.** the dead body of a human being or animal preserved by the ancient Egyptian (or some similar) method of embalming. **2.** a dead body dried and preserved by the agencies of nature. **3.** a withered or shrunken living being. —*v.t.* **4.** to make into or like a mummy; mummify. [ME *mumie,* t. ML: m. *mumia,* t. Ar.: m. *mūmiya,* from Pers. *mūmiyā* asphalt]

mumps (mŭmps), *n.pl.,* construed as *sing. Pathol.* a specific infectious disease characterized by inflammatory swelling of the parotid and (usually) other salivary glands, and sometimes by inflammation of the testicles, ovaries, etc. [orig. meaning "grimace"; imit.]

mun., municipal.

munch (mŭnch), *v.t.* **1.** to chew with steady or vigorous working of the jaws, and often audibly. —*v.i.* **2.** to chew steadily or vigorously, and often audibly. [ME *monche,* nasalized var. of obs. *mouch* eat, chew; orig. unknown] —**munch'er,** *n.*

Mün·chen (myn'kʜən), *n.* German name of **Munich.**

Mün·chen-Glad·bach (myn'kʜən glät'bäkʜ), *n.* former name of **Mönchen-Gladbach.**

Münch·hau·sen (mynkʜ'hou'zən), *n.* **Karl Friedrich Hieronymus** (kärl frē'drĭkʜ hē'ä rō'nʏ mŏōs'), **Baron von** (fən), 1720–97, German soldier, adventurer, and teller of unbelievable tales. English, **Mun·chau·sen** (mŭn chô'zən, mŭnch'hou'zən).

Mun·cie (mŭn'sĭ), *n.* a city in E Indiana. 68,603 (1960).

mun·dane (mŭn'dān), *adj.* **1.** of or pertaining to the world, universe, or earth. **2.** of or pertaining to this world or earth as contrasted with heaven; worldly; earthly: *mundane affairs.* [t. L: m.s. *mundānus* of the world; r. ME *mondeyne,* t. OF] —**mun'dane·ly,** *adv.* —Syn. 2. See **earthly.**

Mu·nich (mū'nĭk), *n.* a city in S West Germany: the capital of Bavaria. 968,233 (est. 1955). German, **München. 2.** any dishonorable appeasement. See **Munich Pact.**

Munich Pact, the pact signed by Germany, Great Britain, France, and Italy on September 29, 1938, by which the Sudetenland was ceded to Germany. Also, **Munich Agreement.**

mu·nic·i·pal (mū nĭs'ə pəl), *adj.* **1.** of or pertaining to the local government of a town or city: *municipal elections.* **2.** pertaining to the internal affairs of a state or nation rather than to international affairs. [t. L: s. *mūnicipālis,* der. *mūniceps* citizen of a privileged (sometimes self-governing) town standing in a certain relation to Rome] —**mu·nic'i·pal·ly,** *adv.*

mu·nic·i·pal·i·ty (mū nĭs'ə păl'ə tĭ), *n., pl.* **-ties. 1.** a city, town, or other district possessing corporate existence. **2.** a community under municipal jurisdiction. **3.** the governing body of such a district or community.

mu·nic·i·pal·ize (mū nĭs'ə pə līz'), *v.t.,* **-ized, -izing. 1.** to make a municipality of. **2.** to bring under municipal ownership or control. —**mu·nic'i·pal·i·za'tion,** *n.*

mu·nif·i·cent (mū nĭf'ə sənt), *adj.* **1.** extremely liberal in giving or bestowing; very generous. **2.** characterized by great generosity, as giving, a gift, etc. [back formation from L *mūnificentia* munificence] —**mu·nif'i·cence,** *n.* —**mu·nif'i·cent·ly,** *adv.* —Ant. 1. niggardly.

mu·ni·ment (mū'nə mənt), *n.* **1.** (*pl.*) *Law.* a document, as a title deed or a charter, by which rights or privileges are defended or maintained. **2.** a defense or protection. [ME, t. ML: s. *mūnimentum* document, title deed, L fortification]

mu·ni·tion (mū nĭsh'ən), *n.* **1.** (*usually pl.*) materials used in war, esp. weapons and ammunition. **2.** material or equipment for carrying on any undertaking. —*v.t.* **3.** to provide with munitions. [t. F, t. L: s. *mūnītio* fortification]

Mun·ká·csy (mōōn'kä chĭ), *n.* **Mihály von** (mĭ'häl'ʏ fən), (*Michael Lieb*) 1844–1900, Hungarian painter.

mun·nion (mŭn'yən), *n.* mullion.

Mun·ro (mən rō'), *n.* **Hector Hugh,** (*Saki*) 1870–1916, British author, born in Burma.

Mun·ster (mŭn'stər), *n.* a province in SW Ireland. 876,620 pop. (prelim. 1956); 9316 sq. mi.

Mün·ster (myn'stər), *n.* a city in NW West Germany; treaty of Westphalia, 1648. 155,694 (est. 1955).

Mün·ster·berg (mĭn'stər bûrg'; *Ger.* myn'stərbĕrkʜ), *n.* **Hugo** (hū'gō; *Ger.* hōō'gō), 1863–1916, German psychologist and philosopher, in America.

munt·jac (mŭnt'jăk), *n.* **1.** any of various small deer constituting the genus *Muntiacus,* of southern and eastern Asia and the adjacent islands, esp. *M. muntjac,* of Java, India, etc., having well-developed horns on bony pedicels. **2.** any of the small deer of the related genus *Elaphodus,* of China and Tibet, having minute horns. Also, **munt'jak.** [t. Javanese]

Muntz metal (mŭnts), *Metall.* an alloy containing approximately 60% copper and 40% zinc, harder and stronger than brass.

mu·ral (myŏōr'əl), *adj.* **1.** of or pertaining to a wall; resembling a wall. **2.** executed on or affixed to a wall. —*n.* **3.** a mural painting. [t. F, t. L: s. *mūrālis*]

mural crown, a golden crown formed with indentations to resemble a battlement, bestowed among the ancient Romans on the soldiers who first mounted the wall of a besieged place and there lodged a standard.

Mu·ra·sa·ki no Shi·ki·bu (mōō'rä sä'kē nō shē'kē-bōō), 11th cent., first Japanese writer of a novel. The English title of her novel is *The Tale of Genji.*

Mu·rat (myrä'), *n.* **Joachim** (zhô ä kēm'), 1767–1815, French general, marshal of France, brother-in-law of Napoleon I, and king of Naples, 1808–15.

Mu·rat (mōō rät'), *n.* a river in E Turkey, flowing W to the Euphrates. 425 mi. Also, **Mu·rad Su** (mōō-räd' sōō').

Mur·cia (mōōr'shä; *Sp.* mōōr'thyä, -syä), *n.* **1.** a city in SE Spain. 235,275 (est. 1955). **2.** a region in SE Spain; formerly a kingdom.

mur·der (mûr'dər), *n.* **1.** *Law.* the unlawful killing of another human being with malice aforethought. Special statutory definitions and degrees are common in the U.S. —*v.t.* **2.** *Law.* to kill by an act constituting murder. **3.** to kill or slaughter inhumanly or barbarously. **4.** to spoil or mar by bad execution, representation, pronunciation, etc. —*v.i.* **5.** to commit murder. [ME; var. of MURTHER] —**mur'der·er,** *n.* —**mur'der·ess,** *n. fem.* —Syn. 2. See **kill**[1].

mur·der·ous (mûr'dər əs), *adj.* **1.** of the nature of or involving murder: *a murderous deed.* **2.** guilty of, bent on, or capable of murder. **3.** intentionally deadly. —**mur'der·ous·ly,** *adv.* —**mur'der·ous·ness,** *n.*

Mu·res (mōō'rĕsh), *n.* a river flowing from the Carpathian Mountains in central Rumania W to the Tisza river in S Hungary. ab. 400 mi. Hungarian, **Maros.**

mu·rex (myŏōr'ĕks), *n., pl.* **murices** (myŏōr'ə sēz'), **murexes. 1.** any of the marine gastropods, common in tropical seas, constituting the genus *Murex* or the family *Muricidae,* certain species of which yielded the celebrated purple dye of the ancients. **2.** a shell used as a trumpet, as in representations of Tritons in art. **3.** purplish red. [t. L: the purple fish]

Murex. *Murex tenuispina*

Mur·frees·bor·o (mûr'frĭz bûr'ō), *n.* a city in central Tennessee: the battle of Stone River (or Murfreesboro) was fought near here, Dec. 31, 1862–Jan. 2, 1863. 18,991 (1960).

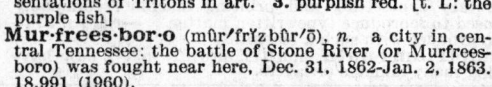

b., blend of, blended; c., cognate with; d., dialect, dialectal; der., derived from; f., formed from; g., going back to; m., modification of; r., replacing; s., stem of; t., taken from; ?, perhaps. See the full key on inside cover.

mu·ri·ate (myŏŏr′ĭ·āt′, -ĭt), *n.* (in industry) any chloride, esp. potassium chloride, KCl, used as a fertilizer. [f. s. L *muria* brine + -ATE²]

mu·ri·at·ed (myŏŏr′ĭ·ā′tĭd), *adj. Obsolesc.* charged with or containing a chloride or chlorides, as mineral waters.

mu·ri·at·ic acid (myŏŏr′ĭ·ăt′ĭk), the commercial name for hydrochloric acid.

Mu·ril·lo (myŏŏ·rĭl′ō; *Sp.* mōō·rē′lyô), *n.* **Bartolomé Esteban** (bär′tô·lô·mā′ ĕs·tĕ′bän), 1617–82, Spanish painter.

mu·rine (myŏŏr′īn, -ĭn), *adj.* **1.** belonging or pertaining to the *Muridae*, the family of rodents that includes the mice and rats, or to the *Murinae*, the subfamily that includes the domestic species. —*n.* **2.** a murine rodent. [t. L: m.s. *mūrīnus* of a mouse]

murk (mûrk), *n.* **1.** darkness. —*adj.* **2.** dark, or with little light, as night, places, etc. Also, **mirk**. [ME *mirke*, OE *myrce*, c. Icel. *myrkr* gloomy]

murk·y (mûr′kĭ), *adj.*, **murkier, murkiest. 1.** intensely dark, gloomy, and cheerless. **2.** obscure or thick with mist, haze, or the like, as the air, etc. Also, **mirky**. —**murk′i·ly**, *adv.* —**murk′i·ness**, *n.* —Syn. **1.** See **dark.** —Ant. **2.** clear.

Mur·man Coast (mŏŏr′män′), an Arctic coastal region in the NW Soviet Union in Europe, on the Kola Peninsula.

Mur·mansk (mŏŏr·mänsk′), *n.* a seaport (ice-free) and railroad terminus in the NW Soviet Union, on the Murman Coast. 168,000 (est. 1956).

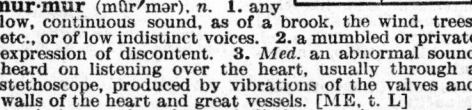

mur·mur (mûr′mər), *n.* **1.** any low, continuous sound, as of a brook, the wind, trees, etc., or of low indistinct voices. **2.** a mumbled or private expression of discontent. **3.** *Med.* an abnormal sound heard on listening over the heart, usually through a stethoscope, produced by vibrations of the valves and walls of the heart and great vessels. [ME, t. L] —*v.i.* **4.** to make a low or indistinct continuous sound. **5.** to speak in a low tone or indistinctly. **6.** to complain in a low tone, or in private. —*v.t.* **7.** to sound by murmurs. **8.** to utter in a low tone. [ME, t. L: s. *murmurāre*] —**mur′mur·er**, *n.* —**mur′mur·ing**, *adj., n.* —**mur′mur·ing·ly**, *adv.*
—Syn. **8.** MURMUR, MUMBLE, MUTTER mean to make sounds which are not fully intelligible. To MURMUR is to utter sounds or words in a low, almost inaudible tone, as in expressing blandishments, affection, dissatisfaction, etc : *to murmur disagreement.* To MUMBLE is to utter imperfect or inarticulate sounds with the mouth partly closed, so that the words can be distinguished only with difficulty: *to mumble the answer to a question.* To MUTTER is to utter words in a low, grumbling way, often voicing complaint or discontent, not meant to be fully audible: *to mutter complaints.* **6.** See **complain.**

mur·mur·ous (mûr′mər·əs), *adj.* **1.** abounding in or characterized by murmurs. **2.** murmuring: *murmurous waters.* —**mur′mur·ous·ly**, *adv.*

mur·phy (mûr′fĭ), *n., pl.* **-phies.** *Slang.* an Irish or white potato. [special use of *Murphy*, Irish surname]

mur·rain (mûr′ĭn), *n.* **1.** any of various diseases of cattle, as anthrax, foot-and-mouth disease, and Texas fever. **2.** *Archaic.* a plague or pestilence (esp. in curses). [ME *moryne*, t. F: m. *morine* plague, der. L *morī* die]

Mur·ray (mûr′ĭ), *n.* **1.** **Sir George Gilbert Aimé** (ā·mā′), 1866–1957, British classical scholar. **2. Sir James Augustus Henry,** 1837–1915, British lexicographer and linguist. **3. Lindley,** 1745–1826, British grammarian, born in the U.S. **4. Philip,** 1886–1952, U.S. labor leader, born in Scotland. **5.** a river in SE Australia, flowing along the border between Victoria and New South Wales and through SE South Australia into the ocean. ab. 1500 mi.

murre (mûr), *n.* **1.** either of two species of northern diving birds of the genus *Uria*, the thick-billed **Brunnich's murre** (*U. omvia*) or the slender-billed **common murre** (*U. aalge*). **2.** *Colloq.* the razor-billed auk.

murre·let (mûr′lĭt), *n.* any of several small, chunky diving birds found principally about the islands and coasts of the north Pacific, as the **marbled murrelet,** *Brachyramphus marmoratus.*

mur·rey (mûr′ĭ), *n.* a dark purplish-red color. [ME *morrey*, t. OF: m. *more*, der. L *mōrum* mulberry]

mur·rhine (mûr′ĭn, -īn), *adj.* pertaining to a stone or substance of Roman times used for wine cups and other vessels. Also, **mur′rine.** [t. L: m.s. *murr(h)īnus*]

murrhine glass, 1. any kind of glassware supposed to resemble the Roman cups of murrhine. **2.** a ware composed of glass in which metals, precious stones, or the like are embedded.

Mur·rum·bidg·ee (mûr′əm·bĭj′ĭ), *n.* a river in SE Australia, flowing W through New South Wales to the Murray river. ab. 1350 mi.

mur·ther (mûr′thər), *n.*, *v.t., v.i. Obs.* murder. [ME *morther*, OE *morthor*, c. Goth. *maurthr*]

Mus., **1.** museum. **2.** music. **3.** musical. **4.** musician.

mu·sa·ceous (mū·zā′shəs), *adj.* belonging to the *Musaceae*, or banana family of plants. [f. s. NL *Mūsāceae* (der. *Musa*, the typical genus, t. Ar.: m. *mawza* banana, prob. of East Ind. orig.) + -OUS]

Mus.B., (L *Musicae Baccalaureus*) Bachelor of Music. Also, **Mus.Bac.**

mus·ca·delle (mŭs′kə·dĕl′), *n.* a grape variety of the aromatic muscat family grown in France. [ME, t. OF: m. *muscadel*, der. Pr. *muscat* MUSCAT]

mus·ca·dine (mŭs′kə·dĭn, -dīn′), *n.* a grape variety, *Vitis rotundifolia*, indigenous to America, esp. scuppernong (white-skinned) and James (black-skinned).

mus·cae vo·li·tan·tes (mŭs′sē vŏl′ĭ·tăn′tēz), specks that seem to dance in the air before the eyes, due to defects in the vitreous humor of the eye or to other causes. [NL: flies flying about]

mus·cat (mŭs′kət, -kăt), *n.* a grape variety with pronounced pleasant sweet aroma and flavor, much used for making wine. [t. F, t. Pr., der. LL *muscus* MUSK]

Mus·cat (mŭs·kăt′), *n.* a seaport in SE Arabia: capital of Muscat and Oman. 5500 (est. 1954). Arabic, **Masqat.**

mus·ca·tel (mŭs′kə·tĕl′, mŭs′kə·tĕl′), *n.* **1.** a sweet wine made from muscat grapes. **2.** the muscat grape. [var. of MUSCADELLE. Cf. OF *muscatel*]

mus·cid (mŭs′ĭd), *adj.* **1.** belonging or pertaining to the *Muscidae*, the family of dipterous insects that includes the common housefly. —*n.* **2.** any muscid fly. [t. NL: s. *Muscidae*, pl., der. L *musca* a fly]

mus·cle (mŭs′əl), *n., v.*, **-cled, -cling.** —*n.* **1.** a discrete bundle or sheet of contractile fibres having the function of producing movement in the animal body. **2.** the tissue of such an organ. **3.** muscular strength; brawn. —*v.i.* **4.** *Colloq.* to make or shove one's way by sheer brawn or force. [t. F, t. L: m.s. *musculus* muscle, lit., little mouse (from the appearance of certain muscles)]

mus·cle-bound (mŭs′əl·bound′), *adj.* having muscles enlarged and inelastic, as from excessive athletics.

muscle plasma, the juice that can be expressed from fresh muscle.

muscle sense, *Psychol., Physiol.* a sense of movement derived from afferent nerves originating in tendons, muscle tissue, skin, and joints.

Muscle Shoals, formerly rapids in the Tennessee river, in NW Alabama: now changed into a lake by Wilson Dam; part of the Tennessee Valley Authority.

muscle spindles, *Anat.* the sensory end organs in skeletal muscle.

mus·cone (mŭs′kōn), *n.* a large cyclic ketone, $C_{16}H_{30}O$, obtained from musk and used in the perfume industry.

mus·co·va·do (mŭs′kə·vä′dō), *n.* raw or unrefined sugar, obtained from the juice of the sugar cane by evaporation and draining off the molasses. [t. Pg.: m. (*açucar*) *mascavado* (sugar) of inferior quality, pp. of *mascavar* diminish]

mus·co·vite (mŭs′kə·vīt′), *n.* common light-colored mica, essentially $KAl_3Si_3O_{10}(OH)_2$, used as an electrical insulator. [formerly called Muscovy glass. See -ITE¹]

Mus·co·vy (mŭs′kə·vĭ), *n.* *Archaic.* Russia. —**Mus′co·vite′,** *n., adj.* —**Mus′co·vit′ic,** *adj.*

Muscovy duck, a large, crested, Neotropical duck, *Cairina moschata*, which has been widely domesticated. Wild birds are glossy-black with a large white patch on each wing. [erroneous var. of *musk-duck*]

mus·cu·lar (mŭs′kyə·lər), *adj.* **1.** of or pertaining to muscle or the muscles. **2.** dependent on or affected by the muscles: *muscular strength.* **3.** having well-developed muscles; brawny. —**mus·cu·lar·i·ty** (mŭs′kyə·lăr′ə·tĭ), *n.* —**mus′cu·lar·ly,** *adv.* —Syn. **3.** sinewy; strong, powerful; stalwart, sturdy.

muscular dystrophy, a disease of unknown origin which produces a progressive muscular deterioration and wasting, robbing the muscles of all vitality until the patient is completely helpless.

mus·cu·la·ture (mŭs′kyə·lə·chər), *n.* the muscular system of the body or of its parts. [t. F, der. L *musculus* MUSCLE]

Mus.D., (L *Musicae Doctor*) Doctor of Music. Also, **Mus.Doc., Mus.Dr.**

muse (mūz), *v.*, **mused, musing.** —*v.i.* **1.** to reflect or meditate in silence, as on some subject, often as in a reverie. **2.** to gaze meditatively or wonderingly. —*v.t.* **3.** to meditate on. [ME *muse*(n), t. OF: m. *muser* ponder, loiter, trifle (cf. AMUSE), der. *muse* muzzle] —**mus′er,** *n.*

Muse (mūz), *n.* **1.** *Class. Myth.* **a.** any of the nine sister goddesses, daughters of Zeus and Mnemosyne, presiding over poetry and song, the drama, dancing, astronomy, etc.: Calliope, Clio, Erato, Euterpe, Melpomene, Polyhymnia, Terpsichore, Thalia, Urania. **b.** some other goddess supposed to preside over a particular field. **2.** (*sometimes l.c.*) the goddess or the power regarded as inspiring a poet. **3.** (*l.c.*) a poet's characteristic genius or powers. [ME, t. OF, t. L: m. *mūsa*, t. Gk.: m. *Moûsa*]

muse·ful (mūz′fəl), *adj.* deeply thoughtful.

mu·sette bag (mū·zĕt′), a small leather or canvas bag for personal belongings of army officers, carried by a shoulder strap. [*musette*, t. F]

mu·se·um (mū·zē′əm), *n.* a building or place for the keeping and exhibition of works of art, scientific specimens, etc. [t. L, t. Gk.: m. *mouseîon* seat of the Muses, place of study, library]

mush¹ (mŭsh), *n.* **1.** *U.S.* meal, esp. corn meal, boiled in water or milk until it forms a thick, soft mass. **2.** any thick, soft mass. **3.** anything unpleasantly lacking in firmness, force, dignity, etc. **4.** *Colloq.* weak or maudlin sentiment or sentimental language. [b. (obs.) *moose* thick vegetable porridge (t. D: m. *moes*) and MASH, n.]

mush² (mŭsh), *v.t.* **1.** to go or travel on foot, esp. over the snow with a dog team. —*interj.* **2.** an order to start or speed up a dog team. —*n.* **3.** a march on foot, esp. over the snow with a dog team. [? t. F: m. *marche* or *marchons,* impr. of *marcher* advance] —**mush′er,** *n.*

mush·room (mŭsh′rōōm, -rŏŏm), *n.* **1.** any of various fleshy fungi including the toadstools, puffballs, coral fungi, morels, etc. **2.** any of certain edible species belonging to the family *Agaricaceae,* usually of umbrella shape. Cf. **toadstool. 3.** the common **meadow mushroom,** *Agaricus campestris,* or related forms grown for the market. **4.** anything of similar shape or correspondingly rapid growth. —*adj.* **5.** of, pertaining to, or made of mushrooms. **6.** resembling or suggesting a mushroom in shape. **7.** of rapid growth and, often, brief duration: *mushroom fame.* —*v.i.* **8.** to gather mushrooms. **9.** to have or assume the shape of a mushroom. **10.** to spread or grow quickly, as mushrooms. [late ME, t. F: m. *mousseron,* g. LL *mussiriōne*]

mush·y (mŭsh′ĭ), *adj.,* **mushier, mushiest. 1.** mushlike; pulpy. **2.** *Colloq.* weakly sentimental: *a mushy valentine.* —**mush′i·ly,** *adv.* —**mush′i·ness,** *n.*

mu·sic (mū′zĭk), *n.* **1.** an art of sound in time which expresses ideas and emotions in significant forms through the elements of rhythm, melody, harmony, and color. **2.** the tones or sounds employed, occurring in single line (melody) or multiple lines (harmony), and sounded or to be sounded by voice(s) or/and instrument(s). **3.** musical work or compositions for singing or playing. **4.** the written or printed score of a musical composition. **5.** such scores collectively. **6.** any sweet, pleasing, or harmonious sounds or sound: *the music of the waves.* **7.** appreciation of or responsiveness to musical sounds or harmonies **8.** *Fox Hunting.* the cries of the hounds. [ME *musik,* t. L: m.s. *mūsica,* t. Gk.: m. *mousikē (téchnē)* orig., any art over which the Muses presided]

mu·si·cal (mū′zə kəl), *adj.* **1.** of, pertaining to, or producing music: *a musical instrument.* **2.** of the nature of or resembling music; melodious; harmonious. **3.** fond of or skilled in music. **4.** set to or accompanied by music: *a musical melodrama.* —*n.* **5.** musical comedy. —**mu′si·cal·ly,** *adv.* —**mu′si·cal·ness,** *n.*

musical comedy, a play with music, often of a whimsical or satirical nature, based on a slight plot with singing and dancing in solos and groups.

mu·si·cale (mū′zĭ kăl′), *n.* a program of music forming part of a social occasion. [t. F: (fem.) in phrase *soirée* (or *matinée) musicale* an evening (or afternoon) musical party]

music box, a box or case containing an apparatus for producing music mechanically, as by means of a comblike steel plate with tuned teeth sounded by small pegs or pins in the surface of a revolving cylinder or disk. Also, *Brit.,* **musical box.**

music hall, 1. a hall for musical entertainments. **2.** *Chiefly Brit.* a hall or theater for vaudeville.

mu·si·cian (mū zĭsh′ən), *n.* **1.** one who makes music a profession, esp. as a performer on an instrument. **2.** one skilled in music. —**mu·si′cian·ly,** *adj.*

music of the spheres, a music, imperceptible to human ears, formerly supposed to be produced by the movements of the spheres or heavenly bodies

mu·si·col·o·gy (mū′zĭ kŏl′ə jĭ), *n.* the scholarly or scientific study of music, as in historical research, musical theory, the physical nature of sound, etc. —**mu′si·col′o·gist,** *n.*

mus·ing (mū′zĭng), *adj.* **1.** absorbed in thought; meditative. —*n.* **2.** contemplation. —**mus′ing·ly,** *adv.*

mus·jid (mŭs′jĭd), *n.* masjid.

musk (mŭsk), *n.* **1.** a substance secreted in a glandular sac under the skin of the abdomen of the male musk deer, having a strong odor, and used in perfumery. **2.** an artificial imitation of the substance. **3.** a similar secretion of other animals, as the civet, muskrat, otter, etc. **4.** the odor, or some similar odor. **5.** *Bot.* any of several plants, as the monkey flower, having a musky fragrance. [ME *muske,* var. of *musco,* t. LL, abl. of *muscus,* t. LGk.: m. *móschos,* t. Pers.: m. *mushk*]

musk deer, a small, hornless animal of the deer kind, *Moschus moschiferus,* of central Asia, the male of which secretes musk and has large canine teeth.

musk duck, 1. Muscovy duck. **2.** an Australian duck, *Biziura lobata.*

mus·keg (mŭs′kĕg), *n.* a bog formed in hollows or depressions of the land surface by the accumulation of water and growth of sphagnum mosses. [t. Amer. Ind. (Ojibwa, Kickapoo) grassy bog]

Mus·ke·gon (mŭs kē′gən), *n.* a city in W Michigan; a port on Lake Michigan. 46,485 (1960).

mus·kel·lunge (mŭs′kə lŭnj′), *n., pl.* **-lunge.** a large game fish, *Esox masquinongy,* of the pike family, of the lakes and rivers of eastern and middle western North America. Also, **maskalonge.** [appar. dissimilated var. of *muscanonge, maskinonge,* t. N Amer. Ind. (Ojibwa): m. *mashkinonge,* f. *mash* great + *kinonge* pike]

mus·ket (mŭs′kĭt), *n.* a hand gun for infantry soldiers, introduced in the 16th century, the predecessor of the modern rifle. [t. F: m. *mousquet,* t. It.: m. *moschetto,* orig. a kind of hawk, der. *mosca* a fly, g. L *musca*]

mus·ket·eer (mŭs′kə tĭr′), *n.* a soldier armed with a musket. [f. MUSKET + -EER, modeled on F *mousquetaire*]

mus·ket·ry (mŭs′kĭt rĭ), *n.* **1.** practice in group combat firing with rifles. **2.** muskets collectively. **3.** troops armed with muskets.

Mus·kho·ge·an (mŭs kō′gĭ ən), *n.* a family of American Indian languages of southeastern U.S., including Choctaw, Chickasaw, and Creek (also called **Muskogee** in Oklahoma and **Seminole** in Florida). Also, **Mus·ko′ge·an.**

musk·mel·on (mŭsk′mĕl′ən), *n.* **1.** a kind of melon, of many varieties, a round or oblong fruit with a juicy, often aromatically sweet, edible flesh (yellow, white, or green). **2.** the plant, *Cucumis melo,* bearing it.

Mus·ko·gee (mŭs kō′gĭ), *n.* **1.** a city in E Oklahoma. 38,059 (1960). **2.** See **Muskhogean.**

White-faced musk ox,
Ovibos moschatus
(Ab. 5 ft. high at the shoulder,
total length 8 ft.)

musk ox, a bovine ruminant, *Ovibos moschatus,* between the ox and the sheep in size and anatomy, and having a musky odor. It is native to arctic America.

musk·rat (mŭsk′răt), *n., pl.* **-rats,** (*esp. collectively*) **-rat. 1.** a large aquatic North American rodent, *Ondatra zibethica,* with a musky odor. **2.** its thick light-brown fur.

musk rose, a species of rose, *Rosa moschata,* having fragrant white flowers.

musk·y[1] (mŭs′kĭ), *adj.,* **muskier, muskiest.** of or like musk, as odors; having an odor like that of musk. [f. MUSK + -Y[1]]

mus·ky[2] (mŭs′kĭ), *n., pl.* **muskies.** *Colloq.* muskellunge.

Muskrat, *Ondatra zibethica*
(Total length 22 to 23 in., tail 10 in.

Mus·lem (mŭz′ləm, mŭs′-), *n., adj.* Moslem. Also, **Mus′lim.**

mus·lin (mŭz′lĭn), *n.* **1.** a cotton fabric made in various degrees of fineness, and often printed, woven, or embroidered in patterns; esp., a cotton fabric of plain weave, used for sheets and for a variety of other purposes. **2.** *Naut. Slang.* sails. [t. F: m. *mousseline,* t. It.: m. *mussolina* muslin, der. *Mussolo* Mosul, city in Iraq]

mus·quash (mŭs′kwŏsh), *n.* muskrat. [t. Algonquian languages of Va. (Abnaki, Ojibwa): it is red]

muss (mŭs), *n. Colloq.* **1.** a state of disorder. **2.** an untidy or dirty mess. —*v.t.* **3.** *U.S. Dial.* to put into disorder; make untidy or messy; rumple. [alter. of MESS]

mus·sel (mŭs′əl), *n.* any bivalve mollusk, esp. an edible marine bivalve of the family *Mytilidae* and a freshwater clam of the family *Unionidae.* [ME and OE *muscle,* t. LL: m.s. *muscula,* var. of L *musculus* MUSCLE, mussel]

Mus·set (my sĕ′), *n.* **Alfred de** (ál frĕd′ də), (*Louis Charles Alfred de Musset*) 1810–57, French poet, dramatist, and writer of stories.

Mus·so·li·ni (mŏŏs′ə lē′nĭ; *It.* mōōs′sō lē′nē), *n.* **Benito** (bĕ nē′tō), (*Il Duce*) 1883–1945, Italian Fascist leader and prime minister of Italy, 1922–43.

Mus·sorg·sky (mŏŏ sôrg′skĭ), *n.* **Modest Petrovich** (mŏ dĕst′ pĕ trô′vĭch), Moussorgsky.

Mus·sul·man (mŭs′əl mən), *n., pl.* **-mans.** a Mohammedan. [t. Pers.: m. *musulmān,* der. *muslim* MOSLEM, t. Ar. (with the Pers. pl. ending -ān)]

muss·y (mŭs′ĭ), *adj.,* **mussier, mussiest.** *Colloq.* untidy, messy, or rumpled.

must[1] (mŭst), *aux. v.* **1.** to be bound by some imperative requirement to: *I must keep my word.* **2.** to be obliged or compelled to, as by some constraining force or necessity: *man must eat to live.* **3.** may reasonably be supposed to: *it must be a large sum now.* **4.** to be inevitably certain to: *it must seem strange.* **5.** to have to; ought to; should: *I must go soon.* **6.** (sometimes used with ellipsis of *go, get,* or some similar verb readily understood from the context): *we must away.* —*adj.* **7.** necessary; vital: *must legislation.* —*n.* **8.** anything necessary or vital: *this law is a must.* [ME *most(e),* OE *mōste,* pret. (pres. *mōt*) akin to D *moeten,* G *müssen* be obliged]

—**Syn. 5.** MUST, OUGHT, SHOULD express necessity or duty. MUST expresses necessity, or compulsion: *all men must die, I must answer this letter, soldiers must obey orders.* OUGHT (weaker than MUST) expresses obligation, duty, desirability: *you ought to tell your mother.* SHOULD expresses obligation, expectation, or probability (*you are not behaving as you should; children should be taugh' to speak the truth; they should arrive at one o'clock*); it also expresses the conditional (*I should be glad to play if I could*) and future intention (*I said I should be at home next week*).

must[2] (mŭst), *n.* new wine; the unfermented juice as pressed from the grape or other fruit. [ME and OE, t. L: s. *mustum,* short for *vīnum mustum* fresh wine]

mus·tache (mŭs′tăsh, məs tăsh′), *n.* **1.** the hair growing on the upper lip, or on either half of the upper lip, of men. **2.** hairs or bristles growing near the mouth of an animal. **3.** a stripe of color, or elongated feathers, suggestive of a mustache on the side of the head of a bird. Also, *esp. Brit.,* **moustache.** [t. F: m. *moustache,* t. It.: m. *mostaccio,* ult. t. Gk.: m. *mýstax* upper lip, mustache]

mus·ta·chio (mŭs tä′shō), *n., pl.* **-chios.** a mustache.

Mus·ta·fa Ke·mal Pa·sha (mŏŏs′tä fä kə mäl′ pä-shä′), former name of **Kemal Atatürk.**

mus·tang (mŭs′tăng), n. the small, wild or half-wild horse of the American plains, descended from Spanish stock. [t. Sp.: m. *mestengo* wild]

mus·tard (mŭs′tərd), n. 1. a pungent powder or paste prepared from the seed of the mustard plant, much used as a food seasoning or condiment, and medicinally in plasters, poultices, etc. 2. any of various brassicaceous plants, esp. *Brassica hirta* (B. alba) (**white mustard**), *B. juncea* (**leaf mustard**), *B. nigra* (**black mustard**), and others cultivated for their seed. [ME, t. OF: m. *moustarde*, orig. powdered mustard seed and must, der. *moust*, g. L *mustum* MUST²]

mustard gas, a liquid chemical-warfare agent, (ClCH₂CH₂)₂S, producing burns, blindness, and death, introduced by the Germans in World War I.

mustard oil, oil expressed from the seed of mustard, esp. a carbylamine (a drying oil) used in making soap.

mustard plaster, a powdered, black, mustard and rubber solution mixture placed on a cloth and used as a counterirritant.

mus·tee (mŭs tē′, mŭs′tē), n. 1. the offspring of a white person and a quadroon. 2. a half-breed. [t. Sp.: m. *mestizo*]

mus·te·line (mŭs′tə līn′, -lĭn), adj. 1. belonging or pertaining to the family *Mustelidae*, including the martens, skunks, minks, weasels, badgers, otters, etc. 2. weasellike. 3. tawny or brown, like a weasel in summer. [t. L: m.s. *mustēlinus* belonging to a weasel]

mus·ter (mŭs′tər), v.t. 1. to assemble (troops, a ship's crew, etc.), as for battle, display, inspection, orders, discharge, etc. 2. to gather or summon (often fol. by *up*): *he mustered up all his courage.* 3. *Naut.* to call the roll of. 4. **muster in** (or **out**), to enlist in (or discharge from) military service. —v.i. 5. to assemble for inspection, service, etc., as troops or forces. 6. to come together, collect, or gather. —n. 7. an assembling of troops or men for inspection or other purposes. 8. an assemblage or collection. 9. act of mustering. 10. Also, **muster roll.** (formerly) a list of the men enrolled in a military or naval unit. 11. **pass muster**, to measure up to specified standards. [ME *mostre*(n), t. OF: m. *mosstrer*, g. L *monstrāre* show] —Syn. 1, 2. See **gather.**

mus·ty (mŭs′tĭ), adj., -tier, -tiest. 1. having an odor or flavor suggestive of mold, as old buildings, long-closed rooms, food, etc. 2. staled by time, or antiquated: *musty laws.* 3. dull; apathetic. [var. of *moisty* (f. MOIST + -Y¹), with loss of *i* before *s*] —mus′ti·ly, adv. —mus′ti·ness, n.

mut (mŭt), n. *Slang.* mutt.

mu·ta·ble (mū′tə bəl), adj. 1. liable or subject to change or alteration. 2. given to changing, or ever changing; fickle or inconstant: *the mutable ways of fortune.* [ME, t. L: m.s. *mūtābilis*] —mu·ta·bil′i·ty, mu′ta·ble·ness, n. —mu′ta·bly, adv.

mu·tant (mū′tənt), adj. 1. undergoing mutation; resulting from mutation. —n. 2. a new type of organism produced as the result of mutation. [t. L: s. *mūtans*, ppr., changing]

mu·ta·ro·ta·tion (mū′tə rō tā′shən), n. *Chem.* a change in the optical rotation of fresh solutions of reducing sugars with time.

mu·tate (mū′tāt), v., -tated, -tating. —v.t. 1. to change; alter. 2. *Phonet.* to change by umlaut. —v.i. 3. to change; undergo mutation. —mu·ta·tive (mū′tə tĭv), adj.

mu·ta·tion (mū tā′shən), n. 1. act or process of changing. 2. a change or alternation, as in form, qualities, or nature. 3. *Biol.* a. a sudden departure from the parent type, as when an individual differs from its parents in one or more heritable characteristics, caused by a change in a gene or a chromosome. b. an individual, species, or the like, resulting from such a departure. 4. *Phonet.* umlaut. [ME, t. L: m.s. *mūtātio*] —mu·ta′tion·al, adj. —mu·ta·tive (mū′tə tĭv), adj.

mu·ta·tis mu·tan·dis (mū tä′tĭs mū tăn′dĭs), *Latin.* with the necessary changes.

mutch (mŭch), n. *Scot. and Brit. Dial.* a cap worn by women and young children. [late ME, t. MD: m.s. *mutse*, c. G *mütze* cap]

mutch·kin (mŭch′kĭn), n. *Scot.* a unit of liquid measure equal to a little less than a U.S. liquid pint. [t. early mod. D: m. *mudseken* a measure]

mute (mūt), adj., n., v., muted, muting. —adj. 1. silent; refraining from speech or utterance. 2. not emitting or having sound of any kind. 3. incapable of speech; dumb. 4. *Gram.* (of letters) silent; not pronounced. 5. *Law.* making no response when arraigned, as a prisoner in **to stand mute**, now resulting in the entry of a plea of "not guilty." —n. 6. one unable to utter words. 7. an actor whose part is confined to dumb show. 8. *Law.* a person who makes no response when arraigned. 9. *Brit. Obs.* a hired attendant at a funeral. 10. a mechanical device of various shapes and materials for muffling the tone of a musical instrument. 11. *Phonetics.* a stop. 12. (of a letter) not pronounced. —v.t. 13. to deaden or muffle the sound of (a musical instrument, etc.). [t. L: m.s. *mūtus* silent, dumb; r. ME *muet*, t. OF] —mute′ly, adv. —mute′ness, n. —Syn. 3. See **dumb.**

mu·ti·late (mū′tə lāt′), v.t., -lated, -lating. 1. to deprive (a person or animal, the body, etc.) of a limb or other important part or parts. 2. to injure, disfigure, or make imperfect by removing or irreparably damaging parts. [t. L: m.s. *mutilātus*, pp., cut off, maimed] —mu′ti·la′tion, n. —mu′ti·la′tive, adj. —mu′ti·la′tor, n. —Syn. 1. See **maim.**

mu·ti·neer (mū′tə nĭr′), n. one guilty of mutiny. [t. F (obs.): m. *mutinier*, der. *mutin* rebellious, der. OF *muete* rebellion, orig. pp., der. L *movēre* move]

mu·ti·nous (mū′tə nəs), adj. 1. disposed to, engaged in, or involving revolt against constituted authority. 2. characterized by mutiny; rebellious. —mu′ti·nous·ly, adv. —mu′ti·nous·ness, n.

mu·ti·ny (mū′tə nĭ), n., pl. -nies, v., -nied, -nying. —n. 1. revolt, or a revolt or rebellion, against constituted authority, esp. by soldiers or seamen. —v.i. 2. to commit the offense of mutiny; revolt against constituted authority: *Some of the crew mutinied but they were quickly overpowered.* [f. (obs.) *mutin*, adj., mutinous (t. F) + -Y¹] —mu′ti·ny, mu·tin·ous·ly, adv.

mut·ism (mū′tĭz əm), n. *Psychiatry.* a conscious or unconscious refusal to respond verbally to interrogation, present in some mental disorders. [t. F: m. *mutisme*, der. L *mūtus* mute, adj.]

Mu·tsu·hi·to (mŏŏ′tsŏŏ hē′tō), n. 1852–1912, emperor of Japan, 1867–1912.

mutt (mŭt), n. *Slang.* 1. a dog, esp. a mongrel. 2. a simpleton; a stupid person. Also, **mut.** [orig. obscure; ? shortened from *muttonhead*]

mut·ter (mŭt′ər), v.i. 1. to utter words indistinctly or in a low tone, often in talking to oneself or in making obscure complaints, threats, etc.; murmur; grumble. 2. to make a low, rumbling sound. —v.t. 3. to utter indistinctly or in a low tone. —n. 4. the act or utterance of one that mutters. [ME *moter*(e), ? freq. of (obs.) *moot*, v., speak, murmur, OE *mōtian* speak in public. Cf. d. G *muttern*] —mut′ter·er, n. —mut′ter·ing·ly, adv. —Syn. 1. See **murmur.**

mut·ton (mŭt′ən), n. 1. the flesh of sheep, used as food. 2. the flesh of the well-grown or more mature sheep, as distinguished from lamb. [ME *moton*, t. OF; of Celtic orig.] —mut′ton·y, adj.

mutton chop, 1. a rib piece of mutton having the bone chopped off at the small end, or some similar piece, for broiling or frying. 2. (pl.) side whiskers shaped like a mutton chop, narrow at the top, and broad and trimmed short at the bottom, the chin being shaved both in front and beneath.

Mut·tra (mŭt′rə), n. former name of Mathura.

mu·tu·al (mū′chŏŏ əl), adj. 1. possessed, experienced, performed, etc., by each of two or more with respect to the other or others; reciprocal: *mutual aid.* 2. having the same relation each toward the other or others: *mutual foes.* 3. of or pertaining to each of two or more, or common: *mutual acquaintance.* 4. pertaining to mutual insurance: *a mutual company.* [late ME, f. s. L *mūtuus* reciprocal + -AL¹] —mu′tu·al·ly, adv. —Syn. 1. MUTUAL, RECIPROCAL agree in the idea of an exchange or balance between two or more persons or groups. MUTUAL indicates an exchange of a feeling, obligation,etc., between two or more people, or an interchange of some kind between persons or things: *mutual esteem, in mutual agreement.* It is not properly a synonym for COMMON, though often used in that sense (shared by, or pertaining to two or more things), esp. in the phrase *a mutual friend* (a friend of each of two or more other persons). RECIPROCAL indicates a relation in which one act, thing, feeling, etc., balances or is given in return for another: *reciprocal promises or favors.*

mutual insurance, insurance in which those insured become members of a company who reciprocally engage, by payment of certain amounts into a common fund, to indemnify one another against loss.

mu·tu·al·i·ty (mū′chŏŏ ăl′ə tĭ), n. condition or quality of being mutual; reciprocity; mutual dependence.

mu·tu·al·ize (mū′chŏŏ ə līz′), v., -ized, -izing. —v.t. 1. to make mutual. 2. to incorporate with employee or customer ownership of the major or controlling portion of issued shares. —v.i. 3. to become mutual. —mu′tu·al·i·za′tion, n.

mutual savings bank, a noncapitalized savings bank distributing its profits to depositors.

mu·tule (mū′chŏŏl), n. *Archit.* a projecting flat block under the corona of the Doric cornice, corresponding to the modillion of other orders. [t. F, t. L: m.s. *mūtulus* modillion]

mu·zhik (mŏŏ zhĭk′, mŏŏ′zhĭk), n. a Russian peasant. Also, **moujik, mujik, mu·zjik′.** [t. Russ.]

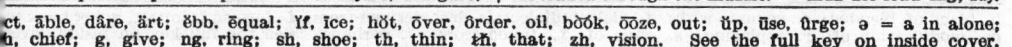

M. Greek mutule

muz·zle (mŭz′əl), n., v., -zled, -zling. —n. 1. the mouth, or end for discharge, of the barrel of a gun, pistol, etc. 2. the projecting part of the head of an animal, including jaws, mouth, and nose. 3. a device, usually an arrangement of straps or wires, placed over an animal's mouth to prevent the animal from biting, eating, etc. —v.t. 4. to put a muzzle on (an animal or its mouth) so as to prevent biting, eating, etc. 5. to restrain from speech or the expression of opinion; gag: *They tried to muzzle him but he insisted on finishing his speech.* [ME *mosel*, t. OF: m. *musel*, der. *muse* muzzle; orig. uncert.] —muz′zler, n.

muz·zle·load·er (mŭz′əl lō′dər), n. a firearm which is loaded through the muzzle. —muz′zle·load′ing, adj.

ct, āble, dâre, ärt; ĕbb, ēqual; Yf, īce; hŏt, ōver, ôrder, oil, bŏŏk, ōōze, out; ŭp, ūse, ûrge; ə = a in alone; th, chief; g, give; ng, ring; sh, shoe; th, thin; ŧħ, that; zh, vision. See the full key on inside cover.

muzzle velocity, *Ordn.* the speed of a projectile in foot-seconds as it leaves a gun muzzle.

muz·zy (mŭz′Y), *adj.,* **-zier, -ziest.** *Colloq.* confused; indistinct. **—muz′zi·ly,** *adv.* **—muz′zi·ness,** *n.*

m.v., (It. *mezza voce*) *Music.* with half the power of the voice; softly.

M.W.A., Modern Woodmen of America.

Mwe·ru (mwā′rōō), *n.* a lake in S Africa between the Belgian Congo and Northern Rhodesia. 68 mi. long.

my (mī), *pron.* **1.** the possessive form corresponding to *I* and *me,* used before a noun: *my house.* **—interj. 2.** *Colloq.* an exclamation of surprise: *Oh, my!* [ME *mī,* apocopated var. of *min,* OE *mīn.* See MINE[1]]

my-, a word element meaning "muscle." Also, **myo-.** [t. Gk., comb. form of *mŷs*]

my·al·gi·a (mīăl′jY′ə), *n.* *Pathol.* pain in the muscles; muscular rheumatism.

my·as·the·ni·a (mī′əsthē′nY′ə), *n.* *Pathol.* muscle weakness.

myc-, a word element meaning "fungus." Also, **myco-.** [comb. form repr. Gk. *mŷkēs*]

my·ce·li·um (mīsē′lY′əm), *n., pl.* **-lia** (-lY′ə). *Bot.* the vegetative part or thallus of the fungi, when composed of one or more filamentous elements, or hyphae. [t. NL, der. Gk. *mŷkēs*] **—my·ce·loid** (mī′sə loid′), *adj.*

My·ce·nae (mīsē′nē), *n.* an ancient city in S Greece, in Argolis: notable ruins.

My·ce·nae·an (mī′sYnē′ən), *adj.* **1.** of or pertaining to the ancient city of Mycenae. **2.** denoting or pertaining to the Aegean civilization which flourished there (c1400 B.C. to c1100 B.C.).

-mycetes, *Bot.* a word element meaning "fungus," as in *myxomycetes.* [comb. form repr. pl. of Gk. *mŷkēs* fungus]

my·ce·to·zo·an (mīsē′tə zō′ən), *adj.* **1.** of or pertaining to the *Mycetozoa.* **—n. 2.** any of the *Mycetozoa,* (*Myxomycetes,* slime molds), a group of very primitive organisms lying near the border line between the plant and animal worlds. [f. *myceto-,* var. of MYC- + -ZOAN]

myco-, var. of **myc-,** before consonants, as in *mycology.*

my·co·bac·te·ri·um (mī′kō băk tYr′Y əm), *n., pl.* **-teria** (-tYr′Y ə). any of a group of bacteria, difficult to stain but which, once stained, hold stain tenaciously and are acid- and alcohol-fast. Mycobacteria produce human and bovine or mammalian tuberculosis, avian tuberculosis, tuberculosis of cold-blooded animals, and leprosy. [t. NL. See MYCO-, BACTERIUM]

my·col·o·gy (mīkŏl′ə jY), *n.* **1.** the branch of botany that treats of fungi. **2.** the fungi found in an area. **—my·col′o·gist,** *n.*

my·co·sis (mīkō′sYs), *n.* **1.** *Pathol.* the presence of parasitic fungi in or on any part of the body. **2.** a disease caused by them. [t. NL. See MYC-, -OSIS] **—my·cot·ic** (mīkŏt′Yk), *adj.*

my·dri·a·sis (mY′drī′ə sYs, mī-), *n.* *Pathol.* excessive dilatation of the pupil of the eye, as the result of disease, drugs, or the like. [t. L, t. Gk.]

myd·ri·at·ic (mYd′rY ăt′Yk), *adj.* **1.** pertaining to or producing mydriasis. **—n. 2.** a mydriatic drug.

myel-, a word element meaning "marrow" or "of the spinal cord." [t. Gk., comb. form of *myelós* marrow]

my·e·len·ceph·a·lon (mī′ə lĕn sĕf′ə lŏn′), *n.* *Anat.* the posterior segment of the brain, practically coextensive with the medulla oblongata; the afterbrain.

my·e·lin (mī′ə lYn), *n.* *Anat.* a soft, white, fatty substance encasing the axis cylinder of certain nerve fibers. Also, **my·e·line** (mī′ə lēn′). [t. G. See MYEL-, -IN[2]]

my·e·li·tis (mī′ə lī′tYs), *n.* *Pathol.* inflammation of the substance of the spinal cord.

my·e·loid (mī′ə loid′), *adj.* *Anat.* **1.** pertaining to the spinal cord. **2.** marrowlike. **3.** pertaining to marrow.

my·lo·nite (mī′lə nīt′, mYl′ə-), *n.* a rock that has been crushed and rolled out to such an extent that the original structure has been destroyed. [f. Gk. *mylōn* mill + -ITE[1]]

my·na (mī′nə), *n.* any of various Asiatic birds of the starling family (*Sturnidae*), esp. those of the genera *Acridotheres* and *Eulabes,* some of which are well-known cage birds and learn to talk. Also, **mina, my′nah.** [t. Hind.: m. *mainā* a starling]

Myn·heer (mīn hâr′, -hYr′), *n.* **1.** the Dutch term of address and title of respect corresponding to *sir* and *Mr.* **2.** (*l.c.*) *Colloq.* a Dutchman. [t. D: m. *mijnheer,* f. *mijn* my + *heer* lord, gentleman]

myo-, var. of **my-,** before consonants.

my·o·car·di·o·graph (mī′ō kär′dY ə grăf′, -gräf′), *n.* *Physiol.* an apparatus which records the movements of the heart muscle.

my·o·car·di·tis (mī′ō kär dī′tYs), *n.* *Pathol.* inflammation of the myocardium. [f. MYOCARD(IUM) + -ITIS]

my·o·car·di·um (mī′ō kär′dY əm), *n.* *Anat.* the muscular substance of the heart. [t. NL. See MYO-, CARDIO-] **—my′o·car′di·al,** *adj.*

my·o·graph (mī′ə grăf′, -gräf′), *n.* *Physiol.* an instrument for taking tracings of muscular contractions and relaxations.

my·ol·o·gy (mīŏl′ə jY), *n.* the science of muscles; the branch of anatomy that treats of muscles.

my·o·ma (mīō′mə), *n., pl.* **-mata** (-mə tə), **-mas** (-məz). *Pathol.* a tumor composed of muscular tissue. [t. NL. See MY-, -OMA] **—my·om·a·tous** (mī ŏm′ə təs, -ō′mə-), *adj.*

my·o·pi·a (mīō′pY′ə), *n.* *Pathol.* a condition of the eye in which parallel rays are focused in front o f the retina, objects being seen distinctly only when near to the eye; near-sightedness (opposed to *hypermetropia*). [t. NL: f. s. Gk. *mŷops* short-sighted + -*ia* -IA] **—my·op·ic** (mīŏp′Yk), *adj.*

my·o·scope (mī′ə skōp′), *n.* an apparatus or instrument for observing muscular contraction.

my·o·sin (mī′ə sYn), *n.* *Biochem.* a globulin occurring in muscle plasma. [f. MY- + -OS(E)[2] + -IN[2]]

my·o·sis (mīō′sYs), *n.* *Pathol.* excessive contraction of the pupil of the eye, as the result of disease, drugs, or the like. [t. NL, f. Gk.: s. *mŷein* close (the eyes) + -*ōsis* -OSIS]

my·o·so·tis (mī′ə sō′tYs), *n.* any plant of the boraginaceous genus *Myosotis,* as the common forget-me-not. Also, **my·o·sote** (mī′ə sōt′). [t. L, t. Gk.: the plant mouse-ear]

my·ot·ic (mīŏt′Yk), *adj.* **1.** pertaining to, producing, or suffering from myosis. **—n. 2.** a myotic drug.

My·ra (mī′rə), *n.* an ancient city in SW Asia Minor, in Lycia.

myr·i·ad (mYr′Y əd), *n.* **1.** an indefinitely great number. **2.** a very great number of persons or things. **3.** ten thousand. **—adj. 4.** of an indefinitely great number; innumerable. **5.** having innumerable phases, aspects, etc.: *the myriad mind of Shakespeare.* **6.** ten thousand. [t. Gk.: s. *mŷriás* a number of ten thousand]

myr·i·a·pod (mYr′Y ə pŏd′), *n.* **1.** any member of the *Myriapoda.* **—adj.** Also, **myr·i·ap·o·dous** (mYr′Y ăp′ə dəs). **2.** belonging or pertaining to the *Myriapoda* or myriapods. **3.** having very numerous legs. [t. NL: s. *Myriapoda,* pl. See MYRIA-, -POD]

Myr·i·ap·o·da (mYr′Y ăp′ə də), *n.pl.* a group of arthropods which have elongate bodies composed usually of many segments, most of which bear three-jointed legs; formerly treated as a class, embracing chiefly the centipedes and millipedes, or *Chilopoda* and *Diplopoda,* which were regarded as orders or subclasses. [NL, f. Gk.: *mŷriá*(s) MYRIAD + s. *poús* foot + -*a,* neut. pl. ending] **—myr′i·ap′o·dan,** *adj.,* *n.*

myr·i·ca (mYrī′kə), *n.* **1.** the bark of the wax myrtle. **2.** the bark of the bayberry. [t. L, t. Gk.: m. *myrīkē*]

myrmeco-, a word element meaning "ant." [t. Gk., comb. form of *mŷrmēx*]

myr·me·col·o·gy (mûr′mY kŏl′ə jY), *n.* the branch of entomology that treats of ants. **—myr·me·co·log·i·cal** (mûr′mY kə lŏj′ə kəl), *adj.* **—myr′me·col′o·gist,** *n.*

myr·me·coph·a·gous (mûr′mY kŏf′ə gəs), *adj.* adapted for feeding on ants or termites, as the jaws, teeth, etc., of various anteaters.

myr·me·co·phile (mûr′mY kō fīl′, -fYl), *n.* any species of foreign insect that lives more or less permanently in an ant colony.

myr·me·coph·i·lous (mûr′mY kŏf′ə ləs), *adj.* **1.** of myrmecophiles. **2.** of plants frequented by ants.

Myr·mi·don (mûr′mə dŏn′, -dən), *n., pl.* **Myrmidons, Myrmidones** (mûr mYd′ə nēz′). **1.** one of the warlike people of ancient Thessaly who accompanied Achilles, their king, to the Trojan War. **2.** (*l.c.*) one who executes without scruple his master's commands.

my·rob·a·lan (mīrŏb′ə lən, mY-), *n.* the dried plumlike fruit of certain tropical trees of the genus *Terminalia,* used in dyeing and making ink. [t. L: s. *myrobalanum,* t. Gk.: m. *myrobálanos* kind of fruit or nut]

My·ron (mī′rən), *n.* fl. c450 B.C., Greek sculptor.

myrrh (mûr), *n.* an aromatic resinous exudation from certain plants of the genus *Commibhora,* esp. *C. Myrrha,* a spiny shrub, used for incense, perfume, etc. [ME *mirre,* OE *myrre,* t. L *myrrha, murra,* t. Gk.: m. *mŷrra,* ult. from Akkadian *murrû;* cf. Heb. *mor,* akin to *mar* bitter]

myr·ta·ceous (mûr tā′shəs), *adj.* **1.** belonging to the *Myrtaceae,* or myrtle family of plants, which includes the myrtle, the clove and allspice trees, the guava, the eucalyptus, etc. **2.** of, pertaining to, or resembling the myrtle. [t. LL: m. *myrtāceus* of myrtle]

myr·tle (mûr′təl), *n.* **1.** any plant of the genus *Myrtus,* esp. *M. communis,* a shrub of southern Europe with evergreen leaves, fragrant white flowers, and aromatic berries. This plant is taken as an emblem of love and was anciently held sacred to Venus. **2.** *U.S.* any of certain plants of other families, as the common periwinkle, *Vinca minor,* and California laurel, *Umbellularia californica.* **3.** Also, **myrtle green.** dark green with bluish tinge. [ME, t. OF: m. *mirtille* myrtle berry, dim. of L *myrtus,* t. Gk.: m. *mŷrtos* myrtle]

my·self (mī sĕlf′), *pron., pl.* **ourselves. 1.** an intensifier of *me* or *I: I myself will go.* **2.** a reflexive substitute for *me: I burned myself.*

My·si·a (mYsh′Y ə), *n.* an ancient country in NW Asia Minor.

My·sore (mīsōr′), *n.* **1.** a state in S India; enlarged in 1956 in conformance with linguistic boundaries. 19,000,-000 pop. (est. 1956); 74,326 sq. mi. *Cap.:* Bangalore. **2.** a city in this state. 244,323 (1951).

mys·ta·gogue (mYs′tə gŏg′, -gôg′), *n.* one who instructs persons before initiation into religious mysteries or before participation in the sacraments. [t. L: m.s *mystagogus,* t. Gk.: m. *mystagōgós* (mYs/tə gō′jY), *n.* **—mys·ta·gog·ic** (mYs′tə gŏj′Yk), *adj.*

mys·te·ri·ous (mYs tYr′Y əs), *adj.* **1.** full of, characterized by, or involving mystery: *a mysterious stranger.* **2.** of obscure nature, meaning, origin, etc.; puzzling

---

inexplicable. **3.** implying or suggesting a mystery: *a mysterious smile.* [f. s. L *mystērium* MYSTERY[1] + -OUS] —**mys·te'ri·ous·ly,** *adv.* —**mys·te'ri·ous·ness,** *n.* —**Syn. 1.** secret, esoteric, occult, cryptic. MYSTERIOUS, INSCRUTABLE, MYSTICAL, OBSCURE refer to that which is not easily comprehended or explained. That which is MYSTERIOUS, by being unknown or puzzling, excites curiosity, amazement, or awe: *a mysterious disease.* INSCRUTABLE applies to that which is impenetrable, so enigmatic that one cannot interpret its significance: *an inscrutable smile.* That which is MYSTICAL has a secret significance, such as that attaching to certain rites, signs, and the like: *mystical symbols.* That which is OBSCURE is discovered or comprehended dimly or with difficulty: *obscure motives.* **2.** unfathomable; enigmatical.

mys·ter·y[1] (mĭs'tər ĭ, -trĭ), *n., pl.* **-ter·ies. 1.** anything that is kept secret or remains unexplained or unknown: *the mysteries of nature.* **2.** any affair, thing, or person that presents features or points so obscure as to arouse curiosity or speculation: *a mystery story.* **3.** obscurity, as of something unexplained or puzzling: *proceedings wrapped in mystery.* **4.** obscure, puzzling, or mysterious quality or character. **5.** any truth unknowable except by divine revelation. **6.** (in the Christian religion) **a.** a sacramental rite. **b.** (*pl.*) the eucharistic elements. **c.** the Eucharist. **7.** an incident or scene in connection with the life of Christ, regarded as of special significance: *the mysteries of the Passion.* **8.** (*pl.*) ancient religions which admitted candidates by secret rites the meaning of which only the initiated might know. **9.** (*pl.*) rites or secrets known only to those specially initiated: *the mysteries of freemasonry.* **10.** a miracle play. [ME *mysterie*, t. L: m. *mystērium*, t. Gk.: m. *mystērion*]

mys·ter·y[2] (mĭs'tər ĭ), *n., pl.* **-ter·ies. 1.** *Archaic.* a craft or trade. **2.** *Archaic or Hist.* a guild, as of craftsmen, merchants, or the like. [ME *misterye*, t. ML: m. *misterium*, L *ministerium* MINISTRY]

mys·tic (mĭs'tĭk), *adj.* **1.** spiritually significant or symbolic, as the *mystic dove* used in religious art to symbolize the Holy Ghost. **2.** of the nature of or pertaining to mysteries known only to the initiated: *mystic rites.* **3.** of occult character, power, or significance: *a mystic formula.* **4.** of obscure or mysterious character or significance. **5.** of or pertaining to mystics or mysticism. —*n.* **6.** one initiated into mysteries. **7.** one who claims to attain, or believes in the possibility of attaining, insight into mysteries transcending ordinary human knowledge, as by immediate intuition in a state of spiritual ecstasy. [ME *mystik*, t. L: m.s. *mysticus*, t. Gk.: m. *mystikós* mystic, secret]

mys·ti·cal (mĭs'tĭ kəl), *adj.* **1.** mystic; occult. **2.** of or pertaining to mystics or mysticism: *mystical doctrines.* **3.** spiritually symbolic. **4.** *Rare.* mysterious. —**mys'ti·cal·ly,** *adv.* —**mys'ti·cal·ness,** *n.* —**Syn. 1.** See **mysterious.**

mys·ti·cism (mĭs'tə sĭz'əm), *n.* **1.** the beliefs, ideas, or mode of thought of mystics. **2.** the doctrine of an immediate spiritual intuition of truths believed to transcend ordinary understanding, or of a direct, intimate union of the soul with the Divinity through contemplation and love. **3.** obscure thought or speculation.

mys·ti·fy (mĭs'tə fī'), *v.t.* **-fied, -fy·ing. 1.** to impose upon (a person) by playing upon his credulity; bewilder purposely. **2.** to involve (a subject, etc.) in mystery or obscurity. [t. F: m. *mystifier*, f. *mysti(que)* mystic + -fier -FY] —**mys'ti·fi·ca'tion,** *n.*

myth (mĭth), *n.* **1.** a traditional or legendary story, usually concerning some superhuman being or some alleged person or event, whether without or with a determinable basis of fact or a natural explanation: esp., a traditional or legendary story usually concerning deities or demigods and the creation of the world and its

inhabitants. **2.** stories or matter of this kind: *in the realm of myth.* **3.** any invented story. **4.** an imaginary or fictitious thing or person. **5.** *Sociol.* a collective belief that is built up in response to the wishes of the group rather than an analysis of the basis of the wishes. [t. NL: s. *mȳthus*, mod. var. of LL *mȳthos*, t. Gk.: word, speech, tale, legend, myth] —**Syn. 1.** See **legend.**

myth., 1. mythological. **2.** mythology.

myth·i·cal (mĭth'ə kəl), *adj.* **1.** pertaining to, of the nature of, or involving a myth or myths. **2.** dealt with in myth, as a period. **3.** dealing with myths, as a writer. **4.** existing only in myth, as a person. **5.** having no foundation in fact; imaginary; fictitious: *his influence at the White House is completely mythical.* Also, **myth'ic.** —**myth'i·cal·ly,** *adv.*

myth·i·cize (mĭth'ə sīz'), *v.t.* **-cized, -cizing.** to turn into, or treat or explain as, a myth.

mytho-, a word element meaning "myth." [t. Gk., comb. form of *mȳthos*]

mythol., 1. mythological. **2.** mythology.

myth·o·log·i·cal (mĭth'ə lŏj'ə kəl), *adj.* of or pertaining to mythology. Also, **myth'o·log'ic.** —**myth'o·log'i·cal·ly,** *adv.*

my·thol·o·gist (mĭ thŏl'ə jĭst), *n.* **1.** an expert in mythology. **2.** a writer of myths.

my·thol·o·gize (mĭ thŏl'ə jīz'), *v.i.* **-gized, -gizing. 1.** to classify, explain, or write about myths. **2.** to construct or relate myths. **3.** to make into or explain as a myth; make mythical. —**my·thol'o·giz'er,** *n.*

my·thol·o·gy (mĭ thŏl'ə jĭ), *n., pl.* **-gies. 1.** a body of myths, as that of a particular people, or that relating to a particular person: *Greek mythology.* **2.** myths collectively. **3.** the science of myths. [ME, t. LL: m.s. *mȳthologia*, t. Gk.: legend]

myth·o·ma·ni·a (mĭth'ə mā'nĭ ə), *n. Psychiatry.* lying or exaggerating to an abnormal degree. —**myth·o·ma·ni·ac** (mĭth'ə mā'nĭ ăk'), *n., adj.*

myth·o·poe·ic (mĭth'ə pē'ĭk), *adj.* myth-making; pertaining to the making of myths. Also, **myth'o·pe'ic.** [f. m.s. Gk. *mȳthopoiós* making myths + -IC] —**myth'o·poe'ism,** *n.* —**myth'o·poe'ist,** *n.*

Myt·i·le·ne (mĭt'ə lē'nĭ; *Gk.* mē'tē lē'nē), *n.* **1.** Also, **Lesbos.** a Greek island in the NE Aegean. 154,795 pop. (1951); 836 sq. mi. **2.** Also, **Kastro.** the capital of this island. 27,125 (1951).

myx-, a word element meaning "slimy." Also, **myxo-.** [t. Gk., comb. form of *mȳxa* slime, mucus]

myx·e·de·ma (mĭk'sĭ dē'mə), *n. Pathol.* a disease characterized by thickening of the skin, blunting of the senses and intellect, labored speech, etc., associated with diminished functional activity of the thyroid gland. Also, **myx'oe·de'ma.** [t. NL. See MYX-, EDEMA] —**myx·e·dem·a·tous** (mĭk'sĭ dĕm'ə təs, -dē'mə təs), *adj.* —**myx·e·dem·ic** (mĭk'sĭ dĕm'ĭk), *adj.*

myx·o·ma·to·sis (mĭk'sə mə tō'sĭs), *n. Vet.* a highly infectious viral disease of rabbits: artificially introduced into Great Britain and Australia to reduce the rabbit population. [f. MYX- + -OMAT(A) + -OSIS]

myx·o·my·cete (mĭk'sō mī sēt'), *n.* any one of the slime molds (*Myxomycetes, Mycetozoa*), primitive organisms whose characters place them at the border line between the plant and animal kingdoms.

myx·o·my·ce·tous (mĭk'sō mī sē'təs), *adj.* belonging or pertaining to the *Myxomycetes*, or slime molds (sometimes regarded as a distinct phylum, *Myxophyta*, and sometimes as a class of *Thallophyta*), having characteristics of both animals and plants. [f. s. NL *Myxomycētes*, pl. (see MYXO-, -MYCETES) + -OUS]

Myx·o·phyc·e·ae (mĭk'sō fĭs'ĭ ē'), *n.pl. Bot.* See **blue-green algae.**

N

N, n (ĕn), *n., pl.* **N's** or **Ns, n's** or **ns. 1.** a consonant, the 14th letter of the English alphabet. **2.** *Math.* an indefinite constant whole number, esp. the degree of a quantic or an equation, or the order of a curve. **3.** *Print.* an en.

N, n, *Chem.* nitrogen. **2.** north. **3.** northern.

N., 1. Nationalist. **2.** Navy. **3.** New. **4.** Noon. **5.** *Chem.* Normal (strength solution). **6.** Norse. **7.** North. **8.** Northern. **9.** November.

n., 1. (L *natus*) born. **2.** nephew. **3.** neuter. **4.** new. **5.** nominative. **6.** noon. **7.** *Chem.* normal (strength solution). **8.** north. **9.** northern. **10.** noun. **11.** number.

na (nä, nə), *Obs. except Dial.* (*chiefly Scot.*). —*adv.* **1.** no. **2.** not. —*conj.* **3.** nor. [Scot. var. of NO]

Na, *Chem.* (L *natrium*) sodium.

N.A., 1. National Army. **2.** North America.

NAACP, National Association for the Advancement

of Colored People. Also, **N.A.A.C.P.**

nab (năb), *v.t.* **nabbed, nabbing.** *Colloq.* **1.** to catch or seize, esp. suddenly. **2.** to capture or arrest. [earlier *nap.* Cf. OE *hnæppan* strike]

Na·blus (nä blōōs'), *n.* modern name of **Shechem.**

na·bob (nā'bŏb), *n.* **1.** an Englishman who has grown rich in India. **2.** any wealthy and luxurious person. **3.** nawab. [t. Hind.: m. *nawwab*. See NAWAB] —**na·bob·er·y** (nā'bŏb'ə rĭ, nā bŏb'ə rĭ), **na'bob·ism,** *n.* —**na'bob·ish,** *adj.*

Na·both (nā'bŏth, -bŏth), *n.* a man of Jezreel whose vineyard was secured for the covetous Ahab by the scheming of Jezebel. I Kings 21.

NACA, National Advisory Committee for Aeronautics.

na·celle (nə sĕl'), *n.* **1.** the enclosed part of an airplane, airship, or dirigible, in which the engine is housed or passengers, etc., are carried. **2.** the car of a balloon. [t. F, g. LL *nāvicella*, dim. of L *nāvis* ship]

na·cre (nā′kər), *n.* mother-of-pearl. [t. F, t. ML: m. *nacrum*, var. of *nacara*, ? t. Pers. (Kurdish): m. *nakára* pearl oyster] —**na·cre·ous** (nā′krĭ əs), *adj.*

Na-Dene (nə dēn′), *n.* an American Indian linguistic phylum including Haida, Tlingit, and Athabascan.

na·dir (nā′dər, nā′dĭr), *n.* **1.** the point of the celestial sphere vertically beneath any place or observer and diametrically opposite to the zenith. **2.** the lowest point, as of adversity. [ME, ult. t. Ar.: m. *naẓīr* corresponding, opposite (i. e., to the zenith)]

nae (nā), *adj., adv. Scot.* **1.** no. **2.** not. [var. of NO]

nae·thing (nā′thĭng), *n., adv. Scot.* nothing.

nae·vus (nē′vəs), *n., pl.* **-vi** (-vī). *Dermatology.* any congenital anomaly, including various types of birthmarks and all types of moles. Also, **nevus.** [t. L] —**nae·void** (nē′void), *adj.*

nag[1] (năg), *v.,* **nagged, nagging.** —*v.t.* **1.** to torment by persistent faultfinding, complaints, or importunities. —*v.i.* **2.** to keep up an irritating or wearisome faultfinding, complaining, or the like (often fol. by *at*). [cf. MLG *naggen* irritate, provoke, Icel. *nagga* grumble, *nagg* grumbling] —**nag′ger,** *n.* —**nag′ging·ly,** *adv.*

nag[2] (năg), *n.* **1.** a small horse or pony, esp. for riding. **2.** *Colloq.* a horse. **3.** an old or inferior horse. [ME *nagge,* c. D *negge*; akin to NEIGH]

na·ga·na (nə gä′nə), *n.* a disease of horses and other animals produced by the action of *Trypanosoma brucei* and carried by a variety of tsetse fly. It occurs only in certain parts of Africa. [native African name]

Na·ga·sa·ki (nä′gä sä′kē), *n.* a seaport in SW Japan, on Kyushu island: the second military use of the atomic bomb, Aug. 9, 1945. 252,630 (1940); 174,141 (1946); 241,805 (1950).

Na·go·ya (nä′gô yä′), *n.* a city in central Japan, on Honshu island. 1,030,635 (1950).

Nag·pur (năg pŏŏr′), *n.* a city in central India: former capital of the Central Provinces and Berar; now in NE Bombay state. 449,099 (1951).

Na·guib (nə gēb′), *n.* **Mohammed,** born 1901, Egyptian general; helped dethrone Farouk in 1952; premier, 1952–54; president from 1953 until ousted in 1954.

Na·gy·vá·rad (nŏd′yə vä′rŏd), *n.* Hungarian name of Oradea.

Nah., Nahum.

Na·hua·tl (nä′wä′təl), *n.* any of a subgroup of Uto-Aztecan languages of central Mexico, including Aztec.

Na·hua·tlan (nä′wät′lən), *n.* the family of Uto-Aztecan languages which includes Aztec.

Na·hum (nā′həm), *n.* **1.** a Hebrew prophet of the late seventh century B.C. **2.** a book of the Old Testament, the seventh among the Minor Prophets. [t. Heb.]

nai·ad (nā′ăd, nī′-), *n., pl.* **-ads, -ades** (-ə dēz′). **1.** (*also cap.*) *Class. Myth.* one of a class of water nymphs fabled to dwell in and preside over streams and springs. **2.** a girl swimmer. **3.** *Bot.* a plant of the genus *Naias,* or the family *Naiadaceae.* [t. L: s. *Nāias,* t. Gk.]

na·if (nä ēf′), *adj.* naïve. [t. F (masc.). See NAIVE]

nail (nāl), *n.* **1.** a slender piece of metal, usually with one end pointed and the other enlarged, for driving into or through wood, etc., as to hold separate pieces together. **2.** a thin, horny plate, consisting of modified epidermis, growing on the upper side of the end of a finger or toe. **3.** a measure of length for cloth, equal to 2¼ inches. **4. hit the nail on the head,** to say or do exactly the right thing. **5. on the nail,** *Colloq.* **a.** of present interest; under discussion. **b.** on the spot, or at once. —*v.t.* **6.** to fasten with a nail or nails: *to nail the cover on a box.* **7.** to stud with or as with nails driven in. **8.** to shut (*up*) within something by driving nails in: *to nail goods up in a box.* **9.** to make fast or keep firmly in one place or position: *surprise nailed him to the spot.* **10.** *Colloq.* to secure by prompt action; catch or seize. **11.** *Colloq.* to catch (a person) in some difficulty, a lie, etc. **12.** *Colloq.* to detect and expose (a lie, etc.). [ME; OE *nægl,* c. D and G *nagel*] —**nail′er,** *n.*

nail file, a small file for trimming fingernails.

nail set, a short rod of steel used to drive a nail below, or flush with, the surface.

nain·sook (nān′sŏŏk, nān′-), *n.* a fine, soft-finished cotton fabric, usually white, used for lingerie and infants' wear. [t. Hind.: m. *nainsukh,* lit., eye pleasure]

Nairn (nârn), *n.* a county in N Scotland. 8300 pop. (est. 1956); 163 sq. mi. *Co. seat:* Nairn. Also, **Nairnshire** (nârn′shĭr, -shər).

Nai·ro·bi (nī rō′bĭ), *n.* the capital of Kenya. 297,000 (1961).

na·ive (nä ēv′), *adj.* having or showing natural simplicity of nature; unsophisticated; ingenuous. Also, **na·ive′.** [t. F, fem. of *naïf,* g. L *nātīvus* native, natural] —**na·ive′ly,** *adv.* —**Syn.** simple, unaffected; unsuspecting.

na·ive·té (nä ēv′tā′), *n.* **1.** the quality of being naïve; artless simplicity. **2.** a naïve action, remark, etc. Also, **na·ive·te′.** [t. F, der. *naïve*]

na·ked (nā′kĭd), *adj.* **1.** without clothing or covering; nude. **2.** without adequate clothing. **3.** bare of any covering, overlying matter, vegetation, foliage, or the like: *naked fields.* **4.** bare, stripped, or destitute (*of* something specified): *trees naked of leaves.* **5.** without a sheath or customary covering: *a naked sword.* **6.** without carpets, hangings, or furnishings, as rooms, walls, etc. **7.** (of the eye, sight, etc.) unassisted by a microscope, telescope, or other instrument. **8.** defenseless or unpro-

tected; unguarded; exposed, as to attack or harm. **9.** simple; unadorned: *the naked truth.* **10.** not accompanied or supplemented by anything else: *a naked outline of facts.* **11.** exposed to view or plainly revealed: *a naked vein.* **12.** plain-spoken; blunt. **13.** *Law.* unsupported, as by authority or consideration: *a naked promise.* **14.** *Bot.* **a.** (of seeds) not enclosed in an ovary. **b.** (of flowers) without a calyx or perianth. **c.** (of stalks, etc.) without leaves. **d.** (of stalks, leaves, etc.) without hairs or pubescence. **15.** *Zool.* having no covering of hair, feathers, shell, etc. [ME *naked(e),* OE *nacod,* c. G *nackt*] —**na′ked·ly,** *adv.* —**na′ked·ness,** *n.*

NAM, National Association of Manufacturers. Also, **N. A. M.**

nam·a·ble (nā′mə bəl), *adj.* that may be named. Also, **nameable.**

Na·man·gan (nä′män gän′), *n.* a city in the SW Soviet Union in Asia, in Uzbek Republic. 104,000 (est. 1956).

Na·ma·qua·land (nə mä′kwə länd′), *n.* a coastal region in the S part of South-West Africa, extending into the Cape of Good Hope province of the Republic of South Africa: inhabited by Hottentots.

nam·ay·cush (năm′ĭ kŭsh′, -ā-), *n.* a lake trout. [t. Algonquian (Cree): m. *namekus,* dim. of *namew* fish]

nam·by-pam·by (năm′bĭ păm′bĭ), *adj., n., pl.* **-bies.** —*adj.* **1.** weakly simple or sentimental; insipid. —*n.* **2.** namby-pamby verse or prose. **3.** a namby-pamby person. **4.** namby-pamby sentiment. [orig. a nickname, *Namby Pamby,* for *Ambrose Philips* (d. 1749), British poet; first used by Henry Carey in 1726 as title of poem ridiculing Philips's verses]

name (nām), *n., v.,* **named, naming.** —*n.* **1.** a word or a combination of words by which a person, place, or thing, a body or class, or any object of thought, is designated or known. **2.** mere designation as distinguished from fact: *king in name only.* **3.** an appellation, title, or epithet, applied descriptively, in honor, abuse, etc.: *to call him bad names.* **4.** a reputation of a particular kind given by common report: *a bad name.* **5.** a distinguished, famous, or great reputation; fame: *to seek name and fortune.* **6.** a widely known or famous person. **7.** a personal or family name as exercising influence or bringing distinction. **8.** a body of persons grouped under one name, as a family or race. **9.** the verbal or other symbolic representation of a thing, event, property, relation, or concept. A **proper name** represents some particular thing or event. A **common name** (e.g. "man") is the name of anything which satisfies certain indicated conditions. **10. in the name of, a.** with appeal to: *in the name of mercy, stop screaming!* **b.** by the authority of: *open in the name of the law.* **c.** on behalf of: *to vote in the name of others.* **d.** under the name of: *money deposited in the name of a son.* **e.** under the designation of: *in the character of: murder in the name of mercy.* **11. to one's name,** belonging to one: *not a nickel to my name.* —*v.t.* **12.** to give a name to: *name a baby.* **13.** to call by a specified name: *to name a child Regina.* **14.** to specify or mention by name: *three persons were named in the report.* **15.** to designate for some duty or office; nominate or appoint: *I have named you for the position.* **16.** to specify: *to name a price.* **17.** to tell the name of: *name the capital of Ohio.* **18.** to speak of. **19.** (in the English Parliament) to cite (a member) for contempt. [ME; OE *nama,* c. G *name*; akin to L *nōmen,* Gk. *ónoma*] —**nam′er,** *n.*

—**Syn. 1.** NAME, TITLE both refer to the label by which a person is known. NAME is the simpler and more general word, for appellation: *the name is John.* A TITLE is an official or honorary term bestowed on a person or the specific designation of a book, article, etc.: *the title of Doctor, Treasure Island is the title of a book.*

name·a·ble (nā′mə bəl), *adj.* namable.

name·less (nām′lĭs), *adj.* **1.** unknown to fame; obscure. **2.** having no name. **3.** left unnamed: *a certain person who shall be nameless.* **4.** anonymous: *a nameless writer.* **5.** having no legitimate paternal name, as a child born out of wedlock. **6.** that cannot be specified or described: *a nameless charm.* **7.** too shocking or vile to be specified. —**name′less·ly,** *adv.* —**name′less·ness,** *n.*

name·ly (nām′lĭ), *adv.* that is to say; to wit: *two cities, namely, Paris and London.*

name·sake (nām′sāk′), *n.* **1.** one having the same name as another. **2.** one named after another. [alter. of *name's sake*]

Na·mur (nä mŏŏr′; *Fr.* nå myr′), *n.* a city in S Belgium on the Sambre and Meuse rivers. 31,807 (1947).

Nan·chang (nän′chäng′), *n.* a city in SE China: the capital of Kiangsi province. 267,000 (est. 1950).

Nan·cy (nän′sĭ; *Fr.* näṅ sē′), *n.* a city in NE France: battles, 1477, 1914, 1944. 124,797 (1954).

Nan·da De·vi (nŭn′dä dā′vē), a peak of the Himalayas in N India, in Uttar Pradesh. 25,661 ft.

nane (nān), *adj., pron., adv. Scot.* none.

Nan·ga Par·bat (nŭng′gə pŭr′bŭt), a peak of the Himalayas in NW Kashmir. 26,660 ft.

Nan·hai (nän′hī′), *n.* a city in SE China, in Kwantung province, near Canton. 96,000 (est. 1950). Also, **Namhoi** (näm′hoi′), **Fatshan.**

nan·keen (nän kēn′), *n.* **1.** a firm, durable, yellow or buff fabric, made orig. from a natural-colored Chinese cotton but now from other cotton and dyed. **2.** (*pl.*) garments made of this material. **3.** a yellow or buff color. **4.** a type of porcelain, blue on a white background. Also, **nan·kin′.** [named after *Nankin* NANKING]

b., blend of, blended; c., cognate with; d., dialect, dialectal; der., derived from; f., formed from; g., going back to; m., modification of; r., replacing; s., stem of; t., taken from; ?, perhaps. See the full key on inside cover.

Nan·king (năn′kĭng′; *Chin.* năn′-), *n.* a former capital of China, in the E part: a port on the Yangtze. 1,020,000 (est. 1954).

Nan Ling (năn′ lĭng′), a mountain range in S China. Also, **Nan Shan.**

Nan·ning (năn′nĭng′; *Chin.* năn′-), *n.* Yungning.

nan·ny (năn′ĭ), *n., pl.* **-nies.** *Brit.* a nurse for children, traditionally pictured as a loyal family retainer.

nanny goat, a female goat.

Nan·sen (năn′sən, năn′-), *n.* **Fridtjof** (frĭt′yŏf), 1861–1930, Norwegian arctic explorer, scientist, and diplomat.

Nan Shan (năn′ shăn′), 1. broad mountain range in W China, in Chinghai and Kansu provinces. 2. Nan Ling.

Nantes (nănts; *Fr.* nänt), *n.* 1. a seaport in W France at the mouth of the Loire river. 222,790 (1954). 2. **Edict of,** a law promulgated by Henry IV of France in 1598, granting considerable religious and civil liberty to the Huguenots: revoked by Louis XIV, 1685.

Nan·ti·coke (năn′tə kōk′), *n.* a city in E Pennsylvania. 20,160 (1950).

Nan·tuck·et (năn tŭk′ĭt), *n.* an island off SE Massachusetts: summer resort. 2,804 (1960); 15 mi. long.

Na·o·mi (nā ō′mĭ, nā′ō mī′, -mĭ), *n.* *Bible.* the mother-in-law of Ruth. Ruth 1:2, etc. [t. Heb.]

na·os (nā′ŏs), *n.* 1. a temple. 2. *Archit.* the central chamber, or cella, of an ancient temple. [t. Gk.: temple]

nap¹ (năp), *v.,* **napped, napping,** *n.* —*v.i.* 1. to have a short sleep; doze. 2. to be off one's guard: *I caught him napping.* —*n.* 3. a short sleep; a doze. [ME *nappe*(n), OE *hnappian,* c. MHG *napfen*]

nap² (năp), *n., v.,* **napped, napping.** —*n.* 1. the short fuzzy ends of fibers on the surface of cloth drawn up in napping. 2. any downy coating, as on plants. —*v.t.* 3. to raise a nap on. [ME *noppe,* OE *-hnoppa* (in *wullcnoppa,* mistake for *wullhnoppa* tuft of wool), c. MD and MLG *noppe;* akin to OE *hnoppian* pluck] —**nap′-less,** *adj.*

nap³ (năp), *n.* napoleon (defs. 2, 3).

na·palm (nā′päm), *n.* *Mil.* a highly incendiary jellylike substance, used in bombs, flame throwers, etc.

nape (nāp, năp), *n.* the back (of the neck). [ME]

na·per·y (nā′pə rĭ), *n.* 1. table linen; tablecloths, napkins, etc. 2. linen for household use. [ME *naperie,* t. OF, der. *nape* tablecloth. See NAPKIN]

Naph·ta·li (năf′tə lī′), *n.* *Bible.* 1. a son of Jacob. Gen. 30:8. 2. one of the 12 tribes of Israel. Num. 1:15, 43.

naph·tha (năp′thə, năf′-), *n.* 1. a colorless, volatile liquid, a petroleum distillate (esp. a product intermediate between gasoline and benzine), used as a solvent, fuel, etc. 2. any of various similar liquids distilled from other products. 3. *Obs.* petroleum. [t. L, t. Gk.]

naph·tha·lene (năf′thə lēn′, năp′-), *n.* *Chem.* a white crystalline hydrocarbon, C₁₀H₈, usually prepared from coal tar, used in making dyes, as a moth repellant, etc. Also, **naph·tha·line′, naph·tha·lin** (năf′thə-lĭn, năp′-). [f. NAPHTH(A) + AL(COHOL) + -ENE]

naph·thene (năf′thēn, năp′-), *n.* *Chem.* any of a group of hydrocarbon ring compounds of the general formula, C°H²ⁿ, derivatives of cyclopentane and cyclohexane, found in certain petroleums.

naph·thol (năf′thŏl, -thôl, năp′-), *n.* *Chem.* 1. either of two isomeric derivatives of naphthalene, having the formula C₁₀H₇OH, and occurring in coal tar, used as antiseptics and in dye manufacture. See betanaphthol. 2. any of certain hydroxyl derivatives of naphthalene. Also, **naph·tol** (năf′tŏl, -tôl, năp′-). [f. NAPHTH(A) + -OL²]

Na·pi·er (nā′pĭ′er, nə pĭr′), *n.* 1. **Sir Charles James,** 1782–1853, British general. 2. **John,** 1550–1617, Scottish mathematician and inventor of logarithms.

Na·pier·i·an logarithm (nə pĭr′ĭ ən), *Math.* a logarithm using the number 2.718281828 + (*symbol: e*) as a base.

Napier of Mag·da·la (măg′də lə), **Robert Cornelis** (kôr nē′lĭs), **Napier, First Baron,** 1810–90, British field marshal.

na·pi·form (nā′pə fôrm′), *adj.* turnip-shaped, as a root. [f. s. L *nāpus* turnip + -(I)FORM]

nap·kin (năp′kĭn), *n.* 1. a rectangular piece of linen or cotton cloth used at table to wipe the lips and hands and to protect the clothes. 2. a square or oblong piece of linen or cotton cloth for some other purpose: **a.** a towel. **b.** *Chiefly Brit.* a diaper. **c.** *Now Scot.* a handkerchief. [late ME *napkyn,* dim. of *nape* tablecloth. t. F: m. *nappe,* g. L *mappa* cloth. Cf. MAP.]

Na·ples (nā′pəlz), *n.* 1. a seaport in SW Italy. 1,059,-000 (est. 1954). 2. **Bay of,** the beautiful bay on which Naples is located. 22 mi. long. Italian, **Napoli.**

Na·po·le·on (nə pō′lĭ ən; *Fr.* nȧ pô lĕ ôn′), *n.* **Louis** (lwē), 1808–73, president of France, 1848–52; as **Napoleon III,** emperor of France, 1852–70 (son of Louis Bonaparte).

na·po·le·on (nə pō′lĭ ən), *n.* 1. a piece of pastry consisting of baked puff paste in layers with a cream filling. 2. a French gold coin, bearing a portrait of Napoleon (I or III), of the value of 20 francs, orig. about $3.86. 3. *Cards.* **a.** a game in which the players bid for the privilege of naming the trump, stating the number of tricks they propose to win. **b.** a bid in this game to take all five tricks of a hand. [named after NAPOLEON]

Napoleon I. See Bonaparte (def. 6).
Napoleon II. See Bonaparte (def. 7).
Napoleon III. See Napoleon, Louis.

Na·po·le·on·ic (nə pō′lĭ ŏn′ĭk), *adj.* pertaining to, resembling, or suggestive of Napoleon I, or, less often, Napoleon III, or their dynasty.

Na·po·li (nä′pô lē′), *n.* Italian name of **Naples.**

nap·per¹ (năp′ər), *n.* 1. one who raises a nap on cloth. 2. a machine for putting a nap on cloth. [f. NAP² + -ER¹]

nap·per² (năp′ər), *n.* one who naps or dozes. [f. NAP¹ + -ER¹]

nap·py¹ (năp′ĭ), *adj.* 1. *Brit.* heady or strong, as ale. 2. *Chiefly Scot.* tipsy. —*n.* 3. *Chiefly Scot.* liquor, esp. ale. [prob. special use of NAPPY³]

nap·py² (năp′ĭ), *n., pl.* **-pies.** a small dish, usually round and often of glass, with a flat bottom and sloping sides, for food, etc. Also, **nap′pie.** [orig. obscure]

nap·py³ (năp′ĭ), *adj.* **-pier, -piest.** covered with nap; downy. [f. NAP² + -Y¹]

na·prap·a·thy (nə prăp′ə thĭ), *n.* a system of treatment based on the belief that all diseases are caused by connective tissue and ligament disorders and can be cured by massage. [f. Czech *napra(va)* correction (cf. Russ. *napravit′* direct, guide) + -PATHY] —**nap·ra·path** (năp′rə păth′), *n.*

Nar·ba·da (nər bŭd′ə), *n.* a river flowing from central India W to the Arabian Sea. ab. 800 mi. Also, **Nerbudda.**

Nar·bonne (nȧr bôn′), *n.* a city in S France: an important port in Roman times. 32,060 (1954).

nar·ce·ine (när′sĭ ēn′, -ĭn), *n.* *Chem.* a bitter, white, crystalline alkaloid, C₂₃H₂₇NO₃, contained in opium, possessing a weak, smooth, muscle-relaxing action. Also, **nar·ce·in** (när′sĭ ĭn). [f. L *narcē* (t. Gk.: m. *nárkē* numbness, torpor) + -INE²]

nar·cis·sism (när′sĭs′ĭz əm), *n.* *Psychoanal.* 1. sexual excitement through admiration of oneself. 2. self-love; erotic gratification derived from admiration of one's own physical or mental attributes: a normal condition at the infantile level of personality development. Also, **nar·cism** (när′sĭz əm). [t. G: m. *Narzissismus.* See NARCISSUS, -ISM] —**nar·cis·sist, nar·cis·sis·tic,** *adj.*

nar·cis·sus (när sĭs′əs), *n., pl.* **-cissuses, -cissi** (-sĭs′ī). 1. any plant of the amaryllidaceous genus *Narcissus,* which comprises bulbous plants bearing showy flowers with a cup-shaped corona, and includes the jonquil and the daffodil. 2. (*cap.*) *Gk. Legend.* a beautiful youth who fell in love with his own image in water, pined away, and was metamorphosed into the narcissus. [t. L, t. Gk.: m. *nárkissos* the plant (so named from its narcotic properties)]

nar·co·lep·sy (när′kə lĕp′sĭ), *n.* *Pathol.* a condition characterized by an uncontrollable desire for, and short attacks of, sleep on all occasions. [b. NARCO(SIS) and (EPI)LEPSY] —**nar′co·lep′tic,** *adj.*

nar·co·sis (när kō′sĭs), *n.* 1. a state of sleep or drowsiness. 2. a temporary state of depression produced by a drug, or by heat, cold, or electricity. [t. NL, t. Gk.: m. *nárkōsis* a benumbing]

nar·co·syn·the·sis (när′kō sĭn′thə sĭs), *n.* a treatment for psychiatric disturbances which uses narcotics.

nar·cot·ic (när kŏt′ĭk), *adj.* 1. having the power to produce narcosis, as a drug. 2. pertaining to or of the nature o. narcosis. 3. pertaining to narcotics or their use. 4. for the use or treatment of narcotic addicts. —*n.* 5. any of a class of substances that blunt the senses, relieving pain, etc., and inducing sleep, and in large quantities producing complete insensibility, often used habitually to satisfy morbid appetite. 6. an individual inclined toward the habitual use of such substances. [t. Gk.: m.s. *narkōtikós* making stiff or numb]

nar·co·tism (när′kə tĭz′əm), *n.* 1. the habit of taking narcotics. 2. the action or influence of narcotics. 3. narcosis. 4. an abnormal inclination to sleep.

nar·co·tize (när′kə tīz′), *v.t.,* **-tized, -tizing.** to subject to a narcotic; stupefy. —**nar′co·ti·za′tion,** *n.*

nard (närd), *n.* 1. an aromatic Himalayan plant, supposedly *Nardostachys Jatamansi* (spikenard), the source of an ointment used by the ancients. 2. the ointment. [ME, t. L: s. *nardus,* t. Gk.: m. *nárdos*]

nar·es (nâr′ēz), *n.pl., sing.* **naris** (nâr′ĭs). *Anat.* the nostrils or the nasal passages. [t. L, pl. of *nāris*]

Na·rew (nä′rĕf), *n.* a river in NE Poland, flowing into the Bug river a little above its junction with the Vistula: battle, 1915. ab. 290 mi. Russian, **Na·rev** (nä′rĕf).

nar·ghi·le (när′gə lĭ), *n.* an Oriental tobacco pipe in which the smoke is drawn through water before reaching the lips; a hookah. Also, **nar′gi·le, nar′gi·leh** (när′gə-lĕ). [t. Pers.: m. *nārgileh,* der. *nārgīl* coconut]

nar·i·al (nâr′ĭ əl), *adj.* *Anat.* of or pertaining to the nares or nostrils. Also, **nar·ine** (nâr′īn, -ĭn).

nark (närk), *Brit. Slang.* —*n.* 1. a stool pigeon. —*v.i.* 2. to act as a stool pigeon. [t. Gipsy: m. *nāk* nose]

Nar·ra·gan·sett (năr′ə găn′sĭt), *n.(pl.)* a North American Indian tribe of the Algonquian family, formerly located on Rhode Island, now extinct. [f. Algonquian: *naiagons* very small point of land + *-et* on, in, along]

Narragansett Bay, an inlet of the Atlantic in E Rhode Island. 28 mi. long.

nar·rate (nă rāt′, năr′āt), *v.,* **-rated, -rating.** —*v.t.* 1. to give an account of or tell the story of (events, experiences, etc.). —*v.i.* 2. to relate or recount events, etc., in speech or writing. [t. L: m.s. *narrātus,* pp.] —**nar·ra′tor, nar·rat′er,** *n.* —Syn. 1. See describe.

nar·ra·tion (nă rā′shən), *n.* 1. an account or story. 2. the act or process of narrating. 3. words or matter narrating something. **4.** *Rhet.* (in a classical speech) the third part, the exposition of the question.

nar·ra·tive (năr′ə tĭv), *n.* **1.** a story of events, experiences, or the like, whether true or fictitious. **2.** narrative matter, as in literary work. **3.** the act or process of narrating. —*adj.* **4.** that narrates: *a narrative poem.* **5.** of or pertaining to narration: *narrative skill.* —**nar′ra·tive·ly,** *adv.*
—**Syn. 1.** NARRATIVE, ACCOUNT, RECITAL, HISTORY are terms for a story of an event or events. NARRATIVE is the general term (for a story long or short; of past, present, or future; factual or imagined; told for any purpose; and with or without much detail). The other three terms apply primarily to factual stories of time already past. An ACCOUNT is usually told informally, often for entertainment, with emphasis on details of action, whether about an incident or a series of happenings. A RECITAL, an extended narrative usually with an informative purpose, emphasizes accuracy and exhaustive details of facts and figures. A HISTORY, usually written and at some length, is characterized by a tracing of causes and effects, and by an attempt to estimate, evaluate, and interpret facts.

nar·row (năr′ō), *adj.* **1.** of little breadth or width; not broad or wide: *a narrow path.* **2.** limited in extent or space, or affording little room: *narrow quarters.* **3.** limited in range or scope. **4.** lacking breadth of view or sympathy, as persons, the mind, ideas, etc. **5.** limited in amount, small, or meager: *narrow resources.* **6.** straitened, as circumstances. **7.** barely sufficient or adequate; being barely that: *a narrow escape.* **8.** careful; minute, as a scrutiny, search, or inquiry. **9.** *Brit. Dial. and Scot.* parsimonious or stingy. **10.** *Phonet.* tense. **11.** noting livestock feeds in which the proportion of protein is higher than ordinary. —*v.i.* **12.** to become narrower. —*v.t.* **13.** to make narrower. **14.** to limit or restrict. **15.** to make narrow-minded. —*n.* **16.** a narrow part, place, or thing. **17.** *(pl.)* a narrow part of a strait, river, ocean current, etc. **18. The Narrows,** the passage from upper to lower New York Bay, between Staten and Long Islands. Least width, 1¼ mi. **19.** a narrow part of a valley, passage, or road. [ME; OE *nearu*, c. OS *naru* narrow, D *naar* unpleasant] —**nar′row·ly,** *adv.* —**nar′row·ness,** *n.*

narrow gauge. See gauge (def. 10).

nar·row-gauge (năr′ō gāj′), *adj.* (of a railroad track) having less than 56½ inches between rails.

nar·row-mind·ed (năr′ō mīn′dĭd), *adj.* having or showing a prejudiced mind, as persons, opinions, etc. —**nar′row-mind′ed·ly,** *adv.* —**nar′row-mind′ed·ness,** *n.* —**Syn.** bigoted; intolerant.

nar·thex (när′thĕks), *n. Archit.* a vestibule along the façade of an early Christian or Byzantine church. [t. LGk.; in Gk., giant fennel]

Nar·va (när′vä), *n.* a seaport in the W Soviet Union, in the Estonian Republic: the Swedes defeated the Russians here, 1700. 20,000 (est. 1948).

Nar·vá·ez (när vä′ĕth), *n.* **Pánfilo de** (päm′fē lô′ dĕ), c1478–1528, Spanish soldier and adventurer in America.

nar·whal (när′wəl), *n.* an arctic cetacean, *Monodon monoceros,* the male of which has a long, spirally twisted tusk extending forward from the upper jaw. Also, **nar′wal,** *narwhale* (när′hwāl). [t. Sw or Dan.: m. *narhval* (f. *nar* + *hval* whale). Cf. Icel. *nāhvalr,* lit., corpse whale (from corpselike color of belly)]

Narwhal, *Monodon monoceros*
(Body 12 ft. long, tusk ab. 9 ft.)

na·sal¹ (nā′zəl), *adj.* **1.** of or pertaining to the nose. **2.** *Phonet.* with the voice issuing through the nose, either partly (as in French nasal vowels) or entirely (as in *m, n,* or the *ng* of song). —*n.* **3.** *Phonet.* a nasal speech sound. [t. NL: s. *nāsālis,* der. L *nāsus* nose. See NOSE] —**na·sal·i·ty** (nā zăl′ə tĭ), *n.* —**na′sal·ly,** *adv.*

na·sal² (nā′zəl), *n.* a part of a helmet, protecting the nose and adjacent parts of the face. [late ME, t. OF, der. L *nāsus* nose]

nasal index, 1. *Craniom.* the ratio of the distance from nasion to the lower margin of the nasal aperture to that of the maximum breadth of the nasal aperture (on the skull). **2.** *Cephalom.* the ratio of the maximum breadth of the external nose to its height from nasal root to where the septum is confluent with the upper lip (on the head).

na·sal·ize (nā′zə līz′), *v.,* -ized, -izing. *Phonet., etc.* —*v.t.* **1.** to pronounce as a nasal sound by allowing some of the voice to issue through the nose. —*v.i.* **2.** to nasalize normally oral sounds. —**na′sal·i·za′tion,** *n.*

nas·cent (năs′ənt, nā′sənt), *adj.* **1.** beginning to exist or develop: *the nascent republic.* **2.** *Chem.* (of an element) being in the nascent state. [t. L: s. *nascens,* ppr., being born] —**nas′cence, nas′cen·cy,** *n.*

nascent state, *Chem.* the condition of an element at the instant it is set free from a combination in which it has previously existed. Also, **nascent condition.**

nase·ber·ry (nāz′bĕr′ĭ), *n., pl.* -ries. **1.** the fruit of the sapodilla, *Achras Zapota.* **2.** the sapodilla (tree). [t. Sp.: m. *nespera* medlar, q. L *mespila.* See MEDLAR]

Nase·by (nāz′bĭ), *n.* a village in central England, in Northamptonshire: Royalist defeat, 1645.

Nash (năsh), *n.* **1. Ogden,** born 1902, U.S. humorist. **2.** Also, **Nashe. Thomas,** 1567–1601, English author.

Nash·u·a (năsh′ōō ə), *n.* a city in S New Hampshire, on the Merrimack river. 39,096 (1960).

Nash·ville (năsh′vĭl), *n.* the capital of Tennessee, in the central part: battle, 1864. 170,874 (1960).

na·si·on (nā′zĭ ŏn′), *n. Craniom.* the intersection of the internasal suture with the nasofrontal suture, in the midsagittal plane. [t. NL, der. L *nāsus* nose] —**na′si·al,** *adj.*

na·so·fron·tal (nā′zō frŭn′təl), *adj.* of or pertaining to the nose and frontal bone.

na·so·phar·ynx (nā′zō făr′ĭngks), *n., pl.* -pharynges (-fə rĭn′jēz), -pharynxes. *Anat.* the part of the pharynx behind and above the soft palate, directly continuous with the nasal passages (distinguished from *oropharynx*).

Nas·sau (năs′ô; *for 2, 3, also Ger.* nä′sou, *Fr.* nà sō′), *n.* **1.** a seaport and the capital of the Bahama Islands. 36,243 (est. 1952). **2.** a district in central West Germany: formerly a duchy, now a part of Hesse. **3.** a European royal family that has reigned in Netherlands since 1815

Nas·ser (nä′sər), *n.* **Gamal Abdel** (gə mäl′ äb′děl), born 1918, Egyptian military leader; member of group that dethroned Farouk in 1952; premier since 1954; President of United Arab Republic since 1958.

Nast (năst), *n.* **Thomas,** 1840–1902, U.S. cartoonist.

nas·tic (năs′tĭk), *adj. Plant Physiol.* of or showing sufficiently greater cellular force or growth on one side of an axis to change the form or position of the axis. [f. s. Gk. *nastós* squeezed together + -ic]

-nastic, a suffix forming adjectives of words ending in **-nasty.** [see NASTIC]

na·stur·tium (nə stûr′shəm, nə-), *n.* any of the garden plants constituting the genus *Tropaeolum,* much cultivated for their showy flowers of yellow, red, and other colors, and for their fruit, which is pickled and used like capers. [t. L: a kind of cress]

nas·ty (năs′tĭ), *adj.,* -tier, -tiest. **1.** physically filthy, or disgustingly unclean. **2.** offensive to taste or smell; nauseous. **3.** offensive; objectionable: *a nasty habit.* **4.** morally filthy; obscene. **5.** vicious, spiteful, or ugly: *a nasty dog.* **6.** bad to deal with, encounter, undergo, etc.: *a nasty cut.* **7.** very unpleasant *nasty weather.* [ME, orig. uncert.] —**nas′ti·ly,** *adv.* —**nas′ti·ness,** *n.*

-nasty, a suffix indicating irregularity of cellular growth because of some pressure. [f. s. Gk. *nastós* squeezed together + -y³]

nat., **1.** national. **2.** native. **3.** natural. **4.** naturalist.

na·tal (nā′təl), *adj.* **1.** of or pertaining to one's birth: *one's natal day.* **2.** presiding over or affecting one at birth: *natal influences.* **3.** *Chiefly Poetic.* (of places) native. [ME, t. L: s. *nātālis*]

Na·tal (nə täl′, -täl′ *for 1*; nä täl′, -tôl′ *for 2*), *n.* **1.** a province of the Union of South Africa, in the E part. 2,571,000 (est. 1955); 35,284 sq. mi. *Cap.:* Pietermaritzburg. **2.** a seaport in E Brazil. 97,736 (est. 1952).

na·tal·i·ty (nā täl′ə tĭ), *n.* birth rate.

na·tant (nā′tənt), *adj.* **1.** swimming; floating. **2.** *Bot.* floating on water, as the leaf of an aquatic plant. [t. L: s. *natans,* ppr.]

na·ta·tion (nā tā′shən), *n.* the act or art of swimming. [t. L: s. *natātio*] —**na·ta·tion·al,** *adj.*

na·ta·to·ri·al (nā′tə tōr′ĭ əl), *adj.* pertaining to, adapted for, or characterized by swimming: *natatorial birds.* Also, **na′ta·to′ry.** [f. s. LL *natātōrius* + -AL¹]

na·ta·to·ri·um (nā′tə tōr′ĭ əm), *n., pl.* -toriums, -toria (-tōr′ĭ ə). a swimming pool. [t. LL]

Natch·ez (năch′ĭz), *n.* **1.** a city in SW Mississippi: a port on the Mississippi. 23,791 (1960). **2.** *(sing. and pl.)* a member of an extinct Muskhogean Indian tribe once living on the lower Mississippi river.

na·tes (nā′tēz), *n.pl.* the buttocks. [t. L, pl. of *natis*]

Na·than (nā′thən), *n.* **George Jean,** 1882–1958, U.S. dramatic critic, editor, and author.

nathe·less (nāth′lĭs, năth′-), *Archaic.* —*adv.* **1.** nevertheless. —*prep.* **2.** notwithstanding. Also, **nath·less** (nāth′lĭs). [ME *natheles,* OE *nāthelǣs,* var. of *nāthȳlǣs,* f. *nā* never + *thȳ* for that + *lǣs* less]

na·tion (nā′shən), *n.* **1.** an aggregation of persons of the same ethnic family, speaking the same language or cognate languages. **2.** a body of people associated with a particular territory who are sufficiently conscious of their unity to seek or to possess a government peculiarly their own. **3.** a member tribe of an Indian confederation. [ME, t. L: s. *nātio* race, people, nation, orig., birth] —**Syn. 2.** See race².

Na·tion (nā′shən), *n.* **Carry,** or **Carrie, Amelia,** (*Carry Amelia Moore*) 1846–1911, U.S. temperance leader.

na·tion·al (năsh′ən əl), *adj.* **1.** of, pertaining to, or maintained by a nation as an organized whole or independent political unit: *national affairs.* **2.** peculiar or common to the whole people of a country: *national customs.* **3.** devoted to one's own nation, its interests, etc.; patriotic. —*n.* **4.** a citizen or subject of a particular nation, entitled to its protection. —**na′tion·al·ly,** *adv.*

national bank, 1. *U.S.* a bank chartered by the national government and formerly authorized to issue notes that served as money. **2.** a governmentally owned and administered bank, as in some European countries.

national church, the church established by law in a nation, generally the prevalent religion.

National City, a city in SW California, near San Diego. 32,771 (1960).

National Guard, State military forces, in part equipped, trained and quartered by the U.S. government, and paid by the U.S. government, which become an active component of the Army when called or ordered into federal service by the president under the authority of the Constitution and implementing laws.

National Guard of the United States, the officers who hold a dual commission, as officers of the National Guard and of the Army of the United States.

national income, *Econ.* the total net value of commodities produced and services rendered by all the people of a nation during a specified period.

na·tion·al·ism (nǎsh'ən əl ĭz'əm), *n.* **1.** national spirit or aspirations. **2.** devotion to the interests of one's own nation. **3.** desire for national advancement or independence. **4.** the policy of asserting the interests of a nation, viewed as separate from the interests of other nations or the common interests of all nations. **5.** an idiom or trait peculiar to a nation. **6.** a form of socialism which advocates the nationalizing of all industries.

na·tion·al·ist (nǎsh'ən əl ĭst), *n.* **1.** one inspired with nationalism. **2.** an advocate of national independence. **—adj. 3.** Also, **na'tion·al·is'tic.** of or pertaining to nationalism or nationalists. **—na'tion·al·is'ti·cal·ly,** *adv.*

Nationalist China, the anti-communist government of China, now on Formosa. Official name: **Republic of China.**

na·tion·al·i·ty (nǎsh'ə nǎl'ə tǐ), *n., pl.* **-ties. 1.** the quality of membership in a particular nation (original or acquired): *the nationality of an immigrant.* **2.** relationship of property, etc., to a particular nation, or to one or more of its members: *the nationality of a ship.* **3.** nationalism. **4.** existence as a distinct nation; national independence. **5.** nation or people: *the various nationalities of America.* **6.** national quality or character.

na·tion·al·ize (nǎsh'ən əl īz'), *v.t.,* **-ized, -izing. 1.** to bring under the control or ownership of a nation, as industries, land, etc. **2.** to make nation-wide. **3.** to naturalize. **4.** to make into a nation. Also, *Brit.,* **na'tion·al·ise'. —na'tion·al·i·za'tion,** *n.* **—na'tion·al·iz'er,** *n.*

national park, a tract of land maintained by the federal government for the use of the people.

National Socialism, the principles and practices of Hitler's **National Socialist German Workers'** (or Nazi) **Party.** See **Nazi. —National Socialist.**

na·tion·wide (nā'shən wīd'), *adj.* extending throughout the nation: *a nation-wide campaign against cancer.*

na·tive (nā'tǐv), *adj.* **1.** being the place or environment in which one was born or a thing came into being: *one's native land.* **2.** belonging to a person or thing by birth or nature; inborn; inherent; natural (often fol. by *to*). **3.** belonging by birth to a people regarded as natives, esp. outside of the general body of white peoples: *native policemen in India.* **4.** of indigenous origin, growth, or production; (often fol. by *to*): *native pottery.* **5.** of, pertaining to, or characteristic of natives: *native customs in Java.* **6.** under the rule of natives: *the native states of India.* **7.** occupied by natives: *the native quarter of Algiers.* **8.** belonging or pertaining to one by reason of one's birthplace or nationality: *one's native language.* **9.** born in a particular place or country: *native American citizens.* **10.** remaining in a natural state; unadorned; untouched by art: *native beauty.* **11.** forming the source or origin of a person or thing. **12.** originating naturally in a particular country or region, as animals or plants. **13.** found in nature rather than produced artificially, as a mineral substance. **14.** occurring in nature pure or uncombined, as metals, etc.: *native copper.* **15.** belonging to one as a possession by virtue of his birth: *native rights.* **16.** *Archaic.* closely related, as by birth. **—n. 17.** one of the original inhabitants of a place or country, esp. as distinguished from strangers, foreigners, colonizers, etc.: *the natives of Chile.* **18.** one born in a particular place or country: *a native of Ohio.* **19.** an animal or plant indigenous to a particular region. **20.** *Brit.* an oyster. **21.** *Astrol.* one born under a particular planet. [t. L: m.s. *nātīvus* native, innate, natural; r. ME *natif,* t. OF] **—na'tive·ly,** *adv.* **—na'tive·ness,** *n.*

na·tive-born (nā'tǐv bôrn'), *adj.* born in a place or country indicated.

na·tiv·ism (nā'tǐ vǐz'əm), *n.* **1.** the policy of protecting the interests of native inhabitants against those of immigrants. **2.** *Philos.* the doctrine of innate ideas. **—na'tiv·ist,** *n.* **—na'tiv·is'tic,** *adj.*

na·tiv·i·ty (nā tǐv'ə tǐ, nə-), *n., pl.* **-ties. 1.** birth. **2.** birth with reference to place or attendant circumstances: *of Irish nativity.* **3.** (*cap.*) the birth of Christ. **4.** (*cap.*) the church festival commemorating the birth of Christ; Christmas. **5.** (*cap.*) a representation of the birth of Christ, as in art. **6.** *Astrol.* a horoscope. [ME *nativite,* t. LL: m.s. *nātīvitas*]

natl., national.

NATO (nā'tō), *n.* North Atlantic Treaty Organization. See **Atlantic Pact.**

na·tri·um (nā'trǐ əm), *n. Obs.* sodium.

na·tro·lite (nǎt'rə līt', nā'trə-), *n.* a zeolite mineral, a hydrous silicate of sodium and aluminum, $Na_2Al_2Si_3O_{10} \cdot 2H_2O$, occurring usually in white or colorless, often acicular crystals. [f. NATRO(N) + -LITE]

na·tron (nā'trŏn), *n.* a mineral, hydrated sodium car-

---

bonate, $Na_2CO_3 \cdot 10H_2O$. [t. F, t. Sp., t. Ar.: m. *naṭrūn,* t. Gk.: m. *nítron* natron. See NITER]

nat·ty (nǎt'ǐ), *adj.,* **-tier, -tiest.** neatly smart in dress or appearance; spruce; trim: *a natty white uniform.* [? akin to NEAT¹] **—nat'ti·ly,** *adv.* **—nat'ti·ness,** *n.*

nat·u·ral (nǎch'ərəl), *adj.* **1.** existing in or formed by nature; not artificial: *a natural bridge.* **2.** based on the state of things in nature; constituted by nature: *the natural day.* **3.** of or pertaining to nature or the created universe: *a natural science.* **4.** occupied with the study of natural science. **5.** in a state of nature; uncultivated, as land. **6.** growing spontaneously, as vegetation. **7.** having a real or physical existence, as opposed to one that is spiritual, intellectual, fictitious, etc., **8.** of, pertaining to, or proper to the nature or essential constitution: *natural ability.* **9.** proper to the circumstances of the case. **10.** free from affection or constraint: *a natural manner.* **11.** essentially pertaining; coming easily or spontaneously: *a manner natural to an aristocrat.* **12.** consonant with the nature or character of. **13.** in accordance with the nature of things: *it was natural that he should hit back.* **14.** based upon the innate moral feeling of mankind: *natural justice.* **15.** *Now Rare.* having or showing the nature, disposition, feelings, etc., befitting a person. **16.** in conformity with the ordinary course of nature; not unusual or exceptional. **17.** happening in the ordinary course of things, without the intervention of accident, violence, etc.: *a natural death.* **18.** by birth merely, and not legally recognized; illegitimate. **19.** based on what is learned from nature, rather than on revelation: *natural religion.* **20.** true to nature, or closely imitating nature. **21.** unenlightened or unregenerate: *the natural man.* **22.** being such by nature; born such: *a natural fool.* **23.** *Music.* **a.** neither sharp nor flat; without sharps or flats. **b.** changed in pitch by the sign ♮. **—n. 24.** *Colloq.* a thing or a person that is by nature satisfactory or successful. **25.** *Music.* **a.** a white key on the pianoforte, etc. **b.** the sign ♮, placed before a note canceling the effect of a previous sharp or flat. **c.** a note affected by a ♮, or a tone thus represented. **26.** an idiot. [ME, t. L: s. *nātūrālis* by birth, in accordance with nature] **—nat'u·ral·ly,** *adv.* **—nat'u·ral·ness,** *n.*

Natural Bridge, a natural limestone bridge in western Virginia. 215 ft. high; 90 ft. span.

Natural Bridges, a national monument in SE Utah: three natural bridges; largest, 222 ft. high; 261 ft. span.

natural gas, combustible gas formed naturally in the earth, as in regions yielding petroleum, and consisting typically of methane with certain amounts of hydrogen and other gases, used as a fuel, etc.

natural history, **1.** the science or study dealing with all objects in nature. **2.** the aggregate of knowledge connected with such objects.

nat·u·ral·ism (nǎch'ərəl ĭz'əm), *n.* **1.** (in art or literature) **a.** an intention on the part of the artist to represent objects as nearly as possible in their natural and everyday forms. **b.** (esp. in literature) a theory, as practiced by Emile Zola, Stephen Crane and others, which applied scientific concepts and methods to such problems as plot development and characterization. **c.** the group of procedures derived from this theory. **2.** action arising from or based on natural instincts and desires alone. **3.** *Philos.* **a.** the view of the world which takes account only of natural elements and forces, excluding the supernatural or spiritual. **b.** the belief that all phenomena are covered by laws of science and that all teleological explanations are therefore without value. **c.** positivism or materialism. **4.** *Theol.* **a.** the doctrine that all religious truth is derived from a study of natural processes, and not from revelation. **b.** the doctrine that natural religion is sufficient for salvation. **5.** adherence or attachment to what is natural.

nat·u·ral·ist (nǎch'ərəl ĭst), *n.* **1.** one who is versed in or devoted to natural history, esp. a zoölogist or botanist. **2.** an adherent of naturalism.

nat·u·ral·is·tic (nǎch'ərəl ĭs'tĭk), *adj.* **1.** imitating nature or usual natural surroundings. **2.** pertaining to naturalists or natural history. **3.** pertaining to naturalism, esp. in art and literature.

nat·u·ral·ize (nǎch'ərəl īz'), *v.,* **-ized, -izing. —v.t. 1.** to invest (an alien) with the rights and privileges of a subject or citizen; confer the rights and privileges of citizenship upon. **2.** to introduce (animals or plants) into a region and cause to flourish as if native. **3.** to introduce or adopt (foreign practices, words, etc.) into a country or into general use: *to naturalize a French phrase.* **4.** to bring into conformity with nature. **5.** to regard or explain as natural rather than supernatural: *to naturalize miracles.* **6.** to adapt or accustom to a place or to new surroundings. **—v.i. 7.** to become naturalized, or as if native. **—nat'u·ral·i·za'tion,** *n.*

natural law, the expression of right reason or of religion, inhering in nature and man, and having ethically a binding force as a rule of civil conduct.

natural logarithm, Napierian logarithm.

natural philosophy, **1.** the study of nature in general. **2.** the branch of physical science which treats of those properties and phenomena of bodies which are unaccompanied by an essential change in the bodies themselves, including the sciences classed under physics.

natural resources, the wealth of a country consisting of land, forests, mines, water, and energy resources.

---

ct, āble, dâre, ärt; ĕbb, ēqual; ĭf, īce; hŏt, ōver, ôrder, oil, bŏŏk, ōōze, out; ŭp, ūse, ûrge; ə = a in alone; th, chief; g, give; ng, ring; sh, shoe; th, thin; th, that; zh, vision. See the full key on inside cover.

natural science, science or knowledge dealing with objects in nature, as distinguished from mental or moral science, abstract mathematics, etc.

natural selection, the elimination of the unfit and the survival of the fit in the struggle for existence, depending upon the adjustment of an organism to a specific environment. Cf. **Darwinism.**

natural sine, tangent, etc., *Math.* the actual value, not the logarithm, of a sine (tangent, etc.).

na·ture (nā′chər), *n.* **1.** the particular combination of qualities belonging to a person or thing by birth or constitution; native or inherent character: *the nature of atomic energy.* **2.** the instincts or inherent tendencies directing conduct: *a man of good nature.* **3.** character, kind, or sort: *a book of the same nature.* **4.** a person of a particular character or disposition. **5.** the material world, esp. as surrounding man and existing independently of his activities. **6.** the universe, with ali its phenomena. **7.** the sum total of the forces at work throughout the universe. **8.** reality, as distinguished from any effect of art: *true to nature.* **9.** the physical being. **10.** the vital powers: *food sufficient to sustain nature.* **11.** a primitive, wild condition; an uncultivated state. **12.** *Theol.* the moral state as unaffected by grace. **13.** by nature, as a result of inherent qualities. **14.** of or in the nature of, having the qualities of. [ME, *natur*, t. L: s. *nātūra* birth, natural character, nature]

nature study, the study of physical nature, esp. on the level of secondary schools.

Nau·cra·tis (nô′krə tĭs), *n.* an ancient Greek city in N Egypt, on the delta of the Nile. Greek, **Nau′kra·tis.**

naught (nôt), *n.* **1.** a cipher (0); zero. **2.** *Now Archaic or Literary.* nothing. **3.** destruction, ruin, or complete failure: *to bring or come to naught.* **4. set at naught,** to regard or treat as of no importance. —*adj. Obs. or Archaic.* **5.** worthless; useless. **6.** lost; ruined. **7.** morally bad; wicked. —*adv.* **8.** *Obs. or Archaic.* in no respect or degree. Also, **nought.** ME; OE *nauht, nāwiht,* f. *nā* NO + *wiht* thing. See NOUGHT, WIGHT¹, WHIT]

naugh·ty (nô′tĭ), *adj.,* **-tier, -tiest. 1.** disobedient; mischievous (esp. in speaking to or about children): *a naughty child.* **2.** improper; obscene: *a naughty word.* **3.** *Obs.* wicked; evil. ɪME, f. NAUGHT (def. 7) + -Y¹] —**naugh′ti·ly,** *adv.* —**naugh′ti·ness,** *n.*

nau·ma·chi·a (nô mā′kĭə), *n., pl.* **-chiae** (-kĭ ē′), **-chias. 1.** a mock sea fight, given as a spectacle among the ancient Romans. **2.** a place for presenting such spectacles. [t. L, t. Gk.]

nau·ma·chy (nô′mə kĭ), *n., pl.* **-chies.** naumachia.

nau·pli·us (nô′plĭ əs), *n., pl.* **-plii** (-plĭ ī′). (in many crustaceans) a larval form with three pairs of appendages and a single median eye, occurring (usually) as the first stage of development after leaving the egg. [t. L: kind of shellfish]

Na·u·ru (nä ōō′rōō), *n.* a Pacific island near the equator, W of the Gilbert Islands: administered by Australia. 3473 pop. (1954); 8¼ sq. mi. Formerly, **Pleasant Island.**

nau·sea (nô′shə, -shĭ ə, -sĭ ə), *n.* **1.** sickness at the stomach; a sensation of impending vomiting. **2.** seasickness. **3.** extreme disgust. [t. L, var. of *nausia,* t. Gk.]

nau·se·ate (nô′shĭ āt′, -sĭ-), *v.,* **-ated, -ating.** —*v.t.* **1.** to affect with nausea; sicken. **2.** to feel extreme disgust at; loathe. —*v.i.* **3.** to become affected with nausea. [t. L: m.s. *nauseātus,* pp., having been seasick] —**nau′se·a′tion,** *n.*

nau·seous (nô′shəs, -shĭ əs), *adj.* **1.** causing nausea, or sickening. **2.** disgusting; loathsome. [t. L: m.s. *nauseōsus*] —**nau′seous·ly,** *adv.* —**nau′seous·ness,** *n.*

Nau·sic·a·ä (nô sĭk′ĭ ə, -ä ə, nou-), *n. Homeric Legend.* the daughter of Alcinoüs, king of the Phaeacians. She led the shipwrecked Ulysses to her father's court.

naut., nautical.

nautch (nôch), *n.* an East Indian exhibition of dancing by professional dancing girls (**nautch girls**). [t. Hind.: m. *nāch,* g. Prakrit *nachcha* dancing]

nau·ti·cal (nô′tə kəl), *adj.* of or pertaining to seamen, ships, or navigation: *nautical terms.* [f. s. L *nauticus* (t. Gk.: m. *nautikós* pertaining to ships or sailors) + -AL¹] —**nau′ti·cal·ly,** *adv.*

nautical mile, mile (def. 1b).

nau·ti·lus (nô′tə ləs), *n., pl.* **-luses, -li** (-lī′). **1.** any of the tetrabranchiate cephalopods that constitute the genus *Nautilus,* having a spiral, chambered shell with pearly septa; pearly nautilus. **2.** the paper nautilus or argonaut. [t. L, t. Gk.: m. *nautilos,* lit., sailor]

nav., 1. naval. 2. navigation.

Nav·a·ho (năv′ə hō′), *n., pl.* **-hos, -hoes. 1.** (*pl.*) the principal tribe of the southern division of the Athabascan stock of North American Indians, located in New Mexico and Arizona, and now constituting the largest tribal group in the U.S. **2.** a member of this tribe. Also, **Nav·a·jo** (năv′ə hō′). [t. Sp.: m. (*Apaches de*) *Navajo,* t. Tewa: m. *Navahu* great fields, applied to former Tewa pueblo and by extension to the Navahos who intruded upon the agricultural pueblos]

na·val (nā′vəl), *adj.* **1.** of or pertaining to ships, esp., and now only, ships of war: *a naval battle.* **2.** belonging to, pertaining to, or connected with, a navy: *naval affairs.* **3.** possessing a navy: *the great naval powers.* [t. L: s. *nāvālis* pertaining to a ship]

naval academy, a collegiate institution for training naval officers.

Na·va·ri·no (nä′vä rē′nô), *n.* a seaport in SW Greece, in the Peloponnesus: the Turkish and Egyptian fleets were defeated in a naval battle near here, 1827.

Na·varre (nə vär′), *n.* a former kingdom in SW France and N Spain. Spanish, **Na·var·ra** (nä-vär′rä).

Kingdom of Navarre, 1492

nave¹ (nāv), *n.* the main body, or middle part, lengthwise, of a church, flanked by the aisles and extending typically from the entrance to the apse or chancel. See diag. under **basilica.** [t. ML: m.s. *nāvis* nave of a church, L ship]

nave² (nāv), *n.* **1.** the central part of a wheel; the hub. **2.** *Obs.* the navel. [ME; OE *nafu,* c. G *nabe*]

na·vel (nā′vəl), *n.* **1.** a pit or depression in the middle of the surface of the belly; the umbilicus. **2.** the central point or middle of any thing or place. **3.** *Her.* nombril. [ME; OE *nafela,* c. G *nabel*] —**na′vel·like′,** *adj.*

navel orange, a kind of orange having at the apex a navellike formation containing a small secondary fruit.

nav·i·cert (năv′ə sûrt′), *n.* a British consulate certificate, specifying the character of a ship's cargo, etc. [f. L *nāvi*(s) ship + CERT(IFICATE)]

na·vic·u·lar (nə vĭk′yə lər), *Anat.* —*adj.* **1.** (of certain bones, etc.) boat-shaped. —*n.* Also, **na·vic·u·la·re** (nə-vĭk′yə lār′ĭ). **2.** the bone at the radial end of the proximal row of the bones of the carpus. **3.** the bone in front of the talus, or anklebone, on the inner side of the foot. [t. LL: s. *nāviculāris* relating to ships]

navig., navigation.

nav·i·ga·ble (năv′ə gə bəl), *adj.* that may be navigated, as waters, or vessels or aircraft. —**nav′i·ga·bil′i·ty, nav′i·ga·ble·ness,** *n.* —**nav′i·ga·bly,** *adv.*

nav·i·gate (năv′ə gāt′), *v.,* **-gated, -gating.** —*v.t.* **1.** to traverse (the sea, a river, etc.) in a vessel, or (the air) in an aircraft. **2.** to direct or manage (a ship or an aircraft) on its course. **3.** to pass over (the sea, etc.), as a ship does. —*v.i.* **4.** to direct or manage a ship or an aircraft on its course. **5.** to travel by using a ship or boat, as over the water; sail. **6.** to pass over the water, as a ship does. [t. L: m.s. *nāvigātus,* pp.]

nav·i·ga·tion (năv′ə gā′shən), *n.* **1.** act or process of navigating. **2.** the art or science of directing the course of a ship or aircraft. —**nav′i·ga′tion·al,** *adj.*

nav·i·ga·tor (năv′ə gā′tər), *n.* **1.** one who navigates. **2.** one who practices, or is skilled in, navigation, whether of ships or aircraft. **3.** one who conducts explorations by sea. **4.** *Brit.* a navvy or laborer. [t. L]

Navigators Islands, former name of Samoa.

nav·vy (năv′ĭ), *n., pl.* **-vies.** *Brit.* a laborer employed in making canals, railroads, etc. [short for NAVIGATOR]

na·vy (nā′vĭ), *n., pl.* **-vies. 1.** the whole body of warships and auxiliaries belonging to a country or ruler. **2.** the department of government charged with their management. **3.** such a body of warships together with their officers and men, equipment, yards, etc. **4.** Also, **navy blue.** a dark blue. **5.** *Archaic.* a fleet of ships. [ME *navie,* t. OF, der. L *nāvis* ship]

navy bean, the common small white bean, used dried for food.

navy yard, a government dockyard where naval vessels are built, repaired, and fitted out, and naval stores and munitions of war are laid up.

na·wab (nə wôb′), *n.* **1.** a viceroy or deputy governor under the former Mogul empire in India. **2.** an honorary title conferred upon Mohammedans of distinction in India. Cf. **rajah. 3.** nabob. [t. Hind.: m. *nawwāb,* t. Ar., pl. of *nā′ib* deputy, viceroy]

Nax·os (năk′sŏs; *Gk.* nä′ksôs), *n.* a Greek island in the S Aegean: the largest of the Cyclades group. 18,593 pop. (1951); 169 sq. mi.

nay (nā), *adv.* **1.** no (used in dissent, denial, or refusal). **2.** also; and not only so; but: *many good, nay, noble qualities.* —*n.* **3.** a denial or refusal. **4.** a negative vote or voter. [ME *nai, nei,* t. Scand.; cf. Icel. *nei* no, f. *ne* not + *ei* ever]

Naz·a·rene (năz′ə rēn′), *n.* **1.** a native or inhabitant of the town of Nazareth, as Jesus Christ (**the Nazarene**). **2.** a Christian (so called by the Jews, Mohammedans, etc.). **3.** one of a sect of early Jewish Christians who retained the Mosaic ritual. —*adj.* **4.** of or pertaining to Nazareth or the Nazarenes. [ME *Nazaren,* t. LL: s. *Nazarēnus,* t. Gk.: m. *Nazarēnós,* der. *Nazarēt* Nazareth]

Naz·a·reth (năz′ə rəth, -rĭth), *n.* a town in N Israel: the childhood home of Jesus. 21,500 (est. 1954).

Naz·a·rite (năz′ə rīt′), *n.* **1.** (among the ancient Hebrews) a religious devotee who had taken certain vows. Num. 6. **2.** *Rare.* a Nazarene. **3.** *Rare.* Christian. **4.** *Rare.* Christ. Also, **Nazirite.** [f. L *Nazar*(*aeus*) (t. Gk.: m. *Nazaraîos,* der. Heb. *nāzar* consecrate) + -ITE¹]

Naze (nāz), *n.* **The,** the Lindesnes.

Na·zi (nä′tsĭ, năt′sĭ), *n., pl.* **-zis,** *adj.* —*n.* **1.** a member of the National Socialist German Workers' party of Germany, which in 1933, under Adolf Hitler, obtained political control of the country, suppressing all opposition and establishing a dictatorship on the principles of one-party control over all cultural, economic, and political activities of the people, belief in the supremacy of

---

b., blend of, blended;   c., cognate with;   d., dialect, dialectal;   der., derived from;   f., formed from;   g., going back to; m., modification of;   r., replacing;   s., stem of;   t., taken from;   ?, perhaps.   See the full key on inside cover.

Hitler as Führer, anti-Semitism, and the establishment of Germany by superior force as a dominant world power. **2.** one who holds similar views elsewhere. —*adj.* **3.** of or pertaining to the Nazis. [t. G, short for *Nazi(onalsozialist)* National Socialist]

Na·zi·mo·va (nä zē′mô vä), *n.* **Alla** (äl′lä), 1879–1945, Russian actress in America.

Naz·i·rite (năz′ərīt′), *n.* Nazarite.

Na·zism (nä′tsĭ′zəm, năt′sĭz-), *n.* the principles or methods of the Nazis. Also, **Na·zi·ism** (nä′tsĭ ĭz′əm, năt′sĭ-).

Nb, *Chem.* niobium.

N. B., **1.** New Brunswick. **2.** Also, **NB** *nota bene.*

N. C., North Carolina.

N. C. O., Noncommissioned Officer.

Nd, *Chem.* neodymium.

n. d., no date.

N. Dak., North Dakota. Also, **N. D.**

Ne, *Chem.* neon.

NE, **1.** northeast. **2.** northeastern. Also, **n.e.**

N. E., **1.** New England. **2.** northeast. **3.** northeastern.

N. E. A., National Education Association.

Ne·an·der·thal (nĭ ăn′dər täl′; *Ger.* nää′n′-), *adj.* *Anthropol.* of or pertaining to the Neanderthal man.

Neanderthal man, *Anthropol.* the species of primeval man widespread in Europe in the paleolithic period. [so called because earliest evidence was discovered at Neanderthal, a valley near Düsseldorf, Germany]

neap¹ (nēp), *adj.* **1.** designating those tides, midway between spring tides, which attain the least height. —*n.* **2.** neap tide. See diag. under **tide.** [ME *neep,* OE *nēp,* in *nēpflōd* neap flood]

neap² 'nēp), *n.* *U.S. Dial.* the pole or tongue of a wagon, etc. [orig. uncert.]

Ne·a·pol·i·tan (nĭ′ə pŏl′ə tən), *adj.* **1.** of or pertaining to Naples. —*n.* **2.** a native or inhabitant of Naples. [ME, t. L: s. *Neāpolītānus*]

Neapolitan ice cream, variously flavored and colored ice cream and ice mixtures frozen in layers.

near (nĭr), *adv.* **1.** close: *near by.* **2.** nigh; at, within, or to a short distance: *to stand near.* **3.** close at hand in time: *New Year's Day is near.* **4.** close in relation; closely with respect to connection, similarity, etc. **5.** *Now Chiefly Colloq. or Dial.* all but; almost: *a period of near thirty years.* **6.** *Naut.* close to the wind. —*adj.* **7.** being close by; not distant: *the near meadows.* **8.** less distant: *the near side.* **9.** short or direct: *the near road.* **10.** close in time: *the near future.* **11.** closely related or connected: *our nearest relation.* **12.** close to an original: *a near translation.* **13.** closely affecting one's interests or feelings: *a matter of near consequence to one.* **14.** intimate or familiar: *a near friend.* **15.** narrow: *a near escape.* **16.** parsimonious or niggardly: *a near man.* **17.** (in riding or driving) on the left (opposed to *off*): *the near wheel.* —*prep.* (*strictly the adverb with "to" understood*). **18.** at, within, or to a short distance, or no great distance, from: *regions near the equator.* **19.** close upon in time: *near the beginning of the year.* **20.** close upon (a condition, etc.): *a task near completion.* **21.** close to in similarity, resemblance, etc.: *near beer.* **22.** close to (doing something): *this act came near spoiling his chances.* —*v.t., v.i.* **23.** to come or draw near (to); approach. [ME *nere,* OE *nēar,* compar. of *nēah* NIGH] —**near′-ness,** *n.*

near·by (nĭr′bī′), *adj.* close at hand; not far off; adjacent; neighboring: *a nearby village.*

Ne·arc·tic (nē ärk′tĭk, -är′-), *adj.* (in zoögeography) belonging to the northern division of the New World (temperate and arctic North America, with Greenland).

Near East, an indefinite geographical or regional term, usually referring to the Balkan States, Egypt and the countries of SW Asia.

near-hand (nĭr′hănd′), *adv.* *Now Brit. Dial. and Scot.* **1.** near at hand. **2.** nearly or almost.

near·ly (nĭr′lĭ), *adv.* **1.** all but; almost: *nearly dead with cold.* **2.** with close approximation. **3.** with close agreement or resemblance: *a case nearly approaching this one.* **4.** with close kinship, interest, or connection; intimately. **5.** with parsimony. —**Syn. 1.** See **almost.**

near-sight·ed (nĭr′sī′tĭd), *adj.* seeing distinctly at a short distance only; myopic. —**near′-sight′ed·ly,** *adv.* —**near′-sight′ed·ness,** *n.*

neat¹ (nēt), *adj.* **1.** in a pleasingly orderly condition: *a neat room.* **2.** habitually orderly in appearance, etc. **3.** of a simple, pleasing appearance: *a neat cottage.* **4.** cleverly effective in character or execution: *a neat scheme.* **5.** clever, dexterous, or apt: *a neat characterization.* **6.** unadulterated or undiluted, as liquors. **7.** net: *neat profits.* [t. F: m. net clean, g. L *nitidus* bright, fine, neat] —**neat′ly,** *adv.* —**neat′ness,** *n.* —**Syn. 1.** NEAT, TIDY, TRIM describe orderliness and an attractive appearance. NEAT suggests order and absence of superfluous details: *a neat desk, dress.* TIDY has workingclass connotations and the idea of making humble things look their best; it suggests a painstaking orderliness, the result of effort and perhaps of habit: *the cottage looked cheerful and tidy.* TRIM suggests a combination of neatness and smartness or stylishness: *a trim new outfit.* —**Ant. 1.** slovenly.

neat² (nēt), *n., pl.* **neat.** *Obs.* cattle of the genus *Bos.* [ME *neet,* OE *nēat,* c. Icel. *naut*]

neath (nēth, nēᵗħ), *prep.* *Poetic or Scot.* beneath. Also, **'neath.**

neat·herd (nēt′hûrd′), *n.* a cowherd.

neat's-foot oil (nēts′fŏŏt′), a pale-yellow fixed oil made by boiling the feet and shinbones of cattle, used chiefly as a dressing for leather. [see NEAT²]

neb (nĕb), *n.* **1.** a bill or beak, as of a bird. **2.** a person's mouth. **3.** the nose, esp. of an animal. **4.** the tip or pointed end of anything. **5.** the nib of a pen. [ME *nebbe,* OE *nebb,* c. MD and MLG *nebbe*]

Neb., Nebraska.

Ne·bi·im (nĕb′ĭ ĭm′; *Heb.* nĕ vē′ĕm′), *n.pl.* (in the Hebrew Bible) the Prophets, the books occurring after the Torah and before the Hagiographa. [t. Heb., pl of *nābhî* prophet]

Ne·bo (nē′bō), *n.* **Mount.** See **Pisgah, Mount.**

Nebr., Nebraska.

Ne·bras·ka (nə brăs′kə), *n.* a State in the central United States. 1,411,330 pop. (1960); 77,237 sq. mi. *Cap.:* Lincoln. *Abbr.:* Nebr. or Neb. —**Ne·bras′kan,** *adj., n.*

neb·ris (nĕb′rĭs), *n.* *Gk. Antiq.* the skin of a fawn, esp. as worn by Bacchus and later, on festival occasions, by his priests and votaries. [t. L, t. Gk.]

Neb·u·chad·nez·zar (nĕb′yŏŏ kəd nĕz′ər, nĕb′ə-), *n.* a king of Babylonia, 604?–561? B.C., and conqueror of Jerusalem. II Kings 24–25. Also, **Neb·u·chad·rez·zar** (nĕb′yŏŏ kəd rĕz′ər, nĕb′ə-).

neb·u·la (nĕb′yə lə), *n., pl.* **-lae** (-lē′), **-las.** **1.** *Astron.* a cloudlike, luminous mass composed of gaseous matter or stars far beyond the solar system. **2.** *Pathol.* **a.** a faint opacity in the cornea. **b.** cloudiness in the urine. [t. L: mist, vapor, cloud] —**neb′u·lar,** *adj.*

nebular hypothesis, *Astron.* the theory that the solar system has been evolved from a mass of nebulous matter (a theory prominent in the 19th century following its precise formulation by Laplace).

neb·u·lize (nĕb′yə līz′), *v.t.,* **-lized, -lizing.** to reduce to fine spray; atomize. —**neb′u·liz′er,** *n.*

neb·u·lose (nĕb′yə lōs′), *adj.* **1.** nebulous; cloudlike. **2.** hazy or indistinct. **3.** having cloudlike markings.

neb·u·los·i·ty (nĕb′yə lŏs′ə tĭ), *n., pl.* **-ties.** **1.** nebulous or nebular matter. **2.** nebulous state.

neb·u·lous (nĕb′yə ləs), *adj.* **1.** hazy, vague, indistinct, or confused: *a nebulous recollection.* **2.** cloudy or cloudlike. **3.** nebular. [ME, t. L: m.s. *nebulōsus*] —**neb′u·lous·ly,** *adv.* —**neb′u·lous·ness,** *n.*

nec·es·sar·i·an (nĕs′ə sâr′ĭ ən), *n., adj.* necessitarian. —**nec′es·sar′i·an·ism,** *n.*

nec·es·sar·i·ly (nĕs′ə sĕr′ə lĭ), *adv.* **1.** by or of necessity: *you need not necessarily go to the party.* **2.** as a necessary result.

nec·es·sar·y (nĕs′ə sĕr′ĭ), *adj., n., pl.* **-saries.** —*adj.* **1.** that cannot be dispensed with: *a necessary law.* **2.** happening or existing by necessity. **3.** acting or proceeding from compulsion or necessity; not free; involuntary: *a necessary agent.* **4.** *Logic.* **a.** (of propositions) denoting that the denial of that proposition involves a self-contradiction (opp. to *contingent*). **b.** (of inferences or arguments) denoting that it is impossible for the premises of an inference or argument to be true and its conclusion false. **5.** *Archaic.* rendering indispensable or useful services. —*n.* **6.** something necessary, indispensable, or requisite. **7.** (*pl.*) *Law.* food, clothing, etc., required by a dependent or incompetent and varying with his social or economic position or that of the person upon whom he is dependent. **8.** a privy or water closet. [ME, t. L: m.s. *necessārius* unavoidable, indispensable] —**Syn. 1.** NECESSARY, ESSENTIAL, INDISPENSABLE, REQUISITE indicate something vital for the fulfillment of a need. NECESSARY applies to that which is inevitable to the fulfillment of a condition, or that which is the inevitable as a consequence to certain causes: *food is necessary to life, multiplicity is a necessary result of division.* INDISPENSABLE applies to that which cannot be done without or removed from the rest of a unitary condition: *food is indispensable to living things; he made himself indispensable as a companion.* That which is ESSENTIAL forms a vital necessary condition of something: *air is essential to red-blooded animals, it is essential to understand the matter clearly.* REQUISITE applies to what is thought necessary to fill out, complete, or perfect something: *he had all the requisite qualifications for a position.*

ne·ces·si·tar·i·an (nə sĕs′ə târ′ĭ ən), *n.* **1.** one who maintains that the action of the will is a necessary effect of antecedent causes (opposed to *libertarian*). —*adj.* **2.** pertaining to necessitarians or necessitarianism.

ne·ces·si·tar·i·an·ism (nə sĕs′ə târ′ĭ ə nĭz′əm), *n.* the doctrine of the determination of the will by antecedent causes, as opposed to that of the freedom of the will.

ne·ces·si·tate (nə sĕs′ə tāt′), *v.t.,* **-tated, -tating.** **1.** to make necessary: *the breakdown of the motor necessitated a halt.* **2.** to compel, oblige, or force: *the rise in prices necessitated greater thrift.* —**ne·ces′si·ta′tion,** *n.* —**ne·ces′si·ta·tive,** *adj.*

ne·ces·si·tous (nə sĕs′ə təs), *adj.* needy or in involving necessity; needy; indigent. —**ne·ces′si·tous·ly,** *adv.* —**ne·ces′si·tous·ness,** *n.*

ne·ces·si·ty (nə sĕs′ə tĭ), *n., pl.* **-ties.** **1.** something necessary or indispensable: *the necessities of life.* **2.** the fact of being necessary or indispensable; indispensableness. **3.** an imperative requirement or need for something: *necessity for a decision.* **4.** state or fact of being necessary or inevitable. **5.** an unavoidable compulsion to do something. **6.** a state of being in difficulty or need; poverty. **7.** *Philos.* **a.** constraint viewed as a principle of universal causation, determining even the action of the will. **b.** the relation of the inevitable to the nature of its conditions; inevitable connection. [ME *necessite*, t. L: m.s. *necessitas* exigency] —**Syn. 1.** See **need.**

neck (nĕk), *n.* **1.** that part of an animal's body which s between the head and the trunk and connects these parts. **2.** the part of a garment covering the neck or extending about it. **3.** the length of the neck of a horse or other animal as a measure in racing. **4.** the slender part of a bottle, retort, or any similar object. **5.** any narrow, connecting, or projecting part suggesting the neck of an animal. **6.** the longer slender part of a violin or the like, extending from the body to the head. **7.** *Anat.* a constricted part of a bone, organ, or the like. **8.** *Dentistry.* junction between enamel of crown and cementum of root of tooth. **9.** *Print.* a beard (def. 5). **10.** *Archit.* the lowest part of the capital of a column, above the astragal at the head of the shaft. See diag. under **column.** **11.** a narrow strip of land, as an isthmus or a cape. **12.** a strait. **13. neck and neck,** just even. **14. neck or nothing,** at every risk; desperately. **15. win by a neck,** *Racing.* to be first by a head and neck; finish closely. —*v.i.* **16.** *U.S. Slang.* to play amorously. —*v.t.* **17.** to strangle or behead. [ME *nekke*, OE *hnecca,* c. D *nek;* akin to G *nacken* nape of the neck]

neck·band (nĕk/bănd/), *n.* **1.** a band of cloth at the neck of a garment. **2.** band worn around the neck.

neck·cloth (nĕk/klŏth/, -klôth/), *n.* cravat.

Neck·er (nĕk/ər; *Fr.* nĕ kĕr/), *n.* **Jacques** (zhäk), 1732–1804, French statesman, born in Switzerland.

neck·er·chief (nĕk/ər chĭf), *n.* a cloth worn round the neck by women or men. [t. NECK + KERCHIEF]

neck·ing (nĕk/ĭng), *n.* **1.** *Archit.* **a.** a molding or group of moldings between the projecting part of a capital of a column and the shaft. **b.** a gorgerin. **2.** *U.S. Slang.* act of playing amorously.

neck·lace (nĕk/lĭs), *n.* an ornament of precious stones, beads, or the like, worn around the neck. Also, **neck·let** (nĕk/lĭt). [f. NECK + LACE string]

neck·piece (nĕk/pēs/), *n.* a scarf made of fur.

neck·tie (nĕk/tī/), *n.* **1.** a narrow band, as of silk or satin, worn around the neck, commonly under a collar, and tied in front. **2.** any band, scarf, or tie fastened at the front of the neck. **3.** *U.S. Slang.* a hangman's rope.

neck·wear (nĕk/wâr/), *n.* articles of dress worn round or at the neck.

necr-, a word element meaning "dead," "corpse," "death." Also, before consonants, **necro-**. [t. Gk.: m. *nekr-, nekro-,* comb. forms of *nekrós* body, dead]

nec·ro·ba·cil·lus (nĕk/rō bə sĭl/əs), *n.* any disease of cattle, horses, sheep, and swine marked by necrotic areas in which a bacillus, *Actinomyces necrophorus,* is found.

ne·crol·a·try (nĕ krŏl/ə trĭ), *n.* worship of the dead.

ne·crol·o·gy (nĕ krŏl/ə jĭ), *n., pl.* -**gies.** **1.** an obituary notice. **2.** a list of persons who have died within a certain time. [t. ML: m.s. *necrologium,* f. Gk. (see NECRO-, -LOGY)] —**nec·ro·log·i·cal** (nĕk/ro lŏj/ə kəl), *adj.* —**nec·ro·log/i·cal·ly,** *adv.* —**ne·crol/o·gist,** *n.*

nec·ro·man·cy (nĕk/rə măn/sĭ), *n.* **1.** magic in general; enchantment; conjuration. **2.** the pretended art of divination through communication with the dead; the black art. [t. L: m.s. *necromantia,* t. Gk.: m. *necromanteia;* r. ME *nigromancie,* t. ML: m. *nigromantia,* alter. of L *necromantia* by assoc. with L *niger* black. Cf. BLACK ART] —**nec/ro·man/cer,** *n.* —**nec/ro·man/tic,** *adj.* —**Syn. 2.** See **magic.**

nec·ro·ma·ni·a (nĕk/rə mā/nĭ ə), *n.* morbid attraction toward dead bodies.

ne·croph·i·lism (nĕ krŏf/ə lĭz/əm), *n.* morbid attraction to corpses. Also, **nec·ro·phil·i·a** (nĕk/ro fĭl/ĭ ə).

nec·ro·pho·bi·a (nĕk/rə fō/bĭ ə), *n.* **1.** morbid fear of death. **2.** a morbid aversion to, or fear of, dead bodies.

ne·crop·o·lis (nĕ krŏp/ə lĭs), *n., pl.* -**lises. 1.** a cemetery, often of large size. **2.** an old or prehistoric burying ground, as of an ancient people. [t. NL, t. Gk.: m. *nekrópolis,* lit., city of the dead]

nec·rop·sy (nĕk/rŏp sĭ), *n., pl.* -**sies.** the examination of a body after death; an autopsy. Also, **ne·cros·co·py** (nĕ krŏs/kə pĭ). [f. NECR- + s. Gk. *ópsis* sight + -Y³]

ne·crose (nĕ krōs/, nĕk/rōs), *v.t., v.i.,* -**crosed, -crosing.** to affect or be affected with necrosis.

ne·cro·sis (nĕ krō/sĭs), *n.* **1.** *Pathol.* death of a circumscribed piece of tissue or of an organ. **2.** *Bot.* a diseased condition in plants resulting from the death of the tissue. [t. NL, t. Gk.: m. *nēkrōsis* a killing] —**ne·crot·ic** (nĕ krŏt/ĭk), *adj.*

necrotic en·ter·i·tis (ĕn/tə rī/tĭs), a disease of swine characterized by extensive ulceration of the intestine.

ne·crot·o·my (nĕ krŏt/ə mĭ), *n., pl.* -**mies. 1.** the excision of necrosed bone. **2.** dissection of dead bodies.

nec·tar (nĕk/tər), *n.* **1.** *Bot.* the saccharine secretion of a plant, which attracts the insects or birds that pollinate the flower, collected by bees, in whose body it is elaborated into honey. **2.** the drink, or, less properly, the food, of the gods of classical mythology. **3.** any delicious drink. [t. L, Gk.: m. *néktar*]

nec·tar·e·ous (nĕk târ/ĭ əs), *adj.* **1.** of the nature of or resembling nectar. **2.** delicious; sweet. Also, **nec·tar·e·an.** [t. L: m. *nectareus,* t. Gk.: m. *nektáreos*]

nec·tar·ine (nĕk/tə rēn/, nĕk/tə rēn), *n.* a form of the common peach, having a skin destitute of down. [n. use of *nectarine,* adj., f. NECTAR + -INE¹]

nec·ta·ry (nĕk/tə rĭ), *n., pl.* -**ries. 1.** *Bot.* an organ or part that secretes nectar. **2.** *Entomol.* one of a pair of small abdominal tubes from which aphids secrete honeydew. —**nec·tar·i·al** (nĕk târ/ĭ al), *adj.*

N.E.D., New English Dictionary (Oxford English Dictionary).

nee (nā), *adj.* born (placed after the name of a married woman to introduce her maiden name): *Madame de Staël, nee Necker.* Also, **née** (nā; *Fr.* nĕ). [t. F, fem. of *né,* pp. of *naître* to be born, g. L *nascī*]

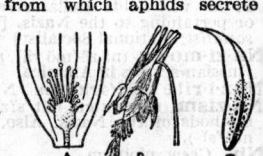

Nectaries (def. 1)
A. Grass of Parnassus, *Parnassia palustris;* B. Columbine, *Aquilegia canadensis;* C. Swamp lily, *Lilium superbum*

need (nēd), *n.* **1.** a case or instance in which some necessity or want exists; a requirement: *to meet the needs of the occasion.* **2.** urgent want, as of something requisite: *he has no need of your kindness.* **3.** necessity arising from the circumstances of a case: *there is no need to worry.* **4.** a situation or time of difficulty; exigency: *a friend in need.* **5.** a condition marked by the lack of something requisite: *the need for leadership.* **6.** destitution; extreme poverty. —*v.t.* **7.** to have need of; require: *to need money.* —*v.i.* **8.** to be necessary: *there needs no apology.* **9.** to be under a necessity (fol. by infinitive, in certain cases without *to;* in the 3d pers. sing. the form is *need,* not *needs*): *he need not go.* **10.** to be in need or want. [ME *nede,* d. OE *nēd;* r. ME *nud*(c), OD *nȳd, nīed;* akin to G *not*] —**need/er,** *n.*

—**Syn. 2.** NEED, NECESSITY imply a want, a lack, or a demand, which must be filled. NEED, a word of Old English origin, has connotations which make it strong in emotional appeal: *the need to be appreciated.* NECESSITY, a word of Latin origin, is more formal and impersonal or objective; though much stronger than NEED in expressing urgency or imperative demand, it is less effective in appealing to the emotions: *water is a necessity for living things.* **6.** See **poverty.**

need·ful (nēd/fəl), *adj.* **1.** necessary: *needful supplies.* **2.** *Rare.* needy. —**need/ful·ly,** *adv.* —**need/ful·ness,** *n.*

need·i·ness (nē/dĭ nĭs), *n.* needy state; indigence.

nee·dle (nē/dəl), *n., v.,* -**dled, -dling.** —*n.* **1.** a small, slender, pointed instrument, now usually of polished steel, with an eye or hole for thread, used in sewing. **2.** a slender, rodlike implement for use in knitting, or one hooked at the end for use in crocheting, etc. **3.** *Med.* a slender, pointed, steel instrument used in sewing or piercing tissues. **4.** any of various objects resembling or suggesting a needle. **5.** a small, slender, pointed instrument, usually of polished steel or some other material, used to transmit vibratory motions as from a phonograph record. **6.** magnetic needle. **7.** a pointed instrument used in engraving, etc. **8.** *Bot.* a needle-shaped leaf, as of a conifer: *a pine needle.* **9.** *Zool.* a slender sharp spicule. **10.** *Chem., Mineral.* a needlelike crystal. **11.** a sharp-pointed mass or pinnacle of rock. **12.** an obelisk, or tapering, four-sided shaft of stone. —*v.t.* **13.** to sew or pierce with or as with a needle. **14.** to prod or goad. **15.** to tease or heckle. —*v.i.* **16.** to form needles in crystallization. **17.** to work with a needle. [ME *nēdle,* d. OE *nǣdl;* r. OE *nǣdl,* G *nadel*] —**nee/dle·like/,** *adj.*

nee·dle·fish (nē/dəl fĭsh/), *n., pl.* -**fishes,** (*esp. collectively*) -**fish. 1.** any fish of the family *Belonidae,* with a long sharp beak and needlelike teeth, found in all warm seas and in some coastal fresh waters; gar. **2.** a pipefish.

nee·dle·ful (nē/dəl fŏol/), *n., pl.* -**fuls.** a suitable length of thread for using at one time with a needle.

needle point, canvas which has been embroidered in a certain manner.

nee·dle-point (nē/dəl point/), *adj.* denoting a kind of lace (**needle-point lace**) in which a needle works out the design upon parchment or paper.

need·less (nēd/lĭs), *adj.* not needed or wanted; unnecessary: *a needless waste of food.* —**need/less·ly,** *adv.* —**need/less·ness,** *n.*

needle valve, *Mach., Eng., etc.* a valve with a needlelike part, a fine adjustment, or a small opening; esp., a valve in which the opening is controlled by a needlelike or conical point which fits into a conical seat.

nee·dle·wom·an (nē/dəl wŏom/ən), *n., pl.* -**women.** a woman who does needlework.

nee·dle·work (nē/dəl wûrk/), *n.* the process or the product of working with a needle as in sewing or embroidery.

need·n't (nēd/nt), contraction of **need not.**

needs (nēdz), *adv.* of necessity; necessarily (usually with *must*). [ME *needes,* OE *nēdes,* orig. gen. of *nēd* need]

need·y (nē/dĭ), *adj.,* **needier, neediest.** in, or characterized by, need or want; very poor: *a needy family.*

neep (nēp), *n. Scot.* and *Brit. Dial.* a turnip. [ME *nepe,* d. OE *nēp;* r. OE *nǣp,* t. L: m.s. *nāpus*]

ne'er (nâr), *adv. Chiefly Poetic.* contraction of **never.**

ne'er-do-well (nâr/dōō wĕl/), *n.* **1.** a worthless person. —*adj.* **2.** worthless; good-for-nothing.

ne·far·i·ous (nĭ fâr/ĭ əs), *adj.* extremely wicked; iniquitous: *nefarious practices.* [t. L: m. *nefārius* impious] —**ne·far/i·ous·ly,** *adv.* —**ne·far/i·ous·ness,** *n.*

Nef·er·ti·ti (nĕf/ər tē/tĭ), *n.* Egyptian queen, wife of Amenhotep IV. Also, **Nofretete.**

neg., **1.** negative. **2.** negatively.

b., blend of, blended; **c.,** cognate with; **d.,** dialect, dialectal; **der.,** derived from; **f.,** formed from; **g.,** going back to; **m.,** modification of; **r.,** replacing; **s.,** stem of; **t.,** taken from; **?,** perhaps. See the full key on inside cover.

ne·gate (nĭ·gāt′, nē′gāt), *v.t.*, **-gated, -gating.** to deny; negative; nullify. [t. L: m.s. *negatus*, pp.]

ne·ga·tion (nĭ·gā′shən), *n.* **1.** the act of denying. **2.** a denial. **3.** a negative thing; a nonentity. **4.** the absence or opposite of what is actual, positive, or affirmative. **5.** a thing, or object of thought, consisting in the absence of something positive.

neg·a·tive (nĕg′ə·tĭv), *adj., n., v.,* **-tived, -tiving.** —*adj.* **1.** expressing or containing negation or denial: *a negative statement.* **2.** expressing refusal to do something. **3.** refusing consent, as to a proposal. **4.** prohibitory, as a command or order. **5.** characterized by the absence of distinguishing or marked qualities or features; lacking positive attributes: *a negative character.* **6.** *Math., Physics.* **a.** involving or denoting subtraction; minus. **b.** measured or proceeding in the opposite direction to that which is considered as positive. **7.** *Bacteriol.* failing to show a positive result in a test for a specific disease caused by either bacteria or viruses. **8.** *Photog.* denoting an image in which the gradations of light and shade are represented in reverse. **9.** *Physiol.* responding in a direction away from the stimulus. **10.** *Elect.* noting or pertaining to the kind of electricity developed on resin, amber, etc., when rubbed with flannel, or that present at the pole from which electrons leave an electric generator or battery, having an excess of electrons. **11.** *Chem.* (of an element or radical) tending to gain electrons and become negatively charged. **12.** *Logic.* (of a proposition) asserting a relation of exclusion between its subject and predicate. —*n.* **13.** a negative statement, answer, word, gesture, etc. **14.** a refusal of assent. **15.** a veto. **16.** that side of a question which denies what the opposite side affirms. **17.** the negative form of statement (opposed to *affirmative*). **18.** a negative quality or characteristic. **19.** *Math.* a negative quantity or symbol. **20.** *Photog.* a negative image, as on a film or plate, used chiefly for printing positive pictures. **21.** *Elect.* the negative plate or element in a voltaic cell. —*v.t.* **22.** to deny; contradict. **23.** to disprove. **24.** to refuse assent or consent to; pronounce against; to veto. **25.** to neutralize or counteract. [ME, t. L: m.s. *negativus* that denies] —**neg′a·tive·ly,** *adv.* —**neg′a·tive·ness, neg′a·tiv′i·ty,** *n.*

neg·a·tiv·ism (nĕg′ə·tĭ·vĭz′əm), *n.* **1.** negativistic behavior. **2.** any system of negative philosophy, such as agnosticism, skepticism, etc. —**neg′a·tiv·ist,** *n.*

neg·a·tiv·is·tic (nĕg′ə·tĭ·vĭs′tĭk), *adj. Psychol.* marked by resistance to a stimulus; tending to react in the opposite way to any suggestion.

neg·a·to·ry (nĕg′ə·tōr′ĭ), *adj.* denying; negative.

neg·a·tron (nĕg′ə·trŏn′), *n. Physics, Chem. Rare.* an electron.

neg·lect (nĭ·glĕkt′), *v.t.* **1.** to pay no attention to; disregard: *a neglected genius.* **2.** to be remiss in care for or treatment of: *to neglect one's family.* **3.** to omit (doing something), through indifference or carelessness. **4.** to fail to carry out or perform (orders, duties, etc.). **5.** to fail to take or use: *to neglect no precaution.* —*n.* **6.** the act or fact of neglecting; disregard. **7.** the fact or state of being neglected; negligence. [t. L: s. *neglectus,* pp., unheeded] —**neg·lect′or, tor,** *n.* —**Syn. 2.** See **slight. 6, 7.** NEGLECT, DERELICTION, NEGLIGENCE, REMISSNESS imply carelessness, failure, or some important omission in the performance of one's duty, a task, etc. NEGLECT and NEGLIGENCE are occasionally interchangeable, but NEGLECT commonly refers to the act, NEGLIGENCE to the habit or trait, of failing to attend to or perform what is expected or required: *gross neglect of duty, negligence in handling traffic problems.* DERELICTION implies culpable or reprehensible neglect or failure in the performance of duty: *dereliction in a position of responsibility.* REMISSNESS implies the omission or the careless or indifferent performance of a duty: *remissness was the cause for tardiness in reporting.* —**Ant. 6.** attention, care.

neg·lect·ful (nĭ·glĕkt′fəl), *adj.* characterized by neglect; disregardful; careless; negligent (often fol. by *of*). —**neg·lect′ful·ly,** *adv.* —**neg·lect′ful·ness,** *n.*

neg·li·gee (nĕg′lə·zhā′, nĕg′lə·zhā′), *n.* **1.** a woman's dressing gown or robe. **2.** easy, informal attire. Also, French, **né·gli·gé** (nā′glē·zhē′). [t. F: m. *négligé,* orig. pp. of *négliger* neglect, t. L: m. *negligere*]

neg·li·gence (nĕg′lə·jəns), *n.* **1.** state or fact of being negligent; neglect. **2.** an instance of being negligent; a defect due to carelessness. **3.** *Law.* the failure to exercise that degree of care which, under the circumstances, the law requires for the protection of those interests of other persons which may be injuriously affected by the want of such care. —**Syn. 1.** See **neglect.**

neg·li·gent (nĕg′lə·jənt), *adj.* guilty of or characterized by neglect, as of duty: *negligent officials.* [ME, t. L: s. *negligens,* ppr., neglecting] —**neg′li·gent·ly,** *adv.*

neg·li·gi·ble (nĕg′lə·jə·bəl), *adj.* that may be neglected or disregarded. —**neg′li·gi·bil′i·ty, neg′li·gi·ble·ness,** *n.* —**neg′li·gi·bly,** *adv.*

ne·go·ti·a·ble (nĭ·gō′shĭ·ə·bəl, -shə·bəl), *adj.* **1.** capable of being negotiated. **2.** (of bills, etc.) transferable by delivery, with or without endorsement, according to the circumstances, the title passing to the transferee. —**ne·go′ti·a·bil′i·ty,** *n.*

ne·go·ti·ant (nĭ·gō′shĭ·ənt), *n.* one who negotiates.

ne·go·ti·ate (nĭ·gō′shĭ·āt′), *v.,* **-ated, -ating.** —*v.i.* **1.** to treat with another or others, as in the preparation of a treaty, or in preliminaries to a business deal.

—*v.t.* **2.** to arrange for or bring about by discussion and settlement of terms: *to negotiate a loan.* **3.** to conduct (an affair, etc.). **4.** *Colloq.* to clear or pass (an obstacle, etc.). **5.** to circulate by endorsement: *to negotiate a bill of exchange.* **6.** to dispose of by sale or transfer: *to negotiate securities.* **7.** to transfer (a bill, etc.) by assignment or delivery. [t. L: m.s. *negotiatus,* pp.] —**ne·go′ti·a′tor,** *n.*

ne·go·ti·a·tion (nĭ·gō′shĭ·ā′shən), *n.* mutual discussion and arrangement of the terms of a transaction or agreement: *the negotiation of a treaty.*

Ne·gri bodies (nā′grĭ), certain microscopic bodies found in the brain cells of animals affected with rabies.

Ne·gril·lo (nĭ·grĭl′ō), *n., pl.* **-los.** a Negrito, esp. of the African division; a pygmy. [t. Sp., dim. of *negro* NEGRO]

Ne·gri Sem·bi·lan (nā′grē sĕm′bē·län′), a state in the former Federation of Malaya: now part of the federation of Malaysia. 364,524 pop. (1957); 2580 sq. mi. *Cap.:* Seremban.

Ne·grit·ic (nĭ·grĭt′ĭk), *adj.* of or pertaining to Negroes or the Negritos.

Ne·gri·to (nĭ·grē′tō), *n., pl.* **-tos, -toes.** a member of any of certain dwarfish Negroid peoples of southeastern Asia and of Africa, esp. of Malaya and the Andaman and Philippine Islands. [t. Sp., dim. of *negro* NEGRO]

Ne·gro (nē′grō), *n., pl.* **-groes,** *adj.* —*n.* **1.** a member of the Negro race. **2.** a person having some Negro ancestry. **3.** a member of any dark-skinned people. —*adj.* **4.** of, denoting or pertaining to the so-called "black" race of Africa and its descendants elsewhere, characterized by a brown-black complexion, broad and flat nose, projecting jaws, everted lips, and crisp or woolly hair. [t. Sp. and Pg.: a black person, Negro, g. L *niger* black] —**Ne·gress** (nē′grĭs), *n. fem.* (often used derogatorily).

Ne·gro (nā′grō; *Sp.* nā′grō), **Río** (rē′ō). **1.** a river flowing from W Colombia through N Brazil into the Amazon. ab. 1400 mi. **2.** a river in S Argentina, flowing from the Andes E to the Atlantic. ab. 700 mi.

Ne·groid (nē′groid), *adj.* **1.** resembling, or akin to, the Negro race and presumably allied to it in origin, as shown by "black" skin and woolly hair. Included are African Negroes, Oceanian Negroes (Papuans and Melanesians), and Negritos, but excluded are Australian blackfellows on account of their nonwoolly hair. —*n.* **2.** a person of a Negroid race.

ne·gro·phile (nē′grə·fīl′, -fĭl), *n.* one who is friendly to and likes Negroes. Also, **ne·gro·phil** (nē′grə·fĭl′).

ne·gro·phobe (nē′grə·fōb′), *n.* one who fears, or has strong antipathy to, Negroes.

ne·gro·pho·bi·a (nē′grə·fō′bĭ·ə), *n.* fear of, or strong antipathy to, Negroes.

Ne·gro·pont (nē′grə·pŏnt′), *n.* Euboea.

Ne·gros (nā′grōs; *Sp.* nĕ′grōs), *n.* one of the Philippine Islands, in the central part of the group. 1,482,219 pop. (1948); 5043 sq. mi.

ne·gus[1] (nē′gəs), *n.* **1.** a royal title in Ethiopia. **2.** (*cap.*) the emperor of Ethiopia. [t. Amharic: king]

ne·gus[2] (nē′gəs), *n. Chiefly Brit.* a beverage made of wine and hot water, with sugar, nutmeg, and lemon. [named after Colonel Francis *Negus* (d. 1732), its reputed inventor]

Neh., Nehemiah.

Ne·he·mi·ah (nē′ə·mī′ə), *n.* **1.** a Hebrew leader of the 5th century B.C.: returned to Jerusalem to rebuild its walls. **2.** a book of the Old Testament. [t. Heb.]

Neh·ru (nē′rōō), *n.* **Jawaharlal** (jə·wə·hər·läl′), 1889–1964, Hindu political leader in India: prime minister of the republic of India, 1950–64.

neigh (nā), *v.i.* **1.** to utter the cry of a horse; whinny. —*n.* **2.** the cry of a horse; a whinny. [ME *neyghe,* OE *hnǣgan,* c. MHG *nēgen.* See NAG[2], *n.*]

neigh·bor (nā′bər), *n.* **1.** one who lives near another. **2.** a person or thing that is near another. **3.** a fellow being subject to the obligations of humanity. —*adj.* **4.** living or situated near to another. —*v.t.* **5.** to place or bring near. **6.** to live or be situated near to; adjoin; border on. —*v.i.* **7.** to associate on the terms of neighbors; be neighborly or friendly (fol. by *with*). **8.** to live or be situated nearby. Also, *Brit.,* **neigh′bour.** [ME *neighebour,* OE *nēahgebūr,* f. *nēah* nigh + *gebūr* dweller, countryman, c. G *nachbar*]

neigh·bor·hood (nā′bər·hŏŏd′), *n.* **1.** the region near or about some place or thing; the vicinity. **2.** a district or locality, often with reference to its character or inhabitants: *a fashionable neighborhood.* **3.** a number of persons living near one another or in a particular locality: *the whole neighborhood was there.* **4.** *Now Rare.* neighborly feeling or conduct. **5.** nearness; proximity. **6.** in the neighborhood of, nearly; about.

neigh·bor·ing (nā′bər·ĭng), *adj.* living or situated near; adjacent.

neigh·bor·ly (nā′bər·lĭ), *adj.* befitting, or acting as befits, a neighbor; friendly. —**neigh′bor·li·ness,** *n.*

Neil·son (nēl′sən), *n.* **William Allan,** 1869–1946, U.S. educator and lexicographer, born in Scotland.

Neis·se (nīs′ə), *n.* a river flowing from NW Czechoslovakia N along part of the boundary between East Germany and Poland to the Oder river. ab. 145 mi.

nei·ther (nē′ŧẖər or, *esp. Brit.,* nī′ŧẖər), *conj.* **1.** not either (a disjunctive connective preceding a series of two or more alternative words, etc., connected by the correlative *nor*): *neither you nor I nor anybody else knows the answer.* **2.** nor yet: *Ye shall not eat of it, neither shall ye touch it.* —*adj.* **3.** not either; not the one or the other: *neither statement is true.* [ME *neither* (f. *ne* not + EITHER); r. ME *nauther*, OE *nāuther*, contr. var. of *nāhwæther*, f. *nā* not + *hwæther* either, WHETHER]

Nejd (nĕzhd, nād), *n.* a former sultanate in central Arabia, forming (with dependencies) with Hejaz the kingdom of Saudi Arabia: inhabited by Wahabis. ab. 3,000,000 pop.; ab. 414,000 sq. mi.

nek·ton (nĕk′tŏn), *n.* the aggregate of actively swimming organisms at the surface of the sea. [t. G, t. Gk.: (neut.) swimming] —**nek·ton′ic**, *adj.*

Nel·son (nĕl′sən), *n.* **1.** Viscount **Horatio**, 1758–1805, British admiral: famous victories over Napoleon I, esp. Trafalgar (1805). **2.** a river in central Canada, from Lake Winnipeg NE to Hudson Bay. ab. 390 mi.

ne·lum·bo (nĭ lŭm′bō), *n.*, *pl.* **-bos.** lotus (def. 3). [t. NL, t. Singhalese: m. *nelumbu*]

nemat-, a word element referring to threadlike things, especially to *nematodes.* Also, before consonants, **nemato-**. [t. Gk., comb. form of *nēma* thread]

nem·a·thel·minth (nĕm′ə thĕl′mĭnth), *n.* any of the *Nemathelminthes*, a phylum of worms (now usually broken up into several phyla), including the nematodes, etc., characterized by an elongated, unsegmented cylindrical body. Also, **nem·a·tel·minth** (nĕm′ə tĕl′mĭnth). [f. Gk.: s. *nēma* thread + s. *hēlmins* worm]

nem·a·to·cyst (nĕm′ə tə sĭst′), *n.* *Zool.* an organ of offense and defense peculiar to coelenterates, consisting of a minute capsule containing a thread capable of being ejected and of causing a sting.

Nem·a·to·da (nĕm′ə tō′də), *n.pl.* the roundworms, a group variously considered a phylum or class. They are elongated smooth worms of cylindroid shape, parasitic or free-living, as ascarids, trichinae, vinegar eels, etc.

nem·a·tode (nĕm′ə tōd′), *n.* any of the *Nematoda.*

Ne·me·a (nē′mĭ ə), *n.* a valley in SE Greece, in ancient Argolis. —**Ne·me·an** (nĭ mē′ən, nē′mĭ-), *adj.*

Nemean games, one of the four national festivals of the ancient Greeks. It was celebrated at Nemea in the 2d and 4th year of each Olympiad.

Nemean lion, *Gk. Legend.* a lion said to have been killed by Hercules.

ne·mer·te·an (nĭ mûr′tĭ ən), *n.* **1.** any of the *Nemertinea.* —*adj.* **2.** belonging or pertaining to the nemerteans. Also, **ne·mer·tine** (nĭ mûr′tĭn). [f. s. NL *Nemertea*, pl. (der. Gk. *Nēmertēs* name of a Nereid) + -AN]

Nem·er·tin·e·a (nĕm′ər tĭn′ĭ ə), *n.pl.* a group of unsegmented marine worms considered either a class of *Platyhelminthes* or an independent phylum, characterized by the long proboscis that can be shot out from the anterior end.

Nem·e·sis (nĕm′ə sĭs), *n.*, *pl.* **-ses** (-sēz′). **1.** the goddess of retribution or vengeance. **2.** (*l.c.*) an agent of retribution or punishment. [t. L, t. Gk.]

ne·mi·ne con·tra·di·cen·te (nĕm′ə nē′ kŏn′trə dĭ-sĕn′tĭ), *Latin.* no one contradicting; unanimously.

ne·mi·ne dis·sen·ti·en·te (nĕm′ə nē′ dĭ sĕn′shĭ ĕn′tĭ), *Latin.* no one dissenting; unanimously.

Ne·mu·nas (nyĕ′mŏŏ näs′), *n.* Lithuanian name of **Niemen.**

N. Eng., Northern England.

neo-, a word element meaning "new", "recent," used in combination, as in *Neo-Darwinism* (a new or modified form of Darwinism), *Neo-Gothic* (Gothic after a new or modern style), *Neo-Hebraic* (pertaining to Hebrew of the modern period), *Neo-Hellenic, Neo-Latin, Neo-Persian.* [t. Gk., comb. form of *néos*]

ne·o·ars·phen·a·mine (nē′ō ärs′fĕn ə mēn′, -fĭ năm′-ĭn), *n.* *Pharm.* a yellow-orange medicinal powder, H₂NC₆H₃(OH)As₂C₆H₃(OH)NHCH₂OSONa, prepared from, but less toxic than, salvarsan.

Ne·o·Cath·o·lic (nē′ō kăth′ə lĭk), *adj.* **1.** of or pertaining to those Anglicans who avowedly prefer the doctrines, rituals, etc., of the Roman Catholic Church to those of the Anglican communion. **2.** (in France) of or pertaining to a person who has left the Roman Catholic Church because of his belief in modernism (def. 3a). —*n.* **3.** a Neo-Catholic person. —**Ne·o·Cath·ol·i·cism** (nē′ō kə thŏl′ə sĭz′əm), *n.*

Ne·o·cene (nē′ə sēn′), *Stratig.* —*adj.* **1.** pertaining to a division of the Tertiary period or system that comprises the Miocene and Pliocene. —*n.* **2.** time or rocks comprising the later half of the Tertiary period or system.

ne·o·clas·sic (nē′ō klăs′ĭk), *adj.* belonging or pertaining to a revival of classic style, as in art or literature. Also, **ne·o·clas′si·cal.**

Ne·o·Dar·win·ism (nē′ō där′wĭ nĭz′əm), *n.* *Biol.* the theory of evolution as expounded by later students of Darwin, esp. Weismann, who hold that natural selection accounts for evolution and deny the inheritance of acquired characteristics.

ne·o·dym·i·um (nē′ō dĭm′ĭ əm), *n.* *Chem.* a rare-earth, metallic, trivalent element occurring with cerium and other rare-earth metals, and having rose- to violet-colored salts. Symbol: Nd; *at. wt.:* 144.27; *at. no.:* 60; *sp. gr.:* 6.9 at 20° C. [t. NL; see NEO-, (DI)DYMIUM]

ne·o·im·pres·sion·ism (nē′ō ĭm prĕsh′ə nĭz′əm), *n.* the theory and methods of certain of the later impressionist painters (from about 1886), characterized by an attempt to make the impressionist methods strictly scientific by employment of the pointillist technique in juxtaposing methodically small dots or squares of pure colors. —**ne′o·im·pres′sion·ist**, *n.*, *adj.*

Ne·o·La·marck·ism (nē′ō lə märk′ĭz əm), *n.* *Biol.* Lamarckism as expounded by later biologists who hold especially that some acquired characters of organisms may be transmitted to descendants, but that natural selection also is a factor in evolution. —**Ne·o·La·marck·i·an** (nē′ō lə märk′ĭ ən), *adj.*, *n.*

Ne·o·Lat·in (nē′ō lăt′ən), *n.* the Latin which became current (notably in scientific literature) after the Renaissance (approximately 1500). Also, **New Latin.**

ne·o·lith (nē′ə lĭth), *n.* a neolithic stone implement.

ne·o·lith·ic (nē′ə lĭth′ĭk), *adj.* *Anthropol.* noting or pertaining to the later part of the Old World Stone Age, characterized by the use of highly finished or polished stone implements and by food raising.

ne·ol·o·gism (nĭ ŏl′ə jĭz′əm), *n.* **1.** a new word or phrase. **2.** the introduction or use of new words, or new senses of words. **3.** a new doctrine. [t. F: m. *néologisme*, der. *néologie.* See NEO-, -LOGY] —**ne·ol′o·gist**, *n.* —**ne·ol′o·gis′tic, ne·ol′o·gis′ti·cal,** *adj.*

ne·ol·o·gy (nĭ ŏl′ə jĭ), *n.*, *pl.* **-gies.** neologism. —**ne·o·log·i·cal** (nē′ə lŏj′ə kəl), *adj.*

ne·o·my·cin (nē′ō mī′sĭn), *n.* a recently developed antibiotic similar to streptomycin but more effective in combating certain microbic infections.

ne·on (nē′ŏn), *n.* *Chem.* a chemically inert gaseous element occurring in small amounts in the earth's atmosphere, and chiefly used in orange-red tubular electrical discharge lamps. Symbol: Ne; *at. wt.:* 20.183; *at. no.:* 10; *weight of one liter of the gas at 0°C. and at 760 mm. pressure:* 0.9002 gr. [t. NL, t. Gk.: (neut.) new]

ne·o·ör·tho·dox·y (nē′ō ôr′thə dŏk′sĭ), *n.* a recent movement in Protestant thought which revives and develops some of the leading doctrines of early theology, such as revelation, the fall, justification by faith, etc.

ne·o·phyte (nē′ə fīt′), *n.* **1.** a converted heathen, heretic, etc. **2.** *Primitive Church.* one newly baptized. **3.** *Rom. Cath. Ch.* a novice. **4.** a beginner. [t. LL: m.s. *neophytus*, t. Gk.: m. *neóphytos* newly planted]

ne·o·plasm (nē′ə plăz′əm), *n.* *Pathol.* a new growth of different or abnormal tissue; a tumor. —**ne·o·plas·tic** (nē′ə plăs′tĭk), *adj.*

ne·o·plas·ty (nē′ə plăs′tĭ), *n.* the repairing or restoration of a part by plastic surgery.

Ne·o·pla·to·nism (nē′ō plā′tə nĭz′əm), *n.* a philosophical system founded chiefly on Platonic doctrine and Oriental mysticism, later influenced by Christianity. It originated in the 3rd century A.D. Also, **Ne·o·Pla′to·nism.** —**Ne·o·pla·ton·ic** (nē′ō plə tŏn′ĭk), *adj.* —**Ne′o·pla′to·nist**, *n.*

ne·o·prene (nē′ə prēn′), *n.* an oil-resistant synthetic rubber made by polymerizing chloroprene.

ne·o·sal·var·san (nē′ō săl′vər săn′), *n.* **1.** neoarsphenamine. **2.** (*cap.*) a trademark for it.

Ne·o·Scho·las·ti·cism (nē′ō skə lăs′tə sĭz′əm), *n.* a contemporary application of scholasticism to modern problems and life. —**Ne·o·Scho·las′tic**, *adj.*

ne·o·style (nē′ə stīl′), *n.*, *v.*, **-styled, -styling.** —*n.* **1.** a type of cyclostyle. —*v.t.* **2.** to reproduce with a neostyle.

ne·ot·e·ny (nĭ ŏt′ə nĭ), *n.* *Zool.* the capacity or phenomenon of becoming sexually mature in the larval state. Cf. **axolotl.** [t. NL: m.s. *neotēnia*, f. Gk.: neo- NEO- + m.s. *teínein* extend + -ia -IA] —**ne·ot′e·nous**, *adj.*

ne·o·ter·ic (nē′ə tĕr′ĭk), *adj.* **1.** modern. —*n.* **2.** a modern writer, thinker, etc. [t. LL: s. *neōtericus*, t. Gk.: m. *neōterikós* youthful] —**ne·o·ter′i·cal·ly**, *adv.*

Ne·o·trop·i·cal (nē′ō trŏp′ə kəl), *adj.* *Zoogeog.* belonging to that part of the New World extending from the tropic of Cancer southward.

ne·o·yt·ter·bi·um (nē′ō ĭ tûr′bĭ əm), *n.* ytterbium.

Ne·o·zo·ic (nē′ə zō′ĭk), *adj.*, *n.* *Obs.* Cenozoic. [f. NEO- + s. Gk. *zōḗ* life + -IC]

NEP (nĕp), *n.* New Economic Policy. Also, **Nep, N.E.P.**

Ne·pal (nə pôl′), *n.* a constitutional monarchy (since 1959) in the Himalayas between N India and Tibet. 8,431,537 (1954); ab. 54,000 sq. mi. *Cap.:* Katmandu.

ne·pen·the (nĭ pĕn′thĭ), *n.* **1.** a drug or draft (in the plant yielding it) mentioned by ancient writers as capable of bringing forgetfulness of sorrow or trouble. **2.** anything inducing easeful forgetfulness. Also, **ne·pen·thes** (nĭ pĕn′thēz). [t. L: m.s. *nēpenthes*, t. Gk.: (neut.) banishing sorrow] —**ne·pen′the·an**, *adj.*

neph·e·line (nĕf′ə lĭn), *n.* a mineral, essentially sodium aluminum silicate, NaAlSiO₄, occurring in alkali-rich volcanic rocks. Also, **neph·e·lite** (nĕf′ə lĭt′). [t. F, f. s. Gk. *nephélē* cloud + -*ine* -INE²]

neph·e·lin·ite (nĕf′ə nĭt′), *n.* *Petrog.* a fine-grained, dark rock of volcanic origin, essentially a basalt containing nepheline but no feldspar and little or no olivine.

neph·e·lom·e·ter (nĕf′ə lŏm′ə tər), *n.* **1.** *Bacteriol.* an apparatus containing a series of barium chloride standards used to determine the number of bacteria in a suspension. **2.** *Chem., etc.* a device for studying the nature of suspensions by the use of diffuse reflected light. [f. s. Gk. *nephélē* cloud + -(O)METER]

neph·ew (nĕf′ū or, esp. Brit., nĕv′ū), *n.* **1.** a son of one's brother or sister. **2.** a son of one's husband's or wife's brother or sister. **3.** (in euphemistic use) an illegitimate son of an ecclesiastic. **4.** *Obs.* a grandson. **5.** *Obs.* a male descendant of more remote degree. [ME *nevew*, t. OF: m. *neveu*, g. L *nepos* grandson, nephew]

---

b., blend of, blended; c., cognate with; d., dialect, dialectal; der., derived from; f., formed from; g., going back to; m., modification of; r., replacing; s., stem of; t., taken from; ?, perhaps. See the full key on inside cover.

nepho-, a word element meaning "cloud." [t. Gk., comb. form of *nephos* cloud]

neph·o·gram (nĕf′ə grăm′), *n.* a photograph of a cloud or clouds.

neph·o·graph (nĕf′ə grăf′, -gräf′), *n.* an instrument for photographing clouds.

ne·phol·o·gy (nĭ fŏl′ə jĭ), *n.* the branch of meteorology that treats of clouds. —**neph·o·log·i·cal** (nĕf′ə lŏj′ə kəl), *adj.*

neph·o·scope (nĕf′ə skōp′), *n.* an instrument for determining the altitude of clouds and the velocity and direction of their motion.

nephr-, var. of nephro-, before vowels.

ne·phral·gi·a (nĭ frăl′jĭ ə), *n.* *Pathol.* pain in the kidney or kidneys.

ne·phrec·to·my (nĭ frĕk′tə mĭ), *n.*, *pl.* **-mies.** *Surg.* excision or removal of a kidney.

neph·ric (nĕf′rĭk), *adj.* renal.

ne·phrid·i·um (nĭ frĭd′ĭ əm), *n.*, *pl.* **-phridia** (-frĭd′ĭ ə). *Zool.* the excretory organ of invertebrates consisting of a tubule with an open or closed motile apparatus at its inner end. [t. NL, f. *nephr-* NEPHR- + *-idium* (dim. suffix)] —**ne·phrid·i·al,** *adj.*

neph·rism (nĕf′rĭzəm), *n.* *Pathol.* the unhealthy state produced by a chronic kidney disease.

neph·rite (nĕf′rīt), *n.* a mineral, a compact or fibrous variety of actinolite, varying from whitish to dark green. See **jade**[1] (def. 1). [t. G: m. *nephrit,* f. *nephr-* NEPHR- + *-it* -ITE[1]]

ne·phrit·ic (nĭ frĭt′ĭk), *adj.* of, pertaining to, or affected with nephritis. [t. LL: s. *nephriticus,* t. Gk.: m. *nephritikós* affected with nephritis]

ne·phri·tis (nĭ frī′tĭs), *n.* *Pathol.* inflammation of the kidneys, esp. in Bright's disease. [t. LL, t. Gk.]

nephro-, a word element referring to the kidneys. Also, **nephr-.** [t. Gk., comb. form of *nephrós* kidney]

neph·ro·lith (nĕf′rə lĭth), *n.* *Pathol.* a renal calculus.

ne·phro·sis (nĭ frō′sĭs), *n.* *Pathol.* kidney disease, esp. marked by non-inflammatory degeneration of the tubular system. [f. NEPHR- +-OSIS] —**ne·phrot·ic** (nĭ frŏt′ĭk), *adj.*

ne·phrot·o·my (nĭ frŏt′ə mĭ), *n.*, *pl.* **-mies.** *Surg.* incision into the kidney, as for the removal of a calculus.

ne plus ul·tra (nē′ plŭs ŭl′trə), *Latin.* **1.** no more beyond; no further (used in prohibiting). **2.** the acme.

nep·man (nĕp′mən), *n.*, *pl.* **-men.** (in Soviet Union) one who, under the NEP, engaged in a private business.

Ne·pos (nē′pŏs, nĕp′ŏs), *n.* **Cornelius,** c99–c24 B.C., Roman biographer and historian.

nep·o·tism (nĕp′ə tĭz′əm), *n.* patronage bestowed in consideration of family relationship and not of merit. [t. F: m. *népotisme,* t. It.: m. *nepotismo,* ult. der. L *nepos* descendant. See -ISM] —**nep·ot·ic** (nĭ pŏt′ĭk), *adj.* —**nep′o·tist,** *n.*

Nep·tune (nĕp′tūn, -tōon), *n.* **1.** *Rom. Myth.* the Roman god of the sea. Cf. **Poseidon. 2.** the sea or ocean. **3.** *Astron.* the eighth planet in order from the sun. Its period of revolution is 164.8 years, its mean distance from the sun is 2,793,500,000 miles, and its diameter is 32,930 miles. It has two satellites. Symbol: Ψ.

Nep·tu·ni·an (nĕp tū′nĭ ən, -tōo′-), *adj.* **1.** pertaining to Neptune or the sea. **2.** pertaining to the planet Neptune. **3.** (*often l.c.*) *Geol.* formed by the action of water.

nep·tu·ni·um (nĕp tū′nĭ əm, -tōo′-), *n.* *Chem.* a radioactive transuranic element, not found in nature, produced artificially by the neutron bombardment of U-238. It decays rapidly to plutonium and then to U-235. *Symbol:* Np; *at. no.:* 93; *at. wt.:* 237.

Ner·bud·da (nər bŭd′ə), *n.* Narbada.

Ne·re·id (nĭr′ĭ ĭd), *n.* *Gk. Myth.* any one of the fifty daughters of the ancient sea god Nereus; a sea nymph. Also, **ne′re·id.** [t. L: s. *Nēreis,* t. Gk.]

Ne·re·is (nĭr′ĭ ĭs), *n.*, *pl.* **Nereides** (nĭ rē′ə dēz′). *Gk. Myth.* Nereid.

Ne·reus (nĭr′ōos), *n.* See **Nereid.**

Ne·ri (nâr′ĭ; *It.* nĕ′rē), *n.* **Saint Philip,** (*Filippo Neri*) 1515–95, Italian priest: founder of Congregation of the Oratory.

Ne·ro (nĭr′ō), *n.* (*Nero Claudius Caesar Drusus Germanicus, Lucius Domitius Ahenobarbus*) A.D. 37–68, Roman emperor, A.D. 54–68, notorious for his cruelty and corruption. —**Ne·ro·ni·an** (nĭ rō′nĭ ən), *adj.*

ne·rol (nĭr′ōl), *n.* a colorless alcohol, C₁₀H₁₈O, contained in neroli oil.

ner·o·li oil (nĕr′ə lĭ, nĭr′-), an essential oil, brown in color, derived from orange blossoms of the tree *Citrus bigardia,* and consisting of citral, limonene, linalool, etc.: used in the perfume industry. [t. F, t. It.; named after an Italian Princess *Neroli*]

Ner·va (nûr′və), *n.* **Marcus Cocceius** (mär′kəs kŏk-sē′yəs), A.D. 32?–98, Roman emperor, A.D. 96–98.

nerv·ate (nûr′vāt), *adj.* *Bot.* (of leaves) having nerves or veins; nerved.

ner·va·tion (nûr vā′shən), *n.* venation.

nerve (nûrv), *n.*, *v.*, **nerved, nerving.** —*n.* **1.** one or more bundles of fibers, forming part of a system which conveys impulses of sensation, motion, etc., between the brain or spinal cord and other parts of the body. **2.** *Dentistry.* **a.** the nerve tissue in the pulp of a tooth. **b.** (popularly but incorrectly) pulp tissue of a tooth. **3.** a sinew or tendon: *to strain every nerve.* **4.** strength, vigor, or energy. **5.** firmness or courage under trying circum-

stances: *a position requiring nerve.* **6.** (*pl.*) nervousness: *a fit of nerves.* **7. get on one's nerves,** to irritate. **8.** *Slang.* impertinent assurance. **9.** *Bot.* a vein, as in a leaf. **10.** a line or one of a system of lines traversing something. —*v.t.* **11.** to give strength, vigor, or courage to. [ME, t. L: m.s. *nervus,* akin to Gk. *neûron* sinew, tendon, nerve]

nerve cell, *Anat., Physiol.* **1.** any of the cells constituting the cellular element of nervous tissue. **2.** one of the essential cells of a nerve center.

nerve center, *Anat., Physiol.* a group of nerve cells closely connected with one another and acting together in the performance of some function.

nerve fiber, *Anat., Physiol.* a process, axone, or dendrite of a nerve cell.

nerve impulse, *Physiol.* a wave of electrical and chemical activity progressing along nerve fibers and acting as a stimulus to muscle, gland, or other nerve cells.

nerve·less (nûrv′lĭs), *adj.* **1.** *Anat., Bot., etc.* without nerves. **2.** lacking strength or vigor; feeble; weak. **3.** lacking firmness or courage; spiritless; pusillanimous. —**nerve′less·ly,** *adv.* —**nerve′less·ness,** *n.*

ner·vine (nûr′vēn, -vĭn), *adj.* **1.** of or pertaining to the nerves. **2.** acting on, or relieving disorders of, the nerves; soothing the nerves. —*n.* **3.** a nervine medicine.

nerv·ing (nûr′vĭng), *n.* *Vet. Sci.* the excision of part of a nerve trunk.

nerv·ous (nûr′vəs), *adj.* **1.** of or pertaining to the nerves. **2.** having or containing nerves of sensation, etc. **3.** affecting the nerves, as diseases. **4.** suffering from, characterized by, or proceeding from disordered nerves. **5.** highly excitable; unnaturally or acutely uneasy or apprehensive. **6.** characterized by or attended with acute uneasiness or apprehension. **7.** sinewy or strong. [ME, t. L: m.s. *nervōsus* sinewy] —**nerv′ous·ly,** *adv.* —**nerv′ous·ness,** *n.*

nervous system, *Anat., Zool.* **1.** the system of nerves and nerve centers in an animal. **2.** a particular part of this system: **a.** the **central** or **cerebrospinal nervous system,** the brain and spinal cord. **b.** the **peripheral nervous system,** the system of nerves and ganglia derived from the central system, comprising the cranial nerves, the spinal nerves, the various sense organs, etc. **c.** the **autonomic nervous system,** the system of nerves and ganglia which supply the walls of the vascular system and the various viscera and glands.

ner·vure (nûr′vyŏór), *n.* *Bot., Zool.* a vein, as of an insect's wing. [t. F, der. L *nervus* NERVE]

nerv·y (nûr′vĭ), *adj.,* **nervier, nerviest. 1.** *U.S. Slang.* audacious; bold. **2.** requiring nerve. **3.** having or showing courage. **4.** strong or vigorous. **5.** *Brit. Colloq.* nervous.

n.e.s., not elsewhere specified.

nes·cience (nĕsh′əns, nĕsh′ĭ əns), *n.* **1.** lack of knowledge; ignorance. **2.** agnosticism. [t. LL: m.s. *nescientia,* der. L *nesciens,* ppr., being ignorant] —**nes′cient,** *adj.*

ness (nĕs), *n.* *Archaic., Dial.,* or *in Place Names.* a headland; a promontory; a cape. [ME *nesse,* OE *ness,* c. MLG *ness;* akin to NOSE]

-ness, a suffix used to form, from adjectives and participles, nouns denoting quality or state (also often, by extension, something exemplifying a quality or state), as in *darkness, goodness, kindness, obligingness, preparedness.* [ME *-nes(se),* OE *-nes(s),* c. G *-niss*]

Nes·sel·rode (nĕs′əl rōd′), *n.* a mixture of preserved fruits, nuts, etc., used in pudding, pie, ice cream, or the like.

Nes·sel·rode (nĕs′əl rōd′; *Russ.* nĕs′səl rō′dĕ), *n.* **Count Karl Robert** (kärl rō′bĕrt′ *or* rō′bĕrt), 1780–1862, Russian diplomat and statesman.

Nes·sus (nĕs′əs), *n.* *Gk. Legend.* a centaur shot by Hercules with a poisoned arrow. Hercules was himself fatally poisoned by a garment stained with the blood of Nessus, sent to him by Deianira, who thought that it would preserve his love for her.

nest (nĕst), *n.* **1.** a structure formed or a place used by a bird for incubation and the rearing of its young. **2.** a place used by insects, fishes, turtles, rabbits, or the like, for depositing their eggs or young. **3.** a number of birds or animals inhabiting one such place. **4.** a snug retreat, or resting place. **5.** an assemblage of things lying or set close together, as a series of boxes, trays, etc., that fit within each other. **6.** a place where something bad is fostered or flourishes: *a nest of vice, a robbers' nest.* **7.** the occupants or frequenters of such a place. —*v.t.* **8.** to settle or place in or as in a nest. **9.** to fit or place one within another. —*v.i.* **10.** to build or have a nest: *the swallows nested under the eaves.* **11.** to settle in or as in a nest. **12.** to search for nests: *to go nesting.* [ME and OE, c. G *nest;* akin to L *nidus*]

n'est-ce pas (nĕs pä′), *French.* isn't that so?

nest egg, 1. an egg (usually artificial) left in a nest to induce a hen to continue laying eggs there. **2.** money saved as the basis of a fund or for emergencies.

nes·tle (nĕs′əl), *v.,* **-tled, -tling.** —*v.i.* **1.** to lie close and snug, like a bird in a nest; snuggle or cuddle. **2.** to lie in a sheltered or pleasant situation. **3.** *Obs.* to make or have a nest. —*v.t.* **4.** to provide with or settle in a nest, as birds. **5.** to settle or ensconce snugly. **6.** to put or press confidingly or affectionately. [ME *nestle*(n), OE *nestlian* (c. D *nestelen*), der. *nest* NEST] —**nes′tler,** *n.*

nest·ling (nĕst′lĭng, nĕs′lĭng), *n.* **1.** a young bird in the nest. **2.** a young child.

Nes·tor (nĕs'tər), *n. Gk. Legend.* the wisest and oldest of the Greeks in the Trojan War.

Nes·to·ri·an (nĕs tōr'ĭən), *n.* one of a sect of Christians, followers of Nestorius, who denied the hypostatic union and were represented as maintaining the existence of two distinct persons in Christ. —**Nes·to'ri·an·ism,** *n.*

Nes·to·ri·us (nĕs tōr'ĭəs), *n.* died A.D. c451, Syrian churchman; patriarch of Constantinople, A.D. 428–431.

net¹ (nĕt), *n., v.,* **netted, netting.** —*n.* 1. a lacelike fabric with a uniform mesh of cotton, silk, rayon, or nylon, often forming the foundation of many kinds of lace. 2. a piece of meshed fabric for any purpose: *a mosquito net.* 3. a bag or other contrivance of strong thread or cord wrought into an open, meshed fabric, for catching fish, birds, or other animals. 4. anything serving to catch or ensnare. 5. any network or reticulated system of filaments, lines, veins, or the like. 6. *Tennis, etc.* a ball that hits the net. —*v.t.* 7. to cover, screen, or enclose with a net or netting. 8. to take with a net: *to net fish.* 9. to set or use nets in (a river, etc.), as for fish. 10. to catch or ensnare. 11. *Tennis, etc.* to hit (the ball) into the net. [ME *net(te)*, OE *net(t)*, c. G *netz*] —**net'like,** *adj.*

net² (nĕt), *adj., n., v.,* **netted, netting.** —*adj.* 1. exclusive of deductions, as for charges, expenses, loss, discount, etc.: *net earnings.* 2. sold at net prices. —*n.* 3. net income, profits, or the like. —*v.t.* 4. to gain or produce as clear profit. [t. F: clean, clear. See NEAT]

Neth., Netherlands.

neth·er (nĕth'ər), *adj.* 1. lying, or conceived as lying, beneath the earth's surface; infernal: *the nether world.* 2. lower or under: *his nether lip.* [ME; OE *neothera,* earlier *ni(o)ther(r)a* (c. G *nieder*), der. *nither,* adv., downward, down, a compar. form]

Neth·er·lands (nĕth'ər ləndz), *n.pl.* **The,** a kingdom in W Europe, bordering on the North Sea, West Germany, and Belgium. 10,888,000 (est. 1956); 13,433 sq. mi. *Capitals:* Amsterdam *and* The Hague. Also, **Holland.**

Netherlands Antilles, possessions of the Netherlands in the West Indies, comprising Curaçao, Aruba, Bonaire, St. Eustatius, Saba, and part of St. Martin. Considered as an integral part of the Dutch realm. 183,-795 (est. 1955); 366 sq. mi. *Cap.:* Willemstad. Also, **Curaçao.** Formerly, **Netherlands West Indies.**

Netherlands East Indies. See **Dutch East Indies.** Also, **Netherlands Indies.**

Netherlands New Guinea, See **West Irian.** Also, **Dutch New Guinea.**

neth·er·most (nĕth'ər mōst', -məst), *adj.* lowest.

nether world, 1. hell. 2. the afterworld.

Né·thou (nĕ tōō'), *n.* **Pic de** (pēk də), a mountain in NE Spain: highest peak of the Pyrenees. 11,165 ft. Spanish, **Pico de Aneto.**

net·ting (nĕt'ĭng), *n.* any of various kinds of net fabric: *fish netting, mosquito netting.*

net·tle (nĕt'əl), *n., v.,* **-tled, -tling.** —*n.* 1. any plant of the genus *Urtica,* comprising widely distributed herbs armed with stinging hairs. 2. any of various allied or similar plants. —*v.t.* 3. to irritate, irk, provoke, or vex. 4. to sting as a nettle does. [ME; OE *netele,* c. G *nessel*]

nettle rash, *Pathol.* urticaria caused by contact with various plants causing local irritation.

net ton, a short ton.

net·work (nĕt'wûrk'), *n.* 1. any netlike combination of filaments, lines, veins, passages, or the like. 2. a netting or net. 3. *Radio.* a group of transmitting stations linked by wire so that the same program can be broadcast by all. 4. *Elect.* a system of interconnected admittances.

Neu·châ·tel (nœ shä tĕl'), *n.* 1. a canton in W Switzerland. 131,500 pop. (est. 1952); 309 sq. mi. 2. the capital of this canton, on the **Lake of Neuchâtel** (92 sq. mi.). 27,998 pop. (1950). German, **Neu·en·burg** (noi'ĕn bŏŏrkʜ').

Neuf·châ·tel cheese (nœ shä tĕl'), a soft, white cheese similar to cream cheese, made from whole or partly skimmed milk in Neufchâtel, a town in N France.

Neuil·ly-sur-Seine (nœ yē svr sĕn'), *n.* a suburb of Paris in N France: treaty of peace between the Allies and Bulgaria, 1919. 66,095 (1954).

neur-, var. of neuro-, before vowels.

neu·ral (nyŏŏr'əl, nŏŏr'-), *adj.* of or pertaining to a nerve or the nervous system.

neu·ral·gia (nyŏŏ räl'jə, nŏŏr'-), *n. Pathol.* sharp and paroxysmal pain along the course of a nerve. —**neu·ral'gic,** *adj.* [t. NL. See NEUR-, -ALGIA]

neu·ras·the·ni·a (nyŏŏr'əs thē'nĭ ə, nŏŏr'-), *n. Pathol.* nervous debility or exhaustion, as from overwork or prolonged mental strain, characterized by vague complaints of a physical nature in the absence of objectively present causes or lesions.

neu·ras·then·ic (nyŏŏr'əs thĕn'ĭk, nŏŏr'-), *adj.* 1. pertaining to or suffering from neurasthenia. —*n.* 2. a person suffering from neurasthenia.

neu·ra·tion (nyŏŏ rā'shən, nŏŏr'-), *n.* venation.

neu·rec·to·my (nyŏŏ rĕk'tə mĭ', nŏŏr'-), *n., pl.* **-mies.** *Surg.* the removal of a nerve or part thereof.

neu·ri·lem·ma (nyŏŏr'ə lĕm'ə, nŏŏr'-), *n. Anat.* the delicate membranous sheath of a nerve fiber. [var. (by

assoc. with LEMMA² husk, outer layer) of *neurilema,* f. NEUR- + m. Gk. *eílēma* covering]

neu·ri·tis (nyŏŏ rī'tĭs, nŏŏ-), *n. Pathol.* 1. inflammation of a nerve. 2. continuous pain in a nerve associated with its paralysis and sensory disturbances. [NL. See NEUR-, -ITIS] —**neu·rit·ic** (nyŏŏ rĭt'ĭk, nŏŏ-), *adj.*

neuro-, a word element meaning "sinew," "tendon," "nerve." Also, **neur-.** [t. Gk., comb. form of *neûron*]

neu·ro·blast (nyŏŏr'ə blăst', nŏŏr'-), *n. Embryol.* one of the cells in the embryonic brain and spinal cord of vertebrates, which are to give rise to nerve cells.

neu·ro·coele (nyŏŏr'ə sēl', nŏŏr'-), *n. Embryol.* the cavity (ventricles and central canal) of the embryonic brain and spinal cord.

neu·rog·li·a (nyŏŏ rŏg'lĭ ə, nŏŏ-), *n. Anat.* the delicate connective tissue which supports and binds together the essential elements of nervous tissue in the central nervous system. [t. NL, f. Gk.: *neu-ro-* NEURO- + *glía* glue]

neu·rol·o·gy (nyŏŏ rŏl'ə jĭ', nŏŏ-), *n.* the science of the nerves or the nervous system, esp. the diseases thereof. —**neu·ro·log·i·cal** (nyŏŏr'ə lŏj'ə kəl, nŏŏr'-), *adj.* —**neu·rol'o·gist,** *n.*

neu·ro·ma (nyŏŏ rō'mə, nŏŏ-), *n., pl.* **-mata** (-mə tə), **-mas.** *Pathol.* a tumor formed of nervous tissue. [t. NL. See NEUR-, -OMA]

neu·ron (nyŏŏr'ŏn, nŏŏr'-), *n.* a nerve cell. Also, **neu·rone** (nyŏŏr'ōn, nŏŏr'-). [t. Gk.: nerve] —**neu·ron·ic** (nyŏŏ rŏn'ĭk, nŏŏ-), *adj.*

Diagram of a neuron
A. Cell; B. Nucleus; C. Dendrites; D. Axis

neu·ro·path (nyŏŏr'ə păth', nŏŏr'-), *n. Psychiatry.* a person subject to or affected with a functional nervous disease; a neurotic person.

neu·ro·path·ic (nyŏŏr'ə păth'ĭk, nŏŏr'-), *adj.* neurotic.

neu·ro·pa·thol·o·gy (nyŏŏr'ō pə thŏl'ə jĭ', nŏŏr'-), *n.* the pathology of the nervous system. —**neu'ro·pa·thol'o·gist,** *n.*

neu·rop·a·thy (nyŏŏ rŏp'ə thĭ', nŏŏ-), *n.* disease of the nervous system. [f. NEURO- + -PATHY]

neu·ro·psy·chi·a·try (nyŏŏr'ō sī kī'ə trĭ', nŏŏr'-), *n.* the branch of medicine dealing with diseases involving the mind and nervous system. —**neu·ro·psy·chi·at·ric** (nyŏŏr'ō sī'kĭ ăt'rĭk, nŏŏr'-), *adj.*

neu·ro·psy·cho·sis (nyŏŏr'ō sĭ kō'sĭs, nŏŏr'-), *n., pl.* **-ses** (-sēz). *Pathol.* mental derangement in association with nervous disease.

neu·rop·ter·ous (nyŏŏ rŏp'tər əs, nŏŏ-), *adj.* belonging to an order of insects, the *Neuroptera,* that includes the ant lions and lacewings, characterized by two pairs of membranous wings with netlike venation. [f. NEURO- + s. Gk. *pterón* wing + -OUS]

neu·ro·sis (nyŏŏ rō'sĭs, nŏŏ-), *n., pl.* **-ses** (-sēz). psychoneurosis.

neu·rot·ic (nyŏŏ rŏt'ĭk, nŏŏ-), *adj.* 1. having a psychoneurosis. 2. pertaining to the nerves or to nervous disease. —*n.* 3. a person affected with psychoneurosis.

neu·rot·o·my (nyŏŏ rŏt'ə mĭ', nŏŏ-), *n., pl.* **-mies.** surgical cutting of a nerve, as to relieve neuralgia.

Neu·satz (noi'zäts), *n.* German name of **Novi Sad.**

Neus·tri·a (nūs'trĭ ə, nōōs'-), *n.* the W part of the kingdom of the Franks, roughly N and NW France.

neut., neuter.

neu·ter (nū'tər, nōō'-), *adj.* 1. *Gram.* **a.** denoting or pertaining to one of the three genders of Latin, German, Greek, etc., or one of the two of Dutch, Swedish, etc.: so termed because few if any nouns denoting males or females belong to it, or (as in German) purely for traditional reasons. For example: Latin *nōmen* "name," *cor* "heart," *bellum* "war" are all neuter gender. **b.** (of verbs) intransitive. 2. *Zool.* having imperfectly developed sexual organs, as the workers among bees and ants. 3. *Bot.* having neither stamens nor pistils; asexual. 4. *Archaic.* neutral. —*n.* 5. *Gram.* **a.** the neuter gender. **b.** a noun of that gender. **c.** another element marking that gender. **d.** an intransitive verb. 6. an animal made sterile by castration. 7. a neuter insect. 8. *Bot.* a plant with neither stamens nor pistils. 9. a neutral. [t. L: neither; r. ME *neutre,* t. OF]

neu·tral (nū'trəl, nōō'-), *adj.* 1. (of a person or state) refraining from taking part in a controversy or war between others. 2. of no particular kind, color, characteristics, etc.; indefinite. 3. gray; without hue; of zero chroma; achromatic. 4. *Biol.* neuter. 5. *Chem.* exhibiting neither acid nor alkaline qualities: *neutral salts.* 6. *Elect., Magnetism.* neither positive nor negative; not electrified; not magnetized. —*n.* 7. a person or a state that remains neutral, as in a war. 8. a citizen of a neutral nation. 9. *Mach.* the position or state of disengaged gears or other interconnecting parts: *in neutral.* [late ME, t. L: s. *neutrālis* neuter] —**neu'tral·ly,** *adv.*

neu·tral·ism (nū'trə lĭz'əm, nōō'-), *n.* the policy of remaining strictly neutral in foreign affairs.

neu·tral·i·ty (nū trăl'ə tĭ', nōō'-), *n.* 1. the state of being neutral. 2. the attitude or status of a nation which does not participate in a war between other nations: *the continuous neutrality of Switzerland.* 3. neutral status, as of a seaport during a war.

neu·tral·ize (nū'trə līz', nōō'-), *v.t.,* **-ized, -izing.** 1. to make neutral. 2. to render ineffective; counteract.

b., blend of, blended; c., cognate with; d., dialect, dialectal; der., derived from; f., formed from; g., going back to; m., modification of; r., replacing; s., stem of; t., taken from; ?, perhaps. See the full key on inside cover.

3. *Mil.* to put out of action or make incapable of action. **4.** to declare neutral; invest with neutrality. **5.** *Chem.* to render inert the peculiar properties of. **6.** *Elect.* to render electrically neutral. **—neu′tral·i·za′tion**, *n.* **—neu′tral·iz′er**, *n.*

neu·tri·no (nū trē′nō, nōō-), *n.*, *pl.* **-nos.** *Physics.* a neutral particle with less mass than the electron. Originally invented to avoid apparent violation of the conservation laws in radioactive disintegration, there is now evidence for its existence.

neu·tron (nū′trŏn, nōō′-), *n.* *Physics.* a neutral particle with approximately the same mass as a proton. [f. NEUTR(AL) neither positive nor negative + -*on* (after ELECTRON, PROTON)]

Nev., Nevada.

Ne·va (nē′və; *Russ.* nĕ vä′), *n.* a river in the NW Soviet Union, flowing from Lake Ladoga through Leningrad into the Gulf of Finland. 40 mi.

Ne·vad·a (nə văd′ə, -vä′də), *n.* a State in the W United States. 285,278 pop. (1960); 110,540 sq. mi. *Cap.*: Carson City. *Abbr.*: Nev. **—Ne·vad′an**, *adj.*, *n.*

né·vé (nā vā′; *Fr.* nĕ vĕ′), *n.* **1.** granular snow accumulated on high mountains and subsequently compacted into glacial ice. **2.** a field of such snow. [t. F, var. of d. F *nevé*, der. O Southeastern F *neif*, g. L *niz* snow]

nev·er (nĕv′ər), *adv.* **1.** not ever; at no time. **2.** not at all: absolutely not; not even. **3.** to no extent or degree. [ME; OE *næfre*, f. *ne* not + *æfre* EVER]

nev·er·more (nĕv′ər môr′), *adv.* never again.

nev·er·the·less (nĕv′ər thə lĕs′), *adv.* none the less; notwithstanding; however. **—Syn.** See but[1].

Ne·vis (nē′vĭs, nĕv′ĭs), *n.* one of the Leeward Islands. 12,761 pop. (1960); 50 sq. mi.

Nev·ski (nĕv′skĭ, nĕf′-), *n.* **Alexander.** See **Alexander Nevski.**

ne·vus (nē′vəs), *n.*, *pl.* **-vi** (-vī). naevus. **—ne·void** (nē′void), *adj.*

new (nū, nōō), *adj.* **1.** of recent origin or production, or having but lately come or been brought into being: *a new book.* **2.** of a kind now existing or appearing for the first time; novel. **3.** having but lately or but now come into knowledge: *a new chemical element.* **4.** unfamiliar or strange (fol. by *to*): *ideas new to us.* **5.** having but lately come to a place, position, status, etc.: *a new minister.* **6.** unaccustomed (fol. by *to*): *men new to such work.* **7.** coming or occurring afresh; further; additional: *new gains.* **8.** fresh or unused: *a new sheet.* **9.** different and better, physically or morally: *the vacation made a new man of him.* **10.** other than the former or the old: *a new era.* **11.** being the later or latest of two or more things of the same kind: *the New Testament.* **12.** (of a language) in its latest known period, esp. as a living language at the present time: *New Latin.* **—adv.** **13.** recently or lately. **14.** freshly; anew or afresh. **15.** something new. [ME and OE *newe*, c. G *neu*, L *novus*, Gk. *néos*] **—new′ness**, *n.*

—Syn. **1.** NEW, FRESH, NOVEL describe that which is not old. NEW applies to that which has not been long in existence: *a new broom, dress* (one recently made or bought). FRESH suggests a condition of newness, not yet affected by use or the passage of time: *a fresh towel, dress* (newly clean). NOVEL suggests newness which has an unexpected quality, or is strange or striking, but generally pleasing: *a novel experience, dress* (a dress of unusual design, or the like).

New Al·ba·ny (ôl′bə nĭ), a city in S Indiana, on the Ohio river. 37,812 (1960).

New Am·ster·dam (ăm′stər dăm′), a former Dutch town on Manhattan Island: the capital of New Netherland; renamed New York by the British, 1664.

New·ark (nū′ərk, nōō′-), *n.* **1.** a city in NE New Jersey, on Newark Bay. 405,220 (1960). **2.** a city in central Ohio. 41,790 (1960).

New Bed·ford (bĕd′fərd), a seaport in SE Massachusetts: formerly a chief whaling port. 102,477 (1960).

New·ber·y Award (nū′bĕr′ĭ, -bərĭ, nōō′-), an annual award for the most distinguished book for juveniles. [named after John *Newbery*, 1713–1767, noted British publisher of books for children]

New·bolt (nū′bōlt, nōō′-), *n.* **Sir Henry John,** 1862–1938, British poet and naval historian.

new·born (nū′bôrn′, nōō′-), *adj.* **1.** recently or only just born. **2.** born anew; reborn.

New Brit·ain (brĭt′ən), **1.** a city in central Connecticut. 82,201 (1960). **2.** an island in the S Pacific, NE of New Guinea: the largest island in the Bismark Archipelago. (Including nearby islands) 87,892 pop. (1954); ab. 14 600 sq. mi. *Cap.*: Rabaul.

New Bruns·wick (brŭnz′wĭk), **1.** a province in SE Canada, E of Maine. 536,000 (est. 1953); 27,985 sq. mi. *Cap.*: Fredericton. **2.** a city in central New Jersey. 40,139 (1960).

New·burgh (nū′bûrg, nōō′-), *n.* a city in SE New York, on the Hudson. 30,979 (1960).

New Cal·e·do·ni·a (kăl′ə dō′nĭ ə, -dōn′yə), **1.** an island in the S Pacific, ab. 800 mi. E of Australia. 46,643 (1952); 6224 sq. mi. **2.** an overseas territory of France comprising this island and other smaller islands: formerly a penal colony. 65,463 (1952); 7200 sq. mi. *Cap.*: Nouméa.

New Cas·tile (kăs tēl′), a region in central Spain: formerly a province. 27,933 sq. mi.

New·cas·tle (nū′kăs′əl, -kä′səl, nōō′-), *n.* **1.** Also, **Newcastle-upon-Tyne** (-tīn′). a seaport in NE England.

on the Tyne river: shipbuilding. 291,724 (1951). **2.** a seaport in SE Australia, in New South Wales. 134,079 (1954).

New Castle, a city in W Pennsylvania. 44,790 (1960).

Newcastle disease, a specific, virus-induced disease of chickens, etc., marked by loss of egg production in old birds and by paralysis in chicks.

New Church, New Jerusalem Church.

New·chwang (nū′chwäng′, nōō′-), *n.* a city in NE China: a river port ab. 30 mi. from the Gulf of Liaotung, in S Manchuria. See **Yingkow.**

New·comb (nū′kəm, nōō′-), *n.* **Simon,** 1835–1909, U.S. astronomer.

new·com·er (nū′kŭm′ər, nōō′-), *n.* one who has newly come; a new arrival.

New Deal, 1. the principles of the progressive wing of the Democratic party, esp. those advocated under the leadership of President Franklin D. Roosevelt. **2.** the Roosevelt administration. **—New Dealer.**

New Delhi, a city in N India, adjacent to (old) Delhi; the capital of the Republic of India. 276,314 (1951).

New Economic Policy, a Soviet Union program, in effect 1921–1928, reviving the wage system and private ownership of some factories and businesses, and abandoning grain requisitions.

new·el (nū′əl, nōō′-), *n.* **1.** a central pillar or upright from which the steps of a winding stair radiate. **2.** a post at the head or foot of a stair, supporting the handrail. [ME *nowell*, t. OF: m. *noiel* kernel, newel (g. LL *nucāle*, neut. of *nucālis* of or like a nut), b. with *noel* bud, trickle-ornament, g. LL *nōdellus*, der. L *nōdus* knot]

New England, six States in the NE United States: Connecticut, Massachusetts, Rhode Island, Vermont, New Hampshire, and Maine. **—New Englander.**

New England aster, a tall aster, *Aster novae-angliae*, of northeastern U.S., with deep-purple rays.

new·fan·gled (nū′făng′gəld, nōō′-), *adj.* **1.** newfashioned; of a new kind: *newfangled ideas.* **2.** fond of novelty. [der. *newfangle*, MEnew*efangel*, f. *newe* NEW + *fangel*, der. ME *fangen* take]

new-fash·ioned (nū′făsh′ənd, nōō′-), *adj.* lately come into fashion; of a new fashion.

New Forest, a forest region in S England, in Hampshire: national park. 145 sq. mi.

New·found·land (nū′-fənd lănd′, nōō′- *for 1*; nū found′lənd, nōō- *for 2*), *n.* **1.** a large island in the eastern part of Canada: became a Canadian province on March 31, 1949. 383,000 (est. 1953); 42,734 sq. mi. (excluding Labrador). **2.** one of a breed of large, shaggy dogs, orig. from Newfoundland, noted for their sagacity, docility, swimming powers, etc.

New·found·land·er (nū-found′lən dər, nōō-), *n.* a native or inhabitant of Newfoundland.

New France, the name of Canada while under French rule.

New Frontier, the principles of the liberal wing of the Democratic party under the leadership of President John F. Kennedy.

Newfoundland
(28 in. high at the shoulder)

New·gate (nū′gāt, -gĭt, nōō′-), *n.* a famous prison in London, England: destroyed, 1902.

New Gra·na·da (grə nä′də), **1.** a former Spanish viceroyalty in NW South America, comprising the present republics of Ecuador, Venezuela, Colombia, and Panama. **2.** early name for Colombia (before the secession of Panama).

New Guin·ea (gĭn′ĭ), **1.** Also, **Papua.** a large island N of Australia: divided into the Indonesian province of West Irian and the merged Australian territories of Papua and New Guinea. 2,722,000 (est. 1961) ab. 316,000 sq. mi. **2. Territory of,** a territory under the trusteeship of Australia, including NE New Guinea, the Bismarck Archipelago, Bougainville, and other islands: merged with the Territory of Papua, 1945. 1,206,749 (1954); including Papua. 1,701,458 (1954); ab. 93,000 sq. mi. (ab. 69,700 sq. mi. mainland).

New Hamp·shire (hămp′shər, -shĭr), **1.** a State in the NE United States. 606,921 pop. (1960); 9304 sq. mi. *Cap.*: Concord. *Abbr.*: N.H. **2.** one of an American breed of domestic fowl, mostly chestnut-red in color, early maturing, and fast-growing.

New Ha·ven (hā′vən), a seaport in S Connecticut, on Long Island Sound. 152,048 (1960).

New Heb·ri·des (hĕb′rə dēz′), an island group in the S Pacific, ab. 1000 mi. NE of Australia: under joint British and French administration. 53,000 pop. (est. 1954); ab. 5700 sq. mi. *Cap.*: Vila.

New Ireland, an island in the S Pacific, in the Bismarck Archipelago, NE of New Guinea. (With adjacent islands) 34,584 pop. (1954); ab. 3800 sq. mi.

new·ish (nū′ĭsh, nōō′-), *adj.* rather new.

New Jer·sey (jûr′zĭ), a State in the E United States, on the Atlantic coast. 6,066,782 pop. (1960); 7836 sq. mi. *Cap.*: Trenton. *Abbr.*: N.J. **—New Jerseyite.**

New Jerusalem, the heavenly city; the abode of God and His saints. Rev. 21:2.

New Jerusalem Church, the church composed of the followers of Swedenborgian. See **Swedenborgian.**

New Kensington, a city in W Pennsylvania. 25,146 (1950).

New Latin, Neo-Latin.

New London, a seaport in SE Connecticut, on the Thames river: naval base. 34,182 (1960).

new·ly (nū′lĭ, nōō′-), *adv.* **1.** recently; lately: *a newly wedded couple.* **2.** anew or afresh: *a newly repeated slander.* **3.** in a new manner or form. [ME; OE nīwlīce]

New·man (nū′mən, nōō′-), *n.* **John Henry,** (*Cardinal Newman*) 1801–90, British theologian and author.

New·mar·ket (nū′mär′kĭt, nōō′-), *n.* **1.** a town in E England, E of Cambridge: horse races. 20,219 (1951). **2.** (*l.c.*) Also, **Newmarket coat.** a long, close-fitting outdoor coat worn by men and women. **3.** (*l.c.*) a kind of card game of the stops family.

New Mexico, a State in the SW United States. 951,023 pop. (1960); 121,666 sq. mi. *Cap.:* Santa Fe *Abbr.:* N. Mex. or N.M. —**New Mexican.**

new moon. See moon (def. 2a).

New Netherland, a Dutch colony on the Hudson (1613) and Delaware rivers: after 1664, included by England in the New York, New Jersey, and Delaware colonies. *Cap.:* New Amsterdam.

New Or·le·ans (ôr′lĭ anz; *older* ôr lēnz′), a seaport in SE Louisiana, on the Mississippi: British defeated by Americans under Andrew Jackson, 1815. 627,525 (1960).

New·port (nū′pôrt, nōō′-), *n.* **1.** a seaport in SW England, near the Severn estuary. 105,285 pop. (1951). **2.** a city in N Kentucky, on the Ohio river, opposite Cincinnati, Ohio. 30,070 (1960). **3.** a seaport and summer resort in SE Rhode Island: naval base. 47,049 (1960). **4.** a city on the Isle of Wight, in S England. 20,426 (1951).

Newport News, a seaport in SE Virginia. 113,662 (1960).

New Ro·chelle (rō shĕl′, rə-), a city in SE New York, near New York City. 76,812 (1960).

news (nūz, nōōz), *n.pl. (now construed as sing.)* **1.** a report of any recent event, situation, etc. **2.** the report of events published in a newspaper. [ME *newes,* pl. of ME and OE *newe* that which is new, n. use of *newe,* adj.]

news·boy (nūz′boi′, nōōz′-), *n.* a boy who sells or delivers newspapers.

news·cast (nūz′kăst′, -käst′, nōōz′-), *n.* a radio broadcast of news reports. —**news′cast′er,** *n.*

news·deal·er (nūz′dē′lər, nōōz′-), *n.* *U.S.* a dealer in newspapers and often magazines, etc. Also, *Brit.,* **news agent.**

New Si·be·ri·an Is·lands (sī bǐr′ĭ ən), a group of islands in the Arctic Ocean, N of the Soviet Union in Asia: part of the Yakutsk Autonomous Republic.

news·let·ter (nūz′lĕt′ər, nōōz′-), *n.* an informal or confidential report and analysis of the news.

news·man (nūz′măn′, -mən, nōōz′-), *n.* **1.** one who sells or distributes newspapers, periodicals, etc. **2.** a newspaper man; a reporter on a newspaper.

news·mon·ger (nūz′mŭng′gər, nōōz′-), *n.* a spreader of news by oral or written means, esp. a gossip.

New South Wales, a state in SE Australia. 3,423,-529 pop. (1954); 309,433 sq. mi. *Cap.:* Sydney.

New Spain, the former Spanish possessions in the Americas, at one time including Mexico, Central America, the West Indies, and parts of the United States.

news·pa·per (nūz′pā′pər, nōōz′-, nŭs′-, nōōs′-), *n.* a printed publication issued at regular intervals, usually daily or weekly, and commonly containing news, comment, features, and advertisements.

news·print (nūz′prĭnt′, nōōz′-), *n.* paper used or made to print newspapers on.

news·reel (nūz′rēl′, nōōz′-), *n.* a short motion picture presenting current news events.

news stall, *Brit.* a newsstand.

news·stand (nūz′stănd′, nōōz′-), *n.* *U.S.* a stand at which newspapers and often magazines, etc., are sold. Also, *Brit.,* **news stall.**

New Style. See style (def. 13).

news·wor·thy (nūz′wûr′thĭ, nōōz′-), *adj.* of sufficient interest to appear in a newspaper.

news·y (nū′zĭ, nōō′-), *adj.,* **newsier, newsiest,** *n., pl.* **newsies.** —*adj.* **1.** *Colloq.* full of news, as on various subjects. —*n.* **2.** *U.S. Colloq.* a newsboy.

newt (nūt, nōōt), *n.* **1.** the salamanders of the genus *Triturus* (or *Triton*), of North America, Europe, and northern Asia. **2.** *Obs.* any of various small, tailed amphibians. [ME *newte,* for *ewte* (an *ewte* being taken as *a newte*), var. of *evet,* OE *efete.* Cf. EFT.]

New Test., New Testament.

New Testament, those books in the Bible which were produced by the early Christian church, and were added to the Jewish scriptures (Old Testament).

New Thought, a system of doctrine and practice based on the theory that through the suggestion of favorable and beneficial ideas all physical and mental

Crested newt,
Triturus cristatus
(4 to 6 in. long)

circumstances of life may be regulated and controlled.

New·ton (nū′tən, nōō′tən), *n.* **1. Sir Isaac,** 1642–1727, British scientist, mathematician, and philosopher, who formulated and proved the law of gravity. **2.** a city in E Massachusetts, near Boston. 92,384 (1960). —**New·to·ni·an** (nū tō′nĭ ən, nōō-), *adj., n.*

New Windsor, Windsor (def. 3).

New World, the Western Hemisphere.

new year, 1. the year approaching or newly begun. **2.** (*caps.*) the first day or days of a year. **3.** (*caps.*) New Year's Day.

New Year's Day, January 1. Also, *esp. U.S.,* **New Year's.**

New Year's Eve, the night of December 31, usually observed with merrymaking.

New York, 1. a State in the NE United States. 16,782,304 pop. (1960); 49,576 sq. mi. *Cap.:* Albany. *Abbr.:* N.Y. **2.** Also, **New York City.** a seaport in SE New York at the mouth of the Hudson: the largest city in the Western Hemisphere, comprising the boroughs of Manhattan, Queens, Brooklyn, The Bronx, and Staten Island. 7,781,984 (1960). —**New York′er.**

New York, Greater, New York City and the counties of Nassau, Suffolk, Rockland, Westchester in New York, and the counties of Bergen, Essex, Hudson, Middlesex, Morris, Passaic, Somerset, Union in New Jersey; the metropolitan area as defined by the U.S. Census. 14,093,535 (1957).

New York Bay, a bay of the Atlantic at the mouth of the Hudson, W of Long Island and E of Staten Island and New Jersey.

New York State Barge Canal, 1. a State waterway system in New York. 575 mi. long. **2.** the main canal of this system, between the Hudson and Lake Erie, consisting of the rebuilt Erie Canal. 352 mi.

New Zea·land (zē′lənd), a member of the British Commonwealth of Nations, consisting of islands (principally North and South Islands) in the S Pacific. 2,174,000 pop. (est. 1956); 103,416 sq. mi. *Cap.:* Wellington. —**New Zea′land·er.**

next (nĕkst), *adj. (superl. of* nigh)*, adv.* —*adj.* **1.** immediately following in time, order, importance, etc.: *the next day.* **2.** nearest in place or position: *the next room.* **3.** nearest in relationship or kinship. —*adv.* **4** in the nearest place, time, importance, etc. **5.** on the first subsequent occasion: *when next we meet.* [ME *nexte,* OE *nēxt,* var. of *nēhst,* superl. of *nēah* NIGH]

next of kin, 1. a person's nearest relative or relatives. **2.** *Law.* the nearest relative(s), to whom the personal property passes upon the death of an intestate.

nex·us (nĕk′səs), *n., pl.* **nexus. 1.** a tie or link; a means of connection. **2.** a connected series. [t. L]

Ney (nā), *n.* **Michel** (mē shĕl′), (*Duke of Elchingen, Prince of the Moskova*) 1769–1815, Marshal of France under Napoleon I.

Nez Per·cé (nĕz′ pûrs′; *Fr.* nĕ pĕr sĕ′), *pl.* **Nez Per·cés** (pûr′sĭz; *Fr.* nĕ pĕr sĕ′). **1.** (*pl.*) a leading North American Indian tribe of the Sahaptan family. **2.** (formerly as used by the French) a number of tribes supposed to pierce the nasal septum for nose ornaments. **3.** a member of one of these tribes. [t. F: lit., pierced nose]

NF, Norman French.

N.F., 1. Newfoundland. **2.** *Banking.* no funds. Also, **n.f. 3.** Norman French.

N.G., 1. National Guard. **2.** no good. Also, **n.g.**

Ngan·hwei (ngän′hwā′), *n.* Anhwei.

NGk., New Greek. Also, **N. Gk.**

N.H., New Hampshire.

Ni, *Chem.* nickel.

N.I., Northern Ireland.

ni·a·cin (nī′ə sĭn), *n.* **1.** nicotinic acid. **2.** (*cap.*) the trademark for this acid. [f. NI(COTINIC) AC(ID) + -IN²]

Ni·ag·a·ra (nī ăg′rə, -ăg′ər ə), *n.* **1.** a river flowing from Lake Erie into Lake Ontario, on the boundary between W New York and Ontario, Canada. 34 mi. **2.** Niagara Falls. **3. Fort,** a fort at the mouth of the Niagara river, in W New York. **4.** *Hort.* a widely grown eastern white grape.

Niagara Falls, 1. the falls of the Niagara river: Horseshoe Falls, in Canada, 158 ft. high; 2600 ft. wide; American Falls, 167 ft. high; 1400 ft. wide. **2.** a city on the New York side of the falls. 102,394 (1960). **3.** a city on the Canadian side. 22,874 (1951).

nib (nĭb), *n. v.,* **nibbed, nibbing.** —*n.* **1.** a bill or beak, as of a bird; a neb. **2.** *Brit.* a pen, for insertion into a penholder. **3.** the point of a pen, or either of its divisions. **4.** a point of anything. **5.** any pointed extremity. —*v.t.* **6.** *Brit.* to furnish with a nib or point. **7.** to mend or trim the nib of. [OE *nybba* point (in a place name), c. Icel. *nibba* sharp point]

nib·ble (nĭb′əl), *v.,* **-bled, -bling,** *n.* —*v.i.* **1.** to bite off small bits. **2.** to eat or feed by biting off small pieces. **3.** to bite slightly or gently (fol. by *at*). —*v.t.* **4.** to bite off small bits of (a thing). **5.** to eat by biting off small pieces. **6.** to bite (*off,* etc.) in small pieces. —*n.* **7.** a small morsel or bit: *each nibble was eaten with the air of an epicure.* **8.** act or an instance of nibbling. [late ME; cf. LG *nibbelen*] —**nib′bler,** *n.*

Ni·be·lung·en·lied (nē′bə lŏong′ən lēt′), *n.* a Middle High German ep.c, given its present form by an unknown author in South Germany during the first half of the 13th century. [t. G. See NIBELUNGS. LIED]

Ni·be·lungs (nē'bə lŏongz'), *n.pl.*, *sing.* **Nibelung.** *Germanic Myth.* **1.** a race of Northern dwarfs who possessed the treasure later captured by Siegfried. They were named from their king, Nibelung. **2.** the followers of Siegfried, who captured the Nibelungs' hoard. **3.** (later, in the *Nibelungenlied*) the Burgundian kings. Also, **Ni·be·lung·en** (nē'bə lŏong'ən).

nib·lick (nĭb'lĭk), *n.* *Golf.* a club with a short, rounded, flat, iron head whose face slopes greatly from the vertical.

Ni·cae·a (nī sē'ə), *n.* an ancient city in N W Asia Minor: Nicene Creed formulated here, A.D. 325.

Ni·cae·an (nī sē'ən), *adj.* Nicene.

Nic·a·ra·gua (nĭk'ə rä'gwə), *n.* **1.** a republic in Central America. 1,245,000 pop. (est. 1955); 57,143 sq. mi. *Cap.:* Managua. **2.** Lake, a lake in SW Nicaragua. 92 mi. long; 34 mi. wide. —**Nic'a·ra'guan,** *adj., n.*

nic·co·lite (nĭk'ə līt'), *n.* a pale copper-red mineral of a metallic luster, nickel arsenide (Ni As), usually occurring massive. [f. s. NL *niccolum* nickel + -ITE[1]]

nice (nīs), *adj.*, **nicer, nicest.** **1.** pleasing; agreeable; delightful: *a nice visit.* **2.** amiably pleasant; kind: *they are always nice to strangers.* **3.** characterized by or requiring great accuracy, precision, skill, or delicacy: *nice workmanship.* **4.** requiring or showing tact or care; delicate. **5.** showing minute differences; minutely accurate, as instruments. **6.** minute, fine, or subtle, as a distinction. **7.** having or showing delicate and accurate perception: *a nice sense of color.* **8.** refined as to manners, language, etc. **9.** suitable or proper: *not a nice song.* **10.** carefully neat as to dress, habits, etc. **11.** dainty or delicious, as food. **12.** dainty as to food. **13.** *Obs.* coy, shy, or reluctant. **14.** *Obs* wanton. **15.** *Obs.* foolish. [ME, t. OF: simple, g. L *nescius* not knowing] —**nice'ly,** *adv.* —**nice'ness,** *n.*

Nice (nēs), *n.* a coastal resort in SE France. 244,360 (1954).

Ni·cene (nī sēn', nī'sēn), *adj.* of or pertaining to Nicaea. Also, **Nicaean.** [ME, t. LL: m.s. *Nicēnus,* der *Nicēa,* t. Gk.: m. *Nikaia,* a town in Bithynia]

Nicene Council, either of two general ecclesiastical councils which met at Nicaea, the first in A.D. 325 to deal with the Arian heresy, the second in A.D. 787 to consider the question of images.

Nicene Creed, 1. a formal statement of the chief tenets of Christian belief, adopted by the first Nicene Council. **2.** a later creed of closely similar form referred, perhaps erroneously, to the Council of Constantinople (A.D. 381) and hence sometimes known as the **Niceno-Constantinopolitan Creed,** received universally in the Eastern Church, and with an addition introduced in the 6th century, accepted generally throughout western Christendom.

ni·ce·ty (nī'sə tĭ), *n.*, *pl.* **-ties. 1.** a delicate or fine point: *niceties of protocol.* **2.** a fine distinction; subtlety. **3.** (*often pl.*) something nice; a refinement or elegance, as of manners or living. **4.** quality of being nice. **5.** delicacy of character, as of something requiring care or tact: *a matter of considerable nicety.* [ME *nycete,* t. OF: m. *nicete,* der. *nice* NICE]

niche (nĭch), *n.*, *v.*, **niched, niching.** —*n.* **1.** an ornamental recess in a wall, etc., usually round in section and arched, as for a statue or other decorative object. **2.** a place or position suitable or appropriate for a person or thing. **3.** *Ecol.* the position or function of an organism in a community of plants and animals. —*v.t.* **4.** to place in a niche. [t. F, der. *nicher* to make a nest, g. Gallo-Rom. *nidicāre,* der. L *nidus* nest]

Nich·o·las (nĭk'ə ləs), *n.* **1.** name of five popes. **2. Grand Duke,** 1856–1929, Russian general in World War I. **3. Saint,** a. Santa Claus. b. fl. 4th cent., bishop in Asia Minor, patron saint of Russia, protector of children.

Nicholas I, 1. Saint, ("*the Great*") died A.D. 867, Italian ecclesiastic; pope, A.D. 858–867. **2.** 1796–1855, czar of Russia, 1825–55.

Nicholas II, 1868–1918, czar of Russia, 1894–1917, executed in the Russian Bolshevik Revolution.

Ni·chrome (nī'krōm), *n.* *Trademark.* a nickel-base alloy, containing chromium and iron, having high electrical resistance and stability at high temperatures.

Ni·ci·as (nĭsh'ĭ əs), *n.* died 414 B.C., Athenian aristocratic statesman and general.

nick (nĭk), *n.* **1.** a notch, groove, or the like, cut into or existing in a thing. **2.** a hollow place produced in an edge or surface, as of a dish, by breaking. **3.** a small groove on one side of the shank of a printing type, serving as a guide in setting or to distinguish different types. See diag. under **type. 4.** the precise moment or time of some occurrence: *in the nick of time.* —*v.t.* **5.** to make a nick or nicks in; notch. **6.** to record by means of a notch or notches. **7.** to cut into or through; to cut short. **8.** to incise certain tendons at the root of (a horse's) tail when setting it, to cause him to carry it higher. **9.** to hit, guess, catch, etc., exactly. **10.** *Brit. Slang.* to capture or arrest. **11.** to trick, cheat, or defraud. [late ME; cf. OE *gehnycted* wrinkled]

Nick (nĭk), *n.* the devil (usually **Old Nick**). [familiar use of *Nicholas,* proper name]

nick·el (nĭk'əl), *n.*, *v.*, **-eled, -eling** or (*esp. Brit.*) **-elled, -elling.** —*n.* **1.** *Chem.* a hard, silvery-white, ductile and malleable metallic element, allied to iron and cobalt, not readily oxidized, and much used in the arts, in making alloys, etc. *Symbol:* Ni; *at. wt.:* 58.6; *at. no.:* 28; *sp. gr.:* 8.9 at 20°C. **2.** *U.S.* a coin composed of

or containing nickel, now a five-cent piece. —*v.t.* **3.** to cover or coat with nickel. [t. Sw., short for *kopparnickel* niccolite, t. G: ha f-trans., half-adoption of *kupfernickel,* said to mean copper demon, since it looks like copper but yields none]

nick·el·ic (nĭk'əl ĭk, nĭ kĕl'-), *adj.* *Chem.* of or containing nickel, esp. in the trivalent state (Ni[+3]).

nick·el·if·er·ous (nĭk'ə lĭf'ər əs), *adj.* containing or yielding nickel.

nick·el·o·de·on (nĭk'ə lō'dĭ ən), *n.* *U.S.* a place of amusement with motion pictures, etc., to which the price of admission is five cents. [f. NICKEL (def. 2) + *odeon,* var. of ODEUM]

nick·el·ous (nĭk'əl əs), *adj.* *Chem.* containing bivalent nickel (Ni[+2]).

nickel plate, thin coating of nickel deposited on the surface of a piece of metal by electroplating or otherwise.

nick·el-plate (nĭk'əl plāt'), *v.t.* **-plated, -plating.** to coat with nickel by electroplating or otherwise.

nickel silver, German silver.

nick·er[1] (nĭk'ər), *n.* one who or that which nicks. [f. NICK + -ER[1]]

nick·er[2] (nĭk'ər), *v.i.*, *n.* *Chiefly Brit. Dial.* **1.** neigh. **2.** laugh; snicker. [appar. var. of *nicher, neigher,* freq. of NEIGH. Cf. LG *gnickern*]

nick·nack (nĭk'năk'), *n.* knickknack.

nick·name (nĭk'nām'), *n.*, *v.*, **-named, -naming.** —*n.* **1.** a name added to or substituted for the proper name of a person, place, etc., as in ridicule or familiarity. **2.** a familiar form of a proper name, as *Jim* for *James.* —*v.t.* **3.** to give a nickname to, or call by a specified nickname. **4.** to call by an incorrect or improper name. [ME *nekename,* for *ekename* (an *ekename* being taken as *a nekename*). See EKE[2], NAME]

Nic·o·bar Islands (nĭk'ə bär'), a group of small islands in the Bay of Bengal, W of the Malay Peninsula: a part of the centrally administered territories of Andaman and Nicobar Islands. 12,009 pop. (1951); 635 sq. mi.

Nic·o·lay (nĭk'ə lā'), *n.* **John George,** 1832–1901, U.S. biographer.

nic·o·tine (nĭk'ə tēn', -tĭn), *n.* a poisonous alkaloid, $C_{10}H_{14}N_2$, the active principle of tobacco, obtained as a colorless or nearly colorless, oily, acrid liquid. Also, **nic·o·tin** (nĭk'ə tĭn). [t. F, der. *Nicot,* who introduced tobacco into France in 1560]

nic·o·tin·ic ac·id (nĭk'ə tĭn'ĭk). *Chem.* an acid derived from the oxidation of nicotine, $(C_5H_4N)COOH$, found in fresh meat, yeast, etc.; niacin. The component of the vitamin B complex which counteracts pellagra.

nic·o·tin·ism (nĭk'ə tēn ĭz'əm, -tĭn-), *n.* a condition due to excessive use of tobacco.

Nic·the·roy (nĭk'tĕ roi'), *n.* Niteroi.

nic·ti·tate (nĭk'tə tāt'), *v.i.*, **-tated, -tating.** to wink. Also, **nic·tate** (nĭk'tāt). [t. ML: m.s. *nictitātus,* pp. of *nictitāre,* freq. of L *nictāre* wink] —**nic'ti·ta'tion,** *n.*

nictitating membrane, a thin membrane, or inner or third eyelid, present in many animals, capable of being drawn across the eyeball, as for protection.

Ni·da·ros (nē'dä rōs'), *n.* former name of **Trondheim.**

nid·der·ing (nĭd'ər ĭng), *Archaic.* —*n.* **1.** a cowardly or base person. —*adj.* **2.** cowardly; base. Also, **nid'er·ing.** [erroneous var. of *nithing,* t. Scand.; cf. Icel. *nidhingr*]

nide (nīd), *n.* a nest or brood, esp. of pheasants. [t. L: m.s. *nīdus* nest]

nid·i·fi·cate (nĭd'ə fə kāt'), *v.i.* **-cated, -cating.** to build a nest. [t. L: m.s. *nīdificātus,* pp.] —**nid'i·fi·ca'tion,** *n.*

nid·i·fy (nĭd'ə fī'), *v.i.*, **-fied, -fying.** nidificate.

ni·dus (nī'dəs), *n.*, *pl.* **-di** (-dī). **1.** a nest, esp. one in which insects, etc., deposit their eggs. **2.** a place or point in a living organism where a germ, whether proper or foreign to the organism, norma. or morbid, may find means of development. [t. L. See NEST]

Nie·buhr (nē'bŏor), *n.* **Barthold Georg** (bär'tôlt gā'ôrкн'), 1776–1831, German historian.

niece (nēs), *n.* **1.** a daughter of one's brother or sister. **2.** a daughter of one's husband's or wife's brother or sister. **3.** (in euphemistic use) an illegitimate daughter of an ecclesiastic [ME *nece, nice,* t. OF: m. *niece,* g. VL *neptia,* r. L *neptis* granddaughter, niece]

Nie·der·sach·sen (nē'dər zäкн'zən), *n.* Lower Saxony.

ni·el·lo (nĭ ĕl'ō), *n.*, *pl.* **nielli** (nĭ ĕl'ī), *v.*, **-loed, -loing.** —*n.* **1.** a black metallic composition, consisting of silver, copper, lead, and sulfur, with which an incised design or ground on metal is filled in to produce an ornamental effect. **2.** ornamental work so produced. **3.** a specimen of such work. —*v.t.* **4.** to decorate by means of niello; treat with niello or by the niello process. [t. It., g. L *nigellus* blackish]

Nie·men (nē'mən; *Pol.* nyĕ'mĕn), *n.* a river in the W Soviet Union, flowing into the Baltic: called **Memel** in its lower course. 565 mi. Lithuanian, **Nemunas.** Russian, **Nyeman.**

Nier·stein·er (nēr'stīn ər, -shtīn ər), *n.* a white Rhine wine. [t. G: f. *Nierstein* place near Mainz + *-er* -ER[1]]

Nie·tzsche (nē'chə), *n.* **Friedrich Wilhelm** (frē'drĭкн vĭl'hĕlm), 1844–1900, German philosopher.

Nie·tzsche·ism (nē'chī ĭz'əm), *n.* the philosophy of Nietzsche, emphasizing self-aggrandizement, or the will to power, as the chief motivating force of both the individual and society. Also, **Nie'tzsche·an·ism.** —**Nie'tzsche·an,** *n., adj.*

ăct, āble, dâre, ärt; ĕbb, ēqual; Ĭf, īce; hŏt, ōver, ôrder, oil, bŏŏk, ōoze, out; ŭp, ūse, ûrge; ə = a in alone; ch, chief; g, give; ng, ring; sh, shoe; th, thin; ŧħ, that; zh, vision. See the full key on inside cover.

nieve (nēv), n. *Archaic except Scot. and Brit. Dial.* a fist. [ME *neve*, t. Scand.; cf. Icel. *hnefi* fist]

Ni·fl·heim (nĭv′əl hām′), n. (in old Scand. cosmogony) the world of fog in the north. Also, **Ni′fel·heim′**. [t. Icel.]

nif·ty (nĭf′tĭ), adj., **-tier, -tiest,** n., pl. **-ties.** *U.S. Slang.* —adj. 1. smart; stylish; fine. —n. 2. a smart or clever remark. [orig. theat. slang]

Ni·ger (nī′jər), n. 1. a river in W Africa rising in S Guinea, flowing NE through the Mali Republic, and then SE through Nigeria into the Gulf of Guinea. ab. 2600 mi. 2. an independent republic in NW Africa: member of the French Community; formerly part of French West Africa. 2,400,000 pop. (est. 1959); 458, 976 sq. mi. *Cap.*: Niamey.

Ni·ge·ri·a (nī jĭr′ĭ·ə), n. a republic in W Africa: member of the Brit. Commonwealth; formerly a British colony and protectorate. 40,000,000 pop. (est. 1961); 360,000 sq. mi. *Cap.*: Lagos. Official name, Federation of Nigeria. —**Ni·ge′ri·an,** adj., n.

nig·gard (nĭg′ərd), n. 1. an excessively parsimonious or stingy person. —adj. 2. niggardly. [ME, f. (obs.) *nig niggard* (t. Scand.; cf. d. Sw. *nygg*) + -ARD]

nig·gard·ly (nĭg′ərd lĭ), adj. 1. parsimonious; stingy. 2. meanly small or scanty: *a niggardly allowance.* —adv. 3. in the manner of a niggard. —**nig′gard·li·ness,** n.

nig·ger (nĭg′ər), n. *Offensive.* 1. a Negro. 2. a member of any dark-skinned race. [var. of *neger,* t. F: m. *nègre,* t. Sp.: m. *negro* NEGRO]

nig·gle (nĭg′əl), v.i., **-gled, -gling.** to trifle; work ineffectively. [appar. t. Scand.; cf. Norw. *nigla*] —**nig′gler,** n. —**nig′gling·ly,** adv.

nigh (nī), adv., adj., **nigher, nighest** or **next,** v., prep. —adv. 1. near in space, time, or relation. 2. *Chiefly Archaic or Dial.* nearly or almost. —adj. 3. being near; not distant; near in relationship. 4. short or direct. 5. (with reference to animals or vehicles) left or near. 6. *Chiefly Archaic or Dial.* parsimonious. —v.i., v.t. 7. *Archaic.* to approach. —prep. 8. *Chiefly Archaic or Dial.* near. [ME *nigh(e), neye,* OE *nēah, nēh,* c. G *nahe*]

night (nīt), n. 1. the interval of darkness between sunset and sunrise. 2. nightfall. 3. the darkness of night; the dark. 4. a state or time of obscurity, ignorance, misfortune, etc. [ME; OE *niht, neaht,* c. G *nacht*]

night blindness, nyctalopia (def. 1).

night-blooming cereus, a typical American species of the genus *Selenicereus* (or *Cereus*), esp. *S. grandiflorus,* bearing large fragrant flowers opening at night.

night·cap (nīt′kăp′), n. 1. a cap for the head, intended primarily to be worn in bed. 2. *Colloq.* an alcoholic drink taken before going to bed.

night clothes, garments designed to be worn in bed.

night club, a restaurant, open until very late, furnishing food, drink, entertainment, etc.

night crawler, *U.S. Dial.* the common large earthworm, which emerges from its burrow at night.

night-dress (nīt′drĕs′), n. 1. dress or clothing for wearing in bed. 2. a nightgown.

night·fall (nīt′fôl′), n. the coming of night.

night·gown (nīt′goun′), n. 1. a loose gown, worn in bed by women or children. 2. a man's nightshirt.

night·hawk (nīt′hôk′), n. 1. any of several long-winged American goatsuckers of the genus *Chordeiles,* all more or less nocturnal and differing from the whippoorwill in having no rictal bristles, as the **common nighthawk,** mosquito hawk, or bullbat (*C. minor*). 2. the European goatsucker or nightjar, *Caprimulgus europaeus.* 3. *Colloq.* one who is habitually up or prowling about at night.

night heron, any of certain thick-billed herons of crepuscular or nocturnal habits, of the genus *Nycticorax* and allied genera, as the **black-crowned night heron** (*Nycticorax nycticorax*) of both New and Old Worlds, and the American **yellow-crowned night heron** (*Nyctanassa violocea*).

night·in·gale (nī′tən gāl′, nī′tĭng-), n. a small Old World migratory bird of the thrush family, esp. the common nightingale, *Luscinia megarhyncha,* of Europe, noted for the melodious song of the male given chiefly at night during the breeding season. [ME *nightyngale,* nasalized var. of *nightegale,* OE *nihtegale,* c. G *nachtigall,* lit., night singer (cf. OE *galan* sing)]

Nightingale,
Luscinia megarhyncha
(6½ in. long)

Night·in·gale (nī′tən gāl′, nī′tĭng-), n. **Florence,** 1820–1910, British nurse: reformer of hospital nursing.

night·jar (nīt′jär′), n. any Old World goatsucker, esp. the common species, *Caprimulgus europaeus,* of England.

night latch, a spring latch for a door or the like, which when adjusted for use, as at night, prevents the door from being opened from outside except by a key.

night letter, a telegram, usually of greater length than an ordinary message, sent at a reduced rate of charge because subject to the priority in transmission and delivery of regular telegrams.

night·long (nīt′lông′, -lŏng′), adj. 1. lasting all night. —adv. 2. throughout the whole night.

night·ly (nīt′lĭ), adj. 1. coming, occurring, appearing, or active at night: *nightly revels.* 2. coming or occurring each night. 3. of, pertaining to, or characteristic of

night. 4. *Obs.* or *Rare.* resembling night. —adv. 5. at or by night. 6. on every night: *performances given nightly.*

night·mare (nīt′mâr′), n. 1. a condition during sleep, or a dream, marked by a feeling of suffocation or distress, with acute fear, anxiety, or other painful emotion. 2. a condition, thought, or experience suggestive of a nightmare in sleep. 3. a monster or evil spirit formerly supposed to oppress persons during sleep. [ME. See NIGHT, MARE²] —**night′mar′ish,** adj.

night owl, *Colloq.* a person who often stays up late.

night raven, 1. *Now Poetic.* a bird that cries in the night. 2. a night heron.

night·rid·er (nīt′rī′dər), n. *Southern U.S.* one of a band of mounted men committing deeds of violence at night, as for purposes of intimidation or vengeance. —**night′rid′ing,** n.

night robe, nightgown.

nights (nīts), adv. *Now Colloq.* or *Dial.* at night.

night school, a school held at night, esp. for those who cannot attend a day school.

night·shade (nīt′shād′), n. 1. any of various plants of the genus *Solanum,* esp. *S. nigrum* (**black nightshade**) or *S. Dulcamara* (**woody nightshade,** or bittersweet). 2. any of various other solanaceous plants, as the **deadly nightshade** (belladonna) or the **stinking nightshade** (henbane). [ME; OE *nihtscada.* See NIGHT, SHADE]

night-shirt (nīt′shûrt′), n. a knee-length shirt or loose garment worn in bed by men or boys.

night soil, the contents of privies, etc., removed at night and used as manure.

night stick, a heavy stick or long club carried by a policeman at night, and sometimes in the daytime.

night·time (nīt′tīm′), n. the time between evening and morning. Also, *Poetic,* **night·tide** (nīt′tīd′).

night·walk·er (nīt′wô′kər), n. one who walks or roves about in the night, as a thief, a prostitute, etc.

night watch, 1. a watch or guard kept during the night. 2. the person or persons keeping such a watch. 3. (*usually pl.*) a period or division of the night.

night·wear (nīt′wâr′), n. clothes for wearing in bed.

ni·gres·cent (nĭ grĕs′ənt), adj. blackish. [t. L: s. *nigrescens,* ppr., becoming black] —**ni·gres′cence,** n.

nig·ri·tude (nĭg′rə tūd′, -tōōd′), n. 1. blackness. 2. something black. [t. L: m. *nigritūdo*]

ni·hil (nī′hĭl), n. nothing; a thing of no value. [t. L]

ni·hil·ism (nī′ə lĭz′əm), n. 1. total disbelief in religion or moral principles and obligations, or in established laws and institutions. 2. *Philos.* a. a belief that there is no objective basis of truth. b. an extreme form of skepticism, denying all real existence. c. nothingness or nonexistence. 3. (*sometimes cap.*) the principles of a Russian revolutionary group, active in the latter half of the 19th century, holding that existing social and political institutions must be destroyed in order to clear the way for a new state of society, and in its extreme measures employing terrorism, assassination, etc. 4. terrorism or revolutionary activity. [f. L *nihil* nothing + -ISM] —**ni′hil·ist,** n. —**ni′hil·is′tic,** adj.

ni·hil·i·ty (nī hĭl′ə tĭ), n. nothingness.

Ni·i·ga·ta (nyē′ē gä′tä), n. a seaport in central Japan, on NW Honshu island. 220,901 (1950).

Ni·jin·sky (nĭ zhĭn′skĭ; *Russ.* nĭ zhēn′-), n. **Waslaw** or **Vaslaw** (väts läf′), 1890–1950, Russian dancer.

Nij·me·gen (nī′mā′gən; *Du.* nī′mā′KHən), n. a city in E Netherlands, on the Waal river: peace treaty, 1678. 106,523 (1947). Also, **Nimwegen.**

Ni·ke (nī′kē, nē′kā), n. 1. *Gk. Myth.* a. the goddess of victory, called by the Romans Victoria, represented as a winged maiden, a palm branch in one hand and a garland in the other, or a fillet outstretched in both hands. b. the goddess Athena as the giver of victory. 2. an anti-aircraft guided missile.

Nik·ko (nyĭk′kō), n. a town in central Japan, on Honshu island: famous for its shrines and temples.

Ni·ko·la·ev (nĭ′kō lä′yĕf), n. a city in the SW Soviet Union. 206,000 (est. 1956). Formerly, **Vernoleninsk.**

nil (nĭl), n. nothing. [t. L, contr. of *nihil*]

Nile (nīl), n. 1. a river in E Africa, flowing N from Lake Victoria to the Mediterranean. 3473 mi. (from the headwaters of the Kagera river, ab. 4000 mi.). 2. **Blue,** a tributary of the Nile, flowing from Lake Tana in Ethiopia into the Nile at Khartoum. 3. **White,** a part of the Nile above Khartoum.

Nile blue, pale greenish blue.

Nile green, pale bluish green.

nil·gai (nĭl′gī), n., pl. **-gais** (*esp. collectively*) **-gai.** a large antelope of E India, *Boselaphus tragocamelus,* the male colored bluish-gray, the hornless female tawny. Also, **nylghau, nylghai.** [t. Hind.: lit., blue cow]

Nil·gi·ri Hills (nĭl′gĭr ĭ), a group of mountains in S India in Madras state. Highest peak, Mt. Dodabetta, 8760 ft.

Nilgai,
Boselaphus tragocamelus
(4 ft. 4 in. to 4 ft. 8 in. high at the shoulder)

nill (nĭl), v.i., v.t. *Archaic.* to be unwilling: *will he, nill he.* [ME *nille(n),* OE *nyllan,* f. *ne* not + *willan* will]

Ni·lom·e·ter (nī lŏm′ə tər), n. a graduated column or the like used to measure the height of the floods of the Nile. [t. Gk.: m.s. *Neilométrion*]

Ni·lot·ic (nī lŏt/ĭk), *adj.* of or pertaining to the river Nile or the inhabitants of the Nile region. [t. L: s. *Nīlōticus*, t. Gk.: m. *Neilōtikós*]

nil si·ne nu·mi·ne (nĭl sĭ/nĭ nū/mĭ nĭ), *Latin.* nothing without the divine will (motto of Colorado).

nim·ble (nĭm/bəl), *adj.*, **-bler, -blest. 1.** quick and light in movement; moving with ease; agile; active; rapid: *nimble feet.* **2.** quick in apprehending, devising, etc.: *nimble wits.* **3.** cleverly contrived. [ME *nymel*, repr. OE var. (unrecorded) of *numol* quick at taking, der. *niman* take] **—nim/ble·ness,** *n.* **—nim/bly,** *adv.*

nim·bo·stra·tus (nĭm/bō strā/təs), *n. Meteorol.* a low, formless cloud layer, of a nearly uniform dark gray; a layer type of rain cloud. [f. *nimbo-* (comb. form of NIMBUS) + STRATUS]

nim·bus (nĭm/bəs), *n.*, *pl.* **-bi** (-bī), **-buses. 1.** a bright cloud anciently conceived of as surrounding a deity of the classical mythology when appearing on earth. **2.** a cloud or atmosphere of some kind surrounding a person or thing. **3.** *Art.* a disk or otherwise shaped figure representing a radiance about the head of a divine or sacred personage, a medieval sovereign, etc. **4.** *Obs.* the type of cloud or mass of clouds, dense, with ragged edges, which yields rain or snow; a rain cloud. [t. L: rainstorm, cloud]

Nîmes (nēm), *n.* a city in S France: famous Roman ruins. 89,130 (1954).

ni·mi·e·ty (nĭ mī/ə tĭ), *n.* excess. [t. LL: m.s. *nimietas*]

nim·i·ny-pim·i·ny (nĭm/ə nĭ pĭm/ə nĭ), *adj.* mincing; affectedly nice or refined. [imit. of a mincing utterance]

Nim·itz (nĭm/ĭts), *n.* **Chester William,** 1885–1966, U.S. admiral.

n'im·porte (năN pôrt/), *French.* it does not matter.

Nim·rod (nĭm/rŏd), *n.* **1.** *Bible.* a "mighty hunter," the great-grandson of Noah. Gen. 10:8, 9. **2.** one expert in or devoted to hunting.

Nim·we·gen (nĭm/vā/ĸнən), *n.* Nijmegen.

nin·com·poop (nĭn/kəm pōōp/), *n.* a fool or simpleton.

nine (nīn), *n.* **1.** a cardinal number, eight plus one. **2.** a symbol for this number, as 9 or IX or VIIII. **3.** a set of nine persons or things. **4.** a team of baseball players. **5.** a playing card with nine pips. **6. The Nine,** the nine Muses. **—***adj.* **7.** amounting to nine in number. [ME; O... *nigen*, var. of *nigon*, c. G *neun*]

nine·fold (nīn/fōld/), *adj.* **1.** nine times as much. **2.** having nine parts. **—***adv.* **3.** nine times as much.

nine·pence (nīn/pəns), *n.* **1.** the sum of nine English pennies. **2.** a coin of this value.

nine·pins (nīn/pĭnz/), *n.pl.* **1.** (*construed as sing.*) a game played with nine wooden pins at which a ball is bowled to knock them down. **2.** (*construed as pl.*) the pins used in this game. **3.** (*construed as sing.*) tenpins played without using a head pin.

nine·teen (nīn/tēn/), *n.* **1.** a cardinal number, ten plus nine. **2.** a symbol for this number, as 19 or XIX or XVIIII. **—***adj.* **3.** amounting to nineteen in number. [ME *nintene*, repr. d. OE var. (unrecorded) of OE *nigontŷne*] **—nine/teenth/,** *adj.*, *n.*

nine·ty (nīn/tĭ), *n.*, *pl.* **-ties,** *adj.* **—***n.* **1.** a cardinal number, ten times nine. **2.** a symbol for this number, as 90 or XC or LXXXX. **—***adj.* **3.** amounting to ninety in number. [ME *nineti*, OE *nigontig*] **—nine·ti·eth** (nīn/tĭ ĭth), *adj.*, *n.*

Nin·e·veh (nĭn/ə və), *n.* the ancient capital of Assyria: its ruins are opposite Mosul, on the Tigris river, in N Iraq. See map under **Babylon.**

Ning·po (nĭng/pō/), *n.* a seaport in E China, in Chekiang province. 240,000 (est. 1951).

Ning·sia (nĭng/shyä/), *n.* a former province in NW China: part of Inner Mongolian Autonomous Region.

nin·ny (nĭn/ĭ), *n.*, *pl.* **-nies.** a fool; a simpleton.

ninth (nīnth), *adj.* **1.** next after the eighth. **2.** being one of nine equal parts. **—***n.* **3.** a ninth part, esp. of one (¹⁄₉). **4.** the ninth member of a series. **5.** *Music.* **a.** a tone distant from another tone by an interval of an octave and a second. **b.** the interval between such tones. **c.** harmonic combination of such tones. **—ninth/ly,** *adv.*

ninth chord, *Music.* a chord formed by the superposition of four thirds.

Ni·nus (nī/nəs), *n.* *Gk. Legend.* the legendary founder of Nineveh: husband of Semiramis.

Ni·o·be (nī/ō bē/), *n.* *Gk. Myth.* the daughter of Tantalus and wife of Amphion of Thebes. She provoked Apollo and Artemis to vengeance by taunting their mother Leto with the number and beauty of her own children. Niobe's children were slain and after Zeus turned her into stone she continued to weep for them.

ni·o·bic (nī ō/bĭk, -ŏb/ĭk), *adj.* *Chem.* **1.** containing pentavalent niobium (Nb⁺⁵), as *niobic acid,* HNbO₃. **2.** of or pertaining to niobium.

ni·o·bi·um (nī ō/bĭ əm), *n.* *Chem.* a steel-gray metallic element resembling tantalum in its chemical properties. Symbol: Nb; *at.no.:* 41; *at.wt.:* 92.91; *sp.gr.:* 8.4 at 20° C. Formerly called columbium. [t. NL; named after *Niobe,* daughter of Tantalus, because found with tantalum. See -IUM]

ni·o·bous (nī ō/bəs), *adj.* *Chem.* **1.** containing trivalent niobium (Nb⁺³), as *niobous chloride,* NbCl₃. **2.** of or pertaining to niobium.

Ni·o·brar·a (nī/ə brär/ə), *n.* a river flowing from E Wyoming E through Nebraska to the Missouri. 431 mi.

nip¹ (nĭp), *v.*, **nipped, nipping,** *n.* **—***v.t.* **1.** to compress sharply between two surfaces or points; pinch or bite. **2.** to take off by pinching, biting, or snipping (usually fol. by *off*). **3.** to check in growth or development: *to nip a plot.* **4.** to affect sharply and painfully or injuriously, as cold does. **5.** *Slang.* to snatch or take suddenly or quickly (fol. by *away, up,* etc.). **6.** *Slang.* to steal. **—***v.i.* **7.** *Brit. Colloq.* to move or go suddenly or quickly, or slip (fol. by *away, off, up,* etc.). **—***n.* **8.** the act of nipping; a pinch. **9.** a sharp or biting remark. **10.** a biting quality, as in cold or frosty air. **11.** sharp cold; a sharp touch of frost. **12.** the biting taste or tang in cheese. **13.** a small bit or quantity of anything. [ME *nyp(pen)*; akin to obs. *nipe,* c. D *nijpen*]

nip² (nĭp), *n.*, *v.*, **nipped, nipping.** **—***n.* **1.** a small drink of liquor; a sip. **2.** a small tankard of ale, about a half pint. **—***v.t., v.i.* **3.** to drink (liquor) in small sips, esp. repeatedly. [short for *nipperkin*; ? t. D or LG]

ni·pa (nē/pə, nĭ/pə), *n.* a palm, *Nipa fruticans,* of the East Indies, the Philippines, etc., whose foliage is much used for thatching, etc. [t. Malay: m. *nĭpah*]

nip and tuck, *U.S.* (in a race or other contest) with one competitor equaling the speed or efforts of the other.

Nip·is·sing (nĭp/ə sĭng), *n.* a lake in SE Canada, in Ontario, N of Georgian Bay. 330 sq. mi.

nip·per (nĭp/ər), *n.* **1.** one who or that which nips. **2.** (*usually pl.*) a device for n.pp.ng, as p.ncers or forceps. **3.** one of the large claws of a crustacean. **4.** (*pl.*) *Slang.* handcuffs. **5.** *Brit. Colloq.* a small boy.

nip·ping (nĭp/ĭng), *adj.* **1.** that nips. **2.** sharp or biting, as cold, etc. **3.** sarcastic. **—nip/ping·ly,** *adv.*

nip·ple (nĭp/əl), *n.* **1.** a protuberance of the mamma or breast where, in the female, the milk ducts discharge; a teat. **2.** something resembling it, as the mouthpiece of a nursing bottle. **3.** a short piece of pipe with threads on each end, used for joining valves, etc. [orig. uncert.]

Nip·pon (nĭp/ŏn/, nĭp/ŏn), *n.* Japanese name of **Japan.**

Nip·pon·ese (nĭp/ə nēz/, -nēs/), *n.*, *pl.* **-ese,** *adj.* Japanese. [f. *Nippon,* native name for Japan, + -ESE]

Nip·pur (nĭp pŏōr/), *n.* an ancient city of Babylonia.

nip·py (nĭp/ĭ), *adj.*, **-pier, -piest. 1.** apt to nip; sharp; biting. **2.** *Chiefly Brit. Colloq.* nimble; active.

nir·va·na (nĭr vä/na, -văn/ə, nər-), *n.* **1.** (*often cap.*) *Buddhism.* **a.** the extinguishment of the restlessness and heat of one's emotions. **b.** the passionless peace of imperturbability, attained through the annihilation of disturbing desires. **2.** freedom from pain, worry, and the external world. [t. Skt.: a blowing out (as of a light)]

Niš (nēsh), *n.* a city in E Yugoslavia: the capital of Serbia. 60,677 (1953). Also, **Nish.**

Ni·san (nī/săn; *Heb.* nē sän/), *n.* (in the Jewish calendar) the seventh month of the civil year and the first of the ecclesiastical year.

Ni·sei (nē/sā/), *n.*, *pl.* **-sei.** a person of Japanese descent, born in the U.S. and loyal to it. [t. Jap.]

Ni·sha·pur (nē/shä pŏōr/), *n.* a town in NE Iran: the birthplace of Omar Khayyam. 24,270 (est. 1949).

ni·si (nī/sī), *conj.* unless (esp. in law, after *decree, order,* etc., to specify some contingency). [t. L]

ni·si pri·us (nī/sī prī/əs), *Law.* **1.** *U.S.* designating a court of first instance. **2.** *Brit.* unless before (formerly used in writs summoning jurors to Westminister "unless before" that day justices came to the assizes). [t. L]

Nis·sen hut (nĭs/ən), a prefabricated shelter with the shape of a long, slightly flattened cylinder, insulated esp. for military troops in arctic regions; Quonset hut.

Nis·tru (nē/strōō), *n.* Rumanian name of **Dniester.**

ni·sus (nī/səs), *n.*, *pl.* **-sus.** effort; impulse. [t. L: effort]

nit (nĭt), *n.* **1.** the egg of a parasitic insect attached to a hair, or fiber of clothing; particularly, the egg of a louse. **2.** the insect while young. [ME *nite,* OE *hnitu,* c. G *niss*]

ni·ter (nī/tər), *n.* **1.** nitrate of potassium, KNO₃, a white salt used in making gunpowder, etc.; saltpeter. **2.** nitrate of sodium, NaNO₃; Chile saltpeter. Also, *esp. Brit.,* **ni/tre.** [ME *nitre,* t. L: m. *nitrum,* t. Gk.: m. *nítron* natron, native sodium carbonate]

Ni·te·roi (nē/tě roi/), *n.* a seaport in SE Brazil, opposite Rio de Janeiro. 174,500 (est. 1952). Also, **Nictheroy.**

ni·ton (nī/tŏn), *n.* *Chem.* an early name for the element radon. Symbol: Nt [t. NL, der. L *nitēre* shine]

nitr-, var. of nitro-, before vowels.

ni·trate (nī/trāt), *n.*, *v.*, **-trated, -trating.** **—***n.* **1.** *Chem.* a salt or ester of nitric acid, or any compound containing the NO₃⁻¹ radical. **2.** fertilizer consisting of potassium nitrate or sodium nitrate. **—***v.t.* **3.** to treat with nitric acid or a nitrate. **4.** to convert into a nitrate. [f. NITER + -ATE²] **—ni·tra/tion,** *n.*

ni·tric (nī/trĭk), *adj.* **1.** *Chem.* containing nitrogen, usually in the pentavalent state (N⁺⁵). **2.** of or pertaining to niter. [t. F: m. *nitrique.* See NITER, -IC]

nitric acid, a corrosive liquid, HNO₃, with powerful oxidizing properties.

nitric bacteria, nitrobacteria.

nitric oxide, a colorless gaseous compound of nitrogen and oxygen, NO, formed when copper is treated with dilute nitric acid.

ni·tride (nī/trīd, nī/trĭd), *n.* *Chem.* a compound, usually containing two elements only, of which the more electronegative one is nitrogen. Also, **ni·trid** (nī/trĭd). [f. NITER + -IDE]

ni·tri·fi·ca·tion (nī′trə fə kā′shən), *n.* **1.** act of nitrifying. **2.** the introduction of an NO_2 radical into an organic compound, usually by means of mixed nitric and sulfuric acids.

ni·tri·fy (nī′trə fī′), *v.t., v.i.,* **-fied, -fying. 1.** to oxidize (ammonia compounds, etc.) to nitrites or nitrates, esp. by bacterial action. **2.** to impregnate (soil, etc.) with nitrates. **3.** to treat or combine with nitrogen or its compounds. **4.** *Obsolesc.* to convert into niter. [t. F: m. *nitrifier.* See NITER -FY]

ni·trile (nī′trĭl, -trēl, -trīl), *n.* any of a class of organic compounds with the general formula RCN. Also, **ni·tril** (nī′trĭl). [f. NITR(OGEN) + -ILE]

ni·trite (nī′trīt), *n. Chem.* a salt of nitrous acid.

nitro-, *Chem.* **1.** a word element indicating the group NO_2. **2.** a misnomer for the nitrate group (NO_3), as in *nitrocellulose.* Also, **nitr-.** [t. Gk., comb. form of *nitron* native sodium carbonate]

ni·tro·bac·te·ri·a (nī′trō băk tĭr′ē ə), *n.pl.* certain bacteria of the soil, concerned in nitrifying processes.

ni·tro·ben·zene (nī′trō běn′zēn, -běn zēn′), *n. Chem.* a light-yellowish liquid, $C_6H_5NO_2$, a derivative of benzene, used in the manufacture of aniline.

ni·tro·cel·lu·lose (nī′trō sĕl′yə lōs′), *n.* cellulose nitrate.

ni·tro·gen (nī′trə jən), *n. Chem.* a colorless, odorless, gaseous element which forms about four fifths of the volume of the atmosphere and is present (combined) in animal and vegetable tissues, chiefly in proteins. It is used in compounds, as fertilizer, in explosives, and in dyes. Symbol: N; *at. wt.:* 14.008; *at. no.:* 7. [t. F: m. *nitrogène.* See NITRO-, -GEN]

nitrogen fixation, 1. any process of combining free nitrogen from the air with other elements, either by chemical means or by bacterial action, used esp. in the preparation of fertilizers, industrial products, etc. **2.** this process as performed by bacteria (**nitrogen fixers**) found in the nodules of leguminous plants, which make the resulting nitrogenous compounds available to their host plants. —**ni′tro·gen-fix′ing,** *adj.*

ni·tro·gen·ize (nī′trə jə nīz′), *v.t.* **-ized, -izing.** to combine with nitrogen or add nitrogenous material to.

ni·trog·e·nous (nī trŏj′ə nəs), *adj.* containing nitrogen.

ni·tro·glyc·er·in (nī′trə glĭs′ər ĭn), *n.* a colorless, highly explosive oil, $C_3H_5(ONO_2)_3$, a principal constituent of dynamites and certain propellent and rocket powders; a nitration product of glycerin. Also, **ni·tro·glyc·er·ine** (nī′trə glĭs′ər ĭn, -ə rēn′).

nitro group, the univalent $-NO_2$ radical.

ni·trol·ic (nī trŏl′ĭk), *adj. Chem.* of or denoting a series of acids of the type, $RC(:NOH)NO_2$, whose salts form deep-red solutions. [f. NITR- + -OL[1] + -IC]

ni·trom·e·ter (nī trŏm′ə tər), *n.* an apparatus for determining the amount of nitrogen or nitrogen compounds in a substance or mixture. [f. NITRO- + -METER]

ni·tro·par·af·fin (nī′trə păr′ə fĭn), *n. Chem.* any of a class of compounds derived from the methane series replacing a hydrogen atom by the nitro group.

ni·tros·a·mine (nī′trōs ə mēn′, nī′trōs ăm′ĭn), *n. Chem.* any of a series of oily compounds with the type formula R_2NNO. Also, **ni·tros·am·in** (nī′trōs ăm′ĭn).

ni·tro·syl (nī trō′sĭl, nī′trə sĕl′, nī′trə sĭl), *n. Chem.* the radical $NO-$. [f. *nitroso-* (comb. form repr. NL *nitrōsus* NITROUS) + -YL]

ni·trous (nī′trəs), *adj. Chem.* **1.** pertaining to compounds obtained from niter, usually containing less oxygen than the corresponding nitric compounds. **2.** containing nitrogen, usually trivalent (N^{+3}). [t. NL: m.s. *nitrōsus* nitrous, L full of natron. See NITER]

nitrous acid, an acid, HNO_2, known only in solution.

nitrous bacteria, nitrobacteria which convert ammonia derivatives into nitrites by oxidation.

nitrous oxide, laughing gas.

Nit·ti (nēt′tē), *n.* **Francesco Saverio** (frän chĕs′kō sä vĕ′ryō), 1868–1953, Italian statesman and publicist.

nit·ty (nĭt′ĭ), *adj.* full of nits.

nit·wit (nĭt′wĭt′), *n.* a slow-witted or foolish person.

Ni·u·e (nĭ′ōō ā), *n.* island in S Pacific between Tonga and Cook islands: possession of New Zealand. 5000 pop. (est. 1956); ab. 100 sq. mi. Also, **Savage Island.**

Ni·ver·nais (nē vĕr nā′), *n.* a former province in central France. *Cap.:* Nevers.

Ni·vôse (nē vōz′), *n.* (in the French Revolutionary calendar) the fourth month of the year. [t. F, t. L: m.s. *nivôsus* snowy]

nix[1] (nĭks), *Slang.* —*n.* **1.** nothing. —*adv.* **2.** no. —*interj.* **3.** (used as a signal warning of someone's approach): *nix, the cops!* [t. G, var. of *nichts* nothing]

nix[2] (nĭks), *n., pl.* **nixes.** *Folklore.* a water spirit, usually small, and either good or bad. [t. G, var. of *nichs,* OHG *nichus,* c. OE *nicor* fabulous sea monster] —**nix·ie** (nĭk′sĭ), *n. fem.*

Nix·on (nĭks′ən), *n.* **Richard Milhous,** born 1913, vice-president of the U.S., 1953–1961.

Ni·zam (nĭ zäm′, nĭ zăm′), *n.* **1.** the title of the ruler of Hyderabad, India. **2.** (*l.c.*) a soldier of the Turkish regular army. [t. Hind. and Turk.]

Nizh·ni Nov·go·rod (nēzh′nĭ nŏv′gŏ rŏt), former name of Gorki. (def. 2.)

Nizhni Ta·gil (tä gĭl′), a city in the W Soviet Union in Asia, on the E slope of the Ural Mts. 297,000 (est. 1956).

N.J., New Jersey.

Njord (nyôrd), *n. Scand. Myth.* the father of Frey and Freya: the dispenser of riches. Also, **Njorth** (nyôrth).

NL, New Latin or Neo-Latin. Also, **NL., N.L.**

n.l., 1. *Print.* new line. **2.** (*L non licet*) it is not permitted. **3.** (*L non liquet*) it is not clear or evident.

N. Lat., north latitude. Also, **N. lat.**

NLRB, National Labor Relations Board.

N.M., New Mexico. Also, **N. Mex.**

NNE, north-northeast. Also, **N.N.E.**

NNW, north-northwest. Also, **N.N.W.**

no[1] (nō), *adv., n., pl.* **noes.** —*adv.* **1. a word used: a.** to express dissent, denial, or refusal, as in response (opposed to *yes*). **b.** to emphasize a previous negative or qualify a previous statement. **2.** not in any degree; not at all (used with a comparative): *he is no better.* **3.** not: *whether or no.* —*n.* **4.** an utterance of the word "no." **5.** a denial or refusal. **6.** a negative vote or voter. [ME; OE *nā* (c. Icel. *nei*), f. *ne* not + *ā ever.* See AY[1]]

no[2] (nō), *adj.* **1.** not any: *no money.* **2.** not at all; very far from being; not at all a: *he is no genius.* [var. NONE[1]]

No[3] (nō), *n., pl.* **No.** a type of Japanese drama, originally religious, with dancing and singing. Also, **Noh.** [t. Jap.]

No., 1. north. **2.** northern. **3.** number. Also, **no.**

No·a·chi·an (nō ā′kĭ ən), *adj.* of the patriarch Noah or his time. Also, **No·ach·ic** (nō ăk′ĭk, -ā′kĭk).

No·ah (nō′ə), *n.* a Hebrew patriarch, the builder of Noah's Ark, in which, with his family and animals of every species, he survived the deluge. Gen. 5–9. [t. Heb.]

nob[1] (nŏb), *n.* **1.** *Slang.* the head. **2.** *Cribbage.* the knave of the same su t as the card turned up, counting one to the holder. [? var. of KNOB]

nob[2] (nŏb), *n. Brit. Slang.* a person of wealth or social distinction. [? special use of NOB[1]]

no-ball (nō′bôl′), *n. Cricket.* an unfairly thrown ball.

nob·ble (nŏb′əl), *v.t.* **-bled, -bling.** *Brit. Slang.* **1.** to disable (a horse), as by drugging it. **2.** to win (a person, etc.) over by underhand means. **3.** to swindle. **4.** to catch. [back formation from *nobbler,* var. of HOBBLER (*an 'obbler* being taken as *a nobbler*)] —**nob′bler,** *n.*

nob·by (nŏb′ĭ), *adj.,* **-bier, -biest.** *Chiefly Brit. Slang.* **1.** fashionable or elegant. **2.** first-rate. [f. NOB[2] + -Y[1]]

No·bel (nō bĕl′), *n.* **Alfred Bernhard** (äl′frĕd bär′närd), 1833–96, Swedish inventor of dynamite and manufacturer of explosives: established Nobel prizes.

no·be·li·um (nō bē′lĭ əm), *n. Chem.* a synthetic, radioactive element. Symbol: No; *at.no.:* 102. [f. NOBEL (*Institute*), where first identified + -IUM]

Nobel prizes, prizes awarded annually from the bequest of Alfred B. Nobel for achievement during the preceding year in physics, chemistry, medicine, literature, and the promotion of peace.

no·bil·i·ar·y (nō bĭl′ĭ ĕr′ĭ), *adj.* of or pertaining to the nobility. [t. F: m. *nobiliaire,* der. L *nōbilis* noble]

no·bil·i·ty (nō bĭl′ə tĭ), *n., pl.* **-ties. 1.** the noble class, or the body of nobles, in a country. **2.** (in Great Britain and Ireland) the peerage. **3.** the state or quality of being noble. **4.** noble birth or rank. **5.** exalted moral excellence. **6.** grandeur. [ME *nobilite,* t. OF, t. L: m.s. *nōbilitas*]

no·ble (nō′bəl), *adj.,* **nobler, noblest,** *n.* —*adj.* **1.** distinguished by birth, rank, or title. **2.** pertaining to persons so distinguished: *noble birth.* **3.** belonging to or constituting a class (the nobility) possessing a hereditary social or political preëminence in a country or state. **4.** of an exalted moral character or excellence: *a noble thought.* **5.** admirable in dignity of conception, or in the manner of expression, execution, or composition: *a noble poem.* **6.** imposing in appearance; stately; magnificent: *a noble monument.* **7.** of an admirably high quality; notably superior. **8.** *Chem.* inert; chemically inactive. **9.** (of some metals, as gold and platinum) that are not altered on exposure to the air, do not rust easily, and are much scarcer and more valuable than the so-called useful metals. **10.** *Falconry.* denoting the long-winged falcons which stoop to the quarry at a single swoop (opposed to *ignoble*). —*n.* **11.** a person of noble birth or rank; a nobleman. **12.** former English gold coin, worth 6 shillings, 8 pence. **13.** (in Great Britain and Ireland) a peer. [ME, t. OF, g. L *nōbilis* well-known, highborn] —**no′ble·ness,** *n.*

—**Syn. 4.** NOBLE, HIGH-MINDED, MAGNANIMOUS agree in referring to lofty principles and loftiness of mind or spirit. NOBLE implies a loftiness of character or spirit that scorns the petty, mean, base, or dishonorable: *a noble deed.* HIGH-MINDED implies having elevated principles and consistently adhering to them: *a high-minded devotion to ideals.* MAGNANIMOUS suggests greatness of mind or soul, esp. as manifested in generosity or in overlooking injuries: *magnanimous toward his former enemies.* —**Ant. 4.** base, mean.

no·ble·man (nō′bəl mən), *n., pl.* **-men.** a man of noble birth or rank; a noble. —**no′ble·wom′an,** *n. fem.*

no·blesse (nō blĕs′), *n.* **1.** noble birth or condition. **2.** the nobility. [ME, t. OF, der. L *nōbilis* noble]

no·blesse o·blige (nō blĕs′ ō blēzh′), *French.* noble rank requires honorable conduct.

no·bly (nō′blĭ), *adv.* **1.** in a noble manner. **2.** courageously. **3.** splendidly; superbly. **4.** of noble ancestry.

no·bod·y (nō′bŏd′ĭ, -bəd ĭ), *pron., n., pl.* **-bodies.** —*pron.* **1.** no person. —*n.* **2.** a person of no importance, esp. socially.

no·cent (nō′sənt), *adj. Now Rare.* **1.** hurtful; harmful; injurious. **2.** guilty. [t. L: s. *nocens,* ppr., harming]

nock (nŏk), *n.* **1.** a metal or plastic piece at the end of an arrow. **2.** a notch or groove at the end of an arrow into which the bowstring fits. **3.** a notch or groove at each end of the bow, to hold the bowstring in place. —*v.t.* **4.** to furnish with a nock. **5.** to adjust (the arrow) to the bowstring, in readiness to shoot. [ME *nocke*; ? t. D: m. *nok*, or LG: m. *nokk* tip or projection]

noc·tam·bu·lism (nŏk tăm′byə lĭz′əm), *n.* somnambulism. Also, **noc·tam·bu·la·tion.** [f. s. L *nox* night + s. *ambulāre* walk about + -ISM] —**noc·tam′bu·list,** *n.*

nocti-, a word element meaning "night." [t. L, comb. form of *nox*]

noc·ti·lu·ca (nŏk′tə lōō′kə), *n., pl.* **-cae** (-sē). a pelagic flagellate protozoan, genus *Noctiluca*, notable for its phosphorescence. [t. L: something that shines by night]

noc·ti·lu·cent (nŏk′tə lōō′sənt), *adj. Meteorol.* (of clouds) very high and cirruslike, visible during the short night of summer and believed to be of meteor dust shining with reflected sunlight.

noc·tu·id (nŏk′chōō ĭd), *n.* **1.** any of the *Noctuidae,* a large family of dull-colored moths, the larvae of which include the highly injurious army worms and cutworms. —*adj.* **2.** belonging or pertaining to the *Noctuidae.* [t. NL: s. *Noctuidae*, pl., der. L *noctua* night owl]

noc·tule (nŏk′chōōl), *n.* a large reddish insectivorous bat, *Nyctalus noctula,* common to Europe and Asia. [t. F, t. It.: m. *nottola* bat, der. *notte* night, g. L *nox*]

noc·tur·nal (nŏk tûr′nəl), *adj.* **1.** of or pertaining to the night. **2.** done, occurring, or coming by night. **3.** active by night, as many animals. **4.** opening by night and closing by day, as certain flowers. [late ME, t. LL: s. *nocturnālis,* der. L *nocturnus* of or in the night] —**noc·tur′nal·ly,** *adv.*

noc·turne (nŏk′tûrn), *n. Music.* **1.** a piece appropriate to the night or evening. **2.** an instrumental composition of a dreamy or pensive character. [t. F, t. LL: m. *nocturna* (fem.) of the night]

noc·u·ous (nŏk′yōō əs), *adj.* injurious; noxious. [t. L: m. *nocuus*] —**noc′u·ous·ly,** *adv.* —**noc′u·ous·ness,** *n.*

nod (nŏd), *v.,* **nodded, nodding,** *n.* —*v.i.* **1.** to make a slight, quick inclination of the head, as in assent, greeting, command, etc. **2.** to let the head fall forward with a sudden, involuntary movement when sleepy. **3.** to grow careless, inattentive, or dull. **4.** (of trees, flowers, plumes, etc.) to droop, bend, or incline with a swaying motion. —*v.t.* **5.** to incline (the head) in a short, quick movement, as of assent, greeting, etc. **6.** to express or signify by such a movement of the head: *to nod assent.* **7.** to summon, bring, or send by a nod of the head. **8.** to incline or cause to lean or sway. —*n.* **9.** a short, quick inclination of the head, as in assent, greeting, command, or drowsiness. **10.** a nap. **11.** a bending or swaying movement of anything. [ME, orig. obscure] —**nod′der,** *n.*

nod·al (nō′dəl), *adj.* of or of the nature of a node.

nod·dle[1] (nŏd′əl), *n. Colloq. and Humorous.* the head. [ME *nodel, nadeul;* orig. uncert.]

nod·dle[2] (nŏd′əl), *v.t., v.i.,* **-dled, -dling.** to nod lightly or frequently. [freq. of NOD]

nod·dy (nŏd′ĭ), *n., pl.* **-dies.** **1.** a white-capped dark-brown tern, *Anous stolidus,* of warm seacoasts of both the New and the Old World common in the West Indies, usually so fearless of man as to seem stupid. **2.** a fool or simpleton. [? n. use of *noddy,* adj., silly; orig. uncert.]

node (nōd), *n.* **1.** a knot, protuberance, or knob. **2.** a complication; difficulty. **3.** a centering point of component parts. **4.** *Bot.* **a.** a joint in a stem. **b.** a part of a stem which normally bears a leaf. **5.** *Geom.* a point on a curve or surface, at which there can be more than one tangent line or plane. **6.** *Physics.* a point, line, or region in a vibrating medium at which there is comparatively no variation of the disturbance which is being transmitted through the medium. **7.** *Astron.* either of the two points at which the orbit of a heavenly body cuts the plane of the ecliptic, equator, or other properly defined plane (that passed as the body goes to the north being called the **ascending node,** and that passed as it goes to the south being called the **descending node**). **8.** *Pathol.* circumscribed swelling. [t. L: m.s. *nōdus* knot]

N, Node on stem of polygonum

nod·i·cal (nŏd′ə kəl, nō′də-), *adj. Astron.* of or pertaining to the nodes: *the nodical month.*

no·dose (nō′dōs, nō dōs′), *adj.* having nodes. [t. L: m.s. *nōdōsus*] —**no·dos·i·ty** (nō dŏs′ə tĭ), *n.*

no·dous (nō′dəs), *adj.* full of knots. [t. L: m.s. *nōdōsus*]

nod·u·lar (nŏj′ə lər), *adj.* having, relating to, or shaped like nodules.

nod·ule (nŏj′ōōl), *n.* **1.** a small node, knot, or knob. **2.** a small rounded mass or lump. **3.** *Bot.* a tubercle. [t. L: m.s. *nōdulus,* dim. of *nōdus* node]

nod·u·lous (nŏj′ə ləs), *adj.* having nodules. Also, **nod·u·lose** (nŏj′ə ləs, nŏj′ə lōs′).

no·dus (nō′dəs), *n., pl.* **-di** (-dī). a difficult or intricate point, situation, plot, etc. [t. L: a knot]

No·el (nō ĕl′), *n.* **1.** Christmas. **2.** (*l.c.*) a Christmas song or carol. [t. F: *noël* Christmas carol, *Noël,* Christmas, g. L *nātālis* birthday, orig. adj.]

no·e·sis (nō ē′sĭs), *n.* **1.** *Philos.* a thing grasped by the intellect alone. **2.** *Psychol.* cognition; the functioning of the intellect. [t. Gk.: a perception]

no·et·ic (nō ĕt′ĭk), *adj.* **1.** of or pertaining to the mind. **2.** originating in and apprehended by the reason.

Nof·re·te·te (nŏf′rə tā′tĭ), *n.* Nefertiti.

nog[1] (nŏg), *n.* **1.** *U.S.* any beverage made with beaten eggs, usually with alcoholic liquor; eggnog. **2.** a kind of strong ale. Also, **nogg.** [orig. uncert.]

nog[2] (nŏg), *n.* **1.** a brick-shaped piece of wood built into a wall. **2.** a wooden peg, pin, or block. [orig. uncert.; ? var. of obs. *knag,* ME *knagge* spur, peg]

nog·gin (nŏg′ĭn), *n.* **1.** a small cup or mug. **2.** a small amount of liquor, usually a gill.

No·gu·chi (nō gōō′chĭ), *n.* **Hideyo** (hē′dĕ yō̄′), 1876–1928, Japanese physician and bacteriologist in U.S.

no·how (nō′hou′), *adv.* (in substandard use) in no manner; not at all.

noil (noil), *n.* a short fiber of wool or silk separated from the long fibers in combing. [orig. uncert.]

noise (noiz), *n., v.,* **noised, noising.** —*n.* **1.** sound, esp. of a loud, harsh, or confused kind: *deafening noises.* **2.** *Physics.* the combination of a nonharmonious group of frequencies of very short duration. **3.** a sound of any kind. **4.** loud shouting, outcry, or clamor. **5.** *Archaic.* rumor. —*v.t.* **6.** to spread the report or rumor of. **7.** to spread (a report, rumor, etc.). —*v.i.* **8.** to talk much or publicly (fol. by *of.*). **9.** to make a noise, outcry, or clamor. [ME, t. OF, g. L *nausea* seasickness] —**Syn. 1.** NOISE, CLAMOR, DIN, HUBBUB, RACKET refer to (usually loud) unmusical or confused sounds. NOISE is the general word, though it may apply to soft, confused sounds as well: *street noises.* CLAMOR and HUBBUB are alike in referring to loud noises resulting from shouting, cries, animated or excited tones, and the like; but in CLAMOR the emphasis is, on the meaning of the shouting, and in HUBBUB the emphasis is on the confused mingling of sounds: *the clamor of an angry crowd, his voice could be heard above the hubbub.* DIN suggests a loud, resonant noise, painful if long continued: *the din of a boiler works.* RACKET suggests a loud, confused noise of the kind produced by clatter or percussion: *she always makes such a racket when she cleans up the dishes.* See **sound**[1].

noise·less (noiz′lĭs), *adj.* making, or attended with, no noise; silent; quiet: *a noiseless step.* —**noise′less·ly,** *adv.* —**noise′less·ness,** *n.* —**Syn.** See **still**[1].

noise·mak·er (noiz′mā′kər), *n.* a person or thing that makes noise, esp. a device used on Hallowe'en, New Year's Eve, etc.

noi·some (noi′səm), *adj.* **1.** offensive or disgusting, often as to odor. **2.** harmful, injurious, or noxious. [ME, f. obs. or prov. *noy* (aphetic var. of ANNOY) + -SOME[1]] —**noi′some·ly,** *adv.* —**noi′some·ness,** *n.*

nois·y (noi′zĭ), *adj.,* **noisier, noisiest.** **1.** making much noise: *a noisy crowd.* **2.** abounding in noise: *a noisy street.* —**nois′i·ly,** *adv.* —**nois′i·ness,** *n.* —**Syn. 1.** See **loud.**

no·lens vo·lens (nō′lĕnz vō′lĕnz), *Latin.* willy-nilly.

no·li-me-tan·ge·re (nō′lĭ mē tăn′jə rĭ), *n. Latin.* **1.** one who or that which must not be touched or interfered with. **2.** a picture representing Jesus appearing to Mary Magdalene after his resurrection. John 20:17. **3.** the touch-me-not. [L: touch me not]

nol·le pros·e·qui (nŏl′ĭ prŏs′ə kwī′), *Law.* an entry made upon the records of a court when the plaintiff or prosecutor will proceed no further in a suit or action. [L: to be unwilling to pursue (prosecute)]

no·lo con·ten·de·re (nō′lō kən tĕn′də rĭ), *Law.* a defendant's pleading which does not admit guilt but subjects him to punishment as though he had pleaded guilty, the determination of guilt remaining open in other proceedings. [L: I am unwilling to contend]

nol. pros., nolle prosequi.

nol-pros (nŏl′prŏs′), *v.t.,* **-prossed, -prossing.** *Law.* to determine by a nolle prosequi.

nom., nominative.

no·ma (nō′mə), *n. Pathol.* a gangrenous ulceration of the mouth and cheeks (and sometimes other parts), occurring mainly in debilitated children. [t. NL, t. Gk.: m. *nomē* a corroding sore]

no·mad (nō′măd, nŏm′ăd), *n.* **1.** one of a race or tribe without fixed abode, but moving about from place to place according to the state of the pasturage or food supply. **2.** any wanderer. —*adj.* **3.** nomadic. [t. L: s. *nomas,* t. Gk.: roaming (like cattle)] —**no′mad·ism,** *n.*

no·mad·ic (nō măd′ĭk), *adj.* of, pertaining to, or characteristic of nomads. —**no·mad′i·cal·ly,** *adv.*

no man's land, a tract of land under dispute, as one between opposing lines of trenches in war.

nom., nominative.

nom·arch (nŏm′ärk), *n.* the governor of a nome or a nomarchy. [t. Gk.: s. *nomárchēs*]

nom·ar·chy (nŏm′är kĭ), *n., pl.* **-chies.** one of the provinces into which modern Greece is divided.

nom·bles (nŭm′bəlz), *n.pl. Archaic.* numbles.

nom·bril (nŏm′brĭl), *n. Her.* the point in an escutcheon between the middle of the base and the fess point. See diag. under **escutcheon.** [t. F: navel]

nom de guerre (nôn də gĕr′), *French.* an assumed name; pseudonym. [F: war name]

nom de plume (nŏm′ də plōōm′; *Fr.* nôn də plŭm′), pen name. [coined in E from F words; lit., pen name]

nome (nōm), *n.* **1.** one of the provinces of ancient Egypt. **2.** nomarchy. [t. Gk.: m.s. *nomós* territorial division]

Nome (nōm), *n.* **1.** a seaport in W Alaska. 2,316 (1960). **2.** Cape, a cape on Seward Peninsula, W of Nome.

no·men·cla·tor (nō′mən klā′tər), *n.* **1.** one who calls or announces things or persons by their names. **2.** one who assigns names, as in scientific classification. [t. L]

no·men·cla·ture (nō'mən klā'chər, nō mĕn'klə-), *n.*
1. a set or system of names or terms, as those used in a particular science or art, by an individual or community, etc. **2.** the names or terms forming a set or system. [t. L: m. *nōmenclātūra*]

nom·i·nal (nŏm'ə nal), *adj.* **1.** being such in name only; so-called: *nominal peace.* **2.** (of a price, consideration, etc.) named as a mere matter of form, being trifling in comparison with the actual value. **3.** of, pertaining to, or consisting in a name or names. **4.** *Gram.* **a.** of, pertaining to, or producing a noun or nouns. **b.** used as or like a noun. **5.** assigned to a person by name: *nominal shares of stock.* **6.** containing, bearing, or giving a name or names. [ME, t. L: s. *nominālis* pert. to names]

nom·i·nal·ism (nŏm'ə nə lĭz'əm), *n. Philos.* the doctrine that universals are reducible to names without any objective existence corresponding to them. In the strict sense, there are no universals either in the mind or in the external world but words operate as symbols. This doctrine shades into conceptualism. —**nom'i·nal·ist,** *n.,* *adj.* —**nom'i·nal·is'tic,** *adj.*

nom·i·nal·ly (nŏm'ə nə lĭ), *adv.* in a nominal manner; by or as regards name; in name; only in name; ostensibly.

nominal value, book or par value; face value.

nominal wages, *Econ.* wages measured in terms of money and not by their ability to command goods and services. Cf. **real wages.**

nom·i·nate (*v.* nŏm'ə nāt'; *adj.* nŏm'ə nĭt), *v.,* **-nat·ed, -nat·ing,** *adj.* —*v.t.* **1.** to propose as a proper person for appointment or election to an office. **2.** to appoint for a duty or office. **3.** *Rare.* to entitle; name. **4.** *Obs.* to specify. —*adj.* **5.** having a particular name. [t. L: m.s. *nōminātus,* pp., named] —**nom'i·na'tor,** *n.*

nom·i·na·tion (nŏm'ə nā'shən), *n.* **1.** act of nominating, esp. to office: *the nomination of candidates for the governorship.* **2.** state of being nominated.

nom·i·na·tive (nŏm'ə nə tĭv, -nā'tĭv, nŏm'nə-), *adj* **1.** *Gram.* **a.** denoting a case which by its form, position or function indicates that it serves as the subject of a finite verb, as in Latin *nauta bonus est* "the sailor is good," *nauta* "sailor" is in the nominative case. **b.** similar to such a case form in function or meaning. **2.** nominated; appointed by nomination. —*n.* **3.** *Gram.* the nominative case, a word in that case, or a form or construction of similar function or meaning. [t. L: m.s. *nōminātivus* serving to name; r. ME *nominatif,* t. OF]

nominative absolute, *Gram.* a group of words including a substantive together with a participial modifier, not grammatically related to any other element in the sentence.

nominative of address, *Gram.* a noun naming the person to whom one is speaking. See **vocative.**

nom·i·nee (nŏm'ə nē'), *n.* one nominated, as to fill an office or stand for election. [f. NOMIN(ATE) + -EE]

no·mism (nō'mĭzəm), *n.* conduct in a religion based on a law or laws. [f. s. Gk. *nómos* law + -ISM] —**no·mis'tic,** *adj.*

nom·o·gram (nŏm'ə grăm, nō'mə-), *n.* a graph containing, usually, three parallel scales graduated for different variables so that when a straight line connects values of any two, the related value may be read directly from the third at the point intersected by the line. Also, **nom'o·graph'** (-grăf', -gräf'). [f. Gk. *nomó(s)* law + -GRAM[1]]

no·mog·ra·phy (nō mŏg'rə fĭ), *n.* **1.** the art of drawing up laws. **2.** the art of making and using a nomogram for solving a succession of nearly identical problems. [t. Gk.: m. *nomographia* a writing of laws]

no·mol·o·gy (nō mŏl'ə jĭ), *n.* **1.** the science of law or laws. **2.** the science of the laws of the mind. [f. nomo- (t. Gk., comb. form of *nómos* law) + -LOGY] —**nom·o·log·i·cal** (nŏm'ə lŏj'ə kəl), *adj.*

no·mos (nō'mŏs), *n. Greek.* nome.

nom·o·thet·ic (nŏm'ə thĕt'ĭk), *adj.* **1.** lawgiving; legislative. **2.** nomistic. **3.** *Psychol.* pertaining to the search for general laws (opposed to *idiographic*). Also, **nom'o·thet'i·cal.** [t. Gk.: m.s. *nomothetikós*]

No·mu·ra (nō'mōō rä'), *n.* Kichisaburo (kē'chē sä' bōō rō'), 1877–1964, Japanese diplomat.

-nomy, a final word element meaning "distribution," "arrangement," "management," or having reference to laws or government, as in *astronomy, economy, taxonomy* [t. Gk.: m.s. *-nomia,* der, *nómos* custom, law. See -IA]

non-, a prefix meaning "not," freely used as an English formative, usually with a simple negative force as implying mere negation or absence of something (rather than the opposite or reverse of it, as often expressed by

un-[1]), as in *nonadherence, noninterference, nonpayment, nonprofessional.* Cf. *unprofessional,* and many other words, mostly self-explanatory, and formed at will to meet the needs. [repr. L *nōn* not; not a L prefix]

non·age (nŏn'ĭj, nō'nĭj), *n.* **1.** the period of legal minority. **2.** any period of immaturity. [ME *nounage,* t. AF, f. *noun-* NON- + *age* AGE]

non·a·ge·nar·i·an (nŏn'ə jə när'ĭ ən, nō'nə jə-), *adj.* **1.** of the age of 90 years, or between 90 and 100 years old. —*n.* **2.** a nonagenarian person. [f. s. L *nōnāgēnārius* containing ninety + -AN]

non·a·gon (nŏn'ə gŏn'), *n.* a polygon having nine angles and nine sides. [f. s. L *nōnus* ninth + -*agon* (after OCTAGON)]

Nonagon

non·al·ler·gen·ic (nŏn'ăl ər jĕn'ĭk), *adj.* not causing an allergic reaction.

non·ap·pear·ance (nŏn'ə pĭr'əns), *n.* failure or neglect to appear, as in a court.

nonce (nŏns), *n.* the one or particular occasion or purpose (chiefly in *for the nonce*). [ME *nones,* in phrase *for the nones,* orig., *for then one(s),* lit., for the once]

nonce word, a word coined and used only for the particular occasion.

non·cha·lance (nŏn'shə ləns, nŏn'shə läns'), *n.* the quality of being nonchalant; cool unconcern or indifference; casualness. [t. F, der. *nonchalant* NONCHALANT]

non·cha·lant (nŏn'shə lənt, nŏn'shə länt'), *adj.* coolly unconcerned, indifferent, or unexcited; casual. [t. F: f. *non* NON- + *chalant* (ppr. of *chaloir* have concern for, g. L *calēre* be hot)] —**non'cha·lant·ly,** *adv.*

non·col·le·giate (nŏn'kə lē'jĭt, -jĭ ĭt), *adj.* **1.** *Brit.* belonging to the body of students in a university not attached to any particular college or hall. **2.** below the level usually associated with college or university study. **3.** (of a university) not composed of colleges.

non·com (nŏn'kŏm'), *n. Colloq.* a noncommissioned officer.

noncom., noncommissioned.

non·com·bat·ant (nŏn kŏm'bə tənt), *n.* **1.** one who is not a combatant; a civilian in time of war. **2.** one connected with a military or naval force in some capacity other than that of a fighter, as a surgeon, a chaplain, etc.

non·com·mis·sioned (nŏn'kə mĭsh'ənd), *adj.* not commissioned (applied esp. to military officers, as sergeants and corporals, ranking below warrant officer).

non·com·mit·tal (nŏn'kə mĭt'əl), *adj.* not committing oneself, or not involving committal, to a particular view, course, or the like: *a noncommittal answer.*

non·com·mu·ni·cant (nŏn'kə mū'nə kənt), *n.* **1.** one who is not a communicant. **2.** one who does not communicate.

non·com·pli·ance (nŏn'kəm plī'əns), *n.* failure or refusal to comply. —**non'com·pli'ant,** *n.*

non com·pos men·tis (nŏn kŏm'pəs mĕn'tĭs), *Latin.* not of sound mind; mentally incapable.

non·con·duc·tor (nŏn'kən dŭk'tər), *n.* a substance which does not readily conduct or transmit heat, sound, electricity, etc.; an insulator. —**non'con·duc'ting,** *adj.*

non·con·form·ance (nŏn'kən fôr'məns), *n.* lack of conformity.

non·con·form·ist (nŏn'kən fôr'mĭst), *n.* **1.** one who refuses to conform, as to an established church. **2.** (*often cap.*) one who refuses to conform to the Church of England. —**non'con·form'ing,** *adj.*

non·con·form·i·ty (nŏn'kən fôr'mə tĭ), *n.* **1.** lack of conformity or agreement. **2.** failure or refusal to conform, as to an established church. **3.** (*often cap.*) refusal to conform to the Church of England.

non·co·öp·er·a·tion (nŏn'kō ŏp'ə rā'shən), *n.* **1.** failure or refusal to coöperate. **2.** a method or practice, established in India by Gandhi, of showing opposition to acts or policies of the government by refusing to participate in civic and political life or to obey governmental regulations. Also, **non'co-op'er·a'tion.** —**non'co·öp'er·a'tive,** *adj.* —**non'co·öp'er·a'tor,** *n.*

non·de·script (nŏn'dĭ skrĭpt'), *adj.* **1.** of no recognized, definite, or particular type or kind: *a nondescript garment.* —*n.* **2.** a person or a thing of no particular type or kind. [f. NON- + s. L *descriptus,* pp., described]

non·dis·junc·tion (nŏn'dĭs jŭngk'shən), *n. Biol.* the failure of chromosomes to follow normal separation into daughter cells at division.

none[1] (nŭn), *pron.* **1.** no one; not one: *there is none to help.* **2.** not any, as of something indicated: *that is none of your business.* **3.** no part; nothing. **4.** (construed as pl.) no, or not any, persons or things: *none come to the*

non'ab·sorb'ent	non-Cath'o·lic	non'con·sec'u·tive	non'cu'mu·la'tive
non'ac·cept'ance	non-cel'lu·lar	non'con·sent'	non'de·cep'tive
non'ad·ja'cent	non-cen'tral	non'con·se·quence'	non'de·cid'u·ous
non'ag·gres'sion	non-Chris'tian	non'con·serv'a·tive	non'de·liv'er·y
non'ag·gres'sive	non-civ'i·lized'	non'con·sti·tu'tion·al	non'dem·o·crat'ic
non'al·co·hol'ic	non-cler'i·cal	non'con·ta'gious	non'de·struc'tive
non'al·lel'ic	non'col·laps'i·ble	non'con·tem'po·rar'y	non'di·ri·gi·ble
non'a·quat'ic	non'com·bat	non'con·tin'u·ance	non'dis·crim'i·na'tion
non'as·sess'a·ble	non'com·bust'i·ble	non'con·tin'u·ous	non'dis·pos'al
non'as·sim'i·la'tion	non'com·mer'cial	non'con·tra'band	non'dis·tinc'tive
non'at·tend'ance	non'com·mu'ni·ca·ble	non'con·tra·dic'to·ry	non'di·ver'gent
non'be·liev'er	non'com·pet'i·tive	non·cor·ro'sive	non'di·vis'i·ble
non'bel·lig'er·ent	non'com·pul'sion	non·crit'i·cal	non'dog·mat'ic
non'break'a·ble	non'con·du'cive	non·crys'tal·line	non'dra·mat'ic

feasts. —*adv.* **5.** to no extent; in no way; not at all: *the supply is none too great.* —*adj.* **6.** not any; no (in later use only before a vowel or *h*): *Thou shalt have none other gods before me.* [ME *non*, OE *nān*, f. *ne* not + *ān* one]

none² (nŏn), *n.* sing. of **nones¹**.

non·ef·fec·tive (nŏn′ə fĕk′tĭv), *adj.* **1.** not effective. **2.** not fit for duty or active service, as a soldier or sailor. —*n.* **3.** a noneffective person.

non·e·go (nŏn ē′gō, -ĕg′ō), *n. Metaphys.* all that is not the ego or conscious self; object as opposed to subject.

non·en·ti·ty (nŏn ĕn′tə tĭ), *n., pl.* **-ties. 1.** a person or thing of no importance. **2.** something which does not exist, or exists only in imagination. **3.** nonexistence. [f. NON- + ENTITY]

nones¹ (nōnz), *n. Eccles.* the fifth of the seven canonical hours, or the service for it, orig. fixed for the ninth hour of the day (or 3 P.M.). [pl. of NONE², OE *nōn*, t. L: s. *nōna* (*hōra*). See NOON]

nones² (nōnz), *n.pl. sing.* **none.** (in the ancient Roman calendar) the ninth day before the ides, both days included, thus being the 7th of March, May, July, and October, and the 5th of the other months. [ME, t. L: m. *nōnae*, orig. fem. pl. of *nōnus* ninth]

non·es·sen·tial (nŏn′ə sĕn′shəl), *adj.* **1.** not essential; not necessary: *nonessential use of gasoline.* —*n.* **2.** a nonessential thing or person.

none·such (nŭn′sŭch′), *n.* **1.** a person or thing without equal; a paragon. **2.** *Bot.* black medic. Also, **nonsuch**.

none·the·less (nŭn′thə lĕs′), *adv.* however; nevertheless.

non·ex·ist·ence (nŏn′ĭg zĭs′təns), *n.* **1.** absence of existence. **2.** a thing that has no existence. —**non′ex·ist′ent**, *adj.*

non·ex·por·ta·tion (nŏn′ĕks pōr tā′shən), *n.* failure or refusal to export.

non·fea·sance (nŏn fē′zəns), *n. Law.* the omission of some act which ought to have been performed.

non·ful·fill·ment (nŏn′fŏŏl fĭl′mənt), *n.* neglect or failure to fulfill.

non·har·mon·ic tone (nŏn′här mŏn′ĭk), *Music.* a tone sounding with a chord of which it is not a chord tone.

non·nil·lion (nō nĭl′yən), *n.* **1.** a cardinal number represented in the U.S. and France by one followed by 30 zeros, and, in Great Britain and Germany, by one followed by 54 zeros. —*adj.* **2.** amounting to one nonillion in number. [t. F f. *non-* (t. L: s. *nōnus* ninth) + (*m*)*illion* million] —**no·nil′lionth**, *n., adj.*

non·im·por·ta·tion (nŏn′ĭm pōr tā′shən), *n.* failure or refusal to import.

non·in·duc·tive (nŏn′ĭn dŭk′tĭv), *adj. Elect.* not inductive: *a noninductive resistance.*

non·in·ter·ven·tion (nŏn′ĭn tər vĕn′shən), *n.* **1.** abstention by a state from interference in the affairs of other states or in those of its own political subdivisions. **2.** failure or refusal to intervene.

non·join·der (nŏn join′dər), *n. Law.* omission to join, as of one who should have been a party to an action.

non·ju·ror (nŏn jŏŏr′ər), *n.* **1.** one who refuses to take a required oath, as of allegiance. **2.** (*often cap.*) one of those clergymen of the Church of England who in 1689 refused to swear allegiance to William and Mary.

non·le·gal (nŏn lē′gəl), *adj.* not (definitely) legal; having no legal aspect (distinguished from *illegal*): *a completely nonlegal controversy.*

non·met·al (nŏn′mĕt′əl), *n. Chem.* **1.** an element not having the character of a metal, as carbon, nitrogen, etc. **2.** an element incapable of forming simple positive ions in solution.

non·me·tal·lic (nŏn′mə tăl′ĭk), *adj.* **Chem. 1.** of or relating to nonmetal. **2.** not of a metallic quality: *a nonmetallic appearance.*

non·mor·al (nŏn mŏr′əl, -môr′-), *adj.* having no relation to morality; neither moral nor immoral: *a completely nonmoral problem of society.*

non·ni·trog·e·nous (nŏn′nī trŏj′ə nəs), *adj.* containing no nitrogen.

non·ob·jec·tive (nŏn′əb jĕk′tĭv), *adj. Fine Arts.* not representing or containing objects known in physical nature; abstract or nonrepresentational.

non ob·stan·te (nŏn ŏb stăn′tĭ), *Latin.* notwithstanding.

non·pa·reil (nŏn′pə rĕl′), *adj.* **1.** having no equal; peerless. —*n.* **2.** a person or thing having no equal; something unique. **3.** a beautifully colored finch, *Passerina ciris*, of the southern U.S.; the painted bunting. **4.** *Print.* **a.** a size of type (6 point). **b.** a slug occupying 6 points of space between lines. [late ME, t. F: f. *non-* NON- + *pareil* equal (ult. der. L *pār*)]

non·par·ous (nŏn păr′əs), *adj. Physiol.* having borne no children.

non·par·tic·i·pat·ing (nŏn′pər tĭs′ə pā′tĭng), *adj. Insurance.* having no right to dividends or to a distribution of surplus.

non·par·ti·san (nŏn păr′tə zən), *adj.* **1.** not partisan; objective. **2.** not supporting any of the established or regular parties. Also, **non·par′ti·zan**.

Nonpartisan League, a political organization of farmers, founded in North Dakota, 1915, and extending to many States west of the Mississippi, with the aim of influencing agricultural legislation in State legislatures.

non·pay·ment (nŏn pā′mənt), *n.* condition of being unpaid; neglect to pay.

non·per·form·ance (nŏn′pər fôr′məns), *n.* failure or neglect to perform.

non·plus (nŏn plŭs′, nŏn′plŭs), *v.,* **-plused, -plusing** or (*esp. Brit.*) **-plussed, -plussing,** *n.* —*v.t.* **1.** to bring to a nonplus; puzzle completely. —*n.* **2.** a state of utter perplexity. [t. L: *nōn plūs* not more, no further]

non pos·su·mus (nŏn pŏs′ə məs), *Latin.* we cannot.

non·pro (nŏn prō′), *n., adj. Slang.* nonprofessional.

non·pro·duc·tive (nŏn′prə dŭk′tĭv), *adj.* **1.** not producing goods directly, as employees in charge of personnel, inspectors, etc. **2.** unproductive. —**non′pro·duc′tive·ness,** *n.*

non·prof·it (nŏn prŏf′ĭt), *adj.* not yielding a return; not entered into for profit: *a nonprofit association.*

non pros., non prosequitur.

non·pros (nŏn′prŏs′), *v.t.* **-prossed, -prossing.** *Law.* to adjudge (a plaintiff) in default.

non pro·se·qui·tur (nŏn prō sĕk′wə tər), *Law.* a judgment entered against the plaintiff in a suit when he does not appear to prosecute it. [L: he does not pursue (prosecute)]

non·rep·re·sen·ta·tion·al (nŏn′rĕp rĭ zĕn tā′shən əl), *adj.* not resembling any object in physical nature: *a nonrepresentational painting.*

non·res·i·dent (nŏn rĕz′ə dənt), *adj.* **1.** not resident in a particular place. **2.** not residing where official duties require one to reside. —*n.* **3.** one who is nonresident. —**non·res′i·dence, non·res′i·den·cy,** *n.*

non·re·sist·ant (nŏn′rĭ zĭs′tənt), *adj.* **1.** not resistant; passively obedient. —*n.* **2.** one who does not resist authority or force. **3.** one who maintains that violence should not be resisted by force. —**non′re·sist′ance,** *n.*

non·re·straint (nŏn′rĭ strānt′), *n.* **1.** *Psychiatry.* the treatment of the mentally ill without mechanical means of restraint. **2.** absence of restraint.

---

non·ed′i·ble	non·her′it·a·ble	non·mar′ry·ing	non·per·pen·dic′u·lar
non·ed′u·ca·ble	non·his·tor′ic	non·mar′tial	non·per·sist′ence
non·ed·u·ca′tion·al	non·hu′man	non·me·chan′i·cal	non·phil·o·soph′i·cal
non·ef·fi′cient	non·hu′mor·ous	non·med′i·cal	non·pi·na′ceous
non·e·las′tic	non·i·den′ti·cal	non·me·dic′i·nal	non·po·et′ic
non·e·mo′tion·al	non·i·den′ti·ty	non·me·lo′di·ous	non·poi′son·ous
non·en·force′ment	non·id·i·o·mat′ic	non·mem′ber	non·po·lit′i·cal
non·e·quiv′a·lent	non·im·mu′ni·ty	non·met′ri·cal	non·po′rous
non·eth′i·cal	non·im·preg′nat·ed	non·mi′gra·to·ry	non·pred′a·to·ry
non′-Eu·clid′e·an	non·in·clu′sive	non·mil′i·tant	non·pre·dict′a·ble
non·ex·change′a·ble	non·in·dict′a·ble	non·mil′i·tar′y	non·pre·hen′si·le
non·ex·clu′sive	non·in·dict′ment	non·mor′tal	non·pre·scrip′tive
non·ex·ist′ing	non·in·dus′tri·al	non·mo′tile	non·pro·duc′ing
non·ex·plo′sive	non·in·fec′tion	non·nat′u·ral	non·pro·fes′sion·al
non·ex·port′a·ble	non·in·fec′tious	non·nav′i·ga·ble	non·prof·it·eer′ing
non·ex·tra·dit′a·ble	non·in·flam′ma·ble	non·ne·ces′si·ty	non·pro·gres′sive
non·fac′tu·al	non·in·form′a·tive	non·ne·go′ti·a·ble	non·pro·tec′tive
non·fad′ing	non·in·her′it·a·ble	non·neu′tral	non′-Prot′es·tant
non·fed′er·al	non·in′ter·course′	non·nu·tri′tious	non·pun′ish·a·ble
non·fed′er·at·ed	non·in·ter·fer′ence	non·o·be′di·ence	non·ra′cial
non·fer′rous	non·in·ter·sect′ing	non·ob·lig′a·to·ry	non·re·al′i·ty
non·fes′tive	non·in·tox′i·cant	non·o′dor·ous	non·re·cip′ro·cal
non·fic′tion	non·in·tox′i·cat′ing	non·of·fi′cial	non·rec·og·ni′tion
non·fic′tion·al	non·ir′ri·ga·ble	non·or′tho·dox′	non·re·cur′rent
non·fis′cal	non·ir′ri·tant	non·par′ish·ion·er	non·re·fill′a·ble
non·fis′sion·a·ble	non·ir′ri·tat′ing	non·par·lia·men′ta·ry	non·re·fu′el·ing
non·flam′ma·ble	non-Jew′	non·pa·ro′chi·al	non·re′gent
non·freez′ing	non-Jew′ish	non·par·tic′i·pa′tion	non·reg′i·ment·ed
non·func′tion·al	non′life	non·pas′ser·i·form′	non·reign′ing
non·gas′e·ous	non·lit′er·ar′y	non·pas′ser·ine	non·re·li′gious
non′green′	non·liv′ing	non·pay′ing	non·re·mu′ner·a·tive
non·hab′it·a·ble	non·lu′mi·nous	non·per′ma·nent	non·re·new′a·ble
non·he·red′i·tar′y	non·mag·net′ic	non·per′me·a·ble	non·res·i·den′tial

---

ăct, āble, dâre, ärt; ĕbb, ēqual; ĭf, īce; hŏt, ōver, ôrder, oil, bŏŏk, ōōze, out; ŭp, ūse, ûrge; ə = a in alone; ch, chief; g, give; ng, ring; sh, shoe; th, thin; ŧh, that; zh, vision. See the full key on inside cover.

non·re·stric·tive (nŏn'rĭ strĭk'tĭv), *adj. Gram.* (of a word or clause) purely descriptive rather than limiting in its application to the sentence element it modifies. "Mr. Owen, *who was here yesterday,* is a farmer" illustrates a nonrestrictive clause. "The man who was here yesterday is a farmer" shows the same clause employed to restrict the meaning *of the man.*

non·rig·id (nŏn rĭj'ĭd), *adj.* 1. not rigid. 2. designating a type of airship having a flexible gas container without a supporting structure and held in shape only by the pressure of the gas within.

non·sec·tar·i·an (nŏn'sĕk târ'ĭ ən), *adj.* not affiliated with any specific religious denomination.

non·sense (nŏn'sĕns), *n.* 1. that which makes no sense or is lacking in sense. 2. words without sense or conveying absurd ideas. 3. senseless or absurd action; foolish conduct, notions, etc.: *to stand no nonsense from a person.* 4. absurdity: *the nonsense of an idea.* 5. stuff, trash, or anything useless. **—non·sen·si·cal** (nŏn-sĕn'sə kəl), *adj.* **—non·sen'si·cal·ly,** *adv.* **—non·sen'-si·cal·ness,** *n.*

non seq., non sequitur.

non se·qui·tur (nŏn sĕk'wə tər), *Latin.* an inference or a conclusion which does not follow from the premises. [L: it does not follow]

non·skid (nŏn'skĭd'), *adj.* having the wheel rim or tire with a ridged or otherwise skid-resistant surface.

non·stop (nŏn'stŏp'), *adj., adv.* without a single stop: *a nonstop flight from New York to Paris.*

non·stri·at·ed (nŏn strī'ā tĭd), *adj.* not striated; unstriped, as muscular tissue.

non·such (nŭn'sŭch'), *n.* nonesuch.

non·suit (nŏn'sōōt'), *Law.* **—n.** 1. a judgment given against a plaintiff who neglects to prosecute, or who fails to show a legal cause of action or to bring sufficient evidence. **—v.t.** 2. to subject to a nonsuit.

non·sup·port (nŏn'sə pōrt'), *n. Law.* omission to support another, as a wife, child, or other dependent, as required by law.

non trop·po (nôn trôp'pō), *Music.* not too much: *non troppo lento* (not too slow). [It.]

non·un·ion (nŏn ūn'yən), *adj.* 1. not belonging to, or not in accordance with the rules of, a trade union. 2. antiunion. **—n.** 3. failure of a broken bone to heal.

non·un·ion·ism (nŏn ūn'yə nĭz'əm), *n.* disregard of or opposition to trade unions. **—non·un'ion·ist,** *n.*

nonunion shop, a shop or business in which the employer fixes terms and conditions of employment unilaterally without recognizing or dealing with a union.

non·vot·er (nŏn vō'tər), *n.* one who does not vote.

noo·dle¹ (nōō'dəl), *n.* a strip or lump of dough or paste, served in soups, etc. [t. G: m. *nudel*]

noo·dle² (nōō'dəl), *n.* 1. the head. 2. a simpleton. [? var. of NODDLE¹ (with *oo* from FOOL)]

nook (nŏŏk), *n.* 1. a corner, as in a room. 2. any retired or obscure corner. 3. any small recess. 4. a remote spot. [ME *noke.* Cf. d. Norw. *nok* hook]

noon (nōōn), *n.* 1. midday. 2. twelve o'clock in the daytime. 3. the highest, brightest, or finest point or part. 4. *Poetic.* midnight. [ME *none,* OE *nōn,* t. L: s. *nōna* ninth hour. See NONES¹]

noon·day (nōōn'dā'), *adj.* 1. of or at noonday. **—n.** 2. midday; noon.

no one, no person; nobody.

noon·ing (nōō'nĭng), *n.* 1. noontime. 2. an interval at noon for rest or food. 3. a rest or meal at noon.

noon·tide (nōōn'tīd'), *n.* 1. the time of noon; midday. 2. the highest or best point or part. 3. *Chiefly Poetic.* midnight. [ME *nonetyde,* OE *nōntīd*]

noon·time (nōōn'tīm'), *n.* the time of noon.

noose (nōōs), *n., v.,* **noosed, noosing. —n.** 1. a loop with a running knot, as in a snare, lasso, hangman's halter, etc., which tightens as the rope is pulled. 2. a tie or bond; a snare. **—v.t.** 3. to secure by or as by a noose. 4. to make a noose with or in (a rope, etc.). [prob. t. OF: m. *nos,* der. *noer* to knit, g. L *nōdāre,* der. *nōdus* knot]

Noot·ka (nōōt'kä), *n.* an American Indian language of Wakashan stock, spoken on Vancouver Island and Cape Flattery, a cape in NW Washington.

no·pal (nō'pəl), *n.* 1. any cactus or fruit of the genera *Opuntia* and *Nopalea.* 2. the prickly pear. [t. Sp., t. Mex.: m. *nopalli* cactus]

no-par (nō'pär'), *adj.* without par, or face value.

No Plays (nō), the highly stylized Japanese classical drama, first developed in the 15th century, employing music, dancing, a chorus, symbolic scenery, and elaborate costumes and masks. Also, **Noh Plays.**

---

nor (nôr; *unstressed* nər), *conj.* 1. a negative conjunction used: **a.** as the correlative to a preceding *neither: he could neither read nor write.* **b.** *Archaic or Poetic.* with omission of a preceding *neither,* its negative force being understood: *he nor I was there.* **c.** *Now Chiefly Poetic.* instead of *neither,* as correlative to a following *nor: nor he nor I was there.* **d.** to continue the force of a negative, such as *not, no, never,* etc., occurring in a preceding clause: *He left and I never saw him again, nor did I regret it.* **e.** after an affirmative clause, or as a continuative, in the sense of *and . . . not: they are happy; nor need we mourn.* 2. *Dial.* than. [ME *nor,* contr. of *nother,* OE *nōther,* f. *ne* not + *ōther* (contr. of *ōhwæther* either)]

nor-, *Chem.* a word element meaning "normal." [short for NORMAL]

Nor., 1. Norman. 2. North. 3. Norway. 4. Norwegian.

Nor·dau (nôr'dou), *n.* **Max Simon** (mäks zē'mōn) 1849–1923, German writer and leading advocate of Zionism.

Nor·den·skjöld (nōōr'dən shœld'), *n.* 1. **Nils Adolf Erik** (nĭls ä'dôlf ā'rĭk), Baron, 1832–1901, Swedish arctic explorer, born in Finland. 2. his nephew, **Nils Otto Gustaf** (nĭls ŏt'tō gŭs'täv), 1869–1928, Swedish arctic and antarctic explorer.

Nordenskjöld Sea, Laptev Sea.

Nord·hau·sen (nōrt'hou'zən), *n.* a city in East Germany: site of a Nazi extermination camp during World War II. 32,848 (1950).

Nor·dic (nôr'dĭk), *adj.* 1. *Ethnol.* designating, or belonging or pertaining to, a race of men or a Caucasian racial subtype characterized by tall stature, blond hair, blue eyes, and elongated head, exemplified most markedly by Scandinavians and Britons and their descendants. **—n.** 2. a member of the Nordic race. [t. F: m. *nordique,* der. *nord* north, t. Gmc., and akin to NORTH. See -IC]

Nord·kyn Cape (nôr'kyn), a cape in N Norway: the northernmost point of the European mainland.

Nord-rhein-West·fal·en (nōrt'rīn věst'fä'lən), *n.* German name of **North Rhine-Westphalia.**

nor'·east·er (nôr ēs'tər), *n.* northeaster.

Nor·folk (nôr'fək), *n.* 1. a seaport in SE Virginia: naval base. 305,872 (1960). 2. a county in E England. 548,062 pop. (1951); 2054 sq. mi. *Co. seat:* Norwich.

Norfolk Island, an island in the S Pacific between New Caledonia and New Zealand: a territory of Australia. 1000 pop. (est. 1955); 13 sq. mi.

Norfolk jacket, a loosely belted single-breasted jacket, with box pleats in front and back. Also, **Norfolk coat.**

Nor·ge (nôr'gə), *n.* Norwegian name of **Norway.**

no·ri·a (nôr'ĭə), *n.* a device consisting of a series of buckets on a wheel, used in Spain and the Orient for raising water. [t. Sp., t. Ar.: m. *nā'ŭra*]

Nor·i·cum (nôr'ĭ kəm, nŏr'-), *n.* an ancient Roman province in central Europe, roughly corresponding to the part of Austria S of the Danube.

nor·land (nôr'lənd), *n. Chiefly Poetic.* northland. [f. *nor* (apocopated var. of NORTH) + LAND]

norm (nôrm), *n.* 1. a standard, model, or pattern 2. *Educ.* a designated standard of average performance of people of a given age, background, etc. [t. L: s. *norma* carpenter's square, rule, pattern]

nor·mal (nôr'məl), *adj.* 1. conforming to the standard or the common type; regular, usual, natural, or not abnormal: *the normal procedure.* 2. serving to fix a standard. 3. *Psychol.* **a.** approximately average in respect to any psychological trait, such as intelligence, personality, emotional adjustment, etc. **b.** without any mental aberrations; sane. 4. *Math.* **a.** being at right angles, as a line; perpendicular. **b.** of the nature of or pertaining to a mathematical normal. 5. *Chem.* **a.** (of a solution) containing one equivalent weight of the constituent in question in one liter of solution. **b.** pertaining to an aliphatic hydrocarbon having a straight unbranched carbon chain, each carbon atom of which is joined to no more than two other carbon atoms. **c.** normal element, a galvanic cell of known and reproducible voltage; standard cell. 6. *Biol., Med.,* etc. **a.** free from any infection or experimental therapy. **b.** of natural occurrence. **—n.** 7. the standard or type. 8. the normal form or state; the average or mean. 9. *Math.* a perpendicular line or plane, esp. one perpendicular to a tangent line of a curve, or a tangent plane of a surface, at the point of contact. [t. L: s. *normālis* made according to a carpenter's square or rule] **—nor·mal·i·ty** (nôr măl'ə tĭ),**nor'mal·ness,** *n.*

normal curve, *Statistics.* a bell-shaped curve giving

---

non·re·strict'ed	non·shrink'a·ble	non·sub·mis'sive	non·trib'u·tar'y
non·re·turn'a·ble	non·sig·nif'i·cant	non·sub·scrib'er	non·typ'i·cal
non·re·vers'i·ble	non·sink'a·ble	non·sub·stan'tial	non·u'nit·ed
non·rhym'ing	non·slip'ping	non·suc·ces'sive	non·us'er
non·rhyth'mic	non·smok'ing	non·sup·port'er	non·ven'om·ous
non·ru'ral	non·so'cial	non·sus·tain'ing	non·ver'ti·cal
non·sal'a·ble	non·spark'ling	non·sym·met'ri·cal	non·vi·o·la'tion
non·sal'a·ried	non·spe·cial·ized'	non·sys·tem·at'ic	non·vis'u·al
non·sci·en·tif'ic	non·spir·it·u·al	non·tax'a·ble	non·vo·cal'ic
non·sea'son·al	non·spore'form'ing	non·teach'a·ble	non·vo·ca'tion·al
non·sec'tion·al	non·stain'a·ble	non·tech'ni·cal	non·vol'a·tile
non·se·lec'tive	non·stan'dard·ized'	non·ter'ri·to'ri·al	non·vol'un·tar'y
non·sen'si·tive	non·stim'u·lat'ing	non·tex'tu·al	non·vot'ing
non·shar'ing	non·strik'er	non·tox'ic	non·work'er
non·shat'ter	non·strik'ing	non·trans·fer'a·ble	non·yield'ing

---

b., blend of, blended; c., cognate with; d., dialect, dialectal; der., derived from; f., formed from; g., going back to; m., modification of; r., replacing; s., stem of; t., taken from; ?, perhaps.   See the full key on inside cover.

the distribution of probability associated with the different values of a variable.

nor·mal·cy (nôr′məl sĭ′), *n.* the character or state of being normal: *back to normalcy.*

nor·mal·ize (nôr′mə līz′), *v.t.*, **-ized, -izing.** to make normal. —**nor′mal·i·za′tion,** *n.* —**nor′mal·iz′er,** *n.*

nor·mal·ly (nôr′məl ĭ), *adv.* as a rule; regularly; according to rule; general custom, etc.

normal school, a school for the preliminary professional education of teachers. [after F *école normale*]

Nor·man (nôr′mən), *n.* **1.** a member of that branch of the Northmen or Scandinavians who in the 10th century conquered Normandy. **2.** one of the mixed Scandinavian and French (**Norman French**) race later inhabiting this region, which conquered England in 1066. **3.** a native or inhabitant of Normandy. **4.** Norman French (language). **5.** a city in central Oklahoma. 33,412 (1960). —*adj.* **6.** of or pertaining to the Normans. **7.** *Archit.* noting or pertaining to a variety of the Romanesque style of architecture which was introduced from Normandy into Great Britain before and at the time of the Norman conquest. [ME, back formation from OF *Normans,* pl. of *Normant.* See NORTHMAN]

Norman Conquest, the conquest of England by the Normans, under William the Conqueror, in 1066.

Nor·man·dy (nôr′mən dĭ), *n.* a region in N France along the English Channel invaded and settled by Northmen in the 10th century; it became a duchy, and later a province; Allied invasion in World War II began June 6, 1944. Its capital was Rouen.

Norman French, 1. the French of the Normans or of Normandy. **2.** the legal jargon of England, now extinct except in phrases, orig. a dialect of Old French.

Nor·man·ize (nôr′mə nīz′), *v.i., v.t.,* **-ized, -izing.** to make or become Norman in customs, language, etc.

nor·ma·tive (nôr′mə tĭv), *adj.* **1.** concerning a norm, esp. an assumed norm regarded as the standard of correctness in speech and writing. **2.** tending or attempting to establish such a norm, esp. by the prescription of rules: *normative grammar.* **3.** reflecting the assumption of such a norm, or favoring its establishment: *a normative attitude.*

nor·mo·cyte (nôr′mə sīt′), *n. Anat.* a red blood cell of normal size.

Norn (nôrn), *n. Scand. Myth.* any one of the goddesses of fate, commonly represented as three in number, whose decrees were irrevocable. [t. Icel.]

Nor·ris (nôr′ĭs, nŏr′-), *n.* **1.** Frank, 1870–1902, U.S. novelist. **2.** George William, 1861–1944, U.S. senator.

Nor·ris·town (nôr′ĭs toun′, nŏr′-), *n.* a borough in SE Pennsylvania, near Philadelphia. 38,925 (1960).

Norr·kö·ping (nôr′chœ′pĭng), *n.* a seaport in SE Sweden. 87,989 (est. 1953).

Norse (nôrs), *adj.* **1.** belonging or pertaining to Norway, esp. ancient Norway with its colonies (as in Iceland), or to ancient Scandinavia generally. —*n.* **2.** (*construed as pl.*) **a.** the Norwegians. **b.** the ancient Norwegians. **c.** the Northmen or ancient Scandinavians generally. **3.** Norwegian (language) esp. in its older forms. See **Old Norse.** [prob. t. D: m. *noorsch,* var. of *noordsch,* der. *noord* north. Cf. Norw., Sw., Dan. *Norsk* Norwegian, Norse]

Norse·man (nôrs′mən), *n., pl.* **-men.** a Northman.

north (nôrth), *n.* **1.** a cardinal point of the compass lying in the plane of the meridian and to the right of a person facing the setting sun or west. **2.** the direction in which this point lies. **3.** (*l.c. or cap.*) a quarter or territory situated in this direction. **4.** (*cap.*) the northern area of the United States, esp. the States which fought with the Union in the Civil War, lying to the north of the Ohio river, Missouri, and Maryland. **5.** (*cap.*) North Country. **6.** *Chiefly Poetic.* the north wind. —*adj.* **7.** lying toward or situated in the north. **8.** directed or proceeding toward the north. **9.** coming from the north, as a w nd. **10.** (*cap.*) designating the northern part of a region, nation, country, etc.: *North America.* —*adv.* **11.** in the direction which is to the right of a person facing the setting sun or west. **12.** toward or in the north. [ME and OE, C. G *nord*]

North (nôrth), *n.* **1.** Christopher, pen name of John Wilson. **2.** Lord Frederick, (*2nd Earl of Guilford*) 1732–92, British statesman: prime minister, 1770–82. **3.** Sir Thomas, 1535?–1601?, English translator.

North Adams, a city in NW Mass. 19,905 (1960).

North America, the northernmost continent of the Western Hemisphere, extending from Central America to the Arctic Ocean. Highest point, Mt. McKinley, 20,300 ft.; lowest, Death Valley, 276 ft. below sea level. (Including Central America) 245,000,000 pop. (est. 1956); ab. 8,440,000 sq. mi. —**North American.**

North·amp·ton (nôr thămp′tən, nôrth hămp′-), *n.* **1.** a city in central England. 104,432 (1951). **2.** a city in central Massachusetts. 30,058 (1960).

North·amp·ton·shire (nôr thămp′tən shĭr′, -shər), *n.* a county in central England. 359,690 pop. (1951); 914 sq. mi. *Co. seat:* Northampton. Also, **Northampton.**

North Atlantic Treaty. See **Atlantic Pact.**

North Bor·ne·o (bôr′nĭ ō′), See **Sabah.**

North Bra·bant (brə bănt′, brä′bənt), a province in S Netherlands 1,332,033 pop. (est. 1954); 1965 sq. mi. *Cap.:* 's Hertogenbosch.

north by east, a point of direction on the mariner's compass, one point east of north.

north by west, a point of direction on the mariner's compass, one point west of north.

North Cape, 1. a point of land on an island at the N tip of Norway: the northernmost point of Europe. **2.** the northern end of North Island, New Zealand.

North Car·o·li·na (kăr′ə lī′nə), a State in the SE United States, on the Atlantic coast. 4,556,155 pop. (1960);52,712 sq. mi. *Cap.:* Raleigh. *Abbr.:* N.C. —**North Car·o·lin·i·an** (kăr′ə lĭn′ĭ ən).

North Cau·ca·sus (kô′kə səs), a region in the S Soviet Union in Europe, E of the Black Sea.

North·cliffe (nôrth′klĭf). *n.* Alfred Charles William Harmsworth, Viscount, 1865–1922, British newspaper publisher.

North Country, 1. the part of England north of the Humber estuary. **2.** Alaska and the Yukon territory of Canada (as a geographical and economic unit).

North Da·ko·ta (də kō′tə), a State in the N central United States. 632,446 pop. (1960). 70,665 sq. mi. *Cap.:* Bismarck. *Abbr.:* N. Dak. —**North Da·ko′tan.**

north·east (nôrth′ēst′; *Naut.* nôr′-), *n.* **1.** the point or direction midway between north and east. **2.** a region in this direction. —*adv.* **3.** in the direction of a point midway between north and east. **4.** from this direction. —*adj.* **5.** lying toward or situated in the northeast. **6.** directed or proceeding toward the northeast. **7.** coming from the northeast, as a wind. —**north′east′ern,** *adj.*

northeast by east, a point of direction on the mariner's compass, one point east of northeast.

northeast by north, a point of direction on the mariner's compass, one point north of northeast.

north·east·er (nôrth′ēs′tər; *Naut.* nôr′-), *n.* a wind or gale from the northeast.

north·east·er·ly (nôrth′ēs′tər lĭ; *Naut.* nôr′-), *adj.* **1.** of or located in the northeast. **2.** toward or from the northeast. —*adv.* **3.** toward or from the northeast.

Northeast Passage, a route for ships along the N coast of Europe and Asia as a possible course for navigation between the Atlantic and Pacific.

north·east·ward (nôrth′ēst′wərd; *Naut.* nôr′-), *adv., adj.* **1.** Also, **north′east′ward·ly.** toward the northeast. —*n.* **2.** the northeast.

north·east·wards (nôrth′ēst′wərdz; *Naut.* nôr′-), *adv.* northeastward.

north·er (nôr′#ər), *n.* **1.** (in the U.S. Gulf Coast region) a cold gale from the north, formed by a vigorous outbreak of continental polar air behind a cold front during the winter. **2.** a wind or storm from the north.

north·er·ly (nôr′#ər lĭ), *adj.* **1.** moving, directed, or situated toward the north. **2.** coming from the north, as a wind. —*adv.* **3.** toward the north. **4.** from the north.

north·ern (nôr′#ərn), *adj.* **1.** lying toward or situated in the north. **2.** directed or proceeding northward. **3.** coming from the north, as a wind. **4.** of or pertaining to the north, esp. (*cap.*) the North of the U.S. **5.** *Astron.* north of the celestial equator or of the zodiac: *a northern constellation.* —*n.* **6.** one living in a northern region or country. [ME and OE *northerne.* See -ERN]

Northern Cross, *Astron.* (in the constellation Cygnus) six stars arranged in the form of a cross.

Northern Crown, *Astron.* Corona Borealis.

north·ern·er (nôr′#ər nər), *n.* a native or inhabitant of the north, esp. (*cap.*) of the Northern U.S.

Northern Hemisphere, the half of the earth between the North Pole and the equator.

Northern Ireland, a political division of the United Kingdom, in the NE part of the island of Ireland. 1,384,000 (est. 1953); 5238 sq. mi. *Cap.:* Belfast.

northern lights, the aurora borealis.

north·ern·most (nôr′#ərn mōst′, -məst), *adj.* furthest north.

Northern Rho·de·sia (rō dē′zhə, -zĭ′ə), former name of Zambia.

Northern Spy, a late-keeping, red-striped American apple.

Northern Territories, a former British protectorate in W Africa; now a part of Ghana, in the N part.

Northern Territory, a territory in N Australia. 16,452 pop. (1954); 523,620 sq. mi. *Cap.:* Darwin.

North Germanic, the Scandinavian subgroup of Germanic languages.

North Holland, a province in W Netherlands. 1,929,620 pop. (est. 1954); 1163 sq. mi. *Cap.:* Haarlem.

north·ing (nôr′#ĭng, -thĭng), *n.* **1.** northward movement or deviation. **2.** distance due north. **3.** distance due north made on any course tending northward.

North Island, northernmost principal island of New Zealand. 1,378,690 pop. (est. 1953); 44,281 sq. mi.

north·land (nôrth′lənd), *n.* **1.** the land or region in the north. **2.** the northern part of a country. **3.** (*cap.*) the peninsula containing Norway and Sweden. [ME and OE, C. G, Dan., Sw. *nordland*] —**north′land·er,** *n.*

North Little Rock, a city in central Arkansas, on the Arkansas river. 58,032 (1960).

ăct, āble, dâre, ärt; ĕbb, ēqual; ĭf, īce; hŏt, ōver, ôrder, oil, bŏŏk, ōōze, out; ŭp, ūse, ûrge; ə = a in alone; ch, chief; g, give; ng, ring; sh, shoe; th, thin; ŧh, that; zh, vision. See the full key on inside cover.

North·man (nôrth'mən), *n.*, *pl.* **-men.** a member of the Scandinavian group which from about the 8th to the 11th century made many raids and settlements on Great Britain, Ireland, and other parts of Europe.

north-north·east (nôrth'nôrth·ēst'; *Naut.* nôr'nôr-ēst'), *adj.* **1.** lying or situated in the direction on the mariner's compass equidistant from north and northeast. —*n.* **2.** this direction. —*adv.* **3.** to or from this direction.

north-north·west (nôrth'nôrth·wĕst'; *Naut.* nôr'-nôr·wĕst'), *adj.* **1.** lying or situated in the direction on the mariner's compass equidistant from north and northwest. —*n.* **2.** this direction. —*adv.* **3.** to or from this direction.

North Platte (plăt), a river flowing from N Colorado through SE Wyoming and W Nebraska into the Platte. 618 mi.

North Pole, 1. *Geog.* that end of the earth's axis of rotation marking the northernmost point on the earth. **2.** *Astron.* the zenith of the earth's north pole, about 1° distant from the North Star.

North Rhine-West·pha·li·a(rīn'wĕst fä'lĭ·ə), a state in W West Germany; formerly a part of Rhine province. 14,989,500 pop. (est. 1956); 13,111 sq. mi. *Cap.*: Düsseldorf. German, **Nordrhein-Westfalen.**

North Rid·ing (rī'dĭng), an administrative county in Yorkshire, England. 525,481 pop. (1951); 2127 sq. mi. *Co. seat*: Northallerton.

North River, that part of the Hudson river below the junction of Spuyten Duyvil Creek.

North Sea, an arm of the Atlantic between Great Britain and the European mainland. ab. 201,000 sq. mi.; greatest depth, 1998 ft. Formerly, **German Ocean.**

North Star, *Astron.* Polaris, the north polar star, situated near the north pole of the heavens.

North Ton·a·wan·da (tŏn'ə wŏn'də), a city in W New York. 34,757 (1960).

North·um·ber·land (nôr thŭm'bər lənd), *n.* a county in NE England. 798,424 pop. (1951); 2019 sq. mi. *Co Seat.*: Newcastle.

North·um·bri·a (nôr thŭm'brĭ·ə), *n.* an early English kingdom extending from the Humber N to the Firth of Forth. See map under **Mercia.**

North·um·bri·an (nôr thŭm'brĭ·ən), *adj.* **1.** of or pertaining to Northumbria, Northumberland, or the inhabitants or dialect of either. —*n.* **2.** a native or inhabitant of Northumbr·a or Northumberland. **3.** the English dialect of Northumbria or Northumberland.

North Vi·et·nam (vē·ĕt·năm'), that part of Vietnam N of ab. 17° N latitude, provisionally controlled by a communist government; formerly a part of French Indochina. ab. 14,500,000 pop. *Cap.*: Hanoi.

north·ward (nôrth'wərd; *Naut.* nôr'thərd), *adv.* **1.** Also, **north'wards.** toward the north. —*adj.* **2.** moving, bearing, facing, or situated toward the north. —*n.* **3.** the northward part, direction, or point. —**north'-ward·ly,** *adj., adv.*

north·west (nôrth'wĕst'; *Naut.* nôr'-), *n.* **1.** the point or direction midway between north and west. **2.** a region in this direction. —*adj.* Also, **north'west'-ern. 3.** lying toward or situated in the northwest. **4.** directed or proceeding toward the northwest. **5.** coming from the northwest, as a wind. —*adv.* **6.** in the direction of a point midway between north and west. **7.** from this direction.

north·west·er (nôrth'wĕs'tər; *Naut.* nôr'-), *n.* a wind or gale from the northwest.

north·west·er·ly (nôrth'wĕs'tər lĭ; *Naut.* nôr'-), *adj., adv.* toward or from the northwest.

North-West Frontier Province, 1. a province in Pakistan, bordering the Punjab and Kashmir on the W. 3,253,000 pop. (1951); 13,560 sq. mi. *Cap.*: Peshawar. **2.** agencies and tribal areas between this province and the Afghanistan frontier. 2,647,000 (1951); 25,699 sq. mi.

Northwest Passage, ship route along the Arctic coast of Canada and Alaska, joining the Atlantic and Pacific oceans.

Northwest Territories, a territory of Canada lying north of the provinces and extending from Yukon territory E to Davis Strait. 16,000 pop. (est. 1953); 1,304,-903 sq. mi.

Northwest Territory, the region north of the Ohio river (Ohio, Indiana, Illinois, Michigan, Wisconsin, and part of Minnesota) organized by Congress in 1787.

Northwest Territory, 1787

north·west·ward (nôrth'-wĕst'wərd; *Naut.* nôr'-), *adv., adj.* **1.** Also, **north'-west'ward·ly.** toward the northwest. —*n.* **2.** the northwest.

north·west·wards (nôrth'wĕst'wərdz; *Naut.* nôr'-), *adv.* northwestward.

Nor·ton (nôr'tən), *n.* **1. Charles Eliot,** 1827–1908, U.S. scholar. **2. Thomas,** 1532–84, English author.

Norw., 1. Norway. **2.** Norwegian.

Nor·walk (nôr'wôk), *n.* a city in SW Connecticut. 67,775 (1960). a city in SW California. 88,739 (1960).

Nor·way (nôr'wā), *n.* a kingdom in N Europe, in the W part of the Scandinavian Peninsula. 3,462,000 pop. (est. 1956); 124,555 sq. mi. *Cap.*: Oslo. Norwegian, **Norge.**

Norway spruce, a spruce introduced from Europe, *Picea Abies,* widely grown as an ornamental.

Nor·we·gian (nôr wē'jən), *adj.* **1.** of or pertaining to Norway, its inhabitants, or their language. —*n.* **2.** a native or inhabitant of Norway. **3.** the speech of Norway in any of its forms, whether Dano-Norwegian, or the local dialects, or the standard language based on these, all being closely related to one another and to the other Scandinavian languages.

nor'·west·er (nôr wĕs'tər), *n.* a seaman's oilskin raincoat.

Nor·wich (nôr'ĭch, -ĭj, nôr'- *for 1*; nôr'wĭch *for 2*), *n.* **1.** a city in E England, in Norfolk: famous cathedral. 121,236 (1951). **2.** a city in SE Connecticut, on the Thames river. 38,506 (1960).

Nor·wood (nôr'wŏŏd'), *n.* a city in SW Ohio, near Cincinnati. 34,580 (1960).

nos-, var. of **noso-,** before vowels.

Nos., numbers. Also, **nos.**

no·sce te ip·sum (nō'sē tē ĭp'səm), *Latin.* know thyself.

nose (nōz), *n., v.,* **nosed, nosing.** —*n.* **1.** the part of the face or head which contains the nostrils, affording passage for air in respiration, etc. **2.** this part as the organ of smell: *the aroma of coffee greeted his nose.* **3.** the sense of smell: *a dog with a good nose.* **4.** a faculty of perceiving or detecting: *a nose for news.* **5.** something regarded as resembling the nose of a person or animal, as a spout or nozzle. **6.** the prow of a ship. **7.** the forward end of an aircraft. **8.** a projecting part of any thing. —*v.t.* **9.** to perceive by or as by the nose or the sense of smell. **10.** to approach the nose to, as in smelling or examining; sniff. **11.** to move or push forward. **12.** to touch or rub with the nose; nuzzle. —*v.i.* **13.** to smell or sniff. **14.** to seek as if by smelling or scent (fol. by *after, for,* etc.); pry (fol. by *about, into,* etc.). **15.** to move or push forward. **16.** to meddle. [ME; OE *nosu,* c. MD and MLG *nose.* Cf. L *nāsus*]

nose·band (nōz'bănd'), *n.* that part of a bridle or halter which passes over the animal's nose.

nose·bleed (nōz'blēd'), *n.* bleeding from the nose.

nose dive, 1. a plunge of an airplane with the fore part of the craft vertically downward. **2.** any sudden drop.

nose-dive (nōz'dīv'), *v.i.* **-dived** or **-dove, -dived, -diving.** to execute a nose dive.

nose·gay (nōz'gā'), *n.* a bunch of flowers; a bouquet; a posy. [ME; lit., a *gay* (obs., something pretty) for the NOSE (i.e., to smell)]

nose·piece (nōz'pēs'), *n.* **1.** a protective cover for the nose. **2.** the part of a microscope where the object slide is attached. **3.** noseband.

nos·ey (nō'zĭ), *adj.*, **nosier, nosiest.** nosy.

no-show (nō'shō'), *n.* *U.S. Colloq.* an airline passenger who fails to use a seat reserved for him on a flight.

nos·ing (nō'zĭng), *n.* a projecting edge, as the part of the tread of a step extending beyond the riser, or a projecting part of a buttress.

noso-, a word element meaning "disease." Also, **nos-.** [t. Gk., comb. form of *nósos*]

nos·o·ge·og·ra·phy (nŏs'ō jĭ·ŏg'rə fĭ), *n.* the study of the causes and occurrence of diseases in terms of geography. —**nos·o·ge·o·graph·ic** (nŏs'ō jē'ə grăf'ĭk), **nos·o·ge·o·graph·i·cal,** *adj.*

no·sog·ra·phy (nō sŏg'rə fĭ), *n.* the systematic description of diseases.

no·sol·o·gy (nō sŏl'ə jĭ), *n.* **1.** the systematic classification of diseases. **2.** the knowledge of a disease. —**nos·o·log·i·cal** (nŏs'ə lŏj'ə kəl), *adj.* —**no·sol'o·gist,** *n.*

nos·tal·gia (nŏs tăl'jə, -jĭ'ə), *n.* homesickness or strong desire for family and friends. [t. NL, f. Gk.: s. *nóstos* a return to home + *-algia* -ALGIA] —**nos·tal'gic,** *adj.*

nos·toc (nŏs'tŏk), *n.* any of the blue-green fresh-water algae constituting the genus *Nostoc,* often found in jellylike colonies in moist places. [t. NL; coined by Paracelsus]

nos·tol·o·gy (nŏs tŏl'ə jĭ), *n.* geriatrics. —**nos·to·log·ic** (nŏs'tə lŏj'ĭk), *adj.*

nos·to·ma·ni·a (nŏs'tō mā'nĭ·ə), *n.* *Psychiatry.* morbid nostalgia or homesickness; an irresistible compulsion to return home.

Nos·tra·da·mus (nŏs'trə dā'məs), *n.* 1503–66, French astrologer.

nos·tril (nŏs'trəl), *n.* one of the external openings of the nose. [ME *nostrill,* OE *nosterl,* var. of *nosthyrl,*f. *nosu* nose + *-thyrel* hole]

nos·trum (nŏs'trəm), *n.* **1.** a patent medicine. **2.** a quack medicine. **3.** a medicine made by the person who recommends it. **4.** a pet scheme or device for effecting something. [t. L, neut. of *noster* our, ours (cf. der. 3)]

nos·y (nō'zĭ), *adj.*, **nosier, nosiest.** *Colloq.* prying; inquisitive. Also, **nosey.**

not (nŏt), *adv.* a word expressing negation, denial, refusal, or prohibition: *not far, you must not do that.* [ME, reduced form of *noht, nouht.* See NOUGHT]

no·ta be·ne (nō'tə bē'nĭ), *Latin.* note well.

no·ta·bil·i·ty (nō'tə bĭl'ə tĭ), *n., pl.* **-ties. 1.** the quality of being notable. **2.** a notable person.

no·ta·ble (nō'tə bəl), *adj.* **1.** worthy of note or notice;

noteworthy: *a notable success.* **2.** prominent, important, or distinguished, as persons. **3.** capable, thrifty, and industrious, as a housewife. —*n.* **4.** a notable person; a prominent or important person. **5.** (*often cap.*) *Fr. Hist.* one of a number of prominent men convoked by the king on extraordinary occasions. **6.** a notable thing. [ME, t. L: m.s. *notābilis*] —**no′ta·ble·ness,** *n.* —**no′ta·bly,** *adv.* —**Syn. 1.** conspicuous, memorable, great.

no·tar·i·al (nō târ′ĭ əl), *adj.* of or pertaining to, or drawn up or executed by, a notary.

no·ta·rize (nō′tə rīz′), *v.t.,* **-rized, -rizing.** to authenticate (a contract, etc.).

no·ta·ry (nō′tər ĭ), *n., pl.* **-ries.** a notary public. [ME, t. L: m.s. *notārius* shorthand writer, clerk, secretary]

notary public, *pl.* **notaries public.** a public officer authorized to authenticate contracts, acknowledge deeds, take affidavits, protest bills of exchange, take depositions, etc.

no·ta·tion (nō tā′shən), *n.* **1.** a system of graphic symbols for a specialized use, other than ordinary writing: *musical notation.* **2.** the process of noting or setting down by means of a special system of signs or symbols. **3.** act of noting, marking, or setting down in writing. **4.** a note, jotting, or record. [t. L: s. *notātio* a marking] —**no·ta′tion·al,** *adj.*

notch (nŏch), *n.* **1.** a more or less angular cut, indentation, or hollow in a narrow object or surface or an edge. **2.** *U.S.* a deep, narrow opening or pass between mountains. **3.** a cut or nick made in a stick or other object for record, as in keeping a score. **4.** *Colloq.* a step, degree, or grade. [n. use of v.] —*v.t.* **5.** to cut or make a notch or notches in. **6.** to make notches in by way of record. **7.** to record by a notch or notches. **8.** to score, as in a game. [t. AF: m. *anocher,* var. of OF *enochier,* der. *oche* notch]

note (nōt), *n., v.,* **noted, noting.** —*n.* **1.** a brief record of something set down to assist the memory, or for reference or development. **2.** (*pl.*) a record of a speech, statement, testimony, etc., or of one's impressions of something. **3.** an explanatory or critical comment, or a reference to authority quoted, appended to a passage in a book or the like. **4.** a brief written or printed statement giving particulars or information. **5.** *Library Science.* additional information about a book, such as its special series or some other significant identification, entered on the library catalogue card. **6.** a short informal letter. **7.** a formal diplomatic or official communication in writing. **8.** a paper acknowledging a debt and promising payment; note of hand. **9.** a piece of paper money. **10.** a certificate, as of a government or a bank, passing current as money. **11.** eminence or distinction: *a man of note.* **12.** importance or consequence: *no other thing of note this year.* **13.** notice, observation, or heed. **14.** a characteristic or distinguishing feature. **15.** a mark, token, or indication of something, or from which something may be inferred. **16.** a musical sound or tone. **17.** *Music.* **a.** a sign or character used to represent a tone, its position and form indicating the pitch and duration of the tone. **b.** a key, as of a piano. **18.** *Archaic or Poetic.* a melody, tune, or song. **19.** a sound of musical quality uttered by a bird. **20.** any call, cry, or sound of a bird, fowl, etc. **21.** a tone sounded on a trumpet or other musical instrument as a signal. **22.** a signal, announcement, or intimation: *a note of warning.* **23.** *Colloq.* a new or unexpected element in a situation. **24.** way of speaking or thinking: *to change one's note.* **25.** a mark or sign, as of punctuation, used in writing or printing. —*v.t.* **26.** to mark down, as in writing; make a memorandum of. **27.** to make particular mention of in a writing. **28.** to annotate. **29.** to observe carefully; give attention or heed to. **30.** to take notice of; perceive. **31.** to set down in or furnish with musical notes. **32.** to indicate or designate; signify or denote. [ME, t. L: m. *nota* a mark] —**not′er,** *n.* —**Syn. 3.** See **remark.**

Notes (def. 17a)
A. Breve; B. Whole note (semibreve); C. Half note (minim); D. Quarter note (crotchet); E. Eighth note (quaver); F. Sixteenth note (semiquaver); G. Thirty-second note (demisemiquaver); H. Sixty-fourth note (hemidemisemiquaver)

note·book (nōt′bŏŏk′), *n.* **1.** a book of or for notes. **2.** a book in which notes of hand are registered.

not·ed (nō′tĭd), *adj.* **1.** celebrated; famous. **2.** specially observed or noticed. —**not′ed·ly,** *adv.* —**not′ed·ness,** *n.*

note·less (nōt′lĭs), *adj.* **1.** of no note; undistinguished; unnoticed. **2.** unmusical or voiceless.

note of hand, a promissory note.

note paper, paper used for correspondence.

note·wor·thy (nōt′wûr′thĭ), *adj.* worthy of note or notice; notable. —**note′wor′thi·ly,** *adv.* —**note′wor′thi·ness,** *n.*

noth·ing (nŭth′ĭng), *n.* **1.** no thing; not anything; naught: *say nothing.* **2.** no part, share, or trace (fol. by *of*): *the place shows nothing of its former magnificence.* **3.** that which is nonexistent. **4.** something of no importance or significance. **5.** a trivial action, matter, circumstance, thing, or remark. **6.** a person of no importance. **7.** that which is without quantity or magnitude. **8.** a cipher or naught. —*adv.* **9.** in no respect or degree; not at all: *it was nothing like what we expected.* [orig. two words. See **NO, THING**]

noth·ing·ness (nŭth′ĭng nĭs), *n.* **1.** state of being nothing. **2.** that which is nonexistent. **3.** nonexistence. **4.** unconsciousness. **5.** utter insignificance, emptiness, or worthlessness; triviality. **6.** something insignificant.

no·tice (nō′tĭs), *n., v.,* **-ticed, -ticing.** —*n.* **1.** information or intelligence: *to give notice of a thing.* **2.** an intimation or warning. **3.** a note, placard, or the like conveying information or warning. **4.** a notification of the termination, at a specified time, of an agreement, as for renting or employment, given by one of the parties to the agreement. **5.** observation, perception, attention, or heed: *worthy of notice.* **6.** interested or favorable attention. **7.** a single observation or perception. **8.** a brief written mention or account, as of a newly published book. —*v.t.* **9.** to pay attention to or take notice of. **10.** to perceive: *did you notice her hat?* **11.** to treat with attention, politeness, or favor. **12.** to acknowledge acquaintance with. **13.** to mention or refer to; point out, as to a person. **14.** to give notice to; serve with a notice. [late ME, t. OF, t. L: m.s. *nōtitia* a being known] —**Syn. 10.** NOTICE, DISCERN, PERCEIVE imply becoming aware of, and paying attention to, something. All are "point-action" verbs. To NOTICE is to become aware of something which has caught one's attention: *to notice the newspaper headline, I'm sorry I didn't notice it.* DISCERN suggests distinguishing (sometimes with difficulty) and recognizing a thing for what it is, discriminating it from its surroundings: *in spite of the fog we finally discerned the outline of the harbor.* PERCEIVE, often used as a formal substitute for "see" or "notice," may convey also the idea of understanding meanings and implications: *after examining the evidence he perceived its real meaning.* —**Ant. 9.** ignore.

no·tice·a·ble (nō′tĭs ə bəl), *adj.* that may be noticed; such as to attract notice. —**no′tice·a·bly,** *adv.*

no·ti·fi·ca·tion (nō′tə fə kā′shən), *n.* **1.** act of notifying, making known, or giving notice. **2.** a formal notifying or informing. **3.** a notice.

no·ti·fy (nō′tə fī′), *v.t.,* **-fied, -fying. 1.** to give notice to, or inform, of something. **2.** *Chiefly Brit.* to make known; give information of: *the sale was notified in the newspapers.* [ME *notifie(n),* t. OF: m. *notifier,* t. L: m. *nōtificāre* make known] —**no′ti·fi′er,** *n.*

no·tion (nō′shən), *n.* **1.** a more or less general, vague or imperfect conception or idea of something: *notions of beauty.* **2.** an opinion, view or belief. **3.** conception or idea. **4.** a fanciful or foolish idea; whim. **5.** a device, contrivance, or ingenious article. **6.** (*pl.*) *U.S.* small wares, esp. pins, needles, thread, tapes, etc. [t. L: s. *nōtio* a becoming acquainted, conception, notion]

no·tion·al (nō′shən əl), *adj.* **1.** pertaining to or expressing a notion or idea. **2.** of the nature of a notion. **3.** abstract or speculative, as reflective thought. **4.** ideal or imaginary, as things. **5.** *U.S.* given to or full of notions, as a person; fanciful. **6.** *Gram.* **a.** relating to the meaning expressed by a linguistic form. **b.** having full lexical meaning, in contrast to relational. **7.** *Semantics.* presentive. —**no′tion·al·ly,** *adv.*

no·to·chord (nō′tə kôrd′), *n.* *Biol.* a rodlike stiffening structure found in the bodies of the protochordates, e.g., along the back of amphioxus, and also found in the embryos of the vertebrates, and presumed to represent an ancestral stage of the spinal column. [f. *noto-* (t. Gk., comb. form of *nōton* back) + CHORD]

No·to·gae·a (nō′tə jē′ə), *n.* *Zoogeog.* a great zoölogical division of the earth's land area, comprising the Austro-colombian, Australasian and Neotropical regions. [NL, f. Gk.: *nōto*(s) the south + m. *gaia* land, earth] —**No′to·gae′an,** *adj.*

no·to·ri·e·ty (nō′tə rī′ə tĭ), *n., pl.* **-ties. 1.** state or character of being notorious or widely known: *a craze for notoriety.* **2.** a widely known or well-known person.

no·to·ri·ous (nō tôr′ĭ əs), *adj.* **1.** widely but unfavorably known: *a notorious gambler.* **2.** publicly or generally known: *notorious crimes.* [t. ML: m. *nōtōrius,* der. L *nōtus,* pp., known] —**no·to′ri·ous·ly,** *adv.* —**no·to′ri·ous·ness,** *n.*

no·tor·nis (nō tôr′nĭs), *n.* any of the rare flightless birds constituting the genus *Notornis,* chiefly of New Zealand. [t. NL, f. Gk.: s. *nōtos* the south + *órnis* bird]

No·tre Dame (nō′trə dăm′, nō′tər; Fr. nô′tr dăm′), famous early Gothic cathedral in Paris (started 1163).

no-trump (nō′trŭmp′), *Bridge.* —*adj.* **1.** denoting a bid or play without any trump suit. **2.** the play, or the bid to play, without any trump suit.

no-trump·er (nō′trŭmp′ər), *n.* *Bridge.* a game or hand played in no-trump.

Not·ting·ham (nŏt′ĭng əm), *n.* **1.** a city in central England. 312,500 (est. 1956). **2.** Nottinghamshire.

Not·ting·ham·shire (nŏt′ĭng əm shĭr′, -shər), *n.* a county in central England. 841,211 pop. (1951); 844 sq. mi. *Co. seat:* Nottingham. Also, **Nottingham** or **Notts** (nŏts).

no·tun·gu·late (nō tŭng′gyə lāt′), *adj.* *Paleontol.* of an order, *Notungulata,* of extinct herbivorous mammals.

not·with·stand·ing (nŏt′wĭth stăn′dĭng, -wĭth-), *prep.* **1.** without being withstood or prevented by; in spite of. —*adv.* **2.** nevertheless; yet. —*conj.* **3.** in spite of the fact that; although. [ME] —**Syn. 1.** NOTWITHSTANDING, DESPITE, IN SPITE OF imply that something is true even though there are obstacles or opposing conditions. The three expressions may be used practically interchangeably. NOTWITHSTANDING suggests, however, a hindrance of some kind: *notwithstanding the long delay, I shall still go.* DESPITE, now literary and somewhat archaic, indicates that there is an active opposition: *despite* *the circulation of slanderous stories about him, the candidate was elected.* IN SPITE OF, the modern equivalent on an informal level, implies meeting strong opposing forces or circumstances which must be taken into account: *he succeeded in spite of all discouragements.*

nou·gat (nōō′gət, nōō′gä), *n.* a pastelike confection containing almonds or other nuts. [t. F. t. Pr., der. *noga,* g. LL *nuca* nut, r. L *nux*]

nought (nôt), *n., adj., adv.* naught. [ME *noht, nouht,* OE *nōht,* syncopated var. of *nōwiht*]

nou·me·non (nōō′mə nŏn′, nou′-), *n., pl.* -na (-nə). 1. (in the Kantian philosophy) that which can be the object only of a purely intellectual (nonsensuous) intuition; essentially, a postulate. 2. the transexperiential object to which a phenomenon is referred as to the basis or cause of its sense content. 3. a thing in itself, as distinguished from a phenomenon or thing as it appears to us. [t. Gk.: m. *nooúmenon,* neut. ppr. pass., (anything) perceived] **—nou′me·nal,** *adj.* **—nou′me·nal·ly,** *adv.* **—nou′me·nal·ism,** *n.* **—nou′me·nal·ist,** *n.*

noun (noun), *n. Gram.* 1. (in most languages) one of the major form classes, or "parts of speech," comprising words denoting person, places, things, and such other words as show similar grammatical behavior, as English *friend, city, desk, whiteness, virtue.* 2. any such word. 3. any word or construction of similar function or meaning. [ME *nowne,* t. AF: m. *noun,* g. L *nōmen* name] **—noun′al,** *adj.* **—noun′al·ly,** *adv.*

nour·ice (nōō′rĭs), *n. Obs.* a nurse.

nour·ish (nûr′ĭsh), *v.t.* 1. to sustain with food or nutriment; supply with what is necessary for maintaining life. 2. to foster or promote. [ME *norische(n),* t. OF: m. *noriss-,* s. *norir,* g. L *nūtrīre* suckle, feed, maintain] **—nour′ish·er,** *n.* **—nour′ish·ing·ly,** *adv.* **—Syn.** 2. See **nurse.**

nour·ish·ment (nûr′ĭsh mənt), *n.* 1. that which nourishes; food, nutriment, or sustenance. 2. act of nourishing. 3. state of being nourished.

nous (nōōs, nous), *n. Gk. Philos.* mind or intellect. [t. Gk., contr. of *nóos*]

nou·veau riche (nōō vō rēsh′), *pl.* **nouveaux riches** (nōō vō rēsh′). *French.* one who has newly become rich.

Nov., November.

no·va (nō′və), *n., pl.* **-vae** (-vē), **-vas.** *Astron.* a new star which makes its appearance suddenly and then gradually grows fainter. [t. NL: (fem.) new]

No·va·chord (nō′və kôrd′), *n.* a trademark for a keyboard instrument resembling in shape an upright piano, operating by electronic tone generation and providing a great variety of tone colors.

no·vac·u·lite (nō văk′yə līt′), *n. Petrog.* a very hard, compact, siliceous rock, probably sedimentary, used for hones, etc. [f. s. L *novācula* sharp knife, razor + -ITE¹]

No·va·lis (nō vä′lĭs), *n* pen name of **Hardenberg, Friedrich von.**

No·va·ra (nō vä′rä), *n.* a city in NW Italy, in Piedmont. 73,000 (est. 1954).

No·va Sco·tia (nō′və skō′shə), a peninsula and province in SE Canada: once a part of the French province of Acadia. 663,000 (est. 1953); 21,068 sq. mi. *Cap.:* Halifax. **—No′va Sco′tian.**

no·va·tion (nō vā′shən), *n.* 1. *Law.* the substitution of a new obligation for an old one, usually by the substitution of a new debtor or of a new creditor. 2. *Now Rare.* the introduction of something new; an innovation.

No·va·ya Zem·lya (nō′vä yä zĕm lyä′). two large islands in the Arctic Ocean, N of the Soviet Union in Europe: a part of the U.S.S.R. ab. 35,000 sq. mi. Also, **No·va Zem·bla** (nō′və zĕm blä′).

nov·el¹ (nŏv′əl), *n.* 1. a fictitious prose narrative of considerable length, portraying characters, actions, and scenes representative of real life in a plot of more or less intricacy. 2. (formerly) a short story, as a novella. [t. It.: m.s. *novella,* t. L (appar. short for *novella narrātio* new kind of story)] **—Syn.** 1. NOVEL, ROMANCE are both long stories. A NOVEL is now a long fictitious story, picturing, in a series of evolving situations, characters and actions that represent real life: *a novel about a war veteran.* A ROMANCE (originally a story told in one of the Romance languages) came to mean a story laid especially in remote or unfamiliar times or places, describing unusual persons, customs, adventures and usually having love as a prominent theme: *a romance about the days of chivalry.*

nov·el² (nŏv′əl), *adj.* of a new kind, or different from anything seen or known before: *a novel idea.* [ME, t. LL: m.s. *novellus* new] **—nov′el·ly,** *adv.* **—Syn.** See **new.**

nov·el³ (nŏv′əl), *n.* 1. *Rom. Law.* **a.** a constitution with imperial authority, subsequent to publication of a code. **b.** (*pl., cap.*) constitutions of Justinian and later emperors before A.D. 582 issued after promulgation of the Justinian Code. 2. *Civil Law.* an amendment to a statute. [t. LL: short for *novella (constitūtio)* new (regulation)]

nov·el·ette (nŏv′ə lĕt′), *n.* a short novel.

nov·el·ist (nŏv′əl ĭst), *n.* a writer of novels.

nov·el·is·tic (nŏv′ə lĭs′tĭk), *adj.* of, pertaining to, or characteristic of novels. **—nov′el·is·ti·cal·ly,** *adv.*

nov·el·ize (nŏv′ə līz′), *v.t.,* -ized, -izing. to put into the form of a novel. **—nov′el·i·za′tion,** *n.*

no·vel·la (nō vĕl′ə), *n., pl.* -le (-lĕ). 1. a tale or short story of the type of those contained in the *Decameron* of Boccaccio, etc. 2. a short story, usually domestic and middle-class in character. [t. It. See NOVEL¹]

nov·el·ty (nŏv′əl tĭ), *n., pl.* -ties. 1. novel character, newness, or strangeness. 2. a novel thing, experience, or proceeding. 3. a new or novel article of trade; a variety of goods differing from the staple kinds. [ME *novelte,* t. OF: m. *novelte,* g. LL *novellitas* newness]

No·vem·ber (nō vĕm′bər), *n.* the eleventh month of the year, containing 30 days. [ME and OE, t. L: the ninth month of the early Roman year]

no·ve·na (nō vē′nə), *n., pl.* -nae (-nē). *Rom. Cath. Ch.* a devotion consisting of prayers or services on nine consecutive days. [t. ML, prop. fem. of L *novēnus* nine each]

no·ver·cal (nō vûr′kəl), *adj.* of, like, or befitting a stepmother. [t. L: s. *novercālis,* der. *noverca* stepmother]

Nov·go·rod (nŏv′gŏ rŏt), *n.* a city in the NW Soviet Union: a former capital of Russia. 50,000 (est. 1948).

nov·ice (nŏv′ĭs), *n.* 1. one who is new to the circumstances, work, etc. in which he is placed; a tyro: *a novice in politics.* 2. one who has been received into a religious order or congregation for a period of probation before taking vows. 3. a person newly become a church member. 4. a recent convert to Christianity. [ME *novise,* t. OF: m. *novice,* t. L: m.s. *novicius* new]

No·vi Sad (nō′vĭ säd′), a city in NE Yugoslavia, on the Danube. 83,233 (1953). German, **Neusatz.**

no·vi·ti·ate (nō vĭsh′ĭ ĭt, -āt′), *n.* 1. state or period of being a novice of a religious order or congregation. 2. the quarters occupied by religious novices during probation. 3. state or period of being a beginner in anything. 4. a novice. Also, **no·vi′ci·ate.** [t. ML: s. *novītiātus,* der. L *novītius* new. See -ATE³]

no·vo·caine (nō′və kān′), *n.* 1. a nonirritant local anesthestic, C₁₃H₂₀N₂O₂HCl, a synthetic and much less toxic substitute for cocaine; procaine. 2. (*cap.*) a trademark for this substance. Also, **no·vo·cain′.** [f. *novo-* (comb. form repr. L *novus* new) + (co)CAINE]

No·vo·kuz·netsk (nō′vō kŏoz netsk′). See **Stalinsk.**

No·vo·ros·siisk (nō′vō rô sēsk′), *n.* a seaport in the SW Soviet Union, on the Black Sea. 110,000 (est. 1948).

No·vo·si·birsk (nō′vō sĭ bērsk′), *n.* a city in the W Soviet Union in Asia, on the Ob. 731,000 (est. 1956). Formerly, **No·vo·ni·ko·la·evsk** (nō′vō nĭ kō lä′yĕfsk).

no·vus or·do se·clo·rum (nō′vəs ôr′dō sĕ klôr′əm), *Latin.* a new order of the ages (is born): motto on the great seal of the United States, adapted from Vergil's *Eclogues,* IV, 5.

now (nou), *adv.* 1. at the present time or moment: *he is here now.* 2. (more emphatically) immediately or at once: *now or never.* 3. at this time or juncture in some period under consideration or in some course of proceedings described: *the case now passes to the jury.* 4. at the time or moment only just past: *I saw him just now on the street.* 5. in these present times; nowadays. 6. under the present or existing circumstances; as matters stand. 7. (often used as a preliminary word before some statement, question, or the like): *Now, what does he mean?* 8. (to strengthen a command, entreaty, or the like): *come, now, stop that!* **9. now and again** or **now and then,** occasionally. **10. now that,** inasmuch as. **—conj. 11. now** that; since, or seeing that: *now you are here, why not stay?* **—n. 12.** the present time or moment. [ME; OE *nū,* c. Icel. and Goth. *nū*]

now·a·days (nou′ə dāz′), *adv.* 1. at the present day; in these times. **—n. 2.** the present. [ME; f. NOW + *adays* by day (f. *a* in + *days* by day, adv. gen.)]

no·way (nō′wā′), *adv.* in no way, respect, or degree; not at all. Also, **no′ways′.**

now·el (nō ĕl′), *n. Archaic.* Noel. [ME, t. OF: m. *no(u)el,* g. L *nātālis* natal]

no·where (nō′hwâr′), *adv.* in, at, or to no place; not anywhere. Also, *U.S. Dial.,* **no′wheres′.** [ME; OE *nāhwær* (also *nōwhær*)]

no·whith·er (nō′hwĭth′ər), *adv.* to no place; nowhere. [ME *nowhider,* OE *nāhwider* (also *nōhwider*)]

no·wise (nō′wīz′), *adv.* in no wise; noway; not at all. [ME; f. NO + WISE; cf. Icel. *naut* NEAT²]

nowt (nout), *n. Scot. and N. Eng.* cattle or oxen. [ME, t. Scand.; cf. Icel. *naut* NEAT²]

Nox (nŏks) *n. Rom. Myth.* the goddess of night. [t. L]

nox·ious (nŏk′shəs), *adj.* 1. harmful or injurious to health or physical well-being: *noxious vapors.* 2. morally harmful; pernicious. [t. L: m.s. *noxius* hurtful] **—nox′ious·ly,** *adv.* **—nox′ious·ness,** *n.*

no·yade (nwä yäd′; *Fr.* nwȧ yȧd′), *n.* destruction or execution by drowning, esp. as practiced at Nantes, France, in 1793–94, during the Reign of Terror. [t. F, der. *noyer* drown, g. L *necāre* kill]

Noyes (noiz), *n.* **Alfred,** 1880–1958, British poet.

noz·zle (nŏz′əl), *n.* 1. a projecting spout, terminal discharging pipe, or the like, as of a bellows or a hose. 2. the socket of a candlestick. 3. the spout of a teapot. 4. *Slang.* the nose. [f. NOSE + -le, dim. suffix]

N.P., Notary Public.

nr., near.

NRA, National Recovery Administration. Also, **N.R.A.**

N.S., 1. New Style. 2. Nova Scotia.

n.s., not specified.

N.S.P.C.A., National Society for the Prevention of Cruelty to Animals.

N.S.P.C.C., National Society for the Prevention of Cruelty to Children.

N.S.W., New South Wales.

Nt, *Chem.* niton.

N.T., 1. New Testament. 2. Northern Territory.

---

b., blend of, blended; c., cognate with d., dialect, dialectal; der., derived from; f., formed from; g., going back to; m., modification of; r., replacing, stem of: t., taken from; ?, perhaps. See the full key on inside cover.

nth (ĕnth), *adj.* **1.** the last in a series of infinitely decreasing or increasing values, amounts, etc. **2. the nth degree** or **power**, a. a high (sometimes, any) degree or power. b. the utmost extent.

nt. wt., net weight.

nu (nū, noo), *n.* the thirteenth letter (N, *ν* = English N, n) of the Greek alphabet.

nu·ance (nū̇äns′, noo-, nū′äns, noo-′; *Fr.* nʏäns′), *n.* a shade of color, expression, meaning, feeling, etc. [t. F, b. OF *muance* variation (der. *muer* to change, g. L *mūtāre*), and *nue* cloud]

nub (nŭb), *n.* **1.** a knob or protuberance. **2.** a lump or small piece. **3.** *U.S. Colloq.* the point or gist of anything. [var. of KNOB]

nub·bin (nŭb′ĭn), *n.* *U.S.* **1.** a small lump or piece. **2.** a small or imperfect ear of maize. **3.** an undeveloped fruit. [dim. of NUB]

nub·ble (nŭb′əl), *n.* **1.** a small lump or piece. **2.** a small knob or protuberance. [f. NUB + -*le*, dim. suffix]

nub·bly (nŭb′lĭ), *adj.* **1.** full of small protuberances. **2.** in the form of small lumps.

nu·bi·a (nū′bĭə, noo-′), *n.* a woman's light knitted woolen scarf. [f. s. L *nūbes* cloud + -IA]

Nu·bi·a (nū′bĭə, noo-′), *n.* a region in what is now S Egypt and the Sudan N of Khartoum, extending from the Ni to the Red Sea.

Nu·bi·an (nū′bĭən, noo-′), *n.* Also, **Nu·ba** (nū′bə, noo-′). **1.** one of a Negroid people, of mixed descent, inhabiting Nubia. **2.** a language of the Nile valley below Khartoum. **3.** a Nubian or Negro slave. **4.** a Nubian horse. —*adj.* **5.** of or pertaining to Nubia.

Nubian Desert, an arid region in the NE Sudan.

nu·bile (nū′bĭl, noo-′), *adj.* marriageable, esp. as to age or physical development. [t. L: m.s. *nūbilis*] —**nu·bil′i·ty**, *n.*

nu·bi·lous (nū′bələs, noo-′), *adj.* **1.** cloudy or foggy. **2.** obscure; indefinite. [t. L: m. *nūbilus* cloudy]

nu·cel·lus (nū̇sĕl′əs, noo-), *n.*, *pl.* **-celli** (-sĕl′ī). *Bot.* the central cellular mass of the body of the ovule, containing the embryo sac. [t. NL, dim. of L *nux* nut]

nu·cha (nū′kə, noo-′), *n.*, *pl.* **-chae** (-kē) the nape of the neck. [ME, t. ML, t. Ar.: m. *nukhā* spinal marrow] —**nu′chal**, *adj.*

nu·cle·ar (nū′klĭ ər, noo-′), *adj.* of, pertaining to, or forming a nucleus. [f. NUCLE(US) + -AR¹]

nuclear fission, the breakdown of an atomic nucleus of an element of relatively high atomic number into two or more nuclei of lower atomic number, with conversion of part of its mass into energy.

nuclear physics, the branch of physics dealing with the nature of atoms.

nu·cle·ate (nū′klĭ ĭt, -āt′, noo-′), *adj.* having a nucleus. [t. L: m.s. *nūcleātus* having a kernel or stone]

nu·cle·i (nū′klĭ ī′, noo-′), *n.* pl. of **nucleus**.

nu·cle·ic acid (nū̇klē′ĭk, noo-), *Biochem.* any of a group of complex acids obtained from the proteins in the cell nucleus, composed of a phosphoric-acid radical, a carbohydrate, two purines, and two pyrimidines.

nu·cle·in (nū′klĭ ĭn, noo-′), *n.* *Biochem.* any of a class of phosphorus-containing protein substances occurring in cell nuclei.

nu·cle·o·lar (nū̇klē′ə lər, noo-), *adj.* *Biol.* relating or pertaining to the nucleolus.

nu·cle·o·lat·ed (nū̇klē′ə lā′tĭd, noo-), *adj.* containing a nucleolus or nucleoli. Also, **nu′cle·o·late′.**

nu·cle·o·lus (nū̇klē′ə ləs, noo-), *n.*, *pl.* **-li** (-lī). *Biol.* a conspicuous, often rounded body within the nucleus of a cell. Also, **nu·cle·ole** (nū′klĭ ōl′, noo-′). See diag. under cell. [t. LL: little nut, dim. of *nūcleus*. See NUCLEUS]

nu·cle·on (nū′klĕ ŏn, noo-′), *n.* one of the elementary particles (protons and neutrons) of atomic nuclei.

nu·cle·on·ics (nū′klĕ ŏn′ĭks, noo-′), *n.* the techniques of applying nuclear science to industry and to biology, physics, chemistry, and other sciences.

nu·cle·o·plasm (nū′klĭ ə plăz′əm, noo-′), *n.* *Biol.* karyoplasm. [f. *nucleo*- (comb. form of NUCLEUS) + -PLASM] —**nu′cle·o·plas′mic**, *adj.*

nu·cle·us (nū′klĭ əs, noo-′), *n.*, *pl.* **-clei** (-klī ī′), **-cle·uses. 1.** a central part or thing about which other parts or things are grouped. **2.** anything constituting a central part, foundation, or beginning. **3.** *Biol.* a differentiated mass (usually rounded) of protoplasm, encased in a delicate membrane, present in the interior of nearly all living cells and forming an essential element in their growth metabolism and reproduction. See diag. under cell. **4.** *Anat.* a mass of gray matter in the brain and spinal cord in which incoming nerve fibers form connections with outgoing fibers. **5.** *Chem.* a fundamental arrangement of atoms, as the benzene ring, which may occur in many compounds by substitution of atoms without a change in structure. **6.** *Physics.* the central core of an atom, composed of protons and neutrons. It has a net positive charge equal to the number of protons. **7.** *Astron.* the more condensed portion of the head of a comet. **8.** *Meteorol.* a particle upon which condensation of water vapor occurs to form water drops. [t. L: nut, kernel, fruit stone]

nude (nūd, nood), *adj.* **1.** naked or unclothed, as a person, the body, etc. **2.** without the usual coverings, furnishings, etc.; bare. **3.** *Law.* unsupported; made without a consideration: *a nude pact.* —*n.* **4. the nude, a.** the condition of being undraped. **b.** the undraped

human figure. **5.** a nude figure as represented in art. [t. L: m.s. *nūdus* bare] —**nude′ly**, *adv.* —**nude′ness**, *n.*

nudge (nŭj), *v.*, **nudged, nudging**, *n.* —*v.t.* **1.** to push slightly or jog, esp. with the elbow, as in calling attention or giving a hint or with sly meaning. —*v.i.* **2.** to give a nudge. —*n.* **3.** a slight push or jog. [orig. obscure]

nudi-, a word element meaning "bare." [t. L, comb. form of *nūdus*]

nu·di·branch (nū′də brăngk′, noo-′), *n.* a shell-less type of marine snail with external respiratory appendages, noted for its beautiful coloring and graceful form. [t. F: m. *nudibranche*, f. *nudi*- NUDI- + *branche* gills, t. L: m. *branchia* BRANCHIA]

nu·di·caul (nū′də kôl′, noo-′), *adj.* *Bot.* having leafless stems. Also, **nu′di·cau′lous.** [f. NUDI- + s. L *caulus* stem]

nud·ism (nū′dĭzəm, noo-′), *n.* the practice of going nude or naked as a measure of healthful living, as by a company of persons. —**nud′ist**, *n.*, *adj.*

nu·di·ty (nū′də tĭ, noo-′), *n.*, *pl.* **-ties. 1.** state or fact of being nude; nakedness. **2.** something nude or naked. **3.** a nude figure, esp. as represented in art.

nu·dum pac·tum (nū′dəm păk′təm), *Latin.* a simple contract or promise with no consideration involved.

Nu·e·ces (noo ā′səs), *n.* a river in S Texas, flowing SE to Corpus Christi Bay, on the Gulf of Mexico. 338 mi.

Nue·vo Le·ón (nwĕ′vō lĕ ŏn′), a state in NE Mexico. 788,386 pop. (est. 1952); 25,136 sq. mi. *Cap.*: Monterrey.

nu·gae (nū′jē), *n.pl.* *Latin.* jests; trifles.

nu·ga·to·ry (nū′gə tōr′ĭ, noo-′), *adj.* **1.** trifling; of no real value; worthless. **2.** of no force or effect; futile; vain. [t. L: m.s. *nūgātōrius* worthless]

nug·get (nŭg′ĭt), *n.* **1.** a lump of something. **2.** a lump of native gold. [appar. der. d. *nug* lump, block]

nui·sance (nū′səns, noo-′), *n.* **1.** a highly obnoxious or annoying thing or person. **2.** something offensive or annoying to individuals or to the community, to the prejudice of their legal rights. [ME *nusance*, t. OF: m. *nuisance*, der. *nuire* harm, g. L *nocēre*]

nuisance tax, a tax paid in small amounts, usually by consumers.

null (nŭl), *adj.* **1.** of no effect, consequence, or significance. **2.** being none, lacking, or nonexistent. **3. null and void**, having no legal force or effect. **4.** zero. [t. L: s. *nullus* no, none]

nul·lah (nŭl′ə), *n.* (in the East Indies) **1.** a ravine. **2.** a watercourse. [t. Hind.: m. *nālā*]

nulli-, a word element meaning "none." [t. L, comb. form of *nullus*]

nul·li·fi·ca·tion (nŭl′ə fə kā′shən), *n.* **1.** act of nullifying. **2.** state of being nullified. **3.** Also, Nul/li·fi·ca′tion. *U.S.* failure of a State to aid in enforcement of Federal laws within its limits. —**nul′li·fi·ca′tion·ist**, *n.*

nul·li·fid·i·an (nŭl′ə fĭd′ĭ ən), *n.* one who has no faith or religion; skeptic. [f. NULLI- + s. L *fides* faith + -IAN]

nul·li·fy (nŭl′ə fī′), *v.t.*, **-fied, -fying. 1.** to make ineffective, futile, or of no consequence. **2.** to render or declare legally void or inoperative: *to nullify a contract.* [t. LL: m. *nullificāre* make null, dispose] —**nul′li·fi′er**, *n.*

nul·lip·a·ra (nə lĭp′ə rə), *n.*, *pl.* **-rae** (-rē′). *Obstet.* a woman who has never borne a child. [t. NL: f. *nulli*- NULLI- + -*para*, fem. of *parus* -PAROUS] —**nul·lip′a·rous**, *adj.*

nul·li·pore (nŭl′ə pōr′), *n.* *Bot.* any of the coralline algae with a crustlike plant body. [f. NULLI- + PORE²]

nul·li·ty (nŭl′ə tĭ), *n.*, *pl.* **-ties. 1.** state of being null; nothingness; invalidity. **2.** something null. **3.** something of no legal force or validity. [t. ML: m.s. *nullitas*]

Num., Numbers.

num., **1.** numeral. **2.** numerals.

Nu·man·ti·a (nū măn′shĭ ə, noo-), *n.* an ancient city in N Spain: besieged and taken by Scipio the Younger, 134–133 B.C.

Nu·ma Pom·pil·i·us (nū′mə pŏm pĭl′ĭ əs, noo′mə), d. 672? B.C., 2nd (legendary) king of Rome (715–672 B.C.), said to have introduced religious worship, having been instructed in it by a nymph, Egeria.

numb (nŭm), *adj.* **1.** deprived of or deficient in the power of sensation and movement: *fingers numb with cold.* **2.** of the nature of numbness: *a numb sensation.* —*v.t.* **3.** to make numb. [ME *nome*, lit., taken, seized, apocopated var. of ME *nomen*, *numen*, OE *numen*, pp. of *niman* take] —**numb′ly**, *adv.* —**numb′ness**, *n.*

num·ber (nŭm′bər), *n.* **1.** the sum, total, count, or aggregate of a collection of units, or any generalization of this concept. **2.** a numeral. **3.** (*pl.*) *Obs.* arithmetic. **4.** the particular numeral assigned to anything in order to fix its place in a series: *a house number.* **5.** a word or symbol, or a combination of words or symbols, used in counting or to denote a total. **6.** one of a series of things distinguished by numerals. **7.** a single part of a book published in parts. **8.** a single issue of a periodical. **9.** any of a collection of poems or songs. **10.** a single part of a program made up of a number of parts. **11.** the full count of a collection or company. **12.** a collection or company. **13.** a quantity (large or small) of individuals. **14.** a certain collection, company, or quantity not precisely reckoned, but usually considerable or large. **15.** (*pl.*) considerable collections or quantities. **16.** numerical strength or superiority. **17.** quantity as composed of units. **18.** *Gram.* (in many languages) a cate-

gory of the inflection of nouns, verbs, and related word classes, usually expressing the number of persons or objects referred to: comprising as subcategories the *singular* and *plural* and in some languages one or two intermediate subcategories (the *dual*, referring to two, and the *trial*, referring to three). **19.** (*pl.*) metrical feet, or verse. **20.** (*pl.*) musical periods, measures, or groups of notes. **21.** a distinct part of an extended musical work, or one in a sequence of compositions. **22.** conformity in music or verse to regular beat or measure; rhythm. **23. number one**, oneself. **24. without number**, of which the number is unknown or too great to be counted: *stars without number.*
—*v.t.* **25.** to ascertain the number of. **26.** to mark with or distinguish by a number or numbers. **27.** to count over one by one. **28.** to mention one by one; enumerate. **29.** to fix the number of, limit in number, or make few in number. **30.** to reckon or include in a number. **31.** to mark with or distinguish by a number or numbers. **32.** to live or have lived (so many years). **33.** to have or comprise in number. **34.** to amount to in number: *a crew numbering fifty men.* **35.** *Obs.* to appoint or allot. —*v.i.* **36.** *Poetic.* to make enumeration; count. **37.** to be numbered or included.
[ME *nombre*, t. OF, g. L *numerus*] —**num'ber·er**, *n.*
—**Syn. 1.** NUMBER, SUM both imply the total of two or more units. NUMBER applies to the result of a count or estimate in which the units are considered as individuals; it is used of groups of persons or things: *a number of persons before the house.* SUM applies to the result of addition, in which only the total is considered: *a large sum of money.*
num·ber·less (nŭm'bərlĭs), *adj.* **1.** innumerable; countless; myriad. **2.** without a number or numbers.
Num·bers (nŭm'bərz), *n.* the fourth book of the Old Testament (so called because it relates the numbering of the Israelites after the exodus from Egypt).
numbers pool, an illegal daily lottery in which money may be wagered on the appearance of certain numbers, usually obtained from daily racing totals.
number theory, *Math.* the study of numbers (integers) and of the relations which hold between them.
numb·fish (nŭm'fĭsh'), *n., pl.* **-fishes**, (*esp. collectively*) **-fish.** an electric ray (fish): so called from its power of numbing its prey by means of electric shocks.
num·bles (nŭm'bəlz), *n.pl.* *Archaic.* certain of the inward parts of an animal, esp. of a deer, used as food. Also, **nom'bles**. [ME *noumbles*, t. OF: m. *nombles*, g. L *lumbulus*, dim. of *lumbus* loin]
nu·men (nū'mĭn, noō'-), *n., pl.* **-mina** (-mə nə). a deity; a divine power or spirit. [t. L]
nu·mer·a·ble (nū'mər ə bəl, noō'-), *adj.* that may be numbered or counted. [t. L: m.s. *numerābilis*]
nu·mer·al (nū'mər əl, noō'-), *n.* **1.** a word or words expressing a number: *cardinal numerals.* **2.** a letter or figure, or a group of letters or figures, denoting a number: *the Roman numerals.* —*adj.* **3.** of or pertaining to number; consisting of numbers. **4.** expressing or denoting number. [t. LL: s. *numerālis*, der. L *numerus* number]
nu·mer·ar·y (nū'mə rĕr'ĭ, noō'-), *adj.* of or pertaining to a number or numbers.
nu·mer·ate (nū'mə rāt', noō'-), *v.t.,* **-ated, -ating. 1.** to number; count; enumerate. **2.** to read (an expression in numbers). [t. L: m.s. *numerātus*, pp.]
nu·mer·a·tion (nū'mə rā'shən, noō'-), *n.* **1.** act, process, or result of numbering or counting. **2.** process or a method of reckoning or calculating. **3.** act, art, or method of reading numbers in numerals or figures.
nu·mer·a·tor (nū'mə rā'tər, noō'-), *n.* **1.** *Math.* that term (usually written above the line) of a fraction which shows how many parts of a unit are taken. **2.** one who or that which numbers. [t. LL: a counter]
nu·mer·i·cal (nū mĕr'ə kəl, noō-), *adj.* **1.** of or pertaining to number; of the nature of number. **2.** denoting number or a number: *numerical symbols.* **3.** bearing, or designated by, a number. **4.** expressed by a number or figure, or by figures, and not by a letter or letters. **5.** *Math.* denoting value or magnitude irrespective of sign: *the numerical value of -10 is greater than that of -5.* Also **nu·mer'ic.** —**nu·mer'i·cal·ly**, *adv.*
nu·mer·ol·o·gy (nū'mə rŏl'ə jĭ', noō'-), *n.* the study of numbers (as one's birth year, etc.), supposedly to determine their influence on one's life and future. [f. s. L *numerus* number + -(o)LOGY] —**nu·mer·o·log·i·cal** (nū'mər ə lŏj'ə kəl, noō'-), *adj.*
nu·mer·ous (nū'mərəs, noō'-), *adj.* **1.** very many; forming a great number. **2.** consisting of or comprising a great number of units or individuals. [t. L: m.s. *numerōsus*]. —**nu'mer·ous·ly**, *adv.* —**nu'mer·ous·ness**, *n.* —**Syn. 1.** See **many.**
Nu·mid·i·a (nū mĭd'ĭ ə, noō-), *n.* an ancient country in N Africa, corresponding generally to modern Algeria. —**Nu·mid'i·an**, *adj., n.*
Numidian crane, demoiselle (def. 2).
numis., **1.** numismatic. **2.** numismatics. Also, **numism.**
nu·mis·mat·ic (nū'mĭz măt'ĭk, -mĭs-, noō'-), *adj.* **1.** of or pertaining to, or consisting of, coins and medals. **2.** pertaining to numismatics. Also, **nu'mis·mat'i·cal.** [t. F: m. *numismatique*, der. L *nomisma* coin, t. Gk.]
nu·mis·mat·ics (nū'mĭz măt'ĭks, -mĭs-, noō'-), *n.* the science of coins and medals. —**nu·mis·ma·tist** (nū-mĭz'mə tĭst, -mĭs'-, noō'-), *n.*
nu·mis·ma·tol·o·gy (nū'mĭz mə tŏl'ə jĭ', -mĭs'-, noō'-), *n.* numismatics. —**nu·mis·ma·tol·o·gist**, *n.*

num·ma·ry (nŭm'ə rĭ), *adj.* **1.** of or pertaining to coins or money. **2.** occupied with coins or money.
num·mu·lar (nŭm'yə lər), *adj.* **1.** pertaining to coins or money; nummary. **2.** coin-shaped. [f. s. L *nummulus* (dim. of *nummus* coin) + -AR[1]]
num·mu·lite (nŭm'yə līt'), *n.* any of the foraminifers (mostly fossil) that constitute the family *Nummulitidae*, having a somewhat coinlike shell. [t. NL: m.s. *nummulītēs*, der. L *nummulus*, dim. of *nummus* coin] —**num·mu·lit·ic** (nŭm'yə lĭt'ĭk), *adj.*
num·skull (nŭm'skŭl'), *n.* *Colloq.* a dull-witted person; a dunce; a dolt. [f. NUMB + SKULL]
nun (nŭn), *n.* **1.** a woman devoted to a religious life under vows. **2.** a woman living in a convent under solemn vows of poverty, chastity, and obedience. [ME and OE *nunne*, t. LL: m. *nonna*, fem. of *nonnus* monk]
Nun (noōn), *n.* the chief mouth of the Niger river, in W Africa.
Nunc Di·mit·tis (nŭngk' dĭ mĭt'ĭs), **1.** the canticle of Simeon (Luke 2:29–32), beginning "Lord, now lettest thou thy servant depart in peace." **2.** (*l.c.*) permission to depart; dismissal; departure. [t. L; the first words as given in the Vulgate]
nun·ci·a·ture (nŭn'shĭ ə chər), *n.* the office or the term of service of a papal nuncio. [t. It.: m. *nunziatura*, der. *nunzio* NUNCIO]
nun·ci·o (nŭn'shĭ ō'), *n., pl.* **-cios.** a permanent diplomatic representative of the Pope at a foreign court or capital. [t. It., g. L *nuntius* messenger]
nun·cle (nŭng'kəl), *n.* *Archaic and Brit. Dial.* uncle.
nun·cu·pa·tive (nŭng'kyə pā'tĭv, nŭng kū'pə tĭv), *adj.* (of wills, etc.) oral, rather than written. [t. LL: m.s. *nuncupātivus* nominal]
Nun·kiang (noōn'jyäng'), *n.* a former province in NE China, in Manchuria. 2,102,100 pop. (1946); 25,856 sq. mi. *Cap.:* Tsitsihar.
nun·ner·y (nŭn'ə rĭ), *n., pl.* **-neries.** a religious house for nuns; a convent.
nun's veiling, a thin, plain-woven, worsted fabric, orig. for nun's veils but now for dresses, etc.
nup·tial (nŭp'shəl), *adj.* **1.** of or pertaining to marriage or the marriage ceremony: *the nuptial day.* —*n.* **2.** (*usually pl.*) marriage; wedding. [t. L: s. *nuptiālis* pertaining to marriage] —**Syn. 2.** See **marriage.**

Nu·rem·berg (nyōōr'əm bûrg', noōr'-), *n.* a city in S West Germany, in Bavaria; war-guilt trials of Nazis, 1945–46. 418,950 (est. 1950). German, **Nurn·berg** (nyrn'bĕrkh).

nurse (nûrs), *n., v.,* **nursed, nursing.** —*n.* **1.** a person (woman or man) who has the care of the sick or infirm. **2.** a woman who has the general care of a child or children. **3.** a woman employed to suckle an infant; wet nurse. **4.** any fostering agency or influence. **5.** a worker that attends the young in a colony of social insects. **6.** *Billiards.* act of nursing the balls. —*v.t.* **7.** to tend in sickness or infirmity. **8.** to seek to cure (a cold, etc.) by taking care of oneself. **9.** to look after carefully so as to promote growth, development, etc.; foster; cherish (a feeling, etc.). **10.** to treat or handle with adroit care in order to further one's own interests. **11.** to bring up, train, or nurture. **12.** to clasp or handle as if fondly or tenderly. **13.** to suckle (an infant). **14.** to feed and tend in infancy. **15.** *Billiards.* to gather and keep (the balls) together for a series of caroms. —*v.i.* **16.** to act as nurse; tend the sick or infirm. **17.** to suckle a child. **18.** (of a child) to take the breast. [ME *norse, nourice,* t. OF, g. LL *nūtrīcia* nurse, prop. fem. of *nūtrīcius* that nourishes] —**nurs'er**, *n.*
—**Syn. 14.** NURSE, NOURISH, NURTURE may be used practically interchangeably to refer to bringing up the young. NURSE, however, suggests particularly attendance and service; NOURISH emphasizes providing whatever is needful for development; and NURTURE suggests tenderness and solicitude in training mind and manners.
nurse·ling (nûrs'lĭng), *n.* nursling.
nurse·maid (nûrs'mād'), *n.* a maidservant employed to take care of children. Also, **nurs'er·y·maid'.**
nurs·er·y (nûr'sə rĭ), *n., pl.* **-eries. 1.** a room or place set apart for young children. **2.** a nursery school. **3.** any place in which something is bred, nourished, or fostered. **4.** any situation, condition, circumstance, practice, etc., serving to foster something. **5.** a place where young trees or other plants are raised for transplanting or for sale.
nurs·er·y·man (nûr'sə rĭ mən), *n., pl.* **-men.** one who owns or conducts a nursery for plants.
nursery rhyme, a short, simple poem or song for children.
nursery school, a prekindergarten school.
nurs·ing bottle (nûr'sĭng), a bottle with a rubber nipple, from which an infant sucks milk, water, etc.
nursing home, *Chiefly Brit.* a private convalescence hospital.
nurs·ling (nûrs'lĭng), *n.* **1.** an infant or child under a nurse's care. **2.** any person or thing under fostering care, influences, or conditions. Also, **nurseling.**

---

b., blend of, blended; c., cognate with; d., dialect, dialectal; der., derived from; f., formed from; g., going back to; m., modification of; r., replacing; s., stem of; t., taken from; ?, perhaps.   See the full key on inside cover.

nur·ture (nûr′chər), v., -tured, -turing, n. —v.t. 1. feed, nourish, or support during the stages of growth, as children or young; rear. 2. to bring up; train; educate. —n. 3. upbringing or training. 4. education; breeding. 5. nourishment or food. [ME, t. OF, var. of *nourriture*, der. s. *nourrir* to nourish, g. L *nūtrīre*] —nur′tur·er, n. —Syn. 1. See *nurse*.

nut (nŭt), n., v. **nutted, nutting.** —n. 1. a dry fruit consisting of an edible kernel or meat enclosed in a woody or leathery shell. 2. the kernel itself. 3. Bot. a hard, indehiscent, one-seeded fruit, as the chestnut or the acorn. 4. a difficult question, problem, or undertaking. 5. any of various devices or parts supposed in some way to resemble a nut. 6. Slang. the head. 7. Slang. a person or fellow. 8. Slang. a foolish or crazy person. 9. a perforated block (usually of metal) with an internal thread or female screw, used to screw on the end of a bolt, etc. 10. (in musical instruments of the violin type) a. the ledge, as of ebony, at the upper end of the finger board, over which the strings pass. b. the movable piece at the lower end of the bow, by means of which the hairs may be slackened or tightened. —v.i. 11. to seek for or gather nuts. [ME *nute*, OE *hnutu*, c. G *nuss*] —nut′like′, adj.

N. Nut (def. 9); B. Bolt

nu·tant (nū′tənt, nōō′-), adj. Bot. drooping; nodding. [t. L: s. *nūtans*, ppr.]

nu·ta·tion (nū tā′shən, nōō-), n. 1. a nodding. 2. Bot. spontaneous movements of plant parts during growth. 3. Astron. the periodic oscillation in the precessional motion of the earth's axis or of the equinoxes. [t. L: s. *nūtātio* a nodding]

nut-brown (nŭt′broun′), adj. brown, as many nuts when ripe.

nut cake, a doughnut or fried cake.

nut-crack·er (nŭt′krăk′ər), n. 1. (often pl.) an instrument for cracking nuts. 2. any of several corvine birds of the genus *Nucifraga* which feed on nuts, as the common nutcracker, *N. caryocatactes*, of Europe.

Nutcracker Suite, a ballet and concert suite (1892), by Tschaikovsky.

nut·gall (nŭt′gôl′), n. 1. a nutlike gall or excrescence, esp. one formed on an oak. 2. the Aleppo nutgall.

nut grass, any of various sedges of the genus *Cyperus*, esp. *C. rotundus*, bearing small nutlike tubers.

nut·hatch (nŭt′hăch′), n. any of numerous small short-tailed sharp-beaked birds constituting the family *Sittidae*, which creep on trees and feed on small nuts and insects. [ME *notehache*, *nuthage*, *nuthake*, lit., nut hacker]

nut·let (nŭt′lĭt), n. 1. a small nut; a small nutlike fruit or seed. 2. the stone of a drupe.

Nut·ley (nŭt′lĭ), n. a city in NE New Jersey. 29,513 (1960).

nut·meat (nŭt′mēt′), n. the edible kernel of a nut.

nut·meg (nŭt′mĕg), n. 1. the hard, aromatic seed of the fruit of an East Indian tree, *Myristica fragrans*, used as a spice. 2. the tree itself. 3. the similar product of certain other trees of the same genus or other genera. [ME *notemuge*, f. *note* nut + OF *mug(u)e* musk, ult. der. LL *muscus*]

nut·pick (nŭt′pĭk′), n. a sharp-pointed table device for removing the meat from nuts.

nut pine, any of various trees of the southwestern U.S. and Rocky Mountains, as *Pinus monophylla*, *P. edulis*, etc., bearing edible nuts.

nu·tri·a (nū′trĭ ə, nōō′-), n. 1. the coypu. 2. the fur of this animal, resembling beaver. [t. Sp.: otter, g. L *lūtra* otter, b. with *enitria*, t. Gk.: m.s. *énydris*]

nu·tri·ent (nū′trĭ ənt, nōō′-), adj. 1. containing or conveying nutriment, as solutions or vessels of the body. 2. nourishing; affording nutriment. —n. 3. a nutrient substance. [t. L: s. *nūtriens*, ppr., nourishing]

nu·tri·ment (nū′trə mənt, nōō′-), n. 1. any matter that, taken into a living organism, serves to sustain it in its existence, promoting growth, replacing loss, and providing energy. 2. that which nourishes; nourishment, food, or aliment. [t. L: s. *nūtrīmentum*]

nu·tri·tion (nū trĭsh′ən, nōō-), n. 1. act or process of nourishing or of being nourished. 2. food; nutriment. 3. the process by which the food material taken into an organism is converted into living tissue, etc. —nu·tri′tion·al, adj. —nu·tri′tion·al·ly, adv.

nu·tri·tion·ist (nū trĭsh′ən ĭst, nōō-), n. one who studies problems of food and nutrition.

nu·tri·tious (nū trĭsh′əs, nōō-), adj. nourishing, esp. in a high degree. [t. L: m. *nūtricius*, *nūtrītius*] —nu·tri′tious·ly, adv. —nu·tri′tious·ness, n.

nu·tri·tive (nū′trə tĭv, nōō′-), adj. 1. serving to nourish; affording nutriment. 2. of or concerned in nutrition. —nu′tri·tive·ly, adv. —nu′tri·tive·ness, n.

nuts (nŭts), Slang. —interj. 1. an expression of defiance, disgust, etc. —adj. 2. crazy; insane.

nut·shell (nŭt′shĕl′), n. 1. the shell of a nut. 2. in a nutshell, in very brief form; in a few words: *Just tell me the story in a nutshell.*

nut·ter (nŭt′ər), n. one who gathers nuts.

nut·ting (nŭt′ĭng), n. act of seeking or gathering nuts.

nut·ty (nŭt′ĭ), adj., -tier, -tiest. 1. abounding in or producing nuts. 2. nutlike, esp. in taste. 3. full of flavor or zest. 4. Slang. crazy. —nut′ti·ness, n.

nut·wood (nŭt′wŏŏd′), n. 1. any one of various species of nut-bearing trees, as hickory, walnut, etc. 2. a tree or the wood of a tree of such a species.

nux vom·i·ca (nŭks vŏm′ə kə), 1. the strychnine-containing seed (used in medicine) of the orangelike fruit borne by an East Indian loganiaceous tree, *Strychnos nux-vomica*. 2. the tree itself. [t. NL: vomiting nut, f. L *nux* nut + NL *vomica*, der. L *vomere* vomit]

nuz·zle[1] (nŭz′əl), v., -zled, -zling. —v.i. 1. to burrow or root with the nose, as an animal does. 2. to thrust the nose (fol. by *at*, *against*, *in*, etc.): *the pup nuzzled up close to the sick child.* —v.t. 3. to root up with the nose. 4. to touch or rub with the nose. 5. to thrust the nose against or into. 6. to thrust (the nose or head), as into something. [ME *nosele*; freq. of NOSE; to some extent confused with NESTLE]

nuz·zle[2] (nŭz′əl), v.t., v.i., -zled, -zling. to snuggle or cuddle. [? special use of NUZZLE[1]]

NW, 1. northwest. 2. northwestern. Also, **N. W., n.w.**

N.W.T., Northwest Territories (Canada).

N.Y., New York.

NYA, National Youth Administration. Also, **N.Y.A.**

Nya·sa (nyä′sä, nĭ äs′ə), n. a lake in SE Africa. ab. 360 mi. long; ab. 11,000 sq. mi. Also, **Nyas′sa.**

Nya·sa·land (nyä′sä länd′, nĭ ăs′ə-), n. former name of Malawi.

N.Y.C., New York City.

nyck·el·har·pa (nĭk′əl här′pə), n. an old-time Swedish stringed musical instrument, similar to the hurdygurdy but sounded with a bow instead of a wheel.

nyct-, a word element meaning "night." [t. Gk.; m. *nykti-*, comb. form of *nýx*]

nyc·ta·gi·na·ceous (nĭk′tə jə nā′shəs), adj. belonging to the *Nyctaginaceae*, or four-o'clock family of plants. [f. s. NL *Nyctago*, former name for genus *Mirabilis* (der. Gk. *nýx* night) + -ACEOUS]

nyc·ta·lo·pi·a (nĭk′tə lō′pĭ ə), n. 1. a condition of the eyes in which sight is normal in the day or in a strong light, but is abnormally poor or wholly gone at night or in a dim light; night blindness. 2. hemeralopia, a condition exactly opposite night blindness; day blindness. [t. LL, f. m.s. Gk. *nyktálops* blind by night + -ia -IA] —nyc·ta·lop·ic (nĭk′tə lŏp′ĭk), adj.

nyc·ti·trop·ic (nĭk′trə trŏp′ĭk), adj. Bot. tending to assume at or just before nightfall positions unlike those maintained during the day, as the leaves of certain plants. [f. *nycti-* (var. of NYCT-) + -TROPIC] —nyc·tit·ro·pism (nĭk tĭt′rə pĭz′əm), n.

Nye (nī), n. Edgar Wilson, ("Bill Nye") 1850-96, U.S. humorist.

Nye·man (nĕ′män), n. Russian name of *Niemen*.

nyl·ghau (nĭl′gô), n. nilgai. Also, **nyl·ghai** (nĭl′gī).

ny·lon (nī′lŏn), n. 1. a synthetic polyamide capable of extrusion when molten into fibers, sheets, etc., of extreme toughness, strength, and elasticity: used for yarn (as for hosiery), for bristles (as for brushes), etc. It is a thermoplastic product, made by interaction of a dicarboxylic acid with a diamine. 2. (cap.) a trademark for this material. 3. (pl.) stockings made of nylon. [coined name]

nymph (nĭmf), n. 1. one of a numerous class of inferior divinities of mythology, conceived as beautiful maidens inhabiting the seas, rivers, woods, trees, mountains, meadows, etc., and frequently mentioned as attending a superior deity. 2. a beautiful or graceful young woman. 3. Chiefly Poetic or Playful. a maiden. 4. Entomol. a. the young of an insect without metamorphosis. b. a pupa. [ME *nimphe*, t. OF, t. L: m. *nympha*, t. Gk.: m. *nýmphe* nymph, pupa] —nymph′al, nym·phe·an (nĭm fē′ən), adj. —Syn. 1. See *sylph*.

nym·pha (nĭm′fə), n., pl. -phae (-fē). 1. (pl.) Anat. the labia minora (see *labium* def. 2b). 2. nymph (def. 4a). [t. L. See NYMPH]

nym·phae·a·ceous (nĭm′fĭ ā′shəs), adj. belonging to the *Nymphaeaceae*, or water-lily family of plants. [f. s. L *nymphaea*, t. Gk.: m. *nymphaia* water lily, prop. fem. of *nymphaios* sacred to the nymphs) + -ACEOUS]

nym·pha·lid (nĭm′fə lĭd), n. any of the numerous butterflies of the family *Nymphalidae*, characterized by small useless forelegs and including the fritillaries, etc. [t. NL: s. *nymphālis*, der. L *nympha* NYMPH + -idae -IDAE]

nym·phet (nĭm fet′), n. a nubile, adolescent girl, esp. as the object of a mature man's love.

nym·pho·lep·sy (nĭm′fə lĕp′sĭ), n., pl. -sies. 1. an ecstasy supposed to be inspired by nymphs. 2. a frenzy of emotion, as for something unattainable. [b. NYMPHOLEPT and EPILEPSY] —nym·pho·lep·tic (nĭm′fə lĕp′tĭk), adj.

nym·pho·lept (nĭm′fə lĕpt′), n. one seized with nympholepsy. [t. Gk.: s. *nymphóleptos* caught by nymphs]

nym·pho·ma·ni·a (nĭm′fə mā′nĭ ə), n. Pathol. morbid and uncontrollable sexual desire in women. [f. Gk. *nympho-* NYMPH + MANIA] —nym·pho·ma·ni·ac (nĭm′fə mā′nĭ ăk′), adj., n.

nys·tag·mus (nĭs tăg′məs), n. Pathol. an involuntary oscillation of the eyeball, usually lateral but sometimes rotatory or vertical: occurring esp. among miners and human albinos and in certain diseases. [t. NL, t. Gk.: m. *nystagmós* nodding] —nys·tag′mic, adj.

Nyx (nĭks), n. Gk. Myth. a goddess, a personification of night.

N.Z., New Zealand. Also, **N. Zeal.**

O

O¹, o (ō), *n., pl.* **O's** or **Os; o's,** or **oes. 1.** a vowel, the 15th letter of the English alphabet. **2.** something resembling the letter O in shape. **3.** the Arabic cipher; zero; naught (0). **4.** a mere nothing.

O² (ō), *interj., n., pl.* **O's.** —*interj.* **1.** a word used before the name in address, esp., as in solemn or poetic language, to lend earnestness to an appeal: *Praise the Lord, O Jerusalem.* **2.** an expression of surprise, pain, longing, gladness, etc. —*n.* **3.** the exclamation "O".

o' (ə, ō), *prep.* **1.** an abbreviated form of *of*, now chiefly *dial.* or *colloq.* except in *o'clock, will-o'-the-wisp,* etc. **2.** an abbreviated form of *on.*

O', a prefix meaning "descendant," in Irish family names: *O'Brien, O'Connor.* [repr. Irish ō descendant]

o-¹, *Chem.* an abridgment of ortho-.

o-², var. of **ob-,** before *m,* as in *omission.*

-o-, an ending for the first element of many compounds, originally found in the combining forms of many Greek words, but often used in English as a connective irrespective of etymology, as in *Franco-Italian, speedometer,* etc.

O, 1. *Chem.* oxygen. **2.** Old.

O, ohm.

O., 1. Ocean. **2.** octavo. **3.** Ohio. **4.** Old. **5.** Ontario.

o., 1. (L *octavus*) pint. **2.** octavo. **3.** off. **4.** old. **5.** only. **6.** order. **7.** *Baseball.* outs or put-outs.

oaf (ōf), *n.* **1.** a simpleton or blockhead. **2.** a lout. **3.** a deformed or idiotic child; an idiot. **4.** a changeling. [var. of *auf,* ME *alfe,* OE *ælf* elf, c. G *alp* nightmare] —**oaf'ish,** *adj.* —**oaf'ish·ly,** *adv.* —**oaf'ish·ness,** *n.*

O·a·hu (ō ä'hōō), *n.* the third largest and most important of the Hawaiian Islands: Honolulu is on Oahu. 345,000 pop. (est. 1950); 589 sq. mi.

oak (ōk), *n.* **1.** any tree or shrub of the large fagaceous genus *Quercus,* including many forest trees with hard, durable wood, bearing the acorn as fruit. **2.** the wood of on oak tree. **3.** the leaves of the oak tree, esp. as worn in a chaplet. **4.** anything made of oak, as furniture, a door, etc. **5.** *sport* **one's oak,** *Oxford and Cambridge Slang.* to indicate one is not at home to visitors by closing an outer door. [ME *ook,* OE *āc,* c. D *eik,* G *eiche*]

oak apple, any of various roundish galls produced on oaks. Also, **oak gall.**

oak·en (ō'kən), *adj.* **1.** made of oak: *the old oaken bucket.* **2.** of or pertaining to the oak.

Oak·land (ōk'lənd), *n.* a seaport in W California, on San Francisco Bay. 367,548 (1960).

oak leaf cluster, a small bronze decoration consisting of a twig bearing four oak leaves and three acorns. It is given to holders of medals for valor, wounds, or distinguished service, in recognition of some act justifying a second award of the same medal.

Oak·ley (ōk'lĭ), *n.* **Annie, 1.** (*Phoebe Anne Oakley Mozee*) 1860–1926, U.S. markswoman. **2.** *U.S. Slang.* a free ticket of admittance. [in allusion to the similarity between a punched ticket and a small target shot through by Annie Oakley]

Oak Park, a village in NE Illinois, near Chicago. 61,093 (1960).

Oak Ridge, a town in E Tennessee, near Knoxville: a center of atomic research. 27,169 (1960).

oa·kum (ō'kəm), *n.* loose fiber obtained by untwisting and picking apart old ropes, used for calking the seams of ships, etc. [ME *okom(e),* OE *ācum(a),* var. of *ācumba,* lit., offcombings. See **comb**]

oar (ōr), *n.* **1.** an instrument for propelling a boat, sometimes used also for steering, consisting of a long shaft of wood with a blade at one end. **2.** something resembling or used for a similar purpose. **3.** an oarsman. —*v.t.* **4.** to propel with or as with oars; row. **5.** to traverse (the sea, etc.), or make (one's way), by or as if by rowing. —*v.i.* **6.** to row. **7.** to move or advance as if by rowing. [ME *ore,* OE *ār,* c. Icel. *ār*] —**oar'less,** *adj.* —**oar'like',** *adj.*

oared (ōrd), *adj.* furnished with oars.

oar·fish (ōr'fĭsh'), *n., pl.* **-fishes,** (*esp. collectively*) **-fish.** any of the pelagic fishes constituting the genus *Regalecus,* characterized by a compressed, tapelike body from 12 to over 20 feet long.

oar·lock (ōr'lŏk'), *n.* a contrivance on a boat's gunwale in or on which the oar rests and swings; rowlock. [ME *orlok,* OE *ārloc.* See **oar, lock¹**]

Oarlock

oars·man (ōrz'mən), *n., pl.* **-men.** an expert in the use of oars; a rower. —**oars'man·ship**, *n.*

oar·y (ōr'ĭ), *adj. Chiefly Poetic.* oarlike.

o·a·sis (ō ā'sĭs, ō'ə sĭs), *n., pl.* **oases** (-sēz, -sēz'). a place in a desert region where ground water brought to the

surface or surface water from other areas provides for humid vegetation. [t. L, t. Gk., ? t. Egyptian: m. *wāh*]

oast (ōst), *n.* *Chiefly Brit.* a kiln for drying hops or malt. [ME *ost,* OE *āst,* c. D *eest*]

oat (ōt), *n.* **1.** (*usually pl.*) a cereal grass, *Avena sativa,* cultivated for its edible seed, which is used in making oatmeal and as a food for horses, etc. **2.** (*pl.*) the seeds. **3.** any species of the same genus, as *A. fatua,* the common **wild oat. 4.** *Poetic.* a musical pipe made of an oat straw. **5. feel one's oats,** *U.S. Slang.* **a.** to feel gay or lively. **b.** to be aware of and use one's importance and power. **6. sow one's wild oats,** to indulge in the excesses or follies of youth. [ME *ote,* OE *āte*]

oat·cake (ōt'kāk'), *n.* a cake, usually thin and brittle, made of oatmeal.

oat·en (ō'tən), *adj.* **1.** made of oats or of oatmeal **2.** of or pertaining to the oat. **3.** made of an oat straw

oat grass, 1. any of certain oatlike grasses. **2.** any wild species of oat.

oath (ōth), *n., pl.* **oaths** (ōthz). **1.** a solemn appeal to God, or to some revered person or thing, in attestation of the truth of a statement or the binding character of a promise: *to testify upon oath.* **2.** a statement or promise strengthened by such an appeal. **3.** a formally affirmed statement or promise accepted as an equivalent. **4.** the form of words in which such a statement or promise is made: *the Hippocratic oath.* **5.** a light or blasphemous use of the name of God or anything sacred. **6.** any profane expression; a curse. [ME *ooth,* OE *āth,* c. G *eid*]

oat·meal (ōt'mēl', ōt'mēl'), *n.* **1.** meal made from oats. **2.** a cooked breakfast food made from this.

Oa·xa·ca (wä hä'kä), *n.* **1.** a state in S Mexico. 1,472,- 381 pop. (est. 1952); 36,375 sq. mi. **2.** the capital of this state. 46,741 (1950).

Ob (ôp), *n.* a river in the W Soviet Union in Asia, ab. 2600 mi. long, flowing NW to the Gulf of Ob (ab. 600 mi. long), an inlet of the Arctic Ocean.

ob-, a prefix meaning "toward," "to," "on," "over," "against," orig. occurring in words from the Latin, but now used also, with the sense of "reversely" or "inversely," to form Neo-Latin and English scientific terms. Also, **o-, oc-, of-, op-.** [t. L, repr. *ob,* prep., toward, to, about, before, on, over, against]

ob., 1. obiit. **2.** (L *obiter*) incidentally. **3.** oboe.

Obad., Obadiah.

O·ba·di·ah (ō'bə dī'ə), *n.* **1.** a Hebrew prophet. **2.** the Old Testament book which bears his name.

obb., obbligato.

ob·bli·ga·to (ŏb'lə gä'tō; *It.* ôb'blē gä'tô), *adj., n., pl.* **-tos, -ti** (-tē). *Music.* —*adj.* **1.** obligatory or indispensable; so important that it cannot be omitted (opposed to *ad libitum*). —*n.* **2.** an obbligato part or accompaniment. Also, **obligato.** [t. It.: obliged]

ob·cor·date (ŏb kôr'dāt), *adj.* *Bot.* heart-shaped, with the attachment at the pointed end, as a leaf.

obdt., obedient.

ob·du·rate (ŏb'dyər ĭt, -də-), *adj.* **1.** hardened against persuasions or tender feelings; hard-hearted. **2.** hardened against moral influence; persistently impenitent: *an obdurate sinner.* [ME, t. L: m.s. *obdūrātus,* pp., hardened] —**ob·du·ra·cy** (ŏb'dyər ə sĭ), **ob'du·rate·ness,** *n.* —**ob'du·rate·ly,** *adj.*

o·be·ah (ō'bĭ ə), *n.* obi². [t. W Afr.]

o·be·di·ence (ō bē'dĭ əns), *n.* **1.** state or fact of being obedient. **2.** act or practice of obeying; dutiful or submissive compliance (fol. by *to*). **3.** a sphere of authority, or a body of persons, etc., subject to some particular authority, esp. ecclesiastical. **4.** authority or rule, esp. ecclesiastical, as over those who should obey.

o·be·di·ent (ō bē'dĭ ənt), *adj.* obeying, or willing to obey; submissive to authority or constraint. [ME, t. L: m.s. *oboediens,* ppr.] —**o·be·di·ent·ly,** *adv.* —**Syn.** compliant, docile, tractable.

o·bei·sance (ō bā'səns, ō bē'-), *n.* **1.** a movement of the body expressing deep respect or deferential courtesy, as before a superior; a bow or curtsy. **2.** deference or homage. [ME *obeisaunce,* t. OF: m. *obeissance* obedience, der. *obeir* **obey**] —**o·bei'sant,** *adj.*

ob·e·lisk (ŏb'ə lĭsk), *n.* **1.** a tapering, four-sided shaft of stone, usually monolithic and having a pyramidal apex, of which notable examples are seen among the monuments of ancient Egypt. **2.** something resembling such a shaft. **3.** *Print.* the dagger (†), used esp. as a

Obelisk

reference mark. [t. L: m.s. *obeliscus*, t. Gk.: m. *obelískos*, dim. of *obelós* OBELUS] —**ob′e·lis′cal,** *adj.*

ob·e·lize (ŏb′ə līz′), *v.t.,* **-lized, -lizing.** to mark (a word or passage) with an obelus.

ob·e·lus (ŏb′ə ləs), *n., pl.* **-li** (-lī′). **1.** a mark (− or +) used in ancient manuscripts to point out spurious, corrupt, doubtful, or superfluous words or passages. **2.** *Print.* the obelisk or dagger (†). [t. LL, t. Gk.: m. *obelós* spit, pointed pillar, obelus]

O·ber·am·mer·gau (ō′bər äm′ər gou′), *n.* a village in S West Germany, SW of Munich: famous for the Passion Play performed every ten years. 5325 (1950).

O·ber·hau·sen (ō′bər hou′zən), *n.* a city in W West Germany, in the lower Ruhr valley. 239,096 (est. 1955).

O·ber·land (ō′bər länt′), *n.* a mountain region in central Switzerland, mostly in S Bern canton.

O·ber·lin (ō′bər lǐn), *n.* a village in N Ohio. 7062 (1950).

O·ber·on (ō′bə rŏn′), *n.* (in medieval folklore and in Shakespeare s *Midsummer Night's Dream*) the king of the fairies and husband of their queen, Titania. [var. of *Auberon,* t. F. Cf. G *Alberich*]

o·bese (ō bēs′), *adj.* excessively fat, as a person or animal, the body, etc.; corpulent. [t. L: m.s. *obēsus,* pp.] —**o·bese′ly,** *adv.* —**o·bese′ness, o·bes·i·ty** (ō bē′sə tǐ, ŏ bĕs′ə-), *n.*

o·bey (ō bā′), *v.t.* **1.** to comply with or fulfill the commands or instructions of: *obey your parents.* **2.** to comply with or fulfill (a command, etc.). **3.** (of things) to respond conformably in action to: *a ship obeys her helm.* **4.** to submit or conform in action to (some guiding principle, impulse, etc.). —*v.i.* **5.** to be obedient. [ME *obei*(*en*), t. OF: m. *obeir,* g. L *oboedīre*] —**o·bey′er,** *n.*

ob·fus·cate (ŏb fǔs′kāt, ŏb′fəs kāt′), *v.t.,* **-cated, -cating. 1.** to confuse or stupefy. **2.** to darken or obscure. [t. LL: m.s. *obfuscātus,* pp.] —**ob′fus·ca′tion,** *n.*

o·bi[1] (ō′bǐ; *Jap.* ō′bē), *n., pl.* **obis.** a long, broad sash worn by Japanese women and children. [t. Jap.]

o·bi[2] (ō′bǐ), *n., pl.* **obis. 1.** a kind of sorcery practiced by the Negroes of Africa, the West Indies, etc. **2.** a fetish or charm used in it. Also, **obeah.** [t. West African]

o·bi·it (ŏb′ǐ ǐt, ō′bǐ-), *Latin.* he (or she) died.

o·bit (ō′bǐt, ŏb′ǐt), *n.* **1.** the date of a person's death. **2.** an obituary notice. [ME, t. L: m.s. *obitus* death]

o·bi·ter dic·tum (ŏb′ə tər dǐk′təm), *pl.* **obiter dicta** (dǐk′tə). **1.** an incidental opinion; a passing remark. **2.** *Law.* an opinion by a judge in deciding a case, upon a matter not essential to the decision, and therefore not binding. [t. L: (something) said by the way]

o·bit·u·ar·y (ō bǐch′ōō ĕr′ǐ), *n., pl.* **-aries,** *adj.* —*n.* **1.** a notice of the death of a person, often with a brief biographical sketch, as in a newspaper. —*adj.* **2.** pertaining to or recording a death: *an obituary notice.* [t. NL: m.s. *obituārius,* der. L *obitus* death]

obj., **1.** object. **2.** objective.

ob·ject (*n.* ŏb′jǐkt; *v.* əb jĕkt′), *n.* **1.** something that may be perceived by the senses, esp. by sight or touch; a visible or tangible thing. **2.** a thing or person to which attention or action is directed: *an object of study.* **3.** any thing that may be presented to the mind: *objects of thought.* **4.** a thing with reference to the impression it makes on the mind: *an object of curiosity.* **5.** the end toward which effort is directed: *the object of our visit.* **6.** a person or thing which arouses feelings of pity, disgust, etc. **7.** *Gram.* (in English and some other languages) the noun or its substitute which represents the goal of an action (in English either *direct* or *indirect*) or the ending point of a relation (in English expressed by a preposition). For example: In *John kicked the ball, ball* is the goal of the action. In *he came to Venice, Venice* is the ending point of the action. In *he gave the boy a coin, coin* is the direct object, *boy* is the indirect object. **8.** *Metaphys.* that toward which a cognitive act is directed; the nonego. —*v.i.* **9.** to offer a reason or argument in opposition. **10.** to express or feel disapproval; be averse. —*v.t.* **11.** to bring as a charge; attribute as a fault. **12.** *Obs.* or *Archaic.* to bring forward or adduce in opposition. [ME, t. ML: s. *objectum,* prop. neut. of L *objectus,* pp., thrown before, presented, exposed, opposed, reproached with] —**ob·jec′tor,** *n.* —**Syn. 5.** purpose, motive, intent. See **aim.**

object., **1.** objection. **2.** objective.

object ball, *Billiards, etc.* the ball which the striker aims to hit with the cue ball; any ball except the striker's.

object glass, objective (def. 3).

ob·jec·ti·fy (əb jĕk′tə fī′), *v.t.,* **-fied, -fying.** to present as an object, esp. of sense; make objective; externalize. [f. s. ML *objectum* an object + -(I)FY] —**ob·jec′ti·fi·ca′tion,** *n.*

ob·jec·tion (əb jĕk′shən), *n.* **1.** something adduced or said in disagreement or disapproval; an adverse reason. **2.** the act of objecting. **3.** a ground or cause of objecting. **4.** a feeling of disapproval or dislike.

ob·jec·tion·a·ble (əb jĕk′shən ə bəl), *adj.* that may be objected to; offensive: *an objectionable passage.* —**ob·jec′tion·a·bly,** *adv.*

ob·jec·tive (əb jĕk′tǐv), *n.* **1.** an end toward which efforts are directed; something aimed at. **2.** *Gram.* **a.** the objective case. **b.** a word in that case. **3.** (in a telescope, microscope, etc.) the lens or combination of lenses which first receives the rays from the object and

forms the image viewed through the eyepiece or photographed. See diag. under **microscope.** —*adj.* **4.** being the object of perception or thought; belonging to the object of thought rather than to the thinking subject (opposed to *subjective*). **5.** free from personal feelings or prejudice; unbiased. **6.** being the object of one's endeavors or actions: *an objective point.* **7.** intent upon or dealing with things external to the mind rather than thoughts or feelings, as a person, a book, etc. **8.** of or pertaining to that which can be known, or to that which is an object or a part of an object. **9.** *Art.* **a.** of or pertaining to an object or objects (opposed to *nonobjective* and *nonrepresentational*). **b.** being, or pertaining to, the object whose perspective delineation is required: *an objective plane.* **10.** *Med.* (of a symptom) discernible to others as well as the patient. **11.** *Gram.* **a.** pertaining to the use of a form as object of a verb or preposition. **b.** (in English and some other languages) denoting a case specialized for that use: in *the boy hit him, him* is in the objective case. **c.** similar to such a case in meaning. [t. ML: m. *objectivus,* adj.] —**ob·jec′tive·ly,** *adv.* —**ob·jec′tive·ness,** *n.*

objective complement, *Gram.* a word or a group of words predicated of a direct object or modifying it.

ob·jec·tiv·ism (əb jĕk′tǐ vǐz′əm), *n.* **1.** a tendency to lay stress on the objective or external elements of cognition. **2.** the tendency to deal with things external to the mind rather than thoughts or feelings, as in a writer. **3.** a doctrine characterized by this tendency. —**ob·jec′tiv·ist,** *n., adj.* —**ob·jec′ti·vis′tic,** *adj.*

ob·jec·tiv·i·ty (ŏb′jĕk tǐv′ə tǐ), *n.* **1.** the state or quality of being objective. **2.** intentness on objects external to the mind. **3.** external reality.

ob·ject·less (ŏb′jǐkt lǐs), *adj.* **1.** having no object. **2.** not directed toward any object; purposeless.

object lesson, **1.** a lesson in which instruction is conveyed by means of a material object. **2.** a practical illustration of a principle.

ob·jet d'art (ŏb zhĕ där′), *pl.* **objets d'art** (ŏb zhĕ där′). *French.* an object of art.

ob·jur·gate (ŏb′jər gāt′, əb jûr′gāt), *v.t.,* **-gated, -gating.** to reproach vehemently; upbraid violently; berate. [t. L: m.s. *objurgātus,* pp.] —**ob′jur·ga′tion,** *n.* —**ob·jur·ga·to·ry** (əb jûr′gə tôr′ǐ), *adj.*

obl., **1.** oblique. **2.** oblong.

ob·lan·ce·o·late (ŏb lăn′sǐ ə lǐt, -lāt′), *adj. Bot.* inversely lanceolate, as a leaf.

ob·late[1] (ŏb′lāt, ŏb lāt′), *adj.* flattened at the poles, as a spheroid generated by the revolution of an ellipse about its shorter axis (opposed to *prolate*). See diag. under **prolate.** [t. NL: m.s. *oblātus,* f. ob- OB- + *-lātus,* modeled on *prolātus* PROLATE] —**ob′late·ly,** *adv.*

ob·late[2] (ŏb′lāt, ŏb lāt′), *n.* **1.** a person offered to the service of a monastery, but not under monastic vows. **2.** a member of any of various Roman Catholic societies devoted to special religious work. [t. ML: m.s. *oblātus,* prop. pp. of *offerre* OFFER]

ob·la·tion (ŏb lā′shən), *n.* **1.** the offering to God of the elements of bread and wine in the Eucharist. **2.** the whole office of the Eucharist. **3.** the act of making an offering, now esp. to God or a deity. **4.** any offering for religious or charitable uses. [ME *oblacion,* t. LL: m.s. *oblātio*] —**ob·la·to·ry** (ŏb′lə tôr′ǐ), *adj.*

ob·li·gate (*v.* ŏb′lə gāt′; *adj.* ŏb′lə gǐt, -gāt′), *v.,* **-gated, -gating,** *adj.* —*v.t.* **1.** to oblige or bind morally or legally: *to obligate oneself to fulfill certain conditions.* —*adj.* **2.** obligated, bound, or constrained. **3.** *Biol.* restricted to a particular condition of life, as certain parasites which must live in close association with their usual hosts in order to survive (opposed to *facultative*). [ME, t. L: m.s. *obligātus,* pp.] —**ob′li·ga′tor,** *n.*

ob·li·ga·tion (ŏb′lə gā′shən), *n.* **1.** a binding requirement as to action or duty: *to fulfill every obligation.* **2.** the binding power or force of a promise, law, duty, agreement, etc. **3.** a binding promise or the like made. **4.** act of binding oneself by a promise, contract, etc. **5.** *Law.* **a.** an agreement enforceable by law, originally applied to promises under seal. **b.** a document containing such an agreement. **c.** a bond containing a penalty, with a condition annexed for payment of money, performance of covenants, etc. **d.** any bond, note, bill, certificate, or the like, as of a government or a corporation, serving as security for payment of indebtedness. **6.** a benefit, favor, or service, for which gratitude is due. **7.** a debt of gratitude. **8.** the state or fact of being indebted for a benefit, favor, or service. —**Syn. 1.** See **duty.**

ob·li·ga·to (ŏb′lə gä′tō), *adj., n., pl.* **-tos, -ti** (-tē). obligato.

ob·lig·a·to·ry (ə blǐg′ə tôr′ǐ, ŏb′lǐg ə-), *adj.* **1.** imposing obligation, morally or legally; binding: *an obligatory promise.* **2.** required as a matter of obligation: *a reply is expected but not obligatory.* **3.** incumbent or compulsory (fol. by *on* or *upon*): *duties obligatory on all.* **4.** creating or recording an obligation, as a writing. [ME, t. LL: m.s. *obligātōrius*] —**ob·lig′a·to′ri·ly,** *adv.*

o·blige (ə blīj′), *v.t.,* **obliged, obliging. 1.** to require or constrain, as the law, a command, duty, or necessity does. **2.** to bind (a person, etc.) by a promise, engagement, or contract. **3.** to bind (a person, etc.) morally or legally, as a promise, contract, or the like does. **4.** to make (an action, course, etc.) incumbent or obligatory. **5.** to place under a debt of gratitude for some benefit,

favor, or service. **6.** to favor or accommodate (fol. by *with*): *he obliged us with a song.* [ME *oblige*(n), t. OF: m. *obligier*, t. L: m. *obligāre* bind or tie around] —**o·blig/-er**, *n.*
—**Syn. 6.** OBLIGE, ACCOMMODATE imply making a gracious and welcome gesture of some kind. OBLIGE emphasizes the idea of conferring a favor or benefit (and often of taking some trouble to do it): *to oblige someone with a loan.* ACCOMMODATE emphasizes doing a service or furnishing a convenience: *to accommodate someone with lodgings and meals.*

ob·li·gee (ŏb/lə jē/), *n.* **1.** *Law.* **a.** one to whom another is bound. **b.** the person to whom a bond is given. **2.** one who is under obligation for a benefit or favor.

o·blig·ing (ə blī/jĭng), *adj.* **1.** disposed to do favors or services, as a person: *the clerk was most obliging.* **2.** that obliges. —**o·blig/ing·ly,** *adv.* —**o·blig/ing·ness,** *n.* —**Syn. 1.** helpful, kind, friendly, accommodating.

ob·li·gor (ŏb/lə gôr/, ŏb/lə gôr/), *n. Law.* **1.** one who is bound to another. **2.** the person who gives a bond.

ob·lique (ə blēk/; *military* ə blīk/), *adj., v.,* **-liqued, -liquing.** —*adj.* **1.** neither perpendicular nor parallel to a given line or surface; slanting; sloping. **2.** (of a solid) not having the axis perpendicular to the plane of the base. **3.** diverging from a given straight line or course. **4.** not straight or direct, as a course, etc. **5.** indirectly stated or expressed: *certain oblique hints.* **6.** indirectly aimed at or reached, as ends, results, etc. **7.** *Rhet.* indirect (applied to discourse in which the original words of a speaker or writer are assimilated to the language of the reporter). **8.** *Gram.* denoting or pertaining to any case of noun inflection except nominative and vocative, or except these two and accusative: *Latin genitive, dative, and ablative cases are said to be oblique.* **9.** morally or mentally wrong; perverse. **10.** *Anat.* pertaining to muscles running obliquely in the body as opposed to those running transversely or longitudinally. **11.** *Bot.* having unequal sides, as a leaf. —*v.i.* **12.** to have or take an oblique direction; slant: *the wall obliques from the gate at a sharp angle.* **13.** *Mil.* to advance obliquely. [ME *oblike*, t. L: m.s. *oblīquus*] —**ob·lique/-ly,** *adv.* —**ob·lique/ness,** *n.*

oblique angle, an angle that is not a right angle.

oblique motion, *Music.* the relative motion of two melodic parts in which one remains in place while the other moves.

oblique sailing, navigation along a course other than directly north, south, east, or west.

ob·liq·ui·ty (ə blĭk/wə tĭ), *n., pl.* **-ties. 1.** the state of being oblique. **2.** divergence from moral rectitude. **3.** a moral delinquency. **4.** mental perversity. **5.** an instance of it. **6.** inclination, or degree of inclination. **7.** *Astron.* **obliquity of the ecliptic,** the angle between the plane of the earth's orbit and that of the earth's equator, equal to about 23° 27′. —**ob·liq/ui·tous,** *adj.*

ob·lit·er·ate (ə blĭt/ə rāt/), *v.t.,* **-ated, -ating. 1.** to remove all traces of; do away with; destroy. **2.** to blot out or render undecipherable (writing, marks, etc); cancel; efface. [t. L: m.s. *oblit*(t)*erātus,* pp., erased] —**ob·lit/er·a/tion,** *n.* —**ob·lit/er·a/tive,** *adj.* —**Syn. 2.** See **cancel.**

ob·liv·i·on (ə blĭv/ĭ ən), *n.* **1.** the state of being forgotten, as by the world. **2.** the forgetting, or forgetfulness, of something: *five minutes of oblivion.* **3.** disregard or overlooking: *oblivion of political offenses.* [ME, t. L: s. *oblīvio*]

ob·liv·i·ous (ə blĭv/ĭ əs), *adj.* **1.** forgetful; without remembrance: *oblivious of my former failure.* **2.** unmindful; unconscious (fol. by *of* or *to*): *she was oblivious of his adoration.* **3.** inducing forgetfulness. [ME, t. L: m.s. *oblīviōsus*] —**ob·liv/i·ous·ly,** *adv.* —**ob·liv/i·ous·ness,** *n.*

ob·long (ŏb/lông, -lŏng), *adj.* **1.** elongated, usually from the square or circular form. **2.** in the form of a rectangle of greater length than breadth. —*n.* **3.** an oblong figure. [ME, t. L: s. *oblongus* rather long, oblong]

Obovate leaf

ob·lo·quy (ŏb/lə kwĭ), *n., pl.* **-quies. 1.** the discredit or disgrace resulting from public blame or revilement. **2.** censure, blame, or abusive language aimed at a person, etc., esp. by numbers of persons or by the public generally. [late ME *obloqui,* t. LL: s. *obloquium,* contradiction]

ob·nounce (ŏb nouns/), *v.i. Rom. Antiq.* to announce an unfavorable omen with reference to a proposed public action.

ob·nox·ious (ab nŏk/shəs), *adj.* **1.** objectionable; offensive; odious: *obnoxious remarks.* **2.** exposed or liable (to harm, evil, or anything objectionable). **3.** *Law.* responsible. **4.** *Obs.* liable to punishment or censure; reprehensible. [t. L: m. *obnoxius* exposed to harm] —**ob·nox/ious·ly,** *adv.* —**ob·nox/ious·ness,** *n.* —**Syn. 1.** See **hateful.**

o·boe (ō/bō, ō/boi), *n.* **1.** a wooden wind instrument in the form of a slender conical tube, in which the tone is produced by a double reed. **2.** a reed stop in an organ which sounds like an oboe. [t. It., t. F: m. *hautbois* HAUTBOY]

Oboe

o·bo·ist (ō/bō ĭst), *n.* a player on the oboe.

ob·ol (ŏb/əl), *n.* an ancient Greek silver coin and weight, ⅙ of a drachma. [see OBOLUS]

ob·o·lus (ŏb/ə ləs), *n., pl.* **-li** (-lī/). **1.** an ancient Greek

unit of weight equal to about 11 grains. **2.** a modern Greek unit of weight equal to 0.1 gram. [t. L, t. Gk.: m. *obolós* a small coin, a weight]

ob·o·vate (ŏb ō/vāt), *adj.* inversely ovate; ovate with the narrow end at the base.

ob·o·void (ŏb ō/void), *adj.* inversely ovoid, ovoid with the narrow end at the base, as certain fruits.

O·bre·gón (ō/brě gôn/), *n.* **Álvaro** (äl/vä-rō/), 1880–1928, Mexican general and statesman: president of Mexico, 1920–24.

O·bre·no·vić (ō brě/nô vět/y), *n.* **1.** a former ruling family of Serbia. **2.** Alexander I of Serbia.

Obs. **1.** observation. **2.** observatory. **3.** obsolete.

ob·scene (ab sēn/, ŏb-), *adj.* **1.** offensive to modesty or decency; indecent; lewd: *obscene pictures.* **2.** *Archaic.* abominable; disgusting; repulsive. [t. L: m.s. *obscēnus, obscaenus* of evil omen, offensive, disgusting] —**ob·scene/ly,** *adv.* —**ob·scene/ness,** *n.*

ob·scen·i·ty (ab sĕn/ə tĭ, -sē/nə-), *n., pl.* **-ties. 1.** obscene quality or character; indecency. **2.** something obscene, as language, a remark, an expression, etc.

ob·scur·ant (ab skyōōr/ənt), *n.* **1.** one who strives to prevent inquiry and enlightenment. **2.** one who obscures. —*adj.* **3.** pertaining to or characteristic of obscurants. [t. L: s. *obscūrans,* ppr.]

ob·scur·ant·ism (ab skyōōr/ən tĭz/əm), *n.* **1.** opposition to inquiry and enlightenment. **2.** the principle or practice of obscurants. —**ob·scur/ant·ist,** *n., adj.*

ob·scu·ra·tion (ŏb/skyōō rā/shən), *n.* **1.** act of obscuring. **2.** state of being obscured.

ob·scure (ab skyōōr/), *adj.,* **-scurer, -scurest,** *v.,* **-scured, -scuring,** *n.* —*adj.* **1.** (of meaning) not clear or plain; uncertain. **2.** (of language, style, a speaker, etc.) not expressing the meaning clearly or plainly. **3.** inconspicuous or unnoticeable: *the obscure beginnings of a great movement.* **4.** of no prominence, note, or distinction. **5.** not readily seen; remote; retired, as a place. **6.** indistinct to the sight, or to some other sense. **7.** dark, as from lack of light or illumination; murky; dim. **8.** enveloped in, concealed by, or frequenting darkness. **9.** dark, dull, or not bright or lustrous, as color or appearance. **10.** not perspicuous. —*v.t.* **11.** to make obscure, dark, dim, indistinct, etc. **12.** to make obscure in sound, as a vowel in pronunciation. —*n.* **13.** obscurity. [ME, t. L: m.s. *obscūrus* dark, dim, unknown, ignoble] —**ob·scure/ly,** *adv.* —**ob·scure/ness,** *n.* —**Syn. 1.** doubtful, dubious, ambiguous. See **mysterious. 9.** See **dark.**

ob·scu·ri·ty (ab skyōōr/ə tĭ), *n., pl.* **-ties. 1.** the state or quality of being obscure. **2.** uncertainty of meaning or expression. **3.** the condition of being unknown. **4.** an unknown or unimportant person or thing. **5.** darkness; dimness; indistinctness.

ob·se·crate (ŏb/sə krāt/), *v.t.,* **-crated, -crating.** to entreat (a person, etc.) solemnly; beseech; supplicate. [t. L: m.s. *obsecrātus,* pp.] —**ob·se·cra/tion,** *n.*

ob·se·qui·ous (ab sē/kwĭ əs), *adj.* **1.** servilely compliant or deferential: *obsequious servants.* **2.** characterized by or showing servile complaisance or deference: *an obsequious bow.* **3.** *Now Rare.* compliant; obedient; dutiful. [ME, t. L: m.s. *obsequiōsus*] —**ob·se/qui·ous·ly,** *adv.* —**ob·se/qui·ous·ness,** *n.* —**Syn. 1.** See **servile.**

ob·se·quy (ŏb/sə kwĭ), *n., pl.* **-quies.** (usually *pl.*) a funeral rite or ceremony. [ME *obsequies,* t. ML: m. *obsequiae,* pl., (L *exsequiae*) funeral rites]

ob·serv·a·ble (ab zûr/və bəl), *adj.* **1.** that may be or is to be noticed; noticeable; noteworthy. **2.** that may be or is to be followed or kept. —**ob·serv/a·bly,** *adv.*

ob·serv·ance (ab zûr/vəns), *n.* **1.** the action of conforming to or following: *observance of laws.* **2.** a keeping or celebration by appropriate procedure, ceremonies, etc. **3.** a procedure, ceremony, or rite, as for a particular occasion: *patriotic observances.* **4.** a rule or custom to be observed. **5.** *Rom. Cath. Ch.* **a.** a rule or discipline for a religious house or order. **b.** such a house or order. **6.** observation. **7.** respectful attention or service. **8.** *Archaic.* attentions or assiduities.

ob·serv·ant (ab zûr/vənt), *adj.* **1.** observing or regarding attentively; watchful. **2.** quick to notice or perceive; alert. **3.** careful in the observing of a law, custom, or the like (fol. by *of*). —*n.* **4.** an observer of law or rule. **5.** Also, **Ob·ser·van·tine** (ŏb zûr/vən tĭn, -tēn/). (*cap.*) a member of a branch of the Franciscan order which in the 15th century separated from the Conventuals and observes strictly the rule of St. Francis. [ME, t. L: s. *observans,* ppr.] —**ob·serv/ant·ly,** *adv.*

ob·ser·va·tion (ŏb/zər vā/shən), *n.* **1.** the act of noticing or perceiving. **2.** the act of regarding attentively or watching. **3.** the faculty or habit of observing or noticing. **4.** notice: *to escape a person's observation.* **5.** the act of viewing or noting something, for some scientific or other special purpose. **6.** the information or record secured thereby. **7.** that which is learned by observing. **8.** an utterance by way of remark or comment. **9.** *Naut.* **a.** the measurement of the altitude or azimuth of a celestial body to deduce a line of position for a vessel at sea. **b.** the result obtained. **10.** *Obs.* or *Rare.* observance, as of law, etc. —**Syn. 8.** See **remark.**

ob·ser·va·tion·al (ŏb/zər vā/shən əl), *adj.* of, pertaining to, or founded on observation, esp. as contrasted with experiment.

observation car, a railroad car usually attached to the rear end of a passenger train, designed to afford passengers an unobstructed view of passing scenery.

observation post, *Mil.* a lookout position from which targets may be observed.

observation train, a train run along a river, etc., to allow the passengers to watch a boat race.

ob·serv·a·to·ry (əb zûr'və tôr'ĭ), *n., pl.* **-ries.** **1.** a place or building set apart and fitted up for making observations of astronomical, meteorological, or other natural phenomena. **2.** an institution which controls or carries on the work of an observatory. **3.** a place or structure for affording an extensive view.

ob·serve (əb zûrv'), *v.,* **-served, -serving.** **—v.t. 1.** to see, perceive, or notice. **2.** to regard with attention, so as to see or learn something. **3.** to make or take an observation of; to watch, view, or note for some scientific, official, or other special purpose: *to observe an eclipse.* **4.** to remark; comment. **5.** to keep or maintain in one's action, conduct, etc.: *you must observe quiet.* **6.** to obey, comply with; conform to: *to observe a law.* **7.** to show regard for by some appropriate procedure, ceremonies, etc.: *to observe a holiday.* **8.** to perform duly, or solemnize (ceremonies, rites, etc.). **—v.i. 9.** to notice. **10.** to act as an observer. **11.** to remark or comment (commonly fol. by *on* or *upon*). [ME *observe(n)*, t. L: m. *observāre* watch, comply with, observe] **—ob·serv'er,** *n.* **—ob·serv'ing·ly,** *adv.*
—Syn. 2. OBSERVE, WITNESS imply paying strict attention to what one sees or perceives. Both are "continuative" in action. To OBSERVE is to mark or be attentive to something seen (heard, etc.); to consider carefully; to watch steadily: *to observe the behavior of birds, a person's pronunciation.* To WITNESS, formerly to be present when something was happening, has added the idea of having observed with sufficient care to be able to give an account as evidence: *to witness an accident.* **—Ant. 1.** disregard, overlook.

ob·sess (əb sĕs'), *v.t.* to beset, trouble, or dominate; haunt: *obsessed by a fear of doctors.* [t. L: s. *obsessus,* pp., besieged, beset] **—ob·ses'sive,** *adj.*

ob·ses·sion (əb sĕsh'ən), *n.* **1.** the besetting or dominating action or influence of a persistent feeling, idea, or the like, which the person cannot escape. **2.** the feeling or idea itself. **3.** the state of being obsessed. **4.** the act of obsessing. **—ob·ses'sion·al,** *adj.*

ob·sid·i·an (əb sĭd'ĭ ən), *n.* a volcanic glass, usually of a very dark color and with a conchoidal fracture. [t. L: s. *Obsidiānus,* prop., *Obsidīnus,* pertaining to *Obsius,* reputed discoverer of a similar mineral]

obsolesc., obsolescent.

ob·so·les·cent (ŏb'sə lĕs'ənt), *adj.* **1.** becoming obsolete; passing out of use, as a word. **2.** tending to become out of date, as machinery, etc. **3.** *Biol.* gradually disappearing or imperfectly developed, as organs, marks, etc. [t. L: s. *obsolescens,* ppr.] **—ob·so·les'cence,** *n.* **—ob·so·les'cent·ly,** *adv.*

ob·so·lete (ŏb'sə lēt'), *adj.* **1.** fallen into disuse, or no longer in use: *an obsolete word.* **2.** of a discarded type; out of date: *an obsolete battleship.* **3.** effaced by wearing down or away. **4.** *Biol.* imperfectly developed or rudimentary in comparison with the corresponding character in other individuals, as of the opposite sex or of a related species. Also, **ob·so·le'tal.** [t. L: m.s. *obsolētus,* pp.] **—ob'so·lete'·ly,** *adv.* **—ob'so·lete'ness,** *n.*

ob·sta·cle (ŏb'stə kəl), *n.* something that stands in the way or obstructs progress. [ME, t. OF, t. L: m.s. *obstāculum*]
—Syn. OBSTACLE, OBSTRUCTION, HINDRANCE, IMPEDIMENT refer to that which interferes with or prevents action or progress. An OBSTACLE is something, material or nonmaterial, which stands in the way of literal or figurative progress: *lack of imagination is an obstacle to one's advancement.* An OBSTRUCTION is something which more or less completely blocks a passage: *a blood clot is an obstruction to the circulation.* A HINDRANCE keeps back by interfering and delaying: *interruptions are a hindrance to one's work.* An IMPEDIMENT interferes with proper functioning: *an impediment in one's speech.* **—Ant.** help.

obstet., **1.** obstetric. **2.** obstetrics.

ob·stet·ric (əb stĕt'rĭk), *adj.* **1.** pertaining to the care and treatment of women in childbirth and during the period before and after delivery. **2.** of or pertaining to obstetrics. Also, **ob·stet'ri·cal.** [t. NL: s. *obstētrīcus,* var. of L *obstētrīcius* pertaining to a midwife] **—ob·stet'·ri·cal·ly,** *adv.*

ob·ste·tri·cian (ŏb'stə trĭsh'ən), *n.* one skilled in obstetrics.

ob·stet·rics (əb stĕt'rĭks), *n.* the branch of medical art or science concerned with caring for and treating woman in, before, and after childbirth; midwifery.

ob·sti·na·cy (ŏb'stə nə sĭ), *n., pl.* **-cies. 1.** the quality or state of being obstinate. **2.** obstinate adherence to purpose, opinion, etc. **3.** stubborn persistence: *the battle continued with incredible obstinacy.* **4.** unyielding nature, as of a disease. **5.** an obstinate action; an instance of being obstinate. [ME, t. ML: m.s. *obstinātia*]

ob·sti·nate (ŏb'stə nĭt), *adj.* **1.** firmly and often perversely adhering to one's purpose, opinion, etc.; not yielding to argument, persuasion, or entreaty. **2.** inflexibly persisted in or carried out: *obstinate resistance.* **3.** not easily controlled: *the obstinate growth of weeds.* **4.** not yielding readily to treatment, as a disease. [ME *obstinal,* t. L: s. *obstinātus,* pp., determined] **—ob'·sti·nate·ly,** *adv.* **—ob'·sti·nate·ness,** *n.* **—Syn. 1.** mulish, obdurate, unyielding. See **stubborn.**

ob·sti·pant (ŏb'stə pənt), *n.* a substance that produces obstipation.

ob·sti·pa·tion (ŏb'stə pā'shən), *n.* obstinate constipation. [t. L: s. *obstipātio*]

ob·strep·er·ous (əb strĕp'ər əs), *adj.* **1.** resisting control in a noisy manner; unruly. **2.** noisy or clamorous; boisterous. [t. L: m. *obstreperus* clamorous] **—ob·strep'er·ous·ly,** *adv.* **—ob·strep'er·ous·ness,** *n.*

ob·struct (əb strŭkt'), *v.t.* **1.** to block or close up, or make difficult of passage, with obstacles, as a way, road, channel, or the like. **2.** to interrupt, make difficult, or oppose the passage, progress, course, etc. of. **3.** to come in the way of (a view, etc.). [t. L: s. *obstructus,* pp.] **—ob·struct'er, ob·struc'tor,** *n.* **—ob·struc'tive,** *adj.* **—ob·struc'tive·ly,** *adv.* **—ob·struc'tive·ness,** *n.* **—Syn. 1.** block, stop, close, choke, clog.

ob·struc·tion (əb strŭk'shən), *n.* **1.** something that obstructs; an obstacle or hindrance: *obstructions to navigation.* **2.** the act of obstructing. **3.** the retarding of business before a legislative group by parliamentary devices, or an attempt at such a retarding. **4.** the state of being obstructed. **—Syn. 1.** See **obstacle.**

ob·struc·tion·ist (əb strŭk'shən ĭst), *n.* a person who obstructs something, esp. legislative business. **—ob·struc'tion·ism,** *n.*

ob·stru·ent (ŏb'strŏŏ ənt), *Med.* **—adj. 1.** (of a substance) producing an obstruction. **—n. 2.** a medicine that closes the natural passages of the body. [t. L: s. *obstruens,* ppr., blocking up]

ob·tain (əb tān'), *v.t.* **1.** to come into possession of; get or acquire; procure, as by effort or request: *he obtained a knowledge of Greek.* **2.** *Obs.* or *Archaic.* to attain or reach. **—v.i. 3.** to be prevalent, customary, or in vogue: *the morals that obtained in Rome.* **4.** *Obs.* or *Archaic.* to succeed. [ME *obteine(n),* t. OF: m. *obtenir,* t. L: m. *obtinēre* take hold of, get, prevail, continue] **—ob·tain'a·ble,** *adj.* **—ob·tain'er,** *n.* **—ob·tain'·ment,** *n.* **—Syn. 1.** See **get.**

ob·tect·ed (ŏb tĕk'tĭd), *adj. Entom.* denoting a pupa in which the antennae, legs, and wings are glued to the surface of the body by a hardened secretion. [f. s. L *obtectus,* pp., covered over + -ED[2]]

ob·test (ŏb tĕst'), *v.t.* **1.** to invoke as witness. **2.** to supplicate earnestly; beseech. **—v.i. 3.** to protest. [t. L: s. *obtestārī* call as a witness] **—ob'tes·ta'tion,** *n.*

ob·trude (əb trŏŏd'), *v.,* **-truded, -truding. —v.t. 1.** to thrust forward or upon a person, esp. without warrant or invitation: *to obtrude one's opinions upon others.* **2.** to thrust forth; push out. **—v.i. 3.** to thrust oneself or itself forward, esp. unduly; intrude. [t. L: m.s. *obtrūdere* thrust upon or into] **—ob·trud'er,** *n.*

ob·tru·sion (əb trŏŏ'zhən), *n.* **1.** the act of obtruding. **2.** something obtruded.

ob·tru·sive (əb trŏŏ'sĭv), *adj.* **1.** having or showing a disposition to obtrude. **2.** (of a thing) obtruding itself: *an obtrusive error.* **—ob·tru'sive·ly,** *adv.* **—ob·tru'sive·ness,** *n.*

ob·tund (ŏb tŭnd'), *v.t.* to blunt; dull; deaden. [ME, t. L: s. *obtundere* beat, strike at] **—ob·tund'ent,** *adj.*

ob·tu·rate (ŏb'tyə rāt', -tə-), *v.t.,* **-rated, -rating. 1.** to stop up; close. **2.** *Ordn.* to close (a hole, joint, or cavity) so as to prevent the flow of gas through it. [t. L: m.s. *obtūrātus,* pp.] **—ob'tu·ra'tion,** *n.* **—ob'tu·ra'tor,** *n.*

ob·tuse (ŏb tūs', -tŏŏs'), *adj.* **1.** blunt in form; not sharp or acute. **2.** (of a leaf, petal, etc.) rounded at the extremity. **3.** not sensitive or observant; stupid; dull in perception, feeling, or intellect. **4.** indistinctly felt or perceived, as pain, sound, etc. [t. L: m.s. *obtūsus,* pp., dulled] **—ob·tuse'·ly,** *adv.* **—ob·tuse'ness,** *n.*

obtuse angle, an angle exceeding 90 degrees but less than 180 degrees.

ADE, Obtuse angle; BDE, Right angle; CDE, Straight angle

ob·verse (*adj.* ŏb vûrs'; *n.* ŏb'vûrs), *n.* **1.** that side of a coin, medal, etc., which bears the principal design (opposed to *reverse*). **2.** the front or principal face of anything. **3.** a counterpart. **4.** *Logic.* a proposition obtained from another by obversion. **—adj. 5.** turned toward or facing one. **6.** corresponding to something else as a counterpart. **7.** having the base narrower than the top, as a leaf. [t. L: m.s. *obversus,* pp., turned toward or against] **—ob·verse'ly,** *adv.*

ob·ver·sion (ŏb vûr'shən, -zhən), *n.* **1.** the act or result of obverting. **2.** *Logic.* a form of inference in which a negative proposition is inferred from an affirmative or an affirmative from a negative.

ob·vert (ŏb vûrt'), *v.t.* **1.** to turn (something) toward an object. **2.** *Logic.* to change (a proposition) by obversion. [t. L: s. *obvertere* turn towards or against]

ob·vi·ate (ŏb'vĭ āt'), *v.t.,* **-ated, -ating.** to meet and dispose of or prevent (difficulties, objections, etc.) by effective measures: *to obviate the necessity of beginning again.* [t. LL: m.s. *obviātus,* pp., met, opposed, prevented] **—ob'vi·a'tion,** *n.*

ob·vi·ous (ŏb'vĭ əs), *adj.* **1.** open to view or knowledge: *an obvious advantage.* **2.** *Obs.* being or standing in the way. [t. L: m. *obvius* in the way, meeting] **—ob·vi·ous·ly,** *adv.* **—ob·vi·ous·ness,** *n.* **—Syn. 1.** plain, manifest, evident. See **apparent.**

ob·vo·lute (ŏb'və lŏŏt'), *adj.* **1.** rolled or turned in. **2.** *Bot.* noting or pertaining to a kind of vernation in

which two leaves are folded together in the bud so that one half of each is exterior and the other interior. [t. L: m.s. *obvolūtus*, pp., wrapped up] —**ob·vo·lu'tion**, *n.*
—**ob'vo·lu·tive**, *adj.*

oc-, var. of ob- (by assimilation) before *c*, as in *Occident*.

Oc., ocean. Also, **oc.**

o·ca·ri·na (ŏk'ə rē'nə), *n.* a simple musical wind instrument shaped somewhat like an elongated egg, with finger holes. [prob. dim. of It. *oca* goose, with reference to the shape]

Ocarina

O'Ca·sey (ō kā'sĭ), *n.* **Sean** (shôn), 1884-1964, Irish dramatist.

Oc·cam (ŏk'əm), *n.* **William of**, died 1349?, English scholastic philosopher. Also, **Ockham.**

occas., **1.** occasional. **2.** occasionally.

oc·ca·sion (ə kā'zhən), *n.* **1.** a particular time, esp. as marked by certain circumstances or occurrences: *on several occasions.* **2.** a special or important time, event, or function. **3.** a convenient or favorable juncture or time; opportunity. **4. on occasion, a.** as occasion or opportunity arises; now and then. **b.** occasionally. **5.** the ground, reason, or incidental cause of some action or result. **6.** *Obs.* need or necessity. **7.** (*pl.*) *Obs.* necessary business matters. —*v.t.* **8.** to give occasion or cause for; bring about. [ME, t. L: s. *occāsio* opportunity, fit time] —Syn. **5.** See **cause.**

oc·ca·sion·al (ə kā'zhən əl), *adj.* **1.** occurring or appearing on one occasion or another or now and then: *an occasional visitor.* **2.** intended for use whenever needed: *an occasional table.* **3.** pertaining to, arising out of, or intended for the occasion: *occasional decrees.* **4.** acting or serving for the occasion or on particular occasions. **5.** serving as the occasion or incidental cause.

oc·ca·sion·al·ism (ə kā'zhən ə lĭz'əm), *n.* *Philos.* the doctrine that the apparent interaction of mind and matter is to be explained by the supposition that God takes an act of the will as the occasion of producing a corresponding movement of the body, and a state of the body as the occasion of producing a corresponding mental state. —**oc·ca'sion·al·ist**, *n.*

oc·ca·sion·al·ly (ə kā'zhən ə lĭ), *adv.* at times; now and then.

Oc·ci·dent (ŏk'sə dənt), *n.* **1.** countries in Europe and America (contrasted with the *Orient*). **2.** the Western Hemisphere. **3.** (*l.c.*) the west; the western regions. [ME, t. L: s. *occidens* the west, sunset, prop. ppr., going down]

oc·ci·den·tal (ŏk'sə dĕn'təl), *adj.* **1.** (*usually cap.*) of, pertaining to, or characteristic of the Occident. **2.** western. —*n.* **3.** (*usually cap.*) a native or inhabitant of the Occident. [ME, t. L: s. *occidentālis* western] —**oc'ci·den'tal·ly**, *adv.*

Oc·ci·den·tal·ism (ŏk'sə dĕn'tə lĭz'əm), *n.* Occidental character or characteristics. —**Oc'ci·den'tal·ist**, *n.*, *adj.*

Oc·ci·den·tal·ize (ŏk'sə dĕn'tə līz'), *v.t.*, **-ized, -izing.** to make Occidental. —**Oc'ci·den'tal·i·za'tion**, *n.*

oc·cip·i·tal (ŏk sĭp'ə təl), *adj.* of or pertaining to the back of the head. [t. ML: s. *occipitālis*, der. *occiput* OCCIPUT]

occipital bone, a compound bone which forms the lower posterior part of the skull. See diag. under **cranium.**

occipito-, a word element meaning "occiput," as in *occipitofrontal* (pertaining to both occiput and forehead), *occipitohyoid* (pertaining to both the occipital and the hyoid bone), *occipitoparietal*, *occipitosphenoid*. [comb. form repr. L *occiput*]

oc·ci·put (ŏk'sə pŭt', -pət), *n.*, *pl.* **occipita** (ŏk sĭp'ə tə). *Anat.* the back part of the head or skull. [ME, t. L]

oc·clude (ə klood'), *v.*, **-cluded, -cluding.** —*v.t.* **1.** to close, shut, or stop up (a passage, etc.). **2.** to shut in, out, or off. **3.** *Chem.* (of certain metals and other solids) to absorb and retain gases or liquids, in minute pores. —*v.i.* **4.** *Dentistry.* to shut or close against each other, as the opposing teeth of the upper and lower jaws. [t. L: m.s. *occlūdere* shut up, close up] —**oc·clu·sion** (ə klooʹzhən), *n.* —**oc·clu·sive** (ə klooʹsĭv), *adj.*

oc·cult (ə kŭlt', ŏk'ŭlt), *adj.* **1.** beyond the bounds of ordinary knowledge; mysterious. **2.** not disclosed; secret; communicated only to the initiated. **3.** (in early science) a. not apparent on mere inspection but discoverable by experimentation. **b.** of a nature not understood, as physical qualities. **c.** dealing with such qualities; experimental: *occult science.* **4.** of the nature of, or pertaining to, certain reputed sciences, as magic, astrology, etc., involving the alleged knowledge or employment of secret or mysterious agencies. **5.** having to do with such sciences. **6.** *Obs. or Rare.* hidden from view. —*n.* **7.** occult studies or sciences. **8.** anything occult. —*v.t.* **9.** to hide; shut off (an object) from view. **10.** *Astron.* to hide (a body) by occultation. —*v.i.* **11.** to become hidden or shut off from view. [t. L: s. *occultus*, pp., covered over, concealed] —**oc·cult'er**, *n.*

oc·cul·ta·tion (ŏk'ŭl tā'shən), *n.* **1.** *Astron.* the passage of one celestial body in front of a second, thus hiding the second from view (applied esp. to the moon's coming between us and a star or planet). **2.** disappearance from view or notice. **3.** act of occulting. **4.** the resulting state.

oc·cult·ism (ə kŭl'tĭzəm), *n.* the doctrine or study of the occult. —**oc·cult'ist**, *n.*, *adj.*

oc·cu·pan·cy (ŏk'yə pən sĭ), *n.* **1.** the act of taking possession. **2.** actual possession. **3.** the term during which one is an occupant. **4.** exercise of dominion over a thing which has no owner so as to become legal owner.

oc·cu·pant (ŏk'yə pənt), *n.* **1.** one who occupies. **2.** a tenant of a house, estate, office, etc. **3.** *Law.* an owner through occupancy. [t. L: s. *occupans*, ppr.]

oc·cu·pa·tion (ŏk'yə pā'shən), *n.* **1.** one's habitual employment; business, trade, or calling. **2.** that in which one is engaged. **3.** possession, as of a place. **4.** act of occupying. **5.** state of being occupied. **6.** tenure, as of an office. **7.** seizure, as by invasion. [ME *occupacion*, t. L: m.s. *occupātio* seizing, employment] —Syn. **1.** OCCUPATION, BUSINESS, PROFESSION, TRADE refer to the activity to which one regularly devotes himself, esp. his regular work, or means of getting a living. OCCUPATION is the general word: *a pleasant or congenial occupation.* BUSINESS esp. suggests a commercial or mercantile occupation: *the printing business.* PROFESSION implies an occupation requiring special knowledge and training in some field of science or learning: *the profession of teaching.* TRADE suggests an occupation involving manual training and skill: *one of the building trades.*

oc·cu·pa·tion·al (ŏk'yə pā'shən əl), *adj.* **1.** of or pertaining to occupation. **2.** of or pertaining to an occupation, trade, or calling: *an occupational disease, occupational guidance.*

occupational therapy, *Med.* a method of treatment consisting of some kind of light work, such as basketry, carpentry, etc., which takes the mind of the patient off himself, and frequently serves to exercise an affected part or to give vocational training.

oc·cu·py (ŏk'yə pī'), *v.*, **-pied, -pying.** —*v.t.* **1.** to take up (space, time, etc.). **2.** to engage or employ (the mind, attention, etc., or the person). **3.** to take possession of (a place), as by invasion. **4.** to hold (a position, office, etc.). **5.** to be resident or established in. —*v.i.* **6.** *Rare or Obs.* to take or hold possession. [ME *occupie(n)*, t. OF: m. *occuper*, t. L: m. *occupāre* take possession of, take up, employ] —**oc'cu·pi'er**, *n.* —Syn. **1-4.** See **have.**

oc·cur (ə kûr'), *v.i.* **-curred, -curring. 1.** to come to pass, take place, or happen. **2.** to be met with or found; present itself; appear. **3.** to suggest itself in thought (commonly fol. by *to*): *an idea occurred to me.* [earlier *occurr*, t. L: s. *occurrere* run against, go up to, meet, befall] —Syn. **1.** See **happen.**

oc·cur·rence (ə kûr'əns), *n.* **1.** the action or fact of occurring. **2.** something that occurs; an event or incident: *a daily occurrence.* —**oc·cur'rent**, *adj.* —Syn. **2.** See **event.**

o·cean (ō'shən), *n.* **1.** the vast body of salt water which covers almost three fourths of the earth's surface. **2.** any of the geographical divisions of this body (commonly given as five: the Atlantic, Pacific, Indian, Arctic, and Antarctic oceans). **3.** a vast expanse or quantity: *an ocean of grass.* [t. L: s. *ōceanus*, t. Gk.: m. *ōkeanós* the ocean, orig. the great stream supposed to encompass the earth (see OCEANUS); r. ME *occean*, t. OF] —**o'cean·like'**, *adj.*

o·cean-gray (ō'shən grā'), *n.*, *adj.* light pearly gray: used by the U.S. Navy for warships in World War II.

O·ce·an·i·a (ō'shĭ ăn'ĭ ə, -ā'nĭ ə), *n.* the islands of the central and S Pacific, including Micronesia, Melanesia, and Polynesia; sometimes also, Australia and the Malay Archipelago. Also, **O·ce·an·i·ca** (ō'shĭ ăn'ə kə). —**O'ce·an'i·an**, *adj.*, *n.*

o·ce·an·ic (ō'shĭ ăn'ĭk), *adj.* **1.** of or belonging to the ocean; pelagic. **2.** oceanlike; vast.

O·ce·a·nid (ō sē'ə nĭd), *n.* *Gk. Myth.* a daughter of Oceanus; an ocean nymph. [t. Gk.: m.s. *Okeanís*]

o·ce·a·nog·ra·phy (ō'shĭ ə nŏg'rə fĭ, ō'shən ŏg'-), *n.* the branch of physical geography dealing with the ocean. —**o'ce·a·nog'ra·pher**, *n.* —**o·ce·a·no·graph·ic** (ō'shĭ ə nə grăf'ĭk, ō'shə nə-), **o'ce·a·no·graph'i·cal**, *adj.* —**o'ce·a·no·graph'i·cal·ly**, *adv.*

O·ce·a·nus (ō sē'ə nəs), *n.* *Gk. Myth.* **1.** the ocean god, and father of the Oceanids. **2.** the great body of water encircling the plain of the earth.

o·cel·lar (ō sĕl'ər), *adj.* pertaining to an ocellus.

oc·el·lat·ed (ŏs'ə lā'tĭd, ō sĕl'ā tĭd), *adj.* **1.** (of a spot or marking) eyelike. **2.** having ocelli, or eyelike spots. Also, **oc·el·late** (ŏs'ə lāt', ō sĕl'ĭt, -āt). [f. s. L *ocellātus* having little eyes + -ED²]

Ocellated marking on feather of peacock

oc·el·la·tion (ŏs'ə lā'shən), *n.* an eyelike spot or marking.

o·cel·lus (ō sĕl'əs), *n.*, *pl.* **ocelli** (ō sĕl'ī). **1.** a type of eye common to invertebrates, consisting of retinal cells, pigments, and nerve fibers. **2.** an eyelike spot, as on a peacock feather. [t. L, dim. of *oculus* eye]

o·ce·lot (ō'sə lŏt', ōs'ə-), *n.* a spotted, leopardlike cat, *Felis pardalis*, some 3 feet in length, ranging from Texas through South America. [t. F, t. Mex.: m. *ocelotl* field tiger]

Ocelot. *Felis pardalis* (Total length 3 ft. or more, tail 1 ft.)

o·cher (ō'kər), *n.*, *adj.*, *v.*, **ochered, ochering.** —*n.* **1.** any of a class of natural earths, mixtures of hydrated oxide of iron with various earthy materials, ranging in color from pale yellow to orange and red, and used as pigments. **2.** *Slang.* money, esp. gold coin. —*adj.* **3.** ranging from a pale-yellow to orange or reddish hue. —*v.t.* **4.** to color or mark with ocher. [ME *oker*, t. OF: m. *ocre*, t. L: m. *ōchra*, t. Gk.: yellow ocher] —**o′cher·ous,** *adj.*

och·loc·ra·cy (ŏk′lŏk′rə sĭ′), *n., pl.* **-cies.** government by the mob; mobocracy; mob rule. [t. Gk.: m.s. *ochlokratía* mob rule] —**och·lo·crat** (ŏk′lə krăt′), *n.* —**och′lo·crat′ic, och·lo·crat′i·cal,** *adj.*

och·one (əкн ōn′), *interj. Irish and Scot.* alas! [t. Irish and Gaelic: m. *ochôin*]

o·chre (ō′kər), *n., adj., v.t.* ochred, ochring. ocher. —**o·chre·ous** (ō′kər əs, ō′krĭ əs), *adj.*

och·re·a (ŏk′rĭ′ə), *n., pl.* **-reae** (-rĭ′ē′). ocrea.

o·chroid (ō′kroid), *adj.* yellow as ocher. [t. Gk.: m.s. *ōchroeidḗs* pallid]

Ochs (ŏks), *n.* **Adolph,** 1858–1935, U.S. newspaper publisher.

-ock, a noun suffix used to make descriptive names, as in *ruddock* (lit., the red one); diminutives, as in *hillock;* etc. [ME *-ok,* OE *-oc, -uc*]

Ock·ham (ŏk′əm), *n.* **William of.** See **Occam.**

o′·clock (ə klŏk′), *of* or by the clock (used in specifying or inquiring the hour of the day): *It is now one o'clock.*

O′Con·nell (ō kŏn′əl), *n.* **Daniel,** 1775–1847, Irish political agitator and orator.

O′Con·nor (ō kŏn′ər), *n.* **Thomas Power,** 1848–1929, Irish journalist, author, and political leader.

o·co·til·lo (ō′kə tē′l̄yō; *Sp.* ō′kō tē′yō), *n., pl.* **-los.** a spiny woody shrub, *Fouqueria splendens,* or candlewood, of arid Mexico and the southwestern U.S. [t. Mex. Sp., dim. of *ocote* kind of pine, t. Aztec: m. *ocotl*]

oc·re·a (ŏk′rĭ′ə, ō′krĭ′ə), *n., pl.* **ocreae** (ŏk′-rĭ′ē′, ō′krĭ′-). *Bot. and Zool.* a sheathing part, as a pair of stipules united about a stem. Also, **ochrea.** [t. L: greave, legging]

oc·re·ate (ŏk′rĭ ĭt, -āt′, ō′krĭ′-), *adj.* having an ocrea or ocreae; sheathed.

Ocrea

oct-, a word element meaning "eight." Also, **octa-.** [t. Gk., comb. form of *oktō*]

Oct., October.

oct., octavo.

oc·tad (ŏk′tăd), *n.* **1.** a group or series of eight. **2.** *Chem.* an element, atom, or radical having a valence of eight. [t. LL: s. *octas,* t. Gk.: m. *oktás*] —**oc·tad′ic,** *adj.*

oc·ta·gon (ŏk′ə gŏn′, -gən), *n.* a polygon having eight angles and eight sides. [t. Gk.: s. *oktágōnos* octangular. See **OCTA-,** **-GON**]

oc·tag·o·nal (ŏk tăg′ə nəl), *adj.* having eight angles and eight sides. —**oc·tag′·o·nal·ly,** *adv.*

oc·ta·he·dral (ŏk′tə hē′drəl), *adj.* having the form of an octahedron.

Octagon

oc·ta·he·drite (ŏk′tə hē′drīt), *n.* anatase.

oc·ta·he·dron (ŏk′tə hē′dran), *n., pl.* **-drons, -dra** (-drə). a solid figure having eight faces. [t. Gk.: m. *oktáedron.* See **OCT-,** **-HEDRON**]

oc·tam·er·ous (ŏk tăm′ər əs), *adj.* **1.** consisting of or divided into eight parts. **2.** *Bot.* (of flowers) having eight members in each whorl. [f. s. Gk. *oktamerḗs* of eight parts + **-OUS**]

Regular octahedrons

oc·tam·e·ter (ŏk tăm′ə tər), *Pros.* —*adj.* **1.** consisting of eight measures or feet. —*n.* **2.** an octameter verse. [t. LL, t. Gk.: m. *oktámetros* of eight measures]

oc·tane (ŏk′tān), *n. Chem.* any of eighteen isomeric saturated hydrocarbons, C_8H_{18}, some of which are obtained in the distillation and cracking of petroleum. [f. OCT- + -ANE]

octane number, (of gasoline) a designation of antiknock quality, numerically equal to the percentage of isooctane (2, 2, 4, trimethyl pentane) by volume in a mixture of isooctane and normal heptane that matches the given gasoline in antiknock characteristics. Also, **octane rating.**

oc·tan·gu·lar (ŏk tăng′gyə lər), *adj.* having eight angles. [f. s. L. *octangulus* eight-angled + -AR¹]

oc·tant (ŏk′tənt), *n.* **1.** the eighth part of a circle. **2.** *Math.* each of the eighths into which three mutually perpendicular planes with a common point divide space. **3.** an instrument having an arc of 45 degrees, used by navigators for measuring angles up to 90°. **4.** the position of one heavenly body when 45 degrees distant from another. [t. L: s. *octans*] —**oc·tan·tal** (ŏk tăn′təl), *adj.*

oc·tar·chy (ŏk′tär kĭ′), *n., pl.* **-chies. 1.** a government by eight persons. **2.** a group of eight states or kingdoms.

oc·tave (ŏk′tĭv, -tāv), *n.* **1.** *Music.* **a.** a tone on the eighth degree from a given tone (counted as the first). **b.** the interval between such tones. **c.** the harmonic combination of such tones. **d.** a series of tones, or of keys of an instrument, extending through this interval. **2.** (in organ building) a stop whose pipes give tones an octave above the normal pitch of the keys used. **3.** a

series or group of eight. **4.** *Pros.* a group or a stanza of eight lines, as the first eight lines of a sonnet. **5.** the eighth of a series. **6.** *Eccles.* **a.** the eighth day from a feast day (counted as the first). **b.** the period of eight days beginning with a feast day. —*adj.* **7.** pitched an octave higher. [ME, t. L: m. *octāva* (fem.) eighth] —**oc·ta·val** (ŏk tā′vəl, ŏk′tə-), *adj.*

Oc·ta·vi·an (ŏk tā′vĭ′ən), *n.* **1.** See **Augustus. 2.** *Brit.* a supporter of Edward VIII, latterly Duke of Windsor.

oc·ta·vo (ŏk tā′vō, -tä′-), *n., pl.* **-vos,** *adj.* —*n.* **1.** a book size (about 6 x 9 inches) determined by printing on sheets folded to form eight leaves or sixteen pages. *Abbr.:* 8vo or 8°. —*adj.* **2.** in octavo. [short for NL phrase *in octāvō* in an eighth (of a sheet)]

oc·ten·ni·al (ŏk těn′ĭ′əl), *adj.* **1.** occurring every eight years. **2.** of or for eight years. [f. s. LL *octennium* a period of eight years + -AL¹] —**oc·ten′ni·al·ly,** *adv.*

oc·tet (ŏk tět′), *n.* **1.** a company of eight singers or players. **2.** a musical composition for eight voices or instruments. **3.** *Pros.* **a.** a group of eight lines of verse. **b.** the first eight lines (octave) of a sonnet. **4.** any group of eight. Also, **oc·tette′.** [f. OCT(o)- + -et as in *duet*]

oc·til·lion (ŏk tĭl′yən), *n.* **1.** a cardinal number represented (in the U.S. and France) by one followed by 27 zeros or (in England and Germany) by one followed by 48 zeros. —*adj.* **2.** amounting to one octillion in number. [t. F: f. *oct-* OCT- + (*m*)*illion* MILLION] —**oc·til′lionth,** *n., adj.*

octo-, a word element meaning "eight." [t. L, Gk., comb. form of L *octo,* Gk. *oktṓ*]

Oc·to·ber (ŏk tō′bər), *n.* **1.** the tenth month of the year, containing 31 days. **2.** *Chiefly Brit.* ale brewed in this month. [ME and OE, t. L: the eighth month of the early Roman year]

oc·to·dec·i·mo (ŏk′tə dĕs′ə mō′), *n., pl.* **-mos,** *adj.* —*n.* **1.** a book size (about 4 x 6¼ inches) determined by printing on sheets folded to form eighteen leaves or thirty-six pages; eighteenmo. *Abbr.:* 18mo or 18°. —*adj.* **2.** in octodecimo. [short for NL phrase *in octōdecimō* in an eighteenth (of a sheet)]

oc·to·ge·nar·i·an (ŏk′tə jə năr′ĭ′ən), *adj.* Also, **oc·tog·e·nar·y** (ŏk tŏj′ə nĕr′ĭ′). **1.** of the age of 80 years. **2.** between 80 and 90 years old. —*n.* **3.** an octogenarian person. [f. s. L *octōgēnārius* containing eighty + -AN]

oc·to·nar·y (ŏk′tə nĕr′ĭ′), *adj., n., pl.* **-naries.** —*adj.* **1.** pertaining to the number eight. **2.** consisting of eight. **3.** proceeding by eights. —*n.* **4.** a group of eight; an ogdoad. **5.** *Pros.* eight lines, as a stanza. [t. L: m.s. *octōnārius* containing eight]

oc·to·pod (ŏk′tə pŏd′), *n.* any of the *Octopoda,* an order or suborder of eight-armed dibranchiate cephalopods that includes the octopuses and paper nautiluses.

oc·to·pus (ŏk′tə pəs), *n., pl.* **-puses, -pi** (-pī′). **1.** any animal of the genus *Octopus,* comprising octopods with a soft, oval body and eight sucker-bearing arms, and living mostly on the sea bottom. **2.** any octopod. **3.** a far-reaching and grasping organization, person, etc. [t. NL, t. Gk.: m. *oktṓpous* eight-footed]

oc·to·roon (ŏk′tə rōōn′), *n.* a person having one-eighth Negro ancestry; offspring of a quadroon and a white. [f. OCTO- + -roon, modeled on QUADROON]

Octopus. *Octopus vulgaris*

oc·to·syl·la·ble (ŏk′tə sĭl′ə bəl), *n.* a word or a line of verse of eight syllables. —**oc·to·syl·lab·ic** (ŏk′tə sĭ-lăb′ĭk), *adj.*

oc·troi (ŏk′troi; *Fr.* ōk trwä′), *n.* **1.** a local tax levied on certain articles, such as foodstuffs, on their admission into a city. **2.** the place at which the tax is collected. **3.** the officials collecting it. [F, der. *octroyer* grant, ult. der. L *auctor* granter, author]

oc·tu·ple (ŏk′tyŏō pəl, -tōō-; ŏk tū′pəl, -tōō′-), *adj., v.,* **-pled, -pling.** —*adj.* **1.** eightfold; eight times as great. **2.** having eight effective units or elements. —*v.t.* **3.** to make eight times as great. [t. L: m.s. *octuplus* eightfold]

oc·u·lar (ŏk′yə lər), *adj.* **1.** of or pertaining to the eye: *ocular movements.* **2.** of the nature of an eye: *an ocular organ.* **3.** performed or perceived by the eye or eyesight. —*n.* **4.** the eyepiece of an optical instrument. [t. LL: s. *oculāris* of the eyes] —**oc′u·lar·ly,** *adv.*

oc·u·list (ŏk′yə lĭst), *n.* a doctor of medicine skilled in the examination and treatment of the eye; an ophthalmologist. [t. F: m. *oculiste,* f. s. L *oculus* eye + *-iste* -IST]

oc·u·lo·mo·tor (ŏk′yə lō mō′tər), *adj.* moving the eyeball. [f. *oculo-* (comb. form repr. L *oculus* eye) + MOTOR]

oculomotor nerve, *Anat.* either of the two cranial nerves which supply most of the muscles of the eyeball.

od (ŏd, ōd), *n.* a hypothetical force formerly held to pervade all nature and to manifest itself in magnetism, mesmerism, chemical action, etc. Also, **odyl, odyle.** [arbitrary name coined by Baron Karl von Reichenbach (1788–1869)]

Od (ŏd), *interj. Archaic or Dial.* reduced form of **God,** used interjectionally and in minced oaths. Also, **′Od, Odd.**

O.D., 1. Officer of the Day. 2. (of military uniform) olive drab. 3. overdraft. 4. overdrawn.

o·da·lisque (ō′dəlĭsk), *n.* a female slave in a harem, esp. in that of the Sultan of Turkey. Also, **o′da·lisk.** [t. F, t. Turk.: m. *ōdalik,* der. *ōdah* room]

odd (ŏd), *adj.* 1. differing in character from what is ordinary or usual: *an odd choice.* 2. singular or peculiar in a freakish or eccentric way, as persons or their manners, etc. 3. fantastic or bizarre, as things. 4. out-of-the-way; secluded. 5. additional to a whole mentioned in round numbers; being a surplus over a definite quantity. 6. additional to what is taken into account. 7. surplus of a lower denomination: *two dollars and some odd cents.* 8. being part of a pair, set, or series of which the rest is lacking: *an odd glove.* 9. leaving a remainder of 1 when divided by 2, as a number (opposed to *even*). 10. remaining after a division into pairs, or into equal numbers or parts. 11. occasional or casual: *odd jobs.* 12. not forming part of any particular group, set, or class: *odd bits of information.* —*n.* 13. that which is odd. 14. *Golf.* a. a stroke more than the opponent has played. b. *Brit.* a stroke taken from a player's total score for a hole in order to give him odds. 15. (*pl.*) odd things, bits, or scraps: *odds and ends.* ee also **odds.** [ME *odde,* t. Scand.; cf. Icel. *odda-tala* odd number] —**odd′ly,** *adv.* —**odd′ness,** *n.* —Syn. 1. See **strange.**

Odd·fel·low (ŏd′fĕl′ō), *n.* a member of a secret social and benevolent society "Independent Order of Oddfellows," originated in England in the 18th century.

odd·ish (ŏd′ĭsh), *adj.* rather odd; queer.

odd·i·ty (ŏd′ə tĭ), *n., pl.* **-ties.** 1. the quality of being odd; singularity or strangeness. 2. an odd characteristic or peculiarity. 3. an odd person or thing.

odd·ment (ŏd′mənt), *n.* 1. an odd article, bit, remnant, or the like. 2. an article belonging to a broken or incomplete set. 3. *Print.* any individual portion of a book excluding the text, as the frontispiece, index, etc.

odd-pin·nate (ŏd′pĭn′āt, -ĭt), *adj. Bot.* pinnate with an odd terminal leaflet.

odds (ŏdz). *n.pl. and sing.* 1. an equalizing allowance, as that given to a weaker side in a contest. 2. the amount by which the bet of one party to a wager exceeds that of the other. 3. balance of probability in favor of something occurring or being the case. 4. advantage or superiority on the side of one of two contending parties: *to strive against odds.* 5. difference in the way of benefit or detriment. 6. the amount of difference. 7. disagreement or strife (chiefly in *at odds*).

ode (ōd), *n.* 1. a lyric poem typically of elaborate or irregular metrical form and expressive of exalted or enthusiastic emotion. 2. (*orig.*) a poem intended to be sung. 3. **regular or Pindaric ode,** a complex poetic type, consisting of strophes and antistrophes identical in form, with contrasting epodes, the three units being repeated in the poem. 4. **irregular, pseudo-Pindaric, or Cowleian ode,** a poetic form in the general style of the regular ode, but lacking its strict complex form and written in a series of irregular strophes. 5. **Horatian or Sapphic ode,** an ode in which one stanzaic form is repeated. [t. F, t. LL: m. *ōda,* t. Gk.: m. *ōidē,* contr. of *aoidē* song]

-ode[1] a suffix of nouns denoting something having some resemblance to what is indicated by the preceding part of the word, as in *phyllode,* as in *phyllode.* [t. Gk.: m. *-ōdēs* like, contr. of *-oeidēs* -OID]

-ode[2] a noun suffix meaning "way," as in *anode, electrode.* [t. Gk.: m. *-odos,* der. *hodós* way]

O·deis·thing (ō′dəlstĭng′), *n.* See **Storthing.**

O·den·se (ō′ᵗhən sä), *n.* a seaport in S Denmark, on Fyn island. 104,344 (est. 1954).

O·der (ō′dər), *n.* a river flowing from the Carpathians in N Czechoslovakia through SW Poland and along the East German-Polish border into the Baltic. ab. 550 mi.

O·der-Neis·se Line (ō′dər nĭs′e), present boundary between Poland and East Germany. See **Germany.**

O·des·sa (ō dĕs′ə; *Russ.* ô dĕ′sä), *n.* 1. a seaport in the SW Soviet Union, on the Black Sea: the principal export center of Ukrainian grain. 607,000 (est. 1956). 2. a city in W Texas. 80,338 (1960).

O·dets (ō dĕts′), *n.* **Clifford,** 1906–1963, U.S. dramatist.

o·de·um (ō dē′əm), *n., pl.* **odea** (ō dē′ə). 1. a hall or structure for musical or dramatic performances. 2. (in ancient Greece and Rome) a roofed building for musical performances. [t. L, t. Gk.: m. *ōideion* music hall]

od·ic[1] (ō′dĭk), *adj.* of an ode. [f. ODE + -IC]

od·ic[2] (ŏd′ĭk, ō′dĭk), *adj.* of or pertaining to the hypothetical force od. [f. OD + -IC]

O·din (ō′dĭn), *n. Scand. Myth.* the chief deity, being the god of wisdom, culture, war, and the dead. Also, **Othin.** [t. Icel.: m. *Odhinn,* c. E *Woden,* G *Wotan*]

o·di·ous (ō′dĭ əs), *adj.* 1. deserving of or exciting hatred; hateful or detestable. 2. highly offensive; disgusting. [ME, t. L: m.s. *odiōsus* hateful] —**o′di·ous·ly,** *adv.* —**o′di·ous·ness,** *n.* —Syn. 1. See **hateful.**

o·di·um (ō′dĭ əm), *n.* 1. hatred; dislike. 2. the reproach, discredit, or opprobrium attaching to something hated or odious. 3. state of being hated. [t. L: hatred]

O·do·a·cer (ō′dō ā′sər), *n.* A.D. 434?–493, first barbarian ruler of Italy, A.D. 476–493. Also, **Odovacar.**

o·do·graph (ō′də grăf′, -gräf′), *n.* 1. an odometer. 2. a pedometer. [var. of *hodograph,* f. Gk. *hodó(s)* way + -GRAPH]

o·dom·e·ter (ō dŏm′ə tər), *n.* an instrument for measuring distance passed over, as by an auto. [prop. *hodometer,* f. Gk. *hodó(s)* way +-METER] —**o·dom′e·try,** *n.*

odont-, a word element meaning "tooth." Also, **odonto-.** [t. Gk., comb. form of *odoús*]

-odont, terminal word element equivalent to **odont-.**

o·don·tal·gi·a (ō′dŏn tăl′jĭ ə), *n. Pathol.* toothache. —**o/don·tal′gic,** *adj.*

o·don·to·blast (ō dŏn′tə blăst′), *n. Anat.* one of a layer of cells which, in the development of a tooth, give rise to the dentin. —**o·don/to·blas′tic,** *adj.*

o·don·to·glos·sum (ō dŏn′tə glŏs′əm), *n.* any of the epiphytic orchids constituting the genus *Odontoglossum,* natives of the mountainous region from Bolivia to Mexico. [t. NL, f. Gk.: *odonto-* ODONTO- + m. *glōssa* tongue]

o·don·to·graph (ō dŏn′tə grăf′, -gräf′), *n.* an instrument for laying out the forms of geared teeth or ratchets.

o·don·toid (ō dŏn′toid), *adj.* 1. noting a toothlike process, as that of the axis, or second cervical vertebra, upon which the atlas rotates. 2. resembling a tooth. [t. Gk.: m.s. *odontoeidēs* toothlike]

o·don·tol·o·gy (ō′dŏn tŏl′ə jĭ, ŏd′ŏn-), *n.* 1. the science or art which treats of the study of the teeth and their surrounding tissues, and of the prevention and cure of their diseases. 2. dentistry. —**o·don·to·log·i·cal** (ō dŏn′tə lŏj′ə kəl), *adj.* —**o/don·tol/o·gist,** *n.*

o·don·to·phore (ō dŏn′tə fōr′), *n. Zool.* a structure in the mouth of most mollusks, over which the radula is drawn backward and forward in the process of breaking up food. [t. Gk.: m.s. *odontophóros* bearing teeth] —**o·don·toph·o·ral** (ō′dŏn tŏf′ə rəl), **o·don·toph·o·rine** (ō′dŏn tŏf′ə rīn′, -rĭn), or **o·don·toph′o·rous,** *adj.*

o·dor (ō′dər), *n.* 1. that property of a substance which affects the sense of smell: *rank odors.* 2. agreeable scent; fragrance. 3. savor characteristic or suggestive of something. 4. repute or estimation: *in ill odor.* Also, *Brit.,* **o′dour.** [ME, t. OF, t. L] —**o/dor·less,** *adj.*

o·dor·if·er·ous (ō′də rĭf′ər əs), *adj.* yielding or diffusing an odor, esp. a fragrant one. [ME, f. L *odorifer* bringing odors +-OUS] —**o/dor·if/er·ous·ly,** *adv.* —**o/dor·if/er·ous·ness,** *n.*

o·dor·ous (ō′dər əs), *adj.* having or diffusing an odor, esp. a fragrant odor. [t. L: m. *odōrus* emitting a scent] —**o/dor·ous·ly,** *adv.* —**o/dor·ous·ness,** *n.*

O·do·va·car (ō′dō vā′kər), *n.* Odoacer.

od·yl (ŏd′ĭl, ō′dĭl), *n.* od. Also, **od′yle.** [f. OD + -YL] —**o·dyl·ic** (ō dĭl′ĭk), *adj.*

-odynia, word element meaning "pain." [t. NL, t. Gk.]

O·dys·seus (ō dĭs′ūs, ō dĭs′Ĭ əs), *n. Gk. Legend.* the son of Laertes, husband of Penelope, and father of Telemachus: wisest and wiliest of the Greek leaders. Latin, **Ulysses.**

Od·ys·sey (ŏd′ə sĭ), *n.* 1. Homer's epic poem describing the ten years' wandering of Odysseus in returning to Ithaca after the Trojan War. 2. (*also l.c.*) any long series of wanderings. [t. Gk.: m.s. *Odýsseia,* der. *Odysseús* Odysseus, Ulysses] —**Od·ys·se·an** (ŏd′ə sē′ən), *adj.*

OE, Old English. Also, **OE., O.E.**

oec·u·men·i·cal (ĕk′yŏō mĕn′ə kəl or, *esp. Brit.,* ē′kyŏō-), *adj.* ecumenical. Also, **oec/u·men/ic.**

O.E.D., Oxford English Dictionary.

Oed·i·pus (ĕd′ə pəs, ē′də-), *n. Gk. Legend.* a son of Laius and Jocasta. Reared by the king of Corinth, he slew his father involuntarily and solved the riddle of the Sphinx, thereby becoming King of Thebes and unwittingly winning the hand of his mother in marriage. When the nature of his deeds became apparent, Jocasta hanged herself, and Oedipus tore out his eyes.

Oedipus complex, *Psychoanal.* 1. the unresolved desire of a child for sexual gratification through the parent of the opposite sex. This involves, first, identification with and, later, hatred for the parent of the same sex, who is considered by the child as a rival. 2. sexual desire of the son for the mother. Cf. **Electra complex.**

oeil-de-boeuf (œ′y də bœf′), *n., pl.* **oeils-de-boeuf** (œ′y də-). *French.* a comparatively small round or oval window, as in a frieze. [F: eye of ox, bull's eye]

oeil·lade (œ yäd′), *n. French.* an amorous glance; ogle. [t. It.: m. *occhiata* glance (der. *occhio* eye, g. L *oculus*)]

oe·nol·o·gy (ē nŏl′ə jĭ), *n.* the science of viniculture. [f. m. Gk. *oíno(s)* wine + -LOGY] —**oe·no·log·i·cal** (ē′nə lŏj′ə kəl), *adj.* —**oe·nol/o·gist,** *n.*

oe·no·mel (ē′nə mĕl′, ĕn′ə-), *n.* 1. a drink made of wine mixed with honey. 2. something combining strength with sweetness. [t. LL: s. *oenomeli,* t. Gk.: m. *oinómeli* wine mixed with honey]

Oe·no·ne (ē nō′nĭ), *n. Gk. Myth.* a nymph living on Mount Ida near Troy. She was the lover of Paris, who later deserted her for Helen.

o'er (ōr), *prep., adv.* Poetic or Dial. over.

oer·sted (ûr′stĕd), *n.* 1. a unit of magnetic intensity equal to the intensity produced by a magnetic pole of unit strength at a distance of one centimeter. 2. *Obs.* the unit of magnetic reluctance equal to the reluctance of a centimeter cube of vacuum between parallel surfaces. [f. H. C. *Oersted* (1777–1851), Danish physicist]

oe·soph·a·gus (ē sŏf′ə gəs), *n., pl.* **-gi** (-jī′). esophagus. —**oe·so·phag·e·al** (ē′sə făj′Ĭ əl), *adj.*

oes·trin (ĕs′trĭn, ēs′trĭn), *n. Biochem.* estrone.

oes·tri·ol (ĕs′trĭ ōl′, -ōl, ēs′trĭ-), *n.* estriol.

oes·tro·gen (ĕs′trə jən, ēs′trə-), *n.* estrogen.

oes·trous (ĕs′trəs, ēs′trəs), *adj.* estrous.

oestrous cycle, estrous cycle.

oes·trus (ĕs′trəs, ēs′trəs), *n.* 1. Also, **oes′trum.** estrus. 2. passion or passionate impulse. 3. a stimulus. [t. L, t. Gk.: m. *oîstros* gadfly, sting, frenzy]

oeu·vre (œ′vr), *n., pl.* **oeuvres** (œ′vr). *French.* work.

of (ŏv, ŭv; *unstressed* əv), *prep.* a particle indicating: 1. distance or direction from, separation, deprivation, riddance, etc.: *within a mile of, to cure of.* 2. derivation, origin, or source: *of good family, the plays of O'Neill.* 3. cause, occasion, or reason: *to die of hunger.* 4. material or substance: *a pound of sugar.* 5. a relation of identity: *the city of Paris.* 6. belonging or possession, connection, or association: *the property of all.* 7. inclusion in a number, class, or whole: *one of us.* 8. objective relation: *the ringing of bells.* 9. reference or respect: *talk of peace.* 10. qualities or attributes: *a man of tact.* 11. time: *of an evening.* 12. to or before (a designated hour of the clock): *twenty minutes of five.* 13. *Chiefly Archaic.* the agent by whom something is done: *beloved of all.* [ME and OE, c. G and L *ab*, Gk. *apó*. See OFF]

Of-, var. of ob-, (by assimilation) before *f*, as in *offend.*

OF, Old French. Also, **OF., O.F.**

off (ôf, ŏf), *adv.* 1. away from a position occupied, or from contact, connection, or attachment: *take off one's hat.* 2. to or at a distance from, or away from, a place: *to run off.* 3. away from or out of association or relation: *to cast off a son.* 4. deviating from, especially from what is normal or regular. 5. as a deduction: *10 percent off on all cash purchases.* 6. away; distant (in future time): *summer is only a week off.* 7. out of operation or effective existence. 8. so as to interrupt continuity or cause discontinuance: *to break off negotiations.* 9. away from employment or service: *to lay off workmen.* 10. so as to exhaust, finish, or complete; completely: *to kill off vermin.* 11. forthwith or immediately: *right off.* 12. with prompt or ready performance: *to dash off a letter.* 13. to fulfillment, or into execution or effect: *the contest came off on the day fixed.* 14. so as to cause or undergo reduction or diminution: *to wear off.* 15. on one's way or journey, as from a place: *to see a friend off on a journey.* 16. *Naut.* away from the land, a ship, the wind, etc. 17. **be or take off,** to depart; leave. 18. **off and on, a.** intermittently: *to work off and on.* **b.** *Naut.* on alternate tacks. 19. **off with** (anything specified), to remove; take or cut off: *off with his head.* —*prep.* 20. away from; so as no longer to be or rest on: *to fall off a horse.* 21. deviating from (something normal or usual): *off one's balance.* 22. from by subtraction or deduction: *25 percent off the marked price.* 23. away or disengaged from (duty, work, etc.). 24. *Slang.* refraining from (some food, activity, etc.): *to be off gambling.* 25. distant from: *a village some miles off the main road.* 26. leading out of: *an alley off 12th Street.* 27. *U.S. Colloq.* from, indicating source: *I bought it off him.* 28. from, indicating material: *to make a meal of fish.* 29. *Naut.* to seaward of. —*adj.* 30. *Now Colloq.* wide of the truth or fact; in error: *you are off on that point.* 31. no longer in contemplation: *the agreement is off.* 32. as to condition, circumstances, supplies, etc.: *better off.* 33. (of time) on which work is suspended: *pastime for one's off hours.* 34. not so good or satisfactory as usual: *an off year for apples.* 35. of less than the ordinary activity, liveliness, or lively interest: *an off season in the woolen trade.* 36. (of a chance) remote. 37. more distant; farther: *the off side of a wall.* 38. (with reference to animals or vehicles) right (opposed to *near* or *left*). 39. *Naut.* farther from the shore. 40. *Cricket.* noting that side of the wicket or of the field opposite which the batsman stands. —*n.* 41. state or fact of being off. 42. *Cricket.* the off side. —*interj.* 43. be off! stand off! off with you! [ME and OE of of, off. See OF]

off., 1. offered. 2. office. 3. officer. 4. official.

of·fal (ôf′əl, ŏf′əl), *n.* 1. the waste parts of a butchered animal, or the inedible portions of food animals, fowl, and fish. 2. refuse in general. [ME, f. of off + *fal* fall]

off·beat (ôf′bēt′), *adj. U.S. Slang.* unusual; unexpected.

off·cast (ôf′kăst′, -käst′, ŏf′-), *adj.* 1. castoff; rejected. —*n.* 2. a castoff person or thing.

off-chance (ôf′chăns′, -chäns′, ŏf′-), *n.* a remote chance or possibility.

off-col·or (ôf′kŭl′ər, ŏf′-), *adj.* 1. defective in color, as a gem. 2. of doubtful propriety: *an off-color story.* Also, *Brit.,* **off′-col′our.**

Of·fen·bach (ôf′ən bäk′, ŏf′-; *also Fr.* ô fĕn bȧk′ *for 1; Ger.* ôf′ən bäκʜ′ *for 2*), *n.* 1. **Jacques** (zhȧk), 1819–80, French composer. 2. a city in central West Germany, on the Main river, near Frankfurt. 104,372 (est. 1955).

of·fend (ə fĕnd′), *v. t.* 1. to irritate in mind or feelings; cause resentful displeasure in. 2. to affect (the sense, taste, etc.) disagreeably. 3. *Obs.* to violate or transgress. 4. *Obs.* (in Biblical use) to cause to sin. —*v.i.* 5. to give offense or cause displeasure. 6. to err in conduct; commit a sin, crime, or fault. [ME *offende(n)*, t. OF: m. *offendre*, t. L: m. *offendere* strike against, displease] —*of·fend′er,* n. —**Syn. 1.** provoke, insult.

of·fense (ə fĕns′), *n.* 1. a transgression; a wrong; a sin. 2. a transgression of law which is not indictable, but is punishable summarily or by the forfeiture of a penalty (**petty offense**). 3. a cause of transgression or wrong. 4. something that offends. 5. act of offending or displeasing. 6. the feeling of resentful displeasure caused

to give offense. 7. act of attacking; attack or assault: *weapons of offense.* 8. the persons, side, etc., attacking. 9. *Obs.* injury, harm, or hurt. Also, *esp. Brit.,* **of·fence′.** [ME *offens,* t. L: s. *offensus*] —**Syn. 1.** See **crime.**

of·fense·less (ə fĕns′lĭs), *adj.* · 1. without offense. 2. incapable of offense or attack. 3. unoffending.

of·fen·sive (ə fĕn′sĭv), *adj.* 1. causing offense or displeasure; irritating; highly annoying. 2. disagreeable to the sense: *an offensive odor.* 3. repugnant to the moral sense, good taste, or the like; insulting. 4. pertaining to offense or attack: *offensive movements.* 5. consisting in or characterized by attack: *offensive warfare.* —*n.* 6. the position or attitude of offense or attack: *to take the offensive.* 7. an offensive movement: *the big Russian offensive.* —**of·fen′sive·ly,** *adv.* —**of·fen′sive·ness,** *n.* —**Syn. 1.** See **hateful.** 2. disagreeable, distasteful, disgusting, repulsive, obnoxious. —**Ant. 1, 2.** pleasing.

of·fer (ôf′ər, ŏf′ər), *v.t.* 1. to present for acceptance or rejection; proffer: *to offer someone a cigarette.* 2. to put forward for consideration: *to offer a suggestion.* 3. to make a show of intention (to do something): *we did not offer to go first.* 4. to propose or volunteer (to do something): *she offered to accompany me.* 5. to proffer (oneself) for marriage. 6. to present solemnly as an act of worship or devotion, as to God, a deity, a saint, etc.; sacrifice. 7. to present; put forward: *she offered no response.* 8. to attempt to inflict, do, or make: *to offer battle.* 9. to do or make (violence, resistance, etc.) actually. 10. to present to sight or notice. 11. to present for sale. 12. to tender or bid as a price: *to offer ten dollars for a radio.* 13. to render (homage, thanks, etc.). —*v.i.* 14. to make an offer. 15. to make an offer of marriage; propose. 16. to present itself; occur: *whenever an occasion offered.* 17. to make an offering as an act of worship or devotion; sacrifice. 18. *Obs. or Rare.* to make an attempt (fol. by *at*). —*n.* 19. act of offering: *an offer of assistance.* 20. a proposal of marriage. 21. a proposal to give or accept something as a price or equivalent for something else; a bid: *an offer of $10,000 for a house.* 22. the condition of being offered: *an offer for sale.* 23. something offered. 24. *Law.* a proposal which requires only acceptance in order to create a contract. 25. an attempt or endeavor. 26. a show of intention. [ME *offre(n),* OE *offrian,* t. L: m. *offerre*] —**of′fer·er, of′fer·or,** *n.*

—**Syn. 1.** OFFER, PROFFER, TENDER mean to present for acceptance or refusal. OFFER is a common word in general use for presenting something to be accepted or rejected: *to offer assistance.* PROFFER, with the same meaning, is now chiefly a literary word: *to proffer one's services.* TENDER (no longer used in reference to concrete objects) is a ceremonious term for a more or less formal or conventional act: *to tender one's resignation.* —**Ant. 1.** withdraw, withhold.

of·fer·ing (ôf′ər Ĭng, ŏf′ər-), *n.* 1. something offered in worship or devotion, as to God, a deity, etc.; an oblation; a sacrifice. 2. a contribution given to or through the church for a particular purpose, as at a service. 3. anything offered; gift. 4. act of one who offers.

of·fer·to·ry (ôf′ər tōr′Ĭ, ŏf′ər-), *n., pl.* **-ries.** 1. *Rom. Cath. Ch.* the oblation of the unconsecrated elements made by the celebrant at this part of the Mass. 2. *Eccles.* **a.** the verses, anthem, or music said, sung, or played while the offerings of the people are received at a religious service. **b.** that part of a service at which offerings are made. **c.** the offerings themselves. [ME *offertorie,* t. LL: m. *offertōrium* place to which offerings were brought, offering, oblation]

off·hand (ôf′hănd′, ŏf′-), *adv.* 1. without previous thought or preparation; extempore: *to decide offhand.* 2. cavalier, curt, or brusque. —*adj.* Also, **off′hand′ed.** 3. done or made offhand. 4. informal or casual.

of·fice (ôf′Ĭs, ŏf′Ĭs), *n.* 1. a room or place for the transaction of business, the discharge of professional duties, or the like: *the doctor's office.* 2. the room or rooms in which the clerical work of an industrial or other establishment is done. 3. the staff or body of persons carrying on work in a business or other office. 4. a building or a set of rooms devoted to the business of a branch of a governmental organization: *the post office.* 5. the body of persons occupying governmental offices. 6. a position of duty, trust, or authority, esp. in the public services, or in some corporation, society, or the like. 7. the duty, function, or part of a particular person or agency: *the office of adviser.* 8. official employment or position: *to seek office.* 9. a service or task to be performed: *little domestic offices.* 10. *Slang.* (prec. by *the*) hint or signal. 11. something (good, or occasionally bad) done for another. 12. *Eccles.* **a.** the prescribed order or form for a service of the church, or for devotional use, or the services so prescribed. **b.** the prayers, readings from Scripture, and psalms that must be recited every day by all who are in major orders. **c.** a ceremony or rite, esp. for the dead. 13. (*pl.*) *Chiefly Brit.* the parts of a house, as the kitchen, pantry, laundry, etc., devoted to household work. 14. *Chiefly Brit.* the stables, barns, cowhouses, etc., of a farm. [ME, t. OF, t. L: m.s. *officium* service, duty, ceremony] —**Syn. 8.** See **appointment.**

office boy, a boy employed in an office for errands, etc.

of·fice·hold·er (ôf′Ĭs hōl′dər, ŏf′Ĭs-), *n.* a person filling a governmental position.

office hours, 1. the hours a person spends working in an office. 2. the hours during which a professional man or an office conducts regular business.

of·fi·cer (ŏf'ə sər, ŏf'ə-), *n.* **1.** one who holds a position of rank or authority in the army, navy, or any similar organization, esp. one who holds a commission in the army or navy. **2.** a policeman or constable. **3.** the master or captain of a merchant vessel or pleasure vessel, or any of his chief assistants. **4.** a person appointed or elected to some position of responsibility and authority in the public service, or in some corporation, society, or the like. **5.** (in some honorary orders) a member of higher rank than the lowest. **6.** *Obs.* an agent. —*v.t.* **7.** to furnish with officers. **8.** to command or direct as an officer does. **9.** to direct, conduct, or manage. [ME, t. OF: m. *officier*, t. ML: m.s. *officiārius*, der. L *officium* office]

officer of the day, *Mil.* an officer who has charge, for the day, of the guard and prisoners of a military force or camp.

officer of the guard, an officer, acting under the officer of the day, who is responsible for the instruction, discipline, and performance of duty of the guard in a post, camp, or station.

office seeker, one who seeks public office.

of·fi·cial (ə fĭsh'əl), *n.* **1.** one who holds an office or is charged with some form of official duty: *police officials.* —*adj.* **2.** of or pertaining to an office or position of duty, trust, or authority: *official powers.* **3.** authorized or issued authoritatively: *an official report.* **4.** holding office. **5.** appointed or authorized to act in a special capacity: *an official representative.* **6.** formal or ceremonious: *an official dinner.* **7.** *Pharm.* authorized by the pharmacopoeia. [t. LL: s. *officiālis*, der. L *officium* office] —**of·fi'cial·ly,** *adv.*

of·fi·cial·dom (ə fĭsh'əl dəm), *n.* **1.** the position or domain of officials. **2.** the official class.

of·fi·cial·ism (ə fĭsh'əl ĭz'əm), *n.* **1.** official methods or system. **2.** excessive attention to official routine. **3.** officials collectively.

of·fi·ci·ant (ə fĭsh'ī ənt), *n.* one who officiates at a religious service or ceremony. [t. ML: s. *officians*, ppr. of *officiāre* OFFICIATE]

of·fi·ci·ar·y (ə fĭsh'ī ĕr'ī), *adj.* **1.** pertaining to or derived from an office, as a title. **2.** having a title or rank derived from an office, as a dignitary.

of·fi·ci·ate (ə fĭsh'ī āt'), *v.i.,* **-ated, -ating. 1.** to perform the duties of any office or position. **2.** to perform the office of a priest or minister, as at divine worship. [t. ML: m.s. *officiātus*, pp. of *officiāre*, der. L *officium* office] —**of·fi'ci·a'tion,** *n.* —**of·fi'ci·a'tor,** *n.*

of·fic·i·nal (ə fĭs'ə nəl), *adj.* **1.** kept in stock by apothecaries, as a drug. Cf. **magistral. 2.** recognized by the pharmacopoeia. —*n.* **3.** an officinal medicine. [t. ML: s. *officinālis*, der. L *officina* workshop, laboratory]

of·fi·cious (ə fĭsh'əs), *adj.* **1.** forward in tendering or obtruding one's services upon others. **2.** marked by or proceeding from such forwardness: *officious interference.* **3.** *Obs.* ready to serve. [t. L: m.s. *officiōsus* obliging, dutiful] —**of·fi'cious·ly,** *adv.* —**of·fi'cious·ness,** *n.*

off·ing (ŏf'ĭng, ôf'ĭng), *n.* **1.** the more distant part of the sea as seen from the shore, beyond the anchoring ground. **2.** position at a distance from the shore. **3. in the offing, a.** not very distant. **b.** close enough to be seen. **c.** ready or likely to happen, appear, etc.

off·ish (ŏf'ĭsh, ôf'ĭsh), *adj. Colloq.* aloof. —**off'ish·ness,** *n.*

off·print (ŏf'prĭnt', ôf'-), *n.* **1.** a reprint in separate form of an article which originally appeared as part of a larger publication. —*v.t.* **2.** to reprint separately, as an article from a larger publication.

off·scour·ing (ŏf'skour'ĭng, ôf'-), *n.* (often *pl.*) that which is scoured off; filth; refuse.

off·set (*v.* ŏf'sĕt', ôf'-; *n., adj.* ŏf'sĕt', ôf'-), *v.,* **-set, -setting,** *n., adj.* —*v.t.* **1.** to balance by something else as an equivalent: *to offset one thing by another.* **2.** to counterbalance as an equivalent does; compensate for: *the gains offset the losses.* **3.** *Print.* **a.** to make an offset of. **b.** to print by the process of offset lithography. **4.** *Archit.* to build with a setoff, as a wall. —*v.i.* **5.** to project as an offset or branch. **6.** *Print.* to make an offset. —*n.* **7.** something that offsets or counterbalances; a compensating equivalent. **8.** the start or outset. **9.** a short lateral shoot by which certain plants are propagated. **10.** any offshoot; branch. **11.** an offshoot from a family or race. **12.** a spur of a mountain range. **13.** *Lithog.* an impression from an inked design or the like on a lithographic stone or metal plate, made on another surface, as a rubber blanket, and then transferred to paper, instead of being made directly on the paper. **14.** *Print.* a faulty transfer of superabundant or undried ink on a printed sheet to any opposed surface, as the opposite page. **15.** *Mach.* a more or less abrupt bend in a pipe, bar, rod, or the like, to serve some particular purpose. **16.** *Archit.* a setoff. **17.** *Survey.* a short distance measured perpendicularly from a line. —*adj.* **18.** *Lithog.* pertaining to, or printed by, offset.

off·shoot (ŏf'shoot', ôf'-), *n.* **1.** a shoot from a main stem, as of a plant; a lateral shoot. **2.** a branch, or a descendant or scion, of a family or race. **3.** anything conceived as springing or proceeding from a main stock: *an offshoot of a mountain range, a railroad, etc.*

off·shore (ŏf'shōr', ôf'-), *adv.* **1.** off or away from the shore. **2.** at a distance from the shore. —*adj.* **3.** moving or tending away from the shore: *an offshore wind.* **4.** being or operating at a distance from the shore: *offshore fisheries or fishermen.*

off·side (ŏf'sīd', ôf'-), *adj. Football, Hockey, etc.* **1.** away from one's own or the proper side, as of the ball or of a player who last played or touched it (a position subject to restrictions or penalties in particular cases). **2.** being or done offside: *an offside play.*

off·spring (ŏf'sprĭng', ôf'-), *n.* **1.** children or young sprung from a particular parent or progenitor. **2.** a child or animal in relation to its parent or parents. **3.** a descendant. **4.** descendants collectively. **5.** the product, result, or effect of something: *the offspring of delirium.* [ME and OE *ofspring.* See OFF, SPRING, v.]

off·stage (ŏf'stāj', ôf'-), *adj.* not in view of the audience; backstage, in the wings, etc.

off·white (ŏf'hwīt', ôf'-), *adj.* white with a slight touch of gray in it.

Of Human Bondage, a novel (1915) by W. Somerset Maugham.

O'Fla·her·ty (ō flä'hər tĭ), *n.* **Liam** (lē'əm), born 1896, Irish novelist.

O.F.M., (L *Ordo Fratrum Minorum*) Order of Friars Minor (Franciscan).

oft (ŏft, ôft), *adv. Chiefly Poetic.* often; frequently. [ME *oft(e)*, OE *oft,* c. G *oft*]

of·ten (ŏf'ən, ôf'ən), *adv.* **1.** many times; frequently. **2.** in many cases. —*adj.* **3.** *Archaic.* frequent. [ME *oftin,* var. (before vowels) of *ofte* OFT] —**Syn. 1, 2.** OFTEN, FREQUENTLY, GENERALLY, USUALLY refer to experiences which are customary. OFTEN and FREQUENTLY may be used interchangeably in most cases, but OFTEN implies numerous repetitions and, sometimes, regularity of recurrence (*we often go there*); FREQUENTLY suggests esp. repetition at comparatively short intervals: *it happens frequently.* GENERALLY refers to place and means "universally" (*it is generally understood; he is generally liked*), but is often used as a colloquial substitute for USUALLY. In this sense, GENERALLY, like USUALLY, refers to time, and means "in numerous instances." GENERALLY, however, extends in range from the merely numerous to a majority of possible instances; whereas USUALLY means "practically always": *the train is generally on time, we usually have hot summers.* —**Ant. 1.** seldom.

of·ten·times (ŏf'ən tĭmz', ôf'ən-), *adv. Archaic.* often. Also, **oft'times'.**

O.G., Officer of the Guard.

o.g., *Philately.* a stamp with original gum; a mint stamp (having gum as issued by the post office).

O·ga·sa·wa·ra Ji·ma (ō'gä sä wä'rä jē'mä), Japanese name of the **Bonin Islands.**

Og·den (ŏg'dən), *n.* a city in N Utah. 70,197 (1960).

og·do·ad (ŏg'dō ăd'), *n.* **1.** the number eight. **2.** group of eight. [t. LL: s. *ogdoas,* t. Gk.: the number eight]

o·gee (ō jē', ō'jē), *n.* **1.** a double curve (like the letter S) formed by the union of a concave and a convex line. **2.** *Archit., etc.* a molding with such a curve for a profile; a cyma. [var. of OGIVE]

ogee arch, *Archit.* a form of pointed arch, each side of which has the curve of an ogee.

O·gil·vie (ō'gəl vĭ), *n.* **John,** 1797–1867, Scottish lexicographer.

o·give (ō'jĭv, ō jīv'), *n. Archit.* **1.** a diagonal groin or rib of a vault. **2.** a pointed arch. **3.** *Statistics.* a curve such that the ordinate for any given value of the abscissa represents the frequency or relative frequency of values of the ordinate less than or equal to the given value. [ME, t. F, also formerly *augive*; orig. uncert.] —**o·gi'val,** *adj.*

Ogee arch
A, Convex curve;
B, Concave curve

o·gle (ō'gəl), *v.,* **ogled, ogling,** *n.* —*v.t.* **1.** to eye with amorous, ingratiating, or impertinently familiar glances. **2.** to eye; look at. —*v.i.* **3.** to cast amorous, ingratiating, or impertinently familiar glances. —*n.* **4.** an ogling glance. [appar. from a freq. (cf. LG *oegeln,* G *äugeln*) of D *oogen* to eye, der. *oog* the eye] —**o'gler,** *n.*

O·gle·thorpe (ō'gəl thôrp'), *n.* **James Edward,** 1696–1785, British general, founder of the colony of Georgia.

Og·pu (ŏg'poō), *n.* Gay-Pay-Oo.

o·gre (ō'gər), *n.* **1.** a monster, commonly represented as a hideous giant, of fairy tales and popular legends, supposed to live on human flesh. **2.** a person likened to such a monster. [t. F] —**o·gre·ish** (ō'gər ĭsh), **o·grish** (ō'grĭsh), *adj.* —**o·gress** (ō'grĭs), *n. fem.*

oh (ō), *interj., n., pl.* **oh's, ohs,** *v.* —*interj.* **1.** an expression of surprise, pain, disappointment, etc. —*n.* **2.** the exclamation "oh." —*v.i.* **3.** to utter or exclaim "oh."

O'Har·a (ō här'ə), *n.* **John,** born 1905, U. S. author.

O'Hare (ō hâr'), *n.* airport in Chicago.

O. Hen·ry (ō hĕn'rĭ), pen name of **William S. Porter.**

OHG, Old High German. Also, **OHG., O.H.G.**

O·hi·o (ō hī'ō), *n.* **1.** a State in the NE central United States: a part of the Midwest. 9,706,397 pop. (1960); 41,222 sq. mi. *Cap.:* Columbus. **2.** a river formed by the confluence of the Allegheny and Monongahela rivers at Pittsburgh, Pennsylvania, flowing SW to the Mississippi in S Illinois. 981 mi. —**O·hi'o·an,** *n., adj.*

ohm (ōm), *n. Elect.* the unit of resistance: the resistance of a conductor in which one volt produces a current of one ampere. [named after G. S. *Ohm* (1787–1854), German physicist] —**ohm·ic** (ō'mĭk), *adj.*

ohm·age (ō'mĭj), *n.* electrical resistance expressed in ohms.

---

b., blend of, blended; c., cognate with; d., dialect, dialectal; der., derived from; f., formed from; g., going back to; m., modification of; r., replacing; s., stem of; t., taken from; ?, perhaps.   See the full key on inside cover.

hm·me·ter (ōm′mē/tər), *n.* an instrument for measuring electrical resistance in ohms.

.H.M.S., On His (or Her) Majesty's Service.

·ho (ō hō′), *interj.* an exclamation expressing surprise, taunting, exultation, etc.

·oid, a suffix used to form adjectives meaning "like" or "resembling," and nouns meaning "something resembling" what is indicated by the preceding part of the word (and often implying an incomplete or imperfect resemblance), as in *alkaloid, anthropoid, cardioid, cuboid, lithoid, ovoid, planetoid.* [t. Gk.: m.s. *-oeidēs*, f. *-o-* (connective vowel from preceding word element) + *-eidēs* having the form of, like, der. *eidos* form. Cf. *-ODE¹*]

·oidea, a suffix used in naming zoölogical classes or entomological superfamilies. [t. NL, der. *-oïdēs* -OID]

·il (oil), *n.* **1.** any of a large class of substances typically unctuous, viscous, combustible, liquid at ordinary temperatures, and soluble in ether or alcohol but not in water: used for anointing, perfuming, lubricating, illuminating, heating, smoothing waves at sea in a storm, etc. **2.** petroleum. **3.** some substance of oily consistency. **4.** *Painting.* **a.** an oil color. **b.** an oil painting. **5.** an oilskin garment. —*v.t.* **6.** to smear, lubricate, or supply with oil. **7.** to bribe. **8.** to make oily or smooth, as in speech. **9.** to convert (butter, etc.) into oil by melting. —*adj.* **10.** pertaining to or resembling oil. **11.** concerned with the production or use of oil. **12.** obtained from oil. [ME *olie, oile,* t. OF, g. L *oleum* (olive) oil]

oil·bird (oil′bûrd′), *n.* the guacharo.

oil cake, a cake or mass of linseed, cottonseed, etc., from which the oil has been expressed, used as a food for cattle or sheep, or as soil fertilizer.

Oil City, a city in NW Pennsylvania, on the Allegheny river. 17,692 (1960).

oil·cloth (oil′klôth′, -kloth′), *n.* **1.** a cotton fabric made waterproof with oil and pigment, and used for tablecloths, etc. **2.** a piece of it.

oil color, a color or paint made by grinding a pigment in oil, usually linseed oil.

oil·er (oi′lər), *n.* **1.** one who oils; a workman employed to oil machinery. **2.** any contrivance for lubricating with oil. **3.** a can with a long spout, used for oiling machinery. **4.** *U.S. Colloq.* an oilskin coat.

oil field, a place where oil is found.

oil of turpentine, a colorless, inflammable, volatile oil, a distillate of turpentine, having a penetrating odor and a pungent, bitterish taste: used in paints, varnishes, and the like, and in medicine as a stimulant, diuretic, rubefacient, etc.

oil of vitriol, sulfuric acid.

oil painting, **1.** the art of painting with oil colors. **2.** a work executed in oil colors.

Oil Rivers, a region in W Africa, comprising the vast Niger river delta: formerly a British protectorate; now a part of Nigeria.

oil·skin (oil′skĭn′), *n.* **1.** a cotton fabric made waterproof by treatment with oil and used for fishermen's clothing and rainwear. **2.** a piece of this. **3.** (*often pl.*) a garment made of it.

oil slick, a slick or smooth place on the surface of water, due to the presence of oil.

oil·stone (oil′stōn′), *n.* a fine-grained whetstone whose rubbing surface is lubricated with oil.

oil well, a well from which oil is obtained.

oil·y (oi′lĭ), *adj.,* oilier, oiliest. **1.** pertaining to oil. **2.** full of or containing oil. **3.** smeared or covered with oil, or greasy. **4.** of the nature of or consisting of oil; resembling oil. **5.** smooth, as in manner or speech; bland; unctuous: *an oily hypocrite.* —*adv.* **6.** in an oily manner. —**oil′i·ly**, *adv.* —**oil′i·ness**, *n.*

oint·ment (oint′mənt), *n.* a soft, unctuous preparation, often medicated, for application to the skin; an unguent. [f. obs. *oint* (aphetic var. of ANOINT) + -MENT; r. ME *oignement,* t. OF]

Oir·each·tas (ĕr′əкн thəs), *n.* **1.** the parliament of Eire (established Dec. 29, 1937), consisting of the President of Eire, the Dáil Eireann (House of Representatives), and the Seanad Eireann (Senate). **2.** a national assembly or festival held annually in Ireland for the encouragement of the use of the Irish language as a literary medium. [t. Irish.: assembly, conference]

Oise (wäz), *n.* a river flowing from S Belgium SW through N France to the Seine near Paris. 186 mi.

O·jib·wa (ō jĭb′wä, -wə). *n., pl.* -wa, -was. **1.** a large tribe of North American Indians of Algonquian family, divided between the United States and Canada in the Lake Superior region. **2.** a member of the Ojibwa tribe. **3.** their language. Also, **O·jib′way, Chippewa.** [t. Amer. Ind., *ojibway* (d.) to roast till puckered up, f. *ojib* to pucker up + *ub-way* to roast; with reference to the puckered seam on their moccasins]

O.K. (*adj., adv.* ō′kā′; *v., n.* ō′kā′), *adv.,., v.* **O.K.'d, O. K.'ing,** *n., pl.* **O.K.'s.** *Colloq. Orig. U.S.* —*adj., adv.* **1.** all right; correct. —*v.t.* **2.** to put "O.K." on (a bill, etc.); endorse; approve. —*n.* **3.** an approval or agreement. Also, **OK, okay.** [origin much debated, but prob. abstracted from "O.K. Club," formed in 1840 by partisans of Martin Van Buren who allegedly named their organization in allusion to "Old Kinderhook," his birthplace being Kinderhook, N.Y.]

o·ka (ō′kə), *n.* **1.** a unit of weight in Turkey and neighboring countries, equal to about 2¾ lbs. **2.** a unit of

liquid measure, equal to about 1¼ U.S. liquid quarts. Also, **oke.** [t. It.: m. *oc(c)a,* t. Turk.: m. *ōqa,* t. Ar.: m. *ūqiyya,* ult. t. Gk. m. *ounkía* = L *uncia*]

O·ka (ō kä′), *n.* a river in the central Soviet Union in Europe, flowing NE to the Volga at Gorki. ab. 950 mi.

o·ka·pi (ō kä′pĭ), *n. pl.* -pis, (*esp. collectively*) -pi. an African forest mammal, *Okapia johnstoni,* closely related to the giraffe, but smaller and with a much shorter neck. [from a Central Afr. language]

o·kay (*adj., adv.* ō′kā′; *v., n.* ō′kā′), *adj., adv., v.t., n. Colloq., Orig. U.S.* O.K.

Okapi, *Okapia 'ohnstoni* (5 ft. high at the shoulder)

O·ka·ya·ma (ō′kä yä′mä), *n.* a seaport in SW Japan, on Honshu island. 162,904 (1950).

oke (ōk), *n.* oka.

O·kee·cho·bee (ō′kĭ chō′bē), *n.* a lake in N part of Everglades, in S Florida. ab. 40 mi. long; ab. 25 mi. wide.

O'Keeffe (ō kēf′), *n.* **Georgia,** born 1887. U.S. painter.

O·ke·fe·no·kee Swamp (ō′kə fə nō′kĭ, -fə nŏk′ĭ), a large wooded swamp area in SE Georgia.

O'Kel·iey (ō kĕl′ĭ), *n.* **Seán Thomas** (shôn, shän), born 1883, Irish statesman; president since 1945.

O·khotsk (ō kŏtsk′; *Russ.* ŏ hŏtsk′), *n.* **Sea of,** an arm of the N Pacific enclosed by Kamchatka Peninsula, the Kurile Islands, Sakhalin, and the Soviet Union in Asia. ab. 582,000 sq. mi.; greatest depth, 10,554 ft.

O·kie (ō′kĭ), *n. Colloq.* **1.** a native or inhabitant of Oklahoma. **2.** a migrant worker, orig. one from Oklahoma, who lost his land or was forced to move because of drought, insect plagues, etc.

O·ki·na·wa (ō′kə nä′wə; *Jap.* ō′kē nä′wä), *n.* the largest of the Ryukyu Islands, in the N Pacific, SW of Japan: taken by U.S. forces in the last major amphibious campaign of World War II, April-June, 1945. 667,545 pop. (est. 1954); 544 sq. mi.

Okla., Oklahoma.

O·kla·ho·ma (ō′klə hō′mə), *n.* a State of the S central United States. 2,328,284 pop. (1960); 69,919 sq. mi. *Cap.:* Oklahoma City. *Abbr.:* Okla. —**O′kla·ho′man,** *adj., n.*

Oklahoma City, the capital of Oklahoma, in the central part. 324,253 (1960).

o·kra (ō′krə), *n.* **1.** a tall plant of the mallow family, *Hibiscus* or *Abelmoschus esculentus,* cultivated for its edible mucilaginous pods, used in soups, etc. **2.** the pod. **3.** the pods collectively. **4.** a dish made with the pods; gumbo. [t. d. West Afr.]

-ol¹, a noun suffix used in the names of chemical derivatives, pharmaceutical compounds, commercial products, etc. representing "alcohol," as in *glycerol, naphthol, phenol,* or sometimes "phenol" or less definitely assignable phenol derivatives. [short for ALCOHOL or PHENOL]

-ol², var. of **-ole.**

O·laf (ō′ləf; *Nor.* ō′läf), *n.* **1.** Saint, A.D. 995–1030, king of Norway, 1015–28. **2.** V, born 1903, king of Norway since 1957.

Olaf Tryg·ves·son (trȳg′vĕs sŏn′), A.D. 969?–1000, king of Norway, A.D. 995?–1000.

Ö·land (œ′länd′), *n.* an island in SE Sweden, separated from the mainland by Kalmar Sound. 26,300 pop. (1946); 519 sq. mi.

-olatry, a word element meaning "worship of," as in *demonolatry.* [see LATRIA]

old (ōld), *adj.,* older, oldest or elder, eldest, *n.* —*adj.* **1.** far advanced in years or life: *a venerable old man.* **2.** of or pertaining to advanced life or persons advanced in years: *to live to a good old age.* **3.** having the appearance or characteristics of advanced age: *prematurely old.* **4.** having reached a specified age: *a man thirty years old.* **5.** advanced in years, in comparison with others or relatively to a scale of age: *the oldest boy.* **6.** having existed long, or made long ago: *old wine.* **7.** long known or in use; familiar: *the same old excuse.* **8.** former, past, or ancient, as time, days, etc.; belonging to a past time: *old kingdoms.* **9.** being the earlier or earliest of two or more things of the same kind, or stages of a thing: *the Old Testament, Old Norse.* **10.** (of colors) dulled, faded or subdued: *old rose.* **11.** deteriorated through age or long use; worn, decayed, or dilapidated. **12.** *Phys. Geog.* (of topographical features) far advanced in reduction by erosion, etc. **13.** of long experience: *an old hand at the game.* **14.** sedate, sensible, or wise, as if from mature years: *an old head on young shoulders.* **15.** Often *Colloq. or Slang.* (implying long acquaintance or friendly feeling): *good old Henry.* **16.** *Colloq.* carried to great lengths; great. —*n.* **17.** old or former time, often time long past. [ME; OE *ald, eald,* c. D *oud,* G *alt;* orig. pp., and akin to Icel. *ala* nourish, bring up, and L *alere* nourish] —**old′ness,** *n.*

—**Syn. 1.** OLD, AGED, ELDERLY all mean well along in years. An OLD person has lived long, nearly to the end of the usual period of life. An AGED person is very far advanced in years, and is usually afflicted with the infirmities of age. An ELDERLY person is somewhat old, but usually has the mellowness, satisfactions, and joys of age before him. **8.** olden, early, primitive, primeval. —**Ant. 1.** young, youthful.

old age, the period of life (generally) after 65.

Old Bai·ley (bā′lĭ), the main criminal court of London.

old boy, *Brit.* an alumnus of a "public school."

Old Cas·tile (käs tēl′), a region in N Spain: formerly a province.

Old-cas·tle (ōld′käs′əl, -käs′əl), *n.* **John.** See **Cobham.**

Old Church Slavic, the extinct language (South Slavic) preserved in religious texts of the Russian Orthodox church. Also, **Old Church Slavonic.**

old country, the country from which an immigrant came, esp. a European country.

Old Curiosity Shop, a novel (1840–41) by Dickens.

Old Dominion, the State of Virginia.

old·en (ōl′dən), *adj. Archaic.* **1.** old. **2.** of old; ancient: *olden days.* **3.** of former days.

Ol·den·burg (ōl′dən bûrg′; *Ger.* -bŏŏrкн′), *n.* **1.** a former state in Germany, including the three scattered provinces of Oldenburg in NW Germany, Birkenfeld in SW Germany, and Lübeck on the Baltic; now a part of Lower Saxony. **2.** a city in NW West Germany, formerly capital of Oldenburg. 120,791 (est. 1955).

Old English, 1. the English of periods before 1100; Anglo-Saxon. **2.** *Print.* the form of black letter used by English printers from the 15th to the 18th century.

old·er (ōl′dər), *adj., compar. of* **old.** of greater age.
—**Syn.** OLDER, ELDER imply having greater age than something or someone else. OLDER is the usual form of the comparative of old: *this building is older than that one.* ELDER, now greatly restricted in application, is used chiefly to indicate seniority in age as between any two people but especially priority of birth as between children born of the same parents: *the elder brother became king.* —**Ant.** newer, younger.

old-fash·ioned (ōld′fāsh′ənd), *adj.* **1.** of an old fashion or a style or type formerly in vogue. **2.** favored or prevalent in former times: *old-fashioned ideas.* **3.** (of persons) having the ways, ideas, or tastes of a former period; out of fashion. —**Syn. 1.** See **ancient.**

old-fo·gy·ish (ōld′fō′gī′Ysh), *adj.* of or like an old fogy; excessively conservative. Also, **old′-fo′gey·ish.**

Old French, the French language of periods before 1400.

Old Glory, the flag of the United States.

Old Guard, 1. the imperial guard created in 1804 by Napoleon. It made the last French charge at Waterloo. **2.** *U.S.* the ultraconservative element of the Republican party. **3.** (*usually l.c.*) the ultraconservative members of any group, country, etc. [trans. of F *Vieille Garde*]

Old·ham (ōl′dəm), *n.* a city in W England, near Manchester. 119,500 (est. 1956).

Old Hickory, nickname of Andrew Jackson.

Old High German, High German of before 1100.

Old Icelandic, the Icelandic of the Middle Ages.

Old Irish, the Irish language before the 11th century.

Old Ironsides, the old U.S. frigate *Constitution.*

old·ish (ōl′dĭsh), *adj.* somewhat old: *an oldish man.*

old-line (ōld′lĭn′), *adj.* **1.** following or supporting conservative or traditional ideas, beliefs, customs, etc. **2.** long established; traditional.

old maid, 1. an elderly or confirmed spinster. **2.** *Colloq.* a person with the alleged characteristics of an old maid, such as primness, prudery, fastidiousness, etc. **3.** a game of cards in which the players draw from one another to match pairs. —**old′-maid′ish,** *adj.*

old master. See **master** (def. 14).

old moon. See **moon** (def. 2d).

Old Nick. See **Nick.**

Old Norse, 1. the language of Norway and Iceland in the Middle Ages. **2.** Old Icelandic.

Old Orchard Beach, a resort town in S Maine. 4593 (1950).

Old Persian, the ancient Iranian of the Persian cuneiforms.

Old Pretender, 1688–1766, James Francis Edward Stuart, son of James II of England.

Old Prussian, a Baltic language extinct since the 17th century.

old-rose (ōld′rōz′), *n., adj.* rose with a purplish or grayish cast.

Old Saxon, the Saxon dialect of Low German as spoken before 1100.

old school tie, *Brit.* **1.** a necktie of the colors of the "public school" that one attended. **2.** the influence wielded by the old public schools in English life.

old sledge, *Cards.* the game of seven-up.

old squaw, a lively, voluble sea duck, *clangula hyemalis,* of northern regions.

old·ster (ōld′stər), *n.* **1.** *Colloq.* an old or older person. **2.** (in the British Navy) a midshipman of four years' standing. [f. OLD + -STER, modeled on YOUNGSTER]

old style, 1. *Print.* a type style differentiated from *modern style* by the more or less uniform thickness of all strokes and the slanted serifs. **2.** (*caps.*) See **style** (def. 13). —**old′-style′,** *adj.*

Old Test., Old Testament.

Old Testament, 1. the collection of Biblical books comprising the Scriptures of "the old covenant." In the Hebrew Bible the three main divisions are the Law, the Prophets, and the Writings. The order in other than Jewish translations follows the Septuagint. In the Vulgate (Latin) translation all but two books of the Apocrypha are included in the Old Testament. **2.** the covenant between God and Israel on Mount Sinai (Ex. 19–24) constituting the basis of the Hebrew religion. See Jer. 31: 31–34; also II Cor. 3: 6, 14.

old-time (ōld′tīm′), *adj.* belonging to or characteristic of old or former times: *old-time sailing ships.*

old-tim·er (ōld′tī′mər), *n. Colloq.* **1.** one whose residence, membership, or experience dates from old times. **2.** one who adheres to old-time ideas or ways.

old-wife (ōld′wīf′), *n., pl.* **-wives. 1.** any of various fishes, as the alewife, the menhaden, or a West Indian fish of the family *Balistidae.* **2.** the old squaw (duck).

Old Wives' Tale, a novel (1908) by Arnold Bennett.

old-wom·an·ish (ōld′wŏŏm′ən Ysh), *adj.* of or like an old woman; excessively fussy.

Old World, 1. Europe, Asia, and Africa. **2.** the Eastern Hemisphere.

old-world (ōld′wûrld′), *adj.* **1.** of or pertaining to the ancient world or to a former period of history. **2.** of or pertaining to the Old World.

-ole, a noun suffix meaning "oil." [repr. L *oleum*]

o·le·a·ceous (ō′lĭ ā′shəs), *adj.* belonging to the Oleaceae, or olive family of plants, which includes the ash, jasmine, etc. [f. s. L *olea* olive + -ACEOUS]

o·le·ag·i·nous (ō′lĭ ăj′ə nəs), *adj.* **1.** having the nature or qualities of oil. **2.** containing oil. **3.** producing oil. **4.** oily or unctuous. [t. L: m. *oleāginus* of the olive] —**o′le·ag′i·nous·ness,** *n.*

O·le·an (ō′lĭ ăn′), *n.* a city in SW New York. 21,868 (1960).

o·le·an·der (ō′lĭ ăn′dər), *n. Bot.* any plant of the apocynaceous genus *Nerium,* esp. *N. oleander,* a poisonous evergreen shrub with handsome rose-colored or white flowers, or *N. ordorum,* a species from India with fragrant flowers. [t. ML, ult. g. LL *lorandrum* (var. of L *rhododendron,* t. Gk.), influenced by form of oil, or *olea* olive]

o·le·as·ter (ō′lĭ ăs′tər), *n.* an ornamental shrub or small tree, *Elaeagnus angustifolia,* of southern Europe and western Asia, w th fragrant yellow flowers and an olivelike fruit. [ME, t. L: the wild olive]

o·le·ate (ō′lĭ āt′), *n. Chem.* an ester or a salt of oleic acid.

o·lec·ra·non (ō lĕk′rə nŏn′, ō′lə krā′nŏn), *n. Anat.* the part of the ulna beyond the elbow joint. [t. Gk.: m. *ōlékranon,* short for *olenokronon* the point of the elbow]

o·le·fin (ō′lə fĭn′), *n. Chem.* any of a series of hydrocarbons homologous with ethylene, having the general formula, C_nH_{2n}, also known as alkenes. Also, **o·le·fine** (ō′lə fĭn, -fēn′). [f. F *olef(iant)* oil-forming (der. L *oleum* oil) + -IN²] —**o′le·fin′ic,** *adj.*

o·le·ic (ō lē′Yk, ō′lĭ Yk), *adj. Chem.* pertaining to or derived from oleic acid. [t. s. L *oleum* oil + -IC]

oleic acid, *Chem.* an oily liquid, $C_{17}H_{33}COOH$, one of the acids present in fats and oils as the glyceride ester.

o·le·in (ō′lĭ Yn), *n. Chem.* **1.** a colorless oily compound, the glyceride of oleic acid and the component of olive oil. **2.** the oily or lower-melting fractions of a fat as distinguished from the solid or higher-melting constituents. [f. s. L *oleum* oil + -IN²]

o·le·o (ō′lĭ ō′), *n.* shortened form of *oleomargarine.*

oleo-, a word element meaning "oil." [t. L, comb. form of *oleum*]

o·le·o·graph (ō′lĭ ə grăf′, -gräf′), *n.* a kind of chromolithograph printed in oil colors. —**o′le·o·graph′ic,** *adj.* —**o·le·og·ra·phy** (ō′lĭ ŏg′rə fĭ), *n.*

o·le·o·mar·ga·rine (ō′lĭ ō mär′jə rēn′, -gə-), *n.* a cooking and table fat made by combining animal oils such as oleo oil and refined lard, and sometimes cottonseed oil, with milk. See **margarine.** Also, **o·le·o·mar·ga·rin** (ō′lĭ ō mär′jə rĭn, -gə-).

oleo oil, a product obtained from beef fat, consisting mainly of a mixture of olein and palmitin: used for making butterlike foods.

o·le·o·res·in (ō′lĭ ō rĕz′ən), *n.* **1.** a natural mixture of an essential oil and a resin. **2.** *Pharm.* an oil holding resin in solution, extracted from a substance (as ginger) by means of alcohol, ether, or acetone.

ol·fac·tion (ŏl făk′shən), *n.* **1.** act of smelling. **2.** the sense of smell. [f. (obs.) *olfact* to smell (t. L: s. *olfactāre*) + -ION]

ol·fac·to·ry (ŏl făk′tə rĭ, -trĭ), *adj., n., pl.* **-ries.** —*adj.* **1.** of or pertaining to the sense of smell: *olfactory organs.* —*n.* **2.** (*usually pl.*) an olfactory organ. [t. L: m.s. *olfactōrius,* adj.; only fem. occurs in n. use]

o·lib·a·num (ō lĭb′ə nəm), *n.* frankincense. [ME, t. ML, var. of LL *lībanus,* t. Gk.: m. *lībanos,* of Semitic orig.; cf. Heb. *lěbhonāh*]

olig-, a word element meaning "few," "little." Also, before consonants, **oligo-.** [t. Gk., comb. form of *olígos* small, (pl.) few]

ol·i·garch (ŏl′ə gärk′), *n.* one of the rulers in an oligarchy.

ol·i·gar·chic (ŏl′ə gär′kĭk), *adj.* of, pertaining to, or having the form of an oligarchy. Also, **ol′i·gar′chi·cal.**

ol·i·gar·chy (ŏl′ə gär′kĭ), *n., pl.* **-chies. 1.** a form of government in which the power is vested in a few, or in a dominant class or clique. **2.** a state so governed. **3.** the ruling few collectively. [t. Gk.: m.s. *oligarchía*]

ol·i·go·car·pous (ŏl′ə gō kär′pəs), *adj. Bot.* not bearing much fruit. [f. OLIGO- + -CARP + -OUS]

Ol·i·go·cene (ŏl′ə gō sēn′), *Stratig.* —*adj.* **1.** pertaining to an early Tertiary epoch or series. —*n.* **2.** a division of the Tertiary that follows Eocene and precedes Miocene. [f. OLIGO- + m.s. Gk. *kainós* new]

ol·i·go·chaete (ŏl′ə gō kēt′), *n.* any of a group of annelids that have locomotory setae sunk directly in the body wall. It includes earthworms and many small fresh-water annelids. —**ol'i·go·chae'tous**, *adj.*

ol·i·go·clase (ŏl'ə gō klās'), *n.* a kind of plagioclase feldspar occurring commonly in crystals of white color, sometimes shaded with gray, green, or red. [f. OLIGO- + m.s. Gk. *klásis* fracture]

ol·i·go·cy·the·mi·a (ŏl'ə gō sī thē'mī ə), *n. Pathol.* a form of anemia in which there is a reduction in the number of red corpuscles in the blood. Also, **ol'i·go·cy·thae'mi·a.** [f. OLIGO- + CYT- + -(H)EMIA]

ol·i·gu·ri·a (ŏl'ə gyŏŏr'ĭ ə), *n. Pathol.* scantiness of urine due to diminished secretion. Also, **ol·i·gu·re·sis** (ŏl'ə gyŏŏ rē'sĭs). [f. OLIG- + URIA]

o·li·o (ō'lĭ ō'), *n., pl.* **olios.** 1. a dish of many ingredients. 2. any mixture of heterogeneous elements. 3. a medley or potpourri (musical, literary, or the like); a miscellany. [t. Sp.: m. *olla* pot, stew. See OLLA]

Ol·i·phant (ŏl'ə fənt), *n.* Margaret, (*Margaret Oliphant Wilson*) 1828–97, British novelist.

ol·i·va·ceous (ŏl'ə vā'shəs), *adj.* of a deep shade of green; olive. [t. NL: m. *olivāceus.* See OLIVE]

ol·i·var·y (ŏl'ə vĕr'ĭ), *adj.* 1. shaped like an olive. 2. *Anat.* noting or pertaining to either of two oval bodies or prominences (**olivary bodies**), made up of nervous tissue, one on each side of the anterior surface of the medulla oblongata. [t. L: m.s. *olivārius* of olives]

ol·ive (ŏl'ĭv), *n.* 1. an evergreen tree, *Olea europaea,* of Mediterranean and other warm regions, cultivated chiefly for its fruit, but yielding also a wood valued for ornamental work. 2. the fruit, a small oval drupe, esteemed as a relish (pickled in brine when either green or ripe), and valuable as a source of oil. 3. any of various related or similar trees. 4. the foliage of the olive tree (*Olea*). 5. an olive branch (an emblem of peace). 6. a wreath of it. 7. a shade of green or yellowish green. —*adj.* 8. of, pertaining to, or made of olives, their foliage, or their fruit. 9. of a dull shade of green or yellowish green. 10. tinged with this color: *an olive complexion.* [ME, t. OF, g. L *oliva;* akin to Gk. *elaia* olive tree]

olive branch, 1. a branch of the olive tree (an emblem of peace). 2. anything offered in token of peace.

olive drab, 1. a deep yellowish green. 2. woolen cloth of this color used for U.S. Army uniforms.

ol·ive-green (ŏl'ĭv grēn'), *n., adj.* green with a yellowish or brownish tinge.

ol·iv·en·ite (ŏl'ĭv ə nīt', ŏl'ə və nīt'), *n.* a mineral, basic copper arsenate, Cu₄As₂O₈(OH) occurring in crystals and in masses, usually olive-green in color. [f. G *oliven(erz)* olive ore + -ITE¹]

olive oil, an oil expressed from the olive fruit, used with food, in medicine, etc.

Ol·i·ver (ŏl'ə vər), *n.* one of the 12 paladins of Charlemagne. See **Roland.** [ME, t. F: m. *Olivier*]

Oliver Twist (twĭst), a novel (1838) by Dickens.

Ol·ives (ŏl'ĭvz), *n.* **Mount of,** a small ridge E of Jerusalem, in what is now Jordan. Highest point, 2737 ft. Also, **Ol·i·vet** (ŏl'ə vĕt', -vĭt).

ol·i·vine (ŏl'ə vēn', ŏl'ə vēn'), *n.* a very common mineral, magnesium iron silicate, (Mg, Fe)₂Si O₄, occurring commonly in olive-green to gray-green masses as an important constituent of basic igneous rocks; rarely, in one variety, transparent and used as a gem. [f. s. L *oliva* olive + -INE²]

ol·la (ŏl'ə; *Sp.* ô'lyä, -yä), *n.* (in Spanish-speaking countries) 1. an earthen pot or jar for holding water or for cooking, etc. 2. a dish of meat and vegetables cooked in such a pot. [t. Sp.: pot. stew, in LL pot, jar]

ol·la-po·dri·da (ŏl'ə pə drē'də; *Sp.* ô'lyä pô drē'dä, ô'yä-), *n.* 1. a Spanish stew of meat and vegetables. 2. any incongruous mixture or miscellaneous collection. [t. Sp.: lit., rotten pot]

ol·o·gy (ŏl'ə jĭ), *n., pl.* **-gies.** *Colloq.* any science or branch of knowledge. [abstracted from words like BIOLOGY, GEOLOGY where the element -LOGY is preceded by -o-. See -o-]

O·lo·mouc (ō'lô mōts'), *n.* a city in central Czechoslovakia, in Moravia. 58,617 (1947). German, **Ol·mütz** (ŏl'mŷts).

O·lym·pi·a (ō lĭm'pĭ ə), *n.* 1. a plain in ancient Elis, Greece, where the Olympic games were held. 2. the capital of Washington, in the W part, on Puget Sound. 18,273 (1960).

O·lym·pi·ad (ō lĭm'pĭ ăd'), *n.* (*often l.c.*) 1. a period of four years reckoned from one celebration of the Olympic games to the next, by which the Greeks computed time from 776 B.C. 2. a celebration of the modern Olympic games. [ME, t. L: s. *olympias,* t. Gk.]

O·lym·pi·an (ō lĭm'pĭ ən), *adj.* 1. pertaining to or dwelling on Mount Olympus, as the greater gods of Greece. 2. pertaining to Olympia in Elis. 3. like the gods of Olympus; grand; imposing. —*n.* 4. an Olympian deity. 5. a contender in the Olympic games.

O·lym·pic (ō lĭm'pĭk), *adj.* 1. pertaining to the Olympic games. 2. pertaining to Olympia, in Greece. 3. pertaining to Mount Olympus, in Greece. —*n.* 4. an Olympic game. 5. **the Olympics,** the Olympic games.

Olympic games, 1. the greatest of the games or festivals of ancient Greece, held every four years in the plain of Olympia in Elis, in honor of Zeus. 2. a modern revival of these games consisting of international competitions in running, jumping, swimming, shooting, etc., held every four years, each time in a different country.

Olympic Mountains, a part of the Coast Range in NW Washington. Highest peak, Mt. Olympus, 7954 ft.

O·lym·pus (ō lĭm'pəs), *n.* **Mount,** 1. a mountain in NE Greece, on the boundary between Thessaly and Macedonia: fabled abode of the greater Grecian gods. 9730 ft. 2. heaven. 3. a peak of the Olympic Mountains in NW Washington. 7954 ft.

O·lyn·thus (ō lĭn'thəs), *n.* an ancient city in NE Greece, on Chalcidice Peninsula.

O.M., *Brit.* Order of Merit.

-oma, *pl.* **-omas, -omata.** a suffix of nouns denoting a morbid condition of growth (tumor), as in *carcinoma, glaucoma, sarcoma.* [t. Gk.]

O·ma·ha (ō'mə hô', -hä'), *n.* 1. a city in E Nebraska, on the Missouri river. 301,598 (1960). 2. an Indian of a Siouan tribe, formerly in Nebraska.

O·man (ō män'), *n.* 1. Also, **Muscat and Oman.** a sultanate of SE Arabia. 550,000 pop. (est. 1954); ab. 82,000 sq. mi. *Cap.:* Muscat. 2. Gulf of, a NW arm of the Arabian Sea, at the entrance to the Persian Gulf.

O·mar Khay·yám (ō'mär kī äm', ō'mər), died 1123?, Persian poet, some of whose poems (*The Rubaiyat*) were translated by Edward FitzGerald.

o·ma·sum (ō mā'səm), *n., pl.* **-sa** (-sə). the third stomach of a ruminant, between the reticulum and the abomasum; the manyplies. See diag. under **ruminant.** [t. NL, in L bullock's tripe]

O·may·yad (ō mī'ăd), *n.* 1. a caliph of the dynasty which ruled at Damascus, A.D. 661 to 750, claiming descent from Omayya, great-uncle of Mohammed the Prophet. 2. an emir (A.D. 756–929) or caliph (A.D. 929–1031) of the Omayyad dynasty of Spain. Also, **Ommiad.**

om·ber (ŏm'bər), *n.* 1. a game at cards, fashionable in the 17th and 18th centuries, played, usually by three persons, with forty cards. 2. the player who undertakes to win the pool in this game. Also, *esp. Brit.,* **om'bre.** [t. F: m. (h)*ombre,* t. Sp.: m. *hombre,* lit., man, g. s. L *homo*]

Om·dur·man (ŏm'dōōr män'), *n.* a city in the Sudan, on the White Nile opposite Khartoum: British victory, 1898. 125,000 (est. 1953).

o·me·ga (ō mē'gə, ō mĕg'ə, ō'mĕg ə), *n.* 1. the last letter (Ω, ω = English long O, o) of the Greek alphabet. 2. the last of any series; the end. [t. Gk.: ō *mega,* lit., great *o.* Cf. OMICRON]

om·e·let (ŏm'lĭt, ŏm'ə lĭt), *n.* eggs beaten with milk and fried or baked, often with other ingredients also, as chopped ham, cheese, jelly, etc. Also, **om'e·lette.** [t. F: m. *omelette,* earlier *amelette,* metathetic form of *alemette,* var. of *alemelle,* lit., thin plate]

o·men (ō'mən), *n.* 1. anything perceived or happening that is regarded as portending good or evil or giving some indication as to the future; a prophetic sign. 2. a prognostic. 3. prophetic significance; presage: *a bird of ill omen.* —*v.t.* 4. to be an omen of; portend. 5. to divine, as if from omens. [t. L] —**Syn.** 1. See **sign.**

o·men·tum (ō mĕn'təm), *n., pl.* **-ta** (-tə). *Anat.* a fold or duplication of the peritoneum passing between certain of the viscera: the **great omentum,** or epiploön (attached to and hanging down from the stomach and the transverse colon); the **lesser omentum** (between the stomach and the liver). [t. L] —**o·men'tal,** *adj.*

o·mer (ō'mər), *n.* a Hebrew unit of dry measure, the tenth part of an ephah. [t. Heb.: m. *'omer*]

om·i·cron (ŏm'ə krŏn', ō'mə-), *n.* the fifteenth letter (O, o = English short O, o) of the Greek alphabet. [t. Gk.: ō *mikrón,* lit., small *o.* Cf. OMEGA]

om·i·nous (ŏm'ə nəs), *adj.* 1. portending evil; inauspicious; threatening: *a dull, ominous rumble.* 2. having the significance of an omen. [t. L: m.s. *ōminōsus* portentous] —**om'i·nous·ly,** *adv.* —**om'i·nous·ness,** *n.*

o·mis·si·ble (ō mĭs'ə bəl), *adj.* that may be omitted.

o·mis·sion (ō mĭsh'ən), *n.* 1. act of omitting. 2. the state of being omitted. 3. something omitted. [ME, t. LL: s. *omissio*]

o·mis·sive (ō mĭs'ĭv), *adj.* neglecting; leaving out.

o·mit (ō mĭt'), *v.t.,* **omitted, omitting.** 1. to leave out: *to omit passages of a text.* 2. to forbear or fail to do, make, use, send, etc.: *to omit a prayer.* [ME *omitte(n),* t. L: m. *omittere* let go, neglect, omit]

om·ma·te·um (ŏm'ə tē'əm), *n. Zool.* a compound eye of arthropods.

om·ma·tid·i·um (ŏm'ə tĭd'ĭ əm), *n., pl.* **-tidia** (-tĭd'ĭ ə). *Zool.* one of the radial elements which make up an ommateum. [Latinization of Gk. *ommatídion,* f. s. *ómma* eye + -*idion* (dim. suffix)] —**om'ma·tid'i·al,** *adj.*

om·mat·o·phore (ō măt'ə fōr'), *n.* a tentacle or movable stalk bearing an eye, as in certain snails. [f. s. Gk. *ómma* eye + -(o)PHORE] —**om·ma·toph·o·rous** (ŏm'ə tŏf'ə rəs), *adj.*

Om·mi·ad (ō mī'ăd), *n., pl.* **-ads, -ades** (-ə dēz'). Omayyad.

omni-, a word element meaning "all," used in combination as in *omniactive* (all-active, active everywhere), *omnibenevolent, omnicompetent, omnicredulous, omniprevalent,* and various other words, mostly of obvious meaning. [t. L, comb. form of *omnis*]

om·ni·a vin·cit a·mor (ŏm'nĭ ə vĭn'sĭt ā'môr), *Latin.* love conquers all.

om·ni·bus (ŏm'nə bŭs', -bəs), *n., pl.* **-buses,** *adj.* —*n.* 1. a bus. 2. a volume of reprinted works by a single author or related in interest or nature. —*adj.* 3. pertaining to or covering numerous objects or items at once: *an omnibus bill.* [t. L: lit., for all (dat. pl. of *omnis*)]

om·ni·far·i·ous (ŏm′nə fâr′ĭ əs), *adj.* of all forms, varieties, or kinds. [t. L: m. *omnifārius* of all sorts] —**om′ni·far′i·ous·ness,** *n.*

om·nif·ic (ŏm nĭf′ĭk), *adj.* creating all things.

om·nip·o·tence (ŏm nĭp′ə təns), *n.* 1. the quality of being omnipotent. 2. (*cap.*) God.

om·nip·o·tent (ŏm nĭp′ə tənt), *adj.* 1. almighty, or infinite in power, as God or a deity. 2. having unlimited or very great authority. —*n.* 3. an omnipotent being. 4. the Omnipotent, God. [ME, t. L: s. *omnipotens* almighty] —**om·nip′o·tent·ly,** *adv.*

om·ni·pres·ent (ŏm′nə prĕz′ənt), *adj.* present everywhere at the same time: *the omnipresent God.* [t. ML: m.s. *omnipraesens.* See OMNI-, PRESENT¹] —**om′ni·pres′·ence,** *n.*

—**Syn.** OMNIPRESENT, UBIQUITOUS refer to the quality of being everywhere. OMNIPRESENT emphasizes the power, usually divine, of being present everywhere at the same time, as though all-enveloping: *divine law is omnipresent.* UBIQUITOUS is applied to that which seems to appear in many and all sorts of places, or humorously is "all over the place," often when unwanted; it is now thus in contrast to the other lofty and dignified expression: *a bore seems to be ubiquitous.*

om·nis·cience (ŏm nĭsh′əns), *n.* 1. the quality of being omniscient. 2. infinite knowledge. 3. (*cap.*) God.

om·nis·cient (ŏm nĭsh′ənt), *adj.* 1. knowing all things, or having infinite knowledge. —*n.* 2. an omniscient being. 3. the Omniscient, God. [f. OMNI- + s. L *sciens,* ppr., knowing] —**om·nis′cient·ly,** *adv.*

om·ni·um-gath·er·um (ŏm′nĭ əm găth′ər əm), *n.* a miscellaneous collection. [f. L *omnium* of all + *gatherum* a gathering, pseudo-L deriv. of GATHER]

om·niv·o·rous (ŏm nĭv′ə rəs), *adj.* 1. eating all kinds of foods indiscriminately. 2. eating both animal and plant foods. 3. taking in everything, as with the mind. [t. L: m. *omnivorus*] —**om·niv′o·rous·ly,** *adv.* —**om·niv′o·rous·ness,** *n.*

o·mo·pha·gi·a (ō′mə fā′jĭ ə), *n.* the eating of raw flesh or raw food. [t.Gk.] —**o·mo·phag·ic** (ō′mə făj′ĭk), **o·moph·a·gous** (ō mŏf′ə gəs), *adj.* —**o·moph·a·gist** (ō mŏf′ə jĭst), *n.*

Om·pha·le (ŏm′fə lē′), *n.* *Gk. Legend.* a Lydian queen whom Hercules served in bondage for three years.

om·pha·los (ŏm′fə ləs), *n.* 1. the navel. 2. the central point. 3. *Gk. Antiq.* a rounded or conical stone in the temple of Apollo at Delphi, reputed to mark the center of the earth.

Omsk (ŏmsk), *n.* a city in the W Soviet Union in Asia, on the Irtish river. 505,000 (est. 1956).

O·mu·ta (ō′mōō tä′), *n.* a seaport in SW Japan, on W Kyushu island. 191,978 (1950). Also, **O·mu·da** (ō′mōō-dä′).

on (ŏn, ôn), *prep.* 1. a particle expressing primarily: **a.** position above and in contact with a supporting surface: *on the table.* **b.** immediate proximity: *to border on absurdity.* **c.** situation, place, etc.: *a scar on the face.* **d.** support, suspension, dependence, or reliance: *on wheels.* **e.** state, condition, course, process, etc.: *on strike.* **f.** ground or basis: *a duty on silk.* **g.** risk or liability: *on pain of death.* **h.** time or occasion: *on Sunday.* **i.** direction or end of motion: *to march on the capital.* **j.** encounter: *to happen on a person.* **k.** object or end of action, thought, desire, etc.: *to gaze on a scene.* **l.** subject, reference, or respect: *views on public matters.* —*adv.* 2. on a thing, place, or person: *put the coffee on.* 3. on oneself or itself: *to put one's coat on.* 4. fast to a thing, as for support: *to hold on.* 5. toward a place, point, or object: *to look on.* 6. forward, onward, or along, as in any course or process: *further on.* 7. with continuous procedure: *to work on.* 8. into or in active operation or performance: *to turn on the gas.* —*adj.* 9. (of a brake) applied, and halting or slowing a vehicle, motor, etc. 10. situated nearer; near. 11. *Cricket.* noting that side of the wicket, or of the field, on which the batsman stands. —*n.* 12. state or fact of being on. 13. *Cricket.* the on side. [ME *on,* *an,* *o,* *a,* OE *on,* *an* on, in, to, c. D *aan,* G *an,* Icel. *ā,* Goth. *ana;* akin to Gk. *aná* up, upon. See ANA-]

On (ŏn), *n.* Biblical name of Heliopolis.

ON, Old Norse. Also, **ON., O.N.**

on·a·ger (ŏn′ə jər), *n.,* *pl.* **-gri** (-grī′), **-gers.** 1. a wild ass, *Equus hemionus,* of southwestern Asia; kiang. 2. an ancient and medieval engine of war for throwing stones. [ME, t. L, t. Gk.: m. *ŏnagros* a wild ass]

on·a·gra·ceous (ŏn′ə grā′-shəs), *adj.* belonging to the Onagraceae (or Oenotheraceae, Ephilobiaceae), the evening-primrose family, including the widespread ornamental fuchsia, the willow herb, etc.

Onager, *Equus hemionus*
(Ab. 4½ ft. high at the shoulder)

o·nan·ism (ō′nə nĭz′əm), *n.* 1. *Psychiatry, Physiol.* withdrawal before occurrence of orgasm. 2. masturbation. [from Onan, son of Judah: see Gen. 38:9. See -ISM] —**o′nan·ist,** *n.* —**o·nan·is′tic,** *adj.*

once (wŭns), *adv.* 1. at one time in the past; formerly: *a once powerful nation.* 2. a single time: *once a day.* 3. even a single time; at any time; ever: *if the facts once become known.* 4. once for all, finally and decisively.

5. once in a while, occasionally. 6. once upon a time, long ago (a favorite beginning of a children's story, etc.). 7. once and again, repeatedly. —*conj.* 8. if or when at any time; if ever. 9. whenever. —*n.* 10. a single occasion: *once is enough.* 11. all at once, suddenly. 12. at once, a. immediately. b. at the same time: *do not all speak at once.* [ME *ones,* OE *ānes,* adv. (orig. genitive of *ān* ONE); r. ME *enes,* OE *ǣnes* once, f. *ǣne* once + -*es,* adv. suffix]

on·col·o·gy (ŏng kŏl′ə jĭ), *n.* the part of medical science that treats of tumors. [f. m. Gk. *ŏnko(s)* bulk, mass + -LOGY]

on·com·ing (ŏn′kŭm′ĭng, ôn′-), *adj.* 1. approaching. —*n.* 2. the approach: *the oncoming of winter.*

on dit (ôn dē′), *French.* they say; it is said.

on·do·gram (ŏn′də grăm′), *n.* an autographic record made on an ondograph.

on·do·graph (ŏn′də grăf′, -gräf′), *n.* an instrument for graphically recording oscillatory variations, as in alternating currents. [irreg. f. F *onde* (g. L *unda*) wave + -o- + -GRAPH]

on·dom·e·ter (ŏn dŏm′ə tər), *n.* an instrument for measuring wave length of radio waves.

one (wŭn), *adj.* 1. being a single unit or individual, rather than two or more; a single: *one apple.* 2. being a person, thing, or individual instance of a number or kind indicated: *one member of the party.* 3. some (day, etc., in the future): *you will see him one day.* 4. single through union, agreement, or harmony: *all were of one mind.* 5. of a single kind, nature, or character; the same: *all our pomp of yesterday is one with Nineveh and Tyre!* 6. a certain (often used in naming a person otherwise unknown or undescribed): *one John Smith was chosen.* 7. a particular (day, night, time, etc., in the past): *one evening last week.* 8. all one, (used predicatively) all the same, as in character, meaning, consequence, etc. —*n.* 9. the first and lowest whole number, or a symbol, as 1, I, or i, representing it; unity. 10. a unit; a single person or thing: *to come one at a time.* 11. at one, in a state of unity, agreement, or accord: *hearts at one.* 12. one by one, singly and in succession. —*pron.* 13. a person or thing of number or kind indicated or understood: *one of the poets.* 14. (in certain pronominal combinations) a person unless definitely specified otherwise: *every one.* 15. (with a defining clause or other qualifying words) a person or a personified being or agency: *the evil one.* 16. a person indefinitely; any one of us all: *as good as one would desire.* 17. a person of the speaker's kind; such as the speaker himself: *to press one's own claims.* 18. (to avoid repetition) a person or thing of the kind just mentioned: *the portraits are fine ones.* [ME *oon,* *oo,* *o,* OE *ān,* c. D *ein,* G *ein*]

-one, a noun suffix used in the names of chemical derivatives, esp. ketones. [t. Gk., abstracted from fem. patronymics in -*ōnē*]

O·ne·ga (ō nē′gə; *Russ.* ŏ nĕ′gä), *n.* a lake in the NW Soviet Union: second largest in Europe. 3764 sq. mi.

one-horse (wŭn′hôrs′), *adj.* 1. using or having only a single horse. 2. *U.S. Colloq.* unimportant; minor; petty.

O·nei·da (ō nī′də), *n.* 1. a tribe of the Iroquois confederacy, former inhabitants of the region east of Oneida Lake, a lake (20 mi. long; 6 mi. wide) in central New York. 2. a member of the Oneida tribe. [t. Iroquois: m. *tiionenyote?* a rock which something set up and which is still standing (with reference to a boulder near an ancient village)]

O'Neill (ō nēl′), *n.* Eugene, 1888–1953, U.S. dramatist.

o·nei·ro·crit·ic (ō nī′rə krĭt′ĭk), *n.* 1. an interpreter of dreams. 2. oneirocriticism. [t. Gk.: m.s. *oneirokritikos,* adj., of or pertaining to the interpretation of dreams] —**o·nei′ro·crit′i·cal,** *adj.*

o·nei·ro·crit·i·cism (ō nī′rə krĭt′ə sĭz′əm), *n.* the art of interpreting dreams.

o·nei·ro·man·cy (ō nī′rə măn′sĭ), *n.* divination through dreams. [f. Gk. *ŏneiro(s)* dream + -MANCY] —**o·nei′ro·man′cer,** *n.*

one·ness (wŭn′nĭs), *n.* 1. the quality of being one; singleness; unity; sameness. 2. agreement; concord; unity of thought, belief, aim, etc.

on·er·ous (ŏn′ər əs), *adj.* burdensome, oppressive, or troublesome: *onerous duties.* [ME, t. L: m.s. *onerōsus.*] —**on′er·ous·ly,** *adv.* —**on′er·ous·ness,** *n.*

one·self (wŭn sĕlf′, wŭnz-), *pron.* a person's self (often used for emphasis or reflexively): *one hurts oneself by such methods.* Also, **one's self.**

one-sid·ed (wŭn′sī′dĭd), *adj.* 1. considering but one side of a matter or question; partial, unjust, or unfair: *a one-sided judgment.* 2. *Law.* unilateral, as a contract. 3. unbalanced; unequal: *a one-sided fight.* 4. existing or occurring on one side only. 5. having but one side, or but one developed or finished side. 6. having one side larger or more developed than the other. 7. having the parts all on one side, as an inflorescence.

one-step (wŭn′stĕp′), *n.* 1. a kind of round dance, danced by couples to ragtime. 2. music for this dance.

one-time (wŭn′tīm′), *adj.* having been (as specified) at one time; former; quondam: *his one-time partner.*

one-track (wŭn′trăk′), *adj.* 1. with but a single track. 2. *Colloq.* restricted: *a one-track mind.*

one-way (wŭn′wā′), *adj.* moving, or allowing motion, in one direction only: *a one-way street.*

on·ion (ŭn'yən), *n.* **1.** a widely cultivated plant of the lily family, *Allium cepa*, having an edible succulent bulb of pungent taste and smell. **2.** the bulb. **3.** any of certain plants similar to the onion, as *A. Fistulosum* (Welsh onion). [ME *onyon*, t. OF: m. *oignon*, g. L *ūnio* large pearl, onion. See UNION]

On·ions (ŭn'yənz), *n.* **Charles Talbut**, born 1873, British lexicographer.

on·ion·skin (ŭn'yən skĭn'), *n.* a translucent, glazed paper.

on·look·er (ŏn'lŏŏk'ər, ôn'-), *n.* a spectator.

on·look·ing (ŏn'lŏŏk'ĭng, ôn'-), *adj.* **1.** looking on; observing; perceiving. **2.** looking onward or foreboding.

on·ly (ōn'lĭ), *adv.* **1.** without others or anything further; alone; solely; exclusively: *only he remained.* **2.** no more than; merely; but; just: *if you would only consent.* **3.** singly; as the only one: *the only begotten Son of God.* —*adj.* **4.** being the single one or the relatively few of the kind, or sole: *an only son.* **5.** single in superiority or distinction. —*conj.* **6.** but (introducing a single restriction, restraining circumstance, or the like): *I would have gone, only you objected.* **7.** *Now Colloq.* except that; but or except for: *only for him you would not be here.* [ME *oonli*(*ch*), OE *ānlíc*, var. of *ænlíc*, f. *ān* one + -*líc* -LY] —Syn. **4.** ONLY, SOLE, SINGLE, UNIQUE are all used to refer to an object (or group of objects) as being without counterpart, alone of its kind, whether temporarily or permanently. SINGLE, SOLE, and ONLY all meant originally alone, unaccompanied, and this is still the meaning of SINGLE: *a huge load drawn by a single horse.* SOLE, however, and ONLY have come to refer to a single representative of a type of which no others exist, though this "type" may be very arbitrarily limited: *the only survivor of a disaster, I am his sole heir.* SOLE, today, is a very formal word and is infrequent outside of a few fixed phrases; in general, it is replaced by ONLY. UNIQUE has always meant existing alone of its kind; today, however, it is mainly used figuratively, to suggest that an object has no equal in excellence, importance, etc.: *a unique occasion.*

on·o·mat·o·poe·ia (ŏn'ə măt'ə pē'ə, ŏnŏm'ə tə-), *n.* **1.** the formation of a name or word by imitating sound associated with the thing designated, e.g., *cuckoo* and *whippoorwill* probably originated in onomatopoeia. **2.** *Obsolesc.* a word so formed. **3.** the use of imitative and naturally suggestive words for rhetorical effect. [t. LL, t. Gk. m. *onomatopoiía* the making of words] —**on'o·mat'o·poe'ic** (ŏn'ə măt'ə pō ĕt'-ĭk), *adj.* —**on'o·mat'o·po·et'i·cal·ly**, *adv.*

On·on·da·ga (ŏn'ən dô'gə, -dä'-), *n.* **1.** a tribe of the Iroquois confederacy, former inhabitants of the region about **Onondaga Lake**, a salt lake (5 mi. long; 1 mi. wide) in central New York. **2.** a member of the Onondaga tribe. [t. Iroquois: m. *ononytā'geh* on top of hill]

on·rush (ŏn'rŭsh', ôn'-), *n.* a strong forward rush, flow, etc.

on·set (ŏn'sĕt', ôn'-), *n.* **1.** an assault or attack: *a violent onset.* **2.** a beginning or start.

on·shore (ŏn'shôr', ôn'-), *adv., adj.* ashore.

on·side (ŏn'sīd', ôn'-), *adj.*, not offside.

on·slaught (ŏn'slôt', ôn'-), *n.* an onset, assault, or attack, esp. a vigorous or furious one.

Ont., Ontario.

On·tar·i·o (ŏn târ'ĭ ō'), *n.* **1.** a province in S Canada, bordering on the Great Lakes. 4,897,000 (est. 1953); 412,582 sq. mi. *Cap.:* Toronto. **2.** Lake, the smallest of the Great Lakes, between New York and Ontario. ab. 190 mi. long; ab. 7540 sq. mi. **3.** a city in SW California, E of Los Angeles. 46,617 (1960). —**On·tar'i·an**, *adj., n.*

on·to (ŏn'tŏŏ, ôn'-; *unstressed* -tə), *prep.* to a place or position on; upon; on: *to get onto a horse.*

on·tog·e·ny (ŏn tŏj'ə nĭ), *n. Biol.* the development of an individual organism (as contrasted with *phylogeny*). Also, **on·to·gen·e·sis** (ŏn'tō jĕn'ə sĭs). [f. Gk. *onto-* (comb. form of *ōn* being) + -GENY] —**on·to·ge·net·ic** (ŏn'tō jə nĕt'ĭk), *adj.* —**on·tog'e·nist,** *n.*

ontological argument, *Metaphys.* the a priori argument for the being of God, founded on the assumption that existence is a property and one discoverable in the very concept of God.

on·tol·o·gism (ŏn tŏl'ə jĭz'əm), *n. Theol.* the doctrine that the human intellect has an immediate cognition of God as its proper object and the principle of all its cognitions.

on·tol·o·gy (ŏn tŏl'ə jĭ), *n.* **1.** the science of being, as such. **2.** the branch of metaphysics that investigates the nature of being and of the first principles, or categories, involved. [t. NL: m. *ontologia*, f. Gk.: *onto-* (comb. form of *ōn* being) + -*logia* -LOGY] —**on·to·log·i·cal** (ŏn'tə lŏj'ə kəl), *adj.* —**on·tol'o·gist,** *n.*

o·nus (ō'nəs), *n.* a burden; a responsibility. [t. L: load, burden]

o·nus pro·ban·di (ō'nəs prō băn'dī), *Latin.* the burden of proof.

on·ward (ŏn'wərd, ôn'-), *adv.* Also, **on'wards. 1.** toward a point ahead or in front; forward, as in space or time. **2.** at a position or point in advance. —*adj.* **3.** directed or moving onward or forward; forward. [ME. See ON, -WARD] —Syn. **1.** See forward.

on·yx (ŏn'ĭks, ō'nĭks), *n.* a quartz consisting of straight layers or bands which differ in color, used for ornament. [ME *onix*, t. L: m. *onyx*, t. Gk.: nail, claw, veined gem]

oö-, a word element meaning "egg." [t. Gk., comb. form of *ōíon*]

o·ö·cyte (ō'ə sīt'), *n. Biol.* a female germ cell in the maturation stage.

o·ö·gen·e·sis (ō'ə jĕn'ə sĭs), *n. Biol.* the genesis or origin and development of the ovum.

o·ö·go·ni·um (ō'ə gō'nĭ əm), *n., pl.* -**nia** (-nĭ ə), -**niums.** **1.** *Biol.* one of the female germ cells at the multiplication stage, preceding the maturation or oöcyte stage. **2.** *Bot.* the one-celled female reproductive organ in certain thallophytic plants, usually a more or less spherical sac containing one or more eggs. [t. NL; see oö-, -GONIUM]

o·ö·lite (ō'ə līt'), *n. Geol.* **1.** a limestone composed of minute rounded concretions resembling fish roe, in some places altered to ironstone by replacement with iron oxide. **2.** (*cap.*) an upper division of the European Jurassic, largely composed of oölitic limestone. [t. F: m. *oolithe*, f. *oo-* oö- + -*lithe* -LITE] —**o·ö·lit·ic** (ō'ə lĭt'ĭk), *adj.*

o·öl·o·gy (ō ŏl'ə jĭ), *n.* the part of ornithology that treats of birds' eggs. —**o·ö·log·i·cal** (ō'ə lŏj'ə kəl), *adj.* —**o·öl'o·gist,** *n.*

oo·long (ōō'lông, -lŏng), *n.* a variety of semifermented brown or amber tea from Formosa. [t. Chinese: m. *wu-lung*, lit., black dragon]

oo·mi·ak (ōō'mĭ ăk'), *n.* umiak.

o·ö·pho·rec·to·my (ō'ə fə rĕk'tə mĭ), *n., pl.* -**mies.** *Surg.* the operation of removal of one or both ovaries. [f. *oöphor-* (t. NL, comb. form of *oöphoron* ovary, t. Gk.: lit., eggbearer) + -ECTOMY]

o·ö·pho·ri·tis (ō'ə fə rī'tĭs), *n. Pathol.* inflammation of an ovary, usually combined with an inflammation of the Fallopian tubes; ovaritis.

o·ö·sphere (ō'ə sfīr'), *n. Bot.* an unfertilized egg within an oögonium.

o·ö·spore (ō'ə spōr'), *n. Bot.* a fertilized egg within an oögonium. Also, *Obs.*, **o·ö·sperm** (ō'ə spûrm'). —**o·ö·spor·ic** (ō'ə spōr'ĭk, -spŏr'-), **o·ös·po·rous** (ō ŏs'pə rəs, ō'ə spō'rəs), *adj.*

Oost (ōst), *n.* **1. Jacob van** (yä'kôp văn), 1600?-71, Flemish painter. **2.** his son, **Jacob van**, 1639?-1713, Flemish painter.

o·ö·the·ca (ō'ə thē'kə), *n., pl.* -**cae** (-sē). a case or capsule containing eggs, as that of certain gastropods and insects. [t. NL, f. Gk.: *ōo-* oö- + m. *thēkē* case]

ooze¹ (ōōz), *v.*, **oozed, ooz·ing,** *n.* —*v.i.* **1.** (of moisture, etc.) to percolate or exude, as through pores or small openings. **2.** (of air, etc.) to pass slowly or gradually as if through pores or small openings. **3.** (of a substance) to exude moisture, etc. **4.** (of information, courage, etc.) to leak or pass (*out*, etc.) slowly or imperceptibly. —*v.t.* **5.** to make by oozing. **6.** to exude (moisture, etc.). [ME *wose*(*n*), der. *wos* OOZE¹, n.] —*n.* **7.** act of oozing. **8.** that which oozes. **9.** an infusion of oak bark, sumac, etc., used in tanning. [ME *wos*, OE *wōs* juice, moisture]

ooze² (ōōz), *n.* **1.** a calcareous mud (chiefly the shells of small organisms) covering parts of the ocean bottom. **2.** soft mud, or slime. **3.** a marsh or bog. [ME *wose*, OE *wāse* mud]

ooze leather, leather, prepared from calfskin or other skin, having a soft, velvety finish on the flesh side.

oo·zy¹ (ōō'zĭ), *adj.* **1.** exuding moisture. **2.** damp with moisture. [f. OOZE¹ + -Y¹]

oo·zy² (ōō'zĭ), *adj.* of or like ooze, soft mud, or slime. [ME *wosie*, der. *wose* mud. See OOZE²] —**oo'zi·ness,** *n.*

op-, var. of **ob-,** (by assimilation) before *p*, as in *oppose.*

op., 1. opera. 2. operation. 3. opposite. 4. opus.

O.P., 1. (L *Ordo Praedicatorum*) Order of Preachers (Dominican). 2. Also, **o.p.** out of print.

OPA, Office of Price Administration

o·pac·i·ty (ō păs'ə tĭ), *n., pl.* -**ties. 1.** state of being opaque. **2.** something opaque. **3.** *Photog.* the ratio of the incident light and that emerging from a photographic density. [t. L: s. *opācitas* shade]

o·pah (ō'pə), *n.* a large, deep-bodied, brilliantly colored, oceanic food fish, *Lampris regius.* [t. West Afr.]

o·pal (ō'pəl), *n.* a mineral, an amorphous form of silica, (SiO₂ with some water), not as hard or as heavy as quartz, found in many varieties and colors (often a milky white), certain of which are iridescent and valued as gems. [t. L: s. *opalus*, t. Gk.: m. *opállios*]

o·pal·esce (ō'pə lĕs'), *v.i.*, -**esced, -esc·ing.** to exhibit a play of colors like that of the opal.

o·pal·es·cent (ō'pə lĕs'ənt), *adj.* **1.** exhibiting a play of colors like that of the opal. **2.** having a milky iridescence. —**o'pal·es'cence,** *n.*

o·pal·ine (ō'pəl ĭn, -pə līn'), *adj.* of or like opal; opalescent.

o·paque (ō pāk'), *adj.* **1.** impenetrable to light; not able to transmit, or not transmitting, light. **2.** not able to transmit, or not transmitting, radiation, sound, heat, etc. **3.** not shining or bright; dark; dull. **4.** hard to understand; not clear or lucid; obscure. **5.** unintelligent; stupid. —*n.* **6.** something opaque. **7.** *Photog.* a coloring matter, usually black or red, used to darken a part of a negative. [ME *opake*, t. L: m. *opācus* shady, darkened] —**o·paque'ly,** *adv.* —**o·paque'ness** *n.*

op. cit., opere citato.

ope (ōp), *adj., v.t., v.i.,* **oped, oping.** *Archaic.* open.

o·pen (ō'pən), *adj.* **1.** not shut, as door, a gate, etc. **2.** not closed, covered, or shut up, as a house, box, drawer, etc. **3.** not enclosed as by barriers, as a space. **4.** that may be entered, used, shared, competed for, etc., by all: *an open session.* **5.** accessible or available (often fol. by *to*): *the only course still open.* **6.** unfilled, as a position. **7.** not engaged, as time. **8.** without prohibition as to hunting or fishing: *open season.* **9.** *U.S. Colloq.* without legal restrictions, or not enforcing legal restrictions, as to saloons, gambling places, etc.: *an open town.* **10.** undecided, as a question. **11.** liable or subject to: *open to question.* **12.** accessible to appeals, ideas, offers, etc. (often fol. by *to*): *to be open to conviction.* **13.** having no cover, roof, etc.: *an open boat.* **14.** not covered or protected; exposed or bare: *to lay open internal parts with a knife.* **15.** unobstructed, as a passage, country, stretch of water, view, etc. **16.** free from ice: *open water in arctic regions.* **17.** free from frost; mild or moderate: *an open winter.* **18.** exposed to general view or knowledge; existing, carried on, etc., without concealment: *open disregard of rules.* **19.** acting publicly or without concealment, as a person. **20.** unreserved, candid, or frank, as persons or their speech, aspect, etc.: *an open face.* **21.** having openings or apertures: *open ranks.* **22.** perforated or porous: *an open texture.* **23.** expanded, extended, or spread out: *an open newspaper.* **24.** generous, liberal, or bounteous: *to give with an open hand.* **25.** *Print.* **a.** (of type) in outline form. **b.** widely spaced or leaded, as printed matter. **26.** not yet balanced or adjusted, as an account. **27.** *Music.* **a.** (of an organ pipe) not closed at the far end. **b.** (of a string) not stopped by a finger. **c.** (of a note) produced by such a pipe or string or, on a wind instrument, without the aid of a slide, key, etc. **28.** *Naut.* free from fog. **29.** not constipated, as the bowels. **30.** *Phonet.* **a.** pronounced with a relatively large opening above the tongue: *"cot"* has a more open vowel than *"caught."* **b.** (of a syllable) ending with its vowel. —*v.t.* **31.** to move (a door, gate, etc.) from a shut or closed position so as to admit of passage. **32.** to make (a house, box, drawer, etc.) open (often fol. by *up*). **33.** to render (any enclosed space) open to passage or access. **34.** to give access to; make accessible or available, as for use. **35.** to recall or revoke, as a judgment or decree, for the purpose of allowing further contest or delay. **36.** to clear of obstructions, as a passage, etc. **37.** to make (bodily passages) clear. **38.** to uncover, lay bare, or expose to view. **39.** to disclose, reveal, or divulge: *to open one's mind.* **40.** to render accessible to knowledge, enlightenment, sympathy, etc. **41.** to expand, extend, or spread out: *to open a map.* **42.** to make less compact, less close together, or the like: *to open ranks.* **43.** to establish for the entrance or use of the public, customers, etc.: *to open an office.* **44.** to set in action, begin, start, or commence (sometimes fol. by *up*): *to open a campaign.* **45.** to cut or break into. **46.** to make an incision or opening in. **47.** to make or produce (an opening) by cutting or breaking, or by pushing aside or removing obstructions: *to open a way through a crowd.* **48.** *Naut.* to come in sight of, or get a view of, as by passing some intervening object. **49.** *Law.* to make the first statement of (a case) to the court or jury. —*v.i.* **50.** to become open, as a door, building, box, enclosure, etc. **51.** to afford access (into, to, etc.): *a door that opened into a garden.* **52.** (of a building, etc.) to open its doors. **53.** to begin a session or term, as a school. **54.** to begin a season or tour, as a theatrical company. **55.** to have an opening, passage, or outlet (into, upon, etc.): *a room that opens into a corridor.* **56.** to have its opening or outlet (fol. by *toward*, *to*, etc.). **57.** to come apart or asunder, or burst open, so as to admit of passage or display the interior. **58.** to become disclosed or revealed. **59.** to come into view, or become more visible or plain, as on nearer approach. **60.** to become receptive to knowledge, sympathy, etc., as the mind. **61.** to disclose or reveal one's knowledge, thoughts, feelings, etc. **62.** to spread out or expand, as the hand or a fan. **63.** to open a book, etc.: *open at page 32.* **64.** to become less compact, less close together, or the like: *ranks open.* **65.** to begin, start, or commence; start operations. **66.** *Hunting.* (of hounds) to begin to bark, as on the scent of game. —*n.* **67.** an open or clear space. **68.** the open air. **69.** the open water, as of the sea. **70.** the situation of one who does not use or seek concealment. **71.** an opening or aperture. **72.** an opening or opportunity. **73. the open,** the unenclosed or unobstructed country. [ME and OE, c. G *offen*] —*o'pen·er,* n. —*o'pen·ly,* adv. —*o'pen·ness,* n. —**Syn. 20.** See **frank.** —**Ant. 20.** reticent.

open air, the unconfined atmosphere; outdoor air.
o·pen-air (ō'pən âr'), adj. existing in, taking place in, or characteristic of the open air; outdoor: *He conducted three open-air concerts last summer.*
o·pen-and-shut (ō'pən ən shŭt'), adj. obvious; easily decided.
open chain, *Chem.* a linking of atoms in an organic molecule which may be represented by a structural formula whose ends do not join to form a ring.
open city, *Mil.* a city which is officially declared to be of no military importance, either in battle or in the movement of troops and matériel, and is therefore not subject to military attack.
open door, 1. the policy of admitting all nations to a country upon equal terms, esp. for trade. **2.** free admission or access; admission to all upon equal terms.

o·pen-eyed (ō'pən īd'), adj. **1.** having the eyes open. **2.** having the eyes wide open as in wonder. **3.** watchful; alert. **4.** done or experienced with the eyes open.
o·pen-faced (ō'pən fāst'), adj. **1.** having a frank or ingenuous face. **2.** (of a watch) having the dial covered only by the crystal.
o·pen-hand·ed (ō'pən hăn'dĭd), adj. generous; free. —o'pen-hand·ed·ly, adv. —o'pen-hand·ed·ness, n.
o·pen-heart·ed (ō'pən här'tĭd), adj. **1.** unreserved, candid, or frank. **2.** kindly. —o'pen-heart·ed·ly, adv. —o'pen-heart·ed·ness, n.
o·pen-hearth (ō'pən härth'), adj. *Metall.* denoting a shallow-hearth reverberatory furnace for steelmaking, with two openings at each end to admit fuel and air. Combustion takes place over the molten metal charge.
open-hearth process, the steelmaking process using an open-hearth furnace.
open house, a house hospitably open to all friends who may wish to visit it or enjoy its entertainment.
o·pen·ing (ō'pən ĭng), n. **1.** a making or becoming open. **2.** act of one who or that which opens (in any sense). **3.** an unobstructed or unoccupied space or place. **4.** an open space in solid matter; a gap, hole, or aperture. **5.** *U.S.* a tract of land thinly wooded as compared with adjoining forest tracts. **6.** act of beginning, starting, or commencing. **7.** the first part or initial stage of anything. **8.** a vacancy. **9.** an opportunity. **10.** a formal beginning of a season's sale of goods. **11.** the first performance of a theatrical production. **12.** *Law.* the statement of the case made by counsel to the court or jury preliminary to adducing evidence. **13.** *Chess, etc.* a mode of beginning a game.
open letter, a letter made public by radio, newspaper, or such, but written as though to a specific person.
o·pen-mind·ed (ō'pən mīn'dĭd), adj. having or showing a mind open to new arguments or ideas. —o'pen-mind·ed·ly, adv. —o'pen-mind·ed·ness, n.
o·pen-mouthed (ō'pən mouᵗʰd', -moutht'), adj. **1.** having the mouth open. **2.** gaping with surprise or astonishment. **3.** greedy, ravenous, or rapacious. **4.** clamoring at the sight of game or prey, as hounds. **5.** vociferous or clamorous. **6.** having a wide mouth, as a vessel.
open policy, *Insurance.* a policy which covers a shifting quantity of goods and which usually requires a monthly computation of premium charges.
open position, *Music.* arrangement of a chord with wide spaces between the parts.
open primary, a direct primary election in which voters need not meet a test of party membership.
Open sesame!, a password or charm at which doors or barriers fly open (from the use of these words to open the door of the robbers' den in "Ali Baba and the Forty Thieves," in *The Arabian Nights' Entertainments*).
open shop, 1. a nonunion shop which may or may not employ union members together with nonmembers, but which does not recognize or deal with a union as the representative of the employees. Cf. **nonunion shop.** **2.** an antiunion shop in which union members are not knowingly employed. **3.** a shop in which a union, because chosen by a majority of the employees, acts as representative of all the employees in making agreements with the employer, but in which union membership is not a condition of employment.
o·pen·work (ō'pən wûrk'), n. any kind of work, esp. ornamental, as of metal, stone, wood, embroidery, lace, etc., showing openings through its substance.
op·e·ra¹ (ŏp'ər ə, ŏp'rə), n. **1.** an extended dramatic composition in which music is an essential and predominant factor, consisting of recitatives, arias, choruses, etc., with orchestral accompaniment, scenery, acting, and sometimes dancing; a musical drama. See **grand opera, comic opera.** **2.** the form or branch of musical and dramatic art represented by such compositions. **3.** the score or the words of a musical drama. **4.** a performance of one. **5.** *Colloq.* an opera house. [t. It., t. L: service, work, a work]
o·pe·ra² (ŏp'ər ə), n. pl. of **opus.**
op·er·a·ble (ŏp'ər ə bəl), adj. **1.** that can be put into practice. **2.** admitting of a surgical operation.
o·pé·ra bouffe (ŏp'ər ə bōōf'; Fr. ō pā rä bōōf'), French. a comic opera, esp. of farcical character.
o·pé·ra co·mique (ō pā rä kō mēk'), French. comic opera.
opera glasses, a small, low-power binocular for use in theaters, etc. Also, **opera glass.**
opera hat, a man's collapsible tall hat, held open or in shape by springs.
opera house, a theater devoted chiefly to operas.
op·er·ant (ŏp'ər ənt), adj. **1.** operating; producing effects. —n. **2.** one who or that which operates. [t. L: s. *operans*]
op·er·ate (ŏp'ə rāt'), v., -ated, -ating. —v.i. **1.** to work or run, as a machine does. **2.** to work or use a machine, apparatus, or the like. **3.** to act effectively; exert force or influence (often fol. by *on* or *upon*): *the same causes are operating for war.* **4.** to perform some process of work or treatment. **5.** *Surg.* to perform some manual act or series of acts upon the body of a patient, usually with instruments, to remedy deformity, injury, or disease. **6.** (of medicines, etc.) to produce the effect intended. **7.** *Mil., Naval.* **a.** to carry on operations in war. **b.** to give orders and accomplish military acts, as distinguished from doing staff work. **8.** to carry on

transactions in securities, or some commodity, esp. speculatively or on a large scale. —*v.t.* **9.** to manage or use (a machine, etc.) at work: *to operate a switchboard.* **10.** to keep (a machine, apparatus, factory, industrial system, etc.) working or in operation. **11.** to bring about, effect, or produce, as by action or the exertion of force or influence. [t. L: m.s. *operātus*, pp., having done work, having had effect] —**op′er·at′a·ble,** *adj.*

op·er·at·ic (ŏp′ərăt′ĭk), *adj.* of or pertaining to opera: *operatic music.* —**op′er·at′i·cal·ly,** *adv.*

op·er·a·tion (ŏp′ərā′shən), *n.* **1.** act, process, or manner of operating. **2.** state of being operative: *a rule no longer in operation.* **3.** the power of operating; efficacy, influence, or virtue. **4.** exertion of force or influence; agency. **5.** a process of a practical or mechanical nature in some form of work or production: *a delicate operation in watchmaking.* **6.** a course of productive or industrial activity: *building operations.* **7.** a particular course or process: *mental operations.* **8.** a business transaction, esp. one of a speculative nature or on a large scale: *operations in oil.* **9.** *Surg.* a process or method of operating on the body of a patient, as with instruments, to remedy injury, etc. **10.** *Math.* **a.** a process such as addition. **b.** the action of applying a mathematical process to a quantity or quantities. **11.** *Mil., Naval.* **a.** the conduct of a campaign. **b.** a campaign. —**op′er·a′tion·al,** *adj.*

op·er·a·tion·al·ism (ŏp′ərā′shən əlĭz′əm), *n. Philos.* the doctrine that scientific concepts secure their meaning from the relevant set of operations involved, stimulated by the relativity theory of Einstein.

operations research, the analysis, usually involving mathematical treatment, of a process, problem, or operation to determine its purpose and effectiveness and to gain maximum efficacy.

op·er·a·tive (ŏp′ərā′tĭv, -ər ə tĭv). *n.* **1.** a worker; one engaged, employed, or skilled in some branch of work, esp. productive or industrial work; a workman, artisan, or factory hand. **2.** a detective. —*adj.* **3.** operating, or exerting force or influence. **4.** having force, or being in effect or operation: *laws operative in a community.* **5.** effective or efficacious. **6.** engaged in, concerned with, or pertaining to work or productive activity. **7.** *Med.* concerned with, involving, or pertaining to remedial operations: *operative surgery.*

op·er·a·tor (ŏp′ərā′tər), *n.* **1.** a worker; one employed or skilled in operating a machine, apparatus, or the like: *a telegraph operator.* **2.** one who conducts some working or industrial establishment, enterprise, or system: *the operators of a mine.* **3.** one who operates in stocks, etc., esp. speculatively or on a large scale. **4.** one who performs a surgical operation.

o·per·cu·late (ō pûr′kyə lĭt, -lāt′), *adj.* having an operculum. Also, **o·per′cu·lat/ed.**

o·per·cu·lum (ō pûr′kyə ləm), *n., pl.* **-la** (-lə), **-lums.** **1.** *Bot., Zool., etc.* a part or organ serving as a lid or cover, as a covering flap on a seed vessel. **2.** *Zool.* **a.** the gill cover of fishes and amphibians. **b.** (in many gastropods) a horny plate which closes the opening of the shell when the animal is retracted. [t. L: a cover, lid]

o·pe·re ci·ta·to (ō′pərē′ sĭ tä′tō). *Latin.* in the work cited or quoted. *Abbr.:* op. cit.

op·er·et·ta (ŏp′ərĕt′ə), *n., pl.* **-erettas, -eretti** (-ərĕt′ē). a short opera, commonly of a light character. [t. It., dim. of *opera* OPERA]

op·er·ose (ŏp′ərōs′), *adj.* **1.** industrious, as a person. **2.** done with or involving much labor. [t. L: m.s. *operōsus*] —**op′er·ose′ly,** *adv.* —**op′er·ose′ness,** *n.*

oph·i·cleide (ŏf′əklīd′), *n.* a musical wind instrument, a development of the old wooden serpent, consisting of a conical metal tube bent double. [t. F, f. Gk.: *ŏphi(s)* serpent + m.s. *kleis* key]

o·phid·i·an (ō fĭd′īən), *adj.* **1.** of, pertaining to, or belonging to the snakes. —*n.* **2.** a snake. [f. s. NL *Ophidia,* pl. (der. Gk. *ŏphis* serpent) + -AN]

oph·i·ol·a·try (ŏf′ĭ ŏl′ə trĭ, ō′fĭ-), *n.* serpent worship. [b. Gk. *ŏphi(s)* snake and (ID)OLATRY] —**oph′i·ol·a·trous,** *adj.*

O·phir (ō′fər), *n.* a country of uncertain location, possibly southern Arabia or the eastern coast of Africa, from which gold and precious stones and trees were brought for Solomon. I Kings 10:11. [t. Heb.]

oph·ite (ŏf′īt, ō′fīt), *n.* a greenish altered diabase. [t. L: m.s. *ophītes,* t. Gk.: serpentlike, serpentine]

o·phit·ic (ō fĭt′ĭk), *adj.* noting or pertaining to a rock texture exhibited by certain ophites (diabases), in which elongate feldspar crystals are embedded in a matrix.

ophthalm., ophthalmology. Also, **ophthalmol.**

oph·thal·mi·a (ŏf thăl′mĭ ə), *n. Pathol.* inflammation of the eye, esp. of its membranes or external structures. [t. LL, t. Gk.: a disease of eyes]

oph·thal·mic (ŏf thăl′mĭk), *adj.* of or pertaining to the eye; ocular.

oph·thal·mi·tis (ŏf′thăl mī′tĭs), *n. Pathol.* inflammation of the eye, esp. of the eyeball in both its external and its internal structures. [t. NL]

ophthalmo-, a word element meaning "eye." [t. Gk., comb. form of *ophthalmós*]

oph·thal·mol·o·gist (ŏf′thăl mŏl′ə jĭst), *n.* a doctor of medicine skilled in ophthalmology.

oph·thal·mol·o·gy (ŏf′thăl mŏl′ə jĭ), *n.* the science dealing with the anatomy, functions, and diseases of the

eye. —**oph·thal·mo·log·i·cal** (ŏf thăl′mə lŏj′ə kəl), *adj.*

oph·thal·mo·scope (ŏf thăl′mə skōp′), *n.* an instrument for viewing the interior of the eye or examining the retina. —**oph·thal·mo·scop·ic** (ŏf thăl′mə skŏp′ĭk), **oph·thal′mo·scop′i·cal,** *adj.*

oph·thal·mos·co·py (ŏf′thăl mŏs′kə pĭ), *n.* the use of an opthalmoscope.

-opia, a word element of nouns denoting a condition of sight or of the visual organs, as in *amblyopia, diplopia, emmetropia, hemeralopia, myopia.* [t. Gk., der. *ŏps* eye]

o·pi·ate (*n., adj.* ō′pĭ ĭt, -āt′; *v.* ō′pĭ āt′), *n., adj., v.,* **-ated, -ating.** —*n.* **1.** a medicine that contains opium and hence has the quality of inducing sleep; a narcotic. **2.** anything that causes dullness or inaction, or that quiets the feelings. —*adj.* **3.** mixed or prepared with opium. **4.** inducing sleep; soporific; narcotic. —*v.t.* **5.** to subject to an opiate; stupefy. **6.** to dull or deaden. [t. ML: m.s. *opiātus,* der. L *opium* OPIUM]

o·pine (ō pīn′), *v.t., v.i.* opined, opining. *Obs. except Humorous.* to think; deem; hold or express an opinion, or as one's opinion. [t. L: m.s. *opīnāri* think, deem]

o·pin·ion (ə pĭn′yən), *n.* **1.** what is thought on any matter or subject; judgment or belief resting on grounds insufficient to produce certainty: *public opinion.* **2.** a particular judgment or belief of this kind; a view or notion (held or expressed): *to give an opinion on tariffs.* **3.** a formal or professional judgment expressed: *a medical opinion.* **4.** a judgment or estimate of a person or thing with respect to character, merit, etc. **5.** a favorable estimate; esteem. [ME, t. OF, t. L: s. *opīnio* supposition]

—**Syn. 1.** OPINION, SENTIMENT, VIEW are terms for one's conclusion about something. An OPINION is a belief or judgment which falls short of absolute conviction, certainty, or positive knowledge; it is a conclusion that certain facts, ideas, etc. are probably true or likely to prove so: *political opinions, an opinion about art, in my opinion this is true.* SENTIMENT (usually pl.) refers to an opinion or judgment arrived at as the result of deliberation and representing a rather fixed conviction; it usually has a tinge of emotion about it: *these are my sentiments.* VIEW is an estimate of something, an intellectual judgment, a critical survey based on a mental examination, particularly of a public matter: *views on governmental planning.* —**Ant. 1.** fact.

o·pin·ion·at·ed (ə pĭn′yə nā′tĭd), *adj.* obstinate or conceited with regard to one's opinions; conceitedly dogmatic. —**o·pin′ion·at′ed·ness,** *n.*

o·pin·ion·a·tive (ə pĭn′yə nā′tĭv), *adj.* **1.** of, pertaining to, or of the nature of opinion. **2.** opinionated. —**o·pin′ion·a′tive·ly,** *adv.* —**o·pin′ion·a′tive·ness,** *n.*

o·pi·um (ō′pĭ əm), *n.* the inspissated juice of a poppy, *Papaver somniferum,* containing morphine and other alkaloids: a stimulant narcotic (in sufficient quantities a powerful narcotic poison) of great value in medicine to relieve pain, induce sleep, etc. [ME, t. L, t. Gk.: m. *ŏpion,* dim. of *opós* juice]

opium eating, the habitual use of opium in some form by eating or swallowing. —**opium eater.**

o·pi·um·ism (ō′pĭ əm ĭz′əm), *n. Pathol.* **1.** the habit of taking opium. **2.** a morbid condition induced by the habitual use of opium.

opium smoking, the practice or habit of smoking opium as a stimulant or intoxicant. —**opium smoker.**

op·o·del·doc (ŏp′ə dĕl′dŏk), *n. Obs.* any of various liniments containing soap, camphor, alcohol, etc. [prob. coined by Paracelsus]

O·por·to (ō pôr′tō), *n.* a city in NW Portugal: a port near the mouth of the Douro river. 281,406 (1950). Portuguese, **Porto.**

o·pos·sum (ə pŏs′əm, pŏs′əm), *n.* **1.** a prehensile-tailed, pouched marsupial mammal, *Didelphis virginiana,* about the size of a large cat, common in the southern U.S., which feigns death when caught. **2.** any of many Neotropical genera of the same family. [t. Algonquian; cf. Renape (of Va.) *apäsum* white beast, Ojibwa *wabä-sim* white dog]

Opossum. *Didelphis virginiana* (Total length 33 in., tail 12 in.)

opossum shrimp, any of the small, shrimplike schizopod crustaceans constituting the family *Mysidae.* The females carry their eggs in a pouch between the legs.

opp., 1. opposed. **2.** opposite.

Op·pen·heim (ŏp′ən hīm′), *n.* E(dward) Phillips, 1866–1946, British novelist.

Op·pen·heim·er (ŏp′ən hī′mər), *n.* J. Robert, born 1904, U.S. nuclear physicist.

op·pi·dan (ŏp′ə dən), *adj.* **1.** of a town; urban. —*n.* **2.** a townsman. [t. L: s. *oppidānus* belonging to a town]

op·pi·late (ŏp′ə lāt′), *v.t.,* **-lated, -lating.** to stop up; fill with obstructing matter; obstruct. [t. L: m.s. *oppīlātus,* pp.] —**op′pi·la′tion,** *n.*

op·po·nen·cy (ə pō′nən sĭ), *n.* **1.** act of opposing. **2.** state of being an opponent.

op·po·nent (ə pō′nənt), *n.* **1.** one who is on the opposite side in a contest, controversy, or the like; an adversary. —*adj.* **2.** being opposite, as in position. **3.** opposing; adverse. **4.** *Anat.* bringing parts into opposition, as the muscles which set the thumb and little finger against each other. [t. L: s. *opponens,* ppr., opposing] —**Syn. 1.** antagonist. OPPONENT, COMPETITOR, RIVAL refer to persons engaged in a contest. OPPONENT is the most impersonal, meaning merely one who opposes; perhaps one who continually blocks and frustrates or one who happens to be on the opposite side in a temporary contest: *an opponent in a debate.* COMPETITOR emphasizes the action in striving against another, or others, for a definite, common goal: *competitors in business.* RIVAL has both personal and emotional connotations; it emphasizes the idea that (usually) two persons are struggling to attain the same object: *rivals for an office.*

op·por·tune (ŏp/ərtūn/, -tōōn/), *adj.* **1.** appropriate or favorable: *an opportune moment.* **2.** occurring or coming at an appropriate time; timely: *an opportune warning.* [ME, t. L: m. *opportūnus*] —**op·por·tune/ly**, *adv.* —**op/por·tune/ness**, *n.*
—**Syn. 2.** OPPORTUNE, SEASONABLE, TIMELY refer to that which is particularly fitting or suitable for a certain time. OPPORTUNE refers to that which is well-timed and meets exactly the demands of the time or occasion: *an opportune remark.* That which is SEASONABLE is right or proper for the time or season or occasion: *seasonable weather.* That which is TIMELY occurs or is done at an appropriate time, esp. in time to meet some need: *timely intervention.* —**Ant. 1.** inappropriate.

op·por·tun·ism (ŏp/ərtū/nĭzəm, -tōō/-), *n.* **1.** the policy or practice, in politics or otherwise, of adapting actions, etc., to expediency or circumstances (often with implication of sacrifice of principle). **2.** an action or proceeding due to this policy. —**op/por·tun·is/tic**, *adj.* —**op/por·tun·is/tic**, *adj.*

op·por·tu·ni·ty (ŏp/ərtū/nətĭ, -tōō/-), *n., pl.* **-ties.** an appropriate or favorable time or occasion.

op·pos·a·ble (əpō/zəbəl), *adj.* **1.** capable of being placed opposite to something else. **2.** that may be opposed. —**op·pos/a·bil/i·ty**, *n.*

op·pose (əpōz/), *v.,* **-posed, -posing.** —*v.t.* **1.** to act or contend in opposition to; drive against; resist; combat. **2.** to stand in the way of; hinder. **3.** to set as an opponent or adversary. **4.** be hostile or adverse to, as in opinion. **5.** to set as an obstacle or hindrance: *to oppose reason to force.* **6.** to set against in some relation, as of offsetting, antithesis, or contrast: *to oppose the advantages to the disadvantages.* **7.** to use or take as being opposite or contrary: *words opposed in meaning.* **8.** to set (something) over against something else in place, or so as to face or be opposite. —*v.i.* **9.** to be or act in opposition. [ME, t. OF: m.s. *opposer,* b. L *oppōnere* set against and F *poser* POSE¹] —**op·pos/er**, *n.*
—**Syn. 1.** OPPOSE, RESIST, WITHSTAND imply setting up a force against something. The difference between OPPOSE and RESIST is somewhat that between offensive and defensive action: to OPPOSE is mainly to fight against, in order to thwart certain tendencies, procedures, of which one does not approve: *he opposed the passage of the bill.* RESIST suggests that the subject is already threatened by the forces, or by the imminent possibility, against which he struggles: *to resist temptation.* Again, whereas OPPOSE always suggests an attitude of great disapproval, RESIST may imply an inner struggle in which the will is divided: *she tried unsuccessfully to resist his charm.* WITHSTAND generally implies successful resistance; it may refer to endurance that allows one to emerge unharmed (*to withstand a shock*), as well as to active resistance: *to withstand an attack.* —**Ant. 9.** comply, submit.

op·po·site (ŏp/əzĭt), *adj.* **1.** placed or lying over against something else or each other, or in a corresponding position from an intervening line, space, or thing: *opposite ends of a room.* **2.** contrary or diametrically different, as in nature, qualities, direction, result, or significance. **3.** *Bot.* a. situated on diametrically opposed sides of an axis, as leaves when there are two on one node. **b.** having one organ vertically above another; superposed. **4.** *Obs.* adverse or inimical. —*n.* **5.** one who or that which is opposite or contrary. **6.** an antonym. **7.** *Rare.* an opponent. [ME, t. L: m. *oppositus,* pp., put before or against, opposed] —**op/po·site·ly**, *adv.* —**op/po·site·ness**, *n.*
—**Syn. 2.** OPPOSITE, CONTRARY, REVERSE imply that two things differ from each other in such a way as to indicate a definite kind of relationship. OPPOSITE suggests symmetrical antithesis in position, action, or character: *opposite ends of a pole, sides of a road, views.* CONTRARY sometimes adds to OPPOSITE the idea of conflict or antagonism: *contrary statements, beliefs.* REVERSE suggests that which faces or moves in the opposite direction: *the reverse side of a coin, a reverse gear.* —**Ant. 2.** same, like.

opposite number, *Chiefly Brit.* a person who holds a corresponding position in another situation.

op·po·si·tion (ŏp/əzĭsh/ən), *n.* **1.** the action of opposing, resisting, or combating. **2.** antagonism or hostility. **3.** an opposing party or body. **4.** the political party opposed to the party in power. **5.** the act of placing opposite. **6.** the state or position of being placed opposite. **7.** the act of opposing or the state of being opposed by way of offset, antithesis, or contrast. **8.** *Logic.* **a.** the relation between two propositions which have the same subject and predicate, but which differ in quantity or quality, or in both. **b.** the relation between two propositions in virtue of which the truth or falsity of one of them determines the truth or falsity of the other. **9.** *Astron.* **a.** the situation of two heavenly bodies when their longitudes or right ascensions differ by 180°. **b.** the opposition of the moon or a planet and the sun, occurring when the earth is directly between them. [t.

Opposite leaves (def. 3a)

L: s. *oppositio;* r. ME *opposicioun,* t. OF: m. *opposicion*] —**op/po·si/tion·al**, *adj.*

op·press (əprĕs/), *v.t.* **1.** to lie heavily upon (the mind, a person, etc.), as care, sorrow, or any disturbing thought does. **2.** to burden with cruel or unjust impositions or restraints; to subject to a burdensome or harsh exercise of authority or power. **3.** to weigh down, as sleep or weariness does. **4.** *Obs.* to put down, subdue or suppress. **5.** *Obs.* to press against or down. [ME *oppresse(n),* t. ML: m. *oppressāre,* freq. of L *opprimere* press against, bear down, subdue] —**op·pres/sor**, *n.*
—**Syn. 1, 2.** OPPRESS, DEPRESS, both having the literal meaning to press down upon, to cause to sink, are today mainly limited to figurative applications. To OPPRESS is usually to subject (a people) to burdens, to undue exercise of authority, and the like; its chief application, therefore, is to a social or political situation: *the tyrant oppressed his subjects.* DEPRESS suggests mainly the psychological effect, upon the individual, of unpleasant conditions, situations, etc., which sadden and discourage: *depressed by the news.* When OPPRESS is sometimes used in this sense, it suggests a psychological attitude of more complete hopelessness: *oppressed by a sense of failure.* —**Ant. 1.** uphold, encourage.

op·pres·sion (əprĕsh/ən), *n.* **1.** the exercise of authority or power in a burdensome, cruel or unjust manner. **2.** act of oppressing. **3.** the state of being oppressed. **4.** the feeling of being oppressed by something weighing down the bodily powers or depressing the mind. —**Syn. 1.** tyranny, despotism, persecution.

op·pres·sive (əprĕs/ĭv), *adj.* **1.** burdensome, unjustly harsh, or tyrannical, as a king, taxes, measures, etc. **2.** causing discomfort because uncomfortably great, intense, elaborate, etc.: *oppressive heat.* **3.** distressing or grievous, as sorrows. —**op·pres/sive·ly**, *adv.* —**op·pres/sive·ness**, *n.*

op·pro·bri·ous (əprō/brĭəs), *adj.* **1.** conveying or expressing opprobrium, as language, a speaker, etc.: *opprobrious invectives.* **2.** disgraceful or shameful; contumelious. [ME, t. LL: m.s. *opprōbriōsus*] —**op·pro/bri·ous·ly**, *adv.* —**op·pro/bri·ous·ness**, *n.*

op·pro·bri·um (əprō/brĭəm), *n.* **1.** the disgrace or the reproach incurred by conduct considered shameful; infamy. **2.** a cause or object of such reproach. [t. L]

op·pugn (əpūn/), *v.t.* **1.** to assail by criticism, argument, or action. **2.** to call in question (rights, judgment, etc.); dispute (statements, etc.). [ME, t. F: s. *oppugner,* t. L: s. *oppugnāre* fight against] —**op·pugn/er**, *n.*

op·pug·nant (əpŭg/nənt), *adj.* opposing; antagonistic; contrary. —**op·pug/nan·cy**, *n.*

Ops (ŏps), *n. Rom. Myth.* the wife of Saturn and goddess of plenty. [t. L: lit., wealth]

-opsis, a word element indicating apparent likeness, as in *coreopsis.* [t. Gk.: appearance, sight]

op·son·ic (ŏpsŏn/ĭk), *adj. Bacteriol.* of, pertaining to, or influenced by opsonin.

opsonic index, the ratio of the number of bacteria taken up by phagocytes in the blood serum of a patient or test animal, to the number taken up in normal blood serum.

op·so·nin (ŏp/sənĭn), *n. Bacteriol.* a constituent of normal or immune blood serum which makes invading bacteria more susceptible to the destructive action of the phagocytes. [f Gk. *opsōn(ion)* provisions + -IN²]

op·so·nize (ŏp/sənīz/), *v.t.,* **-nized, -nizing.** *Immunol.* to increase the susceptibility of (bacteria) to ingestion by phagocytes. —**op/son·i·za/tion**, *n.*

opt (ŏpt), *v.i.* to make a choice; choose. [t. F: s. *opter,* t. L: m. *optāre* choose, wish]

opt., **1.** optative. **2.** optical. **3.** optician. **4.** optics.

op·ta·tive (ŏp/tətĭv), *Gram.* —*adj.* **1.** designating or pertaining to a verb mood (as in Greek) having among its functions the expression of a wish, as Greek *ïoimen* "may we (i.e., we wish we might) go." —*n.* **2.** the optative mood. **3.** a verb in it. [t. LL: m.s. *optātīvus* serving to express a wish] —**op/ta·tive·ly**, *adv.*

op·tic (ŏp/tĭk), *adj.* **1.** pertaining to or connected with the eye as the organ of sight, or sight as a function of the brain. **2.** optical. —*n.* **3.** (*usually pl.*) the eye. [t. ML: s. *opticus,* t. Gk.: m. *optikós* of sight]

op·ti·cal (ŏp/tĭkəl), *adj.* **1.** acting by means of sight or light, as instruments. **2.** constructed to assist the sight, as devices. **3.** pertaining to sight; visual: *an optical illusion.* **4.** pertaining to optics. **5.** dealing with or skilled in optics. —**op/ti·cal·ly**, *adv.*

optical activity, *Phys. Chem.* the property of compounds which consists of rotating the plane of vibration of polarized light.

optic axis, *Crystall.* the direction or directions, uniaxial or biaxial respectively, in a crystal exhibiting double refraction, along which this phenomenon does not occur.

op·ti·cian (ŏptĭsh/ən), *n.* **1.** one who makes glasses for remedying defects of vision, in accordance with the prescriptions of oculists. **2.** a maker or seller of optical glasses and instruments. [t. F: m. *opticien,* der. ML *optica* OPTICS. See -ICIAN]

optic nerve, the nerve of sight, connecting the eye with the brain. See diag. under eye.

op·tics (ŏp/tĭks), *n.* the branch of physical science that deals with the properties and phenomena of light and with vision. [pl. of OPTIC. See -ICS]

optic thalamus, thalamus (def. 1).

op·ti·me (ŏp/təmē/), *n.* (at Cambridge University, England) one of those in the second or third grade of honors in mathematics (**senior optimes** or **junior optimes**), the wranglers constituting the first rank. [t. L: adv., best, very well]

op·ti·mism (ŏp′tə mĭz′əm). *n.* **1.** disposition to hope for the best; tendency to look on the bright side of things. **2.** the belief that good ultimately predominates over evil in the world. **3.** the doctrine that the existing world is the best of all possible worlds. **4.** the belief that goodness pervades reality. [t. NL: s. *optimismus*, der. L *optimus* best]

op·ti·mist (ŏp′tə mĭst). *n.* one given to optimism.

op·ti·mis·tic (ŏp′tə mĭs′tĭk), *adj.* **1.** disposed to take a favorable view of things. **2.** of or pertaining to optimism. Also, **op′ti·mis′ti·cal.** —**op′ti·mis′ti·cal·ly,** *adv.*

op·ti·mize (ŏp′tə mīz′), *v.,* -mized, -mizing. —*v.i.* **1.** to be optimistic. —*v.t.* **2.** to make the best of.

op·ti·mum (ŏp′tə məm). *n., pl.* -ma (-mə), -mums, *adj.* —*n.* **1.** the best or most favorable point, degree, amount, etc., for the purpose, as of temperature, light, moisture, etc., for the growth or reproduction of an organism. —*adj.* **2.** best or most favorable: *optimum conditions.* [t. L: (neut.) best (superl. of *bonus* good)]

op·tion (ŏp′shən), *n.* **1.** power or liberty of choosing; right of freedom of choice. **2.** something which may be or is chosen; choice. **3.** the act of choosing. **4.** a privilege acquired, as by the payment of a premium or consideration, of demanding, within a specified time, the carrying out of a transaction upon stipulated terms. [t. L: s. *optio* choice] —**Syn. 2.** See **choice.**

op·tion·al (ŏp′shən əl), *adj.* **1.** left to one's choice: *attendance is optional.* **2.** leaving something to choice. —**op′tion·al·ly,** *adv.*

op·tom·e·ter (ŏp tŏm′ə tər), *n.* any of various instruments for measuring the refractive error of an eye. [f. OPT(IC) + -(O)METER]

op·tom·e·trist (ŏp tŏm′ə trĭst), *n.* one skilled in optometry.

op·tom·e·try (ŏp tŏm′ə trĭ), *n.* the practice or art of testing the eyes by means of suitable instruments or appliances (usually without the use of drugs), for defects of vision, in order to fit them with glasses.

op·u·lence (ŏp′yə ləns), *n.* **1.** wealth, riches, or affluence. **2.** abundance, as of resources, etc. **3.** the state of being opulent. Also, **op′u·len·cy.**

op·u·lent (ŏp′yə lənt), *adj.* **1.** wealthy, rich, or affluent, as persons or places. **2.** richly supplied; abundant or plentiful: *opulent sunshine.* [t. L: s. *opulens opulentus* rich, wealthy] —**op′u·lent·ly,** *adv.* —**Syn. 1.** See **rich.**

o·pun·ti·a (ō pŭn′shĭ′ə), *n.* **1.** any plant of the cactaceous genus *Opuntia,* comprising fleshy herbs, shrubby plants, and sometimes trees, with branches usually composed of flattened or globose joints, and with (usually) yellow flowers and pear-shaped or ovoid, often edible fruit. **2.** a prickly pear. [t. NL, der. L *Opuntius* pertaining to *Opūs,* a town in Locris, Greece]

o·pus (ō′pəs), *n., pl.* **opera** (ŏp′ə rə). **1.** a work or composition. **2.** a musical composition. **3.** one of the compositions of a composer as numbered according to date of publication. *Abbr.:* Op. [t. L: work, labor, a work]

o·pus·cule (ō pŭs′kūl), *n.* **1.** a small work. **2.** a literary or musical work of small size. [t. L: m.s. *opusculum,* dim. of *opus* work]

o·quas·sa (ō kwăs′ə), *n.* a small trout, *Salvelinus oquassa,* with dark blue coloration, found in Maine. [said to be named after one of the Rangeley Lakes]

or[1] (ôr; *unstressed* ər), *conj.* a particle used: **1.** to connect words, phrases, or clauses representing alternatives: *to be or not to be.* **2.** to connect alternative terms: *the Hawaiian or Sandwich Islands.* **3.** often in correlation: *either . . . or; or . . . or; whether . . . or.* [ME *or,* orig. unstressed member of correlative *other . . . or,* earlier *other . . . other,* OE *āther oththe . . . oththe either . . . or*]

or[2], *prep., conj.* Archaic or Dial. before; ere. [ME *or* before, OE *ār* soon, early (c. Icel. *ār,* Goth. *air* early); akin to OE *ǣr* soon, before, ERE]

or[3] (ôr), *n. Her.* the tincture gold or yellow. [ME, t. F, g. L *aurum* gold]

-or[1], a suffix of nouns denoting action, state or condition, a quality or property, etc. as in *ardor, color, error, honor, labor, odor, tremor, valor, vigor.* [t. L; in some cases r. ME *-our,* t. AF (=F *-eur*), g. L *-or*]

-or[2], a suffix of nouns denoting who or that which does something, or has some particular function or office, as in *actor, confessor, creditor, distributor, elevator, emperor, governor, juror, refractor, tailor, traitor.* This suffix occurs chiefly in nouns originally Latin, or formed from Latin stems. In some cases it is used as an alternative or a substitute for *-er*[1] (a characteristically English suffix), esp. in legal terms (often correlative with forms in *-ee*) or with some other differentiation of sense: *assignor, grantor, lessor, sailor, survivor, vendor.* [t. L; in some cases r. ME *-our,* t. AF: (m.) *-(e)our* (=F *-eur*), g. L *-or, -ātor,* etc.]

or·ach (ôr′əch, ŏr′-), *n.* any of the plants of the genus *Atriplex,* esp. *A. hortensis* (**garden orach**), cultivated for use like spinach. Also, **or′ache.** [ME *orage,* t. OF: m. *arache,* g. L *ātriplex,* t. Gk.: m.s. *atráphaxsi*]

or·a·cle (ôr′ə kəl, ŏr′-), *n.* **1.** (in ancient Greece and elsewhere) an utterance, often ambiguous or obscure, given by a priest or priestess at a shrine as the response of the god to an inquiry. **2.** the agency or medium giving such responses, or a shrine or place at which they were given: *the oracle of Apollo at Delphi.* **3.** a divine communication or revelation. **4.** (*pl.*) the Scriptures. **5.** the holy of holies in the Jewish temple. See I Kings, 6:16, 19–23. **6.** any person or thing serving as an agency of divine communication. **7.** any utterance made or received as authoritative and infallible. **8.** a person who delivers authoritative or highly regarded pronouncements. [ME, t. OF, t. L: m.s. *ōrāculum*]

o·rac·u·lar (ō răk′yə lər), *adj.* **1.** of the nature of, resembling, or suggesting an oracle: *an oracular response.* **2.** giving forth utterances or decisions as if by special inspiration or authority. **3.** uttered or delivered as if divinely inspired or infallible; sententious. **4.** ambiguous or obscure. **5.** portentous. —**o·rac′u·lar·ly,** *adv.*

O·ra·dea (ō rä′dyä), *n.* a city in NW Rumania. 82,282 (1948). Also, **Oradea Ma·re** (mä′rĕ). German, **Grosswardein.** Hungarian, **Nagyvárad.**

o·ral (ōr′əl), *adj.* **1.** uttered by the mouth; spoken: *oral testimony.* **2.** employing speech, as teachers or methods of teaching. **3.** of or pertaining to the mouth: *the oral cavity.* **4.** done, taken, or administered by the mouth: *an oral dose of medicine.* **5.** *Zool.* pertaining to that surface of polyps and marine animals which contains the mouth and tentacles. **6.** *Phonet.* with none of the voice issuing through the nose: *b* and *v* are oral consonants, and the normal English vowels are oral. —*n.* **7.** an oral examination in a college, school, etc. [f. s. L *ōs* mouth + -AL[1]] —**o′ral·ly,** *adv.* —**Syn. 1.** ORAL, VERBAL are not properly synonyms. ORAL is properly applied to that which is uttered by word of mouth, as opposed to what is conveyed in writing: *oral message.* VERBAL is often used for oral: *a verbal agreement.* Literally, however, VERBAL applies to the words, spoken or written, in which thought or feeling is conveyed: *a verbal picture.* —**Ant. 6.** nasal.

oral interpretation, the study and practice of vocally expressing the meaning of the printed page, especially of literature.

O·ran (ō răn′; *Fr.* ō răN′), *n.* a seaport in NW Algeria. 291,671 (1954).

o·rang (ō răng′), *n.* the orang-utan.

or·ange (ôr′ĭnj, ŏr′-). *n.* **1.** a globose reddish-yellow edible citrus fruit of which there are two principal kinds, the bitter and sweet, the latter comprising the most important of the citrus fruits. **2.** any of the white-flowered evergreen rutaceous trees yielding it, as *Citrus aurantium* (**bitter, Seville,** or **sour orange**) and *C. sinensis* (**sweet orange**), cultivated in warm countries. **3.** any of several other citrus trees, as *Poncirus trifoliata* (**trifoliate orange**), a hardy Japanese species cultivated widely in the U.S., largely for hedges. **4.** any of certain trees of other genera, as *Maclura pomifera* (see **Osage orange**), or the fruit. **5.** a color between yellow and red in the spectrum; reddish yellow. —*adj.* **6.** of or pertaining to the orange. **7.** reddish-yellow. [ME *orange,* t. OF, (b. with *or* gold), c. Sp. *naranja,* t. Ar.: m. *nāranj,* t. Pers.: m. *nārang,* prob. of East Indian orig.]

Or·ange (ôr′ĭnj, ŏr′-), *n.* **1.** a city in NE New Jersey, near Newark. 35,789 (1960). **2.** a river in the Union of South Africa, flowing from Basutoland W to the Atlantic. ab. 1300 mi. **3.** a former small principality of W Europe: now in the SE part of France. **4.** a princely family of Europe, rulers of the former principality of Orange. The present royal family of the Netherlands belongs to this family. **5.** a town in SE France, near Avignon: Roman ruins. 17,478 (1954). **6. Fort,** a former Dutch fort near the site of the present capitol in Albany, New York.

or·ange·ade (ôr′ĭnj ād′, ŏr′-), *n.* a drink made of orange juice and sweetened water.

orange blossom, the flower of the orange, much worn in wreaths, etc., by brides.

Orange Free State, a central province of the Union of South Africa: a Boer republic, 1854–1900; a British colony (**Orange River Colony**), 1900–10. 1,129,000 (est. 1955); 49,647 sq. mi. *Cap.:* Bloemfontein.

Or·ange·ism (ôr′ĭnj ĭz′əm, ŏr′-). *n.* the principles and practices of the Orangemen. —**Or′ange·ist,** *n.*

Or·ange·man (ôr′ĭnj mən, ŏr′-), *n., pl.* -men. a member of a secret society formed in the north of Ireland in 1795, having for its object the maintenance of the Protestant religion and political ascendancy.

orange pekoe, 1. a superior black tea composed of only the smallest top leaves and grown in India and Ceylon. **2.** any India or Ceylon tea of good quality.

or·ange·ry (ôr′ĭnj rĭ, ŏr′-), *n., pl.* -ries. a place, as a greenhouse, in which orange trees are cultivated. [t. F: m. *orangerie,* der. *oranger* orange tree, der. *orange* ORANGE]

or·ange·wood (ôr′ĭnj wŏŏd′, ŏr′-), *n.* the hard, fine-grained, yellowish wood of the orange tree, used in inlaid work and fine turnery.

o·rang-u·tan (ō răng′ŏŏ tăn′), *n.* a large, long-armed anthropoid ape, *Pongo pygmaeus,* of arboreal habits, found in Borneo and Sumatra. It is less closely related to man than are the gorilla and chimpanzee. Also, **o·rang-ou·tang** (ō răng′ŏŏ tăng′), **orang.** [ult. Malay: man of the woods]

Orang-utan. *Pongo pygmaeus*
(4½ ft. high, arm spread 7½ ft.)

ăct, āble, dâre, ärt; ĕbb, ēqual; ĭf, īce; hŏt, ōver, ôrder, oil, bŏŏk, ōōze, out; ŭp, ūse, ûrge; ə = a in alone; ch, chief; g, give; ng, ring; sh, shoe; th, thin; ŧh, that; zh, vision. See the full key on inside cover.

o·ra pro no·bis (ōr/ə prō nō/bĭs), *Latin*. pray for us.

o·rate (ōrāt/, ōr/āt), *v.i.*, **orated, orating.** *Chiefly Humorous*. to make an oration; hold forth. [back formation from ORATION]

o·ra·tion (ōrā/shən), *n.* **1.** a formal speech, esp. one delivered on a special occasion, as on an anniversary, at a funeral, or at academic exercises. **2.** a speech whose style, diction, and delivery give a studied, even heightened effect. [ME *oracion*, t. L: m.s. *ōrātio* speech, discourse, prayer] **—Syn. 1.** See **speech.**

or·a·tor (ōr/ə tər, ŏr/-), *n.* **1.** one who delivers an oration; a public speaker, esp. one of great eloquence. **2.** *Law*. a plaintiff. [t. L: speaker, supplicant; r. ME *oratour*, t. AF] **—or·a·tress** (ōr/ə trĭs, ŏr/-), *n. fem.*

or·a·tor·i·cal (ôr/ə tôr/ə kəl, ŏr/ə tŏr/-), *adj.* **1.** of, pertaining to, or character stic of an orator or oratory. **2.** given to oratory. **—or/a·tor/i·cal·ly,** *adv.*

or·a·to·ri·o (ôr/ə tōr/ĭ ō, ŏr/-), *n., pl.* **-rios.** an extended musical composition, with a text more or less dramatic in character and usually based upon a religious theme, for solo voices, chorus, and orchestra, and performed without action, costume, or scenery. [t. It., g. LL *ōrātōrium* ORATORY[2]; so named from the musical services in the church of the Oratory of St. Philip Neri in Rome]

or·a·to·ry[1] (ôr/ə tōr/ĭ, ŏr/-), *n.* **1.** the exercise of eloquence; eloquent speaking. **2.** the art of an orator; the art of public speaking. [t. L: m.s. *ōrātōria*, prop. fem. of *ōrātōrius* of an orator]

or·a·to·ry[2] (ôr/ə tōr/ĭ, ŏr/-), *n., pl.* **-ries. 1.** a place of prayer, as a small chapel or a room for private devotions. **2.** *(cap.)* any of certain religious societies of the Roman Catholic Church, esp. one **(Oratory of St. Philip Neri)** composed of secular priests, not bound by vows, devoted to simple and familiar preaching. [ME, t. LL: m.s. *ōrātōrium* place of prayer, prop. neut. of L *ōrātōrius* oratorical]

orb (ôrb), *n.* **1.** *Chiefly Poetic*. any of the heavenly bodies: *the orb of day* (the sun). **2.** a sphere or globe. **3.** *Chiefly Poetic*. the eyeball or eye. **4.** a globe bearing a cross; the mound, or emblem of sovereignty, esp. as part of the regalia of England. **5.** *Now Rare*. a circle, or anything circular. **6.** *Astron. Obs.* the orbit of a heavenly body. **7.** *Astrol.* the space within which the influence of a planet, etc., is supposed to act. **8.** *Obs.* the earth. **9.** *Obs.* a range or area of action. **—v.t. 10.** to form into a circle or a sphere. **11.** *Poetic*. to encircle; enclose. **—v.i. 12.** to move in an orbit. **13.** *Obs.* to assume the shape of an orb. [t. L: s. *orbis* circle, disk, orb] **—Syn. 2.** See **ball**[1].

or·bic·u·lar (ôr bĭk/yə lər), *adj.* like an orb; circular; ringlike; spherical; rounded. [ME, t. LL: s. *orbiculāris*, der. L *orbiculus*, dim. of *orbis* ORB] **—or·bic/u·lar/i·ty,** *n.* **—or·bic/u·lar·ly,** *adv.*

or·bic·u·late (ôr bĭk/yə lĭt, -lāt/), *adj.* orbicular; rounded. Also, **or·bic/u·lat/ed.** [t. L: m.s. *orbiculātus*, der. *orbiculus*. See ORBICULAR]

or·bit (ôr/bĭt), *n.* **1.** the elliptical or curved path described by a planet, satellite, etc., about a celestial body, as the sun. **2.** a course regularly pursued, as in life. **3.** *Anat.* **a.** the bony cavity of the skull which contains the eye; the eye socket. **b.** the eye. **4.** *Zool.* the part surrounding the eye of a bird or insect. **5.** an orb or sphere. **—v.t. 6.** to describe an orbit. [t. L: s. *orbita* wheel track, course, circuit] **—or·bit·al,** *adj.*

or·bi·ta·le (ôr/bə tā/lĭ), *n.* **1.** *Craniom.* the lowermost point on the lower margin of the left orbit, located instrumentally on the skull. **2.** *Cephalom.* the lowermost point on the lower margin of the left orbit, located by palpation on the head. [t. L: of an orbit (neut.)]

orbital index, *Craniom.* the ratio of the maximum breadth to the maximum height of the orbital cavity.

orb·y (ôr/bĭ), *adj. Rare.* like or pertaining to an orb.

O.R.C., Officers' Reserve Corps.

or·ce·in (ôr/sĭ ĭn), *n. Chem.* a red dye obtained by oxidizing an ammoniacal solution of orcinol, and forming the principal coloring matter of cudbear and orchil. [arbitrary alter. of *orcin*. See ORCINOL]

orch., orchestra.

or·chard (ôr/chərd), *n.* **1.** a piece of ground, usually enclosed, devoted to the cultivation of fruit trees. **2.** a collection of such trees. [ME *orch(i)ard*, OE *orceard*; r. *ortyard*, ME *ortyerd*, OE *ortgeard* (cf. Goth. *aurtigards* garden), f. *ort-* (cf. L *hortus* garden) + *geard* YARD[2]]

or·chard·ist (ôr/chər dĭst), *n.* one who cultivates an orchard.

or·ches·tra (ôr/kĭs trə), *n.* **1.** a company of performers on various musical instruments, including esp. stringed instruments of the violin family, clarinets and flutes, cornets and trombones, drums, cymbals, etc., for playing concert music, as symphonies, operas, and other compositions. **2.** (in a modern theater, etc.) **a.** the space reserved for the musicians, usually the front part of the main floor, **(orchestra pit). b.** the entire main-floor space for spectators. **c.** the parquet. **3.** (in the ancient Greek theater) the circular space in front of the stage, alloted to the chorus. **4.** (in the Roman theater) a similar space reserved for persons of distinction. [t. L, t. Gk.: the space on which the chorus danced]

or·ches·tral (ôr kĕs/trəl), *adj.* **1.** of or pertaining to an orchestra. **2.** composed for or performed by an orchestra. **—or·ches/tral·ly,** *adv.*

or·ches·trate (ôr/kĭs trāt/), *v.t., v.i.,* **-trated, -trating.** to compose or arrange (music) for performance by an orchestra. **—or/ches·tra/tion,** *n.*

or·ches·tri·on (ôr kĕs/trĭ ŏn), *n.* a mechanical musical instrument, resembling a barrel organ but more elaborate, for producing the effect of an orchestra.

or·chid (ôr/kĭd), *n.* **1.** any plant of the family *Orchidaceae*, comprising terrestrial and epiphytic perennial herbs of temperate and tropical regions, with flowers which are usually beautiful and often singular in form. **2.** purple, varying from bluish to reddish. [t. NL: m.s. *Orchideae* (later *Orchidāceae*), der. L *orchis*. See ORCHIS]

or·chi·da·ceous (ôr/kĭ dā/shəs), *adj.* belonging to the *Orchidaceae*, or orchid family of plants, as the vanilla.

or·chid·ol·o·gy (ôr/kĭd ŏl/ə jĭ), *n.* the branch of botany or horticulture that deals with orchids.

or·chil (ôr/kĭl, -chĭl), *n.* **1.** a violet coloring matter obtained from certain lichens, chiefly species of *Roccella*. **2.** any such lichen. Cf. litmus. [late ME, t. OF]

or·chis (ôr/kĭs), *n.* **1.** any orchid. **2.** any of various terrestrial orchids (esp. of the genus *Orchis*) of temperate regions, with spicate flowers. **3.** any orchid of an allied genus, esp. *Blephariglottis*, including the fringed orchis. [t. L, t. Gk.: orig., testicle; so named with reference to the shape of the root]

or·ci·nol (ôr/sə nōl/, -nŏl/), *n. Chem.* a colorless crystalline compound found in many lichens, and also prepared synthetically. Also, **or·cin** (ôr/sĭn). [f. s. NL *orcina* (t. It.: m. *orcello* ORCHIL) + -OL[2]]

Or·cus (ôr/kəs), *n. Rom. Myth.* **1.** the world of the dead; Hades. **2.** the god of the underworld, Pluto.

ord., 1. order. **2.** ordinal. **3.** ordinance. **4.** ordinary. **5.** ordnance.

or·dain (ôr dān/), *v.t.* **1.** *Eccles.* to invest with ministerial or sacerdotal functions; confer holy orders upon. **2.** to appoint authoritatively. **3.** *Obs.* to select or appoint for an office. **4.** to decree; give orders for. **5.** (of God, fate, etc.) to destine or predestine. [ME *ordeine(n)*, t. OF: m. *ordener*, t. L: m. *ordināre* order, arrange, appoint] **—or·dain/er,** *n.* **—or·dain/ment,** *n.*

or·deal (ôr dēl/, -dē/əl, ôr/dēl), *n.* **1.** any severe test or trial; a trying experience. **2.** a primitive form of trial to determine guilt or innocence, as by the effect of fire, poison, or water upon the accused, the result being regarded as a divine or preterhuman judgment. [var. (by correct etym. assoc. with DEAL[1]) of *ordale*, ME and OE *ordāl*, var. of OE *ordēl*, m. *urteil*, c. G *urteil* judgment]

or·der (ôr/dər), *n.* **1.** an authoritative direction, injunction, or mandate. **2.** *Law*. a command of a court or judge. **3.** *Mil.* **a.** order arms: *at the order*. **b.** (pl.) commands or notices issued by the Army, Navy, Air Force, or a military commander to troops under him. **4.** the disposition of things following one after another, as in space, time, etc.; succession or sequence. **5.** a condition in which everything is in its proper place with reference to other things and to its purpose; methodical or harmonious arrangement. **6.** formal disposition or array: *set our men in order*. **7.** proper or satisfactory condition: *my watch is out of order*. **8.** state or condition generally: *affairs are in good order*. **9.** *Gram.* **a.** the arrangement of the elements of a construction in a particular sequence, e.g., the placing of *John* before and of *George* after the verb *saw* in the sentence *John saw George*. **b.** the feature of construction resulting from such an arrangement, e.g., the sentences *John saw George* and *George saw John* differ only in order. **10.** any class, kind, or sort, as of persons or things, distinguished from others by nature or character: *talents of a high order*. **11.** the usual major subdivision of a class or subclass, commonly comprising a plurality of families, e.g., the *Hymenoptera* (ants, bees, etc.). **12.** a rank, grade, or class of the community. **13.** a body of persons of the same profession, occupation, or pursuits: *the clerical order*. **14.** a body or society of persons living by common consent under the same religious, moral, or social regulations. **15.** any of the degrees or grades of the clerical office (the number of which varies in different churches, the Roman Catholic Church, for example, having the **major orders** of bishop, priest, deacon, and subdeacon, and the **minor orders** of acolyte, exorcist, lector, and ostiary, while the Anglican Church recognizes only the three grades of bishop, priest and deacon). **16.** any of the nine grades of angels in medieval angelology (see **angel**, def. 1). **17.** a monastic society or fraternity: *the Franciscan order*. **18.** *(usually pl.)* the rank or status of an ordained Christian minister. **19.** *(usually pl.)* the rite or sacrament of ordination. **20.** a prescribed form of divine service, or of administration of a rite or ceremony. **21.** the service itself. **22.** *Hist.* **a.** a society or fraternity of knights, of combined military and monastic character, as in the Middle Ages, as the Knights Templars, etc. **b.** an institution, partly an imitation of the medieval orders of military monks, having as its purpose the rewarding of meritorious service by the conferring of a dignity: *the Order of the Golden Fleece*. **23.** a modern organization or society more or less resembling the knightly orders: *fraternal orders*. **24.** conformity to law or established authority. **25.** absence of revolt, disturbance, turbulence, unruliness, etc. **26.** customary mode of procedure, or established usage. **27.** the customary or prescribed mode of proceeding in debates or the like, or in the conduct of deliberative or legislative bodies, public meetings, etc. **28.** conformity to this. **29.** prevailing course of things, or an established system or regime: *the old order* *changeth.* **30.** a direction or commission to make, provide or furnish something: *shoes made to order.* **31.** a quantity of goods purchased. **32.** *Chiefly Brit.* a pass for admission to a theater, museum, or the like. **33.** *Archit.* **a.** a series of columns with their entablature arranged in given proportions. **b.** any one of the typical variations of such an arrangement distinguished by proportion, capital types and other characteristics: *the Doric, Ionic, Corinthian, Tuscan, and Composite orders.*

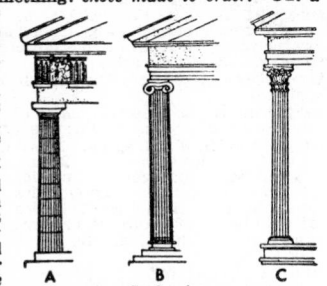

Greek orders
A, Doric; B Ionic; C, Corinthian

34. *Math.* degree, as in algebra. **35. in order,** permissible under the rules of parliamentary procedure. **36. in order that,** to the end that. **37. in order to,** as a means to. **38. in short order,** immediately. **39. on order,** **a.** subject to the order of buyer. **b.** ordered but not yet received. **40. on the order of,** resembling to some extent. **41. out of order,** not in accordance with recognized parliamentary rules. —*v.t.* **42.** to give an order, direction, or command to. **43.** to direct or command to go or come (as specified): *to order a person out of one's house.* **44.** to give an order for. **45.** to prescribe: *a doctor orders a medicine for a patient.* **46.** to direct to be made, supplied, or furnished: *we ordered two steaks.* **47.** to regulate, conduct, or manage. **48.** to arrange methodically or suitably. **49.** to ordain, as God or fate does. **50.** to invest with clerical rank or authority. —*v.i.* **51.** to issue orders. [ME *ordre,* t. OF, t. L: m.s. *ordo* row, rank, regular arrangement] —**or′der·er,** *n.* —**Syn. 42.** See **direct.**

order arms, **1.** a position in the manual of arms in close-order drill, in which the rifle is held at the right side, with the butt on the ground. **2.** (as an interjection) the command to move the rifle to this position.

or·der·ly (ôr′dər lĭ), *adj., adv., n., pl.* **-lies.** —*adj.* **1.** arranged or disposed in order, or regular sequence. **2.** observant of system or method, as persons, the mind, etc. **3.** characterized by or observant of order, rule, or discipline: *an orderly citizen.* **4.** charged with the communication or execution of orders. —*adv.* **5.** according to established order or rule. **6.** *Archaic.* methodically. —*n.* **7.** *Mil.* **a.** a private soldier or a noncommissioned officer attending on a superior officer to carry orders, etc. **b.** See **striker** (def. 5). **8.** an attendant in a hospital, charged with the maintenance of order, cleanliness, etc. —**or′der·li·ness,** *n.* —**Syn.** ORDERLY, METHODICAL, SYSTEMATIC characterize that which is neat, in order and planned. These three words are sometimes used interchangeably. However, ORDERLY emphasizes neatness of arrangement: *an orderly array of books.* METHODICAL suggests a logical plan, a definite order of actions or method from beginning to end: *a methodical examination of something.* SYSTEMATIC suggests thoroughness, an extensive and detailed plan, together with regularity of action: *a systematic review.* —**Ant** 1. chaotic, haphazard.

orderly officer, *Brit. Mil.* officer of the day.

or·di·nal[1] (ôr′də nəl), *adj.* **1.** pertaining to an order, as of animals or plants. —*n.* **2.** an ordinal number or numeral. [ME, t. LL: s. *ordinālis* der. L *ordo* order]

or·di·nal[2] (ôr′də nəl), *n.* **1.** a directory of ecclesiastical services. **2.** a book containing the forms for the ordination of priests, consecration of bishops, etc. [ME, t. ML: m. *ordināle.* See ORDINAL[1]]

ordinal number, any of the numbers *first, second, third,* etc. (in distinction from *one, two, three,* etc. which are called **cardinal numbers**). Also, **ordinal numeral.**

or·di·nance (ôr′də nəns), *n.* **1.** an authoritative rule or law; a decree or command. **2.** a public injunction or regulation. **3.** *Eccles.* **a.** an established rite or ceremony. **b.** a sacrament. **c.** the communion. [ME *ordinaunce,* t. OF: m. *ordenance,* der. *ordener* to order, t. L: m. *ordināre*]

or·di·nar·i·ly (ôr′də nĕr′ə lĭ; *emphatic* ôr′də när′ə lĭ), *adv.* **1.** in ordinary cases; usually: *ordinarily he sleeps until the last possible minute.* **2.** in the ordinary way. **3.** to the usual extent.

or·di·nar·y (ôr′də nĕr′ĭ), *adj., n., pl.* **-naries.** —*adj.* **1.** such as is commonly met with; of the usual kind. **2.** not above, but rather below, the average level of quality; somewhat inferior. **3.** customary; normal: *for all ordinary purposes.* **4.** (of jurisdiction etc.) immediate, as contrasted with that which is delegated. **5.** (of officials, etc.) belonging to the regular staff or the fully recognized class. —*n.* **6.** the ordinary condition, degree, run, or the like: *out of the ordinary.* **7.** something regular, customary, or usual. **8.** *Eccles.* **a.** an order or form for divine service, esp. that for saying Mass. **b.** the service of the Mass exclusive of the canon. **9.** *Obs.* except *Hist.* a clergyman appointed to prepare condemned prisoners for death. **10.** *Brit. Eccl. Law.* a bishop, archbishop, or other ecclesiastic or his deputy, in his capacity as an *ex officio* ecclesiastical authority. **11.** (in some States of the U.S.) a judge of a court of

probate. **12.** *Brit.* a meal regularly served at a fixed price in a restaurant or inn. **13.** *Obs.* a restaurant or inn, or its dining room. **14.** a high bicycle of an early type, with one large wheel in front and one small wheel behind. **15.** *Her.* **a.** any of the simplest and commonest heraldic charges or bearings, usually bounded by straight lines. **b.** any of the more important of these. **16. in ordinary,** (of officials, etc.) in regular service: *a physician in ordinary to a king.* [ME, t. L: m.s. *ordinārius* of the usual order] —**or′di·nar′i·ness,** *n.* —**Syn. 1.** See **common.**

or·di·nate (ôr′də nāt′, -nĭt), *n.* *Math.* the y Cartesian coördinate. [t. L: m.s. *ordinātus,* pp., ordained]

or·di·na·tion (ôr′də nā′shən), *n.* **1.** *Eccles.* act or ceremony of ordaining. **2.** the fact of being ordained. **3.** a decreeing. **4.** act of arranging. **5.** the resulting state. [ME *ordinacion,* t. L: m.s. *ordinātio* ordainment, an ordering]

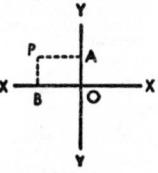

Ordinate
P, Any point; AO and PB′
Ordinate of P; YY, Axis
of ordinate; OB and AP,
Abscissa of P; XX, Axis
of abscissa

ordn., ordnance.

ord·nance (ôrd′nəns), *n.* **1.** cannon or artillery. **2.** military weapons of all kinds with their equipment, ammunition, etc. [var. of ORDINANCE]

or·do (ôr′dō), *n., pl.* **ordines** (ôr′də nēz′). *Rom. Cath. Ch.* a booklet containing short and abbreviated directions for the contents of the office and Mass of each day in the year. [L: row, series, order]

or·don·nance (ôr′də nəns; *Fr.* ôr dô nä̃s′), *n.* **1.** arrangement or disposition of parts, as of a building, a picture, or a literary composition. **2.** an ordinance, decree, or law. [t. F. See ORDINANCE]

Or·do·vi·cian (ôr′də vĭsh′ən), *Stratig.* —*adj.* **1.** pertaining to an early Paleozoic geological period or system equivalent to Lower Silurian of common usage before 1879. —*n* **2.** the period or system following Cambrian and preceding Silurian. [f. s. L *Ordovicēs,* pl., an ancient British tribe in northern Wales + -IAN]

or·dure (ôr′jər, -dyŏŏr), *n.* filth; dung; excrement. [ME, t. OF, der. *ord* filthy, g. L *horridus* horrid]

Or·dzho·ni·kid·ze (ôr jŏ nĭ kēd′zĕ), *n.* a city in the S Soviet Union in Europe, in Caucasia. 159,000 (est. 1956). Also, **Orjonikidze.** Formerly, **Vladikavkaz.**

ore (ôr), *n.* **1.** a metal-bearing mineral or rock, or a native metal, esp. when valuable enough to be mined. **2.** a mineral or natural product serving as a source of some nonmetallic substance, as sulfur. [ME (*o*)*or* metal, ore, OE *ār* brass]

ö·re (œ′rə), *n., pl.* **öre.** a bronze coin and money of account of Denmark, Norway, and Sweden, equal to one hundreth of a krone or krona.

Ore., Oregon.

o·re·ad (ôr′ĭ ăd′), *n.* *Class. Myth.* a mountain nymph. [t. s. *Oreas,* t. Gk.: m. *Oreiăs,* der. *ŏros* mountain]

o·rec·tic (ô rĕk′tĭk), *adj.* *Philos.* of or pertaining to desire; appetitive. [t. Gk.: m.s. *orektikós*]

ore dressing, *Metall.* the art of separating the valuable minerals from an ore without chemical changes.

Oreg., Oregon.

o·reg·a·no (ə rĕg′ə nō′), *n.* a plant of the mint family of the genus *Origanum,* related to but spicier than marjoram, used in cookery.

Or·e·gon (ôr′ə gŏn′, -gən, ôr′-), *n.* a State in the NW United States, on the Pacific coast. 1,768,687 pop. (1960). 96,981 sq. mi. *Cap.:* Salem. *Abbr.:* Oreg. or Ore. —**Or·e·go·ni·an** (ôr′ə gō′nĭ ən, ôr′-), *adj., n.*

Oregon grape, **1.** a small, dark-blue berry of the western coast of the U.S. It is the official flower of Oregon. **2.** the evergreen shrub, *Mahonia aquifolia* (family *Berberidaceae*), on which the berry grows.

Oregon pine, Douglas fir.

Oregon Trail, a route for westward pioneers starting in Missouri and reaching Oregon, much used in the first half of the 19th century. ab. 2000 mi. long.

O·rel (ô rĕl′; *Russ.* ôr yŏl′), *n.* a city in the central Soviet Union in Europe. 128,000 (est. 1956).

O·ren·burg (ô rĕn bŏŏrk′), *n.* Chkalov.

O·res·tes (ô rĕs′tēz), *n.* *Gk. Legend.* son of Agamemnon and Clytemnestra, and brother of Electra: slew his mother and Aegisthus, who had slain Agamemnon.

Ö·re·sund (œ′rə sŏŏn′), *n.* Swedish and Danish name of The Sound.

org., **1.** organic. **2.** organized.

or·gan (ôr′gən), *n.* **1.** a musical instrument (**pipe organ**) consisting of one or more sets of pipes sounded by means of compressed air, played by means of keys arranged in one or more keyboards: in its full modern development the largest and most complicated of musical instruments. **2.** a reed organ, harmonium, or American organ. **3.** a barrel organ or hand organ. **4.** *Obs.* any of various musical instruments, esp. wind instruments. **5.** (in an animal or a plant) a part or member, as the heart, having some specific function. **6.** an instrument or means, as of performance. **7.** a means or medium of communicating thoughts, opinions, etc, as a newspaper serving as the mouthpiece of a political party. [ME, t. L: s. *organum*, t. Gk.: m. *órganon* instrument, tool, bodily organ, musical instrument]

or·gan·dy (ôr′gəndĭ), *n., pl.* **-dies.** a fine, thin, stiff cotton fabric usually having a durable crisp finish, and either white, dyed or printed; used for neckwear, dresses, curtains. Also, **or′gan·die.** [t. F: m. *organdi*; orig. uncert.]

organ grinder, a street musician who plays a hand organ by turning the crank.

or·gan·ic (ôrgăn′ĭk), *adj.* **1.** noting or pertaining to a class of chemical compounds which formerly comprised only those existing in or derived from living organisms (animal or plant), but which now includes these and all other compounds of carbon. **2.** characteristic of, pertaining to, or derived from living organisms: *organic remains found in rocks.* **3.** of or pertaining to an organ or the organs of an animal or a plant. **4.** *Philos.* having a physical organization similar in its complexity to that of living things. **5.** characterized by the systematic arrangement of parts; organized; systematic. **6.** of or pertaining to the constitution or structure of a thing; constitutional; structural. **7.** *Law.* of or pertaining to the constitutional or essential law or laws organizing the government of a state. [t. L: s. *organicus*, t. Gk.: m. *organikós*] —**Syn. 6.** inherent, fundamental, essential.

or·gan·i·cal·ly (ôrgăn′ĭklĭ), *adv.* **1.** in an organic manner; by or with organs. **2.** with reference to organic structure. **3.** by or through organization.

organic chemistry, the branch of chemistry dealing with the compounds of carbon; originally limited to substances found only in living organisms.

organic disease, a disease in which there is a structural alteration (opposed to *functional disease*).

or·gan·i·cism (ôrgăn′əsĭz′əm), *n.* **1.** *Biol., Philos.* the theory that vital activities arise not from any one part of an organism but from its autonomous composition. **2.** *Neurol.* the doctrine that all or the majority of the diseases of the nervous system, including those of the mind, are organic, due to demonstrable changes in the brain or spinal cord. —**or·gan·i·cist** (ôrgăn′əsĭst), *n.*

organic law. See **law** (def. 2).

or·gan·ism (ôr′gənĭz′əm), *n.* **1.** an individual composed of mutually dependent parts constituted for subserving vital processes. **2.** any form of animal or plant life: *microscopic organisms.* **3.** any organized body or system analogous to a living being: *the Korean social organism.* **4.** *Philos.* any thing with a very complex structure and parts which function not only in terms of one another, but also in terms of the whole.

or·gan·ist (ôr′gənĭst), *n.* a player on an organ.

or·gan·i·za·tion (ôr′gənəzā′shən), *n.* **1.** act or process of organizing. **2.** state or manner of being organized. **3.** that which is organized. **4.** organic structure. **5.** any organized whole. **6.** a body of persons organized for some end or work. **7.** the administrative personnel or apparatus of a business. **8.** the functionaries of a political party along with the offices, committees, etc. which they fill. **9.** an organism. —**or·gan·i·za′tion·al,** *adj.*

or·gan·ize (ôr′gənīz′), *v.,* **-ized, -izing.** —*v.t.* **1.** to form as or into a whole consisting of interdependent or coördinated parts, esp. for harmonious or united action: *to organize a party.* **2.** to systematize: *to organize facts.* **3.** to give organic structure or character to. **4.** to build a trade union among: *to organize workers.* **5.** to enlist the employees of into a trade union: *to organize a factory.* —*v.i.* **6.** to combine in an organized company, party, or the like. **7.** to assume organic structure. Also, *esp.* Brit., **or′gan·ise′.** [ME, t. ML: m.s. *organizāre*, der. L *organum* ORGAN] —**or′gan·iz′a·ble,** *adj.* —**or′gan·iz′er,** *n.*

organized ferment. See **ferment** (def. 1a).

organized labor, all workers who are organized in labor unions.

organo-, word element meaning "organ," usually used in the biological sense. [t. Gk., comb. form of *órganon*]

or·ga·nog·ra·phy (ôr′gənŏg′rəfĭ), *n.* the description of the organs of animals or plants.

or·ga·nol·o·gy (ôr′gənŏl′əjĭ), *n.* **1.** the branch of biology that deals with the structure and functions of the organs of animals or plants. **2.** phrenology.

or·ga·non (ôr′gənŏn′), *n., pl.* **-na** (-nə), **-nons. 1.** an instrument of thought or knowledge. **2.** *Philos.* a system of rules or principles of demonstration or investigation. [t. Gk. See **organ**]

or·ga·no·ther·a·py (ôr′gənōthĕr′əpĭ), *n.* that branch of therapeutics which deals with the use of remedies prepared from the organs of animals, as the thyroid gland, the pancreas, the suprarenal bodies, etc. Also, **or·ga·no·ther·a·peu·tics** (ôr′gənō thĕr′ə pū′tĭks).

organ pipe, 1. one of the pipes of a pipe organ. **2.** something resembling such a pipe.

or·ga·num (ôr′gənəm), *n., pl.* **-na** (-nə), **-nums. 1.** an organon. **2.** *Music.* **a.** the doubling, or simultaneous singing, of a melody at an interval of either a fourth, fifth, or octave. **b.** the second part in such singing. [t. L. See **organ**]

or·gasm (ôr′găzəm), *n.* **1.** *Physiol.* a complex series of responses of the genital organs and skin at the culmination of a sexual act. **2.** immoderate excitement. [t. NL:

s. *orgasmus,* t. Gk.: m. *orgasmós,* der. *orgân* swell, be excited] —**or·gas·tic** (ôrgăs′tĭk), *adj.*

or·geat (ôr′zhăt; *Fr.* ôrzhá′), *n.* a syrup or drink made from almonds (orig. from barley), sugar, and a water prepared from orange flowers. [t. F, t. Pr., der. *orge,* g. L *hordeum* barley]

Or·get·o·rix (ôrjĕt′ərĭks), *n.* fl. c60 B.C., Helvetian chieftain.

or·gi·as·tic (ôr′jĭăs′tĭk), *adj.* of, pertaining to, or of the nature of orgies. [t. Gk.: m.s. *orgiastikós*]

or·gy (ôr′jĭ), *n., pl.* **-gies. 1.** wild, drunken, or licentious festivities or revelry. **2.** any proceedings marked by unbridled indulgence of passions: *an orgy of killing.* **3.** (*pl.*) secret rites or ceremonies connected with the worship of certain deities of classical mythology, esp. the rites in honor of Dionysus, celebrated with wild dancing and singing, drinking, etc. [t. L: m.s. *orgia,* pl., t. Gk.]

or·i·bi (ôr′əbĭ, ôr′-), *n., pl.* **-bis.** a small tan-colored antelope, *Ourebia ourebi,* of South and East Africa, with spikelike horns. [t. S Afr. D, t. Hottentot]

o·ri·el (ôr′ĭəl), *n.* a bay window, usually semipolygonal, esp. in an upper story. [ME, t. OF: m. *oriol* porch, passage, gallery, ult. der. L *aureolus* gilded]

Oriel

o·ri·ent (*n., adj.* ôr′ĭ ənt, ôr′ĭ ĕnt′; *v.* ôr′ĭ ĕnt′), *n.* **1.** the east; the eastern regions. **2. The Orient. a.** the East; the countries to the E (and SE) of the Mediterranean. **b.** the countries of Asia generally, especially E Asia. **3.** *Poetic.* shining brightness; radiance. **4.** the luster peculiar to the pearl. **5.** an orient pearl. —*adj.* **6.** rising; appearing as from beneath the horizon: *the orient sun.* **7.** *Now Poetic.* eastern or oriental. **8.** fine or precious, as gems, esp. pearls. —*v.t.* **9.** to place so as to face the east. **10.** to place in any definite position with reference to the points of the compass or other points: *to orient a building north and south.* **11.** to build (a church) with the chief altar to the east and the chief entrance to the west. **12.** to adjust with relation to, or bring into due relation to, surroundings, circumstances, facts, etc.: *to orient one's ideas to new conditions.* **13.** *Survey.* to turn a map or planetable sheet so that the north direction on the map is parallel to the north direction on the ground. **14.** to direct to a particular object. —*v.i.* **15.** to turn toward the east, or in any specified direction. [ME, t. L: s. *oriens* the east, sunrise, n. use of ppr., rising]

o·ri·en·tal (ôr′ĭĕn′təl), *adj.* **1.** (*usually cap.*) of, pertaining to, or characteristic of the Orient or East. **2.** (*cap.*) *Zoogeog.* belonging to a division comprising southern Asia and the Malay Archipelago as far as and including the Philippines, Borneo, and Java. **3.** of the orient or east; eastern. **4.** (of gems) orient. **5.** designating sapphire varieties: *oriental amethyst.* —*n.* **6.** (*usually cap.*) a native or inhabitant of the Orient, esp. one belonging to a native race. [ME, t. L: s. *orientālis*]

O·ri·en·tal·ism (ôr′ĭĕn′təlĭz′əm), *n.* **1.** an Oriental peculiarity. **2.** Oriental character or characteristics. **3.** the knowledge and study of Oriental languages, literature, etc. Also, **orientalism.** —**O′ri·en′tal·ist,** *n.*

O·ri·en·tal·ize (ôr′ĭĕn′təlīz′), *v.t., v.i.,* **-ized, -izing.** to make or become Oriental. Also, **orientalize.**

Oriental rug, any handmade rug or carpet woven, usually in one piece, in the Orient.

o·ri·en·tate (ôr′ĭĕntāt′, ôr′ĭĕntāt′), *v.,* **-tated, -tating.** —*v.t.* **1.** to orient. —*v.i.* **2.** to face or turn toward the east, or in any specified direction; be oriented.

o·ri·en·ta·tion (ôr′ĭĕntā′shən), *n.* **1.** act or process of orienting. **2.** state of being oriented. **3.** *Psychol.* the ability to locate oneself in one's environment with reference to time, place, and people. **4.** the ascertainment of one's true position, as in a novel situation, with reference to new ideas, etc. **5.** *Chem.* **a.** the arrangement of atoms or radicals in a particular position due to electrical charges, etc. **b.** the determination of the position of substituted atoms or radicals in a compound.

O·ri·en·te (ô/rĕ̄ĕn′tĕ̄), *n.* a region in Ecuador, E of the Andes: the border long disputed by Peru.

or·i·fice (ôr′əfĭs, ôr′-), *n.* a mouth or aperture, as of a tube or pipe; a mouthlike opening or hole; a vent. [t. F, t. L: m.s. *ōrificium*]

or·i·flamme (ôr′əflăm′, ŏr′-), *n.* **1.** the red banner of St. Denis, near Paris, carried before the early kings of France as a military ensign. **2.** any ensign or standard. [late ME *oriflam,* t. F: m. *oriflamme,* f. OF *orie* golden (g. L *aureus*) + *flamme* FLAME]

orig., 1. origin. **2.** original. **3.** originally.

or·i·gan (ôr′əgən, ŏr′-), *n.* marjoram, esp. the Old World wild marjoram, *Origanum vulgare.* [ME, t. L: s. *orīganum,* t. Gk.: m. *oríganon*]

Or·i·gen (ôr′əjĕn′, -jən, ŏr′-), *n.* (*Origenes Adamantius*), A.D. c185–c254, Christian theologian, writer, and teacher, at Alexandria.

or·i·gin (ôr′ə jĭn, ŏr′-), *n.* **1.** that from which anything arises or is derived; the source: *to follow a stream to its origin.* **2.** rise or derivation from a particular source: *these and other reports of like origin.* **3.** the first stage of existence; the beginning: *the date of origin of a sect.* **4.** birth; parentage; extraction: *Scottish origin.* **5.** *Anat.* **a.** the point of derivation. **b.** the more fixed portion of a muscle. [t. L: s. *origo* beginning, source, rise]

o·rig·i·nal (ərĭj'ənəl), *adj.* **1.** belonging or pertaining to the origin or beginning of something, or to a thing at its beginning: *the original binding.* **2.** new; fresh; novel: *an original way of advertising.* **3.** arising or proceeding from a thing itself, or independently of anything else. **4.** capable of or given to thinking or acting independently in self-suggested and individual ways: *an original thinker.* **5.** proceeding from a person as the inventor, maker, composer, or author: *original research.* **6.** being that from which a copy, a translation, or the like is made: *the original document is at Washington.* —*n.* **7.** a primary form or type from which varieties are derived. **8.** an original work, writing, or the like, as opposed to any copy or imitation. **9.** the person or thing represented by a picture, description, etc. **10.** one who is original in his ways of thinking or acting. **11.** an eccentric person. **12.** *Archaic.* a source of being; an author or originator.

original gum, *Philately.* the mucilage put on the back of a stamp by the post office.

o·rig·i·nal·i·ty (ərĭj'ənăl'ətĭ), *n., pl.* **-ties. 1.** the state or quality of being original. **2.** ability to think or act in an independent, individual manner. **3.** freshness or novelty, as of an idea, method, or performance.

o·rig·i·nal·ly (ərĭj'ənəlĭ), *adv.* **1.** with respect to origin; by origin. **2.** at the origin; at first. **3.** in the first place; primarily. **4.** from the beginning. **5.** in an original, novel, or distinctively individual manner.

original sin, *Theol.* **1.** a depravity, or tendency to evil, held to be innate in mankind and transmitted from Adam to the race in consequence of his sin. **2.** *Rom. Cath. Theol.* the privation of sanctifying grace in consequence of Adam's sin.

o·rig·i·nate (ərĭj'ənāt'), *v.,* **-nated, -nating.** —*v.i.* **1.** to take its origin or rise; arise; spring. —*v.t.* **2.** to give origin or rise to; initiate; invent. —**o·rig'i·na'tion,** *n.* —**o·rig'i·na'tor,** *n.* —**Syn. 2.** See **discover.**

o·rig·i·na·tive (ərĭj'ənā'tĭv), *adj.* having or characterized by the power of originating; creative. —**o·rig'i·na'tive·ly,** *adv.*

O·ri·no·co (ō'rēnō'kō), *n.* a large river in N South America, flowing from S Venezuela into the Atlantic. ab. 1600 mi.

o·ri·ole (ōr'ĭōl'), *n.* **1.** any bird of the Old World passerine family *Oriolidae,* mostly bright-yellow with black on the head, wings, and tail, as the **golden oriole,** *Oriolus oriolus,* of Europe and Africa. **2.** any of various brightly colored American passerine birds of the family *Icteridae,* not closely related to the true orioles of the Old World, as the Baltimore oriole, *Icterus galbula.* [t. ML: m.s. *oriolus,* var. of L *aureolus* golden]

O·ri·on (ōrī'ən), *n., gen.* **Orionis** (ōrī'ō'nĭs, ŏr'-). **1.** *Gk. Myth.* a giant and a hunter who pursued the Pleiades and was eventually slain by Artemis. He then became the giant constellation. **2.** *Astron.* a constellation, south of Gemini and Taurus, containing the bright supergiant stars Betelgeuse and Rigel, and a remarkable gaseous nebula.

O·ris·ka·ny (ōrĭs'kənĭ), *n.* a village in central New York, near Utica: battle, 1777. 1346 (1950).

or·i·son (ōr'ĭzən, ŏr'-), *n.* a prayer. [ME, t. OF, g. L *ōrātio* prayer. Cf. **oration**]

O·ris·sa (ōrĭs'ə), *n.* a province in E India. 14,645,946 pop. (1951); 60,136 sq. mi. (after 1954). *Cap.:* Cuttack. **-orium.** See **-ory².**

O·ri·za·ba (ō'rēsä'bä), *n.* **1.** a volcano in SE Mexico, in Veracruz state. 18,546 ft. **2.** a city near this peak. 55,531 (1950).

Or·jo·ni·kid·ze (ŏr jŏnĭkēd'zĕ), *n.* Ordzhonikidze.

Ork·ney Islands (ôrk'nĭ), an island group off the NE tip of Scotland, comprising a county in Scotland. 21,258 pop. (1951); 376 sq. mi. *Co. seat:* Kirkwall.

Or·lan·do (ôrlän'dō; *for 1 also It.* ōrlän'dō). *n.* **1. Vittorio Emanuele** (vēt'tō'ryō ĕ'mänwĕ'lĕ), 1860–1952, Italian statesman. **2.** a city in central Florida: resort. 88,135 (1960).

or·le (ôrl), *n. Her.* a narrow band within the shield and following the contour of its edge. [t. F, g. LL *ōrulum,* dim. of L *ōra* border]

Or·lé·a·nais (ôrlĕ'änē'), *n.* a former province in N France. *Cap.:* Orléans.

Or·le·an·ist (ôr'lĭ'ənĭst), *n. French Hist.* an adherent of the Orleans family, which is descended from the younger brother of Louis XIV, and has furnished one sovereign, Louis Philippe (reigned 1830–48).

Or·lé·ans (ôr'lĭ'ənz; *Fr.* ôrlĕ'äN'), *n.* **1.** a city in N France, on the Loire river: siege raised by Joan of Arc, 1428. 76,439 (1954). **2. Louis Philippe Joseph** (lwē fēlēp' zhō'zĕf'), **Duc d'**, (*Philippe Egalité*) 1747–1793, French political leader.

Or·lon (ôr'lŏn), *n. Trademark.* a synthetic acrylic textile fiber of light weight, good wrinkle resistance and high resistance to weathering and many chemicals.

or·lop (ôr'lŏp), *n.* the lowest deck of a ship. [late ME, t. D: m. *overloop,* der. *overloopen* overrun, spread over; so called because it covers the ship's hold]

Or·ly (ôr'lē'), *n.* one of two international airports in Paris. See **Le Bourget.**

Or·mazd (ôr'mazd), *n. Zoroastrianism.* the cosmic principle, spirit, or person, in ceaseless conflict with the spirit of darkness and evil, Ahriman; Ahura Mazda.

Also, **Or'muzd.** [t. Pers., g. Avestan *Ahura Mazda* wise lord]

or·mer (ôr'mər), *n.* **1.** an ear shell, *Haliotis tuberculata,* a gastropod mollusk abundant in the Channel Islands. **2.** any ear shell. [t. F: m. *ormier* (g. L *auris maris* sea ear), b. with *mier* (g. L *merus* pure)]

or·mo·lu (ôr'məlōō'), *n.* **1.** an alloy of copper and zinc, used to imitate gold. **2. a.** gold prepared for use in gilding. **b.** gilded metal. [t. F: m. *or moulu* ground gold, f. *or* (g. L *aurum* gold) + *moulu,* pp. of *moudre* grind (g. L *molere*)]

Or·muz (ôr'mŭz), *n.* **Strait of.** See **Hormuz.**

or·na·ment (*n.* ôr'nəmənt; *v.* ôr'nəmĕnt'), *n.* **1.** an accessory, article, or detail used to beautify the appearance or general effect: *architectural ornaments.* **2.** any adornment or means of adornment. **3.** a person who adds luster, as to surroundings, society, etc. **4.** act of adorning. **5.** state of being adorned. **6.** mere outward display. **7.** *Chiefly Eccles.* any accessory, adjunct, or equipment. **8.** *Music.* a tone or group of tones applied as decoration to a principal melodic tone. —*v.t.* **9.** to furnish with ornaments. **10.** to be an ornament to. **t.** L: s. *ornāmentum* equipment, ornament; r. ME *orne-ment,* t. OF]

or·na·men·tal (ôr'nəmĕn'təl), *adj.* **1.** used for ornament: *ornamental plants.* **2.** such as to ornament; decorative. **3.** of or pertaining to ornament. —*n.* **4.** something ornamental. **5.** a plant cultivated for decorative purposes. —**or·na·men·tal'i·ty,** *n.* —**or·na·men'tal·ly,** *adv.*

or·na·men·ta·tion (ôr'nəmĕntā'shən), *n.* **1.** act of ornamenting. **2.** state of being ornamented. **3.** that with which a thing is ornamented.

or·nate (ôrnāt'), *adj.* **1.** elaborately adorned; sumptuously or showily splendid or fine. **2.** embellished with rhetoric, as a style or discourse. [ME, t. L: m.s. *ornātus,* pp., adorned] —**or·nate'ly,** *adv.* —**or·nate'ness,** *n.*

or·ner·y (ôr'nərĭ), *adj. Chiefly U.S. Dial.* **1.** ugly in disposition or temper. **2.** stubborn. **3.** low or vile. **4.** ordinary; common. [contr. of **ordinary**]

or·nis (ôr'nĭs), *n.* an avifauna. [t. G, t. Gk.: bird]

ornith., **1.** ornithological. **2.** ornithology.

or·nith·ic (ôrnĭth'ĭk), *adj.* of or pertaining to birds. [t. Gk.: m.s. *ornithikós* birdlike]

or·ni·thin (ôr'nəthĭn), *n.* an amino acid, $H_2N(CH_2)_3-CH(NH_2)COOH$, obtained by hydrolysis of arginine.

ornitho-, a word element meaning "bird." Also, **or·nith-.** [t. Gk., comb. form of *órnis*]

or·ni·thoid (ôr'nəthoid'), *adj.* birdlike.

ornithol., **1.** ornithological. **2.** ornithology.

or·ni·thol·o·gy (ôr'nəthŏl'əjĭ), *n.* the branch of zoölogy that deals with birds. —**or·ni·tho·log·i·cal** (ôr'nəthŏlŏj'əkəl), *adj.* —**or·ni·thol'o·gist,** *n.*

or·ni·tho·pod (ôr'nəthəpŏd', ôrnĭ'thə-), *n.* any of the *Ornithopoda,* a group of dinosaurs that walked erect on their hind feet. [t. NL: s. *Ornithopoda,* pl.; or f. **ornitho-** + **-pod**]

or·ni·thop·ter (ôr'nəthŏp'tər), *n.* a heavier-than-air craft sustained in and propelled through the air by flapping wings. [f. **ornitho-** + s. Gk. *pterón* wing]

or·ni·tho·rhyn·chus (ôr'nəthərĭng'kəs), *n.* the duckbill. [t. NL, f. Gk.: *ornitho-* **ornitho-** + m. *rhýnchos* snout, beak]

or·ni·tho·sis (ôr'nəthō'sĭs), *n.* a disease of domestic pigeons and other birds, similar to psittacosis.

oro-, a word element meaning "mountain," as in *orography.* [t. Gk., comb. form of *óros*]

o·ro·ban·cha·ceous (ôr'ōbăngkā'shəs, ôr'ō-), *adj.* belonging to the *Orobanchaceae,* the widespread broomrape family of parasitic herbs. [f. s. L *orobanchē* (t. Gk.: broomrape) + **-aceous**]

o·rog·e·ny (ōrŏj'ənĭ), *n. Geol.* the process of mountain making or upheaval. —**or·o·gen·ic** (ôr'ə jĕn'ĭk, ōr'ə-), *adj.*

o·rog·ra·phy (ōrŏg'rəfĭ), *n.* that branch of physical geography that deals with mountains. —**or·o·graph·ic** (ôr'əgrăf'ĭk, ōr'ə-), **or·o·graph·i·cal,** *adj.*

o·ro·ide (ôr'ōīd'), *n.* an alloy containing copper, tin, etc., used to imitate gold. [t. F: f. *or* (g. L *aurum*) gold + *-oide* **-oid**]

o·rol·o·gy (ōrŏl'əjĭ), *n.* the science of mountains. —**or·o·log·i·cal** (ôr'əlŏj'əkəl, ōr'ə-), *adj.* —**o·rol'o·gist,** *n.*

o·rom·e·ter (ōrŏm'ətər), *n.* an aneroid barometer with a scale giving elevations above sea level, used to determine altitudes of mountains, etc.

O·ron·tes (ōrŏn'tēz), *n.* a river flowing from the Lebanon valley N through NW Syria and SW past Antioch, Turkey, into the Mediterranean. ab. 170 mi.

o·ro·phar·ynx (ôr'ōfăr'ĭngks), *n., pl.* **-pharynges** (-fərĭn'jēz), **-pharynxes.** *Anat.* **1.** the space immediately beneath the mouth cavity. **2.** the pharynx as distinguished from the nasopharynx. [f. *oro-* (comb. form repr. L *ōs* mouth) + **pharynx**]

o·ro·tund (ôr'ətŭnd'), *adj.* **1.** (of the voice or utterance) characterized by strength, fullness, richness, and clearness. **2.** (of a style of utterance) pompous or bombastic. [t. L: m. *ōre rotundō,* lit., with round mouth]

o·ro y pla·ta (ō'rō ē plä'tä), *Spanish.* gold and silver (motto of Montana).

O·roz·co (ōrōs'kō), *n.* José Clemente (hō sĕ' klĕ mĕn'tĕ), 1883–1949, Mexican painter.

ăct, āble, dâre, ärt; ĕbb, ēqual; ĭf, īce; hŏt, ōver, ôrder, oil, bŏŏk, ōoze, out; ŭp, ūse, ûrge; ə = a in alone; ch, chief; g, give; ng, ring; sh, shoe; th, thin; ŧh, that; zh, vision. See the full key on inside cover.

Or·pen (ôr′pən), *n.* **Sir William Newenham Montague,** 1878–1931, British painter.

or·phan (ôr′fən), *n.* **1.** a child bereaved by death of both parents, or, less commonly, of one parent. —*adj.* **2.** of or for orphans: *an orphan asylum.* **3.** bereaved of parents. —*v.t.* **4.** to bereave of parents or a parent. [late ME, t. LL: s. *orphanus,* t. Gk.: m. *orphanós* without parents, bereaved] —**or′phan·hood′,** *n.*

or·phan·age (ôr′fən·ĭj), *n.* **1.** an institution for orphans. **2.** state of being an orphan. **3.** orphans collectively.

Or·phe·us (ôr′fī′əs, -fūs), *n. Gk. Myth.* a son of Apollo and Calliope: a Thracian singer and player of the lyre. He followed his dead wife Eurydice to Hades and was allowed by Pluto, whom he had charmed by his music, to lead her out, provided that he did not look back. At the last moment he looked back and she was lost. —**Or·phe·an** (ôr fē′ən), *adj.*

Or·phic (ôr′fĭk), *adj.* **1.** of or pertaining to Orpheus. **2.** resembling the music attributed to Orpheus; entrancing. **3.** pertaining to a religious or philosophical school maintaining a form of the cult of Dionysus or Bacchus, ascribed to Orpheus as founder: *Orphic mysteries.* **4.** (*cap. or l.c.*) mystic; oracular. [t. Gk.: m.s. *orphikós*]

Or·phism (ôr′fĭz əm), *n.* the religious or philosophical system of the Orphic school.

or·phrey (ôr′frĭ), *n., pl.* **-phreys.** **1.** an ornamental band or border, esp. on an ecclesiastical vestment. **2.** *Now only Hist. or Archaic.* gold embroidery. **3.** *Now only Hist. or Archaic.* rich embroidery of any sort. **4.** a piece of richly embroidered stuff. [ME *orfreis,* t. OF, g. LL *aurifrisium,* for L *aurumphrygium* gold embroidery, lit., Phrygian gold]

or·pi·ment (ôr′pə mənt), *n.* a mineral, arsenic trisulfide, As_2S_3, found usually in soft yellow foliated masses, used as a pigment, etc. [ME, t. OF, t. L: m.s. *auripigmentum* gold pigment]

or·pine (ôr′pĭn), *n.* a crassulaceous perennial, *Sedum telephium,* bearing purplish flowers. Also, **or′pin.** [ME, t. F, back formation from *orpiment* ORPIMENT]

Or·ping·ton (ôr′pĭng tən), *n.* one of a breed of large white-skinned domestic fowls. [named after *Orpington,* town in Kent, southeastern England]

or·ra (ôr′ə, ŏr′ə), *adj. Scot.* odd; extra; occasional.

or·rer·y (ôr′ər ĭ, ŏr′-), *n., pl.* **-reries.** **1.** an apparatus for representing the motions and phases of the planets, etc., in the solar system. **2.** any of certain similar machines, as a planetarium. [named after the Earl of *Orrery* (1676–1731), for whom it was first made]

or·ris (ôr′ĭs, ŏr′-), *n.* any of certain species of iris, as *Iris florentina,* with a fragrant rootstock. Also, **or′rice.** [unexplained var. of IRIS]

or·ris·root (ôr′ĭs root′, -root′, ŏr′-), *n.* the rootstock of the orris, used as a perfume, etc.

ort (ôrt), *n.* (*usually pl.*) a fragment of food left at a meal. [ME, c. LG *ort,* early mod. D *oorete,* f. *oor-* rejected (lit., out, from) + *ete* food. Cf. OE *or-, æt*]

Or·te·gal (ôr′tĕ gäl′), *n.* **Cape,** a cape in NW Spain, on the Bay of Biscay.

Or·te·ga y Gas·set (ôr tĕ′gä ē gäs set′), **José** (hō-sĕ′), 1883–1955, Spanish philosopher and writer.

Orth., Orthodox.

ortho-, **1.** a word element meaning "straight," "upright," "right," "correct," used in combination. **2.** *Chem.* **a.** a prefix indicating that acid of a series which contains most water. Cf. meta-, pyro-. **b.** a prefix applied to a salt of one of these acids: if the acid ends in -*ic*, the corresponding salt ends in -*ate*, as *orthoboric acid* (H_3BO_3) and *potassium orthoborate* (K_3BO_3); if the acid ends in -*ous*, the corresponding salt ends in -*ite*, as *orthoantimonous acid* (H_3SbO_3) and *potassium orthoantimonite* (K_3SbO_3). **c.** a prefix designating the 1.2 position in the benzene ring. [t. Gk., comb. form of *orthós* straight, upright, right, correct]

or·tho·bo·ric acid (ôr′thō bôr′ĭk). See ortho- (def. 2).

or·tho·cen·ter (ôr′thō sĕn′tər), *n. Geom.* the point of intersection of the altitudes of a triangle.

or·tho·ce·phal·ic (ôr′thō sə făl′ĭk), *adj.* having the relation between the height of the skull and the breadth or the length medium or intermediate. Also, **or·tho·ceph·a·lous** (ôr′thō sĕf′ə ləs). —**or′tho·ceph′a·ly,** *n.*

or·tho·chro·mat·ic (ôr′thō krō măt′ĭk), *adj. Photog.* **1.** pertaining to or representing the correct relations of colors, as in nature. **2.** designating a film or plate sensitive to yellow and green as well as to blue and violet.

or·tho·clase (ôr′thə klās′, -klāz′), *n.* a very common mineral of the feldspar group, potassium aluminum silicate, $KAlSi_3O_8$, occurring as an important constituent in many igneous rocks: used in the manufacture of porcelain. [f. ORTHO- + m.s. Gk. *klásis* cleavage]

or·tho·don·tia (ôr′thə dŏn′sha, -shĭ′ə), *n.* the branch of dentistry that is concerned with the straightening of irregular teeth. [t. NL, f. Gk.: *ortho-* + s. *odoús* tooth + -*ia* -IA] —**or′tho·don′tic,** —**or′tho·don′tist,** *n.*

or·tho·dox (ôr′thə dŏks′), *adj.* **1.** sound or correct in opinion or doctrine, esp. theological or religious doctrine. **2.** conforming to the Christian faith as represented in the primitive ecumenical creeds. **3.** (*cap.*) **a.** designating the Eastern or Greek Church. **b.** of or pertaining to the Greek Church. **4.** approved; conventional. [t. LL: s. *orthodoxus,* t. Gk.: m. *orthódoxos* right in opinion] —**or′tho·dox′ly,** *adv.*

Orthodox Church, the Christian church of the countries formerly comprised in the Eastern Roman Empire, and of countries evangelized from it, as Russia; the church or group of local and national Oriental churches in communion or doctrinal agreement with the Greek patriarchal see of Constantinople.

or·tho·dox·y (ôr′thə dŏk′sĭ), *n., pl.* **-doxies.** **1.** orthodox belief or practice. **2.** orthodox character.

or·tho·ë·py (ôr thō′ə pĭ, ôr′thō-), *n.* the study of correct pronunciation. [t. Gk.: m.s. *orthoépeia* correctness of diction] —**or·tho·ëp·ic** (ôr′thō ĕp′ĭk), *adj.* —**or·tho′ë·pist,** *n.*

or·tho·gen·e·sis (ôr′thō jĕn′ə sĭs), *n.* **1.** *Biol.* the evolution of species in definite lines which are predetermined by the constitution of the germ plasm. **2.** *Sociol.* a hypothetical parallelism between the stages through which any culture necessarily passes, in spite of secondary conditioning factors. —**or·tho·ge·net·ic** (ôr′thō jə nĕt′ĭk), *adj.*

or·thog·na·thous (ôr thŏg′nə thəs), *adj. Craniom.* straight-jawed; having the profile of the face vertical or nearly so; having a gnathic index below 98. See diag. under facial angle.

or·thog·o·nal (ôr thŏg′ə nəl), *adj.* **1.** *Math.* pertaining to or involving right angles or perpendicular lines: *an orthogonal projection.* **2.** *Crystall.* referable to a rectangular set of axes. [f. obs. *orthogon*(*ium*) (t. LL, t. Gk.: m. *orthogónion,* neut., right-angled) + -AL¹] —**or·thog′o·nal·ly,** *adv.*

or·thog·ra·pher (ôr thŏg′rə fər), *n.* **1.** one versed in orthography or spelling. **2.** one who spells correctly. Also, **or·thog′ra·phist.**

or·tho·graph·ic (ôr′thə grăf′ĭk), *adj.* **1.** pertaining to orthography. **2.** *Geom., etc.* orthogonal. Also, **or′tho·graph′i·cal.** —**or′tho·graph′i·cal·ly,** *adv.*

or·thog·ra·phy (ôr thŏg′rə fĭ), *n., pl.* **-phies.** **1.** the art of writing words with the proper letters, according to accepted usage; correct spelling. **2.** that part of grammar which treats of letters and spelling. **3.** manner of spelling. **4.** an orthogonal projection, or an elevation drawn by means of it. [ME *orthographie,* t. L: m. *orthographia,* t. Gk.: correct writing]

or·tho·pe·dic (ôr′thə pē′dĭk), *adj.* pertaining to orthopedics. Also, **or′tho·pae′dic.**

or·tho·pe·dics (ôr′thə pē′dĭks), *n.* the correction or cure of deformities and diseases of the spine, bones, joints, muscles, or other parts of the skeletal system in children or in persons of any age. Also, **or′tho·pae′dics, or′tho·pe′dy.** [f. *ortho-* + m.s. Gk. *país* child + -ICS]

or·tho·pe·dist (ôr′thə pē′dĭst), *n.* one skilled in orthopedics. Also, **or′tho·pae′dist.**

or·tho·phos·phor·ic acid (ôr′thō fŏs fôr′ĭk, -fŏr′ĭk), *Chem.* the tribasic acid of phosphorus in its valence of five, H_3PO_4, a colorless, crystalline compound, forming phosphates which are used in fertilizers.

or·tho·psy·chi·a·try (ôr′thō sī kī′ə trĭ), *n.* the science that concerns itself with the study and treatment of behavior disorders, esp. of young people. —**or·tho·psy·chi·at·ric** (ôr′thō sī′kī ăt′rĭk), **or·tho·psy·chi·at·ri·cal,** *adj.* —**or′tho·psy·chi′a·trist,** *n.*

or·thop·ter (ôr thŏp′tər), *n.* ornithopter. [t. NL: s. *Orthoptera,* pl., f. Gk.: *ortho-* ORTHO- + -*pterá* wings]

or·thop·ter·on (ôr thŏp′tə rŏn′, -tər ən), *n.* an orthopterous insect.

or·thop·ter·ous (ôr thŏp′tər əs), *adj.* belonging or relating to the *Orthoptera,* an order of insects that includes the crickets, grasshoppers, cockroaches, etc., characterized usually by leathery forewings and longitudinally folded, membranous hind wings. [t. NL: m. *orthopterus,* f. Gk.: *ortho-* ORTHO- + m. -*pteros* winged] —**or·thop′ter·an,** *adj., n.*

or·thop·tic (ôr thŏp′tĭk), *adj.* pertaining to or producing normal binocular vision.

orthoptic exercises, a method of exercising the eye and its muscles in order to cure strabismus or improve vision.

or·tho·rhom·bic (ôr′thə rŏm′bĭk), *adj. Crystall.* denoting or pertaining to a system of crystallization characterized by three unequal axes intersecting at right angles.

or·tho·scop·ic (ôr′thə skŏp′ĭk), *adj.* pertaining to, characterized by, or produced by normal vision; presenting objects correctly to the eye.

or·thos·ti·chy (ôr thŏs′tə kĭ), *n., pl.* **-chies.** *Bot.* **1.** a vertical rank or row. **2.** an arrangement of members, as leaves, at different heights on an axis so that their median planes coincide. [f. ORTHO- + m.s. Gk. -*stichia* alignment] —**or·thos′ti·chous ,** *adj.*

or·tho·trop·ic (ôr′thə trŏp′ĭk), *adj. Bot.* noting, pertaining to, or exhibiting a mode of growth which is more or less vertical.

or·thot·ro·pism (ôr thŏt′rə pĭz′əm), *n. Bot.* orthotropic tendency or growth.

or·thot·ro·pous (ôr thŏt′rə pəs), *adj. Bot.* (of an ovule) straight and symmetrical, with the chalaza at the evident base and the micropyle at the opposite extremity.

Orthotropous ovule. M. Micropyle; C. Chalaza; O, Ovule

Ort·ler (ôrt′lər), *n.* **1.** a range of the Alps in N Italy. **2.** the highest peak of this range. 12,802 ft.

or·to·lan (ôr′tə lən), *n.* **1.** an Old World bunting, *Emberiza hortulana,* esteemed as a table delicacy. **2.** the bobolink. 3. the sora. [t. F, t. Pr.: lit. gardener (i.e. frequenting gardens), g. L *hortulānus* of gardens]

O·ru·ro (ô rōō′rō), *n.* a city in W Bolivia: a former capital. 58,706 (1950); over 12,000 ft. high.

Or·well (ôr′wĕl), *n.* **George** (*Eric Blair*), 1903–1950, British novelist and essayist.

-ory[1], a suffix of adjectives meaning "having the function or effect of," as in *compulsory, contributory, declaratory, illusory.* [t. L: m.s. *-ōrius* (neut. *-ōrium;* see -ORY[2]), suffix of adjectives associated esp. with agent nouns in *-or.* See -OR[2]]

-ory[2], a suffix of nouns denoting esp. a place or an instrument or thing for some purpose, as in *directory, dormitory, purgatory.* [t. L: m. s. *-ōrium.* See -ORY[1]]

o·ryx (ôr′ĭks), *n., pl.* **oryxes,** (*esp. collectively*) **oryx.** a large African antelope, *Oryx beisa,* grayish with black markings, and having long, nearly straight horns. [ME, t. L, t. Gk.: pickax, oryx]

os[1] (ŏs), *n., pl.* **ossa** (ŏs′ə). *Anat., Zool.* a bone. [t. L]

os[2] (ŏs), *n., pl.* **ora** (ôr′ə). *Anat.* a mouth, opening, or entrance. [t. L: mouth]

os[3] (ŏs), *n., pl.* **osar** (ō′sär). *Geol.* an esker, esp. when of great length. [t. Sw.: m. *as* (pl. *asar*) ridge]

Os, *Chem.* osmium.

OS, Old Saxon. Also, **OS., O.S.**

O/S, Old Style (calendar). Also, **o/s, O.S.**

O.s., out of stock.

O.S.A., Order of St. Augustine (Augustinian).

O·sage (ō′sāj), *n.* **1.** a Siouan language closely related to Omaha. **2.** a river flowing from E Kansas E to the Missouri river in central Missouri. ab. 500 mi.

Osage orange, 1. an ornamental moraceous tree, *Maclura pomifera,* native in Arkansas and adjacent regions, used for hedges. **2.** its fruit, which resembles a warty orange.

O·sa·ka (ō sä′kə; *Jap.* ō′sä kä′), *n.* a seaport in S Japan, on Honshu island. 1,956,136 (1950).

O.S.B., Order of St. Benedict (Benedictine).

Os·born (ŏz′bərn), *n.* **Henry Fairfield,** 1857–1935, U.S. paleontologist and author.

Os·borne (ŏz′bərn), *n.* **Thomas Mott,** 1859–1926, U.S. prison reformer.

Os·can (ŏs′kən), *n.* **1.** an ancient nationality of southcentral Italy constituting a subdivision of the Italic branch (Oscan-Umbrians and Latins) of the Indo-European family. **2.** their language, replaced by Latin.

Os·car II (ŏs′kər), 1829–1907, king of Sweden, 1872–1907, and of Norway, 1872–1905.

Os·ce·o·la (ŏs′ĭ ō′lə), *n.* c1804–38, U. S. Indian chief, of the Seminole tribe.

os·cil·late (ŏs′ə lāt′), *v.i.,* **-lated, -lating. 1.** to swing or move to and fro, as a pendulum does; vibrate. **2.** to fluctuate between states, opinions, purposes, etc. **3.** *Physics.* to have, produce, or generate oscillations: *a vacuum tube oscillates.* [t. L: m. s. *oscillātus,* pp., swung] —**Syn.** 1. See **swing**[1].

os·cil·la·tion (ŏs′ə lā′shən), *n.* **1.** act or fact of oscillating. **2.** a single swing, or movement in one direction, of an oscillating body, etc. **3.** fluctuation between states, opinions, etc. **4.** *Physics.* **a.** a single forward and backward surge of electric charge. **b.** a rapid change in electromotive force. **c.** one complete cycle of an electric wave.

os·cil·la·tor (ŏs′ə lā′tər), *n.* **1.** a device or machine producing oscillations. **2.** one who or that which oscillates.

os·cil·la·to·ry (ŏs′ə lə tôr′ĭ), *adj.* characterized by or involving oscillation.

os·cil·lo·graph (ə sĭl′ə grăf′, -gräf′), *n.* **1.** an instrument for recording oscillations, esp. electric oscillations. **2.** a device for recording the wave forms of changing currents, voltages, or any other quantity which can be translated into electrical energy, as, for example, sound waves. [f. s. L *oscillāre* swing + -(o)GRAPH]

os·cil·lo·scope (ə sĭl′ə skōp′), *n. Physics.* a device which makes the shape of a voltage or current wave visible on the screen of a cathode-ray tube or other device.

os·cine (ŏs′ĭn, -īn), *adj.* of or pertaining to the *Oscines,* a large group of passerine birds, containing those with the most highly developed vocal organs, and commonly termed the singing birds. [back formation from *Oscines,* t.L (see def.)]

os·ci·tant (ŏs′ə tənt), *adj.* **1.** gaping; yawning. **2.** drowsy; inattentive. [t. L: s. *oscitans,* ppr.] —**os′-ci·tan·cy, os′ci·tance,** *n.*

os·cu·lant (ŏs′kyə lənt), *adj.* **1.** united by certain common characteristics. **2.** *Zool.* adhering closely; embracing. [t. L: s. *osculans,* ppr., kissing]

os·cu·lar (ŏs′kyə lər), *adj.* **1.** pertaining to an osculum. **2.** pertaining to the mouth or kissing. [f. s. L *osculum* little mouth, kiss + -AR[1]]

os·cu·late (ŏs′kyə lāt′), *v.,* **-lated, -lating.** —*v.t.* **1.** to kiss. **2.** to bring into close contact or union. **3.** *Geom.* to touch so as to have three or more points in common at the point of contact. —*v.i.* **4.** to kiss each other. **5.** to come into close contact or union. **6.** *Geom.* to osculate each other, as two curves. [t. L: m.s. *osculātus,* pp., kissed] —**os·cu·la·to·ry** (ŏs′kyə lə tôr′ĭ), *adj.*

os·cu·la·tion (ŏs′kyə lā′shən), *n.* **1.** kissing. **2.** a kiss. **3.** close contact. **4.** *Geom.* the contact between two osculating curves or the like.

os·cu·lum (ŏs′kyə ləm), *n., pl.* **-la** (-lə). a small mouthlike aperture, as of a sponge. [t. L, dim. of *ōs* mouth]

O.S.D., Order of St. Dominic (Dominican).

-ose[1], an adjective suffix meaning "full of," "abounding in," "given to," "like," as in *frondose, globose, jocose, otiose, verbose.* [t. L: m. *-ōsus.* Cf. *-ous*]

-ose[2], a noun termination used to form chemical terms, esp. names of sugars and other carbohydrates, as *amylose, fructose, hexose, lactose,* and of protein derivatives, as *proteose.* [abstracted from GLUCOSE]

Ö·sel (œ′zəl), *n.* German name of **Saaremaa.**

O.S.F., Order of St. Francis (Franciscan).

Osh·kosh (ŏsh′kŏsh), *n.* a city in E Wisconsin, on Lake Winnebago. 45,110 (1960).

o·sier (ō′zhər), *Chiefly Brit.* —*n.* **1.** any of various willows, as *Salix viminalis* (the common **basket osier**) and *Salix purpurea* (**red osier**), with tough flexible twigs or branches which are used for wickerwork. **2.** a twig from such a willow. —*adj.* **3.** pertaining to or made of osiers, [ME. t. F; akin to ML *ausaria* willow bed]

O·si·ris (ō sī′rĭs), *n.* one of the principal Egyptian gods, brother and husband of Isis, usually represented as a mummy wearing the crown of Upper Egypt.

-osis, *pl.* **-oses.** a noun suffix denoting action, process, state, condition, etc., as in *metamorphosis,* and in many pathological terms, as *tuberculosis.* [t. Gk., suffix forming nouns from verbs with infinitive in *-ðein, -oûn*]

-osity, a noun suffix equivalent to *-ose* (or *-ous*) plus *-ity.* [f. -OSE + -ITY, repr. s. L *-ōsitas* and F *-osité*]

Os·ler (ŏs′lər, ōz′-), *n.* **Sir William,** 1849–1919, Canadian physician and professor of medicine.

Os·lo (ŏz′lō, ŏs′-; *Nor.* ōōs′lōō), *n.* a seaport in and the capital of Norway, in the SE part at the head of **Oslo Fiord,** an inlet (ab. 75 mi. long) of the Skagerrak. 434,047 (1950). Formerly, **Christiania.**

Os·man (ŏz′mən, ŏs′-; *Turk.* ŏs män′), *n.* 1259–1326, Turkish sultan, founder of the Ottoman dynasty of rulers of Turkey. Also, **Othman.**

Os·man·li (ŏz män′lĭ, ŏs-), *n., pl.* **-lis,** *adj.* —*n.* **1.** an Ottoman. **2.** Ottoman Turkish (language). —*adj.* **3.** Ottoman. [t. Turk. See OTTOMAN]

os·mic (ŏz′mĭk), *adj. Chem.* of or containing osmium in its higher valences, esp. the tetravalent state.

os·mi·ous (ŏz′mĭ əs), *adj. Chem.* of or containing osmium in its lower valences.

os·mi·um (ŏz′mĭ əm), *n. Chem.* a hard, heavy, metallic element used for electric-light filaments, etc., having the greatest density of any known material, and forming octavalent compounds, such as OsO₄, OsF₅. *Symbol:* Os; *at. wt.:* 190.2; *at. no.:* 76; *sp. gr.:* 22.48 at 20°C. [t. NL, der. Gk. *osmḗ* smell, odor; named from the penetrating odor of one of its oxides]

os·mose (ŏz mōs′, ŏs-), *v.,* **-mosed, -mosing.** —*v.i.* **1.** to undergo osmosis. —*v.t.* **2.** to subject to osmosis.

os·mo·sis (ŏz mō′sĭs, ŏs-), *n. Phys. Chem., etc.* **1.** the tendency of a fluid to pass through a semipermeable membrane into a solution where its concentration is lower, thus equalizing the conditions on either side of the membrane. **2.** the diffusion of fluids through membranes or porous partitions. Cf. **endosmosis** and **exosmosis.** [t. NL, der. Gk. *ōsmós* a thrusting] —**os·mot·ic** (ŏz mŏt′-ĭk, ŏs-), *adj.* —**os·mot′i·cal·ly,** *adv.*

Os·na·brück (ŏz′nə brŏŏk′; *Ger.* ŏs′nä bryk′), *n.* a city in N West Germany, in Hanover. 126,586 (est. 1955).

Os·na·burg (ŏz′nə bûrg′), *n.* a heavy coarse cotton in a plain weave used for grain sacks and sports wear.

os·prey (ŏs′prĭ), *n., pl.* **-preys. 1.** a large hawk, *Pandion haliaetus,* which feeds on fish; the fish hawk. **2.** a kind of feather used to trim hats. [ME *ospray*(*e*), t. F: m. *orfraie* (repr. L *ossifraga*), b. with L. See OSSIFRAGE]

Osprey, *Pandion haliaetus* (21 to 26 in. long, winspread 4½ ft.)

OSS, Office of Strategic Services.

Os·sa (ŏs′ə), *n. Gk. Myth.* a mountain in E Greece, in Thessaly. When attacking the Olympian gods, the giants tried to reach heaven by piling Mount Pelion on Mount Olympus and Ossa on Pelion. 6405 ft.

os·se·in (ŏs′ĭ ĭn), *n. Biochem.* the organic basis of bone, which remains after the mineral matter has been removed by treatment with dilute acid. [f. s. L *osseus* bony +-IN[2]]

os·se·ous (ŏs′ĭ əs), *adj.* **1.** composed of, containing, or resembling bone; bony. **2.** ossiferous. [t. L: m. s. *osseus* bony] —**os′se·ous·ly,** *adv.*

Os·se·tia (ŏ sē′shə; *Russ.* ŏ sĕt′ĭ ə), *n.* a region in the S Soviet Union in Europe, in Caucasia. —**Os·se′tian,** *adj.*

Os·sian (ŏsh′ən, ŏs′ĭ ən), *n. Gaelic Legend.* a hero and poet of the third century.

Os·si·an·ic (ŏs′ĭ ăn′ĭk, ŏsh′ĭ-), *adj.* **1.** pertaining to, characteristic of, or resembling the poetry or rhythmic prose published by James Macpherson in 1762–63, as a translation of Ossian. **2.** grandiloquent; bombastic.

os·si·cle (ŏs′ə kəl), *n.* a little bone. [t. L: m.s. *ossiculum,* dim. of os bone]

Os·si·etz·ky (ŏs′ĭ ĕts′kĭ), *n.* **Carl von** (kärl fən), 1889–1938, German pacifist leader.

os·sif·er·ous (ŏ sĭf′ər əs), *adj.* containing bones.

os·si·fi·ca·tion (ŏs/əfəkā/shən), n. 1. act or process of ossifying. 2. the resulting state. 3. that which is ossified.

os·si·frage (ŏs/əfrĭj), n. 1. the osprey. 2. the lammergeier. [t. L: m.s. ossifragus, masc., ossifraga, fem., lit., bonebreaker]

os·si·fy (ŏs/əfī), v., -fied, -fying. —v.t. 1. to convert into, or harden like, bone. —v.i. 2. to become bone or hard like bone. [f. s. L os bone + -(I)FY. Cf. F ossifier]

Os·si·ning (ŏs/ənĭng), n. a village in SE New York, on the Hudson: the site of Sing Sing, a state prison. 18,662 (1960). Formerly, Sing Sing.

os·su·ar·y (ŏs/ŏŏ ĕr/ĭ, ŏsh/-), n., pl. -aries. a place or receptacle for the bones of the dead. [t. LL: m.s. ossuārium, der. L os bone]

os·te·al (ŏs/tĭ əl), adj. osseous. [f. OSTE(O)- + -AL¹]

os·te·i·tis (ŏs/tĭ ī/tĭs), n. Pathol. inflammation of the substance of bone. [f. OSTE(O)- + -ITIS]

Ost·end (ŏst ĕnd/), n. a seaport in NW Belgium. 52,036 (est. 1952). French, Ostende (ŏs täNd/).

os·ten·si·ble (ŏs tĕn/səbəl), adj. given out or outwardly appearing as such; professed; pretended. [t. F, f. s. L ostensus, pp., displayed + -ible -IBLE] —os·ten/si·bly, adv.

os·ten·sive (ŏs tĕn/sĭv), adj. 1. manifestly demonstrative. 2. ostensible. —os·ten/sive·ly, adv.

os·ten·ta·tion (ŏs/tĕn tā/shən), n. 1. pretentious show; display intended to impress others. 2. Obs. a show or display. Also, os/ten·ta/tious·ness. [ME, t. L: s. ostentātio] —Syn. 1. See show.

os·ten·ta·tious (ŏs/tĕn tā/shəs), adj. 1. characterized by or given to ostentation or pretentious show. 2. (of actions, manner, qualities exhibited, etc.) intended to attract notice. —os/ten·ta/tious·ly, adv.

osteo-, a word element meaning "bone." Also, before vowels, oste-. [t. Gk., comb. form of ostéon]

os·te·o·blast (ŏs/tĭə blăst/), n. Anat. a bone-forming cell.

os·te·o·cla·sis (ŏs/tĭ ŏk/lə sĭs), n. 1. Anat. the breaking down or absorption of osseous tissue. 2. Surg. the fracturing of a bone to correct deformity. [t. NL, f. osteo- osteo- + m. Gk. klásis fracture]

os·te·o·clast (ŏs/tĭ ə klăst/), n. 1. Anat. one of the large multinuclear cells in growing bone, and concerned in the absorption of osseous tissue, as in the formation of canals, etc. 2. Surg. an instrument for effecting osteoclasis. [f. OSTEO- + m.s. Gk. klastós broken]

os·te·o·gen·e·sis (ŏs/tĭ ə jĕn/ə sĭs), n. Physiol. the formation of bone.

os·te·oid (ŏs/tĭ oid/), adj. bonelike. [f. OSTE(O)- + -OID]

os·te·ol·o·gy (ŏs/tĭ ŏl/ə jĭ), n. the branch of anatomy that treats of the skeleton and its parts. —os·te·o·log·i·cal (ŏs/tĭ ə lŏj/ə kəl), adj. —os/te·ol/o·gist, n.

os·te·o·ma (ŏs/tĭ ō/mə), n., pl. -mas, -mata (-mə tə). Pathol. a tumor composed of osseous tissue. [t. NL. See OSTEO-, -OMA]

os·te·o·my·e·li·tis (ŏs/tĭ ō mī/ə lī/tĭs), n. Pathol. a purulent inflammation of the bone.

os·te·o·path (ŏs/tĭ ə păth/), n. one who practices osteopathy. Also, os·te·op·a·thist (ŏs/tĭ ŏp/ə thĭst).

os·te·op·a·thy (ŏs/tĭ ŏp/ə thĭ), n. a theory of disease and a method of treatment resting upon the supposition that most diseases are due to deformation of some part of the body and can be cured by some kind of manipulation. —os·te·o·path·ic (ŏs/tĭ ə păth/ĭk), adj.

os·te·o·phyte (ŏs/tĭ ə fīt/), n. Pathol. a small osseous excrescence or outgrowth on bone. —os·te·o·phyt·ic (ŏs/tĭ ə fĭt/ĭk), adj.

os·te·o·plas·tic (ŏs/tĭ ə plăs/tĭk), adj. 1. Surg. pertaining to osteoplasty. 2. Physiol. pertaining to bone formation.

os·te·o·plas·ty (ŏs/tĭ ə plăs/tĭ), n. Surg. the transplanting or inserting of bone, or surgical reconstruction of bone, to repair a defect or loss.

os·te·o·tome (ŏs/tĭ ə tōm/), n. Surg. a double-beveled chisellike instrument for cutting or dividing bone.

os·te·ot·o·my (ŏs/tĭ ŏt/ə mĭ), n., pl. -mies. Surg. the dividing of a bone, or the excision of part of it. —os/te·ot/o·mist, n.

Ö·ster·reich (œ/stər rīKH/), n. German name of Austria.

Os·ti·a (ŏs/tĭ ə; It. ô/styä), n. an ancient city of Latium at the mouth of the Tiber: the port of Rome.

os·ti·ar·y (ŏs/tĭ ĕr/ĭ), n., pl. -aries. 1. Rom. Cath. Ch. one ordained to the lowest of the four minor orders; a porter. 2. a doorkeeper, as of a church. [ME, t. L: m. s. ostiārius doorkeeper]

os·ti·na·to (ŏs/tĭ nä/tō), n., pl. -tos. Music. a constantly recurring melodic fragment. [It.: lit., obstinate]

os·ti·ole (ŏs/tĭ ōl/), n. a small opening or orifice. [t. L: m.s. ostiolum, dim. of ostium door] —os·ti·o·lar (ŏs/tĭ ə lər, ŏs tī/-), adj.

ost·ler (ŏs/lər), n. Now Rare. a hostler. [contr. of ME (h)osteler, t. OF. Cf. HOSTEL]

ost·mark (ŏst/märk), n. the monetary unit of East Germany.

os·to·sis (ŏs tō/sĭs), n. Physiol. the formation of bone; ossification. [t. NL; see OST(EO)- , -OSIS]

Ost·preus·sen (ŏst/proi/sən), n. German name of East Prussia.

os·tra·cism (ŏs/trə sĭz/əm), n. 1. the act of ostracizing. 2. the fact or state of being ostracized. [t. Gk.: m.s. ostrakismós]

os·tra·cize (ŏs/trə sīz/), v.t., -cized, -cizing. 1. to banish (a person) from his native country; expatriate. 2. to exclude by general consent from society, privileges, etc. 3. Ancient Gk. Hist. to banish (a citizen) temporarily by public vote with ballots consisting of potsherds or tablets of earthenware. [t. Gk.: m.s. ostrakizein (def. 3), der. óstrakon potsherd]

os·trich (ŏs/trĭch, ôs/-), n. 1. any of the large two-toed, swift-footed, flightless birds of the ratite genus Struthio, esp. the species S. camelus, the largest of existing birds, a native of Africa and Arabia, now extensively reared for the plumage. 2. a rhea (American ostrich). [ME ostrice, t. OF: m. ostruce, g. LL avi(s) strūthio, f. avis bird + strūthio ostrich, t. Gk.: m. strouthīon]

Ostrich, Struthio camelus (6 ft. long, including tail, 8 ft. high)

Os·tro·goth (ŏs/trə gŏth/), n. a member of the easterly division of the Goths, which maintained a monarchy in Italy from A.D. 493 to 555. [t. LL: s. Ostrogothī, pl., L Austrogotī, t. Goth.] —Os/tro·goth/ic, adj.

Os·ty·ak (ŏs/tĭ äk/), n. a language of western Siberia, one of the Ugric languages of the Finno-Ugric family.

Os·we·go (ŏs wē/gō), n. a city in W New York: a port on Lake Ontario. 22,155 (1960).

Oswego tea, a North American labiate herb, Monarda didyma, bearing showy, bright-red flowers.

OT, Old Testament. Also, OT., O.T.

ot-, var. of oto- before vowels.

o·tal·gi·a (ō tăl/jĭ ə), n. Pathol. earache. [t. NL, t. Gk.] —o·tal/gic, adj.

O·ta·ru (ô/tä rōō/), n. a seaport in N Japan, on Hokkaido island. 178,330 (1950).

O.T.C. 1. Officers' Training Camp. 2. Brit. Officers' Training Corps.

O tem·po·ra! O mo·res! (ō tĕm/pə rə ō mōr/ēz), Latin. O the times! O the customs!

O·thel·lo (ō thĕl/ō, ə-), n. a tragedy by Shakespeare (acted 1604).

oth·er (ŭth/ər), adj. 1. additional or further: he and one other person. 2. different or distinct from the one or ones mentioned or implied: in some other city. 3. different in nature or kind: I would not have him other than he is. 4. being the remaining one of two or more: the other hand. 5. (with plural nouns) being the remaining ones of a number: the other men. 6. former: men of other days. 7. the other day (night, etc.), a day (night, etc.) or two ago. 8. every other, every alternate: a meeting every other week. —pron. 9. the other one: each praises the other. 10. another person or thing. 11. of all others, above or beyond all others. 12. some person or thing else: some day or other. —adv. 13. otherwise. [ME; OE ōther, c. G ander; akin to Skt. antara] —oth/er·ness, n.

oth·er·di·rect·ed (ŭth/ər dĭ rĕk/tĭd), adj. guided by a set of values that is derived from current trends or outward influences rather than from within oneself. —oth/er·di·rect/ed·ness, n. —other direction.

oth·er·guess (ŭth/ərgĕs/), adj. 1. Archaic or Brit. Dial. of another kind. 2. otherwise. [assimilatory var. of othergets, var. of othergates otherwise]

oth·er·wise (ŭth/ər wīz/), adv. 1. under other circumstances. 2. in another manner; differently. 3. in other respects: an otherwise happy life. —adj. 4. other or different; of another nature or kind. 5. that would otherwise be or exist. [ME other wis (two words), OE (on) ōthre wīsan in other manner. See OTHER, WISE²]

other world, the world of the dead; future world.

oth·er·world·ly (ŭth/ər wûrld/lĭ), adj. of, pertaining to, or devoted to another world, as the world of imagination, or the world to come. —oth/er·world/li·ness, n.

O·thin (ō/thĭn), n. Scand. Myth. Odin.

Oth·man (ŏth/mən; for 1 also Arab. ŏŏth män/), n., pl. -mans. 1. Osman. 2. Ottoman (defs. 3, 4).

O·tho I (ō/thō), Otto I.

O·tho I (ō/thō), Otto I.

o·tic (ō/tĭk, ŏt/ĭk), adj. Anat., etc. of or pertaining to the ear; auricular. [t. Gk.: m.s. ōtikós]

-otic, an adjective suffix meaning: 1. "suffering from," as in neurotic. 2. "producing," as in hypnotic. 3. "resembling," as in Quixotic. [t. Gk.: m.s. -ōtikós]

o·ti·ose (ō/shĭ ōs/, -tĭ-), adj. 1. at leisure; idle; indolent. 2. ineffective or futile. 3. superfluous or useless. [t. L: m.s. ōtiōsus] —o/ti·ose/ly, adv. —o·ti·os·i·ty (ō/shĭ ŏs/ ə tĭ, ō/tĭ-), n.

O·tis (ō/tĭs), n. James, 1725–83, American patriot.

o·ti·tis (ō tī/tĭs), n. Pathol. inflammation of the ear.

oto-, a word element meaning "ear." [t. Gk., comb. form of oûs]

o·to·cyst (ō/tə sĭst), n. a statocyst.

o·to·lar·yn·gol·o·gy (ō/tō lăr/ĭng gŏl/ə jĭ), n. the branch of medicine dealing with the ear and throat.

o·to·lith (ō/tə lĭth), n. Anat., Zool. a calcareous concretion in the internal ear of vertebrates and in the balancing organ of some invertebrates.

o·tol·o·gy (ō tŏl/ə jĭ), n. the science of the ear and its diseases. —o·tol/o·gist, n.

o·to·scope (ō'tə skōp'), *n. Med.* **1.** an instrument for examining the external canal and tympanic membrane of the ear. **2.** an instrument for auscultation in the ear.

O·tran·to (ō trän'tō; *It.* ô'trän tô'), *n.* **Strait of,** a strait between SE Italy and Albania, connecting the Adriatic and the Mediterranean. 44 mi. wide.

ot·ta·va ri·ma (ŏt tä'vä rē'mä), *Pros.* an Italian stanza of eight lines, each of eleven syllables (or, in the English adaptation, of ten or eleven syllables), the first six lines riming alternately and the last two forming a couplet with a different rime: used in Keats's *Isabella* and Byron's *Don Juan*. [It.: octave rime]

Ot·ta·wa (ŏt'ə wə), *n.* **1.** the capital of Canada, in SE Ontario. 202,045 (1951); with suburbs, 281,908 (1951). **2.** a river in SE Canada, flowing generally SE along the boundary between Ontario and Quebec into the St. Lawrence at Montreal. 685 mi. **3.** (*pl.*) a tribe of Algonquian Indians of Canada, forced into the Lake Superior and Lake Michigan regions by the Iroquois confederacy. **4.** a member of this tribe. [t. Canadian F: m. *Otana, Otawa,* t. d. Ojibwa (Cree, Ottawa, Chippewa): m. *adaawe* to trade]

ot·ter (ŏt'ər), *n., pl.* **-ters,** (*esp. collectively*) **-ter.** any of the various aquatic, fur-bearing, carnivorous, musteline mammals of the genus *Lutra* and allied genera, with webbed feet adapted for swimming, and a long tail slightly flattened horizontally to act as a rudder, as *L. vulgaris,* of Europe, which in Great Britain is much hunted with dogs, and *L. canadensis,* of the U.S. and Canada, and the sea otter. [ME *oter,* OE *oter, ot(o)r,* c. D and G *otter*]

Otter, *Lutra canadensis*
(Total length 3½ ft., tail 1 ft.)

Ot·ter·burn (ŏt'ər bûrn'), *n.* a village in NE England, in Northumberland: battle of Chevy Chase, 1388.

Ot·to I (ŏt'ō; *Ger.* ôt'ō), ("*the Great*") A.D. 912–973, German king, A.D. 936–973, and emperor of the Holy Roman Empire, A.D. 962–973. Also, **Otho I.**

Ot·to·man (ŏt'ə mən), *adj., n., pl.* **-mans.** —*adj.* **1.** of or pertaining to the Turkish dynasty or empire founded about 1300 by Osman I, and replaced in 1922 by the republic of Turkey under Mustapha Kemal. **2.** of or pertaining to the lands, peoples, and possessions of the Ottoman Empire. —*n.* **3.** a Turk. **4.** a Turk of the family or tribe of Osman. **5.** (*l.c.*) a kind of divan or sofa, with or without a back. **6.** (*l.c.*) a low cushioned seat without back or arms. **7.** (*l.c.*) a cushioned footstool. **8.** (*l.c.*) a corded silk or rayon fabric with large cotton cord for filling. Also, **Othman** for 3, 4. [t. F, t. It.: named after the founder of the empire (Ar. *'Othmān*)]

Ottoman Empire, a former Turkish sultanate which held sway over large dominions in Asia, Africa, and Europe for more than six centuries until its collapse after World War I: at its most extensive it included (with Turkey) the Barbary States, Egypt, Arabia, the Balkan Peninsula, etc.: an area that now contains over 150,000,000 people. *Cap.:* Constantinople. Also, **Turkish Empire.**

Ot·tum·wa (ə tŭm'wə), *n.* a city in SE Iowa, on the Des Moines river. 33,871 (1960).

Ot·way (ŏt'wā), *n.* **Thomas,** 1652–85, British dramatist.

oua·ba·in (wä bä'ĭn), *n. Pharm.* a cardiac glucoside derived from the tree, *Strophanthus gratus.*

Ouach·i·ta (wŏsh'ə tô', wôsh'-), *n.* **1.** a river flowing from W Arkansas SE through NE Louisiana to the Red River. 605 mi. **2.** (*pl.*) a former North American Indian tribe, apparently of the Caddoan stock, of NE Louisiana (not to be confused with the Wichita). Also, **Washita.**

oua·na·niche (wä'nə nēsh'; *Fr.* wà nà-), *n., pl.* **-niche.** a fresh-water salmon, *Salmo Salar ouananiche,* of the Saguenay River, Quebec, and neighboring waters. [t. Canadian F, f. Montsgnais: *awanas* salmon + *-iš* little]

ou·bli·ette (ōō'blĭ ĕt'), *n.* a secret dungeon with an opening only at the top, as in certain old castles. [t. F, der. *oublier* forget, g. Rom. *oblītāre,* der. L *oblīvīscī*]

ouch[1] (ouch), *interj.* an exclamation expressing sudden pain. [t. G: m. *autsch*]

ouch[2] (ouch), *Archaic.* —*n.* **1.** a clasp, buckle, or brooch, esp. one worn for ornament. **2.** the setting of a precious stone. —*v.t.* **3.** to adorn with or as with ouches. [ME *ouche,* for *nouche* (a *nouche* being taken as an *ouche*). Cf. LL *nusca,* OHG *nuscha* buckle, ult. of Celtic orig.]

Oudh (oud), *n.* formerly a part of the United Provinces of Agra and Oudh in N India: now part of Uttar Pradesh.

Oues·sant (wĕ sän'), *n.* French name of **Ushant.**

ought[1] (ôt), *v. aux.* **1.** was (were) or am (is, are) bound in duty or moral obligation: *every citizen ought to help.* **2.** was (am, etc.) bound or required on any ground, as of justice, propriety, probability, expediency, fitness, or the like (usually fol. by an infinitive with *to* or having the infinitive omitted but understood): *he ought to be punished.* —*n.* **3.** duty or obligation. [ME *ought, aught,* etc., OE *āhte,* pret. of *āgan* OWE] —**Syn. 1.** See **must**[1].

ought[2] (ôt), *n.* a cipher (0). [var. of NOUGHT, *a nought* being taken as *an ought*]

ought[3] (ôt), *n., adv.* aught[1].

Oui·da (wē'də), *n.* pen name of **Louise de la Ramée.**

oui·ja (wē'jə), *n.* a device consisting of a small board on legs, which rests on a larger board marked with words, letters of the alphabet, etc., and which, by moving over the larger board and touching the words, letters, etc., while the fingers of mediums or others rest lightly upon it, is employed to give answers, messages, etc. [f. F *oui* yes + G *ja* yes]

ounce[1] (ouns), *n.* **1.** a unit of weight equal to 437.5 grains or ⅟₁₆ lb. avoirdupois. **2.** a unit of 480 grains, ⅟₁₂ lb. troy or apothecaries' weight. **3.** a fluid ounce. **4.** a small quantity or portion. [ME *unce,* t. OF, g. L *uncia* twelfth part, inch, ounce. Cf. INCH]

ounce[2] (ouns), *n.* a long-haired leopardlike feline, *Panthera uncia,* inhabiting the mountain ranges of central Asia; snow leopard. [ME *once,* t. OF, var. of *lonce* (taken as *l'once* the ounce), g. L *lynx* LYNX]

Ounce, *Panthera uncia*
(6 to 6½ ft. long, tail 3 ft.)

our (our), *pron. or adj.* the possessive form corresponding to *we* and *us,* used before a noun. Cf. **ours.** [ME *oure,* OE *ūre,* gen. pl. See **us**]

ou·ra·ri (ōō rä'rē), *n.* curare.

Our Lady, the Virgin Mary.

ours (ourz), *pron.* form of *our* used predicatively or without a noun following.

our·self (our sĕlf'), *pron.* **1.** a form corresponding to *ourselves,* used of a single person, esp. (like *we* for *I*) in the regal or formal style. **2.** the person(s) or thing(s) belonging to us: *books of ours.*

our·selves (our sĕlvz', *pron.pl.* **1.** a substitute for reflexive of *us.* **2.** an intensifier of *we* or *us.*

-ous, **1.** an adjective suffix meaning "full of," "abounding in," "given to," "characterized by," "having," "of the nature of," "like," etc.: *glorious, joyous, mucous, nervous, sonorous, wondrous.* **2.** a suffix used in chemical terms (as compared with *-ic, -ous*) to imply a larger proportion of the element indicated by the word, as *stannous chloride,* SnCl₂, and *stannic chloride,* SnCl₄. In other words, *-ous* implies a lower valence than in the case of a corresponding term in *-ic.* Also, **-eous, -ious.** [ME, t. OF, g. L *-ōsus;* often used to repr. L *-us,* adj., Gk. *-os,* adj.; in a few words (e.g. *wondrous*) it is attached to native stems]

Ouse (ōōz), *n.* **1.** a river in NE England, in Yorkshire, flowing SE to the Humber. 57 mi. **2.** a river in E England, flowing NE to the Wash. ab. 160 mi.

ou·sel (ōō'zəl), *n.* ouzel.

oust (oust), *v.t.* **1.** to expel from a place or position occupied. **2.** *Law.* to eject; dispossess. [t. AF: s. *ouster* remove, g. L *obstāre* be in the way, protect against]

oust·er (ous'tər), *n.* **1.** *Law.* **a.** ejection; dispossession. **b.** a wrongful exclusion from real property. **2.** one who ousts. [t. AF, n. use of inf. See OUST]

out (out), *adv.* **1.** forth from, away from, or not in a place, position, state, etc.: *out of fashion.* **2.** away from one's home, country, etc.: *to set out on a journey.* **3.** to exhaustion, extinction, or conclusion; to the end; so as to finish or exhaust or be exhausted; so as to bring to naught or render useless: *to pump out a well.* **4.** to or at an end or conclusion: *to fight it out.* **5.** no longer or not burning or furnishing light; extinguished: *the lamp went out.* **6.** not in vogue or fashion: *that style has gone out.* **7.** into or in public notice or knowledge: *the book came out in May.* **8.** seeking openly and energetically to do or have: *to try out for the team.* **9.** into or in society: *a young girl who came out last season.* **10.** not in present or personal possession or use; let for hire, or placed at interest: *let out for a year.* **11.** on strike: *the miners are going out.* **12.** so as to project or extend: *to stretch out.* **13.** into or in existence, activity, or outward manifestation: *fever broke out.* **14.** from a source, ground or cause, material, etc. (with *of*): *made out of scraps.* **15.** from a state of composure, satisfaction, or harmony: *to feel put out.* **16.** in or into a state of confusion, vexation, dispute, variance, or unfriendliness: *to fall out about trifles.* **17.** so as to deprive or be deprived (with *of*): *to cheat out of money.* **18.** having used the last (with *of*): *to run out of coal.* **19.** from a number, stock, or store: *to pick out.* **20.** aloud or loudly: *to call out.* **21.** with completeness or effectiveness: *to fit out.* **22.** thoroughly; completely; entirely. **23.** *Colloq.* out along; out on: *out Broadway.* **24.** *Baseball, Cricket, etc.* from a turn at bat: *he struck out.* **25. out and away,** in a preëminent degree; by far. —*adj.* **26.** external; exterior; outer. **27.** outlying. **28.** *Baseball, etc.* not having its inning: *the out side.* **29.** away from one's work: *to be out on account of illness.* **30.** exposed; made bare, as by tears in one's clothing: *out at the knees.* **31.** beyond fixed or regular limits: *the floods are out.* **32.** beyond the usual range: *an out size.* **33.** astray from what is correct: *out in one's calculations.* **34.** not in practice; unskilful from lack of practice: *your bow hand is out.* **35.** at a pecuniary loss: *to be out ten dollars.* **36.** removed from or not in effective operation, play, a turn at bat, or the like, as in a game. **37.** not in office or employment; unemployed; disengaged: *a butler out of service.* **38.** at variance; at odds; unfriendly: *be not out with me.* **39. out of,** foaled by (a dam). **40. out of one's mind,** insane; crazed; crazy after. —*prep.* **41.** out or forth from (now used chiefly after *from* or in certain expressions): *out the door, out the window.* **42.** outside of: on the exterior of; beyond (now chiefly in certain expressions): *out that wall.* —*interj.* **43.** Begone! away! **44.** *Archaic or Dial.* an exclamation of abhorrence, indignation, reproach, or grief: *out upon you!* —*n.* **45.** projection, or projecting corners: *ins and outs.* **46.** a means of escaping from a place, punishment, retribution, responsibility, etc.: *he always left himself an out.* **47.** *Baseball.* **a.** a putout. **b.** an outward curve. **48.** *Tennis.* a return which lands outside the court. **49.** *Polit.* a person not in office or political power (cf. *in*). **50.** *Colloq.* (pl.) odds; bad terms: *at outs with everyone.* **51.** *Printing.* **a.** the omission of a word or words. **b.** that which is omitted. **52.** *Colloq. or Dial.* an outing. —*v.i.* **53.** to go or come out: *murder will out.* **54.** to come out with; bring out; utter. —*v.t.* **55.** to put out; expel; discharge; oust. [ME; OE *ūt*, c. D *uit*, G *aus*, Icel. and Goth. *ūt*]

out-, prefixal use of **out,** *adv., prep.,* or *adj.,* occurring in various senses in compounds, as in *outcast, outcome, outside,* and serving also to form many transitive verbs denoting a going beyond, surpassing, or outdoing in the particular action indicated, as in *outbid, outdo, outgeneral, outlast, outstay, outrate,* and many other words in which the meaning is readily perceived, the more important of these being entered below.

out·age (ou′tĭj), *n.* **1.** an outlet. **2.** a quantity lost or lacking, as from a container. [f. OUT + -AGE]

out-and-out (out′ənd out′), *adj.* thoroughgoing; thorough; complete; unqualified.

out·ar·gue (out är′gū), *v.t.,* **-gued, -guing.** to outdo or defeat in arguing.

out·bal·ance (out băl′əns), *v.t.,* **-anced, -ancing.** to outweigh.

out·bid (out bĭd′), *v.t.,* **-bid, -bidden** or **-bid, -bidding.** to outdo in bidding.

out·board (out′bōrd′), *adv., adj. Naut.* on the outside, or away from the center, of a ship or boat.

outboard motor, a small portable gasoline engine with propeller and tiller, clamped on the stern of a boat.

out·bound (out′bound′), *adj.* outward bound.

out·brave (out brāv′), *v.t.,* **-braved, -braving. 1.** to surpass in daring. **2.** to surpass in beauty, splendor, etc.

out·break (out′brāk′), *n.* **1.** a breaking out; an outburst. **2.** a sudden and active manifestation. **3.** a public disturbance; a riot; an insurrection.

out·breed (out brēd′), *v.t.,* **-bred, -breeding.** to breed outside the limits of the family, within a breed or variety. —**out′breed′ing,** *n.*

out·build (out bĭld′), *v.t.,* **-built, -building.** to exceed in building, or in durability of building.

out·build·ing (out′bĭl′dĭng), *n.* a detached building subordinate to a main building.

out·burst (out′bûrst′), *n.* **1.** a bursting forth. **2.** a sudden and violent outpouring: *an outburst of tears.*

out·cast (out′kăst′, -käst′), *n.* **1.** a person who is cast out, as from home or society. **2.** a vagabond; homeless wanderer. **3.** rejected matter; refuse. **4.** *Scot.* a falling out; quarrel. —*adj.* **5.** cast out, as from one's home or society. **6.** pertaining to or characteristic of an outcast: *outcast misery.* **7.** rejected or discarded.

out·caste (out′kăst′, -käst′), *n.* **1.** a person of no caste. **2.** (in India) one who has forfeited membership in his caste.

out·class (out klăs′, -kläs′), *v.t.* to surpass in class or grade; be distinctly ahead of (a competitor, etc.).

out·come (out′kŭm′), *n.* that which results from something; the consequence or issue. —**Syn.** See end[1].

out·crop (*n.* out′krŏp′; *v.* out krŏp′), *n., v.,* **-cropped, -cropping.** —*n.* **1.** a cropping out, as of a stratum or vein at the surface of the earth. **2.** the emerging part. —*v.i.* **3.** to crop out, as strata.

out·cross·ing (out′krôs′ĭng, -krŏs′ĭng), *n.* breeding of unrelated animals or plants within a variety or breed.

out·cry (*n.* out′krī′; *v.* out krī′), *n., pl.* **-cries,** *v.,* **-cried, -crying.** —*n.* **1.** a crying out. **2.** a cry of distress, indignation, or the like. **3.** loud clamor. **4.** an auction. —*v.t.* **5.** to outdo in crying; cry louder than.

out·curve (out′kûrv′), *n. Baseball.* an outshoot.

out·date (out dāt′), *v.t.,* **-dated, -dating.** to put out of date; make antiquated or obsolete. —**out·dat′ed,** *adj.*

out·dis·tance (out dĭs′təns), *v.t.,* **-tanced, -tancing.** to distance completely; leave far behind; outstrip.

out·do (out dōō′), *v.t.,* **-did, -done, -doing.** to surpass in doing or performance; surpass. —**Syn.** See **excel.**

out·door (out′dōr′), *adj.* **1.** occurring or used out of doors. **2.** *Brit.* outside of a poorhouse, hospital, etc.

out·doors (out dōrz′), *adv.* **1.** out of doors; in the open air. —*n.* **2.** the world outside of houses; open air.

out·er (ou′tər), *adj.* further out; exterior; external; of or pertaining to the outside. [compar. of OUT]

out·er-di·rect·ed (ou′tər dĭ rĕk′tĭd), *adj.* other-directed.

Outer Mongolia, former name of **Mongolian People's Republic.**

out·er·most (ou′tər mōst′, -məst), *adj.* furthest out; remotest from the interior or center. [f. OUTER + -MOST]

out·face (out fās′), *v.t.,* **-faced, -facing. 1.** to face or stare down. **2.** to face or confront boldly; defy.

out·fall (out′fôl′), *n.* the outlet or place of discharge of a river, drain, sewer, etc.

out·field (out′fēld′), *n.* **1.** *Baseball.* **a.** the part of the field beyond the diamond or infield. **b.** the players stationed in it. **2.** *Cricket.* the part of the field farthest from the batsman. **3.** the outlying land of a farm, esp. beyond the enclosed land. **4.** an outlying region.

out·field·er (out′fēl′dər), *n. Baseball, Cricket.* one of the players stationed in the outfield.

out·fit (out′fĭt′), *n., v.,* **-fitted, -fitting.** —*n.* **1.** an assemblage of articles for fitting out or equipping: *an explorer's outfit.* **2.** a set of articles for any purpose: *a cooking outfit.* **3.** *U.S. Colloq.* a group associated in any undertaking, as a military body, etc. **4.** *U.S. Colloq.* a party, company, or set. **5.** the act of fitting out or equipping, as for a voyage, journey, or expedition, or for any purpose. **6.** the mental or moral equipment. —*v.t.* **7.** to furnish with an outfit; fit out; equip. —*v.i.* **8.** to furnish oneself with an outfit. —**out′fit′ter,** *n.*

out·flank (out flăngk′), *v.t.* **1.** to go or extend beyond the flank of (an opposing army, etc.). **2.** to turn the flank of.

out·flow (out′flō′), *n.* **1.** the act of flowing out. **2.** that which flows out. **3.** any outward movement.

out·fly (out flī′), *v.t.,* **-flew, -flown, -flying. 1.** to surpass or outstrip in flying. **2.** to fly out or forth.

out·foot (out fŏŏt′), *v.t.* **1.** (of one boat) to excel (another) in speed. **2.** to surpass in running, walking, dancing, etc.

out·frown (out froun′), *v.t.* to outdo in frowning; frown down.

out·gen·er·al (out jĕn′ər əl), *v.t.,* **-aled, -aling** or (*esp. Brit.*) **-alled, -alling.** to outdo in generalship.

out·go (*n.* out′gō′; *v.* out gō′), *n., pl.* **-goes,** *v.,* **-went, gone, going.** —*n.* **1.** a going out. **2.** expenditure. **3.** that which goes out; outflow. —*v.t.* **4.** to outstrip in going; go faster than. **5.** to go beyond or exceed. **6.** to surpass, excel, or outdo. —*v.i.* **7.** *Obs.* to go out.

out·go·ing (out′gō′ĭng), *adj.* **1.** going out; departing: *outgoing trains.* **2.** interested in and responsive to others: *an outgoing personality.* —*n.* **3.** *Chiefly Brit.* (usually *pl.*) an amount of money expended. **4.** a going out. **5.** that which goes out; an effluence.

out·group (out′grōōp′), *n. Sociol.* everyone not belonging to an in-group.

out·grow (out grō′), *v.t.,* **-grew, -grown, -growing. 1.** to grow too large for. **2.** to leave behind or lose in the changes incident to development or the passage of time: *to outgrow a bad reputation.* **3.** to surpass in growing. —*v.i.* **4.** to grow out; protrude.

out·growth (out′grōth′), *n.* **1.** a natural development, product, or result. **2.** an additional, supplementary result. **3.** a growing out or forth. **4.** that which grows out; an offshoot; an excrescence.

out·guess (out gĕs′), *v.t.* to outwit.

out·haul (out′hôl′), *n. Naut.* a rope used for hauling out a sail on a boom, yard, etc.

out·her·od (out hĕr′əd), *v.t.* to outdo (Herod or any other person) in extravagance or excess.

out·house (out′hous′), *n.* **1.** an outbuilding. **2.** an outside privy.

out·ing (ou′tĭng), *n.* **1.** an excursion or pleasure trip. **2.** the part of the sea out from the shore.

outing flannel, a light cotton flannel with a short nap.

out·land (*n.* out′lănd′, *adj.* out′lănd′, -lənd), *n.* **1.** outlying land, as of an estate. **2.** *Archaic.* a foreign land. —*adj.* **3.** outlying, as districts. **4.** *Archaic.* foreign. [ME; OE *ūtland*]

out·land·er (out′lăn′dər), **1.** a foreigner; an alien. **2.** *Colloq.* an outsider.

out·land·ish (out lăn′dĭsh), *adj.* **1.** freakishly or grotesquely strange or odd; as appearance, dress, objects, ideas, practices, etc.; bizarre; barbarous. **2.** foreign-looking. **3.** out-of-the-way, as places. **4.** *Archaic.* foreign. —**out·land′ish·ly,** *adv.* —**out·land′ish·ness,** *n.*

out·last (out lăst′, -läst′), *v.t.* to last longer than.

out·law (out′lô′), *n.* **1.** one excluded from the benefits and protection of the law. **2.** one under sentence of outlawry. **3.** a habitual criminal. —*v.t.* **4.** to deprive of the benefits and protection of the law. **5.** to remove from legal jurisdiction; deprive of legal force. **6.** to prohibit. [ME *outlawe,* OE *ūtlage,* t. Scand.; cf. Icel. *ūtlagi*]

out·law·ry (out′lô′rĭ), *n., pl.* **-ries. 1.** the act or process of outlawing. **2.** the state of being outlawed. **3.** disregard or defiance of the law.

out·lay (*n.* out′lā′; *v.* out lā′), *n., v.t.,* **-laid, -laying.** —*n.* **1.** an expending; an expenditure, as of money. **2.** an amount expended. —*v.t.* **3.** to expend, as money.

out·let (out′lĕt), *n.* **1.** an opening or passage by which anything is let out; a vent or exit. **2.** *Elect.* **a.** a point on a wiring system at which current is taken to supply electrical devices. **b. outlet box,** the metal box or receptacle designed to facilitate connections to a wiring system. **3.** *Com.* **a.** a market for goods. **b.** (of a wholesaler or manufacturer) a store, merchant, or agency selling one's goods: *he has 50 good outlets.* **4.** discharge.

out·li·er (out′lī′ər), *n.* **1.** one who or that which lies outside. **2.** one residing outside the place of his business, duty, etc. **3.** *Geol.* a part of a formation left detached through the removal of surrounding parts by denudation.

out·line (out′līn′), *n., v.,* **-lined, -lining.** —*n.* **1.** the line, real or apparent, by which a figure or object is defined or bounded; the contour. **2.** a drawing or a style of drawing with merely lines of contour, without shading. **3.** a general sketch, account or report, indicating only the main features, as of a book, a subject, a project or work, facts, events, etc. —*v.t.* **4.** to draw the outline of, or draw in outline, as a figure or object. **5.** to give an outline of (a subject, etc.); sketch the main features of. —Syn. **1.** See **form.**

out·live (outlĭv′), *v.t.*, **-lived, -living. 1.** to live longer than; survive (a person, etc.). **2.** to outlast; live or last through: *the ship outlived the storm.* —Syn. **1.** See **survive.**

out·look (out′loŏk′), *n.* **1.** the view or prospect from a place. **2.** the mental view: *one's outlook upon life.* **3.** prospect of the future: *the political outlook.* **4.** the place from which an observer looks out; a lookout. **5.** a looking out. **6.** a watch kept.

out·ly·ing (out′lī′ĭng), *adj.* **1.** lying at a distance from the center or the main body; remote; out-of-the-way. **2.** lying outside the boundary or limit.

out·man (out mǎn′), *v.t.*, **-manned, -manning. 1.** to surpass in manpower. **2.** to surpass in manliness.

out·ma·neu·ver (out′mə noō′vər), *v.t.* to outdo in or get the better of by maneuvering.

out·march (out märch′), *v.t.* to outstrip or outdo in marching.

out·match (out mǎch′), *v.t.* to surpass; outdo.

out·mode (out mōd′), *v.t.*, **-moded, -moding.** to cause to be out of style. —**out·mod′ed,** *adj.*

out·most (out′mōst′), *adj.* furthest out; outermost.

out·num·ber (out nŭm′bər), *v.t.* to exceed in number.

out-of-date (out′əv dāt′), *adj.* of a previous style or fashion; obsolete.

out-of-doors (out′əv dōrz′), *adj.* **1.** Also, **out′-of-door′.** outdoor. —*adv., n.* **2.** outdoors.

out-of-the-way (out′əv thə wā′), *adj.* **1.** remote from much-traveled ways or frequented or populous regions; secluded. **2.** unusual. **3.** improper.

out·pa·tient (out′pā′shənt), *n.* a patient receiving treatment at a hospital but not being an inmate.

out·play (out plā′), *v.t.* to play better than; defeat.

out·point (out point′), *v.t.* **1.** to excel in number of points, as in a competition or contest. **2.** *Naut.* to sail closer to the wind than (another vessel).

out·post (out′pōst′), *n.* **1.** a station at a distance from the main body of an army to protect it from surprise attack. **2.** the body of troops stationed there.

out·pour (*n.* out′pōr′; *v.* out pōr′), *n.* **1.** an outflow or overflow; that which is poured out. —*v.t.* **2.** to pour out.

out·pour·ing (out′pōr′ĭng), *n.* outflow; effusion.

out·put (out′poŏt′), *n.* **1.** act of turning out; production. **2.** the quantity or amount produced, as in a given time. **3.** the product or yield, as of a mine.

out·rage (out′rāj), *n., v.*, **-raged, -raging.** —*n.* **1.** an act of wanton violence; any gross violation of law or decency. **2.** anything that outrages the feelings. **3.** *Obs.* a passionate or violent outbreak. —*v.t.* **4.** to subject to grievous violence or indignity. **5.** to affect with a sense of offended right or decency; shock. **6.** to offend against (right, decency, feelings, etc.) grossly or shamelessly. **7.** to ravish (a woman). [ME, t. OF, der. *outrer* push beyond bounds, der. *outre,* beyond, g. L *ultrā*]

out·ra·geous (out rā′jəs), *adj.* **1.** of the nature of or involving gross injury or wrong: *an outrageous slander.* **2.** grossly offensive to the sense of right or decency. **3.** passing reasonable bounds; intolerable or shocking: *an outrageous price.* **4.** violent in action or temper. —**out·ra′geous·ly,** *adv.* —**out·ra′geous·ness,** *n.*

ou·trance (oō träNs′), *n. French.* the utmost extremity, as in combat. [ME, t. OF, der. *outrer.* See OUTRAGE]

out·range (out rānj′), *v.t.*, **-ranged, -ranging.** to have a longer or greater range than.

out·rank (out rǎngk′), *v.t.* to rank above.

ou·tré (oō trā′), *adj. French.* passing the bounds of what is usual and considered proper. [F, pp. of *outrer.* See OUTRAGE]

out·reach (*v.* out rēch′; *n.* out′rēch′), *v.t.* **1.** to reach beyond; exceed. **2.** to reach out; extend. —*v.i.* **3.** to reach out. —*n.* **4.** a reaching out. **5.** length of reach.

ou·tre·mer (oō′trə mĕr′), *adv. French.* beyond the sea

out·ride (out rīd′), *v.*, **-rode, -ridden, riding,** *n.* —*v.t.* **1.** to outdo or outstrip in riding. **2.** (of a ship) to last through a storm. —*v.i.* **3.** to ride out. —*n.* **4.** *Pros.* an unaccented syllable or syllables added to a metrical foot, esp. in sprung rhythm.

out·rid·er (out′rī′dər), *n.* **1.** a mounted attendant riding before or beside a carriage. **2.** one who rides out or forth.

out·rig·ger (out′rĭg′ər), *n.* **1.** a framework extended outboard from the side of a boat, esp., as in South Pacific canoes, supporting a float which gives stability. **2.** a bracket extending outward from the side of a racing shell, to support an oarlock. **3.** a spar rigged out from a ship's rail or the like, as for extending a sail. **4.** any of various projecting frames or parts on an airplane, as for supporting a rudder, etc.

Canoe with outrigger

out·right (*adj.* out′rīt′; *adv.* out rīt′), *adj.* **1.** complete or total: *an outright loss.* **2.** downright or unqualified: *an outright refusal.* **3.** directed straight out or

on. —*adv.* **4.** completely; entirely. **5.** without restraint, reserve, or concealment; openly. **6.** at once. **7.** *Obs.* straight out or ahead.

out·root (out roōt′, -roŏt′), *v.t.* to root out; extirpate.

out·run (out rŭn′), *v.*, **-ran, -run, -running. 1.** to outstrip in running. **2.** to escape by or as by running. **3.** to exceed.

out·run·ner (out′rŭn′ər), *n.* **1.** one who or that which runs out or outside. **2.** an attendant who runs before or beside a carriage. **3.** the leader of a team of dogs. **4.** a forerunner.

out·sell (out sĕl′), *v.t.*, **-sold, -selling. 1.** to outdo in selling; sell more than. **2.** to sell or be sold for more than. **3.** to exceed in value.

out·set (out′sĕt′), *n.* the beginning or start.

out·shine (out shīn′), *v.*, **-shone, -shining.** —*v.t.* **1.** to surpass in shining. **2.** to surpass in splendor, excellence, etc. —*v.i.* **3.** to shine forth.

out·shoot (*v.* out shoōt′; *n.* out′shoōt′), *v.*, **-shot, -shooting,** *n.* —*v.t.* **1.** to surpass in shooting. **2.** to shoot beyond. **3.** to shoot or send forth. —*v.i.* **4.** to shoot forth; project. —*n.* **5.** a shooting out. **6.** something that shoots out. **7.** *Baseball.* a curve which shoots or bends out away from the batter as it approaches the home base.

out·side (*n., adj., adv.* out′sīd′; *prep.* out′sīd′), *n.* **1.** the outer side, surface, or part; the exterior. **2.** the external aspect or appearance. **3.** something merely external. **4.** the space without or beyond an enclosure, boundary, etc. **5.** *Chiefly Brit. Colloq.* an outside passenger or place on a coach, etc. **6. the outside,** *Colloq.* the utmost limit: *not more than ten at the outside.* —*adj.* **7.** being, acting, done, or originating beyond an enclosure, boundary, etc.: *outside noises.* **8.** situated on or pertaining to the outside; exterior; external. **9.** not belonging to or connected with an institution, society, etc.: *outside influences.* **10.** extreme: *an outside estimate.* —*adv.* **11.** on or to the outside, exterior, or space without. **12.** *U.S. Colloq.* with the exception (fol. by *of*). —*prep.* **13.** outside of. **14.** *Colloq.* except.

out·sid·er (out′sī′dər), *n.* **1.** one not within an enclosure, boundary, etc. **2.** one not belonging to a particular group, set, party, etc. **3.** one unconnected or unacquainted with the matter in question. **4.** a race horse, etc., not included among the favorites.

out·sing (out sĭng′), *v.*, **-sang, -sung, -singing.** —*v.t.* **1.** to sing better than. **2.** to sing louder than. —*v.i.* **3.** to sing out.

out sister, a nun, especially in a cenobite order, who works outside of the convent in its service.

out·sit (out sĭt′), *v.t.*, **-sat, -sitting. 1.** to sit longer than (another). **2.** to sit beyond the time of.

out·size (out′sīz′), *n.* **1.** an uncommon or irregular size. **2.** a garment of such a size, esp. when larger.

out·skirt (out′skûrt′), *n.* (*often pl.*) an outer or bordering part or district.

out·smart (out smärt′), *v.t. U.S. Colloq.* to prove too clever for.

out·soar (out sōr′), *v.t.* to soar beyond.

out·span (out spǎn′), *v.*, **-spanned, -spanning,** *n. South African.* —*v.t.* **1.** to unyoke or unhitch, as oxen from a wagon. —*v.i.* **2.** to remove the yoke, harness, etc., from animals. —*n.* **3.** the act or place of outspanning. [t. S Afr. D: m. *uitspannen*]

out·speak (out spēk′), *v.*, **-spoke, -spoken, -speaking.** —*v.t.* **1.** to outdo or excel in speaking. **2.** to utter frankly or boldly. —*v.i.* **3.** to speak out.

out·spent (out spĕnt′), *adj.* exhausted.

out·spo·ken (out′spō′kən), *adj.* **1.** uttered or expressed with frankness or lack of reserve: *outspoken criticism.* **2.** free or unreserved in speech: *outspoken people.* —**out′spo′ken·ly,** *adv.* —**out′spo′ken·ness,** *n.* —Syn. **1.** See **frank.**

out·spread (*v.* out sprĕd′; *n., adj.* out′sprĕd′), *v.*, **-spread, -spreading,** *adj.* —*v.t., v.i.* **1.** to spread out; extend. —*adj.* **2.** spread out; stretched out. **3.** diffused abroad. —*n.* **4.** a spreading out. **5.** that which is spread out; an expanse.

out·stand (out stǎnd′), *v.*, **-stood, -standing.** *Now Rare.* —*v.i.* **1.** to be prominent. **2.** (of a ship) to sail out to sea. —*v.t.* **3.** to stay or remain beyond. **4.** to withstand.

out·stand·ing (out stǎn′dĭng), *adj.* **1.** prominent; conspicuous; striking. **2.** that continues in existence; that remains unsettled, unpaid, etc. **3.** standing out; projecting; detached. **4.** that resists or opposes.

out·stare (out stâr′), *v.t.*, **-stared, -staring. 1.** to outdo in staring. **2.** to stare out of countenance.

out·sta·tion (out′stā′shən), *n.* an auxiliary station, esp. on the outskirts of a district.

out·stay (out stā′), *v.t.* **1.** to stay longer than. **2.** to stay beyond the time or duration of.

out·stretch (out strĕch′), *v.t.* **1.** to stretch forth; extend. **2.** to stretch beyond (a limit, etc.). **3.** to stretch out; expand. **4.** to strain.

out·strip (out strĭp′), *v.t.*, **-stripped, -stripping. 1.** to outdo; surpass; excel. **2.** to outdo or pass in running or swift travel. **3.** to get ahead of or leave behind in a race or in any course of competition.

out·stroke (out′strōk′), *n.* **1.** a stroke in an outward direction. **2.** (in an engine) the stroke during which the piston rod moves outward from the cylinder.

out·talk (out tôk′), *v.t.* to outdo or overcome in talking.

out·turn (out′tûrn′), *n.* the quantity produced; output.

out·vote (out vōt′), *v.t.*, **-voted, -voting.** to outdo or defeat in voting.

out·wait (out wāt′), *v.t.* **1.** to lie in ambush longer than. **2.** to surpass in waiting or expecting.

out·walk (out wôk′), *v.t.* to outdo in walking.

out·ward (out′wərd), *adj.* **1.** being, or pertaining to, what is seen or apparent, as distinguished from the underlying nature, facts, etc., or from what is in the mind: *the outward looks.* **2.** pertaining to the outside of the body. **3.** pertaining to the body as opposed to the mind or spirit: *our outward eyes.* **4.** belonging or pertaining to the external world as opposed to the mind or spirit. **5.** belonging or pertaining to what is external to oneself: *a man's outward relations.* **6.** proceeding or directed toward the outside or exterior. **7.** that lies toward the outside; that is on the outer side: *my outward room.* **8.** of or pertaining to the outside, outer surface, or exterior. **9.** not directly concerned or interested. —*n.* **11.** the outward part; the outside or exterior. **12.** that which is without; the external or material world. **13.** outward appearance. **14.** on the outside; without. —*adv.* Also, **out′wards. 15.** toward the outside; out. **16.** away from port: *a ship bound outward.* **17.** visibly; openly. [ME; OE *ūtweard*]

out·ward·ly (out′wərd lī), *adv.* **1.** as regards appearance or outward manifestation. **2.** toward the outside. **3.** on the outside or outer surface.

out·watch (out wŏch′, -wôch′), *v.t.* **1.** to outdo in watching. **2.** to watch until the end of.

out·wear (out wâr′), *v.t.*, **-wore, -worn, -wearing. 1.** to wear or last longer than; outlast. **2.** to outlive or outgrow. **3.** to wear out; consume by wearing. **4.** to exhaust in strength or endurance. **5.** to pass time.

out·weigh (out wā′), *v.t.* **1.** to exceed in value, importance, influence, etc.: *the advantages of the plan outweighed its defects.* **2.** to be too heavy or burdensome for. **3.** to exceed in weight.

out·wit (out wĭt′), *v.t.*, **-witted, -witting. 1.** to get the better of by superior ingenuity or cleverness. **2.** *Archaic.* to surpass in intelligence.

out·work (*v.* out wûrk′, *n.* out′wûrk′), *v.t.*, **-worked** or **-wrought, -working,** *n.* —*v.t.* **1.** to surpass in working; work harder or faster than. **2.** to work out or carry on to a conclusion; finish. —*n.* **3.** *Fort.* a part of the fortifications of a place lying outside the main work.

out·worn (out′wôrn′), *adj.* **1.** outgrown, as opinions. **2.** obsolete; out of date. **3.** worn out, as clothes. **4.** exhausted in strength or endurance, as persons.

ou·zel (ōō′zəl), *n.* **1.** a name used in England for members of the thrush family, esp. the blackbird, *Turdus merula.* **2.** water ouzel. Also, **ousel.** [ME *osel,* OE *ōsle,* c. G *amsel*]

o·va (ō′və), *n.* pl. of **ovum.**

o·val (ō′vəl), *adj.* **1.** having the general form, shape, or outline of an egg; egg-shaped. **2.** ellipsoidal or elliptical. —*n.* **3.** any of various oval things. **4.** a body or a plane figure oval in shape or outline. **5.** an elliptical field, or a field on which an elliptical track is laid out, as for athletic contests. **6.** *Colloq.* a football. [t. NL: s. *ōvālis,* der. L *ōvum* egg. See OVATE] —**o′val·ly,** *adv.* —**o′val·ness,** *n.*

o·var·i·an (ō vâr′ī ən), *adj.* of or pertaining to an ovary.

o·var·i·ot·o·my (ō-vâr′ĭ ŏt′ə mī), *n.*, *pl.* **-mies.** *Surg.* incision into or removal of an ovary.

o·va·ri·tis (ō′və rī′tĭs), *n. Pathol.* oöphoritis.

o·va·ry (ō′və rī), *n.*, *pl.* **-ries. 1.** *Anat., Zool.* the female gonad or reproductive gland, in which the ova, or eggs, and the hormones that regulate female secondary sex characteristics develop. **2.** *Bot.* the enlarged lower part of the pistil in angiospermous plants, enclosing the ovules or young seeds. [t. NL: *ōvārium,* der. L *ōvum* egg]

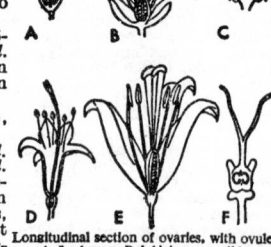

Longitudinal section of ovaries, with ovules A. Larkspur, *Delphinium consolida* B. Chickweed, *Stellaria media*; C, Buttercup, *Ranunculus bulbosus*; D, Fuchsia, *Fuchsia coccinea*; E, Lily, *Lilium superbum*; F, Maple, *Acer rubrum*

o·vate (ō′vāt), *adj.* **1.** egg-shaped. **2.** *Bot.* **a.** having a plane figure like the longitudinal section of an egg. **b.** having such a figure with the broader end at the base, as a leaf. [t. L: m.s. *ōvātus* egg-shaped]

o·va·tion (ō vā′shən), *n.* **1.** an enthusiastic public reception of a person; enthusiastic applause. **2.** a lesser form of triumph accorded to an ancient Roman commander. [t. L: s. *ovātiō* rejoicing]

ov·en (ŭv′ən), *n.* a chamber or receptacle for baking or heating, or for drying with the aid of heat. [ME *ofen,* c. G *ofen*]

Ovate Leaf

ov·en·bird (ŭv′ən bûrd′), *n.* **1.** a well-known American bird, *Seiurus aurocapillus,* which builds an oven-shaped nest of grasses, etc., on the forest floor. It belongs to the wood warbler family, *Compsothlypidae.* **2.** any of the South American passerine birds of the genus *Furnarius.* **3.** a North American warbler, *Seiurus auricapillus,* with a golden-brown color.

ov·en·wood (ŭv′ən wŏŏd′), *n.* brushwood; dead wood fit only for burning.

o·ver (ō′vər), *prep.* **1.** above in place or position; higher up than: *the roof over one's head.* **2.** above and to the other side of: *to leap over a wall.* **3.** above in authority, power, etc.; so as to govern, control, or conquer. **4.** on or upon; so as to rest on or cover. **5.** here and there on or in: *at various places over the country.* **6.** through all parts of; all through: *to look over papers.* **7.** to and fro on or in: *to travel over Europe.* **8.** from side to side of; to the other side of: *to go over a bridge.* **9.** on the other side of: *lands over the sea.* **10.** reaching higher than, so as to submerge. **11.** in excess of, or more than: *over a mile.* **12.** above in degree, etc. **13.** in preference to. **14.** from end to end of: *over the wire.* **15.** until after the end of: *to adjourn over the holidays.* **16.** during the duration of: *over a long term of years.* **17.** in reference to, concerning, or about: *to quarrel over a matter.* **18.** while engaged on or concerned with: *to fall asleep over one's work.* **19.** over all, from one extremity of a thing to the other. **20.** over and above, in addition to; besides. —*adv.* **21.** over the top or upper surface or edge of something. **22.** so as to cover the surface, or affect the whole surface: *to paint a thing over.* **23.** through a region, area, etc.: *to travel all over.* **24.** at some distance, as in a direction indicated: *over by the hill.* **25.** from side to side, or to the other side: *to sail over.* **26.** across any intervening space: *when are you coming over to see us?* **27.** from beginning to end, or all through: *to read a thing over.* **28.** from one person, party, etc., to another: *to make property over to others.* **29.** on the other side, as of a sea, a river, or any space: *over in Europe.* **30.** so as to bring the upper end or side down or under: *to throw a thing over.* **31.** once more; again: *to do a thing over.* **32.** in repetition: *twenty times over.* **33.** in excess or addition: *to pay the full sum and something over.* **34.** remaining beyond a certain amount: *five goes into seven once, with two over.* **35.** throughout or beyond a period of time: *to stay over till Monday.* **36.** Some adverbial phrases are: **all over, 1.** *U.S. Colloq.* everywhere. **2.** thoroughly; entirely. **3.** done with; finished. **all over with,** done with; finished. **over again,** once more; with repetition. **over against, 1.** opposite to; in front of. **2.** as contrasted with or distinguished from: *to set truth over against falsehood.* **over and above, 1.** in addition; besides. **2.** *Colloq.* overmuch; too much; too. **over and over,** repeatedly. **over there,** *U.S. Colloq.* in Europe. —*adj.* **37.** upper; higher up. **38.** higher in authority, station, etc. **39.** serving, or intended, as an outer covering: outer. **40.** in excess or addition; surplus; extra. **41.** too great; excessive. **42.** at an end; done; past: *when the war was over.* —*n.* **43.** an amount in excess or addition; an extra. **44.** *Mil.* a shot which strikes or bursts beyond the target. **45.** *Cricket.* **a.** the number of balls (now usually six) delivered between successive changes of bowlers. **b.** the part of the game played between such changes. —*v.t.* **46.** *Rare.* to go or get over; leap over. —*v.i.* **47.** *Rare.* to go or pass over. [ME; OE *ofer,* c. D *over,* G *über,* akin to Skt. *upari*]

over-, prefixal use of **over,** *prep.,* *adv.,* or *adj.,* occurring in various senses in compounds, as in *overboard, overcoat, overhang, overlap, overlord, overrun, overthrow,* and especially employed, with the sense of "over the limit," "to excess," "too much," "too," to form verbs, adjectives, adverbs, and nouns, as *overact, overcapitalize, overcrowd, overfull, overmuch, oversupply, overweight,* and many others, mostly self-explanatory: a hyphen, which is commonly absent from old or well-established formations, being often used in new coinages, or in any words whose component parts it may be desirable to set off distinctly.

o·ver·a·bound (ō′vər ə bound′), *v.i.* to abound to excess.

o·ver·a·bun·dance (ō′vər ə bŭn′dəns), *n.* excessive abundance: *an overabundance of pie sent poor Tom to bed.* —**o′ver·a·bun′dant,** *adj.*

o·ver·act (ō′vər ăkt′), *v.t.* to act (a part) in an exaggerated manner.

o·ver·ac·tive (ō′vər ăk′tĭv), *adj.* active to excess; too active. —**o′ver·ac·tiv′i·ty,** *n.*

o·ver·age¹ (ō′vər āj′), *adj.* beyond the proper age: *overage for the draft.* [f. OVER- + AGE, n.]

o·ver·age² (ō′vər ĭj), *n. Com.* **1.** an excess supply of merchandise. **2.** the value of goods in excess of amount called for by stock records; money in excess of the amount called for by sales records. [f. OVER- + -AGE]

o·ver·all (ō′vər ôl′), *adj.* **1.** from one extreme limit of a thing to the other: *the overall length of a bridge.* **2.** covering or including everything. —*n.* **3.** (*pl.*) loose, stout trousers, often with a part extending up over the breast, worn over the clothing to protect it, as by workmen and others. **4.** (*pl.*) long waterproof leggings. **5.** *Brit.* a smock or loose housedress.

b., blend of, blended; c., cognate with; d., dialect, dialectal; der., derived from; f., formed from; g., going back to; m., modification of; r., replacing; s., stem of; t., taken from; ?, perhaps. See the full key on inside cover.

o·ver·arch (ō′vər ärch′), *v.t.* **1.** to span with or like an arch. —*v.i.* **2.** to form an arch over something.

o·ver·arm (ō′vər ärm′), *adj. Baseball, etc.* delivered or executed with the arm raised above the shoulder.

o·ver·awe (ō′vər ô′), *v.t.*, **-awed, -awing.** to restrain or subdue by inspiring awe; cow.

o·ver·bal·ance (ō′vər băl′əns) *v.t.*, **-anced, -ancing,** *n.* **1.** to outweigh. **2.** to cause to lose balance or to fall or turn over. —*n.* **3.** overbalancing weight or amount. **4.** something that more thn b alances.

o·ver·bear (ō′vər bâr′), *v.,* **-bore, -borne, -bearing.** —*v.t.* **1.** to bear over or down by weight or force. **2.** to overcome. **3.** to prevail over or overrule (wishes, objections, etc.). **4.** to treat in a domineering way. —*v.i.* **5.** to produce fruit or progeny so abundantly as to impair the health.

o·ver·bear·ing (ō′vər bâr′ĭng), *adj.* domineering; dictatorial; haughtily or rudely arrogant. —**o′ver·bear′ing·ly,** *adv.*

o·ver·bid (*v.* ō′vər bĭd′; *n.* ō′vər bĭd′), *v.,* **-bid, -bid·den** or **-bid, -bidding,** *n.* —*v.t., v.i.* **1.** to bid more than the value of (a thing). **2.** to outbid (a person, etc.). —*n.* **3.** a higher bid.

o·ver·bite (ō′vər bīt′), *n. Dentistry.* occlusion in which the upper incisor teeth overlap the lower.

o·ver·blow (ō′vər blō′), *v.,* **-blew, -blown, -blowing.** —*v.t.* **1.** to blow (clouds, etc.) over or away. **2.** to blow down. **3.** to blow over the surface of, as the wind, sand, or the like does. —*v.i.* **4.** to pass away, as a storm.

o·ver·blown (ō′vər blōn′), *adj.* more than full-blown.

o·ver·board (ō′vər bōrd′), *adv.* over the side of a ship or boat, esp. into or in the water: *to fall overboard.*

o·ver·build (ō′vər bĭld′), *v.t.,* **-built, -building. 1.** to cover or surmount with a building or structure. **2.** to erect too many buildings on (an area). **3.** to build (a structure) on too great or elaborate a scale.

o·ver·bur·den (ō′vər bûr′dən), *v.t.* to load with too great a burden; overload.

o·ver·bur·den·some (ō′vər bûr′dən səm), *adj.* excessively burdensome.

o·ver·buy (ō′vər bī′), *v.,* **-bought, -buying.** —*v.t.* **1.** to purchase in excessive quantities. **2.** *Finance.* to buy on margin in excess of one's ability to provide added security in an emergency, as in a falling market. —*v.i.* **3.** to buy regardless of one's financial ability.

o·ver·call (ō′vər kôl′), *v.t. Cards.* to bid higher than.

o·ver·cap·i·tal·ize (ō′vər kăp′ətə līz′), *v.t.,* **-ized, -izing. 1.** to fix the nominal capital (total amount of securities) of a company in excess of the limits set by law or by sound financial policy. **2.** to overestimate the capital value (of a business property or enterprise). **3.** to provide an excessive amount of capital (for a business enterprise).—**o′ver·cap′i·tal·i·za′tion,** *n.*

o·ver·cast (ō′vər kăst′, -kăst′, ō′vər kăst′, -kăst′), *adj., v.,* **-cast, -casting.** —*adj.* **1.** overspread with clouds, as the sky; cloudy. **2.** dark; gloomy. **3.** *Sewing.* sewn by overcasting. —*v.t.* **4.** to overcloud, darken, or make gloomy. **5.** to sew with stitches passing successively over an edge, esp. long stitches set at intervals to prevent raveling. —*v.i.* **6.** to become cloudy or dark.

o·ver·cast·ing (ō′vər kăs′tĭng, -käs′-), *n.* **1.** act or practice of coating masonry with plaster. **2.** *Sewing.* the stitch used to overcast.

o·ver·cer·ti·fy (ō′vər sûr′tə fī′), *v.t.,* **-fied, -fying.** *Banking.* to issue (a bank check) for an amount greater than the drawer's balance in his account. —**o′ver·cer′ti·fi·ca′tion,** *n.*

o·ver·charge (*v.* ō′vər chärj′; *n.* ō′vər chärj′), *v.,* **-charged, -charging,** *n.* —*v.t.* **1.** to charge (a person) too high a price. **2.** to charge (an amount) in excess of what is due. **3.** to overload; fill too full. **4.** to exaggerate. —*n.* **5.** a charge in excess of a just price. **6.** an excessive load.

o·ver·check (ō′vər chĕk′), *n.* a checkrein passed over a horse's head between the ears.

o·ver·clothes (ō′vər klōz′, -klōᵗẖz′), *n.pl.* clothing worn outside other garments.

o·ver·cloud (ō′vər kloud′), *v.t.* **1.** to overspread with or as with clouds. **2.** to darken; obscure; make gloomy. —*v.i.* **3.** to become clouded over or overcast.

o·ver·coat (ō′vər kōt′), *n.* a coat worn over the ordinary clothing, as in cold weather; a greatcoat.

o·ver·come (ō′vər kŭm′), *v.,* **-came, -come, -coming.** —*v.t.* **1.** to get the better of in a struggle or conflict; conquer; defeat. **2.** to prevail over (opposition, objections, temptations, etc.). **3.** to surmount (difficulties, etc.). **4.** to overpower (a person, etc.) in body or mind, or affect in an overpowering or paralyzing way, as liquor, a drug, excessive exertion, violent emotion, or the like does. **5.** to overwhelm in feeling. **6.** *Archaic.* to overspread or overrun. —*v.i.* **7.** to gain the victory; conquer. [ME; OE *ofercuman*] —Syn. 1. See **defeat.**

o·ver·com·pen·sa·tion (ō′vər kŏm′pən sā′shən), *n. Psychoanal.* the exaggerated striving for any trait to neutralize and conceal strong feelings of an opposite kind.

o·ver·con·fi·dent (ō′vər kŏn′fə dənt), *adj.* too confident. —**o′ver·con′fi·dence,** *n.*

o·ver·crit·i·cal (ō′vər krĭt′ə kəl), *adj.* critical to excess; too critical; hypercritical.

o·ver·crop (ō′vər krŏp′), *v.t.,* **-cropped, -cropping.** *Agric.* to crop (land) to excess; exhaust the fertility of by continuous cropping.

o·ver·crowd (ō′vər kroud′), *v.t., v.i.* to crowd to excess.

o·ver·de·vel·op (ō′vər dĭ vĕl′əp), *v.t.* to develop to excess. —**o′ver·de·vel′op·ment,** *n.*

o·ver·do (ō′vər dōō′), *v.,* **-did, -done, -doing.** —*v.t.* **1.** to do to excess: *to overdo exercise.* **2.** to carry to excess or beyond the proper limit. **3.** to overact (a part); exaggerate. **4.** to overtax the strength of; fatigue; exhaust. —*v.i.* **5.** to do too much.

o·ver·done (ō′vər dŭn′), *v.* **1.** pp. of **overdo.** —*adj.* **2.** (of food, etc.) cooked too much.

o·ver·dose (*n.* ō′vər dōs′; *v.* ō′vər dōs′), *n., v.,* **-dosed, -dosing.** —*n.* **1.** an excessive dose. —*v.t.* **2.** to dose to excess.

o·ver·draft (ō′vər drăft′, -dräft′), *n.* **1.** a draft in excess of one's credit balance, or the amount of the excess. **2.** an excess draft or demand made on anything. **3.** the action of overdrawing an account, as at a bank. **4.** a draft made to pass over a fire, as in a furnace. **5.** a draft passing downward through a kiln.

o·ver·draw (ō′vər drô′), *v.,* **-drew, -drawn, -drawing.** —*v.t.* **1.** to draw upon (an account, allowance, etc.) in excess of the balance standing to one's credit or at one's disposal. **2.** to draw too far; strain, as a bow, by drawing. **3.** to exaggerate in drawing, depicting, or describing. —*v.i.* **4.** to overdraw an account or the like.

o·ver·dress (*v.* ō′vər drĕs′; *n.* ō′vər drĕs′), *v.t., v.i.* to dress to excess or with too much display.

o·ver·drive (*v.* ō′vər drĭv′; *n.* ō′vər drĭv′), *v.,* **-drove, -driven, -driving,** *n.* —*v.t.* **1.** to overwork; push or carry to excess. **2.** to drive too hard. —*n.* **3.** *Mach.* a device containing a gear set at such ratio and arrangement as to provide (when engaged) a propeller speed greater than the engine crankshaft speed.

o·ver·due (ō′vər dū′, -dōō′), *adj.* past due, as a belated train or a bill not paid by the assigned date.

o·ver·eat (ō′vər ēt′), *v.,* **-ate, -eaten, -eating.** —*v.i.* **1.** to eat too much. —*v.t.* **2.** to eat more than is good for (oneself).

o·ver·es·ti·mate (*v.* ō′vər ĕs′tə māt′; *n.* ō′vər ĕs′tə mĭt′), *v.,* **-mated, -mating,** *n.* —*v.t.* **1.** to estimate at too high a value, amount, rate, or the like. —*n.* **2.** an estimate that is too high. —**o′ver·es′ti·ma′tion,** *n.*

o·ver·ex·cite (ō′vər ĭk sīt′), *v.t.,* **-cited, -citing.** to excite too much. —**o′ver·ex·cit′a·ble,** *adj.* —**over·ex·cite′ment,** *n.*

o·ver·ex·ert (ō′vər ĭg zûrt′), *v.t.* to exert too much. —**o′ver·ex·er′tion,** *n.*

o·ver·ex·pose (ō′vər ĭk spōz′), *v.t.,* **-posed, -posing. 1.** to expose too much. **2.** *Photog.* to expose too long.

o·ver·feed (ō′vər fēd′), *v.t., v.i.,* **-fed, -feeding.** to feed to excess.

o·ver·fill (ō′vər fĭl′), *v.t.* **1.** to fill too full so as to cause overflowing. —*v.i.* **2.** to become too full.

o·ver·flow (*v.* ō′vər flō′; *n.* ō′vər flō′), *v.,* **-flowed, -flown, -flowing.** —*v.i.* **1.** to flow or run over, as rivers, water, etc. **2.** to have the contents flowing over, as an overfull vessel. **3.** to discharge a flow of something as from being overfull (fol. by *with*). **4.** to pass from one place or part to another as if flowing from an overfull space: *the population overflowed into the adjoining territory.* **5.** to be filled or supplied in overflowing measure (fol. by *with*): *a heart overflowing with gratitude.* —*v.t.* **6.** to flow over; flood; inundate. **7.** to flow over or beyond (the brim, banks, borders, etc.). **8.** to flow over the edge or brim of (a vessel, etc.). **9.** to fill to the point of running over. —*n.* **10.** an overflowing: *the annual overflow of the Nile.* **11.** that which flows or runs over: *to carry off the overflow from a fountain.* **12.** an excess or superabundance. **13.** a portion passing or crowded out from an overfilled place: *to house the overflow from a museum.* **14.** an outlet for excess liquid.

o·ver·gar·ment (ō′vər gär′mənt), *n.* outer garment.

o·ver·gild (ō′vər gĭld′), *v.t.,* **-gilded** or **-gilt, -gilding.** to cover with gilding.

o·ver·glance (ō′vər glăns′, -gläns′), *v.t.,* **-glanced, -glancing.** to glance over.

o·ver·glaze (ō′vər glāz′), *n.* a glaze or decoration applied over another glaze on pottery.

o·ver·grow (ō′vər grō′), *v.,* **-grew, -grown, -growing.** —*v.t.* **1.** to grow over; cover with a growth of something. **2.** to outdo in growing; choke or supplant by a more exuberant growth. **3.** to grow beyond, grow too large for, or outgrow. —*v.i.* **4.** to grow to excess; grow too large. —**o′ver·grown′,** *adj.*

o′ver·am·bi′tious	o′ver·cau′tious	o′ver·ea′ger	o′ver·fa·mil′iar
o′ver·anx·i′e·ty	o′ver·char′it·a·ble	o′ver·e·mo′tion·al	o′ver·fa·tigue′
o′ver·anx′ious	o′ver·child′ish	o′ver·em′pha·size′	o′ver·fit′
o′ver·bal′last	o′ver·con·serv′a·tive	o′ver·en·thu′si·as′tic	o′ver·fond′
o′ver·bold′	o′ver·cook′	o′ver·ex′er·cise′	o′ver·fre′quent
o′ver·bus′y	o′ver·cu′ri·ous	o′ver·ex·pand′	o′ver·full′
o′ver·care′ful	o′ver·del′i·cate	o′ver·ex·pan′sion	o′ver·gen′er·ous
o′ver·cau′tion	o′ver·dig′ni·fied′	o′ver·ex·po′sure	o′ver·greed′y

o·ver·growth (ō′vərgrōth′), *n.* **1.** a growth overspreading or covering something. **2.** excessive growth.

o·ver·hand (ō′vər hănd′), *adj.* Also, **o′ver·hand′ed.** **1.** done or delivered overhand. **2.** *Cricket, etc.* overarm. *—adv.* **3.** with the hand over the object. **4.** with the hand raised above the shoulder, as in pitching a ball. **5.** *Sewing.* with close, shallow stitches over two selvages. *—n.* **6.** *Sports.* skill in the delivery of overhand strokes. *—v.t.* **7.** to sew overhand.

overhand knot, a simple knot of various uses which slips easily. See illus. under **knot.**

o·ver·hang (*v.* ō′vər hăng′; *n.* ō′vər hăng′), *v.,* **-hung, -hanging,** *n.* *—v.t.* **1.** to hang or be suspended over. **2.** to extend, project, or jut over: *a dark sky overhangs the earth.* **3.** to impend over, or threaten, as danger or evil: *the sadness which overhung him.* **4.** to adorn with hangings. *—v.i.* **5.** to hang over; project or jut out over something below. *—n.* **6.** an overhanging; a projection. **7.** the extent of projection, as of the bow of a vessel. **8.** *Archit.* a projecting upper part of a building as a roof or balcony. **9.** *Aeron.* the amount by which an upper wing of a biplane projects laterally beyond the corresponding lower wing.

o·ver·haul (ō′vər hôl′), *v.t.* **1.** to investigate or examine thoroughly, as for repair. **2.** to haul or turn over for examination. **3.** to gain upon or overtake. **4.** *Naut.* **a.** to slacken (a rope) by hauling in the opposite direction to that in which it was drawn taut. **b.** to release the blocks of (a tackle). *—n.* **5.** a thorough examination.

o·ver·head (*adv.* ō′vər hĕd′; *adj., n.* ō′vər hĕd′), *adv.* **1.** over one's head; aloft; up in the air or sky, esp. near the zenith: *overhead was a cloud.* **2.** so as to be completely submerged or deeply involved: *overhead in debt.* *—adj.* **3.** situated, operating, or passing overhead, aloft, or above. **4.** applicable to one and all; general; average. *—n.* **5.** the general cost of running a business. **6.** the general cost which cannot be assigned to particular products or orders.

overhead railway, *Brit.* an elevated railway.

o·ver·hear (ō′vər hîr′), *v.t.,* **-heard, -hearing.** to hear (speech, etc., or a speaker) without the speaker's intention or knowledge. *—o′ver·hear′er, n.*

o·ver·heat (ō′vər hēt′), *v.t.* **1.** to heat to excess. *—n.* **2.** excessive heat; overheated condition.

o·ver·hung (ō′vər hŭng′), *v.* pt. and pp. of **overhang.**

o·ver·in·dulge (ō′vər ĭn dŭlj′), *v.t., v.i.,* **-dulged, -dulging.** to indulge to excess. *—o′ver·in·dul′gence, n. —o′ver·in·dul′gent, adj.*

o·ver·is·sue (ō′vər ĭsh′ōō), *n.* an excessive issue of stocks or bonds, as in excess of the needs of the business, or in excess of charter authorization.

o·ver·joyed (ō′vər joid′), *adj.* overcome with joy; made exceedingly joyful.

over·kill (ō′vər kĭl′), *n.* **1.** the capacity of a nation to destroy, by nuclear weapons, more of an enemy than would be necessary for a military victory. **2.** an instance of such destruction.

o·ver·lade (ō′vər lād′), *v.t.,* **-laded, -laded** or **-laden, -lading.** to overload (now chiefly in *overladen,* pp.).

o·ver·land (ō′vər lănd′), *adv.* **1.** over or across the land. **2.** by land. *—adj.* **3.** proceeding, performed, or carried on overland: *the overland route.*

overland stage, a stagecoach used in the western U.S. during the middle nineteenth century.

o·ver·lap (*v.* ō′vər lăp′; *n.* ō′vər lăp′), *v.,* **lapped, -lapping,** *n.* *—v.t.* **1.** to lap over (something else or each other); extend over and cover a part of. **2.** to cover and extend beyond (something else). *—v.i.* **3.** to lap over. *—n.* **4.** an overlapping. **5.** the amount of overlapping. **6.** an overlapping part. **7.** the place of overlapping.

o·ver·lay¹ (*v.* ō′vər lā′; *n.* ō′vər lā′), *v.,* **-laid, -laying,** *n.* *—v.t.* **1.** to lay or place (one thing) over or upon another. **2.** to cover, overspread, or surmount with something. **3.** to finish with a layer or applied decoration of something: *wood richly overlaid with gold.* **4.** *Print.* to put an overlay upon. *—n.* **5.** something laid over something else; a covering. **6.** a layer or decoration of something applied: *an overlay of gold.* **7.** *Print.* a shaped piece of paper, or a sheet of paper reinforced at the proper places by shaped pieces, put on the tympan of a press to increase or equalize the impression. **8.** a transparent sheet giving special military information not ordinarily shown on maps, used by being placed over the map on which it is based. **9.** *Scot.* a neckcloth or cravat. [ME, f. OVER- + LAY¹]

o·ver·lay² (ō′vər lā′), *v.* pt. of **overlie.**

o·ver·lie (ō′vər lī′), *v.t.,* **-lay, -lain, -lying. 1.** to lie over or upon, as a covering, stratum, etc. **2.** to smother (an infant) by lying upon it, as in sleep.

o·ver·live (ō′vər lĭv′), *v.,* **-lived, -living.** *—v.t.* **1.** to live longer than; outlast. *—v.i.* **2.** to survive.

o·ver·load (*v.* ō′vər lōd′; *n.* ō′vər lōd′), *v.t.* **1.** to load to excess; overburden. *—n.* **2.** an excessive load.

o·ver·long (ō′vər lông′, -lŏng′), *adj., adv.* too long.

o·ver·look (ō′vər lŏŏk′), *v.t.* **1.** to fail to notice, perceive, or consider: *to overlook a misspelled word.* **2.** to disregard or ignore indulgently, as faults, misconduct, etc. **3.** to look over, as from a higher position. **4.** to

afford a view down over: *a hill overlooking the sea.* **5.** to rise above. **6.** to take no notice of; ignore. **7.** to look over in inspection, examination, or perusal. **8.** to look after, oversee, or supervise. **9.** to look upon with the evil eye; bewitch. *—Syn.* **1.** See **slight.**

o·ver·look·er (ō′vər lŏŏk′ər), *n.* *Brit.* overseer.

o·ver·lord (ō′vər lôrd′), *n.* one who is lord over another or over other lords. *—o′ver·lord′ship, n.*

o·ver·ly (ō′vər lĭ′), *adv.* *Colloq.* overmuch; excessively; too: *a voyage not overly dangerous.*

o·ver·ly·ing (ō′vər lī′ĭng), *v.* ppr. of **overlie.**

o·ver·man (*n.* ō′vər mən *for 1 and 2,* ō′vər măn′ *for 3;* *v.* ō′vər măn′), *n., pl.* **-men,** *v.,* **-manned, -manning.** *—n.* **1.** a foreman or overseer. **2.** an arbiter or umpire. **3.** a superman. *—v.t.* **4.** to oversupply with men, esp. for service. [ME]

o·ver·mas·ter (ō′vər măs′tər, -mäs′tər), *v.t.* to overcome; overpower.

o·ver·match (ō′vər măch′), *v.t.* to outmatch; surpass.

o·ver·much (ō′vər mŭch′), *adj., n., adv.* too much.

o·ver·nice (ō′vər nīs′), *adj.* too nice or fastidious.

o·ver·night (*adv.* ō′vər nīt′; *n., adj.* ō′vər nīt′), *adv.* **1.** during the night: *to stay overnight.* **2.** on the previous evening: *preparations were made overnight.* *—adj.* **3.** done, occurring, or continuing during the night: *an overnight stop.* **4.** designed to be used one night or very few nights: *overnight bag.* **5.** of or pertaining to the previous evening. *—n.* **6.** the previous evening.

o·ver·pass (*n.* ō′vər păs′, -päs′; *v.* ō′vər păs′, -päs′), *n., v.,* **-passed** or **-past, -passing.** *—n.* **1.** a highway or railway bridge crossing some barrier, as another highway. *—v.t.* **2.** to pass over or traverse (a region, space, etc.). **3.** to pass over (bounds, limits, etc.). **4.** to transgress. **5.** to get over (obstacles, etc.). **6.** to go beyond, exceed, or surpass. **7.** to pass through (time, experiences, etc.). **8.** to overlook; disregard; omit.

o·ver·pay (ō′vər pā′), *v.t.,* **-paid, -paying. 1.** to pay more than (an amount due). **2.** to pay in excess. *—o′ver·pay′ment, n.*

o·ver·peo·ple (ō′vər pē′pəl), *v.t.,* **-pled, -pling.** to overstock with people.

o·ver·per·suade (ō′vər pər swād′), *v.t.,* **-suaded, -suading. 1.** to bring over by persuasion. **2.** to persuade (a person) against his inclination or intention.

o·ver·play (ō′vər plā′), *v.t.* **1.** to play (a part, etc.) in an exaggerated manner. **2.** to defeat in playing. **3.** *Golf.* to hit (the ball) past the putting green.

o·ver·plus (ō′vər plŭs′), *n.* **1.** an excess over a particular amount, or a surplus. **2.** superabundance.

o·ver·pop·u·late (ō′vər pŏp′yə lāt′), *v.t.,* **-lated, -lating.** to overpeople. *—o′ver·pop·u·la′tion, n.*

o·ver·pow·er (ō′vər pou′ər), *v.t.* **1.** to overcome or overwhelm in feeling, or affect or impress excessively. **2.** to overcome, master, or subdue by superior force: *to overpower a maniac.* **3.** to overmaster the bodily powers or mental faculties of: *overpowered with wine.* **4.** to furnish or equip with excessive power. *—Syn.* **2.** vanquish, overcome, overwhelm, subjugate.

o·ver·pow·er·ing (ō′vər pou′ər ĭng), *adj.* that overpowers; overwhelming. *—o′ver·pow′er·ing·ly, adv.*

o·ver·print (*v.* ō′vər prĭnt′; *n.* ō′vər prĭnt′), *v.t.* **1.** to print additional material or another color on a form or sheet previously printed. *—n.* **2.** a quantity of printing in excess of that desired; an overrun. **3.** *Philately.* **a.** any word, inscription or device printed across the face of a stamp altering its use or its locality, or overprinted for a special purpose. **b.** a stamp so marked.

o·ver·prize (ō′vər prīz′), *v.t.,* **-prized, -prizing.** to prize too highly; overvalue.

o·ver·pro·duce (ō′vər prə dūs′, -dōōs′), *v.t., v.i.,* **-duced, -ducing.** to produce excessively or in excess of demand.

o·ver·pro·duc·tion (ō′vər prə dŭk′shən), *n.* excessive production; production in excess of the demand.

o·ver·proof (ō′vər prōōf′), *adj.* containing a greater proportion of alcohol than proof spirit does.

o·ver·proud (ō′vər proud′), *adj.* excessively proud.

o·ver·rate (ō′vər rāt′), *v.t.,* **-rated, -rating.** to rate too highly; overestimate: *his fortune has been overrated.*

o·ver·reach (ō′vər rēch′), *v.t.* **1.** to reach or extend over or beyond. **2.** to reach for or aim at but go beyond, as a thing sought, a mark, etc. **3.** to stretch (the arm, etc.) to excess, as by a straining effort. **4.** to defeat (oneself) by overdoing matters, often by excessive eagerness or cunning. **5.** to strain or exert (oneself) to the point of exceeding the purpose. **6.** to get the better of (a person, etc.); cheat. **7.** *Obs.* to overtake. *—v.i.* **8.** to reach or extend over something. **9.** to reach too far. **10.** to cheat others. **11.** (of horses, etc.) to strike, or strike and injure, the forefoot with the hind foot.

o·ver·ride (ō′vər rīd′), *v.t.,* **-rode, -ridden, -riding. 1.** to ride over or across (a region, etc.). **2.** to ride roughshod over. **3.** to pursue one's course in disregard of: *to override one's advisers.* **4.** to prevail over: *a decision that overrides all previous decisions.* **5.** to ride too much. **6.** to exhaust by excessive riding, as a horse. **7.** to pass or extend over. **8.** *Surg.* to overlap, as one piece of a fractured bone over another.

o′ver·hast′y	o′ver·mer′ry	o′ver·o·be′di·ent	o′ver·pow′er·ful
o′ver·high′	o′ver·mod′est	o′ver·please′	o′ver·praise′
o′ver·jeal′ous	o′ver·mourn′ful	o′ver·plump′	o′ver·rash′
o′ver·meas′ure	o′ver·neg′li·gent	o′ver·pop′u·lous	o′ver·re·li′gious

o·ver·ripe (ō′vər·rīp′), *adj.* too ripe; more than ripe.

o·ver·rule (ō′vər·rōōl′), *v.t.*, **-ruled, -ruling. 1.** to rule against or disallow the arguments of (a person). **2.** to rule or decide against (a plea, argument, etc.); disallow. **3.** to prevail over so as to change the purpose or action. **4.** to exercise rule or influence over.

o·ver·run (*v.* ō′vər·rŭn′; *n.* ō′vər·rŭn′), *v.*, **-ran, -run, -running,** *n.* —*v.t.* **1.** to rove over (a country, etc.), as hostile or ravaging invaders. **2.** to swarm over in great numbers, as animals, esp. vermin. **3.** to spread or grow rapidly over, as plants, esp. vines, weeds, etc. **4.** to run over so as to injure or overwhelm. **5.** to spread rapidly throughout, as a new idea, spirit, etc. **6.** to run beyond. **7.** to exceed. **8.** to run over; overflow. **9.** *Print.* **a.** to carry over (letters, words, or lines) to the next line, column, or page. **b.** to carry over words, letters, etc., of. **10.** *Archaic.* to outrun; overtake in running. —*v.i.* **11.** to run over; overthrow. **12.** to extend beyond the proper or desired limit. —*n.* **13.** an overrunning. **14.** an amount overrunning or carried over. [OE *oferyrnan*]

o·ver·score (ō′vər·skôr′), *v.t.*, **-scored, -scoring.** to score over, as with strokes or lines.

o·ver·seas (*adv.* ō′vər·sēz′; *adj.* ō′vər·sēz′), *adv.* **1.** over, across, or beyond the sea. —*adj.* **2.** of or pertaining to passage over the sea: *overseas travel.* **3.** situated beyond the sea: *overseas lands.* **4.** pertaining to countries beyond the sea; foreign: *overseas military service.* Also, **o·ver·sea** (*adv.* ō′vər·sē′; *adj.* ō′vər·sē′).

o·ver·see (ō′vər·sē′), *v.t.*, **-saw, -seen, -seeing. 1.** to direct (work or workers); supervise; manage. **2.** to survey; watch. **3.** *Obs.* to look over; inspect. [OE *ofersēon*]

o·ver·se·er (ō′vər·sē′ər), *n.* **1.** one who oversees; a supervisor. **2.** a minor official of a parish in England (in full, **overseer of the poor**). [ME]

o·ver·sell (ō′vər·sĕl′), *v.t.*, **-sold, -selling. 1.** to sell more of (a stock, etc.) than can be delivered. **2.** to sell to excess.

o·ver·set (*v.* ō′vər·sĕt′; *n.* ō′vər·sĕt′), *v.*, **-set, -setting,** *n.* —*v.t.* **1.** to upset or overturn; overthrow. **2.** to throw into confusion; disorder physically or mentally. —*v.i.* **3.** to become upset, overturned, or overthrown. **4.** *Print.* (of type or copy) **a.** to set in or to excess. **b.** (of space) to set too much type for. —*n.* **5.** act or fact of oversetting; overturn. **6.** *Print.* matter set up in excess of space. [OE *ofersettan*]

o·ver·sew (ō′vər·sō′, ō′vər·sō′), *v.t.*, **-sewed, -sewed** or **-sewn, -sewing.** to sew with stitches passing successively over an edge, esp. closely, so as to cover the edge or make a firm seam.

o·ver·shade (ō′vər·shād′), *v.t.*, **-shaded, -shading. 1.** to cast a shade over. **2.** to make dark or gloomy.

o·ver·shad·ow (ō′vər·shăd′ō), *v.t.* **1.** to diminish the importance of, or render insignificant in comparison. **2.** to tower over so as to cast a shadow over. **3.** to cast a shadow over. **4.** to make dark or gloomy. **5.** to shelter or protect. [OE *ofersceadwian*]

o·ver·shine (ō′vər·shīn′), *v.t.*, **-shone, -shining. 1.** to outshine. **2.** to surpass in splendor, excellence, etc. **3.** to shine over or upon. [OE *oferscinan*]

o·ver·shoe (ō′vər·shōō′), *n.* **1.** a shoe worn over another shoe for protection against wet, cold, etc. **2.** a waterproof outer shoe of India rubber.

o·ver·shoot (ō′vər·shōōt′), *v.*, **-shot, -shooting.** —*v.t.* **1.** to shoot or go over or above (something). **2.** to shoot or go beyond (a point, limit, etc.). **3.** to shoot a missile over or beyond (what is aimed at), thus missing: *to overshoot the mark.* **4.** to go further in any course or matter than is intended or proper, or go too far. **5.** to force or drive (a thing) beyond the proper limit. —*v.i.* **6.** to shoot or go beyond; fly beyond. **7.** to shoot over or too far. [ME]

o·ver·shot (ō′vər·shŏt′), *adj.* **1.** driven by water passing over from above, as a vertical water wheel. **2.** having the upper jaw projecting beyond the lower, as a dog.

o·ver·side (ō′vər·sīd′), *adv.* **1.** over the side, as of a ship. —*adj.* **2.** effected over the side of a ship. **3.** unloading or unloaded over the side.

Overshot water wheel

o·ver·sight (ō′vər·sīt′), *n.* **1.** failure to notice or consider. **2.** an omission or error due to inadvertence. **3.** supervision; watchful care. [ME] —**Syn. 1, 2.** mistake, blunder, slip. **3.** management, direction, control.

o·ver·size (ō′vər·sīz′), *adj.* **1.** of excessive size. **2.** of a size larger than is necessary or required. —*n.* **3.** something that is oversize; an oversize article or object. **4.** a size larger than the proper or usual size.

o·ver·sized (ō′vər·sīzd′), *adj.* of excessive size; over the average size; abnormally large.

o·ver·skirt (ō′vər·skûrt′), *n.* **1.** an outer skirt. **2.** a drapery arranged over or upon a dress skirt.

o·ver·sleep (ō′vər·slēp′), *v.*, **-slept, -sleeping.** —*v.i.* **1.** to sleep beyond the proper time of waking. —*v.t.* **2.** to sleep beyond (a certain hour). [ME]

o·ver·soul (ō′vər·sōl′), *n.* a supreme reality or mind, the spiritual unity of all being: a Platonic concept developed esp. in transcendentalism (def. 2).

o·ver·spend (ō′vər·spĕnd′), *v.*, **-spent, -spending.** —*v.i.* **1.** to spend more than one can afford. —*v.t.* **2.** to spend in excess of. **3.** *Archaic.* to wear out.

o·ver·spread (ō′vər·sprĕd′), *v.t.*, **-spread, -spreading. 1.** to spread (one thing) over another. **2.** to cover (a thing) with something else. **3.** to be spread over (something else). [OE *ofersprædan*]

o·ver·state (ō′vər·stāt′), *v.t.*, **-stated, -stating.** to state too strongly; exaggerate in statement: *to overstate one's case.* —**o·ver·state′ment,** *n.*

o·ver·stay (ō′vər·stā′), *v.t.* **1.** to stay beyond the time or duration of. **2.** *Colloq. Finance.* to remain in (the market) beyond the point where a sale would have yielded the greatest profit.

o·ver·step (ō′vər·stĕp′), *v.t.*, **-stepped, -stepping.** to step or pass over or beyond.

o·ver·stock (*v.* ō′vər·stŏk′; *n.* ō′vər·stŏk′), *v.t.* **1.** to stock to excess. —*n.* **2.** a stock in excess of need.

o·ver·strain (ō′vər·strān′), *v.t.*, *v.i.* to strain to excess.

o·ver·stride (ō′vər·strīd′), *v.t.*, **-strode, -stridden, -striding. 1.** to stride or step over or across. **2.** to stride beyond. **3.** to surpass. **4.** to bestride. [ME]

o·ver·strung (ō′vər·strŭng′), *adj.* too highly strung.

o·ver·stud·y (*v.* ō′vər·stŭd′ĭ; *n.* ō′vər·stŭd′ĭ), *v.*, **-studied, -studying,** *n.* —*v.t.*, *v.i.* **1.** to study too much or too hard. —*n.* **2.** excessive study.

o·ver·stuff (ō′vər·stŭf′), *v.t.* **1.** to force too much into. **2.** *Furnit.* to envelop completely with deep upholstery.

o·ver·stuffed (ō′vər·stŭft′), *adj. Furnit.* having the entire frame covered by stuffing and upholstery, so that only decorative woodwork or the like is exposed.

o·ver·sub·scribe (ō′vər·səb·skrīb′), *v.t.*, **-scribed, -scribing.** to subscribe for in excess of what is available or required. —**o·ver·sub·scrip′tion,** *n.*

o·ver·sup·ply (*n.* ō′vər·sə·plī′; *v.* ō′vər·sə·plī′), *n.*, *pl.* **-plies,** *v.*, **-plied, -plying.** —*n.* **1.** an excessive supply. —*v.t.* **2.** to supply in excess.

o·vert (ō′vûrt, ō·vûrt′), *adj.* **1.** open to view or knowledge; not concealed or secret: *overt hostility.* **2.** *Her.* open, as a purse. [ME, t. OF, pp. of *ovrir* open, g. L. *aperire* open, with o- from *covrir* cover. See COVERT] —**Syn. 1.** plain, manifest, apparent, open, public.

o·ver·take (ō′vər·tāk′), *v.t.*, **-took, -taken, -taking. 1.** to catch up with in traveling or in pursuit. **2.** to come up with in any course of action. **3.** to come upon suddenly (said esp. of night, storm, death, etc.). [ME]

o·ver·task (ō′vər·tăsk′, -täsk′), *v.t.* to impose too heavy a task upon.

o·ver·tax (ō′vər·tăks′), *v.t.* **1.** to tax too heavily. **2.** to make too great demands on: *I had overtaxed my strength.*

o·ver-the-count·er (ō′vər·thə·koun′tər), *adj.* having been sold or purchased other than on an exchange.

o·ver·throw (*v.* ō′vər·thrō′; *n.* ō′vər·thrō′), *v.*, **-threw, -thrown, -throwing,** *n.* —*v.t.* **1.** to cast down as from a position of power; overcome, defeat, or vanquish. **2.** to put an end to by force, as governments or institutions. **3.** to throw over; upset; overturn. **4.** to knock down and demolish. **5.** to subvert, ruin, or destroy. **6.** to destroy the sound condition of (the mind). —*n.* **7.** the act of overthrowing. **8.** the resulting state. **9.** deposition from power. **10.** defeat; destruction; ruin.

o·ver·time (*n.*, *adj.*, *adv.* ō′vər·tīm′; *v.* ō′vər·tīm′), *n.*, *adv.*, *adj.*, *v.*, **-timed, -timing.** —*n.* **1.** time during which one works before or after regularly scheduled working hours; extra time. **2.** pay for such time. —*adv.* **3.** during extra time: *to work overtime.* —*adj.* **4.** of or pertaining to overtime: *overtime pay.* —*v.t.* **5.** to give too much time to, as in photographic exposure.

o·vert·ly (ō′vûrt·lĭ, ō·vûrt′lĭ), *adv.* openly; publicly.

o·ver·tone (ō′vər·tōn′), *n.* **1.** *Acoustics.* any frequency emitted by an acoustical instrument that is higher in frequency than the fundamental. **2.** (*usually pl.*) additional meaning.

o·ver·top (ō′vər·tŏp′), *v.t.*, **-topped, -topping. 1.** to rise over or above the top of. **2.** to rise above in authority; override (law, etc.). **3.** to surpass or excel.

o·ver·trade (ō′vər·trād′), *v.i.*, **-traded, -trading.** to trade in excess of one's capital or the requirements of the market.

o·ver·train (ō′vər·trān′), *v.t.*, *v.i.* to train to excess.

o·ver·trick (ō′vər·trĭk′), *n. Cards.* an extra trick, one over the number necessary to win the game.

o·ver·trump (ō′vər·trŭmp′), *v.t.*, *v.i. Cards.* to trump with a higher trump than has already been played.

o·ver·ture (ō′vər·chər), *n.*, *v.*, **-tured, -turing.** —*n.* **1.** an opening of negotiations, or a formal proposal or offer. **2.** *Music.* **a.** an orchestral composition forming the prelude or introduction to an opera, oratorio, etc. **b.** an independent piece of similar character. **3.** an introductory part, as of a poem. **4.** (in Presbyterian churches) **a.** the action of an ecclesiastical court in submitting a question or proposal to other judicatories for consideration. **b.** the proposal or question so submitted. —*v.t.* **5.** to submit as an overture or proposal.

o′ver·roast′	**o′ver·sim·plic′i·ty**	**o′ver·stu′di·ous**	**o′ver·sweet′**
o′ver·salt′	**o′ver·sim′pli·fy**	**o′ver·sub′tle**	**o′ver·talk′a·tive**
o′ver·scru′pu·lous	**o′ver·skep′ti·cal**	**o′ver·suf·fi′cient**	**o′ver·tech′ni·cal**
o′ver·sen′si·tive	**o′ver·stim′u·late′**	**o′ver·su′per·sti′tious**	**o′ver·thrust′** (*n.* or *adj.*)
o′ver·se′ri·ous	**o′ver·strict′**	**o′ver·sus·pi′cious**	**o′ver·tire′**

6. to make an overture or proposal to. [ME, t. OF, g. L *apertūra* opening, n., with -o- from *overt* OVERT] **—Syn. 1.** See **proposal.**

o·ver·turn (*n.* ō'vər·tûrn'; *n.* ō'vər·tûrn'), *v.t.* **1.** to overthrow; destroy the power of, defeat or vanquish. **2.** to turn over on its side, face, or back; upset. —*v.i.* **3.** to turn on its side, face, or back; upset; capsize. —*n.* **4.** act of overturning. **5.** state of being overturned. **6.** *Com.* a turnover. [ME] **—Syn. 1.** See **upset.**

o·ver·un·der (ō'vər·ŭn'dər), *adj.* **1.** (of double-barreled firearms) with one barrel mounted over the other. —*n.* **2.** such a firearm.

o·ver·val·ue (ō'vər·văl'ū), *v.t.*, **-ued, -uing.** to value too highly; put too high a value on.

o·ver·watch (ō'vər·wŏch', -wŏch'), *v.t.* **1.** to watch over. **2.** to weary by watching.

o·ver·wear (ō'vər·wâr'), *v.t.*, **-wore, -worn, -wearing.** **1.** to wear or use longer than necessary. **2.** to use excessively; grow out of.

o·ver·wea·ry (ō'vər·wir'ĭ), *adj.*, *v.*, **-ried, -rying.** —*adj.* **1.** excessively weary; tired out. —*v.t.* **2.** to weary to excess; overcome with weariness.

o·ver·ween (ō'vər·wēn'), *v.i.* to be conceited or arrogant. [ME]

o·ver·ween·ing (ō'vər·wē'nĭng), *adj.* **1.** conceited, overconfident, or presumptuous: *overweening confidence.* **2.** that overweens. **—o'ver·ween'ing·ly,** *adv.*

o·ver·weigh (ō'vər·wā'), *v.t.* **1.** to exceed in weight; overbalance or outweigh. **2.** to weigh down; oppress.

o·ver·weight (*n.* ō'vər·wāt'; *adj.* ō'vər·wāt'), *n.* **1.** extra weight; excess of weight. **2.** too great weight. **3.** greater weight; preponderance. —*adj.* **4.** weighing more than normally or necessarily required.

o·ver·whelm (ō'vər·hwĕlm'), *v.t.* **1.** to come, rest, or weigh upon overpoweringly; crush. **2.** to overcome completely in mind or feeling. **3.** to load, heap, treat, or address with an overpowering or excessive amount of anything. **4.** to cover or bury beneath a mass of something, a flood, or the like, or cover as a mass or flood does. **5.** *Obs. or Rare.* to overthrow. [ME]

o·ver·whelm·ing (ō'vər·hwĕl'mĭng), *adj.* **1.** that overwhelms. **2.** so great as to render opposition useless: *an overwhelming majority.* **—o'ver·whelm'ing·ly,** *adv.*

o·ver·wind (ō'vər·wīnd'), *v.t.*, **-wound, -winding.** to wind beyond the proper limit; wind too far.

o·ver·work (*v.* ō'vər·wûrk'; *n.* ō'vər·wûrk'), *v.*, **-worked** or **-wrought, -working,** *n.* —*v.t.* **1.** to cause to work too hard or too long; weary or exhaust with work (often reflexively). **2.** to fill (time) too full of work. **3.** to work up, stir up, or excite excessively. **4.** to elaborate to excess. **5.** to work or decorate all over; decorate the surface of. —*v.i.* **6.** to work too hard; work to excess. —*n.* **7.** work beyond one's strength or capacity. **8.** extra work. [OE *oferwyrcan*]

o·ver·write (ō'vər·rīt'), *v.t.*, *v.i.*, **-wrote, -written, -writing.** **1.** to write on top of other writing. **2.** to sacrifice quality to quantity in writing. **3.** to write in an ostentatious or flowery manner.

o·ver·wrought (ō'vər·rôt'), *adj.* **1.** wearied or exhausted by overwork. **2.** worked up or excited excessively. **3.** overworked; elaborated to excess.

ovi-, a word element meaning "egg," as in *oviferous.* [t. L, comb. form of *ōvum*]

Ov·id (ŏv'ĭd), *n.* (*Publius Ovidius Naso*) 43 B.C.–A.D. 17?, Roman poet. **—O·vid·i·an** (ō vĭd'ĭ·an), *adj.*

o·vi·duct (ō'vĭ·dŭkt'), *n. Anat., Zool.* one of a pair of ducts which lead from the body cavity to the exterior in the female and serve to transport and nourish the ova. In higher forms, the distal ends are fused to form the uterus and vagina. [t. NL: s. *ōviductus*, f. L: *ōvi-* ovi- + s. *ductus* DUCT]

O·vie·do (ō vyĕ'dō), *n.* a city in NW Spain. 114,691 (est. 1955).

o·vif·er·ous (ō vĭf'ər əs), *adj. Anat., Zool.* bearing eggs.

o·vi·form (ō'vĭ·fôrm'), *adj.* egg-shaped.

o·vine (ō'vīn, -vĭn), *adj.* pertaining to, of the nature of, or like sheep. [t. LL: m. s. *ovinus*, der. L *ovis* sheep]

o·vi·pa·ra (ō vĭp'ə·rə), *n.pl.* egg-laying animals. [t. NL, t. L: (neut. pl.) egg-laying]

o·vip·a·rous (ō vĭp'ə·rəs), *adj. Zool.* producing ova or eggs which are matured or hatched after being expelled from the body, as birds, most reptiles and fishes, etc. [t. L: m. *ōviparus* egg-laying] **—o·vi·par·i·ty** (ō'vĭ·păr'ə·tĭ), *n.*

o·vi·pos·it (ō'vĭ·pŏz'ĭt), *v.i.* to deposit or lay eggs, esp. by means of an ovipositor. [f. ovi- + s. L *positus*, pp., placed, put] **—o·vi·po·si·tion** (ō'vĭ·pə·zĭsh'ən), *n.*

o·vi·pos·i·tor (ō'vĭ·pŏz'ə·tər), *n.* (in certain insects) an organ at the end of the abdomen, by which eggs are deposited. [f. ovi- + L *positor* placer]

o·vi·sac (ō'vĭ·săk'), *n. Zool.* a sac or capsule containing an ovum or ova.

O, Ovipositor of field cricket

o·void (ō'void), *adj.* **1.** egg-shaped; having the solid form of an egg. **2.** having such a form with the broader end at the base, as a fruit. Cf.

ovate. —*n.* **3.** an ovoid body. [f. s. L *ōvum* egg + -OID]

o·vo·lo (ō'və·lō'), *n.*, *pl.* **-li** (-lē'). *Archit.* a convex molding forming or approximating in section a quarter of a circle or ellipse. See diag. under **column.** [t. It., var. (now obs.) of *uovolo*, dim. of *uovo*, g. L *ōvum* egg]

o·vo·vi·vip·a·rous (ō'vō·vī·vĭp'ə·rəs), *adj. Zool.* producing eggs which are hatched within the body, so that the young are born alive but without placental attachment, as certain reptiles, fishes, etc. [f. *ovo-* (comb. form of OVUM) + VIVIPAROUS]

o·vu·lar (ō'vyə·lər), *adj.* pertaining to or of the nature of an ovule. [t. NL: s. *ōvulāris*]

o·vu·late (ō'vyə·lāt'), *v.i.*, **-lated, -lating.** *Biol.* to shed eggs from an ovary or ovarian follicle. [f. s. NL *ōvulum* little egg + -ATE[1]] **—o'vu·la'tion,** *n.*

o·vule (ō'vūl), *n.* **1.** *Biol.* a small egg. **2.** *Bot.* **a.** a rudimentary seed. **b.** the body which contains the embryo sac and hence the female germ cell, and which after fertilization develops into a seed. [t. NL: m.s. *ōvulum*, dim. of L *ōvum* egg]

o·vum (ō'vəm), *n.*, *pl.* **ova** (ō'və). **1.** *Biol.* **a.** an egg, in a broad biological sense. **b.** the female reproductive cell or gamete of plants. **c.** the female reproductive cell of animals, which (usually only after fertilization) is capable of developing into a new individual. **2.** *Archit.* an egg-shaped ornament. [t. L: egg]

owe (ō), *v.*, **owed, owing.** —*v.t.* **1.** to be indebted or beholden for (usually fol. by *to*). **2.** to be under obligation to pay or repay, or to render (often fol. by *to* or a simple dative): *to owe him interest on a mortgage.* **3.** (by omission of the ordinary direct object) to be in debt to: *he owes not any man.* **4.** to have or cherish (a certain feeling) toward a person: *to owe one a grudge.* **5.** *Obs.* to own or possess. —*v.i.* **6.** to be in debt. [ME *owe(n)*, OE *āgan*, c. OHG *eigan*. Cf. OWN, OUGHT[1]]

Ow·en (ō'ĭn), *n.* **1. Robert,** 1771–1858, British social reformer. **2. Wilfred,** 1893–1918, British poet.

Ow·ens·bor·o (ō'ĭnz·bûr'ō), *n.* a city in NW Kentucky, on the Ohio river. 42,471 (1960).

Ow·en Stan·ley (ō'ĭn stăn'lĭ), a mountain range in SE New Guinea. Highest peak, Mt. Victoria, 13,240 ft.

OWI, Office of War Information.

ow·ing (ō'ĭng), *adj.* **1.** that owes. **2.** owed or due: *to pay what is owing.* **3.** *Obs.* indebted. **4. owing to, a.** on account of; because of. **b.** attributable to.

owl (oul), *n.* **1.** any of numerous birds of prey of the order *Strigiformes,* chiefly nocturnal, with a broad head and with large eyes which are usually surrounded by disks of modified feathers and directed forward. They feed on mice, small birds and reptiles, etc. **2.** a variety of domestic pigeons of owllike appearance. **3.** a person of nocturnal habits. **4.** a person of owllike solemnity of appearance. [ME *oule,* OE *ūle,* c. LG *üle;* akin to G *eule,* Icel. *ugla*] **—owl·like',** *adj.*

owl·et (ou'lĭt), *n.* **1.** a young owl. **2.** a small owl, esp. the **little owl,** *Athene noctua,* of Europe.

owl·ish (ou'lĭsh), *adj.* owllike.

Horned owl, *Bubo virginianus* (23 in long)

owl train, a railroad train which makes its trip during the night.

own (ōn), *adj.* **1.** belonging, pertaining, or relating to oneself or itself (usually used after a possessive to emphasize the idea of ownership, interest, or relation conveyed by the possessive): *his own money.* **2.** (absolutely, with a possessive preceding) own property, relatives, etc.: *to come into one's own.* **3. of one's own,** belonging to oneself. **4. on one's own,** *Colloq.* on one's own account, responsibility, resources, etc. **5. be one's own man,** to be independent. [ME *owen;* OE *āgen,* orig. pp. of *āgan* have, possess. See OWE] —*v.t.* **6.** to have or hold as one's own; possess. **7.** to acknowledge or admit: *to own a fault.* **8.** to acknowledge as one's own. —*v.i.* **9.** to confess: *to own to being uncertain.* [ME *ohnien,* OE *āgnian,* der. *āgen* OWN, adj.] **—Syn. 6.** See **have.** **—Ant. 6.** lack, need.

own·er (ō'nər), *n.* one who owns; a proprietor.

own·er·ship (ō'nər·shĭp'), *n.* **1.** state or fact of being an owner. **2.** legal right of possession; proprietorship.

ox (ŏks), *n.*, *pl.* **oxen. 1.** the adult castrated male of the genus *Bos,* used as a draft animal and for food. **2.** any member of the bovine family. [ME *oxe,* OE *oxa,* c. G *ochse*] **—ox/like/,** *adj.*

Ox., (L *Oxonia*) Oxford.

oxa-, a prefix meaning "oxygen when it replaces carbon."

ox·a·late (ŏk'sə·lāt'), *n. Chem.* a salt or ester of oxalic acid. [f. OXAL(IC) + -ATE[2]]

ox·al·ic acid (ŏks·ăl'ĭk), *Chem.* a white, crystalline, dibasic acid, $H_2C_2O_4 \cdot 2H_2O$, first discovered in the juice of a species of oxalis (wood sorrel), used in textile and dye manufacturing, in bleaching, etc. [*oxalic,* t. F: m. *oxalique,* der. L *oxalis* OXALIS]

ox·a·lis (ŏk'sə·lĭs), *n.* any plant of the large genus *Oxalis,* as the common wood sorrel, *O. Acetosella,* a herb with leaves usually of three heart-shaped leaflets, and white or pink single flowers. [t. L, t. Gk.: sorrel]

o/ver·twist/	o/ver·ve/he·ment	o/ver·vi/gor·ous	o/ver·warmed/
o/ver·val/u·a·tion	o/ver·ven/ture·some	o/ver·vi/o·lent	o/ver·zeal/ous

ox·a·zine (ŏk'sə zēn', -zĭn), *n. Chem.* any of a group of thirteen compounds, C_4H_5NO, containing four carbon atoms, one oxygen atom, and one nitrogen atom, arranged in a six-membered ring. Also, **ox·a·zin** (ŏk'sə zĭn). [f. OX(A)- + -AZINE]

ox·blood (ŏks'blŭd'), *n.* a deep dull red color.

ox·bow (ŏks'bō'), *n. U.S.* **1.** a bow-shaped piece of wood placed under and around the neck of an ox, with its upper ends inserted in the bar of the yoke. **2.** a bow-shaped bend in a river, or the land embraced by it.

ox·cart (ŏks'kärt'), *n.* an ox-drawn cart.

ox·en (ŏk'sən), *n.* pl. of **ox.**

Ox·en·stier·na (ŏk'sən shĕr'nä), *n.* **Count Axel,** (äk'səl), 1583–1654, Swedish statesman. Also, **Ox·en·stiern** (ŏk'sən stĭrn').

ox·eye (ŏks'ī'), *n.* **1.** any of various plants with flowers composed of a disk with marginal rays, as the mayweed, the oxeye daisy, and the false sunflower (*Heliopsis*). **2.** any of several shore birds of the U.S., as the semi-palmated sandpiper (*Ereunetes pusillus*). [ME *oxie,* f. *ox(e)* ox + *ie* EYE]

oxeye daisy. See **daisy** (def. 1).

ox·ford (ŏks'fərd), *n.* **1.** a low shoe laced or buttoned over the instep. **2.** shirting of cotton or rayon in a basket weave. [named after OXFORD, the city]

Ox·ford (ŏks'fərd), *n.* **1.** a city in S England: famous university (founded in the 12th century). 104,500 (est. 1956). **2.** Oxfordshire. **3. Robert Harley, 1st Earl of,** 1661–1724, British statesman. **4.** a large English breed of sheep, hornless, with dark brown face and legs, of the mutton type, noted for its relatively large, heavy market lambs, and heavy fleece of relatively coarse medium wool. [ME *Oxenford,* OE *Oxenaford*]

Oxford corners, *Print.* ruled border lines about the text of a page, etc., that cross and project slightly at the corners.

Oxford gray, medium to dark gray.

Oxford group, Buchmanism.

Oxford movement, a movement toward High-Church principles in the Church of England, which originated at Oxford University about 1833.

Ox·ford·shire (ŏks'fərd shĭr', -shər), *n.* a county in S England. 275,808 pop. (1951); 749 sq. mi. *Co. seat:* Oxford. Also, **Oxford** or **Oxon.**

Oxford shoe, oxford (def. 1). Also, **Oxford tie.**

ox·heart (ŏks'härt'), *n.* any large, heart-shaped variety of sweet cherry.

ox·i·dase (ŏk'sə dās', -dāz'), *n. Biochem.* any of a group of oxidizing enzymes. [f. OXID(E) + -ASE]

ox·i·date (ŏk'sə dāt'), *v.t., v.i.,* **-dated, -dating.** to oxidize. —**ox'i·da'tion,** *n.* —**ox'i·da'tive,** *adj.*

ox·ide (ŏk'sīd, -sĭd), *n. Chem.* a compound, usually containing two elements only, one of which is oxygen, as *mercuric oxide.* Also, **ox·id** (ŏk'sĭd). [t. F (now *oxyde,* f. *ox(ygène)* oxygen + *(ac)ide* acid]

ox·i·dim·e·try (ŏk'sə dĭm'ə trĭ), *n.* a technique of analytical chemistry which utilizes oxidizing agents for titrations.

ox·i·dize (ŏk'sə dīz'), *v.,* **-dized, -dizing.** *Chem.* —*v.t.* **1.** to convert (an element) into its oxide; to combine with oxygen. **2.** to cover with a coating of oxide, or rust. **3.** to take away hydrogen from as by the action of oxygen; to add oxygen or any nonmetal to. **4.** to increase the valence of (an element) in the positive direction. **5.** to remove electrons from. —*v.t.* **6.** to become oxidized. Also, *esp. Brit.,* **ox'i·dise'.** —**ox'i·diz'a·ble,** *adj.* —**ox'i·di·za'tion,** *n.* —**ox'i·diz'er,** *n.*

ox·ime (ŏk'sēm, -sĭm), *n.* any of a group of compounds with the radical -C -NOH (oxime group or radical), prepared by the condensation of ketones or aldehydes with hydroxylamine. Also, **ox·im** (ŏk'sĭm). [f. OX(YGEN) + IM(ID)E]

ox·lip (ŏks'lĭp'), *n.* a species of primrose, *Primula elatior,* with pale-yellow flowers. See SLIP². [ME; OE *oxanslyppe,* f. *oxan* ox's + *slyppe* slime. See SLIP² and cf. COWSLIP]

Ox·nard (ŏks'närd), *n.* a city in SW California, NW of Los Angeles. 28,879 (1956).

Ox·on (ŏk'sŏn), *n.* Oxfordshire.

Oxon., **1.** (L *Oxonia*) Oxford. **2.** (L *Oxoniensis*) of Oxford.

Ox·o·ni·an (ŏk sō'nĭ ən), *adj.* **1.** of or pertaining to Oxford, England, or Oxford University. —*n.* **2.** a member or graduate of Oxford University. **3.** a native or inhabitant of Oxford. [f. s. ML *Oxonia* Oxford + -AN]

ox·o·ni·um compound (ŏk sō'nĭ əm), *Chem.* the product of reaction between an organic compound containing a basic oxygen atom, and a strong acid.

ox·peck·er (ŏks'pĕk'ər), *n.* either of two species of African starlings of the genus *Buphagus.*

ox·tail (ŏks'tāl'), *n.* the skinned tail of an ox used to make a soup.

ox·ter (ŏk'stər), *n. Scot.* the armpit. [appar. der. OE *ōxta* armpit]

ox·tongue (ŏks'tŭng'), *n.* any of various plants with rough, tongue-shaped leaves, as the bugloss, *Anchusa officinalis.*

Ox·us (ŏk'səs), *n.* ancient and modern name of **Amu Darya.**

oxy-¹, a word element meaning "sharp" or "acute." [t. Gk., comb. form of *oxýs* sharp, keen, acid]

oxy-², a combining form of **oxygen** sometimes used as an equivalent of *hydroxy-.*

ox·y·a·cet·y·lene (ŏk'sĭ ə sĕt'ə lēn'), *adj.* of or pertaining to a mixture of oxygen and acetylene, used in a blowtorch (**oxyacetylene blowpipe**) at 3300°C., for cutting steel plates.

ox·y·ac·id (ŏk'sĭ ăs'ĭd), *n. Chem.* an inorganic acid containing oxygen. Also, **oxygen acid.**

ox·y·cal·ci·um (ŏk'sĭ kăl'sĭ əm), *adj.* pertaining to or produced by oxygen and calcium: *the oxycalcium light.*

ox·y·da·tion (ŏk'sə dā'shən), *n.* oxidation.

ox·y·gen (ŏk'sə jən), *n. Chem.* a colorless, odorless gaseous element, constituting about one fifth of the volume of the atmosphere and present in a combined state throughout nature. It is the supporter of combustion in air, and is the standard of atomic, combining, and molecular weights: *Weight of 1 liter at 0°C. and 760 mm. pressure:* 1.4290 grams. Symbol: O; *at. wt.:* 16.0; *at. no.:* 8. [t. F: m. *oxygène,* f. *oxy-* OXY-¹ + *-gène* -GEN]

ox·y·gen·ate (ŏk'sə jə nāt'), *v.t.,* **-ated, -ating.** to treat or combine, esp. to enrich, with oxygen. —**ox'y·gen·a'tion,** *n.*

oxygen-hydrogen welding, welding done at a temperature in excess of 5,000°F. with a blowpipe furnishing oxygen and hydrogen.

ox·y·gen·ize (ŏk'sə jə nīz'), *v.t.,* **-ized, -izing.** oxygenate.

oxygen mask, a masklike device worn by aviators at great altitudes when inhaling supplementary oxygen from an attached tank.

oxygen tent, a small tent for delivering oxygen to a sick person at critical periods.

ox·y·he·mo·glo·bin (ŏk'sĭ hē'mə glō'bĭn), *n.* the substance formed when hemoglobin proper unites loosely with oxygen, present in arterial blood. See **hemoglobin.**

ox·y·hy·dro·gen (ŏk'sĭ hī'drə jən), *n.* a mixture of oxygen and hydrogen, used in a blowtorch (**oxyhydrogen blowpipe**) at 2800°C. for cutting steel plates.

ox·y·mo·ron (ŏk'sĭ môr'ŏn), *n., pl.* **-mora** (-môr'ə). *Rhet.* a figure by which a locution produces an effect by a seeming self-contradiction, as in *cruel kindness* or to *make haste slowly.* [t. NL, t. Gk., neut. of *oxýmōros* pointedly foolish]

ox·y·salt (ŏk'sĭ sôlt'), *n. Chem.* any salt of an oxyacid. [f. OXY-² + SALT]

ox·y·sul·fide (ŏk'sĭ sŭl'fīd, -fĭd), *n. Chem.* a sulfide in which part of the sulfur is replaced by oxygen.

ox·y·to·cic (ŏk'sĭ tō'sĭk, -tŏs'ĭk), *Med.* —*adj.* **1.** of or causing the stimulation of the involuntary muscle of the uterus. **2.** promoting or accelerating parturition. —*n.* **3.** an oxytocic medicine or drug. [f. Gk.: m.s. *oxytókion* a medicine hastening childbirth + -IC]

ox·y·tone (ŏk'sĭ tōn'), *adj.* **1.** (in Greek grammar) having an acute accent on the last syllable. —*n.* **2.** an oxytone word. [t. Gk.: m.s. *oxýtonos*]

O·ya·ma (ō'yä mä'), *n.* **Iwao** (ē'wä ō'), 1842–1916, Japanese field marshal.

o·yer (ō'yər, oi'ər), *n. Law.* **1.** a hearing or trial of (criminal) causes (chiefly in the phrase **oyer and terminer**). **2.** the production in court of some document pleaded by one party and demanded by the other (the party pleading it is said to *make profert* and the other is said to *crave oyer*). [ME, t. AF (prop. inf.), var. of *oir,* g. L *audīre* hear]

oyer and ter·mi·ner (tûr'mə nər), *Law.* **1.** *U.S.* any of various higher criminal courts in some of the States. **2.** *Brit.* **a.** a commission or writ directing the holding of a court to try offenses. **b.** the court itself.

o·yez (ō'yĕs, ō'yĕz), *interj.* **1.** hear! attend! (a cry uttered, usually thrice, by a public or court crier to command silence and attention before a proclamation, etc., is made). —*n.* **2.** a cry of "oyez." Also, **o·yes.** [t. AF: hear ye, 2d pers. pl. impv. of *oyer.* See OYER]

oys·ter (ois'tər), *n.* **1.** any of various edible marine bivalve mollusks (family *Ostreidae*), with irregularly shaped shell, found on the bottom or adhering to rocks, etc., in shallow water, some species being extensively cultivated for the market. **2.** the oyster-shaped bit of dark meat in the front hollow of the side bone of a fowl. **3.** *Slang.* a close-mouthed person. **4.** something from which one may extract or derive advantage. —*v.i.* **5.** to dredge for or otherwise take oysters. [ME *oistre,* t. OF, t. L: m.s. *ostrea, ostreum,* t. Gk.: m. *óstreon*]

oyster bed, a place where oysters breed or are cultivated.

oyster catcher, any of several long-billed, maritime wading birds constituting the genus *Haematopus,* with a plumage chiefly of black and white, as *H. ostralegus,* the common European species.

oyster crab, a crab, *Pinnotheres,* existing commensally in the mantle cavity of oysters.

oyster cracker, a small, round, (usually) salted cracker, served with oysters, soups, etc.

oyster farm, a place where oyster beds are kept.

oys·ter·man (ois'tər mən), *n., pl.* **-men.** **1.** one who gathers, cultivates, or sells oysters. **2.** a container for gathering oysters.

oyster plant, the salsify, whose root has an oyster-like flavor.

oyster white, very light gray.

oz., **1.** ounce. **2.** Also, **ozs.** ounces.

O·zark Mountains (ō'zärk), a group of low mountains in S Missouri, N Arkansas, and NE Oklahoma. Also, **O'zarks.**

o·zo·ce·rite (ō zō′kə rīt′, -sə rīt′, ō′zō sĭr′īt), *n.* wax-like mineral resin; mineral wax. [t. G: m. *ozokerit*, f. Gk. ŏzŏ I smell + s. Gk. *kērós* wax + -*it* -ITE¹]

o·zone (ō′zōn, ō zōn′), *n.* **1.** a form of oxygen, O₃, having three atoms to the molecule, with a peculiar odor suggesting that of weak chlorine, which is produced when an electric spark is passed through air, and in several other ways. It is found in the atmosphere in minute quantities, esp. after a thunderstorm, and is a powerful oxidizing agent, used for bleaching, sterilizing water, etc. **2.** *Colloq.* clear, invigorating, fresh air. [t. F, f. s. Gk. *ŏzein* smell + -*one* -ONE] **—o·zon·ic** (ō zŏn′ĭk, ō zō′nĭk), *adj.*

ozone layer, *Meteorol.* a rather restricted region in the outer portion of the stratosphere at an elevation of about 20 miles, where much of the atmospheric ozone (O₃) is concentrated.

o·zo·nif·er·ous (ō′zə nĭf′ər əs), *adj.* containing ozone.

o·zo·ni·za·tion (ō′zə nə zā′shən), *n.* the treatment of a compound with ozone.

o·zo·nize (ō′zə nīz′), *v.t.,* **-nized, -nizing. 1.** to impregnate or treat with ozone. **2.** to convert (oxygen) into ozone.

o·zo·nol·y·sis (ō′zə nŏl′ə sĭs), *n.* *Chem.* the reaction of ozone with hydrocarbons.

o·zo·nous (ō′zə nəs), *adj.* of or containing ozone.

ozs., ounces.

P

P, p (pē), *n., pl.* **P's** or **Ps, p's** or **ps. 1.** a consonant, the 16th letter of the English alphabet. **2.** *Genetics.* a symbol for the parental generation, P₁ indicating immediate parents, P₂ grandparents, etc. **3.** *mind one's P's and Q's,* to be careful, esp. in behavior. **4.** (in medieval Roman numerals) 400.

P, 1. *Chem.* phosphorus. **2.** *Physics.* pressure. **3.** *Chess.* pawn.

p-, *Chem.* para-¹.

P., 1. (L *Pater*) Father. **2.** (F *Père*) Father. **3.** President. **4.** Prince. **5.** Progressive.

p., 1. page. **2.** part. **3.** participle. **4.** past. **5.** (L *pater*) father. **6.** *Chess.* pawn. **7.** penny. **8.** peseta. **9.** peso. **10.** *Music.* (It. *piano*) softly. **11.** pint. **12.** *Baseball.* pitcher. **13.** population. **14.** (L *post*) after.

pa (pä), *n. Colloq.* papa.

Pa, protoactinium.

Pa., Pennsylvania.

PA, 1. press agent. **2.** public-address (system).

P.A., 1. Passenger Agent. **2.** Post Adjutant. **3.** power of attorney. **4.** Purchasing Agent.

p.a., 1. participial adjective. **2.** per annum. **3.** press agent.

Paa·sen (pä′sən), *n.* **Pierre van** (pyĕr vän, vän), born 1895, U.S. journalist, author, and clergyman, born in the Netherlands.

pab·u·lum (păb′yə ləm), *n.* that which nourishes an animal or vegetable organism; food. [t. L: food, fodder]

Pac., Pacific.

P.A.C., Political Action Committee. Also, **PAC** (păk).

pa·ca (pä′kə, păk′ə), *n.* a large white-spotted, almost tailless, hystricomorphic rodent, *Agouti paca,* of South and Central America; the spotted cavy. [t. Pg. or Sp., both t. Tupi]

Paca. *Agouti paca*
(2½ ft. long, 1 ft. high)

pace¹ (pās), *n., v.,* **paced, pac·ing.** —*n.* **1.** rate of stepping, or of movement in general: *a pace of ten miles an hour.* **2.** a lineal measure of variable extent, representing the space naturally measured by the movement of the foot in walking. The pace of a single step (**military pace**) is reckoned in the U.S. Army at 2½ feet for quick time and 3 feet for double time. The **geometrical** or **great pace** is 5 feet, representing the distance from the place where either foot is taken up, in walking, to that where the same foot is set down. The **Roman pace,** reckoned like the geometrical pace, was equal to 5 Roman feet, or about 58 English inches. **3.** a single step: *she made three paces across the room.* **4.** the distance covered in a step: *stand six paces inside the gates.* **5.** manner of stepping; gait. **6.** a gait of a horse, etc., in which the feet on the same side are lifted and put down together. **7.** any of the gaits of a horse, etc. **8.** a raised step or platform. —*v.t.* **9.** to set the pace for, as in racing. **10.** to traverse with paces or steps: *he paced the floor.* **11.** to measure by paces. **12.** to train to a certain pace; exercise in pacing: *to pace a horse.* —*v.i.* **13.** to take slow, regular steps. **14.** (of a horse) to go at a pace; amble. [ME *pas,* t. OF, g. L *passus* a step, lit., a stretch (of the leg)]
—**Syn. 7.** step, gait, amble, rack, trot, canter, gallop, walk, run, singlefoot **10.** PACE, PLOD, TRUDGE refer to a steady and monotonous kind of walking. PACE suggests steady, measured steps as of one completely lost in thought or impelled by some distraction: *to pace up and down.* PLOD implies a slow, heavy, laborious, weary walk: *the ploughman homeward plods his weary way.* TRUDGE implies a spiritless but usually steady and doggedly persistent walk: *the farmer trudged to his village to buy his supplies.* —**Ant. 10.** scamper, scurry, skip.

pa·ce² (pā′sĭ), *prep. Latin.* with the permission of (a courteous form used to mention one who disagrees). [L, abl. of *pax* peace, pardon, leave]

paced (pāst), *adj.* **1.** having a specified pace: *slow-paced.* **2.** counted out or measured by paces. **3.** *Racing.* run at a pace determined by a pacemaker.

pace·mak·er (pās′mā′kər), *n.* one who sets the pace, as in racing. —**pace′mak′ing,** *n.*

pac·er (pā′sər), *n.* **1.** one who paces. **2.** a pacemaker. **3.** a horse that paces, or whose natural gait is a pace.

pa·cha (pə shä′, päsh′ə), *n.* pasha.

pa·cha·lic (pə shä′lĭk), *n.* pashalik.

pa·chi·si (pə chē′zĭ, pä-), *n.* parcheesi.

Pach·mann (päkн′män), *n.* **Vladimir de** (vlä dē′mĭr də), 1848–1933, Russian pianist.

pach·ou·li (păch′ōō lĭ, pə chōō′lĭ), *n.* patchouli.

Pa·chu·ca (pä chōō′kä), *n.* a city in central Mexico: the capital of Hidalgo state; silver mines. 58,650 (1950).

pach·y·derm (păk′ə dûrm′), *n.* **1.** any of the thick-skinned nonruminant ungulates, as the elephant, hippopotamus, and rhinoceros. **2.** a person who is not sensitive to criticism, ridicule, etc. [t. F: m. *pachyderme,* t. Gk.: m.s. *pachýdermos* thick-skinned] —**pach′y·der′ma·tous, pach′y·der′mous,** *adj.*

pa·cif·ic (pə sĭf′ĭk), *adj.* **1.** tending to make peace; conciliatory: *pacific propositions.* **2.** peaceable; not warlike: *a pacific disposition.* **3.** peaceful; at peace: *pacific state of things.* **4.** (*cap.*) designating, or pertaining to, the Pacific Ocean. **5.** (*cap.*) of or pertaining to the region bordering on the Pacific Ocean: *the Pacific States.* —*n.* **6.** (*cap.*) the Pacific Ocean. Also, **pa·cif′i·cal** for 1–3. [t. L: s. *pācificus* peacemaking] —**pa·cif′i·cal·ly,** *adv.*
—**Syn. 1.** PACIFIC, PEACEABLE, PEACEFUL describe that which is in a state of peace. That which is PACIFIC tends toward the making, promoting, or preserving of peace: *pacific intentions.* That which is PEACEABLE desires to be at peace or is free from the disposition to quarrel: *peaceable citizens.* That which is PEACEFUL is in a calm state, characteristic of, or characterized by, peace: *a peaceful death.* —**Ant. 1** warlike, belligerent.

pa·cif·i·cate (pə sĭf′ə kāt′), *v.t.,* **-cated, -cating.** to pacify. [t. L: m.s. *pācificātus,* pp.] —**pac·i·fi·ca·tion** (păs′ə fə kā′shən), *n.* —**pa·cif′i·ca′tor,** *n.* —**pa·cif·i·ca·to·ry** (pə sĭf′ə kə tōr′ĭ), *adj.*

pa·cif·i·cism (pə sĭf′ə sĭz′əm), *n. Brit.* pacifism. —**pacif′i·cist,** *n.*

pa·ci·fi·co (pä sē′fē kō′), *n., pl.* **-cos** (-kōs′). *Spanish.* **1.** a peaceful person. **2.** a native of Cuba or the Philippine Islands not resisting Spanish occupation of his country. [Sp., t. L: m. *pācificus*]

Pacific Ocean, the largest ocean, between the American continents and Asia and Australia: divided by the equator into the **North Pacific** and the **South Pacific.** ab. 70,000,000 sq. mi.; greatest known depth, 35,433 ft.

Pacific time, See standard time.

pac·i·fi·er (păs′ə fī′ər), *n.* **1.** one who or that which pacifies. **2.** a rubber nipple, etc., given to a baby to suck. **3.** a teething ring.

pac·i·fism (păs′ə fĭz′əm), *n.* the principle or policy of establishing and maintaining universal peace or such relations among all nations that all differences may be adjusted without recourse to war. [f. PACIF(IC) + -ISM] —**pac′i·fist,** *n., adj.* —**pac′i·fis′tic,** *adj.*

pac·i·fy (păs′ə fī′), *v.t.,* **-fied, -fying. 1.** to bring into a state of peace; quiet; calm: *pacify an angry man.* **2.** to appease: *pacify one's appetite.* [late ME, t. L: m.s. *pācificāre* make peace]

pack¹ (păk), *n.* **1.** a quantity of anything wrapped or tied up; parcel (sometimes of fixed amount as a measure): *a pack of cigarettes.* **2.** the quantity of anything, as food, packed or put up at one time or in one season: *salmon pack.* **3.** a set or gang (of people) or a group (of things): *a pack of thieves.* **4.** a company of animals: *a pack of wolves.* **5.** a complete set, as of playing cards, usually 52 in number. **6.** a considerable area of pieces of floating ice driven or packed together. **7.** *Med.* **a.** a wrapping of the body in wet or dry cloths for therapeutic purposes. **b.** the cloths used. **c.** *Obs.* a state of being so wrapped. **8.** a cosmetic treatment similar to this. **9.** *Obs.* a worthless person.

—v.t. 10. to make into a pack or bundle. **11.** to make into a group or compact mass, as animals, ice, etc. **12.** to fill with anything compactly arranged: *pack a trunk.* **13.** to press or crowd together; cram: *a packed gallery.* **14.** to put or arrange in suitable form for the market: *pack fruit.* **15.** to make airtight, vaportight, or watertight by stuffing: *to pack the piston of a steam engine.* **16.** to cover or envelop with something pressed closely around. **17.** to load (a horse, etc.) with a pack. **18.** to carry, esp. as a load. **19.** to send off summarily (sometimes fol. by *off, away*, etc.): *packed off to her mother.* **20.** to put a load upon. **21.** *Boxing Slang.* to be able to make (a forceful blow). **22.** to treat with a therapeutic pack. **—v.i. 23.** to pack goods, etc., into compact form, as for transportation or storage (often fol. by *up*). **24.** to admit of being compactly stowed: *articles that pack well.* **25.** to crowd together, as persons, etc. **26.** to become compacted: *wet snow packs readily.* **27.** to collect into a pack: *grouse began to pack.* **28.** to leave hastily (generally fol. by *off, away*, etc.). **—adj. 29.** transporting, or used in transporting, a pack: *pack horse, pack animals.* **30.** made up of pack animals. **31.** *Chiefly Scot.* (of animals) tame. **32.** compressed into a pack; packed. **33.** used in or adapted for packing. [ME *packe, pakke*, t. Flem., D or LG] **—Syn. 1.** See **package. 4.** See **flock¹. 5.** *Now U.S. only.* deck.

pack² (păk), *v.t.* to collect, arrange, or manipulate (cards, persons, facts, etc.) so as to serve one's own purposes: *pack a jury.* [? var. of PACT]

pack·age (păk′ĭj), *n., v.,* -aged, -aging. **—n. 1.** a bundle or parcel. **2.** that in which anything is packed, as a case, crate, etc. **3.** the packing of goods, etc. **—v.t. 4.** to put into wrappings or a container. **—Syn. 1.** PACKAGE, PACK, PACKET, PARCEL refer to a bundle or to something fastened together. A PACKAGE is a bundle of things packed and wrapped: *a package from the drug store.* A PACK is a large bundle or bale of things put or fastened together, usually wrapped up or in a bag, case, etc., to be carried by a person or a beast of burden: *a peddler's pack.* A PACKET, originally a package of letters or dispatches, is a small package or bundle: *a packet of gems.* A PARCEL is an object or objects wrapped up to form a single, small bundle: *a parcel containing two dresses.*

pack·er (păk′ər), *n.* **1.** one whose business is packing food for the market. **2.** one who or that which packs.

pack·et (păk′ĭt), *n.* **1.** a small pack or package of anything, orig. of letters. **2.** a boat that carries mail, passengers, and goods regularly on a fixed route. **3.** any ship. **—v.t. 4.** to bind up in a package or parcel. [dim. of PACK¹] **—Syn. 1.** See **package.**

pack·ing (păk′ĭng), *n.* **1.** act or work of one who or that which packs. **2.** the preparing and packaging of foodstuffs. **3.** any material used for packing or making watertight, steamtight, etc., as a fibrous substance closing a joint, a metallic ring round a piston, etc.

packing effect, *Physics.* mass defect.

packing house, an establishment in which provisions, esp. beef and pork, are packed for the market.

pack·man (păk′mən), *n., pl.* -men. a peddler.

pack rat, *Zool.* a large, bushy-tailed rodent, *Neotoma cinerea*, of North America, noted for carrying away small articles which it keeps in its nest.

pack·sack (păk′săk′), *n.* a traveling bag, usually of canvas or leather, usually strapped over one's shoulders.

pack·sad·dle (păk′săd′əl), *n.* a saddle specially designed for supporting the load on a pack animal.

pack·thread (păk′thrĕd′), *n.* a strong thread or twine for sewing or tying up packages.

pact (păkt), *n.* an agreement; a compact. [ME, t. L: s. *pactum*, prop. pp. neut., agreed]

pac·tion (păk′shən), *n.* agreement.

Pac·to·lus (păk tō′ləs), *n.* a small river in ancient Lydia: famous for the gold washed from its sands.

pad¹ (păd), *n., v.,* **padded, padding. —n. 1.** a cushionlike mass of some soft material, for comfort, protection, or stuffing. **2.** a cushion used as a saddle; saddle of leather and padding without a tree. **3.** a number of sheets of paper held together at the edge to form a tablet. **4.** a soft ink-soaked block of absorbent material for inking a rubber stamp. **5.** one of the cushionlike protuberances on the underside of the feet of dogs, foxes, and some other animals. **6.** the foot of a fox or other beast of the chase. **7.** *Zool.* a pulvillus, as on the tarsus or foot of an insect. **8.** the large floating leaf of the water lily. **—v.t. 9.** to furnish, protect, fill out, or stuff with a pad or padding. **10.** to expand (writing or speech) with unnecessary words or matter. [special uses of obs. *pad* bundle to lie on, ? b. PACK¹ and BED]

pad² (păd), *n., v.,* **padded, padding. —n. 1.** a dull sound, as of footsteps on the ground. **2.** a road horse, distinguished from a hunter or workhorse. **3.** a highwayman. **4.** *Brit. Dial.* a path or road. **—v.t. 5.** to travel along on foot. **6.** to beat down by treading. **—v.i. 7.** to travel on foot. **8.** to go with a dull sound of footsteps. [t. D or LG (c. PATH); orig. beggars' and thieves' slang]

Pa·dang (pä däng′), *n.* a seaport in Indonesia, in W Sumatra. 120,121 (est. 1952).

pad·ding (păd′ĭng), *n.* **1.** material, as cotton or straw, with which to pad. **2.** unnecessary matter used to expand a speech, etc. **3.** act of one who or that which pads.

Pad·ding·ton (păd′ĭng tən), *n.* a W residential borough of London, England. 125,281 (1951).

pad·dle¹ (păd′əl), *n., v.,* -dled, -dling. **—n. 1.** a short oar held in the hands (not resting in the oarlock) and used esp. for propelling canoes. **2.** one of the broad boards on the circumference of a paddle wheel. **3.** a paddle wheel. **4.** one of the similar projecting blades by means of which a water wheel is turned. **5.** a flipper or limb of a penguin, turtle, whale, etc. **6.** an implement used for beating garments while washing them in running water, as in a stream. **7.** any of various similar implements used in industrial processes. **8.** act of paddling. **—v.i. 9.** to propel, or travel in, a canoe or the like by using a paddle. **10.** to row lightly or gently with oars. **11.** to move by means of paddle wheels, as a steamer. **—v.t. 12.** to propel (a canoe, etc.) with a paddle. **13.** to stir. **14.** *U.S. Colloq.* to beat with or as with a paddle; spank. **15.** to convey by paddling, as in a canoe. [orig. obscure] **—pad′dler¹,** *n.*

pad·dle² (păd′əl), *v.i.,* -dled, -dling. **1.** to dabble or play in or as in shallow water. **2.** to toy with the fingers. **3.** to toddle. [orig. uncert.] **—pad′dler²,** *n.*

paddle box, a box or casing covering the upper part of the paddle wheel of a vessel.

pad·dle·fish (păd′əl fĭsh′), *n., pl.* -fishes, (esp. collectively) -fish. a large ganoid fish, *Polyodon spathula*, remotely allied to the sturgeons, with a long, flat, paddlelike projection of the snout, abundant in the Mississippi river and its larger tributaries.

paddle wheel, a power-driven wheel with floatboards (paddles) on its circumference, for propelling a vessel over the water. **—pad′dle-wheel′,** *adj.*

pad·dock¹ (păd′ək), *n.* **1.** a small field or enclosure, esp. for pasture, near a stable or house. **2.** a turfed enclosure for horses, esp. at a racecourse. **3.** *Australia.* any enclosed field or piece of land. **—v.t. 4.** to confine or enclose in or as in a paddock. [var. of *parrock*, OE *pearroc* enclosure (orig. fence)]

pad·dock² (păd′ək), *n. Now Chiefly Dial. and Scot.* a frog or toad. [ME *paddoke*, f. *pad* toad + *-oke* -OCK]

pad·dy (păd′ĭ), *n., pl.* -dies. **1.** rice. **2.** rice in the husk, uncut or gathered. [t. Malay: m. *pādī*]

Pad·dy (păd′ĭ), *n., pl.* -dies. *Nickname.* an Irishman. [familiar var. of Irish *Padraig* Patrick]

pad·dy·whack (păd′ĭ hwăk′), *n.* **1.** *Brit. Colloq.* an intense anger; a rage. **2.** *U.S. Colloq.* a spanking.

Pa·de·rew·ski (pä′dĕ rĕf′skĭ, păd′ə-), *n. Fr.* **Ignace** (ēnyäs′) or *Pol.* **Ignacy** (ĭg nä′tsĭ) **Jan** (yän) 1860-1941, Polish pianist, composer, and statesman.

Pa·di·shah (pä′dĭ shä′), *n.* great king; emperor (a title applied esp. to the Shah of Iran, formerly also to the Sultan of Turkey, and in India, to the British sovereign as emperor). Also, **padishah.** [t. Pers. (poetical form), f. m. *pati* lord + *shāh* king]

pad·lock (păd′lŏk′), *n.* **1.** a portable or detachable lock having a pivoted or sliding hasp which passes through a staple, ring, or the like and is then made fast. **—v.t. 2.** to fasten with or as with a padlock. [late ME, f. *pad*, var. of POD³, + LOCK¹]

pad·nag (păd′năg′), *n.* an ambling nag. [f. PAD¹+NAG²]

Pa·douk wood (pə dōōk′), an ornamental wood mottled in shades of yellowish red from a Malaysian tree, *Pterocarpus indicus*: used in inlaying and for making small articles; Amboina wood.

pa·dre (pä′drĭ; *Sp.,* It. pä′drĕ), *n.* **1.** father (used esp. with reference to a priest). **2.** (among soldiers and sailors) a chaplain. [t. Sp., Pg., It., g. L *pater* father]

pa·dro·ne (pə drō′nĭ; *It.* pä drō′nĕ), *n., pl.* -ni (-nē) *Italian.* **1.** a master. **2.** one who controls and supplies Italian laborers, as in America. **3.** the master of a vessel. **4.** an innkeeper. [It., der. *padre* father]

Pad·u·a (păj′ōō ə, păd′yōō ə), *n.* a city in NE Italy. 177,000 (est. 1954). Italian, **Pa·do·va** (pä′dō vä′).

pad·u·a·soy (păj′ōō ə soi′), *n., pl.* -soys. **1.** a smooth, strong, rich, silk fabric. **2.** a garment made of it. [appar. alter. of F *pou-de-soie*, by assoc. with *Padua* say serge of PADUA]

Pa·du·cah (pə dū′kə, -dōō′-), *n.* a city in W Kentucky at the junction of the Tennessee and Ohio rivers. 34,479 (1960).

Pa·dus (pä′dəs), *n.* ancient name of Po.

pae·an (pē′ən), *n.* **1.** any song of praise, joy, or triumph. **2.** a hymn of invocation or thanksgiving to Apollo or some other Greek deity. Also, **pean.** [t. L, t. Gk.: m. *paiān* paean, *Paiān*, Homer's name for the physician of the gods, later Apollo]

paed-, var. of ped-². Also, **paedo-.**

pae·di·at·rics (pē′dĭ ăt′rĭks, pĕd′ĭ-), *n. Chiefly Brit.* pediatrics.

pae·do·gen·e·sis (pē′dō jĕn′ə sĭs), *n.* reproduction by animals in the larval state, often by parthenogenesis.

pae·on (pē′ən), *n. Anc. Pros.* a foot of four syllables, one long (in any position) and three short. [t. L, t. Gk.: m. *paiōn* paeon, hymn, Attic var. of *paiān* PAEAN]

Paes·tum (pĕs′təm), *n.* an ancient coastal city of Lucania, in S Italy: the imposing ruins include three Greek temples and a Roman amphitheater.

pa·gan (pā′gən), *n.* **1.** one of a people or community professing some other than the Christian religion (applied to the ancient Romans, Greeks, etc., and sometimes the Jews). **2.** one who is not a Christian, a Jew, or a Mohammedan. **3.** an irreligious or heathenish person. **—adj. 4.** pertaining to the worship or worshipers of any religion which is neither Christian, Jewish, nor Mohammedan. **5.** of, pertaining to, or characteristic ot pagans. **6.** heathen; irreligious. [ME, t. L: s. *pāgānus* civilian; so called (by the Christians) because he was not a soldier of Christ] —**pa′gan·ish**, *adj.* —**Syn. 5.** See **heathen.**

pa·gan·dom (pā′gən dəm), *n.* **1.** the pagan world. **2.** pagans collectively.

Pa·ga·ni·ni (päg′ə nē′nĭ; *It.* pä′gä nē′nē), *n.* **Nicolò** (nē′kô lô′), 1784–1840, Italian violinist.

pa·gan·ism (pā′gə nĭz′əm), *n.* **1.** pagan spirit or attitude in religious or moral questions. **2.** the beliefs or practices of pagans. **3.** the state of being a pagan.

pa·gan·ize (pā′gə nīz′), *v.*, **-ized, -izing.** —*v.t.* **1.** to make pagan. —*v.i.* **2.** to become pagan.

page[1] (pāj), *n.*, *v.*, **paged, paging.** —*n.* **1.** one side of a leaf of a book, manuscript, letter, or the like. **2.** a record: *memory's page.* **3.** any event or period regarded as a matter of history: *a glorious page in Canadian history.* **4.** *Print.* the type set and arranged for a page. —*v.t.* **5.** to paginate. [t. F, g. L *pāgina*]

page[2] (pāj), *n.*, *v.*, **paged, paging.** —*n.* **1.** a boy servant or attendant. **2.** a youth in attendance on a person of rank, sometimes formerly in the course of training for knighthood. **3.** a young male attendant, usually in uniform, in a legislative hall, a hotel, etc. —*v.t.* **4.** *U.S.* to seek (a person) by calling out his name, as a hotel page does. **5.** to attend as a page. [ME, t. OF, t. It.: m. *paggio*, ult. t. Gk.: m. *paidíon* boy, servant]

Page (pāj), *n.* **1.** **Thomas Nelson,** 1853–1922, U.S. novelist and diplomat. **2.** **Walter Hines,** 1855–1918, U.S. editor: ambassador to England, 1913–18.

pag·eant (păj′ənt), *n.* **1.** an elaborate public spectacle, whether processional or at some fitting spot, illustrative of the history of a place, institution, or other subject. **2.** a costumed procession, masque, allegorical tableau, or the like, in public or social festivities. **3.** a splendid or stately procession; a showy display. **4.** a specious show. **5.** *Obs. exc. Hist.* **a.** a platform or stage, usually moving on wheels, on which scenes from the medieval mystery plays were presented. **b.** a stage bearing any kind of spectacle. [ME *pagent*, *pagyn*; orig. obscure]

pag·eant·ry (păj′ən trĭ), *n.*, *pl.* **-ries. 1.** spectacular display; pomp: *the pageantry of war.* **2.** mere show; empty display. **3.** *Obs.* pageants collectively.

Pag·et (păj′ĭt), *n.* **Sir James,** 1814–99, British surgeon and pathologist.

pag·i·nal (păj′ə nal), *adj.* **1.** of or pertaining to pages. **2.** consisting of pages. **3.** page for page: *a paginal reprint.* [t. LL: s. *pāginālis*, der. L *pāgina* PAGE[1]]

pag·i·nate (păj′ə nāt′), *v.t.*, **-nated, -nating.** to indicate the sequence of (pages) by numbers or other characters on each leaf of the book.

pag·i·na·tion (păj′ə nā′shən), *n. Bibliog.* **1.** the number of pages or leaves (or both) of a book identified in bibliographical description or cataloguing of the book. **2.** the figures by which pages are numbered. **3.** act of paging.

Pa·gliac·ci, I (ē pä lyät′chē), an opera (1892) by Leoncavallo.

pa·go·da (pə gō′də), *n.* (in India, Burma, China, etc.) a temple or sacred building, usually more or less pyramidal or forming a tower of many stories. Also, *Archaic,* **pag·od** (păg′əd, pə gŏd′). [t. Pg.: m. *pagode*, orig. uncert.]

Pa·go Pa·go (päng′ō päng′ō), the chief harbor and town of American Samoa, on Tutuila island: naval station. 1586 (1950). Also, **Pagopago.**

pa·gu·ri·an (pə gyŏŏr′ĭ ən), *adj. Zool.* belonging or pertaining to the hermit crab family *Paguridae,* esp. aquatic hermit crabs with short antennules. —*n.* **2.** a pagurian crab. [f. s. NL *Pagurus,* the typical genus (t. Gk.: m. *págouros* kind of crab) + -IAN]

pa·gu·rid (pə gyŏŏr′ĭd, păg′yə rĭd), *n.* a pagurian.

pah (pä, pă), *interj.* an exclamation of disgust.

Pa·hang (pä häng′), *n.* a state in the former Federation of Malaya: now part of the federation of Malaysia. 313,058 pop. (1957); 13,820 sq. mi. *Cap.:* Kuala Lipis.

Pah·la·vi (pä′lə vē′), *n.*, *pl.* **-vis. 1.** the dynasty now ruling in Iran, founded by Riza Shah Pahlavi in 1925. **2.** (*l.c.*) an Iranian gold coin worth 100 rials, in use since 1927. [t. Pers., named after Riza Shah *Pahlavi*]

Pah·la·vi (pä′lə vē′), *n.* the Iranian language of Zoroastrian books, written (3d–10th centuries) in a Semitic script. Also, **Pehlevi.** [t. Pers.: Parthian]

paid (pād), *v.* pt. and pp. of **pay**[1].

paid-in (pād′ĭn′), *adj.* having paid the dues, initiation fees, etc., required by any organization or association: *the union has a paid-in membership of 60,000.*

paid-in surplus, *Accounting.* surplus paid in by purchasers of stock certificates sold at a premium.

pail (pāl), *n.* a container of wood, metal, etc., nearly or quite cylindrical, with a bail or handle, for holding liquids, etc. [ME *payle,* OE *pægel* wine vessel, akin to G *pegel* water gauge] —**pail·ful** (pāl′fŏŏl′), *n.*

pail·lasse (păl′yăs′, păl′yăs), *n. Chiefly Brit.* a mattress of straw or the like. Also, **palliasse.** [t. F, der. *paille* straw, g. L *palea* chaff, straw]

pail·lette (păl yĕt′), *n.* a spangle used in ornamenting a costume. [t. F, dim. of *paille* straw. See PALLET[1]]

pain (pān), *n.* **1.** bodily or mental suffering or distress (opposed to *pleasure*). **2.** a distressing sensation in a particular part of the body. **3.** (*pl.*) laborious or careful efforts; assiduous care: *great pains have been taken.* **4.** (*pl.*) the suffering of childbirth. **5. on pain of death,** liable to the penalty of death. —*v.t.* **6.** to inflict pain on; hurt; distress. —*v.i.* **7.** to cause pain or suffering. [ME *peine,* t. OF, g. L *poena* penalty, pain, t. Gk.: m. *poinē* fine]

—**Syn. 1.** torture, misery. PAIN, ACHE, AGONY, ANGUISH are terms for sensations causing suffering or torment. PAIN and ACHE refer usually to physical sensations (except *heartache*); AGONY and ANGUISH may be physical or mental. PAIN suggests a sudden sharp twinge: *a pain in one's ankle.* ACHE applies to a continuous pain, whether acute or dull: *headache, muscular aches.* AGONY implies a continuous, excruciating, scarcely endurable pain: *in agony from a wound.* ANGUISH suggests not only extreme and long-continued pain, but also a feeling of despair. **3.** See **care. 6.** afflict, torture, torment.

Paine (pān), *n.* **1. Robert Treat,** 1731–1814, American jurist and statesman. **2. Thomas,** 1737–1809, American writer on government and religion, born in England.

pain·ful (pān′fəl), *adj.* **1.** affected with or causing pain: *painful thoughts.* **2.** laborious; difficult. **3.** *Obs.* or *Archaic.* painstaking. —**pain′ful·ly,** *adv.* —**pain′ful·ness,** *n.* —**Syn. 1.** distressing, torturing, agonizing.

pain·less (pān′lĭs), *adj.* without pain; causing no pain. —**pain′less·ly,** *adv.* —**pain′less·ness,** *n.*

pains·tak·ing (pānz′tā′kĭng), *adj.* **1.** assiduously careful; *painstaking work.* —*n.* **2.** careful and assiduous effort. —**pains′tak′ing·ly,** *adv.*

paint (pānt), *n.* **1.** a substance composed of solid coloring matter intimately mixed with a liquid vehicle or medium, and applied as a coating. **2.** the dried surface pigment. **3.** the solid coloring matter alone; a pigment. **4.** color, as rouge, used on the face. **5.** application of color. —*v.t.* **6.** to represent (an object, etc.) or execute (a picture, design, etc.) in colors or pigment. **7.** to depict as if by painting; describe vividly in words. **8.** to coat, cover, or decorate (something) with color or pigment. **9.** to color as if by painting; adorn or variegate. **10.** to apply like paint, as a liquid medicine, etc. —*v.i.* **11.** to coat or cover anything with paint. **12.** to practice painting: *the Queen paints well.* **13.** to put or use artificial colors on the face. [ME *peint(en),* t. OF: m. *peint,* pp. of *peindre,* g. L *pingere* paint, adorn]

paint·brush (pānt′brŭsh′), *n.* **1.** a brush for applying paint. **2.** any of the figwort family of plants.

painted bunting, the nonpareil (def. 3).

painted cup, a plant of the genus *Castilleia,* primarily *C. coccinea,* the scarlet painted cup: so called from the highly colored dilated bracts about the flowers.

painted redstart, a brilliantly colored warbler, *Setophaga picta,* of the southwestern U.S. and Mexico.

paint·er[1] (pān′tər), *n.* **1.** an artist who paints pictures. **2.** a workman who coats surfaces with paint. [ME *peyntour,* t. AF: m. *peintour,* ult. g. L *pictor*]

paint·er[2] (pān′tər), *n.* a rope, usually at the bow, for fastening a boat to a ship, stake, etc. [? var. of d. *panter* noose, ult. t. Gk.: m.s. *panthēra* hunting net]

paint·er[3] (pān′tər), *n.* the American panther, or cougar. [var. of PANTHER]

painter's colic, lead poisoning causing intense pain in the intestines.

paint·ing (pān′tĭng), *n.* **1.** a picture or design executed in paints. **2.** act, art, or work of one who paints.

pair (pâr), *n.*, *pl.* **pairs, pair.** —*n.* **1.** two things of a kind, matched for use together: *a pair of gloves.* **2.** a combination of two parts joined together: *a pair of scissors.* **3.** a married or engaged couple. **4.** two mated animals; a span or team. **5.** *Govt.* **a.** two members on opposite sides in a deliberative body who for convenience (as to permit absence) arrange together to forgo voting on a given occasion. **b.** the arrangement thus made. **6.** *Cards.* **a.** two cards of the same denomination, without regard to suit or color. **b.** (*pl.*) two players who are matched together against different contestants. **7.** *Mech.* two parts or pieces so connected that they mutually constrain relative motion (**kinematic pair**). **8.** *Archaic* or *Dial.* a set or combination of more than two. —*v.t.* **9.** to arrange in pairs. **10.** to join in a pair; match; mate; couple. **11.** to cause to mate. —*v.i.* **12.** to separate into pairs (fol. by *off*). **13.** to form a pair or pairs. **14.** (in a deliberative body) to form a pair to forgo voting. [ME, t. OF: m. *paire,* g. L *pāria,* neut. pl. of *pār* equal]

—**Syn. 1.** PAIR, BRACE, COUPLE, SPAN, YOKE are terms for groups of two. PAIR is used of two things naturally or habitually associated in use, or necessary to each other to make a complete set (*a pair of horses*). It is used also of one thing composed of two similar and complementary parts: *a pair of trousers.* BRACE is a hunter's term, used of a pair of dogs, ducks, etc., or a pair of pistols or slugs: *a brace of partridges.* In COUPLE the idea of combination or interdependence has become greatly weakened; it may be used loosely for two of anything (*a couple of apples*), and even for more than two (= several): *I have to see a couple of people.* SPAN is used of a matched pair of horses harnessed together side by side. YOKE applies to two animals hitched together under a yoke for drawing and pulling: *a yoke of oxen.*

pair-oared (pâr′ōrd′), *adj.* (of racing shells) having two oarsmen, with one oar each.

---

b., blend of, blended; c., cognate with; d., dialect, dialectal; der., derived from; f., formed from; g., going back to; m., modification of; r., replacing; s., stem of; t., taken from; ?, perhaps. See the full key on inside cover.

pair production, *Physics.* the simultaneous creation of a positron and an electron from a high-energy gamma ray.

Pais·ley (pāz′lĭ), *n.* a city in SW Scotland, W of Glasgow: thread factories. 95,200 (est. 1956).

pais·ley (pāz′lĭ), *n., pl.* **-leys. 1.** a soft fabric made from wool and woven with a colorful and minutely detailed pattern. **2.** an article fashioned of paisley. —*adj.* **3.** made of paisley: *a paisley shawl.*

Pai·ute (pī ōōt′), *n.* **1.** (*pl.*) a group of North American Indians of Uto-Aztecan family, dwelling in California, Nevada, Utah, and Arizona. **2.** a member of this group. [orig. name for Corn Creek tribe of Utah]

pa·jam·as (pə jăm′əz, pə jä′məz), *n.pl.* **1.** nightclothes consisting of loose trousers and jacket. **2.** loose trousers, usually of silk or cotton, worn by both sexes in India, etc. Also, *esp. Brit.,* **pyjamas.** [t. Hind., t. Pers.: m. *pāejāmah,* lit., leg garment]

Pa·ki·stan (pä′kĭ stän′), *n.* **1.** a member of the British Commonwealth of Nations in S Asia, divided into **West Pakistan** and **East Pakistan,** 900 miles apart and separated by the republic of India; formerly part of India. 83,603,000 pop. (est. 1956); 364,737 sq. mi. *Provisional Cap.:* Rawalpindi. **2.** (before 1947) the predominantly Moslem areas of the peninsula of India as contrasted to Hindustan, the predominantly Hindu areas.

pal (pǎl), *n., v.,* **palled, palling.** *Colloq.* —*n.* **1.** a comrade; a chum. **2.** an accomplice. —*v.i.* **3.** to associate as pals. [t. Gypsy, dissimilated var. of *plal, pral* brother]

pa·la·bra (pä lä′brä), *n.* Spanish. **1.** a word. **2.** speech; talk. [see PALAVER]

pal·ace (pǎl′ĭs), *n.* **1.** the official residence of a sovereign, a bishop, or some other exalted personage. **2.** a stately mansion or building. **3.** a large place for exhibitions or entertainment. [ME *palais,* t. OF, g. L *palātium* palace, orig. the Palatine Hill in Rome (on which the emperors resided)]

Pa·la·cio Val·dés (pä lä′thyō väl dĕs′), **Armando** (är män′dō), 1853–1938, Spanish novelist and critic.

pal·a·din (pǎl′ə dĭn), *n.* **1.** one of the legendary twelve peers or knightly champions in attendance on Charlemagne. **2.** any knightly or heroic champion. [t. F, t. It.: m. *paladino,* g. L *palātīnus* PALATINE[1]]

palae-, var. of **pale-.** Also, before consonants, **palaeo-.** For words beginning with **palae-,** look under the more common spelling in **pale-.**

pa·laes·tra (pə lĕs′trə), *n., pl.* **-tras, -trae** (trē). *Gk. Antiq.* palestra.

pal·an·quin (pǎl′ən kēn′), *n.* (in India and other Eastern countries) a covered or boxlike litter borne by means of poles resting on men's shoulders. Also, **pal′an·keen′.** [t. Pg. Cf. Skt. *palyanka, paryanka* couch, bed; prob. through Telegu]

Indian palanquin

pal·at·a·ble (pǎl′ət ə bəl), *adj.* **1.** agreeable to the palate or taste; savory. **2.** agreeable to the mind or feelings. —**pal′at·a·bil′i·ty, pal′at·a·ble·ness,** *n.* —**pal′at·a·bly,** *adv.*

pal·a·tal (pǎl′ə tal), *adj.* **1.** *Anat.* of or pertaining to the palate. **2.** *Phonet.* with the tongue held close to the hard palate: the *y* of *yield* is a palatal consonant. —*n.* **3.** *Phonet.* a palatal sound. [f. PALAT(E) + -AL[1]]

pal·a·tal·ize (pǎl′ə tə līz′), *v.t.,* **-ized, -izing.** *Phonet.* to pronounce with the tongue held close to the hard palate so that the sound acquires some of the quality of a *y:* in *million* the *l* sound may or may not be palatalized, but is always followed by a *y* sound. —**pal′a·tal·i·za′tion,** *n.*

pal·ate (pǎl′ĭt), *n.* **1.** the roof of the mouth, consisting of bone (**hard palate**) in front and of a fleshy structure (**soft palate**) at the back. See diag. under **mouth. 2.** this part of the mouth considered (popularly but erroneously) as the organ of taste. **3.** the sense of taste. **4.** mental taste or liking. [ME *palat,* t. L: s. *palātum*]

pa·la·tial (pə lā′shəl), *adj.* pertaining to, of the nature of, or befitting a palace: *palatial homes.* [f. s. L *palātium* PALACE + -AL[1]] —**pa·la′tial·ly,** *adv.*

Pa·lat·i·nate ′pə lăt′ə nāt′, -nĭt), *n.* **1. The,** Also **Lower** or **Rhine Palatinate.** German, *Pfalz.* a district in SW Germany, W of the Rhine, which belonged to Bavaria until 1945; formerly, with portions of the neighboring territory (the **Upper Palatinate**), it constituted an electorate of the Holy Roman Empire; now part of Rhineland-Palatinate state. **2.** a native or inhabitant of the Palatinate. **3.** (*l.c.*) the territory under the jurisdiction of a palatine.

pal·a·tine[1] (pǎl′ə tĭn′, -tīn′), *adj.* **1.** possessing or characterized by royal privileges: *a count palatine.* **2.** pertaining to a count or earl palatine, or to a county palatine. **3.** of or pertaining to a palace; palatial. **4.** (*cap.*) of or pertaining to the Palatinate. —*n.* **5.** a vassal exercising royal privileges in a province; a count or earl palatine. **6.** an officer of an imperial palace. **7.** a high official of an empire. **8.** (*cap.*) a native or inhabitant of the Palatinate. **9.** (*cap.*) Palatine Hill. **10.** a shoulder cape formerly worn by women. [ME, t. L: m.s. *palātīnus* belonging to the palace, imperial (as n., a palace officer)]

pal·a·tine[2] (pǎl′ə tĭn′, -tīn′), *adj.* palatal: *the palatine bones.* [t. F: m. *palatin,* der. L *palātum* PALATE]

Palatine Hill, one of the seven hills on which Rome was built.

Pa·lau Islands (pä lou′), a group of Pacific islands in the W part of the Caroline group: taken by U.S. forces after severe fighting, 1944; formerly a Japanese mandate, now under U.S. trusteeship. 7656 pop. (est. 1955); 171 sq. mi. Also, **Pelew Islands.**

pa·lav·er (pə lǎv′ər, -lä′vər), *n.* **1.** a parley or conference, esp. with much talk, as between travelers and primitive natives. **2.** profuse and plausible talk; flattery. —*v.i.* **3.** to talk profusely and idly. —*v.t.* **4.** to cajole. [t. Pg.: m. *palavra,* g. L *parabola* PARABLE]

Pa·la·wan (pä lä′wän), *n.* one of the Philippine Islands, in the SW part of the group. 106,269 pop. (1948); 5697 sq. mi. *Cap.:* Puerto Princesa.

pale[1] (pāl), *adj.,* **paler, palest,** *v.,* **paled, paling.** —*adj.* **1.** of a whitish appearance; without intensity of color: *pale complexion.* **2.** of a low degree of chroma, saturation or purity; approaching white or gray: *pale yellow.* **3.** lacking in brightness; dim: *the pale moon.* **4.** faint; feeble; lacking vigor. —*v.i., v.t.* **5.** to make or become pale: *He paled when I told him we had found his gun near the house.* [ME, t. OF, t. L: m. *pallidus* pallid] —**pale′ly,** *adv.* —**pale′ness,** *n.*

—Syn. **1.** PALE, PALLID, WAN imply an absence of color, esp. from the human countenance. PALE implies a faintness or absence of color, which may be natural when applied to things (*the pale blue of a violet*) but when applied to the human face, usually unnatural and often temporary as arising from sickness or sudden emotion: *pale cheeks.* PALLID, limited mainly to the human countenance, implies an excessive paleness induced by intense emotion, disease, or death: *the pallid lips of the dying man.* WAN implies a sickly paleness, as after a long illness (*wan and thin*); the suggestion of weakness may be more prominent than that of lack of color: *a wan smile.* —Ant. **1.** rosy, ruddy.

pale[2] (pāl), *n., v.,* **paled, paling.** —*n.* **1.** a stake or picket, as of a fence. **2.** any enclosing or confining barrier. **3.** limits or bounds: *outside the pale of the church.* **4.** the area enclosed by a paling; any enclosed area. **5.** a district or region within fixed bounds. **6.** (*cap.*) a district in E Ireland included in the Angevin Empire of King Henry II and his successors. Also, **English Pale** or **Irish Pale. 7.** *Her.* a broad vertical stripe in the middle of an escutcheon and one third its width. —*v.t.* **8.** to enclose with pales; fence. **9.** to encircle or encompass. [ME, t. F: m. *pal,* t. L: s. *pālus* stake]

pale-, var. of **paleo-,** before most vowels, as in *paleëthnology.*

pa·le·a (pā′lĭə), *n., pl.* **-leae** (-lĭ ē′). *Bot.* **1.** a chafflike scale or bract. **2.** the scalelike, membranous organ in the flowers of grasses which is situated upon a secondary axis in the axil of the flowering glume and envelops the stamens and pistil. [t. L: chaff] —**pa·le·a′ceous** (pā′lĭ ā′shəs), *adj.*

pa·le·ëth·nol·o·gy (pā′lĭ ĕth nŏl′ə jĭ, pǎl′ĭ-), *n.* the branch of ethnology that treats of the earliest or most primitive races of mankind. [f. PALE- + ETHNOLOGY] —**pa·le·ëth·no·log·ic** (pā′lĭ ĕth′nə lŏj′ĭk, pǎl′ĭ-), **pa·le·ëth′no·log′i·cal,** *adj.* —**pa′le·ëth·nol′o·gist,** *n.*

pale·face (pāl′fās′), *n.* a white person (an expression attributed to the American Indians).

Pa·lem·bang (pä′lĕm bäng′), *n.* a city in Indonesia, in SE Sumatra. 237,616 (est. 1952).

Pa·len·que (pä lĕng′kě), *n.* ruins of an ancient Mayan city in SE Mexico, in Chiapas state.

paleo-, a prefix meaning "old," "ancient." Also **pale-, palae-, palaeo-.** [t. Gk.: m. *palaio-,* comb. form of *palaiós*]

pa·le·o·bot·a·ny (pā′lĭ ō bŏt′ə nĭ, pǎl′ĭ-), *n.* the branch of paleontology that treats of fossil plants. —**pa·le·o·bo·tan·i·cal** (pā′lĭ ō bə tǎn′ə kəl, pǎl′ĭ-), **pa·le·o·bo·tan′ic,** *adj.* —**pa′le·o·bot′a·nist,** *n.*

Pa·le·o·cene (pā′lĭ ə sēn′, pǎl′ĭ-), *Stratig.* —*adj.* **1.** pertaining to the oldest series or epoch of the Tertiary. —*n.* **2.** a division of the Tertiary period or system that precedes Eocene.

paleog., paleography.

pa·le·o·ge·og·ra·phy (pā′lĭ ō jĭ ŏg′rə fĭ, pǎl′ĭ-), *n.* representation of earth features belonging to any part of the geologic past. —**pa·le·o·ge·o·graph·ic** (pā′lĭ-ō jĕ′ə grǎf′ĭk, pǎl′ĭ-), **pa′le·o·ge·o·graph′i·cal,** *adj.*

pa·le·o·ge·ol·o·gy (pā′lĭ ō jĭ ŏl′ə jĭ, pǎl′ĭ-), *n.* the science of representing geologic conditions of some given time in past earth history. —**pa·le·o·ge·o·log·ic** (pā′lĭ-ō jē′ə lŏj′ĭk, pǎl′ĭ-), *adj.*

pa·le·og·ra·phy (pā′lĭ ŏg′rə fĭ, pǎl′ĭ-), *n.* **1.** ancient forms of writing, as in documents and inscriptions. **2.** the study of ancient writing, including determination of origin and date, decipherment, etc. —**pa·le·og′ra·pher,** *n.* —**pa·le·o·graph·ic** (pā′lĭ ə grǎf′ĭk, pǎl′ĭ-), **pa′le·o·graph′i·cal,** *adj.*

pa·le·o·lith (pā′lĭ ə lĭth′, pǎl′ĭ-), *n.* a paleolithic stone implement.

pa·le·o·lith·ic (pā′lĭ ə lĭth′ĭk, pǎl′ĭ-), *adj.* noting or pertaining to the earlier part of the Old World Stone Age, marked by exclusive use of chipped stone implements.

paleolithic man, *Anthropol.* any of the primitive species of man (Piltdown, Neanderthal, etc.) living in the paleolithic period.

paleontol., paleontology.

pa·le·on·tol·o·gy (pā′lĭ ən tŏl′ə jĭ, pǎl′ĭ-), *n.* the science of the forms of life existing in former geological periods, as represented by fossil animals and plants. [t.

äct, āble, dâre, ärt; ĕbb, ēqual; ĭf, īce; hŏt, ōver, ôrder, oil, bŏŏk, ōōze, out; ŭp, ūse, ûrge; ə = a in alone; ch, chief; g, give; ng, ring; sh, shoe; th, thin; ŧ͟h, that; zh, vision. See the full key on inside cover.

F: m. *paléontologie;* f. PALE- + ONTOLOGY]. —**pa-le-on-to-log-ic** (pā'lĭ ŏn'/tə lŏj'ĭk, pǎl'Y-), **pa'le-on'/-to-log'i-cal,** *adj.* —**pa'le-on-tol'o-gist,** *n.*

Pa-le-o-zo-ic (pā'lĭ ə zō'ĭk, pǎl'Y-), *Stratig.* —*adj.* **1.** pertaining to the oldest geological era or rocks having abundant fossils; the age of ancient life. —*n.* **2.** the era or rocks comprising divisions from Cambrian to Permian. [f. PALEO- + s. Gk. *zōē* life + -IC]

pa-le-o-zo-öl-o-gy (pā'lĭ ō zō ŏl'ə jĭ, pǎl'Y-), *n.* the branch of paleontology that treats of fossil animals. —**pa-le-o-zo-ö-log-i-cal** (pā'lĭ ō zō'ō lŏj'ə kəl, pǎl'Y-), *adj.*

Pa-ler-mo (pä lĕr'mō), *n.* a seaport in and the capital of Sicily, in the NW part. 528,000 (est. 1954).

Pal-es-tine (pǎl'ə stīn'), *n.* **1.** an ancient country in SW Asia, on the E coast of the Mediterranean. Also, **Holy Land.** Biblical name, **Canaan. 2.** a former British mandate comprising part of this country, now divided between the state of Israel and part of the state of Jordan (**Arab Palestine**). See **Israel.** —**Pal-es-tin-i-an** (pǎl'ə-stĭn'Y ən), *adj., n.*

pa-les-tra (pə lĕs'trə), *n., pl.* **-tras, -trae** (-trē). *Gk. Antiq.* a public place for training or exercise in wrestling or athletics. Also, **palaestra.** [ME, t. L, t. Gk.: m. *palaistra*]

Pa-les-tri-na (pǎl'ə strē'nə; *It.* pä'lĕs trē'nä), *n.* Giovanni Pierluigi da (jō vän'nē pyĕr'lōō ē'jē dä), 1526?–1594, Italian composer of church music.

pal-e-tot (pǎl'ə tō', pǎl'tō), *n.* a loose outer garment or coat. [t. F; OF *paltoc,* of uncert. orig.]

pal-ette (pǎl'ĭt), *n.* **1.** a thin, usually oval or oblong, board or tablet with a thumb hole at one end, used by painters to lay and mix colors on. **2.** the range of colors used by a particular artist. **3.** Also, **pallette.** *Armor.* a small armpit plate. See illustration under **armor.** [t. F: palette, flat-bladed implement, ult. der. L *pāla* spade, shovel]

palette knife, a thin, flexible blade set in a handle, used for mixing painters' colors, etc.

pale-wise (pāl'wīz'), *adv. Her.* in the manner or direction of a pale[2] (def. 7).

Pa-ley (pā'lĭ), *n.* **William,** 1743–1805, British theologian, philosopher, and clergyman.

pal-frey (pôl'frĭ), *n., pl.* **-freys. 1.** a riding horse, as distinguished from a war horse. **2.** a woman's saddle horse. [ME *palefrai,* t. OF: m. *palefrei,* g. LL *paraverēdus,* f. Gk. *pará* beside + L *verēdus* light horse, of Celtic orig.]

Pal-grave (pôl'grāv, pǎl'-), *n.* **Francis Turner,** 1824–97, British critic and poet.

Pa-li (pä'lĭ), *n.* the Prakrit language of the Buddhist scriptures. [t. Skt.: short for *pāli-bhāsā,* lit., canon language]

pal-i-kar (pǎl'Y kär'), *n.* a Greek militiaman in the Greco-Turkish war of 1821–28. Also, **pellekar.** [t. NGk.: m. *palikári* lad, der. Gk. *pállax* youth]

pal-imp-sest (pǎl'Ymp sĕst'), *n.* a parchment or the like from which writing has been partially or completely erased to make room for another text. [t. L: s. *palimpsestus,* t. Gk.: m. *palimpsēstos* scraped again]

pal-in-drome (pǎl'Yn drōm'), *n.* a word, verse, etc., reading the same backward as forward, as *madam, I'm Adam.* [t. Gk.: m.s. *palíndromos* running back]

pal-ing (pā'lĭng), *n.* **1.** a fence of pales. **2.** a pale, as in a fence. **3.** pales collectively. **4.** act of one who builds a fence with pales. [ME, f. PALE[2] + -ING[1]]

pal-in-gen-e-sis (pǎl'Yn jĕn'ə sĭs), *n.* **1.** rebirth; regeneration. **2.** *Biol.* **a.** that development of an individual which reproduces the ancestral features (opposed to *cenogenesis*). **b.** *Obs.* the supposed generation of organisms from others preformed in the germ cells. **3.** baptism in the Christian faith. **4.** the doctrine of transmigration of souls. [f. Gk. *pálin* back, again + -GENESIS]

pal-i-node (pǎl'ə nōd'), *n.* **1.** a poem in which the poet retracts something said in a former poem. **2.** a recantation. [t. LL: m.s. *palinōdia,* t. Gk.: m. *palinōidía*]

pal-i-sade (pǎl'ə sād'), *n., v.,* **-saded, -sading.** —*n.* **1.** a fence of pales or stakes set firmly in the ground, as for enclosure or defense. **2.** one of the pales or stakes, pointed at the top, set firmly in the ground in a close row with others, for defense. **3.** (*pl.*) a line of lofty cliffs. —*v.t.* **4.** to furnish or fortify with a palisade. [t. F: m. *palissade,* der. *palisser* furnish with a paling, der. *palis* paling, der. L *pālus* PALE[2]]

Pal-i-sades (pǎl'ə sādz'), *n.* the cliffs extending almost 40 mi. along the W bank of the lower Hudson river, in NE New Jersey and SE New York: partially included in the **Palisades Interstate Park.**

pal-ish (pā'lĭsh), *adj.* somewhat pale.

pall[1] (pôl), *n.* **1.** a cloth, often of velvet, for spreading over a coffin, bier, or tomb. **2.** something that covers, shrouds, or overspreads, esp. with darkness or gloom. **3.** *Eccles.* **a.** a pallium (vestment). **b.** *Archaic.* a cloth spread upon the altar, esp. a corporal. **c.** a linen cloth, or now usually a square piece of cardboard covered with linen, used to cover the chalice. **4.** *Her.* a bearing representing the front of a pallium (vestment), consisting of a Y-shaped form charged with crosses. **5.** *Obs.* a cloak. —*v.t.* **6.** to cover with or as with a pall. [ME; OE *pæll,* t. L: m.s. *pallium* cloak, covering]

pall[2] (pôl), *v.i.* **1.** to have a wearying effect (fol. by *on* or *upon*). **2.** to become insipid, distasteful, or wearisome.

3. to become satiated or cloyed with something. —*v.t.* **4.** to satiate or cloy. **5.** to make vapid, insipid, or distasteful. [ME *palle(n);* appar. aphetic var. of APPALL]

Pal-la-di-an (pə lā'dĭ ən), *adj.* pertaining to, introduced by, or in the style of Andrea Palladio.

Pal-la-di-an (pə lā'dĭ ən), *adj.* **1.** of or pertaining to the goddess Pallas. **2.** pertaining to wisdom, knowledge, or study.

pal-lad-ic (pə lăd'Yk, -lā'dYk), *adj. Chem.* of or containing palladium, esp. in the tetravalent state (Pd+4).

Pal-la-dio (päl lä'dyō), *n.* **Andrea** (än drě'ä), 1508–80, Italian architect.

Pal-la-di-um (pə lā'dĭ əm), *n., pl.* **-dia** (-dĭ ə). **1.** a statue of Pallas Athene, esp. one on the citadel of Troy on which the safety of the city was supposed to depend. **2.** (*usually l.c.*) anything believed to afford effectual protection or safety. [ME, t. L, t. Gk.: m. *Palládion*]

pal-la-di-um (pə lā'dĭ əm), *n. Chem.* a rare metallic element of the platinum group, silver-white, ductile and malleable. It is harder than platinum and fuses more readily. *Symbol:* Pd; *at. wt.:* 106.7; *at. no.:* 46; *sp. gr.:* 12 at 20°C. [t. NL; named (1803) after the asteroid Pallas, then recently discovered]

pal-la-dous (pə lā'dəs, pǎl'ə dəs), *adj. Chem.* containing divalent palladium (Pd+2).

Pal-las (pǎl'əs), *n.* **1.** a name of Athena (often **Pallas Athene**). **2.** *Astron.* one of the asteroids. [t. L, t. Gk.]

pall-bear-er (pôl'bâr'ər), *n.* one of those who carry or attend one the coffin at a funeral.

pal-let[1] (pǎl'Yt), *n.* **1.** a bed or mattress of straw. **2.** a small or poor bed. [ME *pailet,* t. OF, dim. of *paille* straw, g. L *palea* chaff]

pal-let[2] (pǎl'Yt), *n.* **1.** an implement consisting of a flat blade or plate with a handle, used for shaping by potters, etc. **2.** a flat board or metal plate used to support ceramic articles during drying. **3.** *Horol.* a lever with three projections, two of which intermittently lock and receive impulses from the escape wheel, and one which transmits these impulses to the balance. **4.** a lip or projection on a pawl, that engages with the teeth of a ratchet wheel. **5.** *Gilding.* an instrument used to take up the gold leaves from the pillow, and to apply and extend them. **6.** a platform on which goods are placed for storage or transportation. **7.** a painter's palette. [t. F: m. *palette* PALETTE]

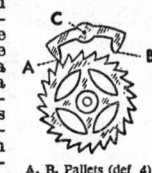

A, B. Pallets (def 4); C, Pivot on which pawl oscillates

pal-lette (pǎl'Yt), *n. Armor.* made pale.

pal-liasse (pǎl yǎs', pǎl'yǎs), *n. Chiefly Brit.* paillasse.

pal-li-ate (pǎl'Y āt'), *v.t.,* **-ated, -ating. 1.** to cause (an offense, etc.) to appear less grave or heinous; extenuate; excuse. **2.** to mitigate or alleviate: *to palliate a disease.* [t. L: m.s. *palliātus,* pp., covered with a cloak] —**pal'-li-a'tion,** *n.* —**pal'li-a'tor,** *n.*

pal-li-a-tive (pǎl'Y ā'tĭv), *adj.* **1.** serving to palliate. —*n.* **2.** something that palliates. —**pal'li-a'tive-ly,** *adv.*

pal-lid (pǎl'Yd), *adj.* pale; deficient in color; wan. [t. L: s. *pallidus*] —**pal'lid-ly,** *adv.* —**pal'lid-ness,** *n.* —**Syn.** See **pale[1].**

pal-li-um (pǎl'Y əm), *n., pl.* **pallia** (pǎl'Y ə), **palliums. 1.** *Rom. Antiq.* a voluminous rectangular mantle worn by men, esp. by philosophers. **2.** *Eccles.* **a.** a woolen vestment worn by the Pope and conferred by him on archbishops, consisting, in its present form, of a narrow ringlike band, which rests upon the shoulders, with two dependent bands or lappets, one in front and one behind. **b.** an altar cloth; a pall. **3.** *Anat.* the entire cortex of the cerebrum. **4.** *Zool.* a mantle. [OE, t. L. See PALL[1]]

Pall Mall (pěl' měl', pǎl' mǎl'), a street in London, England, famed for its clubs. [see PALL-MALL (def. 2)]

pall-mall (pěl'měl'), *n.* **1.** a game formerly played in which a ball of boxwood was struck with a mallet, the object being to drive it through a raised iron ring at the end of an alley. **2.** an alley in which this game was played. [t. F (obs.): m. *pallemaille,* t. It.: m. *pallamaglio* the game, f. *palla* ball (of Gmc. orig.; akin to BALL[1]) + *maglio* mallet, g. L *malleus* hammer]

pal-lor (pǎl'ər), *n.* unnatural paleness, as from fear, ill health, or death; wanness. [t. L]

palm[1] (päm), *n.* **1.** that part of the inner surface of the hand which extends from the wrist to the bases of the fingers. **2.** the corresponding part of the forefoot of an animal. **3.** the part of a glove covering the palm. **4.** a metal shield worn over the palm of the hand by sailmakers to serve instead of a thimble. **5.** a linear measure based on either the breadth of the hand (3 to 4 inches) or its length from wrist to fingertips (7 to 10 inches). **6.** the flat, expanded part of the horn or antler of some deer. **7.** a flat, widened part at the end of an armlike projection. **8.** the blade of an oar. —*v.t.* **9.** to conceal in the palm, as in cheating at cards or dice or in juggling. **10.** to pass fraudulently or deceptively (fol. by *off*). **11.** to impose (something) fraudulently (fol. by *on* or *upon*): *He tried to palm off the broken watch on me.* **12.** to touch or stroke with the palm or hand. **13.** to shake hands with. [t. L: s. *palma* palm, hand, blade of an oar; r. ME *paume,* t. OF, g. L]

---

b., blend of, blended; c., cognate with; d., dialect, dialectal; der., derived from; f., formed from; g., going back to; m., modification of; r., replacing; s., stem of; t., taken from; ?, perhaps. See the full key on inside cover.

palm² (päm), *n.* **1.** any of the plants constituting the large and important *Palmaceae* family, the majority of which are tall, unbranched trees surmounted by a crown of large pinnate or palmately cleft (fan-shaped) leaves. **2.** any of various other trees or shrubs which resemble the palm. **3.** a leaf or branch of a palm tree, esp. as formerly borne as an emblem of victory or as used on festal occasions. **4.** a representation of such a leaf or branch, as on a decoration of honor. **5.** the victor's reward of honor. **6.** victory; triumph. [ME and OE, t. L: s. *palma* palm tree, etymologically identical with PALM¹] —**palm**/like/, *adj.*

Pal·ma (päl′mä), *n.* **1.** a seaport in and the capital of the Balearic Islands, on W Majorca. 147,393 (est. 1955). **2.** one of the Canary Islands, off the NW coast of Africa. 67,225 pop. (1950); 281 sq. mi. *Cap.:* Santa Cruz de la Palma.

pal·ma·ceous (päl mā′shəs), *adj.* belonging to the palm family of plants.

Palma de Mallorca, Palma (def. 1).

pal·mar päl′mər), *adj.* pertaining to the palm of the hand, or to the corresponding part of the forefoot of an animal. [t. L: s. *palmāris*]

Pal·mas (päl′mäs), *n.* **Las** (läs). See **Las Palmas**.

pal·mate (päl′māt, -mĭt), *adj.* **1.** shaped like an open palm, or like a hand with the fingers extended, as a leaf or an antler. **2.** *Bot.* lobed or divided so that the sinuses point to or reach the apex of the petiole, somewhat irrespective of the number of lobes. **3.** *Zool.* web-footed. Also, **pal′·mat·ed.** [t. L: m.s. *palmātus*] —**pal′mate·ly,** *adv.*

Palmate leaf

pal·ma·tion (päl mā′shən), *n.* **1.** palmate state or formation. **2.** a palmate structure.

Palm Beach (päm), a town in SE Florida: seaside winter resort. 6,055 (1960).

palm cat, any of various viverrine animals of southeastern Asia, the East Indies, etc., chiefly arboreal in habit, about the size of the domestic cat, and having a spotted or striped fur and a long curled tail. Also, **palm civet.**

palm·er¹ (pä′mər), *n.* a pilgrim who had returned from the Holy Land, in token of which he bore a palm branch. [ME *palmere,* der. PALM²; translating AF *palmer,* ML *palmārius,* der. L *palma* PALM²]

palm·er² (pä′mər), *n.* one who palms something, as in cheating at cards. [f. PALM¹, v. + -ER¹]

Palm·er (pä′mər), *n.* George Herbert, 1842–1933, U.S. educator, philosopher, and author.

Palmer Peninsula, a large peninsula of Antarctica, S of South America: a dependency of the Falkland Islands. Also, **Graham Land.**

Palm·er·ston (pä′mər stən), *n.* **Henry John Temple, 3rd Viscount,** 1784–1865, British statesman: prime minister, 1855–58 and 1859–65.

palmer worm, the larva of the tineid moth *Ypsilophus ligulellus,* which in eastern parts of the U.S. appears on the leaves of the apple in June, draws them together, and skeletonizes them. [f. PALMER¹ + WORM]

pal·met·to (päl mĕt′ō), *n., pl.* **-tos, -toes.** any of various species of palm with fan-shaped leaves such as *Sabal, Serenoa, Thrinax,* etc. [t. Sp.: m. *palmito,* dim. of *palma,* g. L *palma* PALM²]

palm·is·try (pä′mĭs trĭ), *n.* the art or practice of telling fortunes and interpreting character by the lines and configurations of the palm of the hand. [ME *pawmestry, palmestrie,* appar. der. *palmester* chiromancer, f. *palme* PALM¹ + -STER] —**palm·ist** (pä′mĭst), *n.*

pal·mi·tate (päl′mə tāt′), *n. Chem.* a salt or ester of palmitic acid.

pal·mit·ic acid (päl mĭt′ĭk), *Chem.* a white crystalline acid, $C_{15}H_{31}COOH$, occurring as a glyceride in palm oil and in most solid fats.

pal·mi·tin (päl′mə tĭn), *n.* a colorless fatty substance, $(C_{15}H_{31}COO)_3C_3H_5$, the glyceride of palmitic acid, occurring in palm oil and solid fats, and used in soap manufacture. [t. F: m. *palmitine,* der. L *palma* PALM²]

palm oil, **1.** a yellow, butterlike oil from the fruit of *Elaeis guineensis,* of western Africa, used by the natives as food, and employed also for making soap, candles, etc. **2.** oil obtained from various species of palm.

palm sugar, sugar from the sap of certain palm trees.

Palm Sunday, the Sunday next before Easter, celebrated in commemoration of Christ's triumphal entry into Jerusalem.

palm·y (pä′mĭ), *adj.,* **palmier, palmiest. 1.** glorious, prosperous, or flourishing. **2.** abounding in or shaded with palms; *palmy islands.* **3.** palmlike.

pal·my·ra (päl mī′rə), *n.* a tropical Asian fan palm, *Borassus flabellifer.* Also, **palmyra palm.** [t. Pg.: m. *palmeira,* der. L *palma* PALM²]

Pal·my·ra (päl mī′rə), *n.* **1.** an ancient city in Syria, NE of Damascus: reputedly built by Solomon. Biblical name, **Tadmor. 2.** an atoll in the central Pacific, belonging to the U.S.: airfield. 1½ sq. mi.

Pal·o Al·to (päl′ō äl′tō *for 1;* pä′lō äl′tō *for 2*), **1.** a city in W California, SE of San Francisco. 52,287 (1960). **2.** a battlefield in S Texas, near Brownsville: the first battle of the Mexican War was fought here, 1846.

pal·o·mi·no (päl′ə mē′nō), *n., pl.* **-nos.** a tan or cream-colored horse, bred chiefly in the SW United States. [t. Sp.]

Pa·los (pä′lôs), *n.* a seaport in SW Spain: starting point of Columbus' first voyage westward. 2280 (1950).

palp (pälp), *n.* a palpus. [t. F: m. *palpe,* t. L: m. *palpus* a feeler]

pal·pa·ble (päl′pə bəl), *adj.* **1.** readily or plainly seen, heard, perceived, etc.; obvious: *a palpable lie.* **2.** that can be touched or felt; tangible. **3.** *Med.* perceptible by palpation. [ME, t. LL: m.s. *palpābilis,* der. L *palpāre* touch] —**pal′pa·bil′i·ty,** *n.* —**pal′pa·bly,** *adv.*

pal·pate¹ (päl′pāt), *v.t.* **-pated, -pating.** to examine by the sense of touch, esp. in medicine. [t. L: m.s. *palpātus,* pp., touched, stroked] —**pal·pa′tion,** *n.*

pal·pate² (päl′pāt), *adj. Zool.* having a palpus or palpi. [f. s. L *palpus* a feeler + -ATE¹]

pal·pe·bral (päl′pə brəl), *adj.* of or pertaining to the eyelids. [t. LL: s. *palpebrālis*]

pal·pi (päl′pī), *n. pl.* of **palpus.**

pal·pi·tant (päl′pə tənt), *adj.* palpitating. [t. L: s. *palpitans,* ppr.]

pal·pi·tate (päl′pə tāt′), *v.i.* **-tated, -tating. 1.** to pulsate with unnatural rapidity, as the heart, from exertion, emotion, disease, etc. **2.** to quiver or tremble. [t. L: m.s. *palpitātus,* pp., moved quickly] —**Syn. 1.** See **pulsate.**

pal·pi·ta·tion (päl′pə tā′shən), *n.* **1.** act of palpitating. **2.** rapid or violent beating of the heart.

pal·pus (päl′pəs), *n., pl.* **-pi** (-pī). an appendage attached to an oral part, and serving as an organ of sense, in insects, crustaceans, etc. [t. NL, t. L: a feeler]

pals·grave (pôlz′grāv′, pälz′-), *n.* a German count palatine. [t. D: m. *paltsgrave* (now *paltsgraaf*), c. G *pfalzgraf* palace count]

pals·gra·vine (pôlz′grə vēn′, pälz′-), *n.* the wife or widow of a palsgrave.

pal·sy (pôl′zĭ), *n., pl.* **-sies,** *v.,* **-sied, -sying.** —*n.* **1.** paralysis. —*v.t.* **2.** to paralyze. [ME *parlesie,* t. OF: m. *paralisie,* g. L *paralysis* PARALYSIS] —**pal′sied,** *adj.*

pal·ter (pôl′tər), *v.i.* **1.** to talk or act insincerely; equivocate; deal crookedly. **2.** to haggle. **3.** to trifle. [cf. obs. *palter* mumble, shuffle, b. PALSY and FALTER]

pal·try (pôl′trĭ), *adj.,* **-trier, -triest. 1.** trifling; petty: *a paltry sum.* **2.** trashy or worthless: *paltry rags.* **3.** mean or contemptible: *a paltry coward.* [appar. der. d. *palt* rubbish. Cf. LG *paltrig*] —**pal′tri·ly,** *adv.* —**pal′tri·ness,** *n.* —**Syn. 1.** See **petty.**

pa·lu·dal (pə loo′dəl, päl′yə-), *adj.* **1.** of or pertaining to marshes. **2.** produced by marshes, as miasma or disease. [f. s. L *palus* marsh + -AL¹]

pal·u·dism (päl′yə dĭz′əm), *n. Pathol.* malarial disease.

pal·y¹ (pä′lĭ), *adj. Chiefly Poetic.* pale. [f. PALE¹ + -Y¹]

pal·y² (pä′lĭ), *adj. Her.* divided palewise, or vertically, into equal parts of alternating tinctures. [t. F: m. *palé,* der. *pal* PALE² (see def. 7)]

pam (päm), *n. Cards.* **1.** the knave of clubs, esp. in a form of loo in which it is the best trump. **2.** the game. [for F *pamphile,* orig. proper name, t. Gk.: m. *Pámphilos,* lit., beloved of all]

pam., pamphlet.

Pam·e·la (päm′ə lə), *n.* a novel in letter form by Samuel Richardson, sometimes called the first English novel (1740).

Pa·mirs (pä mĭrz′), *n.pl.* **The,** a lofty plateau in central Asia, where the Hindu Kush, Tien Shan, and Himalayan mountain systems converge. Highest peaks, ab. 25,000 ft. Also, **Pa·mir′.**

Pam·li·co Sound (päm′lĭ kō′), a sound between the North Carolina mainland and coastal islands.

pam·pas (päm′pəz; *attributively* päm′pəs; Sp. päm′-päs), *n. pl.* the vast grassy plains lying in the rain shadow of the Andes and south of the forested lowlands of the Amazon basin, esp. in Argentina. ab. 400 mi. across. [t. Sp., pl. of *pampa,* t. Peruvian] —**pam·pe·an** (päm-pē′ən, päm′pĭ ən), *adj.*

pampas grass, a tall ornamental grass, *Cortaderia Selloana,* native in South America but widely cultivated, having large, thick, feathery, silvery-white panicles.

Pam·pe·lu·na (päm′pĕ loo′nä), *n.* Pamplona.

pam·per (päm′pər), *v.t.* **1.** to indulge (a person, etc.) to the full or to excess: *to pamper a child, one's appetite, etc.* **2.** to indulge with rich food, comforts, etc. [ME *pampren.* Cf. Flem. *pamperen,* G *pampen* cram] —**pam′per·er,** *n.* —**Syn. 1.** gratify, humor, coddle.

pam·pe·ro (päm pâr′ō; Sp. -pě′rō), *n., pl.* **-ros** (-rōz; *Sp.* -rōs). a cold and dry southwesterly wind that sweeps over the pampas of Argentina and northeastward to the Brazilian coast, in the rear of barometric depression. [t. Sp.]

pamph., pamphlet.

pam·phlet (päm′flĭt), *n.* **1.** a short treatise or essay, generally controversial, on some subject of temporary interest: *a political pamphlet.* **2.** a complete publication generally less than 80 pages, stitched and usually enclosed in paper covers. [ME *pamflet,* syncopated var. of *Pamphilet,* popular name for ML poem formally entitled *Pamphilus, seu dē Amōre*]

pam·phlet·eer (päm′flə tĭr′), *n.* **1.** a writer of pamphlets. —*v.i.* **2.** to write and issue pamphlets.

Pam·phyl·i·a (păm fĭl′ĭ ə), *n.* an ancient country and Roman province in S Asia Minor.

Pam·plo·na (păm plō′nä). *n.* a city in N Spain. 78,467 (est. 1955).

pan[1] (păn), *n.*, *v.*, **panned, panning. —*n.* 1.** a dish commonly of metal, usually broad and shallow and often open, used for domestic purposes: *a frying pan.* **2.** any dishlike receptacle or part, as the scales of a balance. **3.** any of various open or closed vessels used in industrial or mechanical processes. **4.** *Metall.* a vessel, usually of cast iron, in which the ores of silver are ground and amalgamated. **5.** a vessel in which gold or other heavy, valuable metals are separated from gravel, etc., by agitation with water. **6.** a depression in the ground, as a natural one containing water, mud, or mineral salts, or an artificial one for evaporating salt water to make salt. **7.** hardpan. **8.** (in old guns) the depressed part of the lock, which holds the priming. —*v.t.* **9.** to wash (auriferous gravel, sand, etc.) in a pan to separate the gold or other heavy valuable metal. **10.** to separate by such washing. **11.** to cook (oysters, etc.) in a pan. **12.** *Colloq.* to criticize or reprimand severely. **13.** *U.S. Colloq.* to get or obtain. —*v.i.* **14.** *Colloq.* to succeed; turn out well (fol. by *out*). **15.** to wash gravel, etc., in a pan, seeking for gold. **16.** to yield gold, as gravel washed in a pan. [ME and OE *panne*, c. G *pfanne*]

pan[2] (păn), *n.* **1.** the leaf of the betel. **2.** the masticatory of which the betel leaf comprises the wrapper. See **betel.** [t. Hind., g. Skt. *parna* feather, leaf]

Pan (păn), *n.* *Gk. Myth.* the god of forests, pastures, flocks, and shepherds, represented with the head, chest, and arms of a man, and the legs and sometimes the horns and ears of a goat.

pan-, a word element or prefix meaning "all," first occurring in words from the Greek, but now used freely as a general formative in English and other languages, esp. in terms implying the union, association, or consideration together, as forming a whole, of all the branches of a race, people, church, or other body, as in *Pan-Anglo-Saxon*, *Pan-Celtic*, *Pan-Christian*, *Pan-Presbyterian*, and other like words of obvious meaning, formed at will, and tending with longer use to lose the hyphen and the second capital, unless these are retained in order to set off clearly the component elements. [t. Gk., comb. form of *pâs* (neut. *pân*)]

Pan., Panama.

pan·a·ce·a (păn′ə sē′ə), *n.* a remedy for all diseases; cure-all. [t. L, t. Gk.: m. *panákeia*] —**pan′a·ce′an,** *adj.*

pa·nache (pə năsh′, -näsh′), *n.* an ornamental plume or tuft of feathers, esp. one worn on a helmet or on a cap. [t. F, t. It.: m. *pennacchio*, der. *penna*, g. L: feather]

pa·na·da (pə nä′də, -nä′-), *n.* a dish made of bread boiled and flavored. [t. Sp., Pr., ult. der. L *pánis* bread]

Pan·a·ma (păn′ə mä′; *Sp.* pä′/nä mä′), *n.* **1.** a republic in S Central America, enclosing, but not including, the Panama Canal. 934,000 (est. 1956); 28,575 sq. mi. **2.** Also, **Panama City.** the capital of Panama, at the Pacific end of the Panama Canal, though not in the Canal Zone. 127,874 (1950). **3. Isthmus of,** (formerly, **Isthmus of Darien**) an isthmus between North and South America. Least width, ab. 30 mi. **4. Gulf of,** the portion of the Pacific in the bend of the Isthmus of Panama. **5.** (*l.c.*) Panama hat. —**Pan·a·ma·ni·an** (păn′ə mä′nĭ ən, -mä′-), *adj., n.*

Panama Canal, a canal extending SE from the Atlantic to the Pacific across the Isthmus of Panama. 40 mi. long.

Panama Canal Zone, Canal Zone.

Panama City, a city in NW Florida. 33,275 (1960).

Panama hat, a fine plaited hat made of the young leaves of a palmlike plant, *Carludovica palmata*, of Central and South America. [named after **Panama**]

Pan-A·mer·i·can (păn′ə mĕr′ə kən), *adj.* of all the countries or people of North, Central, and South America.

Pan-A·mer·i·can·ism (păn′ə mĕr′ə kə nĭz′əm), *n.* the idea or advocacy of a political alliance or union of all the countries of North, Central, and South America.

Pan American Union, an organization of the 21 American republics to further understanding and peace.

Pa·nay (pä nī′), *n.* one of the Philippine Islands, in the central part of the group. 1,310,174 pop. (1948); 4446 sq. mi. *Cap.:* Iloilo.

pan·cake (păn′kāk′), *n.*, *v.*, **-caked, -caking. —*n.* 1.** a flat cake of batter cooked in a pan or on a griddle; a griddlecake; a flapjack. **2.** an airplane landing made by pancaking. —*v.i.* **3.** (of an airplane, etc.) to drop flat to the ground after leveling off a few feet above the ground. —*v.t.* **4.** to cause (an airplane) to pancake.

pan·chro·mat·ic (păn′krō măt′ĭk), *adj.* sensitive to light of all colors, as a photographic film or plate.

pan·cra·ti·um (păn krā′shĭ əm), *n.*, *pl.* **-tia** (-shĭ ə). *Gk. Antiq.* an athletic contest combining wrestling and boxing. [t. L, t. Gk.: m. *pankrátion* complete contest] —**pan·crat·ic** (păn krăt′ĭk), *adj.*

pan·cre·as (păn′krĭ əs, păng′-), *n. Anat., Zool.* a gland situated near the stomach, secreting an important digestive fluid (**pancreatic juice**), discharged into the intestine by one or more ducts. Certain groups of cells (**Islets of Langerhans**) also produce a hormone, insulin. An animal's pancreas, used as food, is called **sweetbread.** [t. NL, t. Gk.: m. *pánkreas* sweetbread] —**pan·cre·at·ic** (păn′krĭ ăt′ĭk, păng′-), *adj.*

pan·cre·a·tin (păn′krĭ ə tĭn, păng′-), *n.* **1.** *Biochem.* a preparation containing all the enzymes of the pancreatic juice. **2.** a commercial preparation of the enzymes in the pancreas of animals, used as a digestive.

pan·cre·a·tot·o·my (păn′krĭ ə tŏt′ə mĭ, păng′-), *n.*, *pl.* **-mies.** *Surg.* the operation of removing part or all of the pancreas.

pan·da (păn′də), *n.* **1.** Also, **lesser panda.** a carnivore, *Aelurus fulgens*, of the Himalayas, somewhat larger than a cat, and having reddish-brown fur darker beneath, face marked with white, and a long, bushy tail marked with pale rings. **2.** Also, **giant panda.** a large bearlike carnivore, *Ailuropoda melanoleuca*, of Tibet and southern China, white with black limbs, shoulders, and ears, and a black ring around each eye, little known in captivity before 1936. [said to be the name (for the animal) current in Nepal]

Giant panda, *Ailuropoda melanoleuca* (5 ft. long, 2 ft. high at the shoulder)

pan·da·na·ceous (păn′də nā′shəs), *adj.* belonging to the *Pandanaceae*, or pandanus family of trees and shrubs.

pan·da·nus (păn dā′nəs). *n.* any plant of the genus *Pandanus*, comprising tropical trees and shrubs, esp. of the islands of the Malay Archipelago and the Indian and Pacific oceans, having a palmlike or branched stem, long, narrow, rigid, spirally arranged leaves, and aerial roots, and bearing edible fruit; a screw pine. [t. NL, t. Malay: m. *pandan*]

Pan·da·rus (păn′də rəs), *n. Gk. Legend.* a leader of the Lycians and an ally of the Trojans in the siege of Troy. In Chaucer, other medieval accounts, and Shakespeare, he is represented as the procurer of Cressida for Troilus.

Pan·de·an (păn dē′ən), *adj.* of or pertaining to the god Pan: *Pandean pipes (Panpipe).*

pan·dect (păn′dĕkt), *n.* **1.** (*pl.*) a complete body or code of laws. **2.** a comprehensive digest. **3. Pandects,** *Rom. Law.* the Digest. [t. L: s. *pandecta*, *pandectēs*, t. Gk.: m. *pandéktēs*, lit., all-receiver]

pan·dem·ic (păn dĕm′ĭk), *adj.* **1.** (of a disease) prevalent throughout an entire country or continent, or the whole world. **2.** general; universal. —*n.* **3.** a pandemic disease. [f. s. Gk. *pandēmos* public, common + -ɪᴄ]

pan·de·mo·ni·um (păn′də mō′nĭ əm), *n.* **1.** (*often cap.*) the abode of all the demons. **2.** hell. **3.** a place of riotous uproar or lawless confusion. **4.** wild lawlessness or uproar. [orig. *Pandaemonium*, Milton's name for the capital of hell. See ᴘᴀɴ-, ᴅᴇᴍᴏɴ, -ɪᴜᴍ]

pan·der (păn′dər), *n.* **1.** a go-between in intrigues of love; a pimp. **2.** one who ministers to the baser passions of others. —*v.t.* **3.** to act as a pander for. —*v.i.* **4.** to act as a pander; cater basely. [var. of *pandar*, generalized use of ME *Pandare* ᴘᴀɴᴅᴀʀᴜs. Cf. Shakespeare's *Troilus and Cressida*, III. 2. 210] —**pan′der·er,** *n.*

Pan·do·ra (păn dōr′ə), *n. Class. Myth.* the first mortal woman, on whom all the gods and goddesses bestowed gifts. She was given by Zeus to Epimetheus to bring misery to mankind because Prometheus had stolen fire from heaven. [t. L, t. Gk.: lit., all-gifted]

pan·do·ra (păn dōr′ə), *n.* bandore. Also, **pan·dore** (păn dōr′, dōr).

Pandora's box, *Class. Myth.* a box or jar, the gift of Zeus to Pandora, containing all human ills, which escaped when she opened it. According to a later version, the box contained all the blessings of the gods, which would have been preserved for the human race had not Pandora opened it, thus letting all the blessings escape, with the exception of hope.

pan·dour (păn′dōōr), *n.* **1.** one of a force of merciless soldiers raised in the 18th century in Croatia, later made a regiment in the Austrian army. **2.** a brutal, marauding soldier. [t. F, t. Hung.: m. *pandúr* infantryman]

pan·dow·dy (păn dou′dĭ), *n.*, *pl.* **-dies.** *U.S.* a pudding or deep pie made with apples, and usually sweetened with molasses.

pan·du·rate (păn′dyə rāt′), *adj.* shaped like a fiddle, as a leaf. Also, **pan·du·ri·form** (păn dyōōr′ə fôrm′, -dōōr′-). [f. s. LL *pandura* (see ᴮᴬɴᴅᴼᴿᴱ) + -ᴀᴛᴇ[1]]

Pandurate leaf

pan·dy (păn′dĭ), *n.*, *pl.* **-dies**, *v.*, **-died, -dying.** *Chiefly Scot.* —*n.* **1.** a stroke on the palm with a cane or strap as a punishment in schools. —*v.t.* **2.** to strike thus. [said to be t. L: m. *pande*, impv., stretch out]

pane (pān), *n.* **1.** one of the divisions of a window, etc., consisting of a single plate of glass in a frame. **2.** a plate of glass for such a division. **3.** a panel, as of a wainscot, ceiling, door, etc. **4.** a flat section, side, or surface, as one of the sides of a bolthead. [ME *pan*, t. OF, g. L *pannus* a cloth, rag]

paned (pānd), *adj.* having panes: *a diamond-paned window.*

pan·e·gyr·ic (păn′ə jĭr′ĭk), *n.* **1.** an oration, dis-

course, or writing in praise of a person or thing; a eulogy. **2.** a formal or elaborate encomium. [t. L: s. *panēgyricus*, t. Gk.: m. *panēgyrikós* festival oration, prop. **adj.**] —**pan·e·gyr·i·cal,** *adj.* —**pan·e·gyr·i·cal·ly,** *adv.*

pan·e·gyr·ist (păn'ə jĭr'ĭst, păn'ə jĭr'ĭst), *n.* one who panegyrizes; a eulogist.

pan·e·gy·rize (păn'ə jə rīz'), *v.,* -**rized,** -**rizing.** —*v.t.* **1.** to pronounce or write a panegyric upon; eulogize. —*v.i.* **2.** to indulge in panegyric; bestow praises.

pan·el (păn'əl), *n.. v.,* -**eled,** -**eling** or (*esp. Brit.*) -**elled,** -**elling.** —*n.* **1.** a distinct portion or division of a wainscot, ceiling, door, shutter, etc., or of any surface sunk below or raised above the general level, or enclosed by a frame or border. **2.** a pane, as in a window. **3.** a comparatively thin, flat piece of wood or the like. **4.** *Painting.* **a.** a flat piece of wood of varying kinds on which a picture is painted. **b.** a picture painted on such a piece of wood. **5.** a photograph much longer in one dimension than the other. **6.** a broad strip of the same or another material set vertically, as for ornament, in or on a woman's skirt. **7.** the section between the two bands on the backbone of a bound book. **8.** *Elect.* a division of a switchboard containing a set of related cords, jacks, relays, etc. **9.** the portion of a truss between adjacent chord joints. **10.** *Law.* **a.** the list of persons summoned for service as jurors. **b.** the body of persons composing a jury. **c.** *Scot. Law.* the person or persons indicted and brought to trial. **11.** any list or group of persons: *a panel to lead a public discussion.* **12.** *Brit.* (in a system of health insurance) a list of doctors to whom the patients may go. **13.** *Aeron.* **a.** a lateral subdivision of an airfoil with internal girder construction. **b.** a section of the hull of a rigid airship marked off by a set of transverse and lateral girders. **14.** *Mining.* an area of a coal seam, separated for mining purposes from adjacent areas by extra thick masses or ribs of coal. **15.** a pad placed under a saddle. **16.** a pad or the like serving as a saddle. **17.** a slip of parchment. —*v.t.* **18.** to arrange in, or furnish with, panels. **19.** to ornament with a panel or panels. **20.** to set in a frame as a panel. **21.** to select (a jury). **22.** *Scot. Law.* to bring to trial. [ME *panel,* t. OF: piece (of anything), ult. der. L *pannus* rag]

panel discussion, an organized discussion, the topic, speakers, etc., being selected beforehand.

pan·el·ing (păn'əl ĭng), *n.* **1.** wood or other material made into panels. **2.** panels collectively. Also, *esp. Brit.,* **pan·el·ling.**

pan·el·ist (păn'əl ĭst), *n.* member of a small group organized for public discussion, etc., as on television.

pan·e·tel·la (păn'ə těl'ə), *n.* a long slender cigar pointed at the end intended for the mouth. [t. Sp.]

pan fish, a fish suitable for frying whole in a pan.

pang (păng), *n.* **1.** a sudden feeling of mental distress. **2.** a sudden, brief, sharp pain, or a spasm or severe twinge of pain: *the pangs of hunger.* [orig. uncert.]

pan·gen·e·sis (păn jĕn'ə sĭs), *n.* *Biol.* a theory advanced by Darwin, according to which a reproductive cell or body contains gemmules or invisible germs which were derived from the individual cells from every part of the organism, and which are the bearers of hereditary attributes. —**pan·ge·net·ic** (păn'jə nĕt'ĭk), *adj.*

Pan-Ger·man·ism (păn'jûr'mə nĭz'əm), *n.* the idea or advocacy of a union of all the German peoples in one political organization or state. —**Pan'-Ger'man,** *adj., n.* —**Pan-Ger·man·ic** (păn'jər măn'ĭk), *adj.*

pan·go·lin (păng gō'lĭn), *n.* any of the scaly anteaters of Africa and tropical Asia, constituting an order of mammals, *Pholidota,* having a covering of broad, overlapping, horny scales. [t. Malay: m. *penggōling* roller]

pan·han·dle¹ (păn'hăn'dəl), *n.* **1.** the handle of a pan. **2.** *U.S.* a narrow projecting strip of land, esp. (*cap.*) part of a State: *the Panhandle of West Virginia, Texas, Oklahoma,* or *Idaho.*

Pangolin, *Smutsia temminckii* (Total length 30 in., tail 14 in.)

pan·han·dle² (păn'hăn'dəl), *v.i.,* -**dled,** -**dling.** *Colloq.* to beg (usually on the street). —**pan'han'dler,** *n.*

Pan·hel·len·ic (păn'hə lĕn'ĭk), *adj.* **1.** pertaining to all Greeks or to Panhellenism. **2.** of or pertaining to collegiate fraternities and sororities. Also, **pan'hel·len'ic.**

Pan·hel·len·ism (păn hĕl'ə nĭz'əm), *n.* the idea or principle of a union of all Greeks in one political body. —**Pan·hel'len·ist,** *n.*

pan·ic¹ (păn'ĭk), *n., adj., v.,* -**icked,** -**icking.** —*n.* **1.** demoralizing terror, with or without clear cause, often as affecting a group of persons or animals. **2.** an instance, outbreak, or period of such fear. **3.** *Finance.* a sudden widespread fear concerning financial affairs leading to credit contraction and widespread sale of securities at depressed prices in an effort to acquire cash. —*adj.* **4.** (of fear, terror, etc.) suddenly destroying the self-control and impelling to some frantic action. **5.** of the nature of, due to, or showing panic: *panic haste.* **6.** (*cap.*) of or pertaining to the god Pan. —*v.t.* **7.** to affect with panic. **8.** *Theat. Slang.* to keep (an audience or the like) highly amused. —*v.i.* **9.** to be stricken with panic. [t. F: m. *panique,* t. L: m. *pānicus,* t. Gk.: m. *Panikós* pertaining to or caused by Pan] —**pan·ick·y,** *adj.* —**pan·ic-strick·en** (păn'ĭk strĭk'ən), **pan·ic-struck** (păn'ĭk-strŭk'), *adj.* —**Syn. 1.** See **terror.**

pan·ic² (păn'ĭk), *n.* **1.** any grass of the genus *Panicum,* many species of which bear edible grain. **2.** the grain. Also, **panic grass.** [OE, t. L: s. *pānicum*]

pan·i·cle (păn'ə kəl), *n. Bot.* **1.** a compound raceme. **2.** any loose, diversely branching flower cluster. [t. L: m.s. *pānicula* tuft on plants, dim. of *pānus* swelling, ear of millet]

pa·nic·u·late (pə nĭk'yə lāt', -lĭt), *adj. Bot.* arranged in panicles. —**pa·nic'u·late'ly,** *adv.*

Pan-Is·lam·ism (păn'ĭs'lə mĭz'əm), *n.* the idea or advocacy of a union of all Mohammedan nations in one political body. —**Pan-Is·lam·ic** (păn'ĭs lăm'ĭk, -lä'mĭk), *adj.*

Branch with panicles

Pan·ja·bi (pŭn jä'bĭ), *n., pl.* -**bis.** **1.** Punjabi. **2.** the Indic language used in the Punjab.

pan·jan·drum (păn jăn'drəm), *n.* a mock title for any important or pretentious official. [a made word, with prefix PAN- and termination simulating Latin; appar. first used by Samuel Foote (1720-77), English dramatist and actor]

Pan·mun·jon (păn'mŏŏn'jŏn'), *n.* a small community along the boundary between North Korea and South Korea: site of the truce talks at the close of the Korean War.

panne (păn), *n.* a soft, lustrous, lightweight velvet with flattened pile. [t. F, g. L *penna* feather]

pan·nier (păn'yər, -ĭr), *n.* **1.** a basket, esp. one of considerable size, for carrying provisions, etc. **2.** a basket for carrying on a person's back, or one of a pair to be slung across the back of a beast of burden. **3.** a puffed arrangement of drapery about the hips. **4.** a framework formerly used for distending the skirt of a woman's dress at the hips. [ME *panier,* t. OF, g. L *pānārium* basket for bread]

pan·ni·kin (păn'ə kĭn), *n. Chiefly Brit.* a small pan or metal cup.

Pan·no·ni·a (pə nō'nĭ ə), *n.* an ancient country and Roman province in central Europe, S and W of the Danube: now mostly in Hungary and Yugoslavia.

pa·no·cha (pə nō'chə), *n.* **1.** a candy made of brown sugar, butter, and milk, usually with nuts. **2.** a coarse grade of sugar made in Mexico. Also, **pa·no·che** (pə nō'chĭ). [t. Mex. Sp.]

pan·o·ply (păn'ə plĭ), *n., pl.* -**plies.** **1.** a complete suit of armor. **2.** a complete covering or array of something. [t. Gk.: m.s. *panoplia* complete suit of armor] —**pan·o·plied** (păn'ə plĭd), *adj.*

pan·op·tic (păn ŏp'tĭk), *adj.* containing all visible objects within sight. Also, **pan·op'ti·cal.**

pan·o·ram·a (păn'ə răm'ə, -rä'mə), *n.* **1.** an unobstructed view or prospect over a wide area. **2.** an extended pictorial representation of a landscape or other scene, often exhibited a part at a time and made to pass continuously before the spectators. **3.** a continuously passing or changing scene. **4.** a comprehensive survey, as of a subject. [f. PAN- + m. Gk. *hórāma* view] —**pan·o·ram·ic,** *adj.* —**pan·o·ram·i·cal·ly,** *adv.*

panoramic sight, a sight for guns that can be swung in a complete circle.

Pan·pipe (păn'pīp'), *n.* a primitive wind instrument consisting of a series of pipes of graduated length, the tones being produced by blowing across the upper ends. Also, **Pan's pipes.**

Pan-Slav·ism (păn'släv'ĭz əm, -släv'-), *n.* the idea or advocacy of a union of all the Slavic races in one political body. —**Pan'-Slav',** **Pan'-Slav'ic,** *adj.*

pan·so·phism (păn'sə fĭz'əm), *n.* the claim or pretension to pansophy. —**pan'so·phist,** *n.*

Panpipe

pan·so·phy (păn'sə fĭ), *n.* universal wisdom or knowledge. [f. PAN- + m.s. Gk. *sophia* wisdom] —**pan·soph·ic** (păn sŏf'ĭk), *adj.* —**pan·soph'i·cal,** *adj.*

pan·sy (păn'zĭ), *n., pl.* -**sies.** **1.** the plant *Viola tricolor,* a species of violet having many cultivated varieties with large, richly and variously colored flowers. **2.** its blossom. **3.** *U.S. Slang.* an effeminate man. [t. F: m. *pensée* pansy, lit., thought, der. *penser* think. See **PENSIVE**]

pant (pănt), *v.i.* **1.** to breathe hard and quickly, as after exertion. **2.** to emit steam or the like in loud puffs. **3.** to gasp, as for air. **4.** to long with breathless or intense eagerness: *he panted for revenge.* **5.** to throb or heave violently or rapidly; palpitate. —*v.t.* **6.** to breathe or utter gaspingly. —*n.* **7.** act of panting. **8.** a short, quick, labored effort of breathing; a gasp. **9.** a puff, as of an engine. **10.** a throb or heave, as of the breast. [ME *panten;* appar. akin to OF *pantaisier,* prob. (with ref. to the feeling of oppression in nightmare) ult. der. L *phantasia* phantasm, idea, **FANTASY**] —**pant'ing·ly,** *adv.*

—**Syn. 1.** PANT, GASP suggest breathing with more effort than usual. PANT suggests rapid, convulsive breathing, as from violent exertion or excitement: *to pant after a run for the train.* GASP suggests catching one's breath in a single quick intake, as from amazement, terror, and the like or a series of such quick intakes of breath as in painful breathing: *to gasp with horror, to gasp for breath.*

Pan·tag·ru·el (păn tăg'rŏŏ ĕl'; *Fr.* păn tå gry ĕl'), *n.*

(in Rabelais' *Gargantua and Pantagruel*), the huge son of Gargantua, represented as dealing with serious matters in a spirit of broad and somewhat cynical good humor. [t. F] —**Pan·ta·gru·el·i·an** (păn/tə grōō ĕl/Y ən), *adj.* —**Pan·ta·gru·el·ism** (păn/tə grōō/ə lĭz/əm, păn tăg/rōō- ə lĭz/əm), *n.* —**Pan/ta·gru/el·ist,** *n.*

pan·ta·iets (păn/tə lĕts/), *n.pl.* **1.** long drawers with a frill or other finish at the bottom of each leg, and extending below the dress, commonly worn by women and girls in the 19th century. **2.** a pair of separate frilled or trimmed pieces for attaching to the legs of women's drawers. Also, **pan/ta·lettes/.** [alter. of PANTALOON, with dim. -ET(TE) substituted for -*oon*]

pan·ta·loon (păn/tə lōōn/), *n.* **1.** (*pl.*) *In U.S.,* *Archaic except Hist.; in England, Formal.* a man's closely fitting garment for the hips and legs, varying in form at different periods; trousers. **2.** (in the modern pantomime) a foolish, vicious old man, the butt and accomplice of the clown. **3.** (*cap. or l.c.*) (in the early Italian comedy) a lean and foolish old Venetian wearing pantaloons and slippers. [t. F: m. *pantalon,* t. It.: m. *pantalone* buffoon (see def. 3), *Pantalone* a Venetian, from St. *Pantaleone* patron of Venice]

pan·tech·ni·con (păn tĕk/nə kŏn/, -kən), *n.* *Brit.* **1.** a furniture van. **2.** a storage warehouse, esp. for furniture. **3.** *Obs.* a bazaar for everything artistic. [f. PAN- + m. Gk. *technikón* (neut. of *technikós* artistic)]

pan·tel·e·graph (păn tĕl/ə grăf/, -gräf/), *n.* a facsimile telegraph.

Pan·tel·le·ri·a (păn tĕl/lĕ rē/ä), *n.* an Italian island in the Mediterranean between Sicily and Tunisia. 10,306 pop. (1951); 32 sq. mi.

Pan-Teu·ton·ism (păn/tū/tən ĭz/əm, -tōō/-), *n.* Pan-Germanism.

pan·the·ism (păn/thē ĭz/əm), *n.* **1.** the doctrine that God is the transcendent reality of which the material universe and man are only manifestations. It involves a denial of God's personality, and expresses a tendency to identify God and nature. Cf. **theism, deism.** **2.** any religious belief or philosophical doctrine which identifies the universe with God. [f. PAN- + s. Gk. *theós* god + -ISM] —**pan/the·ist,** *n.* —**pan/the·is/tic, pan/the·is/ti·cal,** *adj.* —**pan/the·is/ti·cal·ly,** *adv.*

Pan·the·on (păn/thĭ ŏn/, -ən, păn thē/ən), *n.* **1.** a domed circular temple at Rome, erected A.D. 120–124 by Hadrian using an older porch built by Agrippa 27 B.C., and used as a church since A.D. 609. **2.** (*l.c.*). a public building containing tombs or memorials of the illustrious dead of a nation. **3.** (*l.c.*) a temple dedicated to all the gods. **4.** (*l.c.*) the gods of a particular mythology considered collectively. [ME, t. L, t. Gk.: m. *pántheion,* prop. neut. of *pántheios* of all gods]

pan·ther (păn/thər), *n.,* *pl.* **-thers,** (*esp. collectively*) **-ther.** **1.** the cougar or puma, *Felis concolor.* **2.** the leopard, *Panthera pardus.* [t. L: s. *panthēra,* t. Gk.: m. *pánthēr;* r. ME *pantere* (t. OF) and OE *pandher* (t. L)] —**pan·ther·ess** (păn/thər ĭs), *n.* *fem.*

pan·tile (păn/tĭl/), *n.* a roofing tile straight in its length but curved in its width to overlap the next tile. [f. PAN¹ + TILE, n. Cf. G *pfannenziegel*]

Pantiles

panto-, a word element or prefix synonymous with **pan-.** [t. Gk., comb. form of *pâs,* neut. *pân* all]

pan·to·fle (păn/tə fəl, păn tŏf/əl, -tōō/fəl), *n.* a slipper. Also, **pan/tof·fle.** [t. F: m. *pantoufle,* t. OIt.: m. *pantufola,* var. of Sicilian *pantofola,* t. Gk.: m. *pantóphellos* whole cork, through meaning of cork shoe]

pan·to·graph (păn/tə grăf/, -gräf/), *n.* **1.** an instrument for the mechanical copying of plans, diagrams, etc., upon any desired scale. **2.** *Elect.* a current collector transferring current from an overhead wire to a vehicle, usually consisting of two parallel hinged double-diamond frames with a rotatory bar between them.

pan·tol·o·gy (păn tŏl/ə jĭ), *n.* a systematic view of all human knowledge. —**pan·to·log·ic** (păn/tə- lŏj/Yk), **pan/to·log/i·cal,** *adj.* —**pan·tol/o·gist,** *n.*

pan·to·mime (păn/tə mĭm/), *n., v.,* **-mimed, -miming.** —*n.* **1.** a play or entertainment in which the performers express themselves by mute gestures, often to the accompaniment of music. **2.** a form of theatrical spectacle, common in England during the Christmas season, a feature of which is a harlequinade (now sometimes omitted) including pranks of the clown and pantaloon and dancing of the harlequin and columbine. **3.** an actor in dumb show, as in ancient Rome. **4.** significant gesture without speech. —*v.t.* **5.** to represent or express by pantomime. —*v.i.* **6.** to express oneself by pantomime. [t. L: m.s. *pantomīmus,* t. Gk.: m. *pantómimos,* lit., all-imitating] —**pan·to·mim·ic** (păn/- tə mĭm/Yk), *adj.*

pan·to·mim·ist (păn/tə mĭ/mĭst), *n.* **1.** one who acts in pantomime. **2.** the author of a pantomime.

pan·to·then·ic acid (păn/tə thĕn/Yk), *Biochem.* an oily hydroxy acid, HOCH₂C(CH₃)₂CHOHCONHCH₂- CH₂COOH, found in plant and animal tissues, rice bran, etc., and essential for cell growth.

pan·try (păn/trĭ), *n., pl.* **-tries.** a room or closet in which bread and other provisions, or silverware, dishes, etc., are kept. [ME *panetrie,* t. AF, der. OF *panetier* servant in charge of bread, der. L *pānis* bread]

pants (pănts), *n.pl.* **1.** *U.S. Colloq.* trousers. **2.** *Brit.* drawers. [familiar abbr. of PANTALOONS]

pan·tun (păn tōōn/), *n.* a Malay verse form, usually of four lines, the third rhyming with the first, and the fourth with the second. [t. Malay]

Pan·urge (păn ûrj/; *Fr.* pȧ nyrzh/), *n.* (in Rabelais' *Gargantua and Pantagruel*) an irresistible rascal, companion of Pantagruel. [t. F, t. Gk.: m.s. *panoûrgos* ready to do anything]

Pan·za (păn/zə; *Sp.* pän/thä), *n.* See **Sancho Panza.**

pan·zer (păn/zər; *Ger.* păn/tsər), *adj.* German. armored: *a panzer division.*

Pao·shan (bou/shän/), *n.* a city in SW China, in Yünnan province, on the Burma Road.

Pao·ting (bou/tĭng/), *n.* former name of Tsingyuan.

pap¹ (păp), *n.* **1.** soft food for infants or invalids, as bread soaked in water or milk. **2.** *Slang.* profits or favors secured through official patronage. [ME. Cf. LG *pappe,* ML *pappa*]

pap² (păp), *n.* *Archaic or Dial.* **1.** a teat or nipple. **2.** something resembling a teat or nipple. [ME *pappe.* Cf. d. Norw. and Sw. *pappe*]

pa·pa¹ (pä/pə, pə pä/), *n.* father. [t. F, t. L. Cf. It. *pappa,* Gk. *páppas*]

pa·pa² (pä/pä), *n.* papas.

pa·pa·cy (pä/pə sĭ), *n., pl.* **-cies.** **1.** the office, dignity, or jurisdiction of the Pope (of Rome). **2.** the system of ecclesiastical government in which the Pope is recognized as the supreme head. **3.** the time during which a Pope is in office. **4.** the succession or line of the Popes. [ME, t. ML: m.s. *pāpātia,* der. *pāpa* pope. See PAPAS]

pa·pa·in (pə pā/Yn, pä/pə-), *n.* **1.** *Chem.* a proteolytic enzyme contained in the fruit of the papaya tree, *Carica Papaya.* **2.** a commercial preparation of this, used as a digestant. [f. PAPA(YA) + -IN²]

pa·pal (pä/pəl), *adj.* of or pertaining to the Pope, the papacy, or the Roman Catholic Church. [ME, t. ML: s. *pāpālis,* der. *pāpa* pope. See PAPAS]

papal cross, a cross with three horizontal crosspieces. See **cross.**

Papal States, a large district in central Italy ruled as a temporal domain by the Popes from 755 until the final unification of Italy in 1870: partially annexed by Italy, 1860. Also, **States of the Church.**

pa·pas (pä/päs), *n.* **1.** *Gk. Ch.* a parish priest. **2.** the Pope (of Rome or Alexandria). Also, **papa.** [t. ML: pope, LL bishop, t. Gk.: m. *páppas* father (orig. in childish use). See POPE]

pa·pav·er·a·ceous (pə păv/ə rā/shəs), *adj.* belonging to the *Papaveraceae,* or poppy family of plants, a large group of medicinal importance as the source of opium. [f. L *papāver* poppy + -ACEOUS]

pa·pav·er·ine (pə păv/ə rēn/, -ər Yn, pə pā/və-), *n.* a fine, odorless, crystalline, white alkaloid, C₂₀H₂₁NO₄, derived from opium, which relaxes the involuntary muscles of the gastrointestinal tract, and other smooth muscles. Also, **pa·pav·er·in** (pə păv/ər Yn, pə pā/və-).

pa·paw (pô/pô, pə pô/), *n.* **1.** the small fleshy fruit of the temperate North American bush or small tree, *Asimina triloba.* **2.** the tree itself. Also, **pawpaw, f.** Sp. See PAPAYA]

pa·pa·ya (pə pä/yə), *n.* **1.** the large yellow melonlike fruit of the tropical American shrub or small tree, *Carica Papaya,* of the family *Caricaceae,* much prized for its palatable fruits containing a digestive principle. **2.** the tree itself, which is herbaceous. [t. Sp.: *papaya* the fruit, m. *papayo* the tree; of Carib orig.]

Pa·pe·e·te (pä/pY ā/tā), *n.* a seaport in the Society Islands, on Tahiti: capital of the Society Islands and of French Polynesia. 15,214 (1951).

pa·per (pā/pər), *n.* **1.** a substance made from rags, straw, wood, or other fibrous material, usually in thin sheets, for writing or printing on, wrapping things in, decorating walls, etc. **2.** something resembling this substance, as papyrus. **3.** a piece, sheet, or leaf of paper, esp. one bearing writing. **4.** a written or printed document or instrument. **5.** negotiable notes, bills, etc., collectively: *commercial paper.* **6.** a document establishing identity, status, or the like. **7.** (*pl.*) the documents required to be carried by a ship for the manifestation of her ownership, nationality, destination, etc. **8.** a set of questions for an examination, or an individual set of written answers to them. **9.** an essay, article, or dissertation on a particular topic. **10.** a newspaper or journal. **11.** a sheet or card of paper with pins or needles stuck through it in rows. **12.** *Slang.* a free pass to a place of entertainment. —*v.t.* **13.** to write or set down on paper. **14.** to describe in writing. **15.** to fold, enclose, or put up in paper. **16.** to decorate (a wall, room, etc.) with wallpaper. **17.** to supply with paper. —*adj.* **18.** made or consisting of paper: *a paper box.* **19.** paperlike; thin; flimsy; frail. **20.** pertaining to, or carried on by means of, letters, articles, books, etc.: *a paper warfare.* **21.** written or printed on paper. **22.** existing on paper only and not in reality: *paper profits.* **23.** indicating the 1st event of a series, as a wedding anniversary. [ME and OE, t. L: m.s. *papȳrus* paper, PAPYRUS] —**pa/per·like/,** *adj.*

pa·per·back (pā/pər băk/), *n.* a book bound in a flexible paper cover. —**pa/per·back/,** *adj.*

paper birch, the North American birch, *Betula papyrifera,* a tall tree with tough bark and valuable wood.

pa·per·bound (pā′pər bound′), *adj.* (of a book) bound with a flexible paper cover rather than cloth, leather, etc.

pa·per·er (pā′pər ər), *n.* **1.** a paper hanger. **2.** one who papers.

paper hanger, one whose business it is to cover or decorate walls with wallpaper. **—paper hanging.**

paper knife, a knifelike instrument with a blade of metal, ivory, wood, or the like, for cutting open the leaves of books, folded papers, etc.

paper money, currency in paper form, as government and bank notes.

paper nautilus, any dibranchiate cephalopod of the genus *Argonauta,* characterized by the delicate shell of the female; the argonaut.

pa·per·weight (pā′pər wāt′), *n.* a small heavy object laid on papers to keep them from being scattered.

pa·per·y (pā′pər ỹ), *adj.* like paper; thin or flimsy.

pap·e·terie (păp′ə trỹ; *Fr.* påp trē′), *n.* a case or box of paper and other materials for writing. [t. F, der. *papetier* one who makes or sells paper, der. *papier* PAPER]

Pa·phi·an (pā′fĩ ən), *adj.* **1.** of or pertaining to Paphos, an ancient city of Cyprus sacred to Aphrodite. **2.** of love, esp. illicit love or sexual indulgence.

Paph·la·go·ni·a (păf′lə gō′nĩ ə), *n.* an ancient country and Roman province in N Asia Minor, on the S coast of the Black Sea.

Pa·phos (pā′fŏs), *n.* an ancient city in SW Cyprus.

Pa·pia·men·to (pä′pyä měn′tō), *n.* the creolized Spanish of Curaçao, in the Dutch West Indies.

pa·pier col·lé (på pyĕ′ kô lĕ′), *pl.* **papiers collés** (på pyĕ′ kô lĕ′). *French.* an arrangement of various objects and materials pasted on a flat surface to achieve a formal design, used especially in cubism about 1912–14.

pa·pier-mâ·ché (pā′pər mə shā′; *Fr.* på pyĕ′må shĕ′), *n.* a substance made of pulped paper or paper pulp mixed with glue and other materials, or of layers of paper glued and pressed together, molded when moist to form various articles, and becoming hard and strong when dry. [t. F: chewed paper]

pa·pil·i·o·na·ceous (pə pĭl′ĩ ə nā′shəs), *adj. Bot.* **1.** having an irregular corolla shaped somewhat like a butterfly, as the pea and other leguminous plants. **2.** belonging to the family *Papilionaceae* (*Fabaceae*), which is often currently treated as part of a *Leguminosae.* [t. NL: m. *pāpiliōnāceus,* der. L *pāpilio* butterfly]

pa·pil·la (pə pĭl′ə), *n., pl.* **-pillae** (-pĭl′ē). **1.** any small nipplelike process or projection. **2.** one of certain small protuberances concerned with the senses of touch, taste, and smell: *the papillae of the tongue.* **3.** a small vascular process at the root of a hair. **4.** a papule or pimple. **5.** *Bot.* a small nipplelike projection. [t. L: nipple]

Papillonaceous flower of bean, *Phaseolus vulgaris* V, Vexillum; W, Wing; K, Keel, or carina

pap·il·lar·y (păp′ə lĕr′ỹ, pə pĭl′ər ỹ), *adj.* **1.** of or pertaining to, or of the nature of, a papilla or papillae. **2.** provided or furnished with papillae.

pap·il·lo·ma (păp′ə lō′mə), *n., pl.* **-mata** (-mə tə), **-mas.** *Pathol.* a tumor of skin or mucous membrane, consisting of a hypertrophied papilla or group of papillae, as a wart or a corn. [f. PAPILLA + -OMA]

pap·il·lon (păp′ə lŏn′), *n.* a variety of toy spaniel.

pap·il·lose (păp′ə lōs′), *adj.* full of papillae. **—pap·il·los·i·ty** (păp′ə lŏs′ə tỹ), *n.*

pap·il·lote (păp′ə lōt′), *n.* a curled paper, put at the end of the bone of a cutlet or chop. [t. F, der. *papillon* butterfly, t. L: m.s. *pāpilio*]

pa·pist (pā′pĭst), *n.* **1.** an adherent of the Pope. **2.** a member of the Roman Catholic Church (usually in disparagement). **—adj. 3.** papistical. [t. NL: s. *pāpista,* der. L *pāpa* POPE]

pa·pis·ti·cal (pā pĭs′tə kəl, pə-), *adj.* of, pertaining to, or characteristic of papists or papistry (usually in disparagement). Also, **pa·pis·tic.**

pa·pist·ry (pā′pĭs trỹ), *n.* (usually in disparaging use) the systems, doctrines, or practices of papists.

pa·poose (pă pōōs′), *n.* a North American Indian baby or young child. Also, **pap·poose′.** [t. Algonquian (New England): m. *papeisses,* der. *peisses* child]

pap·pose (păp′ōs), *adj. Bot.* **1.** having or forming a pappus. **2.** downy. Also, **pap·pous** (păp′əs).

pap·pus (păp′əs), *n., pl.* **pappi** (păp′ī). *Bot.* a downy, bristly, or other appendage of the achene of certain plants, as the dandelion and the thistle. [t. L, t. Gk.: m. *păppos* down on seeds, orig. grandfather]

pap·py (păp′ỹ), *adj.,* **-pier, -piest.** like pap; mushy.

pap·ri·ka (pă prē′kə, păp′rỹ kə), *n.* the dried fruit of a cultivated form of *Capsicum frutescens,* ground as a condiment, much less pungent than ordinary red pepper. [t. Hung.]

Pap·u·a (păp′yŏō ə, pä′pŏō ä′), *n.* **1.** New Guinea. **2.** Territory of, an Australian territory in SE New Guinea, including the adjacent islands: merged with the Territory of New Guinea, 1945. 494,709 pop. (1954); 90,540 sq. mi. *Cap.:* Port Moresby. **3. Gulf of,** a large gulf of the Coral Sea, on the SE coast of New Guinea. **4.** a Papuan (def. 3). [t. Malay: lit., frizzled]

Pap·u·an (păp′yŏō ən), *adj.* **1.** of or pertaining to Papua. **2.** denoting or pertaining to the native Negroid race of New Guinea, characterized by a black or sooty-brown complexion and crisp, frizzled hair. **—n. 3.** a native or inhabitant of New Guinea. **4.** any of a number of languages of the Southwest Pacific, particularly of New Guinea and New Caledonia.

pap·ule (păp′ūl), *n. Pathol.* a small, somewhat pointed elevation of the skin, usually inflammatory but not suppurative. [t. L: m.s. *papula* pustule, pimple]

pap·y·ra·ceous (păp′ə rā′shəs), *adj.* papery.

pa·py·rus (pə pī′rəs), *n., pl.* **-pyri** (-pī′rī). **1.** a tall aquatic plant, *Cyperus Papyrus,* of the sedge family, found in Ethiopia, Palestine, etc., and formerly abundant in Egypt. **2.** a material for writing on, prepared from thin strips of the pith of this plant laid together, soaked, pressed, and dried, used by the ancient Egyptians, Greeks, and Romans. **3.** an ancient document or manuscript written on this material. [ME, t. L, t. Gk.: m. *păpyros* the plant papyrus, something made from papyrus. Cf. PAPER]

par (pär), *n.* **1.** an equality in value or standing; a level of equality: *the gains and the losses are on a par.* **2.** an average or normal amount, degree, quality, condition, or the like: *above par, below par.* **3.** *Com.* **a.** the legally established value of the monetary unit of one country in terms of that of another using the same metal as a standard of value (**mint par of exchange**). **b.** the state of the shares of any business, undertaking, loan, etc., when they may be purchased at the original price (called **issue par**) or at their face value (called **nominal par**). Such shares or bonds are said to be **at par. 4.** *Golf.* the number of strokes allowed to a hole or course as representing a score made by expert playing. **—adj. 5.** average or normal. **6,** *Com.* at or pertaining to par: *the par value of a bond.* [t. L: equal]

par., **1.** paragraph. **2.** parallel. **3.** parenthesis. **4.** parish.

pa·ra (pä rä′, pä′rä), *n., pl.* **-ras, -ra. 1.** a monetary unit of Turkey, equal to one fortieth of a piaster, or about .11 U.S. cent. **2.** one hundredth of a dinar (of Yugoslavia). [t. Turk. (Pers.): m. *pārah* piece, portion]

Pa·ra (pä rä′), *n.* Pará rubber.

Pa·rá (pä rä′), *n.* **1.** Belém. **2.** an estuary in N Brazil, receiving the Tocantins river and a branch of the Amazon. ab. 200 mi. long; ab. 40 mi. wide.

para-[1], a prefix meaning "beside," "near," "beyond," "aside," "amiss," and sometimes implying alteration or modification, occurring orig. in words from the Greek, but used also as a modern formative, chiefly in scientific words. Also, **par-.** [t. Gk., comb. form of *parắ,* prep.]

para-[2], a prefix of a few words meaning "guard against," as in *parachute.* [t. F, t. It., impv. of *parāre* defend against, g. L: prepare]

Para., Paraguay.

par·a·bi·o·sis (păr′ə bī ō′sĩs), *n. Biol.* experimental or natural union of two individuals with exchange of blood. **—par·a·bi·ot·ic** (păr′ə bĩ ŏt′ĩk), *adj.*

par·a·blast (păr′ə blăst′), *n. Biol.* the nutritive yolk of an ovum or egg.

par·a·ble (păr′ə bəl), *n.* **1.** a short allegorical story, designed to convey some truth or moral lesson. **2.** a discourse or saying conveying the intended meaning by a comparison or under the likeness of something comparable or analogous. [ME *parabil,* t. LL: m.s. *parabola* comparison, parable, proverb, word, t. Gk.: m. *parabolē* a placing beside, comparison]

par·a·bo·la (pə răb′ə lə), *n. Geom.* a plane curve formed by the intersection of a right circular cone with a plane parallel to a generator of the cone. See **conic section** diagram. [t. NL, t. Gk.: m. *parabolē.* See PARABLE]

par·a·bol·ic[1] (păr′ə bŏl′ĩk), *adj.* **1.** having the form or outline of a parabola. **2.** pertaining to or resembling a parabola. [ME, t. LL: s. *parabolicus,* t. LGk.: m. *parabolikós* figurative]

par·a·bol·ic[2] (păr′ə bŏl′ĩk), *adj.* of, pertaining to, or involving a parable. Also, **par′a·bol′i·cal.** [see PARABOLIC[1], PARABLE] **—par′a·bol′i·cal·ly,** *adv.*

Common parabola

AB, Directrix; F, Focus; P, Point on parabola; PQ, Always equal to PF; XX, Axis

par·a·bol·oid (pə răb′ə loid′), *n. Geom.* a solid or surface generated by the revolution of a parabola about its axis, or one of the second degree some of whose plane sections are parabolas. **—par·ab·o·loi·dal** (pə răb′ə loi′dəl, păr′ə bə-), *adj.*

Par·a·cel·sus (păr′ə sĕl′səs), *n.* (*Theophrastus Bombastus von Hohenheim*) 1493?–1541, Swiss-German physician and alchemist.

par·a·chute (păr′ə shōōt′), *n., v.,* **-chuted, -chuting. —n. 1.** an apparatus used in descending safely through the air from a great height, esp. from an aircraft, being umbrellalike in form and rendered effective by the resistance of the air, which expands it during the descent and then reduces the velocity of its motion. **—v.t. 2.** to land (troops, equipment, etc.) by parachute. **—v.i. 3.** to descend by parachute. [t. F: f. *para-* PARA-[2] + *chute* a fall. See CHUTE] **—par′a·chut′ist,** *n.*

par·a·clete (păr′ə klēt′), *n.* **1.** one called in to aid; an advocate or intercessor. **2.** (*cap.*) the Holy Spirit, or Comforter. [t. LL: m.s. *paraclētus,* t. Gk.: m. *parāklētos*]

par·a·cy·mene (păr′ə sĩ′mēn), *n.* the most common

form of cymene, found in several essential oils, as oil of eucalyptus.

pa·rade (pə·rād′), n., v., **-rad·ed, -rad·ing.** —n. 1. a public procession for display: *a political parade.* 2. a ceremony involving the marching of troop units and a mass salute at the lowering of the flag at the end of the day. 3. the orderly assembly of troops for inspection or display. 4. a place where troops regularly assemble for parade. 5. show, display, or ostentation: *to make parade of pain.* 6. *Chiefly Brit.* a promenade. 7. *Chiefly Brit.* a body of promenaders. 8. *Fort.* the level space forming the interior or enclosed area of a fortification. 9. *Fencing.* a parry. —v.t. 10. to walk up and down on or in. 11. to make parade of; display ostentatiously. 12. to cause to march or proceed for display. —v.i. 13. to march or proceed with display. 14. to promenade in a public place to show oneself. 15. to assemble in military order for display. [t. F, t. Sp.: m. *parada,* der. *parar,* g. L *parāre* prepare] —**pa·rad′er,** n.

par·a·di·chlo·ro·ben·zene (păr′ə dī klōr′ō bĕn′zēn, -bĕn zēn′), n. *Chem.* a white crystalline compound, C_6H_4-Cl_2, of the benzene series, used as a moth repellent.

par·a·digm (păr′ə dĭm, -dīm′), n. 1. *Gram.* a. the set of all forms containing a particular element, esp. the set of all inflected forms of a single root, stem, or theme. For example: *boy, boy's, boys, boys'* constitutes the paradigm of the noun *boy.* b. a display in fixed arrangement of such a set. 2. a pattern; an example. [late ME, t. LL: m. *paradīgma,* t. Gk.: m. *parádeigma* pattern] —**par·a·dig·mat·ic** (păr′ə dĭg măt′ĭk), adj.

par·a·di·sa·i·cal (păr′ə dĭ sā′ə kəl), adj. paradisiacal. Also, **par′a·di·sa′ic.** —**par′a·di·sa′i·cal·ly,** adv.

par·a·dise (păr′ə dīs′), n. 1. heaven, as the final abode of the righteous. 2. (according to some) an intermediate place for the departed souls of the righteous awaiting resurrection. 3. the garden of Eden. 4. a place of extreme beauty or delight. 5. supreme felicity. [ME *paradis,* t. LL: s. *paradīsus,* t. Gk.: m. *parádeisos* park, t. OPers.: m. *pairidaēza* enclosure]

paradise fish, a beautiful fish of either of two species of *Macropodus,* often kept in aquariums.

Paradise Lost, an epic poem (1667) by John Milton.

par·a·di·si·a·cal (păr′ə dī sī′ə kəl), adj. of, like, or befitting paradise. Also, **par·a·dis·i·ac** (păr′ə dĭs′Y ăk′). [f. s. LL *paradīsiacus* of paradise + -AL¹] —**par′a·di·si′a·cal·ly,** adv.

par·a·dos (păr′ə dŏs′), n. *Fort.* the bank behind a trench that protects men from fire and from being seen against the skyline. [t. F: f. *para-* PARA-² + *dos* back]

par·a·dox (păr′ə dŏks′), n. 1. a statement or proposition seemingly self-contradictory or absurd, and yet explicable as expressing a truth. 2. a self-contradictory and false proposition. 3. any person or thing exhibiting apparent contradictions. 4. an opinion or statement contrary to received opinion. [t. L: s. *paradoxum,* t. Gk.: m. *parádoxon,* neut. of *parádoxos* contrary to received opinion, incredible] —**par′a·dox′i·cal,** adj. —**par′a·dox′i·cal·ly,** adv. —**par′a·dox′i·cal·ness,** n.

par·aes·the·sia (păr′əs thē′zhə, -zĭ ə), n. *Pathol.* paresthesia. —**par·aes·thet·ic** (păr′əs thĕt′Yk), adj.

par·af·fin (păr′ə fĭn), n. 1. *U.S.* a white or colorless waxy substance (a mixture of hydrocarbons; see def. 2b below), not easily acted upon by reagents, obtained chiefly from crude petroleum, and used for making candles, forming preservative coatings, waterproofing paper, etc. 2. *Chem.* a. any hydrocarbon of the methane series (or **paraffin series**). b. one of the higher members of the methane series, solid at ordinary temperatures, with boiling points above 300°C, which largely constitute commercial paraffin. 3. *Brit.* kerosene. —v.t. 4. to cover or impregnate with paraffin. [t. G, f. (by K. von Reichenbach) L *par(um)* not enough + L *affin(is)* related; so called from its lack of affinity for other substances]

par·af·fine (păr′ə fĭn, -fēn′), n., v.t., **-fined, -fining.** paraffin.

paraffin wax, paraffin in its solid state.

par·a·form·al·de·hyde (păr′ə fôr măl′də hīd′), n. a colorless noncrystalline polymer of formaldehyde, $(CH_2O)_3$, which is utilized as an antiseptic.

par·a·gen·e·sis (păr′ə jĕn′ə sĭs), n. *Geol.* the origin and associations of a mineral or a mineral deposit. Also, **par·a·ge·ne·si·a** (păr′ə jə nē′sĭ ə). [f. PARA-¹ + GENE-SIS] —**par·a·ge·net·ic** (păr′ə jə nĕt′Yk), adj.

par·a·go·ge (păr′ə gō′jĭ), n. (in linguistic change) the addition of a syllable, phoneme, or other element not originally present, at the end of a word, as the substandard pronunciation of *height* as *height-th,* the standard showing no change. [t. LL, t. Gk.: a leading past] —**par·a·gog·ic** (păr′ə gŏj′Yk), adj.

par·a·gon (păr′ə gŏn′, -gən), n. 1. a model or pattern of excellence, or of a particular excellence. 2. *Print.* a type size (20 points). 3. an unusually large round pearl. —v.t. *Archaic or Poetic.* 4. to match or parallel. 5. to compare. 6. to be a match for; equal; rival. 7. to surpass. 8. to regard as a paragon. [t. MF, t. It.: m. *paragone* touchstone, comparison, paragon]

par·a·graph (păr′ə grăf′, -gräf′), n. 1. a distinct portion of written or printed matter dealing with a particular point, and usually beginning (commonly with indention) on a new line. 2. a character (now usually ¶) used to indicate the beginning of a distinct or separate portion of a text, or as a mark of reference. 3. a note, item, or

brief article, as in a newspaper. —v.t. 4. to divide into paragraphs. 5. to write or publish paragraphs about. 6. to express in a paragraph. [t. LL: s. *paragraphus,* t. Gk.: m. *parágraphos* line or mark in the margin]

par·a·graph·er (păr′ə grăf′ər, -gräf′ər), n. one who writes paragraphs, as for a newspaper. Also, *esp. Brit.* **par′a·graph′ist.**

par·a·graph·i·a (păr′ə grăf′Yə), n. *Psychiatry.* a cerebral disorder marked by the writing of words or letters other than those intended, or the loss of ability to express ideas in writing. [t. NL, f. Gk.: *para-* PARA-¹ + -*graphía* writing]

par·a·graph·ic (păr′ə grăf′Yk), adj. 1. of, pertaining to, or forming a paragraph. 2. divided into paragraphs. 3. of or pertaining to paragraphia. Also, **par′a·graph′i·cal.**

Par·a·guay (păr′ə gwā′, -gwī′; Sp. pä′rä gwī′), n. 1. a republic in central South America between Bolivia, Brazil, and Argentina. 1,601,000 pop. (est. 1956); 150,515 sq. mi. *Cap.:* Asunción. 2. a river flowing from W Brazil S through Paraguay to the Paraná. ab. 1500 mi. —**Par′a·guay′an,** adj., n.

Paraguay tea, maté.

par·a·keet (păr′ə kēt′), n. any of numerous small slender parrots, usually with a long, pointed, graduated tail, as the Australian grass **para·keet,** *Melopsittacus undulatus.* Also, **paraquet, paroquet, parrakeet, parroket, parrouqet.** [t. It.: m. *parochito,* var. of *parrochetto,* dim. of *parroco* parson]

par·al·de·hyde (pə răl′də hīd′), n. *Chem.* a colorless liquid, $(CH_3CHO)_3$, formed by polymerization of acetaldehyde, and used as a hypnotic. [f. PAR-+ ALDEHYDE]

par·a·lip·sis (păr′ə lĭp′sĭs), n., pl. **-ses** (-sēz). *Rhetoric.* a pretended ignoring, for rhetorical effect, of something actually spoken of, as in "not to mention other faults." Also, **par·a·leip·sis** (păr′ə lĭp′sĭs). [t. NL, t. Gk.: m. *paráleipsis* a passing over]

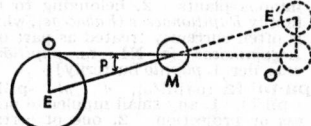

Carolina parakeet, *Conuropsis carolinensis* (1 ft. long)

par·al·lax (păr′ə lăks′), n. 1. the apparent displacement of an object observed, esp. a heavenly body, due to a change or difference in the position of the observer. 2. diurnal or geocentric parallax, the displacement of a body owing to its being observed from the surface instead of from the center of the earth. 3. annual or heliocentric parallax, the displacement of a star owing to its being observed from the earth instead of from the sun. 4. apparent change in the position of cross hairs as viewed through a telescope, when the focusing is imperfect. [t. Gk.: s. *parállaxis* change] —**par·al·lac·tic** (păr′ə lăk′tYk), adj.

Geocentric parallax of the moon
P, Parallax; O, Observer; E, Center of earth; M, Moon; E′, Image of E; O′, Image of O

par·al·lel (păr′ə lĕl′), adj., n., v., **-leled, -leling** or (*esp. Brit.*) **-lelled, -lelling.** —adj. 1. having the same direction, course, or tendency; corresponding; similar; analogous: *parallel forces.* 2. *Geom.* a. (of straight lines) lying in the same plane but never meeting no matter how far extended. b. (of planes) having common perpendiculars. c. (of a single line, figure, etc.) equidistant from another or others at all corresponding points (fol. by *to* or *with*). 3. *Music.* a. (of two voice parts) progressing so that the interval between them remains the same. b. (of a tonality or key) having the same tonic but differing in mode. —n. 4. anything parallel in direction, course, or tendency. 5. a parallel line or plane. 6. *Geog.* a. a circle on the earth surface formed by the intersection of a plane parallel to the plane of the equator, bearing east and west and designated in degrees of latitude north or south of the equator along the arc of any meridian. b. the line representing this circle on a chart or map. 7. a match or counterpart. 8. correspondence or analogy. 9. a comparison of things as if regarded side by side. 10. *Print.* a pair of vertical parallel lines (‖) used as a mark of reference. 11. *Elect.* a connection of two or more circuits in which all ends having the same instantaneous polarity are electrically connected together, and all ends having the opposite polarity are similarly connected. The element circuits are said to be in parallel (opp. to in series). 12. *Fort.* a trench cut in the ground before a fortress, parallel to its defenses, for the purpose of covering a besieging force. —v.t. 13. to make parallel. 14. to furnish a parallel for; find or provide a match for. 15. to form a parallel to; be equivalent to; equal. 16. to compare. [t. L: s. *parallēlus,* t. Gk.: m. *parállēlos* beside one another]

parallel bars, gymnasium apparatus consisting of two wooden bars on uprights, adjustable in height, and used for swinging, vaulting, balancing exercises, etc.

parallel cousin marriage, marriage between the children of two brothers or two sisters.

---

b., blend of, blended; c., cognate with; d., dialect, dialectal; der., derived from; f., formed from; g., going back to; m., modification of; r., replacing; s., stem of; t., taken from; ?, perhaps. See the full key on inside cover.

par·al·lel·e·pi·ped (păr/ə·lĕl/ə·pī/pĭd, -pĭp/ĭd), *n.* a prism with six faces, all parallelograms. Also, **par·al·lel·e·pip·e·don** (păr/ə·lĕl/ə·pĭp/ə·dŏn/, -dŏn). [t. Gk.: s. *parallēlepipedon* body with parallel surfaces]

Parallelepiped

par·al·lel·ism (păr/ə·lĕl/ĭz·əm), *n.* 1. the position or relation of parallels. 2. agreement in direction, tendency, or character. 3. a parallel or comparison. 4. *Metaphys.* the doctrine that mental and bodily processes are concomitant, each varying with variation of the other, but that there is no causal relation or relation of interaction between the two series of changes.

par·al·lel·o·gram (păr/ə·lĕl/ə·grăm/), *n.* a quadrilateral the opposite sides of which are parallel. [t. Gk.: s. *parallēlogrammon*, prop. neut. of *parallēlogrammos* bounded by parallel lines]

Parallelograms

par·a·log·ism (pə·răl/ə·jĭz/əm), *n. Logic.* 1. a piece of false or fallacious reasoning, esp. (as distinguished from *sophism*) one of whose falseness the reasoner is not conscious. 2. reasoning of this kind. [t. Gk.: s. *paralogismós* false reasoning] —**pa·ral/o·gist**, *n.* —**pa·ral/o·gis/tic**, *adj.*

pa·ral·y·sis (pə·răl/ə·sĭs), *n.*, *pl.* **-ses** (-sēz/). 1. *Pathol.* a. loss of power of a voluntary muscular contraction. b. a disease characterized by this; palsy. 2. a more or less complete crippling, as of powers or activities: *a paralysis of trade.* [t. L, t. Gk.: palsy]

paralysis ag·i·tans (ăj/ĭ·tănz/), *Pathol.* Parkinson's disease. [L. PARALYSIS + *agitans* pres. part. of *agitāre* excite]

par·a·lyt·ic (păr/ə·lĭt/ĭk), *n.* 1. one affected with general paralysis. —*adj.* 2. affected with or subject to paralysis. 3. pertaining to or of the nature of paralysis. [f. PARA-¹ + MAGNETIC]

par·a·lyze (păr/ə·līz/), *v.t.* -lyzed, -lyzing. 1. to affect with paralysis. 2. to bring to a condition of helpless inactivity. Also, *esp. Brit.,* **par/a·lyse/.** —**par/a·ly·za/tion**, *n.* —**par/a·lyz/er**, *n.* —Syn. 2. stun. See **shock¹.**

par·a·mag·net (păr/ə·măg/nĭt), *n.* a body or substance having paramagnetic properties. —**par/a·mag/net·ism**, *n.*

par·a·mag·net·ic (păr/ə·măg·nĕt/ĭk), *adj.* denoting or pertaining to a class of substances (e.g., liquid oxygen) which are magnetic like iron, though in a much less degree (distinguished from *ferromagnetic* and opposed to *diamagnetic*). [f. PARA-¹ + MAGNETIC]

Par·a·mar·i·bo (păr/ə·măr/ĭ·bō/), *n.* a seaport in NE South America: capital of Surinam. 86,400 (est. 1952).

par·a·mat·ta (păr/ə·măt/ə), *n.* a light, twilled dress fabric, having a silk or cotton warp and a woolen weft. Also, **parramatta.** [f. *Parramatta* in New South Wales]

par·a·me·ci·um (păr/ə·mē/shĭ·əm, -sĭ·əm), *n.*, *pl.* **-cia** (-shĭ·ə, -sĭ·ə). a ciliate infusorian having an oval body and deep long oral groove, inhabiting fresh water and widely distributed in a number of species, extensively used in experiments on protozoa. [t. NL, der. Gk. *paramēkēs* oblong]

pa·ram·e·ter (pə·răm/ə·tər), *n. Math.* a variable entering into the mathematical form of any distribution such that the possible values of the variable correspond to different distributions.

par·a·mo (pär/ə·mō/; *Sp.* pä/rä·mō/), *n.*, *pl.* **-mos** (-mōz/; *Sp.* -mōs/). a high plateau region in tropical South America, esp. one bare of trees. [t. Sp.]

par·a·morph (păr/ə·môrf/), *n. Mineral.* a pseudomorph formed by a change in crystal structure but not in chemical composition. —**par/a·mor/phic**, *adj.*

par·a·mor·phism (păr/ə·môr/fĭz·əm), *n.* 1. the process by which a paramorph is formed. 2. the state of being a paramorph.

par·a·mount (păr/ə·mount/), *adj.* 1. above others in rank or authority; superior in power or jurisdiction. 2. chief in importance; supreme; preëminent. —*n.* 3. an overlord; a supreme ruler. [t. AF: m. *paramont* above, f. *par* by (g. L *per*) + *amont* upward, up (g. L *ad montem* to the mountain). Cf. AMOUNT] —**par/a·mount/cy**, *n.* —Syn. 2. See **dominant.**

par·a·mour (păr/ə·mŏŏr/), *n.* 1. an illicit lover, esp. of a married person. 2. any lover. 3. a beloved one. [ME, t. OF, orig. phrase *par amour* by love, by way of (sexual) love, f. *par* by (g. L *per*) + *amour* love (g. L *amor*)]

Pa·ra·ná (pä/rə·nä/), *n.* 1. a river flowing from S Brazil along the SE boundary of Paraguay and through E Argentina into the Río de la Plata. 2450 mi. 2. a city in E Argentina, on the Paraná river: the capital of Argentina, 1852–61. 100,000 (est. 1952).

pa·rang (pä/räng), *n.* a large, heavy knife used as a tool or a weapon by the Malays. [t. Malay]

par·a·noi·a (păr/ə·noi/ə), *n. Psychiatry.* mental disorder characterized by systematized delusions and the projection of personal conflicts, which are ascribed to the supposed hostility of others. The disorder often exists for years without any disturbance of consciousness. Also, **par·a·noe·a** (păr/ə·nē/ə). [t. NL, t. Gk.: derangement]

par·a·noi·ac (păr/ə·noi/ăk), *adj.* 1. pertaining to or affected with paranoia. —*n.* 2. a person affected with paranoia. Also, **par/a·noid/, par·a·noe·ac** (păr/ə·nē/ăk).

par·a·nymph (păr/ə·nĭmf), *n.* 1. a groomsman or a bridesmaid. 2. (in ancient Greece) a. a friend who accompanied the bridegroom when he went to bring home the bride. b. the bridesmaid who escorted the bride to the bridegroom. [ult. t. Gk.: s. *paránymphos*, masc., the best man, *paranýmphē*, fem., the bridesmaid]

par·a·pet (păr/ə·pĭt, -pĕt/), *n.* 1. *Fort.* a. a defensive wall or elevation, as of earth or stone, in a fortification. See diag. under **bastion.** b. an elevation raised above the main wall or rampart of a permanent fortification. See diag. under **machicolation.** 2. any protective wall or barrier at the edge of a balcony, roof, bridge, or the like. [t. It.: m. *parapetto*, f. *para-* PARA-³ + *petto*, g. L *pectus* breast] —**par/a·pet·ed**, *adj.*

par·aph (păr/əf), *n.* a flourish made after a signature, as in a document, orig. as a precaution against forgery. [ME *paraf*, t. ML: m.s. *paraphus*, short for L *paragrapus* PARAGRAPH]

par·a·pher·nal·ia (păr/ə·fər·nāl/yə, -fə·nāl/yə), *n.pl.* 1. personal belongings. 2. *Law.* the personal articles, apart from dower, reserved by law to a married woman. 3. (*sometimes construed as sing.*) equipment; apparatus. [t. ML (prop. neut. pl.), der. LL *parapherna*, t. Gk.: bride's belongings other than dowry]

par·a·phrase (păr/ə·frāz/), *n.*, *v.*, **-phrased, -phrasing.** —*n.* 1. a statement of the sense of a text or passage in other words, as for clearness; a free rendering or translation, as of a passage. 2. the act or process of paraphrasing. —*v.t.*, *v.i.* 3. to restate; render in, or make, a paraphrase. [t. F, t. L: m.s. *paraphrasis*, t. Gk.] —**par/a·phras/er**, *n.* —Syn. 1. See **translation.**

par·a·phrast (păr/ə·frăst/), *n.* one who paraphrases.

par·a·phras·tic (păr/ə·frăs/tĭk), *adj.* having the nature of a paraphrase. —**par/a·phras/ti·cal·ly**, *adv.*

pa·raph·y·sis (pə·răf/ə·sĭs), *n.*, *pl.* **-ses** (-sēz/). *Bot.* one of the sterile, usually filamentous, outgrowths often occurring among the reproductive organs in many cryptogamous plants. [t. NL, t. Gk.: offshoot]

par·a·ple·gi·a (păr/ə·plē/jĭ·ə), *n. Pathol.* paralysis of both lower or upper limbs. [t. NL, t. Gk.: paralysis on one side] —**par·a·pleg·ic** (păr/ə·plĕj/ĭk, -plē/jĭk), *adj.*, *n.*

par·a·po·di·um (păr/ə·pō/dĭ·əm), *n.*, *pl.* **-dia** (-dĭ·ə). *Zool.* one of the unjointed lateral locomotor processes or series of rudimentary limbs of many worms, as annelids. [t. NL. See PARA-, -PODIUM]

par·a·psy·chol·o·gy (păr/ə·sī·kŏl/ə·jī), *n.* a division of psychology which investigates psychic phenomena, as clairvoyance, extrasensory perception, and the like.

par·a·quet (păr/ə·kĕt/), *n.* parakeet.

Pa·rá rubber (pä·rä/), India rubber obtained from the euphorbiaceous tree *Hevea brasiliensis* and other species of the same genus, of tropical South America.

par·a·sang (păr/ə·săng/), *n.* a Persian unit of distance, of varying length, anciently about 3 ⅛ miles. [t. L: s. *parasanga*, t. Gk.: m. *parasángēs*; of Pers. orig.]

par·a·se·lene (păr/ə·sĭ·lē/nī), *n.*, *pl.* **-nae** (-nē). *Meteorol.* a bright moonlike spot on a lunar halo; a mock moon. Cf. **parhelion.** [t. NL, f. Gk.: *para-* PARA-¹ + *selēnē* moon]

par·a·shah (păr/ə·shä/), *n.*, *pl.* **parashoth** (păr/ə·shōth/), **parashioth** (păr/ə·shē/ōth). 1. one of the lessons from the Torah or Law read in the Jewish synagogue on Sabbaths and festivals. 2. one of the subsections into which the weekly lessons read on Sabbaths are divided. Cf. **haphtarah.** [t. Heb.: division]

Par·a·shu·ra·ma (păr/ə·shŏŏ·rä/mə), *n. Hindu Myth.* first of the three Ramas, and sixth incarnation of Vishnu.

par·a·site (păr/ə·sīt/), *n.* 1. an animal or plant which lives on or in an organism of another species (the host), from the body of which it obtains nutriment. 2. one who lives on others or another without making any useful and fitting return, esp. one who lives on the hospitality of others. 3. (in ancient Greece) a professional diner-out, who got free meals in return for his amusing or impudent conversation. [t. L: m.s. *parasītus*, t. Gk.: *parásītos* one who eats at the table of another]

par·a·sit·ic (păr/ə·sĭt/ĭk), *adj.* 1. living or growing as a parasite; pertaining to or characteristic of parasites. 2. (of diseases) due to parasites. Also, **par/a·sit/i·cal.** —**par/a·sit/i·cal·ly**, *adv.*

par·a·sit·i·cide (păr/ə·sĭt/ə·sīd/), *adj.* 1. destructive to parasites. —*n.* 2. an agent or preparation that destroys parasites.

par·a·sit·ism (păr/ə·sī·tĭz/əm), *n.* 1. parasitic mode of life or existence. 2. *Zool., Bot.* the vital relation which a parasite bears to its host; parasitic infestation. 3. *Pathol.* diseased condition due to parasites.

par·a·sol (păr/ə·sôl/, -sŏl/), *n.* a woman's small or light sun umbrella; a sunshade. [t. F, t. It.: m. *parasole*, f. *para-* PARA-³ + *sole* (g. L *sōl* sun)]

par·a·stich·y (pə·răs/tə·kĭ), *n.*, *pl.* **-chies** (-kĭz). *Bot.* (in a spiral arrangement of leaves, scales, etc., where the internodes are short and the members closely crowded, as in the houseleek and the pine cone) one of a number of secondary spirals or oblique ranks seen to wind around the stem or axis to the right and left. [f. PARA-¹ + m.s. Gk. *-stichia* alignment]

par·a·sym·pa·thet·ic (păr/ə·sĭm/pə·thĕt/ĭk), *Anat. Physiol.* —*adj.* 1. pertaining to that part of the autonomic nervous system which consists of nerves arising from the cranial and sacral regions, and which opposes the action of the sympathetic system, thus inhibiting heart beat, contracting the pupil of the eye, etc. —*n.* 2. a nerve of the parasympathetic system.

par·a·syn·ap·sis (păr/ə·sĭ·năp/sĭs), *n. Embryol.* the conjugation of chromosomes, side by side; synapsis.

act, āble, dâre, ärt; ĕbb, ēqual; ĭf, īce; hŏt, ōver, ôrder, oil, bŏŏk, ōōze, out; ŭp, ūse, ûrge; ə = a in alone; ch, chief; g, give; ng, ring; sh, shoe; th, thin; ŧh, that; zh, vision. See the full key on inside cover.

par·a·syn·the·sis (păr/ə sĭn/thə sĭs), *n.* *Gram.* the formation of a word by the addition of an affix to a phrase or compound, as *great-hearted*, which is *great heart* plus *-ed* (not *great* plus *hearted*). [f. PARA-¹ + SYNTHESIS] —**par·a·syn·thet·ic** (păr/ə sĭn thĕt/ĭk), *adj.*

par·a·tax·is (păr/ə tăk/sĭs), *n.* the placing together of sentences, clauses, or phrases without a conjunctive word, as *hurry up, it is getting late; I came—I saw—I conquered.* [t. NL, t. Gk.: a placing side by side] —**par·a·tac·tic** (păr/ə tăk/tĭk), **par/a·tac/ti·cal**, *adj.* —**par/a·tac/ti·cal·ly**, *adv.*

par·a·thy·roid (păr/ə thī/roid), *Anat.* —*adj.* 1. situated near the thyroid gland. —*n.* 2. a parathyroid gland.

parathyroid glands, *Anat.* several small glands or oval masses of epithelioid cells, lying near or embedded in the thyroid gland, whose internal secretion governs the calcium content of the blood.

par·a·troop (păr/ə trōōp/), *n.* a force or unit of paratroopers.

par·a·troop·er (păr/ə trōō/pər), *n.* a soldier who reaches battle by landing from a plane by parachute. [f. PARA(CHUTE) + TROOPER]

par·a·ty·phoid (păr/ə tī/foid), *adj.* noting or pertaining to paratyphoid fever.

paratyphoid fever, an infectious disease similar in some ways to typhoid fever but usually milder, and caused by different bacteria.

par·a·vane (păr/ə vān/), *n.* a device, usually torpedo-shaped, for protecting a ship from moored mines. It is towed by a cable and has a device that cuts the mine cable, bringing the mine to the surface to be sunk by gunfire at a safe distance. Paravanes are always used in pairs, one towed from each bow. [f. PARA-¹ + VANE]

par a·vi·on (pàr à vyôN/), *French.* by plane (a label for matter to be sent air mail).

par·boil (pär/boil/), *v.t.* to boil partially, or for a short time; precook. [ME *parboyle*(*n*) boil fully, t. OF: m. *parbouillir*, g. LL *perbullīre*. See PER-, BOIL¹]

par·buck·le (pär/bŭk/əl), *n.*, *v.*, **-led, -ling.** —*n.* 1. a kind of purchase for raising or lowering a cask or similar object along an inclined plane or a vertical surface, consisting of a rope looped over a post or the like, with its two ends passing around the object to be moved. 2. a kind of double sling made with a rope, as around a cask to be raised or lowered. —*v.t.* 3. to raise, lower, or move with a parbuckle. [earlier *parbunkel;* orig. unknown]

Par·cae (pär/sē), *n.pl.* *Rom. Myth.* the Fates. [t. L]

par·cel (pär/səl), *n., v.,* **-celed, -celing** or (*Esp. Brit.*) **-celled, -celing,** *adv.* —*n.* 1. a quantity of something wrapped or put up together; a package or bundle. 2. a quantity of something, as of a commodity for sale; a lot. 3. any group or assemblage of persons or things. 4. a separable, separate, or distinct part or portion or section, as of land. 5. *Chiefly Archaic except Law.* a part or portion of anything. —*v.t.* 6. to divide into or distribute in parcels or portions (usually fol. by *out*). 7. to make into a parcel, or put up in parcels, as goods. 8. *Naut.* to cover or wrap (a rope, etc.) with strips of canvas. —*adv.* 9. partly; in part; partially. [ME *parcelle*, t. OF, t. ML: m.s. *particella,* dim. of L *particula* particle] —**Syn. 1.** See **package.**

parcel post, a branch of a postal service charged with conveying parcels. Also, **parcels post.**

par·ce·nar·y (pär/sə nĕr/ĭ), *n.* *Law.* coheirship; the undivided holding of land by two or more coheirs.

par·ce·ner (pär/sə nər), *n.* *Law.* a joint heir; a coheir. [ME, t. AF, der. *parçon,* g. L *partītio* partition]

parch (pärch), *v.t.* 1. to make dry, esp. to excess, or dry up, as heat, the sun, or a hot wind does. 2. to make (a person, the lips, throat, etc.) dry and hot, or thirsty, as heat, fever, or thirst does. 3. to dry (peas, beans, grain, etc.) by exposure to heat without burning. 4. (of cold, etc.) to dry or shrivel, like heat. —*v.i.* 5. to become parched; undergo drying by heat. 6. to dry (fol. by *up*). 7. to suffer from heat or thirst. [ME *parche*(*n*), *perch*(*en*); orig. uncert.]

par·chee·si (pär chē/zĭ), *n.* 1. a game somewhat resembling backgammon, played in India. 2. a simplified form of this, played elsewhere. Also, **parchesi, par·che/si, par·chi/si.** [t. Hind.: alter. of *pachisi,* der. *pachīs* twenty-five (the highest throw in the game)]

parch·ment (pärch/mənt), *n.* 1. the skin of sheep, goats, etc., prepared for use as a writing material, etc. 2. a manuscript or document on such material. 3. a paper resembling this material. [ME *parchemin,* t. OF, b. LL *pergamēna* parchment (der. *Pergamum,* city in Mysia, Asia Minor, whence parchment was brought) and L *parthica* (*pellis*) Parthian (leather)]

parchment paper, a waterproof and grease-resistant paper obtained by treating a paper with concentrated sulfuric acid.

pard¹ (pärd), *n.* *Archaic.* a leopard or panther. [ME, t. OF, t. L: s. *pardus,* t. Gk.: m. *párdos,* earlier *párdalis;* of Eastern orig.]

pard² (pärd), *n.* *U.S. Slang.* partner. [alter. of PARTNER]

par·di (pär dē/), *adv., interj.* *Archaic.* verily; indeed. Also, **par·die/, pardy, perdie.** [ME *parde,* t. OF: by God]

par·don (pär/dən), *n.* 1. courteous indulgence or allowance, as in excusing fault or seeming rudeness: *I beg your pardon* (a conventional form of apology). 2. *Law.* **a.** a pardoning; a remission of penalty, as by an executive. **b.** the deed or warrant by which such remission

is declared. 3. forgiveness of an offense or offender. 4. *Obs.* a papal indulgence. [ME, t. OF, der. *pardoner.* See below]
—*v.t.* 5. to remit the penalty of (an offense): *he will not pardon your transgressions.* 6. to release (a person) from liability for an offense. 7. to make courteous allowance for, or excuse (an action or circumstance, or a person): *pardon me, madam.* [ME *pardone*(*n*), t. OF: m. *pardoner,* t. LL: m. *perdōnāre* grant, concede, f. L *per-* PER- + *dōnāre* give] —**par/don·a·ble,** *adj.* —**par/don·a·bly,** *adv.* —**Syn. 3.** absolution, remission, amnesty. 5. forgive, absolve, condone, overlook. 6. See **excuse.**

par·don·er (pär/dən ər), *n.* 1. one who pardons. 2. an ecclesiastical official charged with the granting of indulgences.

par·dy (pär dē/), *adv., interj.* *Archaic.* pardi.

pare (pâr), *v.t.,* **pared, paring.** 1. to cut off the outer coating, layer, or part of: *to pare potatoes.* 2. to remove (an outer coating, layer, or part) by cutting (often fol. by *off* or *away*). 3. to reduce or remove by, or as if by, cutting; diminish little by little: *to pare down one's expenses.* [ME *pare*(*n*), t. OF: m. *parer* prepare, trim, g. L *parāre*] —**Syn. 1.** See **peel¹.**

Pa·ré (pà rē/), *n.* **Ambroise** (äN brwàz/), 1510–90, French surgeon.

pa·re·cious (pə rē/shəs), *adj.* *Bot.* paroicous.

par·e·gor·ic (păr/ə gôr/ĭk, -gŏr/ĭk), *Pharm.* —*n.* 1. a soothing medicine; an anodyne. 2. a camphorated tincture of opium, intended primarily to check diarrhea in children. —*adj.* 3. assuaging pain; soothing. [t. LL: s. *parēgoricus,* t. Gk.: m. *parēgorikós* encouraging, soothing]

pa·rei·ra (pə râr/ə), *n.* the root of a South American vine, *Chondodendron tomentosum,* used as a diuretic, etc.; a source of curare. [short for PAREIRA BRAVA]

pa·rei·ra bra·va (pə râr/ə brä/və, brä/və), pareira. [t. Pg.: m. *parreira brava,* lit., wild vine]

paren., parenthesis.

pa·ren·chy·ma (pə rĕng/kĭ mə), *n.* 1. *Bot.* the fundamental (soft) cellular tissue of plants, as in the softer parts of leaves, the pulp of fruits, the pith of stems, etc. 2. *Anat., Zool.* the proper tissue of an animal organ as distinguished from its connective or supporting tissue. 3. *Zool.* a kind of connective tissue in which the cells are numerous. 4. *Pathol.* the functional tissue of a morbid growth. [t. NL, t. Gk.: lit., something poured in beside] —**par·en·chym·a·tous** (păr/ĕng kĭm/ə təs), *adj.*

parens., parentheses.

par·ent (pâr/ənt), *n.* 1. a father or a mother. 2. a progenitor. 3. an author or source. 4. a protector or guardian. 5. any organism that produces or generates another. [ME, t. L: s. *parens*]

par·ent·age (pâr/ən tĭj), *n.* 1. derivation from parents; birth, lineage, or family; origin: *distinguished parentage.* 2. parenthood.

pa·ren·tal (pə rĕn/təl), *adj.* 1. of or pertaining to a parent: *the parental relation.* 2. proper to or characteristic of a parent: *parental feelings.* 3. having the relation of a parent. —**pa·ren/tal·ly,** *adv.*

par·en·ter·al (păr/ĕn/tərəl), *adj.* *Anat., Med., Physiol.* in a manner other than through the digestive canal. [f. PAR(A)-¹ + s. Gk. *énteron* intestine + -AL¹]

pa·ren·the·sis (pə rĕn/thə sĭs), *n.,* *pl.* **-ses** (-sēz/). 1. the upright curves ( ) collectively, or either of them separately, used to mark off an interjected explanatory or qualifying remark. 2. *Gram.* a qualifying or explanatory word (e.g., an appositive), phrase, clause (e.g., a descriptive clause), sentence, or other sequence of forms which interrupts the syntactic construction without otherwise affecting it, having often a characteristic intonation, and shown in writing by commas, parentheses, or dashes. Example: *William Smith—you know him well—will be here soon.* 3. an interval. [t. ML, t. Gk.: a putting in beside]

pa·ren·the·size (pə rĕn/thə sīz/), *v.t.,* **-sized, -sizing.** 1. to insert as or in a parenthesis. 2. to put between marks of parenthesis: *parenthesize the pronunciation.* 3. to interlard with parentheses.

par·en·thet·ic (păr/ən thĕt/ĭk), *adj.* 1. of, pertaining to, or of the nature of a parenthesis: *several unnecessary parenthetic remarks.* 2. characterized by the use of parentheses. Also, **par/en·thet/i·cal.** —**par/en·thet/i·cal·ly,** *adv.*

par·ent·hood (pâr/ənt hŏŏd/), *n.* the position or relation of, or state of being, a parent.

pa·re·sis (pə rē/sĭs, păr/əsĭs), *n.* *Pathol.* 1. incomplete motor paralysis. 2. See **general paralysis.** [t. NL, t. Gk.: a letting go]

par·es·the·sia (păr/əs thē/zhə, -zhĭ ə), *n.* *Pathol.* abnormal sensation, as prickling, itching, etc. Also, **paraesthesia.** [f. PAR(A)-¹ + m. Gk. *aisthēsía* sensation] —**par·es·thet·ic** (păr/əs thĕt/ĭk), *adj.*

pa·ret·ic (pə rĕt/ĭk, pə rē/tĭk), *n.* 1. one who has general paresis. —*adj.* 2. pertaining to, or affected with, paresis.

Pa·re·to (pä rĕ/tô), *n.* **Vilfredo** (vēl frĕ/dô), 1848–1923, Italian sociologist and economist, in Switzerland.

par ex·cel·lence (pär ĕk/sə läns/; *Fr.* pàr ĕk sĕ läNs/), *French.* by excellence or superiority; above all others; preëminently.

par ex·em·ple (pàr ĕg zäN/pl), *French.* for example.

par·fait (pär fā'; *Fr.* pår fĕ'), *n.* a rich frozen preparation of whipped cream and egg, variously flavored. [t. F: lit., perfect]

par·get (pär'jĭt), *n., v.,* **-geted, -geting** or (*esp. Brit.*) **-getted, -getting.** —*n.* **1.** gypsum or plaster stone. **2.** plaster, esp. a kind of mortar formed of lime, hair, and cow dung. **3.** plasterwork, esp. a more or less ornamental facing for exterior walls. —*v.t.* **4.** to cover or decorate with parget. [ME *pargette(n)*, t. OF: m. *parjeter* throw over a surface, f. *par* over + *jeter* throw]

par·get·ing (pär'jĭt ĭng), *n.* **1.** act of one who pargets. **2.** parget. Also, *esp. Brit.*, **par'get·ting.**

par·he·li·a·cal (pär'hĭ lī'ə kəl), *adj.* of or pertaining to or constituting a parhelion or parhelia. Also, **par·he·lic** (pär hē'lĭk, -hĕl'ĭk).

parheliacal ring, *Meteorol.* a white horizontal band passing through the sun, either incomplete or extending round the horizon, produced by the reflection of the sun's rays from the vertical faces of ice prisms in the atmosphere. Also, **parhelic circle.**

par·he·li·on (pär hē'lĭ ən), *n., pl.* **-lia** (-lĭ'ə). *Meteorol.* a bright circular spot on a solar halo; a mock sun; usually, one of two or more such spots seen on opposite sides of the sun, and often accompanied by additional luminous arcs and bands. [t. L: m. *parēlion* (with etymological *-h-*), t. Gk., var. of *parēlios* f. *para-* PARA-[1] + *hēlios* sun]

pa·ri·ah (pə rī'ə, pä'rī'ə, pâr'ĭ ə), *n.* **1.** any person or animal generally despised; an outcast. **2.** (*cap.*) a member of a low caste in southern India. [t. Tamil: m. *pariyar*, pl. of *paraiyan*, lit., drummer (from a hereditary duty of the caste), der. *parai* a festival drum]

Par·i·an (pâr'ĭ ən), *adj.* **1.** of or pertaining to Paros, noted for its white marble. **2.** noting or pertaining to a fine unglazed porcelain resembling this marble. —*n.* **3.** a native or inhabitant of Paros. **4.** Parian porcelain.

par·i·es (pâr'ĭ ēz), *n., pl.* **parietes** (pə rī'ə tēz'). (*usually pl.*) *Biol.* a wall, as of a hollow organ; an investing part. [t. L: wall]

pa·ri·e·tal (pə rī'ə təl), *adj.* **1.** *Anat.* a. referring to the side of the skull, or to any wall or wall-like structure. **b.** noting or pertaining to the parietal bones. **2.** *Biol.* of or pertaining to parietes or structural walls. **3.** *Bot.* pertaining to or arising from a wall: usually applied to ovules when they proceed from or are borne on the walls or sides of the ovary. **4.** *U.S.* pertaining to, or having authority over, those within the walls or buildings of a college. [t. LL: s. *parietālis*, der. L *pariēs* wall]

parietal bones, *Anat.* a pair of bones of the cranium, right and left, developed in membrane, forming most of the top and sides of the skull vault, between the occipital and the frontal bones. See diag. of **cranium.**

parietal lobe, *Anat.* the middle lobe of the cerebrum.

pa·ri·mu·tu·el (pär'ĭ mū'choŏ əl), *n.* **1.** a form of betting, as on horse races, in which those who bet on the winners divide the bets or stakes, less a percentage for the management, taxes, etc. **2.** the apparatus that records the bets. [t. F: mutual bet]

par·ing (pâr'ĭng), *n.* **1.** the act of one who or that which pares. **2.** a piece or part pared off.

pa·ri pas·su (pä'rĭ päs'oŏ, pâr'ī), *Latin.* with equal pace or progress; side by side

par·i·pin·nate (pär'ĭ pĭn'āt), *adj. Bot.* **1.** evenly pinnate. **2.** pinnate without an odd terminal leaflet.

Par·is (pär'ĭs; *Fr.* på rē'), *n.* the capital of France, in the N part, on the Seine. 2,850,189 (1954). [in L *Lutetia Parisiōrum*, in LL *Parisii*, orig. name of the Gallic tribe inhabiting the district] —**Pa·ri·sian** (pə rĭzh'ən, -rĭz'ĭ ən), *adj., n.*

Par·is (pär'ĭs), *n. Gk. Legend.* a Trojan youth, son of King Priam and Hecuba. His abduction of Helen led to the Trojan War, at the end of which he was killed by Philoctetes. See **apple of discord.**

Paris green, an emerald-green pigment prepared from arsenic trioxide and acetate of copper, now used chiefly as an insecticide.

par·ish (pär'ĭsh), *n.* **1.** an ecclesiastical district having its own church and clergyman. **2.** a local church with its field of activity. **3.** *Chiefly Brit.* a civil district or administrative division. **4.** (in Louisiana) a county. **5.** the people of a parish (ecclesiastical or civil). [ME, t. OF: m. *paroisse*, g. LL *parochia*, var. of *paroecia*, t. Gk.: m. *paroikia*]

pa·rish·ion·er (pə rĭsh'ən ər), *n.* one of the community or inhabitants of a parish. [f. earlier *parishion* (t. OF: m. *parochien*) + -ER[1]]

par·i·ty[1] (pär'ə tĭ), *n.* **1.** equality, as in amount, status, or character. **2.** equivalence; correspondence; similarity or analogy. **3.** *Finance.* **a.** equivalence in value in the currency of another country. **b.** equivalence in value at a fixed ratio between moneys of different metals. **4.** *Physics.* a symmetry property of a wave function: if the parity is even (+1), the function is not changed by a mirror reflection of the coördinate system; if the parity is odd (−1), the function changes sign. **5.** a system of regulating prices of farm commodities, usually by government price supports, to provide farmers with the same purchasing power they had in a selected base period. [t. LL: m.s. *pāritas*, der. L *pār* equal]

par·i·ty[2] (pär'ə tĭ), *n. Obstet.* condition or fact of having borne offspring. [f. s. L *parere* bring forth + -ITY]

park (pärk), *n.* **1.** a tract of land set apart, as by a city or a nation, for the benefit of the public: *Central Park, Yellowstone National Park.* **2.** a tract of land set apart

for recreation, sports, etc.: *a baseball park.* **3.** a considerable extent of land forming the grounds of a country house. **4.** *Brit.* an enclosed tract of land for wild beasts. **5.** *U.S.* a high plateaulike valley. **6.** a space where vehicles, esp. automobiles, may be assembled or stationed. **7.** *Mil.* **a.** the space occupied by the assembled guns, tanks, stores, etc., of a body of soldiers. **b.** the assemblage formed. **c.** complete equipment, as of guns, etc. —*v.t.* **8.** to put or leave (an automobile, etc.) for a time in a particular place, as on the street. **9.** *U.S. Colloq.* to put or leave. **10.** to assemble (artillery, etc.) in compact arrangement. **11.** to enclose in or as in a park. —*v.i.* **12.** to park a car, bicycle, etc. [ME *parc*, t. OF; of Gmc. orig., akin to G *pferch* fold, pen, and OE *pearroc* enclosure, and to PADDOCK[1]]

Park (pärk), *n.* **Mungo** (mŭng'gō), 1771–1806?, Scottish explorer in Africa.

par·ka (pär'kə), *n.* **1.** a fur coat, cut like a shirt, worn in northeastern Asia and in Alaska. **2.** a long woolen shirtlike garment with an attached hood. [t. Russ.]

Park Avenue, a street in New York City which, because of its large, expensive apartment houses, has come to represent luxury, the height of fashion, etc.

Par·ker (pär'kər), *n.* **1. Sir Gilbert,** 1862–1932, Canadian novelist and politician in England. **2. Theodore,** 1810–60, U.S. preacher, theologian, and reformer.

Par·kers·burg (pär'kərz bûrg'), *n.* a city in NW West Virginia, on the Ohio river. 44,797 (1960).

Park Forest, a city in NE Illinois. 29,993 (1960).

Par·kin·son's disease (pär'kən sənz), *Pathol.* a form of paralysis characterized by tremor, muscular rigidity, and weakness of movement; also called **paralysis agitans, shaking palsy.** Also, **Par'kin·son·ism.** [named after *James Parkinson*, 1755–1824, British physician who first described it]

park·land (pärk'lănd'), *n.* a grassland region with isolated or grouped trees, usually in temperate regions.

Park·man (pärk'mən), *n.* **Francis,** 1823–93, U.S. historian.

Park Range, a range of the Rocky Mountains in central Colorado. Highest peak, Mt. Lincoln, 14,287 ft.

Park Ridge, a city in NE Illinois. 32,659 (1960).

park·way (pärk'wā'), *n.* a broad thoroughfare with spaces planted with grass, trees, etc.

Parl. **1.** Parliament. **2.** (*also l.c.*) Parliamentary.

par·lance (pär'ləns), *n.* **1.** way of speaking, or language: *legal parlance.* **2.** *Archaic.* talk; parley. [t. AF, der. *parler* speak, der. L *parabola.* See PARABLE]

par·lay (pär'lĭ, pär lā'), *U.S.* —*v.t., v.i.* **1.** to bet (an original amount and its winnings) on a subsequent race, contest, etc. —*n.* **2.** such a bet. [alter. of *paroli*, t. F. t. It., possibly der. Neapolitan *paro* pair]

par·ley (pär'lĭ), *n., pl.* **-leys,** *v.,* **-leyed, -leying.** —*n.* **1.** a discussion; a conference. **2.** an informal conference between enemies under truce, to discuss terms, conditions of surrender, etc. —*v.i.* **3.** to hold an informal conference with an enemy, under a truce, as between active hostilities. **4.** to speak, talk, or confer. Also, *Archaic* or *Brit. Dial.*, **parl.** [t. F: m. *parlée* speech]

par·lia·ment (pär'lə mənt), *n.* **1.** (*usually cap.*) the legislature of Great Britain, historically the assembly of the three estates, now composed of lords spiritual and lords temporal (forming together the **House of Lords**), and representatives of the counties, cities, boroughs, and universities (forming the **House of Commons**). **2.** (*usually cap.*) the legislature of certain British colonies and possessions. **3.** any one of similar legislative bodies in other countries. **4.** (in pre-Revolutionary France) the highest court in each province, succeeding the feudal "parlements", which were both courts and councils. **5.** a meeting or assembly for conference on public or national affairs. Also, *Obs.*, **par'le·ment.** [ME *parlement*, t. OF. der. *parler* speak. See PARLANCE]

par·lia·men·tar·i·an (pär'lə mĕn târ'ĭ ən), *n.* **1.** one skilled in parliamentary procedure or debate. **2.** *Brit.* a member of Parliament. **3.** (*cap.*) a partisan of the British Parliament in opposition to Charles I.

par·lia·men·ta·ry (pär'lə mĕn'tər ĭ), *adj.* **1.** of or pertaining to a parliament. **2.** enacted or established by a parliament. **3.** characterized by the existence of a "parliament". **4.** of the nature of a parliament. **5.** in accordance with the rules and usages of parliaments or deliberative bodies: *parliamentary procedure.*

par·lor (pär'lər), *n.* **1.** a room for the reception and entertainment of visitors; a living room. **2.** a semiprivate room in a hotel, club, or the like for relaxation, conversation, etc.; a lounge. **3.** *U.S.* a room more or less elegantly fitted up for the reception of business patrons or customers: *a tonsorial parlor.* Also, *Brit.,* **par'lour.** [ME *parlur*, t. AF, der. *parler* speak. See PARLANCE]

parlor car, a railroad passenger car for day or evening travel, fitted with individual reserved seats, and more comfortable than ordinary passenger cars.

par·lor·maid (pär'lər mād'), *n.* a maid who takes care of a parlor, waits on guests, etc.

par·lous (pär'ləs), *Archaic.* —*adj.* **1.** perilous; dangerous. **2.** very great. **3.** clever; shrewd. —*adv.* **4.** very. [ME; var. of PERILOUS] —**par'lous·ly,** *adv.*

parl. proc., parliamentary procedure.

Par·ma (pär'mä), *n.* **1.** a city in N Italy. 122,000 (est 1954). **2.** a city in NE Ohio. 82,845 (1960).

Par·men·i·des (pär mĕn'ə dēz'), *n.* fl. c475 B.C., Greek Eleatic philosopher, born in Italy.

Par·me·san (pär'mə zăn'), *adj.* of or from Parma in northern Italy. [t. F, t. It.: m. *parmigiano*, der. *Parma*]

Parmesan cheese, a hard, dry, fine-flavored variety of Italian cheese, made from skim milk.

Par·na·hi·ba (pär'nə ē'bə), *n.* a river in NE Brazil, flowing NE to the Atlantic. ab. 900 mi. Also, **Par'na·hy'ba.**

Par·nas·si·an (pär năs'Yən), *adj.* 1. pertaining to Mount Parnassus, or to poetry. 2. noting or pertaining to a school of French poets, of the latter half of the 19th century, characterized esp. by emphasis of form and by repression of emotion (so called from *Le Parnasse Contemporain,* the title of their first collection of poems, published in 1866). —*n.* 3. a member of the Parnassian school of French poets. [f. s. L *Parnās(s)ius,* (der. *Parnās(s)us*) + -AN. Cf. F *Parnassien*]

Par·nas·sus (pär năs'əs), *n.* 1. **Mount,** Modern, **Liakoura.** a mountain in central Greece, in ancient Phocis: sacred to Apollo and the Muses, and symbolic of poetic inspiration and achievement. 8068 ft. 2. a collection of poems or of elegant literature.

Par·nell (pär'nəl, pär nĕl'), *n.* **Charles Stewart,** 1846–91, Irish political leader.

pa·ro·chi·al (pə rō'kY əl), *adj.* 1. of or pertaining to a parish or parishes. 2. confined to or interested only in one's own parish, or some particular narrow district or field. [ME, t. LL: s. *parochiālis,* der. LL *parochia.* See PARISH] —**pa·ro'chi·al·ly,** *adv.*

pa·ro·chi·al·ism (pə rō'kY ə lĭz'əm), *n.* parochial character, spirit, or tendency; narrowness of interests or view.

parochial school, an elementary or high school maintained and operated by a religious organization.

par·o·dy (păr'ə dĭ), *n., pl.* **-dies,** *v.,* **-died, -dying.** —*n.* 1. a humorous imitation of a serious piece of literature or writing. 2. the kind of literary composition represented by such imitations. 3. a burlesque imitation of a musical composition. 4. a poor imitation; a travesty. —*v.t.* 5. to imitate (a composition, author, etc.) in such a way as to ridicule. 6. to imitate poorly. [t. L: m.s. *parōdia,* t. Gk.: m. *parōidía* burlesque poem] —**par'o·dist,** *n.*

pa·roi·cous (pə roi'kəs), *adj. Bot.* (of certain mosses) having the male and female reproductive organs beside or near each other. Also, **parecious, pa·roe·cious** (pə rē'shəs). [t. Gk.: m. *pároikos* dwelling beside]

pa·rol (pə rōl', păr'əl), *Law.* —*n.* 1. the pleadings in a suit. —*adj.* 2. given by word of mouth; oral; not written (opposed to *documentary,* or given by affidavit): *parol evidence.* [t. AF (legal): m. *parole.* See PAROLE]

pa·role (pə rōl'), *n., v.,* **-roled, -roling.** —*n.* 1. Penol. **a.** the liberation of a person from prison, conditional upon good behavior, prior to the end of the maximum sentence imposed upon that person. **b.** such release or its duration. 2. *Mil.* **a.** the promise of a prisoner of war to refrain from trying to escape, or, if released, to return to custody or to forbear taking up arms against his captors. **b.** a password given by authorized personnel in passing through a guard. 3. word of honor given or pledged. 4. *Law.* parol. —*v.t.* 5. to put on parole. [t. F, g. L *parabola.* See PARABLE]

pa·rol·ee (pə rō'lē'), *n.* one who is released on parole.

par·o·no·ma·si·a (păr'ə nō mā'zhY ə, -zĭ ə), *n. Rhet.* 1. a playing on words; punning. 2. a pun. [t. L, t. Gk.] —**par·o·no·mas·tic** (păr'ə nō măs'tĭk), *adj.*

par·o·nym (păr'ə nĭm), *n. Gram.* a paronymous word.

pa·ron·y·mous (pə rŏn'ə məs), *adj.* (of words) containing the same root or stem, as *wise* and *wisdom.* [t. Gk.: m. *parónymos* derivative]

par·o·quet (păr'ə kĕt'), *n.* parakeet.

Par·os (pâr'ŏs; *Gk.* pä'rŏs), *n.* a Greek island in the S Aegean: one of the Cyclades; noted for its marble. 9022 pop. (1951); 77 sq. mi.

pa·ro·tic (pə rō'tĭk, pə rŏt'Yk), *adj. Anat., Zool.* situated about or near the ear.

pa·rot·id (pə rŏt'Yd), *Anat.* —*n.* 1. either of two saliva-producing glands situated one at the base of each ear. —*adj.* 2. noting, pertaining to, or situated near either parotid. [t. L: s. *parōtis,* t. Gk.: tumor near the ear]

par·o·tit·ic (păr'ə tĭt'Yk), *adj.* having the mumps.

par·o·ti·tis (păr'ə tī'tYs), *n. Pathol.* mumps. Also, **pa·rot·i·di·tis** (pə rŏt'ə dī'tYs). [t. NL; see PAROT(ID), -ITIS]

pa·ro·toid (pə rō'toid), *Zool.* —*adj.* 1. resembling a parotid gland. 2. denoting certain cutaneous glands forming warty masses or excrescences near the ear in certain salientians, as toads. —*n.* 3. a parotoid gland. [f. Gk. *parōt(ís)* (see PAROTID) + -OID]

-parous, an adjective termination meaning "bringing forth," "bearing," "producing," as in *oviparous, viviparous.* [t. L: m. *-parus,* der. *parere* bring forth]

par·ox·ysm (păr'ək sĭz'əm), *n.* 1. any sudden, violent outburst; a fit of violent action or emotion: *paroxysms of rage.* 2. *Pathol.* a severe attack, or increase in violence, of a disease, usually recurring periodically. [t. ML: s. *paroxysmus,* t. Gk.: m. *paroxysmós* irritation] —**par'ox·ys'mal,** *adj.*

par·ox·y·tone (păr ŏk'sə tōn'), *Greek Gram.* —*adj.* 1. having an acute accent on the next to the last syllable. —*n.* 2. a paroxytone word. [t. Gk.: m.s. *paroxýtonos.* See PARA-¹, OXYTONE]

par·quet (pär kā', pär kĕt'), *n., v.,* **-queted, -queting** or

---

(*esp. Brit.*) **-quetted, -quetting.** —*n.* 1. a floor of inlaid design. 2. the part of·the main floor of a theater, etc., between the musicians' space and the parterre or rear division, or (*esp. U.S.*) the entire floor space for spectators. —*v.t.* 3. to construct (a flooring, etc.) of parquetry. 4. to furnish with a floor, etc., of parquetry. [t. F: part of a park, flooring, dim. of *parc* PARK]

parquet circle, a space with curving tiers of seats behind and around the parquet of a theater, etc.

par·quet·ry (pär'kY trY), *n.* mosaic work of wood used for floors, wainscoting, etc. [t. F: m. *parqueterie*]

Parquetry

parr (pär), *n., pl.* **parrs,** (*esp. collectively*) **parr.** 1. a young salmon, having dark crossbars on its sides. 2. the young of some other fishes, as the codfish. [orig. unknown]

Parr (pär), *n.* **Catherine,** 1512–48, sixth wife of Henry VIII of England.

par·ra·keet (păr'ə kēt'), *n.* parakeet. Also, **par·ro·ket** (păr'ə kĕt'), **par'ro·quet'.**

par·ra·mat·ta (păr'ə măt'ə), *n.* paramatta.

Par·ran (păr'ən), *n.* **Thomas,** born 1892, surgeon general of U.S. Public Health Service 1936–1948.

par·rel (păr'əl), *n. Naut.* a sliding ring or collar of rope or iron, which confines a yard or the jaws of a gaff to the mast but allows vertical movement. Also, **par'ral.** [ME *parail,* aphetic var. of *aparail* APPAREL]

par·ri·cide¹ (păr'ə sĭd'), *n.* one who kills either of his parents or any one else to whom he owes reverence. [t. F, t. L: m. *parricīda,* appar. der. *pater* father. See -CIDE¹, PATRICIDE] —**par'ri·cid'al,** *adj.*

par·ri·cide² (păr'ə sĭd'), *n.* the act or crime of killing one's father. [t. F, t. L: m. *parricīdium.* See -CIDE²]

Par·ring·ton (pär'Yng tən), *n.* **Vernon Louis,** 1871–1929, U.S. literary historian and critic.

Par·rish (păr'Ysh), *n.* **Maxfield,** born 1870, U.S. artist.

par·rot (păr'ət), *n.* 1. any of numerous hook-billed, fleshy-tongued, often gaily colored birds which constitute the order *Psittaciformes,* as the cockatoo, lory, macaw, parakeet, etc., valued as cage birds because they can be taught to talk. 2. a person who unintelligently repeats the words or imitates the actions of another. —*v.t.* 3. to repeat or imitate like a parrot. 4. to teach to repeat or imitate thus. [t. F: m. *Perrot, Pierrot,* dim. of *Pierre* Peter]

parrot fever, psittacosis. Also, **parrot disease.**

parrot fish, any of various marine fishes so called because of their coloring or the shape of their jaws, mainly tropical, mostly of the family *Scaridae,* and certain species of the family *Labridae,* esp. *Labrichthys psittacula,* of Australasia and *Halichoeres radiatus* of Florida, the West Indies, etc.

par·ry (păr'Y), *v.,* **-ried, -rying,** *n., pl.* **-ries.** —*v.t.* 1. to ward off (a thrust, stroke, weapon, etc.), as in fencing. 2. to turn aside, evade, or avoid. —*v.i.* 3. to parry a thrust, etc. —*n.* 4. an act or mode of parrying as in fencing. 5. a defensive movement in fencing. [prob. t. F: m. *parez,* impv. of *parer,* t. It.: m. *parare* ward off, protect, g. L: make ready, prepare]

Par·ry (păr'Y), *n.* **William Edward,** 1790–1855, British arctic explorer.

parse (pärs, pärz), *v.t.,* **parsed, parsing.** to describe (a word or series of words) grammatically, telling the part of speech, inflectional form, syntactic relations, etc. [t. L: m. *pars* part, as in *pars ōrātiōnis* part of speech] —**pars'er,** *n.*

par·sec (pär'sĕk'), *n. Astron.* a unit of distance corresponding to a heliocentric parallax of one second of arc, being equal to 206,265 times the distance of the earth from the sun (or about 3.26 light years). [f. PAR(ALLAX) + SEC(OND)²]

Par·see (pär'sē, pär sē'), *n.* one of a Zoroastrian sect in India, descendants of the Persians who settled in India in the 8th century to escape Mohammedan persecution. Also, **Par'si.** [t. Pers. and Hind.: m. *Pārsī* a Persian]

Par·see·ism (pär'sē Yz'əm, pär sē'Yz əm), *n.* the religion and customs of the Parsees. Also, **Par'si·ism.**

Par·si·fal (pär'sə fəl, -fäl'), *n.* 1. a music drama (composed 1877–82; premiere, 1882) by Wagner. 2. *Germanic Myth.* Parzival.

par·si·mo·ni·ous (pär'sə mō'nY əs), *adj.* characterized by or showing parsimony; sparing or frugal, esp. to excess. —**par'si·mo'ni·ous·ly,** *adv.*

par·si·mo·ny (pär'sə mō'nĭ), *n.* 1. extreme or excessive economy or frugality; niggardliness. [ME, t. L: m.s. *parsimōnia, parcimōnia,* lit., sparingness]

pars·ley (pärs'lY), *n.* 1. a garden herb, *Petroselinum crispum,* with aromatic leaves which are much used to garnish or season food. 2. any of certain allied or similar plants. [ME *persely,* b. OF *per(esil)* (g. LL *petrosilium*) and OE *(peter)silie,* t. LL]

pars·nip (pärs'nYp), *n.* 1. a plant, *Pastinaca sativa,* cultivated varieties of which have a large whitish edible root. 2. the root. [ME *pasnepe* (influenced by ME *nepe* NEEP), t. OF: m. *pasnaie,* g. L *pastināca*]

par·son (pär'sən), *n.* 1. a clergyman, minister, or preacher. 2. the holder or incumbent of a parochial benefice. [ME *persone,* t. ML: m. *persōna* parson, in L person. See PERSON]

par·son·age (pär′sən ĭj), *n.* **1.** the residence of a parson or clergyman, as provided by the parish or church. **2.** *Obs. or Legal.* the benefice of a parson.

part (pärt), *n.* **1.** a portion or division of a whole, separate in reality, or in thought only; a piece, fragment, fraction, or section; a constituent. **2.** an essential or integral portion. **3.** a portion, member, or organ of an animal body. **4.** each of a number of equal portions composing a whole: *a third part.* **5.** *Math.* an aliquot part or exact divisor. **6.** an allotted portion; a share. **7.** (*usually pl.*) a region, quarter, or district: *foreign parts.* **8.** one of the sides to a contest, question, agreement, etc. **9.** the dividing line formed in parting the hair. **10.** an extra piece for replacing worn out parts of a tool, machine, etc. **11.** *Music.* **a.** a voice, either vocal or instrumental. **b.** the written or printed matter extracted from the score which a single performer or section uses in the performance of concerted music: *a horn part.* **12.** participation, interest, or concern in something. **13.** one's share in some action; a duty, function, or office: *nature didn't do her part.* **14.** a character sustained in a play or in real life; a role. **15.** the words or lines assigned to an actor. **16.** (*usually pl.*) a personal or mental quality or endowment. **17.** Some special noun phrases are:
for my (his, etc.) **part**, so far as concerns me (him, etc.)
for the most part, as concerns the greatest part; mostly.
in good part, with favor; without offense.
in part, in some measure or degree; to some extent.
part and parcel, an essential part.
take part, to participate.
[ME and OE, t. L: s. *pars* piece, portion, share, role, region, party]
—*v.t.* **18.** to divide (a thing) into parts; break; cleave; divide. **19.** to comb (the hair) away from a dividing line. **20.** to dissolve (a connection, etc.) by separation of the parts, persons, or things involved: *she parted company with her sisters.* **21.** to divide into shares; distribute in parts; apportion. **22.** to put or keep asunder (two or more parts, persons, etc., or one part, person, etc., from another); draw or hold apart; disunite; separate. **23.** *Obs.* to leave. —*v.i.* **24.** to be or become divided into parts; break or cleave: *the frigate parted amidships.* **25.** to go or come apart or asunder, or separate, as two or more things. **26.** to go apart from each other or one another, as persons: *we'll part no more.* **27.** to be or become separated from something else (usually fol. by *from*). **28.** *Naut.* to break or rend, as a cable. **29.** to depart. **30.** to die. **31.** part with, **a.** to give up; relinquish: *I parted with my gold.* **b.** to depart from. [ME *parte(n)*, t. F: m.s. *partir*, g. L *partire*]
—**Syn. 1.** PART, PIECE, PORTION refer to that which is less than the whole. PART is the general word: *part of a house.* A PIECE suggests a part which is itself a complete unit, often of standardized form: *a piece of pie.* A PORTION is a part allotted or assigned to a person, purpose, etc.: *a portion of food.* —**Ant. 1.** whole.

part., **1.** participle. **2.** particular.

par·take (pär tāk′), *v.*, **-took, -taken, -taking.** —*v.i.* **1.** to take or have a part or share in common with others: participate (fol. by *in*). **2.** to receive, take, or have a share (fol. by *of*). **3.** to have something of the nature or character (fol. by *of*): *feelings partaking of both joy and regret.* —*v.t.* **4.** to take or have a part in; share. [back formation from *partaking, partaker,* for *part-taking, part-taker,* trans. of L *participātio, particeps*] —**par·tak′er,** *n.* —**Syn. 1.** See **share¹.**

par·tan (pär′tən), *n. Scot.* a crab. [t. Gael]

part·ed (pär′tĭd), *adj.* **1.** divided into parts; cleft. **2.** put or kept apart; separated. **3.** *Bot.* (of a leaf) separated into rather distinct portions by incisions which extend nearly to the midrib or the base. **4.** *Archaic.* deceased.

par·terre (pär târ′), *n.* **1.** the part of the main floor of a theater, etc., behind the orchestra or parquet, often under the galleries. **2.** an ornamental arrangement of flower beds of different shapes and sizes. [t. F, f. *par* by, on (g. L *per*) + *terre* earth (g. L *terra*)]

par·the·no·gen·e·sis (pär′thə nō jĕn′ə sĭs), *n. Biol.* development of an egg without fertilization. [f. Gk. *parthéno*(s) virgin + GENESIS] —**par·the·no·ge·net·ic** (pär′thə nō jə nĕt′ĭk), *adj.*

Par·the·non (pär′thə nŏn′, -nən), *n.* the temple of Athene on the Acropolis of Athens, completed (structurally) about 438 B.C., regarded as the finest example of Doric temple architecture. [t. L, t. Gk., der. *parthénos* virgin (*Athénē Parthénos* Athene the Virgin)]

Par·then·o·pe (pär thĕn′ə pē′), *n. Gk. Legend.* a Siren who drowned herself when Ulysses remained adamant to her songs.

Par·the·nos (pär′thə nŏs′), *n.* maiden or virgin (applied to some Greek goddesses, esp. Athene).

Par·thi·a (pär′thĭ ə), *n.* an ancient country in W Asia, SE of the Caspian Sea: conquered by the Iranians, A.D. 226; now a part of NE Iran. —**Par′thi·an,** *adj., n.*

Parthian shot, **1.** a rearward shot by a fleeing mounted archer. **2.** any sharp parting remark.

par·tial (pär′shəl), *adj.* **1.** pertaining to or affecting a part. **2.** being such in part only; not total or general; incomplete: *partial blindness.* **3.** *Bot.* secondary or subordinate: *a partial umbel.* **4.** being a part; component or constituent. **5.** biased or prejudiced in favor of

a person, group, side, etc. as in a controversy. **6.** particularly inclined in fondness or liking (fol. by *to*): *I'm partial to sodas.* [ME, t. LL: s. *partiālis,* der. L *pars* PART, n.] —**par′tial·ly,** *adv.* —**Syn. 5.** one-sided, unfair, unjust.

partial fractions, *Alg.* one of the fractions into which a given fraction can be resolved, the sum of such simpler fractions being equal to the given fraction.

par·tial·i·ty (pär shăl′ə tĭ, pär′shĭ ăl′-), *n., pl.* **-ties.** **1.** the state or character of being partial. **2.** favorable bias or prejudice: *the partiality of parents for their own offspring.* **3.** a particular fondness or liking: *he had always shown a partiality for society.*

partial tone, *Chiefly Music.* one of the pure tones forming a part of a complex tone; the fundamental tone or a harmonic.

par·ti·ble (pär′tə bəl), *adj.* that may be parted or divided; divisible.

par·ti·ceps cri·mi·nis (pär′tə sĕps′ krĭm′ə nĭs), *Latin.* an accomplice in a crime.

par·tic·i·pant (pär tĭs′ə pənt), *n.* **1.** one who participates; a participator. —*adj.* **2.** participating; sharing.

par·tic·i·pate (pär tĭs′ə pāt′), *v.,* **-pated, -pating.** —*v.i.* **1.** to take or have a part or share, as with others; share (fol. by *in*): *to participate in profits.* —*v.t.* **2.** to take or have a part or share in; share. [t. L: m.s. *participātus,* pp.] —**par·tic′i·pa′tor,** *n.* —**Syn. 1.** See **share¹.**

par·tic·i·pa·tion (pär tĭs′ə pā′shən), *n.* **1.** the act or fact of participating. **2.** a taking part, as in some action or attempt. **3.** a sharing, as in benefits or profits.

par·ti·cip·i·al (pär′tə sĭp′ĭ əl), *Gram.* —*adj.* **1.** of or pertaining to a participle. **2.** similar to or formed from a participle. —*n.* **3.** a participle. [t. L: s. *participiālis*] —**par′ti·cip′i·al·ly,** *adv.*

par·ti·ci·ple (pär′tə sə pəl, -sĭp′əl), *n. Gram.* (in many languages) an adjective form derived from verbs, which ascribes to a noun participation in the action or state of the verb, without specifying person or number of the subject. For example: *burning* in *a burning candle* or *devoted* in *his devoted friend.* [ME, t. OF, der. *participe* (b. with ending -*ple*), t. L: m.s. *participium* a sharing]

par·ti·cle (pär′tə kəl), *n.* **1.** a minute portion, piece, or amount; a very small bit: *a particle of dust.* **2.** a clause or article, as of a document. **3.** *Rom. Cath. Ch.* **a.** a little piece of the Host. **b.** the small Host given to each lay communicant. **4.** *Gram.* **a.** (in some languages) one of the major form classes, or "parts of speech," consisting of words which are neither nouns nor verbs, or of all uninflected words, or the like. **b.** such a word. **c.** a small word of functional or relational use, such as an article, preposition, or conjunction, whether of a separate form class or not. [ME, t. L: m.s. *particula,* dim. of *pars* PART, n.] —**Syn. 1.** mite, whit, iota, jot, tittle.

par·ti·col·ored (pär′tĭ kŭl′ərd), *adj.* colored differently in different parts, or variegated: *parti-colored dress.* Also, **party-colored.**

par·tic·u·lar (pər tĭk′yə lər), *adj.* **1.** pertaining to some one person, thing, group, class, occasion, etc., rather than to others or all; special, not general: *one's particular interests.* **2.** being a definite one, individual, or single, or considered separately: *each particular item.* **3.** distinguished or different from others or from the ordinary; noteworthy; marked; unusual. **4.** exceptional or especial: *to take particular pains.* **5.** being such in an exceptional degree: *a particular friend of mine.* **6.** dealing with or giving details, as an account, description, etc., or a person; detailed; minute; circumstantial. **7.** attentive to or exacting about details or small points: *to be particular about one's food.* **8.** *Logic.* **a.** not general; not referring to the whole extent of a class, but only to an indefinite part of it: *"some men are wealthy"* is a particular proposition. **b.** partaking of the nature of the individual as opposed to the universal. **9.** *Law.* **a.** denoting an estate which precedes a future or ultimate ownership, as lands devised to a widow during her lifetime, and after that to her children. **b.** denoting the tenant of such an estate. —*n.* **10.** an individual or distinct part, as an item of a list or enumeration. **11.** a point, detail, or circumstance: *a report complete in every particular.* **12.** *Logic.* an individual or a specific group subordinate to a general class or concept. **13. in particular,** particularly; especially: *one book in particular.* [t. L: s. *particulāris* of a part, partial; r. ME *particuler,* t. OF]
—**Syn. 1.** See **special. 7.** PARTICULAR, DAINTY, FASTIDIOUS imply great care, discrimination, and taste in choices, in details about one's person, etc. PARTICULAR implies esp. care and attention to details: *particular about one's clothes.* DAINTY implies delicate taste, and exquisite cleanliness: *a dainty dress.* FASTIDIOUS implies being difficult to please, and critical of small or minor points: *a fastidious taste in styles.* —**Ant. 7.** careless, slovenly, undiscriminating.

par·tic·u·lar·ism (pər tĭk′yə lə rĭz′əm), *n.* **1.** exclusive attention or devotion to one's own particular interests, party, etc. **2.** the principle of leaving each state of a federation free to retain its laws and promote its interests. **3.** *Theol.* the doctrine that divine grace is provided only for the elect. —**par·tic′u·lar·ist,** *n.* —**par·tic′u·lar·ist′ic,** *adj.*

par·tic·u·lar·i·ty (pər tĭk′yə lăr′ə tĭ), *n., pl.* **-ties.** **1.** the quality or fact of being particular. **2.** special, peculiar, or individual character. **3.** detailed, minute, or circumstantial character, as of description or statement. **4.** attentiveness to details or small points, or special carefulness. **5.** fastidiousness. **6.** that which is particular; a particular or characteristic feature or trait.

par·tic·u·lar·ize (pərtĭk′yələrīz′), v., **-ized, -izing.** —v.t. **1.** to make particular (rather than general). **2.** to mention or indicate particularly. **3.** to state or treat in detail. —v.i. **4.** to speak or treat particularly or specifically; mention individuals. **—par·tic′u·lar·i·za′tion,** n. **—par·tic′u·lar·iz′er,** n.

par·tic·u·lar·ly (pərtĭk′yələrlĭ), adv. **1.** in a particular or exceptional degree; especially: he read it with particularly great interest. **2.** in a particular manner; specially; individually. **3.** in detail; minutely. **—Syn. 1.** See especially.

part·ing (pär′tĭng), n. **1.** the act of one who or that which parts. **2.** division; separation. **3.** leave-taking; departure. **4.** death. **5.** a place of division or separation. **6.** something that serves to part or separate things. —adj. **7.** given, taken, done, etc., at parting: a parting shot. **8.** of or pertaining to parting, leave-taking, departure, or death. **9.** departing: the parting day. **10.** dying. **11.** dividing; separating.

parting strip, a strip, as of wood, used to keep two parts separated, as one in each side of the frame of a window to keep the sashes apart when lowered or raised.

par·ti pris (pär tē′ prē′), French. decision taken; foregone conclusion.

par·ti·san[1] (pär′təzən), n. **1.** an adherent or supporter of a person, party, or cause. **2.** Mil. a member of a party of light or irregular troops engaged in harassing the enemy; a guerrilla. —adj. **3.** pertaining to or carried on by military partisans. **4.** of, pertaining to, or characteristic of partisans. Also, **partizan.** [t. F, t. It.: m. partigiano, der. parte part, n., g. L pars] **—par′ti·san·ship′,** n. **—Syn. 1, 2.** See follower.

par·ti·san[2] (pär′təzən), n. a shafted weapon with broad blade and curved basal lobes, esp. carried by bodyguards. Also, **partizan.** [t. F: m. partizane, t. It.: m. partigiana fem., n. use of partigiano, adj., PARTISAN[1]]

par·tite (pär′tīt), adj. **1.** divided into parts. **2.** Bot., etc. parted. [t. L: m.s. partītus, pp.]

par·ti·tion (pärtĭsh′ən), n. **1.** division into or distribution in portions or shares. **2.** separation, as of two or more things. **3.** something that separates. **4.** a part, division, or section. **5.** an interior wall or barrier dividing a building, enclosure, etc. **6.** a septum or dissepiment, as in a plant or animal structure. **7.** Law. **a.** a division of property among joint owners or tenants in common, or a sale of such property followed by a division of the proceeds. **b.** a division of real property held in co-ownership. **8.** Logic. the separation of a whole into its integrant parts. **9.** Math. a mode of separating a positive whole number into a sum of positive whole numbers. **10.** (in a speech organized on classical principles) the second part, usually short, in which a speaker announces the chief lines of thought he proposes to discuss in support of his theme. —v.t. **11.** to divide into parts or portions. **12.** to divide or separate by a partition. **13.** Law. to divide property among several owners, either in specie or by sale and division of the proceeds. [ME, t. L: s. partitio] **—par·ti′tion·er, —par·ti′tion·ment,** n. **—Syn. 1.** See division.

par·ti·tive (pär′tətĭv), adj. **1.** serving to divide into parts. **2.** Gram. denoting part of a whole: the Latin partitive genitive. —n. **3.** Gram. a partitive word or formation, as of the men in half of the men. **—par′ti·tive·ly,** adv.

par·ti·zan (pär′təzən), n., adj. partisan.

part·let (pärt′lĭt), n. Obs. a garment for the neck and shoulders, especially for women. [alter. of patelet, t. OF: m. patelette band of stuff]

part·ly (pärt′lĭ), adv. in part; in some measure; not wholly.

part music, music, esp. vocal music, with parts for two or more independent performers.

part·ner (pärt′nər), n. **1.** a sharer or partaker; an associate. **2.** Law. **a.** one associated with another or others as a principal or a contributor of capital in a business or a joint venture, usually sharing its risks and profits. **b.** See special partner. **3.** See silent partner. **4.** a husband or a wife. **5.** one's companion in a dance. **6.** a player on the same side with another in a game. **7.** (pl.) Naut. a framework of timber round a hole in a ship's deck, to support a mast, capstan, pump, etc. —v.t. **8.** to associate as a partner or partners. **9.** to be, or act as, the partner of. [ME partener, var. of PARCENER, appar. by assoc. with PART, n.] **—Syn. 1.** colleague, accessory, accomplice.

part·ner·ship (pärt′nərshĭp′), n. **1.** the state or condition of being a partner; participation; association; joint interest. **2.** Law. **a.** the relation subsisting between partners. **b.** the contract creating this relation. **c.** an association of persons joined as partners in business.

part of speech, Gram. any of the mutually exclusive major form classes of a language, which taken together include the entire vocabulary, e.g. in Latin, a word is either a noun, verb, pronoun, adjective, adverb, preposition, conjunction, or interjection.

par·took (pärtŏŏk′), v. pt. of **partake.**

par·tridge (pär′trĭj), n., pl. **-tridges,** (esp. collectively) **-tridge. 1.** any of various North American gallinaceous birds as, in New England, the ruffed grouse (Bonasa umbellus); in Virginia, the bob-white quail (Colinus virginianus), etc. **2.** any of various Old World gallinaceous gamebirds of the subfamily Perdicinae, esp. Perdix perdix, the common **gray partridge** of Europe. **3.** any of various South and Central American tinamous. [ME pertrich, t. OF: m. perdriz, perdiz, g. L perdix, t. Gk.]

par·tridge·ber·ry (pär′trĭjbĕr′Ĭ), n., pl. **-ries.** a North American trailing rubiaceous perennial, Mitchella repens, having roundish evergreen leaves, fragrant white flowers, and scarlet berries.

Partridge, Alectoris graeca (14½ in. long)

part song, a song with parts for several voices, esp. one meant to be sung without accompaniment.

par·tu·ri·ent (pärtyŏŏr′Ĭənt, -tŏŏr′-), adj. **1.** bringing forth or about to bring forth young; travailing. **2.** pertaining to parturition. **3.** bringing forth or about to produce something, as an idea. [t. L: s. parturiens, ppr., being in labor] **—par·tu′ri·en·cy,** n.

par·tu·ri·tion (pär′tyŏŏrĭsh′ən, -chŏŏ-), n. the act of bringing forth young; childbirth.

par·ty (pär′tĭ), n., pl. **-ties,** adj. —n. **1.** a group gathered together for some purpose, as for amusement or entertainment. **2.** a social gathering or entertainment, as of invited guests at a private house or elsewhere: to give a party. **3.** a detachment of troops assigned to perform some particular service. **4.** a number or body of persons ranged on one side, or united in purpose or opinion, in opposition to others, as in politics, etc.: the Republican party. **5.** the system of taking sides on public questions or the like. **6.** attachment or devotion to a side or faction; partisanship. **7.** Law. **a.** one of the litigants in a legal proceeding; a plaintiff or defendant in a suit. **b.** a signatory to a legal instrument. **c.** one participating in or otherwise privy to a crime. **8.** one who participates in some action or affair. **9.** U.S. Colloq. **a.** the person under consideration. **b.** a person in general. —adj. **10.** of or pertaining to a party or faction; partisan: party issues. **11.** Her. divided into parts, usually two parts, as a shield. [ME parti(e), t. OF, pp. of partir PART, v.] **—Syn. 1.** See company.

par·ty-col·ored (pär′tĭkŭl′ərd), adj. parti-colored.

party line, 1. a telephone line by which a number of subscribers are connected by one circuit to a central office. **2.** the bounding line between adjoining premises. **3.** the authoritatively announced policies and practices of a group, usually followed without exception: the Communist party line.

party man, a man belonging to a political party, esp. one who adheres strictly to the principles and policy of his party.

party wall, Law. a wall used, or usable, as a part of contiguous structures.

pa·rure (pərŏŏr′; Fr. pä ryr′), n. a set of jewels or ornaments. [ME, t. F, der. parer prepare, adorn. See PARE]

par·ve·nu (pär′vənū′, -nŏŏ′), n. **1.** one who has risen above his class or to a position above his qualifications; an upstart. —adj. **2.** being or resembling a parvenu. **3.** characteristic of a parvenu. [t. F, prop. pp. of parvenir arrive, g. L pervenīre]

par·vis (pär′vĭs), n. **1.** a vacant enclosed area in front of a church. **2.** a colonnade or portico in front of a church. [ME parvys, t. OF: m. parevis, g. LL paradīsus PARADISE]

par·vo·line (pär′vəlēn′, -lĭn), n. Chem. any of several oily isomeric, organic bases, one occurring in coal tar and another in decaying mackerel. Also, **par·vo·lin** (pär′vəlĭn). [f. s. L parvus small (with ref. to its relatively small volatility) + -OL[2] + -INE[2]; modeled on quinoline]

Par·zi·val (pär′tsĬ fäl′), n. the German counterpart of Percival. Also, **Parsifal.**

pas (pä), n. French. **1.** a step or movement in dancing, esp. in ballet. **2.** a dance. **3.** precedence; right of preceding. [see PACE[1]]

Pas·a·de·na (păs′ədē′nə), n. a city in SW California, near Los Angeles. 116,407 (1960).

Pa·sar·ga·dae (pəsär′gədē′), n. an ancient ruined city in S Iran, NE of Persepolis: an early capital of ancient Persia; tomb of Cyrus the Great.

Pas·cal (päs′kəl; Fr. päskál′), n. **Blaise** (blĕz), 1623–1662, French philosopher, mathematician, and physicist.

Pasch (päsk), n. Archaic. **1.** the Passover. **2.** Easter. [ME pasche, t. LL: m. pascha, t. Gk., t. Heb.: m. pesah Passover. Pop. var. of PESACH]

pas·chal (päs′kəl), adj. pertaining to the Passover, or to Easter. [ME paschall, t. LL: m.s. paschālis, der. pascha PASCH]

paschal flower, pasqueflower.

paschal lamb, 1. (among the Jews, during the existence of the Temple) the lamb slain and eaten at the Passover. **2.** (cap.) Christ. **3.** (cap.) any of various symbolical representations of Christ. Cf. **Agnus Dei.**

Pas de Ca·lais (pä də kàlĕ′). See **Dover, Strait of.**

pas de deux (pä də dœ′), French. a dance by two persons.

---

b., blend of, blended; c., cognate with; d., dialect, dialectal; der., derived from; f., formed from; g., going back to; m., modification of; r., replacing; s., stem of; t., taken from; ?, perhaps. See the full key on inside cover.

pash[1] (păsh), *Chiefly Dial.* —*v.t.* 1. to hurl or dash. 2. to smash or shatter. —*v.i.* 3. to dash or strike violently. [ME *pas(s)he(n)*; appar. imit.]

pash[2] (păsh), *n. Chiefly Scot.* the head. [orig. unknown]

pa·sha (pə·shä′, păsh′ə, pä′shə), *n.* a title, placed after the name, formerly borne by civil and military officials of high rank in Turkish dominions, Also, **pacha.** [t. Turk., var of *bāshā*, der. *bash* head, chief]

pa·sha·lik (pə·shä′lĭk), *n.* the territory governed by a pasha. Also, **pachalic, pa·sha′lic.** [t. Turk.: f. *pāshā* PASHA + *-lik*, suffix denoting quality or condition]

Pash·to (pŭsh′tō), *n.* Pushtu.

Pa·siph·a·ë (pə·sĭf′ĭ·ē′), *n. Gk. Legend.* wife of Minos, and mother of Ariadne. She was the mother of the Minotaur, by the white bull given to Minos by Poseidon.

pasque·flow·er (păsk′flou′ər), *n.* 1. an Old World ranunculaceous plant, *Anemone Pulsatilla*, with purple flowers blooming about Easter. 2. a similar plant, *A. ludoviciana*, whose flower is the State flower of South Dakota. [f. *Pasque* (var. spelling of PASCH) + FLOWER (so named by the herbalist Gerarde in 1597); r. *passe-flower*, t. F: m. *passe-fleur*. See PASS, v., FLOWER]

pas·quil (păs′kwĭl), *n.* a pasquinade.

pas·quin·ade (păs′kwĭ·nād′), *n., v.,* **-aded, -ading.** —*n.* 1. a publicly posted lampoon. —*v.t.* 2. to assail in a pasquinade or pasquinades. [t. F, t. It.: m. *pasquinata*, der. *Pasquino*, name given to an antique statue dug up in Rome (1501), which was decorated once a year and posted with verses] —**pas′quin·ad′er,** *n.*

pass (pás, päs), *v.,* **passed** or (*Rare*) **past; passed** or **past; passing;** *n.* —*v.t.* 1. to go by or move past (something). 2. to go by without acting upon or noticing; leave unmentioned. 3. to omit payment of (a dividend, etc.). 4. to go or get through (a channel, barrier, etc.). 5. to go across or over (a stream, threshold, etc.); cross. 6. to undergo successfully (an examination, etc.). 7. to go beyond (a point, degree, stage, etc.); transcend; exceed; surpass. 8. to cause to go or move onward; proceed: *to pass a rope through a hole.* 9. to cause to go by or move past: *to pass troops in review.* 10. to spend, as time. 11. to cause to go about or circulate; give currency to. 12. to cause to be accepted or received. 13. to convey, transfer, or transmit; deliver. 14. to pledge, as one's word. 15. to cause or allow to go through something, as through a test, etc. 16. to discharge or void, as excrement. 17. to sanction or approve: *to pass a bill.* 18. to obtain the approval or sanction of (a legislative body, etc.), as a bill. 19. to express or pronounce, as an opinion or judgment. 20. *Law.* to place legal title or interest in (another) by a conveyance, a will, or other transfer. 21. *Magic.* to perform a pass (def. 59) on (cards, etc.). 22. *Baseball.* to allow (a batter) to reach first base after four balls. —*v.i.* 23. to go or move onward; proceed; make one's or its way. 24. to go away or depart. 25. to elapse or be spent, as time. 26. to come to an end, as a thing in time. 27. to die. 28. *Colloq.* to faint (fol. by *out*). 29. to go on or take place; happen; occur: *to learn what has passed.* 30. to go by or move past, as a procession. 31. to go about or circulate; be current. 32. to be accepted or received (fol. by *for* or *as*): *material that passed for silk.* 33. to be transferred or conveyed. 34. to be interchanged, as between two persons: *sharp words passed between them.* 35. to undergo transition or conversion: *to pass from a solid to a liquid state.* 36. to go or get through something, such as a barrier, test, examination, etc. 37. to go unheeded, uncensured, or unchallenged: *but let that pass.* 38. to express or pronounce an opinion, judgment, verdict, etc. (usually fol. by *on* or *upon*). 39. to be voided, as excrement. 40. to be ratified or enacted, as a bill or law. 41. *Law.* **a.** (of a member of an inquest or other deliberative body) to sit: *to pass on.* **b.** to adjudicate. **c.** to vest title or other legal interest in real or personal property in a new owner. 42. *U.S.* to throw a ball from one to another; play catch. 43. *U.S.* to make a pass, as in football. 44. *Fencing.* to thrust or lunge. 45. *Cards.* **a.** to forgo one's opportunity to bid, play, etc. **b.** to throw up one's hand. 46. Some special verb phrases are:
bring to pass, to cause to happen.
come to pass, to occur.
pass away, 1. to cease to be. 2. to die.
pass off, 1. to put into circulation, or dispose of, esp. deceptively: *to pass off a bad dollar.* 2. to cause to be accepted or received in a false character; *he passed himself off as my servant.*
pass over, 1. to disregard. 2. to omit to notice.
[ME *passe(n)*, t. OF: m. *passer*, ult. der. L *passus* a step] —*n.* 47. a narrow route across a relatively low notch or depression in a mountain barrier separating the headwaters of approaching valleys from either side. 48. a way affording passage, as through an obstructed region or any barrier. [ME *pas*, t. F, g. L *passus* PACE[1]] 49. a navigable channel, as at the mouth or in the delta of a river. 50. a permission or license to pass, go, come, or enter. 51. *Mil.* **a.** a military document granting the right to cross lines, or to enter or leave a military or naval reservation or other area or building. **b.** written authority given a soldier to leave a station or duty for a few hours or days. 52. a free ticket. 53. *Chiefly Brit.* (in a university, course, etc.) the passing of an examination or course, but without honors. 54. the transference of a ball, etc., from one player to another, as in

football. 55. *Baseball.* the right to go to first base after four balls. 56. a thrust or lunge, as in fencing. 57. *Slang.* a jab with the arm, esp. one that misses its mark. 58. *Cards.* an act of not bidding or raising another bid. 59. *Magic, etc.* **a.** a passing of the hand over, along, or before anything. **b.** the transference or changing of objects by or as by sleight of hand; a manipulation, as of a juggler; a trick. 60. a stage in procedure or experience; a particular stage or state of affairs: *things have come to a pretty pass.* 61. the act of passing. 62. *Archaic.* a sally of wit. 63. **make a pass,** to make an amorous overture or gesture (usually fol. by *at*). [ME *passe*; partly n. use of PASS, v.; partly t. F, der. *passer*] —**Syn.** 27. See die[1].

pass., 1. passenger. 2. passive.

pass·a·ble (pás′ə·bəl, päs′-), *adj.* 1. that may be passed. 2. that may be proceeded through or over, or traversed, penetrated, crossed, etc., as a road, forest, or stream. 3. tolerable, fair, or moderate: *a passable knowledge of history.* 4. that may be circulated, or has valid currency, as a coin. 5. that may be ratified or enacted. [ME, t. F, der. *passer* PASS, v.] —**pass′a·ble·ness,** *n.*

pass·a·bly (pás′ə·blĭ, päs′-), *adv.* fairly; moderately.

pas·sa·ca·glia (päs′sä·kä′lyä), *n.* 1. a slow dance of Spanish origin. 2. the music for this dance, based on an ostinato figure.

pas·sade (pə·sād′), *n. Manège.* a turn or course of a horse backward or forward on the same ground.

pas·sa·do (pə·sä′dō), *n., pl.* **-dos, -does** (-dōz). *Fencing. Obs.* or *Archaic.* a forward thrust with the sword, one foot being advanced at the same time. [t. Sp.: m. *pasada,* t. It.: m. *passata,* der. *passare* PASS]

pas·sage[1] (pás′ĭj), *n., v.,* **-saged, -saging.** —*n.* 1. an indefinite portion of a writing, speech, or the like, usually one of no great length; a paragraph, verse, etc.: *a passage of Scripture.* 2. *Music.* **a.** a scalelike or arpeggiolike series of tones introduced as an embellishment; a run, roulade, or flourish. **b.** a phrase or other division of a piece. 3. act of passing. 4. liberty, leave, or right to pass: *to refuse passage through a territory.* 5. that by which a person or thing passes; a means of passing; a way, route, avenue, channel, etc. 6. *Chiefly Brit.* a hall, corridor, or the like. 7. movement, transit, or transition, as from one place or state to another. 8. a voyage across the sea from one port to another: *a rough passage.* 9. the privilege of conveyance as a passenger: *to secure passage for Europe.* 10. lapse, as of time. 11. progress or course, as of events. 12. the passing into law of a legislative measure. 13. an interchange of communications, confidences, etc., between persons. 14. an exchange of blows; an altercation or dispute: *a passage at arms.* 15. the causing of something to pass; transference; transmission. 16. an evacuation of the bowels. 17. *Archaic.* an occurrence, incident, or event. —*v.t.* 18. to make a passage; cross; pass; voyage. [ME, t. OF, der. *passer* PASS, v.]

pas·sage[2] (pás′ĭj), *v.,* **-saged, -saging,** *n. !Manège.* —*v.i.* 1. (of a horse) to move sideways, in obedience to pressure by the rider's leg on the opposite side. 2. (of a rider) to cause a horse to do this. —*v.t.* 3. to cause (a horse) to passage. —*n.* 4. the act of passaging. [t. F: m. s. *passager,* t. It.: m. *passeggiare* to pace, walk, der. *passo* pace, g. L *passus* PACE.]

Passage to India, novel (1924) by E. M. Forster.

pas·sage·way (pás′ĭj·wā′), *n.* a way for passage, as in a building or among buildings, etc.; a passage.

Pas·sa·ic (pə·sā′ĭk), *n.* a city in NE New Jersey. 53,963 (1960).

Pas·sa·ma·quod·dy Bay (pás′ə·mə·kwŏd′ĭ), an inlet of the Bay of Fundy, between Maine and New Brunswick, Canada, at the mouth of the St. Croix river.

pas·sant (pás′ənt), *adj. Her.* (of a beast used as a bearing) walking with one paw raised, and looking forward to the dexter side of the escutcheon. [ME, t. F, ppr. of *passer* PASS, v.]

pass·book (pás′bŏŏk′, päs′-), *n.* 1. a bankbook. 2. a customer's book in which a merchant or trader makes entries of goods sold on credit.

pas·sé (pá·sā′, päs′ā; *Fr.* pá·sĕ′), *adj.* 1. antiquated, or out of date. 2. past. 3. past the prime; aded. [t. F, pp. of *passer* PASS, v.]

passed (pást, päst), *adj.* 1. that has passed or has been passed. 2. having passed an examination or test. 3. *Naval.* having passed an examination for promotion, and awaiting a vacancy in the next grade. 4. *Finance.* denoting a dividend not paid at the usual dividend date.

passed ball, *Baseball.* a pitched ball, not hit by the batsman, which the catcher fails to stop, though it is within his reach, his failure allowing a base runner or base runners to advance.

passe·men·terie (pás·mĕn′trĭ; *Fr.* päs·män·trē′), *n.* trimming made of braid, cord, beads, etc., in various forms. [t. F, der. *passement,* der. *passer* PASS, v.]

pas·sen·ger (pás′ən·jər), *n.* 1. one who travels by some form of conveyance: *the passengers of a ship.* 2. a wayfarer. [ME *passenger,* t. OF: m. *passagier,* der. *passage* PASSAGE[1]; for *-n-,* cf. MESSENGER, etc.]

passenger pigeon, a wild pigeon, *Ectopistes migratorius,* once extraordinarily common in North America but now extinct.

passe par·tout (pás pär·tōō′; *Fr.* päs pär·tōō′), *French.* 1. a kind of ornamental mat for a picture. 2. a frame with such a mat, to receive a photograph or other representation. 3. a picture frame consisting of a piece of glass, under which the picture is placed, affixed to a backing by means of adhesive strips of paper or other material. 4. paper, etc., prepared for this purpose. 5. that which passes, or by means of which one can pass, everywhere. 6. a master key. [F: lit., pass-everywhere]

pass·er (păs/ər, päs/-), *n.* 1. one that passes or causes something to pass. 2. a passer-by.

pass·er-by (păs/ər bī/, päs/-), *n., pl.* **passers-by.** one who passes by.

pas·ser·ine (păs/ər ĭn, -ə rīn/), *adj.* 1. belonging or pertaining to the *Passeriformes*, an order of birds, typically insessorial (perching), embracing more than half of all birds, and including the finches, thrushes, warblers, swallows, crows, larks, etc. —*n.* 2. any bird of the order *Passeriformes.* [t. L: m.s. *passerīnus* of a sparrow]

pas seul (pä sœl/), *French.* a dance performed by one person.

pas·si·ble (păs/ə bəl), *adj.* capable of suffering or feeling; susceptible of sensation or emotion. [ME, t. LL: m.s. *passibilis*] —**pas/si·bil/i·ty,** *n.*

pas·si·flo·ra·ceous (păs/ĭ flō rā/shəs), *adj.* belonging to the *Passifloraceae*, or passionflower family of plants. [f. s. NL *Passiflōra*, the typical genus, (f. L: *passi(o)* passion + -*flōra*, fem. adj., flowering) + -ACEOUS]

pas·sim (păs/ĭm), *adv. Latin.* here and there, as in books or writings.

pass·ing (păs/ĭng, päs/-), *adj.* 1. that passes; going by; elapsing. 2. fleeting or transitory. 3. that is now happening; current. 4. done, given, etc., in passing; cursory: *a passing mention.* 5. surpassing, preëminent, or extreme. 6. indicating that one has passed: *a passing grade on the test.* —*adv.* 7. *Archaic.* surpassingly; exceedingly; very. —*n.* 8. act of one that passes or causes something to pass. 9. a means or place of passage; passage. 10. **in passing,** in the course of passing, going on, or proceeding.

passing bell, 1. a bell tolled to announce a death or funeral. 2. a portent or sign of the passing away of anything.

passing note, *Music.* a note foreign to the harmony, introduced between two successive chord tones in order to produce a melodic transition.

pas·sion (păsh/ən), *n.* 1. any kind of feeling or emotion, as hope, fear, joy, grief, anger, love, desire, etc., esp. when of compelling force. 2. strong amorous feeling or desire. 3. passionate sexual love. 4. an instance or experience of it. 5. a person who is the object of such a feeling. 6. a strong or extravagant fondness, enthusiasm, or desire for anything: *a passion for music.* 7. the object of such a fondness or desire: *accuracy became a passion with him.* 8. a passionate outburst: *she broke into a passion of tears.* 9. violent anger. 10. state or fact of being acted upon or affected by something external (opposed to *action*). 11. (*often cap.*) **a.** the sufferings of Christ on the cross, or his sufferings subsequent to the Last Supper. **b.** the gospel narrative of the sufferings of Christ, as in Mark 14–15, and parallel passages in the other gospels. **c.** a musical setting of it. **d.** a pictorial representation of Christ's sufferings. 12. *Archaic.* the sufferings of a martyr. [ME, t. OF, t. L: s. *passio* suffering] —**Syn.** 1. See **feeling.**

pas·sion·al (păsh/ən əl), *adj.* 1. of or pertaining to passion or the passions. 2. due to passion: *passional crimes.* —*n.* 3. a book containing descriptions of the sufferings of saints and martyrs, for reading on their festivals.

pas·sion·ar·y (păsh/ə něr/ĭ), *n., pl.* -**aries.** passional.

pas·sion·ate (păsh/ən ĭt), *adj.* 1. affected with or dominated by passion or vehement emotion: *a passionate advocate of socialism.* 2. characterized by, expressing, or showing vehement emotion; impassioned: *passionate language.* 3. vehement, as feelings or emotions: *passionate grief.* 4. easily moved to anger; quick-tempered; irascible. [late ME *passionat*, t. ML: s. *passiōnātus*] —**pas/sion·ate·ly,** *adv.* —**pas/sion·ate·ness,** *n.*

pas·sion·flow·er (păsh/ən flou/ər), *n.* any plant of the genus *Passiflora*, which comprises climbing vines or shrubs, mainly American, bearing showy flowers and a pulpy berry or fruit which in some species is edible. [so named from a supposed resemblance of the flower to the wounds, crown of thorns, etc. of Christ]

pas·sion-fruit (păsh/ən frōōt/), *n.* any edible fruit of a passionflower, as the maypop.

pas·sion·less (păsh/ən lĭs), *adj.* without passion; cold; unemotional.

passion play, a dramatic representation of the passion of Christ, such as that given every ten years at the Bavarian village of Oberammergau.

Passion Sunday, the fifth Sunday in Lent, being the second before Easter.

Passion Week, 1. the week preceding Easter; Holy Week. 2. the week before Holy Week, beginning with Passion Sunday.

pas·sive (păs/ĭv), *adj.* 1. not acting, or not attended with or manifested in open or positive action: *passive resistance.* 2. inactive, quiescent, or inert. 3. suffering action, acted upon, or being the object of action (opposed to *active*). 4. receiving, or characterized by the reception of, impressions from without. 5. produced by or due to external agency. 6. suffering, receiving,

or submitting without resistance. 7. characterized by or involving doing this: *passive obedience.* 8. *Gram.* **a.** (in some languages) denoting a voice, or verb inflection, in which the subject is represented as being acted on. For example: Latin *portātur*, "(he, she, it) is carried," is in the passive voice. **b.** denoting a construction similar to this in meaning, as English *he is carried.* 9. *Chem.* inactive, esp. under conditions in which chemical activity is to be expected. 10. *Med.* pertaining to certain unhealthy conditions with insufficient strength; inactive (opp. to *active* or *spontaneous*). —*n.* 11. *Gram.* **a.** the passive voice. **b.** a form or construction therein. [ME, t. L: m.s. *passīvus* capable of feeling] —**pas/sive·ly,** *adv.* —**pas/sive·ness, pas·siv/i·ty,** *n.*

passive immunity, *Immunol.* immunity achieved by injecting immune serum from another organism.

passive resistance, the expression of disapproval of authority or of specific laws by various nonviolent acts, such as public demonstration or (in some cases) voluntary fasting.

pass·key (păs/kē/, päs/-), *n., pl.* -**keys.** 1. a master key. 2. a private key. 3. a latchkey.

Pass·o·ver (păs/ō/vər, päs/-), *n.* 1. an annual feast of the Jews, instituted to commemorate the passing over or sparing of the Hebrews in Egypt when God smote the first-born of the Egyptians (see Ex. 12), but used in the general sense of the Feast of Unleavened Bread (Lev. 23: 5–6) in commemoration of the deliverance from Egypt, beginning on the eve of the 15th day of Nisan, and lasting originally seven days but in later Judaism eight days. 2. (*l.c.*) the paschal lamb. 3. (*l.c.*) Christ. [orig. verbal phrase *pass over*]

pass·port (păs/pōrt, päs/-), *n.* 1. an official document granting permission to the person specified in it to travel, and authenticating his right to protection. 2. an authorization to pass or go anywhere. 3. a document issued to a ship, esp. to neutral merchant vessels in time of war, granting or requesting permission to proceed without molestation in certain waters. 4. a certificate intended to secure admission. 5. anything that gives admission or acceptance. [t. F: m. *passeport*, f. *passe(r)* PASS + *port* PORT¹ (def. 3)]

pas·sus (păs/əs), *n., pl.* -**sus, -suses.** a section or division of a story, poem, etc.; a canto. [t. ML, in L a step, PACE²]

pass·word (păs/wûrd/, päs/-), *n.* a secret word, made known only to authorized persons for their use in passing through a line of guards.

Pas·sy (pà sē/), *n.* **Paul Édouard** (pōl ĕ dwär/). 1859–1940, French phonetician.

past (păst, päst), *v.* 1. pp. and occasional pt. of **pass.** —*adj.* 2. gone by in time. 3. belonging to, or having existed or occurred in, time previous to this. 4. gone by just before the present time; just passed: *the past year.* 5. ago. 6. having served a term in an office: *past master.* 7. *Gram.* designating a tense, or other verb formation or construction, which refers to events or states in time gone by. —*n.* 8. the time gone by: *far back in the past.* 9. the events of that time: *to forget the past.* 10. a past history, life, career, etc.: *a glorious past.* 11. a past career which is kept concealed: *a woman with a past.* 12. *Gram.* **a.** the past tense, as *he ate, he smoked.* **b.** another verb formation or construction with past meaning. **c.** a form therein. —*adv.* 13. so as to pass by or beyond; by: *the troops marched past.* —*prep.* 14. beyond in time; after: *past noon.* 15. beyond in position; further on than: *the house past the church.* 16. beyond in amount, number, etc. 17. beyond the reach, scope, influence, or power of: *past belief.* [see PASS, v.]

paste (pāst), *n., v.,* **pasted, pasting.** —*n.* 1. a mixture of flour and water, often with starch, etc., used for causing paper, etc., to adhere. 2. any material or preparation in a soft or plastic mass: *a tooth paste.* 3. dough, esp. when prepared with shortening, as for making pie crust and other pastry: *puff paste.* 4. any of the various food preparations, made from flour, of the macaroni and noodle kind. 5. any of various sweet confections of doughlike consistence: *fig paste.* 6. *Chiefly Brit.* a preparation of fish, tomatoes, or some other article of food reduced to a smooth, soft mass, as for a relish or for seasoning. 7. a mixture of clay, water, etc., for making earthenware or porcelain. 8. a brilliant, heavy glass, used for making artificial gems. 9. an artificial gem of this material. 10. *Slang.* a smart blow, esp. on the face. —*v.t.* 11. to fasten or stick with paste or the like. 12. to cover with something applied by means of paste. 13. *Slang.* to strike with a smart blow, or beat soundly, as on the face or head. [ME, t. OF, g. LL *pasta*, t. Gk.: m. *pástē* barley porridge]

paste·board (pāst/bōrd/), *n.* 1. a stiff, firm board made of sheets of paper pasted or layers of paper pulp pressed together, used for book covers. 2. *Slang.* a card, as a visiting card or a playing card. 3. *Slang.* a ticket, as for an entertainment. —*adj.* 4. made of pasteboard. 5. unsubstantial or flimsy; sham.

pas·tel¹ (păs tĕl/, păs/tĕl). *n.* 1. a soft subdued shade. 2. a kind of dried paste used for crayons, made of pigments ground with chalk and compounded with gum water. 3. a crayon made with such paste. 4. the art of drawing with such crayons. 5. a drawing so made. 6. a short, slight prose study or sketch. [t. F, t. Pr., der. LL *pasta* PASTE]

pas·tel[2] (păs′tĕl), *n.* **1.** the plant woad. **2.** the dye made from it. [t. F, t. It.: m. *pastello*, dim. der. LL *pasta* PASTE]

pas·tel·ist (păs′tĕl·ĭst, păs·tĕl′ĭst), *n.* an artist who draws with pastels. Also, *esp. Brit.*, **pas′tel·list.**

past·er (pās′tər), *n.* **1.** a slip of paper gummed on the back, to be pasted on or over something, as over a name on a ballot. **2.** one who or that which pastes.

pas·tern (păs′tərn), *n.* **1.** that part of the foot of a horse, etc., between the fetlock and the hoof. See illus. under **horse. 2.** either of two bones of this part, the upper or first phalanx (**great pastern bone**) and the lower or second phalanx (**small pastern bone**), between which is a joint (**pastern joint**). [ME *pastron*, t. F: m. *pasturon*, der. *pasture* shackle for animal while pasturing]

Pas·ter·nak (păs′tər·năk′), *n.* **Boris Leonidovich**, 1890–1960, Russian poet, novelist, and translator.

Pas·teur (păs·tœr′), *n.* **Louis** (lwē), 1822–95, French chemist and bacteriologist.

pas·teur·ism (păs′tə·rĭz′əm), *n.* **1.** a treatment devised by Pasteur for preventing certain diseases, esp. hydrophobia, by inoculations with virus of gradually increasing strength. **2.** the act or process of pasteurizing milk, etc. [named after Louis PASTEUR. See -ISM]

pas·teur·ize (păs′tə·rīz′, păs′chə·rīz′), *v.t.*, **-ized, -iz·ing. 1.** to expose (milk, etc.) to a high temperature, usually about 140° F., in order to destroy certain microörganisms and prevent or arrest fermentation. **2.** to subject to pasteurism in order to prevent certain diseases, esp. hydrophobia. Also, *esp. Brit.*, **pas·teur·ise′. —pas′teur·i·za′tion,** *n.*

pas·tic·cio (păs·tēsh′ō), *n., pl.* **-ci** (-chē). any work of art, literature, or music consisting of motifs borrowed from one or more masters or works of art. [t. It., der. *pasta* PASTE]

pas·tiche (păs·tēsh′, păs-), *n.* a pasticcio. [t. F, t. It.: m. *pasticcio* PASTICCIO]

pas·tille (păs·tēl′, -tĭl′), *n.* **1.** a flavored or medicated lozenge. **2.** a roll or cone of paste containing aromatic substances, burned as a disinfectant, etc. **3.** pastel for crayons. **4.** a crayon made of it. Also, **pas·til** (păs′tĭl). [t. F, t. Sp.: m. *pastilla*, dim. of *pasta* PASTE]

pas·time (păs′tīm′, päs′-), *n.* that which serves to make time pass agreeably; amusement, sport: *to play cards for a pastime.* [late ME, f. PASS, v. + TIME]

past·i·ness (pās′tĭ·nĭs), *n.* pasty quality.

past master, 1. one who has filled the office of master in a guild, lodge, etc. **2.** one who has ripe experience in any profession, art, etc.

Pas·to (päs′tō), *n.* **1.** a city in SW Colombia. 91,520 pop. (est. 1954); ab. 8350 ft. high. **2.** a volcanic peak near this city. 13,990 ft.

pas·tor (păs′tər, päs′-), *n.* **1.** a minister or clergyman with reference to his flock. **2.** one having spiritual care of a number of persons. [t. L: shepherd; r. ME *pastour*, t. AF] **—pas′tor·ship′,** *n.*

pas·to·ral (păs′tə·rəl, päs′-), *adj.* **1.** of or pertaining to shepherds. **2.** used for pasture, as land. **3.** having the simplicity or charm of such country, as scenery. **4.** pertaining to the country or life in the country. **5.** portraying the life of shepherds or of the country, as a work of literature, art, or music. **6.** pertaining to a minister or clergyman, or to his duties, etc. **—n. 7.** a poem, play, or the like, dealing with the life of shepherds, commonly in a conventional or artificial manner, or with simple rural life generally; a bucolic. **8.** a picture or work of art presenting shepherd life. **9.** a pastorale. **10.** a treatise on the duties of a minister or clergyman. **11.** a letter from a spiritual pastor to his people. **12.** a letter from a bishop to his clergy or people. **13.** a pastoral staff, or crosier. [ME,t.L:s. *pastorālis* pertaining to a shepherd] **—pas′to·ral·ism,** *n.* **—pas′to·ral·ist,** *n.* **—pas′to·ral·ly,** *adv.*

pas·to·ra·le (păs′tə·rä′lē; *It.* päs·tō·rä′lĕ), *n., pl.* **-li** (-lē), **-les.** *Music.* **1.** an opera, cantata, or the like, with a pastoral subject. **2.** a piece of music suggestive of pastoral life. [It., der. *pastore* shepherd, g. L *pastor*]

pas·to·rate (păs′tər·ĭt, päs′-), *n.* **1.** the office, or the term of office, of a pastor. **2.** a body of pastors.

pas·to·ri·um (păs·tōr′ĭ·əm, päs-), *n. Southern U.S.* a parsonage. [t. NL, der. L *pastor* PASTOR]

pas·tor·ship (păs′tər·shĭp′, päs′-), *n.* the dignity or office of a pastor.

past participle, *Gram.* a participle with past or perfect meaning; perfect participle, as *fallen, sung, defeated.*

past perfect, *Gram.* pluperfect.

pas·tra·mi (pə·strä′mĭ), *n.* a highly seasoned shoulder cut of smoked beef. [t. Yiddish, t. Polish, ult. t. Turkish]

pas·try (pās′trĭ), *n., pl.* **-tries. 1.** food made of paste, esp. the shortened paste used for pie crust, etc. **2.** articles of food of which such paste forms an essential part, as pies, tarts, napoleons, etc. [f. PASTE + -(E)RY]

pas·tur·a·ble (păs′chər·ə·bəl, päs′-), *adj.* capable of affording pasture, as land.

pas·tur·age (păs′chər·ĭj, päs′-), *n.* **1.** growing grass or herbage for cattle, etc. **2.** grazing ground. **3.** the act or business of pasturing cattle, etc. [t. F, der. *pasture* PASTURE]

pas·ture (păs′chər, päs′-), *n., v.,* **-tured, -tur·ing. —n. 1.** ground covered with grass or herbage, used or suitable for the grazing of cattle, etc.; grassland. **2.** grass or herbage for feeding cattle, etc. **—v.t. 3.** to feed (cattle,

etc.) by putting them to graze on pasture. **4.** (of land) to furnish pasturage for. **5.** (of cattle, etc.) to graze upon. **6.** to put cattle, etc., to graze upon (pasture). [ME, t. OF, g. LL *pastūra*, lit., feeding, grazing]

past·y[1] (pās′tĭ), *adj.,* **pastier, pastiest.** of or like paste in consistency, appearance, etc. [f. PASTE, n. + -Y[1]]

past·y[2] (păs′tĭ, päs′-), *n., pl.* **pasties.** *Chiefly Brit.; Archaic or Hist. in U.S.* a pie filled with game, fish, or the like. [ME *pastee*, t. OF, der. *paste* PASTE]

pat[1] (păt), *v.,* **patted, patting,** *n.* **—v.t. 1.** to strike lightly with something flat, as an implement, the palm of the hand, or the foot. **2.** to stroke gently with the palm or fingers as an expression of affection, approbation, etc. **3.** to strike (the floor, etc.) with lightly sounding footsteps. **—v.i. 4.** to strike lightly or gently. **5.** to walk or run with lightly sounding footsteps. **—n. 6.** a light stroke or blow with something flat. **7.** the sound of a light stroke, or of light footsteps. **8.** a small mass of something, as butter, shaped by patting or other manipulation. [ME; akin to PUTT]

pat[2] (păt), *adj.* **1.** exactly to the point or purpose. **2.** apt; opportune; ready. **—adv. 3.** exactly or perfectly. **4.** aptly; opportunely. **5. stand pat,** *Colloq.* **a.** to stick to one's decision, policy, etc. **b.** (in poker) to play a hand as dealt, without drawing other cards. [appar. akin to PAT[1]] **—pat′ness,** *n.* **—pat′ter,** *n.*

pat., **1.** patent. **2.** patented.

pa·ta·gi·um (pə·tā′jĭ·əm), *n., pl.* **-gia** (-jĭ·ə). **1.** a wing membrane, as of a bat. **2.** the extensible fold of skin of a gliding mammal or reptile, as a flying squirrel. [t. NL, t. L: a gold border on a woman's tunic]

Pat·a·go·ni·a (păt′ə·gō′nĭ·ə), *n.* **1.** the tableland region constituting the S tip of Argentina. **2.** a region in the extreme S part of South America, extending from the Andes to the Atlantic: mostly in S Argentina, partly in S Chile. **—Pat′a·go′ni·an,** *adj., n.*

patch (păch), *n.* **1.** a piece of material used to mend a hole or break, or to strengthen a weak place: *a patch on a sail.* **2.** a piece of material used to cover or protect a wound, an injured part, etc.: *a patch over the eye.* **3.** any of the pieces of cloth sewed together to form patchwork. **4.** a small piece or scrap of anything. **5.** a piece or tract of land. **6.** a small piece of black silk or court plaster worn on the face or elsewhere to hide a defect or to heighten the complexion by contrast. **7.** *U.S. Mil.* an emblem worn on the sleeve to identify the unit to which one belongs. **—v.t. 8.** to mend or strengthen with or as with a patch or patches. **9.** to repair or restore, esp. in a hasty or makeshift way (usually fol. by *up*). **10.** to make by joining patches or pieces together: *to patch a quilt.* **11.** to settle; smooth over: *they patched up their quarrel.* [ME *pacche*; orig. uncert.] **—patch′er,** *n.* **—Syn. 8.** See **mend.**

Patagonia (def. 1)

patch·ou·li (păch′ŏŏ·lĭ, pə·chŏŏ′lĭ), *n.* **1.** the East Indian menthaceous plants, *Pogostemon Heyneanus* and *P. Cablin,* which yield a fragrant oil. **2.** a penetrating perfume derived from it. Also, **pachouli, patch′ou·ly.** [t. vernacular of Madras region of India; orig. uncert.]

patch pocket, a pocket formed by sewing a piece of the material on the outside of a garment.

patch·work (păch′wûrk′), *n.* **1.** work made of pieces of cloth or leather of various colors or shapes sewed together, used esp. for covering quilts, cushions, etc. **2.** work or a product of any kind made up of various pieces or parts put together: *a patchwork of verses.*

patch·y (păch′ĭ), *adj.,* **patchier, patchiest. 1.** marked by patches. **2.** occurring in, forming, or like patches. **—patch′i·ly,** *adv.* **—patch′i·ness,** *n.*

patd., patented.

pate (pāt), *n. Humorous.* **1.** the head. **2.** the crown or top of the head. **3.** brains. [ME; ? var. of PATEN]

pâte (pät), *n. French.* **1.** paste. **2.** porcelain paste used in ceramic work. [see PASTE]

pâ·té (pä·tě′), *n. French.* a form of pastry filled with chicken, sweetbreads, oysters, or the like. [see PASTY[2]]

pâ·té de foie gras (pä·tě′ də fwà grä′), *French.* a paste made with the livers of specially fattened geese.

pa·tel·la (pə·tĕl′ə), *n., pl.* **-tellae** (-tĕl′ē). **1.** *Anat.* the kneecap. See diag. under **skeleton. 2.** *Bot., Zool., etc.* a panlike or cuplike formation. **3.** *Archaeol.* a small pan or shallow vessel. [t. L: small pan, kneepan, dim. of *patina.* See PATINA[2]] **—pa·tel′lar,** *adj.*

pa·tel·late (pə·tĕl′ĭt, -āt), *adj.* **1.** having a patella. **2.** patelliform.

pa·tel·li·form (pə·tĕl′ə·fôrm′), *adj.* having the form of a patella; shaped like a saucer, kneecap, or limpet shell. [f. s. L *patella* small pan + -(I)FORM]

pat·en (păt′ən), *n.* the plate on which the bread is placed in the celebration of the Eucharist. Also, **patin, patine.** [ME *patene,* t. OF, t. L, m. *patena, patina.* See PATINA[2]]

pa·ten·cy (pā′tən·sĭ), *n.* **1.** the state of being patent. **2.** *Med.* the condition of not being blocked or obstructed. **3.** *Phonet.* openness of articulation, found more or less in all phonemes except stops.

pat·ent (păt′ənt *or, esp. Brit.,* pā′tənt for *1–9, 15–19; usually* pāt′ənt for *10–14*), *n.* **1.** a government grant to an inventor, his heirs, or assigns, for a stated period of time, conferring upon him a monopoly of the exclusive right to make, use, and vend the invention or discovery. **2.** an invention, process, etc., which has been patented. **3.** an official document conferring some right, privilege, or the like. **4.** the instrument by which the United States conveys the legal fee-simple title to public land. *—adj.* **5.** of a kind specially protected by a patent. **6.** endowed with a patent, as persons. **7.** belonging as if by a proprietary claim; having a trademark. **8.** conferred by a patent, as a right or privilege. **9.** appointed by a patent, as a person. **10.** open to view or knowledge; manifest; evident; plain. **11.** lying open, or not shut in or enclosed, as a place. **12.** *Chiefly Bot.* expanded or spreading. **13.** open, as a door or a passage. **14.** *Phonet.* open, in various degrees, to the passage of the breath stream (opposed to *stopped* or *occlusive*). **15.** designating certain better grades of flour. *—v.t.* **16.** to take out a patent on; obtain the exclusive rights to (an invention) by a patent. **17.** to originate and establish as one's own. **18.** *Rare.* to grant the exclusive right to (an invention) by a patent. **19.** *Rare.* to grant by a patent (def. 4). [ME, t. L: s. *patens*, ppr., lying open; in some senses, through OF] **—pat′ent·a·ble**, *adj.* **—pat′ent·a·bil′i·ty**, *n.* **—pat′ent·ly**, *adv.* **—Syn.** 10. See **apparent.**

pat·ent·ee (păt′ən tē′), *n.* one to whom a patent is granted.

patent leather, a hard, glossy, smooth leather, usually finished in black.

patent log. See **log** (def. 2c).

patent medicine, a medicine distributed by a company which has a patent on its manufacture.

pat·en·tor (păt′ən tər), *n.* one who grants a patent.

patent right, the exclusive right created by a patent.

pa·ter (pā′tər; *also for 2, 3* păt′ər), *n.* **1.** *Brit. Colloq.* father. **2.** the paternoster or Lord's Prayer. **3.** a recital of it. [ME, t. L: father]

Pa·ter (pā′tər), *n.* **Walter Horatio**, 1839–94, British critic, essayist, and novelist.

pa·ter·fa·mil·i·as (pā′tər fə mĭl′ĭ əs), *n., pl.* **patres·familia** (pā′trēz fə mĭl′ĭ əs). **1.** the head of a family. **2.** *Roman Law.* a free male citizen who has been freed from patria potestas by death of his father or by emancipation. [t. L: f. *pater* father + *familias*, archaic gen. of *familia* family]

pa·ter·nal (pə tûr′nəl), *adj.* **1.** characteristic of or befitting a father; fatherly. **2.** of or pertaining to a father. **3.** related on the father's side. **4.** derived or inherited from a father. [f. s. L *paternus* fatherly + -AL¹] **—pa·ter′nal·ly**, *adv.* **—Syn.** 1. See **fatherly.**

pa·ter·nal·ism (pə tûr′nə lĭz′əm), *n.* the principle or practice, on the part of a government or of any body or person in authority, of managing or regulating the affairs of a country or community, or of individuals, in the manner of a father dealing with his children. **—pater′nal·is′tic**, *adj.* **—pa·ter′nal·is′ti·cal·ly**, *adv.*

pa·ter·ni·ty (pə tûr′nə tĭ), *n.* **1.** derivation from a father. **2.** the state of being a father; fatherhood. **3.** origin or authorship. [ME, t. LL: m.s. *paternitas*, der. L *paternus* fatherly]

pa·ter·nos·ter (pā′tər nŏs′tər, păt′ər-), *n.* **1.** Also, **Pater Noster.** the Lord's Prayer, esp. in the Latin form. **2.** a recital of this prayer as an act of worship. **3.** one of certain beads in a rosary, regularly every eleventh bead, differing in size or material from the rest, and indicating the Lord's Prayer is to be said. **4.** any form of words used as a prayer or charm. [ME and OE, t. L: our father, the first words of the prayer in the Latin version]

Pat·er·son (păt′ər sən), *n.* a city in NE New Jersey. 143,663 (1960).

path (păth, päth), *n.* **1.** a way beaten or trodden by the feet of men or beasts. **2.** a walk in a garden or through grounds. **3.** a route, course, or track in which something moves. **4.** a course of action, conduct, or procedure. [ME; OE *pæth*, c. G *pfad*] **—Syn.** 1. PATH, LANE, TRAIL are passages or routes not so wide as a way or road. A PATH is a way for passing on foot; a track, beaten by feet, not specially constructed, often along the side of a road: *a path through a field.* A LANE is a narrow road or track, generally between fields, often enclosed with fences or trees; sometimes an alley or narrow road between buildings in towns: *a lane leading to a farmhouse, Drury Lane.* A TRAIL is a rough way made or worn through woods, or across mountains, prairies, or other untraveled regions: *an Indian trail.*

path., **1.** pathological. **2.** pathology.

Pa·than (pə tän′, pə hän′), *n.* **1.** an Afghan. **2.** an Afghan dwelling in India. [t. Pushtu]

pa·thet·ic (pə thĕt′ĭk), *adj.* **1.** exciting pity or sympathetic sadness; full of pathos. **2.** affecting or moving the feelings. **3.** pertaining or due to the feelings. Also, **pa·thet′i·cal.** [t. LL: s. *patheticus*, t. Gk.: m. *pathētikós* sensitive] **—pa·thet′i·cal·ly**, *adv.*

pathetic fallacy, the attachment of human traits and feelings to nature.

path·find·er (păth′fīn′dər, päth′-), *n.* one who finds a path or way, as through a wilderness.

-pathia, an obsolete form of **-pathy.**

-pathic, a word element forming adjectives from nouns ending in *-pathy*, as *psychopathic.* [see -PATHY, -IC]

path·less (păth′lĭs, päth′-), *adj.* without paths; trackless. **—path′less·ness**, *n.*

patho-, a word element meaning "suffering," "disease," "feeling." [t. Gk., comb. form of *páthos*]

path·o·gen (păth′ə jən), *n.* a pathogenic or disease-producing organism. Also, **path·o·gene** (păth′ə jēn′).

path·o·gen·e·sis (păth′ə jĕn′ə sĭs), *n.* the production and development of disease. Also, **pa·thog·e·ny** (pə thŏj′ə nĭ). **—path·o·ge·net·ic** (păth′ō jə nĕt′ĭk) *adj.*

path·o·gen·ic (păth′ə jĕn′ĭk), *adj.* disease-producing.

pathol., **1.** pathological. **2.** pathology.

path·o·log·i·cal (păth′ə lŏj′ə kəl), *adj.* **1.** of or pertaining to pathology. **2.** due to or involving disease; morbid. **3.** treating of or concerned with diseases. Also, **path′o·log·ic.** **—path′o·log′i·cal·ly**, *adv.*

pa·thol·o·gy (pə thŏl′ə jĭ), *n., pl.* **-gies.** **1.** the science of the origin, nature, and course of diseases. **2.** the conditions and processes of a disease. **—pa·thol′o·gist**, *n.*

pa·thos (pā′thŏs), *n.* **1.** the quality or power, as in speech, music, etc., of evoking a feeling of pity or sympathetic sadness; touching or pathetic character or effect (opposed to *ethos*). **2.** *Obs.* suffering. [t. Gk.: suffering, disease, feeling]

path·way (păth′wā′, päth′-), *n.* a path.

-pathy, a noun element meaning "suffering," "feeling," as in *anthropopathy, antipathy, sympathy,* and often, esp. in words of modern formation, as "morbid affection," "disease," as in *arthropathy. deuteropathy, neuropathy, psychopathy,* and hence used also in names of systems or methods of treating disease, as in *allopathy, homeopathy, hydropathy, osteopathy.* [t. Gk.: m. s.-*pátheia*]

Pa·ti·a·la (pŭt′ĭ ä′lə), *n.* **1.** a former state in NW India; foremost of the Punjab States; now in Punjab State. **2.** a city in Punjab; formerly capital of state of same name. 97,869 (1951).

pa·tience (pā′shəns), *n.* **1.** calm and uncomplaining endurance, as under pain, provocation, etc. **2.** calmness in waiting: *have patience a little longer.* **3.** quiet perseverance: *to labor with patience.* **4.** *Chiefly Brit.* a card game, usually played by one person alone. Cf. *U.S.* **solitaire** (def. 1). **5.** *Obs.* sufferance. [t. L: m.s. *patientia*; r. ME *pacience*, t. OF] **—Syn.** 1. PATIENCE, ENDURANCE, FORTITUDE, STOICISM imply qualities of calmness, stability, and persistent courage in trying circumstances. PATIENCE may denote calm, self-possessed, and unrepining bearing of pain, misfortune, annoyance, or delay; or painstaking and untiring industry or (less often) application in the doing of something: *to bear afflictions with patience.* ENDURANCE denotes the ability to bear exertion, hardship, or suffering (without implication of moral qualities required or shown): *running a marathon requires great endurance.* FORTITUDE implies not only patience but courage and strength of character in the midst of pain, affliction, or hardship: *to show fortitude in adversity.* STOICISM is calm fortitude, with such repression of emotion as to seem almost like indifference to pleasure or pain: *the American Indians were noted for stoicism under torture.*

pa·tient (pā′shənt), *n.* **1.** one who is under medical or surgical treatment. **2.** a person or thing that undergoes action (opposed to *agent*). **3.** *Obs. or Rare.* a sufferer. *—adj.* **4.** quietly persevering or diligent: *patient workers.* **5.** enduring pain, trouble, affliction, hardship, etc., with fortitude, calmness, or quiet submission. **6.** marked by such endurance. **7.** quietly enduring strain, annoyance, etc.: *patient in a traffic jam.* **8.** disposed to or characterized by such endurance. **9.** enduring delay with calmness or equanimity, or marked by such endurance: *be patient.* **10.** having or showing the capacity for endurance (fol. by *of*). **11.** susceptible (fol. by *of*). **12.** undergoing the action of another (opposed to *agent*). [t. L: s. *patiens*, ppr., suffering, enduring; r. ME *pacient*, t. OF] **—pa′tient·ly**, *adv.* **—Syn.** 5. long-suffering.

pat·in (păt′ən), *n.* paten. Also, **pat′ine.**

pat·i·na¹ (păt′ə nə), *n.* **1.** a film or incrustation, usually green, produced by oxidation on the surface of old bronze, and esteemed as ornamental. **2.** a similar film or coloring on some other substance. **3.** a surface calcification of implements, usually indicating great age. [t. It., t. L: dish, through meaning tarnish (on metal dish)]

pat·i·na² (păt′ə nə), *n., pl.* **-nae** (-nē′). a broad, shallow dish of the ancient Romans. [t. L]

pa·ti·o (pä′tĭ ō′, păt′ĭ ō′; *Sp.* pä′tyō), *n., pl.* **-tios.** **1.** (in Spain and Spanish-American countries) a court, as of a house, esp. an inner court open to the sky. **2.** an area, usually paved, adjoining a house, used for outdoor living. [t. Sp.]

Pat·more (păt′mōr), *n.* **Coventry** (kŏv′ən trĭ, kŭv′-), 1823–96, British poet.

Pat·mos (păt′mŏs, păt′mōs), *n.* one of the Dodecanese Islands, off the SW coast of Asia Minor: St. John is supposed to have been exiled on this island. Rev. 1:9. 2613 pop. (1951); 13 sq. mi. Italian, **Pat·mo** (păt′mō).

Pat·na (păt′nə, pŭt′nä′), *n.* a city in NE India, on the Ganges: the capital of Bihar province. 250,285 (1951).

Pat. Off., Patent Office.

pat·ois (păt′wä; *Fr.* pȧ twä′), *n., pl.* **patois** (păt′wäz; *Fr.* pȧ twä′). any peasant or provincial form of speech. [t. F, der. OF *patoier* handle clumsily, der. *pate* paw]

Pa·tras (pä träs′), *n.* a seaport in W Greece, on the **Gulf of Patras**, an inlet of the Ionian Sea in the NW Peloponnesus. 79,014 (1951). Greek, **Pa·trai** (pä′trē).

---

b., blend of, blended;   c., cognate with;   d., dialect, dialectal;   der., derived from;   f., formed from;   g., going back to; m., modification of;   r., replacing;   s., stem of;   t., taken from;   ?, perhaps.   See the full key on inside cover.

pa·tri·a po·tes·tas (pā/trĭ ə pō tĕs/tăs), *Roman Law.* the power of a man over his children and descendants, which made all their property his and all their transactions void unless he assented. It ended only with the death of the paterfamilias or with emancipation. [L]

pa·tri·arch (pā/trĭ ärk/), *n.* **1.** any of the earlier Biblical personages regarded as the fathers of the human race, comprising those from Adam to Noah (**antediluvian patriarchs**) and those between the Deluge and the birth of Abraham. **2.** one of the three great progenitors of the Israelites: Abraham, Isaac, or Jacob. **3.** one of the sons of Jacob (the **twelve patriarchs**), from whom the tribes of Israel were descended. **4.** (in the early church) a bishop of high rank, esp. one with jurisdiction over metropolitans. **5.** *Gk. Orthodox Ch.* the bishop of the ancient sees of Alexandria, Antioch, Constantinople, and Jerusalem, and in recent years of Russia, Rumania, and Serbia. The bishop of Constantinople is the highest dignitary in the church and bears the title of **ecumenical patriarch. 6.** a bishop of the highest rank or authority in any of the various non-Orthodox churches in the East. **7.** *Rom. Cath. Ch.* **a.** the Pope (**Patriarch of Rome**). **b.** a bishop of the highest rank next after the Pope. **8.** *Mormon Ch.* one of the highest dignitaries who pronounces the blessing of the church; Evangelist. **9.** one of the elders or leading older members of a community. **10.** a venerable old man. **11.** the male head of a family or tribal line. **12.** a person regarded as the father or founder of an order, class, etc. [ME *patriarc,* t. LL: m.s. *patriarcha,* t. Gk.: m. *patriárchēs* head of a family] —**pa/tri·ar/chal,** *adj.* —**pa/tri·ar/chal·ly,** *adv.*

patriarchal cross, a cross with two crossbars. See illus. under **cross.**

pa·tri·ar·chate (pā/trĭ är/kĭt), *n.* **1.** the office, dignity, jurisdiction, province, or residence of an ecclesiastical patriarch. **2.** a patriarchy.

pa·tri·ar·chy (pā/trĭ är/kĭ), *n., pl.* **-archies.** a form of social organization in which the father is head of the family, and in which descent is reckoned in the male line, the children belonging to the father's clan.

pa·tri·cian (pə trĭsh/ən), *n.* **1.** a member of the original senatorial aristocracy in ancient Rome. **2.** (under the later Roman and Byzantine Empires) a title or dignity conferred by the emperor. **3.** a member of an influential and hereditary ruling class in certain medieval German, Swiss, and Italian free cities. **4.** any noble or aristocrat. —*adj.* **5.** of or belonging to the patrician families of ancient Rome. **6.** of high social rank or noble family. **7.** befitting an aristocrat: *patrician aloofness.* [ME, f. s. L *patricius* of the rank of the *patrēs* senators, patricians (lit., fathers, pl. of *pater* father) + -AN]

pa·tri·ci·ate (pə trĭsh/ĭ ĭt, -āt/), *n.* **1.** the patrician class. **2.** patrician rank.

pat·ri·cide¹ (păt/rə sīd/, pā/trə-), *n.* one who kills his father. [f. LL *patri-* father + -CIDE¹] —**pat/ri·cid/al,** *adj.*

pat·ri·cide² (păt/rə sīd/, pā/trə-), *n.* the killing of one's father. [f. LL *patri-* father+ -CIDE²]

Pat·rick (păt/rĭk), *n.* Saint, A.D. c389–c461, English missionary and bishop in Ireland; patron saint of Ireland.

pat·ri·mo·ny (păt/rə mō/nĭ), *n., pl.* **-nies. 1.** an estate inherited from one's father or ancestors. **2.** a heritage. **3.** the aggregate of one's property. **4.** the estate or endowment of a church, religious house, etc. [t. L: m.s. *patrimōnium* paternal estate; r. ME *patrimoygne,* t. OF: m. *patrimoine*] —**pat/ri·mo/ni·al,** *adj.*

pa·tri·ot (pā/trĭ ət, -ŏt/ or, esp. *Brit.,* păt/rĭ ət), *n.* a person who loves his country, zealously supporting and defending it and its interests. [t. LL: s. *patriōta,* t. Gk.: m. *patriōtēs* fellow countryman]

pa·tri·ot·ic (pā/trĭ ŏt/ĭk or, esp. *Brit.,* păt/rĭ-), *adj.* of or like a patriot; inspired by patriotism. —**pa/tri·ot/i·cal·ly,** *adv.*

pa·tri·ot·ism (pā/trĭ ə tĭz/əm or, esp. *Brit.,* păt/rĭ-), *n.* the spirit or action of a patriot; devotion to one's country.

Patriots' Day, the anniversary (April 19) of the battle of Lexington in 1775, observed as a legal holiday in Massachusetts and Maine.

pa·tris·tic (pə trĭs/tĭk), *adj.* of or pertaining to the fathers of the Christian church or their writings. Also, **pa·tris/ti·cal.** —**pa·tris/ti·cal·ly,** *adv.*

Pa·tro·clus (pə trō/kləs), *n. Homeric Legend.* the friend of Achilles, slain by Hector, whose death led Achilles to return to battle. [t. L, t. Gk.: m. *Patroklēs, Pátroklos*]

pa·trol (pə trōl/), *v.,* **-trolled, -trolling,** *n.* —*v.i.* **1.** to go the rounds in a camp or garrison, as a guard. **2.** to traverse a particular district, as a policeman. —*v.t.* **3.** to go about in or traverse for the purpose of guarding or protecting. —*n.* **4.** a person or a body of persons charged with patrolling. **5.** act of patrolling. **6.** a patrol wagon. **7.** (in the Boy Scouts) a unit of eight members. [t. F: m. *patrouiller* patrol, earlier *paddle* or *dabble* in mud, orig., *paw over,* der. OF *pate* paw. Cf PATOIS] —**pa·trol/ler,** *n.*

pa·trol·man (pə trōl/mən), *n., pl.* **-men. 1.** a member of a police force patrolling a certain district. **2.** a man who patrols.

patrol wagon, a wagon used by the police for the conveyance of prisoners.

pa·tron (pā/trən), *n.* **1.** one who supports with his patronage a shop, hotel, or the like. **2.** a protector or supporter, as of a person, cause, institution, art, or enterprise. **3.** one whose support or protection is solicited or acknowledged by the dedication of a book or other work. **4.** a patron saint. **5.** *Roman Hist.* the protector of a dependent or client, often the ex-master of a freedman, still retaining certain rights over him. **6.** *Eccles.* one who has the right of presenting a clergyman to a benefice. [ME, t. L: s. *patrōnus* patron, ML pattern] —**pa/tron·al,** *adj.* —**pa·tron·ess** (pā/trən ĭs, păt/rən-), *n. fem.*

pa·tron·age (pā/trən ĭj, păt/rən-), *n.* **1.** the financial support afforded a shop, hotel, etc., by customers. **2.** the position, encouragement, or support of a patron. **3.** the control of appointments to the public service or of other political favors. **4.** offices or other favors so controlled. **5.** condescending favor: *an air of patronage.* **6.** the right of presentation to an ecclesiastical benefice.

pa·tron·ize (pā/trə nīz/, păt/rə-), *v.t.,* **-ized, -izing. 1.** to favor (a shop, restaurant, etc.) with one's patronage; to trade with. **2.** to treat in a condescending way. **3.** to act as patron toward; support. Also, *esp. Brit.,* **pa/tron·ise/.** —**pa/tron·iz/er,** *n.* —**pa/tron·iz/ing·ly,** *adv.*

patron saint, a saint regarded as the special guardian of a person, trade, place, etc.

pat·ro·nym·ic (păt/rə nĭm/ĭk), *adj.* **1.** (of names) derived from the name of a father or ancestor, esp. by the addition of a suffix or prefix indicating descent. **2.** (of a suffix or prefix) indicating such descent. —*n.* **3.** a patronymic name, such as *Williamson* (son of William) or *Macdonald* (son of Donald). **4.** a family name; surname. [t. LL: s. *patrōnymicus,* t. Gk.: m. *patrōnymikós* pertaining to one's father's name]

pa·troon (pə trōōn/), *n.* one who held an estate in land with certain manorial privileges granted under the old Dutch governments of New York and New Jersey. [t. D, t. L: m.s. *patrōnus* PATRON]

pat·ten (păt/ən), *n.* any of various kinds of footwear, as a wooden shoe, a shoe with a wooden sole, a chopine, etc., to protect the feet from mud or wet. [ME *paten,* t. OF: m. *patin,* der. OF *pate* paw, foot. Cf. PATOIS]

pat·ter¹ (păt/ər), *v.i.* **1.** to strike or move with a succession of slight tapping sounds. —*v.t.* **2.** to cause to patter. **3.** to spatter with something. —*n.* **4.** a pattering sound: *the heavy patter of the rain.* **5.** the act of pattering. [freq. of PAT¹, v.]

pat·ter² (păt/ər), *n.* **1.** the glib speech used by a faker to praise his wares, by a magician while performing tricks, etc.; rapid speech; mere chatter; gabble. **2.** the jargon or cant of any class, group, etc. [var. of PATER (def. 3)] —*v.i.* **3.** to talk glibly or rapidly, esp. with little regard to matter; chatter. **4.** to repeat the paternoster or any prayer, etc., in a rapid, mechanical way. —*v.t.* **5.** to recite or repeat (prayers, etc.) in a rapid, mechanical way. **6.** to repeat or say rapidly or glibly. [v. use of n.] —**pat/ter·er,** *n.*

pat·ter³ (păt/ər), *n.* one who or that which pats.

pat·tern (păt/ərn), *n.* **1.** a decorative design, as for china, wallpaper, textile fabrics, etc. **2.** such a design carried out on something. **3.** a style of marking of natural or chance origin: *patterns of frost on the window.* **4.** style or type in general. **5.** an original or model proposed for or deserving of imitation. **6.** anything fashioned or designed to serve as a model or guide for something to be made: *a paper pattern for a dress.* **7.** *U.S.* a sufficient quantity of material for making a garment. **8.** *Metall.* a model or form, usually of wood or metal, used in a foundry to make a mold. **9.** an example or instance. **10.** a sample or specimen. **11.** *Gun.* **a.** the distribution of shot in a target at which a shotgun or the like is fired. **b.** a diagram showing such distribution. —*v.i.* **12.** to model one's conduct, etc. (fol. by *by* or *after*). —*v.t.* **13.** to make after a pattern; model. **14.** to cover or mark with a pattern. **15.** *Rare.* to take as a pattern. [ME *patron.* See PATRON]

Pat·ti (păt/ĭ; *It.,* *Sp.* däp/tē), *n.* Adelina (ä/dĕ lē/nä), (*Baroness Cederstrom*) 1843–1919, Italian-Spanish soprano opera singer.

Pat·ton (păt/ən), *n.* George Smith, 1885–1945, U.S. general.

pat·ty (păt/ĭ), *n., pl.* **-ties. 1.** a little pie; a pâté: *oyster patties.* **2.** a thin, round piece: *peppermint patties.* [t. F: m. *pâté*]

patty pan, a small pan for baking patties, etc.

pat·u·lous (păch/ə ləs), *adj.* **1.** open; gaping; expanded. **2.** *Bot.* **a.** spreading, as a tree or its boughs. **b.** spreading slightly, as a calyx. **c.** bearing the flowers loose or dispersed, as a peduncle. [t. L: m. *patulus* lying open] —**pat/u·lous·ly,** *adv.* —**pat/u·lous·ness,** *n.*

Pau (pō), *n.* a city in SW France; winter resort. 48.320 (1954).

P.A.U., Pan American Union.

pau·cis ver·bis (pô/sĭs vûr/bĭs), *Latin.* in few words; with or by few words.

pau·ci·ty (pô/sə tĭ), *n.* smallness of quantity; fewness; scantiness: *paucity of material.* [ME, t. L. m. s. *paucitas*]

Paul (pôl for *1, 2, 3,* poul for *4*), *n.* **1.** Saint, died A.D. c67, the great Christian missionary ("Apostle to the Gentiles"), author of several epistles in the New Testament.   2. name six popes.   **3. Elliot Harold**, 1891 –1958, U.S. writer.   **4. Jean** (zhäN). See **Richter**. [t. L: s. *Paulus*; r. ME *Poul* (t. OF) and OE *Paulus* (t. L)]

Paul I, 1754–1801, czar of Russia, 1796–1801, noted for his great cruelty and brutality.

Paul III, (*Alessandro Farnese*) 1468–1549. Italian ecclesiastic; pope, 1534–49.

Paul V, (*Camillo Borghese*) 1552–1621, Italian ecclesiastic; pope, 1605–21.

Paul VI, (*Giovanni Battista Montini*) born 1897, Italian ecclesiastic; pope since 1963.

Paul-Bon·cour (pôl bôn kōōr′), *n*. **Joseph** (zhō zĕf′), born 1873, French statesman; premier, 1932–33.

Paul·ine (pô′lĭn), *adj*. of or pertaining to the Apostle Paul, or his doctrines or writings.

Paul·ing (pôl′ĭng), *n*. **Linus Carl**, born 1901, U.S. chemist; Nobel Prize, 1954.

Paul·ist (pô′lĭst), *n*. a member of the "Missionary Society of St. Paul the Apostle," a community of Roman Catholic priests founded in New York in 1858.

pau·low·ni·a (pô lō′nĭ ə), *n*. **1.** a tree, *Paulownia tomentosa*, of Japan, bearing showy pale-violet or blue flowers, which blossom in early spring. **2.** any other trees of the genus *Paulownia*. [t. NL; named after Anna *Pawlovna*, daughter of Czar Paul I, of Russia]

Pa·u·mo·tu Archipelago (pä′ŏŏ mō′tōō), Tuamotu Archipelago.

paunch (pônch, pänch), *n*. **1.** the belly or abdomen. **2.** a large, prominent belly. **3.** the rumen. [ME *panche*, t. ONF, var. of OF *pance*, der. L *pantex*] —**paunch′y**, *adj*. —**paunch′i·ness**, *n*.

pau·per (pô′pər), *n*. **1.** a very poor person. **2.** one without means of support, who lives as a charge upon the community. [t. L: poor (man)]

pau·per·ism (pô′pə rĭz′əm), *n*. utter poverty.

pau·per·ize (pô′pə rīz′), *v.t.*, **-ized, -izing.** to make a pauper of.

Pau·sa·ni·as (pô sā′nĭ əs), *n*. fl. A.D. c175, Greek traveler and author of a valuable *Description of Greece*.

pause (pôz), *n., v.,* **paused, pausing.** —*n*. **1.** a temporary stop or rest, esp. in speech or action. **2.** a cessation proceeding from doubt or uncertainty. **3.** delay; hesitation; suspense. **4.** a break or rest in speaking or reading as depending on sense, grammatical relations, metrical divisions, etc., or in writing or printing as marked by punctuation. **5.** *Pros*. a caesura. **6.** *Music*. the symbol ‿ or ⌢ placed under or over a note or rest to indicate that it is to be prolonged. —*v.i*. **7.** to make a pause; stop; wait; hesitate. **8.** to dwell or linger (fol. by *upon*). [late ME, t. L: m. *pausa*, t. Gk.: m. *paûsis* cessation] —**paus′er**, *n*. —**Syn. 7.** See **stop**.

pav·an (păv′ən), *n*. **1.** a stately dance in vogue in the 16th century. **2.** the music for it. Also, **pav·ane** (păv′ən; *Fr*. pả våN′), **pavin**. [t. F: m. *pavane*, t. Sp.: m. *pavana*, t. d. It.: Paduan dance]

pave (pāv), *v.t.,* **paved, paving. 1.** to cover or lay (a road, walk, etc.) with stones, bricks, tiles, wood, concrete, etc., so as to make a firm, level surface. **2.** to prepare (the way) for. [ME *pave*(n), t. OF: m. *paver*, g. Rom. *pavāre*, for L *pavīre* beat down] —**pav′er**, *n*.

pa·vé (pả vě′), *n. French*. **1.** a pavement. **2.** a setting in which jewels are placed close together so as to show no metal. [orig. pp. of *paver* PAVE]

pave·ment (pāv′mənt), *n*. **1.** a paved road, etc. **2.** a surface, ground covering, or floor made by paving. **3.** a material used for paving. [ME, t. OF: a floor beaten down, der. *paver* PAVE]

Pa·vi·a (pả vē′ä), *n*. city in N Italy. 67,000 (est. 1954).

pav·id (păv′ĭd), *adj*. frightened; fearful; timid.

pa·vil·ion (pə vĭl′yən), *n*. **1.** a light, more or less open structure for purposes of shelter, pleasure, etc., as in a park. **2.** a projecting element, architecturally defined, in the front or side of a building. **3.** one of a group of buildings forming a hospital. **4.** a tent. **5.** a large tent on posts. **6.** *Jewelry*. the lower part of the stone, taken from the girdle and including the culet. **7.** *Anat*. the auricle of the ear. —*v.t*. **8.** to shelter in or as in a pavilion. **9.** to furnish with pavilions. [ME *pavilioun*, t. OF, g. L *pāpilio* tent, orig. butterfly]

pav·in (păv′ən), *n*. pavan.

pav·ing (pā′vĭng), *n*. **1.** a pavement. **2.** material for paving.

pav·ior (pāv′yər), *n*. a paver. Also, *Brit*., **pav′iour**.

pav·is (păv′ĭs), *n*. a large medieval shield, covering the whole body. Also, **pav′ise**. [ult. der. PAVIA]

pav·is·er (păv′ĭsər), *n*. one armed with or bearing a pavis. Also, **pav′is·or**.

Pav·lov (păv′lôf), *n*. **Ivan Petrovich** (ĭ′vän′ pĕ trō′vĭch), 1849–1936, Russian physiologist and physician.

Pav·lo·va (păv′lō vä), *n*. **Anna** (än′nä), 1885–1931, Russian ballet dancer.

pav·o·nine (păv′ə nīn′, -nĭn), *adj*. **1.** of or like the peacock. **2.** resembling the peacock's feathers, as in coloring. [t. L: m.s. *pāvōnīnus* pertaining to a peacock]

paw (pô), *n*. **1.** the foot of an animal with nails or claws. **2.** the foot of any animal. **3.** *Humorous or Contemptuous*. the human hand. —*v.t*. **4.** to strike or scrape with the paws or feet. **5.** *Colloq*. to handle clumsily, rudely, or overfamiliarly. —*v.i*. **6.** to beat or scrape the ground, etc., with the paws or feet. **7.** *Colloq*. to use the hands clumsily or rudely on something. [ME *powe*, t. OF, of Gmc. orig.; cf. G *pfote*]

pawk·y (pô′kĭ), *adj.,* **pawkier, pawkiest.** *Scot. and Brit. Dial*. cunning; sly. [f. *pawk* trick, artifice + -y[1]]

pawl (pôl), *n*. a pivoted bar adapted to engage with the teeth of a ratchet wheel or the like so as to prevent movement or to impart motion. [? t. D: m. *pal*]

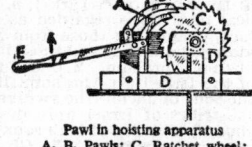

Pawl in hoisting apparatus A, B, Pawls; C, Ratchet wheel; D, Frame; E, Handle. Arrows indicate direction of motion.

pawn[1] (pôn), *v.t*. **1.** to deposit as security, as for money borrowed: *to pawn a watch*. **2.** to pledge or stake: *I pawn my honor*. —*n*. **3.** state of being deposited or held as security: *jewels in pawn*. **4.** something given or deposited as security, as for money borrowed. **5.** any thing or person serving as security. **6.** the act of pawning. [late ME, t. OF: m. *pan*. Cf. G *pfand*] —**pawn·er** (pô′nər), **pawn·or** (pô′nər, pôn ôr′), *n*.

pawn[2] (pôn), *n*. **1.** *Chess*. one of the 16 pieces of lowest value, usually moving one square straight ahead, but capturing diagonally. **2.** an unimportant person used as the tool of another. [ME *poune*, t. AF, var. of OF *peon*, g. s. LL *pedo* foot soldier]

pawn·bro·ker (pôn′brō′kər), *n*. one who lends money at interest on pledged personal property. —**pawn′bro′king**, *n*.

Paw·nee (pô nē′), *n*. **1.** (*pl.*) a confederacy of North American Plains Indians of Caddoan stock, formerly located in Platte river valley, Nebr.; now living in northern Oklahoma. **2.** a member of this group. [? der. Pawnee *parika* horn, term used for dressing of scalp lock to resemble a horn]

pawn·shop (pôn′shop′), *n*. a pawnbroker's shop.

paw·paw (pô′pô), *n*. papaw.

Paw·tuck·et (pô tŭk′ĭt), *n*. a city in NE Rhode Island. 81,001 (1960).

pax (păks), *n*. *Rom. Cath. Ch*. a small tablet bearing a representation of the Crucifixion or some other sacred subject, formerly kissed by the celebrating priest and the congregation at Mass. [ME, t. L: peace]

Pax (păks), *n*. *Rom. Myth*. the goddess of Peace, the counterpart of the Greek goddess, Irene.

pax vo·bis·cum (păks vō bĭs′kəm). *Latin*. peace be with you.

pax·wax (păks′wăks′), *n*. *Now Brit. Dial*. neck ligament. [ME *faxwax*, f. OE *feax* hair + *weax*(an) grow]

pay[1] (pā), *v.,* **paid** or (*Obs*. except for def. 12a) **payed**, **paying,** *n., adj*. —*v.t*. **1.** to discharge (a debt, obligation, etc.), as by giving or doing something. **2.** to give (money, etc.) as in discharge of debt or obligation. **3.** to satisfy the claims of (a person, etc.) as by giving money due. **4.** to defray (cost or expense). **5.** to give compensation for. **6.** to yield a recompense or return to; be profitable to: *it pays me to be honest*. **7.** to yield as a return: *the stock pays four percent*. **8.** to requite, as for good, harm, offense, etc. **9.** to retaliate upon or punish (often fol. by *off* or *out*). **10.** to give or render (attention, regard, court, compliments, etc.) as if due or fitting. **11.** to make (a call, visit, etc.). **12.** *Naut., etc*. **a.** to let out (a rope, etc.) as by slackening (fol. by *out* or *away*). **b.** to apply a weather helm to (a vessel) letting it fall off to leeward. —*v.i*. **13.** to give money, etc., due: *to pay for goods*. **14.** to discharge debt. **15.** to yield a return or profit; be advantageous or worthwhile. **16.** to give compensation, as for damage or loss sustained. **17.** to suffer, or be punished, as for something; make amends. **18.** *Naut*. to fall (*off*) to leeward. **19. pay up**, to pay in full. —*n*. **20.** payment, as of wages. **21.** wages, salary, or stipend. **22.** a person in respect to his solvency or reputation for meeting obligations: *he is good pay*. **23.** paid employ: *in the pay of the enemy*. **24.** requital; reward or punishment. —*adj*. **25.** (of earth, etc.) containing a sufficient quantity of metal or other value to be profitably worked by the miner. **26.** having a mechanism for payment when used: *a pay telephone*. [ME *paie*(n), t. F: m. *payer*, g. L *pācāre* pacify] —**Syn. 1.** settle, liquidate. **3.** reward, reimburse, indemnify. **21.** remuneration, emolument, fee.

pay[2] (pā), *v.t.,* **payed, paying.** *Naut*. to coat or cover (seams, a ship's bottom, etc.) with pitch, tar, or the like. [t. ONF: m. *peier*, g. L *picāre* cover with pitch]

pay·a·ble (pā′ə bəl), *adj*. **1.** that is to be paid; due. **2.** that may be paid. **3.** profitable. **4.** *Law*. imposing an immediate obligation on the debtor.

pay·box (pā′bŏks′), *n*. *Brit*. box office.

pay·day (pā′dā′), *n*. the day when payment is made, or to be made; the day on which wages are paid.

pay·ee (pā ē′), *n*. one to whom money is paid, or to be paid.

pay·er (pā′ər), *n*. **1.** one who pays. **2.** the person named in a bill or note who has to pay the holder.

pay·load (pā′lōd′), *n*. the income-producing part of a cargo.

pay·mas·ter (pā′măs′tər, -mäs′-), *n*. an officer or an official responsible for the payment of wages or salaries.

pay·ment (pā′mənt), *n*. **1.** act of paying. **2.** that which is paid; compensation; recompense. **3.** requital.

Payne (pān), *n*. **John Howard**, 1791–1852, U.S. actor and writer; author of "Home, Sweet Home."

---

b., blend of, blended; c., cognate with; d., dialect, dialectal; der., derived from; f., formed from; g., going back to; m., modification of; r., replacing; s., stem of; t., taken from; ?, perhaps.   See the full key on inside cover.

pay·nim (pā′nĭm), *n.* *Archaic.* **1.** a pagan or heathen. **2.** a Mohammedan. [ME *painime*, t. OF: m. *paieni(s)me*, g. LL *pāgānismus* heathenism]

pay-off (pā′ôf′, -ŏf′), *n.* **1.** the payment of a salary. **2.** the time when it is paid. **3.** *Colloq.* a final consequence; a settlement: *the pay-off was that they fired him.*

pay·o·la (pā ō′lə), *n.* a bribe, esp. for the promotion of a commercial product through the abuse of one's position or influence.

pay roll, 1. a roll or list of persons to be paid, with the amounts due. **2.** the aggregate of these amounts.

payt., payment.

Pb, *Chem.* (L *plumbum*) lead.

P.B., 1. (L *Pharmacopoeia Britannica*) British Pharmacopoeia. **2.** Prayer Book.

P/C, 1. petty cash. **2.** price current. Also, **p/c**

pc., 1. (*pl.* **pcs.**) piece. **2.** prices.

P.C., 1. Past Commander. **2.** *Brit.* Police Constable. **3.** Post Commander. **4.** *Brit.* Privy Council. **5.** *Brit.* Prince Consort.

p.c. 1. percent. **2.** petty cash. **3.** postal card. **4. price current.**

pct., percent.

Pd, *Chem.* palladium.

pd., paid.

P.D., 1. per diem. **2.** Police Department.

p.d., 1. per diem. **2.** potential difference.

Pd.B., Bachelor of Pedagogy.

Pd.D., Doctor of Pedagogy.

Pd.M., Master of Pedagogy.

P.E. 1. Presiding Elder. **2.** *Statistics.* probable error. **3.** Professional Engineer. **4.** Protestant Episcopal.

pea (pē), *n., pl.* **peas,** (*Archaic or Brit. Dial.*) **pease. 1.** the round, highly nutritious seed of *Pisum sativum,* a hardy plant in wide circulation. **2.** the plant bearing such seeds. **3.** any of various related or similar plants, or their seed, as the chickpea. **4.** something small as a pea. **—pea′like′,** *adj.* [back formation from PEASE (orig. sing., but later taken as pl.)]

Pea·bod·y (pē′bŏd′Y, -bəd Y), *n.* **1.** a city in NE Massachusetts. 22,645 (1950). **2.** George, 1795–1869, U.S. merchant, banker, and philanthropist in England.

peabody bird, the white-throated sparrow.

peace (pēs), *n.* **1.** freedom from war or hostilities. **2.** an agreement between contending parties to abstain from further hostilities. **3.** freedom from strife or dissension. **4.** freedom from civil commotion; public order and security: *a justice of the peace.* **5.** freedom from mental disturbance: *peace of mind.* **6. make one's peace,** to effect reconciliation for oneself, or for another person. **—v.i. 7.** *Obs. exc. as imperative.* to be or become silent. [ME *pais*, t. OF, g. L *pax* peace] **—Syn. 2.** armistice, truce. **3.** harmony, amity. **5.** calm, quiet.

peace·a·ble (pē′sə bəl), *adj.* **1.** disposed to peace; inclined to avoid strife or dissension: *peaceable intentions.* **2.** peaceful: *a peaceable adjustment.* **—peace′a·ble·ness,** *n.* **—peace′a·bly,** *adv.* **—Syn. 1.** See pacific.

Peace Corps, a benevolent civilian organization sponsored by the U.S. government to carry out useful, esp. technological, works abroad, esp. in underdeveloped countries.

peace·ful (pēs′fəl), *adj.* **1.** characterized by peace; free from strife or commotion; tranquil: *a peaceful reign.* **2.** pertaining to or characteristic of a state of peace: *peaceful uses of atomic energy.* **3.** peaceable. **—peace′-ful·ly,** *adv.* **—peace′ful·ness,** *n.* **—Syn. 2.** PEACEFUL, PLACID, SERENE, TRANQUIL refer to what is characterized by lack of strife or agitation. PEACEFUL today is rarely applied to persons; it refers to situations, scenes and activities free of disturbances, or, occasionally, of warfare: *a peaceful life.* PLACID, SERENE, TRANQUIL are used mainly of persons; when used of things (usually elements of Nature) there is a touch of personification. PLACID suggests an unruffled calm that verges on complacency: *a placid disposition; a placid stream.* SERENE is a somewhat nobler word; when used of persons it suggests dignity, composure, and graciousness (*a serene old age*); when applied to Nature there is a suggestion of mellowness (*the serene landscapes of Autumn*). TRANQUIL implies a command of emotions, often because of strong faith, which keeps one unagitated even in the midst of excitement or danger.

peace·mak·er (pēs′mā′kər), *n.* one who makes peace, as by reconciling parties at variance.

peace offering, 1. an offering or sacrifice prescribed by the Levitical law (see Lev. 3, 7) as thanksgiving to God. **2.** any offering made to procure peace.

peace officer, a civil officer appointed to preserve the public peace, as a sheriff or constable.

peace pipe, the calumet or pipe smoked by the North American Indians in token or ratification of peace.

Peace River, a river in W Canada, flowing from the Rocky Mountains in E British Columbia NE through Alberta to the Slave river. ab. 1050 mi.

peace·time (pēs′tīm′), *n.* **1.** a period of peace. **—adj.** **2.** of or for such a period: *peacetime uses of atomic energy.*

peach [1] (pēch), *n.* **1.** the subacid, juicy drupaceous fruit of a tree, *Prunus Persica,* of many varieties, widely cultivated in temperate climates. **2.** the tree itself. **3.** a light pinkish yellow, as of a peach. **4.** *Slang.* a person or thing especially admired or liked. **—adj. 5.** of the color peach. [ME *peche,* t. OF; r. OE *persic,* t. L: s. *persicum,* t. Gk.: m. *Persikón,* lit., Persian (apple)]

peach [2] (pēch), *v.i.* **1.** *Now Slang.* to inform against an accomplice or associate. **—v.t. 2.** *Now Rare.* to inform against. [aphetic var. of *appeach,* ME *apeche*(n), t. AF: m. *apecher,* var. of OF *empechier* hinder. See IMPEACH]

peach-blow (pēch′blō′), *n.* a delicate purplish pink. [f. PEACH [1] + BLOW, [3] n.]

peach·y (pē′chY), *adj.,* **peachier, peachiest. 1.** peachlike, as in color or appearance. **2.** *Slang.* excellent; wonderful.

pea·cock (pē′kŏk′), *n., pl.* **-cocks,** (*esp. collectively*) **cock. 1.** the male of the peafowl, esp. of the common peafowl, *Pavo cristatus,* a native of India but now widely domesticated, distinguished for its long, erectile, ocellated tail coverts with rich iridescent coloring of green, blue, and gold, and taken as a proverbial type of vainglory, and as a symbol of immortality. **2.** any peafowl. **3.** a vain person. **—v.i. 4.** to strut like a peacock; make a vainglorious display. [ME *pecok,* f. *pe* (OE *pēa* peafowl, t. L: m. *pavo*) + *cok* COCK[1]] **—pea′-cock′ish, pea′cock′y,** *adj.*

Blue peacock. *Pavo cristatus*
(Total length ab. 6½ ft., body 3 ft.)

Pea·cock (pē′kŏk′), *n.* Thomas Love, 1785–1866, British novelist and poet.

peacock blue, a lustrous greenish blue as of certain peacock feathers.

peacock ore, bornite.

pea·fowl (pē′foul′), *n.* any of the gallinaceous birds constituting the genus *Pavo;* a peacock or peahen.

peag (pēg), *n.* wampum.

pea green, a medium green or yellowish green.

pea·hen (pē′hĕn′), *n.* the female peafowl.

pea jacket, a short coat of thick woolen cloth worn esp. by seamen. [t. D: Anglicization of *pij-jakker*]

peak [1] (pēk), *n.* **1.** the pointed top of a mountain. **2.** a mountain with a pointed summit. **3.** the pointed top of anything. **4.** the highest point: *the peak of his career.* **5.** the maximum point or degree of anything. **6.** *Elect., Mech., etc.* **a.** the maximum value of a quantity during a specified time: *a voltage peak.* **b.** the maximum power consumed or produced by a unit or group of units in a stated period of time. **7.** a projecting point: *the peak of a man's beard.* **8.** widow's peak. **9.** a projecting front piece, or vizor, of a cap. **10.** *Naut.* **a.** the contracted part of a ship's hold at the bow or the stern. **b.** the upper after corner of a sail that is extended by a gaff. **c.** the outer extremity of a gaff. **—v.t. 11.** *Naut.* to raise the after end of a yard, gaff, etc. to or toward an angle above the horizontal. **—v.i. 12.** to project in a peak. [b. PIKE[2] (or PICK[1]) and BEAK[1]]

peak [2] (pēk), *v.i.* to become weak, thin, and sickly. [orig. uncert.]

peaked [1] (pēkt, pē′kĭd), *adj.* having a peak. [f. PEAK,[1] n. + -ED[2]]

peak·ed [2] (pē′kĭd), *adj.* thin; emaciated. [f. PEAK[2] + -ED[2]]

peal (pēl), *n.* **1.** a loud, prolonged sound of bells, or of cannon, thunder, applause, laughter, etc. **2.** a set of bells tuned to one another. **3.** a series of changes rung on a set of bells. **—v.t. 4.** to give forth loudly and sonorously. **5.** *Obs.* to assail with loud sounds. **—v.i. 6.** to sound forth in a peal; resound. [ME *pele;* akin to *peal, pell,* v., strike, beat]

Peale (pēl), *n.* Charles Willson, 1741–1827, U.S. portrait painter.

pea·nut (pē′nŭt′), *n.* **1.** the fruit (pod) or the edible seed of *Arachis hypogaea,* a leguminous plant, the pod of which is forced underground in growing, where it ripens. **2.** the plant.

peanut butter, a smooth paste made from finely ground roasted peanuts, used as a spread, etc.

pear (pâr), *n.* **1.** the edible fruit, typically rounded but elongated and growing smaller toward the stem, of a rosaceous tree, *Pyrus communis,* familiar in cultivation. **2.** the tree itself. [ME *peere,* OE *pere,* t. LL: m. *pirum*]

pearl [1] (pûrl), *n.* **1.** a hard, smooth, often highly lustrous concretion, a mass of nacre, white or variously colored, and rounded, pear-shaped, or irregular (baroque) in form, secreted as a morbid product within the shell of various bivalve mollusks, and often valuable as a gem. **2.** nacre, or mother-of-pearl. **3.** something similar in form, luster, etc., as a dewdrop or a capsule of medicine. **4.** something precious or choice; the finest example of anything. **5.** a very pale gray approaching white but commonly with bluish tinge. **6.** *Print.* a size of type (5 point). **—v.t. 7.** to adorn or stud with or as with pearls. **8.** to make like pearls, as in form or color. **—v.i. 9.** to seek for pearls. **10.** to take a pearl-like form or appearance. **—adj. 11.** of the color or luster of pearl; nacreous. **12.** of, pertaining to, or inlaid with pearls. **13.** reduced to small rounded grains: *pearl barley.* [ME *perle,* t. OF, t. ML: m. *perla,* ? b. L *perna* a kind of mussel and *sphaerula* little sphere] **—pearl′er,** *n.*

pearl [2] (pûrl), *v.t., v.i., n.* purl[2].

pearl·ash (pûrl′ăsh′), *n.* commercial carbonate of potassium.

pearl gray, a very pale bluish gray.

Pearl Harbor, a harbor near Honolulu, on the island

of Oahu in the Hawaiian Islands: surprise attack by Japan on the U.S. naval base there, Dec. 7, 1941.

pearl·ite (pûr′līt), *n.* **1.** *Metall.* an iron carbon alloy containing approximately 0.86 percent carbon, and consisting of alternate layers of ferrite and cementite. **2.** *Petrog.* perlite. [f. PEARL¹ + -ITE¹]

pearl millet, a tall grass, *Pennisetum glaucum,* cultivated in Africa, the Orient, and the southern U.S., for its edible seeds and as a forage plant.

Pearl River, 1. a river flowing from central Mississippi into the Gulf of Mexico. ab. 350 mi. **2.** Chu-Kiang.

pearl·y (pûr′lĭ), *adj.,* **pearlier, pearliest. 1.** like a pearl or like pearl. **2.** adorned with or abounding in pearls or pearl.

pearly nautilus, nautilus (def. 1).

pear·main (pâr′mān), *n.* any of several varieties of apple. [ME *parmayn,* t. OF: m. *parmain* pear (? orig. adj., der. *Parma* PARMA)]

Pear·son (pîr′sən), *n.* **Lester B**(owles), born 1897, prime minister of Canada since 1963.

peart (pĭrt), *adj.* **1.** lively or brisk; cheerful. **2.** clever. [var. of PERT]

Pea·ry (pîr′ĭ), *n.* **Robert Edwin,** 1856–1920. U.S. naval officer and explorer: discovered North Pole (1909).

peas·ant (pĕz′ənt), *n.* **1.** one of a class of persons, as in European countries, of inferior social rank, living in the country and engaged usually in agricultural labor. **2.** a rustic or countryman. [late ME, t. AF: m. *paisant,* der. *pais* country, g. LL *pāgensis,* adj., der. L *pāgus* district. Cf. PAGAN]

peas·ant·ry (pĕz′ən trĭ), *n.* **1.** peasants collectively. **2.** the status or character of a peasant.

pease (pēz), *n., pl.* **pease.** *Archaic or Brit. Dial.* **1.** a pea. **2.** *(pl.)* peas collectively. **3.** pl. of **pea.** [ME *pese,* OE *peose, pise,* t. LL: m. *pīsa,* orig. pl. of *pīsum,* t. Gk.: m. *pīson* pulse, pea]

pease·cod (pēz′kŏd′), *n.* the pod of the pea. Also, **peas′cod′.** [ME; f. PEASE + cod²]

peat¹ (pēt), *n.* **1.** a highly organic soil (more than fifty percent combustible) of partially decomposed vegetable matter, in marshy or damp regions, drained and cultivated, cut out and dried for use as fuel. **2.** such vegetable matter as a substance or fuel. [ME *pete* in Anglo-L *peta*); orig. uncert.] —**peat′y,** *adj.*

peat² (pēt), *n. Archaic.* a pet or darling. [orig. uncert.]

pea·vey (pē′vĭ), *n., pl.* **-veys.** a lumberman's cant hook with a spike at the end. [named after Joseph *Peavey,* the inventor]

Peavey

pea·vy (pē′vĭ), *n., pl.* **-vies.** peavey.

peb·ble (pĕb′əl), *n., v.,* **-bled, -bling.** —*n.* **1.** a small, rounded stone, esp. one worn by the action of water. **2.** pebbled leather, or its granulated surface. **3.** a transparent colorless rock crystal used for the lenses of eyeglasses. **4.** a lens made of it. —*v.t.* **5.** to prepare (leather, etc.) so as to have a granulated surface. **6.** to pelt with or as with pebbles. [ME *puble-,* etc., OE *pæbbel* (in place names)] —**peb′bly,** *adj.*

pe·can (pĭ kän′, pĭ kǎn′, pē′kǎn), *n.* **1.** a hickory tree, *Carya illinoensis* (C. Pecan), indigenous to the lower Mississippi valley and grown in the southern U.S. for its oval, smooth-shelled nut with a sweet, oily, edible kernel. **2.** the nut. [t. Amer. Ind. (Algonquian), der. *pukan, pakan* hard-shelled nut]

pec·ca·ble (pĕk′ə bəl), *adj.* liable to sin or err. [t. ML: m.s. *peccābilis*] —**pec′ca·bil′i·ty,** *n.*

pec·ca·dil·lo (pĕk′ə dĭl′ō), *n., pl.* **-loes, -los.** a petty sin or offense; a trifling fault. [t. Sp.: m. *pecadillo,* dim. of *pecado,* g. L *peccātum* a sin]

pec·cant (pĕk′ənt), *adj.* **1.** sinning or offending. **2.** faulty. [t. L: s. *peccans,* ppr., sinning] —**pec′can·cy,** *n.* —**pec′cant·ly,** *adv.*

pec·ca·ry (pĕk′ə rĭ), *n., pl.* **-ries,** *(esp. collectively)* **-ry.** any of a number of gregarious, piglike American ungulates, occurring in two genera, *Pecari,* the collared peccaries, and *Tayassu,* the white-lipped peccaries, ranging from Paraguay to Texas and constituting the artiodactylous family *Tayassuidae,* related to the hog. [t. Carib: m. *pakira*]

Collared peccary, *Pecari angulatus* (Ab. 3 ft. long, 15 to 17 in. high at the shoulders)

pec·ca·vi (pĕ kä′vĭ, -kä′vē), **1.** I have sinned (confession of King David). —*n.* **2.** *(pl.* **-vis)** any avowal of guilt. [t. L]

Pe·cho·ra (pĕ chô′rä), *n.* a river in the NE Soviet Union in Europe, flowing from the Ural Mountains into the Arctic Ocean. ab. 1100 mi.

peck¹ (pĕk), *n.* **1.** a dry measure of 8 quarts; the fourth part of a bushel. **2.** a container for measuring this quantity. **3.** a considerable quantity: *a peck of trouble.* [ME *pek,* orig. unknown]

peck² (pĕk), *v.t.* **1.** to strike or indent with the beak, as a bird does, or with some pointed instrument, esp. with quick, repeated movements. **2.** to make (a hole, etc.) by such strokes. **3.** to take (food, etc.) bit by bit, with or as with the beak. —*v.i.* **4.** to make strokes with the beak or a pointed instrument. **5.** to pick or nibble at food. **6.** to carp or nag (fol. by *at*). —*n.* **7.** a pecking

stroke. **8.** a hole or mark made by or as by pecking. [ME *pekke*(n); ? var. of PICK¹] —**peck′er,** *n.*

Peck·snif·f·i·an (pĕk snĭf′ĭ ən), *adj.* making a hypocritical parade of benevolence or high principle. [after Mr. *Pecksniff* in Dickens' *Martin Chuzzlewit*]

Pe·cos (pā′kəs, -kōs), *n.* a river flowing from N New Mexico SE through W Texas to the Rio Grande. 735 mi.

Pe·cos Bill (pā′kōs bĭl′), the legendary cowboy of the American frontier who performed such fabulous feats as digging the Rio Grande River.

Pecs (pāch), *n.* a city in SW Hungary. 87,140 (est. 1954). German, **Fünfkirchen.**

pec·tase (pĕk′tās), *n. Chem.* an enzyme found in various fruits, and concerned with the formation of pectic acid from pectin. [f. PECT(IN) + -ASE]

pec·tate (pĕk′tāt), *n. Chem.* a salt of pectic acid.

pec·ten (pĕk′tən), *n., pl.* **-tines** (-tə nēz′). *Zool., Anat.* **1.** a comblike part or process. **2.** a pigmented vascular membrane with parallel folds suggesting the teeth of a comb, projecting into the vitreous humor of the eye in birds and reptiles. [ME, t. L: a comb]

pec·tic (pĕk′tĭk), *adj.* pertaining to pectin. [t. Gk.: m.s. *pēktikós* congealing, curdling]

pectic acid, *Chem.* any of several water-insoluble products of the hydrolysis of pectin esters.

pec·tin (pĕk′tĭn), *n. Chem.* an amorphous, colloidal material which occurs in ripe fruits, esp. in apples, currants, etc., and which dissolves in boiling water, forming a jelly upon subsequent evaporation. [f. PECT(IC) + -IN²]

pec·ti·nate (pĕk′tə nāt′), *adj.* comblike; formed into or with teeth like a comb. Also, **pec′ti·nat′ed.** [t. L: m.s. *pectinātus* comblike, pp.] —**pec′ti·na′tion,** *n.*

pec·to·ral (pĕk′tərəl), *adj.* **1.** of or pertaining to the breast or chest; thoracic. **2.** worn on the breast or chest: *the pectoral cross of a bishop.* **3.** proceeding from the heart or inner consciousness. **4.** *Speech.* (of a vocal quality) appearing to come from resonance in the chest; full or deep. —*n.* **5.** something worn on the breast for ornament, protection, etc., as a breastplate. **6.** a pectoral fin. [late ME. t. L: s. *pectorālis* pertaining to the breast]

pectoral arch, 1. (in vertebrates) a bony or cartilaginous arch supporting the forelimbs. **2.** (in man) the bony arch, formed by the collarbone and shoulder blade, which attaches the upper extremity to the axial skeleton. Also, **pectoral girdle.**

pectoral fin, (in fishes) either of a pair of fins situated usually behind the head, one on each side, and corresponding to the forelimbs of higher vertebrates. See illus. under **ventral fin.**

pectoral sandpiper, an American shore bird, *Erolia melanotos,* so called because the male, when courting, inflates its chest conspicuously.

pec·u·late (pĕk′yə lāt′), *v.i., v.t.,* **-lated, -lating.** to embezzle (public money); appropriate dishonestly (money or goods entrusted to one's care). [t. L: m.s. *pecūlātus,* pp., having embezzled] —**pec′u·la′tion,** *n.* —**pec′u·la′tor,** *n.*

pe·cu·li·ar (pĭ kūl′yər), *adj.* **1.** strange, odd, or queer: *a peculiar old man.* **2.** uncommon; unusual: *a peculiar hobby.* **3.** distinguished in nature or character from others. **4.** belonging characteristically (fol. by *to*): *an expression peculiar to Canadians.* **5.** belonging exclusively to a person or thing. —*n.* **6.** a peculiar property or privilege. **7.** *Brit.* a particular parish or church which is exempted from the jurisdiction of the ordinary or bishop in whose diocese it lies and is governed by another. [late ME, t. L: s. *pecūliāris* pertaining to one's own, der. *pecūlium* property] —**pe·cul′iar·ly,** *adv.* —**Syn. 1.** eccentric, bizarre. See **strange. 5.** individual, personal, particular, special.

pe·cu·li·ar·i·ty (pĭ kū′lĭ ăr′ə tĭ), *n., pl.* **-ties. 1.** an odd trait or characteristic. **2.** singularity or oddity. **3.** peculiar or characteristic quality. **4.** a distinguishing quality or characteristic. —**Syn. 4.** See **feature.**

pe·cu·li·um (pĭ kū′lĭ əm), *n.* **1.** private property. **2.** *Rom. Law.* property given by a paterfamilias to those subject to him, or by a master to his slave, to be treated as though the property of the recipient. [t. L: property]

pe·cu·ni·ar·y (pĭ kū′nĭ ĕr′ĭ), *adj.* **1.** consisting of or given or exacted in money: *pecuniary penalties.* **2.** of or pertaining to money: *pecuniary affairs.* **3.** (of an offense, etc.) entailing a money penalty. [t. L: m.s. *pecūniārius* pertaining to money] —**Syn. 1.** See **financial.**

ped-¹, var. of **pedi-²,** as in *pedagogic.* Also, **paed-.**

ped-², var. of **pedi-¹.**

-ped, a word element meaning "foot," serving to form adjectives and nouns, as *aliped, biped, breviped, quadruped.* Cf. **-pod.** [t. L, comb. form of *pēs* foot]

ped., 1. pedal. **2.** pedestal.

ped·a·gog·ic (pĕd′ə gŏj′ĭk, -gō′jĭk), *adj.* of or pertaining to a pedagogue or pedagogy. Also, **ped′a·gog′i·cal.** [t. Gk.: m.s. *paidagōgikós,* der. *paidagōgós* pedagogue] —**ped′a·gog′i·cal·ly,** *adv.*

ped·a·gog·ics (pĕd′ə gŏj′ĭks), *n.* the science or art of teaching or education; pedagogy.

ped·a·gog·ism (pĕd′ə gŏg′ĭz əm, -gŏg′-), *n.* the principles, manner, method, or characteristics of pedagogues. Also, **ped·a·gogu·ism** (pĕd′ə gŏg′ĭz əm, -gŏg′-).

ped·a·gogue (pĕd′ə gŏg′, -gŏg′), *n.* **1.** a teacher of children; a schoolteacher. **2.** a person who is pedantic, dogmatic, and formal. Also, **ped′a·gog′.** [ME *peda-*

goge, t. OF, t. L: m. *paedagōgus*, t. Gk.: m. *paidagōgós* a teacher of boys]

ped·a·go·gy (pĕd′ə gō′jĭ, -gŏj′Ĭ), n. **1.** the function, work, or art of a teacher; teaching. **2.** instruction.

ped·al (pĕd′əl for *1–5, 7, 8*; pē′dəl *for 6*), n., v., **-aled**, **-aling** or (*esp. Brit.*) **-alled, -alling**, adj. —n. **1.** a lever worked by the foot, in various musical instruments, as the organ, piano, and harp, and having various functions. **2.** a keyboard attached to the organ, harpsichord, etc., operated by the feet. **3.** pedal point. **4.** a lever-like part worked by the foot, in various mechanisms, as the sewing machine, bicycle, etc.; a treadle. —v.i., v.t. **5.** to work or use the pedals (of), as in playing an organ or propelling a bicycle. [t. F: m. *pédale*, t. It., t. L: (something) pertaining to the foot] —adj. **6.** of or pertaining to a foot or the feet. **7.** of or pertaining to a pedal or pedals. **8.** consisting of pedals: *a pedal keyboard*. [t. L: s. *pedālis* pertaining to the foot]

pedal point, *Music*. **1.** a tone sustained by one of the parts (usually the bass) while other parts progress without reference to it. **2.** a passage containing it.

ped·ant (pĕd′ənt), n. **1** one who makes an excessive or tedious show of learning or learned precision; one who possesses mere book learning without practical wisdom. **2.** *Obs.* a schoolmaster. [t. It.: m. *pedante* teacher, pedant, der. It. *ped-*, *piede* foot (in meaning of servile follower)] —**pe·dan·tic** (pĭ dăn′tĭk), **pe·dan′ti·cal**, adj. —**pe·dan′ti·cal·ly**, adv.

ped·ant·ry (pĕd′ən trĭ), n., pl. **-ries**. **1.** the character or practice of a pedant; an undue display of learning. **2.** slavish attention to rules, details, etc.

ped·ate (pĕd′āt), adj. **1.** having feet. **2.** footlike. **3.** having divisions like toes. **4.** *Bot.* (of a leaf) palmately parted or divided with the lateral lobes or divisions cleft or divided. [t. L: m.s. *pedātus* having feet] —**ped′ate·ly**, adv.

pedati-, a word element meaning "pedate." [comb. form repr. L *pedātus*]

pe·dat·i·fid (pĭ dăt′ə fĭd, -dā′tə-), adj. *Bot.* pedately cleft.

ped·dle (pĕd′əl), v., **-dled, -dling**. —v.t. **1.** to carry about for sale at retail; hawk. **2.** to deal out in small quantities. —v.i. **3.** to travel about retailing small wares. **4.** to occupy oneself with trifles; trifle. [appar. a back formation from PEDDLER, and in part confused with PIDDLE]

ped·dler (pĕd′lər), n. one who peddles. Also, **pedlar, pedler**. [ME *pedlere*, appar. der. *pedle*, dim. of *ped* basket]

ped·dler·y (pĕd′lər Ĭ), n. **1.** the business of a peddler. **2.** peddlers' wares. **3.** trumpery.

ped·dling (pĕd′lĭng), adj. trifling; paltry; piddling.

-pede, a word element meaning "foot," as in *centipede*. [t. F: m. *-pède*, t. L: m. *-peda*, a comb. form of *pēs* foot]

ped·er·ast (pĕd′ə răst′, pē′də-), n. one who practices pederasty.

ped·er·as·ty (pĕd′ə răs′tĭ, pē′də-), n. unnatural sex relations between males. —**ped′er·as′tic**, adj. —**ped′er·as′ti·cal·ly**, adv.

ped·es·tal (pĕd′Ĭs təl), n., v., **-taled, -taling** or (*esp. Brit.*) **-talled, -talling**. —n. **1.** an architectural support for a column, statue, vase, or the like. **2.** a supporting structure or piece; a base. **3. set on a pedestal**, to idealize. —v.t. **4.** to set on or supply with a pedestal. [t. F: m. *piédestal*, t. It.: m. *piedestallo*, f. *piede* foot (g. L *pēs*) + *di* of (g. L *dē*) + *stallo* (of Gmc. orig. cf. STALL¹)]

pe·des·tri·an (pə dĕs′trĭ ən), n. **1.** one who goes or travels on foot; a walker. —adj. **2.** going or performed on foot; walking. **3.** pertaining to walking. **4.** commonplace; prosaic; dull. [f. s. L *pedester* on foot + -IAN]

pe·des·tri·an·ism (pə dĕs′trĭ ə nĭz′əm), n. **1.** the exercise or practice of walking. **2.** pedestrian manner or traits.

pedi-¹, a word element meaning "foot," as in *pediform*. Also, **ped-²**. [t. L, comb. form of *pēs*]

pedi-², a word element meaning "child." Also, **paed-, paedo-, ped-¹**. [t. Gk.: m. *paidi-*, comb. form of *pais*]

pe·di·a·tri·cian (pē′dĭ ə trĭsh′ən, pĕd′Ĭ-), n. a physician who specializes in pediatrics. Also, **pe·di·at·rist** (pē′dĭ ăt′rĭst, pĕd′Ĭ-).

pe·di·at·rics (pē′dĭ ăt′rĭks, pĕd′Ĭ-), n. the science of the medical and hygienic care of, or the diseases of, children. Also, **paediatrics**. [pl. of *pedi·atric* (f. PED-¹ + m.s. Gk. *iātrikós* of medicine). See -ICS] —**pe′di·at′ric**, adj.

ped·i·cel (pĕd′ə səl), n. **1.** *Bot.* **a.** a small stalk. **b.** an ultimate division of a common peduncle. **c.** one of the subordinate stalks in a branched inflorescence, bearing a single flower. **2.** *Zool., Anat.* **a.** a small stalk or stalklike part; a peduncle. **b.** a little foot or footlike part. [t. NL: m.s. *pedicellus*, dim. of L *pediculus* PEDICLE]

A. Pedicel; B. Peduncle

ped·i·cel·late (pĕd′ə səl ĭt, -lāt′), adj. having a pedicel or pedicels.

ped·i·cle (pĕd′ə kəl), n. *Bot., Zool., etc.* a small stalk or stalklike support; a pedicel or peduncle. [t. L: m.s. *pediculus*, dim. of *pēs* foot]

pe·dic·u·lar (pĭ dĭk′yə lər), adj. of or pertaining to lice. [t. L: s. *pediculāris*, der. *pediculus* louse]

pe·dic·u·late (pĭ dĭk′yə lĭt, -lāt′), adj. **1.** of or relating to the *Pediculati*, a group of teleost fishes, characterized by the elongated basis of their pectoral fins simulating an arm or peduncle. —n. **2.** a member of this group. [f. s. L *pediculus* footstalk + -ATE¹]

pe·dic·u·lo·sis (pĭ dĭk′yə lō′sĭs), n. *Pathol.* the state of being infested with lice. [t. NL, f. s. L *pediculus* louse + -ōsis -OSIS] —**pe·dic·u·lous** (pĭ dĭk′yə ləs), adj.

ped·i·cure (pĕd′ə kyŏŏr′), n. **1.** professional care or treatment of the feet. **2.** one who makes a business of caring for the feet; a chiropodist. [t. F, f. L: *pedi-* PEDI-¹ + m. *cūra* care. Cf. MANICURE]

ped·i·form (pĕd′ə fôrm′), adj. in the form of a foot.

ped·i·gree (pĕd′ə grē′), n. **1.** an ancestral line, or line of descent, esp. as recorded; lineage. **2.** a genealogical table: *a family pedigree*. **3.** a line, family, or race. **4.** derivation, as from a source: *the pedigree of a word*. [ME *pedegru*, appar. t. OF: m. *pied de grue*, lit., foot of crane, said to refer to a mark having three branching lines, used in old genealogical tables] —**Syn. 2.** PEDIGREE, GENEALOGY refer to an account of ancestry. A PEDIGREE is a table or chart recording a line of ancestors, either of persons or (more especially) of animals, as horses, cattle, and dogs; in the case of animals, such a table is used as proof of superior qualities: *a detailed pedigree*. A GENEALOGY is an account of the descent of a person or family traced through a series of generations, usually from the first known ancestor: *a genealogy that includes a king*.

ped·i·greed (pĕd′ə grēd′), adj. having known purebred ancestry.

ped·i·ment (pĕd′ə mənt), n. *Archit.* **1.** a low triangular gable crowned with a projecting cornice, in the Greek, Roman, or Renaissance style, esp. over a portico or porch or at the ends of a gabled-roofed building. **2.** any member of similar outline and position, as over an opening. [?. t. L: m.s. *pedamentum* a prop for a vine] —**ped·i·men·tal** (pĕd′ə mĕn′təl), adj.

Pediment

ped·lar (pĕd′lər), n. peddler. Also, **ped′ler**.

pe·do·bap·tism (pē′dō băp′tĭz′əm), n. the baptism of infants. [f. *pedo-* (var. of PEDI-²) + BAPTISM]

pe·dol·o·gy¹ (pĭ dŏl′ə jĭ), n. the more fundamental aspects of soil science, particularly the genesis and classification of soils. [f. Gk. *pédo(n)* soil + -LOGY]

pe·dol·o·gy² (pĭ dŏl′ə jĭ), n. **1.** the scientific study of the nature and development of children. **2.** pediatrics. [f. *pedo-* (var. of PEDI-²) + -LOGY]

pe·dom·e·ter (pĭ dŏm′ə tər), n. an instrument for recording the number of steps taken in walking, and thus showing approximately the distance traveled. [t. F: m. *pédomètre*, f. *pedo-* PEDI-¹ + *-mètre* -METER]

pe·dro (pē′drō), n., pl. **-dros**. *Cards*. **1.** any of several varieties of seven-up in which the five of trumps counts at its face value. **2.** the five of trumps. [t. Sp.: special use of *Pedro* Peter]

pe·dun·cle (pĭ dŭng′kəl), n. **1.** *Bot.* **a.** a flower stalk, supporting either a cluster or a solitary flower. **b.** the stalk bearing the fructification in fungi, etc. **2.** *Zool.* a stalk or stem; a stalk-like part or structure. **3.** *Anat.* a stalklike structure composed of white matter connecting various regions of the brain. [t. NL: m.s. *pedunculus*, dim. of L *pēs* foot] —**pe·dun′cled, pe·dun·cu·lar** (pĭ dŭng′kyə lər), adj.

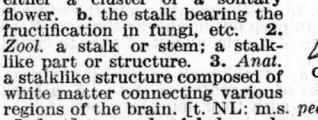

One-flowered peduncle of periwinkle, *Vinca minor*

pe·dun·cu·late (pĭ dŭng′kyə lĭt, -lāt′), adj. **1.** having a peduncle. **2.** growing on a peduncle. Also, **pe·dun′cu·lat·ed**.

Pee·bles (pē′bəlz), n. a county in S Scotland. 14,300 pop. (est. 1956); 347 sq. mi. *Co. seat:* Peebles. Also, **Pee·bles·shire** (pē′bəlz shĭr′, -shər) or Tweeddale.

Pee Dee (pē′ dē′), a river flowing through central North Carolina and NE South Carolina into the Atlantic. 435 mi. Called **Yadkin** in North Carolina.

peek (pēk), v.i. **1.** to peep; peer. —n. **2.** a peeking look; a peep. [ME *pike(n)*, ? dissimilated var. of *kike* peep; akin to LG *kiken*] —**Syn. 1.** See peep¹.

peel¹ (pēl), v.t. **1.** to strip off the skin, rind, bark, etc.; decorticate. **2.** to strip off (skin, etc.). **3. keep (one's) eye peeled**, *Slang*. to keep a close watch. —v.i. **4.** (of skin, etc.) to come off. **5.** to lose the skin, rind, bark, etc. **6.** *Slang*. to undress. —n. **7.** the skin or rind of a fruit, etc. [ME *pelen*, phonetic var. of *pilen* PILL²] —**Syn. 1.** PEEL, PARE agree in meaning to remove the skin or rind from something. PEEL means to pull or strip off the natural external covering or protection of something: *to peel an orange*. PARE is used of trimming off chips, flakes, or superficial parts from something, as well as of cutting off the skin or rind: *to pare the nails, to pare a potato*.

peel² (pēl), n. a shovellike implement for putting bread, pies, etc., into the oven or taking them out. [ME *pele*, t. OF: shovel, g. L *pāla* spade]

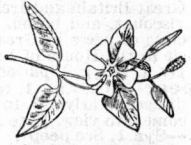

peel[3] (pēl), *n.* one of a class of fortified towers for residence or safe resort, common in the border counties of England and Scotland in the 16th century. [ME *pel*, t. OF: stake, g. L *pālus* PALE[2]]

Peel (pēl), *n.* **1. Sir Robert,** 1788–1850, British prime minister, 1834–35 and 1841–46. **2.** a seaport on the W coast of the Isle of Man: castle; resort. 2582 (1951).

Peele (pēl), *n.* **George,** 1558?–97?, English dramatist.

peel·er[1] (pē'lər), *n.* one who or that which peels. [f. PEEL[1] + -ER[1]]

peel·er[2] (pē'lər), *n. Obsolesc. Irish and Brit. Slang.* a policeman. [named after Sir Robert Peel, secretary for Ireland (1812–18) under whom the Irish constabulary was founded. Cf. BOBBY]

peel·ing (pē'lĭng), *n.* **1.** act of one who or that which peels. **2.** that which is peeled from something, as a piece of the skin or rind of a fruit peeled off.

peen (pēn), *n.* **1.** the sharp, spherical, or otherwise modified end of the head of a hammer, opposite to the face. —*v.t.* **2.** to treat by striking regularly all over with the peen of a hammer. [earlier *pen;* orig. uncert.]

peep[1] (pēp), *v.i.* **1.** to look through or as through a small aperture. **2.** to ,ook slyly, pryingly, or furtively. **3.** to peer, as from a hiding place. **4.** to come partially into view; begin to appear. —*v.t.* **5.** to show or protrude slightly. —*n.* **6.** a peeping look or glance. **7.** the first appearance, as of dawn. **8.** an aperture for looking through. [? assimilated var. of PEEK]
—**Syn. 1, 2.** PEEP, PEEK, PEER mean to look through, over, or around something. To PEEP or PEEK is usually to give a quick look through a narrow aperture or small opening, often furtively, slyly, or pryingly; or to look over or around something curiously or playfully: *to peep over a wall, to peek into a room.* PEEK is often associated with children's games. To PEER is to look continuously and narrowly for some time, esp. in order to penetrate obscurity or to overcome some obstacle in the way of vision: *the sun peers through the clouds.*

peep[2] (pēp), *n.* **1.** a peeping cry or sound. **2.** any of various small shore birds. —*v.i.* **3.** to utter the shrill little cry of a young bird, a mouse, etc.; cheep; squeak. **4.** to speak in a thin, weak voice. [ME *pēpe(n),* also *pipen.* Cf. OF *piper,* L *pīpāre,* D and G *piepen,* all imit.]

peep·er[1] (pē'pər), *n.* the maker of a peeping sound. [f. PEEP[2], v. + -ER[1]]

peep·er[2] (pē'pər), *n.* **1.** a prying or spying person. **2.** *Slang.* an eye. [f. PEEP[1], v. + -ER[1]]

peep·hole (pēp'hōl'), *n.* a hole through which to peep.

Peeping Tom, a prying, furtive observer, often for sexual gratification (in allusion to the man who peeped at Lady Godiva riding through Coventry).

peep show, an exhibition of objects or pictures viewed through an aperture usually fitted with a magnifying lens.

peep sight, a plate containing a small hole through which a gunner peeps in sighting.

peer[1] (pîr), *n.* **1.** a person of the same civil rank or standing; an equal before the law. **2.** one who ranks with another in respect to endowments or other qualifications; an equal in any respect. **3.** a nobleman. **4.** a member of any of the five degrees of the nobility in Great Britain and Ireland, namely, duke, marquis, earl, viscount, and baron. **5. peer of the realm,** any of a class of peers in Great Britain and Ireland entitled to sit in the House of Lords. **6.** *Obs.* a companion. [ME *per,* t. OF, g. L *pār* equal]

peer[2] (pîr), *v.i.* **1.** to look narrowly, as in the effort to discern clearly. **2.** to peep out or appear slightly. **3.** to come into view. [late ME, orig. uncert., ? akin to PERK]
—**Syn. 1.** See peep[1].

peer·age (pîr'ĭj), *n.* **1.** the rank or dignity of a peer. **2.** the body of peers of a country or state. **3.** a book giving a list of peers, with their genealogy, etc.

peer·ess (pîr'ĭs), *n.* **1.** the wife of a peer. **2.** a woman having in her own right the rank of a peer.

Peer Gynt (pîr' gĭnt'; *Nor.* pâr' gynt'), a drama (1867) by Henrik Ibsen.

peer·less (pîr'lĭs), *adj.* having no peer or equal; matchless. —**peer'less·ly,** *adv.* —**peer'less·ness,** *n.*

peet·weet (pēt'wēt), *n. U.S.* the spotted sandpiper. See sandpiper. [imit. Cf. PEWIT]

peeve (pēv), *v.* peeved, peeving, *n.* —*v.t.* **1.** *Colloq.* to render peevish. —*n.* **2.** an annoyance: *my pet peeve.* [back formation from PEEVISH]

pee·vish (pē'vĭsh), *adj.* **1.** cross, querulous, or fretful, as from vexation or discontent. **2.** *Obs.* perverse. [ME *pevysh;* orig. unknown] —**pee'vish·ly,** *adv.* —**pee'-vish·ness,** *n.* —**Syn. 1.** See cross.

peg (pĕg), *n., v.,* pegged, pegging. —*n.* **1.** a pin of wood or other material driven or fitted into something, as to fasten parts together, to hang things on, to make fast a rope or string on, to stop a hole, or to mark some point. **2.** *Colloq.* a leg, sometimes one of wood. **3.** an occasion; reason: *a peg to hang a grievance on.* **4.** *Colloq.* a degree: *to come down a peg.* **5.** a pin of wood or metal to which one end of a string of a musical instrument is fastened, and which may be turned in its socket to adjust the string's tension. **6.** *Brit. and Anglo-Indian.* a drink usually made of whiskey or brandy and soda water. —*v.t.* **7.** to drive or insert a peg into. **8.** to fasten with or as with pegs. **9.** to mark with pegs. **10.** to strike or pierce with or as with a peg. **11.** *Colloq.* to aim or throw. —*v.i.* **12.** to work persistently, or

keep on energetically (fol. by *away, along, on,* etc.). **13.** *Croquet.* to strike a peg. [ME *pegge.* Cf. OE *pecg* (in a place name), d. D *peg,* LG *pigge*]

Peg·a·sus (pĕg'ə·səs), *n.* **1.** *Class. Myth.* a winged horse, sprung from the blood of Medusa when slain by Perseus, who with a stroke of his hoof caused the spring Hippocrene to well forth on Mount Helicon, causing his modern association with the Muses and poetry. **2.** *Astron.* a northern constellation represented as the forward half of a flying horse.

Pegasus

peg·ma·tite (pĕg'mə·tīt'), *n.* **1.** a graphic intergrowth of quartz and feldspar; graphic granite. **2.** a coarsely crystalline granite or other rock occurring in veins or dikes. [f. s. Gk. *pēgma* something fastened together + -ITE[1]]

peg top, 1. a child's wooden top spinning on a metal peg. **2.** *(pl.)* peg-top trousers. **3.** a peg-top skirt.

peg-top (pĕg'tŏp'), *adj.* shaped like a top, as men's trousers or women's skirts wide at the hips and narrowing to the ankle.

Peh·le·vi (pā'lə·vē'), *n.* Pahlavi (language).

P.E.I., Prince Edward Island.

peign·oir (pān wär', pān'wär), *n.* **1.** a dressing gown. **2.** a woman's loose robe for wearing while the hair is being combed. [t. F, der. *peigner,* g. L *pectināre* comb]

Pei·ping (bā'pǐng'), *n.* former name of Peking: used when city was not capital of China.

Pei·pus (pī'pəs; *Ger.* -pŏŏs), *n.* former name of Chudskoe. Also, Estonian, **Peip·si** (pāp'sǐ).

Pei·rae·us (pīrē'əs), *n.* Piraeus.

Pei·rai·evs (pē'rĕ'ĕfs'), *n.* Greek name of Piraeus.

Peirce (pûrs), *n.* **Charles Sanders,** 1839–1914, U.S. logician, mathematician, and physicist.

pe·jo·ra·tive (pē'jə·rā'tĭv, pǐ jōr'ə·tĭv, pǐ jŏr'-), *adj.* **1.** depreciative. **2.** having a disparaging force, as certain derivative word forms. —*n.* **3.** a pejorative form or word, as *poetaster.* [f. s. L *pējōrātus,* pp., having been made worse + -IVE[1]] —**pe'jo·ra'tive·ly,** *adv.*

pek·an (pĕk'ən), *n.* the fisher, *Martes pennanti.* [t. Canadian F, t. Algonquian (Abnakĭ): m. *pékanĕ*]

Pe·kin (pē'kǐn), *n.* a hardy yellow-white duck developed in China. [named after *Peking*]

Pe·kin (pē'kǐn), *n.* a city in central Illinois. 28,146 (1960).

Pe·king (pē'kǐng'; *Chin.* bā'jǐng'), *n.* traditional capital of China, in NE part. 2,900,000 (est. 1954). City named Peiping during and immediately following World War II.

Pekinese
(8 to 14 in. high at the shoulder)

Pe·king·ese (pē'kǐng·ēz'), *n.* **1.** small, long-haired Chinese dog prized as a pet. **2.** standard Chinese (language). **3.** the dialect of Peking. **4.** a native of Peking. —*adj.* **5.** pertaining to Peking. Also, **Pe·kin·ese** (pē'kə·nēz').

Peking man, an extinct human species of which skeletal remains were found in a cave N of Peking, China.

pe·koe (pē'kō *or, esp. Brit.,* pĕk'ō), *n.* a superior kind of black tea from Ceylon, India, and Java, made from leaves smaller than those used for orange pekoe. [t. Chinese (Amoy dialect): m. *pek-ho* white down]

pel·age (pĕl'ĭj), *n.* the hair, fur, wool, or other soft covering of a mammal. [t. F, der. *poil,* g. L *pilus* hair]

Pe·la·gi·an (pə·lā'jǐ'ən), *n.* a follower of Pelagius, a British monk (fl. about A.D. 400–418), who denied original sin and maintained the freedom of the will and its power to attain righteousness. —**Pe·la'gi·an·ism,** *n.*

pe·lag·ic (pə·lăj'ǐk), *adj.* **1.** of or pertaining to the seas or oceans. **2.** living at or near the surface of the ocean, far from land, as certain animals or plants. [t. L: s. *pelagicus,* t. Gk.: m. *pelagikós* pertaining to the sea]

pel·ar·gon·ic acid (pĕl'är gŏn'ĭk, -gō'nĭk), *Chem.* an oily organic acid, $C_9H_{18}O_2$, occurring as an ester in a volatile oil in species of pelargonium.

pel·ar·go·ni·um (pĕl'är gō'nǐ əm), *n.* any plant of the genus *Pelargonium,* the cultivated species of which are usually called geranium. See geranium (def. 2). [t. NL, der. Gk. *pelargós* stork]

Pe·las·gi·an (pə·lăz'jǐ'ən), *adj.* **1.** of or pertaining to the Pelasgi, an ancient race inhabiting Greece and the islands and coasts of the Aegean Sea and the eastern Mediterranean in prehistoric times. —*n.* **2.** a member of this race.

Pe·las·gic (pə·lăz'jǐk), *adj.* Pelasgian.

Pe·lée (pə·lā'), *n.* **Mount,** a volcano in the West Indies, on the island of Martinique: eruption, 1902. 4428 ft.

pel·er·ine (pĕl'ə·rēn'), *n.* a woman's cape, esp. a narrow cape with long descending ends in front. [t. F: pilgrim's cape or mantle, special use of fem. of *pèlerin* pilgrim, g. L *peregrīnus* wandering]

Pe·leus (pē'lūs, -lǐ əs), *n. Gk. Legend.* a king of the Myrmidons, son of Aeacus, and father of Achilles.

b., blend of, blended; c., cognate with; d., dialect, dialectal; der., derived from; f., formed from; g., going back to; m., modification of; r., replacing; s., stem of; t., taken from; ?, perhaps. See the full key on inside cover.

Pe·lew Islands (pēlōō′), Palau Islands.

pelf (pĕlf), *n.* *Usually Contemptuous.* money or riches. [ME, t. OF: m. *pelfre* spoil; orig. uncert. Cf. PILFER]

Pe·li·as (pē′lĭ as, pĕl′ĭ-), *n.* *Gk. Legend.* a son of Poseidon, who sent Jason and the Argonauts to recover the Golden Fleece.

pel·i·can (pĕl′ə kən), *n.* any of various large, totipalmate birds of the family *Pelecanidae*, having a large fish-catching bill with distensible pouch beneath into which the young stick their heads when feeding. [ME and OE, t. LL: s. *pelicānus*, var. of *pelecānus*, t. Gk.: m. *pelekán*]

American white pelican, *Pelecanus erythrorhynchos* (5 ft. long)

Pe·li·on (pē′lĭ ən; *Gk.* -lē-ŏn′), *n.* Mount, 1. a mountain near the E coast of Greece, in Thessaly. ab. 5330 ft. 2. *Gk. Myth.* See Ossa.

pe·lisse (pə lēs′), *n.* 1. an outer garment lined or trimmed with fur. 2. a woman's long cloak with arm openings. [t. F, g. LL *pellicia* fur garment, prop. fem. of LL *pelliceus* made of skins]

pe·lite (pē′līt), *n.* any clay rock. Cf. psephite and psammite. [f. s. Gk. *pēlós* clay, earth + -ITE¹]

Pel·la (pĕl′ə), *n.* a ruined city in N Greece, NW of Salonica: the capital of ancient Macedonia; birthplace of Alexander the Great.

pel·la·gra (pə lā′grə, pə lăg′rə), *n.* *Pathol.* a chronic, noncontagious disease caused by deficient diet, characterized by skin changes, severe nervous dysfunction, and diarrhea. [t. It., ? orig. *pelle agra* rough skin] —**pel·la′grous**, *adj.*

Pel·lé·as et Mé·li·sande (pĕlē ás′ ĕ mĕlē zänd′) an opera (1902) by Debussy, based on a play by Maeterlinck.

pel·le·kar (pĕl′ə kär′), *n.* palikar.

Pel·les (pĕl′ēz), *n.* Sir, *Arthurian Romance.* the father of Elaine, the mother of Galahad.

pel·let (pĕl′ĭt), *n.* 1. a round or spherical body, esp. one of small size; a little ball, as of food or medicine. 2. a ball, usually of stone, formerly used as a missile. 3. a bullet or one of a charge of small shot, as for a shotgun. 4. an imitation bullet, as of wax or paper. —*v.t.* 5. to form into pellets. 6. to hit with pellets. [ME *pelet*, t. OF: m. *pelote*, der. L *pila* ball]

pel·li·cle (pĕl′ə kəl), *n.* a thin skin or membrane; a film; a scum. [t. L: m.s. *pellicula*, dim. of *pellis* skin] —**pel·lic·u·lar** (pə lĭk′yə lər), *adj.*

pel·li·to·ry (pĕl′ə tŏr′ĭ), *n.*, *pl.* -ries. an asteraceous plant, *Anacyclus Pyrethrum*, of Algeria, etc., whose root is used as a local irritant (**pellitory of Spain**). [alter. with change of suffix of ME *peletre*, t. AF, g. L *pyrethrum* pellitory of Spain, t. Gk.: m. *pýrethron* feverfew]

pell-mell (pĕl′mĕl′), *adv.* 1. in an indiscriminate medley; in a confused mass or crowd. 2. in disorderly, headlong haste. —*adj.* 3. indiscriminate; disorderly; tumultuous. —*n.* 4. an indiscriminate medley. 5. violent disorder. Also, **pell′mell′**. [t. F: m. *pêle-mêle*, in OF *pesle mesle*, appar. der. *mesler* mix]

pel·lu·cid (pə lōō′sĭd), *adj.* 1. allowing the passage of light; translucent. 2. clear or limpid, as water. 3. clear in meaning. [t. L: s. *pellūcidus* transparent] —**pel·lu·cid·i·ty** (pĕl′ōō sĭd′ə tĭ), **pel·lu′cid·ness**, *n.* —**pel·lu′cid·ly**, *adv.*

Pe·lop·i·das (pĭ lŏp′ə dəs), *n.* died 364 B.C., Greek general and statesman of Thebes.

Peloponnesian War, a war between Athens and Sparta from 431 to 404 B.C. which resulted in the transfer of hegemony in Greece from Athens to Sparta.

Pel·o·pon·ne·sus (pĕl′ə pə nē′səs), *n.* the S peninsula of Greece: the seat of the early Mycenaean civilization and of the powerful city-states of Sparta, Argos, etc. 1,129,222 pop. (1951); 8356 sq. mi. Also, **Pel′o·pon·ne′sos** or **Morea**. —**Pel·o·pon·ne·sian** (pĕl′ə pə nē′shən, -zhən), *adj.*, *n.*

Pe·lops (pē′lŏps), *n.* *Gk. Legend.* a son of Tantalus. He was restored to life after Tantalus served him as meat to the gods.

pe·lo·ri·a (pə lōr′ĭ ə), *n.* *Bot.* regularity of structure occurring abnormally in flowers normally irregular. [t. NL, f. Gk. *pelōr* monster + -*ia* -IA] —**pe·lor·ic** (pə lōr′ĭk, -lŏr′-), *adj.*

pe·lo·ta (pĕ lō′tä), *n.* a Basque and Spanish game played in a court with a ball and a curved wicker racket. [Sp., aug. of *pella*, g. L *pila* ball. Cf. PELLET]

pelt¹ (pĕlt), *v.t.* 1. to assail with repeated blows or (now usually) with missiles. 2. to throw (missiles). 3. to drive, put, etc., by blows or missiles. 4. to assail with abuse. —*v.i.* 5. to strike blows; beat with force or violence. 6. to throw missiles. 7. to cast abuse. 8. to hurry. —*n.* 9. act of pelting. 10. a vigorous stroke. 11. a blow with something thrown. 12. speed. [orig. uncert.; ? akin to PELLET] —**pelt′er**, *n.*

pelt² (pĕlt), *n.* 1. the skin of a beast with or without the hair. 2. *Humorous.* the human skin, esp. when hairy. [ME, appar. a back formation from PELTRY] —**Syn.** 1. See skin.

pel·tast (pĕl′tăst), *n.* an ancient Greek soldier armed with a light shield. [t. L: s. *peltasta*, t. Gk.: m. *peltastḗs*]

pel·tate (pĕl′tāt), *adj.* *Bot.* (of a leaf, etc.) having the stalk or support attached to the lower surface at a distance from the margin; shield-shaped. [t. L: m.s. *peltātus* armed with a light shield] —**pel′tate·ly**, *adv.*

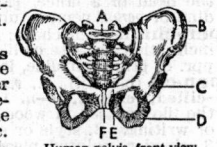
Peltate leaf

pelt·ing (pĕl′tĭng), *adj.* *Archaic.* paltry; petty; mean. [cf. obs. *peltry*, var. of PALTRY]

pelt·ry (pĕl′trĭ), *n.*, *pl.* -ries. 1. fur skins; pelts collectively. 2. a pelt. [ME *peltre*, t. OF: m. *peleterie*, ult. der. *pel* skin, g. L *pellis*]

pel·vic (pĕl′vĭk), *adj.* of or pertaining to the pelvis.

pelvic arch, 1. (in vertebrates) a bony or cartilaginous arch supporting the hind limbs or analogous parts. 2. (in man) the arch, formed by the innominate bones, which attaches the lower extremity to the axial skeleton. Also, **pelvic girdle**.

pel·vis (pĕl′vĭs), *n.*, *pl.* -ves (-vēz). *Anat.*, *Zool.* 1. the basinlike cavity in the lower part of the trunk of many vertebrates, formed in man by the innominate bones, sacrum, etc. 2. the bones forming this cavity. 3. the cavity of the kidney which receives the urine before it is passed into the ureter. [t. L: basin]

Human pelvis, front view
A. Upper base of sacrum; B. Crest of ilium; C. Acetabulum; D. Ischium; E. Pubis; F. Pubic symphysis

Pem·ba (pĕm′bə), *n.* an island near the E coast of equatorial Africa, in Zanzibar protectorate. 114,587 pop. (1948); 380 sq. mi.

Pem·broke (pĕm′brŏŏk), *n.* 1. Pembrokeshire. 2. a variety of the Welsh Corgi breed of dogs. See Welsh Corgi.

Pem·broke·shire (pĕm′brŏŏk shĭr′, -shər), *n.* a county in SW Wales. 90,906 pop. (1951); 614 sq. mi. *Co. seat:* Pembroke. Also, **Pembroke**.

pem·mi·can (pĕm′ə kən), *n.* dried meat pounded into a paste with melted fat and dried fruits, pressed into cakes, orig. prepared by North American Indians. Also, **pem′i·can**. [t. N Amer. Ind. (Cree): m. *pimikan* manufactured grease, der. *pimikew* he makes grease (by boiling fat)]

pem·phi·gus (pĕm′fə gəs, pĕm fī′-), *n.* *Pathol.* a serious disease, commonly fatal, characterized by vesicles and bullae on the skin and mucous membranes. [t. NL, f. s. Gk. *pemphis* bubble + -*us* (n. ending)]

pen¹ (pĕn), *n.*, *v.*, penned, penning. —*n.* 1. any instrument for writing with ink. 2. a small instrument of steel or other metal, with a split point, used, when fitted into a penholder, for writing with ink. 3. the pen and penholder together. 4. a quill pointed and split at the nib, used for writing with ink. 5. the pen as the instrument of writing or authorship: *the pen is mightier than the sword.* 6. style or quality of writing. 7. a writer or author. 8. the profession of writing or literature: *men of the pen.* 9. *Ornith.* a. a large feather of the wing or tail; a quill feather; a quill. b. a pinfeather of a bird. 10. a female mute swan. 11. something resembling or suggesting a feather or quill. 12. *Zool.* an internal, corneous or chitinous, feather-shaped structure in certain cephalopods, as the squid. —*v.t.* 13. to write with a pen; set down in writing. [ME *penne*, t. OF, g. L *penna* feather, LL pen]

pen² (pĕn), *n.*, *v.*, penned or pent, penning. —*n.* 1. a small enclosure for domestic animals. 2. animals so enclosed. 3. any place of confinement or safekeeping. —*v.t.* 4. to confine in or as in a pen. [ME *penne*, OE *penn*; orig. uncert.]

Pen., peninsula.

P.E.N., International Association of Poets, Playwrights, Editors, Essayists, and Novelists.

pe·nal (pē′nəl), *adj.* 1. of or pertaining to punishment, as for offenses or crimes. 2. prescribing punishment: *penal laws.* 3. constituting punishment: *penal servitude.* 4. used as a place of punishment: *a penal settlement.* 5. subject to or incurring punishment: *a penal offense.* 6. payable or forfeitable as a penalty: *a penal sum.* [ME, t. L: m.s. *poenālis* pertaining to punishment]

penal code, *Law.* the aggregate of statutory enactments dealing with crimes and their punishment.

pe·nal·ize (pē′nə līz′, pĕn′ə-), *v.t.*, -ized, -izing. 1. to subject to a penalty, as a person. 2. to declare penal, or punishable by law, as an action. 3. to lay under a disadvantage. Also, *esp. Brit.*, **pe′nal·ise′**. —**pe′nal·i·za′tion**, *n.*

pen·al·ty (pĕn′əl tĭ), *n.*, *pl.* -ties. 1. a punishment imposed or incurred for a violation of law or rule. 2. a loss or forfeiture to which one subjects himself by nonfulfillment of an obligation. 3. that which is forfeited, as a sum of money. 4. consequence or disadvantage attached to any action, condition, etc. 5. *Sports.* a disadvantage imposed upon a competitor or side for infraction of the rules. 6. **on** or **under penalty**, with the liability of incurring a penalty in case of nonfulfillment of a specified condition, injunction, etc. [f. PENAL + -TY²]

pen·ance (pĕn'əns), *n.* **1.** punishment undergone in token of penitence for sin. **2.** a penitential discipline imposed by church authority. **3.** a sacrament, as in the Roman Catholic Church, consisting in a confession of sin with sorrow and the purpose of amendment followed by the forgiveness of sin. [ME *penaunce*, t. OF: m. *peneance*, g. L *poenitentia*. See PENITENCE]

Pe·nang (pĕ'năng'), *n.* **1.** an island in SE Asia, off the W coast of the Malay Peninsula. 262,705 pop. (1947); 110 sq. mi. **2.** a state including this island and parts of the adjacent mainland: now part of the Federation of Malaysia, formerly one of the Straits Settlements and in the former Federation of Malaya. 616,294 pop. (1959); 400 sq. mi. *Cap.:* George Town. **3.** George Town.

pe·na·tes (pə nā'tēz), *n.pl. Rom. Myth.* tutelary deities of the household and of the state, worshiped in close association with the lares. Also, **Pe·na'tes**. [t. L, der. *penus* innermost part of a temple. Cf. PENETRATE]

pence (pĕns), *n. Brit.* pl. of *penny*, when value is indicated: *he gave two pennies for twopence worth.*

pen·cel (pĕn'səl), *n. Archaic.* a small pennon, as at the head of a lance. [ME, t. AF, contr. of *penoncel*, dim. of *penon* pennon, ult. der. L *penna* feather]

pen·chant (pĕn'chənt; *Fr.* päṅ shäṅ'), *n.* a strong inclination; a taste or liking for something. [t. F, orig. ppr. of *pencher* incline, lean, der. L *pendre* hang]

pen·cil (pĕn'səl), *n., v.,* **-ciled, -ciling** or (*esp. Brit.*) **-cilled, -cilling.** —*n.* **1.** a strip of graphite, chalk, or the like incased in wood, metal, etc., used for drawing or writing. **2.** style or skill in painting or delineation. **3.** slender, pointed piece of some marking substance. **4.** a stick of cosmetic coloring material for use on the eyebrows, etc. **5.** a similarly shaped piece of some other substance, as lunar caustic. **6.** a set of lines, light rays, or the like diverging from or converging to a point. **7.** *Archaic.* an artist's paintbrush, esp. for fine work. —*v.t.* **8.** to use a pencil on. **9.** to execute, draw, or write with or as with a pencil. **10.** to mark or color with or as with a pencil. [ME *pencel*, t. OF: m. *pincel*, g. VL var. of L *pēnicillum*, dim. of *pēniculus* brush] —**pen'cil·er**; *esp. Brit.*, **pen'cil·ler,** *n.*

pend (pĕnd), *v.i.* **1.** to remain undecided. **2.** to hang. **3.** *Obs.* to depend. [late ME, t. L: s. *pendēre* hang, depend]

pend·ant (pĕn'dənt), *n.* **1.** a hanging ornament, as of a necklace or earring or of a vaulted roof. **2.** a chandelier. **3.** that by which something is suspended, as the ringed stem of a watch. **4.** a match or parallel. —*adj.* **5.** pendent. [ME *pendaunte*, t. OF: m. *pendant*, ppr., hanging, der. *pendre* hang, g. L *pendēre*]

pend·ent (pĕn'dənt), *adj.* **1.** hanging or suspended. **2.** overhanging; jutting or leaning over. **3.** impending. **4.** pending or undecided. —*n.* **5.** pendant. [t. L: s. *pendens*, ppr., hanging; r. ME *penda(u)nt*, t. OF: m. *pendant*, g. L] —**pend'en·cy,** *n.* —**pend'ent·ly,** *adv.*

pen·den·te li·te (pĕn dĕn'tĭ lī't), *Law.* during litigation; while a suit is in progress. [L]

pen·den·tive (pĕn dĕn'tĭv), *n. Archit.* **1.** a triangular segment of the lower part of a hemispherical dome, between two penetrating arches. **2.** a similar segment of a groined vault, resting on a single pier or corbel. [f. PENDENT + -IVE, translating F *pendentif*]

pend·ing (pĕn'dĭng), *prep.* **1.** while awaiting; until: *pending his return.* **2.** in the period before the decision or conclusion of; during: *pending the negotiations.* —*adj.* **3.** remaining undecided; awaiting decision. **4.** hanging; impending. [f. PEND(ENT) + -ING²]

pen·drag·on (pĕn drăg'ən), *n.* chief leader (a title of ancient British chiefs). [t. Welsh: f. *pen* head + *dragon* dragon (used as symbol), leader] —**pen·drag'on·ship',** *n.*

Pen·drag·on (pĕn drăg'ən), *n.* either of two kings of ancient Britain. See Uther.

pen·du·lous (pĕn'jə ləs), *adj.* **1.** hanging. **2.** swinging freely. **3.** vacillating. [t. L: m. *pendulus* hanging, swinging] —**pen'du·lous·ly,** *adv.* —**pen'du·lous·ness,** *n.*

pen·du·lum (pĕn'jə ləm, pĕn'də-), *n.* **1.** a body so suspended from a fixed point as to move to and fro by the action of gravity and acquired momentum. **2.** a swinging device used for controlling the movement of clockwork. [t. NL, prop. neut. of L *pendulus* hanging, swinging]

Pe·nel·o·pe (pə nĕl'ə pĭ), *n.* **1.** the wife of Odysseus in the *Odyssey*, who, during her husband's long absence, remained faithful to him in spite of numerous suitors. **2.** a faithful wife.

pe·ne·plain (pē'nə plān', pĕ'nə plān'), *n. Geol.* an area reduced almost to a plain by erosion. Also, **pe'ne·plane'.** [f. L *pēne* almost + PLAIN]

pen·e·tra·ble (pĕn'ə trə bəl), *adj.* capable of being penetrated. [ME, t. L: m.s. *penetrābilis*.] —**pen'e·tra·bil'i·ty,** *n.* —**pen'e·tra·bly,** *adv.*

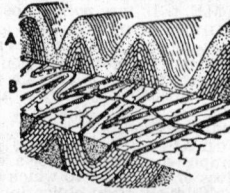

Cross section of peneplain
A. Original land structure;
B. Peneplain with residual ridges

pen·e·tra·li·a (pĕn'ə trā'lĭ ə), *n. pl.* the innermost parts or recesses of a place or thing. [t. L, prop. neut. pl. of *penetrālis* inner, orig. penetrating]

pen·e·trate (pĕn'ə trāt'), *v.,* **-trated, -trating.** —*v.t.* **1.** to pierce into or through. **2.** to enter the interior of. **3.** to enter and diffuse itself through; permeate. **4.** to affect or impress deeply. **5.** to arrive at the meaning of; understand. —*v.i.* **6.** to enter, reach, or pass through, as by piercing. [t. L: m.s. *penetrātus*, pp.] —**Syn. 1.** See **pierce. 5.** comprehend, fathom.

pen·e·trat·ing (pĕn'ə trā'tĭng), *adj.* **1.** that penetrates; piercing; sharp. **2.** acute; discerning. **3.** *Surg.* denoting a wound produced by an agent or missile such that depth is its salient feature, as a wound entering a member. Also, **pen·e·trant** (pĕn'ə trənt). —**pen'e·trat'ing·ly,** *adv.* —**Syn. 2.** See **acute.**

pen·e·tra·tion (pĕn'ə trā'shən), *n.* **1.** the act or power of penetrating. **2.** the extension, usually peaceful, of the influence of one country in the life of another. **3.** mental acuteness, discernment, or insight: *a scholar of rare penetration.* **4.** *Gun.* the depth to which a projectile goes into the target.

pen·e·tra·tive (pĕn'ə trā'tĭv), *adj.* tending to penetrate; piercing; acute; keen. —**pen'e·tra'tive·ly,** *adv.*

Pe·ne·us (pĭ nē'əs), *n.* ancient name of **Salambria.**

pen·gö (pĕn'gœ'), *n., pl.* **-gö, -gös** (-gœz'). **1.** the monetary unit for Hungary stabilized in 1925 at 17.49 cents in U.S. and equal to 100 fillér: no longer the basis of coinage system. **2.** the Hungarian silver coin equal to 17.49 cents in U.S. [t. Hung., ppr. of *pengeni* sound]

Pen·gu (pĕn'gōō'), *n.* Pescadores.

pen·guin (pĕn'gwĭn, pĕng'-), *n.* **1.** any of various flightless aquatic birds (family *Spheniscidae*) of the southern hemisphere, with webbed feet, and wings reduced to flippers. **2.** *Obs.* the great auk. **3.** *Aeron.* an airplane which merely rolls along the ground, enabling a beginner to learn certain manipulations safely. [Cf. F *pingouin*, earlier *penguyn* auk; of disputed orig.]

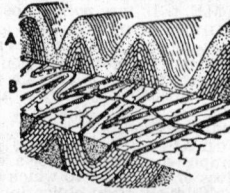

Emperor penguin. *Aptenodytes forsterii* (Total length 4 ft.)

pen·hold·er (pĕn'hōl'dər), *n.* **1.** a holder in which a pen point is placed. **2.** a rack for a pen or pens.

pen·i·cil (pĕn'ə sĭl), *n.* a small brushlike tuft of hairs, as on a caterpillar. [t. L: m.s. *pēnicillus*, paint brush, pencil]

pen·i·cil·late (pĕn'ə sĭl'ĭt, -āt), *adj.* having a penicil or penicils. [t. NL: m.s. *pēnicillātus*, der. L *pēnicillus* pencil] —**pen'i·cil·late·ly,** *adv.* —**pen'i·cil·la'tion,** *n.*

pen·i·cil·lin (pĕn'ə sĭl'ĭn), *n.* a powerful antibacterial substance produced by molds of the genus *Penicillium*. [f. PENICILL(IUM) + -IN²]

pen·i·cil·li·um (pĕn'ə sĭl'ĭ əm), *n., pl.* **-cilliums, -cillia** (-sĭl'ĭ ə). any member of the fungus genus *Penicillium*, known usually as the green molds, embracing species used in cheesemaking (*P. Camemberti, P. Roqueforti*) and species (especially *P. notatum*) from which penicillin is extracted. [f. s. L *pēnicillus* small brush, lit., small tail + -IUM]

pen·in·su·la (pə nĭn'sə lə, -syə lə), *n.* **1.** a piece of land almost surrounded by water, esp. one connected with the mainand by only a narrow neck or isthmus. **2. the Peninsula. a.** Iberia: so called in connection with the **Peninsular War** waged there by the British, Spanish, and Portuguese against the French, 1808–14. **b.** a district in SE Virginia between the York and James rivers: Civil War battles. [t. L: m. *paeninsula*] —**pen·in'su·lar,** *adj.*

pe·nis (pē'nĭs), *n., pl.* **-nes** (-nēz), **-nises** (-nĭs'ĭz). the male organ of copulation. [t. L: orig., tail]

pen·i·tence (pĕn'ə təns), *n.* state of being penitent; repentance; contrition. —**Syn.** See **regret.**

pen·i·tent (pĕn'ə tənt), *adj.* **1.** repentant; contrite; sorry for sin or fault and disposed to atonement and amendment. —*n.* **2.** a penitent person. **3.** *Rom. Cath. Ch.* one who confesses sin and submits to a penance. [t. L: m.s. *paenitens* ppr., repenting; r. ME *penitaunt*, t. AF] —**pen'i·tent·ly,** *adv.*

pen·i·ten·tial (pĕn'ə tĕn'shəl), *adj.* **1.** of or pertaining to, proceeding from, or expressive of penitence or repentance. —*n.* **2.** a penitent. **3.** a book or code of canons relating to penance, its imposition, etc. [t. ML: m.s. *poenitentiālis*] —**pen'i·ten'tial·ly,** *adv.*

pen·i·ten·tia·ry (pĕn'ə tĕn'shə rĭ), *n., pl.* **-ries,** *adj.* —*n.* **1.** a place for imprisonment and reformatory discipline. **2.** U.S. a State prison. **3.** *Rom. Cath. Ch.* **a.** an officer appointed to deal with cases of conscience reserved for a bishop or for the Holy See. **b.** an office of the Holy See (presided over by the **cardinal grand penitentiary**) having jurisdiction over such cases. —*adj.* **4.** (of an offense) punishable by imprisonment in a penitentiary. **5.** pertaining to or intended for penal confinement and discipline. **6.** penitential. [ME, t. ML: m.s. *poenitentiārius*, der. L *poenitentia* penitence]

pen·knife (pĕn'nīf'), *n., pl.* **-knives** (-nīvz'). a small pocketknife, orig. for making and mending quill pens.

pen·man (pĕn'mən), *n., pl.* **-men. 1.** one who uses a pen. **2.** expert in penmanship. **3.** a writer or author.

pen·man·ship (pĕn'mən shĭp'), *n.* the use of the pen in writing; the art of handwriting; manner of writing.

Penn (pĕn), *n.* **1. Sir William,** 1621–70, British admiral. **2.** his son, **William,** 1644–1718, British Quaker who founded the colony of Pennsylvania.

Penn., Pennsylvania. Also, **Penna.**

pen·na (pĕn′ə), *n.*, *pl.* **pennae** (pĕn′ē). *Ornith.* a contour feather, as distinguished from a down feather, plume, etc. [t. L: feather]

pen name, a name assumed to write under; an author's pseudonym; nom de plume.

pen·nant (pĕn′ənt), *n.* **1.** a flag of distinctive form and special significance, borne on naval or other vessels or used in signaling, etc. **2.** any flag serving as an emblem, as of success in an athletic contest. **3.** *Music.* hook (def. 12). [var. of PENDANT; assoc. also with PENNON]

pen·nate (pĕn′āt), *adj.* winged; feathered. [t. L: m.s. *pennātus* winged]

Pen·nell (pĕn′əl), *n.* **Joseph**, 1860–1926. U.S. etcher. illustrator, and writer.

pen·ni (pĕn′ī), *n.*, *pl.* **pennia** (pĕn′ī·ə). a Finnish coin and money of account equivalent to one hundredth of a mark. [Finnish, t. G: m. *pfennig*]

pen·ni·less (pĕn′ī·lĭs), *adj.* without a penny; destitute of money. —**Syn.** See **poor.**

Pen·nine Alps (pĕn′īn), a mountain range on the Swiss-Italian border. Highest peak, Monte Rosa.

pen·non (pĕn′ən), *n.* **1.** a distinctive flag in various forms (tapering, triangular, swallow-tailed, etc.), orig. one borne on the lance of a knight. **2.** a pennant. **3.** any flag or banner. **4.** *Poetic.* a wing or pinion. [ME *penon*, t. OF, der. *penne*, g. L *penna* feather]

pen·non·cel (pĕn′ən·sĕl′), *n.* *Archaic.* pencel.

Penn·syl·va·ni·a (pĕn′səl·vā′nĭ·ə, -vān′yə), *n.* a State in E United States. 11,319,366 pop. (1960); 45,333 sq. mi. *Cap.:* Harrisburg. *Abbr.:* Pa., Penn., or Penna.

Pennsylvania Dutch, 1. the descendants of 18th-century settlers in Pennsylvania from southwestern Germany. **2.** a German dialect spoken mainly in eastern Pennsylvania, developed from the language of these settlers. —**Penn′syl·va′ni·a-Dutch′**, *adj.*

Penn·syl·va·ni·an (pĕn′səl·vā′nĭ·ən, -vān′yən), *adj.* **1.** of or pertaining to the State of Pennsylvania. **2.** *Stratig.* pertaining to a late Paleozoic geological period or a system of rocks equivalent to the Upper Carboniferous of usage outside of North America. —*n.* **3.** a native or inhabitant of Pennsylvania. **4.** *Stratig.* the period or system following Mississippian and preceding Permian, characterized by abundance of coal deposits.

pen·ny (pĕn′ī), *n.*, *pl.* **pennies**, (*esp. collectively*) **pence** for **1b. 1.** any of various coins, as **a.** the U.S. and Canadian cent. **b.** an English coin, $^1/_{12}$ of the shilling (about 1 U.S. cent), but once of greater value. **2.** a sum of money. [ME *peni*, OE *penig, pening, pending*, i.e. (coin) of King Penda of Mercia. Cf. G *pfennig*]

-penny, a suffix forming adjectives that denote price or value, as in *fourpenny, fivepenny*, etc. (as used in *fourpenny nails, fivepenny nails*, etc., formerly meaning "nails costing fourpence, fivepence, etc., a hundred," but now nails of certain arbitrary sizes).

pen·ny-a-lin·er (pĕn′ī·ə·lī′nər), *n.* *Chiefly Brit.* a hack writer.

penny dreadful, *Chiefly Brit.* a piece of cheap popular literature; dime novel.

pen·ny·roy·al (pĕn′ī·roi′əl), *n.* any of several labiate herbaceous plants, as the one found in the Old World, *Mentha Pulegium*, or the American **mock pennyroyal**, *Hedeoma pulegioides*, used medicinally and yielding a pungent aromatic oil. [f. *penny* (? alter. of OF *puliol*, der. L *pūlegium* pennyroyal) + ROYAL]

pen·ny·weight (pĕn′ī·wāt′), *n.* (in troy weight) a unit of 24 grains or one twentieth of an ounce.

pen·ny-wise (pĕn′ī·wīz′), *adj.* wise or saving in regard to small sums: *penny-wise and pound-foolish.*

pen·ny·wort (pĕn′ī·wûrt′), *n.* any of several plants with round or roundish leaves, as the **marsh pennywort**, of the genus *Hydrocotyle*, the navelwort, *Cotyledon umbilicus*, the Kenilworth ivy, *Cymbalaria muralis* (see ivy), and a small American plant, *Obolaria virginica*, of the gentian family.

pen·ny·worth (pĕn′ī·wûrth′), *n.* **1.** as much as may be bought for a penny. **2.** a small quantity. **3.** a bargain.

Pe·nob·scot (pə·nŏb′skŏt), *n.* **1.** a river flowing from N Maine S to **Penobscot Bay**, an island-studded inlet (ab. 30 mi. long) of the Atlantic. ab. 350 mi. **2.** (*pl.*) an Algonquian Indian tribe of the Abnaki confederacy located on both sides of Penobscot Bay and river. **3.** a member of this tribe. [t. Algonquian, der. *pannawanbskek* it forks on the white rocks; or *penaubsket* it flows on rocks; or *penops* rock (locative); or *penabskat* plenty stones]

pe·nol·o·gy (pē·nŏl′ə·jī), *n.* **1.** the science of the punishment of crime, in both its deterrent and its reformatory aspects. **2.** the science of the management of prisons. [f. PEN(AL) + -(o)LOGY] —**pe·no·log·i·cal** (pē′nə·lŏj′ə·kəl), *adj.* —**pe·nol·o·gist** (pē·nŏl′ə·jĭst), *n.*

Pen·sa·co·la (pĕn′sə·kō′lə), *n.* a seaport in NW Florida, on Pensacola Bay, an inlet of the Gulf of Mexico; naval aviation station. 56,752 (1960).

pen·sile (pĕn′sĭl), *adj.* **1.** hanging, as the nests of certain birds. **2.** building a hanging nest. [t. L (neut.): hanging down]

pen·sion (pĕn′shən; *for 3 Fr.* päN·syôN′), *n.* **1.** a fixed periodical payment made in consideration of past services, injury or loss sustained, merit, poverty, etc.

2. an allowance or annuity. **3.** (in France and elsewhere on the Continent) a boarding house or school. —*v.t.* **4.** to grant a pension to. **5.** to cause to retire on a pension (fol. *by off*). [t. L: s. *pensio* payment; r. ME *pensioun*, t. OF: m. *pensiun*] —**pen′sion·a·ble**, *adj.*

pen·sion·ar·y (pĕn′shə·nĕr′ī), *n.*, *pl.* **-aries**, *adj.* —*n.* **1.** a pensioner. **2.** hireling. —*adj.* **3.** of the nature of a pension. **4.** receiving a pension.

pen·sion·er (pĕn′shən·ər), *n.* **1.** one who receives a pension. **2.** a hireling. **3.** a student at Cambridge University who pays for his commons, etc., and is not supported by any foundation. **4.** *Obs. except Hist.* a gentleman-at-arms.

pen·sive (pĕn′sĭv), *adj.* **1.** deeply, seriously, or sadly thoughtful. **2.** expressing thoughtfulness or sadness. [t. F (fem.), der. *penser* think; r. ME *pensif*, t. F (masc.)] —**pen′sive·ly**, *adv.* —**pen′sive·ness**, *n.*
—**Syn. 1.** PENSIVE, MEDITATIVE, REFLECTIVE suggest quiet modes of apparent or real thought. PENSIVE, the weakest of the three, suggests dreaminess or wistfulness, and may involve little or no thought to any purpose: *a pensive, faraway look.* MEDITATIVE involves thinking of certain facts or phenomena—perhaps in the religious sense of "contemplation"—without necessarily having a goal of complete understanding or of action: *meditative but unjudicial.* REFLECTIVE has a strong implication of orderly, perhaps analytic, processes of thought, usually with a definite goal of understanding: *a careful and reflective critic.* —**Ant. 1.** thoughtless.

pen·stock (pĕn′stŏk′), *n.* **1.** a pipe conducting water from the head gates to a water wheel. **2.** a conduit for conveying water to a power plant. **3.** a sluicelike contrivance used to control the flow of water.

pent (pĕnt), *v.* **1.** a pt. and pp. of **pen**[2]. —*adj.* **2.** shut in. **3.** confined.

pent-, a word element meaning "five." Also, before consonants, **penta-**. [t. Gk., comb. forms of *pénte*]

pen·ta·cle (pĕn′tə·kəl), *n.* **1.** a pentagram. **2.** some more or less similar figure, as a hexagram. [prob. t. F, or t. ML: m. *pentaculum*. See PENTA-, -CLE]

pen·tad (pĕn′tăd), *n.* **1.** a period of five years. **2.** *Chem.* a pentavalent element or radical. **3.** a group of five. **4.** the number five. [t. Gk.: s. *pentás* a group of five]

pen·ta·gon (pĕn′tə·gŏn′), *n.* **1.** a polygon having five angles and five sides. **2.** the **Pentagon**, the building in Arlington, Va., containing most U.S. Defense Department offices. [t. L: s. *pentagōnum*, t. Gk.: m. *pentágōnon*, prop. neut adj. used as noun] —**pen·tag·o·nal** (pĕn·tăg′ə·nəl), *adj.* —**pen·tag′o·nal·ly**, *adv.*

Pentagon

pen·ta·gram (pĕn′tə·grăm′), *n.* a five-pointed star-shaped figure made by extending the sides of a regular pentagon until they meet (a symbolical figure used by the Pythagoreans and later philosophers, by magicians, and others). [t. Gk.: m.s. *pentágrammon* (prop. neut. of *adj.*) figure consisting of five lines]

pen·ta·he·dron (pĕn′tə·hē′drən), *n.*, *pl.* **-drons, -dra** (-drə). a solid figure having five faces. —**pen′ta·he′dral**, *adj.*

Pentagram

pen·tam·er·ous (pĕn·tăm′ər·əs), *adj.* **1.** consisting of or divided into five parts. **2.** *Bot.* (of flowers) having five members in each whorl. [t. NL: m. *pentamerus*, t. Gk.: m. *pentamerēs*]

pen·tam·e·ter (pĕn·tăm′ə·tər), *Pros.* —*n.* **1.** a verse of five feet. **2.** *Anc. Pros.* a verse consisting of two dactyls, one long syllable, two more dactyls, and another single syllable (**elegiac pentameter**). **3.** unrhymed iambic pentameter; heroic verse. —*adj.* **4.** consisting of five metrical feet. [t. L, t. Gk.: m.s. *pentámetros*]

pen·tane (pĕn′tān), *n.* *Chem.* a hydrocarbon, C_5H_{12}, of the methane series, existing in three isomeric forms. [f. Gk. *pént(e)* five + -ANE]

pen·tar·chy (pĕn′tär·kī), *n.*, *pl.* **-chies. 1.** a government by five persons. **2.** a governing body of five persons. **3.** a group of five states or kingdoms, each under its own ruler. [t. Gk.: m.s. *pentarchia*]

pen·ta·stich (pĕn′tə·stĭk′), *n.* *Pros.* a strophe, stanza, or poem consisting of five lines or verses. [t. NL: s. *pentastichus*, t. Gk.: m. *pentástichos* of five lines]

Pen·ta·teuch (pĕn′tə·tūk′, -tōōk′), *n.* the first five books of the Old Testament, regarded as a group. [t. L: s. *Pentateuchus*, t. Gk.: m. *pentáteuchos* consisting of five books] —**Pen′ta·teuch′al**, *adj.*

pen·tath·lon (pĕn·tăth′lən), *n.* an athletic contest comprising five different exercises or events, and won by the contestant having the highest total score. [t. Gk.]

pen·ta·va·lent (pĕn′tə·vā′lənt, pĕn·tăv′ə-), *adj.* *Chem.* possessing a valence of 5: *pentavalent arsenic.*

Pen·te·cost (pĕn′tə·kôst′, -kŏst′), *n.* **1.** a Christian festival commemorating the descent of the Holy Ghost upon the apostles on the day of the Jewish festival; Whitsunday. **2.** a Jewish harvest festival observed on the fiftieth day from the second day of Passover. [ME *pentecoste*, OE *pentecosten*, t. LL: m. *pentecoste*, t. Gk.: m. *pentēkostē* fiftieth (day)] —**Pen′te·cos′tal**, *adj.*

Pen·tel·i·cus (pĕn·tĕl′ə·kəs), *n.* a mountain in SE Greece, near Athens: noted for its fine marble. 3640 ft. Also, **Pen·tel·i·kon** (pĕn·tĕl′ə·kŏn′).

pent·house (pĕnt′hous′), *n.* **1.** a separate apartment or dwelling on a roof. **2.** a structure on a roof for housing elevator machinery, etc. **3.** a shed with a sloping roof, or a sloping roof, projecting from a wall or the side of a building, as to shelter a door. **4.** any rooflike shelter or overhanging part. [ME *pentis*, appar. t. OF: m. *apentis*, der. L *appendere* hang to or on, append]

pen·tom·ic (pĕn·tŏm′ĭk), *adj. Mil.* of, pertaining to, or characterizing the organization of an army division into five units geared to the requirements of combat with atomic weapons. [PENT- + (AT)OMIC]

pen·to·san (pĕn′tə·săn′), *n. Chem.* any of a class of polysaccharides which occur in plants, humus, etc., and form pentoses upon hydrolysis.

pen·tose (pĕn′tōs), *n. Chem.* a monosaccharide containing five atoms of carbon, or produced from pentosans by hydrolysis. [f. PENT(A)- + -OSE²]

Pen·to·thal Sodium (pĕn′tə·thôl′), *Trademark.* sodium pentothal.

pent·ste·mon (pĕnt·stē′mən), *n.* any plant of the scrophulariaceous genus *Pentstemon*, chiefly of North America, including species cultivated for their variously colored flowers with long-tubed corolla. [t. NL, f. Gk.: *pent*(e) five + *stēmon* warp, thread]

pent-up (pĕnt′ŭp′), *adj.* confined; restrained: *pent-up rage*.

pe·nuch·le (pē′nŭk′əl), *n.* pinochle. Also, **pe′·nuck′le**.

pe·nult (pē′nŭlt, pĭ·nŭlt′), *n.* the last syllable but one in a word. Also, **pe·nul·ti·ma** ((pĭ·nŭl′tə·mə). [t. L: m. *paenultima* (fem.) last but one]

pe·nul·ti·mate (pĭ·nŭl′tə·mĭt), *adj.* **1.** next to the last. **2.** of the penult. —*n.* **3.** the penult.

pe·num·bra (pĭ·nŭm′brə), *n., pl.* **-brae** (-brē), **-bras.** *Astron.* **1.** the partial or imperfect shadow outside the complete shadow (umbra) of an opaque body, as a planet, where the light from the source of illumination is only partly cut off. **2.** the grayish marginal portion of a sunspot. [t. NL, f. m. L *paene* almost + *umbra* shade, shadow] —**pe·num′bral**, *adj.*

pe·nu·ri·ous (pə·nyŏŏr′ĭ·əs, -nŏŏr′-), *adj.* meanly parsimonious; stingy. —**pe·nu′ri·ous·ly**, *adv.* —**pe·nu′ri·ous·ness**, *n.*

pen·u·ry (pĕn′yər·ĭ), *n.* **1.** extreme poverty; destitution. **2.** dearth or insufficiency. [ME, t. L: m.s. *pēnūria* want, scarcity. Cf. Gk. *penia* poverty, need]

Pe·nu·ti·an (pə·nōō′tĭ·ən, -shən), *n.* a tentatively established North American Indian linguistic stock which includes several linguistic families formerly regarded as unrelated, distributed from California northward through Oregon and British Columbia.

Pen·za (pĕn′zä), *n.* a city in the central Soviet Union in Europe. 231,000 (est. 1956).

Pen·zance (pĕn·zăns′), *n.* a seaport in SW England, in Cornwall: resort. 20,648 (1951).

pe·on¹ (pē′ən), *n.* **1.** *Spanish America.* **a.** a day laborer. **b.** one who tends a horse or mule. **2.** *Chiefly Mexico.* one held in servitude to work off debts, etc. [t. Sp.: m. *peón*, g. s. L *pedo* foot soldier. See PAWN]

pe·on² (pē′ən), *n. India.* **1.** a foot soldier. **2.** a messenger or attendant. **3.** a native soldier. [t. Pg.: m. *peao*, and t. F: m. *pion* foot soldier, pedestrian, day laborer. See PEON¹]

pe·on·age (pē′ən·ĭj), *n.* **1.** the condition or service of a peon. **2.** the practice of holding persons in servitude or partial slavery, as to work off debt or (under a convict lease system) a penal sentence. Also, **pe′on·ism.**

pe·o·ny (pē′ən·ĭ), *n., pl.* **-nies. 1.** any plant of the ranunculaceous genus *Paeonia*, which comprises perennial herbs and a few shrubs with large showy flowers, familiar in gardens. **2.** the flower. [t. L: m.s. *paeōnia* t. Gk.: m. *paiōnia*, der. *Paiōn* the physician of the gods (because the plant was used in medicine); r. ME *pione*, t. ONF, t. L, t. Gk.; r. OE *peonie*. t. L, t. Gk]

peo·ple (pē′pəl), *n., pl.* **-ple, -ples** for 1, *v.,* **-pled, -pling.** —*n.* **1.** the whole body of persons constituting a community, tribe, race, or nation: *the people of England.* **2.** the persons of any particular group, company, or number: *the people of a parish.* **3.** persons in relation to a ruler, leader, etc.: *the king and his people.* **4.** one's family or relatives: *to visit one's people.* **5.** the members of any group or number to which one belongs. **6.** the body of enfranchised citizens of a state: *representatives chosen by the people.* **7.** the commonalty or populace: *a man of the people.* **8.** persons indefinitely, whether men or women: *people may say what they please.* **9.** human beings as distinguished from animals. **10.** *Chiefly Poetic.* living creatures. —*v.t.* **11.** to furnish with people; populate. **12.** to stock with animals, etc. [ME *peple*, t. AF: m. *poeple*, g. L *populus* people] —**peo·pler** (pē′plər), *n.* —**Syn. 1.** See **race².**

People's charter. See **chartism.**

Peo·ple's party (pē′pəlz), *U.S. Pol.* See **Populist.**

Pe·o·ri·a (pĭ·ōr′ĭə), *n.* a city in central Illinois, on the Illinois river. 103,162 (1960).

pep (pĕp), *n., v.,* **pepped, pepping.** *U.S. Slang.* —*n.* **1.** spirit or animation; vigor; energy. —*v.t.* **2.** to give spirit or vigor to (fol. by *up*). [short for PEPPER]

Pep·in (pĕp′ĭn), *n.* ("*Pepin the Short*") died A.D. 768, king of the Franks, 751–768 (father of Charlemagne).

pep·los (pĕp′ləs), *n.* a voluminous outer garment worn draped in folds about the person by women in ancient Greece. Also, **pep′lus.** [t. Gk.]

pep·lum (pĕp′ləm), *n., pl.* **-lums, -la** (-lə). **1.** a short full flounce or an extension of the waist, covering the

hips. **2.** a short skirt attached to a bodice or coat. **3.** a peplos. [t. L: (m.) *peplum, peplus.* See PEPLOS]

pe·po (pē′pō), *n., pl.* **-pos.** the characteristic fruit of cucurbitaceous plants, having a fleshy, many-seeded interior, and a hard or firm rind, as the gourd, melon, cucumber, etc. [t. L: melon, pumpkin, t. Gk.: m. *pēpōn* kind of gourd or melon eaten when ripe, orig. adj., ripe]

pep·per (pĕp′ər), *n.* **1.** a pungent condiment obtained from various plants of the genus *Piper*, esp. from the dried berries, either whole or ground (affording the **black pepper** and **white pepper** of commerce), of *P. nigrum*, a tropical climbing shrub. **2.** any plant of the genus *Piper* or family *Piperaceae*. **3.** cayenne (**red pepper**), prepared from species of *Capsicum*. **4.** any species of *Capsicum*, esp. *C. frutescens* (the common pepper of the garden) or its fruit (green or red, hot or sweet). —*v.t.* **5.** to season with or as with pepper. **6.** to sprinkle as with pepper; dot; stud. **7.** to sprinkle like pepper. **8.** to pelt with shot or missiles. **9.** to discharge shot or missiles at something. [ME *peper*, OE *piper*, t. L, t. Gk.: m. *piperi* pepper; of Eastern orig.]

pep·per-and-salt (pĕp′ər·ən·sôlt′), *adj.* composed of a fine mixture of black with white, as cloth.

pep·per·corn (pĕp′ər·kôrn′), *n.* **1.** the berry of the pepper plant, *Piper nigrum*, often dried and used in pickling. **2.** anything very small, insignificant, or trifling. [ME *pepercorn*, OE *piporcorn*. See PEPPER, CORN²]

pep·per·grass (pĕp′ər·grăs′, -gräs′), *n.* any plant of the genus *Lepidium*, as L. *sativum* (**garden cress**), pungent in flavor and used as a potherb or salad vegetable. Also, **pep·per·wort** (pĕp′ər·wûrt′).

pep·per·idge (pĕp′ər·ĭj), *n.* the tupelo.

pep·per·mint (pĕp′ər·mĭnt′), *n.* **1.** a labiate herb, *Mentha piperita*, cultivated for its aromatic pungent oil. **2.** this oil, or some preparation of it. **3.** a lozenge or confection flavored with it.

pepper pot, 1. a West Indian stew, the principal flavoring of which is cassareep, with meat or fish and vegetables. **2.** a kind of soup made of tripe and highly seasoned, sometimes containing small balls of dough.

pepper tree, any of several evergreen trees, members of the genus *Schinus*, mostly native of South America and cultivated in subtropical regions as ornamentals because of evergreen foliage and bright-red fruits.

pep·per·y (pĕp′ər·ĭ), *adj.* **1.** resembling pepper; full of pepper; pungent. **2.** of or pertaining to pepper. **3.** sharp or stinging, as speech. **4.** irascible or irritable, as persons or their temper. —**pep′per·i·ness**, *n.*

pep·py (pĕp′ĭ), *adj.,* **-pier, -piest.** *Slang.* energetic. —**pep′pi·ness**, *n.*

pep·sin (pĕp′sĭn), *n. Biochem.* an enzyme produced in the stomach which, in the presence of hydrochloric acid, splits proteins into proteoses and peptones. Also, **pep′sine.** [f. s. Gk. *pépsis* digestion + -IN²]

pep·sin·ate (pĕp′sə·nāt′), *v.t.,* **-ated, -ating.** to treat, prepare, or mix with pepsin.

pep·sin·o·gen (pĕp·sĭn′ə·jən), *n. Biochem.* the substance in the gastric glands which produces pepsin.

pep·tic (pĕp′tĭk), *adj.* **1.** pertaining to or concerned in digestion; digestive. **2.** promoting digestion. **3.** of pepsin. —*n.* **4.** a substance promoting digestion. [t. L: s. *pepticus*, t Gk.: m. *peptikós* able to digest]

pep·tide (pĕp′tīd, -tĭd), *n. Biochem.* a compound containing two or more amino acids in which the carboxyl group of one acid is linked to the amino group of the other. [f. PEPT(IC) + -IDE]

pep·tize (pĕp′tīz), *v.t.,* **-tized, -tizing.** to disperse (a substance) into colloidal form, as in a liquid medium.

pep·tone (pĕp′tōn), *n. Biochem.* any of a class of diffusible, soluble substances into which proteins are converted by hydrolysis. [t. G: m. *pepton*, t. Gk.: (neut. adj.) cooked, digested] —**pep·ton·ic** (pĕp·tŏn′ĭk), *adj.*

pep·to·nize (pĕp′tə·nīz′), *v.t.,* **-nized, -nizing. 1.** to convert into a peptone. **2.** to hydrolyze or dissolve by a proteolytic enzyme, such as pepsin. **3.** to subject (food) to an artificial partial digestion by pepsin or pancreatic extract, to aid digestion. —**pep/to·ni·za′tion**, *n.*

Pep·ys (pēps, pĕps, pĕp′ĭs), *n.* **Samuel,** 1633–1703, British government official and diarist. —**Pep·ys·i·an** (pĕp′sĭ·ən, pĕp′-), *adj.*

Pe·quot (pē′kwŏt), *n.* **1.** (*pl.*) a former tribe of Algonquian Indians in southern New England in the early 17th century. **2.** a member of this tribe. [t. Algonquian, contr. of *Paquatauog* destroyers]

per (pûr, pər), *prep.* through; by; for each: *per annum* (by the year), *per diem* (by the day), *per yard* (for each yard), etc. [t. L. Cf. PER-]

per-, 1. a prefix meaning "through," "thoroughly," "utterly," "very," as in *pervert, pervade, perfect.* **2.** *Chem.* a prefix applied: **a.** to inorganic acids to indicate they possess excess of the designated element: *perboric* (HBO₃ or H₂B₄O₈), *percarbonic* (H₂C₂O₅), *permanganic* (HMnO₄), and *persulfuric* (H₂S₂O₅) *acids.* **b.** to salts of these acids (the name ending in *-ate*): *potassium perborate* (K₂B₄O₈), *potassium permanganate* (KMnO₄), and *potassium persulfate* (K₂S₂O₅). [t. L (in some words, t. OF or F), repr. *per*, prep., through, by; akin to Gk. *parā*]

per., 1. period. **2.** person.

Pe·ra (pē′rä), *n.* the modern, foreign section of Istanbul, Turkey, N of the Golden Horn. 280,318 (1950).

per·ad·ven·ture (pûr′əd věn′chər, pĕr′-), adv. 1. it may be; maybe; possibly. —n. 2. chance; uncertainty. 3. doubt or question. [ME peraventure, t. OF: m. par aventure, f. par by (t. L: m. per) + aventure ADVENTURE]

Pe·rae·a (pərē′ə), n. a region in ancient Palestine, E of the Jordan and the Dead Sea.

Pe·rak (pā′räk; Malay pĕ′rä), n. a state in the former Federation of Malaya: now part of the federation of Malaysia. 1,327,120 pop. (1959); 7980 sq. mi. Cap.: Taiping.

per·am·bu·late (pərăm′byəlāt′), v., -lated, -lating. —v.t. 1. to walk through, about, or over; travel through; traverse. 2. to traverse and examine or inspect. —v.i. 3. to walk or travel about; stroll. [t. L: m.s. perambulātus, pp.] —per·am′bu·la′tion, n. —per·am·bu·la·to·ry (pərăm′byələ tôr′ĭ), adj.

per·am·bu·la·tor (pərăm′byəlā′tər), n. Brit. a baby carriage, usually small and pushed by hand from behind.

per an., per annum.

per an·num (pər ăn′əm), Latin. by the year; yearly.

per·bo·rate (pərbōr′āt), n. Chem. a salt of perboric acid, containing the radicals BO_3^{-1} or $B_4O_8^{-2}$, as sodium perborate, $NaBO_2·4H_2O$, used for bleaching, disinfecting, etc. [f. PER- + BORATE]

per·cale (pərkāl′), n. closely woven, smooth-finished cambric, plain or printed. [t. F, t. Pers.: m. pārgālä]

per·ca·line (pûr′kəlēn′), n. a fine, lightweight cotton fabric, usually finished with a gloss and dyed in one color: used esp. for linings. [t. F, dim. of percale PERCALE]

per cap·i·ta (pər kăp′ə tə), Latin. by individuals.

per·ceiv·a·ble (pərsē′vəbəl), adj. capable of being perceived; perceptible. —per·ceiv′a·bly, adv.

per·ceive (pərsēv′), v.t., -ceived, -ceiving. 1. to gain knowledge of through one of the senses; discover by seeing, hearing, etc. 2. to apprehend with the mind; understand. [ME perceyve(n), t. OF: m. perceivre, g. L percipere seize, receive, understand] —Syn. 1. See notice.

per·cent (pərsĕnt′), n. by the hundred; for or in every hundred (used in expressing proportions, rates of interest, etc.): to get 3 percent interest. Symbol: % Also, per cent [orig. per cent., abbr. of L per centum by the hundred]

per·cent·age (pərsĕn′tĭj), n. 1. a rate or proportion per hundred. 2. an allowance, duty, commission, or rate of interest on a hundred. 3. a proportion in general. 4. Slang. gain; advantage.

per·cen·tile (pərsĕn′tĭl, -tīl), Statistics. —n. 1. one of the values of a variable which divides the distribution of the variable into 100 groups having equal frequencies. Thus, there are 100 percentiles: the first, second, etc., percentile. —adj. 2. of or pertaining to a percentile or a division of a distribution by percentiles. [f. PER CENT + -ile, modeled on BISSEXTILE]

per cen·tum (pər sĕn′təm), Latin. percent.

per·cept (pûr′sĕpt), n. 1. the mental result or product of perceiving, as distinguished from the act of perceiving. 2. that which is perceived; the object of perception. [t. L: s. perceptum, neut. pp., (a thing) perceived]

per·cep·ti·ble (pərsĕp′təbəl), adj. capable of being perceived; cognizable; appreciable: quite a perceptible time. —per·cep′ti·bil′i·ty, per·cep′ti·ble·ness, n. —per·cep′ti·bly, adv.

per·cep·tion (pərsĕp′shən), n. 1. the action or faculty of perceiving; cognition; a taking cognizance, as of a sensible object. 2. an immediate or intuitive recognition, as of a moral or aesthetic quality. 3. the result or product of perceiving, as distinguished from the act of perceiving; a percept. 4. Psychol. a single unified meaning obtained from sensory processes while a stimulus is present. [late ME, t. L: s. perceptio a receiving, hence apprehension] —per·cep′tion·al, adj.

per·cep·tive (pərsĕp′tĭv), adj. 1. having the power or faculty of perceiving. 2. of or pertaining to perception. 3. of ready or quick perception. —per·cep′tive·ly, adv. —per′cep·tiv′i·ty, per·cep′tive·ness, n.

per·cep·tu·al (pərsĕp′chŏŏ əl), adj. pertaining to perception.

Per·ce·val (pûr′sə vəl), n. Arthurian Romance. Percival.

perch[1] (pûrch), n. 1. a pole or rod usually fixed horizontally to serve as a roost for birds. 2. any thing or place serving for a bird, or for anything else, to alight or rest upon. 3. an elevated position or station. 4. a small elevated seat on a vehicle, for the driver. 5. a pole connecting the fore and hind running parts of a spring carriage or other vehicle. 6. a rod, or linear measure of 5½ yards or 16½ feet. 7. a square rod (30½ square yards). 8. a solid measure for stone, etc., commonly 16½ feet by 1½ feet by 1 foot. 9. Obs. or Dial. any pole, rod, or the like. —v.i. 10. to alight or rest upon a perch, as a bird. 11. to settle or rest in some elevated position, as if on a perch. —v.t. 12. to set or place on, or as if on, a perch. [ME perche, t. OF, g. L pertica pole, measuring rod]

perch[2] (pûrch), n., pl. perches, (esp. collectively) perch. 1. a spiny-finned, fresh-water food fish of the genus Perca, as P. flavescens (yellow perch) of the U.S., or P. fluviatilis of Europe. 2. any of various other spiny-rayed fishes of the same and other families, often marine. [ME perche, t. OF, g. L perca, t. Gk.: m. pérkē perch. Cf. Gk. perknós dark-colored]

per·chance (pərchăns′, -chäns′), adv. Poetic or Archaic. 1. maybe; possibly. 2. by chance. [ME per chance, t. AF: m. par chance by chance]

Perche (pĕrsh), n. a former division of N France.

perch·er (pûr′chər), n. 1. one who or that which perches. 2. a bird whose feet are adapted for perching.

Per·che·ron (pûr′chə rŏn′, -shə-), n. one of a breed of draft horses, orig. raised in Perche, France. [t. F]

per·chlo·rate (pərklôr′āt), n. Chem. a salt of perchloric acid, as potassium perchlorate.

per·chlo·ric acid (pərklôr′ĭk), Chem. an acid of chlorine, $HClO_4$, containing one more oxygen atom than chloric acid, and occurring as a colorless syrupy liquid. [f. PER- + CHLOR(INE) + -IC]

per·chlo·ride (pərklôr′īd, -ĭd), n. Chem. that chloride of any particular element or radical with maximum proportion of chlorine. Also, **per·chlo·rid** (pərklôr′ĭd).

per·cip·i·ent (pərsĭp′ĭ ənt), adj. 1. perceiving. 2. having perception. —n. 3. one who or that which perceives. [t. L: s. percipiens, ppr., perceiving] —**per·cip′i·ence**, **per·cip′i·en·cy**, n.

Per·ci·val (pûr′sə vəl), n. Arthurian Romance. a knight of King Arthur's court who sought the Holy Grail. Also, **Perceval**, **Per′ci·vale**.

per·coid (pûr′koid), adj. 1. belonging to the Percoidea, a group of acanthopterygian fishes comprising the true perches and related families, and constituting one of the largest natural groups of fishes. 2. resembling a perch. —n. 3. a percoid fish. Also, **per·coi·de·an** (pərkoi′dĭ ən). [f. s. L perca perch + -OID]

per·co·late (v. pûr′kəlāt′; n. pûr′kəlĭt, -lāt′), v., -lated, -lating, n. —v.t. 1. to cause (a liquid) to pass through a porous body; filter. 2. (of a liquid) to filter through; permeate. —v.i. 3. to pass through a porous substance; filter; ooze: the coffee started to percolate. —n. 4. a percolated liquid. [t. L: m.s. percolātus, pp., strained through] —**per′co·la′tion**, n.

per·co·la·tor (pûr′kəlā′tər), n. 1. a kind of coffee pot in which boiling water is forced up a hollow stem, filters through ground coffee, and returns to the pot below. 2. that which percolates.

per con·tra (pər kŏn′trə), Latin. to the opposite side of an account.

per·cuss (pərkŭs′), v.t. 1. to strike (something) so as to shake or cause a shock to. 2. Med. to strike or tap for diagnostic or therapeutic purposes. [t. L: s. percussus, pp., struck through]

per·cus·sion (pərkŭsh′ən), n. 1. the striking of one body against another with some violence; impact. 2. Med. the striking or tapping of a part of the body for diagnostic or therapeutic purposes. 3. the striking of musical instruments to produce tones. 4. a sharp light blow, esp. one for setting off a cap formerly used to discharge small arms. 5. the act of percussing.

percussion cap, a small metallic cap or cup containing fulminating powder, formerly exploded by percussion so as to fire the charge of small arms.

percussion instrument, a musical instrument, as drum, cymbal, piano, etc., which is struck to produce a sound, as distinguished from string or wind instruments.

per·cus·sive (pərkŭs′ĭv), adj. of, pertaining to, or characterized by percussion.

Per·cy (pûr′sĭ), n. 1. Sir Henry, ("Hotspur") 1364–1403, English military leader, killed near Shrewsbury in a rebellion he led against Henry IV of England. 2. Thomas, 1729–1811, British bishop who edited a collection of popular ballads.

Per·di·do (pĕrdē′dô), n. Monte (môn′tĕ). See Perdu, Mont.

per·die (pərdē′), adv., interj. pardi.

per di·em (pər dī′əm), 1. Latin. by the day. 2. a daily allowance, usually for living expenses while traveling in connection with one's work.

per·di·tion (pərdĭsh′ən), n. 1. a condition of final spiritual ruin or damnation. 2. the future state of the wicked. 3. hell. 4. utter destruction or ruin. [ME, t. L: s. perditio act of destroying]

per·du (pərdū′, -dōō′), adj. 1. hidden or concealed. —n. 2. Obs. a soldier placed in a dangerous position. Also, **per·due′**. [t. F, pp. of perdre lose, g. L perdere lose, destroy]

Per·du (pĕrdy′), n. Mont (môN), a peak of the Pyrenees, in NE Spain. 10,994 ft. Spanish, Monte Perdido.

per·dur·a·ble (pərdyŏŏr′ə bəl, -dōōr′-), adj. permanent; everlasting; imperishable. [ME, t. LL: s.s. perdūrābilis, der. L perdūrāre last, hold out] —**per·dur′a·bly**, adv.

père (pĕr), n. French. 1. father. 2. Senior: Dumas père.

per·e·gri·nate (pĕr′ə grə nāt′), v., -nated, -nating. —v.i. 1. to travel or journey. —v.t. 2. to travel over; traverse. [t. L: m.s. peregrīnātus, pp., having traveled] —**per′e·gri·na′tor**, n.

per·e·gri·na·tion (pĕr′ə grə nā′shən), n. 1. traveling from one place to another. 2. a course of travel; journey.

per·e·grine (pĕr′ə grĭn, -grīn′), adj. 1. foreign; alien; coming from abroad. —n. 2. a spirited falcon, Falco peregrinus, formerly much used in Europe for hawking, of which there are several varieties, including the American duck hawk, F. p. anatum. Also, **per·e·grin** (pĕr′ə grĭn). [ME, t. L: m.s. peregrīnus coming from foreign parts; as n., a foreigner]

---

per·emp·to·ry (pərĕmp′tərĭ, pěr′əmptōr′ĭ), *adj.* **1.** leaving no opportunity for denial or refusal; imperative: *a peremptory command.* **2.** imperious or dictatorial. **3.** *Law.* **a.** that precludes or does not admit of debate, question, etc.: *a peremptory edict.* **b.** decisive or final. **c.** in which a command is absolute and unconditional: *a peremptory writ.* **4.** positive in speech, tone, manner, etc. [t. L: m.s. *peremptōrius* destructive, decisive] —**per·emp′to·ri·ly,** *adv.* —**per·emp′to·ri·ness,** *n.*

peremptory exception, *Law.* a plea in bar of an action. Also, **peremptory plea.**

per·en·ni·al (pərĕn′ĭəl), *adj.* **1.** lasting for an indefinitely long time; enduring. **2.** *Bot.* having a life cycle lasting more than two years. **3.** lasting or continuing throughout the year, as a stream. **4.** perpetual; everlasting. —*n.* **5.** a perennial plant. [f. L *perenni(s)* lasting through the year + -AL¹] —**per·en′ni·al·ly,** *adv.*

perf., **1.** perfect. **2.** perforated.

per·fect (*adj., n.* pûr′fĭkt; *v.* pərfĕkt′, pûr′fĭkt), *adj.* **1.** in a state proper to a thing when completed; having all essential elements, characteristics, etc., lacking in no respect; complete. **2.** in a state of complete excellence; without blemish or defect; faultless. **3.** completely skilled. **4.** completely corresponding to a type or description; exact: *a perfect sphere.* **5.** correct in every detail: *a perfect copy.* **6.** thorough; unqualified: *perfect strangers.* **7.** pure or unmixed: *perfect yellow.* **8.** *Chiefly Colloq.* unmitigated or utter. **9.** *Obs.* assured or certain. **10.** *Bot.* **a.** having all parts or members present. **b.** monoclinous. **11.** *Gram.* **a.** denoting action or state brought to a close prior to some temporal point of reference, in contrast to imperfect or uncompleted action. **b.** designating a tense, or other verb formation or construction, with such meaning. **12.** *Music.* **a.** applied to the consonances of unison, octave, fifth, and fourth, as distinguished from those of a third and sixth, which are called imperfect. **b.** applied to the intervals, harmonic or melodic, of an octave, fifth, and fourth in their normal form, as opposed to augmented and diminished. —*n.* **13.** *Gram.* **a.** the perfect tense. **b.** another verb formation or construction with perfect meaning. **c.** a form therein: as English *he had cooked the meal before six o'clock,* or Latin *ōrāculum audīvī* "I heard the oracle." —*v.t.* **14.** to bring to completion, complete, or finish. **15.** to make perfect or faultless, bring to perfection. **16.** to bring nearer to perfection; improve. **17.** to make fully skilled. [t. L: s. *perfectus,* pp., performed, completed; r. ME *parfit,* t. OF] —**per·fect′er,** *n.* —**Syn. 1, 2.** See **complete.**

perfect cadence, *Music.* a cadence in which the tonic chord has its root in both bass and soprano.

per·fect·i·ble (pərfĕk′təbəl), *adj.* capable of becoming, or being made, perfect. —**per·fect′i·bil′i·ty,** *n.*

per·fec·tion (pərfĕk′shən), *n.* **1.** the state or quality of being perfect. **2.** the highest degree of proficiency, as in some art. **3.** a perfect embodiment of something. **4.** a quality, trait, or feature of a high degree of excellence. **5.** the highest or most perfect degree of a quality or trait. **6.** the act or fact of perfecting.

per·fec·tion·ism (pərfĕk′shənĭz′əm), *n.* any of various doctrines holding that religious, moral, social, or political perfection is attainable. —**per·fec′tion·ist,** *n.*

per·fec·tive (pərfĕk′tĭv), *adj.* **1.** tending to make perfect; conducive to perfection. **2.** *Gram.* denoting an aspect of the verb rather than a tense, as in Russian, which indicates completion of the action or state of the verb prior to a temporal point of reference. —*n.* **3.** *Gram.* **a.** the perfective aspect. **b.** a verb therein. —**per·fec′tive·ly,** *adv.* —**per·fec′tive·ness,** *n.*

per·fect·ly (pûr′fĭktlĭ), *adv.* in a perfect manner or degree.

per·fec·to (pərfĕk′tō), *n., pl.* **-tos.** a rather thick, medium-sized cigar tapering toward both ends. [t. Sp.: lit., perfect]

perfect participle, past participle.

perfect rhyme, **1.** rhyme of two words spelled or pronounced identically but differing in meaning, as *rain, reign;* rich rhyme. **2.** correct or faultless rhyme.

per·fer·vid (pərfûr′vĭd), *adj.* very fervid.

per·fid·i·ous (pərfĭd′ĭəs), *adj.* guilty of perfidy; deliberately faithless; treacherous. [t. L: m.s. *perfidiōsus*] —**per·fid′i·ous·ly,** *adv.* —**per·fid′i·ous·ness,** *n.*

per·fi·dy (pûr′fĭdĭ), *n., pl.* **-dies.** base breach of faith or trust; faithlessness; treachery. [t. L: m.s. *perfidia* faithlessness] —**Syn.** See **disloyalty.**

per·fo·li·ate (pərfō′lĭĭt, -āt′), *adj. Bot.* having the stem apparently passing through the leaf, owing to congenital union of the basal edges of the leaf round the stem: *a perfoliate leaf.* [t. NL: m.s. *perfoliātus,* f. L: *per* through + *foli(um)* leaf + -ātus -ATE¹] —**per·fo′li·a′tion,** *n.*

per·fo·rate (*v.* pûr′fərāt′; *adj.* pûr′fərĭt, -fərāt′), *v.,* **-rated, -rating,** *adj.* —*v.t.* **1.** to make a hole or holes through by boring, punching or other process. **2.** to pierce through or to the interior of; penetrate. —*v.i.* **3.** to make its way through or into something; penetrate. —*adj.* **4.** perforated. [t. L: s. *perforātus,* pp., having been pierced through] —**per′fo·ra·tive,** *adj.* —**per′fo·ra′tor,** *n.*

Perfoliate leaves

per·fo·rat·ed (pûr′fərā′tĭd), *adj.* **1.** pierced with a hole or holes. **2.** *Philately.* having perforations by which one stamp can be separated from others in the sheet.

per·fo·ra·tion (pûr′fərā′shən), *n.* **1.** a hole, or one of a number of holes, bored or punched through something, as those between individual postage stamps of a sheet to facilitate separation. **2.** a hole made or passing through a thing. **3.** the act of perforating. **4.** the state of being perforated.

per·force (pərfōrs′), *adv.* of necessity. [ME *par force,* t. OF: by force, f. *par* by (g. L *per*) + *force* FORCE]

per·form (pərfôrm′), *v.t.* **1.** to carry out; execute; do: *to perform miracles.* **2.** to go through or execute in due form: *to perform a ceremony.* **3.** to carry into effect; fulfil. **4.** to act (a play, a part, etc.), as on the stage. **5.** to render (music), as by playing or singing. **6.** to execute (any skill or ability) before an audience. **7.** *Obs.* to complete. —*v.i.* **8.** to fulfil a command, promise, or undertaking. **9.** to execute or do something. **10.** to act in a play. **11.** to perform music. **12.** to go through any performance. [ME *parfourme(n),* t. AF: m. *parfourmer* (appar. for OF *parfournir* complete, accomplish), influenced by *fourme* form, g. L *forma*] —**per·form′a·ble,** *adj.* —**per·form′er,** *n.* —**Syn. 1.** PERFORM, DISCHARGE, EXECUTE, TRANSACT mean to carry to completion a prescribed course of action. PERFORM is the general word, often applied to ordinary activity as a more formal expression than *do,* but usually implying regular, methodical, or prolonged application or work: *to perform an exacting task.* DISCHARGE implies carrying out an obligation, often a formal or legal one: *to discharge one's duties as a citizen.* EXECUTE means either to carry out an order, or to carry through a plan or a program: *to execute a maneuver.* TRANSACT, meaning to conduct or manage, has commercial connotations: *to transact business.*

per·form·ance (pərfôr′məns), *n.* **1.** a musical, dramatic, or other entertainment. **2.** the performing of ceremonies, or of music, or of a play, part, or the like. **3.** execution or doing, as of work, acts, or feats. **4.** a particular action, deed, or proceeding. **5.** an action or proceeding of a more or less unusual or spectacular kind. **6.** the act of performing.

performance test, *Psychol.* a test to be responded to by manual or other behavioral performance rather than verbally.

per·fume (*n.* pûr′fūm, pərfūm′; *v.* pərfūm′), *n., v.,* **-fumed, -fuming.** —*n.* **1.** a substance, extract, or preparation (now esp. liquid) for diffusing or imparting a sweet smell. **2.** the scent, odor, or volatile particles emitted by sweet-smelling substances. —*v.t.* **3.** (of substances, flowers, etc.) to impart fragrance to. **4.** to impregnate with a sweet odor; scent. [t. F: m. *parfum,* der. *parfumer* to scent, f. *par-* PER- + *fumer* smoke] —**Syn. 2.** redolence, scent, odor, smell. PERFUME, AROMA, FRAGRANCE all refer to agreeable odors. PERFUME often indicates a strong, rich smell, natural or manufactured: *the perfume of flowers.* FRAGRANCE is best used of fresh, delicate, and delicious odors, esp. from growing things: *fragrance of new-mown hay.* AROMA is restricted to a somewhat spicy smell: *the aroma of coffee.* —**Ant. 2.** stench.

per·fum·er (pərfū′mər), *n.* **1.** one who or that which perfumes. **2.** a maker or seller of perfumes.

per·fum·er·y (pərfū′mərĭ), *n., pl.* **-eries. 1.** perfumes collectively. **2.** a perfume. **3.** the art or business of a perfumer. **4.** the place of business of a perfumer. **5.** the preparation of perfumes.

per·func·to·ry (pərfŭngk′tərĭ), *adj.* **1.** performed merely as an uninteresting or routine duty; mechanical; indifferent, careless, or superficial: *perfunctory courtesy.* **2.** acting as if merely to get rid of a duty or matter. [t. LL: m.s. *perfunctōrius,* der. L *perfunctus,* pp., performed] —**per·func′to·ri·ly,** *adv.* —**per·func′to·ri·ness,** *n.*

per·fuse (pərfūz′), *v.t.,* **-fused, -fusing. 1.** to overspread with moisture, color, etc. **2.** to diffuse (a liquid, etc.) through or over something. [t. L: m.s. *perfūsus,* pp., poured through] —**per·fu·sion** (pərfū′zhən), *n.* —**per·fu·sive** (pərfū′sĭv), *adj.*

Per·ga·mum (pûr′gəməm), *n.* an ancient city in W Asia Minor: the capital of ancient Mysia.

per·go·la (pûr′gələ), *n.* **1.** an arbor formed of horizontal trelliswork supported on columns or posts, over which vines or other plants are trained. **2.** an architectural construction resembling such an arbor. [t. It., t. L: m. *pergula* shed, vine arbor]

Per·go·le·si (pĕr′gōlĕ′sē), *n.* Giovanni Battista (jō-vän′nē bät tēs′tä), 1710–36, Italian composer.

perh., perhaps.

per·haps (pərhăps′), *adv.* **1.** maybe; possibly. **2.** *Now Rare.* perchance. [ME *per happes* by chances]

pe·ri (pĭr′ĭ), *n., pl.* **-ris. 1.** one of a race of beautiful fairylike beings of Persian mythology, represented as descended from fallen angels and excluded from paradise till their penance is accomplished. **2.** any lovely, graceful creature. [t. Pers., g. Avestan *pairika* female demon]

peri-, a prefix meaning "around," "about," "beyond," or having an intensive force, occurring in words from the Greek, and used also as a modern formative, esp. in scientific terms. [t. Gk. (prefix and prep.)]

per·i·anth (pĕr′ĭănth), *n. Bot.* the envelop of a flower, whether calyx or corolla or both. [short for *perianthium,* t. NL. See PERI-, ANTHO-, -IUM]

per·i·apt (pĕr′ĭăpt), *n.* an amulet. [t. F: m. *périapte,* t. Gk.: m.s. *periapton* (neut.), lit., hung around]

per·i·blem (pĕr′ə blĕm′), *n. Bot.* the histogen in plants which gives rise to the cortex. [t. Gk.: m. *perí-blēma* anything thrown or put around]

per·i·car·di·al (pĕr′ə kär′dY əl), *adj.* of or pertaining to the pericardium. Also, **per·i·car·di·ac′.**

per·i·car·di·tis (pĕr′ə kär dī′tYs), *n. Pathol.* inflammation of the pericardium.

per·i·car·di·um (pĕr′ə kär′dY əm), *n., pl.* **-dia** (-dY ə). *Anat.* the membranous sac enclosing the heart. [t. NL., t. Gk.: m. *perikárdion*]

per·i·carp (pĕr′ə kärp′), *n. Bot.*
1. the walls of a ripened ovary or fruit, sometimes consisting of three layers, the epicarp, mesocarp, and endocarp. **2.** a membranous envelope around the cystocarp of red algae. **3.** a seed vessel. [t. NL: m.s. *pericarpium,* t. Gk.: m. *peri-kárpion* pod, husk] **—per·i·car·pi·al** (pĕr′ə kär′pY əl), *adj.*

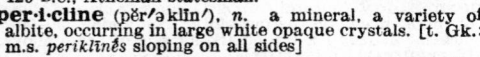

per·i·chon·dri·um (pĕr′ə kŏn′drY əm), *n., pl.* **-dria** (-drY ə). *Anat.* the membrane of fibrous connective tissue covering the surface of cartilages except at the joints. [f. PERI- + s. Gk. *chóndros* cartilage + -IUM] **—per·i·chon·dri·al,** *adj.*

Per·i·cle·an (pĕr′ə klē′ən), *adj.* of or pertaining to Pericles, or his age, the period of the intellectual and material preëminence of Athens.

Pericarps (def. 1)
A. Section and capsule of poppy; B. Section and cone of pine; C. Section and drupe of plum

Per·i·cles (pĕr′ə klēz′), *n.* c490-429 B.C., Athenian statesman.

per·i·cline (pĕr′ə klīn′), *n.* a mineral, a variety of albite, occurring in large white opaque crystals. [t. Gk.: m.s. *periklīnēs* sloping on all sides]

per·i·cra·ni·um (pĕr′ə krā′nY əm), *n., pl.* **-nia** (-nY ə).
1. *Anat.* the external periosteum of the cranium. **2.** *Colloq.* the skull or brain. [t. NL, t. Gk.: m. *perikrā-nion* (neut.) around the skull] **—per·i·cra·ni·al,** *adj.*

per·i·cy·cle (pĕr′ə sī′kəl), *n. Bot.* the outmost cell layer of the stele frequently becoming a multilayered zone. [t. Gk.: m. *perikyklos* all around, used as n.]

per·i·derm (pĕr′ə dûrm′), *n. Bot.* the cork-producing tissue of stems together with the cork layers and other tissues derived from it.

pe·rid·i·um (pĭ rĭd′Y əm), *n., pl.* **-ridia** (-rĭd′Y ə). *Bot.* the outer enveloping coat of the fruit body in many fungi, sometimes itself differentiated into outer and inner layers, exoperidium and endoperidium respectively. [t. NL, t. Gk.: m. *pērídion,* dim. of *pēra* leather pouch, wallet] **—pe·rid′i·al,** *adj.*

per·i·dot (pĕr′ə dŏt′), *n.* a green variety of chrysolite used as a gem. [ME, t. F; orig. uncert.] **—per·i·dot′ic,** *adj.*

per·i·do·tite (pĕr′ə dō′tīt), *n.* any of a group of igneous rocks of granitic texture, composed chiefly of olivine with an admixture of various other minerals, but nearly or wholly free from feldspar.

per·i·gee (pĕr′ə jē′), *n. Astron.* the point in the orbit of a heavenly body, now usually of the moon, that is nearest to the earth (opposed to *apogee*). See diag. under apogee. [t. F, t. NL: m.s. *perigēum,* t. Gk.: m. *perígeion,* (neut.) close around the earth] **—per·i·ge′al, per·i·ge′an,** *adj.*

pe·rig·y·nous (pə rĭj′ə nəs), *adj. Bot.*
1. situated around the pistil on the edge of a cuplike receptacle, as stamens, etc. **2.** having stamens, etc., so arranged, as a flower. [t. NL: m. *perígynus,* der. Gk.: peri- PERI- + *gynē* woman, female]

pe·rig·y·ny (pə rĭj′ə nĭ), *n.* perigynous condition.

per·i·he·li·on (pĕr′ə hē′lĬ ən), *n., pl.* **-lia** (-lĬ ə). *Astron.* the point of a planet's or comet's orbit nearest to the sun (opposed to *aphelion*). See diag. under aphelion. [t. NL: m. *perthēlium,* t. Gk.: peri- PERI- + m. *hēlios* sun]

Section of perigynous flower

per·il (pĕr′əl), *n., v.,* **-iled, -iling** or (*esp. Brit.*) **-illed, -illing.** **—n. 1.** exposure to injury, loss, or destruction; risk; jeopardy; danger. **—v.t. 2.** to imperil. [ME, t. F, g. L *periculum*] **—Syn. 1.** See danger.

per·il·ous (pĕr′ə ləs), *adj.* full of or attended with peril; hazardous; dangerous. [ME, t. AF: m. *perillous,* g. L *periculōsus*] **—per′il·ous·ly,** *adv.*

pe·rim·e·ter (pə rĭm′ə tər), *n.* **1.** the circumference, border, or outer boundary of a two-dimensional figure. **2.** the length of such a boundary. **3.** *Ophthalm.* an instrument for determining the extent and defects of the visual field. [t. L: m. *perimetros,* t. Gk.] **—per·i·met·ric** (pĕr′ə mĕt′rĭk), **per·i·met′ri·cal,** *adj.* **—per′i·met·ri·cal·ly,** *adv.*

per·i·morph (pĕr′ə môrf′), *n.* a mineral enclosing another mineral (opposed to *endomorph*). [f. PERI- + s. Gk. *morphē* form] **—per·i·mor′phic, per·i·mor′phous,** *adj.*

per·i·neph·ri·um (pĕr′ə nĕf′rY əm), *n. Anat.* the capsule of connective tissue which envelops the kidney. [f. PERI- + s. Gk. *nephrós* kidney + -IUM]

per·i·ne·um (pĕr′ə nē′əm), *n., pl.* **-nea** (-nē′ ə). *Anat.* **1.** the urogenital triangle in front of the anus which is bounded by the rami of the pubis, including the vulva

or the roots of the penis. **2.** the diamond-shaped area corresponding to the outlet of the pelvis, containing the anus and vulva or the roots of the penis. [t. NL, t. Gk.: m. *perínaion*] **—per·i·ne′al,** *adj.*

per·i·neu·ri·tis (pĕr′ə nyŏŏ rī′tĬs, -nŏŏ-). *n. Pathol.* inflammation of the perineurium.

per·i·neu·ri·um (pĕr′ə nyŏŏr′Ĭ əm, -nŏŏr′-), *n., pl.* **-neuria** (-nyŏŏr′Ĭ ə, -nŏŏr′-). *Anat.* the sheath of connective tissue which incloses a bundle of nerve fibers. [t. NL, f. *peri-* PERI- + s. Gk. *neûron* nerve + -ium -IUM]

pe·ri·od (pĭr′Y əd), *n.* **1.** an indefinite portion of time, or of history, life, etc., characterized by certain features or conditions. **2.** any specified division or portion of time. **3.** *Educ.* a session of classroom study devoted to a single subject. **4.** *Sports, etc.* a definite, timed part of a game: *a rest between periods.* **5.** *Music.* a division of a composition, usually a passage of eight or sixteen measures, complete or satisfactory in itself, commonly consisting of two or more contrasted or complementary phrases ending with a conclusive cadence. **6.** *Geol.* a main division of a geological era, characterized by distinctness of its remains of life and generally delimited by interruptions in sedimentation. **7.** *Physics.* the time of one complete oscillation or cycle of a periodic quantity or motion; the time between a given phase and its next recurrence. **8.** *Astron.* the time in which a planet or satellite revolves about its primary. **9.** *Chronol.* a round of time or series of years by which time is measured. **10.** a round of time marked by the recurrence of some phenomenon or occupied by some recurring process of action. **11.** (*also pl.*) *Physiol.* menstruation. **12.** the time during which anything runs its course. **13.** the present time. **14.** the point of completion of a round of time or course of duration or action. **15.** the point or character (.) used to mark the end of a complete declarative sentence, indicate an abbreviation, etc. **16.** a full pause such as is made at the end of a complete sentence. **17.** a complete sentence. **18.** (*pl.*) rhetorical language. **19.** *Anc. Pros.* a group of two or more cola. [ME *peryod,* t. L: m.s. *periodus,* t. Gk.: m. *periodos* a going around, cycle, period] **—Syn. 1.** See age.

per·i·o·date (pərī′ə dāt′), *n.* a salt of periodic acid.

pe·ri·od·ic (pĭr′Y ŏd′Yk), *adj.* **1.** characterized by periods or rounds of recurrence. **2.** occurring or appearing at regular intervals. **3.** intermittent. **4.** *Physics.* recurring after equal intervals of time. **5.** *Astron.* **a.** characterized by a series of successive circuits or revolutions, as the motion of a planet or satellite. **b.** of or pertaining to a period, as of the revolution of a heavenly body. **6.** pertaining to or characterized by rhetorical periods or periodic sentences. **7.** (of a sentence) having the sense incomplete until the end is reached. [t. L: s. *periodicus,* t. Gk.: m. *periodikós*] **—pe′ri·od′i·cal·ly,** *adv.*

per·i·od·ic acid (pûr′Ĭ ŏd′Yk), *Chem.* any of a series of acids derived from I_2O_7 by the addition of *n* molecules of water, where *n* has values from 1 to 7. [f. PER- + IODIC]

pe·ri·od·i·cal (pĭr′Y ŏd′ə kəl), *n.* **1.** a periodical publication. **—adj. 2.** (of magazines, etc.) issued at regularly recurring intervals (of more than one day). **3.** of or pertaining to such publications. **4.** periodic.

pe·ri·o·dic·i·ty (pĭr′Y ə dĬs′ə tĭ), *n., pl.* **-ties.** periodic character; tendency to recur at regular intervals.

pe·ri·od·ic law (pĭr′Y ŏd′Yk), *Chem.* **1.** (after the discovery of a means of establishing atomic numbers by Moseley) the law that the properties of the elements are periodic functions of their atomic numbers. **2.** (originally) the statement that the chemical and physical properties of the chemical elements recur periodically when the elements are arranged in the order of their atomic weights.

periodic system, *Chem.* a system of classification of the elements based on the periodic law.

periodic table, *Chem.* a table illustrating the periodic system, in which the chemical elements, arranged in the order of their atomic weights (now, atomic numbers) are shown in related groups.

per·i·o·dide (pərī′ə dīd′, -dYd), *n. Chem.* an iodide with the maximum proportion of iodine.

per·i·os·te·um (pĕr′Y ŏs′tĬ əm), *n., pl.* **-tea** (-tĬ ə). *Anat.* the normal investment of bone, made up of a dense outer fibrous tissue layer and a more delicate inner or cambian layer: the layer of bone regeneration. [t. NL, var. of LL *periosteon,* t. Gk.: (neut.) around the bones] **—per′i·os·te·al,** *adj.*

per·i·os·ti·tis (pĕr′Y ŏs tī′tYs), *n. Pathol.* inflammation of the periosteum. [f. PERIOST(EUM) + -ITIS] **—per·i·os·tit·ic** (pĕr′Y ŏs tĭt′Yk), *adj.*

pe·ri·o·tic (pĕr′Y ō′tYk, -ŏt′Yk), *adj. Anat.* **1.** surrounding the ear. **2.** noting or pertaining to certain bones or bony elements which form or help to form a protective capsule for the internal ear, being usually confluent or fused, and in man constituting part of the temporal bone. [f. Gk.: peri- PERI- + m.s. *ōtikós* of the ear]

Per·i·pa·tet·ic (pĕr′ə pə tĕt′Yk), *adj.* **1.** of or pertaining to the philosophy or the followers of Aristotle, who taught while walking in the Lyceum of ancient Athens. **2.** (*l.c.*) *Chiefly Humorous.* walking or traveling about; itinerant. **—n. 3.** a member of the Aristotelian school. **4.** (*l.c.*) *Chiefly Humorous.* one who walks or travels about. [ME, t. L: s. *peripatēticus,* t. Gk.: m. *peripatētikós* walking about]

pe·riph·er·al (pərĭf′ərəl), *adj.* **1.** pertaining to, situated in, or constituting the periphery. **2.** *Anat.* outside of; external (as distinguished from *central*). **—pe·riph′er·al·ly**, *adv.*

pe·riph·er·y (pərĭf′ərĭ), *n., pl.* **-eries. 1.** the external boundary of any surface or area. **2.** the external surface of a body. **3.** *Anat.* the area in which nerves end. [t. LL: m. s. *peripheria*, t. Gk.: m. *periphéreia*]

pe·riph·ra·sis (pərĭf′rəsĭs), *n., pl.* **-ses** (-sēz′). **1.** a roundabout way of speaking; circumlocution. **2.** a roundabout expression. Also, **per·i·phrase** (pĕr′əfrāz′). [t. L, t. Gk.]

per·i·phras·tic (pĕr′əfrăs′tĭk), *adj.* **1.** circumlocutory; roundabout. **2.** *Gram.* **a.** denoting a construction of two or more words with a class meaning which in other languages or in other forms of the same language is expressed by inflectional modification of a single word. For example: *The son of Mr. Smith* is periphrastic; *Mr. Smith's son* is inflectional. **b.** denoting a class meaning expressed by a construction of two or more words. **—per′i·phras′ti·cal·ly**, *adv.*

pe·rique (pərēk′), *n.* a rich-flavored tobacco produced in Louisiana. [t. Louisiana F]

per·i·sarc (pĕr′əsärk′), *n. Zool.* the horny or chitinous outer case or covering with which the soft parts of hydrozoans are often protected. [f. PERI- + m.s. Gk. *sárx* flesh]

per·i·scope (pĕr′əskōp′), *n.* an optical instrument consisting essentially of a tube with an arrangement of prisms or mirrors by which a view at the surface of water, the top of a parapet, etc., may be seen from below or behind. [t. Gk.: m.s. *periskopein* look around]

per·i·scop·ic (pĕr′əskŏp′ĭk), *adj.* **1.** (of certain lenses in special microscopes, cameras, etc.) giving distinct vision obliquely, or all around, as well as, or instead of, in a direct line. **2.** pertaining to periscopes or their use. Also, **per·i·scop·i·cal.**

per·ish (pĕr′ĭsh), *v.i.* **1.** to suffer death, or lose life through violence, privation, etc.: *to perish in battle.* **2.** to pass away; decay and disappear. **3.** to suffer destruction: *whole cities perish in an earthquake.* **4.** to suffer spiritual death. [ME *perisse*(n), t. OF: m. *periss-*, s. *perir*, g. L *perīre* pass away, perish] **—Syn. 1.** See die[1].

per·ish·a·ble (pĕr′ĭshəbəl), *adj.* **1.** liable to perish; subject to decay or destruction. **—n. 2.** (*usually pl.*) a perishable thing, as food. **—per·ish·a·ble·ness, per′ish·a·bil′i·ty**, *n.*

per·i·spore (pĕr′əspōr′), *n. Bot.* a membrane surrounding a spore.

per·is·so·dac·tyl (pĕr′ĭs·ō·dăk′tĭl), *adj.* **1.** having an uneven number of toes or digits on each foot. **—n. 2.** any animal of the mammalian order *Perissodactyla*, which comprises the odd-toed hoofed quadrupeds: the tapirs, the rhinoceroses, and all the horses (*Equidae*), sometimes classified as a suborder of ungulates. Also, **pe·ris′so·dac′tyle**. [t. NL: s. *perissodactylus*, f. Gk.: *perissó*(*s*) odd, uneven + m. *dáktylos* finger or toe] **—pe·ris′so·dac′ty·lous**, *adj.*

per·i·stal·sis (pĕr′əstăl′sĭs), *n., pl.* **-ses** (-sēz). *Physiol.* peristaltic movement. [t. NL, f. Gk.: *peri-* PERI- + *stálsis* compression]

per·i·stal·tic (pĕr′əstăl′tĭk), *adj. Physiol.* noting or pertaining to the alternate waves of constriction and dilation of a tubular muscle system or cylindrical structure, as the wavelike circular contractions of the alimentary canal. [t. Gk.: m.s. *peristaltikós* compressing]

per·i·stome (pĕr′əstōm′), *n.* **1.** *Bot.* the one or two circles of small, pointed, toothlike appendages around the orifice of the capsule or urn of mosses, appearing when the lid is removed. **2.** *Zool.* any of various structures or sets of parts which surround, or form the walls, etc., of a mouth or mouthlike opening. [t. NL: m. *peristoma*, f. Gk.: *peri-* PERI- + *stóma* mouth]

per·i·style (pĕr′əstīl′), *n. Archit.* **1.** a range or ranges of columns surrounding a building, court, or the like. **2.** a space or court so enclosed. [t. F, t. L: m.s. *peristylum*, t. Gk.: m. *peristylon*, neut. of *peristylos* having columns all around] **—per′i·sty′lar**, *adj.*

per·i·the·ci·um (pĕr′ə·thē′shĭəm, -sĭ′əm), *n., pl.* **-cia** (-shĭ′ə, -sĭ′ə). *Bot.* the fructification of certain fungi, typically a minute, more or less completely closed, globose or flask-shaped body enclosing the asci. [t. NL, f. Gk.: *peri-* PERI- + m. *thēkion*, dim. of *thēkē* case]

per·i·to·ne·um (pĕr′ə·tə·nē′əm), *n., pl.* **-nea** (-nē′ə). *Anat.* the serous membrane lining the abdominal cavity and investing its viscera. Also, **per′i·to·nae′um**. [t. LL, t. Gk.: m. *peritónaion* lit., stretched over] **—per′i·to·ne′al**, *adj.*

per·i·to·ni·tis (pĕr′ə·tə·nī′tĭs), *n. Pathol.* inflammation of the peritoneum. [t. NL, f. s. Gk. *peritonos* stretched around or over + -*ĭtis* -ITIS. See PERITONEUM]

per·i·tri·cha (pərĭt′rəkə), *n.pl.* bacteria having the organs of locomotion all around the body. Cf. **monotricha, amphitricha**. **—pe·rit′ri·chous**, *adj.*

per·i·wig (pĕr′əwĭg′), *n.* a peruke or wig. [alter. of *perruck*, t. F: m. *perruque*. See PERUKE]

per·i·win·kle¹ (pĕr′ə·wĭng′kəl), *n.* **1.** any of various marine gastropods or sea snails, esp. *Littorina littorea*, used for food in Europe. **2.** the shell of any of various other small univalves. [OE *pinewincle*, f. *pine* (t. L: m. *pīna* kind of mussel) + *wincle* (c. Dan. *vinkel* snail shell)]

per·i·win·kle² (pĕr′ə·wĭng′kəl), *n.* any plant of the apocynaceous genus *Vinca*, as *V. minor* (lesser peri-

winkle) or *V. major* (**greater periwinkle**), trailing evergreen plants with blue flowers. [ME *perwynke*, OE *perwince*, t. L: m. *pervinca*]

per·jure (pûr′jər), *v.t.*, **-jured, -juring. 1.** to render (oneself) guilty of swearing falsely, or of willfully making a false statement under oath or solemn affirmation. **2.** to be found guilty of, or be tainted with, perjury. [late ME, t. L: m.s. *perjūrāre*] **—per′jur·er**, *n.*

per·jured (pûr′jərd), *adj.* **1.** guilty of perjury. **2.** characterized by or involving perjury: *perjured testimony.*

per·ju·ry (pûr′jərĭ), *n., pl.* **-ries.** *Law.* the willful utterance of a false statement under oath or affirmation, before a competent tribunal, upon a point material to a legal inquiry. [ME, t. AF: m. *perjurie*, t. L: m. *perjūrium*]

perk (pûrk), *v.i.* **1.** to carry oneself, lift the head, or act in a jaunty manner. **2.** to become lively or vigorous, as after depression or sickness (fol. by *up*). **3.** to put oneself forward briskly or presumptuously. **4.** to percolate. **—v.t. 5.** to raise smartly or briskly (often fol. by *up*). **6.** to dress smartly, or deck (sometimes fol. by *up* or *out*). **—adj. 7.** perky. [ME *perke*(n); ? akin to PEER²]

Per·kin (pûr′kĭn), *n.* **Sir William Henry**, 1838–1907, British chemist: first to produce a synthetic dye (1856).

Per·kins (pûr′kĭnz), *n.* **Frances**, 1882–1965, U.S. sociologist: secretary of labor, 1933–45.

perk·y (pûr′kĭ), *adj.*, **perkier, perkiest.** jaunty; brisk; pert.

Per·lis (pûr′lĭs), *n.* a state in the former Federation of Malaya: now part of the federation of Malaysia. 101,357 pop. (est. 1961); 310 sq. mi. *Cap.*: Kangar.

per·lite (pûr′līt), *n. Petrog.* a form of obsidian or other vitreous rock, usually appearing as a mass of enamellike globules. [t. F] **—per·lit·ic** (pərlĭt′ĭk), *adj.*

Perm (pĕrm), *n.* Molotov (def. 2).

perm·al·loy (pûrm′ăl′oi), *n.* **1.** one of a class of alloys of high magnetic permeability, containing 30–90% nickel. **2.** (*cap.*) a trademark for one of these alloys. [f. PERM(EABLE) + ALLOY]

per·ma·nence (pûr′mənəns), *n.* the condition or quality of being permanent; continued existence.

per·ma·nen·cy (pûr′mənənsĭ), *n., pl.* **-cies. 1.** permanence. **2.** a permanent person, thing, or position.

per·ma·nent (pûr′mənənt), *adj.* **1.** lasting or intended to last indefinitely; remaining unchanged; not temporary; enduring; abiding: *a permanent employee.* **—n. 2.** a permanent wave. [ME, t. L: s. *permanens*, ppr., remaining throughout] **—per′ma·nent·ly**, *adv.*

Permanent Court of Arbitration, the official name of the Hague Tribunal.

Permanent Court of International Justice, former official name of the World Court.

permanent magnet, *Physics.* a magnet which retains its magnetism without the action of external electric or magnetic fields.

permanent wave, a wave set into the hair by a special technique and remaining for a number of months.

per·man·ga·nate (pərmăng′gənāt′), *n. Chem.* a salt of permanganic acid, for disinfecting, oxidizing, etc.

per·man·gan·ic acid (pûr′măngăn′ĭk), *Chem.* an acid, $HMnO_4$, containing manganese.

per·me·a·bil·i·ty (pûr′mĭəbĭl′ətĭ), *n.* **1.** the property or state of being permeable. **2.** specific permeance; the magnetic permeance of a material compared with that of air (**magnetic permeability**). **3.** *Aeron.* the rate at which gas is lost through the envelope of an aerostat, usually expressed as the number of liters thus diffused in one day through a square meter.

per·me·a·ble (pûr′mĭəbəl), *adj.* capable of being permeated. [t. L: m.s. *permeābilis*]

per·me·ance (pûr′mĭəns), *n.* **1.** act of permeating. **2.** the conducting power of a magnetic circuit for magnetic flux, or the reciprocal of magnetic reluctance.

per·me·ant (pûr′mĭənt), *adj.* permeating; pervading.

per·me·ate (pûr′mĭāt′), *v.*, **-ated, -ating. —v.t. 1.** to pass through the substance or mass of. **2.** to penetrate through the pores, interstices, etc., of. **3.** to be diffused through; pervade; saturate. **—v.i. 4.** to penetrate; diffuse itself. [t. L: m.s. *permeātus*, pp., passed through] **—per′me·a′tion**, *n.* **—per′me·a′tive**, *adj.*

per men·sem (pər mĕn′səm), *Latin.* by the month.

Per·mi·an (pûr′mĭən), *Stratig.* **—adj. 1.** pertaining to the latest Paleozoic geological period or system. **—n. 2.** the period or system following Pennsylvanian (or Carboniferous) and preceding Triassic, characterized by prominence of salt deposits and, in the southern hemisphere, by extensive glaciation. **3.** a subgroup of two closely related Finno-Ugric languages of Russia, i.e. Zyrian, or Syryenian, and Votyak. [f. PERM (where such strata occur) + -IAN]

per mill, per thousand. Also, **per mil.**

per·mis·si·ble (pərmĭs′əbəl), *adj.* allowable. **—per·mis′si·bil′i·ty**, *n.* **—per·mis′si·bly**, *adv.*

per·mis·sion (pərmĭsh′ən), *n.* **1.** the act of permitting; formal or express allowance or consent. **2.** liberty or license to do something. [ME, t. L: s. *permissio*]

per·mis·sive (pərmĭs′ĭv), *adj.* **1.** permitting or allowing. **2.** permitted or allowed; optional. **—per·mis′sive·ly**, *adv.*

per·mit (*v.* pərmĭt′; *n.* pûr′mĭt, pərmĭt′), *v.*, **-mitted, -mitting**, *n.* **—v.t. 1.** to allow (a person, etc.) to do something: *permit me to explain.* **2.** to let (something) be

done or occur: *the law permits the sale of such drugs.*
3. to tolerate; agree to. **4.** to afford opportunity for, or admit of: *vents permitting the escape of gases.* —*v.i.*
5. to grant permission; allow liberty to do something.
6. to afford opportunity or possibility: *write when time permits.* **7.** to allow or admit (fol. by *of*): *statements that permit of no denial.* —*n.* **8.** a written order granting leave to do something. **9.** an authoritative or official certificate of permission; a license. **10.** permission. [late ME, t. L: m.s. *permittere* to let go through] —**per·mit′-ter,** *n.* —Syn. 1. See allow.

per·mu·ta·tion (pûr′myə tā′shən), *n.* **1.** *Math.* a. the act of changing the order of individuals arranged in a particular order (as, *abc* into *acb, bac,* etc.), or of arranging a number of individuals in groups made up of equal numbers of the individuals in different orders (as, *a* and *b* in *ab* and *ba*). b. any of the resulting arrangements or groups. **2.** the act of permuting; alteration. —**per·mute** (pər mūt′), *v.t.,* -**muted,** -**muting. 1.** to alter. **2.** *Math.* to subject to permutation. [ME *permute*(n), t. L: m. *permūtāre*] —**per·mut′a·ble,** *adj.*

Per·nam·bu·co (pûr′nəm bū′kō; *Port.* pĕr′nəm bōō′-kōō), *n.* Recife.

per·ni·cious (pər nĭsh′əs), *adj.* **1.** ruinous; highly hurtful: *pernicious teachings.* **2.** deadly; fatal. **3.** evil or wicked. [t. L: m.s. *perniciōsus*] —**per·ni′cious·ly,** *adv.* —**per·ni′cious·ness,** *n.*

pernicious anemia, *Pathol.* a macrocytic anemia produced by deficient maturation of the red blood cells, and associated with subacute degenerative lesions in the posterior and lateral columns of the spinal cord, glossitis, gastric disturbances, and atrophy of the gastric mucosa.

per·nick·et·y (pər nĭk′ə tĭ), *adj. Colloq.* **1.** fastidious; fussy. **2.** requiring painstaking care. [orig. Scot.]

Pe·rón (pĕ rōn′), *n.* **Juan Domingo** (hwän dô mĭng′gō), born 1902, president of Argentina from 1946 to 1955.

per·o·ne·al (pĕr′ə nē′əl), *adj. Anat.* pertaining or proximate to the fibula. [f. NL *peronē* fibula (t. Gk.: pin, brooch) + -AL¹]

per·o·rate (pĕr′ə rāt′), *v.i.,* -**rated,** -**rating. 1.** to speak at length; make a speech. **2.** to bring a speech to a close with a formal conclusion. [t. L: m.s. *perōrātus,* pp., spoken at length]

per·o·ra·tion (pĕr′ə rā′shən), *n.* the concluding part of a speech or discourse, in which the speaker or writer recapitulates the principal points and urges them with greater earnestness and force. [late ME, t. L: s. *perōrātio*]

per·ox·ide (pər ŏk′sīd), *n., v.,* -**ided,** -**iding.** —*n.* Also, **per·ox·id** (pər ŏk′sĭd). **1.** *Chem.* a. an oxide derived from hydrogen peroxide which contains the -O-O- group; generally that oxide of an element or radical which contains an unusually large amount of oxygen. **b.** hydrogen peroxide, H₂O₂. —*v.t.* **2.** to use peroxide (def. 1b) on (the hair) as a bleach.

per·ox·y·ac·id (pər ŏk′sĭ ăs′ĭd), *n.* an acid containing oxygen in the form of peroxide.

per·ox·y·bo·ric acid (pər ŏk′sĭ bōr′ĭk), *Chem.* the hypothetical acid, HBO₃, known by its salts (perborates).

per·pend¹ (pûr′pənd), *n. Masonry.* a large stone passing through the entire thickness of a wall so as to show on both sides, and forming a border. Also, **perpent.** [t. OF: m. *perpain,* g. LL *perpannius* extending to the visible portion of the wall, influenced by PEND]

per·pend² (pər pĕnd′), *Archaic.* —*v.t.* **1.** to consider. —*v.i.* **2.** to ponder; deliberate. [t. L: s. *perpendere*]

per·pen·dic·u·lar (pûr′pən dĭk′yə lər), *adj.* **1.** vertical; upright. **2.** *Geom.* meeting a given line or surface at right angles. **3.** *Archit.* noting or pertaining to a style of architecture, the last stage of English Gothic, in which a large proportion of the chief lines of the tracery intersect at right angles. —*n.* **4.** a perpendicular line or plane. **5.** an instrument for indicating the vertical line from any point. **6.** upright position. **7.** rectitude. [t. L: s. *perpendicularis;* r. ME *perpendiculer,* t. OF] —**per′pen-dic·u·lar′i·ty,** *n.* —**per′pen·dic′u·lar·ly,** *adv.* —Syn. 1. See upright.

per·pent (pûr′pənt), *n. Masonry.* perpend.

per·pe·trate (pûr′pə trāt′), *v.t.,* -**trated,** -**trating.** to perform, execute, or commit (something bad): *to perpetrate a crime.* [t. L: m.s. *perpetrātus,* pp.] —**per′pe·tra′tion,** *n.* —**per′pe·tra′tor,** *n.*

per·pet·u·al (pər pĕch′ōō əl), *adj.* **1.** continuing or enduring forever or indefinitely: *perpetual snows.* **2.** continuing or continued without intermission or interruption: *a perpetual stream of visitors.* **3.** *Hort.* blooming more or less continuously throughout the season or the year. —*n.* **4.** a hybrid rose that is perpetual. [ME *perpetuall,* t. L: m.s. *perpetuālis*] —**per·pet′u·al·ly,** *adv.* —Syn. 1. everlasting, permanent. See eternal. **2.** continuous, ceaseless, incessant, constant.

per·pet·u·ate (pər pĕch′ōō āt′), *v.t.,* -**ated,** -**ating.** to make perpetual. [t. L: m.s. *perpetuātus,* pp.] —**per·pet′u·a′tion, per·pet·u·ance** (pər pĕch′ōō əns), *n.* —**per·pet′u·a′tor,** *n.*

per·pe·tu·i·ty (pûr′pə tū′ĭ tĭ, -tōō′-), *n., pl.* -**ties.**
1. endless or indefinitely long duration or existence.
2. something that is perpetual. **3.** a perpetual annuity.

4. *Law.* (of property) an interest under which property is less than completely alienable for longer than the law allows. **5. in perpetuity,** forever. [ME *perpetuite,* t. F, t. L: m.s. *perpetuitas*]

Per·pi·gnan (pĕr pē nyäN′), *n.* a city in S France. 70,051 (1954).

per·plex (pər plĕks′), *v.t.* **1.** to confuse mentally, bewilder, or puzzle over what is not understood or certain. **2.** to make complicated or confused, as a matter, question, etc. **3.** to hamper with complications, confusion, or uncertainty. [back formation from PERPLEXED] —**per·plex′ing·ly,** *adv.* —Syn. 1. See puzzle.

per·plexed (pər plĕkst′), *adj.* **1.** bewildered or puzzled. **2.** tangled; involved. [ME *perplex* intricate, bewildered (t. L: s. *perplexus* involved) + -ED²] —**per·plex·ed·ly** (pər plĕk′sĭd lĭ), *adv.*

per·plex·i·ty (pər plĕk′sə tĭ), *n., pl.* -**ties. 1.** perplexed or puzzled condition; uncertainty as to what to think or do. **2.** something that perplexes. **3.** tangled, involved, or confused condition.

per·qui·site (pûr′kwə zĭt), *n.* **1.** an incidental emolument, fee, or profit over and above fixed income, salary, or wages. **2.** *Chiefly Brit.* anything customarily supposed to be allowed or left to an employee or servant as an incidental advantage of the position held. **3.** something advantageous specially belonging. [late ME, t. ML: m.s. *perquisitum,* neut. pp., sought for]

Per·rault (pĕ rō′), *n.* **Charles** (shärl), 1628–1703, French critic and writer: famous for his "Mother Goose."

per·ron (pĕr′ən; *Fr.* pĕ rôN′), *n. Archit.* an outside platform upon which the entrance door of a building opens, with steps leading to it. [ME *peroun,* t. OF: m. *perron,* der. *pierre* rock, g. L *petra*]

per·ry (pĕr′ĭ), *n. Brit.* a fermented beverage, similar to cider, made from the juice of pears. [ME *pereye,* t. OF, ult. der. L *pirum.* See PEAR]

Per·ry (pĕr′ĭ), *n.* **1. Bliss,** 1860–1954, U.S. educator, literary critic, and editor. **2. Oliver Hazard,** 1785–1819, U.S. naval officer: defeated the British in the battle of Lake Erie (1813). **3. Matthew Calbraith** (kăl′-brĕth), 1794–1858, U.S. naval officer: persuaded Japan to open trade with American merchant ships (brother of Oliver Hazard). **4. Ralph Barton,** 1876–1957, U.S. philosopher and educator.

Pers., **1.** Persia. **2.** Persian.

pers., **1.** person. **2.** personal.

per·salt (pûr′sôlt′), *n. Chem.* (in a series of salts of a given metal or radical) that salt in which the metal or radical has a high, or the highest apparent, valence.

perse (pûrs), *adj.* of a very deep shade of blue or purple. [ME *pers,* t. OF, g. LL *persus;* orig. uncert.]

per se (pûr sē′), *Latin.* by or in itself; intrinsically.

per·se·cute (pûr′sə kūt′), *v.t.,* -**cuted,** -**cuting. 1.** to pursue with harassing or oppressive treatment; harass persistently. **2.** to oppress with injury or punishment for adherence to principles or religious faith. **3.** to annoy by persistent attentions, importunities, or the like. [back formation from PERSECUTION, conformed to L *persecūtus,* pp., having pursued] —**per′se·cu′tive, per·se·cu·to·ry** (pûr′sə kū tō rĭ, pûr′sə kū′-), *adj.* —**per′se·cu′tor,** *n.* —Syn. 3. worry, badger, vex.

per·se·cu·tion (pûr′sə kū′shən), *n.* **1.** act of persecuting. **2.** state of being persecuted. [ME, t. L: s. *persecūtio*] —**per′se·cu′tion·al,** *adj.*

Per·se·id (pûr′sĭ ĭd), *n. Astron.* any of a shower of meteors appearing in August, and radiating from a point in the constellation Perseus. [t. Gk.: s. *Persēides,* pl. of *Persēis* daughter of Perseus]

Per·seph·o·ne (pər sĕf′ə nĭ), *n.* **1.** Also, *Latin,* **Proserpina.** *Gk. Myth.* daughter of Zeus and Demeter, kidnapped by Pluto (or Hades) to be his wife and queen of the lower world, but allowed to return every year. **2.** a personification of spring.

Per·sep·o·lis (pər sĕp′ə lĭs), *n.* an ancient capital of Persia: its imposing ruins in S Iran, ab. 30 mi. NE of Shiraz. See map under **Media.**

Per·seus (pûr′sūs, pûr′sĭ əs), *n.* **1.** *Gk. Myth.* a hero, the son of Zeus and Danaë, who slew the Gorgon Medusa, and afterward saved Andromeda from a sea monster. **2.** *Astron.* one of the northern constellations, containing the remarkable variable star Algol.

per·se·ver·ance (pûr′sə vĭr′əns), *n.* **1.** steady persistence in a course of action, a purpose, a state, etc. **2.** *Theol.* continuance in a state of grace to the end, leading to eternal salvation.
—Syn. **1.** PERSEVERANCE, PERSISTENCE, TENACITY, PERTINACITY imply resolute and unyielding holding on, in following a course of action. PERSEVERANCE commonly suggests activity maintained in spite of difficulties; steadfast and long continued application: *endurance and perseverance combined to win in the end.* It is regularly used in a favorable sense. PERSISTENCE, which may be used in either a favorable or an unfavorable sense, implies unremitting (and sometimes annoying) perseverance: *persistence in a belief, in talking when others wish to be quiet* TENACITY, with the original meaning of adhesiveness, as of glue, is a dogged and determined holding on. Whether used literally or figuratively it has favorable implications: *a bulldog quality of tenacity, the tenacity of one's memory.* PERTINACITY, unlike its related word, is used chiefly in an unfavorable sense, that of overinsistent tenacity: *the pertinacity of the social climber.*

per·se·vere (pûr′sə vĭr′), *v.i.,* -**vered,** -**vering.** to persist in anything undertaken; maintain a purpose in spite of difficulty or obstacles; continue steadfastly. [ME *persevere(n)*, t. F: m. *persévérer*, t. L: m. *persevērāre* continue steadfastly] —**per′se·ver′ing·ly,** *adv.*

Per·shing (pûr′shĭng), *n.* **John Joseph,** 1860–1948, U.S. general; commander of the A.E.F. in World War I.

Per·sia (pûr′zhə, -shə), *n.* **1.** an ancient empire centering in W and SW Asia: at its peak it extended from Egypt and the Aegean to India; conquered by Alexander the Great, 334–331 B.C. **2.** former official name (until 1935) of **Iran.**

Per·sian (pûr′zhən, -shən), *adj.* **1.** of or pertaining to Iran, its people, or their language. —*n.* **2.** a member of the native race of Iran, now a mixed race descended in part from the ancient Iranians. **3.** an Iranian language, the principal language of Iran, in its historical (Old Persian, Avestan, and Pahlavi) and modern forms. **4.** (*usually pl.*) Persian blinds.

Persian blinds, **1.** outside window shutters made of thin, movable horizontal slats. **2.** Venetian blinds.

Persian carpet, a large one-piece carpet having a pile of wool, sometimes of silk, twisted by hand with a special knot over the warp.

Persian Gulf, an arm of the Arabian Sea, extending NW between Arabia and Iran. ab. 600 mi. long.

Persian lamb, **1.** the lamb which furnishes caracul. **2.** its skin, bearing closely curled lustrous hairs, usually dyed black; caracul.

Persian walnut, English walnut.

per·si·ennes (pûr′zĭ ĕnz′; *Fr.* pĕr syĕn′), *n.pl.* Persian blinds. [t. F, pl. of fem. adj.: Persian]

per·si·flage (pûr′sə fläzh′; *Fr.* pĕr sĕ fläzh′), *n.* **1.** light, bantering talk. **2.** a frivolous style of treating a subject. [t. F, der. *persifler* banter lightly, f. *per-* PER- + *siffler* whistle, hiss, g. L *sifilāre, sibilāre*]

per·sim·mon (pər sĭm′ən), *n.* **1.** any of various trees of the genus *Diospyros*, esp. *D. virginiana* of North America, with astringent plumlike fruit becoming sweet and edible when thoroughly ripe, and *D. Kaki*, of Japan and China, with soft, rich red or orange fruits, often 3 inches across. **2.** the fruit. [t. Algonquian (Delaware): m *pasimenan* (artificially) dried fruit]

per·sist (pər sĭst′, -zĭst′), *v.i.* **1.** to continue steadily or firmly in some state, purpose, course of action, or the like, esp. in spite of opposition, remonstrance, etc. **2.** to last or endure. **3.** to be insistent in a statement or question. [t. L: s. *persistere* to continue steadfastly]

per·sist·ence (pər sĭs′təns, -zĭs′-), *n.* **1.** the action or fact of persisting. **2.** the quality of being persistent. **3.** continued existence or occurrence. **4.** the continuance of an effect after its cause is removed. Also, **per·sist′en·cy.** —**Syn. 1.** See **perseverance.**

per·sist·ent (pər sĭs′tənt, -zĭs′-), *adj.* **1.** persisting, esp. in spite of opposition, etc.; persevering. **2.** lasting or enduring. **3.** continued; constantly repeated. **4.** *Biol.* continuing or permanent. **5.** *Zool.* perennial; holding to morphological character, or continuing in function or activity. —**per·sist′ent·ly,** *adv.* —**Syn. 1.** indefatigable, pertinacious, tenacious. See **stubborn.**

per·son (pûr′sən), *n.* **1.** a human being, whether man, woman, or child: *four persons saw him.* **2.** a human being as distinguished from an animal or a thing. **3.** *Sociol.* a human being who is conscious of his social relations to other human beings toward whom he acts. **4.** *Philos.* a self-conscious or rational being. **5.** the actual self or individual personality of a human being: *to assume a duty in one's own person.* **6.** the living body of a human being. **7.** the body in its external aspect. **8. in person,** in one's own bodily presence: *to apply in person.* **9.** a character, part, or role, in a play, story, or in real life, etc. **10.** an individual of distinction or importance. **11.** one not entitled to social recognition or respect. **12.** *Law.* an individual human being (**natural person**) or a body corporate (**artificial person**) having rights and duties before the law. **13.** *Gram.* **a.** (in some languages) a category of verb inflection and of pronoun classification, distinguishing between the speaker (**first person**), the one addressed (**second person**), and anyone or anything else (**third person**), sometimes with further subdivisions of the third, as *I* and *we* (first person), *you* (second person), and *he, she, it* and *they* (third person). **b.** any of these three (or more) divisions. **14.** *Theol.* any of the three hypostases or modes of being in the Trinity (Father, Son, and Holy Ghost). [ME *persone*, t. OF, g. L *persōna* actor's mask, character acted, personage, being]
—**Syn. 1.** PERSON, INDIVIDUAL, PERSONAGE are terms applied to human beings. PERSON is the most general and common word: *the average person.* INDIVIDUAL views a person (rarely a thing) as standing alone or as a single member of a group: (*the characteristics of the individual*); its implication is sometimes derogatory: *a disagreeable individual.* PERSONAGE is used (sometimes ironically) of an outstanding or illustrious person: *a distinguished personage as a visitor.*

per·so·na (pər sō′nə), *n.*, *pl.* **-nae** (-nē). *Latin.* person.

per·son·a·ble (pûr′sən ə bəl), *adj.* of pleasing personal appearance; comely; presentable.

per·son·age (pûr′sən ĭj), *n.* **1.** a person of distinction or importance. **2.** any person. **3.** a character in a play, story, etc. [late ME, t. OF] —**Syn. 1.** See **person.**

per·so·na gra·ta (pər sō′nə grā′tə), *Latin.* **1.** an acceptable person. **2.** a diplomatic representative acceptable to the government to which he is accredited. [LL]

per·son·al (pûr′sən əl), *adj.* **1.** of or pertaining to a particular person; individual; private: *a personal matter.* **2.** relating to, directed to, or aimed at, a particular person: *a personal favor.* **3.** referring or directed to a particular person in a disparaging or offensive sense or manner: *personal remarks.* **4.** making personal remarks or attacks: *to become personal in a dispute.* **5.** done, affected, held, etc., in person: *a personal conference, personal service.* **6.** pertaining to or characteristic of a person or self-conscious being. **7.** of the nature of an individual rational being: *a personal God.* **8.** pertaining to the person, body, or bodily aspect: *personal cleanliness.* **9.** *Gram.* **a.** denoting grammatical person. For example: in Latin *portō* "I carry," *portās* "you carry," *portat* "he, she or it carries," *-ō*, *-s* and *-t* are said to be personal endings. **b.** denoting a class of pronouns classified as referring to the speaker, the one addressed, and anyone or anything else. **10.** *Law.* noting or pertaining to estate or property consisting of movable chattels, money, securities and choses in action (distinguished from *real*). —*n.* **11.** *U.S.* a short news paragraph in a newspaper, referring to a particular person or particular persons. [ME, t. L: s. *persōnālis*]

personal effects, *Law.* clothing, books, and similar personalty, usually of a decedent.

personal equation, personal tendency to deviation or error, for which allowance must be made.

per·son·al·ism (pûr′sən ə lĭz′əm), *n.* *Philos.* a movement which finds ultimate value and reality in persons, human or divine; usually favoring democracy, self psychology, theism, and idealism, while opposing naturalism, dualism, and irrationalism. —**per′son·al·ist,** *n.* —**per′son·al·ist′ic,** *adj.*

per·son·al·i·ty (pûr′sə năl′ə tĭ), *n.*, *pl.* **-ties.** **1.** distinctive or notable personal character: *a man with personality.* **2.** a person as an embodiment of an assemblage of qualities. **3.** *Psychol.* **a.** all the constitutional, mental, emotional, social, etc., characteristics of an individual. **b.** an organized pattern of all the characteristics of an individual. **c.** a pattern of characteristics consisting of two or more usually opposing, types of behavior: *multiple personality.* **4.** the quality of being a person; existence as a self-conscious being; personal identity. **5.** the essential character of a person as distinguished from a thing. **6.** application or reference to a particular person or particular persons, often in disparagement or hostility. **7.** a disparaging or offensive statement referring to a particular person. **8.** *Geog.* the distinguishing or peculiar characteristics of a region. —**Syn. 1.** See **character.**

per·son·al·ize (pûr′sən ə līz′), *v.t.*, **-ized, -izing.** **1.** to make personal. **2.** to personify.

per·son·al·ly (pûr′sən ə lĭ), *adv.* **1.** as regards oneself: *personally I don't care to go.* **2.** as an individual person: *he hates me personally.* **3.** in person. **4.** as (if) intended personally: *don't take his bluntness personally.*

personal pronoun, *Gram.* any one of the subject pronouns (*I, we, thou, you, he, she, it, they*).

per·son·al·ty (pûr′sən əl tĭ), *n.*, *pl.* **-ties.** *Law.* personal estate or property.

per·so·na non gra·ta (pər sō′nə nŏn grā′tə), *Latin.* an unacceptable person, esp. a diplomatic representative.

per·son·ate[1] (pûr′sə nāt′), *v.*, **-ated, -ating.** —*v.t.* **1.** to act or present (a character in a play, etc.). **2.** to assume the character or appearance of; pass oneself off as, esp. in England, in order to vote fraudulently. **3.** (in the arts) to represent in terms of personal properties. —*v.i.* **4.** to act or play a part. [t. L: m.s. *persōnātus*, pp.] —**per′son·a′tion,** *n.* —**per′son·a′tive,** *adj.* —**per′son·a′tor,** *n.*

per·son·ate[2] (pûr′sən ĭt, -sə nāt′), *adj.* *Bot.* **1.** (of a bilabiate corolla) masklike. **2.** having the lower lip pushed upward so as to close the hiatus between the lips, as in the snapdragon. See illus. under **corolla.** [t. L: m.s. *persōnātus* masked]

per·son·i·fi·ca·tion (pər sŏn′ə fə kā′shən), *n.* **1.** the attribution of personal nature or character to inanimate objects or abstract notions, esp. as a rhetorical figure. **2.** the representation of a thing or abstraction in the form of a person, as in art. **3.** the person or thing embodying a quality or the like; an embodiment. **4.** an imaginary person or creature conceived or figured to represent a thing or abstraction. **5.** act of personifying.

per·son·i·fy (pər sŏn′ə fī′), *v.t.*, **-fied, -fying.** **1.** to attribute personal nature or character to (an inanimate object or an abstraction), as in speech or writing. **2.** to represent (a thing or abstraction) in the form of a person, as in art. **3.** to embody (a quality, idea, etc.) in a real person or a concrete thing. **4.** to be an embodiment of; typify. **5.** to personate. [f. PERSON + -(I)FY, appar. modeled on F *personnifier*] —**per·son′i·fi′er,** *n.*

per·son·nel (pûr′sə nĕl′), *n.* the body of persons employed in any work, undertaking, or service (distinguished from *matériel*). [t. F, n. use of adj.]

per·sorp·tion (pər sôrp′shən), *n.* *Phys. Chem.* adsorption in pores only slightly wider than the diameter of the adsorbed molecule.

per·spec·tive (pər spĕk′tĭv), *n.* **1.** the art of depicting on a flat surface, various objects, architecture, landscape, etc., in such a way as to express dimensions and spatial relations. **2.** the relation of parts to one another and to the whole, in a mental view or prospect. **3.** a visible scene, esp. one extending to a distance; a vista. **4.** the appearance of objects with reference to relative position, distance, etc. **5.** a mental view or prospect. **6.** *Obs.* an optical glass. —*adj.* **7.** of or pertaining to the

b., blend of, blended; c., cognate with; d., dialect, dialectal; der., derived from; f., formed from; g., going back to; m., modification of; r., replacing; s., stem of; t., taken from; ?, perhaps. See the full key on inside cover.

art of perspective, or represented according to its laws. [ME, t. ML: m. *perspectīva (ars)* science of optics, der. L *perspectus* see through] **—per·spec′tive·ly,** *adv.*

per·spi·ca·cious (pûr′spə kā′shəs), *adj.* **1.** having keen mental perception; discerning. **2.** *Archaic.* having keen sight. [f. PERSPICACI(TY) + -OUS] **—per′spi·ca′-cious·ly,** *adv.*

per·spi·cac·i·ty (pûr′spə kăs′ə tĭ), *n.* **1.** keenness of mental perception; discernment; penetration. **2.** *Archaic.* keenness of sight. [t. L: m.s. *perspicācitas*] **—Syn.** **1.** See perspicuity. **—Ant. 1.** obtuseness.

per·spi·cu·i·ty (pûr′spə kū′ə tĭ), *n.* **1.** clearness or lucidity, as of a statement. **2.** quality of being perspicuous. **3.** perspicacity. [late ME, t. L: m.s. *perspicuitas*] **—Syn. 1.** PERSPICUITY and PERSPICACITY are not properly synonyms, but for several centuries the first has been confused with the second, by less careful writers. Both are derived from a Latin word meaning to see through clearly: PERSPICACITY refers to the power of seeing clearly; to clearness of insight or judgment: *a man of acute perspicacity, the perspicacity of his judgment.* PERSPICUITY refers to that which can be seen through, i. e., to lucidity, clearness of style or exposition, freedom from obscurity: *the perspicuity of his argument.* **—Ant. 1.** obscurity.

per·spic·u·ous (pər spĭk′yŏŏ əs), *adj.* **1.** clear to the understanding. **2.** clear in expression or statement; lucid. **3.** perspicacious. [late ME, t. L: m. *perspicuus*] **—per·spic′u·ous·ly,** *adv.* **—per·spic′u·ous·ness,** *n.*

per·spi·ra·tion (pûr′spə rā′shən), *n.* **1.** the act or process of perspiring. **2.** that which is perspired; sweat. **—Syn. 2.** PERSPIRATION, SWEAT refer (primarily) to moisture exuded (by animals and people) from the pores of the skin. PERSPIRATION is the more refined and elegant word, and is often used overfastidiously by those who consider SWEAT coarse; but SWEAT is a strong word and in some cases obviously more appropriate: *a light perspiration; the sweat of his brow.* SWEAT is always used when referring to animals or objects: *sweat drips from a dog's tongue;* it may also be used metaphorically of objects: *sweat forms on apples after they are gathered.*

per·spir·a·to·ry (pər spĭr′ə tōr′ĭ), *adj.* of, pertaining to or stimulating perspiration.

per·spire (pər spīr′), *v.,* **-spired, -spiring. —v.i. 1.** to excrete watery fluid through the pores; sweat. *—v.t.* **2.** to emit through pores; exude. [t. L: m.s. *perspīrāre,* lit., breathe through]

per·suade (pər swād′), *v.t.,* **-suaded, -suading. 1.** to prevail on (a person, etc.), by advice, urging, reasons, inducements, etc., to do something: *we could not persuade him to wait.* **2.** to induce to believe; convince. [t. L: m.s. *persuādēre*] **—per·suad′a·ble,** *adj.* **—per·suad′er,** *n.* **—Syn. 1.** PERSUADE, INDUCE, CONVINCE imply influencing someone's thoughts or actions. PERSUADE and INDUCE (followed by the infinitive) are used today mainly in the meaning of winning over a person to a certain course of action: *it was I who persuaded him to call a doctor; I induced him to do this.* They differ in that PERSUADE suggests appealing more to the reason and understanding: *I persuaded him to go back to his wife* (though it is often lightly used: *can't I persuade you to stay to supper?*); INDUCE emphasizes only the idea of successful influence, whether achieved by argument or by promise of reward: *What can I say that will induce you to stay at your job?* Owing to this idea of compensation, INDUCE may be used in reference to the influence of factors as well as of persons: *the prospect of a raise of salary was what induced him to stay.* CONVINCE means to satisfy the understanding of a person with regard to a truth or a statement: *to convince one by quoting statistics.* Only when followed by a *that-* clause may CONVINCE refer to winning a person to a course of action: *I convinced her that she should go.* **—Ant. 1.** dissuade.

per·sua·si·ble (pər swā′sə bəl), *adj.* open to persuasion.

per·sua·sion (pər swā′zhən), *n.* **1.** act of persuading or seeking to persuade. **2.** power of persuading; persuasive force. **3.** the state or fact of being persuaded or convinced. **4.** a conviction or belief. **5.** a form or system of belief, esp. religious belief, or the body of persons adhering to it. **6.** sect or denomination. **7.** *Colloq.* kind or sort. [ME, t. L: s. *persuāsio*]

per·sua·sive (pər swā′sĭv), *adj.* **1.** able, fitted, or intended to persuade. **—n. 2.** something that persuades. **—per·sua′sive·ly,** *adv.* **—per·sua′sive·ness,** *n.*

per·sul·fate (pər sŭl′fāt), *n. Chem.* a salt of persulfuric acid. See per- (def. 2).

per·sul·fu·ric acid (pûr′sŭl fyŏŏr′ĭk). See per- (def. 2a).

pert (pûrt), *adj.* **1.** bold, forward, or impertinent; saucy. **2.** *Now Dial.* lively; sprightly; in good health. **3.** *Obs.* clever. [ME, aphetic var. of *apert,* appar. b. OF *apert* open (g. L *apertus*) and OF *a(s)pert* skilled (g. L *expertus*)] **—pert′ly,** *adv.* **—pert′ness,** *n.*

pert., pertaining.

per·tain (pər tān′), *v.i.* **1.** to have reference or relation; relate: *documents pertaining to the case.* **2.** to belong or be connected as a part, adjunct, possession, attribute, etc. **3.** to belong properly or fittingly; be appropriate. [ME *partene(n),* t. OF: m. *partenir,* g. L *pertinēre* extend, reach, relate]

Perth (pûrth), *n.* **1.** Also, **Perthshire.** a county in central Scotland. 126,800 pop. (est. 1956); 2493 sq. mi. **2.** its county seat: a port on the Tay river. 41,000 (est. 1956). **3.** a city in SW Australia: the capital of Western Australia. 97,350 (1954); with suburbs, 348,596 (1954).

Perth Am·boy (pûrth′ ăm′boi), a seaport in E New Jersey. 38,007 (1960).

Perth·shire (pûrth′shĭr, -shər), *n.* Perth (def. 1).

per·ti·na·cious (pûr′tə nā′shəs), *adj.* **1.** holding tenaciously to a purpose, course of action, or opinion. **2.** extremely persistent: *pertinacious efforts.* [f. s. L *pertinācia* + -OUS] **—per′ti·na′cious·ly,** *adv.* **—per′ti·na′-cious·ness,** *n.*

per·ti·nac·i·ty (pûr′tə năs′ə tĭ), *n.* the quality of being pertinacious. **—Syn.** See perseverance.

per·ti·nent (pûr′tə nənt), *adj.* pertaining or relating to the matter in hand; relevant; apposite: *pertinent details.* [ME, t. L: s. *pertinens,* ppr.] **—per′ti·nence, per′ti·nen·cy,** *n.* **—per′ti·nent·ly,** *adv.* **—Syn.** See apt.

per·turb (pər tûrb′), *v.t.* **1.** to disturb or disquiet greatly in mind; agitate. **2.** to disturb greatly; throw into disorder; derange. **3.** *Astron.* to induce perturbation of. [ME, t. L: s. *perturbāre*] **—per·turb′a·ble,** *adj.*

per·tur·ba·tion (pûr′tər bā′shən), *n.* **1.** act of perturbing. **2.** state of being perturbed. **3.** mental disquiet or agitation. **4.** a cause of mental disquiet. **5.** *Astron.* deviation of a celestial body from regular motion around its primary due to some force other than the gravitational attraction of a spherical primary.

per·tus·sis (pər tŭs′ĭs), *n. Pathol.* whooping cough. [t. NL: f. per- PER- + L *tussis* cough] **—per·tus′sal,** *adj.*

Pe·ru (pə rōō′; *Sp.* pě-), *n.* a republic in W South America. 9,651,000 pop. (est. 1956); 482,258 sq. mi. *Cap.:* Lima. **—Pe·ru·vi·an** (pə rōō′vĭ ən), *adj., n.*

Pe·ru·gia (pě rōō′jä), *n.* a city in central Italy, in Umbria. 99,000 (est. 1954).

Pe·ru·gi·no, Il (ēl pě′rōō jē′nô), (*Pietro Vannucci*) 1446–1524, Italian painter.

pe·ruke (pə rōōk′), *n.* a wig, esp. of the kind worn by men in the 17th and 18th centuries; a periwig. [t. F: m. *perruque,* back formation from Pr. *perucat* well-preened, orig., like a parrot, der. *perruca* parrot. Cf. PERIWIG]

Man wearing a peruke

per·rus·al (pə rōō′zəl), *n.* **1.** a reading. **2.** act of perusing; survey or scrutiny.

pe·ruse (pə rōōz′), *v.t.,* **-rused, -rusing. 1.** to read through, as with thoroughness or care. **2.** to read. **3.** *Archaic.* to survey or examine in detail. [late ME; orig., use up, f. PER- + USE, V.] **—pe·rus′a·ble,** *adj.* **—pe·rus′er,** *n.*

Peruvian bark, cinchona (def.2).

per·vade (pər vād′), *v.t.,* **-vaded, -vading. 1.** to extend its presence, activities, influence, etc., throughout: *spring pervaded the air.* **2.** to go everywhere throughout (a place), as a person. **3.** to go, pass, or spread through. [t. L: m.s. *pervādere*] **—per·vad′er,** *n.* **—per·va·sion** (pər vā′zhən), *n.* **—per·va·sive** (pər vā′sĭv), *adj.* **—per·va′sive·ly,** *adv.* **—per·va′sive·ness,** *n.* **—Syn. 1.** PERVADE, PERMEATE suggest a slow diffusion and an ultimate saturation of something. PERVADE is now found chiefly in figurative uses: *the perfume of roses pervades the air, a spirit of uneasiness pervaded the city.* PERMEATE is found in both concrete and figurative senses: *water permeated the soil, ideas of democracy permeated the group.*

per·verse (pər vûrs′), *adj.* **1.** willfully determined or disposed to go counter to what is expected or desired; contrary. **2.** characterized by or proceeding from such a determination: *a perverse mood.* **3.** wayward; cantankerous. **4.** persistent or obstinate in what is wrong. **5.** turned away from what is right, good, or proper; wicked. [ME, t. L: m.s. *perversus,* pp., turned the wrong way, awry] **—per·verse′ly,** *adv.* **—per·verse′ness,** *n.* **—Syn. 4.** stubborn, headstrong. See willful.

per·ver·sion (pər vûr′zhən, -shən), *n.* **1.** act of perverting. **2.** state of being perverted. **3.** a perverted form of something. **4.** *Psychiatry.* perverted or abnormal condition of the sexual instincts (**sexual perversion**). **5.** *Pathol.* change to what is unnatural or abnormal: *a perversion of function, taste, etc.*

per·ver·si·ty (pər vûr′sə tĭ), *n., pl.* **-ties. 1.** the quality of being perverse. **2.** an instance of it.

per·ver·sive (pər vûr′sĭv), *adj.* tending to pervert.

per·vert (*v.* pər vûrt′; *n.* pûr′vûrt), *v.t.* **1.** to turn away from the right course. **2.** to lead astray morally. **3.** to lead into mental error or false judgment. **4.** to bring over to a religious belief regarded as false or wrong. **5.** to turn to an improper use; misapply. **6.** to distort. **7.** to bring to a less excellent state, vitiate, or debase. **8.** *Pathol.* to change to what is unnatural or abnormal. **9.** to affect with perversion. **—n. 10.** *Pathol.* one affected with perversion. **11.** one who has been perverted. [ME, t. L: s. *pervertere*] **—per·vert′er,** *n.* **—per·vert′i·ble,** *adj.*

per·vert·ed (pər vûr′tĭd), *adj.* **1.** *Pathol.* changed to or being of an unnatural or abnormal kind: *a perverted appetite.* **2.** turned from what is right; wicked; misguided; misapplied; distorted. **3.** affected with or due to perversion. **—per·vert′ed·ly,** *adv.*

per·vi·ous (pûr′vĭ əs), *adj.* **1.** admitting of passage or entrance; permeable: *pervious soil.* **2.** accessible to reason, feeling, etc. [t. L: m. *pervius*] **—per′vi·ous·ness,** *n.*

Pe·sach (pä′säкн), *n.* the Passover. Also, **Pe′sah.** [t. Heb.: m. *pesaḥ*]

Pes·ca·do·res (pěs′kä dô′rěs), *n.pl.* a group of small islands off the SE coast of China, in Formosa Strait: ceded to Japan, 1895; returned to China, 1945. 84,502 pop. (est. 1954); ab. 50 sq. mi. Also, **Pengu.**

ăct, āble, dâre, ärt; ĕbb, ēqual; ĭf, īce; hŏt, ōver, ôrder, oil, bŏŏk, ōōze, out; ŭp, ūse, ûrge; ə = a in alone; ch, chief; g, give; ng, ring; sh, shoe; th, thin; ŧh, that; zh, vision. See the full key on inside cover.

pe·se·ta (pə sā′tə; *Sp.* pě sě′tä), *n.* a silver coin and monetary unit of Spain, equivalent to 1½ U.S. cents. [dim. of *pesa* weight. See PESO]

Pe·sha·war (pě shä′wər), *n.* a city in Pakistan, near the Khyber Pass: the capital of North-West Frontier Province. 151,776 (1951).

Pe·shit·ta (pə shět′tä), *n.* the principal Syriac version of the Bible. [t. Syriac: m. *p'shittā* the simple]

pes·ky (pěs′kĭ), *adj.,* **-kier, -kiest.** *U.S. Colloq.* troublesome; annoying. [b. *pesty* (der. PEST) and RISKY]

pe·so (pā′sō; *Sp.* pě′sō), *n., pl.* **-sos** (-sōz; *Sp.* -sōs). **1.** the monetary unit and a silver coin of Mexico, equivalent since 1954 to 8 U.S. cents. **2.** the monetary unit and a gold or silver coin of Cuba, equal to 100 centavos, worth about 30 U.S. cents. **3.** any of various monetary units and coins of Spanish America. **4.** the monetary unit and a silver coin of the Philippine Islands, worth about 28 U.S. cents. **5.** an old Spanish gold or silver coin. [Sp.: lit., weight , g. L *pensum,* pp., weighed]

pes·sa·ry (pěs′ə rĭ), *n., pl.* **-ries.** *Med.* **1.** an instrument worn in the vagina to remedy uterine displacement. **2.** a vaginal suppository. **3.** a contraceptive device worn in the vagina or uterine cervix. [ME, t. LL: m.s. *pessārium,* der. L *pessus,* t. Gk.: m. *pessós,* orig., oval stone used in a game]

pes·si·mism (pěs′ə mĭz′əm), *n.* **1.** disposition to take the gloomiest possible view. **2.** the doctrine that the existing world is the worst of all possible worlds, or that all things naturally tend to evil. **3.** the belief that the evil and pain in the world are not compensated for by the good and happiness. [f. s. L *pessimus* worst + -ISM, modeled on OPTIMISM]

pes·si·mist (pěs′ə mĭst), *n.* **1.** one who looks on the gloomy side of things. **2.** an adherent of pessimism.

pes·si·mis·tic (pěs′ə mĭs′tĭk), *adj.* pertaining to or characterized by pessimism. —**pes′si·mis′ti·cal·ly,** *adv.* —**Syn.** See CYNICAL.

pest (pěst), *n.* **1.** a noxious, destructive, or troublesome thing or person; nuisance. **2.** a deadly epidemic disease; a pestilence. **3.** a disease produced by the plague bacillus. [t. L: s. *pestis* plague, disease]

Pest (pěst; *Hung.* pěsht), *n.* See Budapest.

Pes·ta·loz·zi (pěs′tä lŏt′sĭ), *n.* **Johann Heinrich** (yō′-hän hĭn′rĭKH), 1746–1827, Swiss educational reformer.

pes·ter (pěs′tər), *v.t.* to harass with petty annoyances, vexing importunities, or the like; torment. [? t. OF: m. *empestrer* hobble (a horse); later associated with PEST]

pest·hole (pěst′hōl′), *n.* a location prone to epidemic disease.

pest·house (pěst′hous′), *n.* a house or hospital for persons infected with pestilential disease.

pest·i·cide (pěs′tə sĭd′), *n.* a chemical substance for destroying pests, such as mosquitos, flies, etc.

pes·tif·er·ous (pěs tĭf′ər əs), *adj.* **1.** bearing pests. **2.** pestilential. **3.** pernicious in any way. **4.** *Colloq.* mischievous; troublesome or annoying. [f. L *pestifer* plague-bringing + -ous] —**pes·tif′er·ous·ly,** *adv.*

pes·ti·lence (pěs′tə ləns), *n.* **1.** a deadly epidemic disease. **2.** that which produces or tends to produce epidemic disease. **3.** the bubonic plague.

pes·ti·lent (pěs′tə lənt), *adj.* **1.** infectious, as a disease; pestilential. **2.** producing or tending to produce infectious disease. **3.** destructive to life; deadly; poisonous. **4.** injurious to peace, morals, etc. **5.** troublesome or annoying. **6.** pernicious or mischievous. [ME, t. L: s. *pestilens,* ppr.] —**pes′ti·lent·ly,** *adv.*

pes·ti·len·tial (pěs′tə lěn′shəl), *adj.* **1.** producing or tending to produce pestilence. **2.** pertaining to or of the nature of pestilence, specif. bubonic plague. **3.** pernicious; harmful. **4.** mischievous. [ME, t. ML: s. *pestilentiālis*]

pes·tle (pěs′əl, pěs′təl), *n., v.,* **-tled, -tling.** —*n.* **1.** an instrument for braying or triturating substances in a mortar. See illus. under **mortar. 2.** any of various appliances for pounding, stamping, etc. —*v.t.* **3.** to pound or triturate with or as with a pestle. —*v.i.* **4.** to work with a pestle. [ME, t. OF: m. *pestel,* ult. der. L *pistum,* pp., pounded]

pet¹ (pět), *n., adj., v.,* **petted, petting.** —*n.* **1.** any domesticated or tamed animal that is kept as a favorite and cared for affectionately. **2.** a person especially cherished or indulged; a favorite. **3.** a thing particularly cherished. —*adj.* **4.** treated as a pet, as an animal. **5.** especially cherished or indulged, as a child or other person. **6.** favorite: *a pet theory.* **7.** showing affection: *a pet name.* —*v.t.* **8.** to treat as a pet; fondle; indulge. **9.** *U.S. Slang.* to fondle or caress (one of the opposite sex). [? back formation from *pet lamb* cade lamb, itself ? syncopated var. of *petty lamb* little lamb, where *petty* marks affection. Cf. PETCOCK]

pet² (pět), *n.* **1.** a fit of peevishness. —*v.i.* **2.** to be peevish; sulk. [appar. back formation from PETTISH]

Pet., Peter.

Pé·tain (pě tăN′), *n.* **Henri Philippe** (äNrē′ fēlēp′), 1856–1951, French general: convicted of treason after World War II.

pet·al (pět′əl), *n. Bot.* one of the members of a corolla. See diag. under **flower.** [t. NL: s. *petalum* petal (L metal plate), t. Gk.: m. *pétalon* leaf, prop. neut. adj., outspread] —**pet′aled, pet′alled,** *adj.*

pet·al·if·er·ous (pět′ə lĭf′ər əs), *adj.* bearing petals.

pet·al·ine (pět′əl ĭn, -ə lĭn′), *adj.* pertaining to or resembling a petal.

pet·a·lo·dy (pět′ə lō′dĭ), *n. Bot.* a condition in flowers, in which certain organs, as the stamens in most double flowers, assume the appearance of or become metamorphosed into petals. [f. s. Gk. *petalṓdēs* leaflike +-Y³]

pet·al·oid (pět′ə loid′), *adj.* having the form or appearance of a petal.

pet·al·ous (pět′ə ləs), *adj.* having petals.

pe·tard (pĭ tärd′), *n.* **1.** an engine of war or an explosive device formerly used to blow in a door or gate, form a breach in a wall, etc. **2. hoist on one's own petard,** caught in one's own trap. **3.** a kind of firecracker. [t. F, der. *péter* break wind, explode, der. *pei* (noun), g. L *pēditum,* der. *pēdere* break wind]

pet·a·sus (pět′ə səs), *n.* a low-crowned, broad-brimmed hat worn by ancient Greeks and Romans, often represented as worn by Hermes or Mercury. [t. L, t. Gk.: m. *pétasos*]

pet·cock (pět′kŏk′), *n.* a small valve or faucet, as for draining off excess or waste material from the cylinder of a steam engine or an internal-combustion engine. Also, **pet cock.** [f. PET(TY) + cock¹]

Pe·ter (pē′tər), *n.* **1.** died A.D. 67?, one of the twelve apostles, a fisherman on the Sea of Galilee and leader of the group of apostles. He was the reputed author of two New Testament epistles bearing his name. Also called **Simon Peter** or **Saint Peter. 2.** one of the two Epistles of Peter. [ME, t. L: m. s. *Petrus,* t. Gk.: m. *Pétros* stone, trans. of Syriac *kēfā*]

pe·ter (pē′tər), *v.i. U.S. Colloq.* to diminish gradually and then disappear or cease .(fol. by *out).* [orig. unknown]

Peter I, 1. ("the Great") 1672–1725, czar of Russia, 1682–1725. **2.** (*Peter Karageorgevich*) 1844–1921, king of Serbia, 1903–21.

Peter II, born 1923, king of Yugoslavia, 1934–1945.

Peter III, 1728–1762, the weak-minded husband of Catherine II of Russia: ascended the throne (1762) but was deposed by his wife and a group of nobles and assassinated.

Pe·ter·bor·ough (pē′tər bûr′ō, -bə rə), *n.* **1.** a city in E England, in Northamptonshire. 53,412 (1951). **2.** a city in SE Canada, in Ontario. 38,272 (1951). **3. Soke of** (sōk), an administrative county in E England: a part of Northamptonshire. 63,791 pop. (1951); 84 sq. mi.

Pe·ter·mann Peak (pā′tər män′), a mountain in E Greenland. ab. 10,000 ft.

Pe·ter Pan (pē′tər păn′), **1.** a play (1904) by Sir J. M. Barrie about a boy who never grew up. **2.** this boy.

Pe·ters·burg (pē′tərz bûrg′), *n.* a city in SE Virginia: besieged by Union forces, 1864–65. 36,750 (1960).

pe·ter·sham (pē′tər shəm), *n.* **1.** a kind of heavy woolen cloth used for overcoats, etc. **2.** a kind of heavy overcoat formerly in fashion. [named after Viscount *Petersham* (1780–1851)]

Peter's pence, 1. an annual tax or tribute, orig. of a penny from each householder, formerly paid by the people of certain countries to the papal see at Rome. **2.** a voluntary contribution to the Pope, made by Roman Catholics everywhere. Also, **Peter pence.**

Peter the Hermit, c1050–1115, French monk; a preacher of the first Crusade.

pet·i·o·lar (pět′ĭ ə lər), *adj. Bot.* of, pertaining to, or growing from a petiole.

pet·i·o·late (pět′ĭ ə lāt′), *adj. Zool.* having a petiole or peduncle. Also, **pet′i·o·lat′ed.**

pet·i·ole (pět′ĭ ōl′), *n.* **1.** *Bot.* the slender stalk by which a leaf is attached to the stem; a leafstalk. **2.** *Zool.* a stalk or peduncle, as that connecting the abdomen and thorax in wasps, etc. [t. F, t. L: m.s. *petiolus* little foot, stem, stalk, dim. of *pēs* foot]

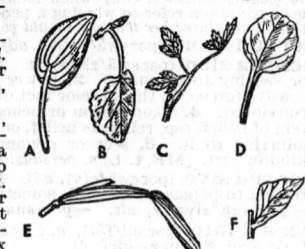

Petioles
A. Terete; B. Flat; C. Dilated at the base; D. Winged; E. Forming a sheath; F Leaflike (the so-called phyllode)

pet·it (pět′ĭ; *Fr.* pə tē′), *adj.* (now only in legal phrases) small; petty; minor. [ME, t. F, der. Rom. stem *pit-* small]

pe·tite (pə tēt′), *adj. French.* little; of small size; tiny.

pet·it four (pět′ĭ fôr′; *Fr.* pə tē fōōr′), *pl.* **petits fours** (pět′ĭ fōrz′; *Fr.* pə tē fōōr′). a small tea cake, variously frosted and decorated. [F: little oven]

pe·ti·tion (pə tĭsh′ən), *n.* **1.** a formally drawn-up request addressed to a person or a body of persons in authority or power, soliciting some favor, right, mercy, or other benefit. **2.** a request made for something desired, esp. a respectful or humble request, as to a superior or to one or those in authority: *a petition for aid.* **3.** that which is sought by request or entreaty. **4.** *Law.* an application for an order of court or for some judicial action. **5.** a supplication or prayer, as to God. —*v.t.* **6.** to entreat, supplicate, or beg, as for something desired. **7.** to address a formal petition to (a sovereign, a legislative body, etc.). **8.** to ask by petition for (something) (fol. by *that*). —*v.i.* **9.** to present a petition. **10.** to address or present a formal petition. [ME, t. L: s. *petitio*] —**pe·ti′tion·er,** *n.* —**Syn. 9.** See **appeal.**

pe·ti·tion·ar·y (pə tĭsh′ə nĕr′ĭ), *adj.* **1.** of the nature of or expressing a petition. **2.** *Obs.* or *Archaic.* petitioning or supplicant.

pe·ti·ti·o prin·ci·pi·i (pĭ tĭsh′ĭ ō′ prĭn sĭp′ĭ ī′), *Logic.* a fallacy in reasoning resulting from the assumption of that which in the beginning was set forth to be proved; begging the question. [L, trans. of Gk. *tò en archêi aiteîsthai* an assumption at the outset]

pet·it jury (pĕt′ĭ), petty jury. —**petit juror.**

petit larceny, petty larceny.

pe·tits pois (pə tē pwä′), *French.* small green peas.

Pe·tra (pē′trə), *n.* an ancient city in SW Jordan: unusual ruined buildings, carved out of varicolored stratified rock.

Pe·trarch (pē′trärk), *n.* (*Francesco Petrarca*) 1304–74. Italian poet and scholar.

pet·rel (pĕt′rəl), *n.* **1.** any of numerous sea birds of the family *Procellariidæ*. **2.** any of various small, long-winged, usually black-and-white oceanic birds known as Mother Carey's chickens, esp. the stormy or storm petrel, *Hydrobates pelagicus*. **3.** a person whose coming is supposed to portend trouble or strife. [t. F, earlier *pétérel,* der. *péter* break wind. See PETARD]

Pe·trie (pē′trĭ), *n.* **Sir Flinders** (flĭn′dərz), 1853–1942. British Egyptologist and archaeologist.

pet·ri·fac·tion (pĕt′rə făk′shən), *n.* **1.** act or process of petrifying. **2.** state of being petrified. **3.** something petrified. Also, **pet·ri·fi·ca·tion** (pĕt′rə fə kā′shən). —**pet′ri·fac′tive,** *adj.*

Petrified Forest, a national monument in E Arizona: forests turned to stone by the action of mineral-laden water. 40 sq. mi.

pet·ri·fy (pĕt′rə fī′), *v.,* **-fied, -fying.** —*v.t.* **1.** to convert into stone or a stony substance. **2.** to make rigid, stiffen, or benumb; deaden; make inert. **3.** to stupefy or paralyze with astonishment, horror, or other strong emotion. —*v.i.* **4.** to become petrified. [t. F: m.s. *pétrifier,* f. *pétri-* (repr. L *petra* rock, stone. t. Gk.) + *-fier* -FY]

Pe·trine (pē′trīn, -trĭn), *adj.* of or pertaining to the apostle Peter or the Epistles bearing his name.

petro-, a word element meaning "stone" or "rock." [t. Gk., comb. form of *pétra* rock, *pétros* stone]

pet·ro·chem·i·cal (pĕt′rō kĕm′ə kal), *n.* a chemical made from petroleum. [f. PETRO (LEUM) + CHEMICAL]

petrog., petrography.

pet·ro·glyph (pĕt′rə glĭf), *n.* a drawing or carving on rock made by prehistoric or primitive people. [t. F: m. *pétroglyphe,* f. Gk.: petro- PETRO- + *glyphé* carving]

Pet·ro·grad (pĕt′rə grăd′), *Russ.* pĕ trô grät′), *n.* former name of **Leningrad** (1914–24).

pe·trog·ra·phy (pĭ trŏg′rə fĭ), *n.* the scientific description and classification of rocks. —**pe·trog′ra·pher,** *n.* —**pet·ro·graph·ic** (pĕt′rə grăf′ĭk), **pet′ro·graph′i·cal,** *adj.*

pet·rol (pĕt′rəl), *n., v.,* **-rolled, -rolling.** —*n.* **1.** *Brit.* gasoline. **2.** *Obs.* petroleum. —*v.t.* **3.** *Brit.* to clean with gasoline. [t. F: m. *pétrole,* t. ML: m.s. *petroleum* PETROLEUM]

petrol., petrology.

pet·ro·la·tum (pĕt′rə lā′təm), *n.* a soft or semisolid unctuous substance obtained from petroleum, used as a basis for ointments and as a protective dressing. [t. NL. See PETROL, -ATE²]

pe·tro·le·um (pə trō′lĭ əm), *n.* an oily, usually dark-colored liquid (a form of bitumen or mixture of various hydrocarbons), occurring naturally in various parts of the world, and commonly obtained by boring: used (in its natural state or after certain treatment) as a fuel, or separated by distillation into gasoline, naphtha, benzine, kerosene, paraffin, etc. [t. ML: f. petro- PETRO- + L *oleum* oil (t. Gk.: m. *élaion*)]

petroleum ether, an inflammable low-boiling hydrocarbon mixture produced by the fractional distillation of petroleum, used as a solvent.

pé·tro·leur (pĕ trô lœr′), *n. French.* an incendiary who uses petroleum, esp. an adherent of the Commune who set fire to public buildings in Paris, May, 1871.

pe·trol·ic (pə trŏl′ĭk), *adj.* relating to, resembling, or produced from petroleum: *petrolic ether.*

pe·trol·o·gy (pĭ trŏl′ə jĭ), *n., pl.* **-gies.** the scientific study of rocks, including their origin, structure, changes, etc. —**pet·ro·log·ic** (pĕt′rə lŏj′ĭk), **pet′ro·log′i·cal,** *adj.* —**pet′ro·log′i·cal·ly,** *adv.* —**pe·trol′o·gist,** *n.*

pet·ro·nel (pĕt′rə nəl), *n.* a 15th century firearm which was fired with the butt resting against the breast. [t. F: m. *petrinal,* orig. adj., for the breast, ult. der. L *pectus* breast]

Pe·tro·ni·us (pĭ trō′nĭ əs), *n.* **Gaius** (gā′əs), ("*Petronius Arbiter*") died A.D. c66, Roman writer.

pe·tro·sal (pĭ trō′səl), *adj. Anat.* **1.** petrous. —*n.* **2.** a bone forming the pyramidal part of the temporal bone. [t. s. L *petrōsus* stony, rocky + -AL¹. See PETROUS]

Pe·trouch·ka (pə trōōsh′kə), *n.* ballet music (1911) by Igor Stravinski.

pet·rous (pĕt′rəs, pē′trəs), *adj.* **1.** *Anat.* noting or pertaining to the hard, dense portion of the temporal bone, containing the internal auditory organs; petrosal. **2.** like stone in hardness; stony; rocky. [t. L: m. *petrōsus,* der. *petra* rock, t. Gk.]

Pet·sa·mo (pĕt′sä mô′), *n.* a seaport in the extreme NW Soviet Union, on the Arctic Ocean: ice-free the year round; ceded by Finland, 1944.

pet·ti·coat (pĕt′ĭ kōt′), *n.* **1.** a skirt, esp. an underskirt, worn by women and children. **2.** any skirtlike part or covering. **3.** *Chiefly Humorous.* a woman or girl. **4.** *Elect.* the skirt-shaped portion of an insulator. —*adj.* **5.** female or feminine. **6.** wearing petticoats. [ME; see PETTY, COAT]

pet·ti·fog (pĕt′ĭ fŏg′, -fôg′), *v.i.,* **-fogged, -fogging. 1.** to carry on a petty or shifty law business. **2.** to practice chicanery of any sort. [back formation from *pettifogger,* f. PETTY + *fogger* (of obscure orig.)] —**pet′ti·fog′ger,** *n.* —**pet′ti·fog·er·y,** *n.*

pet·ti·fog·ging (pĕt′ĭ fŏg′ĭng, -fôg′-), *adj.* petty; mean; paltry.

pet·tish (pĕt′ĭsh), *adj.* peevish; petulant: *a pettish refusal.* [? f. PET¹ + -ISH¹, orig., like a spoiled child] —**pet′tish·ly,** *adv.*

pet·ti·toes (pĕt′ĭ tōz′), *n.pl.* **1.** the feet of a pig, esp. as food. **2.** the human feet, esp. those of a child.

pet·to (pĕt′tō), *n., pl.* **-ti** (-tē). *Italian.* the breast. See **in petto.** [It., g. L *pectus* breast]

pet·ty (pĕt′ĭ), *adj.,* **-tier, -tiest. 1.** of small importance; trifling; trivial: *petty grievances.* **2.** of lesser or secondary importance, merit, etc. **3.** having or showing narrow ideas, interests, etc.: *petty minds.* **4.** mean or ungenerous in nature or of trifling things: *a petty revenge.* [ME *pety,* t. OF: m. *petit.* See PETIT] —**pet′ti·ly,** *adv.* —**pet′ti·ness,** *n.*

—**Syn. 1.** PETTY, PALTRY, TRIFLING, TRIVIAL apply to that which is so insignificant as to be almost unworthy of notice. PETTY implies contemptible insignificance and littleness, inferiority and small worth: *petty quarrels.* PALTRY is applied to that which is beneath one's notice, even despicable: *a paltry amount.* That which is TRIFLING is so unimportant and inconsiderable as to be practically negligible: *a trifling error.* That which is TRIVIAL is slight, insignificant, and even in incongruous contrast to that which is significant or important: *a trivial remark, a trivial task.*

petty cash, a small cash fund set aside to meet incidental expenditures, as for office supplies.

petty jury, (in a civil or criminal proceeding) a jury, usually of 12 persons, impaneled to determine the facts and render a verdict pursuant to the court's instructions on the law. Also, **petit jury.** —**petty juror.**

petty larceny. See **larceny.**

petty officer, an enlisted man in the navy holding an official rank corresponding to that of a noncommissioned officer in the army.

petty sessions, *Brit.* a court held before a justice of the peace.

pet·u·lance (pĕch′ə ləns), *n.* **1.** petulant spirit or behavior. **2.** state or quality of being petulant. **3.** a petulant speech or action.

pet·u·lan·cy (pĕch′ə lən sĭ), *n., pl.* **-cies.** petulance.

pet·u·lant (pĕch′ə lənt), *adj.* moved to or showing sudden, impatient irritation, esp. over some trifling annoyance: *a petulant toss of the head.* [t. L: s. *petulans* forward, pert, wanton, der. *petere* fall on, assail] —**pet′u·lant·ly,** *adv.*

pe·tu·ni·a (pə tū′nĭ ə, -tōō′-), *n.* **1.** any of the herbs constituting the solanaceous genus *Petunia,* native to tropical America but cultivated elsewhere, bearing funnel-shaped flowers of various colors. **2.** a deep reddish purple. [t. NL, f. Amer. Ind. *petun* tobacco + *-ia* -IA]

pe·tun·tse (pĕ tŏŏn′tsě; *Chin.* bĭ′dŭn′dzü′), *n.* a Chinese rock reduced mechanically to a fine powder and used as one of the ingredients of certain kinds of porcelain. Also, **pe·tun′tze.** [t. Chinese: f. *pe* (d. var. of *pai*) white + *tun* mound, stone + *tze* (a formative element)]

peu à peu (pœ ä pœ′), *French.* little by little.

peu de chose (pœd shôz′), *French.* a small matter.

pew (pū), *n.* **1.** (in a church) one of an assemblage of fixed benchlike seats (with backs), accessible by aisles, for the use of the congregation. **2.** an enclosed seat in a church, or an enclosure with seats, appropriated to the use of a family or other worshipers. [ME *puwe,* t. OF: m. *puie* balcony, g. L *podia,* pl. of *podium* elevated place, balcony. See PODIUM]

pe·wee (pē′wē), *n.* **1.** wood pewee. **2.** the phoebe.

pe·wit (pē′wĭt, pū′ĭt), *n.* **1.** the lapwing, *Vanellus vanellus.* **2.** the phoebe. **3.** the European black-headed gull, *Larus ridibundus.* [imit. of its cry]

pew·ter (pū′tər), *n.* **1.** any of various alloys in which tin is the chief constituent, orig. one of tin and lead. **2.** a vessel or utensil made of such an alloy. **3.** such utensils collectively. —*adj.* **4.** consisting or made of pewter: *a pewter mug.* [ME *peutre,* t. OF: orig. uncert.]

pew·ter·er (pū′tər ər), *n.* a maker of pewter utensils.

pe·yo·te (pā yō′tē), *n.; pl.* -**tes** (-tēz); *Sp.* pā yō′tĕ), *n.* **1.** a cactus, *Lophophora williamsii,* containing a narcotic prized by the Indians of Mexico and certain regions of the southwestern U.S. **2.** (in Mexico) any of several related or unrelated cacti. [t. Amer. Sp., t. Nahuatl: m. *peyotl*]

---

caterpillar (referring to the downy center of the peyote button)]

pf., 1. pfennig. 2. preferred.

p.f., (It. *piu forte*) *Music.* louder.

Pfalz (pfälts), *n.* German name of **The Palatinate.**

Pfc., *Mil.* private first class.

pfd., preferred.

pfen·nig (pfĕn′ĭg), *n., pl.* **-nigs, -nige** (-ʸgə). a small bronze coin and money of account of Germany, the hundredth part of a mark, normally equivalent to about one fourth of a U.S. cent. [G. See PENNY]

pfg., pfennig.

Pforz·heim (pfôrts′hīm), *n.* a city in SW West Germany, in Baden-Württemberg 62,000 (est. 1953).

Pg., 1. Portugal. 2. Portuguese.

pg., page.

Ph, *Chem.* phenyl.

pH, *Chem.* the symbol for the logarithm of the reciprocal of hydrogen ion concentration in gram atoms per liter. For example, a pH of 5 indicates a concentration of .00001 or 10⁻⁵ gram atoms of hydrogen ions in one liter of solution.

P.H., Public Health.

Phae·a·cia (fē ā′shə), *n. Homeric Legend.* a land visited by Ulysses after the fall of Troy. —**Phae·a′cian,** *n., adj.*

Phae·dra (fē′drə), *n. Gk. Legend.* the daughter of Minos and Pasiphaë, sister of Ariadne, and wife of Theseus. See **Hippolytus.**

Phae·drus (fē′drəs), *n.* fl. A.D. c40, Roman writer of fables.

Pha·ë·thon (fā′ə thən), *n. Class. Myth.* the son of Helios, the sun god. For one day he was allowed to drive his father's chariot, but drove too near earth, and had not Zeus struck him down with a thunderbolt, would have set the world on fire. [t. L, t. Gk.: lit., shining]

pha·e·ton (fā′ə tən *or, esp. Brit.,* fā′tən), *n.* 1. a light four-wheeled carriage, with or without a top, having one or (more commonly) two seats facing forward, and made in various forms. 2. an automobile of the touring-car type. 3. the body of such a car. Also, **pha′ë·ton.** [t. F: m. *phaëton,* t. L: m. *Phaëthon* PHAETHON]

Phaeton (def. 1)

-phag, a word element meaning "eating," "devouring," used in biology to refer to phagocytes. [t. L: s. *-phagus,* t. Gk.: m. *-phagos.* See -PHAGOUS]

-phage, var. of **-phag,** as in *bacteriophage.* [t. F]

phag·e·de·na (făj′ə dē′nə), *n. Pathol.* a severe destructive eroding ulcer. Also, **phag′e·dae′na.** [t. L: m. *phagedaena,* t. Gk.: m. *phagēdaina* an eating ulcer]

phago-, a word element referring to eating. [t. Gk.]

phag·o·cyte (făg′ə sīt′), *n. Physiol.* a blood cell which ingests and destroys particles, bacteria, and other cells. —**phag·o·cyt·ic** (făg′ə sĭt′ĭk), *adj.*

phagocytic index, the average number of bacteria ingested per leucocyte under standard conditions.

phag·o·cy·to·sis (făg′ə sī tō′sĭs), *n.* the ingestion of particlelike matter by cells, in contrast to the entrance of dissolved substance. [t. NL. See PHAGOCYTE, -OSIS]

-phagous, a word element used as an adjective termination meaning "eating," "feeding on," "devouring," as in *creophagous, hylophagous, rhizophagous.* [t. L: m. *-phagus,* t. Gk.: m. *-phagos*]

-phagy, a word element used as a noun termination meaning "eating," "devouring," esp. as a practice or habit, as in *allotriophagy, anthropophagy.* [t. Gk.: m.s. *-phagia,* der. *-phagos* -PHAGOUS]

pha·i·no·pep·la (fā ī′nō pĕp′lə, fā′ə-), *n.* a crested passerine bird, *Phainopepla nitens,* of the southwestern U.S. and Mexico. [t. NL, f. Gk.: m. *phaeinó(s)* shining + m. *péplos* robe]

phal·ange (făl′ənj, fə lănj′), *n. Anat., etc.* a phalanx. [back formation from PHALANGES]

pha·lan·ge·al (fə lăn′jĭ əl), *adj. Anat., etc.* pertaining to, or of the nature of, a phalanx or phalanges.

pha·lan·ger (fə lăn′jər), *n.* any of numerous arboreal marsupials constituting the family *Phalangeridae,* of the Australian region, esp. those of the genus *Phalanger* (or *Cuscus*), as *P. maculatus* (**spotted phalanger**). See **flying phalanger.** [t. NL, der. Gk. *phálanx* bone of finger or toe; with reference to the webbed digits of the hind feet]

pha·lan·ges (fə lăn′jēz), *n. pl.* of **phalanx.**

phal·an·ster·y (făl′ən stĕr′ĭ), *n., pl.* **-steries.** 1. (in Fourierism) **a.** the buildings occupied by a phalanx. **b.** the community itself. 2. any similar association, or the buildings they occupy. [t. F: m. *phalanstère,* b. *phalange* phalanx and *monastère* monastery] —**phal·an·ste·ri·an** (făl′ən stîr′ĭ ən), *adj., n.*

pha·lanx (fā′lăngks, făl′ăngks), *n., pl.* **phalanxes** (fā′lăngk sĭz), **phalanges** (fə lăn′jēz). 1. (in ancient Greece) a body of heavy-armed infantry formed in ranks and files close and deep, with shields joined and long spears overlapping. 2. any body of troops in close array. 3. a compact or closely massed body of persons, animals, or things. 4. a number of persons, etc., united for a common purpose. 5. (in Fourierism) a group of about 1800 persons, living together and holding their property in common. 6. *Anat., Zool.* any of the bones of

the fingers or toes. See diag. under **skeleton.** 7. *Bot.* a bundle of stamens, joined by their filaments. [t. L, t. Gk. (def. 1, 2, 6)]

phal·a·rope (făl′ə rōp′), *n.* any of three species of small aquatic birds constituting the family *Phalaropodidae,* resembling sandpipers but having lobate toes, as *Phalaropus fulicarius* of both Old and New Worlds. [t. F, t. NL: m. *Phalaropūs* (genus name), f. *phalaro-* (comb. form repr. Gk. *phalārīs* coot) + *-pūs* (t. Gk.: m. *poús* foot)]

phal·lic (făl′ĭk), *adj.* of or pertaining to the phallus or phallicism. Also, **phal′li·cal.** [t. Gk.: m.s. *phallikós*]

phal·li·cism (făl′ə sĭz′əm), *n.* worship of the phallus. Also, **phal′lism.** —**phal′li·cist,** *n.*

phal·lus (făl′əs), *n., pl.* **phalli** (făl′ī). 1. an image of the male reproductive organ, symbolizing in certain religious systems the generative power in nature, esp. that carried in procession in ancient festivals of Dionysus or Bacchus. 2. *Anat.* the penis, clitoris, or the sexually undifferentiated embryonic organ out of which each develops. [t. L, t. Gk.: m. *phallós*]

-phane, a word element indicating apparent similarity to some particular substance. [t. Gk.: m. *phan-,* s. *phaínein* shine, (in pass.) appear]

phan·er·o·gam (făn′ər ə găm′), *n. Bot.* any of the *Phanerogamia,* an old primary division of plants comprising those having reproductive organs (stamens and pistils); a flowering plant or seed plant (opposed to *cryptogam*). [t. NL: s. *phanerogamus,* f. Gk.: *phaneró(s)* visible + m. *gámos* marriage] —**phan·er·o·gam′ic, phan·er·og·a·mous** (făn′ə rŏg′ə məs), *adj.*

phan·tasm (făn′tăzəm), *n.* 1. an apparition or specter. 2. a creation of the imagination or fancy. 3. an illusive likeness of something. 4. *Philos.* a mental image or representation of a real object. 5. *Archaic.* an illusive likeness of something. Also, **fantasm.** [t. LL: m. *phantasma,* t. Gk. Cf. PHANTOM] —**Syn.** 1. See **apparition.**

phan·tas·ma (făn tăz′mə), *n., pl.* **-mata** (-mətə). phantasm.

phan·tas·ma·go·ri·a (făn tăz′mə gôr′ĭ ə), *n.* 1. a shifting series of phantasms, illusions, or deceptive appearances, as in a dream or as created by the imagination. 2. a changing scene made up of many elements. 3. an exhibition of optical illusions produced by a magic lantern or the like, as one in which figures increase or diminish in size, dissolve, pass into each other, etc. [t. NL, f. Gk.: *phántasma* phantasm + (appar.) m. *agorá* assembly] —**phan·tas′ma·go′ri·al, phan·tas·ma·gor·ic** (făn tăz′mə gôr′ĭk, -gŏr′ĭk), *adj.*

phan·tas·ma·go·ry (făn tăz′mə gôr′ĭ), *n., pl.* **-ries.** phantasmagoria.

phan·tas·mal (făn tăz′məl), *adj.* pertaining to or of the nature of a phantasm; unreal; illusive; spectral: *he was surrounded by beings of some weird phantasmal scene.* Also, **phan·tas′mic.**

phan·ta·sy (făn′tə sĭ, -zĭ), *n., pl.* **-sies.** fantasy.

phan·tom (făn′təm), *n.* 1. an image appearing in a dream or formed in the mind. 2. an apparition or specter. 3. a thing or person that is little more than an appearance or show. 4. an appearance without material substance. —*adj.* 5. of the nature of a phantom; unreal; illusive; spectral. Also, **fantom.** [ME *fantosme,* t. OF, var. of *fantasme,* g. LL *phantasma* PHANTASM] —**Syn.** 1. See **apparition.**

-phany, a noun termination meaning "appearance," "manifestation," as of deity or a supernatural being, as in *angelophany, Christophany, epiphany, satanophany.* [t. Gk.: m.s. *-pháneia* (sometimes *-phánia*). See -PHANE]

Phar., 1. pharmaceutical. 2. pharmacopoeia. 3. pharmacy. Also, **phar.**

Phar·aoh (fâr′ō, fâr′ʸ ō′), *n.* a title of the ancient Egyptian kings. [ME *Pharao,* OE *Pharaon,* t. L, t. Gk., t. Heb.: m. *Phar′ōh,* t. Egyptian: m. *per-′o* great house] —**Phar·a·on·ic** (fâr′ʸ ŏn′ĭk), *adj.*

Phar. B., Bachelor of Pharmacy.

Phar. D., Doctor of Pharmacy.

Phar·i·sa·ic (fâr′ə sā′ĭk), *adj.* 1. of or pertaining to the Pharisees. 2. *(l.c.) New Testament.* Also, **phar′i·sa′i·cal.** practicing or advocating strict observance of external forms and ceremonies of religion without regard to its spirit; self-righteous; hypocritical. —**phar′i·sa′i·cal·ly,** *adv.*

Phar·i·sa·ism (fâr′ə sā′ĭz′əm), *n.* 1. the doctrine and practice of the Pharisees. 2. *(l.c.)* rigid observance of external forms of religion without genuine piety; hypocrisy. Also, **Phar·i·see·ism** (fâr′ə sē′ĭz′əm).

Phar·i·see (fâr′ə sē′), *n.* 1. one of an ancient Jewish sect which believed in the validity of the oral law and in the free interpretation of the written law by seeking to discover its inner meaning. 2. *(l.c.)* a pharisaic, self-righteous, or hypocritical person. [ME *pharise,* ME and OE *farisē,* t. L: (m.)s. *pharisēus,* t. Gk.: m. *pharisaíos,* t. Aram.: m. *p'rīshāiyā* separated]

Pharm., 1. pharmaceutic. 2. pharmacopoeia. 3. pharmacy. Also, **pharm.**

phar·ma·ceu·tic (fär′mə sōō′tĭk), *adj.* pertaining to pharmacy. Also, **phar′ma·ceu′ti·cal.** [t. L: s. *pharmaceuticus,* t. Gk.: m. *pharmakeutikós*] —**phar′ma·ceu′ti·cal·ly,** *adv.*

phar·ma·ceu·tics (fär′mə sōō′tĭks), *n.* pharmacy (def. 1). [pl. of PHARMACEUTIC. See -ICS]

b., blend of, blended; c., cognate with; d., dialect, dialectal; der., derived from; f., formed from; g., going back to; m., modification of; r., replacing; s., stem of; t., taken from; ?, perhaps. See the full key on inside cover.

phar·ma·cist (fär′məsĭst), *n.* one skilled in pharmacy; a druggist or pharmaceutical chemist. Also, **phar·ma·ceu·tist** (fär′məsōō′tĭst).

phar·ma·col·o·gy (fär′məkŏl′əjĭ), *n.* the science of drugs, their preparation, uses, and effects. [t. NL: m.s. *pharmacologia*, f. Gk.: m. *phármako(n)* drug + *-logia* -LOGY] —**phar·ma·co·log·i·cal** (fär′məkəlŏj′əkəl), *adj.* —**phar·ma·col′o·gist,** *n.*

phar·ma·co·poe·ia (fär′məkəpē′ə), *n.* **1.** a book, esp. one published by authority, containing a list of drugs and medicines and describing their preparation, properties, uses, etc. **2.** a stock of drugs. [t. NL, t. Gk.: m. *pharmakopoiía* art of preparing drugs] —**phar′-ma·co·poe′ial,** *adj.*

phar·ma·cy (fär′məsĭ), *n., pl.* **-cies. 1.** the art or practice of preparing and dispensing drugs and medicines. **2.** the occupation of a druggist. **3.** a drug store. [t. LL: m.s. *pharmacia*, t. Gk.: m. *pharmakeía* the practice of a druggist; r. ME *fermacie,* t. OF]

Pharm. D., Doctor of Pharmacy.

Pharm. M., Master of Pharmacy.

Pha·ros (fâr′ŏs, fā′rŏs), *n.* **1.** a small peninsula in N Egypt at Alexandria: in ancient times it was an island on which a large lighthouse was built. **2.** this lighthouse. See **Seven Wonders of the World. 3.** any lighthouse or beacon to direct seamen.

Phar·sa·lus (fär·sā′ləs), *n.* an ancient city in central Greece, in Thessaly: site of Pompey's defeat by Caesar, 48 B.C. Modern, **Phar·sa·la** (fär′sä lä′).

pha·ryn·ge·al (fərĭn′jĭ′əl, fär′ĭn jē′əl), *adj.* of, pertaining to, or connected with the pharynx. Also, **pha·ryn·gal** (fərĭng′gəl).

phar·yn·gi·tis (fär′ĭn jĭ′tĭs), *n. Pathol.* inflammation of the mucous membrane of the pharynx. [t. NL: f. s. Gk. *phárynx* throat + -*ītis* -ITIS]

pharyngo-, a word element meaning "pharynx." [t. Gk., comb. form of *phárynx* throat]

phar·yn·gol·o·gy (fär′ĭng gŏl′ə jĭ), *n.* the science of the pharynx and its diseases.

pha·ryn·go·scope (fərĭng′gəskōp′), *n.* an instrument for inspecting the pharynx.

phar·ynx (fär′ĭngks), *n., pl.* **pharynges** (fərĭn′jēz), **pharynxes.** *Anat.* the tube or cavity, with its surrounding membrane and muscles, which connects the mouth and nasal passages with the esophagus. [t. NL, t. Gk.: m. throat]

phase (fāz), *n.* **1.** any of the appearances or aspects in which a thing of varying modes or conditions manifests itself to the eye or mind. **2.** a stage of change or development. **3.** *Astron.* **a.** the particular appearance presented by a planet, etc., at a given time. **b.** one of the recurring appearances or states of the moon or a planet in respect to the form, or the absence, of its illuminated disk: *the phases of the moon.* **4.** *Biol.* an aspect of or stage in meiosis or mitosis. **5.** *Zool.* a color period. **6.** *Chem.* a mechanically separate, homogeneous part of a heterogeneous system: *the solid, liquid, and gaseous phases of a substance.* **7.** *Physics.* a particular stage or point of advancement in a cycle; the fractional part of the period through which the time has advanced, measured from some arbitrary origin. [back formation from *phases,* pl. of PHASIS]

phase modulation, *Electronics.* radio transmission in which the carrier wave is modulated by changing its phase to transmit the amplitude and pitch of the signal.

-phasia, a word element referring to disordered speech, as in *aphasia.* Also, **-phasy.** [t. Gk., der. *phánai* speak]

pha·sis (fā′sĭs), *n., pl.* **-ses** (-sēz). a phase; an appearance; a manner, stage, or aspect of being. [t. L. t. Gk.]

Ph. B., (L *Philosophiae Baccalaureus*) Bachelor of Philosophy.

Ph. C., Pharmaceutical Chemist.

Ph. D., (L *Philosophiae Doctor*) Doctor of Philosophy.

pheas·ant (fĕz′ənt), *n.* **1.** any of various large, long-tailed gallinaceous birds of the genus *Phasianus* and allied genera, orig. natives of Asia, esp. the ring-necked pheasant (*P. colchicus torquatus*). **2.** any of various gallinaceous birds, as, in the southern U.S., the ruffed grouse. [ME *fesant,* t. AF, var. of OF *faisan,* t. Pr., t. L: m.s. *phāsiānus,* t. Gk.: m. *phāsiānós* Phasian (bird)]

Golden pheasant
Chrysolophus pictus
(Total length ab. 3½ ft.)

Phei·dip·pi·des (fīdĭp′ədēz′), *n.* the Athenian runner who secured aid from Sparta in the struggle between the Athenians and the Persians, 490 B.C. Also, **Phidippides.**

phel·lo·derm (fĕl′ədûrm′), *n. Bot.* a layer of tissue in certain plants, formed from the inner cells of phellogen, and consisting usually of chlorenchyma. [f. Gk. *phelló(s)* cork + -DERM] —**phel′lo·der′mal,** *adj.*

phel·lo·gen (fĕl′ə jən), *n. Bot.* cork cambium, a layer of tissue or secondary meristem external to the true cambium and giving rise to cork tissue on the outside and phelloderm on the inside. [f. Gk. *phelló(s)* cork + -GEN] —**phel·lo·ge·net·ic** (fĕl′ə jə nĕt′ĭk) **phel·lo·gen·ic** (fĕl′ə jĕn′ĭk), *adj.*

Phelps (fĕlps), *n.* **William Lyon** (lī′ən), 1865–1943, U.S. educator and literary critic.

phen-, a word element used in chemical terms to indicate derivation from benzene: sometimes used with particular reference to phenol. Also, **pheno-.** [t. Gk.: m. *phaino-* shining; with reference orig. to products from the manufacture of illuminating gas]

phe·na·caine (fē′nəkān′, fĕn′ə-), *n. Pharm.* a local anesthetic, $C_{18}H_{22}N_2O_2HCl$, resembling cocaine in its action, used chiefly for the eye. [f. PHEN- + A(CET)- + (CO)CAINE]

phe·nac·e·tin (fənăs′ətĭn), *n. Pharm.* a crystalline organic compound used as an antipyretic, etc. Also, **phe·nac′e·tine.**

phen·a·cite (fĕn′əsīt′), *n.* a vitreous mineral, beryllium silicate, Be_2SiO_4, occurring in crystals, sometimes used as a gem. [f. m.s. Gk. *phénax* cheat, impostor + -ITE¹]

phe·nan·threne (fənăn′thrēn), *n. Chem.* a colorless shiny crystalline isomer of anthracene, $C_{14}H_{10}$, derived from coal tar, and used in the dye and drug industries. [f. PHEN- + ANTHR(ACITE) + -ENE]

phen·a·zine (fĕn′əzēn′, -zĭn), *n. Chem.* a yellowish crystalline organic compound, $C_{12}H_8N_2$, some derivatives of which are important dyes. Also, **phen·a·zin** (fĕn′ə zĭn). [f. PHEN- + AZ(O)- + -INE²]

phe·net·i·dine (fənĕt′ədēn′, -dĭn), *n. Chem.* a liquid organic compound, $C_8H_{11}NO$, a derivative of phenetole, used in making phenacetin, etc. Also, **phe·net·i·din** (fə nĕt′ə dĭn). [f. PHENET(OL) + -ID² + -INE²]

phen·e·tole (fĕn′ətōl′, -tŏl′), *n. Chem.* the ethyl ether of phenol, $C_6H_5OC_2H_5$, a colorless volatile aromatic liquid. Also, **phen′e·tol′.** [f. PHEN(YL) + ET(HYL) + -OLE]

Phe·ni·cia (fənĭsh′ə), *n.* Phoenicia.

phe·nix (fē′nĭks), *n.* phoenix.

pheno-, var. of **phen-,** before consonants.

phe·no·bar·bi·tal (fē′nō bär′bətăl′, -tŏl′), *n.* a hypnotic, $C_{12}H_{12}O_3N_2$, a white, odorless powder; Luminal.

phe·no·cryst (fē′nəkrĭst, fĕn′ə-), *n. Geol.* any of the conspicuous crystals in a porphyritic rock. [f. PHENO- + CRYST(AL)]

phe·nol (fē′nōl, -nŏl), *n. Chem.* **1.** carbolic acid, C_6H_5OH, a hydroxyl derivative of benzene used as a disinfectant, antiseptic, and in organic synthesis. **2.** any analogous hydroxyl derivative of benzene. [f. PHEN- + -OL¹] —**phe·no·lic** (fē nō′lĭk, -nŏl′ĭk), *adj.*

phe·no·late (fē′nəlāt′), *n. Chem.* a salt of phenol.

phe·nol·o·gy (fĭnŏl′ə jĭ), *n.* the science dealing with the influence of climate on the recurrence of such annual phenomena of animal and plant life as bird migrations, budding, etc. [short for PHENOMENOLOGY] —**phe·no·log·i·cal** (fē′nə lŏj′ə kəl), *adj.* —**phe·nol′o·gist,** *n.*

phe·nol·phthal·ein (fē′nŏl thăl′ēn, -fthăl′Ĭ′ĭn, fē′-nŏl-), *n.* a white crystalline compound, $C_{20}H_{14}O_4$, used as an indicator in acid-base titration and as a laxative.

phe·nom·e·na (fĭ nŏm′ə nə), *n.* pl. of **phenomenon.**

phe·nom·e·nal (fĭ nŏm′ə nəl), *adj.* **1.** extraordinary or prodigious: *phenomenal speed.* **2.** of or pertaining to a phenomenon or phenomena. **3.** of the nature of a phenomenon; cognizable by the senses. —**phe·nom′e·nal·ly,** *adv.*

phe·nom·e·nal·ism (fĭ nŏm′ə nə lĭz′əm), *n. Philos.* **1.** the manner of thinking that considers things as phenomena only. Cf. **positivism. 2.** the philosophical doctrine that phenomena are the only objects of knowledge, or that phenomena are the only realities. —**phe·nom′e·nal·ist,** *n.* —**phe·nom′e·nal·is′tic,** *adj.*

phe·nom·e·nol·o·gy (fĭ nŏm′ə nŏl′ə jĭ), *n. Philos.* **1.** the science of phenomena, as distinguished from ontology or the science of being. **2.** the school of Husserl, which stresses the careful description of phenomena in all domains of experience without regard to traditional epistemological questions.

phe·nom·e·non (fĭ nŏm′ə nŏn′), *n., pl.* **-na** (-nə). **1.** a fact, occurrence, or circumstance observed or observable: *the phenomena of nature.* **2.** something that impresses the observer as extraordinary; a remarkable thing or person. **3.** *Philos.* **a.** an appearance or immediate object of awareness in experience. **b.** (in Kantian philosophy) a thing as it appears to, and is constructed by, us, as distinguished from a noumenon, or thing in itself. [t. LL: m. *phaenomenon,* t. Gk.: m. *phainómenon,* prop. neut. ppr. (that which is) appearing] —**Syn. 2.** prodigy, marvel, wonder.

phe·no·type (fē′nə tīp′), *n. Genetics.* the observable hereditary characters arising from the interaction of the genotype with its environment. Organisms with the same phenotype look alike but may breed differently because of dominance. [f. PHENO(MENON) + TYPE]

phe·nox·ide (fĭ nŏk′sīd), *n. Chem.* phenolate.

phen·yl (fĕn′ĭl, fē′nĭl), *n. Chem.* a univalent radical, C_6H_5, from benzene. [t. F: m. *phényle.* See PHEN, -YL]

phen·yl·ene (fĕn′ə lēn′, fē′nə-), *n. Chem.* a bivalent organic radical, C_6H_4, derived from benzene by removal of two of its hydrogen atoms.

phew (fū, pfū), *interj.* an exclamation of disgust, impatience, exhaustion, surprise, etc.

Ph. G., Graduate in Pharmacy.

phi (fī, fē), *n.* the twenty-first letter (Φ, φ) of the Greek alphabet.

phi·al (fī′əl), *n.* vial (def. 1).

Phi Be·ta Kap·pa (fī′ bā′tə kăp′ə, bē′tə), an honorary collegiate society, membership being based on high scholarship records. It is the oldest American fraternity, founded in 1776.

Phid·i·an (fĭd′ĭən), *adj.* of, associated with, or following the style of Phidias, exemplified in the Parthenon.

Phid·i·as (fĭd′ĭəs), *n.* c500–c432 B.C., Greek sculptor.

Phi·dip·pi·des (fĭdĭp′ədēz′), *n.* Pheidippides.

phil-, a word element meaning "loving," as in *philanthropy.* Also, **philo-.** [t. Gk., comb. form of *phílos* loving, dear]

-phil, var. of **-phile,** as in *eosinophil.*

Phil., 1. Philemon. 2. Philip. 3. Philippians. 4. Philippine.

phil., 1. philosophical. 2. philosophy.

Phila., Philadelphia.

Phil·a·del·phi·a (fĭl′ədĕl′fĭə), *n.* a city in SE Pennsylvania, on the Delaware river; Declaration of Independence, July 4, 1776. 2,002,512 (1960).

Philadelphia lawyer, *U.S. Slang.* a lawyer of outstanding ability in matters involving fine points and technicalities.

Phi·lae (fī′lē), *n.* an island in the Nile, in Upper Egypt: the site of ancient temples; submerged except during months of the sluices of the Aswan dam are open.

phi·lan·der (fĭ lăn′dər), *v.i.* (of a man) to make love, esp. without serious intentions; carry on a flirtation. [t. Gk.: m. s. *philandros* man-loving (person), later used in fiction as proper name, given to a lover] **—phi·lan′·der·er,** *n.*

phil·an·throp·ic (fĭl′ən thrŏp′ĭk), *adj.* of, pertaining to, or characterized by philanthropy; benevolent. Also, **phil′an·throp′i·cal. —phil′an·throp′i·cal·ly,** *adv.*

phi·lan·thro·pist (fĭ lăn′thrə pĭst), *n.* one who practices philanthropy. [t. PHILANTHROP(Y) + -IST]

phi·lan·thro·py (fĭ lăn′thrə pĭ), *n., pl.* **-pies.** 1. love of mankind, esp. as manifested in deeds of practical beneficence. 2. a philanthropic action, work, institution, or the like. [t. LL: m.s. *philanthrōpía,* t. Gk.]

phi·lat·e·ly (fĭ lăt′əlĭ), *n.* the collecting and study of postage stamps, revenue stamps, stamped envelopes, postmarks, post cards, covers and similar material relating to postal history. [t. F: m. *philatélie,* f. *phil-* PHIL- + m. Gk. *atéleia* exemption from charge] **—phil·a·tel·ic** (fĭl′ə tĕl′ĭk), **phil′a·tel′i·cal,** *adj.* **—phil′a·tel′i·cal·ly,** *adv.* **—phi·lat·e·list** (fĭ lăt′ə lĭst), *n.*

-phile, a word element meaning "loving," "friendly," or "lover," "friend," serving to form adjectives and nouns, as *Anglophile, bibliophile, demophile.* Also, **-phil.** [t. L: m.s. *-philus, -phila,* t. Gk.: m. *-phílos* dear, beloved, occurring in proper names. Cf. F *-phile*]

Philem., Philemon.

Phi·le·mon (fĭ lē′mən), *n.* 1. *Gk. Legend.* See **Baucis and Philemon.** 2. the Epistle of Paul to Philemon, a brief New Testament epistle, written by Paul.

phil·har·mon·ic (fĭl′här mŏn′ĭk, fĭl′ər-), *adj.* fond of music; music-loving: used esp. in the name of certain musical societies (**Philharmonic Societies**) and hence applied to their concerts (**philharmonic concerts**). [t. F: m. *philharmonique.* See PHIL-, HARMONIC]

phil·hel·lene (fĭl hĕl′ēn), *n.* a friend or supporter of the Greeks. Also, **phil·hel·len·ist** (fĭl hĕl′ən ĭst, fĭl′hĕ-lē′nĭst). **—phil·hel·len·ic** (fĭl′hĕ lĕn′ĭk, -lē′nĭk), *adj.* **—phil·hel·len·ism** (fĭl hĕl′ən ĭz′əm), *n.*

phil·i·beg (fĭl′ə bĕg′), *n.* filibeg.

Phil·ip (fĭl′ĭp), *n.* 1. one of the twelve apostles, Mark 3:18; John 1:43–48, 6:5–7, etc. 2. one of "the Seven" appointed to oversee the Hellenists in the Jerusalem Church (Acts 6); later an evangelist or missionary (Acts 8:26–40). 3. King, (*Metacom, Metacomet*) died 1676, American Indian chief; leader in a war against the New England colonists, 1675–76 (son of Massasoit). 4. **Prince,** (*Duke of Edinburgh*) born 1921, husband of Queen Elizabeth II of England.

Philip II, 1. 382–336 B.C., king of Macedonia, 359–336 B.C. (father of Alexander the Great). 2. Also, **Philip Augustus.** 1165–1223, King of France, 1180–1223. 3. 1527–98, king of Spain, 1556–98, who sent the Armada against England; husband of Mary I of England.

Philip IV, ("*Philip the Fair*") 1268–1314, king of France, 1285–1314.

Philip V, 1683–1746, king of Spain, 1700–46.

Philip VI, 1293–1350, king of France, 1328–50, the first of the Valois family of French rulers.

Philip., Philippians.

Phi·lippe (fē lēp′), *n.* French name for **Philip.**

Phi·lip·pi (fĭ lĭp′ī), *n.* a ruined city in NE Greece, in Macedonia: Octavian and Mark Antony defeated Brutus and Cassius here, 42 B.C.; the site of one of the first Christian Churches in Europe, founded by St. Paul. **—Phi·lip·pi·an** (fĭ lĭp′ĭ ən), *adj., n.*

Phi·lip·pi·ans (fĭ lĭp′ĭ ənz), *n.* the epistle of the apostle Paul to the Christian community in Philippi, in the New Testament.

Phi·lip·pic (fĭ lĭp′ĭk), *n.* 1. any of the orations delivered by Demosthenes, the Athenian orator, in the 4th century B.C., against Philip, king of Macedon. 2. (*l.c.*) any discourse or speech of bitter denunciation. [t. L: s. *Philippicus,* t. Gk.: m. *Philippikós* pertaining to Philip]

Phil·ip·pine (fĭl′ə pēn′), *adj.* of or pertaining to the Philippine Islands or their inhabitants. Also, **Filipine.** [t. Sp.: m. *Filipino*]

Philippine Islands, an archipelago of 7083 islands

in the Pacific, SE of China: formerly under the guardianship of the U.S.; now an independent republic known as **the Philippines.** 22,265,000 (est. 1956); 114,830 sq. mi. *Cap.:* Manila. (See **Quezon City**). Official name, **Republic of the Philippines.** Formerly (1935–46), **Commonwealth of the Philippines.**

Phi·lip·pop·o·lis (fĭl′ə pŏp′ə lĭs), *n.* Greek name of Plovdiv.

Phil·ips (fĭl′ĭps), *n.* **Ambrose,** 1675?–1749, British poet and dramatist.

Philip the Good, 1396–1467, duke of Burgundy, 1419–67.

Phi·lis·ti·a (fĭ lĭs′tĭ ə), *n.* an ancient country on the E coast of the Mediterranean.

Phi·lis·tine (fĭ lĭs′tĭn, fĭl′ə stēn′, -stĭn′), *n.* 1. a member of a non-Semitic people who settled on the coast of Palestine about 1200 B.C., and with whom the history of Israel is intimately connected. 2. one looked down upon as lacking in and indifferent to culture, esthetic refinement, etc., or contentedly commonplace in ideas and tastes. —*adj.* 3. lacking in culture; commonplace. 4. of or belonging to the ancient Philistines. [ME, t. LL: m.s. *Philistīni,* pl., t. LGk.: m. *Philistīnoi,* t. Heb.: m. p'*lishtīm*] **—Phi·lis·tin·ism** (fĭ lĭs′tĭ nĭz′əm, fĭl′ə stī-), *n.*

Philistia. c950—700 B.C.

Phil·lips (fĭl′ĭps), *n.* 1. **David Graham,** 1867–1911, U.S. novelist. 2. **Stephen,** 1868–1915, British poet and dramatist. 3. **Wendell** (wĕn′dəl), 1811–84, U.S. orator and reformer.

Phil·lips·burg (fĭl′ĭps bûrg′), *n.* a city in NW New Jersey, on the Delaware river. 18,919 (1950).

philo-, var. of **phil-,** before consonants, as in *philosopher.*

Phil·oc·te·tes (fĭl′ŏk tē′tēz), *n. Gk. Legend.* the armor bearer of Hercules, and the archer whose poisoned arrow caused the death of Paris in the Trojan War.

phil·o·den·dron (fĭl′ə dĕn′drən), *n.* a tropical American climbing plant of the family *Araceae,* usually with smooth, shiny, evergreen leaves, often used as an ornamental house plant. [t. NL. See PHILO-, -DENDRON]

phi·log·y·ny (fĭ lŏj′ənĭ), *n.* love of women. [t. Gk.: m.s. *philogynía*] **—phi·log′y·nist,** *n.* **—phi·log′y·nous,** *adj.*

Phi·lo Ju·dae·us (fī′lō jōō dē′əs), c20 B.C.–c50 A.D., Jewish philosopher, influenced by Greek philosophy.

philol., 1. philological. 2. philology.

phil·o·lo·gi·an (fĭl′ə lō′jĭ ən), *n.* a philologist.

phi·lol·o·gy (fĭ lŏl′ə jĭ), *n.* 1. the study of written records, the establishment of their authenticity and their original form, and the determination of their meaning. 2. linguistics. [ME *philologie,* t. L: m. *philologia,* t. Gk.: love of learning and literature] **—phil·o·log·i·cal** (fĭl′ə lŏj′ə kəl), **phil′o·log′ic,** *adj.* **—phi·lol·o·gist,** **phi·lol′o·ger,** *n.*

phil·o·mel (fĭl′ə mĕl′), *n. Poetic.* the nightingale. Also, **phil′o·me·la.** [ME, t. L: s. *philomēla,* t. Gk.]

Phil·o·me·la (fĭl′ə mē′lə), *n.* 1. *Gk. Legend.* the daughter of a king of Athens. Tereus, her sister Procne's husband, raped her and cut out her tongue. Philomela was turned into a nightingale. 2. (*l.c.*) philomel. [cf. PHILOMEL]

phil·o·pe·na (fĭl′ə pē′nə), *n.* 1. a friendly or playful practice by which when two persons have by agreement shared a nut with two kernels, or the like, the person who fails subsequently to meet certain conditions is bound to pay the other a forfeit. 2. the thing shared. 3. the forfeit paid. Also, **fillipeen.** [alter. of G *vielliebchen* sweetheart. Cf. F *philippine*]

phil·o·pro·gen·i·tive (fĭl′ō prō jĕn′ə tĭv), *adj.* fond of young children, esp. one's own.

philos., 1. philosopher. 2. philosophical. 3. philosophy.

phi·los·o·pher (fĭ lŏs′ə fər), *n.* 1. one versed in philosophy. 2. a person who regulates his life, actions, judgments, utterances, etc., by the light of philosophy or reason. 3. one who is philosophic, esp. under trying circumstances. 4. an alchemist or occult scientist. [ME *philosophre,* t. AF; r. OE *philosoph,* t. L: s. *philosophus,* t. Gk.: m. *philósophos* lover of wisdom]

philosophers stone, *Alchemy.* an imaginary substance or preparation believed capable of transmuting baser metals into gold or silver, and of prolonging life.

phil·o·soph·i·cal (fĭl′ə sŏf′ə kəl), *adj.* 1. of or pertaining to philosophy: *philosophical studies.* 2. versed in or occupied with philosophy, as persons. 3. proper to or befitting a philosopher. 4. rationally or sensibly calm under trying circumstances: *a philosophical acceptance of necessity.* 5. (formerly) of or pertaining to natural philosophy or physical science. Also, **phil′o·soph′ic. —phil′o·soph′i·cal·ly,** *adv.*

phi·los·o·phism (fĭ lŏs′ə fĭz′əm), *n.* 1. philosophizing. 2. the affectation of philosophy; spurious philosophy.

phi·los·o·phize (fĭ lŏs′ə fīz′), *v.i.* **-phized, -phizing.** 1. to speculate or theorize; moralize. 2. to think or reason as a philosopher. Also, *esp. Brit.,* **phi·los′o·phise′. —phi·los′o·phiz′er,** *n.*

phi·los·o·phy (fĭ lŏs′ə fĭ), *n., pl.* **-phies.** 1. the study or science of the truths or principles underlying all knowledge and being (or reality). 2. any one of the three branches (natural philosophy, moral philosophy, and metaphysical philosophy) accepted as composing this science. 3. a system of philosophical doctrine: *the philosophy of Spinoza.* 4. metaphysical science;

metaphysics. **5.** the study or science of the principles of a particular branch or subject of knowledge: *the philosophy of history.* **6.** a system of principles for guidance in practical affairs. **7.** philosophical spirit or attitude; wise composure throughout the vicissitudes of life. [ME *philosophie*, t. L: m. *philosophia*, t. Gk.: lit., love of wisdom]

-philous, a word element used as an adjective termination meaning "loving," as in *anthophilous, dendrophilous, heliophilous.* [t. L: m. *-philus,* t. Gk.: m. *-philos*]

phil·ter (fĭl′tər), *n., v.,* **-tered, -tering. —n. 1.** a potion, drug, or the like, supposed to induce love. **2.** a magic potion for any purpose. —*v.t.* **3.** to charm with a philter. [t. F: m. *philtre,* t. L: m. *philtrum,* t. Gk.: m. *philtron* love charm]

phil·tre (fĭl′tər), *n., v.t.,* **-tred, -tring.** *Chiefly Brit.* philter.

phle·bi·tis (flĭ bī′tĭs), *n. Pathol.* inflammation of a vein. [t. NL, f. Gk.: s. *phlĕps* vein + *-ītis*-ITIS]

phleb·o·scle·ro·sis (flĕb′ō sklĭ rō′sĭs), *n. Pathol.* sclerosis or hardening of the walls of veins. [f. *phlebo-* (t. Gk., comb. form of *phlĕps* vein) + SCLEROSIS]

phle·bot·o·mize (flĭ bŏt′ə mīz′), *v.t.,* **-mized, -mizing.** to subject to phlebotomy; bleed.

phle·bot·o·my (flĭ bŏt′ə mĭ), *n., pl.* **-mies.** *Med.* act or practice of opening a vein for letting blood; bleeding. [ME *flebotomie,* t. LL: m. *phlebotomia,* t. Gk.] —**phle-bot′o·mist,** *n.*

Phleg·e·thon (flĕg′ə thŏn′, flĕj′-), *n.* **1.** *Gk. Myth.* a fabled river of fire in Hades. **2.** (*cap.* or *l.c.*) a stream of fire or fiery light. [t. Gk.: lit., burning, blazing]

phlegm (flĕm), *n.* **1.** *Physiol.* the thick mucus secreted in the respiratory passages and discharged by coughing, etc., esp. that occurring in the lungs and throat passages during a cold, etc. **2.** (in the old physiology) that one of the four humors supposed when predominant to cause sluggishness or apathy. **3.** sluggishness or apathy. **4.** coolness or self-possession. [ME *fleume,* t. OF, g. LL *phlegma,* t. Gk.: flame, clammy humor] —**phlegm′y,** *adj.*

phleg·mat·ic (flĕg măt′ĭk), *adj.* **1.** not easily excited to action or feeling; sluggish or apathetic. **2.** cool or self-possessed. **3.** of the nature of or abounding in phlegm. Also, **phleg·mat′i·cal.** [t. LL: s. *phlegmaticus,* t. Gk.: m. *phlegmatikós*] —**phleg·mat′i·cal·ly,** *adv.*

phlo·em (flō′ĕm), *n. Bot.* that part of a vascular bundle not included in the xylem, including sieve tubes and companion cells, parenchyma, secretory cells, etc.; bast tissue. Also, **phlo′ëm.** [t. G, f. Gk.: s. *phlóos* bark + *-ēm*(a) (passive suffix)]

phlo·gis·tic (flō jĭs′tĭk), *adj.* **1.** *Pathol.* inflammatory. **2.** *Old Chem.* pertaining to or consisting of phlogiston.

Portions of phloem, showing oblique and transvers striation of the cell walls

phlo·gis·ton (flō jĭs′tŏn, -tən), *n. Old Chem.* a nonexistent chemical which, previous to the discovery of oxygen, was thought to be released during combustion. [t. NL, t. Gk.: (neut.) inflammable]

phlog·o·pite (flŏg′ə pīt′), *n.* a mica, KMg₃AlSi₃O₁₀- (OH)₂, usually yellowish-brown, but sometimes reddish-brown. [f. s. Gk. *phlogōpós* fiery-looking + -ITE¹]

phlor·i·zin (flôr′ə zĭn, flôr′-, flə rī′zĭn), *n. Chem.* a bitter, crystalline glucoside, C₂₁H₂₄O₁₀, obtained from the root bark of the apple, pear, cherry, etc., and at one time used as a tonic and antiperiodic. [f. s. Gk. *phlóos* bark + m.s. Gk. *rhíza* root + -IN²]

phlox (flŏks), *n. Bot.* **1.** any of the herbs constituting the polemoniaceous genus *Phlox,* native in North America, many of which are cultivated for their showy flowers of various colors. **2.** the flower of these plants. [t. L, t. Gk.: kind of plant, orig., flame]

phlyc·te·na (flĭk tē′nə), *n., pl.* **-nae** (-nē). *Pathol.* a small vesicle, blister, or pustule. Also, **phlyc·tae′na.** [t. NL, t. Gk.: m. *phlýktaina*]

Phnom Penh (nŏm pĕn), Pnom Penh.

-phobe, a word element used as a noun termination meaning "one who fears or dreads," and often implying aversion or hatred, as in *Anglophobe, Russophobe.* [t. F, t. L: m. *-phobus* fearing, t. Gk.: m. *-phobos*]

pho·bi·a (fō′bĭ ə), *n.* any obsessing or morbid fear or dread. [independent use of -PHOBIA] —**pho′bic,** *adj.*

-phobia, a word element used as a noun termination meaning "fear" or "dread," often morbid, or with implication of aversion or hatred, as in *ailurophobia, Anglophobia, hydrophobia, monophobia.* [t. L, t. Gk.]

pho·cine (fō′sīn, -sĭn), *adj.* **1.** of or pertaining to the seals. **2.** belonging to the *Phocinae,* the pinniped subfamily that includes the typical seals. [f. s. L *phŏca* (t. Gk.: m. *phṓkē* seal) + -INE¹]

Pho·ci·on (fō′shĭ ən), *n.* c402–317 B.C., Athenian statesman and general.

Pho·cis (fō′sĭs), *n.* an ancient country in central Greece, N of Gulf of Corinth: site of Delphic oracle.

Phoe·be (fē′bĭ), *n.* **1.** *Gk. Myth.* Artemis (Diana) as goddess of the moon. **2.** *Poetic.* the moon personified. [t. L, t. Gk.: m. *Phoíbē,* prop. fem. of *Phoíbos* PHOEBUS]

phoe·be (fē′bĭ), *n.* any of certain small American flycatchers of the genus *Sayornis,* esp. the familiar phoebe, *S. phoebe,* of eastern North America; pewit; pewee. [imit. of its cry; spelling conformed to PHOEBE]

Phoe·bus (fē′bəs), *n.* **1.** *Gk. Myth.* Apollo as the sun god. **2.** *Poetic.* the sun personified. [ME *Phebus,* t. L: m. *Phoebus,* t. Gk.: m. *Phoîbos,* lit., bright]

Phoe·ni·cia (fĭ nĭsh′ə), *n.* an ancient maritime country on the E coast of the Mediterranean. Also, **Phenicia.**

Phoe·ni·cian (fĭ nĭsh′ən), *n.* **1.** a native or inhabitant of Phoenicia. **2.** the extinct Semitic language of the Phoenicians. —*adj.* **3.** of or pertaining to Phoenicia.

phoe·nix (fē′nĭks), *n.* **1.** Also, **Phoe′nix,** a mythical bird of great beauty, the only one of its kind, fabled to live 500 or 600 years in the Arabian wilderness, to burn itself on a funeral pile, and to rise from its ashes in the freshness of youth and live through another cycle of years (often an emblem of immortality). **2.** a person or thing of peerless beauty or excellence; a paragon. Also, **phenix.** [ME and OE *fēnix,* t. ML: m. *phēnix,* L *phoenix,* t. Gk.: m. *phoînix*]

Phoe·nix (fē′nĭks), *n.* the capital of Arizona, in the central part. 439,170 (1960).

Phoenix Islands, eight coral islands forming part of the British Gilbert and Ellice Islands colony: two of the group are under U.S.-British control. 16 sq. mi.

phon-, a word element meaning "voice," "sound." Also, **phono-.** [t. Gk., comb. form of *phōnē*]

phon., phonetics.

pho·nate (fō′nāt), *v.t., v.i.,* **-nated, -nating.** to produce (sound) by vibration of the vocal bands; vocalize. —**pho·na′tion,** *n.*

phone¹ (fōn), *n., v.t., v.i.,* **phoned, phoning.** *Colloq.* telephone. [short for TELEPHONE]

phone² (fōn), *n. Phonet.* an individual speech sound. [t. Gk. See PHON-]

-phone, a word element meaning "sound," especially used in names of instruments, as in *xylophone, megaphone, telephone.* [comb. form repr. Gk. *phōnē*]

pho·neme (fō′nēm), *n. Phonet.* the smallest distinctive group or class of phones in a language. The phonemes of a language contrast with one another; e.g., in English, *pip* differs from *nip, pin, tip, pit, bib,* etc., and *rumple* from *rumble;* by contrast of a phoneme (p) with other phonemes. In writing, the same symbol can be used for all the phones belonging to one phoneme without causing confusion between words: the (r) consonant phoneme includes the voiceless fricative *r* phone of *tree,* the voiced *r* phone of *red,* etc. [t. Gk.: m. *phṓnēma* a sound]

pho·ne·mic (fō nē′mĭk), *adj.* **1.** of or pertaining to phonemes: *a phonemic system.* **2.** of or pertaining to phonemics; concerning or involving the discrimination of distinctive speech sounds: *a phonemic contrast.*

pho·ne·mics (fō nē′mĭks), *n.* the science of phonemic systems and contrasts. —**pho·ne·mi·cist** (fō nē′mə-sĭst), *n.*

phonet., phonetics.

pho·net·ic (fō nĕt′ĭk), *adj.* **1.** of or pertaining to speech sounds and their production. **2.** agreeing with or corresponding to pronunciation: *phonetic transcription.* Also, **pho·net′i·cal.** [t. NL: s. *phoneticus,* t. Gk.: m. *phōnētikós*] —**pho·net′i·cal·ly,** *adv.*

pho·net·ics (fō nĕt′ĭks), *n.* **1.** the science of speech sounds and their production. **2.** the phonetic system, or the body of phonetic facts, of a particular language. —**pho·ne·ti·cian** (fō′nə tĭsh′ən), *n.*

pho·ne·tist (fō′nə tĭst), *n.* one who uses or advocates phonetic spelling.

Phone·vi·sion (fōn′vĭzh′ən), *n. Trademark.* a system of subscription television in which programs are broadcast in coded form for use only by subscribers.

pho·ney (fō′nĭ), *adj.,* **-nier, -niest,** *n., pl.* **-neys.** *U.S. Slang.* phony.

phon·ic (fŏn′ĭk, fō′nĭk), *adj.* of or pertaining to speech sounds.

phon·ics (fŏn′ĭks, fō′nĭks), *n.* **1.** a method of teaching reading, pronunciation, and spelling based upon the phonetic interpretation of ordinary spelling. **2.** *Obs.* phonetics.

phono-, var. of phon-, before consonants, as in *phonogram.*

pho·no·gram (fō′nə grăm′), *n.* a unit symbol of a phonetic writing system, standing for a speech sound, syllable, or other sequence of speech sounds, without reference to meaning. —**pho′no·gram′ic,** *adj.*

pho·no·graph (fō′nə grăf′, -gräf′), *n.* any sound-reproducing machine using records, whether cylinders or disks. —**pho′no·graph′ic,** *adj.* —**pho′no·graph′i·cal·ly,** *adv.*

pho·nog·ra·phy (fō nŏg′rə fĭ), *n.* **1.** phonetic spelling, writing, or shorthand. **2.** a system of phonetic shorthand invented by Sir Isaac Pitman in 1837.

phonol., phonology.

pho·no·lite (fō′nə līt′), *n.* a fine-grained volcanic rock composed chiefly of alkali feldspar and nepheline, some varieties of which split into pieces which ring on being struck. —**pho·no·lit·ic** (fō′nə lĭt′ĭk), *adj.*

pho·nol·o·gist (fō nŏl′ə gĭst), *n.* a phonetician or phonemicist.

pho·nol·o·gy (fō nŏl′ə jĭ), *n.* **1.** phonetics or phonemics, or both together. **2.** the phonetic and phonemic system, or the body of phonetic and phonemic facts, of a language. —**pho·no·log·ic** (fō′nə lŏj′ĭk), **pho′no·log′i·cal,** *adj.* —**pho′no·log′i·cal·ly,** *adv.*

ăct, āble, dâre, ärt; ĕbb, ēqual; ĭf, īce; hŏt, ōver, ôrder, oil, bŏŏk, ōōze, out; ŭp, ūse, ûrge; ə = a in alone; ch, chief; g, give; ng, ring; sh, shoe; th, thin; t͟h, that; zh, vision. See the full key on inside cover.

pho·no·scope (fō'nəskōp'), *n.* **1.** a device by which sound is indicated by the optical phenomena it is made to produce. **2.** a device for testing the quality of strings for musical instruments.

pho·no·type (fō'nətīp'), *n.* **1.** a type bearing a phonetic character or symbol. **2.** phonetic type or print.

pho·no·typ·y (fō'nətī'pĭ), *n.* a phonetic shorthand developed by Sir Isaac Pitman. —**pho'no·typ'ist,** *n.*

pho·ny (fō'nĭ), *adj.,* **-nier, -niest,** *n., pl.* **-nies.** *U.S. Slang.* —*adj.* **1.** not genuine; spurious, counterfeit, or bogus; fraudulent. —*n.* **2.** a counterfeit or fake. **3.** a faker. Also, **phoney.** [var. of *fawney* ring (used in confidence game), t. Irish: m. *fáinne*]

-phony, a word element used in abstract nouns related to **-phone,** as in *telephony.* [t. Gk.: m.s. *-phōnia*]

-phore, a word element used as a noun termination meaning "bearer," "thing or part bearing (something)," as in *anthophore, gonophore, ommatophore.* [t. NL: m.s. *-phorus,* t. Gk.: m. *-phoros* bearing. Cf. F. *-phore*]

-phorous, a word element used as an adjective termination meaning "bearing," "having," as in *anthophorous.* [t. NL: m. *-phorus,* t. Gk.: m. *-phoros* bearing]

phos·gene (fŏs'jēn), *n. Chem.* carbonyl chloride, $COCl_2$, a poisonous gas used in chemical warfare and in organic synthesis. [f. Gk. *phōs* light + -GENE]

phos·ge·nite (fŏs'jənīt'), *n.* a mineral, lead chlorocarbonate, $Pb_2Cl_2CO_3$, occurring in crystals.

phosph-, var. of **phospho-,** before vowels, as in *phosphate.*

phos·pha·tase (fŏs'fətās'), *n. Biochem.* an enzyme found in body tissues which breaks up compounds made of carbohydrates and phosphates. [f. PHOSPHAT(E) + -ASE]

phos·phate (fŏs'fāt), *n.* **1.** *Chem.* **a.** (loosely) a salt or ester of phosphoric acid. **b.** the tertiary salt of orthophosphoric acid: *sodium phosphate.* **2.** *Agric.* a fertilizing material containing compounds of phosphorus. **3.** a carbonated drink of water and fruit syrup containing a little phosphoric acid. [t. F. See PHOSPH-, -ATE[2]]

phos·phat·ic (fŏsfăt'ĭk), *adj.* pertaining to, of the nature of, or containing phosphates: *phosphatic slag.*

phos·pha·tide (fŏs'fətīd', -tĭd), *n. Biochem.* one of a group of fatty compounds found in cellular organisms made up of phosphoric esters, as lecithin.

phos·pha·tize (fŏs'fətīz'), *v.t.,* **-tized, -tizing.** **1.** to treat with phosphates. **2.** to change to phosphate.

phos·pha·tu·ri·a (fŏs'fətyŏŏr'ĭə, -tōōr'-), *n. Pathol.* the presence of an excessive quantity of phosphates in the urine. [f. s. NL *phōsphātum* phosphate + -URIA] — **phos'pha·tu'ric,** *adj.*

phos·phene (fŏs'fēn), *n. Physiol.* a luminous image produced by mechanical stimulation of the retina, as by pressing the eyeball with the finger when the lid is closed. [t. F, f. Gk.: m. *phōs* light + m.s. *phaínein* show, shine]

phos·phide (fŏs'fīd, -fĭd), *n. Chem.* a compound of phosphorus with a basic element or radical.

phos·phine (fŏs'fēn, -fĭn), *n. Chem.* **1.** a colorless, poisonous, ill-smelling gas, PH_3, which is spontaneously inflammable. **2.** any of certain organic derivatives of this compound.

phos·phite (fŏs'fīt), *n. Chem.* **1.** (loosely) a salt of phosphorous acid. **2.** the tertiary salt of orthophosphorous acid.

phospho-, a word element representing **phosphorus,** as in *phosphoprotein.* Also, **phosph-.**

phos·pho·ni·um (fŏs fō'nĭəm), *n. Chem.* the radical PH_4^{+3}, analogous to ammonium (NH_4^{+2}). [f. PHOSPH-(OROUS) + (AMM)ONIUM]

phos·pho·pro·te·in (fŏs'fō prō'tē ĭn, -tēn), *n. Biochem.* a protein composed of a molecule of protein linked with a substance other than nucleic acid or lecithin and containing phosphorous.

phos·phor (fŏs'fər), *n.* **1.** phosphorus. **2.** a composition of matter which radiates light (usually visible) upon impact of light of a different wave length, usually ultraviolet. [special use of PHOSPHOR]

Phos·phor (fŏs'fər), *n. Poetic.* the morning star; Lucifer. Also, **Phos·phore** (fŏs'fōr). [t. L: s. *Phōsphorus.* See PHOSPHORUS]

phos·pho·rate (fŏs'fərāt'), *v.t.,* **-rated, -rating.** *Chem.* to combine or impregnate with phosphorus.

phos·pho·resce (fŏs'fərĕs'), *v.i.,* **-resced, -rescing.** to be luminous without sensible heat, as phosphorus. [f. PHOSPHOR(US) + -ESCE]

phos·pho·res·cence (fŏs'fərĕs'əns), *n.* **1.** the property of being luminous at temperatures below incandescence, as from slow oxidation, in the case of phosphorus, or after exposure to light or other radiation. **2.** this luminous appearance. **3.** any radiation emitted by a substance after the removal of the exciting agent.

phos·pho·res·cent (fŏs'fərĕs'ənt), *adj.* exhibiting phosphorescence.

phos·phor·et·ed (fŏs'fərĕt'ĭd), *adj.* phosphureted. Also, **phos'phor·et'ted.**

phos·phor·ic (fŏsfôr'ĭk, -fŏr'-), *adj. Chem.* pertaining to or containing the element phosphorus, esp. in its pentavalent state (P^{+5}).

phosphoric acid, any of three acids, orthophosphoric acid, H_3PO_4, metaphosphoric acid, HPO_3, or pyrophosphoric acid, $H_4P_2O_7$, derived from phosphorus pentoxide, P_2O_5, with various amounts of water.

phos·pho·rism (fŏs'fərĭz'əm), *n. Pathol.* condition of chronic phosphorus poisoning.

phos·pho·rite (fŏs'fərīt'), *n.* **1.** a massive form of the mineral apatite: the principal source of phosphate for fertilizers. **2.** any of various compact or earthy, more or less impure varieties of calcium phosphate.

phos·phor·o·scope (fŏsfôr'əskōp', -fŏr'-), *n.* an instrument for measuring the duration of evanescent phosphorescence in different substances. [f. PHOSPHOR-(US) + -(O)SCOPE]

phos·pho·rous (fŏs'fərəs, fŏsfōr'əs), *adj. Chem.* containing trivalent phosphorus (P^{+3}).

phos·pho·rus (fŏs'fərəs), *n., pl.* **-ri** (-rī'). **1.** *Chem.* a solid nonmetallic element existing in at least two allotropic forms, one yellow (poisonous, inflammable, and luminous in the dark), the other red (less poisonous, and less inflammable). *Symbol:* P; *at. wt.:* 30.98; *at. no.:* 15; *sp. gr.:* (yellow) 1.82 at 20°C., (red) 2.20 at 20°C. The element is used in forming smoke screens; its compounds are used in matches and in phosphate fertilizers. It is a necessary constituent in plant and animal life, in bones, nerves, and embryos. **2.** *Now Rare.* any phosphorescent substance. **3.** (*cap.*) Phosphor. [t. NL, special use of L *Phosphorus,* the morning star, t. Gk.: m. *Phōsphóros,* lit., lightbringer]

phosphorus-32, *Chem.* a radioactive isotope of phosphorus, used as a chemotherapeutic agent.

phos·phor·y·lase (fŏsfôr'əlās', -fŏr'-), *n.* an enzyme which breaks up carbohydrates and phosphoric acid, as in muscle contraction.

phos·phu·ret·ed (fŏs'fyərĕt'ĭd), *adj. Chem.* combined with phosphorus, esp. in its lowest valence state. Also, **phos'phu·ret'ted, phosphoreted, phosphoretted.** [f. *phosphuret* phosphide (t. NL: m.s. *phosphorētum,* with -u- from *phosphure*) + -ED[3]]

phot (fŏt, fōt), *n. Physics.* a unit of illumination, equal to 1 lumen per sq. cm. [t. Gk.: s. *phōs* light]

pho·tic (fō'tĭk), *adj.* **1.** of or pertaining to light. **2.** pertaining to the generation of light by organisms, or their excitation by means of light.

pho·to (fō'tō), *n., pl.* **-tos.** *Colloq.* photograph.

photo-, a word element meaning "light" (sometimes used to represent "photographic" or "photograph"). [t. Gk., comb. form of *phōs* light]

pho·to·ac·tin·ic (fō'tōăktĭn'ĭk), *adj.* emitting radiation having the chemical effects of light and ultraviolet rays, as on a photographic film.

pho·to·bath·ic (fō'təbăth'ĭk). *adj.* in or relating to the stratum of ocean depth penetrated by sunlight.

pho·to·cell (fō'təsĕl'), *n.* a phototube.

pho·to·chem·is·try (fō'təkĕm'ĭstrĭ), *n.* the branch of chemistry that deals with the chemical action of light. —**pho·to·chem·i·cal** (fō'təkĕm'əkəl), *adj.*

pho·to·chro·my (fō'təkrō'mĭ), *n.* the art of producing photographs showing objects in natural colors.

pho·to·chron·o·graph (fō'təkrŏn'əgrăf', -gräf'), *n.* **1.** a device for taking instantaneous photographs at regular and generally short intervals of time, as of a bird, a horse, a projectile, etc., in motion. **2.** a picture taken by such a device. **3.** a chronograph in which the tracing or record is made by a pencil of light on a sensitized surface. **4.** an instrument for measuring small intervals of time by the photographic trace of a pencil of light.

pho·to·dra·ma (fō'tədrä'mə, -drăm'ə), *n.* a photoplay.

pho·to·dy·nam·ics (fō'tədīnăm'ĭks, -dĭ-), *n.* the science dealing with light in its relation to movement in plants.

pho·to·e·lec·tric (fō'tōĭlĕk'trĭk), *adj.* pertaining to the electronic or other electrical effects produced by light. Also, **pho'to·e·lec'tri·cal.**

photoelectric cell, *Electronics.* **1.** a device incorporated in an electric circuit to make the resistance or electromotive force of part of the circuit variable in accordance with variations in the intensity of light or similar radiation falling upon it, and so to make operations controlled by the circuit dependent on variations in illumination, in a beam of radiation, etc. **2.** a phototube.

photoelectric meter, *Photog.* an exposure meter using a photoelectric cell for the measurement of light intensity.

pho·to·e·lec·tro·type (fō'tōĭlĕk'trətīp'), *n.* an electrotype made by the aid of photography.

pho·to·en·grave (fō'tōĕngrāv'), *v.t.,* **-graved, -graving.** to make a photoengraving of. —**pho'to·en·grav'er,** *n.*

pho·to·en·grav·ing (fō'tōĕngrā'vĭng), *n.* **1.** a process of preparing printing plates for letterpress printing. **2.** a process of photographic reproduction by which a relief-printing surface is obtained for letterpress printing. **3.** a plate so produced. **4.** a print made from it.

photo finish, *Racing.* a close race in which the decision is made from a photograph of the contestants as they crossed the finish line.

pho·to·flash lamp (fō'təflăsh'), *Photog.* a flash bulb.

pho·to·flood lamp (fō'təflŭd'). *Photog.* an incandescent tungsten lamp, in which high intensity is obtained by overloading the voltage.

---

photog., 1. photographic. **2.** photography.

pho·to·gene (fō′tə jēn′), *n.* an afterimage on the retina.

pho·to·gen·ic (fō′tə jĕn′ĭk), *adj.* **1.** *Photog.* (of a person) suitable for being photographed for artistic purposes, etc. **2.** *Biol.* producing or emitting light as certain bacteria; luminiferous; phosphorescent. **3.** *Rare.* produced by light. —**pho′to·gen′i·cal·ly,** *adv.*

pho·to·gram·me·try (fō′tə grăm′ə trĭ), *n.* the process of making surveys and maps utilizing photographs. [f. PHOTO- + -GRAM (for -GRAPH) + -METRY]

pho·to·graph (fō′tə grăf′, -gräf′), *n.* **1.** a picture produced by photography. —*v.t.* **2.** to take a photograph of. —*v.i.* **3.** to practice photography.

pho·tog·ra·pher (fə tŏg′rə fər), *n.* one who takes photographs or practices photography.

pho·to·graph·ic (fō′tə grăf′ĭk), *adj.* **1.** of or pertaining to photography. **2.** used in or produced by photography. **3.** suggestive of a photograph; extremely realistic and detailed: *photographic accuracy.* **4.** mechanically imitative, with lack of artistic feeling. Also, **pho′to·graph′i·cal.** —**pho′to·graph′i·cal·ly,** *adv.*

pho·tog·ra·phy (fə tŏg′rə fĭ), *n.* the process or art of producing images of objects on sensitized surfaces by the chemical action of light or of other forms of radiant energy, as x-rays, gamma rays, cosmic rays, etc.

pho·to·gra·vure (fō′tə grə vyŏor′, fō′tə grā′vyər), *n.* **1.** any of various processes, based on photography, by which an intaglio engraving is formed on a metal plate, from which ink reproductions are made. **2.** the plate. **3.** a print made from it. [t. F: f. *photo-* PHOTO- + *gravure* engraving]

pho·to·ki·ne·sis (fō′tə kĭ nē′sĭs, -kī-), *n.* *Physiol.* movement occurring upon exposure to light. —**pho·to·ki·net·ic** (fō′tə kĭ nĕt′ĭk, -kī-), *adj.*

pho·to·lith·o·graph (fō′tə lĭth′ə grăf′, -gräf′), *n.* **1.** a lithograph printed from a stone, etc., upon which a picture or design has been formed by photography. —*v.t.* **2.** to make a photolithograph of.

pho·to·li·thog·ra·phy (fō′tə lĭ thŏg′rə fĭ), *n.* the technique or art of making photolithographs. —**pho·to·lith·o·graph·ic** (fō′tə lĭth′ə grăf′ĭk), *adj.*

pho·tol·y·sis (fō tŏl′ə sĭs), *n.* the breakdown of materials under the influence of light. [t. NL, f. Gk.: *phōto-* PHOTO- + *lýsis* a loosing] —**pho·to·lyt·ic** (fō′təlĭt′ĭk), *adj.*

photom., photometry.

pho·to·me·chan·i·cal (fō′tō mə kăn′ə kəl), *adj.* noting or pertaining to any of various processes for printing in ink from plates or surfaces prepared by the aid of photography. —**pho′to·me·chan′i·cal·ly,** *adv.*

pho·tom·e·ter (fō tŏm′ə tər), *n.* an instrument for measuring the intensity of light or the relative illuminating power of different lights.

pho·tom·e·try (fō tŏm′ə trĭ), *n.* **1.** the measurement of the intensity of light or of relative illuminating power. **2.** the science dealing with this. —**pho·to·met·ric** (fō′tə mĕt′rĭk), **pho′to·met′ri·cal,** *adj.* —**pho·tom′e·trist,** *n.*

pho·to·mi·cro·graph (fō′tə mī′krə grăf′, -grăf′), *n.* **1.** a photograph of a microscopic object, taken through a microscope. **2.** a microphotograph. —**pho·to·mi·crog·ra·phy** (fō′tə mī krŏg′rə fĭ), *n.*

pho·to·mon·tage (fō′tə mŏn täzh′, -môn-), *n.* *Photog.* a combination of several photographs joined together for artistic effect or to show more of the subject than can be disclosed in a single photograph.

pho·to·mu·ral (fō′tə myŏŏr′əl), *n.* a very large photograph covering most of a wall as decoration.

pho·ton (fō′tŏn), *n.* *Physics.* a quantum of light energy, the energy being proportional to the frequency of the radiation. [der. PHOTO-; modeled on ELECTRON, PROTON]

pho·to·off·set (fō′tō ôf′sĕt′, -ŏf′-), *n.* *Print.* a method of printing similar to offset lithography (see **offset** def. 13), in which the text or designs are impressed on metal plates by photography.

pho·toph·i·lous (fō tŏf′ə ləs), *adj.* thriving in strong light, as a plant.

pho·to·pho·bi·a (fō′tə fō′bĭ ə), *n.* *Pathol.* a morbid dread or intolerance of light, as in iritis. [t. NL. See PHOTO-, -PHOBIA]

pho·to·play (fō′tə plā′), *n.* a play presented, or arranged to be presented, in moving pictures.

pho·to·sen·si·tive (fō′tə sĕn′sə tĭv), *adj.* sensitive to light or similar radiation.

pho·to·spec·tro·scope (fō′tə spĕk′trə skōp′), *n.* a spectrograph (def. 2).

pho·to·sphere (fō′tə sfĭr′), *n.* **1.** a sphere of light. **2.** *Astron.* the luminous envelope of gas surrounding the sun. —**pho·to·spher·ic** (fō′tə sfĕr′ĭk), *adj.*

pho·to·stat (fō′tə stăt′), *n.* **1.** (*cap.*) a special camera for making facsimile copies of maps, drawings, pages of books or manuscripts, etc., which photographs directly as a positive on sensitized paper. **2.** a copy or photograph made with it. —*v.t., v.i.* **3.** to make a photostatic copy or copies (of). —**pho′to·stat′ic,** *adj.*

pho·to·syn·the·sis (fō′tə sĭn′thə sĭs), *n.* *Bot., Biochem.* the synthesis of complex organic materials by plants from carbon dioxide, water, and inorganic salts using sunlight as the source of energy and with the aid of a catalyst such as chlorophyll; commonly used in the more restricted sense of the synthesis of carbohydrates. [t. NL: See PHOTO-, SYNTHESIS] —**pho·to·syn·thet·ic** (fō′tə sĭn thĕt′ĭk), *adj.*

pho·to·tax·is (fō′tə tăk′sĭs), *n.* *Biol.* a movement of an organism toward or away from a source of light. Also, **pho′to·tax′y.** [t. NL. See PHOTO-, -TAXIS]

pho·to·te·leg·ra·phy (fō′tō tə lĕg′rə fĭ), *n.* the electric transmission of facsimiles of photographs, etc.; telephotography. —**pho·to·tel·e·graph·ic** (fō′tə tĕl′ə grăf′ĭk), *adj.*

pho·to·ther·a·peu·tics (fō′tə thĕr′ə pū′tĭks), *n.* that branch of therapeutics which deals with the curative use of light rays. —**pho′to·ther′a·peu′tic,** *adj.*

pho·to·ther·a·py (fō′tə thĕr′ə pĭ), *n.* treatment of disease by means of light rays.

pho·to·ther·mic (fō′tə thûr′mĭk), *adj.* **1.** pertaining to the thermal effects of light. **2.** pertaining to or involving both light and heat.

pho·tot·o·nus (fō tŏt′ə nəs), *n.* *Biol.* **1.** the normal condition of sensitiveness to light in leaves, etc. **2.** the irritability exhibited by protoplasm when exposed to light of a certain intensity. [t. NL, f. Gk.: *phōto-* PHOTO- + m. *tónos* tension] —**pho·to·ton·ic** (fō′tə tŏn′ĭk), *adj.*

pho·to·trop·ic (fō′tə trŏp′ĭk), *adj.* *Bot.* **1.** taking a particular direction under the influence of light. **2.** growing toward or away from the light. —**pho·to·trop′i·cal·ly,** *adv.*

pho·tot·ro·pism (fō tŏt′rə pĭz′əm), *n.* *Bot.* phototropic tendency or growth.

pho·to·tube (fō′tə tūb′, -tōōb′), *n.* *Electronics.* a two-element tube in which light falling on the light-sensitive cathode causes electrons to be emitted, the electrons being collected by the plate.

pho·to·type (fō′tə tīp′), *n.* **1.** a plate with a (relief) printing surface produced by photography. **2.** any process for making such a plate. **3.** a print made from it.

pho·to·ty·pog·ra·phy (fō′tō tī pŏg′rə fĭ), *n.* the art of making printing surfaces by light or photography, by any of a large number of processes.

pho·to·typ·y (fō′tə tī′pĭ, fō tŏt′ə pĭ), *n.* the art or process of producing phototypes.

pho·to·vol·ta·ic (fō′tō vŏl tā′ĭk), *adj.* providing a source of electric current under the influence of light or similar radiation.

pho·to·zin·cog·ra·phy (fō′tō zĭng kŏg′rə fĭ), *n.* a type of photoengraving using a sensitized zinc plate.

phr., phrase.

phras·al (frā′zal), *adj.* of the nature of, or consisting of, a phrase.

phrase (frāz), *n., v.,* **phrased, phrasing.** —*n.* **1.** *Gram.* **a.** a sequence of two or more words arranged in a grammatical construction and acting as a unit in the sentence. **b.** (in English) such a sequence which is smaller than a clause, e.g., consisting of preposition plus noun or pronoun, adjective plus noun, adverb plus verb, etc. (but not usually of noun plus verb). **2.** *Speech.* a word or group of spoken words which the mind focuses on momentarily as a meaningful unit and which is preceded and followed by pauses. **3.** way of speaking, mode of expression, or phraseology. **4.** a characteristic, current, or proverbial expression. **5.** a brief utterance or remark. **6.** *Music.* a division of a composition, commonly a passage of four or eight measures, forming part of a period. **7.** *Dance.* a sequence of motions making up a choreographic pattern. —*v.t.* **8.** to express or word in a particular way. **9.** to express in words. **10.** *Music.* **a.** to mark off or bring out the phrases of (a piece), esp. in execution. **b.** to group (notes) into a phrase. [back formation from *phrases,* pl. of LL *phrasis,* t. Gk.: speech, phraseology, expression]

phra·se·o·gram (frā′zĭ ə grăm′), *n.* a written symbol, as in shorthand, representing a phrase. [f. PHRASEO- (LOGY) + -GRAM]

phra·se·o·graph (frā′zĭ ə grăf′, -grăf′), *n.* a phrase for which there is a phraseogram.

phra·se·ol·o·gist (frā′zĭ ŏl′ə jĭst), *n.* **1.** one who treats of phraseology. **2.** one who affects a particular phraseology.

phra·se·ol·o·gy (frā′zĭ ŏl′ə jĭ), *n.* **1.** manner or style of verbal expression; characteristic language: *the phraseology of lawyers.* **2.** phrases or expressions: *medical phraseology.* [t. NL:m.s. *phraseologia,* t. Gk.] —**phra·se·o·log·i·cal** (frā′zĭ ə lŏj′ə kəl), *adj.* —Syn. 1. See **diction.**

phra·try (frā′trĭ), *n., pl.* **-tries. 1.** a grouping of clans or other social units within a tribe. **2.** (in ancient Greece) a subdivision of a phyle. [t. Gk.: m. *phratría*]

phren., 1. phrenological. **2.** phrenology.

phre·net·ic (frĭ nĕt′ĭk), *adj.* **1.** delirious; insane; frenetic. **2.** filled with extreme emotion, esp. in religious matters. **3.** a phrenetic individual. [ME *frenetike,* t. OF, t. L: m. *phrenēticus,* t. LGk.: m. *phrenētikós*] —**phre·net′i·cal·ly,** *adv.*

phren·ic (frĕn′ĭk), *adj.* **1.** *Anat.* of or pertaining to the diaphragm. **2.** *Physiol.* relating to the mind or mental activity. [t. NL: s. *phrenicus,* f. s. Gk. *phrēn* diaphragm, mind + -*icus* -IC]

phrenol., 1. phrenological. **2.** phrenology.

phre·nol·o·gy (frĕ nŏl′ə jĭ), *n.* the theory that one's mental powers are indicated by the shape of the skull. [f. *phreno-* (comb. form repr. Gk. *phrēn* mind) + -LOGY] —**phren·o·log·ic** (frĕn′ə lŏj′ĭk), **phren·o·log′i·cal,** *adj.* —**phre·nol′o·gist,** *n.*

phren·sy (frĕn′zĭ), *n.*, *pl.* **-sies**, *v.t.*, **-sied**, **-sying**. frenzy.

Phryg·i·a (frĭj′ĭ ə), *n.* an ancient country in central and NW Asia Minor. —**Phryg′i·an**, *adj.*, *n.*

PHS., Public Health Service.

phthal·ein (thăl′ēn, -ĭn, fthăl′-), *n.* *Chem.* any of a group of compounds (certain of whose derivatives are important dyes) formed by treating phthalic anhydride with phenols. [f. (NA)PHTHALE(NE) + -IN²]

phthal·ic (thăl′ĭk, fthăl′-), *adj.* *Chem.* 1. noting or pertaining to any of three isomeric acids, $C_6H_4(COOH)_2$, derived from benzene, esp. one which is prepared by oxidizing naphthalene, which forms an anhydride. 2. noting this anhydride. [f. (NA)PHTHAL(ENE) + -IC]

phthal·in (thăl′ĭn, fthăl′-), *n.* *Chem.* any of a group of compounds obtained by reduction of the phthaleins.

phthi·o·col (thī′ə kŏl′, -kŏl′), *n.* *Biochem.* a yellow pigment, the vitamin K properties of which counteract hemorrhage.

phthis·ic (tĭz′ĭk), *n.* *Pathol.* a wasting disease of the lungs; phthisis. [ME *tisike*, t. OF, t. L: m. *phthisica*, fem. of *phthisicus*, t. Gk.: m. *phthisikós* consumptive]

phthis·i·cal (tĭz′ə kəl), *adj.* pertaining to, of the nature of, or affected by phthisis. Also, **phthis′ick·y**.

phthi·sis (thī′sĭs, fthī′-), *n.* *Pathol.* 1. a wasting away. 2. tuberculosis of the lungs; consumption. [t. L, t. Gk.]

-phyceae, a combining form used in names of algae. [NL, der. Gk. *phýkos* seaweed]

phy·col·o·gy (fī kŏl′ə jĭ), *n.* the branch of botany that deals with algae. [f. m. Gk. *phýko(s)* seaweed + -LOGY] —**phy·col′o·gist**, *n.*

phy·co·my·ce·tous (fī′kō mī sē′təs), *adj.* *Bot.* belonging or pertaining to the Phycomycetes, the lowest of the three primary subdivisions of the fungi, whose members more closely resemble algae than do the higher fungi. [f. s. NL *Phycomycētes*, pl., (f. Gk.: *phýko(s)* seaweed + pl. of *mýkēs* fungus) + -ous]

Phyfe (fīf), *n.* **Duncan** (dŭng′kən), 1768–1854, U.S. furniture maker.

-phyl, a word element used as a noun termination meaning "leaf," as in *chlorophyl*, *cladophyl*, *lithophyl*. Also, **-phyll**. [t. Gk.: m.s. *phýllon*]

phy·lac·ter·y (fə lăk′tə rĭ), *n.*, *pl.* **-teries**. 1. either of two small leather cases containing slips inscribed with certain texts from the Pentateuch, worn by Jews, one on the head and one on the left arm, during prayer to remind them to keep the law. Deut. 6:8, 11:18. 2. (in early Christianity) a receptacle containing a holy relic. 3. a reminder. 4. an amulet, charm, or safeguard. [t. LL: m.s. *phylactērium*, t. Gk.: m. *phylaktḗrion* outpost, safeguard, amulet; r. ME *philaterie*, t. OF]

phy·le (fī′lē), *n.*, *pl.* **-lae** (-lē). (in ancient Greece) a tribe or clan, based on supposed kinship. [t. NL, t. Gk.]

phy·let·ic (fī lĕt′ĭk), *adj.* *Biol.* pertaining to race or species; phylogenic; racial. [t. Gk.: m.s. *phyletikós*]

-phyll, var. of -phyl.

Phyl·lis (fĭl′ĭs), *n.* a name, orig. in pastoral literature, for a country girl or a sweetheart.

phyl·lite (fĭl′īt), *n.* a slaty rock with lustrous cleavage planes due to minute scales of mica. [f. PHYLL(O)- + -ITE¹]

phyllo-, a word element meaning "leaf." Also, before vowels, **phyll-**. [t. Gk., combining form of *phýllon*]

phyl·lo·clade (fĭl′ə klād′), *n.* *Bot.* 1. a flattened stem or branch having the function of a leaf. 2. cladophyll. [f. PHYLLO- + m.s. Gk. *kládos* branch]

phyl·lode (fĭl′ōd), *n.* *Bot.* an expanded petiole resembling, and having the function of, a leaf. [t. F, t. NL: m.s. *phyllōdium*, t. Gk.: m. *phyllṓdēs* leaflike. See -ODE¹]

phyl·loid (fĭl′oid), *adj.* leaflike.

phyl·lome (fĭl′ōm), *n.* *Bot.* 1. a leaf of a plant. 2. a structure corresponding to it. [t. NL: m. *phyllṓma*, t. Gk.] —**phyl′lom·ic** (fī lŏm′ĭk, -lō′mĭk), *adj.*

phyl·lo·pod (fĭl′ə pŏd′), *n.* 1. any of the Phyllopoda, an order of crustaceans characterized by leaflike swimming appendages. —*adj.* 2. pertaining to the phyllopods. 3. belonging to the Phyllopoda. Also, **phyl·lop·o·dan** (fī lŏp′ədən). [t. NL: s. *Phyllopoda*, pl. See PHYLLO-, -POD]

phyl·lo·tax·is (fĭl′ə tăk′sĭs), *n.* *Bot.* 1. the arrangement of leaves on a stem or axis. 2. the principles governing such arrangement. Also **phyl′lo·tax′y**. [t. NL. See PHYLLO-, -TAXIS]

-phyllous, a word element used as an adjective termination meaning "having leaves," "leaved," or implying some connection with a leaf, as in *diphyllous*, *epiphyllous*, *monophyllous*, *polyphyllous*. [t. Gk.: m. *-phyllos* pertaining to a leaf]

phyl·lox·e·ra (fĭl′ək sîr′ə, fĭ lŏk′sərə), *n.*, *pl.* **phylloxerae** (fĭl′ək sîr′ē, fĭ lŏk′sə rē′). any of the plant lice constituting the genus *Phylloxera*, esp. *P. vastatrix*, very destructive to European grape vines. [t. NL, f. Gk.: *phyllo-* PHYLLO- + m. *xērós* dry]

phylo-, a word element meaning "tribe." [t. Gk., comb. form of *phýlon* race, tribe]

phy·log·e·ny (fī lŏj′ə nĭ), *n.*, *pl.* **-nies**. *Biol.* the development or evolution of a kind or type of animal or plant; racial history. Cf. *ontogeny*. Also, **phy·lo·gen·e·sis** (fī′lə jĕn′ə sĭs). —**phy·lo·ge·net·ic** (fī′lə jə nĕt′ĭk), **phy′lo·gen′ic**, *adj.* —**phy′lo·ge·net′i·cal·ly**, *adv.*

phy·lum (fī′ləm), *n.*, *pl.* **-la** (-lə). 1. *Biol.* a primary division of the animal or vegetable kingdom: e.g., the *arthropods*, the *mollusks*, the *spermatophytes*. 2. (in the classification of languages) a group of linguistic stocks or families having no known congeners outside the group. [t. NL, t. Gk.: m. *phýlon* race, tribe, akin to *phylé*. See PHYLE]

-phyre, a word element used to form names of porphyritic rocks, as in *granophyre*. [t. Gk.: m. *-phyr*, for *porphyr* porphyry]

phys., 1. physical. 2. physician. 3. physics. 4. physiological. 5. physiology.

phys. chem., physical chemistry.

phys. geog., physical geography.

phys·ic (fĭz′ĭk), *n.*, *v.*, **-icked**, **-icking**. —*n.* 1. a medicine that purges; a cathartic. 2. any medicine; a drug or medicament. 3. *Archaic.* the medical art or profession. 4. *Obs.* natural science. —*v.t.* 5. to treat with physic or medicine. 6. to treat with or to act upon as, a cathartic; purge. 7. to work upon as a medicine does; relieve or cure. [ME *fisyke*, t. L: m. *physica* natural (ML medical) science, t. Gk.: m. *physikḗ* science of nature, prop. fem. adj., pertaining to nature]

phys·i·cal (fĭz′ə kəl), *adj.* 1. pertaining to the body; bodily: *physical exercise*. 2. of or pertaining to material nature; material. 3. denoting or pertaining to the properties of matter and energy other than those that are chemical or peculiar to living matter; pertaining to physics. 4. denoting or pertaining to the properties of matter and energy other than those peculiar to living matter; pertaining to physical science. [ME, t. ML: s. *physicālis*, der. *physica* PHYSIC] —**phys′i·cal·ly**, *adv.* —**Syn.** 1. PHYSICAL, BODILY, CORPOREAL, CORPORAL agree in pertaining to the body. PHYSICAL indicates connected with, pertaining to, the animal or human body as a material organism: *physical strength, exercise of an animal or man*. BODILY means belonging to, concerned with, the human body as distinct from the mind or spirit: *bodily pain or suffering*. CORPOREAL, a more poetic and philosophical word than BODILY, refers esp. to the mortal substance of which the human body is composed as opposed to spirit: *this corporeal habitation* CORPORAL is now usually reserved for reference to whippings, etc., inflicted on the human body: *corporal punishment*.

physical anthropology, the science concerned with: 1. evolutionary changes in man's bodily structure and the classification of modern races, in which mensurational and descriptive techniques are employed. 2. physical growth from infancy to adulthood.

physical chemistry, that branch of chemistry which deals with the relations between the physical (i.e. electrical, optical, etc.) properties of substances and their chemical composition and transformations.

physical education, gymnastic and hygienic instruction and allied subjects as a division of instruction.

physical geography, that part of geography concerned with natural features and phenomena of the earth's surface, as land forms, drainage features, climates, ocean currents, soils, vegetation, and animal life.

physical science, the study of natural laws and processes other than those peculiar to living matter, as in physics, chemistry, astronomy, etc.

physical therapy, physiotherapy.

phy·si·cian (fə zĭsh′ən), *n.* 1. one legally qualified to practice medicine. 2. one engaged in general medical practice as distinguished from one specializing in surgery. 3. one who is skilled in the art of healing. [ME *fisicien*, t. OF, der. ML *physica* PHYSIC. See -IAN]

phys·i·cist (fĭz′ə sĭst), *n.* a person versed in physics and its methods.

phys·ics (fĭz′ĭks), *n.* the science dealing with natural laws and processes, and the states and properties of matter and energy, other than those restricted to living matter and to chemical changes. [pl. of PHYSIC. See -ICS]

physio-, a word element representing physical, physics. [t. Gk., comb. form of *phýsis* nature]

phys·i·o·crat (fĭz′ĭ ə krăt′), *n.* one of a school of political economists, followers of Quesnay, who recognized an inherent natural order as properly governing society, regarded land as the basis of wealth and taxation, and advocated freedom of industry and trade. [t. F: m. *physiocrate*. See PHYSIO-, -CRAT] —**phys·i·o·crat′ic**, *adj.*

phys·i·og·no·my (fĭz′ĭ ŏg′nə mĭ, -ŏn′ə mĭ), *n.*, *pl.* **-mies**. 1. the face or countenance, esp. as considered as an index to the character. 2. the art of determining character or personal characteristics from the features of the face or the form of the body. 3. the general or characteristic appearance of anything. [t. Gk.: m.s. *physiognōmonia* the judging of one's nature; r. ME *fisonomie*, t. ML: m. *phisonomia*] —**phys·i·og·nom·ic** (fĭz′ĭ ŏg nŏm′ĭk, fĭz′ĭ ə nŏm′ĭk), **phys′i·og·nom′i·cal**, *adj.* —**phys′i·og·nom′i·cal·ly**, *adv.* —**phys′i·og′no·mist**, *n.*

phys·i·og·ra·phy (fĭz′ĭ ŏg′rə fĭ), *n.* 1. physical geography. 2. U.S. geomorphology. 3. the systematic description of nature in general. —**phys′i·og′ra·pher**, *n.* —**phys·i·o·graph·ic** (fĭz′ĭ ə grăf′ĭk), **phys′i·o·graph′i·cal**, *adj.*

physiol., 1. physiological. 2. physiologist. 3. physiology.

phys·i·o·log·i·cal (fĭz′ĭ ə lŏj′ə kəl), *adj.* *Physiol.* 1. of or relating to physiology. 2. consistent with the normal functioning of an organism. Also, **phys′i·o·log′ic.** —**phys′i·o·log′i·cal·ly**, *adv.*

phys·i·ol·o·gy (fĭz′ĭ·ŏl′ə·jĭ), *n.* the science dealing with the functions of living organisms or their parts. [t. L: m.s. *physiologia*, t. Gk.] —**phys′i·ol′o·gist,** *n.*

phys·i·o·ther·a·py (fĭz′ĭ·ō·thĕr′ə·pĭ), *n.* the treatment of disease or bodily weaknesses or defects by physical remedies, such as massage, gymnastics, etc. (rather than by drugs).

phy·sique (fĭ·zēk′), *n.* physical or bodily structure, organization, or development. [t. F, prop. adj., physical, t. L: m.s. *physicus*, t. Gk.: m. *physikós*]

phy·so·clis·tous (fĭ′sō·klĭs′təs), *adj.* Ichthyol. having the air bladder closed off from the mouth. [f. s. NL *Physóclistī*, genus name (f. *physō-* (comb. form repr. Gk. *phýsa* bladder) + m. Gk. *kleistoī* (pl.) shut) + -ous]

phy·so·stig·mine (fĭ′sō·stĭg′mēn, -mĭn), *n.* Chem. a poisonous alkaloid, C15H21N3O2, constituting the active principle of the Calabar bean, used in medicine as a myotic, etc. Also, **phy·so·stig·min** (fĭ′sō·stĭg′mĭn). [f. m. NL *Phýsostigma* (f. Gk.: m. *phýsa* bellows + *stígma* stigma) + -INE²]

phy·sos·to·mous (fĭ·sŏs′tə·məs), *adj.* Ichthyol. having the mouth and air bladder connected by an air duct. [f. s. NL *Phýsostomī*, a genus name (f. Gk.: m. *phýsa* bellows + m. *-stomos* mouthed) + -ous]

-phyte, a word element used as a noun termination meaning "a growth," "plant," as in *epiphyte, halophyte, lithophyte, osteophyte.* [comb. form repr. Gk. *phytón*]

phy·tin (fī′tĭn), *n.* an organic compound containing phosphorus, occurring in seeds, tubers, and rhizomes as a reserve material. [f. PHYT- + -IN²]

phyto-, a word element meaning "plant." Also, before vowels, **phyt-,** as in *phytin.* [t. Gk., comb. form of *phytón* plant]

phy·to·gen·e·sis (fī′tō·jĕn′ə·sĭs), *n.* the origin and development of plants. Also, **phy·tog·e·ny** (fī·tŏj′ə·nĭ). —**phy·to·ge·net·ic** (fī′tō·jə·nĕt′ĭk), **phy′to·ge·net′i·cal,** *adj.* —**phy′to·ge·net′i·cal·ly,** *adv.*

phy·to·gen·ic (fī′tō·jĕn′ĭk), *adj.* of plant origin.

phy·to·ge·og·ra·phy (fī′tō·jĭ·ŏg′rə·fĭ), *n.* the science treating of the geographical relationships of plants.

phy·tog·ra·phy (fī·tŏg′rə·fĭ), *n.* that branch of botany which deals with the description of plants.

phy·tol·o·gy (fī·tŏl′ə·jĭ), *n.* Obs. botany.

phy·toph·a·gous (fī·tŏf′ə·gəs), *adj.* herbivorous.

pi¹ (pī), *n., pl.* **pis.** 1. the sixteenth letter (Π, π) of the Greek alphabet. 2. Math. **a.** the letter π, used as the symbol for the ratio (3.141592+) of the circumference of a circle to its diameter. **b.** the ratio itself. [t. Gk., in def. 2 the initial letter of *periphéreia* PERIPHERY]

pi² (pī), *n., v.,* **pied, piing.** U.S. —*n.* 1. printing types mixed together indiscriminately. —*v.t.* 2. to reduce (printing types) to a state of confusion. Also, **pie.** [orig. uncert.]

P.I., Philippine Islands.

Pia·cen·za (pyä·chĕn′tsä), *n.* a city in N Italy, on the Po river. 76,000 (est. 1954).

pi·ac·u·lar (pī·ăk′yə·lər), *adj.* 1. expiatory. 2. requiring expiation; sinful; wicked. [t. L: s. *piăculāris*]

piaffe (pyăf), *v.i.*, **piaffed, piaffing.** 1. (of a horse) to lift each pair of diagonally opposite legs in succession, as in the trot, but without going forward, backward, or sideways. 2. to move slowly forward, backward, or sideways in this manner. [t. F. See PIAFFER]

piaf·fer (pyăf′ər), *n.* act of piaffing. [t. F (inf.). t. Pr.: m. *piafa* prance, make merry, b. with *pialhà* scream (der. L *pīca* magpie) and *pifrà* play the bagpipes, ult. of Gmc. orig.]

pi·a ma·ter (pī′ə mā′tər), *Anat.* the delicate, fibrous, and highly vascular membrane forming the innermost of the three meninges enveloping the brain and spinal cord. [ME, t. ML: tender mother, an inexact rendering of Arabic *umm raqīqah* thin or tender mother. Cf. DURA MATER]

pi·a·nis·si·mo (pē′ä·nĭs′ə·mō; It. pyä·nēs′sē·mô′), *adj., adv., n., pl.* **-mos, -mi** (-mē). Music. —*adj.* 1. very soft. —*adv.* 2. very softly. —*n.* 3. a passage or movement played in this way. [It., superl. of *piano,* g. L *plānus.* See PIANO²]

pi·an·ist (pĭ·ăn′ĭst, pē′ə·nĭst), *n.* a performer on the piano.

pi·an·o¹ (pĭ·ăn′ō), *n.* 1. a musical instrument in which hammers, operated from a keyboard, strike upon metal strings. 2. **grand piano,** a piano with a harp-shaped body supported horizontally, called **concert grand piano** in the largest size. 3. **square piano,** a piano with a rectangular body supported horizontally. 4. **upright piano,** a piano with a rectangular body placed vertically. [t. It., short for *pianoforte* or *fortepiano* PIANOFORTE]

pi·a·no² (pĭ·ä′nō), *Music.* —*adj.* 1. soft; subdued. —*adv.* 2. softly. Abbr.: p. [It., g. L *plānus* PLAIN²]

pi·an·o·for·te (pĭ·ăn′ə·fôr′tĭ, pĭ·ăn′ə·fôrt′), *n.* the piano. [t. It.: f. *piano* soft + *forte* loud, strong]

pi·as·sa·va (pē′ə·sä′və), *n.* a coarse, woody fiber obtained from the palms *Leopoldinia piassaba* and *Attalea funifera* of South America, used in making brooms, etc. 2. either of these trees. Also, **pi·as·sa′ba.** [t. Pg., t. Tupi: m. *piaçaba*]

pi·as·ter (pĭ·ăs′tər), *n.* 1. the monetary coin unit of Turkey, at one time equivalent to about 4.4 U.S. cents. 2. the old Spanish peso or dollar. 3. any of the various coins based on it. Also, **pi·as′tre.** [t. F: m. *piastre,* t. It.: m. *piastra* metal plate (coin), g. L *emplastrum* a plaster. See PLASTER]

Pia·ti·gorsk (pyä′tĭ·gôrsk′), *n.* Pyatigorsk.

Pia·ve (pyä′vě), *n.* a river in NE Italy, flowing into the Adriatic: scene of bitter fighting, 1917–18. 137 mi.

pi·az·za (pĭ·ăz′ə; Brit. pĭ·ăt′sə, -ăd′zə; It. pyät′tsä), *n., pl.* **piazzas,** It. **piazze** (pyät′tsě). 1. an open square or public place in a city or town. 2. Chiefly U.S. a veranda of a house. 3. Chiefly British. an arcade or covered walk or gallery, as around a public square or in front of a building. [t. It., g. L *platēa,* t. Gk.: m. *plateîa* broad street. See PLACE]

pi·broch (pē′brŏкн), *n.* (in the Scottish Highlands) a kind of musical piece performed on the bagpipe, comprising a series of variations on a ground theme, usually martial in character, but sometimes used as a dirge or otherwise. [t. Gaelic: m. *piobaireachd* pipe music, the art of playing a bagpipe, der. *piobair* PIPER]

pi·ca¹ (pī′kə), *n.* Print. 1. a type (12 point) of a size between **small pica** (11 point) and English. 2. the depth of this type size (about one sixth of an inch) as a unit of linear measurement for type, etc. [t. AL: book of rules for Church services, appar. the same word as L *pīca* magpie. See PIE³]

pi·ca² (pī′kə), *n.* Pathol. depraved or perverted appetite or craving for unnatural food, as chalk, clay, etc., common in chlorosis, pregnancy, etc. [t. NL or ML *pīca* magpie, with reference to its omnivorous feeding]

pic·a·dor (pĭk′ə·dôr′; Sp. pē′kä·dôr′), *n.* one of the horsemen who open a bullfight by irritating and enraging the bull with pricks of lances, without disabling him. [Sp., der. *picar* prick, pierce]

Pic·ar·dy (pĭk′ər·dĭ), *n.* a region in N France: formerly a province.

pic·a·resque (pĭk′ə·rĕsk′), *adj.* of or pertaining to rogues: applied to a type of fiction, of Spanish origin, with a rogue or adventurer for hero. [t. F., t. Sp.: m. *picaresco,* der. *picara* rogue, t. F: m. *Picard* native of Picardy]

pic·a·roon (pĭk′ə·rōōn′), *n.* 1. a rogue, thief, or brigand. 2. a pirate or corsair. —*v.i.* 3. to act or cruise as a brigand or pirate. [t. Sp.: m. *picarón,* aug. of *pícaro* rogue. See PICARESQUE]

Pi·cas·so (pē·käs′sō), *n.* Pablo (pä′blō), born 1881, Spanish-French painter and sculptor.

pic·a·yune (pĭk′ĭ·ūn′), *n.* 1. (formerly in Florida, Louisiana, etc.) the Spanish half real, equal to about 6 U.S. cents. 2. U.S. any small coin, as a five-cent piece. 3. Colloq. an insignificant person or thing. —*adj.* 4. Colloq. Also, **pic′a·yun′ish.** of little value or account; small; petty. [t. Pr.: m. *picaioun,* old copper coin of Piedmont, ult. der. L *pecūnia* money]

Pic·ca·dil·ly (pĭk′ə·dĭl′ĭ), *n.* a street in London, England, noted for its shops, clubs, and residences.

pic·ca·lil·li (pĭk′ə·lĭl′ĭ), *n., pl.* **-lis.** a highly seasoned pickle, of East Indian origin, made of chopped vegetables.

Pic·card (pē·kär′), *n.* **Auguste** (ō·gyst′), 1884–1962, Belgian physicist, born in Switzerland: stratosphere balloon ascent to 55,500 ft. (1932).

pic·co·lo (pĭk′ə·lō), *n., pl.* **-los.** a small flute, sounding an octave higher than the ordinary flute. [t. It.: small]

pic·co·lo·ist (pĭk′ə·lō·ĭst), *n.* a player on the piccolo.

pice (pīs), *n., pl.* **pice.** a British Indian bronze coin and money of account equal to one fourth of an anna (about one half of a U.S. cent). [t. Hind.: m. *paisā*]

pic·e·ous (pĭs′ĭ·əs, pī′sĭ·əs), *adj.* 1. of, pertaining to, or resembling pitch. 2. inflammable or combustible. 3. Zool. black or nearly black as pitch. [t. L: m. *piceus*]

pich·i·ci·a·go (pĭch′ə·sĭ′ä′gō, -ä′gō), *n., pl.* **-gos.** the smallest of the armadillos, of the genera *Chlamydophorus* and *Burmeisteria* of southern South America. [t. S Amer. Sp.: m. *pichiciego,* f. Guarani *pichey* small armadillo + Sp. *ciego* blind (g. L *caecus*)]

pick¹ (pĭk), *v.t.* 1. to choose or select; select carefully. 2. to choose (one's way or steps), as over rough ground or through a crowd. 3. to seek and find occasion for: *to pick a quarrel.* 4. to seek or find (flaws) in a spirit of faultfinding. 5. to steal the contents of (a person's pocket, purse, etc.). 6. to open (a lock) with a pointed instrument, a wire, or the like, as for robbery. 7. to pierce, indent, dig into, or break up (something) with a pointed instrument. 8. to form (a hole, etc.) by such action. 9. to use a pointed instrument, the fingers, the teeth, the beak, etc., on (a thing), in order to remove something. 10. to clear (a thing) of something by such action: *to pick one's teeth.* 11. to prepare for use by removing feathers, hulls, or other parts: *to pick a fowl.* 12. to detach or remove with the fingers, the beak, or the like, esp. with the fingers. 13. to pluck or gather: *to pick flowers.* 14. (of birds or other animals) to take up (small bits of food) with the bill or teeth. 15. to eat in small morsels or daintily. 16. to separate, pull apart, or pull to pieces (fibers, etc.). 17. Music. **a.** to pluck (the strings of an instrument). **b.** to play (a stringed instrument) by plucking with the fingers.

—*v.i.* 18. to strike with or use a pointed instrument or the like on something. 19. to eat with dainty bites.

20. to choose; make careful or fastidious selection. **21.** to pilfer. **22.** Special verb phrases are: **pick at,** *Colloq.* to nag at. **pick off,** to single out and shoot. **pick on,** *Colloq.* to annoy; tease; criticize or blame. **pick out, 1.** to choose. **2.** to distinguish (a thing) from surrounding or accompanying things. **3.** to make out (sense or meaning). **4.** to discover by combining separate fragments of information. **5.** to extract by picking. **pick up, 1.** to take up: *to pick up a stone.* **2.** to pluck up, recover, or regain (courage, etc.). **3.** to gain by occasional opportunity: *to pick up a livelihood.* **4.** to learn by occasional opportunity or without special teaching. **5.** to get casually. **6.** to become acquainted with informally or casually. **7.** *Colloq.* to improve. **8.** to take (a person or thing) into a car, ship, etc., or along with one. **9.** to bring into the range of reception, observation, etc.: *to pick up Rome on one's radio.* **10.** to accelerate, esp. in speed. *—n.* **23.** choice or selection. **24.** that which is selected. **25.** the choicest or most desirable part, example, or examples. **26.** the right of selection. **27.** an act of picking. **28.** the quantity of a crop picked at a particular time. **29.** *Print.* a speck of dirt, hardened ink, or extra metal on set type or a plate. **30.** a stroke with something pointed. **31.** a plectrum. [ME *picke* (c. G *picken*), var. of *pike*, v. (now d.), ME *piken.* Cf. OE *picung* pricking] **—Syn. 1.** See **choose.**

pick² (pĭk), *n.* **1.** a hand tool consisting of an iron bar, usually curved, tapering to a point at one or both ends, mounted on a wooden handle, and used for loosening and breaking up soil, rock, etc. **2.** any pointed or other tool or instrument for picking. [ME *pikk(e)*, OE *pīc*]

pick³ (pĭk), *Weaving.* *—v.t.* **1.** to cast (a shuttle). *—n.* **2.** (in a loom) one passage of the shuttle. **3.** a single filling yarn. [var. of PITCH¹]

pick·a·back (pĭk′ə băk′), *adv.* on the back or shoulders like a pack: *she rode pickaback on her father till he was exhausted.*

pick·a·nin·ny (pĭk′ə nĭn′ĭ), *n., pl.* **-nies. 1.** a Negro or colored child. **2.** a small child. [t. Negro pidgin E: child, t. Pg.: m. *pequenino* very little]

pick·ax (pĭk′ăks′), *n.* **1.** a pick, esp. a mattock. *—v.t.* **2.** to cut or clear away with a pickax. *—v.i.* **3.** to use a pickax. [f. PICK¹ + AX; r. ME *picois*, t. OF (cf. OF *pic*, OE *pīc* PIKE⁵)]

pick·axe (pĭk′ăks′), *n., v.t., v.i.,* **-axed, -axing.** pickax.

picked¹ (pĭkt), *adj.* **1.** specially chosen or selected: *a crew of picked men.* **2.** cleared or cleaned, as of refuse parts, by picking. [f. PICK¹, v. + -ED²]

pick·ed² (pĭk′ĭd, pĭkt), *adj. Now Archaic or Dial.* pointed. [f. PICK² + -ED²]

Pick·ens (pĭk′ənz), *n.* **1. Andrew,** 1739–1817, American Revolutionary general. **2. Fort,** a fort at the entrance of Pensacola Bay in NW Florida: in Union hands throughout the Civil War.

pick·er¹ (pĭk′ər), *n.* **1.** one who picks. **2.** one who plucks or gathers fruit, flowers, etc. [f. PICK¹, v. + -ER¹]

pick·er² (pĭk′ər), *n. Weaving.* **1.** a tool or instrument for picking. **2.** the piece that throws the shuttle of the loom through the warp. **3.** one who works a picker. [f. PICK³, v. + -ER¹]

pick·er·el (pĭk′ər əl), *n., pl.* **-els,** (*esp. collectively*) **-el. 1.** *U.S., Canada.* any of various species of pike, esp. one of the smaller species, as the **chain pickerel,** *Esox niger,* and the **mud pickerel,** *Esox vermiculatus.* **2.** the pike perch. **3.** *Brit.* a young pike. [ME *pykerel,* f. PIKE¹ + -REL]

pick·er·el·weed (pĭk′ər əl wēd′), *n.* any plant of the American genus *Pontederia,* esp., *P. cordata,* a blue-flowered herb common in shallow fresh water.

Pick·er·ing (pĭk′ər ĭng), *n.* **1. Edward Charles,** 1846–1919, U.S. astronomer. **2.** his brother, **William Henry,** 1858–1938, U.S. astronomer.

pick·et (pĭk′ĭt), *n.* **1.** a pointed post, stake, pale, or peg, as for driving into the ground in making a stockade, for placing vertically to form the main part of a fence **(picket fence),** for driving into the ground to fasten something to, etc. **2.** a person or a body of persons stationed by a trade union or the like before a place of work and attempting to dissuade or prevent workers or shoppers from entering the building during a strike. **3.** *Mil.* a small detached body of troops, posted out from a force to warn against an enemy's approach. *—v.t.* **4.** to enclose, fence, or make secure with pickets. **5.** to fasten or tether to a picket. **6.** to place pickets at, as during a strike. **7.** *Mil.* **a.** to guard, as a camp, by or as pickets. **b.** *Obs.* to post as a picket. *—v.i.* **8.** to stand or march by a place of employment as a picket. [t. F: m. *piquet* pointed stake, military picket, dim. of *pic* a pick; in other senses connected with *piquer* prick, pierce, with dim. suffix. See -ET] **—pick′et·er,** *n.*

Pick·ett (pĭk′ĭt), *n.* **George Edward,** 1825–75, Confederate general in the Civil War.

Pick·ford (pĭk′fərd), *n.* **Mary,** (*Gladys Smith*) born 1893, U.S. motion picture actress, born in Canada.

pick·ing (pĭk′ĭng), *n.* **1.** act of one who or that which picks. **2.** that which is or may be picked or picked up. **3.** the amount picked. **4.** (*pl.*) things, portions, or scraps remaining and worth picking up or appropriating. **5.** (*pl.*) pilferings, or perquisites gotten by means not strictly honest. [f. PICK¹ + -ING¹]

pick·le (pĭk′əl), *n., v.,* **-led, -ling.** *—n.* **1.** a pickled cucumber. **2.** (*often pl.*) vegetables, as cucumbers, cauliflower, etc., preserved in vinegar and eaten as a relish. **3.** something preserved in a pickling brine. **4.** a liquid prepared with salt or vinegar for preserving or flavoring fish, meat, vegetables, etc.; marinade. **5.** *Metall.* an acid or other chemical solution in which metal objects are dipped to remove oxide scale or other adhering substances. **6.** *Colloq.* a condition or situation, esp. a disagreeable one. **7.** *Colloq.* a mischievous child. *—v.t.* **8.** to preserve or steep in pickle. **9.** to treat with a chemical pickle. [ME *pykyl, pekille,* t. MD or MLG: m. *pekel(e).* Cf. G *pökel* brine]

pick·lock (pĭk′lŏk′), *n.* **1.** a person who picks locks. **2.** a thief. **3.** an instrument for picking locks.

pick·pock·et (pĭk′pŏk′ĭt), *n.* one who steals from pockets.

pick·up (pĭk′ŭp′), *n.* **1.** *U.S. Slang.* an informal or casual acquaintance. **2.** *Auto.* **a.** capacity for rapid acceleration. **b.** a small, open-body delivery truck, built on a chassis comparable to that of a passenger car. **3.** *U.S. Slang.* improvement. **4.** *U.S. Slang.* a stimulant. **5.** *Sports.* the act of fielding a ball after it hits the ground. **6.** *Radio.* **a.** the act of receiving sound waves in the transmitting set in order to change them into electrical waves. **b.** a receiving or recording device. **c.** the place at which a broadcast is being transmitted. **d.** interference. **7.** *Television.* **a.** the change of light energy into electrical energy in the transmitting set. **b.** the device used. **8.** *Radio.* Also, **cartridge.** a device which generates electric or acoustic impulses in accordance with the mechanical variations impressed upon a phonograph record **(phonograph pickup).**

pickup arm, tone arm.

Pick·wick (pĭk′wĭk), *n.* **Samuel,** (in Dickens' *Pickwick Papers*) the benevolent, naïve founder of the Pickwick Club.

Pick·wick·i·an (pĭk wĭk′ĭ ən), *adj.* of, pertaining to, or characteristic of Mr. Pickwick.

pic·nic (pĭk′nĭk), *n., v.,* **-nicked, -nicking.** *—n.* **1.** an outing or excursion in which those taking part, usually carrying food with them, share a meal in the open air. **2.** *Slang.* an enjoyable experience or time. *—v.i.* **3.** to hold, or take part in, a picnic. [t. F: m. *pique-nique;* orig. unknown] **—pic′nick·er,** *n.*

Pi·co del·la Mi·ran·do·la (pē′kō děl′lä mē rän′dō-lä′), **Count Giovanni** (jō vän′nē), 1463–94, Italian humanist and writer.

Pi·co de Tei·de (pē′kō dě tā′dě). See **Teide.**

pic·o·line (pĭk′ə lēn′, -lĭn), *n. Chem.* any of three isomeric derivatives of pyridine, C_6H_7N, obtained from coal tar as colorless oily liquids with a strong odor. [f. s. L *pix* pitch + L *ol(eum)* oil + -INE²]

pi·cot (pē′kō), *n.* one of a number of ornamental loops in embroidery, or along the edge of lace, ribbon, etc. [t. F, dim. of *pic* a pick, something pointed. See PIKE⁵]

pic·o·tee (pĭk′ə tē′), *n. Chiefly Brit.* a variety of carnation whose petals have an outer margin of another color, usually red. [t. F: m. *picoté,* pp. of *picoter* mark with pricks or spots. See PICOT]

pic·rate (pĭk′rāt), *n. Chem.* a salt or ester of picric acid.

pic·ric acid (pĭk′rĭk), *Chem.* an intensely bitter yellow acid, $C_6H_3N_3O_7$, used as a dye and as an explosive. [f. m. s. Gk. *pikrós* bitter + -IC]

pic·rite (pĭk′rīt), *n.* a granular igneous rock composed chiefly of olivine and augite, but containing small amounts of feldspar. [f. m.s. Gk. *pikrós* bitter + -ITE¹]

Pict (pĭkt), *n.* one of a race of people of disputed origin who formerly inhabited parts of northern Britain, and in the 9th century became united with the Scots. [ME *Pictes,* pl. (t. L: m. *Picti*); r. ME *Peghttes,* OE *Peohtas,* earlier *Pihtas,* t. L (as above)]

Pict·ish (pĭk′tĭsh), *n.* **1.** the language of the Picts. *—adj.* **2.** of or pertaining to the Picts.

pic·to·graph (pĭk′tə gräf′, -gräf′), *n.* **1.** a record consisting of pictorial symbols. **2.** a pictorial sign or symbol. [f. s. L *pictus,* pp., painted, represented pictorially + -o- + -GRAPH] **—pic′to·graph′ic,** *adj.*

pic·tog·ra·phy (pĭk tŏg′rə fĭ), *n.* the use of pictographs; picture writing.

pic·to·ri·al (pĭk tōr′ĭ əl), *adj.* **1.** pertaining to, expressed in, or of the nature of, a picture or pictures: *pictorial writing.* **2.** illustrated by or containing pictures: *a pictorial history.* **3.** of or pertaining to a painter or maker of pictures. **4.** suggestive of, or representing as if by, a picture; graphic. *—n.* **5.** a periodical in which pictures are the leading feature. [f. s. LL *pictōrius* (der. L *pictor* painter) + -AL¹] **—pic·to′ri·al·ly,** *adv.*

pic·ture (pĭk′chər), *n., v.,* **-tured, -turing.** *—n.* **1.** a painting, drawing, photograph, or other representation, as of a person, object, or scene, executed on a flat surface. **2.** any visible image, however produced: *the picture we see in a mirror.* **3.** a mental image. **4.** a graphic or vivid description or account: *Gibbon's picture of ancient Rome.* **5.** a tableau, as in theatrical representation **(living picture). 6.** a motion picture. **7.** a person, thing, group, or scene regarded as resembling a work of pictorial art. **8.** the image or counterpart: *the picture of his father.* **9.** a visible or concrete embodiment of some quality or the like: *the picture of health.* **10.** *Pathol.* the assemblage of conditions presented in a case of disease. *—v.t.* **11.** to represent in a picture or pictorially. **12.** to form a mental picture of; imagine. **13.** to depict in words; describe graphically. **14.** to present to the eye as in a picture. [ME, t. L: m. *pictūra*]

picture hat, a woman's hat having a broad brim and decorated with ostrich feathers, etc.

pic·tur·esque (pĭk/chə rĕsk/), *adj.* **1.** of a character such as to suggest a picture; strikingly interesting; colorful: *a picturesque costume.* **2.** (of language, etc.) strikingly graphic or vivid. **3.** having pleasing or interesting pictorial qualities; strikingly effective in appearance. [f. PICTURE + -ESQUE, modeled on F *pittoresque*, t. It.: m. *pittoresco*, der. *pittore* painter, g. L *pictor*] —**pic/-tur·esque/ly,** *adv.* —**pic/tur·esque/ness,** *n.*
—**Syn. 2.** PICTURESQUE, GRAPHIC, VIVID apply to descriptions that produce a strong, especially a visual impression. PICTURESQUE is a less precise term than the other two. A PICTURESQUE account, though striking and interesting, may be inaccurate or may reflect personal ideas: *he called the landscape picturesque.* A GRAPHIC account is more objective and factual; it produces a clear, definite impression, and carries conviction. A VIVID account is told with liveliness and intenseness; the description is so interesting, or even exciting, that the hearer may be emotionally stirred.

picture tube, a kinescope, def. 1.

picture window, a large window in a home, usually dominating the room, and sometimes designed to frame an attractive outside view.

picture writing, 1. the art of recording events or expressing ideas by pictures, or pictorial symbols, as practiced by preliterate peoples. **2.** pictorial symbols forming a record or communication.

pic·ul (pĭk/ŭl), *n.* (in China and elsewhere in the East) a weight equal to 100 catties, or from about 133 to about 143 pounds avoirdupois. [t. Malay-Javanese: m. *pikul* a man's load]

pid·dle (pĭd/əl), *v.i.*, **-dled, -dling.** to do anything in a trifling or ineffective way. [cf. Norw. *pydla* pout]

pid·dling (pĭd/lĭng), *adj.* trifling; petty.

pid·dock (pĭd/ək), *n.* any of the bivalve mollusks of the genus *Pholas* or the family *Pholadidae*, mostly marine, with long ovate shell, and burrowing in soft rock, wood, etc. [cf. OE *puduc* wart]

pidg·in (pĭj/ĭn, -ən), *n.* a jargon. Also, **pigeon.** [for BUSINESS (Chinese pron.)]

pidgin English, 1. an English jargon used in commerce in Chinese ports. **2.** any of several similar jargons used in other areas, e.g., Melanesia or West Africa. Also, **pigeon English.**

pie[1] (pī), *n.* **1.** a baked dish consisting of fruit, meat, oysters, or the like, with an under or an upper crust of pastry, or both. **2.** a layer cake with a filling of cream, jelly, or the like. [ME; orig. uncert.] —**pie/like/,** *adj.*

pie[2] (pī), *n.* magpie. [ME, t. OF, g. L *pīca* magpie]

pie[3] (pī), *n.*, *v.*, **pied, pieing.** *U.S.* pi[2]. [orig. uncert.]

pie[4] (pī), *n. Eccles.* (in England before the Reformation) a book of rules for finding the particulars of the service for the day. Also, **pye.** [trans. of L *pīca* magpie; see PICA[1]]

pie[5] (pī), *n.* an East Indian bronze coin, equal to one twelfth of an anna, and equivalent to about one sixth of a U.S. cent. [t. Hind.: m. *pā'ī*]

pie·bald (pī/bôld/), *adj.* **1.** having patches of black and white or of other colors; parti-colored. —*n.* **2.** a piebald animal, esp. a horse. [f. PIE[2] (see PIED) + BALD]

piece (pēs), *n.*, *v.*, **pieced, piecing.** —*n.* **1.** a limited portion or quantity of something: *a piece of land.* **2.** a quantity of some substance or material forming a single mass or body. **3.** a more or less definite quantity. **4.** a particular length, as some goods as put up for the market: *cloth sold only by the piece.* **5.** an amount of work forming a single job: *to work by the piece.* **6.** a specimen of workmanship, esp. of artistic production, as a picture or a statue. **7.** a literary composition, in prose or verse, usually short. **8.** a literary selection for recitation. **9.** a musical composition, usually a short one. **10.** one of the parts which, assembled together, form a combined whole: *the pieces of a machine.* **11.** an individual article of a set or collection: *a set of dishes of 100 pieces.* **12.** *Chess, Checkers, etc.* **a.** one of the figures, disks, blocks, or the like, of wood, ivory or other material, used in playing, as on a board or table. **b.** (in chess) a superior man, as distinguished from a pawn. **13.** an individual thing of a particular class or kind: *a piece of furniture.* **14.** an example, specimen, or instance of something: *a fine piece of work.* **15.** a specimen of humanity. **16.** one of the parts into which a thing is divided or broken; a portion, part, fragment, or shred: *to tear a letter into pieces.* **17.** *Mil.* **a.** a shoulder firearm; a rifle. **b.** cannon. **18.** a coin: *a five-cent piece.* **19.** *Dial.* **a.** a while. **b.** a short distance. **20. a piece of one's mind,** a bluntly expressed, uncomplimentary opinion. **21. of a** (or **one**) **piece,** of the same kind. —*v.t.* **22.** to mend (a garment, etc.) by applying a piece or pieces; patch. **23.** to complete, enlarge, or extend by an added piece or something additional; eke (out) with something added. **24.** to make by joining pieces together. **25.** to join together, as pieces or parts. **26.** to join as a piece or addition to something. [ME *pece*, t. OF, g. Rom. *pettia* broken piece, piece of land, of Celtic orig.] —**Syn. 1.** section, segment, scrap, fragment. See **part.**

pièce de ré·sis·tance (pyĕs də rē zēs tän s/), *French.* **1.** the principal dish of a meal. **2.** the principal event, incident, article, etc., of a series.

piece-dyed (pēs/dīd/), *adj.* dyed after weaving.

piece goods, goods or fabrics woven in lengths suitable for retail sale by the usual linear measure.

piece·meal (pēs/mēl/), *adv.* **1.** piece by piece; gradually. **2.** done piece by piece. **3.** into pieces or fragments. [ME *pecemele* (r. OE *styccemǣlum*). See PIECE]

piece of eight, the old Spanish dollar or peso, of the value of 8 reals.

piece rate, compensation based on output or production, usually a fixed sum per piece of work turned out.

piece·work (pēs/wûrk/), *n.* work done and paid for by the piece. —**piece/work/er,** *n.*

pied (pīd), *adj.* **1.** having patches of two or more colors, as various birds and other animals. **2.** wearing parti-colored clothes. [f. PIE[2] (with reference to the black-and-white plumage of the magpie) + -ED[3]]

pied-à-terre (pyĕ dà tĕr/), *n. French.* a lodging for temporary use. [F: lit., foot (footing) on ground]

Pied·mont (pēd/mŏnt), *n.* **1.** a plateau between the coastal plain and the Appalachian Mountains, including parts of Virginia, North Carolina, South Carolina, Georgia, and Alabama. **2.** Italian, **Piemonte.** a department in NW Italy. 3,536,169 pop. (est. 1952); 11,335 sq. mi. **3.** (*l.c.*) a district lying along or near the foot of a mountain range. —*adj.* **4.** (*l.c.*) lying along or near the foot of a mountain range. [t. It.: m. *Piedmonte*, lit., foothill (region)] —**Pied·mon·tese** (pēd/mŏn tēz/, -tēs/), *adj., n.*

Pie·mon·te (pyĕ môn/tě), *n.* Italian name of **Piedmont** (def. 2).

pie·plant (pī/plănt/), *n. U.S.* the common garden rhubarb: so called from its use in pies.

pier (pĭr), *n.* **1.** a structure built out into the water to serve as a landing place for ships. **2.** a support at the point where the ends of two adjacent bridge spans meet. **3.** a square pillar. **4.** a portion of wall between doors, windows, etc. **5.** a pillar or post on which a gate or door is hung. **6.** a support of masonry or the like for sustaining vertical pressure. See diag. under **arch.** [ME *per(e)*, t. ML: m. *pera*]

pierce (pĭrs), *v.*, **pierced, piercing.** —*v.t.* **1.** to penetrate or run into or through (something), as a sharp-pointed instrument, a jag of rock, a missile, or the like does. **2.** to make a hole or opening in. **3.** to bore into or through; tunnel. **4.** to perforate. **5.** to make (a hole, etc.) by or as by boring or perforating. **6.** to force or make a way into or through: *to pierce a wilderness.* **7.** to penetrate with the eye or mind; see into or through. **8.** to affect sharply with some sensation or emotion, as of cold, pain, grief, etc. **9.** to sound sharply through (the air, stillness, etc.), as a cry. —*v.i.* **10.** to force or make a way into or through something; penetrate. [ME *perce(n)*, *persche(n)*, t. OF: m. *percier*, ult. der. L *pertūsus*, pp., pierced] —**pierc/er,** *n.* —**pierc/ing·ly,** *adv.*
—**Syn. 1.** PIERCE, PENETRATE suggest the action of one object passing through another or making a way through and into another. The terms are used both concretely and figuratively. To PIERCE is to perforate quickly, as by stabbing; it suggests the use of a sharp-pointed instrument which is impelled by force: *to pierce the flesh with a knife, a scream pierces one's ears.* PENETRATE suggests a slow or difficult movement: *no ordinary bullet can penetrate an elephant's hide, to penetrate the depths of one's ignorance.*

Pierce (pĭrs), *n.* **Franklin,** 1804–69, 14th president of the U.S., 1853–57.

pier glass, a tall mirror such as is used to fill the pier or space between two windows.

Pi·e·ri·a (pī ĭr/ĭə), *n.* a coastal region including Mt. Olympus, in ancient Macedonia: the legendary birthplace of Orpheus and the Muses.

Pi·e·ri·an (pī ĭr/ĭən), *adj.* of or pertaining to Pieria or to the Muses. [f. s. L *Pīerius* of Pieria + -AN]

pi·er·i·dine (pī ĕr/ə dīn/, -dĭn), *adj.* of or denoting a butterfly of the family *Pieridae*, which includes various white, yellow, and orange species. [t. NL: m. *Pieridīnae*, pl., der. *Pieris* the typical genus, t. Gk.: a Muse]

Pierre (pĭr), *n.* the capital of South Dakota, in the central part, on the Missouri river. 5715 (1950).

Pi·er·rot (pē/ə rō/; *Fr.* pyĕ rō/), *n.* **1.** a male character in certain French pantomime, having a whitened face and wearing a loose white fancy costume. **2.** (*l.c.*) a masquerader or buffoon so made up. [F, dim. of *Pierre*, man's name. See PETER]

pier table, a table or low bracket for occupying the space against a pier between two windows, often used under a pier glass.

Pie·ter·mar·itz·burg (pē/tər mâr/ĭts bûrg/), *n.* a city in the E Republic of South Africa: the capital of Natal province. With suburbs, 73,189 (1951).

Pi·e·tism (pī/ə tĭz/əm), *n.* **1.** a movement inaugurated during the latter part of the 17th century for the revival and advancement of piety in the Lutheran churches in Germany. **2.** the principles and practices of the Pietists. **3.** (*l.c.*) depth of religious feeling; godliness of life. **4.** (*l.c.*) exaggeration or affectation of piety. [t. NL(G): m. *Pietismus*] —**Pi/e·tist,** *n.* —**pi/e·tis/tic,** *adj.*

pi·e·ty (pī/ə tĭ), *n., pl.* **-ties. 1.** reverence for God, or regard for religious obligations. **2.** the quality or fact of being pious. **3.** dutiful respect or regard for parents or others. **4.** a pious act, remark, belief, or the like. [ME, t. L: m.s. *pietas*] —**Syn. 2.** godliness, devoutness.

pi·e·zo·e·lec·tric·i·ty (pī ē/zō ĭ lĕk/trĭs/ə tĭ, -ē/l k-), *n.* electricity produced by pressure, as in a crystal subjected to compression along a certain axis. [f. *piezo*-(comb. form repr. Gk. *piézein* press, squeeze) + ELECTRICITY] **—pi·e·zo·e·lec·tric** (pī ē/zō ĭ lĕk/trĭk), *adj.* **—pi·e·zo·e·lec/tri·cal·ly**, *adv.*

pi·e·zom·e·ter (pī/ə zŏm/ə tər), *n.* any of various instruments for measuring pressure. **—pi·e·zo·met·ric** (pī ē/zə mĕt/rĭk), pi·e/zo·met/ri·cal, *adj.*

pi·e·zom·e·try (pī/ə zŏm/ə trĭ), *n.* the measurement of pressure or compressibility.

pif·fle (pĭf/əl), *n.*, *v.*, **-fled, -fling.** *Colloq.* **—n. 1.** nonsense. **—v.i. 2.** to talk nonsense. [cf. OE *pyff* PUFF]

pig (pĭg), *n.*, *v.*, **pigged, pigging. —n. 1.** a young swine of either sex weighing less than 120 pounds. **2.** any swine or hog. **3.** the flesh of swine; pork. **4.** *Colloq.* a person or animal of piggish character or habits. **5.** *Metall.* **a.** an oblong mass of metal that has been run while still molten into a mold of sand or the like, esp. such a mass of iron from a blast furnace. **b.** one of the molds for such masses of metal. **c.** metal in the form of such masses. **d.** pig iron. **—v.i. 6.** to bring forth pigs. **7.** to live, lie, etc., as if in a pigsty. [ME *pigge*, OE *picg* (in *pic*(*g*)-*bred* pig-bread, mast). Cf. D *big* young pig]

pig bed, a bed of sand for molding pigs into which molten metal is poured.

pi·geon[1] (pĭj/ən), *n.* **1.** any member of the family *Columbidae*, comprising birds characterized by a compact body and short legs, and existing in several hundred species widely distributed throughout the world; a dove. **2.** a domesticated member of this family, as one of the varieties of the rock dove or rock pigeon, *Columba livia.* **3.** *Slang.* a simpleton, dupe, or gull. [ME *pejon*, t. OF: m. *pijon*, g. s. LL *pipio* squab]

pi·geon[2] (pĭj/ĭn), *n.* pidgin.

pigeon breast, *Pathol.* chicken breast.

Pigeon English, pidgin English.

pigeon hawk, a small American true falcon, *Falco columbarius*, closely related to the merlin.

pi·geon-heart·ed (pĭk/ən här/tĭd), *adj.* timid; meek.

pi·geon·hole (pĭj/ən hōl/), *n.*, *v.*, **-holed, -holing. —n. 1.** one of a series of small compartments in a desk, cabinet, or the like, used for papers, etc. **2.** a hole or recess, or one of a series of recesses, for pigeons to nest in. **—v.t. 3.** to put away in the proper place for later reference. **4.** to assign a definite place in some orderly system. **5.** to put aside for the present, esp. with the intention of ignoring or forgetting. **6.** to place in a pigeonhole or pigeonholes.

pigeon pox, a disease affecting pigeons, similar to fowl pox.

pi·geon-toed (pĭj/ən tōd/), *adj.* having the toes or feet turned inward.

pi·geon·wing (pĭj/ən wĭng/), *n.* *U.S.* **1.** a particular figure in skating, outlining the spread wing of a pigeon. **2.** a similar fancy step or evolution in dancing.

pig·fish (pĭg/fĭsh/), *n.*, *pl.* **-fishes,** (*esp. collectively*) **-fish.** any of various fishes, as a grunt, *Orthopristis chrysopterus*, a food fish of the S Atlantic coast of the U.S.

pig·ger·y (pĭg/ə rĭ), *n.*, *pl.* **-geries.** *Chiefly Brit.* a place where pigs are kept.

pig·gin (pĭg/ĭn), *n.* a small wooden pail or tub with a handle formed by continuing one of the staves above the rim. [? der. *pig* pot, jar]

pig·gish (pĭg/ĭsh), *adj.* like or befitting a pig; greedy or filthy. **—pig/gish·ly,** *adv.* **—pig/gish·ness,** *n.*

pig·gy (pĭg/ĭ), *n.*, *pl.* **-gies.** a small or young pig. Also, **pig/gie.**

pig·gy·back (pĭg/ĭ băk/), *adv.* **1.** pickaback. **—adj. 2.** of or pertaining to a truck trailer, plane, etc., carried part of the way by a larger vehicle.

pig·gy·back·ing (pĭg/ĭ băk/ĭng), *n.* the transporting of loaded truck trailers, especially on railroad flat cars.

pig·head·ed (pĭg/hĕd/ĭd), *adj.* stupidly obstinate.

pig iron, **1.** iron produced in a blast furnace, poured into special molds, and used to make wrought iron, cast iron, or steel. **2.** such iron, whether molten or in pigs.

pig lead, lead molded in pigs.

pig·let (pĭg/lĭt), *n.* a little pig.

pig·ling (pĭg/lĭng), *n.* a young or small pig.

pig·ment (pĭg/mənt), *n.* **1.** a coloring matter or substance. **2.** a dry substance, usually pulverized, which when mixed with a liquid vehicle in which it is insoluble becomes a paint, ink, etc. **3.** *Biol.* any substance whose presence in the tissues or cells of animals or plants colors them. [ME, t. L: s. *pigmentum*]

pig·men·tar·y (pĭg/mən tĕr/ĭ), *adj.* of pigment.

pig·men·ta·tion (pĭg/mən tā/shən), *n.* *Biol.* coloration or deposition of pigment.

Pig·my (pĭg/mĭ), *n.*, *pl.* **-mies,** *adj.* Pygmy.

pig·nus (pĭg/nəs), *n.*, *pl.* **pignora** (pĭg/nə rə). *Roman and Civil Law.* **1.** property held as security for a debt. **2.** the contract containing such a pledge. [t. L: pledge]

pig·nut (pĭg/nŭt/), *n.* **1.** the nut of the brown hickory, *Carya glabra*, of North America. **2.** the tree itself. **3.** the tuber of a European plant, *Conopodium denudatum*, a kind of earthnut.

pig·pen (pĭg/pĕn/), *n.* **1.** *Chiefly Brit.* a pen for pigs; a pigsty. **2.** a dirty place.

pig·skin (pĭg/skĭn/), *n.* **1.** the skin of a pig. **2.** leather made from it. **3.** *Colloq.* a saddle. **4.** *Colloq.* a football.

pig·stick (pĭg/stĭk/), *v.i.* to go wild boar hunting using a spear. **—pig/stick/er,** *n.* **—pig/stick/ing,** *n.*

pig·sty (pĭg/stī/), *n.*, *pl.* **-sties.** a sty for pens for pigs.

pig·tail (pĭg/tāl/), *n.* **1.** a braid of hair hanging down the back of the head. **2.** tobacco in a thin twisted roll.

pig·weed (pĭg/wēd/), *n.* **1.** any of the goosefoots of the genus *Chenopodium*, esp. **white pigweed,** *C. album.* **2.** any of certain amaranths, as *Amaranthus retroflexus.*

pi·ka (pī/kə), *n.* any of various small mammals allied to the rabbits and inhabiting alpine regions of the northern hemisphere, as *Ochotona princeps* of North America. [t. native Siberian: m. *piika*]

pike[1] (pīk), *n.*, *pl.* **pikes,** (*esp. collectively*) **pike. 1.** any of various large, slender, voracious fresh-water fishes of the genus *Esox*, having a long snout, esp. the **northern pike,** *E. lucius.* **2.** any of various superficially similar fishes, as *Stizostedion vitreum*. See **pike perch.** [ME, short for *pikefish*, so called from its pointed snout. See PIKE[2]] **—pike/like/,** *adj.*

pike[2] (pīk), *n.*, *v.*, **piked, piking. —n. 1.** *Hist.* an infantry weapon with long shaft and comparatively small metal head usually leaf- or diamond-shaped. **—v.t. 2.** to pierce, wound, or kill with or as with a pike. [t. F: m. *pique*, akin to *pic* a pick (cf. PIKE[5]) and *piquer* prick (see PIQUE, v.)]

pike[3] (pīk), *n.* **1.** a turnpike road, or country highway. **2.** a turnpike or tollgate. **3.** the toll paid at a tollgate. [short for TURNPIKE]

pike[4] (pīk), *n.* *Brit. Dial.* a hill or mountain with a pointed summit. [special use of PIKE[5]. Cf. OE *hornpic* pinnacle]

pike[5] (pīk), *n.* **1.** a sharp point; a spike. **2.** the pointed end of anything, as of an arrow or a spear. [ME, t. OF: m. *pic* a pick or pickax, a point. See PIKE[2]]

pike[6] (pīk), *v.i.*, **piked, piking.** *Slang.* to go quickly. [orig. uncert.]

Pike (pīk), *n.* Zebulon Montgomery (zĕb/yōō lən), 1779–1813, U.S. General and explorer of the west.

pike·man (pīk/mən), *n.*, *pl.* **-men.** a soldier armed with a pike.

pike perch, any of several pikelike fishes of the perch family, as *Stizostedion vitreum* (**walleye**) of North America.

pik·er (pī/kər), *n.* *U.S. Slang.* **1.** one who gambles, speculates, etc., in a small cautious way. **2.** one who does anything in a contemptibly small or cheap way.

Pike's Peak (pīks), a mountain peak of the Rocky Mountains in central Colorado: ascended by a cog railway and an auto road. 14,108 ft.

pike·staff (pīk/stăf/, -stäf/), *n.*, *pl.* **-staves** (-stāvz/). **1.** the staff or shaft of a pike (weapon). **2.** a foot traveler's staff with a metal point or spike at the lower end.

pi·las·ter (pĭ lăs/tər), *n.* *Archit.* a square or rectangular pillar, with capital and base, engaged in a wall from which it projects. [t. F: m. *pilastre*, t. It.: m. *pilastro*, der. L *pila* pillar]

Pi·late (pī/lət), *n.* Pontius (pŏn/shəs, pŏn/tĭ əs), Roman governor of Judea, A.D. 26–36?, when Christ was crucified.

Pi·la·tus (pē lä/tōōs), *n.* a mountain of the Alps in central Switzerland, near Lucerne: cable railway. 6998 ft.

pi·lau (pĭ lô/, -lō/), *n.* an oriental dish consisting of rice boiled with mutton, fowl, or the like, and flavored with spices, etc. Also, **pi·laf** (pĭ läf/), **pi·laff/, pi·law** (pĭ lô/). [t. Pers.: (m). *piläw*]

pil·chard (pĭl/chərd), *n.* **1.** a small southern European marine fish, the sardine, *Arengus pilchardus*, allied to the herring but smaller and rounder. **2.** any of several related fishes, as the California sardine, *Sardinops caeruleus.*

Pil·co·ma·yo (pēl/kō mä/yō), *n.* a river flowing from S Bolivia SE along the boundary between Paraguay and Argentina to the Paraguay river at Asunción. 1000 mi.

pile[1] (pīl), *n.*, *v.*, **piled, piling. —n. 1.** an assemblage of things laid or lying one upon another in a more or less orderly fashion: *a pile of boxes.* **2.** *Colloq.* a large number, quantity, or amount of anything: *a pile of good sense.* **3.** a heap of wood on which a dead body, a living person, or a sacrifice is burned. **4.** a lofty or large building or mass of buildings. **5.** *Colloq.* a large accumulation of money. **6.** a bundle of pieces of iron ready to be welded and drawn out into bars; fagot. **7.** *Nuclear Physics.* a latticework of uranium and various moderating substances used to produce plutonium in the original harnessing of atomic energy. It is essentially a means of controlling the nuclear chain reaction. **—v.t. 8.** to lay or dispose in a pile (often fol. by *up*). **9.** to accumulate (fol. by *up*). **10.** to cover or load, with a pile or piles. **—v.i. 11.** to accumulate, as money, debts, evidence, etc. (fol. by *up*). **12.** *Colloq.* to get somewhere (fol. by *in, into, out, off, down*, etc.) in a body and more or less confusedly. **13.** to gather or rise in a pile or piles, as snow, etc. [ME, t. OF, t. L: m. *pila* pillar, pier, mole]

pile[2] (pīl), *n.*, *v.*, **piled, piling. —n. 1.** a heavy timber, stake or pole, sometimes pointed at the lower end, driven vertically into the ground or the bed of a river, etc., to support a superstructure or form part of a wall. **2.** any steel or concrete member similarly used. **3.** *Her.* a bearing in the form of a wedge, usually with its point downward. **—v.t. 4.** to furnish, strengthen, or support with piles. **5.** drive piles into. [ME and OE *pĭl* shaft, stake, t. L: s. *pīlum* javelin]

Pikeman, early 17th century

Pilaster

pile³ (pīl), *n.* **1.** hair, esp. soft, fine hair or down. **2.** wool, fur, or pelage. **3.** a fabric with a surface of upright cut or looped yarns, as velvet, Turkish toweling, etc. **4.** such a surface. **5.** one of the strands in such a surface. [ME *pilus*, t. L: hair]

pile⁴ (pīl), *n.* (*usually pl.*) a hemorrhoid. [ME *pyle*]

pil·e·ate (pīl′ī·āt′, pīl′ī-), *adj.* capped, as a mushroom. [t. L: m.s. *pīleātus* capped. See PILEUS]

pil·e·at·ed (pīl′ī·ā′tĭd, pīl′ī-), *adj. Ornith.* crested.

pileated woodpecker, a large black-and-white North American woodpecker, *Ceophloeus pileatus*, with prominent red crest.

piled (pīld), *adj.* having a pile, as velvet and other fabrics. [f. PILE³ + -ED³]

pile driver, a machine for driving down piles, usually a tall framework in which a heavy weight of iron is raised between guides to a height, as by steam, and then allowed to fall upon the head of the pile.

pil·e·ous (pīl′ī·əs), *adj.* **1.** of or pertaining to hair. **2.** hairy. [f. PILE³ + -OUS]

pil·e·um (pīl′ī·əm, pĭl′ī·əm), *n., pl.* **pilea** (pīl′ī·ə, pĭl′-ī·ə). the top of the head of a bird, from the base of the bill to the nape. [t. NL, t. L, var. of *pilleum*. See PILEUS]

pil·e·us (pīl′ī·əs, pĭl′ī·əs), *n., pl.* **pilei** (pīl′ī·ī′, pĭl′ī·ī′). **1.** *Bot.* the horizontal portion of a mushroom, bearing gills, tubes, etc. on its underside; a cap. **2.** a felt skullcap worn by the ancient Romans and Greeks. [t. L, more correctly *pilleus*, also *pilleum* felt cap; akin to L *pilus* hair, Gk. *pîlos* felt, felt cap]

pile·wort (pīl′wûrt′), *n.* **1.** (in the New World) **a.** the amaranthaceous weed, *Amaranthus cruentus*, native of Asia. **b.** fireweed. **2.** (in the Old World) the lesser celandine, *Ranunculus Ficaria*. [f. PILE⁴ + WORT; formerly used medicinally]

pil·fer (pĭl′fər), *v.i., v.t.* to steal, esp. in small quantities; obtain by, or practice, petty theft. [appar. t. AF or OF: m.s. *pelfrer* pillage, rob. Cf. PELF] —**pil′fer·er,** *n.*

pil·fer·age (pĭl′fər·ĭj), *n.* **1.** act or practice of pilfering; petty theft. **2.** that which is pilfered.

pil·grim (pĭl′grĭm), *n.* **1.** one who journeys, esp. a long distance, to some sacred place as an act of devotion. **2.** a traveler or wanderer. **3.** an original settler in a region. **4.** (*cap.*) one of the Pilgrim Fathers. **5.** *Western U.S.* a newcomer (person or animal) in a region. [ME *pelegrim*, t. AF (unrecorded), t. ML: m.s. *peregrīnus* pilgrim, L foreigner. See PEREGRINE] —Syn. **2.** wayfarer, sojourner.

pil·grim·age (pĭl′grə·mĭj), *n.* **1.** a journey, esp. a long one, made to some sacred place, as an act of devotion. **2.** any long journey. [ME, t. AF: m. *pilgrymage*, var. of OF *peligrinage*. See PILGRIM] —Syn. **1.** See trip.

Pilgrim Fathers, *U.S. Hist.* the English separatists who founded the colony of Plymouth, Massachusetts, in 1620.

Pilgrim's Progress, an allegory (1678), by John Bunyan.

pi·li (pē′lē′), *n., pl.* **-lis. 1.** a Philippine burseraceous tree, *Canarium ovatum*, the seeds of which are edible, resembling a sweet almond. **2.** its seeds (**pili nuts**). [t. Tagalog]

pi·lif·er·ous (pī·lĭf′ər·əs), *adj.* having hair. [f. *pili-* (comb. form repr. L *pilus* hair) + -FEROUS]

pil·i·form (pĭl′i·fôrm′), *adj.* having the form of a hair.

pil·ing (pī′lĭng), *n.* **1.** piles collectively. See pile². **2.** a structure composed of piles. [f. PILE² + -ING¹]

pill¹ (pĭl), *n.* **1.** a small globular or rounded mass of medicinal substance, to be swallowed whole. **2.** something unpleasant that has to be accepted or endured. **3.** *Slang.* a disagreeable or unpleasant person. **4.** *Sports Slang.* a ball, esp. in golf and baseball. **5.** (*pl.*) *Brit. Slang.* billiards. —*v.t.* **6.** to dose with pills. **7.** *Slang.* to blackball. [late ME, prob. t. MD or MLG: s. *pille*, t. L: m. *pilula*, dim. of *pila* ball]

pill² (pĭl), *v.t., v.i.* **1.** *Archaic* or *Dial.* to peel. **2.** *Obs.* to make or become bald. [partly ME *pilen*, OE *pilian* peel, skin, t. L: m.s. *pilāre* deprive of hair; also ME *pille*(*n*), *pylle*(*n*), t. OF: m. *piller* plunder, mishandle, g. L *pilleāre* flay]

pill³ (pĭl), *v.t. Archaic* to rob, plunder, or pillage. [ME, prob. akin to PILL²]

pil·lage (pĭl′ĭj), *v.,* **-laged, -laging,** *n.* —*v.t.* **1.** to strip of money or goods by open violence, as in war; plunder. **2.** to take as booty. —*v.i.* **3.** to rob with open violence; take booty. [v. use of PILLAGE, n.] —*n.* **4.** the act of plundering, esp. in war. **5.** booty or spoil. [ME *pilage*, t. OF: m. *pillage*, der. *piller* PILL²] —**pil′lag·er,** *n.*

pil·lar (pĭl′ər), *n.* **1.** an upright shaft or structure, of stone, brick, or other material, relatively slender in proportion to its height, and of any shape in section, used as a support, or standing alone, as for a monument. **2.** an upright supporting part. **3.** a person who is a chief supporter of a state, institution, etc.: *a pillar of society.* **4. from pillar to post,** from one predicament or difficulty to another. —*v.t.* **5.** to provide or support with pillars. [ME *pylere*, t. OF: m. *piler*, der. L *pīla* pillar, PILE¹] —Syn. **1.** See column.

pillar box, *Brit.* a pillarlike box in which letters are deposited for collection by mailmen.

Pillars of Hercules, the two promontories on opposite sides of the Strait of Gibraltar: the Rock of Gibraltar in Europe, and the Jebel Musa in Africa are fabled to have been raised by Hercules. [trans. of L *Columnae Herculis*, Gk. *Hērakleíou stêlai*]

pill·box (pĭl′bŏks′), *n.* **1.** a small, low structure of reinforced concrete, enclosing machine guns, and employed as a minor fortress in warfare. **2.** a box, usually shallow and often round, for holding pills.

pill bug, any of various small terrestrial isopods, esp. of the genus *Armadillo*, which can roll themselves up into a ball like a pill.

pil·lion (pĭl′yən), *n.* **1.** a pad or cushion attached behind a saddle, esp. as a seat for a woman. **2.** *Brit.* an extra saddle behind the driver's seat on a motorcycle. [appar. t. Gaelic: m. *pillean*, *pillin*, dim. of *pell* cushion, t. L: s. *pellis* skin, pelt]

pil·lo·ry (pĭl′ə·rĭ), *n., pl.* **-ries,** *v.,* **-ried, -rying.** —*n.* **1.** a wooden framework erected on a post, with holes for securing the head and hands, used to expose an offender to public derision. —*v.t.* **2.** to set in the pillory. **3.** to expose to public ridicule or abuse. [ME *pillori*, t. OF, t. Pr.: m. *espi*(*n*)*glóri*, t. ML: alter. of *speculum* in *glóriam Dei* court (lit., mirror) to the glory of God]

Pillory

pil·low (pĭl′ō), *n.* **1.** a bag or case filled with feathers, down, or other soft material, commonly used as a support for the head during sleep or rest. **2.** a cushion or pad, as the cushion on which pillow lace is made. **3.** a supporting piece or part, as the block on which the inner end of a bowsprit rests. —*v.t.* **4.** to rest on or as on a pillow. **5.** to support with pillows. **6.** to serve as a pillow for. —*v.i.* **7.** to rest as on a pillow. [ME *pilwe*, OE *pyle*, *pylu*, pre-E **pulvi*(*n*), t. L: m.s. *pulvīnus*] —**pil′low·like′,** *adj.* —Syn. **1.** See cushion.

pillow block, *Mach.* a metal box or case for supporting the end of a revolving shaft or journal.

pil·low·case (pĭl′ō·kās′), *n.* a removable case, usually of white cotton or linen, drawn over a pillow. Also, **pil·low·slip** (pĭl′ō·slĭp′).

pillow lace, lace made on a pillow with threads wound on bobbins.

pillow sham, an ornamental cover laid over a bed pillow.

pil·low·y (pĭl′ō·ĭ), *adj.* pillowlike; soft; yielding: *a pillowy clump of sod.*

pi·lo·car·pine (pī′lō·kär′pēn, -pĭn, pĭl′ō·-), *n. Chem.* an alkaloid, $C_{11}H_{16}N_2O_2$, obtained from the leaflets of species of a South American shrub, *Pilocarpus* (jaborandi), used as a diaphoretic and diuretic. Also, **pi·lo·car·pin** (pī′lō·kär′pĭn, pĭl′ō·-). [f. s. NL *Pilocarpus* (f. Gk.: *pîlo*(*s*) cap + m. *karpós* fruit) + -INE²]

pi·lose (pī′lōs), *adj.* covered with hair, esp. soft hair; furry. [t. L: m.s. *pilōsus*] —**pi·los·i·ty** (pī·lŏs′ə·tĭ), *n.*

pi·lot (pī′lət), *n.* **1.** one duly qualified to steer ships into or out of a harbor or through certain difficult waters. **2.** the steersman of a ship. **3.** *Aeron.* one duly qualified to operate an airplane, balloon, or other aircraft. **4.** a guide or leader. **5.** *Mach.* a smaller element acting in advance of another or principal element, and causing the latter to come into play when desired: *the pilot on a gas stove.* —*v.t.* **6.** to steer. **7.** to guide or conduct, as through unknown places, intricate affairs, etc. **8.** to act as pilot on, in, or over. [t. F: m. *pilote*, t. It.: m. *pilota*, t. MGk.: m. **pēdótēs*, der. *pēdá*, pl., rudder]

pi·lot·age (pī′lət·ĭj), *n.* **1.** act of piloting. **2.** the fee paid to a pilot for his services. [t. F]

pilot balloon, a balloon used for the visual observation of upper-air wind currents, etc.

pilot biscuit, hardtack. Also, **pilot bread.**

pilot engine, a locomotive sent on ahead of a railroad train to see that the way is clear and the track is safe.

pilot fish, 1. any of various marine fishes supposed to lead sharks or ships, including *Naucrates, Seriola* and *Kyphosus.* **2.** a whitefish, *Prosopium cylindraceum,* of the Great Lakes and other northern waters.

pi·lot·house (pī′lət·hous′), *n.* an enclosed place on the deck of a vessel, for the steering gear and the pilot.

pilot lamp, an electric lamp, used in association with a control, which by means of position or color indicates the functioning of the control; an indicator light or a control light.

pilot light, 1. a small light kept burning continuously, as beside a large gas burner, to relight a main light whenever desired. **2.** a pilot lamp. Also, **pilot burner.**

pilot plant, a small factory in which processes planned for full-scale operation are tested in advance to eliminate problems, etc.

pi·lous (pī′ləs), *adj.* hairlike. [t. L: m. s. *pilōsus*]

Pil·sen (pĭl′zən), *n.* a city in W Czechoslovakia, in Bohemia. 117,814 (1947). Czech, Plzen.

Pil·sud·ski (pĭl·sōōt′skĭ), *n.* Józe**f** (yōō′zĕf), 1867-1935, Polish marshal and statesman: president, 1918-22; premier, 1926-28, 1930.

Pilt·down (pĭlt′doun′), *n. Anthropol.* a station used by Paleolithic man near Sussex, England, where parts of a skull were found.

Piltdown man, a very early type of man (earlier than the Neanderthaloid type), whose existence was inferred from fragments of a skull discovered at Piltdown in 1912, but whose authenticity is now generally doubted.

ăct, āble, dâre, ärt; ĕbb, ēqual; Ĭf, īce; hŏt, ōver, ôrder, oil, bŏŏk, ōōze, out; ŭp, ūse, ûrge; ə = a in alone; ch, chief; g, give; ng, ring; sh, shoe; th, thin; ŧ̱h, that; zh, vision. See the full key on inside cover.

pil·u·lar (pĭl′yə lər), *adj.* of, pertaining to, or characteristic of pills. [f. s. L *pilula* pill + -AR¹]

pil·ule (pĭl′ūl), *n.* a pill; a little pill. [ME, t. L: m. *pilula* pill, dim. of *pila* ball]

Pi·man (pē′mən), *n.* **1.** a subdivision of the Uto-Aztecan linguistic stock. **2.** *pl.* a tribe of North American Indians of southern Arizona and northwestern Mexico. —*adj.* **3.** of or pertaining to the Pimans.

pi·men·to (pĭ mĕn′tō), *n.*, *pl.* **-tos.** **1.** the dried fruits of *Pimenta officinalis;* allspice. **2.** the tropical American myrtaceous tree yielding it. **3.** the pimiento. [t. Sp.: m. *pimienta* pepper, *pimiento* capsicum, g. L *pigmentum* pigment, in ML spice]

pimento cheese, a processed cheese made from Neufchâtel, cream, or cheddar cheese and pimientos. Also, **pimiento cheese.**

pi·mien·to (pĭ myĕn′tō), *n.*, *pl.* **-tos,** a garden pepper, used as a vegetable, a relish, etc. [t. Sp. See PIMENTO]

pim·o·la (pĭ mō′lə), *n.* an olive stuffed with red sweet pepper; stuffed olive.

pimp (pĭmp), *n.* a pander. [cf. OE *Pimpern* (place name)]

pim·per·nel (pĭm′pər nĕl′, -nəl), *n.* a primulaceous herb of the genus *Anagallis,* esp. the **scarlet pimpernel,** *A. arvensis,* a species with scarlet, purplish, or white flowers that close at the approach of bad weather. [ME, t. OF: m. *pimprenele,* earlier *piprenelle,* der. L *piperīnus* consisting of peppercorns; r. OE *pipeneale,* of Rom. orig.]

pimp·ing (pĭm′pĭng), *adj.* **1.** petty. **2.** weak; sickly.

pim·ple (pĭm′pəl), *n.* a small, usually inflammatory swelling or elevation of the skin; a papule or pustule. [ME; cf. OE *piplian* be pimpled]

pim·ply (pĭm′plĭ), *adj.*, **-plier, -pliest.** having many pimples. Also, **pim·pled** (pĭm′pəld).

pin (pĭn), *n.*, *v.*, pinned, pinning. —*n.* **1.** a small, slender, often pointed piece of wood, metal, etc., used to fasten, support, or attach things. **2.** a short, slender piece of wire with a point at one end and a head at the other, for fastening things together. **3.** any of various forms of fastening or ornament consisting essentially or in part of a pointed penetrating bar: *a safety pin.* **4.** a badge having a pointed bar or pin attached, by which it is fastened to the clothing. **5.** a linchpin, serving to keep a wheel on its axle. **6.** that part of the stem of a key which enters the lock. **7.** a clothespin. **8.** a rolling pin. **9.** a peg, nail, or stud marking the center of a target. **10.** one of the bottle-shaped pieces of wood knocked down in ninepins, tenpins, etc. **11.** *Golf.* the flag staff which identifies a hole. **12.** *Colloq.* a leg. **13.** *Music.* a peg. **14.** *Naut.* **a.** a thole pin. **b.** a belaying pin. **15.** a very small amount; a trifle. **16. on pins and needles,** very nervous and upset. —*v.t.* **17.** to fasten or attach with a pin or pins, or as if with a pin. **18.** to hold fast in a spot or position: *the debris pinned him down.* **19.** to bind or hold to a course of action, a promise, etc. (often fol. by *down*). **20.** to transfix with a pin or the like. **21.** *Slang.* to seize or nab. [ME *pinne,* OE *pinn* peg (c. G *pinne*)]

pi·ña (pē′nyä), *n.* Spanish. **1.** pineapple. **2.** (esp. in Latin America) a pineapple drink. [S Amer. Sp., formerly *pinna,* t. L: m. *pinea* pine cone]

pi·na·ceous (pī nā′shəs), *adj.* belonging to the *Pinaceae,* or pine family of trees and shrubs, which includes the pine, spruce, fir, etc. [f. s. NL *Pināceae* (der. L *pinus* pine) the pine family + -OUS]

piña cloth, a fine, sheer fabric, made from the fiber of pineapple leaves.

pin·a·coid (pĭn′ə koid′), *n.* Crystall. a form whose faces are parallel to two of the axes. [f. m.s. Gk. *pinax* slab + -OID]

pin·a·fore (pĭn′ə fōr′), *n.* **1.** a child's apron, usually one large enough to cover most of the dress. **2.** *Brit.* an apron for grownups. [f. PIN, v., + AFORE, adv.]

Pi·nar del Rí·o (pē när′ dĕl rē′ō), a city in W Cuba. 87,960 pop. (est. 1951).

pi·nas·ter (pī năs′tər, pĭ-), *n.* a pine, *Pinus pinaster,* of southern Europe, having the cones arranged around the branches in radiating clusters. [t. L: wild pine]

pin·ball (pĭn′bôl′), *n.* any of various games played on a sloping board, the object usually being either to shoot a ball, driven by a spring, up a side passage and cause it to roll back down against pins or bumpers and through channels which electrically record the score, or to shoot a ball into pockets at the back of the board.

pince-nez (păns′nā′, păns′-; Fr. păns nĕ′), *n.* a pair of eyeglasses kept in place by a spring which pinches the nose. [t. F: pinch nose]

pin·cers (pĭn′sərz), *n.pl. or sing.* **1.** a gripping tool consisting of two pivoted limbs forming a pair of jaws and a pair of handles (often called a **pair of pincers**). **2.** *Zool.* a grasping organ or pair of organs resembling this. [ME *pynceours,* t. OF: der. *pincier* PINCH]

pinch (pĭnch), *v.t.* **1.** to compress between the finger and thumb, the teeth, the jaws of an instrument, or the like. **2.** to compress, constrict, or squeeze painfully, as a tight shoe does. **3.** to cramp within narrow bounds or quarters. **4.** to render (the face, etc.) unnaturally thin and drawn, as pain or distress does. **5.** to nip (plants) injuriously, as frost does. **6.** to affect with sharp discomfort or distress, as cold, hunger, or need does. **7.** to straiten in means or circumstances. **8.** to stint in al-lowance of money, food, or the like. **9.** to hamper or inconvenience by lack of something specified. **10.** *Dial.* to stint the supply or amount of (a thing). **11.** to put a pinch or small quantity of (a powder, etc.) into something. **12.** *Slang.* to steal. **13.** *Slang.* to arrest. **14.** to move (a heavy object) by means of a pinch or pinch bar. **15.** *Naut.* to sail (a vessel) so close to the wind that her sails shake slightly and her speed is reduced. —*v.i.* **16.** to exert a sharp or painful compressing force. **17.** to cause sharp discomfort or distress: *when hunger pinches.* **18.** to stint oneself; economize unduly; be stingy or miserly. **19.** *Mining.* (of a vein of ore, etc.) to become narrower or smaller, or to give (*out*) altogether. —*n.* **20.** act of pinching; nip; squeeze. **21.** as much of anything as can be taken up between the finger and thumb: *a pinch of salt.* **22.** a very small quantity of anything. **23.** sharp or painful stress, as of hunger, need, or any trying circumstances. **24.** a situation or time of special stress; an emergency. **25.** a pinch bar. **26.** *Slang.* a raid or an arrest. **27.** *Slang.* a theft. [ME *pinche(n),* t. OF: m. *pincier,* g. LL *punctiāre* (der. *punctio* act of pricking), b. with stem *pic-* PIKE²]

pinch bar, a kind of crowbar or lever with a projection which serves as a fulcrum.

pinch·beck (pĭnch′bĕk), *n.* **1.** an alloy of copper and zinc, used in imitation of gold. **2.** something spurious. —*adj.* **3.** made of pinchbeck. **4.** sham or spurious. [named after the inventor, Christopher *Pinchbeck* (died 1732), a London clockmaker]

pinch·cock (pĭnch′kok′), *n.* a clamp for compressing a flexible pipe, as an India-rubber tube, in order to regulate or stop the flow of a fluid.

pinch effect, *Physics.* the constriction of a stream of charged particles resulting from the magnetic field associated with the current carried by the particles.

pinch·er (pĭn′chər), *n.* **1.** one who or that which pinches. **2.** (*pl.*) pincers.

pinch-hit (pĭnch′hĭt′), *v.i.,* **-hit, -hitting. 1.** *Baseball.* to serve as a pinch hitter. **2.** to substitute for someone.

pinch hitter, 1. *Baseball.* a substitute who, usually at some critical moment of the game, bats for another. **2.** any substitute for another, esp. in an emergency.

Pinck·ney (pĭngk′nĭ), *n.* **Charles Cotesworth** (kōts′-wûrth) 1746–1825, American patriot and statesman.

pin·cush·ion (pĭn′kŏŏsh′ən), *n.* a small cushion in which pins are stuck, in readiness for use.

Pin·dar (pĭn′dər), *n.* c522–c443 B.C., Greek lyric poet.

Pin·dar·ic (pĭn där′ĭk), *adj.* **1.** of, pertaining to, or after the manner of Pindar. **2.** of elaborate or regular metrical structure, as an ode or verse. —*n.* **3.** Pindaric ode. See **ode** (def. 3).

pin·dling (pĭn′dlĭng), *adj.* U.S. Dial. puny; sickly.

Pin·dus (pĭn′dəs), *n.* a mountain range in central Greece. Highest peak, 7665 ft.

pine¹ (pīn), *n.* **1.** any member of the genus *Pinus,* comprising evergreen coniferous trees varying greatly in size, with long needle-shaped leaves, including many species of economic importance for their timber and as a source of turpentine, tar, pitch, etc. **2.** any of various coniferous pinelike trees, in regions where the genus *Pinus* is not found. **3.** the wood of the pine tree. **4.** *Colloq.* the pineapple. [ME; OE *pīn,* t. L s. *pīnus*] —**pine′like′,** *adj.*

pine² (pīn), *v.,* pined, pining. —*v.i.* **1.** to suffer with longing, or long painfully (fol. by *for*). **2.** to fail gradually in health or vitality from grief, regret, or longing. **3.** to languish, droop, or waste away. **4.** to repine or fret. —*v.t.* **5.** Archaic. to suffer grief or regret over. —*n.* **6.** *Obs. or Archaic.* painful longing. [ME; OE *pīnian* to torture, der. *pīn.* n., torture, t. VL: m.s. *pēna,* L *poena* punishment]

pin·e·al (pĭn′ĭ əl), *adj.* **1.** pertaining to the pineal body. **2.** resembling a pine cone in shape. [t. NL: s. *pineālis,* der. L *pīnea* pine cone]

pineal body, a body of unknown function present in the brain of all vertebrates having a cranium, believed to be a vestigial sense organ. Also, **pineal gland.**

pine·ap·ple (pīn′ăp′əl), *n.* **1.** the edible juicy fruit (somewhat resembling a pine cone) of a tropical bromeliaceous plant, *Ananas comosus,* being a large collective fruit developed from a spike or head of flowers, and surmounted by a crown of leaves. **2.** the plant itself, a native of tropical South America, now widely cultivated throughout the tropics, having a short stem and rigid, spiny-margined, recurved leaves. **3.** *Mil. Slang.* a bomb or hand grenade made with dynamite.

Pine Bluff, a city in central Arkansas, on the Arkansas river. 44,037 (1960).

pine cone, the cone or strobile of a pine tree.

pine·drops (pīn′drŏps′), *n.sing. and pl.* **1.** a slender, leafless North American ericaceous herb, *Pterospora andromedea,* with nodding white flowers, found growing under pines. **2.** beechdrops.

pi·nene (pī′nēn), *n.* Chem. a terpene, $C_{10}H_{16}$, forming the principal constituent of oil of turpentine and occurring also in other essential oils. [f. PIN(E)¹ + -ENE]

pine needle, the needlelike leaf of the pine tree.

Pi·ne·ro (pə nĭr′ō, -nēr′-), *n.* **Sir Arthur Wing,** 1855–1934, British dramatist.

pin·er·y (pī′nə rĭ), *n.*, *pl.* **-eries. 1.** a place in which pineapples are grown. **2.** a forest or grove of pine trees.

Pines (pīnz), *n.* **Isle of,** an island in the Caribbean, south of and belonging to Cuba. 9812 pop. (1943); 1182 sq. mi.

pine siskin, a small, conifer-inhabiting North American finch, *Spinus pinus*, having yellow markings on the wings and tail. Also, **pine finch**.

pine tar, the residue left after the destructive distillation of pine wood, used medicinally in dermatology and for colds.

pi·ne·tum (pī·nē′təm), n., pl. **-ta** (-tə). an arboretum of pines and coniferous trees. [t. L: pine grove]

pine warbler, a warbler, *Dendroica pinus*, found principally in pine forests of the southeastern U.S.

pin·ey (pī′nĭ), adj., **pinier, piniest**. piny.

pin·feath·er (pĭn′fĕth′ər), n. *Ornith.* 1. an undeveloped feather, before the web portions have expanded. 2. a feather just coming through the skin.

pin·fish (pĭn′fĭsh′), n., pl. **-fishes** (*esp. collectively*) **-fish**. a small fish, *Lagodon rhomboides*, of the porgy family, abounding in the bays of the South Atlantic and Gulf coasts of the U.S.

pin·fold (pĭn′fōld′), n. 1. a pound for stray animals. 2. a fold, as for sheep or cattle. —v.t. 3. to confine in or as in a pinfold. [f. *pin(d)* impound + FOLD²; r. ME *ponfold*, OE *pundfald*]

ping (pĭng), v.i. 1. to produce a sound like that of a bullet striking an object. —n. 2. a pinging sound. [imit.]

ping-pong (pĭng′pŏng′), n. 1. a variety of tennis played on a table with small rackets and a hollow celluloid ball. 2. (*cap.*) a trademark for this game. [der. PING, n., on model of *ding-dong*, etc.]

pin·guid (pĭng′gwĭd), adj. fat; oily; unctuous. [f. s. L *pinguis* fat + -ID⁴] —**pin·guid·i·ty**, n.

pin·head (pĭn′hĕd′), n. 1. the head of a pin. 2. something very small or insignificant. 3. *Slang.* a stupid person.

pin·hole (pĭn′hōl′), n. a small hole made by or as by a pin.

pin·ion¹ (pĭn′yən), n. *Mach.* 1. a small cogwheel engaging with a larger cogwheel or with a rack. 2. an arbor or spindle with teeth which engage with a cogwheel. [t. F: m. *pignon* pinion, OF battlement. der. L *pinna* pinnacle]

pin·ion² (pĭn′yən), n. 1. the distal or terminal segment of a bird's wing (the carpus, metacarpus, and phalanges). 2. the wing of a bird. 3. a feather. 4. *Chiefly Poetic.* the flight feathers collectively. —v.t. 5. to cut off the pinion of (a wing) or bind (the wings), as in order to prevent a bird from flying. 6. to disable or restrain (a bird) thus. 7. to bind (a person's arms or hands) so as to deprive him of the use of them. 8. to disable thus; shackle. 9. to bind or hold fast, as to a thing. [ME, t. OF: m. *pignon* feather. der. L *pinna*]

pin·ite (pĭn′īt, pī′nīt), n. a micalike material, essentially a hydrous silicate of aluminum and potassium. [t. G: m. *pinit*; named after the *Pini* mine in Saxony. See -ITE²]

pink¹ (pĭngk), n. 1. a light tint of crimson; pale reddish purple. 2. any plant of the caryophyllaceous genus *Dianthus*, as *D. plumarius* (the common **garden pink**), *D. chinensis* (**China pink**), or *D. Caryophyllus* (**clove pink**, or carnation). 3. the flower of such a plant; a carnation. 4. the highest type or example of excellence. 5. the highest form or degree: *in the pink of condition*. 6. (*often cap.*) a person with radical, but not extreme, political opinions. 7. *Brit.* scarlet, or scarlet cloth, as worn by fox hunters. 8. *Brit.* a fox hunter. —adj. 9. of the color pink. [orig. uncert.]

pink² (pĭngk), v.t. 1. to pierce with a rapier or the like; stab. 2. to finish at the edge with a scalloped, notched, or other ornamental pattern. 3. to punch (cloth, leather, etc.) with small holes or figures for ornament. 4. *Chiefly Brit. Dial.* to deck or adorn (often fol. by *out* or *up*). [ME *pynke(n)* make points (marks) or holes (with a sharp instrument). Cf. OE *pynca* point. der. *pyng-* (s. *pyngan* to prick)]

pink³ (pĭngk), n. a kind of vessel with a narrow stern. [ME *pinck*, t. MD: m. *pincke* fishing boat]

Pink·er·ton (pĭngk′ər·tən), n. Allan, 1819–84. U.S. detective, born in Scotland.

pink·eye (pĭngk′ī′), n. *Pathol.* a contagious form of conjunctivitis: from the color of the inflamed eye.

Pin·kiang (bĭn′jyäng′), n. Harbin.

pink·ie¹ (pĭngk′ĭ), n. *U.S. Naut.* a type of Atlantic fishing boat. [f. PINK³ + -IE; or ? t. MD: m. *pincke*]

pink·ie² (pĭngk′ĭ), n. *Chiefly Eastern U.S.* the little (fifth) finger. [orig. uncert.]

pink·ish (pĭngk′ĭsh), adj. somewhat pink.

pink rhododendron, *Bot.* a rhododendron, *Rhododendron macrophyllum*, common on the west coast of the U.S.: floral emblem of the State of Washington.

pink·root (pĭngk′rōōt′, -rŏŏt′), n. 1. the root of any of various plants of the loganiaceous genus *Spigelia*, esp. that of *S. marilandica* of the U.S., which is used as a vermifuge. 2. any of these plants.

Pink·ster (pĭngk′stər), n. *U.S. Dial.* Whitsuntide. [t. D: Easter, ult. t. Gk.: alter. of *pentekostē* PENTECOST]

pinkster flower, pinxter flower.

pink tea, *U.S. Colloq. or Slang.* a stylish or elegant reception or person.

pin money, 1. any small sum set aside for non-

essential minor expenditures. 2. an allowance of money to a wife for personal expenditures.

pin·na (pĭn′ə), n., pl. **pinnae** (pĭn′ē), **pinnas**. 1. *Bot.* one of the primary divisions of a pinnate leaf. 2. *Zool.* a. a feather, wing, or winglike part. b. a fin or flipper. 3. *Physiol.* the auricle of the ear. [t. L: feather (pl. wing), also fin] —**pin′nal**, adj.

pin·nace (pĭn′ĭs), n. 1. a light sailing ship, esp. one formerly used in attendance on a larger vessel. 2. any of various kinds of ship's boats. [t. F: m. *pinace*, t. It.: m. *pinaccia*, t. Sp.: m. *pinaza*, der. L *pinus* pine tree]

pin·na·cle (pĭn′ə·kəl), n., v., **-cled, -cling**. —n. 1. a lofty peak. 2. a lofty eminence or position. 3. the highest or culminating point: *the pinnacle of fame*. 4. any pointed, towering part or formation, as of rock. 5. *Archit.* a relatively small upright structure, commonly terminating in a gable, a pyramid, or a cone, rising above the roof or coping of a building or capping a tower, buttress, or other projecting architectural member. —v.t. 6. to place on or as on a pinnacle. 7. to form a pinnacle on; crown. [ME *pinacle*, t. OF; t. LL: m. *pinnāculum*, dim. of L *pinna* pinnacle, usually identified with *pinna* PINNA] —**Syn.** 3. apex, acme.

pin·nate (pĭn′āt, -ĭt), adj. 1. resembling a feather. 2. having parts arranged on each side of a common axis. 3. *Bot.* (of a leaf) having leaflets or primary divisions arranged on each side of a common petiole. Also, **pin′nat·ed**. [t. L: m.s. *pinnātus* feathered, pinnate] —**pin′nate·ly**, adv.

pinnati-, a word element meaning "pinnate." [comb. form repr. L *pinnātus*]

pin·nat·i·fid (pĭ·năt′ə·fĭd), adj. *Bot.* (of a leaf) pinnately cleft, with clefts reaching halfway or more to the midrib. [t. NL: s. *pinnātifidus*, f. *pinnāti-* PINNATI- + *-fidus* cleft]

pin·nat·i·lo·bate (pĭ·năt′ə·lō′bāt), adj. *Bot.* (of a leaf) pinnately lobed, with the divisions extending less than halfway to the midrib. Also, **pin·nat·i·lobed** (pĭ·năt′ə·lōbd′).

pin·na·tion (pĭ·nā′shən), n. *Bot.* pinnate condition or formation.

pin·nat·i·par·tite (pĭ·năt′ə·pär′tīt), adj. *Bot.* (of a leaf) parted in a pinnate manner.

pin·nat·i·ped (pĭ·năt′ə·pĕd′), adj. *Ornith.* having lobate feet.

pin·nat·i·sect (pĭ·năt′ə·sĕkt′), adj. *Bot.* (of a leaf) divided in a pinnate manner.

pin·ner (pĭn′ər), n. 1. one who or that which pins. 2. a headdress with a long hanging flap pinned on at each side.

pin·ni·grade (pĭn′ə·grād′), adj. 1. moving by means of finlike parts or flippers, as the seals and walruses. —n. 2. a pinnigrade animal.

pin·ni·ped (pĭn′ə·pĕd′), adj. belonging to the *Pinnipedia*, a suborder of carnivores with limbs adapted to an aquatic life, including the seals and walruses. [f. *pinni-*, t. L, comb. form of *pinna* feather, fin) + -PED] —**pin·ni·pe·di·an** (pĭn′ə·pē′dĭ·ən), adj., n.

pin·nu·la (pĭn′ yə·lə), n., pl. **-lae** (-lē′). 1. a pinnule. 2. barb of a feather. [t. L, dim. of *pinna* feather, fin]

pin·nu·late (pĭn′yə·lāt′), adj. having pinnules. Also, **pin′nu·lat′ed**.

pin·nule (pĭn′ūl), n. 1. *Zool.* a. a part or organ resembling a barb of a feather, or a fin or the like. b. a finlet. c. one of the lateral branchlets of the arms of a crinoid. 2. *Bot.* a secondary pinna, one of the pinnately disposed divisions of a bipinnate leaf. [t. L: m. *pinnula* PINNULA] —**pin·nu·lar** (pĭn′yə·lər), adj.

pi·noch·le (pē′nŭk·əl), n. 1. a card game played by two, three, or four persons, with a 48-card deck. 2. the combination of the queen of spades and the jack of diamonds in this game. Also, **penuchle, penuckle, pi′·noc′le**. [orig. uncert.]

pi·no·le (pē·nō′lĕ), n. corn (or wheat) dried, ground, and sweetened (usually with the flour of mesquite beans). [t. Sp., t. Aztec: m. *pinolli*]

pi·ñon (pĭn′yən, pēn′yŏn; Sp. pē·nyôn′), n. 1. any of various pines, esp. of the southern Rocky Mountain region, producing large edible seeds. 2. the seed. [t. Sp., der. *piña* pine cone. See PINA]

pin·point (pĭn′point′), n. 1. the point of a pin. 2. a trifle. —v.t. 3. to locate or describe exactly. —adj. 4. exact, precise.

pint (pīnt), n. a liquid and also dry measure of capacity, equal to one half of a liquid and dry quart respectively. [ME *pynte*, t. F: m. *pinte*, t. MD: plug]

pin·ta (pĭn′tə; Sp. pēn′tä), n. a disease prevalent in Mexico, Central and South America, and elsewhere, marked by spots of various colors on the skin. [t. Sp.: spot, g. L *pi(n)cta*, fem. pp., painted]

Pin·ta (pĭn′tə), n. one of the three ships under Columbus when he first discovered America.

pin·ta·do (pĭn′tä′dō), n., pl. **-dos, -does**. the Spanish mackerel. Also, **pin·ta·da**. [t. Sp. and Pg.: painted, pp. of *pintar* paint, der. *pinta* a spot. See PINTA]

pin·tail (pĭn′tāl′), n. 1. a long-necked river duck, *Dafila acuta*, of the Old and New Worlds, having long narrow middle tail feathers. 2. the American ruddy duck, *Erismatura jamaicensis rubida*. 3. the sharp-tailed grouse, *Pedioecetes phasianellus*, of North America. 4. an Old World sand grouse, *Pteroclurus alchatus*.

pin·ta·no (pĭn tä′nō), n., pl. **-nos.** the cow pilot (fish).

pin·tle (pĭn′tal), n. **1.** a pin or bolt, esp. one upon which something turns, as in a hinge. **2.** a pin, bolt, or hook on the rear of the towing vehicle, to which a gun or the like, is attached. [ME and OE *pintel* penis, f. *pint* (c. D and G *pint*) + *-el*, dim. suffix]

pin·to (pĭn′tō, pēn′-), adj., n., pl. **-tos.** —adj. **1.** piebald; mottled; spotted: *a pinto horse.* —n. **2.** *Western U.S.* a pinto horse. **3.** pinto bean. [t. Sp.: painted, short for *pintado*, pp. of *pintar* paint. See PINTADO, PINTA]

pinto bean, *Western U.S.* a variety of the common bean, *Phaseolus vulgaris*, having mottled or spotted seeds.

Pintsch gas (pĭnch), gas with high illuminating power made from shale oil or petroleum, used in floating buoys, lighthouses, and railroad cars. [named for Richard *Pintsch*, 1840–1919, German inventor]

pin·up (pĭn′ŭp′), *U.S. Slang.* —n. **1.** a picture of a very attractive girl, hung on a wall, usually by personally unknown admirers. **2.** the girl in such a picture. —adj. **3.** of or in such a picture: *a pinup girl.*

pin·weed (pĭn′wēd′), n. any plant of the cistaceous genus *Lechea*, so called from the slender stems and narrow leaves.

pin·wheel (pĭn′hwēl′), n. **1.** a child's toy consisting of a paper wheel fixed by a pin to a stick so as to revolve in the wind. **2.** a kind of firework supported on a pin and revolving rapidly when ignited. **3.** *Mach.* a wheel with pins, usually on the periphery as cogs. Also, **pin wheel.**

pin·worm (pĭn′wûrm′), n. a small nematode worm, *Enterobius vermicularis*, infesting the intestine and migrating to the rectum and anus, esp. in children.

pinx., pinxit.

pinx·it (pĭnk′sĭt), *Latin.* he (or she) painted it.

pinx·ter flower (pĭngk′star), a wild azalea, *Rhododendron nudiflorum* (*Azalea nudiflora*), of the U.S., with pink or purplish flowers. Also, **pinkster flower.**

pin·y (pī′nĭ), adj., **pinier, piniest. 1.** abounding in or covered with pine trees. **2.** consisting of pine trees. **3.** pertaining to or suggestive of pine trees. Also, **piney.**

pin·yon jay (pĭn′yan, pēn′yōn), a grayish-blue, uncrested jay, *Gymnorhinus cyanocephalus*, found in mountainous parts of the western U.S.

Pin·zón (pēn thōn′), n. **1. Martín Alonso** (mär tēn′ ä lōn′sō), c1440–93? Spanish navigator with Columbus. **2.** his brother, **Vicente Yáñez** (vē thĕn′tĕ yä′nyĕth), c1460–c1524, Spanish navigator with Columbus.

pi·o·neer (pī′ə nĭr′), n. **1.** one of those who first enter or settle a region, thus opening it for occupation and development by others. **2.** one of those who are first or earliest in any field of inquiry, enterprise, or progress: *pioneers in cancer research.* **3.** one of a body of foot soldiers detailed to make roads, dig intrenchments, etc., in advance of the main body. **4.** *Ecol.* a plant or animal which successfully invades and becomes established in a bare area. —v.i. **5.** to act as a pioneer. —v.t. **6.** to open or prepare (a way, etc.), as a pioneer does. **7.** to open a way for. **8.** to be a pioneer in. [t. F: m. *pionnier* pioneer, der. OF *peon* foot soldier. See PEON, PAWN²]

pi·ous (pī′əs), adj. **1.** having or showing a dutiful spirit of reverence for God or an earnest regard for religious obligations. **2.** practiced or used from religious motives (real or pretended), or for some good object: *a pious deception.* **3.** sacred as distinguished from secular: *pious literature.* **4.** *Archaic.* having or showing due respect or regard for parents or others. [t. L: m. *pius*] —**pi′ous·ly,** adv. —**pi′ous·ness,** n. —Syn. **1.** devout, godly. See **religious.**

pip¹ (pĭp), n. **1.** *Chiefly Brit.* one of the spots on dice, playing cards, or dominoes. **2.** each of the small segments into which the surface of a pineapple is divided. **3.** *Brit. Slang.* metal insigne of rank on the shoulders of commissioned officers. **4.** *Hort.* **a.** an individual rootstock of a plant, esp. of lily of the valley. **b.** a portion of the rootstock or root of several other plants, as the peony. [earlier *peep*; orig. unknown]

pip² (pĭp), n. **1.** a contagious disease of birds, esp. poultry, characterized by the secretion of a thick mucus in the mouth and throat. **2.** *Chiefly Humorous.* any minor ailment in a person. [ME *pippe*, appar. t. MD, t. VL: m.s. *pipita*, for L *pītuīta* phlegm, pip]

pip³ (pĭp), n. a small seed, esp. of a fleshy fruit, as an apple or orange. [short for PIPPIN]

pip⁴ (pĭp), v., **pipped, pipping.** —v.i. **1.** to peep or chirp. —v.t. **2.** (of a young bird) to crack or chip a hole through (the shell). [var. of PEEP²]

pip·age (pī′pĭj), n. **1.** conveyance, as of water, gas, or oil, by means of pipes. **2.** the pipes so used. **3.** the sum charged for the conveyance.

pi·pal (pē′pəl), n. a species of fig tree, *Ficus religiosa*, of India, somewhat resembling the banian. Cf. **bo tree.** [t. Hind., g. Skt. *pippala*]

pipe¹ (pīp), n., v., **piped, piping.** —n. **1.** a hollow cylinder of metal, wood, or other material, for the conveyance of water, gas, steam, etc., or for some other purpose; a tube. **2.** any of various tubular or cylindrical objects, parts, or formations. **3.** a tube of wood, clay, hard rubber, or other material, with a small bowl at one end, used for smoking tobacco, opium, etc. **4.** a quantity, as of tobacco, that fills the bowl. **5.** *Music.* **a.** a tube used as, or to form an essential part of, a musical wind instrument. **b.** a musical wind instrument consisting of a single tube of straw, reed, wood, or other material, as a flute, clarinet, or oboe. **c.** one of the wooden or metal tubes from which the tones of an organ are produced. **d.** (pl.) any musical wind instrument. **e.** (pl.) any woodwind instrument. **f.** (usually pl.) bagpipe. **g.** (usually pl.) a set of flutes, as Panpipes. **h.** a small primitive type of flute, played with one hand and usually accompanied by a drum which is struck by the other hand (used chiefly in ancient military music). **6.** *Naut.* a boatswain's whistle. **b.** the sounding of it as a call. **7.** the note or call of a bird, etc. **8.** the voice, esp. as used in singing. **9.** a tubular organ or passage in an animal body. **10.** (pl.) *Colloq.* the respiratory passages. **11.** *Mining.* **a.** a cylindrical vein or body of ore. **b.** one of the vertical cylindrical masses of bluish rock, of eruptive origin, in which diamonds are found embedded in South Africa. **12.** *Bot.* the stem of a plant. —v.i. **13.** to play on a pipe. **14.** *Naut.* to announce orders, etc. by a boatswain's pipe or other signal. **15.** to speak shrilly. **16.** to make or utter a shrill sound like that of a pipe. **17.** *Mining.* to carve forming a cylindrical cavity. **18.** to form cylindrical or conical holes during molding, as in casting steel ingots. —v.t. **19.** to convey by means of pipes. **20.** to supply with pipes. **21.** to play (music) on a pipe or pipes. **22.** to summon, order, etc., by sounding the boatswain's pipe or whistle: *all hands were piped on deck.* **23.** to bring, lead, etc., by playing on a pipe. **24.** to utter in a shrill tone. **25.** to trim or finish (a garment, etc.) with piping. [ME and OE *pīpe* (c. LG *pīpe*, G *pfeife*), ult. der. L *pīpāre* chirp] —**pipe′like′,** adj.

pipe² (pīp), n. **1.** a large cask, of varying capacity, for wine, etc. **2.** such a cask as a measure of capacity for wine, etc., equal to 4 barrels, 2 hogsheads, or half a tun, and containing 126 wine gallons. **3.** such a cask with its contents. [t. OF, ult. same as PIPE¹]

pipe clay, a fine white clay used for making tobacco pipes, whitening parts of military or other dress, etc.

pipe dream, *Slang.* any fantastic notion, story, etc.

pipe·fish (pīp′fĭsh′), n., pl. **-fishes,** (esp. collectively) **-fish.** an elongate fish belonging to the *Syngnathidae*, a family of lophobranch fishes with an elongated tubular snout and a slender body of angular section, encased in a bony armor.

pipe·ful (pīp′fŏŏl′), n., pl. **-fuls.** a quantity sufficient to fill the bowl of a pipe.

pipe line, 1. a conduit of pipe for the transportation of petroleum, petroleum products, natural gas, etc. **2.** a channel of information, usually confidential. Also, **pipe′line′.**

pipe of peace, a calumet.

pipe organ, an organ with pipes, as distinguished from a reed organ. See **organ** (def. 1).

pip·er (pī′par), n. **1.** one who plays on a pipe. **2.** a bagpiper. **3. pay the piper,** to bear the consequences, usually of some pleasure.

pip·er·a·ceous (pĭp′ə rā′shəs, pī′pə-), adj. belonging to the *Piperacae*, or pepper family of plants, which includes the spice-bearing pepper, *Piper nigrum*, the betel and cubeb plants, etc. [f. L *piper* pepper + -ACEOUS]

pi·per·i·dine (pī pĕr′ĭ dēn′, pĭp′ərə-, -dĭn), n. *Chem.* a volatile liquid, $C_5H_{11}N$, with the odor of an amine, obtained from the alkaloid piperine or from pyridine. [f. L *piper* pepper + -ID(E) + -INE²]

pip·er·ine (pĭp′ərēn′, -ərĭn), n. *Chem.* a white crystalline alkaloid, $C_{17}H_{19}NO_3$, obtained from pepper and other piperaceous plants, and also prepared synthetically. [t. F, t. It.: m. *peperino* a cement of volcanic ashes, der. L *piper* pepper]

pip·er·o·nal (pĭp′ərə näl′), n. *Chem.* a white crystalline aldehyde, $C_8H_6O_3$, a benzene derivative, with an odor resembling that of heliotrope: used in perfumery.

pipe·stem (pīp′stĕm′), n. the stem of a tobacco pipe.

pipe·stone (pīp′stōn′), n. a reddish argillaceous stone, used by North American Indians for making tobacco pipes.

pi·pette (pĭ pĕt′), n. a slender graduated tube for measuring and transferring liquids from one vessel to another. Also, **pi·pet′.** [t. F, dim. of *pipe* PIPE¹]

pip·ing (pī′pĭng), n. **1.** pipes collectively. **2.** material formed into a pipe or pipes. **3.** the act of one who or that which pipes. **4.** the sound of pipes. **5.** shrill sound. **6.** the music of pipes. **7.** a cordlike ornamentation made of icing, used on pastry. **8.** a tubular band of material, sometimes containing a cord, for trimming garments, etc., as along edges and seams. —adj. **9.** characterized by the music of the peaceful pipe (rather than the martial fife or trumpet). **10.** playing on a musical pipe. **11.** that pipes. **12.** emitting a shrill sound: *a piping voice.* **13. piping hot,** very hot.

pip·it (pĭp′ĭt), n. any of various small passerine birds of the genus *Anthus* (family *Motacillidae*) bearing a superficial resemblance to the larks. [imit. of its note]

pip·kin (pĭp′kĭn), n., **1.** a small earthen pot. **2.** a piggin. [? f. PIPE² + -KIN]

pip·pin (pĭp′ĭn), n. **1.** any of numerous varieties of apple, generally characterized by substantial, roundish oblate, blocky fruit. **2.** *Bot.* a seed. [ME *pypyn*, t. OF: m. *pepin* fruit seed, pip; orig. uncert.]

pip·sis·se·wa (pĭp sĭs′ə wə), n. an evergreen herb of the ericaceous genus *Chimaphila*, esp. *C. umbellata*, the

b., blend of, blended; c., cognate with; d., dialect, dialectal; der., derived from; f., formed from; g., going back to; m., modification of; r., replacing; s., stem of; t., taken from; ?, perhaps. See the full key on inside cover.

leaves of which are used medicinally for their tonic, diuretic, and astringent properties. [t. Cree: m. *pipisisikew* it reduces stone in the bladder to particles]

pip·y (pī′pī), *adj.* **pipier, pipiest. 1.** pipelike; tubular. **2.** piping; shrill.

pi·quant (pē′kənt), *adj.* **1.** agreeably pungent or sharp in taste or flavor; biting; tart. **2.** agreeably stimulating, interesting, or attractive. **3.** of a smart or racy character: *piquant wit*. **4.** *Archaic.* sharp or stinging, esp. to the feelings. [t. F: pricking, pungent, ppr. of *piquer*. See PIQUE, v.] —**pi′quan·cy,** *n.* —**pi′quant·ly,** *adv.*

pique (pēk), *v.*, **piqued, piquing,** *n.* —*v.t.* **1.** to affect with sharp irritation and resentment, esp. by some wound to pride: *to be piqued at a refusal.* **2.** to wound (the pride, vanity, etc.). **3.** to excite (interest, curiosity, etc.). **4.** to affect with a lively interest or curiosity. **5.** to pride or plume (oneself). **6.** *Aeron.* to dive at. [t. F: m.s. *piquer* prick, sting] —*n.* **7.** a state of irritated feeling between persons. **8.** a feeling of sharp irritation and resentment, esp. from some wound to pride, self-esteem; offense or umbrage taken. [t. F, der. *piquer* prick, sting] —**Syn. 1.** offend, sting, nettle, vex. **3.** stimulate, excite, prick, goad.

pi·qué (pī kā′), *n.* **1.** a fabric woven lengthwise with raised cords, of cotton, spun rayon, or silk. —*adj.* **2.** (of glove seams and gloves) stitched through lapping edges. [t. F: stitched. quilted, pp. of *piquer*. See PIQUE]

pi·quet (pī ket′), *n.* a card game played by two persons with a pack of 32 cards, the cards from deuces to sixes being excluded. [t. F, orig. uncert]

pi·ra·cy (pī′rəsī), *n., pl.* **-cies. 1.** robbery or illegal violence at sea or on the shores of the sea. **2.** the unauthorized appropriation or use of a copyrighted or patented work, idea, etc. [t. ML: m.s. *pirātia*, t. Gk.: s. m. *peirāteia*]

Pi·rae·us (pī rē′əs), *n.* a seaport in SE Greece: the port of Athens. 186,014 (1951). Also, **Peiraeus.** Greek, **Peiraievs.**

pi·ra·gua (pī rä′gwə, -räg′wə), *n.* pirogue. [t. Sp., t. Carib: a dugout. Cf. PIROGUE]

Pi·ran·del·lo (pē′rän del′lō), *n.* Luigi (lōō ē′jē), 1867–1936, Italian dramatist, novelist, and poet.

pi·ra·nha (pī rän′yə), *n.* any small (hand-sized) South American characin fish of the subfamily *Serraosalminae,* noted for voracious habits, dangerous even to human swimmers. [t. Pg.]

pi·rate (pī′rət), *n., v.*, **-rated, -rating.** —*n.* **1.** one who robs or commits illegal violence at sea or on the shores of the sea. **2.** a vessel employed by such persons. **3.** any plunderer. **4.** one who appropriates and reproduces, without authorization as for his own profit, the literary artistic, or other work or any invention of another. —*v.t.* **5.** to commit piracy upon; rob or plunder as a pirate does. **6.** to take by piracy. **7.** to appropriate and reproduce (literary work, etc.) without authorization or legal right. —*v.i.* **8.** to commit or practice piracy. [ME, t. L: m. *pirāta*, t. Gk.: m. *peirātēs*] —**pi·rat·i·cal** (pī rat′ə kəl), *adj.* —**pi·rat′i·cal·ly,** *adv.*

Pirates of Penzance, an operetta (1879) by Gilbert and Sullivan.

Pi·rith·o·us (pī rith′ō əs), *n.* *Gk. Legend.* one of the Lapithae. He went to Hades with Theseus to abduct Persephone but perished in the attempt. See **Lapithae.**

pi·rogue (pī rōg′), *n.* **1.** a canoe hollowed from the trunk of a tree. **2.** a native boat, especially an American dugout. **3.** a canoe of any kind. Also, **piragua.** [t. F, prob. t. Galibi, Carib d. of Cayenne. Cf. PIRAGUA]

pir·ou·ette (pīr′ōō ět′), *n., v.*, **-etted, -etting.** —*n.* **1.** a whirling about on one foot or on the points of the toes, as in dancing. —*v.i.* **2.** to perform a pirouette; whirl, as on the toes. [t. F: top, whirligig, whirl, b. with *pivot* pivot and *girouette* weathervane (der. s. *girer* to turn)]

Pi·sa (pē′zə; *It.* -sä), *n.* a city in NW Italy, on the Arno river: leaning tower. 81,000 (est. 1954).

pis al·ler (pē zà lě′), *French.* the last resort. [F: worst going]

Pi·sa·no (pē sä′nō), *n.* **1.** Giovanni (jō vän′nē) c1245–c1320, Italian sculptor and architect. **2.** his father, Niccola (nēk kô′lä), c1220–78, Italian sculptor and architect.

pis·ca·ry (pīs′kə rī), *n., pl.* **-ries. 1.** *Law.* the right or privilege of fishing in particular waters. **2.** a fishing place. [late ME, t. ML: m.s. *piscāria,* prop. fem. of L *piscārius* pertaining to fish]

pis·ca·to·ri·al (pīs′kə tōr′ī əl), *adj.* **1.** of or pertaining to fishermen or fishing. **2.** given or devoted to fishing. Also, **pis·ca·to·ry** (pīs′kə tōr′ī). [f. s. L *piscātorius* + -AL[1]]

Pis·ces (pīs′ēz), *n.pl., gen.* **Piscium** (pīsh′ī əm). **1.** the Fishes, a northern zodiacal constellation. **2.** the twelfth sign of the zodiac. See diag. under **zodiac.3.** *Zool.* the class of vertebrates that includes the fishes (*teleosts*), exclusive of elasmobranchs, dipnoans, and marsipobranchs. [t. L, pl. of *piscis* fish]

pisci-, a word element meaning "fish." [t. L, comb. form of *piscis*]

pis·ci·cul·ture (pīs′ī kŭl′chər), *n.* the breeding, rearing, and transplantation of fish by artificial means.

pis·ci·na (pī sī′nə, pī sē′-), *n., pl.* **-nae** (-nē). *Eccles.* a basin with a drain used for certain ablutions, now generally in the sacristy. [t. L: orig. fishpond] —**pis·ci·nal** (pīs′ī nəl), *adj.*

pis·cine (pīs′īn, -īn), *adj.* of or pertaining to fishes. [f. s. L *piscis* fish + -INE[1]]

pis·civ·o·rous (pī sīv′ə rəs), *adj.* fish-eating.

Pis·gah (pīz′gə), *n.* **Mount,** a mountain ridge of ancient Palestine, NE of the Dead Sea (now in Jordan): from its summit, Mt. Nebo, Moses viewed the Promised Land.

pish (pīsh, psh), *interj.* **1.** an exclamation of contempt or impatience. —*n.* **2.** an exclamation of "pish!" —*v.i.* **3.** to say "pish." —*v.t.* **4.** to say "pish" at or to.

Pi·sid·i·a (pī sīd′ī ə), *n.* an ancient country in S Asia Minor: later a Roman province.

pis·i·form (pī′sə fôrm′), *adj.* **1.** having the form of a pea. **2.** *Anat., Zool.* pertaining to the pealike bone on the ulnar side of the carpus. [t. NL: s. *pisiformis,* f. *pīsi-* (comb. form repr. L *pīsum* pea) + *-formis* -FORM]

Pi·sis·tra·tus (pī sīs′trə təs, pī sīs′-), *n.* c605–527 B.C., tyrant of Athens.

pis·mire (pīs′mīr′), *n.* an ant. [cf. Dan. *myre* ant]

pi·so·lite (pī′sə līt′, pīz′ə-), *n.* limestone composed of rounded concretions about the size of a pea. [t. NL: m.s. *pisolithus,* f. Gk.: *pīso(s)* pea + m. *-lithos* -LITE] —**pi·so·lit·ic** (pī′sə lĭt′ĭk, pīz′ə-), *adj.*

Pis·sar·ro (pē sà rō′), *n.* **Camille** (kà mē′y), 1830?–1903, French impressionist painter.

pis·ta·chi·o (pīs tä′shī ō′, pīs täsh′ī ō′), *n., pl.* **-chios. 1.** the stone (nut) of the fruit of a small anacardiaceous tree, *Pistacia vera,* of southern Europe and Asia Minor. **2.** its edible greenish kernel, used for flavoring. **3.** the tree itself. **4.** pistachio nut flavor. **5.** light yellowish green. Also, **pis·ta·che** (pīs täsh′; *Fr.* päsh′). [t. It.: m. *pistacchio,* t. L: m. *pistācium,* t. Gk.: m. *pistákion*]

pis·ta·reen (pīs′tə rēn′), *n.* **1.** (in Spanish America) the old Spanish peseta. —*adj.* **2.** having little value. [appar. a pop. deriv. of Sp. *peseta,* dim. of *peso* PESO]

pis·til (pīs′tĭl), *n.* *Bot.* **1.** the ovule-bearing or seed-bearing organ of a flower, consisting when complete of ovary, style and stigma. **2.** such organs collectively, where there are more than one in a flower. **3.** a gynoecium. [t. NL: m.s. *pistillum* pistil, L pestle]

pis·til·late (pīs′tə lĭt, -lāt′), *adj.* *Bot.* **1.** having a pistil or pistils. **2.** having a pistil or pistils but no stamens.

Pis·to·ia (pē stô′yä), *n.* a city in N Italy, in Tuscany. 79,000 (est. 1954).

pis·tol (pīs′təl), *n., v.*, **-toled, -toling** or (*esp. Brit.*) **-tolled, -tolling.** —*n.* **1.** a short firearm intended to be held and fired with one hand. —*v.t.* **2.** to shoot with a pistol. [t. F: m. *pistole* pistol, also pistole, t. G, t. Czech: m. *pišt'al*]

pis·tole (pīs tōl′), *n.* **1.** a former gold coin of Spain, worth about $4. **2.** any of various other obsolete European gold coins. [t. F: a coin, transferred use of *pistole* PISTOL, on the analogy of *écu* meaning both shield and coin]

pis·to·leer (pīs′tə lĭr′), *n.* one who uses a pistol. [t. F m. *pistolier*]

pis·ton (pīs′tən), *n.* **1.** a movable disk or cylinder fitting closely within a tube or hollow cylinder, and capable of being driven alternately forward and backward in the tube by pressure, as in a gasoline engine, thus imparting reciprocatory motion to a rod (**piston rod**) attached to it on one side, or of being driven thus by the rod, as in a pump. **2.** a pumplike valve used to change the pitch in a cornet or the like. [t. F, t. It.: m. *pistone,* der. *pistare* pound, der. L *pistus,* pp., pounded]

piston ring, a metallic ring, usually one of a series, and split so as to be expansible, placed around a piston in order to maintain a tight fit, as inside the cylinder of an internal-combustion engine.

pit[1] (pīt), *n., v.*, **pitted, pitting.** —*n.* **1.** a hole or cavity in the ground. **2.** a covered or concealed excavation in the ground to serve as a trap; pitfall. **3.** *Mining.* **a.** an excavation made in digging for some mineral deposit. **b.** the shaft of a coal mine. **c.** the mine itself. **4.** the abode of evil spirits and lost souls; hell, or a part of it. **5.** a hollow or indentation in a surface. **6.** a natural hollow or depression in the body: *the pit of the stomach.* **7.** a small depressed scar such as one of those left on the skin after smallpox. **8.** an inclosure for combats, as of dogs or cocks. **9.** *U.S.* that part of the floor of an exchange devoted to a special kind of business: *the grain pit.* **10.** *Archit.* **a.** all that part of the main floor of a theater behind the musicians. **b.** *Brit.* a section of the main floor of a theater behind the orchestra and in front of the parquet, parterre, or orchestra stalls, usually of unreserved seats. **c.** the persons occupying this section. —*v.t.* **11.** to mark with pits or depressions. **12.** to place or bury in a pit. **13.** to set in active opposition, as one against another. **14.** to set (animals) in a pit or inclosure to fight. —*v.i.* **15.** to become marked with pits or depressions. **16.** *Pathol.* to retain for a time the mark of pressure by the finger, etc., as the skin. [ME and OE *pytt,* ult. t. L: m. *puteus* well, pit, shaft]

pit[2] (pīt), *n., v.*, **pitted, pitting.** *U.S.* —*n.* **1.** the stone of a fruit, as of a cherry, peach, or plum. —*v.t.* **2.** to take out the pit from (a fruit, etc.). [t. D: kernel]

pi·ta (pē′tə), *n.* **1.** a fiber obtained from species of *Agave, Aechmea,* or related genera, used for cordage, etc. **2.** one of these plants. [t. Sp., t. Kechua]

pit·a·pat (pĭt′ə·păt′), *adv.*, *n.*, *v.*, **-patted, -patting.** —*adv.* 1. with a quick succession of beats or taps. —*n.* 2. the movement or the sound of something going pitapat. —*v.i.* 3. to go pitapat. [imit.]

Pit·cairn Island (pĭt′kârn), a small British island in the S Pacific, SE of Tuamotu Archipelago: settled by mutineers of the *Bounty* in 1790. 135 (est. 1955); 2 sq. mi.

pitch¹ (pĭch), *v.t.* 1. to set up or erect (a tent, camp, or the like). 2. to put, set, or plant in a fixed or definite place or position. 3. to fix firmly, as in the ground. 4. to throw, fling, hurl, or toss. 5. *Baseball.* to deliver or serve (the ball) to the batter. 6. to set at a certain point, degree, level, etc. 7. *Obs. except in pp.* to set in order; to arrange, as a field of battle. 8. *Music.* to set at a particular pitch, or determine the key or keynote of (a tune, etc.). 9. *Cards.* a. to lead (a card of a particular suit), thereby fixing that suit as trump. b. to determine (the trump) thus. —*v.i.* 10. to plunge or fall forward or headlong. 11. to lurch. 12. to throw or toss. 13. *Baseball.* a. to deliver or serve the ball to the batter. b. to fill the position of pitcher. 14. to slope downward; dip. 15. to plunge with alternate fall and rise of bow and stern, as a ship (opposed to *roll*). 16. to fix a tent or temporary habitation; encamp. 17. to settle. 18. to fix or decide (fol. by *on* or *upon*), often casually or without particular consideration. 19. **pitch in,** *Colloq.* to begin vigorously. 20. **pitch into,** *Colloq.* to attack vigorously. —*n.* 21. point, position, or degree, as in a scale. 22. height in general (now chiefly in certain specific uses): *pitch of an arch.* 23. the highest point or greatest height. 24. *Music, Speech, etc.* degree of height (acuteness) or depth (gravity) of a tone or of sound, depending upon the relative rapidity of the vibrations by which it is produced. 25. a particular tonal standard with which given tones may be compared in respect to their relative level. 26. *Acoustics.* the apparent predominant frequency sounded by an acoustical source. 27. act or manner of pitching. 28. a throw or toss, as of a baseball. 29. the pitching movement, or a plunge forward, of a ship or the like. 30. downward inclination or slope. 31. a sloping part or place. 32. a quantity of something pitched or placed somewhere. 33. *Cricket.* the central part of the cricket field. 34. a spot where a person or thing is placed or stationed, esp., in England, the established location of a street peddler, singer, etc. 35. *Aeron.* a. (of an airplane) nosing up or down about a transverse axis. b. (of a propeller) the distance which a propeller would advance in one revolution. 36. *Geol., Mining.* the inclination of the axis of a fold from the horizontal. 37. *Archit.* the slope or steepness of a roof. 38. *Mach.* a. the distance between the centers of two adjacent teeth in a toothed wheel or rack. b. the distance between two things, esp. in a series, as between two threads of a screw, two rivets in a girder, etc. 39. *Cards.* a variety of seven-up, in which the trump suit for a deal is set by the first card led. [ME *picche(n)*; ? akin to PICK¹] —**Syn.** 4. See throw.

pitch² (pĭch), *n.* 1. any of various dark-colored tenacious or viscous substances used for covering the seams of vessels after calking, for making pavements, etc., as the residuum left after the distillation of coal tar (coal-tar pitch), or a product derived similarly from wood tar (wood pitch). 2. any of certain bitumens: *mineral pitch* (asphaltum). 3. any of various resins. 4. the sap or crude turpentine which exudes from the bark of pines. —*v.t.* 5. to smear or cover with pitch. [ME *pich,* OE *pic,* t. L: s. *piz;* akin to Gk. *píssa*] —**pitch′like′,** *adj.*

pitch·blende (pĭch′blĕnd′), *n.* an impure uraninite, occurring in black pitchlike masses: the principal ore of uranium and radium. [half trans., half adoption of G *pechblende.* See PITCH², BLENDE]

pitch circle, an imaginary circle concentric with the axis of a toothed wheel, at such a distance from the base of the teeth that it is in contact with and rolls upon a similar circle of another toothed wheel engaging with the first.

pitch-dark (pĭch′därk′), *adj.* black or dark as pitch.

pitched battle (pĭcht), (formerly) a battle in which all forces of both antagonists are engaged.

pitch·er¹ (pĭch′ər), *n.* 1. a container, usually with a handle and spout or lip, for holding and pouring liquids. 2. *Bot.* a. a pitcherlike modification of the leaf of certain plants. b. an ascidium. [ME *picher,* t. OF: m. *pichier;* ? akin to BEAKER] —**pitch′er·like′,** *adj.*

pitch·er² (pĭch′ər), *n.* 1. one who pitches. 2. *Baseball.* the player who delivers or throws the ball to the batter. 3. *Golf.* a lightweight iron golf club with a broad, greatly lofted face. [f. PITCH¹, v. + -ER¹]

pitcher plant, any of various plants with leaves modified into a pitcherlike receptacle, or ascidium, as the plants of the genera *Sarracenia* and *Darlingtonia.*

pitch·fork (pĭch′fôrk′), *n.* 1. a fork for lifting and pitching hay, etc. —*v.t.* 2. to pitch or throw with or as with a pitchfork.

Pitch Lake, a deposit of asphalt on Trinidad, in the British West Indies.

California pitcher plant, *Darlingtonia californica*

pitch line, 1. a pitch circle. 2. a corresponding straight line on a toothed rack.

pitch·man (pĭch′mən), *n.* 1. an itinerant salesman of small wares which are usually carried in a case with col-

lapsible legs, allowing it to be set up or removed quickly. 2. any high-pressure salesman, usually of goods of dubious quality. [f. PITCH¹ + MAN]

pitch pine, any of several species of pine from which pitch or turpentine is obtained.

pitch pipe, a small pipe sounded with the breath to give the pitch for singing, tuning an instrument, etc.

pitch·stone (pĭch′stōn′), *n.* a glassy igneous rock having a resinous luster and resembling hardened pitch. [f. PITCH², n., + STONE, trans. of G *pechstein*]

pitch·y (pĭch′Y), *adj.,* **pitchier, pitchiest.** 1. full of or abounding in pitch. 2. smeared with pitch. 3. of the nature of pitch; resembling pitch. 4. black; dark as pitch. —**pitch′i·ness,** *n.*

pit·e·ous (pĭt′Yəs), *adj.* 1. such as to excite or deserve pity, or appealing strongly for pity; pathetic. 2. *Archaic.* compassionate. [f. *pite* PITY + -OUS; r. ME *pitous,* t. AF, ult. der. L *pietas* piety] —**pit′e·ous·ly,** *adv.* —**pit′e·ous·ness,** *n.* —**Syn.** 1. affecting, distressing, lamentable, woeful, sad. See pitiful.

pit·fall (pĭt′fôl′), *n.* 1. a concealed pit prepared as a trap for animals or men to fall into. 2. any trap or danger for the unwary. —**Syn.** 1, 2. See trap¹.

pith (pĭth), *n.* 1. any soft, spongy tissue or substance: *the pith of an orange.* 2. *Bot.* the central cylinder of parenchymatous tissue in the stems of dicotyledonous plants. 3. *Zool.* the soft inner part of a feather, a hair, etc. 4. the important or essential part; essence. 5. strength, force, or vigor. —*v.t.* 6. to take the pith from (plants, etc.). 7. to destroy the spinal cord or brain of. 8. to slaughter, as cattle, by severing the spinal cord. [ME; OE *pitha* pith. Cf. D *pit* pith, PIT²]

pith·e·can·thrope (pĭth′ə·kăn′thrōp), *n.* a member of the genus *Pithecanthropus.*

Pith·e·can·thro·pus (pĭth′ə·kăn·thrō′pəs, -kăn′thrə-pəs), *n., pl.* **-pi** (-pĭ, -pī). an extinct genus of "apelike" men, esp. *Pithecanthropus erectus* of the Pleistocene of Java (the **Java man**). [t. NL, f. Gk.: m.s. *píthēkos* ape + m. *ánthropos* man]

pith·y (pĭth′Y), *adj.,* **pithier, pithiest.** 1. full of vigor, substance, or meaning; terse; forcible: *a pithy criticism.* 2. of, like, or abounding in pith. —**pith′i·ly,** *adv.* —**pith′i·ness,** *n.*

pit·i·a·ble (pĭt′Yəbəl), *adj.* 1. deserving to be pitied; such as justly to excite pity; lamentable; deplorable. 2. such as to excite a contemptuous pity; miserable; contemptible. —**pit′i·a·ble·ness,** *n.* —**pit′i·a·bly,** *adv.* —**Syn.** 1, 2. See pitiful.

pit·i·er (pĭt′Yər), *n.* one who pities.

pit·i·ful (pĭt′Yfəl), *adj.* 1. such as to excite or deserve pity: *a pitiful fate.* 2. such as to excite contempt by smallness, poor quality, etc.: *pitiful attempts.* 3. full of pity or compassion; compassionate. —**pit′i·ful·ly,** *adv.* —**pit′i·ful·ness,** *n.* —**Syn.** 1. lamentable, deplorable, woeful. 1, 2. PITIFUL, PITIABLE, PITEOUS apply to that which excites pity (with compassion or with contempt). That which is PITIFUL is touching and excites pity or is mean and contemptible: *a pitiful leper; a pitiful exhibition of cowardice.* PITIABLE may mean lamentable, or wretched and paltry: *a pitiable hovel.* PITEOUS refers only to that which exhibits suffering and misery, and is therefore heart-rending: *piteous poverty.*

pit·i·less (pĭt′Ylĭs), *adj.* feeling or showing no pity; merciless. —**pit′i·less·ly,** *adv.* —**pit′i·less·ness,** *n.* —**Syn.** See cruel.

pit·man (pĭt′mən), *n., pl.* **-men** for 1, **-mans** for 2. 1. one who works in a pit, as in coal mining. 2. *Mach.* a connecting rod. [f. PIT¹ + MAN]

Pit·man (pĭt′mən), *n.* **Sir Isaac,** 1813–97, British inventor of a system of shorthand.

pi·ton (pē′tŏn′), *n. Mountain Climbing.* a metal spike with an eye through which a rope may be passed.

Pi·tot tube (pē′tō′), an instrument for measuring fluid velocity by means of the differential pressure between the tip (dynamic) and side (static) openings.

pit·saw (pĭt′sô′), *n.* a saw operated by two men, one on the log and the other below it, often in a pit. Also, **pit saw.**

Pitt (pĭt), *n.* 1. **William,** (1st Earl of Chatham), 1708–1778, British statesman. 2. his son, **William,** 1759–1806, British statesman; prime minister, 1783–1801 and 1804–1806.

pit·tance (pĭt′əns), *n.* 1. a small allowance or sum for living expenses. 2. a scanty income or remuneration. [ME *pita(u)nce,* t. OF, der. *pitie* pity. See PIETY, PITY]

pit·ter-pat·ter (pĭt′ər·păt′ər), *n.* 1. a rapid succession of light beats or taps, as of rain. —*adv.* 2. with a rapid succession of light beats or taps, as of rain.

Pitts·burgh (pĭts′bûrg), *n.* a city in SW Pennsylvania: a port where the Allegheny and Monongahela rivers converge to form the Ohio; steel. 604,332 (1960).

Pittsburg Landing, a village in SW Tennessee, on the Tennessee river: battle of Shiloh, 1862.

Pitts·field (pĭts′fēld′), *n.* a city in W Massachusetts. 57,879 (1960).

pi·tu·i·tar·y (pĭ·tū′ə·tĕr′Y, -tōō′-), *n., pl.* **-taries,** *adj.* —*n.* 1. *Anat.* the pituitary gland. 2. *Med.* the extract obtained from either the anterior or posterior lobes of the pituitary. The anterior lobe substance regulates growth of the skeleton; that of the posterior lobe increases blood pressure, contracts the smooth muscles, etc. —*adj. Anat.* 3. of the pituitary gland. 4. noting a physical type of abnormal size with overgrown extremities resulting from excessive pituitary secretion. [t. L: m.s. *pituitārius* pertaining to, or secreting phlegm]

---

b., blend of, blended; c., cognate with; d., dialect, dialectal; der., derived from; f., formed from; g., going back to; m., modification of; r., replacing; s., stem of; t., taken from; ?, perhaps. See the full key on inside cover.

pituitary gland, *Anat.* a small, oval, endocrine gland attached to the base of the brain and situated in a depression of the sphenoid bone, which secretes several hormones, and was formerly supposed to secrete mucus. Also, **pituitary body.**

pit·y (pĭt′ĭ), *n.*, *pl.* **pities,** *v.*, **pitied, pitying.** —*n.* **1.** sympathetic or kindly sorrow excited by the suffering or misfortune of another, often leading one to give relief or aid or to show mercy: *to weep from pity, to take pity on a person.* **2.** a cause or reason for pity, sorrow, or regret: *What a pity you could not go!* —*v.t.* **3.** to feel pity or compassion for; be sorry for; commiserate. —*v.i.* **4.** to feel pity; have compassion. [ME *pite*, t. OF, t. L. m.s. *pietas* piety] —**pit′y·ing·ly,** *adv* —**Syn. 1.** commiseration, sympathy, compassion.

pit·y·ri·a·sis (pĭt′ə rī′ə sĭs), *n.* **1.** *Pathol.* any of various skin diseases marked by the shedding of branlike scales of epidermis. **2.** *Vet. Sci.* a skin disease in various domestic animals marked by dry scales. [t. NL, t. Gk.: branlike eruption]

più (pū), *adv. Music.* more; somewhat. [It.]

Pi·us (pī′əs), *n.* name of twelve popes.

Pius VII, (*Luigi Barnaba Chiaramonti*) 1740–1823, Italian ecclesiastic; pope, 1800–23.

Pius IX, (*Giovanni Maria Mastai-Ferretti*), 1792–1878, Italian ecclesiastic; pope, 1846–78.

Pius X, (*Giuseppe Sarto*) 1835–1914. Italian ecclesiastic; pope, 1903–14.

Pius XI, (*Achille Ratti*) 1857–1939. Italian ecclesiastic; pope, 1922–39.

Pius XII, (*Eugenio Pacelli*) 1876–1958. pope, 1939-58.

Pi·ute (pī ōōt′), *n.* Paiute.

piv·ot (pĭv′ət), *n.* **1.** a pin or short shaft on the end of which something rests and turns, or upon and about which something rotates or oscillates **2.** the end of a shaft or arbor, resting and turning in a bearing. **3.** that on which something turns, hinges, or depends. **4.** the person upon whom a line, as of troops, wheels about. —*v.i.* **5.** to turn on or as on a pivot. —*v.t.* **6.** to mount on, attach by, or provide with a pivot or pivots. [t. F; orig. uncert.]

piv·ot·al (pĭv′ət əl), *adj.* **1.** of, pertaining to, or serving as a pivot. **2.** of critical importance. —**piv′ot·al·ly,** *adv.*

pix (pĭks), *n.* pyx.

pix·i·lat·ed (pĭk′sə lā′tĭd), *adj.* amusingly eccentric. [der. PIXY, modeled on TITILLATED]

pix·y (pĭk′sĭ), *n.*, *pl.* **pixies.** a fairy or sprite. Also. **pix′ie.** [orig. uncert.]

Pi·zar·ro (pĭ zär′ō; *Sp.* pē thär′rō. -sär′-), *n.* **Francisco** (frän thĕs′kō), 1471 or 1475–1541. Spanish conqueror of Peru.

pizz., *Music.* pizzicato.

piz·za (pēt′sə; *It.* -tsä), *n. Italian.* a pielike dish, prepared with tomatoes and cheese, in a thin bottom crust.

piz·zi·ca·to (pĭt′sə kä′tō; *It.* pēt′tsä kä′tō), *adj.*, *n.*, *pl.* **-ti** (-tĭ; *It.* -tē). *Music.* —*adj.* **1.** played by plucking the strings with the finger instead of using the bow, as on a violin. —*n.* **2.** a note or passage so played. [It., pp. of *pizzicare* pick, twang (a stringed instrument)]

pk., *pl.* **pks. 1.** pack. **2.** park. **3.** peak. **4.** peck.

pkg., *pl.* **pkgs.** package.

pkt., packet.

pl., 1. place. **2.** plate. **3.** plural.

pla·ca·ble (plā′kə bəl, plăk′ə-), *adj.* capable of being placated or appeased; forgiving: *he seemed mild and placable.* [ME, t. L: m.s. *plācābilis*] —**pla′ca·bil′i·ty, pla′ca·ble·ness,** *n.* —**pla′ca·bly,** *adv.*

plac·ard (*n.* plăk′ärd; *v.* plə kärd′, plăk′ärd), *n.* **1.** a written or printed notice to be posted in a public place; a poster. —*v.t.* **2.** to post placards on or in. **3.** to give notice of by means of placards. **4.** to post as a placard. [t. F, der. *plaque*, t. D: m. *plak* flat board] —**pla-card′er,** *n.*

pla·cate (plā′kāt, plăk′āt), *v.t.*, **-cated, -cating.** to appease; pacify: *to placate an angry person.* [t. L: m.s. *plācātus,* pp.] —**pla·ca·tion** (plā kā′shən), *n.*

pla·ca·to·ry (plā′kə tôr′ĭ, plăk′ə-), *adj.* tending or intended to placate. [t. L: m.s. *plācātōrius*]

place (plās), *n.*, *v.*, **placed, placing.** —*n.* **1.** a particular portion of space, of definite or indefinite extent. **2.** space in general (chiefly in connection with *time*). **3.** the portion of space occupied by anything. **4.** a space or spot, set apart or used for a particular purpose: *a place of worship.* **5.** any part or spot in a body or surface: *a decayed place in a tooth.* **6.** a particular passage in a book or writing. **7.** a space or seat for a person, as in a theater, train, etc. **8.** the space or position customarily or previously occupied by a person or thing. **9.** position, situation, or circumstances: *if I were in your place.* **10.** a proper or appropriate location or ground. **11.** a job, post, or office. **12.** a function or duty. **13.** position or standing in the social scale, or in any order of merit, estimation, etc. **14.** high position or rank. **15.** official employment or position. **16.** a region. **17.** *Now Rare.* an open space, or square, in a city or town. **18.** a short street, a court, etc. **19.** a portion of space used for habitation, as a city, town, or village. **20.** a building. **21.** a part of a building. **22.** a residence, dwelling, or house. **23.** stead, or lieu: *use water in place of milk.* **24.** a step or point in order of proceeding: *in the first place.* **25.** a fitting opportunity. **26.** a reasonable ground or occasion. **27.** *Arith.* **a.** the position of a figure in a series, as in decimal notation. **b.** (*pl.*) the figures of the series. **28.** *Drama.* one of three unities. See **unity** (def. 11). **29.** *Astron.* the position of a heavenly body at any instant. **30.** *Sports.* **a.** a position among the leading competitors, usually the first three, at the finish of a race. **b.** the position of the second (opposed to *win*). **31. take place,** to happen; occur. —*v.t.* **32.** to put in the proper position or order; arrange; dispose. **33.** to put in a certain or suitable place, or into particular or proper hands, for some purpose: *to place an order for a car.* **34.** to appoint (a person) to a post or office. **35.** to find a place, situation, etc., for (a person). **36.** to determine or indicate the place of. **37.** to assign a certain position or rank to. **38.** to assign a position to (a horse, etc.) among the leading competitors, usually the first three, at the finish of a race. **39.** to put or set in a particular place, position, situation, or relation. **40.** to identify by connecting with the proper place, circumstances, etc.: *to be unable to place a person.* **41.** to sing or speak with consciousness of the bodily point of emphasis of resonance of each tone or register. —*v.i.* **42.** *Racing.* to finish among the three winners, usually second. [ME; OE *plætse*, *plæce*, t. L: m.s. *platēa* street, area, t. Gk.: m. *plateîa* broad way, prop. fem. of *platýs* broad] —**Syn. 11.** See **position.** **32.** See **put.**

pla·ce·bo (plə sē′bō), *n.*, *pl.* **-bos, -boes. 1.** *Rom. Cath. Ch.* the vespers of the office for the dead, so called from the initial word of the first antiphon, taken from Psalm 114:9 of the Vulgate. **2.** *Med.* a medicine given merely to please the patient. [ME, t. L: I shall be pleasing, acceptable]

place kick, *Football.* a kick given the ball after it has been held in place on the ground. Cf. **drop kick** and **punt.**

place·man (plās′mən), *n.*, *pl.* **-men.** *Chiefly Brit.* one who holds a place or office, esp. under a government (often depreciatory).

place·ment (plās′mənt), *n.* **1.** act of placing. **2.** act of employment office or employer in filling a job or position. **3.** the state of being placed. **4.** location; arrangement. **5.** *Football.* **a.** the placing of the ball on the ground in attempting (not after a touchdown) a place kick. **b.** the position of the ball.

pla·cen·ta (plə sĕn′tə), *n.*, *pl.* **-tae** (-tē). **-tas.** **1.** *Zoöl.*, *Anat.* the organ formed in the lining of the mammalian uterus by the union of the uterine mucous membrane with the membranes of the fetus to provide for the nourishment of the fetus and the elimination of its waste products. **2.** *Bot.* **a.** that part of the ovary of flowering plants which bears the ovules. **b.** (in ferns, etc.) the tissue giving rise to sporangia. [t. NL: something having a flat circular form, L a cake, t. Gk.: m. *plakoûnta,* acc. of *plakoûs* flat cake] —**pla·cen′tal,** *adj.*

pla·cen·tate (plə sĕn′tāt), *adj.* having a placenta.

plac·en·ta·tion (plăs′ən tā′shən), *n.* **1.** *Zool.*, *Anat.* **a.** the formation of a placenta. **b.** the manner of the disposition or construction of a placenta. **2.** *Bot.* the disposition or arrangement of a placenta or placentas.

plac·er[1] (plăs′ər), *n.* *Mining.* **1.** a superficial gravel or similar deposit containing particles of gold or the like (distinguished from *lode*). **2.** a place where such a deposit is washed for gold, etc. (**placer mining**). [t. Amer. Sp.: sand-bank; akin to *plaza*. See PLACE]

plac·er[2] (plā′sər), *n.* one who places. [f. PLACE, v. + -ER[1]]

pla·cet (plā′sĭt), *n.* an expression or vote of assent or sanction by the Latin word *placet* it pleases.

plac·id (plăs′ĭd), *adj.* pleasantly calm or peaceful; unruffled; tranquil; serene. [t. L: s. *placidus*] —**pla·cid·i·ty** (plə sĭd′ə tĭ), **plac′id·ness,** *n.* —**plac′id·ly,** *adv.* —**Syn.** See **peaceful.**

plack·et (plăk′ĭt), *n.* **1.** the opening or slit from the top of a skirt, or in a dress or blouse, to facilitate putting it on and off. **2.** a pocket, esp. one in a woman's skirt.

plac·oid (plăk′oid), *adj.* platelike, as the scales or dermal investments of sharks. [f. m.s. Gk. *pláx* something flat, tablet + -OID]

pla·fond (plə fôn′), *n.* *Archit.* a ceiling, whether flat or arched, esp. one of decorative character. [t. F: f. *plat* flat + *fond* bottom. See PLATE[1], FUND]

pla·gal (plā′gəl), *adj.* Gregorian *Music.* having the final tone or keynote in the middle of the compass, as a mode. [t. ML: s. *plagālis,* der. *plaga* plagal mode, appar. back formation from *plagius,* t. MGk.: m. *plágios,* in Gk., oblique]

plagal cadence, *Modern Music.* a cadence in which the chord of the tonic is preceded by that of the subdominant.

pla·gia·rism (plā′jĭ ə rĭz′əm, plā′jə-), *n.* **1.** copying or imitating the language, ideas, and thoughts of another author and passing off the same as one's original work. **2.** something appropriated and put forth in this manner. —**pla′gia·rist,** *n.* —**pla′gi·a·ris′tic,** *adj.*

pla·gia·rize (plā′jĭ ə rīz′, plā′jə-), *v.*, **-rized, -rizing.** —*v.t.* **1.** to appropriate by plagiarism. **2.** to appropriate ideas, passages, etc., from by plagiarism. —*v.i.* **3.** to commit plagiarism. Also, *Brit.,* **pla′gia·rise′.** —**pla′gia·riz′er,** *n.*

pla·gia·ry (plā′jĭ ə rĭ, plā′jə-), *n.*, *pl.* **-ries. 1.** plagiarism. **2.** a plagiarist. [t. L: m.s. *plagiārius* one who abducts the child or slave of another]

pla·gi·o·clase (plā′jĭ ə klās′), *n.* any of the feldspar minerals varying in composition from $NaAlSi_3O_8$ to $CaAl_2Si_2O_8$, important constituents of many igneous rocks. [f. Gk.: *plágio(s)* oblique + m. *klásis* fracture] —**pla·gi·o·clas·tic** (plā′jĭ ə klás′tĭk), *adj.*

pla·gi·o·trop·ic (plā′jĭ ə trŏp′ĭk), *adj. Bot.* noting, pertaining to, or exhibiting a mode of growth which is more or less divergent from the vertical. [f. Gk.: *plágio(s)* oblique + m.s. *tropikós* inclined] —**pla′gi·o·trop′i·cal·ly,** *adv.*

pla·gi·ot·ro·pism (plā′jĭ ŏt′rə pĭz′əm), *n. Bot.* plagiotropic tendency or growth.

plague (plāg, plĕg), *n., v.,* **plagued, plaguing.** —*n.* **1.** an epidemic disease of high mortality; a pestilence. **2.** an infectious, epidemic disease, occurring in several forms (**bubonic, pneumonic,** and **septicemic**), known in history as the **Black Death** of the 14th century, the **Great Plague of London** in 1664–65, and the **Oriental Plague. 3.** an affliction, calamity, or evil, esp. one regarded as a visitation from God: *the ten plagues.* **4.** any cause of trouble or vexation. —*v.t.* **5.** to trouble or torment in any manner. **6.** to annoy, bother, or pester. **7.** to smite with a plague. **8.** to infect with a plague. **9.** to afflict with any evil. [ME *plage,* t. L: m. *plāga* blow, wound, LL affliction, pestilence; akin to Gk. *plēgē* stroke] —**pla′guer,** *n.* —**Syn. 4.** nuisance, trouble, bother. **6.** harass, vex. See **bother.**

pla·guy (plā′gĭ, plĕg′ĭ). *Colloq.* —*adj.* **1.** such as to plague, torment, or annoy; vexatious. —*adv.* **2.** vexatiously or excessively. Also, **pla′guey.** —**pla′gui·ly,** *adv.*

plaice (plās), *n., pl.* **plaice. 1.** a. European flatfish, *Pleuronectes platessa,* an important food fish. **2.** any of various American flatfishes or flounders. [ME *plais,* t. OF, g. LL *platessa* flatfish, der. Gk. *platŷs* flat]

plaid (plăd; *Scot.* plād), *n.* **1.** any fabric woven of different colored yarns in a crossbarred pattern. **2.** a pattern of this kind. **3.** a long, rectangular piece of cloth, usually with such a pattern, worn about the shoulders by Scottish Highlanders. —*adj.* **4.** having the pattern of a plaid. [t. Gaelic: m. *plaide* blanket, plaid]

plaid·ed (plăd′ĭd; *Scot.* plā′dĭd), *adj.* **1.** wearing a plaid. **2.** made of plaid, or having a similar pattern.

plain¹ (plān), *adj.* **1.** clear or distinct to the eye or ear: *leaving a plain trail.* **2.** clear to the mind; evident, manifest, or obvious: *to make one's meaning plain.* **3.** conveying the meaning clearly or simply; easily understood: *plain talk.* **4.** downright; sheer: *plain folly.* **5.** free from ambiguity or evasion; candid; outspoken. **6.** without special pretensions, superiority, elegance, etc.: *plain people.* **7.** not beautiful; homely: *plain face.* **8.** without intricacies or difficulties. **9.** ordinary, simple, or unostentatious. **10.** with little or no embellishment, decoration, or enhancing elaboration: *plain clothes.* **11.** without pattern, device, or coloring. **12.** not rich, highly seasoned, or elaborately prepared, as food. **13.** flat or level: *plain country.* **14.** (*Dial.* except in *plain sight*) unobstructed, clear, or open, as ground, a space, etc. **15.** *Cards.* **a.** not a court card. **b.** not a trump. —*adv.* **16.** clearly or intelligibly. **17.** candidly. —*n.* **18.** an area of land not significantly higher than adjacent areas and with relatively minor differences in elevation within the area (commonly less than 500 feet). **19. the Plain,** a popular name for the more moderate party in the legislatures of the French Revolution. **20. The Plains,** the Great Plains. [ME, t. OF, g. L *plānus* flat, level, plane] —**plain′ly,** *adv.* —**plain′ness,** *n.* —**Syn. 5.** blunt. **10.** See **simple.**

plain² (plān), *v.i. Archaic or Brit. Dial.* to complain. [ME *plei(g)ne,* t. OF: m.s. *plaindre,* g. L *plangere* beat (the breast, etc.), lament]

plain-clothes man (plān′klōz′, -klōᵺz′), a detective.

Plain·field (plān′fēld′), *n.* a city in N New Jersey. 45,330 (1960).

plain-laid (plān′lād′), *adj.* (of a rope) made by laying three strands together with a right-handed twist.

Plains Indian, a member of any of the American Indian tribes which once inhabited the Great Plains, of the Algonquian, Athabascan, Caddoan, Kiowa, Siouan, and Uto-Aztecan linguistic stocks. All were more or less nomadic, following the buffalo in their movements, and were often in touch with one another, so that the development among them of common culture traits is notable. Also, **Buffalo Indian.**

plains·man (plānz′mən), *n., pl.* **-men.** a man or inhabitant of the plains.

Plains of Abraham. a high plain adjoining the city of Quebec in Canada: battlefield where English under Wolfe defeated French under Montcalm, 1759.

plain·song (plān′sông′, -sŏng′), *n.* **1.** the unisonous vocal music used in the Christian church from the earliest times. **2.** model liturgical music; Gregorian chant. Also, **plain chant.** [trans. of ML *cantus plānus*]

plain song, 1. a cantus firmus or theme chosen for contrapuntal development. **2.** any simple and unadorned melody or air.

plain-spo·ken (plān′spō′kən), *adj.* candid; blunt.

plaint (plānt), *n.* **1.** a complaint. **2.** *Law.* a statement of grievance made to a court for the purpose of asking redress. **3.** *Archaic and Poetic.* lament. [ME *plainte,* t. OF, g. L *planctus* lamentation. See PLAIN²]

plain·tiff (plān′tĭf), *n. Law.* one who brings suit in a court (opposed to *defendant*). [ME *plaintif* complaining, t. OF. See PLAINTIVE]

plain·tive (plān′tĭv), *adj.* expressing sorrow or melancholy discontent; mournful: *plaintive music.* [ME *plaintif,* t. OF. See PLAINT] —**plain′tive·ly,** *adv.* —**plain′tive·ness,** *n.* —**Syn.** wistful, sorrowful, sad.

plais·ter (plās′tər), *n., v.t. Obs.* plaster.

plait (plāt), *n.* **1.** a braid, as of hair or straw; a plat. **2.** a pleat or fold, as of cloth. —*v.t.* **3.** to braid (one's hair, etc.). **4.** to make (a mat, etc.) by braiding. **5.** to pleat (cloth, etc.). [ME *pleyt,* t. OF: m. *pleit,* g. L *plicitum,* pp. neut., folded. See PLY]

plan (plăn), *n., v.,* **planned, planning.** —*n.* **1.** a scheme of action or procedure: *a plan of operations.* **2.** a design or scheme of arrangement. **3.** a project or definite purpose: *plans for the future.* **4.** a drawing made to scale to represent the top view or a horizontal cut of a structure or a machine, as a floor plan of a building. **5.** a representation of a thing drawn on a plane, as a map or diagram: *a floor plan.* **6.** one of several planes in front of a represented object, and perpendicular to the line between the object and the eye. —*v.t.* **7.** to arrange a plan or scheme for (any work, enterprise, or proceeding). **8.** to form a plan, project, or purpose of: *to plan a visit.* **9.** to draw or make a plan of (a building, etc.). —*v.i.* **10.** to make plans. [t. F, n. use of *plan* flat, plane, t. L: s. *plānus.* See PLANE¹, PLAIN¹]

—**Syn. 1.** PLAN, PROJECT, DESIGN, SCHEME imply a formulated method of doing something. PLAN refers to any method of thinking out acts and purposes beforehand: *what are your plans for today?* A PROJECT is a proposed or tentative plan, often elaborate or extensive: *an irrigation project.* DESIGN suggests art, dexterity, or craft (sometimes evil and selfish) in the elaboration or execution of a plan, and often tends to emphasize the purpose in view: *a misunderstanding brought about by design.* A SCHEME is apt to be either a speculative, possibly impractical, plan, or a selfish or dishonest one: *a scheme to swindle someone.*

plan-, var. of **plano-,** before vowels, as in *planarian.*

pla·nar·i·an (plə nâr′ĭ ən), *n. Zool.* a free-living flatworm having a trifid intestine. [f. s. NL *Plānāria,* the typical genus (prop. fem. of LL *plānārius* level, flat, der. L *plānus*) + -AN]

planch (plănch, plänch), *n.* **1.** a flat piece of metal, stone, or baked clay, used as a tray in an enameling oven. **2.** *Brit. Dial.* **a.** a floor. **b.** a plank. Also, **planche.** [ME *plaunche,* t. OF: m. *planche.* See PLANK]

planch·et (plăn′chĭt), *n.* a flat piece of metal for stamping as a coin; a coin blank. [f. PLANCH + -ET]

plan·chette (plăn chĕt′), *n. Chiefly Brit.* a small board on two casters and a vertical pencil, said to write messages without conscious effort by persons whose fingers rest lightly on the board. [t. F, dim. of *planche* PLANCH]

Planck (plängk), *n.* **Max** (mäks), 1858-1947, German physicist: formulated the quantum theory.

Planck's constant, *Physics.* a universal constant (approx. 6.624×10^{-27} erg-seconds; *Symbol-h*) expressing the proportion of the energy of any form of wavelike radiation to its frequency.

plane¹ (plān), *n., adj., v.,* **planed, planing.** —*n.* **1.** a flat or level surface. **2.** a level of dignity, character, existence, development, or the like: *a high moral plane.* **3.** an airplane or a hydroplane. **4.** *Aeron.* a thin, flat, or curved, extended member of an airplane or a hydroplane, affording a supporting surface. —*adj.* **5.** flat or level, as a surface. **6.** of plane figures: *plane geometry.* —*v.i.* **7.** to glide. **8.** to lift partly out of water when running at high speed, as a racing boat does. [t. L: m.s. *plānum* level ground. See PLAIN¹] —**plane′ness,** *n.*

plane² (plān), *n., v.,* **planed, planing.** —*n.* **1.** a tool with an adjustable blade for paring, truing, smoothing, or finishing the surface of wood, etc. **2.** a tool resembling a trowel for smoothing the surface of the clay in a brick mold. —*v.t.* **3.** to smooth or dress with or as with a plane or a planer. **4.** to remove by or as by means of a plane (fol. by *away* or *off*). —*v.i.* **5.** to work with a plane. **6.** to function as a plane. [ME, t. F, g. LL *plāna*]

Planes (def. 1)
A. Iron jack plane; B. Wooden jointing plane; C. Wooden intermediate plane; D. Wooden smoothing plane

plane³ (plān), *n. Brit.* a plane tree. [ME, t. F, g. L *platanus,* t. Gk.: m. *plátanos,* der. *platŷs* broad (with reference to the leaves)]

plane angle, *Math.* an angle between two intersecting lines.

plane geometry, *Math.* the geometry of figures whose parts all lie in one plane.

plan·er (plā′nər), *n. Carp.* a power machine for removing the rough or excess surface from a board.

planer saw, *Carp.* a type of circular saw which saws so smoothly that planing is unnecessary.

planer tree, a small ulmaceous tree, *Planera aquatica,* growing in moist ground in the southern U.S., bearing a small, ovoid, nutlike fruit and affording a compact light-brown wood.

plan·et (plăn′ĭt), *n.* **1.** *Astron.* **a.** any one of the solid heavenly bodies revolving about the sun and shining by reflected light. There are nine major planets (Mercury, Venus, the Earth, Mars, Jupiter, Saturn, Uranus, Neptune, and Pluto, in their order from the sun) and thousands of **minor planets** or asteroids between the orbit of Mars and Jupiter. **Inferior planets** are those nearer to the sun than the earth is; **superior planets** are those farther from the sun than the earth is. **b.** (orig.) a celestial body moving in the sky, as distinguished from a fixed star, formerly applied also to the sun and moon. **2.** *Astrol.* a heavenly body regarded as exciting influence on mankind and events. **3.** anything thought to have such influence. [ME *planete*, t. LL: m. *planēta*, t. Gk.: m. *planētēs*, lit. wanderer]

plane table, *Surveying.* a drawing board mounted on a tripod by means of which survey data may be obtained and plotted in the field.

plan·e·tar·i·um (plăn'ə târ'ĭəm), *n.*, *pl.* **-tariums,** **-taria** (-târ'ĭə). **1.** an apparatus or model representing the planetary system. **2.** an optical device which projects a representation of the heavens upon a dome through the use of many stereopticons in motion. **3.** the structure in which such a planetarium is housed. [t. NL, prop. neut. of L *planetārius* planetary]

plan·e·tar·y (plăn'ə těr'ĭ), *adj.* **1.** of, pertaining to, of the nature of, or resembling a planet or the planets. **2.** wandering or erratic. **3.** terrestrial or mundane. **4.** *Mach.* noting or pertaining to a form of transmission (consisting of an epicyclic train of gears) for varying the speed in automobiles. [t. L: m.s. *planetārius*]

plan·e·tes·i·mal (plăn'ə těs'ə məl), *adj.* **1.** of or pertaining to minute bodies in the solar system or in similar systems, which, according to the **planetesimal hypothesis,** move in planetary orbits and gradually unite to form the planets and satellites of the system. —*n.* **2.** one of the minute bodies of the planetesimal hypothesis. [der. PLANET modeled on INFINITESIMAL]

plan·et·oid (plăn'ə toid'), *n.* a minor planet; an asteroid. —**plan'et·oi'dal,** *adj.*

plane tree, any tree of the genus *Platanus,* esp. *P. orientalis,* which is found wild from Italy to Persia and is much used in Europe for ornament, or *P. occidentalis,* the buttonwood or sycamore of North America.

plan·et-struck (plăn'ĭt strŭk'), *adj.* **1.** stricken by the supposed influence of a planet; blasted. **2.** panicstricken. Also, **plan·et-strick·en** (plăn'ĭt strĭk'ən).

planet wheel, any of the wheels in an epicyclic train, whose axes revolve around the common center.

plan·gent (plăn'jənt), *adj.* **1.** beating or dashing, as waves. **2.** resounding loudly. [t. L: s. *plangens,* ppr., beating, lamenting. Cf. PLAIN²] —**plan'gen·cy,** *n.*

plani-, var. of plano-, as in *planimeter.*

pla·nim·e·ter (plə nĭm'ə tər), *n.* an instrument for measuring mechanically the area of plane figures.

pla·nim·e·try (plə nĭm'ə trĭ), *n.* the measurement of plane areas. —**plan·i·met·ric** (plăn'ə mĕt'rĭk), **plan·i·met'ri·cal,** *adj.*

plan·ish (plăn'ĭsh), *v.t.* **1.** to flatten or smooth (metal) by hammering, rolling, etc. **2.** to finish off (metal, paper, etc.) with a polished surface. [ME, t. F (obs.): m. *planiss-,* s. *planir,* for *planner.* See PLANE², v.]

plan·i·sphere (plăn'ə sfîr'), *n.* **1.** a map of half or more of the celestial sphere with a device for indicating the part visible at a given time. **2.** a projection or representation of the whole or a part of a sphere on a plane. [f. PLANI- + SPHERE; r. ME *planisperie,* t. ML: m. *plānisphaerium*]

plank (plăngk), *n.* **1.** a long, flat piece of timber thicker than a board. **2.** timber in such pieces. **3.** something to stand on or to cling to for support. **4.** an article of a platform of political or other principles. —*v.t.* **5.** to lay, cover, or furnish with planks. **6.** *Colloq.* to lay, put, or pay (fol. by *down,* etc.). **7.** to bake or broil and serve (fish, chicken, etc.) on a board. [ME *planke,* t. ONF, g. L *planca.* Cf. PLANCH]

plank·ing (plăngk'ĭng), *n.* **1.** planks collectively, as in a floor. **2.** act of laying or covering with planks.

plank-sheer (plăngk'shîr'), *n.* *Naut.* a timber around a vessel's hull at the deck line.

plank·ton (plăngk'tən), *n.* *Biol.* the small animal and plant organisms that float or drift in the water, esp. at or near the surface. [t. G, t. Gk.: (neut.) wandering] —**plank·ton·ic** (plăngk tŏn'ĭk), *adj.*

plan·ner (plăn'ər), *n.* one who plans.

plano-, a word element meaning "flat," "plane." Also, **plan-,** **plani-.** [comb. form repr. L *plănus*]

pla·no-con·cave (plā'nō kŏn'kāv), *adj.* (of lenses) plane on one side and concave on the other. See **lens.**

pla·no-con·vex (plā'nō kŏn'věks), *adj.* (of lenses) plane on one side and convex on the other. See **lens.**

pla·nom·e·ter (plə nŏm'ə tər), *n.* a flat plate, usually of cast iron, used as a gauge for plane surfaces.

plant (plănt, plänt), *n.* **1.** any member of the vegetable group of living organisms. **2.** a vegetable. **3.** an herb or other small vegetable growth, in contrast with a tree or a shrub. **4.** a seedling or a growing slip, esp. one ready for transplanting. **5.** the equipment, including the fixtures, machinery, tools, etc., and often the buildings, necessary to carry on any industrial business: *a manufacturing plant.* **6.** the complete equipment or apparatus for a particular mechanical process or operation: *the power plant of an automobile.* **7.** the buildings, equipment, etc., of an institution: *the sprawling plant of the university.* **8.** *Slang.* something intended to trap, decoy, or lure, as criminals. **9.** *Slang.* a scheme to trap, trick, swindle, or defraud.

—*v.t.* **10.** to put or set in the ground for growth, as seeds, young trees, etc. **11.** to furnish or stock (land) with plants. **12.** to implant (ideas, sentiments, etc.); introduce and establish (principles, doctrines, etc.). **13.** to introduce (a breed of animals) into a country. **14.** to deposit (young fish, or spawn) in a river, lake, etc. **15.** to bed (oysters). **16.** to insert or set firmly in or on the ground or some other body or surface. **17.** to put or place. **18.** *Slang.* to deliver (a blow, etc.). **19.** to post or station. **20.** to locate or situate. **21.** to establish or set up (a colony, city, etc.); found. **22.** to settle (persons), as in a colony. **23.** *Slang.* to hide or conceal, as stolen goods. **24.** *Slang.* to put (gold dust, ore, etc.) in a mine or the like to create a false impression of the value of the property. [ME and OE *plante,* t. L: m. *planta* sprout, slip, graft]

Plan·tag·e·net (plăn tăj'ə nĭt), *n.* one of the line of English sovereigns from Henry II through Richard III. [t. F: lit., sprig of broom]

plan·tain¹ (plăn'tĭn), *n.* **1.** a tropical herbaceous plant, *Musa paradisiaca,* very similar to the banana, usually requiring cooking. **2.** its fruit. [t. Sp.: m. *plántano* plantain, also planetree, t. L: m. *pla(n)tanus.* See PLANE³]

plan·tain² (plăn'tĭn), *n.* any plant of the widespread genus *Plantago,* esp. *P. major,* a common weed with large, spreading leaves close to the ground and long, slender spikes of small flowers. [ME *planteine,* t. OF: m. *plantain,* g. s. L *plantāgo*]

plan·tar (plăn'tər), *adj.* *Anat., Zool.* of or pertaining to the sole of the foot. [t. L: s. *plantāris*]

plan·ta·tion (plăn tā'shən), *n.* **1.** a farm or estate, esp. in a tropical or semitropical country, on which cotton, tobacco, coffee, or the like is cultivated, usually by resident laborers. **2.** *Chiefly Brit.* a group of planted trees or plants. **3.** *Now only Hist.* **a.** a colony. **b.** the establishment of a colony, etc. **4.** *Now Rare.* the planting of seeds, etc. [late ME, t. L: s. *plantātio* a planting]

plant·er (plăn'tər, plän'-), *n.* **1.** one who plants. **2.** an implement or machine for planting seeds in the ground. **3.** the owner or occupant of a plantation. **4.** *Now only Hist.* a colonist. **5.** a decorative container, of a variety of sizes and shapes, for plants, ferns, etc.

plan·ti·grade (plăn'tə grād'), *adj.* **1.** walking on the whole sole of the foot, as man, the bears, etc. —*n.* **2.** a plantigrade animal. [t. NL: m.s. *plantigradus,* f. L: m. *planta* sole + *-gradus* walking]

plant louse, aphid.

plan·u·la (plăn'yə lə), *n.*, *pl.* **-lae** (-lē'). *Zool.* the ciliated, free-swimming larva of a coelenterate, characterized by the solid interior. [t. NL, dim. of L *plānus* flat, plane] —**plan'u·lar,** *adj.*

plaque (plăk), *n.* **1.** a thin, flat plate or tablet of metal, porcelain, etc., intended for ornament, as on a wall, or set in a piece of furniture. **2.** a platelike brooch or ornament, esp. one worn as the badge of an honorary order. **3.** *Anat., Zool.* a small flat, rounded formation or area. [t. F, t. D: m. *plak* flat board. See PLACK]

plash¹ (plăsh), *n.* **1.** a splash. **2.** a pool or puddle. —*v.t., v.i.* **3.** to splash. [ME *plasch,* OE *plæsc,* c. D and LG *plas,* prob. of imit. orig.]

plash² (plăsh), *v.t.* **1.** to interweave (branches, etc., bent over and often cut partly through), as for a hedge or an arbor. **2.** to make or renew (a hedge, etc.) by such interweaving. [ME, t. OF: m. *plaissier,* der. L *plectere* plait. Cf. PLEACH]

plash·y (plăsh'ĭ), *adj.,* **plashier, plashiest. 1.** marshy; wet. **2.** splashing.

-plasia, a word element meaning "biological cellular growth," as in *hypoplasia.* Also, **-plasis.** [t. NL, der. Gk. *plásis* a molding]

-plasm, a word element used as a noun termination meaning "something formed or molded" in biological and other scientific terms, as in *bioplasm, metaplasm, neoplasm, protoplasm.* [comb. form repr. Gk. *plásma*]

plas·ma (plăz'mə), *n.* **1.** *Anat., Physiol.* the liquid part of blood or lymph, as distinguished from the corpuscles. **2.** *Biol.* protoplasm. **3.** whey. **4.** a green, faintly translucent chalcedony. **5.** *Physics.* a stream of ionized particles. Also, **plasm** (plăz'əm). [t. LL, t. Gk.: something formed or molded] —**plas·mat·ic** (plăz măt'ĭk), **plas'mic,** *adj.*

plas·mo·chin (plăz'mə kĭn), *n.* *Pharm.* a synthetic antimalarial drug, $C_{19}H_{29}N_3O.$ Also, **plasmoquine.**

plas·mo·di·um (plăz mō'dĭəm), *n.,* *pl.* **-dia** (-dĭ ə). **1.** *Biol.* a mass or sheet of protoplasm formed by the fusion or contact of a number of amoeboid bodies. **2.** *Zool.* a parasitic protozoan organism of the genus *Plasmodium* (malaria parasites). [t. NL, f. *plasma* PLASMA + *-ōdium* -ODE¹]

plas·mol·y·sis (plăz mŏl'ə sĭs), *n.* *Bot.* contraction of the protoplasm in a living cell when water is removed by exosmosis. [f. *plasmo-* (comb. form repr. Gk. *plásma* PLASMA) + -LYSIS]

Plasmodium (def. 2). *Plasmodium vivax* (tertian form)

A. Young form within a red corpuscle; B. Developing pigmented form within corpuscle; C. Full-grown body; D. Segmenting body; E. Degenerating form undergoing vacuolation

plas·mo·quine (plăz′mə kwĭn′), *n. Pharm.* plasmochin.

plas·mo·some (plăz′mə sōm′), *n. Biol.* a true nucleolus which is stained by cytoplasmic dyes. Cf. **karyosome**. [f. *plasmo-* (comb. form repr. Gk. *plásma* PLASMA) + m. Gk. *sōma* body]

Plas·sey (plăs′ĭ), *n.* a village in NE India, ab. 80 mi. N of Calcutta: Clive's victory over a Bengal army here (1757) led to the establishment of British power in India.

-plast, a word element used as a noun termination, meaning "formed," "molded," esp. in biological and botanical terms, as in *bioplast, chloroplast, mesoplast, protoplast.* [comb. form repr. Gk. *plastós*]

plas·ter (plăs′tər, pläs′-), *n.* 1. a pasty composition, as of lime, sand, water, and often hair, used for covering walls, ceilings, etc., where it hardens in drying. 2. gypsum powdered but not calcined. 3. calcined gypsum **(plaster of Paris)**, a white powdery material which swells when mixed with water and sets rapidly, used for making casts, molds, etc. 4. a solid or semisolid preparation for spreading upon cloth or the like and applying to the body for some remedial or other purpose. —*v.t.* 5. to cover (walls, etc.) with plaster. 6. to treat with gypsum or plaster of Paris. 7. to lay flat like a layer of plaster. 8. to daub or fill with plaster or something similar. 9. to apply a plaster to (the body, etc.). 10. to overspread with anything, esp. thickly or to excess: *a wall plastered with posters.* [ME and OE, t. VL and ML: m.s. *plastrum* plaster (both medical and builder's senses), g. L *emplastrum,* t. Gk.: m. *émplastron* salve] **—plas′ter·er,** *n.* **—plas′ter·ing,** *n.* **—plas′ter·y,** *adj.*

plas·ter·board (plăs′tər bōrd′, pläs′-), *n.* plaster and felt in paper-covered sheets, used for walls.

plaster cast, 1. any piece of sculpture cast in plaster of Paris. 2. *Surg.* See **cast** (def. 48).

plas·tic (plăs′tĭk), *adj.* 1. concerned with or pertaining to molding or modeling: *plastic arts.* 2. capable of being molded or of receiving form: *plastic substances.* 3. produced by molding: *plastic figures.* 4. having the power of molding or shaping formless or yielding material. 5. *Biol., Pathol.* formative. 6. *Surg.* concerned with or pertaining to the remedying or restoring of malformed, injured, or lost parts: *plastic surgery.* 7. pliable; impressionable: *the plastic mind of youth.* —*n.* 8. any of a group of synthetic or natural organic materials which may be shaped when soft and then hardened, including many types of resins, resinoids, polymers, cellulose derivatives, casein materials, and proteins. Plastics are used in place of such other materials as glass, wood, and metals in construction and decoration, for making many articles, as coatings, and, drawn into filaments, for weaving. They are usually known by trademark names as *Bakelite, Vinylite, Lucite,* etc. [t. L: s. *plasticus* that may be molded, t. Gk.: m. *plastikós*] **—plas′ti·cal·ly,** *adv.*

-plastic, a word element forming adjectives related to *-plast, -plasty,* as in *protoplastic.* [see PLASTIC]

plas·tic·i·ty (plăs tĭs′ə tĭ), *n.* 1. the quality of being plastic. 2. capability of being molded, receiving shape, or being brought to a definite form.

plas·ti·ciz·er (plăs′tə sī′zər), *n.* any of a group of substances which are used in plastics or the like, to impart softness and viscous quality to the finished product.

plas·tid (plăs′tĭd), *n. Biol.* 1. a morphological unit consisting of a single cell. 2. any of certain small specialized masses of protoplasm (as chloroplasts, chromoplasts, etc.) in certain cells. See diag. under **cell**. [t. G, short for *plastidion,* f. Gk.: *plast(ós)* formed + *-idion,* dim. suffix]

plas·tral (plăs′trəl), *adj. Zool.* relating to the plastron.

plas·tron (plăs′trən), *n.* 1. *Armor.* a medieval metal breastplate worn under the hauberk. 2. a protective shield of leather for the breast of a fencer. 3. an ornamental front piece of a woman's bodice. 4. the starched front of a shirt. 5. *Zool.* the ventral part of the shell of a turtle. [F, t. It.: m. *piastrone,* aug. of *piastra* metal plate. See PLASTER. Cf. PIASTER]

-plasty, a word element used as a noun termination meaning "formation," occurring in the names of processes of plastic surgery, as *autoplasty, cranioplasty, dermatoplasty, neoplasty, rhinoplasty,* and occasionally in other words, as *galvanoplasty.* [t. Gk.: m.s. *-plastia,* comb. form der. *plastós* formed]

-plasy, var. of **-plasia.**

plat[1] (plăt), *n., v.,* **platted, platting.** —*n.* 1. a plot of ground, usually small. 2. *U.S.* a plan or map, as of land. —*v.t.* 3. *U.S.* to make a plat of; plot. [ME (in place names), c. Goth. *plat* patch]

plat[2] (plăt), *n.* plait or braid. [var. of PLAIT]

plat., 1. plateau. 2. platoon.

Pla·ta (plä′tä), *n.* **Río de la** (rē′ō dĕ lä), an estuary on the SE coast of South America between Argentina and Uruguay, formed by the Uruguay and Paraná rivers. ab. 185 mi. long. Also, **Plata River;** *Brit.,* **River Plate** (plāt).

Pla·tae·a (plə tē′ə), *n.* an ancient Boeotian city NW of Athens: Greeks defeated Persians here, 479 B.C.

plat·an (plăt′ən), *n.* a plane tree.

plate[1] (plāt), *n., v.,* **plated, plating.** —*n.* 1. a shallow, usually circular dish, now usually of earthenware or porcelain, from which food is eaten. 2. the contents of such a dish. 3. a service of food for one person at table. 4. an entire course on one dish. 5. *Chiefly Brit.* domestic

dishes, utensils, etc., of gold or silver. 6. a dish, as of metal or wood, used for collecting offerings in a church, etc. 7. a thin, flat sheet or piece of metal or other material, esp. of uniform thickness. 8. metal in such sheets. 9. a flat, polished piece of metal on which something may be or is engraved. 10. a sheet of metal for printing from, formed by stereotyping or electrotyping a page of type, or metal or plastic formed by molding, etching, or photographic development. 11. a printed impression from such a piece, or from some similar piece, as a woodcut. 12. such a piece engraved to print from. 13. a full-page inserted illustration forming part of a book. 14. plated metallic ware. 15. wrought metal, or a piece of it, used in making armor. 16. armor composed of such pieces. 17. *Dentistry.* a piece of metal, vulcanite, or plastic substance, with artificial teeth attached, to replace lost or missing natural teeth. 18. *Baseball.* the home base, at which the batter stands and which he must return to and touch, after running around the bases, in order to score a run. 19. plate glass. 20. *Photog.* a sensitized sheet of glass, metal, etc., on which to take a photograph or make a reproduction by photography. 21. *Anat., Zool., etc.* a platelike part, structure, or organ. 22. a thin piece or cut of beef at the lower end of the ribs. 23. *Electronics.* one of the interior elements of an electron tube, toward which electrons are attracted by virtue of its positive charge; the anode. 24. *Archit.* a timber laid horizontally, as in a wall, to receive the ends of other timbers. 25. a gold or silver cup or the like awarded as a prize in horse racing, etc. 26. a horse race or other contest for such a prize. —*v.t.* 27. to coat (metal) with a thin film of gold, silver, nickel, etc., by mechanical or chemical means. 28. to cover or overlay with metal plates for protection, etc. 29. *Print.* to make a stereotype or electrotype plate from (type). 30. *Papermaking.* to give a high gloss to (paper), as on supercalendered paper. [ME, t. OF: flat piece, plate, prob. der. OF *plat* flat, g. LL *plattus,* t. Gk.: m. *platýs* broad, flat] **—plate′like′,** *adj.*

plate[2] (plāt), *n. Obs.* a coin, esp. of silver. [ME, t. OF; etymologically same as PLATE[1]]

pla·teau (plă tō′ *or, esp. Brit.,* plăt′ō), *n., pl.* **-teaus, -teaux** (-tōz′). 1. a tabular surface of high elevation, deeply cut by narrow stream valleys or canyons but with the greater part of the surface consisting of broad and nearly level interstream areas. 2. *Psychol.* a period of little or no progress in an individual's learning, marked by temporary constancy in speed, number of errors committed, etc., and indicated by a flat stretch in his learning curve or graph. [t. F, in OF flat object, der. *plat* flat]

plat·ed (plā′tĭd), *adj.* (of a knitted fabric) made of two yarns, as wool on the face and cotton on the back.

plate·ful (plāt′fǒol′), *n., pl.* **-fuls.** as much as a plate will hold.

plate glass, a soda-lime-silica glass formed by rolling the hot glass into a plate which is subsequently ground and polished: used in large windows, mirrors, etc.

plate·let (plāt′lĭt), *n.* a microscopic, disk occurring in profusion in the blood: important aid in coagulation. [f. PLATE[1] + -LET]

plat·en (plăt′ən), *n.* 1. a flat plate in a printing press, which presses the paper against the inked type, thus securing an impression. 2. a rotating cylinder used for the same purpose. 3. the roller of a typewriter. [ME *plateyne,* t. OF: m. *platine* flat piece of metal, also pop. alter. of *patene* paten, from its form]

plat·er (plā′tər), *n.* 1. one who or that which plates. 2. an inferior race horse.

plate rail, a rail or narrow shelf placed along a wall to hold plates, etc.

plat·form (plăt′fôrm), *n.* 1. a raised flooring or structure, as in a hall or meeting place, for use by public speakers, performers, etc. 2. a landing in a flight of stairs. 3. the raised area between or alongside the tracks of a railroad station, from which the cars of the train are entered. 4. *U.S.* the open entrance area, or the vestibule, at the end of a railroad passenger car. 5. a level place for mounting guns, as in a fort. 6. a flat elevated piece of ground. 7. a body of principles on which a party or the like takes its stand in appealing to the public. 8. a public statement of the principles and policy of a political party, esp. as put forth by the representatives of the party in a convention to nominate candidates for an election. 9. a plan or set of principles. 10. *Now Rare.* a scheme of religious principles or doctrines. [t. F: m. *plateforme,* lit., flat form, plan, flat area, terrace. See PLATE[1]] **—Syn.** 1. stage, dais, rostrum, pulpit.

platform car, a railroad freight car having no enclosing sides or top; a flatcar.

plat·i·na (plăt′ə nə, plə tē′nə), *n.* a native alloy of platinum with palladium, iridium, osmium, etc. [t. NL or Sp. See PLATINUM]

plat·ing (plā′tĭng), *n.* 1. a thin coating of gold, silver, etc. 2. an external layer of metal plates. 3. act of one who or that which plates.

pla·tin·ic (plə tĭn′ĭk), *adj. Chem.* of or containing platinum, esp. in its tetravalent state (Pt+4).

plat·i·rid·i·um (plăt′ən ĭ rĭd′ĭ əm, -ĭ rĭd′-), *n.* a natural alloy composed chiefly of platinum and iridium. [f. PLATIN(UM) + IRIDIUM]

plat·i·nize (plăt′ə nīz′), *v.t.,* **-nized, -nizing.** to coat or plate with metallic platinum.

●**latino-**, a combining form of **platinum**.

●**lat·i·no·cy·an·ic acid** (plăt/ə nō sĭ ăn/ĭk). *Chem.* an acid containing platinum and the radical cyanogen.

●**lat·i·no·cy·a·nide** (plăt/ə nō sī/ə nīd/, -nĭd), *n. Chem.* a salt of platinocyanic acid. Also, **plat·i·no·cy·a·nid** (plăt/ə nō sī/ə nĭd).

●**lat·i·noid** (plăt/ə noid/), *adj.* **1.** resembling platinum: *the platinoid elements.* —*n.* **2.** any of the metals (palladium, iridium, etc.) with which platinum is usually associated. **3.** an alloy of copper, zinc, and nickel, to which small quantities of such elements as tungsten or aluminum have been added; used in electrical work, etc.

●**lat·i·no·type** (plăt/ə nō tīp/), *n. Photog.* **1.** a process of printing in which a platinum salt is employed, yielding more permanent prints than those obtainable with silver salts. **2.** a print made by such a process.

●**lat·i·nous** (plăt/ə nəs), *adj. Chem.* containing divalent platinum (Pt+2).

●**lat·i·num** (plăt/ə nəm), *n.* **1.** *Chem.* a heavy, grayish-white, highly malleable and ductile metallic element, resistant to most chemicals, practically unoxidizable save in the presence of bases, and fusible only at extremely high temperatures, used esp. for making chemical and scientific apparatus, as a catalyst in the oxidation of ammonia to nitric acid, and in jewelry. *Symbol:* Pt; *at. wt.:* 195.23; *at.no.:* 78: *sp.gr.:* 21.5 at 20°C. **2.** a light metallic gray with very slight bluish tinge when compared with silver. [t. NL. earlier *platina*, t. Sp., der. *plata* silver]

●**latinum black**, a black powder consisting of very finely divided metallic platinum, used as a catalyst, esp. in organic synthesis.

●**lat·i·tude** (plăt/ə tūd/, -tŏōd/), *n.* **1.** a flat, dull, or trite remark, esp. one uttered as if it were fresh and profound. **2.** flatness, dullness, or triteness. [t. F, der. *plat* flat. Cf. F and E *latitude*, altitude. See PLATE¹] —**TUDE]

●**plat·i·tu·di·nize** (plăt/ə tū/də nīz/, -tŏō/-), *v.i.*, -nized, -nizing. to utter platitudes.

●**plat·i·tu·di·nous** (plăt/ə tū/də nəs, -tŏō/-), *adj.* **1.** characterized by or given to platitudes. **2.** of the nature of a platitude.

Pla·to (plā/tō), *n.* 427?–347 B.C., Greek philosopher.

Pla·ton·ic (plə tŏn/ĭk, plā-), *adj.* **1.** of or pertaining to Plato or his doctrines: *the Platonic philosophy.* **2.** of or pertaining to love which, in Platonic philosophy, transcends the feeling for the individual and rises to a contemplation of the ideal or pattern. **3.** (*l.c. or cap.*) purely spiritual; free from sensual desire: *platonic love.* **4.** (*l.c. or cap.*) (of persons) feeling or professing such love. —**Pla·ton/i·cal·ly**, *adv.*

Pla·to·nism (plā/tə nĭz/əm), *n.* **1.** the philosophy or doctrines of Plato or his followers. **2.** a Platonic doctrine or saying. **3.** the belief that physical objects are but impermanent representations of unchanging ideas, and that these ideas alone give true knowledge as they are known by the mind. **4.** (*l.c. or cap.*) the doctrine or the practice of platonic love. —**Pla/to·nist**, *n., adj.*

Pla·to·nize (plā/tə nīz/), *v.*, -nized, -nizing. —*v.i.* **1.** to follow the opinions or doctrines of Plato. **2.** to reason like Plato. —*v.t.* **3.** to give a Platonic character to. **4.** to explain in accordance with Platonic principles.

pla·toon (plə tŏōn/), *n.* **1.** a military unit consisting of two or more squads or sections and a headquarters. **2.** a small unit of a police force. **3.** a company or set of persons. [t. F: m. *peloton* little ball, group, platoon, dim. of *pelote* ball. See PELLET]

Platt·deutsch (plăt/doich/), *n.* the colloquial Low German of northern Germany. [G: f. *platt* flat (see PLATE¹) + *deutsch* German]

Platte (plăt), *n.* a river flowing from the junction of the North and South Platte rivers in central Nebraska E to the Missouri river S of Omaha. 310 mi.

Plat·ten See (plăt/ən zā/), German name of **Balaton**.

plat·ter (plăt/ər), *n.* a large, shallow dish, commonly oval, for holding or serving meat, etc. [ME *plater*, t. AF, der. OF *plat* plate, dish]

Platts·burgh (plăts/bûrg), *n.* a city in N E New York, on Lake Champlain: battle, 1814. 20,172 (1960).

plat·y·hel·minth (plăt/ĭ hěl/mĭnth), *n. Zool.* a member of the Platyhelminthes; a flatworm. [t. NL: s. *Platyhelmintha*, f. Gk.: m. *platýs* broad, flat + m.s. *hélmins* worm]

Plat·y·hel·min·thes (plăt/ĭ hěl mĭn/thēz), *n.pl. Zool.* a phylum of worms, the flatworms, having bilateral symmetry and a soft, solid, usually flattened body, including the planarians, flukes, tapeworms, and others.

plat·y·pus (plăt/ə pəs), *n., pl.* -puses, -pi (-pī/). the duckbill. [t. NL, t. Gk.: m. *platýpous* flat-footed]

plat·yr·rhine (plăt/ə rīn/, -rĭn), *adj. Zool., Anthropol.* having a broad, flat-bridged nose. [f. *platy-* (t. Gk., comb. form of *platýs* broad) + m.s. Gk. *rhís* nose]

plau·dit (plô/dĭt), *n.* (*usually pl.*) **1.** a demonstration or round of applause, as for some approved or admired performance. **2.** any enthusiastic expression of approval. [t. L: alter. of *plaudite*, impv., APPLAUD]

Plau·en (plou/ən), *n.* a city in S East Germany, in Karl-Marx-Stadt district. 81,998 (est.1955).

plau·si·ble (plô/zə bəl), *adj.* **1.** having an appearance of truth or reason; seemingly worthy of approval or acceptance; specious: *a plausible story.* **2.** fair-spoken and apparently worthy of confidence: *a plausible ad-*

venturer. [t. L: m.s. *plausibilis*] —**plau/si·bil/i·ty, plau/si·ble·ness**, *n.* —**plau/si·bly**, *adv.*

—**Syn. 1.** PLAUSIBLE, SPECIOUS describe that which has a fair appearance but is completely deceptive. The person or thing that is PLAUSIBLE strikes the superficial judgment favorably; it may or may not be intentionally deceptive: *a plausible argument* (one which omits or glosses over important points). SPECIOUS definitely implies deceit or hypocrisy; the surface appearances are quite different from what is beneath: *a specious pretense of honesty, a specious argument* (one deliberately deceptive, probably for selfish or evil purposes). —**Ant. 1.** honest, sincere.

plau·sive (plô/sĭv), *adj.* **1.** *Rare.* applauding. **2.** *Obs.* plausible.

Plau·tus (plô/təs), *n.* **Titus Maccius** (tī/təs măk/sĭ əs), c254–c184 B.C., Roman comic dramatist.

play (plā), *n.* **1.** a dramatic composition or piece; a drama. **2.** a dramatic performance, as on the stage. **3.** exercise or action by way of amusement or recreation. **4.** fun, jest, or trifling, as opposed to earnest: *he said it merely in play.* **5.** a pun. **6.** the playing, or carrying on, of a game. **7.** manner or style of playing. **8.** an act or performance in playing: *a stupid play.* **9.** turn to play: *it is your play.* **10.** the state, as of a ball, of being played with or in use in the active playing of a game: *in play; out of play.* **11.** a playing for stakes; gambling. **12.** *Obs.* (except in *fair play*, etc.) action, conduct, or dealing of a specified kind. **13.** action, activity, or operation: *the play of fancy.* **14.** brisk movement or action: *a fountain with a leaping play of water.* **15.** elusive change, as of light or colors. **16.** a space in which a thing, as a piece of mechanism, can move. **17.** freedom of movement, as within a space, as of a part of a mechanism. **18.** freedom for action, or scope for activity: *full play of the mind.* [ME; OE *plega, plæga*] —*v.t.* **19.** to act the part of (a person or character) in a dramatic performance: *to play Lady Macbeth.* **20.** to perform (a drama, etc.) on or as on the stage. **21.** to act or sustain (a part) in a dramatic performance or in real life. **22.** to sustain the part or character of in real life: *to play the fool.* **23.** to give performances in, as a theatrical company does: *to play the larger cities.* **24.** to engage in (a game, pastime, etc.). **25.** to contend against in a game. **26.** to employ (a player, etc.) in a game. **27.** to use as if in playing a game, as for one's own advantage: *play off one person against another.* **28.** to play an extra game or round in order to settle (a tie) (fol. by *off*). **29.** to stake or wager, as in playing. **30.** to lay a wager or wagers on (something). **31.** to represent or imitate in sport: *to play school.* **32.** to perform on (a musical instrument). **33.** to perform (music) on an instrument. **34.** to do, perform, bring about, or execute: *to play tricks.* **35.** to cause to move or change lightly or quickly: *play colored lights on a fountain.* **36.** to operate, or cause to operate, esp. continuously or with repeated action: *to play a hose on a fire.* **37.** to allow (a hooked fish) to exhaust itself by pulling on the line. **38.** to bring to an end; use up (fol. by *out*). **39. play the game**, *Colloq.* **a.** to play in accordance with the rules. **b.** to play one's part.

—*v.i.* **40.** to exercise or employ oneself in diversion, amusement, or recreation. **41.** to do something only in sport, which is not to be taken seriously. **42.** to amuse oneself or toy; trifle (fol. by *with*). **43.** to take part or engage in a game. **44.** to take part in a game for stakes; gamble. **45.** to act, or conduct oneself, in a specified way: *to play fair.* **46.** to act on or as on the stage; perform. **47.** to perform on a musical instrument. **48.** (of the instrument or the music) to sound in performance. **49.** to move freely, as within a space, as a part of a mechanism. **50.** to move about lightly or quickly. **51.** to present the effect of such motion, as light or the changing colors of an iridescent substance. **52.** to operate continuously or with repeated action, often on something. **53. play into the hands of,** to act in such a way as to give an advantage to. **54. play on** or **upon,** to work on (the feelings, weaknesses, etc., of another) for one's own purpose. **55. play up to,** to attempt to get into the favor of. [ME *pleye*(n), OE *plegan*, c. MD *pleyen* dance, leap for joy, G *pflegen* take care of, look after]

—**Syn. 3.** PLAY, GAME, SPORT refer to forms of diverting activity. PLAY is the general word for any such form of activity, often undirected, spontaneous, or random: *childhood should be a time for play.* GAME refers to a recreational contest, mental or physical, usually governed by set rules: *a game of chess.* Besides referring to an individual contest, GAME may refer to a pastime as a whole: *golf is a good game.* If, however, the pastime is one (usually an outdoor one) depending chiefly on physical strength, though not necessarily a contest, the word SPORT is applied: *football is a vigorous sport.* **13.** movement, action, exercise. **21.** personate, impersonate. **40.** sport, frolic, romp, revel. —**Ant. 3.** work, toil.

pla·ya (plä/yä), *n. Western U.S.* the sandy, salty, or mud-caked floor of a desert basin with interior drainage, usually occupied by a shallow lake during the rainy season or after prolonged, heavy rains. [t. Sp.: shore, beach, g. LL *plāgia*, der. *plāga* region, tract]

play·a·ble (plā/ə bəl), *adj.* **1.** capable of or suitable for being played. **2.** (of ground) fit to be played on.

play·back (plā/băk/), *n.* **1.** the act of operating a phonograph, tape-recorder, etc., so as to hear the reproduction of a recording. —*adj.* **2.** of or pertaining to a device used in reproducing a recording.

play·bill (plā/bĭl/), *n.* a program or announcement of a play.

play·boy (plā′boi′), *n.* *U.S. Colloq.* a wealthy, care-free person who spends most of his time at parties, nightclubs, etc.

Playboy of the Western World, The, a satiric comedy (1907) by John Millington Synge.

play·day (plā′dā′), *n.* a holiday.

play·er (plā′ər), *n.* **1.** one who or that which plays. **2.** one who takes part or is skilled in some game. **3.** *Brit.* a person engaged in playing a game professionally. **4.** one who plays parts on the stage; an actor. **5.** a performer on a musical instrument. **6.** a mechanical device by which a musical instrument, esp. a piano (**player piano**), is played automatically. **7.** a gambler.

play·fel·low (plā′fĕl′ō), *n.* a playmate.

play·ful (plā′fəl), *adj.* **1.** full of play; sportive; frolic-some. **2.** pleasantly humorous: *a playful remark.* —**play′ful·ly,** *adv.* —**play′ful·ness,** *n.*

play·go·er (plā′gō′ər), *n.* one who often or habitually attends the theater.

play·ground (plā′ground′), *n.* **1.** ground used specifi-cally for open-air recreation, as one attached to a school. **2.** any place of open-air recreation, as a park.

play·house (plā′hous′), *n.* **1.** a theater. **2.** a small house for children to play in. **3.** a toy house. [OE *pleghūs* theater]

playing card, **1.** one of the conventional set of 52 cards, in 4 suits (diamonds, hearts, spades, and clubs), used in playing various games of chance and skill. **2.** one of any set or pack of cards used in playing games.

playing field, *Brit.* an athletic ground; a ball park.

play·let (plā′lĭt), *n.* a short dramatic play.

play·mate (plā′māt′), *n.* a companion in play.

play·off (plā′ôf′, -ŏf′), *n.* the playing off of a tie, as in games or sports.

play on words, a pun.

play·pen (plā′pĕn′), *n.* a small enclosure in which a young child can play safely by himself without constant supervision.

play·thing (plā′thĭng′), *n.* a thing to play with; a toy.

play·time (plā′tīm′), *n.* time for play or recreation.

play·wright (plā′rīt′), *n.* a writer of plays; a drama-tist. [f. PLAY + WRIGHT]

pla·za (plä′zə, plăz′ə), *n.* a public square or open space in a city or town. [t. Sp., g. L *platēa.* See PLACE]

plea (plē), *n.* **1.** that which is alleged, urged, or pleaded in defense or justification. **2.** an excuse; a pretext. **3.** *Law.* **a.** an allegation made by, or on behalf of, a party to a legal suit, in support of his claim or defense. **b.** a defendant's answer to a legal declaration or charge. **c.** (in courts of equity) a plea which admits the truth of the declaration, but alleges special or new matter in avoidance. **d.** a suit or action at law: *to hold pleas* (*to try actions at law*). **4.** an appeal or entreaty: *a plea for mercy.* [ME *plaid, plai,* t. OF: g. L *placitum* (thing which) seemed good, prop. pp. neut., pleased; in ML, court, plea. See PLEASE]

pleach (plēch), *v.t.* **1.** to plash or interweave (growing branches, vines, etc.), as for a hedge or arbor. **2.** to interlace or entwine. [ME *pleche*(n), var. of PLASH²]

plead (plēd), *v.,* **pleaded** or **plead** (plĕd) or **pled,** **plead-ing.** —*v.i.* **1.** to make earnest appeal or entreaty. **2.** to use arguments or persuasions, as with a person, for or against something. **3.** to afford an argument or ap-peal: *his youth pleads for him.* **4.** *Law.* **a.** to make any allegation or plea in an action at law. **b.** to put forward an answer on the part of a defendant to a legal declaration or charge. **c.** to address a court as an advo-cate. **d.** *Obs.* to prosecute a suit or action at law. —*v.t.* **5.** to allege or urge in defense, justification, or excuse: *to plead ignorance.* **6.** *Law.* **a.** to maintain (a cause, etc.) by argument before a court. **b.** to allege or set forth (something) formally in an action at law. **c.** to allege or cite in legal defense: *to plead a statute of limitations.* [ME *plaide*(n), t. OF: m. *plaidier* go to law, plead, g. VL *placitāre,* der. L *placitum* thing which pleases]

plead·a·ble (plē′də bəl), *adj.* capable of being pleaded.

plead·er (plē′dər), *n.* one who pleads, esp. at law.

plead·ing (plē′dĭng), *n.* **1.** act of one who pleads. **2.** *Law.* **a.** the advocating of a cause in a court of law. **b.** the art or science of setting forth or drawing pleas in legal causes. **c.** *Chiefly Brit.* a formal statement (now usually written) setting forth the cause of action or the defense of a case at law. **d.** (*pl.*) the successive state-ments delivered alternately by plaintiff and defendant until issue is joined. —**plead′ing·ly,** *adv.*

pleas·ance (plĕz′əns), *n.* **1.** a space laid out with trees, walks, etc. **2.** *Archaic.* pleasure. [ME, t. OF: m. *plaisance,* der. *plaisant* PLEASANT]

pleas·ant (plĕz′ənt), *adj.* **1.** pleasing, agreeable, or affording enjoyment; pleasurable: *pleasant news.* **2.** (of persons, manners, disposition, etc.) agreeable socially. **3.** (of weather, etc.) fair. **4.** gay, sprightly, or merry. **5.** jocular or facetious. [ME *plesaunt,* t. OF: m. *plaisant,* ppr. OF *plaisir* PLEASE] —**pleas′ant·ly,** *adv.* —**pleas′ant·ness,** *n.* —Syn. **2.** delightful, congenial.

Pleasant Island, former name of Nauru.

pleas·ant·ry (plĕz′ən trĭ), *n., pl.* -ries. **1.** good-hu-mored raillery; pleasant humor in conversation. **2.** a humorous or jesting remark. **3.** a humorous action.

please (plēz), *v.,* **pleased, pleasing.** —*v.t.* **1.** to act to the pleasure or satisfaction of: *to please the public.* **2.** to be the pleasure or will of; seem good to: *may it please*

God. 3. (as a polite addition to requests, etc.) if you are willing: *please come here.* **4.** to find something agreeable; like, wish, or choose: *go where you please.* —*v.i.* **5.** to be agreeable; give pleasure or satisfaction. **6.** if you please, **a.** if you like; if it be your pleasure. **b.** (in stat-ing some surprising fact): *in his pocket, if you please, was the letter!* [ME *plese,* t. OF: m. *plaisir,* g. L *placēre* please, seem good]

pleas·ing (plē′zĭng), *adj.* that pleases; giving pleas-ure; agreeable; gratifying; likable. —**pleas′ing·ly,** *adv.* —**pleas′ing·ness,** *n.* —Syn. See interesting.

pleas·ur·a·ble (plĕzh′ər ə bəl), *adj.* such as to give pleasure; agreeable; pleasant. —**pleas′ur·a·ble·ness,** *n.* —**pleas′ur·a·bly,** *adv.*

pleas·ure (plĕzh′ər), *n., v.,* **-ured, -uring.** —*n.* **1.** the state or feeling of being pleased. **2.** enjoyment or satis-faction derived from what is to one's liking; gratifica-tion; delight. **3.** worldly or frivolous enjoyment: *the pursuit of pleasure.* **4.** sensual gratification. **5.** a cause or source of enjoyment or delight: *it was a pleasure to see you.* **6.** pleasurable quality. **7.** one's will, desire, or choice: *to make known one's pleasure.* —*v.t.* **8.** to give pleasure to; gratify; please. —*v.i.* **9.** to take pleasure; delight. **10.** *Colloq.* to seek pleasure, as by taking a holi-day. [ME *plesir,* t. OF: m. *plaisir* PLEASE] —Syn. **1.** happiness, gladness, delectation. PLEASURE, EN-JOYMENT, DELIGHT, JOY refer to the feeling of being pleased and happy. PLEASURE is the general term: *to take pleasure in beautiful scenery.* ENJOYMENT is a quiet sense of well-being and pleasurable satisfaction: *enjoyment at sitting in the shade on a warm day.* DELIGHT is a high degree of pleasure, usually leading to active expression of it: *delight at receiving a hoped-for letter.* JOY is a eeling of delight so deep and so lasting that one radiates happiness and expresses it spontaneously: *joy at unexpected good news.* —Ant. **1.** discomfort, sorrow, grief.

pleasure principle, *Psychoanal.* an automatic mental drive or instinct seeking to avoid pain and to ob-tain pleasure.

pleat (plēt), *n.* **1.** a fold of definite, even width made by doubling cloth or the like upon itself, and pressing, stitch-ing, or otherwise fastening in place. —*v.t.* **2.** to fold or arrange in pleats. [var. of PLAIT]

pleb (plĕb), *n.* a plebeian or commoner.

plebe (plĕb), *n.* (at the U.S. Military and Naval Acad-emies) a member of the lowest class. [short for PLEBEIAN]

ple·be·ian (plĭ bē′ən), *adj.* **1.** belonging or pertaining to the Roman plebs. **2.** belonging or pertaining to the common people. **3.** common, commonplace, or vulgar. —*n.* **4.** a member of the Roman plebs. **5.** a plebeian person. [f. s. L *plēbēius* belonging to the plebs + -AN] —**ple·be′ian·ism,** *n.*

pleb·i·scite (plĕb′ə sīt′, -sĭt), *n.* **1.** a direct vote of the qualified electors of a state in regard to some important public question. **2.** the vote by which the people of a political unit determine autonomy or affiliation with an-other country. [t. L: m.s. *plēbiscītum*]

plebs (plĕbz), *n., pl.* **plebes** (plē′bēz). **1.** (in ancient Rome) the commons as contrasted with the patricians, the later senatorial nobility, or the equestrian order. **2.** the common people; the populace. [t. L]

plec·tog·nath (plĕk′tŏg năth′), *adj.* belonging to the *Plectognathi,* a group of teleost fishes having the jaws ex-tensively ankylosed and including the filefishes, globe-fishes, etc. [t. NL: s. *Plectognathī,* pl., f. Gk.: m. *plektó* plaited, twisted + m. *gnáthos* jaw]

plec·tron (plĕk′trŏn), *n., pl.* **-tra** (-trə). plectrum.

plec·trum (plĕk′trəm), *n., pl.* **-tra** (-trə), **-trums.** a small piece of wood, metal, ivory, etc., for plucking strings of a lyre, mandolin, etc. [t. L, t. Gk.: m. *plēktron*]

pled (plĕd), *v.* a pt. and pp. of **plead.**

pledge (plĕj), *n., v.,* **pledged, pledging.** —*n.* **1.** a sol-emn promise of something, or to do or refrain from doing something: *a pledge of aid.* **2.** a piece of personal prop-erty delivered as security for the payment of a debt or the discharge of some obligation, and liable to forfeiture. **3.** the state of being given or held as security: *to put a thing in pledge.* **4.** *Law.* **a.** the act of delivering goods, etc., to another for security. **b.** the resulting legal rela-tionship. **5.** anything given or regarded as a security of something. **6.** *Obs.* **a.** a hostage. **b.** one who becomes bail or surety for another. **7.** a person accepted for membership in a club, fraternity, etc., but not yet for-mally approved. **8.** an assurance of support or good will conveyed by drinking a person's health; a toast. **9.** the solemn, formal vow to abstain from intoxicating drink: *to take the pledge.* —*v.t.* **10.** to bind by or as by a pledge: *to pledge hearers to secrecy.* **11.** to promise solemnly, or engage to give, maintain, etc.: *to pledge one's support.* **12.** to give or deposit as a pledge; pawn. **13.** to plight or stake, as one's honor, etc. **14.** to secure by a pledge; give a pledge for. **15.** to accept as a pledge (def. 7). **16.** to drink a health or toast to. [ME *plege,* t. OF, g. ML *plevium, plebium;* of Gmc. orig.] —**pledg′er,** *n.*

pledg·ee (plĕ jē′), *n.* the person with whom something is deposited as a pledge.

pledg·et (plĕj′ĭt), *n.* a small, flat mass of lint, absorb-ent cotton, or the like, for use on a wound, sore, etc.

pledg·or (plĕj ôr′), *n.* *Law.* one who deposits personal property as a pledge.

-plegia, a word element used as a noun termination in pathological terms denoting forms of paralysis, as in *paraplegia.* [t. Gk., comb. form der. *plēgē* blow, stroke]

Ple·iad (plē′əd, plī′əd), *n.* any of the Pleiades.

Ple·ia·des (plē′ə dēz′, plī′-), *n.pl.* **1.** *Class. Myth.* the seven daughters of Atlas and a nymph, pursued by Orion and transformed into the group of stars bearing their name (one star, missing, being the traditional **Lost Pleiad.** 2. *Astron.* a conspicuous group or cluster of stars in the constellation Taurus, commonly spoken of as seven, though only six are plain to the average naked eye.

plein-air (plăn′âr′; *Fr.* plĕn′ĕr′), *adj.* pertaining to a movement in art, originating in France about 1870 and concerned with rendering effects of atmosphere and light in nature, as seen out of doors, rather than in the artificial light of studios. [F: *plein air* open air]

Plei·o·cene (plī′ə sēn′), *adj., n. Stratig.* Pliocene.

Pleis·to·cene (plīs′tə sēn′), *Stratig.* —*adj.* 1. pertaining to the earlier division of the Quaternary period or system (the glacial epoch or Ice Age). —*n.* 2. the epoch or series of the Quaternary that follows Pliocene and precedes Recent. [f. Gk. *pleísto(s)* most (superl. of *polýs* much) + -CENE]

ple·na·ry (plē′nə rǐ, plĕn′ə rǐ), *adj.* 1. full; complete; entire; absolute; unqualified. 2. attended by all qualified members, as a council; fully constituted. [late ME, t. LL: m.s. *plēnārius*] —**ple′na·ri·ly,** *adv.*

plenary indulgence, *Rom. Cath. Ch.* remission of the total temporal punishment which is still due to sin after sacramental absolution. See **indulgence** (def. 5).

ple·nip·o·tent (plə nǐp′ə tənt), *adj.* invested with or possessing full power. [t. LL: s. *plēnipotens,* f. L *plēni-* full + *potens* potent]

plen·i·po·ten·ti·a·ry (plĕn′ǐ pō tĕn′shǐ ĕr′ǐ, -shə rǐ), *n., pl.* -**aries,** *adj.* —*n.* 1. a person, esp. a diplomatic agent, invested with full power or authority to transact business. —*adj.* 2. invested with full power or authority, as a diplomatic agent. 3. bestowing full power, as a commission. 4. absolute or full, as power. [t. ML: m.s. *plēnipotentiārius,* der. LL *plēnipotens*]

plen·ish (plĕn′ǐsh), *v.t. Chiefly Scot.* to fill up; stock; furnish. [late ME *plenyss,* t. OF: m. *pleniss-,* s. *plenir,* der. *plen-,* g. L *plēnus* full]

plen·i·tude (plĕn′ə tǐd′, -tōōd′), *n.* 1. fullness in quantity, measure, or degree; abundance. 2. the condition of being full. [t. L: m. *plēnitūdo*]

ple·no ju·re (plē′nō jŏŏr′ǐ), *Latin.* with full right.

plen·te·ous (plĕn′tǐ əs), *adj.* 1. plentiful; copious; abundant: *a plenteous supply of corn.* 2. yielding abundantly. —**plen′te·ous·ly,** *adv.* —**plen′te·ous·ness,** *n.*

plen·ti·ful (plĕn′tǐ fəl), *adj.* 1. existing in great plenty. 2. amply supplied with something. 3. yielding abundantly. —**plen′ti·ful·ly,** *adv.* —**plen′ti·ful·ness,** *n.* —**Syn.** 1. bountiful, ample.

plen·ty (plĕn′tǐ), *n., pl.* -**ties,** *adj., adv.* —*n.* 1. a full or abundant supply: *there is plenty of time.* 2. abundance: *resources in plenty.* 3. a time of abundance. —*adj.* 4. *Now Chiefly Colloq.* existing in ample quantity or number (usually in the predicate): *this is plenty.* —*adv.* 5. *Colloq.* fully: *plenty good enough.* [ME *plente(th),* t. OF: m. *plente(t),* g. s. L *plēnitas* fullness, abundance] —**Syn.** 2. plenteousness, copiousness. PLENTY, ABUNDANCE, PROFUSION refer to a large quantity or supply. PLENTY suggests a supply that is fully adequate to any demands: *plenty of money.* ABUNDANCE implies a great plenty, an ample and generous oversupply: *an abundance of rain.* PROFUSION applies to such a lavish and excessive abundance as often suggests extravagance or prodigality: *luxuries in great profusion.*

ple·num (plē′nəm), *n., pl.* -**nums,** -**na** (-nə). 1. a container of air, or other gas, under greater than the surrounding pressure. 2. the whole of space regarded as being filled with matter. 3. a full assembly, as a joint legislative assembly. [t. L, prop. neut. of *plēnus* full, filled, complete, abundant]

ple·o·chro·ic (plē′ə krō′ǐk), *adj.* (of a biaxial crystal) exhibiting different colors in three different directions when viewed by transmitted light. [f. m. Gk. *pleíon* more + Gk. *chró(s)* color + -IC] —**ple·och·ro·ism** (plī′ŏk′rō ǐz′əm), *n.*

ple·o·nasm (plē′ə năz′əm), *n.* 1. the use of more words than are necessary to express an idea; redundancy. 2. an instance of this. 3. a redundant word or expression. [t. L: s. *pleonasmus,* t. Gk.: m. *pleonasmós*] —**ple·o·nas′tic,** *adj.* —**ple·o·nas′ti·cal·ly,** *adv.*

ple·o·pod (plē′ə pŏd′), *n. Zool.* a swimmeret. [f. Gk. *pléo(n),* ppr., swimming + -POD]

ple·si·o·saur (plē′sǐ ə sôr′), *n.* any member of the extinct genus *Plesiosaurus* (and of the order *Sauropterygia*), comprising marine reptiles with small head, very long neck, short tail, and four large paddles, which existed in the Jurassic and Cretaceous. Also, **ple·si·o·sau·rus** (plē′sǐ ə sôr′əs). [t. NL: s. *plēsiosaurus,* f. Gk.: *plēsío(s)* near + m. *saûros* lizard]

ples·sor (plĕs′ər), *n.* plexor.

pleth·o·ra (plĕth′ə rə), *n.* 1. overfullness; superabundance. 2. *Pathol., Obs.* a morbid condition due to excess of red corpuscles in the blood or increase in the quantity of blood. [t. NL, t. Gk.: m. *plēthōrē* fullness]

ple·thor·ic (plē thôr′ǐk, -thŏr′-, plĕth′ə rǐk), *adj.* 1. overfull; turgid; inflated. 2. characterized by plethora. —**ple·thor′i·cal·ly,** *adv.*

pleur-, a word element meaning "side," "pleura," sometimes "rib." Also, before consonants, **pleuro-.** [t. Gk., comb. form of *pleurá* side, rib, or *pleurón* rib; or abstracted from PLEURA]

pleu·ra (plŏŏr′ə), *n., pl.* **pleurae** (plŏŏr′ē). a delicate serous membrane investing each lung in mammals and

folded back as a lining of the corresponding side of the thorax. [t. NL, t. Gk.: rib, side] —**pleu′ral,** *adj.*

pleu·ri·sy (plŏŏr′ə sǐ), *n. Pathol.* inflammation of the pleura, with or without a liquid effusion. [ME, t. OF: m. *pleurisie,* t. LL: m. *pleurisis,* for L *pleurītis,* t. Gk.] —**pleu·rit·ic** (plŏŏ rǐt′ǐk), *adj.*

pleurisy root, 1. a North American milkweed, *Asclepias tuberosa,* whose root was used as a popular remedy for pleurisy. 2. the root.

pleu·ro·dont (plŏŏr′ə dŏnt′), *adj.* 1. ankylosed or attached to the inner edge of the jaw, as a tooth. 2. having teeth so ankylosed, as certain lizards. —*n.* 3. a pleurodont animal. [f. PLEUR- + -ODONT]

pleu·ron (plŏŏr′ŏn), *n., pl.* **pleura** (plŏŏr′ə). *Entomol.* the lateral plate or plates of a thoracic segment of an insect. [t. Gk.: side]

pleu·ro·pneu·mo·ni·a (plŏŏr′ō nū mō′nǐ ə, -nŏŏ-), *n. Pathol.* pleurisy conjoined with pneumonia.

Plev·en (plĕv′ĕn), *n.* a city in N Bulgaria: siege of 143 days, 1877. 38,997 (1946). Also, **Plev·na** (plĕv′nä).

plex·i·form (plĕk′sə fôrm′), *adj.* in the form of a plexus. [f. PLEX(US) + -(I)FORM]

Plex·i·glas (plĕk′sə glăs′, -gläs′), *n. Trademark.* a thermoplastic notable for its permanent transparency, light weight, and resistance to weathering. Bent to any shape when hot, it returns to its original shape if reheated.

plex·i·glass (plĕk′sə glăs′, -gläs′), *n.* Plexiglas.

plex·im·e·ter (plĕk sǐm′ə tər), *n. Med.* a small, thin plate, as of ivory, to receive the blow of a plexor. [f. Gk. *plēxi(s)* stroke, percussion + -METER]

plex·or (plĕk′sər), *n. Med.* a small hammer with a soft rubber head or the like, used in percussion for diagnostic purposes. Also, **plessor.** [f. Gk. *plēx(is)* stroke, percussion + -OR²]

plex·us (plĕk′səs), *n., pl.* **plexuses, plexus.** a network, as of nerves or blood vessels. [t. L: an interweaving, twining]

plf., plaintiff. Also, **plff.**

pli·a·ble (plī′ə bəl), *adj.* 1. easily bent; flexible; supple. 2. easily influenced; yielding; adaptable. [t. F, der. *plier* fold, bend. See PLY²] —**pli′a·bil′i·ty, pli′a·ble·ness,** *n.* —**pli′a·bly,** *adv.*

pli·ant (plī′ənt), *adj.* 1. bending readily; flexible; supple. 2. easily inclined or influenced; yielding; compliant. [ME, t. OF, ppr. of *plier* fold, bend. See PLY²] —**pli′an·cy, pli′ant·ness,** *n.* —**pli′ant·ly,** *adv.* —**Syn.** 1, 2. See **flexible.**

pli·ca (plī′kə), *n., pl.* **plicae** (plī′sē). 1. *Zool., Anat.* a fold or folding. 2. *Pathol.* a matted, filthy condition of the hair, caused by disease, etc. [t. ML: a fold, der. L *plicāre* fold]

pli·cate (plī′kāt), *adj.* folded like a fan; pleated. Also, **pli′cat·ed.** [t. L: m.s. *plicātus,* pp., folded] —**pli′cate·ly,** *adv.*

pli·ca·tion (plī kā′shən, plǐ-), *n.* 1. a folding or fold. 2. plicate form or condition. Also, **plic·a·ture** (plǐk′ə chər).

pli·er (plī′ər), *n.* 1. (*pl., sometimes construed as sing.*) small pincers with long jaws, for bending wire, holding small objects, etc. (often called a **pair** of **pliers**). 2. one who or that which plies.

Plicate leaf

plight¹ (plīt), *n.* condition, state, or situation (good, bad, or as specified, now usually bad). [ME *plit,* t. AF, var. of OF *pleit* fold, manner of folding, condition (see PLAIT); ? influenced by PLIGHT² in archaic sense of danger] —**Syn.** See **predicament.**

plight² (plīt), *v.t.* 1. to pledge (one's troth) in engagement to marry. 2. to bind by a pledge, now esp. of marriage. 3. to give in pledge; pledge (one's honor, etc.). —*n.* 4. *Now Rare,* pledge. [ME; OE *pliht* danger, risk, c. G *pflicht* duty, obligation] —**plight′er,** *n.*

Plim·soll line (plǐm′sŏl, -səl), a line or mark required to be placed on the hull of all British merchant vessels, showing the depth to which they may be submerged through loading. Also, **Plimsoll mark.**

plinth (plǐnth), *n. Archit.* 1. the lower square part of the base of a column. See diag. under **column.** 2. a square base or a lower block, as of a pedestal. 3. a course of stones, as at the base of a wall, forming a continuous plinthlike projection. [t. L: s. *plinthus,* t. Gk.: m. *plinthos* plinth, squared stone] —**plinth′like′,** *adj.*

Plin·y (plǐn′ǐ), *n.* 1. ("*the Elder,*" *Gaius Plinius Secundus*) A.D. 23–79, Roman naturalist, encyclopedist, and writer. 2. his nephew ("*the Younger,*" *Gaius Plinius Caecilius Secundus*) A.D. 62?–c113, Roman writer, statesman, and orator.

Pli·o·cene (plī′ə sēn′), *Stratig.* —*adj.* 1. pertaining to the latest principal division of the Tertiary period or system. —*n.* 2. the epoch or series of the Tertiary that follows Miocene and precedes Pleistocene. Also, **Pleiocene.** [f. m. Gk. *pleíon* more (compar. of *polýs* much) + -CENE]

plod (plŏd), *v.,* **plodded, plodding,** *n.* —*v.i.* 1. to walk heavily; trudge; move laboriously. 2. to work with dull perseverance; drudge. —*v.t.* 3. to walk heavily over or along. —*n.* 4. the act or a course of plodding. 5. a sound of or as of a heavy tread. [? imit.] —**plod′der,** *n.* —**plod′ding·ly,** *adv.* —**Syn.** 1. See **pace¹.**

Plo·es·ti (plŏ yĕsht′), *n.* a city in S Rumania: the center of a rich oil-producing region. 95,632 (1948).

-ploid, a word element used in cytology and genetics referring to the number of chromosomes. [f. s. Gk. *-ploos* (equivalent to E suffix *-fold*) + -(o)ID]

plop (plŏp), *v.,* **plopped, plopping,** *n.* —*v.i.* **1.** to make a sound like that of a flat object striking water without a splash. **2.** to fall plump with such a sound. —*n.* **3.** a plopping sound or fall. **4.** the act of plopping. [imit.]

plo·sion (plō'zhən), *n. Phonet.* explosion (def. 6).

plo·sive (plō'sĭv), *adj., n. Phonet.* explosive (defs. 3, 5).

plot[1] (plŏt), *n., v.,* **plotted, plotting.** —*n.* **1.** a secret plan or scheme to accomplish some purpose, esp. a hostile, unlawful, or evil purpose. **2.** the plan, scheme, or main story of a play, novel, poem, or the like. **3.** *Artillery.* a calculated graph: *a plot of shots.* —*v.t.* **4.** to plan secretly (something hostile or evil): *to plot mutiny.* **5.** to mark on a plan, map, or chart, as a ship's course, etc. **6.** to make a plot, plan, or map of, as a tract of land, a building, etc. **7.** to determine and mark (points), as on plotting paper, by means of measurements or co-ordinates. **8.** to draw (a curve) by means of points so marked. **9.** to represent by means of such a curve. **10.** to devise the plot of (a play, etc.). **11.** to make (a calculation) by graph. —*v.i.* **12.** to form secret plots; conspire. [aphetic var. of COMPLOT] —**plot'ter,** *n.* —**Syn. 1.** intrigue, conspiracy, cabal. **4.** devise, contrive, concoct. **12.** PLOT, CONSPIRE, SCHEME imply secret, cunning, and often unscrupulous planning to gain one's own ends. To PLOT is to contrive a secret plan of a selfish and often treasonable kind: *to plot against someone's life.* To CONSPIRE is to unite with others in an illicit or illegal machination: *to conspire to seize a government.* To SCHEME is to plan ingeniously, subtly, and often craftily for one's own advantage: *to scheme how to gain power.*

plot[2] (plŏt), *n., v.,* **plotted, plotting.** —*n.* **1.** a small piece or area of ground: *a garden plot.* In the U.S. *lot* is usually preferred. **2.** *Chiefly U.S.* a plan, map, or diagram, as of land, a building, etc. —*v.t.* **3.** to divide (land) into plots. [ME and OE; orig. uncert.]

Plo·ti·nus (plō tī'nəs), *n.* A.D. 205?–270?, Neoplatonic philosopher in Rome, born in Egypt.

plotting paper, paper ruled into small squares or spaces, used in plotting points, curves, etc.

plough (plou), *n., v.t., v.i. Chiefly Brit.* plow.

Plov·div (plŏv'dĭf), *n.* a city in S Bulgaria, on the Maritsa river. 150,000 (est. 1953). Greek, **Philippopolis.**

plov·er (plŭv'ər, plō'vər), *n.* **1.** any of various limicoline birds of the family *Charadriidae,* esp. those with a short tail and a bill like that of a pigeon, as the American killdeer plover, *Charadrius vociferus.* **2.** any of various shore birds, as the **upland plover,** *Bartramia longicauda,* of the New World. [ME, t. AF, der. L *pluvia* rain (cf. PLUVIAL); the connection of the bird with rain being uncert.]

plow (plou), *n.* **1.** an agricultural implement for cutting furrows in and turning up the soil, as for sowing or planting. **2.** any of various implements resembling or suggesting this, as a kind of plane for cutting grooves or a contrivance for clearing away snow from a road or track. **3.** (*cap.*) *Astron.* **a.** the whole constellation Ursa Major. **b.** the Big Dipper. —*v.t.* **4.** to make furrows in or turn up (the soil) with a plow. **5.** to make (a furrow, etc.) with a plow. **6.** to furrow, remove, etc., or make (a furrow, groove, etc.), as if with a plow. **7.** *Naut.* **a.** to cleave the surface of (the water). **b.** to make (a way) or follow (a course) thus. —*v.i.* **8.** to till the soil with a plow; work with a plow. **9.** to take plowing in a specified way: *land that plows easily.* **10.** to move through anything in the manner of a plow. **11.** to move through water by cleaving the surface. Also, *esp. Brit.,* **plough.** [ME; OE *plōh* plowland, c. G *pflug* plow] —**plow'er,** *n.*

plow·boy (plou'boi'), *n.* **1.** a boy who leads or guides a team drawing a plow. **2.** a country boy.

plow·man (plou'mən), *n., pl.* **-men.** **1.** a man who plows. **2.** a farm laborer or a rustic.

plow·share (plou'shâr'), *n.* the share of a plow which cuts the slice of earth and raises it to the moldboard.

ploy (ploi), *n.* a maneuver or stratagem, as in conversation, to gain the advantage. [t. F: s. *ployer,* g. L *plicāre* fold]

plu., plural.

pluck (plŭk), *v.t.* **1.** to pull off or out from the place of growth, as fruit, flowers, feathers, etc. **2.** to give a pull at. **3.** to pull with sudden force or with a jerk. **4.** to pull by force (fol. by *away, off, out,* etc.). **5.** to pull off the feathers, hair, etc., from. **6.** *Slang.* to rob, plunder, or fleece. **7.** to sound (the strings of a musical instrument) by pulling at them with the fingers or a plectrum. **8.** *Brit. Univ. Slang.* to reject, as after an examination. **9.** **pluck up, a.** to pull up; uproot; eradicate. **b.** to rouse (courage, spirit, etc.). —*v.i.* **10.** to pull sharply; tug (*at*). **11.** to snatch (*at*). —*n.* **12.** act of plucking; a pull, tug, or jerk. **13.** the heart, liver, and lungs, esp. of an animal used for food. **14.** courage or resolution in the face of difficulties. [ME *plukke,* OE *pluccian,* c. MLG *plucken;* akin to G *pflücken*] —**pluck'er,** *n.*

pluck·y (plŭk'ĭ), *adj.,* **pluckier, pluckiest.** having or showing pluck or courage; brave. —**pluck'i·ly,** *adv.* —**pluck'i·ness,** *n.*

plug (plŭg), *n., v.,* **plugged, plugging.** —*n.* **1.** a piece of wood or other material used to stop up a hole or aperture, to fill a gap, or to act as a wedge. **2.** *Elect.* **a.** a tapering piece of conducting material designed to be inserted between contact surfaces and so establish connection be-

tween elements of an electric current connected to the respective surfaces. **b.** a device to which may be attached the conductors of a cord and which by insertion in a jack, or by screwing into a receptacle, establishes contact. **3.** a spark plug. **4.** a fireplug. **5.** a cake of pressed tobacco. **6.** a piece of tobacco cut off for chewing, etc. **7.** *Chiefly U.S. Slang.* a worn-out or inferior horse. **8.** *U.S. Slang.* the favorable mention of a product, as in a lecture, radio show, etc. **9.** *Slang.* a man's tall silk hat (**plug hat**). **10.** *Colloq.* a shopworn or unsalable article. **11.** *Slang.* a punch. —*v.t.* **12.** to stop or fill with or as with a plug. **13.** to insert or drive a plug into. **14.** to secure by a plug. **15.** to insert (something) as a plug. **16.** *U.S. Slang.* to mention (a product) favorably, as in a lecture, radio show, etc. **17.** *Slang.* to punch. **18.** *Slang.* to shoot. **19.** to connect (an electrical device) with an outlet (fol. by *in*). —*v.i.* **20.** *Colloq.* to work steadily or doggedly. **21.** *Slang.* to strike; shoot. [t. MD: m. *plugge* (D *plug*) plug, peg; akin to G *pflock*] —**plug'ger,** *n.*

plug-ug·ly (plŭg'ŭg'lĭ), *n., pl.* **-lies.** *U.S. Slang.* a ruffian; a rowdy; a tough.

plum[1] (plŭm), *n.* **1.** the drupaceous fruit of any of various trees of the rosaceous genus *Prunus,* closely related to the cherry but with an oblong stone. **2.** a tree bearing such fruit. **3.** any of various other trees with a plumlike fruit. **4.** the fruit itself. **5.** a sugarplum. **6.** a raisin as in a cake or pudding. **7.** anything resembling a plum, as in taste or shape. **8.** a deep purple varying from bluish to reddish. **9.** a good or choice thing, as one of the best parts of anything, a fine situation or appointment, etc. **10.** *Finance,* an extra dividend, generally large. [ME; OE *plūme* (c. G *pflaume*), ult. t. Gk.: m. *proúmnon*] —**plum'like,** *adj.*

plum[2] (plŭm), *adj., adv.* plumb (defs. 3–7).

plum·age (plōō'mĭj), *n.* **1.** the entire feathery covering of a bird. **2.** feathers collectively. [late ME, t. OF: f. *plume* feather + *-age* -AGE]

plu·mate (plōō'māt, -mĭt), *adj. Zool.* resembling a feather, as a hair or bristle which bears smaller hairs. [t. L: m.s. *plūmātus,* pp., covered with feathers]

plumb (plŭm), *n.* **1.** a small mass of lead or heavy material, used for various purposes. **2.** the position of a plumb line when freely suspended; the perpendicular: *out of plumb.* —*adj.* **3.** true according to a plumb line; perpendicular. **4.** *Colloq.* downright or absolute. —*adv.* **5.** in a perpendicular or vertical direction. **6.** exactly, precisely, or directly. **7.** *Colloq.* completely or absolutely. —*v.t.* **8.** to test or adjust by a plumb line. **9.** to make vertical. **10.** to sound (the ocean, etc.) with, or as with, a plumb line. **11.** to measure (depth) by sounding. **12.** to sound the depths of, or penetrate to the bottom of. **13.** to seal with lead. Also, **plum** for 3–7. [ME *plumbe,* t. OF: m. *plomb,* g. L *plumbum* lead]

plum·bag·i·na·ceous (plŭm băj'ə nā'shəs), *adj.* belonging to the *Plumbaginaceae,* or leadwort family of plants, certain of which, as *Plumbago* and *Statice,* are in wide cultivation as ornamentals.

plum·ba·go (plŭm bā'gō), *n., pl.* **-gos.** **1.** graphite. **2.** a drawing made by an instrument with a lead point. [t. L: lead, ore]

plumb bob (bŏb), plummet (def. 1).

plum·be·ous (plŭm'bĭ əs), *adj.* leaden. [t. L: m. *plumbeus*]

plumb·er (plŭm'ər), *n.* **1.** one who installs and repairs piping, fixtures, appliances, and appurtenances in connection with the water supply, drainage systems, etc., both in and out of buildings. **2.** a worker in lead or similar metals. [ME, t. OF: m. *plombier,* g. LL *plumbārius,* der. L *plumbum* lead]

plumb·er·y (plŭm'ər ĭ), *n., pl.* **-eries.** **1.** a plumber's workshop. **2.** plumber's work. **3.** working in lead.

plum·bic (plŭm'bĭk), *adj. Chem.* containing lead, esp. in the tetravalent state (Pb+4). [f. s. L *plumbum* lead + -IC]

plum·bif·er·ous (plŭm bĭf'ər əs), *adj.* yielding or containing lead. [f. s. L *plumbum* lead + -(I)FEROUS]

plumb·ing (plŭm'ĭng), *n.* **1.** the system of pipes and other apparatus for conveying water, liquid wastes, etc., as in a building. **2.** the work or trade of a plumber. **3.** the act of one who plumbs, as in ascertaining depth.

plum·bism (plŭm'bĭz əm), *n. Pathol.* chronic lead poisoning.

plumb line, **1.** a cord to one end of which is attached a metal bob, used to determine perpendicularity, find the depth of water, etc. **2.** a plumb rule.

plum·bous (plŭm'bəs), *adj. Chem.* containing divalent lead (Pb+2). [t. L: m.s. *plumbōsus*]

plumb rule, a device used by builders, etc., for determining perpendicularity, consisting of a narrow board fitted with a plumb line and bob.

plum·bum (plŭm'bəm), *n. Chem.* lead. *Abbr.:* Pb [t. L]

plum duff, a kind of flour pudding containing raisins or currants, steamed, or boiled in a cloth or bag.

plume (plōōm), *n., v.,* **plumed, pluming.** —*n.* **1.** a feather. **2.** a large, long, or conspicuous feather: *the plume of an ostrich.* **3.** a soft, fluffy feather. **4.** any plumose part or formation. **5.** a feather, a tuft of feathers, or some substitute, worn as an ornament on the hat, helmet, etc. **6.** an ornament; a token of honor or distinction. **7.** *Now Chiefly Poetic.* plumage. —*v.t.* **8.** to furnish, cover, or adorn with plumes or feathers. **9.** (of a bird) to preen (itself or its feathers). **10.** to display or feel satisfaction with or pride in (oneself); pride (oneself) complacently (fol. by *on* or *upon*). [t. OF, g. L *pluma* feather; r. OE *plūm*, t. L: s. *plūma*] —**plume´-like´,** *adj.*

plume·let (plōōm´lĭt), *n.* a small plume.

plum·met (plŭm´ĭt), *n.* 1. Also, **plumb bob**, a piece of lead or some other weight attached to a line, used for determining perpendicularity, for sounding, etc.; the bob of a plumb line. 2. a plumb rule. 3. something that weighs down or depresses. —*v.i.* 4. to plunge. [ME *plomet*, t. OF: m. *plommet, plombet*, dim. of *plomb* lead]

plum·my (plŭm´ĭ), *adj.* 1. full of or resembling plums. 2. *Chiefly Brit. Colloq.* choice, good, or desirable.

plu·mose (plōō´mōs), *adj.* 1. having feathers or plumes; feathered. 2. feathery or plumelike. [t. L: m.s. *plūmōsus*] —**plu·mos·i·ty** (plōō mŏs´ə tĭ), *n.*

plump[1] (plŭmp), *adj.* 1. well filled out or rounded in form; somewhat fleshy or fat; chubby. —*v.i.* 2. to become plump (often fol. by *up* or *out*). —*v.t.* 3. to make plump (fol. by *up* or *out*). [ME *plompe* dull, rude, c. MLG *plump* blunt, thick, rude] —**plump´ly,** *adv.* —**plump´ness,** *n.* —**Syn.** 1. See **stout.**

plump[2] (plŭmp), *v.i.* 1. to fall heavily or suddenly and directly; drop, sink, or come abruptly, or with direct impact. 2. to vote exclusively for one candidate, at an election, instead of distributing or splitting one's votes among a number. —*v.t.* 3. to drop or throw heavily or suddenly. 4. to utter or say bluntly (often fol. by *out*). —*n.* 5. a heavy or sudden fall. —*adv.* 6. with a heavy or sudden fall or drop. 7. directly or bluntly, as in speaking. 8. straight. 9. with sudden encounter. 10. with direct impact. —*adj.* 11. direct; downright; blunt. [ME *plumpen*, c. D *plompen*; prob. imit.]

plump[3] (plŭmp), *n. Archaic or Brit. Dial.* a group or cluster. [orig. uncert.]

plump·er[1] (plŭmp´ər), *n.* 1. a plumping or falling heavily. 2. the vote of one who plumps. 3. a voter who plumps. [f. PLUMP[2], v. + -ER[1]]

plump·er[2] (plŭmp´ər), *n.* 1. something that plumps, or makes plump. 2. something carried in the mouth to fill out hollow cheeks. [f. PLUMP[1], v. + -ER[1]]

plum pudding, a rich steamed or boiled pudding containing raisins, currants, citron, spices, etc.

plu·mule (plōō´mūl), *n.* 1. *Bot.* the bud of the ascending axis of a plant while still in the embryo. 2. *Ornith.* a down feather. [t. L: m. *plūmula*, dim. of *plūma* feather]

plum·y (plōō´mĭ), *adj.* 1. having plumes or feathers. 2. adorned with a plume or plumes: *a plumy helmet.* 3. plumelike or feathery.

plun·der (plŭn´dər), *v.t.* 1. to rob of goods or valuables by open force, as in war, hostile raids, brigandage, etc.: *to plunder a town.* 2. to rob, despoil, or fleece: *to plunder the public treasury.* 3. to take by pillage or robbery. —*v.i.* 4. to take plunder; pillage. —*n.* 5. plundering, pillage, or spoliation. 6. that which is taken in plundering; loot. 7. anything taken by robbery, theft, or fraud. [t. G: m. *plündern*] —**plun´der·er,** *n.*

plun·der·age (plŭn´dər yĭj), *n.* 1. the act of plundering; pillage. 2. *Maritime Law.* **a.** the embezzlement of goods on board a ship. **b.** the goods embezzled.

plunge (plŭnj), *v.*, **plunged, plunging,** *n.* —*v.t.* 1. to cast or thrust forcibly or suddenly into a liquid, a penetrable substance, a place, etc.; immerse; submerge: *to plunge a dagger into one's heart.* 2. to bring into some condition, situation, etc.: *to plunge a country into war.* 3. to immerse mentally, as in thought. —*v.i.* 4. to cast oneself, or fall as if cast, into water, a deep place, etc. 5. to rush or dash with headlong haste: *to plunge through a doorway.* 6. *Slang.* to bet or speculate recklessly. 7. to throw oneself impetuously or abruptly into some condition, situation, matter, etc.: *to plunge into war.* 8. to descend abruptly or precipitously, as a cliff, a road, etc. 9. to pitch violently forward, esp. with the head downward, as a horse, a ship, etc. —*n.* 10. act of plunging. 11. a leap or dive into water or the like. 12. a headlong or impetuous rush or dash. 13. a sudden, violent pitching movement. 14. a place for plunging or diving, as a swimming tank. [ME, t. OF: m. *plungier*, ult. der. L *plumbum* lead] —**Syn.** 1. See **dip.**

plung·er (plŭn´jər), *n.* 1. *Mach.* a device or a part of a machine which acts with a plunging or thrusting motion; a piston; a ram. 2. *Auto.* a pistonlike part in the valve of a pneumatic tire. 3. one who or that which plunges; a diver. 4. *Slang.* a reckless bettor or speculator.

plung·ing (plŭn´jĭng), *adj.* 1. that plunges. 2. *Mil.* (of fire) directed downward from pieces situated above the plane of the object fired at.

plunk (plŭngk), *Colloq. except def. 1.* —*v.t.* 1. to pluck (a stringed instrument or its strings); twang. 2. to throw, push, put, etc., heavily or suddenly. —*v.i.* 3. to give forth a twanging sound. 4. to drop down heavily or suddenly; plump. —*n.* 5. act or sound of plunking. 6. a direct, forcible blow. —*adv.* 7. with a plunking sound. [imit.]

plu·per·fect (plōō pûr´fĭkt), *Gram.* —*adj.* 1. perfect with respect to a temporal point of reference in the past. Example: In "He had done it when I came," *had done*

is pluperfect (completed action) in relation to *came.* 2. designating a tense, or other verb formation or construction, with such meaning. Latin *portāveram* "I had carried" etc., is in the pluperfect tense. —*n.* 3. the pluperfect tense, or other verb formation or construction with such meaning. 4. a form therein. [t. L, contr. of *plūs quam perfectum* more than perfect]

plupf., pluperfect.

plur., 1. plural. 2. plurality.

plu·ral (plōōr´əl), *adj.* 1. consisting of, containing, or pertaining to more than one. 2. pertaining to or involving a plurality of persons or things. 3. being one of such a plurality: *a plural wife.* 4. *Gram.* (in many languages) designating the number category that normally implies more than one person, thing, or collection, as English, *men, things, they.* —*n.* 5. *Gram.* the plural number. 6. a form therein. [ME, t. L: s. *plūrālis*]

plu·ral·ism (plōōr´ə lĭz əm), *n.* 1. *Philos.* a theory or system that recognizes more than one ultimate substance or principle. Cf. **monism, dualism.** 2. *Chiefly Brit.* the holding by one person of two or more offices, esp. ecclesiastical benefices, at the same time. 3. the character of being plural. —**plu´ral·ist,** *n.* —**plu´ral·is´tic,** *adj.*

plu·ral·i·ty (plōō răl´ə tĭ), *n., pl.* **-ties.** 1. (when there are three or more candidates) the excess of votes received by the leading candidate over those received by the next candidate (esp. in distinction from a *majority*). 2. more than half of the whole; the majority. 3. a number greater than unity. 4. the fact of being numerous. 5. a large number, or a multitude. 6. state or fact of being plural. 7. pluralism (def. 2). 8. any of the offices or benefices so held.

plu·ral·ize (plōōr´ə līz), *v.t.,* **-ized, -izing.** 1. to make plural. 2. to express in the plural form.

plu·ral·ly (plōōr´ə lĭ), *adv.* as a plural; in a plural sense.

pluri-, a word element meaning "several," "many." [t. L, comb. form of *plūrēs*, pl.]

plus (plŭs), *prep.* 1. more by the addition of; increased by: *ten plus two.* 2. with the addition of; with. —*adj.* 3. involving or denoting addition. 4. positive: *a plus quantity.* 5. *Colloq.* with something in addition. 6. more (by a certain amount). 7. *Elect.* positive or to be connected to the positive: *the plus terminal.* 8. *Bot.* designating, in the absence of morphological difference, one of the two strains or mycelia in fungi which must unite in the sexual process. —*n.* 9. a plus quantity. 10. the plus sign (+). 11. something additional. 12. a surplus or gain. [t. L: more]

plus fours, baggy knickers, as for sports wear.

plush (plŭsh), *n.* a fabric of silk, cotton, wool, etc., having a longer pile than that of velvet. [t. F: m. *pluche, peluche*, ult. der. L *pilus* hair]

plus sign, the symbol (+) indicating summation or a positive quantity.

Plu·tarch (plōō´tärk), *n.* A.D. c 46–c120, Greek biographer.

Plu·to (plōō´tō), *n.* 1. *Gk. Myth.* **a.** Hades, the lord of the dead and the lower world. **b.** a nymph, mother of Tantalus. 2. *Astron.* the ninth and outermost planet from the sun, discovered in 1930. Period of revolution: 248.42 years; mean distance from sun: 3,671,000,000 miles; diameter probably a little smaller than earth's. [t. L, t. Gk.: m. *Ploútōn*]

plu·toc·ra·cy (plōō tŏk´rə sĭ), *n., pl.* **-cies.** 1. the rule or power of wealth or of the wealthy. 2. a government or state in which the wealthy class rules. 3. a class or group ruling, or exercising power or influence, by virtue of its wealth. [t. Gk.: m. *ploutokratia.* See -CRACY]

plu·to·crat (plōō´tə krăt´), *n.* a member of a plutocracy.

plu·to·crat·ic (plōō´tə krăt´ĭk), *adj.* of, pertaining to, or indicative of, a plutocracy or plutocrats. Also, **plu´to·crat´i·cal.**

plu·ton (plōō´tŏn), *n. Geol.* any body of igneous rock that solidified far below the earth's surface. [named after PLUTO]

Plu·to·ni·an (plōō tō´nĭ ən), *adj.* 1. of or pertaining to Pluto; infernal. 2. (*cap. or l.c.*) *Geol.* pertaining to the theory that the present condition of the earth's crust is mainly due to igneous action.

plu·ton·ic (plōō tŏn´ĭk), *adj.* 1. *Geol.* noting a class of igneous rocks which have solidified far below the earth's surface. 2. (*cap. or l.c.*). Plutonian.

plu·to·ni·um (plōō tō´nĭ əm), *n.* a radioactive element, capable of self-maintained explosive fission, isolated during research on the atomic bomb in 1940. It is formed by deuteron bombardment of neptunium, and has an isotope of major importance (Pu[239]), which is fissionable and can be produced in chain-reacting units from uranium 238, by neutron capture followed by the spontaneous emission of two beta particles. Symbol: Pu; at. no.: 94. [f. m. Gk. *Ploútōn* PLUTO + -IUM]

Plu·tus (plōō´təs), *n. Class. Myth.* a personification of wealth, the son of Demeter, and associated with peace. [t. L, t. Gk.: m. *Ploûtos* god of riches, lit., wealth]

plu·vi·al (plōō´vĭ əl), *adj.* 1. of or pertaining to rain; rainy. 2. *Geol.* due to rain. [t. L: s. *pluviālis*]

plu·vi·om·e·ter (plōō´vĭ ŏm´ə tər), *n.* an instrument for measuring rainfall. [f. s. L *pluvia* rain + -(o)METER] —**plu·vi·o·met·ric** (plōō´vĭ ə mĕt´rĭk), **plu·vi·o·met´-ri·cal,** *adj.* —**plu·vi·om´e·try,** *n.*

B.   P. Plumules
A. Rhubarb, *Rheum moorcroftianum;*
B. Bean, *Vicia faba;*
C. Sedge, *Cyperus niculata*

act, āble, dâre, ärt; ĕbb, ēqual; ĭf, īce; hŏt, ōver, ôrder, oil, bŏŏk, ōōze, out; ŭp, ūse, ûrge; ə = a in alone; ch, chief; g, give; ng, ring; sh, shoe; th, thin; ŧh, that; zh, vision. See the full key on inside cover.

Plu·vi·ôse (plōō′vYōs′; *Fr.* plγ vyōz′), *n.* (in the calendar of the first French republic) the fifth month of the year, extending from Jan. 20 to Feb. 18. [t. F: m. *pluviôse*, t. L: m. *pluviôsus* rainy]

plu·vi·ous (plōō′vY əs), *adj.* **1.** rainy. **2.** pertaining to rain. [t. L: m. *pluviôsus*]

ply[1] (plī), *v.*, **plied, plying.** —*v.t.* **1.** to use; employ busily, or work with or at: *to ply the needle*. **2.** to carry on, practice, or pursue: *to ply a trade*. **3.** to treat with something repeatedly applied: *I plied the fire with fresh fuel*. **4.** to assail persistently: *to ply horses with a whip*. **5.** to supply with something pressingly offered: *to ply a person with drink*. **6.** to address persistently or importunately, as with questions, solicitations, etc.; importune. **7.** to traverse (a river, etc.), esp. on regular trips. —*v.i.* **8.** to travel or run regularly over a fixed course or between certain places, as a boat, a stage, etc. **9.** to perform one's or its work or office busily or steadily: *to ply with the oars*. **10.** to pursue or direct the course, on the water or otherwise. [ME *plye(n)*, aphetic var. of ME *aplye(n)* APPLY]

ply[2] (plī), *n.*, *pl.* **plies,** *v.*, **plied, plying.** —*n.* **1.** a fold; a thickness. **2.** a unit of yarn: *single ply*. **3.** bent, bias, or inclination. —*v.t.* **4.** *Now Chiefly Brit. Dial.* to bend, fold, or mold. —*v.i.* **5.** *Obs.* to bend, incline, or yield. [ME *plien*, t. OF: m. *plier* fold, bend, g. L *plicāre* fold]

-ply, suffixal use of **ply**[2] (thickness), as in *three-ply*.

Plym·outh (plĭm′əth), *n.* **1.** a seaport in SW England, on the English Channel: naval base; the departing point of the *Mayflower* (1620). 216,200 (est. 1956). **2.** a city in SE Massachusetts: the oldest town in New England; founded by the Pilgrims, 1620. 6,488 (1960).

Plymouth Brethren, a religious sect which originated in the 1820's in the British Isles, in Plymouth, Bristol, and Dublin.

Plymouth Colony, the colony established in SE Massachusetts by the English Pilgrims in 1620.

Plymouth Rock, 1. a rock at Plymouth, Massachusetts, on which the Pilgrim Fathers are said to have landed in 1620. **2.** one of an American breed of domestic fowls, of moderate size, usually well-fleshed.

ply·wood (plī′wŏŏd′), *n.* a material consisting of an odd number of thin sheets or strips of wood glued together with the grains (usually) at right angles, used in building, cabinetwork, and airplane construction.

Plzen (pŭl′zĕn′y), *n.* Czech name of **Pilsen.**

P.M., 1. Past Master. **2.** Paymaster. **3.** Police Magistrate. **4.** Postmaster. **5.** post meridiem. **6.** postmortem. **7.** Prime Minister. **8.** Provost Marshal.

p.m., 1. post meridiem. **2.** post-mortem.

P.M.G., 1. Postmaster General. **2.** Provost Marshal General.

P/N, promissory note. Also, **p.n.**

pneum., 1. pneumatic. **2.** pneumatics.

pneu·ma (nū′mə, nōō′-), *n. Gk. Philos., etc.,* the vital spirit; the soul. [t. Gk.]

pneu·mat·ic (nū măt′ĭk, nōō-), *adj.* **1.** of or pertaining to air, or gases in general. **2.** pertaining to pneumatics. **3.** operated by air, or by pressure or exhaustion of air. **4.** containing air; filled with compressed air, as a tire. **5.** equipped with pneumatic tires. **6.** *Theol.* of or pertaining to the spirit; spiritual. **7.** *Zool.* containing air or air cavities. —*n.* **8.** a pneumatic tire. **9.** a vehicle having wheels with such tires. [t. L: s. *pneumaticus*, t. Gk.: m. *pneumatikós*] —**pneu·mat′i·cal·ly,** *adv.*

pneu·mat·ics (nū măt′Yks, nōō-), *n.* the branch of physics that deals with the mechanical properties of air and other gases. [pl. of PNEUMATIC, adj. See -ICS]

pneumato-, a word element, used chiefly in scientific terms, referring to air, breath, spirit. [t. Gk., comb. form of *pneûma*]

pneu·ma·tol·o·gy (nū′mə tŏl′ə jY, nōō-), *n.* **1.** *Theol.* **a.** the doctrine of the Holy Spirit. **b.** the belief in intermediary spirits between men and God. **2.** the doctrine or theory of spiritual beings. **3.** *Archaic.* psychology. **4.** *Obs.* pneumatics.

pneu·ma·tol·y·sis (nū′mə tŏl′ə sYs, nōō-), *n. Geol.* the process by which minerals and ores are formed by the action of vapors given off from igneous magmas.

pneu·ma·to·lyt·ic (nū′mə tə lYt′Yk, nōō-), *adj. Geol.* pertaining to or formed by pneumatolysis.

pneu·ma·tom·e·ter (nū′mə tŏm′ə tər, nōō-), *n. Physiol.* an instrument for measuring the quantity of air inhaled or exhaled during a single inspiration or expiration, or the force of inspiration or expiration.

pneu·ma·to·phore (nū′mə tō fōr′, -fôr′, nōō-), *n.* **1.** *Bot.* a specialized structure developed from the root in certain plants growing in swamps and marshes, and serving as a respiratory organ. **2.** *Zool.* the air sac of a siphonophore, serving as a float.

pneu·ma·to·ther·a·py (nū′mə tō thĕr′ə pY, nōō′-), *n.* the use of compressed or rarefied air in treating disease.

pneumo-, a word element referring to the lungs or to respiration. [comb. form repr. Gk. *pneúmōn* lung, or, less often, *pneûma* wind, air, breath]

pneu·mo·ba·cil·lus (nū′mō bə sĭl′əs, nōō′-), *n.*, *pl.* **-cilli** (-sĭl′ī). a bacillus, *Bacillus mucosus*, the causative agent of certain respiratory diseases, esp. pneumonia. [t. NL. See PNEUMO-, BACILLUS]

pneu·mo·coc·cus (nū′mə kŏk′əs, nōō′-), *n.*, *pl.* **-cocci** (-kŏk′sī). a bacterium, *Micrococcus lanceolatus*, a

rather large pear-shaped coccus, occurring in pairs and surrounded by a wide capsule: the cause of acute lobar pneumonia and **pneumococcal meningitis.** [t. NL. See PNEUMO-, COCCUS]

pneu·mo·dy·nam·ics (nū′mō dī năm′Yks, nōō′-, -dY-), *n.* pneumatics.

pneu·mo·gas·tric (nū′mə găs′trYk, nōō′/-), *n.* **1.** the vagus nerve. —*adj.* **2.** pertaining to the lungs and stomach.

pneu·mo·nec·to·my (nū′mə nĕk′tə mY, nōō′/-), *n.*, *pl.* **-mies.** the removal of an entire lung by surgery. [f. Gk. *pneúmōn* lung + -ECTOMY]

pneu·mo·nia (nū mō′nyə -nY ə, nōō-), *n. Pathol.* **1.** inflammation of the lungs. **2.** an acute affection of the lungs, **croupous pneumonia or lobar pneumonia,** regarded as due to the pneumococcus. [t. NL, t. Gk.]

pneu·mon·ic (nū mŏn′Yk, nōō-), *adj.* **1.** of, pertaining to, or affecting the lungs; pulmonary. **2.** pertaining to or affected with pneumonia.

pneu·mo·tho·rax (nū′mō thŏr′ăks, nōō′/-), *n. Pathol.* the presence of air or gas in the pleural cavity.

Pnom Penh (nŏm′pĕn′; *local* pnŏŏm pĕn′y), *n.* a city in SE Asia, capital of Cambodia. 375,000 (est. 1953). Also, **Pnom′-Penh′, Phnom Penh, Pnom′penh′.**

pnxt., pinxit.

Po (pō), *n.* a river flowing from the Alps in NW Italy E to the Adriatic. 418 mi. Ancient, **Padus.**

Po, *Chem.* polonium.

po., *Baseball.* put-outs.

P.O., 1. petty officer. **2.** postal order. **3.** post office.

po·a·ceous (pō ā′shəs), *adj.* belonging to the *Poaceae* (or *Gramineae*), the grass family of plants. [f. s. NL *Poa* the typical genus (t. Gk.: grass) + -ACEOUS]

poach[1] (pōch), *v.i.* **1.** *Chiefly Brit.* to trespass on another's land, etc., esp. in order to steal game. **2.** to take game or fish illegally. **3.** (of land) to become broken up or slushy by being trampled. —*v.t.* **4.** to trample. **5.** to mix with water and reduce to a uniform consistency, as clay. [t. MF: m. *pocher* thrust or put out (eyes), dig out with the fingers, prob. t. Gmc.; akin to POKE[1]] —**poach′er,** *n.*

poach[2] (pōch), *v.t.* to cook (an egg) by dropping it whole (without the shell) into hot liquid and simmering till done. [t. F: m.s. *pocher*; cf. *poche* cooking spoon, g. LL *popia*; of Gaelic orig.; ult. c. L *coquere* to cook]

POB, Post Office Box. Also, **P.O.B.**

Po·ca·hon·tas (pō′kə hŏn′təs), *n.* (*Rebecca Rolfe*) 1595?-1617, American Indian girl who is said to have prevented the execution of Captain John Smith.

Po·ca·tel·lo (pō′kə tĕl′ō), *n.* a city in SE Idaho. 28,534 (1960).

po·chard (pō′chərd, -kərd), *n.* **1.** an Old World diving duck, *Aythya ferina*, with a chestnut-red head. **2.** any of various related ducks, as the American redhead. [orig. uncert.]

pock (pŏk), *n.* **1.** a pustule on the body in an eruptive disease, as smallpox. **2.** a mark or spot left by or resembling such a pustule. [ME *pokke*, OE *poc*, c. G *pocke*; ? akin to OE *pocca* bag. See POKE[2]]

pock·et (pŏk′Yt), *n.* **1.** a small bag inserted in a garment, for carrying a purse or other small articles. **2.** a bag or pouch. **3.** money, means, or financial resources. **4.** any pouchlike receptacle, hollow, or cavity. **5.** a cavity in the earth, esp. one containing gold or other ore. **6.** a small ore body or mass of ore, frequently isolated. **7.** *Mining.* **a.** a bin for ore or rock storage. **b.** a raise or small slope fitted with chute gates. **8.** a small bag or net at the corner or side of a billiard table. **9.** *Racing.* a position in which a contestant is so hemmed in by others that his progress is impeded. **10.** *Naut.* a holder consisting of a strip of sailcloth sewed to a sail, to contain a thin wooden batten which stiffens the leech of the sail. —*adj.* **11.** suitable for carrying in the pocket. **12.** small enough to go in the pocket; diminutive. —*v.t.* **13.** to put into one's pocket. **14.** to take possession of as one's own, often dishonestly. **15.** to submit to or endure without protest or open resentment. **16.** to conceal or suppress: *to pocket one's pride*. **17.** to enclose or confine as in a pocket. **18.** to drive (a ball) into a pocket, as in billiards. **19.** *U.S.* (of the President or a legislative executive) to retain (a bill) without action on it and thus prevent it from becoming a law. **20.** to hem in (a contestant) so as to impede progress, as in racing. [ME *poket*, t. AF: m. *pokete*, dim. of ONF *poke*, var. of F *poche* bag. See POKE[2], POUCH]

pocket battleship, a small, heavily armed and armored warship serving as a battleship because of limitations imposed by treaty.

pock·et·book (pŏk′Yt bŏŏk′), *n.* **1.** a small bag or case, as of leather, for papers, money, etc., usually carried by a handle or in the pocket. **2.** pecuniary resources. **3.** a book, usually paperbound and small enough for the pocket.

pocket borough, an English borough whose parliamentary representation (before 1832) was practically in the hands of some individual or family.

pock·et·ful (pŏk′Yt fŏŏl′), *n.*, *pl.* **-fuls.** as much as a pocket will hold.

pock·et·knife (pŏk′Yt nīf′), *n.*, *pl.* **-knives** (-nīvz′). a knife with one or more blades which fold into the handle, suitable for carrying in the pocket.

pocket money, money for small current expenses.

pocket veto, 1. the retaining, without action, past the time of the adjournment of Congress, by the President of the U.S., of a bill presented to him for signature within ten days of the end of a session, which is equivalent to a veto. **2.** a similar action on the part of any legislative executive.

pock·mark (pŏk′märk′), *n.* a mark or pit left by a pustule in smallpox or the like. —**pock′-marked′,** *adj.*

pock·y (pŏk′ĭ), *adj.* having pocks; marked by pocks.

po·co (pô′kô), *adj. Music.* somewhat: *poco presto* (*somewhat fast*). [It.: little, g. L *paucus* few]

po·co a po·co (pô′kô ä pô′kô), *Music.* gradually. [It.]

po·co·cu·ran·te (pô′kô kōō rän′tĭ; *It.* pô′kô kōō rän′-tĕ), *n.* **1.** a careless or indifferent person. —*adj.* **2.** caring little; indifferent; nonchalant. [t. It.: f. *poco* little + *curante* caring. g. s. L *curans,* ppr.] —**po·co·cu·ran·tism** (pô′kô kōō rän′tĭz əm, -rän′-), *n.*

pod[1] (pŏd), *n., v.* **podded, podding.** —*n.* **1.** a more or less elongated, two-valved seed vessel, as that of the pea or bean. **2.** a dehiscent fruit or pericarp with several seeds. —*v.i.* **3.** to produce pods. **4.** to swell out like a pod. [appar. back formation from *podder* peasecod gatherer. Cf. *podder,* var. of *podware,* unexplained var. of *codware* podded vegetables (f. COD[1] pod, bag + *-ware* crops, vegetables)]

pod[2] (pŏd), *n.* **1.** a small herd or school, esp. of seals or whales. **2.** a small flock of birds. [orig. uncert.]

pod[3] (pŏd), *n.* the straight groove or channel in the body of certain augers or bits. [cf. OE *pād* covering, cloak]

pod-, a word element meaning "foot." Also, before consonants, **podo-.** [t. Gk., comb. form of *poús*]

-pod, a word element meaning "footed," as in *cephalopod.* Cf. **-poda.** [t. Gk.: s. *-podos,* der. *poús* foot]

P.O.D. 1. pay on delivery. **2.** Post Office Department.

-poda, pl. of **-pod,** as in *cephalopoda.*

po·dag·ra (pō dăg′rə, pŏd′ə grə), *n.* gout in the foot. [t. L, t. Gk.: lit., a trap for the feet]

po·des·ta (pō dĕs′tə; *It.* pô′dĕ stä′), *n.* **1.** any of certain magistrates in Italy, as the chief magistrate in medieval towns and republics. **2.** a Fascist city official (mayor) in Italy, appointed by the party. [t. It., g. L *potestas* power, magistrate]

podg·y (pŏj′ĭ), *adj.,* **podgier, podgiest.** *Chiefly Brit.* pudgy.

po·di·a·try (pō dī′ə trĭ), *n. Med.* the investigation and treatment of foot disorders. [f. POD- + -IATRY] —**po·di′a·trist,** *n.*

po·di·um (pō′dĭ əm), *n., pl.* **-di·a** (-dĭ ə). **1.** a small platform for the conductor of an orchestra, for a public speaker, etc. **2.** *Archit.* **a.** a continuous projecting base of a building usually of considerable height and forming the front of the basement of the foundation behind it. **b.** a low continuous structure serving as a base or terrace wall. **c.** the stylobate or the structure under the stylobate of a temple. **d.** a raised platform surrounding the arena of an ancient amphitheater. **3.** *Zool., Anat.* a foot. **4.** *Bot.* a footstalk or stipe. [t. L: elevated place, balcony, t. Gk.: m. *pódion,* dim. of *poús* foot. Cf. PEW]

-podium, a word element meaning "footlike," used in nouns. [t. NL. See PODIUM]

pod·o·phyl·lin (pŏd′ə fĭl′ĭn), *n.* a resin obtained from podophyllum and used as a cathartic.

pod·o·phyl·lum (pŏd′ə fĭl′əm), *n.* the dried rhizome of the May apple, *Podophyllum peltatum.* [t. NL. f. Gk.: *podo-* (see POD-) + m. *phýllon* leaf]

-podous, a word element used as an adjective termination, corresponding to **-pod.** [t. Gk.: m. *-podos* footed, der. *poús* foot]

Po·dunk (pō′dŭngk), *n. U.S.* a humorous name for any small or insignificant place.

pod·zol (pŏd′zŏl), *n.* a forest soil, notably acidic, having an upper layer that is greyish-white or ash-colored and depleted of colloids and iron and aluminum compounds, and a lower layer, brownish in color, in which those have accumulated; an infertile soil difficult to cultivate, found over vast areas in northern North America and Eurasia. [t. Russ.: adj., resembling ashes] —**pod·zol′ic,** *adj.*

Poe (pō), *n.* **Edgar Allan,** 1809–49, U. S. poet, writer of tales, and critic.

po·em (pō′ĭm), *n.* **1.** a composition in verse, esp. one characterized by artistic construction and imaginative or elevated thought: *a lyric poem.* **2.** a composition which, though not in verse, is characterized by great beauty of language or thought: *a prose poem.* **3.** a work in poetry rather than prose. **4.** something having qualities suggestive of or likened to those of poetry. [t. L: s. *poēma,* t. Gk.: m. *poíēma,* poem, something made]

po·e·sy (pō′ə sĭ, -zĭ), *n., pl.* **-sies. 1.** *Poetic.* poetry in general. **2.** *Archaic.* the work or the art of poetic composition. **3.** *Archaic.* poetry or verse. **4.** *Obs.* a verse or poetry or the like used as a motto. See **posy** (def. 2). **5.** *Obs.* a poem. [ME *poesie,* t. OF, t. L: m. *poēsis,* t. Gk.: m. *poíēsis* poetic composition, poetry, a making]

po·et (pō′ĭt), *n.* **1.** one who composes poetry. **2.** one having the gift of poetic thought, imagination, and creation, together with eloquence of expression. [ME *poete,* t. L: m. *poēta,* t. Gk.: m. *po(i)ētēs* poet, maker]

poet., 1. poetic. **2.** poetical. **3.** poetry.

po·et·as·ter (pō′ĭt ăs′tər), *n.* an inferior poet; a writer of indifferent verse. [t. ML or NL. See POET, -ASTER]

po·et·ess (pō′ĭt ĭs), *n.* a female poet.

po·et·ic (pō ĕt′ĭk), *adj.* Also, **po·et·i·cal. 1.** possessing the qualities or the charm of poetry: *poetic descriptions of nature.* **2.** of or pertaining to a poet or poets. **3.** characteristic of or befitting a poet: *poetic feeling.* **4.** endowed with the faculty or feeling of a poet, as a person. **5.** having or showing the sensibility of a poet. **6.** of or pertaining to poetry: *poetic license.* **7.** of the nature of poetry: *a poetic composition.* **8.** celebrated in poetry, as a place. **9.** affording a subject for poetry. **10.** of or pertaining to literature in verse form. —*n.* **11.** poetics. **12.** versification or the study of prosody. [t. L: s. *poēticus,* t. Gk.: m. *po(i)ētikós*] —**po·et′i·cal·ly,** *adv.*

poetic justice, an ideal distribution of rewards and punishments such as is common in poetry and fiction.

poetic license, license or liberty taken by a poet in deviating from rule, conventional form, logic, or fact, in order to produce a desired effect.

po·et·ics (pō ĕt′ĭks), *n.* **1.** literary criticism treating of the nature and laws of poetry. **2.** a treatise on poetry: the "Poetics" of Aristotle.

po·et·ize (pō′ĭ tīz′), *v.,* **-ized, -izing.** —*v.i.* **1.** to compose poetry. —*v.t.* **2.** to write about in poetry; express in poetic form. **3.** to make poetic: *he poetized his letter to her.*

poet laureate, *pl.* **poets laureate. 1.** (in Great Britain) an officer of the royal household, of whom no special duty is required, but who formerly was expected to write odes, etc., in celebration of court and national events. **2.** (in certain States of the U.S.) a title officially conferred upon some native or resident poet of the State. **3.** (formerly) a title given to any eminent poet.

po·et·ry (pō′ĭt rĭ), *n.* **1.** the art of rhythmical composition, written or spoken, for exciting pleasure by beautiful, imaginative, or elevated thoughts. **2.** literary work in metrical form; verse. **3.** prose with poetic qualities. **4.** poetic qualities however manifested. **5.** poetic spirit of feeling. **6.** something suggestive of or likened to poetry. [ME *poetrie,* t. LL: m. *poētria*] —**Syn. 2.** POETRY, VERSE agree in referring to the work of a poet. The difference between POETRY and VERSE is usually the difference between substance and form. POETRY is lofty thought or impassioned feeling expressed in imaginative words: *Elizabethan poetry.* VERSE is any expression in words which conforms to accepted metrical rules and structure: *the differences between prose and verse.* —**Ant. 2.** prose.

po·go·ni·a (pə gō′nĭ ə, -gōn′yə), *n.* a plant of the genus *Pogonia,* comprising terrestrial orchids of North America. [t. NL, t. Gk.: m. *pōgōnías* bearded (with reference to the frequently fringed lip)]

po·grom (pō′grəm, pō grŏm′), *n.* an organized massacre, esp. of Jews. [t. Russ.: devastation, destruction]

po·gy (pō′gĭ, pŏg′ĭ), *n., pl.* **-gies. 1.** a porgy. **2.** a viviparous perch, *Holiconotus rhodoterus,* caught in the surf of the West Coast of the U.S. **3.** the menhaden.

Po·hai (pō′hī′; *Chin.* bô′-), *n.* a NW arm of the Yellow Sea, forming a gulf on the NE coast of China. Formerly, **Gulf of Chihli.**

poi (poi, pō′ĭ), *n.* a Hawaiian dish made of the root of the taro baked, pounded, moistened, and fermented.

-poietic, a word element meaning "productive," as in *hematopoietic.* [t. Gk.: m.s. *poiētikós* creative, active]

poign·ant (poin′ənt, poin′yənt), *adj.* **1.** keenly distressing to the mental or physical feelings: *poignant regret, poignant suffering.* **2.** keen or strong in mental appeal: *a subject of poignant interest.* **3.** pungent to the taste or smell: *poignant sauces.* [ME *poynaunt,* t. OF: m. *poignant,* ppr. of *poindre,* g. L *pungere* prick, pierce. Cf. PUNGENT] —**poign′an·cy,** *n.* —**poign′ant·ly,** *adv.*

poi·ki·lo·ther·mal (poi′kə lō thûr′məl), *adj. Zool.* having a body temperature that fluctuates with the temperature of the environment. [f. Gk. *poikílo(s)* various + THERMAL]

poi·lu (pwä′lōō; *Fr.* pwà lȳ′), *n.* a French common soldier. [t. F: hairy, der. *poil* hair, g. L. *pilus*]

Poin·ca·ré (pwän kà rĕ′), *n.* **1. Jules Henri** (zhyl än rē′), 1854–1912, French mathematician. **2.** his cousin, **Raymond** (rĕ mōn′), 1860–1934, French statesman; president of France, 1913–20.

poin·ci·a·na (poin′sĭ ā′nə), *n.* **1.** a plant of the caesalpiniaceous genus *Poinciana,* of the warmer parts of the world, comprising trees or shrubs with showy orange or scarlet flowers. **2.** a tree, *Delionix regia* (**royal poinciana**), native in Madagascar but now widely cultivated, remarkable for its showy scarlet flowers. [t. NL, named after M. de *Poinci,* governor of the French West Indies in the 17th century]

poind (poind; *Scot. also* pȳnd), *Scot.* —*v.t.* **1.** to seize and sell property of a debtor under a warrant. **2.** to impound. —*n.* **3.** distraint. [ME (Scot. d.) *pund, poynd,* OE *pyndan* enclose. See POUND[2], n.]

poin·set·ti·a (poin sĕt′ĭ ə), *n.* an euphorbiaceous perennial, *Euphorbia* (*Poinsettia*) *pulcherrima,* native to Mexico and Central America, with variously lobed leaves and brilliant scarlet bracts, associated in the U.S. with Christmas festivities. [t. NL, named after J. R. *Poinsett,* 1779–1851, U.S. minister to Mexico, who discovered the plant there in 1828]

ăct, āble, dâre, ärt; ĕbb, ēqual; ĭf, īce; hŏt, ōver, ôrder, oil, bŏŏk, ōōze, out; ŭp, ūse, ûrge; ə = a in alone; ch, chief; g, give; ng, ring; sh, shoe; th, thin; ŧħ, that; zh, vision. See the full key on inside cover.

point (point), *n.* **1.** a sharp or tapering end, as of a dagger. **2.** a projecting part of anything. **3.** a tapering extremity, as a cape. **4.** something having a sharp or tapering end. **5.** a pointed weapon, as a dagger. **6.** a pointed tool or instrument, as an etching needle. **7.** a mark made as with the sharp end of something; a dot. **8.** a mark of punctuation. **9.** the period. **10.** a decimal point, etc. **11.** *Phonet., etc.* a diacritical mark indicating a vowel or other modification of sound. **12.** one of the embossed dots used in certain systems of writing and printing for the blind. **13.** something that has position but not extension, as the intersection of two lines. **14.** a place of which the position alone is considered; a spot. **15.** any definite position, as in a scale, course, etc.: *the boiling point.* **16. a.** each of the 32 positions indicating direction marked at the circumference of the card of a compass. **b.** the interval of 11° 15′ between any two adjacent positions. **17.** a degree or stage: *frankness to the point of insult.* **18.** a particular instant of time. **19.** the critical position in a course of affairs. **20.** a decisive state of circumstances. **21.** the important or essential thing: *the point of the matter.* **22.** the salient feature of a story, epigram, joke, etc. **23.** a particular aim, end, or purpose: *he carried his point.* **24.** a hint or suggestion: *points on getting a job.* **25.** a single or separate article or item, as in an extended whole; a detail or particular. **26.** an individual part or element of something: *noble points in her character.* **27.** a distinguishing mark or quality, esp. one of an animal, used as a standard in stockbreeding, etc. **28.** (*pl.*) the extremities of a horse, pig, etc. **29.** a single unit, as in counting, measuring rations allowed, etc. **30.** a unit of count in the score of a game. **31.** (in the game craps) the number which must be thrown to win: *your point is 4.* **32.** the position of one of the players in various games, as, **a.** *Lacrosse.* that of the player who stands a short distance in front of the goalkeeper. **b.** *Cricket.* that of the fielder who stands a short distance in front and to the off side of the batsman. **c.** the player himself. **33.** *Boxing.* the edge of the chin. **34.** *Hunting.* the position taken by a pointer or setter when he locates the game. **35.** *Sports.* **a.** a run across country. **b.** a scoring unit used in boxing, wrestling, diving, etc. **36.** one of the narrow tapering spaces marked on a backgammon board. **37.** *Educ.* a single credit, usually corresponding to an hour's class work per week for one semester. **38.** *Elect.* **a.** either of a pair of contacts tipped with tungsten or platinum that make or break current flow in a distributor. **b.** *Brit.* an outlet or socket. **39.** *Com.* a unit of price quotation, as in the U. S., one dollar in stock transactions, one hundredth of a cent in cotton and coffee, or one cent in oil, grain, pork, etc. **40.** *Mil.* **a.** a patrol or reconnaissance unit that goes ahead of the advance party of an advance guard, or follows the rear party of the rear guard. **b.** the stroke in bayonet drill or combat. **41.** *Print.* a unit of measurement being about 1/72 (.0138+) of an inch in the U.S. system. **42.** a vaccine point. **43.** point lace. **44.** *Obs. or Rare.* an end or conclusion. **45.** *Obs.* condition. **46.** any lace made by hand. **47.** *Archaic.* a tagged ribbon or cord, formerly much used in dress, as for tying or fastening parts. **48.** *Railroads.* **a.** the vertex of the angle formed at a frog by two rails, the intersection of gauge lines in a switch or frog. **b.** *Brit.* a tapering moveable rail, as in a railroad switch. **49.** act of pointing.
50. Some special noun phrases are:
at the point, close to.
in point, pertinent: *a case in point.*
in point of, as regards: *in point of fact.*
make a point of, to insist upon.
on the point of, on the verge of: *on the point of leaving England.*
strain, or stretch, a point, **1.** to make a special concession. **2.** to become unreasonable.
to the point, pertinent.
[ME, t. OF (two words): *point* dot, mark, place, moment (g. L *punctum*) and *pointe* sharp end (g. L *puncta*); both L words prop. pp. forms of *pungere* prick, stab]
—*v.t.* **51.** to direct (the finger, a weapon, the attention, etc.) at, to, or upon something. **52.** to indicate the presence or position of, as with the finger (now usually fol. by *out*); direct attention to (fol. by *out*). **53.** to furnish with a point or points; sharpen: *to point a lead pencil.* **54.** to mark with one or more points, dots, or the like. **55.** to punctuate, as writing. **56.** *Phonet., etc.* to mark (letters) with points. **57.** to separate (figures) by dots or points. **58.** to give point or force to (speech, action, etc.). **59.** (of a pointer, setter or some spaniels) to indicate game by standing rigid, with the muzzle usually directed toward it. **60.** to fill the joints of (brickwork, etc.) with mortar or cement, smoothed with the point of the trowel.
—*v.i.* **61.** to indicate position or direction, or direct attention, with or as with the finger. **62.** to direct the mind or thought in some direction: *everything points to his guilt.* **63.** to aim. **64.** to have a tendency, as toward something. **65.** to have a specified direction. **66.** to face in a particular direction, as a building. **67.** (of a pointer or setter) to point game. **68.** *Naut.* to sail close to the wind. **69.** (of an abscess) to come to a head.
[ME, t. OF: m. *pointer,* der. *point(e),* n.]

point-blank (point′blăngk′), *adj.* **1.** aimed or fired straight at the mark; direct. **2.** straightforward, plain, or explicit. **—*adv.*** **3.** with a direct aim; directly; straight. **4.** bluntly. **5.** without deliberation or forethought. [f. POINT, V. + BLANK (def. 15)]

point d'ap·pui (pwăN dȧ pwē′), *French.* **1.** a prop; a stay. **2.** *Mil.* a point of support for a battle line.

point-de·vice (point′dĭ vīs′), *Archaic.* **—*adv.*** **1.** completely; perfectly; exactly. **—*adj.*** **2.** perfect; precise; scrupulously nice or neat. [ME *at poynt devys* (cf. OF or AF *devis* devised, arranged). See POINT, DEVISE]

point duty, *Brit.* traffic control by a policeman at an intersection, etc.

point·ed (poin′tĭd), *adj.* **1.** having a point or points: *a pointed arch.* **2.** sharp or piercing: *pointed wit.* **3.** having point or force: *pointed comment.* **4.** directed; aimed. **5.** directed particularly, as at a person. **6.** marked; emphasized. **—point′ed·ly,** *adv.* **—point′ed·ness,** *n.*

pointed fox, a red fox fur having badger hairs glued to the fur near the skin, in order to simulate silver fox.

point·er (poin′tər), *n.* **1.** one who or that which points (sharpens, points out or indicates, or directs or aims). **2.** a long, tapering stick used by teachers, lecturers, etc. in pointing things out on a map, blackboard, or the like. **3.** the hand on a watch, machine, or instrument. **4.** *Mil.* an individual who aims a piece of artillery. **5.** *Naval.* a member of a gun crew who brings the gun or turret to the correct elevation. **6.** one of a breed of short-haired hunting dogs trained to point game. **7.** *U.S. Colloq.* a hint or suggestion. **8.** (*cap., pl.*) *Astron.* the two outer stars in the bowl of the Big Dipper, the line joining which points toward the pole star.

Pointer
(26 in. more or less at the shoulder)

Point Four, program of U. S. technical aid to underdeveloped areas in the world: proposed by Truman on Jan. 20, 1949; approved by Congress in May, 1950.

poin·til·lism (pwăn′tə lĭz′əm), *n.* a method of painting, an offshoot of French impressionism, in which luminosity is produced by laying on the colors in points or small dots of unmixed color, which are blended by the eye. [t. F: m. *pointillisme,* der. *pointiller* mark with points] **—poin′til·list,** *n.*

point lace, lace made with a needle rather than with bobbins; needle point.

point·less (point′lĭs), *adj.* **1.** without a point. **2.** blunt, as an instrument. **3.** without force, meaning, or relevance, as a remark. **4.** without a point scored, as in a game. **—point′less·ly,** *adv.* **—point′less·ness,** *n.*

point of honor, something that affects one's honor, reputation, etc.

point of order, (in deliberative bodies) a question raised as to whether proceedings are in order, or in conformity with parliamentary law.

point of view, **1.** a point from which things are viewed. **2.** a mental position or viewpoint.

point system, **1.** *Print.* a system for grading the sizes of type bodies, leads, etc., which employs the point as a unit of measurement. See **point** (def. 41). **2.** any of certain systems of writing and printing for the blind which employ embossed symbols for letters, etc. **3.** a system of promoting students by an evaluation of their work on the basis of points representing quality of achievement.

poise (poiz), *n., v.,* **poised, poising.** **—*n.*** **1.** a state of balance or equilibrium, as from equality or equal distribution of weight; equipoise. **2.** composure; self-possession. **3.** steadiness; stability. **4.** suspense or indecision. **5.** the way of being poised, held, or carried. **6.** a state or position of hovering: *the poise of a bird in the air.* **—*v.t.*** **7.** to balance evenly; adjust, hold, or carry in equilibrium. **8.** to hold supported or raised, as in position for casting, using, etc.: *to poise a spear.* **9.** to hold or carry in a particular manner. **10.** *Obs.* to weigh. **—*v.i.*** **11.** to be balanced; rest in equilibrium. **12.** to hang supported or suspended. **13.** to hover, as a bird in the air. [late ME, t. OF: m. *peser* (OF 3d pers. sing. pres. ind. *poise*), g. L *pensāre,* freq. of *pendere* weigh]

poi·son (poi′zən), *n.* **1.** any substance (liquid, solid, or gaseous) which by reason of an inherent deleterious property tends to destroy life or impair health. **2.** anything harmful, fatal, baneful, or highly pernicious, as to character, happiness, or well-being: *the poison of slander.* **—*v.t.*** **3.** to administer poison to (a person or animal). **4.** to kill or injure with poison, or as poison does. **5.** to put poison into or upon; impregnate with poison: *to poison food.* **6.** to ruin, vitiate, or corrupt: *to poison the mind.* **7.** *Phys. Chem.* to destroy or diminish the activity of (a catalyst or enzyme). **—*adj.*** **8.** poisonous; causing poisoning. [ME, t. OF: potion, draft, poison, g. L *pōtio.* See POTION] **—poi′son·er,** *n.*
—Syn. 1. POISON, TOXIN, VENOM, VIRUS are terms for any substance that injures the health or destroys life when absorbed into the system esp. of a higher animal. POISON is the general word: *a poison for insects.* A TOXIN is a poison produced in animal tissues by the action of microörganisms; it is a medical term for the albuminous secretion of microbes, which causes certain diseases: *a toxin produces diphtheria.* VENOM is esp. used of the poisons secreted by certain animals, usually injected by bite or sting: *the venom of a snake.* VIRUS is a medical term for the active organic element or poison which infects with and produces contagious disease: *the virus of scarlet fever.*

poison dogwood, poison sumac. Also, **poison elder.**

b., blend of, blended; c., cognate with; d., dialect, dialectal; der., derived from; f., formed from; g., going back to; m., modification of; r., replacing; s., stem of; t., taken from; ?, perhaps. See the full key on inside cover.

poison gas, any of various deadly gases, esp. those used in warfare, as chlorine, phosgene, etc.

poison hemlock, hemlock.

poison ivy, any of several North American shrubs of the anacardiaceous genus *Rhus,* or *Toxicodendron,* poisonous to the touch, with shiny trifoliate leaves, green flowers, and whitish berries, esp. a climbing species, *R. radicans,* growing on fences, rocks, trees, etc.

Poison ivy

poison oak, 1. any of several shrubs of the genus *Rhus* (or *Toxicodendron*). **2.** poison sumac. **3.** common poison ivy.

poi·son·ous (poi/zən əs), *adj.* **1.** full of or containing poison. **2.** having the properties or effects of a poison. **—poi/son·ous·ly,** *adv.* **—poi/son·ous·ness,** *n.*

poison sumac, a highly poisonous shrub or small tree, *Rhus* (or *Toxicodendron*) *Vernix,* a sumac with pinnate leaves and whitish berries, growing in swamps.

Pois·son distribution (pwä sôn/), *Statistics.* a limiting form of the binomial probability distribution for small values of the probability of success and for large numbers of trials. It is particularly useful in industrial quality-control work and in radiation and bacteriological problems. [named after Siméon Denis *Poisson* (1781–1840), French mathematician]

Poi·tiers (pwä tyē/), *n.* a city in W France: Roman ruins; battles, A.D. 507, A.D. 732, 1356. 52,633 (1954).

Poi·tou (pwä tōō/), *n.* **1.** a former province in W France. *Cap.:* Poitiers. **2.** Gate of, a wide pass near Poitiers.

poke¹ (pōk), *v.,* poked, poking, *n.* —*v.t.* **1.** to thrust against or into (something) with the finger or arm, a stick, etc.: *to poke a person in the ribs.* **2.** to make (a hole, one's way, etc.) by or as by thrusting. **3.** to thrust or push: *poke his stick through the carpet.* **4.** to force or drive (*away, in, out,* etc.) by or as by thrusting or pushing. **5.** to direct (fun), esp. covertly or slyly, at a person or thing. **6.** to thrust obtrusively: *to poke one's nose into everything.* —*v.i.* **7.** to make a thrust or thrusts with the finger, a stick, etc. **8.** to thrust itself or stick (fol. by *out*). **9.** to thrust oneself obtrusively, as into a matter. **10.** to pry; search curiously. **11.** to go or proceed in a slow or aimless way. —*n.* **12.** a thrust or push. **13.** *Colloq.* a slow or dawdling person. [ME *poken,* c. LG and D *poken.* Cf. POACH¹]

poke² (pōk), *n.* **1.** *Now Chiefly Dial.* a bag or sack. **2.** *Archaic.* a pocket. [ME *poke,* c. MD *poke;* akin to OE *pocca, pohha* pocket, bag. Cf. ONF *poke* (t. D) and *pouche* POUCH]

poke³ (pōk), *n.* **1.** a projecting brim at the front of a woman's bonnet or hat. **2.** a bonnet (**poke bonnet**) or hat with such a brim. [appar. special use of POKE¹]

Poke³ (def. 2)

poke⁴ (pōk), *n.* pokeweed. [t. Algonquian (Va.): m. *puccoon* plant used in dyeing]

poke·ber·ry (pōk/běr/ĭ), *n., pl.* -ries. **1.** the berry of the pokeweed. **2.** the plant. [f. POKE⁴ + BERRY]

pok·er¹ (pō/kər), *n.* **1.** one who or that which pokes. **2.** a metal rod for poking or stirring a fire. [f. POKE¹, v. + -ER¹]

pok·er² (pō/kər), *n.* a card game played by two or more persons, in which the players bet on the value of their hands, the winner taking the pool. [orig. uncert. Cf. G *pochspiel,* a similar game, der. *pochen* poke]

poker face, *Colloq.* an expressionless face.

poke·weed (pōk/wēd/), *n.* a tall herb, *Phytolacca americana,* of North America, having juicy purple berries and a purple root used in medicine, and young edible shoots resembling asparagus. Also, **poke·root** (pōk/-rōōt/,-rŏŏt/). [f. POKE⁴ + WEED]

pok·e·y (pō/kĭ), *adj.* **pokier, pokiest.** *Colloq.* poky.

pok·y (pō/kĭ), *adj.,* **pokier, pokiest.** *Colloq.* **1.** puttering; slow; dull. **2.** (of a place) small and cramped. **3.** (of dress, etc.) dowdy. [f. POKE¹ + -Y¹]

Pol., 1. Poland. **2.** Polish.

pol., 1. political. **2.** politics.

Po·la (pō/lä), *n.* a seaport in NW Yugoslavia, on the Istrian peninsula. 28,089 (1953). Yugoslavian, **Pula.**

Po·lack (pō/lăk, -läk), *n.* **1.** (in contemptuous use) a person of Polish descent. **2.** *Archaic.* a Pole.

Po·land (pō/lənd), *n.* a republic in C Europe. 27,680,000 est. (1956); ab. 121,000 sq. mi. (1946). *Cap.:* Warsaw.

Poland China, one of an American breed of black swine with white markings.

po·lar (pō/lər), *adj.* **1.** of or pertaining to a pole, as of the earth, a magnet, an electric cell, etc. **2.** opposite in character or action. **3.** existing as ions; ionized. **4.** central. **5.** analogous to the polestar as a guide; guiding. [t. ML: s. *polāris,* der. L *polus* POLE²]

polar bear, a large white bear, *Thalarctos maritimus,* of the arctic regions.

polar body, *Biol.* one of the minute cells arising by the very unequal meiotic divisions of the ovum at or near the time of fertilization.

Polar bear, *Thalarctos maritimus* (7 to 8 ft. long)

polar circles, the Arctic and Antarctic circles.

polar coördinates, *Math.* a system of plane coördinates in which the position of a point is determined by the length of its radius vector from a fixed origin and the angle this vector makes with a fixed line.

polar distance, *Astron.* codeclination.

polar front, the transition region, or belt, between the cold polar easterly winds and the relatively warm southwesterly winds of the middle latitudes.

po·lar·im·e·ter (pō/lə rĭm/ə tər), *n.* **1.** an instrument for measuring the amount of polarized light, or the extent of polarization, in the light received from a given source. **2.** a form of polariscope for measuring the angular rotation of the plane of polarization. [f. ML *polāri(s)* polar + -METER]

Po·lar·is (pō lâr/ĭs), *n. Astron.* the polestar or North Star, a star of the second magnitude situated close to the north pole of the heavens, in the constellation Ursa Minor: the outermost star in the handle of the Little Dipper. [short for ML *stella polāris* Polar star]

po·lar·i·scope (pō lâr/ə skōp/), *n.* an instrument for exhibiting or measuring the polarization of light, or for examining substances in polarized light.

po·lar·i·ty (pō lăr/ə tĭ), *n.* **1.** *Physics.* **a.** the possession of an axis with reference to which certain physical properties are determined; the possession of two poles. **b.** the power or tendency of a magnetized bar, etc., to orient itself along the lines of force. **c.** positive or negative polar condition. **2.** the possession or exhibition of two opposite or contrasted principles or tendencies.

po·lar·i·za·tion (pō/lər ə zā/shən), *n.* **1.** *Optics.* **a.** state, or the production of a state, in which rays of light, or similar radiation, exhibit different properties in different directions, e.g. when they are passed through a crystal of tourmaline, which transmits rays in which the vibrations are confined to a single plane. **2.** *Elect.* the process by which gases produced during electrolysis are deposited on the electrodes of a cell. **3.** the production or acquisition of polarity.

po·lar·ize (pō/lə rīz/), *v.t.,* -ized, -izing. to cause polarization in. Also, *esp. Brit.,* **po/lar·ise/.** [t. F: m.s. *polariser*] **—po/lar·iz/a·ble,** *adj.* **—po/lar·iz/er,** *n.*

po·lar·ize (pō/lə rīz/), *v.t.,* -ized, -izing. to give polarity to. Also, *esp. Brit.,* **po/lar·ise/.** [f. POLAR + -IZE] **—po/lar·iz/a·ble,** *adj.* **—po/lar·iz/er,** *n.*

polar lights, the aurora borealis or the aurora australis.

po·lar·o·graph (pō lăr/ə grăf/, -gräf/), *n.* an instrument that automatically measures and records the concentration, solubility, constituents, equilibrium, etc., of an electrolytic solution.

Po·lar·oid (pō/lə roid/), *n. Trademark.* a material which polarizes light, consisting of a pane compounded of a sheet of plastic holding oriented iodo-quinine crystals between two panes of protecting glass.

Polar Regions, the regions within the Arctic and Antarctic circles.

pol·der (pōl/dər), *n.* a tract of low land, esp. in the Netherlands, reclaimed from the sea or other body of water and protected by dikes. [t. D]

pole¹ (pōl), *n., v.,* **poled, poling.** —*n.* **1.** a long, slender piece of wood or other material. **2.** the long tapering piece of wood extending from the front axle of a vehicle, between the animals drawing it. **3.** *Naut.* a light spar. **4.** a unit of length equal to 16½ ft.; a rod. **5.** a square rod, 30¼ sq. yards. —*v.t.* **6.** to furnish with poles. **7.** to push, strike, propel, etc., with a pole. **8.** *Metall.* to stir (a molten bath or copper) with green wood poles, thus introducing carbon which reacts with the oxygen present to effect deoxidation. —*v.i.* **9.** to propel a boat, etc., with a pole. [ME; OE *pāl,* t. L: s. *pālus* stake. Cf. PALE²]

pole² (pōl), *n.* **1.** each of the extremities of the axis of the earth or of any more or less spherical body. **2.** each of the two points in which the axis of the earth produced cuts the celestial sphere, about which the stars seem to revolve (**celestial pole**). **3.** *Physics.* each of the two regions or parts of a magnet, electric battery, etc., at which certain opposite forces are manifested or appear to be concentrated. **4.** *Biol.* **a.** either end of an ideal axis in a nucleus, cell, or ovum, about which parts are more or less symmetrically arranged. **b.** either end of a spindle-shaped figure formed in a cell during mitosis. **5.** *Anat.* the point in a nerve cell where a process forming an axis cylinder begins. [ME *pol,* t. L: s. *polus,* t. Gk.: m. *pólos* pivot, axis, pole]

Pole (pōl), *n.* a native or inhabitant of Poland. [t. G. sing. of *Polen,* t. Pol.: m. *Poljane* Poles, lit., field-dwellers, der. *pole* field]

Pole (pōl), *n.* Reginald, 1500–58, English cardinal and last Roman Catholic archbishop of Canterbury.

pole·ax (pōl/ăks/), *n.* **1.** a medieval shafted weapon with blade combining ax, hammer, and apical spike, used for fighting on foot. **2.** an ax used in felling or stunning animals. —*v.t.* **3.** to fell with a poleax. [ME *pollax,* lit., head-ax. Cf. MLG *poleze* and see POLL¹ (def. 10)]

pole·axe (pōl/ăks/), *n., v.,* -axed, -axing. poleax.

pole·cat (pōl/kăt/), *n.* **1.** an ill-smelling, long-haired member of the weasel family, *Putorius putorius,* resembling a marten. The domestic ferret is believed to be derived from it. **2.** any of various North American skunks. [ME *polcat; pol-* of uncert. orig.]

Pol. Econ., political economy. Also, **pol. econ.**

pole horse, a horse harnessed to the tongue of a vehicle; a poler; wheeler.

pole jump, pole vault.

pole-jump (pōl′jŭmp′), v.i. pole-vault. —**pole′-jump′er**, n.

po·lem·ic (pō lĕm′ĭk), n. 1. a controversial argument; argumentation against some opinion, doctrine, etc. 2. one who argues in opposition to another; a controversialist, esp. in theology. —adj. 3. Also, **po·lem′i·cal**. of or pertaining to disputation or controversy; controversial. [t. Gk.: m.s. *polemikós* of or for war] —**po·lem′i·cal·ly**, adv.

po·lem·ics (pō lĕm′ĭks), n. the art or practice of disputation or controversy, esp. in theology.

pol·e·mist (pŏl′ə mĭst), n. one engaged or versed in polemics. Also, **po·lem·i·cist** (pō lĕm′ə sĭst).

pol·e·mo·ni·a·ceous (pŏl′ə mō′nĭ ā′shəs), adj. belonging to the *Polemoniaceae*, a family of plants including the Jacob's-ladder, phlox, etc. [f. s. NL *Polemōnium*, the typical genus (t. Gk.: m. *polemōnion* kind of plant) + -ACEOUS]

po·len·ta (pō lĕn′tə), n. a thick mush of corn meal, much used in Italy. [t. It., g. L: peeled or pearl barley]

pol·er (pō′lər), n. 1. one who or that which poles. 2. a pole horse.

pole·star (pōl′stär′), n. 1. Polaris. 2. that which serves as a guide; a lodestar. 3. a guiding principle.

pole vault, Sports. a leap over a horizontal bar with the help of a long pole.

pole-vault (pōl′vôlt′), v.i. to execute a pole vault. —**pole′-vault′er**, n.

po·lice (pə lēs′), n., v., -liced, -licing. —n. 1. an organized civil force for maintaining order, preventing and detecting crime, and enforcing the laws. 2. (construed as pl.) the members of such a force. 3. the regulation and control of a community, esp. with reference to the maintenance of public order, safety, health, morals, etc. 4. the department of the government concerned with this, esp. with the maintenance of order. 5. any body of men officially maintained or employed to keep order, enforce regulations, etc. 6. Mil. (in the U.S. Army) a. the cleaning and keeping clean of a camp, post, station, etc. b. the condition of a camp, post, station, etc., with reference to cleanliness. —v.t. 7. to regulate, control, or keep in order by or as by police, or as police do. 8. Mil. to clean and keep clean (a camp, etc.). [t. F: government, civil administration, police, t. ML: m. *politia*, var. of L *polītīa* POLITY. Cf. POLICY[1]]

police court, an inferior court with summary jurisdiction for the trial of persons accused of any certain minor offenses, and with power to examine those charged with more serious offenses and hold them for trial in a superior court or for a grand jury.

police dog, 1. a sheep dog of wolflike appearance, used in police work, as guide for the blind, etc. 2. a dog of any of various kinds used or trained to assist the police.

Police dog. German shepherd (Ab. 2 ft. high at the shoulder)

po·lice·man (pə lēs′mən), n., pl. -men. a member of a body or force of police. —**po·lice′wom′an**, n. fem.

pol·i·clin·ic (pŏl′ĭ klĭn′ĭk), n. a department of a hospital at which outpatients are treated. Cf. **polyclinic**. [t. G: m. *poliklinik*, f. Gk.: *pŏli*(s) city + s. *klīnikē* clinic art]

pol·i·cy[1] (pŏl′ə sĭ), n., pl. -cies. 1. a definite course of action adopted as expedient or from other considerations: *a business policy.* 2. a course or line of action adopted and pursued by a government, ruler, political party, or the like: *the foreign policy of a country.* 3. action or procedure conforming to, or considered with reference to, prudence or expediency: *it was good policy to consent.* 4. prudence, practical wisdom, or expediency. 5. sagacity; shrewdness. 6. Rare. government; polity. [ME *policie*, t. OF: government, civil administration, t. L: m. *polītīa* POLITY. Cf. POLICE]

pol·i·cy[2] (pŏl′ə sĭ), n., pl. -cies. 1. a document embodying a contract of insurance. 2. U.S. a method of gambling in which bets are made on numbers to be drawn by lottery. [t. F: m. *police*, t. It.: m. *polizza*, g. ML *apodixa*, ult. t. Gk.: m. *apódeixis* a showing or setting forth]

pol·i·cy·hold·er (pŏl′ə sĭ hōl′dər), n. one who has an insurance policy in his possession or under his control.

policy racket. See **policy[2]** (def. 2).

pol·i·o·my·e·li·tis (pŏl′ĭ ō mī′ə lī′tĭs), n. Pathol. infantile spinal paralysis. Also, Colloq., **po·li·o** (pō′lĭ ō′). [t. NL, f. Gk.: *polio*(s) gray + s. *myelos* marrow + -itis -ITIS]

-polis, a word element meaning "city," as in *metropolis* (lit., "the mother city"). [t. Gk., comb. form of *pólis*]

pol·ish (pŏl′ĭsh), v.t. 1. to make smooth and glossy, esp. by friction: *to polish metal.* 2. to render finished, refined or elegant: *his speech needs polishing.* 3. to take or bring by smoothing or refining (fol. by *away, off, out*, etc.). 4. Slang. to finish, or dispose of, quickly (fol. by *off*): *to polish off an opponent.* 5. Slang. to improve (fol. by *up*). —v.i. 6. to become smooth and glossy; take on

a polish. 7. to become refined or elegant. —n. 8. a substance used to give smoothness or gloss: *shoe polish.* 9. act of polishing. 10. state of being polished. 11. smoothness and gloss of surface. 12. superior or elegant finish imparted; refinement; elegance: *the polish of literary style.* [ME *polische*(n), t. F: m. *poliss-*, s. *polir*, g. L *polīre*] —**pol′ish·er**, n.

—Syn. 11. POLISH, GLOSS, LUSTER, SHEEN refer to a smooth, shining or bright surface from which light is reflected. POLISH suggests the smooth and shining quality given to a surface by friction: *a high polish on a varnished surface.* GLOSS suggests a superficial, hard smoothness such as characterizes a lacquered surface: *a gloss on oilcloth.* LUSTER denotes the characteristic quality of the light reflected from the surfaces of certain materials (pearls, silk, wax, freshly cut metals, etc.): *an opaline luster.* SHEEN, sometimes poetical, is a glistening brightness such as that reflected from the surface of silk or velvet, or from furniture oiled and hand polished: *a rich velvety sheen.*

Pol·ish (pō′lĭsh), adj. 1. of or pertaining to the Poles or Poland. —n. 2. a Slavic language, the principal language of Poland.

Polish Corridor, the strip of land near the mouth of the Vistula river, formerly separating Germany from East Prussia, given Poland in the Treaty of Versailles to provide her with access to the Baltic.

Polish Corridor, 1938

pol·ished (pŏl′ĭsht), adj. 1. made smooth and glossy. 2. naturally smooth and glossy. 3. refined, cultured, or elegant. 4. flawless or excellent.

polit., 1. political. 2. politics.

Po·lit·bu·ro (pō lĭt′byoor′ō), n. a committee in the Communist Party of the Soviet Union, which examines every question before it is referred to the government, and sometimes issues orders independently.

po·lite (pə līt′), adj. 1. showing good manners toward others, as in behavior, speech, etc.; courteous; civil: *a polite reply.* 2. refined or cultured: *polite society.* 3. of a refined or elegant kind: *polite learning.* [late ME, t. L: m.s. *polītus*, pp., polished] —**po·lite′ly**, adv. —**po·lite′ness**, n. —Syn. 1. well-bred, gracious. See civil.

pol·i·tesse (pŏl′ĭ tĕs′; Fr. pô lē tĕs′) n. Now chiefly as French, politeness. [F, t. It.: m. *pulitezza*, der. *pulito* polished, pp. of *pulire*, g. L *polīre*]

Po·li·tian (pō lĭsh′ən), n. (Angelo Poliziano) 1454–94, Italian classical scholar, teacher, and poet.

pol·i·tic (pŏl′ə tĭk), adj. 1. characterized by policy; sagacious or prudent. 2. shrewd; artful. 3. in keeping with policy; expedient, or judicious. 4. political (now chiefly in *body politic*, which see). [ME, t. L: s. *polīticus*, t. Gk.: m. *polītikós* pertaining to citizens or to the state] —**pol′i·tic·ly**, adv. —Syn. 1. See diplomatic.

po·lit·i·cal (pə lĭt′ə kəl), adj. 1. pertaining to or dealing with the science or art of politics: *political writers.* 2. pertaining to or connected with a political party, or its principles, aims, activities, etc.: *a political campaign.* 3. exercising or seeking power in the governmental or public affairs of a state, municipality, or the like: *a political party.* 4. of or pertaining to the state or its government: *political measures.* 5. affecting or involving the state or government: *a political offense.* 6. engaged in or connected with civil administration: *political office.* 7. having a definite policy or system of government: *a political community.* 8. of or pertaining to citizens: *political rights.* —**po·lit′i·cal·ly**, adv.

political economy, economics. —**political economist.**

political science, the science of politics, or of the principles and conduct of government.

pol·i·ti·cian (pŏl′ə tĭsh′ən), n. 1. one who is active in party politics. 2. one who, in seeking or conducting public office, is more concerned to win favor or to retain power than to maintain principles. 3. one who holds a political office. 4. one skilled in political government or administration; a statesman. 5. Now Rare. an expert in politics or political government. [f. POLITIC + -IAN]

—Syn. 4. POLITICIAN, STATESMAN refer to one skilled in politics. These terms differ particularly in their connotations; POLITICIAN is more often derogatory, and STATESMAN laudatory. POLITICIAN suggests the schemes and devices of one who engages in (esp. small) politics for party ends or his own advantage: *a dishonest politician.* STATESMAN suggests the eminent ability, foresight, and unselfish devotion to the interests of his country of one dealing with (esp. important or great) affairs of state: *a distinguished statesman.*

po·lit·i·cize (pə lĭt′ə sīz′), v., -cized, -cizing. —v.t. 1. to make political. —v.i. 2. to engage in, or talk about, politics.

po·lit·i·co (pə lĭt′ə kō′), n., pl. -cos. a politician. [t. It. or Sp.]

politico-, a word element meaning "political," used in combination, as in *politico-military* (political and military), *politico-religious*, *politico-social*. [comb. form repr. Gk. *politikós*]

pol·i·tics (pŏl′ə tĭks), n. 1. the science or art of political government. 2. the practice or profession of conducting political affairs. 3. political affairs. 4. political methods or maneuvers. 5. (construed as pl.) political principles or opinions.

pol·i·ty (pŏl′ətĭ), *n.*, *pl.* **-ties.** **1.** a particular form or system of government (civil, ecclesiastical, or other). **2.** the condition of being constituted as a state or other organized community or body. **3.** government or administrative regulation. **4.** a state or other organized community or body. [t. F (obs.): m. *politie*, t. L: m. *politia*, t. Gk.: m. *polīteía* citizenship, government, form of government, commonwealth]

Polk (pōk), *n.* **James Knox,** 1795–1849, the 11th president of the United States, 1845–49.

pol·ka (pōl′kə, pō′kə), *n.*, *v.* **-kaed, -kaing.** —*n.* **1.** a lively round dance of Bohemian origin, with music in duple time. **2.** a piece of music for such a dance or in its rhythm. —*v.i.* **3.** to dance the polka. [t. F and G, t. Czech: m. *pulka* half step]

polka dot, 1. a dot or round spot (printed, woven, or embroidered) repeated to form a pattern on a textile fabric. **2.** a pattern of, or a fabric with such dots.

poll[1] (pōl), *n.* **1.** the registering of votes, as at an election. **2.** the voting at an election. **3.** the number of votes cast. **4.** the numerical result of the voting. **5.** an enumeration or a list of individuals, as for purposes of taxing or voting. **6.** (*usually pl.*) the place where votes are taken. **7.** a poll tax. **8.** a person or individual in a number or list. **9.** an analysis of public opinion on a subject, usually by selective sampling. **10.** the head, esp. the part of it on which the hair grows. **11.** the back of the head. **12.** the broad end or face of a hammer. —*v.t.* **13.** to receive at the polls, as votes. **14.** to enroll in a list or register, as for purposes of taxing or voting. **15.** to take or register the votes of, as persons. **16.** to deposit or cast at the polls, as a vote. **17.** to bring to the polls, as voters. **18.** to cut off or cut short the hair, etc., of (a person, etc.); crop; clip; shear. **19.** to cut off or cut short (hair, etc.). **20.** to cut off the top of (a tree, etc.); pollard. **21.** to cut off or cut short the horns of (cattle). —*v.i.* **22.** to vote at the polls; give one's vote. [ME *pol(le)*, c. MD and LG *polle*. Cf. d. Sw. *pull* crown of the head, Dan. *pul*]

poll[2] (pōl), *n.* (at Cambridge University, England) those students who read for or obtain a "pass" degree, as distinguished from an "honours" degree. [appar. t. Gk.: s. *pollo*í, in *hoi pollo*í the many]

pol·lack (pōl′ək), *n.*, *pl.* **-lacks,** (*esp. collectively*) **-lack. 1.** a darkly colored North Atlantic food fish, *Pollachius virens*, of the cod family. **2.** a similar North Pacific cod, *Theragra chalcograma*. Also, *esp. Brit.* **pollock.**

pol·lard (pōl′ərd), *n.* **1.** a tree cut back nearly to the trunk, so as to produce a dense mass of branches. **2.** an animal, as a stag, ox, or sheep, without horns. —*v.t.* **3.** to convert into a pollard. [appar. f. POLL[1], v. + -ARD]

polled (pōld), *adj.* hornless, as the Aberdeen Angus.

pol·len (pōl′ən), *n.* the fertilizing element of flowering plants, consisting of fine, powdery, yellowish grains or spores, sometimes in masses. [t. L: fine flour, dust]

pol·len·o·sis (pŏl′ə nō′sĭs), *n. Pathol.* pollinosis.

Grains of Pollen

A. Evening primrose, *Oenothera biennis*; B. Scotch pine, *Pinus sylvestris*; C. Chicory, *Chicorium intybus*; D. Hibiscus, *Hibiscus moscheutos*; E. Passionflower, *Passiflora caerulea*

poll evil (pōl), an acute swelling on the top of the head of a horse originating in an inflamed bursa which underlies the great neck ligament there.

pol·lex (pŏl′ĕks), *n.*, *pl.* **-lices** (-ə sēz′). the innermost digit of the forelimb; the thumb. [t. L: thumb]

pol·li·nate (pŏl′ə nāt′), *v.t.*, **-nated, -nating.** *Bot.* to convey pollen for fertilization to; shed pollen on.

pol·li·na·tion (pŏl′ə nā′shən), *n. Bot.* the transfer of pollen from the anther to the stigma.

polling booth (pō′lĭng), a booth used in voting.

polling place, a place of voting.

pol·li·nif·er·ous (pŏl′ə nĭf′ər əs), *adj.* **1.** *Bot.* producing or bearing pollen. **2.** *Zool.* fitted for carrying pollen. [f. s. L *pollen* dust + -IFEROUS]

pol·lin·i·um (pə lĭn′ĭ əm), *n.*, *pl.* **-linia** (-lĭn′ĭ ə). *Bot.* an agglutinated mass or body of pollen grains, characteristic of orchidaceous and asclepiadaceous plants. [t. NL: f. s. L *pollen* dust + -IUM]

pol·li·no·sis (pŏl′ə nō′sĭs), *n. Pathol.* hay fever. Also, **pollenosis.** [t. NL: f. s. L *pollen* dust + -ōsis -OSIS]

pol·li·wog (pŏl′ĭ wŏg′), *n.* a tadpole. Also, **pollywog.** [cf. ME *polwygle*, f. POLL[1] (def. 10) + WIGGLE]

pol·lock (pŏl′ək), *n. Chiefly Brit.* pollack.

Pol·lock (pŏl′ək), *n.* **Sir Frederick,** 1845–1937, British legal scholar and author.

poll·ster (pōl′stər), *n.* *Often derogatory.* one whose occupation is the taking of public opinion polls.

poll tax, a capitation tax, the payment of which is a prerequisite to exercise of the right of suffrage.

poll-tax·er (pōl′tăk′sər), *n. U.S. Slang.* **1.** an advocate of the poll tax. **2.** a Congressman from a State having a poll tax.

pol·lute (pə lōōt′), *v.t.*, **-luted, -luting. 1.** to make foul or unclean; dirty. **2.** to make morally unclean; defile. **3.** to render ceremonially impure; desecrate. [t. L: m.s. *pollūtus*, pp.] —**pol·lut′er,** *n.* —**pol·lu′tion** (pə lōō′shən), *n.*

Pol·lux (pŏl′əks), *n.* **1.** *Gk. Myth.* See **Castor and Pollux. 2.** *Astron.* the brightest star in the constellation Gemini. [t. L, t. Gk.: m. *Polydeúkēs*]

Pol·ly·an·na (pŏl′ĭ ăn′ə), *n.* a blindly optimistic person. [from the name of the heroine in a novel by Eleanor Porter, 1868–1920, U.S. writer]

pol·ly·wog (pŏl′ĭ wŏg′), *n.* polliwog.

po·lo (pō′lō), *n.* **1.** a game resembling hockey, played on horseback with long-handled mallets and a wooden ball. **2.** some game more or less resembling this, as water polo. [t. Balti, c. Tibetan *pulu*] —**po′lo·ist,** *n.*

Po·lo (pō′lō), *n.* **Marco** (mär′kō), c1254–c1324. Venetian traveler in Asia, esp. at the court of Kublai Khan.

po·lo·naise (pŏl′ə nāz′, pō′lə-), *n.* **1.** a slow dance of Polish origin, in triple rhythm, consisting chiefly of a march or promenade in couples. **2.** a piece of music for, or in the rhythm of, such a dance. **3.** a woman's overdress combining a bodice and a cutaway overskirt. [t. F: (fem.) Polish]

po·lo·ni·um (pə lō′nĭ əm), *n. Chem.* a radioactive element discovered by M. and Mme. Curie in 1898; radium F. *Symbol:* Po; *at. no.:* 84. *at. wt.:* about 210. [f. ML *Polon*(*ia*) Poland + -ium -IUM]

Po·lo·ni·us (pə lō′nĭ əs), *n.* the sententious father of Ophelia in Shakespeare's *Hamlet*.

Pol·ta·va (pŏl tä′vä), *n.* a city in the SW Soviet Union: Russian defeat of Swedes, 1709. 129,000 (est. 1956).

pol·ter·geist (pōl′tər gīst′), *n.* a ghost or spirit which manifests its presence by noises, knockings, etc. [t. G: lit., noise-ghost]

Pol·to·ratsk (pŏl tŏ rätsk′), *n.* former name of **Ashkhabad.**

pol·troon (pŏl trōōn′), *n.* a wretched coward; a craven. [t. F: m. *poltron*, t. It.: m. *poltrone*, der. *poltro* lazy (as n., bed; cf. *poltrire* lie lazily in bed), t. Gmc.; cf. OHG *polstar* BOLSTER]

pol·troon·er·y (pŏl trōō′nə rĭ), *n.* cowardice.

pol·y-, a word element or prefix, meaning "much," "many," first occurring in words from the Greek (as *polyandrous*), but now used freely as a general formative, esp. in scientific or technical words. Cf. **mono-.** [t. Gk., comb. form of *polýs* much, many; akin to L *plēnum* full, and to FULL[1]]

poly., polytechnic.

pol·y·an·drous (pŏl′ĭ ăn′drəs), *adj.* **1.** having more than one husband at one time. **2.** characterized by plurality of husbands for one wife. **3.** *Bot.* **a.** having the stamens indefinitely numerous. **b.** having twenty or more free stamens.

pol·y·an·dry (pŏl′ĭ ăn′drĭ, pŏl′ĭ ăn′-), *n.* **1.** the practice or condition of having more than one husband at one time; marriage with several husbands. **2.** *Bot.* the fact of being polyandrous. [t. Gk.: m.s. *polyandría*]

pol·y·an·thus (pŏl′ĭ ăn′thəs), *n.* **1.** a hybrid primrose, *Primula polyantha*. **2.** a narcissus, *Narcissus Tazetta*, in many varieties, bearing small white or yellow flowers. [t. NL, t. Gk.: m. *polýanthos* having many flowers]

pol·y·ba·sic (pŏl′ĭ bā′sĭk), *adj. Chem.* (of an acid) having two or more atoms of replaceable hydrogen.

pol·y·ba·site (pŏl′ĭ bā′sīt, pə lĭb′ə sīt′), *n.* a blackish mineral, Ag₉SbS₆: a minor ore of silver. [t. G: m. *polybasit*. See POLY-, BASIS, -ITE[1]]

Po·lyb·i·us (pə lĭb′ĭ əs), *n.* c205–c123 B.C., Greek historian who wrote a history of Rome.

Pol·y·carp (pŏl′ĭ kärp′), *n.* **Saint,** A.D. 69?–155, bishop of Smyrna and Christian martyr.

pol·y·chaete (pŏl′ĭ kēt′), *Zool.* —*n.* **1.** any of the *Polychaeta*, a group or division of annelids having unsegmented swimming appendages with many chaetae or bristles, and including most of the common marine worms. —*adj.* **2.** pertaining to the polychaetes. [t. NL: m.s. *Polychaeta*, t. Gk.: m. *polychaítēs* having much hair] —**pol·y·chae′tous,** *adj.*

pol·y·cha·si·um (pŏl′ĭ kā′zhĭ əm, -zĭ əm), *n.*, *pl.* **-sia** (-zhĭ ə, -zĭ ə). *Bot.* a form of cymose inflorescence in which each axis produces more than two lateral axes. [t. NL, f. *poly-* POLY- + s. Gk. *chásis* separation + -*ium* -IUM]

pol·y·chro·mat·ic (pŏl′ĭ krō măt′ĭk), *adj.* having many colors; exhibiting a variety of colors. Also, **pol·y·chro·mic** (pŏl′ĭ krō′mĭk).

pol·y·chrome (pŏl′ĭ krōm′), *adj.* **1.** being of many or various colors. **2.** decorated or executed in many colors, as a statue, a vase, a mural painting, a printed work, etc. [t. F, t. Gk.: m. *polýchrōmos* many-colored]

pol·y·chro·my (pŏl′ĭ krō′mĭ), *n.* polychrome coloring; decoration or execution in many colors.

pol·y·clin·ic (pŏl′ĭ klĭn′ĭk), *n.* a clinic or hospital dealing with various diseases. Cf. **policlinic.**

Pol·y·cli·tus (pŏl′ĭ klī′təs), *n.* fl. c450–c420 B.C., Greek sculptor. Also, **Pol·y·clei′tus, Pol·y·cle·tus** (pŏl′ĭ klē′təs).

pol·y·con·ic projection (pŏl′ĭ kŏn′ĭk), *Cartography.* a conic projection in which the parallels are arcs of circles that are not concentric but are equally spaced along the central straight meridian, all other meridians being curves equally spaced along the parallels.

Po·lyc·ra·tes (pə lĭk′rə tēz′), *n.* died 522? B.C., Greek tyrant of Samos.

pol·y·dac·tyl (pŏl′ĭ dăk′tĭl), *adj.* **1.** having many or several digits. **2.** having more than the normal number of fingers or toes. —*n.* **3.** a polydactyl animal. —**pol′y·dac′tyl·ism,** *n.*

ăct, āble, dâre, ärt; ĕbb, ēqual; ĭf, īce; hŏt, ōver, ôrder, oil, bŏŏk, ōōze, out; ŭp, ūse, ûrge; ə = a in alone; ch, chief; g, give; ng, ring; sh, shoe; th, thin; ŧħ, that; zh, vision. See the full key on inside cover.

Pol·y·do·rus (pŏl'ĭ dōr'əs), *n.* fl. 1st cent. B.C., Greek sculptor.

pol·y·em·bry·o·ny (pŏl'ĭ ĕm'brĭ ō' nĭ, -brĭ ə nĭ), *n. Embryol.* the production of more than one embryo from one egg.

pol·y·eth·yl·ene (pŏl'ĭ ĕth'ə lēn), *n. Chem.* a plastic polymer of ethylene used for containers, electrical insulation, packaging, etc. Also, *Brit.*, **polythene.**

pol·y·foil (pŏl'ĭ foil'), *Archit.* —*adj.* 1. having many, esp. more than five, foils: *a polyfoil window.* —*n.* 2. a polyfoil ornament or decorative feature.

po·lyg·a·la (pə lĭg'ə lə), *n.* any of the herbs and shrubs, commonly known as milkworts, which constitute the genus *Polygala,* as *P. paucifolia* (**fringed polygala**), of North America. [t. Gk., pl. of *polýgalon* milkwort]

po·lyg·a·mist (pə lĭg'ə mĭst), *n.* one who practices or favors polygamy.

po·lyg·a·mous (pə lĭg'ə məs), *adj.* 1. of, pertaining to, characterized by, or practicing polygamy. 2. *Bot.* bearing both unisexual and hermaphrodite flowers on the same or on different plants. [t. Gk.: m. *polýgamos*] —**po·lyg'a·mous·ly,** *adv.*

po·lyg·a·my (pə lĭg'ə mĭ), *n.* 1. the practice or condition of having many or several spouses, esp. wives, at one time. 2. *Zool.* the habit of mating with more than one of the opposite sex.

pol·y·gen·e·sis (pŏl'ĭ jĕn'ə sĭs), *n. Biol.* the descent of a species or race from more than one ancestral species.

pol·y·ge·net·ic (pŏl'ĭ jə nĕt'ĭk), *adj.* 1. *Biol.* relating to or exhibiting polygenesis. 2. formed by several different causes, in several different ways, or of several different parts.

pol·y·gen·ic inheritance (pŏl'ĭ jĕn'ĭk), *Genetics.* the heredity of complex characters based on their development from a large number of genes, each one ordinarily with a relatively small effect.

pol·y·glot (pŏl'ĭ glŏt'), *adj.* 1. knowing many or several languages, as a person. 2. containing, made up of, or in several languages: *a polyglot Bible.* —*n.* 3. a mixture or confusion of languages. 4. a person with a command of a number of languages, whether as to reading or speaking, or both. 5. a book or writing, esp. a Bible, containing the same text in several languages. [t. ML: m.s. *polyglōttus,* t. Gk.: m. *polýglōttos* many-tongued]

Pol·yg·no·tus (pŏl'ĭg nō'təs), *n.* fl. c450 B.C., Greek painter.

pol·y·gon (pŏl'ĭ gŏn'), *n.* a figure, esp. a closed plane figure, having many (more than four) angles and sides. [t. L: s. *polygōnum,* t. Gk.: m. *polýgōnon* (neut.) many-angled] —**po·lyg·o·nal** (pəlĭg'ənəl), *adj.* —**po·lyg'o·nal·ly,** *adv.*

pol·y·go·na·ceous (pŏl'ĭ gə nā'shəs), *adj.* belonging to the *Polygonaceae,* or buckwheat family of plants, including the knotgrass, jointweed, dock, etc.

pol·yg·o·num (pə lĭg'ə nəm), *n.* a plant of the genus *Polygonum,* which consists chiefly of herbs, often with knotty, jointed stems, and which includes the knotgrass, bistort, smartweed, etc. [t. NL, t. Gk.: m. *polýgonon* knot grass]

pol·y·graph (pŏl'ĭ grăf', -gräf'), *n.* 1. an apparatus for multiplying copies of a drawing or writing. 2. a prolific or versatile author. [t. Gk.: s. *polygráphos* writing much] —**pol·y·graph'ic,** *adj.*

pol·yg·y·nous (pə lĭj'ə nəs), *adj.* 1. having more than one wife at a time. 2. characterized by plurality of wives for one husband. 3. *Bot.* having many pistils or styles.

po·lyg·y·ny (pə lĭj'ə nĭ), *n.* 1. the practice or the condition of having more than one wife at one time. 2. marriage of one man to several women. 3. *Bot.* the fact of having many pistils or styles. [f. Gk. *polygýn(aios)* having many wives + -Y³]

pol·y·he·dral (pŏl'ĭ hē'drəl), *adj.* many-faced.

pol·y·he·dron (pŏl'ĭ hē'drən), *n., pl.* -**drons, -dra** (-drə), a solid figure having many faces. [t. Gk.: m. *polýedron* (neut.) having many bases. See HEDRON]

pol·y·his·tor (pŏl'ĭ hĭs'tər), *n.* a person of great and varied learning. —**pol·y·his·tor'ic,** *adj.*

pol·y·hy·drox·y (pŏl'ĭ hī drŏk'sĭ), *adj. Chem.* containing a number of hydroxyl groups.

Pol·y·hym·ni·a (pŏl'ĭ hĭm'nĭ ə), *n.* the Muse of sublime hymns or serious sacred songs. [t. L, t. Gk.: m. *Polýmnia* to agree with L *hymnus* HYMN]

pol·y·mer (pŏl'ĭ mər), *n. Chem.* 1. a compound of high molecular weight derived either by the combination of many smaller molecules or by the condensation of many smaller molecules eliminating water, alcohol, etc. 2. any of two or more polymeric compounds. 3. a product of polymerization. [t. Gk.: s. *polymerēs* of many parts]

pol·y·mer·ic (pŏl'ĭ mĕr'ĭk), *adj. Chem.* (of compounds, or of one compound in relation to another) having the same elements combined in the same proportions by weight, but differing in molecular weight: more recently extended to include high molecular weight substances resulting from condensation.

po·lym·er·ism (pə lĭm'ər ĭz'əm, pŏl'ĭ mə-), *n.* 1. *Chem.* polymeric state. 2. *Biol., Bot.* polymerous state.

po·lym·er·i·za·tion (pə lĭm'ərə zā'shən, pŏl'ĭ mər-), *n. Chem.* 1. act or process of forming a polymer or polymeric compound. 2. the union of two or more molecules of a compound to form a more complex compound with a higher molecular weight. 3. the conversion of one compound into another by such a process.

po·lym·er·ize (pŏl'ĭ mə rīz', pə lĭm'ə rīz'), *v.t., v.i.* -**ized, -izing.** 1. to combine so as to form a polymer. 2. to subject to or undergo polymerization.

po·lym·er·ous (pə lĭm'ər əs), *adj.* 1. *Biol.* composed of many parts. 2. *Bot.* having numerous members in each whorl.

pol·y·morph (pŏl'ĭ mŏrf'), *n.* 1. *Zool., etc.* a polymorphous organism or substance. 2. *Cryst.* one of the forms assumed by a polymorphous substance. [t. Gk.: s. *polýmorphos,* adj., multiform]

pol·y·mor·phism (pŏl'ĭ mŏr'fĭz əm), *n.* 1. polymorphous state or condition. 2. *Cryst.* crystallization into two or more chemically identical but crystallographically distinct forms. 3. *Zool., Bot.* existence of an animal or plant in several form or color varieties.

pol·y·mor·phous (pŏl'ĭ mŏr'fəs), *adj.* having, assuming, or passing through many or various forms. stages, or the like. Also, **pol·y·mor'phic.**

Pol·y·ne·sia (pŏl'ĭ nē'shə, -zhə), *n.* one of the three principal divisions of Oceania, comprising those island groups in the Pacific lying E of Melanesia and Micronesia and extending from the Hawaiian Islands 8 to New Zealand. [t. NL, t. F: m. *Polynésie,* f. *poly-* POLY- + *-nésie,* der. Gk. *nêsos* island]

Pol·y·ne·sian (pŏl'ĭ nē'shən, -zhən), *adj.* 1. of or pertaining to Polynesia, its inhabitants, or their languages. —*n.* 2. any of a "brown" people, variably classified as to race, of distinctive customs, speaking closely related Austronesian languages, and inhabiting Polynesia. 3. the easternmost group of the Austronesian languages, including Maori, Tahitian, Samoan, Hawaiian, and the language of Easter Island.

Pol·y·ni·ces (pŏl'ə nī'sēz), *n. Gk. Legend.* the son of Oedipus. The expedition of the Seven against Thebes was organized to restore him to the throne of Thebes.

pol·y·no·mi·al (pŏl'ĭ nō'mĭ əl), *adj.* 1. consisting of or characterized by many or several names or terms. —*n.* 2. a polynomial name or the like. 3. *Alg.* an expression consisting of two or more terms, as $2x^3 = 7x^2 + 4x + 2$. 4. *Zool., Bot.* a species name containing more than two terms. [f. POLY- + *-nomial* as in BINOMIAL]

pol·y·nu·cle·ar (pŏl'ĭ nū'klĭ ər. -nōō'-), *adj.* multinuclear.

pol·yp (pŏl'ĭp), *n.* 1. *Zool.* **a.** a sedentary type of animal form characterized by a more or less fixed base, columnar body, and free end with mouth and tentacles, esp. as applied to coelenterates. **b.** an individual zoöid of a compound or colonial organism. 2. *Pathol.* a projecting growth from a mucus surface, as of the nose, being either a tumor or a hypertrophy of the mucous membrane. [t. F: m. *polype,* t. L: m.s. *polypus,* t. Gk.: m. *polýpous* octopus, also *polyp* (def. 2)]

pol·y·par·y (pŏl'ĭ pĕr'ĭ), *n., pl.* -**paries.** the common supporting structure of a colony of polyps, as corals.

pol·y·pep·tide (pŏl'ĭ pĕp'tīd), *n. Chem.* one of a group of compounds having two or more amino acids and one or more peptide radicals. See **peptide.**

pol·y·pet·al·ous (pŏl'ĭ pĕt'əl əs), *adj. Bot.* having many or (commonly) separate petals. See **corolla.**

pol·y·pha·gi·a (pŏl'ĭ fā'jĭ ə), *n.* 1. *Pathol.* excessive desire to eat. 2. *Zool.* the habit of subsisting on many different kinds of food. [t. NL, t. Gk.] —**po·lyph·a·gous** (pə lĭf'ə gəs), *adj.*

pol·y·phase (pŏl'ĭ fāz'), *adj. Elect.* 1. having more than one phase. 2. denoting or pertaining to a system combining two or more alternating currents which differ from one another in phase.

Pol·y·phe·mus (pŏl'ĭ fē'məs), *n. Gk. Legend.* a chief among the Cyclopes, blinded by Odysseus who thus escaped him.

Polyphemus moth, a large North American silkworm moth, *Telea polyphemus,* of a buff and pink coloration and with eyespots on the hind wings.

pol·y·phone (pŏl'ĭ fōn'), *n. Phonet.* a polyphonic letter or symbol.

pol·y·phon·ic (pŏl'ĭ fŏn'ĭk), *adj.* 1. consisting of many voices or sounds. 2. *Music.* **a.** having two or more voices or parts, each with an independent melody, but all harmonizing; contrapuntal (opposed to *homophonic*). **b.** of music of this kind. **c.** capable of producing more than one tone at a time, as an organ or a harp. 3. *Phonet.* having more than one phonetic value, as a letter. [f. s. Gk. *polýphōnos* having many tones + -IC]

po·lyph·o·ny (pə lĭf'ə nĭ), *n.* 1. *Music.* polyphonic composition; counterpoint. 2. *Phonet.* representation of different sounds by the same letter or symbol. [t. Gk.: m.s. *polyphōnía* variety of tones or speech] —**po·lyph'o·nous,** *adj.*

pol·y·phy·let·ic (pŏl'ĭ fī lĕt'ĭk), *adj.* developed from more than one ancestral type, as a group of animals. [t. POLY- + m.s. Gk. *phyletikós* of the same tribe]

pol·y·ploid (pŏl'ĭ ploid'), *Genetics.* —*n.* 1. an organism with more than twice the haploid number of chromosomes. —*adj.* 2. of a chromosome number which is some multiple of the haploid number. —**pol·y·ploi'dy,** *n.*

pol·y·po·dy (pŏl'ĭ pō'dĭ), *n., pl.* -**dies.** any fern of the genus *Polypodium,* as *P. vulgare,* a common species with creeping rootstocks, deeply pinnatifid evergreen fronds, and round, naked sori. [t. L: m.s. *polypodium,* t. Gk.: m. *polypódion*]

pol·yp·tych (pŏl'ĭp tĭk), *n.* a painted or sculptured

ensemble, usually an altarpiece, composed of several separate parts. [t. LL: s. *polyptycha* (neut. pl.) account books, t. Gk.: having many folds]

pol·y·pus (pŏl′ə pəs), *n.*, *pl.* **-pi** (-pī′). *Pathol.* a polyp. [t. L. See POLYP]

pol·y·sac·cha·ride (pŏl′ĭ săk′ə rīd′, -rĭd), *n. Chem.* a carbohydrate, as starch, inulin, cellulose, etc., containing more than three monosaccharide units per molecule, the units being attached to each other in the manner of acetals, and therefore capable of hydrolysis by acids or enzymes to monosaccharides. Also, **pol·y·sac·cha·rid** (pŏl′ĭ săk′ə rĭd).

pol·y·sty·rene (pŏl′ĭ stī′rēn), *n. Chem.* a polymer of styrene used in making synthetic rubber.

pol·y·sul·fide (pŏl′ĭ sŭl′fīd, -fĭd), *n. Chem.* a sulfide containing more than the ordinary quantity of sulfur.

pol·y·syl·lab·ic (pŏl′ĭ sĭ lăb′ĭk), *adj.* 1. consisting of many, or more than three, syllables, as a word. 2. characterized by such words, as language, etc. Also, **pol·y·syl·lab·i·cal**. [f. s. ML *polysyllabus* (t. Gk.: m. *polysýllabos* of many syllables) + -IC]

pol·y·syl·la·ble (pŏl′ĭ sĭl′ə bəl), *n.* a polysyllabic word.

pol·y·syn·de·ton (pŏl′ĭ sĭn′də tŏn′), *n. Rhet.* the use of a number of conjunctions in close succession, as in Rom. 8:38, 39. Cf. **asyndeton**. [t. NL, f. Gk.: *poly-* POLY- + *sýndeton* (neut.) bound together]

pol·y·tech·nic (pŏl′ĭ těk′nĭk), *adj.* 1. pertaining to or dealing with various arts. —*n.* 2. an institution or school in which instruction in technical subjects is given. [t. F: m. *polytechnique*, f. s. Gk. *polýtechnos* + *-ique* -IC]

pol·y·the·ism (pŏl′ĭ thē′ĭz′əm), *n.* the doctrine of, or belief in, many gods or more gods than one. [t. F: m. *polythéisme*, f. s. Gk. *polýtheos* of many gods + *-isme* -ISM] —**pol′y·the′ist**, *n.* —**pol′y·the·is′tic**, *adj.*

pol·y·thene (pŏl′ə thēn′), *n. Chem.* the British name for polyethylene.

pol·y·to·nal·i·ty (pŏl′ĭ tō năl′ə tĭ), *n. Music.* the use of more than one key at the same time.

pol·y·typ·ic (pŏl′ĭ tĭp′ĭk), *adj.* having or involving many or several types. Also, **pol′y·typ′i·cal**.

pol·y·ure·thane (pŏl′ĭ yŏor′ə thān′), *n. Chem.* a polymer of urethane used in making rigid foam products for insulation, decoration, etc.

pol·y·u·ri·a (pŏl′ĭ yŏor′ĭ ə), *n. Pathol.* the passing of an excessive quantity of urine, as in diabetes, certain nervous diseases, etc. [t. NL. See POLY-, -URIA] —**pol′y·u′ric**, *adj.*

pol·y·va·lent (pŏl′ĭ vā′lənt, pə lĭv′ə lənt), *adj.* 1. *Chem.* having more than one valence. 2. *Bacteriol.* noting a serum which contains antibodies against a group of similar diseases and is capable of attacking their different antigens. [f. POLY- + -VALENT] —**pol′y·va′lence**, *n.*

pol·y·vi·nyl acetate (pŏl′ĭ vī′nĭl), a transparent thermoplastic resin used as an adhesive, as an interlayer of safety glass, etc.

Po·lyx·e·na (pə lĭk′sə nə), *n. Gk. Legend.* daughter of Priam and Hecuba and bride of Achilles.

pol·y·zo·an (pŏl′ĭ zō′ən), *n. Zool.* one of the *Polyzoa* or *Bryozoa*, a phylum of small aquatic animals forming branching, gelatinous, or incrusting colonies. [f. POLY- + -ZO(A) + -AN] —**pol′y·zo′an**, *adj.*

pol·y·zo·ar·i·um (pŏl′ĭ zō âr′ĭ əm), *n.*, *pl.* **-aria** (-âr′ĭ ə). *Zool.* a polyzoan colony, or its supporting skeleton.

pom·ace (pŭm′ĭs), *n.* 1. the pulpy residue from apples or similar fruit after crushing and pressing, as in cider making. 2. any crushed or ground pulpy substance. [ME, t. ML: m.s. *pōmācium* cider, der. L *pōmum* fruit]

po·ma·ceous (pō mā′shəs), *adj.* pertaining to pomes, as the apple, pear, and quince. [t. NL: m. *pōmāceus*, der. L *pōmum* fruit]

po·made (pō mād′, -măd′), *n.*, *v.*, **-maded**, **-mading**. —*n.* 1. a scented ointment, used for the scalp and hair. —*v.t.* 2. to anoint or dress with pomade. [t. F: m. *pommade*, t. It.: m. *pommata* (so called because orig. made with apples), der. L *pōmum* fruit. Cf. POMATUM]

po·man·der (pō′măn dər, pō măn′dər), *n.* 1. a mixture of aromatic substances, often in the form of a ball, formerly carried on the person for perfume or as a guard against infection. 2. the case in which it was carried. [earlier *pomeamber*, f. POME + AMBER]

po·ma·tum (pō mā′təm, -mä′-), *n.* pomade. [t. NL, der. L *pōmum* fruit]

pome (pōm), *n. Bot.* the characteristic fruit of the apple family, as an apple, pear, quince, etc. [ME, t. OF, g. LL *pōma* (neut. pl.) fruit] —**pome′like′**, *adj.*

pome·gran·ate (pŏm′grăn′ĭt, pŭm′-, pəm grăn′ĭt), *n.* 1. a several-chambered, many-seeded, globose fruit of medium size, with a tough rind (usually red) and surmounted by a crown of calyx lobes, the edible portion consisting of pleasantly acid flesh developed from the outer seed coat. 2. the shrub or small tree, *Punica Granatum*, which yields it, native in southwestern Asia but widely cultivated in warm regions. [ME *pomegarnet*, t. OF: m. *pome grenate* (f. *pome* apple, fruit + *grenate*, t. L: m. *grānāta* (fem.) having grains or seeds). See POME, GRAIN]

pom·e·lo (pŏm′ə lō′), *n.*, *pl.* **-los.** the grapefruit.

Pom·er·a·ni·a (pŏm′ə rā′nĭ ə, -răn′yə), *n.* a former province of NE Germany, now mostly in NW Poland. German, **Pommern**.

Pom·er·a·ni·an (pŏm′ə rā′nĭ ən), *adj.* 1. of or pertaining to Pomerania, on the south coast of the Baltic Sea. —*n.* 2. one of a breed of medium-sized or small dogs with sharp nose, pointed ears, and long, thick silky hair. 3. a native or inhabitant of Pomerania.

Pomeranian
(14 in. or less high at the shoulder)

po·mi·cul·ture (pō′mĭ kŭl′chər), *n.* the cultivation or growing of fruit. [f. *pōmi-* (comb. form of L *pōmum* fruit) + CUL- TURE] —**po′mi·cul′tur·ist**, *n.*

po·mif·er·ous (pō mĭf′ər əs), *adj. Bot.* bearing pomes or pomelike fruits. [f. L *pōmifer* fruit-bearing + -OUS]

pom·mel (pŭm′əl, pŏm′əl), *n.*, *v.*, **-meled**, **-meling** or (*esp. Brit.*) **-melled**, **-melling.** —*n.* 1. a knob, as on the hilt of a sword, etc. 2. the protuberant part at the front and top of a saddle. See illus. under **saddle.** —*v.t.* 3. to strike or beat with or as with the pommel or with the fist. Also, **pummel.** [ME *pomel*, t. OF, ult. der. L *pōmum* fruit]

Pom·mern (pŏm′ərn), *n.* German name of **Pomerania**.

po·mol·o·gy (pō mŏl′ə jĭ), *n.* the science that deals with fruits and fruit growing. [t. NL: m.s. *pōmologia*. See POME, -LOGY] —**po·mo·log·i·cal** (pō′mə lŏj′ə kəl), *adj.* —**po·mol′o·gist**, *n.*

Po·mo·na (pə mō′nə), *n.* 1. *Rom. Myth.* the goddess of fruit trees. 2. a city in SW California, E of Los Angeles, 67,157 (1960). 3. Also, **Mainland.** an island N of Scotland: the largest of the Orkney Islands. 13,352 pop. (1951); 190 sq. mi.

pomp (pŏmp), *n.* 1. stately or splendid display; splendor; magnificence. 2. ostentatious or vain display, esp. of dignity or importance. 3. (*pl.*) pompous displays or things. 4. *Obs.* a stately or splendid procession; pageant. [ME *pompe*, t. OF, t. L: m. *pompa*, t. Gk.: m. *pompḗ*, orig., a sending.] —**Syn. 1.** See **show.**

pom·pa·dour (pŏm′pə dōr′, -dŏor′), *n.* 1. an arrangement of a man's hair, brushed up from the forehead. 2. an arrangement of a woman's hair in which it is raised above the forehead, often over a pad. 3. a shade of pink or of crimson. [named after the Marquise de *Pompadour*]

Pom·pa·dour (pŏN pä dōor′), *n.* **Marquise de,** (*Jeanne Antoinette Poisson Le Normant D'Etioles*) 1721–64, mistress of Louis XV of France.

pom·pa·no (pŏm′pə nō′), *n.*, *pl.* **-nos.** 1. a deep-bodied food fish of the genus *Trachinotus*. 2. a prized food fish, *Palometus simillimus*, of California. [t. Sp.: m. *pampano*, g. L *pampinus*]

Pom·pe·ii (pŏm pā′ē), *n.* an ancient city in SW Italy at the foot of Mount Vesuvius: buried by an eruption, A.D. 79. —**Pom·pe·ian** (pŏm pā′ən, -pē′ən), *adj.*, *n.*

Pom·pey (pŏm′pĭ), *n.* ("*The Great,*" *Gnaeus Pompeius Magnus*) 106–48 B.C., Roman general and statesman; a member of the first triumvirate.

pom-pom (pŏm′pŏm′), *n.* an automatic anti-aircraft cannon. [imit.]

pom·pon (pŏm′pŏn; *Fr.* pôN pôN′), *n.* 1. an ornamental tuft or ball of feathers, wool, or the like, used in millinery, etc. 2. a tuft of wool or the like worn on a shako, a sailor's cap, etc. 3. *Hort.* a form of small, globe-shaped flower head that characterizes a class or type of various flowering plants, especially chrysanthemums and dahlias. [t. F, ult. der. *pompe* POMP]

pom·pos·i·ty (pŏm pŏs′ə tĭ), *n.*, *pl.* **-ties.** 1. the quality of being pompous. 2. pompous parade of dignity or importance. 3. ostentatious loftiness of language or style. [ME, t. ML: m.s. *pompōsitas*]

pomp·ous (pŏm′pəs), *adj.* 1. characterized by an ostentatious parade of dignity or importance: *a pompous bow.* 2. (of language, style, etc.) ostentatiously lofty. 3. characterized by pomp, stately splendor, or magnificence. [ME, t. LL: s. *pompōsus*] —**pomp′ous·ly**, *adv.* —**pomp′ous·ness**, *n.*

Pon·ce (pôn′sĕ), *n.* a seaport in S Puerto Rico, 65,182 (1950); municipality, 105,116 (1950).

Ponce de Le·ón (pŏns′ də lē′ən; *Sp.* pôn′thĕ dĕ lĕ·ôn′, pôn′sĕ), **Juan** (hwän), c1460–1521, Spanish explorer of Florida.

pon·cho (pŏn′chō), *n.*, *pl.* **-chos.** a blanketlike cloak with a hole in the center to put on over the head, worn orig. in South America, now by soldiers and sportsmen as a raincoat. [t. S Amer. Sp., t. Araucanian: m. *pontho*]

pond (pŏnd), *n.* a body of water smaller than a lake, often once artificially formed, as by a dam. [ME, anomalous var. of POUND³]

pon·der (pŏn′dər), *v.i.* 1. to consider deeply; meditate. —*v.t.* 2. to weigh carefully in the mind, or consider carefully. [ME *pondre(n)*, t. OF: m. *ponderer*, t. L: m. *ponderāre* ponder, weigh] —**Syn. 1.** reflect, cogitate, deliberate, ruminate.

pon·der·a·ble (pŏn′dərə bəl), *adj.* capable of being weighed; having appreciable weight. —**pon′der·a·bil′i·ty**, *n.*

pon·der·ous (pŏn′dərəs), *adj.* 1. of great weight; heavy; massive: *a ponderous mass of iron.* 2. without graceful lightness or ease; dull: *a ponderous dissertation.* [ME, t. L: m.s. *ponderōsus*] —**pon′der·ous·ly**, *adv.* —**pon′der·ous·ness, pon·der·os·i·ty** (pŏn′dərŏs′ə tĭ), *n.*

Pon·di·che·ry (pŏn´dē shĕr´ē´), *n.* **1.** a former province of French India, on the Coromandel Coast; now a centrally-administered territory of India. 293,000 pop. (est. 1954, with Mahé, Karikal, and Yanaon); 200 sq. mi. **2.** a seaport in and capital of the territory. 58,600 (est. 1952). Also, **Pon·di·cher·ry** (pŏn´də chĕr´ĭ, -shĕr´ĭ). See **French India.**

pond lily, a water lily.

pond scum, any free-floating fresh-water alga that forms a green scum on water.

pond·weed (pŏnd´wēd´), *n.* any of the aquatic plants constituting the genus *Potamogeton*, most of which grow in ponds and quiet streams.

pone (pōn), *n. Southern U.S.* **1.** bread, esp. of a plain or simple kind, made of corn meal. **2.** a loaf or cake of it. [t. Powhatan: m. *ápan* something baked]

pon·gee (pŏn jē´), *n.* **1.** silk of a plain weave made from filaments of wild silk woven in natural tan color. **2.** a cotton or rayon fabric imitating it. [? t. North Chinese: m. *pun-chu*, Mandarin *pun-ki* own loom]

pon·iard (pŏn´yərd), *n.* **1.** a dagger. —*v.t.* **2.** to stab with a poniard. [t. F: m. *poignard*, der. *poing*, g. L *pugnus* fist]

pons (pŏnz), *n., pl.* **pontes** (pŏn´tēz). *Anat.* a connecting part. [t. L: bridge]

Pons (pŏnz; *Fr.* pôNs), *n.* **Lily** (lĭl´ĭ; *Fr.* lē lē´), born 1904, U.S. operatic soprano, born in France.

pons as·i·no·rum (pŏnz´ ăs´ə nōr´əm), the geometrical proposition (Euclid, 1:5) that if a triangle has two of its sides equal, the angles opposite these sides are also equal: so named from the difficulty experienced by beginners in mastering it. [L: bridge of asses]

pons Va·ro·li·i (pŏnz´ və rō´lĭ ī´). *Anat.* a band of nerve fibers in the brain connecting the lobes of the cerebellum, as well as the medulla and cerebrum. [named after *Varoli*, Italian anatomist (16th cent.)]

Pon·ta Del·ga·da (pŏn´tə dĕl gä´də), a seaport in the Azores, on São Miguel island. 22,448 (1950).

Pont·char·train (pŏn´chər trān´), *n.* **Lake,** a shallow extension of the Gulf of Mexico in SE Louisiana, N of New Orleans. ab. 40 mi. long; ab. 22 mi. wide.

Pon·te·fract (pŏn´tĭ frăkt´; *local* pŭm´frĭt, pŏm´-), *n.* a city in N England, SE of Leeds: ruins of a 12th century castle. 23,173 (1951).

Pon·ti·ac (pŏn´tĭ ăk´), *n.* **1.** a city in SE Michigan. 82,233 (1960). **2.** c1720–69, American Indian chief, of the Ottawa tribe.

Pon·tic (pŏn´tĭk), *adj.* pertaining to the Pontus Euxinus (Black Sea) or to Pontus (an ancient country south of it). [t. L: s. *Ponticus*, t. Gk.: m. *Pontikós*]

pon·ti·fex (pŏn´tə fĕks´), *n., pl.* **pontifices** (pŏn tĭf´ə sēz´). a member of the principal college of priests in ancient Rome, whose head was the **Pontifex Maximus,** or chief priest. [L: a Roman high priest]

pon·tiff (pŏn´tĭf), *n.* **1.** an ancient Roman pontifex. **2.** a high or chief priest. **3.** *Eccles.* **a.** a bishop. **b.** the bishop of Rome (the Pope). [t. L: m. *pontifex*]

pon·tif·i·cal (pŏn tĭf´ə kəl), *adj.* **1.** of, pertaining to, or characteristic of a pontiff: *pontifical Mass.* **2.** pertaining to the Pope; papal. —*n.* **3.** (in the Western Church) a book containing the forms for the sacraments and other rites and ceremonies to be performed by bishops. **4.** (*pl.*) the vestments and other insignia of a pontiff, esp. a bishop. [ME, t. L: s. *pontificālis*] —**pon·tif´i·cal·ly,** *adv.*

Pontifical College, 1. the chief body of priests in ancient Rome. **2.** the chief hieratic body of the Roman Catholic Church.

pon·tif·i·cate (pŏn tĭf´ə kĭt´, -kāt´), *n., v.,* **-cated, -cating.** —*n.* **1.** the office, or term of office, of a pontiff. —*v.i.* **2.** to speak in a pompous manner. **3.** to serve as a bishop, esp. in a pontifical Mass. [t. ML: m.s. *pontificātus,* pp.]

pon·til (pŏn´tĭl), *n.* punty.

Pon·tine Marshes (pŏn´tĭn, -tīn), an area in W Italy, SE of Rome: formerly marshy, now drained.

Pon·tius (pŏn´shəs, -tĭ əs), *n.* family name of **Pilate.**

pont·lev·is (pŏnt lĕv´ĭs; *Fr.* pôN lĕ vē´), *n.* a drawbridge.

pon·to·nier (pŏn´tə nĭr´), *n. Mil.* an officer or soldier in charge of bridge equipment or construction of pontoon bridges. [t. F: m. *pontonnier*, der. *ponton* PONTOON[1]]

pon·toon[1] (pŏn tōōn´), *n.* **1.** *Mil.* a boat, or some other floating structure, used as one of the supports for a temporary bridge over a river. **2.** *Nav.* a floating cubical structure to serve as a temporary dock. **3.** a watertight box or cylinder used in raising a submerged vessel, etc. **4.** a seaplane float. Also, **pon·ton** (pŏn´tən). [t. F: m. *ponton*, g. s. L *ponto* bridge, pontoon, punt]

pon·toon[2] (pŏn tōōn´), *n. Brit.* a card game similar to blackjack. [(? humorous) mispron. of F *vingt-un*]

pontoon bridge, a bridge supported by pontoons.

Pon·tus (pŏn´təs), *n.* an ancient country in NE Asia Minor, bordering on the Black Sea: became a Roman province, A.D. 62.

Pontus Eux·i·nus (ūk sī´nəs), ancient name of the Black Sea.

po·ny (pō´nĭ), *n., pl.* **-nies,** *v.,* **-nied, -nying.** —*n.* **1.** a horse of a small type, usually not over 14 hands high. **2.** a horse of any small type or breed. **3.** *U.S. Slang.* a translation or other illicit aid, used instead of doing one's own work. Cf. *Brit.* **crib. 4.** something small of

its kind. **5.** *Colloq.* a small glass for liquor. **6.** *Colloq.* the amount of liquor it will hold. **7.** *Brit. Slang.* the sum of £25.8. —*v.t., v.i. U.S. Slang.* **8.** to prepare (lessons) by means of a pony. **9.** to pay (money), as in settling an account (fol. by *up*) [var. of *powney*, t. F: m *poulenet*, ult. der. L *pullus* young animal. See FOAL]

pony express, *U.S.* a system of carrying mail and express by relays of horsemen in the American West. 1860–61.

pooch (pōōch), *n. Slang.* a dog, esp. a mongrel.

pood (pōōd), *n.* a Russian weight equal to about 36 pounds avoirdupois. [t. Russ.: t. LG or Scand.: m. *pund* POUND]

poo·dle (pōō´dəl), *n.* one of a breed of intelligent pet dogs, of numerous varieties, with thick curly hair often trimmed in an elaborate manner, as with pompons. [short for *poodle dog*, half adoption, half trans. of G *pudelhund*, lit., splash-dog (because the poodle is a water dog). Cf. PUDDLE]

French poodle
(15 in. or more high at the shoulder)

pooh (pōō, pŏŏ), *interj.* **1.** an exclamation of disdain or contempt (often repeated). —*n.* **2.** an exclamation of "pooh."

pooh-pooh (pōō´pōō´), *v.t.* to express disdain or contempt for; make light of; dismiss as unworthy of consideration.

pool[1] (pōōl), *n.* **1.** a small body of standing water **2.** a small pond. **3.** a puddle. **4.** any small collection of liquid on a surface: *a pool of blood.* **5.** a still, deep place in a stream. **6.** a tank or large basin of water to swim or bathe in. [ME and OE *pōl*, c. G *pfuhl*]

pool[2] (pōōl), *n.* **1.** an association of competitors who agree to control the production, market, and price of a commodity for mutual benefit, although they appear to be rivals. **2.** *Finance.* a combination of persons to manipulate one or more securities. **3.** a combination of interests, funds, etc., for common advantage. **4.** the combined interests or funds. **5.** the persons or parties involved. **6.** the stakes in certain games. **7.** a game played by two or more persons on a billiard table with six pockets, the object of the players being to pocket balls of ivory or other hard material by means of cues. **8.** *Brit.* a billiard game. **9.** the total amount staked by a combination of betters, as on a race, to be awarded to the successful better or betters. **10.** the combination of such betters. **11.** *Fencing.* a match in which each teammate successively plays against each member of the opposing team. —*v.t.* **12.** to put (interests, money, etc.) into a pool, or common stock or fund, as for a financial venture, according to agreement. **13.** to form a pool of. **14.** to make a common interest of. —*v.i.* **15.** to enter into or form a pool. [t. F: m. *poule*, lit., hen: prob. at first slang for booty]

pool·room (pōōl´rōōm´, -rŏŏm´), *n.* an establishment or room in which pool or billiards is played.

pool table, a billiard table with six pockets, on which pool is played.

poon (pōōn), *n.* any of several East Indian trees of the tropical genus *Calophyllum*, which yield a light, hard wood used for masts, spars, etc. **2.** the wood. [t. Singhalese or Telugu: m. *puna*]

Poo·na (pōō´nə), *n.* a city in W India. 75 mi. SE of Bombay. 480,982 (1951).

poop (pōōp), *n.* **1.** the aftermost part, or stern, of a ship. **2.** a deck above the ordinary deck in that part, often forming the roof of a cabin, etc. —*v.t.* **3.** (of a wave) to break over the stern of (a ship). **4.** to take (seas) over the stern. [ME *pouppe,* t. OF: m. *poupe,* t. It.: m. *poppa,* g. L *puppis*]

poop deck, a raised deck built on the stern of a ship above the main deck.

Po·o·pó (pō´ō pô´), *n.* a lake in SW Bolivia, in the Andes. ab. 80 mi. long; ab. 12,000 ft. high.

poor (pŏŏr), *adj.* **1.** having little or nothing in the way of wealth, goods, or means of subsistence. **2.** *Law.* dependent upon charity. **3.** (of a country, institution, etc.) meagerly supplied or endowed with resources or funds. **4.** (of the circumstances, life, home, dress, etc.) characterized by or showing poverty. **5.** deficient or lacking in something specified: *a region poor in mineral deposits.* **6.** faulty or inferior, as in construction. **7.** deficient in desirable ingredients, qualities, or the like: *poor soil.* **8.** lean or emaciated, as cattle. **9.** of an inferior, inadequate, or unsatisfactory kind; not good: *poor health.* **10.** deficient in aptitude or ability: *a poor cook.* **11.** deficient in moral excellence; cowardly, abject, or mean. **12.** scanty, meager, or paltry in amount or number: *a poor pittance.* **13.** humble: *deign to visit our poor house.* **14.** unfortunate or hapless (much used to express pity): *the poor mother was in despair* —*n.* **15.** poor persons collectively (usually prec. by *the*). [ME *povere,* t. OF: m. *povre,* g. L *pauper.* Cf. PAUPER] —**poor´ness,** *n.*

—**Syn. 1.** needy, indigent, necessitous, straitened, destitute, penniless, poverty-stricken. POOR, IMPECUNIOUS, IMPOVERISHED, PENNILESS refer to those lacking money. POOR is the simple term for the condition of lacking means to obtain the comforts of life: *a very poor family.* IMPECUNIOUS often suggests that the poverty is a consequence of unwise habits: *an impecunious actor.* IMPOVERISHED often implies a former state of greater plenty, from which one has been re-

---

b., blend of, blended; c., cognate with; d., dialect, dialectal; der., derived from; f., formed from; g., going back to; m., modification of; r., replacing; s., stem of; t., taken from; ?, perhaps. See the full key on inside cover

duced: *the impoverished aristocracy.* PENNILESS may mean destitute, or it may apply simply to a temporary condition of being without funds: *the widow was left penniless with three small children.* —**Ant. 1.** rich, wealthy.

poor farm, a farm maintained at public expense for the housing and support of paupers.

poor·house (poŏr′hous′), *n.* a house in which paupers are maintained at the public expense.

poor law, a law or system of laws providing for the relief or support of the poor at the public expense.

poor·ly (poŏr′lĭ), *adv.* **1.** in a poor manner or way. —*adj.* **2.** *Chiefly Colloq.* in poor health; somewhat ill.

poor-spir·it·ed (poŏr′spĭr′ĭt′ĭd), *adj.* having or showing a poor, cowardly, or abject spirit.

poor white, *Usually Derogatory.* an ignorant, shiftless, poverty-stricken, Southern white (*usually collective or pl.*).

poor white trash, *Usually Derogatory.* poor whites collectively.

pop[1] (pŏp), *v.,* **popped, popping,** *n., adv.* —*v.i.* **1.** to make a short, quick, explosive sound or report: *the cork popped.* **2.** to burst open with such a sound, as chestnuts or corn in roasting. **3.** to come or go quickly, suddenly, or unexpectedly (*in, into, out, off, up, etc.*). **4.** to shoot with a firearm: *to pop at a mark.* —*v.t.* **5.** to cause to make a sudden, explosive sound. **6.** to cause to burst open with such a sound. **7.** to put or thrust quickly, suddenly, or unexpectedly (fol. by *in, into, out, up, etc.*). **8.** *Colloq.* to fire (a gun, etc.). **9.** to shoot (fol. by *down, etc.*). **10.** *Brit. Slang.* to pawn. **11. pop corn,** *U.S.* to parch or roast the kernels of certain varieties of maize until they burst open. **12. pop the question,** *Colloq.* to propose marriage. —*n.* **13.** a short, quick, explosive sound. **14.** a popping. **15.** a shot with a firearm. **16.** an effervescent beverage, esp. an unintoxicating one. —*adv.* **17.** with a pop or explosive sound. **18.** quickly, suddenly, or unexpectedly. [ME; imit.]

pop[2] (pŏp), *adj. Colloq.* popular: *a pop concert.* [short for POPULAR]

pop., **1.** popular. **2.** popularly. **3.** population.

pop·corn (pŏp′kôrn′), *n.* **1.** any of several varieties of corn whose kernels burst open and puff out when subjected to dry heat. **2.** popped corn.

pope (pōp), *n.* **1.** (*cap.* or *l.c.*) the bishop of Rome as head of the Roman Catholic Church. **2.** one considered as having or assuming a similar position or authority. [ME; OE *pāpa,* t. ML: bishop, pope, orig. father, t. Gk.: m. *pápas,* var. of *páppas* father]

Pope (pōp), *n.* **1. Alexander,** 1688–1744, British poet. **2. John,** 1822–92, Union general in the Civil War.

pope·dom (pōp′dəm), *n.* **1.** the office or dignity of a pope. **2.** the tenure of office of a pope. **3.** the papal government. **4.** a system resembling the papacy.

pop·er·y (pō′pər̆ĭ), *n.* the doctrines, customs, etc., of the Roman Catholic Church (used in a hostile sense).

pop·gun (pŏp′gŭn′), *n.* a child's toy gun from which a pellet is shot with a loud pop by compressed air.

pop·in·jay (pŏp′ĭn jā′), *n.* **1.** a vain, chattering person; a coxcomb; a fop. **2.** a figure of a parrot formerly used as a target. **3.** a woodpecker, esp. the green woodpecker (*Picus viridis*) of Europe. **4.** *Archaic.* a parrot. [ME *papejay,* t. OF: m. *papegai* parrot, t. Sp.: m. *papagayo,* t. Ar.: m. *babbaghā′,* t. Pers.]

pop·ish (pō′pĭsh), *adj.* of or pertaining to the Roman Catholic Church (used in a hostile sense). —**pop′ish·ly,** *adv.* —**pop′ish·ness,** *n.*

pop·lar (pŏp′lər), *n.* **1.** any of various rapidly growing trees constituting the salicaceous genus *Populus,* yielding a useful, light, soft wood, as *P. nigra italica* (**Lombardy poplar**), a tall tree of striking columnar or spire-shaped outline due to the fastigiate habit of its branches. **2.** the wood itself. **3.** any of various trees resembling these in some respect, as the tulip tree (**yellow poplar**). **4.** the wood of any such tree. [ME *popler,* t. OF: m. *poplier;* r. OE *pōpul,* t. L: s. *pōpulus*]

pop·lin (pŏp′lĭn), *n.* a corded fabric of cotton, wool, rayon, or silk, used for women's dresses, etc. [t. F: m. *popeline,* t. It.: m. *papalina,* fem. of *papalino* papal; so called from being made at the papal city of Avignon]

pop·lit·e·al (pŏp lĭt′ē əl, pŏp′lə tē′əl), *adj. Anat.* of or pertaining to the ham, or part of the leg back of the knee. [f. s. NL *popliteus* (der. L *poples* the ham) + -AL[1]]

Po·po·ca·te·petl (pō′pə kät′ə pĕt′əl; *native* pō pō kä′tē pĕt′l), *n.* a volcano in S central Mexico, ab. 40 mi. SE of Mexico City. 17,887 ft.

pop·o·ver (pŏp′ō′vər), *n.* a kind of muffin so light as to overflow its pan in cooking.

Pop·pae·a Sa·bi·na (pŏ pē′ə sə bī′nə), died A.D. 65?, second wife of the Roman emperor Nero.

pop·per (pŏp′ər), *n.* **1.** one who or that which pops. **2.** a utensil for popping corn.

pop·pet (pŏp′ĭt), *n.* **1.** Also, **poppet valve.** a valve which in opening is lifted bodily from its seat instead of being hinged at one side. **2.** *Brit. Dial.* a term of endearment for a girl or child. [earlier form of PUPPET]

pop·pied (pŏp′ĭd), *adj.* **1.** covered or adorned with poppies. **2.** affected by or as by opium; listless.

pop·ping crease (pŏp′ĭng), *Cricket.* the line designating the batsman's position.

pop·ple (pŏp′əl), *v.,* **-pled, -pling,** *n.* —*v.i.* **1.** to move in a tumbling, irregular manner, as boiling water. —*n.* **2.** a poppling motion. [ME *pople*(n); prob. imit.]

pop·py (pŏp′ĭ), *n., pl.* **-pies.** **1.** any plant of the genus

Papaver, comprising herbs with showy flowers of various colors, as *P. somniferum,* the source of opium. **2.** an extract, as opium, from such a plant. **3.** orangeish red; scarlet. [ME; OE *popæg, papig,* t. VL: m. *papāvum,* for L *papāver*]

pop·py·cock (pŏp′ĭ kŏk′), *n. Colloq.* nonsense; bosh.

pop·py·head (pŏp′ĭ hĕd′), *n. Archit.* a finial or other ornament, often richly carved, as at the top of the upright end of a bench or pew.

poppy seed, seed of the poppy plant, used as a topping for breads, rolls, and cookies.

Pop·sic·le (pŏp′sĭ′kəl), *n. Trademark.* a flavored, frozen confection on a stick.

pop·u·lace (pŏp′yə lĭs), *n.* the common people of a community, as distinguished from the higher classes. [t. F, t. It.: m. *popolaccio,* pejorative of *popolo* PEOPLE]

pop·u·lar (pŏp′yə lər), *adj.* **1.** regarded with favor or approval by associates, acquaintances, the general public, etc.: *a popular preacher.* **2.** of, pertaining to, or representing the people, or the common people: *popular discontent.* **3.** prevailing among the people generally: *a popular superstition.* **4.** suited to or intended for ordinary people. **5.** adapted to the ordinary intelligence or taste: *popular lectures on science.* **6.** suited to the means of ordinary people: *popular prices.* [t. L: s. *populāris*] —**Syn. 1.** favorite, approved. **2.** common, prevailing, current. See **general.**

popular front, an alliance (not necessarily permanent) of leftwing, labor, and liberal parties against reactionary government or dictatorship.

pop·u·lar·i·ty (pŏp′yə lăr′ə tĭ), *n.* **1.** the quality or fact of being popular. **2.** favor enjoyed with the people, the public generally, or a particular set of people.

pop·u·lar·ize (pŏp′yə lə rīz′), *v.t.,* **-ized, -izing.** to make popular. Also, *esp. Brit.,* **pop′u·lar·ise′.** —**pop′u·lar·i·za′tion,** *n.* —**pop′u·lar·iz′er,** *n.*

pop·u·lar·ly (pŏp′yə lər lĭ), *adv.* **1.** by the people as a whole; generally. **2.** in a popular manner.

pop·u·late (pŏp′yə lāt′), *v.t.,* **-lated, -lating.** **1.** to inhabit. **2.** to furnish with inhabitants, as by colonization; people. [t. ML: m.s. *populātus,* pp., inhabited]

pop·u·la·tion (pŏp′yə lā′shən), *n.* **1.** the total number of persons inhabiting a country, city, or any district or area. **2.** the body of inhabitants of a place. **3.** the number or body of inhabitants of a particular race or class in a place. **4.** *Statistics.* an aggregate of statistical items. **5.** *Biol.* the assemblage of organisms living in a region. **6.** *Biometry.* the assemblage of all the organisms under consideration. **7.** act or process of populating.

population parameter, *Statistics.* a variable entering into the mathematical form of the distribution of a population such that the possible values of the variable correspond to different distributions: *the mean and variance of a population are population parameters.*

population pyramid, *Sociol.* a graph showing the distribution of a population in terms of sex, age, etc.

Pop·u·list (pŏp′yə lĭst), *n. U.S. Pol.* a member of the People's party, a political organization formed in 1891, advocating expansion of the currency, state control of railroads, the placing of restrictions upon the ownership of land, etc. [f. s. L *populus* people + -IST] —**Pop′u·lism,** *n.* —**Pop′u·lis′tic,** *adj.*

pop·u·lous (pŏp′yə ləs), *adj.* full of people or inhabitants, as a region; well populated. —**pop′u·lous·ly,** *adv.* —**pop′u·lous·ness,** *n.*

por·bea·gle (pôr′bē′gəl), *n.* a shark of the genus *Lamna,* esp. *L. nasus,* a large voracious species of the North Atlantic and North Pacific oceans. [orig. Cornish]

por·ce·lain (pôr′sə lĭn, pôrs′lĭn), *n.* **1.** a vitreous, more or less translucent, ceramic body or ware; china. **2.** a vessel or object made of this material. [t. F: m. *porcelaine,* t. It.: m. *porcellana* orig., a kind of shell, der. *porcella,* dim. of *porca,* of uncert. orig. (? akin to PORK)]

porcelain enamel, a glass which has been or can be used to adhere to a metal or another enamel by proper application and fusion.

porch (pôrch), *n.* **1.** an exterior appendage to a building, forming a covered approach or vestibule to a doorway, esp., in England, of a church. **2.** *U.S.* a veranda. **3.** a portico. **4. the Porch,** a public ambulatory in ancient Athens to which the Stoic philosopher Zeno of Citium and his followers resorted. [ME *porche,* t. OF, g. L *porticus* porch, portico]

por·cine (pôr′sīn, -sĭn), *adj.* **1.** of or resembling swine. **2.** swinish, hoggish, or piggish. [t. L: m.s. *porcīnus*]

por·cu·pine (pôr′kyə pīn′), *n.* any of various rodents covered with stout, erectile spines or quills, as the African porcupine, *Hystrix cristata,* with long spines, and the common porcupine of U.S. and Canada, *Erethizon dorsatum,* with short spines or quills partially concealed by the fur. [ME *porkepyn,* t. OF: m. *porcespin,* lit., spine-pig. See PORK, SPINE]

porcupine anteater, an echidna, or spiny anteater.

pore[1] (pōr), *v.t.,* **pored, poring.** **1.** to meditate or ponder intently (usually fol. by *over, on,* or *upon*). **2.** to gaze ear-

American porcupine,
Erethizon dorsatum
(Total length 3 to 3½ ft.
tail 6 in., quills 1 or 2 in. long)

nestly or steadily. **3.** to read or study with steady attention or application. [ME *pouren, puren;* orig. uncert.]

pore² (pōr), *n.* **1.** a minute opening or orifice, as in the skin or a leaf, for perspiration, absorption, etc. **2.** a minute interstice in a rock, etc. [ME, t. F, t. L: m. *porus,* t. Gk.: m. *póros* passage]

por·gy (pôr'gĭ), *n., pl.* **-gies,** (*esp. collectively*) **-gy.** any of numerous sparoid fishes, esp. a sea bream, *Pagrus pagrus,* of Mediterranean and Atlantic waters of Europe (**red porgy**). [cf. Sp. *porgo*]

Po·rif·er·a (pō rĭf'ər ə), *n. pl. Zool.* the phylum that comprises the sponges.

po·rif·er·ous (pō rĭf'ər əs), *adj.* bearing or having pores. [f. s. L *porus* pore + -(i)FEROUS]

po·ri·on (pōr'ĭ ŏn′), *n., pl.* **poria** (pōr'ĭ ə). *Craniom.* the most lateral point in the roof of the bony external auditory meatus (or earhole). [t. NL, der. Gk. *póros* passage, way]

po·rism (pōr'ĭz əm), *n. Math.* a form of proposition among the Greeks which has been variously defined, esp. as a proposition affirming the possibility of finding such conditions as will render a certain problem indeterminate, or capable of innumerable solutions. [t. L: m. *porisma,* t. Gk.: a corollary, a problem]

pork (pôrk), *n.* **1.** the flesh of hogs used as food. **2.** *U.S. Slang.* appropriations, appointments, etc., by the government for political reasons rather than for public necessity, as for public buildings, river improvements, etc. [ME *porc,* t. OF, g. L *porcus* hog, pig. See FARROW¹] —**pork·like′,** *adj.*

pork barrel, *U.S. Slang.* a government appropriation, bill, or policy which supplies funds for local improvements designed to ingratiate legislators with their constituents. [f. PORK federal money for local improvements secured on a political patronage basis + BARREL]

pork·er (pôr'kər), *n.* a swine, esp. one fatted for killing.

pork·y (pôr'kĭ), *adj.* **1.** porklike. **2.** fat: *a snub-nosed, porky little brat.*

por·nog·ra·phy (pôr nŏg'rə fĭ), *n.* obscene literature or art. [f. s. Gk. *pornográphos* writing of prostitutes + -y³] —**por·no·graph·ic** (pôr′nə grăf′ĭk), *adj.*

po·ros·i·ty (pō rŏs′ə tĭ), *n.* state or quality of being porous. [ME, t. ML: m.s. *porōsitas*]

po·rous (pōr'əs), *adj.* **1.** full of pores. **2.** permeable by water, air, or the like. —**po'rous·ness,** *n.*

por·phy·rin (pôr'fə rĭn), *n. Biochem.* any of a group of pyrrole derivatives, iron-free or magnesium-free, decomposition products of hematin and chlorophyll. They are found in all plant and animal protoplasm.

por·phy·rit·ic (pôr′fə rĭt′ĭk), *adj.* **1.** of, pertaining to, containing, or resembling porphyry. **2.** noting or pertaining to, or resembling the texture or structure characteristic of porphyry.

por·phy·roid (pôr′fə roid′), *n.* **1.** a rock resembling porphyry. **2.** a sedimentary rock which has been altered by some metamorphic agency so as to take on a slaty and more or less perfectly developed porphyritic structure.

por·phy·ry (pôr'fə rĭ), *n., pl.* **-ries.** **1.** a very hard rock, anciently quarried in Egypt, having a dark purplish-red ground mass containing small crystals of feldspar. **2.** any rock of similar texture. [ME *porfirie,* t. AF, ult. der. Gk. *pórphyros* purple. Cf. L *porphyrītēs* porphyry, t. Gk.]

por·poise (pôr'pəs), *n., pl.* **-poises,** (*esp. collectively*) **-poise.** **1.** any of the gregarious cetaceans constituting the genus *Phocaena* (family *Delphinidae*), five to eight feet long, usually blackish above and paler beneath, and having a blunt, rounded snout, esp. the common porpoise, *P. phocaena,* of both the North Atlantic and Pacific. **2.** any of several other small cetaceans, as the common dolphin, *Delphinus delphis.* [ME *porpeys,* t. OF: m. *porpeis,* g. LL *porcus piscis* hog fish, for L *porcus marinus*]

Common porpoise
Phocaena phocaena
(5½ to 6 ft. long)

por·ridge (pôr'ĭj, pŏr'-), *n. Chiefly Brit.* a food made of oatmeal, or some other meal or cereal, boiled to a thick consistency in water or milk. [var. of POTTAGE]

por·rin·ger (pôr'ĭn jər, pŏr'-), *n.* a dish, deeper than a saucer, from which soup, porridge, etc., may be eaten. [alter. of earlier *potager,* t. OF, der. *potage* POTTAGE]

Por·se·na (pôr'sə nə), *n.* **Lars** (lärz), a legendary Etruscan king, said to have attacked Rome in order to restore the banished Tarquinius Superbus to the throne. Also, **Por·sen·na** (pôr sĕn′ə).

port¹ (pōrt), *n.* **1.** a town or place where ships load or unload. **2.** a place along the coast where ships may take refuge from storms. **3.** *Law.* any place where persons and merchandise are allowed to pass (by water or land) into and out of a country and where customs officers are stationed to inspect or appraise imported goods; port of entry. [ME and OE, t. L: s. *portus* harbor, haven] —**Syn. 1.** See **harbor.**

port² (pōrt), *Naut.* —*n.* **1.** the side of a ship left of a person facing the bow (opp. to *starboard*). See illus. under **aft.** —*adj.* **2.** pertaining to the port. **3.** on the left side of a vessel. —*v.t., v.i.* **4.** to turn or shift to the port or left side. [orig. uncert.; ? because the larboard side was customarily next to the shore in port]

port³ (pōrt). *n.* any of a class of very sweet wines, mostly dark-red, orig. from Portugal. [from *Oporto* (Pg. *o porto* the port), city in Portugal]

port⁴ (pōrt), *n.* **1.** *Naut.* a. a porthole. **b.** the covering for a porthole. **2.** *Mech.* an aperture in the surface of a cylinder, for the passage of steam, air, water, etc. **3.** *Chiefly Scot.* a gate or portal, as of a town or fortress. [ME and OE, t. L: s. *porta* gate]

port⁵ (pōrt), *v.t.* **1.** *Mil.* to carry (a rifle, etc.), with both hands, in a slanting direction across the front of the body, with the barrel or like part near the left shoulder. —*n.* **2.** *Mil.* the position of a rifle or other weapon when ported. **3.** manner of bearing oneself; carriage or bearing. [t. F: s. *porter,* g. L *portāre* carry. See FARE]

Port., **1.** Portugal. **2.** Portuguese.

port·a·ble (pōr'tə bəl), *adj.* **1.** capable of being carried in the hand or on the person. **2.** easily carried or conveyed. **3.** *Obs.* endurable. [ME, t. LL: m.s. *portābilis*] —**port'a·bil'i·ty,** *n.*

por·tage (pōr'tĭj), *n.* **1.** the act of carrying; carriage. **2.** the carrying of boats, goods, etc., overland from one navigable waterway to another. **3.** place or course over which this is done. **4.** cost of carriage. [ME, t. F, der. *porter* carry]

por·tal¹ (pōr'təl), *n.* a door, gate, or entrance, esp. one of imposing appearance, as in a palace. [ME *portale,* t. ML, der. L *porta* gate]

por·tal² (pōr'təl), *Anat.* —*adj.* **1.** noting or pertaining to the transverse fissure of the liver. —*n.* **2.** portal vein. [t. ML: s. *portālis* of a gate]

por·tal-to-por·tal pay (pōr'təl tə pōr'təl), payment for time spent between the entrance to a factory, etc., and one's assigned place.

portal vein, *Anat.* the large vein conveying blood to the liver from the veins of the stomach, intestine, spleen, and pancreas.

por·ta·men·to (pōr'tə mĕn'tō; *It.* pôr'tä mĕn'tô), *n., pl.* **-ti** (-tē). *Music.* a passing or gliding from one pitch or tone to another with a smooth progression. [It.: a bearing, carrying, der. *portar* carry, g. L]

por·tance (pōr'təns), *n. Archaic.* bearing; behavior. [t. F (obs.)]

Port Ar·thur (är'thər), **1.** Japanese, *Ryojunko.* a seaport on the Yellow Sea in NE China, in Liaoning province, Manchuria: formerly a possession of Japan (1905–1945); now nominally under joint Russian-Chinese control. 210,000 (est. 1954). **2.** a seaport in SE Texas, on Sabine Lake. 66,676 (1960).

por·ta·tive (pōr'tə tĭv). *adj.* **1.** portable. **2.** having or pertaining to the power or function of carrying. [ME *portatif,* t. OF, der. *porter* carry. See -IVE]

Port-au-Prince (pōrt'ō prĭns′; *Fr.* pôr tō prăns′), *n.* a seaport in and the capital of Haiti. 134,117 (1950).

port authority, a government commission having jurisdiction over the regulations of a port.

Port Blair (blâr), a seaport in and the capital of the Andaman and Nicobar Islands. 3496 (1951).

Port Ches·ter (chĕs′tər), a city in SE New York, on Long Island Sound. 24,960 (1960).

port·cul·lis (pōrt kŭl′ĭs). *n.* a strong grating, as of iron, made to slide in vertical grooves at the sides of a gateway of a fortified place, and let down to prevent passage. [ME *portcullise,* t. OF: m. *porte coleice,* f. *porte* PORT⁴ (def. 3) + *coleice,* fem. of *coleis* flowing, sliding, ult. der. L *cōlātus,* pp., strained]

Portcullis

Porte (pōrt), *n.* the Ottoman Turkish court and government; (officially) Sublime Porte. [short for *Sublime Porte,* lit. High Gate, F trans. of the Turkish official title, with reference to the palace gate at which justice was administered]

porte-co·chere (pōrt′kō shâr′; *Fr.* pôrt kō shĕr′). *n.* **1.** a covered carriage entrance leading into a courtyard. **2.** a porch at the door of a building for sheltering persons entering and leaving carriages. Also, **porte'-co·chère′.** [t. F: gate for coaches]

Port E·liz·a·beth (ĭ lĭz′ə bĕth), a seaport in the S Republic of South Africa, in Cape of Good Hope province. With suburbs, 169,277 (1951).

porte-mon·naie (pōrt′mŭn′ĭ; *Fr.* pôrt mô nĕ′), *n. French.* a purse or pocketbook. [F: lit., money-carrier]

por·tend (pōr tĕnd′), *v.t.* **1.** to indicate beforehand, or presage, as an omen does. **2.** *Obs.* to signify; mean. [ME, t. L: s. *portendere* point out, indicate, portend]

por·tent (pōr'tĕnt), *n.* **1.** an indication or omen of something about to happen, esp. something momentous. **2.** ominous significance: *an occurrence of dire portent.* **3.** a prodigy or marvel. [t. L: s. *portentum,* prop. neut. pp., presaged] —**Syn. 1.** See **sign.**

por·ten·tous (pōr tĕn′təs), *adj.* **1.** of the nature of a portent; ominous; ominously indicative. **2.** marvelous; amazing. **3.** extraordinary; prodigious. —**por·ten′·tous·ly,** *adv.* —**por·ten′tous·ness,** *n.*

por·ter¹ (pōr'tər), *n.* **1.** one employed to carry burdens or baggage, as at a railroad station or a hotel. **2.** *U.S.*

---

b., blend of, blended; c., cognate with; d., dialect, dialectal; der., derived from; f., formed from; g., going back to; m., modification of; r., replacing; s., stem of; t., taken from; ?, perhaps. See the full key on inside cover.

an attendant in a parlor car or sleeping car. [ME *portour*, t. OF: m. *porteour*, ult. der. L *portāre* carry]

por·ter² (pōr′tər), *n.* **1.** one who has charge of a door or gate; a doorkeeper; a janitor. **2.** *Rom. Cath.* an ostiary. [ME, t. AF, g. LL *portārius*, der. L *porta* gate]

por·ter³ (pōr′tər), *n.* a heavy, dark-brown beer made with malt browned by drying at a high temperature. [short for porter's ale, appar. orig. brewed for porters]

Por·ter (pōr′tər), *n.* **1.** David, 1780–1843, U.S. naval officer. **2.** his son, **David Dixon**, 1813–91, Union naval officer in the Civil War, later an admiral. **3. Noah**, 1811–92, U.S. educator, writer, and lexicographer. **4. William Sidney**, (*O. Henry*) 1862–1910, U.S. short-story writer.

por·ter·age (pōr′tər ĭj), *n.* **1.** the work of a porter or carrier. **2.** the charge for such work.

por·ter·house (pōr′tər hous′), *n.* **1.** a house at which porter and other liquors are retailed. **2.** a chophouse. **3.** Also, **porterhouse steak**, a choice cut of beef from between the prime ribs and the sirloin.

port·fo·li·o (pōrt fō′lĭ ō′), *n.*, *pl.* -**lios**. **1.** a portable case for detached papers, prints, etc. **2.** such a case for carrying documents of a state department. **3.** the office or post of a minister of state or member of a cabinet. **4.** an itemized account; the securities, discount paper, etc., of an investment organization, bank, or other investor. [t. It.: m. *portafoglio*, f. *porta*, impv. of *portare* (g. L) carry + *foglio* (g. L *folium*) leaf, sheet]

port·hole (pōrt′hōl′), *n.* **1.** an aperture in the side of a ship, as for discharging cannon through or for admitting light and air. **2.** an opening in a wall, door, etc., as one through which to shoot.

Port Hud·son (hŭd′sən), a village in SE Louisiana, on the Mississippi, N of Baton Rouge: siege, 1863.

Port Hu·ron (hyōōr′ən), a city in SE Michigan: a port on the St. Clair river at the S end of Lake Huron. 36,084 (1960).

Por·tia (pōr′shə, -shĭ′ə), *n.* **1.** the heroine of Shakespeare's *Merchant of Venice*, who, in one scene, disguises herself as a lawyer. **2.** a woman lawyer.

por·ti·co (pōr′tə kō′), *n.*, *pl.* -**coes**, -**cos**. a structure consisting of a roof supported by columns or piers, usually attached to a building as a porch, but sometimes detached. [t. It., t. L: m. *porticus* porch, portico]

por·tiere (pōr tyâr′, -tĭ′âr′; *Fr.* pōr tyĕr′), *n.* a curtain hung at a doorway, either to replace the door or merely for decoration. Also, **por·tière′**. [t. F]

por·tion (pōr′shən), *n.* **1.** a part of any whole, whether actually separated from it or not: *a portion of the manuscript is illegible*. **2.** the part of a whole allotted to or belonging to a person or group; a share. **3.** a quantity of food served for one person. **4.** the part of an estate that goes to an heir or next of kin. **5.** the money, goods, or estate which a woman brings to her husband at marriage; a dowry. **6.** that which is allotted to a person by God or fate. —*v.t.* **7.** to divide into or distribute in portions or shares; parcel (fol. by *out*). **8.** to furnish with a portion, inheritance, or dowry. **9.** to provide with a lot or fate. [ME *porcion*, t. OF, t. L: m.s. *portio* share, part; akin to L *pars* part] —**por′-tion·less**, *adj.* —**Syn. 1.** See **part**.

por·tion·er (pōr′shən ər), *n.* one who divides or holds in shares.

Port Jack·son (jăk′sən), an inlet of the Pacific in SE Australia, forming the excellent harbor of Sydney.

Port·land (pōrt′lənd), *n.* **1.** a seaport in NW Oregon at the confluence of the Willamette and Columbia rivers. 372,676 (1960). **2.** a seaport in SW Maine, on Casco Bay. 72,566 (1960).

Portland cement, a kind of hydraulic cement usually made by burning a mixture of limestone and clay in a kiln. [named for Portland Peninsula, Dorsetshire, England]

Port Lou·is (lōō′ĭs, lōō′ĭ), a seaport in and the capital of Mauritius, in the Indian Ocean, E of Madagascar. 94,638 (1955).

port·ly (pōrt′lĭ), *adj.*, -**lier**, -**liest**. **1.** large in person; stout; corpulent. **2.** stately, dignified, or imposing: *she was a portly and impressive lady*. [f. PORT⁵, n. + -LY] —**port′li·ness**, *n.*

port·man·teau (pōrt măn′tō), *n.*, *pl.* -**teaus**, -**teaux**. *Chiefly Brit.* a bag or case to carry clothing, etc., in when traveling, orig. one designed for carrying on horseback. [t. F: m. *portemanteau* cloak carrier. See PORT, MANTLE]

portmanteau word, a word made by telescoping or blending two other words, as *brunch* for *breakfast* and *lunch*. See **blend** (def. 8).

Port Mores·by (mōrz′bĭ), a seaport in SE New Guinea: capital of the merged Australian territories of Papua and New Guinea; important Allied base in World War II. 3688 (1954).

Por·to (pōr′tōō), *n.* Portuguese name of **Oporto**.

Por·to A·le·gre (pōr′tōō ä lĕ′grə), a seaport in S Brazil. 450,000 (est. 1952).

Por·to·bel·lo (pōr′tō bĕl′ō), *n.* a small seaport on the Caribbean coast of Panama, NE of Colón: harbor discovered and named by Columbus, 1502; a principal city of Spanish colonial America.

port of entry, port¹ (def. 3).

Port-of-Spain (pōrt′əv spān′), *n.* the capital of Trinidad and Tobago; seaport of Trinidad. 93,954 (1960).

Por·to No·vo (pōr′tō nō′vō), a seaport in W Africa; former capital of Dahomey. 31,500 (1957).

Por·to Ri·co (pōr′tō rē′kō), Puerto Rico.

Port Phil·lip Bay (fĭl′ĭp), a bay in SE Australia: the harbor of Melbourne. 31 mi. long; ab. 20 mi. wide.

por·trait (pōr′trāt, -trĭt), *n.* **1.** a likeness of a person, especially of the face, usually made from life. **2.** a verbal picture, now usually of a person. [t. F, orig. pp. of *portraire*, g. L *prōtrahere* portray, bring forward]

por·trait·ist (pōr′trā tĭst), *n.* a portrait painter.

por·trai·ture (pōr′trĭ chər), *n.* **1.** the art of portraying. **2.** a pictorial representation; a portrait. **3.** a verbal picture. [ME *purtreyture*, t. OF: m. *portraiture*, der. *portrait* PORTRAIT]

por·tray (pōr trā′), *v.t.* **1.** to represent by a drawing, painting, carving, or the like. **2.** to represent dramatically, as on the stage. **3.** to depict in words; describe graphically. [ME, t. OF: s. *portraire*, g. LL *prōtrahere* depict, L draw forth] —**por·tray′a·ble**, *adj.* —**por·tray′er**, *n.* —**Syn. 1, 3.** picture, delineate. See **depict**.

por·tray·al (pōr trā′əl), *n.* **1.** the act of portraying. **2.** a representation portraying something.

por·tress (pōr′trĭs), *n.* a female porter or doorkeeper.

Port Roy·al (roi′əl), **1.** a village in S South Carolina, on Port Royal island: colonized by French Huguenots, 1562. **2.** a historic town in SE Jamaica at the entrance of Kingston harbor: a former capital of Jamaica. **3.** the name of Annapolis Royal while under French rule.

Port Sa·id (sä ēd′), a seaport in NE Egypt at the Mediterranean end of the Suez Canal. 186,300 (est. 1952).

Ports·mouth (pōrts′məth), *n.* **1.** a seaport in S England, on the English Channel: chief British naval station. 233,545 (est. 1951). **2.** a seaport in SE Virginia: navy yard. 114,773 (1960). **3.** a seaport in SE New Hampshire: naval base; Russian-Japanese peace treaty, 1905. 25,833 (1960). **4.** a city in S Ohio, on the Ohio river. 33,637 (1960).

Por·tu·gal (pōr′chə gəl; *Port.* pōr′tōō gäl′), a republic in SW Europe, on the Iberian Peninsula W of Spain. (Including the Azores and the Madeira Islands) 8,837,000 (est. 1956); 35,414 sq. mi. *Cap.:* Lisbon.

Por·tu·guese (pōr′chə gēz′, -gēs′), *adj.* **1.** of or pertaining to Portugal, its people, or their language. —*n.* **2.** a native or inhabitant of Portugal. **3.** the Romance language of Portugal and Brazil.

Portuguese East Africa, Mozambique (def. 1).

Portuguese Guinea, a Portuguese overseas territory on the W coast of Africa between Guinea and Senegal. 540,000 (est. 1954); 13,948 sq. mi. *Cap.:* Bissau.

Portuguese India, a Portuguese overseas territory on the W coast of India, consisting of the districts of Gôa, Damão, and Diu. 643,000 (est. 1954); 1538 sq. mi. *Cap.:* Gôa.

Portuguese man-of-war, any of several large oceanic hydrozoans of the genus *Physalia*, having a large, bladderlike structure by which they are buoyed up and from which depend numerous processes.

Portuguese West Africa, Angola.

por·tu·lac·a (pōr′chə lăk′ə), *n.* any plant of the genus *Portulaca*, which comprises herbs with thick, succulent leaves and variously colored flowers, as *P. grandiflora*, cultivated in gardens, and *P. oleracea*, the common purslane. [NL, t. L: purslane]

por·tu·la·ca·ceous (pōr′chə lə kā′shəs), *adj.* belonging to the *Portulacaceae*, or portulaca family of plants.

pos., **1.** positive. **2.** possessive.

po·sa·da (pō sä′dä), *n.* Spanish. lodging; an inn.

pose¹ (pōz), *v.*, **posed**, **posing**, *n.* —*v.i.* **1.** to affect a particular character as with a view to the impression made on others. **2.** to present oneself before others: *to pose as a judge of literature*. **3.** to assume or hold a position or attitude for some artistic purpose. —*v.t.* **4.** to place in a suitable position or attitude for a picture, tableau, or the like: *to pose a group for a photograph*. **5.** to assert, state, or propound: *to pose a hard problem*. **6.** *Archaic.* to put or place. —*n.* **7.** attitude or posture of body: *her pose had a kind of defiance in it*. **8.** attitude assumed in thought or conduct. **9.** the act or period of posing, as for a picture. **10.** a position or attitude assumed in posing, or exhibited by a figure in a picture, sculptural work, tableau, or the like. **11.** a studied attitude or mere affectation, as of some character, quality, sentiment, or course: *his liberalism is all a pose*. [ME t. OF: m. *poser*, g. LL *pausāre* lay down (same due to confusion with L *pōnere* place, put), in L halt, cease] —**Syn. 7.** See **position**.

pose² (pōz), *v.t.*, **posed**, **posing**. **1.** to embarrass by a difficult question or problem. **2.** *Obs.* to examine by putting questions. [aphetic var. of. obs. *appose*, var. of OPPOSE, used in sense of L *appōnere* put to]

Po·sei·don (pō sī′dən), *n.* the Greek god of the sea, identified by the Romans with Neptune.

Po·sen (pō′zən), a city in W Poland, on the Warta river. 355,000 (est. 1954). Polish, *Poznań*.

pos·er¹ (pō′zər), *n.* one who poses. [f. POSE¹ + -ER¹]

pos·er² (pō′zər), *n.* a question or problem that poses. [f. POSE² + -ER¹]

po·seur (pō zûr′; *Fr.* pō zœr′), *n.* one who affects a particular pose (def. 11) to impress others. [t. F, der. *poser* POSE¹]

pos·it (pŏz′ĭt), *v.t.* **1.** to place, put, or set. **2.** to lay down or assume as a fact or principle; affirm; postulate. [t. L: s. *positus*, pp., placed]

po·si·tion (pəzĭsh′ən), *n.* **1.** condition with reference to place; location. **2.** a place occupied or to be occupied; site: *a fortified position.* **3.** proper or appropriate place: *out of position.* **4.** situation or condition, esp. with relation to circumstances: *to be in an awkward position.* **5.** status or standing. **6.** high standing, as in society. **7.** a post of employment: *a position in a bank.* **8.** manner of being placed, disposed, or arranged: *the relative position of the hands of a clock.* **9.** posture or attitude of body. **10.** mental attitude; way of viewing a matter: *one's position on a public question.* **11.** condition (of affairs, etc.). **12.** the act of positing. **13.** that which is posited. **14.** *Anc. Pros.* the situation of a short vowel before two or more consonants or their equivalent, making the syllable metrically long. —*v.t.* **15.** to put in a particular or appropriate position; place. **16.** to determine the position of; locate. [ME, t. L: s. *positio.* Cf. POSIT, POSE[1]] —**po·si′tion·al,** *adj.*

—**Syn. 1.** station, place, locality, spot. **7.** POSITION, JOB, PLACE, SITUATION refer to a post of employment. POSITION is any employment, though usually above manual labor: *position as clerk.* JOB is colloquial for POSITION, and applies to any work from lowest to highest in an organization: *a job as fireman, as manager.* PLACE and SITUATION are both mainly used today in reference to a POSITION that is desired or being applied for; SITUATION is the general word in the business world *Situations Wanted;* PLACE is used rather of domestic employment: *she is looking for a place as a housekeeper.* —**Syn. 9.** POSITION, POSTURE, ATTITUDE, POSE refer to an arrangement or disposal of the body or its parts. POSITION is the general word for the arrangement of the body: *in a sitting position.* POSTURE is usually an assumed arrangement of the body: *an erect posture, a relaxed posture.* ATTITUDE is often a posture assumed for imitative effect or the like, but may be one adopted for a purpose (as that of a fencer or a tightrope walker): *an attitude of prayer.* A POSE is an attitude assumed, in most cases, for artistic effect: *an attractive pose.*

pos·i·tive (pŏz′ətĭv), *adj.* **1.** explicitly laid down or expressed: *a positive declaration.* **2.** arbitrarily laid down; determined by enactment or convention (opposed to *natural*): *positive law.* **3.** admitting of no question: *positive proof.* **4.** stated; express; emphatic. **5.** confident in opinion or assertion, as a person; fully assured. **6.** overconfident or dogmatic. **7.** without relation to or comparison with other things; absolute (opposed to *relative* and *comparative*). **8.** *Colloq.* downright; out-and-out. **9.** possessing an actual force, being, existence, etc. **10.** *Philos.* **a.** constructive and sure, rather than skeptical. **b.** concerned with or based on matters of experience: *positive philosophy.* See **positivism** (def. 3). **11.** practical; not speculative or theoretical. **12.** consisting in or characterized by the presence or possession of distinguishing or marked qualities or features (opposed to *negative*): *light is positive, darkness negative.* **13.** denoting the presence of such qualities, as a term. **14.** measured or proceeding in a direction assumed as that of increase, progress, or onward motion. **15.** *Elect.* denoting or pertaining to the kind of electricity developed on glass when rubbed with silk, or the kind of electricity present at that pole where electrons enter, or return to, an electric generator; having a deficiency of electrons. **16.** *Chem.* (of an element or radical) basic. **17.** *Photog.* showing the lights and shades as seen in the original, as a print from a negative. **18.** *Gram.* **a.** denoting the initial degree of the comparison of adjectives and adverbs, as English *smooth* in contrast to *smoother* and *smoothest.* **b.** having or pertaining to the function or meaning of this degree of comparison. **19.** *Math.* denoting a quantity greater than zero. **20.** measured or proceeding in a direction assumed as that of increase, progress, or onward motion. **21.** *Biol.* oriented or moving towards the focus of excitation: *a positive tropism.* **22.** *Bacteriol.* (of blood, affected tissue, etc.) showing the presence of an organism which causes a disease. **23.** *Mach.* noting or pertaining to a process or machine part having a fixed or certain operation, esp. as the result of elimination of play, free motion, etc.: *positive lubrication.*
—*n.* **24.** something positive. **25.** a positive quality or characteristic. **26.** a positive quantity or symbol. **27.** *Photog.* a positive picture. **28.** *Gram.* **a.** the positive degree. **b.** a form in it.
[t. L: m.s. *positīvus;* r. ME *positif,* t. OF] —**pos′i·tive·ly,** *adv.* —**pos′i·tive·ness,** *n.* —**Syn. 1.** See **sure.**

pos·i·tiv·ism (pŏz′ətĭvĭz′əm), *n.* **1.** state or quality of being positive; definiteness; assurance. **2.** dogmatism. **3.** a philosophical system founded by Comte, concerned with positive facts and phenomena, and excluding speculation upon ultimate causes or origins. —**pos′i·tiv·ist,** *adj., n.* —**pos′i·tiv·is′tic,** *adj.*

pos·i·tron (pŏz′ətrŏn′), *n. Physics.* a particle of positive electricity with a mass equal to that of the electron.

poss., **1.** possession. **2.** possessive.

pos·se (pŏs′ĭ), *n.* **1.** posse comitatus. **2.** a body or force armed with legal authority. [t. ML: power, force, n. use of L inf., to be able, have power. See POTENT]

pos·se com·i·ta·tus (pŏs′ĭ kŏm′ətā′təs), **1.** the body of men that a peace officer is empowered to call to assist him in preserving the peace, making arrests, and serving writs. **2.** a body of men so called into service. [ML: force of the county]

pos·sess (pəzĕs′), *v.t.* **1.** to have as property; to have belonging to one. **2.** to hold or to occupy. **3.** to have as a faculty, quality, or the like: *to possess courage.* **4.** to have knowledge of. **5.** to impart; inform; familiarize. **6.** *Archaic.* to seize or take. **7.** *Archaic.* to gain or win. **8.** to keep or maintain (oneself, one's mind, etc.) in a certain state, as of peace, patience, etc. **9.** to maintain control over (oneself, one's mind, etc.). **10.** (of a spirit, esp. an evil one) to occupy and control, or dominate from within, as a person. **11.** (of a feeling, idea, etc.) to dominate or actuate after the manner of such a spirit. **12.** to make (one) owner, holder, or master, as of property, information, etc. **13.** to cause to be dominated or influenced, as by a feeling, idea, etc.; imbue (*with*). [back formation from *possessor,* ME *possessour,* t. L: m. *possessor*] —**pos·ses′sor,** *n.* —**pos·ses′sor·ship′,** *n.*

pos·ses·sion (pəzĕsh′ən), *n.* **1.** act or fact of possessing. **2.** state of being possessed. **3.** ownership. **4.** *Law.* actual holding or occupancy, either with or without rights of ownership. **5.** a thing possessed. **6.** (*pl.*) property or wealth. **7.** a territorial dominion of a state. **8.** control over oneself, one's mind, etc. **9.** domination or actuation by a feeling, idea, etc. **10.** the feeling or idea itself. [ME, t. L: s. *possessio*] —**Syn. 2.** See **custody.**

pos·ses·sive (pəzĕs′ĭv), *adj.* **1.** of or pertaining to possession or ownership. **2.** *Gram.* **a.** denoting a possessor: *a possessive pronoun or adjective.* **b.** (in some languages) denoting a case that indicates possession and similar relations, as *John's hat, your book.* **c.** similar to such a case form in function or meaning, as *the head of the horse.* See **periphrastic.** —*n.* **3.** *Gram.* **a.** possessive form. **b.** the possessive case. —**pos·ses′sive·ly,** *adv.* —**pos·ses′sive·ness,** *n.*

pos·ses·so·ry (pəzĕs′ərĭ), *adj.* **1.** pertaining to a possessor or to possession. **2.** arising from possession: *a possessory interest.* **3.** having possession.

pos·set (pŏs′ĭt), *n.* a drink made of hot milk curdled with ale, wine, or the like, often sweetened and spiced. [late ME *poshote, possot,* ? OE **poswǣt* drink good for cold, f. *pos* cold in the head + *wǣt* drink]

pos·si·bil·i·ty (pŏs′əbĭl′ətĭ), *n., pl.* **-ties.** **1.** state or fact of being possible: *the possibility of error.* **2.** a possible thing or person.

pos·si·ble (pŏs′əbəl), *adj.* **1.** that may or can be, exist, happen, be done, be used, etc.: *no possible cure.* **2.** that may be true or a fact, or may perhaps be the case, as something concerning which one has no knowledge to the contrary: *it is possible that he went.* [ME, t. L: m.s. *possibilis*]
—**Syn. 1.** POSSIBLE, FEASIBLE, PRACTICABLE refer to that which may come about or take place without prevention by serious obstacles. That which is POSSIBLE is naturally able or even likely to happen, other circumstances being equal: *a new source of plutonium may be possible.* FEASIBLE refers to the ease with which something can be done and implies a high degree of desirability for doing it: *this plan is the most feasible.* PRACTICABLE applies to that which can be done with the means which are at hand, and conditions being what they are: *we ascended the slope as far as was practicable.*

pos·si·bly (pŏs′əblĭ), *adv.* **1.** perhaps or maybe. **2.** in a possible manner. **3.** by any possibility.

pos·sum (pŏs′əm), *n.* **1.** *U.S. Colloq.* opossum. **2. play possum,** *U.S. Colloq.* to feign; dissemble. **3.** *Australian.* any of many kinds of phalangers, esp. of the genus *Trichosurus.*

post[1] (pōst), *n.* **1.** a strong piece of timber, metal, or the like, set upright as a support, a point of attachment, a place for displaying notices, etc. —*v.t.* **2.** to affix (a notice, etc.) to a post, wall, or the like. **3.** to bring to public notice by or as by a placard: *to post a reward.* **4.** to denounce by a public notice or declaration: *to post a person as a coward.* **5.** to enter the name of in a published list. **6.** to publish the name of (a ship) as missing or lost. **7.** to placard (a wall, etc.) with notices or bills. [ME and OE, t. L: s. *postis*]

post[2] (pōst), *n.* **1.** a position of duty, employment, or trust to which one is assigned or appointed: *a diplomatic post.* **2.** the station, or the round or beat, of a soldier, sentry, or other person on duty: *the nurse's post.* **3.** a military station with permanent buildings. **4.** the body of troops occupying a military station. **5.** *U.S.* a local unit of a veterans' organization. **6.** a trading post. **7.** a place in the stock exchange where a particular stock is traded in. **8.** (in the British army) either of two bugle calls (**first post** and **last post**) giving notice of the hour for retiring, as for the night. —*v.t.* **9.** to station at a post or place as a sentry or for some other purpose. **10.** *Mil., Naval.* (formerly) to appoint to a post of command. [t. F: m. *poste,* t. It.: m. *posto,* g. L *positus,* pp., placed, put. Cf. POSITION] —**Syn. 2.** See **appointment.**

post[3] (pōst), *n.* **1.** *Chiefly Brit.* a single dispatch or delivery of mail. **2.** *Chiefly Brit.* the mail itself. **3.** *Chiefly Brit.* the letters, etc., coming to a single person or recipient. **4.** *Chiefly Brit.* an established service or system for the conveyance of letters, etc., esp. under governmental authority. **5.** *Brit.* a post office. **6.** *Brit.* a mailbox. **7.** a title of a newspaper: *the Washington Post.* **8.** one of a series of stations along a route, for furnishing relays of men and horses for carrying letters, etc. **9.** one who travels express, esp. over a fixed route with letters, etc. **10.** (*Brit.* except in *post octavo*) a size of paper, about 16 by 20 inches.
—*v.t.* **11.** *Chiefly Brit.* to place in a post office or a mailbox for transmission; to mail. **12.** *Bookkeeping.* **a.** to transfer (an entry or item), as from the journal to the

b., blend of, blended; c., cognate with; d., dialect, dialectal; der., derived from; f., formed from; g., going back to; m., modification of; r., replacing; s., stem of; t., taken from; ?, perhaps. See the full key on inside cover.

ledger. **b.** to enter (an item) in due place and form. **c.** to make all the requisite entries in (the ledger, etc.). —*v.i.* **13.** to travel with post horses, by carriage, etc. **14.** to travel with speed; go or pass rapidly; hasten. **15.** to supply with up-to-date information; to inform: *to be well posted on current events.* —*adv.* **16.** by post or courier. **17.** with post horses, or by posting. **18.** with speed or haste; post haste. [t. F: m. *poste*, t. It.: m. *posta*, g. *posita*, pp., fem., placed, put. Cf. POST]

post-, a prefix meaning "behind," "after," occurring orig. in words from the Latin, but now freely used as an English formative: *post-Elizabethan, postfix, postgraduate.* Cf. ante- and pre-. [t. L, repr. *post*, adv. and prep.]

Post (pōst), *n.* **1.** George Browne, 1837–1913. U.S. architect. **2.** Emily Price, 1873(?)–1960. U.S. writer on social etiquette.

post·age (pōs′tĭj), *n.* the charge for the conveyance of a letter or other matter sent by post or mail (ordinarily prepaid by means of a stamp or stamps).

postage stamp, an official stamp in the form of a design on an envelope, etc., or a printed adhesive label to be affixed to a letter, etc., as evidence of prepayment of a designated postage.

post·al (pōs′təl), *adj.* **1.** of or pertaining to the post or mail service. —*n.* **2.** U.S. *Colloq.* a postal card.

postal card, **1.** a card with a printed governmental stamp, for correspondence at a rate lower than that for letters. **2.** an unofficial post card.

post·ax·i·al (pōst ăk′sĭ əl), *adj. Anat., Zool.* behind the body axis, as the posterior part of the limb axis.

post bel·lum (pōst bĕl′əm), after the war. [L]

post-bel·lum (pōst bĕl′əm), *adj.* occurring after the war, esp. the U.S. Civil War.

post·boy (pōst′boi′), *n.* **1.** a boy or man who rides post or carries mail. **2.** a postilion.

post card, **1.** a postal card with a printed governmental stamp. **2.** an unofficial card, often pictorial, mailable when bearing an adhesive postage stamp.

post chaise, a chaise or four-wheeled coach for hire, for speedy traveling: used in the 18th and early in the 19th centuries

post·date (p st′dāt′), *v.t.*, **-dated, -dating. 1.** to give a later date to othan the true date. **2.** to date (an instrument such as a check or invoice) with a date later than the current date. **3.** to follow in time.

post·di·lu·vi·an (pōst′dĭ lōō′vĭ ən), *adj.* **1.** existing or occurring after the Flood. —*n.* **2.** one who has lived since the Flood.

post·er[1] (pōs′tər), *n.* **1.** a placard or bill posted or for posting in some public place. **2.** one who posts bills, etc. [f. POST[1] v. + -ER[1]]

post·er[2] (pōs′tər), *n.* a post horse. [f. POST[3]- + ER[1]]

poste res·tante (pōst′ rĕs tänt′; *Fr.* pōst rĕs tänt′), **1.** a direction written on mail which is to remain at the post office until called for. **2.** *Chiefly Brit.* a department in charge of such mail. [F: standing post]

pos·te·ri·or (pŏs tĭr′ĭ ər), *adj.* **1.** situated behind, or hinder (opposed to *anterior*). **2.** coming after in order, as in a series. **3.** coming after in time; later; subsequent (sometimes fol. by *to*). **4.** *Zool.* pertaining to the caudal end of the body. **5.** *Anat.* of or pertaining to the dorsal side of man. **6.** *Bot.* (of an axillary flower) on the side next to the main axis. —*n.* **7.** (*sometimes pl.*) the hinder parts of the body; the buttocks. [t. L, compar. of *posterus* coming after] —**pos·te′ri·or·ly,** *adv.* —Syn. **1.** See back[1].

pos·te·ri·or·i·ty (pŏs tĭr′ĭ ôr′ə tĭ, -ŏr′-), *n.* posterior position or date.

pos·ter·i·ty (pŏs tĕr′ə tĭ), *n.* **1.** succeeding generations collectively. **2.** descendants collectively. [ME *posterite*, t. L: m.s. *posteritas*]

pos·tern (pōs′tərn, pŏs′-), *n.* **1.** a back door or gate. **2.** any lesser or private entrance. —*adj.* **3.** like or pertaining to a postern. [ME, t. OF: m. *posterne*, for *posterle*, g. LL *posterula*, dim. of L *posterus* behind]

Post Exchange, *U.S. Army.* a retail store on an army post selling extra provisions, etc.

post·ex·il·i·an (pōst′ĭg zĭl′ĭ ən, -ĭk sĭl′-), *adj.* subsequent to the Babylonian exile or captivity of the Jews. Also, **post′ex·il′ic.**

post·fix (*v.* pōst fĭks′; *n.* pōst′fĭks), *v.t.* **1.** to affix at the end of something; append; suffix. —*n.* **2.** something postfixed. **3.** *Rare.* a suffix. [f. POST- + FIX, modeled on PREFIX]

post-free (pōst′frē′), *Brit.* postpaid.

post·grad·u·ate (pōst grăj′ŏŏ ĭt, -āt′), *adj.* **1.** pertaining to or pursuing a course of study after graduation. —*n.* **2.** a postgraduate student.

post·haste (pōst′hāst′), *adv.* **1.** with all possible speed or expedition: *to come posthaste.* **2.** with the haste of a post. —*n.* **3.** *Archaic.* great haste. [f. POST[3] + HASTE]

post hoc, er·go prop·ter hoc (pōst hŏk′, ûr′gō prŏp′tər hŏk′), *Latin.* after this, therefore because of it (a formula designating an error in logic: taking for a cause something merely earlier in time).

post horse, a horse kept, as at a station on a post road, for the use of persons riding post or for hire by travelers.

post·hu·mous (pŏs′chŏŏ məs), *adj.* **1.** published after the death of the author. **2.** born after the death of the father. **3.** arising, existing, or continuing after one's death. [t. L: m. *posthumus*, erroneously (by assoc.

with *humus* earth, ground, as if referring to burial) for *postumus* last, posthumous (superl. adj.)] —**post′hu·mous·ly,** *adv.*

pos·tiche (pōs tēsh′), *adj.* **1.** superadded, esp. inappropriately, as a sculptural or architectural ornament. **2.** artificial, counterfeit, or false. —*n.* **3.** an imitation or substitute. **4.** pretense. [F, t. It.: m. (*ap*)*posticcio,* g. L *appositicius* put on, factitious, false]

pos·ti·cous (pōs tī′kəs), *adj. Bot.* hinder; posterior. [t. L: m. *posticus*]

pos·til·ion (pōs tĭl′yən, pŏs-), *n.* one who rides the near horse of the leaders when four or more horses are used to draw a carriage, or who rides the near horse when only one pair is used. Also, *esp. Brit.*, **pos·til′lion.** [t. F: m. *postillon,* t. It.: m. *postiglione,* der. *posta* POST[3]]

post·im·pres·sion·ism (pōst′ĭm prĕsh′ə nĭz əm), *n.* the varied doctrines and methods of certain modern painters developed between 1875 and 1890, which rejected the casual and momentary effects and the naturalistic tendency of the impressionists, but accepted their use of pure color as a means of intensifying permanence and solidity (Cézanne), movement (Van Gogh), pattern (Gauguin), etc. —**post′im·pres′sion·ist,** *n.,* *adj.* —**post′im·pres′sion·is′tic,** *adj.*

post·lim·i·ny (pōst lĭm′ə nĭ), *n. Internat. Law.* the right by which persons and things taken in war are restored to their former status when coming again under the power of the nation to which they belonged. [t. L: m.s. *postliminium*]

post·lude (pōst′lōōd′), *n. Music.* **1.** a concluding piece or movement. **2.** a voluntary at the end of a church service. [f. POST- + m.s. L *lūdus* game; modeled on PRELUDE]

post·man (pōst′mən), *n., pl.* **-men. 1.** a postal employee who carries and delivers mail. **2.** *Obs.* courier.

post·mark (pōst′märk′), *n.* **1.** an official mark stamped on a letter or other mail, to cancel the postage stamp, indicate the place and date of sending or of receipt, etc. —*v.t.* **2.** to stamp with a postmark.

post·mas·ter (pōst′măs′tər, -mäs′tər), *n.* **1.** the official in charge of a post office. **2.** the master of a station for furnishing post horses for travelers. —**post′mas′ter·ship′,** *n.*

postmaster general, *pl.* **postmasters general.** the executive head of the postal system of a country.

post·me·rid·i·an (pōst′mə rĭd′ĭ ən), *adj.* **1.** occurring after noon. **2.** of or pertaining to the afternoon.

post me·rid·i·em (pōst mə rĭd′ĭ ĕm′), after noon. used in specifying the hour, usually in the abbreviated form P.M. or p.m.: *10 P.M.* [L]

post·mil·len·ni·al (pōst′mə lĕn′ĭ əl), *adj.* of or pertaining to the period following the millennium.

post·mil·len·ni·al·ism (pōst′mə lĕn′ĭ ə lĭz′əm), *n.* the doctrine or belief that the second coming of Christ will follow the millennium. —**post′mil·len′ni·al·ist,** *n.*

post·mis·tress (pōst′mĭs′trĭs), *n.* a female postmaster (def. 1).

post-mor·tem (pōst môr′təm), *adj.* **1.** subsequent to death, as an examination of the body. —*n.* **2.** a postmortem examination. [t. L: after death]

post-mortem examination, *Med.* an autopsy.

post·na·tal (pōst nā′təl), *adj.* subsequent to birth.

post-o·bit (pōst ō′bĭt, -ŏb′ĭt), *adj.* effective after a particular person's death. [short for POST OBITUM]

post-obit bond, a bond paying a sum of money after the death of some specified person.

post ob·i·tum (pōst ŏb′ə təm), *Latin.* after death.

post office, **1.** an office or station of a governmental postal system, for receiving, distributing, and transmitting mail, selling postage stamps, and other service. **2.** (*often cap.*) the governmental department charged with the conveyance of letters, etc., by post.

post·or·bit·al (pōst ôr′bĭ təl), *adj. Anat., Zool.* located behind the orbit or socket of the eye.

post·paid (pōst′pād′), *adj.* with the postage prepaid.

post·pone (pōst pōn′), *v.,* **-poned, -poning.** —*v.t.* **1.** to put off to a later time; defer: *he postponed his departure an hour.* **2.** to place after in order of importance or estimation; subordinate: *to postpone private ambitions to the public welfare.* —*v.i.* **3.** *Med.* to be put off to a later time. [t. L: m.s. *postpōnere*] —**post·pon′a·ble,** *adj.* —**post·pone′ment,** *n.* —**post·pon′er,** *n.* —Syn. **1.** See defer.

post·po·si·tion (pōst′pə zĭsh′ən), *n.* **1.** the act of placing after. **2.** the state of being so placed. **3.** *Gram.* a word placed after another as a modifier or to show its relation to other parts of the sentence. Examples: *attorney general, the man afloat.* [f. POST- + POSITION. Cf. PREPOSITION]

post·pos·i·tive (pōst pŏz′ə tĭv), *Gram.* —*adj.* **1.** placed after. —*n.* **2.** a postposition. —**post·pos′i·tive·ly,** *adv.*

post·pran·di·al (pōst prăn′dĭ əl), *adj.* after-dinner. [f. POST- + s. L *prandium* meal + -AL[1]]

post·rid·er (pōst′rī′dər), *n.* one who rides post; a mounted mail carrier.

post road, **1.** a road with stations for furnishing horses for postriders, mail coaches, or travelers. **2.** a road or route over which mail is carried.

post·script (pōst′skrĭpt′, pōs′skrĭpt′), *n.* **1.** a paragraph added to a letter which has already been concluded and signed by the writer. **2.** any supplementary part. [t. L: s. *postscriptum,* pp. neut., written after]

pos·tu·lant (pŏs′chə lənt), n. **1.** one who asks or applies for something. **2.** a candidate, esp. for admission into a religious order. [t. L: s. *postulans*, ppr., demanding]

pos·tu·late (v. pŏs′chə lāt′; n. pŏs′chə lĭt, -lāt′), v., **-lated, -lating,** n. —v.t. **1.** to ask, demand, or claim. **2.** to claim or assume the existence or truth of, esp. as a basis for reasoning. **3.** to assume without proof, or as self-evident; take for granted. **4.** Geom. to assume; to take as an axiom. —n. **5.** something postulated or assumed without proof as a basis for reasoning or as self-evident. **6.** a fundamental principle. **7.** a necessary condition; a prerequisite. [t. L: m.s. *postulātum*, prop. pp. neut., thing requested] —**pos′tu·la′tion,** n.

pos·ture (pŏs′chər), n., v., **-tured, -turing.** —n. **1.** the relative disposition of the various parts of anything. **2.** the position of the body and limbs as a whole: *a change in posture, a sitting posture.* **3.** an affected or unnatural attitude, or a contortion of the body: *antic postures and gestures.* **4.** mental or spiritual attitude. **5.** position, condition, or state, esp. of affairs. —v.t. **6.** to place in a particular posture or attitude; dispose in postures. —v.i. **7.** to assume a particular posture. **8.** to assume affected or unnatural postures; bend or contort the body in various ways, specif. in public performing. **9.** to act in an affected or artificial way, as if for show; pose for effect. [t. F, g. L *positūra*] —**pos′tur·al,** adj. —**pos′tur·er,** n. —Syn. 2. See **position.**

pos·tur·ize (pŏs′chə rīz′), v.i., **-ized, -izing.** to posture; pose.

post·war (pōst′wôr′), adj. after the war: *postwar trade.*

po·sy (pō′zĭ), n., pl. **-sies. 1.** a flower; a nosegay or bouquet. **2.** Archaic. a brief motto or the like, such as is inscribed within a ring. [syncopated var. of POESY]

pot¹ (pŏt), n., v., **potted, potting.** —n. **1.** an earthen, metallic, or other container, usually round and deep, used for domestic or other purposes. **2.** such a vessel with its contents. **3.** a potful. **4.** a potful of liquor. **5.** liquor or drink. **6.** a wicker vessel for trapping fish or crustaceans. **7.** Brit. a chimney pot. **8.** Slang. a large sum of money. **9.** the aggregate of bets at stake at one time, as in cardplaying, esp. poker. **10.** a pot shot. **11.** a liquid measure, usually equal to a pint or quart. **12. go to pot,** to deteriorate. —v.t. **13.** to put into a pot. **14.** to put up and preserve (food) in a pot. **15.** to cook in a pot; stew. **16.** Hunting. **a.** to shoot (game birds) on the ground or water, or (game animals) at rest, instead of in flight or running. **b.** to shoot for food, not for sport. **17.** Colloq. to capture, secure, or win. —v.i. **18.** Slang. to take a pot shot; shoot. [ME and OE *pott*, c. MLG *pot*. Cf. F *pot* (? t. G)]

pot² (pŏt), n. Scot. and N. Eng. a deep hole; a pit. [ME; ? same as POT¹]

pot., potential.

po·ta·ble (pō′tə bəl), adj. **1.** fit or suitable for drinking. —n. **2.** (usually pl.) anything drinkable. [t. LL: m.s. *pōtābilis*, der. L *pōtāre* drink]

po·tage (pō täzh′; Fr. pô täzh′), n. French. soup.

po·tam·ic (pō tăm′ĭk), adj. of or pertaining to streams.

pot·ash (pŏt′ăsh′), n. **1.** potassium carbonate, esp. the crude impure form obtained from wood ashes. **2.** caustic potash. **3.** the oxide of potassium, K₂O. **4.** potassium: *carbonate of potash.* [earlier *pot-ashes*, pl., trans. of early D *potasschen*]

po·tas·sic (pə tăs′ĭk), adj. of, pertaining to, or containing potassium.

po·tas·si·um (pə tăs′ĭ əm), n. Chem. a silvery-white metallic element, which oxidizes rapidly in the air, and whose compounds are used as fertilizer and in special hard glasses. Symbol: K; at. wt.: 39.096; at. no.: 19; sp. gr.: 0.86 at 20°C. [t. s. NL *potassa* (t. F: m. *potasse*, a former equivalent of POTASH) + -IUM]

potassium bromide, a white crystalline compound, KBr, used in photography and medicinally as a sedative.

potassium carbonate, a white solid, K₂CO₃. used in the manufacture of glass, etc.

potassium cyanide, a white, crystalline, poisonous compound, KCN, used in metallurgy, medicine, and photography.

potassium dichromate, an orange-red crystalline compound, K₂Cr₂O₇, used in dyeing, photography, etc.

potassium hydroxide, a white caustic solid, KOH, used in making soft soap, etc.

potassium nitrate, saltpeter; a crystalline compound, KNO₃, used in gunpowder, fertilizers, preservatives, and medicinally as a diaphoretic. It is produced by nitrification in soil.

potassium permanganate, a nearly black crystalline compound, KMnO₄, forming red-purple solutions in water: used as an oxidizing agent, disinfectant, etc.

po·ta·tion (pō tā′shən), n. **1.** the act of drinking. **2.** a drink or draft, esp. of alcoholic liquor. [t. L: s. *pōtātio*; r. ME *potacioun*, t. OF]

po·ta·to (pə tā′tō), n., pl. **-toes. 1.** the edible tuber (white potato or Irish potato) of a cultivated plant, *Solanum tuberosum.* **2.** the plant itself. **3.** sweet potato. [t. Sp.: m. *patata* white potato, var. of *batata* sweet potato, t. Haitian]

potato beetle, a widely distributed leaf beetle, *Leptinotarsa decemlineata*, one of the most serious agricultural pests in the world. Also, **potato bug.**

potato chip, a thin slice of potato fried until crisp, and usually salted and eaten cold.

po·ta·to·ry (pō′tə tōr′ĭ), adj. **1.** of, pertaining to, or given to drinking. **2.** Rare. potable. [t. L: m.s. *pōtātōrius*]

pot-au-feu (pô tō fœ′), n. French. boiled beef, broth, and vegetables. [F: lit., pot on the fire.]

pot·bel·ly (pŏt′bĕl′ĭ), n., pl. **-lies.** a distended or protuberant belly. —**pot′bel′lied,** adj.

pot·boil·er (pŏt′boi′lər), n. Colloq. a work of literature or art produced merely for the necessaries of life.

pot·boy (pŏt′boi′), n. Chiefly Brit. **1.** a boy or man who carries pots of beer, ale, etc., to customers. **2.** an assistant in a tavern, etc.

pot cheese, cottage cheese.

po·teen (pō tēn′), n. (in Ireland) illicitly distilled whiskey. Also, **potheen.** [t. Irish: m. *poitīn* small pot, dim. of *pota* pot]

Po·tem·kin (pō tĕm′kĭn; Russ. pŏ tyôm′kĭn), n. **Prince Grigori Aleksandrovich** (grĭ gô′rĭ ä lĕ ksän′drə vĭch), 1739–91, Russian statesman and favorite of Catherine II.

po·ten·cy (pō′tən sĭ), n., pl. **-cies. 1.** the quality of being potent. **2.** power or authority. **3.** powerfulness or effectiveness. **4.** strength or efficacy, as of a drug. **5.** a person or thing exerting power or influence. **6.** capability of development, or potentiality. Also, **po′tence.** [t. L: m.s. *potentia*]

po·tent (pō′tənt), adj. **1.** powerful; mighty. **2.** cogent, as reasons, motives, etc. **3.** producing powerful physical or chemical effects, as a drug. **4.** possessed of great power or authority. **5.** exercising great moral influence. **6.** having sexual power. [t. L: s. *potens*, ppr., being able, powerful] —**po′tent·ly,** adv. —**po′tent·ness,** n. —Syn. 1. See **powerful.**

po·ten·tate (pō′tən tāt′), n. one who possesses great power; a sovereign, monarch, or ruler. [t. L: m.s. *potentiātus* potentate, L power, dominion]

po·ten·tial (pə tĕn′shəl), adj. **1.** possible as opposed to actual. **2.** capable of being or becoming; latent. **3.** Gram. expressing possibility, as of a mode or model construction, as, I can go. **4.** Physics. denoting energy which is due to position or the like and not to motion, as that possessed by a raised weight (opposed to *kinetic*). **5.** Now Rare. potent. —n. **6.** a possibility or potentiality. **7.** Gram. a potential mode or construction, or a form therein. **8.** Elect. **a.** the electrification of a point near or within an electrified body, represented by the work hypothetically necessary to bring a unit of positive electricity from an infinite distance to that point. **b.** the relative electrification of a point or body with respect to some other electrification, e.g., that of the ground nearby or of the earth in general, taken as a base of reference. **9.** Math., Physics. a type of function from which the intensity of a field may be derived, usually by differentiation. [ME, t. ML: s. *potentiālis*] —Syn. 2. See **latent.**

po·ten·ti·al·i·ty (pə tĕn′shĭ ăl′ə tĭ), n., pl. **-ties. 1.** potential state or quality; possibility; latent power or capacity. **2.** something potential. [t. ML: m.s. *potentiālitas*]

po·ten·tial·ly (pə tĕn′shəl ĭ), adv. not actually, but possibly.

po·ten·til·la (pō′tən tĭl′ə), n. any plant of the rosaceous genus *Potentilla*, comprising herbs, or small shrubs, abundant in north temperate regions. [t. NL, f. s. L *potens* potent + -*illa* (dim. suffix)]

po·ten·ti·om·e·ter (pə tĕn′shĭ ŏm′ə tər), n. Elect. an instrument for measuring electromotive force or difference in potential. [f. POTENTI(AL), n., + -(o)-METER] —**po·ten·ti·o·met·ric** (pə tĕn′shĭ ō mĕt′rĭk), adj.

po·theen (pō thēn′), n. poteen.

poth·er (pŏth′ər), n. **1.** commotion; uproar. **2.** a disturbance or fuss. **3.** a choking or suffocating cloud, as of smoke or dust. —v.t., v.i. **4.** to worry; bother. [orig. uncert.]

pot·herb (pŏt′ûrb′, -hûrb′), n. any herb prepared as food by cooking in a pot, as spinach, or added as seasoning in cookery, as thyme.

pot·hole (pŏt′hōl′), n. **1.** a deep hole; a pit. **2.** a more or less cylindrical hole formed in rock by the grinding action of the detrital material in eddying water.

pot·hook (pŏt′hŏŏk′), n. **1.** a hook for suspending a pot or kettle over an open fire. **2.** an iron rod, usually curved, with a hook at the end, used to lift hot pots, irons, stove lids, etc. **3.** an S-shaped stroke in writing, esp. as made by children in learning to write.

pot·house (pŏt′hous′), n. Brit. a place where ale, beer, etc., is retailed; an alehouse.

pot·hunt·er (pŏt′hŭn′tər), n. **1.** one who hunts merely for food or profit, regardless of the rules of sport. **2.** one who takes part in contests merely to win prizes.

po·tiche (pō tēsh′), n., pl. **-tiches** (-tēsh′), a vase or jar, as of porcelain, with rounded or polygonal body narrowing at the top. [t. F, der. *pot* POT¹]

po·tion (pō′shən), n. **1.** a drink or draft, esp. one of a medicinal, poisonous, or magical kind. **2.** Rare. a beverage. [t. L: m.s. *pōtio*; r. ME *pocioun*, t. OF]

pot·latch (pŏt′lăch), n. **1.** (among some American Indians of the northern Pacific coast) **a.** a distribution of gifts. **b.** a winter celebration. **2.** a ceremonial feast at which gifts are bestowed on the guests and property destroyed in a competitive show of wealth. [t. N. Amer. Ind.: metathetic var. of Chinook *potshatl* gift]

---

b., blend of, blended; c., cognate with; d., dialect, dialectal; der., derived from; f., formed from; g., going back to;
m., modification of; r., replacing; s., stem of; t., taken from; ?, perhaps. See the full key on inside cover.

pot·luck (pŏt'lŭk'), n. whatever food happens to be at hand without special preparation or buying.

pot·man (pŏt'mən), n., pl. -men. Brit. a waiter.

pot marigold, the common marigold, *Calendula officinalis*, the flower heads of which are sometimes used in cookery for seasoning.

Po·to·mac (pə tō'mək), n. a river flowing from the Allegheny Mountains in West Virginia, between Maryland and Virginia, and past Washington, D.C., into Chesapeake Bay. 287 mi. from junction of forks.

po·to·roo (pō'tə rōō'), n. kangaroo rat.

Po·to·sí (pō'tō sē'), n. a city in S Bolivia: once a rich silver-mining center. 43,579 (1950); 13,022 ft. high.

pot·pie (pŏt'pī'), n. 1. a baked meat pie. 2. a stew, as of chicken or veal, with dumplings.

pot·pour·ri (pŏt pŏŏr'ī; Fr. pō pŏŏ rē'), n., pl. -ris. 1. a mixture of dried petals of roses or other flowers with spices, etc., kept in a jar for the fragrance. 2. a musical medley. 3. a collection of miscellaneous literary extracts. [t. F: rotten pot, trans. of Sp. *olla podrida*. See OLLA]

pot roast, beef which is browned, then cooked slowly in a covered pot, with very little water.

Pots·dam (pŏts'dăm; Ger. pōts'däm), n. a city in East Germany, near Berlin: formerly the residence of the German emperors; wartime conference of Truman, Churchill (later, Attlee), and Stalin, July–Aug., 1945. 117,571 (est. 1955).

pot·sherd (pŏt'shûrd'), n. a fragment or broken piece of earthenware. [f. POT¹ + *sherd*, var. of SHARD]

pot shot, 1. a shot fired at game merely for food, with little regard to skill or the rules of sport. 2. a shot at an animal or person within easy range, as from ambush.

pot·stone (pŏt'stōn'), n. a kind of soapstone, sometimes used for making pots and other household utensils.

pot·tage (pŏt'ĭj), n. a thick soup made of vegetables, without or with meat. [ME *potage*, t. OF, der. *pot* pot]

pot·ted (pŏt'ĭd), adj. 1. placed in a pot. 2. preserved or cooked in a pot. 3. Slang. drunk.

pot·ter¹ (pŏt'ər), n. one who makes earthen pots or other vessels. [ME; OE *pottere*, f. *pott* POT¹ + -*ere* -ER¹]

pot·ter² (pŏt'ər), v.i., n. Chiefly Brit. or Literary in U.S. putter¹. [appar. freq. of obs. or prov. *pote* push, poke, OE *potian* push, thrust. See PUT] —**pot'ter·er,** n. —**pot'ter·ing·ly,** adv.

Pot·ter (pŏt'ər), n. Paul, 1625–54, Dutch painter.

potter's field, a piece of ground reserved as a burial place for strangers and the friendless poor. See Matt. 27:7.

potter's wheel, a device with a rotating horizontal disk upon which clay is molded by a potter.

pot·ter·y (pŏt'ə rĭ), n., pl. -teries. 1. ware fashioned from clay or other earthy material and hardened by heat (sometimes used esp. of the coarser kinds): *Mexican pottery*. 2. a place where earthen pots or vessels are made. 3. the art or business of a potter; ceramics. [late ME, t. F: m. *poterie*, der. *potier* potter, der. *pot* pot]

pot·tle (pŏt'əl), n. 1. a former liquid measure equal to two quarts. 2. a pot or tankard of this capacity. 3. the wine, etc., in it. 4. liquor. 5. Chiefly Brit. a small container or basket, as for fruit. [ME *potel*, t. OF, dim. of *pot* POT¹]

Pott's disease (pŏts), Pathol. caries of the bodies of the vertebrae, often resulting in marked curvature of the spine, and usually associated with a tuberculosis infection. [named after Percival *Pott* (1714–88), British surgeon, who described it]

Potts·town (pŏts'toun'), n. a borough in SE Pennsylvania. 26,144 (1960).

Potts·ville (pŏts'vĭl), n. a city in E Pennsylvania. 21,659 (1960).

pot·ty (pŏt'ĭ), adj. Brit. Colloq. 1. paltry. 2. slightly insane.

pot-val·iant (pŏt'văl'yənt), adj. brave only when drunk.

pot-wal·lop·er (pŏt'wŏl'əpər, pŏt'wŏl'-), n. (before 1832, in some English boroughs) a man qualified for a parliamentary vote as a householder, the test being possession of his own fireplace. [alter. of *potwaller*, lit., potboiler, after *wallop*, v., boil vigorously]

pouch (pouch), n. 1. a bag, sack, or similar receptacle, esp. one for small articles. 2. a small moneybag. 3. (formerly) a bag or case for powder. 4. a cartridge box. 5. a bag for carrying mail. 6. something shaped like or resembling a bag or pocket. 7. Chiefly Scot. a pocket in a garment. 8. a baggy fold of flesh under the eye. 9. Anat., Zool. a baglike or pocketlike part; a sac or cyst, as the sac beneath the bill of pelicans, the saclike dilation of the cheeks of gophers, or (esp.) the receptacle for the young of marsupials. 10. Bot. a baglike cavity. —v.t. 11. to put into or enclose in a pouch, bag, or pocket; pocket. 12. to arrange (something) in pouchlike form. 13. Colloq. to supply the purse or pocket of, provide with money, or give a present of money to. 14. to submit to without protest. 15. (of a fish or bird) to swallow. —v.i. 16. to form a pouch or pouchlike cavity. [ME *pouche*, t. ONF, var. of OF *poche*, also *poque, poke* bag. Cf. POKE²]

pouched (poucht), adj. having a pouch, as the pelicans, gophers, and marsupials.

pouf (pŏŏf), n. 1. a kind of headdress worn by women in the latter part of the 18th century. 2. an arrangement of the hair over a pad. 3. a puff of material as an ornament in a dress or headdress. [t. F. Cf. PUFF]

Pough·keep·sie (pə kĭp'sĭ), n. a city in SE New York, on the Hudson: regatta. 38,330 (1960).

pou·lard (pŏŏ lärd'), n. 1. a hen spayed to improve the flesh for use as food. 2. a fatted hen. [t. F, der. *poule* hen. See PULLET]

poult (pōlt), n. the young of the domestic fowl, the turkey, the pheasant, or a similar bird. [ME *pult(e)*, syncopated var. of PULLET]

poul·ter·er (pōl'tərər), n. Chiefly Brit. a dealer in poultry. Also, Rare or Obs., **poul'ter.** [f. *poulter* poultry dealer (t. F: m. *pouletier*) + -ER¹]

poul·tice (pōl'tĭs), n., v., -ticed, -ticing. —n. 1. a soft, moist mass of bread, meal, herbs, etc., applied as a medicament to the body. —v.t. 2. to apply a poultice to. [orig. *pultes*, appar. pl. of L *puls* thick pap]

poul·try (pōl'trĭ), n. domestic fowls collectively, as chickens, turkeys, guinea fowls, ducks, and geese. [ME *pult(e)rie*, t. OF: m. *pouleterie*, ult. der. *poulet* fowl]

pounce¹ (pouns), v., pounced, pouncing, n. —v.i. 1. to swoop down suddenly and lay hold, as a bird does on its prey. 2. to spring, dash, or come suddenly. —v.t. 3. to seize with the talons. 4. to swoop down upon and seize suddenly, as a bird of prey does. —n. 5. the claw or talon of a bird of prey. 6. a sudden swoop, as on prey. [orig. uncert.]

pounce² (pouns), v.t., pounced, pouncing. to emboss (metal) by hammering on an instrument applied on the reverse side. [prob. same as POUNCE¹]

pounce³ (pouns), n., v., pounced, pouncing. —n. 1. a fine powder, as of cuttlebone, formerly used to prevent ink from spreading in writing, as over an erasure or an unsized paper, or to prepare parchment for writing. 2. a fine powder, usually charcoal, rubbed through a perforated pattern, for transferring a design. —v.t. 3. to sprinkle, smooth, or prepare with pounce. 4. to trace (a design) with pounce. 5. to finish the surface of (hats) by rubbing with sandpaper or the like. [t. F: m. *ponce*, ult. g. L *pūmex* PUMICE] —**pounc'er,** n.

pounce box, a small box with perforated lid for holding pounce powder for transferring designs, or for use in writing.

poun·cet box (poun'sĭt), a small perfume box with a perforated lid. [der. POUNCE² or POUNCE³]

pound¹ (pound), v.t. 1. to strike repeatedly and with great force, as with an instrument, the fist, heavy missiles, etc. 2. to produce (sound) by striking or thumping, or with an effect of thumping (often fol. by *out*): *to pound out a tune on a piano*. 3. to force (a way) by battering. 4. to crush by beating, as with an instrument; bray, pulverize, or triturate. —v.i. 5. to strike heavy blows repeatedly: *to pound on a door*. 6. to beat or throb violently, as the heart. 7. to give forth a sound of or as of thumps: *the drums pounded loudly*. 8. to walk or go with heavy steps; move along with force or vigor. —n. 9. act of pounding. 10. a heavy or forcible blow. 11. a thump. [ME *pounen*, OE *pūnian*; akin to D *puin* rubbish, LG *pün* fragments] —**pound'er,** n. —Syn. 1. See beat.

pound² (pound), n., pl. pounds, (collectively) pound. 1. a unit of weight and of mass, varying in different periods and countries. 2. (in the British Empire and the U.S.) either of two legally fixed units, the **pound avoirdupois** (of 7,000 grains, divided into 16 ounces) used for ordinary commodities, or the **pound troy** (of 5,760 grains, divided into 12 ounces) used for gold, silver, etc., and also serving as the basis of apothecaries' weight. 3. a British money of account (**pound sterling**) of the value of 20 shillings and equivalent at present to about $2.80 (denoted by the symbol £ before the numeral or sometimes *l.* after it, and orig. equivalent to a pound of silver). 4. a former Scottish money of account (**pound Scots**), orig. the equivalent of the pound sterling, but at the union of the crowns of England and Scotland in 1603 worth only one twelfth of the pound sterling. 5. the monetary unit of Israel, Lebanon, Syria, Egypt, and several countries in the British Commonwealth. 6. formerly, the Turkish lira. [ME and OE *pund*, t. L. m. *pondo* a pound, orig. *libra pondō* a pound in weight]

pound³ (pound), n. 1. an enclosure maintained by authority for confining trespassing or stray cattle, dogs, etc., or for keeping goods seized by distress. 2. an enclosure for sheltering, keeping, confining, or trapping animals. 3. an enclosure or trap for fish. 4. a place of confinement or imprisonment. —v.t. 5. to shut up in or as in a pound; impound; imprison. [ME and OE *pund*-. Cf. obs. *pind*, v., enclose, OE *pyndan*]

Pound (pound), n. 1. Ezra Loomis, born 1885, U.S. poet. 2. Louise, 1872–1958, U.S. scholar and linguist. 3. her brother, Roscoe, 1870–1964, U.S. legal scholar and writer.

pound·age¹ (poun'dĭj), n. a tax, commission, rate, etc., of so much per pound sterling or per pound weight. [f. POUND² + -AGE]

pound·age² (poun'dĭj), n. 1. confinement within an enclosure or within certain limits. 2. the fee demanded to free animals from a pound. [f. POUND³ + -AGE]

pound·al (poun'dəl), n. Physics. a unit of force: the force which, acting for one second on a mass of one pound, gives it a velocity of one foot per second.

ăct, āble, dâre, ärt; ĕbb, ēqual; ĭf, īce; hŏt, ōver, ôrder, oil, bŏŏk, ōōze, out; ŭp, ūse, ûrge; ə = a in alone; ch, chief; g, give; ng, ring; sh, shoe; th, thin; ŧh, that; zh, vision. See the full key on inside cover.

pound·cake (pound/kāk/), *n.* a rich, sweet cake made with a pound each of butter, sugar, and flour.

pound·er[1] (poun/dər), *n.* one who or that which pounds, pulverizes, or beats. [f. POUND[1] + -ER[1]]

pound·er[2] (poun/dər), *n.* **1.** a person or thing having, or associated with, a weight or value of a pound or a specified number of pounds. **2.** a gun that discharges a missile of a specified weight in pounds. **3.** a person possessing, receiving an income of, or paying a specified number of pounds. [f. POUND[2] + -ER[1]]

pound-fool·ish (pound/fōō/lĭsh), *adj. Chiefly Brit.* foolish in regard to large sums. Cf. **penny-wise.**

pound net, a kind of weir or fish trap of netting having a pound or enclosure with a contracted opening.

pour (pōr), *v.t.* **1.** to send (a liquid or fluid, or anything in loose particles) flowing or falling, as from a container or into, over, or on something. **2.** to emit or discharge (a liquid, etc.) in a stream. **3.** to send forth (words, etc.) as in a stream or flood (often fol. by *out* or *forth*). —*v.i.* **4.** to issue, move, or proceed in great quantity or number. **5.** to flow forth or along. —*n.* **6.** a pouring. **7.** an abundant or continuous flow or stream. **8.** a heavy fall of rain. [ME *poure(n)*; orig. uncert.] —**pour/-er,** *n.* —**pour/ing·ly,** *adv.*

pour·boire (pōōr bwȧr/), *n.* a tip or gratuity, esp. one to be spent on drink. [F: lit., for drinking]

pour le mé·rite (pōōr lə mě rēt/), *French.* for merit.

pour·par·ler (pōōr pȧr lā/), *n.* an informal preliminary conference. [F, n. use of OF *pourparler* discuss, f. *pour-* for, before (g. L *prō*) + *parler* speak]

pour·point (pōōr/point/), *n.* a stuffed and quilted doublet worn by men from the 14th to 17th centuries. [t. F, orig. pp. of *pourpoindre* quilt, perforate, f. *pour-*, for *par-* (g. L *per ad*) through + *poindre* (g. L *pungere* prick, pierce; r. ME *purpont,* t. ML: m.s. *purpunctum,* for *perpunctum.*]

pousse-ca·fé (pōōs kȧ fā/), *n.*, *pl.* **-fés** (-fā/). **1.** a small glass of liqueur served after coffee. **2.** a glass of various liqueurs arranged in layers. [F: lit., coffee-pusher]

pous·sette (pōō sět/), *n.*, *v.*, **-setted, -setting.** —*n.* **1.** a dance step in which a couple or several couples dance around the ballroom, holding hands, used in country dances. —*v.i.* **2.** to perform a poussette, as a couple in a country dance. [t. F, der. *pousser* push]

Pous·sin (pōō săn/), *n.* **Nicolas** (nēkō lä/), 1594–1655, French painter.

pou sto (pōō/ stō/, pou/), a place to stand on; a basis of operation. [Gk.: where I may stand; from the alleged saying of Archimedes, "Give me where I may stand, and I will move the earth."]

pout[1] (pout), *v.i.* **1.** to thrust out or protrude the lips, esp. in displeasure or sullenness. **2.** to look sullen. **3.** to swell out or protrude, as lips. —*v.t.* **4.** to protrude (lips, etc.). **5.** to utter with a pout. —*n.* **6.** a protrusion of the lips, as in pouting. **7.** a fit of sullenness. [ME *poute(n),* c. d. Sw. *puta* be inflated]

pout[2] (pout), *n.*, *pl.* **pouts,** (*esp. collectively*) **pout. 1.** the horned pout. **2.** an eelpout. **3.** a northern marine food fish, *Gadus luscus.* [OE *-pūte* in *ælepūte* eel pout, c. D *puit* frog]

pout·er (pou/tər), *n.* **1.** one who pouts. **2.** one of a breed of long-legged domestic pigeons which puff out the crop, sometimes to surprising size.

pov·er·ty (pŏv/ər tĭ), *n.* **1.** the condition of being poor with respect to money, goods, or means of subsistence. **2.** deficiency or lack of something specified: *poverty of ideas.* **3.** deficiency of desirable ingredients, qualities, etc.: *poverty of soil.* **4.** scantiness; scanty amount. [ME *poverte,* t. OF, g. s. L *paupertas.* Cf. POOR, PAUPER] —**Syn. 1.** POVERTY, DESTITUTION, NEED, WANT imply a state of privation and lack of necessities. POVERTY denotes serious lack of the means for proper existence: *living in a state of extreme poverty.* DESTITUTION, a somewhat more literary word, implies a state of having absolutely none of the necessaries of life: *widespread destitution in countries at war.* NEED emphasizes the fact that help or relief is necessary: *most of the people were in great need.* WANT emphasizes privations, esp. lack of food and clothing: *families were suffering from want.* —**Ant. 1.** riches, wealth, plenty.

pov·er·ty-strick·en (pŏv/ər tĭ strĭk/ən), *adj.* suffering from poverty; very poor: *poverty-stricken exiles.*

pow (pō, pou), *n. Scot. and N. Eng.* the poll; the head.

POW, prisoner of war.

pow·der[1] (pou/dər), *n.* **1.** any solid substance in the state of fine, loose particles, as produced by crushing, grinding, or disintegration; dust. **2.** a preparation in this form for some special purpose, as gunpowder, a medicinal powder, a cosmetic or toilet powder, etc. —*v.t.* **3.** to reduce to powder; pulverize. **4.** to sprinkle or cover with powder. **5.** to apply powder to (the face, skin, etc.) as a cosmetic. **6.** to sprinkle or strew as with powder. **7.** to ornament with small objects scattered over a surface. —*v.i.* **8.** to use powder as a cosmetic. **9.** to become pulverized. [ME *poudre,* t. OF, g. s. L *pulvis* dust] —**pow/der·er,** *n.*

pow·der[2] (pou/dər), *v.i. Brit. Dial.* to rush. [orig. uncert.]

powder blue, pale gray blue; blue diluted with gray.

powdered sugar, a sugar produced by grinding coarse granulated sugar. **Powdered sugar** (symbol, XX), made of the coarser particles, is used for fruits or beverages; **confectioners' sugar** (symbol, XXXX) is used in icings, confections, etc.

powder flask, a flask or case for gunpowder.

powder horn, a powder flask made of horn.

powder magazine, a compartment for the storage of ammunition and explosives.

powder metallurgy, the art or science of manufacturing useful articles by compacting metal and other powders in a die, followed by sintering.

powder monkey, 1. a boy formerly employed on warships, etc., to carry powder. **2.** *Humorous,* a man in charge of explosives in any operation requiring their use.

powder puff, a soft, feathery ball or pad, as of down, for applying powder to the skin.

pow·der·y (pou/də rĭ), *adj.* **1.** of the nature of, or consisting of, powder. **2.** easily reduced to powder. **3.** sprinkled or covered with powder.

pow·er (pou/ər), *n.* **1.** ability to do or act; capability of doing or effecting something. **2.** (*usually pl.*) a particular faculty of body or mind. **3.** political or national strength: *the balance of power in Europe.* **4.** great or marked ability to do or act; strength; might; force. **5.** the possession of control or command over others; dominion; authority; ascendancy or influence. **6.** politica. ascendancy or control in the government of a country, etc.: *the party in power.* **7.** legal ability, capacity, or authority. **8.** delegated authority; authority vested in a person or persons in a particular capacity. **9.** a written statement, or a document, conferring legal authority. **10.** one who or that which possesses or exercises authority or influence. **11.** a state or nation having international authority or influence: *the great powers of the world.* **12.** *Archaic.* a military or naval force. **13.** (*often pl.*) a deity or divinity. **14.** *Theol.* (*pl.*) an order of angels. **15.** *Colloq.* a large number or amount. **16.** *Physics.* the time rate of transferring or transforming energy; work done, or energy transferred, per unit of time. **17.** *Mech.* energy or force available for application to work. **18.** mechanical energy as distinguished from hand labor. **19.** a particular form of mechanical energy. **20.** a simple machine. **21.** *Math.* the product obtained by multiplying a quantity by itself one or more times: *4 is the second, 8 the third, power of 2.* **22.** *Optics.* the magnifying capacity of a microscope, telescope, etc., expressed as ratio of diameters, of image and object. [ME *poer,* t. AF, prop. inf., be able, g. VL *potēre,* for L *posse*] —**pow/ered,** *adj.* —**Syn. 4.** See **strength.**

pow·er·boat (pou/ər bōt/), *n.* **1.** a boat propelled by mechanical power. **2.** a motorboat.

power drill, a drill operated by a motor.

pow·er·ful (pou/ər fəl), *adj.* **1.** having or exerting great power or force. **2.** strong physically, as a person. **3.** producing great physical effects, as a machine or a blow. **4.** potent, as a drug. **5.** having great influence, as a speech, speaker, description, reason, etc. **6.** having great power, authority, or influence, as a nation; mighty. **7.** *Colloq.* great in number or amount: *a powerful lot of money.* —**pow/er·ful·ly,** *adv.* —**pow/er·ful·ness,** *n.* —**Syn. 1.** POWERFUL, MIGHTY, POTENT suggest great force or strength. POWERFUL suggests capability of exerting great force or overcoming strong resistance: *a powerful machine like a bulldozer.* MIGHTY, now chiefly rhetorical, implies uncommon or overwhelming strength of power: *a mighty army.* POTENT, a dignified word, implies great natural or inherent power: *a potent influence.* **5.** convincing, forcible, cogent. —**Ant. 1.** weak.

pow·er·house (pou/ər hous/), *n. Elect.* a generating station.

pow·er·less (pou/ər lĭs), *adj.* **1.** lacking power or ability; unable to produce any effect. **2.** of or pertaining to inability to act with legal effect. —**pow/er·less·ly,** *adv.* —**pow/er·less·ness,** *n.*

power loading. See **loading** (def. 4).

power loom, a loom worked by machinery.

power of appointment, *Law.* the right granted by one person (the donor) to another (the donee or appointer) to dispose of the donor's property or create rights therein.

power of attorney, *Law.* a written document given by one person or party to another authorizing the latter to act for the former.

power plant, 1. a plant (including engines, dynamos, etc., with the building or buildings) for the generation of power. **2.** the apparatus for supplying power for a particular mechanical process or operation.

power politics, international diplomacy based on the use, or threatened use, of military or naval power.

power station, *Elect.* a generating station.

Pow·ha·tan (pou/hə tăn/), *n.* c1550–1618, Indian chief in Virginia, father of Pocohantas.

pow·wow (pou/wou/), *n.* **1.** (among North American Indians) a ceremony, esp. one accompanied by magic, feasting, and dancing, performed for the cure of disease, success in a hunt, etc. **2.** a council or conference (of or with Indians). **3.** *U.S. Colloq.* any conference or meeting. —*v.i.* **4.** to hold a powwow. **5.** *U.S. Colloq.* to confer. [t. Algonquian (Narragansett): m. *pow waw* or *po-wah.* Cf. Micmac *bu*ᵘ*in* priest, shaman, Ojibwa *pawaana* he dreams of him]

Pow·ys (pō/ĭs), *n.* **1. John Cowper** (kou/pər), born 1872, British author. **2.** his brother, **Llewelyn** (lōō ĕl/ĭn), 1884–1939, British author. **3.** his brother, **Theodore Francis,** 1875–1953, British author.

pox (pŏks), *n.* **1.** a disease characterized by multiple skin pustules, as smallpox. **2.** syphilis (**great pox** or **French pox**). [for *pocks,* pl. of POCK]

b., blend of, blended; c., cognate with; d., dialect, dialectal; der., derived from; f., formed from; g., going back to; m., modification of; r., replacing; s., stem of; t., taken from; ?, perhaps. See the full key on inside cover.

Po·yang (pô′yäng′), *n.* a lake in E China, in Kiangsi province. ab. 90 mi. long; ab. 20 mi. wide.

Poz·nań (pôz′nän′y), *n.* Polish name of **Posen.**

Po·zsony (pô′zhôn′y), *n.* Hungarian name of **Bratislava.**

poz·zuo·la·na (pŏt′swə·lä′nə; *It.* pôt′tzwô·lä′nä), *n.* a porous variety of volcanic tuft or ash used in making hydraulic cement. Also, **poz·zo·la·na** (pŏt′sə·lä′nə; *It.* pŏt′tsô·lä′nä). [t. It., use of adj., belonging to *Pozzuoli* (L *Puteolī*), lit., little springs]

Poz·zuo·li (pŏt·tswô′lē), *n.* a seaport in SW Italy, near Naples; Roman ruins. 41,843 (1951).

pp., 1. pages. 2. past participle. 3. pianissimo. 4. privately printed.

P.P., 1. parcel post. 2. Parish Priest.

p.p., 1. parcel post. 2. past participle. 3. postpaid.

ppl., participial. Also, **p.pl.**

ppr., present participle. Also, **p.pr.**

P.P.S., (L *post postscriptum*) a second postscript.

P.Q., Province of Quebec.

p.q., previous question.

Pr, *Chem.* praseodymium.

Pr., 1. preferred (stock). 2. Prince. 3. Provençal.

pr., *pl.* **prs.** 1. pair. 2. pairs. 3. paper. 4. power. 5. preference. 6. preferred (stock). 7. present. 8. price. 9. priest. 10. printing. 11. pronoun.

P.R., 1. Proportional Representation. 2. Puerto Rico.

prac·tic (prăk′tĭk), *adj. Archaic.* practical. [ME *practik*, t. LL: m.s. *practicus*, t. Gk.: m. *praktikós* practical]

prac·ti·ca·ble (prăk′tə·kə·bəl), *adj.* 1. capable of being put into practice, done, or effected, esp. with the available means or with reason or prudence; feasible. 2. capable of being used or traversed, or admitting of passage: *a practicable road.* [f.s. ML *practicāre* PRACTICE + -ABLE] —**prac′ti·ca·bil′i·ty, prac′ti·ca·ble·ness,** *n.* —**prac′ti·ca·bly,** *adv.*
—**Syn.** 1. See **possible.** PRACTICABLE, PRACTICAL, though not properly synonyms, often cause confusion. PRACTICABLE means possible or feasible, able to be done, capable of being put into practice or of being used: *a practicable method of communication.* PRACTICAL (applied to persons) means sensible and businesslike, (applied to things) efficient and workable, as contrasted with theoretical: *practical measures.* —**Ant.** 1. unfeasible; inefficient, theoretical.

prac·ti·cal (prăk′tə·kəl), *adj.* 1. pertaining or relating to practice or action: *practical agriculture.* 2. consisting of, involving, or resulting from practice or action: *a practical application of a rule.* 3. pertaining to or connected with the ordinary activities, business, or work of the world: *practical affairs.* 4. adapted for actual use: *a practical method.* 5. engaged or experienced in actual practice or work: *a practical politician.* 6. inclined toward or fitted for actual work or useful activities: *a practical man.* 7. mindful of the results, usefulness, advantages or disadvantages, etc., of action or procedure. 8. matter-of-fact; prosaic. 9. being such in practice or effect; virtual: *a practical certainty.* [f. PRACTIC + -AL¹] —**prac′ti·cal·i·ty, prac′ti·cal·ness,** *n.*
—**Syn.** 1. See **practicable.** 7. PRACTICAL, JUDICIOUS, SENSIBLE refer to good judgment in action, conduct, and the handling of everyday matters. PRACTICAL suggests the ability to adopt means to an end or to turn what is at hand to account: *to adopt practical measures for settling problems.* JUDICIOUS implies the possession and use of discreet judgment, discrimination and balance: *a judicious use of one's time.* SENSIBLE implies the possession and use of sound reason and shrewd common sense: *a sensible suggestion.* —**Ant.** 7. ill-advised, unwise, foolish.

practical joke, a joke or jest carried out in action; a trick played upon a person.

prac·ti·cal·ly (prăk′tĭk·lĭ), *adv.* 1. in effect; virtually. 2. in a practical manner. 3. from a practical point of view.

practical nurse, a woman who has practical nursing experience, but does not have formalized nursing training or the diploma of a registered nurse.

prac·tice (prăk′tĭs), *n., v.* **-ticed, -ticing.** —*n.* 1. habitual or customary performance. 2. a habitual performance; a habit or custom. 3. repeated performance or systematic exercise for the purpose of acquiring skill or proficiency: *practice makes perfect.* 4. skill gained by experience or exercise. 5. the action or process of performing or doing something (opposed to *theory* or *speculation*); performance; operation. 6. the exercise of a profession or occupation, esp. law or medicine. 7. the business of a professional man: *a lawyer with a large practice.* 8. plotting, intriguing, or trickery. 9. a plot or intrigue. 10. a stratagem or maneuver. 11. *Law.* the established method of conducting legal proceedings. [n. use of v., substituted for earlier *practise*, n.] —*v.t.* 12. to carry out, perform, or do habitually or usually, or make a practice of. 13. to follow, observe, or use habitually or in customary practice. 14. to exercise or pursue as a profession, art, or occupation: *to practice law.* 15. to perform or do repeatedly in order to acquire skill or proficiency. 16. to exercise (a person, etc.) in something in order to give proficiency; train or drill. —*v.i.* 17. to act habitually; do something habitually or as a practice. 18. to pursue a profession, esp. law or medicine. 19. to exercise oneself by performance tending to give proficiency: *to practice at shooting.* 20. *Rare.* to plot or conspire. Also, **practise** for 12–20. [ME, t. OF: m.s. *pra(c)tiser*, ult. der. LL *practicus* PRACTICAL] —**prac′tic·er,** *n.* —**Syn.** 2. See **custom.** 3. See **exercise.**

prac·ticed (prăk′tĭst), *adj.* 1. experienced; expert; proficient. 2. acquired or perfected through practice. Also, **prac′tised.**

prac·tise (prăk′tĭs), *v.t., v.i.* **-tised, -tising.** practice.

prac·ti·tion·er (prăk·tĭsh′ən·ər), *n.* 1. one engaged in the practice of a profession or the like: *a medical practitioner.* 2. one who practices something specified. [f.m. *practician* (f. PRACTIC + -IAN) + -ER¹]

prae-, var. of **pre-.**

prae·di·al (prē′dĭ·əl), *adj.* 1. pertaining to or consisting of land or its products; real; landed. 2. arising from or consequent upon the occupation of land. 3. attached to land. Also, **predial.** [t. ML: m.s. *praediālis,* der. L *praedium* farm, estate]

prae·fect (prē′fĕkt), *n.* prefect.

prae·mu·ni·re (prē′myōō·nī′rē), *n. Eng. Law.* 1. a writ charging the offense of resorting to a foreign court or authority, as that of the Pope, and thus calling in question the supremacy of the English Crown. 2. the offense. 3. the penalty of forfeiture, imprisonment, outlawry, etc., incurred. [t. ML: a word used in the writ (by confusion with L *praemūnīre* fortify, protect) for L *praemonēre* forewarn, admonish. See PREMONISH]

prae·no·men (prē·nō′mĕn), *n., pl.* **-nomina** (-nŏm′ə·nə). the first or personal name of a Roman citizen, as in "Caius Julius Caesar." [t. L: f. *prae* before + *nōmen* name] —**prae·nom·i·nal** (prē·nŏm′ə·nəl), *adj.*

prae·pos·tor (prē·pŏs′tər), *n.* (at various English public schools) any of certain senior pupils to whom authority is delegated for the government of the others. Also, **prepositor, prepostor.** [t. ML: m. *praepositor,* der. L *praepositus,* pp., set before]

prae·tor (prē′tər), *n. Rom. Hist.* 1. the title of a consul as leader of the army. 2. one of a number of elected magistrates, engaged chiefly in the administration of justice. Also, **pretor.** [ME, t. L: leader, chief, head] —**prae·to·ri·al** (prē·tōr′ĭ·əl), *adj.*

prae·to·ri·an (prē·tōr′ĭ·ən), *Hist.* —*adj.* 1. of or pertaining to a praetor. 2. (*often cap.*) designating or pertaining to the Praetorian Guard. —*n.* 3. a man having the rank of a praetor or ex-praetor. 4. (*often cap.*) a soldier of the Praetorian Guard. Also, **pretorian.**

Praetorian Guard, *Hist.* the bodyguard of a Roman military commander, esp. the imperial guard stationed in Rome.

prag·mat·ic (prăg·măt′ĭk), *adj.* Also, **prag·mat′i·cal.** 1. treating historical phenomena with special reference to their causes, antecedent conditions, and results. 2. *Philos.* of or pertaining to pragmatism. 3. concerned with practical consequences or values. 4. pertaining to the affairs of a state or community: *pragmatic sanction.* 5. busy or active. 6. officiously busy; meddlesome. 7. conceited; opinionated; dogmatic. —*n.* 8. a pragmatic sanction. [t. L: s. *pragmaticus,* t. Gk.: m. *pragmatikós* active, versed in state affairs; as n., a man of business or action] —**prag·mat′i·cal·ly,** *adv.*

pragmatic sanction, 1. any one of various imperial decrees with the effect of fundamental law. 2. the decrees of a council of French clergy.

prag·ma·tism (prăg′mə·tĭz′əm), *n.* 1. pragmatic character or conduct. 2. *Philos.* a tendency, movement, or more or less definite system of thought in which stress is placed upon practical consequences and values as standards for explicating philosophic concepts, and as tests for determining their value and truth. 3. officiousness; dogmatism; practicality. —**prag′ma·tist,** *n., adj.*

Prague (präg; *older* prāg), *n.* the capital of Czechoslovakia, in the W part, on the Moldau: also the capital of Bohemia. 932,024 (1951). Czech, **Pra·ha** (prä′hä). German, **Prag** (präkh).

Prai·ri·al (prĕ·rē·àl′), *n.* (in the calendar of the first French republic) the ninth month of the year, extending from May 20 to June 18. [F, der. *prairie* meadow. See PRAIRIE]

prai·rie (prâr′ĭ), *n.* 1. an extensive level or slightly undulating treeless tract of land in the Mississippi valley, characterized by a highly fertile soil and originally covered with coarse grasses 2. a meadow; a tract of grassland. 3. *U.S. Dial.* a small open space in a forest. [t. F, der. *pré* field, g. L *prātum* meadow]

prairie chicken, a North American gallinaceous bird, *Tympanuchus cupido,* inhabiting prairies and valued as game. Also, **prairie hen.**

prairie dog, any of certain gregarious burrowing rodents (genus *Cynomys*) of American prairies, which utter a barklike cry.

Prairie Provinces, the provinces of Manitoba, Saskatchewan, and Alberta, in W Canada.

prairie schooner, a small covered wagon, copied from the Conestoga wagon, used by pioneers in crossing the prairies and plains of North America.

prairie wolf, the coyote.

Prairie dog.
Cynomys ludovicianus
(14 to 16 in. long,
tail 2½ to 3 in.)

praise (prāz), *n., v.* **praised, praising.** —*n.* 1. act of praising; commendation; laudation. 2. the offering of grateful homage in words or song, as an act of worship. 3. state of being praised. 4. *Archaic.* a ground for praise, or a merit. 5. *Obs.* an object of praise. —*v.t.*

6. to express approbation or admiration of; commend; extol. **7.** to offer grateful homage to (God or a deity), as in words or song. [ME *preise(n)*, t. OF: m. *preisier* value, prize, ult. der. L *pretium* price. Cf. PRIZE²] —**prais'er,** *n.* —**Syn. 1.** acclamation, plaudit, compliment. **6.** See **approve. 7.** glorify, magnify, exalt.

praise·wor·thy (prāz'wûr'thǐ), *adj.* deserving of praise; laudable. —**praise'wor'thi·ly,** *adv.* —**praise'- wor'thi·ness,** *n.*

Pra·ja·dhi·pok (prə chä'tǐ pŏk'), *n.* 1893–1941, king of Siam, 1925 until his abdication in 1935.

Pra·krit (prä'krǐt), *n.* any of the vernacular Indic languages of the ancient and medieval periods, as distinguished from Sanskrit. [t. Skt.: m. *prākrta* natural, common, vulgar. Cf. SANSKRIT]

pra·line (prä'lēn), *n.* any of various confections of almonds or other nut kernels cooked in a syrup. [t. F; named after Marshal du Plessis-*Praslin* (1598–1675), whose cook invented them]

prall·tril·ler (präl'trǐl'ər), *n. Music.* a melodic embellishment consisting of a rapid alternation of a principal tone with a supplementary tone one degree above it; an inverted mordent. [G: lit., rebounding quaver]

pram (präm), *n. Brit. Colloq.* perambulator.

prance (präns, präns), *v.,* **pranced, pranc·ing,** *n.* —*v.i.* **1.** to spring, or move by springing, from the hind legs, as a horse. **2.** to ride on a horse doing this. **3.** to ride gaily, proudly, or insolently. **4.** to move or go in an elated manner; swagger. **5.** to caper or dance. —*v.t.* **6.** to cause to prance. —*n.* **7.** act of prancing; a prancing movement. [ME *pra(u)nce,* ? alliterative alter. of DANCE. Cf. *prick* and *prance* (Gower)] —**pranc'er,** *n.* —**pranc'ing·ly,** *adv.*

pran·di·al (prăn'dǐ əl), *adj.* of or pertaining to a meal, esp. dinner. [f. s. L *prandium* luncheon, meal + -AL¹] —**pran'di·al·ly,** *adv.*

prank¹ (prăngk), *n.* **1.** a trick of a frolicsome nature. **2.** a trick of a malicious nature. [orig. uncert.]

prank² (prăngk), *v.t.* **1.** to dress or deck in a showy manner; adorn. —*v.i.* **2.** to make an ostentatious show or display. [cf. D *pronk* show, finery, MLG *prank* pomp]

prank·ish (prăngk'ĭsh), *adj.* **1.** of the nature of a prank. **2.** full of pranks.

prase (prāz), *n.* a leek-green cryptocrystalline variety of chalcedony. [ME, s. F, t. L: m.s. *prasius* a leek-green stone, t. Gk.: m. *prásios* leek-green]

pra·se·o·dym·i·um (prā'zĭ ō dǐm'ĭ əm, prā'sǐ-), *n. Chem.* a rare-earth, metallic, trivalent element: so named from its green salts. Symbol: Pr; *at. wt.:* 140.92; *at. no.:* 59; *sp. gr.:* 6.5 at 20°C. [f. *praseo-* (comb. form repr. PRASE) + (DI)DYMIUM]

prate (prāt), *v.,* **prated, prat·ing,** *n.* —*v.i.* **1.** to talk much or long and to little purpose. —*v.t.* **2.** to utter in empty or foolish talk. —*n.* **3.** act of prating. **4.** empty or foolish talk. [late ME *prate,* c. D and LG *praten*] —**prat'er,** *n.* —**prat'ing·ly,** *adv.*

prat·in·cole (prăt'ĭng kōl', prā'tǐn-), *n.* any of the limicoline birds of the eastern hemisphere which constitute the genus *Glareola,* resembling the swallows. [t. NL: m. *prātincola,* f. s. L *prātum* meadow + *incola* inhabitant]

pra·tique (prä tēk', prăt'ĭk; *Fr.* prȧ tēk'), *n. Com.* license or permission to use a port, given to a ship after quarantine or on showing a clean bill of health. [t. F: lit., practice, t. ML: m.s. *practica*]

prat·tle (prăt'əl), *v.,* **-tled, -tling,** *n.* —*v.i.* **1.** to talk or chatter in a simple-minded or foolish way; babble. —*v.t.* **2.** to utter by chattering or babbling. —*n.* **3.** act of prattling. **4.** mere chatter. **5.** a babbling sound. [freq. and dim. of PRATE] —**prat'tler,** *n.* —**prat'- tling·ly,** *adv.*

prawn (prôn), *n.* **1.** any of various shrimplike decapod crustaceans of the genera *Palaemon, Penaeus,* etc. (suborder *Macrura*), certain of which are used as food. —*v.i.* **2.** to catch prawns, as for food. [ME *pra(y)ne;* orig. unknown] —**prawn'er,** *n.*

Prawn. *Palaemon serratus* (3 to 4 in. long)

prax·is (prăk'sĭs), *n.* **1.** practice, esp. as opposed to theory. **2.** a set of examples for practice. [t. ML, t. Gk.]

Prax·it·e·les (prăk sǐt'ə lēz'), *n.* fl. c350 B.C., Greek sculptor.

pray (prā), *v.t.* **1.** to make earnest petition to (a person, etc.). **2.** to make devout petition to (God or an object of worship). **3.** to make petition or entreaty for; crave. **4.** to offer (a prayer). **5.** to bring, put, etc., by praying. —*v.i.* **6.** to make entreaty or supplication, as to a person or for a thing. **7.** to make devout petition to God or to an object of worship. **8.** to enter into spiritual communion with God or an object of worship through prayer. [ME *preie(n),* t. OF: m. *preier,* ult. g. L *precāri* beg, pray; akin to OE *fricgan,* G *fragen* ask]

prayer¹ (prâr), *n.* **1.** a devout petition to, or any form of spiritual communion with, God or an object of worship. **2.** act, action, or practice of praying to God or an object of worship. **3.** a spiritual communion with God or an object of worship, as in supplication, thanksgiving, adoration, or confession. **4.** a form of words used in or appointed for praying: *the Lord's Prayer.*

5. a religious observance, either public or private, consisting wholly or mainly of prayer. **6.** that which is prayed for. **7.** a petition or entreaty. **8.** the section of a bill in equity, or of a petition, setting forth the complaint or the action desired. [ME *preiere,* t. OF, g. Rom. *pre-cāria,* orig. neut. pl. of L *precārius* obtained by entreaty]

pray·er² (prā'ər), *n.* one who prays. [f. PRAY + -ER¹]

prayer book (prâr), **1.** a book of forms of prayer. **2.** (*usually caps.*) the Book of Common Prayer.

prayer·ful (prâr'fəl), *adj.* given to, characterized by, or expressive of prayer; devout. —**prayer'ful·ly,** *adv.* —**prayer'ful·ness,** *n.*

prayer wheel (prâr), a wheel or cylinder inscribed with or containing prayers, used chiefly by Buddhists of Tibet as a mechanical aid to continual praying, each revolution counting as an uttered prayer.

praying mantis, the mantis.

pre-, a prefix applied freely to mean "prior to," "in advance of" (*preschool, prewar*), also "early," "beforehand" (*prepay*), "before," "in front of" (*preoral, prepeduncle*), and in many figurative meanings, often attached to stems not used alone (*prevent, preclude, preference, precedent*). [t. L: m. *prae-,* repr. *prae,* prep., adv.]

preach (prēch), *v.t.* **1.** to advocate or inculcate (religious or moral truth, right conduct, etc.) in speech or writing. **2.** to proclaim or make known by sermon (the gospel, good tidings, etc.). **3.** to deliver (a sermon or the like). —*v.i.* **4.** to deliver a sermon. **5.** to give earnest advice, as on religious subjects. **6.** to do this in an obtrusive or tedious way. [ME *preche(n),* t. OF: m. *preēchier,* g. LL *praedicāre.* See PREDICATE]

preach·er (prē'chər), *n.* **1.** one whose occupation or function it is to preach the gospel. **2.** one who preaches.

preach·i·fy (prē'chə fī'), *v.i.,* **-fied, -fying.** *Colloq.* to preach in an obtrusive or tedious way (used in disparagement). [f. PREACH + -(I)FY]

preach·ing (prē'chǐng), *n.* **1.** the act or practice of one who preaches. **2.** the art of delivering sermons. **3.** a sermon. **4.** a public religious service with a sermon. —**preach'ing·ly,** *adv.*

preach·ment (prēch'mənt), *n.* **1.** the act of preaching. **2.** a sermon or other discourse, esp. when obtrusive or tedious.

pre·ad·am·ite (prē ăd'ə mīt'), *n.* **1.** a person supposed to have existed before Adam. **2.** a person who believes that there were men in existence before Adam. —*adj.* **3.** existing before Adam. **4.** of the preadamites.

pre·ad·o·les·cent (prē'ăd ə lěs'ənt), *adj.* pertaining to the period just before adolescence.

pre·al·lot·ment (prē'ə lŏt'mənt), *n.* an allotment given in advance.

pre·al·tar (prē ôl'tər), *adj.* in front of the altar.

pre·am·ble (prē'ăm'bəl), *n.* **1.** an introductory statement; a preface; an introduction. **2.** the introductory part of a statute, deed, or the like, stating the reasons and intent of what follows. **3.** a preliminary or introductory fact or circumstance. [ME, t. F: m. *préam-bule,* t. ML: m.s. *praeambulum,* prop. neut. of LL *prae-ambulus* walking before]

pre·am·pli·fi·er (prē'ăm'plə fī'ər), *n.* a device in the amplifier circuit of a radio or phonograph which increases the strength of a weak signal for detection and amplification. Also, **pre·amp** (prē'ămp').

pre·ap·point (prē'ə point'), *v.t.* to appoint beforehand.

pre·ar·range (prē'ə rānj'), *v.t.,* **-ranged, -ranging.** to arrange beforehand. —**pre'ar·range'ment,** *n.*

pre·ax·i·al (prē ăk'sǐ əl), *adj. Anat.* before the body axis; pertaining to the radial side of the arm and the tibial side of the leg.

preb·end (prĕb'ənd), *n. Brit.* **1.** a stipend allotted from the revenues of a cathedral or a collegiate church to a canon or member of the chapter. **2.** the land yielding such a stipend. **3.** a prebendary. [ME *prebende,* t. ML: m. *prēbenda,* var. of *praebenda* prebend, LL allowance, prop. neut. pl. ger. of L *prae(hi)bēre* offer, furnish] —**pre·ben·dal** (prǐ bĕn'dəl), *adj.*

preb·en·dar·y (prĕb'ən dĕr'ĭ), *n., pl.* **-daries.** *Brit.* a canon or clergyman who for special services at a cathedral or collegiate church is entitled to a prebend.

Pre·ble (prĕb'əl), *n.* Edward, 1761–1807, U.S. naval officer.

prec., **1.** preceding. **2.** preceded.

Pre-Cam·bri·an (prē kăm'brǐ ən), *Stratig.* —*adj.* **1.** pertaining to time or rocks older than the Cambrian. —*n.* **2.** time or rocks older than the Cambrian, characterized by almost complete lack of fossils.

pre·can·cel (prē kăn'səl), *v.,* **-celed, -celing** or (esp. *Brit.*) **-celled, -celling,** *n. Philately.* —*v.t.* **1.** to cancel a stamp before placing it on mail matter. —*n.* **2.** a precanceled stamp.

pre·car·i·ous (prǐ kâr'ĭ əs), *adj.* **1.** dependent on circumstances beyond one's control; uncertain; unstable; insecure: *a precarious livelihood.* **2.** dependent on the will or pleasure of another; liable to be withdrawn or lost at the will of another: *precarious tenure.* **3.** exposed to or involving danger; dangerous; perilous; risky: *a precarious life.* **4.** having insufficient, little, or no foundation: *a precarious assumption.* [t. L: m. *pre-cārius* obtained by entreaty or by mere favor, hence uncertain, precarious] —**pre·car'i·ous·ly,** *adv.* —**pre-car'i·ous·ness,** *n.* —**Syn. 1.** See **uncertain.**

prec·a·to·ry (prĕk'ə·tōr'ĭ), *adj.* pertaining to or of the nature of, or expressing entreaty or supplication. Also, **prec·a·tive** (prĕk'ə·tĭv). [t. LL: m.s. *precātōrius*]

pre·cau·tion (prĭ·kô'shən), *n.* **1.** a measure taken beforehand to ward off possible evil or secure good results. **2.** caution employed beforehand; prudent foresight. [t. LL: m.s. *praecautio*, der. L *praecavēre* guard against]

pre·cau·tion·ar·y (prĭ·kô'shə·nĕr'ĭ), *adj.* **1.** pertaining to or of the nature of precaution or a precaution. **2.** expressing or advising precaution. Also, **pre·cau'tion·al**.

pre·cau·tious (prĭ·kô'shəs), *adj.* using or displaying precaution.

pre·cede (prē·sēd'), *v.* **-ced·ed, -ced·ing.** —*v.t.* **1.** to go before, as in place, order, rank, importance, or time. **2.** to introduce by something preliminary; preface. —*v.i.* **3.** to go or come before. [ME *precede(n*, t. L: m. *praecēdere*]

pre·ced·ence (prĭ·sē'dəns, prĕs'ə·dəns), *n.* **1.** act or fact of preceding. **2.** priority in order, rank, importance, etc. **3.** priority in time. **4.** the right to precede others in ceremonies or social formalities. **5.** the order to be observed ceremonially by persons of different ranks. Also, **pre·ced·en·cy** (prĭ·sē'dən·sĭ, prĕs'ə·dən·sĭ).

prec·e·dent¹ (prĕs'ə·dənt), *n.* **1.** a preceding instance or case which may serve as an example for or a justification in subsequent cases. **2.** *Law.* a legal decision or form of proceeding serving as an authoritative rule or pattern in future similar or analogous cases. [n. use of PRECEDENT²]

prec·ed·ent² (prĭ·sē'dənt, prĕs'ə·dənt), *adj.* preceding. [ME, t. L: m.s. *praecēdens* going before]

prec·e·den·tial (prĕs'ə·dĕn'shəl), *adj.* **1.** of the nature of or constituting a precedent. **2.** having precedence.

pre·ced·ing (prē·sē'dĭng), *adj.* that precedes; previous.

pre·cent (prē·sĕnt'), *v.i.* to act as precentor. [back formation from PRECENTOR]

pre·cen·tor (prĭ·sĕn'tər), *n.* one who leads a church choir or congregation in singing. [t. LL: m. *praecentor* leader in music, der. L *praecinere* sing before] —**pre·cen·to·ri·al** (prē'sĕn·tōr'ĭ·əl). —**pre·cen'tor·ship'**,*n.*

pre·cept (prē'sĕpt), *n.* **1.** a commandment or direction given as a rule of action or conduct. **2.** an injunction as to moral conduct; a maxim. **3.** a rule, as for the performance of some technical operation. **4.** *Law.* **a.** a writ or warrant. **b.** a written order issued pursuant to law, as a sheriff's order for an election. [ME, t. L: m.s. *praeceptum*, prop. neut. pp., instructed]

pre·cep·tive (prĭ·sĕp'tĭv), *adj.* **1.** of the nature of or expressing a precept; mandatory. **2.** giving instructions; instructive. —**pre·cep'tive·ly**, *adv.*

pre·cep·tor (prĭ·sĕp'tər), *n.* **1.** an instructor, a teacher; a tutor. **2.** the head of a preceptory. [t. L: m. *praeceptor*] —**pre·cep·tor·ate** (prĭ·sĕp'tər·ĭt), *n.* —**pre·cep·to·ri·al** (prē'sĕp·tōr'ĭ·əl), **pre·cep'to·ral**, *adj.* —**pre·cep·tress** (prĭ·sĕp'trĭs), *n. fem.*

pre·cep·to·ry (prĭ·sĕp'tər·ĭ), *n., pl.* **-ries.** a subordinate house or community of the Knights Templars. [t. ML: m.s. *praeceptōria*, der. L *praeceptor* PRECEPTOR]

pre·ces·sion (prē·sĕsh'ən), *n.* **1.** act or fact of preceding; precedence. **2.** *Astron.* **a.** the precession of the equinoxes. **b.** the related motion of the earth's axis of rotation. [ME, t. LL: m.s. *praecessio*, der. L *praecessus*. pp., gone before]

pre·ces·sion·al (prē·sĕsh'ən·əl), *adj.* pertaining to or resulting from the precession of the equinoxes.

precession of the equinoxes, *Astron.* the earlier occurrence of the equinoxes in each successive sidereal year because of a slow retrograde motion of the equinoctial points along the ecliptic caused by the combined action of the sun and moon on the mass of matter accumulated about the earth's equator. A complete revolution of the equinoxes requires about 26,000 years.

pre·cinct (prē'sĭngkt), *n.* **1.** a district for governmental, administrative, or other purposes: *a police precinct.* **2.** a small electoral area containing one polling place. **3.** a space or place of definite or understood limits. **4.** (*often pl.*) an inclosing boundary or limit. **5.** (*pl.*) the parts or regions immediately about any place; the environs: *the precincts of a town.* **6.** *Chiefly Brit.* the ground immediately surrounding a church, temple, or the like. **7.** a walled or otherwise bounded or limited space within which a building or place is situated. [ME, t. ML: m.s. *praecinctum*, prop. neut. of L *praecinctus*, pp., girded about, surrounded]

pre·ci·os·i·ty (prĕsh'ĭ·ŏs'ə·tĭ), *n., pl.* **-ties.** fastidious or carefully affected refinement, as in language, style, or taste. [ME *preciosite*, t. OF, t. L: m.s. *pretiōsitas*]

pre·cious (prĕsh'əs), *adj.* **1.** of great price or value; valuable; costly: *precious metals.* **2.** of great moral or spiritual worth. **3.** dear or beloved. **4.** choice, fine, or pretty (used ironically). **5.** egregious, arrant, or gross. **6.** *Colloq.* very great. **7.** affectedly or excessively delicate, refined, or nice. —*n.* **8.** precious one; darling. —*adv.* **9.** *Colloq.* extremely; very. [ME, t. OF: m. *precios*, t. L: m.s. *pretiōsus* costly] —**pre'cious·ly**, *adv.* —**pre'cious·ness**, *n.* —**Syn. 1.** See **valuable**.

precious stone, a gem distinguished for its beauty and rarity, used in jewelry, etc.

prec·i·pice (prĕs'ə·pĭs), *n.* **1.** a cliff with a vertical, or nearly vertical, or overhanging face. **2.** a situation of great peril. [t. F, t. L: m.s. *praecipitium*]

pre·cip·i·tan·cy (prĭ·sĭp'ə·tən·sĭ), *n., pl.* **-cies.** **1.** the quality or fact of being precipitant. **2.** headlong or rash haste. **3.** (*pl.*) hasty or rash acts. Also, **pre·cip'i·tance.**

pre·cip·i·tant (prĭ·sĭp'ə·tənt), *adj.* **1.** falling headlong. **2.** rushing headlong, rapidly, or hastily onward. **3.** hasty; rash. **4.** unduly sudden or abrupt. —*n.* **5.** *Chem.* anything that causes precipitation. [t. L: m.s. *praecipitans*, ppr., falling headlong] —**pre·cip'i·tant·ly**, *adv.*

pre·cip·i·tate (*v.* prĭ·sĭp'ə·tāt'; *adj., n.* prĭ·sĭp'ə·tāt', -tĭt), *v.* **-tat·ed, -tat·ing,** *adj., n.* —*v.t.* **1.** to hasten the occurrence of; bring about in haste or suddenly: *to precipitate a quarrel.* **2.** *Chem.* to separate (a substance) out in solid form from a solution, as by means of a reagent. **3.** *Physics, Meteorol.* to condense (moisture) from a state of vapor in the form of rain, dew, etc. **4.** to cast down headlong; fling or hurl down. **5.** to cast, plunge, or send, violently or abruptly: *to precipitate oneself into a struggle.* —*v.i.* **6.** to separate from a solution as a precipitate. **7.** *Physics, Meteorol.* to be condensed as rain, dew, etc. **8.** to be cast down or falling headlong. —*adj.* **9.** headlong. **10.** rushing headlong or rapidly onward. **11.** proceeding rapidly or with great haste: *a precipitate retreat.* **12.** exceedingly sudden or abrupt. **13.** acting, or done or made, in sudden haste, or without due deliberation; overhasty; rash. —*n.* **14.** *Chem.* a substance precipitated from a solution. **15.** *Physics, Meteorol.* moisture condensed in the form of rain, dew, etc. [t. L: m.s. *praecipitātus*, pp., cast headlong] —**pre·cip'i·tate·ly**, *adv.* —**pre·cip'i·tate·ness**, *n.* —**pre·cip'i·ta'tive**, *adj.* —**pre·cip'i·ta'tor**, *n.*

pre·cip·i·ta·tion (prĭ·sĭp'ə·tā'shən), *n.* **1.** act of precipitating. **2.** state of being precipitated. **3.** a casting down or falling headlong. **4.** a hastening or hurrying in movement, procedure, or action. **5.** sudden haste. **6.** unwise or rash rapidity. **7.** *Chem., Physics.* the precipitating of a substance from a solution. **8.** *Meteorol.* **a.** falling products of condensation in the atmosphere, as rain, snow, hail. **b.** the amount precipitated at a given place within a given period, usually expressed in inches of rain or snow, etc. **9.** *Spiritualism, materialization.*

pre·cip·i·tin (prĭ·sĭp'ə·tĭn), *n.* a substance developed in certain blood serums, capable of precipitating albuminous substances, etc. [f. PRECIPIT(ATE) + -IN²]

pre·cip·i·tous (prĭ·sĭp'ə·təs), *adj.* **1.** of the nature of a precipice, or characterized by precipices: *a precipitous wall of rock.* **2.** extremely or impassably steep. **3.** precipitate. [f. PRECIPIT(ATE), adj., + -OUS] —**pre·cip'i·tous·ly**, *adv.* —**pre·cip'i·tous·ness**, *n.*

pré·cis (prā·sē', prā'sē), *n., pl.* **-cis,** *v.* —*n.* **1.** an abstract or summary. —*v.t.* **2.** to make a précis of. [t. F n. use of adj., cut short, PRECISE]

pre·cise (prĭ·sīs'), *adj.* **1.** definite or exact; definitely or strictly stated, defined, or fixed: *precise directions.* **2.** being exactly that, and neither more nor less: *the precise amount.* **3.** being just that, and not some other. **4.** definite or exact in statement, as a person. **5.** carefully distinct, as the voice. **6.** exact in measuring, recording, etc., as an instrument. **7.** excessively or rigidly particular; puritanical. [t. L: m.s. *praecīsus*, pp., cut short, brief] —**pre·cise'ly**, *adv.* —**pre·cise'ness**, *n.* —**Syn. 1.** See **correct**.

pre·ci·sian (prĭ·sĭzh'ən), *n.* **1.** one who adheres punctiliously to the observance of rules or forms, esp. in matters of religion. **2.** one of the English Puritans of the 16th and 17th centuries. —**pre·ci'sian·ism**, *n.*

pre·ci·sion (prĭ·sĭzh'ən), *n.* **1.** the quality or state of being precise. **2.** accuracy. **3.** mechanical exactness. **4.** punctiliousness. —**pre·ci'sion·ist**, *n.*

pre·clin·i·cal (prē·klĭn'ə·kəl), *adj.* *Med.* pertaining to the period prior to the appearance of the symptoms.

pre·clude (prĭ·klood'), *v.t.* **-clud·ed, -clud·ing.** **1.** to shut out or exclude; prevent the presence, existence, or occurrence of; make impossible. **2.** to shut out, debar, or prevent (a person, etc.) from something. [t. L: m.s. *praeclūdere* shut off, close] —**pre·clu·sion** (prĭ·kloo'zhən), *n.* —**pre·clu·sive** (prĭ·kloo'sĭv), *adj.* —**pre·clu'sive·ly**, *adv.*

pre·co·cial (prĭ·kō'shəl), *adj.* (of birds) active, down-covered, and able to move about freely when hatched. [f. PRECOCI(OUS) + -AL¹]

pre·co·cious (prĭ·kō'shəs), *adj.* **1.** forward in development, esp. mental development, as a child. **2.** prematurely developed, as the mind, faculties, etc. **3.** pertaining to or showing premature development. **4.** *Bot.* **a.** flowering, fruiting, or ripening early, as plants or fruit. **b.** bearing blossoms before leaves, as plants. **c.** appearing before leaves, as flowers. [f. PRECOCI(TY) (t. F: m. *précocité* early maturity) + -OUS] —**pre·co'cious·ly**, *adv.* —**pre·co'cious·ness, pre·coc·i·ty** (prĭ·kŏs'ə·tĭ), *n.*

pre·con·ceive (prē'kən·sēv'), *v.t.*, **-ceived, -ceiv·ing.** to conceive beforehand; form an idea of in advance.

pre·con·cep·tion (prē'kən·sĕp'shən), *n.* **1.** a conception or opinion formed beforehand. **2.** bias; predilection.

pre·con·cert (prē'kən·sûrt'), *v.t.* to arrange beforehand.

pre·con·demn (prē'kən·dĕm'), *v.t.* to condemn beforehand.

pre·co·nize (prē'kə·nīz'), *v.t.*, **-nized, -niz·ing.** **1.** to proclaim; commend publicly. **2.** to summon publicly. **3.** *Rom. Cath. Ch.* (of the Pope) to declare solemnly in consistory the appointment of (a new bishop). [ME, t. ML: m. *praecōnizāre*, der. L *praeco* crier, herald]

pre·con·tract (prē·kŏn′trăkt), *n.* a preëxisting contract of marriage.

pre·crit·i·cal (prē·krĭt′ə·kəl), *adj.* *Med.* anteceding a crisis.

pre·cur·sor (prĭ·kûr′sər), *n.* **1.** one who or that which precedes; a predecessor. **2.** one who or that which indicates the approach of another or something else. [t. L: m. *praecursor*]

pre·cur·so·ry (prĭ·kûr′sə·rĭ), *adj.* **1.** of the nature of a precursor; introductory. **2.** indicative of something to follow; premonitory. Also, **pre·cur·sive** (prĭ·kûr′sĭv).

pred., predicate.

pre·da·cious (prĭ·dā′shəs), *adj.* predatory. Also, **pre·da′ceous.** [f. m.s. L *praedāri* take booty + -ACIOUS] —**pre·da′cious·ness, pre·dac·i·ty** (prĭ·dăs′ə·tĭ), *n.*

pre·date (prē·dāt′), *v.t.,* -**dated,** -**dating.** **1.** to date before the actual time: *he predated the check by three days.* **2.** to precede in date.

pred·a·tor (prĕd′ə·tər), *n.* a predatory person, organism, or thing. [t. L: m. *praedātor*]

pred·a·to·ry (prĕd′ə·tōr′ĭ), *adj.* **1.** of, pertaining to, or characterized by plundering, pillaging, or robbery. **2.** addicted to or living by plundering or robbery: *predatory bands.* **3.** *Zool.* habitually preying upon other animals. [t. L: m.s. *praedātōrius*] —**pred′a·to·ri·ly,** *adv.* —**pred′a·to·ri·ness,** *n.*

pre·de·cease (prē′dĭ·sēs′), *v.t.,* -**ceased,** -**ceasing.** to die before (a person or an event).

pred·e·ces·sor (prĕd′ə·sĕs′ər, prĕd′ə·sĕs′ər or, esp. Brit., prē′də-), *n.* **1.** one who precedes another in an office, position, etc. **2.** anything to which something else has succeeded. **3.** an ancestor or forefather. [ME *predecessour,* t. LL: m. *praedēcessor*]

pre·des·ig·nate (prē·dĕz′ĭg·nāt′, -dĕs′-), *v.t.,* -**nated,** -**nating.** to designate beforehand. —**pre′des·ig·na′tion,** *n.*

pre·des·ti·nar·i·an (prĭ·dĕs′tə·nâr′ĭ·ən), *adj.* **1.** of or pertaining to predestination. **2.** believing in predestination. —*n.* **3.** one who holds the doctrine of predestination. —**pre·des′ti·nar′i·an·ism,** *n.*

pre·des·ti·nate (*v.* prĭ·dĕs′tə·nāt′; *adj.* prĭ·dĕs′tə·nĭt, -tə·nāt′), *v.,* -**nated,** -**nating,** *adj.* —*v.t.* **1.** to foreordain; predetermine. **2.** *Theol.* to foreordain by divine decree or purpose. —*adj.* **3.** predestinated. [ME, t. L: m.s. *praedestinātus,* pp., appointed beforehand]

pre·des·ti·na·tion (prĭ·dĕs′tə·nā′shən, prē′dĕs-), *n.* **1.** act of predestinating or predestining. **2.** the resulting state. **3.** fate or destiny. **4.** *Theol.* **a.** the action of God in foreordaining from eternity whatever comes to pass. **b.** the decree of God by which men are foreordained to everlasting happiness (election) or misery.

pre·des·tine (prĭ·dĕs′tĭn), *v.t.,* -**tined,** -**tining.** to destine beforehand; foreordain; predetermine: *he seemed almost predestined for the ministry.*

pre·de·ter·mi·nate (prē′dĭ·tûr′mə·nĭt, -nāt′), *adj.* determined beforehand.

pre·de·ter·mine (prē′dĭ·tûr′mĭn), *v.t.,* -**mined,** -**mining.** **1.** to determine or decide beforehand. **2.** to ordain beforehand; predestine. **3.** to direct or impel beforehand to something. —**pre′de·ter′mi·na′tion,** *n.* —**pre′de·ter′mi·na′tive,** *adj.*

pre·di·al (prē′dĭ·əl), *adj.* praedial.

pred·i·ca·ble (prĕd′ə·kə·bəl), *adj.* **1.** that may be predicated or affirmed; assertable. —*n.* **2.** that which may be predicated; an attribute. **3.** *Logic.* any one of the various kinds of predicate that may be used of a subject (in Aristotelian logic: genus, species, difference, property, and accident). —**pred′i·ca·bil′i·ty, pred′i·ca·ble·ness,** *n.* —**pred′i·ca·bly,** *adv.*

pre·dic·a·ment (prĭ·dĭk′ə·mənt), *n.* **1.** an unpleasant, trying, or dangerous situation. **2.** a particular state, condition, or situation. **3.** one of the classes or categories of logical predications. [ME, t. LL: m.s. *praedicāmentum,* der. L *praedicāre* proclaim] —**pre·dic·a·men′tal** (prĭ·dĭk′ə·mĕn′təl), *adj.*

—**Syn. 1.** PREDICAMENT, DILEMMA, PLIGHT, QUANDARY refer to unpleasant or puzzling situations. PREDICAMENT and PLIGHT stress more the unpleasant nature, QUANDARY and DILEMMA the puzzling nature of the situation. PREDICAMENT and PLIGHT are sometimes interchangeable; PLIGHT, however, though originally meaning peril, danger, is seldom used today except laughingly: *when his suit failed to come from the cleaners, he was in a terrible plight.* PREDICAMENT, though likewise capable of being used lightly, may also refer to a really crucial situation: *unexpected company for supper, and no food: what a predicament!* DILEMMA, in popular use, means a position of doubt or perplexity in which one is faced by two equally undesirable alternatives: *the dilemma of a hostess who must choose between shocking her strait-laced guest or disappointing those who expected cocktails.* QUANDARY (hardly used outside of the expression: *to be in a quandary*) is the state of mental perplexity of one faced with a difficult situation: *there seemed to be no way out of the quandary.*

pred·i·cant (prĕd′ə·kənt), *adj.* **1.** preaching. —*n.* **2.** a preacher.

pred·i·cate (*n., adj.* prĕd′ə·kĭt; *v.* prĕd′ə·kāt′), *v.,* -**cated,** -**cating,** *adj., n.* —*v.t.* **1.** to proclaim; declare; affirm or assert. **2.** to affirm or assert (something) of the subject of a proposition. **3.** to make (a term) the predicate of such a proposition. **4.** to connote or imply. **5.** *U.S.* to found or base (a statement, action, etc.) on something. —*v.i.* **6.** to make an affirmation or assertion.

—*adj.* **7.** predicated. **8.** *Gram.* belonging to the predicate: *a predicate noun.* —*n.* **9.** *Gram.* (in many languages) the active verb in a sentence or clause along with all the words it governs and those which modify it, e.g., *is here* in *Jack is here.* **10.** *Logic.* that which is predicated or said of the subject in a proposition. [t. L: m.s. *praedicātus,* pp., declared publicly, asserted, LL preached] —**pred′i·ca′tion,** *n.* —**pred′i·ca′tive,** *adj.* —**pred′i·ca′tive·ly,** *adv.*

predicate adjective, (in English and certain other languages, when one of a particular group of verbs is used) an adjective of the predicate bearing a sort of attributive relation to the subject (e.g. *he is dead*) or to the direct object (e.g., *it made him sick*).

predicate noun, (in English and some other languages) a noun following one of a certain group of verbs and designating the same entity as the subject (*he is the king*) or the direct object (*they made him king*).

pred·i·ca·to·ry (prĕd′ə·kə·tōr′ĭ), *adj.* pertaining to preaching.

pre·dict (prĭ·dĭkt′), *v.t.* **1.** to foretell; prophesy. —*v.i.* **2.** to foretell the future. [t. L: m.s. *praedictus,* pp.] —**pre·dict′a·ble,** *adj.* —**pre·dic′tive,** *adj.* —**pre·dic′tive·ly,** *adv.* —**pre·dic′tor,** *n.*

—**Syn. 1.** PREDICT, PROPHESY, FORESEE, FORECAST mean to know or tell (usually correctly) beforehand what will happen. To PREDICT is usually to foretell with precision of calculation, knowledge, or shrewd inference from facts or experience (*the astronomers can predict an eclipse*); it may, however, be used quite lightly: *I predict she'll be a success at the party.* PROPHESY may have the solemn meaning of predicting future events by the aid of divine or supernatural inspiration (*Merlin prophesied the two knights would meet in conflict*); this verb, too, may be used loosely: *I prophesy he'll be back in the old job.* To FORESEE refers specifically not to the uttering of predictions but to the mental act of seeing ahead; there is often (but not always) a practical implication of preparing for what will happen: *he was clever enough to foresee this shortage of materials.* FORECAST has much the meaning of FORESEE, except that conjecture rather than real insight or knowledge is apt to be involved; it is used today particularly of the weather: *rain and snow are forecast for tonight.*

pre·dic·tion (prĭ·dĭk′shən), *n.* **1.** the act of predicting. **2.** an instance of this; a prophecy.

pre·di·gest (prē′dĭ·jĕst′, -dī-), *v.t.* to treat (food), before introduction into the body, by an artificial process similar to digestion, in order to make it more easily digestible. —**pre′di·ges′tion,** *n.*

pre·di·lec·tion (prē′də·lĕk′shən, prĕd′ə-), *n.* a prepossession of the mind in favor of something; a partiality. [f. PRE- + s. L *dīlectio* love, choice]

pre·dis·pose (prē′dĭs·pōz′), *v.t.,* -**posed,** -**posing.** **1.** to dispose beforehand. **2.** to dispose of beforehand. **3.** to give a previous inclination or tendency to. **4.** to render subject, susceptible, or liable: *poor health predisposed them to infection.*

pre·dis·po·si·tion (prē′dĭs·pə·zĭsh′ən), *n.* **1.** the condition of being predisposed. **2.** *Pathol.* a condition in which a slight exciting cause may produce a disease.

pre·dom·i·nance (prĭ·dŏm′ə·nəns), *n.* the quality of being predominant; prevalence over others. Also, **pre·dom′i·nan·cy.**

pre·dom·i·nant (prĭ·dŏm′ə·nənt), *adj.* **1.** having ascendancy, power, authority, or influence over others; ascendant. **2.** prevailing. —**pre·dom′i·nant·ly,** *adv.* —**Syn. 1, 2.** See **dominant.**

pre·dom·i·nate (prĭ·dŏm′ə·nāt′), *v.,* -**nated,** -**nating.** —*v.i.* **1.** to be the stronger or leading element; preponderate; prevail. **2.** to have or exert controlling power (often fol. by *over*). **3.** to surpass others in authority or influence. **4.** to tower (*over*). —*v.t.* **5.** to dominate over. **6.** to prevail over. [f. PRE- + m.s. L *dominātus,* pp., ruled, dominated] —**pre·dom′i·nat′ing·ly,** *adv.* —**pre·dom′i·na′tion,** *n.* —**pre·dom′i·na′tor,** *n.*

pre·em·i·nence (prĭ·ĕm′ə·nəns), *n.* the state or character of being preëminent. Also, **pre·em′i·nence.**

pre·em·i·nent (prĭ·ĕm′ə·nənt), *adj.* eminent before or above others; superior to or surpassing others; distinguished beyond others. Also, **pre·em′i·nent.** [ME, t. L: m.s. *praeēminens,* ppr., standing out, rising above] —**pre·em′i·nent·ly,** *adv.* —**Syn.** See **dominant.**

pre·empt (prĭ·ĕmpt′), *v.t.* **1.** to occupy (land) in order to establish a prior right to buy. **2.** to acquire or appropriate beforehand. Also, **pre·empt′.** [back formation from PREEMPTION] —**pre·emp′tive, pre·emp·to·ry** (prĭ·ĕmp′tə·rĭ), *adj.* —**pre·emp·tor** (prĭ·ĕmp′tor), *n.*

pre·emp·tion (prĭ·ĕmp′shən), *n.* the act or right of purchasing before or in preference to others. Also, **pre·emp′tion.** [f. PRE- + s. L *emptio* a buying]

preen (prēn), *v.t.* **1.** to trim or dress with the beak, as a bird does its feathers. **2.** to prepare, dress, or array (oneself) carefully in making the toilet. [prob. var. of PRUNE³] —**preen′er,** *n.*

pre·en·gage (prē′ĕn·gāj′), *v.t., v.i.,* -**gaged,** -**gaging.** to engage beforehand. Also, **pre′-en·gage′.**

pre-Eng·lish (prē′ĭng′glĭsh), *n.* **1.** the ancient Germanic dialect which by differentiation from its sister dialects eventually became English. **2.** the languages current in Britain before the English settlement. —*adj.* **3.** pertaining to the ancestral Germanic dialect from which English grew, and to its speakers. **4.** pertaining to the languages and peoples of Britain before the English settlement.

---

b., blend of, blended; **c.,** cognate with; **d.,** dialect, dialectal; **der.,** derived from; **f.,** formed from; **g.,** going back to; **m.,** modification of; **r.,** replacing; **s.,** stem of; **t.,** taken from; **?,** perhaps. See the full key on inside cover.

pre·es·tab·lish (prē'ĕs·tăb'lĭsh), *v.t.* to establish beforehand. Also, **pre'-es·tab'lish.** —**pre'es·tab'lish·ment,** *n.*

pre·ex·il·i·an (prē'ĕg·zĭl'ĭ·ən, prē'ĕk·sĭl'-), *adj.* before the Babylonian exile or captivity of the Jews. Also, **pre'-ex·il'i·an, pre'ex·il'ic, pre'-ex·il'ic.** [f. PRE- + s. L *exilium* exile + -AN]

pre·ex·ist (prē'ĭg·zĭst'), *v.i.* 1. to exist beforehand. 2. to exist in a previous state. Also, **pre'-ex·ist'.** —**pre'·ex·ist'ence,** *n.* —**pre'ex·ist'ent,** *adj.*

pref., 1. preface. 2. preference. 3. preferred. 4. prefix.

pre·fab (prē'făb'), *adj., n., v.,* **-fabbed, -fabbing.** —*adj.* 1. prefabricated. —*n.* 2. something prefabricated. —*v.t.* 3. to prefabricate.

pre·fab·ri·cate (prē·făb'rə·kāt'), *v.t.,* **-cated, -cating.** 1. to fabricate or construct beforehand. 2. to manufacture (houses, etc.) in standardized parts or sections ready for rapid assembling and erection. —**pre·fab'ri·cat'ed,** *adj.* —**pre·fab·ri·ca'tion,** *n.*

pref·ace (prĕf'ĭs), *n., v.,* **-aced, -acing.** —*n.* 1. a preliminary statement by the author or editor of a book, setting forth its purpose and scope, expressing acknowledgment of assistance from others, etc. 2. an introductory part, as of a speech. 3. something preliminary or introductory. 4. *Eccles.* a prayer of thanksgiving, the introduction to the canon of the Mass, ending with the Sanctus. —*v.t.* 5. to provide with or introduce by a preface. 6. to serve as a preface to. [ME, t. OF, t. ML: m. *prefātia,* r. L *praefātio* a saying beforehand] —**Syn.** 1. See **introduction.**

pref·a·to·ry (prĕf'ə·tōr'ĭ), *adj.* of the nature of a preface; preliminary. —**pref'a·to·ri·ly,** *adv.*

pre·fect (prē'fĕkt), *n.* 1. a person appointed to any of various positions of command, authority, or superintendence, as a chief magistrate in ancient Rome, or the chief administrative official of a department of France and Italy. 2. the dean in a Jesuit school or college. Also, **praefect.** [ME, t. L: m.s. *praefectus* overseer, director, prop. pp., appointed as a superior]

pre·fec·ture (prē'fĕk·chər), *n.* the office, jurisdiction, territory, or official residence of a prefect. [t. L: m. *praefectūra*] —**pre·fec·tur·al** (prĭ·fĕk'chər·əl), *adj.*

pre·fer (prĭ·fûr'), *v.t.,* **-ferred, -ferring.** 1. to set or hold before or above other persons or things in estimation; like better; choose rather: *to prefer Hemingway to Steinbeck.* 2. *Law.* to give priority, as to one creditor over another. 3. to put forward or present (a statement, suit, charge, etc.) for consideration or sanction. 4. to put forward or advance, as in rank or office. [ME *preferre,* t. L: m. *praeferre* bear before, set before, prefer] —**pre·fer'rer,** *n.* —**Syn.** 1. See **choose.**

pref·er·a·ble (prĕf'ər·ə·bəl), *adj.* 1. worthy to be preferred. 2. more desirable. —**pref'er·a·bil'i·ty, pref'er·a·ble·ness,** *n.* —**pref'er·a·bly,** *adv.*

pref·er·ence (prĕf'ər·əns), *n.* 1. act of preferring; estimation of one thing above another; prior favor or choice. 2. state of being preferred. 3. that which is preferred; the object of prior favor or choice. 4. a practical advantage given to one over others. 5. a prior right or claim, as to payment of dividends, or to assets upon dissolution. 6. the favoring of one country or group of countries by granting special advantages over others in international trade. —**Syn.** 3. See **choice.**

pref·er·en·tial (prĕf'ə·rĕn'shəl), *adj.* 1. pertaining to or of the nature of preference. 2. showing or giving preference. 3. receiving or enjoying preference. —**pref'er·en'tial·ism,** *n.* —**pref'er·en'tial·ist,** *n.* —**pref'er·en'tial·ly,** *adv.*

preferential shop, a shop in which union members are preferred, usually by agreement of an employer with a union.

preferential voting, a system in which the voter expresses ranked alternative choices among candidates to allow a majority choice at one balloting.

pre·fer·ment (prĭ·fûr'mənt), *n.* 1. act of preferring. 2. state of being preferred. 3. advancement or promotion, as in rank. 4. a position or office giving social or pecuniary advancement.

preferred stock, stock which has a preference, with respect to dividends, and often as to assets.

pre·fig·u·ra·tion (prē·fĭg'yə·rā'shən), *n.* 1. the act of prefiguring. 2. that in which something is prefigured.

pre·fig·ure (prē·fĭg'yər), *v.t.,* **-ured, -uring.** 1. to represent beforehand by a figure or type; foreshow; foreshadow. 2. to figure or represent to oneself beforehand. [late ME, t. LL: m.s. *praefigūrāre.* See PRE-, FIGURE, v.] —**pre·fig·ur·a·tive** (prē·fĭg'yər·ə·tĭv), *adj.* —**pre·fig'ure·ment,** *n.*

pre·fix (*n.* prē'fĭks; *v.* prē·fĭks'), *n.* 1. *Gram.* an affix which is put before a word, stem, or word element to add to or qualify its meaning (as *un-* in *unkind*), strictly speaking an inseparable form, but usually applied to prepositions and adverbs also, as in German *mitgehen,* or English *withstand.* 2. something prefixed, as a title before a person's name. [t. NL: m.s. *praefixum*] —*v.t.* 3. to fix or put before or in front. 4. *Gram.* to add as a prefix. 5. to fix, settle, or appoint beforehand. [ME, t. L: m.s. *praefixus,* pp., fixed before] —**pre·fix·al** (prē'fĭk·səl, prē·fĭk'səl), *adj.* —**pre'fix·al·ly,** *adv.*

pre·form (prē·fôrm'), *v.t.* to form beforehand.

pre·for·ma·tion (prē'fôr·mā'shən), *n.* 1. previous formation. 2. *Biol.* a theoretical concept according to which the individual, with all its parts, preëxists in the germ and grows from microscopic to normal proportions during embryogenesis (opposed to *epigenesis*).

preg·na·ble (prĕg'nə·bəl), *adj.* 1. capable of being taken or won by force, as a fortress. 2. open to attack; assailable. [late ME *prenable,* t. OF, der. s. *prendre,* g. L *pre(he)ndre* seize, take] —**preg'na·bil'i·ty,** *n.*

preg·nan·cy (prĕg'nən·sĭ), *n., pl.* **-cies.** the condition or quality of being pregnant.

preg·nant (prĕg'nənt), *adj.* 1. being with child or young, as a woman or female animal. 2. fraught, filled, or abounding (fol. by *with*): *words pregnant with meaning.* 3. fertile or rich (fol. by *in*): *a mind pregnant in ideas.* 4. full of meaning; highly significant: *a pregnant utterance.* 5. full of possibilities, involving important issues or results, or momentous. 6. teeming with ideas or imagination: *a pregnant wit.* [ME, t. L: m.s. *praegnans*] —**preg'nant·ly,** *adv.*

pre·heat (prē·hēt'), *v.t.* to heat before using or before submitting to some process.

pre·hen·sile (prĭ·hĕn'sĭl), *adj.* 1. adapted for seizing, grasping, or laying hold of anything. 2. fitted for grasping by folding or wrapping round an object. [t. F, f. s. L *prehensus,* pp., seized + *-ile* -ILE] —**pre·hen·sil·i·ty** (prē'hĕn·sĭl'ə·tĭ), *n.*

pre·hen·sion (prĭ·hĕn'shən), *n.* 1. the act of seizing, grasping, or taking hold. 2. mental apprehension. [t. L: s. *prehensio*]

pre·his·tor·ic (prē'hĭs·tôr'ĭk, -tŏr'-), *adj.* of or belonging to a period prior to that of recorded history. Also, **pre·his·tor·i·cal.** —**pre·his·tor'i·cal·ly,** *adv.*

pre·his·to·ry (prē·hĭs'tə·rĭ), *n.* course of events in preliterate times, known mainly by archaeology.

pre·ig·ni·tion (prē'ĭg·nĭsh'ən), *n.* ignition of the charge in an internal-combustion engine earlier in the cycle than is compatible with proper operation.

pre·judge (prē·jŭj'), *v.t.,* **-judged, -judging.** 1. to judge beforehand. 2. to pass judgment on prematurely or in advance of due investigation. —**pre·judg'er,** *n.* —**pre·judg'ment;** *esp. Brit.,* **pre·judge'ment,** *n.*

prej·u·dice (prĕj'ə·dĭs), *n., v.,* **-diced, -dicing.** —*n.* 1. an unfavorable opinion or feeling formed beforehand or without knowledge, thought, or reason. 2. any preconceived opinion or feeling, favorable or unfavorable. 3. disadvantage resulting from some judgment or action of another. 4. resulting injury or detriment. 5. **without prejudice,** *Law.* without dismissing, damaging, or otherwise affecting a legal interest or demand. —*v.t.* 6. to affect with a prejudice, favorable or unfavorable: *these facts prejudiced us in his favor.* 7. to affect disadvantageously or detrimentally. [ME, t. F, t. L: m.s. *praejūdicium*] —**Syn.** 1. See **bias.**

prej·u·di·cial (prĕj'ə·dĭsh'əl), *adj.* causing prejudice or disadvantage; detrimental. —**prej'u·di·cial·ly,** *adv.*

prel·a·cy (prĕl'ə·sĭ), *n., pl.* **-cies.** 1. the office or dignity of a prelate. 2. the order of prelates. 3. the body of prelates collectively. 4. the system of church government by prelates (often opprobrious).

prel·ate (prĕl'ĭt), *n.* an ecclesiastic of a high order, as an archbishop, bishop, etc.; a church dignitary. [ME *prelat,* t. ML: m.s. *praelātus,* a civil or ecclesiastical dignitary; in L, pp., set before, preferred] —**prel'ate·ship',** *n.* —**pre·lat·ic** (prĭ·lăt'ĭk), *adj.*

prel·a·tism (prĕl'ə·tĭz'əm), *n.* prelacy or episcopacy. —**prel'a·tist,** *n.*

prel·a·ture (prĕl'ə·chər), *n.* 1. the office of a prelate. 2. the order of prelates. 3. prelates collectively. [t. ML: m. *praelātūra,* der. L *praelātus.* See PRELATE]

pre·lect (prĭ·lĕkt'), *v.i.* to lecture or discourse publicly. —**pre·lec·tion** (prĭ·lĕk'shən), *n.* —**pre·lec'tor,** *n.*

pre·li·ba·tion (prē'lĭ·bā'shən), *n.* a foretaste. [t. LL: m.s. *praelibātio,* der. L *praelibāre* taste beforehand]

prelim., preliminary.

pre·lim·i·nar·y (prĭ·lĭm'ə·nĕr'ĭ), *adj., n., pl.* **-naries.** —*adj.* 1. preceding and leading up to the main matter or business; introductory; preparatory. —*n.* 2. something preliminary; introductory or preparatory step, measure, or the like. [t. NL: m. *praelimināris,* f. L: *prae-* PRE- + *limināris* of a threshold] —**pre·lim'i·nar'i·ly,** *adv.* —**Syn.** 1. PRELIMINARY, INTRODUCTORY both refer to that which comes before the principal subject of consideration. That which is PRELIMINARY is in the nature of preparation or of clearing away details which would encumber the main subject or problem; it often deals with arrangements and the like, which have to do only incidentally with the principal subject: *preliminary negotiations.* That which is INTRODUCTORY leads with natural, logical, or close connection, directly into the main subject of consideration: *introductory steps.* —**Ant.** 1. concluding.

pre·lit·er·ate (prē·lĭt'ər·ĭt), *adj.* not leaving or having written records: *a preliterate culture.*

prel·ude (prĕl'ūd, prē'lōōd), *n., v.,* **-uded, -uding.** —*n.* 1. a preliminary to an action, event, condition, or work of broader scope and higher importance. 2. preliminary action, remarks, etc. 3. *Music.* a. a relatively short, independent instrumental composition, free in form and of an improvised character. b. a piece which precedes a more important movement. c. the overture to an opera. d. an independent piece, of moderate length, sometimes used as an introduction to a fugue. e. music opening a church service; an introductory voluntary. —*v.t.* 4. to serve as a prelude or introduction to. 5. to introduce by a prelude. 6. to play as a prelude. —*v.i.* 7. to serve as a prelude. 8. to give a prelude. 9. to play a prelude. [t. F, t. ML: m.s.

praelūdium, der. L *praelūdere* play beforehand] **—pre·lud·er** (prĭ lōō'dər, prĕl'yə dər), *n.*

pre·lu·sion (prĭ lōō'zhən), *n.* a prelude. [t. L: m. s. *praelūsio*]

pre·lu·sive (prĭ lōō'sĭv), *adj.* introductory. Also, **pre·lu·so·ry** (prĭ lōō'sə rĭ). **—pre·lu'sive·ly,** *adv.*

prem., premium.

pre·ma·ture (prē'mə tyŏŏr', -tŏŏr', prē'mə chŏŏr'), *adj.* **1.** coming into existence or occurring too soon. **2.** mature or ripe before the proper time. **3.** overhasty, as in action. [t. L: m.s. *praemātūrus*] **—pre'ma·ture'ly,** *adv.* **—pre'ma·ture'ness, pre'ma·tu'ri·ty,** *n.*

pre·max·il·la (prē'măk sĭl'ə), *n., pl.* **-maxillae** (-măk-sĭl'ē). *Anat., Zool.* one of a pair of bones of the upper jaw of vertebrates, situated in front of and between the maxillary bones. [t. NL: m. *praemaxilla,* f. L: *prae-* + *maxilla* jaw-bone] **—pre·max·il·lar·y** (prē-măk'sə lĕr'ĭ), *adj.*

pre·med·i·cal (prē mĕd'ə kəl), *adj.* pertaining to the preparation for the study of medicine.

pre·med·i·tate (prĭ mĕd'ə tāt'), *v.t., v.i.,* **-tated, -tating.** to meditate, consider, or plan beforehand. [t. L: m.s. *praemeditātus,* pp., meditated beforehand] **—pre·med'i·ta'tive,** *adj.* **—pre·med'i·ta'tor,** *n.* **—Syn.** See **deliberate.**

pre·med·i·ta·tion (prē'mĕd ə tā'shən), *n.* **1.** the act of premeditating. **2.** *Law.* sufficient forethought to impute deliberation and intent to commit the act.

pre·mier (*n.* prĭ mĭr', prē'mĭ ər; *adj.* prē'mĭ ər), *n.* **1.** the prime minister, or first minister of state, in France, Great Britain, etc. **2.** a chief officer. **—*adj.* 3.** first in rank; chief; leading. **4.** earliest. [t. F: first, g. L *prī-mārius* of the first rank] **—pre·mier·ship** (prĭ-mĭr'shĭp, prē'mĭ'ər shĭp'), *n.*

pre·mière (prĭ mĭr'; *Fr.* prə myĕr'), *n.* **1.** a first public performance of a play, etc. **2.** the leading woman, as in a drama. [F: lit., first (fem.)]

pre·mil·le·nar·i·an (prē'mĭl ə nâr'ĭ ən), *n.* a believer in premillennialism. **—pre·mil·le·nar'i·an·ism,** *n.*

pre·mil·len·ni·al (prē'mə lĕn'ĭ əl), *adj.* of or pertaining to the period preceding the millennium.

pre·mil·len·ni·al·ism (prē'mə lĕn'ĭ ə lĭz'əm), *n.* the doctrine or belief that the second coming of Christ will precede the millennium. **—pre·mil·len'ni·al·ist,** *n.*

prem·ise (prĕm'ĭs), *n., v.,* **-ised, -ising.** *—n.* Also, **prem'iss.** **1.** (*pl.*) **a.** the property forming the subject of a conveyance. **b.** a tract of land. **c.** a house or building with the grounds, etc., belonging to it. **2.** *Logic.* a proposition (or one of several) from which a conclusion is drawn. **3.** *Law.* **a.** a basis, stated or assumed, on which reasoning proceeds. **b.** an earlier statement in a document. **c.** (in a bill in equity) the statement of facts upon which the complaint is based, the parties, etc. *—v.t.* **4.** to set forth beforehand, as by way of introduction or explanation. **5.** to assume, whether explicitly or implicitly, a proposition as a premise for some conclusion. *—v.i.* **6.** to state or assume a premise. [*premiss,* ra. ML: m.s. *praemissa,* prop. fem. pp., sent before; *premise,* b. F (obs.), lit., a sitting before; the E spoken form is always *premiss*]

pre·mi·um (prē'mĭ əm), *n.* **1.** a prize to be won in a competition. **2.** a bonus, gift, or sum additional to price, wages, interest, or the like. **3.** the amount paid or agreed to be paid, in one sum or periodically, as the consideration for a contract of insurance. **4.** *Econ.* the excess value of one form of money over another of the same nominal value. **5.** a sum above the nominal or par value of a thing. **6.** *Stock Market.* the amount paid by the borrower of a stock to the lender of it for the use of the stock. **7.** a fee paid for instruction in a trade or profession. **8.** (formerly) interest paid for the loan of money. **9. at a premium,** in high esteem; in demand. [t. L: m. *praemium* profit, reward] **—Syn. 2.** See **bonus.**

pre·mo·lar (prē mō'lər), *adj.* noting or pertaining to certain of the permanent teeth in mammals (in man, usually called bicuspid teeth) in front of the molar teeth.

pre·mon·ish (prĭ mŏn'ĭsh), *v.t.* to forewarn. [f. s. L *praemonēre* forewarn + *-ish,* modeled on ADMONISH]

pre·mo·ni·tion (prē'mə nĭsh'ən), *n.* **1.** a forewarning. **2.** a presentiment. [t. F (obs.), t. LL: m.s. *praemonitio*]

pre·mon·i·to·ry (prĭ mŏn'ə tōr'ĭ), *adj.* giving premonition; serving to warn beforehand.

pre·morse (prĭ môrs'), *adj. Biol.* having the end irregularly truncate, as if bitten or broken off. [t. L: m.s. *praemorsus,* pp., bitten off in front]

pre·mun·dane (prē mŭn'dān), *adj.* antemundane.

pre·na·tal (prē nā'təl), *adj.* previous to birth: *prenatal care.* **—pre·na'tal·ly,** *adv.*

pre·nom·i·nate (prĭ nŏm'ə nāt', -nĭt), *adj. Archaic.* forementioned. [t. L: m.s. *praenōmĭnātus,* pp., named before]

pre·no·tion (prē nō'shən), *n.* a preconception. [t. L: m.s. *praenōtio*]

pren·tice (prĕn'tĭs), *adj., n. Colloq.* apprentice. [ME]

pre·oc·cu·pan·cy (prĭ ŏk'yə pən sĭ), *n.* **1.** previous occupancy. **2.** state of being preoccupied.

pre·oc·cu·pa·tion (prĭ ŏk'yə pā'shən), *n.* **1.** the state of being preoccupied. **2.** the act of preoccupying.

pre·oc·cu·pied (prĭ ŏk'yə pīd'), *adj.* **1.** completely engrossed in thought; absorbed. **2.** occupied previously. **3.** *Biol.* already used as a name for some species, genus, etc., and not available as a designation for any other.

pre·oc·cu·py (prĭ ŏk'yə pī'), *v.t.,* **-pied, -pying. 1.** to absorb or engross to the exclusion of other things. **2.** to occupy or take possession of beforehand or before others.

pre·o·ral (prē ōr'əl), *adj. Zool.* situated in front of or before the mouth. **—pre·o'ral·ly,** *adv.*

pre·or·dain (prē'ôr dān'), *v.t.* to ordain beforehand; foreordain. **—pre·or·di·na·tion** (prē'ôr də nā'shən), *n.*

prep (prĕp), *Colloq. —adj.* **1.** preparatory: *a prep school.* *—n.* **2.** a preparatory school.

prep., **1.** preparatory. **2.** preposition.

prep·a·ra·tion (prĕp'ə rā'shən), *n.* **1.** a proceeding, measure, or provision by which one prepares for something: *preparations for a journey.* **2.** any proceeding, experience, or the like considered as a mode of preparing for the future. **3.** act of preparing. **4.** state of being prepared. **5.** something prepared, manufactured, or compounded. **6.** a specimen, as an animal body, prepared for scientific examination, dissection, etc. **7.** *Music.* **a.** the preparing of a dissonance, by introducing the dissonant tone as a consonant tone in the preceding chord. **b.** the tone so introduced. **8.** *New Testament.* the day before the Sabbath or some other feast day.

pre·par·a·tive (prĭ păr'ə tĭv), *adj.* **1.** preparatory. *—n.* **2.** something that prepares. **3.** a preparation.

pre·par·a·to·ry (prĭ păr'ə tōr'ĭ), *adj.* **1.** serving or designed to prepare or make ready: *preparatory arrangements.* **2.** preliminary or introductory. **3.** undergoing preparation for entering college (or, in England, a public school), as a student.

pre·pare (prĭ pâr'), *v.,* **-pared, -paring.** *—v.t.* **1.** to make ready, or put in due condition, for something. **2.** to get ready for eating, as a meal, by due assembling, dressing, or cooking. **3.** to manufacture, compound, or compose. **4.** *Music.* to lead up to (a discord, an embellishment, etc.) by some preliminary tone or tones. *—v.i.* **5.** to put things or oneself in readiness; get ready: *to prepare for war.* [t. L: m.s. *praeparāre* make ready beforehand] **—pre·par·ed·ly** (prĭ pâr'ĭd lĭ), *adv.* **—Syn. 1.** PREPARE, CONTRIVE, DEVISE imply planning for, and making ready for something expected or thought possible. To PREPARE is to make ready beforehand for some approaching event, need, and the like: *to prepare a room, a speech.* CONTRIVE and DEVISE emphasize the exercise of ingenuity and inventiveness. The first word suggests a shrewdness that borders on trickery, but this is absent from DEVISE: *to contrive a means of escape; to devise a time-saving method.*

pre·par·ed·ness (prĭ pâr'ĭd nĭs, -pârd'nĭs), *n.* **1.** state of being prepared; readiness. **2.** possession of an adequate army and navy.

pre·pay (prē pā'), *v.t.,* **-paid, -paying. 1.** to pay beforehand. **2.** to pay the charge upon in advance. **—pre·pay'ment,** *n.*

pre·pense (prĭ pĕns'), *adj.* premeditated: *malice prepense.* [earlier *prepenst, prepensed,* pp. of obs. *prepense* meditate beforehand; r. ME *purpense,* t. OF]

pre·pon·der·ance (prĭ pŏn'dər əns), *n.* the quality or fact of being preponderant; superiority in weight, power, number, etc. Also, **pre·pon'der·an·cy.**

pre·pon·der·ant (prĭ pŏn'dər ənt), *adj.* preponderating; superior in weight, force, influence, number, etc.; predominant. **—pre·pon'der·ant·ly,** *adv.*

pre·pon·der·ate (prĭ pŏn'də rāt'), *v.i.,* **-ated, -ating. 1.** to exceed something else in weight; be the heavier. **2.** to incline downward or descend, as one scale or end of a balance, because of greater weight; be weighed down. **3.** to be superior in power, force, influence, number, amount, etc.; predominate. [t. L: m.s. *praeponde-rātus,* pp. See PONDER] **—pre·pon'der·at'ing,** *adj.* **—pre·pon·der·at'ing·ly,** *adv.* **—pre·pon'der·a'tion,** *n.*

prep·o·si·tion (prĕp'ə zĭsh'ən), *n. Gram.* **1.** (in some languages) one of the major form-classes, or "parts of speech," comprising words placed before nouns to indicate their relation to other words or their function in the sentence. *By, to, in, from* are prepositions in English. **2.** any such word, as *by, to, in, from.* **3.** any word or construction of similar function or meaning, as *on top of* (=*on*). [ME, t. L: m.s. *praepositio*] **—prep'o·si'-tion·al,** *adj.* **—prep'o·si'tion·al·ly,** *adv.*

pre·pos·i·tive (prē pŏz'ə tĭv), *adj.* **1.** put before; prefixed. *—n.* **2.** *Gram.* a word placed before another as a modifier or to show its relation to other parts of the sentence. *Red* in *red book* is a prepositive adjective. *John's* in *John's book* is a prepositive genitive.

pre·pos·i·tor (prē pŏz'ə tər), *n.* praepostor. Also, **pre·pos·tor** (prē pŏs'tər). **—pre·pos·i·to·ri·al** (prē pŏz'ə-tōr'ĭ əl), *adj.*

pre·pos·sess (prē'pə zĕs'), *v.t.* **1.** to possess or dominate mentally beforehand, as a prejudice does. **2.** to prejudice or bias, esp. favorably. **3.** to impress favorably beforehand or at the outset.

pre·pos·sess·ing (prē'pə zĕs'ĭng), *adj.* that prepossesses, esp. favorably. **—pre·pos·sess'ing·ly,** *adv.*

pre·pos·ses·sion (prē'pə zĕsh'ən), *n.* **1.** state of being prepossessed. **2.** a prejudice, esp. in favor of a person or thing.

pre·pos·ter·ous (prĭ pŏs'tər əs), *adj.* directly contrary to nature, reason, or common sense; absurd, senseless, or utterly foolish. [t. L: m. *praeposterus* with the hinder part foremost] **—pre·pos'ter·ous·ly,** *adv.* **—pre·pos'ter·ous·ness,** *n.* **—Syn.** See **absurd.**

pre·po·ten·cy (prĭ pō'tən sĭ), *n. Genetics.* the ability of one parent to impress its hereditary characters on its progeny because it possesses more homozygous, dominant, or epistatic genes.

---

b., blend of, blended; **c.,** cognate with; **d.,** dialect, dialectal; **der.,** derived from; **f.,** formed from; **g.,** going back to; **m.,** modification of; **r.,** replacing; **s.,** stem of; **t.,** taken from; **?,** perhaps. See the full key on inside cover.

pre·po·tent (prĭ pō'tənt), *adj.* **1.** preëminent in power, authority, or influence, predominant. **2.** *Genetics.* denoting, pertaining to, or having prepotency. [t. L: m.s. *praepotens*, ppr., having superior power. See **potent**] —**pre·po'tent·ly,** *adv.*

pre·print (prē'prĭnt'). *n.* an advance printing, usually of a portion of a book or of an article in a periodical.

pre·puce (prē'pūs). *n. Anat.* the fold of skin which covers the head of the penis or clitoris; foreskin. [ME, t. F, t. L: m.s. *praepūtium*] —**pre·pu·tial** (prĭ pū'shəl), *adj.*

Pre-Raph·a·el·ite (prē rǎf'ẏə lĭt', -rā'fĭ'-), *n.* **1.** one of a group of English artists (the **Pre-Raphaelite Brotherhood,** formed in 1848, and including Holman Hunt, John Everett Millais, and Dante Gabriel Rossetti) who aimed to revive the style and spirit of the Italian artists before the time of Raphael. Their work was delicate in color and finish and imbued with poetic sentiment. —*adj.* **2.** of, pertaining to, or characteristic of the Pre-Raphaelites. —**Pre-Raph'a·el·it'ism,** *n.*

pre·req·ui·site (prē rěk'wə zĭt), *adj.* **1.** required beforehand; requisite as an antecedent condition. —*n.* **2.** something prerequisite: *three courses in economics were the only prerequisites for admission to his seminar.*

pre·rog·a·tive (prĭ rŏg'ə tĭv). *n.* **1.** an exclusive right or privilege attaching to an office or position, as theoretically that of a sovereign. **2.** a prior, peculiar, or exclusive right or privilege. **3.** *Obs.* precedence. —*adj.* **4.** having or exercising a prerogative. **5.** pertaining to, characteristic of, or existing by virtue of, a prerogative. **6.** *Law.* pertaining to a prerogative court. [ME, t. L: m. *praerogātīva,* prop. fem. adj., voting first] —**Syn. 1.** See **privilege.**

prerogative court, 1. a former ecclesiastical court in England and Ireland for the trial of certain testamentary cases. **2.** the court of probate in New Jersey.

Pres., President.

pres., **1.** present. **2.** presidency.

pre·sa (prě'sä), *n., pl.* **prese** (prě'sě). *Music.* a mark, as :S:, +, or ※, used in a canon, round, etc., to indicate where the successive voice parts are to take up the theme. [It.: a taking, fem. of *preso,* pp. of *prendere* take, g. L *prehendere*]

pres·age (*n.* prěs'ĭj, *v.* prĭ sāj'), *n., v.,* **-aged, -aging.** —*n.* **1.** a presentiment or foreboding. **2.** a prophetic impression. **3.** something that portends or foreshadows a future event; an omen, prognostic, or warning indication. **4.** prophetic significance; augury. **5.** a forecast or prediction. —*v.t.* **6.** to have a presentiment of. **7.** to portend, foreshow, or foreshadow. **8.** to forecast; predict. —*v.i.* **9.** to have a presentiment. **10.** to make a prediction. [ME, t. L: m.s. *praesāgium*] —**pre·sag'er,** *n.*

Presb., Presbyterian.

pres·by·o·pi·a (prěz'bĭ ō'pẏə, prěs'-), *n. Pathol.* a defect of vision incident to advancing age, in which near objects are seen with difficulty. [f. *presby-* (t. Gk., comb. form of *presbys* old man) + -OPIA] —**pres·by·op·ic** (prěz'bĭ ŏp'ĭk, prěs'-), *adj.*

pres·by·ter (prěz'bə tər, prěs'-), *n.* **1.** (in the early Christian church) an office bearer exercising teaching, priestly and administrative functions. **2.** (in hierarchical churches) a priest. [t. LL, t. Gk.: s. *presbýteros,* prop. adj., older] —**pres·byt·er·al** (prěz bĭt'ər əl, prěs'-), *adj.*

pres·byt·er·ate (prěz bĭt'ər ĭt, -ə rāt', prěs'-), *n.* **1.** the office of presbyter or elder. **2.** a body of presbyters.

pres·by·te·ri·al (prěz'bə tĭr'ĭ əl, prěs'-), *adj.* **1.** of or pertaining to a presbytery. **2.** presbyterian (def. 1).

pres·by·te·ri·an (prěz'bə tĭr'ĭ ən, prěs'-), *adj.* **1.** pertaining to or based on the principle of ecclesiastical government by presbyters or presbyteries. **2.** (*cap.*) designating or pertaining to various churches having this form of government and holding more or less modified forms of Calvinism. —*n.* **3.** (*cap.*) a member or adherent of a Presbyterian church. [f. s. L *presbyterium* presbytery + -AN]

Pres·by·te·ri·an·ism (prěz'bə tĭr'ĭ ə nĭz'əm, prěs'-), *n.* **1.** church government by presbyters or elders, equal in rank and organized into graded administrative courts. **2.** the doctrines of Presbyterian churches.

pres·by·ter·y (prěz'bə tĕr'ĭ, prěs'-), *n., pl.* **-teries.** **1.** a body of presbyters or elders. **2.** (in Presbyterian churches) a judicatory consisting of all the ministers (teaching elders) and representative lay or ruling elders from the congregations within a district. **3.** the churches under the jurisdiction of a presbytery. **4.** the part of a church appropriated to the clergy. **5.** (now only in Roman Catholic use) a clergyman's or priest's house. [ME, t. LL: m.s. *presbyterium,* t. Gk.: m. *presbytērion*]

pre·school (prē'skōōl'), *adj.* noting, pertaining to, or taught prior to entrance into a school.

pre·sci·ence (prē'shĭ əns, prěsh'ĭ-), *n.* knowledge of things before they exist or happen; foreknowledge; foresight. [ME, t. LL: m. *praescientia,* der. L *praesciens,* ppr., knowing before] —**pre'sci·ent,** *adj.* —**pre'sci·ent·ly,** *adv.*

pre·scind (prĭ sĭnd'), *v.t.* **1.** to separate in thought; abstract. **2.** to remove. —*v.i.* **3.** to withdraw the attention (*from*). **4.** to turn aside in thought. [t. L: m.s. *praescindere* cut off in front]

Pres·cott (prěs'kət). *n.* **William Hickling,** 1796–1859, U.S. historian.

pre·scribe (prĭ skrīb'), *v.,* **-scribed, -scribing.** —*v.t.* **1.** to lay down, in writing or otherwise, as a rule or a course to be followed; appoint, ordain, or enjoin. **2.** *Med.* to designate or order for use, as a remedy or treatment. **3.** *Law.* to render invalid or outlawed by negative prescription. —*v.i.* **4.** to lay down rules, direct, or dictate. **5.** *Med.* to designate remedies or treatment to be used. **6.** *Law.* **a.** to claim a right or title by virtue of long use and enjoyment (esp. with *for* or *to*). **b.** to become invalid or outlawed by negative prescription, or through lapse of time, as a claim or action. [t. L: m.s. *praescribere* write before, direct] —**pre·scrib'er,** *n.*

pre·script (*adj.* prĭ skrĭpt', prē'skrĭpt; *n.* prē'skrĭpt), *adj.* **1.** prescribed. —*n.* **2.** that which is prescribed; a rule; a regulation. [t. L: m.s. *praescriptum,* n. use of pp., (thing) prescribed]

pre·scrip·ti·ble (prĭ skrĭp'tə bəl), *adj.* **1.** subject to effective prescription. **2.** depending on or derived from prescription, as a claim or right.

pre·scrip·tion (prĭ skrĭp'shən), *n.* **1.** *Med.* **a.** a direction (usually written) by the physician to the pharmacist for the preparation and use of a medicine or remedy. **b.** the medicine prescribed. **2.** the act of prescribing. **3.** that which is prescribed. **4.** *Law.* **a.** a long or immemorial use of some right with respect to a thing so as to give a right to continue such use. **b.** the process of acquiring rights by uninterrupted assertion of the right over a long period of time. [ME, t. L: m.s. *praescriptio*]

pre·scrip·tive (prĭ skrĭp'tĭv), *adj.* **1.** that prescribes; giving directions or injunctions. **2.** depending on or arising from effective prescription, as a right or title. —**pre·scrip'tive·ly,** *adv.*

pres·ence (prěz'əns), *n.* **1.** the state or fact of being present, as with others or in a place. **2.** attendance or company. **3.** immediate vicinity; close proximity: *in the presence of witnesses.* **4.** *Chiefly Brit.* the immediate personal vicinity of a great personage giving audience or reception. **5.** personal appearance or bearing, esp. of a dignified or imposing kind: *a man of fine presence.* **6.** a person, esp. of dignified or fine appearance. **7.** a divine or spiritual being. **8.** *Obs.* a presence chamber. [ME, t. OF, t. L: m. *praesentia*]

presence chamber, *Chiefly Brit.* the room in which a great personage, as a sovereign, receives guests, etc.

presence of mind, alert, calm state of mind in emergencies.

pres·ent¹ (prěz'ənt), *adj.* **1.** being, existing, or occurring at this time or now: *the present ruler.* **2.** for the time being: *articles for present use.* **3.** *Gram.* **a.** denoting action or state in process at the moment of speaking. Example: "*knows*" *is a present form in* "*he knows that.*" **b.** designating a tense, or other verb formation or construction, with such meaning. **4.** being with one or others, or in the specified or understood place (opposed to *absent*): *to be present at a wedding.* **5.** being here or there, rather than elsewhere. **6.** existing in a place, thing, combination, or the like: *carbon is present in many minerals.* **7.** being actually or here under consideration. **8** being before the mind. **9.** *Obs. or Rare.* mentally alert and calm esp. in emergencies. **10.** *Obs.* immediate or instant. —*n.* **11.** the present time. **12.** *Gram.* the present tense, or other verb formation or construction with present meaning, or a form therein. **13.** (*pl.*) *Law.* the present writings, or this document, used in a deed of conveyance, a lease, etc., to denote the document itself: *know all men by these presents.* **14.** *Obs.* the matter in hand. [ME, t. L: m.s. *praesens,* ppr., lit., being before (one)] —**Syn. 1.** See **current.**

pre·sent² (*v.* prĭ zěnt'; *n.* prěz'ənt), *v.t.* **1.** to furnish or endow with a gift or the like, esp. by formal act: *to present someone with a gold watch.* **2.** to bring, offer, or give, often in a formal or ceremonious way: *to present a message, one's card, etc.* **3.** afford or furnish (an opportunity, possibility, etc.). **4.** to hand or send in, as a bill or a check for payment. **5.** to bring (a person, etc.) before, or into the presence of, another, esp. a superior. **6.** to bring before or introduce to the public: *to present a new play.* **7.** to come to show (oneself) before a person, in or at a place, etc. **8.** to show or exhibit. **9.** to bring before the mind; offer for consideration. **10.** to set forth in words: *to present arguments.* **11.** to represent, personate, or act, as on the stage. **12.** to direct, point, or turn to something or in a particular way. **13.** to level or aim (a weapon, esp. a firearm). **14.** *Law.* **a.** to bring a formal charge against, as a person. **b.** to bring formally to the notice of the proper authority, as an offense. **15.** *Brit. Eccles.* to offer or recommend (a clergyman) to the bishop for institution to a benefice. —*n.* **16.** a thing presented as a gift; a gift: *Christmas presents.* [ME *presente(n),* t. OF: m. *presenter,* t. L: m. *praesentāre*] —**pre·sent'er,** *n.*

—**Syn. 1.** See **give. 5.** See **introduce. 16.** PRESENT, GIFT, DONATION, BONUS refer to something freely given. PRESENT and GIFT are both used of something given as an expression of affection, friendship, interest, or respect. PRESENT is the less formal; GIFT is generally used of something conferred (esp. with ceremony) on an individual, a group, or an institution: *a birthday present; a gift to a bride.* DONATION applies to an important gift, usually of considerable size, though the term is often used, to avoid the suggestion of charity, in speaking of small gifts to or for the needy: *a donation to an endowment fund,* to the Red Cross. BONUS applies to something given in addition to what is due, esp to employees who have worked

---

āct, āble, dâre, ärt; ĕbb, ēqual; ĭf, īce; hŏt, ōver, ôrder, oil, bŏŏk, ōōze, out; ŭp, ūse, ûrge; ə = a in alone; ch, chief; g, give; ng, ring; sh, shoe; th, thin; ŧh, that; zh, vision. See the full key on inside cover.

for a long time or particularly well: *a bonus at the end of the year.*

pre·sent·a·ble (prĭ zĕn′tə bəl), *adj.* **1.** that may be presented. **2.** suitable as in appearance, dress, manners, etc., for being introduced into society or company. **3.** of sufficiently good appearance, or fit to be seen. —**pre·sent′a·bil′i·ty, pre·sent′a·ble·ness,** *n.* —**pre·sent′a·bly,** *adv.*

present arms, *Mil.* position of salute in the manual of arms of close-order drill in which the rifle is held in both hands vertically in front of the body, with the muzzle up and the trigger side of the gun forward.

pres·en·ta·tion (prĕz′ən tā′shən, prē′zĕn-), *n.* **1.** the act of presenting. **2.** the state of being presented. **3.** introduction as of a person at court. **4.** exhibition or representation, as of a play. **5.** offering, delivering, or bestowal, as of a gift. **6.** a gift. **7.** *Com.* the presentment of a bill, note, or the like. **8.** *Med.* the appearance of a particular part of the fetus at the mouth of the uterus during labor. **9.** *Brit. Eccles.* the act or the right of presenting a clergyman to the bishop for institution to a benefice.

pres·en·ta·tion·al (prĕz′ən tā′shən əl, prē′zĕn-), *adj.* **1.** of or pertaining to presentation. **2.** presentive.

pres·en·ta·tion·ism (prĕz′ən tā′shə nĭz′əm, prē′zĕn-), *n.* the doctrine that perception is an immediate cognition of ideas. —**pres·en·ta′tion·ist,** *n., adj.*

pres·ent·a·tive (prĭ zĕn′tə tĭv), *adj.* **1.** presented or causing to be presented. **2.** *Eccles.* admitting of or pertaining to presentation.

pres·ent-day (prĕz′ənt dā′), *adj.* current.

pres·en·tee (prĕz′ən tē′), *n.* **1.** one to whom something is presented. **2.** one who is presented.

pre·sen·ti·ment (prĭ zĕn′tə mənt), *n.* a feeling or impression of something about to happen, esp. something evil; a foreboding. [t. F (obs.) der. L *praesentīre* perceive beforehand] —**pre·sen′ti·men′tal,** *adj.*

pre·sen·tive (prĭ zĕn′tĭv), *adj. Semantics.* (esp. formerly) belonging to a class of words which express clear concepts, as distinct from *symbolic* words, which express relations between concepts; notional. —**pre·sen′tive·ly,** *adv.* —**pre·sen′tive·ness,** *n.*

pres·ent·ly (prĕz′ənt lĭ), *adv.* **1.** in a little while or soon. **2.** *Archaic or Dial.* immediately. —**Syn.** See **immediately.**

pre·sent·ment (prĭ zĕnt′mənt), *n.* **1.** the act of presenting. **2.** the state of being presented. **3.** presentation. **4.** a representation, picture, or likeness. **5.** *Com.* the presenting of a bill, note, or the like, as for acceptance or payment. **6.** *Law.* the written statement of an offense by a grand jury, of their own knowledge or observation, when no indictment has been laid before them. [ME, t. OF: m. *presentement,* der. *presenter* PRESENT²]

present participle, a participle with present meaning, e.g. *growing* in "a growing boy."

present perfect, 1. (in English) the tense form constructed by using the present tense of *have* with a past participle, and denoting that the action of the verb was completed prior to the present, e.g., *I have finished.* **2.** (in some other languages) a tense form of similar construction. **3.** a verb in this tense.

pre·serv·a·tive (prĭ zûr′və tĭv), *n.* **1.** something that preserves or tends to preserve. **2.** a chemical substance used to preserve foods, etc., from decomposition or fermentation. **3.** a medicine that preserves health or prevents disease. —*adj.* **4.** tending to preserve.

pre·serve (prĭ zûrv′), *v.,* -**served,** -**serving,** *n.* —*v.t.* **1.** to keep alive or in existence; make lasting. **2.** to keep safe from harm or injury; save. **3.** to keep up; maintain. **4.** to keep possession of; retain: *to preserve one's composure.* **5.** to prepare (food or any perishable substance) so as to resist decomposition or fermentation. **6.** to prepare (fruit, etc.) by cooking with sugar. **7.** *Chiefly Brit.* to keep (game, etc.) undisturbed for personal use in hunting or fishing. —*v.i.* **8.** to preserve fruit, etc.; make preserves. **9.** to maintain a preserve for game animals. —*n.* **10.** something that preserves. **11.** that which is preserved. **12.** (*usually pl.*) fruit, etc., prepared by cooking with sugar. **13.** *Chiefly Brit.* a place set apart for the protection and propagation of game or fish for sport, etc. [ME *preserve(n),* t. LL: m. *praeservāre,* f. L *prae-* + *servāre* keep] —**pre·serv′a·ble,** *adj.* —**pres·er·va·tion** (prĕz′ər vā′shən), *n.* —**pre·serv′er,** *n.* —**Syn. 2.** See **defend.**

pre·side (prĭ zīd′), *v.i.,* -**sided,** -**siding. 1.** to occupy the place of authority or control, as in an assembly; act as chairman or president. **2.** to exercise superintendence or control. [t. L: m.s. *praesidēre* sit before, guard, preside over] —**pre·sid′er,** *n.*

pres·i·den·cy (prĕz′ə dən sĭ), *n., pl.* -**cies. 1.** the office, function, or term of office of a president. **2.** (*often cap.*) the office of President of the United States. **3.** *Mormon Ch.* **a.** a local governing body consisting of a council of three. **b.** the highest administrative body (**First Presidency**), composed of the prophet and his two councilors. **4.** the former designation of any of the three original provinces of British India: Bengal, Bombay, and Madras.

pres·i·dent (prĕz′ə dənt), *n.* **1.** (*often cap.*) the highest executive officer of a modern republic. **2.** an officer appointed or elected to preside over an organized body of persons. **3.** the chief officer of a college, university, society, corporation, etc. **4.** one who presides. [ME, t. L: m.s. *praesidens,* ppr., presiding, ruling]

pres·i·dent-e·lect (prĕz′ə dənt ĭ lĕkt′), *n.* a president after election but before induction into office.

pres·i·den·tial (prĕz′ə dĕn′shəl), *adj.* **1.** of or pertaining to a president or presidency. **2.** of the nature of a president. [t. ML: m.s. *praesidentiālis*]

presidential primary, a direct primary for the choice of state delegates to a national party convention and the expression of preference for a presidential nominee.

pres·i·dent·ship (prĕz′ə dənt shĭp′), *n. Brit.* presidency.

pre·sid·i·o (prĭ sĭd′ĭ ō′; *Sp.* prē sē′dyō), *n., pl.* -**sidios** (-sĭd′ĭ ōz′; *Sp.* -sē′dyōs). **1.** a garrisoned fort; a military post. **2.** a penal settlement. [t. Sp., g. L *praesidium* guard, garrison, post] —**pre·sid′i·al, pre·sid·i·ar·y** (prĭ sĭd′ĭ ĕr′ĭ), *adj.*

pre·sid·i·um (prĭ sĭd′ĭ əm), *n.* (in the Soviet Union) an administrative committee, usually permanent and governmental. [t. L: m. *praesidium* a sitting before]

pre·sig·ni·fy (prē sĭg′nə fī′), *v.t.,* -**fied,** -**fying.** to signify or indicate beforehand; foreshow. [t. L: m. *praesignificāre*]

press¹ (prĕs), *v.t.* **1.** to act upon with weight or force. **2.** to move by weight or force in a certain direction or into a certain position. **3.** to compress or squeeze, as to alter in shape or size. **4.** to weigh heavily upon; to subject to pressure. **5.** to hold closely, as in an embrace; clasp. **6.** to iron (clothes, etc.). **7.** to extract juice, etc., from by pressure. **8.** to squeeze out or express, as juice. **9.** to form hot glass into ware (**pressed ware**) by means of iron mold and plunger, operated by hand or mechanically. **10.** to beset or harass. **11.** to oppress or trouble; to put to straits, as by lack of something: *they were pressed for time.* **12.** to urge or impel, as to a particular course; constrain or compel. **13.** to urge onward; hurry; hasten. **14.** to urge (a person, etc.), importune, beseech, or entreat. **15.** to insist on: *to press the payment of a debt, to press one's theories.* **16.** to plead with insistence: *to press a claim.* **17.** to push forward. **18.** *Archaic.* to crowd upon or throng. —*v.i.* **19.** to exert weight, force, or pressure **20.** to iron clothes, etc. **21.** to bear heavily, as upon the mind. **22.** to compel haste: *time presses.* **23.** to demand immediate attention. **24.** to use urgent entreaty: *to press for an answer.* **25.** to push forward with force, eagerness, or haste. **26.** to crowd or throng. [ME *pressen,* v., der. *presse,* n.; but cf. OF *presser,* g. L *pressāre,* freq. of *premere* press]
—*n.* **27.** printed publications collectively, esp. newspapers and periodicals. **28.** the body or class of persons engaged in writing for or editing newspapers or periodicals. **29.** the critical comment of newspapers, etc., on some matter of current public interest. **30.** *Print.* **a.** machine used for printing, as a **flat-bed cylinder press,** one in which a flat bed holding the printing form moves against a revolving cylinder which carries the paper. **b. rotary press,** one in which the types or plates to be printed are fastened upon a rotating cylinder and are impressed on a continuous roll of paper. **31.** an establishment for printing books, etc. **32.** the process or art of printing. **33.** any of various instruments or machines for exerting pressure. **34.** act of pressing; pressure. **35.** a pressing or pushing forward. **36.** a pressing together in a crowd, or a crowding or thronging. **37.** a crowd, throng, or multitude. **38.** pressed state. **39.** a crease caused by pressing. **40.** pressure or urgency, as of affairs or business. **41.** an upright case, or piece of furniture, for holding clothes, books, etc. [ME *presse,* OE *press,* t. ML: s. *pressa*]

press² (prĕs), *v.t.* **1.** to force into service, esp. naval or military service; to impress. **2.** to make use of in a manner different from that intended or desired. —*n.* **3.** impressment into service, esp. naval or military service. [back formation from *prest,* pp. of obs. *prest,* v., take (men) for military service, v. use of obs. *prest,* n., enlistment, loan, t. OF, der. *prester* furnish, lend, g. L *praestāre* perform, vouch for, excel]

press agent, a person employed to attend to the advertising and publicity of a theater, performer, etc., through advertisements and other notices in the press.

press·board (prĕs′bōrd′), *n.* a kind of millboard or pasteboard.

Press·burg (prĕs′bŏŏrкн), *n.* German name of **Bratislava.**

press·er (prĕs′ər), *n.* one who or that which presses, or applies pressure.

press gang, a body of men under the command of an officer, formerly employed to impress other men for service, esp. in the navy or army. Also, **pressgang.** [PRESS² + GANG]

press·ing (prĕs′ĭng), *adj.* urgent; demanding immediate attention: *a pressing need.* —**press′ing·ly,** *adv.*

press·man (prĕs′mən), *n., pl.* -**men. 1.** a man who operates or has charge of a printing press. **2.** *Brit.* a writer or reporter for the press.

press·mark (prĕs′märk′), *n. Library Science.* a mark put upon a volume to indicate its location in the library.

press of sail, *Naut.* as much sail as the wind, etc., will permit a ship to carry. Also, **press of canvas.**

pres·sor (prĕs′ər), *adj. Physiol.* increasing pressure, as in the circulatory system.

pressor nerve, *Physiol.* a nerve whose stimulation causes an increase of blood pressure.

---

b., blend of, blended; c., cognate with; d., dialect, dialectal; der., derived from; f., formed from; g., going back to; m., modification of; r., replacing; s., stem of; t., taken from; ?, perhaps. See the full key on inside cover.

press·room (prĕs/rōōm/, -rŏŏm/), n. the room in a printing establishment containing the presses.

pres·sure (prĕsh/ər), n. 1. the exertion of force upon a body by another body in contact with it; compression. 2. Physics. the force per unit area exerted at a given point. 3. Elect. electromotive force. 4. the act of pressing. 5. the state of being pressed. 6. harassment; oppression. 7. a state of trouble or embarrassment. 8. a constraining or compelling force or influence. 9. urgency, as of affairs or business. 10. Obs. that which is impressed. [ME, t. F (obs.), t. L: m. pressūra]

pressure cooker, a strong, closed vessel in which liquids, meats, vegetables, etc., may be heated above the boiling point under pressure.

pressure gauge, 1. an apparatus for measuring the pressure of gases or liquids, as of steam in a boiler. 2. an instrument used to determine the pressure in the bore or chamber of a gun when the charge explodes.

pressure gradient, Meteorol. the decrease in atmospheric pressure per unit of horizontal distance in the direction in which pressure decreases most rapidly.

pressure group, a group, such as business or labor, which attempts to protect or advance its interests in state or national legislative bodies.

pressure head, Physics. the pressure of a fluid at a given point in a system divided by the unit weight of the fluid.

pres·su·rize (prĕsh/ər īz/), v.t., v.i., -rized, -rizing. 1. to maintain normal air pressure in (the cockpit or cabin of) an airplane designed to fly at high altitudes. 2. to compress (a gas or liquid) to a pressure greater than normal. —**pres/su·ri·za/tion,** n.

press·work (prĕs/wûrk/), n. 1. the working or management of a printing press. 2. the work done by it.

prest (prĕst), adj. Obs. ready. [ME, t. OF, g. VL or LL praestus]

pres·ter (prĕs/tər), n. priest. [ME, t. OF: m. prestre. See PRIEST]

Pres·ter John (prĕs/tər), a supposed Christian monk and potentate of the Middle Ages, said to have had a kingdom in some remote part of Asia or Africa and associated with fabulous narratives of travel.

pres·ti·dig·i·ta·tion (prĕs/tə dĭj/ə tā/shən), n. sleight of hand; legerdemain. [t. F, der. s. L praestīgiātor juggler, b. with preste lively (t. It.: m. presto, g. L praesto) and with L digitus finger] —**pres/ti·dig/i·ta/tor,** n.

pres·tige (prĕs tēzh/, prĕs/tĭj), n. 1. reputation or influence arising from success, achievement, rank, or other circumstances. 2. distinction or reputation attaching to a person or thing and dominating the mind of others or of the public. [t. F: illusion, glamour, t. L: m.s. praestigium illusion, der. praestīgiae, pl., jugglers' tricks]

pres·tis·si·mo (prĕs tĭs/ə mō/), adv. Music. in the most rapid tempo. [t. It., der. presto PRESTO]

pres·to (prĕs/tō), adv., adj., n., pl. -tos. —adv. 1. quickly, rapidly, or immediately. 2. Music. in quick tempo. —adj. 3. quick or rapid. 4. Music. in quick tempo. —n. 5. Music. a movement or piece in quick tempo. [t. It.: quick, quickly, g. LL praestus, adj., ready, L praestō, adv., at hand]

Pres·ton (prĕs/tən), n. a seaport in NW England, in Lancashire. 119,250 (1951).

Pres·ton·pans (prĕs/tən pănz/), n. a seaside resort in SE Scotland, E of Edinburgh: battle, 1745. 7593 (1951).

Prest·wick (prĕst/wĭk), n. international airport in W Scotland, ab. 25 miles from Glasgow.

pre·sum·a·ble (prĭ zōō/mə bəl), adj. capable of being taken for granted; probable. —**pre·sum/a·bly,** adv.

pre·sume (prĭ zōōm/), v., -sumed, -suming. —v.t. 1. to take for granted, assume, or suppose: I presume you're tired. 2. Law. to assume as true in the absence of proof to the contrary. 3. to undertake, with unwarrantable boldness. 4. to undertake or venture (to do something) as by taking a liberty: to presume to speak for another. —v.i. 5. to take something for granted; suppose. 6. to act or proceed with unwarrantable or impertinent boldness. 7. to rely (on or upon) in acting unwarrantably or taking liberties. [ME, t. L: m.s. praesūmere take beforehand, venture] —**pre·sum·ed·ly** (prĭ zōō/mĭd lĭ), adv. —**pre·sum/er,** n.

pre·sump·tion (prĭ zŭmp/shən), n. 1. the act of presuming. 2. assumption of something as true. 3. belief on reasonable grounds or probable evidence. 4. that which is presumed; an assumption. 5. a ground or reason for presuming or believing. 6. Law. an inference required or permitted by law as to the existence of one fact from proof of the existence of other facts. 7. Logic. an inference in accordance with the common experience of mankind and the established principles of logic (frequently used for arguments by analogy). 8. unwarrantable, unbecoming, or impertinent boldness.

pre·sump·tive (prĭ zŭmp/tĭv), adj. 1. affording ground for presumption. 2. based on presumption: a presumptive title. 3. regarded as such by presumption: an heir presumptive. —**pre·sump/tive·ly,** adv.

pre·sump·tu·ous (prĭ zŭmp/chōō əs), adj. 1. full of, characterized by, or showing presumption or readiness to presume in conduct or thought. 2. unwarrantedly or impertinently bold; forward. 3. Obs. presumptive. [ME presumptuose, t. LL: m. praesumptuōsus, var. of praesumptiōsus] —**pre·sump/tu·ous·ly,** adv. —**pre·sump/tu·ous·ness,** n. —Syn. 2. See bold.

pre·sup·pose (prē/sə pōz/), v.t., -posed, -posing. 1. to

suppose or assume beforehand; to take for granted in advance. 2. (of a thing) to require or imply as an antecedent condition: an effect presupposes a cause. —**pre·sup·po·si·tion** (prē/sŭp ə zĭsh/ən), n.

pre·sur·mise (prē/sər mīz/), n. a surmise previously formed.

pret., preterit.

pre·tence (prĭ tĕns/, prē/tĕns). n. Chiefly Brit. pretense.

pre·tend (prĭ tĕnd/), v.t. 1. to put forward a false appearance of; feign: to pretend illness. 2. to venture or attempt falsely (to do something). 3. to allege or profess, esp. insincerely or falsely. —v.i. 4. to make believe. 5. to lay claim (fol. by to). 6. to make pretensions (fol. by to). 7. to aspire, as a suitor or candidate (fol. by to). [ME pretende(n), t. L: m. praetendere stretch forth, put forward, pretend] —Syn. 1. PRETEND, AFFECT, ASSUME, FEIGN imply an attempt to create a false appearance. To PRETEND is to create an imaginary characteristic or to play a part: to pretend to be ill. To AFFECT is to make a consciously artificial show of having qualities which one thinks would look well and impress others: to affect shyness. To ASSUME is to take on or put on a specific outward appearance, often (but not always) with intent to deceive: to assume an air of indifference. To FEIGN implies using ingenuity in pretense, and some degree of imitation of appearance or characteristics: to feign surprise.

pre·tend·ed (prĭ tĕn/dĭd), adj. 1. insincerely or falsely professed. 2. feigned, fictitious, or counterfeit. 3. alleged or asserted; reputed. —**pre·tend/ed·ly,** adv.

pre·tend·er (prĭ tĕn/dər), n. 1. one who pretends; one who makes false professions. 2. an aspirant or candidate. 3. a claimant to a throne.

pre·tense (prĭ tĕns/, prē/tĕns), n. 1. pretending or feigning; make-believe: my sleepiness was all pretense. 2. a false show of something: a pretense of friendship. 3. a piece of make-believe. 4. the act of pretending or alleging, now esp. falsely. 5. an alleged or pretended reason or excuse, or a pretext. 6. insincere or false profession. 7. the putting forth of a claim. 8. the claim itself. 9. pretension (fol. by to): destitute of any pretense to wit. 10. pretentiousness. Also, esp. Brit., pretence. [ME, t. AF: m. pretensse, t. ML: m. praetensa, prop. fem. (r. L praetenta) of pp. of praetendere pretend]

pre·ten·sion (prĭ tĕn/shən), n. 1. a laying claim to something. 2. a claim or title to something. 3. (often pl.) a claim made, esp. indirectly or by implication, or right to some quality, merit, or the like: pretensions to superior judgment. 4. claim to dignity, importance, or merit. 5. pretentiousness. 6. the act of pretending or alleging. 7. an allegation. 8. a pretext.

pre·ten·tious (prĭ tĕn/shəs), adj. 1. full of pretension. 2. characterized by assumption of dignity or importance. 3. making an exaggerated outward show; ostentatious. [f. m. L praetenti(o) pretension + -ous] —**pre·ten/tious·ly,** adv. —**pre·ten/tious·ness,** n.

preter-, a prefix meaning "beyond," "more than." [t. L: m. praeter-, repr. praeter, adv., prep.]

pre·ter·hu·man (prē/tər hū/mən), adj. beyond what is human.

pret·er·it (prĕt/ər ĭt), n. 1. Gram. (esp. in Germanic grammar) a past. 2. a preterit tense. c. a verb form in this tense. —adj. 2. Gram. denoting past action or state. 3. bygone; past. Also, pret/er·ite. [ME, t. L: m.s. praeteritus, pp., gone by]

pret·er·i·tion (prĕt/ə rĭsh/ən), n. 1. the act of passing by or over; omission; neglect. 2. Law. the passing over by a testator of an heir otherwise entitled to a portion. 3. Calvinistic Theol. the passing over by God of those not elected to salvation or eternal life. [t. LL: m.s. praeteritio a passing over. See PRETERIT]

pret·er·i·tive (prĭ tĕr/ə tĭv), adj. 1. preterit. 2. (of verbs) limited to past tenses.

pre·ter·mit (prē/tər mĭt/), v.t., -mitted, -mitting. 1. to let pass without notice; disregard. 2. to leave undone; neglect; omit. [t. L: m.s. praetermittere let pass] —**pre·ter·mis·sion** (prē/tər mĭsh/ən), n.

pre·ter·nat·u·ral (prē/tər năch/ə rəl), adj. 1. out of the ordinary course of nature; abnormal. 2. supernatural. —**pre/ter·nat/u·ral·ism,** n. —**pre/ter·nat/u·ral·ly,** adv. —Syn. 1. See miraculous.

pre·text (prē/tĕkst), n. 1. that which is put forward to conceal a true purpose or object; an ostensible reason. 2. an excuse; a pretense. [t. L: m.s. praetextus]

pre·tor (prē/tər), n. Roman Hist. praetor. —**pre·to·ri·an** (prē tōr/ĭ ən), adj., n.

Pre·to·ri·a (prĭ tōr/ĭ ə), n. a city in the NE Republic of South Africa: the capital of Transvaal and seat of the executive government of the Republic of South Africa. 230,243 (1951).

pret·ti·fy (prĭt/ə fī/), v.t., -fied, -fying. to make pretty (often in a disparaging sense). [f. PRETT(Y) + -(I)FY]

pret·ty (prĭt/ĭ), adj., -tier, -tiest, n., pl. -ties, adv. —adj. 1. fair or attractive to the eye in a feminine or childish way: a pretty face. 2. (of things, places, etc.) pleasing to the eye, esp. without grandeur. 3. pleasing to the ear: a pretty tune. 4. pleasing to the mind or aesthetic taste: some pretty little story. 5. fine, pleasant, or excellent (much used ironically): a pretty mess. 6. Colloq. or Dial. considerable; fairly great. 7. Archaic or Scot. brave; hardy. 8. Archaic. smart; elegant. —n. 9. (usually pl.) a pretty thing, as a trinket or ornament. 10. a pretty one (used esp. in address). —adv. 11. moderately: *her work was pretty good.* **12.** quite; very: *the wind blew pretty hard.* **13.** *Chiefly Dial.* prettily. [ME *prety, praty,* OE *prættig* cunning, wily, der. OE *prætt,* n., wile, trick; akin to D *part* trick, prank, Icel. *prettr* trick, *prettugr* tricky] —**pret′ti·ly,** *adv.* —**pret′ti·ness,** *n.* —**pret′ty·ish,** *adj.* —**Syn. 1.** See **beautiful.**

pre·typ·i·fy (prē tĭp′ə fī′). *v.t.* **-fied, -fying.** to typify beforehand; prefigure.

pret·zel (prĕt′səl), *n.* a crisp, dry biscuit, usually in the form of a knot or stick, salted on the outside. [t. G, var. of *bretzel.* Cf. ML *bracellus* bracelet]

Preus·sen (proi′sən), *n.* German name of **Prussia.**

pre·vail (prĭ vāl′), *v.i.* **1.** to be widespread or current; to exist everywhere or generally: *dead silence prevailed.* **2.** to appear or occur as the more important or frequent feature or element; predominate: *green tints prevail in the picture.* **3.** to be or prove superior in strength, power, or influence. **4.** to operate effectually; to be efficacious. **5.** to use persuasion or inducement successfully (fol. by *on, upon,* or *with*). [ME *prevaylle(n).* t. L: m. *praevalēre* be more able]

pre·vail·ing (prĭ vā′lĭng), *adj.* **1.** predominant. **2.** generally current. **3.** having superior power or influence. **4.** effectual. —**pre·vail′ing·ly,** *adv.* —**pre·vail′ing·ness,** *n.* —**Syn. 2.** See **current.**

prev·a·lent (prĕv′ə lənt), *adj.* **1.** widespread; of wide extent or occurrence; in general use or acceptance. **2.** *Rare.* having the superiority or ascendancy. **3.** *Now Rare.* effectual or efficacious. [t. L: m.s. *praevalens,* ppr., prevailing] —**prev′a·lence,** *n.* —**prev′a·lent·ly,** *adv.* —**Syn. 1.** See **current.**

pre·var·i·cate (prĭ văr′ə kāt′), *v.i.,* **-cated, -cating.** to act or speak evasively; equivocate; quibble. [t. L: m.s. *praevāricātus,* pp., walked crookedly, deviated] —**pre·var′i·ca′tion,** *n.* —**pre·var′i·ca′tor,** *n.*

pre·ven·ient (prĭ vēn′yənt), *adj.* **1.** coming before; antecedent. **2.** anticipatory. **3.** preventive. [t. L: m.s. *praeveniens,* ppr.] —**prev·e·nance** (prĕv′ə nəns), **pre·ven·ience** (prĭ vēn′yəns), *n.*

pre·vent (prĭ vĕnt′), *v.t.* **1.** to keep from occurring; hinder. **2.** to hinder (a person, etc.), as from doing something: *there is nothing to prevent us from going.* **3.** *Rare.* to cut off beforehand or debar (a person, etc.) as from something. **4.** *Obs.* to precede. **5.** *Obs.* to anticipate. —*v.i.* **6.** to interpose a hindrance: *he will come if nothing prevents.* [ME, t. L: m.s. *praeventus,* pp., lit., come before] —**pre·vent′a·ble, pre·vent′i·ble,** *adj.* —**pre·vent′er,** *n.* —**Syn. 1.** PREVENT, HAMPER, HINDER, IMPEDE refer to complete or partial stoppage of action or progress. To PREVENT is to stop something effectually by forestalling action and rendering it impossible: *to prevent the sending of a message.* To HAMPER is to clog or entangle or put an embarrassing restraint upon: *to hamper preparations for a trip.* To HINDER is to keep back by delaying or stopping progress or action: *to hinder the progress of an expedition.* To IMPEDE is to make difficult the movement or progress of anything by interfering with its proper functioning: *to impede a discussion by demanding repeated explanations.* —**Ant. 1.** help, assist.

pre·ven·tion (prĭ vĕn′shən) *n.* **1.** the act of preventing; effectual hindrance. **2.** a preventive.

pre·ven·tive (prĭ vĕn′tĭv), *adj.* **1.** *Med.* warding off disease. **2.** serving to prevent or hinder. —*n.* **3.** *Med.* a drug, etc., for preventing disease. **4.** a preventive agent or measure. Also, esp. for defs. 2 and 4, **pre·vent·a·tive** (prĭ vĕn′tə tĭv). —**pre·ven′tive·ly,** *adv.* —**pre·ven′tive·ness,** *n.*

pre·view (prē′vū′), *n.* **1.** a previous view: a view in advance, as of a moving picture. —*v.t.* **2.** to view beforehand or in advance. Also, *U.S.,* **prevue.**

pre·vi·ous (prē′vĭ əs) *adj.* **1.** coming or occurring before something else; prior. **2.** *Colloq.* done, occurring, etc., before the proper time; premature. [t. L: m. *praevius*] —**pre′vi·ous·ly,** *adv.* —**pre′vi·ous·ness,** *n.*

previous question, *Parl. Proc.* the question whether a vote shall be taken on a main question, moved before the main question is put, resorted to (esp. in the U.S.) in order to cut off debate.

pre·vise (prĭ vīz′), *v.t.,* **-vised, -vising. 1.** to foresee. **2.** to forewarn. [t. L: m.s. *praevīsus,* pp., foreseen]

pre·vi·sion (prĭ vĭzh′ən), *n.* **1.** foresight, foreknowledge, or prescience. **2.** an anticipatory vision or perception. [f. PRE- + VISION] —**pre·vi′sion·al,** *adj.*

pre·vo·ca·tion·al (prē′vō kā′shən əl). *adj.* consisting of or pertaining to preliminary vocational training.

Pré·vost (prā vō′). *n.* **Marcel** (mȧr sĕl′), 1862–1941, French novelist and dramatist.

Pré·vost d′Ex·iles (prā vō′ dĕg zēl′). **Antoine François** (ȧN twȧn′ frȧn swȧ′). ("*Abbé Prevost*") 1697–1763, French novelist.

pre·vue (prē′vū′), *n., v.t. U.S.* preview.

pre·war (prē′wôr′), *adj.* before the war.

prey (prā), *n.* **1.** an animal hunted or seized for food, esp. by a carnivorous animal. **2.** a person or thing that falls a victim to an enemy, a sharper, a disease, or any adverse agency. **3.** the action or habit of preying: *beast of prey.* **4.** *Rare.* booty or plunder. —*v.i.* **5.** to seek for and seize prey, as an animal does. **6.** to take booty or plunder. **7.** to make profit by activities on a victim. **8.** to exert a harmful or destructive influence: *these worries preyed upon his mind.* [ME *preye,* t. OF, g. L *praeda* booty, prey] —**prey′er,** *n.*

Pri·am (prī′əm), *n. Gk. Legend.* son of Laomedon, hus-

band of Hecuba, and father of Hector and Paris. He was the last king of Troy, at the capture of which he was slain.

Pri·a·pus (prī ā′pəs), *n. Gk. and Rom. Relig.* the personification as a god of the male procreative power. He is the deity of gardens and vineyards, but is a comparatively late addition to the pantheon. [t. L, t. Gk.: m. *Priāpos*] —**Pri·a·pe·an** (prī′ə pē′ən), *adj.*

Prib·i·lof Islands (prĭb′ĭ lôf′). a group of islands in the Bering Sea, SW of Alaska, and belonging to the U.S.: the breeding ground of fur seals.

price (prīs), *n., v.,* **priced, pricing.** —*n.* **1.** the sum or amount of money or its equivalent for which anything is bought, sold, or offered for sale. **2.** a sum offered for the capture of a person alive or dead: *a price on a man's head.* **3.** the sum of money, or other consideration, for which a person's support, consent, etc., may be obtained: *he has his price.* **4.** that which must be given, done, or undergone in order to obtain a thing: *to gain a victory at a heavy price.* **5.** value; worth. **6.** at any price, at any cost, no matter how great. **7.** beyond or without price, unobtainable; priceless. **8.** *Archaic* value or worth. **9.** *Archaic.* great value or worth. —*v.t* **10.** to fix the price of. **11.** *Colloq.* to ask the price of **12.** to set a price on, for capture alive or dead. [ME, t OF: m. *pris,* g. L *pretium* price, value, worth] —**Syn. 1, 4.** PRICE, CHARGE, COST, EXPENSE refer to outlay or expenditure required in buying or maintaining something. PRICE is used mainly of single, concrete objects offered for sale; CHARGE, of services: *what is the price of that coat? a small charge for mailing packages.* COST is mainly a purely objective term, often used in financial calculations: *the cost of building a new annex was estimated at $10,000.* EXPENSE suggests cost plus incidental expenditure: *the expense of a journey was more than the contemplated cost.* Only CHARGE is not used figuratively. PRICE, COST, and sometimes EXPENSE may be used to refer to the expenditure of mental energy, what one "pays" in anxiety, suffering, etc.

price cutting, the act of selling an article at a price under the usual or advertised price.

price·less (prīs′lĭs), *adj.* **1.** having a value beyond all price; invaluable: *she was a priceless help to him.* **2.** *Chiefly Brit. Colloq.* delightfully amusing; absurd.

price list, a list of articles for sale, with prices.

Prich·ard (prĭch′ərd), *n.* a city in S Alabama. 47,371 (1960).

prick (prĭk), *n.* **1.** a puncture made by a needle, thorn, or the like. **2.** act of pricking: *the prick of a needle.* **3.** the state or sensation of being pricked. **4.** *Obs.* a small or minute mark, a dot, or a point. **5.** *Archaic.* a goad for oxen. **6.** *Obs.* any pointed instrument or weapon. **7.** kick against the pricks, to hurt oneself by vain resistance. [ME *prike,* OE *prica* dot, c. LG *prik* point] —*v.t.* **8.** to pierce with a sharp point; puncture. **9.** to affect with sharp pain, as from piercing. **10.** to cause sharp mental pain to; to sting, as with remorse or sorrow: *his conscience pricked him suddenly.* **11.** to urge on with, or as with, a goad or spur: *my duty pricks me on.* **12.** to mark (a surface) with pricks or dots in tracing something. **13.** to mark or trace (something) on a surface by pricks or dots. **14.** to cause to stand erect or point upward: *to prick up one's ears.* **15.** *Farriery.* **a.** to lame (a horse) by driving a nail improperly into its hoof. **b.** to nick: *to prick a horse's tail.* **16.** to measure (distance, etc.) on a chart with dividers (fol. by *off*). —*v.i.* **17.** to perform the action of piercing or puncturing something. **18.** to have a sensation of being pricked. **19.** to rise erect or point upward, as the ears of an animal (fol. by *up*). **20.** *Archaic.* to spur or urge a horse on; ride rapidly. **21.** to transplant seedlings from their original beds to larger boxes (fol. by *off* or *out*). [ME *priken,* OE *prician,* der. *prica* puncture] —**prick′er,** *n.* —**prick′ing·ly,** *adv.*

prick·et (prĭk′ĭt), *n.* **1.** a sharp metal point on which to stick a candle. **2.** a candlestick with one or more such points. **3.** a buck in his second year. [ME, f. PRICK + -ET]

prick·le (prĭk′əl), *n., v.,* **-led, -ling.** —*n.* **1.** a sharp point. **2.** a small, pointed process growing from the bark of a plant. **3.** *Colloq.* a pricking sensation. —*v.t.* **4.** to pick. **5.** to cause a pricking sensation in. —*v.i.* **6.** to rise or stand erect like prickles. **7.** to tingle as if pricked. [ME *prykel,* OE *pricel,* f. *pric(a)* prick + -*el,* n. suffix]

prick·ly (prĭk′lĭ), *adj.,* **-lier, -liest. 1.** full of or armed with prickles. **2.** full of troublesome points. **3.** prickling; smarting. —**prick′li·ness,** *n.*

prickly ash, a rutaceous shrub or small tree (*Zanthoxylum americanum*) with aromatic leaves and branches usually armed with strong prickles.

prickly heat, *Pathol.* a cutaneous eruption accompanied by a prickling and itching sensation, due to an inflammation of the sweat glands.

prickly pear, **1.** the pear-shaped or ovoid, often prickly and sometimes edible, fruit of any of certain species of cactus (genus *Opuntia*). **2.** the plant itself.

prickly poppy, a poppy, *Argemone mexicana,* with prickly pods and leaves, and yellow or white flowers.

prick song, *Archaic or Hist.* written music.

---

b., blend of, blended; c., cognate with; d., dialect, dialectal; der., derived from; f., formed from; g., going back to; m., modification of; r., replacing; s., stem of; t., taken from; ?, perhaps. See the full key on inside cover

pride (prīd), *n., v.,* **prided, priding.** —*n.* **1.** high or inordinate opinion of one's own dignity, importance, merit, or superiority, whether as cherished in the mind or as displayed in bearing, conduct, etc. **2.** the state or feeling of being proud. **3.** becoming or dignified sense of what is due to oneself or one's position or character; self-respect; self-esteem. **4.** pleasure or satisfaction taken in something done by or belonging to oneself or conceived as reflecting credit upon oneself: *civic pride.* **5.** that of which a person or a body of persons is proud: *he was the pride of the family.* **6.** the best or most admired part of anything. **7.** the most flourishing state or period: *in the pride of manhood.* **8.** mettle in a horse. **9.** *Archaic.* splendor, magnificence, or pomp. **10.** *Archaic.* ornament or adornment. **11.** *Obs.* sexual desire. —*v.t.* **12.** to indulge or plume (oneself) in a feeling of pride (usually fol. by *on* or *upon*). [ME; OE *prȳde* (c. Icel. *prȳdhi* bravery), der. *prūd* proud] —**pride′ful,** *adj.* —**pride′ful·ly,** *adv.*
—**Syn. 1.** PRIDE, CONCEIT, SELF-ESTEEM, VANITY imply an unduly favorable idea of one's own appearance, advantages, achievements, etc., and often apply to offensive characteristics. PRIDE is a lofty and often arrogant assumption of superiority in some respect: *pride must have a fall.* CONCEIT implies an exaggerated estimate of one's own abilities or attainments, together with pride: *blinded by conceit.* SELF-ESTEEM implies an estimate of oneself more complimentary than that held by others: *a ridiculous self-esteem.* VANITY implies self-admiration and an excessive desire to be admired by others: *his vanity was easily flattered.* —**Ant. 1.** humility.
Pride (prīd), *n.* **Thomas,** died 1658, British soldier and regicide.
Pride and Prejudice, a novel (1813) by Jane Austen (written 1796–97).
pride of China, the chinaberry tree (def. 1).
Pride's Purge, the exclusion from the House of Commons in Dec., 1648, of about 100 members who favored compromise with the royal party. It was carried out by a force under Colonel Thomas Pride.
prie-dieu (prēdyœ′), *n.* a piece of furniture for kneeling on during prayer, having a rest above, as for a book. [F: pray God]
pri·er (prī′ər), *n.* one who looks or searches curiously or inquisitively into something. Also, **pryer.** [f. PRY + -ER¹]
priest (prēst), *n.* **1.** one whose office it is to perform religious rites, and esp. to make sacrificial offerings. **2.** (in Christian use) **a.** one ordained to the sacerdotal or pastoral office; a clergyman; a minister. **b.** (in hierarchical churches) a clergyman of the order next below that of bishop, authorized to carry out the Christian ministry. **3.** a minister of any religion. [ME *preest,* OE *prēost,* ult. (through VL) t. L: m. *presbyter.* See PRESBYTER]
priest·craft (prēst′kräft′, -kräft′), *n.* priestly arts.
priest·ess (prēs′tĭs), *n.* a woman who officiates in sacred rites.
priest·hood (prēst′hŏŏd), *n.* **1.** the condition or office of a priest. **2.** priests collectively. [ME; OE *prēosthād.* See PRIEST, -HOOD]
Priest·ley (prēst′lĭ), *n.* **1. John Boynton** (boin′tən), born 1894, British novelist. **2. Joseph,** 1733–1804, British chemist, author, and clergyman.
priest·ly (prēst′lĭ), *adj.,* **-lier, -liest. 1.** of or pertaining to a priest; sacerdotal. **2.** characteristic of or befitting a priest. —**priest′li·ness,** *n.*
priest-rid·den (prēst′rĭd′ən), *adj.* managed or governed by priests; dominated by priestly influence.
prig¹ (prĭg), *n.* one who is precise to an extreme in attention to principle or duty, esp. in a self-righteous way. [formerly, coxcomb; ? akin to PRINK]
prig² (prĭg), *v.,* **prigged, prigging,** *n.* —*v.t.* **1.** *Slang.* to steal. **2.** *Scot. and N. Eng.* to haggle. —*v.i.* **3.** *Scot.* to make entreaty. —*n.* **4.** *Slang.* a thief. [orig. cant]
prig·ger·y (prĭg′ərĭ), *n., pl.* **-geries.** the conduct or character of a prig.
prig·gish (prĭg′ĭsh), *adj.* excessively precise, esp. in an affectedly superior or high-minded way. —**prig′gish·ly,** *adv.* —**prig′gish·ness,** *n.*
prig·gism (prĭg′ĭz əm), *n.* priggish character or ideas.
prim (prĭm), *adj.,* **primmer, primmest,** *v.,* **primmed, primming.** —*adj.* **1.** affectedly precise or proper, as persons, behavior, etc.; stiffly neat. —*v.i.* **2.** to draw up the mouth in an affectedly nice or precise way. —*v.t.* **3.** to make prim, as in appearance. **4.** to purse (the mouth, etc.) into a prim expression. [orig. obscure] —**prim′ly,** *adv.* —**prim′ness,** *n.*
prim., primitive.
pri·ma·cy (prī′məsĭ), *n., pl.* **-cies. 1.** state of being first in order, rank, importance, etc. **2.** *Brit. Eccles.* the office, rank, or dignity of a primate. **3.** *Rom. Cath. Ch.* the jurisdiction of the pope as supreme bishop. [ME, t. ML: m.s. *prīmātia,* der. L *prīmas* PRIMATE]
pri·ma don·na (prē′mə dŏn′ə; *It.* prē′mä dôn′nä), *pl.* **prima donnas, prime donne** (*It.* prē′mĕ dôn′nĕ). **a.** first or principal female singer of an operatic company. [t. It.: first lady]
pri·ma fa·ci·e (prī′mə fā′shĭ ē′, fā′shĭ), *Latin.* at first appearance; at first view, before investigation. —**pri′ma-fa′ci·e,** *adj.*
prima-facie evidence, *Law.* evidence sufficient to establish a fact, or to raise a presumption of fact, unless rebutted.
pri·mage (prī′mĭj), *n.* a small allowance formerly paid by a shipper to the master and crew of a vessel for the loading and care of the goods: now charged with the freight and retained by the shipowner. [f. PRIME, V., load + -AGE]
pri·mal (prī′məl), *adj.* **1.** first; original; primeval. **2.** of first importance; fundamental: [t. ML: s. *prīmālis,* der. L *primus* first]
pri·ma·ri·ly (prī′mĕr′ə lĭ, prī′mərə lĭ; *emphatically* prī mâr′ə lĭ), *adv.* **1.** in the first place; chiefly; principally. **2.** in the first instance; at first; originally.
pri·ma·ry (prī′mĕr′ĭ, -mə rĭ), *adj., n., pl.* **-ries.** —*adj.* **1.** first or highest in rank or importance; chief; principal. **2.** first in order in any series, sequence, etc. **3.** first in time; earliest; primitive. **4.** constituting, or belonging to, the first stage in any process. **5.** of the nature of the ultimate or simpler constituents of which something complex is made up. **6.** original, not derived or subordinate; fundamental; basic. **7.** immediate or direct, or not involving intermediate agency. **8.** *Ornith.* pertaining to any of the set of flight feathers situated on the distal segment of a bird's wing. **9.** *Elect.* noting or pertaining to the inducing circuit, coil, or current in an induction coil or the like. **10.** *Chem.* **a.** involving, or obtained by replacement of, one atom or radical. **b.** denoting or containing a carbon atom united to no other or to only one other carbon atom in a molecule. **11.** *Gram.* **a.** (of derivation) with a root or other unanalyzable element as underlying form. **b.** (of Latin, Greek, Sanskrit tenses) having reference to present or future time. —*n.* **12.** that which is first in order, rank, or importance. **13.** *Pol.* **a.** *U.S.* a meeting of the voters of a political party in an election district for nominating candidates for office, choosing delegates for a convention, etc. **b.** a preliminary election in which voters of each party nominate candidates for office, party officers, etc. **14.** one of any set of primary colors. See **primary colors. 15.** *Ornith.* a primary feather. **16.** *Elect.* a primary circuit or coil. **17.** *Astron.* a body in relation to a smaller body or smaller bodies revolving around it, as a planet in relation to its satellites. [late ME, t. L: m.s. *prīmārius* of the first rank. See PRIME, -ARY]
—**Syn. 4.** See **elementary.**
primary accent, *Phonet.* the principal or strongest stress of a word.
primary cell, *Elect.* a cell designed to produce electric current through an electrochemical reaction which is not efficiently reversible and hence the cell, when discharged cannot efficiently be recharged by an electric current.
primary colors, red, green, and blue lights, which, when properly selected and mixed can produce any hue, even white, grays, and purples. These are the **additive primary colors.** In mixing dyes and pigments the colors act subtractively; the **subtractive primary colors** are carelessly named as red, yellow, and blue, but actually the red must be a purple and the blue must be a bluegreen. More than 100 different hues have been detected in the spectrum, but only four of them (red, yellow, green, and blue) contain no suggestion of another hue. From the viewpoint of sensation, therefore, these four may be considered primary colors. To these, white and black may be added for the same reason.
primary election, primary (def. 13b).
primary group, *Sociol.* a group of individuals living in close, intimate, and personal relationship.
primary school, 1. a school for elementary instruction. **2.** *Chiefly U.S.* a school covering the first part, usually the first four years, of the public school course.
pri·mate (prī′mĭt, -māt), *n.* **1.** *Brit. Eccles.* an archbishop or bishop ranking first among the bishops of a province, country, etc. **2.** any mammal of the order *Primates,* that includes man, the apes, the monkeys, the lemurs, etc. **3.** *Rare.* a chief or leader. [ME, t. ML: m.s. *primas* chief bishop, in LL, chief, head, n. use of L *primas,* adj., of first rank] —**pri′mate·ship′,** *n.* —**pri·ma·tial** (prī mā′shəl), *adj.*
prime (prīm), *adj., n., v.,* **primed, priming.** —*adj.* **1.** first in importance, excellence, or value. **2.** first or highest in rank, dignity, or authority; chief; principal; main: *the prime minister.* **3.** first in comparison with others. **4.** of the first grade or best quality: *prime ribs of beef.* **5.** first in order of time, existence, or development; earliest; primitive. **6.** original; fundamental. **7.** *Math.* **a.** not divisible without remainder by any number except itself and unity: *5 is a prime number.* **b.** having no common divisor except unity: *2 is prime to 9.* [late ME, t. L: m.s. *primus* first (superl. of *prior* PRIOR¹)] —*n.* **8.** the most flourishing stage or state. **9.** the time of early manhood or womanhood: *prime of youth.* **10.** the period or state of greatest perfection or vigor of human life: *in the prime of life.* **11.** the choicest or best part of anything. **12.** the beginning or earliest stage of any period. **13.** the spring of the year. **14.** the first hour or period of the day, after sunrise. **15.** *Eccles.* the second of the seven canonical hours or the service for it, orig. fixed for the first hour of the day. **16.** *Math.* **a.** a prime number. **b.** one of the equal parts into which a unit is primarily divided. **c.** the mark (′) indicating such a division (also variously used as a distinguishing mark). **17.** *Fencing.* the first of eight defensive positions. **18.** *Music.* **a.** unison. **b.** (in a scale) the tonic or keynote. [ME; OE *prīm* (def. 15), t. L: s. *prima* (*hōra*) first (hour). Cf. F *prime*]
—*v.t.* **19.** to prepare or make ready for a particular purpose or operation. **20.** to supply (a firearm) with

powder for communicating fire to a charge. **21.** to lay a train of powder to (any charge, a mine, etc.). **22.** to pour water into (a pump) so as to swell the sucker and so act as a seal, making it work effectively. **23.** to cover (a surface) with a preparatory coat or color, as in painting. **24.** to supply or equip with information, words, etc., for use. **25.** (of a boiler or a steam engine) to operate so that water is carried over into the cylinder with the steam. [orig. doubtful] **—prime′ness,** *n.* **—Syn. 5.** PRIME, PRIMEVAL, PRIMITIVE have reference to that which is first. PRIME means first in numerical order or order of development: *prime meridian; prime cause.* PRIMEVAL means belonging to the first or earliest ages: *the primeval forest.* PRIMITIVE suggests the characteristics of the origins or early stages of a development, and hence implies the simplicity of original things: *primitive tribes, conditions, ornaments, customs, tools.*

prime cost, that part of the cost of a commodity deriving from the labor and materials directly utilized in its construction.

prime·ly (prīm′lĭ), *adv. Colloq.* excellently.

prime meridian, a meridian from which longitude east and west is reckoned, usually that of Greenwich, England.

prime minister, the first or principal minister of certain governments: the chief of the cabinet or ministry: *the British prime minister.* **—prime ministry.**

prime mover, 1. *Mech.* **a.** the initial agent which puts a machine in motion, as wind, electricity, etc. **b.** a machine, as a water wheel or steam engine, which receives and modifies energy as supplied by some natural source. **2.** means of towing a cannon, as an animal, truck, or tractor. **3.** *Aristotelian Philos.* that which is the first cause of all movement and does not itself move.

prim·er[1] (prĭm′ər), *n.* **1.** an elementary book for teaching children to read. **2.** any small book of elementary principles: *a primer of phonetics.* **3. great primer,** a printing type (18 point). **4. long primer,** a printing type (10 point). [ME, t. ML: m.s. *prīmārium,* prop. neut. adj., PRIMARY]

prim·er[2] (prī′mər), *n.* **1.** one who or that which primes. **2.** a cap, cylinder, etc., containing a compound which may be exploded by percussion or other means, used for firing a charge of powder. [f. PRIME, v. + -ER[1]]

pri·me·ro (prĭ′mâr′ō), *n.* a card game fashionable in England in the 16th and 17th centuries. [t. Sp.: alter. of *primera,* fem. of *primero* first, g. L *prīmārius* PRIMARY]

pri·me·val (prī·mē′vəl), *adj.* of or pertaining to the first age or ages, esp. of the world: *primeval forms of life.* [f. m.s. L *prīmaevus* young + -AL[1]] **—pri·me′val·ly,** *adv.* **—Syn.** See **prime.**

pri·mi·ge·ni·al (prī′mə jē′nĭ əl), *adj.* **1.** of a primitive type; primordial. **2.** *Obs.* first generated or produced. [f. s. L *prīmigenius* original + -AL[1]]

pri·mine (prī′mĭn), *n. Bot.* the outer integument of an ovule. Cf. **secundine.** [f. s. L *prīmus* first + -INE[2]]

prim·ing (prī′mĭng), *n.* **1.** the powder or other material used to ignite a charge. **2.** act of one who or that which primes. **3.** a first coat or layer of paint, size, etc., given to any surface as a ground. [see, PRIME v.]

pri·mip·a·ra (prī·mĭp′ə rə), *n., pl.* **-rae** (-rē). *Obstet.* a woman who has borne but one child or who is parturient for the first time. [t. L: f. *prīmi-* (comb. form of *prīmus* first) + *-para* (fem.) -PAROUS] **—pri·mi·par·i·ty** (prī′mĭ păr′ə tĭ), *n.* **—pri·mip′a·rous,** *adj.*

prim·i·tive (prĭm′ə tĭv), *adj.* **1.** being the first or earliest of the kind or in existence, esp. in an early age of the world: *primitive forms of life.* **2.** early in the history of the world or of mankind. **3.** characteristic of early ages or of an early state of human development: *primitive art.* **4.** *Anthropol.* of or pertaining to a race, group, etc., having cultural or physical similarities with their early ancestors. **5.** unaffected or little affected by civilizing influences. **6.** being in its or the earliest period; early. **7.** old-fashioned. **8.** original or radical (as opposed to *derivative*): *a primitive word.* **9.** primary (as opposed to *secondary*). **10.** *Biol.* **a.** rudimentary; primordial. **b.** denoting species, etc., only slightly evolved from early antecedent types. **c.** of early formation and temporary, as a part that subsequently disappears. **—n. 11.** something primitive. **12.** *Art.* **a.** an artist, esp. a painter, belonging to an early period in the development of a style, esp. that preceding the Renaissance. **b.** a provincial or naïve painter. **c.** a work of art by such an artist. **13.** *Math.* a geometrical or algebraic form or expression from which another is derived. **14.** the form from which a given word or other linguistic form has been derived, by either morphological or historical processes, as *take* in *undertake.* [t. L: m.s. *prīmitīvus* first of its kind; r. ME *primitif,* t. OF] **—prim′i·tive·ly,** *adv.* **—prim′i·tive·ness,** *n.* **—Syn. 1.** See **prime.**

prim·i·tiv·ism (prĭm′ə tĭv ĭz′əm), *n.* a recurrent theory or belief, as in philosophy, art, etc., that the qualities of primitive or chronologically early cultures are superior to those of contemporary civilization. **—prim′i·tiv·ist,** *n.*

Pri·mo de Ri·ve·ra (prē′mō dĕ rē vĕ′rä), **Miguel** (mē gel′), 1870–1930, Spanish general: dictator of Spain.

pri·mo·gen·i·tor (prī′mə jĕn′ə tr), *n.* **1.** a first parent or earliest ancestor. **2.** a forefather or ancestor. [t. ML, f. L: *prīmō* at first + *genitor* male parent]

pri·mo·gen·i·ture (prī′mə jĕn′ə chər), *n.* **1.** state or fact of being the first-born among the children of the same parents. **2.** *Law.* the principle of inheritance or succession by the first-born, specif. the eldest son. [t. ML: m. *prīmōgenitūra,* der. L *prīmōgenitus* first-born]

pri·mor·di·al (prī môr′dĭ əl), *adj.* **1.** constituting a beginning; giving origin to something derived or developed; original; elementary. **2.** *Biol.* primitive; initial; first; specif., in *Embryol.,* of determined but incompletely differentiated character: *primordial germ cells.* **3.** pertaining to or existing at or from the very beginning: *primordial matter.* [ME, t. LL: s. *prīmordiālis,* der. L *prīmordium* beginning] **—pri·mor′di·al·ly,** *adv.*

pri·mor·di·um (prī môr′dĭ əm), *n.,pl.* **-dia** (-dĭ ə). *Embryol.* the first recognizable, histologically undifferentiated stage in the development of an organ. [prop. neut. of L *prīmordius* original]

primp (prĭmp), *v.t.* **1.** to dress or deck with nicety. **—v.i. 2.** *Dial.* or *Colloq.* to primp oneself; to prink. [akin to PRIM, v.]

prim·rose (prĭm′rōz′), *n.* **1.** any plant of the genus *Primula* (family *Primulaceae*), comprising perennial herbs with variously colored flowers, as *P. vulgaris,* a common yellow-flowered European species cultivated in many varieties, or *P. sinensis,* with flowers of various colors. **2.** evening primrose. **3.** pale yellow. **—adj. 4.** pertaining to the primrose. **5.** abounding in primroses. **6.** pleasant; being that of pleasure: *the primrose path.* **7.** of a pale yellow. [ME *primerose,* t. ML: m. *prīma rosa* first rose]

prim·u·la (prĭm′yə lə), *n.* a primrose (def. 1). [t. ML: kind of flower; short for *prīmula vēris,* lit., first (flower) of spring]

prim·u·la·ceous (prĭm′yə lā′shəs), *adj.* belonging to the *Primulaceae,* a family of plants of which the primrose or primula is the type. [f. PRIMUL(A) + -ACEOUS]

pri·mum mo·bi·le (prī′məm mŏb′ə lē′), *Latin.* **1.** *Ptolemaic Astronomy.* the outermost of the ten concentric spheres of the universe, making a complete revolution every twenty-four hours and causing all the others to do likewise. **2.** a prime mover. [L: lit., first moving thing]

prin., principal.

prince (prĭns), *n.* **1.** a nonreigning male member of a royal family. **2.** *Hist.* a sovereign or monarch; a king. **3.** (in Great Britain) a son, or a grandson (if the child of a son), of a king or queen. **4.** the English equivalent of certain titles of nobility of varying importance or rank in certain continental European (or other) countries. **5.** a holder of such a title. **6.** the ruler of a small state, as one actually or nominally subordinate to a suzerain. **7.** one who or that which is chief or preëminent in any class, group, etc.: *a merchant prince.* **8.** (formerly) a queen. [ME, t. OF, t. L: m.s. *princeps* principal person, prop. adj., first, principal] **—prince′li·ness,** *n.*

Prince Albert, a double-breasted, long frock coat.

Prince Albert National Park, a national park in W Canada, in central Saskatchewan. 1869 sq. mi.

prince consort, a prince who is the husband of a reigning female sovereign. **2.** (*caps.*) **Albert,** 1819–61, Prince of Saxe-Coburg-Gotha, husband of Queen Victoria.

prince·dom (prĭns′dəm), *n.* **1.** the position, rank, or dignity of a prince. **2.** a principality (territory). **3.** (*pl.*) the principalities (angels).

Prince Edward Island, an island in the Gulf of St. Lawrence, forming a province of Canada: fox farms. 106,000 pop. (est. 1953); 2184 sq. mi. *Cap.* Charlottetown.

prince·kin (prĭns′kĭn), *n.* a little or minor prince. Also, **prince·let** (prĭns′lĭt), **prince·ling** (prĭns′lĭng).

prince·ly (prĭns′lĭ), *adj.,* **-lier, -liest. 1.** greatly liberal; lavish. **2.** like or befitting a prince; magnificent. **3.** of or pertaining to a prince; royal; noble; magnificent. **—prince′li·ness,** *n.*

Prince of Darkness, the devil; Satan.

Prince of Peace, Christ. Isa. 9:6.

Prince of Wales, 1. a title conferred on the eldest son, or heir apparent, of the British sovereign. **2. Cape,** a cape in W Alaska, on Bering Strait opposite the Soviet Union: the westernmost point of North America.

prince regent, a prince who is regent of a country.

prince royal, the eldest son of a king or queen.

Prince Ru·pert (rōō′pərt), a seaport and railway terminus in W Canada, in British Columbia. 8546 (1951).

prince's-feath·er (prĭn′sĭz fĕth′ər), *n.* a tall, showy, garden annual, a variety of *Amaranthus hybridus,* bearing thick crowded spikes of small red flowers.

prin·cess (prĭn′sĭs), *n.* **1.** a nonreigning female member of a royal family. **2.** a female sovereign. **3.** the consort of a prince. **4.** (in Great Britain) a daughter, or a granddaughter (if the child of a son), of a king or queen. [ME *princesse,* t. F, fem. of *prince* PRINCE]

prin·cesse dress (prĭn sĕs′, prĭn′sĭs), a woman's close-fitting dress cut in one piece from shoulder to hem, thus combining bodice and skirt. Also, **princess dress.**

Prince·ton (prĭns′tən), *n.* a borough in central New Jersey: battle, 1777. 12,230 (1950).

prin·ci·pal (prĭn′sə pəl), *adj.* **1.** first or highest in rank, importance, value, etc.; chief; foremost. **2.** of the nature of principal, or a capital sum. **—n. 3.** a chief or head. **4.** a governing or presiding officer, as of a school or (*esp. Brit.*) a college. **5.** one who takes a leading part;

---

a chief actor or doer. **6.** the first player of a division of instruments in an orchestra (excepting the leader of the first violins). **7.** something of principal or chief importance. **8.** *Law.* **a.** a person authorizing another (an agent) to represent him. **b.** a person directly responsible for a crime, either as actual perpetrator or as abettor present at its commission. Cf. **accessory. 9.** a person primarily liable for an obligation, in contrast, usage, with endorser. **10.** the main body of an estate, etc., as distinguished from income. **11.** *Com.* a capital sum, as distinguished from interest or profit. **12.** *Music.* **a.** an organ stop otherwise called diapason. **b.** the subject of a fugue (opposed to *answer*). **13.** the central structure of a roof which determines its shape and supports it. **14.** each of the combatants in a duel, as distinguished from the seconds. [ME, t. L: s. *principālis* first, chief] **—prin′ci·pal·ship′**, *n.* —Syn. **1.** prime, paramount, leading, main. See **capital¹.**

principal clause, main clause.

prin·ci·pal·i·ty (prĭn′sə păl′ə tĭ), *n.*, *pl.* -ties. **1.** a state ruled by a prince, usually a relatively small state or a state that falls within a larger state such as an empire. **2.** the position or authority of a prince or chief ruler; sovereignty; supreme power. **3.** the rule of a prince of a small or subordinate state. **4. the principality,** *(often cap.)* Brit. Wales. **5.** *(pl.) Theol.* an order of angels. See **angel** (def. 1). **6.** *Obs.* preëminence.

prin·ci·pal·ly (prĭn′sə pəl ĭ, -sĭp lĭ), *adv.* chiefly; mainly. —Syn. See **especially.**

principal parts, *Gram.* a set of inflected forms of a verb from which all the other inflected forms can be inferred (theoretically, the smallest such set) as *sing, sang, sung; smoke, smoked.*

prin·ci·pate (prĭn′sə pāt′), *n.* chief place or authority.

prin·cip·i·um (prĭn sĭp′Y əm), *n.*, *pl.* -cipia (-sĭp′Y ə). a principle. [t. L]

prin·ci·ple (prĭn′sə pəl), *n.* **1.** an accepted or professed rule of action or conduct: *a man of good principles.* **2.** a fundamental, primary, or general truth, on which other truths depend: *the principles of government.* **3.** a fundamental doctrine or tenet; a distinctive ruling opinion: *the principles of the Stoics.* **4.** *(pl.)* right rules of conduct. **5.** guiding sense of the requirements and obligations of right conduct: *a man of principle.* **6.** fixed rule or adopted method as to action. **7.** a rule or law exemplified in natural phenomena, in the construction or operation of a machine, the working of a system, or the like: *the principle of capillary attraction.* **8.** the method of formation, operation, or procedure exhibited in a given case: *a community organized on the principle of one great family.* **9.** a determining characteristic of something; essential quality of character. **10.** an originating or actuating agency or force. **11.** an actuating agency in the mind or character, as an instinct, faculty, or natural tendency. **12.** *Chem.* a constituent of a substance, esp. one giving to it some distinctive quality or effect. **13.** *Obs.* beginning or commencement. **14. in principle,** according to the rule generally followed. **15. on principle, a.** according to fixed rule, method, or practice. **b.** according to the personal rule for right conduct, as a matter of moral principle. [ME, f. F *principe* (t. L: m. *principium*) + -le, n. suffix (cf. SYLLABLE, etc.)] —Syn. **1, 2.** PRINCIPLE, CANON, RULE imply something established as a standard or test, for measuring, regulating, or guiding conduct or practice. A PRINCIPLE is a general and fundamental truth which may be used in deciding conduct or choice: *to adhere to principle.* CANON, originally referring to an edict of the Church (a meaning which it still retains), is used of any principle, law, or critical standard which is officially approved, particularly in aesthetics and scholarship: *canons of literary criticism.* A RULE, usually something adopted or enacted, is often the specific application of a principle: *the golden rule.*

prin·ci·pled (prĭn′sə pəld), *adj.* imbued with or having principles: *high-principled.*

principle of relativity. See **relativity** (def. 2).

prink (prĭngk), *v.t.* **1.** to deck or dress for show. —*v.i.* **2.** to deck oneself out. **3.** to fuss over one's dress, esp. before the looking glass. [appar. akin to PRANK², v.] —**prink′er,** *n.*

print (prĭnt), *v.t.* **1.** to produce (a book, picture, etc.) by applying inked types, plates, blocks, or the like, with direct pressure to paper or other material. **2.** to cause (a manuscript, etc.) to be reproduced in print. **3.** to write in letters like those commonly used in print. **4.** to indent or mark (a surface, etc.) by pressing something into or on it. **5.** to produce or fix (an indentation, mark, etc.) as by pressure. **6.** to impress on the mind, memory, etc. **7.** to apply (a thing) with pressure so as to leave an indentation, mark, etc. **8.** *Photog.* to produce a positive picture from (a negative) by the transmission of light. —*v.i.* **9.** to take impressions from type, etc., as in a press. **10.** to produce books, etc., by means of a press. **11.** to give an impression on paper, etc., as types, plates, etc. **12.** to write in characters such as are used in print. **13.** to follow the vocation of a printer. —*n.* **14.** state of being printed. **15. in print, a.** in printed form; published. **b.** (of a book, etc.) still available for purchase from the publisher. **16. out of print,** (of a book, etc.) no longer available for purchase from the publisher; sold out by the publisher. **17.** printed lettering, esp. with reference to character, style, or size. **18.** printed matter. **19.** a printed publication, as a newspaper. **20.** newsprint. **21.** a picture, design, or

the like, printed from an engraved or otherwise prepared block, plate, etc. **22.** an indentation, mark, etc., made by the pressure of one body or thing on another. **23.** something with which an impression is made; a stamp or die. **24.** a design usually in color pressed on woven cotton with engraved rollers. **25.** the cloth so treated. **26.** something that has been subjected to impression, as a pat of butter. **27.** *Photog.* a picture made from a negative. [ME *priente*, t. OF: impression, print, pp. of *preindre*, g. L *premere* press] —**print′a·ble,** *adj.* —**print′er,** *n.*

print., printing.

print·er's devil (prĭn′tərz), devil (def. 4).

print·er·y (prĭn′tər Y). *n.*, *pl.* -eries. **1.** an establishment for typographic printing. **2.** an establishment for the printing of calico or the like.

print·ing (prĭn′tĭng), *n.* **1.** the art, process, or business of producing books, newspapers, etc., by impression from movable types, plates, etc.; typography. **2.** act of one who or that which prints. **3.** words, etc., in printed form. **4.** printed matter. **5.** the whole number of copies of a book, etc., printed at one time. **6.** writing in which the letters are like those commonly used in print.

printing press, a machine for printing on paper or the like from type, plates, etc. Cf. **press** (def. 30).

print·less (prĭnt′lĭs), *adj.* making, retaining, or showing no print or impression.

print shop, 1. a shop where prints or engravings are sold. **2.** a shop for typographic printing.

pri·or¹ (prī′ər), *adj.* **1.** preceding in time, or in order; earlier or former; anterior or antecedent: *a prior agreement.* **2. prior to,** preceding: *prior to that time.* —*adv.* **3.** previous (fol. by *to*): *this happened prior to the year 1900.* [t. L: former, earlier]

pri·or² (prī′ər), *n.* **1.** an officer in a monastic order or religious house, sometimes next in rank below an abbot. **2.** a chief magistrate, as in the medieval republic of Florence. [ME and OE, t. ML: superior, head] —**pri′or·ship′,** *n.*

Pri·or (prī′ər), *n.* **Matthew,** 1664–1721, British poet.

pri·or·ate (prī′ər Yt), *n.* **1.** the office, rank, or term of office of a prior. **2.** a priory.

pri·or·ess (prī′ər Ys), *n.* a woman holding a position corresponding to that of a prior, sometimes ranking next below an abbess.

pri·or·i·ty (prī ŏr′ə tY, -ŏr′-), *n.*, *pl.* -ties. **1.** state of being earlier in time, or of preceding something else. **2.** precedence in order, rank, etc. **3.** the having of certain rights before another.

pri·o·ry (prī′ər Y), *n.*, *pl.* -ries. a religious house governed by a prior or prioress, often dependent upon an abbey. [ME *priorie*, t. ML: m. *priória*]

Pris·ci·an (prĭsh′ən, prĭsh′Yən), *n.* fl. A.D. c500, Latin grammarian.

prise (prīz), *v.t.*, **prised, prising,** *n.* prize³.

prism (prĭz′əm), *n.* **1.** *Optics.* a transparent prismatic body (esp. one with triangular bases) used for decomposing light into its spectrum or for reflecting light beams. **2.** *Geom.* a solid whose bases or ends are any congruent and parallel polygons, and whose sides are parallelograms. **3.** *Crystall.* **a.** a form consisting of faces which are parallel to the vertical axis and intersect the horizontal axes. **b.** a dome (**horizontal prism**). [t. LL: m. *prisma*, t. Gk.: lit., something sawed]

Prism (def. 1)

pris·mat·ic (prĭz măt′Yk), *adj.* **1.** of, pertaining to, or like a prism. **2.** formed by, or as if by, a transparent prism. **3.** varied in color; brilliant. Also, **pris·mat′i·cal.** —**pris·mat′i·cal·ly,** *adv.*

prismatic colors, the components of ordinary white or near-white light as separated by a prism.

pris·on (prĭz′ən), *n.* **1.** a public building for the confinement or safe custody of criminals and others committed by law. **2.** state prison. **3.** a place of confinement or involuntary restraint. **4.** imprisonment. [ME, t. OF, g. s. L *pre(he)nsio* seizure, arrest]

pris·on·er (prĭz′ə nər, prĭz′nər), *n.* **1.** one who is confined in prison or kept in custody, esp. as the result of legal process. **2.** one taken by an enemy in war (**prisoner of war**). **3.** one who or something that is deprived of liberty or kept in restraint.

prisoner's base, an old game variously played, esp. by boys.

prison psychosis, *Psychiatry.* a state of mental confusion, transitory or permanent, precipitated by incarceration or by the anticipation of imprisonment.

pris·sy (prĭs′Y), *adj.*, -sier, -siest. *U.S. Colloq.* or *Dial.* precise; prim; affectedly nice. [b. PRIM and SISSY]

pris·tine (prĭs′tēn, -tYn, -tīn), *adj.* **1.** of or pertaining to the earliest period or state; original; primitive. **2.** having its original purity. [t. L: m.s. *pristinus* early]

prith·ee (prĭth′Y), *interj.* *Archaic.* (I) pray thee.

priv., privative.

pri·va·cy (prī′və sY; *also* Brit. prĭv′ə sY), *n.*, *pl.* -cies. **1.** state of being private; retirement or seclusion. **2.** secrecy. **3.** *Rare.* a private place. [f. PRIV(ATE) + -ACY]

Pri·vat·do·cent (prē vät′dō tsĕnt′), *n.* (in German and certain other universities) a private teacher or lecturer recognized by the university but receiving no compensation from it, being remunerated by fees. Also, **Pri·vat′do·zent′.** [G: private instructor]

pri·vate (prī′vYt), *adj.* **1.** belonging to some particular person or persons; belonging to oneself; being one's own:

private property. **2.** pertaining to or affecting a particular person or a small group of persons; individual; personal: *for your private satisfaction.* **3.** confined to or intended only for the person or persons immediately concerned; confidential: *a private communication.* **4.** not holding public office or employment, as a person. **5.** not of an official or public character: *to retire to private life.* **6.** removed from or out of public view or knowledge; secret. **7.** not open or accessible to people in general: *a private road.* **8.** without the presence of others; alone; secluded. **9.** of lowest military rank. —*n.* **10.** a private soldier. **11.** *U.S. Army* a soldier of one of the three lowest ranks (**Private 1, Private 2, Private first class**). **12. in private,** in secret; not publicly. [ME, t. L: m.s. *prīvātus,* pp., lit., separated] —**pri'vate·ly,** *adv.* —**pri'vate·ness,** *n.*

pri·va·teer (prī/və tǐr/), *n.* **1.** a privately owned and manned armed vessel, commissioned by a government in time of war to fight the enemy, esp. his commercial shipping. **2.** the commander, or one of the crew, of such a vessel. —*v.i.* **3.** to cruise as a privateer. [f. PRIVATE + -EER, modeled on VOLUNTEER]

pri·va·teers·man (prī/və tǐrz/mən), *n., pl.* **-men.** an officer or seaman of a privateer.

private secretary, a person who handles the individual or confidential correspondence, etc., of a person or business organization.

pri·va·tion (prī vā/shən), *n.* **1.** lack of the usual comforts or necessaries of life, or an instance of this: *to lead a life of privation.* **2.** a depriving. **3.** state of being deprived. [ME *privacion,* t. L: m.s. *prīvātio*] —**Syn. 1.** See **hardship.**

priv·a·tive (prĭv/ə tǐv), *adj.* **1.** having the quality of depriving. **2.** consisting in or characterized by the taking away of something, or the loss or lack of something properly present. **3.** *Gram.* indicating negation or absence. —*n.* **4.** *Gram.* a privative element, as *a-* in *asymmetric = without symmetry.* **5.** that which is privative. [t. L: m.s. *prīvātivus*] —**priv'a·tive·ly,** *adv.*

priv·et (prĭv/ĭt), *n.* **1.** a European oleaceous shrub, *Ligustrum vulgare,* with evergreen leaves and small white flowers, much used for hedges. **2.** any of various other species of the genus *Ligustrum.* **3.** any of certain other plants, as *Forestiera (Adelia) acuminata* (**swamp privet**), an oleaceous shrub of the southern U.S. [orig. uncert.]

priv·i·lege (prĭv/ə lĭj), *n., v.,* **-leged, -leging.** —*n.* **1.** a right or immunity enjoyed by a person or persons beyond the common advantages of others. **2.** a special right or immunity granted to persons in authority or office; a prerogative. **3.** a prerogative, advantage, or opportunity enjoyed by anyone in a favored position (as distinct from a right). **4.** a grant to an individual, a corporation, etc., of a special right or immunity, sometimes in derogation of the common right. **5.** the principle or condition of enjoying special rights or immunities. **6.** any of the more sacred and vital rights common to all citizens under a modern constitutional government. **7.** *Stock Exchange.* a speculative contract covering a call, put, spread, or straddle. —*v.t.* **8.** to grant a privilege to. **9.** to exempt (fol. by *from*). **10.** to authorize or to license (something otherwise forbidden). [ME *privileg(i)e,* t. L: m. *prīvilēgium,* orig., a law in favor of or against an individual. Se PRIVITY.] LEX —**Syn. 1.** PRIVILEGE, PREROGATIVE refer to some special advantage which one person has over others. A PRIVILEGE is a benefit or advantage conferred or attained justly or unjustly: *the privilege of paying half fare.* A PREROGATIVE is a particular or official privilege assumed or granted as a right, and thought suitable and proper for one of a certain rank, descent, office, etc.: *the prerogative of a king.*

privileged communication, *Law.* confidential communication.

priv·i·ly (prĭv/ə lǐ), *adv.* in a privy manner; secretly.

priv·i·ty (prĭv/ə tǐ), *n., pl.* **-ties. 1.** participation in the knowledge of something private or secret, esp. as implying concurrence or consent. **2.** *Law.* the relation between privies. **3.** *Obs.* privacy. [ME *privete, privite,* t. OF, der. L *privus* private. See PRIVATE, -ITY]

priv·y (prĭv/ĭ), *adj., n., pl.* **privies.** —*adj.* **1.** participating in the knowledge of something private or secret (usually fol. by *to*): *many persons were privy to the plot.* **2.** private; assigned to private uses: *the privy purse.* **3.** belonging or pertaining to some particular person or persons, now esp. with reference to a sovereign. **4.** *Archaic.* secret, concealed, hidden, or secluded. **5.** *Archaic.* acting or done in secret. —*n.* **6.** an outhouse serving as a toilet. **7.** *Law.* one participating directly in a legal transaction, or claiming through or under such a one. [ME, t. OF: m. *prive,* adj. and n., g. L *prīvātus,* pp., separated, private]

privy chamber, 1. a private apartment in a royal residence. **2.** *Archaic.* a room reserved for the private or exclusive use of some particular person or persons.

privy council, 1. a board or select body of personal advisers, as of a sovereign. **2.** (in Great Britain) a body of advisers, selected theoretically by the sovereign, whose function of advising the crown in matters of state is, except in a formal sense, now discharged by the cabinet, committees, etc. **3.** any similar body, as one appointed to assist the governor of a British dominion. —**privy councilor.**

privy seal, (in Great Britain) the seal affixed to grants, etc., which are to pass the great seal, and to documents which do not require the great seal.

prize¹ (prīz), *n.* **1.** a reward of victory or superiority, as in a contest or competition. **2.** that which is won in a lottery or the like. **3.** anything striven for, worth striving for, or much valued. **4.** a taking or capturing at sea. **5.** a capturing. **6.** something seized or captured, esp. an enemy's ship with the property in it taken at sea under the law of war. **7.** *Archaic.* a contest or match. —*adj.* **8.** that has gained a prize. **9.** worthy of a prize. **10.** given or awarded as a prize. [ME *prise,* t. OF: a taking, pp. of *prendre* take, capture, g. L *pre(he)ndere;* influenced by ME *pris, prise* reward, prize, PRICE] —**Syn. 1.** See **reward.**

prize² (prīz), *v.t.,* **prized, prizing. 1.** to value or esteem highly. **2.** to estimate the worth or value of. [ME *prise(n),* t. OF: m. *prisier* praise, g. L *pretiāre* prize] —**Syn. 1.** See **appreciate.**

prize³ (prīz), *v.,* **prized, prizing.** *n.* —*v.t.* **1.** *Chiefly Brit.* to raise, move, or force with or as with a lever. [v. use of n.] —*n.* **2.** leverage. **3.** *Dial.* a lever. Also, **prise.** [ME *prise,* t. F: a taking hold, ult. g. L *pre(he)nsa,* fem. pp., seized]

prize court, a court whose function it is to adjudicate on prizes taken in war.

prize fight, a contest between boxers for a prize. —**prize fighter.** —**prize fighting.**

prize money, a portion of the money from the sale of a prize, esp. an enemy's vessel, divided among the captors.

priz·er (prī/zər), *n.* *Archaic.* a competitor for a prize.

prize ring, 1. a ring or enclosed square area for prize fighting. **2.** prize fighting.

pro¹ (prō), *adv., n., pl.* **pros.** —*adv.* **1.** in favor of a proposition, opinion, etc. (opposed to *con*). —*n.* **2.** a proponent of an issue; one who upholds the affirmative in a debate. **3.** an argument, consideration, vote, etc., for something. [t. L: prep., in favor of, for]

pro² (prō), *n., pl.* **pros,** *adj. Colloq.* professional.

pro-¹, 1. prefix indicating favor for some party, system, idea, etc., without identity with the group, e.g., *pro-British, pro-Communist, proslavery,* having *anti-* as its opposite. **2.** prefix of priority in space or time having especially a meaning of advancing or projecting forward or outward, having also extended figuration meanings, including substitution, attached widely to stems not used as words, e.g., *provision, prologue, proceed, produce, protract, procathedral, proconsul.* [t. L, repr. *prō,* prep., before, for, in favor of, on behalf of]

pro-², **a prefix identical in meaning with **pro-¹, occurring in words taken from Greek (as *prodrome*) or formed of Greek (and occasionally Latin) elements. [t. Gk., repr. *prŏ* for, before, in favor of]

pro·a (prō/ə), *n.* **1.** any of various types of South Pacific boat. **2.** a swift Malay sailing boat built with the lee side flat and balanced by a single outrigger. [also *prau,* t. Malay: m. *prāū*]

prob., 1. probably. **2.** problem.

prob·a·bi·lism (prŏb/ə bə lǐz/əm), *n.* **1.** *Philos.* the doctrine that certainty is impossible, and that probability suffices to govern faith and practice. **2.** *Rom. Cath. Theol.* a theory that in cases of doubt as to the lawfulness or unlawfulness of an action, it is permissible to follow a soundly probable opinion favoring its lawfulness. —**prob'a·bi·list,** *n., adj.*

prob·a·bil·i·ty (prŏb/ə bǐl/ə tǐ), *n., pl.* **-ties. 1.** the quality or fact of being probable. **2.** a likelihood or chance of something: *there is a probability of his coming.* **3.** a probable event, circumstance, etc.: *to regard a thing as a probability.* **4.** *Statistics.* the relative frequency of the occurrence of an event as measured by the ratio of the number of cases or alternatives favorable to the event to the total number of cases or alternatives. **5. in all probability,** likely; very probably.

probability curve, *Statistics.* **1.** a curve which describes the distribution of probability over the values of a variable. **2.** the normal curve.

prob·a·ble (prŏb/ə bəl), *adj.* **1.** likely to occur or prove true. **2.** having more evidence for than against, or evidence which inclines the mind to belief but leaves some room for doubt. **3.** affording ground for belief: *probable evidence.* [ME, t. L: m.s. *probābilis*]

probable cause, *Law.* reasonable ground for belief, esp. on defense to action for malicious prosecution.

probable error, *Statistics.* a value such that the error in an error distribution is equally likely to be greater or smaller than it.

prob·a·bly (prŏb/ə blǐ), *adv.* in a probable manner; with probability; in all likelihood.

pro·bang (prō/băng), *n. Surg.* a long, slender, elastic rod with a sponge, ball, or the like, at the end, to be introduced into the esophagus, etc., as for removing foreign bodies, or for introducing medication. [orig. *provang,* b. obs. *prov(et)* probe and (F)ANG, n. or v.]

pro·bate (prō/bāt), *n., adj., v.,* **-bated, -bating.** —*n.* **1.** *Law.* the official proving of a will as authentic or valid. **2.** *Law.* an officially certified copy of a will so proved. —*adj.* **3.** of or pertaining to probate or a court of probate. —*v.t.* **4.** to establish the authenticity or validity of (a will). [ME, t. L: m.s. *probātum,* neut. pp., (a thing) proved]

probate court, a special court limited to the administration of decedent estates, the probate of wills, etc.

pro·ba·tion (prō bā/shən), *n.* **1.** act of testing. **2.** the testing or trial of a person's conduct, character, qualifications, or the like. **3.** the state or period of such testing or trial. **4.** *Law.* **a.** a method of dealing with offenders, esp. young persons guilty of minor crimes or first offenses, by allowing them to go at large conditionally under supervision, as that of a person (**probation officer**) appointed for such duty. **b.** the state of having been conditionally released. **5.** *Educ.* a trial period or condition of students in certain educational institutions who are being permitted to redeem faults, misconduct, etc. **6.** the testing or trial of a candidate for membership in a religious body or order, for holy orders, etc. **7.** *Rare.* proof. [ME *probacion*, t. L: m.s. *probātio*] —**pro·ba'tion·al, pro·ba·tion·ar·y** (prō bā'shə nĕr'Ỹ), *adj.*

pro·ba·tion·er (prō bā'shən ər), *n.* one undergoing probation or trial. —**pro·ba'tion·er·ship'**, *n.*

pro·ba·tive (prō'bə tĩv, prōb'ə-), *adj.* **1.** serving or designed for testing or trial. **2.** affording proof or evidence. Also, **pro·ba·to·ry** (prō'bə tōr'Ỹ).

probe (prōb), *v.*, **probed, probing,** *n.* —*v.t.* **1.** to search into or examine thoroughly; question closely. **2.** to examine or explore as with a probe. —*v.i.* **3.** to penetrate with or as with a probe. [der. **PROBE,** n.] —*n.* **4.** act of probing. **5.** a slender surgical instrument for exploring the depth or direction of a wound, sinus, or the like. **6.** *U.S.* an investigation, esp. by a legislative committee, of suspected illegal activity. [t. ML: m. *proba* test, LL proof. See **PROOF**] —**prob'er,** *n.*

pro·bi·ty (prō'bə tỹ, prŏb'ə-), *n.* integrity; uprightness; honesty. [t. L: m.s. *probitas*]

prob·lem (prŏb'ləm), *n.* **1.** any question or matter involving doubt, uncertainty, or difficulty. **2.** a question proposed for solution or discussion. **3.** *Math.* anything requiring something to be done. —*adj.* **4.** difficult to train or guide; unruly: *a problem child.* **5.** *Literature.* dealing with choices of action difficult either for an individual or for society at large: *a problem play.* [ME *probleme,* t. L: m. *problēma,* t. Gk.]

prob·lem·at·ic (prŏb'lə măt'Ỹk), *adj.* of the nature of a problem; doubtful; uncertain; questionable. Also, **prob'lem·at'i·cal.** —**prob'lem·at'i·cal·ly,** *adv.*

pro bo·no pu·bli·co (prō bō'nō pŭb'lỸ kō'), *Latin.* for the public good or welfare.

pro·bos·cid·e·an (prō'bə sỸd'Ỹ ən), *adj.* **1.** pertaining to or resembling a proboscis. **2.** having a proboscis. **3.** belonging or pertaining to the *Proboscidea,* the order of mammals that consists of the elephants and their extinct allies. Also, **pro'bos·cid'i·an,** [f. m.s. NL *Proboscidea,* pl. (see **PROBOSCIS**) + -**AN**]

pro·bos·cis (prō bŏs'Ỹs), *n., pl.* -**boscises** (-bŏs'Ỹs Ỹz), -**boscides** (-bŏs'ə dēz'). **1.** an elephant's trunk. **2.** any long flexible snout, as of the tapir. **3.** *Entomol.* **a.** an elongate but not rigid feeding organ of certain insects formed of the mouth parts, as in the *Lepidoptera* and *Diptera.* **b.** any elongate or snoutlike feeding organ. **4.** *Humorous.* human nose. [t. L, t. Gk.: m. *proboskis*]

proc., **1.** proceedings. **2.** procedure. **3.** process.

pro·caine (prō kān', prō'kān), *n.* novocaine. [f. **PRO-** + (co)**CAINE**]

pro·cam·bi·um (prō kăm'bỸ əm), *n. Bot.* the meristem from which vascular bundles are developed. [t. NL. See **PRO-**[1], **CAMBIUM**] —**pro·cam'bi·al,** *adj.*

pro·carp (prō'kärp), *n. Bot.* a carpogonium plus certain cells intimately associated with it.

pro·ca·the·dral (prō'kə thē'drəl), *n.* a church used temporarily as a cathedral.

pro·ce·dure (prə sē'jər), *n.* **1.** the act or manner of proceeding in any action or process; conduct. **2.** a particular course or mode of action. **3.** mode of conducting legal, parliamentary, or other business, specif. litigation and judicial proceedings. [t. F, der. *procéder* **PROCEED**] —**pro·ce'dur·al,** *adj.* —**Syn. 2.** See **process.**

pro·ceed (*v.* prə sēd'; *n.* prō'sēd), *v.i.* **1.** to move or go forward or onward, esp. after stopping. **2.** to go on with or carry on any action or process. **3.** to go on (to do something). **4.** to continue one's discourse. **5.** *Law.* **a.** to begin and carry on a legal action. **b.** to take legal proceedings (fol. by *against*). **6.** to be carried on, as an action, process, etc. **7.** to go or come forth; issue. **8.** to arise, originate, or result. —*n.* **9.** that which results or accrues. **10.** (*usually pl.*) the sum derived from a sale or other transaction. [ME *procede*(*n*), t. L: m. *prōcēdere*] —**Syn. 1.** See **advance.**

pro·ceed·ing (prə sē'dỸng), *n.* **1.** a particular action or course of action. **2.** action, course of action, or conduct. **3.** act of one who or that which proceeds. **4.** (*pl.*) records of the doings of a society. **5.** *Law.* **a.** the instituting or carrying on of an action at law. **b.** a legal step or measure: *to institute proceedings against a person.* —**Syn. 1, 2, 4.** See **process.**

proc·e·leus·mat·ic (prŏs'ə lōōs măt'Ỹk), *adj.* **1.** inciting, animating, or inspiriting. **2.** *Pros.* **a.** denoting a metrical foot of four short syllables. **b.** pertaining to or consisting of feet of this kind. —*n.* **3.** *Pros.* a proceleusmatic foot. [t. LL: s. *proceleusmaticus,* t. Gk.: m. *prokeleusmatikós*]

proc·ess (prŏs'ĕs or, esp. *Brit.,* prō'sĕs), *n.* **1.** a systematic series of actions directed to some end: *the process of making butter.* **2.** a continuous action, operation, or series of changes taking place in a definite manner: *the process of decay.* **3.** *Law.* **a.** the summons, mandate, or writ by which a defendant or thing is brought before court for litigation. **b.** the total of such summoning writs. **c.** the whole course of the proceedings in an action at law. **4.** *Photog.* **a.** photomechanical or photoengraving methods collectively. **b.** a system of superimposing background in motion pictures, or otherwise creating a picture by combining elements not ordinarily united: *a process shot.* **5.** *Biol.* a natural outgrowth, projection, or appendage: *a process of a bone.* **6.** a prominence or protuberance. **7.** the action of going forward or on. **8.** the condition of being carried on. **9.** course or lapse, as of time. **10.** in (the) **process of,** during the course of. —*v.t.* **11.** to treat or prepare by some particular process, as in manufacturing. **12.** to convert (an agricultural commodity) into marketable form by some special process. **13.** to institute a legal process against. **14.** to serve a process or summons on. —*adj.* **15.** prepared or modified by an artificial process: *process cheese.* **16.** pertaining to, made by or using, or used in, photomechanical or photoengraving methods. [ME *proces,* t. F, t. L: m.s. *prōcessus* a going forward]

—**Syn. 1.** **PROCESS, PROCEDURE, PROCEEDING** apply to something which goes on or takes place. A **PROCESS** is a series of progressive and interdependent steps by which an end is attained: *a chemical process.* **PROCEDURE** usually implies a formal or set order of doing a thing, a method of conducting affairs: *parliamentary procedure.* **PROCEEDING** (usually pl.) applies to what goes on or takes place on a given occasion: to a certain behavior, or transaction (or, the records of a transaction): *Proceedings of the Royal Academy of Sciences.*

processing tax, a tax levied by the government at an intermediate stage in the production of goods.

pro·ces·sion (prə sĕsh'ən), *n.* **1.** the proceeding or moving along in orderly succession, in a formal or ceremonious manner, of a line or body of persons, animals, vehicles, or other things. **2.** the line or body of persons or things moving along. **3.** *Eccles.* an office, litany, etc., said or sung in a religious procession. **4.** *Theol.* the relation of the Holy Spirit to the Father and later, in the Western church, to the Son; distinguished from the "generation" of the son and the "unbegottenness" of the Father. John 15, 26. **5.** act of proceeding forth from a source. —*v.i.* **6.** to go in procession. [early ME, t. ML: s. *prōcessio* a religious procession, L a marching on]

pro·ces·sion·al (prə sĕsh'ən əl), *adj.* **1.** of or pertaining to a procession. **2.** of the nature of a procession. **3.** characterized by processions. **4.** sung or recited in procession, as a hymn. **5.** a processional hymn. —*n.* **6.** an office book containing hymns, litanies, etc., for use in religious processions.

process printing, a method of printing practically any color by using four separate halftone plates for red, yellow, blue, and black ink.

process server, *Law.* one who serves legal documents such as a subpoena, writ, or warrant, etc., requiring appearance in court or before a notary, etc.

pro·cès-ver·bal (prō sā'vĕr băl'; *Fr.* prō sĕ vĕr bäl'), *n., pl.* -**baux** (-bō'). **1.** a report of proceedings, as of an assembly. **2.** *French Law.* an authenticated written account of facts in connection with a criminal or other charge. [F]

pro·chein (prō'shĕn), *adj. Law.* nearest: *prochein ami* (next friend). Also, *French,* **pro·chain** (prō shăn'). [t. F: m. *prochain,* ult. der. L *prope* near]

pro·claim (prō klām'), *v.t.* **1.** to announce or declare publicly or officiously: *to proclaim one s opinions.* **2.** to announce or declare, publicly and officially: *to proclaim war.* **3.** (of things) to indicate or make known. **4.** to declare (a district, etc.) subject to particular legal restrictions. **5.** to declare to be an outlaw, evildoer, or the like. **6.** to denounce or prohibit publicly. —*v.i.* **7.** to make proclamation. [ME *proclame*(*n*), t. L: m. *prōclāmāre*] —**pro·claim'er,** *n.* —**Syn. 1.** See **announce.**

proc·la·ma·tion (prŏk'lə mā'shən), *n.* **1.** that which is proclaimed; a public and official announcement. **2.** act of proclaiming.

pro·clit·ic (prō klỸt'Ỹk), *Gram.* —*n.* **1.** an element similar to a prefix but of more independent status, approaching that of a separate word. —*adj.* **2.** having the nature of a proclitic. [t. NL: s. *procliticus,* der. Gk. *proklīnein* lean forward. Cf. **ENCLITIC**]

pro·cliv·i·ty (prō klỸv'ə tỸ), *n., pl.* -**ties.** natural or habitual inclination or tendency; propensity; predisposition: *a proclivity to faultfinding.* [t. L: m. *prōclīvitas* tendency, propensity. Cf. F *proclivité*]

Proc·ne (prŏk'nỸ), *n. Gk. Legend.* the wife of Tereus and sister of Philomela, later turned into a swallow.

pro·con·sul (prō kŏn'səl), *n.* **1.** (among the ancient Romans) a governor or military commander of a province with duties and powers similar to those of a consul. **2.** any appointed administrator over a dependency or an occupied area: *MacArthur is U.S. proconsul in Japan.* [ME, t. L] —**pro·con'su·lar,** *adj.*

pro·con·su·late (prō kŏn'sə lỸt), *n. Hist.* the office or term of office of a proconsul. Also, **pro·con'sul·ship'.**

Pro·co·pi·us (prō kō'pỸ əs), *n.* A.D. c490–c562, Greek historian of the Byzantine Empire.

pro·cras·ti·nate (prō krăs'tə nāt'), *v.,* -**nated,** -**nating.** **1.** to defer action; delay: *to procrastinate until an opportunity is lost.* —*v.t.* **2.** to put off till another day or time; defer; delay. [t. L: m.s. *prōcrastinātus,* pp., put off till the morrow] —**pro·cras'ti·na'tion,** *n.* —**pro·cras'ti·na'tor,** *n.*

pro·cre·ant (prō′krĭ ənt), *adj.* **1.** procreating; generating. **2.** pertaining to procreation. [t. L: s. *prōcreans,* ppr.]

pro·cre·ate (prō′krĭ āt′), *v.t.,* **-ated, -ating. 1.** to beget or generate (offspring). **2.** to produce; bring into being. [t. L: m.s. *prōcreātus,* pp.] **—pro′cre·a′tion,** *n.* **—pro′cre·a′tive,** *adj.* **—pro′cre·a′tor,** *n.*

Pro·crus·te·an (prō krŭs′tĭ ən), *adj.* **1.** pertaining to or suggestive of Procrustes. **2.** tending to produce conformity by violent or arbitrary means.

Pro·crus·tes (prō krŭs′tēz), *n.* a fabled robber of ancient Greece who stretched or mutilated his victims to make them conform to the length of his bed.

proc·tor (prŏk′tər), *n.* **1.** (in a university or college) **a.** *Chiefly Brit.* an official charged with various duties, esp. with the maintenance of good order. **b.** one appointed to keep watch over students at examinations. **2.** *Law.* a person employed to manage another's cause in a court of civil or ecclesiastical law, or to collect tithes for the owner of them. **3.** *—v.t.* to act as a proctor (def. 1b). [contracted var. of PROCURATOR] **—proc·to·ri·al** (prŏk tōr′ĭ əl), *adj.* **—proc′tor·ship′,** *n.*

proc·to·scope (prŏk′tə skōp′), *n.* an instrument for examining the interior of the rectum. [f. *procto-* (t. Gk.: m. *prōkto-,* comb. form of *prōktós* anus) + -SCOPE]

pro·cum·bent (prō kŭm′bənt), *adj.* **1.** lying on the face; prone; prostrate. **2.** *Bot.* (of a plant or stem) lying along the ground, but without putting forth roots. [t. L s. *prōcumbens,* ppr., falling forward]

pro·cur·a·ble (prō kyŏŏr′ə bəl), *adj.* obtainable.

pro·cur·ance (prō kyŏŏr′əns), *n.* act of bringing something about; agency.

proc·u·ra·tion (prŏk′yə rā′shən), *n.* **1.** the appointment of a procurator, agent, or attorney. **2.** the authority given. **3.** a document whereby the authority is given. **4.** act of obtaining or getting; procurement. **5.** management for another; agency.

proc·u·ra·tor (prŏk′yə rā′tər), *n.* **1.** (among the ancient Romans) any of various imperial officers with fiscal or administrative powers. **2.** *Law. Now Rare.* an agent, deputy, or attorney. [ME *procuratour,* t. L: m. *prōcūrātor*] **—proc·u·ra·to·ri·al** (prŏk′yə rə tōr′ĭ əl), **proc·u·ra·to·ry** (prŏk′yə rə tōr′ĭ, prō kyŏŏr′ə tōr′ĭ), *adj.*

pro·cure (prō kyŏŏr′), *v.,* **-cured, -curing. —v.t. 1.** to obtain or get by care, effort, or the use of special means: *to procure evidence.* **2.** to bring about; effect; cause: *to procure a person's death.* **3.** to obtain (women) for the gratification of lust. *—v.i.* **4.** to act as a procurer (pander) or procuress. [ME, t. L: m.s. *prōcūrāre* take care of, manage] **—pro·cure′ment,** *n.* **—Syn. 1.** acquire, gain, win, secure. See get.

pro·cur·er (prō kyŏŏr′ər), *n.* **1.** one who procures. **2.** a pander or pimp. **—pro·cur·ess** (prō kyŏŏr′ĭs), *n. fem.*

Pro·cy·on (prō′sĭ ŏn′), *n. Astron.* a star of the first magnitude in the constellation Canis Minor.

prod (prŏd), *v.,* **prodded, prodding,** *n.* *—v.t.* **1.** to poke or jab with something pointed: *to prod an animal with a stick.* **2.** to seek to rouse or incite as if by poking. *—n.* **3.** act of prodding; a poke or jab. **4.** any of various pointed instruments, such as a goad. [OE *prod-* in *prodbor* auger] **—prod′der,** *n.*

prod., produced.

prod·i·gal (prŏd′ə gəl), *adj.* **1.** wastefully or recklessly extravagant: *prodigal expenditure.* **2.** giving or yielding profusely; lavish (fol. by *of*): *prodigal of smiles.* **3.** lavishly abundant; profuse. *—n.* **4.** one who spends, or has spent, his money or substance with wasteful extravagance; a spendthrift. [back formation from PRODIGALITY] **—prod′i·gal·ly,** *adv.* **—Syn. 1.** See lavish.

prod·i·gal·i·ty (prŏd′ə găl′ə tĭ), *n., pl.* **-ties. 1.** quality or fact of being prodigal; wasteful extravagance in spending. **2.** an instance of it. **3.** lavish abundance. [ME *prodigalite,* t. ML: m.s. *prōdigālitas*]

pro·di·gious (prə dĭj′əs), *adj.* **1.** extraordinary in size, amount, extent, degree, force, etc.: *a prodigious noise.* **2.** wonderful or marvelous: *a prodigious feat.* **3.** abnormal; monstrous. **4.** *Obs.* ominous. [t. L: m. *prōdigiōsus*] **—pro·di′gious·ly,** *adv.* **—pro·di′gious·ness,** *n.* **—Syn. 1.** enormous, immense, huge. **2.** amazing, stupendous.

prod·i·gy (prŏd′ə jĭ), *n., pl.* **-gies. 1.** a person endowed with extraordinary gifts or powers: *a musical prodigy.* **2.** a marvelous example (fol. by *of*): *that prodigy of learning.* **3.** something wonderful or marvelous; a wonder. **4.** something abnormal or monstrous. **5.** something extraordinary regarded as of prophetic significance. [t. L: m.s. *prōdigium* prophetic sign]

pro·drome (prō′drōm), *n. Pathol.* a premonitory symptom. [t. F, t. NL: m.s. *prodromus,* t. Gk.: m. *pródromos* running before] **—prod·ro·mal** (prŏd′rə məl), *adj.*

pro·duce (*v.* prə dūs′, -dōōs′; *n.* prŏd′ūs, -dōōs, or prō′- dūs, -dōōs), *v.,* **-duced, -ducing.** *—v.t.* **1.** to bring into existence; to give rise to; to cause: *to produce steam.* **2.** to bring into being by mental or physical labor, as a work of literature or art. **3.** *Econ.* to create (something having an exchangeable value). **4.** to bring forth, bear, or yield, as young or natural products; to give forth; to furnish; to supply: *a mine producing silver.* **5.** to yield; to cause to accrue: *money producing interest.* **6.** to bring forward; to present to view or notice; to

exhibit. **7.** to bring (a play, etc.) before the public. **8.** to extend or prolong, as a line. *—v.i.* **9.** to bring forth or yield appropriate offspring, products, etc. **10.** *Econ.* to create value; bring crops, goods, etc., into a state in which they will command a price. *—n.* **11.** that which is produced; yield; product. **12.** agricultural or natural products collectively. [t. L: m.s. *prōdūcere* lead or bring forward, extend, prolong, bring forth, produce] **—pro·duc′i·ble,** *adj.* **—Syn. 11.** See crop.

pro·duc·er (prə dū′sər, -dōō′-), *n.* **1.** one who produces. **2.** *Econ.* one who creates value, or produces goods and services (opposed to *consumer*). **3.** the person who exercises general supervision over the production of a play, motion picture, etc. **4.** an arrangement for making producer gas.

producer gas, a vaporous fuel produced by gasifying cheap solid fuel with steam, used in the place of gasoline natural gas, etc.

producers′ goods, *Econ.* goods that are used in the process of creating final consumer goods, as machinery, raw materials, etc.

prod·uct (prŏd′əkt, -ŭkt), *n.* **1.** a thing produced by any action or operation, or by labor; an effect or result. **2.** something produced; a thing produced by nature or by a natural process. **3.** *Chem.* a substance obtained from another substance through chemical change. **4.** *Math.* the result obtained by multiplying two or more quantities together. [ME, t. L: s. *prōductum,* neut. pp., (thing) produced]

pro·duc·tion (prə dŭk′shən), *n.* **1.** act of producing; creation; manufacture. **2.** that which is produced; a product. **3.** a work of literature or art. **4.** *Econ.* the creation of value; the producing of articles having an exchangeable value. [ME, t. L: s. *prōductio*]

pro·duc·tive (prə dŭk′tĭv), *adj.* **1.** having the power of producing; generative; creative. **2.** producing readily or abundantly; fertile; prolific. **3.** *Econ.* producing or tending to produce goods and services having exchangeable value. **—pro·duc′tive·ly,** *adv.* **—pro·duc·tiv·i·ty** (prō′dŭk tĭv′ə tĭ), **pro·duc′tive·ness,** *n.* **—Syn. 2.** PRODUCTIVE, FERTILE, FRUITFUL apply to that which is capable of generating or producing (abundantly). PRODUCTIVE meaning that which produces, refers to continued activity, past, present, and future: *productive soil, a productive influence.* FERTILE refers to that in which seeds may be expected to take root: *fertile soil, a fertile suggestion.* FRUITFUL refers to that which has produced: *fruitful soil, discovery, theory. Fertile soil, properly cultivated, has become fruitful, and is now steadily productive.* **—Ant. 2.** sterile.

pro·em (prō′ĕm), *n.* an introductory discourse; an introduction; a preface; a preamble. [t. L: m.s. *pro- oemium,* t. Gk.: m. *prooímion*; r. ME *proheme,* t. OF] **—pro·e·mi·al** (prō ē′mĭ əl), *adj.*

Prof., Professor. Also, **prof.**

prof·a·na·tion (prŏf′ə nā′shən), *n.* act of profaning; desecration; defilement; debasement.

pro·fan·a·to·ry (prō făn′ə tōr′ĭ), *adj.* tending to desecrate; profaning.

pro·fane (prə fān′), *adj., v.,* **-faned, -faning.** *—adj.* **1.** characterized by irreverence or contempt for God or sacred things; irreligious, esp. speaking or spoken in manifest or implied contempt for sacred things. **2.** not sacred, or not devoted to sacred purposes; unconsecrated; secular: *profane history.* **3.** unholy; heathen; pagan. **4.** not initiated into religious rites or mysteries, as persons. **5.** common or vulgar. *—v.t.* **6.** to misuse (anything that should be held in reverence or respect); defile; debase; employ basely or unworthily. **7.** to treat (anything sacred) with irreverence or contempt. [ME *prophane,* t. F, t. L: m. *profānus,* lit., before (outside of) the temple] **—pro·fane′ly,** *adv.* **—pro·fane′ness,** *n.* **—pro·fan′er,** *n.*

pro·fan·i·ty (prə făn′ə tĭ), *n., pl.* **-ties. 1.** the quality of being profane; irreverence. **2.** profane conduct or language; a profane act or utterance.

pro·fert (prō′fərt), *n. Law.* an exhibition of a record or paper in open court. [L: he brings forward]

pro·fess (prə fĕs′), *v.t.* **1.** to lay claim to (a feeling, etc.), often insincerely; pretend to: *he professed extreme regret.* **2.** to declare openly; announce or affirm; avow or acknowledge: *to profess one's satisfaction.* **3.** to affirm faith in or allegiance to (a religion, God, etc.). **4.** to declare oneself skilled or expert in; claim to have knowledge of; make (a thing) one's profession or business. **5.** to receive or admit into a religious order. *—v.i.* **6.** to make profession. **7.** to take the vows of a religious order. [back formation from PROFESSED]

pro·fessed (prə fĕst′), *adj.* **1.** alleged; pretended. **2.** avowed; acknowledged. **3.** professing to be qualified; professional (rather than amateur). **4.** having taken the vows of or been received into, a religious order. [ME (def. 4), f. s. L *professus,* pp., + -ED[2]]

pro·fess·ed·ly (prə fĕs′ĭd lĭ), *adv.* **1.** allegedly. **2.** avowedly. **3.** ostensibly.

pro·fes·sion (prə fĕsh′ən), *n.* **1.** a vocation requiring knowledge of some department of learning or science, esp. one of the three vocations of theology, law, and medicine (formerly known specifically as the **professions** or **the learned professions**): *the profession of teaching.* **2.** the body of persons engaged in an occupation or calling: *to be respected by the profession.* **3.** act of professing; avowal; a declaration, whether true or false: *professions of love.* **4.** the declaration of belief in or acceptance of religion or a faith: *the profession of Christian-*

ity. **5.** a religion or faith professed. **6.** the declaration made on entering a religious order. [ME, t. L: s. *professio*] —Syn. **1.** See **occupation.**

pro·fes·sion·al (prə fĕsh′ən əl), *adj.* **1.** following an occupation as a means of livelihood or for gain: *a professional actor.* **2.** pertaining or appropriate to a profession: *professional studies.* **3.** engaged in one of the learned professions: *a professional man.* **4.** following as a business an occupation ordinarily engaged in as a pastime: *a professional golfer.* **5.** making a business of something not properly to be regarded as a business: *a professional politician.* **6.** undertaken or engaged in as a means of livelihood or for gain: *professional baseball.* —*n.* **7.** one belonging to one of the learned or skilled professions. **8.** one who makes a business of an occupation, etc., esp. of an art or sport in which amateurs engage for amusement or recreation. **9.** *Golf.* the person, usually an expert player, who manages a golf links. —**pro·fes′-sion·al·ly,** *adv.*

pro·fes·sion·al·ism (prə fĕsh′ən əl ĭz′əm), *n.* **1.** professional character, spirit, or methods. **2.** the standing, practice, or methods of a professional as distinguished from an amateur.

pro·fes·sor (prə fĕs′ər), *n.* **1.** a teacher of the highest rank, usually in a particular branch of learning, in a university or college. **2.** a teacher. **3.** an instructor in some popular art, as boxing. **4.** one who professes his sentiments, beliefs, etc. [ME, t. L] —**pro·fes·so·ri·al** (prō′fĕ sōr′ĭ əl, prŏf′ə-), *adj.* —**pro′fes·so′ri·al·ly,** *adv*

pro·fes·sor·ate (prə fĕs′ər ĭt), *n.* **1.** the office or the period of service of a professor. **2.** a group of professors.

pro·fes·so·ri·ate (prō′fĕ sōr′ĭ ĭt, prŏf′ə-), *n.* **1.** a group of professors. **2.** the office or post of professor.

pro·fes·sor·ship (prə fĕs′ər shĭp′), *n.* the office or post of a professor.

prof·fer (prŏf′ər), *v.t.* **1.** to put before a person for acceptance; offer. —*n.* **2.** act of proffering. **3.** an offer. [ME *profre(n)*, t. AF: m. *profrer*, var. of OF *poroffrir*, f. *por-* PRO¹ + *ofrir* (g. LL *offerīre*, var. of L *offerre* offer)] —Syn. **1.** See **offer.**

pro·fi·cien·cy (prə fĭsh′ən sĭ), *n., pl.* **-cies.** state of being proficient; skill; expertness: *proficiency in music.*

pro·fi·cient (prə fĭsh′ənt), *adj.* **1.** well advanced or expert in any art, science, or subject; skilled. —*n.* **2.** an expert. [t. L: s. *proficiens,* ppr., making progress. See PROFIT] —**pro·fi′cient·ly,** *adv.*

pro·file (prō′fīl), *n., v.,* -**filed,** -**filing.** —*n.* **1.** the outline or contour of anything, as the human face, esp. as seen from the side. **2.** *Archit., Engin.* a drawing of a section, esp. a vertical section, through something. **3.** a vivid and concise sketch of the biography and personality of an individual. —*v.t.* **4.** to draw a profile of. **5.** to shape as to profile. [t. It.: m. *profilo,* der. *profilare* draw in outline, f. L *pro-* PRO¹ + LL *fīlāre* spin]

prof·it (prŏf′ĭt), *n.* **1.** (*often pl.*) pecuniary gain resulting from the employment of capital in any transaction: **a. gross profit,** gross receipts less the immediate costs of production. **b. net profit,** amount remaining after deducting all costs from gross receipts. **c.** the ratio of such pecuniary gain to the amount of capital invested. **2.** (*often pl.*) returns, proceeds, or revenue, as from property or investments. **3.** *Econ.* the surplus left to the producer or employer after deducting wages, rent, cost of raw materials, etc. **4.** (*usually pl.*) such additional charges as interest on capital, insurance, etc. **5.** advantage; benefit; gain. —*v.i.* **6.** to gain advantage or benefit. **7.** to make profit. **8.** to be of advantage or benefit. **9.** to take advantage. **10.** *Obs.* to make progress. —*v.t.* **11.** to be of advantage or profit to. [ME, t. OF, g. L *profectus* progressed, profited] —**prof′it·less,** *adj.* —Syn. **2.** dividend, revenue, proceeds, returns. **5.** good, welfare. See **advantage.**

prof·it·a·ble (prŏf′ĭt ə bəl), *adj.* **1.** yielding profit; remunerative. **2.** beneficial or useful. —**prof′it·a·ble·ness,** *n.* —**prof′it·a·bly,** *adv.*

profit and loss, the gain and loss arising from commercial or other transactions, applied esp. to an account in bookkeeping showing gains and losses in business. —**prof′it-and-loss′,** *adj.*

prof·it·eer (prŏf′ə tĭr′), *n.* **1.** one who seeks or exacts exorbitant profits as by taking advantage of public necessity. —*v.i.* **2.** to act as a profiteer.

profit sharing, the sharing of profits, as between employer and employee, esp. in such a way that the laborer receives, in addition to his wages, a share in the profits of the business. —**prof′it-shar′ing,** *adj.*

prof·li·ga·cy (prŏf′lə gə sĭ), *n.* **1.** shameless dissoluteness. **2.** reckless extravagance. **3.** great abundance.

prof·li·gate (prŏf′lə gĭt, -gāt′), *adj.* **1.** utterly and shamelessly immoral; thoroughly dissolute. **2.** recklessly prodigal or extravagant. —*n.* **3.** a profligate person. [t. L: m. *prōflīgātus,* pp., overthrown, ruined] —**prof′li·gate·ly,** *adv.* —**prof′li·gate·ness,** *n.*

prof·lu·ent (prŏf′lōō ənt), *adj.* flowing smoothly along. [ME, t. L: s. *prōfluens,* ppr., flowing forth]

pro for·ma (prō fôr′mə; *Brit.* -mā), *Latin.* according to form; as a matter of form.

pro·found (prə found′), *adj.* **1.** penetrating or entering deeply into subjects of thought or knowledge: *a profound thinker.* **2.** intense; extreme: *profound sleep.* **3.** being or going far beneath what is superficial, external, or obvious: *profound insight.* **4.** of deep mean-

ing; abstruse: *a profound book.* **5.** extending, situated, or originating far down, or far beneath the surface. **6.** low: *a profound bow.* **7.** deep. —*n. Poetic.* **8.** that which is profound. **9.** the deep sea; ocean. **10.** depth; abyss: [ME, t. OF: m. *profond,* g. L *profundus*] —**pro·found′-ly,** *adv.* —**pro·found′ness,** *n.*

pro·fun·di·ty (prə fŭn′də tĭ), *n., pl.* **-ties. 1.** quality of being profound; depth. **2.** a profoundly deep place; an abyss. **3.** (*pl.*) profound or deep matters. [ME *profundite,* t. LL: m.s. *profunditas*]

pro·fuse (prə fūs′), *adj.* **1.** spending or giving freely and in large amount, often to excess; extravagant (fol. by *of* or *in*). **2.** made or done freely and abundantly: *profuse apologies.* **3.** abundant; in great amount. [ME, t. L: m.s. *profūsus,* pp., poured forth] —**pro·fuse′ly,** *adv.* —**pro·fuse′ness,** *n.* —Syn. **1.** See **lavish.**

pro·fu·sion (prə fū′zhən), *n.* **1.** abundance; abundant quantity. **2.** a great quantity or amount (fol. by *of*). **3.** lavish spending; extravagance. —Syn. **1.** See **plenty.**

prog (prŏg), *v.,* **progged, progging,** *n. Slang or Dial.* —*v.i.* **1.** to search or prowl about, as for plunder or food; forage. —*n.* **2.** food or victuals. [? b. PROD and BEG]

Prog., Progressive.

pro·gen·i·tive (prō jĕn′ə tĭv), *adj.* producing offspring; reproductive.

pro·gen·i·tor (prō jĕn′ə tər), *n.* a direct ancestor; forefather. [ME *progenitour,* t. L: m. *prōgenitor*]

prog·e·ny (prŏj′ə nĭ), *n., pl.* **-nies.** offspring; issue; descendants. [ME *progenie,* t. OF, t. L: m. *prōgenies*]

pro·ges·ter·one (prō jĕs′tə rōn′), *n. Biochem.* a hormone of the corpus luteum of the ovary, $C_{21}H_{30}O_2$, which prepares the uterus for the fertilized ovum and maintains pregnancy. Also, **pro·ges·tine** (prō jĕs′tĭn).

pro·glot·tis (prō glŏt′ĭs), *n., pl.* **-glottides** (-glŏt′ə dēz′). *Zool.* one of the segments or joints of a tapeworm, containing complete reproductive systems, usually both male and female. Also, **pro·glot·tid** (prō-glŏt′ĭd). [t. NL, t. Gk.: m. *proglōssis* point of the tongue (with reference to shape)] —**pro·glot′tic,** *adj.*

prog·na·thous (prŏg′nə thəs, prŏg nā′-), *adj.* **1.** (of a jaw) protruding; with a gnathic index over 103. **2.** (of a skull or a person) having protrusive jaws. See diag. under facial angle. Also, **prog·nath·ic** (prŏg năth′ĭk). [f. PRO-² + s. Gk. *gnáthos* jaw + -ous] —**prog·na·thism** (prŏg′nə thĭz′əm), **prog·na·thy** (prŏg′nə thĭ), *n.*

prog·no·sis (prŏg nō′sĭs), *n., pl.* **-noses** (-nō′sēz). *Med.* **1.** a forecasting of the probable course and termination of a disease. **2.** a particular forecast made. [t. LL, t. Gk.: foreknowledge]

prog·nos·tic (prŏg nŏs′tĭk), *adj.* **1.** of or pertaining to prognosis. **2.** indicating something in the future. [t. ML: s. *prognōsticus,* t. Gk.: m. *prognōstikós* foreknowing] —*n.* **3.** a forecast or prediction. [t. L: s. *prognōsticon,* t. Gk.: m. *prognōstikon* a prognostic; r. ME *pronostike,* t. F]

prog·nos·ti·cate (prŏg nŏs′tə kāt′), *v.,* **-cated, -cating.** —*v.t.* **1.** to forecast or predict (something future) from present indications or signs; to prophesy. —*v.i.* **2.** to make a forecast; to prophesy. —**prog·nos′ti·ca·tive,** *adj.* —**prog·nos′ti·ca′tor,** *n.*

prog·nos·ti·ca·tion (prŏg nŏs′tə kā′shən), *n.* **1.** the act of prognosticating. **2.** a forecast or prediction.

pro·gram (prō′grăm, -grəm), *n.* **1.** a plan to be followed. **2.** a list of items, pieces, performers, etc., in a musical, theatrical, or other entertainment; a playbill. **3.** an entertainment with reference to its pieces or numbers. **4.** a prospectus or syllabus. Also, *esp. Brit.,* **pro·gramme.** —*v.i.* **5.** to plan a program. —*v.t.* **6.** to schedule as part of a program. **7.** *App. Math.* to organize and arrange data relevant to a problem so that it can be solved by a computer. [t. LL: m. *programma,* t. Gk.: public notice in writing]

program music, music intended to convey an impression of a definite series of images, scenes, or events.

prog·ress (*n.* prŏg′rĕs or, *esp. Brit.,* prō′grĕs; *v.* prə-grĕs′), *n.* **1.** a proceeding to a further or higher stage, or through such stages successively: *the progress of a scholar in his studies.* **2.** advancement in general. **3.** growth or development; continuous improvement. **4.** *Sociol.* the development of an individual or group in a direction considered as beneficial and to a degree greater than that yet attained. **5.** *Biol.* increasing differentiation and perfection in the course of ontogeny or phylogeny. **6.** forward or onward movement in space or course. **7.** course of action, of events, of time, etc. **8. in progress,** taking place; happening. —*v.i.* **9.** to advance. **10.** to go forward or onward. [ME, t L: s. *prōgressus* a going forward] —Syn. **9.** develop, improve, grow.

pro·gres·sion (prə grĕsh′ən), *n.* **1.** act of progressing; forward or onward movement. **2.** a passing successively from one member of a series to the next; succession; sequence. **3.** *Astron.* (of a planet) direct, as opposed to retrograde, motion. **4.** *Math.* a succession of quantities in which there is a constant relation between each member and the one succeeding it. Cf. **arithmetic progression** and **geometric progression. 5.** *Music.* the manner in which chords or melodic tones follow one another. —**pro·gres′sion·al,** *adj.*

pro·gres·sion·ist (prə grĕsh′ən ĭst), *n.* one who believes in or advocates progress, as in politics. —**pro·gres′sion·ism,** *n.*

prog·ress·ist (prŏg′rĕs ĭst, prō′grĕs ĭst), *n.* one favoring progress, as in politics; a progressive.

pro·gres·sive (prə grĕs′ĭv), *adj.* **1.** favoring or advocating progress, improvement, or reform, esp. in political matters. **2.** progressing or advancing; making progress toward better conditions, more enlightened or liberal ideas, the use of new and advantageous methods, etc.: *a progressive community.* **3.** characterized by such progress, or by continuous improvement. **4.** (*cap.*) of the Progressive party. **5.** going forward or onward; passing successively from one member of a series to the next; proceeding step by step. **6.** *Govt.* noting or pertaining to a form of taxation in which the rate increases with certain increases in the amount taxed. **7.** *Gram.* denoting a verb aspect, or other verb category, which indicates action or state going on at a temporal point of reference: *the progressive form of "is doing" in "he is doing it."* **8.** *Med.* continuously increasing in extent or severity, as a disease. —*n.* **9.** one who is progressive, or who favors progress or reform, esp. in political matters. **10.** (*cap.*) a member of the Progressive party. **11.** a prisoner of war who is influenced by or collaborates with his Communist captives. —**pro·gres′sive·ly,** *adv.* —**pro·gres′sive·ness,** *n.*

Progressive party, 1. a party formed in 1912 under the leadership of Theodore Roosevelt, advocating popular control of government, direct primaries, the initiative, the referendum, woman suffrage, etc. **2.** a similar party formed in 1924 under the leadership of Robert M. La Follette. **3.** a political party formed in 1948 under the leadership of Henry A. Wallace.

pro·gres·siv·ism (prə grĕs′ĭv ĭz′əm), *n.* the principles and practices of progressives.

pro·hib·it (prō hĭb′ĭt), *v.t.* **1.** to forbid (an action, a thing) by authority: *smoking is prohibited.* **2.** to forbid (a person) from doing something. **3.** to prevent; to hinder. [ME, t. L: s. *prohibitus,* pp., held back, restrained] —**Syn. 1.** See **forbid.**

pro·hi·bi·tion (prō′ə bĭsh′ən), *n.* **1.** the interdiction by law of the manufacture and sale of alcoholic drinks for common consumption. **2.** act of prohibiting. **3.** a law or decree that forbids. —**Syn. 3.** interdiction.

pro·hi·bi·tion·ist (prō′ə bĭsh′ən ĭst), *n.* **1.** one who favors or advocates prohibition. **2.** (*cap.*) a member of the Prohibition party.

Prohibition party, a national U.S. party organized in 1869, advocating the legislative prohibition of the manufacture and sale of alcoholic drinks.

pro·hib·i·tive (prō hĭb′ə tĭv), *adj.* **1.** that prohibits or forbids something. **2.** serving to prevent the use, purchase, etc., of something. —**pro·hib′i·tive·ly,** *adv.*

pro·hib·i·to·ry (prō hĭb′ə tôr′ĭ), *adj.* prohibitive.

pro·ject (*n.* prŏj′ĕkt; *v.* prə jĕkt′), *n.* **1.** something that is contemplated, devised, or planned; a plan; a scheme. **2.** a specific task of investigation, esp. in scholarship. **3.** *Educ.* an educational assignment necessitating personal initiative on the part of a student. —*v.t.* **4.** to propose, contemplate, or plan. **5.** to throw, cast, or impel forward or onward. **6.** to throw or cause to fall upon a surface or into space, as a ray of light, a shadow, etc. **7.** to cause (a figure or image) to appear as on a background. **8.** to visualize or regard (an idea, etc.) as an objective reality. **9.** to cause to jut out or protrude. **10.** to throw forward (a figure, etc.) by straight lines or rays (parallel or from a center) which pass through all points of it and reproduce it on a surface or other figure. **11.** to delineate by any system of correspondence between points. **12.** to transform the points of (one figure) into those of another by any correspondence between points. —*v.i.* **13.** to extend or protrude beyond something else. [ME, t. L: s. *prōjectum,* pp. neut., (thing) thrown out] —**Syn. 1.** See **plan.**

pro·jec·tile (prə jĕk′tĭl), *n.* **1.** *Mil.* an object fired from a gun with an explosive propelling charge, such as a bullet, shell, rocket, or grenade. **2.** a body projected or impelled forward, as through the air. —*adj.* **3.** impelling or driving forward, as a force. **4.** caused by impulse, as motion. **5.** capable of being impelled forward, as a missile. **6.** *Zool.* protrusile, as the jaws of a fish. [t. NL, neut. of *prōjectilis,* adj., projecting]

pro·jec·tion (prə jĕk′shən), *n.* **1.** a projecting or protruding part. **2.** the state or fact of jutting out or protruding. **3.** a causing to jut out or protrude. **4.** *Geom., etc.* the act, process, or result of projecting. **5.** *Cartog.* a systematic drawing of lines representing meridians and parallels on a plane surface on which the earth surface (or the celestial sphere) or some portion of it may be drawn. **6.** *Photog.* **a.** the projection of an image by optical means, as in the projection of lantern slides or motion pictures or the making of enlargements. **b.** the representation or picture formed. **7.** the act of visualizing and regarding an idea or the like as an objective reality. **8.** that which is so visualized and regarded. **9.** *Psychol.* **a.** the tendency to attribute to another person, or to the environment, what is actually within oneself. **b.** *Psychoanal.* (usually) such an attribution relieving the ego of guilt feelings. **10.** the act of planning or scheming. **11.** *Alchemy.* the casting of the powder of the philosophers' stone upon metal in fusion, to transmute it into gold or silver. [t. L: s. *prōjectio*]

projection machine, a device which projects motion pictures.

pro·jec·tive (prə jĕk′tĭv), *adj.* **1.** of or pertaining to projection. **2.** produced, or capable of being produced, by projection. **3.** *Psychol.* **a.** pertaining to projection,

b. (in certain tests) pertaining to the ways in which the person projects his inner attributes into or upon prepared test materials. See **projective technique.** —**pro·jec·tiv·i·ty** (prō′jĕk tĭv′ə tĭ), *n.*

projective geometry, the geometric study of projective properties.

projective property, a geometric property which is unaltered by projection.

projective technique, *Psychol.* a method of detecting hidden motives or underlying personality structure by allowing a subject to express himself in free play, theatricals, response to pictures, etc.

pro·jec·tor (prə jĕk′tər), *n.* **1.** an apparatus for throwing an image on a screen, as a magic lantern, a motion-picture projector, etc. **2.** a device for projecting a beam of light. **3.** one who forms projects or plans; a schemer.

pro·jet (prō zhĕ′), *n.* **1.** a project. **2.** a draft of a proposed treaty or other instrument. [F. See PROJECT, n.]

Pro·kof·iev (prŏ kôf′yĕf), *n.* **Sergei Sergeevich** (sĕr′gā′ sĕr gā′yə vĭch), 1891–1953, Russian composer.

Pro·ko·pi·evsk (prŏ kô′pĭ ĕfsk′), *n.* a city in the S Soviet Union in Asia, SE of Novosibirsk. 260,000 (est. 1956).

pro·lac·tin (prō lăk′tĭn), *n.* *Biochem.* an anterior pituitary hormone which regulates milk secretion in mammals and the activity of the crop glands in birds.

pro·lan (prō′lăn), *n.* *Biochem.* a sex hormone found in high concentration in pregnancy urine, making possible the diagnosis of early pregnancy. [contr. of PROLACTIN]

pro·lapse (prō lăps′), *n., v.,* **-lapsed, -lapsing.** —*n.* Also, **pro·lap·sus** (prō lăp′səs). **1.** *Pathol.* a falling down of an organ or part, as the uterus, from its normal position. —*v.i.* **2.** *Chiefly Pathol.* to fall or slip down or out of place. [t. LL: m.s. *prōlapsus* a falling down]

pro·late (prō′lāt), *adj.* elongated along the polar diameter, as a spheroid generated by the revolution of an ellipse about its longer axis (opposed to *oblate*). [t. L: m.s. *prōlātus,* pp., brought forward, extended]

A   B
Spheroids
A. Prolate; B. Oblate

pro·leg (prō′lĕg′), *n.* one of the abdominal ambulatory processes of caterpillars and other larvae, as distinct from the true or thoracic legs. [f. PRO¹⁻ + LEG]

pro·le·gom·e·non (prō′lə gŏm′ə nŏn′, -nən), *n., pl.* **-gomena** (-gŏm′ə nə). a preliminary observation, as on the subject of a book (usually *pl.,* as applied to an introduction to a book). [t. NL, t. Gk.: (neut. ppr. pass.) being said beforehand]

Proleg (to the right) of larva of milkweed butterfly, *Anosia plexippus*

pro·le·gom·e·nous (prō′lə gŏm′ə nəs), *adj.* **1.** prefatory; preliminary. **2.** characterized by unnecessary or lengthy prologuizing.

pro·lep·sis (prō lĕp′sĭs), *n., pl.* **-ses** (-sēz). **1.** *Rhet.* an anticipation of objections in order to answer them in advance. **2.** the assigning of an event, etc., to a period earlier than its actual date. **3.** the use of an epithet in anticipation of its becoming applicable. [t. L, t. Gk.: anticipation, preconception] —**pro·lep′tic,** *adj.*

pro·le·tar·i·an (prō′lə târ′ĭ ən), *adj.* **1.** pertaining or belonging to the proletariat. **2.** (in ancient Rome) belonging to the lowest or poorest class of the people, regarded as contributing nothing but offspring to the state. —*n.* **3.** a member of the proletariat. [f. s. L *prōlētārius* a Roman citizen of the lowest class + -AN]

pro·le·tar·i·at (prō′lə târ′ĭ ət), *n.* **1.** the unpropertied class; that class which is dependent for support on daily or casual employment. **2.** the working class, or wage earners in general. [t. F, f. s. L *prōlētārius* a Roman citizen of the lowest class + -*at* -AT(E)³]

pro·le·tar·y (prō′lə tĕr′ĭ), *adj., n., pl.* **-taries.** a proletarian person. See **proletarian,** def. 2.

pro·lif·er·ate (prō lĭf′ə rāt′), *v.i., v.t.,* **-ated, -ating.** to grow or produce by multiplication of parts, as in budding or cell division. —**pro·lif′er·a′tion,** *n.*

pro·lif·er·ous (prō lĭf′ər əs), *adj.* **1.** proliferating. **2.** *Bot.* **a.** producing new individuals by budding or the like. **b.** producing an organ or shoot from an organ which is itself normally ultimate, as a shoot or a new flower from the midst of a flower. [f. ML *prōlifer* (f. L *prōli-* offspring + -*fer* bearing) + -OUS]

pro·lif·ic (prō lĭf′ĭk), *adj.* **1.** producing offspring, young, fruit, etc., esp. abundantly; fruitful. **2.** producing much or abundantly: *a prolific writer.* **3.** abundantly productive of or fruitful in something specified. **4.** characterized by, involving, or causing abundant production. [t. ML: s. *prōlificus,* f. L *prōli-* offspring + -*ficus* -FIC] —**pro·lif·i·ca·cy** (prō lĭf′ə kə sĭ), **pro·lif′ic·ness,** *n.* —**pro·lif′i·cal·ly,** *adv.*

pro·line (prō′lēn, -lĭn), *n.* *Biochem.* an alcohol-soluble amino acid found in all proteins. [contr. of *pyrroline,* f. PYRROLE + -INE²]

pro·lix (prō′lĭks′, prō′lĭks), *adj.* **1.** extended to great, unnecessary, or tedious length; long and wordy. **2.** speaking or writing at great or tedious length. [ME, t. L: s. *prolixus* extended, long] —**pro·lix·i·ty** (prō lĭk′sə tĭ), **pro·lix′ness,** *n.* —**pro·lix′ly,** *adv.*

pro·loc·u·tor (prō lŏk/yə tər), *n.* **1.** a presiding officer of an assembly; a chairman. **2.** *Ch. of Eng.* the chairman of the lower house of a convocation. [t. L] —**pro·loc/-u·tor·ship/**, *n.*

pro·logue (prō/lôg, -lŏg), *n., v.,* **-logued, -loguing.** —*n.* **1.** an introductory speech, often in verse, calling attention to the theme of a play. **2.** the actor who delivers it. **3.** an introductory act of a dramatic performance. **4.** a preliminary discourse; a preface or introductory part of a discourse, poem, or novel. **5.** any introductory proceeding, event, etc. —*v.t.* **6.** to introduce with, or as with, a prologue. Also, **pro/log.** [ME *prolog,* t. L: s. *prólogus,* t. Gk.: m. *prólogos*]

pro·logu·ize (prō/lôg ĭz/, -lŏg-), *v.i.,* **-ized, -izing.** to compose or deliver a prologue. Also, **pro·log·ize** (prō/-lŏg ĭz/, -lŏg-, prō/lə jīz/). —**pro/logu·iz/er,** *n.*

pro·long (prə lông/. -lŏng/), *v.t.* **1.** to lengthen out in time; to extend the duration of; to cause to continue longer: *to prolong one's life.* **2.** to make longer in spatial extent: *to prolong a line.* [late ME *prolonge*(n), t. LL: m. *prolongāre*] —**pro·long/er,** *n.* —**pro·long/ment,** *n.* —**Syn. 1.** See **lengthen.**

pro·lon·gate (prə lông/gāt, -lŏng/-), *v.t.,* **-gated, -gating.** *Rare.* to prolong.

pro·lon·ga·tion (prō/lông gā/shən, -lŏng-), *n.* **1.** the act of prolonging: *the prolongation of a line.* **2.** the state of being prolonged. **3.** a prolonged or extended form. **4.** an added part.

pro·longe (prō/lônj/; *Fr.* prô lônzh/), *n. Mil.* a rope having a hook at one end and a toggle at the other, used for various purposes, as to draw a gun carriage. [t. F, der. *prolonger* PROLONG]

pro·lu·sion (prō lōō/zhən), *n.* **1.** a preliminary written article. **2.** an essay preliminary to a more profound work, or of an introductory or slight nature. [t. L: s. *prōlūsio* preliminary exercise]

pro·lu·so·ry (prō lōō/sə rĭ), *adj.* **1.** serving for prolusion. **2.** of the nature of a prolusion.

prom (prŏm), *n. Colloq.* (in American schools) a ball or dance. [short for PROMENADE (def. 4)]

prom., promontory.

pro me·mo·ri·a (prō mə mōr/ĭ ə), *Latin.* for memory (used in diplomacy to recall rights which have lapsed for a long time).

prom·e·nade (prŏm/ə nād/, -näd/), *n., v.,* **-naded, -nading.** —*n.* **1.** a walk, esp. in a public place, as for pleasure or display. **2.** a space on an upper deck (**promenade deck**) of a passenger ship for the use of passengers. **3.** prom. **4.** a march of guests into a ballroom constituting the opening of a formal ball. **5.** a march of dancers in folk or square dancing. —*v.i.* **6.** to take a promenade. —*v.t.* **7.** to take a promenade through or about. **8.** to take or conduct on or as on a promenade; parade. [t. F, der. *promener* lead out, take for a walk or airing] —**prom/e·nad/er,** *n.*

Pro·me·the·an (prə mē/thĭ ən), *adj.* **1.** of or suggestive of Prometheus. **2.** creative; boldly original. —*n.* **3.** one who resembles Prometheus in spirit or actions.

Pro·me·theus (prə mē/thōŏs, -thĭ əs), *n. Gk. Myth.* a Titan fabled to have made men out of clay, to have stolen fire for them from Olympus, and to have taught them various arts, in punishment for which he was chained by order of Zeus to a rock in the Caucasus, where his liver was daily gnawed by a vulture. He was freed when Hercules killed the vulture.

pro·me·thi·um (prə mē/thĭ əm), *n. Chem.* a rare-earth, metallic, trivalent element. *Symbol:* Pm; *at.no.:* 61.

prom·i·nence (prŏm/ə nəns), *n.* **1.** Also, **prom/i·nen·cy.** the state of being prominent; conspicuousness. **2.** that which is prominent; a projection or protuberance: *the prominence of a rock or cliff, the prominences of a face.* **3.** *Astron.* a cloud of gas high above the surface of the sun, especially when seen in silhouette at the sun's limb.

prom·i·nent (prŏm/ə nənt), *adj.* **1.** standing out so as to be easily seen; conspicuous; especially noticeable: *a prominent feature.* **2.** standing out beyond the adjacent surface or line; projecting. **3.** important; leading; well-known: *a prominent citizen.* [t. L: s. *prōminens,* ppr., jutting out] —**prom/i·nent·ly,** *adv.*

prom·is·cu·i·ty (prŏm/ĭs kū/ə tĭ, prō/mĭs-), *n., pl.* **-ties.** **1.** the state of being promiscuous. **2.** promiscuous sexual union. **3.** indiscriminate mixture.

pro·mis·cu·ous (prə mĭs/kyōŏ əs), *adj.* **1.** consisting of parts, elements, or individuals of different kinds brought together without order. **2.** characterized by or involving indiscriminate mingling or association. **3.** indiscriminate; without discrimination. **4.** *Colloq.* casual; without particular plan or reason. [t. L: m. *prōmiscuus*] —**pro·mis/cu·ous·ly,** *adv.* —**pro·mis/cu·ous·ness,** *n.* —**Syn. 1.** See **miscellaneous.**

prom·ise (prŏm/ĭs), *n., v.,* **-ised, -ising.** —*n.* **1.** a declaration made, as to another person, with respect to the future, giving assurance that one will do, not do, give, not give, etc., something. **2.** an express assurance on which expectation is to be based. **3.** something that has the effect of an express assurance; indication of what may be expected. **4.** indication of future excellence or achievement: *a writer that shows promise.* **5.** that which is promised. —*v.t.* **6.** to engage or undertake by promise (with an infinitive or a clause): *to promise not to interfere.* **7.** to make a promise of: *to promise help.* **8.** to make a promise of (something) to. **9.** to afford ground for expecting. **10.** to engage to give in marriage. **11.** *Col-*

loq. to assure (used in emphatic declarations). —*v.i.* **12.** to afford ground for expectation (often fol. by *well* or *fair).* **13.** to make a promise. [ME, t. L: m.s. *prōmissum* a promise, prop. neut. pp. of *prōmittere* to promise] —**prom/is·er;** *Law,* **prom·i·sor** (prŏm/ə sôr/), *n.*

Promised Land, 1. Canaan, the land promised by God to Abraham and his descendants. Gen. 12:7. **2.** Heaven.

prom·is·ee (prŏm/ə sē/), *n. Law.* one to whom a promise is made.

prom·is·ing (prŏm/ə sĭng), *adj.* giving promise; likely to turn out well: *a promising young man.* —**prom/is·ing·ly,** *adv.*

prom·is·so·ry (prŏm/ə sôr/ĭ), *adj.* **1.** containing or implying a promise. **2.** of the nature of a promise. **3.** *Insurance.* of or denoting preliminary agreements and representations, made in drawing up a contract of insurance. [t. ML: m.s. *prōmissōrius,* der. L *prōmissor*]

promissory note, a written promise to pay a specified sum of money to a person designated or to his order, or to the bearer, at a time fixed or on demand.

prom·on·to·ry (prŏm/ən tōr/ĭ), *n., pl.* **-ries. 1.** a high point of land or rock projecting into the sea or other water beyond the line of coast; a headland. **2.** *Anat.* a prominent or protuberant part. [t. ML: m.s. *prōmontōrium,* for L *prōmunturium*]

pro·mote (prə mōt/), *v.t.,* **-moted, -moting. 1.** to further the growth, development, progress, etc., of; further; encourage. **2.** to advance in rank, dignity, position, etc. **3.** *Educ.* to put ahead to the next higher stage or grade of a course or series of classes. **4.** to aid in organizing (financial undertakings). [ME, t. L: m.s. *prōmōtus,* pp., moved forward, advanced]

pro·mot·er (prə mō/tər), *n.* **1.** one who initiates or takes part in the organizing of a company, development of a project, etc. **2.** one who or that which promotes. **3.** *Obs.* an informer.

pro·mo·tion (prə mō/shən), *n.* **1.** advancement in rank or position. **2.** furtherance or encouragement. **3.** the act of promoting. **4.** the state of being promoted.

pro·mo·tive (prə mō/tĭv), *adj.* tending to promote.

prompt (prŏmpt), *adj.* **1.** done, performed, delivered, etc., at once or without delay: *a prompt reply.* **2.** ready in action; quick to act as occasion demands. **3.** ready and willing. —*v.t.* **4.** to move or incite to action. **5.** to suggest or induce (action, etc.); inspire or occasion. **6.** to assist (a person speaking) by suggesting something to be said. **7.** *Theat.* to supply (an actor or reciter) with his cue from off stage if he has missed it, or his line if he has forgotten it. —*v.i.* **8.** *Theat.* to supply off-stage cues and effects. —*n.* **9.** *Com.* a limit of time given for payment for merchandise purchased, the limit being stated on a note of reminder called a **prompt note. b.** the contract setting the time limit. **10.** act of prompting. **11.** something that prompts. [ME, t. L: s. *promptus,* pp., taken out, at hand] —**prompt/ly,** *adv* —**prompt/ness,** *n.*

prompt·er (prŏmp/tər), *n.* **1.** *Theat.* one who follows a play in progress from the book, off stage, to repeat missed cues and supply actors with forgotten lines. **2.** one who or that which prompts.

promp·ti·tude (prŏmp/tə tōōd/, -tŏŏd/), *n.* promptness. [late ME, t. LL: m. *promptitūdō*]

pro·mul·gate (prō mŭl/gāt *or. esp. Brit.,* prŏm/əl gāt/), *v.t.,* **-gated, -gating. 1.** to make known by open declaration; to publish; to proclaim formally or put into operation (a law or rule of court or decree). **2.** to set forth or teach publicly (a creed, doctrine, etc.). [t. L: m.s. *prōmulgātus,* pp., made publicly known, published] —**prom·ul·ga·tion** (prō/mŭl gā/shən, prŏm/əl-), *n.* —**pro·mul·ga·tor** (prō mul/gā tər, prŏm/əl-), *n.*

pro·mulge (prō mŭlj/), *v.t.,* **-mulged, -mulging.** *Archaic.* to promulgate.

pro·my·ce·li·um (prō/mī sē/lĭ əm), *n., pl.* **-lia** (-lĭ ə) *Bot.* a short filament produced in the germination of a spore, which bears small spores and then dies. —**pro/-my·ce/li·al,** *adj.*

pron., 1. pronominal. **2.** pronoun. **3.** pronounced. **4.** pronunciation.

pro·nate (prō/nāt), *v.,* **-nated, -nating.** *Physiol.* —*v.t.* **1.** to render prone; to rotate or place (the hand or forelimb) so that the palmar surface is downward when the limb is stretched forward horizontally. Cf. **supinate.** —*v.i.* **2.** to become pronated. [t. LL: s. *prōnātus,* pp., bent forward, der. L *prōnus* PRONE] —**pro·na/tor,** *n.*

pro·na·tion (prō nā/shən), *n. Physiol.* **1.** a rotation of the hand which leaves the palm facing downwards and the bones of the forearm crossed (opposed to *supination*). **2.** a comparable motion of the foot consisting of abduction followed by eversion. **3.** the position assumed as the result of this rotation.

prone (prōn), *adj.* **1.** having a natural inclination or tendency to something; disposed; liable: *to be prone to anger.* **2.** having the front or ventral part downward; lying face downward. **3.** lying flat; prostrate. **4.** having a downward direction or slope. **5.** having the palm downward, as the hand. [ME, t. L: m.s. *prōnus* turned or leaning forward, inclined downward, disposed, prone] —**prone/ly,** *adv.* —**prone/ness,** *n.*

pro·neph·ros (prō nĕf/rŏs), *n. Embryol.* a primitive kidney functioning in lower vertebrates but vestigial in higher vertebrates and man. Cf. **mesonephros.** [t. NL. f. Gk.: pro- PRO-² + *nephrós* kidney]

prong (prông, prŏng), *n.* **1.** one of the pointed divisions or tines of a fork. **2.** any pointed projecting part, as of an antler. —*v.t.* **3.** to pierce or stab with a prong. **4.** to supply with prongs. [? b. PRICK and TONG[1]]

prong·horn (prông′hôrn′, prŏng′-), *n.* a fleet antelopelike ruminant, *Antilocapra americana*, of the plains of western North America.

pro·nom·i·nal (prō nŏm′ə nəl), *adj.* pertaining to or having the nature of a pronoun. [t. LL: s. *prōnōminālis*, der. L *prōnōmen* pronoun] —**pro·nom′i·nal·ly,** *adv.*

Pronghorn.
Antilocapra americana
(Ab. 3 ft. high at the shoulder, total length 5½ ft.)

pro·noun (prō′noun′), *n. Gram.* **1.** (in many languages) one of the major form classes, or "parts of speech," comprising words used as substitutes for nouns. **2.** any such word, as *I, you, he, this, who, what.* **3.** a word of similar function or meaning, whether member of a special form class or not. [t. F: m. *pronom,* t. L: m. *prōnōmen*]

pro·nounce (prə nouns′), *v.* **-nounced, -nouncing.** —*v.t.* **1.** to enunciate or articulate (words, etc.). **2.** to utter or sound in a particular manner in speaking. **3.** to declare (a person or thing) to be as specified. **4.** to utter or deliver formally or solemnly. **5.** to announce authoritatively or officially. —*v.i.* **6.** to pronounce words, etc. **7.** to make a statement or assertion, esp. an authoritative statement. **8.** to give an opinion or decision. [ME, t. OF: m. *prononcier,* t. L: m. *prōnuntiāre* proclaim, announce, recite, utter] —**pro·nounce′a·ble,** *adj.* —**pro·nounc′er,** *n.*

pro·nounced (prə nounst′), *adj.* **1.** strongly marked. **2.** clearly indicated. **3.** decided: *to have very pronounced views.* —**pro·nounc·ed·ly** (prə noun′sĭd lĭ), *adv.*

pro·nounce·ment (prə nouns′mənt), *n.* **1.** a formal or authoritative statement. **2.** an opinion or decision. **3.** act of pronouncing.

pron·to (prŏn′tō), *adv. U.S. Slang.* promptly; quickly. [t. Sp. (adj. and adv.), g. L *promptus.* See PROMPT]

pro·nu·cle·us (prō nū′klĭ əs, -nōō′-), *n., pl.* **-clei** (-klĭ-ī′). *Embryol.* either of the gametic nuclei which after fertilization unite and form a double nucleus.

pro·nun·ci·a·men·to (prə nŭn′sĭ ə men′tō, -shĭ ə-), *n., pl.* **-tos.** a proclamation; manifesto. [t. Sp.: f. *pronuncia*(*r*) (t. L: m. *prōnuntiāre* proclaim) + *-mento* (noun suffix)]

pro·nun·ci·a·tion (prə nŭn′sĭ ā′shən, -shĭ ā′-), *n.* the act or the result of producing the sounds of speech, including articulation, vowel formation, accent, inflection, and intonation, often with reference to the correctness or acceptability of the speech sounds. [ME, t. L: m.s. *prōnuntiātio*]

proof (prōōf), *n.* **1.** evidence sufficient to establish a thing as true, or to produce belief in its truth. **2.** anything serving as such evidence. **3.** act of testing or making trial or anything; test; a trial: *to put a thing to the proof.* **4.** the establishment of the truth of anything; demonstration. **5.** *Law.* (in judicial proceedings) evidence having probative weight. **6.** the effect of evidence in convincing the mind. **7.** an arithmetical operation serving to check the correctness of a calculation. **8.** a test to determine the quality, etc., of materials used in manufacture. **9.** the state of having been tested and approved. **10.** proved strength, as of armor. **11. a.** the arbitrary standard strength, as of alcoholic liquors. **b.** strength with reference to this standard, indicated on a scale on which **100 proof** signifies a proof spirit. **12.** *Photog.* a trial print from a negative. **13.** *Print.* **a.** a trial impression as of composed type, taken to correct errors and make alterations. **b.** one of a number of early and superior impressions taken before the printing of the ordinary issue. **14.** *Engraving, etc.* an impression taken from a plate or the like to show its state during the process of execution. —*adj.* **15.** impenetrable, impervious, or invulnerable: *proof against temptation.* **16.** of tested or proved strength or quality: *proof armor.* **17.** used for testing or proving; serving as proof. **18.** of standard strength, as an alcoholic liquor. **19.** referring to pieces of pure gold and silver which the United States assay and mint offices use as standards. [ME *preove,* t. OF: m. *prueve,* g. LL *proba* proof, der. L *probāre* PROVE] —**Syn. 1.** See *evidence.*

proof·read (prōōf′rēd′), *v.t., v.i.* **-read, -reading.** to read (printers' proofs, etc.) in order to detect and mark errors to be corrected. —**proof′read′er,** *n.* —**proof′read′ing,** *n.*

proof sheet, a printer's proof.

proof spirit, an alcoholic liquor, or mixture of alcohol and water, containing a standard amount of alcohol: **1.** *U.S.* one with a specific gravity of .93353 (containing one half of its volume of alcohol of a specific gravity of .7939 at 60° Fahrenheit). **2.** *Brit.* one with a specific gravity of .91984.

prop[1] (prŏp), *v.,* **propped, propping,** *n.* —*v.t.* **1.** to support, or prevent from falling, with or as with a prop: *to prop a roof.* **2.** to rest (a thing) against support. **3.** to support or sustain. —*n.* **4.** a stick, rod, pole, beam, or other rigid support. **5.** a person or thing serving as a support or stay. [ME *proppe,* c. MD *proppe* prop, support; orig. uncert.]

prop[2] (prŏp), *n. Theat.* property (def. 8).
prop[3] (prŏp), *n. Colloq.* a propeller.
prop., **1.** properly. **2.** property. **3.** proposition.

pro·pae·deu·tic (prō′pə dū′tĭk, -dōō′-), *adj.* Also, **pro′pae·deu′ti·cal. 1.** pertaining to or of the nature of preliminary instruction. **2.** introductory to some art or science. —*n.* **3.** a propaedeutic subject or study. **4.** (*pl.*) the preliminary body of knowledge and rules necessary for the study of some art or science. [f. PRO-[2] beforehand + m.s. Gk. *paideutikós* pertaining to teaching]

prop·a·ga·ble (prŏp′ə gə bəl), *adj.* capable of being propagated.

prop·a·gan·da (prŏp′ə găn′də), *n.* **1.** the particular doctrines or principles propagated by an organization or concerted movement. **2.** such an organization or concerted movement. **3.** College of Propaganda, a committee of cardinals, established in 1622 by Pope Gregory XV, having supervision of the foreign missions of the Roman Catholic Church and of the training of priests for these missions. [t. NL: short for *congregātio dē propāgandā fidē* congregation for propagating the faith]

prop·a·gan·dism (prŏp′ə găn′dĭz əm), *n.* **1.** zealous propagation of particular doctrines or principles. **2.** the practice or spirit of a propaganda.

prop·a·gan·dist (prŏp′ə găn′dĭst), *n.* **1.** one devoted to the propagation of particular doctrines or principles. **2.** a member or agent of a propaganda. —*adj.* **3.** pertaining to propaganda or propagandists.

prop·a·gan·dize (prŏp′ə găn′dīz), *v.,* **-dized, -dizing.** —*v.t.* **1.** to propagate or spread (principles, etc.) by a propaganda. —*v.i.* **2.** to carry on a propaganda.

prop·a·gate (prŏp′ə gāt′), *v.,* **-gated, -gating.** —*v.t.* **1.** to cause (plants, animals, etc.) to multiply by any process of natural reproduction from the parent stock. **2.** to reproduce (itself, its kind, etc.), as a plant or an animal does. **3.** to transmit (traits, etc.) in reproduction, or through offspring. **4.** to spread (a report, doctrine, practice, etc.) from person to person; to disseminate. **5.** to cause to increase in number or amounts. **6.** to cause to extend to a greater distance, or transmit through space or a medium: *to propagate sound.* —*v.i.* **7.** to multiply by any process of natural reproduction, as plants or animals; to breed. [t. L: m.s. *propāgātus,* pp., propagated (orig. referring to plants by layers or slips)] —**prop′a·ga′tive,** *adj.* —**prop′a·ga′tor,** *n.*

prop·a·ga·tion (prŏp′ə gā′shən), *n.* **1.** the act of propagating. **2.** the fact of being propagated. **3.** multiplication by natural reproduction. **4.** increase; transmission; dissemination.

pro·pane (prō′pān), *n. Chem.* a gaseous hydrocarbon, C_3H_8, of the methane series, found in petroleum. [PROP(IONIC) + -ANE]

pro·par·ox·y·tone (prō′păr ŏk′sə tōn′), *Gk. Gram.* —*adj.* **1.** having an acute accent on the antepenult. —*n.* **2.** a proparoxytone word. [t. Gk.: m.s. *proparoxýtonos*] —**pro·par·ox·y·ton·ic** (prō′păr ŏk′sə tŏn′ĭk), *adj.*

pro pa·tri·a (prō pā′trĭ ə), *Latin.* for one's country.

pro·pel (prə pĕl′), *v.t.,* **-pelled, -pelling. 1.** to drive, or cause to move, forward: *a boat propelled by oars.* **2.** to impel or urge onward. [t. L: m.s. *prōpellere*]

pro·pel·lant (prə pĕl′ənt), *n.* **1.** a propelling agent. **2.** *Mil.* the charge of explosive used in a cannon to make the shell travel to the target.

pro·pel·lent (prə pĕl′ənt), *adj.* **1.** propelling; driving forward. —*n.* **2.** a propelling agent.

pro·pel·ler (prə pĕl′ər), *n.* **1.** a device having a revolving hub with radiating blades, for propelling a steamship, airship, etc. **2.** one who or that which propels.

pro·pend (prō pĕnd′), *v.i. Obs.* to incline or tend. [t. L: s. *prōpendere*]

pro·pen·si·ty (prə pĕn′sə tĭ), *n., pl.* **-ties. 1.** natural or habitual inclination or tendency: *a propensity to find fault.* **2.** *Obs.* favorable disposition or partiality. Also, *Rare.,* **pro·pen·sion** (prə pĕn′shən).

prop·er (prŏp′ər), *adj.* **1.** adapted or appropriate to the purpose or circumstances; fit; suitable: *the proper time to plant.* **2.** conforming to established standards of behavior or manners; correct or decorous. **3.** fitting; right. **4.** strictly belonging or applicable: *the proper place for a stove.* **5.** belonging or pertaining exclusively or distinctly to a person or thing. **6.** strict; accurate. **7.** strictly so-called; in the strict sense of the word (now usually following the noun): *shellfish do not belong to the fishes proper.* **8.** *Gram.* **a.** (of a name, noun, or adjective) designating a particular person or thing, written in English with an initial capital letter: *John, Chicago, Monday, American.* **b.** having the force or function of a proper name: *a proper adjective.* **9.** normal or regular. **10.** *Her.* (of an object used as a bearing) represented in its natural color or colors: *an eagle proper.* **11.** *Eccles.* used only on a particular day or festival: *the proper introit.* **12.** *Chiefly Brit. Colloq.* complete or thorough: *a proper thrashing.* **13.** *Archaic or Dial.* **a.** excellent; capital; fine. **b.** good-looking or handsome. **14.** *Archaic.* belonging to oneself or itself; own. **15.** *Archaic.* of good character; respectable. —*n.* **16.** *Eccles.* a special office or special parts of an office appointed for a particular day or time. [ME *propre,* t. OF, t. L: m.s. *proprius* one's own]

proper fraction, *Math.* a fraction having the numerator less, or lower in degree, than the denominator.

b., blend of, blended; c., cognate with; d., dialect, dialectal; der., derived from; f., formed from; g., going back to; m., modification of; r., replacing; s., stem of; t., taken from; ?, perhaps. See the full key on inside cover.

prop·er·ly (prŏp′ər lĭ′), *adv.* **1.** in a proper manner. **2.** correctly. **3.** appropriately. **4.** decorously. **5.** accurately. **6.** justifiably. **7.** *Colloq.* completely.

proper name. See **name** (def. 9).

proper noun, *Gram.* a noun that is not usually preceded by an article or other limiting modifier, in meaning applicable only to a single person or thing, or to several persons or things which do not constitute a class save by virtue of having the same name: *Lincoln, New York*, in contrast to *man. city*. See **common noun**.

prop·er·tied (prŏp′ər tĭd), *adj.* owning property

Pro·per·ti·us (prō pûr′shĭ əs, -shəs), *n.* **Sextus** (sĕk′stəs) c50-c15 B.C., Roman poet.

prop·er·ty (prŏp′ər tĭ), *n., pl.* **-ties. 1.** that which one owns; the possession or possessions of a particular owner. **2.** goods, lands, etc., owned: *a man of property* **3.** a piece of land or real estate: *property on Main Street.* **4.** ownership; right of possession, enjoyment, or disposal of anything, esp. of something tangible: *to have property in land.* **5.** something at the disposal of a person, a group of persons, or the community or public: *the secret became common property.* **6.** an essential or distinctive attribute or quality of a thing or (formerly) a person. **7.** *Logic.* **a.** any attribute or characteristic. **b.** (according to Aristotelian usage) an attribute which, though not part of the essential nature of a species, is necessarily connected with it: *bitterness is a property of wormwood.* **8.** *Theat.* an item of furniture, ornament, or decoration in a stage setting; any object handled or used by an actor in performance. [ME *proprete*, f. *propre* PROPER (def. 7 and 14) + *-te* -TY²] —**Syn. 1.** PROPERTY, CHATTELS, EFFECTS, ESTATE, GOODS are terms for material things which are owned. PROPERTY is the general word: *he owns a great deal of property* (land, etc.). *he said that the umbrella was his property.* CHATTELS is a term for pieces of personal property or movable possessions; it may be applied to livestock, automobiles, etc.. *a mortgage on chattels.* EFFECTS is a legal term for personal property, including even things of the least value: *all his effects were insured against fire.* ESTATE refers to property of any kind which has been, or is capable of being handed down to descendants or disposed of otherwise in a will: *he left most of his estate to his nephew.* It may consist of personal estate (money, valuables, securities, chattels, etc.), or real estate (land and buildings). GOODS refers to household possessions or other movable property, esp. that comprising the stock in trade of a business: *a store arranges its goods conveniently for sale.* **6.** See **quality**.

pro·phase (prō′fāz′), *n. Biol.* the first mitotic stage wherein the chromatin condenses to form chromosomes which arrange themselves in the equatorial plane of the cell. Simultaneously, the achromatic spindle forms.

proph·e·cy (prŏf′ə sĭ), *n., pl.* **-cies. 1.** foretelling or prediction (orig. by divine inspiration) of what is to come. **2.** that which is declared by a prophet; a prediction. **3.** divinely inspired utterance or revelation. **4.** the action, function, or faculty of a prophet. [ME *prophecie*, t. OF, t. LL: m. *prophētīa*. t. Gk.: m. *prophēteĩa*]

proph·e·sy (prŏf′ə sĭ), *v.,* **-sied, -sying.** —*v.t.* **1.** to foretell or predict: *to prophesy a storm.* **2.** to indicate beforehand. **3.** to declare or foretell by or as by divine inspiration. **4.** to utter in prophecy or as a prophet. —*v.i.* **5.** to make predictions. **6.** to make inspired declarations of what is to come. **7.** to speak as a mediator between God and man or in God's stead. **8.** to teach religious subjects or material. [v. use of var of PROPHECY] —**proph′e·si′er,** *n.* —**Syn. 1.** See **predict**.

proph·et (prŏf′ĭt), *n.* **1.** one who speaks for God or a deity, or by divine inspiration. **2.** one of a class of persons in the early church, next on order after the apostles, recognized as inspired to utter special revelations and predictions. 1 Cor. 12: 28. **3. the Prophet, a.** Mohammed, the founder of Islam. See **Koran. b.** *Mormon Ch.* Joseph Smith. **4. the Prophets,** the books which form the second of the three Jewish divisions of the Old Testament, comprising **a.** Joshua, Judges, I and II Samuel, and I and II Kings; **b.** Isaiah, Jeremiah, and Ezekiel (**Major Prophets**); **c.** Hosea, Joel, Amos, Obadiah, Jonah, Micah, Nahum, Habakkuk, Zephaniah, Haggai, Zechariah, and Malachi (**Minor Prophets**). Group **a** is called the **Former Prophets**; groups **b** and **c** together the **Latter Prophets**. Cf. **law** (def. 16), **Hagiographa. 5.** one regarded as, or claiming to be, an inspired teacher or leader. **6.** one who foretells or predicts what is to come: *a weather prophet.* **7.** a spokesman or proclaimer of some doctrine, cause, or the like. [ME *prophete*, t. L: m. *prophēta*, t. Gk.: m. *prophētēs* (prŏf′ĭt ĭs), *n. fem.* —**proph′et·hood′,** *n.*

pro·phet·ic (prə fĕt′ĭk), *adj.* **1.** of or pertaining to a prophet: *prophetic inspiration.* **2.** of the nature of or containing prophecy: *prophetic writings.* **3.** having the function or powers of a prophet, as a person. **4.** predictive; presageful; ominous. Also, **pro·phet′i·cal.** —**pro·phet′i·cal·ly,** *adv.*

pro·phy·lac·tic (prō′fə lăk′tĭk, prŏf′ə-), *adj.* **1.** defending or protecting from disease, as a drug. **2.** preventive; preservative; protective. —*n.* **3.** a prophylactic medicine or measure. **4.** a preventative. [t. Gk.: m.s. *prophylaktikós*]

pro·phy·lax·is (prō′fə lăk′sĭs, prŏf′ə-), *n.* **1.** the preventing of disease. **2.** the prevention of a specific dis-

ease, as by studying the biological behavior, transmission, etc. of its causative agent and applying a series of measures against it. **3.** prophylactic treatment. [t. NL, f. Gk.: pro- PRO-¹ + *phylaxis* a watching, guarding]

pro·pin·qui·ty (prō pĭng′kwə tĭ), *n.* **1.** nearness in place; proximity. **2.** nearness of relation; kinship. **3.** affinity of nature; similarity. **4.** nearness in time. [ME *propinquite*, t. L: m.s. *propinquitas*]

pro·pi·o·nate (prō′pĭ ə nāt′), *n. Chem.* an ester or salt derived from propionic acid.

pro·pi·on·ic acid (prō′pĭ ŏn′ĭk, -ō′nĭk), *Chem.* a liquid organic acid, C_2H_5COOH. [f. PRO-² + Gk. *pĩon* fat + -IC]

pro·pi·ti·ate (prə pĭsh′ĭ āt′), *v.t.,* **-ated, -ating.** to make favorably inclined; appease; conciliate. [t. L: m.s. *propitiātus,* pp.] —**pro·pi·ti·a·ble** (prə pĭsh′ĭ ə bəl), *adj.* —**pro·pi′ti·a′tive,** *adj.* —**pro·pi′ti·a′tor,** *n.* —**Syn.** See **appease**.

pro·pi·ti·a·tion (prə pĭsh′ĭ ā′shən), *n.* **1.** the act of propitiating; conciliation. **2.** that which propitiates.

pro·pi·ti·a·to·ry (prə pĭsh′ĭ ə tōr′ĭ), *adj.* **1.** serving or intended to propitiate. **2.** making propitiation; conciliatory. —*n.* **3.** *Jewish Antiq.* the mercy seat.

pro·pi·tious (prə pĭsh′əs), *adj.* **1.** presenting favorable conditions; favorable: *propitious weather.* **2.** indicative of favor: *propitious omens.* **3.** favorably inclined; disposed to bestow favors or forgive. [late ME *propicius,* t. L: m. *propitius*] —**pro·pi′tious·ly,** *adv.* —**pro·pi′tious·ness,** *n.*

prop·o·lis (prŏp′ə lĭs), *n.* a reddish resinous cement collected by bees from the buds of trees, used to stop up crevices in the hives, strengthen the cells, etc. [t. L, t. Gk.]

pro·po·nent (prə pō′nənt), *n.* **1.** one who puts forward a proposition or proposal. **2.** *Law.* one who argues in favor of; specif., one who seeks to obtain probate of a will. **3.** one who supports a cause or doctrine.

pro·por·tion (prə pôr′shən), *n.* **1.** comparative relation between things or magnitudes as to size, quantity, number, etc.; ratio: *a house tall in proportion to its width.* **2.** proper relation between things or parts. **3.** relative size or extent. **4.** (*pl.*) dimensions: *a rock of gigantic proportions.* **5.** a portion or part in its relation to the whole: *a large proportion of the total.* **6.** a portion or part. **7.** relation, comparison, or analogy. **8.** symmetry; harmony; agreement. **9.** *Math.* **a.** a relation of four quantities such that the first divided by the second is equal to the third divided by the fourth; the equality of ratios. **b.** the rule of three. —*v.t.* **10.** to adjust in proper proportion or relation, as to size, quantity, etc. **11.** to adjust the proportions of. [ME *proporcioun,* t. L: m.s. *prōportiō*] —**pro·por′tion·er,** *n.*

pro·por·tion·a·ble (prə pôr′shən ə bəl), *adj.* being in due proportion; proportional.

pro·por·tion·al (prə pôr′shən əl), *adj.* **1.** having due proportion; corresponding. **2.** being in or characterized by proportion. **3.** of or pertaining to proportion; relative. **4.** *Math.* having the same or a constant ratio or relation. —**pro·por′tion·al′i·ty,** *n.* —**pro·por′tion·al·ly,** *adv.*

proportional representation, a method of voting by which political parties are given legislative representation in proportion to their popular strength.

pro·por·tion·ate (*adj.* prə pôr′shən ĭt; *v.* prə pôr′shə nāt′), *adj., v.,* **-ated, -ating.** —*adj.* **1.** proportioned; being in due proportion; proportional. —*v.t.* **2.** to make proportionate. —**pro·por′tion·ate·ly,** *adv.* —**pro·por′tion·ate·ness,** *n.*

pro·por·tion·ment (prə pôr′shən mənt), *n.* **1.** act of proportioning. **2.** state of being proportioned.

pro·pos·al (prə pō′zəl), *n.* **1.** act of proposing for acceptance, adoption, or performance. **2.** a plan or scheme proposed. **3.** an offer, specif. of marriage. —**Syn. 2.** PROPOSAL, OVERTURE, PROPOSITION refer to something in the nature of an offer. A PROPOSAL is a plan, a scheme, an offer to be accepted or rejected: *to make proposals for peace.* An OVERTURE is a friendly approach, an opening move (perhaps involving a proposal) tentatively looking toward the settlement of a controversy, or else preparing the way for a proposal, etc.: *to make overtures to an enemy.* PROPOSITION, used in mathematics to refer to a formal statement of truth, and often including the proof or demonstration of the statement, has something of this same meaning when used nontechnically (particularly in business): a PROPOSITION is a PROPOSAL in which the terms are clearly stated and their advantageous nature emphasized: *his proposition involved a large discount to the retailer*

pro·pose (prə pōz′), *v.,* **-posed, -posing.** —*v.t.* **1.** to put forward (a matter, subject, case, etc.) for consideration, acceptance, or action: *to propose a new method; to propose a toast.* **2.** to put forward or suggest as something to be done: *he proposed that a messenger be sent.* **3.** to present (a person) for some position, office, membership, etc. **4.** to put before oneself as something to be done; to design; to intend. **5.** to present to the mind or attention; to state. **6.** to propound (a question, riddle, etc.). —*v.i.* **7.** to make a proposal, esp. of marriage. **8.** to form or entertain a purpose or design. [ME, t. F: m.s. *proposer,* f. pro- PRO-¹ + *poser* put (see POSE¹), but assoc. with derivatives of L *prōpōnere* set forth] —**pro·pos′er,** *n.* —**Syn. 4.** See **intend**.

prop·o·si·tion (prŏp′ə zĭsh′ən), *n.* **1.** the act of proposing, or a proposal of, something to be considered, accepted, adopted, or done. **2.** a plan or scheme proposed. **3.** a thing presented for purchase, or considered with reference to its value to the purchaser or owner. **4.** an offer of terms for a transaction, as in business. **5.** *U.S. Slang.* a thing, matter, or person considered as something dealt with or encountered in experience. **6.** anything stated or affirmed for discussion or illustration. **7.** *Rhet.* that which is offered near the beginning as the subject for an argument or discourse. **8.** *Logic.* a statement in which something is affirmed or denied of a subject. **9.** *Math.* a formal statement of either a truth to be demonstrated or an operation to be performed; a theorem or a problem. [ME *proposicioun,* t. L: s. *prōpositio* a setting forth] **—prop'o·si'tion·al,** *adj.* **—prop'o·si'tion·al·ly,** *adv.* **—Syn. 2.** See **proposal.**

pro·pound (prə pound'), *v.t.* to put forward for consideration, acceptance, or adoption. [later var. of ME *propone,* t. L: m.s. *prōpōnere* set forth. Cf. COMPOUND, EXPOUND] **—pro·pound'er,** *n.*

pro·prae·tor (prō prē'tər), *n. Rom. Hist.* an officer who, after having served as praetor in Rome, was sent to govern a province with praetorial authority. Also, **pro·pre'tor.** [t. L]

pro·pri·e·tar·y (prə prī'ə tĕr'Ĭ), *adj., n., pl.* **-taries.** **—adj. 1.** belonging to a proprietor or proprietors. **2.** being a proprietor or proprietors; holding property: *the proprietary class.* **3.** pertaining to property or ownership: *proprietary rights.* **4.** belonging or controlled as property; manufactured and sold only by the owner of the patent, formula, brand name, or trademark associated with the product: *proprietary medicine.* **—n. 5.** an owner or proprietor. **6.** a body of proprietors. **7.** *Amer. Hist.* the grantee or owner, or one of the grantees or owners, of a proprietary colony. **8.** ownership. **9.** something owned. **10.** a proprietary medicine. [ME, t. LL: m.s. *proprietārius,* der. L *proprietas* ownership]

proprietary colony, *Amer. Hist.* a colony granted by the British crown to particular persons, with full rights of government.

pro·pri·e·tor (prə prī'ə tər), *n.* **1.** the owner (or manager) of a business establishment, a hotel business, etc. **2.** one who has the exclusive right or title to something; an owner, as of property. **3.** proprietary (def. 6). [f. PROPRIET(Y) (in obs. sense of property) + -OR²] **—pro·pri'e·tor·ship',** *n.* **—pro·pri·e·tress** (prə prī'ə trĬs), *n. fem.*

pro·pri·e·ty (prə prī'ə tĬ), *n., pl.* **-ties. 1.** conformity to established standards of behavior or manners. **2. the proprieties,** the conventional standards or requirements of proper behavior. **3.** appropriateness to the purpose or circumstances; or suitability. **4.** rightness or justness. **5.** *Obs.* a property, peculiarity, or characteristic of something. [ME *propriete,* t. L: m.s. *proprietas* peculiarity, ownership] **—Syn. 1.** See **etiquette.**

pro·pri·o·cep·tive (prō'prĬ ə sĕp'tĬv), *adj. Physiol.* referring to sensory excitations originating in muscles, tendons and joints, as in the kinesthetic sense. [f. *proprio-* (comb. form of L *proprius* one's own) + (RE)CEPTIVE]

pro·pri·o·cep·tor (prō'prĬ ə sĕp'tər), *n. Physiol.* the sensory end organ in muscles, tendons and joints responding to certain activities of these parts. [f. PROPRIOCEPT(IVE) + -OR²]

prop root, *Bot.* a root that supports the plant, as the aerial roots of the mangrove tree or corn.

prop·to·sis (prŏp tō'sĬs), *n. Med.* forward displacement of the eyeball. [t. NL, t. Gk.: a fall forward]

pro·pul·sion (prə pŭl'shən), *n.* **1.** the act of propelling or driving forward or onward. **2.** the state of being propelled. **3.** propulsive force; impulse given. [f. s. L *prōpulsus,* pp., driven forward + -ION] **—pro·pul·sive** (prə pŭl'sĬv), *adj.*

pro·pyl (prō'pĬl), *n. Chem.* the univalent radical, C₃H₇, derived from propane. [f. PROP(IONIC) + -YL]

prop·y·lae·um (prŏp'ə lē'əm), *n., pl.* **-laea** (-lē'ə). (commonly *pl.*) a vestibule or entrance to a temple area or other enclosure, esp. when elaborate or of architectural importance. [t. L, t. Gk.: m. *propȳlaion* (neut.) before the gate]

propyl alcohol, *Chem.* a colorless liquid alcohol, C₃H₇OH, used in organic syntheses and as a solvent.

pro·pyl·ene (prō'pə lēn'), *n. Chem.* a colorless, unsaturated, gaseous hydrocarbon gas, C₃H₆.

prop·y·lite (prŏp'ə lĬt'), *n. Petrog.* an altered form of andesite or some allied rock, usually containing secondary minerals such as chlorite and calcite. [f. s. Gk. *prŏpylon* gateway + -ITE¹; so named because supposed to open the tertiary volcanic epoch]

pro ra·ta (prō rā'tə, rä'tə), in proportion; according to a certain rate. [ML: according to rate]

pro·rate (prō rāt', prō'rāt'), *v.,* **-rated, -rating. —v.i. 1.** to make an arrangement on a basis of proportional distribution. **—v.t. 2.** to divide or distribute proportionately. [der. PRO RATA] **—pro·rat'a·ble,** *adj.*

pro re na·ta (prō rē nā'tə), *Latin.* for an unexpected contingency.

pro·rogue (prō rōg'), *v.t.,* **-rogued, -roguing. 1.** to discontinue a session of (the British Parliament or a similar body). **2.** *Rare.* to defer; postpone. [late ME *proroge,* t. F: m.s. *proroguer,* t. L: m. *prōrogāre* prolong, protract, defer] **—pro·ro·ga·tion** (prō'rə gā'shən), *n.*

pros., prosody.

pro·sa·ic (prō zā'Ĭk), *adj.* **1.** commonplace or dull; matter-of-fact or unimaginative: *the prosaic type of mind.* **2.** having the character or spirit of prose as opposed to

poetry, as verse or writing. Also, **pro·sa'i·cal.** [t. ML: s. *prōsaicus,* der. L *prōsa* PROSE] **—pro·sa'i·cal·ly,** *adv.* **—pro·sa'ic·ness,** *n.*

pro·sa·ism (prō'zā'Ĭz'əm), *n.* **1.** prosaic character. **2.** a prosaic expression. Also, **pro·sa·i·cism** (prō zā'ə sĬz'əm), *n.*

pro·sce·ni·um (prō sē'nĬ əm), *n., pl.* **-nia** (-nĬ ə). **1.** (in the modern theater) **a.** that part of the stage in front of the curtain often including the curtain and the framework which holds it. **b.** the decorative arch or opening between the stage and the auditorium. **2.** (in the ancient theater) the stage. [t. L, t. Gk.: m. *proskēnion*]

pro·scribe (prō skrīb'), *v.t.,* **-scribed, -scribing. 1.** to denounce or condemn (a thing) as dangerous; to prohibit. **2.** to put out of the protection of the law; to outlaw. **3.** to banish or exile. **4.** to announce the name of (a person) as condemned to death and subject to confiscation of property. [t. L: m.s. *prōscribere* write before, publish, proscribe] **—pro·scrib'er,** *n.*

pro·scrip·tion (prō skrĬp'shən), *n.* **1.** act of proscribing. **2.** state of being proscribed. **3.** outlawry; interdiction. **—pro·scrip·tive** (prō skrĬp'tĬv), *adj.* **—pro·scrip'tive·ly,** *adv.*

prose (prōz), *n., adj., v.,* **prosed, prosing. —n. 1.** the ordinary form of spoken or written language, without metrical structure (as distinguished from poetry or verse). **2.** matter-of-fact, commonplace, or dull expression, quality, discourse, etc. **3.** *Liturg.* a hymn sung after the gradual, originating from a practice of setting words to the jubilatio of the alleluia. **—adj. 4.** consisting of or pertaining to prose. **5.** prosaic. **—v.t. 6.** to turn into prose. **—v.i. 7.** to write or talk in a dull or prosy manner. [ME, t. F, t. L: m. *prōsa* (*ōrātio*), lit., straightforward (speech), fem. of *pro(r)sus,* for *proversus,* pp., turned forward]

pro·sec·tor (prō sĕk'tər), *n.* one who dissects cadavers for the illustration of anatomical lectures or the like. [t. LL: anatomist, der. L *prōsectus,* pp., cut off]

pros·e·cute (prŏs'ə kūt'), *v.,* **-cuted, -cuting. —v.t. 1.** *Law.* **a.** to institute legal proceedings against (a person, etc.). **b.** to seek to enforce or obtain by legal process. **c.** to conduct criminal proceedings in court against. **2.** to follow up or go on with something undertaken or begun: *to prosecute an inquiry.* **3.** to carry on or practice. **—v.i. 4.** *Law.* **a.** to institute and carry on a legal prosecution. **b.** to act as prosecutor. [ME, t. L: m.s. *prōsecūtus,* pp., pursued, continued]

prosecuting attorney, *Law.* (in some States) a local prosecutor for a county or district.

pros·e·cu·tion (prŏs'ə kū'shən), *n.* **1.** *Law.* **a.** the institution and carrying on of legal proceedings against a person. **b.** the party by whom such proceedings are instituted and carried on. **2.** the following up of any matter in hand; pursuit.

pros·e·cu·tor (prŏs'ə kū'tər), *n.* **1.** *Law.* **a.** one who institutes and carries on legal proceedings in a court of justice, esp. in a criminal court. **b.** an officer charged with the conduct of criminal prosecution in the interest of the public: *public prosecutor.* **2.** one who prosecutes.

pros·e·lyte (prŏs'ə līt'), *n., v.,* **-lyted, -lyting. —n. 1.** one who has come over or changed from one opinion, religious belief, sect, or the like to another; a convert. **—v.t. 2.** to make a proselyte of; convert. **—v.i. 3.** to make proselytes. [ME, t. LL: m.s. *prosēlytus,* t. Gk.: m. *prosēlytos* newcomer, proselyte]

pros·e·lyt·ism (prŏs'ə līt'Ĭz əm), *n.* **1.** state or condition of a proselyte. **2.** practice of making proselytes.

pros·e·lyt·ize (prŏs'ə līt Īz', -lĬ tīz'), *v.t., v.i.,* **-ized, -izing.** proselyte. Also, *Brit.,* **pros'e·lyt·ise'.**

pros·en·ceph·a·lon (prŏs'ĕn sĕf'ə lŏn'), *n., pl.* **-la** (-lə). *Anat.* **1.** the anterior segment of the brain, consisting of the cerebral hemispheres (or their equivalent) and certain adjacent parts. **2.** the forebrain. [t. NL, f. Gk.: *prŏs* before + m. *enkĕphalon* brain] **—pros·en·ce·phal·ic** (prŏs'ĕn sə făl'Ĭk), *adj.*

pros·en·chy·ma (prŏs ĕng'kĬ mə), *n. Bot.* the tissue characteristic of the woody and bast portions of plants, consisting typically of long, narrow cells with pointed ends. [t. NL, f. Gk.: *prŏs* toward, to + *ĕnchyma* infusion; modeled on PARENCHYMA] **—pros·en·chym·a·tous** (prŏs'ĕng kĬm'ə təs), *adj.*

pros·er (prō'zər), *n.* one who talks or writes prosaically.

Pro·ser·pi·na (prō sûr'pə nə), *n.* the Roman counterpart of Persephone. Also, **Pro·ser·pi·ne** (prō sûr'pə nē', prŏs'ər pīn'). [t. L, t. Gk.: alter. of *Persephŏnē*]

pro·sit (prō'sĬt), *interj. Latin.* (as a toast) may it do good!

pro·slav·er·y (prō slā'vər Ĭ), *adj.* **1.** favoring slavery. **2.** *U.S. Hist.* favoring the continuance of the institution of Negro slavery, or opposed to interference with it. **—n. 3.** the favoring or support of slavery.

pros·o·dist (prŏs'ə dĬst), *n.* one versed in prosody.

pros·o·dy (prŏs'ə dĬ), *n.* **1.** the science or study of poetic meters and versification. **2.** a particular or distinctive system of metrics and versification: *Milton's prosody.* [late ME, t. L: m.s. *prosōdia,* t. Gk.: m. *prosōidia* tone or accent, modulation of voice, song sung to music] **—pro·so·di·ac** (prō sō'dĬ ăk'), **pros·o·di·a·cal** (prŏs'ə dī'ə kəl), **pro·sod·ic** (prō sŏd'Ĭk), **pro·sod'i·cal,** *adj.*

pro·so·po·poe·ia (prō sō'pə pē'ə), *n. Rhet.* **1.** personification, as of inanimate things. **2.** representation of an imaginary or absent person as speaking or acting. Also, **pro·so·po·pe'ia.** [t. L: m. *prosōpopoeia*, t. Gk.: m. *prosōpopoiía*]

pros·pect (prŏs'pĕkt), n. 1. (*usually pl.*) an apparent probability of advancement, success, profit, etc. 2. a mental looking forward, or contemplation of something future or expected. 3. the outlook for the future: *good business prospects.* 4. something in view as a source of profit. 5. a prospective customer, as in business. 6. a view or scene presented to the eye, esp. of scenery 7. outlook or view over a region or in a particular direction. 8. a mental view or survey, as of a subject or situation. 9. *Mining.* a. an apparent indication of metal, etc. b. a spot giving such indications. c. excavation or workings in search of ore. 10. *Archaic.* sight; range of vision. —*v.t.* 11. to search or explore (a region), as for gold. 12. to work (a mine or claim) experimentally in order to test its value. —*v.i.* 13. to search or explore a region for gold or the like. [ME, t. L: s. *prospectus* outlook, view] —**pros·pec·tor** (prŏs'pĕk·tər, prə·spĕk'tər), n. —Syn. 6. See **view.**

pro·spec·tive (prə·spĕk'tĭv), adj. in prospect or expectation; expected; future. —**pro·spec'tive·ly,** adv.

pro·spec·tus (prə·spĕk'təs), n. a statement which describes or advertises a forthcoming literary work, a new enterprise, or the like. [t. L: outlook, view]

pros·per (prŏs'pər), v.i. 1. to be prosperous or successful; to thrive. —*v.t.* 2. to make prosperous or successful. [late ME, t. L: s. *prosperāre* make prosperous] —Syn. 1. See **succeed.**

pros·per·i·ty (prŏs·pĕr'ə·tĭ), n., pl. **-ties.** 1. prosperous, flourishing, or thriving condition; good fortune; success. 2. (*pl.*) prosperous circumstances.

Pros·per·o (prŏs'pə·rō'), n. (in Shakespeare's *The Tempest*) the father of Miranda and rightful duke of Milan.

pros·per·ous (prŏs'pər·əs), adj. 1. having or characterized by continued good fortune; flourishing; successful: *a prosperous business.* 2. well-to-do or well-off: *a prosperous family.* 3. favorable or propitious. [late ME, t. L: m. *prosperus*] —**pros'per·ous·ly,** adv. —**pros'per·ous·ness,** n.

pros·tate (prŏs'tāt), *Anat.* —n. 1. the prostate gland. —adj. 2. designating or pertaining to the prostate gland. [t. ML: m. *prostata*, t. Gk.: m. *prostátēs* one standing before] —**pro·stat·ic** (prō·stăt'ĭk), adj.

prostate gland, *Anat.* the composite gland which surrounds the urethra of males at the base of the bladder, subject to enlargement in old age.

pros·the·sis (prŏs'thə·sĭs), n. *Surg.* the addition of an artificial part to supply a defect of the body [t. LL, t. Gk.: a putting to, addition] —**pros·thet·ic** (prŏs·thĕt'ĭk), adj.

pros·thi·on (prŏs'thĭ·ŏn'), n. *Craniom.* the most forward projecting point of the anterior surface of the upper jaw (maxilla), in the midsagittal plane. [t. Gk. m. *prosthéon* running forward]

pros·tho·don·ti·a (prŏs'thə·dŏn'shĭ·ə), n. the branch of dentistry concerned with the reconstruction and replacement of missing teeth. [f. Gk. *prósth*(*en*) forwards + -ODONT + -IA] —**pros·tho·don·tist** (prŏs'thə·dŏn'tĭst), n.

pros·ti·tute (prŏs'tə·tūt', -tōōt'), n., v., **-tuted, -tuting.** —n. 1. a woman who engages in sexual intercourse for money as a livelihood; a harlot. 2. a base hireling —*v.t.* 3. to submit to sexual intercourse for money as a livelihood. 4. to put to any base or unworthy use. [t L: m.s. *prōstitūtus*, pp., placed before, exposed publicly prostituted] —**pros'ti·tu'tor,** n.

pros·ti·tu·tion (prŏs'tə·tū'shən, -tōō'-), n. 1. the act or practice of prostituting. 2. devotion to any base or unworthy use.

pros·trate (prŏs'trāt), v., **-trated, -trating,** adj. —*v.t.* 1. to cast (oneself) down in humility or adoration. 2. to lay flat, as on the ground. 3. to throw down level with the ground. 4. to overthrow, overcome, or reduce to helplessness. 5. to reduce to physical weakness or exhaustion. —adj. 6. lying flat or at full length, as on the ground. 7. lying with the face to the ground, as in token of submission or humility. 8. overthrown, overcome, or helpless: *a prostrate country.* 9. in a state of physical weakness or exhaustion 10. submissive. 11. lying or bowed low, as in adoration or worship. 12. *Bot.* (of a plant or stem) lying flat on the ground [ME *prostrat*, t. L: s. *prōstrātus*, pp., spread out]

pros·tra·tion (prŏs·trā'shən), n. 1. the act of prostrating. 2. the state of being prostrated. 3. extreme mental depression or dejection. 4. extreme physical weakness or exhaustion: *nervous prostration.*

pro·style (prō'stīl), *Archit.* —adj. 1. having a portico in front, standing from the walls of the building, as a temple. —n. 2. a prostyle building.

pros·y (prō'zĭ), adj., **prosier, prosiest.** 1. of the nature of or resembling prose. 2. prosaic; commonplace, dull, or wearisome. —**pros'i·ly,** adv. —**pros'i·ness,** n.

prot-, var. of **proto-,** before some vowels, as in *protamine.*

Prot., Protestant.

pro·tac·tin·i·um (prō'tăk·tĭn'ĭ·əm), n. *Chem.* a radioactive, metallic element. Symbol: Pa; at. no.: 91 Formerly, **protoactinium.** [f. PROT(O)- + ACTINIUM]

pro·tag·o·nist (prō·tăg'ə·nĭst), n. 1. the leading character in a play. 2. any leading character or personage. [t. Gk.: s. *prōtagōnistés*]

Pro·tag·o·ras (prō·tăg'ə·rəs), n. c481–411? B.C., Greek Sophist and philosopher.

pro·ta·mine (prō'tə·mēn', -mĭn), n. *Biochem.* any of a group of basic, simple proteins which do not coagulate by heat, are soluble in ammonia, and upon hydrolysis form amino acids. [f. PROT- + AMINE]

prot·a·sis (prŏt'ə·sĭs), n. 1. the clause expressing the condition in a conditional sentence, in English usually beginning with *if.* Cf. **apodosis.** 2. *Anc. Drama.* the first part of the play, in which the characters are introduced and the subject is proposed. [t. L, t. Gk.]

pro·te·an (prō'tĭ·ən, prō·tē'ən), adj. 1. readily assuming different forms or characters; exceedingly variable. 2. (*cap.*) of, like, or suggestive of Proteus.

pro·te·ase (prō'tĭ·ās'), n. *Biochem.* any enzyme that acts upon proteins. [f. PROTE(IN) + -ASE]

pro·tect (prə·tĕkt'), v.t. 1. to defend or guard from attack, invasion, annoyance, insult, etc.; cover or shield from injury or danger. 2. *Econ.* to guard against the competition of foreign productions by import duties on the latter: *to protect home industries.* 3. *Com.* to provide funds for the payment of (a draft, etc.). [t. L s. *prōtectus*, pp., covered over] —Syn. 1. See **defend.**

pro·tec·tion (prə·tĕk'shən), n. 1. the act of protecting. 2. the state of being protected. 3. preservation from injury or harm. 4. something that protects. 5. *Econ.* the system or theory of fostering or developing home industries by protecting them from foreign competition through duties imposed on importations from foreign countries. 6. a treaty, safe-conduct, passport, or other writing which secures from molestation the person, persons, or property specified in it. 7. a document given by notaries to a person traveling abroad certifying that the holder is a citizen of the United States. 8. patronage. —Syn. 4. See **cover.**

pro·tec·tion·ism (prə·tĕk'shə·nĭz'əm), n. the economic system or theory of protection. —**pro·tec'tion·ist,** n.

pro·tec·tive (prə·tĕk'tĭv), adj. 1. having the quality of protecting. 2. tending to protect. 3. designed to protect economically: *a protective tariff.* 4. pertaining to economic protection. —**pro·tec'tive·ly,** adv.

protective tariff, a tariff for the protection of domestic production rather than for revenue.

pro·tec·tor (prə·tĕk'tər), n. 1. one who or that which protects; a defender; a guardian. 2. *Eng. Hist.* a. one in charge of the kingdom during the sovereign's minority, incapacity, or absence. b. (*cap.*) the title (more fully **Lord Protector**) of the head of the executive during the period of the Protectorate (held by Oliver Cromwell, 1653–58, and by Richard Cromwell, 1658–59). —**pro·tec'tor·ship',** n. —**pro·tec·tress** (prə·tĕk'trĭs), n. *fem.*

pro·tec·tor·ate (prə·tĕk'tər·ĭt), n. 1. the relation of a strong state toward a weaker state or territory which it protects and partly controls. 2. a state or territory so protected. 3. the office or position, or the term of office, of a protector. 4. the government of a protector. 5. (*cap.*) *Eng. Hist.* the period during which Oliver and Richard Cromwell held the title of Lord Protector.

pro·tec·to·ry (prə·tĕk'tə·rĭ), n., pl. **-ries.** an institution for the care of destitute or delinquent children.

pro·té·gé (prō'tə·zhā'; Fr. prō'tĕ·zhē'), n., pl. **-gés.** one who is under the protection or friendly patronage of another [t. F, pp. of *protéger* protect, t. L: m. *prōtegere*] —**pro'té·gée,** n. *fem.*

pro·te·in (prō'tēn, prō'tē·ĭn), n. 1. *Biochem.* any of a group of nitrogenous organic compounds of high molecular weight, synthesized by plants from simple substances, and undergoing hydrolysis by enzymes to yield amino acids, which in animal metabolism are required for all life processes. 2. (formerly) a substance thought to be the essential nitrogenous component of all organic bodies. Also, **pro·te·id** (prō'tē·ĭd). [t. G, f. m.s. Gk. *prōteíos* primary + -*in* -IN²]

pro·te·in·ase (prō'tē·ĭn·ās', -tēn-), n. *Biochem.* any of several enzymes which are capable of hydrolyzing proteins.

pro tem (prō tĕm'), pro tempore.

pro tem·po·re (prō tĕm'pə·rē'), *Latin.* 1. temporarily; for the time being. 2. temporary.

pro·te·ol·y·sis (prō'tĭ·ŏl'ə·sĭs), n. *Biochem.* the hydrolysis or breaking down of proteins into simpler compounds, as in digestion. [f. *proteo-* (comb. form repr PROTEIN) + -LYSIS] —**pro·te·o·lyt·ic** (prō'tĭ·ə·lĭt'ĭk), adj.

pro·te·ose (prō'tĭ·ōs'), n. *Biochem.* any of a class of soluble compounds derived from proteins by the action of gastric juice, etc. [f. PROTE(IN) + -OSE²]

Prot·er·o·zo·ic (prŏt'ər·ə·zō'ĭk), *Stratig.* —adj. 1. pertaining to a geological era or rocks preceding the Paleozoic and equivalent to the Algonquian. —n. 2. the era or rocks intervening between Archeozoic and Paleozoic, presumed to be characterized by relative prominence of sedimentary rocks which do not contain fossils. [f. Gk. *prótero*(s) being before + s. Gk. *zōé* life + -IC]

pro·test (n. prō'tĕst; v. prō·tĕst'), n. 1. the formal expression of objection or disapproval, often in opposition to something which one is powerless to prevent or avoid: *to submit under protest.* 2. *Com.* a. a formal notarial certificate attesting the fact that a check, note, or bill of exchange has been presented for acceptance or payment and that it has been refused. b. the action taken to fix the liability for a dishonored bill of exchange or note. 3. *Law.* a. (upon one's payment of a tax or other state or city exaction) a formal statement protesting the legality of the demand. **b.** a written and attested declaration made by the master of a ship stating the circumstances under which some injury has happened to the ship or cargo, or other circumstances involving the liability of the officers, crew, etc. **4.** *Sports.* a formal expression of objection or complaint placed with an official. [ME, t. ML: s. *prōtestum* declaration] —*v.i.* **5.** to give formal expression to objection or disapproval; remonstrate. **6.** to make solemn declaration. —*v.t.* **7.** to make a protest or remonstrance against. **8.** to say in protest or remonstrance. **9.** to declare solemnly or formally; affirm; assert. **10.** to make a formal declaration of the nonacceptance or nonpayment of (a bill of exchange or note). **11.** to object to as disqualified, as a player on an opposing football team. **12.** *Obs.* to call to witness. [late ME, t. F: s. *protester*, t. L: m. *prōtestārī* declare publicly] —**pro·test′er**, *n.* —**pro·test′ing·ly**, *adv.* —*Syn.* 6. See **declare.**

Prot·es·tant (prŏt′ĭs tɔnt), *n.* **1.** any Western Christian not an adherent of the Roman Catholic Church. **2.** an adherent of any of those Christian bodies which separated from the Church of Rome at the Reformation, or of any group descended from them. **3.** (*orig.*) any of the German princes who protested against the decision of the Diet of Spires in 1529, which had denounced the Reformation. **4.** (*l.c.*) one who protests. —*adj.* **5.** belonging or pertaining to Protestants or their religion. **6.** (*l.c.*) protesting. [sing. of *protestants* for L *prōtestantēs*, pl. ppr. of *protestārī* protest]

Protestant Episcopal Church, the church in the United States inheriting the doctrine, discipline, and worship of the Church of England: in 1789 became an independent body within the Anglican communion.

Prot·es·tant·ism (prŏt′ĭs tən tĭz′əm), *n.* **1.** the religion of Protestants. **2.** the Protestant churches, collectively. **3.** Protestants. **4.** adherence to Protestant principles.

Protestant Reformation. See **reformation** (def. 3).

prot·es·ta·tion (prŏt′əs tā′shən), *n.* **1.** the act of protesting or affirming. **2.** a solemn declaration or affirmation. **3.** the formal expression of objection or disapproval. **4.** a protest, or formal statement of objection.

Pro·teus (prō′tūs, prō′tĭ əs), *n.* **1.** a sea god of classical mythology who had the power of assuming different forms. **2.** a person or thing capable of taking on various aspects or characters.

pro·tha·la·mi·on (prō′thə lā′mĭ ŏn′, -ən), *n.*, *pl.* **-mia** (-mĭ ə). a song or poem written to celebrate a marriage. [f. PRO-² + s. Gk. *thálamos* bridal chamber + -ION; coined by Spenser, after Gk. *epithalámion* EPITHALAMIUM]

pro·tha·la·mi·um (prō′thə lā′mĭ əm), *n.*, *pl.* **-mia** (-mĭ ə). prothalamion.

pro·thal·li·um (prō thăl′ĭ əm), *n.*, *pl.* **-thallia** (-thăl′Y ə). *Bot.* **1.** the gametophyte of ferns, etc. **2.** the analogous rudimentary gametophyte of seed-bearing plants. [NL, f. Gk.: pro- PRO-² + m. *thallion*, dim. of *thallós* young shoot] —**pro·thal′li·al**, *adj.*

proth·e·sis (prŏth′ə sĭs), *n.* **1.** the addition of a phoneme or syllable at the beginning of a word, as in Spanish *escala* (ladder) from Latin *scala.* **2.** *Gk. Orth. Ch.* **a.** the preparation and preliminary oblation of the eucharistic elements. **b.** the table on which this is done. **c.** the part of the bema or sanctuary where this table stands. [t. LL, t. Gk.: a putting before] —**pro·thet·ic** (prō thĕt′Yk), *adj.* —**pro·thet′i·cal·ly**, *adv.*

pro·thon·o·tar·y (prō thŏn′ə tĕr′Y, prō′thə nō′tə rY), *n.*, *pl.* **-taries. 1.** a principal clerk in some courts. **2.** *Rom. Cath. Ch.* **a.** one of a college of ecclesiastics of superior rank charged with the registry of pontifical acts, canonizations, etc. **b.** any of certain prelates of similar rank. **3.** *Gk. Orth. Ch.* the chief secretary of the patriarch of Constantinople. Also, **protonotary.** [t. ML: m.s. *prōthonotārius*, LL *prōtonotārius*, t. Gk.: m. *prōtonotārios*] —**pro·thon·o·tar·i·al** (prō thŏn′ə târ′Y əl), *adj.*

pro·tho·rax (prō thōr′ăks), *n.*, *pl.* **-thoraxes, -thoraces** (-thōr′ə sēz′). the anterior division of an insect's thorax, bearing the first pair of legs. See illus. under **coleopter.** —**pro·tho·rac·ic** (prō′thō răs′Yk), *adj.*

pro·throm·bin (prō thrŏm′bĭn), *n.* *Biochem.* one of the blood-clotting factors in the blood, believed to be the forerunner of thrombin.

pro·tist (prō′tĭst), *n.* *Biol.* any of the single-celled organisms, including all the unicellular animals and plants. [t. NL: s. *protista*, pl., t. Gk.: m. *prōtistos* the very first, superl. of *prōtos* first] —**pro·tis·tan** (prō tĭs′tən), *adj.*, *n.* —**pro·tis′tic**, *adj.*

pro·ti·um (prō′tY əm, -shY əm), *n.* *Chem.* the common isotope of hydrogen, of atomic weight 1.008. *Symbol:* H¹.

proto-, a word element meaning "first," "earliest form of," especially used in chemistry of the first of a series of compounds, or of the one containing the minimum amount of an element. Also, **prot-.** [t. Gk., comb. form of *prōtos* first]

pro·to·ac·tin·i·um (prō′tō ăk tĭn′Y əm), *n.* *Chem.* protactinium.

pro·to·chor·date (prō′tō kôr′dāt), *n.* *Zool.* any of the nonvertebrate chordates, as the tunicates, cephalochordates, and hemichordates.

pro·to·col (prō′tə kŏl′), *n.* **1.** an original draft, minute, or record from which a document, esp. a treaty, is prepared. **2.** a supplementary international agreement. **3.** an agreement between states. **4.** an annex to a treaty giving data relating to it. **5.** the customs and regulations dealing with the ceremonies and etiquette of the diplomatic corps and others at a court or capital. [earlier *protocoll*, t. ML: s. *prōtocollum*, t. LGk.: m. *protókollon*, orig., a first leaf glued to the front of a manuscript containing notes as to contents]

pro·to·gine (prō′tə jĭn, -jēn), *n.* a gneissoid granite, occurring chiefly in the Alps. [t. F, irreg. f. Gk.: *prōto*-PROTO- + *gine*(*sthai*) be born or produced]

pro·to·lith·ic (prō′tə lĭth′Yk), *adj.* Anthropol. denoting or pertaining to stone implements selected according to fitness of form, and shaped by wear without definite shaping on the part of the operator. Cf. **technolithic.**

pro·to·mar·tyr (prō′tō mär′tər), *n.* **1.** the first Christian martyr (Stephen). **2.** the first martyr in any cause.

pro·to·mor·phic (prō′tə môr′fYk), *adj.* *Biol.* having a primitive character or structure. —**pro′to·morph′**, *n.*

pro·ton (prō′tŏn), *n.* *Physics, Chem.* a subatomic particle bearing a unitary, or electronic, positive charge of electricity, and one of the constituents of every atomic nucleus, the number of protons in the nucleus being different for each element and called the *atomic number* of that element. [t. Gk., neut. of *prōtos* first]

pro·to·ne·ma (prō′tə nē′mə), *n.*, *pl.* **-mata** (-mə tə). *Bot.* a primary, usually filamentous structure produced by the germination of the spore in mosses and certain related plants, and upon which the leafy plant which bears the sexual organs arises as a lateral or terminal shoot. [t. NL, f. Gk.: *prōto*- PROTO- + *nēma* thread]

pro·ton·o·tar·y (prō tŏn′ə tĕr′Y, prō′tə nō′tə rY), *n.*, *pl.* **-teries.** prothonotary.

pro·to·path·ic (prō′tə păth′Yk), *adj.* *Physiol.* **1.** denoting general, nondiscriminating sensory reception (opposed to *epicritic*). **2.** primitive; primary.

pro·to·plasm (prō′tə plăz′əm), *n.* *Biol.* **1.** a complex substance (typically colorless and semifluid) regarded as the physical basis of life, having the power of spontaneous motion, reproduction, etc.; the living matter of all vegetable and animal cells and tissues. **2.** (formerly) cytoplasm. [t. NL: m. *prōtoplasma*, ML first thing made, first creature, f. Gk.: *prōto*- PROTO- + *plásma* something formed] —**pro′to·plas′mic**, *adj.*

pro·to·plast (prō′tə plăst′), *n.* **1.** *Biol.* **a.** the protoplasm within a cell considered as a fundamental entity. **b.** the primordial living unit or cell. **2.** one who or that which is first formed; the original. **3.** the hypothetical first individual or one of the supposed first pair of a species or the like. [t. LL: s. *prōtoplastus* the first man, t. Gk.: m. *prōtóplastos* formed first] —**pro′to·plas′tic**, *adj.*

pro·to·ste·le (prō′tə stē′lY, -stēl′), *n.* *Bot.* the solid stele of most roots, having a central core of xylem enclosed by phloem. —**pro·to·ste·lic** (prō′tə stē′lĭk), *adj.*

pro·to·troph·ic (prō′tə trŏf′Yk), *adj.* **1.** *Physiol.* using the energy from light in the synthesis of protoplasm. **2.** having the nutritional requirements of the prototype. [f. PROTO- + s. Gk. *trophē* nourishment + -IC]

pro·to·type (prō′tə tĭp′), *n.* **1.** the original or model after which anything is formed. **2.** *Biol.* an archetype; a primitive form regarded as the basis of a group. [t. NL: m.s. *prōtotypon*, t. Gk.: (neut.) original, primitive] —**pro·to·typ·al** (prō′tə tī′pəl), **pro·to·typ·ic** (prō′tə tYp′Yk), *adj.*

Pro·to·zo·a (prō′tə zō′ə), *n.pl.* a phylum comprising all those animals that consist of one cell or of a colony of like or similar cells. [t. NL, pl. of *prōtozōön*, f. Gk.: *prōto*- PROTO- + m. *zōïon* animal]

pro·to·zo·an (prō′tə zō′ən), *adj.* **1.** belonging or pertaining to the *Protozoa.* —*n.* **2.** any of the *Protozoa.*

pro·tract (prō trăkt′), *v.t.* **1.** to draw out or lengthen in time; extend the duration of. **2.** *Anat.*, *etc.* to extend or protrude. **3.** *Survey.*, *etc.* to plot; to draw by means of a scale and protractor. [t. L: s. *prōtractus*, pp., drawn forth, drawn out] —**pro·trac′tive**, *adj.* —*Syn.* **1.** See **lengthen.** —*Ant.* **1.** shorten.

pro·trac·tile (prō trăk′tYl), *adj.* capable of being protracted or lengthened out, or being protruded.

pro·trac·tion (prō trăk′shən), *n.* **1.** the act of protracting. **2.** extension in time or space. **3.** that which is protracted.

pro·trac·tor (prō trăk′tər), *n.* **1.** one who or that which protracts. **2.** *Math.*, *etc.* an instrument, a graduated arc, for plotting or for measuring angles on paper. **3.** *Anat.* a muscle which causes a part to protrude.

Protractor (def. 2)

pro·trude (prō trōōd′), *v.*, **-truded, -truding.** —*v.i.* **1.** to project. —*v.t.* **2.** to thrust forward; cause to project. [t. L: m.s. *prōtrūdere*] —**pro·trud′ent**, *adj.* —**pro·tru·si·ble** (prō trōō′sə bəl), *adj.*

pro·tru·sile (prō trōō′sYl), *adj.* capable of being thrust forth or extended, as a limb, etc. [f. s. L *prōtrūsus*, pp., thrust forth + -ILE]

pro·tru·sion (prō trōō′zhən), *n.* **1.** act of protruding. **2.** state of being protruded. **3.** that which protrudes or projects.

pro·tru·sive (prō trōō′sYv), *adj.* **1.** thrusting forward. **2.** obtrusive. **3.** projecting. —**pro·tru′sive·ly**, *adv.*

---

b., blend of, blended; c., cognate with; d., dialect, dialectal; der., derived from; f., formed from; g., going back to; m., modification of; r., replacing; s., stem of; t., taken from; ?, perhaps. See the full key on inside cover.

pro·tu·ber·ance (prō tū/bər əns, -tōō/-), *n.* **1.** protuberant state or form. **2.** a protuberant part; a rounded projection.

pro·tu·ber·an·cy (prō tū/bər ən sĭ, -tōō/-), *n., pl.* **-cies.** protuberance.

pro·tu·ber·ant (prō tū/bər ənt, -tōō/-), *adj.* bulging out beyond the surrounding surface. [t. LL: s. *prō̆tūberans*, ppr., swelling] —**pro·tu/ber·ant·ly,** *adv.*

proud (proud), *adj.* **1.** feeling pleasure or satisfaction over something conceived as highly honorable or creditable to oneself (often fol. by *of,* an infinitive, or a clause). **2.** having or cherishing, or proceeding from or showing, a high, esp. an inordinately high, opinion of one's own dignity, importance, or superiority. **3.** having or showing self-respect or self-esteem. **4.** highly gratifying to the feelings or self-esteem. **5.** highly honorable or creditable: *a proud achievement.* **6.** (of things) stately, majestic, or magnificent: *proud cities.* **7.** of lofty dignity or distinction: *a proud name, proud nobles.* **8.** *Poetic.* full of vigor or spirit. **9.** *Obs.* brave. [ME; late OE *prūd*, c. Icel. *prūdhr* magnificent, stately, gallant, appar. t. VL. Cf. OF *prud, prod* gallant, g. L *prōd-* in *prōdesse* be of worth] —**proud/ly,** *adv.*
—**Syn. 2.** PROUD, ARROGANT, HAUGHTY imply a consciousness of, or a belief in, one's superiority in some respect. PROUD implies sensitiveness, lofty self-respect, or jealous preservation of one's dignity, station, and the like. (It may refer to an affectionate admiration or a justifiable pride concerning someone else: *proud of his son.*) ARROGANT applies to insolent or overbearing behavior, arising from an exaggerated belief in one's importance: *arrogant rudeness.* HAUGHTY implies lofty reserve and confident, often disdainful assumption of superiority over others: *the haughty manner of an ill-bred debutante.* —**Ant. 1.** humble. **2.** modest.

proud flesh, *Pathol.* granulation tissue.

Prou·dhon (prōō dôn/), *n.* **Pierre Joseph** (pyĕr zhō zĕf/), 1809–65, French socialist and writer.

Proust (prōōst), *n.* **Marcel** (mȧr sĕl/), 1871–1922. French novelist.

prous·tite (prōōs/tīt), *n. Mineral.* a mineral, silver arsenic sulfide, Ag₃AsS₃, occurring in scarlet crystals and masses: a minor ore of silver; ruby silver.

Prov., **1.** Provençal. **2.** Provence. **3.** Proverbs. **4.** Province. **5.** Provost.

prov., **1.** province. **2.** provincial. **3.** provisional.

prove (prōōv), *v.,* **proved, proved** or **proven, proving.** —*v.t.* **1.** to establish the truth or genuineness of, as by evidence or argument: *to prove one's contention.* **2.** *Law.* to establish the authenticity or validity of (a will); probate. **3.** to give demonstration of by action. **4.** to put to the test; try or test. **5.** *Math.* to verify the correctness of (some statement). **6.** *Print., etc.* to take a trial impression of (type, etc.). **7.** to determine the characteristics of by scientific analysis: *to prove ore.* **8.** *Archaic.* to experience. —*v.i.* **9.** to turn out: *the report proved to be false.* **10.** to be found by trial or experience, or in the event, to be. **11.** *Archaic.* to make trial. [ME, t. OF: m. *prover,* g. L *probāre* try, test, prove, approve] —**prov/a·ble,** *adj.* —**prov/er,** *n.*

prov·e·nance (prŏv/ə nəns), *n.* the place of origin, as of a work of art, etc. [t. F. der. *provenir,* t. L: m. *prō̆venīre* come forth]

Pro·ven·çal (prō/vən säl/, *Fr.* prō vän sȧl/), *adj.* **1.** of or pertaining to Provence, in France, or its people, or their language. —*n.* **2.** a native or inhabitant of Provence. **3.** a Romance language, the language of Provence. [t. F. der. *Provence,* g. L *prōvincia* province]

Pro·vence (prō väns/), *n.* a region in SE France, bordering on the Mediterranean: formerly a province; famous in the Middle Ages for poetry and chivalry.

prov·en·der (prŏv/ən dər), *n.* **1.** dry food for beasts, as hay; fodder. **2.** *Colloq. and Humorous.* food or provisions. [ME *provendre,* t. OF, var. of *provende* prebend, provender, g. LL *prōbenda,* b. *praebenda* prebend and *prō̆videre* look out for] —**Syn. 1.** See **feed.**

pro·ve·ni·ence (prō vē/nĭ əns, -vĕn/yəns), *n.* provenance; origin. [der. *provenient,* t. L: s. *prō̆veniens,* ppr., coming forth]

prov·erb (prŏv/ərb), *n.* **1.** a short popular saying, long current, embodying some familiar truth or useful thought in expressive language. **2.** a wise saying or precept; a didactic sentence. **3.** a person or thing that has become proverbial. **4.** *Bible.* a profound saying or oracular utterance requiring interpretation. **5.** **Proverbs,** one of the books of the Old Testament, made up of sayings of wise men of Israel, including Solomon. —*v.t.* **6.** to utter in the form of a proverb. **7.** to make (something) the subject of a proverb. **8.** to make a byword of. [ME *proverbe,* t. OF, t. L: m. *prōverbium*]
—**Syn. 1.** PROVERB, MAXIM are terms for short pithy sayings. A PROVERB is such a saying popularly known and repeated, usually expressing simply and concretely, though often metaphorically, a truth based on common sense or the practical experience of mankind: *"A stitch in time saves nine."* A MAXIM is a brief statement of a general and practical truth, esp. one that serves as a rule of conduct or a precept: *"It is wise to risk no more than one can afford to lose."*

pro·ver·bi·al (prə vûr/bĭ əl), *adj.* **1.** pertaining to or characteristic of a proverb: *proverbial brevity.* **2.** expressed in a proverb or proverbs: *proverbial wisdom.* **3.** of the nature of or resembling a proverb: *proverbial sayings.* **4.** having been made the subject of a proverb. **5.** having become an object of common mention or reference. —**pro·ver/bi·al·ly,** *adv.*

pro·vide (prə vīd/), *v.,* **-vided, -viding.** —*v.t.* **1.** to

furnish or supply. **2.** to afford or yield. **3.** to get ready, prepare, ensure, or procure beforehand. **4.** *Law.* to arrange for or stipulate beforehand, as by a provision or proviso. —*v.i.* **5.** to take measures with due foresight (fol. by *for* or *against*). **6.** to make arrangements for supplying means of support, money, etc. (fol. by *for*). **7.** to supply means of support, etc. (often fol. by *for*). [ME, t. L: m.s. *prō̆vidēre* foresee, look after, provide for] —**pro·vid/er,** *n.*

pro·vid·ed (prə vī/dĭd), *conj.* it being stipulated or understood (that); on the condition or supposition (that): *to consent, provided* (or *provided that*) *all the others agree.* —**Syn.** See **if.**

prov·i·dence (prŏv/ə dəns), *n.* **1.** the foreseeing care and guardianship of God over His creatures. **2.** (*cap.*) God. **3.** a manifestation of the divine care or direction. **4.** provident or prudent management of resources; economy. **5.** *Rare.* foresight; provident care.

Prov·i·dence (prŏv/ə dəns), *n.* a seaport in and the capital of Rhode Island, in the NE part, at the head of Narragansett Bay. 207,498 (1960).

prov·i·dent (prŏv/ə dənt), *adj.* **1.** having or showing foresight; careful in providing for the future. **2.** characterized by or proceeding from foresight: *provident care.* **3.** mindful in making provision (fol. by *of*). **4.** economical or frugal. [ME, t. L: s. *prō̆videns,* ppr., looking for, providing] —**prov/i·dent·ly,** *adv.*

prov·i·den·tial (prŏv/ə dĕn/shəl), *adj.* **1.** of, pertaining to, or proceeding from divine providence: *providential care.* **2.** opportune, fortunate, or lucky: *a providential occurrence.* —**prov/i·den/tial·ly,** *adv.*

pro·vid·ing (prə vī/dĭng), *conj.* provided. —**Syn.** See **if.**

prov·ince (prŏv/ĭns), *n.* **1.** an administrative division or unit of a country: *the provinces of Spain.* **2.** the **Provinces, a.** the parts of a country outside of the capital or the largest cities. **b.** (in England) all parts of the country outside of London. **3.** a country, territory, district, or region. **4.** *Geog.* an area lower in rank than a region. **5.** a department or branch of learning or activity: *the province of mathematics.* **6.** the sphere or field of action of a person, etc.; one's office, function, or business. **7.** the major subdivision of British India. **8.** an ecclesiastical territorial division, as that within which an archbishop or a metropolitan exercises jurisdiction. **9.** (formerly) **a.** those North American colonies of Great Britain now forming provinces of Canada. **b.** certain of those colonies which after the Revolutionary War united to form the United States. **10.** a country or territory outside of Italy, brought under the ancient Roman dominion, and administered by a governor sent from Rome. [ME, t. F, t. L: m.s. *prōvincia* province, official charge]

Prov·ince·town (prŏv/ĭns toun/), *n.* a resort town at the tip of Cape Cod, in SE Massachusetts: the first landing place of the Pilgrims in the New World, 1620. 3,346 (1960).

pro·vin·cial (prə vĭn/shəl), *adj.* **1.** belonging or peculiar to some particular province or provinces; local: *provincial customs.* **2.** of or pertaining to the provinces: *the provincial press.* **3.** having or showing the manners characteristic of inhabitants of a province or the provinces; countrified or rustic. **4.** narrow or illiberal. **5.** *Hist.* of or pertaining to any of the American provinces of Great Britain. —*n.* **6.** one who lives in or comes from the provinces. **7.** a provincial or countrified person. **8.** *Eccles.* **a.** the head of an ecclesiastical province. **b.** a member of a religious order presiding over his order in a given district or province. —**pro·vin/cial·ly,** *adv.*

pro·vin·cial·ism (prə vĭn/shə lĭz/əm), *n.* **1.** provincial character or peculiarity. **2.** manner, habit of thought, etc., characteristic of a province or the provinces. **3.** a word, expression, or mode of pronunciation peculiar to a province. **4.** devotion to one's own province before the nation as a whole.

pro·vin·ci·al·i·ty (prə vĭn/shĭ ăl/ə tĭ), *n., pl.* **-ties.** **1.** provincial character. **2.** a provincial characteristic.

pro·vi·sion (prə vĭzh/ən), *n.* **1.** a clause in a legal instrument, a law, etc., providing for a particular matter; a stipulation; a proviso. **2.** the providing or supplying of something, as of necessaries or food. **3.** arrangement or preparation beforehand, as for the doing of something, the meeting of needs, the supplying of means, etc. **4.** something provided; a measure or other means for meeting a need. **5.** a supply or stock of something provided. **6.** (*pl.*) supplies of food. **7.** *Eccles.* **a.** appointment to an ecclesiastical office. **b.** appointment by the pope to a see or benefice not yet vacant. —*v.t.* **8.** to supply with provisions, or stores of food. [ME, t. L: s. *prōvisio*] —**pro·vi/sion·er,** *n.* —**Syn. 6.** See **food.**

pro·vi·sion·al (prə vĭzh/ən əl), *adj.* Also, **pro·vi/sion·ar/y. 1.** pertaining to or of the nature of a temporary arrangement: *a provisional agreement.* **2.** provided for the time being: *a provisional government.* **3.** temporary. —*n.* **4.** *Philately* a stamp which serves temporarily pending the appearance of the regular issue, or during a temporary shortage of the regular stamps. —**pro·vi/sion·al·ly,** *adv.*

pro·vi·so (prə vī/zō), *n., pl.* **-sos, -soes. 1.** a clause in a statute, contract, or the like, by which a condition is introduced. **2.** a stipulation or condition. [late ME, t. ML: *prōvīsō* (*quod*) it being provided that]

pro·vi·so·ry (prə vī/zə rĭ), *adj.* **1.** provisional. **2.** containing a proviso or condition; conditional.

pro·vi·ta·min (prō vī'tə mǐn). *n. Biochem.* a substance which an organism can transform into a vitamin, as carotene which is converted to Vitamin A in the liver.

Pro·vo (prō'vō), *n.* a city in central Utah. 36,047 (1960).

prov·o·ca·tion (prŏv'ə kā'shən). *n.* **1.** the action of provoking. **2.** something that incites, instigates, angers, or irritates. **3.** *Crim. Law.* words or conduct leading to a killing in hot passion and without deliberation. [ME, t. L: s. *prŏvocātio* a calling forth]

pro·voc·a·tive (prə vŏk'ə tǐv), *adj.* **1.** tending or serving to provoke; inciting, stimulating, irritating, or vexing. —*n.* **2.** something provocative. **—pro·voc'a·tive·ly,** *adv.* **—pro·voc'a·tive·ness,** *n.*

pro·voke (prə vōk'), *v.t.,* **-voked, -voking. 1.** to anger, enrage, exasperate, or vex. **2.** to stir up, arouse, or call forth. **3.** to incite or stimulate (a person, etc.) to action. **4.** to give rise to, induce, or bring about. **5.** *Obs.* to summon. [ME, t. L: m. *prŏvocāre* call forth, challenge, provoke] **—pro·vok'er,** *n.* **—pro·vok'ing,** *adj.* **—pro·vok'ing·ly,** *adv.* **—Syn. 1.** See **irritate.**

prov·ost (prŏv'əst), *n.* **1.** one appointed to superintend or preside, as: **a.** the head (sometimes, **Lord Provost**) of a Scottish burgh, etc. **b.** *Chiefly Brit.* the head of certain colleges or churches. **c.** (in American universities) an officer who assists the chief executive in administering certain phases of the institutional program. **2.** *Eccles.* the chief dignitary of a cathedral or collegiate church. **3.** *Obs.* a prison warden. [ME; OE *profost,* t. ML: m.s. *prōpositus,* lit., one placed before, president] **—prov'ost·ship',** *n.*

pro·vost marshal (prō'vō), **1.** (in the army) an officer acting as head of police in a camp or area, and charged with the maintenance of order, etc. **2.** (in the navy) an officer charged with the safekeeping of a prisoner pending trial by court-martial.

prow (prou), *n.* **1.** the forepart of a ship or boat; the bow. **2.** the front end of an airship. **3.** *Poetic.* a ship. [t. F: m. *proue,* t. d. It. (Genoese): m. *proa,* g. L *prōra,* t. Gk.: m. *prōira*]

prow·ess (prou'ĭs), *n.* **1.** valor; bravery. **2.** martial daring and skill; valorous achievement. **3.** a valiant or daring deed. [ME *prowesse,* t. OF: m. *proec(c)e,* der. *proue* good, valiant, g. L *prōd-* in *prōdesse* be useful]

prowl (proul), *v.i.* **1.** to rove or go about stealthily in search of prey, plunder, etc. —*v.t.* **2.** to rove over or through in search of what may be found. —*n.* **3.** act of prowling. [ME *proll(en);* orig. uncert.] **—prowl'er,** *n.* **—Syn. 1.** See **lurk.**

prowl car, a police automobile which patrols a district, receiving instructions from headquarters by short-wave radio.

prox., (L *proximo* [*mense*]) proximo.

prox·i·mal (prŏk'sə məl), *adj.* situated toward the point of origin or attachment, as of a limb or bone (opposed to *distal*). [f. s. L *proximus* next + -AL[1]] **—prox'i·mal·ly,** *adv.*

prox·i·mate (prŏk'sə mǐt), *adj.* **1.** next; nearest. **2.** closely adjacent; very near. **3.** fairly accurate; approximate. **4.** next in a chain of relation. [t. LL: m.s. *proximātus,* pp., approached] **—prox'i·mate·ly,** *adv.*

prox·im·i·ty (prŏk sǐm'ə tǐ), *n.* nearness in place, time, or relation. [late ME, t. L: m.s. *proximitas*]

prox·i·mo (prŏk'sə mō'), *adv.* in or of the next or coming month: *on the 1st proximo.* Cf. **ultimo.** *Abbr.:* prox. [L: in the next (month), abl. of *proximus* next. See **PROXIMAL**]

prox·y (prŏk'sǐ), *n., pl.* **proxies. 1.** the agency of a person deputed to act for another. **2.** the person so deputed; an agent; a substitute. **3.** a written authorization empowering another to vote or act for the signer. [ME *prokecye,* contr. of *procuracy* (see **PROCURATOR**)]

prs., pairs.

prude (prōōd), *n.* a person who affects extreme modesty or propriety. [t. F: a prude, as adj., prudish, back formation from OF *preudefeme, prodefeme* worthy or respectable woman]

pru·dence (prōō'dəns), *n.* **1.** cautious practical wisdom; good judgment; discretion. **2.** the quality or fact of being prudent. **3.** regard for one's own interests. **4.** provident care in management; economy or frugality. **—Syn. 1.** PRUDENCE, CALCULATION, FORESIGHT, FORETHOUGHT imply attempted provision against possible contingencies. PRUDENCE is care, caution, and good judgment, as well as wisdom in looking ahead: *sober prudence in handling one's affairs.* CALCULATION suggests a disposition to get a large return for as small an outlay as possible (lit. or fig.) and willingness to benefit at the expense of others (lit. and fig.): *cold calculation.* FORESIGHT implies a prudent looking ahead rather far into the future: *admirable foresight in planning.* FORETHOUGHT emphasizes the adequacy of preparation for the future: *complete forethought.* **—Ant. 1.** rashness.

pru·dent (prōō'dənt), *adj.* **1.** wise, judicious, or wisely cautious in practical affairs, as a person; sagacious or judicious; discreet or circumspect. **2.** careful of one's own interests; provident, or careful in providing for the future. **3.** characterized by or proceeding from prudence, as conduct, action, etc. [ME, t. L: s. *prūdens,* foreseeing, knowing, contr. of *prōvidens* PROVIDENT] **—pru'dent·ly,** *adv.*

pru·den·tial (prōō dĕn'shəl), *adj.* **1.** of, pertaining to, or characterized by prudence. **2.** exercising prudence. **3.** having discretionary charge of certain matters. **—pru·den'tial·ly,** *adv.*

prud·er·y (prōō'də rǐ), *n., pl.* **-eries. 1.** extreme modesty or propriety. **2.** (*pl.*) prudish actions or speeches.

prud·ish (prōō'dǐsh), *adj.* **1.** extremely modest or proper. **2.** characteristic of a prude. **—prud'ish·ly,** *adv.* **—prud'ish·ness,** *n.* **—Syn. 1.** See **modest.**

pru·i·nose (prōō'ə nōs'), *adj. Biol.* covered with a frostlike bloom or powdery secretion, as a plant surface. [t. L: m.s. *pruīnōsus* frosty]

prune[1] (prōōn), *n.* **1.** a variety of plum which dries without spoiling, hence one used for drying. **2.** a dried plum used for eating, cooked or uncooked. **3.** a plum. [late ME, t. F, g. LL *prūna,* for L *prūnum* plum (*prūnus* plum tree), t. Gk.: m. *proûnon* plum]

prune[2] (prōōn), *v.t.,* **pruned, pruning. 1.** to cut or lop off (twigs, branches, or roots). **2.** to cut or lop superfluous or undesired twigs, branches, or roots from; to trim. **3.** to rid or clear of anything superfluous or undesirable. **4.** to remove (superfluities, etc.). [ME *prouyne(n),* t. OF: m. *proignier* prune (vines), g. L *prōvīneāre,* der. *vīnea* a vine] **—prun'er,** *n.*

prune[3] (prōōn), *v.t.,* **pruned, pruning.** *Archaic.* **1.** (of persons) to arrange or dress carefully. **2.** to preen. [ME *prune(n), pruyne(n), proyne(n)*]

pruning hook, an implement with a hooked blade, used for pruning vines, etc.

pru·ri·ent (prōōr'ǐ ənt), *adj.* **1.** inclined to or characterized by lascivious thought. **2.** morbidly uneasy, as desire or longing. **3.** *Rare.* itching. [t. L: s. *prūriens,* ppr., itching] **—pru'ri·ence, pru'ri·en·cy,** *n.* **—pru'ri·ent·ly,** *adv.*

pru·rig·i·nous (prōō rǐj'ə nəs), *adj. Med.* itching. [t. LL: m.s. *prūrīginōsus*]

pru·ri·go (prōō rī'gō), *n. Pathol.* a skin affection characterized by itching papules. [t. L: an itching]

pru·ri·tus (prōō rī'təs), *n. Pathol.* itching. [t. L: an itching. See **PRURIENT**] **—pru·rit·ic** (prōō rǐt'ĭk), *adj.*

Prus., 1. Prussia. **2.** Prussian.

Prus·sia (prŭsh'ə), *n.* a former state in N Germany: as a former kingdom (with its capital at Berlin) it was the central state in the formation of the German Empire: dissolved March, 1947. German, **Preussen.**

Prussia, 1871–1914.

Prus·sian (prŭsh'ən), *adj.* **1.** of or pertaining to Prussia or its inhabitants. —*n.* **2.** a native or inhabitant of Prussia. **3.** any of the German dialects of East or West Prussia. **4.** Old Prussian. **5.** (orig.) one of a Lettic people formerly inhabiting territory along and near the coast at the southeastern corner of the Baltic Sea.

Prussian blue, a dark-blue, crystalline, insoluble pigment, $Fe_4[FeFe(CN)_6]_3 \cdot 10H_2O$, formed in testing for the ferric ion, and produced by aging **soluble Prussian blue,** $KFe_2(CN)_6$.

Prus·sian·ism (prŭsh'ə nǐz'əm), *n.* **1.** the spirit, system, policy, or methods of the Prussians. **2.** Prussian militarism and the despotic characteristics attributed to it, especially since Frederick the Great (ruled 1740–86).

prus·si·ate (prŭsh'ǐ āt', -ǐt, prŭs'-), *n. Chem.* **1.** a ferricyanide or ferrocyanide. **2.** a salt of prussic acid; a cyanide. [t. F: f. *prussi(que)* PRUSSIC + -ate -ATE[2]]

prus·sic acid (prŭs'ĭk), *Chem.* hydrocyanic acid. [*prussic,* t. F: m. *prussique,* der. *Prusse* Prussia]

Prut (prōōt), *n.* a river flowing from the Carpathian Mountains in the SW Soviet Union SE along the border between the Soviet Union and Rumania into the Danube. ab. 500 mi. German, **Pruth** (prōōt).

pry[1] (prī), *v.,* **pried, prying,** *n., pl.* **pries.** —*v.i.* **1.** to look closely or curiously, peer, or peep. **2.** to search or inquire curiously or inquisitively into something: *to pry into the affairs of others.* —*v.t.* **3.** to ferret or find (*out*) by curious searching or inquiry. —*n.* **4.** the act of prying; a prying glance. **5.** an inquisitive person. [ME *prye(n), prie(n);* orig. uncert.]

pry[2] (prī), *v.,* **pried, prying,** *n., pl.* **pries.** —*v.t.* **1.** to raise, open, or move by force of leverage. **2.** to get or obtain with difficulty: *to pry a secret out of someone.* —*n.* **3.** any instrument for raising or moving a thing by leverage, as a crowbar. **4.** the leverage exerted. [back formation from PRIZE[3], n. (taken as pl.)]

pry·er (prī'ər), *n.* prier.

pry·ing (prī'ĭng), *adj.* **1.** that pries; looking or searching curiously. **2.** unduly curious; inquisitive. **—pry'ing·ly,** *adv.* **—Syn. 2.** See **curious.**

Prze·myśl (pshĕ'mǐsh əl), *n.* a city in SE Poland: occupied by the Russians, 1915. 36,838 (1946).

Ps., 1. Psalm. **2.** Psalms.

ps., pieces.

P.S., 1. Also, **p.s.** postscript. **2.** Privy Seal. **3.** Public School.

Psa., Psalm; Psalms.

psalm (säm), *n.* **1.** a sacred or solemn song, or hymn. **2.** (*cap.*) any of the 150 songs, hymns, and prayers which together form a book of the Old Testament (**Book of Psalms**). **3.** a metric version or paraphrase of any of these. **4.** a poem of like character. —*v.t.* **5.** to celebrate in psalms; hymn. [ME *psalme*, OE *ps(e)alm*, *sealm*, t. LL: m.s. *psalmus*, t. Gk.: m. *psalmós* song sung to the harp, orig., a plucking, as of strings]

psalm·ist (sä′mĭst), *n.* **1.** the author of a psalm or psalms. **2. the Psalmist**, David, the traditional author of the Psalms.

psal·mo·dy (sä′mə dĭ, săl′mə dĭ), *n., pl.* **-dies. 1.** the arrangement of the Psalms for singing. **2.** psalms or hymns collectively. **3.** the act, practice, or art of singing psalms or hymns. [ME, t. LL: m.s. *psalmōdia*, t. Gk.: m. *psalmōidía* singing to the harp] —**psal′mo·dist,** *n.*

Psal·ter (sôl′tər), *n.* **1.** the Book of Psalms. **2.** (*sometimes l.c.*) a book containing the Psalms for liturgical or devotional use. [t. LL: m.s. *psaltērium* the Psalter, L a psaltery, t. Gk.: m. *psaltērion* a stringed instrument; r. ME *sauter* (t. AF) and OE *saltere* (t. LL: m.s. *psaltērium*]

psal·te·ri·um (sôl tĭr′ĭ əm, săl-), *n., pl.* **-teria** (-tĭr′ĭ ə). *Zool.* the omasum or manyplies. [t. LL: the Psalter (the folds of the omasum being likened to the leaves of a book), t. Gk.: m. *psaltērion*]

psal·ter·y (sôl′tər ĭ), *n., pl.* **-teries. 1.** an ancient musical instrument consisting of a flat sounding box with numerous strings which were plucked with the fingers or struck with a plectrum. **2.** (*cap.*) the Psalter. [t. L: m.s. *psaltērium* psaltery, LL the Psalter, t. Gk.: m. *psaltērion* psaltery, later the Psalter; r. ME *sautrie*, t. OF]

Man playing a psaltery, 12th century

psam·mite (săm′ĭt), *n. Geol.* any sandstone (contrasted with *psephite* and *pelite*). [f. s. Gk. *psámmos* sand + -ITE¹] —**psam·mit·ic** (să mĭt′ĭk), *adj.*

pse·phite (sē′fĭt, psē′-), *n. Geol.* any coarse fragmental rock, as breccia (contrasted with *psammite* and *pelite*). [f. s. Gk. *psḗphos* pebble + -ITE¹]

pseud., pseudonym.

pseu·dax·is (soo dăk′sĭs), *n. Bot.* sympodium. [f. PSEUD(o)- + AXIS]

pseu·de·pig·ra·pha (soo′də pĭg′rə fə), *n.pl.* certain writings (other than the canonical books and the Apocrypha) professing to be Biblical in character, but not considered canonical or inspired. [NL, t. Gk., neut. pl. of *pseudepígraphos* falsely inscribed, bearing a false title] —**pseu·dep·i·graph·ic** (soo′dĕp ə grăf′ĭk), **pseu·de·pig·ra·phous** (soo′də pĭg′rə fəs), *adj.*

pseu·do (soo′dō), *adj.* false; counterfeit; spurious; sham; pretended. [ME; independent use of PSEUDO-]

pseudo-, a word element meaning "false," "pretended"; in scientific use, denoting close or deceptive resemblance to the following element, used sometimes in chemical names of isomers. Also, before vowels, **pseud-.** [t. Gk., comb. form of *pseudḗs* false]

pseu·do·a·quat·ic (soo′dō ə kwăt′ĭk, -kwŏt′-), *adj.* not aquatic but indigenous to moist regions.

pseu·do·carp (soo′dō kärp′), *n. Bot.* a fruit which includes other parts in addition to the mature ovary and its contents, as the apple, pineapple, etc. —**pseu′do·car′pous,** *adj.*

pseu·do·clas·sic (soo′dō klăs′ĭk), *adj.* falsely or spuriously classic. —**pseu·do·clas·si·cism** (soo′dō klăs′ə sĭz′əm), *n.*

pseu·do·learn·ed (soo′dō lûr′nĭd), *adj.* **1.** characterized by erroneous or defective learning. **2.** exhibiting unnecessary or misguided antiquarianism, as in adding *b* in the spelling of *debt* after the Latin source *debitum,* for Middle English *det.*

pseu·do·morph (soo′də môrf′), *n.* **1.** a false or deceptive form. **2.** *Mineral.* a substance or structure of definite or characteristic form which is represented or defined by another substance to which the form does not properly belong: *Limonite is often a pseudomorph after pyrite.* —**pseu·do·mor′phic, pseu·do·mor′phous,** *adj.* —**pseu·do·mor′phism,** *n.*

pseu·do·nym (soo′də nĭm), *n.* an assumed name adopted by the author to conceal his identity; pen name. [t. Gk.: s. *pseudónymon* false name]

pseu·do·nym·i·ty (soo′də nĭm′ə tĭ), *n.* pseudonymous character. **2.** the use of a pseudonym.

pseu·don·y·mous (soo dŏn′ə məs), *adj.* **1.** bearing a false name. **2.** writing or written under an assumed name. [t. Gk.: m. *pseudṓnymos*] —**pseu·don′y·mous·ly,** *adv.*

pseu·do·po·di·um (soo′də pō′dĭ əm), *n., pl.* **-dia** (-dĭ ə). a temporary protrusion of the protoplasm of a protozoan, serving as an organ of locomotion, prehension, etc. Also, **pseu·do·pod** (soo′də pŏd′). [NL, f. Gk.: *pseudo-* PSEUDO- + *pódion,* dim. of *poús* foot]

pshaw (shô), *interj.* **1.** an exclamation expressing impatience, contempt, etc. —*n.* **2.** an exclamation of "pshaw!" —*v.i.* **3.** to say "pshaw." —*v.t.* **4.** to say "pshaw" at or to.

psi¹ (sī, psē), *n.* the twenty-third letter (Ψ, ψ) of the Greek alphabet.

psi² (sī, psī), pounds per square inch.

psi·lan·thro·pism (sī lăn′thrə pĭz′əm), *n.* the doctrine that Jesus Christ was a mere man. Also, **psi·lan′thro·py.** [f. Gk. *psilánthropos* merely human + -ISM]

psi·lom·e·lane (sī lŏm′ə lān′), *n.* a common mineral, a hydrated barium manganate, occurring in smooth, black to steel-gray, botryoidal or stalactitic forms and in

masses: an ore of manganese. [f. Gk.: *psiló(s)* bare, mere + m. *mélan* (neut.) black]

Psi·lo·ri·ti (psē′lô rē′tē) *n.* Mount. See **Ida, Mount** (def. 2).

psi·lo·sis (sī lō′sĭs), *n. Pathol.* sprue. [NL, t. Gk.]

psit·ta·co·sis (sĭt′ə kō′sĭs), *n.* a severe infectious disease characterized by high fever and pulmonary involvement recently introduced into the U.S. by parrots, and easily transmissible from parrots to man; parrot fever [NL, f. m.s. Gk. *psittakós* parrot + *-ōsis* -OSIS]

Pskov (pskôf), *n.* **1.** a lake in the W Soviet Union, forming the S part of Lake Peipus. **2.** a city near this lake. 60,000 (est. 1948).

pso·as (sō′əs), *n. Anat.* a muscle of the loin, arising internally from the sides of the spinal column and fitting into the upper end of the thighbone. [NL, t. Gk. acc. pl. of *psóa* a muscle of the loins]

pso·ra·le·a (sō rā′lĭ ə), *n.* any plant of the leguminous genus *Psoralea,* esp. the breadroot, *P. esculenta.* [NL, t. Gk.: (neut. pl.) scabby: with reference to the glandular dots on the plant]

pso·ri·a·sis (sō rī′ə sĭs), *n. Pathol.* a common chronic skin disease characterized by scaly patches. [t. NL, t. Gk.] —**pso·ri·at·ic** (sôr′ĭ ăt′ĭk), *adj.*

P.SS., (L *postscripta*) postscripts. Also, **p.ss.**

P.S.T., Pacific Standard Time.

psych-, var. of **psycho-,** before some vowels, as in *psychasthenia.*

psych., 1. psychological. **2.** psychology.

psy·chas·the·ni·a (sī′kăs thē′nĭ ə, -thə nī′ə), *n.* **1.** *Psychiatry.* a neurosis marked by fear, anxiety, phobias, etc. **2.** *Pathol.* mental weakness or exhaustion. [NL. See PSYCH-, ASTHENIA]

Psy·che (sī′kĭ), *n.* **1.** *Gk. Myth.* the soul, sometimes represented in art as a butterfly or a tiny winged being, and in the late classical era as a beautiful girl loved by Eros or Cupid. **2.** (*l.c.*) the human soul, spirit, or mind.

Psyche knot, a knot or knotted arrangement of a woman's hair projecting from the back of the head.

psy·chi·a·trist (sī kī′ə trĭst), *n.* one who is versed in or practices psychiatry. Also, **psy·chi·a·ter** (sī kī′ə tər).

psy·chi·a·try (sī kī′ə trĭ), *n.* the practice or the science of treating mental diseases. [f. PSYCH- + m.s. Gk. *iatreía* healing] —**psy·chi·at·ric** (sī′kĭ ăt′rĭk), **psy·chi·at′ri·cal,** *adj.*

psy·chic (sī′kĭk), *adj.* Also, **psy′chi·cal. 1.** of or pertaining to the human soul or mind; mental (opposed to *physical*). **2.** *Psychol.* pertaining to super- or extrasensory mental functioning, such as clairvoyance, telepathy. See **parapsychology. 3.** exerted by or proceeding from some nonphysical agency. **4.** of the nature of such an agency. **5.** associated with or attributed to such agencies, as phenomena, etc. **6.** of or pertaining to the class of phenomena associated with such agencies: *psychic research.* **7.** specially susceptible to psychic influences. —*n.* **8.** a person specially susceptible to psychic influences. [t. Gk.: m.s. *psýchikos* of the soul] —**psy′chi·cal·ly,** *adv.*

psycho-, a word element representing **psyche** (as in *psychological*) and **psychological** (as in *psychoanalysis*). Also, **psych-.** [t. Gk., comb. form of *psychḗ* breath, spirit, soul, mind]

psychoanal., psychoanalysis.

psy·cho·anal·y·sis (sī′kō ə năl′ə sĭs), *n.* **1.** a systematic structure of theories concerning the relation of conscious and unconscious psychological processes. **2.** a technical procedure for investigating unconscious mental processes, and for treating psychoneuroses. —**psy·cho·an·a·lyt·ic** (sī′kō ăn′ə lĭt′ĭk), **psy·cho·an·a·lyt′i·cal,** *adj.* —**psy·cho·an·a·lyt′i·cal·ly,** *adv.*

psy·cho·an·a·lyst (sī′kō ăn′ə lĭst), *n.* one who is versed in or practices psychoanalysis.

psy·cho·an·a·lyze (sī′kō ăn′ə līz), *v.t.,* **-lyzed, -lyzing.** to investigate or treat by psychoanalysis. —**psy′cho·an′a·lyz′er,** *n.*

psy·cho·bi·ol·o·gy (sī′kō bī ŏl′ə jĭ), *n.* **1.** that branch of biology which treats of the relations or interactions between body and mind, esp. as exhibited in the nervous system, receptors, effectors, or the like. **2.** psychology as studied by biological methods or in terms of biology —**psy·cho·bi·o·log·i·cal** (sī′kō bī′ə lŏj′ə kəl), *adj.* —**psy′cho·bi·ol′o·gist,** *n.*

psy·cho·gen·e·sis (sī′kō jĕn′ə sĭs), *n.* **1.** (in animal evolution) hypothetical origin or development due to psychic or mental activity. **2.** genesis of the psyche. **3.** the origin of physical or psychological states, normal or abnormal, out of the interplay of conscious and unconscious psychological forces. —**psy·cho·ge·net·ic** (sī′kō jə nĕt′ĭk), *adj.*

psy·cho·gen·ic (sī′kō jĕn′ĭk), *adj.* of psychic origin, or dependent on psychic conditions or processes, as a mental disorder.

psy·chog·no·sis (sī kŏg′nə sĭs), *n. Psychiatry.* a complete examination of the mind.

psy·cho·graph (sī′kə grăf′, -gräf′), *n. Psychol.* the graphic representation of the relative strength of the various traits of a personality.

psychol., 1. psychological. **2.** psychology.

psy·cho·log·i·cal (sī′kə lŏj′ə kəl), *adj.* **1.** of or pertaining to psychology. **2.** pertaining to the mind or to mental phenomena as the subject matter of psychology. Also, **psy′cho·log′ic.** —**psy′cho·log′i·cal·ly,** *adv.*

psychological moment, the most appropriate moment for effect on the mind; the critical moment: *at the psychological moment he announced his resignation.*

psy·chol·o·gist (sĭ kŏl'ə jĭst), *n.* one trained in psychology.

psy·chol·o·gize (sĭ kŏl'ə jīz'), *v.i.* **-gized, -gizing.** to make psychological investigations or speculations.

psy·chol·o·gy (sĭ kŏl'ə jĭ), *n., pl.* **-gies.** 1. the science of mind, or of mental states and processes; the science of human nature. 2. the science of human and animal behavior. 3. the mental states and processes of a person or of a number of persons, esp. as determining action: *the psychology of the fighting man in war.* [t. NL: m. s. *psȳchologia,* f. Gk.: *psȳcho-* PSYCHO- + *-logȋa* -LOGY]

psy·cho·man·cy (sī'kō măn'sĭ), *n.* occult communication between souls or with spirits.

psy·chom·e·try (sī kŏm'ə trĭ), *n.* 1. Also, **psy·chom·et·rics** (sī'kō mĕt'rĭks). *Psychol.* the measurement of mental states, mental processes, and their relationships. 2. the alleged art or faculty of divining the properties of an object, or matters associated with it, through contact with or proximity to it.

psy·cho·neu·ro·sis (sī'kō nyŏŏ rō'sĭs, -nŏŏ-), *n., pl.* **-ses** (-sēz). an emotional disorder in which feelings of anxiety, obsessional thoughts, compulsive acts, and physical complaints without objective evidence of disease, in various patterns, dominate the personality. [t. NL. See PSYCHO-, NEUROSIS] —**psy·cho·neu·rot·ic** (sī'kō nyŏŏ rŏt'ĭk, -nŏŏ-), *adj.*

psy·cho·path (sī'kə păth'), *n.* one affected with psychopathy.

psy·cho·path·ic (sī'kə păth'ĭk), *adj.* 1. pertaining to or of the nature of, affected with, or engaged in treating psychopathy. 2. pertaining to a psychosis or psychoneurosis, or to any other mental disorder.

psy·cho·pa·thol·o·gy (sī'kō pa thŏl'ə jĭ), *n.* mental pathology; the science of diseases of the mind. —**psy·cho·path·o·log·i·cal** (sī'kō păth'ə lŏj'ə kəl), *adj.* —**psy·cho·pa·thol'o·gist,** *n.*

psy·chop·a·thy (sī kŏp'ə thĭ), *n.* 1. mental disease or disorder. 2. the treatment of disease by mental or psychic influence.

psy·cho·phys·ics (sī'kō fĭz'ĭks), *n.* that department of psychology which deals with the measurement of relationships between attributes of the stimulus and of the sensation. —**psy·cho·phys·i·cal** (sī'kō fĭz'ə kəl), *adj.* —**psy·cho·phys·i·cist** (sī'kō fĭz'ə sĭst), *n.*

psy·cho·pomp (sī'kō pŏmp'), *n.* one who conducts spirits or souls to the other world, as Hermes or Charon. [f. PSYCHO- + s. Gk. *pompós* conductor]

psy·cho·sis (sī kō'sĭs), *n., pl.* **-ses** (-sēz). 1. *Pathol.* any major, severe form of mental affection or disease. 2. *Rare.* the state of consciousness at a given time. [t. NL, t. LGk.] —**psy·chot·ic** (sī kŏt'ĭk), *adj., n.*

psy·cho·so·mat·ic (sī'kō sō măt'ĭk), *adj.* denoting a physical disorder which is caused by or notably influenced by the emotional state of the patient.

psychosomatic medicine, the application of the principles of psychology in the study and treatment of physical diseases.

psy·cho·ther·a·peu·tics (sī'kō thĕr'ə pū'tĭks), *n.* therapeutics concerned with the treatment of disease by psychic influence, as by mental suggestion. —**psy·cho·ther'a·peu'tic,** *adj.* —**psy·cho·ther'a·peu'tist,** *n.*

psy·cho·ther·a·py (sī'kō thĕr'ə pĭ), *n.* the science or art of curing psychological abnormalities and disorders by psychological techniques. —**psy·cho·ther'a·pist,** *n.*

psy·chrom·e·ter (sī krŏm'ə tər), *n.* an instrument used to determine atmospheric humidity by the reading of two thermometers, the bulb of one of which is kept moistened and ventilated. [f. *psychro-* (t. Gk., comb. form of *psȳchrós* cold) + -METER]

Pt, *Chem.* platinum.

pt., 1. part. 2. payment. 3. pint. 4. pints. 5. point. 6. port. 7. preterit.

P.T., Pacific time.

p.t., pro tempore.

P.T.A., Parent-Teacher Association.

Ptah (ptä, ptäᴋʜ), *n.* an Egyptian deity of high rank, worshiped especially at Memphis, and reverenced as the creative force. [t. Egypt.]

ptar·mi·gan (tär'mə gən), *n.* any of various species of grouse of the genus *Lagopus,* characterized by feathered feet, and found in mountainous and cold regions. [t. Gaelic.: m. *tarmachan,* orig. unknown]

PT boat, *U.S.* a small speedy boat used chiefly to torpedo enemy shipping. It generally has no protective armor, and its armament consists of light weapons. [from the initial letters of *p(ropeller) t(orpedo)* boat]

pter·i·dol·o·gy (tĕr'ə dŏl'ə jĭ), *n.* the branch of botany that treats of ferns. [f. *pterido-* (comb. form repr. Gk. *pteris* fern) + -LOGY] —**pter·i·do·log·i·cal** (tĕr'ə dō lŏj'ə kəl), *adj.* —**pter·i·dol'o·gist,** *n.*

pter·i·do·phyte (tĕr'ə dō fīt'), *n.* any of the *Pteridophyta,* a primary division of the vegetable kingdom comprising plants (as the ferns and fern allies) which are without seeds, have vascular tissue, and are differentiated into root, stem, and leaf. It includes ferns, horsetails, and club mosses. [t. NL: m. *Pteridophyta,* pl., f. Gk.: *pterido-* (comb. form repr. Gk. *pteris* fern) + m. *phytá* plants] —**pter·i·do·phyt·ic** (tĕr'ə dō fĭt'ĭk), **pter·i·doph·y·tous** (tĕr'ə dŏf'ə təs), *adj.*

pte·ri·on (tĭr'Ῑ ŏn', tĕr'-), *n. Craniom.* the craniometric point at the side of the sphenoidal fontanelle.

pter·o·dac·tyl (tĕr'ə dăk'tĭl), *n.* any member of the *Pterosauria,* an order of extinct (Jurassic to Cretaceous) flying reptiles, having the outside digit of the forelimb greatly elongated and supporting a wing membrane. [t. NL: s. *Pterodactylus,* genus name, f. Gk.: m. *pteró(n)* wing + m. *dáktylos* digit]

pter·o·pod (tĕr'ə pŏd'), *adj.* belonging or pertaining to the *Pteropoda,* a group of mollusks which have the lateral portions of the foot expanded into winglike lobes. [t. NL: s. *Pteropoda,* pl., t. Gk., neut. pl. of *pterópous* wing-footed]

-pterous, an adjectival word element meaning "winged," as in *dipterous.* [t. Gk.: m. *-pteros,* comb. form der. *pterón* feather, wing]

pter·y·goid (tĕr'ə goid'), *adj.* 1. winglike. 2. *Anat.* denoting or pertaining to the pterygoid process. —*n.* 3. *Anat.* the muscles, nerves, blood vessels, etc., of the pterygoid process. [t. Gk.: m.s. *pterygoeidḗs* winglike]

pterygoid process, *Anat.* 1. either of two processes descending, one on each side, from the point where the body of the sphenoid bone joins a bone of a temporal wing, each process consisting of two plates (**external pterygoid plate** and **internal pterygoid plate**) separated by a notch. 2. either of these two plates.

ptg., printing.

ptis·an (tĭz'ən, tĭ zăn'), *n.* a nourishing decoction, often having a slight medicinal quality, originally one made from barley. [t. L: s. *ptisana,* t. Gk.: m. *ptisáne* peeled barley, barley water; r. ME *tisane,* t. F]

p.t.o., please turn over.

Ptol·e·ma·ic (tŏl'ə mā'ĭk), *adj.* of or pertaining to Ptolemy.

Ptolemaic system, *Astron.* a system elaborated by Ptolemy and subsequently modified by others, according to which the earth was the fixed center of the universe, with the heavenly bodies moving about it.

Ptol·e·ma·ist (tŏl'ə mā'ĭst), *n.* a believer in the Ptolemaic system of astronomy.

Ptol·e·my (tŏl'ə mĭ), *n.* 1. (*Claudius Ptolemaeus*) fl. A.D. 127–151, Greek mathematician, astronomer, and geographer, at Alexandria. 2. any of a Macedonian family of rulers of Egypt, 323-30 B.C.

Ptolemy I, (surnamed *Soter*) 367?–283 B.C., king of Egypt, 306–285 B.C., born in Macedonia, founder of Macedonian dynasty in Egypt.

Ptolemy II, (surnamed *Philadelphus*) 309?–247? B.C., king of Egypt, from 285–247? B.C. (son of Ptolemy I).

pto·maine (tō'mān, tō mān'), *n.* any of a class of basic nitrogenous substances, some of them very poisonous, produced during putrefaction of animal or plant proteins (**ptomaine poisoning**). Also, **pto'main.** [t. It.: m. *ptomaina,* f. Gk. *ptȏma* dead body + *-ina* -INE²]

pto·sis (tō'sĭs), *n. Pathol.* a dropping of the upper eyelid. [NL, t. Gk.: a *falling*] —**pto·tic** (tō'tĭk), *adj.*

pts., 1. parts. 2. payments. 3. pints. 4. points. 5. ports.

pty·a·lin (tī'ə lĭn), *n. Biochem.* an enzyme in the saliva of man and certain of the lower animals, possessing the property of converting starch into dextrin and maltose. [f. s. Gk. *ptýalon* spittle, saliva + -IN²]

pty·a·lism (tī'ə lĭz'əm), *n. Pathol.* excessive secretion of saliva. [t. Gk.: s. *ptyalismós* expectoration]

pub (pŭb), *n. Brit. Slang.* a tavern. [short for PUBLIC HOUSE]

pub., 1. public. 2. publication. 3. published. 4. publisher. 5. publishing.

pu·ber·ty (pū'bər tĭ), *n.* sexual maturity; the earliest age at which a person is capable of procreating offspring (in common law, presumed to be 14 years in the male and 12 years in the female). [ME *puberte,* t. L: m.s. *pūbertas*]

pu·bes (pū'bēz), *n. Anat.* 1. the lower part of the abdomen, esp. the region between the right and left iliac regions. 2. the hair appearing on the lower part of the abdomen at puberty. [t. L: *pubic hair, groin*]

pu·bes·cent (pū bĕs'ənt), *adj.* 1. arriving or arrived at puberty. 2. *Bot., Zool.* covered with down or fine short hair. [t. L: s. *pūbescens,* ppr., reaching puberty, becoming hairy or downy] —**pu·bes'cence,** *n.*

pu·bic (pū'bĭk), *adj.* pertaining to the pubes or pubis.

pu·bis (pū'bĭs), *n., pl.* **-bes** (-bēz). *Anat.* that part of either innominate bone which, with the corresponding part of the other, forms the front of the pelvis. See diag. under **pelvis.** [short for NL *os pūbis* bone of the pubes]

pub·lic (pŭb'lĭk), *adj.* 1. of, pertaining to, or affecting the people as a whole, the community, state, or nation: *public affairs.* 2. done, made, acting, etc., for the people or community as a whole: *a public prosecutor.* 3. open to all the people: *a public meeting.* 4. pertaining to or engaged in the affairs or service of the community or nation: *a public official.* 5. maintained at the public expense, under public control, and open to the public generally: *a public library.* 6. open to the view or knowledge of all; existing, done, etc., in public: *the fact became public.* 7. having relations with or being known to the public generally: *a public character.* 8. *Rare.* international: *public law.* —*n.* 9. the people constituting a community, state, or nation. 10. a particular section of the people: *the novel-reading public.* 11. public view or access: *in public.* 12. *Brit. Colloq.* a public house. [t. L: s. *publicus;* r. ME *publique,* t. F (fem.)]

b., blend of, blended; c., cognate with; d., dialect, dialectal; der., derived from; f., formed from; g., going back to; m., modification of; r., replacing; s., stem of; t., taken from; ?, perhaps. See the full key on inside cover.

pub·lic-ad·dress system (pŭb′lĭk ə drĕs′), a combination of electronic devices designed to transmit, amplify, and reproduce speech and/or music so as to render it audible to many people at the same time.

pub·li·can (pŭb′lə kən), n. 1. *Brit.* the keeper of a public house. 2. *Ancient Rome.* who farmed the public revenues; a tax gatherer. 3. any collector of toll, tribute, or the like. [ME, t. L: s. *publicānus*]

pub·li·ca·tion (pŭb′lə kā′shən), n. 1. the publishing of a book, periodical, map, piece of music, engraving, or the like. 2. the act of publishing. 3. the state or fact of being published. 4. that which is published, as a book or the like. [ME, t. L: s. *pūblicātio*]

public domain, *Law.* 1. the status of productions of authorship upon which the copyrights have expired and of works which have been published without copyright protection. 2. land owned by the government.

public enemy, 1. a person who is a danger or menace to the public, usually as shown by his criminal record. 2. a nation or government at war with one's own.

public house, 1. *Brit.* a tavern. 2. an inn. —Syn. 1. See hotel.

pub·li·cist (pŭb′lə sĭst), n. 1. one who is expert in or writes on current public or political affairs. 2. an expert in public or international law. 3. a press agent or public relations man.

pub·lic·i·ty (pŭb lĭs′ə tĭ′), n. 1. the state of being public, or open to general observation or knowledge. 2. public notice as the result of advertising or other special measures. 3. the state of being brought to public notice by announcements (aside from advertisements) by mention in the press, on the radio, or any means serving to effect the purpose. 4. the measures, process, or business of securing public notice.

pub·li·cize (pŭb′lĭ sīz′), v.t., -cized, -cizing. to give publicity to; bring to public notice; advertise: *they publicized the meeting as best they could.*

public liability insurance, insurance which protects the policyholder against risks involving liability to the public for legal damages occasioned by negligence.

pub·lic·ly (pŭb′lĭk lĭ), adv. 1. in a public or open manner. 2. by the public. 3. in the name of the community. 4. by public action or consent.

public opinion, the collective opinion that is formed around an issue of difference.

public opinion poll, a poll by sampling to predict election results or to estimate public attitudes on issues.

public school, 1. *U.S.* a school maintained at the public expense for the education of the children and youth of a community or district, as part of a system of public (and usually free) education, commonly forming one of a series of graded schools including primary schools, grammar schools, and high schools. The primary schools and grammar schools together are known as elementary or common schools; the high schools, as distinguished from these, are known as secondary schools. See also high school. 2. *England.* a. any of certain large, endowed boarding schools, patronized esp. by the wealthy, which prepare pupils mainly for the universities or public service. b. *Hist.* a grammar school founded or endowed for the benefit of the public and carried on under some form of public control.

public servant, one holding a government office.

public service corporation, an incorporated public utility.

pub·lic-spir·it·ed (pŭb′lĭk spĭr′ĭt ĭd), adj. having or showing an unselfish desire for the public good: *a public-spirited citizen.*

public utility, 1. a business enterprise performing an essential public service, as supplying gas and electricity or transportation, and either operated or regulated by the federal, state, or local government. 2. (*usually pl.*) *Stock Exchange.* shares issued by public utilities.

public works, constructions as roads, dams, post offices, etc., out of government funds for public use.

pub·lish (pŭb′lĭsh), v.t. 1. to issue or cause to be issued, in copies made by printing or other process, for sale or distribution to the public, as a book, periodical, map, piece of music, engraving, or the like. 2. *Law.* (in the law of defamation) to communicate (the defamatory statement in some form) to some person or persons other than the person defamed. 3. to announce formally or officially; proclaim; promulgate. 4. to make publicly or generally known. [ME, f. F *publ*(*ier*) + -ISH²] —pub/lish·a·ble, adj. —Syn. 3. See announce.

pub·lish·er (pŭb′lĭsh ər), n. 1. one whose business is the publishing of books, periodicals, engravings, or the like. 2. the business head of a newspaper organization, commonly the owner or the representative of the owner.

pub·lish·ment (pŭb′lĭsh mənt), n. publication.

Puc·ci·ni (pŏŏt chē′nē), n. **Giacomo** (jä′kō mô′), 1858–1924, Italian operatic composer.

puc·coon (pə kōōn′), n. 1. any of certain plants which yield a red dye, as the bloodroot (*Sanguinaria canadensis*) and certain herbs of the boraginaceous genus *Lithospermum.* 2. the dye itself. [t. N Amer. Ind. (Algonquian d.)]

puce (pūs), adj. 1. of a dark or purplish brown. —n. 2. dark or purplish brown. [t. F: lit., flea, g. L *pūlex*]

Puck (pŭk), n. 1. a particular mischievous or tricksy sprite or fairy (called also Hobgoblin and Robin Goodfellow) who appears as a character in Shakespeare's

Midsummer Night's Dream. 2. (*l.c.*) a malicious or mischievous demon or spirit; a goblin. 3. (*l.c.*) a rubber disk used in place of a ball in ice hockey. [ME *pouke*, OE *pūca*, c. Icel *pūki* a mischievous demon]

puck·a (pŭk′ə), adj. pukka.

puck·er (pŭk′ər), v.t., v.i. 1. to draw or gather into wrinkles or irregular folds. —n. 2. a wrinkle; an irregular fold. 3. a puckered part, as of cloth tightly or crookedly sewed. 4. *Colloq.* a state of agitation or perturbation. [appar. a freq. form connected with POKE² (bag). Cf. PURSE, v.]

puck·er·y (pŭk′ər ĭ), adj. 1. puckered. 2. puckering. 3. tending to pucker.

puck·ish (pŭk′ĭsh), adj. (*also cap.*) mischievous·impish.

pud·ding (pŏŏd′ĭng), n. a dish made in many forms and of various materials, as flour (or rice, tapioca, or the like), milk, and eggs, with fruit or other ingredients or seasoning, and commonly sweetened. [ME *puddyng*, *poding*; orig. uncert. Cf. LG *pudde-wurst* black pudding]

pudding stone, *Geol.* a conglomerate.

pud·dle (pŭd′əl), n., v. -dled, -dling. —n. 1. a small pool of water, esp. dirty water, as in a road after rain. 2. a small pool of any liquid. 3. clay, or a similar material, which has been mixed with water and tempered, used as a watertight canal lining, etc. —v.t. 4. to mark or fill with puddles. 5. to wet with dirty water, etc. 6. to make (water) muddy or dirty. 7. to muddle or confuse. 8. to make (clay, etc.) into puddle. 9. to cover with pasty clay or puddle. 10. to subject (molten iron) to the process of puddling. 11. to destroy the granular structure of (soil) by agricultural operations on it when it is too wet. [ME *puddel*, *podel*, appar. der. OE *pudd* ditch] —pud/dler, n. —pud/dly, adj.

pud·dling (pŭd′lĭng), n. 1. act of one who puddles. 2. the conversion of pig iron into wrought iron by heating and stirring the molten metal in a reverberatory furnace, with an oxidizing agent. 3. act or method of making puddle of clay or a similar material. 4. puddle (pasty clay, etc.).

pu·den·cy (pū′dən sĭ), n. shamefacedness; modesty. [t. LL: m. s. *pudentia*]

pu·den·dum (pū dĕn′dəm), n., pl. -da (-də). (*also pl.*) *Anat.* the external genital organs, esp. those of the female; the vulva. [t. L, prop. neut. ger., that about which one should have a feeling of modesty]

pudg·y (pŭj′ĭ), adj., pudgier, pudgiest. short and fat or thick. Also, *esp. Brit.*, podgy. [orig. obscure] —pudg/i·ly, adv. —pudg/i·ness, n.

Pue·bla (pwĕ′blä), n. 1. a state in S central Mexico. 1,702,115 pop. (est. 1952); 13,124 sq. mi. 2. the capital of this state. 211,285 (1950).

pueb·lo (pwĕb′lō; *also for* 3, 4, Sp. pwĕ′blō), n., pl. -los. 1. *U.S.* a. an apartment house village of certain Southwestern Indians: the communal house or group of houses, built of adobe or stone. b. (*cap.*) any sedentary, farming, peace-loving Indians of four linguistic groups (Tanoan, Keresan, Zuñi, Hopi) living prehistorically and now in pueblos in New Mexico and Arizona. 2. an Indian village. 3. *Spanish America.* a town or village. 4. *Philippine Islands.* a town or a township. [t. Sp.: people, g. L *populus*]

Pueb·lo (pwĕb′lō), n. a city in central Colorado. 91,181 (1960).

pu·er·ile (pū′ər ĭl; *Brit.* -ə rīl′), adj. 1. of or pertaining to a child or boy. 2. childishly foolish, irrational, or trivial: *a piece of puerile writing.* [t. L, neut. of *puerilis*] —pu/er·ile·ly, adv.

pu·er·il·ism (pū′ər ə lĭz′əm), n. *Psychoanal.* childishness (the stage following infantilism).

pu·er·il·i·ty (pū′ə rĭl′ə tĭ′), n., pl. -ties. 1. the quality of being puerile; childish foolishness or triviality. 2. something puerile; a puerile act, idea, remark, etc.: *an inexcusable puerility.*

pu·er·per·al (pū ûr′pər əl), adj. 1. of or pertaining to a woman in childbirth. 2. pertaining to or consequent on childbirth: *puerperal fever.* [t. NL: s. *puerperālis*, der. L *puerperus* bringing forth children]

puerperal fever, an infection occurring during the puerperium; childbed fever.

pu·er·pe·ri·um (pū′ər pĭr′ĭ əm), n. *Obstet.* the state of a woman at and just after childbirth. [t. L]

Puer·to Ca·bel·lo (pwĕr′tō kä bĕ′yō), a seaport in N Venezuela. 34,382 (1950).

Puer·to Ri·co (pwĕr′tō rē′kō; Sp. pwĕr′tō rē′kō), an island in the West Indies: a commonwealth associated with the U.S. 2,221,000 pop. (est. 1954); 3435 sq. mi. *Cap.:* San Juan. Former official name (until 1932), Porto Rico. —Puer/to Ri/can.

puff (pŭf), n. 1. a short, quick blast, as of wind or breath. 2. an abrupt emission of air, vapor, etc. 3. a whiff, as at a pipe. 4. the sound of an abrupt emission of air, etc. 5. a small quantity of vapor, smoke, etc., emitted at one blast. 6. an inflated or distended part of a thing; a swelling; a protuberance. 7. a commendation, esp. an exaggerated one, of a book, an actor's performance, etc. 8. inflated or exaggerated praise, esp. as uttered or written from interested motives: seller's talk. 9. a powder puff. 10. a form of light pastry with a filling of cream, jam, or the like. 11. a portion of material gathered and held down at the edges but left full in the middle, as in a dress, etc. 12. a

cylindrical roll of hair. **13.** a comforter, usually down-filled. **14.** *Dial.* a puffball. [ME; OE *pyff*]
—*v.i.* **15.** to blow with short, quick blasts, as the wind. **16.** to be emitted in a puff. **17.** to emit a puff or puffs; to breathe quick and hard, as after violent exertion. **18.** to go with puffing or panting. **19.** to emit puffs or whiffs of vapor or smoke. **20.** to move with such puffs. **21.** to take puffs at a cigar, etc. **22.** to become inflated or distended (usually fol. by *up*).
—*v.t.* **23.** to send forth (air, vapor, etc.) in short quick blasts. **24.** to drive or impel by puffing, or with a short quick blast. **25.** to blow or put (*out*) by a puff: *to puff out a light.* **26.** to smoke (a cigar, etc.). **27.** to inflate or distend, esp. with air. **28.** to inflate with pride, etc. **29.** to praise in exaggerated language. **30.** to advertise with exaggerated commendation. **31.** to apply powder to (the face, etc.) with a powder puff. **32.** to apply (powder) with a powder puff. **33.** to arrange in puffs, as the hair. [ME *puffen*, OE *pyffan*; of imit. orig]

puff adder, a large, venomous African snake, *Bitis arietans*, which puffs up its body when irritated.

puff·ball (pŭf′bôl′), *n.* any of various basidiomycetous fungi, esp. genus *Lycoperdon* and allied genera, characterized by a ball-like fruit body which emits a cloud of spores when broken.

puff·er (pŭf′ər), *n.* **1.** one who or that which puffs. **2.** any of various fishes of the family *Tetraodontidae*, capable of inflating the body with water or air until it resembles a globe, with the spines in the skin erected.

puff·er·y (pŭf′ər ĭ), *n.*, *pl. *-eries. **1.** act of praising unduly. **2.** exaggerated commendation.

puf·fin (pŭf′ĭn), *n.* any of various sea birds (genera *Fratercula* and *Lunda*) of the auk family, with a curious bill, as *F. arctica*, the common species, which abounds on both coasts of the northern Atlantic, nesting in holes in the ground. [ME *poffin*, *pophyn*; orig. uncert.]

puff·ing adder (pŭf′ĭng), hognose snake.

Common puffin,
Fratercula arctica
(13 in. long)

puff paste, a very light, flaky, rich paste for pies, tarts, etc.

puff·y (pŭf′ĭ), *adj.*, puffier, puffiest. **1.** gusty. **2.** short-winded. **3.** inflated or distended. **4.** fat. **5.** conceited. **6.** bombastic. —**puff′i·ness,** *n.*

pug[1] (pŭg), *n.* **1.** one of a breed of dogs, slightly resembling the bulldog, but much smaller. **2.** a pug nose. **3.** the fox. [orig. unknown]

pug[2] (pŭg), *v.t.*, pugged, pugging. **1.** to knead (clay, etc.) with water to make it plastic, as in brickmaking. **2.** to stop or fill in with clay or the like. **3.** to pack or cover with mortar, etc., to deaden sound. **4.** to mix with water, forming a paste. [orig. uncert.]

pug[3] (pŭg), *n.* *Slang.* pugilist. [short for PUGILIST]

pug[4] (pŭg), *n.*, *v.*, pugged, pugging. *Anglo-Indian.* —*n.* **1.** a footprint, as of an animal. —*v.i.* **2.** to track (game, etc.) by footprints. [t. Hind.: m. *pag*]

Puss[1] (def. 1)
(12 in. high at the shoulder)

pug·dog (pŭg′dôg′), *n.* pug[1].

Pu·get Sound (pū′jĭt), a long, irregularly-shaped arm of the Pacific in NW Washington.

pugh (pōō, pŏŏ), *interj.* an exclamation of contempt or disgust.

pu·gil·ism (pū′jə lĭz′əm), *n.* the art or practice of fighting with the fists; boxing. [f. L *pugil* boxer (akin to *pugnus* fist, and *pugnāre* fight) + -ISM]

pu·gil·ist (pū′jə lĭst), *n.* one who fights with the fists; a boxer, usually a professional. —**pu′gil·is′tic,** *adj.*

pug·na·cious (pŭg nā′shəs), *adj.* given to fighting; quarrelsome. [f. *pugnaci(ty)* (t. L: m.s. *pugnācitas* combativeness) + -OUS] —**pug·na′cious·ly,** *adv.* —**pug·nac·i·ty** (pŭg nǎs′ə tĭ), pug·na′cious·ness, *n.*

pug nose, a short nose turning abruptly up at the tip. —**pug-nosed** (pŭg′nōzd′), *adj.*

pug·ree (pŭg′rē), *n.* **1.** a light turban worn by natives in India. **2.** a scarf of silk or cotton wound round a hat or helmet and falling down behind, as a protection against the sun. [t. Hind.: m. *pagri* turban]

puis·ne (pū′nĭ), *adj.* **1.** *Law.* younger; inferior in rank; junior, as in appointment. —*n.* **2.** an associate judge as distinguished from a chief justice. [archaic form of *puny*, t. OF: f. *puis* after (g. var. of L *posteā*) + *ne* born, pp. of *naistre* come into existence (g. L *nascere*)]

puis·sance (pū′ə səns, pū ĭs′əns, pwĭs′əns), *n.* Archaic or Poetic. power, might, or force. [ME, t. OF, der. *puissant* PUISSANT]

puis·sant (pū′ə sənt, pū ĭs′ənt, pwĭs′ənt), *adj.* Archaic. powerful; mighty; potent. [ME, t. OF, ppr. of *pouvoir* be able, g. var. of L *potens*, ppr., being able, having power] —**pu′is·sant·ly,** *adv.*

puke (pūk), *v.i.*, *v.t.*, puked, puking, *n.* vomit. [orig. uncert.]

puk·ka (pŭk′ə), *adj.* Anglo-Indian. reliable; good. Also, pucka. [t. Hind.: m. *pakkā* cooked, ripe, mature]

Pu·la (pōō′lä), *n.* Yugoslavian name of **Pola.**

Pu·las·ki (pōō lǎs′kĭ, -kĭ, pə-; *Pol.* pōō lä′skĕ), *n.* **1.** Count Casimir (kăz′ə mĭr′), 1748–79, Polish patriot; general in the American Revolutionary army. **2.** Fort, a fort at the mouth of the Savannah river, in E Georgia: taken by Union forces, 1862.

pul·chri·tude (pŭl′krə tūd′, -tōōd′), *n.* beauty; comeliness. [ME, t. L: m. *pulchritūdo*]

pul·chri·tu·di·nous (pŭl′krə tū′də nəs, -tōō′-), *adj.* beautiful.

pule (pūl), *v.i.*, puled, puling. to cry in a thin voice, as a child; whimper; whine. [? of imit. orig.] —**pul′er,** *n.*

pul·ing (pū′lĭng), *adj.* whining: *a puling child.* —**pul′ing·ly,** *adv.*

Pu·litz·er (pū′lĭt sər, pŏŏl′ĭt sər), *n.* **Joseph,** 1847–1911, U.S. journalist and publisher, born in Hungary.

Pulitzer Prize, *U.S.* one of a group of annual prizes in journalism and letters established by Joseph Pulitzer.

pull (pŏŏl), *v.t.* **1.** to draw or haul toward oneself or itself, in a particular direction, or into a particular position: *to pull a sled up a hill.* **2.** to draw or tug at with force: *to pull a person's hair.* **3.** to draw, rend, or tear (apart, to pieces, etc.). **4.** to draw or pluck away from a place of growth, attachment, etc.: *to pull a tooth.* **5.** to strip of feathers, hair, etc., as a bird, a hide, etc. **6.** *Slang.* to draw out for use, as a knife or a pistol. **7.** *Slang.* to put or carry through (something attempted). **8.** *Slang.* to arrest (a person). **9.** *Golf.* to play (the ball) with a curve to the left (or, if a left-handed player, to the right). **10.** to bring (a horse) to a stand by pulling on the reins. **11.** *Print.* to take (an impression or proof) from type, etc. **12.** to be provided with, or rowed with (a certain number of oars), as a boat. **13.** to propel by rowing, as a boat. **14.** *Sports.* to strain, as a ligament. **15.** *Racing.* to hold in or check (a horse), esp. so as to keep it from winning. **16.** *Cricket.* to hit (a ball pitched on the wicket or on the off side) to the on side. —*v.i.* **17.** to exert a drawing, tugging, or hauling force (often fol. by *at*). **18.** to inhale through a pipe, cigarette, etc. **19.** to make the way or get (fol. by *in*, etc.) as by a pull or effort: *to pull through.* **20.** to become or come as specified, by pulling: *a rope pulls apart.* **21.** to row. **22.** to proceed by rowing. **23.** to move toward the front in a race or other contest.
—*n.* **24.** act of pulling or drawing. **25.** force used in pulling; pulling power. **26.** *Colloq.* a drawing of a liquid into the mouth; a drink. **27.** a part or thing to be pulled, as a handle or the like. **28.** an instrument or device for pulling something. **29.** a spell at rowing. **30.** a stroke of an oar. **31.** a pulling of the ball in cricket or golf. **32.** *Slang.* an advantage over another or others. **33.** *Slang.* influence, as with persons able to grant favors.
[ME *pulle*(n), OE *pullian* pull, pluck. Cf. MLG *pülen* strip off husks, pick, Icel. *pūla* work hard] —**pull′er,** *n.*
—Syn. 2. See **draw.** —Ant. 2. push.

pul·let (pŏŏl′ĭt), *n.* a young hen, less than one year old. [ME *poullet*, t. OF: m. *poulette* young hen, dim. of *poule* hen, g. LL *pulla* young animal, chicken]

pul·ley (pŏŏl′ĭ), *n.*, *pl. *-leys. **1.** a wheel with a grooved rim for carrying a line, turning in a frame or block and serving to change the direction of or transmit power, as in pulling at one end of the line to raise a weight at the other end. **2.** a combination of such wheels in a block, or of such wheels or blocks in a tackle, to increase the power applied. **3.** a wheel driven by or driving a belt or the like, as in the transmission of power. [ME, t. OF: m. *poulie*, ult. from a deriv. of Gk. *pólos* axle]

Pull·man (pŏŏl′mən), *n.*, *pl. *-mans. *Railroads.* a sleeping car or parlor car. Also, pull′man, Pullman car. [named after George M. *Pullman* (1831–97), the originator]

pul·lo·rum disease (pə lōr′əm), an egg-transmitted bacterial disease, frequently a cause of heavy death losses in very young poultry. [*pullorum*, gen. pl. of L *pullus* cockerel]

pull·o·ver (pŏŏl′ō′vər), *n.* a sweater which is drawn over the head when it is put on.

pul·lu·late (pŭl′yə lāt′), *v.i.*, -lated, -lating. **1.** to come forth in growth; sprout. **2.** to send forth sprouts, buds, etc. **3.** to spring up abundantly. **4.** to breed; multiply; teem. **5.** to be produced as offspring. [t. L: m. s. *pullulātus*, pp., sprouted] —**pul′lu·la′tion,** *n.*

pul·mo·nar·y (pŭl′mə nĕr′ĭ), *adj.* **1.** of or pertaining to the lungs. **2.** of the nature of a lung; lunglike. **3.** affecting the lungs. **4.** having lungs or lunglike organs. **5.** pertaining to or affected with disease of the lungs. [t. L: m.s. *pulmōnārius*, der. *pulmo* lung, akin to Gk. *pleúmōn*, later *pneúmōn* lung]

pulmonary artery, an artery conveying (venous) blood from the right ventricle of the heart to the lungs. See diag. under **heart.**

pulmonary vein, a vein conveying (arterial) blood from the lungs to the left auricle of the heart.

pul·mo·nate (pŭl′mə nāt′, -nĭt), *adj.* **1.** having lungs or lunglike organs. **2.** belonging to the *Pulmonata*, an order or group of gastropod mollusks usually breathing by means of a lunglike sac, and including most of the terrestrial snails and the slugs and certain aquatic snails. —*n.* **3.** a pulmonate gastropod. [t. NL: m.s. *pulmōnātus*, der. L *pulmo* lung]

pul·mon·ic (pŭl mŏn′ĭk), *adj.* **1.** pulmonary. **2.** pneumonic. [t. F: m. *pulmonique*, der. L *pulmo* lung]

---

b., blend of, blended; c., cognate with; d., dialect, dialectal; der., derived from; f., formed from; g., going back to; m., modification of; r., replacing; s., stem of; t., taken from; ?, perhaps.   See the full key on inside cover.

pul·mo·tor (pŭl′mō′tər, pŏŏl′-), *n.* **1.** a mechanical device for artificial respiration where respiration has ceased through asphyxiation, drowning, etc., which forces oxygen into the lungs. **2.** (*cap.*) a trademark for this device. [f. L *pul(mo)* lung + MOTOR]

pulp (pŭlp), *n.* **1.** the succulent part of a fruit. **2.** the pith of the stem of a plant. **3.** a soft or fleshy part of an animal body. **4.** the inner substance of the tooth containing arteries, veins, and lymphatic and nerve tissue which communicate with their respective vascular and lymph and nerve systems of the body. **5.** any soft, moist, slightly cohering mass, as that into which linen, wood, etc., are converted in the making of paper. **6.** a magazine printed on rough paper, usually devoted to sensational and lurid stories, articles, etc. **7.** *Mining.* **a.** ore pulverized and mixed with water. **b.** dry crushed ore. —*v.t.* **8.** to reduce to pulp. **9.** to remove the pulp from. —*v.i.* **10.** to become reduced to pulp. [t. L: s. *pulpa*]

pul·pit (pŏŏl′pĭt), *n.* **1.** a platform or raised structure in a church, from which the clergyman delivers the sermon or conducts the service. **2. the pulpit, a.** preachers collectively. **b.** the Christian ministry. **3.** preaching. [ME, t. L: s. *pulpitum* stage, platform, ML pulpit]

pul·pit·eer (pŏŏl′pĭ tēr′), *n.* a preacher by profession (usually contemptuous). Also, **pul·pit·er** (pŏŏl′pĭt ər).

pulp·wood (pŭlp′wŏŏd′), *n.* spruce or other soft wood suitable for making paper.

pulp·y (pŭl′pĭ), *adj.*, **pulpier, pulpiest.** of the nature of or resembling pulp; fleshy; soft. —**pulp′i·ness,** *n.*

pul·que (pŏŏl′kĭ; *Sp.* pōōl′kĕ), *n.* a fermented milkish drink made from the juice of certain species of agave in Mexico. [Mex. Sp.]

pul·sate (pŭl′sāt), *v.i.*, **-sated, -sating. 1.** to expand and contract rhythmically, as the heart; beat; throb. **2.** to vibrate; quiver. [t. L: m.s. *pulsātus*, pp., pushed, struck, beaten. See PULSE[1]]
—**Syn. 1.** PULSATE, BEAT, PALPITATE, THROB refer to the recurrent vibratory movement of the heart, the pulse, etc. To PULSATE is to move in a definite rhythm, temporarily or for a longer duration: *blood pulsates in the arteries.* To BEAT is to repeat a vibration or pulsation regularly for some time: *one's heart beats many times a minute.* To PALPITATE is to beat at a rapid rate, often producing a flutter: *to palpitate with excitement.* To THROB is to beat with so much force as often to cause pain: *to throb with terror.*

pul·sa·tile (pŭl′sə tĭl), *adj.* pulsating; throbbing.

pul·sa·tion (pŭl sā′shən), *n.* **1.** act of pulsating; beating or throbbing. **2.** a beat or throb, as of the pulse. **3.** vibration or undulation. **4.** a single vibration.

pul·sa·tive (pŭl′sə tĭv), *adj.* pulsating.

pul·sa·tor (pŭl sā′tər), *n.* **1.** something that pulsates, beats, or strikes. **2.** a pulsometer (def. 2). [t. L: striker]

pul·sa·to·ry (pŭl′sə tôr′ĭ), *adj.* pulsating; pulsatile.

pulse[1] (pŭls), *n., v.,* **pulsed, pulsing.** —*n.* **1.** the regular throbbing of the arteries caused by the successive contractions of the heart, esp. as felt in an artery at the wrist. **2.** a single beat or throb of the arteries or the heart. **3.** the rhythmic recurrence of strokes, vibrations, or undulations. **4.** a single stroke, vibration, or undulation. **5.** a throb of life, emotion, etc. **6.** vitality. **7.** feeling, sentiment, or tendency. —*v.i.* **8.** to beat or throb; pulsate. **9.** to beat, vibrate, or undulate. [t. L: m. *pulsus* a pushing, beating, pulse; r. ME *pous,* t. OF]

pulse[2] (pŭls), *n.* **1.** the edible seeds of certain leguminous plants, as peas, beans, lentils, etc. **2.** a plant producing such seeds. [ME *puls,* t. OF: m. *po(u)ls,* g. L *puls* thick pap of meal, pulse, etc. Cf. POULTICE]

pulse-time modulation, *Electronics.* radio transmission in which the carrier is modulated to produce a series of pulses timed to transmit amplitude and pitch of the signal.

pul·sim·e·ter (pŭl sĭm′ə tər), *n.* an instrument for measuring the strength or quickness of the pulse. [f. *pulsi-* (comb. form repr. PULSE[1]) + -METER]

pul·som·e·ter (pŭl sŏm′ə tər), *n.* **1.** a pulsimeter. **2.** a vacuum pump. [f. *pulso-* (comb. form repr. PULSE[1]) + -METER]

pul·ver·a·ble (pŭl′vər ə bəl), *adj.* pulverizable.

pul·ver·ize (pŭl′və rīz′), *v.,* **-ized, -izing.** —*v.t.* **1.** to reduce to dust or powder, as by pounding, grinding, etc. **2.** to demolish. —*v.i.* **3.** to become reduced to dust. Also, *esp. Brit.,* **pul′ver·ise′.** [ME, t. LL: m.s. *pulverizāre,* der. L *pulvis* dust] —**pul′ver·iz·a·ble,** *adj.* —**pul′ver·i·za′tion,** *n.* —**pul′ver·iz′er,** *n.*

pul·ver·u·lent (pŭl vĕr′yə lənt, -ə lənt), *adj.* **1.** consisting of dust or fine powder. **2.** crumbling to dust. **3.** covered with dust or powder. [t. L: s. *pulverulentus* dusty]

pul·vil·lus (pŭl vĭl′əs), *n., pl.* **-villi** (-vĭl′ī). *Entom.* a cushionlike pad or process on insect's foot. [t. L, dim. of *pulvīnus* cushion]

pul·vi·nate (pŭl′və nāt), *adj.* **1.** cushion-shaped. **2.** having a pulvinus. Also, **pul′vi·nat′ed.** [t. L: m.s. *pulvīnātus* made into or like a cushion]

pul·vi·nus (pŭl vī′nəs), *n., pl.* **-ni** (-nī). *Bot.* a cushionlike swelling at the base of a leaf or leaflet, at the point of junction with the axis. [t. L: cushion]

pu·ma (pyōō′mə), *n.* **1.** the cougar. **2.** its fur. [t. Sp., t. Kechua]

pum·ice (pŭm′ĭs), *n., v.,* **-iced, -icing.** —*n.* **1.** Also, **pumice stone.** a porous or spongy form of volcanic glass, used, esp. when powdered, as an abrasive, etc. —*v.t.* **2.** to rub, smooth, clean, etc., with pumice. [ME *pomis,* t. OF, g. s. L *pūmex;* r. OE *pumic(stān)* pumice (stone), from L] —**pu·mi·ceous** (pyōō mĭsh′əs), *adj.*

pum·mel (pŭm′əl), *n., v.t.,* **-meled, -meling** or (*esp. Brit.*) **-melled, -melling.** pommel.

pump[1] (pŭmp), *n.* **1.** an apparatus or machine for raising, driving, exhausting, or compressing fluids, as by means of a piston, plunger, or rotating vanes. —*v.t.* **2.** to raise, drive, etc., with a pump. **3.** to free from water, etc., by means of a pump. **4.** to inflate by pumping (often fol by *up*): *to pump up a tire.* **5.** to operate by action like that on a pump handle. **6.** to supply with air, as an organ, by means of a pumplike device. **7.** to drive, force, etc., as if from a pump: *they pumped ten bullets into him.* **8.** to subject to a process likened to pumping, in order to extract something: *to pump one's brains for ideas.* **9.** to seek to elicit information from, as by artful questioning. **10.** to elicit (information) by questioning. —*v.i.* **11.** to work a pump; raise or move water, etc., with a pump. **12.** to operate as a pump does. **13.** to move up and down like a pump handle. **14.** to exert oneself in a manner likened to pumping. **15.** to seek to elicit information from a person. [ME *pumpe,* c. G *pumpe;* orig. uncert.] —**pump′er,** *n.* —**pump′like′,** *adj.*

pump[2] (pŭmp), *n.* a light, low slipperlike shoe worn by men and women, orig. for dancing. [orig. uncert.]

pum·per·nick·el (pŭm′pər nĭk′əl; *Ger.* pōōm′-), *n.* a coarse, slightly sour bread made of unbolted rye. [t. G]

pump gun, *Hunting.* a repeating shotgun, operated by sliding a handle back and forth along the magazine.

pump·kin (pŭmp′kĭn, pŭng′kĭn), *n.* **1.** a large orange-yellow fruit borne by a coarse, decumbent vine, *Cucurbita Pepo,* much used for making pies and as food for cattle. **2.** the vine. **3.** certain varieties of *Cucurbita Pepo.* [alter. of *pumpion,* t. F: m. *pompon* a melon, ult. der. L *pepo,* t. Gk.: m. *pēpōn*]

pump·kin-seed (pŭmp′kĭn sēd′, pŭng′kĭn-), *n.* **1.** the seed of the pumpkin. **2.** a fresh-water sunfish, *Lepomis gibbosus,* of eastern North America.

pump·well (pŭmp′wĕl), *n.* a well having a pump.

pun (pŭn), *n., v.,* **punned, punning.** —*n.* **1.** the humorous use of a word in such a manner as to bring out different meanings or applications, or of words alike or nearly alike in sound but different in meaning; a play on words. —*v.i.* **2.** to make puns. [orig. uncert.]

pu·na (pōō′nä), *n.* **1.** a high, cold, arid plateau, as in the Peruvian Andes. **2.** *South Amer.* mountain sickness. [t. Peruvian]

punch[1] (pŭnch), *n.* **1.** a thrusting blow, esp. with the fist. **2.** *Slang.* a vigorous, telling effect or force. —*v.t.* **3.** to give a sharp thrust or blow to, esp. with the fist. **4.** *Western U.S.* to drive (cattle). **5.** to poke or prod, as with a stick. [? var. of POUNCE] —**punch′er,** *n.*

punch[2] (pŭnch), *n.* **1.** a tool or apparatus for piercing, perforating, or stamping materials, impressing a design, forcing nails beneath a surface, driving bolts out of holes, etc. **2.** the solid tool used in a punch press in conjunction with a corresponding hollow die for blanking out shaped pieces of sheet metal; the upper die. —*v.t.* **3.** to cut, stamp, pierce, form, or drive with a punch (tool). [short for PUNCHEON[2] (def. 3)]

punch[3] (pŭnch), *n.* **1.** a beverage consisting of wine or spirits mixed with water, milk, etc., and flavored with sugar, lemon, spices, etc. **2.** a beverage of two or more fruit juices, sugar and water, often carbonated. [? short for PUNCHEON[1]; if so, a metonymic use]

Punch (pŭnch), *n.* **1.** the chief character in the puppet show called "Punch and Judy," a grotesque, hook-nosed, humpbacked figure who strangles his child, beats his wife (Judy) to death, etc. **2. pleased as Punch,** delighted; highly pleased. [short for PUNCHINELLO]

punch bowl, a bowl in which punch is mixed, and from which it is served by means of a ladle.

punch-drunk (pŭnch′drŭngk′), *adj.* having cerebral concussion so that one's movements resemble those of a drunken person, a condition sometimes found in boxers.

pun·cheon[1] (pŭn′chən), *n.* **1.** a large cask of varying capacity, but usually 111.6 gals. **2.** its volume as a measure. [t. F, ult. identical with PUNCHEON[2]]

pun·cheon[2] (pŭn′chən), *n.* **1.** a slab of timber, or a piece of a split log, with the face roughly dressed, used for flooring, etc. **2.** a short upright timber in a framing. **3.** (in goldsmith work) **a.** any of various pointed instruments; a punch. **b.** a stamping tool. [ME *punchon,* t. OF: m. *po(i)nchon,* ult. der. L *punctus,* pp., pricked, pierced. Cf. PUNGENT]

pun·chi·nel·lo (pŭn′chə nĕl′ō), *n., pl.* **-los, -loes. 1.** the chief character in a puppet show of Italian origin, being the prototype of Punch. **2.** any similar grotesque or absurd person or thing. [It.: m. *Pulcinella,* prob. orig. dim. of *pulcino* chicken, ult. der. L *pullus* young animal]

punching bag, an inflated or stuffed bag, usually suspended, punched with the fists as an exercise.

punch press, *Mach.* a power-driven machine used to cut, draw, or otherwise shape material, esp. metal sheets, with dies, under pressure or by heavy blows.

punc·tate (pŭngk′tāt), *adj.* marked with points or dots; having minute spots or depressions. Also, **punc′-tat·ed.** [t. NL: m.s. *punctātus,* der. L *punctum* point]

punc·ta·tion (pŭngk tā′shən), *n.* **1.** punctate condition or marking. **2.** one of the marks or depressions.

punc·til·i·o (pŭngk tĭl′ĭ ō′), *n., pl.* **-tilios. 1.** a fine point, particular, or detail, as of conduct, ceremony, or procedure. **2.** strictness or exactness in the observance of forms. [t. It.: m. *puntiglio*, t. Sp.: m. *puntillo*, dim. of *punto* point, t. L: m. *punctum*]

punc·til·i·ous (pŭngk tĭl′ĭ əs), *adj.* attentive to punctilios; strict or exact in the observance of forms in conduct or actions. —**punc·til′i·ous·ly**, *adv.* —**punc·til′i·ous·ness**, *n.* —Syn. See **scrupulous.**

punc·tu·al (pŭngk′chŏŏ əl), *adj.* **1.** strictly observant of an appointed or regular time; not late. **2.** prompt, as an action: *punctual payment.* **3.** of or pertaining to a point: *punctual coördinates* (the coördinates of a point). **4.** *Obs.* punctilious. [ME, t. ML: s. *punctuālis*, der. L *punctus* a pricking, a point] —**punc′tu·al·ly**, *adv.* —**punc′tu·al·ness**, *n.*

punc·tu·al·i·ty (pŭngk′chŏŏ ăl′ə tĭ), *n.* **1.** the quality or state of being punctual. **2.** strict observance in keeping engagements, etc.; promptness.

punc·tu·ate (pŭngk′chŏŏ āt′), *v.*, **-ated, -ating.** —*v.t.* **1.** to mark or divide with punctuation marks, as a sentence, etc., in order to make the meaning clear. **2.** to interrupt at intervals, as a speech by cheers. **3.** to give point or emphasis to. —*v.i.* **4.** to insert or use marks of punctuation. [t. ML: m.s. *punctuātus*, pp., pointed, der. L *punctus* a point] —**punc′tu·a′tor**, *n.*

punc·tu·a·tion (pŭngk′chŏŏ ā′shən), *n.* **1.** the practice, art, or system of inserting marks or points in writing or printing in order to make the meaning clear; the punctuating of written or printed matter with commas, semicolons, colons, periods, etc. (**punctuation marks**). **2.** act of punctuating.

punc·ture (pŭngk′chər), *n., v.,* **-tured, -turing.** —*n.* **1.** act of pricking or perforating as with a pointed instrument or object. **2.** a mark or hole so made. **3.** *Zool.* a small pointlike depression. —*v.t.* **4.** to prick, pierce, or perforate: *to puncture the skin with a pin.* **5.** to make (a hole, etc.) by pricking or perforating. **6.** *Colloq.* to make a puncture in: *to puncture a tire.* —*v.i.* **7.** to admit of being punctured. [t. L: m. *punctūra*] —**punc′tur·a·ble**, *adj.*

pun·dit (pŭn′dĭt), *n.* **1.** a Hindu scholar or learned man. **2.** a learned man. [t. Hind.: m. *pandit*, g. Skt. *pandita* learned man, as adj., learned]

pung (pŭng), *n.* *U.S. Dial.* a sleigh with a boxlike body on runners. [short for *tom-pung*, alter. of TOBOGGAN, of N Amer. Ind. orig. (cf. Montagnais *utápŏn* and Abnaki *udabagan* what is used for dragging)]

pun·gent (pŭn′jənt), *adj.* **1.** sharply affecting the organs of taste, as if by a penetrating power; biting; acrid. **2.** acutely distressing to the feelings or mind; poignant. **3.** caustic, biting, or sharply expressive, as speech, etc. **4.** mentally stimulating or appealing. **5.** *Biol.* piercing or sharp-pointed. [t. L: s. *pungens*, ppr., pricking. Cf. POIGNANT, POINT, PUNCHEON[2], etc.] —**pun′gen·cy**, *n.* —**pun′gent·ly**, *adv.*

Pu·nic (pū′nĭk), *adj.* **1.** of or pertaining to the ancient Carthaginians. **2.** (in the Roman view of the Carthaginians) treacherous; perfidious. —*n.* **3.** the language of ancient Carthage, a form of late Phoenician. [t. L: s. *Pūnicus*, earlier *Poenicus* Carthaginian, prop. Phoenician, t. Gk.: m. *Phoînix*]

Punic Wars, the three wars waged by Rome against Carthage, 264–241, 218–201, and 149–146 B.C., resulting in the overthrow and annexation of Carthage to Rome.

pun·ish (pŭn′ĭsh), *v.t.* **1.** to subject to a penalty, or to pain, loss, confinement, death, etc., for some offense, transgression, or fault: *to punish a criminal.* **2.** to inflict a penalty for (an offense, fault, etc.): *to punish theft.* **3.** *Colloq.* to handle severely or roughly, as in a fight. **4.** *Colloq.* to put to painful exertion, as a horse in racing. **5.** *Colloq.* to make a heavy inroad on (a supply, etc.). —*v.i.* **6.** to inflict punishment. [ME *punische(n)*, t. OF: m. *puniss-*, s. *punir*, g. L *pūnīre*] —**pun′ish·er**, *n.* —Syn. **1.** PUNISH, CORRECT, DISCIPLINE refer to making evident, by penalties, public or private disapproval of violations of law, wrongdoing, or refusal to obey rules or regulations. To PUNISH is chiefly to inflict penalty or pain as a retribution for misdeeds, with little or no expectation of correction or improvement: *to punish a thief.* To CORRECT is to reprove or inflict punishment for faults, specifically with the idea of bringing about improvement: *to correct a rebellious child.* To DISCIPLINE is to give a kind of punishment which will educate or will establish useful habits: *to discipline a careless driver.* —Ant. **1.** reward.

pun·ish·a·ble (pŭn′ĭsh ə bəl), *adj.* liable to or deserving of punishment. —**pun′ish·a·bil′i·ty**, *n.*

pun·ish·ment (pŭn′ĭsh mənt), *n.* **1.** act of punishing. **2.** fact of being punished, as for an offense or fault. **3.** that which is inflicted as a penalty in punishing. **4.** *Colloq.* severe handling or treatment.

pu·ni·tive (pū′nə tĭv), *adj.* serving for, concerned with, or inflicting punishment: *punitive laws.* Also, **pu·ni·to·ry** (pū′nə tôr′ĭ).

Pun·jab (pŭn jäb′, pŭn′jäb), *n.* a former province in NW India: now divided between Punjab (in India) and West Punjab (in Pakistan). **2.** a state in NW India. 16,000,000 pop. (est. 1956); 47,456 sq. mi. *Cap.* Chandigarh.

Pun·ja·bi (pŭn jä′bĭ), *n.* **1.** a native of Punjab, India. **2.** Panjabi. [t. Hind.: m. *Panjābī*]

Punjab States, a former group of states in NW India; amalgamated with Punjab state (in India) in 1956.

punk (pŭngk), *n.* **1.** a preparation that will smolder, used in sticks, as for lighting fireworks. **2.** decayed wood used as tinder. —*adj.* **3.** *U.S. Slang.* poor or bad in quality. [orig. uncert. Cf. Lenape *punk* living ashes, Shawnee *pekwi* ashes, Ojibwa *pinkoš* sand fly]

pun·kah (pŭng′kə), *n.* *East Indies.* a fan, esp. a large, swinging, screenlike fan hung from the ceiling and kept in motion by a servant or by machinery. Also, **pun′ka.** [t. Hind.: m. *pankhā* a fan, g. Skt. *pakshaka*]

punk·ie (pŭng′kĭ), *n.* a very minute biting gnat. [f. obs. *ponk* kind of insect (lit., ashes. See PUNK) + -IE]

pun·ster (pŭn′stər), *n.* one given to making puns.

punt[1] (pŭnt), *n.* **1.** *Football.* a kick given to a dropped ball before it touches the ground. **2.** *Brit.* a shallow, flat-bottomed, square-ended boat, usually propelled by thrusting with a pole against the bottom. —*v.t.* **3.** *Football.* to kick (a dropped ball) before it touches the ground. **4.** to propel (a punt or other boat) by thrusting with a pole against the bottom. **5.** to convey (a person, etc.) in, or as in, a punt. —*v.i.* **6.** to punt a football. **7.** *Brit.* to propel, or travel in, a punt. [OE *punt*, t. L: m. *ponto* punt, PONTOON] —**punt′er**, *n.*

punt[2] (pŭnt), *v.i.* **1.** to lay a stake against the bank, as at faro. —*n.* **2.** one who lays such a stake. [t. F: m.s. *ponter*, der. *ponte* punter, t. Sp.: m. *punto* point, t. L: m. *punctum*] —**punt′er**, *n.*

Pun·ta A·re·nas (pŏŏn′tä ä rě′näs), a seaport in S Chile, on the Strait of Magellan: the southernmost city in the world. 48,000 (est. 1954). Also, **Magallanes.**

pun·ty (pŭn′tĭ), *n., pl.* **-ties.** an iron rod used in glassmaking for handling the hot glass. Also, **pontil.** [t. It.: m. *ponte* bridge]

pu·ny (pū′nĭ), *adj.,* **-nier, -niest. 1.** of less than normal size and strength; weakly. **2.** petty; insignificant. **3.** *Obs.* puisne. [var. of PUISNE]

pup (pŭp), *n., v.,* **pupped, pupping.** —*n.* **1.** a young dog, under one year; a puppy. **2.** a young seal. —*v.i.* **3.** to bring forth pups. [apocopated var. of PUPPY]

pu·pa (pū′pə), *n., pl.* **-pae** (-pē), **-pas.** an insect in the nonfeeding, usually immobile, transformation stage between the larva and the imago. [NL, in L girl, doll, puppet. Cf. PUPIL, PUPPET] —**pu′pal**, *adj.*

pu·par·i·um (pū pâr′ĭ əm), *n.* *Entomol.* a pupal case formed of the cuticula of a preceding larval instar. [NL: f. *pupa* PUPA + -*ārium*; modeled on HERBARIUM]

pu·pate (pū′pāt), *v.i.,* **-pated, -pating.** to become a pupa. —**pu·pa′tion**, *n.*

pu·pil[1] (pū′pəl), *n.* **1.** one who is under an instructor or teacher; a student. **2.** *Civil Law.* a person under twenty-five (under puberty, in Roman law), orphaned or emancipated, and under the care of a guardian. [ME *pupille*, t. OF, t. L: m. *pūpillus* (masc.) *pūpilla* (fem.) orphan, ward, dims. of *pūpus* boy, *pūpa* girl] —Syn. **1.** PUPIL, DISCIPLE, SCHOLAR, STUDENT refer to one who is studying, usually in a school. A PUPIL is one under the close supervision of a teacher, either because of his youth or of specialization in some branch of study: *a grade-school pupil, the pupil of a famous musician.* A DISCIPLE is one who follows the teachings or doctrines of a person whom he considers to be a master or authority: *a disciple of Swedenborg.* SCHOLAR, once meaning the same as PUPIL, is today usually applied to one who has acquired wide erudition in some field of learning: *a great Latin scholar.* A STUDENT is one attending a higher institution of learning, or one who has devoted much attention to a particular problem: *a college student, a student of politics.*

pu·pil[2] (pū′pəl), *n.* *Anat.* the expanding and contracting opening in the iris of the eye, through which light passes to the retina. [t. L: m.s. *pūpilla*, lit., little doll. See PUPA]

pu·pil·age (pū′pə lĭj), *n.* the state or period of being a pupil.

pu·pil·lar·i·ty (pū′pə lăr′ə tĭ), *n.* *Civil and Sc. Law.* the period between birth and puberty, or until attaining majority. Also, **pu/pi·lar/i·ty.**

pu·pil·lar·y[1] (pū′pə lĕr′ĭ), *adj.* pertaining to a pupil or student. [t. L: m. *pūpillāris*]

pu·pil·lar·y[2] (pū′pə lĕr′ĭ), *adj. Anat.* pertaining to the pupil of the eye. [f. s. L *pūpilla* PUPIL[2] + -ARY[1]]

Pu·pin (pū pēn′; *Hung.* pōō′pēn), *n.* **Michael Idvorsky** (ĭd vôr′skĭ), 1858–1935, U.S. physicist, born in Hungary of Serbian parents.

pu·pip·a·rous (pū pĭp′ə rəs), *adj.* **1.** bringing forth pupae. **2.** of or belonging to the *Pupipara*, a division of dipterous insects, including the sheep tick, etc., in which the young are born ready to become pupae. [t. NL: m. *pūpiparus*, f. *pūpi-* PUPA + -*parus* -PAROUS]

pup·pet (pŭp′ĭt), *n.* **1.** a doll. **2.** an artificial figure with jointed limbs, moved by wires, etc., on a miniature stage; a marionette. **3.** a person whose actions are prompted and controlled by another or others. [earlier *poppet*, ME *popet*, appar. der. MLG *poppe* doll, of Rom. orig.; cf. LL *puppa*]

pup·pet·ry (pŭp′ĭt rĭ), *n., pl.* **-ries. 1.** the art of making puppets perform. **2.** the action of puppets. **3.** mummery; mere show. **4.** puppets collectively.

pup·py (pŭp′ĭ), *n., pl.* **-pies. 1.** a young dog. **2.** the young of certain other animals, as the shark. **3.** a presuming, conceited, or empty-headed young man. [f. m. *poupée* doll, ult. der. LL *puppa*. See PUPPET]

pur (pûr), *v.i., v.t.,* purred, purring, *n.* purr.

pur·blind (pûr′blīnd′), *adj.* **1.** nearly blind; partially blind; dim-sighted. **2.** dull in discernment or understanding. **3.** *Obs.* totally blind. [ME *pur blind* completely blind. See PURE, formerly used as adv., entirely] —**pur′blind′ly,** *adv.* —**pur′blind′ness,** *n.* —**Syn. 2.** See **blind.**

Pur·cell (pûr′səl), *n.* **Henry,** 1658?–95, British composer.

pur·chas·a·ble (pûr′chəs ə bəl), *adj.* **1.** capable of being bought. **2.** that may be won over by bribery; venal. —**pur′chas·a·bil′i·ty,** *n.*

pur·chase (pûr′chəs), *v.,* **-chased, -chasing,** *n.* —*v.t.* **1.** to acquire by the payment of money or its equivalent; buy. **2.** to acquire by effort, sacrifice, flattery, etc. **3.** to win over by a bribe. **4.** (of things) to be sufficient to buy. **5.** *Law.* to acquire, as an estate in lands, otherwise than by inheritance. **6.** to haul, draw, or raise, esp. by the aid of a mechanical power. **7.** to get a leverage on. **8.** to apply a purchase to. **9.** *Obs.* to procure, acquire, or obtain. —*n.* **10.** acquisition by the payment of money or its equivalent; buying, or a single act of buying. **11.** something which is purchased or bought. **12.** a (good, bad, etc.) bargain. **13.** *Law.* the acquisition of an estate in lands, etc., otherwise than by inheritance. **14.** acquisition by means of effort, labor, etc. **15.** a means of increasing power or influence. **16.** the annual return or rent from land. **17.** a tackle or lever to multiply power. **18.** leverage. **19.** *Obs.* booty. [ME, t. AF: m. *purchacer* seek to obtain, procure, f. *pur-* PRO-¹ + *chacer* CHASE] —**pur′chas·er,** *n.* —**Syn. 1.** See **buy.** —**Ant. 1.** sell.

pur·dah (pûr′də), *n.* *India, etc.* **1.** a screen hiding women from the sight of men or strangers. **2.** the system of such seclusion. [t. Hind. (Urdū): curtain, t. Pers.: m. *pardah*]

pure (pyŏŏr), *adj.,* **purer, purest. 1.** free from extraneous matter, or from mixture with anything of a different, inferior, or contaminating kind: *pure gold.* **2.** unmodified by an admixture; simple or homogeneous: *a pure color.* **3.** of unmixed descent. **4.** free from foreign or inappropriate elements: *pure Attic Greek.* **5.** (of language) idiomatic, and unmixed with foreign elements. **6.** (of literary style) straightforward; unaffected. **7.** abstract or theoretical (opposed to *applied*): *pure science.* **8.** without discordant quality, or clear and true, as musical tones, etc. **9.** *Phonet.* monophthongal. **10.** unqualified, absolute, utter, or sheer: *pure ignornace.* **11.** being that and nothing else; mere: *a pure accident.* **12.** clean, spotless, or unsullied: *pure hands.* **13.** untainted with evil; innocent; chaste: *pure in heart.* **14.** ceremonially clean. **15.** free or without guilt (fol. by *from*). **16.** guiltless (fol. by *of*). **17.** independent of sense or experience: *pure knowledge.* **18.** *Biol., Genetics.* **a.** homozygous. **b.** containing but one characteristic for a trait. [ME *pur,* t. OF, g. L *pūrus* clean, unmixed, plain, pure] —**pure′ness,** *n.* —**Syn. 1.** unmixed, unadulterated, unalloyed. See **clean. 4.** genuine, faultless. **13.** virtuous, undefiled.

pure·bred (pyŏŏr′brĕd′), *adj.* **1.** noting an animal the ancestors of which are all of the same standard breed. **2.** of such an animal.

pure culture, a nutrient medium and a single bacterial or other species cultivated on it.

pu·rée (pyŏŏ rā′, pyŏŏr′ā; *Fr.* py rĕ′), *n.* a cooked and sieved vegetable or fruit used for soups or other foods. [t. F, der. *purer* strain, der. *pur* PURE]

pure line, *Genetics.* a uniform strain of organisms which is relatively pure genetically because of continued inbreeding coupled with selection.

pure·ly (pyŏŏr′lĭ), *adv.* **1.** in a pure manner; without admixture. **2.** merely; entirely: *purely accidental.* **3.** exclusively. **4.** cleanly; innocently; chastely.

pur·fle (pûr′fəl), *v.,* **-fled, -fling,** *n.* —*v.t.* **1.** to finish with an ornamental border. —*n.* **2.** Also, **pur′fling,** an ornamental border. [ME *purfile(n),* t. OF: m. *porfiler,* f. *por-* PRO-¹ + *filer* spin, der. *fil* thread, g. L *filum*]

pur·ga·tion (pûr gā′shən), *n.* the act of purging.

pur·ga·tive (pûr′gə tĭv), *adj.* **1.** purging; cleansing; specif., causing evacuation of the bowels. —*n.* **2.** a purgative medicine or agent. [ME, t. LL: m.s. *purgātīvus,* pp., cleansed] —**pur′ga·tive·ly,** *adv.*

pur·ga·to·ri·al (pûr′gə tōr′ĭ əl), *adj.* **1.** removing sin; purifying. **2.** of, pertaining to, or like purgatory.

pur·ga·to·ry (pûr′gə tōr′ĭ), *n., pl.* **-ries,** *adj.* —*n.* **1.** (in the belief of Roman Catholics and others) a condition or place in which the souls of those dying penitent are purified from venial sins, or undergo the temporal punishment which, after the guilt of mortal sin has been remitted, still remains to be endured by the sinner. **2.** any condition, situation, or place of temporary suffering, expiation, or the like. —*adj.* **3.** serving to purge, cleanse, or purify; expiatory. [ME *purgatorye,* t. LL: m. *purgātōrius,* adj., der. *purgāre* cleanse]

purge (pûrj), *v.,* **purged, purging,** *n.* —*v.t.* **1.** to cleanse; rid of whatever is impure or undesirable; purify. **2.** to rid or clear (fol. by *of*) or free (fol. by *from*): *to purge a party of undesirable members.* **3.** to clear (a person, etc.) of imputed guilt. **4.** to clear away or wipe out legally (an offense, accusation, etc.) by atonement or other suitable action. **5.** to remove by cleansing or purifying (often fol. by *away, off,* or *out*). **6.** to clear or empty (the bowels, etc.) by causing evacuation. **7.** to cause evacuation of the bowels of (a person). —*v.i.* **8.** to become cleansed or purified. **9.** to undergo or cause purging of the bowels. —*n.* **10.** act or a process of purging. **11.** something that purges, as a purgative medicine or dose. [ME, t. OF: m. *purgier,* g. L *purgāre* cleanse] —**purg′er,** *n.*

Pu·ri (pōō′rē, pōō rē′), *n.* a seaport in E India, on the Bay of Bengal: a place of pilgrimage (temple of Krishna). 49,057 (1951). See **Juggernaut** (def. 1 b).

pu·ri·fy (pyŏŏr′ə fī′), *v.,* **-fied, -fying.** —*v.t.* **1.** to make pure; free from extraneous matter, or from anything that debases, pollutes, or contaminates: *to purify metals.* **2.** to free from foreign or objectionable elements: *to purify a language.* **3.** to free from whatever is evil or base. **4.** to clear or purge (fol. by *of* or *from*). **5.** to make ceremonially clean. Lev. 12:4. —*v.i.* **6.** to become pure. [ME *puryfie(n),* t. OF: m. *purifier,* t. L: m. *pūrificāre*] —**pu′ri·fi·ca′tion,** *n.* —**pu·rif·i·ca·to·ry** (pyŏŏ rĭf′ə kə tōr′ĭ), *adj.* —**pu′ri·fi′er,** *n.*

Pu·rim (pyŏŏr′ĭm, pŏŏr′ĭm; *Heb.* pōō rēm′), *n.* Jewish festival, observed in February or March, in commemoration of the deliverance of the Jews from the massacre planned by Haman. Esther 9. [t. Heb., pl. of *pūr,* said to mean lot]

pu·rine (pyŏŏr′ēn, -ĭn), *n.* *Chem.* a white crystalline compound, $C_5H_4N_4$, regarded as the parent substance of a group of compounds including uric acid, xanthine, caffeine, etc. Also, **pu·rin** (pyŏŏr′ĭn). [b. PURE and URINE, modeled on G *purin*]

pur·ism (pyŏŏr′ĭz əm), *n.* **1.** scrupulous or excessive observance of or insistence on purity in language, style, etc. **2.** an instance of this. [f. PURE + -ISM] —**pur′ist,** *n.* —**pu·ris′tic,** *adj.*

Pu·ri·tan (pyŏŏr′ə tən), *n.* **1.** one of a class of Protestants who arose in the 16th century within the Church of England, demanding further reforms in doctrine and worship, and greater strictness in religious discipline, and during part of the 17th century constituting a powerful political party. **2.** (*l.c.*) one who affects great purity or strictness of life and religious principles. —*adj.* **3.** of or pertaining to the Puritans or (*l.c.*) puritans. [f. LL *pūrit(as)* purity + -AN]

pu·ri·tan·i·cal (pyŏŏr′ə tăn′ə kəl), *adj.* **1.** having the character of a puritan; excessively strict, rigid, or austere. **2.** of, pertaining to, or characteristic of puritans or (*cap.*) the Puritans. Also, **pu′ri·tan′ic.** —**pu′ri·tan′i·cal·ly,** *adv.* —**pu′ri·tan′i·cal·ness,** *n.*

Pu·ri·tan·ism (pyŏŏr′ə tə nĭz′əm), *n.* **1.** the principles and practices of the Puritans. **2.** (*l.c.*) strictness in matters of conduct or religion; puritanical austerity.

pu·ri·ty (pyŏŏr′ə tĭ), *n.* **1.** the condition or quality of being pure; freedom from extraneous matter or from anything that debases or contaminates: *the purity of drinking water.* **2.** freedom from any admixture or modifying addition. **3.** freedom from foreign or inappropriate elements; careful correctness: *purity of language.* **4.** (of color) chroma; saturation; degree of freedom from white. **5.** cleanness or spotlessness, as of garments. **6.** ceremonial cleanness. **7.** freedom from evil or guilt; innocence; chastity. [t. L: m.s. *pūritas;* r. ME *pur(e)te,* t. OF]

purl¹ (pûrl), *v.i.* **1.** to flow with curling or rippling motions, as a shallow stream does over stones. **2.** to flow with a murmuring sound. **3.** to pass in a manner or with a sound likened to this. —*n.* **4.** the action or sound of purling. **5.** a circle or curl made by the motion of water; a ripple; eddy. [cf. Norw. *purla* bubble up, gush]

purl² (pûrl), *v.t.* **1.** to knit with inversion of the stitch. **2.** to finish with loops or a looped edging. —*n.* **3.** a stitch used in hand knitting to make a rib effect. **4.** one of a series of small loops along the edge of lace braid. **5.** thread made of twisted gold or silver wire. Also, **pearl.** [orig. uncert. Cf. obs. or prov. *pirl* twist (threads, etc.) into a cord]

pur·lieu (pûr′lōō), *n.* **1.** a piece of land on the border of a forest. **2.** any bordering, neighboring, or outlying region or district. **3.** *Eng.* a piece of land which, after having been included in a royal forest, was restored to private ownership, though still subject, in some respects, to the operation of the forest laws. **4.** (*pl.*) neighborhood. **5.** a place where one may range at large; one's bounds. **6.** one's haunt or resort. [alter. (simulating F *lieu* place) of earlier *purlewe, purley, puraley* purlieu of a forest, t. AF: m. *purale(e)* a going through.]

pur·lin (pûr′lĭn), *n.* a timber or piece laid horizontally on the principal rafters of a roof to support the common rafters. Also, **pur′line.** [orig. uncert.]

pur·loin (pər loin′), *v.t.* **1.** to take dishonestly or steal. —*v.i.* **2.** to commit theft. [ME *purloyne(n),* t. AF: m. *purloigner* put off, remove, der. *pur-* PRO-¹ + *loin* far off (g. L *longē*)] —**pur·loin′er,** *n.*

pur·ple (pûr′pəl), *n., adj., v.,* **-pled, -pling.** —*n.* **1.** any color having components of both red and blue, such as lavender, magenta, orchid, or rose. **2.** cloth or clothing of this hue, esp. as formerly worn distinctively by persons of imperial, royal, or other high rank: *born to the purple.* **3.** the rank or office of a cardinal, in allusion to his scarlet official dress. **4.** the office of a bishop. **5.** imperial or lofty rank or position. —*adj.* **6.** of the color of purple. **7.** imperial or regal. **8.** brilliant or gorgeous. **9.** full of literary devices and effects: *a purple passage.* —*v.t., v.i.* **10.** to make or become purple. [ME *purpel,* OE (Northumbrian) *purpl(e),* var. of OE *purpur(e),* t. L: m. *purpura,* t. Gk.: m. *porphýra* kind of shellfish yielding purple dye]

ăct, āble, dâre, ärt; ĕbb, ēqual; ĭf, īce; hŏt, ōver, ôrder, oil, bŏŏk, ōōze, out; ŭp, ūse, ûrge; ə = a in alone; ch, chief; g, give; ng, ring; sh, shoe; th, thin; th, that; zh, vision. See the full key on inside cover.

pur·ple-fringed orchid (pûr′pəl frĭnjd′), either of two orchids of genus *Habenaria* (*Blephariglottis*) of eastern North America, the smaller (*H. psychodes*) having dark-purple cut fringed flowers, and the larger (*H. fimbriata*) lighter flowers.

purple gallinule, a purple, blue, green, and white gallinule, *Porphyrula martinica*, having a bright red, yellow, and blue bill, and lemon-yellow legs and feet, and inhabiting warmer parts of the New World.

Purple Heart, *U.S. Army*. a medal awarded to anyone wounded by enemy action while in service.

purple martin, a large American swallow, *Progne subis*. The male is blue-black.

purple medic, lucerne, or alfalfa.

pur·plish (pûr′plĭsh), *adj*. of a purple hue. Also, **pur′ply.**

pur·port (*v*. pər pōrt′, pûr′pōrt; *n*. pûr′pōrt), *v.t.* **1.** to profess or claim, as by the tenor: *a document purporting to be official.* **2.** to convey to the mind as the meaning or thing intended; express; imply. —*n.* **3.** tenor, import, or meaning. [late ME, t. AF: s. *purporter* convey, f. *pur-*PRO-¹ + *porter* (g. L *portāre*) carry] —**Syn.** 3. See **meaning.**

pur·pose (pûr′pəs), *n., v.* **-posed, -posing.** —*n.* **1.** the object for which anything exists or is done, made, used, etc. **2.** an intended or desired result; end or aim. **3.** intention or determination. **4.** that which one puts before oneself as something to be done or accomplished. **5.** the subject in hand; the point at issue: *to the purpose.* **6.** practical result, effect, or advantage: *to good purpose.* **7. on purpose, a.** by design; intentionally. **b.** with the particular purpose specified. —*v.t.* **8.** to put before oneself as something to be done or accomplished; propose. **9.** to determine on the performance of; design, intend. **10.** to be resolved. [ME *purpos*, t. OF, der. *purposer*, var. of *proposer* PROPOSE] —**pur′pose·less,** *adj.* —**pur′pose·less·ly,** *adv.* —**Syn.** 1. See **intention.**

pur·pose·ful (pûr′pəs fəl), *adj.* having a purpose. —**pur′pose·ful·ly,** *adv.* —**pur′pose·ful·ness,** *n.*

pur·pose·ly (pûr′pəs lĭ), *adv.* **1.** intentionally: *to do a thing purposely.* **2.** with the particular purpose specified; expressly.

pur·pos·ive (pûr′pəs ĭv), *adj.* **1.** acting with, characterized by, or showing a purpose, intention, or design. **2.** adapted to a purpose or end. **3.** serving some purpose. **4.** characterized by purpose, determination, or resolution. **5.** of or of the nature of purpose. —**pur′pos·ive·ly,** *adv.* —**pur′pos·ive·ness,** *n.*

pur·pu·ra (pûr′pyŏŏ rə), *n. Pathol.* a disease characterized by purple or livid spots on the skin or mucous membrane, caused by the extravasation of blood. [t. NL, special use of L *purpura*. See PURPLE]

pur·pure (pûr′pyŏŏr), *n. Her.* purple. [OE, t. L: m. *purpura*. See PURPLE] —**pur·pu·ric** (pər pyŏŏr′ĭk), *adj.*

purr (pûr), *v.i.* **1.** to utter a low, continuous murmuring sound expressive of satisfaction, as a cat does. **2.** (of things) to make a sound suggestive of the purring of a cat. —*v.t.* **3.** to express by, or as if by, purring. —*n.* **4.** act of purring. **5.** sound of purring. Also, **pur.** [imit.]

purse (pûrs), *n., v.,* **pursed, pursing.** —*n.* **1.** a small bag, pouch, or case for carrying money on the person. **2.** a purse with its contents. **3.** money, resources, or wealth. **4.** a sum of money collected as a present or the like. **5.** a sum of money offered as a prize. **6.** any baglike receptacle. —*v.t.* **7.** to contract into folds or wrinkles; pucker. **8.** *Rare.* to put into a purse. [ME and OE *purs*, b. *pusa* bag and *burs*, t. LL: s. *bursa* bag, t. Gk.: m. *byrsa* hide, leather]

purse-proud (pûrs′proud′), *adj.* proud of one's wealth.

purs·er (pûr′sər), *n.* an officer, esp. on board a ship, charged with keeping accounts, etc.

purse strings, 1. the strings by which a purse is closed. **2.** the power to spend or withhold money.

purs·lane (pûrs′lān, -lĭn), *n.* **1.** a widely distributed, yellow-flowered species of portulaca, *Portulaca oleracea*, used as a salad plant and potherb. **2.** any other portulacaceous plant. [ME *purcelan(e)*, t. OF: m. *porcelaine*, appar. b. L *porcilāca* (for *portulāca* purslane) and It. *porcellana* porcelain]

pur·su·ance (pər sŏŏ′əns), *n.* the following or carrying out of some plan, course, injunction, or the like.

pur·su·ant (pər sŏŏ′ənt), *adj.* **1.** proceeding conformably (fol. by *to*). **2.** pursuing. —*adv.* Also, **pur·su′ant·ly. 3.** according (fol. by *to*): *to do something pursuant to an agreement.* **4.** in a manner conformable (fol. by *to*).

pur·sue (pər sŏŏ′), *v.,* **-sued, -suing.** —*v.t.* **1.** to follow with the view of overtaking, capturing, killing, etc.; chase. **2.** to follow close upon; go with; attend: *bad luck pursued him.* **3.** to strive to gain; seek to attain or accomplish (an end, object, purpose, etc.). **4.** to proceed in accordance with (a method, plan, etc.). **5.** to carry on (a course of action, train of thoughts, etc.). **6.** to prosecute (inquiries, studies, etc.). **7.** to practice (an occupation, pastime, etc.). **8.** to continue to discuss (a subject, topic, etc.). **9.** to follow (a path, etc.). **10.** to continue on (one's way, course, etc.); go on with or continue (a journey, etc.). —*v.i.* **11.** to follow in pursuit. **12.** to continue. [ME *pursue(n)*, t. AF: m. *pursuer*, g. L *prosequī* follow, continue. Cf. PROSECUTE] —**pur·su′a·ble,** *adj.* —**pur·su′er,** *n.*

pur·suit (pər sŏŏt′), *n.* **1.** act of pursuing: *in pursuit of the fox.* **2.** the effort to secure; quest: *the pursuit of happiness.* **3.** any occupation, pastime, or the like, regularly or customarily pursued: *literary pursuits.* [ME *pursuit*, t. AF: m. *purseute*, der. *pursuer* PURSUE]

pursuit plane, *Mil.* an armed airplane designed for speed and maneuverability in fighting enemy aircraft.

pur·sui·vant (pûr′swĭ vənt), *n.* **1.** a heraldic officer of the lowest class, ranking below a herald. **2.** an official attendant on heralds. **3.** any attendant. [ME *purs(ev)-aunt*, t. OF: m. *poursuivant*, prop. ppr. of *poursuivre* PURSUE]

pur·sy (pûr′sĭ), *adj.,* **-sier, -siest. 1.** short-winded, esp. from corpulence or fatness. **2.** corpulent or fat. [earlier *pursive*, ME *pursif*, t. AF: m. *porsif*, var. of OF *polsif*, der. *polser* pant, heave. See PUSH] —**pur′si·ness,** *n.*

pur·te·nance (pûr′tə nəns), *n. Archaic.* the heart, liver, and lungs of an animal. Ex. 12:9. [ME; aphetic var. of APPURTENANCE]

pu·ru·lence (pyŏŏr′ə ləns, pyŏŏr′yə-), *n.* **1.** the condition of containing or forming pus. **2.** pus. Also, **pu′ru·len·cy.**

pu·ru·lent (pyŏŏr′ə lənt, pyŏŏr′yə-), *adj.* **1.** full of, containing, forming, or discharging pus; suppurating: *a purulent sore.* **2.** attended with suppuration: *purulent appendicitis.* **3.** of the nature of or like pus: *purulent matter.* [t. L: as *pūrulentus*] —**pu′ru·lent·ly,** *adv.*

Pu·rús (pŏŏ rŏŏs′), *n.* a river flowing from E Peru NE through W Brazil to the Amazon. ab. 2000 mi.

pur·vey (pər vā′), *v.t. Chiefly Brit.* to provide, furnish, or supply (esp. food or provisions). [ME *porveie(n)*, t. AF: m. *porveier*, g. L *prōvidēre* foresee, provide for]

pur·vey·ance (pər vā′əns), *n.* **1.** act of purveying. **2.** that which is purveyed, as provisions. **3.** *Eng. Law.* a prerogative of the crown, abolished in 1660, of taking provisions, supplies or services for the sovereign or the royal household at an appraised value.

pur·vey·or (pər vā′ər), *n.* **1.** *Chiefly Brit.* one who purveys, provides, or supplies. **2.** *Eng. Hist.* an officer who, by purveyance, provided or exacted provisions, etc., for the sovereign under the prerogative of purveyance.

pur·view (pûr′vū), *n.* **1.** range of operation, activity, concern, etc. **2.** range of vision; view. **3.** that which is provided or enacted in a statute, as distinguished from the preamble. **4.** the full scope or compass of a statute or law, or of any document, statement, book, subject, etc. [ME *purveu*, t. AF: provided, pp. of *porveier* PURVEY]

pus (pŭs), *n.* a yellow-white, more or less viscid substance produced by suppuration and found in abscesses, sores, etc., consisting of a liquid plasma in which leucocytes, etc., are suspended. [t. L; akin to Gk. *pýon* pus. See PYIN, FOUL] —**pus′like,** *adj.*

Pu·san (pŏŏ′sän′), *n.* a seaport in SE South Korea. 473,619 (1949). Formerly, **Fusan.**

Pu·sey (pū′zĭ), *n.* **Edward Bouverie** (bŏŏ′və rĭ), 1800–82, British clergyman.

Pu·sey·ism (pū′zĭ ĭz′əm), *n.* Tractarianism. —**Pu·sey·ite** (pū′zĭ īt′), *n.*

push (pŏŏsh), *v.t.* **1.** to exert force upon or against (a thing) in order to move it away. **2.** to move (*away, off,* etc.) by exerting force thus; shove; thrust; drive. **3.** to make by thrusting obstacles aside: *to push one's way through the crowd.* **4.** to press or urge (a person, etc.) to some action or course. **5.** to press (an action, etc.) with energy and insistence. **6.** to carry (an action or thing) further, to a conclusion or extreme, too far, etc. **7.** to press the adoption, use, sale, etc., of. **8.** to press or bear hard upon (a person, etc.) as in dealings. **9.** to put to straits (fol. by *for*): *we're pushed for time.* —*v.i.* **10.** to exert a thrusting force upon something. **11.** to use steady force in moving a thing away; shove. **12.** to move from the shore, etc., as the result of a push (often fol. by *off*). **13.** to make one's way with effort or persistence, as against difficulty or opposition. **14.** to put forth vigorous or persistent efforts. —*n.* **15.** act of pushing; a shove or thrust. **16.** a contrivance or part to be pushed in order to operate a mechanism. **17.** a vigorous onset or effort. **18.** a determined pushing forward or advance. **19.** the pressure of circumstances. **20.** an emergency. **21.** *Colloq.* persevering energy; enterprise. **22.** *Slang.* a crowd, company, or set of persons. [ME *posshe(n)*, t. OF: m. *poulser*, g. L *pulsāre*. See PULSATE]

—**Syn.** 1. PUSH, SHOVE, THRUST is to move or attempt to move something by exerting force against it. To PUSH is to move or attempt to move something in the direction in which a force is exerted: *to push a wheelbarrow.* To SHOVE, sometimes a more colloquial word, is to cause to move by sliding, or to push roughly: *to shove a person aside.* To THRUST is a formal word, meaning to shove with one quick, strong movement, usually with the effect of penetrating into or through something: *to thrust a sword through a body.*

push·ball (pŏŏsh′bôl′), *n.* **1.** a game played with a large, heavy ball, usually about 6 feet in diameter, which two sides of players endeavor to push toward opposite goals. **2.** the ball used in this game.

push button, a device designed to close or open an electric circuit when a button or knob is depressed, and to return to a normal position when it is released.

push-but·ton (pŏŏsh′bŭt′ən), *adj.* operated by, or as by, push buttons: *push-button tuning.*

push·cart (pŏŏsh′kärt′), *n.* a light cart to be pushed by hand, used by street venders, etc.

push·er (poŏosh'ər), n. **1.** one who or that which pushes. **2.** Aeron. an airplane which has its propeller behind the main supporting planes.

push·ing (poŏosh'ĭng), adj. **1.** that pushes. **2.** enterprising; energetic. **3.** aggressive; presuming.

Push·kin (poŏosh'kĭn), n. **Aleksander Sergeevich** (ä'lĕksän'dər sĕr gĕ'ə vĭch), 1799 -1837, Russian poet and short story writer.

push-o·ver (poŏosh'ō'vər), n. Slang. **1.** anything done easily. **2.** an easily defeated person or a team.

push·pin (poŏosh'pĭn'), n. **1.** a children's game played with pins. **2.** child's play; triviality.

push-pull (poŏosh'poŏl'), n. Radio. a two-tube symmetrical arrangement in which the grid excitation voltages are opposite in phase.

Push·tu (pŭsh'too), n. an Iranian language, the principal language of Afghanistan. Also, **Pashto.**

pu·sil·la·nim·i·ty (pū'sə lə nĭm'ə tĭ), n. state or condition of being pusillanimous; timidity; cowardliness.

pu·sil·lan·i·mous (pū'sə lăn'ə məs), adj. **1.** lacking strength of mind or courage; faint-hearted; cowardly. **2.** proceeding from or indicating a cowardly spirit. ιt. LL: m. pusillanimis, f. L: s. pusillus very small, petty + -animis -spirited] —**pu'sil·lan·i·mous·ly,** adv.

puss¹ (poŏos), n. **1.** a cat. **2.** Brit. a hare. **3.** a girl or woman. [cf. D poes, LG puus-katte, d. Sw. katte-pus]

puss² (poŏos), n. Slang. **1.** face. **2.** mouth. [orig. obscure]

puss·y¹ (poŏos'ĭ), n., pl. **pussies. 1.** puss¹. **2.** the game of tipcat. **3.** the "cat" used in it. [dim. of PUSS¹]

pus·sy² (pŭs'ĭ), adj. Med. puslike. [f. PUS + -Y¹]

puss·y·foot (poŏos'ĭ foŏot'), v.i. **1.** to go with a soft, stealthy tread like that of a cat. **2.** U.S. Slang. to act cautiously or timidly, as if afraid to commit oneself on a point at issue. —n. **3.** a person with a catlike, or soft and stealthy, tread. **4.** U.S. Slang. one who pussyfoots. **5.** Chiefly Brit. a teetotaler; a prohibitionist.

puss·y willow (poŏos'ĭ), **1.** a small American willow, Salix discolor, with silky catkins. **2.** any of various similar willows.

pus·tu·lant (pŭs'chə lənt), adj. **1.** causing the formation of pustules. —n. **2.** a medicament or agent causing pustulation. [t. LL: s. pustulans, ppr.]

pus·tu·lar (pŭs'chə lər), adj. **1.** of, pertaining to, or of the nature of pustules. **2.** characterized by pustules. [t. NL: s. pustulāris]

pus·tu·la·tion (pŭs'chə lā'shən), n. the formation or breaking out of pustules.

pus·tule (pŭs'choŏol), n. **1.** Pathol. a small elevation of the skin containing pus. **2.** any pimplelike or blisterlike swelling or elevation. [ME, t. L: m. pustula]

Pussy willow, Salix discolor

put (poŏot), v., **put, putting,** n. —v.t. **1.** to move or place (anything) so as to get it into or out of some place or position: to put money in one's purse. **2.** to bring into some relation, state, etc.: put everything in order. **3.** to place in the charge or power of a person, etc.: to put oneself under a doctor's care. **4.** to subject to the endurance or suffering of something: to put a person to death. **5.** to set to a duty, task, action, etc.: to put one to work. **6.** to force or drive to some course or action: to put an army to flight. **7.** to render or translate, as into another language. **8.** to assign or attribute: to put a certain construction upon an action. **9.** to set at a particular place, point, amount, etc., in a scale of estimation: he puts the distance at five miles. **10.** to express or state: to put a thing in writing. **11.** to apply, as to a use or purpose. **12.** to set, give, or make: to put an end to a practice. **13.** to propose or submit for answer, consideration, deliberation, etc.: to put a question. **14.** to impose, as a burden, charge, or the like: to put a tax on an article. **15.** to lay the blame of (fol. by on, to, etc.). **16.** to throw or cast, esp. with a forward motion of the hand when raised close to the shoulder: to put the shot. **17.** Dial. to push. —v.i. **18.** to go, move, or proceed: to put to sea. **19.** Colloq. to make off: to put for home. **20.** Dial. to shoot out or grow, or send forth shoots or sprouts. **21.** Some special verb phrases are:

put about, Naut. to change direction, as on a course.
put aside, away, or **by,** to save or store up.
put down, 1. to write. **2.** to repress or suppress. **3.** Brit. to destroy (an animal).
put in, Naut. to enter a port or harbor, esp. in turning aside from the regular course for shelter, repairs, provisions, etc.
put off, 1. to postpone. **2.** to bid or cause to wait until later. **3.** to get rid of (a person, demand, etc.) by delay or evasive shifts. **4.** to lay aside. **5.** Naut. to start out, as on a voyage.
put on, 1. to assume or take on airs. **2.** to assume insincerely or falsely: his sorrow is only put on.
put out, 1. to extinguish (fire, etc.). **2.** to confuse or embarrass. **3.** to distract, disturb, or interrupt. **4.** to subject to inconvenience. **5.** to annoy, irritate, or vex. **6.** Sports. to cause to be removed from an opportunity to reach base or score. **7.** Naut. to go out to sea.
put up, 1. to erect. **2.** to preserve (jam, etc.). **3.** to arrange (hair, etc.). **4.** to provide (money, etc.). **5.** to lodge. **6.** to show. **7.** Archaic. to sheathe one's sword, stop fighting. —n. **22.** a throw or cast. **23.** Finance. the privilege of

delivering a certain amount of stock, at a specified price, within a specified time to the maker of the contract. [ME putten, pūten push, thrust, put. Cf. OE putung an impelling, inciting, potian push, thrust, also Dan. putte put, put in]

—**Syn. 1.** PUT, PLACE, LAY, SET mean to bring or take an object (or cause to go) to a certain location or position, there to leave it. PUT is the general word: to put the dishes on the table, to put one's hair up. PLACE is a more formal word, suggesting precision of movement or definiteness of location: he placed his hand on the Bible. LAY, meaning originally to cause to lie, and SET, meaning originally to cause to sit, are used particularly to stress the position in which an object is put: LAY usually suggests putting an object rather carefully into a horizontal position: to lay a pattern out on the floor. SET usually means to place upright: to set a child on a horse.

pu·ta·men (pū tā'mĭn), n., pl. **-tamina** (-tăm'ə nə). Bot. a hard or stony endocarp, as a peach stone. [t. L: that which is removed in pruning]

pu·ta·tive (pū'tə tĭv), adj. commonly regarded as such; reputed; supposed. [late ME, t. LL: m.s. putātīvus, der. L putāre think] —**pu'ta·tive·ly,** adv.

put·log (poŏot'lŏg', -lŏg', pŭt'-), n. one of the short horizontal timbers that support the floor of a scaffolding.

Put·nam (pŭt'nəm), n. **Israel,** 1718–90, American Revolutionary general.

put-out (poŏot'out'), n. Baseball. an act of putting a player out. See **out** (def. 24).

pu·tre·fac·tion (pū'trə făk'shən), n. act or process of putrefying; rotting. —**pu'tre·fac'tive,** adj.

pu·tre·fy (pū'trə fī), v., **-fied, -fying.** —v.t. **1.** to render putrid; cause to rot or decay with an offensive odor. —v.i. **2.** to become putrid; rot. **3.** to become gangrenous. [ME putrefie(n), t. OF: m. putrefier, t. L: m. putrefierī rot] —**pu'tre·fi'er,** n.

pu·tres·cent (pū trĕs'ənt), adj. becoming putrid; in process of putrefaction. [t. L: s. putrescens, ppr., growing rotten] —**pu·tres'cence,** n.

pu·tres·ci·ble (pū trĕs'ə bəl), adj. **1.** liable to become putrid. —n. **2.** a putrescible substance.

pu·tres·cine (pū trĕs'ēn, -ĭn), n. Biochem. a colorless, liquid ptomaine, C₄H₁₂N₂, with a disagreeable odor, derived from decayed animal tissue.

pu·trid (pū'trĭd), adj. **1.** in a state of foul decay or decomposition, as animal or vegetable matter; rotten. **2.** attended with or pertaining to putrefaction. **3.** having the odor of decaying flesh. **4.** thoroughly corrupt, depraved, or bad. **5.** offensively or disgustingly objectionable or bad. [t. L: s. putridus] —**pu·trid'i·ty, pu'trid·ness,** n. —**pu'trid·ly,** adv.

Putsch (poŏoch), n. German. a minor revolt or uprising.

putt (pŭt), Golf. —v.t., v.i. **1.** to strike (the ball) gently and carefully so as to make it roll along the putting green into the hole. —n. **2.** an act of putting. **3.** a stroke made in putting. [var. of PUT]

put·tee (pŭt'ĭ), n. **1.** a long strip of cloth wound spirally round the leg from ankle to knee, worn by sportsmen, soldiers, etc., as a protection or support. **2.** a kind of gaiter or legging of leather or other material, worn by soldiers, riders, etc. Also, **putty.** [t. Hind.: m. patti bandage. Cf. Skt. patta strip of cloth, bandage]

put·ter¹ (pŭt'ər), v.i. **1.** to busy or occupy oneself in an ineffective manner: to putter over a task. **2.** to move or go (about, along, etc.) with ineffective action or little energy or purpose. **3.** to move or go slowly or aimlessly; loiter. —n. **4.** puttering or ineffective action; dawdling. Also, esp. Brit. or Literary in U.S., **potter.** [var. of POTTER²]

put·ter² (pŭt'ər), n. Golf. **1.** one who putts. **2.** a club with a relatively short, stiff shaft and a wooden or iron head, used in putting. [f. PUTT + -ER¹]

put·ti·er (pŭt'ĭ ər), n. one who putties, as a glazier.

put·ting green (pŭt'ĭng), n. Golf. **1.** that part of the course within 20 yards of a hole, excepting hazards. **2.** a practice area for putting practice.

put·ty¹ (pŭt'ĭ), n., pl. **-ties,** v., **-tied, -tying.** —n. **1.** a kind of cement, of doughlike consistency, made of whiting and linseed oil and used for securing panes of glass, stopping up holes in woodwork, etc. **2.** any of various more or less similar preparations, prepared from other ingredients and used for the same or other purposes. **3.** a substance consisting of linseed oil and various other materials (as ferric oxide and red and white lead), employed in sealing the joints of tubes, pipes, etc. **4.** Plastering, etc. a very fine cement made of lime only. **5.** any person or thing easily molded, influenced, etc. **6.** light brownish or yellowish gray. —v.t. **7.** to secure, cover, etc., with putty. [t. F: m. potée, prop., a potful]

put·ty² (pŭt'ĭ), n., pl. **-ties.** puttee.

put·ty·root (pŭt'ĭ root', -root'), n. an American orchidaceous plant, Aplectrum hyemale, having a slender naked rootstock which produces each spring a scape with a loose raceme of brownish flowers.

Pu·tu·ma·yo (poŏo'too mä'yō), n. a river forming the boundary between S Colombia and N Peru, flowing into the Amazon in NW Brazil. ab. 900 mi. Called **Içá** in Brazil.

put-up (poŏot'ŭp'), adj. Colloq. planned beforehand in a secret or crafty manner: a put-up job.

Pu·vis de Cha·vannes (py vē' də shä vän'), **Pierre Cécile** (pyĕr sĕ sēl'), 1824–98, French painter.

Puy-de-Dôme (pwē də dōm'), n. a mountain in central France. 4805 ft.

Pu-yi (pōō′yē′), *n.* **Henry,** born 1906, last emperor of China, 1908 until his abdication in 1912; dictator of Manchukuo, 1932–34; emperor (as Kang Te) of Manchukuo, 1934 until his abdication in 1945.

puz·zle (pŭz′əl), *n., v.* **-zled, -zling.** —*n.* **1.** a toy or other contrivance designed to amuse by presenting difficulties to be solved by ingenuity or patient effort. **2.** something puzzling; a puzzling question, matter, or person. **3.** puzzled or perplexed condition. [appar. der. PUZZLE, v.] —*v.t.* **4.** to render at a loss what to do or say. **5.** to render at a loss what to think or understand; perplex: *the long silence puzzled him.* **6.** to render confused, intricate, involved, or complicated. **7.** to exercise (oneself, one's brain, etc.) over some problem or matter. **8.** to make, as something obscure, by careful study or effort (fol. by *out*): *to puzzle out the meaning of a sentence.* —*v.i.* **9.** to be in perplexity. **10.** to ponder or study over some perplexing problem or matter. [ME *poselet* puzzled, confused, OE *puslian* pick (out), c. D *peuzelen* pick, piddle, Norw. *pusla* be careful or fussy. For meaning, cf. E slang *fussed* confused]
—**Syn. 2.** PUZZLE, RIDDLE, ENIGMA refer to something baffling or confusing which is to be solved. A PUZZLE is a question or problem, intricate enough to be perplexing to the mind; it is sometimes a contrivance made purposely perplexing to test one's ingenuity: *the reason for their behavior remains a puzzle; a crossword puzzle.* A RIDDLE is an intentionally obscure statement or question, the meaning of or answer to which is to be arrived at only by guessing: *the famous riddle of the Sphinx.* ENIGMA, originally meaning riddle, now refers to some baffling problem with connotations of mysteriousness: *he will always be an enigma to me.* **4.** PUZZLE, BEWILDER, PERPLEX imply mental confusion and consequent inability to decide or to act. PUZZLE suggests mental embarrassment amid a complexity of possible decisions: *one may be puzzled over a problem.* BEWILDER suggests complete bafflement, the mind being lost in a multiplicity of considerations and alternatives: *bewildered by an unexpected situation.* PERPLEX suggests such an entanglement of one's judgment that he is uncertain as to what to think or how to act: *perplexed as to a decision.*

puz·zle·ment (pŭz′əl mənt), *n.* **1.** puzzled state; perplexity. **2.** something puzzling.

puz·zler (pŭz′lər), *n.* **1.** a person who puzzles. **2.** a baffling question or problem.

Pvt., Private.

P.W.A., Public Works Administration.

P.W.D., Public Works Department.

pwt., pennyweight.

PX, Post Exchange.

pxt., pinxit.

py·ae·mi·a (pī ē′mī ə), *n. Pathol.* pyemia.

Pya·ti·gorsk (pyä′tĭ gôrsk′), *n.* a city in the S Soviet Union in Europe, in Caucasia. 62,875 (1939). Also, **Piatigorsk.**

pyc·nid·i·um (pĭk nĭd′ī əm), *n., pl.* **-nidia** (-nĭd′ĭə). *Bot.* (in certain ascomycetes and *Fungi Imperfecti*) an asexual (imperfect) fruit body, commonly globose or flask-shaped and bearing conidia on conidiophores. [NL, f. Gk.: m.s. *pyknós* close, thick, dense + m. *-idion* (dim. suffix)]

pyc·nom·e·ter (pĭk nŏm′ə tər), *n.* a flask holding a definite volume, used in determining relative density or specific gravity. [f. m. Gk. *pyknó(s)* dense + -METER]

Pyd·na (pĭd′nə), *n.* an ancient town of Pieria, in Macedonia, W of the Gulf of Salonika: decisive Roman victory over the Macedonians, 168 B.C.

pye (pī), *n. Eccles.* pie⁴.

py·e·li·tis (pī′ə lī′tĭs), *n. Pathol.* inflammation of the pelvis or outlet of the kidney. [NL, f. Gk.: s. *pýelos* basin + -*itis* -ITIS. Cf. L *pelvis* basin, PELVIS]

py·e·lo·gram (pī′ə lə grăm′), *n.* a Roentgenograph produced by pyelography. Also, **py·e·lo·graph** (pī′ə lə gräf′, -gräf′). [f. Gk. *pýelo(s)* basin + -GRAM]

py·e·log·ra·phy (pī′ə lŏg′rə fĭ), *n.* the art of making photographs of the kidneys and ureter by means of the Roentgen rays, after the injection of an opaque solution or of a radio-opaque dye. —**py·e·lo·graph·ic** (pī′ə lə grăf′ĭk), *adj.*

py·e·mi·a (pī ē′mĭ ə), *n. Pathol.* the growth, in different tissues, of multiple metastatic abscesses, developing from emboli disseminated in the blood stream as fragments of a disintegrating infective thrombus. Also, **pyaemia.** [NL. See PYO-, -EMIA]

Pyg·ma·li·on (pĭg mā′lĭ ən, -māl′yən), *n. Gk. Legend.* **1.** a sculptor and king of Cyprus, who fell in love with an ivory statue which he had made and which came to life in answer to his prayer. **2.** a drama (1912) by G. B. Shaw.

Pyg·my (pĭg′mĭ), *n., pl.* **-mies.** **1.** any member of any of various Negroid races of small stature, of Africa, of southeastern Asia, the Andaman and Philippine Islands. **2.** (*l.c.*) a small or dwarfish person. **3.** (*l.c.*) anything very small of its kind. **4.** (*l.c.*) one who is of small importance, or who has some quality, etc., in very small measure. **5.** one of a race of dwarfs in ancient history and tradition. —*adj.* **6.** of or pertaining to the Pygmies. **7.** (*l.c.*) of very small size, capacity, power, etc. Also, **Pigmy.** [ME *pigmey,* t. L: m.s. *Pygmaeī,* pl., t. Gk.: m. *Pygmaîoi,* prop. pl. of *Pygmaîos* dwarfish] —**Syn. 1.** See **dwarf.**

py·in (pī′ĭn), *n. Biochem.* an albuminous constituent of pus. [f. s. Gk. *pýon* pus + -IN²]

py·jam·as (pə jä′məz, -jăm′əz), *n.pl. Brit.* pajamas.

Pyle (pīl), *n.* **1. Ernest,** ("*Ernie*") 1900–45, U.S. war correspondent and journalist. **2. Howard,** 1853–1911, U.S. illustrator and author.

py·lon (pī′lŏn), *n.* **1.** a marking post or tower for guiding aviators, frequently used in races. **2.** a relatively tall structure at either side of a gate, bridge, or avenue, marking an entrance or approach. **3.** any architectural form of a projecting nature which flanks an entrance. **4.** a steel tower or mast carrying high-tension, telephonic or other cables and lines. **5.** *Egypt. Archit.* **a.** a monumental gateway to an Egyptian temple or edifice, in the shape of a truncated pyramid through which the passage for the gate was pierced. **b.** a combination of two such truncated pyramidal structures connected by a lower architectural member, in which was the gate proper. [t. Gk.: gateway]

py·lo·rec·to·my (pī′lə rĕk′tə mĭ), *n., pl.* **-mies.** *Surg.* removal of the pylorus. [f. PYLOR(US) + -ECTOMY]

py·lo·rus (pī lōr′əs, pī-), *n., pl.* **-lori** (-lōr′ī). *Anat.* the opening between the stomach and the intestine. See diag. under **intestine.** [t. LL, t. Gk.: m. *pylōrós,* lit., gatekeeper] —**py·lor·ic** (pī lôr′ĭk, -lŏr′-, pī-), *adj.*

Pym (pĭm), *n.* **John,** 1584–1643, English statesman: championed rights of Parliament against King Charles I.

pyo-, a word element meaning "pus." [t. Gk., comb. form of *pýon*]

py·o·gen·e·sis (pī′ə jĕn′ə sĭs), *n. Pathol.* the generation of pus; the process of the formation of pus.

py·o·gen·ic (pī′ə jĕn′ĭk), *adj. Pathol.* **1.** producing or generating pus. **2.** attended with or pertaining to the formation of pus.

py·oid (pī′oid), *adj. Pathol.* pertaining to pus; puslike. [t. Gk.: m.s. *pyoeidḗs* puslike]

py·or·rhe·a (pī′ə rē′ə), *n. Pathol.* a disease occurring in various forms and degrees of severity, characterized in its severe forms by the formation of pus in the pockets between the root of the tooth and its surrounding tissues, and frequently accompanied by the loss of the teeth; Riggs' disease. Also, **pyorrhea al·ve·o·lar·is** (ăl-vē′ə lâr′ĭs), **py·or·rhoe·a.** [t. NL. See PYO-, -RRHEA] —**py′or·rhe′al,** *adj.*

py·o·sis (pī ō′sĭs), *n. Pathol.* the formation of pus; suppuration. [NL, t. Gk.]

pyr-, var. of **pyro-,** used occasionally before vowels or *h,* as in *pyran.*

pyr·a·mid (pĭr′ə mĭd), *n.* **1.** *Archit.* a massive structure built of stone, with square (or polygonal) base, and sloping sides meeting at an apex, such as those built by the ancient Egyptians as royal tombs or by the Mayas as platforms for their sanctuaries. **2.** anything of such form. **3.** a number of things heaped up or arranged in this form. **4.** *Geom.* a solid having a triangular, square, or polygonal base, and triangular sides which meet in a point. **5.** *Crystall.* any form the planes of which intersect all three of the axes. **6.** *Anat., Zool.* any of various parts or structures of pyramidal form. **7.** *Stock Exchange.* the series of transactions in which a speculator increases his holdings by using the rising market value of those holdings as margin for further purchases. **8.** a tree pruned, or trained to grow, in pyramidal form. —*v.i.* **9.** to be disposed in the form or shape of a pyramid. **10.** *Stock Exchange.* (in speculating on margin) to enlarge one's operations in a series of transactions, as on a continued rise or decline in price, by using profits in transactions not yet closed, and consequently not yet in hand, as margin for additional buying or selling in the next transaction. —*v.t.* **11.** to arrange in the form of a pyramid. **12.** to raise or increase (costs, wages, etc.) by increasing additions, as if building up a pyramid. **13.** (in speculating on margin) to operate in, or employ in, pyramiding. [t. L: s. *pyramis,* t. Gk., of Egypt. orig.; r. ME *pyramis,* t. L] —**pyr′a·mid·like′,** *adj.*

Pyramids (def. 4)

py·ram·i·dal (pĭ răm′ə dəl), *adj.* **1.** of or pertaining to a pyramid: *the pyramidal form.* **2.** of the nature of a pyramid; pyramidlike. —**py·ram′i·dal·ly,** *adv.*

pyr·a·mid·i·cal (pĭr′ə mĭd′ə kəl), *adj.* pyramidal. Also, **pyr′a·mid′ic.** [f. m.s. Gk. *pyramidikós* + -AL¹] —**pyr′a·mid′i·cal·ly,** *adv.*

Pyr·a·mus (pĭr′ə məs), *n. Class. Legend.* a youth of Babylon, the lover of Thisbe (which see).

py·ran (pī′răn, pī răn′), *n. Chem.* either of two compounds, C₅H₆O, containing one oxygen and five carbon atoms arranged in a six-membered ring. [f. PYR- + -AN. Cf. PYRONE]

py·rar·gy·rite (pī rär′jə rīt′), *n.* a blackish mineral, silver antimony sulfide (AgSbS₃), showing (when transparent) a deep ruby-red color by transmitted light; an ore of silver. [t. G: m. *pyrargyrit,* f. Gk. *pýr* fire + s. Gk. *árgyron* silver + -*it* -ITE¹]

pyre (pīr), *n.* **1.** a pile or heap of wood or other combustible material. **2.** such a pile for burning a dead body. [t. L: m. *pyra,* t. Gk.]

py·rene (pī′rēn), *n. Bot.* a putamen or stone, esp. when there are several in a single fruit; a nutlet. [t. NL: m. *pýrēna,* t. Gk.: m. *pýrēn* fruit stone]

Pyr·e·nees (pĭr′ə nēz′), *n.pl.* a mountain range between Spain and France. Highest peak, Pic de Néthou, 11,165 ft. —**Pyr′e·ne′an,** *adj.*

py·ret·ic (pī rĕt′ĭk), *adj.* of, pertaining to, affected by,

b., blend of, blended; c., cognate with; d., dialect, dialectal; der., derived from; f., formed from; g., going back to; m., modification of; r., replacing; s., stem of; t., taken from; ?, perhaps. See the full key on inside cover.

or producing fever. [t. NL: s. *pyreticus*, der. Gk. *pyretós* fever]

pyr·e·tol·o·gy (pĭr′ə tŏl′ə jĭ, pī′rə-), *n.* the branch of medicine that treats of fevers. [f. Gk. *pyretó(s)* fever + -LOGY]

Py·rex (pī′rĕks), *n. Trademark.* a heat-resistant glassware for baking, frying, etc.

py·rex·i·a (pī rĕk′sī′ə), *n. Pathol.* 1. fever. 2. feverish condition. [NL, t. Gk.: m. *pyrexis* feverishness.] —**py·rex**/**i·al, py·rex**/**ic,** *adj.*

pyr·he·li·om·e·ter (pĭr hē′lĭ ŏm′ə tər, pī′r-), *n. Astrophysics.* an instrument for measuring the total intensity of the sun's energy radiation. [f. Gk. *pỹr* fire + HELIO- + -METER]

pyr·i·ben·za·mine (pĭr′ə bĕn′zə mēn′, -mĭn), *n.* a recently developed antihistamine, used esp. in the treatment of allergic disorders.

pyr·i·dine (pĭr′ə dēn′, -dĭn), *n. Chem.* a liquid organic base, C_5H_5N, with a pungent odor, found in coal tar, bone oil, etc., and the parent substance of many compounds: used as a solvent and as an amine. [f. Gk. *pỹr* fire + -ID² + -INE²] —**py·rid·ic** (pī rĭd′ĭk), *adj.*

pyr·i·dox·ine (pĭr′ə dŏk′sēn, -sĭn), *n. Biochem.* vitamin B₆; a derivative of pyridine, known to counteract dermatitis in rats. In human beings, pyridoxine apparently plays a part in preventing pellagra and in the formation of hemoglobin.

pyr·i·form (pĭr′ə fôrm), *adj.* pear-shaped. [t. NL: s. *pyriformis*, f. *pyri-* (for *piri-* pear) + -*formis* -FORM]

py·rim·i·dine group or **nucleus** (pī rĭm′ə dēn′, pĭr′ə mə dēn′, -dĭn), *Chem.* heterocyclic ring compound, $C_4H_4N_2$, an important constituent of several biochemical substances, as thiamine.

py·rite (pī′rīt), *n.* a very common brass-yellow mineral, iron disulfide (FeS₂), with a metallic luster, burned to sulfur dioxide in the manufacture of sulfuric acid; fool's gold. [t. L: m. *pyrītes*. See PYRITES] —**py·rit·ic** (pī rĭt′ĭk, pə-), **py·rit**/**i·cal,** *adj.*

py·ri·tes (pī rī′tēz, pə-, pī′rīts), *n.* 1. pyrite (sometimes called **iron pyrites**). 2. marcasite (**white iron pyrites**). 3. any of various other sulfides, as of copper, tin, etc. [t. L, t. Gk.: orig. adj., of or in fire]

pyro-, *Chem.* 1. a word element: **a.** used before the name of an inorganic acid, indicating that its water content is intermediate between that of the corresponding ortho- (more water) and meta- (least water) acids: *pyroantimonic,* H₄Sb₂O₇, *pyroarsenic* H₄As₂O₇, *and pyrosulfuric,* H₂S₂O₇, *acids.* **b.** applied to salts of these acids. If the acid ends in -*ic,* the corresponding salt ends in -*ate,* as *pyroboric acid,* H₂B₄O₇ and *potassium pyroborate,* K₂B₄O₇, or *pyrosulfuric,* H₂S₂O₇, and *pyrosulfate,* N₂S₂O₇. If the acid ends in -*ous,* the corresponding salt ends in -*ite: pyrophosphorous acid,* H₄P₂O₅, *potassium pyrophosphite,* K₄P₂O₅. 2. *Geol.* used in the names of minerals, rocks, etc., indicating a quality produced by the action of fire. 3. used to mean "of, relating to, or concerned with fire." [t. Gk., comb. form of *pỹr* fire]

py·ro·cat·e·chol (pī′rə kăt′ə kôl, -chôl, -kōl, pĭr′ə-), *n.* catechol. Also, **py·ro·cat·e·chin** (pī′rə kăt′ə chĭn, -kĭn, pĭr′ə-).

py·ro·chem·i·cal (pī′rə kĕm′ə kəl, pĭr′ə-), *adj.* pertaining to or producing chemical change at high temperatures. —**py·ro·chem**/**i·cal·ly,** *adv.*

py·ro·clas·tic (pī′rə klăs′tĭk, pĭr′ə-), *adj. Geol.* composed chiefly of fragments of volcanic origin, as agglomerate, tuff, and certain other rocks.

py·ro·crys·tal·line (pī′rə krĭs′tə lĭn, -līn′, pĭr′ə-), *adj. Petrog.* crystallized from a molten magma or highly heated solution.

py·ro·e·lec·tric (pī′rō′ĭ lĕk′trĭk, pĭr′ō-), *adj.* of, subject to, or manifesting, pyroelectricity.

py·ro·e·lec·tric·i·ty (pī′rō′ĭ lĕk′trĭs′ə tĭ, -ē′lĕk-, pĭr′ō-), *n.* the electrified state, or electric polarity, in some crystals produced by and changing with temperature.

py·ro·gal·late (pī′rə găl′āt, pĭr′ə-), *n. Chem.* a salt or ether of pyrogallol.

py·ro·gal·lol (pī′rə găl′ōl, -ŏl, -gə lōl′, pĭr′ə-), *n. Chem.* a white crystalline phenolic compound, C₆H₃(OH)₃, obtained by heating gallic acid, and used as a photographic developer. Also, **pyrogallic acid.** —**py·ro·gal**/**lic,** *adj.*

py·ro·gen (pī′rə jən, pĭr′ə-), *n. Chem.* a substance which produces a rise of temperature in an animal body.

py·ro·gen·ic (pī′rə jĕn′ĭk, pĭr′ə-), *adj.* 1. producing heat or fever. 2. produced by fire, as igneous rocks.

py·rog·e·nous (pī rŏj′ə nəs, pĭ-), *adj. Geol.* produced by the action of fire.

py·rog·nos·tics (pī′rəg nŏs′tĭks, pĭr′əg-), *n.pl.* those properties of a mineral which it exhibits when heated, alone or with fluxes, in the blowpipe flame, as the fusibility, intumescence, or other phenomena of fusion, flame coloration, etc. [pl. of *pyrognostic,* f. PYRO- + m.s. Gk. *gnōstikós* pertaining to knowledge. See -ICS]

py·rog·ra·phy (pī rŏg′rə fĭ, pĭ-), *n.* the process of burning designs on wood, leather, etc., with a heated tool. —**py·rog**/**ra·pher,** *n.* —**py·ro·graph·ic** (pī′rə grăf′ĭk, pĭr′ə-), *adj.*

py·ro·lig·ne·ous (pī′rə lĭg′nĭ əs, pĭr′ə-), *adj.* produced by the distillation of wood. Also, **py·ro·lig·nic.** [f. PYRO- + m. L *ligneus* of wood]

pyroligneous acid, an acidic distillate obtained from wood and containing about 10% acetic acid.

pyroligneous alcohol, methyl alcohol.

py·ro·lu·site (pī′rə lōō′sīt, pī rōl′yə sīt′), *n.* a common mineral, manganese dioxide, MnO₂, the principal ore of manganese, used in various manufactures, as a decolorizer of brown or green tints in glass, as a depolarizer in dry-cell batteries, etc. [f. PYRO- + m.s. Gk. *loûsis* washing + -ITE¹]

py·rol·y·sis (pī rŏl′ə sĭs), *n. Chem.* the subjection of organic compounds to very high temperatures and the resulting decomposition. —**py·ro·lyt·ic** (pī′rə lĭt′ĭk, pĭr′ə-), *adj.*

py·ro·mag·net·ic (pī′rō măg nĕt′ĭk, pĭr′ō-), *adj.* 1. pertaining to or depending upon the combined action of heat and magnetism. 2. relating to magnetic properties as changing with the temperature.

py·ro·man·cy (pī′rə măn′sĭ, pĭr′ə-), *n.* divination by fire, or by forms appearing in fire. [ME *piromancie,* t. ML: m. *pyromantia,* t. Gk.: m. *pyromanteia*]

py·ro·ma·ni·a (pī′rə mā′nĭ ə, pĭr′ə-), *n.* a mania for setting things on fire. —**py/ro·ma**/**ni·ac**/, *n.* —**py·ro·ma·ni·a·cal** (pī′rō mən nī′ə kəl, pĭr′ō-), *adj.*

py·ro·met·al·lur·gy (pī′rə mĕt′ə lûr′jĭ, pĭr′ə-), *n.* the practice of refining ores by the use of heat which serves to accelerate chemical reactions, to cause the metal to melt, or to liquefy the slag or nonmetallics.

py·rom·e·ter (pī rŏm′ə tər), *n.* an apparatus for determining high temperatures which depends commonly on observation of color or measurement of electric current produced by heating of dissimilar metals. —**py·ro·met·ric** (pī′rə mĕt′rĭk, pĭr′ə-), **py·ro·met**/**ri·cal,** *adj.*

py·ro·mor·phite (pī′rə môr′fīt, pĭr′ə-), *n.* a mineral, lead chlorophosphate, Pb₅P₃O₁₂Cl, occurring in crystals and massive, and of a green, yellow, or brown color: a minor ore of lead. [t. G: m. *pyromorphit.* See PYRO-, MORPH-, -ITE¹]

py·rone (pī′rōn, pĭ rōn′), *n. Chem.* either of two heterocyclic ketones, C₅H₄O₂. [f. PYR- fire + -ONE]

py·rope (pī′rōp), *n.* a mineral, magnesium-aluminum garnet, Mg₃Al₂Si₃O₁₂, occurring in crystals of varying shades of red, and frequently used as a gem. [ME *pirope,* t. OF, t. L: m. *pyrōpus* gold-bronze, t. Gk.: m. *pyrōpós* fiery (eyed), gold-bronze. Cf. G *pyrop*]

py·ro·phos·phor·ic acid (pī′rō fŏs fôr′ĭk, -fōr′ĭk, pĭr′ō-), *Chem.* the acid H₄P₂O₇, formed by the union of one molecule of phosphorus pentoxide with two molecules of water. It is a water-soluble crystalline powder.

py·ro·pho·tom·e·ter (pī′rō fō tŏm′ə tər, pĭr′ō-), *n.* a form of pyrometer which measures temperature by optical or photometric means.

py·ro·phyl·lite (pī′rə fĭl′īt, pĭr′ə-), *n.* a mineral, hydrous aluminum silicate, AlSi₂O₅(OH)₄, usually having a white or greenish color, and occurring in either foliated or compact masses, the latter variety being used like soapstone. [t. G: m. *pyrophyllit;* so called from its exfoliating when heated. See PYRO-, PHYLL(O)-, -ITE¹]

py·ro·sis (pī rō′sĭs), *n. Pathol.* an affection characterized by a burning sensation in the stomach, often extending to the esophagus, and the eructation of a watery, often acrid fluid; heartburn. [NL, t. Gk.]

py·ro·stat (pī′rə stăt′, pĭr′ə-), *n.* a thermostat for high temperatures.

py·ro·sul·fate (pī′rə sŭl′fāt, pĭr′ə-), *n. Chem.* See pyro-.

py·ro·tech·nic (pī′rə tĕk′nĭk, pĭr′ə-), *adj.* 1. of or pertaining to pyrotechny or pyrotechnics. 2. pertaining to, resembling, or suggesting fireworks. Also, **py/ro·tech/ni·cal.**

py·ro·tech·nics (pī′rə tĕk′nĭks, pĭr′ə-), *n.* 1. the art of making fireworks. 2. the making and use of fireworks for display, military purposes, etc. 3. a brilliant or sensational display, as of rhetoric, etc. Also, **py/ro·tech/ny** for 1, 2.

py·ro·tech·nist (pī′rə tĕk′nĭst, pĭr′ə-), *n.* one skilled in pyrotechnics.

py·ro·tox·in (pī′rə tŏk′sĭn, pĭr′ə-), *n.* pyrogen.

py·rox·ene (pī′rŏk sēn′), *n.* a very common group of minerals of many varieties, silicates of magnesium, iron, calcium, and other elements, occurring as important constituents of many kinds of rocks, chiefly igneous. [t. F, f. Gk.: *pyro-* fire + m.s. *xénos* stranger; orig. supposed to be a foreign substance when found in igneous rocks] —**py·rox·en·ic** (pī′rŏk sĕn′ĭk, pĭr′ə-), *adj.*

py·rox·e·nite (pī rŏk′sə nīt′), *n.* any rock composed essentially, or in large part, of pyroxene of any kind.

py·rox·y·lin (pī rŏk′sə lĭn), *n.* a nitrocellulose compound containing fewer nitro groups than guncotton and used as collodion, and in the artificial silk, leather, oilcloth industries, etc. Also, **py·rox/y·line.** [f. PYRO- + Gk. *xýlon* wood + -IN²]

Pyr·rha (pĭr′ə), *n. Gk. Legend.* wife of Deucalion.

Pyr·rhic (pĭr′ĭk), *adj.* of or pertaining to Pyrrhus, king of Epirus.

pyr·rhic¹ (pĭr′ĭk), *Pros.* —*adj.* 1. consisting of two short or unaccented syllables. 2. composed of or pertaining to pyrrhics. —*n.* 3. a pyrrhic foot. [t. L: m.s. *pyrrhichius,* t. Gk.: m. *pyrrhíchios* pertaining to the *pyrrhichē* PYRRHIC²]

pyr·rhic² (pĭr′ĭk), *n.* 1. an ancient Grecian warlike dance in which the motions of actual warfare were imitated. —*adj.* 2. of or pertaining to this dance. [t. L: m.s. *pyrrhicha,* t. Gk.: m. *pyrrichē* a dance; said to be named after Pyrrhichus, the inventor]

Pyrrhic victory, a victory gained at too great a cost, as that of Pyrrhus over the Romans at Apulum (modern Ascoli Satriano in SE Italy) in 279 B.C.

Pyr·rho (pĭr′ō), n. c365–c275 B.C., Greek Skeptic philosopher.

Pyr·rho·nism (pĭr′ə nĭz′əm), n. **1.** the doctrines or system of the Greek Skeptic philosopher Pyrrho (c365–c275 B.C.) and his followers. **2.** absolute or universal skepticism.

pyr·rho·tite (pĭr′ə tīt′), n. a common mineral, iron sulfide (nearly FeS), occurring in crystals and massive, of a bronze color and metallic luster, and generally slightly magnetic. Also, **pyr·rho·tine** (pĭr′ə tĭn). [for earlier *pyrrhotine*, f. s. Gk. *pyrrhótēs* redness + INE²]

pyr·rhu·lox·i·a (pĭr′ə lŏk′sĭ ə), n. a cardinallike grosbeak, *Pyrrhuloxia sinuata*, inhabiting the southwestern U.S. and Mexico, and having a bill superficially resembling that of a parrot.

Pyr·rhus (pĭr′əs), n. **1.** c318–272 B.C., king of Epirus, c300–272 B.C. **2.** Gk. *Legend.* son of Achilles.

pyr·role (pĭr′ōl′, pĭr′ōl), n. Chem. a five-membered ring system, C₄H₅N, containing four carbon atoms and a nitrogen atom. Chlorophyll, hemin, and many other important naturally occurring substances are built up of pyrrole rings. [f. Gk. *pyrr(hós)* red + -OLE]

pyr·rol·i·dine (pĭr rōl′ə dēn′, -dĭn, -rōl′ə-), n. Chem. a compound, C₄H₉N, derived from proline and some alkaloids, and present in tobacco.

py·ru·vic acid (pī rōō′vĭk, pĭ-), Chem. an acid, CH₃COCOOH, important in many biochemical processes, prepared by heating tartaric acid. [f. PYR(O)- + L *ūv(a)* grape + -IC + ACID]

pyruvic aldehyde, Chem. an organic compound, CH₃COCHO, containing both an aldehyde and a ketone group, usually obtained in a polymeric form.

Py·thag·o·ras (pī thăg′ə rəs), n. c582–c500 B.C., Greek philosopher, mathematician, and religious reformer.

Py·thag·o·re·an (pī thăg′ə rē′ən), adj. **1.** pertaining to Pythagoras, to whom the doctrine of metempsychosis is attributed, or to his teaching or school. —n. **2.** a follower of Pythagoras. **—Py·thag′o·re′an·ism,** n.

Pyth·i·a (pĭth′ĭ ə), n. Gk. *Myth.* the priestess of Apollo at Delphi who delivered the oracles. [t. L, t. Gk., prop. fem. of *Pȳthios* Pythian]

Pyth·i·ad (pĭth′ĭ ăd′), n. the period of four years between two celebrations of the Pythian games.

Pyth·i·an (pĭth′ĭ ən), adj. **1.** of or pertaining to Delphi, in ancient Greece. **2.** of or pertaining to Apollo, with reference to his oracle at Delphi. Also, **Pyth′ic.** [f. s. L *Pȳthius* (t. Gk.: m. *Pȳthios* of Delphi) + -AN]

Pythian games, one of the great national festivals of ancient Greece, held every four years at Delphi in honor of Apollo.

Pyth·i·as (pĭth′ĭ əs), n. See **Damon.**

py·thon¹ (pī′thŏn, -thən), n. **1.** a possessing spirit or demon. **2.** one who is possessed by a spirit and prophesies by its aid. [t. LGk.; relation to PYTHON not clear]

py·thon² (pī′thŏn, -thən), n. any of various large, nonvenomous, Old World tropical snakes, genus *Python*, which kill by constriction. [t. L, t. Gk.]

Py·thon (pī′thŏn, -thən), n. Gk. *Myth.* a huge serpent or monster fabled to have been slain by Apollo near Delphi.

py·tho·ness (pī′thə nĭs, pĭth′ə-), n. **1.** a woman supposed to be possessed by a soothsaying spirit, as the priestess of Apollo at Delphi. **2.** a woman with power of divination; a witch. [f. PYTHON + -ESS; r. ME *phytonesse*, t. OF]

py·thon·ic¹ (pī thŏn′ĭk, pī-), adj. prophetic; oracular. [t. L: s. *pythōnicus*, t. Gk.: m. *pythōnikós* prophetic]

py·thon·ic² (pī thŏn′ĭk, pī-), adj. **1.** of or pertaining to pythons². **2.** pythonlike. [f. PYTHON + -IC]

py·u·ri·a (pī yŏŏr′ĭ ə), n. Pathol. the presence of pus in the urine. [f. PY(O)- + URIA]

pyx (pĭks), n. **1.** Eccles. **a.** the box or vessel in which the reserved Eucharist or Host is kept. **b.** a watch-shaped container for carrying the Eucharist to the sick. **2.** a box or chest at a mint, in which specimen coins are deposited and reserved for trial by weight and assay. Also, **pix.** [ME, t. L: s. *pyxis*, t. Gk.: a box, orig., made of boxwood]

pyx·id·i·um (pĭk sĭd′ĭ əm), n., pl. **pyxidia** (pĭk sĭd′ĭ ə). Bot. a seed vessel which dehisces transversely, the top part acting as a lid, as in the purslane. [NL, t. Gk.: m. *pyxídion*, dim. of *pyxis* box]

pyx·ie (pĭk′sĭ), n. **1.** either of two trailing, shrubby, evergreen plants, *Pyxidanthera barbulata* or *P. brevifolia*, of the eastern U. S., bearing numerous small, starlike blossoms. **2.** Bot. pyxidium. [short for *Pyxidanthera* (see def.)]

Pyxidium

pyx·is (pĭk′sĭs), n., pl. **pyxides** (pĭk′sə dēz′). **1.** a small box or boxlike vase. **2.** a casket. **3.** Bot. a pyxidium. [ME, t. L. See PYX]

Q

Q, q (kū), n., pl. **Q's** or **Qs, q's** or **qs.** a consonant, the 17th letter of the English alphabet.

Q., **1.** pl. **Qq.** quarto. **2.** Quebec. **3.** Queen. **4.** question.

q., **1.** (L *quadrans*) farthing. **2.** quart; quarts. **3.** query. **4.** question. **5.** quintal. **6.** quire.

QB, Chess. queen's bishop.

Q.B., **1.** Queen's Bench. **2.** Also, **q.b.** Football. quarterback.

Q.C., Queen's Counsel.

Q.E.D., quod erat demonstrandum.

Q.E.F., quod erat faciendum.

Q-fe·ver (kū′fē′vər), n. a fever exhibiting pneumonialike symptoms, and caused by *Rickettsia diaphorica.*

Qishm (kĭsh′əm), n. an island S of, and belonging to, Iran, in the Strait of Hormuz. ab. 25,000 pop.; 68 mi. long; ab. 510 sq. mi.

Qkt, Chess. queen's knight.

ql., quintal.

Q.M., Quartermaster.

Q.M.C., Quartermaster Corps.

Q.M.G., Quartermaster-General. Also, **Q.M.Gen.**

q. pl., (L *quantum placet*) as much as you please.

qq. v., (L *quae vide*) which (words, etc.) see.

QR, Chess. queen's rook.

qr., pl. **qrs.** **1.** (L *quandrans*, pl. *quadrantes*) farthing. **2.** quarter. **3.** quire.

q.s., **1.** quantum sufficit. **2.** quarter section.

qt, **1.** quantity. **2.** (pl. **qt., qts.**) quart.

q.t., Slang. quiet.

qu., **1.** quart. **2.** quarter. **3.** quarterly. **4.** queen. **5.** query. **6.** question.

qua (kwā, kwä), adv. as; as being; in the character or capacity of: *he spoke qua judge.* [t. L, orig. abl. fem. of *qui* who]

quack¹ (kwăk), v.i. **1.** to utter the cry of a duck, or a sound resembling it. —n. **2.** the cry of a duck, or some similar sound. [imit. Cf. D *kwakken*, G *quacken*]

quack² (kwăk), n. **1.** an ignorant or fraudulent pretender to medical skill. **2.** one who pretends professionally or publicly to skill, knowledge, or qualifications which he does not possess; a charlatan. —adj. **3.** being a quack: *a quack doctor.* **4.** pertaining to or befitting a quack. **5.** involving quackery: *quack methods.* —v.i. **6.** to play the quack. [short for QUACKSALVER]

quack·er·y (kwăk′ə rĭ), n., pl. **-eries.** **1.** the practice or methods of a quack. **2.** an instance of this.

quack grass, couch grass, *Agropyron repens.*

quack·sal·ver (kwăk′săl′vər), n. **1.** a quack in medicine. **2.** Archaic. a charlatan. [t. early mod. D. Cf. QUACK¹, SALVE]

quad¹ (kwŏd), n. Colloq. a quadrangle, orig. of a college. [short for QUADRANGLE; orig. collegiate slang]

quad² (kwŏd), n. Print. a piece of type metal of less height than the lettered types, serving to cause a blank in printed matter, used for spacing, etc. [short for QUADRAT]

quad³ (kwŏd), n. Chiefly Brit. Slang. quod.

quad⁴ (kwŏd), n. Colloq. quadruplet.

quad., quadrangle.

quadr-, var. of quadri-, before vowels, as in *quadrangle.*

Quad·ra·ges·i·ma (kwŏd′rə jĕs′ə mə), n. **1.** the first Sunday in Lent (more fully, **Quadragesima Sunday**). **2.** Obs. the forty days of Lent. [ML, short for L *quadrāgēsima dies* fortieth day]

Quad·ra·ges·i·mal (kwŏd′rə jĕs′ə məl), adj. **1.** pertaining to, or suitable for, Lent. **2.** (*sometimes l.c.*) lasting forty days, as the fast of Lent.

quad·ran·gle (kwŏd′răng′gəl), n. **1.** a plane figure having four angles and four sides, as a square. **2.** a quadrangular space or court wholly or nearly surrounded by a building or buildings. **3.** the building or buildings about such a space or court. **4.** the area shown on one of the standard topographic sheets of the U.S. Geological Survey (approximately 17 miles north to south and from

15 to 11 miles east to west). [ME, t. LL: m.s. *quadrangulum* (neut.), lit., four-cornered (thing)] —**quad·ran·gu·lar** (kwŏd′răng/gyə lər), *adj.*

quad·rant (kwŏd′rənt), *n.* **1.** the quarter of a circle; an arc of 90°. **2.** the area included between such an arc and two radii drawn one to each extremity. **3.** something shaped like a quarter of a circle, as a part of a machine. **4.** *Geom.* one of the four parts into which a plane is divided by two perpendicular lines. **5.** an instrument, usually containing a graduated arc of 90°, used in astronomy, navigation, etc., for measuring altitudes. [ME, t. L: s. *quadrans* fourth part] —**quad·ran·tal** (kwŏd răn′təl), *adj.*

Quadrants
Arc AC (def. l);
Segment ABC (def. 2)

quad·rat (kwŏd′rət), *n. Print.* a quad². [var. of QUADRATE]

quad·rate (*adj.*, *n.* kwŏd′rāt, -răt; *v.* kwŏd′rāt), *adj.*, *n.*, *v.*, **-rated, -rating** —*adj.* **1.** square; rectangular. **2.** *Zool.* of or pertaining to the quadrate. —*n.* **3.** a square, or something square or rectangular. **4.** *Zool.* one of a pair of bones in the skulls of many lower vertebrates, to which the lower jaw is articulated. —*v.t.* **5.** to conform; adapt. —*v.i.* **6.** to agree; conform. [ME *quadrat*, t. L: s. *quadrātus*, pp., made square]

quad·rat·ic (kwŏd răt′Yk), *adj.* **1.** square. **2.** *Alg.* involving the square and no higher power of the unknown quantity; the second degree: *a quadratic equation.* —*n.* *Alg.* a quadratic equation.

quad·rat·ics (kwŏd răt′Yks), *n.* the branch of algebra that treats of quadratic equations.

quad·ra·ture (kwŏd′rə char), *n.* **1.** act of squaring. **2.** act or process of finding a square equal in area to a given surface, esp. a surface bounded by a curve. **3.** *Astron.* **a.** the situation of two heavenly bodies when their longitudes differ by 90°. **b.** either of the two points in the orbit of a body, as the moon, midway between the syzygies. **c.** (of the moon) those points or moments at which a half moon is visible. [t. L: m. *quadrātūra*]

quadrature of the circle, *Math.* the geometrically insoluble problem of constructing a square equal in area to a given circle.

quad·ren·ni·al (kwŏd rĕn′Yəl), *adj.* **1.** occurring every four years. **2.** of or for four years. [earlier *quadriennial*, f. L *quadrienni(s)* + -AL¹] —**quad·ren·ni·al·ly,** *adv.*

quad·ren·ni·um (kwŏd rĕn′Yəm), *n.*, *pl.* **-renniums, -rennia** (-rĕn′Yə). a period of four years. [NL, alter. of L *quadriennium*]

quadri-, a word element meaning "four." Also, **quadr-.** [t. L; cf. L *quattuor* four]

quad·ric (kwŏd′rYk), *Math.* —*adj.* **1.** of the second degree: said esp. of functions with more than two variables. —*n.* **2.** a surface such as an ellipsoid or paraboloid as defined by a second degree equation in three real variables. [f. s. L *quadra* a square + -IC]

quad·ri·cen·ten·ni·al (kwŏd′rY sĕn tĕn′Yəl), *adj.* **1.** of, pertaining to, or marking the completion of a period of four hundred years. —*n.* **2.** a quadricentennial anniversary. **3.** its celebration.

quad·ri·ceps (kwŏd′rə sĕps′), *n. Anat.* the great muscle of the front of the thigh, which extends the leg and is considered as having four heads or origins. [NL, f. L: *quadri-* QUADRI- + *-ceps* headed. Cf. BICEPS]

quad·ri·cy·cle (kwŏd′rə sī′kəl), *n.* a vehicle similar to the bicycle and tricycle but having four wheels.

quad·ri·fid (kwŏd′rə fĭd), *adj.* cleft into four parts or lobes. [t. L: s. *quadrifidus*. See QUADRI-, -FID]

quad·ri·ga (kwŏd rī′gə), *n.*, *pl.* **-gae** (-jē). *Class. Antiq.* a two-wheeled chariot drawn by four horses harnessed abreast. [L, earlier pl., *quadrigae*, contr. of *quadrijugae* a team of four]

quad·ri·lat·er·al (kwŏd′rə lăt′ər əl), *adj.* **1.** having four sides. —*n.* **2.** a plane figure having four sides and four angles. **3.** something of this form. **4.** *Geom.* a figure formed by four straight lines which have six points of intersection (**complete quadrilateral**). **5.** the space enclosed between and defended by four fortresses. [f. s. L *quadrilaterus* four-sided + -AL¹]

Quadrilaterals
A. Simple (def. 2);
B. Complete (def. 4)

quad·ri·lin·gual (kwŏd′rə-lYng′gwəl), *adj.* using or involving four languages. [f. QUADRI- + s. L *lingua* tongue + -AL¹]

qua·drille¹ (kwədrYl′, kə-), *n.* **1.** a square dance for four couples, consisting of five parts or movements, each complete in itself. **2.** some similar dance. **3.** the music for such a dance. [t. F, t. Sp.: m. *cuadrilla* company, troop, dim. of *cuadra* square, g. L *quadra*]

qua·drille² (kwədrYl′, kə-), *n.* a game at cards played by four persons. [t. F, t. Sp.: m. *cuartillo*, der. *cuarto* fourth, g. L *quartus*]

quad·ril·lion (kwŏd rYl′yən), *n.* **1.** a cardinal number represented by one followed by 15 zeros in the U.S. and France, or 24 zeros in Great Britain and Germany. —*adj.* **2.** amounting to one quadrillion in number. [t. F, f. L *quadr-* QUADR- + F (m)*illion* MILLION]

quad·ri·no·mi·al (kwŏd′rə nō′mYəl), *Alg.* —*adj.* **1.** consisting of four terms. —*n.* **2.** a quadrinomial expression.

quad·ri·par·tite (kwŏd′rə pär′tĭt), *adj.* **1.** divided into or consisting of four parts. **2.** involving four participants: *a quadripartite treaty.* [t. L: m.s. *quadripartītus*]

quad·ri·syl·la·ble (kwŏd′rə sY'l ə bəl), *n.* a word of four syllables. —**quad·ri·syl·lab·ic** (kwŏd′rə sY lăb′Yk), *adj.*

quad·ri·va·lent (kwŏd′rə vā′lənt, kwŏd rYv′ə-), *adj. Chem.* **1.** having a valence of four; tetravalent. **2.** exercising four different valences, as antimony with valences 5, 4, 3, and −3. —**quad·ri·va·lence, quad·ri·va·len·cy,** *n.*

quad·riv·i·al (kwŏd rYv′Yəl), *adj.* **1.** having four ways or roads meeting in a point. **2.** (of ways or roads) leading in four directions. [ME, t. ML: s. *quadriviālis*, der. L *quadrivium*. See QUADRIVIUM]

quad·riv·i·um (kwŏd rYv′Yəm), *n.* (during the Middle Ages) the more advanced division of the seven liberal arts, comprising arithmetic, geometry, astronomy, and music. [t. LL, special use of L *quadrivium* place where four ways meet]

quad·roon (kwŏd rōōn′), *n.* a person who is one fourth Negro; the offspring of a mulatto and white. [t. Sp.: m. *cuarterón*, der. *cuarto* fourth, g. L *quartus*]

quad·ru·ma·nous (kwŏd rōō′mə nəs), *adj.* four-handed; having all four feet adapted for use as hands, as animals of the monkey kind. [t. NL: m. *quadrumanus*]

quad·ru·ped (kwŏd′rōō pĕd′), *adj.* **1.** four-footed. —*n.* **2.** an animal, esp. a mammal, having four feet. [t. L: s. *quadrupēs*] —**quad·ru·pe·dal** (kwŏd rōō′pə dəl, kwŏd′rōō pĕd′əl), *adj.*

quad·ru·ple (kwŏd′rōō pəl, kwŏd rōō′pəl), *adj.*, *n.*, *v.*, **-pled, -pling.** —*adj.* **1.** fourfold; consisting of four parts: *a quadruple alliance.* **2.** four times as great. —*n.* **3.** a number, amount, etc., four times as great as another. —*v.t.*, *v.i.* **4.** to make or become four times as great. [ME, t. L: m.s. *quadruplus*]

quad·ru·plet (kwŏd′rōō plĭt, kwŏd rōō′-), *n.* **1.** any group or combination of four. **2.** (*pl.*) four children born at a birth. **3.** one of four children born at a birth.

quadruple time, 1. a measure consisting of four beats or pulses with accent on the first and third. **2.** the rhythm created by use of this measure.

quad·ru·plex (kwŏd′rōō plĕks′, kwŏd rōō′plĕks), *adj.* **1.** fourfold; quadruple. **2.** noting or pertaining to a system of telegraphy by which four messages may be transmitted simultaneously over one wire or communications channel. [t. L]

quad·ru·pli·cate (*v.* kwŏd rōō′plə kāt′; *adj.*, *n.*, kwŏd rōō′plə kĭt, -kāt/), *v.*, **-cated, -cating,** *adj.*, *n.* —*v.t.* **1.** to make fourfold; quadruple. —*adj.* **2.** fourfold; quadruple. —*n.* **3.** one of four things. [t. L: m.s. *quadruplicātus*, pp., quadrupled] —**quad·ru/pli·ca/tion,** *n.*

quae·re (kwYr′Y), *v. imperative.* **1.** ask; inquire (used to introduce or suggest a question). —*n.* **2.** a query or question. [L, impv. of *quaerere* seek, ask. Cf. QUERY]

quaes·tor (kwĕs′tər, kwēs/tər), *n.* (in ancient Rome) **1.** one of two subordinates of the consuls serving as public prosecutors in certain criminal cases. **2.** (later) one of the public magistrates in charge of the state funds, as treasury officers or attached to the consuls and provincial governors. Also, **questor.** [t. L] —**quaes·to·ri·al** (kwĕs tōr′Yəl, kwĕs-), *adj.* —**quaes/tor·ship/**, *n.*

quaff (kwăf, kwäf, kwôf), *v.i.* **1.** to drink wine or the like in large drafts, as with hearty enjoyment. —*v.t.* **2.** to drink (wine, etc.) copiously and heartily. —*n.* **3.** a quaffing. [earlier *quaft*, b. QUENCH and DRAUGHT] —**quaff/er,** *n.*

quag·ga (kwăg/ə), *n.* a South African equine mammal, *Equus quagga*, extinct since about 1875, related to the zebra, but striped only on the fore part of the body and the head. [t. S Afr. (Zulu), ? der. *quag* striped]

quag·gy (kwăg/Y, kwŏg/Y), *adj.*, **-gier, -giest.** of the nature of or resembling a quag or quagmire; boggy.

quag·mire (kwăg/mīr′, kwŏg/-), *n.* **1.** a piece of miry or boggy ground whose surface yields under the tread; a bog. **2.** a situation from which extrication is difficult. Also, *Brit.*, **quag.** [f. *quag-* (? b. QUAKE and SAG) + MIRE]

qua·hog (kwō/hŏg, -hôg, kwə hŏg′, -hôg/), *n.* an edible American clam, *Venus mercenaria*, the round clam or hard clam of the Atlantic coast. Also, **qua/haug.** [t. N Amer. Ind. (Narragansett), aphetic var. of *poquauhock*]

Quai d'Or·say (kĕ dôr sĕ′), **1.** the quay along the south bank of the Seine in Paris, on which are the department of foreign affairs and other government offices. **2.** the French foreign office, or the government in general. [F: lit., quay of Orsay (a French general)]

quail¹ (kwāl), *n.*, *pl.* **quails,** (*esp. collectively*) **quail. 1.** a small migratory Old World gallinaceous game bird, *Coturnix coturnix*. **2.** any of various New World gallinaceous game birds of the genus *Colinus* and allied genera, many of which are locally known as partridges, esp. the bobwhite, *C. virginianus*. [ME *quaille*, t. OF; of Gmc. orig. Cf. D *kwakkel* quail, and MD, MLG *quackele*, akin to QUACK¹]

quail² (kwāl), *v.i.* to lose heart or courage in difficulty or danger; shrink with fear. [ME; orig. uncert.]

Bobwhite quail,
Colinus virginianus
(10 in. long)

quaint (kwānt), *adj.* **1.** strange or odd in an interesting, pleasing, or amusing way: *the quaint streets of Quebec.* **2.** oddly picturesque; having an old-fashioned attractiveness or charm: *a quaint old house.* **3.** *Archaic.* wise; skilled. **4.** strange; odd. [ME *queinte*, t. OF, var. of *cointe* pretty, pleasing, g. L *cognitus*, pp., known] —**quaint′ly,** *adv.* —**quaint′ness,** *n.*

quake (kwāk), *v.,* **quaked, quaking,** *n.* —*v.i.* **1.** (of persons) to shake from cold, weakness, fear, anger, or the like. **2.** (of things) to shake or tremble, as from shock, internal convulsion, or instability. —*n.* **3.** an earthquake. **4.** a trembling or tremulous agitation. [ME; OE *cwacian* shake, tremble] —**Syn. 1.** shudder, tremble. See **shiver¹.**

Quak·er (kwā′kər), *n.* a member of the Society of Friends. The term *Quaker* is not used by members of the group. [f. QUAKE, v. + -ER¹; first used because George Fox, the founder, bade them "tremble at the word of the Lord"] —**Quak′er·ess,** *n. fem.* —**Quak′er·ish,** *adj.*

Quaker gun, a dummy gun, as in a ship or fort (so named in allusion to the Quakers' opposition to all war).

Quak·er·ism (kwā′kə rĭz′əm), *n.* the principles and customs of the Quakers.

Qua·ker-la·dies (kwā′kər lā′dĭz), *n.pl.* bluet (def. 2).

Quak·er·ly (kwā′kər lĭ), *adj.* **1.** like a Quaker. —*adv.* **2.** in the manner of the Quakers.

qual·i·fi·ca·tion (kwŏl′ə fə kā′shən), *n.* **1.** a quality, accomplishment, etc., which qualifies or fits for some function. **2.** a required circumstance or condition for acquiring or exercising a right, holding an office, or the like. **3.** act of qualifying. **4.** state of being qualified. **5.** modification, limitation, or restriction; an instance of this: *to assert a thing without any qualification.*

qual·i·fied (kwŏl′ə fīd′), *adj.* **1.** possessed of qualities or accomplishments which fit one for some function or office. **2.** having qualifications required by law or custom. **3.** modified, limited, or restricted in some way: *a qualified statement.* —**qual′i·fied′ly,** *adv.*

qual·i·fi·er (kwŏl′ə fī′ər), *n.* **1.** one who or that which qualifies. **2.** *Gram.* a word which qualifies the meaning of another, as an adjective or adverb.

qual·i·fy (kwŏl′ə fī′), *v.,* **-ied, -fying.** —*v.t.* **1.** to invest with proper or necessary qualities; make competent. **2.** to attribute some quality or qualities to; to characterize, call, or name. **3.** *Law.* **a.** to furnish with legal power or capacity: *by filing a bond he qualified himself as executor.* **b.** to make legally capable by the administration of an oath. **4.** to modify in some way; limit; make less strong or positive: *to qualify a statement.* **5.** *Gram.* to modify. **6.** to make less violent, severe, or unpleasant; moderate; mitigate. **7.** to modify or alter the strength or flavor of. —*v.i.* **8.** to make or show oneself competent for something. **9.** to obtain competent power or capacity, as by fulfilling necessary conditions or taking an oath. **10.** *U.S.* to make oath to any fact. **11.** *Sports.* to demonstrate the necessary ability in an initial contest. [t. ML: m.s. *quālificāre.* See -FY] —**Syn. 1.** fit. **4.** See **modify. 6.** reduce, diminish, temper, soften.

qual·i·ta·tive (kwŏl′ə tā′tĭv), *adj.* pertaining to or concerned with quality or qualities. —**qual′i·ta·tive·ly,** *adv.*

qualitative analysis, *Chem.* the analysis of a substance in order to ascertain the nature of its constituents.

qual·i·ty (kwŏl′ə tĭ), *n., pl.* **-ties. 1.** a characteristic, property, or attribute: *useful qualities.* **2.** character or nature, as belonging to or distinguishing a thing: *the quality of a sound.* **3.** character with respect to excellence, fineness, etc., or grade of excellence: *food of poor quality.* **4.** high grade; superior excellence: *goods of quality.* **5.** native excellence or superiority. **6.** an accomplishment or attainment. **7.** *Archaic.* social status or position. **8.** good or high social position: *a man of quality.* **9.** the superiority or distinction associated with high social position. **10.** *Archaic or Dial.* persons of high social position. **11.** *Acoustics.* the texture of a tone, dependent on its overtone content, which distinguishes it from others of the same pitch and loudness. **12.** *Phonet.* the timbre or tonal color which distinguishes one speech sound from another and remains essentially constant for each sound, even in different voices. **13.** *Logic.* the character of a proposition as affirmative or negative. [ME *qualite*, t. L: m.s. *quālitas*] —**Syn. 1.** trait, character, feature. QUALITY, ATTRIBUTE, PROPERTY agree in meaning a particular characteristic (of a person or thing). A QUALITY is a characteristic, innate or acquired, which, in some particular, determines the nature and behavior of a person or thing: *kindness as a quality, the quality of cloth.* An ATTRIBUTE was originally a quality attributed, usually to a person or something personified; more recently it has meant a fundamental or innate characteristic: *an attribute of God, attributes of a logical mind.* PROPERTY applies only to things; it means a characteristic belonging specifically in the constitution of, or found (invariably) in, the behavior of a thing: *a property of hydrogen, of limestone.* **3.** nature, kind, grade.

qualm (kwäm, kwôm), *n.* **1.** an uneasy scruple or a pang of compunction as to conduct. **2.** a sudden misgiving, or feeling of apprehensive uneasiness. **3.** a sudden sensation of faintness or illness, now esp. of nausea. [OE *cwealm* torment, pain, plague]

qualm·ish (kwä′mĭsh, kwô′-), *adj.* **1.** inclined to have, or having, qualms, esp. of nausea. **2.** character-

ized by qualms. **3.** of the nature of a qualm. **4.** apt to cause qualms. —**qualm′ish·ly,** *adv.* —**qualm′ish·ness,** *n.*

quam·ash (kwŏm′ăsh, kwə măsh′), *n.* camass.

quan·da·ry (kwŏn′də rĭ, -drĭ), *n., pl.* **-ries.** a state of embarrassing perplexity or uncertainty, esp. as to what to do; a dilemma. [orig. obscure] —**Syn.** See **predicament.**

quand même (kän mĕm′), *French.* just the same.

quan·dong (kwŏn′dŏng′), *n.* **1.** a santalaceous tree, *Fusanus acuminatus,* of Australia, yielding an edible drupaceous fruit whose seed (**quandong nut**) has an edible kernel. **2.** the fruit, or the seed or nut. Also **quan·dang** (kwŏn′dŏng′). [native Australian]

quant (kwänt, kwŏnt), *Brit.* —*n.* **1.** a pole having a flange near its tip, used for punting. —*v.t., v.i.* **2.** to propel or be propelled with the aid of a quant.

quan·ta (kwŏn′tə), *n.* pl. of **quantum.**

quan·tic (kwŏn′tĭk), *n.* *Math.* a rational, integral, homogeneous function of two or more variables. [f. s. L *quantus* how great + -IC]

quan·ti·fi·er (kwŏn′tĭ fī′ər), *n.* *Logic.* an expression, such as "all" or "some," which indicates the quantity of a proposition.

quan·ti·fy (kwŏn′tə fī′), *v.t.,* **-fied, -fying. 1.** to determine the quantity of; measure. **2.** *Logic.* to make explicit the quantity of. [t. ML: m.s. *quantificāre.* See -FY] —**quan′ti·fi·ca′tion,** *n.*

quan·ti·ta·tive (kwŏn′tə tā′tĭv), *adj.* **1.** that is or may be estimated by quantity. **2.** of or pertaining to the describing or measuring of quantity. **3.** of or pertaining to the metrical system in classical poetry based on feet of long and short, rather than accented and unaccented, syllables. **4.** of or pertaining to the length or quantity of a vowel. —**quan′ti·ta′tive·ly,** *adv.* —**quan′ti·ta′tive·ness,** *n.*

quantitative analysis, *Chem.* the analysis of a substance in order to determine the amounts and proportions of its constituents.

quan·ti·ty (kwŏn′tə tĭ), *n., pl.* **-ties. 1.** a particular, indefinite, or considerable amount of anything: *a small quantity of water.* **2.** amount or measure: *food in great quantity.* **3.** considerable or great amount: *to extract ore in quantity.* **4.** *Math.* **a.** an entity subject to treatment in accordance with a set of consistent rules. **b.** the property of magnitude involving comparability with other magnitudes. **c.** something having magnitude, as size, extent, amount, or the like. **d.** magnitude, size, volume, area, or length. **5.** *Music.* the length or duration of a note. **6.** *Logic.* the character of a proposition as universal or particular. **7.** *Philos.* that in terms of which a thing is more or less. **8.** *Pros., Phonet.* (of sounds or syllables) character as to being long or short, with reference to the time required in uttering them. A long or accented syllable takes about twice the time, in practice and theory, of a short or unaccented syllable. **9.** *Law.* length or duration in time. [ME *quantite,* t. L: m.s. *quantitas*]

quan·tum (kwŏn′təm), *n., pl.* **-ta** (-tə). **1.** quantity or amount. **2.** a particular amount. **3.** a share or portion. **4.** *Physics.* **a.** one of the discrete quantities of energy or momentum of an atomic system which are characteristic of the quantum theory. **b.** this amount of energy regarded as a unit. [t. L: (neut.) how great, how much]

quan·tum suf·fi·cit (kwŏn′təm sŭf′ə sĭt), *Latin.* as much as suffices; enough.

quantum theory, *Physics.* a theory that energetic physical processes, especially changes of energy in molecules and atoms, are discontinuous, involving discrete quantities of energy called quanta.

quar., **1.** quarter. **2.** quarterly.

quar·an·tine (kwôr′ən tēn′, kwŏr′-), *n., v.,* **-tined, -tining.** —*n.* **1.** a strict isolation designed to prevent the spread of disease: *a house in quarantine for scarlet fever.* **2.** a period, orig. forty days, of detention or isolation imposed upon ships, persons, etc., on arrival at a port or place, when liable or suspected to be bringing some infectious or contagious disease. **3.** a system of measures maintained by public authority at ports, on frontiers, etc., for preventing the spread of disease. **4.** the branch of the public service concerned with such measures. **5.** a place or station at which such measures are carried out. **6.** the detention or isolation enforced. **7.** the port or place where the ships are detained. **8.** the place (esp. a hospital) where people are detained. **9.** a period of forty days. —*v.t.* **10.** to put in or subject to quarantine. **11.** to isolate politically and commercially. [t. It.: m. *quarantina,* der. *quaranta,* g. L *quadrāgintā* forty]

Quarles (kwôrlz, kwärlz), *n.* **Francis,** 1592–1644, British poet.

Quar·ne·ro (kwär nĕ′rō), *n.* **Gulf of,** an arm of the Adriatic Sea, E of the Istrian peninsula, in NW Yugoslavia.

quar·rel¹ (kwôr′əl, kwŏr′-), *n., v.,* **-reled, -reling** or (*esp. Brit.*) **-relled, -relling.** —*n.* **1.** an angry dispute or altercation; a disagreement marked by a break in friendly relations. **2.** a cause of complaint or hostile feeling against a person, etc. —*v.i.* **3.** to disagree angrily, squabble, or fall out. **4.** to dispute angrily; wrangle. **5.** to raise a complaint, or find fault. [ME *querele,* t. OF, g. L *querēl(l)a* complaint] —**quar′rel·er;** *esp. Brit.* **quar′rel·ler,** *n.* —**Syn. 1.** dispute, contention, disagreement, controversy.

dissension. QUARREL, FEUD apply to a more or less hostile demonstration or a situation of enmity existing between individuals or groups. A QUARREL varies in degrees of seriousness from a slight, brief, and petty difference or dispute (usually between individuals), to an angry, violent altercation resulting in deep-seated hostility: *a domestic quarrel*. A FEUD is an enduring hostility between families or groups (rarely individuals), often resulting in acts of violence and efforts at retaliation and revenge: *a bitter feud between the Hatfields and McCoys.* 3. disagree, differ, bicker, squabble.

quar·rel² (kwôr′əl, kwŏr′-). *n.* **1.** a square-headed bolt or arrow, formerly used with a crossbow. **2.** a small square or diamond-shaped pane of glass, as used in latticed windows. **3.** any of certain tools, as a stonemason's chisel. [ME *quarel*, t. OF, t. ML: m.s. *quadrellus*, dim. of L *quadrus* square]

quar·rel·some (kwôr′əl səm, kwŏr′-), *adj.* inclined to quarrel. —**quar′rel·some·ly**, *adv.* —**quar′rel·some·ness**, *n.*

quar·ri·er (kwôr′ĭər, kwŏr′-), *n.* one who quarries stone.

quar·ry¹ (kwôr′ĭ, kwŏr′ĭ), *n., pl.* **-ries**, *v.,* **-ried, -rying.** —*n.* **1.** an excavation or pit, usually open to the air, from which building stone, slate, or the like is obtained by cutting, blasting, etc. —*v.t.* **2.** to obtain (stone, etc.) from, or as from, a quarry. **3.** to make a quarry in. [ME *quarey*, t. ML: m.s. *quareia*, var. of *quareria*, VL *quadrāria* place where stone is squared, der. L *quadrāre* to square]

quar·ry² (kwôr′ĭ, kwŏr′ĭ), *n., pl.* **-ries. 1.** a beast or bird hunted or pursued. **2.** game, esp. game hunted with hounds or hawks. **3.** any object of pursuit or attack. [ME *querre*, t. OF: m. *cuiree*, der. *cuir* skin, hide, g. L *corium*]

quar·ry³ (kwôr′ĭ, kwŏr′ĭ), *n., pl.* **-ries. 1.** a small square or diamond-shaped pane of glass. **2.** a square stone or tile. [n. use of obs. *quarry*, adj., square, t. OF: m. *quarre*]

quart¹ (kwôrt), *n.* **1.** a liquid and also dry measure of capacity, equal to one fourth of a gallon or one eighth of a peck respectively (of varying content in different systems, places, and times). **2.** a vessel or measure holding a quart. [ME, t. F: m. *quarte*, t. ML: m. *quarta* (fem.) fourth]

quart² (kärt), *n.* **1.** *Cards.* (in piquet) **a.** a sequence of four cards. **b. quart major,** the sequence of the highest four cards in any suit. **2.** *Fencing.* quarte. [t. F: m. *quarte* (fem.) fourth, g. L *quarta*]

quart., 1. quarter. 2. quarterly.

quar·tal harmony (kwôr′təl), *Music.* harmony based on chords constructed of fourths instead of thirds.

quar·tan (kwôr′tən), *adj.* **1.** (of a fever, ague, etc.) characterized by paroxysms which recur every fourth day, both days of consecutive occurrence being counted. —*n.* **2.** a quartan fever or ague. [ME *quartaine*, t. F, g. L (*febris*) *quartāna* quartan fever, (fever) of the fourth]

quarte (kärt; *Fr.* kàrt), *n. Fencing.* the fourth of eight defensive positions; carte. [t. F, t. It.: m. *quarta* fourth]

quar·ter (kwôr′tər), *n.* **1.** one of the four equal or equivalent parts into which anything is or may be divided: *a quarter of an apple.* **2.** *U.S. and Canada.* one fourth of a dollar (25 cents). **3.** a silver coin of this value. **4.** one fourth of an hour (15 minutes). **5.** the moment marking this period. **6.** one fourth of a year. **7.** *Astron.* **a.** a fourth of the moon's period or monthly revolution, being that portion of its period or orbital course between a quadrature and a syzygy. **b.** either quadrature of the moon. **c. first quarter,** that fourth of the moon's period coming between the new moon and the last half moon. See diag. under **moon.** **d. last quarter,** that fourth of the moon's period coming between the second half moon and the new moon. See diag. under **moon.** **8.** (in colleges and universities) one of the periods into which instruction is organized, generally 10 to 12 weeks in length. **9.** *Sports.* any one of the four periods that make up some games. **10.** one fourth of a pound. **11.** a fourth of a mile; two furlongs. **12.** the fourth part of a yard; 9 inches. **13.** a unit of weight, chiefly British, the fourth part of a hundredweight; 25 or 28 pounds. **14.** a British measure of capacity for grain, etc., equal to 8 bushels, or, locally, to more or less than this. **15.** the region of any of the four principal points of the compass or divisions of the horizon. **16.** such a point or division. **17.** any point or direction of the compass. **18.** a region, district, or place. **19.** a particular district of a city or town, esp. one appropriated to or occupied by a particular class or group of people. **20.** (*usually pl.*) a place of stay, residence, or lodgment, esp. in military use, the buildings, houses, barracks, or rooms in which officers or enlisted men live, including those occupied by families. **21.** a certain part or member of the community, etc., without reference to locality: *information from a high quarter.* **22.** mercy or indulgence, esp. as shown to a vanquished enemy in sparing his life and accepting his surrender. **23.** one of the four parts, each including a leg, of the body or carcass of a quadruped. **24.** *Vet. Sci.* either side of a horse's hoof, between heel and toe. **25.** *Shoemaking.* the part of a boot or shoe on either side of the foot, from the middle of the back to the vamp. **26.** *Naut.* **a.** the after part of a ship's side, usually from about the aftermost mast to the stern. **b.** the general horizontal direction 45° from the stern of a ship on either side: *land in* *sight on the port quarter.* **c.** one of the stations to which crew members are called for battle, emergencies, or drills. **d.** the part of a yard between the slings and the yardarm. **27.** *Her.* **a.** one of the four (or more) parts into which a shield may be divided by horizontal and vertical lines. **b.** a charge occupying one fourth of the shield, placed in chief. **c.** a quartering, or one of various coats of arms marshaled upon one shield. —*v.t.* **28.** to divide into four equal or equivalent parts. **29.** to divide into parts fewer or more than four. **30.** to cut the body of (a person) into quarters, esp. in executing for treason or the like. **31.** *Mach.* to make holes in, fix, etc., a quarter of a circle apart. **32.** to station or lodge in a particular place. **33.** to impose (soldiers) on persons, etc., to be lodged and fed. **34.** to assign to a particular position for living purposes, action, etc., as on a ship. **35.** to traverse (the ground) from left to right and right to left while advancing, as dogs in search of game. **36.** *Her.* **a.** to divide a shield into four (or more) parts by horizontal and vertical lines. **b.** to place or bear quarterly upon a shield, as different coats of arms. **c.** to add (a coat of arms) thus to one's own. —*v.i.* **37.** to take up or be in quarters; lodge. **38.** to range to and fro, as dogs in search of game. —*adj.* **39.** being one of the four equal (or approximately equal) parts into which anything is or may be divided. **40.** being equal to only about one fourth of the full measure. [ME, t. OF, g. L *quartārius* fourth part.]

quar·ter·age (kwôr′tər ĭj), *n.* a quarterly payment, charge, or allowance. [ME, t. OF]

quar·ter·back (kwôr′tər bǎk′), *n. Football.* **1.** one of the players behind the forward line. **2.** the player who directs his team on attack.

quarter day, one of the four days (in England), Lady Day, Midsummer Day, Michaelmas, and Christmas or (in Scotland), Candlemas, Whitsunday, Lammas, and Martinmas, regarded as marking off the quarters of the year, on which tenancies begin and end, quarterly payments fall due, etc.

quar·ter·deck (kwôr′tər dĕk′), *n. Naut.* the upper deck between the mainmast and the poop or stern.

quar·tered (kwôr′tərd), *adj.* **1.** divided into quarters. **2.** furnished with quarters or lodging. **3.** (of oak, sycamore, gum, etc.) quartersawed. **4.** *Her.* **a.** divided or arranged quarterly. **b.** (of a cross) having a square piece missing in the center.

quar·ter·fi·nal (kwôr′tər fī′nəl), *adj. Sports.* of or pertaining to the contest preceding the semifinals in a tournament.

quar·ter·hour (kwôr′tər our′), *n.* **1.** a period of fifteen minutes. **2.** a point fifteen minutes after or before the hour.

quar·ter·ing (kwôr′tər ĭng), *n.* **1.** act of one who or that which quarters. **2.** the assigning of quarters or lodgings. **3.** *Her.* **a.** the division of a shield into (four or more) quarters. **b.** the marshaling of various coats of arms upon one shield, as to indicate family alliances. **c.** (*chiefly pl.*) one of the coats so marshaled. —*adj.* **4.** that quarters. **5.** lying at right angles. **6.** *Naut.* (of a wind) blowing on a ship's quarter.

quar·ter·ly (kwôr′tər lĭ), *adj., n., pl.* **-lies,** *adv.* —*adj.* **1.** occurring, done, etc., at the end of every quarter of a year. **2.** pertaining to or consisting of a quarter. —*n.* **3.** a periodical issued every three months. —*adv.* **4.** by quarters; once in a quarter of a year. **5.** *Her.* **a.** with division into quarters. **b.** in the quarters of a shield.

quar·ter·mas·ter (kwôr′tər mǎs′tər, -mäs′tər), *n.* **1.** *Mil.* an officer charged with providing quarters, clothing, fuel, transportation, etc., for a body of troops. **2.** *Naval.* a petty officer having charge of signals, navigating apparatus, etc.

quar·tern (kwôr′tərn), *n. Chiefly Brit.* a quarter, or fourth part, esp. of certain weights and measures, as of a pound, ounce, peck, or pint. [ME *quarteroun*, t. OF: m. *quarteron*, der. *quart* fourth. See QUART¹]

quarter note, *Music.* a note equivalent to one fourth of a whole note; a crotchet. See illus. under **note.**

quar·ter·phase (kwôr′tər fāz′), *adj. Elect.* noting a combination of circuits energized by alternating electromotive forces which differ in phase by a quarter of a cycle; two-phase.

quarter point, the fourth part of the distance between any two adjacent points of the 32 marked on a compass, being 2° 48′ 45″.

quar·ter·saw (kwôr′tər sô′), *v.t.,* **-sawed, -sawed** or **-sawn, -sawing.** to saw (lumber) into quarters so that the faces coincide with radii of the log.

quarter section, (in surveying and homesteading) a square tract of land, half a mile on each side, thus containing ¼ sq. mi. or 160 acres.

quarter sessions, *Law.* **1.** an English court of general criminal jurisdiction held quarterly. **2.** *U.S.* a similar court in New Jersey.

quar·ter·staff (kwôr′tər stǎf′, -stäf′). *n., pl.* **-staves** (-stāvz′, -stävz′, -stävz′). **1.** a former English weapon consisting of a stout pole 6 to 8 feet long, tipped with iron. **2.** exercise or fighting with this weapon.

Heraldic quarter (def. 27b)

Quarrels² (def. 2)

Quartered arms² (def. 4a)

ǎct, āble, dâre, ärt; ĕbb, ēqual; ĭf, īce; hŏt, ōver, ôrder, oil, bŏŏk, ōoze, out; ŭp, ūse, ûrge; ə = a in alone; ch, chief; g, give; ng, ring; sh, shoe; th, thin; ᵺ, that; zh, vision. See the full key on inside cover.

quarter tone, *Music.* an interval equivalent to half of a semitone.

quar·tet (kwôr·tĕt′), *n.* **1.** any group of four persons or things. **2.** a company of four singers or players. **3.** a musical composition for four voices or instruments. Also, *esp. Brit.,* **quar·tette′.** [t. F: m. *quartette,* t. It.: m. *quartetto,* der. *quarto* fourth, g. L *quartus*]

quar·tile (kwôr′tīl, -tĭl), *adj.* **1.** *Astrol.* noting or pertaining to the aspect of two heavenly bodies when their longitudes differ by 90°. —*n.* **2.** *Astrol.* a quartile aspect. **3.** *Statistics.* (in a frequency distribution) one of the values of a variable which divides the distribution of the variable into four groups having equal frequencies. [t. ML, neut. of *quartilis,* der. L *quartus* fourth]

quar·to (kwôr′tō), *n., pl.* **-tos,** *adj.* —*n.* **1.** a volume printed from sheets folded twice to form four leaves or eight pages; book size about 9½ x 12 inches. *Abbr.:* 4to or 4° —*adj.* **2.** in quarto. [short for NL *in quartō* in fourth]

quartz (kwôrts), *n.* one of the commonest minerals, silicon dioxide, SiO_2, having many varieties which differ in color, luster, etc., occurring in crystals (rock crystal, amethyst, citrine, etc.) or massive (agate, bloodstone, chalcedony, jasper, etc.), an important constituent of many rocks. It is piezoelectric and is cut into wafers used to control the frequencies of radio transmitters. [t. G: m. *quarz;* orig. unknown]

quartz glass, a glass composed entirely of silica.

quartz·if·er·ous (kwôrts·ĭf′ər·əs), *adj.* containing quartz; consisting of quartz. [f. QUARTZ + -(I)FEROUS]

quartz·ite (kwôrts′īt), *n.* a granular rock consisting essentially of quartz in interlocking grains.

quartz plate, *Elect.* a carefully cut quartz crystal which is piezoelectrically active. See **crystal** (def. 10).

quash¹ (kwŏsh), *v.t.* to put down or suppress completely; subdue. [ME *quasche(n),* t. OF: m. *quasser,* t. L: m. *quassāre* shake, freq. of *quatere*]

quash² (kwŏsh), *v.t.* to make void, annul, or set aside (a law, indictment, decision, etc.). [ME *quasche(n),* t. OF: m. *quasser,* t. L: m. *quassāre* shake, but influenced by LL *cassāre* annul. der. L *cassus* empty, void]

qua·si (kwā′sī, -zī, kwä′sĭ), *adj.* **1.** resembling; as it were. —*adv.* **2.** seemingly, but not actually. [ME, t. L]

quasi-, a prefix form of "quasi," *adj.* and *adv.,* as in **quasi-official, quasi-deify.**

quasi contract, *Law.* an obligation imposed by law in the absence of a contract to prevent unjust enrichment.

qua·si·ju·di·cial (kwā′sī·jōō·dĭsh′əl, -zī-, kwä′sĭ-), *adj.* having characteristics of a judicial act but performed by an administrative agency.

quass (kväs), *n.* a Russian beer made from barley, malt, and rye. Also, **kvass.** [t. Russ.: m. *kvas*]

quas·sia (kwŏsh′ə, -Y·ə), *n.* **1.** a plant of the simaroubaceous genus *Quassia* or of the genus *Picrasma,* esp. *Q. amara,* a tree of tropical America. **2.** the bitter wood of this tree and certain other trees. **3.** a medicinal preparation made from it. [NL; named after *Quassi,* a Surinam Negro, who (ab. 1730) used the bark as a fever remedy]

qua·ter·na·ry (kwə·tûr′nə·rĭ), *adj., n., pl.* **-ries.** —*adj.* **1.** consisting of four. **2.** arranged in fours. **3.** (*cap.*) *Stratig.* pertaining to the most recent geological period or system of rocks, which constitutes the later principal division of the Cenozoic era. —*n.* **4.** a group of four. **5.** the number four. **6.** (*cap.*) *Stratig.* the period or system following the Tertiary. [ME, t. L: m.s. *quaternārius*]

qua·ter·ni·on (kwə·tûr′nĭ·ən), *n.* **1.** a group or set of four persons or things. **2.** *Math.* **a.** the quotient of two vectors considered as depending on four geometrical elements and as expressible by an algebraic quadrinomial. **b.** (*pl.*) the calculus of such quantities. [ME, t. LL: s. *quaternio* the number four, a group of four, der. L *quaternī* four together]

quat·rain (kwŏt′rān), *n.* a stanza or poem of four lines, usually with alternate rhymes. [t. F, der. *quatre* four. See QUATRE]

qua·tre (kä′tər; *Fr.* kȧ′tr), *n.* **1.** four. **2.** the four at cards, dice, or the like. [t. F, g. L *quattuor* four]

Qua·tre Bras (kä′trə brä′; *Fr.* kȧ′tr brä′), a village in central Belgium, near Brussels: a battle preliminary to the battle of Waterloo was fought here, 1815.

quat·re·foil (kăt′ər·foil′, kăt′rə-), *n.* **1.** a leaf composed of four leaflets, as sometimes a leaf of clover. **2.** *Archit.* an ornament or decorative feature having four foils or lobes. [late ME *quater foyl(e),* f. MF. See QUATRE, FOIL²]

quat·tro·cen·to (kwät′trō·chĕn′tō), *n.* the 15th century, used in reference to Italian art of that time. [It.: four hundred, short for *mille quattrocento* one thousand four hundred]

Architectural quatrefoils

qua·ver (kwā′vər), *v.i.* **1.** to shake tremulously, quiver, or tremble (now said usually of the voice). **2.** to sound, speak, or sing tremulously. **3.** to perform quavers, shakes, or trills in singing or on a musical instrument. —*v.t.* **4.** to utter, say, or sing with a quavering or tremulous voice. —*n.* **5.** a quavering or tremulous shake, esp. in the voice. **6.** a quavering tone or utterance. **7.** *Brit.* (in music) an eighth note. [ME; b. QUAKE and WAVER] —**qua′ver·y,** *adj.*

quay (kē), *n.* an artificial landing place, as of masonry built along navigable water, for vessels unloading or loading cargo, etc. [later spelling (after F *quai*) of earlier *kay,* also *key* (whence the mod. pronunciation), t. OF: m. *kay, cay;* akin to Sp. *cayo* shoal. See KEY²]

quay·age (kē′ĭj), *n.* **1.** quays collectively. **2.** space appropriated to quays. **3.** a charge for the use of a quay or quays. [t. F, der. *quay* QUAY]

Que., Quebec.

quean (kwēn), *n.* **1.** a bold, impudent woman; a shrew; a hussy. **2.** a prostitute. **3.** *Scot. and Brit. Dial.* a girl or young woman. [ME *quene,* OE *cwene,* c. OHG *quena* woman; akin to Gk. *gynē* woman. Cf. QUEEN]

quea·sy (kwē′zĭ), *adj.,* **-sier, -siest. 1.** inclined to nausea, as the stomach, a person, etc. **2.** tending to cause nausea, as articles of food. **3.** uneasy or uncomfortable, as feelings, the conscience, etc. **4.** squeamish; excessively fastidious. [late ME; orig. obscure] —**quea′si·ly,** *adv.* —**quea′si·ness,** *n.*

Que·bec (kwĭ·bĕk′), *n.* **1.** a province in E Canada. 4,269,000 (est. 1953); 594,860 sq. mi. **2.** the capital of this province: a seaport on the St. Lawrence; the capital of New France from 1663 to 1759, when it was taken by the English; wartime conferences, 1943, 1944. 164,016; with suburbs, 274,827 (1951).

que·bra·cho (kā·brä′chō; *Sp.* kĕ·brä′chō), *n., pl.* **-chos. 1.** the anacardiaceous trees *Schinopsis Lorentzii* and *S. Balansae,* the wood and bark of which are important in tanning and dyeing. **2.** the apocynaceous tree *Aspidosperma quebrachoblanco,* yielding a medicinal bark. **3.** any of several hard-wooded South American trees. **4.** the wood or bark of any of these trees. [t. Sp., der. *quebrar* break, g. L *crepāre* burst]

Quech·ua (kĕch′wä), *n.* Kechua. —**Quech·uan** (kĕch′wən), *adj., n.*

queen (kwēn), *n.* **1.** the wife or consort of a king. **2.** a female sovereign or monarch. **3.** a woman, or something personified as a woman, that is chief or preëminent in any respect. **4.** a playing card bearing a picture of a queen. **5.** *Chess.* the most powerful piece, moving any distance in any straight or diagonal line. **6.** a fertile female of ants, bees, or termites, frequently the mother of the entire colony. —*v.i.* **7.** to reign as queen. **8.** to play the queen. **9.** to have queenly preëminence (usually fol. by indefinite *it*). [ME *quene,* OE *cwēn* wife, queen, c. OS *quān,* Goth. *qēns* woman, wife; akin to QUEAN]

Queen Anne, *Archit.* denoting or of a style which obtained in England under the reign of Queen Anne (1702–1714), combining classical designs and plans with baroque decorative motifs.

Queen Anne's lace, an umbelliferous plant, *Daucus Carota,* with large lacy umbels of white minute flowers, the central one mostly dark purple.

Queen Char·lotte Islands (shär′lət), a group of islands off the W coast of Canada, in British Columbia. 2389 pop. (1951); 3970 sq. mi.

queen consort, the wife of a king.

queen·dom (kwēn′dəm), *n.* **1.** the position or dignity of a queen. **2.** the realm of a queen.

queen dowager, the widow of a king.

queen·hood (kwēn′hŏŏd′), *n.* the rank of a queen.

queen of the prairie, a tall perennial herb, *Filipendula rubra,* found in meadows and prairies.

queen·ly (kwēn′lĭ), *adj.,* **-lier, -liest,** *adv.* **1.** belonging or proper to a queen: *queenly rank.* **2.** befitting, or suggestive of, a queen: *queenly dignity.* —*adv.* **3.** in a queenly manner. —**queen′li·ness,** *n.*

Queen Mab (măb), *Irish and English Folklore.* a mischievous, tantalizing fairy who governs and produces the dreams of men.

Queen Maud Land (môd), a large coastal region of Antarctica, south of Africa: Norwegian explorations.

Queen Maud Range (môd), a mountain range S of the Ross Sea, in Ross Dependency, Antarctica.

queen mother, a queen dowager who is also mother of a reigning sovereign.

queen olive, **1.** any large-fruited, meaty olive suitable for pickling or processing. **2.** such an olive from the area of Seville, Spain.

queen post, one of a pair of timbers or posts extending vertically upward from the tie beam of a roof truss or the like, one on each side of the center.

Queen-post roof
A. Queen post; B. Tie beam; C. Strut; D. Straining piece

queen regnant, a queen who reigns in her own right.

Queens (kwēnz), *n.* an E borough of New York City, on Long Island. 1,809,578 (1960); 113.1 sq. mi.

Queen's Bench, King's Bench.

queen's English, king's English.

queen's evidence, king's evidence.

Queens·land (kwēnz′lănd′, -lənd), *n.* a state in NE Australia. 3,423,529 pop. (1954); ab. 670,500 sq. mi. *Cap.:* Brisbane.

Queen's Remembrancer. See **remembrancer** (def. 4a).

---

b., blend of, blended; c., cognate with; d., dialect, dialectal; der., derived from; f., formed from; g., going back to; m., modification of; r., replacing; s., stem of; t., taken from; ?, perhaps. See the full key on inside cover.

Queens·town (kwēnz′toun′), *n.* former name of **Cóbh.**

queer (kwĭr), *adj.* **1.** strange from a conventional point of view; singular or odd: *a queer notion.* **2.** *Colloq.* of questionable character; suspicious; shady. **3.** out of the normal state of feeling physically; giddy, faint, or qualmish: *to feel queer.* **4.** *Colloq.* mentally unbalanced or deranged. **5.** *Slang.* bad, worthless, or counterfeit. **6.** *Slang.* homosexual. —*v.t. Slang.* **7.** to bring to confusion; spoil; ruin. **8.** to put (a person) in a hopeless situation as to success, favor, etc. —*n.* **9.** *Slang.* a homosexual. [t. G: m. *quer* oblique, cross, adverse] —**queer′ly,** *adv.* —**queer′ness,** *n.* —Syn. 1. curious.

quell (kwĕl), *v.t.* **1.** to suppress (disorder, mutiny, etc.); put an end to; extinguish. **2.** to vanquish; subdue. **3.** to quiet or allay (feelings, etc.). [ME; OE *cwellan* kill, causative of *cwelan* die; akin to D *kwellen,* G *quälen*] —**quell′er,** *n.* —Syn. 1. crush, quash, overpower.

Quel·part (kwĕl′pärt′), *n.* Cheju.

Que·moy (kē′moi′), a Chinese island off the SE coast of China. With Matsu, important in the defense of Formosa. Pop. & area of both: 56,349 (est. 1956); ab. 67 sq. mi.

quench (kwĕnch), *v.t.* **1.** to suppress or stifle; put an end to; slake, as thirst. **2.** to put out or extinguish (fire, light, etc.). **3.** to cool suddenly, as by plunging into water, as steel in tempering it. [ME *quench(en),* OE *-cwencan,* causative of *-cwincan.* Cf. Fris. *kwinka* be put out] —**quench′a·ble,** *adj.* —**quench′er,** *n.*

quench·less (kwĕnch′lĭs), *adj.* that cannot be quenched; inextinguishable.

que·nelle (kə něl′), *n. Cookery.* a ball of minced chicken, veal, or the like, blended with egg and crumbs and boiled in stock. [t. F, f. G: m. *knödel*]

quer·ce·tin (kwûr′sə tĭn), *n.* a yellow crystalline powder, $C_{15}H_{10}O_7$, obtained from the bark of the quercitron and from other vegetable substances: used as a yellow dye. [appar. f. s. L *quercētum* oak-wood $+ -IN^2$] —**quer·cet·ic** (kwər sĕt′ĭk, -sē′tĭk), *adj.*

quer·cine (kwûr′sĭn, -sīn), *adj.* of or pertaining to the oak. [t. LL: m.s. *quercīnus,* der. L *quercus* oak]

quer·cit·ron (kwûr′sĭt′ron), *n.* **1.** a species of oak, *Quercus velutina,* of eastern North America, whose inner bark yields a yellow dye. **2.** the bark itself. **3.** the dye obtained from it. [abbr. for *querci-citron,* f. *querci-* (comb. form repr. L *quercus* oak) + CITRON]

Quer·cus (kwûr′kəs), *n.* a genus of dicotyledonous, apetalous plants, the oaks, of the family *Fagaceae,* native to all north temperate regions, and having a durable wood.

Que·ré·ta·ro (kē rĕ′tä rō′), *n.* **1.** a state in central Mexico. 295,413 (est. 1952); 4432 sq. mi. **2.** the capital of this state: republican forces executed Emperor Maximilian here, 1867. 49,209 (1950).

que·rist (kwĭr′ĭst), *n.* one who puts a query. [f. m.s. L *quaerere* ask + -IST]

quer·u·lous (kwĕr′ə ləs, kwĕr′yə-), *adj.* **1.** full of complaints; complaining. **2.** characterized by, or uttered in, complaint; peevish: *a querulous tone.* [t. L: m. *querulus*] —**quer′u·lous·ly,** *adv.* —**quer′u·lous·ness,** *n.*

que·ry (kwĭr′ĭ), *n., pl.* **-ries,** *v.,* **-ried, -rying.** —*n.* **1.** a question; an inquiry. **2.** doubt. **3.** *Print.* a question or interrogation point (?), esp. as added on a manuscript, proof sheet, or the like, with reference to some point in the text. —*v.t.* **4.** to ask or inquire. **5.** to question (a statement, etc.) as doubtful or obscure. **6.** *Print.* to mark with a query. **7.** to ask questions of. [earlier *quere,* t. ML, for L *quaere,* impv. of *quaerere* ask]

Ques·nay (kě ně′), *n.* François (frän swä′), 1694-1774, French economist and physician.

quest (kwĕst), *n.* **1.** a search or pursuit made in order to find or obtain something: *a quest for gold.* **2.** *Medieval Romance.* a knight′y expedition undertaken to secure or achieve something: *the quest of the Holy Grail.* **3.** those engaged in such an expedition. **4.** an inquest. **5.** *Now Rare.* a jury of inquest. —*v.i.* **6.** to search; seek. **7.** to go on a quest. **8.** *Hunting.* (of dogs, etc.) **a.** to search for game. **b.** to bay or give tongue in pursuit of game. —*v.t.* **9.** to search or seek for; pursue. [ME *queste,* t. OF, g. L *quaesitus,* pp., sought, asked] —**quest′er,** *n.*

ques·tion (kwĕs′chən), *n.* **1.** a sentence in an interrogative form, addressed to someone in order to elicit information. **2.** a problem for discussion or under discussion; a matter for investigation. **3.** a matter or point of uncertainty or difficulty; a case (fol. by *of*): *to be a question of time.* **4.** a subject of dispute or controversy. **5.** a proposal to be debated or voted on, as in a meeting or a deliberative assembly. **6.** the procedure of putting a proposal to vote. **7.** *Pol.* a problem of public policy submitted to the voters for an expression of opinion. **8.** *Law.* **a.** a controversy which is submitted to a judicial tribunal or administrative agency for decision. **b.** the interrogation by which information is secured. **c.** *Obs.* judicial examination or trial. **9.** act of asking or inquiring; interrogation; query. **10.** inquiry into, or discussion of, some problem or doubtful matter. **11. beyond (all) question,** beyond dispute; indisputably. **12. in question. a.** under consideration. **b.** in dispute. **13. out of the question,** not to be considered. **14. call in question. a.** to dispute, question, or challenge. **b.** to cast doubt upon. —*v.t.* **15.** to ask a question or questions of; interrogate. **16.** to ask or inquire. **17.** to make a question of; doubt. **18.** to call in question; dispute. —*v.i.* **19.** to ask a question or questions. [ME *questiun,* t. AF, t. L m.s. *quaestio*] —**ques′tion·er,** *n.* —**ques′tion·ing·ly,** *adv.* —Syn. 16. See inquire.

ques·tion·a·ble (kwĕs′chən ə bəl), *adj.* **1.** of doubtful propriety, honesty, morality, respectability, etc. **2.** open to question or dispute; doubtful or uncertain: *whether this is true is questionable.* **3.** open to question as to being such: *a questionable privilege.* —**ques′tion·a·ble·ness, ques′tion·a·bil′i·ty,** *n.* —**ques′tion·a·bly,** *adv.* —Syn. 2. debatable, disputable, controvertible.

ques·tion·ar·y (kwĕs′chə nĕr′ĭ), *n., pl.* **-aries.** a questionnaire.

ques·tion·less (kwĕs′chən lĭs), *adj.* **1.** unquestionable. **2.** unquestioning. —*adv.* **3.** without question.

question mark, a mark indicating a question: usually, as in English, the mark (?) placed after the question; interrogation point.

ques·tion·naire (kwĕs′chə nâr′), *n.* a list of questions, as for statistical purposes, or for governmental use, or to obtain opinions on some subject. [t.F]

ques·tor (kwĕs′tər, kwĕs′-), *n.* quaestor.

Quet·ta (kwĕt′ä), *n.* a city in Pakistan: formerly the capital of British Baluchistan; almost totally destroyed by an earthquake. 1935. 84,334 (1951).

quet·zal (kĕt säl′), *n.* **1.** a Central American bird, *Pharomacrus mocinno,* having golden-green and scarlet plumage, and, in the male, long flowing upper tail coverts (the national bird of Guatemala). **2.** the monetary unit of Guatemala, a gold coin worth about one U. S. dollar. Also, **que·zal** (kě säl′). [t. Sp., t. Mex. (Aztec): m. *quetzalli* tail-feather of the bird *quetzaltototl*]

Quet·zal·co·a·tl (kĕt säl′kō ä′tl), *n.* the feathered serpent god of the Aztec and Toltec cultures.

queue (kū), *n., v.,* **queued, queuing.** —*n.* **1.** a braid of hair worn hanging down behind. **2.** *Chiefly Brit.* a file or line of persons, etc. —*v.i.* **3.** *Brit.* to form in a line while waiting for something. [t. F, g. L *cōda* tail, r. *cauda*] —**queu′er,** *n.*

Que·zal·te·nan·go (kě säl′tě näng′gō), *n.* a city in SW Guatemala: earthquake, 1902. 31,352 (est. 1953).

Que·zon y Mo·li·na (kā′zŏn ē mō lē′na: *Sp.* kě′sŏn ē mō lē′nä, -thōn), *n.* Manuel L. (mä nwĕl′), 1878-1944, Filipino political leader; 1st president of the Philippine Commonwealth, 1935-44.

Quezon City, a city in the Philippines, on Luzon Island NE of Manila; designated the national capital in 1948, though Manila remains the traditional capital and center of administration. 107,977 (1948).

quib·ble (kwĭb′əl), *n., v.,* **-bled, -bling.** —*n.* **1.** a use of ambiguous, prevaricating, or irrelevant language or arguments to evade a point at issue. **2.** the use of such arguments. —*v.i.* **3.** to use a quibble or quibbles; evade the point or the truth by a quibble. [? der. *quib* gibe, appar. var. of QUIP] —**quib′bler,** *n.* —Syn. 1. evasion, equivocation, sophism, shift.

Qui·be·ron (kēb rŏn′), *n.* a peninsula (6 mi. long) in NW France, on the S coast of Brittany, partially enclosing **Quiberon Bay:** British naval victory over the French, 1759.

Qui·ché (kē chā′), *n.* an important American Indian language of Guatemala, of the Mayan stock.

quick (kwĭk), *adj.* **1.** done, proceeding, or occurring with promptness or rapidity, as an action, process, etc.; prompt; immediate: *a quick answer.* **2.** that is over or completed within a short space of time. **3.** moving with speed. **4.** swift or rapid, as motion. **5.** hasty; impatient: *a quick temper.* **6.** lively or keen, as feelings. **7.** having a high degree of vigor, energy, or activity. **8.** prompt in action; acting with swiftness or rapidity. **9.** prompt or swift (to do something): *quick to respond.* **10.** prompt to perceive: *a quick eye.* **11.** prompt to understand, learn, etc.; of ready intelligence. **12.** consisting of living plants: *a quick hedge.* **13.** brisk, as fire, flames, heat, etc. **14.** *Finance.* readily convertible into cash; liquid, as assets. **15.** *Mining.* containing ore, or productive, as veins. **16.** *Archaic* or *Dial.* endowed with life. **17.** *Archaic* or *Dial.* living, as persons, animals, plants, etc. —*n.* **18.** living persons: *the quick and the dead.* **19.** *Chiefly Brit.* living plants (esp. hawthorn) as set to form a hedge. **20.** a single such plant. **21.** the tender sensitive flesh of the living body, esp. that under the nails: *nails bitten down to the quick.* **22.** the vital or most important part. —*adv.* **23.** quickly. [ME; OE *cwic, cwicu* living, c. OS *quik,* G *queck, keck,* Icel. *kvikr;* akin to L *vīvus* living] —**quick′ness,** *n.* —Syn. 3. QUICK, FAST, SWIFT, RAPID describe speedy tempo. QUICK applies particularly to something practically instantaneous, an action or reaction, perhaps, of very brief duration: *to give a quick look around, to make a quick change of clothes.* FAST and SWIFT refer to actions, movements, etc., which continue for a time, and usually to those which are uninterrupted: when used of communication, transportation, and the like, they suggest a definite goal and a continuous trip. SWIFT, the more formal—even poetic—word suggests the greater speed: *a fast train, a swift message.* RAPID, less speedy than the others, applies to a rate or movement or action, and usually to a series of actions of movements, related or unrelated: *rapid calculation, a rapid walker.* 11. See **sharp.**

quick assets, *Accounting.* liquid assets including cash, receivables and marketable securities.

quick·en (kwĭk′ən), *v.t.* **1.** to make more rapid; accelerate; hasten: *he quickened her pace.* **2.** to make quick or alive; restore life to. **3.** to give or restore vigor or activity to; stir up, rouse, or stimulate: *to quicken the imagination.* —*v.i.* **4.** to become more active, sensitive, etc. **5.** to become alive; receive life. **6.** (of the mother) to enter that stage of pregnancy in which the child gives indications of life. **7.** (of a child in the womb) to begin to manifest signs of life. —**quick′en·er,** *n.*

quick fire, fast firing used against a moving target.

quick-fire (kwĭk′fīr′), *adj.* shooting, or capable of shooting, rapidly. Also, **quick′-fir′ing.**

quick-freeze (kwĭk′frēz′), *v.t.* **-froze, -frozen, -freezing.** to subject food, cooked or uncooked, to rapid refrigeration, permitting it to be stored almost indefinitely at freezing temperatures. —**quick-fro·zen** (kwĭk′frō′zən), *adj.*

quick grass, couch grass, *Agropyron repens.*

quick·ie (kwĭk′ĭ), *n. U.S. Slang.* **1.** a book, story, etc., usually trivial in quality, requiring only a short time to produce. **2.** anything of extremely short duration.

quick·lime (kwĭk′līm′), *n.* unslaked lime. See **lime.**

quick·ly (kwĭk′lĭ), *adv.* with speed; rapidly; very soon.

quick·sand (kwĭk′sănd′), *n.* an area of soft or loose, wet sand of considerable depth, as on a coast or inland, yielding under weight and hence apt to engulf persons, animals, etc., coming upon it.

quick·set (kwĭk′sĕt′), *n. Chiefly Brit.* **1.** a plant or cutting (esp. of hawthorn) set to grow, as in a hedge. **2.** such plants collectively. **3.** a hedge of such plants. —*adj.* **4.** formed of quickset, or of growing plants.

quick·sil·ver (kwĭk′sĭl′vər), *n.* the metallic element mercury. [ME *qwyksilver,* OE *cwicseolfor* living silver, c. G *quecksilber,* after L *argentum vīvum* living silver]

quick·step (kwĭk′stĕp′), *n.* **1.** (formerly) a lively step used in marching. **2.** music adapted to such a march, or in a brisk march rhythm. **3.** a lively dance step.

quick-tem·pered (kwĭk′tĕm′pərd), *adj.* easily moved to anger.

quick time, 1. a quick rate of marching. **2.** *U.S. Army.* a normal rate of marching in which 120 paces, each of 30 inches, are taken in a minute.

quick trick, *Bridge.* a card, or group of cards, that will probably win the first or second trick in a suit, regardless of who plays it or at what declaration.

quick-wit·ted (kwĭk′wĭt′ĭd), *adj.* having a nimble, alert intelligence. —**quick′-wit′ted·ly,** *adv.* —**quick′-wit·ted·ness,** *n.*

quid[1] (kwĭd), *n.* a portion of something, esp. tobacco, for holding in the mouth and chewing. [OE *cwidu* CUD]

quid[2] (kwĭd), *n., pl.* **quid.** *Brit. Slang.* a sovereign. [orig. uncert.]

quid·di·ty (kwĭd′ə tĭ), *n., pl.* **-ties. 1.** that which makes a thing what it is; the essential nature. **2.** a trifling nicety of subtle distinction, as in argument. [t. ML: m.s. *quidditas,* der. L *quid* what]

quid·nunc (kwĭd′nŭngk′), *n.* one who is curious to know all the news and gossip. [t. L: *quid nunc* what now?]

quid pro quo (kwĭd′ prō kwō′), *Latin.* one thing in return for another. [L: something for something]

¿quién sa·be? (kyĕn sä′bĕ), *Spanish.* who knows?

qui·es·cent (kwĭ ĕs′ənt), *adj.* being at rest, quiet, or still; inactive or motionless. [t. L: s. *quiescens,* ppr., keeping quiet] —**qui·es′cent·ly,** *adv.* —**qui·es′cence,** **qui·es′cen·cy,** *n.*

qui·et[1] (kwī′ət), *n.* **1.** freedom from disturbance or tumult; tranquillity; rest; repose: *to live in quiet.* **2.** peace; peaceful condition of affairs. [ME *quiet(e),* t. L: s. *quies* rest, repose, quiet]

qui·et[2] (kwī′ət), *adj.* **1.** making no disturbance or trouble; not turbulent; peaceable. **2.** free from disturbance or tumult; tranquil; peaceful: *a quiet life.* **3.** free from disturbing emotions, etc.; mentally peaceful. **4.** being at rest. **5.** refraining or free from activity, esp. busy or vigorous activity: *a quiet evening at home.* **6.** motionless or still; moving gently: *quiet waters.* **7.** making no noise or sound, esp. no disturbing sound: *quiet neighbors.* **8.** free, or comparatively free, from noise: *a quiet street.* **9.** silent: *be quiet!* **10.** restrained in speech, manner, etc.; saying little. **11.** said, expressed, done, etc., in a restrained or unobtrusive way. **12.** of an inconspicuous kind; not showy; subdued. **13.** *Com.* commercially inactive. —*v.t.* **14.** to make quiet. **15.** to make tranquil or peaceful; pacify. **16.** to calm mentally, as a person. **17.** to allay, as tumult, doubt, fear, etc. **18.** to silence. —*v.i.* **19.** to become quiet. [ME, t. L: s. *quiētus,* pp., rested] —**qui′et·er,** *n.* —**qui′et·ly,** *adv.* —**qui′et·ness,** *n.* —Syn. **8.** See **still**[1].

qui·et·en (kwī′ə tən), *Brit. and U.S. Dial.* —*v.i.* **1.** to become quiet. —*v.t.* **2.** to make quiet.

qui·et·ism (kwī′ə tĭz′əm), *n.* **1.** a form of religious mysticism taught by Molinos, a Spanish priest, in the latter part of the 17th century, requiring extinction of the will, withdrawal from worldly interests, and passive meditation on God and divine things. **2.** some similar form of religious mysticism. **3.** quietness of mind or life. [t. It.: m. *quietismo*] —**qui′et·ist,** *n.*

qui·e·tude (kwī′ə tūd′, -tōōd′), *n.* state of being quiet; tranquillity; calmness; stillness; quiet. [t. LL: m. *quiētūdo,* der. L *quiētus*]

qui·e·tus (kwī ē′təs), *n.* **1.** a finishing stroke; anything that effectually ends or settles: *to give a quietus to a rumor.* **2.** discharge or release from life. [t. ML: quit (in *quiētus est* he is quit, a formula of acquittance), L he is quiet, at rest. See QUIET[2], *adj.* Cf. QUIT[1], *adj.*]

quill (kwĭl), *n.* **1.** one of the large feathers of the wing or tail of a bird. **2.** the hard, tubelike part of a feather, nearest the body, extending to the superior umbilicus.

3. a feather, as of a goose, formed into a pen for writing. **4.** one of the hollow spines on a porcupine or hedgehog. **5.** a device for plucking the strings of a musical instrument (as of a harpsichord), made from the quill of a feather. **6.** (*pl.*) *Archaic.* a musical instrument made of pieces of reed or cane of different lengths. **7.** a roll of bark, as of cinnamon, as formed in drying. **8.** a reed or other hollow stem on which yarn is wound. **9.** a bobbin or spool. [ME *quil.* Cf. LG *quiele,* G *kiel*]

quil·lai (kĭ lī′), *n.* soapbark (def. 1). [t. Chilean (Araucanian)]

quillai bark, soapbark (def. 2).

Quil·ler-Couch (kwĭl′ər kōōch′), *n.* **Sir Arthur Thomas,** ("*Q*") 1863–1944, British novelist and critic.

quil·let (kwĭl′ĭt), *n. Archaic.* a subtlety; a quibble.

quill·wort (kwĭl′wûrt′), *n.* any of the aquatic and paludal pteridophytic plants constituting the genus *Isoëtes,* characterized by clustered, quill-like leaves bearing sporangia in their bases.

quilt (kwĭlt), *n.* **1.** a coverlet for a bed, made by stitching together two thicknesses of fabric with some soft substance, as wool, between them. **2.** anything quilted or resembling a quilt. **3.** a bedspread or counterpane. **4.** *Obs.* a kind of mattress. —*v.t.* **5.** to stitch together (two pieces of cloth with a soft interlining), usually in an ornamental pattern. **6.** to sew up between pieces of material. **7.** to pad or line with some material. —*v.i.* **8.** to make quilts or quilted work. [ME *quilte,* t. OF: m. *cuilte,* q. L *culcita* mattress, cushion]

quilt·ing (kwĭl′tĭng), *n.* **1.** act of one who quilts. **2.** material for making quilts.

quilting bee, *U.S.* a social gathering of women to make a quilt or quilts.

quin·a·crine (kwĭn′ə krēn′), *n.* atabrine.

qui·na·ry (kwī′nə rĭ), *adj.* **1.** pertaining to or consisting of five. **2.** arranged in fives. [t. L: m.s. *quīnārius* containing five]

quince (kwĭns), *n.* **1.** the hard, yellowish, acid fruit of a small, hardy, rosaceous tree (*Cydonia oblonga*). **2.** the tree itself. [ME *quince,* appar. orig. pl., taken as sing. of ME *quyne, coyn,* t. OF: m. *cooin,* q. L *cotōneum,* for *cydōnium,* t. Gk.: m. *kydōnion* quince, lit., (apple) of *Cydonia* (ancient city of Crete)]

quin·cun·cial (kwĭn kŭn′shəl), *adj.* **1.** noting or pertaining to a quincunx. **2.** *Bot.* noting a five-ranked arrangement of leaves.

quin·cunx (kwĭn′kŭngks), *n.* **1.** an arrangement of five objects (as trees) in a square or rectangle, one at each corner and one in the middle. **2.** *Bot.* an imbricated arrangement of five petals or leaves, in which two are interior, two are exterior, and one is partly interior and partly exterior. [t. L: orig., five twelfths (a Roman coin worth five twelfths of the as, and marked with a quincunx of spots)]

Quin·cy (kwĭn′zĭ for 1, 2; kwĭn′sĭ for 3), *n.* **1. Josiah** (jō sī′ə), 1744–75, American patriot and writer. **2.** a city in E Massachusetts, near Boston. 87,409 (1960). **3.** a city in W Illinois, on the Mississippi. 43,793 (1960).

quin·dec·a·gon (kwĭn dĕk′ə gŏn′), *n. Geom.* a polygon with fifteen angles and fifteen sides. [f. L *quindec*(im) fifteen + -*agon* (abstracted from DECAGON)]

quin·de·cen·ni·al (kwĭn′dĭ sĕn′ĭ əl), *adj.* **1.** of or pertaining to a period of fifteen years or the fifteenth occurrence of a series, as an anniversary. —*n.* **2.** a fifteenth anniversary. [f. L *quindec*(im) fifteen + -*ennial,* as in DECENNIAL]

quin·ic acid (kwĭn′ĭk), *Chem.* a white crystalline organic acid, $C_6H_7(OH)_4CO_2H$, present in cinchona bark, coffee beans, and the leaves of many plants. [f. Sp. *quin*(a), (t. Kechua: m. *kina* bark) + -IC + ACID]

quin·i·dine (kwĭn′ə dēn′, -dĭn), *n. Pharm.* a colorless crystalline alkaloid isomeric with quinine, $C_{20}H_{24}N_2O_2$, derived from the bark of the cinchona species: used to regulate the heart rhythm, and to treat malaria.

qui·nine (kwī′nīn *or, esp. Brit.,* kwĭ nēn′), *n. Chem.* **1.** a bitter colorless alkaloid, $C_{20}H_{24}N_2O_2$, having needlelike crystals, which is used in medicine as a stimulant and to treat malaria; originally derived from the bark of species of *Cinchona.* **2.** a salt of this alkaloid, esp. the sulfate. Also, **quin·in** (kwĭn′ĭn). [f. Sp. *quin*(a) (t. Kechua: m. *kina* bark) + -INE[2]]

quin·nat salmon (kwĭn′ăt), chinook salmon. [t. N. Amer. Ind. (Upper Chinook): m. *igúnat*]

quin·oid (kwĭn′oid), *n. Chem.* a quinonoid substance.

qui·noi·dine (kwĭ noi′dēn, -dĭn), *n. Pharm.* a brownish-black resinous substance consisting of a mixture of alkaloids, obtained as a by-product in the manufacture of quinine and used as a cheap substitute for it. Also, **qui·noi·din** (kwĭ noi′dĭn). [f. QUIN(INE) + -OID + -INE[2]]

quin·o·line (kwĭn′ə lēn′, -lĭn), *n. Chem.* a nitrogenous organic base, C_9H_7N, a colorless liquid with a pungent odor, occurring in coal tar, and obtained by oxidation of a mixture of aniline and glycerol, and used in preparing other compounds. Also, **quin·o·lin** (kwĭn′ə lĭn). [f. quinone (f. Sp. *quin*(a) quinine bark + -OLE) + -INE[2]]

qui·none (kwĭ nōn′, kwĭn′ōn), *n. Chem.* **1.** a yellow crystalline unsaturated cyclic diketone, $C_6H_4O_2$, formed by oxidizing aniline or hydroquinone, and used in tanning leather. **2.** any of a class of compounds of which this is the type. [f. Sp. *quin*(a) quinine bark + -ONE]

quin·o·noid (kwĭn′ə noid′, kwĭ nō′noid), *adj. Chem.* of or resembling quinone. [f. QUINON(E) + -OID]

quin·qua·ge·nar·i·an (kwĭn′kwə jə när′ĭ ən), *adj.* **1.**

of the age of 50 years.   2. between 50 and 60 years old. —**n.** 3. a quinquagenarian person. [f. s. L *quinquā-genārius* consisting of fifty + -AN]

Quin·qua·ges·i·ma (kwĭn'kwə jĕs'ə mə), *n.* the Sunday before Lent (more fully, **Quinquagesima Sunday**), being the fiftieth day before Easter (reckoning inclusively); Shrove Sunday. [ME, t. ML, short for L *quinquāgesima dies* fiftieth day]

quinque-, a word element meaning "five." [t. L, comb. form of *quinque*]

quin·que·fo·li·o·late (kwĭn'kwə fō'lĭ ə lāt, -lāt'), *adj. Bot.* having five leaves or leaflets.

quin·quen·ni·al (kwĭn kwĕn'ĭ əl), *adj.* 1. of or for five years. 2. occurring every five years. —**n.** 3. something that occurs every five years. 4. a fifth anniversary. 5. a five-year term in office. [late ME, f.L *quinquenni(s)* of five years + -AL[1]]

quin·quen·ni·um (kwĭn kwĕn'ĭ əm), *n., pl.* **-quenni·ums, -quennia** (-kwĕn'ĭ ə). a period of five years. Also, **quin·quen·ni·ad** (kwĭn kwĕn'ĭ ăd'). [t. L]

quin·que·par·tite (kwĭn'kwə pär'tīt), *adj.* divided into or consisting of five parts.

quin·que·va·lent (kwĭn'kwə vā'lənt, kwĭn kwĕv'ə lənt), *adj. Chem.* 1. pentavalent. 2. exercising five different valences, as phosphorus with valences 5, 4, 3, 1, and —3. —**quin·que·va·lence** (kwĭn'kwə vā'ləns, kwĭn kwĕv'ə ləns), **quin·que·va·len·cy,** *n.*

quin·sy (kwĭn'zĭ), *n., pl.* **-sies.** *Pathol.* a suppurative inflammation of the tonsils; suppurative tonsillitis. [ME *qwinaci,* t. ML: m. *quinancia,* der. LL *cynanchē,* t. Gk.: m. *kynánchē* sore throat]

quint[1] (kwĭnt, kĭnt), *n.* 1. an organ stop sounding a fifth higher than the corresponding digitals. 2. *Piquet.* a series of five cards, all of the same suit. [t. F: m. *quinte* (fem.), t. L: m. *quinta* fifth]

quint[2] (kwĭnt), *n. Colloq.* a quintuplet.

quin·tain (kwĭn'tĭn), *n.* 1. (during the Middle Ages and later) a post, or an object mounted on a post, for tilting at as a knightly or other exercise. 2. such exercise or sport. [ME *quyntaine,* t. OF: m. *quintaine,* t. ML: m. *quintāna* quintain, L street in a camp]

quin·tal (kwĭn'təl), *n.* 1. a unit of weight in the metric system, equal to 100 kilograms, and equivalent to 220.462 avoirdupois pounds. 2. a hundredweight. [late ME, t.ML: s. *quintāle,* t. Ar.: m. *qinṭār* weight of a hundred pounds, prob. ult. der. L *centēnārius,* der. *centum* hundred. Cf. KANTAR]

Movable quintain, 14th century

quin·tan (kwĭn'tən), *adj.* 1. (of a fever, ague, etc.) characterized by paroxysms which recur every fifth day, both days of consecutive occurrence being counted. —**n.** 2. a quintan fever or ague. [t. L: s. *quintāna (febris)* (fever) belonging to the fifth]

quinte (kăNt), *n. Fencing.* the fifth of eight defensive positions. [F]

Quin·te·ro (kēn tě'rō), *n.* See **Álvarez Quintero.**

quin·tes·sence (kwĭn tĕs'əns), *n.* 1. the pure and concentrated essence of a substance. 2. the most perfect embodiment of something. 3. the fifth essence or element of ancient and medieval philosophy (in addition to earth, water, air, and fire), supposed to constitute the heavenly bodies, to permeate the material world, and to be capable of extraction. [ME, t. ML: alter. of *quinta essentia* fifth essence] —**quin·tes·sen·tial** (kwĭn'tə sĕn'shəl), *adj.*

quin·tet (kwĭn tĕt'), *n.* 1. any set or group of five persons or things. 2. a set of five singers or players. 3. a musical composition for five voices or instruments. Also, *esp. Brit.,* **quin·tette.** [t. F: m.] *quintette,* t. It.: m. *quintetto,* der. *quinto* fifth, g. L *quintus* fifth]

quin·tile (kwĭn'tĭl), *Astrol.* —*adj.* 1. pertaining to the aspect of two heavenly bodies distant from each other the fifth part of the zodiac, or 72°. —**n.** 2. a quintile aspect. [t. L, neut. of *quintilis* fifth]

Quin·til·ian (kwĭn tĭl'yən, -Yən), *n.* (*Marcus Fabius Quintilianus*) A.D. c35–c95, Roman rhetorician.

quin·til·lion (kwĭn tĭl'yən), *n.* a cardinal number represented by one followed by 18 zeros in the U.S. and France, or 30 zeros in Gt. Britain and Germany (usually prec. by *one* or *a*). —*adj.* 2. amounting to one quintillion in number. [f. s. L *quintus* fifth + (M)ILLION]

quin·tu·ple (kwĭn'tyŏŏ pəl, -tŏŏ-, kwĭn tū'pəl, -tŏŏ'-), *adj., n., v.,* **-pled, -pling.** —*adj.* 1. fivefold; consisting of five parts. 2. five times as great. —**n.** 3. a number, amount, etc., five times as great as another. —*v.t., v.i.* 4. to make or become five times as great. [t. F, f. *quint* fifth + -*uple* (abstracted from *quadruple* QUADRUPLE)]

quin·tu·plet (kwĭn'tyŏŏ plĭt, -tŏŏ-, kwĭn tū'plĭt, -tŏŏ'-, -tŭp'lĭt), *n.* 1. any group or combination of five. 2. (*pl.*) five offspring born at a birth. 3. one of five children born at a birth.

quip (kwĭp), *n., v.,* **quipped, quipping.** —*n.* 1. a sharp, sarcastic remark; a cutting jest. 2. a clever or witty saying. 3. a quibble. 4. an odd or fantastic action or thing. —*v.i.* 5. to use quips. [back formation from *quippy* quip, t. L *quippe* indeed]

quip·ster (kwĭp'stər), *n.* one given to quips.

qui·pu (kē'pŏŏ, kwĭp'ŏŏ), *n.* (among the ancient Peruvians) a device consisting of a cord with knotted strings

of various colors attached, for recording events, keeping accounts, etc. [t. Peruvian (Kechua): lit., knot]

quire[1] (kwīr), *n.* 1. a set of 24 uniform sheets of paper. 2. *Bookmaking.* the section of leaves or pages in proper sequence after the printed sheet or sheets have been folded; a gathering. [ME *quayer,* t. OF: m. *quaier,* g. VL *quaternum* set of four sheets, der. L *quaterni* four each]

quire[2] (kwīr), *n., v.i., v.t.,* **quired, quiring.** *Archaic.* choir.

Quir·i·nal (kwĭr'ə nəl), *n.* 1. one of the seven hills of Rome. 2. a palace built upon this hill. 3. the Italian royal court or government (as distinguished from the Vatican). —*adj.* 4. denoting or pertaining to the Quirinal. 5. of or pertaining to Quirinus. [t. L: s. *Quirinālis,* der. *Quirīnus* an ancient Italian war god identified by the Romans with Romulus]

Qui·ri·nus (kwĭ rī'nəs), *n.* an early Roman god of war, identified with the deified Romulus.

Qui·ri·tes (kwĭ rī'tēz), *n.pl.* the citizens of ancient Rome considered in their civil capacity. [t. L, pl. of *Quiris,* orig. an inhabitant of the Sabine town *Cures,* later a Roman citizen]

quirk (kwûrk), *n.* 1. a trick or peculiarity. 2. a shift or evasion; a quibble. 3. a sudden twist, turn, or curve. 4. a flourish, as in writing. 5. an acute angle or a channel, as one separating a convex part of a molding from a fillet. —*adj.* 6. formed with a quirk or channel, as a molding. [orig. obscure] —**quirk'y,** *adj.*

quirt (kwûrt), *n.* 1. a riding whip consisting of a short, stout stock and a lash of braided leather. —*v.t.* 2. to strike with a quirt. [? t. Sp.: m. *cuerda* cord]

quis·ling (kwĭz'lĭng), *n.* a person who undermines his own country from within; a fifth columnist. [from Vidkun *Quisling,* 1887–1945, pro-Nazi leader in Norway]

quis se·pa·ra·bit (kwĭs sĕp'ə rā'bĭt), *Latin.* who shall separate (us)? (a motto of South Carolina).

quit (kwĭt), *v.,* **quit** or **quitted, quitting,** *adj.* —*v.t.* 1. to stop, cease, or discontinue. 2. to depart from; leave. 3. to give up; let go; relinquish. 4. to let go one's hold of (something grasped). 5. *Archaic.* to acquit (oneself). —*v.i.* 6. to cease from doing something; stop. 7. to depart or leave. —*adj.* 8. released from obligation, penalty, etc.; free, clear, or rid (fol. by *of*). [ME *quitte(n), quite(n),* t. OF: m. *quit(t)er,* t. ML: m. *quittāre, quiētāre* release, discharge, LL QUIET[3], v.] —**Syn.** 6. See **stop.**

quitch (kwĭch), *n.* couch grass. Also, **quitch grass.** [OE *cwice,* c. D *kweek,* Norw. *kvike;* akin to QUICK, adj.]

quit·claim (kwĭt'klām'), *n. Law.* 1. a transfer of all one's interest, as in a parcel of real estate. 2. **quitclaim deed,** the instrument making such a transfer (as distinguished from a *warranty deed*). —*v.t.* 3. to quit or give up claim to (a possession, etc.). [ME *quitclayme,* t. AF: m. *quiteclame,* der. *quiteclamer* declare quit. See QUIT, adj., CLAIM]

quite (kwīt), *adv.* 1. completely, wholly, or entirely: *quite the reverse.* 2. actually, really, or truly: *quite a sudden change.* 3. *Colloq.* to a considerable extent or degree: *quite pretty.* [ME; adv. use of ME *quite,* adj., QUIT]

Qui·to (kē'tō), *n.* the capital of Ecuador, in the N part. 212,873 (est. 1954); 9348 ft. high.

qui trans·tu·lit sus·ti·net (kwī trăns'tyŏŏ lĭt sŭs'tə nĕt'), *Latin.* he who transplanted (the vine) sustains (it) (motto of Connecticut).

quit·rent (kwĭt'rĕnt'), *n.* rent paid by a freeholder or copyholder in lieu of services which might otherwise have been required of him. [f. QUIT, adj. + RENT[1]]

quits (kwĭts), *adj.* on equal terms by repayment or retaliation. [cf. QUIT, adj.; -s of uncert. orig.]

quit·tance (kwĭt'əns), *n.* 1. recompense or requital. 2. discharge from debt or obligation. 3. a document certifying this; a receipt.

quit·ter (kwĭt'ər), *n. Colloq.* one who quits or gives up easily.

quit·tor (kwĭt'ər), *n. Vet. Sci.* any of various infections of the foot in which tissues degenerate and form a slough, possibly involving tendons and bone as well as skin. [ME, t. OF: m. *culture* cooking]

qui va là? (kē vä lä'), *French.* who goes there?

quiv·er[1] (kwĭv'ər), *v.i., v.t.,* 1. to shake with a slight but rapid motion; vibrate tremulously; tremble. —*n.* 2. act or state of quivering; a tremble; a tremor. [ME; c. MD *quieren* tremble] —**Syn.** 1. See **shake.**

quiv·er[2] (kwĭv'ər), *n.* a case for holding arrows. 2. the contents of such a case. [ME, t. AF: m. *quiveir,* var. of OF *quivre;* ? of Gmc. orig.; cf. OE *cocer* quiver]

qui vive (kē vēv'), *French.* 1. who goes there? 2. **on the qui vive,** on the alert. [F: (long) live who?—as if calling for such a reply as *Vive le roi!* Long live the king!]

Qui·xo·te (kĭ hō'tĭ, kwĭk'sət; *Sp.* kē hō'tě), *n.* See **Don Quixote.**

quix·ot·ic (kwĭks ŏt'ĭk), *adj.* 1. (*sometimes cap.*) resembling or befitting Don Quixote. 2. extravagantly chivalrous or romantic; visionary; impracticable. Also, **quix·ot'i·cal.** [f. (DON) QUIXOTE + -IC] —**quix·ot'i·cal·ly,** *adv.*

quix·ot·ism (kwĭk'sə tĭz'əm), *n.* 1. (*sometimes cap.*) quixotic character or practice. 2. a quixotic idea or act.

quiz (kwĭz), *v.,* **quizzed, quizzing,** *n., pl.* **quizzes.** —*v.t.* 1. to examine informally or coach (a student or class) by questions. 2. to question. 3. *Chiefly Brit.* to make fun

ăct, āble, dâre, ärt; ĕbb, ēqual; ĭf, īce; hŏt, ōver, ôrder, oil, bŏŏk, ōōze, out; ŭp, ūse, ûrge; ə = a in alone; ch, chief; g, give; ng, ring; sh, shoe; th, thin; th, that; zh, vision. See the full key on inside cover.

of; ridicule; chaff. —*n.* **4.** an informal examination or test of a student or class. **5.** a questioning. **6.** a practical joke; a hoax. [orig. uncert.] —**quiz′zer,** *n.*

quiz·zi·cal (kwĭz′ə kəl), *adj.* **1.** odd, queer, or comical. **2.** quizzing, ridiculing, or chaffing: *a quizzical smile.* —**quiz′zi·cal·ly,** *adv.*

quo·ad hoc (kwō′ăd hŏk′), *Latin.* as much as this; to this extent.

quod (kwŏd), *n.* *Chiefly Brit. Slang.* jail. Also, **quad.**

quod e·rat de·mon·stran·dum (kwŏd ĕr′ăt dĕm′- ən străn′dəm), *Latin.* which was to be shown or proved.

quod e·rat fa·ci·en·dum (kwŏd ĕr′ăt fā′shĭ ĕn′- dəm), *Latin.* which was to be done.

quoin (koin, kwoin), *n.* **1.** an external solid angle of a wall or the like. **2.** one of the stones forming it; a cornerstone. **3.** a wedge-shaped piece of wood, stone, or other material, used for any of various purposes. **4.** *Print.* a wedge of wood or metal for securing type in a chase, etc. —*v.t.* **5.** to provide with quoins, as a corner of a wall. **6.** to secure or raise with a quoin or wedge. [var. of COIN]

Quoins

quoit (kwoit), *n.* **1.** a flattish iron or other ring thrown in play to encircle a peg stuck in the ground or to come as close to it as possible. **2.** (*pl.*, construed as *sing.*) the game so played. —*v.t.* **3.** to throw as or like a quoit. [ME *coyte;* orig. unknown]

quon·dam (kwŏn′dăm), *adj.* that formerly was or existed; former: *his quondam partner.* [t. L: formerly]

Quon·set hut (kwŏn′sĭt), a compact and serviceable metal shelter or hut resembling a more or less semicircular arch in cross section. [named from *Quonset,* R.I.]

quo·rum (kwōr′əm), *n.* **1.** the number of members of a body required to be present to transact business legally. **2.** the number of judges of a court required to be present to enable the court to act. **3.** a particularly chosen group. [t. L: of whom; from a use of the word in commissions written in Latin]

quot., quotation.

quo·ta (kwō′tə), *n.* **1.** the proportional part or share of a total which is due from, or is due or belongs to, a particular district, state, person, etc. **2.** a proportional part or share of a fixed total amount or quantity. [t. ML, short for L *quota pars* how great a part?]

quo·ta·tion (kwō tā′shən), *n.* **1.** that which is quoted;

a passage quoted from a book, speech, etc. **2.** act or practice of quoting. **3.** *Com.* **a.** the statement of the current or market price of a commodity or security. **b.** the price so stated.

quotation mark, one of the marks used to indicate the beginning and end of a quotation, in English usually consisting of two inverted commas (") at the beginning and two apostrophes (") at the end, or, for a quotation within a quotation, of single marks of this kind: "*He said, 'I will go.*' " Frequently, esp. in Great Britain, single marks are used instead of double, the latter being then used for a quotation within a quotation.

quote (kwōt), *v.,* quoted, quoting, *n.* —*v.t.* **1.** to repeat (a passage, etc.) from a book, speech, etc., as the words of another, as by way of authority, illustration, etc. **2.** to repeat words from (a book, author, etc.). **3.** to bring forward, adduce, or cite. **4.** to enclose (words) within quotation marks. **5.** *Com.* **a.** to state (a price). **b.** to state the current price of. —*v.i.* **6.** to make a quotation or quotations, as from a book or author. —*n.* **7.** a quotation. **8.** a quotation mark. [ME, t. ML: m. *quotāre* divide into chapters and verses, der. L *quot* how many] —**quot′a·ble,** *adj.*

quoth (kwōth), *v.t.* *Archaic.* said: used with nouns, and with first and third person pronouns, and always placed before the subject: *quoth the raven, "Never more.*" [pret. of *quethe* (otherwise obs.), OE *cwethan* say. Cf. BEQUEATH]

quoth·a (kwō′thə), *interj.* *Archaic.* indeed! (used ironically or contemptuously in quoting another). [for *quoth a* quoth he]

quo·tid·i·an (kwō tĭd′ĭ ən), *adj.* **1.** daily. **2.** everyday; ordinary. **3.** (of a fever, ague, etc.) characterized by paroxysms which recur daily. —*n.* **4.** something recurring daily. **5.** a quotidian fever or ague. [t. L: s. *quotīdiānus* daily; r. ME *cotidien,* t. OF]

quo·tient (kwō′shənt), *n.* *Math.* the result of division; the number of times one quantity is contained in another. [ME, t L: m. *quotiens* how many times]

quo war·ran·to (kwō wô răn′tō, wŏ-), *Law.* **1.** an ancient writ calling upon a person to show by what warrant he claims an office, privilege, franchise, or liberty. **2.** (now) a similar proceeding upon an information of this nature of quo warranto or under statutory provisions. **3.** the pleading initiating such trial. **4.** the trial. [ME: by what warrant]

q.v., (L *quod vide*) which see.

Qy., query. Also, **qy.**

R

R, r (är), *n., pl.* **R's** or **Rs, r's** or **rs.** **1.** the 18th letter of the English alphabet. **2.** See the **three R's.**

R, **1.** *Physics, Chem.* gas constant. **2.** *Chem.* radical. **3.** *Math.* ratio. **4.** *Elect.* resistance. **5.** *Chess.* rook. **6.** *pl.* **Rs.** rupee.

R., **1.** rabbi. **2.** Radical. **3.** railroad. **4.** railway. **5.** Réaumur (thermometer). **6.** rector. **7.** redactor. **8.** Regina. **9.** Republican. **10.** response. **11.** Rex. **12.** (in stage directions) right. **13.** River. **14.** Road. **15.** Royal.

r, **1.** *Elect.* resistance. **2.** ruble. **3.** *pl.* **rs.** rupee.

r., **1.** radius. **2.** rare. **3.** *Com.* received. **4.** recipe. **5.** replacing. **6.** residence. **7.** rises. **8.** rod. **9.** ruble. **10.** *Baseball.* runs. **11.** *pl.* **rs.** rupee.

Ra (rä), *n.* the great sun god of the Egyptians, the sovereign god of historical Egypt, in art typically represented as a hawk-headed man bearing on his head the solar disk and the royal uraeus. Also, **Re.** [t. Egypt.]

RA, Regular Army.

Ra, *Chem.* radium.

R.A., **1.** Rear Admiral. **2.** *Astron.* right ascension. **3.** Royal Academician. **4.** Royal Academy.

Ra·bat (rä bät′), *n.* a seaport in and capital of Morocco, in NW part. 156,209 (1952).

rab·bet (răb′ĭt), *n., v.,* -beted, -beting. —*n.* **1.** a cut, groove, or recess made on the edge or surface of a board or the like, as to receive the end or edge of another board or the like similarly shaped. **2.** a joint so made. —*v.t.* **3.** to cut or form a rabbet in (a board, etc.). **4.** to join by rabbets. —*v.i.* **5.** to join by a rabbet (fol. by *on* or *over*). Also, **rebate.** [ME *rabit,* prob. t. OF: m. *rabat* a beating down, or *rabot* a joiner's plane]

Rabbets

rab·bi (răb′ī), *n., pl.* **-bis.** **1.** *Jewish Relig.* a graduate of a rabbinical school, a preacher, or any religious functionary. **2.** *Hist.* a Jewish title for a doctor or expounder of the law. [ME and OE, t. L, t. Heb.: my master]

rab·bin (răb′ĭn), *n.* rabbi. [t. ML: s. *rabbinus*]

Rab·bin·ic (rə bĭn′ĭk), *n.* the Hebrew language as used by the rabbis in their writings; the later Hebrew.

rab·bin·i·cal (rə bĭn′ə kəl), *adj.* of or pertaining to the rabbis or their learning, writings, etc. Also, **rab·bin′ic.**

rab·bin·ist (răb′ĭ nĭst), *n.* among the Jews, one who adheres to the Talmud and the traditions of the rabbis. —**rab′bin·is′tic, rab′bin·is′ti·cal,** *adj.*

rab·bit (răb′ĭt), *n.* **1.** any of various rodentlike, lagomorph mammal of the genus *Sylvilagus,* esp. the cottontail. **2.** a small, long-eared, burrowing lagomorph, *Lepus cuniculus,* of the hare family. **3.** the skin of any member of the rabbit family, usually prepared to imitate another fur. **4.** Welsh rabbit. [ME *rabet.* Cf. Walloon *robett,* Flem. *robbe*]

rabbit fever, *Med.* tularemia.

rabbit punch, *Boxing.* a short cutting blow to the nape of the neck or the lower part of the skull.

rab·bit·ry (răb′ĭt rĭ), *n., pl.* **-ries. 1.** a collection of rabbits. **2.** a place where rabbits are kept.

rabbit's foot, **1.** the foot of a rabbit, carried as a good-luck piece. **2.** a clover, *Trifolium arvense.*

rab·ble¹ (răb′əl), *n., v.,* -bled, -bling. —*n.* **1.** a disorderly crowd; a mob. **2.** (in contemptuous use) the lowest class of people (prec. by *the*). —*v.t.* **3.** to beset as a rabble does; mob. [ME *rabel;* ? akin to RABBLE²]

rab·ble² (răb′əl), *n., v.,* -bled, -bling. *Metall.* —*n.* **1.** a tool or mechanically operated device used for stirring or mixing a charge in a roasting furnace. —*v.t.* **2.** to stir (the charge) in a roasting furnace. [t. F: m. *râble,* g. L *rutābulum* fire shovel] —**rab′bler,** *n.*

rab·ble³ (răb′əl), *v.t., v.i.,* -bled, -bling. *Scot.* and *Brit. Dial.* to utter, read, or speak in a rapid, confused manner. [late ME *rable,* c. G *rabbeln*]

Rab·e·lais (răb′ə lā′; *Fr.* rà blĕ′), *n.* François (frän- swä′), c1490–1553, French satirist and humorist.

Rab·e·lai·si·an (răb′ə lā′zĭ ən, -zhən), *adj.* **1.** of, pertaining to, or suggesting François Rabelais, whose work is characterized by broad, coarse humor and keen satire. —*n.* **2.** one who admires or studies the works of Rabelais.

Ra·bi (rä′bĭ), *n.* **Isidor Isaac,** born 1898, U.S. physicist.

rab·id (răb′ĭd), *adj.* **1.** irrationally extreme in opinion or practice: *a rabid isolationist.* **2.** furious or raging; violently intense: *rabid hunger.* **3.** affected with or pertaining to rabies; mad. [t. L: s. *rabidus* raving, mad] —**ra·bid/i·ty, rab/id·ness.** *n.* —**rab/id·ly,** *adv.*

ra·bies (rā/bēz, -bĭ ēz/), *n.* a fatal, infectious disease of the brain which occurs in all warm-blooded animals including man, and is due to a specific virus which occurs in saliva and is transmitted to new victims by the bite of the afflicted animal, generally the dog; hydrophobia. [t. L: madness, rage]

rac·coon (ră koon/), *n.* 1. a small nocturnal carnivore, *Procyon lotor,* of North America, arboreal in habit, and having a sharp snout and a bushy ringed tail. 2. the thick gray to brown underfur of the raccoon, with silver gray guard hairs tipped with black. Also, **ra·coon.** [t. N Amer. Ind. (Algonquian, Virginia): m. *ärähkunem* he scratches with the hands)]

Eastern raccoon.
Procyon lotor
(Total length 2½ ft.,
tail 10 in.)

raccoon dog, a small wild dog of eastern Asia, of the genus *Nycteritus,* having dark marks around the eyes that give it some resemblance to a raccoon.

race[1] (rās), *n., v.,* **raced, racing.** —*n.* 1. a contest of speed, as in running, riding, driving, sailing, etc. 2. (*pl.*) a series of horse races run at a set time over a regular course. 3. any contest or competition: *an armament race, the race for the presidency.* 4. onward movement; an onward or regular course. 5. the course of time. 6. the course of life, or of a part of life. 7. *Geol.* a. a strong or rapid current of water, as in the sea or a river. b. the channel or bed of such a current, or of any stream. 8. an artificial channel, leading water to or from a place where its energy is utilized. 9. the current of water in such a channel. 10. *Mach.* a channel, groove, or the like, for a sliding or rolling part, as for ball bearings. 11. *Aeron.* the air projected to the rear by a propeller; slip stream. —*v.i.* 12. to engage in a contest of speed; run a race. 13. to run horses in races; engage in or practice horse racing. 14. to run, move, or go swiftly. 15. (of an engine, wheel, etc.) to run with undue or uncontrolled speed when the load is diminished without corresponding diminution of fuel, power, etc. —*v.t.* 16. to run a race with; try to beat in a contest of speed. 17. to cause to run in a race or races. 18. to cause to run, move, or go swiftly: *to race a motor.* [ME *ras(e),* t. Scand.; cf. Icel. *rās* a running, race, rush of liquid, c. OE *rǣs* a running, rush]

race[2] (rās), *n.* 1. a group of persons connected by common descent, blood, or heredity. 2. a population so connected. 3. *Ethnol.* a subdivision of a stock, characterized by a more or less unique combination of physical traits which are transmitted in descent. 4. a group of tribes or peoples forming an ethnic stock. 5. the state of belonging to a certain ethnic stock. 6. the distinguishing characteristics of special ethnic stocks. 7. the human race or family, or mankind. 8. *Zool.* a variety; a subspecies. 9. a natural kind of living creature: *the human race, the race of fishes.* 10. any group, class, or kind, esp. of persons. 11. lofty or noble extraction or lineage. 12. (of speech, writing, etc.) characteristic quality, esp. liveliness or piquancy. 13. the characteristic taste or flavor of wine. [t. F, t. It.: m. *razza* race, breed, lineage; orig. uncert.]
—**Syn.** 1. RACE, NATION, PEOPLE are terms for a large body of persons who may be thought of as a unit because of common characteristics. RACE refers to a large body of persons, animals, or plants characterized by community of descent: *the white race.* NATION considers a body of persons as living under an organized government, occupying a fixed area, and dealing as a unit in matters of peace and war with other similar groups: *the English nation.* Whereas RACE and NATION are objective, PEOPLE have emotional connotations similar to those of *family.* PEOPLE refers to the persons composing a race, nation, tribe, etc. as members of a body with common interests and a unifying culture: *we are one people, any people on any continent, the peoples of the world.*

Race (rās), *n.* **Cape,** a cape at the SE extremity of Newfoundland.

race·course (rās/kōrs/), *n.* 1. *Chiefly Brit.* a race track. 2. a millrace or the like.

race horse, a horse bred or kept for racing.

ra·ceme (rā sēm/, rə-), *n. Bot.* 1. a simple indeterminate inflorescence in which the flowers are borne on short pedicels lying along a common axis, as in the lily of the valley. 2. a compound inflorescence in which the short pedicels with single flowers of the simple raceme are replaced by racemes (**compound raceme**). [t. L: m.s. *racēmus* cluster of grapes. See RAISIN]
—**race·mif·er·ous** (rās/ə mĭf/ər əs), *adj.*

ra·ce·mic (rā sē/mĭk, -sĕm/ĭk, rə-), *adj. Chem.* noting or pertaining to any of various organic compounds in which racemism occurs. [f. s. L *racēmus* cluster of grapes + -IC]

Raceme
of lily of
the valley,
*Convallaria
majalis*

racemic acid, *Chem.* an isomeric modification of tartaric acid, which is sometimes found in the juice of grapes in conjunction with the common dextrorotatory form, and which is optically inactive, but can be separated into the two usual isomeric forms, dextrorotatory and levorotatory.

ra·ce·mism (rās/ə mĭz/əm, rā sē/mĭz əm), *n. Chem.* the character of an optically inactive substance (as racemic acid) separable into two other substances, of the same

chemical composition as the original substance, one of which is dextrorotatory and the other levorotatory.

rac·e·mi·za·tion (rās/ə mə zā/shən), *n. Chem.* the conversion of substances which are optically active into ones which are optically inactive.

rac·e·mose (rās/ə mōs/), *adj. Bot.* 1. having the form of a raceme. 2. arranged in racemas. [t. L: m.s. *racē-mōsus* clustering]

rac·er (rā/sər), *n.* 1. one who or that which races, or takes part in a race, as a race horse, or a bicycle, yacht, etc., used for racing. 2. anything having great speed. 3. a turntable on which a heavy gun is turned. 4. any of the North American snakes of the genus *Coluber.*

race riot, *U.S.* an act of mob violence resulting from racial animosity.

race suicide, the extinction of a race or people which tends to result when, through the unwillingness or forbearance of its members to have children, the birth rate falls below the death rate.

race track, 1. a plot of ground laid out for horse-racing. 2. the course for any race.

race·way (rās/wā/), *n. Chiefly Brit.* a passage or channel for water, as a millrace.

Ra·chel (rā/chəl), *n. Bible.* Jacob's favorite wife, and mother of Joseph and Benjamin. Gen. 29–35.

ra·chis (rā/kĭs), *n., pl.* **rachises** (rā/kĭs ĭz), **rachides** (rāk/ə dēz/, rā/kə-). 1. *Bot.* a. the axis of an inflorescence when somewhat elongated, as in a raceme. b. (in a pinnately compound leaf or frond) the prolongation of the petiole along which the leaflets are disposed. c. any of various axial structures. 2. *Zool.* the shaft of a feather, esp. that part, anterior to the superior umbilicus, bearing the web, as distinguished from the *quill.* 3. *Anat.* the spinal column. Also, **rhachis.** [NL, t. Gk.]

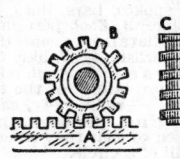

R. Rachis

ra·chi·tis (rə kī/tĭs), *n. Pathol.* rickets. [NL, t. Gk.: disease of the spine] —**ra·chit·ic** (rə-kĭt/ĭk), *adj.*

R. Rachis
(def. 1a) of
rye grass

Rach·ma·ni·noff (räкн mä/nĭ nôf/), *n.* **Sergei Wassilievitch** (sĕr gā/ väs sē/lyə vĭch), 1873–1943, Russian pianist and composer. Also, **Rach·ma/ni·nov/.**

ra·cial (rā/shəl), *adj.* pertaining to or characteristic of race or extraction, or a race or races. —**ra/cial·ly,** *adv.*

ra·cial·ism (rā/shə lĭz/əm), *n.* the belief or the practice of the doctrine of racism.

Ra·cine (rà sēn/ for 1; rə sēn/ for 2), *n.* 1. **Jean Baptiste** (zhän bà tēst/), 1639–99, French tragic dramatist. 2. a city in SE Wisconsin. 89,144 (1960).

rac·ism (rā/sĭz əm), *n.* 1. a belief that human races have distinctive make-ups that determine their respective cultures, usually involving the idea that one's own race is superior and has the right to rule others. 2. a policy of enforcing such asserted right. 3. a system of government and society based upon it. —**rac/ist,** *n.*

rack[1] (răk), *n.* 1. a framework of bars, wires, or pegs on which articles are arranged or deposited (used esp. in composition): *a hat rack.* 2. a spreading framework set on a wagon for carrying hay, straw, or the like in large loads. 3. *Print.* an upright framework with side cleats or other supports for the storing of cases, of boards or of galleys of type, etc. 4. *Mach.* a. a bar with teeth on one of its sides, adapted to engage with the teeth of a pinion or the like, as for converting circular into rectilinear motion or vice versa. b. a similar bar with notches over which the projections of such devices as pawls operate. 5. an apparatus or instrument formerly in use for torturing persons by stretching the body. 6. a cause or state of intense suffering of body or mind. 7. torment, anguish. 8. violent strain. 9. **on the rack,** a. in great pain, distress, or anxiety. b. under the strain of great effort. —*v.t.* 10. to torture; distress acutely; torment. 11. to strain in mental effort: *to rack one's brains.* 12. to strain by physical force or violence; shake violently. 13. to strain beyond what is normal or usual. 14. to stretch the joints of (a person) in torture by means of a rack. [ME *rekke, rakke,* t. MD or MLG] —**Syn.** 7, 10. See **torment.**

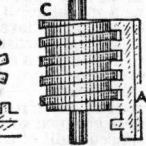

A. Rack (def. 4)
B. with pinion gear; C. with worm gear

rack[2] (răk), *n.* wreck; destruction: *to go to rack and ruin.* [var. of WRACK]

rack[3] (răk), *n.* 1. the gait of a horse in which the legs move in lateral pairs but not quite simultaneously; the single-foot. 2. the pace. —*v.i.* 3. (of a horse) to go with a gait, similar to a pace, in which the legs move in lateral pairs but not quite simultaneously; single-foot. 4. to pace. [? var. of ROCK, v.]

rack[4] (răk), *n.* 1. flying, broken clouds; a mass of clouds driven by the wind. —*v.i.* 2. to drive or move, esp. before the wind. [ME *rak, rakke;* prob. t. Scand.; cf. Icel. *rek* rack, wreckage, *reka* drive]

rack[5] (răk), *v.t.* to draw off (wine, cider, etc.) from the lees. [late ME; cf. obs. F *raqué* of wine, pressed from the marc of grapes, Pr. *arracar* to rack, *raca* dregs]

rack[6] (răk), *n.* the neck portion of mutton, pork, or veal. [cf. G *rachen* throat]

rack·et[1] (răk′ĭt), n. 1. a loud noise, esp. of a disturbing or confusing kind; din; uproar; clamor or noisy fuss. 2. social excitement, gaiety, or dissipation. 3. *U.S. Slang.* an organized illegal activity such as bootlegging, or extorting money by threat or violence from legitimate businessmen. 4. *U.S. Slang.* a dishonest scheme, trick, etc. —*v.i.* 5. to make a racket or noise. 6. to indulge in social gaiety or dissipation. [metathetic var. of d. *rattick*. See RATTLE[1]] —Syn. 1. See noise.

rack·et[2] (răk′ĭt), n. 1. a light bat having a network of cord or catgut stretched in a more or less elliptical frame, used in tennis, etc. 2. (*pl. construed as sing.*) a game of ball, played in a walled court, in which such bats are used. 3. a snowshoe made in the manner of a tennis racket. Also, **rack′ett, racquet.** [t. F: m. *raquette;* orig. uncert.]

rack·et·eer (răk′ə tĭr′), *U.S.* —n. 1. one engaged in a racket. —*v.i.* 2. to engage in a racket. [f. RACKET[1] (defs. 3, 4) + -EER] —**rack′et·eer′ing,** n.

rack·et·y (răk′ĭt ĭ), adj. 1. making or causing a racket; noisy. 2. fond of excitement or dissipation.

Rack·ham (răk′əm), n. Arthur, 1867–1939, British illustrator and water-color painter.

rack rail, (in an inclined-plane or mountain-climbing railway) a rail between the running rails having cogs or teeth with which cogwheels on the locomotive engage.

rack railway, a steep railway fitted with a rack rail.

rack-rent (răk′rĕnt′), n. 1. a rent for land equal or nearly equal to its full annual value. —*v.t.* 2. to exact the highest possible rent for. 3. to demand rack-rent from. [f. RACK[1], v. + RENT[1]] —**rack′-rent′er,** n.

rack·work (răk′wûrk′), n. a mechanism in which a rack is used; a rack and pinion or the like.

rac·on·teur (răk′ŏn tûr′), n. a person skilled in relating stories and anecdotes. [t. F. See RECOUNT]

ra·coon (ră kōōn′), n. raccoon.

rac·quet (răk′ĭt), n. racket[2].

rac·y (rā′sĭ), adj., **racier, raciest.** 1. vigorous; lively; spirited. 2. sprightly; piquant; pungent: *a racy style.* 3. having an agreeably peculiar taste or flavor, as wine, fruits, etc. 4. suggestive; risqué: *a racy story.* [f. RACE[1] + -Y[1]] —**rac′i·ly,** adv. —**rac′i·ness,** n.

rad., 1. *Math.* radical. 2. radix.

ra·dar (rā′där), n. *Electronics.* a device to determine the presence and location of an object by measuring the time for the echo of a radio wave to return from it, and the direction from which it returns. [short for ra(dio) d(etecting) a(nd) r(anging)]

ra·dar·scope (rā′där skōp′), n. the viewing screen of radar equipment.

rad·dle[1] (răd′əl), v.t., **-dled, -dling.** *Now Prov. Eng.* to interweave; wattle. [v. use of *raddle* lath, t. AF: m. *reidele* thick stick]

rad·dle[2] (răd′əl), n., v., **-dled, -dling.** —n. 1. ruddle. —*v.t.* 2. to paint with ruddle. 3. to color coarsely. Also, **reddle.** [var. of RUDDLE]

Ra·detz·ky (rä dĕts′kĭ), n. **Count Joseph** (yō′zĕf), 1766–1858, Austrian field marshal.

Rad·ford (răd′fərd), n. **Arthur W.,** born 1896, U.S. admiral; chairman, Joint Chiefs of Staff, 1953–57.

ra·di·al (rā′dĭ əl), adj. 1. arranged like radii or rays. 2. having spokes, bars, lines, etc., arranged like radii, as a machine. 3. *Zool.* pertaining to structures that radiate from a central point, as the arms of a starfish. 4. of, like, or pertaining to a radius or a ray. 5. *Anat.* referring to the radius or more lateral of the two bones of the forearm. —**ra′di·al·ly,** adv.

radial engine, an engine having cylinders grouped so that they resemble equally spaced radii of a circle.

Radial arrangement of spokes of a wheel

ra·di·an (rā′dĭ ən), n. *Math.* an angle at the center of a circle, subtending an arc of the circle equal in length to the radius: equal to 57.2958°.

ra·di·ance (rā′dĭ əns), n. 1. radiant brightness or light: *radiance of the tropical sun, radiance lit her face.* 2. radiation. Also, **ra′di·an·cy.**

ra·di·ant (rā′dĭ ənt), adj. 1. emitting rays of light; shining; bright: *the radiant sun, radiant colors.* 2. bright with joy, hope, etc.: *radiant smiles.* 3. *Physics.* emitted in rays, or by radiation. —n. 4. a point or object from which rays proceed. 5. *Astron.* the point in the heavens from which a shower of meteors appears to radiate. [late ME, t. L: s. *radians,* ppr., emitting rays] —**ra′di·ant·ly,** adv. —Syn. 1. See bright.

radiant energy, *Physics.* the energy propagated through a medium as a wave, as heat, light, sound, etc.

ra·di·ate (rā′dĭ āt′), v., **-ated, -ating,** adj. —*v.i.* 1. to spread or move like rays or radii from a center. 2. to emit rays, as of light or heat; irradiate. 3. to issue or proceed in rays. —*v.t.* 4. to emit in rays; disseminate as from a center. —adj. 5. radiating from a center. 6. represented with rays proceeding from it, as a head on a coin, in art, etc. [t. L: m.s. *radiātus,* pp.] —**ra′di·a′tive,** adj.

ra·di·a·tion (rā′dĭ ā′shən), n. 1. the emission and diffusion of rays of heat, light, electricity, or sounds. 2. radiant energy or a particular form of it. 3. the giving off of one or more rays by a radioactive substance. 4. act or process of radiating. 5. that which is radiated; a ray or rays. 6. radial arrangement of parts.

ra·di·a·tor (rā′dĭ ā′tər), n. 1. one who or that which radiates. 2. any of various heating devices, as a series

or coil of pipes through which steam or hot water passes. 3. a device constructed from thin-walled tubes and metal fins, used for cooling circulating water, as on an automobile. 4. *Radio.* a form of antenna.

rad·i·cal (răd′ə kəl), adj. 1. going to the root or origin; fundamental: *a radical change.* 2. thoroughgoing or extreme, esp. in the way of reform. 3. (*often cap.*) belonging or pertaining to a political party favoring drastic reforms. 4. forming the basis or foundation. 5. existing inherently in a thing or person: *radical defects of character.* 6. *Math.* a. pertaining to or forming a root. b. denoting or pertaining to the radical sign. 7. *Gram.* of or pertaining to a root. 8. *Bot.* of or arising from the root or the base of the stem. —n. 9. one who holds or follows extreme principles; an extremist. 10. (*often cap.*) one who advocates fundamental and drastic political reforms or changes by direct and uncompromising methods. 11. *Math.* a. a quantity expressed as a root of another quantity. b. a radical sign. 12. *Chem.* an atom or group of atoms regarded as an important constituent of a molecule, which remains unchanged and behaves as a unit in many reactions. 13. *Gram.* a root. [ME, t. LL: s. *rādicālis,* der. L *rādix* root] —**rad′i·cal·ness,** n.

—Syn. 2. RADICAL, EXTREME, FANATICAL denote that which goes beyond moderation or even to excess in opinion, belief, action, etc. RADICAL emphasizes the idea of going to the root of a matter, and this often seems immoderate in its thoroughness or completeness: *radical ideas, radical changes, reforms.* EXTREME applies to excessively biased ideas, intemperate conduct, or repressive legislation: *to use extreme measures.* FANATICAL is applied to a person who has extravagant views, esp. in matters of religion or morality, which render him incapable of sound judgments; and excessive zeal which leads him to take violent action against those who have other views: *fanatical in persecuting others.*

radical axis, *Geom.* (of two circles) the line such that tangents drawn from any point of the line to the two circles are equal in length.

rad·i·cal·ism (răd′ə kəl ĭz′əm), n. 1. the holding or following of radical or extreme views or principles. 2. the principles or programs of radicals.

rad·i·cal·ly (răd′ĭk lĭ), adv. 1. with regard to origin or root. 2. in a complete or basic manner.

radical sign, *Math.* the symbol √ or √ (initially the first letter of *radix*) indicating extraction of a root of the following quantity: $\sqrt{a^2} = \pm a$, $\sqrt[3]{a^3b^3} = ab$.

rad·i·cel (răd′ə sĕl′), n. *Bot.* a minute root; a rootlet. [t. NL: m.s. *rādicella,* dim. of L *rādix* root]

rad·i·cle (răd′ə kəl), n. *Bot.* 1. the lower part of the axis of an embryo; the primary root. 2. a rudimentary root; a radicel or rootlet. 3. *Chem.* a radical. 4. *Anat.* a small rootlike part, as the beginning of a nerve fiber. [t. L: m. *rādicula,* dim. of *rādix* root]

ra·di·i (rā′dĭ ī′), n. pl. of radius.

ra·di·o (rā′dĭ ō′), n., pl. **-dios,** adj., v., **-dioed, -dioing.** —n. 1. wireless telegraphy or telephony: *speeches broadcasted by radio.* 2. an apparatus for receiving radio broadcasts. 3. a message transmitted by radio. —adj. 4. pertaining to, used in, or sent by radio. 5. pertaining to or employing radiations, as of electrical energy. —*v.t.* 6. to transmit (a message, etc.) by radio. 7. to send a message to (a person) by radio. —*v.i.* 8. to transmit a message, etc., by radio. [short for *radiotelegraphic* (or *telephonic*) *instrument, message,* or *transmission*]

radio-, a word element meaning: 1. radio. 2. a radial. 3. radium, radioactive, or radiant energy. [orig., comb. form of RADIUS]

ra·di·o·ac·tive (rā′dĭ ō ăk′tĭv), adj. *Physics, Chem.* 1. having the property of emitting particles or radiation from an atomic nucleus such as alpha rays, beta rays, or gamma rays, as is the case with radium, uranium, thorium, etc. 2. pertaining to this property.

radioactive series, *Physics, Chem.* the series of isotopes of various elements through which a radioactive substance decays before it reaches a stable state. The three known spontaneous series start with thorium and two different isotopes of uranium and each ends at a stable isotope of lead.

ra·di·o·ac·tiv·i·ty (rā′dĭ ō ăk tĭv′ə tĭ), n. the property of being radioactive.

ra·di·o·as·tron·o·my (rā′dĭ ō ə strŏn′ə mĭ), n. the study of celestial bodies through energy received from them at radio frequencies.

radio beacon, a radio station for sending a characteristic signal so as to enable ships or airplanes to determine their position or bearing by a receiving instrument (**radio compass**).

radio beam, beam (def. 13).

ra·di·o·broad·cast (rā′dĭ ō brŏd′kăst′, -käst′), n., v., **-cast** or **-casted, -casting.** —n. 1. a broadcast by radio. —*v.t., v.i.* 2. to broadcast by radio. —**ra′di·o·broad′cast′er,** n. —**ra′di·o·broad′cast′ing,** n.

ra·di·o·car·bon (rā′dĭ ō kär′bən), n. *Chem.* a radioactive isotope of carbon with atomic weight 14 and a half-life of ab. 5760 years: widely used in the dating of organic materials. Also, **carbon 14, carbon-14.** [f. RADIO- + CARBON]

radiocarbon dating, the determination of the age of objects of plant or animal origin by means of their radiocarbon content.

ra·di·o·chem·is·try (rā′dĭ ō kĕm′ĭs trĭ), n. the chemical study of radioactive elements, both natural and artificial, and their use in the study of other chemical processes.

ra·di·o·fre·quen·cy (rā/dĭ ō frē/kwən sĭ), n., pl. **-cies.** 1. the frequency of the transmitting waves of a given radio message or broadcast. 2. a frequency within the range of radio transmission, i.e. from about 15,000 to 10^{11} cycles per second. Also, **radio frequency.**

ra·di·o·gram (rā/dĭ ō grăm/), n. 1. a message transmitted by radiotelegraphy. 2. Brit. an x-ray.

ra·di·o·graph (rā/dĭ ō grăf/, -gräf/), n. 1. an image or picture produced by the action of x-ray or other rays (as from radioactive substances) on a photographic plate. —v.t. 2. to make a radiograph of.

ra·di·og·ra·phy (rā/dĭ ŏg/rə fĭ), n. the production of radiographs. —**ra/di·og/ra·pher,** n. —**ra·di·o·graph·ic** (rā/dĭ ō grăf/ĭk), adj.

ra·di·o·i·so·tope (rā/dĭ ō ī/sə tōp/), n. a radioactive isotope, usually artificially produced, of a normally inert chemical element, used in physical and biological research, therapeutics, etc.

ra·di·o·lar·i·an (rā/dĭ ō lâr/Ĭ ən), n. any of the *Radiolaria,* an extensive group or order of minute marine protozoans, having amoebalike bodies with fine radiating pseudopodia, and usually elaborate skeletons. [f. NL *Radiolāria,* pl., (der. L *radiolus,* dim. of *radius* ray) + -(A)N]

ra·di·o·log·i·cal (rā/dĭ ō lŏj/ə kəl), adj. involving radioactive materials: *radiological warfare.*

ra·di·ol·o·gy (rā/dĭ ŏl/ə jĭ), n. 1. the science dealing with x-rays or rays from radioactive substances, esp. for medical uses. 2. examining or photographing organs, etc., with such rays. —**ra/di·ol/o·gist,** n.

ra·di·o·me·te·or·o·graph (rā/dĭ ō mē/tĭ ər ə grăf/, -gräf/), n. radiosonde.

ra·di·om·e·ter (rā/dĭ ŏm/ə tər), n. 1. an instrument for indicating the transformation of radiant energy into mechanical work, consisting of an exhausted glass vessel containing vanes which revolve about an axis when exposed to radiant energy. 2. an instrument based on the same principle, but used for detecting and measuring small amounts of radiant energy. —**ra·di·o·met·ric** (rā/dĭ ō mĕt/rĭk), adj. —**ra/di·om/e·try,** n.

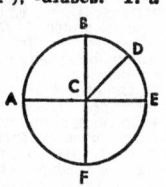
Radiometer (def. 1)

ra·di·o·paque (rā/dĭ ō pāk/), adj. opaque to radiation, hence, visible in x-ray photographs and under fluoroscopy.

ra·di·o·phone (rā/dĭ ō fōn/), n. 1. any of various devices for producing sound by the action of radiant energy. Thus, light falling on a phototube will vary an electric current which can actuate a loud-speaker. 2. a radiotelephone.

ra·di·os·co·py (rā/dĭ ŏs/kə pĭ), n. the examination of opaque objects by means of the x-rays or rays emitted by radioactive substances. —**ra·di·o·scop·ic** (rā/dĭ ō skŏp/ĭk), **ra/di·o·scop/i·cal,** adj.

ra·di·o·sonde (rā/dĭ ō sŏnd/), n. Meteorol. an instrument carried aloft by a balloon and sending, by means of a small radio transmitter, the atmospheric temperature, pressure, and humidity encountered. [appar. f. RADIO- + ME *sonde,* OE *sond* messenger]

radio spectrum, the wave length range of electromagnetic waves (approximately 30,000 meters to 1 millimeter or 10 kilocycles to 300,000 megacycles).

radio station, 1. a combination of devices for radio transmitting and/or receiving. 2. a complete installation for radio broadcasting, including transmitting apparatus, broadcasting studios, etc. 3. an organization or unit in an organization whose business it is to carry on commercial broadcasting, having a radiofrequency assigned to it by the FCC.

ra·di·o·tel·e·gram (rā/dĭ ō tĕl/ə grăm/), n. a message transmitted by radiotelegraphy.

ra·di·o·tel·e·graph (rā/dĭ ō tĕl/ə grăf/, -gräf/), n. 1. a wireless telegraph. —v.t., v.i. 2. to telegraph by radiotelegraphy. —**ra/di·o·tel/e·graph/ic,** adj.

ra·di·o·te·leg·ra·phy (rā/dĭ ō tə lĕg/rə fĭ), n. wireless telegraphy, in which messages are transmitted through space by means of the radiated energy of electromagnetic waves.

ra·di·o·tel·e·phone (rā/dĭ ō tĕl/ə fōn/), n., v., -phoned, -phoning. —n. 1. a wireless telephone. —v.t., v.i. 2. to telephone by radiotelephony. —**ra·di·o·tel·e·phon·ic** (rā/dĭ ō tĕl/ə fŏn/ĭk), adj.

ra·di·o·te·leph·o·ny (rā/dĭ ō tə lĕf/ə nĭ), n. wireless telephony.

radio telescope, a large parabolic reflector used to gather radio signals emitted by celestial bodies and focus them for reception by a receiver. See **radio astronomy.**

ra·di·o·ther·a·py (rā/dĭ ō thĕr/ə pĭ), n. treatment of disease by means of the x-rays or of radioactive agencies.

ra·di·o·ther·my (rā/dĭ ō thûr/mĭ), n. therapy which utilizes the heat from a short-wave radio apparatus or diathermy machine.

ra·di·o·tho·ri·um (rā/dĭ ō thôr/Ĭ əm), n. a disintegration product of thorium. [NL. See RADIO-,THORIUM]

radio tube, a type of electron tube.

radio wave, Radio. an electromagnetic wave, propagated through the atmosphere.

rad·ish (răd/Ĭsh), n. 1. the crisp, pungent, edible root of a cruciferous plant, *Raphanus sativus.* 2. the plant. [late ME; OE *rædic,* t. L: m.s. *rādix* root, radish]

ra·di·um (rā/dĭ əm), n. Chem. a radioactive metallic element which undergoes spontaneous atomic disintegration, the first products formed being the element radon (**radium emanation**) and alpha rays (which are regarded as positively charged particles of helium): discovered by M. and Mme. Curie in 1898. The disintegration of radium is understood to be a process by which an atom of radium breaks down into an atom of helium (the material of alpha rays) and an atom of radon (the material of the radium emanation), and by which an atom of radon loses an atom of helium and becomes radium A, and by which subsequent products are formed. *Symbol:* Ra; *at. wt.:* 226.05; *at. no.:* 88. [NL, der. L *radius* ray]

radium A, a substance, formed from radon by disintegration, which gives rise to radium B.

radium B, an isotope of lead, formed from radium A by disintegration, which gives rise to an isotope of bismuth called **radium C,** from which **radium D, radium E,** and **radium F** (polonium) are derived.

ra·di·um·ther·a·py (rā/dĭ əm thĕr/ə pĭ), n. treatment of disease by means of radium.

ra·di·us (rā/dĭ əs), n., pl. **-dii** (-dĭ ī/), **-diuses.** 1. a straight line extending from the center of a circle or sphere to the circumference or surface. 2. the length of such a line. 3. any radial or radiating part. 4. a circular area of an extent indicated by the length of the radius of its circumscribing circle: *every house within a radius of fifty miles.* 5. field or range of operation or influence. 6. extent of possible operation, travel, etc., as under a single supply of fuel: *the flying radius of an airplane.* 7. Anat. that one of the two bones of the forearm which is on the thumb side. See **shoulder.** 8. Zool. a corresponding bone in the forelimb of other vertebrates. 9. Mach. the throw of an eccentric wheel or cam. [t. L: staff, rod, spoke of a wheel, radius, ray or beam of light]

Radii: CA, CB, CD, CE, CF

radius vec·tor (vĕk/tər), pl. **radii vectores** (vĕk tōr/ēz), **radius vectors.** 1. Math. the length of the line segment joining a fixed point or origin to a variable point. 2. Astron. a line (or distance) from the sun or the like taken as a fixed point or origin, to a planet or the like as a variable point. [see RADIUS, VECTOR]

ra·dix (rā/dĭks), n., pl. **radices** (răd/ə sēz/, rā/də-), **radixes.** 1. Math. a number taken as the base of a system of numbers, logarithms, or the like. 2. Bot. a root; a radical. 3. Gram. a root (def. 11). [t. L: root]

Rad·nor·shire (răd/nər shĭr/, -shər), n. a county in E Wales. 19,993 pop. (1951); 471 sq. mi. Co. seat: Presteigne. Also, **Rad/nor.**

Ra·dom (rä/dôm), n. a city in E Poland. 117,000 (est. 1955).

ra·don (rā/dŏn), n. Chem. a rare, chemically inert, radioactive gaseous element produced in the disintegration of radium. *Symbol:* Rn; *at. no.:* 86; *at. wt.:* 222. [f. RAD(IUM) + -on, modeled on ARGON, NEON]

rad·u·la (răj/ŏŏ lə), n., pl. **-lae** (-lē/). a chitinous band in the mouth of most mollusks, set with numerous minute horny teeth, and drawn backward and forward over the odontophore in the process of breaking up food. [t. L: a scraper] —**rad/u·lar,** adj.

Rae·burn (rā/bərn), n. Sir Henry, 1756–1823, Scottish portrait painter.

R.A.F., Royal Air Force.

raff (răf), n. 1. the riffraff; the rabble. 2. Scot. and Brit. Dial. trash. [appar. abstracted from RIFFRAFF]

raf·fi·a (răf/Ĭ ə), n. 1. a species of palm, Raphia pedunculata, of Madagascar, bearing long, plumelike, pinnate leaves, the leafstalks of which yield an important fiber. 2. the fiber, much used for tying plants, cut flowers, small packages, etc., and for making matting, baskets, hats, and the like. 3. some other palm of the same genus. 4. its fiber. [t. Malagasy]

raf·fi·nose (răf/ə nōs/), n. Chem. a colorless crystalline trisaccharide, $C_{18}H_{32}O_{16} \cdot 5H_2O$, with little or no sweetness, occurring in the sugar beet, cottonseed, etc., and breaking down to fructose, glucose, and galactose on hydrolysis. [f. s. F *raffiner* refine + -OSE²]

raff·ish (răf/Ĭsh), adj. disreputable; vulgar. [f. RAFF + -ISH¹] —**raff/ish·ly,** adv. —**raff/ish·ness,** n.

raf·fle¹ (răf/əl), n., v., -fled, -fling. —n. 1. a form of lottery in which something put up as a prize goes to some one among a number of persons buying chances to win it. —v.t. 2. to dispose of by a raffle (often fol. by off): *to raffle off a watch.* —v.i. 3. to take part in a raffle. [ME *rafle,* t. OF: m. *raffle* kind of game at dice, net, plundering, der. *rafler* scratch, t. D: m. *rafelen* ravel] —**raf/fler,** n.

raf·fle² (răf/əl), n. 1. rubbish. 2. Naut. a tangle, as of ropes, canvas, etc. [der. RAFF (def. 2)]

raft¹ (răft, räft), n. 1. a more or less rigid floating platform made of buoyant materials. 2. a collection of logs, planks, casks, etc., fastened together for floating on water in an emergency. —v.t. 3. to transport on a raft. 4. to form (logs, etc.) into a raft. 5. to travel or cross by a raft. —v.i. 6. to use a raft; go or travel on a raft. [ME *rafte* beam, rafter, t. Scand.; cf. Icel. *raptr* log]

raft² (răft, räft), n. Colloq. a great quantity; a lot: *a raft of trouble.* [var. of *raff* large number (ME abundance, plenty). See RAFF]

raft·er (răf′tər, räf′-), *n.* one of the sloping timbers or members sustaining a roof sheeting or covering. See diag. under **curb roof.** [ME; OE *ræfter,* c. MLG *rafter.* See RAFT[1]]

rafts·man (răfts′mən, räfts′-), *n., pl.* **-men.** a man who manages, or is employed on, a raft.

rag[1] (răg), *n.* **1.** a comparatively worthless fragment of cloth, esp. one resulting from tearing or wear. **2.** (*pl.*) ragged or tattered clothing. **3.** a shred, scrap, or fragmentary bit of anything. **4.** (in contemptuous or humorous use) an article of cloth, paper, etc., such as a handkerchief, a theater curtain, a newspaper, or a piece of paper money. **5.** (in contemptuous use) a beggarly, worthless person. **6.** *Colloq.* a song or a piece of instrumental music in ragtime. **7.** the axis and carpellary walls of a citrus fruit. [ME *ragg(e),* t. Scand.; cf. Icel. *rögg* shag]

rag[2] (răg), *v.,* **ragged, ragging,** *n. Slang.* —*v.t.* **1.** to scold. **2.** to tease. **3.** *Brit.* to play rough jokes on. —*n.* **4.** *Brit.* act of ragging. [cf. Icel. *ragna* curse, swear]

rag·a·muf·fin (răg′əmŭf′ĭn), *n.* **1.** a ragged, disreputable person; a tatterdemalion. **2.** a ragged child.

rage (rāj), *n., v.,* **raged, raging.** —*n.* **1.** angry fury; violent anger: *to fall into a rage.* **2.** fury or violence of wind, waves, fire, disease, etc. **3.** violence of feeling, desire, or appetite: *the rage of thirst.* **4.** a violent desire or passion. **5.** ardor; fervor; enthusiasm: *poetic rage.* **6.** the object of widespread enthusiasm: *chess became all the rage.* **7.** *Obs.* insanity. —*v.i.* **8.** to act or speak with fury; show or feel violent anger. **9.** to move, rush, dash, or surge furiously. **10.** to proceed, continue, or prevail with great violence: *the battle raged ten days.* **11.** (of feelings, etc.) to hold sway with unabated violence. [ME, t. OF g. VL *rabia,* for L *rabies* madness, rage. See RABIES] —**Syn. 1.** frenzy, passion. See **anger. 6.** vogue, fad, fashion, craze. **8.** rave, fume.

rag·ged (răg′ĭd), *adj.* **1.** clothed in tattered garments. **2.** torn or worn to rags; tattered: *ragged clothing.* **3.** shaggy, as an animal, its coat, etc. **4.** having loose or hanging shreds or fragmentary bits: *a ragged wound.* **5.** full of rough or sharp projections; jagged: *ragged stones.* **6.** in a wild or neglected state: *a ragged garden.* **7.** rough, imperfect, or faulty: *a ragged piece of work.* **8.** harsh, as sound, the voice, etc. —**rag′ged·ly,** *adv.* —**rag′ged·ness,** *n.*

ragged robin, a caryophyllaceous plant, *Lychnis loscuculi,* bearing pink or white flowers with dissected petals.

rag·i (răg′ĭ), *n.* a cereal grass, *Eleusine coracana,* cultivated in Asia, etc., for its grain. Also, **rag′gee, rag′gy.** [t. Hind.: m. *rāgī*]

rag·lan (răg′lən), *n.* a loose overcoat the sleeves of which are cut so as to continue up to the collar. [named after Lord **Raglan** (1788–1855), British field marshal]

rag·man (răg′măn′, -mən), *n., pl.* **-men** (-měn′, -mən). a man who gathers, or deals in, rags.

Rag·na·rok (răg′nərŏk′), *n. Scand. Myth.* the destruction of the gods and all things in a great battle with evil powers. Also, **Rag·na·rök** (răg′nə rœk′).

ra·gout (răgōō′), *n., v.,* **-gouted** (-gōōd′), **-gouting** (-gōō′ĭng). —*n.* **1.** a highly seasoned stew of meat and vegetables. —*v.t.* **2.** to make into a ragout. [t. F, der. *ragoûter* restore the appetite of, der. *re-* RE- + *à* (g. L *ad*) + *goût* (g. L *gustus*) taste]

rag·pick·er (răg′pĭk′ər), *n.* one who picks up rags and other waste material from the streets, refuse heaps, etc., for a livelihood.

ragtag and bobtail, the riffraff.

rag·time (răg′tīm′), *n. Colloq.* (in music) **1.** rhythm marked by frequent syncopation, such as is common in Negro dance music. **2.** music in this rhythm. [prob. alter. of *ragged time*]

Ra·gu·sa (rägōō′zä), *n.* Italian name of **Dubrovnik.**

rag·weed (răg′wēd′), *n.* **1.** any of the composite herbs constituting the genus *Ambrosia,* whose air-borne pollen is the most prevalent cause of autumnal hay fever, as the common ragweed, *A. artemisiifolia,* and the giant ragweed, *A. trifida.* **2.** *U.S. Dial.* marsh elder. **3.** *Brit.* the ragwort.

rag·wort (răg′wûrt′), *n.* any of various composite plants of the genus *Senecio,* as *S. Jacobaea,* a yellow-flowered Old World herb with irregularly lobed leaves, or a North American species, *S. aureus* (**golden ragwort**), also bearing yellow flowers.

rah (rä), *interj.* an exclamation. [short for HURRAH]

ra·ia (rä′yə, rī′ə), *n. Obs.* rayah.

raid (rād), *n.* **1.** a sudden onset or attack, as upon something to be seized or suppressed: *a police raid on a gambling house.* **2.** a sudden attack on the enemy, esp. by airplanes or by a small force. **3.** *Finance.* a concerted attempt of speculators to force stock prices down. —*v.t.* **4.** to make a raid on. —*v.i.* **5.** to engage in a raid. [ME *raide,* OE *rād* expedition, lit., riding. See ROAD] —**raid′er,** *n.* —**Syn. 2.** incursion, invasion, inroad.

rail[1] (rāl), *n.* **1.** a bar of wood or metal fixed horizontally for any of various purposes, as for a support, barrier, fence, railing, etc. **2.** a fence; a railing. **3.** one of a pair of steel bars that provide the running surface for the wheels of locomotives and cars. **4.** the railroad, as a means of transportation: *to travel by rail.* **5.** (*pl.*) stocks, bonds, etc., of railroads. **6.** *Naut.* the upper part of the bulwarks of a ship. **7.** a horizontal timber or piece in a

framework or in paneling. —*v.t.* **8.** to furnish or enclose with a rail or rails. [ME *raylle,* t. OF: m. *reille,* g. L *rēgula* rule, straight stick, bar. See RULE]

rail[2] (rāl), *v.i.* **1.** to utter bitter complaint or vehement denunciation (often fol. by *at* or *against*): *to rail at fate.* —*v.t.* **2.** to bring, force, etc., by railing. [late ME, t. F: m.s. *railler* deride, t. Pr.: m. *ralhar* chatter ult. der. L *ragere* shriek] —**rail′er,** *n.*

rail[3] (rāl), *n.* any of numerous wading birds constituting the subfamily *Rallinae* (family *Rallidae*), characterized by short wings, a narrow body, strong legs, long toes, and a harsh cry, and abounding in marshes in most parts of the world, as the European **water rail** (*Rallus aquaticus*), the **Virginia rail** (*R. limicola*), and the **Carolina rail** or **sora** (*Porzana carolina*). [late ME, t. OF: m. *raale,* c. Pr. *rascla,* prob. ult. der. L *rādere* scratch]

Virginia rail.
Rallus limicola
(9½ in. long)

rail·head (rāl′hĕd′), *n.* **1.** the farthest point to which the rails of a railroad have been laid. **2.** *Mil.* a railroad depot at which supplies are unloaded to be distributed or forwarded by truck or other means.

rail·ing (rā′lĭng), *n.* **1.** a barrier made of rails, rails and supports, etc. **2.** rails collectively.

rail·ler·y (rā′lə rĭ), *n., pl.* **-leries. 1.** good-humored ridicule; banter. **2.** a bantering remark. [t. F: m. *raillerie.* See RAIL[2]]

rail·road (rāl′rōd′), *n. Chiefly U.S.* **1.** a permanent road or way, laid or provided with rails, commonly in one or more pairs of continuous lines forming a track or tracks, on which locomotives and cars are run for the transportation of passengers, freight, express, and mails. **2.** such a road together with its rolling stock, buildings, etc.; the entire railway plant, including fixed and movable property. **3.** the company of persons owning or operating it. —*v.t.* **4.** *U.S.* to transport by means of a railroad. **5.** to supply with railroads. **6.** *U.S. Colloq.* to send or push forward with great or undue speed: *to railroad a bill through a legislature.* **7.** *Slang.* to imprison on a false charge in order to be rid of.

rail·road·ing (rāl′rō′dĭng), *n.* the construction or operation of railroads.

rail·way (rāl′wā′), *n.* **1.** a rail line with lighter-weight equipment and roadbed than a main-line railroad. **2.** *Chiefly Brit.* a railroad. **3.** any line or lines of rails forming a road for flanged-wheel equipment.

rai·ment (rā′mənt), *n. Archaic or Poetic.* clothing; apparel; attire. [ME *rayment,* aphetic var. of *arrayment.* See ARRAY]

rain (rān), *n.* **1.** water in drops falling from the sky to the earth, being condensed from the aqueous vapor in the atmosphere. **2.** a rainfall, rainstorm, or shower. **3.** (*pl.*) the seasonal rainfalls, or the rainy season, in some regions, as India. **4.** a large quantity of anything falling thickly: *a rain of blows.* —*v.i.* **5.** (of rain) to fall: *it rained all night.* **6.** to fall like rain: *tears rained from her eyes.* **7.** to send down or let fall rain (said of God, the sky, the clouds, etc.). —*v.t.* **8.** to send down (rain, etc.). **9.** to offer, bestow, or give abundantly: *to rain blows upon a person.* [ME *rein,* OE *regn,* c. D and G *regen,* Icel. *regn*]

rain·band (rān′bănd′), *n. Physics.* a dark band in the solar spectrum, due to water vapor in the atmosphere.

rain·bow (rān′bō′), *n.* **1.** a bow or arc of prismatic colors appearing in the heavens opposite the sun, due to the refraction and reflection of the sun's rays in drops of rain. **2.** a similar bow of colors, esp. one appearing in the spray of cataracts, etc. [ME *reinbowe,* OE *regnboga,* c. OHG *reginbogo,* Icel. *regnbogi*]

Rainbow Bridge, a natural stone bridge in S Utah: a national monument. 309 ft. high; 278 ft. span.

rainbow trout, a trout, *Salmo gairdnerii,* native in the coastal waters and streams from Lower California to Alaska but introduced elsewhere.

rain check, a ticket for future use given to spectators at a baseball game, track meet, etc., stopped by rain.

rain·coat (rān′kōt′), *n.* a waterproof coat, worn as a protection from rain.

rain·drop (rān′drŏp′), *n.* a drop of rain.

rain·fall (rān′fôl′), *n.* **1.** a fall or shower of rain. **2.** the amount of water falling in rain, snow, etc., within a given time and area, ordinarily expressed as a hypothetical depth of coverage: *a rainfall of 70 inches a year.*

rain gauge, an instrument for measuring rainfall. Also, **rain gage.**

Rai·nier (rā nîr′, rā′nîr; *locally* rə nîr′), *n.* **Mount,** a mountain in W Washington, in the Cascade Range. 14,408 ft. Also, **Mount Tacoma.**

rain·proof (rān′prōōf′), *adj.* **1.** proof against rain; impervious to rain. —*v.t.* **2.** to make impervious to rain.

rain·storm (rān′stôrm′), *n.* a storm of rain.

rain water, water fallen as rain.

rain·y (rā′nĭ), *adj.,* **rainier, rainiest. 1.** characterized by rain: *rainy weather, a rainy region.* **2.** wet with rain: *rainy streets.* **3.** bringing rain: *rainy clouds.* **4.** a rainy day, a time of need or emergency in the future. —**rain′i·ness,** *n.*

raise (rāz), *v.,* **raised, raising,** *n.* —*v.t.* **1.** to move to a higher position; lift up; elevate: *to raise one's hand.*

2. to set upright; lift up. **3. to cause** to rise or stand up; rouse. **4. to** build; erect: *to raise a monument.* **5. to set** up the framework of (a house, etc.). **6. to cause** to be or appear: *to raise a tempest.* **7. to cause** or promote the growth of, as crops, plants, animals, etc. **8. to give** rise to; bring up or about: *to raise a question.* **9. to put** forward, as an objection **or** a claim. **10.** *Law.* to begin or institute, as a suit at law. **11. to restore** to life: *to raise the dead.* **12. to stir** up: *to raise a rebellion.* **13. to give** vigor to; animate. **14. to advance** in rank, dignity, etc.: *to raise a man to the peerage.* **15. to gather** together; collect: *to raise an army.* **16. to increase** in height. **17. to increase** in degree, intensity, pitch, or force. **18. to utter** (a cry, etc.) in a loud voice. **19. to cause** (the voice) to be heard: *to raise one's voice in opposition.* **20. to cause** (dough or bread) to rise by expansion and become light, as by the use of yeast. **21. to increase** in amount, as rent, prices, wages, etc. **22. to increase** the value or price, as a commodity or security. **23.** *Poker, etc.* to wager more than (another player's bet, or another player). **24. to increase** the amount specified in (a check or the like), by fraudulent alteration. **25. to bring** up; rear: *to raise six children.* **26.** *Mil.* **a. to end** (a siege) by withdrawing the investing forces. **b. to end** (a siege) by compelling the investing forces to withdraw. **27. to remove** (a prohibition, etc.). **28.** *Naut.* **a. to cause** (something) to rise above the visible horizon by approaching nearer to it. **b. to come** in sight of (land, a whale, etc.). —*v.i.* **29.** *Colloq.* to cough up mucous or phlegm. —*n.* **30.** an increase in amount, as of wages. **31.** the amount of such an increase. **32.** a raising, lifting, etc. **33.** a raised piece. [ME *reise(n)*, t. Scand.; cf. Icel. *reisa*, c. OE *rǣran* raise, causative of OE *rīsan* RISE. See REAR²] —**rais′er,** *n.* —**Syn. 1, 2.** RAISE, LIFT, HEAVE, HOIST imply bringing something up above its original position. RAISE, the most general word, may mean to bring something to or towards an upright position with one end resting on the ground; or it may be used like LIFT of moving an object generally a comparatively short distance upward, but breaking completely its physical contact with the place where it has been: *to raise a ladder; to lift a package.* HEAVE implies lifting with effort or exertion: *to heave a huge box onto a truck.* HOIST implies lifting slowly and gradually something of considerable weight, usually with mechanical help, such as a crane or derrick: *to hoist steel beams to the top of the framework of a building.* See **rise.** —**Ant. 1.** lower.

raised (rāzd), *adj.* **1.** fashioned or made as a surface design in relief. **2.** *Cookery.* made light by the use of yeast or other ferment, but not with baking powder, soda, or the like. **3.** that is or has been raised.

rai·sin (rā′zən), *n.* **1.** a grape of some sweet variety, suitable for the purpose, dried in the sun or artificially and used in cookery, etc. **2.** dark bluish purple. [ME *razin,* t. OF, g. L *racēmus* cluster of grapes]

rai·son d'é·tat (rě zōN′ dě tá′), *French.* reason of state; for the good of the country as a whole.

rai·son d'ê·tre (rě zōN′ dě′tr), *French.* reason for being or existence.

raj (räj), *n. India.* rule; dominion: *the British raj.*

ra·jah (rä′jə), *n.* **1.** *India.* **a.** a king or prince. **b.** a chief or dignitary. **c.** an honorary title conferred on Hindus in India. **2.** a title of rulers, princes, or chiefs in Java, Borneo, etc. Also, **ra′ja.** [t. Hind.: m. *rājā,* c. L *rex* king]

Ra·jas·than (rä′jə stän), *n.* a state in NW India; formerly Rajputana and a group of small states. 15,970,000 pop. (est. 1956); 132,078 sq. mi. *Cap.*: Jaipur.

Raj·put (räj′pōōt), *n.* a member of a Hindu race claiming descent from the ancient Kshatriya or warrior caste and noted for their military spirit. [t. Hind., f. Skt. *rāj* king + *put(ra)* son. See RAJAH, RAJ]

Raj·pu·ta·na (räj′pōō tä′nə), *n.* a former region in NW India, now making up the preponderant part of Rajasthan state.

rake¹ (rāk), *n., v.,* **raked, raking.** —*n.* **1.** an implement with teeth or tines for gathering together hay or the like, breaking and smoothing the surface of ground, etc. **2.** any of various implements having a similar form, as a croupier's implement for gathering in money on a gaming table. **3.** a long, forcible sweep or onset. —*v.t.* **4. to gather** together, draw, or remove with a rake: *to rake dead leaves from a lawn.* **5. to clear,** smooth, or prepare with a rake: *to rake a garden bed.* **6. to clear** (a fire, etc.) by stirring with a poker or the like. **7. to gather** or collect, often with effort or difficulty: *to rake in the money.* **8. to revive:** *to rake up an old scandal.* **9. to search** thoroughly through. **10. to scrape;** scratch; graze. **11. to fire** guns lengthwise on (a place, troops, a ship, etc.). **12. to sweep** with the eyes. —*v.i.* **13. to use** a rake. **14. to search** as with a rake. **15. to scrape** or sweep (fol. by *against, over,* etc.). [ME; OE *raca*]

rake² (rāk), *n.* a profligate or dissolute person; a roué. [short for RAKEHELL]

rake³ (rāk), *v.,* **raked, raking.** —*v.i.* **1. to incline** from the vertical (as a mast) or from the horizontal. —*n.* **2.** inclination or slope away from the perpendicular or the horizontal. **3.** *Aeron.* the angle measured between the tip edge of an airfoil and the plane of symmetry. **4.** *Mach.* the angle between the cutting face of a tool and a plane perpendicular to the surface of the work at the cutting point. [orig. uncert.]

rake⁴ (rāk), *v.i.,* **raked, raking. 1.** *Hunting.* **a.** (of a hawk) to fly along after the game, or to fly wide of it.

b. (of a dog) to hunt with the nose close to the ground. **2.** *Dial.* to go or proceed, esp. with speed. [OE *racian* go, proceed, hasten, c. Sw. *raka* run, rush]

rake·hell (rāk′hĕl′), *n. Archaic.* a roué; a rake. [f. RAKE¹ (def. 9) + HELL; r. ME *rakel,* adj., rash, rough, coarse, hasty, der. RAKE⁴]

rake·hell·y (rāk′hĕl′ȳ), *adj. Archaic.* profligate.

rake·off (rāk′ôf′, -ŏf′), *n. U.S. Slang.* **1.** a share or portion, as of a sum involved or of profits. **2.** a share or amount taken or received illicitly, as in connection with a public enterprise.

ra·ki (rä kē′, rāk′ȳ), *n.* a spirituous liquor distilled from grain, grapes, plums, etc., in southeastern Europe and the Near East. [t. Turk.: m. *rāqī*]

rak·ish¹ (rā′kĭsh), *adj.* **1.** smart; jaunty; dashing. **2.** like a rake; dissolute. [f. RAKE² + -ISH¹] —**rak′ish·ly,** *adv.* —**rak′ish·ness,** *n.*

rak·ish² (rā′kĭsh), *adj.* (of ships) having an appearance suggestive of speed and dash. [f. RAKE³ + -ISH¹]

râle (räl), *n. Pathol.* an abnormal sound accompanying the normal respiratory murmur, as in pulmonary diseases. [t. F, der. *râler* rattle when breathing, der. *râle* RAIL³]

Ra·leigh (rô′lȳ), *n.* **1.** Also, **Ra′legh. Sir Walter,** 1552?–1618, English explorer, favorite of Queen Elizabeth, and author. **2.** the capital of North Carolina, in the central part. 93,931 (1960).

rall., rallentando.

ral·len·tan·do (räl′lĕn tän′dō), *adj. Music.* slackening; becoming slower. [It., ppr. of *rallentare* abate]

ral·li·form (răl′ə fôrm′), *adj. Zool.* raillike in shape, anatomy, etc. [t. NL: s. *ralliformis.* See RAIL³]

ral·line (răl′īn, -ȳn), *adj.* belonging or pertaining to the subfamily *Rallinae,* or the family *Rallidae,* which includes the rails and their near relatives. [f. s. NL *Rallus* typical genus of rails + -INE¹]

ral·ly¹ (răl′ȳ), *v.,* **-lied, -lying,** *n., pl.* **-lies.** —*v.t.* **1. to bring** together or into order again: *to rally an army.* **2. to draw** or call (persons) together for common action. **3. to concentrate** or revive, as one's strength, spirits, etc. —*v.i.* **4. to come** together for common action. **5. to come** together or into order again. **6. to come** to the assistance of a person, party, or cause. **7. to recover** partially from illness. **8. to acquire** fresh strength or vigor: *the stock market rallied today.* **9.** *Tennis, etc.* to engage in a rally. —*n.* **10.** a recovery from dispersion or disorder, as of troops. **11.** the signal for this. **12.** a renewal or recovery of strength, activity, etc. **13.** a partial recovery of strength during illness. **14.** a drawing or coming together of persons, as for common action, as in a mass meeting. **15.** *Finance.* a sharp rise in price and active trading, after a declining market. **16.** *Tennis, etc.* the return of the ball by both sides a number of times consecutively. **17.** *Boxing.* an exchange of blows. [t. F: m.s. *rallier.* See RE-, ALLY]

ral·ly² (răl′ȳ), *v.t.,* **-lied, -lying.** to ridicule good-humoredly; banter. [t. F: m.s. *railler* RAIL²]

ram (răm), *n., v.,* **rammed, ramming.** —*n.* **1.** a male sheep. **2.** (*cap.*) the zodiacal constellation or sign Aries. **3.** any of various devices for battering, crushing, driving, or forcing something. **4.** a battering ram. **5.** a heavy beak or spur projecting from the bow of a warship, for penetrating an enemy's ship. **6.** a vessel so equipped. **7.** the heavy weight which strikes the blow in a pile driver or the like. **8.** a piston, as on a hydraulic press. **9.** a hydraulic ram. —*v.t.* **10. to drive** or force by heavy blows. **11. to strike** with great force; dash violently against. **12. to cram;** stuff. **13. to push** firmly. **14. to force** (a charge) into a firearm, as with a ramrod. [ME and OE, c. D and LG *ram,* G *ramm*]

ram-, an intensive prefix, as in *ramshackle.* [cf. Icel. *ram-* very, special use of *rammr* strong, akin to RAM]

R.A.M., Royal Academy of Music.

Ra·ma (rä′mə), *n.* the name of three avatars of Vishnu and heroes of Hindu mythology: Balarama, Parashurama, and Ramachandra (esp. the last). [Skt.]

Ra·ma·chan·dra (rä′mə chŭn′drə), *n.* the hero of the Ramayana, and a character in the Mahabharata.

Ram·a·dan (răm′ə dän′), *n.* **1.** the ninth month of the Mohammedan year. **2.** the daily fast which is rigidly enjoined from dawn until sunset during this month. [t. Ar.: m. *Ramaḍān*]

Ra·ma·ya·na (rä mä′yə nə), *n.* one of the two great epics of India (the other being the Mahabharata). It is ascribed to the poet Valmiki, and was probably composed early in the Christian era. [Skt.]

ram·ble (răm′bəl), *v.,* **-bled, -bling,** *n.* —*v.i.* **1. to wander** about in a leisurely manner, without definite aim or direction. **2. to take** a course with many turns or windings, as a growing plant, a stream, or path. **3. to talk** or write discursively or without sequence of ideas. —*n.* **4.** a walk without a definite route, taken merely for pleasure. [? freq. of ROAM, but cf. Icel. *ramba* sway to and fro] —**Syn. 1.** stroll, saunter, stray. See roam.

ram·bler (răm′blər), *n.* **1.** one who or that which rambles. **2.** any of various climbing roses, esp. the **crimson rambler,** an ornamental hybrid with bright crimson flowers.

ram·bling (răm′blĭng), *adj.* **1.** wandering about aimlessly. **2.** taking an irregular course; straggling. **3.** spread out irregularly in various directions: *a rambling mansion.* **4.** straying from one subject to another.

Ram·bouil·let (răm/bŏŏ lā/; *Fr.* răN bŏŏ yĕ/), *n.* a variety of Merino sheep yielding good mutton and wool, the most popular fine-wool breed of sheep in the western U.S. [named after *Rambouillet*, France]

ram·bunc·tious (răm bŭngk/shəs), *adj. U.S. Colloq.* 1. boisterous; noisy. 2. obstreperous; perverse; unruly. [f. RAM- + var. of BUMPTIOUS]

ram·bu·tan (răm bŏŏ/tən), *n.* 1. the bright-red oval fruit of a Malayan sapindaceous tree, *Nephelium lappaceum*, covered with soft spines or hairs, and containing a pulp of pleasant subacid taste. 2. the tree. [t. Malay]

Ra·mée (rə mā/), *n.* **Louise de la,** ("Ouida") 1839–1908, British novelist.

ram·e·kin (răm/ə kĭn), *n.* 1. a small, separately cooked portion of some cheese preparation, or other food mixture, baked in a small dish. 2. the dish. Also, **ram/e·quin.** [t. F: m. *ramequin*, t. D. Cf. G *rahm* cream]

Ram·e·ses (răm/ə sēz/), *n.* Rameses.

ra·mi (rā/mī), *n.* pl. of *ramus*.

ram·ie (răm/ĭ), *n.* 1. an Asiatic urticaceous shrub, *Boehmeria nivea*, yielding a fiber used in making textiles, etc. 2. the fiber itself. [t. Malay: m. *rāmī*]

ram·i·fi·ca·tion (răm/ə fə kā/shən), *n.* 1. act, process, or manner of ramifying. 2. a branch: *the ramifications of a nerve.* 3. a division or subdivision springing or derived from a main stem or source: *to pursue a subject in all its ramifications.* 4. *Bot.* **a.** a structure formed of branches. **b.** a configuration of branching parts.

ram·i·form (răm/ə fôrm/), *adj.* 1. having the form of a branch; branchlike. 2. branched. [. *rami-* (t. L, comb. form of *rāmus* branch) + -FORM]

ram·i·fy (răm/ə fī/), *v.t., v.i.,* **-fied, -fying.** to divide or spread out into branches or branchlike parts. [t. F: m.s. *ramifier*, t. ML: m. *rāmificāre*, f. L: *rāmi-* (comb. form of *rāmus* branch) + *-ficāre* make]

Ra·mil·lies (rȧ mē yĕ/), *n.* a village in central Belgium: Marlborough's defeat of the French, 1706.

ram·jet (răm/jĕt/), *n.* a jet-propulsion engine operated by the injection of fuel into a stream of air compressed by the forward speed of the aircraft.

ram·mer (răm/ər), *n.* one who or that which rams.

ram·mish (răm/ĭsh), *adj.* 1. like a ram. 2. rank.

ra·mose (rā/mōs, rə mōs/), *adj.* 1. having many branches. 2. branching. [t. L: m.s. *rāmōsus*]

ra·mous (rā/məs), *adj.* 1. ramose. 2. like branches.

ramp (rămp), *n.* 1. a sloping surface connecting two different levels. 2. a short concave slope or bend, as one connecting the higher and lower parts of a staircase railing at a landing. 3. any extensive sloping walk or passageway. 4. act of ramping. [t. F: m. *rampe*] —*v.i.* 5. to rise or stand on the hind legs, as a quadruped, esp. a lion (often one represented in heraldry or sculpture). 6. to rear as if to spring. 7. to leap or dash with fury (fol. by *about*, etc.). 8. to act violently; rage; storm. [ME, t. F: s. *ramper* creep, crawl, climb]

ram·page (*n.* răm/pāj; *v.* răm pāj/), *n., v.,* **-paged, -paging.** —*n.* 1. violent or excited behavior. 2. an instance of this: *to go on a rampage.* —*v.i.* 3. to rush, move, or act furiously or violently. [orig. Scot.; appar. dissimilated var. of *ramp-rage*. See RAMP (def. 8), RAGE (def. 10)]

ram·pa·geous (răm pā/jəs), *adj.* violent; unruly; boisterous. —**ram·pa/·geous·ness,** *n.*

ramp·an·cy (răm/pən sĭ), *n.* rampant condition or position.

ramp·ant (răm/pənt), *adj.* 1. violent in action, spirit, opinion, etc.; raging; furious. 2. in full sway; prevailing unbridled: *anarchy reigned rampant.* 3. standing on the hind legs; ramping. 4. (of a lion, bear, etc., as depicted in heraldry) standing on its left hind leg with the forelegs elevated, the right higher than the left, and, unless otherwise specified, with the head in profile. 5. *Archit.* (of an arch or vault) springing at one side from one level of support and resting at the other on a higher level. [ME *rampaunt*, t. OF: m. *rampant,* ppr. of *ramper* climb, RAMP] —**ramp/ant·ly,** *adv.*

Heraldic lion rampant

ram·part (răm/pärt, -pərt), *n.* 1. *Fort.* **a.** a broad elevation or mound of earth raised as a fortification about a place, and usually having a stone or earth parapet built upon it. **b.** such an elevation together with the parapet. 2. anything serving as a bulwark or defense. —*v.t.* 3. to furnish with or as with a rampart. [t. F: m. *rempart,* der. *remparer* fortify] —**Syn.** 2. bulwark, breastwork, barricade.

Rampant arch in staircase

ram·pi·on (răm/pǐ ən), *n.* 1. a European campanula, *Campanula Rapunculus,* having an edible white tuberous root used for salad in Europe. 2. any of the plants of the campanulaceous genus *Phyteuma,* bearing heads or spikes of blue flowers. [cf. It. *ramponzolo*]

ram·rod (răm/rŏd/), *n.* 1. a rod for ramming down the charge of a muzzleloading firearm. 2. a cleaning rod for the barrel of a rifle, etc.

Ram·say (răm/zĭ), *n.* 1. **Allan,** 1686–1758, Scottish poet. 2. **James Andrew Broun.** See **Dalhousie.** 3. **Sir William,** 1852–1916, British chemist.

Ram·ses (răm/sēz), *n.* name of several kings of ancient Egypt. Also, **Rameses.**

Ramses II, died 1225? B.C., king of ancient Egypt.

Ramses III, died 1167? B.C., king of ancient Egypt.

Rams·gate (rămz/gāt/; *Brit.* -gǐt), *n.* a seaport in SE England, in Kent: seaside resort. 35,748 (1951).

ram·shack·le (răm/shăk/əl), *adj.* loosely made or held together; rickety; shaky: *a ramshackle house.* [earlier *ramshackled,* f. RAM- + *shackled,* pp. of *shackle,* freq. of SHAKE, V.]

ram·son (răm/zən, -sən), *n.* 1. a species of garlic, *Allium ursinum,* with broad leaves. 2. (*usually pl.*) its bulbous root, used as a relish. [orig. pl. taken as sing.: ME *ramsyn,* OE *hramsan,* pl. of *hramsa* kind of garlic]

ram·til (răm/tĭl), *n.* Niger seed. [t. Bengali]

ram·u·lose (răm/yə lōs/), *adj. Bot., Zool.* having many small branches. Also, **ram·u·lous** (răm/yə ləs). [t. L: m.s. *rāmulōsus*]

ra·mus (rā/məs), *n., pl.* **-mi** (-mī). *Bot., Anat., etc.* a branch, as of a plant, a vein, a bone, etc. [t. L]

ran (răn), *v.* pt. of **run.**

Ran (răn), *n. Scand. Myth.* the sea goddess, who caught drowning men in her net; wife of Aegir.

rance (răns), *n.* a variety of marble from Belgium, dull red with white and blue graining. [t. F]

ranch (rănch), *n.* 1. an establishment maintained for production of livestock under range conditions where grass is the main source of feed. 2. the persons employed or living on it. 3. any farm or farming establishment. —*v.i.* 4. to conduct, or work on, a ranch. [t. Sp.: m. *rancho.* See RANCHO]

ranch·er (răn/chər), *n.* one who owns or works on a ranch.

ran·che·ro (răn châr/ō; *Sp.* rän chĕ/rō), *n., pl.* **-che·ros** (-châr/ōz; *Sp.* -chĕ/rōs). (in Spanish America and the southwestern U.S.) rancher. [t. Sp.]

ranch·man (rănch/mən), *n., pl.* **-men.** rancher.

ran·cho (răn/chō, rän/-; *Sp.* rän/chō), *n., pl.* **-chos** (-chōz; *Sp.* -chōs). (in Spanish America and the southwestern U.S.) 1. a hut or collection of huts for herdsmen, laborers, or travelers. 2. a ranch. [t. Sp.: mess, group of persons who eat together, in Sp. Amer. applied to the huts occupied by herdsmen and laborers]

ran·cid (răn/sĭd), *adj.* 1. having a rank, unpleasant, stale smell or taste: *rancid butter.* 2. rank in this manner: *a rancid smell.* [t. L: s. *rancidus*] —**ran/cid·ness,** *n.*

ran·cid·i·ty (răn sĭd/ə tĭ), *n.* 1. rancid state or quality. 2. a rancid odor or taste.

ran·cor (răng/kər), *n.* bitter, rankling resentment or ill will; hatred; malice. Also, *Brit.,* **ran/cour.** [ME, t. OF, g. LL *rancor* rank smell or taste, der. L *rancere* to be rank] —**Syn.** See **malevolence.**

ran·cor·ous (răng/kər əs), *adj.* full of or showing rancor. —**ran/cor·ous·ly,** *adv.* —**ran/cor·ous·ness,** *n.*

rand (rănd), *n.* 1. *Shoemaking.* a strip of leather, for leveling, set in a shoe at the heel before the lifts are attached. 2. *Scot.* or *Brit. Dial.* a border or margin. [ME and OE, c. D and G *rand* border, margin]

Rand (rănd), *n.* **The,** Witwatersrand.

R. & I., 1. (L *Regina et Imperatrix*) Queen and Empress. 2. (L *Rex et Imperator*) King and Emperor.

Rand·ers (răn/ərs), *n.* a seaport in Denmark, in E Jutland. 41,177 (est. 1954).

ran·dom (răn/dəm), *adj.* 1. going, made, occurring, etc., without definite aim, purpose, or reason. —*n.* 2. **at random,** in a haphazard way; without definite aim, purpose, or method. [ME *randon,* t. OF: rushing movement, disorder] —**ran/dom·ly,** *adv.* —**Syn.** 1. haphazard, chance, casual, stray, aimless.

random sampling, *Statistics.* the drawing of a sample from a statistical population in which all members of the population have equal probabilities of being included in the sample.

ra·nee (rä/nĭ), *n. India, etc.* 1. the wife of a rajah, king, or prince. 2. a reigning queen or princess. Also, **rani.** [t. Hind.: m. *rānī*]

rang (răng), *v.* pt. of **ring²**.

range (rānj), *n., adj., v.,* **ranged, ranging.** —*n.* 1. the extent to which, or the limits between which, variation is possible: *the range of prices for a commodity.* 2. the extent or scope of the operation or action of something: *within range of vision.* 3. the distance to which a projectile is or may be sent by a gun, etc. 4. the distance of the target from the gun, etc. 5. a place with targets for practice in shooting: *a rifle range.* 6. the distance of something to be located from some point of operation, as in sound ranging. 7. *Statistics.* the difference between the smallest and largest varieties in a statistical distribution. 8. the compass of a musical instrument or a voice. 9. *Survey.* **a.** the extension or prolongation of a line to intersect a transit line usually employed for location of physical features. **b.** a line established by markers on shore for the location of soundings. 10. (in U.S. public-land surveys) one of a series of divisions numbered east or west from the principal meridian of the survey, and consisting of a row of townships, each six miles square, which are numbered north or south from a base line. 11. a rank, class, or order. 12. a row, range, or series, as of persons or things. 13. act of ranging, or moving about, as over an area or region. 14. an area or tract that is or may be ranged over. 15. the region over which something is distributed, is found, or occurs: *the range of a plant.* **16.** a chain of mountains; a mountain range. **17.** an extensive stretch of grazing ground. **18.** a form of large stove, portable or stationary, for cooking, now usually having one or more ovens, and openings on the top for heating various articles at once. —*adj.* **19.** of, or grazing on, a range. [ME, t. OF, der. *ranger* RANGE, v.] —*v.t.* **20.** to draw up or dispose (persons or things) in a row or line, in rows or lines, or in a particular position, company, or group. **21.** to dispose systematically; set in order; arrange. **22.** to place in a particular class; classify. **23.** to make straight, level, or even, as lines of type. **24.** to pass over or through (an area or region) in all directions, as in exploring or searching. **25.** to pasture (cattle) on a range. **26.** to train, as a telescope, upon an object. **27.** to obtain the range of (something aimed at or to be located). **28.** *Naut.* to lay out (an anchor cable) so that the anchor may descend smoothly. —*v.i.* **29.** to vary within certain limits: *prices ranging from $5 to $10.* **30.** to have range of operation. **31.** to have a particular range, as a gun or a projectile. **32.** to find the range, as of something aimed at or to be located. **33.** to stretch out or extend in a line, as things. **34.** to extend, run or go in a certain direction: *a boundary ranging east and west.* **35.** to lie or extend in the same line, or the same plane, as one thing with another or others. **36.** to take up a position in a line or in order. **37.** to take up or occupy a particular place or position. **38.** to move about or through a region in all directions, as persons, animals, etc. **39.** to rove, roam, or wander: *the talk ranged over a variety of matters.* **40.** to extend, be found, or occur over an area or throughout a period, as animals, plants, etc.: *a plant which ranges from Canada to Mexico.* [ME *range(n)* v., t. OF: m. *ranger* arrange in line, der. *reng* line. See RANK[1]] —**Syn. 1.** RANGE, COMPASS, LATITUDE, SCOPE refer to extent or breadth, with or without limits. RANGE emphasizes extent and diversity: *the range of one's interests.* COMPASS suggests definite limits: *within the compass of one's mind.* LATITUDE emphasizes the idea of freedom from narrow confines; thus breadth or extent: *granted latitude of action.* SCOPE suggests great freedom but a proper limit: *the scope of one's activities or of one's obligations.* **39.** See roam.

range finder, any of various instruments for determining the range or distance of an object, as in order that a gun may be accurately sighted when firing at it.

Range·ley Lakes (rānj/lĭ), a group of lakes in W Maine.

rang·er (rān/jər), *n.* **1.** a warden employed to patrol a tract of forest. **2.** one of a body of armed men employed in ranging over a region. **3.** (*cap.*) a U.S. soldier in World War II specially trained for making surprise raids and attacks in small groups. Cf. *Brit.* **Commando.** **4.** *Brit.* a keeper of a royal forest or park. **5.** one who or that which ranges. —**rang/er·ship/,** *n.*

Ran·goon (răng·gōōn/), *n.* a seaport in and the capital of Burma, in the S part. 711,520 (prelim. 1953).

rang·y (rān/jĭ), *adj.,* **rangier, rangiest. 1.** slender and long-limbed, as animals or persons. **2.** given to or fitted for ranging or moving about, as animals. **3.** *Australia.* having a mountain range; mountainous.

ra·ni (rä/nĭ), *n., pl.* **-nis.** ranee.

Ran·jit Singh (rŭn/jĭt sĭn/hə), 1780–1839, Indian ruler of the Punjab in India.

rank[1] (răngk), *n.* **1.** a number of persons forming a separate class in the social scale or in any graded body: *he was a favorite among all ranks.* **2.** position or standing in the social scale or in any graded body: *the rank of colonel.* **3.** high position or station in the social or some similar scale: *pride of rank.* **4.** a class in any scale of comparison. **5.** relative position or standing: *a writer of the highest rank.* **6.** a row, line, or series of things or persons. **7.** (*pl.*) the lines or body of an army or other force or organization. **8.** the general body of any party, society, or organization apart from the officers or leaders. **9.** orderly arrangement; array. **10.** a line of persons, esp. soldiers, standing abreast in close-order formation (distinguished from *file*). **11.** (*pl.*) enlisted men as distinguished from commissioned officers: *to rise from the ranks.* **12.** *Chess.* one of the horizontal lines of squares on a chessboard. —*v.t.* **13.** to arrange in a rank or row, or in ranks, as things or persons. **14.** to dispose in suitable order; arrange; classify. **15.** to draw up (persons, esp. soldiers) in a rank or in ranks. **16.** to assign to a particular position, station, class, etc. **17.** *U.S.* to outrank. —*v.i.* **18.** to form a rank or ranks. **19.** to stand in rank. **20.** to take up or occupy a place in a particular rank, class, etc. **21.** to have rank or standing. **22.** to be the senior in rank: *the major ranks here.* [t. F (obs.): m. *ranc,* OF *renc, reng,* of Gmc. orig.; cf. OE *hring* RING[1]]

rank[2] (răngk), *adj.* **1.** growing with excessive luxuriance; vigorous and tall of growth: *tall rank grass.* **2.** producing an excessive and coarse growth, as land. **3.** having an offensively strong smell or taste: *a rank cigar.* **4.** offensively strong, as smell or taste. **5.** utter; absolute: *a rank outsider, rank treachery.* **6.** highly offensive; disgusting. **7.** grossly coarse or indecent. [ME; OE *ranc* proud, bold, c. Icel. *rakkr* erect] —**rank/ly,** *adv.* —**rank/ness,** *n.*

rank and file, 1. the lines of soldiers from side to side and from front to rear. **2.** the body of an army, or any other organization, apart from officers or leaders.

Ran·ke (räng/kə), *n.* **Leopold von,** (lā/ō pōlt/ fən), 1795–1886, German historian.

rank·er (răngk/ər), *n.* **1.** one who ranks. **2.** *Brit.* a soldier in the ranks or a commissioned officer promoted from the ranks. [f. RANK[1], n., + -ER[1]]

ran·kle (răng/kəl), *v.i.,* **-kled, -kling.** (of unpleasant feelings, experiences, etc.) to keep up within the mind keen irritation or bitter resentment; fester; be painful. [ME *rancle(n),* t. OF: m. (*d*)*raoncler,* der. ML *dracunculus* ulcer, dim. of L *draco* serpent, DRAGON]

ran·sack (răn/săk), *v.t.* **1.** to search thoroughly or vigorously through (a house, receptacle, etc.). **2.** to search (a place, etc.) for plunder; pillage. [ME *ransake(n),* t. Scand.; cf. Icel. *rannsaka* search (a house), f. *rann* house + *-saka,* akin to *sækja* SEEK] —**ran/sack·er,** *n.*

ran·som (răn/səm), *n.* **1.** the redemption of a prisoner, slave, kidnapped person, captured goods, etc., for a price. **2.** the sum or price paid or demanded. **3.** a means of delivering or rescuing, esp., in religious use, from sin and its consequences. —*v.t.* **4.** to redeem from captivity, bondage, detention, etc., by paying a price demanded. **5.** to release or restore on receipt of a ransom. **6.** to deliver or redeem from sin and its consequences. [ME *ransome,* t. OF: m. *rançon,* g. s. L *redemptio* REDEMPTION] —**ran/som·er,** *n.* —**Syn. 4.** See redeem.

rant (rănt), *v.i.* **1.** to speak or declaim extravagantly or violently; talk in a wild or vehement way: *a ranting actor.* —*v.t.* **2.** to utter or declaim in a ranting manner. —*n.* **3.** ranting, extravagant, or violent declamation. **4.** a ranting utterance. [t. MD: s. *ranten* rave, c. G *ranzen* frolic] —**rant/er,** *n.* —**rant/ing,** *adj.*

ra·nun·cu·la·ceous (rə nŭng/kyə lā/shəs), *adj.* belonging to the *Ranunculaceae,* the crowfoot or buttercup family of plants, which includes also the marsh marigold, aconite, black hellebore, anemone, hepatica, clematis, columbine, larkspur, peony, etc. [f. RANUNCUL(US) + -ACEOUS]

ra·nun·cu·lus (rə nŭng/kyə ləs), *n., pl.* **-luses, -li** (-lī/). any plant of the large and widely distributed genus *Ranunculus,* comprising herbs with leaves mostly divided and flowers, commonly yellow, with five petals; a crowfoot; a buttercup. [t. L, orig., dim. of *rana* frog]

rap[1] (răp), *v.,* **rapped, rapping,** *n.* —*v.t.* **1.** to strike, esp. with a quick, smart, or light blow. **2.** to produce or announce by raps (fol. by *out,* and used esp. of communications ascribed to spirits). **3.** to utter sharply or vigorously: *to rap out an oath.* —*v.i.* **4.** to knock smartly or lightly, esp. so as to make a noise: *to rap on a door.* —*n.* **5.** a quick, smart, or light blow. **6.** (in modern spiritualism) a sound as of knocking, ascribed to the agency of disembodied spirits. [ME; cf. Sw. *rappa* beat, drub, G *rappeln* rattle]

rap[2] (răp), *n.* **1.** the least bit: *I don't care a rap.* **2.** a counterfeit coin, worth about half a farthing, which formerly passed current in Ireland for a halfpenny. [cf. G *rappe* small coin]

ra·pa·cious (rə pā/shəs), *adj.* **1.** given to seizing for plunder or the satisfaction of greed. **2.** inordinately greedy; predatory; extortionate: *a rapacious disposition.* **3.** (of animals) subsisting by the capture of living prey; predacious. [f. RAPACI(TY) (t. L: m.s. *rāpācitus* greediness) + -OUS] —**ra·pa/cious·ly,** *adv.* —**ra·pac·i·ty** (rə păs/ə tĭ), **ra·pa/cious·ness,** *n.*

Ra·pal·lo (rä päl/lō), *n.* a seaport in NW Italy, on the Gulf of Genoa: treaties, 1920, 1922. 14,037 (1951).

Ra·pa Nu·i (rä/pä nōō/ĭ), native name of **Easter Island.**

rape[1] (rāp), *n., v.,* **raped, raping.** —*n.* **1.** act of seizing and carrying off by force. **2.** the crime of violating a woman forcibly. —*v.t.* **3.** to seize, take, or carry off by force. **4.** to plunder (a place). **5.** to commit the crime of rape on. —*v.i.* **6.** to commit rape. [ME *rape(n),* t. L: m. *rapere* seize, carry off] —**rap/ist,** *n.*

rape[2] (rāp), *n.* a brassicaceous plant, *Brassica Napus,* whose leaves are used as a food for sheep, etc., and whose seeds yield rape oil. [ME, t. L: m. *rāpum, rāpa* turnip]

rape[3] (rāp), *n.* the refuse of grapes, after the juice has been extracted, used as a filter in making vinegar. [t. F, g. LL *raspa,* der. *raspāre* grate, t. Gmc.; cf. OHG *raspōn*]

rape oil, a brownish-yellow oil obtained from rapeseed, used as a lubricant, etc.; colza oil.

rape·seed (rāp/sēd/), *n.* **1.** the seed of the rape. **2.** the plant itself.

Raph·a·el (răf/ĭ əl, rā/fĭ-), *n.* **1.** (*Raffaello Santi* or *Sanzio*) 1483–1520, Italian painter. **2.** one of the archangels. [(def. 2) ult. t. Heb.: m. *Rĕfā'ēl* God healed]

ra·phe (rā/fē), *n., pl.* **-phae** (-fē). **1.** *Anat.* a seamlike union between two parts or halves of an organ or the like. **2.** *Bot.* **a.** (in certain ovules) a ridge connecting the hilum with the chalaza. **b.** a median line or slot on a cell wall of a diatom. [NL, t. Gk.: seam, suture]

raph·i·des (răf/ə dēz/), *n.pl.* *Bot.* acicular crystals, usually composed of calcium oxalate, which occur in bundles in the cells of many plants. [NL (pl.), t. Gk.: needles]

rap·id (răp/ĭd), *adj.* **1.** occurring with speed; coming about within a short time: *rapid growth.* **2.** moving or acting with great speed; swift: *a rapid worker.* **3.** characterized by speed, as motion. —*n.* **4.** (*usually pl.*) a part of a river where the current runs very swiftly, as over a steep slope in the bed. [t. L: s. *rapidus*] —**rap′-id·ly**, *adv.* —**Syn. 2.** See **quick.**

Rap·i·dan (răp′ə dăn′), *n.* a river in N Virginia, flowing from the Blue Ridge Mountains into the Rappahannock: the scene of severe fighting in the Civil War.

Rapid City, a city in SW South Dakota. 42,399 (1960).

rap·id-fire (răp′ĭd fīr′), *adj.* **1.** characterized by or delivered or occurring in rapid procedure, esp. in speech: *rapid-fire questions.* **2.** *Ordn.* noting or pertaining to any of various mounted guns of moderate caliber which can be fired rapidly. **3.** *Mil.* firing shots in rapid succession. Also, **rap′id-fir′ing.** —**rap′id-fir′er,** *n.*

ra·pid·i·ty (rə pĭd′ə tĭ), *n.* rapid state or quality. —**Syn.** swiftness, fleetness, speed, velocity, celerity.

ra·pi·er (rā′pĭ ər), *n.* **1.** a sword, with highly developed hilt, and long, slender, pointed blade used only for thrusting. **2.** (orig.) a long, narrow, two-edged sword, used chiefly for thrusting. [t. F: m. *rapière,* orig. adj., der. *râpe* grater. See RAPE³]

rap·ine (răp′ĭn), *n.* the violent seizure and carrying off of property of others; plunder. [ME, t.L: m. *rapina*]

Rap·pa·han·nock (răp′ə hăn′ək), *n.* a river flowing from N Virginia SE to Chesapeake Bay: battle, 1863. 185 mi.

rap·pa·ree (răp′ə rē′), *n.* **1.** an armed Irish freebooter or plunderer, esp. of the 17th century. **2.** a freebooter or robber. [t. Irish: m. *rapaire*]

rap·pee (ră pē′), *n.* a strong snuff made from the darker and ranker kinds of tobacco leaves. [t. F: m. *râpé* grated, pp. of *râper.* See RAPE¹, RASP]

rap·per (răp′ər), *n.* **1.** the knocker of a door. **2.** one who or that which raps or knocks. [f. RAP¹ + -ER¹]

rap·port (ră pôrt′; Fr. ră pôr′), *n.* relation; connection, esp. harmonious or sympathetic relation (usually in the phrases *to be en,* or *in, rapport with*). [t. F, der. *rapporter* bring back, refer, f. re- RE- + *apporter* (t. L: m. *apportāre* bring to)]

rap·proche·ment (ră prôsh män′), *n.* an establishment or reëstablishment of harmonious relations. [F, der. *rapprocher* bring near. See APPROACH]

rap·scal·lion (răp skăl′yən), *n.* a rascal; rogue; scamp. [ult. der. RASCAL]

rapt (răpt), *adj.* **1.** deeply engrossed or absorbed: *rapt in thought.* **2.** transported with emotion; enraptured: *rapt with joy.* **3.** showing or proceeding from rapture: *a rapt smile.* **4.** carried off to another place, sphere of existence, etc. [first used as pp., ME, t. L: s. *raptus,* pp., seized, transported. See RAPE¹]

rap·to·ri·al (răp tōr′ĭ əl), *adj.* **1.** preying upon other animals; predatory. **2.** adapted for seizing prey, as the beak or claws of a bird. **3.** belonging or pertaining to the *Raptores,* an order consisting of birds of prey, as the eagles, hawks, etc. [f. s. NL *Raptōrēs* (pl. of L *raptor* robber, plunderer) + -(I)AL]

rap·ture (răp′chər), *n.* **1.** ecstatic joy or delight; joyful ecstasy. **2.** (often *pl.*) an utterance or expression of ecstatic delight. **3.** the carrying of a person to another place or sphere of existence. **4.** *Obs.* act of carrying off. [f. RAPT + -URE]

Head and foot of raptorial bird
Golden eagle.
Aquila chrysaetos

rap·tur·ous (răp′chər əs), *adj.* **1.** full of, feeling, or manifesting ecstatic joy or delight. **2.** characterized by, attended with, or expressive of such rapture: *rapturous surprise.* —**rap′tur·ous·ly,** *adv.* —**rap′tur·ous·ness,** *n.*

ra·ra a·vis (râr′ə ā′vĭs), *pl.* **rarae aves** (râr′ē ā′vēz). *Latin.* a rare person or thing. [L: a rare bird]

rare¹ (râr), *adj.,* **rarer, rarest. 1.** coming or occurring far apart in time; unusual; uncommon: *rare occasions, a rare smile, a rare disease.* **2.** thinly distributed over an area, or few and widely separated: *rare lighthouses.* **3.** having the component parts not closely compacted together: *rare gases.* **4.** unusually great: *sympathetic in a rare degree.* **5.** unusually excellent; admirable; fine: *rare tact.* [ME, t. L: m.s. *rārus*] —**rare′ness,** *n.*

—**Syn. 1.** RARE, SCARCE characterize that which is hard to find, exists in small quantities, or is uncommon. A thing is RARE which is seldom to be met with and is therefore often sought after; the word often implies exceptional quality or value: *a rare book; a rare beauty.* SCARCE is applied to that of which there is an insufficient supply; it usually implies a previous or usual condition of greater abundance: *food is scarce, fruit is scarce this year.* —**Ant. 1.** abundant.

rare² (râr), *adj.,* **rarer, rarest.** (of meat) not thoroughly cooked; underdone. [ME *rere,* OE *hrēre* lightly boiled (said of eggs)]

rare·bit (râr′bĭt), *n.* Welsh rabbit.

rare book, a book which is distinctive by virtue of its early printing date, limited copies, special character of the edition, binding, historical interest, or the like.

rare earth, *Chem.* the oxide of any of the rare-earth elements, contained in various minerals.

rare-earth elements (râr′ûrth′), *Chem.* a group of closely related metallic elements of atomic number 57 to 71 inclusive, often divided into three groups: **cerium metals** (lanthanum, cerium, praseodymium, neodym-

ium, promethium, and samarium); **terbium metals** (europium, gadolinium, and terbium), and **yttrium metals** (dysprosium, holmium, erbium, thulium, yttrium, ytterbium, and lutecium).

rar·ee show (râr′ē), **1.** a peep show. **2.** any show or spectacle. [? repr. foreigners′ pronunciation of *rare show*]

rar·e·fac·tion (râr′ə făk′shən), *n.* **1.** act or process of rarefying. **2.** state of being rarefied. —**rar′e·fac′tive,** *adj.*

rar·e·fy (râr′ə fī), *v.,* **-fied, -fying.** —*v.t.* **1.** to make rare, more rare, or less dense. **2.** to make less gross; refine. —*v.i.* **3.** to become rare or less dense; become thinned. [t. L: m. *rārēfacere*]

rare·ly (râr′lĭ), *adv.* **1.** on rare occasions; infrequently: *he is rarely late.* **2.** exceptionally; in an unusual degree. **3.** unusually or remarkably well or excellent.

rar·i·ty (râr′ə tĭ), *n., pl.* **-ties. 1.** something rare, unusual, or uncommon. **2.** something esteemed or interesting as being rare, uncommon, or curious. **3.** rare state or quality. **4.** rare occurrence; infrequency. **5.** unusual excellence. **6.** thinness, as of air or a gas.

Ra·ro·tong·a (rä′rō tŏng′ä), *n.* one of the Cook Islands, in the S Pacific. 6417 (1956); 26 sq. mi.

ras·cal (răs′kəl), *n.* **1.** a base, dishonest person. **2.** any person or animal: *you little rascal.* **3.** *Obs.* a person belonging to the rabble. —*adj.* **4.** knavish; dishonest. **5.** *Obs.* belonging to or being the rabble. [ME *rascayl,* t. OF: m. *rascaille* rabble, ult. der. L *rādere* scratch] —**Syn. 1.** See **knave.**

ras·cal·i·ty (răs kăl′ə tĭ), *n., pl.* **-ties. 1.** rascally or knavish character or conduct. **2.** a rascally act.

ras·cal·ly (răs′kə lĭ), *adj.* **1.** being, characteristic of, or befitting a rascal or knave; dishonest; mean: *a rascally trick.* **2.** (of places, etc.) wretchedly bad or unpleasant. —*adv.* **3.** in a rascally manner.

rase (rāz), *v.t.,* **rased, rasing.** raze.

rash¹ (răsh), *adj.* **1.** acting too hastily or without due consideration. **2.** characterized by or showing too great haste or lack of consideration: *rash promises.* [ME *rasch,* c. D and G *rasch* quick, brisk] —**rash′ly,** *adv.* —**rash′ness,** *n.* —**Syn. 1.** hasty, impetuous, reckless.

rash² (răsh), *n.* an eruption or efflorescence on the skin. [t. F: m. *rache,* ult. der. L *rādere* scratch]

rash·er (răsh′ər), *n.* a thin slice of bacon or ham for frying or broiling. [cf. OE *ræscettan* crackle]

Ras·mus·sen (räs′mŏŏ sən), *n.* **Knud Johan Victor** (knŏŏth yŏō hän′ vēk′tŏr), 1879–1933, Danish arctic explorer.

ra·so·ri·al (rə sōr′ĭ əl), *adj.* given to scratching the ground for food, as poultry; gallinaceous. [f. NL *Rasōrēs* (pl.) lit., scratchers, der. L *rāsus* scraped, scratched + -(I)AL]

rasp (răsp, räsp), *v.t.* **1.** to scrape or abrade with a rough instrument. **2.** to scrape or rub roughly. **3.** to grate upon or irritate (the nerves, feelings, etc.). **4.** to utter with a grating sound. —*v.i.* **5.** to scrape or grate. **6.** to make a grating sound. —*n.* **7.** act of rasping. **8.** a rasping sound. **9.** a coarse form of file, having separate pointlike teeth. [ME *raspe(n),* t. OF: m. *rasper* scrape, grate, t. Gmc.; cf. obs. G *raspen* grate]

Foot of rasorial bird

rasp·ber·ry (răz′bĕr′ĭ, räz′-), *n., pl.* **-ries. 1.** the fruit of several shrubs of the rosaceous genus *Rubus,* consisting of small juicy drupelets, red, black, or pale-yellow, forming a detachable cap about a convex receptacle, being thus distinguished from the blackberry. **2.** any of these plants, as the **red raspberry,** *R. Idaeus* (of Europe) and its var. *R. strigosus* (of the U.S.), the blackcap or **black raspberry,** *R. occidentalis,* or the purple cane, a **purple raspberry,** cross of the red and the black raspberries. **3.** dark reddish purple. **4.** *Slang.* a sound expressing derision or contempt made with the tongue and lips. [f. *rasp(is)* raspberry (orig. uncert.) + BERRY]

rasp·er (răs′pər, räs′-), *n.* one who or that which rasps, as a machine for rasping sugar cane.

rasp·ing (răs′pĭng, räs′-), *adj.* harsh: *a rasping voice.*

Ras·pu·tin (răs pū′tĭn; *Russ.* räs pŏō′tĭn), *n.* **Grigori Efimovich** (grĭ gô′rĭ ĕ fē′mŏ vĭch), 1871–1916, Siberian peasant who posed as a monk and exerted great influence over Czar Nicholas II.

rat (răt), *n., v.,* **ratted, ratting.** —*n.* **1.** any of certain long-tailed rodents of the genus *Rattus* and allied genera (family *Muridae*), distinguished from the mouse by being larger. **2.** any rodent of the same family, or any of various similar animals, e.g., the pack or wood rats, of the genus *Neotoma,* of North America, etc. **3.** *Slang.* one who abandons his party or associates, esp. in time of trouble. **4.** *U.S. Colloq.* a roll of hair or other material used as a pad by women to puff out the hair. —*v.i.* **5.** *Slang.* to desert one′s party or associates, esp. in time of trouble. **6.** *Slang.* to behave like a mean, cowardly person. **7.** to hunt or catch rats. [ME *ratte,* OE *ræt,* c. G *ratz, ratte*]

rat·a·ble (rā′tə bəl), *adj.* **1.** capable of being rated or appraised. **2.** proportional. **3.** *Brit.* liable to rates or local taxes. Also, **rateable.** —**rat′a·bil′i·ty, rat′a·ble·ness,** *n.* —**rat′a·bly,** *adv.*

rat·a·fi·a (răt′ə fē′ə), *n.* a cordial or liqueur flavored with fruit kernels, fruit, or the like. Also, **rat·a·fee** (răt′ə fē′). [f. F]

ratafia biscuit, *Brit.* a macaroon.

rat·al (rā′təl), *n. Brit.* the amount on which rates or taxes are assessed. [f. RAT(E)[1] + -AL[1]]

ra·tan (rǎ tǎn′), *n.* rattan.

rat·a·plan (rǎt′ə plǎn′), *n., v.,* **-planned, -planning.** —*n.* 1. a sound of or as of the beating of a drum; a rubadub. —*v.t., v.i.* 2. to play by or play a rataplan. [t. F]

rat·bite fever (rǎt′bīt′), a relapsing fever, widely distributed geographically, caused by infection with a spirillum transmitted by rats. Also, **ratbite disease.**

ratch (rǎch), *n.* ratchet. [var. of RATCHET. Cf. G *ratsche*]

ratch·et (rǎch′ĭt), *n.* 1. a toothed bar with which a pawl engages. 2. the pawl used with such a device. 3. a mechanism consisting of such a bar or wheel with the pawl. 4. a ratchet wheel. [t. F: m. *rochet* ratchet, bobbin, t. It.: m. *rocchetto,* der. *rocca* distaff, t. Gmc.; cf. obs. E *rock* distaff]

ratchet wheel, a wheel with teeth on the edge, into which a pawl drops or catches, so as to prevent reversal of motion or convert reciprocating into rotatory motion.

Ratchet wheel
A. Wheel; B. Pawl preventing reversal of motion; C, Pawl conveying motion to wheel; D, Reciprocating lever

rate[1] (rāt), *n., v.,* **rated, rating.** —*n.* 1. the amount of a charge or payment with reference to some basis of calculation: *the rate of interest.* 2. a certain quantity or amount of one thing considered in relation to a unit of another thing and used as a standard or measure: *at the rate of 60 miles an hour.* 3. a fixed charge per unit of quantity: *a rate of 10 cents a pound.* 4. price: *to cut rates.* 5. degree of speed, progress, etc.: *to work at a rapid rate.* 6. degree or comparative extent of action or procedure: *the rate of increase.* 7. relative condition or quality; grade, class, or sort. 8. assigned position in any of a series of graded classes, or rating. 9. *Insurance.* the premium charge per unit of insurance. 10. a charge by a common carrier for transportation, sometimes including certain services involved in rendering such service. 11. (*usually pl.*) *Brit.* a tax on property for some local purpose. 12. **at any rate, a.** under any circumstances; in any case; at all events. **b.** at least. —*v.t.* 13. to estimate the value or worth of; appraise. 14. to esteem, consider, or account: *he was rated one of the rich men of the city.* 15. to fix at a certain rate, as of charge or payment. 16. to value for purposes of taxation, etc. 17. to make subject to the payment of a certain rate or tax. 18. to place in a certain class, etc., as a ship or a seaman; give a certain rating to. 19. to arrange for the conveyance of (goods) at a certain rate. —*v.i.* 20. to have value, standing, etc. 21. to have position in a certain class. [ME, t. ML: m. *rata* fixed amount or portion, rate, prop. fem. of L *ratus,* pp., fixed by calculation, determined. See RATIO]

rate[2] (rāt), *v.t., v.i.,* **rated, rating.** to chide vehemently; scold. [ME; appar. c. Sw. *rata* find fault]

rate·a·ble (rā′tə bəl), *adj.* ratable. —**rate′a·bil′i·ty, rate′a·ble·ness,** *n.* —**rate′a·bly,** *adv.*

ra·tel (rā′təl, rǎ′-), *n.* a badgerlike carnivore, *Mellivora capensis,* of Africa and India. [t. S Afr. D]

Ratel, *Mellivora capensis*
(Total length 3 ft., tail 9 in.)

rate of exchange, the ratio at which the unit of currency of one country can be exchanged for the unit of currency of another country.

rate·pay·er (rāt′pā′ər), *n. Brit.* a payer of rates.

rathe (rāth), *adj.* 1. *Archaic and Poetic.* growing, blooming, or ripening early in the year or season. —*adv.* 2. *Archaic.* quickly. 3. *Archaic and Dial.* early. [ME; OE *hræth,* c. OHG *hrad,* Icel. *hradhr* quick]

Ra·the·nau (rä′tə nou′), *n.* Walther (väl′tər), 1867–1922, German industrialist, writer, and statesman (assassinated).

rath·er (rǎth′ər, räth′ər), *adv.* 1. in a measure; to a certain extent; somewhat: *rather good.* 2. (with verbs) in some degree (used either literally to modify a statement, or ironically to lend emphasis). 3. more properly or justly; with better reason: *the contrary is rather to be supposed.* 4. sooner or more readily or willingly: *to die rather than yield, I would rather go today.* 5. in preference; as a preferred or accepted alternative. 6. more properly or correctly speaking; more truly. 7. on the contrary. 8. *Chiefly Brit.* (as a response, a colloquial equivalent of an emphatic affirmative): *Is it worth going to? Rather!* [ME; OE *hrathor,* compar. of *hrathe* quickly]

raths·kel·ler (räts′kĕl′ər), *n.* 1. (in Germany) the cellar of a town hall, often used as a beer hall or restaurant. 2. any saloon or restaurant of the German type, usually in a cellar or basement. [t. G, old. sp. of *ratskeller,* lit., town-hall cellar]

rat·i·fi·ca·tion (rǎt′ə fə kā′shən), *n.* 1. act of ratifying; confirmation; sanction. 2. state of being ratified.

rat·i·fy (rǎt′ə fī′), *v.t.,* **-fied, -fying.** 1. to confirm by expressing consent, approval, or formal sanction. 2. to approve (something done or arranged by an agent or by representatives) by such action. [ME *ratifie(n),* t. OF:

ratifier, t. ML: m. *ratificāre,* f. *rati-* (comb. form repr. L *ratus* fixed; see RATE[1]) + L *-ficāre* make] —**rat′i·fi′er,** *n.*

ra·ti·né (rǎt′ə nā′; *Fr.* rȧ tē nĕ′), *n.* a loosely woven fabric made with nubby or knotty yarns. [t. F]

rat·ing[1] (rā′tĭng), *n.* 1. classification according to grade or rank. 2. *Naut.* **a.** assigned position in a particular class or grade, or relative standing, as of a ship or a seaman. **b.** (*pl.*) men of certain ratings, esp., in the British Navy, an enlisted man without rank. 3. a person's or firm's credit standing. 4. an amount fixed as a rate. 5. *Brit.* apportioning of a tax. 6. *Elect.* (of a machine, apparatus, etc.) a designated limit of operating characteristics, as voltage, amperes, frequency, etc., based on definite conditions. [f. RATE[1] + -ING[1]]

rat·ing[2] (rā′tĭng), *n.* angry reprimand or rebuke; a scolding. [f. RATE[2] + -ING[1]]

ra·tio (rā′shō, -shĭ ō′), *n., pl.* **-tios.** 1. the relation between two similar magnitudes in respect to the number of times the first contains the second: *the ratio of 5 to 2, which may be written 5 : 2,* or ⁵⁄₂. 2. proportional relation; rate; quotient of two numbers. 3. *Finance.* the relative value of gold and silver in a bimetallic currency system. [t. L: reckoning, relation, reason]

ra·ti·oc·i·nate (rǎsh′ĭ ŏs′ə nāt′), *v.i.,* **-nated, -nating.** to reason; carry on a process of reasoning. [t. L: m.s. *ratiōcinātus,* pp., calculated] —**ra′ti·oc′i·na′tor,** *n.*

ra·ti·oc·i·na·tion (rǎsh′ĭ ŏs′ə nā′shən), *n.* reasoning, or a process of reasoning. —**ra′ti·oc′i·na′tive,** *adj.*

ra·tion (rǎsh′ən, rā′shən), *n.* 1. a fixed allowance of provisions or food: *rations of coal and coffee.* 2. the daily allowance assigned to a soldier or sailor. —*v.t.* 3. to apportion or distribute as rations or by some method of allowance. 4. to put on: or restrict to, rations. 5. to supply with ration, as of food: *to ration an army.* [t. F, t. ML: s. *ratio* allowance of provisions, L account. See RATIO] —**ra′tion·ing,** *n.* —Syn. 1. See food.

ra·tion·al (rǎsh′ən əl), *adj.* 1. agreeable to reason; reasonable; sensible. 2. having or exercising reason, sound judgment, or good sense. 3. being in or characterized by full possession of one's reason; sane; lucid: *the patient appeared perfectly rational.* 4. endowed with the faculty of reason: *man is a rational animal.* 5. of or pertaining to reason: *the rational faculty.* 6. proceeding or derived from reason, or based on reasoning: *a rational explanation.* 7. *Arith.* expressible as the quotient of two integers. 8. *Math.* (of functions) expressible as the quotient of two polynomials. 9. *Gk. and Lat. Pros.* capable of measurement in terms of the metrical unit (mora). [t. L: s. *ratiōnālis*] —**ra′tion·al·ly,** *adv.* —Syn. 2. intelligent, wise, judicious, discreet. 6. See reasonable.

ra·tion·ale (rǎsh′ə nǎl′, -nā′lĭ, -nā′lĭ), *n.* 1. a statement of reasons. 2. a reasoned exposition or principles. 3. the fundamental reasons serving to account for something [t. L, neut. of *ratiōnālis* rational]

ra·tion·al·ism (rǎsh′ən ə lĭz′əm, rǎsh′nə-), *n.* 1. the principle or habit of accepting reason as the supreme authority in matters of opinion, belief, or conduct. 2. *Philos.* the theory that reason is in itself a source of knowledge, independent of the senses. 3. *Theol.* the doctrine that human reason, unaided by divine revelation, is an adequate or the sole guide to all attainable religious truth. —**ra′tion·al·ist,** *n., adj.* —**ra′tion·al·is′tic, ra′tion·al·is′ti·cal,** *adj.* —**ra′tion·al·is′ti·cal·ly,** *adv.*

ra·tion·al·i·ty (rǎsh′ə nǎl′ə tĭ), *n., pl.* **-ties.** 1. the quality of being rational. 2. the possession of reason. 3. reasonableness. 4. the exercise of reason. 5. a rational or reasonable view, practice, etc.

ra·tion·al·ize (rǎsh′ən ə līz′, rǎsh′nə-), *v., -ized, -izing.* —*v.t.* 1. *Psychol.* to invent a rational, acceptable explanation for behavior which has its origin in the unconscious; to justify unconscious behavior. 2. to remove unreasonable elements from. 3. to make rational or conformable to reason. 4. to treat or explain in a rational or rationalistic manner. —*v.i.* 5. to employ reason; think in a rational or rationalistic manner. 6. *Brit.* to reorganize and integrate (an industry). —**ra′tion·al·i·za′tion,** *n.* —**ra′tion·al·iz′er,** *n.*

rational number, *Math.* a number which can be expressed as the quotient of two positive or negative integers.

Rat·is·bon (rǎt′ĭs bŏn′, -ĭz-), *n.* Regensburg.

rat·ite (rǎt′īt), *adj.* 1. without a carina, as a breastbone. 2. having a flat breastbone, as the ostrich, cassowary, emu, moa, etc. (contrasted with *carinate*). [t. s. L *ratis* raft + -ITE[2]]

rat·line (rǎt′lĭn), *n. Naut.* 1. any of the small ropes or lines which traverse the shrouds horizontally, serving as steps for going aloft. 2. the kind of rope or line from which these are made. Also, **rat′-lin.** [late ME *ratling, radelyng;* orig. uncert.]

ra·toon (rǎ tōōn′), *n.* 1. a sprout or shoot from the root of a plant (esp. a sugar cane) after it has been cropped. —*v.i., v.t.* 2. to put forth or cause to put forth ratoons. Also, **rattoon.** [t. Sp.: m. *retoño,* t. Hind.: m. *ratun*]

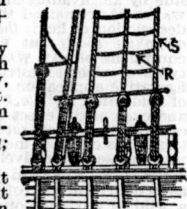

R. Ratline; S Shroud.

rats·bane (răts′bān′), *n.* **1.** rat poison. **2.** the trioxide of arsenic. [earlier *rats bane*. See RAT, BANE]

rat·tan (ră tăn′), *n.* **1.** any of various climbing palms of the genus *Calamus*, or allied genera. **2.** the tough stems of such palms, used for wickerwork, canes, etc. **3.** a stick or switch of this material. Also, **ratan**. [var. of *rotang*, t. Malay: m. *rōtan*]

rat·teen (ră tēn′), *n. Obs.* ratiné.

rat·ter (răt′ər), *n.* **1.** one who or that which catches rats, as a terrier. **2.** *Slang.* deserter or betrayer.

rat·tish (răt′ĭsh), *adj.* **1.** of, pertaining to, characteristic of, or resembling a rat. **2.** infested with rats.

rat·tle[1] (răt′əl), *v.*, **-tled, -tling,** *n.* —*v.i.* **1.** to give out a rapid succession of short, sharp sounds, as in consequence of agitation and repeated concussions: *the windows rattled in their frames.* **2.** to cause such sounds, as by knocking on something or by causing things to strike together. **3.** to be filled with such sounds, as a place. **4.** to move or go, esp. rapidly, with such sounds. **5.** to talk rapidly; chatter. —*v.t.* **6.** to cause to rattle: *he rattled the doorknob violently.* **7.** to drive, send, bring, etc., esp. rapidly, with rattling. **8.** to utter or perform in a rapid or lively manner: *to rattle off a speech.* **9.** *Colloq.* to disconcert or confuse (a person). **10.** *Hunting.* **a.** to stir up (a cover). **b.** to pursue (game) strongly. —*n.* **11.** a rapid succession of short, sharp sounds, as from the collision of hard bodies. **12.** an instrument contrived to make a rattling sound, as a child's toy. **13.** the series of horny pieces or rings at the end of a rattlesnake's tail, with which it produces a rattling sound. **14.** a rattling sound in the throat, as the death rattle. [ME *ratele(n)*, c. D *ratelen*, G *rasseln*; imit.]

rat·tle[2] (răt′əl), *v.t.*, **-tled, -tling.** *Naut.* to furnish with ratlines (usually fol. by *down*). [back formation from RATLINE, taken as a verbal n.]

rat·tle·brain (răt′əl brān′), *n.* a giddy, empty-headed chatterer. Also, **rat·tle·pate** (răt′əl pāt′).

rat·tler (răt′lər), *n.* **1.** a rattlesnake. **2.** one who or that which rattles. **3.** *Colloq.* a fast freight train.

rat·tle·snake (răt′əl snāk′), *n.* any of various venomous American snakes of the genera *Crotalus* and *Sistrurus*, having several loosely articulated horny pieces or rings at the end of the tail, which produce a rattling or whirring sound when shaken.

rattlesnake plantain, any of several low terrestrial orchids, as *Goodyera repens* of northern temperate regions or *G. pubescens*.

rattlesnake root, 1. any of certain plants of the genus *Prenanthes*, whose roots or tubers have been regarded as a remedy for snake bites, as *P. serpentaria* or *P. alba*. **2.** the root or tuber. **3.** the Seneca snakeroot, *Polygala Senega*. **4.** its root. **5.** the liliaceous plant, *Trillium cernuum*.

rattlesnake weed, 1. a hawkweed, *Hieracium venosum*, of eastern North America, whose leaves and root are thought to possess medicinal virtue. **2.** a carrotlike weed, *Daucus pusillus*, of S and W North America. **3.** any of certain other plants, as the umbelliferous plant *Eryngium aquaticum*. **4.** a rattlesnake plantain.

rat·tle·trap (răt′əl trăp′), *n.* **1.** a shaky, rattling object, as a rickety vehicle. **2.** *Slang.* a garrulous person. **3.** *Slang.* the mouth.

rat·tly (răt′lĭ), *adj.* **1.** apt to rattle. **2.** making or having a rattling sound.

rat·toon (ră tōōn′), *n.*, *v.i.*, *v.t.* ratoon.

rat·trap (răt′trăp′), *n.* **1.** a device for catching rats. **2.** a difficult and involved set of circumstances.

rat·ty (răt′ĭ), *adj.*, **-tier, -tiest. 1.** full of rats. **2.** of or characteristic of a rat. **3.** *Slang.* wretched; shabby.

rau·cous (rô′kəs), *adj.* hoarse; harsh of voice or sound. [t. L: m. *raucus*] —**rau′cous·ly,** *adv.* —**rau′cous·ness, rau·ci·ty** (rô′sə tĭ), *n.*

rau·wol·fi·a (rô wōōl′fĭ ə), *n.* **1.** *Bot.* a genus of trees or shrubs of the family *Apocynum*, esp. *R. serpentina.* **2.** *Pharm.* an extract from the roots of the rauwolfia with many medicinal uses in its various purified forms. Also called **snakeroot.** [named after *Leonhart Rauwolf*, 16th cent. German botanist and physician]

rav·age (răv′ĭj), *n.*, *v.*, **-aged, -aging.** —*n.* **1.** devastating or destructive action. **2.** havoc; ruinous damage: *the ravages of war.* —*v.t.* **3.** to work havoc upon; damage or mar by ravages: *a face ravaged by grief.* —*v.i.* **4.** to work havoc; do ruinous damage. [t. F, der. *ravir*. See RAVISH] —**rav′ag·er,** *n.*

—**Syn. 3.** RAVAGE, DEVASTATE, LAY WASTE all refer, in their literal application, to the wholesale destruction of a countryside by an invading army (or something comparable). LAY WASTE has remained the closest to the original meaning of destruction of land: *the invading army laid waste the towns along the coast;* but RAVAGE and DEVASTATE (the Latin equivalent of LAY WASTE) are used in reference to other types of violent destruction and may also have a purely figurative application. RAVAGE is often used of the results of epidemics: *the Black Plague ravaged 14th-century Europe,* and even of the effect of disease or suffering on the human countenance: *a face ravaged by despair.* DEVASTATE, in addition to its concrete meaning (*east areas devastated by bombs*), may be used figuratively: *a devastating wit.*

rave (rāv), *v.*, **raved, raving,** *n.* —*v.i.* **1.** to talk wildly, as in delirium. **2.** (of wind, water, storms, etc.) to make a wild or furious sound; rage. **3.** *Colloq.* to talk with extravagant enthusiasm. —*v.t.* **4.** to utter as if in madness. —*n.* **5.** act of raving. [ME, prob. t. OF: m.s. *raver* wander; be delirious]

rav·el (răv′əl), *v.*, **-eled, -eling** or (*esp. Brit.*) **-elled, -elling,** *n.* —*v.t.* **1.** to disengage the threads or fibers of (a woven or knitted fabric, a rope, etc.). **2.** to tangle or entangle. **3.** to involve; confuse; perplex. **4.** to make plain or clear (often fol. by *out*). —*v.i.* **5.** to become disjoined thread by thread or fiber by fiber; fray. **6.** to become tangled. **7.** to become confused or perplexed. —*n.* **8.** a tangle or complication. **9.** an unraveled thread or fiber. [appar. t. MD: s. *ravelen* entangle] —**rav′el·er;** *esp. Brit.*, **rav′el·ler,** *n.*

Ra·vel (rä vĕl′), *n.* **Maurice** (mō rēs′), 1875–1937, French composer.

rave·lin (răv′lĭn), *n. Fort.* a triangular outwork, outside the main ditch, having two embankments forming a projecting angle. [t. F, earlier *revellin*, t. D: m. *regeling* framework]

rav·el·ing (răv′əl ĭng), *n.* something raveled out, as a thread drawn from a knitted or woven fabric. Also, *esp. Brit.*, **rav′el·ling.**

AA Ravelin: DD, Main ditch of fortress; C, Passage giving access from fortress to ravelin; B, Redoubt; EE, Ditch

rav·el·ment (răv′əl mənt), *n.* entanglement; confusion.

ra·ven[1] (rā′vən), *n.* **1.** any of several large corvine birds with lustrous black plumage and raucous voice, esp. the raven, *Corvus corax*, of the New and Old Worlds, which has from time immemorial been considered a bird of ill omen. **2.** the divine culture hero and trickster of the North Pacific Coast Indians. **3.** (*cap.*) *Astron.* the southern constellation Corvus. —*adj.* **4.** lustrous black: *raven locks.* [ME; OE *hræfn*, c. OHG *hraban*, MD *rāven*]

rav·en[2] (răv′ən), *v.i.* **1.** to seek plunder or prey. **2.** to eat or feed voraciously or greedily. **3.** to have a ravenous appetite. —*v.t.* **4.** to seize as spoil or prey. **5.** to devour voraciously. —*n.* **6.** rapine; robbery. **7.** plunder or prey. Also, **ravin.** [ME *ravine*, t. F, g. L *rapina* RAPINE]

Raven, *Corvus corax* (Ab. 2 ft. long)

rav·en·ing (răv′ən ĭng), *adj.* **1.** rapacious; voracious. —*n.* **2.** rapacity. —**Syn. 1.** See **ravenous.**

Ra·ven·na (rə vĕn′ə; *It.* rä vĕn′nä), *n.* a city in NE Italy: the capital of Italy under the Byzantine Empire; tomb of Dante. 95,000 (est. 1954).

rav·en·ous (răv′ən əs), *adj.* **1.** extremely hungry. **2.** extremely rapacious. **3.** voracious or gluttonous. **4.** given to seizing prey in order to devour it, as animals. [ME, t. OF: m. *ravinos*. See RAVEN[2]] —**rav′en·ous·ly,** *adv.* —**rav′en·ous·ness,** *n.*

—**Syn. 1.** RAVENOUS, RAVENING, VORACIOUS suggest a greediness for food and usually intense hunger. RAVENOUS implies extreme hunger, or a famished condition: *ravenous wild beasts.* RAVENING adds the idea of fierceness and savagery, esp. as shown in a violent manner of acquiring food: *ravening wolves.* VORACIOUS implies the eating of a great deal of food, or the disposition to eat a great deal, without reference to the degree of hunger (*a voracious small boy incessantly eating*) or figuratively (*a voracious reader*).

rav·in (răv′ən), *n.*, *v.t.*, *v.i.* raven[2].

ra·vine (rə vēn′), *n.* a long, deep, narrow valley, esp. one worn by water. [t. F: torrent of water, ravine]

rav·ing (rā′vĭng), *adj.* **1.** that raves; delirious; frenzied. **2.** *Colloq.* extraordinary or remarkable: *she's no raving beauty.* —*n.* **3.** irrational, incoherent talk.

ra·vi·o·li (rä′vĭ ō′lĭ, răv′ĭ′–; *It.* rä vyô′lē), *n. pl.* small squares or otherwise-shaped pieces of paste enclosing forcemeat (and often spinach), cooked, and served in a sauce. [t. It., der. d. It. *rava*, ult. g. L *rāpum* turnip, beet]

rav·ish (răv′ĭsh), *v.t.* **1.** to fill with strong emotion, esp. joy. **2.** to seize and carry off by force. **3.** to carry off (a woman) by force. **4.** to rape (a woman). [ME *ravisshe(n)*, t. OF: m. *raviss–*, s. *ravir*, der. L *rapere* seize, carry off. Cf. RAPE[1], RAPTURE] —**rav′ish·er,** *n.*

rav·ish·ing (răv′ĭsh ĭng), *adj.* entrancing; enchanting. —**rav′ish·ing·ly,** *adv.*

rav·ish·ment (răv′ĭsh mənt), *n.* **1.** rapture or ecstasy. **2.** violent removal. **3.** the forcible abduction of a woman. **4.** rape.

raw (rô), *adj.* **1.** not having undergone processes of preparing, dressing, finishing, refining, or manufacture: *raw silk.* **2.** uncooked, as articles of food. **3.** unnaturally or painfully exposed, as flesh, etc., by removal of the skin or natural integument. **4.** painfully open, as a sore, wound, etc. **5.** crude in quality or character; not tempered or refined by art or taste. **6.** ignorant, inexperienced, or untrained: *a raw recruit.* **7.** brutally or grossly frank: *a raw portrayal of human passions.* **8.** *Slang.* brutally harsh or unfair: *a raw deal.* **9.** disagreeably damp and chilly, as the weather, air, etc. **10.** not diluted, as spirits. —*n.* **11.** the raw, sore or naked flesh. **12.** unrefined sugar, etc. [ME; OE *hrēaw, hræw,* c. D *rauw,* G *roh*; akin to L *crūdus* raw, *cruor* blood, Gk. *krĕas* raw flesh] —**raw′ly,** *adv.* —**raw′ness,** *n.*

—**Syn.** **1.** RAW, CRUDE, RUDE refer to something not in a finished or highly refined state. RAW applies particularly to material not yet changed by a process, by manufacture, or by preparation for consumption: *raw cotton, leather*. CRUDE refers to that which still needs refining: *crude petroleum*. RUDE refers to what is still in a condition of rough simplicity or in a makeshift form: *rude agricultural implements*. —**Ant. 1.** manufactured, polished, refined.

Ra·wal·pin·di (rä/wəl pǐn/dǐ), *n.* a city in Pakistan, in W Punjab. 237,219 (1951).

raw·boned (rô/bōnd/), *adj.* having little flesh; gaunt.

raw fibers, textile fibers which have not been carded or spun.

raw·hide (rô/hīd/), *n.*, *v.*, -**hided**, -**hiding.** —*n.* **1.** untanned skin of cattle or other animals. **2.** a rope or whip made of this. —*v.t.* **3.** to whip with a rawhide.

Raw·lin·son (rô/lǐn sən), *n.* **1.** George, 1812–1902, British historian. **2.** his brother, **Sir Henry Creswicke** (krěz/ǐk), 1810–95, British archaeologist, diplomat, and soldier.

raw material, the unprocessed material obtained from nature for processing and manufacture.

ray¹ (rā), *n.* **1.** a narrow beam of light. **2.** a gleam, or slight manifestation, of intelligence, comfort, etc.: *a ray of hope*. **3.** a raylike line or stretch of something. **4.** *Poetic.* light or radiance. **5.** a line of sight. **6.** *Physics.* **a.** any of the lines or streams in which light or radiant energy appears to issue from a luminous object. **b.** the straight line perpendicular to the wave front in the propagation of radiant energy. **c.** a stream of material particles moving in the same line. **7.** *Math.* one of a system of straight lines emanating from a point. **8.** any of a system of parts radially arranged. **9.** *Zool.* **a.** one of the branches or arms of a starfish or other radiate animal. **b.** one of the jointed supports of the soft fins of fishes. **10.** *Bot.* **a.** a ray flower. **b.** one of the branches of an umbel. **c.** a medullary ray. **d.** (in certain composite plants) the marginal part of the flower head. **11.** *Astron.* one of many long bright streaks radiating from the large lunar craters. —*v.i.* **12.** to emit rays. **13.** to issue in rays. —*v.t.* **14.** to send forth in rays. **15.** to throw rays upon; irradiate. **16.** to subject to the action of rays, as in radiotherapy. **17.** *Colloq.* to make a radiograph of. **18.** to furnish with rays or radiating lines. [ME *raye*, t. OF: m. *rai*, g. L *radius*. See RADIUS] —Syn. **1.** See **gleam**.

Rays on fin of fish
A. Dorsal, with 10 spines;
B. Ventral, with 1 spine;
C. Anal, with 3 spines

ray² (rā), *n.* an elasmobranch fish, with flat (depressed) body fitted for life on the sea bottom, distinguished by having the gill openings on the lower surface. [ME *raye*, t. F: m. *raie*, g. L *raia*]

ra·yah (rä/yə, rī/ə), *n.* any subject of the Sultan of Turkey who is not a Mohammedan. Also, **ra/ya.** [t. Ar.: m. *ra-'iyah* flock, peasants]

ray flower, *Bot.* one of the marginal florets surrounding the disk of tubular florets in the flower heads of certain composite plants. Also, **ray floret.**

Ray·leigh (rā/lǐ), *n.* **John William Strutt** (strŭt), **3rd Baron,** 1842–1919, British physicist.

ray·less (rā/lǐs), *adj.* **1.** without rays. **2.** unillumined, dark, or gloomy.

ray·on (rā/ŏn), *n.* **1.** any textile made from cellulose by passing an appropriate solution of it through spinnerets to form filaments which are used in yarns for making cloth. **2.** fabric made with the product. [t. F: ray, der. OF *rai* RAY¹]

raze (rāz), *v.t.*, **razed, razing.** to tear down, demolish, or level to the ground. Also, **rase.** [ME *rase(n)*, t. F: m. *raser*, g. VL *rāsāre*, der. L *rāsus*, pp., scraped] —**Syn.** See **destroy.**

ra·zee (rä zē/), *n.*, *v.*, -**zeed**, -**zeeing.** —*n.* **1.** a ship, esp. a warship, reduced in height by the removal of the upper deck. —*v.t.* **2.** to cut down (a ship) by removing the upper deck. [t. F: m. *rasé*, pp. of *raser* RAZE]

ra·zor (rā/zər), *n.* a sharp-edged instrument used esp. for shaving the face. [ME *rasour*, t. OF: m. *rasor*, der. *raser* scrape, shave, RAZE]

ra·zor·back (rā/zər băk/), *n.* **1.** a finback or rorqual. **2.** a wild or semiwild hog with a ridgelike back, common in the southern U.S.

razz (răz), *U.S. Slang.* —*v.t.* **1.** to deride; make fun of. —*n.* **2.** severe criticism; derision. [short for RASPBERRY]

Rb, *Chem.* rubidium.

R.C., 1. Red Cross. **2.** Reserve Corps. **3.** Roman Catholic.

r-col·ored (är/kŭl/ərd), *adj. Phonet.* pronounced with a special articulation, usually retroflex, which produces an *r* quality. —**r/-col/or,** *n.*

Rd, *Chem.* radium.

Rd., Road.

rd., 1. rendered. **2.** road. **3.** rod; rods. **4.** round.

R.D., Rural Delivery.

re¹ (rā, rē), *n. Music.* the syllable used for the second tone of a scale and sometimes for the tone D. See **sol-fa.** [see GAMUT]

re² (rē), *prep. Chiefly Law and Com.* in the case of; with reference to. [t. L, abl. of *rēs* thing, matter]

Re (rā), *n.* Ra.

Re, *Chem.* rhenium.

re-, 1. a prefix indicating repetition, as in *reprint, rebirth.* **2.** a prefix indicating withdrawal or backward motion, often figurative like "back," applied often to stems not used as words, as in *revert, retract.* [t. L]

Re., rupee. Also, **re.**

R.E., 1. Reformed Episcopal. **2.** Right Excellent.

r.e., *Football.* right end.

REA, Rural Electrification Administration.

reach (rēch), *v.t.* **1.** to get to, or get as far as, in moving, going, traveling, etc.: *the boat reached the shore.* **2.** to come to or arrive at in some course of progress, action, etc.: *his letter reached me.* **3.** to succeed in touching or seizing with an outstretched hand, a pole, etc.: *to reach a book on a high shelf.* **4.** to stretch or hold out; extend. **5.** to stretch or extend so as to touch or meet: *the bookcase reaches the ceiling.* **6.** to establish communication with. **7.** to amount to, as in the sum or total: *the cost will reach millions.* **8.** to carry to (a point, etc.), as the eye, a gun, etc. **9.** to succeed in striking or hitting, as with a weapon or missile. **10.** to succeed in influencing, impressing, interesting, convincing, etc. —*v.i.* **11.** to make a stretch, as with the hand or arm. **12.** to become outstretched, as the hand or arm. **13.** to make a movement or effort as if to touch or seize something: *to reach for a weapon.* **14.** to extend in operation or effect: *power that reaches throughout the land.* **15.** to stretch in space; extend in direction, length, distance, etc.: *a coat reaching to the knee.* **16.** to extend or continue in time. **17.** to get or come to a specified place, person, condition, etc. (often fol. by *to*). **18.** to amount (fol. by *to*): *sums reaching to a considerable total.* **19.** to carry, as the eye, a gun, etc. **20.** *Naut.* **a.** to sail on a reach. **b.** to sail with the wind from somewhere near abeam, i.e., neither ahead nor dead astern. —*n.* **21.** act of reaching: *to make a reach for a weapon.* **22.** the extent or distance of reaching: *within reach of his voice.* **23.** range of effective action, power, or capacity. **24.** a continuous stretch or extent of something: *a reach of woodland.* **25.** a level portion of a canal, between locks. **26.** *Naut.* a point of sailing where the wind is coming from within a few points of abeam. In a *close reach,* the wind is forward of the beam; in a *broad reach* it is abaft the beam; in a *beam reach* it is abeam or nearly so. **27.** the pole connecting the rear axle of a wagon to the transverse bar or bolster over the front axle supporting the wagon bed. **28.** a portion of a river between bends. [ME *reche*, OE *rǣcan*, c. G *reichen*] —**reach/er,** *n.* —**Syn. 22, 23.** See **grasp.**

re·act (rǐ ăkt/), *v.i.* **1.** to act in return on an agent or influence; act reciprocally upon each other, as two things. **2.** to act in a reverse direction or manner. **3.** to act in opposition, as against some force. **4.** to respond to a stimulus in a particular manner. [f. RE- (def. 2) + ACT, v.]

re·act (rē ăkt/), *v.t.* to act or perform again. [f. RE- (def. 1) + ACT, v.]

re·act·ance (rǐ ăk/təns), *n. Elect.* that part of the impedance of an alternating-current circuit which is due to inductance and capacity. [f. REACT + -ANCE]

re·ac·tion (rǐ ăk/shən), *n.* **1.** a reverse movement or tendency, especially in the direction of political conservatism. **2.** action in a reverse direction or manner. **3.** action in response to some influence, event, etc.: *his reaction to the President's speech.* **4.** *Physiol.* action in response to a stimulus, as of the system, or of a nerve, muscle, etc. **5.** *Med.* **a.** the action caused by the resistance to another action. **b.** a return to the opposite physical condition, as after shock, exhaustion, or chill. **6.** *Bacteriol., Immunol.* the specific cellular effect produced by a foreign matter, as in testing for allergies. **7.** *Chem.* the reciprocal action of chemical agents upon each other; a chemical change. **8.** *Mech.* a force called into existence along with another force, being equal and opposite to it. **9.** *Com.* a drop in the market after an advance in prices.

re·ac·tion·ar·y (rǐ ăk/shə něr/ǐ), *adj.*, *n.*, *pl.* -**aries.** —*adj.* **1.** of, pertaining to, marked by, or favoring reaction, as in politics. —*n.* **2.** one who favors or inclines to reaction. Also, **re·ac/tion·ist.**

re·ac·tive (rǐ ăk/tǐv), *adj.* **1.** tending to react. **2.** pertaining to or characterized by reaction.

re·ac·tor (rǐ ăk/tər), *n.* **1.** substance or person undergoing a reaction. **2.** *Elect.* a device, the primary purpose of which is to introduce reactance into a circuit. **3.** *Immunol., Vet. Sci.* a patient or animal that reacts positively towards a foreign material. **4.** *Physics.* any arrangement of component parts for the creation and controlled release of atomic energy, consisting of a device capable of bringing about nuclear fission and a group of materials or machines to inhibit the consequent chain reaction.

read¹ (rēd), *v.*, **read** (rěd), **reading.** —*v.t.* **1.** to observe, and apprehend the meaning of (something written, printed, etc.): *to read a book.* **2.** to utter aloud;

| re/a·ban/don | re/ab·sorp/tion | re/ac·cept/ | re/ac·com/pa·ny |
| re/ab·sorb/ | re/ac·cede/ | re/ac·com/mo·date/ | re/ac·cuse/ |

render in speech (something written, printed, etc.). **3.** to have such knowledge of (a language) as to be able to understand things written in it: *to be able to read French.* **4.** to apprehend the meaning of (signs, characters, etc.) otherwise than with the eyes, as by means of the fingers. **5.** to make out the significance of, by scrutiny or observation: *to read the sky.* **6.** to foresee, foretell, or predict: *to read a person's fortune.* **7.** to make out the character, etc., of (a person, etc.), as by the interpretation of outward signs. **8.** to understand or take (something read or observed) in a particular way. **9.** to introduce (something not expressed or directly indicated) into what is read or considered. **10.** to adopt or give as a reading in a particular passage: *for "one thousand" another version reads "ten thousand."* **11.** to register or indicate, as a thermometer or other instrument does. **12.** *Now Brit.* to study, as by perusing books: *to read law.* **13.** to learn by, or as if by, perusal: *to read a person's thoughts.* **14.** to bring, put, etc. by reading: *to read oneself to sleep.* **15.** to give one (a lecture or lesson) by way of admonition or rebuke. **16.** to discover or explain the meaning of (a riddle, a dream, etc.). —*v.i.* **17.** to read or peruse writing, printing, etc., or papers, books, etc. **18.** to utter aloud, or render in speech, written or printed words that one is perusing: *to read to a person.* **19.** to give a public reading or recital. **20.** to inspect and apprehend the meaning of written or other signs or characters. **21.** to occupy oneself seriously with reading or study. **22.** to obtain knowledge or learn of something by reading. **23.** to admit of being read, esp. properly or well. **24.** to have a certain wording. **25.** to admit of being read or interpreted (as stated): *a rule that reads two different ways.* [ME *rede*(n), OE *rædan* counsel, consider, read, c. D *raden*, G *raten*, Icel. *rāðha* REDE]

read² (rĕd), *adj.* having knowledge gained by reading: *a well-read person.* [prop. pp. of READ¹]

read·a·ble (rē′də bəl), *adj.* **1.** easy or interesting to read. **2.** capable of being read; legible. —**read′a·bil′i·ty, read′a·ble·ness,** *n.* —**read′a·bly,** *adv.*

Reade (rēd), *n.* **Charles,** 1814–84, British novelist.

read·er (rē′dər), *n.* **1.** one who reads. **2.** a schoolbook for instruction and practice in reading. **3.** one employed to read critically manuscripts, etc., offered for publication, in order to report on their merits. **4.** one who reads or recites before an audience; an elocutionist. **5.** one authorized to read the lessons, etc., in a church service. **6.** *Chiefly Brit.* a lecturer or instructor, as in certain universities. **7.** an assistant to a professor, who grades examinations, etc. —**read′er·ship′,** *n.*

read·i·ly (rĕd′ə lǐ), *adv.* **1.** promptly; quickly; easily. **2.** in a ready manner; willingly.

read·i·ness (rĕd′ǐ nǐs), *n.* **1.** the condition of being ready. **2.** ready action or movement; promptness; quickness; ease; facility. **3.** willingness; inclination; cheerful consent: *a readiness to help others.*

read·ing (rē′dǐng), *n.* **1.** the action or practice of one who reads. **2.** *Speech.* the oral interpretation of written language. **3.** the rendering given to a dramatic part, musical composition, etc., by a particular person. **4.** the extent to which one has read; literary knowledge: *a man of wide reading.* **5.** matter read or for reading: *a novel that makes good reading.* **6.** the form or version of a given passage in a particular text: *the various readings of a line in Shakespeare.* **7.** an interpretation given to anything: *what is your reading of the situation?* **8.** the indication of a graduated instrument. —*adj.* **9.** pertaining to, or used for, reading. **10.** given to reading: *the reading public.*

Read·ing (rĕd′ǐng), *n.* **1. Rufus Daniel Isaacs, 1st Marquis of,** 1860–1935, lord chief justice of England, 1913–21; viceroy of India, 1921–26. **2.** a city in SE Pennsylvania. 98,177 (1960). **3.** a city in S England: the county seat of Berkshire. 117,900 (est. 1956).

read·ing desk, **1.** a desk for use in reading, esp. by a person standing. **2.** (in church) a lectern.

reading room, a room appropriated for reading, as in a library or a club.

re·ad·just (rē′ə jŭst′), *v.t.* to adjust again or anew; rearrange. —**re′ad·just′er,** *n.*

re·ad·just·ment (rē′ə jŭst′mənt), *n.* **1.** a readjusting or state of being readjusted. **2.** *Finance.* important changes in the financial structure of a corporation (often less drastic than in *reorganization*).

read·y (rĕd′ǐ), *adj.,* **readier, readiest,** *v.,* **readied, readying,** *n.* —*adj.* **1.** completely prepared or in due condition for immediate action or use: *troops ready for battle, dinner is ready.* **2.** duly equipped, completed, adjusted, or arranged, as for the occasion or purpose. **3.** willing: *ready to forgive.* **4.** prompt or quick in perceiving, comprehending, speaking, writing, etc. **5.** proceeding from or showing such quickness: *a ready reply.* **6.** prompt or quick in action, performance, manifestation, etc. **7.** inclined, disposed, or apt: *too ready to criticize others.* **8.** in such a condition as to be about; likely or liable at any moment (to do something): *a tree ready to fall.* **9.** immediately available for use: *ready money.* **10.** pertaining to prompt payment. **11.** present or convenient (to hand, or the hand, etc.): *to lie ready to one's hand.*

—*v.t.* **12.** to make ready; prepare. —*n.* **13.** *Colloq.* **ready money.** **14.** condition or position of being ready: *to bring a rifle to the ready.* [ME *redy,* early ME *rædig,* f. OE *ræde* ready + *-ig* -Y¹]

read·y-made (rĕd′ǐ mād′), *adj.* **1.** made for sale to any purchaser, rather than to order: *ready-made shoes.* **2.** made for immediate use. **3.** unoriginal; conventional.

read·y-to-wear (rĕd′ǐ tə wâr′), *adj.* (of clothing) made in standard sizes to fit a large number of people.

read·y-wit·ted (rĕd′ǐ wǐt′ǐd), *adj.* having a quick wit or intelligence.

re·a·gent (rē ā′jənt), *n.* a substance which, on account of the reactions it causes, is used in chemical analysis.

re·al¹ (rē′əl, rēl), *adj.* **1.** true (rather than merely ostensible, nominal, or apparent): *the real reason for an act.* **2.** existing or occurring as fact; actual (rather than imaginary, ideal, or fictitious): *a story taken from real life.* **3.** being an actual thing, with objective existence (rather than merely imaginary). **4.** being actually such (rather than merely so called): *a real victory.* **5.** genuine; not counterfeit, artificial, or imitation: *a real antique, a real diamond, real silk.* **6.** unfeigned or sincere: *real sympathy.* **7.** *Philos.* **a.** existent or pertaining to the existent as opposed to the nonexistent. **b.** actual as opposed to possible or potential. **c.** independent of experience as opposed to phenomenal or apparent. **8.** *Law.* denoting or pertaining to immovable property of a freehold type, as lands and tenements excluding leaseholds (opposed to *personal*). **9.** *Optics.* (of an image) formed by the actual convergence of rays, as the image produced in a camera (opposed to *virtual*). —*n.* **10.** **the real, a.** that which is real or actually exists. **b.** reality in general. [ME, t. LL: s. *reālis,* der. L *rēs* thing, matter] —**re′al·ness,** *n.*

—**Syn. 2.** REAL, ACTUAL, TRUE suggest a faithful rendering of facts, whether those existing in nature or those created by human action. REAL applies particularly to facts rooted in nature: *sunshine and rain are real.* ACTUAL applies to facts as they now are or have become, implying that one may have previously had a different idea of them or that the facts themselves may have been changed by circumstances: *the actual facts of natural science are different today since new elements have been created.* TRUE may be used of that which conforms to either the real or the actual.

re·al² (rē′əl, rēl; *Sp.* rĕ äl′), *n., pl.* **reals** (rē′əlz, rēlz), *Sp.* **reales** (rĕ ä′lēs). **1.** a former Spanish silver coin and money of account, still current in certain Spanish-American countries, equal to one eighth of a peso, or about 12½ U.S. cents. **2.** a former Spanish monetary unit equal to one quarter of a peseta, or about 5 U.S. cents. [t. Sp.: lit., royal, g. L *rēgālis* regal]

re·al³ (rē′əl), *n.* sing. of **reis.**

real estate, 1. ownership of or property in lands, etc. **2.** land and whatever by nature or artificial annexation is a part of it or is the means of its enjoyment, as minerals, trees, buildings, fences, etc.

re·al·gar (rǐ äl′gər), *n.* arsenic disulfide, As₂S₂, found native as an orange-red mineral and also prepared artificially: used in pyrotechnics. [ME, t. ML, t. Ar.: m. *rehj al-ghār* powder of the mine]

re·al·ise (rē′ə līz′), *v.,* **-ised, -ising.** *Chiefly Brit.* realize.

re·al·ism (rē′ə lǐz′əm), *n.* **1.** interest in or concern for the actual or real as distinguished from the abstract, speculative, etc. **2.** the tendency to view or represent things as they really are. **3.** the treatment of subjects in literature or art with fidelity to nature or to real life (opposed to *idealism*). **4.** *Philos.* **a.** the doctrine that universals have a real objective existence (medieval **realism**). Cf. **nominalism** and **conceptualism. b.** the doctrine that objects of sense perception have an existence independent of the act of perception. Cf. **idealism.**

re·al·ist (rē′əl ǐst), *n.* **1.** one who tends to view or represent things as they really are, esp. a writer or artist. **2.** *Philos.* an adherent of realism.

re·al·is·tic (rē′ə lǐs′tǐk), *adj.* **1.** interested in or concerned with what is real or practical. **2.** pertaining to, characterized by, or given to the representation in literature or art of things as they really are: *a realistic novel.* **3.** of or pertaining to realists or realism in philosophy. —**re′al·is′ti·cal·ly,** *adv.*

re·al·i·ty (rǐ äl′ə tǐ), *n., pl.* **-ties. 1.** state or fact of being real. **2.** resemblance to what is real. **3.** a real thing or fact. **4.** *Philos.* **a.** that which exists independently of ideas concerning it. **b.** that which exists independently of all other things; an ultimate thing which produces derivatives. **5.** that which is real. **6.** that which constitutes the real or actual thing, as distinguished from that which is merely apparent. **7. in reality,** really; actually; in fact or truth.

re·al·i·za·tion (rē′əl ə zā′shən), *n.* **1.** the making or being made real of something imagined, planned, etc. **2.** the result of such a process: *the realization of a project.* **3.** act of realizing. **4.** state of being realized. **5.** an instance or result of realizing.

re·al·ize (rē′ə līz′), *v.,* **-ized, -izing.** —*v.t.* **1.** to grasp or understand clearly. **2.** to make real, or give reality to (a hope, fear, plan, etc.). **3.** to bring vividly before the mind. **4.** to convert into cash or money: *to realize securities.* **5.** to obtain as a profit or income for oneself

re′a·dapt′	**re′ad·journ′ment**	**re′ad·mit′tance**	**re′af·fir·ma′tion**
re′ad·dress′	**re′ad·mis′sion**	**re·a·dopt′**	**re′a·lign′**
re′ad·journ′	**re′ad·mit′**	**re′af·firm′**	**re′a·lign′ment**

by trade, labor, or investment. **6.** to bring as proceeds, as from a sale: *the goods realized $1,000.* —*v.i.* **7.** to convert property or goods into cash or money. **8.** to realize a profit. Also, *esp. Brit.*, **realise.** —**re'al·iz'a·ble,** *adj.* —**re'al·iz'er,** *n.* —Syn. **1.** conceive, comprehend. **3.** See **imagine.**

re·al·iz·ing (rē'əlī'zĭng), *adj.* **1.** that realizes. **2.** clear in apprehending or understanding.

re·al·ly (rē'əlĭ, rē'lĭ), *adv.* **1.** in reality; actually: *to see things as they really are.* **2.** genuinely or truly: *a really honest man.* **3.** indeed: *really, this is too much.*

realm (rĕlm), *n.* **1.** a royal domain; kingdom: *the realm of England.* **2.** the region, sphere, or domain within which anything rules or prevails: *the realm of dreams.* **3.** the special province or field of something: *the realm of physics.* [ME *realme,* t. OF: m. *reialme,* der. *reial regal,* g. L *rēgālis*] —Syn. **1.** See **kingdom.**

real number, *Math.* a rational number or the limit of a sequence of rational numbers, as opposed to complex numbers.

Re·al·po·li·tik (rā'äl'pō'lĭ'tēk'), *n.* German. political realism, esp. policy based on power rather than on ideals.

re·al·tor (rē'əl tər, -tôr'), *n.* a real estate broker, esp. one who belongs to the National Association of Real Estate Boards. [f. REALT(Y) + -OR²; coined by C.N. Chadbourn, of Minneapolis, formally adopted by the Association in 1916]

re·al·ty (rē'əl tĭ), *n.* real property or real estate. [f. REAL¹ (def. 8) + -TY²]

real wages, wages estimated not in money but in their purchasing power. Cf. **nominal wages.**

ream¹ (rēm), *n.* **1.** a standard quantity among paper dealers meaning 20 quires or 500 sheets (formerly 480 sheets). A **printer's ream** consists of 516 sheets. **2.** (*pl.*) *Colloq.* a large quantity: *to write reams and reams of poetry.* [ME *rem,* t. OF: m. *rayme,* through Sp., t. Ar.: m. *razmah, rizmah* bundle or bale]

ream² (rēm), *v.t.* to enlarge (a hole or opening) to size by means of a reamer. [ME *reme,* OE *rēman* open up]

ream·er (rē'mər), *n.* one of many rotating finishing tools with spiral or straight fluted cutting edges for finishing a hole to size and shape. [f. REAM² + -ER¹]

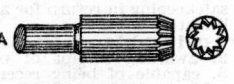

Reamers and sections
A. Head of machinist's reamer, with cross-section;
B. Head of flatsided reamer, or broach, with cross-section.

re·an·i·mate (rēăn'ə māt'), *v.t.,* **-mated, -mating. 1.** to restore to life; resuscitate. **2.** to give fresh vigor, spirit, or courage to. **3.** to stimulate to renewed activity. —**re'an·i·ma'tion,** *n.*

reap (rēp), *v.t.* **1.** to cut (grain, etc.) with a sickle or other implement or a machine, as in harvest. **2.** to gather or take (a crop, harvest, etc.). **3.** to get as a return, recompense, or result: *to reap large profits.* —*v.i.* **4.** to reap grain, etc. [ME *repe(n),* OE *repan,* c. MLG *repen* ripple (flax); akin to RIPE]

reap·er (rē'pər), *n.* **1.** a machine for cutting standing grain; a reaping machine. **2.** one who reaps.

reaping machine, any of various machines for reaping grain, often fitted with a device for automatically throwing out bundles of the cut grain.

rear¹ (rĭr), *n.* **1.** the back of anything, as opposed to the front. **2.** the space or position behind anything. **3.** the hindmost portion of an army, fleet, etc. —*adj.* **4.** situated at or pertaining to the rear: *the rear door.* [aphetic var. of ARREAR, n.] —Syn. **4.** See **back¹.**

rear² (rĭr), *v.t.* **1.** to care for and support up to maturity: *to rear a child.* **2.** to raise by building; erect. **3.** to raise to an upright position: *to rear a ladder.* **4.** to lift or hold up; elevate: raise. —*v.i.* **5.** to rise on the hind legs, as a horse or other animal. **6.** (of persons) to start up in angry excitement, hot resentment, or the like (commonly fol. by *up*). **7.** to rise high or tower aloft, as a building. [ME *rere(n),* OE *rǣran* RAISE, c. Goth. *-raisjan,* Icel. *reisa*] —**rear'er,** *n.*

rear admiral, a naval officer next in rank below a vice-admiral.

rear guard, a part of an army or military force detached from the main body to bring up and guard the rear from surprise attack, esp. in a retreat.

re·arm (rēärm'), *v.t.* **1.** to arm again. **2.** to furnish with new or better weapons: *they rearmed the troops as soon as possible.* —**re·ar·ma·ment** (rē är'mə mənt), *n.*

rear·most (rĭr'mōst'), *adj.* farthest in the rear; last.

rear sight, the sight nearest the breech of a firearm.

rear·ward (rĭr'wərd), *adj., adv.* toward or in the rear.

rear·wards (rĭr'wərdz), *adv.* rearward.

rea·son (rē'zən), *n.* **1.** a ground or cause, as for a belief, action, fact, event, etc.: *the reason for declaring war.* **2.** a statement in justification or explanation of belief or action. **3.** the mental powers concerned with drawing conclusions or inferences. **4.** sound judgment or good sense. **5.** normal or sound powers of mind; sanity. **6.** *Logic.* a premise of an argument. **7.** (as used by Kant) the faculty by which we attain the knowledge of first principles (distinguished from *understanding*). **8. by reason of,** on account of; because of. **9. in reason,** in accordance with reason; justly or properly. —*v.i.* **10.** to think or argue in a logical manner. **11.** to draw conclusions or inferences from facts or premises. **12.** to urge reasons which should determine belief or action. —*v.t.* **13.** to think out (a problem, etc.) logically (often fol. by *out*). **14.** to conclude or infer (fol. by *that*). **15.** to bring, persuade, etc., by reasoning. **16.** to support with reasons. [ME *reisun,* t. OF: m. *raison,* g. L *ratio* reckoning, account] —**rea'son·er,** *n.* —Syn. **1.** REASON, CAUSE, MOTIVE are terms for a circumstance (or circumstances) which brings about or explains certain results. A REASON is an explanation of a situation or circumstance which made certain results seem possible or appropriate: *the reason for the robbery was the victim's display of his money.* The CAUSE is the way in which the circumstances produce the result; that is, make a specific action seem necessary or desirable: *the cause was the robber's extreme need of money.* A MOTIVE is the hope, desire, or other force which starts the action (or an action) in an attempt to produce specific results: *the motive was to get money to buy food for his family.*

rea·son·a·ble (rē'zən ə bəl, rēz'nə-), *adj.* **1.** agreeable to reason or sound judgment: *a reasonable choice.* **2.** not exceeding the limit prescribed by reason; not excessive: *reasonable terms.* **3.** moderate, or moderate in price: *the coat was reasonable but not cheap.* **4.** endowed with reason. —**rea'son·a·ble·ness, rea'son·a·bil'i·ty,** *n.* —**rea'son·a·bly,** *adv.* —Syn. **1.** REASONABLE, RATIONAL refer to the faculty of reasoning. RATIONAL is the more technical or more abstract term, concerned always with pure reason. It is applied to statements (etc.) which reflect or satisfy highly logical thinking: *her conclusions are always of a rational, never an emotional, nature.* REASONABLE has taken on more and more the pragmatic idea of simple common sense: *a reasonable supposition is one which appeals to our common sense.*

rea·son·ing (rē'zən ĭng), *n.* **1.** act or process of one who reasons. **2.** the process of drawing conclusions or inferences from facts or premises. **3.** the reasons, arguments, proofs, etc., resulting from this process.

rea·son·less (rē'zən lĭs), *adj.* **1.** not according to reason: *an utterly reasonless display of temper.* **2.** not endowed with reason.

re·as·sure (rē'ə shŏŏr'), *v.t.,* **-sured, -suring. 1.** to restore (a person, etc.) to assurance or confidence: *his remarks reassured me.* **2.** to assure again. **3.** to reinsure. —**re'as·sur'ance,** *n.* —**re'as·sur'ing·ly,** *adv.*

Réaum., Réaumur (thermometer).

Ré·au·mur (rā'ə myŏŏr'), *adj.* designating, or in accordance with, the thermometric scale introduced by de Reaumur in which the freezing point of water is at 0°, and the boiling point at 80°. See illus. under **thermometer.** *Abbr.:* R. Also, **Re'au·mur'.**

Ré·au·mur (rā'ə myŏŏr'; *Fr.* rě ō myr'), *n.* **René Antoine Ferchault de** (rənē' än twän' fěr shō' də), 1683–1757, French physicist and inventor.

reave¹ (rēv), *v.t.,* **reaved** or **reft, reaving.** *Archaic.* to deprive forcibly, strip, or rob. [ME *reve(n),* OE *rēafian,* c. G *rauben* ROB]

reave² (rēv), *v.t., v.i.,* **reaved** or **reft, reaving.** *Archaic.* to rend; break; tear. [appar. special use of REAVE¹ by assoc. with RIVE]

re·bate¹ (rē'bāt, rĭ bāt'), *n., v.,* **-bated, -bating.** —*n.* **1.** a return of part of an original amount paid for some service or merchandise. **2.** repayment, as of a part of charges. —*v.t.* **3.** to allow as a discount. **4.** to deduct (a certain amount), as from a total. [ME, t. OF: m. *rabatre* beat or put down, f. *re-* RE- + *abbatre* ABATE]

re·bate² (rē'bāt, răb'ĭt), *n., v.t., v.i.,* **-bated, -bating.** *Archit.* rabbet. [var. of RABBET]

re·bec (rē'bĕk), *n.* a small medieval fiddle having commonly a pear-shaped body and three strings, and played with a bow. Also, **re'beck.** [t. F; ME *ribibe,* ult. t. Ar.: m. *rabāb* primitive one- or two-stringed viol]

Re·bec·ca (rĭ bĕk'ə), *n. Bible.* the sister of Laban, wife of Isaac, and mother of Esau and Jacob. Gen. 24–27. Also, **Re·bek'ah.**

reb·el (*n., adj.* rĕb'əl; *v.* rĭ bĕl'), *n., adj., v.,* **-belled, -belling.** —*n.* **1.** one who refuses allegiance to, resists, or rises in arms against, the established or rightful government or ruler. **2.** one who or that which resists any authority or control. —*adj.* **3.** rebellious. **4.** of or pertaining to rebels. [ME, t. L: m.s. *rebellis*] —*v.i.* **5.** to rise in arms or active resistance against one's government or ruler. **6.** to resist any authority. **7.** to manifest or feel utter repugnance: *her very soul rebelled at going back.* [ME *rebell(en),* t. OF: m. *rebeller,* t.

Rebec

re'a·noint'	re'ap·por'tion·ment	re'as·sess'	re'at·tach'
re'ap·pear'	re'ar·range'	re'as·sign'	re'at·tach'ment
re'ap·pear'ance	re'ar·range'ment	re'as·sign'ment	re'at·tain'
re'ap·pli·ca'tion	re'as·cend'	re'as·sim'i·late'	re'at·tain'ment
re'ap·ply'	re'as·sem'ble	re'as·sim'i·la'tion	re'at·tempt'
re'ap·point'	re'as·sem'bly	re'as·so'ci·ate'	re'a·wak'en
re'ap·point'ment	re'as·sert'	re'as·sume'	re'bap'tism
re'ap·por'tion	re'as·ser'tion	re'as·sump'tion	re'bap·tize'

L: m. *rebellāre* wage war again (as conquered people)] —**Syn.** 1. insurgent, insurrectionist, mutineer. 6. revolt, mutiny.

reb·el·dom (rĕb′əl dəm), *n.* 1. a region controlled by rebels. 2. rebels collectively. 3. rebellious conduct.

re·bel·lion (rĭ bĕl′yən), *n.* 1. open, organized, and armed resistance to one's government or ruler. 2. resistance against or defiance of any authority or control. 3. act of rebelling. [ME, t. L: s. *rebellio*] —**Syn.** 1. insurrection, mutiny, sedition, revolution. See **revolt.** 2. insubordination, disobedience.

re·bel·lious (rĭ bĕl′yəs), *adj.* 1. defying lawful authority; insubordinate; disposed to rebel. 2. pertaining to or characteristic of rebels or rebellion. 3. (of things) resisting treatment; refractory. [ME, f. REBELLI(ON) + -OUS] —**re·bel′lious·ly,** *adv.* —**re·bel′lious·ness,** *n.* —**Syn.** 1. insurgent, mutinous, seditious.

re·birth (rē bûrth′, rē′bûrth′), *n.* 1. being born again; a second birth. 2. a renaissance; a new activity or growth.

reb·o·ant (rĕb′ō ənt), *adj.* bellowing in return; resounding loudly. [t. L: s. *reboans,* ppr.]

re·born (rē bôrn′), *adj.* born again.

re·bound (*v.* rĭ bound′; *n.* rē′bound′, rĭ bound′), *v.i.* 1. to bound or spring back from force of impact. —*v.t.* 2. to cause to bound back; cast back. —*n.* 3. act of rebounding; recoil. [ME, t. OF: m.s. *rebondir*]

re·broad·cast (rē brôd′kăst′, -käst′), *v.,* **-cast** or **-casted, -casting,** *n.* 1. to broadcast again from the same station. 2. to relay a broadcast received from another station. —*n.* 3. a program that is rebroadcast.

re·buff (rĭ bŭf′), *n.* 1. a blunt or abrupt check, as to one making advances. 2. a peremptory refusal of a request, offer, etc.; a snub. 3. a check to action or progress. —*v.t.* 4. to give a rebuff to; check; repel; refuse; drive away. [t. F (obs.): m. *rebuffe,* t. It: m. *ributfo*]

re·buke (rĭ būk′), *v.t.,* **-buked, -buking.** —*v.t.* 1. to reprove or reprimand. —*n.* 2. a reproof; a reprimand. [ME, t. AF: m. *rebuker,* var. of OF *rebuchier* beat back] —**re·buk′er,** *n.* —**Syn.** 1. censure, upbraid, chide. See **reproach.**

re·bus (rē′bəs), *n.* an enigmatical representation of a word or phrase by pictures, symbols, etc., suggesting the word elements or words: *two gates and a head is a rebus for Gateshead.* [t. L, abl. pl. of *rēs* thing]

Rebus of Bishop Oldham ("owldom")

re·but (rĭ bŭt′), *v.t.,* **-butted, -butting.** 1. to refute by evidence or argument. 2. to oppose by contrary proof. [ME *rebute*(n), t. AF: m. *reboter,* f. re- RE- + *boter* BUTT V.]

re·but·tal (rĭ bŭt′əl), *n.* act of rebutting, esp. in law.

re·but·ter[1] (rĭ bŭt′ər), *n.* one who or that which rebuts. [REBUT + -ER[1]]

re·but·ter[2] (rĭ bŭt′ər), *n. Law.* a defendant's answer to a plaintiff's surrejoinder. [t. AF: m. *rebuter,* inf. used as noun]

rec., 1. receipt. 2. recipe. 3. record. 4. recorder.

re·cal·ci·trant (rĭ kăl′sə trənt), *adj.* 1. resisting authority or control; not obedient or compliant; refractory. —*n.* 2. a recalcitrant person. [t. L: s. *recalcitrans,* ppr., lit., kicking back] —**re·cal′ci·trance, re·cal′ci·tran·cy,** *n.*

re·cal·ci·trate (rĭ kăl′sə trāt′), *v.i.,* **-trated, -trating.** to make resistance or opposition; show strong objection or repugnance. —**re·cal′ci·tra′tion,** *n.*

re·ca·lesce (rē′kə lĕs′), *v.i.,* **-lesced, -lescing.** to become hot again (said esp. of cooling iron, which glows with increased brilliancy upon passing certain temperatures). [t. L: m.s. *recalescere*] —**re′ca·les′cence,** *n.* —**re′ca·les′cent,** *adj.*

re·call (*v.* rĭ kôl′; *n.* rĭ kôl′, rē′kôl′), *v.t.* 1. to recollect or remember. 2. to call back; summon to return. 3. to bring back in thought or attention, as to present circumstances. 4. to revoke, take back, or withdraw: *to recall a promise.* 5. *Poetic.* to revive. —*n.* 6. act of recalling. 7. the act or possibility of revoking something. 8. the removal, or the right of removal, of a public official from office by a vote of the people taken upon petition of a specified number of the qualified electors. 9. a signal flag used to recall a boat to a ship, etc. —**re·call′a·ble,** *adj.* —**Syn.** 1. See **remember.**

Ré·ca·mier (rē kå myā′), *n.* Madame, (*Jeanne Françoise Julie Adélaïde Bernard*) 1777–1849, French social leader in the literary and political circles of Paris.

re·cant (rĭ kănt′), *v.t.* 1. to withdraw or disavow (a statement, etc.), esp. formally; retract. —*v.i.* 2. to disavow an opinion, etc., esp. formally. [t. L: s. *recantāre*] —**re·can·ta·tion** (rē′kăn tā′shən), *n.* —**re·cant′er,** *n.*

re·cap (rē′kăp′, rē kăp′), *v.t.,* **-capped, -capping.** to recondition (a worn automobile tire) by cementing on a strip of prepared rubber and vulcanizing by subjecting to heat and pressure in a mold.

re·cap·i·tal·i·za·tion (rē kăp′ə təl ə zā′shən), *n.* a revision of a corporation's capital structure by an exchange of securities.

re·cap·i·tal·ize (rē kăp′ə tə līz′), *v.t.,* **-ized, -izing.** to renew or change the capital of.

re·ca·pit·u·late (rē′kə pĭch′ə lāt′), *v.,* **-lated, -lating.** —*v.t.* 1. to review by way of an orderly summary, as at the end of a speech or discourse. 2. *Zool.* (of a young animal) to repeat (ancestral evolutionary stages) in its development. —*v.i.* 3. to sum up statements or matters. [t. LL: m.s. *recapitulātus,* pp.] —**re′ca·pit′u·la′tion,** *n.* —**re′ca·pit·u·la·tive, re·ca·pit·u·la·to·ry** (rē′kə pĭch′ə lə tōr′ĭ), *adj.* —**Syn.** 1. See **repeat.**

re·cap·ture (rē kăp′chər), *v.,* **-tured, -turing,** *n.* —*v.t.* 1. to capture again; recover by capture; retake. 2. (of the government) to take by recapture. —*n.* 3. recovery or retaking by capture. 4. the taking by the government of a fixed part of all earnings in excess of a certain percentage of property value, as in the case of a railroad. 5. *Internat. Law.* the lawful reacquisition of a former possession. 6. fact of being recaptured.

re·cast (*v.* rē kăst′, -käst′; *n.* rē′kăst′, -käst′), *v.,* **-cast, -casting,** *n.* —*v.t.* 1. to cast again or anew. 2. to form, fashion, or arrange again. 3. to remodel or reconstruct (a literary work, a document, a sentence, etc.) —*n.* 4. a recasting. 5. a new form produced by recasting.

recd., received. Also, **rec'd.**

re·cede[1] (rĭ sēd′), *v.i.,* **-ceded, -ceding.** 1. to go or move back, to or toward a more distant point. 2. to become more distant. 3. to slope backward: *a receding chin.* 4. to draw back or withdraw from a position taken in a matter, or from an undertaking, promise, etc. [ME, t. L: m.s. *recēdere* go back]

re·cede[2] (rē sēd′), *v.t.,* **-ceded, -ceding.** to cede back; yield or grant to a former possessor. [f. RE- + CEDE]

re·ceipt (rĭ sēt′), *n.* 1. a written acknowledgment of having received money, goods, etc., specified. 2. (*pl.*) the amount or quantity received. 3. act of receiving. 4. state of being received. 5. that which is received. 6. a recipe. —*v.t.* 7. to acknowledge in writing the payment of (a bill). 8. to give a receipt for (money, goods, etc.). —*v.i.* 9. to give a receipt, as for money or goods. [ME *receite,* t. AF, g. L *recepta,* fem. pp., received]

re·ceipt·or (rĭ sē′tər), *n.* 1. one who receipts. 2. *Law.* a person to whom attached property is delivered for safekeeping in return for a bond to produce it when the litigation ends.

re·ceiv·a·ble (rĭ sē′və bəl), *adj.* 1. fit for acceptance. 2. awaiting receipt of payment: *accounts receivable.* 3. capable of being received. —*n.* 4. (*pl.*) business assets in the form of obligations due from others.

re·ceive (rĭ sēv′), *v.,* **-ceived, -ceiving.** —*v.t.* 1. to take into one's hand or one's possession (something offered or delivered). 2. to have (something) bestowed, conferred, etc.: *to receive an honorary degree.* 3. to have delivered or brought to oneself: *to receive a letter.* 4. to get or learn: *to receive notice, to receive news.* 5. to become the support of; sustain. 6. to hold or contain. 7. to take into the mind; apprehend mentally. 8. to take from another by hearing or listening: *a priest received his confession.* 9. to meet with; experience: *to receive attention.* 10. to suffer or undergo: *to receive an affront.* 11. to have inflicted upon one: *to receive a broken arm.* 12. to be at home to (visitors). 13. to greet or welcome (guests, etc.) upon arriving. 14. to admit (a person) to a place. 15. to admit to a state or condition, a privilege, membership, etc.: *to receive someone into the church.* 16. to accept as authoritative, valid, true, or approved: *a principle universally received.* —*v.i.* 17. to receive something. 18. to receive visitors or guests. 19. *Radio.* to convert incoming electromagnetic waves into the original signal, as sound waves or light on a kinescope screen. 20. to receive the eucharist. [ME *receve,* t. ONF: m. *receivre,* ult. g. L *recipere* take back, take to one's self, receive]

re·ceiv·er (rĭ sē′vər), *n.* 1. one who or that which receives. 2. a device or apparatus which receives electrical signals, waves, or the like, and renders them perceptible to the senses, as the part of a telephone held to the ear, a radio receiving set, or a television receiving set. 3. *Law.* a person appointed by a court to take charge of a business or property of others, pending litigation. 4. *Com.* one appointed to receive money due. 5. one who, for purposes of profit or concealment, knowingly receives stolen goods. 6. a receptacle; a device or apparatus for receiving or holding something. 7. *Chem.* a vessel for collecting and containing a distillate.

re·ceiv·er·ship (rĭ sē′vər shĭp′), *n. Law.* 1. the condition of being in the hands of a receiver. 2. the position or function of being a receiver in charge of administering the property of others.

receiving set, *Radio.* a mechanism for the reception of electromagnetic waves.

re·cen·sion (rĭ sĕn′shən), *n.* 1. a revision of an early work on the basis of critical examination of the text and the sources used. 2. a version of a text resulting from such revision. [t. L: s. *recensio*]

re·cent (rē′sənt), *adj.* 1. of late occurrence, appearance, or origin; lately happening, done, made, etc.: *recent events.* 2. not long past, as a period. 3. belonging to such a period; not remote or primitive. 4. (*cap.*) *Stratig.* pertaining to the later division of the Quaternary period or system, succeeding the Pleistocene, and regarded as the present or existing geological division. [t. L: s. *recens*] —**re′cen·cy, re′cent·ness,** *n.* —**re′cent·ly,** *adv.* —**Syn.** 1. See **modern.**

re·bill′	re·build′	re·bur′y	re·cel′e·brate′
re·bind′	re·built′	re·car′ry	re·cel·e·bra′tion

b., blend of, blended; c., cognate with; d., dialect, dialectal; der., derived from; f., formed from; g., going back to; m., modification of; r., replacing; s., stem of; t., taken from; ?, perhaps. See the full key on inside cover.

re·cept (rē'sĕpt), *n. Psychol.* an idea formed by the repetition of similar percepts, as successive percepts of the same object. [t. L: s. *receptum*, neut. pp., taken back]

re·cep·ta·cle (rĬ·sĕp'tə·kəl), *n.* **1.** that which serves to receive or hold something; a repository; a container. **2.** *Bot.* the modified or expanded portion of an axis, which bears the organs of a single flower or the florets of a flower head. **3.** *Elect.* a contact device installed at an outlet for the connection of a portable lamp or appliance by means of a plug and flexible cord. [late ME, t. L: m.s. *receptāculum*]

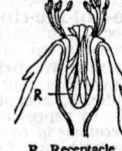

R. Receptacle
(Longitudinal section)

re·cep·tion (rĬ·sĕp'shən), *n.* **1.** act of receiving. **2.** fact of being received. **3.** a manner of being received: *the book met with a favorable reception.* **4.** a function or occasion when persons are formally received. **5.** *Radio.* the quality or fidelity attained in receiving under given circumstances. [ME *recepcion*, t. L: m.s. *receptio*]

re·cep·tion·ist (rĬ·sĕp'shən·Ĭst), *n.* a person employed to receive callers, as in an office.

reception room, a room for receiving visitors, clients, etc.

re·cep·tive (rĬ·sĕp'tĬv), *adj.* **1.** having the quality of receiving, taking in, or admitting. **2.** able or quick to receive ideas, etc.: *a receptive mind.* **3.** having, or characterized by, a disposition to receive a suggestion, offer, or the like with favor: *a receptive frame of mind.* **4.** of or pertaining to reception or receptors: *a receptive end organ.* —**re·cep'tive·ly,** *adv.* —**re·cep·tiv·i·ty** (rē'sĕp·tĬv'ə·tĬ), **re·cep'tive·ness,** *n.*

re·cep·tor (rĬ·sĕp'tər), *n. Physiol.* the end organs of sensory or afferent neurons, specialized to be sensitive to stimulating agents. [t. L: s. *receiver*]

re·cess (*n.* rĬ·sĕs', rē'sĕs; *v.* rĬ·sĕs'), *n.* **1.** withdrawal or cessation for a time from the usual occupation, work, or activity. **2.** a period of such withdrawal. **3.** a receding part or space, as a bay or alcove in a room. **4.** an indentation in a line or extent of coast, hills, forest, etc. **5.** (*pl.*) a secluded or inner place or part: *in the recesses of the palace.* —*v.t.* **6.** to place or set in a recess. **7.** to set or form as or like a recess; make a recess or recesses in: *to recess a wall.* —*v.i.* **8.** to take a recess. [t. L: s. *recessus* a going back]

re·ces·sion[1] (rĬ·sĕsh'ən), *n.* **1.** act of receding or withdrawing. **2.** a receding part of a wall, etc. **3.** a procession at the end of a service. **4.** a temporary decline in business occurring during a period of generally increasing economic prosperity, esp. during a period of recovery after a depression. [t. L: s. *recessio*]

re·ces·sion[2] (rē·sĕsh'ən), *n.* returning ownership to a former possessor. [f. RE- + CESSION]

re·ces·sion·al (rĬ·sĕsh'ən·əl), *adj.* **1.** of or pertaining to a recession of the clergy and choir after the service. **2.** of or pertaining to a recess, as of a legislative body. —*n.* **3.** a recessional hymn, or music for it.

recessional hymn, a hymn sung at the close of a church service while the clergy and choir retire from the chancel to the vestry.

re·ces·sive (rĬ·sĕs'Ĭv), *adj.* **1.** tending to recede; receding. **2.** *Biol.* pertaining to or exhibiting a recessive, as opposed to a dominant, character. **3.** (of accent) showing a tendency to recede from the end toward the beginning of a word. —*n. Biol.* **4.** a hereditary character resulting from a gene which possesses lesser biochemical activity than another termed the dominant, and hence is suppressed more or less completely by it when in a heterozygous condition. **5.** an individual exhibiting such character.

ré·chauf·fé (rē·shō·fā'), *n., pl.* -**fés** (-fā'). *French.* **1.** a warmed-up dish of food. **2.** anything old or stale brought out again. [F: warmed again]

re·cher·ché (rə·shâr'shā; *Fr.* rə·shĕr·shĕ'), *adj.* **1.** sought out with care. **2.** rare or choice. **3.** of studied refinement or elegance. [t. F, pp. of *rechercher.* See RE-SEARCH, *v.*]

re·cid·i·vism (rĬ·sĬd'ə·vĬz'əm), *n.* **1.** repeated or habitual relapse into crime. **2.** *Psychiatry.* the chronic tendency toward repetition of criminal or antisocial behavior patterns. [f. s. L *recidīvus* relapsing + -ISM] —**re·cid'i·vist,** *n.* —**re·cid'i·vis'tic, re·cid'i·vous,** *adj.*

Re·ci·fe (rē·sē'fə), *n.* a seaport in E Brazil. 522,466 (est. 1952). Also, **Pernambuco.**

rec·i·pe (rĕs'ə·pē'), *n.* **1.** any formula, esp. one for preparing a dish in cookery. **2.** a medical prescription. **3.** a method to attain a desired end. [ME, t. L: take, impv. of *recipere* (see RECEIVE), as used at the head of prescriptions]

re·cip·i·ence (rĬ·sĬp'Ĭ·əns), *n.* **1.** act of receiving; reception. **2.** state or quality of being receptive; receptiveness. Also, **re·cip'i·en·cy.**

re·cip·i·ent (rĬ·sĬp'Ĭ·ənt), *n.* **1.** one who or that which receives; a receiver. —*adj.* **2.** receiving or capable of receiving. [t. L: s. *recipiens,* ppr., receiving]

re·cip·ro·cal (rĬ·sĬp'rə·kəl), *adj.* **1.** given, felt, etc., by each to or toward each, or mutual: *reciprocal affection.* **2.** given, performed, felt, etc., in return: *reciprocal aid.* **3.** *Gram.* expressing mutual relation, as *each other, one*

another, etc. (sometimes opposed to, but often including, *reflexive* when referring to plural subjects). **4.** *Math.* denoting various types of mutual relations. —*n.* **5.** a thing that is reciprocal to something else; an equivalent; a counterpart; a complement. **6.** *Math.* that by which a given quantity is multiplied to produce unity. [f. s. L. *reciprocus* returning, reciprocal + -AL[1]] —**re·cip'ro·cal'i·ty,** *n.* —**re·cip'ro·cal·ly,** *adv.* —**Syn. 2.** See **mutual.**

reciprocal ohm, *Elect.* a mho.

reciprocal translocation, *Genetics.* an atypical interchange of parts of two or more pairs of non-homologous chromosomes, ordinarily giving a ring of such chromosomes.

re·cip·ro·cate (rĬ·sĬp'rə·kāt'), *v.,* -**cated,** -**cating.** —*v.t.* **1.** to give, feel, etc., in return. **2.** to give and receive reciprocally; interchange: *to reciprocate favors.* **3.** to cause to move alternately backward and forward. —*v.i.* **4.** to make return, as for something given. **5.** to make interchange. **6.** to be correspondent. **7.** to move alternately backward and forward. [t. L: m.s. *reciprocātus,* pp.] —**re·cip'ro·ca'tive,** *adj.* —**re·cip'ro·ca'tor,** *n.*

reciprocating engine, an engine characterized by the movement of the pistons in the cylinders back and forth in a straight line.

re·cip·ro·ca·tion (rĬ·sĬp'rə·kā'shən), *n.* **1.** act or fact of reciprocation. **2.** a making return for something. **3.** a mutual giving and receiving. **4.** state of being reciprocal or corresponding.

rec·i·proc·i·ty (rĕs'ə·prŏs'ə·tĬ), *n.* **1.** reciprocal state or relation. **2.** reciprocation; mutual exchange. **3.** that relation or policy in commercial dealings between countries by which corresponding advantages or privileges are granted by each country to the citizens of the other.

re·ci·sion (rĬ·sĬzh'ən), *n.* an invalidating or rescinding. [t. L: s. *recisio*]

re·cit·al (rĬ·sī'təl), *n.* **1.** a musical entertainment given usually by a single performer, or consisting of selections from a single composer. **2.** act of reciting. **3.** a detailed statement. **4.** an account, narrative, or description. —**Syn. 4.** See **narrative.**

rec·i·ta·tion (rĕs'ə·tā'shən), *n.* **1.** act of reciting. **2.** a reciting or repeating of something from memory, esp. formally or publicly. **3.** a reciting of a prepared lesson by pupils before a teacher. **4.** a separate part of classroom instruction. **5.** an elocutionary delivery of a piece of poetry or prose, without the text, before an audience. **6.** a piece so delivered or for such delivery. [t. L: s. *recitātio*]

rec·i·ta·tive[1] (rĕs'ə·tā'tĬv, rĬ·sī'tə-), *adj.* pertaining to or of the nature of recital, as of facts. [f. RECITE + -ATIVE]

rec·i·ta·tive[2] (rĕs'ə·tə·tēv'), *Music.* —*adj.* **1.** of the nature of or resembling recitation or declamation. —*n.* **2.** a style of vocal music intermediate between speaking and singing. **3.** a passage, part, or piece in this style. [t. It.: m. *recitativo,* der. *recitare* RECITE]

re·cite (rĬ·sīt'), *v.,* -**cited,** -**citing.** —*v.t.* **1.** to repeat the words of, as from memory, esp. in a formal manner: *to recite a lesson.* **2.** to repeat (a piece of poetry or prose) before an audience, as for entertainment. **3.** to give an account of: *to recite one's adventures.* **4.** to enumerate. —*v.i.* **5.** to recite a lesson, or part of a lesson, before a teacher. **6.** to recite or repeat something from memory. [late ME, t. L: m. s. *recitāre* read aloud, repeat] —**re·cit'er,** *n.* —**Syn. 2, 3.** See **relate.**

reck (rĕk), *v.i.* **1.** to have care, concern, or regard (often fol. by *of, with,* or a clause). **2.** to take heed. **3.** *Archaic.* to be of concern or importance, or matter: *it recks not.* —*v.t.* **4.** to have regard for; mind; heed. [ME *rekke(n),* OE *reccan,* var. of *rēcan,* c. G *(ge)ruhen* deign]

reck·less (rĕk'lĬs), *adj.* **1.** utterly careless of the consequences of action; without caution (fol. by *of*). **2.** characterized by or proceeding from such carelessness: *reckless extravagance.* [ME *rekles,* OE *reccelēas,* var. *rēcelēas* careless (c. G *ruchlos*)] —**reck'less·ly,** *adv.* —**reck'less·ness,** *n.*

reck·on (rĕk'ən), *v.t.* **1.** to count, compute, or calculate as to number or amount. **2.** to esteem or consider (as stated): *to be reckoned a wit.* **3.** *Colloq.* or *Dial.* to think or suppose. —*v.i.* **4.** to count; make a computation or calculation. **5.** to settle accounts, as with a person. **6.** to count, depend, or rely (*on*), as in expectation. **7.** to deal (*with*), as with something to be taken into account or entering into a case. [ME *reken(e),* OE *(ge)recenian,* c. G *rechnen*] —**Syn. 1.** enumerate. **2.** regard, account, deem.

reck·on·er (rĕk'ən·ər), *n.* **1.** one who reckons. **2.** a collection of mathematical and other tables for ready calculation.

reck·on·ing (rĕk'ən·Ĭng), *n.* **1.** count, computation, or calculation. **2.** the settlement of accounts, as between parties. **3.** a statement of an amount due; bill. **4.** an accounting, as for things received or done: *a day of reckoning.* **5.** See **dead reckoning.**

re·claim (rĬ·klām'), *v.t.* **1.** to bring (wild, waste, or marshy land) into a condition for cultivation or other use. **2.** to recover (substances) in a pure or usable

| re·chal/lenge | re·char/ter | re·choose/ | re·cir/cle |
| re·charge/ | re·check/ | re·chris/ten | re·cir/cu·late/ |

form from refuse matter, articles, etc. **3.** to bring back to right courses, living, principles, ideas, etc. —*n.* **4.** reclamation: *beyond reclaim.* [ME *reclaime(n)*, t. OF: m. *reclaimer*, g. L *reclāmāre* cry out against] —**re-claim'a-ble**, *adj.* —**re-claim'er**, *n.* —**Syn. 2.** See recover.

re-claim' (rĭ klām'), *v.t.* to claim or demand the return or restoration of. [f. RE- + CLAIM]

re-claim-ant (rĭ klā'mənt), *n.* a person who makes appeals to reclaim.

rec-la-ma-tion (rĕk'lə mā'shən), *n.* **1.** the reclaiming of waste, desert, marshy, or submerged land for cultivation or other use. **2.** act or process of reclaiming. **3.** state of being reclaimed. **4.** the process or industry of deriving useable materials from waste products. [t. L: s. *reclāmātio*]

ré-clame (rĕ kläm'), *n. French.* **1.** publicity; advertisement. **2.** seeking for publicity.

re-cline (rĭ klīn'), *v.,* **-clined, -clining.** —*v.i.* **1.** to lean or lie back; rest in a recumbent position. —*v.t.* **2.** to cause to lean back on something; place in a recumbent position. [late ME, t. L: m.s. *reclīnāre*] —**re-clin'er**, *n.*

rec-luse (*n.* rĕk'lōōs, rĭ klōōs'; *adj.* rĭ klōōs'), *n.* **1.** a person who lives in seclusion or apart from society, often for religious meditation. **2.** a religious voluntarily immured or remaining for life within a cell. —*adj.* **3.** shut off or apart from the world, or living in seclusion, often for religious reasons. **4.** characterized by seclusion. [ME *reclus*, t. OF, g. LL *reclūsus*, pp., shut up] —**re-clu'sive**, *adj.*

re-clu-sion (rĭ klōō'zhən), *n.* **1.** the condition or life of a recluse. **2.** a shutting or a being shut up in seclusion.

rec-og-ni-tion (rĕk'əg nĭsh'ən), *n.* **1.** act of recognizing. **2.** state of being recognized. **3.** the perception of something as identical with something previously known or in the mind. **4.** the perception of something as existing or true; realization. **5.** the acknowledgement of something as valid or as entitled to consideration: *the recognition of a claim.* **6.** the acknowledgment of kindness, service, merit, etc. **7.** the expression of this by some token of appreciation. **8.** formal acknowledgment conveying approval or sanction. **9.** acknowledgment of right to be heard or given attention. **10.** *Internat. Law.* an official act by which one state acknowledges the existence of another state or government, or of belligerency or insurgency. [late ME, t. L: s. *recognitio*] —**re-cog-ni-to-ry** (rĭ kŏg'nə tôr'ĭ), *adj.*

re-cog-ni-zance (rĭ kŏg'nə zəns, -kŏn'ə-), *n.* **1.** act of recognizing; recognition. **2.** *Law.* **a.** a bond or obligation of record entered into before a court of record or a magistrate, binding a person to do a particular act. **b.** the sum pledged as surety on such a bond. [ME *reconissance*, t. OF. See RECOGNIZE]

rec-og-nize (rĕk'əg nīz'), *v.,* **-nized, -nizing.** —*v.t.* **1.** to know again; perceive to be identical with something previously known: *he had changed so much that one could scarcely recognize him.* **2.** to identify from knowledge of appearance or character. **3.** to perceive as existing or true; realize: *to be the first to recognize a fact.* **4.** to acknowledge as the person entitled to speak at the particular time. **5.** to acknowledge formally as existing or as entitled to consideration: *one government recognizes another.* **6.** to acknowledge or accept formally as being something stated: *to recognize a government as a belligerent.* **7.** to acknowledge or treat as valid: *to recognize a claim.* **8.** to acknowledge acquaintance with (a person, etc.) as by a salute. **9.** to show appreciation of (kindness, service, merit, etc.) as by some reward or tribute. —*v.i.* **10.** *Law.* to enter into a recognizance. Also, *esp. Brit.,* **rec'og-nise'.** [appar. f. *recogn(ition)* + -IZE; r. late ME (Scot.) *racunnys*, t. OF] —**rec'og-niz'a-ble**, *adj.* —**rec'og-niz'er**; *Law.* **re-cog-ni-zor** (rĭ kŏg'nə zôr', rĭ kŏn'-), *n.*

re-coil (rĭ koil' *for 1–3;* rē- *for 4;* rē'koil' *for 5), *v.i.* **1.** to draw back; start or shrink back, as in alarm, horror, or disgust. **2.** to spring or fly back, as in consequence of force of impact or the force of the discharge, as a firearm. **3.** to spring or come back; react (fol. by *on* or *upon*). —*n.* **4.** act of recoiling. **5.** the length through which a weapon moves backwards after its discharge. [ME *recuyel(l)e(n)*, t. OF: m. *reculer*, der. L *re*- RE- + *cūlus* the posteriors]

re-coil-less (rĭ koil'lĭs, rē'koil'-), *adj.* without recoil: *recoilless artillery.*

re-col-lect (rĕk'ə lĕkt'), *v.t.* **1.** to recall to mind, or recover knowledge of by an act or effort of memory; remember. —*v.i.* **2.** to have a recollection; remember. [from the same source as RE-COLLECT, but distinguished in sense and pronunciation] —**rec'ol-lec'tive**, *adj.* —**Syn. 1.** See remember.

re-col·lect (rē'kə lĕkt'), *v.t.* **1.** to collect, gather together, or assemble again (what is scattered). **2.** to rally (one's faculties, powers, spirits, etc.); recover or compose (oneself). [orig. t. L: s. *recollectus*, pp., collected again, but later taken as f. RE- + COLLECT]

rec-ol-lec-tion (rĕk'ə lĕk'shən), *n.* **1.** act or power of recollecting, or recalling to mind; remembrance. **2.** that which is recollected: *recollections of one's childhood.* [f. RECOLLECT + -ION]

re-col-lec-tion (rē'kə lĕk'shən), *n.* **1.** act of re-collecting, or gathering together again. **2.** state of being re-collected. [f. RE-COLLECT + -ION]

rec-om-mend (rĕk'ə mĕnd'), *v.t.* **1.** to commend by favorable representations; present as worthy of confidence, acceptance, use, etc.: *to recommend a book.* **2.** to represent or urge as advisable or expedient: *to recommend caution.* **3.** to advise (a person, etc., to do something): *to recommend one to wait.* **4.** to make acceptable or pleasing: *a plan that has very little to recommend it.* [ME *recommende(n)*, t. ML: m. *recommendāre*, f. L: *re*- RE- + *commendāre* commend] —**rec'om-mend'er**, *n.*

rec-om-men-da-tion (rĕk'ə mĕn dā'shən), *n.* **1.** act of recommending. **2.** a letter or the like recommending a person or thing. **3.** representation in favor of a person or thing. **4.** anything that serves to recommend a person or thing or induce acceptance or favor.

rec-om-mend-a-to-ry (rĕk'ə mĕn'də tôr'ĭ), *adj.* **1.** serving to recommend; recommending. **2.** serving as, or of the nature of, a recommendation.

re-com-mit (rē'kə mĭt'), *v.t.,* **-mitted, -mitting. 1.** to commit again. **2.** to refer again to a committee. —**re'com-mit'ment, re'com-mit'tal**, *n.*

rec-om-pense (rĕk'əm pĕns'), *v.,* **-pensed, -pensing**, *n.* —*v.t.* **1.** to make compensation to (a person, etc.); repay, remunerate, reward, or requite for service, aid, etc. **2.** to make compensation for; make a return or requital for. —*n.* **3.** compensation made, as for service, loss, injury, or wrong: *to make recompense.* **4.** repayment or requital. **5.** remuneration or a reward. [ME, t. LL: m. *recompensāre*, f. L: *re*- RE- + *compensāre* compensate] —**Syn. 3.** See reward.

re-com-pose (rē'kəm pōz'), *v.t.,* **-posed, -posing. 1.** to compose again; reconstitute; rearrange. **2.** to restore to composure or calmness. —**re-com-po-si-tion** (rē'kŏm pə zĭsh'ən), *n.*

rec-on-cil-a-ble (rĕk'ən sī'lə bəl), *adj.* **1.** that can be reconciled. **2.** capable of reconciliation. —**rec'on-cil'a-bil'i-ty, rec'on-cil'a-ble-ness**, *n.* —**rec'on-cil'a-bly**, *adv.*

rec-on-cile (rĕk'ən sīl'), *v.t.,* **-ciled, -ciling. 1.** to render no longer opposed; bring to acquiescence (fol. by *to*): *to reconcile someone to his fate.* **2.** to win over to friendliness: *to reconcile a hostile person.* **3.** to compose or settle (a quarrel, difference, etc.). **4.** to bring into agreement or harmony; make compatible or consistent: *to reconcile differing statements.* [ME, t. L: m.s. *reconciliāre*] —**rec'on-cile'ment**, *n.* —**rec'on-cil'er**, *n.*

rec-on-cil-i-a-tion (rĕk'ən sĭl'ĭ ā'shən), *n.* **1.** act of reconciling. **2.** state of being reconciled. **3.** the process of making consistent or compatible.

rec-on-cil-i-a-to-ry (rĕk'ən sĭl'ĭ ə tôr'ĭ), *adj.* tending to reconcile.

rec-on-dite (rĕk'ən dīt', rĭ kŏn'dīt), *adj.* **1.** dealing with abstruse or profound matters: *a recondite treatise.* **2.** removed from ordinary knowledge or understanding; abstruse; profound: *recondite principles.* **3.** little known; obscure. [earlier *recondit*, t. L: s. *reconditus*, pp., put away, hidden] —**rec'on-dite'ly**, *adv.* —**rec'on-dite'ness**, *n.*

re-con-di-tion (rē'kən dĭsh'ən), *v.t.* to restore to a good or satisfactory condition; repair; make over.

re-con-nais-sance (rĭ kŏn'ə səns), *n.* **1.** act of reconnoitering. **2.** *Mil.* a search made for useful military information in the field, esp. by examining the ground. **3.** *Engin.* a preliminary examination of a region as to its general natural features, before a more exact survey for triangulation, etc. **4.** *Geol.* an examination or survey of the general geological characteristics of a region. Also, **re-con'nois-sance**. [t. F. See RECOGNIZANCE]

re-con-noi-ter (rē'kə noi'tər, rĕk'ə-), *v.t.* **1.** to inspect, observe, or survey (the enemy, the enemy's strength or position, a region, etc.) in order to gain information for military purposes. **2.** to examine or survey (a region, etc.) for engineering, geological, or other purposes. —*v.i.* **3.** to make a reconnaissance. [t. F: m. *reconnoître*, earlier form of *reconnaître* reconnoiter, RECOGNIZE] —**re'con-noi'ter-er**, *n.*

re-con-noi-tre (rē'kə noi'tər, rĕk'ə-), *v.t., v.i.,* **-tred, -tring.** *Chiefly Brit.* reconnoiter. —**re'con-noi'trer**, *n.*

re-con-sid-er (rē'kən sĭd'ər), *v.t.* **1.** to consider again. **2.** to consider again with a view to a change of decision or action: *to reconsider a refusal.* **3.** (in parliamentary use) to take up for consideration a second time, as a motion or a vote, as with the view of reversing or modifying action taken. —*v.i.* **4.** to reconsider a matter. —**re'con-sid'er-a'tion**, *n.*

re-con-sign-ment (rē'kən sīn'mənt), *n.* **1.** a consigning again. **2.** *Com.* a change in the route, point of delivery, or consignee as stated in the original bill of lading.

re-clasp'	re-col'or	re'con-ceal'	re'con-firm'
re-clothe'	re'com-bi-na'tion	re'con-cen'trate'	re'con-quer'
re-coin'	re'com-bine'	re'con-cen-tra'tion	re'con-quest'
re-coin'age	re'com-mence'	re'con-den-sa'tion	re'con-se'crate'
re-col'o-nize'	re'com-mence'ment	re'con-dense'	re'con-se-cra'tion

re·con·sti·tute (rēkŏn′stətūt′, -tōōt′), *v.t.*, **-tuted,** **-tuting.** to constitute again; reconstruct; recompose. —re′con·sti·tu′tion, *n.*

re·con·struct (rē′kən strŭkt′), *v.t.* to construct again; rebuild; make over.

re·con·struc·tion (rē′kən strŭk′shən), *n.* **1.** act of reconstructing. **2.** (*cap.*) *U.S. Hist.* the process by which the States which had seceded were reorganized as a part of the Union after the Civil War.

Reconstruction Acts, *U.S. Hist.* acts of Congress (March 2 and 23, 1867) providing for military government for ten Southern States and setting forth the process by which they might be restored to representation in Congress.

re·con·struc·tive (rē′kən strŭk′tĭv), *adj.* tending to reconstruct.

re·con·vey (rē′kən vā′), *v.t.* to convey again or back. —re′con·vey′ance, *n.*

re·cord (*v.* rĭ′kôrd′; *n., adj.* rĕk′ərd), *v.t.* **1.** to set down in writing or the like, as for the purpose of preserving evidence. **2.** to cause to be set down or registered: *to record one's vote.* **3.** to serve to relate or to tell of, as a written statement does. **4.** to set down or register in some permanent form, as instruments do. **5.** to set down, register, or fix by characteristic marks, incisions, magnetism, etc., for the purpose of reproduction by a phonograph, or magnetic reproducer. —*v.i.* **6.** to record something. —*n.* **7.** act of recording. **8.** state or fact of being recorded, as in writing. **9.** an account in writing or the like preserving the memory or knowledge of facts or events. **10.** information or knowledge preserved in writing or the like. **11.** a report, list, or aggregate of actions or achievements, as in the case of a person, an organization, a horse, a ship, etc.: *to have a good record.* **12.** any thing or person serving as a memorial. **13.** the tracing, marking, or the like made by a recording instrument. **14.** a cylinder, disk, or other device having characteristic markings or the like for reproducing sound, as in a phonograph. **15.** a notable recorded degree of achievement or attainment: *to hold the record.* **16.** the highest or furthest recorded degree attained; the best rate, amount, etc., attained, as in some form of sport: *to break the record in the high jump.* **17.** an official writing intended to be preserved. **18.** *Law.* **a.** the commitment to writing, as authentic evidence, of something having legal importance, esp. as evidence of the proceedings or verdict of a court. **b.** evidence preserved in this manner. **c.** an authentic or official written report of proceedings of a court of justice. —*adj.* **19.** making or affording a record. **20.** notable in the degree of attainment: *a record year for sales.* [ME *recorde(n),* t. OF: m. *recorder,* g. L *recordārī* call to mind, remember]

rec·ord-chang·er (rĕk′ərd chān′jər), *n.* a device which automatically changes the records in a phonograph.

re·cord·er (rĭ′kôr′dər), *n.* **1.** one who records, esp. as an official duty. **2.** *Law.* (in England) **a.** a judge having criminal jurisdiction. **b.** (formerly) the chief magistrate of a city or district. **3.** a recording or registering apparatus or device. **4.** a device to record sound by varying the magnetism in a moving steel wire or tape. The sound is recovered by moving the steel wire past an inductance coil, and may be erased by demagnetizing. **5.** a soft-toned flute with a plug in the mouthpiece, played in vertical position. —re·cord′er·ship′, *n.*

re·count (rĭ′kount′), *v.t.* **1.** to relate or narrate; tell in detail; give the facts or particulars of. **2.** to narrate in order. **3.** to tell one by one; enumerate. [late ME *recompte(n),* t. AF: m. *reconter* repeat, relate, f. *re-* RE- + *conter* tell, count¹] —**Syn. 1.** See relate.

re-count (*v.* rēkount′; *n.,* rē′kount′, rēkount′), *v.t.* **1.** to count again. —*n.* **2.** a second or additional count, as of votes in an election. [f. RE- + COUNT¹]

re-count·al (rĭ′koun′təl), *n.* act of recounting.

re·coup (rĭ′kōōp′), *v.t.* **1.** to provide or be an equivalent for; compensate for: *to recoup one's losses.* **2.** to yield in return; return an amount equal to. **3.** to reimburse or indemnify: *to recoup a person for expenses.* —*n.* **4.** act of recouping. [ME, t. F: s. *recouper* cut again, f. *re-* RE- + *couper* cut] —re·coup′ment, *n.*

re·course (rē′kôrs, rĭ′kōrs), *n.* **1.** resort or application to a person or thing for help or protection, as when in difficulty: *to have recourse to someone.* **2.** a person or thing resorted to for help or protection. **3.** *Com.* the right to resort to a person for pecuniary compensation. An endorsement **without recourse** is one by which a payee or holder of a negotiable instrument, by writing "without recourse" with his name, merely transfers the instrument without assuming any liability upon it. [ME *recours,* t. OF, g. L *recursus* a running back]

re·cov·er (rĭ′kŭv′ər), *v.t.* **1.** to get again, or regain (something lost or taken away): *to recover lost property.* **2.** to make up for or make good (loss, damage, etc., to oneself). **3.** to regain the strength, composure, balance, etc., of (oneself). **4.** *Law.* **a.** to obtain by judgment in a court of law, or by legal proceedings: *to recover damages for a wrong.* **b.** to acquire title to through judicial process: *to recover land.* **5.** to reclaim from a bad state, practice, etc. **6.** to regain (a substance) in usable form, as from refuse material or from a waste product or by-product of manufacture; reclaim. **7.** (in military use) to bring back (a weapon) to a certain position, as after use. —*v.i.* **8.** to regain health after sickness, a wound, etc. (often fol. by *from*): *to recover from an illness.* **9.** to regain a former (and better) state or condition: *the city soon recovered from the effects of the explosion.* **10.** to regain one's composure, balance, etc. **11.** *Law.* to obtain a favorable judgment in a suit for something. **12.** *Fencing. Rowing, etc.* to make a recovery. [ME *recovere,* t. AF: m. *recoverer,* g. L *recuperāre* recuperate] —re·cov′er·a·ble, *adj.* —re·cov′er·er. *n.* —**Syn. 1.** RECOVER, RECLAIM, RETRIEVE is to regain literally or figuratively something or someone. To RECOVER is to obtain again what one has lost possession of: *to recover a stolen watch.* To RECLAIM is to bring back from error or wrongdoing, or from a rude or undeveloped state: *to reclaim desert land by irrigation.* To RETRIEVE is to bring back or restore, esp. something to its former, prosperous state: *to retrieve one's fortune.* —**Ant. 1.** lose.

re-cov·er (rēkŭv′ər), *v.t.* to cover again or anew.

re·cov·er·y (rĭ′kŭv′ər ĭ), *n., pl.* **-eries.** **1.** act of recovering. **2.** the regaining of something lost or taken away, or the possibility of this. **3.** restoration or return to health from sickness. **4.** restoration or return to a former (and better) state or condition. **5.** time required for recovery. **6.** that which is gained in recovering. **7.** the regaining of substances in usable form, as from refuse material or waste products. **8.** *Law.* the obtaining of right to something by verdict or judgment of a court of law. **9.** *Fencing.* the movement to the position of guard after a lunge. **10.** *Rowing.* a return to a former position for making the next stroke.

rec·re·ant (rĕk′rĭ ənt), *adj.* **1.** cowardly or craven. **2.** unfaithful, disloyal, or false. —*n.* **3.** a coward or craven. **4.** an apostate; a traitor. [ME, t. OF, der. *recreire,* yield in a contest, f. *re-* back + *creire,* g. L *crēdere* believe] —rec′re·ance, rec′re·an·cy, *n.* —rec′re·ant·ly, *adv.*

rec·re·ate (rĕk′rĭ āt′), *v.,* **-ated, -ating.** —*v.t.* **1.** to refresh by means of relaxation and enjoyment, as after work. **2.** to restore or refresh physically or mentally. —*v.i.* **3.** to take recreation. [late ME, t. L: m.s. *recreātus,* pp. of *recreāre* restore, f. *re-* RE- + *creāre* create]

re-cre·ate (rē′krĭ āt′), *v.t.,* **-ated, -ating.** to create anew. [f. RE- + CREATE]

rec·re·a·tion (rĕk′rĭ ā′shən), *n.* **1.** refreshment by means of some pastime, agreeable exercise, or the like. **2.** a pastime, diversion, exercise, or other resource affording relaxation and enjoyment. **3.** act of recreating. **4.** state of being recreated. [ME, t. L: s. *recreātio*] —rec′re·a′tion·al, *adj.*

re-cre·a·tion (rē′krĭ ā′shən), *n.* **1.** act of creating anew. **2.** a thing created anew. [f. RE- + CREATION]

re·cre·ment (rĕk′rə mənt), *n. Physiol.* a secretion which, after having been separated from the blood, is returned to it, as the saliva. —re·cre·men′tal, *adj.*

re·crim·i·nate (rĭ′krĭm′ə nāt′), *v.,* **-nated, -nating.** —*v.i.* **1.** to bring a countercharge against an accuser. —*v.t.* **2.** to accuse in return. [t. ML: m.s. *recrīminātus,* pp.] —re·crim′i·na′tion, *n.* —re·crim′i·na′tive, re·crim·i·na·to·ry (rĭ′krĭm′ə nə tô′rĭ), *adj.*

re·cru·desce (rē′krōō dĕs′), *v.i.,* **-desced, -descing.** to break out afresh, as a sore or a disease, or anything that has been quiescent. [t. L: m.s. *recrūdescere*]

re·cru·des·cence (rē′krōō dĕs′əns), *n.* a breaking out afresh, or into renewed activity; revival or reappearance in active existence. —re′cru·des′cent, *adj.*

re·cruit (rĭ′krōōt′), *n.* **1.** a newly enlisted or drafted soldier or sailor. **2.** a newly secured member of any body or class. —*v.t.* **3.** to enlist (men) for military or naval service. **4.** to raise (a force) by enlistment. **5.** to strengthen or supply (an army, etc.) with new men. **6.** to furnish or replenish with a fresh supply; renew. **7.** to renew or restore (the health, strength, etc.). —*v.i.* **8.** to enlist or raise men for military or naval service. **9.** to recover health, strength, etc. **10.** to gain new supplies of anything lost or wasted. [t. F: m.s. *recruter,* der. *recrue* a new growth, prop. pp. of *recroître* grow again, f. *re-* RE- + *croître* (g. L *crescere*) grow] —re·cruit′er, *n.* —re·cruit′ment, *n.*

rect., **1.** receipt. **2.** rector. **3.** rectory.

rec·tal (rĕk′təl), *adj.* of or pertaining to the rectum.

rec·tan·gle (rĕk′tăng′gəl), *n.* a parallelogram with all its angles right angles. [t. LL: m.s. *rectangulum,* neut. of *rectangulus* right-angled]

rec·tan·gu·lar (rĕk tăng′gyə lər), *adj.* **1.** shaped like a rectangle. **2.** having the base or section in the form of a rectangle. **3.** having right angles or a right angle. **4.** forming a right angle. —rec·tan′gu·lar′i·ty, *n.* —rec·tan′gu·lar·ly, *adv.*

Rectangle

recti-, a word element meaning "straight," "right." Also, before vowels, **rect-.** [t. L, comb. form of *rectus*]

rec·ti·fi·er (rĕk′tə fī′ər), *n.* **1.** one who or that which rectifies. **2.** *Elect.* an apparatus or contrivance which changes an alternating current into a direct current, without an intermediate transformation of energy.

re′con·sol′i·date′	re′con·ver′sion	re·cop′y	re·crown′
re′con·sol′i·da′tion	re′con·vert′	re′cor·o·na′tion	re′crys·tal·li·za′tion
re′con·vene′	re′con·vert′er	re·cross′	re·crys′tal·lize′

rec·ti·fy (rĕk′tə fī′), v.t., **-fied, -fying. 1.** to make, put, or set right; remedy; correct. **2.** to put right by adjustment or calculation, as an instrument or a course at sea. **3.** Chem. to purify (esp. a spirit or liquor) by repeated distillation. **4.** Elect. to change (an alternating current) into a direct current. **5.** to determine the length of (a curve). **6.** Astron., Geog. to adjust (a globe) for the solution of any proposed problem. [ME, t. LL: m.s. rectificāre. See RECTI-. -FY] —**rec′ti·fi′a·ble,** adj. —**rec′ti·fi·ca′tion,** n. —Syn. 2. adjust, regulate.

rec·ti·lin·e·ar (rĕk′tə lĭn′ĭ ər), adj. **1.** forming a straight line. **2.** formed by straight lines. **3.** characterized by straight lines. **4.** moving in a straight line. Also, **rec′ti·lin′e·al.** —**rec′ti·lin′e·ar·ly,** adv.

rec·ti·tude (rĕk′tə tūd′, -tōōd′), n. **1.** rightness of principle or practice: the rectitude of one's motives. **2.** correctness: rectitude of judgment. **3.** Rare. straightness. [ME, t. LL: m. rectitūdo, der. L rectus. See RECTI-, -TUDE]

rec·to (rĕk′tō), n., pl. **-tos.** Print. a right-hand page of an open book or manuscript; the front of a leaf (opposed to verso). [t. L, short for rectō foliō on right-hand leaf]

rec·to·cele (rĕk′tə sēl′), n. a hernia of the rectum into the vagina. [f. recto- (comb. form of RECTUM) + -CELE]

rec·tor (rĕk′tər), n. **1.** U.S. a clergyman in charge of a parish in the Protestant Episcopal Church. **2.** Rom. Cath. Ch. an ecclesiastic in charge of a college, religious house, or congregation. **3.** Anglican Ch. a clergyman who has the charge of a parish with full possession of all its rights, tithes, etc. **4.** the permanent head in certain universities, colleges, and schools. [ME, t. L: ruler] —**rec·to·ri·al** (rĕk tōr′ĭ əl), adj.

rec·tor·ate (rĕk′tər ĭt), n. the office, dignity, or term of a rector.

rec·tor·y (rĕk′tər ĭ), n., pl. **-ries. 1.** a rector's house; a parsonage. **2.** Brit. a benefice held by a rector.

rec·trix (rĕk′trĭks), n., pl. **rectrices** (rĕk trī′sēz). Ornith. a large tail feather of a bird. [t. L: director]

rec·tum (rĕk′təm), n., pl. **-ta** (-tə). Anat. the comparatively straight, terminal section of the intestine, ending in the anus. See diag. under **intestine.** [t. NL, short for L rectum intestinum straight intestine]

rec·tus (rĕk′təs), n., pl. **-ti** (-tī). Anat. any of several straight muscles, as of the abdomen, thigh, eye, etc. [NL, short for L rectus musculus straight muscle]

re·cum·bent (rĭ kŭm′bənt), adj. **1.** lying down; reclining; leaning. **2.** inactive; idle. **3.** Zool., Bot. noting a part that leans or reposes upon anything. [t. L: s. recumbens, ppr.] —**re·cum′ben·cy,** n. —**re·cum′bent·ly,** adv.

re·cu·per·ate (rĭ kū′pə rāt′), v., **-ated, -ating.** —v.i. **1.** to recover from sickness or exhaustion; regain health or strength. **2.** to recover from pecuniary loss. —v.t. **3.** to restore to health, vigor, etc. [t. L: m.s. recuperātus, pp., regained, recovered.] —**re·cu′per·a′tion,** n.

re·cu·per·a·tive (rĭ kū′pər ə tīv′), adj. **1.** that recuperates. **2.** having the power of recuperating. **3.** pertaining to recuperation: recuperative powers. Also, **re·cu·per·a·to·ry** (rĭ kū′pər ə tōr′ĭ). —**re·cu′per·a′tive·ness,** n.

re·cu·per·a·tor (rĭ kū′pə rā′tər), n. **1.** one who or that which recuperates. **2.** a system of thin-walled refractory ducts for exchange of heat between gases.

re·cur (rĭ kûr′), v.i., **-curred, -curring. 1.** to occur again, as an event, experience, etc. **2.** to return to the mind: recurring ideas. **3.** to come up again for consideration, as a question. **4.** to return in action, thought, etc.: to recur to a subject. **5.** Rare. to have recourse. [late ME, t. L: m.s. recurrere run back]

re·cur·rence (rĭ kûr′əns), n. **1.** act or fact of recurring. **2.** return to a state, habit, subject, etc. **3.** recourse.

re·cur·rent (rĭ kûr′ənt), adj. **1.** that recurs; occurring or appearing again, esp. repeatedly or periodically. **2.** Anat., etc. turned back so as to run in a reverse direction, as a nerve, artery, branch, etc. [t. L: s. recurrens] —**re·cur′rent·ly,** adv.

recurring decimal, Math. a circulating decimal.

re·cur·vate (rĭ kûr′vĭt, -vāt), adj. recurved. [t.L: m.s. recurvātus, pp.]

re·curve (rĭ kûrv′), v.t., v.i., **-curved, -curving.** to curve or bend back or backward.

re·cu·san·cy (rĕk′yə zən sĭ, rĭ kū′-), n. **1.** state of being recusant. **2.** obstinate refusal or opposition. [der. RECUSANT. See -CY]

re·cu·sant (rĕk′yə zənt, rĭ kū′zənt), adj. **1.** refusing to submit, comply, etc. **2.** obstinate in refusal. **3.** Eng. Hist. refusing to attend services of the Church of England. —n. **4.** one who is recusant. **5.** Eng. Hist. a person, esp. a Roman Catholic, who refused to attend the services of the Church of England. [t. L: s. recūsans, ppr., refusing]

re·cuse (rĭ kūz′), v.t., **-cused, -cusing.** Rare. Law. to reject or challenge (a judge or juror) as disqualified to act. [ME, t. L: m.s. recūsāre reject, refuse]

red (rĕd), adj., **redder, reddest,** n. —adj. **1.** of a spectral hue beyond orange in the spectrum. **2.** having red clothing, etc. **3.** ultraradical politically. —n. **4.** any of the hues adjacent to orange in the spectrum such as

scarlet, vermilion, cherry. **5.** something red. **6.** (cap.) an ultraradical in politics, esp. a communist. **7.** see **red,** Colloq. to become angry or infuriated. **8.** the **red,** **a.** red ink as used in bookkeeping and accounting practice for recording losses and deficits in financial statements. **b.** loss or deficit: to be in or out of the red. [ME red(e), OE rēad, c. G rot, akin to L rūfus, ruber]

-red, a noun suffix denoting condition, as in hatred, kindred. [ME -rede, OE -rǣden]

re·dact (rĭ dăkt′), v.t. **1.** to bring into presentable literary form; revise; edit. **2.** to draw up or frame (a statement, etc.). [t. L: s. redactus, pp., brought back, reduced] —**re·dac′tion,** n. —**re·dac′tor,** n.

red algae, algae of the class Rhodophyceae, in which the chlorophyll is masked by a red or purplish pigment.

re·dan (rĭ dăn′), n. Fort. a work consisting of two parapets forming a salient angle. [t. F, var. of redent, a double notching or jagging, f. re- RE- + dent tooth, g. s. L dens]

Red Army, the official name of the Soviet Army.

red-bait (rĕd′bāt′), v.i. to denounce or deprecate as a political radical. —**red′bait′er,** n. —**red′bait′ing,** adj., n.

red·bird (rĕd′bûrd′), n. **1.** the cardinal grosbeak, Richmondena cardinalis. **2.** any of various unrelated red birds, as the scarlet tanager, Piranga olivacea, and summer tanager or **summer redbird,** P. rubra, of America.

red-blood·ed (rĕd′blŭd′ĭd), adj. vigorous; virile.

red·breast (rĕd′brĕst′), n. **1.** the European or American robin. **2.** either of two shore birds in breeding plumage, the dowitcher or knot. **3.** a freshwater sunfish, Lepomis auritus, of the eastern U. S.

red·bud (rĕd′bŭd′), n. **1.** the leguminous American Judas tree, Cercis canadensis, bearing small, budlike, pink flowers. **2.** any of various related trees.

red·bug (rĕd′bŭg′), n. a chigger.

red·cap (rĕd′kăp′), n. **1.** U.S. a porter, esp. in a railroad station. **2.** Brit. Colloq. a military policeman. **3.** the European goldfinch, Carduelis carduelis.

red cedar, 1. an American coniferous tree, Juniperus virginiana, with a fragrant, reddish wood used for making lead pencils, etc. **2.** an arbor vitae, Thuja plicata, a giant pinaceous tree of western U.S. **3.** the wood of these trees.

red cent, U.S. Colloq. a cent (used esp. in negative expressions): not worth a red cent.

red clover, the common clover, Trifolium pratense, a leguminous plant with red flowers: widely cultivated as a forage plant.

red-coat (rĕd′kōt′), n. a British soldier.

Red Cross, 1. an international philanthropic organization (**Red Cross Society**) formed, in consequence of the Geneva Convention of 1864, to care for the sick and wounded in war, and secure the neutrality of nurses, hospitals, etc., and active also in relieving suffering occasioned by pestilence, floods, fire, and other calamities. **2.** a branch of it: the American Red Cross. **3.** the English national emblem of St. George's cross. **4.** Geneva cross.

redd (rĕd), v.t., **redd, redded, redding.** Colloq. to put in order; tidy. [special use of obs. redd to free, rescue (OE hreddan), confused with obs. rede, OE rǣdan put in order. Cf. READY]

red deer, 1. a species of deer, Cervus elaphus, native in the forests of Europe and Asia, and formerly very abundant in England. **2.** the common American deer, Odocoileus virginianus, in its summer coat.

red·den (rĕd′ən), v.t. **1.** to make or cause to become red. —v.i. **2.** to become red. **3.** to blush; flush.

red·dish (rĕd′ĭsh), adj. somewhat red; tending to red; tinged with red.

red·dle (rĕd′əl), n., v.t., **-dled, -dling.** raddle[2].

red drum, a large drumfish, Sciaenops ocellata, an important food fish of the Atlantic coast of the U.S.

rede (rēd), v.t. Archaic or Dial. **1.** to counsel; advise. **2.** to explain. **3.** to tell. —n. **4.** counsel; advice. **5.** a plan; scheme. **6.** a tale; story. **7.** interpretation. [ME rede(n), OE rǣdan; the same word as READ[1]]

re·deem (rĭ dēm′), v.t. **1.** to buy or pay off; clear off by payment: to redeem a mortgage. **2.** to buy back, as after a tax sale or a mortgage foreclosure. **3.** to recover (something pledged or mortgaged) by payment or other satisfaction: to redeem a pawned watch. **4.** to convert paper money into specie. **5.** to discharge or fulfill (a pledge, promise, etc.). **6.** to make up for; make amends for: a redeeming feature. **7.** to obtain the release or restoration of, as from captivity, by paying a ransom. **8.** to deliver from sin and its consequences by means of a sacrifice offered for the sinner. [late ME, t. L: m.s. redēm-, perfect s. of redimere buy back] —Syn. 1. REDEEM, RANSOM mean literally to buy back. REDEEM is wider in its application than RANSOM, and means to buy back, regain possession, or improve the condition of anything; as by money, endeavor, devotion, sacrifice, or the like: to redeem one's property. To RANSOM is to redeem a person from captivity by paying a stipulated price, or (theol.) to redeem by sacrifice: to ransom a kidnapped child. —Ant. 1. abandon.

re′de·cay′	re′de·cide′	re′dec·o·ra′tion	re·ded′i·cate′
re′de·ceive′	re′de·cline′		re·ded·i·ca′tion

re·deem·a·ble (rǐ dē'mə bəl), *adj.* 1. capable of being redeemed. 2. that is to be redeemed: *bonds redeemable in 1960.* Also, **re·demp·ti·ble** (rǐ dĕmp'tə bəl).

re·deem·er (rǐ dē'mər), *n.* 1. one who redeems. 2. (*cap.*) Jesus Christ.

re·de·liv·er (rē'dǐ lǐv'ər), *v.t.* 1. to deliver again. 2. to deliver back; return.

re·de·mand (rē'dǐ mănd', -mänd'), *v.t.* 1. to demand again. 2. to demand back; demand the return of.

re·demp·tion (rǐ dĕmp'shən), *n.* 1. act of redeeming. 2. state of being redeemed. 3. deliverance; rescue. 4. repurchase, as of something sold. 5. paying off, as of a mortgage, bond, or note. 6. recovery by payment, as of something pledged. 7. convertibility of paper money into specie. [ME *redempcio(u)n*, t. L: m.s. *redemptio*, der. *redemptus*, pp. of *redimere* buy back]

re·demp·tive (rǐ dĕmp'tǐv), *adj.* serving to redeem.

Re·demp·tor·ist (rǐ dĕmp'tər ǐst), *n. Rom. Cath. Ch.* a member of the "Congregation of the Most Holy Redeemer," founded by St. Alphonsus Liguori in 1732.

re·demp·to·ry (rǐ dĕmp'tə rǐ), *adj.* 1. of or pertaining to redemption. 2. redemptive.

re·de·vel·op (rē'dǐ vĕl'əp), *v.t.* 1. to develop (something) again. 2. *Photog.* to intensify or tone by a second developing process. —*v.i.* 3. to develop again. —**re'·de·vel'op·er,** *n.* —**re'de·vel'op·ment,** *n.*

red·fin (rĕd'fǐn'), *n.* any of various small fresh-water minnows with red fins, esp. a shiner, *Notropis umbratilis,* of eastern and central North America.

red fir, 1. any of certain pinaceous trees, as *Abies magnifica,* of western U.S. 2. their wood. 3. Douglas fir.

red fire, any of various combustible preparations (as one containing strontium nitrate) burning with a vivid red light, used in pyrotechnic displays, signaling, etc.

red·fish (rĕd'fǐsh'), *n., pl.* **-fishes,** (*esp. collectively*) **-fish.** 1. one of the Pacific salmon, the red or sockeye salmon, *Oncorhynchus nerka.* 2. the rosefish.

red flag, 1. the recognized symbol of an extreme revolutionary party. 2. a danger signal. 3. something certain to arouse, anger, etc.

red fox. See **fox** (def. 1).

red grouse. See **grouse**[1].

red-hand·ed (rĕd'hăn'dǐd), *adj.* in the very act of a crime: *catch a thief red-handed.* —**red'-hand'ed·ly,** *adv.*

red hat, 1. the official hat, or the office or dignity, of a cardinal. 2. a cardinal.

red·head (rĕd'hĕd'), *n.* 1. a person having red hair. 2. an American diving duck, *Aythya americana,* the male of which has a bright chestnut-red head.

red·head·ed (rĕd'hĕd'ǐd), *adj.* 1. having red hair, as a person. 2. having a red head, as a bird.

red-headed woodpecker, a well-known woodpecker, *Melanerpes erythrocephalus,* of eastern and middle North America.

red heat, 1. the temperature of a red-hot body. 2. condition of being red-hot.

red herring, 1. something to divert attention; a false clue. 2. a smoked herring.

red hind (hīnd), a serranoid food fish, *Epinephelus guttatus,* of Florida, the West Indies, etc.

red-hot (rĕd'hŏt'), *adj.* 1. red with heat; very hot. 2. very excited or enthusiastic. 3. violent; furious: *red-hot anger.* 4. fresh; new; most recent: *red-hot tip.*

Red Indian, an aborigine of North America.

red·in·gote (rĕd'ǐng gōt'), *n.* 1. a full-length coat or dress open along entire front to show a dress or underdress. 2. a man's outer coat with long skirts. [t. F, t. E: m. *riding coat*]

red·in·te·grate (rĕd ǐn'tə grāt'), *v.t.,* **-grated, -grating.** to make whole again; restore to a perfect state; renew; reëstablish. —**red·in'te·gra'tive,** *adj.*

red·in·te·gra·tion (rĕd ǐn'tə grā'shən), *n.* 1. act or process of redintegrating. 2. *Psychol.* the tendency, when a response has occurred to a complex stimulus, to make that same response later to any part of that stimulus.

re·di·rect (rē'də rĕkt', -dī-), *v.t.* 1. to direct again. —*adj.* 2. *Law.* pertaining to the examination of a witness by the party calling him, after cross-examination. —**re'di·rec'tion,** *n.*

re·dis·count (rē dǐs'kount), *v.t.* 1. to discount again. —*n.* 2. an act of rediscounting. 3. (*usually pl.*) commercial paper which is discounted a second time.

re·dis·trict (rē dǐs'trǐkt), *v.t.* to divide anew into districts, as for administrative or electoral purposes.

red lattice, *Archaic.* an alehouse.

red lead (lĕd), a heavy, earthy substance, Pb₃O₄, orange to red in color, used as a paint pigment in the manufacture of glass and glazes; minium.

red lead ore, crocoite.

red-let·ter (rĕd'lĕt'ər), *adj.* 1. marked by red letters, as festival days in the church calendar. 2. memorable; especially happy: *a red-letter day.*

red light, a red lamp, used as a traffic signal to mean "stop."

red-light district, a neighborhood with many houses of prostitution, sometimes indicated by red lights.

red man, a North American Indian.

Red·mond (rĕd'mənd), *n.* **John Edward,** 1856–1918, Irish political leader.

red mullet, a goatfish or surmullet.

red·ness (rĕd'nǐs), *n.* the quality or state of being red.

red oak, 1. any of several oak trees, as *Quercus velutina* or *Q. borealis,* common to North America. 2. the hard cross-grained wood of these trees.

red ocher, any of the red natural earths, mixtures of hematite, which are used as pigments.

red·o·lent (rĕd'ə lənt), *adj.* 1. having a pleasant odor; fragrant. 2. odorous or smelling (fol. by *of*). 3. suggestive; reminiscent (fol. by *of*): *stories redolent of mystery.* [ME, t. L: s. *redolens,* ppr., giving back an odor] —**red'o·lence,** *n.* —**red'o·lent·ly,** *adv.*

Re·don·do Beach (rə dŏn'dō), a city in SW California. 46,986 (1960).

red osier, 1. a willow, *Salix purpurea,* with tough, flexible twigs or branches used for wickerwork. 2. any willow with reddish branches. 3. *U.S.* a dogwood, *Cornus stolonifera,* sending up osierlike shoots.

re·dou·ble (rē dŭb'əl), *v.,* **-bled, -bling,** *n.* —*v.t.* 1. to double; make twice as great: *to redouble one's efforts.* 2. to repeat. 3. to echo or reëcho. 4. *Bridge.* to double the double of (an opponent). —*v.i.* 5. to be doubled; become twice as great. 6. to be echoed; resound. 7. *Bridge.* to double the double of an opponent. —*n.* 8. *Bridge.* act of doubling one's opponent's double. [late ME, t. F: m. *redoubler*]

re·doubt (rǐ dout'), *n. Fort.* 1. an isolated work forming a complete enclosure of any form used to defend a prominent point. See diag. under **ravelin.** 2. an independent earthwork built within a permanent fortification to reinforce it. [t. F: m. *redoute,* t. It.: m. *ridotto,* g. LL *reductus* a refuge, L, pp., retired]

re·doubt·a·ble (rǐ dou'tə bəl), *adj.* 1. that is to be feared; formidable. 2. commanding respect. [ME *redoutable,* t. OF, der. *redouter* fear, der. *douter* DOUBT] —**re·doubt'a·ble·ness,** *n.* —**re·doubt'a·bly,** *adv.*

re·doubt·ed (rǐ dou'tǐd), *adj.* 1. dreaded; formidable. 2. respected; renowned.

re·dound (rǐ dound'), *v.i.* 1. to have an effect or result, as to the advantage, disadvantage, credit, or discredit of a person or thing. 2. to result or accrue, as to a person. 3. to come back or recoil, as upon a person. 4. to proceed, issue, or arise. —*n.* 5. the fact of redounding or resulting. [ME *redounde,* t. OF: m. *redonder,* t. L: m. *redundāre* overflow]

red·o·wa (rĕd'ə wə, -ō), *n.* a Bohemian dance in two forms, one, the more common, resembling the waltz or the mazurka, the other resembling the polka. [G, t. Czech: m. *reydovák,* der. *reydovati* turn or whirl round]

red pepper, 1. the condiment cayenne. 2. any of the hot peppers, *Capsicum frutescens* and botanical varieties, the yellow or red pods of which are used for flavoring, sauces, etc.

red·poll (rĕd'pōl'), *n.* 1. any of various small fringilline birds of the genus *Acanthis,* the adults of which usually have a crimson crown patch. 2. one of a breed of polled, red, dual-purpose cattle, originating in England, having a coat of short hair.

re·draft (rē drăft', -dräft'), *n.* 1. a second draft or drawing. 2. *Com.* a draft on the drawer or endorsers of a protested bill of exchange for the amount of the bill plus the costs and charges.

re·dress (*n.* rē'drĕs, rǐ drĕs'; *v.* rǐ drĕs'), *n.* 1. the setting right of what is wrong: *redress of abuses.* 2. relief from wrong or injury. —*v.t.* 3. to set right; remedy or repair (wrongs, injuries, etc.). 4. to correct or reform (abuses, evils, etc.). 5. to remedy or relieve (suffering, want, etc.). 6. to adjust evenly again, as a balance. [ME *redresse,* t. F. See RE-, DRESS] —**re·dress'er, re·dres'sor,** *n.*

—**Syn.** 1. REDRESS, REPARATION, RESTITUTION suggest making amends or giving indemnification for a wrong. REDRESS may refer either to the act of setting right an unjust situation (as by some power), or to satisfaction sought or gained for a wrong suffered: *the redress of grievances.* REPARATION means compensation or satisfaction for a wrong or loss inflicted. The word may have the moral idea of amends (*to make reparation for one's neglect*), but more frequently it refers to financial compensation (which is asked for, rather than given): *the reparations demanded of the aggressor nations.* RESTITUTION means literally the restoration of what has been taken from the lawful owner (*he demanded restitution of his land*); it may also refer to restoring the equivalent of what has been taken: *the servant convicted of robbery made restitution to his employer.*

re·dress (rē drĕs'), *v.t.* to dress again.

Red River, 1. a river flowing from NW Texas along the S boundary of Oklahoma into the Mississippi in E Louisiana. ab. 1200 mi. 2. Also, **Red River of the North.** a river flowing along the Minnesota-North Dakota boundary N to Lake Winnipeg in S Canada. 545 mi. 3. Songka.

re/de·feat/	re/dem/on·strate/	re/de·scribe/	re/dis·trib/ute
re/de·fend/	re/dem·on·stra/tion	re/de·ter/mine	re/dis·tri·bu/tion
re/de·fine/	re/de·ny/	re/di·gest/	re/di·vide/
re/de·fy/	re/de·pos/it	re/dis·cov/er	re·do/
re/de·lete/	re/de·scend/	re/dis·cov/er·y	re·draw/
re/de·liv/e·ry	re/de·scent/	re/dis·till/	re·draw/er

red·root (rĕd'rōōt', -rŏŏt'), n. 1. a North American plant, *Lachnanthes tinctoria*, having sword-shaped leaves, woolly flowers, and a red root. 2. any of various other plants with red roots, as the alkanet, *Alkanna tinctoria*, and pigweed, *Amaranthus retroflexus*.

red rose, *Hist.* See rose (def. 9b).

Red Sea, a long narrow arm of the Indian Ocean, extending NW between Africa and Arabia: connected with the Mediterranean by the Suez Canal. ab. 1450 mi. long; ab. 178,000 sq. mi.; greatest depth, 7254 ft.

red shift, *Physics.* the spectrometric shift of light from the galaxies toward longer wavelengths: interpreted as indicating that the galaxies are receding and the universe expanding. See **Doppler effect.**

red-short (rĕd'shôrt'), adj. *Metall.* brittle when at a red heat, as iron or steel containing too much sulfur. [t. Sw.: m. *rödskört* (sc. *jern* iron), neut. of *rödskör*, f. *röd* red + *skör* brittle]

red·skin (rĕd'skĭn'), n., adj. North American Indian.

red squirrel, a reddish arboreal squirrel, *Tamiasciurus hudsonius*, common to North America.

red·start (rĕd'stärt'), n. 1. a small European bird, *Phoenicurus phoenicurus*, with reddish-brown tail. 2. a red, black, and white fly-catching warbler, *Setophaga ruticilla*, of America. [f. RED + *start* tail, OE *steort*]

red tape, 1. tape of a red color, much used for taping up official papers. 2. excessive attention to formality and routine. —**red'-tape'**, adj.

red·top (rĕd'tŏp'), n. a grass, *Agrostis alba*, certain forms of which have a reddish panicle.

re·duce (rĭ dūs', -dōōs'), v., **-duced, -ducing.** —v.t. 1. to bring down to a smaller extent, size, amount, number, etc. 2. to lower in degree, intensity, etc.: *to reduce speed.* 3. to bring down to a lower rank, dignity, etc. 4. to lower in price. 5. to bring to a certain state, condition, arrangement, etc.: *to reduce glass to powder.* 6. to bring under control or authority. 7. *Photog.* to treat so as to make less dense, as a negative. 8. to adjust or correct by making allowances, as an astronomical observation. 9. *Math.* to change the denomination or form of. 10. *Chem.* a. to deoxidize. b. to add hydrogen to. c. to change (a compound) so that the valence of the positive element is lower. 11. *Chem., Metall.* to bring into the metallic state by separating from nonmetallic constituents; smelt. 12. (of paints, etc.) to thin with oil or turpentine. 13. *Biol.* to cause (a cell) to undergo meiotic division, halving the number of chromosomes. 14. *Surg.* to restore to the normal place, relations, or condition, as a dislocated organ or a fractured bone with separation of the fragment ends. —v.i. 15. to become reduced. [ME, t. L. m. *redūcere* bring back, restore, replace] —**re·duc'i·ble,** adj. —**re·duc'i·bil'i·ty,** n. —**re·duc'i·bly,** adv. —**Syn.** 1. diminish, decrease, shorten, abridge, curtail, retrench.

re·duced (rĭ dūst', -dōōst'), adj. 1. that is or has been reduced. 2. *Math.* denoting an equation in which the second highest power is missing.

re·duc·er (rĭ dū'sər, -dōō'-), n. 1. one who or that which reduces. 2. *Photog.* a. an oxidizing solution used to reduce a negative in density. b. developing agent.

reducing agent, *Chem.* a substance that causes another substance to undergo reduction and is oxidized in the process.

re·duc·tase (rĭ dŭk'tās, -tāz), n. *Biochem.* any enzyme acting as a reducing agent. [f. REDUCT(ION) + -ASE]

re·duc·ti·o ad ab·sur·dum (rĭ dŭk'shĭ ō' ăd ăb sûr'dəm), *Latin.* a reduction to an absurdity; the refutation of a proposition by demonstrating the absurd inevitable conclusion to which it would logically lead.

re·duc·tion (rĭ dŭk'shən), n. 1. act of reducing. 2. state of being reduced. 3. the amount by which something is reduced or diminished. 4. a form produced by reducing; a copy on a smaller scale. 5. *Biol.* meiosis. 6. *Chem.* the converse of oxidation. [t. L: s. *reductio*] —**re·duc'tion·al,** adj. —**re·duc'tive,** adj.

re·duc·tor (rĭ dŭk'tər), n. a tube with a stopcock at one end, filled with granulated zinc, for reducing iron to a ferrous state for analysis.

re·dun·dan·cy (rĭ dŭn'dən sĭ), n., pl. **-cies.** 1. state of being redundant. 2. a redundant thing, part, or amount; a superfluity. Also, **re·dun'dance.**

re·dun·dant (rĭ dŭn'dənt), adj. 1. being in excess; exceeding what is usual or natural: *a redundant part.* 2. characterized by or using too many words to express the ideas: *a redundant style.* 3. having some unusual or extra part or feature. 4. characterized by superabundance or superfluity. [t. L: s. *redundans,* ppr., overflowing] —**re·dun'dant·ly,** adv.

re·dupl. reduplication.

re·du·pli·cate (v. rĭ dū'plə kāt', -dōō'-; adj. rĭ dū'plə kĭt, -kāt', -dōō'-), v., **-cated, -cating.** —v.t. 1. to double; repeat. 2. *Gram.* to form (a derivative or an inflected form) by doubling a specified syllable or other portion of the primitive, sometimes with fixed modifications, as in Greek *lĕloipa* "I have left;" *leipo* "I leave."

—v.i. 3. to become doubled. 4. *Gram.* to become reduplicated. —adj. 5. doubled. 6. *Bot.* valvate, with the edges folded back so as to project outward. [t. LL: m.s. *reduplicātus,* pp., doubled. See REDUPLICATE]

re·du·pli·ca·tion (rĭ dū'plə kā'shən, -dōō'-), n. 1. act of reduplicating. 2. state of being reduplicated. 3. something resulting from reduplication. 4. *Gram.* a. reduplicating as a grammatical pattern. b. the added element in a reduplicated form. c. a form containing a reduplicated element.

re·du·pli·ca·tive (rĭ dū'plə kā'tĭv, -dōō'-), adj. 1. tending to reduplicate. 2. pertaining to or marked by reduplication. 3. *Bot.* reduplicate.

red·ware[1] (rĕd'wâr'), n. a type of pottery made by the Pennsylvania Dutch. [f. RED + WARE[1]]

red·ware[2] (rĕd'wâr'), n. *Obs.* a large brown seaweed, *Laminaria digitata,* common off northern Atlantic coasts. [f. RED + *ware* (ME; OE *wār*) seaweed]

red·wing (rĕd'wĭng'), n. 1. a European thrush, *Turdus musicus,* having chestnut-red flank and axillary feathers. 2. an American blackbird, *Agelaius phoeniceus,* the male of which has a scarlet patch on the wing.

red·wood (rĕd'wŏŏd'), n. 1. a coniferous tree, *Sequoia sempervirens,* of California, remarkable for its height (commonly from 200 to over 300 feet). 2. its valuable brownish-red timber. 3. a red-colored wood. 4. any of various trees with a reddish wood. 5. any tree whose wood produces a red dyestuff. 6. its wood.

Redwood City, city in W California. 46,290 (1960).

red-yel·low (rĕd'yĕl'ō), adj. orange.

re·ech·o (rē ĕk'ō), v., **-echoed, -echoing,** n., pl. **-echoes.** —v.i. 1. to echo back, as a sound. 2. to give back an echo; resound. —v.t. 3. to echo back. 4. to repeat like an echo. —n. 5. a repeated echo. Also, **re-ech'o.**

reed (rēd), n. 1. the straight stalk of any of various tall grasses, esp. of the genera *Phragmites* and *Arundo,* growing in marshy places. 2. the stalk of *Phragmites communis.* 3. any of the plants themselves. 4. such stalks or plants collectively. 5. anything made from such a stalk or from something similar, as an arrow. 6. *Music.* a. a pastoral or rustic musical pipe made from a reed or from the hollow stalk of some other plant. b. a small flexible piece of cane or metal which, attached to the mouths of some wind instruments (**reed instruments**), is set into vibration by a stream of air and, in turn, sets into vibration the air column enclosed in the tube of the instrument. c. any instrument with such a device, as the oboe, clarinet, etc. 7. *Archit., Carp., etc.* a small convex molding. 8. (in a loom) the series of parallel strips of wires which force the weft up to the web and separate the threads of the warp. 9. *Bible.* a Hebrew unit of length, equal to 6 cubits. —v.t. 10. to decorate with reed. 11. to thatch with or as with reed. [ME; OE *hrēod,* c. D and G *riet*]

Reed (rēd), n. 1. **John,** 1887–1920, U.S. journalist and poet. 2. **Walter C.,** 1851–1902, U.S. army surgeon who discovered that yellow fever is transmitted by a certain species of mosquitoes (*Aëdes aegypti*).

reed·bird (rēd'bûrd'), n. the American bobolink.

reed·buck (rēd'bŭk'), n., pl. **-bucks,** (esp. collectively) **-buck.** any of various yellowish African antelopes, genus *Redunca,* about the size of a small deer. The males have short, forward-curving horns. [trans. of D *rietbok*]

reed bunting, a well-known Old World fringilline bird, *Emberiza schoeniclus,* inhabiting marshy places.

reed·ing (rē'dĭng), n. 1. a small convex or semicylindrical molding, resembling a reed. 2. a set of such moldings, as on a column, where they resemble small convex fluting. 3. ornamentation consisting of such moldings. [f. REED, v. + -ING[1]]

reed·ling (rēd'lĭng), n. a small European bird, *Panurus biarmicus,* frequenting reedy places, and characterized in the male by a tuft of black feathers on each side of the chin. [f. REED, n. + -LING[1]]

reed mace, the cattail (def. 1).

reed organ, a musical keyboard instrument resembling the pipe organ but having the tones produced by small metal reeds.

reed pipes, the pipes of a reed organ.

reed stop, a set of reed pipes (opposed to *flue stop*).

re·ed·u·cate (rē ĕj'ŏŏ kāt'), v.t. **-cated, -cating.** 1. to educate again. 2. to educate for resumption of normal activities, as a cripple. Also, **re-ed·u'cate.** —**re·ed'u·ca'tion,** n.

reed warbler, a small Old World warbler, *Acrocephalus scirpaceus,* inhabiting marshy places.

reed·y (rē'dĭ), adj. **reedier, reediest.** 1. full of reeds. 2. consisting or made of a reed or reeds: *a reedy pipe.* 3. like a reed or reeds: *reedy grass.* 4. noting or having a tone like that of a reed instrument. —**reed'i·ness,** n.

reef[1] (rēf), n. 1. a narrow ridge of rocks or sand, often of coral debris, at or near the surface of the water. 2. *Mining.* a lode or vein. [earlier *riff(e),* t. D or LG: m. *rif,* t. Scand.; cf. Icel. *rif* rib, reef]

reef[2] (rēf), *Naut.* —n. 1. a part of a sail which is rolled and tied down to reduce the area exposed to the wind. —v.t. 2. to shorten (sail) by tying in one or more reefs. 3. to reduce the length of (a topmast, a bowsprit, etc.), as by lowering, sliding inboard, or the like. [ME *riff,* t. Scand.; cf. Icel. *rif* rib, reef]

re·droop'	**re·drug'**	**re·dye'**	**re·ed'it**
re·drop'	**re·dry'**	**re·ed'i·fy'**	**re·ed'i·tor**

reef·er[1] (rē′fər), *n.* **1.** *Naut.* one who reefs. **2.** a short coat or jacket of thick cloth. [f. REEF[2] + -ER[1]]

reef·er[2] (rē′fər), *n.* *U.S. Slang.* a marijuana cigarette. [same as REEF[2], in generalized sense of rolled object]

reef knot, *Naut.* a kind of square knot, so called because used in tying reef points.

reef point, *Naut.* a short piece of line fastened through a sail, used to tie in a reef.

reek (rēk), *n.* **1.** a strong, unpleasant smell. **2.** vapor or steam. —*v.i.* **3.** to smell strongly and unpleasantly. **4.** to be strongly pervaded with something unpleasant or offensive. **5.** to give off steam, smoke, etc. **6.** to be wet with sweat, blood, etc. —*v.t.* **7.** to expose to or treat with smoke. **8.** to emit (smoke, fumes, etc.). [ME *rek(e)*, OE *rēc*, c. G *rauch*] —**reek′er,** *n.* —**reek′y,** *adj.*

reel[1] (rēl), *n.* **1.** a cylinder, frame, or other device, turning on an axis, on which to wind something. **2.** a rotatory device attached to a fishing rod at the butt, for winding up or letting out the line. **3.** *Chiefly Brit.* a roller or bobbin for thread used in sewing; spool. **4.** a quantity of something wound on a reel. **5.** *Photog.* **a.** the spool, usually metal, on which (esp. motion-picture) film is wound. **b.** a roll of celluloid bearing a series of photographs to be exhibited with a motion-picture machine. —*v.t.* **6.** to wind on a reel, as thread, yarn, etc. **7.** to draw with a reel, or by winding: *to reel in a fish.* **8.** to say, write, or produce in an easy, continuous way (fol. by *off*). [ME *rele.* OE *hrēol*] —**reel′er,** *n.*

reel[2] (rēl), *v.i.* **1.** to sway or rock under a blow, shock, etc.: *to reel under a heavy blow.* **2.** to fall back; waver, as troops. **3.** to sway about in standing or walking, as from dizziness, intoxication, etc.; stagger. **4.** to turn round and round; whirl. **5.** to have a sensation of whirling: *his brain reeled.* —*v.t.* **6.** to cause to reel. —*n.* **7.** act of reeling; a reeling or staggering movement. [ME *rele(n)*, der. *rele* REEL[1]] —**Syn.** 3. See **stagger.**

reel[3] (rēl), *n.* **1.** a lively dance popular in Scotland. **2.** Virginia reel. **3.** music for either of these. [special use of REEL[2] (def. 7)]

re·ën·force (rē′ĕn fôrs′), *v.t.,* **-forced, -forcing.** reinforce. Also, **re′-en·force′.**

re·ën·ter (rē ĕn′tər), *v.t.* **1.** to come or go into again. **2.** to record again, as in a list or account. —*v.i.* **3.** to come or go into again. Also, **re-en′ter.** —**re·ën·trance** (rē ĕn′trəns), *n.*

reëntering angle, an angle directed back inward, rather than extending outward, as an exterior angle of less than 180° in a closed polygon.

Reentering angle

reëntering polygon, a polygon having one or more reëntering angles.

re·ën·trant (rē ĕn′trənt), *adj.* **1.** reëntering: *a reëntrant angle.* **2.** a reëntering angle or part.

re·ën·try (rē ĕn′trĭ), *n., pl.* **-tries. 1.** act of reëntering. **2.** *Law.* the retaking of possession under a right reserved in a prior conveyance. Also, **reëntry card.** *Whist and Bridge.* a card which will win a trick and thereby permit one to take the lead once again. **4.** the return from outer space into the earth's atmosphere of an artificial satellite, rocket, etc.

reeve[1] (rēv), *n.* **1.** an administrative officer of a town or district. **2.** *Chiefly Brit. Dial.* a bailiff, steward, or overseer. **3.** *Brit.* (formerly) one of high rank representing the crown. **4.** *Canada.* the presiding officer of a village or town council. **5.** the female of the European ruff, *Philomachus pugnax.* [ME *ireve*, OE *gerēfa* high official, lit., head of a *rōf* array number (of soldiers)]

reeve[2] (rēv), *v.t.,* **reeved** or **rove, reeving.** *Naut.* **1.** to pass (a rope, etc.) through a hole, ring, or the like. **2.** to fasten by placing through or around something. **3.** to pass a rope through (a block, etc.). [orig. obscure]

re·ëx·am·ine (rē′ĭg zăm′ĭn), *v.t.,* **-ined, -ining. 1.** to examine again. **2.** *Law.* to examine (a witness) again after a previous examination. Also, **re′-ex·am′ine.** —**re′ex·am′i·na′tion,** *n* —**re′ëx·am′in·er,** *n.*

re·ëx·port (*v.* rē′ĭks pôrt′, rē ĕks′pôrt; *n.* rē ĕks′pôrt), *v.t.* **1.** to export again, as imported goods. —*n.* **2.** a reëxporting. **3.** that which is reëxported. Also, **re′-export′.** —**re′ëx·por·ta′tion,** *n.*

ref., 1. referee. 2. reference. 3. referred. 4. reformation. 5. reformed.

re·face (rē fās′), *v.t.,* **-faced, -facing. 1.** to renew, restore, or repair the face or surface of (buildings, stone, etc.). **2.** to provide (a garment, etc.) with a new facing.

re·fect (rĭ fĕkt′), *v.t. Archaic.* to refresh, esp. with food or drink. [t. L: s. *refectus,* pp., restored]

re·fec·tion (rĭ fĕk′shən), *n.* **1.** refreshment, esp. with food or drink. **2.** a portion of food or drink; repast. [ME, t. L: s. *refectio*]

re·fec·to·ry (rĭ fĕk′tər ĭ), *n., pl.* **-ries.** a dining hall in a religious house, a college, or other institution. [t. ML: m.s. *refectōrium,* der. L *reficere* restore]

re·fer (rĭ fûr′), *v.,* **-ferred, -ferring.** —*v.t.* **1.** to direct the attention or thoughts of *the asterisk refers the reader*

to a footnote. **2.** to direct for information or for anything required: *to refer students to books on a subject.* **3.** to hand over or submit for information, consideration, decision, etc.: *to refer a cause to arbitration.* **4.** to assign to a class, period, etc.; regard as belonging or related. —*v.i.* **5.** to direct attention, as a reference mark does. **6.** to direct anyone for information, esp. about one's character, abilities, etc.: *to refer to a former employer.* **7.** to have relation; relate; apply. **8.** to have recourse or resort; turn, as for aid or information: *to refer to one's notes.* **9.** to direct a remark or mention; make reference or allusion, as a speaker or writer does. [ME *referre,* t. L: lit., carry back] —**ref·er·a·ble** (rĕf′ər ə bəl), **re·fer·ra·ble** (rĭ fûr′ə bəl), *adj.* —**re·fer′ral,** *n.* —**re·fer′rer,** *n.* —**Syn.** 4. attribute, ascribe. 9. advert, allude.

ref·er·ee (rĕf′ə rē′), *n., v.,* **-eed, -eeing.** —*n.* **1.** one to whom something is referred, esp. for decision or settlement; arbitrator; umpire. **2.** a judge in certain games having functions fixed by the rules. **3.** *Law.* **a.** a person selected by a court to take testimony in a case and return it to the court with recommendations as to the decision. **b.** a person selected to hear and decide controversies pending before administrative agencies. —*v.t.* **4.** to preside over as referee; act as referee in. —*v.i.* **5.** to act as referee. —**Syn.** 1. See **judge.**

ref·er·ence (rĕf′ər əns), *n.* **1.** act or fact of referring. **2.** direction of the attention: *marks of reference.* **3.** a mention; allusion. **4.** a direction in a book or writing to some book, passage, etc.: *to look up a reference.* **5.** a note indicating this. **6.** direction or a direction to some source of information. **7.** use or recourse for purposes of information: *a library for public reference.* **8.** a person to whom one refers for testimony as to one's character, abilities, etc. **9.** a written testimonial as to character, abilities, etc. **10.** relation, regard, or respect: *all persons, without reference to age.*

reference book, a publication consulted to identify certain facts or for background information, as an encyclopedia, dictionary, yearbook, atlas, etc.

ref·er·en·dum (rĕf′ə rĕn′dəm), *n., pl.* **-dums, -da** (-də). **1.** the principle or procedure of referring or submitting measures already passed on by the legislative body to the vote of the electorate for approval or rejection. **2.** an instance of this procedure. [t. L, gerund (or neut. gerundive) of *referre* refer]

ref·er·ent (rĕf′ər ənt), *n.* *Rhet., Semantics.* the object to which a term of discourse refers.

re·fill (*v.* rē fĭl′; *n.* rē′fĭl′), *v.t.* **1.** to fill again. —*n.* **2.** the material replacing a used-up product which was in an original purchase: *a refill for a lipstick.* —**re·fill′a·ble,** *adj.*

re·fi·nance (rē fī′năns, rē′fĭ năns′), *v.i., v.t.,* **-nanced, -nancing.** to sell securities in order to redeem (existing bonds or preferred stock).

re·fine (rĭ fīn′), *v.,* **-fined, -fining.** —*v.t.* **1.** to bring to a fine or a pure state; free from impurities: *to refine metal, sugar, petroleum, etc.* **2.** to purify from what is coarse, vulgar, or debasing; make elegant or cultured. **3.** to bring by purifying, as to a finer state or form. **4.** to make more fine, nice, subtle, or minutely precise. —*v.i.* **5.** to become pure. **6.** to become more fine, elegant, or polished. **7.** to make fine distinctions in thought or language. **8. refine on** or **upon,** a. to reason or discourse with subtlety. b. to improve (*on*) by superior fineness, excellence, etc. [f. RE- + FINE[1], v.] —**re·fin′er,** *n.*

re·fined (rĭ fīnd′), *adj.* **1.** imbued with or showing nice feeling, taste, etc.: *refined people.* **2.** freed or free from coarseness, vulgarity, etc.: *refined taste.* **3.** freed from impurities: *refined sugar.* **4.** subtle: *refined distinctions.* **5.** minutely precise; exact.

re·fine·ment (rĭ fīn′mənt), *n.* **1.** fineness of feeling, taste, etc. **2.** elegance of manners or language. **3.** an instance of refined feeling, manners, etc. **4.** act of refining. **5** state of being refined. **6.** improvement on something else. **7.** an instance or result of this. **8.** a subtle point or distinction. **9.** subtle reasoning. **10.** an improved, higher, or extreme form of something.

re·fin·er·y (rĭ fī′nə rĭ), *n., pl.* **-eries.** an establishment for refining something, as metal, sugar, or petroleum.

re·fit (rē fĭt′), *v.,* **-fitted, -fitting,** *n.* —*v.t.* **1.** to fit, prepare, or equip again. —*v.i.* **2.** to renew supplies or equipment. **3.** to get refitted. —*n.* **4.** act of refitting.

refl., 1. reflection. 2. reflective. 3. reflex. 4. reflexive.

re·flect (rĭ flĕkt′), *v.t.* **1.** to cast back (light, heat, sound, etc.) after incidence. **2.** to give back or show an image of; mirror. **3.** to throw or cast back; cause to return or rebound. **4.** to reproduce; show: *followers reflecting the views of the leader.* **5.** to serve to cast or bring (credit, discredit, etc.). **6.** to think carefully; meditate on. —*v.i.* **7.** to be turned or cast back, as light. **8.** to cast back light, heat, etc. **9.** to be reflected or mirrored. **10.** to give back or show an image. **11.** to serve or tend to bring reproach or discredit. **12.** to serve to give a particular aspect or impression: *his speech reflects no credit on his candidacy.* **13.** to think, ponder, or meditate. [late ME, t. L: s. *reflectere* bend

re′·ë·lect′	re·ëm′pha·size′	re′·ën·gage′	re′·ën·tab′lish·ment
re′·ë·lec′tion	re′·ën·act′	re′·ën·gage′ment	re′·ëx·am′i·na′tion
re′·ëm·bark′	re′·ën·ac′tion	re′·ën·grave′	re′·ëx·hib′it
re′·ë·merge′	re′·ën·act′ment	re′·ën·list′	re·fash′ion
re′·ë·mer′gence	re′·ën·cour′age	re′·ën·list′ment	re·fas′ten
re′·ëm′i·grate′	re′·ën·cour′age·ment	re′·ës·tab′lish	re·fer′ti·lize′

back] —**Syn. 6.** ruminate, ponder, deliberate, muse, consider, cogitate, contemplate. See **study.**

reflecting telescope, a telescope using a mirror instead of a lens to form the principal image.

re·flec·tion (rĭ flĕk′shən), n.   **1.** act of reflecting. **2.** state of being reflected. **3.** an image; representation; counterpart. **4.** a fixing of the thoughts on something; careful consideration. **5.** a thought occurring in consideration or meditation. **6.** an unfavorable remark or observation. **7.** the casting of some imputation or reproach. **8.** *Physics.* **a.** the casting back, or the change of direction, of light, heat, sound, etc., after striking a surface. **b.** something so reflected, as heat, or esp. light. **9.** reflexion. —**re·flec′tion·al,** adj. —**Syn. 4.** meditation, rumination, deliberation, cogitation, study. **6.** imputation, aspersion.

re·flec·tive (rĭ flĕk′tĭv), adj. **1.** that reflects; reflecting. **2.** of or pertaining to reflection. **3.** cast by reflection. **4.** given to or concerned with meditation. —**re·flec′tive·ly,** adv. —**re·flec′tive·ness, re·flec·tiv·i·ty** (rē′flĕk tĭv′ə tĭ), n. —**Syn. 4.** See **pensive.**

re·flec·tor (rĭ flĕk′tər), n. **1.** one who or that which reflects. **2.** a body, surface, or device that reflects light, heat, sound, or the like. **3.** a reflecting telescope.

re·flet (rə flĕ′), n. an effect of luster, color, or iridescence on an object (as a piece of pottery) due to reflection of light. [F: reflection]

re·flex (adj., n. rē′flĕks; v. rĭ flĕks′), adj. **1.** *Physiol.* noting or pertaining to an involuntary response in which an impulse evoked by a stimulus is transmitted along an afferent nerve to a nerve center, and from there through one or more synapses to an efferent nerve, calling into play muscular or other activity. **2.** occurring in reaction; responsive. **3.** designating a radio apparatus in which the same part performs two functions, as in a **reflex klystron,** in which one resonator acts as buncher and catcher. **4.** cast back; reflected, as light, etc. **5.** bent or turned back. —n. **6.** *Physiol.* a reflex action or movement. **7.** *Psychol.* an immediate response to a stimulus, inborn and often unaccompanied by consciousness, as eyeblink, perspiring, sneezing, etc. **8.** the reflection or image of an object, as exhibited by a mirror or the like. **9.** a reproduction as if in a mirror. **10.** a copy; adaptation. **11.** *Rare.* reflected light, color, etc. **12.** a reflex radio receiving apparatus or set. —v.t. **13.** to subject to a reflex process. **14.** to bend, turn, or fold back. **15.** to arrange in reflex system. [t. L: s. *reflexus,* pp., reflected, bent back]

reflex angle, *Geom.* an angle greater than a straight angle.

re·flex·ion (rĭ flĕk′shən), n. **1.** *Chiefly Anat.* the bending or folding back of a thing upon itself. **2.** reflection.

re·flex·ive (rĭ flĕk′sĭv), adj. *Gram.* **1.** (of a verb) having identical subject and object, as *shave* in *he shaved himself.* **2.** (of a pronoun) indicating identity of object with subject, as *himself* in the example above. —n. **3.** a reflexive verb or pronoun, as *himself* in *he deceived himself.* —**re·flex′ive·ly,** adv. —**re·flex′ive·ness, re·flex·iv·i·ty** (rē′flĕk sĭv′ə tĭ), n.

ref·lu·ent (rĕf′lŏŏ ənt), adj. flowing back; ebbing, as the waters of a tide. [ME, t. L: s. *refluens,* ppr.] —**ref′lu·ence,** n.

re·flux (rē′flŭks′), n. a flowing back; ebb. [f. RE- + FLUX. Cf. F *reflux*]

re·for·est (rē fôr′ĭst, -fŏr′-), v.t. to replant with forest trees. —**re′for·est·a′tion,** n.

re·form¹ (rĭ fôrm′), n. **1.** the improvement or amendment of what is wrong, corrupt, etc.: *social reform.* **2.** an instance of this. **3.** the amendment of conduct, etc. —v.t. **4.** to restore to a former and better state; improve by alteration, substitution, abolition, etc. **5.** to cause (a person) to abandon wrong or evil ways of life or conduct. **6.** to put an end to (abuses, disorders, etc.). —v.i. **7.** to abandon evil conduct or error. [ME *reforme,* t. L: m. *reformāre*] —**re·form′a·ble,** adj. —**re·form′a·tive,** adj. —**re·form′er,** n. —**Syn. 4.** better, rectify, correct.

re·form² (rē fôrm′), v.t., v.i. to form again.

ref·or·ma·tion (rĕf′ər mā′shən), n. **1.** act of reforming. **2.** state of being reformed. **3.** (*cap.*) the great religious movement in the 16th century which had for its object the reform of the Western Catholic Church, and which led to the establishment of the Protestant churches. —**ref′or·ma′tion·al,** adj. —**Syn. 1.** improvement, betterment, correction.

re·form·a·to·ry (rĭ fôr′mə tōr′ĭ), adj., n., pl. -ries. —adj. **1.** serving or designed to reform: *reformatory schools.* —n. **2.** Also, **reform school.** a penal institution for the reformation of young offenders.

re·formed (rĭ fôrmd′), adj. **1.** amended by removal of faults, abuses, etc. **2.** improved in conduct, morals, etc. **3.** (*cap.*) noting or pertaining to Protestant churches, esp. Calvinist as distinguished from Lutheran.

re·fract (rĭ frăkt′), v.t. **1.** to subject to refraction. **2.** to determine the refractive condition of (an eye, a lens). [t. L: s. *refractus,* pp., broken up]

refracting telescope, a telescope consisting essentially of a lens for forming an image and an eyepiece for viewing it. See **telescope** (def. 1).

re·frac·tion (rĭ frăk′shən), n. **1.** *Physics.* the change of direction of a ray of light, heat, or the like, in passing obliquely from one medium into another in which its speed is different. **2.** *Optics.* **a.** the ability of the eye to refract light which enters it so as to form an image on the retina. **b.** the determining of the refractive condition of the eye. —**re·frac′tion·al,** adj.

re·frac·tive (rĭ frăk′tĭv), adj. **1.** of or pertaining to refraction. **2.** having power to refract. **3.** refracting. —**re·frac′tive·ly,** adv. —**re·frac′tive·ness, re·frac·tiv·i·ty** (rē′frăk tĭv′ə tĭ), n.

refractive index, the specific refractive power of a substance.

re·frac·tom·e·ter (rē′frăk tŏm′ə tər), n. an instrument for measuring or determining refraction. [f. REFRACT + -(o)METER]

re·frac·tor (rĭ frăk′tər), n. **1.** something that refracts. **2.** a refracting telescope.

re·frac·to·ry (rĭ frăk′tə rĭ), adj., n., pl. -ries. —adj. **1.** stubborn; unmanageable: *a refractory child.* **2.** resisting ordinary methods of treatment. **3.** difficult to fuse, reduce, or work, as an ore or metal. —n. **4.** a material having the ability to retain its physical shape and chemical identity when subjected to high temperatures. **5.** (pl.) bricks of various shapes used in lining furnaces. **6.** *Physiol.* a momentary state of reduced excitability following a response: *the refractory period of a nerve.* —**re·frac′to·ri·ly,** adv. —**re·frac′to·ri·ness,** n.

re·frain¹ (rĭ frān′), v.i. **1.** to keep oneself from. —v.t. **2.** *Rare.* to curb. [ME *refreyne(n),* t. OF: m. *refrener,* t. L: m. *refrēnāre* to bridle] —**re·frain′er,** n.

re·frain² (rĭ frān′), n. **1.** a phrase or verse recurring at intervals in a song or poem, esp at the end of each stanza; chorus. **2.** a musical setting for the refrain of a poem. [ME *refreyne,* t. OF: m. *refrain,* der. *refraindre,* g. VL *refrangere,* r. L *refringere* refract]

re·fran·gi·ble (rĭ frăn′jə bəl), adj. capable of being refracted, as rays of light. [f. RE- + s. L *frangere* break + -IBLE] —**re·fran′gi·ble·ness, re·fran′gi·bil·i·ty,** n.

re·fresh (rĭ frĕsh′), v.t. **1.** to reinvigorate by rest, food etc. (often reflexive). **2.** to stimulate (the memory). **3.** to make fresh again; reinvigorate or cheer (a person, the mind, spirits, etc.). **4.** to freshen in appearance, color, etc., as by a restorative. —v.i. **5.** to take refreshment, esp. food or drink. **6.** to become fresh or vigorous again; revive. [ME, t. OF: m.s. *refrescher,* der. *re-* RE- + *fresche* FRESH] —**re·fresh′ing,** adj. —**re·fresh′ing·ly,** adv.

re·fresh·er (rĭ frĕsh′ər), adj. **1.** serving as a review of material previously studied: *a refresher course.* —n., **2.** one who or that which refreshes. **3.** *Brit.* an interim fee paid to a lawyer.

re·fresh·ment (rĭ frĕsh′mənt), n. **1.** that which refreshes, esp. food or drink. **2.** (pl.) articles or portions of food or drink, esp. for a light meal. **3.** act of refreshing. **4.** state of being refreshed.

re·frig·er·ant (rĭ frĭj′ər ənt), adj. **1.** refrigerating; cooling. **2.** reducing bodily heat or fever. —n. **3.** a refrigerant agent, as in a drug. **4.** a liquid capable of vaporizing at a low temperature, as ammonia, used in mechanical refrigeration. **5.** a cooling substance, as ice, solid carbon dioxide, etc., used in a refrigerator.

re·frig·er·ate (rĭ frĭj′ə rāt′), v.t., -ated, -ating. **1.** to make or keep cold or cool. **2.** to freeze or near-freeze (food, etc.) for preservation. [t. L: m.s. *refrigerātus,* pp., made cool again] —**re·frig′er·a·tive, re·frig·er·a·to·ry** (rĭ frĭj′ər ə tōr′ĭ), adj.

re·frig·er·a·tion (rĭ frĭj′ə rā′shən), n. **1.** the process of producing low temperatures, usually throughout an appreciable volume. **2.** the resulting state.

re·frig·er·a·tor (rĭ frĭj′ə rā′tər), n. **1.** a box, room, or cabinet in which food, drink, etc., are kept cool, as by means of ice or mechanical refrigeration. **2.** the element of a refrigerating system consisting of the space or medium to be cooled.

re·frin·gent (rĭ frĭn′jənt), adj. refracting; refractive. [t. L: s. *refringens,* ppr.]

reft (rĕft), v. pt. and pp. of **reave.**

re·fu·el (rē fū′əl), v., -eled, -eling or (esp. Brit.) -elled, -elling. —v.t. **1.** to supply again with fuel: *to refuel an airplane.* —v.i. **2.** to take on a fresh supply of fuel: *they refueled at Paris and flew on.*

ref·uge (rĕf′ūj), n., v., -uged, -uging. —n. **1.** shelter or protection from danger, trouble, etc.: *to take refuge from a storm.* **2.** a place of shelter, protection, or safety. **3.** anything to which one has recourse for aid, relief, or escape. **4.** *Brit.* a platform in the center of a street for the use of pedestrians in crossing; island (def. 5). —v.t. **5.** *Archaic.* to afford refuge to. —v.i. **6.** *Archaic.* to take refuge. [ME, t. OF, t. L: m.s. *refugium*] —**Syn. 2.** asylum, retreat, sanctuary.

ref·u·gee (rĕf′yŏŏ jē′), n. one who flees for refuge or safety. esp. to a foreign country, as in time of political upheaval, war, etc. [t. F: m. *refugié,* pp. of *refugier* take refuge, der. *refuge* REFUGE]

S, Q
P
Q R L
Refraction
SP, Ray of light;
SPL. Original direction;
SPR. Refracted ray;
QQ. Perpendicular

re·flow′	re·forge′	re·for′ti·fy	re·frac′ture
re·fold′	re′for·ti·fi·ca′tion	re·for′ward	re·frame′

re·ful·gent (rǐ fŭl′jənt), *adj.* shining; radiant; glowing. [t. L: s. *refulgens*, ppr.] —**re·ful′gence**, *n.* —**re·ful′gent·ly**, *adv.*

re·fund¹ (*v.* rǐ fŭnd′; *n.* rē′fŭnd), *v.t.* **1.** to give back or restore (esp. money); repay. **2.** to make repayment to; reimburse. —*v.i.* **3.** to make repayment. —*n.* **4.** a repayment. [ME, t. L: s. *refundere*, lit., pour back]

re·fund² (rē fŭnd′), *v.t.* **1.** to fund anew. **2.** *Finance.* **a.** to meet (a matured debt structure) by new borrowing, esp. through issuance of bonds. **b.** to replace (an old issue) with a new, esp. with one bearing a lower rate of interest. [f. RE- + FUND]

re·fur·bish (rē fûr′bǐsh), *v.t.* to furbish again; renovate; polish up again; brighten: *the theater lobby was fully refurbished.*

re·fus·al (rǐ fū′zəl), *n.* **1.** act of refusing. **2.** priority in refusing or taking something; option.

re·fuse¹ (rǐ fūz′), *v.*, -**fused**, -**fusing.** —*v.t.* **1.** to decline to accept (something offered): *to refuse an office.* **2.** to decline to give; deny (a request, demand, etc.). **3.** to express a determination not (to do something): *to refuse to discuss the question.* **4.** to decline to submit to. **5.** (of a horse) to decline to leap over (a fence, water, etc.). **6.** *Mil.* to bend or curve back (the flank units of a military force) so that they face generally to the flank rather than the front. **7.** *Obs.* to renounce. —*v.i.* **8.** to decline acceptance, consent, or compliance. [ME, t. OF: m. *refuser*, g. VL *refusāre*, der. L *refusus*, pp., lit., poured back] —**re·fus′er**, *n.*
—**Syn. 1.** REFUSE, DECLINE, REJECT, SPURN all imply nonacceptance of something. To DECLINE is milder and more courteous than to REFUSE, which is direct and often emphatic in expressing determination not to accept what is offered or proposed: *to refuse a bribe, to decline an invitation.* To REJECT is even more positive and definite than refuse: *to reject a suitor.* To SPURN is to reject with scorn: *to spurn a bribe.* —Ant. 1. accept, welcome.

ref·use² (rĕf′ūs), *n.* **1.** that which is discarded as worthless or useless; rubbish. —*adj.* **2.** rejected as worthless; discarded: *refuse matter.* [ME, t. OF: m. *refus*, pp., refused. See REFUSE¹]

ref·u·ta·tion (rĕf′yŏŏ tā′shən), *n.* act of refuting a statement, charge, etc.; disproof. Also, **re·fut·al** (rǐ fū′təl).

re·fute (rǐ fūt′), *v.t.*, -**futed**, -**futing.** **1.** to prove to be false or erroneous, as an opinion, charge, etc. **2.** to prove (a person) to be in error. [t. L: m.s. *refūtāre* repel, refute] —**re·fut′a·ble** (rĕf′yə təl, rǐ fū′tə-), *adj.* —**ref′u·ta·bly**, *adv.* —**re·fut′er**, *n.* —**Syn. 1.** disprove, rebut.

reg., **1.** regiment. **2.** register. **3.** registered. **4.** registrar. **5.** registry. **6.** regular. **7.** regularly. **8.** regulation.

re·gain (rǐ gān′), *v.t.* **1.** to get again; recover. **2.** to succeed in reaching again; get back to: *to regain the shore.* —**re·gain′er**, *n.*

re·gal (rē′gəl), *adj.* **1.** of or pertaining to a king; royal: *the regal power.* **2.** befitting or resembling a king. **3.** stately; splendid. [ME, t. L: s. *rēgālis*] —**re′gal·ly**, *adv.* —**Syn. 2.** See **kingly.**

re·gale (rǐ gāl′), *v.*, -**galed**, -**galing**, *n.* —*v.t.* **1.** to entertain agreeably; delight. **2.** to entertain with choice food or drink. —*v.i.* **3.** to feast. —*n. Obs.* **4.** a choice feast. **5.** a choice article of food or drink. **6.** refreshment. [t. F: s. *régaler*, der. OF *regale* feast, der. *gale* pleasure, t. MD: m. *wale* wealth] —**re·gale′ment**, *n.*

re·ga·li·a (rǐ gā′lǐ ə, -gāl′yə), *n.pl.* **1.** the rights and privileges of a king. **2.** the ensigns or emblems of royalty, as the crown, scepter, etc. **3.** the decorations or insignia of any office or order. [t. ML, prop. neut. pl. of L *rēgālis* regal]

re·gal·i·ty (rē gǎl′ə tǐ), *n.*, *pl.* -**ties.** **1.** royalty, sovereignty, or kingship. **2.** a right or privilege pertaining to a king. **3.** a kingdom. **4.** (in Scotland) **a.** territorial jurisdiction of a royal nature formerly conferred by the king. **b.** a territory subject to such jurisdiction.

re·gard (rǐ gärd′), *v.t.* **1.** to look upon or think of with a particular feeling: *to regard a person with favor.* **2.** to have or show respect or concern for. **3.** to think highly of. **4.** to take into account; consider. **5.** to look at; observe. **6.** to relate to; concern. **7.** *Obs.* to show attention to; guard. —*v.i.* **8.** to pay attention. **9.** to look or gaze. —*n.* **10.** reference; relation: *to err in regard to facts.* **11.** a point or particular: *quite satisfactory in this regard.* **12.** thought; attention; concern. **13.** look; gaze. **14.** respect; deference: *due regard to authority.* **15.** kindly feeling; liking. **16.** (*pl.*) sentiments of esteem or affection: *give them my regards.* **17.** *Obs.* aspect. [ME *regard*, n., t. F, der. *regarder*, v., f. re- RE- + *garder* GUARD] —**Syn. 3.** esteem, respect.

re·gard·ant (rǐ gär′dənt), *adj. Her.* looking backward. [t. F, ppr. of *regarder* REGARD]

re·gard·ful (rǐ gärd′fəl), *adj.* **1.** observant; attentive; heedful (often fol. by *of*). **2.** considerate or thoughtful; respectful. —**re·gard′ful·ly**, *adv.* —**re·gard′ful·ness**, *n.*

re·gard·ing (rǐ gär′dǐng), *prep.* with regard to; respecting; concerning: *he knew nothing regarding the lost watch.*

re·gard·less (rǐ gärd′lǐs), *adj.* **1.** having or showing no regard; heedless; unmindful; careless (often fol. by

of). **2.** *Colloq.* without regard to expense, danger, etc. —*adv.* **3.** anyway. —**re·gard′less·ly**, *adv.* —**re·gard′less·ness**, *n.* —**Syn. 1.** inattentive, negligent, neglectful, indifferent.

re·gat·ta (rǐ gǎt′ə), *n.* **1.** a boat race, as of rowboats, yachts, or other vessels. **2.** an organized series of such races. **3.** (orig.) a gondola race in Venice. [t. It. (Venetian): m. *regata*, der. *regatar* compete]

re·ge·late (rē′jə lāt′, rē′jə lāt′), *v.i.*, -**lated**, -**lating.** to freeze together, as two pieces of ice pressed together near the freezing point. [t. L: m.s. *regelātus*] —**re′ge·la′tion**, *n.*

re·gen·cy (rē′jən sǐ), *n.*, *pl.* -**cies**, *adj.* —*n.* **1.** the office, jurisdiction, or control of a regent or body of regents exercising the ruling power during the minority, absence, or disability of a sovereign. **2.** a body of regents. **3.** a government consisting of regents. **4.** a territory under the control of a regent or regents. **5.** the term of office of a regent. **6.** (*cap.*) *Brit. Hist.* the period (1811–20) during which George (later, George IV) was regent. **7.** (*cap.*) *Fr. Hist.* the period (1715–23) during which Philip, Duke of Orleans, was regent, in the minority of Louis XV. **8.** the office or function of a regent or ruler. —*adj.* **9.** pertaining to a regency. **10.** (*cap.*) of or pertaining to the Regency in French or English history.

re·gen·er·a·cy (rǐ jĕn′ər ə sǐ), *n.* regenerate state.

re·gen·er·ate (*v.* rǐ jĕn′ə rāt′; *adj.* rǐ jĕn′ər ǐt), *v.*, -**ated**, -**ating**, *adj.* —*v.t.* **1.** to effect a complete moral reform in. **2.** to re-create, reconstitute, or make over, esp. in a better form or condition. **3.** to generate or produce anew; bring into existence again. **4.** *Physics.* to restore (a substance) periodically to a favorable thermal state or physical condition from which it later departs while performing a desired function. **5.** *Electronics.* to magnify the amplification of, by relaying part of the output circuit power into the input circuit. **6.** *Theol.* to cause to be born again spiritually. —*v.i.* **7.** to come into existence or be formed again. **8.** to reform; become regenerate. **9.** to produce a regenerative effect. —*adj.* **10.** reconstituted or made over in a better form. **11.** reformed. **12.** *Theol.* born again spiritually. [late ME, t. L: m.s. *regenerātus*, pp., made over, produced anew]

re·gen·er·a·tion (rǐ jĕn′ə rā′shən), *n.* **1.** act of regenerating. **2.** state of being regenerated. **3.** *Electronics.* a feedback process in which energy fed back to the grid circuit reinforces the input. **4.** *Embryol.* the restitution of a lost part through growth and differentiation of residual blastemic cell. **5.** *Theol.* spiritual rebirth.

re·gen·er·a·tive (rǐ jĕn′ə rā′tǐv), *adj.* **1.** pertaining to regeneration. **2.** tending to regenerate. —**re·gen′er·a·tive·ly**, *adv.*

re·gen·er·a·tor (rǐ jĕn′ə rā′tər), *n.* **1.** one who or that which regenerates. **2.** *Mech.* (in a regenerative furnace, etc.) the device for heating the incoming air or fuel gas.

Re·gens·burg (rā′gəns bŏŏrкн), *n.* a city in West Germany, in Bavaria: battle, 1809. 124,000 (est. 1955). Also, **Ratisbon.**

re·gent (rē′jənt), *n.* **1.** one who exercises the ruling power in a kingdom during the minority or other disability of the sovereign. **2.** *U.S.* a member of the governing board of certain universities and other institutions. **3.** *U.S.* a university officer who exercises a general supervision over the conduct and welfare of the students. **4.** (in certain Catholic universities) a member of the religious order who is associated in the administration of a school or college with a layman who is its dean or director. **5.** (in old universities) a member of certain governing and teaching bodies. **6.** *Rare.* a ruler or governor. —*adj.* **7.** acting as regent of a country. **8.** exercising vicarious ruling authority: *a prince regent.* **9.** holding the position of a regent in a university. **10.** *Rare.* ruling. [ME, t. L: s. *regens*, ppr., ruling] —**re′gent·ship′**, *n.*

Reg·gio Ca·la·bri·a (rĕd′jô kä lä′brē ä′), a seaport in S Italy, on the Strait of Messina: almost totally destroyed by an earthquake, 1908. 144,000 (est. 1954).

Reg·gio E·mi·lia (rĕd′jô ĕ mē′lyä), a city in N Italy. 109,000 (est. 1954).

reg·i·cide¹ (rĕj′ə sīd′), *n.* one who kills a king; one responsible for the death of a king (esp. applied to the judges who condemned Charles I of England to death). [f. regi- (comb. form. repr. L *rex* king) + -CIDE¹] —**reg′i·cid′al**, *adj.*

reg·i·cide² (rĕj′ə sīd′), *n.* the killing of a king. [f. regi- (comb. form repr. L *rex* king) + -CIDE²]

re·gime (rā zhēm′, rǐ-), *n.* **1.** a mode or system of rule or government. **2.** a ruling or prevailing system. **3.** *Med.* regimen. Also, **ré·gime′.** [t. F, t. L: m. *regimen* direction, government]

reg·i·men (rĕj′ə mən′, -mən), *n.* **1.** *Med.* a regulated course of diet, exercise, or manner of living, intended to preserve or restore health or to attain some result. **2.** rule or government. **3.** a particular form or system of government. **4.** a prevailing system. **5.** *Gram. Obsolesc.* government: *the regimen of the verb by its subject.* [ME, t. L.]

reg·i·ment (*n.* rĕj′ə mənt; *v.* rĕj′ə mĕnt′), *n.* **1.** *Mil.* a unit of ground forces, consisting of two or more

| re·fur′nish | re·gam′ble | re·gear′ | re′ger·mi·na′tion |
| re·gal′van·ize′ | re·gath′er | re·ger′mi·nate′ | re·gild′ |

battalions, a headquarters unit, and certain supporting units. **2.** *Obs.* government. —*v.t.* **3.** to form into a regiment or regiments. **4.** to assign to a regiment or group. **5.** to form into an organized body or group; organize or systematize. **6.** to group together and treat in a uniform manner; subject to strict discipline. [ME, t. LL: s. *regimentum* rule] —**reg·i·men·ta′tion,** *n.*

re·gi·men·tal (rĕj′ə·mĕn′təl), *adj.* **1.** of or pertaining to a regiment. —*n.* **2.** *(pl.)* the uniform of a regiment.

re·gi·na (rĭ·jī′nə), *n.* Latin. queen.

Re·gi·na (rĭ·jī′nə), *n.* a city in SW Canada: the capital of Saskatchewan. 71,319 (1951).

re·gion (rē′jən), *n.* **1.** any more or less extensive, continuous part of a surface or space. **2.** a part of the earth's surface (land or sea) of considerable and usually indefinite extent: *tropical regions.* **3.** a district without respect to boundaries or extent. **4.** a part or division of the universe, as the heavens: *celestial regions.* **5.** an administrative division of a city or territory. **6.** *Zoögeog.* a large faunal area of the earth's surface, sometimes one regarded as a division of a larger area. **7.** *Anat.* a place in, or a division of, the body or a part of the body: *the abdominal region.* [ME, t. L: s. *regio* line, district]

re·gion·al (rē′jən·əl), *adj.* **1.** of or pertaining to a region of considerable extent; not merely local. **2.** of or pertaining to a particular region, district, area, or part; sectional; local. —**re′gion·al·ly,** *adv.*

reg·is·ter (rĕj′ĭs·tər), *n.* **1.** a book in which entries of acts, occurrences, names, or the like are made for record. **2.** any list of such entries; a record of acts, occurrences, etc. **3.** an entry in such a book, record, or list. **4.** *Com.* an official document issued to a ship as evidence of its nationality, etc. **5.** registration or registry. **6.** a mechanical device by which certain data are automatically recorded. **7.** *Music.* **a.** the compass or range of a voice or an instrument. **b.** a particular series of tones, esp. of the human voice, produced in the same way and having the same quality: *the head register.* **c.** (in an organ) a stop. **8.** a contrivance for regulating the passage of warm air, or the like, esp. a closable perforated plate in a duct of a heating or ventilating system. **9.** *Photog.* proper relationship between two plane surfaces in photography, as corresponding plates in photoengraving, etc. **10.** *Print., etc.* **a.** a precise adjustment or correspondence, as of lines, columns, etc., esp. on the two sides of a leaf. **b.** correct relation or exact superimposition, as of colors in color printing. —*v.t.* **11.** to enter or have entered formally in a register. **12.** to cause to be recorded for purposes of safety, as letters or packages at a post office, for security in transmission, by payment of a special fee. **13.** to indicate by a record, as instruments do. **14.** to indicate or show, as on a scale. **15.** *Print., etc.* to adjust so as to secure exact correspondence; cause to be in register. **16.** *Mil.* to adjust (fire) on a known point. **17.** to show (surprise, joy, anger, etc.), as by facial expression or by actions. —*v.i.* **18.** to enter one's name, or cause it to be entered, in a register; enroll. **19.** to apply for and obtain inclusion of one's name on the list of voters. **20.** *Print., etc.* to be in register. **21.** to show surprise, joy, etc. [ME *registre,* t. ML: m. *registrum,* for *regestum,* neut. of L *regestus,* pp., recorded] —**reg′is·ter·er,** *n.* —**reg′is·tra·ble,** *adj.* —**Syn. 2.** roll, roster, catalogue.

reg·is·tered (rĕj′ĭs·tərd), *adj.* **1.** recorded, as in a register or book; enrolled. **2.** *Com.* officially listing the owner's name with the issuing corporation and suitably inscribing the certificate, as with bonds to evidence title. **3.** officially or legally certified by a government officer or board: *a registered patent.* **4.** denoting cattle, horses, dogs, etc., having pedigrees verified and filed by authorized associations of breeders.

register of wills, (in some States) the official charged with the probate of wills or with the keeping of the records of the probate court.

reg·is·trar (rĕj′ĭs·trär′, rĕj′ĭs·trär′), *n.* one who keeps a record; an official recorder. [f. REGISTER, v. + -AR²]

reg·is·tra·tion (rĕj′ĭs·trā′shən), *n.* **1.** act of registering. **2.** an instance of this. **3.** an entry in a register. **4.** the group or number registered.

reg·is·try (rĕj′ĭs·trĭ), *n., pl.* **-tries. 1.** act of registering; registration. **2.** a place where a register is kept; an office of registration. **3.** a register. **4.** state of being registered.

registry office, Brit. **1.** an office where civil marriages are performed. **2.** an employment bureau.

re·gi·us (rē′jĭ·əs), *adj.* **1.** of or belonging to a king. **2.** royal (applied to professors in British universities who hold chairs founded by the sovereign). [t. L]

reg·let (rĕg′lĭt), *n.* **1.** *Archit.* a narrow, flat molding. **2.** *Print.* **a.** a thin strip, usually of wood, less than type-high, used to produce a blank in or about a page of type. **b.** such strips collectively. [t. F, dim. of *regle,* g. L *regula* rule]

reg·ma (rĕg′mə), *n., pl.* **-mata** (-mə·tə). *Bot.* a dry fruit consisting of three or more carpels which separate from the axis at maturity. [NL, t. Gk.: m. *rhēgma* rupture, abscess]

reg·nal (rĕg′nəl), *adj.* of or pertaining to reigning, sovereignty, or a reign: *the second regnal year.* [t. ML: s. *regnālis,* der. L *regnum* kingdom]

reg·nant (rĕg′nənt), *adj.* **1.** reigning; ruling: *a queen regnant.* **2.** exercising sway or influence; predominant. **3.** prevalent; widespread. [t. L: s. *regnans,* ppr., ruling] —**reg·nan·cy** (rĕg′nən·sĭ), *n.*

reg·nat po·pu·lus (rĕg′năt pŏp′yə·ləs), *Latin.* the people rule (motto of Arkansas).

reg·o·lith (rĕg′ə·lĭth), *n.* *Phys. Geog.* mantle rock.

re·gorge (rĭ·gôrj′), *v.,* **-gorged, -gorging.** —*v.t.* **1.** to disgorge; cast up again. —*v.i.* **2.** to rush back again; gush: *the waters regorged.* [t. F: m.s. *regorger,* or f. RE- + GORGE, v., after L *regurgitāre* regurgitate]

re·grate (rĭ·grāt′), *v.t.* **-grated, -grating. 1.** to buy up (grain, provisions, etc.) in order to sell again at a profit in or near the same market. **2.** to sell again (commodities so bought); retail. [ME, t. OF: m. *re·grater,* ? der. *grater* GRATE²] —**re·grat′er,** *n.*

re·gress (*v.* rĭ·grĕs′; *n.* rē′grĕs), *v.i.* **1.** to move in a backward direction; go back. —*n.* **2.** act of going back; return. **3.** backward movement or course; retrogression. [ME, t.L: s. *regressus* a going back] —**re·gres′sive,** *adj.* —**re·gres′sive·ly,** *adv.* —**re·gres′sor,** *n.*

re·gres·sion (rĭ·grĕsh′ən), *n.* **1.** act of going back; return; backward movement. **2.** retrogradation; retrogression. **3.** *Biol.* reversion to an earlier or less advanced state or form or to a common or general type. **4.** *Pyscho·anal.* the reversion to a chronologically earlier or less adapted pattern of behavior and feeling.

regression coefficient, *Statistics.* a constant by which a given value of a variable may be multiplied to obtain the best estimate of the value of a second variable corresponding to this value.

re·gret (rĭ·grĕt′), *v.,* **-gretted, -gretting,** *n.* —*v.t.* **1.** to feel sorry about (anything disappointing, unpleasant, etc.). **2.** to think of with a sense of loss: *to regret one's vanished youth.* —*n.* **3.** a sense of loss, disappointment, dissatisfaction, etc. **4.** the feeling of being sorry for some fault, act, omission, etc., of one's own. **5.** *(pl.)* feelings of sorrow over what is lost, gone, done, etc. **6.** *(pl. or sing.)* a polite and formal expression of regretful feelings. [ME *regrette,* t. OF: m. *regretter,* ? der. M grete GREET²] —**re·gret′ta·ble,** *adj.* —**re·gret′ta·bly,** *adv.* —**re·gret′ter,** *n.*

—**Syn. 2.** deplore, lament. **4.** REGRET, PENITENCE, REMORSE imply a sense of sorrow about events in the past, usually wrongs committed or errors made. REGRET is distress of mind, sorrow for what has been done: *to have no regrets.* PENITENCE implies a sense of sin or misdoing, a feeling of contrition and determination not to sin again: *a humble sense of penitence.* REMORSE implies pangs, qualms of conscience, a sense of guilt, regret, and repentance for sins committed, wrongs done, or duty not performed: *a deep sense of remorse.*

re·gret·ful (rĭ·grĕt′fəl), *adj.* full of regret; sorrowful because of what is lost, gone, done. —**re·gret′ful·ly,** *adv.* —**re·gret′ful·ness,** *n.*

Regt., 1. regent. **2.** regiment.

reg·u·lar (rĕg′yə·lər), *adj.* **1.** usual; normal; customary: *to put something in its regular place.* **2.** conforming in form or arrangement; symmetrical: *regular teeth.* **3.** characterized by fixed principle, uniform procedure, etc.: *regular breathing.* **4.** recurring at fixed times; periodic: *regular meals.* **5.** adhering to rule or procedure: *to be regular in one's diet.* **6.** observing fixed times or habits: *regular customer.* **7.** orderly; well-ordered: *a regular life.* **8.** conforming to some accepted rule, discipline, etc. **9.** carried out in accordance with an accepted principle; formally correct. **10.** properly qualified for or engaged in an occupation. **11.** *Colloq.* complete; thorough: *a regular rascal.* **12.** (of a flower) having the members of each of its floral circles or whorls normally alike in form and size. **13.** *Gram.* conforming to the most prevalent pattern of formation, inflection, construction, etc. **14.** *Math.* governed by one law throughout: *a regular polygon has all its angles and sides equal.* **15.** *Mil.* denoting or belonging to the permanently organized or standing army of a state. **16.** *Internat. Law.* denoting soldiers recognized as legitimate combatants in warfare. **17.** *Eccles.* subject to a religious rule, or belonging to a religious or monastic order (opposed to *secular*): *regular clergy.* **18.** *U.S. Pol.* of, pertaining to, or selected by the recognized agents of a political party: *the regular ticket.* —*n.* **19.** *Eccles.* a member of a duly constituted religious order under a rule. **20.** *Mil.* a regular soldier. **21.** *U.S. Pol.* a party member who faithfully stands by his party. [t. L: s. *rēgulāris;* r. ME *reguler,* t. OF] —**reg′u·lar′i·ty,** *n.*

Regular Army, *U.S.* the permanent army maintained in peace as well as in war; the standing army: one of the major components of the Army of the United States.

reg·u·lar·ize (rĕg′yə·lə·rīz′), *v.t.* **-ized, -izing.** to make regular. —**reg′u·lar·i·za′tion,** *n.*

reg·u·lar·ly (rĕg′yə·lər·lĭ), *adv.* **1.** at regular times or intervals. **2.** according to plan, custom, etc.

reg·u·late (rĕg′yə·lāt′), *v.t.,* **-lated, -lating. 1.** to control or direct by rule, principle, method, etc. **2.** to adjust to some standard or requirement, as amount, degree, etc.: *to regulate the temperature.* **3.** to adjust so as to ensure accuracy of operation: *to regulate a watch.* **4.** to put in good order: *to regulate the digestion.* [t. LL:

re·gird′	**re·glo′ri·fy′**	**re·grab′**	**re·grant′**
re·glaze′	**re·glue′**	**re·grade′**	**re·group′**

b., blend of, blended; c., cognate with; d., dialect, dialectal; der., derived from; f., formed from; g., going back to; m., modification of; r., replacing; s., stem of; t., taken from; ?, perhaps.   See the full key on inside cover.

m.s. *regulātus*, pp., der. L *regula* rule] —**reg′u·la′-tive, reg·u·la·to·ry** (rĕg′yə lə tōr′Y), *adj.* —**Syn. 1.** rule, direct, manage, order, adjust, arrange.

reg·u·la·tion (rĕg′yə lā′shən), *n.* **1.** a rule or order, as for conduct, prescribed by authority; a governing direction or law. **2.** act of regulating. **3.** state of being regulated. —**Syn. 2.** direction, management, control.

reg·u·la·tor (rĕg′yə lā′tər), *n.* **1.** one who or that which regulates. **2.** *Horol.* **a.** a device in a clock or a watch for causing it to go faster or slower. **b.** a master clock, esp. one of great accuracy, against which other clocks are checked. **3.** *Mach.* **a.** a governor. **b.** a governor employed to control the closing of the port opening for admission of steam to the cylinder of a steam engine. **c.** a reducing valve for regulating steam pressure. **4.** *Elect.* a device which functions to maintain a designated characteristic, as voltage or current, at a predetermined value, or to vary it according to a predetermined plan.

reg·u·lus (rĕg′yə ləs), *n.*, *pl.* **-luses, -li** (-lī′). **1.** (*cap.*) *Astron.* a star of the first magnitude in the constellation Leo. **2.** *Metall.* **a.** the metallic mass which forms beneath the slag at the bottom of the crucible or furnace in smelting ores. **b.** an impure intermediate product obtained in smelting ores. [t. L: a little king, dim. of *rex* king; in early chemistry, antimony, so called because it readily combines with gold (the king of metals)]

Reg·u·lus (rĕg′yə ləs), *n.* **Marcus Atilius** (mär′kəs ə tĭl′Yəs), died 250? B.C., Roman general.

re·gur·gi·tate (rē gûr′jə tāt′), *v.*, **-tated, -tating.** —*v.i.* **1.** to surge or rush back, as liquids, gases, undigested food, etc. —*v.t.* **2.** to cause to surge or rush back. [t. ML: m.s. *regurgitātus*, pp., surged back] —**re·gur′gi·tant** (rē gûr′jə tənt), *adj.*

re·gur·gi·ta·tion (rē gûr′jə tā′shən), *n.* **1.** act of regurgitating. **2.** *Med.* voluntary or involuntary return of partly digested food from the stomach to the mouth. **3.** *Physiol.* the reflux of blood through leaking heart valves.

re·ha·bil·i·tate (rē′hə bĭl′ə tāt′), *v.t.*, **-tated, -tating. 1.** to restore to a good condition; regenerate, or make over in an improved form. **2.** to reëstablish in good repute or accepted respectability, as a person or the character, name, etc., after disrepute. **3.** to restore formally to a former capacity or standing, or to rank, rights, or privileges lost or forfeited. [t. ML: m.s. *rehabilitātus*, pp., restored] —**re·ha·bil′i·ta′tion**, *n.*

re·hash (*v.* rē hăsh′; *n.* rē′hăsh′), *v.t.* **1.** to work up (old material) in a new form. —*n.* **2.** act of rehashing. **3.** something rehashed.

re·hears·al (rĭ hûr′səl), *n.* **1.** a performance beforehand by way of practice or drill. **2.** act of going through a dramatic, musical, or other performance in private, for practice, before going through it publicly or on some formal occasion. **3.** a repeating or relating: *a rehearsal of grievances.*

re·hearse (rĭ hûrs′), *v.*, **-hearsed, -hearsing.** —*v.t.* **1.** to recite or act (a play, part, etc.) in private by way of practice, before a public performance. **2.** to drill or train (a person, etc.) by rehearsal, as for some performance or part. **3.** to go through (any performance) in private beforehand, for practice: *to rehearse a symphony.* **4.** to relate the facts or particulars of; enumerate. —*v.i.* **5.** to rehearse a play, part, etc. [ME *reherce*(n), t. OF: m. *rehercier*, appar. f. re- RE-² + *hercier* harrow] —**re·hears′er**, *n.* —**Syn. 4.** See relate.

rei (rā), *n.* occasional singular of reis.

Reich (rīk; *Ger.* rīKH), *n.* **1.** Germany. **2.** the Holy Roman Empire, until its dissolution in 1806 (**First Reich**). **3.** the Empire, 1871–1919 (**Second Reich**). **4.** the German federal republic, 1919–33. **5.** the Nazi state, 1933–45 (**Third Reich**). [G]

Reichs·bank (rīks′băngk′; *Ger.* rīKHs′băngk′), *n.* the German national bank.

reichs·mark (rīks′märk′; *Ger.* rīKHs′-), *n.*, *pl.* **-marks, -mark.** the reconstituted German mark introduced in November, 1924, having a gold value of 23.8 U.S. cents: monetary unit of Germany until 1948. See **Deutsche mark** and **Ostmark.**

reichs·pfen·nig (rīKHs′pfĕn′Yg), *n.* a minor bronze German coin valued at ¹⁄₁₀₀ of a reichsmark.

Reichs·rath (rīKHs′rät′), *n.* **1.** the national council (Council of the Reich) of the German Republic, composed of members appointed to represent the component states, and corresponding to some extent to the former Bundesrat. Cf. **Reichstag.** **2.** *Hist.* the legislature or parliament in the Austrian division of Austria-Hungary. Also, **Reichs·rat′.**

Reichs·tag (rīks′täg′; *Ger.* rīKHs′täKH′), *n.* the elective legislative assembly of Germany.

re·i·fy (rē′ə fī′), *v.t.*, **-fied, -fying.** to convert into or regard as a concrete thing: *to reify an abstract concept.* [f. L *rē*(s) thing + -(I)FY]

reign (rān), *n.* **1.** the period or term of ruling, as of a sovereign. **2.** royal rule or sway. **3.** dominating power or influence: *the reign of law.* —*v.i.* **4.** to possess or exercise sovereign power or authority. **5.** to hold the position and name of sovereign without exercising the ruling power. **6.** to have ascendancy; predominate. [ME *reyne*, t. OF: m. *regne*, t. L: m. *regnum*] —**Syn. 2.** dominion, sovereignty.

Reign of Terror, a period of the French Revolution, from about March, 1793, to July, 1794, during which many persons were ruthlessly executed by the ruling faction.

reign style, the designation of a period of rule under the dynastic system of China and Japan, the name of the ruler himself not being used because of taboo.

re·im·burse (rē′Ym bûrs′), *v.t.*, **-bursed, -bursing. 1.** to make repayment or for expense or loss incurred. **2.** to pay back; refund; repay. [f. RE- + *imburse* (t. ML: m.s. *imbursāre*, der. L *in-* IN-² + ML *bursa* purse, bag)] —**re·im·burse′ment,** *n.*

re·im·port (rē′Ym pōrt′), *v.t.* to import back into the country of exportation. —**re·im·por·ta′tion,** *n.*

re·im·pres·sion (rē′Ym prĕsh′ən), *n.* **1.** a second or repeated impression. **2.** a reprinting or a reprint.

Reims (rēmz; *Fr.* răns), *n.* a city in NE France: cathedral; unconditional surrender of Germany, May 7, 1945. 121,145 (1954). Also, **Rheims.**

rein (rān), *n.* **1.** a long, narrow strap or thong, fastened to the bridle or bit, by which a rider or driver restrains and guides a horse or other animal. See illus. under **harness. 2.** any of certain other straps or thongs forming part of a harness, as a checkrein. **3.** any means of curbing, controlling, or directing; a check; restraint. **4.** (*often pl.*) complete license; free scope: *to give free rein to one's imagination.* —*v.t.* **5.** to furnish with a rein or reins, as a horse. **6.** to check or guide (a horse, etc.) by pulling at the reins. **7.** to curb; restrain; control. —*v.i.* **8.** to obey the reins: *a horse that reins well.* **9.** to rein a horse (fol. by *in* or *up*). [ME *rene*, t. OF, var. of *resne* (AF *redne*), ult. der. L *retinēre* hold back]

re·in·car·nate (rē′Yn kär′nāt), *v.t.*, **-nated, -nating.** to give another body to; incarnate again.

re·in·car·na·tion (rē′Yn kär nā′shən), *n.* **1.** the belief that the soul, upon death of the body, moves to another body or form. **2.** rebirth of the soul in a new body. **3.** a new incarnation or embodiment, as of a person. —**re′in·car·na′tion·ist,** *n.*

rein·deer (rān′dYr′), *n.*, *pl.* **-deer,** (*occasionally*) **-deers.** any of various species of large deer of the genus *Rangifer,* with branched antlers in both males and females, found in northern or arctic regions, and often domesticated. See **caribou.** [ME *raynedere*, t. Scand.; cf. Icel. *hreindȳr*]

European reindeer, *Rangifer tarandus* (Ab. 4½ ft. high at the shoulder)

Reindeer Lake, a lake in central Canada, mostly in NE Saskatchewan province. ab. 2000 sq. mi.

re·in·force (rē′Yn fōrs′), *v.t.*, **-forced, -forcing. 1.** to strengthen with some added piece, support, or material: *to reinforce a wall.* **2.** to strengthen with additional men or ships for military or naval purposes: *to reinforce a garrison.* **3.** to strengthen; make more forcible or effective: *to reinforce efforts.* **4.** to augment; increase: *to reinforce a supply.* Also, **reënforce, re-enforce.** [f. RE- + *inforce,* var. of ENFORCE]

reinforced concrete, concrete poured to embody steel bars for greater strength.

re·in·force·ment (rē′Yn fōrs′mənt), *n.* **1.** act of reinforcing. **2.** state of being reinforced. **3.** something that reinforces or strengthens. **4.** (*often pl.*) an additional supply of men, ships, etc., for a military or naval force. **5.** a system of steel bars used to strengthen concrete.

Rein·hardt (rīn′härt′), *n.* **Max,** 1873–1943, German theater director, producer, and actor, born in Austria.

reins (rānz), *n.pl. Archaic.* **1.** the kidneys. **2.** the region of the kidneys, or the lower part of the back. **3.** the seat of the feelings or affections, formerly identified with the kidneys (esp. in Biblical use). [ME, t. OF; r. ME *reenes,* OE *rēnys,* t. L: m. *rēnēs,* pl., kidneys, loins]

re·in·state (rē′Yn stāt′), *v.t.*, **-stated, -stating.** to put back or establish again, as in a former position or state. —**re′in·state′ment,** *n.*

re·in·sure (rē′Yn shŏŏr′), *v.t.*, **-sured, -suring. 1.** to insure again. **2.** to insure under a contract by which a first insurer relieves himself from a part or from all of the risk and devolves it upon another insurer. —**re′in·sur′-ance,** *n.* —**re′in·sur′er,** *n.*

re·han′dle	re·im·print′	re′in·fect′	re′in·spect′
re·heat′	re·im·pris′on	re′in·fec′tion	re′in·spec′tion
re·heel′	re·im·pris′on·ment	re′in·flame′	re′in·spire′
re·ig′nite	re·im·aug′u·rate′	re′in·form′	re′in·stall′
re·im·pose′	re′in·cite′	re′in·fuse′	re′in·stal·la′tion
re′im·po·si′tion	re′in·cor′po·rate′	re′in·scribe′	re′in·stall′ment
re′im·preg′nate	re′in·cur′	re′in·sert′	re′in·stal′ment
re′im·press′	re′in·duce′	re′in·ser′tion	re′in·struct′

reis (rās), *n. pl.*, *sing.* **real** (rĕ äl′). a former Portuguese and a Brazilian money of account, being a multiple (varying according to the particular case) of an amount equivalent in the respective cases to about ¹/₉ and ¹/₁₈ of a U.S. cent. Cf. **milreis**. [t. Pg., pl. of *rei* king]

re·it·er·ate (rē ĭt′ə rāt′), *v.t.*, **-ated, -ating.** to repeat; say or do again or repeatedly. [t. L: m.s. *reiterātus*, pp.] —**re·it′er·a′tion,** *n.* —**re·it′er·a·tive,** *adj.* —**Syn.** See **repeat.**

re·ject (*v.* rĭ jĕkt′; *n.* rē′jĕkt), *v.t.* **1.** to refuse to have, take, recognize, etc. **2.** to refuse to grant (a demand, etc.). **3.** to refuse to accept (a person); rebuff. **4.** to throw away, discard, or refuse as useless or unsatisfactory. **5.** to cast out or eject; vomit. **6.** to cast out or off. —*n.* **7** something rejected, as an imperfect article. [t. L: s. *rējectus*, pp., thrown back] —**re·ject′er,** *n.* —**Syn. 1.** See **refuse¹. 4.** REJECT, DISCARD imply refusing to take or to keep something as being unsatisfactory or unworthy. To REJECT is to refuse to accept something that is offered or to make a distinction between something acceptable and something not acceptable: *to reject the offer of a position.* To DISCARD is to cast aside as no longer useful something which has served one: *to discard old magazines.* —**Ant. 1.** accept, keep.

re·jec·ta·men·ta (rĭ jĕk′tə mĕn′tə), *n.pl.* things or matter rejected as useless or worthless. [NL, pl. of *rējectāmentum*, der. L *rējectus*, pp., thrown away. See **-MENT**]

re·jec·tion (rĭ jĕk′shən), *n.* **1.** act of rejecting. **2.** state of being rejected. **3.** that which is rejected.

re·joice (rĭ jois′), *v.*, **-joiced, -joicing.** —*v.i.* **1.** to be glad; take delight (*in*). —*v.t.* **2.** to make joyful; gladden. [ME, t. OF: m. *rejoiss-*, stem of *rejoir*, f. *re-* RE- + *joir* joy] —**re·joic′er,** *n.*

re·joic·ing (rĭ joi′sĭng), *n.* **1.** act of one who rejoices. **2.** the feeling or the expression of joy. **3.** (*often pl.*) an occasion for expressing joy.

re·join¹ (rē join′), *v.t.* **1.** to come again into the company of: *to rejoin a party after a brief absence.* **2.** to join together again; reunite. —*v.i.* **3.** to become joined together again. [f. RE- + JOIN]

re·join² (rĭ join′), *v.t.* **1.** to say in answer. —*v.i.* **2.** to answer. **3.** *Law.* to answer the plaintiff's replication. [late ME *rejoyne*, t. AF: m. *rejoyner,* F *rejoindre,* f. *re-* RE- + *joindre* JOIN]

re·join·der (rĭ join′dər), *n.* **1.** an answer to a reply; response. **2.** *Law.* the defendant's answer to the plaintiff's replication. Cf. **replication** and **surrejoinder.** [late ME *rejoyner,* t. AF, inf. used as n.; cf. F *rejoindre*]

re·ju·ve·nate (rĭ jōō′və nāt′), *v.t.*, **-nated, -nating.** **1.** to make young again; restore to youthful vigor, appearance, etc. **2.** *Phys. Geog.* **a.** to renew the activity, erosive power, etc., of (a stream) by the uplifting of the region it drains, or by removal of a barrier in the bed of the stream. **b.** to impress again the characters of youthful topography on (a region) by the action of rejuvenated streams. [f. LL *rejuven(escere)* become young again + -ATE¹] —**re·ju′ve·na′tion,** *n.* —**re·ju′ve·na′tor,** *n.*

re·ju·ve·nes·cent (rĭ jōō′və nĕs′ənt), *adj.* **1.** becoming young again. **2.** making young again; rejuvenating. —**re·ju′ve·nes′cence,** *n.*

re·ju·ve·nize (rĭ jōō′və nīz′), *v.t.*, **-nized, -nizing.** to rejuvenate.

-rel, a noun suffix having a diminutive or pejorative force, as in *cockerel, wastrel.* Also, **-erel.** [ME, t. OF: m. *-erel, -erelle*]

rel., 1. relating. **2.** relative. **3.** relatively. **4.** religion. **5.** religious.

re·lapse (rĭ lăps′), *v.*, **-lapsed, -lapsing,** *n.* —*v.i.* **1.** to fall or slip back into a former state, practice, etc.: *to relapse into silence.* **2.** to fall back into illness after convalescence or apparent recovery. **3.** to fall back into wrongdoing or error; backslide. —*n.* **4.** act of relapsing. **5.** a return of a disease or illness after partial recovery. [t. L: m.s. *relapsus,* pp., slipped back] —**re·laps′er,** *n.*

relapsing fever, one of a group of fevers characterized by relapses, occurring in many tropical countries, and caused by several species of spirochetes transmitted by several species of lice and ticks.

re·late (rĭ lāt′), *v.*, **-lated, -lating.** —*v.t.* **1.** to tell. **2.** to bring into or establish association, connection, or relation. —*v.i.* **3.** to have reference (*to*). **4.** to have some relation (*to*). [t. L: m.s. *relātus,* pp., reported, carried back] —**re·lat′er,** *n.* —**Syn. 1.** RELATE, RECITE, RECOUNT, REHEARSE mean to tell, report, or describe in some detail an occurrence or circumstance. To RELATE is to give an account of happenings, events, circumstances, etc.: *to relate one's adventures.* To RECITE may mean to give details consecutively, but more often applies to the repetition from memory of something learned with verbal exactness: *to recite a poem.* To RECOUNT is usually to set forth consecutively the details of an occurrence, argument, experience, etc., to give an account in detail: *to recount an unpleasant experience.* REHEARSE implies some formality and exactness in telling, sometimes with repeated performance as for practice before final delivery: *to rehearse one's part in a play.*

re·lat·ed (rĭ lā′tĭd), *adj.* **1.** associated; connected. **2.** allied by nature, origin, kinship, marriage, etc. **3.** narrated. **4.** (of tones) belonging to a melodic or harmonic series, so as to be susceptible of close connection.

re·la·tion (rĭ lā′shən), *n.* **1.** an existing connection; a particular way of being related: *the relation between cause and effect.* **2.** (*pl.*) the various connections between peoples, countries, etc.: *commercial or foreign relations.* **3.** (*pl.*) the various connections in which persons are brought together, as by common interests. **4.** the mode or kind of connection between one person and another, between man and God, etc. **5.** connection between persons by blood or marriage. **6.** a relative. **7.** reference; regard; respect: *to plan with relation to the future.* **8.** the action of relating, narrating, or telling; narration. **9.** a narrative; account. **10.** *Law.* the statement or complaint of a relator at whose instance an action or special proceeding is brought. [ME, t. L: s. *relātio* a bringing back, report] —**Syn. 5.** relationship, connection. **9.** recital, report.

re·la·tion·al (rĭ lā′shən əl), *adj.* **1.** of or pertaining to relations. **2.** indicating or specifying some relation. **3.** *Gram.* serving to indicate relations between other elements in a sentence, as prepositions, conjunctions, etc. Cf. **notional.**

re·la·tion·ship (rĭ lā′shən shĭp′), *n.* **1.** connection; a particular connection. **2.** connection by blood or marriage. **3.** an emotional connection between people. —**Syn. 2.** RELATIONSHIP, KINSHIP refer to connection with others by blood or by marriage. RELATIONSHIP can be applied to connection either by birth or by marriage: *relationship to a ruling family.* KINSHIP generally denotes common descent, and implies a more intimate connection than relationship: *the ties and obligations of kinship.*

rel·a·tive (rĕl′ə tĭv), *n.* **1.** one who is connected with another or others by blood or marriage. **2.** something having, or standing in, some relation to something else. **3.** *Gram.* a relative pronoun, adjective, or adverb. —*adj.* **4.** considered in relation to something else; comparative: *the relative merits of democracy and monarchy.* **5.** existing only by relation to something else; not absolute or independent. **6.** having relation or connection: *relative phenomena.* **7.** having reference or regard; relevant; pertinent (fol. by *to*). **8.** correspondent; proportionate: *value is relative to demand.* **9.** (of a term, name. etc.) depending for significance upon something else: *better is a relative term.* **10.** *Gram.* **a.** designating words which introduce subordinate clauses and refer to some element of the principal clause (the antecedent), as *who* in "He's the man *who saw you.*" **b.** (of a clause) introduced by such a word. [ME, t. LL: m.s. *relātīvus,* der. L *relātus* carried back] —**rel′a·tive·ness,** *n.*

relative frequency, 1. *Math.* the ratio of the number of times an event occurs to the number of occasions on which it might occur in the same period. **2.** *Statistics.* the number of items of a certain type divided by the number of all the items considered.

rel·a·tive·ly (rĕl′ə tĭv lĭ), *adv.* **1.** in a relative manner: *a relatively small difference.* **2.** with reference (fol. by *to*): *the value of one thing relatively to other things.* **3.** in proportion (fol. by *to*).

relative humidity. *Meteorol.* See **humidity** (def. 2).

relative major, *Music.* the major key whose tonic is the third degree of a given minor key.

relative minor, *Music.* the minor key whose tonic is the sixth degree of a given major key.

relative pronoun, a pronoun with a relative function. See **relative** (def. 10a).

rel·a·tiv·ism (rĕl′ə tĭ vĭz′əm), *n.* the theory of knowledge or ethics which holds that criteria of judgment are relative, varying with the individual, time, and circumstance. —**rel′a·tiv·ist,** *n.* —**rel′a·tiv·is′tic,** *adj.*

rel·a·tiv·i·ty (rĕl′ə tĭv′ə tĭ), *n.* **1.** state or fact of being relative. **2. principle of relativity,** *Physics.* the principle that there is no absolute motion, or motion with respect to some absolute space filled with ether, but that all motion observable is relative, being that of one portion or manifestation of matter with respect to another portion of matter—a principle which is confirmed by the fact that the velocity of light is constant and is independent of the motion of the source. Among the conclusions resulting from this principle are: that there can be no transmission of energy with a velocity greater than that of light; that the mass of a moving body increases with its velocity, and depends upon its content of internal energy; that time, like motion, is relative and not absolute, so that we cannot speak of the absolute simultaneity of events which occur in different places; that time and space are dependent on each other, time forming with the three dimensions of space a single four-dimensional manifold; that the presence of matter in space is associated with a "warping" of the manifold in its neighborhood, so that a freely moving body describes, not a straight line, but a curve (this effect being what is known as gravitation), and that rays of light will be deflected or curved, when passing through a gravitational field. When all the velocities considered are very small

re·in′te·grate′	re′in·tro·duce′	re′in·vig′or·ate′	re·kin′dle
re·in′te·gra′tion	re′in·tro·duc′tion	re′in·vig′or·a′tion	re·la′bel
re′in·ter′	re′in·vent′	re′in·vite′	re·lace′
re′in·ter′ment	re′in·vest′	re′in·volve′	re·lac′quer
re′in·ter′ro·gate′	re′in·ves′ti·gate′	re·is′sue	re·lance′
re′in·trench′	re′in·vest′ment	re·judge′	re·latch′

b., blend of, blended; **c.,** cognate with; **d.,** dialect, dialectal; **der.,** derived from; **f.,** formed from; **g.,** going back to; **m.,** modification of; **r.,** replacing; **s.,** stem of; **t.,** taken from; **?,** perhaps.   See the full key on inside cover.

compared with the velocity of light, the results of this theory are practically indistinguishable from those of previously accepted principles. For velocities approaching that of light, they are very great. The theory was developed by H. A. Lorentz and Albert Einstein in their **restricted theory of relativity**, dealing with uniform motion, and by Einstein in his **general theory of relativity** (1915), dealing with gravitation. **3.** *Philos.* existence only in relation to a thinking mind.

relativity of knowledge, *Philos.* the doctrine that all human knowledge is relative to the human mind, or that the mind can know concerning things only the effects which they produce upon it and not what the things themselves are.

re·la·tor (rĭ lā′tər), *n.* **1.** one who relates or narrates. **2.** *Law.* a private person on whose suggestion or complaint an action or special proceeding in the name of the state is brought, to try a question involving both public and private right. [t. L. Cf. F *relateur*]

re·lax (rĭ lăks′), *v.t.* **1.** to make lax, or less tense, rigid, or firm: *to relax the muscles.* **2.** to diminish the force of. **3.** to slacken or abate. as effort, attention, etc. **4.** to make less strict or severe, as rules, discipline, etc. —*v.i.* **5.** to become less tense, rigid, or firm. **6.** to become less strict or severe; grow milder. **7.** to slacken in effort, application, etc.; take relaxation. [ME, t. L: s. *relaxāre*] —**re·lax′er,** *n.*

re·lax·a·tion (rē′lăk sā′shən), *n.* **1.** abatement or relief of bodily or mental effort or application. **2.** something affording such relief; a diversion or entertainment. **3.** a loosening or slackening. **4.** diminution or remission of strictness or severity.

re·lay (rē′lā, rĭ lā′), *n.* **1.** a set of persons relieving others or taking turns; a shift. **2.** a fresh set of dogs or horses posted in readiness for use in a hunt, on a journey, etc. **3.** *Athletics.* **a.** relay race. **b.** one of the lengths, or legs, of a relay race. **4.** a device that extends or reinforces the action or effect of an apparatus. **5.** *Elect.* **a.** a device by means of which a change of current or voltage in one circuit can be made to produce a change in the electrical condition of another circuit. **b.** a device that is operative by a variation in the conditions of one electric circuit to effect the operation of other devices in the same or another electric circuit. —*v.t.* **6.** to carry forward by or as by relays: *to relay a message.* **7.** to provide with or replace by fresh relays. **8.** *Elect.* to retransmit by means of a telegraphic relay, or as such a relay does. —*v.i.* **9.** *Elect.* to relay a message. [ME, t. OF: m. *relais,* orig., hounds in reserve along the line of the hunt, der. *relaier* leave behind]

relay race, a race of two or more teams of contestants, each contestant running but part of the distance and being relieved by a teammate.

re·lease (rĭ lēs′), *v.,* **-leased, -leasing,** *n.* —*v.t.* **1.** to free from confinement, bondage, obligation, pain, etc.; let go. **2.** to free from anything that restrains, fastens, etc. **3.** to allow to become known, be issued or exhibited: *to release an article for publication.* **4.** *Law.* give up, relinquish, or surrender (a right, claim, etc.). —*n.* **5.** a freeing or releasing from confinement, obligation, pain, etc. **6.** liberation from anything that restrains or fastens. **7.** some device for effecting such liberation. **8.** the releasing of something for publication or public exhibition or sale, as a written article. **9.** the article so released. **10.** *Law.* **a.** the surrender of a right or the like to another. **b.** a document embodying such a surrender. **11.** *Obs. or Law.* a remission, as of a debt, tax, or tribute. **12.** *Mach.* a control mechanism for starting or stopping a machine, esp. by removing some restrictive apparatus. **13.** *Engin.* **a.** (in a steam engine) the opening of the exhaust port of the cylinder at or near the end of the working stroke of the piston. **b.** the moment at which the exhaust port is opened. [ME *relesse*(n), t. OF: m. *relesser,* g. L *relaxāre* relax]

—**Syn. 1.** RELEASE, FREE, DISMISS, DISCHARGE may all mean to set at liberty, let loose, or let go. RELEASE, meaning to set loose, and FREE, when applied to persons, always suggest a helpful action. Both may be used (not always interchangeably) of delivering a person from confinement or obligation: *to free or release prisoners.* FREE (less often, RELEASE) is also used for delivering a person from pain, etc.: *to free someone from fear.* DISMISS, meaning to send away, usually has the meaning of forcing to go unwillingly (*to dismiss a servant*), but may refer to giving permission to go: *the teacher dismissed the class early.* DISCHARGE, meaning originally to relieve of a burden (*to discharge a gun*), has come to refer to that which is sent away and is often a close synonym to DISMISS; it is used in the meaning permit to go, in connection with courts and the army: *the court discharged a man accused of robbery.* **2.** loose, extricate, disengage. **6.** deliverance, emancipation. —**Ant. 1.** bind, restrain.

re·lease (rē lēs′), *v.t.,* **-leased, -leasing. 1.** to lease again. **2.** *Law.* to make over (land, etc.), as to another.

rel·e·gate (rĕl′ə gāt′), *v.t.,* **-gated, -gating. 1.** to send or consign to some obscure position, place, or condition. **2.** to consign or commit (a matter, task, etc.), as to a person. **3.** to assign or refer (something) to a particular class or kind. **4.** to send into exile; banish. [t. L: s. *relēgātus,* pp., sent back] —**rel′e·ga′tion,** *n.*

re·lent (rĭ lĕnt′), *v.i.* **1.** to soften in feeling, temper, or determination; become more mild, compassionate, or

forgiving. —*v.t.* **2.** *Obs.* to cause to relent. [ME *relente* melt, appar. t. L: m. *relentescere* grow slack or soft]

re·lent·less (rĭ lĕnt′lĭs), *adj.* that does not relent; unrelenting: *a relentless enemy.* —**re·lent′less·ly,** *adv.* —**re·lent′less·ness,** *n.* —**Syn.** See **inflexible**.

rel·e·vant (rĕl′ə vant), *adj.* bearing upon or connected with the matter in hand; to the purpose; pertinent: *a relevant remark.* [t. ML: s. *relevans,* prop. ppr. of L *relevāre* raise up] —**rel′e·vance, rel′e·van·cy,** *n.* —**rel′e·vant·ly,** *adv.* —**Syn.** applicable, germane, apposite, appropriate, suitable, fitting. See **apt**.

re·li·a·ble (rĭ lī′ə bəl), *adj.* that may be relied on; trustworthy: *reliable sources of information.* —**re·li·a·bil′i·ty, re·li′a·ble·ness,** *n.* —**re·li′a·bly,** *adv.* —**Syn.** trusty, dependable. RELIABLE, INFALLIBLE, TRUSTWORTHY apply to one who or that which can be depended upon with certainty. The person who or that which is RELIABLE can be relied upon; from such a one, satisfactory performance may be expected with complete confidence (it may also have the suggestion of honesty): *a reliable formula.* One who or that which is INFALLIBLE is incapable of making mistakes and is never in error: *an infallible test.* One who or that which is TRUSTWORTHY is worthy of being trusted and believed in, usually because of steadiness and honesty: *trustworthy and accurate reports.* —**Ant.** undependable, questionable, deceitful.

re·li·ance (rĭ lī′əns), *n.* **1.** confident or trustful dependence. **2.** confidence. **3.** something relied on.

re·li·ant (rĭ lī′ənt), *adj.* **1.** having or showing reliance. **2.** confident; trustful. **3.** self-reliant.

rel·ic (rĕl′ĭk), *n.* **1.** a surviving memorial of something past. **2.** an object having interest by reason of its age or its association with the past: *a museum of historic relics.* **3.** a surviving trace of something: *a custom which is a relic of paganism.* **4.** (*pl.*) remaining parts or fragments. **5.** something kept in remembrance. **6.** *Eccles.* (esp. in the Roman Catholic and Greek churches) the body, a part of the body, or some personal memorial of a saint, martyr, or other sacred person, preserved as worthy of veneration. **7.** (*pl.*) the remains of a deceased person. [ME *relik,* OE *relic,* short for *reliquium,* t. L]

rel·ict (rĕl′ĭkt), *n.* **1.** *Ecol.* a plant or animal species living in an environment which has changed from that which is typical for it. **2.** *Archaic or Rare.* a widow. [late ME, t. ML: s. *relicta* widow, prop. fem. of L *relictus,* pp., left behind]

re·lief (rĭ lēf′), *n.* **1.** deliverance, alleviation, or ease through the removal of pain, distress, oppression, etc. **2.** a means or thing that relieves pain, distress, anxiety, etc. **3.** help or assistance given, as to those in poverty or need. **4.** something affording a pleasing change, as from monotony. **5.** release from a post of duty, as by the coming of a substitute or replacement. **6.** the person or persons thus bringing release. **7.** the deliverance of a besieged town, etc., from an attacking force. **8.** prominence, distinctness, or vividness due to contrast. **9.** the projection of a figure or part from the ground or plane on which it is formed, in sculpture or similar work. **10.** a piece or work in such projection: *high relief.* **11.** an apparent projection of parts in a painting, drawing, etc., giving the appearance of the third dimension. **12.** *Phys. Geog.* the departure of the land surface in any area from that of a level surface. **13.** *Engraving.* any printing process by which the printing ink is transferred to paper, etc., from areas that are higher than the rest of the block. **14.** *Feudal Law.* a fine or composition which the heir of a feudal tenant paid to the lord for the privilege of succeeding to the estate. [ME *relief,* t. OF, der. *relever* RELIEVE] —**Syn. 1.** mitigation, assuagement, comfort. **3.** succor, aid, redress.

Assyrian relief. 7th century

relief map, a map showing the relief of an area, usually by generalized contour lines.

re·lieve (rĭ lēv′), *v.t.,* **-lieved, -lieving. 1.** to ease or alleviate (pain, distress, anxiety, need, etc.). **2.** to free from anxiety, fear, pain, etc. **3.** to deliver from poverty, need, etc. **4.** to bring efficient aid to (a besieged town, etc.). **5.** to ease (a person) of any burden, wrong, or oppression, as by legal means. **6.** to make less tedious, unpleasant, or monotonous; break or vary the sameness of. **7.** to bring into relief or prominence; heighten the effect of. **8.** to release (one on duty) by coming as or providing a substitute. [ME *releve,* t. OF: m. *relever,* g. L *relevāre* raise again, assist] —**re·liev′a·ble,** *adj.* —**re·liev′er,** *n.* —**Syn. 1.** mitigate, assuage, allay, lighten. See **comfort**.

re·lie·vo (rĭ lē′vō), *n., pl.* **-vos.** relief (defs. 9, 10). [t. It., der. *rilevare* raise, modeled on F *relief*]

relig., religion.

re·li·gieuse (rə lē zhyœz′), *n., pl.* **-gieuses** (-zhyœz′). *French.* a woman belonging to a religious order, etc.

re·li·gieux (rə lē zhyœ′), *adj., n., pl.* **-gieux** (-zhyœ′). *French.* —*adj.* **1.** religious; devout; pious. —*n.* **2.** person bound by monastic vows.

re·li·gion (rĭ lĭj′ən), *n.* **1.** the quest for the values of the ideal life, involving three phases: the ideal, the practices for attaining the values of the ideal, and the the-

| **re·launch′** | **re·laun′der** | **re·learn′** | **re·light′** |

ăct, āble, dâre, ärt; ĕbb, ēqual; ĭf, īce; hŏt, ōver, ôrder, oil, bŏŏk, ōōze, out; ŭp, ūse, ûrge; ə = a in alone; ch, chief; g, give; ng, ring; sh, shoe; th, thin; ᵺ, that; zh, vision.   See the full key on inside cover.

ology or world view relating the quest to the environing universe. **2.** a particular system in which the quest for the ideal life has been embodied: *the Christian religion.* **3.** recognition on the part of man of a controlling superhuman power entitled to obedience, reverence, and worship. **4.** the feeling or the spiritual attitude of those recognizing such a controlling power. **5.** the manifestation of such feeling in conduct or life. **6.** a point or matter of conscience: *to make a religion of doing something.* **7.** *Obs.* the practice of sacred rites or observances. **8.** (*pl.*) *Obs.* religious rites. [ME, t. L: s. *religio* fear of the gods, religious awe, sacredness, scrupulousness]

re·li·gion·ism (rĭlĭj′ənĭz′əm), *n.* **1.** excessive or exaggerated religious zeal. **2.** affected or pretended religious zeal. —**re·li′gion·ist,** *n.*

re·lig·i·os·i·ty (rĭlĭj′ĭŏs′ətĭ), *n.* **1.** the quality of being religious; piety; devoutness. **2.** affected or excessive devotion to religion.

re·li·gious (rĭlĭj′əs), *adj.* **1.** of, pertaining to, or concerned with religion. **2.** imbued with or exhibiting religion; pious; devout; godly. **3.** scrupulously faithful; conscientious: *religious care.* **4.** belonging to a religious order, as persons. **5.** pertaining to or connected with a monastic or religious order. **6.** appropriate to religion or to sacred rites or observances. —*n.* **7.** a member of a religious order, congregation, etc.; a monk, friar, or nun. **8.** (*pl.*) such persons collectively [ME, t. L: m.s. *religiōsus*] —**re·li′gious·ly,** *adv.* —**re·li′gious·ness,** *n.* —**Syn. 2.** RELIGIOUS, DEVOUT, PIOUS indicate a spirit of reverence toward God. RELIGIOUS is a general word, applying to whatever pertains to faith or worship: *a religious ceremony.* DEVOUT indicates a fervent spirit, usually genuine and often independent of outward observances: *a deeply devout though unorthodox church member.* PIOUS implies such constant attention to, and extreme conformity with, outward observances as often to suggest sham or hypocrisy: *a pious hypocrite.* —**Ant. 2.** irreligious, scoffing.

re·lin·quish (rĭlĭng′kwĭsh), *v.t.* **1.** to renounce or surrender (a possession, right, etc.). **2.** to give up; put aside or desist from: *to relinquish a plan.* **3.** to let go: *to relinquish one's hold.* [ME, t. OF: m. *relinquiss-,* s. *relinquir,* g. L *relinquere*] —**re·lin′quish·er,** *n.* —**re·lin′quish·ment,** *n.* —**Syn. 2.** yield, cede, waive, forgo, abdicate, leave, quit. See **abandon**[1].

rel·i·qua·ry (rĕl′əkwĕr′ĭ), *n., pl.* **-quar·ies.** a repository or receptacle for a relic or relics. [t. ML: m.s. *reliquiārium,* der. L *reliquiae,* pl., remains. See RELIC]

rel·ique (rĕl′ĭk; *Fr.* rəlēk′), *n.* *Archaic.* relic. [F]

re·liq·ui·ae (rĭlĭk′wĭ ē′), *n.pl.* remains, as those of fossil organisms. [t. L]

rel·ish (rĕl′ĭsh), *n.* **1.** liking for the taste of something, or enjoyment of something eaten. **2.** pleasurable appreciation of anything; liking: *no relish for such jokes.* **3.** something appetizing or savory added to a meal, as pickles or olives. **4.** a pleasing or appetizing flavor. **5.** a pleasing or enjoyable quality. **6.** a taste or flavor. **7.** a smack, trace, or touch of something. —*v.t.* **8.** to take pleasure in; like; enjoy. **9.** to make pleasing to the taste. **10.** to like the taste or flavor of. —*v.i.* **11.** to have taste or flavor. **12.** to be agreeable or pleasant. [ME *reles,* t. OF: what is left, remainder, der. *relaisser* leave behind] —**rel′ish·a·ble,** *adj.*

rel. pron., relative pronoun.

re·lu·cent (rĭlōō′sənt), *adj.* *Rare.* shining; bright. [t. L:s. *relūcens,* ppr., shining back; r. ME *relusant,* t. OF]

re·luct (rĭlŭkt′), *v.i.* *Archaic or Rare.* **1.** to struggle against something; resist. **2.** to object; show reluctance. [back formation from RELUCTANCE, RELUCTANT]

re·luc·tance (rĭlŭk′təns), *n.* **1.** unwillingness; disinclination: *reluctance to speak.* **2.** *Elect.* the resistance offered to the passage of magnetic lines of force, being numerically equal to the magnetomotive force divided by the magnetic flux. Also, **re·luc′tan·cy.**

re·luc·tant (rĭlŭk′tənt), *adj.* **1.** unwilling; disinclined. **2.** *Rare.* struggling in opposition. [t. L: s. *reluctans,* ppr., struggling against] —**re·luc′tant·ly,** *adv.* —**Syn. 1.** hesitant. RELUCTANT, LOATH, AVERSE describe disinclination toward something. RELUCTANT implies some sort of mental struggle, as between disinclination and a sense of duty: *reluctant to expel students.* LOATH describes extreme disinclination: *loath to part from a friend.* (RELUCTANT and LOATH are used with the infinitive.) AVERSE, used with "to" and a noun or a gerund, describes a long-held dislike or unwillingness, though not a particularly strong feeling: *averse to an idea, averse to getting up early.*

re·luc·tiv·i·ty (rĕl′əktĭv′ətĭ), *n.* *Elect.* a specific reluctance, or the magnetic reluctance of a material compared with that of air.

re·lume (rĭlōōm′), *v.t.* **-lumed, -luming.** to light or illuminate again. [t. LL: m.s. *relūmināre.* See RE-, ILLUMINE]

re·ly (rĭlī′), *v.i.,* **-lied, -lying.** to depend confidently; put trust in (fol. by *on* or *upon*). [ME *relie,* t. OF: m. *relier* bind together, g. L *religāre* bind back]

rem (rĕm), *n.* the quantity of ionizing radiation whose biological effect is equal to that produced by one roentgen of x-rays. [f. R(OENTGEN) E(QUIVALENT) M(AN)]

re·main (rĭmān′), *v.i.* **1.** to continue in the same state; continue to be (as specified): *to remain at peace.* **2.**

to stay in a place: *to remain at home.* **3.** to be left after the removal, loss, etc., of another or others. **4.** to be left to be done, told, etc. **5.** to be reserved or in store. —*n.* (*always pl.*) **6.** that which remains or is left; a remnant. **7.** miscellaneous, fragmentary, or other writings collected after the author's death. **8.** traces of some quality, condition, etc. **9.** that which remains of a person after death; a dead body. **10.** parts or substances remaining from animal or plant life, occurring in the earth's crust or strata: *fossil remains, organic remains.* [ME *remayn,* t. AF: m.s. *remaindre,* g. L *remanēre*] —**Syn. 1.** stay. See **continue.** **2.** wait, tarry. **3.** endure, abide.

re·main·der (rĭmān′dər), *n.* **1.** that which remains or is left: *the remainder of the day.* **2.** a remaining part. **3.** *Arith.* the quantity that remains after subtraction or division. **4.** *Law.* a future interest so created as to take effect at the end of another estate, as when property is conveyed to A for life and then to B. **5.** (*pl.*) *Philately.* the quantities of stamps on hand after they have been demonetized or otherwise voided for postal use. **6.** a copy of a book remaining in the publisher's stock when the sale has practically ceased, frequently sold at a reduced price. —*adj.* **7.** remaining; left. —*v.t.* **8.** to dispose of or sell as a publisher's remainder. [late ME *remaindre,* t. AF, prop. inf. See REMAIN] —**Syn. 1.** residuum, remnant, excess, rest. **2.** REMAINDER, BALANCE, RESIDUE, SURPLUS refer to a portion left over. REMAINDER is the general word (*the remainder of one's life*); it may refer in particular to the mathematical process of subtraction: *7 minus 5 leaves a remainder of 2.* BALANCE, originally a bookkeeper's term referring to the amount of money left to one's account, is often used colloquially as a synonym for REMAINDER: *a bank balance.* RESIDUE is used particularly to designate what remains as the result of a process; this is usually a chemical process, but the word may also refer to a legal process concerning inheritance: *a residue of ash left from burning leaves.* SURPLUS suggests that what remains is in excess of what was needed: *a surplus of goods.*

re·man (rēmăn′), *v.t.,* **-manned, -manning. 1.** to man again; furnish with a fresh supply of men. **2.** to restore the manliness or courage of.

re·mand (rĭmănd′, -mänd′), *v.t.* **1.** to send back, remit, or consign again. **2.** *Law.* **a.** to send back (a case) to a lower court from which it was appealed, with instructions as to what further proceedings should be had. **b.** (of a court or magistrate) to send back (a prisoner or accused person) into custody, as to await further proceedings. —*n.* **3.** act of remanding. **4.** state of being remanded. —*n.* **5.** a person remanded. [late ME *remaund(en),* t. LL: m. *remandāre* to send back word, repeat a command]

rem·a·nent (rĕm′ənənt), *adj.* *Rare.* remaining; left behind. [late ME, t. L: s. *remanens*]

re·mark (rĭmärk′), *v.t.* **1.** to say casually, as in making a comment. **2.** to note; perceive. **3.** *Obs.* to mark distinctively. —*v.i.* **4.** to make a remark or observation (fol. by *on* or *upon*). —*n.* **5.** act of remarking; notice. **6.** comment: *to let a thing pass without remark.* **7.** a casual or brief expression of thought or opinion. **8.** *Engraving.* a remarque. [t. F: m.s. *remarquer* note, heed, f. *re-* RE- + *marquer* mark] —**Syn. 7.** REMARK, COMMENT, NOTE, OBSERVATION imply giving special attention, an opinion, or a judgment. A REMARK is usually a casual and passing expression of opinion: *a remark about a play.* A COMMENT expresses judgment or explains a particular point: *a comment on the author's scholarship.* A NOTE is a memorandum or explanation, as in the margin of a page: *a note explaining a passage.* OBSERVATION suggests a note based on judgment and experience: *an observation on customary usages.*

re·mark·a·ble (rĭmär′kəbəl), *adj.* **1.** notably or conspicuously unusual, or extraordinary: *a remarkable change.* **2.** worthy of remark or notice. —**re·mark′a·ble·ness,** *n.* —**re·mark′a·bly,** *adv.* —**Syn. 2.** notable, noteworthy, striking, extraordinary, wonderful, unusual.

re·marque (rĭmärk′), *n.* *Engraving.* **1.** a distinguishing mark or peculiarity indicating a particular stage of a plate. **2.** a small sketch engraved on the margin of a plate, and usually removed after a number of early proofs have been printed. **3.** a plate so marked. [t. F]

Re·marque (rəmärk′), *n.* **Erich Maria** (ā′rĭKH märē′ä), born 1897, German novelist, in the U.S.

Rem·brandt (rĕm′brănt; *Du.* rĕm′bränt), *n.* (*Rembrandt Harmenszoon van Rijn* or *van Ryn*) 1606–69, Dutch painter and etcher.

re·me·di·a·ble (rĭmē′dĭəbəl), *adj.* capable of being remedied. —**re·me′di·a·bly,** *adv.*

re·me·di·al (rĭmē′dĭəl), *adj.* affording remedy; tending to remedy something. [t. L: s. *remediālis*] —**re·me′di·al·ly,** *adv.*

rem·e·di·less (rĕm′ədĭlĭs; *older* rĭmĕd′əlĭs), *adj.* not admitting of remedy, as disease, trouble, damage, etc.

rem·e·dy (rĕm′ədĭ), *n., pl.* **-dies,** *v.,* **-died, -dying.** —*n.* **1.** something that cures or relieves a disease or bodily disorder; a healing medicine, application, or treatment. **2.** something that corrects or removes an evil of any kind. **3.** *Law.* legal redress; the legal means of enforcing a right or redressing a wrong. **4.** *Coinage.* a cer-

re·line′	re·load′	re·made′	re·mar′shal
re·liq′ui·date′	re·loan′	re·make′	re·mas′ter
re·liq·ui·da′tion	re·lo′cate	re·mar′riage	re·match′
re·live′	re·lo·ca′tion	re·mar′ry	re·meas′ure

tain allowance at the mint for deviation from the standard weight and fineness of coins; tolerance. —*v.t.* 5. to cure or heal. 6. to put right, or restore to the natural or proper condition: *to remedy a matter.* 7. to counteract or remove: *to remedy an evil.* [ME, t. L: m.s. *remedium*] —**Syn.** 1. cure, restorative, specific, medicament. 2. corrective, antidote. 5. repair, correct, redress. See **cure.**

re·mem·ber (rĭ mĕm'bər), *v.t.* 1. to recall to the mind by an act or effort of memory. 2. to retain in the memory; bear in mind. 3. to have (something) come into the mind again. 4. to bear (a person) in mind as deserving a gift, reward, or fee. 5. to reward; tip. 6. to mention to another as sending kindly greetings. 7. *Archaic or Dial.* to remind. —*v.i.* 8. to possess or exercise the faculty of memory. 9. *Archaic.* to have memory or recollection (fol. by *of*). [ME *remembre(n),* t. OF: m. *remembrer,* g. LL *rememorāri,* f. L: re- RE- + *memorāre* call to mind] —**re·mem'ber·er,** *n.*
—**Syn.** 1. REMEMBER, RECALL, RECOLLECT refer to bringing back before the conscious mind things which exist in the memory. REMEMBER implies that a thing exists in the memory, though not actually present in the thoughts at the moment, and that it can be called up without effort: *to remember the days of one's childhood.* RECALL, the more conversational word, implies a voluntary effort, though not a great one: *to recall the words of a song.* RECOLLECT implies an earnest voluntary effort to remember some definite, desired fact or thing: *I cannot recollect the exact circumstances.* —**Ant.** 1. forget.

re·mem·brance (rĭ mĕm'brəns), *n.* 1. a mental impression retained. 2. act or fact of remembering. 3. the power or faculty of remembering. 4. the length of time over which recollection or memory extends. 5. state of being remembered; commemoration. 6. something that serves to bring to or keep in mind. 7. *(pl.)* greetings. —**Syn.** 6. keepsake, trophy, souvenir.

Remembrance of Things Past, a long novel (French publication, 1913–1927) by Marcel Proust.

re·mem·bran·cer (rĭ mĕm'brən sər), *n.* 1. one who reminds another of something. 2. one engaged to do this. 3. a reminder; memento; souvenir. 4. *(usually cap.)* **a.** (in England) the **King's** (or **Queen's**) **Remembrancer,** an official collecting debts due to the king and an officer of the Supreme Court. **b.** (formerly) one of certain officials of the Court of Exchequer. 5. an officer of the corporation of the City of London.

re·mex (rē'mĕks), *n., pl.* **remiges** (rĕm'ə jēz'). *Ornith.* a flight feather. [t. L: lit., oarsman (pl., *rēmigēs*), der. *rēmus* oar] —**re·mig·i·al** (rĭ mĭj'ĭ əl), *adj.*

re·mind (rĭ mīnd'), *v.t.* to cause (one) to remember. [f. RE- + MIND, v.] —**re·mind'er,** *n.*

re·mind·ful (rĭ mīnd'fəl), *adj.* 1. reviving memory of something; reminiscent. 2. retaining memory of something; mindful.

Rem·ing·ton (rĕm'ĭng tən), *n.* **Frederic,** 1861–1909, U.S. painter and sculptor.

rem·i·nisce (rĕm'ə nĭs'), *v.i.,* -nisced, -niscing. to indulge in reminiscence; recall past experiences. [back formation from REMINISCENCE]

rem·i·nis·cence (rĕm'ə nĭs'əns), *n.* 1. act or process of remembering one's past. 2. a mental impression retained and revived. 3. *(often pl.)* a recollection narrated or told. 4. something that recalls or suggests something else. 5. *Platonic Philos.* the source and cognition of ideas without appeal to sensible experience. [t. L: m. *reminiscentia*]

rem·i·nis·cent (rĕm'ə nĭs'ənt), *adj.* 1. awakening memories of something else; suggestive (fol. by *of*). 2. characterized by or of the nature of reminiscence or reminiscences. 3. given to reminiscence, as a person. [t. L: s. *reminiscens,* ppr., remembering] —**rem'i·nis'cent·ly,** *adv.*

re·mise (rĭ mīz'), *v.t.,* -mised, -mising. *Law.* to give up a claim to; surrender by deed. [t. OF, pp. (fem.) of *remettre* put back, deliver, f. re- RE- + *mettre* put (g. L *mittere* send)]

re·miss (rĭ mĭs'), *adj.* 1. not diligent, careful, or prompt in duty, business, etc. 2. characterized by negligence or carelessness. 3. lacking force or energy; languid; sluggish. [ME, t. L: s. *remissus,* pp., lit., sent back] —**re·miss'ly,** *adv.* —**re·miss'ness,** *n.*

re·mis·si·ble (rĭ mĭs'ə bəl), *adj.* that may be remitted. —**re·mis'si·bil'i·ty,** *n.*

re·mis·sion (rĭ mĭsh'ən), *n.* 1. act of remitting. 2. pardon; forgiveness, as of sins or offenses. 3. abatement or diminution, as of diligence, labor, intensity, etc. 4. the relinquishment of a payment, obligation, etc. 5. a temporary decrease or subsidence of manifestations of a disease. 6. *Obs.* relaxation.

re·miss·ness (rĭ mĭs'nĭs), *n.* state or character of being remiss; slackness. —**Syn.** See **neglect.**

re·mit (rĭ mĭt'), *v.,* -mitted, -mitting, *n.* —*v.t.* 1. to transmit or send (money, etc.) to a person or place. 2. to refrain from inflicting or enforcing, as a punishment, sentence, etc. 3. to refrain from exacting, as a payment or service. 4. to pardon or forgive (a sin, offense, etc.). 5. to slacken; abate: *to remit watchfulness.* 6. to give back: *to remit a fine.* 7. *Law.* to send back (a case) to an inferior court for further action. 8. to put back into a previous position or condition. 9. to put off; postpone. 10. *Obs.* to set free; release. 11. *Obs.* to send back to prison or custody. 12. *Obs.* to give up;

surrender. —*v.i.* 13. to transmit money, etc., as in payment. 14. to abate for a time or at intervals, as a fever. 15. to slacken; abate. —*n.* 16. *Law.* a transfer of the record of an action from one tribunal to another, particularly from an appellate court to the court of original jurisdiction. [ME, t. L: m.s. *remittere* send back] —**re·mit'ta·ble,** *adj.*

re·mit·tal (rĭ mĭt'əl), *n.* remission.

re·mit·tance (rĭ mĭt'əns), *n.* 1. the remitting of money, etc., to a recipient at a distance. 2. money or its equivalent sent from one place to another.

re·mit·tent (rĭ mĭt'ənt), *adj.* 1. abating for a time or at intervals: used esp. of a fever in which the symptoms diminish considerably at intervals without disappearing entirely. —*n.* 2. a remittent fever. —**re·mit'tence, re·mit'ten·cy,** *n.* —**re·mit'tent·ly,** *adv.*

re·mit·ter (rĭ mĭt'ər), *n.* *Law.* 1. the principle or operation by which a person who enters on an estate by a defective title, and who previously had an earlier and more valid title to it, is adjudged to hold it by the earlier and more valid one. 2. act of remitting a case to another court for decision. 3. restoration, as to a former right or condition.

re·mit·tor (rĭ mĭt'ər), *n.* *Law.* one who makes a remittance.

rem·nant (rĕm'nənt), *n.* 1. a part, quantity, or number (usually small), remaining. 2. a fragment or scrap, esp. an odd piece of cloth, lace, etc., unsold or unused. 3. a trace; vestige: *remnants of former greatness.* —*adj.* 4. remaining. [ME; syncopated var. of ME *remenant,* t. OF, ppr. of *remenoir* remain] —**Syn.** 1. remainder, residue.

re·mod·el (rē mŏd'əl), *v.t.,* -eled, -eling or *(esp. Brit.)* -elled, -elling. 1. to model again. 2. to reconstruct; make over.

re·mo·lade (rā'mə lād'), *n.* rémoulade.

re·mon·e·tize (rē mŭn'ə tīz', -mŏn'-), *v.t.,* -tized, -tizing. to restore to use as legal tender: *to remonetize silver.* —**re·mon'e·ti·za'tion,** *n.*

re·mon·strance (rĭ mŏn'strəns), *n.* 1. act of remonstrating; expostulation. 2. a protest: *deaf to remonstrances.* [late ME t. ML: m.s. *remonstrantia*]

re·mon·strant (rĭ mŏn'strənt), *adj.* 1. remonstrating; expostulatory. —*n.* 2. one who remonstrates. 3. *(cap.)* one of the Dutch Arminians whose doctrinal differences from strict Calvinists were set forth in 1610.

re·mon·strate (rĭ mŏn'strāt), *v.,* -strated, -strating. —*v.t.* 1. to say in remonstrance; protest. 2. *Obs.* to point out; show. —*v.i.* 3. to present reasons in complaint; plead in protest. [t. ML: m.s. *remonstrātus,* pp., exhibited] —**re·mon·stra·tion** (rē'mŏn strā'shən, rĕm'ən-), *n.* —**re·mon·stra·tive** (rĭ mŏn'strə tĭv), *adj.* —**re·mon·stra·tor** (rĭ mŏn'strā tər), *n.*

re·mon·tant (rĭ mŏn'tənt), *adj.* 1. blooming more than once in a season: said of certain roses. —*n.* 2. a remontant rose. [t. F, ppr. of *remonter* REMOUNT]

rem·o·ra (rĕm'ə rə), *n.* 1. any of various fishes (family Echeneididae) having on the top of the head a sucking disk by which they can attach themselves to sharks, turtles, ships, and other moving objects. 2. *Obs.* or *Archaic.* an obstacle, hindrance, or obstruction. [t. L: name of an fish, lit., delay, hindrance]

Remora, Echeneis naucrates (24 to 30 in. long)

re·morse (rĭ môrs'), *n.* 1. deep and painful regret for wrongdoing; compunction. 2. **remorse of conscience,** mental distress due to conscience. 3. *Obs.* pity; compassion. [ME *remors,* t. L: s. *remorsus* a biting back] —**Syn.** 1. penitence, contrition. See **regret.**

re·morse·ful (rĭ môrs'fəl), *adj.* 1. full of remorse. 2. characterized by or due to remorse: *a remorseful mood.* —**re·morse'ful·ly,** *adv.* —**re·morse'ful·ness,** *n.*

re·morse·less (rĭ môrs'lĭs), *adj.* without remorse; relentless; pitiless. —**re·morse'less·ly,** *adv.* —**re·morse'less·ness,** *n.*

re·mote (rĭ mōt'), *adj.,* -moter, -motest. 1. far apart; far distant in space. 2. out-of-the-way; retired; secluded: *a remote village.* 3. distant in time: *remote antiquity.* 4. distant in relationship or connection: *a remote ancestor.* 4. far removed; alien: *remote from common experience.* 5. far off; removed: *principles remote from actions.* 6. by intervention; not proximate: *remote control.* 7. slight or faint: *not the remotest idea.* 8. separated; abstracted. [ME, t. L: m.s. *remōtus,* pp., removed] —**re·mote'ly,** *adv.* —**re·mote'ness,** *n.*

re·mo·tion (rĭ mō'shən), *n.* 1. act of removing; removal. 2. *Obs.* departure.

ré·mou·lade (rā'mə läd'; *Fr.* rĕ mōō läd'), *n.* a dressing for salads. Also, **remolade.** [t. F, t. It.: m. *remolata*]

re·mount (rē mount'), *v.i., v.t.* 1. to mount again; reascend. —*n.* 2. a fresh horse, or a supply of fresh horses. [ME, t. OF: m.s. *remonter.* See RE-, MOUNT[1]]

re·mov·a·ble (rĭ mōō'və bəl), *adj.* that may be removed. —**re·mov'a·bil'i·ty, re·mov'a·ble·ness,** *n.* —**re·mov'a·bly,** *adv.*

re·mov·al (rĭ mōō'vəl), *n.* 1. act of removing. 2. change of residence, position, etc. 3. dismissal, as from an office.

re·mi/grate	re·mil/i·ta·rize/	re·mod/i·fi·ca/tion	re·mold/
re·mil/i·ta·ri·za/tion	re·mix/	re·mod/i·fy/	re·mol/li·fy/

re·move (rĭ mōōv′), v., **-moved, -moving,** n. —v.t.
1. to move from a place or position; take away; take off
2. to move or shift to another place or position. **3.** to
put out; send away: *to remove a tenant.* **4.** to displace
from a position or office. **5.** to take, withdraw, or separate (from). **6.** to do away with; put an end to: *to remove a stain.* **7.** to kill; assassinate. —v.i. **8.** to move
from one place to another, esp. to another locality or
residence. **9.** *Poetic.* to go away; depart; disappear.
—n. **10.** act of removing. **11.** a removal from one place,
as of residence, to another. **12.** the distance by which
one place or thing is separated from another. **13.** a step
or degree, as in a graded scale. **14.** *Brit.* a promotion
of a pupil to a higher class or division at school. [ME,
t. OF: m. *remouvoir,* g. L. *removēre*] —**re·mov′er,** n.
—Syn. **2.** transfer, displace.

re·moved (rĭ mōōvd′), adj. **1.** remote; separate; not
connected with; distinct from. **2.** distant: used in expressing degrees of relationship: *a first cousin twice removed is a cousin's grandchild.*

Rem·sen (rĕm′sən), n. **Ira** (ī′rə), 1846–1927, U.S.
chemist and educator.

re·mu·ner·ate (rĭ mū′nə rāt′), v.t., **-ated, -ating. 1.** to
pay, recompense, or reward for work, trouble, etc. **2.** to
yield a recompense for (work, services, etc.). [t. L: m.s.
remūnerātus, pp., given back]

re·mu·ner·a·tion (rĭ mū′nə rā′shən), n. **1.** act of re-
munerating. **2.** that which remunerates; reward; pay:
little remuneration for his services.

re·mu·ner·a·tive (rĭ mū′nə rā′tĭv, -nər ə tĭv), adj. **1.**
affording remuneration; profitable: *remunerative work.*
2. that remunerates. —**re·mu′ner·a·tive·ly,** adv.

Re·mus (rē′məs), n. **1.** *Rom. Legend.* the twin brother
of Romulus (which see). **2. Uncle.** See **Uncle Remus.**

ren·ais·sance (rĕn′ə säns′, -zäns′, rĭ nā′səns; Fr. rə-
nĕ säns′), n. **1.** a new birth; a revival. **2.** (*cap.*) **a.** the
activity, spirit, or time of the great revival of art, letters,
and learning in Europe during the 14th, 15th, and 16th
centuries, marking the transition from the medieval to
the modern world. **b.** the forms and treatments in art
used during this period. **c.** any similar revival in the
world of art and learning. [t. F, der. *renaître* be born
again. See RENASCENT]

Renaissance architecture, the style of building
and decoration succeeding the medieval, based upon
clarity and mathematical relationship of plan and design, and employing to this end the forms and ornaments
of classical Roman art. It originated in Italy in the
early 15th century.

re·nal (rē′nəl), adj. of or pertaining to the kidneys or
the surrounding regions. [t. LL: s. *rēnālis,* der. L *rēn*
kidney]

renal capsule, *Anat.* suprarenal gland. Also, **renal
gland.**

Re·nan (rĭ nän′; Fr. rə nän′), n. **Ernest** (ĕr nĕst′),
1823–92, French philologist, historian, and critic.

Ren·ard (rĕn′ərd), n. Reynard.

re·nas·cence (rĭ näs′əns), n. **1.** rebirth; revival: *a
period of moral renascence.* **2.** (*cap.*) the Renaissance.

re·nas·cent (rĭ näs′ənt), adj. being reborn; springing
again into being or vigor: *a renascent interest in Henry
James.* [t. L: s. *renascens,* ppr.]

ren·coun·ter (rĕn koun′tər), v.t., v.i. **1.** to meet hostilely. **2.** to encounter casually. —n. Also, **ren·con·tre**
(rĕn kŏn′tər; Fr. rän kôn′tr). **3.** a hostile meeting; a
battle. **4.** a contest of any kind. **5.** a casual meeting.
[t. F: m. *rencontrer,* f. re- RE- + *encontrer* ENCOUNTER]

rend (rĕnd), v., **rent, rending.** —v.t. **1.** to separate into
parts with force or violence: *rent to pieces.* **2.** to tear
apart, split, or divide. **3.** to pull or tear violently (fol. by
away, off, up, etc.). **4.** to tear (one's garments or hair)
in grief, rage, etc. **5.** to disturb (the air) sharply with
loud noise. **6.** to harrow or distress (the heart, etc.) with
painful feelings. —v.i. **7.** to render or tear something.
8. to become rent or torn. [ME *rende(n),* OE *rendan,* c.
OFris. *renda*] —Syn. **2.** rip, rive, sunder, sever, cleave,
chop, fracture. See tear[2].

ren·der (rĕn′dər), v.t. **1.** to make, or cause, to be or
become: *to render someone helpless.* **2.** to do; perform: *to
render a service.* **3.** to furnish: *to render aid.* **4.** to exhibit or show (obedience, attention, etc.). **5.** to present
for consideration, approval, payment, action, etc., as an
account. **6.** *Law.* to return; to make a payment in
money, kind, or service, as by a tenant to his superior.
7. to pay as due (a tax, tribute, etc.). **8.** to deliver officially, as judgment. **9.** to reproduce in another language;
translate. **10.** to represent; depict, as in painting.
11. to represent (a perspective view of a projected building) in drawing or painting. **12.** to bring out the meaning of by performance or execution, or interpret, as a
part in a drama, a piece of music, a subject in representational art, etc. **13.** to give in return or requital.
14. to give back; restore (often fol. by *back*). **15.** to
give up; surrender. **16.** *Bldg. Trades.* to cover (brickwork or stone) with a first coat of plaster. **17.** to melt
(fat, etc.); clarify or extract by melting; try out. —n.
18. *Bldg. Trades.* the first coat of plaster applied to
brickwork or stone. [ME *rendre(n),* t. OF, g. Rom. *ren-
dere* give back (b. *prendere,* L *prehendere* take and L
reddere give back)] —**ren′der·a·ble,** adj. —**ren′der·er,**
n. —Syn. **3.** give, supply, contribute.

ren·dez·vous (rän′də vōō′; Fr. rän dĕ vōō′), n., pl.
-vous (-vōōz′; Fr. -vōō′), v., **-voused** (-vōōd′), **-vousing**
(-vōō′ĭng). —n. **1.** an appointment or engagement
made between two or more persons to meet at a fixed
place and time. **2.** a place for meeting or assembling,
esp. of troops or ships. —v.i., v.t. **3.** to assemble at a
place previously appointed. [t. F, n. use of *rendez vous*
present or betake yourself (yourselves)]

ren·di·tion (rĕn dĭsh′ən), n. **1.** act of rendering.
2. translation. **3.** interpretation, as of a role or a piece
of music. **4.** *Obs. or Rare.* surrender. [t. obs. F, t. L: m.s.
redditio, with -n- from *rendre* RENDER]

ren·e·gade (rĕn′ə gād′), n. **1.** one who deserts a party
or cause for another. **2.** an apostate from a religious
faith. —adj. **3.** of or like a renegade; traitorous. [t. Sp.,
Pg.: m. *renegado,* der. *renegar* renounce, t. ML: m. *renegāre,* der. L *negāre* deny]

ren·e·ga·do (rĕn′ə gā′dō), n., pl. **-does.** *Archaic.* a
renegade.

re·nege (rĭ nĭg′, -nĕg′), v., **-neged, -neging,** n.
—v.i. **1.** *Cards.* to play a card that is not of the suit led or
to break a rule of play. **2.** *Colloq.* to go back on one's
word. —v.t. **3.** *Archaic.* to deny; disown; renounce.
—n. **4.** *Cards.* an act or instance of reneging. [t. ML:
m.s. *renegāre,* f. L: re- RE- + *negāre* deny] —**re·neg′er,** n.

re·new (rĭ nū′, -nōō′), v.t. **1.** to begin or take up again,
as acquaintance, conversation, etc. **2.** to make effective
for an additional period: *to renew a lease.* **3.** to restore or
replenish: *to renew a stock of goods.* **4.** to make, say, or
do again. **5.** to revive; reëstablish. **6.** to recover (youth
strength, etc.). **7.** to make new, or as if new, again; restore to a former state. —v.i. **8.** to begin again; recom-
mence. **9.** to renew a lease, note, etc. **10.** to become
new, or as if new, again. —**re·new′a·ble,** adj.
—Syn. **7.** re-create, rejuvenate, regenerate. RENEW,
RENOVATE, REPAIR, RESTORE suggest making something the
way it formerly was. To RENEW means to bring back to an
original condition of freshness and vigor: *to renew one's
enthusiasm.* RENOVATE means to make good any dilapida-
tions: *to renovate an old house.* To REPAIR is to put into good
or sound condition; to make good any injury, damage,
wear and tear, decay, etc.; to mend: *to repair the roof of a
house.* To RESTORE is to bring back to its former place or
position something which has faded, disappeared, been lost,
etc.; to reinstate a person in a rank or position: *to restore a
king to his throne.*

re·new·al (rĭ nū′əl, -nōō′-), n. **1.** act of renewing.
2. state of being renewed. **3.** an instance of this.

Ren·frew (rĕn′frōō), n. a county in SW Scotland.
318,400 pop. (est. 1946); 225 sq. mi.: *Co. seat:* Renfrew.
Also, **Ren·frew·shire** (rĕn′frōō shĭr′, -shər).

Re·ni (rē′nē), n. **Guido** (gwē′dô), 1575–1642, Italian painter.

ren·i·form (rĕn′ə fôrm′, rē′nə-), adj.
kidney-shaped: *a reniform leaf,* hematite in reniform masses. [f. reni- (comb.
form repr. L rēn kidney) + -FORM]

Reniform leaf

re·ni·tent (rĭ nī′tənt, rĕn′ə-), adj. **1.**
resisting pressure; resistant. **2.** persistently opposing; recalcitrant. [t. L:
s. *renitens,* ppr., struggling, resisting] —**re·ni′ten·cy,** n.

Rennes (rĕn), n. a city in NW France: formerly capital
of Brittany; scene of Dreyfus trial. 124,122 (1954).

ren·net (rĕn′ĭt), n. **1.** the lining membrane of the
fourth stomach of a calf, or of the stomach of certain
other young animals. **2.** *Biochem.* the substance from
the stomach of the calf which contains rennin. **3.** a
preparation or extract of the rennet membrane, used to
curdle milk, as in making cheese, junket, etc. [ME, f.
renne run + -et (OE -et), n. suffix]

ren·nin (rĕn′ĭn), n. *Biochem.* a coagulating enzyme
occurring in the gastric juice of the calf, forming the active principle of rennet, and able to curdle milk.

Re·no (rē′nō), n. a city in W Nevada: divorce courts.
51,470 (1960).

Re·noir (rə nwär′), n. **Pierre Auguste** (pyĕr ō gyst′),
1841–1919, French painter.

re·nounce (rĭ nouns′), v., **-nounced, -nouncing.** —v.t.
1. to give up or put aside voluntarily. **2.** to give up by
formal declaration: *to renounce a claim.* **3.** to repudiate;
disown. —v.i. **4.** *Cards.* to play a card of a different
suit from that led. **5.** *Cards.* to renounce a suit led.
[ME, t. F: m.s. *renoncer,* g. L *renuntiāre* make known,
report] —**re·nounce′ment,** n. —Syn. **1.** forsake,
forgo, relinquish. See **abandon**[1].

ren·o·vate (rĕn′ə vāt′), v., **-vated, -vating,** adj. —v.t.
1. to make new or as if new again; restore to good condition; repair. **2.** to reinvigorate; refresh; revive. —adj.
3. *Archaic.* renovated. [t. L: m.s. *renovātus,* pp.] —**ren′-
o·va′tion,** n. —**ren′o·va′tor,** n. —Syn. **1.** See renew.

re·nown (rĭ noun′), n. **1.** widespread and high repute;
fame. **2.** *Rare.* report or rumor. [ME, t. AF: m. *renoun,*
der. OF *renommer* name over again (frequently), der.
nommer name, g. L *nōmināre*] —Syn. **1.** celebrity,
glory, distinction, note.

re·nowned (rĭ nound′), adj. celebrated; famous.

rens·se·laer·ite (rĕn′sə lĕr′ĭt, rĕn′sə lər′ĭt), n. a variety of talc. [named after Stephen Van *Rensselaer*
(1764–1839) of New York]

rent[1] (rĕnt), n. **1.** a return or payment made periodically by a tenant to an owner or landlord for the use of

re·name′	re·nom′i·nate′	re·no′tice	re·nour′ish
re·nav′i·gate′	re·nom′i·na′tion	re·no′ti·fy′	re·nour′ish·ment

b., blend of, blended; c., cognate with; d., dialect, dialectal; der., derived from; f., formed from; g., going back to;
m., modification of; r., replacing; s., stem of; t., taken from; ?, perhaps. **See the full key on inside cover.**

land or building. **2.** a similar return or payment for the use of property of any kind. **3.** *Econ.* the excess of the produce or return yielded by a given piece of cultivated land over the cost (labor, capital, etc.) of production; the yield from a piece of land or real estate. **4.** profit or return derived from any differential advantage in production. **5.** *Obs.* revenue or income. —*v.t.* **6.** to grant the possession and enjoyment of (property) in return for payments to be made at agreed times. **7.** to take and hold (property) in return for payments to be made at agreed times. —*v.i.* **8.** to be leased or let for rent. [ME, t. OF: m. *rente*, g. Rom. *rendita*, g. L *reddita* (*pecūnia*) paid (money), with -*n*- from *pre*(*he*)*n-dere* take] —**rent′a·ble,** *adj.* —**Syn. 7.** See **hire.**

rent² (rěnt), *n.* **1.** an opening made by rending or tearing; slit; fissure. **2.** a breach of relations or union. [n. use of *rent*, v., var. of REND] —*v.* **3.** pt. and pp. of **rend.**

rent·al (rěn′təl), *n.* **1.** an amount received or paid as rent. **2.** an income arising from rents received. —*adj.* **3.** pertaining to rent. [ME *rentall*, t. AF: m. *rental*, or t. Anglo-L: m. *rentale.* See RENT, -AL²]

rental library, a collection of popular current books available for loan upon payment of a small fee.

rente (ränt), *n.* French. **1.** revenue or income, or the instrument evidencing a right to such periodic receipts. **2.** (*pl.*) perpetual bonds issued by the French government. [see RENT¹]

rent·er (rěn′tər), *n.* **1.** one who rents. **2.** one who holds, or has the use of, property by payment of rent.

ren·tier (rän tyē′), *n.* French. one who has a fixed income, as from lands, bonds, etc. [F, der. *rente* RENTE]

rent-seck (rěnt′sěk′), *n.* a right to rent in which the renter does not have the usual power of collection by seizure of the tenant's goods. [late ME, t. AF: m. *rente secque,* lit., dry rent]

re·nun·ci·a·tion (rǐ nǔn′sǐ ā′shən, -shǐ-), *n.* **1.** the formal abandoning of a right, title, etc. **2.** a voluntary giving up, esp. at a sacrifice. —**re·nun·ci·a·tive** (rǐ nǔn′shǐ ā′tǐv, -sǐ-), **re·nun·ci·a·to·ry** (rǐ nǔn′shǐ ə tōr′ǐ, -sǐ-), *adj.*

re·o·pen (rē ō′pən), *v.t., v.i.* **1.** to open again. **2.** to start again; resume: *to reopen an argument, an attack, etc.*

re·or·der (rē ôr′dər), *v.t.* **1.** to put in order again. **2.** *Com.* to give a reorder for. —*n.* **3.** *Com.* a second or repeated order for the same goods from the same dealer.

re·or·gan·i·za·tion (rē′ôr gən ə zā′shən), *n.* **1.** act or process of reorganizing. **2.** state of being reorganized. **3.** *Finance.* a thorough or drastic reconstruction of a business corporation, including a marked change in capital structure, often following a failure and receivership or bankruptcy trusteeship.

re·or·gan·ize (rē ôr′gə nīz′), *v.t., v.i.,* **-ized, -izing.** to organize again. Also, *esp. Brit.,* **re·or·gan·ise′.** —**re·or′gan·iz′er,** *n.*

rep¹ (rěp), *n.* a transversely corded fabric of wool, silk, rayon, or cotton. Also, **repp.** [t. F: m. *reps*]

rep² (rěp), *n.* *Slang.* reputation. [a shortened form]

Rep., **1.** Representative. **2.** Republic. **3.** Republican.

rep., **1.** report. **2.** reported. **3.** reporter.

re·paint (rē pānt′), *v.t.* **1.** to paint again. —*n.* **2.** a part repainted, esp. a part of a picture by a restorer.

re·pair¹ (rǐ pâr′), *v.t.* **1.** to restore to a good or sound condition after decay or damage; mend: *to repair a motor.* **2.** to restore or renew by any process of making good, strengthening, etc.: *repair a broken constitution.* **3.** to remedy; make good; make up for: *to repair damage, a loss, a deficiency, etc.* **4.** to make amends for: *repair a wrong done.* —*n.* **5.** act, process, or work of repairing: *repair of a building.* **6.** (*usually pl.*) an instance, operation, or piece of repairing: *to make repairs.* **7.** the good condition resulting from repairing: *to keep in repair.* [ME *repaire*(*n*), t. L: m. *reparāre* put in order] —**re·pair′a·ble,** *adj.* —**re·pair′er,** *n.* —**Syn. 1.** remodel, renovate. See **renew.**

re·pair² (rǐ pâr′), *v.i.* **1.** to betake oneself or go, as to a place: *he soon repaired in person to Washington.* **2.** to go frequently or customarily. —*n.* **3.** *Archaic.* a resort or haunt. [ME *repaire*(*n*), t. OF: m. *repairer* return, g. LL *repatriāre* return to one's country]

re·pair·man (rǐ pâr′măn′, -mən), *n., pl.* **-men.** one whose occupation is repairing things.

re·pand (rǐ pǎnd′), *adj. Bot.* **1.** having the margin slightly wavy, as a leaf. **2.** slightly wavy. [t. L: s. *repandus* bent back]

rep·a·ra·ble (rěp′ə rə bəl), *adj.* capable of being repaired or remedied. Also, **re·pair·a·ble** (rǐ pâr′ə bəl). [t. L: m.s. *reparābilis*] —**rep′a·ra·bly,** *adv.*

Repand leaf

rep·a·ra·tion (rěp′ə rā′shən), *n.* **1.** the making of amends for wrong or injury done: *a wrong which admits of no reparation.* **2.** (*usually pl.*) compensation in money, material, labor, etc. by a defeated nation (as Germany and her allies after World War I) for damage to civilian population and property during war. **3.** restoration to good condition. **4.** repairs. [ME *reparacion,* t. L: m.s. *reparātio*] —**Syn. 1.** See **redress.**

re·par·a·tive (rǐ pǎr′ə tǐv), *adj.* **1.** tending to repair. **2.** pertaining to or involving reparation. Also, **re·par·a·to·ry** (rǐ pǎr′ə tōr′ǐ).

rep·ar·tee (rěp′ər tē′), *n.* **1.** a ready and witty reply. **2.** speech or talk characterized by quickness and wittiness of reply. **3.** skill in making witty replies. [t. F: m. *repartie* an answering thrust, prop. pp. of *repartir* reply promptly, f. re- RE- + *partir* divide (cf. F *jeu parti* question and answer poem or contest)]

re·par·ti·tion (rē′pär tǐsh′ən, -pär-), *n.* **1.** distribution; partition. **2.** redistribution. —*v.t.* **3.** to divide up.

re·pass (rē păs′, -päs′), *v.t., v.i.* to pass back or again. —**re·pas·sage** (rē păs′ǐj), *n.*

re·past (rǐ păst′, -päst′), *n.* **1.** a quantity of food taken or provided for one occasion of eating: *to eat a light repast.* **2.** a taking of food; a meal: *the evening repast.* **3.** *Archaic.* the taking of food, as at a meal. **4.** *Obs.* food. [ME, t. OF, t. LL: s. *repastus,* prop. pp. of *repascere* feed regularly]

re·pa·tri·ate (*v.* rē pā′trǐ āt′; *n.* rē pā′trǐ ǐt), *v.t., v.i.,* **-ated, -ating,** *n.* —*v.t.* **1.** to bring or send back (a person) to his own country, esp. (prisoners of war, refugees, etc.) to the land of citizenship. —*n.* **2.** one who has been repatriated. [t. LL: m.s. *repatriātus,* pp.] —**re·pa′tri·a′tion,** *n.*

re·pay (rǐ pā′), *v.,* **-paid, -paying.** —*v.t.* **1.** to pay back or refund (money, etc.). **2.** to make return for: *repaid with thanks.* **3.** to make return to in any way: *feel repaid for sacrifices made.* **4.** to return: *repay a visit.* —*v.i.* **5.** to make repayment or return. —**re·pay′a·ble,** *adj.* —**re·pay′ment,** *n.* —**Syn. 1.** reimburse, indemnify.

re·peal (rǐ pēl′), *v.t.* **1.** to revoke or withdraw formally or officially: *to repeal a grant.* **2.** to revoke or annul (a law, tax, duty, etc.) by express legislative enactment; abrogate. —*n.* **3.** act of repealing; revocation; abrogation. [ME *repele*(*n*), t. AF: m. *repel*(*l*)*er,* f. re- RE- + *apeler* APPEAL] —**re·peal′a·ble,** *adj.* —**re·peal′er,** *n.*

re·peat (rǐ pēt′), *v.t.* **1.** to say or utter again (something one has already said): *to repeat a word for emphasis.* **2.** to say or utter in reproducing the words, etc., of another: *repeat a sentence after the teacher.* **3.** to reproduce (utterances, sounds, etc.) as an echo, a phonograph, or the like does. **4.** to tell (something heard) to another or others. **5.** to do, make, perform, etc. again: *to repeat an action, a ceremony, a passage of music, etc.* **6.** to go through or undergo again: *to repeat an experience.* —*v.i.* **7.** to do or say something again. **8.** *U.S.* to vote more than once at the same election (a form of fraud). —*n.* **9.** act of repeating. **10.** something repeated. **11.** a duplicate or reproduction of something. **12.** *Music.* **a.** a passage to be repeated. **b.** a sign, as a vertical arrangement of dots, calling for the repetition of a passage. [ME *repete*(*n*), t. L: m. *repetere* do or say again] —**Syn. 1, 5.** REPEAT, RECAPITULATE, REITERATE refer to saying a thing more than once. To REPEAT is to do or say something over again: *to repeat a question, an order.* To RECAPITULATE is to restate in brief form, to summarize, often by repeating the principal points in a discourse: *to recapitulate an argument.* To REITERATE is to do or say something over and over again, to repeat insistently: *to reiterate a refusal, a demand.*

re·peat·ed (rǐ pē′tǐd), *adj.* done, made, or said again and again: *repeated attempts.* —**re·peat′ed·ly,** *adv.*

re·peat·er (rǐ pē′tər), *n.* **1.** one who or that which repeats. **2.** a repeating firearm. **3.** a watch or clock, esp. a watch, which may be made to strike the hour (and sometimes the quarter-hour, etc.) last past. **4.** *Educ.* a pupil who repeats a course or group of courses, in which he has previously failed. **5.** *U.S.* one who fraudulently votes more than once at an election.

repeating decimal, *Math.* circulating decimal.

repeating rifle or **firearm,** a rifle or firearm capable of discharging a number of shots without reloading.

re·pel (rǐ pěl′), *v.,* **-pelled, -pelling.** —*v.t.* **1.** to drive or force back (an assailant, invader, etc.). **2.** to thrust back or away: *he repelled the medicine the nurse offered.* **3.** to resist effectually (an attack, onslaught): *repel the invader's attack.* **4.** to keep off or out; fail to mix with: *water and oil repel each other.* **5.** to put away from one; refuse to have to do with: *repel temptation.* **6.** to refuse to accept or admit; reject: *to repel a suggestion.* **7.** to discourage the advances of (a person): *he repelled her with his harshness.* **8.** to excite feelings of distaste or aversion: *her untidy appearance repels me.* **9.** *Mech.* to push back or away by a force, as one body acting upon another (opposed to *attract*). —*v.i.* **10.** to act with a force that drives or keeps away something. **11.** to cause distaste or aversion. [ME *repelle,* t. L: m. *repellere* drive back] —**re·pel′lence, re·pel′len·cy,** *n.* —**re·pel′ler,** *n.* —**Syn. 1.** repulse, parry, ward off.

re·pel·lent (rǐ pěl′ənt), *adj.* **1.** causing distaste or aversion; repulsive. **2.** repelling; driving back. —*n.* **3.** something that repels. **4.** a medicine that serves to prevent or reduce swellings, tumors, etc. **5.** a kind of water-resistant fabric.

re·pent¹ (rǐ pěnt′), *v.i.* **1.** to feel self-reproach, compunction, or contrition for past conduct; change one's mind with regard to past action in consequence of dis-

re·num′ber	re·oc·cu·pa′tion	re·pac′i·fy	re·pave′
re·nu′mer·ate′	re·oc·cu·py′	re·pack′	re·pawn′
re·ob·tain′	re·op·pose′	re·pack′er	re·ped′dle
re·ob·tain′a·ble	re·or·di·na′tion	re·paid′	re·pe′nal·ize′

satisfaction with it or its results (often fol. by *of*). **2.** to feel such sorrow for sin or fault as to be disposed to change one's life for the better; be penitent (often fol. by *of*). —*v.t.* **3.** to remember or regard with self-reproach or contrition: *to repent one's injustice to another.* **4.** to feel sorry for; regret: *to repent one's words.* [ME *repenten*, t. OF: m. *repentir*, f. re- RE- + Rom. *penitīre* (r. L *poenitēre*)] —**re·pent/er,** n.

re·pent² (rē/pənt), *adj.* **1.** *Bot.* creeping. **2.** *Zool.* reptant. [t. L: s. *rēpens*, ppr., creeping]

re·pent·ance (rǐ pĕn/təns), n. **1.** compunction or contrition for wrongdoing or sin. **2.** regret for any past action. —**Syn.** 1. contriteness, penitence, remorse. 2. sorrow, regret.

re·pent·ant (rǐ pĕn/tənt), *adj.* **1.** repenting; experiencing repentance. **2.** characterized by or showing repentance: *a repentant mood.* [ME, t. OF, ppr. of *repentir* REPENT] —**re·pent/ant·ly,** *adv.*

re·peo·ple (rē pē/pəl), *v.t.,* -pled, -pling. **1.** to furnish again with people. **2.** to restock with animals. [t. OF: m. *repeupler.* See RE-, PEOPLE, v.]

re·per·cus·sion (rē/pər kŭsh/ən), n. **1.** an after effect, often an indirect result, of some event or action: *the repercussions of the first World War are still felt.* **2.** the state of being driven back by a resisting body. **3.** a rebounding or recoil of something after impact. **4.** reverberation; echo. **5.** *Music.* (in a fugue) the point after the development of an episode at which the subject and answer appear again. [ME, t. L: s. *repercussio*]

re·per·cus·sive (rē/pər kŭs/ĭv), *adj.* **1.** causing repercussion; reverberating. **2.** reflected; reverberated.

rep·er·toire (rĕp/ər twär/, -twôr/), n. the list of dramas, operas, parts, pieces, etc., which a company, actor, singer, or the like, is prepared to perform. [t. F, t. L: m. *repertōrium* inventory, catalogue]

rep·er·to·ry (rĕp/ər tōr/ĭ), n., *pl.* -ries. **1.** repertoire. **2.** a type of theatrical producing organization wherein one company prepares several plays, operas, etc., and produces them alternately. **3.** a store or stock of things available. **4.** storehouse. [t. L: m.s. *repertōrium*]

rep·e·tend (rĕp/ə tĕnd/, rĕp/ə tĕnd/), n. **1.** *Math.* that part of a circulating decimal repeated indefinitely. **2.** *Music.* a phrase or sound which is repeated. [t. L: s. *repetendum,* neut. ger., (that) which is to be repeated]

rep·e·ti·tion (rĕp/ə tĭsh/ən), n. **1.** act of repeating; repeated action, performance, production, or presentation. **2.** repeated utterance; reiteration. **3.** something made by or resulting from repeating. **4.** a reproduction, copy, or replica. [t. L: s. *repetitio*]

rep·e·ti·tious (rĕp/ə tĭsh/əs), *adj.* abounding in repetition; characterized by undue and tedious repetition. —**rep/e·ti/tious·ly,** *adv.* —**rep/e·ti/tious·ness,** n.

re·pet·i·tive (rǐ pĕt/ə tĭv), *adj.* pertaining to or characterized by repetition.

re·phrase (rē frāz/), *v.t.,* -phrased, -phrasing. to phrase again or differently: *he rephrased the statement to give it more informality.*

re·pine (rǐ pīn/), *v.i.,* -pined, -pining. to be fretfully discontented; fret; complain. [appar. f. RE- + PINE², v.]

re·place (rǐ plās/), *v.t.,* -placed, -placing. **1.** to fill or take the place of; substitute for (a person or thing): *electricity has replaced gas as a means of illumination.* **2.** to provide a substitute or equivalent in the place of: *to replace a broken vase or dish.* **3.** to restore; return; make good: *to replace a sum of money borrowed.* **4.** to restore to a former or the proper place: *the stolen paintings were replaced in the museum.* —**re·place/a·ble,** *adj.* —**re·plac/er,** n.

—**Syn.** 1. REPLACE, SUPERSEDE, SUPPLANT refer to putting one thing or person in place of another. To REPLACE is to take the place of, to succeed: *Mr. A. will replace Mr. B. as president.* SUPERSEDE implies that that which is replacing another is an improvement: *the typewriter has superseded the pen.* SUPPLANT implies that that which takes the other's place has ousted the former holder, and usurped the position or function esp. by art or fraud: *to supplant a former favorite.* 3. refund, repay.

re·place·ment (rǐ plās/mənt), n. **1.** act of replacing. **2.** *Mil.* a reinforcement. **3.** *Geol.* the process of practically simultaneous removal and deposition by which a new mineral of partly or wholly differing chemical composition grows in the body of an old mineral or mineral aggregate. **4.** *Crystall.* the replacing of an angle or edge by one face or more.

re·plead·er (rē plē/dər), n. *Law.* **1.** a second pleading. **2.** the right or privilege of pleading again. [f. RE- + PLEAD + -ER³. Cf. OF *repledoier,* F *replaider*]

re·plen·ish (rǐ plĕn/ĭsh), *v.t.* **1.** to bring back to a state of fullness or completeness, as by supplying what is lacking: *to replenish a stock of goods.* **2.** to supply (a fire, stove, etc.) with fresh fuel. **3.** to fill again or anew. [ME *replenys,* t. OF: m. *repleniss-,* s. *replenir* fill up again, f. re- RE + *plenir* fill, der. *plein* full, g. L *plēnus*] —**re·plen/ish·er,** n. —**re·plen/ish·ment,** n.

re·plete (rǐ plēt/), *adj.* **1.** abundantly supplied or provided (fol. by *with*). **2.** stuffed or gorged with food and drink. [ME, t. L: m. *replētus,* pp., filled] —**re·plete/ness,** n.

re·ple·tion (rǐ plē/shən), n. **1.** condition of being replete; fullness. **2.** overfullness resulting from eating or drinking to excess.

re·plev·in (rǐ plĕv/ǐn), *Law.* —n. **1. a.** the recovery of goods or chattels wrongfully taken or detained, on security given that the issue shall be tried at law and the goods returned in case of an adverse decision. **b.** the common law action or writ by which goods are replevied. —*v.t.* **2.** to replevy. [late ME, t. AF, der. OF *replevir;* whence also Anglo-L *replevina*]

re·plev·i·sa·ble (rǐ plĕv/ə sə bəl), *adj. Law.* capable of being replevied. Also, **re·plev·i·a·ble** (rǐ plĕv/ǐ ə bəl).

re·plev·y (rǐ plĕv/ǐ), *v.,* -plevied, -plevying, n., *pl.* -plevies. *Law.* —*v.t.* **1.** to recover possession of by an action of replevin. —*v.i.* **2.** to take possession of goods or chattels under a replevin order. —n. **3.** a seizure in replevin. [late ME, t. OF: m. *replevir,* AF *replever,* f. re- RE- + *plevir* PLEDGE]

rep·li·ca (rĕp/lə kə), n. **1.** a copy or reproduction of a work of art by the maker of the original. **2.** a copy or reproduction. [t. It., der. *replicare.* See REPLY, v.]

rep·li·cate (rĕp/lə kǐt), *adj.* folded; bent back on itself. Also, **rep·li·cat·ed** (rĕp/lə kā/tǐd). [t. L: m.s. *replicātus,* pp.]

rep·li·ca·tion (rĕp/lə kā/shən), n. **1.** a reply. **2.** a reply to an answer. **3.** *Law.* the reply of the plaintiff or complainant to the defendant's plea or answer. **4.** reverberation; echo. **5.** a copy.

re·ply (rǐ plī/), *v.,* -plied, -plying, n., *pl.* -plies. —*v.i.* **1.** to make answer in words or writing; answer; respond: *reply to me.* **2.** to respond by some action, performance, etc.: *reply to the enemy's fire.* **3.** to return a sound; echo. **4.** *Law.* to answer a defendant's plea. —*v.t.* **5.** to return as an answer: *he replied that no consideration would induce him to accept.* —n. **6.** an answer or response in words or writing. **7.** a response made by some action, performance, etc. [ME *replye(n),* t. OF: m. s. *replier* fold again, turn back, reply, g. L *replicāre* unfold, reply] —**re·pli/er,** n. —**Syn.** 6. See **answer.**

ré·pon·dez s'il vous plaît (rā pôN dā/ sēl vōō plĕ/), French. please reply. *Abbr.:* R.S.V.P.

re·port (rǐ pōrt/), n. **1.** an account brought back or presented; a statement submitted in reply to inquiry as the result of investigation, or by a person authorized to examine and bring or send information. **2.** an account of a speech, debate, meeting, etc., esp. as taken down for publication. **3.** a statement of a judicial opinion or decision, or of a case argued and determined in a court of justice. **4.** *(pl.) Law.* a collection of adjudications: *New York reports.* **5.** a statement or announcement. **6.** a statement generally circulated; rumor. **7.** repute; reputation. **8.** a loud noise, as from an explosion. —*v.t.* **9.** to carry and repeat as an answer or message; repeat as what one has heard. **10.** to relate as what has been learned by observation or information. **11.** to give or render a formal account or statement of: *to report a deficit.* **12.** to make a formal report on (a bill, etc., officially referred). **13.** to lay a charge against (a person), as to a superior. **14.** to make known the presence or whereabouts of (oneself); present (oneself) to a person in authority, as in accordance with requirements. **15.** to take down (a speech, etc.) in writing. **16.** to write an account of (an event, situation, etc.), as for publication in a newspaper. **17.** to relate or tell. —*v.i.* **18.** to make a report; draw up or submit a formal report. **19.** to act as a reporter, as for a newspaper. **20.** to report oneself, as to one in authority. **21.** to present oneself duly, as at a place. [ME *reporte(n),* t. OF: m. *reporter,* g. L *reportāre*] —**re·port/a·ble,** *adj.*

re·port·er (rǐ pōr/tər), n. **1.** one who reports. **2.** one employed to gather and report news for a newspaper or news agency. **3.** one who prepares official reports, as of legal or legislative proceedings.

rep·or·to·ri·al (rĕp/ər tōr/ǐ əl), *adj.* of or pertaining to a reporter.

re·pos·al (rǐ pō/zəl), n. act of reposing.

re·pose¹ (rǐ pōz/), n., *v.,* -posed, -posing. —n. **1.** state of reposing or resting; rest; sleep. **2.** peace or tranquility. **3.** dignified calmness, as of manner or demeanor. **4.** absence of movement, animation, etc. —*v.i.* **5.** to lie at rest; take rest. **6.** to be at peace or in tranquillity, as a land; lie in quiet. **7.** to lie or rest on something. **8.** to depend or rely on a person or thing. —*v.t.* **9.** to lay to rest; rest, refresh by rest (often used reflexively). [late ME, t. F: m.s. *reposer,* g. L *repausāre*]

re·pose² (rǐ pōz/), *v.t.,* -posed, -posing. **1.** to put (confidence, trust, etc.) in a person or thing. **2.** *Obs. or Rare.* to deposit. [t. L: m. *repos-* (in *reposuī, repositus,* forms of *repōnere* replace), modeled on DISPOSE, etc.]

re·pose·ful (rǐ pōz/fəl), *adj.* full of repose; calm; quiet. —**re·pose/ful·ly,** *adv.* —**re·pose/ful·ness,** n.

re·pos·it (rǐ pŏz/ĭt), *v.t.* **1.** to put back; replace. **2.** to lay up or store; deposit. [t. L: s. *repositus,* pp., put back in place]

re·po·si·tion (rē/pə zĭsh/ən, rĕp/ə-), n. **1.** act of depositing or storing. **2.** replacement, as of a bone.

re·pos·i·to·ry (rǐ pŏz/ə tōr/ǐ), n., *pl.* -tories. **1.** a receptacle or place where things are deposited, stored, or

re·plant/	re·pledge/	re/pol·ar·i·za/tion	re/pop/u·late/
re/plan·ta/tion	re·plume/	re·pol/ish	re/pop·u·la/tion
re·play/	re·plunge/	re·pop/u·lar·ize/	re/por·tion

b., blend of, blended; c., cognate with; d., dialect, dialectal; der., derived from; f., formed from; g., going back to; m., modification of; r., replacing; s., stem of; t., taken from; ?, perhaps. See the full key on inside cover.

offered for sale, esp., in England, a storage warehouse. 2. a place in which a dead body is deposited. 3. a person to whom something is intrusted or confided. [t. L: m.s. *repositōrium*]

re·pos·sess (rē'pə zĕs'), v.t. 1. to possess again; regain possession of. 2. to put again in possession of something. —**re·pos·ses·sion** (rē'pə zĕsh'ən), n.

re·pous·sé (rə pōō sā'), adj. 1. (of a design) raised in relief by hammering on the reverse side. 2. ornamented or made in this kind of raised work. [F, pp. of *repousser*, f. re- BE- + *pousser* PUSH, v.]

repp (rĕp), n. rep[1].

Rep·plier (rĕp'līr), n. **Agnes,** 1855–1950, U.S. essayist.

repr., 1. represented. 2. representing. 3. reprint. 4. reprinted.

rep·re·hend (rĕp'rĭ hĕnd'), v.t. to reprove or find fault with; rebuke; censure; blame. [ME, t. L: s. *reprehendere*]

rep·re·hen·si·ble (rĕp'rĭ hĕn'sə bəl), adj. deserving to be reprehended; blameworthy. —**rep're·hen'si·bil'i·ty, rep're·hen'si·ble·ness,** n. —**rep're·hen'si·bly,** adv. —**Ant.** praiseworthy.

rep·re·hen·sion (rĕp'rĭ hĕn'shən), n. act of reprehending; reproof; censure. —**rep·re·hen·sive** (rĕp'rĭ hĕn'sĭv), adj. —**rep're·hen'sive·ly,** adv.

rep·re·sent (rĕp'rĭ zĕnt'), v.t. 1. to serve to express, designate, stand for, or denote, as a word, symbol, or the like does; symbolize. 2. to express or designate by some term, character, symbol, or the like: *to represent musical sounds by notes.* 3. to stand or act in the place of, as a substitute, proxy, or agent does. 4. to speak and act for by delegated authority: *to represent one's government in a foreign country.* 5. to act for (a constituency, etc.) by deputed right in exercising a voice in legislation or government. 6. to portray, depict, or figure; present the likeness or semblance of, as a picture, image, or the like does. 7. to present to the mind; place clearly before or picture to the mind. 8. to present in words; set forth; describe; state. 9. to set forth or describe as having a particular character (fol. by *as, to be*, etc.). 10. to set forth clearly or earnestly with a view to influencing opinion or action or making protest. 11. to present, produce, or perform (a play, etc.), as on the stage. 12. to impersonate (a character, etc.), as in acting. 13. to serve as an example or specimen of; exemplify: *a genus represented by two species.* 14. to be the equivalent of; correspond to: *the llama represents the camel in the New World.* [ME *represente(n)*, t. L: m. *repraesentāre*] —**rep're·sent'a·ble,** adj. —**Syn.** 13. typify, symbolize.

re·pre·sent (rē'prĭ zĕnt'), v.t. to present again or anew.

rep·re·sen·ta·tion (rĕp'rĭ zĕn tā'shən), n. 1. act of representing. 2. state of being represented. 3. the expression or designation by some term, character, symbol, or the like. 4. the representing of a person, body, business house, district, or the like by an agent, deputy, or representative. 5. state or fact of being so represented: *to demand representation on a directing board.* 6. *Govt.* the state, fact, or right of being represented by delegates having a voice in legislation or government. 7. the body or number of representatives, as of a constituency. 8. *Diplomacy.* a. speaking and acting for a state. b. an utterance on behalf of a state. 9. presentation to the mind; a mental image or idea presented. 10. act of portrayal, picturing, or other rendering in visible form. 11. a picture, figure, statue, etc. 12. the production, or a performance, of a play or the like, as on the stage. 13. (*often pl.*) a description or statement, as of things true or alleged. 14. a statement of facts, reasons, etc., made in appealing or protesting; a protest or remonstrance. 15. *Law.* an implication or statement of fact to which legal liability may attach if material: *a representation of authority.* —**rep're·sen·ta'tion·al,** adj.

rep·re·sent·a·tive (rĕp'rĭ zĕn'tə tĭv), n. 1. one who or that which represents another or others. 2. an agent or deputy: *a legal representative.* 3. one who represents a constituency or community in a legislative body, esp. a member of the lower house in the U.S. Congress **(House of Representatives)** or in a State legislature. 4. an example or specimen; type; typical embodiment, as of some quality. —*adj.* 5. serving to represent; representing. 6. standing or acting for another or others. 7. representing a constituency or community or the people generally in legislation or government: *a representative assembly.* 8. characterized by, founded on, or pertaining to representation of the people in government: *representative of government.* 9. exemplifying a class; typical: *a representative selection of Elizabethan plays.* 10. corresponding to or replacing some other species or the like, as in a different locality. —**rep're·sent'a·tive·ly,** adv. —**rep're·sent'a·tive·ness,** n.

re·press (rĭ prĕs'), v.t. 1. to keep under control, check, or suppress (desires, feelings, action, tears, etc.). 2. to keep down or suppress (anything objectionable). 3. to put down or quell (sedition, disorder, etc.). 4. to reduce (persons) to subjection. [ME, t. L: s. *repressus*, pp.] —**re·pressed** (rĭ prĕst'), adj. —**re·press'er,** n. —**re·press'i·ble,** adj. —**Syn.** 1. See **check.**

re·pres·sion (rĭ prĕsh'ən), n. 1. act of repressing. 2. state of being repressed. 3. *Psychoanal.* the rejection

from consciousness of painful or disagreeable ideas, memories, feelings, and impulses.

re·pres·sive (rĭ prĕs'ĭv), adj. tending or serving to repress. —**re·pres'sive·ly,** adv. —**re·pres'sive·ness,** n.

re·prieve (rĭ prēv'), v., -prieved, -prieving, n. —v.t. 1. to respite (a person) from impending punishment, esp. to grant a delay of the execution of (a condemned person). 2. to relieve temporarily from any evil. —n. 3. respite from impending punishment, esp. from execution of a sentence of death. 4. a warrant authorizing this. 5. any respite or temporary relief. [ME *repreven* REPROVE, appar. taken in literal sense of test again (involving postponement)]

rep·ri·mand (rĕp'rə mănd', -mänd'), n. 1. a severe reproof, esp. a formal one by a person in authority. —v.t. 2. to reprove severely, esp. in a formal way. [t. F: m. *réprimande*, der. *réprimer* repress, reprove]

re·print (v. rē prĭnt'; n. rē'prĭnt'), v.t. 1. to print again; print a new impression of. —n. 2. a reproduction in print of matter already printed. 3. *Philately.* an impression from the original plate after the issuance of the stamps has ceased and their use for postage has been voided. 4. a new impression, without alteration, of any printed work. —**re·print'er,** n.

re·pris·al (rĭ prī'zəl), n. 1. the infliction of similar or severer injury on the enemy in warfare, in retaliation for some injury, as by the punishment or execution of prisoners of war. 2. an instance of this. 3. act or practice of using force, short of war, against another nation, to secure redress of a grievance. 4. retaliation, or an act of retaliation. 5. (orig.) the forcible seizing of property or subjects in retaliation. [ME *reprisail*, t. AF: m. *reprisaille*, der. *repris(e)*, pp., taken back] —**Syn.** 1. See **revenge.**

re·prise (rĭ prīz' for 1; rĭ prīz', rə prēz' for 2), n. 1. *Law.* (*usually pl.*) an annual deduction, duty, or payment out of a manor or estate, as an annuity or the like. 2. *Music.* a. a repetition. b. a return to the first theme or subject. [ME, t. F, fem. pp. of *reprendre* take back, g. L *reprehendere*]

re·proach (rĭ prōch'), v.t. 1. to find fault with (a person, etc.); blame; censure. 2. to upbraid (fol. by *with*). 3. to be a cause of blame or discredit to. —n. 4. blame or censure conveyed by reproaching: *a term of reproach.* 5. an expression of upbraiding, censure, or reproof. 6. disgrace, discredit, or blame incurred: *to bring reproach on one's family.* 7. a cause or occasion of disgrace or discredit. 8. an object of scorn or contempt. [late ME *reproche*, t. F: m. *reprocher*, g. deriv. of L *reprobāre* REPROVE] —**re·proach'a·ble,** adj. —**re·proach'a·ble·ness,** n. —**re·proach'a·bly,** adv. —**re·proach'er,** n.

—**Syn.** 1. chide, abuse, reprimand, condemn, criticize. RE- PROACH, REBUKE, SCOLD, REPROVE imply calling one to account for something done or said. REPROACH is censure (often about personal matters, obligations, and the like) given with an attitude of fault finding and some intention of shaming: *to reproach one for neglect.* REBUKE suggests sharp or stern reproof given usually formally or officially and approaching reprimand in severity: *he rebuked him strongly for laziness in his accounts.* SCOLD suggests that censure is given at some length, harshly, and more or less abusively; it implies irritation, which may be with or without justification: *to scold a boy for wanting a dog.* A word of related meaning, but suggesting a milder or more kindly censure, often intended to correct the fault in question, is REPROVE: *to reprove one for inattention.* —**Ant.** 1. praise.

re·proach·ful (rĭ prōch'fəl), adj. 1. full of or expressing reproach or censure; upbraiding: *a reproachful look.* 2. *Obs.* deserving reproach; shameful. —**re·proach'ful·ly,** adv. —**re·proach'ful·ness,** n.

re·proach·less (rĭ prōch'lĭs), adj. irreproachable.

rep·ro·bate (rĕp'rə bāt'), n., adj., v., -bated, -bating. —n. 1. an abandoned, unprincipled, or reprehensible person: *a penniless drunken reprobate.* 2. a reprobate person; one rejected by God or beyond hope of salvation. —adj. 3. morally depraved; unprincipled; bad. 4. rejected by God; excluded from the number of the elect. —v.t. 5. to disapprove, condemn, or censure. 6. (of God) to reject (a person), as for sin; exclude from the number of the elect or from salvation. [ME, t. LL: m.s. *reprobātus*, pp., reproved]

rep·ro·ba·tion (rĕp'rə bā'shən), n. 1. disapproval, condemnation, or censure. 2. rejection. 3. *Theol.* rejection by God, as of persons excluded from the number of the elect or from salvation.

rep·ro·ba·tive (rĕp'rə bā'tĭv), adj. reprobating; expressing reprobation. —**rep'ro·ba'tive·ly,** adv.

re·proc·essed (rē prŏs'ĕst), adj. (of wool) previously spun and woven but not used, as tailor's clippings.

re·pro·duce (rē'prə dūs', -dōōs'), v., -duced, -ducing. —v.t. 1. to make a copy, representation, duplicate, or close imitation of: *to reproduce a picture, voice, etc.* 2. to produce again or anew by natural process: *to reproduce a torn claw.* 3. to produce another or more individuals of (some animal or plant kind) by some process of generation or propagation, sexual or asexual. 4. to cause or foster the reproduction of (animals or plants). 5. to produce, form, make, or bring about again or anew in any manner. 6. to call up again before the mind or represent mentally (a past scene, etc.) as by the aid of memory or imagination. 7. to produce again (a play,

re·pos'tu·late'	**re·pour'**	**re·prime'**	**re·proc'ess**
re'/post·pone'	**re·press'**	**re'/pro·ceed'**	**re'/pro·claim'**

etc., produced at an earlier time). —*v.i.* 8. to reproduce its kind, as an animal or plant does; propagate. 9. to turn out (well, etc.) when copied. —**re/pro·duc/er,** *n.* —**re/pro·duc/i·ble,** *adj.* —**Syn.** 3. generate, beget, propagate. 5. duplicate, repeat. See **imitate.**

re·pro·duc·tion (rē/prə dŭk/shən), *n.* 1. act or process of reproducing. 2. state of being reproduced. 3. that which is made by reproducing; a copy or duplicate, esp. of a picture or the like made by photoengraving or some similar process. 4. the natural process among animals and plants by which new individuals are generated and the species perpetuated.

re·pro·duc·tive (rē/prə dŭk/tĭv), *adj.* 1. serving to reproduce. 2. concerned with or pertaining to reproduction. —**re/pro·duc/tive·ly,** *adv.* —**re/pro·duc/-tive·ness,** *n.*

re·proof (rĭ prōōf/), *n.* 1. act of reproving, censuring, or rebuking. 2. an expression of censure or rebuke.

re·prov·a·ble (rĭ prōōv/ə bəl), *adj.* deserving of reproof.

re·prov·al (rĭ prōō/vəl), *n.* 1. act of reproving. 2. a reproof.

re·prove (rĭ prōōv/), *v.*, **-proved, -proving.** —*v.t.* 1. to address words of disapproval to (a person, etc.); rebuke; blame. 2. to express disapproval of (actions, words, etc.). 3. *Obs.* to disprove or refute. —*v.i.* 4. to speak in reproof; administer a reproof. [ME, t. OF: m. *re-prover*, g. L *reprobāre*] —**re·prov/er,** *n.* —**re·prov/-ing·ly,** *adv.* —**Syn.** 1. censure, reprimand, upbraid, chide. See **reproach.**

rept., report.

rep·tant (rĕp/tənt), *adj.* 1. *Zool.* creeping. 2. *Bot.* repent² [t. L: s. *rēptans*, ppr., creeping]

rep·tile (rĕp/tĭl *or, esp. Brit.,* -tīl), *n.* 1. any of various creeping or crawling animals, as the lizards, snakes, etc. 2. any of the *Reptilia.* 3. a groveling, mean, or despicable person. —*adj.* 4. creeping or crawling. 5. groveling, mean, or malignant. [ME, t. LL, neut. of *reptilis,* adj.]

Rep·til·i·a (rĕp tĭl/ĭ ə), *n.pl.* a class of cold-blooded vertebrates, including the lizards, snakes, turtles, alligators, and rhynchocephalians, together with various extinct types. Reptiles are now relatively unimportant, but before the development of birds and mammals, they were the dominant class of land animals, appearing as fossils in a great variety of forms. They are distinguished from the *Amphibia* chiefly by adaptations to a more completely terrestrial life, without the further elaborations characteristic of the birds and mammals. [NL, neut. pl. of LL *reptilis* creeping, der. *reptāre* creep]

rep·til·i·an (rĕp tĭl/ĭ ən), *adj.* 1. belonging or pertaining to the *Reptilia.* 2. reptilelike. 3. mean; base; malignant. —*n.* 4. any of the *Reptilia;* a reptile.

Repub., 1. Republic. 2. Republican.

re·pub·lic (rĭ pŭb/lĭk), *n.* 1. a state in which the supreme power rests in the body of citizens entitled to vote and is exercised by representatives chosen directly or indirectly by them. 2. any body of persons, etc., viewed as a commonwealth. 3. a state, especially a democratic state, in which the head of the government is an elected or nominated president, not a hereditary being (distinguished from a state like Great Britain with a *limited monarchy*). [t. L: m.s. *rēspublica* (abl. *rēpublicā*) state, lit., public matter]

re·pub·li·can (rĭ pŭb/lə kən), *adj.* 1. of, pertaining to, or of the nature of a republic. 2. favoring a republic. 3. (*cap.*) of or pertaining to the Republican party. —*n.* 4. one who favors a republican form of government. 5. (*cap.*) a member of the Republican party.

re·pub·li·can·ism (rĭ pŭb/lə kə nĭz/əm), *n.* 1. republican government. 2. republican principles or adherence to them. 3. (*cap.*) the principles or policy of the Republican party.

re·pub·li·can·ize (rĭ pŭb/lə kə nīz/), *v.t.,* **-ized, -izing.** to make republican. —**re·pub/li·can·i·za/tion,** *n.*

Republican party, one of the two major political parties of the United States, originated (1854–56) to combat slavery.

Republican river, a river flowing from E Colorado through Nebraska and Kansas into the Kansas river. ab. 500 mi.

re·pub·li·ca·tion (rē/pŭb lə kā/shən), *n.* 1. publication anew. 2. a book or the like published again.

republic of letters, 1. the collective body of literary people. 2. literature.

re·pu·di·ate (rĭ pū/dĭ āt/), *v.t.,* **-ated, -ating.** 1. to reject as having no authority or binding force, as a claim, etc. 2. to cast off or disown: *to repudiate a son.* 3. to reject with disapproval or condemnation, as a doctrine, etc. 4. to reject with denial, as a charge, etc. 5. to refuse to acknowledge and pay, as a debt (said specif. of a state, municipality, etc.). [t. LL: m.s. *re-pudiātus,* pp., rejected, divorced] —**re·pu/di·a/tive,** *adj.* —**re·pu/di·a/tor,** *n.* —**Ant.** 1. acknowledge.

re·pu·di·a·tion (rĭ pū/dĭ ā/shən), *n.* 1. act of repudiating. 2. state of being repudiated. 3. refusal, as by a state or municipality, to pay a debt lawfully contracted.

re·pugn (rĭ pūn/), *v.t., v.i. Obs. or Rare.* to resist. [ME *repugne(n),* t. OF: m. *repugner,* g. L *repugnāre* fight against]

re·pug·nance (rĭ pŭg/nəns), *n.* 1. state of being repugnant. 2. objection, distaste, or aversion. 3. contradictoriness or inconsistency. Also, **re·pug/nan·cy.** —**Syn.** 2. See **dislike.**

re·pug·nant (rĭ pŭg/nənt), *adj.* 1. distasteful or objectionable. 2. making opposition; objecting; averse. 3. opposed or contrary, as in nature or character. [t. L: s. *repugnans,* ppr., fighting against] —**re·pug/-nant·ly,** *adv.*

re·pulse (rĭ pŭls/), *v.,* **-pulsed, -pulsing.** —*v.t.* 1. to drive back, or repel, as an assailant, etc. 2. to repel with denial, discourtesy, or the like; refuse or reject. —*n.* 3. act of repelling. 4. fact of being repelled, as in hostile encounter. 5. refusal or rejection. [t. L: m.s. *repulsus,* pp., repelled] —**re·puls/er,** *n.*

re·pul·sion (rĭ pŭl/shən), *n.* 1. act of repelling or driving back. 2. state of being repelled. 3. the feeling of being repelled; distaste, repugnance, or aversion. 4. *Physics.* a situation in which bodies are forced apart (opposed to *attraction*).

re·pul·sive (rĭ pŭl/sĭv), *adj.* 1. causing repugnance or aversion. 2. tending to repel by denial, discourtesy, or the like. 3. *Physics.* a. of the nature of or characterized by physical repulsion. b. tending to repel or drive back. —**re·pul/sive·ly,** *adv.* —**re·pul/sive·ness,** *n.*

re·pur·chase (rē pūr/chəs), *v.,* **-chased, -chasing,** *n.* —*v.t.* 1. to buy again; regain by purchase. —*n.* 2. act of repurchasing. —**re·pur/chas·er,** *n.*

rep·u·ta·ble (rĕp/yə tə bəl), *adj.* held in good repute; honorable; respectable; estimable. —**rep/u·ta·bil/i·ty,** *n.* —**rep/u·ta·bly,** *adv.*

rep·u·ta·tion (rĕp/yə tā/shən), *n.* 1. the estimation in which a person or thing is held, esp. by the community or the public generally; repute: *a man of good reputation.* 2. favorable repute; good name: *to ruin one's reputation by misconduct.* 3. a favorable and publicly recognized name or standing for merit, achievement, etc.: *to build up a reputation.* 4. the estimation or name of being, having, having done, etc., something specified. —**Syn.** 1. REPUTATION, CHARACTER are often confused. REPUTATION, however, is the word which refers to the position one occupies or the standing that he has in the opinion of others, in respect to attainments, integrity, and the like: *a fine reputation, a reputation for honesty.* CHARACTER is the combination of moral and other traits which make one the kind of person he actually is (as contrasted with what others think of him): *honesty is an outstanding trait of his character.* 2. fame, distinction, renown. 3. See **credit.**

re·pute (rĭ pūt/), *n., v.,* **-puted, -puting.** —*n.* 1. estimation in the view of others; reputation: *persons of good repute.* 2. favorable reputation; good name; credit or note. —*v.t.* 3. to consider or esteem (a person or thing) to be as specified; account or regard (commonly in the passive): *he was reputed to be a millionaire.* [late ME, t. L: m.s. *reputāre* reckon, think] —**Syn.** 2. See **credit.**

re·put·ed (rĭ pū/tĭd), *adj.* accounted or supposed to be such: *the reputed author of a book.* —**re·put/ed·ly,** *adv.*

req., 1. required. 2. requisition.

re·quest (rĭ kwĕst/), *n.* 1. act of asking for something to be given, or done, esp. as a favor or courtesy; solicitation or petition: *a dying request.* 2. that which is asked for: *to obtain one's request.* 3. state of being much asked for; demand: *to be in great request as an after-dinner speaker.* —*v.t.* 4. to ask for, solicit (something), esp. politely or formally. 5. to ask or beg (used with a clause or an infinitive): *to request that he leave, to request to be excused.* 6. to make request to, ask, or beg (a person, etc.) to do something: *he requested me to go.* [ME *requeste,* t. OF, g. Gallo-Rom. *requaesita,* pp., (things) asked for, der. LL *requaerere* seek, r. L *requīrere*] —**Syn.** 5. See **beg.**

Re·qui·em (rē/kwĭ əm, rĕk/wĭ-), *n.* 1. *Rom. Cath. Ch.* a. the mass celebrated for the repose of the souls of the dead. b. a celebration of this mass (**Requiem Mass**). c. a musical setting of this mass. 2. any musical service, hymn, or dirge for the repose of the dead. Also, **re/qui·em.** [ME, t. L, acc. of *requies* rest, the first word of the introit of the Latin mass for the dead]

re·qui·es·cat (rĕk/wĭ ĕs/kăt), *n.* a wish or prayer for the repose of the dead. [L: short for *requiescat in păce* may he (or she) rest in peace]

re·qui·es·cat in pa·ce (rĕk/wĭ ĕs/kăt ĭn pā/sĭ), *Lat. in.* rest in peace.

re·quire (rĭ kwīr/), *v.,* **-quired, -quiring.** —*v.t.* 1. to have need of; need: *he requires medical care.* 2. to call on authoritatively, order, or enjoin (a person, etc.) to do something: *to require an agent to account for money spent.* 3. to ask for authoritatively or imperatively; demand. 4. to impose need or occasion for; make necessary or indispensable: *the work required infinite patience.* 5. to call for or exact as obligatory: *the law requires annual income-tax returns.* 6. to place under an obligation or necessity. 7. *Brit.* to wish to have: *will you require tea at four o'clock?* —*v.i.* 8. to make demand; impose obligation or need: *to do as the law requires.* [ME, t. L: m.s. *requīrere* search for, require] —**Syn.** 2. See **demand.**

re·quire·ment (rĭ kwīr/mənt), *n.* 1. that which is required; a thing demanded or obligatory: *a knowledge of Spanish is among the requirements.* 2. the act or an in-

re/pro·mul/gate	re·prove/	re·pur/i·fy/	re/pur·sue/
re/pro·mul·ga/tion	re·pub/lish	re·pur/pose	re·quick/en

stance of requiring. **3.** a need: *to meet the requirements of daily life.*
—Syn. 1. REQUIREMENT, REQUISITE refer to that which is necessary. A REQUIREMENT is some quality or performance demanded of a person in accordance with certain fixed regulations: *requirements for admission to college.* A REQUISITE is nothing imposed from outside; it is a factor which is judged necessary according to the nature of things, or to the circumstances of the case: *this system combines the two requisites of efficacy and economy.* REQUISITE may also refer to a concrete object judged necessary: *the requisites for perfect grooming.*

req·ui·site (rĕk′wə zĭt), *adj.* **1.** required by the nature of things or by circumstances; indispensable: *he has the requisite qualifications.* **—n. 2.** something requisite; a necessary thing. [late ME, t. L: m.s. *requisitus,* pp., sought for] **—req′ui·site·ly,** *adv.* **—req′ui·site·ness,** *n.* **—Syn. 1.** See **necessary.** **2.** See **requirement.**

req·ui·si·tion (rĕk′wə zĭsh′ən), *n.* **1.** act of requiring or demanding. **2.** a demand made. **3.** the demanding authoritatively or formally of something to be done, given, furnished, etc. **4.** an authoritative or official demand. **5.** state of being required for use or called into service. **6.** a requirement, or essential condition. **—v.t. 7.** to require or take for use; press into service. **8.** to demand or take as by authority for military purposes, public needs, etc.: *to requisition supplies.*

re·quit·al (rĭ kwī′təl), *n.* **1.** act of requiting. **2.** return or reward for service, kindness, etc. **3.** retaliation for a wrong, injury, etc. **4.** repayment; something given or serving to requite.

re·quite (rĭ kwīt′), *v.t.,* **-quited, -quiting. 1.** to make repayment or return for (service, benefits, etc.). **2.** to make retaliation for (a wrong, injury, etc.). **3.** to make return to (a person) for service, etc. **4.** to make retaliation on (a person) for a wrong, etc. **5.** to give or do in return. [f. RE- + *quite,* obs. var. of QUIT, v.] **—re·quite′ment,** *n.* **—re·quit′er,** *n.* **—Syn. 1.** repay.

re·ra·di·a·tion (rē′rā dĭ ā′shən), *n. Physics.* radiation emitted as a consequence of a previous absorption of radiation.

rere·dos (rĭr′dŏs), *n. Chiefly Brit.* a screen or a decorated part of the wall behind an altar in a church. [ME, t. AF, aphetic var. of *areredos,* f. *arere* REAR + *dos* back]

re·run (*v.* rē′rŭn′; *n.* rē′rŭn′), *v.,* **-ran, -run, -running,** *n.* **—v.t. 1.** to run again. **—n. 2.** act of rerunning. **3.** a reshowing of a movie.

res., **1.** reserve. **2.** residence. **3.** resigned.

Re·sa·ca de la Pal·ma (rā sä′kə dĕ lä päl′mə), a locality in S Texas, near Brownsville: battle, 1846.

re·sail (rē sāl′), *v.i.* to sail back or again.

re·sale (rē′sāl′, rē sāl′), *n.* act of reselling.

re·scind (rĭ sĭnd′), *v.t.* **1.** to abrogate; annul, revoke; repeal. **2.** to invalidate (an act, measure, etc.) by a later action or a higher authority. [t. L: s. *rescindere* cut off, annul] **—re·scind′a·ble,** *adj.* **—re·scind′er,** *n.*

re·scis·si·ble (rĭ sĭs′ə bəl), *adj.* able to be rescinded.

re·scis·sion (rĭ sĭzh′ən), *n.* act of rescinding.

re·scis·so·ry (rĭ sĭs′ə rĭ,-sĭz′ə-), *adj.* serving to rescind. [t. LL: m.s. *rescissōrius,* der. L *rescissus,* pp., annulled]

re·script (rē′skrĭpt′), *n.* **1.** a written answer, as of a Roman emperor or a pope, to a query or petition in writing. **2.** any edict, decree, or official announcement. **3.** act, or the product, of rewriting. [t. L: s. *rēscriptum,* prop. neut. pp., rescribed, written back. Cf. OF *rescrit*]

res·cue (rĕs′kū), *v.,* **-cued, -cuing,** *n.* **—v.t. 1.** to free or deliver from confinement, violence, danger, or evil. **2.** *Law.* to liberate or take by forcible or illegal means from lawful custody. **—n. 3.** act of rescuing. [ME *rescoue,* t. OF: m. *rescoure,* der. L *re-* RE- + *excutere* shake out or off] **—res′cu·er,** *n.* **—Syn. 1.** liberate, release, save. **2.** liberation, deliverance.

re·search (rĭ sûrch′, rē′sûrch), *n.* **1.** (*often pl.*) diligent and systematic inquiry or investigation into a subject in order to discover facts or principles: *research in nuclear physics.* **—v.i. 2.** to make researches; investigate carefully. [t. F (obs.): m. *recherche.* See RE-, SEARCH, v.] **—re·search′er,** *n.* **—Syn. 1.** See **investigation.**

research library, a library which concentrates on materials for specialists and scholars in certain fields.

re·seat (rē sēt′), *v.t.* **1.** to provide with a new seat or new seats. **2.** to seat again.

re·seau (rĕ zō′), *n., pl.* **-seaux** (-zō′). **1.** a network. **2.** a netted or meshed ground in lace. **3.** *Astron.* a network of fine lines on a glass plate, used in a photographic telescope in order to produce a corresponding network (for measuring purposes) on photographs of the stars. [F, dim. of OF *roiz,* g. L *rēte* net]

re·sect (rĭ sĕkt′), *v.t. Surg.* to cut away or pare off; excise a portion of. [t. L: s. *resectus,* pp., cut back, cut off] **—re·sec′tion,** *n.*

re·se·da (rĭ sē′də), *n.* **1.** any plant of the genus *Reseda,* esp. *R. odorata,* the garden mignonette. **—adj. 2.** grayish green, like the flowers of the mignonette plant.

[L: plant name; said to be special use of impv. of *resedāre* heal]

res·e·da·ceous (rĕs′ə dā′shəs), *adj.* belonging to the *Resedaceae,* or mignonette family of plants.

re·sem·blance (rĭ zĕm′bləns), *n.* **1.** state or fact of resembling; similarity. **2.** a degree, kind, or point of likeness. **3.** the likeness, appearance, or semblance of something. [ME, t. AF; see RESEMBLE, -ANCE] **—Syn. 1.** RESEMBLANCE, SIMILARITY imply that there is a likeness between two or more people or things. RESEMBLANCE indicates primarily a likeness in appearance, either a striking one or one which merely serves as a reminder to the beholder: *the boy has a strong resemblance to his father.* SIMILARITY may imply a surface likeness, but usually suggests also a likeness in other characteristics: *there is a similarity in their tastes and behavior.* **—Ant. 1.** difference.

re·sem·ble (rĭ zĕm′bəl), *v.t.,* **-bled, -bling. 1.** to be like or similar to. **2.** *Archaic.* to liken or compare. [ME, t. OF: m. *resembler,* f. *re-* RE- + *sembler* be like, g. L *simulāre* simulate, imitate, copy] **—re·sem′bler,** *n.*

re·send (rē sĕnd′), *v.t.,* **-sent, -sending. 1.** to send again. **2.** to send back.

re·sent (rĭ zĕnt′), *v.t.* to feel or show displeasure or indignation at, from a sense of injury or insult. [t. F: m.s. *ressentir,* f. *re-* RE- + *sentir,* g. L *sentīre* feel]

re·sent·ful (rĭ zĕnt′fəl), *adj.* full of, or marked by, resentment. **—re·sent′ful·ly,** *adv.* **—re·sent′ful·ness,** *n.*

re·sent·ment (rĭ zĕnt′mənt), *n.* the feeling of displeasure or indignation at something regarded as an injury or insult, or against the author or source of it.

res·er·pine (rĕs′ər pĭn, -pēn, rə sûr′-), *n.* originally, a purified extract from the root of *Rauwolfia serpentina;* now made synthetically: widely used as a tranquilizer and in the treatment of hypertension and various psychogenic illnesses.

res·er·va·tion (rĕz′ər vā′shən), *n.* **1.** a keeping back, withholding, or setting apart. **2.** the making of some exception or qualification; an exception or qualification made, expressly or tacitly: *a mental reservation.* **3.** *U.S.* a tract of public land set apart for a special purpose, as for the use of an Indian tribe. **4.** (*often pl.*) the allotting or the securing of accommodations at a hotel, on a train or boat, etc., as for a traveler: *to write for reservations.* **5.** the record or assurance of such an arrangement.

re·serve (rĭ zûrv′), *v.,* **-served, -serving,** *n., adj.* **—v.t. 1.** to keep back or save for future use, disposal, treatment, etc. **2.** to retain or secure by express stipulation. **3.** to set apart for a particular use, purpose, service, etc.: *ground reserved for gardening.* **4.** to keep for some fate, lot, experience, etc. **5.** *Eccles.* to save or set aside (the Eucharistic Hosts) to be administered outside the Mass or communion service. **—n. 6.** an amount of capital retained, as by a banker, to meet probable demands. **7.** something reserved, as for some purpose or object; a store or stock. **8.** a tract of public land set apart for a special purpose: *a forest reserve.* **9.** a reservation, exception, or qualification. **10.** act of reserving. **11.** the state of being reserved, as for future use or for some purpose or person: *money in reserve.* **12.** *Mil.* **a.** a fraction of a military force held in readiness to sustain the attack or defense made by the rest of the force. **b.** the part of a country's fighting force not in active service. **c.** (*pl.*) the enrolled but not regular components of the Army of the U.S. **13.** avoidance of familiarity in social relationships; self-restraint in action or speech. **14.** reticence or silence. **—adj. 15.** kept in reserve; forming a reserve: *a reserve fund or supply.* [ME, t. L: m. *reservāre* keep back] **—Syn. 1.** retain. See **keep.**

reserve bank, *U.S.* one of the twelve principal banks of the Federal Reserve System.

re·served (rĭ zûrvd′), *adj.* **1.** kept in reserve; set apart for a particular use or purpose. **2.** kept by special arrangement for some person or persons: *a reserved seat.* **3.** self-restrained in action or speech; disposed to keep one's feelings, thoughts, or affairs to oneself. **4.** characterized by reserve, as the disposition, manner, etc. **—re·serv·ed·ly** (rĭ zûr′vĭd lĭ), *adv.* **—re·serv′ed·ness,** *n.*

re·serv·ist (rĭ zûr′vĭst), *n.* one who belongs to a reserve military force of a country.

res·er·voir (rĕz′ər vôr′, -vwär′), *n.* **1.** a natural or artificial place where water is collected and stored for use, esp. water for supplying a community, irrigating land, furnishing power, etc. **2.** a receptacle or chamber for holding a liquid or fluid, as oil or gas. **3.** *Biol.* a cavity or part which holds some fluid or secretion. **4.** a place where anything is collected or accumulated in great amount. **5.** a great supply, store, or reserve of something. [t. F, der. *reserver* keep, reserve]

re·set (*v.* rē sĕt′; *n.* rē′sĕt′), *v.,* **-set, -setting,** *n.* **—v.t. 1.** to set again. **—n. 2.** act of resetting. **3.** that which is reset. **4.** a plant which is replanted.

res ges·tae (rēz jĕs′tē), *Latin.* achievements.

re·shape (rē shāp′), *v.t.* **-shaped, -shaping.** to shape again or into different form.

re·ra′di·ate′	re·route′	re·seed′	re·sell′er
re·rate′	re·sad′dle	re·seek′	re·serve′
re·read′	re·sal′a·ble	re·seg′re·gate′	re·set′tle
re·reel′	re·sa·lute′	re·seize′	re·set′tle·ment
re·rise′	re·seal′	re·sei′zure	re·shake′
re·roll′	re·search′	re·sell′	re·sharp′en

re·ship (rē shĭp′), v., **-shipped, -shipping.** —v.t. **1.** to ship again. **2.** to transfer from one ship to another. —v.i. **3.** to go on a ship again. **4.** (of a member of a ship's crew) to sign up for another voyage. —**re·ship′-ment,** n.

Resht (rĕsht), n. a city in NW Iran, near the Caspian Sea. 111,978 (est. 1950).

re·side (rĭ zīd′), v.i., **-sided, -siding. 1.** to dwell permanently or for a considerable time; have one's abode for a time: *he resided in Boston.* **2.** (of things, qualities, etc.) to abide, lie, or be present habitually; exist or be inherent (fol. by *in*). **3.** to rest or be vested, as powers, rights, etc. (fol. by *in*). [late ME, t. L: m.s. *residēre*] —**Syn. 1.** live, abide, sojourn, stay, lodge.

res·i·dence (rĕz′ə dəns), n. **1.** the place, esp. the house, in which one resides; dwelling place; dwelling. **2.** a large house. **3.** act or fact of residing. **4.** living or staying in a place of official or other duty. **5.** the time during which one resides in a place. —**Syn. 1, 2.** See **house.**

res·i·den·cy (rĕz′ə dən sĭ), n., pl. **-cies. 1.** residence. **2.** the official residence in India of a representative of the British governor general at a native court. **3.** an administrative division of the Dutch East Indies.

res·i·dent (rĕz′ə dənt), n. **1.** one who resides in a place. **2.** a diplomatic representative, inferior in rank to an ambassador, residing at a foreign court. **3.** a representative of the British governor general at a native court in India. **4.** the governor of a residency in the Dutch East Indies. —adj. **5.** residing; dwelling in a place. **6.** living or staying at a place in discharge of duty. **7.** (of qualities) existing; intrinsic. **8.** (of birds, etc.) not migratory. [ME, t. L: s. *residens*]

res·i·den·tial (rĕz′ə dĕn′shəl), adj. **1.** of or pertaining to residence or residences. **2.** adapted or used for residence: *a residential section.*

res·i·den·ti·ar·y (rĕz′ə dĕn′shĭ ĕr′ĭ, -shə rĭ), adj., n., pl. **-aries.** —adj. **1.** residing; resident. **2.** bound to or involving official residence. —n. **3.** a resident. **4.** an ecclesiastic bound to official residence.

re·sid·u·al (rĭ zĭj′ŏŏ əl), adj. **1.** pertaining to or constituting a residuum; remaining; left over. **2.** *Math.* formed by the subtraction of one quantity from another: *a residual quantity.* —n. **3.** a residual quantity; a remainder. **4.** *Math.* **a.** the deviation of one of a set of observations or numbers from the mean of the set. **b.** the deviation between an empirical and a theoretical result. [f. RESIDU(E) + -AL¹]

re·sid·u·ar·y (rĭ zĭj′ŏŏ ĕr′ĭ), adj. **1.** entitled to the residue of an estate: *a residuary legatee.* **2.** pertaining to or of the nature of a residue, remainder, or residuum. [f. RESIDU(UM) + -ARY]

res·i·due (rĕz′ə dū, -dōō′), n. **1.** that which remains after a part is taken, disposed of, or gone; remainder; rest. **2.** *Chem.* a quantity of matter remaining after evaporation, combustion, or some other process; a residuum. **b.** an atom or group of atoms considered as a radical or part of a molecule. **c.** that part remaining as a solid on a filter paper after a liquid passes through in the filtration procedure. **3.** *Law.* the part of a testator's estate that remains after the payment of all debts, charges, devises, and bequests. [ME, t. F: m. *residu,* t. L: s. *residuum*] —**Syn. 1.** See **remainder.**

re·sid·u·um (rĭ zĭj′ŏŏ əm), n., pl. **-sidua** (-zĭj′ŏŏ ə). **1.** the residue, remainder, or rest of something. **2.** *Chem.* a quantity or body of matter remaining after evaporation, combustion, distillation, or the like. **3.** any residual product. **4.** *Law.* the residue of an estate. [t. L]

re·sign (rĭ zīn′), v.i. **1.** to give up an office or position (often fol. by *from*). **2.** to submit; yield. —v.t. **3.** to give up (an office, position, etc.) formally. **4.** to relinquish, as a right or claim. **5.** to submit (oneself, one's mind, etc.) without resistance. [ME *resignen,* t. OF: m. *resigner,* t. L: m. *resignāre* unseal, annul] —**Syn. 4.** give up, surrender, renounce, abdicate.

res·ig·na·tion (rĕz′ĭg nā′shən), n. **1.** act of resigning. **2.** the formal statement, document, etc. stating that one resigns an office, position, etc. **3.** state of being submissive; submission; unresisting acquiescence. [ME, t. ML: s. *resignātio*] —**Syn. 3.** meekness, patience.

re·signed (rĭ zīnd′), adj. **1.** submissive or acquiescent. **2.** characterized by or indicative of resignation. —**re·sign·ed·ly** (rĭ zī′nĭd lĭ), adv. —**re·sign′ed·ness,** n.

re·sile (rĭ zīl′), v.i., **-siled, -siling. 1.** to spring back; rebound; resume the original form or position, as an elastic body. **2.** to shrink back; recoil. [t. L: m.s. *resilīre*]

re·sil·i·ence (rĭ zĭl′ĭ əns), n. **1.** resilient power; elasticity. **2.** resilient action; rebound; recoil. Also, **re·sil′i·en·cy.**

re·sil·i·ent (rĭ zĭl′ĭ ənt), adj. **1.** springing back; rebounding. **2.** returning to the original form or position after being bent, compressed, or stretched. **3.** readily recovering, as from depression; buoyant; cheerful. [t. L: s. *resiliens,* ppr., rebounding] —**re·sil′i·ent·ly,** adv.

res·in (rĕz′ĭn), n. **1.** any of a class of nonvolatile, solid or semisolid organic substances (copal, mastic, etc.) obtained directly from certain plants as exudations or prepared by polymerization of simple molecules, and used in medicine and in the making of varnishes and plastics. **2.** a substance of this type obtained from cer-

tain pines; rosin. —v.t. **3.** to treat or rub with resin. [ME *resyn,* t. L: m.s. *resīna,* c. Gk. *rhētínē*] —**res′in·like′,** adj.

res·in·ate (rĕz′ə nāt′), v.t., **-ated, -ating.** to treat with resin, as by impregnation.

res·in·if·er·ous (rĕz′ə nĭf′ər əs), adj. yielding resin.

res·in·oid (rĕz′ə noid′), adj. **1.** resinlike. —n. **2.** a resinoid substance. **3.** a resinous substance synthetically compounded. **4.** gum resin.

res·in·ous (rĕz′ə nəs), adj. **1.** full of or containing resin. **2.** of the nature of or resembling resin. **3.** pertaining to or characteristic of resin. Also, **res·in·y** (rĕz′ə nĭ). [t. L: m.s. *resīnōsus*]

re·sist (rĭ zĭst′), v.t. **1.** to withstand, strive against, or oppose: *to resist infection.* **2.** to withstand the action or effect of: *gold resists rust.* **3.** to refrain or abstain from: *to resist a smile.* —v.i. **4.** to make a stand or make efforts in opposition; act in opposition; offer resistance. —n. **5.** a substance applied to a surface to enable it to resist corrosion or the like. [ME *resisten,* t. L: m. *resistere* withstand] —**re·sist′er,** n. —**Syn. 1.** See **oppose.** —**Ant. 4.** submit.

re·sist·ance (rĭ zĭs′təns), n. **1.** act or power of resisting, opposing, or withstanding. **2.** the opposition offered by one thing, force, etc., to another. **3.** *Elect.* **a.** that property of a conductor by virtue of which the passage of a current is opposed, causing electric energy to be transformed into heat (**true** or **ohmic resistance**). **b.** a conductor or coil offering such opposition; a resistor. **c.** impedance (**apparent resistance**). [late ME, t. F; r. ME *resistence,* t. OF, t. LL: m.s. *resistentia*]

re·sist·ant (rĭ zĭs′tənt), adj. **1.** resisting. —n. **2.** one who or that which resists.

re·sist·i·ble (rĭ zĭs′tə bəl), adj. that may be resisted. —**re·sist′i·bil′i·ty,** n.

re·sis·tive (rĭ zĭs′tĭv), adj. resisting; capable of or inclined to resistance.

re·sis·tiv·i·ty (rē′zĭs tĭv′ə tĭ), n. **1.** the power or property of resistance. **2.** *Elect.* the resistance between opposite faces of a one-centimeter cube of a given material (the reciprocal of *conductivity*).

re·sist·less (rĭ zĭst′lĭs), adj. **1.** irresistible. **2.** unresisting. —**re·sist′less·ly,** adv. —**re·sist′less·ness,** n.

re·sis·tor (rĭ zĭs′tər), n. *Elect.* a device, the primary purpose of which is to introduce resistance into an electric circuit.

res ju·di·ca·ta (rĕz jŏŏ′də kā′tə), *Latin.* a thing adjucated; a case that has been decided.

res·na·tron (rĕz′nə trŏn′), n. *Electronics.* a tetrode vacuum tube with the grid connected to form a drift space for the electrons, used to generate large power at very high frequency.

re·sole (rē sōl′), v.t., **-soled, -soling.** to put a new sole on (a shoe, etc.).

res·o·lu·ble (rĕz′ə lŏŏ′bəl), adj. capable of being resolved. [t. LL: m.s. *resolūbilis*] —**res·o·lu·bil′i·ty,** n. —**res′o·lu·ble·ness,** n.

res·o·lute (rĕz′ə lŏŏt′), adj. **1.** firmly resolved or determined; set in purpose or opinion. **2.** characterized by firmness and determination, as the temper, spirit, actions, etc. [ME, t. L: m.s. *resolūtus,* pp., resolved] —**res′o·lute′ly,** adv. —**res′o·lute′ness,** n. —**Syn. 1.** firm, steadfast. See **earnest.**

res·o·lu·tion (rĕz′ə lŏŏ′shən), n. **1.** a formal determination, or expression of opinion, of a deliberative assembly or other body of persons. See **concurrent resolution, joint resolution. 2.** a resolve or determination: *to make a firm resolution to do something.* **3.** act of resolving or determining as to action, etc. **4.** the mental state or quality of being resolved or resolute; firmness of purpose. **5.** the act or process of resolving or separating into constituent or elementary parts. **6.** the resulting state. **7.** solution or explanation, as of a problem, a doubtful point, etc. **8.** *Music.* **a.** progression of a voice part or of the harmony as a whole from a dissonance to a consonance, or sometimes to another dissonance. **b.** the note or chord to which this is effected. **9.** reduction to a simpler form; conversion. **10.** *Med.* the reduction or disappearance of a swelling or inflammation without suppuration. [ME *resolucion,* t. L: m.s. *resolūtio*]

Resolution (def. 8)
A. Dissonance;
B. Consonance

res·o·lu·tion·er (rĕz′ə lŏŏ′shən ər), n. one joining in or subscribing to a resolution. Also, **res′o·lu′tion·ist.**

re·solv·a·ble (rĭ zŏl′və bəl), adj. that may be resolved. —**re·solv′a·bil′i·ty, re·solv′a·ble·ness,** n.

re·solve (rĭ zŏlv′), v., **-solved, -solving.** —v.t. **1.** to fix or settle on by deliberate choice and will; determine (to do something). **2.** to separate into constituent or elementary parts, break up, or disintegrate; separate or break up (fol. by *into*). **3.** to reduce or convert by or as by breaking up or disintegration (fol. by *into* or *to*). **4.** to convert or transform by any process (often reflexive). **5.** to reduce by mental analysis (fol. by *into*). **6.** to settle, determine, or state formally in a vote or resolution, as of a deliberative assembly. **7.** to deal with (a question, a matter of uncertainty, etc.) conclusively; explain; solve (a problem). **8.** to clear away

re·shoul′der	**re·sift′**	**re·smooth′**	**re·sol′der**
re·shuf′fle	**re·sight′**	**re·soak′**	**re·so·lid′i·fy′**

b., blend of, blended; **c.,** cognate with; **d.,** dialect, dialectal; **der.,** derived from; **f.,** formed from; **g.,** going back to; **m.,** modification of; **r.,** replacing; **s.,** stem of; **t.,** taken from; **?,** perhaps.　See the full key on inside cover.

or dispel (doubts, etc.). **9.** *Chem.* to separate (a racemic mixture) into its optically active components. **10.** *Music.* to cause (a voice part or the harmony as a whole) to progress from a dissonance to a consonance. **11.** *Optics.* to separate and make visible the individual parts of (an image); to distinguish between. **12.** *Med.* to cause (swellings, inflammation, etc.) to disappear without suppuration. —*v.i.* **13.** to come to a determination; make up one's mind; determine (often fol. by *on* or *upon*). **14.** to break up or disintegrate. **15.** to be reduced or changed by breaking up or otherwise (fol. by *into* or *to*). **16.** *Music.* to progress from a dissonance to a consonance. —*n.* **17.** a resolution or determination made, as to follow some course of action. **18.** determination; firmness of purpose. [ME, t. L: m. *resolvere* loosen, dissolve] —**re·solv'er,** *n.* —Syn. 1. See decide.

re·solved (rĭ zŏlvd/), *adj.* determined; firm in purpose; resolute. —**re·solv·ed·ly** (rĭ zŏl/vĭd lĭ), *adv.*

re·sol·vent (rĭ zŏl/vənt), *adj.* **1.** resolving; causing solution; solvent. —*n.* **2.** something resolvent. **3.** *Med.* a remedy that causes resolution, as of swellings, etc. [t. L: s. *resolvens,* ppr., resolving]

resolving power, *Optics.* the ability of an optical device to produce separate images of close objects.

res·o·nance (rĕz/ə nəns), *n.* **1.** state or quality of being resonant. **2.** the prolongation of sound by reflection; reverberation. **3.** the amplification of vocal tone by the bones of the head and upper chest and by the air cavities of the pharynx, mouth, and nasal passages. **4.** *Physics.* **a.** an abnormally large response of a system having a natural frequency to a periodic external stimulus of the same, or nearly the same, frequency. **b.** the increase of intensity of sound by the sympathetic vibration of other bodies. **c.** the prolongation or increase of a wave by the sympathetic vibration of other bodies: used to describe an atom which gives off rays of the same wave length as it has absorbed. **5.** *Elect.* that condition of a circuit with respect to a given frequency or the like in which the total reactance is zero and the current flow a maximum. **6.** *Chem.* the condition exhibited by a molecule when the actual arrangement of its valence electrons is intermediate between two or more arrangements having nearly the same energy, and the positions of the atomic nuclei are identical. **7.** *Med.* a sound produced when air is present (in percussing for diagnostic purposes).

res·o·nant (rĕz/ə nənt), *adj.* **1.** resounding or reëchoing, as sounds, places, etc. **2.** deep and full of resonance: *resonant voice.* **3.** pertaining to resonance. **4.** having the property of increasing the intensity of sound by sympathetic vibration. [t. L: s. *resonans,* ppr., resounding] —**res/o·nant·ly,** *adv.*

res·o·nate (rĕz/ə nāt), *v.i.,* **-nated, -nating. 1.** to resound. **2.** to act as a resonator; exhibit resonance. **3.** *Electronics.* to reinforce oscillations because the natural frequency of the device is the same as the frequency of the source. **4.** to amplify vocal sound by the sympathetic vibration of air in certain cavities and bony structures. [t. L: m.s. *resonātus,* pp., resounded] —**res/o·na/tion,** *n.*

res·o·na·tor (rĕz/ə nā/tər), *n.* **1.** anything that resonates. **2.** an appliance for increasing sound by resonance. **3.** an instrument for detecting the presence of a particular frequency by means of resonance. **4.** *Electronics.* **a.** a hollow enclosure made of conducting material of such dimensions that electromagnetic radiation of a certain frequency will resonate. **b.** any circuit having this frequency characteristic. [t. NL. See RESONATE, -OR²]

re·sorb (rĭ sôrb/), *v.t.* to absorb again, as an exudation. [t. L: s. *resorbēre* suck back] —**re·sorp·tion** (rĭ sôrp/shən), *n.*

res·or·cin·ol (rĕz ôr/sĭ nōl/, -nŏl/), *n.* *Chem.* a colorless crystalline benzene derivative, $C_6H_4(OH)_2$, originally obtained from certain resins, used in medicine and in making dyes. Also, **res·or·cin.** [f. *resorcin* (f. RES(IN) + ORCIN) + -OL²]

re·sort (rĭ zôrt/), *v.i.* **1.** to have recourse for use, service, or help: *to resort to war.* **2.** to go, esp. frequently or customarily: *a beach to which many people resort.* —*n.* **3.** a place frequented, esp. by the public generally: *a summer resort.* **4.** a habitual or general going, as to a place or person. **5.** a resorting to some person or thing for aid, service, etc.; recourse: *to have resort to force.* **6.** a person or thing resorted to for aid, service, etc. [ME *resorte*(*n*), t. OF: m. *resortir,* f. re- RE- + *sortir* issue, go out]

re·sound¹ (rĭ zound/), *v.i.* **1.** to reëcho or ring with sound, as a place. **2.** to make an echoing sound, or sound loudly, as a thing. **3.** to be echoed, or ring, as sounds. **4.** to be famed or celebrated. —*v.t.* **5.** to reëcho (a sound). **6.** to give forth or utter loudly. **7.** to proclaim loudly (praises, etc.). [ME *resoun*(*en*), f. re- RE- + *soun*(*en*) SOUND¹, after L *resonāre*] —**re·sound'ing·ly,** *adv.*

re·sound² (rē′sound/), *v.t., v.i.* to sound again. [f. RE- + SOUND¹]

re·source (rĭ sôrs/, rē/sôrs), *n.* **1.** a source of supply, support, or aid. **2.** (*pl.*) the collective wealth of a country, or its means of producing wealth. **3.** (often *pl.*) money, or any property which can be converted into money; assets. **4.** available means afforded by the mind or the personal capabilities. **5.** an action or measure to which one may have recourse in an emergency; expedient. **6.** capability in dealing with a situation or in meeting difficulties. [t. F: m. *ressource,* der. OF *res*(*s*)*sourdre* (f. re- RE- + *sourdre*), g. L *resurgere* rise again]

re·source·ful (rĭ sôrs/fəl), *adj.* full of resource; fertile in expedients. —**re·source/ful·ly,** *adv.* —**re·source/ful·ness,** *n.*

resp., **1.** respective. **2.** respectively. **3.** respondent.

re·spect (rĭ spĕkt/), *n.* **1.** a particular, detail, or point (in phrases prec. by *in*): *to be defective in some respect.* **2.** relation or reference: *inquiries with respect to a route.* **3.** esteem or deferential regard felt or shown. **4.** the condition of being esteemed or honored. **5.** (*pl.*) deferential, respectful, or friendly compliments, as paid by making a call on a person or otherwise: *to pay one's respects.* **6.** discrimination or partiality in the regarding of persons or things. **7.** *Archaic.* consideration. —*v.t.* **8.** to hold in esteem or honor: *to respect one's elders.* **9.** to show esteem, regard, or consideration for: *to respect someone's wishes.* **10.** to refrain from interfering with: *to respect a person's privacy.* **11.** to relate or have reference to. [ME, t. L: s. *respectus,* pp., having been regarded] —**re·spect/er,** *n.*
—Syn. 3. RESPECT, ESTEEM, VENERATION imply recognition of personal qualities by approbation, deference, and more or less affection. RESPECT is commonly the result of admiration and approbation, together with deference: *to feel respect for a great scholar.* ESTEEM is deference combined with admiration and often with affection: *to hold a friend in great esteem.* VENERATION is an almost religious attitude of deep respect, reverence, and love, such as we feel for persons or things of outstanding superiority, endeared by long association: *veneration for one's grandparents, for noble traditions.*

re·spect·a·bil·i·ty (rĭ spĕk/tə bĭl/ə tĭ), *n., pl.* **-ties. 1.** state or quality of being respectable. **2.** respectable social standing, character, or reputation. **3.** respectable people. **4.** (*pl.*) things accepted as respectable.

re·spect·a·ble (rĭ spĕk/tə bəl), *adj.* **1.** worthy of respect or esteem; estimable; worthy: *a respectable citizen.* **2.** of good social standing, reputation, etc.: *a respectable neighborhood.* **3.** pertaining or appropriate to such standing; proper or decent: *respectable language.* **4.** of moderate excellence; fairly good; fair: *a respectable performance.* **5.** considerable in size, number, or amount: *a respectable navy.* —**re·spect/a·ble·ness,** *n.* —**re·spect/a·bly,** *adv.*

respecter of persons, one who is unduly influenced in his dealings by the social standing, importance, etc., of persons.

re·spect·ful (rĭ spĕkt/fəl), *adj.* full of, characterized by, or showing respect: *a respectful reply.* —**re·spect/ful·ly,** *adv.* —**re·spect/ful·ness,** *n.* —Syn. courteous, polite.

re·spect·ing (rĭ spĕk/tĭng), *prep.* regarding; concerning.

re·spec·tive (rĭ spĕk/tĭv), *adj.* pertaining individually or severally to each of a number of persons, things, etc.; particular: *the respective merits of the candidates.*

re·spec·tive·ly (rĭ spĕk/tĭv lĭ), *adv.* with respect to each of a number: *labeled respectively A, B, and C.*

re·spell (rē spĕl/), *v.t.* to spell again or anew.

Re·spi·ghi (rĕ spē/gē), *n.* Ottorino (ôt/tō rē/nō), 1879–1936, Italian composer.

re·spir·a·ble (rĭ spīr/ə bəl, rĕs/pə rə bəl), *adj.* **1.** capable of being respired. **2.** capable of respiring.

res·pi·ra·tion (rĕs/pə rā/shən), *n.* **1.** act of respiring; inhalation and exhalation of air; breathing. **2.** (in living organisms) the process by which oxygen and carbohydrates are assimilated into the system and the oxidation products (carbon dioxide and water) are given off.

res·pi·ra·tor (rĕs/pə rā/tər), *n.* **1.** a device, usually of gauze, worn over the mouth, or nose and mouth, to prevent the inhalation of noxious substances, etc. **2.** *Brit.* a gas mask. **3.** an apparatus to produce artificial respiration.

re·spir·a·to·ry (rĭ spīr/ə tōr/ĭ, rĕs/pə rə tōr/ĭ), *adj.* pertaining to or serving for respiration: *the respiratory system of mammals.*

re·spire (rĭ spīr/), *v.,* **-spired, -spiring.** —*v.i.* **1.** to inhale and exhale air for the purpose of maintaining life; breathe. **2.** to breathe freely again, after anxiety, trouble, etc. —*v.t.* **3.** to breathe; inhale and exhale. **4.** *Rare.* to exhale. [ME, t. L: m. *respīrāre*]

res·pite (rĕs/pĭt), *n., v.,* **-pited, -piting.** —*n.* **1.** a delay or cessation for a time, esp. of anything distressing or trying; an interval of relief: *to toil without respite.* **2.** temporary suspension of the execution of a person condemned to death; a reprieve. —*v.t.* **3.** to relieve temporarily, esp. from anything distressing or trying; give an interval of relief from. **4.** to grant delay in the carrying out of (a punishment, obligation, etc.). [ME *respit,* t. OF, g. LL *respectus* delay, der. L *respectāre* look for, wait for]

re·splend·ence (rĭ splĕn/dəns), *n.* resplendent state; splendor. Also, **re·splend/en·cy.**

re·splend·ent (rĭ splĕn/dənt), *adj.* shining brilliantly; gleaming; splendid: *resplendent in white uniforms.* [t. L: s. *resplendens,* ppr., shining] —**re·splend/ent·ly,** *adv.*

ăct, āble, dâre, ärt; ĕbb, ēqual; ĭf, īce; hŏt, ōver, ôrder, oil, bŏŏk, ōoze, out; ŭp, ūse, ûrge; ə = a in alone; ch, chief; g, give; ng, ring; sh, shoe; th, thin; th̷ that; zh, vision. See the full key on inside cover.

re·spond (rĭ spŏnd′), *v.i.* **1.** to answer; give a reply in words: *to respond briefly to a question.* **2.** to make a return by some action as if in answer: *to respond generously to a charity drive.* **3.** *Physiol.* to exhibit some action or effect as if in answer; react: *nerves respond to a stimulus.* **4.** to correspond (fol. by *to*). —*v.t.* **5.** to say in answer; reply. [t. L: s. *respondēre*]
—*n.* **6.** *Archit.* a half pillar or the like engaged in a wall to support an arch. **7.** *Eccles.* **a.** a short anthem chanted at intervals during the reading of a lection. **b.** responsory. **c.** response. [ME, t. OF, der. *respondre* respond]

re·spond·ence (rĭ spŏn′dəns), *n.* act of responding; response: *respondence to a stimulus.* Also, **re·spond′-en·cy.**

re·spond·ent (rĭ spŏn′dənt), *adj.* **1.** answering; responsive. —*n.* **2.** one who responds or makes reply. **3.** *Law.* a defendant, esp. in appellate and divorce cases. [t. L: s. *respondens*, ppr., answering]

re·sponse (rĭ spŏns′), *n.* **1.** answer or reply, whether in words, in some action, etc. **2.** *Biol.* any behavior of a living organism which results from stimulation. **3.** *Eccles.* **a.** a verse, sentence, phrase, or word said or sung by the choir or congregation in reply to the officiant. **b.** responsory. [t. L: m.s. *responsum*, neut. of *responsus*, pp., answered; r. ME *respouns(e)*, t. OF: m. *respuns*, *respons* (masc.), *response* (fem.)] —**Syn. 1.** See **answer.**

re·spon·si·bil·i·ty (rĭ spŏn′sə bĭl′ə tĭ), *n.*, *pl.* **-ties. 1.** state or fact of being responsible. **2.** an instance of being responsible. **3.** a particular burden of obligation upon one who is responsible: *to feel the responsibilities of one's position.* **4.** something for which one is responsible: *a child is a responsibility to its parents.* **5.** ability to meet debts or payments. **6. on one's own responsibility,** on one's own initiative or authority.

re·spon·si·ble (rĭ spŏn′sə bəl), *adj.* **1.** answerable or accountable, as for something within one's power, control, or management (often fol. by *to* or *for*). **2.** involving accountability or responsibility: *a responsible position.* **3.** chargeable with being the author, cause, or occasion of something (fol. by *for*). **4.** having a capacity for moral decisions and therefore accountable; capable of rational thought or action. **5.** able to discharge obligations or pay debts. **6.** reliable in business or other dealings; showing reliability. —**re·spon′si·ble·ness,** *n.* —**re·spon′si·bly,** *adv.*

re·spon·sion (rĭ spŏn′shən), *n.* **1.** act of responding or answering. **2.** (*pl.*) the first examination at Oxford University which candidates for the degree of B.A. have to pass. [late ME, t. L: s. *responsio*]

re·spon·sive (rĭ spŏn′sĭv), *adj.* **1.** making answer or reply, esp. responding readily to influences, appeals, efforts, etc. **2.** *Physiol.* acting in response, as to some stimulus. **3.** characterized by the use of responses: *responsive worship.* —**re·spon′sive·ly,** *adv.*

re·spon·sive·ness (rĭ spŏn′sĭv nĭs), *n.* **1.** quality or state of being responsive. **2.** *Mach.* the capacity of a device, esp. if subject to oscillation, to stabilize without undue delay.

re·spon·so·ry (rĭ spŏn′sə rĭ), *n.*, *pl.* **-ries.** *Eccles.* an anthem sung after a lection by a soloist and choir alternately. [ME, t. LL: m.s. *responsoria*, pl.]

res pu·bli·ca (rēz pŭb′lə kə), *Latin.* the state; republic; commonwealth.

rest¹ (rĕst), *n.* **1.** the refreshing quiet or repose of sleep: *a good night's rest.* **2.** refreshing ease or inactivity after exertion or labor: *to allow an hour for rest.* **3.** relief or freedom, esp. from anything that wearies, troubles, or disturbs. **4.** mental or spiritual calm; tranquillity: *to set one's mind at rest.* **5.** the repose of death: *to lay the dead to rest.* **6.** cessation or absence of motion: *to bring a machine to rest.*
7. at rest, inactive or quiescent: *a volcano at rest.* **8.** *Music.* **a.** an interval of silence between tones. **b.** a mark or sign indicating it. **9.** *Pros.* a short pause in reading; a caesura. **10.** an establishment for providing shelter or lodging for some class of persons. **11.** a piece or thing for something to rest on: *a foot rest.* **12.** a support; a supporting device. **13.** *Billiards.* bridge (def. 10). [ME and OE, akin to G *rast*]
—*v.i.* **14.** to refresh oneself, as by sleeping, lying down, or relaxing. **15.** to relieve weariness by cessation of exertion or labor. **16.** to be at ease; have tranquillity or peace. **17.** to repose in death. **18.** to be quiet or still. **19.** to cease from motion, come to rest, or stop. **20.** to become or remain inactive. **21.** to remain without further action or notice: *to let a matter rest.* **22.** to lie, sit, lean, or be set (fol. by *in*, *on*, *against*, etc.): *his arm rested on the table.* **23.** *Agric.* to lie fallow or unworked: *to let land rest.* **24.** to be imposed as a burden or responsibility (fol. by *on* or *upon*). **25.** to rely (fol. by *on* or *upon*). **26.** to be based or founded (fol. by *on* or *upon*). **27.** to be found or be (where specified): *the blame rests with them.* **28.** to be present; dwell; linger (fol. by *on* or *upon*): *a light rests upon the altar.* **29.** to be fixed or directed on something, as the

Rests (def. 8b)
A. Double whole; B. Whole; C. Half;
D. Quarter; E. Eighth; F. Sixteenth;
G. Thirty-second; H. Sixty-fourth

gaze, eyes, etc. **30.** *Law.* to terminate voluntarily the introduction of evidence in a case.
—*v.t.* **31.** to give rest to; refresh with rest: *to rest oneself.* **32.** to lay or place for rest, ease, or support: *to rest one's back against a tree.* **33.** to direct (the eyes, etc.): *to rest one's eyes on someone.* **34.** to base, or let depend, as on some ground of reliance. **35.** to bring to rest; halt; stop. **36.** *Law.* to terminate voluntarily the introduction of evidence on: *to rest one's case.* [ME *resten*, OE *restan*, c. OHG *restan*, akin to G *rasten*]

rest² (rĕst), *n.* **1.** that which is left or remains; the remainder: *the rest of the money is his.* **2.** the others: *all the rest are going.* **3.** *Brit. Banking.* the reserve funds or surplus. [late ME *reste*, t. F, der. *rester*, v. (see below)]
—*v.i.* **4.** to continue to be; remain (as specified): *rest assured.* [late ME, t. F: s. *rester*, g. L *rēstāre* remain]

rest³ (rĕst), *n.* *Medieval Armor.* a lance rest. [ME, aphetic var. of *arest* ARREST, n.]

re·state (rē stāt′), *v.t.*, **-stated, -stating.** to state again or in a new way. —**re·state′ment,** *n.*

res·tau·rant (rĕs′tə rənt, -ränt′), *n.* an establishment where meals are served to customers. [t. F, special use of ppr. of *restaurer* RESTORE]

res·tau·ra·teur (rĕs′tə rə tûr′; *Fr.* rĕs tô râ tœr′), *n.* the keeper of a restaurant. [F, der. *restaurer* RESTORE]

rest cure, *Med.* a treatment for nervous disorders, consisting of a complete rest, usually combined with systematic diet, massage, etc.

rest·ful (rĕst′fəl), *adj.* **1.** full of, or giving, rest. **2.** being at rest; quiet; tranquil; peaceful. —**rest′ful·ly,** *adv.* —**rest′ful·ness,** *n.* —**Ant. 1.** disturbing.

rest·har·row (rĕst′hăr′ō), *n.* a low, pink-flowered, leguminous European shrub, *Ononis spinosa,* with tough roots which hinder the plow or harrow. [f. REST¹ + HARROW]

res·ti·form bodies (rĕs′tə fôrm′), *Anat.* a pair of cordlike bundles of nerve fibers lying one on each side of the medulla oblongata and connecting it with the cerebellum. [t. NL: s. *restiformis,* f. L: *resti(s)* rope, cord + *-formis* -FORM]

rest·ing (rĕs′tĭng), *adj.* **1.** that rests. **2.** *Bot.* dormant (applied esp. to spores or seeds which germinate after a period of dormancy).

res·ti·tu·tion (rĕs′tə tū′shən, -tōō′-), *n.* **1.** reparation made by giving an equivalent or compensation for loss, damage, or injury caused; indemnification. **2.** the restoration of property or rights previously taken away, conveyed, or surrendered. **3.** restoration to the former or original state or position. **4.** *Physics.* the return of an elastic to its original form when released from strain. [ME *restitucion,* t. L: m.s. *restitūtio* a restoring] —**Syn. 1.** See **redress.**

res·tive (rĕs′tĭv), *adj.* **1.** restless; uneasy; impatient of control, restraint, or delay, as persons. **2.** refractory. **3.** refusing to go forward, as a horse. [f. REST² (def. 4) + -IVE; r. ME *restif* stationary, balking, t. OF: inert] —**res′tive·ly,** *adv.* —**res′tive·ness,** *n.*

rest·less (rĕst′lĭs), *adj.* **1.** characterized by or showing inability to remain at rest: *a restless mood.* **2.** unquiet or uneasy, as a person, the mind, heart, etc. **3.** never at rest, motionless, or still; never ceasing. **4.** without rest; without restful sleep: *a restless night.* **5.** characterized by unceasing activity; averse to quiet or inaction, as persons. —**rest′less·ly,** *adv.* —**rest′less·ness,** *n.*

restless cavy, a wild guinea pig. See **cavy.**

re·stock (rē stŏk′), *v.t.*, *v.i.* to stock again; replenish.

res·to·ra·tion (rĕs′tə rā′shən), *n.* **1.** act of restoring; renewal, revival, or reëstablishment. **2.** state or fact of being restored. **3.** a bringing back to a former, original, normal, or unimpaired condition. **4.** restitution of something taken away or lost. **5.** something which is restored. **6.** a representation or reconstruction of an ancient building, extinct animal, or the like, showing it in its original state. **7.** a putting back into a former position, dignity, etc. **8. the Restoration, a.** the reëstablishment of the monarchy in England with the return of Charles II in 1660. **b.** the period of the reign of Charles II (1660–85), sometimes extended to include the reign of James II (1685–88).

re·stor·a·tive (rĭ stôr′ə tĭv), *adj.* **1.** serving to restore; pertaining to restoration. **2.** capable of renewing health or strength. —*n.* **3.** a restorative agent. **4.** a means of restoring a person to consciousness.

re·store (rĭ stôr′), *v.t.*, **-stored, -storing. 1.** to bring back into existence, use, or the like; reëstablish: *to restore order.* **2.** to bring back to a former, original, or normal condition, as a building, statue, or painting. **3.** bring back to a state of health, soundness, or vigor. **4.** to put back to a former place, or to a former position, rank, etc. **5.** to give back; make return or restitution of (anything taken away or lost). **6.** to reproduce, reconstruct, or represent (an ancient building, extinct animal, etc.) in the original state. [ME, t. OF: m.s. *restorer,* g. L *rēstaurāre* restore, repair] —**re·stor′er,** *n.* —**Syn. 2.** See **renew.**

re·strain (rĭ strān′), *v.t.* **1.** to hold back from action; keep in check or under control; keep down; repress. **2.** to deprive of liberty, as a person. [ME *restreyn(en),* t. OF: m. *restrei(g)n-,* s. *restreindre,* g. L *restringere*] —**re·strain′a·ble,** *adj.* —**re·strain·ed·ly** (rĭ strā′nĭd lĭ), *adv.* —**Syn. 1.** curb, bridle. See **check.**

re·spread′ re·sprin·kle	re·squan·der re·stab′	re·stack′ re·stamp′	re·start′ re·stip′u·late′

b., blend of, blended; c., cognate with; d., dialect, dialectal; der., derived from; f., formed from; g., going back to; m., modification of; r., replacing; s., stem of; t., taken from; ?, perhaps. See the full key on inside cover.

re·strain·er (rĭ strā′nər), *n.* **1.** one who or that which restrains. **2.** a chemical, as potassium bromide, added to a photographic developer to retard its action.

re·straint (rĭ strānt′). *n.* **1.** restraining action or influence: *freedom from restraint.* **2.** a means of restraining. **3.** act of restraining, or holding back, controlling, or checking. **4.** state or fact of being restrained; deprivation of liberty; confinement. **5.** constraint or reserve in feelings. [ME *restraynte*, t. OF: m. *restraint(e)*, n. use of pp. of *restraindre* restrain] **—Ant. 4.** liberty.

restraint of trade, action tending to interrupt the free flow of goods in commerce.

re·strict (rĭ strĭkt′), *v.t.* to confine or keep within limits, as of space, action, choice, quantity, etc. [t. L: s. *restrictus*, pp., restrained, restricted] **—re·strict′ed,** *adj.* **—re·strict′ed·ly,** *adv.* **—Syn.** curb, circumscribe, abridge.

re·stric·tion (rĭ strĭk′shən), *n.* **1.** something that restricts; a restrictive condition or regulation; a limitation. **2.** act of restricting. **3.** state of being restricted.

re·stric·tive (rĭ strĭk′tĭv), *adj.* **1.** tending or serving to restrict. **2.** of the nature of a restriction. **3.** expressing or implying restriction or limitation of application, as terms, expressions, etc. **—re·stric′tive·ly,** *adv.*

restrictive clause, *Gram.* a relative clause, usually not set off by commas, which identifies the person or object named by the antecedent (opposed to *descriptive clause*).

re·sult (rĭ zŭlt′), *n.* **1.** that which results; the outcome, consequence, or effect. **2.** *Math.* a quantity, value, etc., obtained by calculation. **—v.i. 3.** to spring, arise, or proceed as a consequence from actions, circumstances, premises, etc.; be the outcome. **4.** to terminate or end in a specified manner or thing. [late ME, t. L: s. *resultāre* spring back] **—Syn. 1.** See effect. **3.** See follow. **—Ant. 1.** cause.

re·sult·ant (rĭ zŭl′tənt), *adj.* **1.** that results; following as a result or consequence. **2.** resulting from the combination of two or more agents: *a resultant force.* **—n. 3.** *Physics.* a force, velocity, etc. equal in result or effect to two or more such forces, velocities, etc. **4.** that which results.

re·sume (rĭ zōōm′), *v.* **-sumed, -suming. —v.t. 1.** to take up or go on with again after interruption: *to resume a journey.* **2.** to take or occupy again: *to resume one's seat.* **3.** to take, or take on, again: *to resume one's maiden name.* **4.** to take back. **—v.i. 5.** to go on or continue after interruption. **6.** to begin again. [late ME, t. L: m.s. *resūmere* take up again] **—re·sum′a·ble,** *adj.* **—re·sum′er,** *n.*

ré·su·mé (rĕz′oŏ mā′), *n.* a summing up; a summary. [t. F, prop. pp. of *resumer* RESUME.]

re·sump·tion (rĭ zŭmp′shən), *n.* **1.** act of resuming; a taking back, as of something previously granted. **2.** a taking up or going on with again, as of something interrupted. **3.** a taking, or taking on, again, as of something given up or lost. [late ME, t. L: s. *resumptio*]

re·su·pi·nate (rĭ sōō′pə nāt′), *adj.* **1.** bent backward. **2.** *Bot.* inverted; appearing as if upside down. [t. L: m.s. *resupīnātus*, pp., bent back]

re·su·pi·na·tion (rĭ sōō′pə nā′shən), *n.* resupinate condition.

re·su·pine (rĕ′sōō pīn′), *adj.* lying on the back; supine. [t. L: m.s. *resupīnus*]

re·sur·face (rē sûr′fĭs), *v.t.,* **-faced, -facing.** to give a new surface to.

re·sur·gam (rĭ sûr′găm), *Latin.* I shall rise again.

re·surge (rĭ sûrj′), *v.i.,* **-surged, -surging.** to rise again, as from the dead. [t. L: m.s. *resurgere* rise again]

re·sur·gent (rĭ sûr′jənt), *adj.* rising or tending to rise again. **—re·sur′gence,** *n.*

res·ur·rect (rĕz′ə rĕkt′), *v.t.* **1.** to raise from the dead; bring to life again. **2.** to bring back into use, practice, etc.: *to resurrect an ancient custom.* **—v.i. 3.** to rise from the dead. [back formation from RESURRECTION]

res·ur·rec·tion (rĕz′ə rĕk′shən), *n.* **1.** act of rising again from the dead. **2.** (*cap.*) the rising again of Christ after His death and burial. **3.** (*cap.*) the rising again of men on the judgment day. **4.** state of those risen from the dead. **5.** a rising again, as from decay, disuse, etc.; revival. [ME *resur(r)ectioun*, t. LL: m.s. *resurrectio*] **—res·ur·rec′tion·al,** *adj.*

res·ur·rec·tion·ar·y (rĕz′ə rĕk′shə nĕr′ĭ), *adj.* **1.** pertaining to or of the nature of resurrection. **2.** pertaining to resurrectionism.

res·ur·rec·tion·ism (rĕz′ə rĕk′shə nĭz′əm), *n.* exhuming and stealing of dead bodies, esp. for dissection.

res·ur·rec·tion·ist (rĕz′ə rĕk′shən ĭst), *n.* **1.** one who brings something to life or view again. **2.** a believer in resurrection. **3.** *Rom. Cath. Ch.* a member of the "Congregation of the Resurrection" founded in 1836. **4.** one who exhumes and steals dead bodies, esp. for dissection.

re·sus·ci·tate (rĭ sŭs′ĭ tāt′), *v.t.,* **-tated, -tating.** to revive, esp. from apparent death or from unconsciousness. [t. L: m.s. *resuscitātus*, pp., revived] **—re·sus·ci·ta·ble** (rĭ sŭs′ĭ tə bəl), *adj.* **—re·sus·ci·ta′tion,** *n.* **—re·sus′ci·ta·tive,** *adj.* **—re·sus′ci·ta·tor,** *n.*

Resz·ke (rĕsh′kĕ), *n.* **Jean de** (zhäɴ də), 1850–1925, Polish (tenor) opera singer.

ret (rĕt), *v.t.,* **retted, retting.** to expose to moisture or soak in water, as flax, in order to soften by partial rotting. [ME *retten, reten,* akin to D *reten.* Cf. also D *roten,* c. d. E *rait,* t. Scand.; cf. Sw. *röta* ret]

ret., **1.** retired. **2.** returned.

re·ta·ble (rĭ tā′bəl), *n.* a decorative structure raised above an altar at the back, often forming a frame for a picture, bas-relief, or the like, and sometimes including a shelf or shelves, as for ornaments. [t. F, f. OF *rere* at the back + *table* TABLE]

re·tail (rē′tāl for 1–3, 5; rĭ tāl′ for 4), *n.* **1.** the sale of commodities to household or ultimate consumers, usually in small quantities (opposed to *wholesale*). **—adj. 2.** pertaining to, connected with, or engaged in sale at retail: *the retail price.* **—v.t. 3.** to sell at retail; to sell directly to the consumer. **4.** to relate or repeat in detail to others: *to retail scandal.* **—v.i. 5.** to be sold at retail: *it retails at 50 cents.* [late ME, t. AF: a cutting, der. *retailler* cut, clip, pare, f. re- RE- + *tailler* cut] **—re′tail·er,** *n.*

re·tain (rĭ tān′), *v.t.* **1.** to keep possession of. **2.** to continue to use, practice, etc.: *to retain an old custom.* **3.** to continue to hold or have: *this cloth retains its color.* **4.** to keep in mind; remember. **5.** to hold in place or position. **6.** to engage, esp. by the payment of a preliminary fee, as a lawyer. [ME *reteyne,* t. OF: m. *retenir,* g. Rom. *retenēre,* r. L *retinēre* hold back, keep. Cf. CONTAIN, DETAIN] **—re·tain′a·ble,** *adj.* **—re·tain′ment,** *n.* **—Syn. 1.** See keep. **—Ant. 1.** relinquish.

retained object, *Gram.* an object in a passive construction identical with the direct or indirect object in the corresponding active construction, as *me* in *the picture was shown me* (corresponding active construction: *they showed me the picture*).

re·tain·er¹ (rĭ tā′nər), *n.* **1.** one who or that which retains. **2.** *Hist.* one attached to a noble household and owing it occasional service. **3.** *Mach.* the groove or frame in which roller bearings operate. [f. RETAIN + -ER¹]

re·tain·er² (rĭ tā′nər), *n.* **1.** act of retaining in one's service. **2.** fact of being so retained. **3.** a fee paid to secure services, as of a lawyer. [t. F: m. *retenir,* inf. used as n. See RETAIN]

retaining wall, **1.** a wall built to hold back a mass of earth, etc. **2.** revetment.

R. Retaining wall

re·take (*v.* rē tāk′; *n.* rē′-tāk′), *v.,* **-took, -taken, -taking,** *n.* **—v.t. 1.** to take again; take back. **2.** to recapture. **3.** *Motion Pictures.* to film again. **—n. 4.** a retaking, as of a picture. **5.** a scene, sequence, etc., which is to be or has been filmed again. **—re·tak′er,** *n.*

re·tal·i·ate (rĭ tăl′ĭ āt′), *v.,* **-ated, -ating. —v.i. 1.** to return like for like, esp. evil for evil: *to retaliate for an injury.* **—v.t. 2.** to make return for or requite (now usually wrong, injury, etc.) with the like. [t. LL: m.s. *retāliātus,* pp., requited] **—re·tal′i·a·tive, re·tal·i·a·to·ry** (rĭ tăl′ĭ ə tôr′ĭ), *adj.*

re·tal·i·a·tion (rĭ tăl′ĭ ā′shən), *n.* act of retaliating; return of like for like; reprisal.

re·tard (rĭ tärd′), *v.t.* **1.** to make slow; delay the progress of (an action, process, etc.); hinder or impede. **—v.i. 2.** to be delayed. **—n. 3.** retardation; delay. [t. L: s. *retardāre*] **—re·tard′er,** *n.* **—Ant. 1.** accelerate.

re·tar·da·tion (rē′tär dā′shən), *n.* **1.** act of retarding. **2.** state of being retarded. **3.** that which retards; a hindrance. **4.** *Music.* a form of suspension which is resolved upwards. Also, **re·tard′ment.** **—re·tard·a·tive** (rĭ tär′də tĭv), **re·tard·a·to·ry** (rĭ tär′də tôr′ĭ), *adj.*

retch (rĕch), *v.i.* to make efforts to vomit. [OE *hrǣcan* clear the throat (der. *hrāca* clearing of the throat), c. Icel. *hrækja* hawk, spit]

retd., **1.** retained. **2.** returned.

re·te (rē′tē), *n., pl.* **retia** (rē′shĭ ə, -tĭ ə). a network, as of fibers, nerves, or blood vessels. [ME *riet,* t. L: m. *rēte* net]

re·tene (rē′tēn, rĕt′ēn), *n. Chem.* a crystalline hydrocarbon, $C_{18}H_{18}$, obtained from the tar of resinous woods, certain fossil resins, etc. [t. Gk.: m. *rhētīnē* resin. See -ENE]

re·ten·tion (rĭ tĕn′shən), *n.* **1.** act of retaining. **2.** state of being retained. **3.** power to retain; capacity for retaining. **4.** act or power of remembering things; memory. [ME, t. L: s. *retentio*]

re·ten·tive (rĭ tĕn′tĭv), *adj.* **1.** tending or serving to retain something. **2.** having power or capacity to retain. **3.** having power or ability to remember; having a good memory. **—re·ten′tive·ness,** *n.*

re·ten·tiv·i·ty (rē′tĕn tĭv′ĭ tĭ), *n.* **1.** power to retain; retentiveness. **2.** the ability to retain magnetization after the removal of the magnetizing field.

re·strength′en	re·string′	re·sum′mon	re′sur·vey′
re·stress′	re·strive′	re·sum·mons	re·teach′
re·strike′	re·stud′y	re·sup·ply′	re·tell′

re·te·pore (rē′tə pōr′), *n.* any of the *Reteporidae*, a family of polyzoans which form colonies with a network-like structure. [t. NL: m. *Rētepora*, the typical genus, f. L *rēte* net + *-pora* (t. Gk.: m. *póros* PORE]

re·ti·ar·i·us (rē′shĭ âr′ĭ əs), *n., pl.* **-arii** (-âr′ĭ ī′). *Rom. Hist.* a gladiator equipped with a net for casting over his opponent. [t. L, der. *rēte* net]

re·ti·ar·y (rē′shĭ ĕr′ĭ), *adj.* 1. using a net or any entangling device. 2. netlike. 3. making a net or web, as a spider.

ret·i·cent (rĕt′ə sənt), *adj.* disposed to be silent; not inclined to speak freely; reserved. [t. L: s. *reticens*, ppr., keeping silent] **—ret′i·cence,** *n.* **—ret′i·cent·ly,** *adv.*

ret·i·cle (rĕt′ə kəl), *n.* a network of fine lines, wires, or the like, placed in the focus of the objective of a telescope. [t. L: m.s. *rēticulum*, dim. of *rēte* net. Cf. RETICULE]

re·tic·u·lar (rĭ tĭk′yə lər), *adj.* 1. having the form of a net; netlike. 2. intricate or entangled. [t. NL: s. *rēticulāris*, der. L *rēticulum* small net]

re·tic·u·late (*adj.* rĭ tĭk′yə lĭt, -lāt′; *v.* rĭ tĭk′yə lāt′), *adj., v.,* **-lated, -lating.** **—***adj.* 1. netted; covered with a network. 2. netlike. 3. *Bot.* (of leaves, etc.) having the veins or nerves disposed like the threads of a net. **—***v.t.* 4. to form into a network. 5. to cover or mark with a network. **—***v.i.* 6. to form a network. [t. L: m.s. *rēticulātus* made like a net]

re·tic·u·la·tion (rĭ tĭk′yə lā′shən), *n.* reticulated formation, arrangement, or appearance; a network.

ret·i·cule (rĕt′ə kūl′), *n.* 1. a small purse or bag, orig. of network but later of silk, etc. 2. *Physics.* reticle. [t. F, t. L: m.s. *rēticulum*, dim. of *rēte* net]

re·tic·u·lum (rĭ tĭk′yə ləm), *n., pl.* **-la** (-lə). 1. a network; any reticulated system or structure. 2. *Anat.* reticular endothelial tissue. 3. *Zool.* the second stomach of ruminating animals, between the rumen and the omasum. See diag. under **ruminant.** [t. L: little net]

re·ti·form (rē′tĭ fôrm′, rĕt′ĭ-), *adj.* netlike; reticulate. [t. NL: s. *rētiformis,* f. L *rēti-* (comb. form of *rēte* net) + *-formis* -FORM]

ret·i·na (rĕt′ə nə, rĕt′nə), *n., pl.* **-nas, -nae** (-nē′). *Anat.* the innermost coat of the posterior part of the eyeball, consisting of a layer of light-sensitive cells connecting with the optic nerve by way of a record layer of nerve cells, and serving to receive the image. See diag. under **eye.** [ME, t. ML, ? der. L *rēte* net] **—ret′i·nal,** *adj.*

ret·i·nite (rĕt′ə nīt′), *n.* any of various fossil resins, esp. one of those derived from brown coal. [t. F, f. m.s. Gk. *rhētínē* resin + *-ite* -ITE[1]]

ret·i·ni·tis (rĕt′ə nī′tĭs), *n.* *Pathol.* inflammation of the retina. [NL. See RETINA, -ITIS]

ret·i·nol (rĕt′ə nōl′, -nŏl′), *n.* a yellowish oil obtained by the distillation of resin, used as a solvent, a mild antiseptic, etc. [f. *retin-* (m.s. Gk. *rhētínē* resin) + -OL[2]]

ret·i·no·scope (rĕt′ə nə skōp′), *n.* *Med.* a skiascope.

ret·i·nos·co·py (rĕt′ə nŏs′kə pĭ, rĕt′ə nə skō′pĭ), *n.* an objective method of determining the refractive error of an eye. [f. *retino-* (comb. form repr. RETINA) + -SCOPY] **—ret·i·no·scop·ic** (rĕt′ə nə skŏp′ĭk), *adj.*

ret·i·nue (rĕt′ə nū′, -nōō′), *n.* a body of retainers in attendance upon an important personage; a suite. [ME, t. OF: m. *retenue,* fem. pp. of *retenir* RETAIN]

re·tire (rĭ tīr′), *v.,* **-tired, -tiring.** **—***v.i.* 1. to withdraw, or go away or apart, to a place of abode, shelter, or seclusion. 2. to go to bed. 3. to withdraw from office, business, or active life: *to retire at the age of sixty.* 4. to fall back or retreat, as from battle or danger. 5. to withdraw, go away, or remove oneself. **—***v.t.* 6. to withdraw from circulation by taking up and paying, as bonds, bills, etc. 7. to withdraw or lead back (troops, etc.), as from battle or danger; retreat. 8. to remove from active service or the usual field of activity, as an officer in the army or the navy. 9. *Baseball, etc.* to put out (a batter). [t. F: m.s. *retirer* withdraw, f. re- RE- + *tirer* draw] **—Syn. 5. See depart.**

re·tired (rĭ tīrd′), *adj.* 1. withdrawn from or no longer occupied with one's business or profession: *a retired sea-captain.* 2. due or given a retired person: *retired pay.* 3. withdrawn; secluded or sequestered.

re·tire·ment (rĭ tīr′mənt), *n.* 1. act of retiring. 2. state of being retired. 3. removal or retiring from service, office, or business. 4. withdrawal into privacy or seclusion. 5. privacy or seclusion. 6. a private or secluded place. 7. retreat of a military force. 8. repurchase of its own securities by a corporation.

re·tir·ing (rĭ tīr′ĭng), *adj.* 1. that retires. 2. withdrawing from contact with others; reserved; shy.

re·tor·sion (rĭ tôr′shən), *n.* *Internat. Law.* retaliation or reprisal by one state identical or similar to an act by an offending state, such as high tariffs or discriminating duties. Also, **retortion.** [t. ML: s. *retorsio* RETORTION]

re·tort[1] (rĭ tôrt′), *v.t.* 1. to reply in retaliation; make a retort or retorts; reply in kind to. 2. to return (an accusation, epithet, etc.) upon the person uttering it. 3. to answer (an argument or the like) by another to the contrary. **—***n.* 4. a severe, incisive, or witty reply, esp. one that counters a first speaker's statement, argument, etc. 5. act of retorting. [t. L: s. *retortus,* pp., twisted back] **—Syn. 4. See answer.**

re·tort[2] (rĭ tôrt′), *n.* 1. *Chem.* a vessel, commonly a glass bulb with a long neck bent downward, used for distilling or decomposing substances by heat. 2. *Metall.* a vessel, generally cylindrically shaped, within which an ore is heated so that the metal may be removed by distillation or sublimation. [t. ML: s. *retorta,* prop. fem. pp., twisted back. See RETORT[1], v.]

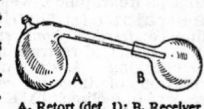

A. Retort (def. 1); B, Receiver

re·tor·tion (rĭ tôr′shən), *n.* 1. act of turning or bending back. 2. retaliation. 3. *Internat. Law.* retorsion. [t. ML: s. *retortio,* der. L *retortus,* pp., twisted back]

re·touch (rē tŭch′), *v.t.* 1. *Photog.* to correct or improve (a negative or print) by the use of a pencil, scraping knife, etc. 2. to improve by new touches or the like, as a painting. **—***n.* 3. an added touch to a painting, etc., by way of improvement or alteration. **—re·touch′er,** *n.*

re·trace (rĭ trās′), *v.t.* **-traced, -tracing.** 1. to trace backward; go back over: *to retrace one's steps.* 2. to go back over with the memory. 3. to go over again with the sight or attention. [t. F: m.s. *retracer,* f. re- RE- + *tracer* TRACE[1]] **—re·trace′a·ble,** *adj.*

re·trace (rētrās′), *v.t.* **-traced, -tracing.** to trace again, as lines in writing or drawing. [f. RE- + TRACE[1] (defs. 18, 19)]

re·tract[1] (rĭ trăkt′), *v.t.* to draw back or in. [late ME, t. L: s. *retractus,* pp., drawn back]

re·tract[2] (rĭ trăkt′), *v.t.* 1. to withdraw (a statement, opinion, etc.) as unjustified. 2. to withdraw or revoke (a decree, promise, etc.). **—***v.i.* 3. to draw or shrink back. 4. to withdraw a promise, etc. 5. to make disavowal of a statement, opinion, etc., or recant. [t. L: s. *retractāre* recall] **—re·tract′a·ble,** *adj.* **—re·trac·ta·tion** (rē′trăk tā′shən), *n.*

re·trac·tile (rĭ trăk′tĭl), *adj.* *Zool.* capable of being drawn back or in, as the head of a tortoise; exhibiting the power of retraction. **—re′trac·til′i·ty,** *n.*

re·trac·tion (rĭ trăk′shən), *n.* 1. act of retracting. 2. state of being retracted. 3. withdrawal of a promise, statement, opinion, etc.: *his retraction of the libel came too late.* 4. retractile power.

re·trac·tive (rĭ trăk′tĭv), *adj.* tending or serving to retract.

re·trac·tor (rĭ trăk′tər), *n.* 1. one who or that which retracts. 2. *Anat.* a muscle that retracts an organ or protruded part, etc. 3. *Surg.* an instrument or appliance for drawing back an impeding part.

re·tread (*v.* rē trĕd′; *n.* rē′trĕd′), *v.,* **-treaded, -treading,** *n.* **—***v.t.* 1. to put a new tread on (a worn pneumatic tire casing) either by recapping or by cutting fresh treads in the smooth surface; regroove. **—***n.* 2. a retreaded tire. [f. RE- + TREAD[2]]

re·tread (rē trĕd′), *v.t., v.i.,* **-trod, -trodden** or **-trod, -treading.** to tread again. [f. RE- + TREAD[1]]

re·treat (rĭ trēt′), *n.* 1. the forced or strategic retirement of an armed force before an enemy, or the withdrawing of a ship or fleet from action. 2. act of withdrawing, as into safety or privacy; retirement; seclusion. 3. a place of refuge, seclusion, or privacy. 4. an asylum, as for the insane. 5. a retirement, or a period of retirement, for religious exercises and meditation. 6. a signal given in the army or navy by drum, bugle, or trumpet, at sunset. [ME *retret,* t. OF, var. of *retrait,* prop. pp. of *retraire* draw back, g. L *retrahere*] **—***v.i.* 7. to withdraw, retire, or draw back, esp. for shelter or seclusion. 8. to make a retreat, as an army. 9. to slope backward; recede: *a retreating chin.* **—***v.t.* 10. to draw or lead back. [ME *retrete(n),* der. *retret,* n., retreat] **—Syn. 7. See depart.** **—Ant. 1.** advance.

re·trench (rĭ trĕnch′), *v.t.* 1. to cut down, reduce, or diminish; curtail (expenses). 2. to cut off or remove. 3. *Mil.* to protect by a retrenchment. **—***v.i.* 4. to economize; reduce expenses: *they retrenched by eliminating half of the workers.* [t. F (obs.): s. *retrencher.* See RE-, TRENCH]

re·trench·ment (rĭ trĕnch′mənt), *n.* 1. act of retrenching; a cutting down or off; reduction of expenses. 2. *Fort.* **a.** an interior work which cuts off a part of a fortification from the rest, and to which a garrison may retreat. **b.** entrenchment.

ret·ri·bu·tion (rĕt′rə bū′shən), *n.* 1. requital according to merits or deserts, esp. for evil. 2. something given or inflicted in such requital. 3. *Theol.* the distribution of rewards and punishments in a future life. [ME, t. L: s. *retribūtio*] **—Syn. 2. See revenge.**

re·trib·u·tive (rĭ trĭb′yə tĭv), *adj.* characterized by or involving retribution. Also, **re·trib·u·to·ry** (rĭ trĭb′yə tōr′ĭ).

re·triev·al (rĭ trē′vəl), *n.* 1. act of retrieving. 2. chance of recovery or restoration: *lost beyond retrieval.*

re·trieve (rĭ trēv′), *v.,* **-trieved, -trieving,** *n.* **—***v.t.* 1. to recover or regain. 2. to bring back to a former and better state; restore: *to retrieve one's fortunes.* 3. to make amends for (an error, etc.). 4. to make good; repair (a loss, etc.). 5. *Hunting.* (of dogs) to find and fetch (killed or wounded game). 6. to rescue or save. **—***v.i.*

re·test′	re·think′	re·told′	re′trans·late′
re·tes′ti·fy′	re·tie′	re·trans′fer	re·tri′al

b., blend of, blended; c., cognate with; d., dialect, dialectal; der., derived from; f., formed from; g., going back to; m., modification of; r., replacing; s., stem of; t., taken from; ?, perhaps. See the full key on inside cover.

7. *Hunting.* to retrieve game. —*n.* **8.** act of retrieving; recovery. **9.** possibility of recovery. [ME *retreve,* t. OF: m. *retroev-,* stressed stem of *retrouver,* f. re- RE- + *trouver* find. See TROVER] —**re·triev′a·ble,** *adj.* —Syn. **1.** See recover.

re·triev·er (rĭ trē′vər), *n.* **1.** one who or that which retrieves. **2.** any of several breeds of dog developed esp. in America and England for retrieving game. **3.** any dog trained to retrieve game.

Labrador retriever (2 ft. or more high at the shoulder)

retro-, a prefix meaning "backwards" in space or time, e.g., *retrogression, retrospect.* [t. L, prefix repr. *retrō,* adv., backward, back, behind]

ret·ro·ac·tion (rĕt′rō ăk′shən), *n.* **1.** action which is opposed or contrary to the preceding action. **2.** *Law.* (of a past or still operative event or act) the impingement of a later law or agreement.

ret·ro·ac·tive (rĕt′rō ăk′tĭv), *adj.* operative with respect to past occurrences, as a statute; retrospective. —**ret′ro·ac′tive·ly,** *adv.* —**ret′ro·ac·tiv′i·ty,** *n.*

ret·ro·cede¹ (rĕt′rō sēd′), *v.i.,* **-ceded, -ceding.** to go back; recede; retire. [t. L: m. *retrōcēdere* yield, go back] —**ret·ro·ces·sion** (rĕt′rō sĕsh′ən), *n.*

ret·ro·cede² (rĕt′rō sēd′), *v.t.,* **-ceded, -ceding.** to cede back (territory, etc.). [f. RETRO- + CEDE] —**ret·ro·ces·sion** (rĕt′rō sĕsh′ən, *n.*

ret·ro·choir (rĕt′rə kwīr′), *n.* that part of a church behind the choir or the main altar. [f. RETRO- + CHOIR, after ML *retrōchorus*]

ret·ro·flex (rĕt′rə flĕks′), *adj.* **1.** bent backward; exhibiting retroflexion. **2.** *Phonet.* with the tip of the tongue raised or tilted upward: *burn* has a retroflex vowel in a common American pronunciation. [t. L: s. *retrōflexus,* pp., bent back. See FLEX]

ret·ro·flex·ion (rĕt′rə flĕk′shən), *n.* **1.** a bending backward. **2.** *Pathol.* a bending backward of the body of the uterus. **3.** *Phonet.* **a.** retroflex articulation. **b.** the acoustic quality resulting from retroflex articulation; r-color.

ret·ro·gra·da·tion (rĕt′rō grā dā′shən), *n.* **1.** backward movement. **2.** decline or deterioration.

ret·ro·grade (rĕt′rə grād′), *adj., v.,* **-graded, -grading.** —*adj.* **1.** moving backward; having a backward motion or direction; retiring or retreating. **2.** inverse or reversed, as order. **3.** *Chiefly Biol.* exhibiting degeneration or deterioration. **4.** *Astron.* **a.** noting an apparent or actual motion in a direction contrary to the order of the signs of the zodiac, or from east to west. **b.** moving in an orbit in the direction opposite to that of the earth in its revolution round the sun. —*v.i.* **5.** to move or go backward; retire or retreat. **6.** *Chiefly Biol.* to decline to a worse condition; degenerate. **7.** *Astron.* to have a retrograde motion. [ME *retrograd,* t. L: s. *retrōgradus* going backward]

ret·ro·gress (rĕt′rə grĕs′), *v.i.* **1.** to go backward into a worse or earlier condition. **2.** to move backward.

ret·ro·gres·sion (rĕt′rə grĕsh′ən), *n.* **1.** act of retrogressing; backward movement. **2.** *Biol.* degeneration; retrograde metamorphosis; passing from a more complex to a simpler structure.

ret·ro·gres·sive (rĕt′rə grĕs′ĭv), *adj.* characterized by retrogression; degenerating. —**ret′ro·gres′sive·ly,** *adv.* —Ant. progressive.

re·trorse (rĭ trôrs′), *adj.* turned backward. [t. L: m. s. *retrōrsus,* contr. of *retrōversus* bent or turned backward] —**re·trorse′ly,** *adv.*

ret·ro·spect (rĕt′rə spĕkt′), *n.* **1.** contemplation of the past; a survey of the past time, events, etc. **2.** in retrospect, looking backwards. —*v.i.* Rare. **3.** to look back in thought. **4.** to refer back (fol. by *to*). —*v.t.* **5.** *Rare.* to look back upon, contemplate, or think of (something past). [back formation from RETROSPECTION]

ret·ro·spec·tion (rĕt′rə spĕk′shən), *n.* action or faculty of looking back on things past; a survey of past events or experiences. [f. s. L *retrōspectus* (pp. of *retrōspicere* look back at) + -ION]

ret·ro·spec·tive (rĕt′rə spĕk′tĭv), *adj.* **1.** directed to the past; contemplative of past events, etc. **2.** looking or directed backward. **3.** retroactive, as a statute. —**ret′ro·spec′tive·ly,** *adv.*

ret·rous·sé (rĕt′rōō sā′; *Fr.* rə trōō sě′), *adj.* (esp. of the nose) turned up. [t. F, pp. of *retrousser,* f. re- RE- + *trousser* TRUSS]

ret·ro·ver·sion (rĕt′rə vûr′zhən, -shən), *n.* **1.** a looking or turning back. **2.** the resulting state or condition. **3.** *Pathol.* a tilting or turning backward of an organ or part: *retroversion of the uterus.* [f. s. L *retrōversus* turned back + -ION]

re·turn (rĭ tûrn′), *v.i.* **1.** to go or come back, as to a former place, position, state, etc. **2.** to revert to a former owner. **3.** to revert or recur in thought or discourse. **4.** to make reply; retort. —*v.t.* **5.** to put, bring, take, give, or send back: *return a book to its shelf.* **6.** to send or give back in reciprocation, recompense, or requital: *return shot for shot.* **7.** to reciprocate, repay,

or requite (something sent, given, done, etc.) with something similar: *return the enemy's fire.* **8.** *Law.* **a.** to return to a judge or official (a statement or a writ of actions done). **b.** to render (a verdict, etc.). **9.** to reflect (light, sound, etc.). **10.** to yield (a profit, revenue, etc.), as in return for labor, expenditure, or investment. **11.** to report or announce officially. **12.** to elect, as to a legislative body. **13.** *Mil.* to put (a weapon) back into its holder. **14.** *Cards.* to respond to (a suit lead) by a similar lead. **15.** to turn back or in the reverse direction. **16.** *Chiefly Archit.* to turn away from, or at an angle to, the previous line of direction. —*n.* **17.** act or fact of returning; a going or coming back; a bringing, sending, or giving back. **18.** a recurrence: *many happy returns of the day.* **19.** reciprocation, repayment, or requital: *profits in return for outlay.* **20.** response or reply. **21.** one who or that which is returned: *returns of mill goods.* **22.** the gain realized on an exchange of goods. **23.** *(often pl.)* a yield or profit, as from labor, land, business, investment, etc. **24.** a report, esp. a formal or official report: *tax returns; election returns.* **25.** the report or statement of financial condition. **26.** *Colloq.* a round-trip railroad ticket. **27.** *Archit.* **a.** the continuation of a molding, projection, etc., in a different direction. **b.** a side or part which falls away from the front of any straight work. **28.** *Tennis, Cricket, etc.* **a.** the process of returning a ball. **b.** the ball which is returned. **29.** *Econ.* yield per unit as compared to the cost per unit involved in a specific industrial process. **30.** *Law.* **a.** the bringing or sending back of various documents, such as a writ, summons, or subpoena, with a brief written report usually indorsed upon it, by a sheriff, etc., to the court from which it issued. **b.** a certified return by a great variety of officers, such as assessors, collectors, and election officers. **c.** the report or certificate indorsed on such documents. **31.** *Cards.* a lead which responds to a partner's lead. —*adj.* **32.** of or pertaining to return or returning: *a return trip.* **33.** sent, given, or done in return: *a return shot.* **34.** done or occurring again: *a return engagement of the opera.* **35.** denoting a person or thing which is returned or returning to a place: *return cargo.* **36.** changing in direction; doubling or returning on itself: *return bend in the road.* [ME *retorne(n),* t. OF: m. *retorner.* See RE-, TURN, v.]

re·turn·a·ble (rĭ tûr′nə bəl), *adj.* **1.** that may be returned. **2.** required to be returned.

return ticket, a round-trip ticket.

re·tuse (rĭ tūs′, -tōōs′), *adj.* (of a leaf, etc.) having an obtuse or rounded apex with a shallow notch. [t. L: m.s. *retūsus,* pp., blunted]

Retuse leaf

Reu·ben (rōō′bĭn), *n.* **1.** the eldest son of Jacob and Leah. Gen. 29, 30, etc. **2.** one of the 12 tribes of Israel. Num. 32. [t. Heb.]

Reuch·lin (roĭкH′lēn, roĭ кH lēn′), *n.* **Johann** (yō′hän), 1455–1522, German humanist and scholar.

re·un·ion (rē ūn′yən), *n.* **1.** act of uniting again. **2.** state of being united again. **3.** a gathering of relatives, friends, or associates after separation: *a family reunion.*

Ré·un·ion (rē ūn′yən; *Fr.* rě ynyôN′), *n.* an island in the Indian Ocean, E of Madagascar: a department of France. 274,370 pop. (1954); 970 sq. mi. *Cap.:* St. Denis.

re·un·ion·ist (rē ūn′yən ĭst), *n.* one who advocates the reunion of the Anglican Church with the Roman Catholic Church. —**re·un′ion·ism,** *n.* —**re·un′ion·is′tic,** *adj.*

re·u·nite (rē′ū nīt′), *v.t., v.i.,* **-nited, -niting.** to unite again, as after separation. —**re′u·nit′a·ble,** *adj.* —**re′u·nit′er,** *n.*

re·used (rē ūzd′), *adj.* denoting wool which has been spun, woven, and used once before.

Reu·ters (roi′tərz), *n.* a British news-gathering agency, founded in London by Baron Paul Julius von Reuter (1816–99).

Reu·ther (rōō′thər), *n.* **Walter Philip,** born 1907, U.S. labor leader, president of the C.I.O. since 1952.

rev (rĕv), *n., v.,* **revved, revving.** *Colloq.* —*n.* **1.** a revolution (in an engine or the like). —*v.t.* **2.** to change the speed of (in a specified way): *to rev a motor up.* —*v.i.* **3.** to undergo revving. [short for REVOLUTION]

Rev., **1.** Revelation. **2.** Revelations. **3.** Reverend.

rev., **1.** revenue. **2.** reverse. **3.** review. **4.** revise. **5.** revised. **6.** revision. **7.** revolution. **8.** revolving.

Re·val (rā′väl), *n.* German name of Tallinn.

re·val·ue (rē văl′ū), *v.t.,* **-ued, -uing.** to value again.

re·vamp (rē vămp′), *v.t.* to vamp afresh; renovate.

re·veal (rĭ vēl′), *v.t.* **1.** to make known; disclose; divulge: *to reveal a secret.* **2.** to lay open to view; display; exhibit. —*n.* **3.** a revealing; revelation; disclosure. **4.** *Archit.* **a.** that part of a jamb, or vertical face of an opening for a window or door, included between the face of the wall and that of the frame containing the window or door. **b.** the whole jamb or vertical face of an opening. **5.** the framework or edge of an automobile window. [ME *revele,* t. L: m. *revēlāre* unveil, reveal] —**re·veal′a·ble,** *adj.* —**re·veal′er,** *n.*

—Syn. **1, 2.** REVEAL, DISCLOSE, DIVULGE is to make known something previously concealed or secret. To REVEAL is to uncover as if by drawing away a veil: *the fog lifted and revealed the harbor.* To DISCLOSE is to lay open and thereby

re·try′	re·use′	re·ut′ter	re′val·u·a′tion
re·type′	re·u′ti·lize′	re·val′u·ate′	re·var′nish

invite inspection: *to disclose the plans of an organization.* To DIVULGE is to communicate, sometimes to a large number, what was at first intended to be private, confidential, or secret: *to divulge the terms of a contract.* —**Ant.** 2. conceal, hide.

re·veal·ment (rĭ vēl′mənt), *n.* act of revealing; revelation.

re·veg·e·tate (rē vĕj′ə tāt′), *v.i.*, **-tated, -tating. 1.** to grow again, as plants. **2.** to put forth vegetation again, as plants.

rev·eil·le (rĕv′ə lĭ), *n.* a signal, as of a drum or bugle, sounded at a prescribed hour, to waken soldiers or sailors for the day's duties. [t. F: m. *réveillez,* impv. pl. of *réveiller* awaken, f. re- RE- + *veiller,* g. L *vigilāre* keep watch]

rev·el (rĕv′əl), *v.,* **-eled, -eling** or (*esp. Brit.*) **-elled, -elling,** *n.* —*v.i.* **1.** to take great pleasure or delight (fol. by *in*). **2.** to make merry; indulge in boisterous festivities. —*n.* **3.** boisterous merrymaking or festivity; revelry. **4.** (*often pl.*) an occasion of merrymaking or noisy festivity with dancing, masking, etc. [ME *revel(en),* t. OF: m. *reveler,* orig., to make noise, rebel, g. L *rebellāre.* See REBEL] —**rev′el·er;** *esp. Brit.,* **rev′el·ler,** *n.*

Re·vel (rĕ′vĕl′y), *n.* Russian name of Tallinn.

rev·e·la·tion (rĕv′ə lā′shən), *n.* **1.** act of revealing or disclosing; disclosure. **2.** something revealed or disclosed, esp. a striking disclosure, as of something not before realized. **3.** *Theol.* **a.** God's disclosure of himself and of his will to his creatures. **b.** an instance of such communication or disclosure. **c.** something thus communicated or disclosed. **d.** that which contains such disclosure, as the Bible. **4. Revelation,** (*often pl.*) "the Revelation of St. John the Divine." [ME, t. L: s. *revēlātio*]

rev·e·la·tion·ist (rĕv′ə lā′shən ĭst), *n.* one who believes in revelation.

Revelation of St. John the Divine, The, the last book in the New Testament; the Apocalypse.

rev·e·la·tor (rĕv′ə lā′tər), *n.* one who makes a revelation.

rev·el·ry (rĕv′əl rĭ), *n., pl.* **-ries.** reveling; boisterous festivity: *the sound of their revelry could be heard across the river.*

rev·e·nant (rĕv′ə nənt), *n.* **1.** one who returns. **2.** one who returns as a spirit after death; a ghost. [t. F, prop, ppr. of *revenir* return, f. re- RE- + *venir* come, g. L *venīre*]

re·venge (rĭ vĕnj′), *n., v.,* **-venged, -venging.** —*n.* **1.** act of revenging; retaliation for injuries or wrongs; vengeance. **2.** something done in revenging. **3.** the desire to revenge; vindictiveness. **4.** an opportunity for retaliation or satisfaction. —*v.t.* **5.** to take vengeance or exact expiation on behalf of (a person, etc.) or for (a wrong, etc.), esp. in a resentful or vindictive spirit. —*v.i.* **6.** *Obs.* to take revenge. [ME, t. OF: m.s. *revengier,* f. re- RE- + *vengier* VENGE] —**re·veng′er,** *n.*
—**Syn. 1.** REVENGE, REPRISAL, RETRIBUTION, VENGEANCE suggest a punishment, or injury inflicted in return for one received. REVENGE is the carrying out of a bitter desire to injure another for a wrong done to oneself or to those who seem a part of oneself: *to plot revenge.* REPRISAL, formerly any act of retaliation, is used specifically in warfare for retaliation upon the enemy for his (usually unlawful) actions: *to make a raid in reprisal for one by the enemy.* RETRIBUTION suggests just or deserved punishment, often without personal motives, for some evil done: *a just retribution for wickedness.* VENGEANCE is usually wrathful, vindictive, furious revenge: *implacable vengeance.* **5.** See avenge.

re·venge·ful (rĭ vĕnj′fəl), *adj.* full of revenge; vindictive. —**re·venge′ful·ly,** *adv.* —**re·venge′ful·ness,** *n.* —**Syn.** See spiteful.

rev·e·nue (rĕv′ə nū′, -nōō′), *n.* **1.** the income of a government from taxation, excise duties, customs, or other sources, appropriated to the payment of the public expenses. **2.** the government department charged with the collection of such income. **3.** (*pl.*) the collective items or amounts of income of a person, a state, etc. **4.** the return or yield from any kind of property; income. **5.** an amount of money regularly coming in. **6.** a particular item or source of income. [late ME, t. F, orig. fem. pp. of *revenir* return, f. re- RE- + *venir* come]

revenue cutter. See cutter (def. 4).

revenue stamp, a stamp showing that a government tax has been paid.

re·ver·ber·ant (rĭ vûr′bər ənt), *adj.* reverberating; reëchoing.

re·ver·ber·ate (rĭ vûr′bər āt′), *v.,* **-ated, -ating.** —*v.i.* **1.** to reëcho or resound. **2.** *Physics.* to be reflected many times, as sound waves from the walls, etc. of a confined space. **3.** to rebound or recoil. **4.** to be deflected, as flame in a reverberatory furnace. —*v.t.* **5.** to echo back or reëcho (sound). **6.** to cast back or reflect (light, etc.). **7.** to treat (a substance) in a reverberatory furnace or the like. **8.** to deflect (flame or heat) on something, as in a reverberatory furnace. [t. L: m. *reverberātus,* pp., beaten back] —**re·ver′ber·a′tive,** *adj.* —**re·ver′ber·a′tor,** *n.*

re·ver·ber·a·tion (rĭ vûr′bə rā′shən), *n.* **1.** a reëchoed sound. **2.** the fact of being reverberated or reflected. **3.** that which is reverberated. **4.** act or instance of reverberating. **5.** *Physics.* multiple reflection of sound in a room, causing a sound to persist after the stopping of the source. **6.** the action or process of subjecting something to reflected heat as in a reverberatory furnace. [ME, t. L: s. *reverberātio*]

re·ver·ber·a·to·ry (rĭ vûr′bər ə tōr′ĭ), *adj., n., pl.* **-ries.** —*adj.* **1.** characterized or produced by reverberation. **2.** denoting a furnace, kiln, or the like, in which the fuel is not in direct contact with the ore, metal, etc., to be heated, but furnishes a flame that plays over the material, esp. by being deflected downward from the roof. **3.** deflected, as flame. —*n.* **4.** any device, as a furnace, embodying reverberation.

Section of reverberatory furnace

re·vere¹ (rĭ vĭr′), *v.t.,* **-vered, -vering.** to regard with respect tinged with awe; venerate. [t. L: m.s. *reverērī* feel awe of, fear, revere]

re·vere² (rĭ vĭr′), *n.* revers.

Re·vere (rĭ vĭr′), *n.* **1. Paul,** 1735-1818, American patriot, famous for his night horseback ride to warn Massachusetts colonists of the coming of British troops. **2.** a city in E Massachusetts, on Massachusetts Bay, near Boston: seaside resort. 40,080 (1960).

rev·er·ence (rĕv′ər əns), *n., v.,* **-enced, -encing.** —*n.* **1.** the feeling or attitude of deep respect tinged with awe; veneration. **2.** the outward manifestation of this feeling: *to pay reverence.* **3.** a gesture indicative of deep respect; an obeisance, bow, or curtsy. **4.** state of being revered. **5.** (*cap.*) a title used in addressing or mentioning a clergyman (prec. by *your* or *his*). —*v.t.* **6.** to regard or treat with reverence; venerate. [ME, t. L: m. *reverentia*]
—**Syn. 1.** REVERENCE, WORSHIP imply sentiments of respect and homage. REVERENCE is a strong feeling of deference, respect, and esteem: *reverence shown to the venerable and wise.* WORSHIP, which is associated with an exalted religious feeling of reverence and love, refers primarily not to the feeling itself but to its manifestation in certain practices: *the worship of idols.* Thus, even in such expressions as *worship of beauty,* there is the suggestion of a way of behavior. —**Ant. 1.** irreverence, contempt.

rev·er·end (rĕv′ər ənd), *adj.* **1.** an epithet of respect applied to, or prefixed to the name of, a clergyman. **2.** worthy to be revered; entitled to reverence. **3.** pertaining to or characteristic of the clergy. —*n.* **4.** *Colloq.* a clergyman. [t. L: s. *reverendus,* ger. of *reverērī* revere]

rev·er·ent (rĕv′ər ənt), *adj.* feeling, exhibiting, or characterized by reverence; deeply respectful. [t. L: s. *reverens,* ppr., feeling awe of] —**rev′er·ent·ly,** *adv.*

rev·er·en·tial (rĕv′ə rĕn′shəl), *adj.* of the nature of or characterized by reverence; reverent: *reverential awe.* —**rev′er·en′tial·ly,** *adv.*

rev·er·ie (rĕv′ə rĭ), *n.* **1.** a state of dreamy meditation or fanciful musing: *lost in reverie.* **2.** a day dream. **3.** a fantastic, visionary, or unpractical idea. **4.** *Music.* an instrumental composition of a vague and dreamy character. Also, **revery.** [t. F, der. *rêver* to dream]

re·vers (rə vĭr′, -vâr′), *n., pl.* **-vers** (-vĭrz′, -vârz′). **1.** a part of a garment turned back to show the lining or facing, as a lapel. **2.** a trimming simulating such a part. **3.** the facing shown. Also, **re·vere′.** [t. F. See REVERSE]

re·ver·sal (rĭ vûr′səl), *n.* **1.** act of reversing. **2.** an instance of this. **3.** state of being reversed. **4.** *Law.* the revocation of a lower court's decision by an appellate court.

re·verse (rĭ vûrs′), *adj., n., v.,* **-versed, -versing.** —*adj.* **1.** opposite or contrary in position, direction, order, or character: *an impression reverse to what was intended.* **2.** acting in a manner opposite or contrary to that which is usual, as an appliance or apparatus. **3.** with the rear part toward one: *reverse side of a coin.* **4.** producing a rearward motion: *reverse drive.* **5.** *Auto.* of or pertaining to reverse (gear ratio). —*n.* **6.** the opposite or contrary of something. **7.** the back or rear of anything. **8.** *Coins.* **a.** that side of a coin, medal, etc., which does not bear the principal design (opposed to *obverse*). **b.** (in ancient coins) the side struck with the upper or punch die. **9.** an adverse change of fortune, a misfortune, check, or defeat: *to meet with an unexpected reverse.* **10.** *Auto.* a transmission gear ratio driving a car backwards. **11.** *Mach.* a reversing mechanism, etc. —*v.t.* **12.** to turn in an opposite position; transpose. **13.** to turn inside out or upside down. **14.** to turn in the opposite direction; send on the opposite course. **15.** to turn in the opposite order: *to reverse the usual order.* **16.** to alter to the opposite in character or tendency, or change completely. **17.** to revoke or annul (a decree, judgment, etc.). **18.** *Mach.* to cause to revolve or act in an opposite or contrary direction or manner. —*v.i.* **19.** to turn or move in the opposite or contrary direction, as in dancing. **20.** (of an engine) to reverse the action of the mechanism. [ME *revers,* t. L: s. *reversus,* pp., turned about] —**re·verse′ly,** *adv.* —**re·vers′er,** *n.*
—**Syn. 1.** See **opposite. 12.** REVERSE, INVERT agree in meaning to change into a contrary position, order, or relation. To REVERSE is to place or move something so that it is facing in the opposite direction from the one faced previously: *to reverse from right to left; to reverse a decision.* To INVERT is to turn upside down: *to invert a stamp in printing, to invert a bowl over a plate.*

re·vers·i·ble (rĭ vûr′sə bəl), *adj.* **1.** capable of being reversed or of reversing. **2.** capable of reëstablishing the original condition after a change by the reverse of the change. **3.** (of a fabric) woven or printed so that either side may be exposed. —*n.* **4.** a garment, esp. a coat, that may be worn with either side exposed. —**re·vers'i·bil'i·ty, re·vers'i·ble·ness,** *n.* —**re·vers'i·bly,** *adv.*

re·ver·sion (rĭ vûr'zhən, -shən), *n.* **1.** act of turning something the reverse way. **2.** state of being so turned; reversal. **3.** act of reverting; return to a former practice, belief, condition, etc. **4.** *Biol.* **a.** reappearance of ancestral characters that have been absent in intervening generations. **b.** return to an earlier or primitive type; atavism. **5.** *Law.* **a.** the returning of an estate to the grantor or his heirs after the interest granted expires. **b.** an estate which so returns. **c.** the right of succeeding to an estate, etc. [ME, t. L: s. *reversio* a turning back]

re·ver·sion·ar·y (rĭ vûr'zhə nĕr'ĭ, -shə-), *adj.* of, pertaining to, or involving a reversion. Also, **re·ver'sion·al.**

re·ver·sion·er (rĭ vûr'zhən ər, -shən-), *n.* *Law.* one who possesses a reversion.

re·vert (rĭ vûrt'), *v.i.* **1.** to return to a former habit, practice, belief, condition, etc. **2.** to go back in thought or discourse, as to a subject. **3.** *Biol.* to return to an earlier or primitive type. **4.** *Law.* to go back or to return to the former owner or his heirs. [ME *reverte(n)*, t. OF: m. *revertir*, g. LL *revertīre*, r. L *revertere*] —**re·vert'i·ble,** *adj.*

rev·er·y (rĕv'ər ĭ), *n.*, *pl.* **-eries.** reverie.

re·vest (rē vĕst'), *v.t.* **1.** to vest (a person, etc.) again, as with ownership or office; reinvest; reinstate. **2.** to vest (powers, etc.) again. —*v.i.* **3.** to become vested again in a person; go back again to a former owner.

re·vet (rĭ vĕt'), *v.t.*, **-vetted, -vetting.** to face, as an embankment, with masonry or other material. [t. F: m.s. *revêtir*, lit., clothe. See REVEST]

re·vet·ment (rĭ vĕt'mənt), *n.* **1.** a facing of masonry or the like, esp. for protecting an embankment. **2.** a retaining wall. [t. F: m. *revêtement.* See REVET, -MENT]

re·view (rĭ vū'), *n.* **1.** a critical article or report, as in a periodical, on some literary work, commonly some work of recent appearance; a critique. **2.** a periodical publication containing articles on current events or affairs, books, art, etc.: *a literary review.* **3.** a viewing again; a second or repeated view of something. **4.** the process of going over a subject again in study or recitation in order to fix it in the memory or summarize the facts, or an exercise of this kind. **5.** an inspection, or examination by viewing, esp. a formal inspection of any military or naval force, parade, or the like. **6.** a viewing of the past; contemplation or consideration of past events, circumstances, or facts. **7.** a general survey of something, esp. in words; a report or account of something. **8.** a judicial reëxamination, as by a higher court, of the decision or proceedings in a case. **9.** *Theat.* revue. [t. F: m. *revue*, orig. pp. fem. of *revoir* see again, g. L *revidēre*] —*v.t.* **10.** to view, look at, or look over again. **11.** to go over (lessons, studies, work, etc.) in review. **12.** to inspect, esp. formally or officially. **13.** to look back upon; view retrospectively. **14.** to survey mentally; take a survey of: *to review the situation.* **15.** to present a survey of in speech or writing. **16.** to discuss (a book, etc.) in a critical review; write a critical report upon. **17.** *Law.* to reëxamine judicially. —*v.i.* **18.** to write reviews; review books, etc., as for some periodical. [v. use of REVIEW, n.] —**re·view'a·ble,** *adj.* —**Syn. 1.** REVIEW, CRITICISM imply carefully examining something, making a judgment, and putting the judgment into (usually) written form. A REVIEW is a survey over a whole subject or division of it; or esp. an article making a critical reconsideration and summary of something written: *a review of the latest book on Chaucer.* A CRITICISM is a judgment, usually in an article, either favorable or unfavorable or both: *a criticism of a proposed plan.*

re·view·al (rĭ vū'əl), *n.* act of reviewing.

re·view·er (rĭ vū'ər), *n.* **1.** one who reviews. **2.** one who writes reviews of new books, etc.

re·vile (rĭ vīl'), *v.*, **-viled, -viling.** —*v.t.* **1.** to assail with contemptuous or opprobrious language; address, or speak of, abusively. —*v.i.* **2.** to speak abusively. [ME *revile(n)*, t. OF: m. *reviler* treat or regard as vile, der. *re-* RE- + *vil* VILE] —**re·vile'ment,** *n.* —**re·vil'er,** *n.* —**re·vil'ing·ly,** *adv.*

re·vis·al (rĭ vī'zəl), *n.* act of revising; revision.

re·vise (rĭ vīz'), *v.*, **-vised, -vising,** *n.* —*v.t.* **1.** to amend or alter: *to revise one's opinion.* **2.** to alter after one or more typings or printings: *to revise a manuscript, proof, or book.* —*n.* **3.** a revising. **4.** a revised form of something. **5.** *Print.* a proof sheet taken after alterations have been made, for further examination or correction. [t. F: m.s. *reviser*, t. L: m. *revisere* go see again, look back on] —**re·vis'er,** *n.*

Revised Version of the Bible, a recension of the King James Version of the Bible, prepared by a committee of British and American scholars, the Old Testament being published in 1885, and the New Testament in 1881.

re·vi·sion (rĭ vĭzh'ən), *n.* **1.** act or work of revising. **2.** a process of revising. **3.** a revised form or version, as of a book. [t. LL: s. *revīsio*] —**re·vi'sion·al, re·vi'sion·ar'y,** *adj.*

re·vi·sion·ist (rĭ vĭzh'ən ĭst), *n.* **1.** an advocate of revision, esp. of some political or religious doctrine. **2.** a reviser. —**re·vi'sion·ism',** *n.*

re·vi·so·ry (rĭ vī'zə rĭ), *adj.* pertaining to or for the purpose of revision.

re·viv·al (rĭ vī'vəl), *n.* **1.** act of reviving. **2.** state of being revived. **3.** restoration to life, consciousness, vigor, strength, etc. **4.** restoration to use, acceptance, or currency: *the revival of old customs.* **5.** the production anew of an old play. **6.** Also, **revival of religion.** an awakening, in a church or a community, of interest in and care for matters relating to personal religion. **7.** a service or a series of services for the purpose of effecting a religious awakening: *to hold a revival.* **8.** *Law.* the reëstablishment of legal force and effect.

re·viv·al·ism (rĭ vī'və lĭz'əm), *n.* **1.** the tendency to revive what belongs to the past. **2.** that form of religious activity which manifests itself in revivals.

re·viv·al·ist (rĭ vī'vəl ĭst), *n.* **1.** one who revives former customs or methods. **2.** one who promotes or holds religious revivals.

Revival of Learning, the Renaissance in its relation to learning.

re·vive (rĭ vīv'), *v.*, **-vived, -viving.** —*v.t.* **1.** to set going or in activity again: *to revive old feuds.* **2.** to make operative or valid again. **3.** to bring back into notice, use, or currency: *to revive a subject of discussion.* **4.** to produce (an old play) again. **5.** to restore to life or consciousness. **6.** to reanimate or cheer (the spirit, heart, etc., or a person). **7.** to quicken or renew in the mind; bring back: *to revive memories.* **8.** *Chem.* to restore or reduce to its natural or uncombined state, as a metal. —*v.i.* **9.** to return to life, consciousness, vigor, strength, or a flourishing condition. **10.** to recover from depression. **11.** to be quickened, restored, or renewed, as hope, confidence, suspicions, memories, etc. **12.** to return to notice, use, or currency, as a subject, practice, doctrine, etc. **13.** to become operative or valid again. **14.** *Chem.* to recover its natural or uncombined state, as a metal. [ME, t. L: m. *revivere* live again] —**re·viv'er,** *n.*

re·viv·i·fy (rē vĭv'ə fī'), *v.t.*, **-fied, -fying.** to restore to life; give new life to; revive; animate anew. —**re·viv·i·fi·ca·tion** (rē vĭv'ə fə kā'shən), *n.*

rev·i·vis·cence (rĕv'ə vĭs'əns), *n.* act or state of being revived; revival; reanimation. Also, **rev'i·vis'cen·cy.** —**rev'i·vis'cent,** *adj.*

rev·o·ca·ble (rĕv'ə kə bəl), *adj.* that may be revoked. Also, **re·vok·a·ble** (rĭ vō'kə bəl). [late ME, t. L: m.s. *revocābilis*] —**rev'o·ca·bil'i·ty,** *n.* —**rev'o·ca·bly,** *adv.*

rev·o·ca·tion (rĕv'ə kā'shən), *n.* **1.** act of revoking; annulment. **2.** *Law.* the nullification or withdrawal of an offer to contract. [late ME, t. L: s. *revocātio*] —**rev'o·ca·to·ry** (rĕv'ə kə tōr'ĭ), *adj.*

re·voice (rē vois'), *v.t.*, **-voiced, -voicing. 1.** to voice again or in return; echo. **2.** to readjust the tone of.

re·voke (rĭ vōk'), *v.*, **-voked, -voking,** *n.* —*v.t.* **1.** to take back or withdraw; annul, cancel, or reverse; rescind or repeal: *to revoke a decree.* **2.** *Now Rare.* to recall (what is past). —*v.i.* **3.** *Cards.* to fail to follow suit when one can and should do so. —*n.* **4.** *Cards.* an act or instance of revoking. [ME, t. L: m. *revocāre* call back] —**re·vok'er,** *n.*

re·volt (rĭ vōlt'), *v.i.* **1.** to break away from or rise against constituted authority, as by open rebellion; cast off allegiance or subjection to those in authority; rebel; mutiny. **2.** to turn away in mental rebellion, utter disgust, or abhorrence (fol. by *from*); rebel in feeling (fol. by *against*); feel disgust or horror (fol. by *at*). —*v.t.* **3.** to affect with disgust or abhorrence. —*n.* **4.** act of revolting; an insurrection or rebellion. **5.** aversion, disgust, or loathing. **6.** state of those revolting: *to be in revolt.* [t. F: m. *révolte*, t. It.: m. *rivolta* revolt, turning, der. *rivoltare* turn, g. Rom. *revoltāre*, der. L *revolvere* overturn, revolve] —**re·volt'er,** *n.* —**Syn.** REVOLT, INSURRECTION, REBELLION, REVOLUTION refer to risings in active resistance against civil or governmental authority. A REVOLT is a casting off of allegiance or subjection to rulers or authorities; it is usually a vigorous outbreak, whether brief or prolonged, and may arise from general turbulence or from opposition to tyranny or oppression: *a revolt because of unjust government.* An INSURRECTION may be local or general, and is often unorganized: *a popular insurrection in one province.* A REBELLION is on a larger scale than either of the foregoing, is generally better organized, and has for its object the securing of independence or the overthrow of government: *a widespread rebellion.* A REVOLUTION is a rebellion or any public movement (with or without actual fighting) that succeeds in overthrowing one government or political system and establishing another: *the American Revolution.* Accordingly, it may be used metaphorically of any development that upsets the established order: *the Industrial Revolution.*

re·volt·ing (rĭ vōl'tĭng), *adj.* **1.** rebellious. **2.** disgusting; repulsive. —**re·volt'ing·ly,** *adv.*

rev·o·lute (rĕv'ə lōōt'), *adj.* *Biol.* rolled backward or downward; rolled backward at the tip or margin, as a leaf. [t. L: m.s. *revolūtus*, pp., revolved]

| **re·ve'to** | **re·vict'ual** | **re'vin·di·ca'tion** | **re'vis·it·a'tion** |
| **re·vi'brate** | **re·vin'di·cate'** | **re·vis'it** | **re·vi'tal·ize'** |

A. Revolute margined leaf; B. Transverse section

ăct, āble, dâre, ärt; ĕbb, ēqual; ĭf, īce; hŏt, ōver, ôrder, oil, bŏŏk, ōōze, out; ŭp, ūse, ûrge; ə = a in alone; ch, chief; g, give; ng, ring; sh, shoe; th, thin; ŧħ, that; zh, vision. See the full key on inside cover.

rev·o·lu·tion (rĕv/ə-lōō/shən), *n.* **1.** a complete overthrow of an established government or political system, as the English Revolution (1688), the American Revolution (1775), the French Revolution (1789), the Chinese Revolution (1911), or the Russian Revolution (1917). **2.** a complete or marked change in something. **3.** procedure or course as if in a circuit, as back to a starting point in time. **4.** a single turn of this kind. **5.** *Mech.* **a.** a turning round or rotating, as on an axis. **b.** a moving in a circular or curving course, as about a central point. **c.** a single cycle in such a course. **6.** *Astron.* **a.** (of a heavenly body) the action or fact of going round in an orbit. **b.** a single course of such movement. **c.** an apparent movement around the earth. **7.** round or cycle of events in time, or a recurring period of time. [ME *revolucion,* t. L: m.s. *revolūtio*] —**Syn. 1.** See **revolt.**

rev·o·lu·tion·ar·y (rĕv/ə-lōō/shə-nĕr/ĭ), *adj., n., pl.* **-aries.** —*adj.* **1.** pertaining to, characterized by, or of the nature of a revolution, or complete or marked change. **2.** subversive to established procedure, principles, etc. **3.** revolving. —*n.* **4.** a revolutionist.

Revolutionary calendar, the calendar of the first French republic.

Revolutionary War, the American Revolution.

rev·o·lu·tion·ist (rĕv/ə-lōō/shən-ĭst), *n.* one who advocates or takes part in a revolution.

rev·o·lu·tion·ize (rĕv/ə-lōō/shə-nīz/), *v.t.,* **-ized, -izing. 1.** to bring about a revolution in; effect a radical change in. **2.** to subject to a political revolution. Also, *esp. Brit.,* **rev/o·lu·tion·ise/.**

re·volve (rĭ-vŏlv/), *v.,* **-volved, -volving.** —*v.i.* **1.** to turn round or rotate, as on an axis. **2.** to move in a circular or curving course, or orbit. **3.** to proceed in a round or cycle. **4.** to come round in the process of time. **5.** to be revolved in the mind. —*v.t.* **6.** to cause to turn round, as on an axis. **7.** to cause to move in a circular or curving course, as about a central point. **8.** to think about; consider. [ME, t. L: m. *revolvere* roll, turn] —**re·volv/a·ble,** *adj.* —**Syn. 1.** See **turn.**

re·volv·er (rĭ-vŏl/vər), *n.* **1.** a pistol having a revolving chambered cylinder for holding a number of cartridges which may be discharged in succession without reloading. **2.** one who or that which revolves.

re·volv·ing (rĭ-vŏl/vĭng), *adj.* **1.** that revolves. **2.** *Mach.* noting or pertaining to a radial engine, whose cylinders revolve about a stationary crankshaft, such as a helicopter motor, or the blades of a propeller.

revolving fund, 1. any loan fund intended to be maintained by the repayment of past loans. **2.** a U.S. government fund, with loans and repayments equalized, used to aid businesses affected with the public interest, as public utilities.

re·vue (rĭ-vū/), *n.* **1.** a form of theatrical entertainment in which recent events, popular fads, etc., are parodied. **2.** any group of skits, dances, and songs. [t. F. See REVIEW, n.]

re·vul·sion (rĭ-vŭl/shən), *n.* **1.** a sudden and violent change of feeling or reaction in sentiment. **2.** *Med.* the diminution of morbid action in one part of the body by irritation in another. **3.** act of drawing something back or away. **4.** fact of being so drawn. [t. L: s. *revulsio* a plucking away]

re·vul·sive (rĭ-vŭl/sĭv), *adj.* tending to alter the distribution of blood by causing congestion, esp. in the intestine.

Rev. Ver., Revised Version (of the Bible).

re·ward (rĭ-wôrd/), *n.* **1.** something given or received in return or recompense for service, merit, hardship, etc. **2.** a sum of money offered for the detection or capture of a criminal, the recovery of lost or stolen property, etc. —*v.t.* **3.** to recompense or require (a person, etc.) for service, merit, achievement, etc. **4.** to make return for or requite (service, merit, etc.); recompense. [ME *rewarde,* t. ONF: m. *rewarder,* var. of OF *regarder.* See REGARD] —**re·ward/er,** *n.*
—**Syn. 1.** REWARD, PRIZE, RECOMPENSE imply something given in return for good. A REWARD is something given or done in return for good (or, more rarely, evil) received; it may refer to something abstract or concrete: *a $50 reward, her devotion was his reward.* PRIZE refers to something concrete offered as a reward of merit, or to be contested for and given to the winner: *to win a prize for an essay.* A RECOMPENSE is something given or done, whether as reward or punishment, for acts performed, services rendered, etc.; or something given in compensation for loss or injury suffered, etc.: *renown was his principal recompense for years of hard work.*

re·wire (rē-wīr/), *v.t.,* **-wired, -wiring.** to provide with new wiring: *to rewire a house, radio, lamp, etc.*

re·word (rē-wûrd/), *v.t.* **1.** to put into other words. **2.** to repeat.

re·write (*v.* rē-rīt/; *n.* rē/rīt/), *v.,* **-wrote, -written, -writing,** *n.* —*v.t.* **1.** to write again or in a different form. **2.** *U.S.* to write (the news submitted by a reporter) into a form for inclusion in the newspaper. —*n.* **3.** *U.S.* the article thus written.

rex (rĕks), *n., pl.* **reges** (rē/jēz). *Latin.* king.

Rey·kja·vik (rā/kyə-vēk/), *n.* a seaport in and the capital of Iceland, in the SW part. 60,024 (est. 1953).

Rey·mont (rā/mônt), *n.* **Wladyslaw Stanislaw** (vlä-dĭ/släf stä-nē/släf), (*Ladislas Regmont*) 1868–1925, Polish novelist.

Reyn·ard (rĕn/ərd, rā/närd), *n.* a name given to the fox, orig. in the medieval beast epic, *Reynard the Fox.* Also, **Renard.**

Rey·naud (rĕ-nō/), *n.* **Paul** (pōl), born 1878, French public official and statesman; premier of France, 1940.

Reyn·olds (rĕn/əldz), *n.* **Sir Joshua,** 1723–92, British portrait painter.

rf., *Baseball.* right fielder.

r.f., 1. radio frequency. **2.** rapid-fire.

R.F.D., Rural Free Delivery.

r.g., *Football.* right guard.

Rh, 1. *Chem.* rhodium. **2.** See **RH factor.**

R.H., Royal Highness.

r.h., right hand.

rhab·do·man·cy (răb/də-măn/sĭ), *n.* divination by means of a rod or wand, esp. in discovering ores, springs of water, etc. [t. LL: m.s. *rhabdomantīa,* t. Gk.: m. *rhabdomanteía*] —**rhab/do·man/tist,** *n.*

rhab·do·my·o·ma (răb/dō·mī·ō/ma), *n., pl.* **-mata** (-mə-tə), **-mas.** *Pathol.* a tumor made up of striated muscular tissue. Cf. **leiomyoma.** [t. NL, f. Gk. *rhábdo(s)* rod + NL *myōma* MYOMA]

rha·chis (rā/kĭs), *n., pl.* **rhachises, rhachides** (răk/ə-dēz/, rā/kə-). rachis.

Rhad·a·man·thus (răd/ə-măn/thəs), *n.* **1.** *Gk. Myth.* a son of Zeus and Europa, rewarded for the justice he exemplified on earth by being made, after his death, a judge in the lower world, where he served with his brothers Minos and Aeacus. **2.** an inflexibly just or severe judge. —**Rhad·a·man·thine** (răd/ə·măn/thĭn), *adj.*

Rhae·ti·a (rē/shĭ-ə), *n.* an ancient Roman province in central Europe, comprising what is now E Switzerland and a part of the Tyrol: later extended to the Danube.

Rhae·tian (rē/shən), *adj.* **1.** of or pertaining to Rhaetia. **2.** Rhaeto-Romanic.

Rhaetian Alps, a chain of the Alps in E Switzerland and W Austria. Highest peak, Mt. Bernina, 13,295 ft.

Rhae·tic (rē/tĭk), *adj. Stratig.* pertaining to certain strata, extensively developed in the Rhaetian Alps, having features of the Triassic and Jurassic but generally classed as belonging to the former. Also, **Rhetic.**

Rhae·to-Ro·man·ic (rē/tō·rō·măn/ĭk), *n.* **1.** a group of closely similar Romance languages, comprising Swiss Romansh, Tyrolese Ladino, and Friulian. —*adj.* **2.** noting or pertaining to these languages.

-rhagia, a word element meaning "bursting forth." Also, **-rhage, -rrhagia, -rrhage, -rrhagy.** [t. Gk.: (m.) *-rrhagia*]

rham·na·ceous (răm-nā/shəs), *adj.* belonging to the *Rhamnaceae,* or buckthorn family of plants. [f. s. NL *Rhamnus,* the typical genus, (t. Gk.: m. *rhámnos* a prickly shrub) + -ACEOUS]

rhap·sod·i·cal (răp-sŏd/ə-kəl), *adj.* **1.** pertaining to, characteristic of, or of the nature of rhapsody. **2.** extravagantly enthusiastic; ecstatic. Also, **rhap·sod/ic.** —**rhap·sod/i·cal·ly,** *adv.*

rhap·so·dist (răp/sə-dĭst), *n.* **1.** one who rhapsodizes. **2.** a reciter of epic poetry among the ancient Greeks, esp. a professional reciter of the Homeric poems.

rhap·so·dize (răp/sə-dīz/), *v.,* **-dized, -dizing.** —*v.i.* **1.** to speak or write rhapsodies. **2.** to talk rhapsodically. —*v.t.* **3.** to recite as a rhapsody.

rhap·so·dy (răp/sə-dĭ), *n., pl.* **-dies. 1.** an exalted or exaggerated expression of feeling or enthusiasm. **2.** an epic poem, or a part of such a poem, as a book of the *Iliad,* suitable for recitation at one time. **3.** a similar piece of modern literature. **4.** an unusually intense or irregular poem or piece of prose. **5.** *Music.* an instrumental composition irregular in form and suggestive of improvisation: *Liszt's Hungarian Rhapsodies.* [t. L: m.s. *rhapsōdia,* t. Gk.: m. *rhapsōidía* epic recital]

rhat·a·ny (răt/ə-nĭ), *n., pl.* **-nies. 1.** a procumbent South American leguminous shrub, *Krameria triandra,* the root of which is used as an astringent and tonic in medicine and also to color port wine. **2.** some other plant of this genus, esp. *K. argentea.* **3.** the roots of these plants. [t. Pg.: m. *rhatanhia,* or t. Sp.: m. *ratania;* from Peruvian]

r.h.b., *Football.* right halfback.

Rhe·a (rē/ə), *n.* **1.** *Gk. Myth.* a daughter of Uranus and Gaea, wife of Cronus, and mother of Zeus and other major deities. She was called "Mother of the Gods" and identified with Cybele. **2.** (*l.c.*) a bird of the genus *Rhea,* which consists of South American ratite birds resembling the African ostrich but smaller and having three toes instead of two. [t. L, t. Gk.]

-rhea, a word element meaning "flow," "discharge," as in *gonorrhea.* Also, **-rrhea.** [t. Gk.: m. *-rrhoia*]

Rhe·a Sil·vi·a (rē/ə sĭl/vĭ·ə), *Rom. Legend.* a vestal virgin; mother by Mars of Romulus and Remus.

Rhea. *Rhea americana* (Total length 4½ ft., 5 ft. high)

Rhee (rē), *n.* **Syngman,** born 1875, president of Korea 1948–1960.

| re·vote/ | re·warm/ | re·wa/ter | re·wind/ |
| re·voy/age | re·wash/ | re·weigh/ | re·work/ |

Rheims (rēmz; *Fr.* räNs), *n.* Reims.

Rhein (rīn), *n.* German name of **Rhine**.

Rhein·gold (rīn′gōld′), *n.* See **Ring of the Nibelung.** Also, **Rheingold.**

Rhein·land (rīn′länt′), *n.* German name of **Rhineland.**

Rhein·land-Pfalz (rīn′länt pfälts), *n.* German name of Rhineland-Palatinate.

rhe·mat·ic (rĭ mät′ĭk), *adj.* **1.** pertaining to the formation of words. **2.** pertaining to or derived from a verb. [t. Gk.: m.s. *rhēmatikós* belonging to a verb, a word]

rhe·nic (rē′nĭk), *adj. Chem.* of or containing rhenium.

Rhen·ish (rĕn′ĭsh), *adj.* **1.** of the river Rhine or the regions bordering on it. —*n.* **2.** Rhine wine. [f. L *Rhēn(us)* Rhine + -ISH; r. ME *Rinisch(e)*, t. MHG]

rhe·ni·um (rē′nĭ əm), *n. Chem.* a rare metallic element of the manganese subgroup, used, because of its high melting point, in platinum-rhenium thermocouples. *Symbol:* Re; *at. no.:* 75; *at. wt.:* 186.31. [f. s. L *Rhēnus* the Rhine + -IUM]

rheo-, a word element meaning "something flowing," "a stream," "current." [comb. form repr. Gk. *rhéos*]

rheo., rheostat; rheostats.

rhe·ol·o·gy (rĭ ŏl′ə jĭ), *n.* the study of the deformation and flow of matter. [f. RHEO- + -LOGY]

rhe·om·e·ter (rē ŏm′ə tər), *n.* an instrument for measuring the velocity of flow of fluids (e.g., blood flow).

rhe·o·scope (rē′ə skōp′), *n.* an instrument which indicates the presence of an electric current. —**rhe·o·scop·ic** (rē′ə skŏp′ĭk), *adj.*

rhe·o·stat (rē′ə stăt′), *n. Elect.* an adjustable resistor so constructed that its resistance may be changed without opening the circuit in which it may be connected. —**rhe′o·stat′ic,** *adj.*

rhe·o·tax·is (rē′ə tăk′sĭs), *n. Biol.* the property in a cell or organism of responding by movement to the stimulus of a current of water.

rhe·ot·ro·pism (rē ŏt′rə pĭz′əm), *n.* the effect of a current of water upon the direction of plant growth.

rhe·sus (rē′səs), *n.* **1.** a macaque, *Macacus rhesus,* common in India, much used in experimental medicine. **2.** (*cap.*) *Gk. Myth.* a Thracian ally of Troy whose horses were stolen by Odysseus and Diomedes. An oracle had declared that if his horses drank from the Xanthus river Troy would not fall. See **Diomedes.** [t. L, t. Gk.: m. *Rhēsos* (def. 2)]

Rhe·sus factor (rē′səs), Rh factor.

rhet., **1.** rhetoric. **2.** rhetorical.

Rhe·tic (rē′tĭk), *adj. Geol.* Rhaetic.

rhe·tor (rē′tər), *n.* **1.** a master or teacher of rhetoric. **2.** an orator. [t. L, t. Gk.; r. ME *rethor* t. ML]

rhet·o·ric (rĕt′ə rĭk), *n.* **1.** the art or science of all specially literary uses of language in prose or verse, including the figures of speech. **2.** the art of prose in general as opposed to verse. **3.** (in prose or verse) the use of exaggeration or display, in an unfavorable sense. **4.** (orig.) the art of oratory. **5.** (in classical oratory) the art of influencing the thought and conduct of one's hearers. [ME *retorik,* t. L: m.s. *rhetorica,* t. Gk.: m. *rhētorikē* (*téchnē*) the rhetorical (art)]

rhe·tor·i·cal (rĭ tôr′ə kəl, -tŏr′-), *adj.* **1.** belonging to or concerned with mere style or effect. **2.** having the nature of rhetoric. —**rhe·tor′i·cal·ly,** *adv.*

rhetorical question, a question designed to produce an effect and not to draw an answer.

rhet·o·ri·cian (rĕt′ə rĭsh′ən), *n.* **1.** one versed in the art of rhetoric. **2.** one given to display in language. **3.** a person who teaches rhetoric.

rheum (rōōm), *n.* **1.** *Med.* a thin serous or catarrhal discharge. **2.** catarrh; a cold. [ME *rewme,* t. OF: m. *reume,* t. L: m. *rheuma,* t. Gk.: a flow, rheum]

rheu·mat·ic (rōō măt′ĭk), *adj.* **1.** pertaining to or of the nature of rheumatism. **2.** affected with or subject to rheumatism. —*n.* **3.** one affected with or subject to rheumatism. [ME *r(e)umatyk(e),* t. L: m.s. *rheumaticus,* t. Gk.: m. *rheumatikós*]

rheumatic fever, *Pathol.* a serious prevalent disease usually afflicting children and marked by fever, inflammation of the joints, generalized muscle pains, and frequently associated with pathological changes in the heart and the different serous membranes.

rheu·ma·tism (rōō′mə tĭz′əm), *n.* **1.** *Pathol.* a disease commonly affecting the joints and accompanied by constitutional disturbances, now usually thought to be due to a microörganism; (in a growing child) rheumatic fever. **2.** any of various ailments of the joints or muscles, as certain chronic disabilities of the joints (**chronic rheumatism**) and certain painful affections of the muscles (**muscular rheumatism**). [t. LL: s. *rheumatismus,* t. Gk.: m. *rheumatismós* liability to rheum]

rheu·ma·toid (rōō′mə toid′), *adj.* **1.** resembling rheumatism. **2.** rheumatic. Also, **rheu′ma·toi′dal.**

rheumatoid arthritis, *Med.* a chronic disease marked by signs and symptoms of inflammation of the joints, frequently accompanied by marked deformities, and ordinarily associated with manifestations of a general or systemic affliction.

Rheydt (rīt), *n.* a city in West Germany, in the Rhineland, adjacent to Mönchen-Gladbach. 84,500 (est. 1953).

Rh factor, *Biochem.* an agglutinogen often present in human blood. Blood containing this factor (**Rh positive**) may cause hemolytic reactions, esp. during pregnancy or

---

after repeated transfusions with blood lacking it (**Rh negative**). In infants it may cause hemolytic anemias. In full, **Rhesus factor.** [so called because first found in the blood of rhesus monkeys]

rhig·o·lene (rĭg′ə lēn′), *n.* an extremely volatile liquid obtained from petroleum: used to produce local anesthesia by freezing. [f. s. Gk. *rhigos* cold + -OLE + -ENE]

rhin-, var. of **rhino-**, before vowels, as in *rhinencephalon.*

rhi·nal (rī′nəl), *adj.* of or pertaining to the nose; nasal. [f. RHIN- + -AL¹]

Rhine (rīn), *n.* a river flowing from SE Switzerland through West Germany and the Netherlands into the North Sea: branches off into the **Waal, Lek,** and **Ijssel** in its lower course. ab. 810 mi. German, **Rhein.** French, **Rhin** (răN). Dutch, **Rijn.**

Rhine·gold (rīn′gōld′), *n.* Rheingold.

Rhine·land (rīn′land′), *n.* that part of West Germany W of the Rhine. German, **Rheinland.**

Rhine·land-Palatinate (rīn′land pə lät′ə nāt′,-nĭt), *n.* a state in W West Germany; formerly part of Rhine Province. 3,324,900 pop. (est. 1956); 7655 sq. mi. *Cap.:* Mainz. German, **Rheinland-Pfalz.**

rhi·nen·ceph·a·lon (rī′nĕn sĕf′ə lŏn′), *n., pl.* -la (-lə). *Anat.* the olfactory portion of the brain. [f. RHIN- + ENCEPHALON] —**rhi·nen·ce·phal·ic** (rī′nĕn sə făl′ĭk), *adj.*

Rhine Palatinate, Palatinate (def. 1).

Rhine Province, a former province in W Germany, mostly W of the Rhine; now divided between Rhineland-Palatinate and North Rhine-Westphalia. Also, **Rhineland,** German, **Rheinland.**

rhine·stone (rīn′stōn′), *n.* an artificial gem made of paste or strass, often cut to imitate the diamond. [trans. of F *caillou du Rhin* pebble of the Rhine]

Rhine wine, 1. wine (of many varieties) produced in the valley of the Rhine. **2.** any of a class of white wines, mostly light, still, and dry.

rhi·ni·tis (rī nī′tĭs), *n. Pathol.* inflammation of the nose or its mucous membrane.

rhi·no (rī′nō), *n., pl.* **-nos. 1.** *Colloq.* rhinoceros. **2.** *Brit. Slang.* money.

rhino-, a word element meaning "nose." Also, **rhin-.** [t. Gk., comb. form of *rhis*]

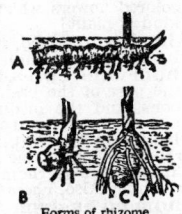

Indian rhinoceros.
Rhinoceros unicornis
(10 ft. long, 5½ to 6½ ft. high at the shoulder, horn 1 to 2 ft.)

rhi·noc·er·os (rī nŏs′ər əs), *n., pl.* **-oses,** (*esp. collectively*) **-os.** any of various large, ungainly, thick-skinned, perissodactyl mammals, family Rhinocerotidae, with one or two upright horns on the snout. Five species are still extant. [ME *rinoceros,* t. LL, t. Gk.: m. *rhinókerōs,* f. *rhino-* RHINO- + *kerōs* horned]

rhi·nol·o·gy (rī nŏl′ə jĭ), *n.* the science dealing with the nose and its diseases. —**rhi·nol′o·gist,** *n.*

rhi·no·plas·ty (rī′nō plăs′tĭ), *n. Med.* plastic surgery of the nose. —**rhi′no·plas′tic,** *adj.*

rhi·no·scope (rī′nə skōp′), *n. Med.* an instrument for examining the nasal passages.

rhi·nos·co·py (rī nŏs′kə pĭ), *n. Med.* the investigation of the nasal passages.

rhizo-, a word element meaning "root." [t. Gk., comb. form of *rhiza*]

rhi·zo·bi·um (rī zō′bĭ əm), *n., pl.* -bia (-bĭ ə). *Bacteriol.* any bacterium of a genus (*Rhizobium*) characterized by a rodlike shape, found as nitrogen fixers in nodules on the roots of the bean, clover, etc. [NL, f. *rhizo-* RHIZO- + m. Gk. *bios* life]

rhi·zo·car·pous (rī′zō kär′pəs), *adj. Bot.* having the root perennial but the stem annual, as perennial herbs.

rhi·zo·ceph·a·lous (rī′zō sĕf′ə ləs), *adj. Zool.* belonging to the *Rhizocephala,* a group of degenerate hermaphrodite crustaceans which are parasitic chiefly on crabs. [f. s. NL *Rhizocephala,* pl. (f. *rhizo-* RHIZO- + m. Gk. *kephalē* head) + -ous]

rhi·zo·gen·ic (rī′zō jĕn′ĭk), *adj. Bot.* producing roots, as certain cells. Also, **rhi·zog·e·nous** (rī zŏj′ə nəs).

rhi·zoid (rī′zoid), *adj.* **1.** rootlike. —*n.* **2.** (in mosses, etc.) one of the rootlike filaments by which the plant is attached to the substratum. [f. RHIZ(O)- + -OID] —**rhi·zoi′dal,** *adj.*

rhi·zome (rī′zōm), *n. Bot.* a rootlike subterranean stem, commonly horizontal in position, which usually produces roots below and sends up shoots progressively from the upper surface. [t. Gk.: m. *rhízōma* mass of roots] —**rhizom·a·tous** (rī zŏm′ə təs, -zō′mə-), *adj.*

rhi·zo·mor·phous (rī′zō môr′fəs), *adj. Bot.* rootlike in form.

rhi·zoph·a·gous (rī zŏf′ə gəs), *adj.* feeding on roots.

rhi·zo·pod (rī′zə pŏd′), *n.* any of the *Rhizopoda,* a class of protozoans having pseudopodia. [t. NL: s. *Rhizopoda,* pl. See RHIZO-, -POD] —**rhi·zop·o·dan** (rī zŏp′ə dən), *adj., n.* —**rhi·zop′o·dous,** *adj.*

Forms of rhizome
A. Solomon's seal,
Polygonatum commutatum;
B. Jack-in-the-pulpit,
Arisaema triphyllum;
C. Trillium,
Trillium sessile

ăct, āble, dâre, ärt; ĕbb, ēqual; ĭf, īce; hŏt, ōver, ôrder, oil, bŏŏk, ōōze, out; ŭp, ūse, ûrge; ə = a in alone; ch, chief; g, give; ng, ring; sh, shoe; th, thin; ŧħ, that; zh, vision.   See the full key on inside cover.

rhi·zo·pus (rī′zō pəs), n.   Bot. any fungus of the phycomycetous genus *Rhizopus*, of which the bread mold, *R. nigricans*, is best known. [NL, f. *rhizo-* RHIZO- + m. Gk. *poús* foot]

rhi·zot·o·my (rī zŏt′ə mĭ), n., pl. -mies.   Surg. the surgical section or cutting of the spinal nerve roots, usually posterior or sensory roots, to eliminate pain or paralysis.

Rh negative.   See **Rh factor.**

rho (rō), n. the 17th letter (P, ρ) of the Greek alphabet.

Rho.,   Rhodesia. Also, **Rhod.**

·rhod-,   var. of **rhodo-,** before vowels, as in *rhodamine*.

rho·da·mine (rō′də mēn′, -mĭn), n.   Chem. 1. a red dye obtained by heating an alkyl aminophenol with phthalic anhydride. 2. any of various related dyes. [f. RHOD- + AMINE]

Rhode Island (rōd), a state of the NE United States, on the Atlantic coast: a part of New England; the smallest state in the U.S. 859,488 pop. (1960); 1214 sq. mi. *Cap.*: Providence. *Abbr.*: R.I.   —**Rhode Islander.**

Rhode Island Red, one of an American variety of the domestic fowl having dark reddish-brown feathers.

Rhodes (rōdz), n. **1.** Ceci John, 1853-1902, British colonial capitalist and government administrator in S Africa. **2. James Ford,** 1848-1927 U.S. historian. **3.** Italian **Rodi,** Greek, **Rhodos.** an island in the Aegean, off the SW coast of Turkey: the largest of the Dodecanese Islands. 58,946 (1951); 542 sq. mi. **4.** Italian, **Rodi,** Greek, **Rhodos.** a seaport on this island. 24,186 (1951). **5. Colossus of,** a huge bronze statue of Apollo that stood (c280 B.C.–224 B.C.) at the entrance of Rhodes harbor: one of the Seven Wonders of the World.

Rho·de·sia (rō dē′zhə), n. **1.** a region in S Africa, that comprised the British territories of Northern Rhodesia (now Zambia) and Southern Rhodesia, forming part of the Federation of Rhodesia and Nyasaland. **2.** See **Southern Rhodesia.**

Rhodesia and Nyasaland, Federation of, a former grouping of British territories comprising Southern Rhodesia, Northern Rhodesia, Nyasaland.

Rhodes scholarship, one of the scholarships at Oxford University established by the will of Cecil Rhodes, for selected students (**Rhodes scholars**) from the British Commonwealth and the United States.

Rho·di·an (rō′dĭ ən), adj. **1.** of or pertaining to the island, Rhodes. —n. **2.** a native or inhabitant of Rhodes.

rho·dic (rō′dĭk), adj.   Chem. of or containing rhodium, esp. in the tetravalent state (Rh+4).

rho·di·um (rō′dĭ əm), n.   Chem. a silvery-white metallic element of the platinum family, forming salts which give rose-colored solutions and used recently to electroplate microscopes and instrument parts to prevent corrosion. *Symbol*: Rh; *at. wt.*: 102.91; *at. no.*: 45; *sp. gr.*: 12.5 at 20° C. [t. NL. See RHOD-, -IUM]

rhodo-, a word element meaning "rose." Also, **rhod-.** [t. Gk., comb. form of *rhódon*]

rho·do·chro·site (rō′də krō′sīt), n. a mineral, manganese carbonate, MnCO₃, commonly containing some iron and calcium, and usually rose-red in color; a minor ore of manganese. [t. G: m. *rhodochrosit,* f. Gk. *rhodóchrōs* rose-colored + -*it* -ITE¹]

rho·do·den·dron (rō′də dĕn′drən), n. Bot. any plant of the ericaceous genus *Rhododendron,* comprising evergreen and deciduous shrubs and trees with pink, purple, or white flowers and oval or oblong leaves, as *R. maximum* (**great rhododendron**), and *R. catawbiense,* cultivated for ornament. [t. NL, t. Gk.: lit., rose tree]

rho·do·lite (rō′də līt′), n. a rose-red variety of pyrope garnet, sometimes used as a gem.

rho·do·nite (rō′də nīt′), n. a mineral, manganese metasilicate, MnSiO₃, occurring usually in rose-red masses, sometimes used as an ornamental stone. [t. G: m. *rhodonit,* f. Gk. *rhódon* rose + -*it* -ITE¹]

Rhod·o·pe (rŏd′ə pĭ; Gk. rŏ dô′pē), n. a mountain range in SW Bulgaria. Highest peak, Mus Allah, 9595 ft.

rho·do·ra (rō dōr′ə), n. a low ericaceous shrub, *Rhododendron canadense,* of North America, with rose-colored flowers which appear before the leaves. [t. L: kind of plant]

Rho·dos (rō′t̸hŏs), n. See **Rhodes** (defs. 3 and 4).

rhomb (rŏm, rŏmb), n. rhombus.

rhom·ben·ceph·a·lon (rŏm′bĕn sĕf′ə lŏn′), n. Anat. the part of the brain made up of the cerebellum, the pons, and the medulla oblongata; the hindbrain. [f. RHOMB + ENCEPHALON]

rhom·bic (rŏm′bĭk), adj. **1.** having the form of a rhombus. **2.** having a rhombus as base or cross section. **3.** bounded by rhombs, as a solid. **4.** Crystall. orthorhombic. Also, **rhom′bi·cal.**

rhom·bo·he·dron (rŏm′bə hē′drən), n., pl. -drons, -dra (-drə). a solid bounded by six rhombic planes. [f. *rhombo-* (comb. form of Gk. *rhómbos* rhombus) + -HEDRON] —**rhom′bo·he′dral,** adj.

rhom·boid (rŏm′boid), n. **1.** an oblique-angled parallelogram with only the opposite sides equal. —adj. **2.** Also, **rhom·boi′dal.**

Rhomboid

having a form like, or approaching that of, a rhombus; shaped like a rhomboid. [t. LL: s. *rhomboides,* t. Gk.: m.s. *rhomboeidēs*]

rhom·bus (rŏm′bəs), n., pl. -buses, -bi (-bī). **1.** an oblique-angled equilateral parallelogram. **2.** rhombohedron. [t. L, t. Gk.: m. *rhómbos*]

rhombus

rhon·chus (rŏng′kəs), n., pl. -chi (-kī). Pathol. a râle, esp. when produced in the bronchial tubes. [t. L, t. Gk.: m. (unrecorded) *rhónchos,* var. of *rhénchos* snoring]   —**rhon·chi·al** (rŏng′kĭ əl), **rhon·chal** (rŏng′kəl), adj.

Rhon·dda (rŏn′də), n. a city in SE Wales. 107,400 (est. 1956).

Rhone (rōn), n. a river flowing from the Alps in S Switzerland through the Lake of Geneva and SE France into the Mediterranean. 504 mi. French, **Rhône.**

Rh positive.   See **Rh factor.**

rhu·barb (rōō′bärb), n. **1.** any of the herbs constituting the polygonaceous genus *Rheum,* as *R. officinale,* a plant with a medicinal rhizome, and *R. Rhaponticum,* a garden plant with edible leafstalks. **2.** the rhizome of any medicinal species of this plant, forming a combined cathartic and astringent. **3.** the edible fleshy leafstalks of any of the garden species, used in making pies, etc. **4.** *U.S. Slang.* a quarrel or squabble. [ME *rubarbe,* t. OF: m. *reubarbe,* t. ML: m.s. *reubarbarum,* t. Gk.: m. *rhéon bárbaron* foreign rhubarb]

rhumb (rŭm, rŭmb), n. **1.** a rhumb line. **2.** *Archaic.* a point of the compass. [t. Sp.: m. *rumbo,* t. L: m. *rhombus* RHOMBUS]

rhumb·a·tron (rŭm′bə trŏn′), n. Electronics. a cavity resonator.

rhumb line, a loxodromic curve; a curve on the surface of a sphere which cuts all meridians at the same angle. It is the path taken by a ship which maintains a constant compass direction.

rhyme (rīm), n., v., **rhymed, rhyming.** —n. **1.** agreement in the terminal sounds of lines of verse, or of words. **2.** a word agreeing with another in terminal sound. **3.** verse or poetry having correspondence in the terminal sounds of the line. **4.** a poem or piece of verse having such correspondence. —v.t. **5.** to treat in rhyme, as a subject; turn into rhyme, as something in prose. **6.** to compose (verse, etc.) in metrical form with rhymes. **7.** to use (a word) as a rhyme to another word; use (words) as rhymes. —v.i. **8.** to make rhyme or verse; versify. **9.** to use rhyme in writing verse. **10.** to form a rhyme, as one word or line with another. **11.** to be composed in metrical form with rhymes, as verse. Also, **rime.** (The spelling *rime* is strongly preferred by many because it is the etymologically direct form). [ME *rime,* t. OF, der. *rimer* to rhyme, g. Gallo-Rom. *rimāre* put in a row, der. OHG *rīm* series, row; prob. not connected with L *rhythmus* rhythm]   —**rhym′er,** n.

rhyme royal, *Pros.* a form of verse introduced into English by Chaucer, consisting of seven-line stanzas of iambic pentameter in which there are three rhymes, the first line rhyming with the third, the second with the fourth and fifth, and the sixth with the seventh.

rhyme scheme, the pattern of rhymes used in a poem, usually marked by letters, as rhyme royal, ababbcc.

rhyme·ster (rīm′stər), n. a maker of rhyme or verse, esp. of an inferior order; a poetaster. Also, **rimester.**

rhyn·cho·ce·pha·lian (rĭng′kō sə fāl′yən), adj. **1.** belonging to the *Rhynchocephalia,* an order of lizard-shaped reptiles, now extinct except for the *Sphenodon* of New Zealand. —n. **2.** a rhynchocephalian reptile. [f. s. NL *Rhynchocephalia,* n. pl. (f. Gk.: *rhyncho-,* comb. form of *rhýnchos* snout + m. *kephalē* head) + -AN]

rhy·o·lite (rī′ə līt′), n. a kind of volcanic rock containing an abundance of silica. [f. *rhyo-* (irreg. comb. form of Gk. *rhýax* stream) + -LITE]

rhythm (rĭt̸h′əm), n. **1.** movement or procedure with uniform recurrence of a beat, accent, or the like. **2.** measured movement, as in dancing. **3.** *Music.* **a.** the pattern of regular or irregular pulses caused in music by the occurrence of strong and weak melodic and harmonic beats. **b.** a particular form of this: *duple rhythm, triple rhythm.* **4.** *Pros.* **a.** metrical or rhythmical form; meter. **b.** a particular kind of metrical form. **c.** metrical movement. **5.** *Art.* a proper relation and interdependence of parts with reference to one another and to an artistic whole. **6.** procedure marked by the regular recurrence of particular elements, phases, etc. **7.** regular recurrence of elements in a system of motion. [t. L: s. *rhythmus,* t. Gk.: m. *rhythmós*]

rhyth·mic (rĭt̸h′mĭk), adj. **1.** rhythmical. —n. **2.** rhythmics.

rhyth·mi·cal (rĭt̸h′mə kəl), adj. **1.** periodic, as motion, etc. **2.** having a flowing rhythm. **3.** of or pertaining to rhythm: *an excellent rhythmical sense.* —**rhyth′mi·cal·ly,** adv.

rhyth·mics (rĭt̸h′mĭks), n. the science of rhythm and rhythmic forms.

rhyth·mist (rĭt̸h′mĭst), n. **1.** one versed in, or having a fine sense of, rhythm. **2.** one who uses rhythm in a certain way: *a good rhythmist.*

R.I., 1. (L *Regina et Imperatrix*) Queen and Empress. **2.** (L *Rex et Imperator*) King and Emperor. **3.** Rhode Island.

ri·al (rī′əl), n. the monetary unit of Iran, a silver coin equal to 100 dinars and worth about 1 U.S. cent.

b., blend of, blended; c., cognate with; d., dialect, dialectal; der., derived from; f., formed from; g., going back to; m., modification of; r., replacing; s., stem of; t., taken from; ?, perhaps.   See the full key on inside cover.

ri·al·to (rĭ ăl′tō), n., pl. **-tos.** an exchange or mart.

Ri·al·to (rĭ ăl′tō; *also for 1, 2, It.* rē äl′tō), n. **1.** a commercial center in Venice, Italy, consisting of an island and the surrounding district. **2.** a bridge, constructed of marble about 1590, spanning the Grand Canal in Venice. **3.** theater district of New York City, along Broadway.

ri·ant (rī′ənt), adj. laughing; smiling; cheerful; gay. [t. F, ppr. of *rire*, g. L *rīdēre* laugh] **—ri′ant·ly,** adv.

ri·a·ta (rĭ ä′tə), n. lariat. [t. Sp.: m. *reata*, der. *reatar* tie again, f. *re- + atar*, g. L *aptāre* fit, v.]

rib[1] (rĭb), n., v., **ribbed, ribbing.** —n. **1.** one of a series of long, slender, curved bones, occurring in pairs, more or less enclosing the thoracic cavity, and articulated with the vertebrae. See diag. under **skeleton. 2.** a cut of meat, as beef, containing a rib. **3.** some thing or part resembling a rib in form, position, or use, as a supporting or strengthening part. **4.** an arch or arched member, plain or molded, forming a support of a vault, or a merely decorative feature of like appearance on the surface of a vault or ceiling. **5.** a structural member which supports the shape of something: *an umbrella rib.* **6.** one of the curved timbers or members in a ship's frame which spring upward and outward from the keel. **7.** a primary vein of a leaf. **8.** a ridge, as in poplin or rep, caused by heavy yarn. **9.** a wife (in humorous allusion to the creation of Eve. Gen. 2:21–22). —v.t. **10.** to furnish or strengthen with ribs. **11.** to enclose as with ribs. **12.** to mark with riblike ridges or markings. [ME and OE, t. G *rippe*] **—ribbed,** adj.

rib[2] (rĭb), v.t., **ribbed, ribbing.** Slang. to tease; ridicule; make fun of. [appar. short for *rib-tickle*, v.]

rib·ald (rĭb′əld), adj. **1.** offensive or scurrilous in speech, language, etc.; coarsely mocking or abusive; wantonly irreverent. —n. **2.** a ribald person. [ME *ribaut*, t. OF, der. *riber* dissipate, t. MHG: m. *riben* be in heat, copulate, or der. MD *ribe* whore]

rib·ald·ry (rĭb′əl drĭ), n. **1.** ribald character, as of language; scurrility. **2.** ribald speech.

rib·and (rĭb′ənd), n. Archaic and Brit. ribbon.

rib·band (rĭb′bănd′, -ənd, -ən), n. Shipbuilding. a lengthwise timber or the like used to secure a ship's ribs in position while the outside planking or plating is being put on. [appar. f. RIB[1] + BAND]

rib·bing (rĭb′ĭng), n. **1.** ribs collectively. **2.** an assemblage or arrangement of ribs.

rib·bon (rĭb′ən), n. **1.** a woven strip or band of fine material, as silk, rayon, etc., finished off at the edges, and varying in width, used for ornament, tying, etc. **2.** material in such strips. **3.** anything resembling or suggesting a ribbon or woven band. **4.** (pl.) torn or ragged strips; shreds: *clothes torn to ribbons.* **5.** a long, thin, flexible band of metal, as for a spring, a band saw, a tapeline, etc. **6.** a band of material charged with ink, or supplying ink, for the impression in a typewriter. **7.** Shipbuilding. ribband. **8.** a badge of an order of knighthood or other distinction: *the red ribbon of the French Legion of Honor.* **9.** (pl.) Colloq. reins for driving. —v.t. **10.** to adorn with ribbon. **11.** to streak or mark with something suggesting ribbon. **12.** to separate into or reduce to ribbonlike strips. —v.i. **13.** to form in ribbonlike strips. [ME *riban*, t. OF, var. of *r(e)uban*, ? t. Gmc.; see RUDDY, BAND[2]] **—rib′bon·like′,** adj.

rib·bon·fish (rĭb′ən fĭsh′), n., pl. **-fishes,** (esp. collectively) **-fish.** any of certain marine fishes with a long, compressed, ribbonlike body, as the dealfish.

Ri·be·ra (rē bĕ′rä), n. **José** (hô sĕ′), ("Lo Spagnoletto") 1588–1656, Spanish painter.

ri·bo·fla·vin (rī′bō flā′vĭn), n. Biochem. a factor of the vitamin B complex, $C_{17}H_{20}N_4O_6$, found in milk, fresh meat, eggs, fresh vegetables, etc., necessary for growth; lactoflavin; vitamin B_2; vitamin G. [f. RIBO(SE) + s. L *flāvus* yellow + -IN[2]]

ri·bose (rī′bōs), n. Chem. a pentose sugar, $C_5H_{10}O_5$, existing in some nucleic acids. [f. *rib(onic acid)* (ult. irreg. der. GUM ARABIC) + (PENT)OSE]

rib·wort (rĭb′wûrt′), n. **1.** a plantain, *Plantago lanceolata*, having narrow leaves with prominent ribs. **2.** any of various similar plantains.

Ri·car·do (rĭ kär′dō), n. **David,** 1772–1823, British economist.

Ric·cio (rēt′chō), n. **David.** See **Rizzio.**

rice (rīs), n., v., **riced, ricing.** —n. **1.** the starchy seeds or grain of a species of grass, *Oryza sativa*, cultivated in warm climates and constituting an important food. **2.** the plant itself. —v.t. **3.** to reduce to a form resembling rice: *to rice potatoes.* See **ricer.** [ME *rys*, t. OF: m. *ris*, t. It.: m. *riso*, ult. (through MGk.) from Gk. *óryza*; of Eastern orig.]

Rice (rīs), n. **Elmer,** born 1892, U.S. dramatist.

rice·bird (rīs′bûrd′), n. **1.** Southern U.S. the bobolink. **2.** the Java sparrow.

rice paper, 1. a thin paper made from the straw of rice, in China, etc. **2.** a Chinese paper consisting of the pith of certain plants cut and pressed into thin sheets.

ric·er (rī′sər), n. an implement for ricing potatoes, etc., by pressing them through small holes.

rich (rĭch), adj. **1.** having wealth or great possessions; abundantly supplied with resources, means, or funds: *a rich man or nation.* **2.** abounding in natural resources: *a rich territory.* **3.** having wealth or valuable resources (fol. by *in*): *a tract rich in minerals.* **4.** abounding (fol. by *in* or *with*): *a country rich in traditions.* **5.** of great value or worth; valuable: *a rich harvest.* **6.** costly; expensively elegant or fine, as dress, jewels, etc. **7.** sumptuous, as a feast. **8.** of valuable materials or elaborate workmanship, as buildings, furniture, etc. **9.** abounding in desirable elements or qualities. **10.** (of food) containing good, nutritious, or choice ingredients, as butter, cream, sugar, etc. **11.** (of wine, etc.) strong and finely flavored. **12.** (of color) deep, strong, or vivid. **13.** (of sound, the voice, etc.) full and mellow in tone. **14.** (of odor) strongly fragrant. **15.** producing or yielding abundantly: *a rich soil.* **16.** abundant, plentiful, or ample: *a rich supply.* **17.** Colloq. highly amusing. **18.** Colloq. ridiculous, absurd, or preposterous. —n. **19.** rich people collectively (usually prec. by *the*). [ME; OE *rīce*, c. G *reich*, of Celtic origin; akin to L *rex* king] **—rich′ly,** adv. **—rich′ness,** n.

—Syn. 1. well-to-do, moneyed. RICH, AFFLUENT, OPULENT, WEALTHY agree in indicating abundance of possessions. RICH is the general word; it may imply that possessions are newly acquired: *a rich oil man.* WEALTHY suggests permanence, stability, and appropriate surroundings: *a wealthy banker.* AFFLUENT and OPULENT both suggest the possession of great wealth; AFFLUENT especially connoting a handsome income and free expenditure of resources; OPULENT suggesting display or luxuriousness: *an affluent family, opulent circumstances.* **15.** fruitful, productive. **—Ant. 1.** poor.

Richard I (rĭch′ərd), ("Richard the Lion-Hearted," "Richard Coeur de Lion") 1157–99, king of England, 1189–99.

Richard II, 1367–1400, king of England, 1377–99 (successor and grandson of Edward III, and son of the Black Prince).

Richard III, (Duke of Gloucester) 1452–85, king of England, 1483–85.

Rich·ard·son (rĭch′ərd sən), n. **1. Henry Hobson,** 1838–86, U.S. architect. **2. Samuel,** 1689–1761, British novelist.

Rich·e·lieu (rĭsh′ə lōō′; Fr. rē shə lyœ′), n. **1. Armand Jean du Plessis** (àr män′ zhän′ dü plĕ sē′), **Duc de,** 1585–1642, French cardinal and statesman. **2.** a river in SE Canada, in Quebec, flowing from Lake Champlain N to the St. Lawrence. ab. 210 mi.

rich·es (rĭch′ĭz), n.pl. abundant and valuable possessions; wealth. [ME, t. OF: m. *richesse* wealth, der. *riche* (of Gmc. orig.) RICH]

Rich·field (rĭch′fēld′), n. a city in E Minnesota, near Minneapolis. 42,523 (1960).

Rich·mond (rĭch′mənd), n. **1.** the capital of Virginia, in the E part: port on James river; capital of the Confederacy, 1861–65. 219,958 (1960). **2.** a SW borough of New York City, comprising Staten Island. 221,991 (1960); 60.3 sq. mi. **3.** a city in SE England, on the Thames, near London: site of Kew Gardens. 41,945 (1951). **4.** a city in E Indiana. 39,539 (1950). **5.** a seaport in W California, on San Francisco Bay. 71,854 (1960).

rich rhyme, complete identity in sound but not in sense, of the rhyming syllables, as *bare, bear* or *mind, undermined.*

Rich·ter (rĭkH′tər), n. **Jean Paul Friedrich** (zhän poul frē′drĭKH), ("Jean Paul") 1763–1825, German author.

Richt·ho·fen (rĭkHt′hō′fən), n. **Baron Manfred von** (män′frät fən), 1892–1918, German aviator.

ri·cin (rī′sĭn, rĭs′ĭn), n. Chem. a white, toxic protein from the bean of the castor-oil plant. [t. NL: s. *ricinus* a genus of plants, t. L (Pliny)]

ri·cin·o·le·ic acid (rĭs′ĭ nō lē′ĭk, -ĭ nō′lĭ ĭk), Chem. an unsaturated hydroxy acid, $C_{17}H_{32}(OH)COOH$, occurring in castor oil in the form of the glyceride. [f. RICIN + -OLE + -IC]

ri·cin·o·le·in (rĭs′ĭ nō′lĭ ĭn), n. Chem. the glyceride of ricinoleic acid, the chief constituent of castor oil.

rick (rĭk), Chiefly Brit. —n. **1.** a stack of hay, straw, or the like, esp. one thatched or covered for protection. —v.t. **2.** to pile in ricks. [ME *rek(e)*, OE *hrēac*, c. D *rook*]

Rick·en·back·er (rĭk′ən băk′ər), n. **Edward Vernon,** born 1890, U.S. aviator and aviation executive.

rick·ets (rĭk′ĭts), n. Pathol. a disease of childhood, characterized by softening of the bones as a result of malnutrition (ordinarily lack of Vitamin D), or insufficient ingestion of calcium, or both, and often resulting in deformities. [orig. uncert.]

Rick·ett·si·a (rĭ kĕt′sĭ ə), n.pl. bacterialike microörganisms, apparently members of a single group or genus, which are found living as parasites in arthropods and are the cause of certain human diseases, as Rocky Mountain spotted fever. **—rick·ett′si·al,** adj.

rick·et·y (rĭk′ĭt ĭ), adj. **1.** liable to fall or collapse; shaky: *a rickety chair.* **2.** feeble in the joints; tottering; infirm. **3.** irregular, as motion or action. **4.** affected with or suffering from rickets. **5.** pertaining to or of the nature of rickets. [f. RICKET(S) + -Y[1]]

rick·ey (rĭk′ĭ), n., pl. **-eys.** a drink made principally of spirituous liquor (esp. gin), lime juice, and carbonated water. [named after a Colonel Rickey]

rick·rack (rĭk′răk′), n. a kind of openwork trimming made, with needle and thread, out of a narrow zigzag braid. [dissimilated reduplication of RACK[1]]

rick·shaw (rĭk′shô), n. jinrikisha. Also, **rick′sha.**

ric·o·chet (rĭk′ə shā′, -shĕt′), n., v., **-cheted** (-shād′), **-cheting** (-shā′ĭng) or (esp. Brit.) **-chetted** (-shĕt′ĭd), **-chetting** (-shĕt′ĭng). —n. **1.** the motion of an object or projectile which rebounds one or more times from a flat surface over which it is passing. —*v.i.* 2. to move in this way, as a projectile. [t. F; orig. uncert.]

rid[1] (rĭd), *v.t.*, **rid** or **ridded, ridding.** 1. to clear, disencumber, or free of something objectionable (fol. by *of*). 2. to disembarrass or relieve (fol. by *of*): *to rid the mind of doubt.* 3. **get rid of, a.** to get free, or relieved of. **b.** to get (a thing or person) off one's hands. **c.** to do away with. 4. *Obs.* or *Archaic.* to deliver, rescue, or save (fol. by *out of, from,* etc.). [ME *rydde,* OE *geryddan* clear (land), c. Icel. *rydhja* clear, empty] —**rid′der,** *n.*

rid[2] (rĭd), *v. Archaic.* pt. and pp. of **ride.**

rid·a·ble (rī′də bəl), *adj.* 1. capable of being ridden, as a horse. 2. capable of being ridden over, through, etc., as a road or a stream.

rid·dance (rĭd′əns), *n.* 1. a clearing away or out, as of anything undesirable. 2. a relieving or deliverance from something. 3. **good riddance,** a welcome relief or deliverance from something.

rid·den (rĭd′ən), *v.* pp. of **ride.**

rid·dle[1] (rĭd′əl), *n., v.,* -dled, -dling. —*n.* 1. a question or statement so framed as to exercise one's ingenuity in answering it or discovering its meaning; conundrum. 2. a puzzling question, problem, or matter. 3. a puzzling thing or person. 4. any enigmatic or dark saying or speech. —*v.i.* 5. to propound riddles; to speak enigmatically. [ME *redele,* OE *rǣdelle,* var. of *rǣdels* enigma (c. G *rätsel*), der. *rǣdan* READ[1]] —**Syn.** 1. See **puzzle.**

rid·dle[2] (rĭd′əl), *v.,* -dled, -dling, *n.* —*v.t.* 1. to pierce with many holes suggesting those of a sieve. 2. to sift through a riddle, as gravel. 3. to impair or refute completely by persistent verbal attacks: *to riddle a person's reputation.* —*n.* 4. a coarse sieve, as one for sifting sand in the foundry. [ME *riddil,* OE *hriddel,* dissimilated var. of *hridder,* akin to L *crībrum* sieve]

ride (rīd), *v.,* **rode** or (*Archaic*) **rid; ridden** or (*Archaic*) **rid; riding;** *n.* —*v.i.* 1. to sit on and manage a horse or other animal in motion; be carried on the back of an animal. 2. to be carried on something as if on horseback. 3. to be borne along on or in a vehicle or any kind of conveyance. 4. to move along in any way; be carried or supported: *distress riding among the people.* 5. to move or float on the water. 6. to lie at anchor, as a ship. 7. to appear to float in space, as a heavenly body. 8. to turn or rest on something. 9. to extend or project over something, as the edge of one thing over the edge of another thing. 10. to work or move (*up*) from the proper position, as a part of the dress. 11. to have a specified character for riding purposes: *the car rides smoothly.* —*v.t.* 12. to sit on and manage (a horse or other animal, or a bicycle or the like) so as to be carried along. 13. to sit or be mounted on (something) as if on horseback; be carried or borne along on. 14. to rest on, esp. by overlapping. 15. to control, dominate, or tyrannize over: *a land that was king-ridden.* 16. *Slang.* to harass or torment. 17. to ride over, along or through (a road, boundary, region, etc.). 18. to execute by riding: *to ride a race.* 19. to cause to ride. 20. to carry (a person) on something as if riding on a horse: *to ride a person on a rail as punishment.* 21. to keep (a vessel) at anchor or moored. 22. **ride out, a.** to sustain (a gale, etc.) without damage, as while riding at anchor. **b.** to sustain or endure successfully. —*n.* 23. a journey or excursion on a horse, etc., or on or in a vehicle. 24. a way, road, etc., made esp. for riding. [ME *ride(n),* OE *rīdan,* c. D *rijden,* G *reiten,* Dan. *ride*] —**Syn.** 3. See **drive.**

ri·dent (rī′dənt), *adj.* laughing; smiling; cheerful. [t. L: s. *rīdens,* ppr.]

rid·er (rī′dər), *n.* 1. one who rides a horse or other animal, or a bicycle or the like. 2. one who or that which rides. 3. any of various objects or devices straddling, mounted on, or attached to something else. 4. an additional clause, usually unrelated to the main body, attached to a legislative bill in passing it. 5. an addition or amendment to a document, etc.

ridge (rĭj), *n., v.,* **ridged, ridging.** —*n.* 1. a long, narrow elevation of land, or a chain of hills or mountains. 2. the long and narrow upper part or crest of something, as of an animal's back, a hill, a wave, etc. 3. the back of an animal. 4. any raised narrow strip, as on cloth, etc. 5. the horizontal line in which the tops of the rafters of a roof meet. 6. (on a weather chart) a narrow elongated area of high pressure. —*v.t.* 7. to provide with or form into a ridge or ridges. 8. to mark with or as with ridges. —*v.i.* 9. to form ridges. [ME *rigge,* OE *hrycg* spine, crest, ridge, c. D *rug*]

ridge·ling (rĭj′lĭng), *n. Vet. Sci.* a colt with undescended testicles.

ridge·pole (rĭj′pōl′), *n.* 1. the horizontal timber or member at the top of a roof, to which the upper ends of the rafters are fastened. 2. the horizontal pole at the top of a tent.

ridg·y (rĭj′ĭ), *adj.* rising in a ridge or ridges.

rid·i·cule (rĭd′i kūl′), *n., v.,* -culed, -culing. —*n.* 1. words or actions intended to excite contemptuous laughter at a person or thing; derision. —*v.t.* 2. to deride; make fun of. [t. F, L: m. *rīdiculum* laughable (thing), prop. neut. adj.] —**rid′i·cul′er,** *n.*
—**Syn.** 1. mockery, gibes, jeers. 2. banter, rally, chaff, twit. RIDICULE, DERIDE, MOCK, TAUNT imply making game of a person, usually in an unkind, jeering way. To RIDICULE is to make fun of, either sportively and good-humoredly, or unkindly with the intention of humiliating: *to ridicule a pretentious person.* To DERIDE is to assail with scornful laugh-

ter: *to deride a statement of belief.* To MOCK is sometimes playfully, sometimes insultingly, to imitate and caricature the appearance or actions of another: *to mock the seriousness of his expression.* To TAUNT is maliciously and exultingly to press upon one's attention (and often on the notice of others) some annoying or humiliating fact: *to taunt a person defeated in a contest.* —**Ant.** 1. praise.

ri·dic·u·lous (rĭ dĭk′yə ləs), *adj.* 1. such as to excite ridicule or derision; absurd, preposterous, or laughable. —*n.* 2. that which is ridiculous (prec. by *the*). —**ri·dic′u·lous·ly,** *adv.* —**ri·dic′u·lous·ness,** *n.* —**Syn.** 1. nonsensical, ludicrous, funny. See **absurd.**

rid·ing[1] (rī′dĭng), *n.* 1. act of one who or that which rides. —*adj.* 2. used in traveling or in riding. [f. RIDE + -ING[1]]

rid·ing[2] (rī′dĭng), *n.* 1. each of the three administrative divisions into which Yorkshire, England, is divided: *the North Riding, East Riding,* and *West Riding.* 2. each of a like group elsewhere. [ME *triding,* t. Scand.; cf. Icel. *thridhjungr* third part; *t-* for *th-* by assimilation to *-t* in *east* and *west;* later *-t t-* simplified to *-t*]

Rid·ley (rĭd′lĭ), *n.* **Nicholas,** c1500-55, English bishop, reformer, and Protestant martyr.

ri·dot·to (rĭ dŏt′ō), *n., pl.* **-tos.** a public ball or social gathering, often in masquerade (common in the 18th century). [t. It.: a retreat, resort. See REDOUBT]

Rie·mann (rē′män), *n.* **Georg Friedrich Bernhard** (gā′ōrkн′ frē′drĭкн bĕrn′härt), 1826-66, German mathematician.

Ri·en·zi (rē ĕn′zĭ; *It.* ryĕn′tsē), *n.* **Cola di** (kō′lä dē′), (*Nicholas Gabrini* 1313?-54, Roman orator and tribune of the people. Also, **Ri·en·zo** (rē ĕn′zō; *It.* ryĕn′tsō).

Rif (rĭf), *n.* **Er** (ĕr), a mountainous coastal region in N Morocco. Also, **Riff.**

ri·fa·ci·men·to (rē fä′chē mĕn′tō), *n., pl.* **-ti** (-tē). a recast or adaptation, as of a literary or musical work. [It.: a remaking, der. *rifare* make over, f. *ri-* RE- + *fare* make, g. L *facere*]

rife (rīf), *adj.* 1. of common or frequent occurrence; prevalent; in widespread existence, activity, or use. 2. current in speech or report. 3. abundant, plentiful, or numerous. 4. abounding (fol. by *with,* formerly *in*). [ME; late OE *rȳfe,* c. MD *riff*] —**Ant.** 3. scarce.

Riff (rĭf), *n.* a member of the primitive northern African people of Barbary and the Sahara. —**Riff·i·an** (rĭf′ĭən), *adj., n.*

riff (rĭf), *n. Colloq.* a melodic phrase, constantly repeated, which often serves as the main theme or the background in a piece of swing music. [short for REFRAIN]

rif·fle (rĭf′əl), *n., v.,* -fled, -fling. —*n.* 1. *U.S.* **a.** a rapid, as in a stream. **b.** a ripple, as upon the surface of water. 2. *Mining.* **a.** the lining at the bottom of a sluice or the like, made of blocks or slats of wood, or stones, arranged in such a manner that grooves or openings are left between them for catching and collecting particles of gold. **b.** one of the slats of wood or the like so used. **c.** one of the grooves or openings formed. 3. the method of riffling cards. —*v.t., v.i.* 4. to cause or become a riffle. 5. to flutter and shift, as pages. 6. to shuffle (cards) by dividing the deck in two, raising the corners slightly, and allowing them to fall alternately together. [b. RIPPLE and RUFFLE[1]]

riff·raff (rĭf′răf′), *n.* 1. the worthless or disreputable element of society; the rabble: *the riffraff of the city.* 2. worthless or low persons: *a pack of riffraff.* 3. *Dial.* trash; rubbish. [ME *rif* and *raf* every particle, things of small value, t. OF: m. *rif et raf, rifle rafle,* der. OF *rifler* spoil, *raffler* ravage, snatch away]

ri·fle[1] (rī′fəl), *n., v.,* -fled, -fling. —*n.* 1. a shoulder firearm with spiral grooves cut in the inner surface of the gun barrel to give the bullet a rotatory motion and thus render its flight more accurate. 2. one of the grooves. 3. a cannon with such grooves. 4. (*pl.*) certain military units or bodies equipped with rifles. —*v.t.* 5. to cut spiral grooves within (a gun barrel, etc.). [t. LG: m.s. *rifeln* to groove, der. *rive, riefe* groove, flute, furrow; akin to OE *rifelede* wrinkled, *rīf* violent]

ri·fle[2] (rī′fəl), *v.t.,* -fled, -fling. 1. to ransack and rob (a place, receptacle, etc.). 2. to search and rob (a person). 3. to plunder or strip bare of. 4. to steal or take away. [ME *rifel,* t. OF: s. *rifler* scrape, graze, plunder, t. D: m. *riffelen* scrape, c. RIFLE[1], v.] —**ri′fler,** *n.* —**Syn.** 1. See **rob.**

ri·fle·man (rī′fəl mən), *n., pl.* **-men.** 1. a soldier armed with a rifle. 2. one skilled in the use of a rifle.

rifle pit, a pit or short trench affording shelter to riflemen in firing at an enemy.

rifle range, 1. target practice ground. 2. the distance covered by the bullet discharged from a rifle.

ri·fling (rī′flĭng), *n.* 1. act or process of cutting spiral grooves in a gun barrel, etc. 2. the system of spiral grooves so cut.

rift (rĭft), *n.* 1. an opening made by riving or splitting; a fissure; a cleft; a chink. —*v.i., v.t.* 2. to burst open; split. [ME, t. Scand.; cf. Dan. *rift* cleft; akin to RIVE, v.]

rig (rĭg), *v.,* **rigged, rigging.** —*v.t.* 1. *Chiefly Naut.* **a.** to put in proper order for working or use. **b.** to fit (a vessel, a mast, etc.) with the necessary shrouds, stays, etc. **c.** to fit (shrouds, stays, sails, etc.) to the mast, yard, or the like. 2. to furnish or provide with equipment, etc.; fit (usually fol. by *out* or *up*). 3. to prepare or put together, esp. as a makeshift (often fol. by *up*). 4. *Colloq.* to fit or deck with clothes, etc. (often fol. by *out* or *up*). **5.** *Colloq.* to manipulate fraudulently: *to rig prices.* —*n.* **6.** the arrangement of the masts, spars, sails, etc., on a boat or ship. **7.** apparatus for some purpose; equipment; outfit. **8.** *U.S. Colloq.* a vehicle with a horse or horses, as for driving. **9.** the equipment used in drilling an oil well. **10.** *Colloq.* costume or dress, esp. when odd or conspicuous. [prob. t. Scand.; cf. d. Sw. *rigga pa* to harness] —**rigged,** *adj.*

Ri·ga (rē′gä), *n.* **1.** a seaport in the W Soviet Union, on the Gulf of Riga: capital of the Latvian Republic. 565,-000 (est. 1956). **2.** Gulf of, an arm of the Baltic between the Latvian and Estonian Republics of the Soviet Union. ab. 100 mi. long; ab. 60 mi. wide.

rig·a·doon (rĭg′ə dōōn′), *n.* **1.** a lively dance, formerly popular, for one couple, characterized by a peculiar jumping step, and usually in quick duple rhythm. **2.** a piece of music for this dance, or in its rhythm. [t. F: m. *rigaudon*; named after *Rigaud*, the originator]

Ri·gel (rī′jəl, -gəl), *n.* *Astron.* Beta Orionis, a bluish star of the first magnitude in the constellation Orion.

rig·ger (rĭg′ər), *n.* **1.** one who rigs. **2.** one whose occupation is the fitting of the rigging of ships. **3.** one who works with hoisting tackle, etc. **4.** a protective structure around a construction operation. **5.** *Aeron.* a mechanic skilled at assembling and repairing airplane wings, fuselages, and sometimes control mechanisms.

rig·ging (rĭg′ĭng), *n.* **1.** the ropes, chains, etc., employed to support and work the masts, yards, sails, etc., on a ship. **2.** tackle in general. **3.** *Colloq.* clothing.

Riggs' disease (rĭgz), *Pathol.* pyorrhea. [named after John M. *Riggs* (1810–85), U.S. dentist]

right (rīt), *adj.* **1.** in accordance with what is just or good: *right conduct.* **2.** in conformity with fact, reason, or some standard or principle; correct: *the right solution.* **3.** correct in judgment, opinion, or action. **4.** sound or normal, as the mind, etc; sane, as persons. **5.** in good health or spirits, as persons: *he is all right again.* **6.** in a satisfactory state; in good order: *to put things right.* **7.** principal, front, or upper: *the right side of cloth.* **8.** most convenient, desirable, or favorable. **9.** fitting or appropriate: *to say the right thing.* **10.** genuine; legitimate: *the right owner.* **11.** belonging or pertaining to the side of a person or thing which is turned toward the east when the face is toward the north (opposed to left). **12.** (of political opinion, etc.) approaching the reactionary position. **13.** straight: *a right line.* **14.** formed by, or with reference to, a line or a plane extending to another line or a surface by the shortest course: *a right angle.* **15.** *Geom.* having the axis perpendicular to the base: *a right cone.*
—*n.* **16.** a just claim or title, whether legal, prescriptive, or moral. **17.** that which is due to any one by just claim: *to give one his right or his rights.* **18.** *Finance.* **a.** the privilege, usually preëmptive, which accrues to the owners of the stock of a corporation to subscribe for stock at an advantageous price to additional shares of stock or securities convertible into stock. **b.** (*often pl.*) a privilege of subscribing for a stock or bond. **19.** that which is ethically good and proper and in conformity with the moral law. **20.** that which accords with fact, reason, or propriety. **21.** the right or proper way of thinking: *to be in the right.* **22.** the right side: *to turn to the right.* **23.** what is on the right side. **24.** the starboard of a ship. **25.** the Right, (*often l.c.*) **a.** that part of a legislative assembly in continental Europe which sits on the right of the president, a position customarily assigned to the conservatives. **b.** a party holding such views. **26.** to rights, into proper condition: *to set a room to rights.*
—*adv.* **27.** in a right or straight line; straight; directly (fol. by *to, into, through,* etc.): *right to the bottom.* **28.** quite or completely: *his hat was knocked right off.* **29.** immediately: *right after dinner.* **30.** exactly, precisely, or just: *right here.* **31.** uprightly or righteously. **32.** correctly or accurately: *to guess right.* **33.** properly or fittingly: *to behave right, it serves you right.* **34.** advantageously, favorably, or well: *to turn out right.* **35.** toward the right hand; to the right. **36.** *Colloq.* or *Dial.* extremely: *I was right glad to be there.* **37.** very (used in certain titles): *the right reverend.*
—*v.t.* **38.** to bring or restore to an upright or the proper position. **39.** to set in order or put right. **40.** to bring into conformity with fact, or correct. **41.** to do justice to. **42.** to redress (wrong, etc.).
—*v.i.* **43.** to resume an upright or the proper position. [ME; OE *reht, riht,* c. D and G *recht,* Icel. *rēttr,* Goth. *raihts*; akin to L *rectus*] —**Syn. 1.** equitable. **2.** accurate, true. **8.** proper, suitable, convenient. **19.** virtue.

right-a·bout (rīt′ə bout′), *n.* the opposite direction as faced after turning about to the right.

right about face, *Mil.* a command to turn so as to face the opposite direction.

right angle, the angle formed by two perpendicular lines intercepting a quarter of a circle drawn about its vertex. See diag. under **angle.** —**right′-an′gled,** *adj.*

right ascension, *Astron.* **1.** the rising of a star or point above the horizon on the celestial sphere. **2.** the arc of the celestial equator measured eastward from the vernal equinox to the foot of the great circle passing through the celestial poles and the point on the celestial sphere in question, and expressed in degrees or time.

right·eous (rī′chəs), *adj.* **1.** characterized by uprightness or morality: *a righteous act.* **2.** morally right or justifiable: *righteous indignation.* **3.** in accordance with

right; upright or virtuous: *a righteous and godly man.* —*n.* **4.** righteous people collectively (prec. by *the*). [earlier *rightwos(e), rightwis(e),* OE *rihtwis,* f. *riht* RIGHT + *wis* WISE²] —**right′eous·ly,** *adv.* —**right′eous·ness,** *n.* —**Ant. 3.** evil, wicked.

right face, *Mil.* a command to face to the right in a prescribed manner while standing.

right·ful (rīt′fəl), *adj.* **1.** having a right, or just claim, as to some possession or position: *the rightful owner.* **2.** belonging by right, or just claim: *one's rightful property.* **3.** equitable or just, as actions, etc.: *a rightful cause.* —**right′ful·ly,** *adv.* —**right′ful·ness,** *n.*

right hand, the most efficient help or resource.

right-hand (rīt′hănd′), *adj.* **1.** on or to the right. **2.** of, for, or with the right hand. **3.** most efficient or useful as a helper: *one's right-hand man.* **4.** plain-laid.

right-hand·ed (rīt′hăn′dĭd), *adj.* **1.** having the right hand or arm more serviceable than the left; preferably using the right hand. **2.** adapted to or performed by the right hand. **3.** *Mach.* moving or rotating from left to right, or in the same direction as the hands of a clock. **4.** right-handed helix or spiral, one that is turned in this way and runs upward from left to right when viewed from the side with the axis vertical, as the thread of a right-handed screw.

right·ist (rī′tĭst), *adj.* **1.** having conservative or reactionary political views. —*n.* **2.** a conservative or reactionary.

right·ly (rīt′lĭ), *adv.* **1.** in accordance with truth or fact; correctly. **2.** in accordance with morality or equity; uprightly. **3.** properly, fitly, or suitably. [ME; OE *rihtlīce.* See RIGHT, -LY]

right-mind·ed (rīt′mīn′dĭd), *adj.* having right opinions or principles. —**right′-mind′ed·ness,** *n.*

right·ness (rīt′nĭs), *n.* **1.** correctness or accuracy. **2.** propriety or fitness. **3.** straightness or directness.

right·o (rīt′ō′), *interj.* *Brit.* yes; all right.

right of search, *Law.* a privilege of a nation at war to search neutral ships on the high seas for contraband or other matters in violation of neutrality which may subject the ship to seizure.

right of way, **1.** a common law or statutory right to proceed ahead of another. **2.** a path or route which may lawfully be used. **3.** a right of passage, as over another's land. **4.** the strip of land acquired for use by a railroad for tracks. **5.** land covered by a public road. **6.** land over which a power line passes.

right triangle, a triangle with a right angle.

right whale, any of various large toothless whales, genus *Balaena,* including those hunted commercially.

right wing, **1.** members of a conservative or reactionary political party, or those opposing extensive political reform. **2.** such a political party, or a group of such parties. —**right′-wing′,** *adj.* —**right′-wing′er,** *n.*

Ri·gi (rē′gē), *n.* a mountain in central Switzerland, near the Lake of Lucerne. 5906 ft.

rig·id (rĭj′ĭd), *adj.* **1.** stiff or unyielding; not pliant or flexible; hard. **2.** firmly fixed, set, or not moving. **3.** inflexible, strict, or severe: *a rigid discipline or disciplinarian.* **4.** rigorously strict regarding opinion or observance. **5.** severely exact; rigorous: *a rigid examination.* **6.** *Aeron.* **a.** (of an airship or dirigible) having its form maintained by a rigid structure contained within the envelope. **b.** pertaining to a helicopter rotor which is fixedly held at its root. [t. L: *rigidus*] —**ri-gid′i·ty, rig′id·ness,** *n.* —**rig′id·ly,** *adv.* —**Syn. 1.** unbending, firm. **3.** rigorous, stringent, austere, stern. See **strict.** —**Ant. 1.** elastic. **3.** lax.

rig·ma·role (rĭg′mə rōl′), *n.* a succession of confused or foolish statements; incoherent or rambling discourse. [alter. of obs. *ragman roll* a roll, list, or catalogue, f. *ragman,* in same sense (of obscure orig.) + ROLL]

Ri·o·let·to (rē′gə lĕt′ō; *It.* rē′gō lĕt′tô), *n.* an opera (1851) by Verdi.

rig·or (rĭg′ər), *n.* **1.** strictness, severity, or harshness, as in dealing with persons. **2.** the full or extreme severity of laws, rules, etc.: *the rigor of the law.* **3.** severity of life; hardship. **4.** a severe or harsh act, circumstance, etc. **5.** severity of weather or climate, or an instance of this: *the rigors of winter.* **6.** *Pathol.* a sudden coldness, as that preceding certain fevers; a chill. **7.** *Physiol.* a state in living tissues in which they are unable to react to a stimulus. **8.** stiffness or rigidity. Also, *Brit., chiefly Brit.* **rigour.** [ME *rigour,* t. OF, t. L: m. *rigor*]

rig·or·ism (rĭg′ə rĭz′əm), *n.* **1.** extreme strictness. **2.** *Rom. Cath. Theol.* the theory that in doubtful cases of conscience the strict course is always to be followed. —**rig′or·ist,** *n.* —**rig′or·is′tic,** *adj.*

ri·gor mor·tis (rī′gôr môr′tĭs; rĭg′ər), the stiffening of the body after death. [L: lit., stiffness of death]

rig·or·ous (rĭg′ər əs), *adj.* **1.** characterized by rigor; rigidly severe or harsh, as persons, rules, discipline, etc.: *rigorous laws.* **2.** severely exact or rigidly accurate: *rigorous accuracy.* **3.** severe or sharp, as weather or climate. —**rig′or·ous·ly,** *adv.* —**rig′or·ous·ness,** *n.* —**Syn. 1.** stern, austere. See **strict.** **3.** inclement, bitter.

rig·our (rĭg′ər), *n.* *Brit.* rigor.

Rigs·dag (rĭgz′däg′), *n.* *Danish.* the parliament of Denmark. [cf. RIKSDAG, REICHSTAG]

rigs·da·ler (rĭgz′dä′lər), *n.* an obsolete Danish silver coin worth sixteen skillings. [see RIX-DOLLAR]

Rig-Ve·da (rĭg′vā′də, -vē′də), *n.* *Hinduism.* the Veda of Verses, or Psalms (totaling 1028); the oldest document among the sacred scriptures of the world's living religions, dating not later than the second millennium B.C. See **Veda.** [t. Skt., f. *ric* praise + *veda* knowledge]

Riis (rēs), *n.* **Jacob August,** 1849–1914, U.S. journalist and social reformer, born in Denmark.

Ri·je·ka (rē yĕ′kä), *n.* a seaport in NW Yugoslavia, at the head of the Gulf of Quarnero; seized by d'Annunzio, 1919; a part of Italy, 1924–47. 75,112 (1952). Formerly, **Fiume.**

Rijn (rīn), *n.* Dutch name of the **Rhine.**

Riks·dag (rĭks′däg′), *n.* the parliament of Sweden.

rile (rīl), *v.t.,* **riled, riling.** *Colloq. or Dial.* **1.** to irritate or vex. **2.** *U.S.* to roil (water, etc.). [var. of ROIL]

Ri·ley (rī′lĭ), *n.* **James Whitcomb** (hwĭt′kəm), 1849–1916, U.S. poet.

ri·lie·vo (rē lyĕ′vō), *n., pl. -vi* (-vē). *Sculpture, Painting, etc.* relief (defs. 9, 10). [It.: relief]

Ril·ke (rĭl′kə), *n.* **Rainer Maria** (rī′nər mä rē′ä), 1875–1926, German poet and author, born in Prague.

rill[1] (rĭl), *n.* a small rivulet or brook. [cf. D, Fris., and LG *ril,* G *rille*]

rill[2] (rĭl), *n.* *Astron.* any of certain long, narrow trenches or valleys observed on the surface of the moon. Also, **rille.** [t. G. See RILL[1]]

rill·et (rĭl′ĭt), *n.* a little rill; a streamlet.

rim (rĭm). *n., v.,* **rimmed, rimming.** —*n.* **1.** the outer edge, border, or margin, esp. of a circular object. **2.** any edge or margin, often a raised one. **3.** the circular part of a wheel, furthest from the axle. **4.** a circular strip of metal forming the connection between an automobile wheel and tire, and either permanently attached to or removable from the wheel. **5.** *Basketball.* the metal ring in front of the backboard from which the goal net is suspended. —*v.t.* **6.** to furnish with a rim, border, or margin. **7.** *Golf.* to roll around the edge of (a hole). [ME; OE *rima,* c. Icel. *rimi* raised strip of land. ridge]
—**Syn. 1.** RIM, BRIM refer to the boundary of a circular or curved area. A RIM is a line or surface bounding such an area; an edge or border: *the rim of a glass.* BRIM usually means the inside of the rim, at the top of a hollow object (except of a hat); and is used particularly when the object contains something: *the cup was filled to the brim.*

Rim·baud (răn bō′), *n.* **Arthur** (àr tyr′), 1854–91, French symbolist poet.

rime[1] (rīm), *n., v.t., v.i.,* **rimed, riming.** rhyme.

rime[2] (rīm). *n., v.,* **rimed, riming.** *Meteorol.* —*n.* **1.** a rough, white icy covering deposited on trees, etc., somewhat resembling white frost, but formed only from fog or vapor-bearing air. —*v.t.* **2.** to cover with rime or hoarfrost. [ME; OE *hrīm,* c. D *rijm*]

rime·ster (rīm′star), *n.* rhymester.

Rim·i·ni (rĭm′ə nĭ′; *It.* rē′mē nē′), *n.* a seaport in NE Italy, on the Adriatic. 76,739 (1951).

ri·mose (rī′mōs, rī mōs′), *adj.* full of chinks or crevices. [t. L: *m. s. rīmōsus* full of fissures]

Rim·ski-Kor·sa·kov (rĭm′skĭ′kôr′sə kôf′; *Russ.* rēm′-skĭ′ kôr sä kôf′), *n.* **Nikolai Andreevich** (nĭ′kŏ lī′ ăn-drē′ə vĭch), 1844–1908, Russian composer.

rim·y (rī′mĭ), *adj.,* **rimier, rimiest.** covered with rime.

rind (rīnd), *n.* a thick and firm outer coat or covering, as of animals, plants, fruits, cheeses, etc. [ME and OE *rind(e),* c. G *rinde*]

rin·der·pest (rĭn′dər pĕst′), *n.* *Vet. Sci.* an acute, usually fatal, infectious disease of cattle, sheep, etc., characterized by high fever, diarrhea, lesions of the skin and mucous membranes, etc. [t. G: cattle pest]

ring[1] (rĭng), *n., v.,* **ringed, ringing.** —*n.* **1.** a circular band of metal or other material, esp. one of gold or other precious metal, often set with gems, for wearing on the finger as an ornament, a token of betrothal or marriage, etc. **2.** anything having the form of a circular band. **3.** a circular line or mark. **4.** a circular course: *to dance in a ring.* **5.** the outside edge of a circular body, as a wheel. **6.** a single turn in a spiral or helix or in a spiral course. **7.** *Geom.* the area or space between two concentric circles. **8.** one of the concentric layers of wood produced yearly in the trunks of exogenous trees. **9.** a circle of bark cut from around a tree. **10.** a number of persons or things placed in a circle. **11.** an enclosed circular or other area, as one in which some sport or exhibition takes place: *the ring of a circus.* **12.** an enclosure in which prize fights take place (now usually a square area marked off by stakes and ropes). **13.** prize fighting. **14.** a space devoted to betting at a racecourse. **15.** competition; contest: *to toss one's hat in the election ring.* **16.** a group of persons cooperating for selfish or illicit purposes, as to control a business, etc. **17.** *Chem.* a number of atoms so united that they may be graphically represented in cyclic form.
—*v.t.* **18.** to surround with a ring; encircle. **19.** to form into a ring. **20.** to put a ring in the nose of (an animal). **21.** to hem in (animals) by riding or circling about them. **22.** to cut away the bark in a ring about (a tree, branch, etc.). **23.** (in ring toss games) to hurl a ring over (the goal).
—*v.i.* **24.** to form a ring or rings. **25.** to move in a ring or a constantly curving course.
[ME; OE *hring,* c. D and G *ring,* Icel. *hringr.* Cf. RANK[1]]
—**ring′like′,** *adj.*
—**Syn. 2.** circlet, circle, hoop. **16.** RING and CLIQUE are terms applied with disapproving connotations to groups of persons. RING suggests a small and intimately related

group, combined for selfish and often dishonest purposes: *a gambling ring.* A CLIQUE is a small group which prides itself on its congeniality and exclusiveness: *cliques in a school.*

ring[2] (rĭng). *v.,* **rang, rung, ringing.** *n.* —*v.i.* **1.** to give forth a clear, resonant sound when set in sudden vibration by a blow or otherwise, as a bell, glass, etc. **2.** to seem (true, false, etc.) in the effect produced on the mind: *his words ring true.* **3.** to cause a bell or bells to sound, esp. as a summons: *ring for a messenger.* **4.** to sound loudly; be loud or resonant; resound. **5.** to be filled with sound; reëcho with sound, as a place. **6.** (of the ears) to have the sensation of a continued humming sound. **7.** *Falconry.* to fly upward in a spiral manner. —*v.t.* **8.** to cause to ring, as a bell, etc. **9.** to produce (sound) by or as if by ringing. **10.** to announce or proclaim, usher in or out, summon, signal, etc., by or as by the sound of a bell: *to ring a person's praises.* **11.** to test (coin, etc.) by the sound produced in striking on something. **12.** *Brit.* to telephone (usually fol. by *up*). **13.** *Slang.* to bring or put (in) artfully or fraudulently: *to ring someone in.* —*n.* **14.** a ringing sound, as of a bell, etc.: *the ring of sleigh bells.* **15.** a sound or tone resembling the ringing of a bell: *there was a ring in his voice.* **16.** any loud sound; sound continued, repeated, or reverberated. **17.** a set or peal of bells. **18.** a telephone call: *give me a ring tomorrow.* **19.** an act of ringing a bell. **20.** a characteristic sound, as of a coin. **21.** a characteristic quality, indicating genuineness or not. [ME; OE *hringan,* c. Icel. *hringja,* G *ringen*]

ring·bolt (rĭng′bōlt′), *n.* a bolt with a ring fitted in an eye at its head.

ring·bone (rĭng′bōn′), *n.* *Vet. Sci.* a morbid bony growth on the pastern bones of a horse, often resulting in lameness.

ring·dove (rĭng′dŭv′), *n.* **1.** the European wood pigeon, *Columba palumbus,* with two whitish patches on the neck. **2.** Also, **ringed turtledove.** a small Old World pigeon, *Streptopelia risoria,* with a black half ring around the neck.

ringed (rĭngd), *adj.* **1.** having or wearing a ring or rings. **2.** marked or decorated with a ring or rings. **3.** surrounded by a ring or rings. **4.** formed of or with rings; ringlike or annular.

rin·gent (rĭn′jənt), *adj.* **1.** gaping. **2.** *Bot.* having widely spread lips, as some corollas. [t. L: s. *ringens,* ppr.]

ring·er[1] (rĭng′ər), *n.* **1.** one who or that which rings, encircles, etc. **2.** a quoit or horseshoe so thrown as to encircle the peg. **3.** the throw itself. [f. RING[1] + -ER[1]]

ring·er[2] (rĭng′ər), *n.* **1.** one who or that which rings a bell, etc. **2.** *Slang.* an athlete, horse, etc., entered in a competition under false representations as to identity or ability. **3.** *Slang.* a person or thing that closely resembles another. [f. RING[2] + -ER[1]]

ring·lead·er (rĭng′lē′dər), *n.* one who leads others in opposition to authority or law, or in anything deemed objectionable. [der. phrase *to lead the ring* to be first]

ring·let (rĭng′lĭt), *n.* **1.** a small ring or circle. **2.** a curled lock of hair. —**ring·let·ed** (rĭng′lĭt ĭd), *adj.*

ring·mas·ter (rĭng′măs′tər, -mäs′-), *n.* one in charge of the performances in the ring of a circus.

ring·neck (rĭng′nĕk′), *n.* any of various birds having a ring of distinctive color about the neck, as the ring-necked pheasant, the mallard, etc.

ring-necked pheasant (rĭng′nĕkt′), a gallinaceous Asiatic bird, *Phasianus colchicus,* now acclimated esp. in Great Britain and the U.S.

Ring of the Ni·be·lung (nē′bə lŏŏng′), Wagner's tetralogy of music dramas: *Das Rheingold* (completed 1869), *Die Walküre* (completed 1870), *Siegfried* (completed 1876), and *Götterdämmerung* (completed 1876). The cycle was first performed at Bayreuth, 1876.

ring·side (rĭng′sīd′), *n.* **1.** the space immediately surrounding an arena, as the first row of seats around a prize-fight ring. **2.** any place providing a close view.

ring·ster (rĭng′stər), *n.* *U.S. Colloq.* a member of a ring, esp. a political ring.

ring-streaked (rĭng′strēkt′), *adj.* having streaks or bands of color round the body.

ring·tail (rĭng′tāl′). *n.* any phalanger of the genus *Pseudocheirus,* related by the structure of the molar teeth to the koala.

ring·worm (rĭng′wûrm′), *n.* *Pathol.* any of certain contagious skin diseases due to vegetable parasites and characterized by the formation of ring-shaped eruptive patches.

rink (rĭngk). *n.* **1.** a sheet of ice for skating, often one artificially prepared and under cover. **2.** a smooth floor for roller-skating. **3.** a building or enclosure containing a surface prepared for skating. **4.** an area of ice marked off for the game of curling. **5.** a section of a bowling green where a match can be played. **6.** a set of players on one side in bowling or curling. [orig. Sc.; ME *renk,* appar. t. OF: m. *renc* RANK[1]]

rinse (rĭns), *v.,* **rinsed, rinsing,** *n.* —*v.t.* **1.** to wash lightly, as by pouring water into or over or by dipping in water. **2.** to put through clean water, as a final stage in cleansing. **3.** to remove (impurities, etc.) thus. —*n.* **4.** a rinsing. **5.** a final application of water to remove impurities. **6.** the water or the like used. [ME *rynce,* t. OF: m. *reincer,* g. Rom. *recentiāre* make fresh, der. s. L *recens* fresh, recent] —**rins′er,** *n.*

rins·ing (rĭn'sĭng), *n.* **1.** act of one who rinses. **2.** (*chiefly pl.*) the liquid with which anything has been rinsed.

Rí·o Bra·vo (rē'ō brä'vō), Mexican name of **Rio Grande** (def. 1).

Ri·o de Ja·nei·ro (rē'ō də zhə när'ō; *Port.* rē'ŏŏ də zhə nĕ'rŏŏ), a seaport in and the former capital of Brazil, in the SE part: excellent harbor. 3,220,225 (est. 1960). Also, **Rio.**

Ri·o de O·ro (rē'ō dĕ ō'rō), **1.** a Spanish colony on the NW coast of Africa. 1476 pop. (est. 1951). ab. 70,000 sq. mi. *Cap.:* Villa Cisneros. **2.** Former name of **Spanish Sahara.**

Ri·o Grande (rē'ō gränd', grän'dĭ *for 1*; rē'ŏŏ grän'də *for 2, 3*), **1.** Mexican, **Rio Bravo.** a river flowing from SW Colorado through central New Mexico and along the Texas-Mexico boundary into the Gulf of Mexico. ab. 1800 mi. **2.** a river flowing from SE Brazil W to the Paraná river. ab. 600 mi. **3.** Also, **Rio Grande do Sul** (dŏŏ sŏŏl'). a seaport in S Brazil. 64,241 (est. 1952).

Rí·o Mu·ni (rē'ō mŏŏ'nē), the mainland portion of Spanish Guinea. 156,785 (est. 1955). 10,040 sq. mi.

ri·ot (rī'ət), *n.* **1.** a disturbance of the peace by an assembly of persons. **2.** *Law.* the execution of a violent and unlawful purpose by three or more persons acting together, to the terror of the people. **3.** violent or wild disorder or confusion. **4.** loose or wanton living; unrestrained revelry. **5.** an unbridled outbreak, as of emotions, passions, etc. **6.** a brilliant display: *a riot of color.* **7. run riot, a.** to act without control or restraint; disregard all limits. **b.** to grow luxuriantly or wildly. —*v.i.* **8.** to take part in a riot or disorderly public outbreak. **9.** to live in a loose or wanton manner; indulge in unrestrained revelry. **10.** to indulge unrestrainedly; run riot. —*v.t.* **11.** to spend (money, etc.) or pass (time, etc.) in riotous living (fol. by *away* or *out*). [ME, t. OF: m. *riote* debate, dispute, quarrel, der. *r(u)ihoter* to quarrel, dim. of *ruir* make an uproar, g. L *rugīre* roar] —**ri'ot·er,** *n.* —**Syn. 1.** outbreak, disorder, brawl.

Riot Act, an English statute of 1715 providing that if twelve or more persons assemble unlawfully and riotously, to the disturbance of the public peace, and refuse to disperse upon proclamation (called **reading the Riot Act),** they shall be considered guilty of felony.

ri·ot·ous (rī'ətəs), *adj.* **1.** characterized by or of the nature of rioting, or disturbance of the peace, as actions. **2.** inciting to or taking part in a riot, as persons. **3.** given to or marked by unrestrained revelry; loose; wanton. **4.** boisterous or uproarious: *riotous laughter.* —**ri'ot·ous·ly,** *adv.* —**ri'ot·ous·ness,** *n.*

rip¹ (rĭp), *v.,* **ripped, ripping,** *n.* —*v.t.* **1.** to cut or tear apart in a rough or vigorous manner; slash; slit. **2.** to cut or tear away in a rough or vigorous manner. **3.** to saw (wood) in the direction of the grain. —*v.i.* **4.** to become torn apart or split open. **5.** *Colloq.* to move along with violence or great speed. **6.** *Colloq.* to break (*out*) angrily, as with an oath. —*n.* **7.** a rent made by ripping; a tear. [late ME; c. Fris. *rippe,* Flem. *rippen* rip; akin to d. E *ripple,* v., scratch] —**Syn. 1.** See **tear².**

rip² (rĭp), *n.* a stretch of broken water at sea or in a river. [see RIP¹, v., RIPPLE]

rip³ (rĭp), *n.* *Colloq.* **1.** a dissolute or worthless person. **2.** a worthless or worn-out horse. **3.** anything of little or no value. [OE *rypa,* var. of *reopa* bundle of corn, sheaf, akin to *rīpan* reap]

R.I.P., (L *requiescat* or *requiescant in pace*) may he or she (or they) rest in peace.

ri·par·i·an (rĭ pâr'ĭ ən, rī-), *adj.* **1.** of, pertaining to, or situated or dwelling on the bank of a river or other body of water. —*n.* **2.** *Law.* one who owns land on the bank of a natural watercourse or body of water. [f. s. L *rīpārius* belonging to a river bank or shore + -AN]

riparian right, (*usually pl.*) *Law.* a right, as fishing or use of water for irrigation or power, enjoyed by one who owns riparian property.

rip cord, *Aeron.* **1.** a cord or ring which opens a parachute during a descent. **2.** a cord fastened in the bag of a balloon or dirigible so that a sharp pull upon it will rip or open the bag and let the gas escape, thus causing the balloon to descend rapidly.

ripe (rīp), *adj.,* **riper, ripest. 1.** ready for reaping or gathering, as grain, fruits, etc.; complete in natural growth or development, as when arrived at the stage most fit for eating or use. **2.** resembling ripe fruit, as in ruddiness and fullness. **3.** fully grown or developed, as animals when ready to be killed and used for food. **4.** advanced to the point of being in the best condition for use, as cheese, beer, etc. **5.** arrived at the highest or a high point of development or excellence; mature. **6.** of mature judgment or knowledge. **7.** characterized by full development of body or mind: *of ripe years.* **8.** advanced in years: *a ripe old age.* **9.** ready for action, execution, etc. **10.** fully prepared or ready to do or undergo something, or for some action, purpose, or end. **11.** ready for some operation or process: *a ripe abscess.* **12.** (of time) fully or sufficiently advanced. [ME and OE; c. D *riip,* G *reif:* akin to OE *rīpan* reap] —**ripe'ly,** *adv.* —**ripe'ness,** *n.*

—**Syn. 1.** RIPE, MATURE, MELLOW refer to that which is no longer in an incomplete stage of development. RIPE implies completion reached beyond which the processes of decay begin: *a ripe harvest.* MATURE means fully grown and developed, of living organisms: *a mature animal or tree.*

MELLOW denotes complete absence of sharpness or asperity, with sweetness and richness such as characterize ripeness or age: *mellow fruit or flavor.*

rip·en (rī'pən), *v.i., v.t.* **1.** to become or make ripe. **2.** to come or bring to maturity, the proper condition, etc.; mature. [ME *ripe(n),* OE *rīpian* (c. D *rijpen*), der. *ripe* RIPE] —**rip'en·er,** *n.*

Rip·ley (rĭp'lĭ), *n.* George, 1802-80, U.S. literary critic, author, and editor: helped found Brook Farm.

ri·poste (rĭ pōst'), *n., v.,* **-posted, -posting.** —*n.* **1.** *Fencing.* a quick thrust given after parrying a lunge. **2.** a quick, sharp return. —*v.i.* **3.** to make a riposte. **4.** to reply or retaliate. Also, **ri·post'.** [t. F, t. It.: m. *risposta* response, der. *rispondere* answer, g. L *respondēre*]

rip·per (rĭp'ər), *n.* **1.** one who or that which rips. **2.** Also, **ripper bill, ripper act.** *U.S.* a legislative bill or act for taking powers of appointment to and removal from office away from the usual holders of these powers and conferring them unrestrictedly on a chief executive, as a governor or a mayor, or on a board of officials. **3.** a double-ripper. **4.** *Chiefly Brit. Slang.* something especially strong, fine, or good of its kind.

rip·ping (rĭp'ĭng), *adj.* **1.** that rips. **2.** *Chiefly Brit. Slang.* excellent, splendid, or fine.

rip·ple¹ (rĭp'əl), *v.,* **-pled, -pling,** *n.* —*v.i.* **1.** to form small waves or undulations on the surface, as water when agitated by a gentle breeze or by running over a rocky bottom. **2.** to flow with a light ruffling of the surface. **3.** to form or have small undulations. **4.** (of sound) to go on or proceed with an effect like that of water flowing in ripples. —*v.t.* **5.** to form small waves or undulations on; agitate lightly. **6.** to mark as with ripples; give a wavy form to. —*n.* **7.** a small wave or undulation, as on water. **8.** any similar movement or appearance; a small undulation, as in hair. **9.** *U.S.* a small rapid. **10.** a ripple mark. **11.** a sound as of water flowing in ripples: *a ripple of laughter.* [orig. uncert.] —**rip'pling·ly,** *adv.* —**Syn. 7.** See **wave.**

rip·ple² (rĭp'əl), *n., v.,* **-pled, -pling.** —*n.* **1.** a toothed or comblike device for removing seeds or capsules from flax, etc. —*v.t.* **2.** to remove the seeds or capsules from (flax, etc.) with a ripple. [ME *rypel;* akin to G *riffel*]

ripple mark, one of the wavy lines or ridges produced on sand, etc., by waves, wind, or the like.

rip·pler (rĭp'lər), *n.* **1.** one who ripples flax, etc. **2.** an instrument for rippling; ripple.

rip·plet (rĭp'lĭt), *n.* a little ripple.

rip·ply (rĭp'lĭ), *adj.* **1.** characterized by ripples; rippling. **2.** sounding as rippling water.

rip·rap (rĭp'răp'), *n., v.,* **-rapped, -rapping.** —*n.* **1.** broken stones used for foundations, etc. **2.** a foundation or wall of stones thrown together irregularly. —*v.t.* **3.** to construct with or strengthen by stones, either loose or fastened with mortar. [varied reduplication of RAP]

rip·roar·ing (rĭp'rōr'ĭng), *adj.* *Slang.* riotous; wild and noisy: *to have a rip-roaring time.*

rip·saw (rĭp'sô'), *n.* a saw used for sawing timber with the grain. [f. RIP¹, v. + SAW¹]

rip·tide (rĭp'tīd'), *n.* *U.S.* a tide which opposes another or other tides, causing a violent disturbance in the sea. —**Syn.** See **undertow.**

Ri·pu·ar·i·an (rĭp'yŏŏ âr'ĭ ən), *adj.* **1.** designating or pertaining to the group of Franks who dwelt along the Rhine in the neighborhood of Cologne, or the code of laws observed by them. —*n.* **2.** a Ripuarian Frank. [f. s. ML *ripuārius* (orig. uncert.) pertaining to the Ripuarian Franks + -AN]

Rip Van Win·kle (rĭp' văn wĭng'kəl), **1.** (in a story by Washington Irving) a ne'er-do-well who sleeps 20 years and wakes to find everything changed. **2.** the story itself, published in the *Sketch-Book* (1819).

rise (rīz), *v.,* **rose, risen, rising,** *n.* —*v.i.* **1.** to get up from a lying, sitting, or kneeling posture; assume a standing position. **2.** to get up from bed: *to rise early.* **3.** to become erect and stiff, as the hair. **4.** to get up after falling or being thrown down. **5.** to become active in opposition or resistance; revolt or rebel. **6.** to be built up, erected, or constructed. **7.** to spring up or grow, as plants. **8.** to become prominent on a surface, as a blister. **9.** to come into existence; appear. **10.** to come into action, as a wind, storm, etc. **11.** to occur: *a quarrel rose between them.* **12.** to originate, issue, or be derived; to have its spring or source. **13.** to move from a lower to a higher position; move upward; ascend: *a bird rises in the air.* **14.** to come above the horizon, as a heavenly body. **15.** to extend directly upward: *the tower rises to the height of 60 feet.* **16.** to have an upward slant or curve: *the walk rises as it approaches the house.* **17.** to attain higher rank, importance, etc. **18.** to advance to a higher level of action, thought, feeling, expression, etc. **19.** to prove oneself equal to a demand, emergency, etc.: *to rise to the occasion.* **20.** to become animated or cheerful, as the spirits. **21.** to become stirred or roused: *to feel one's temper rising.* **22.** to increase in height, as water: *the river sometimes rose 30 feet in eight hours.* **23.** to swell or puff up, as dough from the action of yeast. **24.** to increase in amount, as prices, etc. **25.** to increase in price or value, as commodities. **26.** to increase in degree, intensity, or force, as color, fever, etc. **27.** to become louder or of higher pitch, as the voice. **28.** to adjourn, or close a session, as a deliberative body or court. **29.** to return from the dead. —*v.t.* **30.** to cause to rise. **31.** *Naut.* to cause (some-

thing) to rise above the visible horizon by approaching nearer to it; raise.
—**n. 32.** act of rising; upward movement or ascent. **33.** appearance above the horizon, as of the sun or moon. **34.** elevation or advance in rank, position, fortune, etc.: *the rise and fall of ancient Rome.* **35.** an increase in height, as of water. **36.** the amount of such increase. **37.** an increase in amount, as of prices. **38.** an increase in price or value, as of commodities. **39.** *Chiefly Brit.* raise (def. 30). **40.** an increase in degree or intensity, as of temperature. **41.** an increase in loudness or in pitch, as of the voice. **42.** the vertical height included in a flight of steps. **43.** the vertical height of a riser (def. 2). **44.** origin, source, or beginning: *the rise of a stream in a mountain.* **45.** occasion: *to give rise to suspicion.* **46.** a coming into existence or notice. **47.** extension upward. **48.** the amount of this. **49.** upward slope, as of ground or a road. **50.** a piece of rising or high ground.
[ME; OE *rīsan*, c. D *rijzen*, G *reisen*. Cf. RAISE]
—**Syn. 30.** RISE, RAISE are not synonyms, though the forms of RAISE are commonly and mistakenly used as if they also meant RISE. RISE, the verb with irregular forms, never takes an object: *one rises from a chair.* RAISE, with regular forms (raised, have raised, raising), originally meaning "to cause something to rise," has to have an object, either a concrete one or an abstract one: *one raises his hat, had raised a question.*

ris·er (rī′zər), *n.* **1.** one who rises, esp. from bed: *to be an early riser.* **2.** the vertical face of a stair step.
ris·i·bil·i·ty (rĭz′ə bĭl′ə tĭ), *n., pl.* **-ties. 1.** ability or disposition to laugh: *he was a man of infinite risibility.* **2.** (*often pl.*) faculty of laughing.
ris·i·ble (rĭz′ə bəl), *adj.* **1.** having the faculty or power of laughing; inclined to laughter. **2.** pertaining to or connected with laughing. **3.** capable of exciting laughter; laughable or ludicrous. [t. LL: m.s. *rīsibilis*, der. L *rīsus*, pp., laughed at]
ris·ing (rī′zĭng), *adj.* **1.** that rises; advancing, ascending, or mounting. **2.** growing; or advancing to adult years: *the rising generation.* —*prep.* **3.** *Colloq.* somewhat more than; above. —*n.* **4.** act of one who or that which rises. **5.** an insurrection or revolt. **6.** something that rises; a projection or prominence. **7.** a period of leavening of dough preceding baking. **8.** *Dial.* a morbid swelling, as an abscess, boil, etc.
risk (rĭsk), *n.* **1.** exposure to the chance of injury or loss; a hazard or dangerous chance: *to run risks.* **2.** *Insurance.* **a.** the hazard or chance of loss. **b.** the degree of probability of such loss. **c.** the amount which the insurance company may lose. **d.** a person or thing with reference to the risk involved in insuring him or it. **e.** the type of loss, as life, fire, marine disaster, earthquake, etc., against which insurance policies are drawn. —*v.t.* **3.** to expose to the chance of injury or loss, or hazard: *to risk one's life to save another.* **4.** to venture upon; take or run the risk of: *to risk a fall in climbing, to risk a battle.* [t. F: m. *risque*, t. It.: m. *risc*(*hi*)*o*, der. *risicare* to risk, dare, der. Gk. *rhīza* cliff, root (through meaning of to sail around a cliff)] —**Syn. 1.** venture, peril, jeopardy.
risk·y (rĭs′kĭ), *adj.*, **riskier, riskiest. 1.** attended with or involving risk; hazardous: *a risky undertaking.* **2.** risqué.
Ri·sor·gi·men·to (rē sôr′jē mĕn′tô), *n., pl.* **-ti** (-tē). *Italian.* the period of renewed energy and reforms attending the unification of Italy, 1750–1870.
ri·sot·to (rē sôt′tô), *n.* *Italian.* a dish of rice with grated cheese and other seasoning. [It., der *riso* RICE]
ris·qué (rĭs kā′; *Fr.* rēs kē′), *adj.* daringly close to indelicacy or impropriety: *a risqué story.* [t. F, pp. of *risquer* RISK]
ris·sole (rĭs′ōl; *Fr.* rē sôl′), *n.* a small fried ball, roll, or cake of minced meat or fish mixed with bread crumbs, egg, etc., and usually enclosed in paste. [t. F, ? ult. der. VL *russeola* (fem. adj.) reddish]
rit., *Music.* ritardando. Also, **ritard.**
ri·tar·dan·do (rē′tär dän′dô), *adj. Music.* becoming gradually slower. [It., gerund of *ritardare* RETARD]
rite (rīt), *n.* **1.** a formal or ceremonial act or procedure prescribed or customary in religious or other solemn use: *rites of baptism, sacrificial rites.* **2.** a particular form or system of religious or other ceremonial practice: *the Roman rite, the Scottish rite in freemasonry.* **3.** (*often cap.*) (historically) one of the versions of the Eucharistic service: *the Anglican rite.* **4.** (*often cap.*) liturgy. **5.** (*sometimes cap.*) *Eastern & Western Churches.* a division or differentiation of churches according to liturgy. **6.** any customary observance or practice. [ME, t. L: m.s. *rītus* ceremony] —**Syn. 1.** See ceremony.
rit·u·al (rĭch′ŏŏ əl), *n.* **1.** a form or system of religious or other rites. **2.** observance of set forms in public worship. **3.** a book of rites or ceremonies. **4.** a book containing the offices to be used by priests in administering the sacraments and for visitation of the sick, burial of the dead, etc. **5.** a ritual proceeding or service: *the ritual of the dead.* **6.** ritual acts or features collectively, as in religious services. —*adj.* **7.** of the nature of, or practiced as, a rite or rites: *a ritual dance.* **8.** of or pertaining to rites: *ritual laws.* [t. L: s. *rītuālis*, adj.] —**rit′-u·al·ly,** *adv.* —**Syn. 1.** See ceremony.
rit·u·al·ism (rĭch′ŏŏ ə lĭz′əm), *n.* **1.** adherence to or insistence on ritual. **2.** the study of ritual practices or religious rites. **3.** fondness for ritual.

rit·u·al·ist (rĭch′ŏŏ əl ĭst), *n.* **1.** a student of or authority on ritual practices or religious rites. **2.** one who practices or advocates observance of ritual, as in religious services. —**rit′u·al·is′tic,** *adj.* —**rit′u·al·is′ti·cal·ly,** *adv.*
riv., river.
riv·age (rĭv′ĭj), *n. Archaic.* a bank, shore, or coast. [ME, t. OF, der. *rive* bank, g. L *rīpa.* See -AGE]
ri·val (rī′vəl), *n., adj., v.,* **-valed, -valing** or (*esp. Brit.*) **valled, -valling.** —*n.* **1.** one who is in pursuit of the same object as another, or strives to equal or outdo another; a competitor. **2.** one who or that which is in a position to dispute preëminence or superiority with another: *a stadium without a rival.* **3.** *Obs.* a companion in duty. —*adj.* **4.** being a rival; competing or standing in rivalry: *rival suitors, rival business houses.* —*v.t.* **5.** to compete with in rivalry; strive to equal or outdo. **6.** to prove to be a worthy rival of: *he soon rivaled the others in skill.* **7.** to equal (something) as if in rivalry. —*v.i.* **8.** *Archaic.* to engage in rivalry; compete (*with*). [t. L: s. *rīvālis*, orig., one living by or using the same stream as another] —**Syn. 1.** competitor, contestant, emulator, antagonist. See opponent. —**Ant. 1.** partner.
ri·val·ry (rī′vəl rĭ), *n., pl.* **-ries.** the action, position, or relation of a rival or rivals; competition; emulation: *rivalry between Yale and Harvard.*
rive (rīv), *v.,* **rived, rived** or **riven, riving.** —*v.t.* **1.** to tear or rend apart. **2.** to strike asunder; split; cleave. **3.** to rend, harrow, or distress (the heart, etc.). —*v.i.* **4.** to become rent or split apart. [ME *rive*(n), t. Scand.; cf. Icel. *rīfa.* See RIFT]
riv·en (rĭv′ən), *v.* **1.** pp. of **rive.** —*adj.* **2.** rent or split apart.
riv·er[1] (rĭv′ər), *n.* **1.** a considerable natural stream of water flowing in a definite course or channel or series of diverging and converging channels. **2.** a similar stream of something other than water. **3.** any abundant stream or copious flow: *rivers of lava, blood, etc.* [ME, OF: m. *riv*(*i*)*ere*, ult. der. L *rīpa* bank]
riv·er[2] (rī′vər), *n.* a person who rives. [f. RIVE + -ER¹]
Ri·ve·ra (rē vĕ′rä), *n.* **Diego** (dyĕ′gô), 1886–1957, Mexican painter, esp. of murals.
Ri·ve·ra y Or·ba·ne·ja (rē vĕ′rä ē ôr′bä nĕ′hä). See Primo de Rivera.
river basin, *Phys. Geog.* the area drained by a river and its branches.
riv·er·head (rĭv′ər hĕd′), *n.* the spring or source of a river.
river horse, hippopotamus.
riv·er·ine (rĭv′ə rīn′, -ər ĭn), *adj.* **1.** of or pertaining to a river. **2.** situated or dwelling beside a river.
Riv·ers (rĭv′ərz), *n.* **William Halse** (hôls), 1865–1922, British physiologist and anthropologist.
riv·er·side (rĭv′ər sīd′), *n.* **1.** the bank of a river. —*adj.* **2.** on the bank of a river.
Riv·er·side (rĭv′ər sīd′), *n.* a city in SW California. 84,332 (1960).
riv·et (rĭv′ĭt), *n.* **1.** a metal pin or bolt for passing through holes in two or more plates or pieces to hold them together, usually made with a head at one end, the other end being hammered into a head after insertion. —*v.t.* **2.** to fasten with a rivet or rivets. **3.** to hammer or spread out the end of (a pin, etc.), in order to form a head and secure something; clinch. **4.** to fasten or fix firmly: *to stand riveted to the spot.* **5.** to hold (the eye, attention, etc.) firmly. [ME *ryvette,* t. OF: m. *rivet,* der. *river* fix, clinch, g. Rom. *rīpāre* make firm, come to shore, der. L *rīpa* shore] —**riv′et·er,** *n.*
Riv·i·er·a (rĭv′ĭ âr′ə; *It.* rē vyĕ′rä), *n.* a famous resort region along the Mediterranean coast, extending from Marseilles, in SE France, to La Spezia, in NW Italy.
ri·vière (rē vyĕr′), *n.* a necklace of diamonds or other gems, esp. in more than one string. [F: lit., river]
riv·u·let (rĭv′yə lĭt), *n.* a small stream; a streamlet; a brook. [earlier *rivolet,* t. It.: m. *rivoletto,* dim. of *rivolo,* g. L *rīvulus* small stream]
rix·dol·lar (rĭks′dŏl′ər), *n.* any of various silver coins of the Netherlands, Denmark, Germany, etc., now mostly disused, varying in value but commonly worth about $1. See **rigsdaler.** [t. D: m. *rijcksdaler* (now *rijksdaalder*). c. G. *reichsthaler* national dollar]
Ri·yadh (rē yäd′), *n.* a city in central Arabia: the capital of Nejd, and one of the two capitals of Saudi Arabia. 80,000 (est. 1954).
Ri·zal (rē säl′), *n.* **José** (hô sĕ′), 1861–96, Filipino patriot, novelist, poet, and physician.
Riz·zio (rēt′tsyô), *n.* **David** (dä′vĕd), c1533–66, Italian secretary and favorite adviser of Mary, Queen of Scots. Also, **Riccio.**
RM, reichsmark. Also, **r.m.**
rm., *pl.* **rms. 1.** ream. **2.** room.
R.M.S., 1. Railway Mail Service. **2.** Royal Mail Service. **3.** Royal Mail Steamship.
r.m.s., root mean square.
Rn, *Chem.* radon.
R.N., 1. Registered Nurse. **2.** Royal Navy.
roach[1] (rōch), *n.* a cockroach.
roach[2] (rōch), *n., pl.* **roaches,** (*esp. collectively*) **roach. 1.** a European fresh-water fish, *Rutilus rutilus,* of the carp family. **2.** any of various similar fishes, as the golden shiner, *Notemigonus crysoleucas,* of eastern North

---

b., blend of, blended; c., cognate with; d., dialect, dialectal; der., derived from; f., formed from; g., going back to; m., modification of; r., replacing; s., stem of; t., taken from; ?, perhaps. See the full key on inside cover.

America. **3.** a fresh-water sunfish, genus *Lepomis*, of eastern North America. [ME *roche*, t. OF; orig. uncert.]

road (rōd), *n.* **1.** an open way for passage or travel, usually one wide enough for vehicles, and esp. one between distant points; a highway. **2.** *U.S.* a railroad. **3.** a way or course: *the road to peace*. **4.** (*often in pl.*) a protected place near the shore where ships may ride at anchor. **5. on the road, a.** traveling, esp. as a salesman. **b.** on tour, as a theatrical company. **6.** all places outside New York City where theatrical companies perform (prec. by *the*). [ME *rode*, OE *rād* a riding, journey on horseback (akin to *rīdan* ride), c. G *reede*]

road·a·bil·i·ty (rōd′ə bĭl′ə tĭ), *n.* ability of an automobile to ride smoothly and comfortably under adverse road conditions.

road agent, *U.S.* highwayman.

road·bed (rōd′bĕd′), *n.* **1.** the bed or foundation structure of a railroad, on which ties, rails, etc., rest. **2.** a layer of crushed rock, cinders, gravel, or other ballast directly beneath the ties. **3.** the whole material (foundation, etc.) of an ordinary road.

road·block (rōd′blŏk′), *n.* an obstruction (as barricades, police cars, etc.) across a road to control traffic, as to capture a pursued car, inspect trucks for safety violations, etc.

road·house (rōd′hous′), *n.* an inn, hotel, dance hall, etc., usually on a highway outside the city.

road metal, broken stone, etc., used for making roads.

road runner, a terrestrial cuckoo, *Geococcyx californianus*, of America.

road·side (rōd′sīd′), *n.* **1.** the side or border of the road; the wayside. —*adj.* **2.** on the side of a road.

road·stead (rōd′stĕd′), *n. Naut.* road (def. 4). [f. ROAD + STEAD]

road·ster (rōd′stər), *n.* **1.** an automobile of the open-car type for use on ordinary roads, having a single seat for two or more persons, and often a rumble seat as well. **2.** a horse for riding or driving on the road.

road·way (rōd′wā′), *n.* **1.** a way used as a road; a road. **2.** the central part of a road, used by vehicles, etc.

roam (rōm), *v.i.* **1.** to walk, go, or travel about without fixed purpose or direction; ramble; wander; rove. —*v.t.* **2.** to wander over or through: *to roam the country-side.* —*n.* **3.** act of roaming; a ramble. [ME *romen*; orig. obscure] —**roam′er,** *n.*
—**Syn. 1.** stray, stroll, prowl. ROAM, RAMBLE, RANGE, ROVE imply wandering about over (usually) a considerable amount of territory. ROAM implies a wandering or traveling over a large area, esp. as prompted by restlessness or curiosity: *to roam through a forest.* RAMBLE implies pleasant, carefree moving about, walking with no specific purpose or for a limited distance: *to ramble through fields near home.* RANGE usually implies wandering over a more or less defined but extensive area in search of something: *cattle range over the plains.* ROVE sometimes implies wandering with specific incentive or aim, as an animal for prey: *bandits rove through these mountains.*

roan (rōn), *adj.* **1.** (chiefly of horses) of a sorrel, chestnut, or bay color sprinkled with gray or white. **2.** prepared from roan (leather). —*n.* **3.** a roan horse or other animal. **4.** a soft, flexible sheepskin leather, used in bookbinding, often made in imitation of morocco. [ME. t. F, t. Sp.: m. *roano*, ult. der. L *rāvidus* yellow-gray]

Ro·a·noke (rō′ə nōk′), *n.* **1.** a city in western Virginia. 97,110 (1960). **2.** a river flowing from western Virginia SE to Albemarle Sound in North Carolina. ab. 380 mi.

Roanoke Island, an island off the NE coast of North Carolina, S of Albemarle Sound: Raleigh's unsuccessful colonial attempts, 1585–87.

roar (rōr), *v.i.* **1.** to utter a loud, deep sound, esp. of excitement, distress, or anger. **2.** to laugh loudly or boisterously. **3.** to make a loud noise in breathing, as a horse. **4.** to make a loud noise or din, as thunder, cannon, waves, wind, etc. **5.** to function or move with a roar, as a vehicle: *the automobile roared away.* —*v.t.* **6.** to utter or express in a roar. **7.** to bring, put, make, etc. by roaring: *to roar oneself hoarse.* —*n.* **8.** the sound of roaring; a loud, deep sound, as of a person or persons, or of a lion or other large animal. **9.** a loud outburst of laughter. **10.** a loud noise, as of thunder, waves, etc.: *the roar of the surf.* [ME *rore(n)*, OE *rārian*, c. G *rehren*; ult. orig. obscure] —**roar′er,** *n.* —**Syn. 1.** See **cry.** **4.** resound, boom, thunder, peal.

roar·ing (rōr′ĭng), *n.* **1.** act or one who or that which roars. **2.** a loud, deep cry or sound. **3.** *Vet. Sci.* a disease of horses causing them to make a loud noise in breathing under exertion. —*adj.* **4.** that roars, as a person, thunder, etc. **5.** *Colloq.* brisk or highly successful, as trade.

roast (rōst), *v.t.* **1.** to bake (meat or other food) by dry heat, as in an oven. **2.** to prepare (meat or other food) for eating by direct exposure to dry heat, as on a spit. **3.** to brown by exposure to heat, as coffee. **4.** to embed in hot coals, embers, etc., to cook. **5.** to heat (any material) more or less violently. **6.** to heat (an ore, etc.) with access of air, as to cause oxidation. **7.** to warm (oneself, etc.) at a hot fire. **8.** *Slang.* to ridicule or criticize severely or mercilessly. —*v.i.* **9.** to roast meat, etc. **10.** to undergo the process of becoming roasted. —*n.* **11.** a piece of roasted meat; roasted meat. **12.** a piece of meat for roasting. **13.** something that is roasted. **14.** act or operation of roasting. **15.** *Slang.* severe criticism. —*adj.* **16.** roasted: *roast beef.* [ME *roste(n)*, t. OF: m. *rostir*, t. Gmc.; cf. D *roosten*]

roast·er (rōs′tər), *n.* **1.** a contrivance for roasting something. **2.** a pig, chicken, or other animal or article fit for roasting. **3.** one who or that which roasts.

roast·ing (rōs′tĭng), *adj.* **1.** that roasts. **2.** exceedingly hot; scorching.

rob (rŏb), *v.,* **robbed, robbing.** —*v.t.* **1.** to deprive of something by unlawful force or threat of violence; commit robbery upon. **2.** to deprive of something legally belonging or due. **3.** to plunder or rifle (a house, etc.). **4.** to deprive of something unjustly or injuriously: *the shock robbed him of speech.* —*v.i.* **5.** to commit or practice robbery. [ME *robbe(n)*, t. OF: m. *robber*, t. OHG: m. *roubōn*, c. REAVE]
—**Syn. 1.** ROB, RIFLE, SACK refer to seizing possessions which belong to others. ROB is the general word for taking possessions by unlawful force or violence: *to rob a bank, a house, a train.* A term with a more restricted meaning is RIFLE, to make a thorough search for what is valuable or worthwhile, usually within a small space: *to rifle a safe.* On the other hand, SACK is a term for robbery on a huge scale, during war; it suggests destruction accompanying pillage, and often includes the indiscriminate massacre of civilians: *to sack a town or district.* **2.** defraud, cheat.

rob·a·lo (rŏb′ə lō′, rō′bə-), *n., pl.* **-los,** (*esp. collectively*) **-lo.** any of the marine fishes constituting the family *Centropomidae*, esp. *Centropomus undecimalis*, a valuable food fish of Florida, the West Indies, etc. [t. Pg., t. Catalan: m. *elobarro*, ult. der. L *lupus* wolf]

rob·and (rŏb′ənd), *n. Naut.* a short piece of spun yarn or other material, used to secure a sail to a yard, gaff, or the like. [southern form answering to northern E *raband*, t. D, f. *rā* sailyard + *band* BAND]

rob·ber (rŏb′ər), *n.* one who robs. —**Syn.** See **thief.**

robber baron, *Hist.* a noble who robbed travelers passing through his lands.

robber fly, any of the swift, often large, flies constituting the family *Asilidae*, that prey on other insects.

rob·ber·y (rŏb′ər ĭ), *n., pl.* **-beries. 1.** the action or practice, or an instance, of robbing. **2.** *Law.* the felonious taking of the property of another from his person or in his immediate presence, against his will, by violence or intimidation. [ME *roberie*, t. OF, der. *rober* ROB]

Rob·bia (rŏb′byä), *n.* Luca della (lŏo′kä dĕl′lä), 1400?–82, Italian artist, esp. in enameled terra cotta.

robe (rōb), *n., v.,* **robed, robing.** —*n.* **1.** a long, loose or flowing gown or outer garment worn by men or women, esp. for formal occasions; an official vestment, as of a judge. **2.** any long, loose garment: *a bathrobe.* **3.** a woman's gown or dress, esp. of a more elaborate kind. **4.** (*pl.*) apparel in general; dress; costume. **5.** a piece of fur, cloth, knitted work, etc., used as a covering or wrap: *a buffalo robe; a lap robe.* —*v.t.* **6.** to clothe or invest in a robe or robes; dress or apparel. —*v.i.* **7.** to put on a robe. [ME, t. OF: orig., spoil, booty. See ROB]

robe-de-cham·bre (rôb də shäɴ′br), *n. French.* a dressing gown.

Rob·ert I (rŏb′ərt), **1.** ("*Robert the Bruce*"), 1274–1329, king of Scotland 1306–29, who preserved the independence of Scotland by his victory over the English at Bannockburn in 1314. **2.** ("*Robert the Devil*") died 1035, duke of Normandy.

Ro·bert Guis·card (rō bĕr′ gēs kär′). See **Guiscard.**

Rob·erts (rŏb′ərts), *n.* **1.** Elizabeth Madox (măd′-əks), 1886–1941, U.S. poet and novelist. **2.** Frederick Sleigh (slā), Earl, 1832–1914, British field marshal. **3.** Kenneth, 1885–1957, U.S. author.

Rob·ert·son (rŏb′ərt sən), *n.* **1.** William, 1721–93, Scottish historian. **2. Sir William Robert,** 1860–1933, British field marshal.

Robes·pierre (rōbz′pĭr; *Fr.* rô bĕs pyĕr′), *n.* Maximilien François Marie Isidore de (mák sē mē lyäɴ′ frän swä′ má rē′ ē zē dôr′ də), 1758–94, French lawyer and revolutionary leader.

rob·in (rŏb′ĭn), *n.* **1.** a large American thrush, *Merula migratoria*, with chestnut-red breast and belly. **2.** a small European bird, *Erithacus rubecula*, with a yellowish-red breast. Also, **robin redbreast.** [ME *Robyn*, t. OF: m. *Robin*, dim. of *Robert* Robert]

Robin Good·fel·low (gŏod′fĕl′ō), the fairy Puck.

Robin Hood, a traditional English outlaw of the 12th century, a popular hero in many ballads, who robbed the rich to give to the poor. A popular model of courage, generosity, justice, and skill in archery, Robin Hood and his band of followers lived chiefly in Sherwood Forest.

rob·in's-egg blue (rŏb′ĭnz ĕg′), a medium tint of greenish blue, as that of the robin's eggshell.

Rob·in·son (rŏb′ĭn sən), *n.* **1.** Edwin Arlington, 1869–1935, U.S. poet. **2.** James Harvey, 1863–1936, U.S. historian.

Robinson Cru·soe (krŏo′sō), **1.** (in a novel by Defoe) a mariner of York who, shipwrecked, lives adventurously for years upon a small island. **2.** the novel itself (1719).

ro·ble (rō′blā), *n.* **1.** a Californian white oak, *Quercus lobata.* **2.** any of several other trees, esp. of the oak and beech families. [t. Sp. and Pg., g. L *rōbur* oak tree]

rob·o·rant (rŏb′ə rənt), *Med.* —*adj.* **1.** strengthening. —*n.* **2.** a tonic. [t. L: s. *rōborans* ppr., strengthening]

Robber fly,
Asilus sericeus
(Ab. 1 in. long)

ro·bot (rō′bət, rŏb′ət), n. 1. a manufactured or machine-made man. 2. a merely mechanical being; an automaton. [first used in the play *R. U. R.* (by CAPEK), appar. back formation from Czech *robotnik* serf] —**ro′bot·ism**, n. —**ro·bot·is·tic** (rō′bə tĭs′tĭk, rŏb′ə-), adj.

Rob·son (rŏb′sən), n. **Mount**, a mountain in SW Canada, in E British Columbia: highest peak in the Canadian Rockies. 12,972 ft.

ro·bust (rō bŭst′, rō′bŭst), adj. 1. strong and healthy, hardy, or vigorous. 2. strongly or stoutly built: *his robust frame*. 3. suited to or requiring bodily strength or endurance. 4. rough, rude, or boisterous. [t. L: s. *rōbustus*] —**ro·bust′ly**, adv. —**ro·bust′ness**, n. —Syn. 1. sturdy, stalwart. See **strong.** —Ant. 1. feeble.

ro·bus·tious (rō būs′chəs), adj. *Archaic or Humorous.* 1. rough, rude, or boisterous. 2. robust, strong, or stout. —**ro·bus′tious·ly**, adv.

roc (rŏk), n. *Arabian Myth.* a fabulous bird of enormous size and strength. [t. Ar.: m. *rukhkh*, prob. t. Pers.]

Ro·ca (rō′kä), n. **Cape**, a cape in W Portugal, near Lisbon: the western extremity of continental Europe.

roc·am·bole (rŏk′əm bōl′), n. a European liliaceous plant, *Allium Scorodoprasum*, used like garlic. [t. F, t. G: m. *rockenbolle*, lit., distaff bulb (from its shape)]

Ro·cham·beau (rō shän bō′), n. **Jean Baptiste Donatien de Vimeur** (zhän bá tēst′ dō nà syän′ də vē-mœr′), **Count de**, 1725–1807, French general, marshal, and commander of the French army in the American Revolutionary War.

Roch·dale (rŏch′dāl′), n. a city in W England, near Manchester: one of the earliest coöperative societies was formed there, 1844. 86,260 (est. 1956).

Ro·chelle (rō shěl′), n. **La** (lä). See **La Rochelle.**

Ro·chelle powder (rō shěl′), Seidlitz powder.

Rochelle salt, a tartrate of sodium and potassium, used as a laxative. [named after (La) *Rochelle*]

roche mou·ton·née (rōsh mōō tô nē′), *French.* a knob of rock rounded and smoothed by glacial action.

Roch·es·ter (rŏch′ĕs′tər, -ĭs tər), n. 1. a city in W New York, on the Genesee river. 318,611 (1960). 2. a town in SE Minnesota. 40,663 (1960). 3. a city in SE England, in Kent. 43,700; with suburbs, 175,000 (1951).

roch·et (rŏch′ĭt), n. a vestment of linen or lawn, resembling a surplice, worn esp. by bishops and abbots. [ME, t. OF, der. *roc* outer garment, t. Gmc.; cf. OE *rocc* outer garment]

rock[1] (rŏk), n. 1. a large mass of stone forming an eminence, cliff, or the like. 2. *Geol.* a mineral matter of various composition, consolidated or unconsolidated, assembled in masses or considerable quantities in nature, as by the action of heat (*igneous rock*) or of water (*aqueous rock*). **b.** a particular kind of such matter. 3. stone in the mass. 4. something resembling or suggesting a rock. 5. a firm foundation or support: *the Lord is my rock.* 6. *Chiefly Brit.* a kind of hard candy, variously flavored. 7. (*usually pl.*) *U.S. Slang.* a piece of money. 8. *Dial. or Colloq.* a stone of any size. 9. **on the rocks**, **a.** on rocks, as a shipwrecked vessel. **b.** *Colloq.* into or in a state of disaster or ruin. **c.** *Colloq.* without funds or bankrupt. [ME *rokk(e)*, OE *-rocc*, t. ML: s. *rocca*] —**rock′like′**, adj.

rock[2] (rŏk), v.i. 1. to move or sway to and fro or from side to side. 2. to be moved or swayed powerfully with emotion, etc. 3. *Mining.* to be rocked or panned with a rocker: *this ore rocks slowly.* —v.t. 4. to move or sway to and fro or from side to side, esp. gently and soothingly. 5. to lull in security, hope, etc. 6. to move or sway powerfully with emotion, etc. 7. *Engraving.* to roughen the surface of (a copperplate) with a rocker preparatory to scraping a mezzotint. 8. *Mining.* to pan with a cradle: *to rock gravel for gold.* —n. 9. a rocking movement. [ME *rocken*, OE *roccian*, c. MD *rocken*; akin to Icel. *rykkja* jerk] —Syn. 1. See **swing**[1].

rock[3] (rŏk), n. the striped bass. [short for ROCKFISH]

Rockaway

rock-and-roll (rŏk′ən rōl′), n. rock 'n' roll.

rock·a·way (rŏk′ə wā′), n. a light four-wheeled carriage with two (or three) seats and a standing top. [appar. named after *Rockaway*, N.J.]

rock bass, an eastern North American fresh-water food fish, *Ambloplites rupestris*, of the sunfish family, *Centrarchidae*.

rock bottom, the lowest level: *to touch rock bottom.*

rock-bot·tom (rŏk′bŏt′əm), adj. at the lowest limit; extreme lowest: *rock-bottom prices.*

rock-bound (rŏk′bound′), adj. hemmed in by rocks; rocky: *a rock-bound coast.*

rock brake, a fern of the genus *Pellaea.*

rock candy, sugar in large hard cohering crystals.

rock cod, 1. rockfish (def. 3). 2. a small cod, caught about the rocks.

rock crystal, transparent quartz, esp. of the colorless kind.

rock dove, a European pigeon, *Columba livia*, from which most domestic pigeons have been developed.

Rock·e·fel·ler (rŏk′ə fěl′ər), n. 1. **John Davison**, 1839–1937, U.S. capitalist and philanthropist. 2. his son, **John Davison**, 1874–1960, U.S. capitalist and philanthropist. 3. his grandson, **Nelson Aldrich**, born 1908,

U.S. philanthropist; governor of New York since 1959.

rock·er (rŏk′ər), n. 1. one of the curved pieces on which a cradle or a rocking chair rocks. 2. a rocking chair. 3. any of various devices that operate with a rocking motion. 4. *Engraving.* a small steel plate with one curved and toothed edge for roughening a copperplate to make a mezzotint. 5. *Mining.* a cradle (def. 6). 6. an ice skate which has a curved blade.

rocker arm, *Mach.* armlike attachment to a rockshaft.

rock·er·y (rŏk′ə rĭ), n., pl. **-eries**. a mound of rocks and earth for growing ferns or other plants.

rock·et[1] (rŏk′ĭt), n. 1. a cylindrical tube containing combustibles which on being ignited liberate gases whose action propels the tube through the air: used for pyrotechnic effect, signaling, carrying a life line, etc., and for hurling explosives on the enemy. —v.i. 2. to move like a rocket. 3. (of game birds) to fly straight up rapidly when flushed. [t. F: m. *roquet*, or t. It.: m. *rocchetta*, appar. a dim. of *rocca* ROCK[1] with reference to its shape]

rock·et[2] (rŏk′ĭt), n. 1. a European plant, *Eruca sativa*, eaten as a salad. 2. a noxious weed, *Barbarea vulgaris*, in parts of U.S. 3. any of various other (chiefly cruciferous) plants, esp. *Hesperis matronalis*, a garden plant with white, pinkish, or purple flowers which are fragrant after dark. [t. F: m. *roquette*, t. Pr.: m. *rouqueto*, ult. der. L *ērūca* kind of colewort]

rocket gun, any weapon which uses a rocket as a projectile, as a rocket launcher or bazooka.

rocket launcher, *Mil.* a cylindrical weapon used by infantrymen to fire rockets capable of penetrating several inches of armor plate.

rock·et·ry (rŏk′ĭt rĭ), n. the science of rocket design, development, and flight.

Rock fever, undulant fever. [named after the Rock of Gibraltar, where it is prevalent]

rock·fish (rŏk′fĭsh′), n., pl. **-fishes**, (*esp. collectively*) **-fish**. 1. any of various fishes found about rocks. 2. the striped bass, *Roccus saxatilis*. 3. any of the North Pacific marine fishes of the genus *Sebastodes*; rock cod. 4. any other fish of the family *Scorpaenidae*.

rock flower, any of the handsome shrubs of the genus *Crossosoma* (family *Crossosomataceae*), native to the arid regions of the southwestern U.S.

Rock·ford (rŏk′fərd), n. a city in N Illinois. 126,706 (1960).

rock garden, a garden on rocky ground or among rocks, for the growing of alpine or other plants.

Rock·ies (rŏk′ĭz), n.pl. Rocky Mountains.

rocking chair, a chair mounted on rockers, or on springs, so as to permit a rocking back and forth.

rocking horse, a toy horse, as of wood, mounted on rockers, on which children play at riding.

Rock Island, a city in NW Illinois: a port on the Mississippi; government arsenal. 49,641 (1956).

rock 'n' roll, 1. a style of popular music with a heavily accented rhythm, related to hillbilly and blues forms. 2. a dance performed to this music, usually with vigorous, exaggerated movements. 3. of or pertaining to this music. Also, **rock′-and-roll′**, **rock′n roll**.

rock oil, *Chiefly Brit.* petroleum.

rock-ribbed (rŏk′rĭbd′), adj. 1. having ribs or ridges of rock: *the rock-ribbed coast of Maine*. 2. unyielding: *a rock-ribbed conservative*.

rock·rose (rŏk′rōz′), n. 1. any plant of the genus *Cistus* or some allied genus, as *Helianthemum*. 2. any cistaceous plant.

rock salt, common salt (sodium chloride), occurring in extensive, irregular beds in rocklike masses.

rock·shaft (rŏk′shăft′), n. *Mach.* a shaft that rocks or oscillates on its journals instead of revolving, as the shaft of a bell or a pendulum, or a shaft operating the valves of a steam engine.

Rockville Centre Village, a city in SE New York, on Long Island. 26,355 (1960).

rock·weed (rŏk′wēd′), n. a fucoid seaweed growing on rocks exposed at low tide.

rock wool, an insulating material consisting of wool-like fibers made from molten rock or slag by forcing a blast of steam through the liquid.

rock wren, an American wren, *Salpinctes obsoletus*, found principally in the foothills, badlands and mesa country of the western U.S. and Mexico.

rock·y[1] (rŏk′ĭ), adj., **rockier**, **rockiest**. 1. full of or abounding in rocks. 2. consisting of rock. 3. rocklike. 4. firm as a rock. 5. (of the heart, etc.) hard or unfeeling. [f. ROCK[1] + -Y[1]] —**rock′i·ness**, n.

rock·y[2] (rŏk′ĭ), adj., **rockier**, **rockiest**. 1. inclined to rock; tottering or shaky. 2. unpleasantly uncertain. 3. *Colloq. or Slang.* weak; shaky; dizzy. [f. ROCK[2] + -Y[1]]

Rocky Mount, a city in NE North Carolina. 32,147 (1960).

Rocky Mountain goat, a long-haired, white, goatlike, bovid ruminant, *Oreamnos montanus*, of the western North American mountains. It has short black horns.

Rocky Mountain National Park, a national park (405 sq. mi.) in N Colorado. Highest peak, Longs Peak, 14,255 ft.

Rocky Mountains, the chief mountain system in North America, extending from N Mexico to Alaska.

---

b., blend of, blended; c., cognate with; d., dialect, dialectal; der., derived from; f., formed from; g., going back to; m., modification of; r., replacing; s., stem of; t., taken from; ?, perhaps. See the full key on inside cover.

Highest peak, Mt. McKinley (in Alaska), 20,300 ft.; Elbert Peak, 14,431 ft. Also, **Rockies.**

Rocky Mountain spotted fever, *Pathol.* a disease of the typhus-rickettsia group characterized by high fever, pains in joints, bones, and muscles, and a cutaneous eruption, and caused by Rickettsia transmitted by ticks. It was first found in the Rocky Mountain area, but is now more widely distributed.

ro·co·co (rəkō′kō; *Fr.* rô kôkô′), *n.* **1.** a style of architecture and decoration, originating in France about 1720, evolved from baroque types and distinguished by its elegant refinement in using different materials (stucco, metal, wood, mirrors, tapestries) for a delicate overall effect and by its ornament of shellwork, foliage, etc. —*adj.* **2.** in the rococo style. **3.** tastelessly or clumsily florid. **4.** antiquated. [t. F, said to be der. *rocaille* rockwork, pebble- or shellwork, der. *roc* rock[1]]

rod (rŏd), *n.* **1.** a stick, wand, staff, shaft, or the like, of wood, metal, or other material. **2.** a straight, slender shoot or stem of any woody plant, whether growing upon or cut from the plant. **3.** a pole used in angling or fishing. **4.** a stick used to measure with. **5.** a linear measure of 5½ yards or 16½ feet; a perch or pole. **6.** a square perch or pole (30¼ square yards). **7.** a stick, or a bundle of sticks or switches bound together, used as an instrument of punishment. **8.** punishment or chastisement. **9.** a wand or staff carried as a symbol of office, authority, power, etc. **10.** authority; sway; tyrannical rule. **11.** (in Biblical use) an offshoot or branch of a family; a scion; a tribe. **12.** *U.S. Slang.* a pistol or revolver. **13.** *Anat.* one of the rodlike cells in the retina of the eye which respond to dim light. **14.** *Bacteriol.* any microörganism which is neither spherical nor spiral, but elongated. See illus. under **bacteria.** [ME and OE *rodd*; appar. akin to Icel. *rudda* kind of club]

rode (rōd), *v.* pt. of **ride.**

ro·dent (rō′dənt), *adj.* **1.** belonging or pertaining to the *Rodentia*, the order of gnawing or nibbling mammals, that includes the mice, squirrels, beavers, etc. **2.** gnawing. —*n.* **3.** a rodent mammal. [t. L: s. *rōdens*, ppr., gnawing] —**ro′dent·like′,** *adj.*

ro·de·o (rō′dĭ ō′, rōdā′ō), *n., pl.* **-deos.** *U.S.* **1.** an exhibition of the skills of cowboys for public entertainment. **2.** a roundup of cattle. [t. Sp.: cattle ring, der. *rodear* go round, der. *rueda* wheel, g. L *rota*]

Ro·di (rō′dē), *n.* Italian name of **Rhodes** (defs. 3 and 4).

Ro·din (rōdăn′), *n.* **Auguste** (ōgyst′), 1840–1917, French sculptor.

rod·man (rŏd′mən), *n., pl.* **-men.** **1.** one who handles a rod. **2.** the man who carries the leveling rod in surveying.

Rod·ney (rŏd′nĭ), *n.* **George Brydges** (brĭj′ĭz), **Baron,** 1718–92, British admiral.

rod·o·mon·tade (rŏd′ə mŏn tād′, -tăd′), *n., adj., v.,* **-taded, -tading.** —*n.* **1.** vainglorious boasting or bragging; pretentious, blustering talk. —*adj.* **2.** bragging. —*v.i.* **3.** to boast; brag; talk big. [t. F, it. It.: m. *rodomontata*]

roe[1] (rō), *n.* **1.** the mass of eggs, or spawn, within the ovarian membrane of the female fish (**hard roe**). **2.** the milt or sperm of the male fish (**soft roe**). **3.** the eggs of various crustaceans, as the coral of the lobster. [ME *row(e)*, c. OHG *rogo*]

roe[2] (rō), *n., pl.* **roes,** (*esp. collectively*) **roe.** the roe deer. [ME *roo,* OE *rā,* earlier *rāha,* c. G *reh*]

roe·buck (rō′bŭk′), *n.* a male roe deer.

roe deer, a small, agile Old World deer, *Capreolus capreolus,* the male of which has three-pointed antlers. [OE *rāh-dēor.* See ROE[2], DEER]

European roe deer,
Capreolus capreolus
(2½ ft. high at the shoulder)

Roent·gen (rĕnt′gən; *Ger.* rœnt′gən), *n.* **1. Wilhelm Konrad** (vĭl′hĕlm kŏn′rät), 1845–1923, German physicist, discoverer of x-rays. **2.** (*l.c.*) the amount of x- or gamma-radiation that will produce ions in air containing a quantity of positive or negative electricity equal to one electrostatic unit in 0.001293 grams of air. —*adj.* **3.** (*sometimes l.c.*) pertaining to Roentgen rays. **4.** pertaining to Wilhelm Konrad Roentgen. Also, **Röntgen.**

roent·gen·ize (rĕnt′gə nīz′), *v.t.,* **-ized, -izing.** to subject to the action of Roentgen rays.

roent·gen·o·gram (rĕnt′gə nə grăm′), *n.* a photograph made with Roentgen rays.

roent·gen·o·graph (rĕnt′gə nə grăf′, -gräf′), *n.* roentgenogram. —**roent·gen·og·ra·phy** (rĕnt′gə nŏg′rə fĭ), *n.*

roent·gen·ol·o·gy (rĕnt′gə nŏl′ə jĭ), *n.* that branch of medicine concerned with diagnosis and therapeutics through Roentgen rays. —**roent′gen·ol′o·gist,** *n.*

roent·gen·o·paque (rĕnt′gən ō pāk′), *adj.* not permitting the passage of Roentgen rays.

roent·gen·o·par·ent (rĕnt′gən ō pâr′ənt), *adj.* visible in Roentgen rays.

roent·gen·o·ther·a·py (rĕnt′gən ō thĕr′ə pĭ), *n.* treatment of disease by means of Roentgen rays.

Roentgen ray, (*sometimes l.c.*) x-ray. Also, **Röntgen ray.**

Roe·rich (rœ′rĭкн), *n.* **Nicholas Konstantinovitch** (nĭk′ə ləs kôn′stän tē′nô vĭch), 1874–1947, U.S. painter, born in Russia.

ro·ga·tion (rōgā′shən), *n.* **1.** (*usually pl.*) *Eccles.* solemn supplication, esp. as chanted during procession on the three days (**Rogation Days**) before Ascension Day. **2.** *Rom. Hist.* **a.** the proposing by the consuls or tribunes of a law to be passed by the people. **b.** a law so proposed. [ME *rogacio(u)n,* t. L: m.s. *rogātio*]

rog·a·to·ry (rŏg′ə tôr′ĭ), *adj.* pertaining to asking or requesting: *a rogatory commission.* [t. ML: m.s. *rogātōrius,* f. L *rogātor* asker, solicitor]

rog·er (rŏj′ər), *interj. U.S. Slang.* **1.** all right; O.K. **2.** received.

Rog·ers (rŏj′ərz), *n.* **Will,** 1879–1935, U.S. actor and humorist.

rogue (rōg), *n., v.,* **rogued, roguing.** —*n.* **1.** a dishonest person. **2.** a rascal or scamp. **3.** a playfully mischievous person. **4.** an elephant or other animal of savage disposition and solitary life. **5.** *Biol.* an individual varying markedly from the normal, usually inferior. —*v.i.* **6.** to live or act like a rogue. —*v.t.* **7.** to cheat. **8.** to uproot or destroy, as plants which do not conform to a desired standard. **9.** to perform this operation upon: *to rogue a field.* [appar. short for obs. *roger* begging vagabond, b. ROAMER and BEGGAR] —**Syn. 1.** See **knave.**

ro·guer·y (rō′gər ĭ), *n., pl.* **-gueries. 1.** roguish conduct; rascality. **2.** a rascally act; playful mischief.

rogues′ gallery, a collection of portraits of criminals, as at police headquarters.

rogue′s march, derisive music played to accompany a person's expulsion from a regiment, community, etc.

ro·guish (rō′gĭsh), *adj.* **1.** pertaining to, characteristic of, or acting like a rogue; knavish or rascally. **2.** playfully mischievous: *a roguish smile.* —**ro′guish·ly,** *adv.* —**ro′guish·ness,** *n.*

roil (roil), *v.t.* **1.** to render (water, etc.) turbid by stirring up sediment. **2.** to disturb or disquiet; irritate; vex. [t. obs. F: m. *ruiler* mix up mortar, der. OF *rieule* mason's formboard, g. L *rēgula* rule]

roil·y (roil′ĭ), *adj.* turbid; muddy.

roist·er (rois′tər), *v.i.* **1.** to act in a swaggering, boisterous, or uproarious manner. **2.** to revel noisily or without restraint. [v. use of *roister,* n., t. F: m. *ru(i)stre* ruffian, boor, der. *ru(i)ste* RUSTIC, n.] —**roist′er·er,** *n.* —**roist′er·ous,** *adj.*

Ro·land (rō′lənd), *n.* Charlemagne's greatest legendary paladin, famous for his prowess and death in the battle of Roncesvalles (A.D. 778), and also for his five days' combat with Oliver, another paladin, in which neither gained the advantage (whence **a Roland for an Oliver** for an equally effective retort or retaliation).

role (rōl), *n.* **1.** the part or character which an actor presents in a play. **2.** proper or customary function: *the teacher's role in society.* Also, **rôle.** [t. F: prop., the roll. (as of paper) containing an actor's part]

roll (rōl), *v.i.* **1.** to move along a surface by turning over and over, as a ball or a wheel. **2.** to move or be moved on wheels, as a vehicle or its occupants. **3.** to move onward or advance in a stream or with an undulating motion, as water, waves, or smoke. **4.** to extend in undulations, as land. **5.** to move (fol. by *on,* etc.) or pass (fol. by *away,* etc.), as time. **6.** to move (fol. by *round*) as in a cycle, as seasons. **7.** to perform a periodical revolution in an orbit, as a heavenly body. **8.** to continue with or have a deep, prolonged sound, as thunder, etc. **9.** to trill, as a bird. **10.** to turn over, or over and over, as a person or animal lying down. **11.** *Colloq.* to luxuriate or abound (in wealth, etc.). **12.** to turn round in different directions, as the eyes in their sockets. **13.** to sway or rock from side to side, as a ship (opposed to *pitch*). **14.** to sail with a rolling motion. **15.** to walk with a rolling or swaying gait. **16.** to form into a roll, or curl up from itself. **17.** to admit of being rolled up, as a material. **18.** to spread out from being rolled up (fol. by *out,* etc.). **19.** to spread out as under a roller. **20.** to cast the dice in a game of craps. —*v.t.* **21.** to cause to move along a surface by turning over and over, as a ball, a ball, or a hoop. **22.** to move along on wheels or rollers; to convey in a wheeled vehicle. **23.** to drive, impel, or cause to flow onward with a sweeping motion. **24.** to utter or give forth with a full, flowing, continuous sound. **25.** to trill: *to roll one's r's.* **26.** to turn over, or over and over. **27.** to turn round in different directions, as the eyes. **28.** to cause to sway or rock from side to side, as a ship. **29.** to wrap round an axis, round upon itself, or into a roll, ball, or the like. **30.** to make by forming a roll: *to roll a cigarette.* **31.** to spread out from being rolled up (fol. by *out,* etc.). **32.** to wrap, infold, or envelop, as in some covering. **33.** to operate upon with a roller or rollers. **34.** to spread out, level, compact, or the like, with a rolling pin, cylinder, etc. **35.** to beat (a drum) with rapid, continuous strokes. **36.** *Print.* to apply ink with a roller or series of rollers. —*n.* **37.** a piece of parchment, paper, or the like, as for writing, etc., which is or may be rolled up; a scroll. **38.** a list, register, or catalogue. **39.** a list containing the names of the persons belonging to any company, class, society, etc. **40.** anything rolled up in cylindrical form. **41.** a number of papers or the like rolled up to-

---

ăct, āble, dâre, ärt; ĕbb, ēqual; Yf, Ice; hŏt, ōver, ôrder, oil, bŏŏk, ōōze; out; ŭp, ūse, ûrge; ə = a in alone; ch, chief; g, give; ng, ring; sh, shoe; th, thin; ŧħ, that; zh, vision. See the full key on inside cover.

gether. **42.** a quantity of cloth, wallpaper, or the like, rolled up in cylindrical form (often forming a definite measure). **43.** a cylindrical or rounded mass of something: *rolls of fat.* **44.** some article of cylindrical or rounded form, as a molding. **45.** a cylindrical piece upon which something is rolled along to facilitate moving. **46.** a cylinder upon which something is rolled up. **47.** a roller with which something is spread out, leveled, crushed, compacted, or the like. **48.** *Cookery.* **a.** a thin cake spread with jelly or the like and rolled up. **b.** a small cake of bread, orig. and still often rolled or doubled on itself before baking. **c.** food which is rolled up. **d.** meat rolled up and cooked. **49.** act of rolling. **50.** undulation of surface: *the roll of a prairie.* **51.** sonorous or rhythmical flow of words. **52.** a deep, prolonged sound, as of thunder, etc.: *the deep roll of a breaking wave.* **53.** the trill of certain birds. **54.** the continuous sound of a drum rapidly beaten. **55.** a rolling motion, as of a ship. **56.** a rolling or swaying gait. **57.** *Aeron.* a single complete rotation of an airplane around the axis of the fuselage with little loss of altitude or change of direction. **58.** *U.S. Slang.* a wad of paper currency. **59.** *U.S. Slang.* any amount of money. [ME *roll(en)*, t. OF: m. *roller*, ult. der. L *rotula*, dim. of *rota* wheel] —**Syn. 39.** See *list*[1].

Rol·land (rôlän′), *n.* **Romain** (rô mǎn′), 1866–1944, French novelist, music critic, and dramatist.

roll·back (rōl′bǎk′), *n.* a return to a lower level of prices, wages, etc., as by government order.

roll call, 1. the calling of a list of names, as of soldiers or students, to find out who is absent. **2.** a military signal for this, as one given by a drum.

roll·er (rō′lər), *n.* **1.** one who or that which rolls; a cylinder, wheel, or the like, upon which something is rolled along. **2.** a cylindrical body, revolving on a fixed axis, esp. one to facilitate the movement of something passed over or around it. **3.** a cylindrical body upon which cloth or other material is rolled up. **4.** a cylindrical body for rolling over something to be spread out, leveled, crushed, compacted, impressed, inked, etc. **5.** any of various other revolving cylindrical bodies, as the barrel of a music box. **6.** a long, swelling wave advancing steadily. **7.** a rolled bandage. **8.** *Ornith.* **a.** a variety of tumbler pigeon. **b.** any of the Old World nonpasserine birds constituting the family *Coraciidae*, esp. the **common roller,** *Coracias garrulus.* **c.** a variety of canary bird, remarkable for rolling or trilling.

roller bearing, *Mach.* a bearing in which the shaft or journal turns upon a number of steel rollers running in an annular track.

roller coaster, a twining, sloping railway with open cars ridden for the thrills of speed and rapid turns.

roller mill, any mill which pulverizes or otherwise changes material by passing it between rolls.

roller skate, a form of skate with small wheels or rollers instead of a runner, for use on a smooth floor, etc.

roll·er-skate (rōl′ər skāt′), *v.i.* **-skated, -skating.** to glide about by means of roller skates.

roller towel, a long towel sewed together at the ends and hung on a roller.

roll film, *Photog.* a rolled strip of sensitized film for taking successive still pictures.

rol·lick (rŏl′ĭk), *v.i.* to move or act in a careless, frolicsome manner; behave in a free, hearty, gay, or jovial way. [b. ROMP and FROLIC]

rol·lick·ing (rŏl′ĭk ĭng), *adj.* swaggering and jolly: *a pair of rollicking drunken sailors.* Also, **rol·lick·some** (rŏl′ĭk səm).

roll·ing (rō′lĭng), *n.* **1.** the action, motion, or sound of anything that rolls. —*adj.* **2.** that rolls. **3.** rising and falling in gentle slopes, as land. **4.** moving in undulating billows, as clouds or waves. **5.** rocking or swaying from side to side. **6.** turning or folding over, as a collar. **7.** producing a deep, continuous sound.

rolling hitch, a kind of hitch which is made round a spar or the like with the end of a rope, and which jams when the rope is pulled.

rolling mill, 1. a mill or establishment where (heated) iron or other metal is rolled into sheets, bars, or the like. **2.** a machine or set of rollers for rolling out or shaping metal, etc.

rolling pin, a cylinder of wood or other material for rolling out dough, etc.

rolling stock, the wheeled vehicles of a railroad, including locomotives, cars, etc.

Rol·lo (rŏl′ō), *n.* died A.D. 932?, Scandinavian chieftain: first duke of Normandy. Also, **Hrolf.**

roll-top (rōl′tŏp′), *adj.* fitted with a cover that moves on rollers: *a roll-top desk.*

roll·way (rōl′wā′), *n.* **1.** a place on which things are rolled or moved on rollers. **2.** a place where logs are rolled into a stream for transportation. **3.** a pile of logs at the side of a stream awaiting transportation.

Röl·vaag (rœl′väg), *n.* Ole Edvart (ō′lə ĕd′värt), 1876–1931, U.S. novelist, born in Norway.

ro·ly-po·ly (rō′lĭ pō′lĭ), *adj., n., pl.* **-lies.** —*adj.* **1.** short and plumply round, as a person, a young animal, etc. —*n.* **2.** a roly-poly person or thing. **3.** *Chiefly Brit.* a sheet of biscuit dough spread with jam, fruit, or the like, rolled up and steamed or baked. [earlier *rowle powle,* ? var. of *roll ye, poll ye.* See ROLL, v., POLL, v. (def. 19)] —**Ant. 1.** scrawny.

Rom. 1. Roman. **2.** Romance; Romanic. **3.** Romans (New Testament).

rom., roman type.

Ro·ma (rō′mä), *n.* Italian name of **Rome** (def. 1).

Ro·ma·gna (rô mä′nyä), *n.* a former province of the Papal States, in NE Italy. *Cap.:* Ravenna.

Ro·ma·ic (rō mā′ĭk), *n.* Modern Greek. [t. Gk.: m.s. *Rhōmaïkós* Roman, used of the Eastern empire]

ro·maine (rō mān′), *n.* a variety of cos with long, comparatively narrow, crisp leaves. [t. F, fem. of *romain* ROMAN]

Ro·mains (rô mǎn′), *n.* **Jules** (zhȳl), born 1885, French novelist, poet, and dramatist.

Ro·man (rō′man), *adj.* **1.** of or pertaining to Rome, ancient or modern, or its inhabitants. **2.** of a kind or character regarded as typical of the ancient Romans. **3.** (*usually l.c.*) designating or pertaining to the style of printing types most commonly used in modern books, etc., of which the text of this dictionary is an example. **4.** of or pertaining to the Roman Catholic Church. —*n.* **5.** a native, inhabitant, or citizen of ancient or modern Rome. **6.** the Itali.an of Rome. **7.** (*usually l.c.*) roman type or letters. **8** Latin. **9.** *Colloq.* a member of the Roman Catholic Church. [OE, t. L: s. *Rōmānus*; r. ME *Romain*, t. OF]

ro·man (rō mǎn′), *n. French.* a metrical narrative, esp. in medieval French literature.

ro·man à clef (rô mǎn′ à klĕ′), *French.* a novel in which actual persons and events are disguised as fiction. [F: lit., novel with a key]

Roman arch, a semicircular arch.

Roman architecture, the architecture of the ancient Romans, characterized by rational design and planning, the use of vaulting and concrete masonry, and the use of the classical orders only sporadically for purposes of architectural articulation and decoration.

Roman calendar, the ancient Roman calendar, the ancestor of our present calendars.

Roman candle, a kind of firework consisting of a tube which sends out a shower of sparks and a succession of balls of fire.

Roman Catholic, 1. of or pertaining to the Roman Catholic Church. **2.** a member of the Roman Catholic Church.

Roman Catholic Church, the Christian church of which the Pope, or Bishop of Rome, is the supreme head.

Roman Catholicism, the faith, practice, membership, and government of the Roman Catholic Church.

ro·mance[1] (*n.* rō mǎns′, rō′mǎns; *v.* rō mǎns′), *n., v.,* **-manced, -mancing,** *adj.* —*n.* **1.** a tale depicting heroic or marvelous achievements, colorful events or scenes, chivalrous devotion, unusual, even supernatural, experiences, or other matters of a kind to appeal to the imagination. **2.** the world, life, or conditions depicted in such tales. **3.** a medieval tale, orig. one in verse and in some Romance dialect, treating of heroic personages or events: *the Arthurian romances.* **4.** a made-up story; fanciful or extravagant invention or exaggeration. **5.** romantic spirit or sentiment. **6.** romantic character or quality. **7.** a romantic affair or experience; a love affair. —*v.i.* **8.** to invent or relate romances; indulge in fanciful or extravagant stories. **9.** to think or talk romantically. —*adj.* **10.** (*cap.*) pertaining to the Romance languages. [ME *romanz,* t. OF, g. VL *Rōmānicē,* adv., in Romance (i.e., in one of the Romance languages), der. L *Rōmānicus* Romanic] —**ro·manc′er,** *n.* —**Syn. 1.** See **novel**[1].

ro·mance[2] (rō mǎns′), *n.* **1.** *Music.* a short, simple melody, vocal or instrumental, of tender character. **2.** *Spanish Lit.* a short epic narrative poem; historical ballad. [t. F, t. Sp.: kind of poem, ballad, t. OF: m. *romanz.* See ROMANCE[1]]

Romance language, any of the group of languages which have developed out of Latin, in their historical (from 800) or modern forms, principally, Sardinian, Dalmatian (extinct), Rumanian, Italian, Rhaeto-Romanic, French, Provençal, Catalan, Spanish, and Portuguese. [t. OF: from the phrase *langue romance* (now *langues romanes*), lit., Romanic language]

Roman Curia, 1. the judicial and executive organizations of the papal see comprising the government of the Catholic Church. **2.** the court of the papal see.

Roman Empire, 1. the lands and peoples subject to the authority of ancient Rome. **2.** the form of government established in ancient Rome in 27 B.C., comprising the Principate or Early Empire (27 B.C. to A.D. 284) and the Autocracy or Later Empire (from A.D. 284). **3.** a later empire, as that of Charlemagne or the Byzantine Empire, regarded as a restoration or continuation of the ancient Roman empire or one of its branches.

Roman Empire, A.D. 180

Ro·man·esque (rō′mə nĕsk′), *adj.* **1.** noting or pertaining to the style of architecture which, developing from earlier medieval and Near Eastern types, prevailed in western and southern Europe from the late 10th until the 12th and 13th centuries, characterized by the rich

---

b., blend of, blended; c., cognate with; d., dialect, dialectal; der., derived from; f., formed from; g., going back to; m., modification of; r., replacing; s., stem of; t., taken from; ?, perhaps. See the full key on inside cover.

outline of the exterior (towers), the clear organization of the interior (bays), heavy walls, small windows, and the use of open timber roofs and groin, barrel, or rib vaults. **2.** noting or pertaining to the corresponding styles of sculpture, ornament, and painting. **3.** (*l.c.*) of or pertaining to fanciful or extravagant literature, as romance or fable; fanciful. —*n.* **4.** the Romanesque style of art or architecture. [f. ROMAN + -ESQUE. Cf. F *romanesque* romantic]

ro·man-fleuve (rô mäN′ flœv′), *n.* French. See **saga novel**. [F: lit., stream-novel]

Ro·mâ·nia (rō mä′nyə; *Rum.* rô mœ′nyä), *n.* Rumanian name of **Rumania**.

Ro·man·ic (rō măn′ĭk), *adj.* **1.** derived from the Romans. **2.** pertaining to the Romance languages. —*n.* **3.** Romance language. [t. L: s. *Rōmānicus* (def. 1)]

Ro·man·ism (rō′mə nĭz′əm), *n.* (usually in derogatory use) Roman Catholicism.

Ro·man·ist (rō′mən ĭst), *n.* **1.** a member of the Roman Catholic Church. **2.** one versed in Roman institutions, law, etc.

Ro·man·ize (rō′mə nīz′), *v.*, **-ized, -izing.** —*v.t.* **1.** to render Roman Catholic. **2.** to make Roman in character. —*v.i.* **3.** to conform to Roman Catholic doctrine, etc.; become Roman Catholic. **4.** to follow Roman practices. —**Ro′man·i·za′tion,** *n.*

Roman law, the system of jurisprudence elaborated by the ancient Romans, forming the basis of civil law in many countries.

Roman nose, a nose having a prominent upper part or bridge.

Roman numerals, the numerals in the ancient Roman system of notation, still used for certain limited purposes. The common basic symbols are I(=1), V(=5), X(=10), L(=50), C(=100), D(=500), and M(=1000). Integers are written according to these two rules: If a letter is immediately followed by one of equal or lesser value, the two values are added; thus, XX equals 20, XV equals 15, VI equals 6. If a letter is immediately followed by one of greater value, however, the first is subtracted from the second; thus IV equals 4, XL equals 40, CM equals 900. Examples: XLVII(=47), CXVI (=116), MCXX(=1120), MCMXIV(=1914). The Roman numerals for one to nine are: I, II, III, IV, V, VI, VII, VIII, IX. Roman numerals may be written in lower-case letters, though they appear more commonly in capitals. A bar over a letter multiplies it by 1000; thus X̄ equals 10,000.

Ro·ma·nov (rō′mə nôf′, -nôf′; *Russ.* rŏ mä′nŏf), *n.* **1.** the imperial dynasty which ruled Russia from 1613 to the abdication of Nicholas II in 1917. **2.** Mikhail Feodorovich (mĭ hä ēl′ fĭ ô′dŏ rō′vĭch), 1596–1645, Czar of Russia, 1613–45. **3.** family of rulers in Russia, 1613–1917. Also, **Ro′ma·noff′.**

Roman punch, a lemon water ice flavored with rum or other spirit.

Roman rite, the liturgical forms of Mass and sacrament used in the Roman Catholic Church.

Ro·mans (rō′mənz), *n.* (in the New Testament) one of the most important doctrinal epistles of Paul, written to the Christian community at Rome.

Ro·mansh (rō mänsh′, -mänsh′), *n.* **1.** a Rhaeto-Romanic language spoken in the Swiss canton Grisons. It has equal standing with German, French, and Italian as one of the official languages of Switzerland. **2.** Rhaeto-Romanic in general. [t. Rhaetian: m. *romansch* Romanic]

ro·man·tic (rō măn′tĭk), *adj.* **1.** of, pertaining to, or of the nature of romance; characteristic or suggestive of the world of romance: *a romantic adventure.* **2.** proper to romance rather than to real or practical life; fanciful; unpractical; quixotic: *romantic ideas.* **3.** imbued with or dominated by the ideas, spirit, or sentiment prevailing in romance. **4.** of or pertaining to a style of literature and art characterized by freedom of treatment, subordination of form to matter, imagination, picturesqueness, etc. (opposed to **classical**). **5.** imaginary, fictitious, or fabulous. —*n.* **6.** a romantic person. **7.** a romanticist. **8.** (*pl.*) romantic ideas, ways, etc. [f. F: m. *romantique,* der. *romant* older form of *roman* romance, novel. See ROMANCE¹] —**ro·man′ti·cal·ly,** *adv.*

ro·man·ti·cism (rō măn′tə sĭz′əm), *n.* **1.** romantic spirit or tendency. **2.** the romantic style or movement in literature and art, or adherence to its principles (as contrasted with *classicism*).

ro·man·ti·cist (rō măn′tə sĭst), *n.* an adherent of romanticism in literature or art.

ro·man·ti·cize (rō măn′tə sīz′), *v.t.*, **-cized, -cizing.** to make romantic; invest with a romantic character: *she romanticized her work as an editor.*

Romantic Movement, the late 18th- and early 19th-century movement in France, Germany, England, and America to establish romanticism in art and literature.

Rom·a·ny (rŏm′ə nĭ), *n.*, *pl.* **-nies,** *adj.* —*n.* **1.** a Gypsy. **2.** Gypsies collectively. **3.** the Indic language of the Gypsies, its various forms differing greatly because of local influences. —*adj.* **4.** pertaining to Gypsies, their language, or customs. [t. Gypsy: m. *Romani,* fem. and pl. of *Romano,* adj., der. *Rom* gypsy, man, husband]

ro·maunt (rō mänt′, -mônt′), *n.* Archaic. a romance, or romantic poem or tale. [t. AF, var. of OF *romant* ROMANCE¹]

Rom·berg (rŏm′bûrg), *n.* **Sigmund** (sĭg′mənd), 1887–1951, Hungarian composer of light opera in U.S.

Rom. Cath., Roman Catholic.

Rom. Cath. Ch., Roman Catholic Church.

Rome (rōm), *n.* **1.** Italian, **Roma.** the capital of Italy, in the central part, on the Tiber: the ancient capital of the Roman Empire; the site of Vatican City, seat of authority of the Roman Catholic Church. 1,751,000 (est. 1954). **2.** the Roman Catholic Church. **3.** Roman Catholicism. **4.** a city in central New York, E of Oneida Lake. 51,646 (1960). **5.** a city in NW Georgia. 32,226 (1960).

Ro·me·o and Juliet (rō′mĭ ō′), a tragedy (produced between 1591 and 1596), by Shakespeare.

Rom·ish (rō′mĭsh), *adj.* (often in derogatory use) of or pertaining to Rome as the center of the Roman Catholic Church; Roman Catholic.

Rom·ma·ny (rŏm′ə nĭ), *n.*, *pl.* **-nies,** *adj.* Romany.

Rom·mel (rŭm′əl; *Ger.* rôm′əl), *n.* **Erwin** (ĕr′vĕn), 1891–1944, German field marshal; commander of German forces in North Africa in World War II.

Rom·ney (rŏm′nĭ, rŭm′-), *n.* **George,** 1734–1802, British painter.

romp (rŏmp), *v.i.* **1.** to play or frolic in a lively or boisterous manner. **2.** to run or go rapidly and without effort, as in racing. —*n.* **3.** a romping frolic. **4.** a romping person, esp. a girl. [var. of obs. *ramp* rough woman, lit., one who ramps. See RAMP, v.]

romp·ers (rŏm′pərz), *n.pl.* a loose outer garment combining a waist and knickerbockers, worn by young children.

romp·ish (rŏm′pish), *adj.* given to romping. —**romp′-ish·ness,** *n.*

Rom·u·lus (rŏm′yə ləs), *n.* *Rom. Legend.* the founder of Rome (753 B.C.) and its first king. The son of Mars by Rhea Silvia, he and his twin brother Remus (whom he eventually killed) were abandoned as infants but suckled by a wolf. The Romans deified him as Quirinus.

Ron·ces·valles (rŏn′sə vălz′; *Sp.* rōn′thĕs vä′lyĕs), *n.* a village in N Spain, in the Pyrenees: defeat of part of Charlemagne's army and the death of Roland, A.D. 778. French, **Ronce·vaux** (rôNs vō′).

ron·deau (rŏn′dō, rŏn dō′), *n.*, *pl.* **-deaux.** French Pros. a short poem of fixed form, consisting of thirteen (or ten) lines on two rhymes and having the opening words or phrase used in two places as an unrhymed refrain. [see RONDEL]

ron·del (rŏn′dəl), *n.* Pros. a short poem of fixed form, consisting usually of fourteen lines on two rhymes, of which four are made up of the initial couplet repeated in the middle and at the end (the second line of the couplet sometimes being omitted at the end). [ME *rondeal,* t. OF: m. *rondel, rondeau,* dim. of *rond* round]

ron·de·let (rŏn′də lĕt′), *n.* a short poem of fixed form, consisting of five lines on two rhymes, and having the opening words or word used after the second and fifth lines as an unrhymed refrain.

ron·do (rŏn′dō, rŏn dō′), *n.*, *pl.* **-dos.** Music. a work or movement, often the last movement of a sonata, having one principal subject which is stated at least three times in the same key and to which return is made after the introduction of each subordinate theme. [t. It., t. F.: m *rondeau.* See RONDEL]

ron·dure (rŏn′jər), *n.* Poetic. **1.** a circle. **2.** roundness. [t. F: m. *rondeur,* der. *rond* round]

Ron·sard (rôN sär′), *n.* **Pierre de** (pyĕr də), 1524–85, French poet.

Rönt·gen (rĕnt′gən; *Ger.* rœnt′gən), *adj.* Roentgen.

Röntgen ray, Roentgen ray.

rood (rōōd), *n.* **1.** a crucifix, esp. a large one at the entrance to the choir or chancel of a medieval church, often supported on a rood beam or rood screen. **2.** Archaic. the cross on which Christ died. **3.** a cross as used in crucifixion. **4.** a unit of length varying locally from 5½ to 8 yards. **5.** a unit of land measure, equal to 40 square rods or ¼ acre. **6.** a unit of 1 square rod, or thereabouts. [ME; OE *rōd,* akin to G *rute.* See ROD]

rood beam, a beam extending across the entrance to the choir or chancel of a church to support the rood, and usually forming the head of a rood screen.

rood loft, a loft or gallery over a rood screen.

rood screen, a screen, often of elaborate design, and properly surmounted by a rood, separating the nave from the choir or chancel of a church.

roof (rōōf, rŏof), *n.* **1.** the external upper covering of a house or other building. **2.** a house. **3.** the highest part or summit. **4.** something which in form or position resembles the roof of a house, as the top of a car, the upper part of the mouth, etc. —*v.t.* **5.** to provide or cover with a roof. [ME; OE *hrōf,* akin to G D roof cover, cabin]

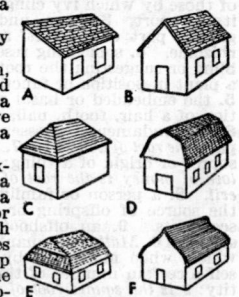

Types of roofs
A. Lean-to; B. Saddle or ridge; C. Hip; D. Gambrel; E. Mansard; F. Ogee

roof·er (rōōf′ər, rŏof′-), *n.* one who makes or repairs roofs.

ăct, āble, dâre, ärt; ĕbb, ēqual; ĭf, īce; hŏt, ōver, ôrder, oil, bŏŏk, ōoze, out; ŭp, ūse, ûrge; ə = a in alone; ch, chief; g, give; ng, ring; sh, shoe; th, thin; ŧħ, that; zh, vision. See the full key on inside cover.

roof garden, 1. a garden on the flat roof of a house or other building. **2.** the top, or top story, of a building, having a garden, restaurant, or the like.

roof·ing (rōōf′ĭng, rŏŏf′-), *n.* **1.** act of covering with a roof. **2.** material for roofs. **3.** a roof.

roof·less (rōōf′lĭs, rŏŏf′-), *adj.* **1.** having no roof. **2.** without the shelter of a house.

roof·tree (rōōf′trē′, rŏŏf′-), *n.* **1.** the ridgepole of a roof. **2.** the roof itself. **3.** a shelter or home.

rook[1] (rŏŏk), *n.* **1.** a black European crow, *Corvus frugilegus,* of a gregarious disposition and given to nesting in colonies in trees about buildings. **2.** a sharper, as at cards or dice; a swindler. —*v.t.* **3.** to cheat; fleece; swindle. [ME *roke,* OE *hrōc,* c. G *ruch*]

rook[2] (rŏŏk), *n. Chess.* a piece having the power to move any unobstructed distance in a straight line forward, backward, or sidewise; a castle. [ME *rok,* t. OF, ult. t. Pers.: m. *rukhkh*]

rook·er·y (rŏŏk′ər·ĭ), *n., pl.* **-eries.** *Brit.* **1.** a colony of rooks. **2.** a place where rooks congregate to breed. **3.** a breeding place or colony of other birds or animals, as penguins, seals, etc. **4.** a crowded tenement house.

rook·ie (rŏŏk′ĭ), *n. Slang.* a raw recruit, orig. in the army, and hence in any service.

rook·y (rŏŏk′ĭ), *adj.* full of or frequented by rooks.

room (rōōm, rŏŏm), *n.* **1.** a portion of space within a building or other structure, separated by walls or partitions from other parts: *a dining room.* **2.** (*pl.*) lodgings or quarters, as in a house or building. **3.** the persons present in a room: *the whole room laughed.* **4.** space, or extent of space, occupied by or available for something: *the desk takes up too much room.* **5.** opportunity or scope for or to do something: *room for improvement or doubt.* —*v.i.* **6.** to occupy a room or rooms; lodge. [ME *roume,* OE *rūm,* c. D *ruim,* G *raum*]

room·er (rōōm′ər, rŏŏm′-), *n. U.S.* a lodger.

room·ette (rōōm·ĕt′, rŏŏm-), *n.* a small private compartment in the sleeping car of a train, usually for one person, containing its own washroom facilities and a bed that folds against the wall when not in use. [f. ROOM + -ETTE]

room·ful (rōōm′fŏŏl′, rŏŏm′-), *n., pl.* **-fuls.** an amount or number sufficient to fill a room.

rooming house, a lodging house.

room·mate (rōōm′māt′, rŏŏm′-), *n.* one who shares a room with another or others.

room·y (rōōm′ĭ, rŏŏm′ĭ), *adj.* **roomier, roomiest.** affording ample room; spacious; large. —**room′i·ly,** *adv.* —**room′i·ness,** *n.*

roor·back (rŏŏr′băk), *n. U.S.* a false and more or less damaging report circulated for political effect. [from *Roorback,* a pretended traveler in whose alleged book of his experiences in the U.S. occurred an account of an incident damaging to the character of James K. Polk]

roose (rōōz; *Scot. also* rœz), *v.t., v.i.,* **roosed, roosing,** *n. Chiefly Scot.* praise. [t. Scand.; cf. Icel. *hrōsa* praise]

Roo·se·velt (rō′zə vĕlt′, -vält′), *n.* **1.** (**Anna**) **Eleanor,** 1884–1962, U.S. diplomat and writer (wife of F. D. Roosevelt). **2. Franklin Delano** (dĕl′ə nō′), 1882–1945, 32nd president of the U.S., 1933–45. **3. Theodore,** 1858–1919, 26th president of the U.S., 1901–09. **4. Río.** Formerly, **Río da Duvida.** a river flowing from W Brazil N to the Madeira river. ab. 550 mi.

Roosevelt Dam, a dam on the Salt River, in central Arizona. 284 ft. high; 1080 ft. long.

roost (rōōst), *n.* **1.** a perch upon which domestic fowls rest at night. **2.** a house or place for fowls or birds to roost in. **3.** a place for sitting, resting, or staying. —*v.i.* **4.** to sit or rest on a roost, perch, etc. **5.** to settle or stay, esp. for the night. [ME *rooste,* OE *hrōst,* c. MD and Flem. *roest*]

roost·er (rōōs′tər), *n.* a male chicken. [f. ROOST + -ER[1]]

root[1] (rōōt, rŏŏt), *n.* **1.** a part of the body of a plant which, typically, develops from the radicle, and grows downward into the soil, fixing the plant and absorbing nutriment and moisture. **2.** a similar organ developed from some other part of the plant, as one of those by which ivy clings to its support. **3.** any underground part of a plant, as a rhizome. **4.** something resembling or suggesting the root of a plant in position or function. **5.** the embedded or basal portion of a hair, tooth, nail, etc. **6.** the fundamental or essential part: *the root of a matter.* **7.** the source or origin of a thing: *the love of money is the root of all evil.* **8.** a person or family as the source of offspring or descendants. **9.** an offshoot or scion. **10.** *Math.* a. a quantity which, when multiplied by itself a certain number of times, produces a given quantity: *2 is the square root of 4, the cube root of 8, and the fourth root of 16.* b. a quantity which, when substituted for the unknown quantity in an algebraic equation, satisfies the equation. **11.** *Gram.* a. a morpheme which underlies an inflectional paradigm or is used itself as a word or element of a compound. Thus, *dance* is the root

Types of roots
A. Tap (sweet clover, *Melilotus alba*); B. Fibrous (meadow grass, *Poa annua*); C. Fleshy (carrot, *Daucus Carota*); D. Tuberous (rue anemone, *Anemonella thalictoides*); E. Aerial (orchid, *Oncidium ciliatum*)

of *dancer, dancing.* In German, *seh* is the root of *gesehen.* **b.** such a morpheme as posited for a parent language, such as proto-Indo-European, on the basis of comparison of extant forms in daughter languages. **12.** *Music.* **a.** the fundamental tone of a compound tone or of a series of harmonies. **b.** the lowest tone of a chord when arranged as a series of thirds; the fundamental. **13. take** (or **strike**) **root,** a. to send out roots and begin to grow. **b.** to become fixed or established. —*v.i.* **14.** to send out roots and begin to grow. **15.** to become fixed or established. —*v.t.* **16.** to fix by, or as if by, roots. **17.** to implant or establish deeply. **18.** to pull, tear, or dig (fol. by *up, out,* etc.) by the roots. **19.** to extirpate; exterminate (with *up, out,* etc.). [ME; OE *rōt,* t. Scand.] —**root′less,** *adj.*

root[2] (rōōt, rŏŏt), *v.i.* **1.** to turn up the soil with the snout, as swine. **2.** to poke, pry, or search, as if to find something. —*v.t.* **3.** to turn over with the snout (often fol. by *up*). **4.** to unearth; bring to light (fol. by *up,* etc.). [var. of obs. *wroot,* OE *wrōtan,* akin to *wrōt* snout] —**root′er,** *n.*

root[3] (rōōt, rŏŏt), *v.i. U.S. Slang.* to give encouragement to, or applaud, a contestant, etc. [? var. of *rout* make a loud noise. Cf. Norw. *ruta*] —**root′er,** *n.*

Root (rōōt), *n.* **Elihu** (ĕl′ə hū′), 1845–1937, U. S. lawyer and statesman.

root·age (rōōt′ĭj, rŏŏt′-), *n.* **1.** act of taking root. **2.** firm fixture by means of roots.

root beer, a drink containing the extracted juices of various roots, as of sarsaparilla, sassafras, etc.

root hair, *Bot.* an elongated tubular extension of an epidermal cell of the root serving to absorb water and minerals from the soil.

root·let (rōōt′lĭt, rŏŏt′-), *n. Bot.* **1.** a little root. **2.** a small or fine branch of a root. **3.** one of the adventitious roots by which ivy or the like clings to rocks, etc.

root·stalk (rōōt′stôk′, rŏŏt′-), *n. Bot.* a rhizome.

root·stock (rōōt′stŏk′, rŏŏt′-), *n.* **1.** *Hort.* a root used as a stock in plant propagation. **2.** *Bot.* rhizome.

root·y (rōōt′ĭ, rŏŏt′ĭ), *adj.,* **rootier, rootiest.** abounding in roots. —**root′i·ness,** *n.*

rope (rōp), *n., v.,* **roped, roping.** —*n.* **1.** a strong, thick line or cord, commonly one composed of twisted or braided strands of hemp, flax, or the like, or of wire or other material. **2.** lasso. **3.** (*pl.*) the cords used to enclose a prize ring or other space. **4.** a hangman's cord or halter. **5.** death by hanging as a punishment. **6.** a quantity of material or a number of things twisted or strung together in the form of a thick cord: *a rope of tobacco.* **7.** a stringy, viscid, or glutinous formation in a liquid. —*v.t.* **8.** to tie, bind, or fasten with a rope. **9.** to enclose or mark off with a rope. **10.** to catch with a lasso. **11.** *U.S. Slang.* to draw, entice, or inveigle into something (fol. by *in*). —*v.i.* **12.** to be drawn out into a filament of thread; become ropy. [ME; OE *rāp,* c. D *reep,* G *reif*]

rope·danc·er (rōp′dăn′sər, -dän′-), *n.* one who dances, walks, etc., on a rope stretched at some height above the floor or ground.

rope·mak·ing (rōp′mā′kĭng), *n.* the art, act, or process of making rope.

rope·walk (rōp′wôk′), *n.* a long, usually covered, course, or a long, low building, where ropes are made.

rope·walk·er (rōp′wô′kər), *n.* a ropedancer.

rope yarn. See yarn (def. 3).

rop·y (rō′pĭ), *adj.,* **ropier, ropiest. 1.** resembling a rope or ropes. **2.** forming viscid or glutinous threads, as a liquid. —**rop′i·ness,** *n.*

roque (rōk), *n.* a difficult form of croquet. [arbitrary var. of CROQUET]

Roque·fort cheese (rōk′fərt), a strongly flavored cheese, veined with mold, made wholly or in part of sheep's milk and ripened in caves at Roquefort, a town in S France.

roq·ue·laure (rŏk′ə lôr′, rŏk lōr′), *n.* a cloak reaching to the knees, much worn by men during the 18th century. [t. F. after Duc de *Roquelaure*(1656–1738)]

ro·quet (rō kā′), *v.,* **-queted** (-kād′), **-queting** (-kā′ĭng), *n. Croquet and Roque.* —*v.t.* **1.** to cause one's ball to strike (another player's ball). **2.** (of a ball) to strike (another ball). —*v.i.* **3.** to roquet a ball. —*n.* **4.** act of roqueting. [? alter. of CROQUET]

ror·qual (rôr′kwəl), *n. Zool.* any of the whalebone whales, some being very large, that constitute the genus *Balaenoptera,* having a dorsal fin; a finback. [t. F. t. Norw.: m. *röyrkval* finner-whale]

Common Antarctic rorqual, *Balaenoptera rostrata* (30 ft. long)

Ror·schach test (rôr′shäкн), *Psychol.* a test devised for the analysis of personality, calling for responses to ink blots and drawings. [named after Hermann *Rorschach,* 1884–1922, Swiss psychiatrist]

Ro·sa (rō′zä), *n.* **Monte** (mōn′tě), a mountain between Switzerland and Italy, in the Pennine Alps: second highest peak of the Alps. 15,217 ft.

ro·sa·ceous (rō zā′shəs), *adj.* **1.** belonging to the *Rosaceae,* or rose family of plants, which includes also the blackberry, strawberry, agrimony, spiraea, etc. **2.** having a corolla of five broad petals, like that of a rose. **3.** roselike. **4.** rose-colored; rosy. [t. L: m. *rosaceus*]

ros·an·i·line (rō zǎn'ə lǐn, -lēn'), *n. Chem.* **1.** a red dye, $C_{20}H_{19}N_3 \cdot HCl$, derived from aniline and ortho-toluidine: a constituent of fuchsin. **2.** the base, $C_{20}H_{21}$, N_3O, which with hydrochloric acid forms this dye. [f. ROSE[1] + ANILINE]

Ro·sa·rio (rō sä'ryō), *n.* a city in E Argentina: a port on the Paraná river. 483,000 (est. 1952).

ro·sa·ry (rō'zə rǐ), *n., pl.* **-ries. 1.** *Rom. Cath. Ch.* **a.** a series of prayers consisting (in the usual form) of fifteen decades of aves, each decade being preceded by a pater-noster and followed by a gloria (Gloria Patri), one of the mysteries or events in the life of Christ and of the Virgin Mary being recalled at each decade. **b.** a string of beads used for counting the prayers in the recitation of these prayers. **2.** (among other religious bodies) a string of beads similarly used in praying. **3.** a rose garden; a bed of roses. [ME, t. L: m.s. *rosārium* rose garden, ML rosary, prop. neut. of *rosārius* of roses]

rose[1] (rōz), *n., v.,* **rosed, rosing. —n. 1.** any of the wild or cultivated, usually prickly-stemmed, showy-flowered shrubs constituting the genus *Rosa*, having in the wild state a corolla of five roundish petals. **2.** any of various related or similar plants. **3.** the flower of any such shrub, of a red, pink, white, or yellow color, and often fragrant. **4.** an ornament shaped like or suggesting a rose; a rosette of ribbon or the like. **5.** purplish red; pinkish red; light crimson; rose color. **6.** rosy color in the cheek. **7.** a rose window. **8.** bed of roses, a situation of luxurious ease; an easy and highly agreeable position. **9.** *Hist.* **a.** white rose, the emblem of the house of York. **b.** red rose, the emblem of the house of Lancaster. **c.** Wars of the Roses, the civil struggle between the houses of Lancaster and York, begun in 1455 and ending in the accession of Henry VII and the union of the two houses. **10.** the compass card of the mariners' compass as printed on charts. **11.** a form of cut gem formerly much used with a triangularly faceted top and flat underside: *a rose diamond.* **12.** a perforated cap or plate at the end of a water pipe or the spout of a watering pot, etc., to break a flow of water into a spray. —*adj.* **13.** of the color rose. —*v.t.* **14.** to make rose-colored. **15.** to flush (the cheeks, face, etc.). [ME and OE, t.. L: m *rosa*] —**rose'like,** *adj.*

rose[2] (rōz), *v.* pt. of rise.

rose acacia, a small tree, *Robinia hispida*, of the southern Allegheny Mountains, having large, dark rose-colored, inodorous flowers in racemes.

ro·se·ate (rō'zǐ ǐt, -āt'), *adj.* **1.** tinged with rose; rosy. **2.** bright or promising. **3.** optimistic. [f. s. L *roseus* rosy + -ATE[1]] —**ro'se·ate·ly,** *adv.*

rose·bay (rōz'bā'), *n.* **1.** the oleander. **2.** the rhodo-dendron. **3.** *Brit.* the willow herb (def. 1).

rose beetle, a scarabaeid beetle, the British *Cetonia aurata* or the American *Macrodactylus subspinosus*, which destroys rose plants.

Rose·ber·y (rōz'bə rǐ), *n.* **Archibald Philip Prim-rose, Earl of,** 1847–1929, British statesman and author.

rose-breast·ed grosbeak (rōz'brěst'ǐd), an American finch, *Hedymeles endovicianus*, the male of which, in breeding plumage, has a rose-pink triangular breast patch.

rose·bud (rōz'bǔd'), *n.* the bud of a rose.

rose·bush (rōz'bŏŏsh'), *n.* a shrub which bears roses.

rose campion, 1. a cultivated plant (*Lychnis coronaria*) of the pink family, with crimson flowers. **2.** the red-flowering corn cockle.

rose cold, a form of hay fever caused by the pollen of roses. Also, **rose fever.**

rose color, pinkish red; purplish red; light crimson.

rose-col·ored (rōz'kǔl'ərd), *adj.* **1.** of rose color; rosy; rosaceous. **2.** promising, cheerful, or optimistic.

Rose·crans (rōz'krǎns), *n.* **William Starke,** 1819–1898, Union general in the Civil War.

rose·fish (rōz'fǐsh'), *n., pl.* **-fishes,** (*esp. collectively*) **-fish.** a north Atlantic rock cod, *Sebastes marinus*, an important food fish in New England.

rose geranium, any of a class of geraniums (*Pelargonium*) cultivated for their fragrant, lobed or narrowly subdivided leaves rather than for their small pink flowers.

rose mallow, 1. any of various plants of the malvaceous genus *Hibiscus*, bearing rose-colored flowers. **2.** the hollyhock, *Althaea rosea.*

rose·mar·y (rōz'mâr'ǐ), *n., pl.* **-maries.** an evergreen menthaceous shrub, *Rosmarinus officinalis*, native in the Mediterranean region, and yielding a fragrant essential oil. It is a traditional symbol of remembrance. [ME *rose mary*, t. L: m. *rōs mare*, lit., dew of the sea; in E the final *-s* mistaken for pl. sign]

rose moss, the portulaca, esp. the garden variety, *Portulaca grandiflora.*

rose of Jericho, an Asiatic cruciferous plant, *Anastatica hierochuntica*, which, after drying and curling up, expands when moistened.

rose of Sharon, 1. the althea, *Hibiscus syriacus*. **2.** a St.-John's-wort, *Hypericum calacinum*. **3.** a plant mentioned in the Bible (see Cant. 2:1).

ro·se·o·la (rō zē'ə lə), *n. Pathol.* a kind of rose-colored rash. [t. NL, f. L *rose(us)* rosy + dim. suffix -*ola*]

Ro·set·ta (rō zět'ə), *n.* a town in N Egypt at a mouth of the Nile. 28,698 (1947). See **Rosetta stone.**

Rosetta stone, a stone slab, found in 1799 near Rosetta, bearing parallel inscriptions in Greek and in Egyptian hieroglyphic and demotic characters, making possible the decipherment of ancient Egyptian writing.

ro·sette (rō zět'), *n.* **1.** any arrangement, part, object, or formation more or less resembling a rose. **2.** a rose-shaped arrangement of ribbon or other material, used as an ornament or badge. **3.** an architectural ornament resembling a rose or having a generally circular combination of parts. **4.** *Bot.* a circular cluster of leaves or other organs. [t. F, dim. of *rose* ROSE[1]]

Architectural rosette

rose water, water tinctured with the essential oil of roses.

rose-wa·ter (rōz'wô'tər, -wŏt'ər), *adj.* **1.** having the odor of rose water. **2.** affectedly delicate, nice, or fine; sentimental.

rose window, a circular window with roselike tracery or radiating mullions.

rose·wood (rōz'wŏŏd'), *n.* **1.** any of various reddish cabinet woods (sometimes with a roselike odor) yielded by certain fabaceous tropical trees, esp. of the genus *Dalbergia*. **2.** a tree yielding such wood.

Rosh Ha·sha·na (rōsh hə shä'nə, rōsh), the two-day Jewish holiday celebrated at the start of the Jewish New Year, when the shophar is blown. Also, **Rosh Ha·sho·na** (hə shō'nə). [t. Heb.: f. *rōsh* head + *hash-shānāh* the year]

Ro·si·cru·cian (rō'zə krōō'shən, rŏz'ə-), *n.* **1.** one of a number or body of persons (an alleged secret society) prominent in the 17th and 18th centuries, laying claim to various forms of occult knowledge and power and professing esoteric principles of religion. **2.** a member of any of several later or modern bodies or societies professing doctrines derived from or attributed to the earlier Rosicrucians, esp. of an organization known as the **Rosicrucian Order** or the **Ancient Mystic Order Rosae Crucis** (AMORC) which is active in America. —*adj.* **3.** of, pertaining to, or characteristic of the Rosicrucians. [f. *Rosicruc-* (Latinized form of G *Rosenkreuz*, name of supposed founder) + -IAN] —**Ro'si·cru'cian·ism,** *n.*

ros·i·ly (rō'zə lǐ), *adv.* **1.** with a rosy color. **2.** in a rosy manner.

ros·in (rŏz'ǐn), *n.* **1.** the hard, brittle resin left after distilling off the oil of turpentine from the crude oleo-resin of the pine, used in making varnish, for rubbing on violin bows, etc. **2.** resin. —*v.t.* **3.** to cover or rub with rosin. [ME, t. OF: m. *rosine*, var. of *resine* RESIN]

Ros·i·nan·te (rŏz'ə nǎn'tǐ), *n.* **1.** the old, worn horse of Don Quixote. **2.** (*l.c.*) a broken-down, old horse. [t. Sp.: m. *Rocinante* (ult. der. Rom. *runcinus* strong low-class horse)]

ros·in·weed (rŏz'ǐn wēd'), *n.* **1.** any of the coarse North American composite plants with resinous juice which constitute the genus *Silphium*. **2.** the compass plant, *S. laciniatum.*

ro·so·lio (rō zō'lyō), *n.* a cordial made from raisins, etc., popular in southern Europe. [t. It., var. of *rosoli*, g. L *rōs sōlis* dew of the sun]

Ross (rôs, rŏs), *n.* **1. Betsy,** 1752–1836, American woman who designed and made the first U.S. flag. **2. Sir James Clark,** 1800–62, British naval officer and explorer of the Arctic and Antarctic. **3.** his uncle, **Sir John,** 1777–1856, British naval officer and arctic explorer. **4. Sir Ronald,** 1857–1932, British physician.

Ross and Crom·ar·ty (krŏm'ər tǐ, krŭm'-), a county in NW Scotland. 59,600 pop. (est. 1956); 3089 sq. mi. Co. seat: Dingwall.

Ross Dependency, a British territory in Antarctica. including **Ross Island,** the coasts of the Ross Sea, and adjacent islands: a dependency of New Zealand. ab. 175,000 sq. mi.

Ros·set·ti (rō sět'ǐ, -zět'ǐ), *n.* **1. Christina Georgina,** 1830–94, British poet. **2.** her brother, **Dante Gabriel,** 1828–82, British poet and painter.

Ross Ice Shelf, an ice barrier filling the S part of the Ross Sea.

Ros·si·ni (rō sē'nǐ; *It.* rôs·sē'nē), *n.* **Gioachino Antonio** (jō'ä kē'nō än tô'nyō), 1792–1868, Italian composer.

Ross Sea, an arm of the Antarctic Ocean, S of New Zealand, extending into Antarctica.

Ros·tand (rôs tän'), *n.* **Edmond** (ĕd môn'), 1868–1918, French dramatist and poet.

ros·tel·late (rŏs'tə lāt', -lǐt), *adj. Bot.* having a ros-tellum.

ros·tel·lum (rŏs tĕl'əm), *n., pl.* **-la** (-lə). *Bot.* **1.** any small, beaklike process. **2.** a modification of the stigma in many orchids. [t. L, dim. of *rōstrum* beak]

ros·ter (rŏs'tər), *n.* **1.** a list of persons or groups with their turns or periods of duty. **2.** any list, roll, or register. [t. D: m. *rooster* list, orig., gridiron (der. *roosten* roast), from the ruled paper used]

Ros·tock (rŏs'tŏk; *Ger.* rôs'tôk), *n.* a Baltic seaport in N East Germany, in Rostock District. 150,000 (est. 1955).

Ros·tov (rŏ stôf′), n.   a seaport in the S Soviet Union in Europe, on the Don river, near the Sea of Azov. 552,000 (est. 1956). Also, **Rostov-on-Don** (-dôn′; *Russ.* -dôn′).

Ro·stov·tzeff (rŏ stôf′tsĕf), n.   **Michael Ivanovich** (mĭ′kəl ĭ vä′nə vĭch), 1870–1952, U.S. historian, born in Russia.

ros·tral (rŏs′trəl), adj.   of or pertaining to a rostrum. [t. LL: s. *rōstrālis*, f. s. L *rōstrum* beak + -*ālis* -AL¹]

ros·trate (rŏs′trāt), adj.   furnished with a rostrum.

ros·trum (rŏs′trəm), n., pl. **-tra** (-trə), **-trums.** 1. any platform, stage, or the like, for public speaking. 2. a pulpit. 3. a beaklike projection from the prow of a ship, esp. one on an ancient warship for ramming an enemy ship. 4. the platform or elevated place (adorned with the beaks of captured warships) in the ancient Roman forum, from which orations, pleadings, etc., were delivered. 5. *Biol.* a beaklike process or extension of some part. [L: beak, in pl., speakers′ platform (cf. def. 4)]

Ros·well (rŏz′wĕl), n.   a city in SE New Mexico. 39,593 (1960).

ros·y (rŏ′zĭ), adj., **rosier, rosiest.** 1. pink or pinkish-red; roseate. 2. (of persons, the cheeks, lips, etc.) having a fresh, healthy redness. 3. bright or promising: *a rosy future.* 4. cheerful or optimistic: *rosy anticipations.* 5. made or consisting of roses. —**ros′i·ly,** adv. —**ros′i·ness,** n.
—**Syn.** 1. ROSY, RUBICUND, RUDDY are descriptive of a red color. ROSY suggests a charming warm pink or blooming red: *rosy cheeks, a rosy child.* RUBICUND, today applied only to the complexion, suggests an unnatural red in the face or some part of it, esp. as a result of high living or intemperance in drink: *the rubicund nose of a sot.* RUDDY indicates a deep and healthy red such as is associated with life out of doors: *the ruddy face of a woodsman.* —**Ant.** 2. pale.

rot (rŏt), v., **rotted, rotting,** n., interj.   —v.i. 1. to undergo decomposition; decay. 2. to pass or fall by decay (fol. by *away, off,* etc.). 3. to become morally corrupt or offensive. —v.t. 4. to cause to rot. 5. to ret (flax, etc.). —n. 6. the process of rotting. 7. state of being rotten; decay; putrefaction. 8. rotting or rotten matter. 9. *Pathol.* any disease characterized by malodorous decay. 10. *Plant Pathol.* any of various diseases or forms of decay produced by fungi or bacteria. 11. *Chiefly Brit. Slang.* nonsense. —interj. 12. an exclamation of distaste or disgust. [ME, t. Scand.; cf. Icel. *rot,* n., akin to OE *rotian* to rot] —**Syn.** 1. See decay.

ro·ta (rŏ′tə), n.   1. *Chiefly Brit.* a round, as of duty. 2. a roster. 3. (cap.) *Rom. Cath. Ch.* an ecclesiastical tribunal forming a court of final appeal. [t. L: wheel]

ro·ta·ry (rŏ′tə rĭ), adj., n., pl. **-ries.** —adj. 1. turning round as on an axis, as an object. 2. taking place round an axis, as motion. 3. having a part or parts that rotate, as a machine. 4. noting or pertaining to an internal-combustion engine for an airplane, having radially arranged cylinders which move about a stationary crankshaft. —n. 5. *Elect.* synchronous converter. [t. LL: m.s. *rotārius,* der. L *rota* wheel. See -ARY]

Rotary Club, an international organization, originated at Chicago in 1905, devoted to service to the community and to the advance of world peace. —**Ro·tar·i·an** (rŏ târ′ĭən), n.   —**Ro·tar′i·an·ism,** n.

rotary hoe, an implement with many fingerlike wheels, pulled over the ground for early crop cultivation and destruction of weeds.

rotary plow, a series of swinging knives mounted on a horizontal power-driven shaft which pulverize unplowed soil, for planting, in one operation. Also, **rotary tiller.**

rotary press. See press¹ (def. 30b).

ro·tate¹ (rŏ′tāt, rŏ tāt′), v., **-tated, -tating.** —v.t. 1. to cause to turn round like a wheel on its axis. 2. to cause to go through a round of changes; cause to pass or follow in a fixed routine of succession: *to rotate crops.* —v.i. 3. to turn round as on an axis. 4. to proceed in a fixed routine of succession. [t. L: m.s. *rotātus,* pp., swung round, revolved] —**ro′tat·a·ble,** adj.
—**Syn.** 1. See turn.

ro·tate² (rŏ′tāt), adj.   wheel-shaped (applied esp. to a gamopetalous short-tubed corolla with a spreading limb). [f. s. L *rota* wheel + -ATE¹]

ro·ta·tion (rŏ tā′shən), n.   1. act of rotating; a turning round as on an axis. 2. the turning of the earth daily on its own axis. 3. regularly recurring succession, as of officials. 4. *Agric.* the process or method of varying, in a definite order, the crops grown on the same ground. —**ro·ta′tion·al,** adj.

Rotate corolla of potato, Solanum tuberosum

ro·ta·tive (rŏ′tə tĭv), adj.   1. rotating; pertaining to rotation. 2. producing rotation. 3. happening in regular succession.

ro·ta·tor (rŏ′tā tər, rŏ tā′-), n., pl. **rotators** for 1, **rotatores** (rŏ′tə tôr′ēz) for 2.   1. one who or that which rotates. 2. *Anat.* a muscle serving to rotate a part of the body. [t. L]

ro·ta·to·ry (rŏ′tə tôr′ĭ), adj.   1. pertaining to or of the nature of rotation: *rotatory motion.* 2. rotating, as an object. 3. passing or following in rotation or succession. 4. causing rotation, as a muscle.

R.O.T.C., Reserve Officers′ Training Corps.

rotche (rŏch), n.   dovekie. [var. of *rotge;* cf. D *rotje* petrel]

rote¹ (rōt), n.   1. routine; fixed or mechanical course of procedure. 2. **by rote,** in a mechanical way without thought of the meaning. [ME; orig. uncert.]

rote² (rōt), n.   *Music.* a kind of medieval stringed instrument. [ME, t. OF; of Celtic orig.]

ro·te·none (rō′tə nōn′), n.   *Chem.* a crystalline heterocyclic compound, $C_{23}H_{23}O_6$: possessing ketone, olefin, and ether functional groups: the poisonous principle of certain insecticides derived from the tropical derris plant.

Roth·er·ham (rŏth′ər əm), n.   a city in central England, near Sheffield. 82,850 (est. 1956).

Roth·schild (rŏth′chĭld, rŏths′-; *Ger.* rōt′shĭlt), n. 1. **Meyer Anselm** (mī′ər än′sĕlm), c1743–1812, German banker: founder of international banking firm (House of Rothschild). 2. his son, **Nathan Meyer, Baron de,** 1777–1836, banker in London.

ro·ti·fer (rō′tĭ fər), n.   any of the animalcules constituting the phylum *Rotifera,* found in fresh and salt water, and characterized by a ciliary apparatus on the anterior end; a wheel animalcule. [NL, f. *roti-* (comb. form repr. L *rota* wheel) + -*fer* bearing] —**ro·tif′-er·al, ro·tif′er·ous,** adj.

ro·tis·ser·ie (rō′tĭs′ə rī), n.   small electric broiler with motor-driven spit, for barbecuing fowl, beef, etc. [t. F: roasting-place]

rot·l (rŏt′əl), n., pl. **artal** (är′təl). 1. a unit of weight used in Mohammedan countries, varying widely in value, but of the order of the pound. 2. a varying unit of dry measure, used in the same areas. [t. Ar.: m. *ratl,* ult. from Gk. *litra* or L *libra* pound]

A rotifer, Floscularia ornata (greatly magnified)

ro·to·gra·vure (rō′tə grə vyoor′, -grā′vyər), n.   1. a photomechanical process in which pictures, letters, etc., are printed from an engraved copper cylinder, the ink-bearing lines, etc., which print being depressed (etched in) instead of raised as in ordinary metal type, etc. 2. a print made by this process. 3. *U.S.* roto section. [f. *roto-* (comb. form of L *rota* wheel) + F *gravure* engraving]

ro·tor (rō′tər), n.   1. *Elect.* the rotating member of a machine (opposed to *stator*). 2. *Aeron.* a system of rotating airfoils, usually horizontal, as those of a helicopter. 3. *Naut.* a high, towerlike, cylindrical structure of metal, rising above the deck and rotated by a small motor, which so operates in connection with the wind so as to propel the ship (**roto ship**). [short for ROTATOR]

ro·to section (rō′tō), pages of a newspaper containing pictures and text printed by the rotogravure process.

rot·ten (rŏt′ən), adj.   1. in a state of decomposition or decay; putrid; tainted, foul, or ill-smelling. 2. corrupt or offensive morally, politically, or otherwise. 3. *Slang.* wretchedly bad, unsatisfactory, or unpleasant: *to feel rotten, rotten work.* 4. contemptible: *a rotten little snob.* 5. (of soil, rocks, etc.) soft, yielding, or friable as the result of decomposition. [ME *roten,* t. Scand.; cf. Icel. *rotinn*] —**rot′ten·ly,** adv. —**rot′ten·ness,** n. —**Syn.** 1. decomposed, decayed, putrefied, putrescent.

rotten borough, (formerly) any of certain English boroughs which had only a few voters, but still sent members to Parliament.

rot·ten·stone (rŏt′ən stōn′), n.   a friable stone resulting from the decomposition of a siliceous limestone, used as a powder for polishing metals.

rot·ter (rŏt′ər), n.   *Brit. Slang.* a thoroughly bad, worthless, or objectionable person.

Rot·ter·dam (rŏt′ər däm′; *Du.* rôt′ər däm′), n.   a seaport in SW Netherlands: severely bombed by the Germans, May, 1940. 704,646 (est. 1954).

ro·tund (rŏ tŭnd′), adj.   1. rounded; plump. 2. full-toned or sonorous: *rotund speeches.* [t. L: s. *rotundus*] —**ro·tun′di·ty, ro·tund′ness,** n. —**ro·tund′ly,** adv.

ro·tun·da (rŏ tŭn′də), n.   1. a round building, esp. one with a dome. 2. a large and high circular hall or room in a building, esp. one surmounted by a dome. [t. L, fem. of *rotundus* rotund]

ro·tu·rier (rō′tr ryĕ′), n., pl. **-riers** (-ryĕ′).   *French.* a person of low rank; a plebeian. [F, der. *roture* plebeian tenure, g. L *ruptūra* a breaking]

Rou·ault (roo ō′, *Fr.* rwō), n.   **Georges** (zhôrzh), 1871–1958, French expressionist painter.

Rou·baix (roo bĕ′), n.   a city in N France. 110,067 (1954).

rou·ble (roo′bəl), n.   ruble.

rou·é (roo ā′), n.   a debauchee or rake. [t. F, pp. of *rouer* break on the wheel, first applied to the profligate companions of the Duc d′ Orléans (c. 1720)]

Rou·en (roo än′; *Fr.* rwän), n.   a city in N France, on the Seine: famous cathedral; execution of Joan of Arc, 1431. 116,540 (1954).

rouge (roozh), n., v., **rouged, rouging.** —n. 1. any of various red cosmetics for coloring the cheeks or lips. 2. a reddish powder, chiefly ferric oxide, used for polishing metal, etc. —v.t. 3. to color with rouge. —v.i. 4. to use rouge. [t. F: prop. adj., red, g. L *rubeus*]

rouge et noir (roozh′ ĕ nwär′), *French.* a gambling game at cards, played at a table marked with two red and two black diamond-shaped spots on which the players place their stakes. [F: red and black]

Rou·get de Lisle (roo zhĕ′ də lēl′), **Claude Joseph** (klōd zhō zĕf′), 1760–1836, French soldier who wrote the "Marseillaise." Also, **de l′Isle.**

---

b., blend of, blended; c., cognate with; d., dialect, dialectal; der., derived from; f., formed from; g., going back to; m., modification of; r., replacing; s., stem of; t., taken from; ?, perhaps.   See the full key on inside cover.

rough (rŭf), *adj.* **1.** uneven from projections, irregularities, or breaks of surface; not smooth: *rough boards, a rough road.* **2.** shaggy: *a dog with a rough coat.* **3.** acting with or characterized by violence. **4.** violently disturbed or agitated, as the sea, water, etc. **5.** violently irregular, as motion. **6.** stormy or tempestuous, as wind, weather, etc. **7.** sharp or harsh: *a rough temper.* **8.** unmannerly or rude. **9.** disorderly or riotous. **10.** *Colloq.* severe, hard, or unpleasant: *to have a rough time of it.* **11.** harsh to the ear, grating, or jarring, as sounds. **12.** harsh to the taste, sharp, or astringent, as wines. **13.** coarse, as fare, food, materials, etc. **14.** lacking culture or refinement. **15.** without refinements, luxuries, or ordinary comforts or conveniences. **16.** requiring exertion or strength rather than intelligence or skill, as work. **17.** unpolished, as language, verse, style, etc.; not elaborated, perfected, or corrected: *a rough draft.* **18.** made or done without any attempt at exactness, completeness, or thoroughness: *a rough guess.* **19.** crude, unwrought, undressed, or unprepared: *a rough diamond, rough rice.* **20.** *Phonet.* with aspiration; having the sound of *h.*
—*n.* **21.** that which is rough; rough ground. **22.** *Golf.* any part of the course bordering the fairway on which the grass, weeds, etc., are not trimmed. **23.** the rough, hard, or unpleasant side or part of anything. **24.** *Chiefly Brit.* a rough person; rowdy. **25. in the rough,** in a rough, crude, unwrought, or unfinished state.
—*adv.* **26.** in a rough manner; roughly.
—*v.t.* **27.** to make rough; roughen. **28.** to treat roughly or harshly. **29.** to subject to some rough preliminary process of working or preparation. **30.** to cut, shape, or sketch roughly (fol. by *in* or *out*): *to rough out a plan, to rough in the outlines of a face.* **31.** *Football.* to expose (a member of the opposing team) to unnecessary and premeditated roughness.
—*v.i.* **32.** to become rough, as a surface. **33.** to behave roughly. **34.** to live without even the ordinary comforts or conveniences (fol. by indefinite *it*): *we roughed it all month long.*
[ME; OE *rūh,* c. D *ruig,* G *rauh*] —**rough′ly,** *adv.* —**rough′ness,** *n.* —**Syn. 1.** irregular, rugged, jagged. **3.** disorderly, turbulent, boisterous. —**Ant. 1.** smooth. **3.** gentle.

rough·age (rŭf′ĭj), *n.* **1.** rough or coarse material. **2.** the coarser kinds or parts of fodder or food, of less nutritive value, as distinguished from those affording more concentrated nutriment.

rough-and-read·y (rŭf′ən rĕd′ĭ), *adj.* **1.** rough, rude, or crude, but good enough for the purpose: *in a rough-and-ready fashion.* **2.** exhibiting or showing rough vigor rather than refinement or delicacy: *a rough-and-ready person.*

rough-and-tum·ble (rŭf′ən tŭm′bəl), *adj.* **1.** characterized by rough tumbling, falling, struggling, etc.: *a rough-and-tumble fight.* **2.** given to such action.

rough breathing, *Gram.* an aspirate mark (ʽ) placed over initial vowels to indicate a preceding *h* sound. [trans. of L *spiritus asper*]

rough·cast (rŭf′kăst′, -käst′), *n., v.,* **-cast, -casting.**
—*n.* **1.** a coarse plaster for outside surfaces, usually thrown against the wall. **2.** a crudely formed pattern or model. —*v.t.* **3.** to cover or coat with roughcast. **4.** to make, shape, or prepare in a rough form: *to roughcast a story.* —**rough′cast′er,** *n.*

rough-dry (rŭf′drī′), *v.t.,* **-dried, -drying.** to dry (clothes, etc.) after washing, without smoothing, ironing, etc.

rough·en (rŭf′ən), *v.t., v.i.* to make or become rough.

rough·er (rŭf′ər), *n.* one who roughs or roughs out.

rough-hew (rŭf′hū′), *v.t.,* **-hewed, -hewed** or **-hewn, -hewing. 1.** to hew (timber, stone, etc.) roughly or without smoothing or finishing. **2.** to shape roughly; give crude form to.

rough·house (rŭf′hous′), *n., v.,* **-housed, -housing.** *Slang.* —*n.* **1.** rough, disorderly behavior or play; rowdy conduct. —*v.i.* **2.** to engage or take part in roughhouse. —*v.t.* **3.** to disturb or harass by roughhouse.

rough·ish (rŭf′ĭsh), *adj.* rather rough: *a roughish sea.*

rough·neck (rŭf′nĕk′), *n.* *Slang.* a rough, coarse person.

rough·rid·er (rŭf′rī′dər), *n.* **1.** one who breaks horses to the saddle. **2.** one accustomed to rough or hard riding.

Rough Riders, the members of a volunteer regiment of cavalry, organized by Theodore Roosevelt and Leonard Wood for service in the Spanish-American War of 1898.

rough·shod (rŭf′shŏd′), *adj.* **1.** shod with horseshoes having projecting nails or points. **2. ride roughshod over,** to override harshly or domineeringly.

rou·lade (rōō läd′), *n.* **1.** a musical embellishment consisting of a rapid succession of tones sung to a single syllable. **2.** a slice of meat rolled about a filling of minced meat and cooked. [t. F, der. *rouler* ROLL]

rou·leau (rōō lō′), *n., pl.* **-leaux, -leaus** (-lōz′). **1.** a roll of something. **2.** a number of coins put up in cylindrical form in a paper wrapping. [t. F, der. *rôle* roll]

Rou·lers (rōō lârs′; *Fr.* rōō lĕr′), *n.* a city in NW Belgium: battles, 1914, 1918. 33,210 (1947).

rou·lette (rōō lĕt′), *n., v.,* **-letted, -letting.** —*n.* **1.** a wheel or revolving disk used in playing a game of chance. **2.** a game of chance played at a table in the center of which is a revolving disk (**roulette wheel**) with numbered compartments, alternately red and black, into one of which a ball in motion finally comes to rest. **3.** a small wheel, esp. one with sharp teeth, mounted in a handle, for making lines of marks, dots, or perforations: *engravers' roulettes,* a roulette for perforating sheets of postage stamps. **4.** *Philately.* short consecutive cuts in the paper between the individual stamps of the sheet so that they may be readily separated from each other. It differs from perforation in that no paper is removed. —*v.t.* **5.** to mark, impress, or perforate with a roulette. [t. F, dim. of *rouelle* wheel. See ROWEL]

Roulettes (def 3)

Rou·ma·ni·a (rōō mā′nĭ ə, -mān′yə), *n.* Rumania. —**Rou·ma′ni·an,** *adj., n.*

Rou·me·li·a (rōō mē′lĭ ə), *n.* Rumelia.

round (round), *adj.* **1.** circular, as a disk. **2.** ring-shaped, as a hoop. **3.** curved like part of a circle, as an outline. **4.** having a circular cross section, as a cylinder. **5.** spherical or globular, as a ball. **6.** rounded more or less like a part of a sphere. **7.** free from angularity; plump, as parts of the body. **8.** executed with or involving circular motion: *a round dance.* **9.** completed by passing through a course which finally returns to the place of starting: *a round trip.* **10.** full, complete, or entire: *a round dozen.* **11.** forming, or expressed by, an integer or whole number (with no fraction). **12.** expressed in tens, hundreds, thousands, or the like: *in round numbers.* **13.** roughly correct: *a round guess.* **14.** considerable in amount: *a good round sum of money.* **15.** brought to completeness or perfection. **16.** full and sonorous, as sound. **17.** vigorous, brisk, or smart: *a round trot.* **18.** plain, honest, or straightforward. **19.** candid or outspoken. **20.** unmodified, as an oath; positive or unqualified, as an assertion.
—*n.* **21.** something round; a circle, ring, curve, etc.; a circular, ring-shaped, or curved object; a rounded form. **22.** something circular in cross section, as a rung of a ladder. **23.** a completed course of time, a series of events, operations, etc., ending at a point corresponding to that at which it began. **24.** any complete course, series, or succession. **25.** a circuit of any place, series of places, etc., as of a policeman, mailman, etc. **26.** a going about from place to place in a more or less definite course. **27.** a completed course or spell of activity, commonly one of a series, in some play or sport. **28.** a recurring period or time, succession of events, duties, etc.: *the daily round.* **29.** a single outburst of applause, cheers, etc. **30.** a single discharge of shot by each of a number of guns, rifles, etc., or by a single piece. **31.** a charge of ammunition for a single shot. **32.** a portion of drink, etc., served to all the members of a company. **33.** a dance with the dancers arranged or moving in a circle or ring. **34.** movement in a circle or about an axis. **35.** a form of sculpture in which figures are executed apart from any background (contrasted with *relief*). **36.** the portion of the thigh of beef below the rump and above the leg. **37.** *Brit.* (of bread) a slice. **38.** *Archery.* a specified number of arrows shot from a specified distance from the target in accordance with the rules. **39.** one of a series of three-minute periods (separated by one-minute rests) making up a prize fight. **40.** *Music.* **a.** a short rhythmical canon at the unison, in which the several voices enter at equal intervals of time. **b.** (*pl.*) the order followed in ringing a peal of bells in diatonic sequence from the highest to the lowest. **41.** *Golf.* a number of holes or period of play in a match.
—*adv.* **42.** in a circle, ring, or the like, or so as to surround something. **43.** on all sides, or about, whether circularly or otherwise. **44.** in all directions from a center. **45.** in the region about a place: *the country round.* **46.** in circumference: *a tree 40 inches round.* **47.** in a circular or rounded course: *to fly round and round.* **48.** through a round, circuit, or series, as of places or persons: *to show a person round.* **49.** through a round, or recurring period, of time, esp. to the present or particular time: *when the time rolls round.* **50.** throughout, or from beginning to end of, a recurring period of time: *all the year round.* **51.** by a circuitous or roundabout course. **52.** to a place or point as by a circuit or circuitous course: *to get round into the navigable channel.* **53.** *Chiefly U.S.* in circulation, action, etc.; about. **54.** with a rotating course or movement: *the wheels went round.* **55.** with change to another or opposite direction, course, opinion, etc.: *to sit still without looking round.*
—*prep.* **56.** so as to encircle, surround, or envelop: *to tie paper round a package.* **57.** on the circuit, border, or outer part of. **58.** around; about. **59.** in all or various directions from: *to look round one.* **60.** in the vicinity of: *the country round Boston.* **61.** in a round, circuit, or course through. **62.** to all or various parts of: *to wander round the country.* **63.** throughout (a period of time): *a resort visited all round the year.* **64.** here and there in: *there are mailboxes all round the city.* **65.** so as to make a turn or partial circuit about or to the other side of: *to sail round a cape.* **66.** reached by making a turn or partial circuit about (something): *the church round the corner.* **67.** so as to revolve or rotate about (a center or axis): *the earth's motion round its axis.*
—*v.t.* **68.** to make round. **69.** to free from angularity; fill out symmetrically; make plump. **70.** to bring to

completeness or perfection; finish off. **71.** to drive or bring (cattle, etc.) together (commonly fol. by *up*). **72.** to end (a sentence, etc.) with something specified. **73.** to encircle or surround. **74.** to make the complete circuit of; pass completely round. **75.** to make a turn or partial circuit about, or to the other side of: *to round a cape.* **76.** to cause to move in a circle or turn round. **77.** *Phonet.* to pronounce with the lips forming an approximately oval opening: *"boot" has a rounded vowel.* —*v.i.* **78.** to become round. **79.** to become free from angularity; become plump. **80.** to develop to completeness or perfection. **81.** to take a circular course; make a circuit; go the round, as a guard. **82.** to make a turn or partial circuit about something. **83.** to turn round as on an axis: *to round on one's heels.* [ME, t. OF: m. *rond,* g. L *rotundus* wheel-shaped] —**round′ish,** *adj.* —**round′ness,** *n.*

round·a·bout (round′ə bout′), *adj.* **1.** circuitous or indirect, as a road, journey, method, statement, person, etc. **2.** cut circularly at the bottom, without tails or the like, as a coat or jacket. —*n.* **3.** a short, closely fitting coat or jacket, without skirts, for men or boys. **4.** *Chiefly Brit.* a merry-go-round. **5.** a circuitous or indirect road, method, etc. **6.** *Brit.* a traffic circle.

round dance, 1. a dance performed by couples and characterized by circular or revolving movement, as the waltz. **2.** (orig.) a dance with the dancers arranged in or moving about in a circle or ring.

round·ed (roun′dĭd), *adj.* **1.** reduced to simple curves; made round. **2.** *Phonet.* labialized.

roun·del (roun′dəl), *n.* **1.** something round or circular. **2.** a small round pane or window. **3.** a decorative plate, panel, tablet, or the like, round in form. **4.** *Armor.* **a.** a disk of metal which protects the armpit. **b.** a disk of metal on a hafted weapon or a dagger to protect the hand. **5.** *Pros.* **a.** a rondel or rondeau. **b.** a modification of the rondeau consisting of nine lines with two refrains. **6.** a dance in a circle or ring. [ME *roundele,* t. OF: m. *rondel,* der. *rond* ROUND, *adj.*]

roun·de·lay (roun′də lā′), *n.* **1.** a song in which a phrase, line, or the like is continually repeated. **2.** the music for such a song. **3.** a dance in a circle. [f. ROUNDEL (def. 5) + LAY⁴]

round·er (roun′dər), *n.* **1.** one who or that which rounds something. **2.** one who makes a round. **3.** *U.S. Slang.* a habitual drunkard or criminal; an idle frequenter of public resorts. **4.** (*cap.*) *Brit.* a Methodist minister who travels a circuit among his congregations. **5.** (*pl. construed as sing.*) *Brit.* a game somewhat resembling baseball.

round hand, a style of handwriting in which the letters are round, full, and clearly separated.

Round·head (round′hĕd′), *n. Eng. Hist.* a member or adherent of the Parliamentarians or Puritan party during the civil wars of the 17th century (so called in derision by the Cavaliers because they wore their hair cut short).

round·house (round′hous′), *n.* **1.** a building for locomotives, usually round or semicircular, and built about a turntable. **2.** *Naut.* a cabin on the after part of a quarterdeck.

round·let (round′lĭt), *n.* a small circle or circular object. [ME *rondlet,* t. OF: m. *rondelet,* dim. of *rondel.* See ROUNDEL]

round·ly (round′lĭ), *adv.* in a round manner; vigorously or briskly; outspokenly, severely, or unsparingly.

round of beef, the thigh meat found below the aitchbone, or between the leg and the rump.

round robin, a petition, remonstrance, or the like, having the signatures arranged in circular form, so as to disguise the order of signing.

round-shoul·dered (round′shōl′dərd), *adj.* having the shoulders bent forward, giving a rounded form to the upper part of the back.

rounds·man (roundz′mən), *n., pl.* **-men.** **1.** one who makes rounds, as of inspection; (esp. in England) a deliveryman of milk, bread, etc. **2.** a police officer who inspects the policemen on duty in a particular district.

round steak, the beef cut directly above the hind leg.

round table, 1. a number of persons seated, or conceived as seated, about a round (or other) table, esp. for discussion of some subject. **2.** (*cap.*) *Arthurian Romance.* **a.** the celebrated table, made round to avoid quarrels as to precedence, about which King Arthur and his knights sat. **b.** King Arthur and his knights as a body.

round trip, a trip to a given place and back again, but applied in England to a circular tour only. —**round′-trip′,** *adj.*

round-up (round′ŭp′), *n.* **1.** the driving together of cattle, etc., for inspection, branding, or the like, as in the western U.S. **2.** the men and horses who do this. **3.** the herd so collected. **4.** any similar driving or bringing together.

round·worm (round′wûrm′), *n.* any nematode, esp. *Ascaris lumbricoides,* infesting the human intestine, or other ascarids in other animals.

roup (rōōp), *n.* **1.** *Vet. Sci.* any kind of a catarrhal inflammation of the eyes and nasal passages of poultry. **2.** hoarseness or huskiness. [orig. uncert.]

roup·y (rōō′pĭ), *adj.* **1.** affected with the disease roup. **2.** hoarse or husky.

rouse¹ (rouz), *v.,* **roused, rousing,** *n.* —*v.t.* **1.** to bring out of a state of sleep, unconsciousness, inactivity, fancied security, apathy, depression, etc. **2.** to stir to strong indignation or anger. **3.** to cause (game) to start from a covert or lair. **4.** *Naut.* to pull by main strength; haul. —*v.i.* **5.** to come out of a state of sleep, unconsciousness, inaction, apathy, depression, etc. **6.** to start up from a covert or lair, as game. —*n.* **7.** a rousing. **8.** a signal for rousing; the reveille. [orig. uncert.] —**rous′er,** *n.* —**Syn. 1.** stir, excite, animate, kindle, stimulate, awaken.

rouse² (rouz), *n. Archaic.* a carouse. [? var. of CAROUSE (*drink carouse* being wrongly analyzed as *drink a rouse*)]

rous·ing (rou′zĭng), *adj.* **1.** that rouses; stirring: *a rousing song.* **2.** stirringly active or vigorous: *a rousing campaign.* **3.** brisk; lively: *a rousing trade.* **4.** *Colloq.* great, extraordinary, or outrageous: *a rousing lie.*

Rous·seau (rōō sō′), *n.* **1. Henri** (än rē′), (*Le Douanier*), 1844–1910, French painter. **2. Jean Jacques** (zhän zhäk), 1712–78, French philosopher, author, and social reformer, born in Switzerland. **3. Pierre Étienne Theodore** (pyĕr ĕ tyĕn′ tĕ ô dôr′), 1812–1867, French landscape painter.

roust·a·bout (rous′tə bout′), *n. U.S.* **1.** a wharf laborer or deck hand, as on the Mississippi river. **2.** an unskilled laborer who lives by odd jobs.

rout¹ (rout), *n.* **1.** a defeat attended with disorderly flight; dispersal of a defeated force in complete disorder: *to put an army to rout.* **2.** a tumultuous or disorderly crowd of persons. **3.** a rabble or mob. **4.** *Law.* an assembly of three or more persons doing some act towards a violent and unlawful purpose, to the terror of the people. **5.** *Archaic.* a troop, company, or band. **6.** *Archaic.* a large evening party or social gathering. —*v.t.* **7.** to disperse in defeat and disorderly flight: *to rout an army.* **8.** to defeat. [ME, t. AF: m. *rute,* g. L *rupta,* pp. (fem.), broken]

rout² (rout), *v.i.* **1.** to root, as swine. **2.** to poke, search, or rummage. —*v.t.* **3.** to turn over or dig up with the snout, as swine. **4.** to bring or get in poking about, searching, etc. (fol. by *out*). **5.** to cause to get from bed (fol. by *up* or *out*). **6.** to force or drive out. **7.** to hollow out or furrow, as with a scoop, gouge, or machine. [see ROOT², and cf. MD *ruten* root out]

route (rōōt, rout), *n., v.,* **routed, routing.** —*n.* **1.** a way or road for passage or travel. **2.** a customary or regular line of passage or travel. **3.** *Med.* the area of the body through which a curative is introduced: *the digestive route.* —*v.t.* **4.** to fix the route of. **5.** to send or forward by a particular route. [ME, t. F, ult. g. L *rupta* (*via*) broken (road)]

rout·er (rou′tər), *n.* **1.** any of various tools or machines for routing, hollowing out, or furrowing. **2.** a carpentry plane designed for working out the bottom of a rectangular cavity. **3.** a tool or machine for routing out parts of an etched plate, electrotype, etc.

rou·tine (rōō tēn′), *n.* **1.** a customary or regular course of procedure: *the routine of an office.* **2.** regular, unvarying, or mechanical procedure. —*adj.* **3.** of the nature of, proceeding by, or adhering to routine: *routine duties.* [t. F, der. *route* ROUTE]

rou·tin·ism (rōō tē′nĭz əm), *n.* adherence to routine. —**rou·tin·ist** (rōō tē′nĭst), *n.*

roux (rōō), *n.* a mixture of fat and flour used to thicken sauces. [t. F: browned, reddish, g. L *russus*]

rove¹ (rōv), *v.,* **roved, roving.** —*v.i.* **1.** to wander about without definite destination; move hither and thither at random, esp. over a wide area. —*v.t.* **2.** to wander over or through; traverse: *to rove the woods.* [ME, t. Scand.; cf. Icel. *ráfa*] —**Syn. 1.** see **roam.**

rove² (rōv), *v.* a pt. and pp. of **reeve²**.

rove³ (rōv), *v.t.,* **roving, roving.** to form (slivers of wool, cotton, etc.) into slightly twisted strands in a preparatory process of spinning. [orig. obscure]

rove beetle, any beetle of the family *Staphylinidae,* which comprises numerous insects having long, slender bodies and very short elytra, and capable of running swiftly.

rove-o·ver (rōv′ō′vər), *adj. Pros.* (in sprung rhythm) of or pertaining to the completion of a metrical foot, incomplete at the end of one line, completed with a syllable or syllables from the beginning of the next line.

rov·er¹ (rō′vər), *n.* **1.** one who roves; a wanderer. **2.** *Archery.* **a.** a mark selected at random. **b.** any of a group of set marks at a long distance. **c.** one who starts from a distance. **3.** *Croquet.* a ball that has gone through all the arches and needs only to strike the winning peg to be out of the game. **4.** *Brit.* (at concerts, etc.) a person who has a ticket for standing room only. **5.** *Brit. Rugby.* an outside player of no fixed position. **6.** *Brit.* an older boy scout, of eighteen years or above. [f. ROVE¹ + -ER¹]

rov·er² (rō′vər), *n. Archaic.* **1.** a sea robber or pirate. **2.** a pirate ship. [t. MD or MLG, der. *roven* rob]

rov·er³ (rō′vər), *n.* **1.** a roving or routing machine. **2.** a roving-machine operator. [f. ROVE³ + -ER¹]

rov·ing (rō′vĭng), *n.* a strand of loosely assembled fibers, wool, cotton, etc., preparatory to spinning.

row¹ (rō), *n.* **1.** a number of persons or things arranged in a line, esp. a straight line. **2.** a line of adjacent seats facing the same way, as in a theater. **3.** a street formed by two continuous lines of buildings. —*v.t.* **4.** to put in

a row (often fol. by *up*). [ME *row(e)*, OE *rāw*, akin to Lithuanian *raiwe* stripe]

row[2] (rō). *v.i.* **1.** to use oars or the like for propelling a boat. —*v.t.* **2.** to propel (a boat, etc.) by or as by the use of oars. **3.** to convey in a boat, etc., so propelled. **4.** to convey or propel (something) in a manner suggestive of rowing. **5.** to employ (a number of oars): *the captain's barge rowed twenty oars.* **6.** to use (oars or oarsmen) for rowing. **7.** to perform (a race, etc.) by rowing. **8.** to row against in a race. —*n.* **9.** act of rowing; a turn at the oars. **10.** an excursion in a rowboat: *to go for a row.* [ME; OE *rōwan*, c. Icel. *rōa*; akin to L *rēmus*, Gk. *eretmòn.* Cf. RUDDER] —**row'er**, *n.*

row[3] (rou), *n.* **1.** a noisy dispute or quarrel; commotion. **2.** *Colloq.* noise or clamor. —*v.i.* **3.** *Colloq.* to make or engage in a noisy quarrel. —*v.t.* **4.** *Colloq.* to assail roughly; upbraid severely. [orig. uncert.]

row·an (rō'ən, rou'-), *n.* **1.** the European mountain ash, *Sorbus Aucuparia*, a tree with red berries. **2.** either of two American mountain ashes, *S. americana* and *S. sambucifolia.* **3.** the berry of any of these trees. [t. Scand.; cf. Norw. *raun*]

row·boat (rō'bōt'), *n.* a boat propelled by rowing.

row·dy (rou'dĭ), *n., pl.* -**dies**, *adj.,* -**dier**, -**diest**. —*n.* **1.** a rough, disorderly person. —*adj.* **2.** of the nature of or characteristic of a rowdy; rough and disorderly. [orig. obscure] —**row'di·ly**, *adv.* —**row'di·ness**, *n.*

row·dy·ish (rou'dĭ'ĭsh), *adj.* **1.** like or characteristic of a rowdy. **2.** disposed to or characterized by rowdyism. —**row'dy·ish·ness**, *n.*

row·dy·ism (rou'dĭ'ĭz/əm), *n.* rowdy conduct.

row·el (rou'əl). *n., v..* -**eled**, -**eling** or (*esp. Brit.*) -**elled**, -**elling**. **1.** a small wheel with radiating points, forming the extremity of a horseman's spur. **2.** *Vet. Sci.* a piece of leather or the like inserted beneath the skin of a horse or other animal to cause a discharge. —*v.t.* **3.** to prick, or urge, with a rowel. **4.** *Vet. Sci.* to insert a rowel in. [ME, t. OF: m. *roel*, dim. of *roe, roue,* g. L *rota* wheel]

Spur with rowel

row·en (rou'ən), *n.* the second crop of grass or hay in a season; the aftermath. [ME *rewayn*, t. ONF, c. F *regain*]

row·ing boat (rō'ĭng), *Brit.* rowboat.

row·lock (rō'lŏk', rŭl'ək), *n. Chiefly Brit.* oarlock. [var. of *oarlock*, by assoc. with ROW[2]]

Ro·xas (rō'häs), *n.* **Manuel** (mä nwĕl'), 1892–1948, Philippine statesman; first president of the Philippine Republic, 1946–48.

Rox·ourgh (rŏks'bûr'ō, -bə rə), *n.* a county in SE Scotland. 45,500 pop. (est. 1956); 666 sq. mi. *Co. seat:* Jedburgh. Also, **Rox·burgh·shire** (rŏks'bûr'ō shĭr', -shər, -bə rə-).

roy·al (roi'əl), *adj.* **1.** of or pertaining to a king, queen, or sovereign: *royal power, a royal palace, the royal family.* **2.** belonging to the royal family: *a royal prince.* **3.** having the rank of a king or queen. **4.** established or chartered by, or existing under the patronage of, a sovereign: *a royal society.* **5.** proceeding from or performed by a sovereign: *a royal warrant.* **6.** befitting, appropriate to, a sovereign; kinglike or princely; magnificent; splendid: *royal splendor.* **7.** *Colloq.* fine, first-rate, or excellent: *in royal spirits.* **8.** beyond the common or ordinary in size, quality, etc. —*n.* **9.** *Naut.* a sail set on the royal mast. See illus. under SAIL. [ME, t. OF: m. *roial*, g. L *rēgālis*] —**roy'al·ly**, *adv.* —**Syn. 1.** regal, majestic. See **kingly**.

Royal Academy, a society founded in 1768 by George III of England for the establishment of a school of design and the holding of an annual exhibition of the works of living artists.

royal blue, deep blue, often with faint reddish tinge.

royal fern, a fern, *Osmunda regalis*, with tall fronds.

royal flush, *Poker.* the five highest cards of a suit.

roy·al·ist (roi'əl ĭst), *n.* **1.** a supporter or adherent of a king or a royal government, esp. in times of rebellion or civil war. **2.** (*cap.*) a Cavalier adherent of Charles I. **3.** (*cap.*) *Amer. Hist.* a Tory. **4.** (*cap.*) an adherent of the house of Bourbon in France. —*adj.* **5.** of or pertaining to royalists. —**roy'al·ism**, *n.* —**roy'al·is'tic**, *adj.*

royal mast, *Naut.* the mast next above the topgallant mast.

Royal Oak, a city in SE Michigan, near Detroit. 80,195 (1960).

royal palm, any of various tall decorative feather palms of the genus *Roystones*, including *R. regia* and others.

royal purple, a deep bluish purple.

roy·al·ty (roi'əl tĭ), *n., pl.* -**ties**. **1.** royal persons collectively. **2.** royal status, dignity, or power; sovereignty. **3.** a prerogative or right belonging to a king or sovereign. **4.** a royal domain; a kingdom; a realm. **5.** character or quality proper to or befitting a sovereign; kingliness; nobility; generosity. **6.** a compensation or portion of proceeds paid to the owner of a right, as a patent, for the use of it. **7.** a fixed portion of the proceeds from his work, paid to an author, composer, etc. **8.** a royal right, as over minerals, granted by a sovereign to a person or corporation. **9.** the payment made for such a right. [ME *roialte*, t. OF. See ROYAL]

Royce (rois), *n.* **Josiah** (jō sī'ə), 1855–1916, U.S. philosopher and educator.

R.P., **1.** Reformed Presbyterian. **2.** Regius Professor.

r.p.m., revolutions per minute.

r.p.s., revolutions per second.

rpt., report.

R.Q., respiratory quotient.

R.R., **1.** Railroad. **2.** Right Reverend.

-rrhagia, var. of **-rhagia**. Also, **-rrhage, -rrhagy**.

-rrhea, var. of **-rhea**.

RSFSR, Russian Soviet Federated Socialist Republic. Also, **R.S.F.S.R.**

R.S.V.P., (French, *répondez s'il vous plaît*) please reply.

rt., right.

r.t., *Football.* right tackle.

Rt. Hon., Right Honorable.

Rt. Rev., Right Reverend.

Ru, *Chem.* ruthenium.

Ru·an·da-U·run·di (rōō än'dä ōō rōōn'dĭ), *n.* a former territory in central Africa, E of the Republic of the Congo: formerly part of German East Africa; administered by Belgium as a League of Nations mandate (1923–46) and as a U.N. trust territory (1946–62). Now divided into the independent states of Rwanda and Burundi.

rub (rŭb), *v.,* **rubbed, rubbing**, *n.* —*v.t.* **1.** to subject (an object) to pressure and friction, esp. in order to clean, smooth, polish, etc. **2.** to move, spread, or apply (something) with pressure and friction over something else. **3.** to move (things) with pressure and friction over each other (fol. by *together*, etc.). **4.** to force, etc., by rubbing (fol. by *over, in, into*, etc.). **5.** to remove by rubbing (fol. by *off, out*, etc.): *to rub off rust.* **6. rub it in**, to emphasize or reiterate something unpleasant. —*v.i.* **7.** to exert pressure and friction on something. **8.** to move with pressure against something. **9.** to proceed, continue in a course, or keep going, with effort or difficulty (fol. by *on, along, through*, etc.). **10.** to admit of being rubbed (*off.* etc.). —*n.* **11.** act of rubbing. **12.** something irritating to the feelings; a reproof, gibe, sarcasm, or the like. **13.** an annoying experience or circumstance. **14.** an obstacle, impediment, or difficulty. **15.** a rough or abraded spot due to rubbing. [ME *rubbe*, c. LG *rubben*, of uncert. orig.]

rub-a-dub (rŭb'ə dŭb'), *n.* the sound of a drum when beaten. [imit.]

Ru·bái·yát (rōō'bĭ yät', -bĭ-), *n.* **1.** the best-known work of Omar Khayyám, familiar in English through the version by Edward FitzGerald in quatrains, rhyming *aaba.* **2.** *Pros.* a stanza of the kind in the *Rubáiyát.* [t. Pers., t. Ar., fem. pl. of *rubā'ī* quatrain]

Rub' al Kha·li (rōōb' äl KHä'lĭ), the large desert of S Arabia, N of the Hadhramaut and extending from Yemen to Oman.

ru·basse (rōō bäs', -bäs'), *n.* a variety of rock crystal containing minute flakes of iron ore which impart a bright-red color, used as a decorative stone, but imitated with dyes in crackled quartz. [t. F, der. *rubis* ruby, der. L *rubeus* red]

ru·ba·to (rōō bä'tō), *adj., n., pl.* -**tos.** *Music.* —*adj.* **1.** having certain notes arbitrarily lengthened while others are correspondingly shortened, or vice versa. —*n.* **2.** a rubato phrase or passage. **3.** rubato performance. [It., for *tempo rubato* stolen time]

rub·ber (rŭb'ər), *n.* **1.** an elastic material derived from the latex of *Hevea* and *Ficus* species; caoutchouc; India rubber. **2.** something made of India rubber, as an elastic band for holding things together. **3.** a piece of India rubber for erasing pencil marks, etc. **4.** (*usually pl.*) overshoe (def. 2). **5.** an instrument tool, etc., used for rubbing something. **6.** one who rubs, as in order to smooth or polish something. **7.** *Brit.* a dishcloth. **8.** one who practices massage, as at a bath. **9.** one who massages horses, as those used for racing. **10.** *Baseball.* the restraining line from which the pitcher delivers the ball, made (properly) of whitened rubber. **11.** a coarse file. **12.** (in certain games as bridge or whist) **a.** a series of games, usually three, decided when either opposing side wins two games. **b.** the decisive game in a series of this kind. —*v.i.* **13.** to stretch the neck or turn the head in order to look at something. [f. RUB + -ER]

rub·ber·ize (rŭb'ə rīz'), *v.t.,* -**ized, -izing**. to coat or impregnate with India rubber or some preparation of it.

rub·ber·neck (rŭb'ər nĕk'), *U.S. Slang.* —*n.* **1.** one who strains to look at things, esp. in curiosity. —*adj.* **2.** pertaining to or for such people. —*v.i.* **3.** to look at things in this manner.

rubber plant, **1.** a moraceous plant, *Ficus elastica,* with oblong, shining, leathery leaves, growing native as a tall tree in India, the Malay Archipelago, etc., and much cultivated in Europe and America as an ornamental house plant. **2.** any plant yielding caoutchouc.

rubber stamp, **1.** a device of rubber for imprinting dates, etc., by hand. **2.** *Colloq.* one who gives approval without consideration.

rub·ber-stamp (rŭb'ər stămp'), *v.t.* **1.** to imprint with a rubber stamp. **2.** *Colloq.* to give approval without consideration.

rub·ber·y (rŭb'ə rĭ), *adj.* like rubber; elastic; tough.

rub·bing (rŭb'ĭng), *n.* **1.** act of one who or that which rubs. **2.** a reproduction of an incised or sculptured surface made by laying paper or the like upon it and rubbing with some marking substance.

rub·bish (rŭb'ĭsh), *n.* **1.** waste or refuse material; debris; litter. **2.** worthless stuff; trash. **3.** nonsense. [ME *robous, robys*; orig. obscure. Cf. RUBBLE] —**rub'bish·y**, *adj.*

rub·ble (rŭb/əl), *n.* **1.** rough fragments of broken stone, formed by geological action, in quarrying, etc., and sometimes used in maso ry. **2.** masonry built of rough fragments of broken stone. **3.** any solid substance, as ice, in irregularly broken pieces. [ME *robyl, robel;* orig. obscure. Cf. RUBBISH] —**rub/bly,** *adj.*

rub·ble·work (rŭb/əl wûrk/), *n.* masonry built of rubble or roughly dressed stones.

rub·down (rŭb/doun/), *n.* massage.

rube (rōōb), *n. Slang.* an unsophisticated countryman. [short for *Reuben,* man's name]

ru·be·fa·cient (rōō/bə fā/shənt), *adj.* **1.** producing redness of the skin, as a medicinal application. —*n.* **2.** *Med.* a rubefacient application, as a mustard plaster. [t. L: s. *rubefaciens,* ppr., making red]

ru·be·fac·tion (rōō/bə făk/shən), *n.* **1.** a making red, esp. with a rubefacient. **2.** redness of the skin produced by a rubefacient.

ru·bel·la (rōō bĕl/ə), *n.* German measles. [NL, prop. neut. pl. of L *rubellus* reddish]

ru·bel·lite (rōō bĕl/īt), *n.* a deep-red variety of tourmaline, used as a gem. [f. s. L *rubellus* reddish + -ITE[1]]

Ru·bens (rōō/bənz; *Flem.* rŷ/bəns), *n.* **Peter Paul** (pä/tər poul), 1577–1640, Flemish painter.

ru·be·o·la (rōō bē/ə lə), *n. Pathol.* **1.** measles. **2.** German measles. [NL, dim. (neut. pl.) of L *rubeus* red] —**ru·be/o·lar,** *adj.*

ru·bes·cent (rōō bĕs/ənt), *adj.* becoming red; blushing. [t. L: s. *rubescens,* ppr.] —**ru·bes/cence,** *n.*

ru·bi·a·ceous (rōō/bĭ ā/shəs), *adj.* belonging to the *Rubiaceae,* or madder family of plants, including also the coffee, cinchona, and ipecac plants, the gardenia, partridgeberry, houstonia, bedstraw, etc. [f. s. NL *Rubiāceae* (der. L *rubia* madder) + -OUS]

Ru·bi·con (rōō/bĭ kŏn/), *n.* **1.** the river in N Italy forming the southern boundary of Caesar's province of Cisalpine Gaul, by crossing which, in 49 B.C., he began a civil war with Pompey. **2. pass, or cross, the Rubicon,** to take a decisive, irrevocable step.

ru·bi·cund (rōō/bə kŭnd/), *adj.* red or reddish. [t. L: s. *rubicundus*] —**ru/bi·cun/di·ty,** *n.* —**Syn.** See **rosy.**

ru·bid·i·um (rōō bĭd/ĭ əm), *n. Chem.* a silver-white metallic, active element resembling potassium, with no commercial uses. *Symbol:* Rb; *at. wt.:* 85.48; *at. no.:* 37; *sp. gr.:* 1.53 at 20°C. [NL, f. s. L *rubidus* red (in allusion to the two red lines in its spectrum) + -*ium* -IUM]

ru·big·i·nous (rōō bĭj/ə nəs), *adj.* rusty; rust-colored; brownish-red. [f. s. L *rūbīgo* rust + -OUS]

Ru·bin·stein (rōō/bĭn stīn/; *Russ.* rōō bĭn shtīn/), *n.* **Anton** (än tôn/), 1829–94, Russian pianist and composer.

ru·bi·ous (rōō/bĭ əs), *adj. Rare or Poetic.* ruby-colored.

ru·ble (rōō/bəl), *n.* the monetary unit and a silver coin of Russia, equal to 100 kopecks, and currently equivalent to about 25 U.S. cents. Also, **rouble.** [t. Russ.; orig. uncert.]

ru·bric (rōō/brĭk), *n.* **1.** a title, heading, direction, or the like, in a manuscript, book, etc., written or printed in red or otherwise distinguished from the rest of the text. **2.** the title or a heading of a statute, etc. (orig. written in red). **3.** a direction for the conduct of divine service or the administration of the sacraments, inserted in liturgical books. [t. L: s. *rubrica* red earth; r. ME *rubriche,* t. OF]

ru·bri·cal (rōō/brə kəl), *adj.* **1.** reddish; marked with red. **2.** of, pertaining to, or enjoined by liturgical rubrics. —**ru/bri·cal·ly,** *adv.*

ru·bri·cate (rōō/brə kāt/), *v.t.,* -**cated,** -**cating.** **1.** to mark or color with red. **2.** to furnish with or regulate by rubrics. [t. L: m.s. *rubricātus,* pp.] —**ru/bri·ca/tion,** *n.* —**ru/bri·ca/tor,** *n.*

ru·bri·cat·ed (rōō/brə kā/tĭd), *adj.* (in ancient manuscripts, early printed books, etc.) having titles, catchwords, etc., distinctively colored.

ru·bri·cian (rōō brĭsh/ən), *n.* an expert in rubrics.

ru·by (rōō/bĭ), *n., pl.* -**bies.** **1.** a red variety of corundum, highly prized as a gem **(true ruby** or **oriental ruby). 2.** a piece of this stone. **3.** deep red; carmine. **4.** *Brit. Print.* a type (about 5½ point) nearly corresponding in size to American agate. —*adj.* **5.** rubycolored: *ruby lips.* [ME, t. OF: m. *rubi(s),* ult. der. L *rubeus* red]

ruby silver, **1.** proustite. **2.** pyrargyrite.

ruche (rōōsh), *n.* a full pleating or frilling of lace, net, muslin, ribbon, etc., used as a trimming or finish for women's dress. [t. F: lit., beehive, g. LL *rusca*]

ruch·ing (rōō/shĭng), *n.* **1.** material made into a ruche. **2.** ruches collectively.

ruck[1] (rŭk), *n.* **1.** a large number or quantity; a crowd or throng. **2.** the great mass of undistinguished or inferior persons or things. [ME *ruke,* prob. t. Scand.; cf. Norw. *ruka* in same senses; akin to RICK, n.]

ruck[2] (rŭk), *n., v.t., v.i.* fold, crease, or wrinkle. [t. Scand.; cf. Icel. *hrukka*]

ruck·sack (rŭk/săk/; *Ger.* rŏŏk/zäk/), *n.* a kind of knapsack carried by hikers, etc. [t. G: lit., back sack]

ruc·tion (rŭk/shən), *n. Colloq.* a disturbance, quarrel or row. [cf. obs. *ructation* belching, vomiting, aphetic var. of ERUCTATION]

rud·beck·i·a (rŭd bĕk/ĭ ə), *n.* any of the showy-flowered composite herbs constituting the genus *Rud-beckia,* as *R. hirta,* the yellow daisy, whose flower head has a dark disk and yellow rays; a coneflower. [NL; named after O. *Rudbeck,* Swedish botanist]

rudd (rŭd), *n.* a European fresh-water fish, *Scardinius erythrophthalmus,* of the carp family. [appar. special use of *rud* (now d.), OE *rudu* redness]

rud·der (rŭd/ər), *n.* **1.** a movable flat piece hinged vertically at the stern of a boat or ship as a means of steering. **2.** a device like a ship's rudder for steering an airplane, etc., hinged vertically (for right-and-left steering). [ME *roder, rother,* OE *rōthor,* c. G *ruder.* See ROW[2]]

rud·der·post (rŭd/ər pōst/), *n. Naut.* **1.** Also, **rud·der·stock** (rŭd/ər stŏk/). the vertical member at the forward end of a rudder which is hinged to the stern-post and attached to the helm or steering gear. **2.** the vertical member abaft the screw, in single-screw vessels, which holds the rudder.

R, Rudder (def. 1)

rud·dle (rŭd/əl), *n., v.,* -**dled,** -**dling.** —*n.* **1.** a red variety of ocher, used for marking sheep, coloring, etc. —*v.t.* **2.** to mark or color with ruddle. [der. *rud,* OE *rudu* a red cosmetic]

rud·dock (rŭd/ək), *n.* the European robin, *Erithacus rubecula.* [ME *ruddoc,* OE *rudduc,* der. *rudu* redness]

rud·dy (rŭd/ĭ), *adj.,* -**dier,** -**diest. 1.** of or having a fresh, healthy red color. **2.** reddish. [ME *rudi,* OE *rudig,* der. *rudu* redness] —**rud/di·ness,** *n.* —**Syn. 1.** See **rosy.**

ruddy duck, a stiff-tailed North American fresh-water duck, *Erismatura jamaicensis rubida,* the adult male of which has a brownish-red body, black crown, and white cheeks.

rude (rōōd), *adj.,* **ruder, rudest. 1.** discourteous or impolite: *a rude reply.* **2.** without culture, learning, or refinement. **3.** rough in manners or behavior; unmannerly. **4.** rough, harsh, or ungentle: *rude hands.* **5.** roughly wrought, built, or formed; of a crude make or kind. **6.** unwrought, raw, or crude. **7.** harsh to the ear, as sounds. **8.** without artistic elegance; of a primitive simplicity. **9.** violent or tempestuous, as the waves. **10.** robust, sturdy, or vigorous: *rude strength.* [ME, t. L: m. *rudis*] —**rude/ly,** *adv.* —**rude/ness,** *n.* —**Syn. 1.** uncivil. **2.** rough, unfinished, unrefined. **6.** See **raw.**

ru·di·ment (rōō/də mənt), *n.* **1.** the elements or first principles of a subject: *the rudiments of grammar.* **2.** (*usually pl.*) a mere beginning, first slight appearance, or undeveloped or imperfect form of something. **3.** *Biol.* an organ or part incompletely developed in size or structure, as one in an embryonic stage, one arrested in growth, or one with no functional activity, as a vestige. [t. L: s. *rudimentum* beginning]

ru·di·men·ta·ry (rōō/də mĕn/tə rĭ, -trĭ), *adj.* **1.** pertaining to rudiments or first principles; elementary. **2.** of the nature of a rudiment; undeveloped. **3.** vestigial; abortive. Also, **ru/di·men/tal.** —**ru/di·men/ta·ri·ly,** *adv.* —**ru/di·men/ta·ri·ness,** *n.* —**Syn. 1.** See **elementary. 2.** See **imperfect.**

Ru·dolf (rōō/dŏlf), *n.* **Lake,** a lake in E Africa, in N Kenya colony. ab. 180 mi. long. ab. 3500 sq. mi.

Ru·dolph I (rōō/dŏlf; *Ger.* -dŏlf), 1218–91, German king and emperor of the Holy Roman Empire, 1273–91: founder of the Hapsburg dynasty. Also, **Ru/dolf.**

rue[1] (rōō), *v.,* **rued, ruing.** —*v.t.* **1.** to feel sorrow over; repent of; regret bitterly. **2.** to wish (that something might never have been done, taken place, etc.): *to rue the day one was born.* —*v.i.* **3.** to feel sorrow; be repentant. **4.** to feel regret. —*n. Archaic.* **5.** sorrow; repentance; regret. **6.** pity or compassion. [ME *rue, rewe,* OE *hrēowan,* c. G *reuen*]

rue[2] (rōō), *n.* any of the strongly scented plants constituting the genus *Ruta,* esp. *R. graveolens,* a yellow-flowered herb with decompound leaves formerly much used in medicine. [ME, t. OF and F, g. L *rūta,* t. Gk.: m. *rhytē*]

rue anemone, a small ranunculaceous plant, *Anemonella thalictoides,* of North America, bearing white or pinkish flowers.

rue·ful (rōō/fəl), *adj.* **1.** such as to cause sorrow or pity; deplorable; pitiable: *a rueful plight.* **2.** feeling, showing, or expressing sorrow or pity; mournful; doleful. —**rue/ful·ly,** *adv.* —**rue/ful·ness,** *n.*

ru·fes·cent (rōō fĕs/ənt), *adj.* somewhat reddish; tinged with red; rufous. [t. L: s. *rūfescens,* ppr., becoming reddish] —**ru·fes/cence,** *n.*

ruff[1] (rŭf), *n.* **1.** a neckpiece or collar of lace, lawn, etc., gathered or drawn into deep, full, regular folds, much worn in the 16th century by both men and women. **2.** something resembling such a piece in form or position. **3.** a collar, or set of lengthened or specially marked hairs or feathers, on the neck of an animal. **4.** an Old World shore bird, *Philomachus pugnax,* the male of which has an enormous frill of feather on the neck during the breeding season. The female is called a *reeve.* [? n. use of ROUGH, adj.] —**ruffed,** *adj.*

Ruff, 16th century

ruff[2] (rŭf), *n.* **1.** *Cards.* act of trumping when one cannot follow suit. **2.** *Obs.* an old game at cards, resem-

---

b., blend of, blended; c., cognate with; d., dialect, dialectal; der., derived from; f., formed from; g., going back to; m., modification of; r., replacing; s., stem of; t., taken from; ?, perhaps. See the full key on inside cover.

bling whist. —*v.t., v.i.* **3.** *Cards.* to trump when unable to follow suit. [prob. t. F: m. *ro(u)ffle,* c. It. *ronfa* a card game]

ruff[3] (rŭf), *n.* a small European fresh-water fish, *Acerina cernua,* of the perch family. [ME *ruf, roffe;* ? special use of ROUGH, adj.]

ruffed grouse, a North American game bird, *Bonasa umbellus,* having a tuft of feathers on each side of the neck (called *partridge* in the northeastern U.S., *birch partridge* in Canada, and *pheasant* in the southern U.S.).

ruf·fi·an (rŭf/ĭ ən, -yən), *n.* **1.** a tough, lawless person; a brutal bully. —*adj.* **2.** Also, **ruf/fi·an·ly.** tough; lawless; brutal. [earlier *rufian,* t. F]

ruf·fi·an·ism (rŭf/ĭ ə nĭz/əm, rŭf/yə-), *n.* **1.** conduct befitting a ruffian. **2.** ruffianly character.

ruf·fle[1] (rŭf/əl), *v.,* **-fled, -fling,** *n.* —*v.t.* **1.** to destroy the smoothness or evenness of: *the wind ruffled the sand.* **2.** to erect (the feathers), as in anger, as a bird. **3.** to disturb, discompose, or irritate. **4.** to turn over (the pages of a book) rapidly. **5.** to pass (cards) through the fingers rapidly. **6.** to draw up (cloth, lace, etc.) into a ruffle by gathering along one edge. —*v.i.* **7.** to be or become ruffled. —*n.* **8.** a break in the smoothness or evenness of some surface. **9.** a strip of cloth, lace, etc., drawn up by gathering along one edge, and used as a trimming on dress, etc. **10.** some object resembling this, as the ruff of a bird. **11.** a disturbing experience; an annoyance or vexation. **12.** a disturbed state of the mind; perturbation. [ME; c. LG *ruffelen* crumple, rumple; cf. Icel. *hrufla* scratch] —**Syn. 3.** upset, agitate, annoy, vex.

ruf·fle[2] (rŭf/əl), *n., v.,* **-fled, -fling.** —*n.* **1.** a low, continuous beating of a drum, less loud than a roll. —*v.t.* **2.** to beat (a drum) in this manner. [der. *ruff* in same sense. ? imit.]

ru·fous (ro͞o/fəs), *adj.* reddish; rufescent; tinged with red; brownish-red. [t. L: m. *rūfus* red, reddish]

rug (rŭg), *n.* **1.** a square or oblong piece of carpeting, used as a floor covering or a hanging. **2.** *Chiefly Brit.* a piece of thick, warm cloth used as a coverlet, lap robe, etc. [t. Scand.; cf. d. Norw. *rugga* coarse covering (for bed or body)]

ru·ga (ro͞o/gə), *n., pl.* **-gae** (-jē). a wrinkle, fold, or ridge. [t. L]

ru·gate (ro͞o/gāt, -gĭt), *adj.* wrinkled; rugose.

Rug·by (rŭg/bĭ), *n.* **1.** a city in central England, in Warwickshire. 45,418 (1951). **2.** a famous boys' school located there: founded, 1567.

Rugby football, an English form of football (of which the common American game is a development) in which handling and carrying of the ball are permitted. Also, *Brit. Slang,* **Rug·ger** (rŭg/ər). Cf. **soccer.** [named after RUGBY (def. 2)]

rug·ged (rŭg/ĭd), *adj.* **1.** roughly broken, rocky, hilly, or otherwise difficult of passage: *rugged ground.* **2.** wrinkled or furrowed: *a rugged face.* **3.** roughly irregular, heavy, or hard in outline or form: *Lincoln's rugged features.* **4.** rough, harsh, or stern, as persons, the nature, etc. **5.** severe, hard, or trying: *a rugged life.* **6.** tempestuous, as weather. **7.** harsh to the ear, as sounds. **8.** rude, uncultivated, or unrefined. **9.** homely or plain. **10.** *U.S.* robust or vigorous. [ME, t. Scand.; cf. Sw. *rugga* roughen and see RUG] —**rug/ged·ly,** *adv.* —**rug/ged·ness,** *n.* —**Ant. 1.** smooth. **4.** mild. **10.** frail.

ru·gose (ro͞o/gōs, ro͞o gōs/), *adj.* **1.** having wrinkles; wrinkled; ridged. **2.** *Bot.* rough and wrinkled (applied to leaves in which the reticulate venation is very prominent beneath with corresponding creases on the upper side). [t. L: m.s. *rūgōsus* wrinkled] —**ru/gose·ly,** *adv.* —**ru·gos·i·ty** (ro͞o gŏs/ə tĭ), *n.*

Ruhm·korff coil (ro͞om/kôrf), an induction coil.

Ruhr (ro͝or), *n.* **1.** a river in W West Germany, flowing into the Rhine. 144 mi. **2.** an important mining and industrial region centering in the Ruhr river valley.

ru·in (ro͞o/ĭn), *n.* **1.** (*pl.*) the remains of a fallen building, town, etc., or of anything in a state of destruction or decay: *the ruins of an ancient city.* **2.** a ruined building, town, etc. **3.** fallen and wrecked or decayed state; ruinous condition: *a building falls to ruin.* **4.** the downfall, decay, or destruction of anything. **5.** the complete loss of means, position, or the like. **6.** something that causes downfall or destruction. **7.** the downfall of a person. **8.** a person as the wreck of his former self. **9.** the seduction of a woman. —*v.t.* **10.** to reduce to ruin. **11.** to bring (a person, etc.) to financial ruin. **12.** to injure (a thing) irretrievably. **13.** to seduce. —*v.i.* **14.** to fall into ruins. **15.** to come to ruin. [ME *ruine,* t. OF, t. L: m. *ruīna* overthrow, ruin] —**ru/in·a·ble,** *adj.* —**ru/ined,** *adj.* —**ru/in·er,** *n.*

—**Syn. 3.** dilapidation, decay, ruination, perdition. RUIN, DESTRUCTION, HAVOC imply irrevocable and often widespread damage. DESTRUCTION may be on a large or small scale (*destruction of tissue, of enemy vessels*); it emphasizes particularly the act of destroying, while RUIN and HAVOC emphasize the resultant state. RUIN, from the verb meaning to fall to pieces, suggests a state of decay or disintegration (or an object in that state) which is apt to be more the result of the natural processes of time and change, than of sudden violent activity from without (*the house has fallen in ruins*); only in its figurative application is it apt to suggest the result of destruction from without: *the ruin of her hopes.* HAVOC, originally a cry which served as the signal for pillaging, has changed its reference from that of spoliation to devastation, being used particularly of the destruction following in the wake of natural calamities: *the havoc wrought by flood and pestilence.* Today it is used figuratively to refer to the destruction of hopes and plans: *this sudden turn of events played havoc with her carefully laid designs.* **10.** See **spoil.**

ru·in·a·tion (ro͞o/ə nā/shən), *n.* **1.** act of ruining. **2.** state of being ruined. **3.** something that ruins.

ru·in·ous (ro͞o/ə nəs), *adj.* **1.** bringing or tending to bring ruin; destructive; disastrous: *a ruinous war.* **2.** fallen into ruin; dilapidated. **3.** consisting of ruins. —**ru/in·ous·ly,** *adv.* —**ru/in·ous·ness,** *n.*

Ruis·dael (rois/däl; *Du.* rœĭs/-), *n.* **Jacob van.** See **Ruysdael.**

rule (ro͞ol), *n., v.,* **ruled, ruling.** —*n.* **1.** a principle or regulation governing conduct, action, procedure, arrangement, etc. **2.** the code of regulations observed by a religious order or congregation. **3.** that which customarily or normally occurs or holds good: *the rule rather than the exception.* **4.** control, government, or dominion. **5.** tenure or conduct of reign or office. **6.** a prescribed mathematical method for performing a calculation or solving a problem. **7.** ruler (def. 2). **8.** *Print.* a thin, type-high strip of metal, usually brass, for printing a line or lines. **9.** *Law.* **a.** a formal order or direction made by a court and limited in application to the case for which it is given (**special rule**). **b.** an order or regulation governing the procedure of a court (**general rule**). **c.** a proposition of law. **10.** (*pl.*) **a.** a fixed area in the neighborhood of certain prisons, within which certain prisoners were allowed to live on giving security. **b.** the freedom of such an area. —*v.t.* **11.** to control or direct; exercise dominating power or influence over. **12.** to exercise authority or dominion over; govern. **13.** to decide or declare judicially or authoritatively; decree. **14.** to mark with lines, esp. parallel straight lines, with the aid of a ruler or the like. **15.** to mark out or form (a line) by this method. —*v.i.* **16.** to exercise dominating power or influence. **17.** to exercise authority, dominion, or sovereignty. **18.** to make a formal decision or ruling, as on a point at law. **19.** to prevail or be current, as prices. [ME, t. OF: m. *riule,* g. L *rēgula* straight stick, pattern]

—**Syn. 1.** standard, law, canon. See **principle. 12.** RULE, ADMINISTER, COMMAND, GOVERN, MANAGE mean to exercise authoritative guidance or direction. RULE implies the exercise of authority as by a sovereign: *to rule a kingdom.* ADMINISTER places emphasis on the planned and orderly procedures used: *to administer the finances of an institution.* COMMAND suggests military authority and the power to exact obedience; to be in command of: *to command a ship.* TO GOVERN is authoritatively to guide or direct persons or things, esp. in the affairs of a large administrative unit: *to govern a state.* TO MANAGE is to conduct affairs, i.e., to guide them in a unified way toward a definite goal; or to direct or control people, often by tact, address, or artifice: *to manage a business.*

rule of three, *Math.* the method of finding the fourth term in a proportion when three terms are given.

rule of thumb, **1.** a rule based on experience or practice rather than on scientific knowledge. **2.** a rough, practical method of procedure.

rul·er (ro͞o/lər), *n.* **1.** one who or that which rules or governs; a sovereign. **2.** a strip of wood, metal, or other material with a straight edge, used in drawing lines, measuring, etc. **3.** one who or that which rules paper, etc. —**rul/er·ship/,** *n.*

rul·ing (ro͞o/lĭng), *n.* **1.** an authoritative decision, as by a judge on a point at law. **2.** act of drawing straight lines with a rule. **3.** ruled lines. —*adj.* **4.** that rules; governing. **5.** predominating. **6.** prevalent.

rum[1] (rŭm), *n.* **1.** an alcoholic liquor or spirit distilled from molasses or some other sugar-cane product. **2.** alcoholic drink in general; intoxicating liquor. [? short for obs. *rumbullion.* Cf. F *rebouillir* boil again]

rum[2] (rŭm), *adj. Slang.* **1.** *Chiefly Brit.* odd, strange, or queer. **2.** *Archaic.* good or fine. [earlier *rome, room* great, of unknown orig.]

Rum (ro͞om), *n.* Arabic name of Rome, once used to designate the Byzantine Empire.

Rum., **1.** Rumania. **2.** Rumanian.

Ru·ma·ni·a (ro͞o mā/nĭ ə -mān/yə), *n.* a republic in SE Europe, bordering on the Black Sea; one of the Balkan States. 17,490,000 pop. (est. 1956); 91,654 sq. mi. *Cap.:* Bucharest. Also, **Roumania,** Rumanian, **Romănia.**

Ru·ma·ni·an (ro͞o mā/nĭ ən, -mān/yən), *adj.* **1.** of Rumania, its inhabitants, or their language. —*n.* **2.** a native or inhabitant of Rumania. **3.** the language of Rumania (a Romance language). Also, **Roumanian.**

rum·ba (rŭm/bə; *Sp.* ro͞om/bä), *n.* **1.** a dance, Cuban Negro in origin and complex in rhythm. **2.** an imitation or adaptation of this dance in the U.S. **3.** the music for this dance or in its rhythm. [t. Sp., prob. of Afr. orig.]

rum·ble (rŭm/bəl), *v.,* **-bled, -bling,** *n.* —*v.i.* **1.** to make a deep, heavy, continuous, jarring sound, as thunder, etc. **2.** to move or travel with such a sound: *the train rumbled on.* —*v.t.* **3.** to give forth or utter with a rumbling sound. **4.** to cause to make or move with a rumbling sound. **5.** to subject to the action of a rumble or tumbling box, as for the purpose of polishing. —*n.* **6.** a rumbling sound, as of thunder or a heavy vehicle. **7.** a smaller open-air seat (in full, **rumble seat**) behind the principal roofed seat in an automobile. **8.** a rear part of a carriage containing seating accommodations as for servants or space for baggage. **9.** a tumbling box. **10.** *U.S. Slang.* a fight between juvenile gangs. [ME. Cf. D *rommelen,* prob. of imit. orig.]

ăct, āble, dâre, ärt; ĕbb, ēqual; ĭf, īce; hŏt, ōver, ôrder, oil, bo͝ok, o͞oze, out; ŭp, ūse, ûrge; ə = a in alone; ch, chief; g, give; ng, ring; sh, shoe; th, thin; ŧh, that; zh, vision. See the full key on inside cover.

rum·bly (rŭm′blĭ), *adj.* **1.** rumbling. **2.** attended with, making, or causing a rumbling sound.

Ru·me·li·a (rōō mē′lĭ ə), *n.* **1.** a division of the former Turkish Empire, in the Balkan Peninsula: it included Albania, Macedonia, and Thrace. **2. Eastern,** a former autonomous province within this division, which later became S Bulgaria. Also, **Roumelia.**

ru·men (rōō′mĕn), *n., pl.* **-mina** (-mə nə). **1.** the first stomach of ruminating animals, lying next to the reticulum. See diag. under **ruminant. 2.** the cud of a ruminant. [t. L: throat, gullet]

Rum·ford (rŭm′fərd), *n.* Count. See **Thompson, Benjamin.**

ru·mi·nant (rōō′mə nənt), *n.* **1.** any animal of the artiodactyl suborder or division, *Ruminantia,* which comprises the various "cloven-hoofed" and cud-chewing quadrupeds: cattle, bison, buffalo, sheep, goats, chamois, deer, antelopes, giraffes, camels, chevrotains, etc. —*adj.* **2.** ruminating; chewing the cud. **3.** given to or characterized by meditation; meditative. [t. L: s. *rūminans,* ppr., ruminating]

Ruminant stomach
A. Duodenum; B. Abomasum;
C. Omasum; D. Esophagus;
E. Reticulum; F. Rumen

ru·mi·nate (rōō′mə nāt′), *v.,* **-nated, -nating.** —*v.i.* **1.** to chew the cud, as a ruminant. **2.** to meditate or muse; ponder. —*v.t.* **3.** to chew again. **4.** to meditate on; ponder. [t. L: m.s. *rūmĭnātus,* pp.] —**ru′mi·nat′ing·ly,** *adv.* —**ru′mi·na′tion,** *n.* —**ru′mi·na′tive,** *adj.* —**ru′mi·na′tor,** *n.*

rum·mage (rŭm′ĭj), *v.,* **-maged, -maging,** *n.* —*v.t.* **1.** to search thoroughly or actively through (a place, receptacle, etc.), esp. by moving about, turning over, or looking through contents. **2.** to bring or fetch (*out* or *up*) by searching. —*v.i.* **3.** to search actively, as in a place or receptacle, or among contents, etc. —*n.* **4.** miscellaneous articles; odds and ends. **5.** a rummaging search. [ult. t. (older) F: m. *arrumage,* n., der. *arrumer* stow goods in hold of ship; orig. uncert.] —**rum′mag·er,** *n.*

rummage sale, a sale of unclaimed goods at a wharf or warehouse, or of odds and ends of merchandise at a shop, of miscellaneous articles (old or new) contributed to raise money for charity, etc.

rum·mer (rŭm′ər), *n.* a large drinking glass or cup. [cf. Flem. *rummer,* G *romer;* orig. uncert.]

rum·my¹ (rŭm′ĭ), *n.* a card game in which the object is to match cards into sets and sequences. [orig. uncert.]

rum·my² (rŭm′ĭ), *n., pl.* **-mies. 1.** *Slang.* a drunkard. —*adj.* **2.** of or like rum. [f. RUM¹ + -Y¹]

rum·my³ (rŭm′ĭ), *adj.,* **-mier, -miest.** *Chiefly Brit. Slang.* odd; queer. [f. RUM² + -Y¹]

ru·mor (rōō′mər), *n.* **1.** a story or statement in general circulation without confirmation or certainty as to facts. **2.** unconfirmed gossip. —*v.t.* **3.** to circulate, report, or assert by a rumor. [ME *rumour,* t. OF, t. L: m. *rūmor*] —**Syn. 1.** talk, gossip, hearsay.

rump (rŭmp), *n.* **1.** the hinder part of the body of an animal. **2.** *Chiefly Brit.* a cut of beef from this part of the animal, behind the loin and above the round. **3.** the buttocks. **4.** the last and unimportant or inferior part; fag end. **5. the Rump,** *Eng. Hist.* the remnant of the Long Parliament established by the expulsion of the Presbyterian members in 1648, dismissed by force in 1653, and restored briefly in 1659–60. [ME *rumpe,* t. Scand.; cf. Dan. *rumpe* rump, c. G *rumpf* trunk]

Rum·pel·stilts·kin (rŭm′pəl stĭlt′skĭn; *Ger.* rōōm′pəl shtĭlts′kĭn), *n.* the dwarf in German legend who agreed to spin great quantities of flax required by the king of his new bride. The girl-bride in return agreed to go off with the dwarf if she should not guess his name within a month. At the last moment she succeeded and he vanished.

rum·ple (rŭm′pəl), *v.,* **-pled, -pling,** *n.* —*v.t.* **1.** to draw or crush into wrinkles; crumple: *a rumpled sheet of paper.* **2.** to ruffle; tousle (often fol. by *up*). —*v.i.* **3.** to become wrinkled or crumpled. —*n.* **4.** a wrinkle or irregular fold; crease. [t. MD: m. *rompel* n., or t. MLG: m. *rumpel*]

rum·pus (rŭm′pəs), *n.* *Colloq.* **1.** disturbing noise; uproar. **2.** a noisy or violent disturbance or commotion.

rum·run·ner (rŭm′rŭn′ər), *n.* *U.S. Colloq.* a person or a ship engaged in smuggling liquor.

Rum·sey (rŭm′zĭ), *n.* **James,** 1743–92, U.S. inventor (of steam-driven boat).

run (rŭn), *v.,* **ran, run, running,** *n., adj.* —*v.i.* **1.** to move the legs quickly, so as to go more rapidly than in walking (in bipedal locomotion, so that for an instant in each step neither foot is on the ground). **2.** to move swiftly by other means of locomotion than legs. **3.** to move swiftly, as a vessel, vehicle, etc. **4.** to make off quickly; take to flight. **5.** to make a rapid journey for a short stay at a place: *to run up to New York.* **6.** *Racing.* **a.** to take part in a race. **b.** to finish a race in a certain (numerical)position: *he ran second.* **7.** to stand as a candidate for election. **8.** to migrate, as fish: *to run huge shoals.* **9.** to migrate upstream or inshore from deep water to spawn. **10.** to sail or be driven (ashore, aground, etc.), as a vessel or those on board. **11.** to

ply between places, as a vessel or conveyance. **12.** to go about without restraint (often fol. by *about*): *to run about at will.* **13.** to move easily, freely, or smoothly: *a rope runs in a pulley.* **14.** to flow, as a liquid. **15.** to flow along, esp. strongly, as a stream, the sea, etc.: *with a strong tide running.* **16.** to melt and flow, as varnish, etc. **17.** to spread on being applied to a surface, as a liquid. **18.** to spread over a material when exposed to moisture: *the colors in a fabric run.* **19.** to flow, stream, or be wet with a liquid. **20.** to discharge, or give passage to, a liquid or fluid. **21.** to overflow or leak, as a vessel. **22.** to creep, trail, or climb, as vines, etc. **23.** to pass quickly: *a thought ran through his mind.* **24.** to continue in or return to the mind persistently: *a tune running through one's head.* **25.** to come undone or unravel, as stitches or a fabric. **26.** to be in operation, or continue operating, as machinery. **27.** *Com.* **a.** to accumulate, follow, or become payable in due course, as interest on a debt. **b.** to make many withdrawals in rapid succession. **28.** *Law.* **a.** to have legal force or effect, as a writ. **b.** to continue to operate. **c.** to go along with: *the easement runs with the land.* **29.** to pass or go by, as time. **30.** to keep the stage or be played continuously, as a play. **31.** to go or proceed: *so the story runs.* **32.** to extend or stretch: *shelves ran round the walls.* **33.** to have a specified character, quality, form, etc.: *potatoes running large.* **35.** to pass into a certain state or condition; get; become: *to run into debt.*
—*v.t.* **36.** to run along (a way, path, etc.). **37.** to traverse in running: *to run the streets.* **38.** to perform by or as by running: *to run a race.* **39.** to contend with in a race. **40.** to enter (a horse, etc.) in a race. **41.** to run or get past or through: *to run a blockade.* **42.** to bring into a certain state by running: *to run oneself out of breath.* **43.** to pursue, or hunt (game, etc.). **44.** to cause to ply between places, as a vessel or conveyance. **45.** to convey or transport, as in a vessel or vehicle. **46.** to cause to pass quickly: *to run one's eyes over a letter.* **47.** to keep operating or going, as a machine. **48.** to expose oneself to, or be exposed to (a chance, risk, etc.). **49.** to put up (a person) as a candidate for election. **50.** to sew (fabric) by passing the needle in and out repeatedly with even stitches in a line. **51.** (in some games, as billiards) to complete a series of successful strokes, shots, etc. **52.** to bring, lead, or force into some state, action, etc.: *to run oneself into debt.* **53.** to cause (a liquid) to flow. **54.** to give forth or flow with (a liquid). **55.** to pour forth or discharge. **56.** to cause to move easily, freely, or smoothly: *to run up a sail.* **57.** to pierce or stab (fol. by *through*). **58.** to drive, force, or thrust. **59.** to conduct, as a business, an establishment, etc. **60.** to extend (a thing), as in a particular direction: *to run a partition across a room.* **61.** to draw or trace, as a line. **62.** to melt, fuse, or smelt, as ore. **63.** to smuggle (contraband goods).
—*n.* **64.** act or spell of running, as in hastening to some point or in rapid flight: *to be on the run.* **65.** a running pace. **66.** act or spell of moving rapidly, as in sailing, moving on wheels, etc. **67.** the distance covered. **68.** a rapid journey for a short stay at a place: *to take a run up to New York.* **69.** a spell or period of causing something, as a machine, to run or continue operating. **70.** the amount of anything produced in such a period. **71.** a line or place in knitted work where a series of stitches have slipped out or come undone. **72.** a continuous course of performances, as of a play. **73.** onward movement, progress, course, etc. **74.** the direction of something: *the run of the grain of wood.* **75.** the particular course or tendency of something: *the run of events.* **76.** freedom to range over, go through, or use: *to have the run of the house.* **77.** any rapid or easy course or progress. **78.** a continuous course of some condition of affairs, etc.: *a run of bad luck.* **79.** a continuous extent of something, as a vein of ore. **80.** a continuous series of something. **81.** a set of things in regular order, as a sequence at cards. **82.** any continued or extensive demand, call, or the like. **83.** a spell of being in demand or favor with the public. **84.** a spell of causing something liquid to run or flow. **85.** the amount which runs. **86.** a flow or rush of water, etc. **87.** a small stream; brook; rivulet. **88.** a kind or class, as of goods. **89.** the ordinary or average kind. **90.** that in or on which something runs or may run. **91.** *Chiefly Brit.* an enclosure within which domestic animals may range about: *a chicken run.* **92.** a way, track, or the like, along which something runs or moves. **93.** a trough or pipe through which water, etc., runs. **94.** the movement of a number of fish upstream or inshore from deep water. **95.** large numbers of fish in motion, esp. inshore from deep water or up a river for spawning. **96.** a number of animals moving together. **97.** *Music.* a rapid succession of tones; a roulade. **98.** a series of sudden and urgent demands, as on a bank, for payment. **99.** a series of successful shots, strokes, or the like, in a game. **100.** *Baseball.* the score unit, made by successfully running around all the bases and reaching the home plate. **101.** *Cricket.* the score unit, made by the successful running of both batsmen from one wicket to the other. **102.** *Naut.* the extreme after part of a ship's bottom. —*adj.* **103.** melted or liquefied. **104.** poured in a melted state; run into and cast in a mold. [ME *rinne(n),* OE *rinnan,* c. G *rinnen,* Icel. *rinna.* form *run* orig. pp., later extended to present tense]

run·a·bout (rŭn′ə bout′), *n.* **1.** an automobile of the open-car type intended to accommodate two persons; roadster. **2.** one who runs about from place to place.

run·a·gate (rŭn′ə gāt′), *n. Archaic.* **1.** a fugitive or runaway. **2.** a vagabond or wanderer. [f. RUN, v. + obs. *agate* away; sense devel. influenced by contam. with obs. *renegate* (ME *renegat,* t. ML: s. *renegātus* RENEGADE)]

run-a·round (rŭn′ə round′), *n.* **1.** *Slang.* equivocation; evasion. **2.** *Print.* an arrangement of type using a temporarily narrower column around a picture, etc.

run·a·way (rŭn′ə wā′), *n.* **1.** one who runs away; a fugitive; a deserter. **2.** a horse or team which has broken away from control. **3.** act of running away. —*adj.* **4.** having run away; escaped; fugitive. **5.** (of a horse, etc.) having escaped from the control of the rider or driver. **6.** pertaining to or accomplished by running away or eloping: *a runaway marriage.* **7.** easily won, as a race. **8.** Com. characterized by a rapid price rise: *runaway inflation.*

run·ci·ble spoon (rŭn′sə bəl), a utensil with two broad prongs (like a fork) and one sharp, curved prong (like a spoon).

run·ci·nate (rŭn′sĭ nĭt, -nāt′), *adj. Bot.* (of a leaf, etc.) pinnately incised, with the lobes or teeth curved backward. [t. NL: m.s. *runcīnātus,* der. L *runcina* plane (once thought to mean saw)]

run·dle (rŭn′dəl), *n.* **1.** a rung of a ladder. **2.** a wheel or similar rotating object. [var. of ROUNDEL]

Runcinate leaf

rund·let (rŭnd′lĭt), *n. Archaic.* an old British measure of capacity, about 18 wine gallons. [ME *rondelet,* t. OF, der. *rondelle,* der. *rond* ROUND]

run-down (rŭn′doun′), *adj.* **1.** fatigued; weary. **2.** fallen into disrepair. **3.** (of a spring-operated timepiece) not running because not wound. —*n.* **4.** a quick review or summary of main points of information, usually oral: *this brief run-down of past events will bring you up to date.*

rune¹ (rōōn), *n.* **1.** any of the characters of an alphabet used by the ancient Germanic-speaking peoples, esp. the Scandinavians. **2.** something written or inscribed in such characters. [t. Icel.: m. *rūn*]

Runes, 9th century

rune² (rōōn), *n. Poetic.* a poem, song, or verse. [t. Finnish: m. *runo* poem or canto, t. Scand. See BUNE¹]

rung¹ (rŭng), *v.* pt. and pp. of ring².

rung² (rŭng), *n.* **1.** one of the rounded crosspieces forming the steps of a ladder. **2.** a rounded or shaped piece fixed horizontally, for strengthening purposes, as between the legs of a chair. **3.** a stout stick, rod, or bar, esp. one of rounded section, forming a piece in something framed or constructed: *the rungs of a wheel.* [ME; OE *hrung,* c. G *runge*]

ru·nic¹ (rōō′nĭk), *adj.* **1.** consisting of or set down in runes: *runic inscriptions.* **2.** (of ornamental knots, figures, etc.) of an interlaced form seen on ancient monuments, metalwork, etc., of the northern European peoples. [f. RUNE¹ + -IC]

ru·nic² (rōō′nĭk), *adj.* of the ancient Scandinavian class or type, as literature, poetry, etc. [f. RUNE² + -IC]

run-in (rŭn′ĭn′), *n.* **1.** *Colloq.* disagreement; slight quarrel. **2.** *Printing.* matter that is added to a text, esp. without indenting or making a new paragraph.

Run·jeet Singh (rŭn′jĭt sĭn′hə), Ranjit Singh.

run·let (rŭn′lĭt), *n.* a runnel. [f. RUN, n., + -LET]

run·nel (rŭn′əl), *n.* **1.** a small stream or brook, or a rivulet. **2.** a small channel, as for water. [OE *rynel(e),* var. of *rinelle* rindle]

run·ner (rŭn′ər), *n.* **1.** one who or that which runs; a racer. **2.** a messenger. **3.** a messenger of a bank or brokerage house. **4.** one whose business it is to solicit patronage or trade. **5.** one acting as collector, agent, or the like for a bank, broker, etc. **6.** something in or on which something else runs or moves. **7.** either of the long pieces of wood or metal on which a sled or the like slides. **8.** the blade of a skate. **9.** a sharp curved blade used to open a furrow for placing seed. **10.** the rotating system of blades driven by the fluid passing through a reaction turbine. **11.** a roller on which something moves along. **12.** an operator or manager, as of a machine. **13.** a long, narrow rug, suitable for a hall or passageway. **14.** a long, narrow strip of linen, embroidery, lace, or the like, placed across a table. **15.** *Bot.* **a.** a slender, prostrate stem which throws out roots at its nodes or end, thus producing new plants. **b.** a plant that spreads by such stems. **16.** *Metall.* gate (def. 9). **17.** a smuggler. **18.** a smuggling vessel. **19.** *Ichthyol.* a jurel, *Caranx crysos,* ranging from Cape Cod to Brazil.

Runner of strawberry

runner bean, *Brit.* string bean.

run·ner-up (rŭn′ər ŭp′), *n.* the competitor, player, or team finishing in second place.

run·ning (rŭn′ĭng), *n.* **1.** act of one who or that which runs. **2.** competition, as in a race: *to be out of the run-*

ning. **3.** managing or directing: *the running of a business.* —*adj.* **4.** that runs; moving or passing rapidly. **5.** (of a horse) **a.** going or proceeding rapidly at the gait of a run. **b.** taught to proceed at a run. **6.** creeping or climbing, as plants. **7.** moving or proceeding easily or smoothly. **8.** moving when pulled or hauled, as a rope. **9.** slipping or sliding easily, as a knot or a noose. **10.** operating, as a machine. **11.** (of measurement) linear; straight-line. **12.** cursive, as handwriting. **13.** flowing, as a stream. **14.** liquid or fluid. **15.** current: *the running month.* **16.** prevalent, as a condition, etc. **17.** going or carried on continuously; sustained: *a running commentary.* **18.** extending or repeated continuously: *a running pattern.* **19.** following in succession (placed after the noun): *for three nights running.* **20.** performed with or during a run: *a running leap.* **21.** discharging matter, as a sore.

running board, a small ledge, step, or footboard, beneath the doors of an automobile, to assist passengers entering or leaving the car.

running gear, the frame, wheels, axles, and power developing and transmitting components of a motor or steam-driven vehicle, and their attachments and accessories, as distinguished from the body.

running head, *Print.* a descriptive heading repeated at the top of (usually) each page. Also, **running title.**

running knot, a knot made round and so as to slide along a part of the same rope, thus forming a noose (**running noose**) which tightens as the rope is pulled.

running mate, 1. a horse used to establish the pace for another horse in a race. **2.** a candidate for an office linked with another and more important office, as the vice-presidency.

running shed, *Brit.* a railroad roundhouse.

Run·ny·mede (rŭn′ĭ mēd′), *n.* a meadow on the S bank of the Thames, W of London, England: the supposed place of the signing of the Magna Charta by King John, 1215.

run-off (rŭn′ôf′, -ŏf′), *n.* **1.** something which runs off, as rain which flows off from the land in streams. **2.** a deciding final contest held after a principal one. **3.** a deciding final race held after a dead heat.

run-off primary, a second election, in most Southern States, between the two highest candidates of the primary, to provide nomination by majority rather than by plurality.

run-on (rŭn′ŏn′, -ôn′), *adj.* of or designating something which is added on or run on: *a run-on entry in a dictionary.*

run·round (rŭn′round′), *n.* run-around.

runt (rŭnt), *n.* **1.** an undersized, stunted animal, person, or thing, esp. one that is small as compared with others of its kind. **2.** a vague term of opprobrium for a person. [OE **hrunta* (in *Hrunting* name of sword in *Beowulf,* der. *hrung* RUNG²]

run-through (rŭn′thrōō′), *n.* the performing of a sequence of designated actions, esp. as a trial prior to their official performance; rehearsal.

runt·y (rŭn′tĭ), *adj.* **runtier, runtiest.** stunted; dwarfish: *dominated by his runty wife.* —**runt′·i·ness,** *n.*

run·way (rŭn′wā′), *n.* **1.** a way along which something runs. **2.** a paved or cleared strip on which planes land and take off; airstrip. **3.** a similar strip for cars, trucks, etc. **4.** the beaten track of deer or other animals. **5.** a run (def. 91). **6.** the bed of a stream. **7.** *Bowling.* a path over which the bowls are sent back to the bowlers.

ru·pee (rōō pē′), *n.* a silver coin and the monetary unit of India, equal to 16 annas, and at present equivalent to about 21 U.S. cents. [t. Hind. (Urdū): m. *rupiyah,* g. Skt. *rūpya* wrought silver]

Ru·pert (rōō′pərt; *Ger.* -pĕrt), *n.* Prince, 1619–82, German prince who aided his uncle, Charles I of England, in the English Civil War.

rup·ture (rŭp′chər), *n., v.,* **-tured, -turing.** —*n.* **1.** act of breaking or bursting. **2.** state of being broken or burst. **3.** a breach of harmonious, friendly, or peaceful relations. **4.** *Pathol.* hernia, esp. abdominal hernia. —*v.t.* **5.** to break or burst (a blood vessel, etc.). **6.** to cause a breach of (relations, etc.). **7.** *Pathol.* to affect with hernia. —*v.i.* **8.** to suffer a break or rupture. [t. L: m. *ruptūra*] —**rup′tur·a·ble,** *adj.*

ru·ral (rōōr′əl), *adj.* **1.** of, pertaining to, or characteristic of the country (as distinguished from towns or cities), country life, or country people; rustic. **2.** living in the country. **3.** of or pertaining to agriculture: *rural economy.* [ME, t. L: s. *rūrālis*] —**ru′ral·ism,** *n.* —**ru′ral·ist,** *n.* —**ru′ral·ly,** *adv.*

—Syn. **1.** RURAL and RUSTIC are terms which refer to the country. RURAL is the official term: *rural education.* It may be used subjectively, and usually in a favorable sense: *the charm of rural life.* RUSTIC, however, may have either favorable or unfavorable connotations. In a derogatory sense, it means rough, boorish, or crude; in a favorable sense, it may suggest a homelike unsophistication or ruggedness: *rustic simplicity.* —Ant. **1.** urban.

rural free delivery, free mail delivery in outlying country areas. *Abbr.:* R.F.D.

ru·ral·i·ty (rōō rāl′ə tĭ), *n., pl.* **-ties. 1.** rural character. **2.** a rural characteristic, matter, or scene.

ru·ral·ize (rōōr′ə līz′), *v.,* **-ized, -izing.** —*v.t.* **1.** to make rural. —*v.i.* **2.** to spend time in the country; rusticate. —**ru′ral·i·za′tion,** *n.*

Ru·rik (rŏŏr′ĭk), n. died A.D. 879, Scandinavian prince: founder of the Russian monarchy.

ruse (rōōz), n. a trick, stratagem, or artifice. [ME, n. use of obs. *ruse* to detour, t. F: m. *ruser*. See RUSH]

rush[1] (rŭsh), v.i. **1.** to move or go with speed, impetuosity, or violence. **2.** to dash; dash forward for an attack or onslaught. **3.** to go or plunge with headlong or rash haste. **4.** to go, come, pass, etc., rapidly: *tears rushed to her eyes.* —v.t. **5.** to send or drive with speed or violence. **6.** to carry or convey with haste: *to rush an injured person to the hospital.* **7.** to send, push, force, etc., with unusual speed or undue haste: *to rush a bill through Congress.* **8.** to attack with a rush. **9.** to overcome or take (a person, force, place, etc.). **10.** *U.S. Slang.* to heap attentions on. **11.** *Football.* to move (the ball) forward by one or several rushes. —n. **12.** act of rushing; a rapid, impetuous, or headlong onward movement. **13.** a hostile attack. **14.** an eager rushing of numbers of persons to some region to be occupied or exploited, esp. to a new mine field. **15.** a sudden coming or access: *a rush of blood to his face.* **16.** hurried activity; busy haste: *the rush of city life.* **17.** a hurried state, as from pressure of affairs: *to be in a rush.* **18.** press of work, business, traffic, etc., requiring extraordinary effort or haste. **19.** *Football.* **a.** an attempt to carry the ball through the opposing line. **b.** a player in the forward line who makes such attempts. **20.** *U.S.* a scrimmage held as a form of sport between classes or bodies of students in colleges. **21.** (pl.) *Motion Pictures.* the first prints made after shooting a scene or scenes. —adj. **22.** requiring haste: *a rush order.* **23.** characterized by press of work, traffic, etc.: *rush season.* [ME *rusche(n)*, t. AF: m. *russher*, *russer*, var. of OF *re(h)usser*, *re(h)user*, *ruser*, g. LL *recūsāre* push back, L *refuse*] —Syn. **1.** RUSH, HURRY, DASH, SPEED imply swiftness of movement. RUSH implies haste and sometimes violence in motion through some distance: *to rush to the store.* HURRY suggests a sense of strain or agitation, a breathless rushing to get to a definite place by a certain time: *to hurry to an appointment.* DASH implies impetuosity or spirited, swift movement for a short distance: *to dash to the neighbor's.* SPEED means to go fast, usually by means of some type of transportation, and with some smoothness of motion: *to speed to a nearby city.*

rush[2] (rŭsh), n. **1.** any plant of the genus *Juncus* (family *Juncaceae*), which comprises grasslike herbs with pithy or hollow stems, found in wet or marshy places. **2.** any plant of the same family. **3.** any of various similar plants. **4.** a stem of such a plant, used for making chair bottoms, mats, baskets, etc. **5.** something of little or no value: *not worth a rush.* [ME *russhe*, OE *rysc(e)*, c. D and G *rusch*] —**rush′like′**, adj.

Rush (rŭsh), n. **Benjamin,** 1745–1813, U.S. physician and patriot.

rush candle, a candle made by dipping a dried and peeled pithy-stemmed rush in tallow. Also, **rush light.**

rush·er (rŭsh′ər), n. **1.** one who or that which rushes. **2.** *Football.* a player in the forward line.

rush hour, the morning or evening period when large numbers of people are going to work or returning home. —**rush-hour** (rŭsh′our′), adj.

rush line, *Football.* the forward line of players.

rush·y (rŭsh′ĭ), adj., **rushier, rushiest. 1.** abounding with rushes. **2.** covered or strewed with rushes. **3.** consisting or made of rushes. **4.** rushlike.

ru·sine antler (rōō′sĭn, -sĭn) an antler resembling that of the sambar.

rus in ur·be (rŭs′ ĭn ûr′bē), *Latin.* the country in the city.

rusk (rŭsk), n. **1.** a slice of sweet raised bread dried and browned in the oven; zwieback. **2.** light, soft, sweetened biscuit. [t. Sp. or Pg.: m. *rosca* twist of bread, lit., screw]

Rus·kin (rŭs′kĭn), n. **John,** 1819–1900, British author, art critic, and social reformer.

Russ (rŭs), n., pl. **Russ,** adj. —n. **1.** a Russian. —adj. **2.** Russian. [t. Russ.: m. *Rusi*]

Russ., **1.** Russia. **2.** Russian.

Rus·sell (rŭs′əl), n. **1. Bertrand, third Earl,** born 1872, British philosopher, mathematician, and writer. **2. (Elizabeth) Mary Annette Russell, Countess,** 1866–1941, British novelist. **3. George William,** (*AE*) 1867–1935, Irish poet and painter. **4. John Russell, 1st Earl,** (*Lord John Russell*) 1792–1878, British statesman; prime minister, 1846–52 and 1865–66. **5. Lillian,** (*Helen Louise Leonard*) 1861–1922, U.S. singer and actress.

rus·set (rŭs′ĭt), n. **1.** yellowish brown; light brown; reddish brown. **2.** a coarse reddish-brown or brownish homespun cloth formerly in use. **3.** a winter apple with a rough brownish skin. —adj. **4.** yellowish-brown; light-brown; reddish-brown. [ME, t. OF: m. *rousset*, dim. of *rous* red, g. L *russus*]

Rus·sia (rŭsh′ə), n. **1.** Also, **Russian Empire.** a former empire in E Europe and N and W Asia: overthrown by the Russian Revolution, 1917. *Cap.*: St. Petersburg (Petrograd). **2.** the Soviet Union.

Russia leather, a fine, smooth leather produced by careful tanning and dyeing, esp. in dark red: orig. prepared in Russia, but imitated elsewhere. Also, **russia.**

Rus·sian (rŭsh′ən), adj. **1.** of or pertaining to Russia, its people, or their language. —n. **2.** a native or inhabitant of Russia. **3.** a member of the dominant

Slavic race of Russia. **4.** the principal Slavic language, belonging to the East Slavic subgroup, and the predominant language of the Soviet Union. See **Great Russians, Little Russians, White Russians.**

Russian Church, the national church of Russia (before 1918), a branch of the Orthodox Eastern Church.

Russian dressing, a sharp mayonnaise dressing prepared by the addition of chopped pickles, chili sauce, pimientos, etc.

Russian Empire, Russia (def. 1).

Rus·sian·ize (rŭsh′ə nīz′), v.t., **-ized, -izing.** to make Russian; impart Russian characteristics to.

Russian Revolution, 1. the uprising of March 12, 1917, by which the Czar's government was abolished and replaced by a constitutional government. **2.** the overthrow of this provisional government by a coup d'état on Nov. 7, 1917, establishing the Soviet Union.

Russian Soviet Federated Socialist Republic, the largest of the constituent republics of the Soviet Union, including over three fourths of the total area. 113,200,000 (est. 1956); ab. 6,442,700 sq. mi. *Cap.*: Moscow. *Abbr.*: RSFSR or R.S.F.S.R. Also, **Soviet Russia.**

Russian thistle, an annual tumbleweed, *Salsola tragus,* growing 2 to 3 feet in diameter, with small-leafed, spiny branches.

Russian wolfhound, a large dog of a Russian breed, resembling the deerhound in general build but having much softer hair; borzoi.

Russian Zone, zone in Germany controlled by Soviet Union since 1945. Also, **East Germany.**

Russian wolfhound
(28 to 31 in. high at the shoulder)

Russo-, a word element representing Russia, as in *Russophobe, Russophile.*

Rus·so·phile (rŭs′ō fĭl′), n. one who admires or favors Russia or anything Russian.

Rus·so·phobe (rŭs′ō fōb′), n. one who fears or hates anything Russian. —**Rus·so·pho·bi·a** (rŭs′ō fō′bĭ ə), n.

rust (rŭst), n. **1.** the red or orange coating which forms on the surface of iron when exposed to air and moisture, consisting chiefly of ferric hydroxide and ferric oxide. **2.** any film or coating on metal due to oxidation, etc. **3.** a stain resembling iron rust. **4.** any growth, habit, influence, or agency tending to injure the mind, character, abilities, usefulness, etc. **5.** *Plant Pathol.* **a.** of the various plant diseases caused by fungi, in which the leaves and stems become spotted and acquire a red to brown color. **b.** Also, **rust fungus.** a fungus producing such a disease. **6.** rust color; reddish yellow; reddish brown; yellowish red. —v.i. **7.** to grow rusty, as iron does. **8.** to contract rust. **9.** to deteriorate or become impaired, as through inaction or disuse. **10.** to become rust-colored. —v.t. **11.** to affect with rust. **12.** to impair as if with rust. **13.** to make rust-colored. [ME and OE, c. G *rost*] —**rust′a·ble,** adj.

rust-col·ored (rŭst′kŭl′ərd), adj. of the color of iron rust. See **rust** (def. 6).

rus·tic (rŭs′tĭk), adj. **1.** of, pertaining to, or living in the country as distinguished from towns or cities; rural. **2.** simple, artless, or unsophisticated. **3.** uncouth, rude, or boorish. **4.** made of roughly dressed limbs or roots of trees, as garden seats, etc. **5.** *Masonry.* having the surface rough or irregular, or the joints deeply sunk or chamfered. —n. **6.** a country person. **7.** an unsophisticated country person. [late ME, t. L: s. *rusticus*] —**rus′ti·cal·ly,** adv. —Syn. **1.** See rural.

rus·ti·cate (rŭs′tə kāt′), v.i., **-cated, -cating.** —v.i. **1.** to go to the country. **2.** to stay or sojourn in the country. —v.t. **3.** to send to or domicile in the country. **4.** to make rustic, as persons, manners, etc. **5.** to construct or finish (masonry, etc.) in the rustic manner. **6.** *Brit.* to suspend (a student) from a university as punishment. [t. L: m.s. *rusticātus,* pp., having lived in the country] —**rus′ti·ca′tion,** n. —**rus′ti·ca′tor,** n.

rus·tic·i·ty (rŭs tĭs′ə tĭ), n., pl. **-ties. 1.** state or quality of being rustic. **2.** rural character or life.

rus·tle (rŭs′əl), v., **-tled, -tling,** n. —v.i. **1.** to make a succession of slight, soft sounds, as of parts rubbing gently one on another, as leaves, silks, papers, etc. **2.** to cause such sounds by moving or stirring something. **3.** *U.S. Slang.* to move, proceed, or work energetically or vigorously. —v.t. **4.** to move or stir so as to cause a rustling sound: *the wind rustled the leaves.* **5.** *U.S. Slang.* to move, bring, get, etc., by energetic action. **6.** *Western U.S.* to steal (cattle, etc.). —n. **7.** the sound made by anything that rustles: *the rustle of leaves.* [ME; OE *hrūtlian* make a noise] —**rus′tling·ly,** adv.

rus·tler (rŭs′lər), n. **1.** one who or that which rustles. **2.** *U.S. Slang.* an active, energetic person. **3.** *Western U.S.* a cattle thief.

rust·less (rŭst′lĭs), adj. **1.** free from rust. **2.** rustproof.

rust-proof (rŭst′prōōf′), adj. not subject to rusting.

rust·y[1] (rŭs′tĭ), adj., **rustier, rustiest. 1.** covered or affected with rust. **2.** consisting of or produced by rust. **3.** of the color of rust; rust-colored; tending toward rust. **4.** faded or shabby; impaired by time or wear, as clothes, etc. **5.** impaired through disuse or neglect: *my Latin is rusty.* **6.** having lost agility or alertness; out of practice. **7.** (of plants) affected with the rust disease. [ME; OE *rustig,* c. G *rostig*] —**rust′i·ly,** adv. —**rust′i·ness,** n.

b., blend of, blended; c., cognate with; d., dialect, dialectal; der., derived from; f., formed from; g., going back to; m., modification of; r., replacing; s., stem of; t., taken from; ?, perhaps. See the full key on inside cover.

rust·y² (rŭs'tĭ), *adj.* **1.** restive; refractory. **2.** ill-tempered; cross. [appar. special use of RUSTY¹ in sense of rough, churlish; but cf. E *resty* RESTIVE]

rut¹ (rŭt), *n., v.,* **rutted, rutting.** —*n.* **1.** a furrow or track in the ground, esp. one made by the passage of a vehicle or vehicles. **2.** any furrow, groove, etc. **3.** a fixed or established mode of procedure or course of life: *to get into a rut.* —*v.t.* **4.** to make a rut or ruts in; furrow. [orig. uncert.; ? var. of ROUTE]

rut² (rŭt), *n., v.,* **rutted, rutting.** —*n.* **1.** the periodically recurring sexual excitement of the deer, goat, sheep, etc. —*v.i.* **2.** to be in the condition of rut. [ME *rutte,* t. OF: m. *rut,* var. of *ruit,* g. L *rugitus* a roaring]

ru·ta·ba·ga (rōō'tə bā'gə, -bĕg'ə), *n.* the Swedish or yellow turnip, *Brassica Napobrassica.* [t. d. Sw.: m. *rotabagge*]

ru·ta·ceous (rōō tā'shəs), *adj.* **1.** of or like rue². **2.** belonging to the *Rutaceae,* a family of plants including the rue, dittany, angostura bark tree, orange, lemon, shaddock, kumquat, etc., having pellucid dotted leaves. [t. L: m. *rūtāceus*]

Ruth (rōōth), *n. Bible.* **1.** a Moabite woman who married Boaz in Bethlehem and was an ancestress of David. **2.** a book of the Old Testament. [LL, t. Heb.]

Ruth (rōōth), *n.* **George Herman,** (*"Babe"*) 1895–1948, U.S. baseball player.

ruth (rōōth), *n. Archaic.* **1.** pity or compassion. **2.** sorrow or grief. [ME *r(e)uthe,* der. *rewe* RUE¹, or *rewe,* n., pity, OE *hrēow*]

Ru·the·ni·a (rōō thē'nĭ ə), *n.* a former province in E Czechoslovakia. See **Carpatho-Ukraine.**

Ru·the·ni·an (rōō thē'nĭ ən), *adj.* **1.** of or pertaining to the Little Russians, esp. a division of them dwelling in Galicia, Ruthenia, and neighboring regions. —*n.* **2.** one of the Ruthenian people. **3.** a Slavic language spoken in Ruthenia.

ru·then·ic (rōō thĕn'ĭk, -thē'nĭk), *adj. Chem.* containing ruthenium in a higher valence state than the corresponding ruthenious compound.

ru·the·ni·ous (rōō thē'nĭ əs), *adj. Chem.* containing divalent ruthenium (Ru+²).

ru·the·ni·um (rōō thē'nĭ əm), *n. Chem.* a difficultly fusible, steel-gray, rare metallic element, belonging to the platinum group of metals, and very little acted on by aqua regia. *Symbol:* Ru; *at. wt.:* 101.7; *at. no.:* 44; *sp. gr.:* 12.2 at 20°C. [NL, f. s. ML *Ruthenia* Russia (so named because it was first found in ores from the Ural Mountains) + *-ium* -IUM]

Ruth·er·ford (rŭth'ər fərd), *n.* **Ernest Rutherford, 1st Baron,** 1871–1937, British physicist, born in New Zealand.

ruth·ful (rōōth'fəl), *adj. Archaic.* **1.** compassionate or sorrowful. **2.** such as to excite sorrow or pity. —**ruth'·ful·ly,** *adv.* —**ruth'ful·ness,** *n.*

ruth·less (rōōth'lĭs), *adj.* without pity or compassion; pitiless; merciless. —**ruth'less·ly,** *adv.* —**ruth'less·ness,** *n.* —Syn. See **cruel.**

ru·ti·lant (rōō'tə lənt), *adj. Rare.* glowing; shining; glittering. [t. L: s. *rutilans,* ppr.]

ru·tile (rōō'tĕl, -tĭl), *n.* a common mineral, titanium dioxide, TiO₂, having a brilliant metallic-adamantine luster, and usually of a reddish-brown color. It occurs usually in crystals and is used to coat welding rods. [t. F, t. G: m. *rutil,* t. L: s. *rutilus* red]

Rut·land (rŭt'lənd), *n.* **1.** a city in W Vermont. 18,325 (1960) **2.** Rutlandshire.

Rut·land·shire (rŭt'lənd shĭr', -shər), *n.* a county in central England. 20,510 pop. (est. 1956); 152 sq. mi. *Co. seat:* Oakham. Also, **Rutland.**

Rut·ledge (rŭt'lĭj), *n.* **1. Edward,** 1749–1800, American patriot. **2.** his brother, **John,** 1739–1800, American statesman and jurist; associate justice of U.S. Supreme Court, 1789–91.

rut·tish (rŭt'ĭsh), *adj.* lustful. [f. RUT² + -ISH¹]

rut·ty (rŭt'ĭ), *adj.,* **-tier, -tiest.** full of or abounding in ruts, as a road. —**rut'ti·ness,** *n.*

Ru·wen·zo·ri (rōō'wĕn zōr'ĭ), *n.* a mountain group in central Africa between Lake Albert and Lake Edward: sometimes identified with Ptolemy's "Mountains of the Moon." Highest peak, Mt. Stanley, 16,790 ft.

Ruys·dael (rois'däl; *Du.* rœĭs'-), *n.* **Jacob van** (yä'kōp vän), 1628?–82, Dutch painter. Also, **Ruisdael.**

Ruy·ter (roi'tər; *Du.* rœĭ'-), *n.* **Michel Adriaanszoon de** (mĭ'кнəl ä'drĭ än'sōn də), 1607–76, Dutch admiral.

RV, Revised Version (of the Bible).

R.W., **1.** Right Worshipful. **2.** Right Worthy.

Rwan·da (rōō än'dä), *n.* a republic in central Africa, E of the Republic of the Congo: formerly comprising the northern part of the Belgian trust territory of Ruanda-Urundi; became independent on July 1, 1962. 2,634,451 pop. (1962); 10,169 sq. mi. *Cap.:* Kigali.

Ry., Railway.

-ry, a suffix of abstract nouns of condition, practice (*heraldry, husbandry, dentistry*), and of collectives (*tenantry, jewelry*). [short form of -ERY]

Rya·zan (ryä zän'), *n.* a city in the central Soviet Union in Europe, on the Oka river. 136,000 (est. 1956).

Ry·binsk (rwē'bĭnsk), *n.* former name of **Shcherbakov.**

Ry·der (rī'dər), *n.* **Albert Pinkham** (pĭngk'əm), 1847–1917, U.S. painter.

rye¹ (rī), *n.* **1.** a widely cultivated cereal grass, *Secale cereale,* with one-nerved glumes (differing from wheat which is many-nerved) and two- or three-flowered spikelets. **2.** the seeds or grain of this plant, used for making flour, for livestock feed, and for whiskey. **3.** a straight whiskey distilled from a mash containing 51% or more rye grain. **4.** (*Eastern U.S.*) a blended whiskey. [ME; OE *ryge,* c. Icel. *rugr,* akin to D *rogge,* G *roggen*]

rye² (rī), *n.* a gentleman: *Romany rye.* [t. Gypsy]

rynd (rīnd, rĭnd), *n.* a piece of iron running across the hole of an upper millstone and serving to support the stone. [ME *rynd(e),* c. d. D *ryn,* LG *rīn*]

Ryo·jun·ko (ryō'jōōn kō'), *n.* Japanese name of **Port Arthur** (def. 1). Also, **Ryo·jun** (ryō'jōōn').

ry·ot (rī'ət), *n.* (in India) **1.** a peasant. **2.** one who holds land as a cultivator of the soil. [t. Hind. (Urdū): m. *raiyat*]

Rys·wick (rĭz'wĭk), *n.* a village in SW Netherlands, near The Hague: Treaty of Ryswick, 1697.

Ryu·kyu (rū'kū'), *n.* a chain of 55 islands in the W Pacific between Japan and Formosa. Islands S of 28° N lat. under U. S. administration; islands N of 28° returned to Japan. 914,937 pop. (1950); 2046 sq. mi.

S

S, s (ĕs), *n., pl.* **S's** or **Ss, s's** or **ss.** a consonant, the 19th letter of the English alphabet.

-s¹, a suffix serving to form adverbs, as *always, betimes, needs, unawares.* Cf. **-ways.** [ME and OE *-es,* orig. gen. sing. ending.]

-s², an ending which marks the third person sing. indicative active of verbs, as in *hits.* [northern ME and OE *-(e)s* (orig. ending of second person, as in L and Gk.); r. ME and OE *-(e)th*]

's¹, an ending which marks the possessive sing. of nouns, as in *man's.* [ME and OE *-es*]

's², an ending which marks the possessive plur. of nouns, as in *men's.* [pl. use of poss. sing. ending]

's³, colloquial reduction of: **a.** is: *he's here.* **b.** has: *he's just gone.* **c.** us: *let's go.*

S, 1. Saxon. **2.** South. **3.** Southern. **4.** *Chem.* sulfur.

S., 1. Sabbath. **2.** Saint. **3.** Saturday. **4.** School. **5.** Sea. **6.** Senate. **7.** September. **8.** *Pharm.* (L *signa*) mark; label. **9.** (*Ital.*) Signor. **10.** (L *Socius*) Fellow. **11.** South. **12.** Southern. **13.** Sunday.

s., 1. second. **2.** section. **3.** (L *solidus*) shilling. **4.** (L *solidi*) shillings. **5.** singular. **6.** son. **7.** south. **8.** southern. **9.** stem. **10.** stem of. **11.** substantive.

Sa, *Chem.* samarium.

S.A., 1. Salvation Army. **2.** South Africa. **3.** South America. **4.** South Australia.

s.a., 1. semiannual. **2.** (L *sine anno*) without year or date. **3.** subject to approval. **4.** sex appeal.

Saa·di (sä dē'), *n.* c1184–1291?, Persian poet. Also, **Sadi.**

Saar (zär), *n.* **1.** a territory in W West Germany, in the Saar river valley: governed by the League of Nations, 1919–1935; returned to Germany 1935 as a result of a plebiscite. Under French economic control following World War II until 1956. 986,858 (est. 1954); 743 sq. mi. Also, **Saar Basin; Saar·land** (zär'länt). **2.** a river flowing from the Vosges Mountains in NE France N to the Moselle river in W West Germany. ab. 150 mi. French, **Sarre** (sär).

Saar·brück·en (zär brŏŏk'ən; *Ger.* zär brȳk'ən), *n.* a city in W West Germany: the chief city of the Saar. 116,395 (est. 1953).

Saa·re·maa (sä'rĕ mä'), *n.* an island in the Baltic at the mouth of the Gulf of Riga, forming part of the Estonian Republic of the Soviet Union. ab. 60,000; 1144 sq. mi. Also, **Saa·re** (sä'rĕ). German, **Osel.**

Sab., Sabbath.

Sa·ba (sä'bä), *n.* **1.** an island in the Netherlands Antilles. 1131 (1955); 5 sq. mi. **2.** Sheba.

sab·a·dil·la (săb'ə dĭl'ə), *n.* **1.** a liliaceous plant of Mexico, *Schoenocaulon officinale,* with long grasslike leaves and bitter seeds. **2.** the seeds, which are used medicinally and as a source of veratrine and veratridine. [t. Sp.: m. *cebadilla,* dim. of *cebada* barley]

Sa·bae·an (sə bē'ən), *adj., n.* Sabean.

Sa·bah (sä'bä'), *n.* formerly, **British North Borneo,** a crown colony in NE Borneo: now part of the federation of Malaysia. 449,461 pop. (1960); 29,347 sq. mi. *Cap.:* Jesselton.

Sab·a·oth (săb'ȳ ŏth, -ŏth', sə bā'ŏth), *n.pl.* armies; hosts. [t. LL, t. Gk., t. Heb.: m. ç'bhāōth pl. of çābhā army]

Sab·a·ti·ni (săb'ə tē'nĭ; *It.* sä'bä tē'nē), *n.* **Rafael** (räf'ĭ əl), 1875–1950, Italian-English writer.

ăct, āble, dâre, ärt; ĕbb, ēqual; ĭf, īce; hŏt, ōver, ôrder, oil, bŏŏk, ōōze, out; ŭp, ūse, ûrge; ə = a in alone; ch, chief; g, give; ng, ring; sh, shoe; th, thin; ŧh, that; zh, vision. See the full key on inside cover.

Sab·ba·tar·i·an (săb′ə târ′Ĭ ən), *n.* **1.** one who observes the seventh day of the week (Saturday) as the Sabbath. **2.** one who adheres to or favors a strict observance of Sunday. [f. obs. *Sabbatary* (t. L: m.s. *sabbatārius* pertaining to the Sabbath) + -AN] —**Sab′·ba·tar′i·an·ism,** *n.*

Sab·bath (săb′əth), *n.* **1.** the seventh day of the week (Saturday) as the day of rest and religious observance among the Jews and certain Christian sects. See Ex. 20:8–11. **2.** the first day of the week (Sunday), similarly observed by most Christians in commemoration of the resurrection of Christ. [ME *sabath,* var. of ME and OE *sabat,* t. L: m.s. *sabbatum,* t. Gk.: m. *sábbaton,* t. Heb.: m. *shabbāth*] —**Syn. 2.** See **Sunday.**

Sabbath School, 1. a Sunday school. **2.** (among Seventh Day Adventists) such a school held on Saturday, their holy day.

Sab·bat·ic (sə băt′Ĭk), *adj., n.* Sabbatical. [t. Gk.: m.s. *sabbatikós*]

Sab·bat·i·cal (sə băt′ə kəl), *adj.* **1.** of, pertaining to, or appropriate to the Sabbath. **2.** (*l.c.*) bringing a period of rest: *a sabbatical leave.* —*n.* **3.** (*l.c.*) a sabbatical year. [f. SABBATIC + -AL¹] —**Sab·bat′i·cal·ly,** *adv.*

sabbatical year, 1. (in certain universities, etc.) a year, usually every seventh, of freedom from teaching, granted to a professor, as for study or travel. **2.** (among ancient Jews) every seventh year, during which fields were to be left untilled, debtors were to be released, etc.

Sa·be·an (sə bē′ən), *adj.* **1.** of or pertaining to Saba (Biblical Sheba). —*n.* **2.** an inhabitant of Saba. Also, **Sabaean.** [f. m.s. L *Sabaeus* t. Gk.: m. *Sabatos,* der. *Sába,* t. Ar., c. Heb. *Sh′bha*) + -AN]

sa·ber (sā′bər), *n.* **1.** a heavy one-edged sword, usually slightly curved, used esp. by cavalry. **2.** a soldier armed with such a sword. —*v.t.* **3.** to strike, wound, or kill with a saber. Also, *Brit.,* **sabre.** [t. F: m. *sabre, sable,* t. G: m. *sabel* (now *säbel;* ? of Oriental orig.] —**sa′ber·like′,** *adj.*

sa·ber-toothed (sā′bər tōōtht′), *adj.* having saberlike teeth, as some extinct feline mammals whose long upper canine teeth sometimes extended below the margin of the lower jaw.

saber-toothed tiger, any of a subfamily, *Machaerodontinae,* of fossil felines characterized by greatly elongated, saberlike upper canine teeth, found widely distributed in the Oligocene and into the Pleistocene.

Saber-toothed tiger.
Smilodon californicus
(6 ft. long)

Sa·bine (sā′bĭn), *adj.* **1.** belonging or pertaining to an ancient people of central Italy who lived chiefly in the Apennines to the northeast of Rome and who were subjugated by the Romans about 290 B.C. —*n.* **2.** one of the Sabine people.

Sa·bine (sə bēn′), *n.* a river flowing from NE Texas along the boundary between Louisiana and Texas, widening to form Sabine Lake (18 mi. long; 9 mi. wide) 5 mi. from its outflow into the Gulf of Mexico. 403 mi.

sa·ble (sā′bəl), *n.* **1.** an Old World weasellike mammal, *Mustela zibellina,* of cold regions, valued for its dark-brown fur. **2.** a marten, esp. *Mustela americana.* **3.** the fur of the sable. **4.** some similar fur, used as a substitute. **5.** the color black, often one of the heraldic colors. **6.** (*pl.*) mourning garments. —*adj.* **7.** made of the fur or hair of the sable. **8.** *Poetic.* black; very dark. [ME, t. OF, ult. t. Slavic; cf. Russ. *sobol*]

Sable, *Mustela zibellina*
(Total length 28 in., tail 9½ in.)

Sa·ble (sā′bəl), *n.* Cape, **1.** a cape on a small island at the SW tip of Nova Scotia, Canada: lighthouse. **2.** a cape at the S tip of Florida.

sable antelope, a large antelope, *Hippotragus niger,* of Africa, with long, saberlike horns.

sa·ble·fish (sā′bəl fĭsh′), *n., pl.* **-fishes,** (*esp. collectively*) **-fish.** a large, dark food fish, *Anoplopoma fimbria,* of the North Pacific Ocean.

sab·ot (săb′ō; *Fr.* sȧ bō′), *n.* **1.** a wooden shoe made of a single piece of wood hollowed out, worn by peasants in France, Belgium, etc. **2.** a shoe with a thick wooden sole and sides, and top of coarse leather. [t. F, in OF *çabot,* der. *savate* old shoe (ult. t. Ar.: m. *sabbāt* sandal), b. with *botte* boot]

sab·o·tage (săb′ə täzh′; *Fr.* sȧ bō tȧzh′), *n., v.,* **-taged, -taging.** —*n.* **1.** malicious injury to work, tools, machinery, etc., or any underhand interference with production or business, by enemy agents during wartime, by employees during a trade dispute, etc. **2.** any malicious attack on or undermining of a cause. —*v.t.* **3.** to injure or attack by sabotage. [t. F, der. *saboter* make a noise with sabots, do work badly, der. *sabot* SABOT]

sab·o·teur (săb′ə tûr′; *Fr.* sȧ bō tœr′), *n.* one who commits or practices sabotage.

sa·bre (sā′bər), *n., v.t.,* **-bred, -bring.** *Brit.* saber.

sa·bre·tache (sā′bər tăsh′, săb′ər-), *n.* a case, as of leather, suspended by long straps from the sword belt of a cavalryman and hanging beside the saber. [t. F, t. G: m. *säbel′ asche* saber pocket]

sab·u·lous (săb′yə ləs), *adj.* sandy; gritty. [t. L: m.s. *sabulōsus*] —**sab·u·los·i·ty** (săb′yə lŏs′ə tĬ), *n.*

sac (săk), *n.* a baglike structure in an animal or plant, as one containing fluid. [t. L: m.s. *saccus.* See SACK¹] —**sac′like′,** *adj.*

Sac (săk, sôk), *n.* **1.** (*pl.*) a tribe of Algonquian-speaking Indians, formerly of N Wisconsin and Iowa, now in Iowa and Oklahoma. **2.** a member of this tribe. Also, **Sauk.**

S.A.C., Strategic Air Command.

sac·a·ton (săk′ə tōn′), *n.* a grass, *Sporobolus wrightii,* used in the semiarid southwestern U.S. for pasture or hay. [t. Amer. Sp.: m. *zacatón,* aug. of *zacate* grass, hay, t. Aztec: m. *zacatl*]

sac·cate (săk′Ĭt, -āt), *adj.* in the form of, or having, a sac. [t. ML: m.s. *saccātus,* der. L *saccus.* See SAC]

sacchar-, a word element referring to sugar or saccharine. Also, **saccharo-.** [comb. form repr. Gk. *sákchar, sákcharon,* etc., sugar]

sac·cha·rate (săk′ə rāt′), *n. Chem.* **1.** a salt of saccharic acid. **2.** a compound formed by interaction of sucrose with a metallic oxide, usually lime, and useful in the purification of sugar.

sac·char·ic acid (sə kăr′Ĭk), the dicarboxylic acid formed by oxidation of glucose.

sac·char·i·fy (sə kăr′ə fĬ′, săk′ə rə fĬ′), *v.t.,* **-fied, -fying.** to convert (starch, etc.) into sugar. —**sac·char·i·fi·ca·tion** (sə kăr′ə fə kā′shən), *n.*

sac·cha·rim·e·ter (săk′ə rĬm′ə tər), *n.* an optical instrument for determining the strength of sugar solutions by measuring polarization of light through them. [t. F: m. *saccharimètre.* See SACCHAR-, -I-, -METER]

sac·cha·rin (săk′ə rĬn), *n.* a crystalline compound, $C_7H_5NO_3S$, obtained from toluene. It is some 400 times as sweet as cane sugar and is used as a sweetening agent in cases of diabetes and obesity.

sac·cha·rine (săk′ə rĬn, -rĬn′), *adj.* **1.** of a sugary sweetness: *a saccharine smile.* **2.** pertaining to, of the nature of, or containing sugar. —*n.* **3.** saccharin. —**sac·cha·rin·i·ty** (săk′ə rĬn′ə tĬ), *n.*

sac·cha·rize (săk′ə rĬz′), *v.t.,* **-rized, -rizing. 1.** to convert into sugar; saccharify. **2.** to convert (the starches in grain) to fermentable sugars during mashing. —**sac′cha·ri·za′tion,** *n.*

saccharo-, var. of **sacchar-,** before consonants.

sac·cha·roid (săk′ə roid′), *adj. Geol.* having a granular texture like that of loaf sugar. Also, **sac′cha·roi′dal.**

Sac·co (săk′ō; *It.* säk′kō), *n.* **Nikola** (nē kō′lä), 1891–1927, Italian political radical in U.S., executed for murder along with Bartolomeo Vanzetti after a trial which caused protests from liberals who believed political considerations had influenced the verdict.

sac·cu·late (săk′yə lāt′), *adj.* formed into or with a saccule, sac, or saclike dilations. Also, **sac′cu·lat′ed.**

sac·cule (săk′ūl), *n.* **1.** *Anat.* the smaller of two sacs in the membranous labyrinth of the internal ear. **2.** a little sac. [t. L: m.s. *sacculus,* dim. of *saccus* SAC]

sac·cu·lus (săk′yə ləs), *n., pl.* **-li** (-lĬ′). saccule. [t. L. See SACCULE]

sac·er·do·tal (săs′ər dō′təl), *adj.* of priests; priestly. [t. L: s. *sacerdōtālis*] —**sac′er·do·tal·ly,** *adv.*

sac·er·do·tal·ism (săs′ər dō′tə lĬz′əm), *n.* **1.** the system, spirit, or methods of the priesthood. **2.** *Derogatory.* priestcraft.

sa·chem (sā′chəm), *n.* **1.** (among some tribes of American Indians) **a.** the chief. **b.** the chief of a confederation of Indians. **2.** a member of the governing body of the League of the Iroquois. **3.** one of the high officials in the Tammany Society. [t. Algonquian (Narragansett): chief, (Massachusetts Indians) head chief]

sa·chet (să shā′ *or, esp. Brit.,* săsh′ā), *n.* **1.** a small bag, case, pad, etc., containing perfuming powder or the like. **2.** the powder. [t. F, dim. of *sac,* g. L *saccus.* See SACK¹]

Sachs (zäks), *n.* **Hans** (häns), 1494–1576, German cobbler, famous as a writer of poems and plays.

Sach·sen (zäk′sən), *n.* German name of **Saxony** (defs. 1, 2, and 3).

sack¹ (săk), *n.* **1.** a large bag of stout woven material, as for grain, potatoes, coal, etc. **2.** the amount which a sack will hold, a varying unit of measure. **3.** *U.S.* any bag: *a sack of candy.* **4.** Also, **sacque.** a loose-fitting coat or jacket, esp. for women and children. **5.** *Brit. Slang.* dismissal or discharge, as from employment. —*v.t.* **6.** to put into a sack or sacks. **7.** *Brit. Slang.* to dismiss or discharge, as from employment. [ME *sak,* OE *sacc,* t. L: s. *saccus* bag, sackcloth, t. Gk.: m. *sákkos,* t. Heb.: m. *saq*] —**Syn. 1.** See **bag.**

sack² (săk), *v.t.* **1.** to pillage or loot after capture; plunder: *to sack a city.* —*n.* **2.** the plundering of a captured place; pillage: *the sack of Troy.* [t. F: m. *sac,* t. It.: m. *sacco,* der. LL *saccāre,* t. Gmc. (cf. MLG *schäken* rob), b. with L *saccus* SACK¹] —**sack′er,** *n.* —**Syn. 1.** See **rob.**

sack³ (săk), *n.* any of various strong light-colored wines formerly brought from Spain, the Canary Islands, etc. [t. F: m. (*vin*) *sec* dry (wine), g. L *siccus* dry]

sack·but (săk′bŭt′), *n.* **1.** a medieval form of the trombone. **2.** (in Biblical usage) an ancient stringed musical instrument. Dan. 3. [t. F: m. *saquebute,* ONF *saqueboute,* lit., pull-push]

---

b., blend of, blended; c., cognate with; d., dialect, dialectal; der., derived from; f., formed from; g., going back to; m., modification of; r., replacing; s., stem of; t., taken from; ?, perhaps. See the full key on inside cover.

sack·cloth (săk′klôth′, -klŏth′), *n.* **1.** sacking. **2.** coarse cloth worn as a sign of mourning or penitence.

sack coat, a man's short, more or less loose-fitting coat for ordinary wear.

sack·ful (săk′fŏŏl′), *n.*, *pl.* **-fuls.** the amount that fills a sack.

sack·ing (săk′ĭng), *n.* stout or coarse woven material of hemp, jute, or the like, used for making sacks, etc.

sack·less (săk′lĭs), *adj.* **1.** *Scot.* lacking energy; dispirited. **2.** *Scot.* feeble-minded. **3.** *Archaic.* guiltless. [ME *sak(e)les*, OE *sacleas*. See SAKE[1], -LESS]

Sack·ville (săk′vĭl), *n.* **Thomas.** See **Dorset, 1st Earl of.**

Sack·ville-West (săk′vĭl wĕst′), *n.* **Victoria Mary,** 1892–1962, British novelist and poet.

sacque (săk), *n.* a woman's sack (coat or jacket).

sa·cral[1] (sā′krəl), *adj.* of or pertaining to sacred rites or observances. [f. s. L *sacrum* sacred rite (prop. neut. adj.) + -AL[1]]

sa·cral[2] (sā′krəl), *adj.* of or pertaining to the sacrum. [t. NL: s. *sacrālis*. See SACRUM]

sac·ra·ment (săk′rə mənt), *n.* **1.** *Eccles.* a visible sign instituted by Jesus Christ to confer grace or Divine Life on those who worthily receive it. The sacraments of the Protestant Churches are baptism and the Lord's Supper; the sacraments of the Roman and Greek Catholic Churches are baptism, confirmation, the Eucharist, matrimony, penance, holy orders, and extreme unction. **2.** (*often cap.*) the Eucharist, or Lord's Supper. **3.** the consecrated elements of the Eucharist, esp. the bread (the Blessed Sacrament). **4.** something regarded as possessing a sacred character or a mysterious significance. **5.** a sign, token, or symbol. **6.** an oath; solemn pledge. [ME, t. L: s. *sacrāmentum* oath, solemn engagement]

sac·ra·men·tal (săk′rə mĕn′təl), *adj.* **1.** of, pertaining to, or of the nature of a sacrament, esp. the sacrament of the Eucharist. **2.** peculiarly sacred: *a sacramental obligation.* —*n.* **3.** *Rom. Cath. Ch.* a sacramentlike ritual, object, etc., which the church institutes and uses for obtaining a spiritual effect, such as the sign of the cross, the use of holy water, etc.

sac·ra·men·tal·ist (săk′rə mĕn′təl ĭst), *n.* one who holds strong convictions about the importance and efficacy of the sacrament.

Sac·ra·men·tar·i·an (săk′rə mĕn târ′ĭ ən), *n.* **1.** one of the Protestant theologians, as Zwingli, maintaining that the bread and wine of the Eucharist can be said to be the body and blood of Christ only in a sacramental (that is, symbolical or metaphorical) sense. **2.** (*l.c.*) a sacramentalist. —*adj.* **3.** (*l.c.*) pertaining to the sacraments or (*cap.*) to the Sacramentarians.

Sac·ra·men·to (săk′rə mĕn′tō), *n.* **1.** the capital of California, in the central part: a port on the Sacramento river. 191,667 (1960). **2.** a river flowing from N California S to San Francisco Bay. 382 mi.

sa·crar·i·um (sə krâr′ĭ əm), *n.*, *pl.* **-craria** (-krâr′ĭ ə). **1.** *Rom. Cath. Ch.* a piscina. **2.** *Eccles.* the sanctuary or chancel. **3.** *Rom. Hist.* a shrine; a sanctuary. [t. L]

sa·cred (sā′krĭd), *adj.* **1.** appropriated or dedicated to a deity or to some religious purpose; consecrated. **2.** entitled to veneration or religious respect by association with divinity or divine things; holy. **3.** pertaining to or connected with religion (opposed to *profane* and *secular*): *sacred music.* **4.** reverently dedicated to some person or object: *a monument sacred to her memory.* **5.** regarded with reverence: *the sacred memory of a dead hero.* **6.** secured against violation, infringement, etc., by reverence, sense of right, etc.: *sacred oaths, sacred rights.* **7.** properly immune from violence, interference, etc., as a person or his office. [ME, pp. of *sacren* render holy, t. L: m. *sacrāre*] —**sa′cred·ly,** *adv.* —**sa′cred·ness,** *n.* —Syn. 2. See **holy.**

Sacred College, *Rom. Cath. Ch.* the College of Cardinals.

sac·ri·fice (săk′rə fīs′), *n.*, *v.*, **-ficed, -ficing.** —*n.* **1.** the offering of life (animal, plant, or human) or some material possession, etc., to a deity, as in propitiation or homage. **2.** that which is so offered. **3.** the surrender or destruction of something prized or desirable for the sake of something considered as having a higher or more pressing claim. **4.** the thing so surrendered or devoted. **5.** a loss incurred in selling something below its value. —*v.t.* **6.** to make a sacrifice or offering of. **7.** to surrender or give up, or permit injury or disadvantage to, for the sake of something else. **8.** to dispose of (goods, etc.) regardless of profit. —*v.i.* **9.** *Baseball.* to gain a base by a sacrifice hit. **10.** to offer or make a sacrifice. [ME, t. F, t. L: m.s. *sacrificium*] —**sac′ri·fic′er,** *n.*

sacrifice hit, *Baseball.* a hit which allows a runner to gain a base while the batter is (or could be) put out before reaching first base.

sac·ri·fi·cial (săk′rə fĭsh′əl), *adj.* pertaining to or concerned with sacrifice. —**sac′ri·fi′cial·ly,** *adv.*

sac·ri·lege (săk′rə lĭj), *n.* **1.** the violation or profanation of anything sacred or held sacred. **2.** an instance of this. **3.** the stealing of anything consecrated to the service of God. [ME, t. OF, t. L: m.s. *sacrilegium*]

sac·ri·le·gious (săk′rə lĭj′əs, -lē′jəs), *adj.* **1.** guilty of sacrilege: *a sacrilegious person.* **2.** involving sacrilege: *sacrilegious practices.* [f. s. L *sacrilegium* sacrilege + -OUS] —**sac′ri·le′gious·ly,** *adv.* —**sac′ri·le′gious·ness,** *n.*

sa·cring (sā′krĭng), *n. Archaic.* act or ceremony of consecrating, esp. the consecrating of the Eucharistic elements in the Mass.

sac·ris·tan (săk′rĭs tən), *n.* **1.** an official in charge of the sacred vessels, vestments, etc., of a church or a religious house. **2.** *Obs.* or *Archaic.* a sexton. [ME, t. ML: s. *sacristānus*]

sac·ris·ty (săk′rĭs tĭ), *n.*, *pl.* **-ties.** an apartment in or a building connected with a church or a religious house, in which the sacred vessels, vestments, etc., are kept. [t. ML: m.s. *sacristia*]

sacro-, a word element: **1.** meaning "holy." **2.** referring to the sacrum. [t. L, comb. form of *sacer* (neut. *sacrum*) holy]

sa·cro·il·i·ac (sā′krō ĭl′ĭ ăk, săk′rō-), *Anat.* —*n.* **1.** the joint where the sacrum and ilium meet. —*adj.* **2.** pertaining to this joint. [f. SACRO- + ILIAC]

sac·ro·sanct (săk′rō săngkt′), *adj.* especially or superlatively sacred or inviolable. [t. L: s. *sacrōsanctus*] —**sac′ro·sanc′ti·ty,** *n.*

sa·cro·sci·at·ic (sā′krō sī ăt′ĭk), *adj. Anat.* pertaining to the sacrum and the ischium: *the sacrosciatic ligament.*

sa·crum (sā′krəm), *n.*, *pl.* **-cra** (-krə). *Anat.* a bone resulting from the ankylosis of two or more vertebrae between the lumbar and the coccygeal regions, in man composed (usually) of five fused vertebrae and forming the posterior wall of the pelvis. See diag. under **pelvis.** [t. NL, short for L (*os*) *sacrum*, lit., sacred (bone): so called because used in sacrifices]

sad (săd), *adj.*, **sadder, saddest. 1.** sorrowful or mournful: *to feel sad.* **2.** expressive of or characterized by sorrow: *sad looks.* **3.** causing sorrow: *a sad disappointment.* **4.** (of color) somber, dark, or dull. **5.** *Often Humorous.* deplorably bad; shocking: *a sad attempt.* **6.** *Dial.* soggy or doughy: *sad bread.* **7.** *Archaic.* firm or steadfast. [ME; OE *sæd*, c. G *satt*, Goth. *saths* full, sated; akin to L *sat, satis* enough, *satur* sated, Gk. *hádēn* enough] —**sad·ly** (săd′lĭ), *adv.*

—Syn. **1.** unhappy, despondent, disconsolate. SAD, DEPRESSED, DEJECTED, MELANCHOLY describe states of low spirits. SAD, the general term, varies in its suggestion from a slight, momentary unhappiness to deep-felt grief, or to a continuous state of combined pensiveness, wistfulness, and resignation: *sorrowful and sad, sad and lonely.* DEPRESSED refers to a temporary lapse in natural buoyancy because of fatigue, unhappiness, a sense of being unable to change unsatisfactory conditions, or the like: *depressed by a visit to the slums.* DEJECTED, though also referring to a temporary state of discouragement caused by some definite event or circumstance, implies lower spirits, being cast down by disappointment, frustration, and the like: *dejected over losing one's position.* MELANCHOLY describes a state caused rather by temperament and a chronically gloomy outlook than by any external reason: *habitually melancholy.*

sad·den (săd′ən), *v.t.*, *v.i.* to make or become sad.

sad·dle (săd′əl), *n.*, *v.*, **-dled, -dling.** —*n.* **1.** a seat for a rider on the back of a horse or other animal. **2.** a similar seat on a bicycle, machine, etc. **3.** a part of a harness laid across the back of an animal and girded under the belly, to which the terrets and checkhook are attached. See illus. under **harness. 4.** something resembling a saddle in shape or position. **5.** (of mutton, venison, etc.) a cut including part of the backbone and both loins. **6.** (of poultry) the posterior part of the back. **7.** the saddle of an animal prepared for food. **8.** a ridge connecting two higher elevations. **9.** the bearing on the journal of the axle of a railroad-car wheel. **10.** *Ordn.* the support for the trunnion on some gun carriages. —*v.t.* **11.** to put a saddle upon (a horse, etc.). **12.** to load or charge, as with a burden. **13.** to impose as a burden or responsibility. —*v.i.* **14.** to get into the saddle. [ME *sadel*, OE *sadol*, c. G *sattel*]

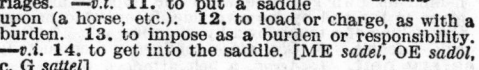

Western Saddle
A. Pommel; B. Seat; C. Cantle; D. Flap; E. Stirrup

sad·dle-backed (săd′əl băkt′), *adj.* **1.** having the back or upper surface curved like a saddle. **2.** having a saddlelike marking on the back, as certain birds.

sad·dle·bag (săd′əl băg′), *n.* a large bag, usually one of a pair, hung from or laid over a saddle.

sad·dle·bow (săd′əl bō′), *n.* the arched front part of a saddle or saddletree.

sad·dle·cloth (săd′əl klôth′, -klŏth′), *n.* a cloth placed between a horse's back and the saddle.

saddle horse, any type of horse which has a strong back and trained gait and is therefore used for riding.

sad·dler (săd′lər), *n.* one who makes or deals in saddlery.

saddle roof, a roof having two gables. See illus. under **roof.**

sad·dler·y (săd′lə rĭ), *n.*, *pl.* **-dleries. 1.** saddles and other articles pertaining to the equipment of horses, etc. **2.** the work, business, or shop of a saddler.

saddle soap, a soap, usually consisting chiefly of Castile, used for cleaning and preserving saddles and other leather articles.

sad·dle·tree (săd′əl trē′), *n.* the frame of a saddle.

Sad·du·cee (săj′ə sē′), *n.* one of an ancient Jewish sect or party whose views and practices were opposed to those of the Pharisees, and who denied the authority

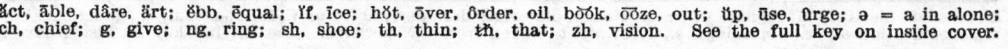

of oral tradition, the resurrection of the dead, the existence of angels, etc. [ME *saduces* (pl.), OE *sadducēas* (pl.), t. LL: m. *Sadducaeus*, t. LGk.: m. *Saddoukaios*, t. Heb.: m. *Caddûqî*, der. *Cadduq* Zadok, name of Hebrew high priest under David] —**Sad/du·cee/an**, *adj.*, *n.* —**Sad/du·cee/ism**, *n.*

Sa·di (sä dē/), *n.* Saadi.

sad·i·ron (săd/ī/ərn), *n.* a solid flatiron. [f. **SAD** (def. 7) + **IRON**]

sad·ism (săd/ĭzəm, sä/dĭzəm), *n. Psychiatry.* 1. sexual gratification gained through causing physical pain and humiliation. 2. any morbid enjoyment in being cruel. [t. F: m. *sadisme*, from the Count de *Sade*, notorious for the character of his books] —**sad/ist**, *n.*, *adj.* —**sa·dis·tic** (sä dĭs/tĭk, sä-), *adj.* —**sa·dis/ti·cal·ly**, *adv.*

sad·ness (săd/nĭs), *n.* 1. quality of being sad; unhappiness. 2. state of being sad; grief. —Ant. 1, 2. joy.

Sa·do·wa (sä/dô vä/), *n.* a village in W Czechoslovakia, in NE Bohemia: Prussian victory over Austrians, 1866.

sad sack, *U.S. Slang.* an ineffective person who always blunders despite good intentions, esp. a soldier.

S.A.E., Society of Automotive Engineers.

sa·fa·ri (sə fär/ĭ), *n.*, *pl.* **-ris.** (in eastern Africa) 1. a journey; an expedition, esp. for hunting. 2. the persons, animals, etc., forming such an expedition. [t. Ar.]

Sa·fa·vi (sä fä/wē), *adj.* of the Persian dynasty which ruled from 1500 to 1736. Also, **Sa·fa·vid** (sä fä/wĕd).

safe (sāf), *adj.*, **safer, safest**, *n.* —*adj.* 1. secure from liability to harm, injury, danger, or risk: *a safe place.* 2. free from hurt, injury, danger, or risk: *to arrive safe and sound.* 3. involving no risk of mishap, error, etc.: *a safe estimate.* 4. dependable or trustworthy: *a safe guide.* 5. cautious in avoiding danger: *a safe player.* 6. placed beyond the power of doing harm; in secure custody: *a criminal safe in jail.* —*n.* 7. a steel or iron box or repository for money, jewels, papers, etc. 8. any receptacle or structure for the storage or preservation of articles: *a meat safe.* [ME *sauf*, t. OF, g. L *salvus* uninjured] —**safe/ly**, *adv.* —**safe/ness**, *n.*
—Syn. 1. **SAFE**, **SECURE** may both imply that something can be regarded as free from danger. These words are frequently interchangeable. **SAFE**, however, is rather applied to a person or thing that is out of, or has passed beyond, the reach of danger: *the ship is safe in port.* **SECURE** is applied to that about which there is no need to fear or worry: *to feel secure about the future, the foundation of the house does not seem very secure.* —Ant. 3. unsure, dangerous.

safe·blow·er (sāf/blō/ər), *n.* a burglar who breaks open safes by means of explosives.

safe·break·er (sāf/brā/kər), *n.* a burglar who robs safes.

safe·con·duct (sāf/kŏn/dŭkt), *n.* 1. a document securing a safe passage through a region, esp. in time of war. 2. this privilege. 3. a conducting in safety.

safe·de·pos·it (sāf/dĭ pŏz/ĭt), *adj.* providing safekeeping for valuables: *a safe-deposit vault or box.*

safe·guard (sāf/gärd/), *n.* 1. something serving as a protection or defense, or ensuring safety. 2. a permit for safe passage. 3. a guard or convoy. 4. a mechanical device for ensuring safety. —*v.t.* 5. to guard; protect; secure. [ME *saufegard*, t. OF: m. *sauvegarde*, f. *sauve* (fem. of *sauf*) + *garde*. See **SAFE**, **GUARD**]

safe hit, *Baseball.* a hit by which the batter reaches first base without any fielding errors.

safe·keep·ing (sāf/kē/pĭng), *n.* protection; care.

safe·ty (sāf/tĭ), *n.*, *pl.* **-ties.** 1. state of being safe; freedom from injury or danger. 2. quality of insuring against hurt, injury, danger, or risk. 3. a contrivance or device to prevent injury or avert danger. 4. a locking or cutoff device that prevents a gun from being fired accidentally. 5. the action of keeping safe. 6. *Football.* an action of a player in touching the ball down behind his own goal line when the impetus has been given to the ball by his own side, in order to prevent the making of a touchdown by the other side. 7. *Baseball.* safe hit. 8. *Obs.* close confinement or custody.

safety belt, 1. *Aeron.* a belt attached to the seat, used for securing the passenger or pilot against sudden turns, bumps, etc. 2. a lifebelt.

safety bicycle, a bicycle with two low, equal wheels.

safety glass, a pane made by joining two plates or panes of glass with a layer of plastic or artificial resin between them which retains the fragments if the glass is broken.

Safety Islands, a group of three French islands off the coast of French Guiana, in South America.

safety lamp, a miner's lamp in which the flame is protected by wire gauze, thus preventing immediate ignition of explosive gases.

safety match, a match designed to ignite only when rubbed on a specially prepared surface.

safety pin, a pin bent back on itself to form a spring, with a guard to cover the point.

safety razor, a razor provided with a guard or guards to prevent cutting the skin.

safety valve, 1. a valve in a steam boiler or the like, which, when the pressure becomes abnormal or dangerous, opens and allows the steam or fluid to escape. 2. a harmless outlet for emotion, nervousness, etc.

saf·flow·er (săf/lou/ər), *n.* 1. a thistlelike composite herb, *Carthamus tinctorius*, a native of the Old World, bearing large orange-red flower heads. 2. its dried florets, used medicinally or as a red dyestuff. [t. D: m.

saf·floer, t. OF: m. *saffleur*, t. It.: m. *saffiore*; ult. orig. uncert.]

saf·fron (săf/rən), *n.* 1. a crocus, *Crocus sativus*, with handsome purple flowers. 2. an orange-colored product consisting of its dried stigmas, used to color confectionery, for flavoring, etc., in rolls and buns and in chicken-rice dishes. 3. Also, **saffron yellow.** yellow orange. [ME, t. F: m. *safran*, ult. t. Ar.: m. *za'farān*]

Sa·fid Rud (sä fēd/ rōōd/), a river flowing from NW Iran into the Caspian Sea. ab. 450 mi.

S.Afr., 1. South Africa. 2. South African.

saf·ra·nine (săf/rə nēn/, -nĭn), *n. Chem.* 1. any of a class of (chiefly red) organic dyes, phenazine derivatives, used for dyeing wool, silk, etc. 2. a dye, $C_{18}H_{14}N_4$. [var. of *safranin*, t. G, f. *safran* saffron + -in -**INE**[2]]

S. Afr. D., South African Dutch (Afrikaans).

saf·role (săf/rōl), *n. Chem.* a colorless or faintly yellow liquid, $C_{10}H_{10}O_2$, obtained from oil of sassafras, etc., and used for flavoring and in perfumery. Also, **saf·rol** (săf/rōl, -rŏl). [f. (SAS)SAFR(AS) + -OLE]

sag (săg), *v.*, **sagged, sagging**, *n.* —*v.i.* 1. to sink or bend downward by weight or pressure, in the middle. 2. to hang down unevenly: *a sagging skirt.* 3. to droop; hang loosely: *sagging shoulders.* 4. to yield through weakness, lack of effort, or the like. 5. to decline, as in price. 6. *Naut.* to drift out of the intended course. —*v.t.* 7. to cause to sag. —*n.* 8. act of sagging. 9. the degree of sagging. 10. a place where anything sags; a depression. 11. moderate decline in prices. 12. *Naut.* leeway. [ME *sagge*; prob. akin to MD *zakken* subside]

sa·ga (sä/gə), *n.* 1. a medieval Icelandic or Norse prose narrative of achievements and events in the history of a personage, family, etc. 2. any narrative or legend of heroic exploits. [t. Icel.: story, history; c. SAW[3]]

sa·ga·cious (sə gā/shəs), *adj.* 1. having acute mental discernment and keen practical sense; shrewd: *a sagacious author.* 2. *Obs.* keen-scented. [f. SAGACI(TY) + -OUS] —**sa·ga/cious·ly**, *adv.* —**sa·ga/cious·ness**, *n.*

sa·gac·i·ty (sə găs/ə tĭ), *n.*, *pl.* **-ties.** acuteness of mental discernment and soundness of judgment. [t. L: m. *sagācitas*]

sag·a·more (săg/ə môr/), *n.* (among the American Indians of New England) a chief or great man.

saga novel, a form of novel, characteristically French (**roman-fleuve**) but also written in English, in which the members or generations of a family or social group are chronicled in a long and leisurely narrative.

sage[1] (sāj), *n.*, *adj.*, **sager, sagest.** —*n.* 1. a profoundly wise man; a man famed for wisdom. 2. a man venerated for his wisdom, judgment, and experience: *the seven sages of ancient Greece.* —*adj.* 3. wise, judicious, or prudent: *sage conduct.* 4. *Obs.* grave or solemn. —**sage/ly**, *adv.* —**sage/ness**, *n.* [ME, t. OF, g. L -*sapius* wise]

sage[2] (sāj), *n.* 1. any species of salvia, as *S. splendens*, a garden plant with scarlet flowers (**scarlet sage**). 2. a perennial herb, *Salvia officinalis*, whose grayish-green leaves are used in medicine and for seasoning in sausage making, cookery, etc. 3. the leaves themselves. 4. sagebrush. [ME *sauge*, t. OF, g. L *salvia*]

Sage (sāj), *n.* Russell, 1816–1906, U.S. financier.

sage·brush (sāj/brŭsh/), *n.* any of various sagelike bushy plants of the composite genus *Artemisia*, common on the dry plains of the western U. S.

sage hen, a large grouse, *Centrocercus urophasianus*, of the sagebrush regions of western North America.

sage sparrow, a small gray finch, *Amphispiza nevadensis*, of western North America.

sag·gar (săg/ər), *n.* 1. a box or case made of refractory baked clay in which the finer ceramic wares are enclosed and protected while baking. —*v.t.* 2. to place in or upon a saggar. Also, **sag/ger.** [prob. contr. of SAFEGUARD]

Sag·i·naw (săg/ə nô/), *n.* a city in E Michigan: a port on the Saginaw river, 15 mi. from Saginaw Bay, an arm (ab. 55 mi. long) of Lake Huron. 98,265 (1960). [t. Amer. Ind.: m. *sāginawa* mouth of the river]

Sa·git·ta (sə jĭt/ə), *n.* a northern constellation, near Aquila, the Arrow.

sag·it·tal (săj/ə təl), *adj.* 1. *Anat.* a. denoting, or pertaining to, the suture between the parietal bones of the skull, or to a venous channel within the skull and parallel to this suture. See diag. under **cranium.** b. (in direction or location) from front to back in the median plane, or in a plane parallel to the median. 2. pertaining to or resembling an arrow or arrowhead. [t. NL: s. *sagittālis*, der. L *sagitta* arrow]

Sag·it·ta·ri·us (săj/ə târ/ĭəs), *n.* 1. the Archer (a centaur drawing a bow), a zodiacal constellation. 2. the ninth sign of the zodiac. See diag. under **zodiac.** [t. L]

sag·it·tate (săj/ə tāt/), *adj.* shaped like an arrowhead. Also, **sa·git·ti·form** (sə jĭt/ə-fôrm/, săj/ə tə fôrm/). [t. NL: m.s. *sagittātus*, der. L *sagitta* arrow]

sa·go (sä/gō), *n.* a starchy foodstuff derived from the soft interior of the trunk of various palms and cycads, used in making puddings, etc. [t. Malay: m. *sāgū*]

Sagittate leaf

Sa·guache (sə wäch/), *n.* Sawatch.

sa·gua·ro (sə gwä/rō, -wä/rō), *n.*, *pl.* **-ros.** an extremely tall cactus, *Carnegiea* (or *Cereus*) *gigantea*, of Arizona and neighboring regions, yielding a useful wood and an edible fruit. [t. Sp.; cf. Amer. Ind. orig.]

Sag·ue·nay (săg/ə nā/), *n.* a river in SE Canada, in Quebec province, flowing from Lake St. John SE to the St. Lawrence: in its lower course it is a fiord ¾–2 mi. wide. 125 mi.

Sa·gun·to (sä gōōn/tô), *n.* a city in E Spain, N of Valencia: besieged by Hannibal, 219–218 B.C. 20,253 (1950). Ancient, **Sa·gun·tum** (sə gŭn/təm).

Sa·hap·tan (sä hăp/tən), *n.* **1.** an American Indian linguistic stock of central Idaho and adjoining parts of Oregon and Washington, including Nez Percé. —*adj.* **2.** of or pertaining to the Sahaptan Indian tribes. [t. Amer. Ind. (Salish): m. *sáptini*, in pl. *Saháptini*]

Sa·har·a (sə hâr/ə, sə hä/rə), *n.* **1.** a great desert in N Africa, extending from the Atlantic to the Nile valley. ab. 3,500,000 sq. mi. **2.** any arid waste.

Sa·ha·ran·pur (sə hä/rən pŏŏr/), *n.* a city in N India, in Uttar Pradesh. 142,665 (1951).

sa·hib (sä/īb), *n.* (in India) a term of respect applied by natives to a European. [t. Hind., t. Ar.: m. *çāhib* master, lit., friend]

said (sĕd), *v.* **1.** pt. and pp. of **say.** —*adj.* **2.** *Chiefly Law.* named or mentioned before: *said witness, said sum.*

Sa·i·da (sä/ē dä), *n.* a seaport in SW Lebanon: the site of ancient Sidon. 60,000 (est. 1953).

sai·ga (sī/gə), *n.* an antelope, *Saiga tartarica,* of western Asia and eastern Russia. [t. Russ.]

Sai·gon (sī gŏn/; Fr. så ē gôN/), *n.* capital of and seaport in S South Vietnam. With suburbs, 1,614,200 (est. 1953).

sail (sāl), *n.* **1.** an expanse of canvas or similar material spread to the wind to make a vessel move through the water. It is called a **square sail** when quadrilateral and extended by a yard, usually at right angles to the masts, and a **fore-and-aft sail** when set on a mast, boom, gaff, or stay, more or less in line with the keel. **2.** some similar piece or apparatus, as the part of an arm of a windmill which catches the wind. **3.** a voyage or excursion, esp. in a sailing vessel. **4.** a sailing vessel or ship. **5.** sailing vessels collectively: *the fleet numbered thirty sail.* **6.** sails for a vessel or vessels, collectively. **7. make sail,** *Naut.* **a.** to set the sail or sails of a boat, or increase the amount of sail already set. **b.** to set out on a voyage. **8. set sail,** to start a voyage. **9. under sails,** with sails set. —*v.i.* **10.** to travel in a vessel conveyed by the action of wind, steam, etc. **11.** to move along or be conveyed by wind, steam, etc.: *steamships sailing to Lisbon.* **12.** to manage a sailboat, esp. for sport. **13.** to begin a journey by water: *sailing at dawn.* **14.** to move along in a manner suggestive of a sailing vessel: *clouds sailing overhead.* **15.** to travel through the air, as an airship. **16.** to move along with dignity: *to sail into a room.* **17.** *Colloq.* to go boldly into action (fol. by *in*). —*v.t.* **18.** to sail upon, over, or through: *to sail the seven seas.* **19.** to navigate (a ship, etc.). [ME, OE *segl,* c. G *segel*]

Sails on full-rigged merchant sailing ship

1, Foresail; 2. Mainsail; 3. Crossjack; 4. Fore lower topsail; 5. Main lower topsail; 6. Mizzen lower topsail; 7. Fore upper topsail; 8. Main upper topsail; 9. Mizzen upper topsail; 10. Fore-topgallant sail; 11. Main-topgallant sail; 12. Mizzen-topgallant sail; 13. Fore royal; 14. Main royal; 15. Mizzen royal; 16. Fore skysail; 17. Main skysail; 18. Mizzen skysail; 19. Spanker; 20. Mizzen staysail; 21. Fore-topmast staysail; 22. Main lower topmast staysail; 23. Main upper topmast staysail; 24. Mizzen-topmast staysail; 25. Jib; 26. Flying jib; 27. Jib topsail; 28. Main-topgallant staysail; 29. Mizzen-topgallant staysail; 30. Main-royal staysail; 31. Mizzen-royal staysail; 32. Lower studding sail; 33. Fore-topmast studding sail; 34. Main-topmast studding sail; 35. Fore-topgallant studding sail; 36. Main-topgallant studding sail; 37. Fore-royal studding sail; 38. Main-royal studding sail.

sail·boat (sāl/bōt/), *n.* a boat propelled by sails.

sail·cloth (sāl/klôth/, -klŏth/), *n.* canvas or other material such as is used for making sails.

sail·er (sā/lər), *n.* **1.** a vessel propelled by a sail or sails. **2.** a vessel with reference to its powers or manner of sailing.

sail·fish (sāl/fĭsh/), *n.,* *pl.* -fishes (*esp. collectively*) -fish. any of the large marine fishes constituting the genus *Istiophorus,* characterized by a very large dorsal fin likened to a sail, and related to the swordfishes, as *I. americanus,* of the warmer parts of the Atlantic.

sail·ing (sā/lĭng), *n.* **1.** act of one who or that which sails. **2.**

Florida sailfish, *Istiophorus americanus* (Ab. 7 ft. long)

the procedure of solving problems of courses, distances, and positions in navigating a ship, without the use of celestial observations.

sailing boat, *Brit.* sailboat.

sail·or (sā/lər), *n.* **1.** one whose occupation is sailing or navigation; a mariner; a seaman. **2.** a seaman below the rank of officer. **3.** a person, with reference to freedom from seasickness: *a bad sailor.* **4.** a flat-brimmed straw hat with a low, flat crown. [ME *sailer* one who sails] —**Syn. 1.** SAILOR, MARINER, SALT, SEAMAN, TAR are terms for one who leads a seafaring life. A SAILOR or SEAMAN is one whose occupation is on board a ship at sea; one of a ship's crew below the rank of petty officer: *a sailor before the mast, an able-bodied seaman.* MARINER is a term now found only in certain technical expressions: *master mariner* (captain in merchant service), *mariner's compass;* formerly used much as "sailor" or "seafaring man" now are, the word seems elevated or quaint: *Rime of the Ancient Mariner.* SALT and TAR are familiar and colloquial terms for old and experienced sailors: *an old salt, a jolly tar.*

sail·or·ly (sā/lər lĭ), *adj.* like or befitting a sailor.

sail·or's-choice (sā/lərz chois/), *n.,* *pl.* -choice. any of several fishes of the Atlantic coast of the U. S., esp. a pinfish, *Lagodon rhomboides,* ranging from Massachusetts to Texas, and a grunt, *Haemulon parra,* ranging from Florida to Brazil.

sain (sān), *v.t.* *Archaic or Dial.* **1.** to make the sign of the cross on as to protect against evil influences. **2.** to safeguard by prayer. **3.** to bless. [ME; OE *segnian* (c. G *segnen*), ult. t. L: m. *signāre*]

sain·foin (sān/foin), *n.* a European fabaceous herb, *Onobrychis sativa,* cultivated as a forage plant. [t. F, f. *sain* wholesome (or *saint* holy) + *foin* hay, g. L *faenum*]

saint (sānt), *n.* **1.** one of certain persons of exceptional holiness formally recognized by the Christian Church as having attained an exalted position in heaven and as being entitled to veneration on earth; a canonized person. **2.** (in certain religious bodies) a designation applied by the members to themselves. **3.** a person of great holiness. —*v.t.* **4.** to enroll formally among the saints recognized by the church. **5.** to give the name of saint to; reckon as a saint. —*adj.* **6.** sacred; holy. [ME, t. OF, g. L *sanctus,* pp., consecrated]

Saint Ag·nes's Eve (ăg/nĭs Iz), the night of Jan. 20, the traditional time for rites to reveal a woman's future husband.

Saint Andrew's Cross, an X-shaped cross. See illus. under **cross.**

Saint Anthony's Cross, a T-shaped cross. See illus. under **cross.**

Sainte-Beuve (săn bœv/), *n.* Charles Augustin (shärl ō gys tăN/), 1804–69, French critic.

Saint Bernard, one of a breed of large dogs with a massive head, noted for their intelligence: named from the hospice of St. Bernard, on the pass of the Great St. Bernard in the Alps, where they are kept by the monks for rescuing travelers from the snow.

Saint Bernard
(25 to 28 n. high at the shoulder)

saint·ed (sān/tĭd), *adj.* **1.** enrolled among the saints. **2.** being a saint in heaven. **3.** sacred or hallowed. **4.** saintly.

Saint-Ex·u·pé·ry (săN tĕg zy pĕ rē/), *n.* Antoine de (äN twăn/ də), 1900–45, French author and aviator.

Saint-Gau·dens (sānt gô/dənz), *n.* Augustus (ô gŭs/təs), n. 1848–1907, U. S. sculptor, born in Ireland.

Saint George's cross, the Greek cross as used in the flag of Great Britain. See illus. under **cross.**

saint·hood (sānt/hŏŏd), *n.* **1.** the character or status of a saint. **2.** saints collectively.

Saint John, 1. a seaport in SE Canada, in New Brunswick, on the Bay of Fundy. 85,121 (1951). **2.** a river forming part of the boundary between Maine and Canada, flowing S and E through New Brunswick to the Bay of Fundy. ab. 450 mi.

Saint-Just (săN zhyst/), *n.* Louis Antoine Léon de (lwē äN twăn/ lē ôN/ də), 1767–94, French writer and revolutionary leader.

saint·ly (sānt/lĭ), *adj.* -lier, -liest. like, proper to, or befitting a saint: *saintly lives.* —**saint/li·ness,** *n.*

Saint Nicholas, fl. 4th century, bishop of Asia Minor, patron saint of Russia, and protector of children.

Saint Patrick's Day, March 17, observed by the Irish in honor of St. Patrick, the patron saint of Ireland.

Saint-Pierre (săN pyĕr/), *n.* Jacques Henri Bernardin de (zhàk äN rē/ bĕr när dăN/ də), 1737–1814, French writer.

Saint-Saëns (săN säNs/), *n.* Charles Camille (shärl kà mē/y), 1835–1921, French composer and pianist.

Saints·bur·y (sānts/bər ĭ), *n.* George Edward Bateman, 1845–1933, British literary critic and historian.

saint·ship (sānt/shĭp), *n.* qualities of a saint.

Saint-Si·mon (săN sē môN/), *n.* **1.** Claude Henri (klōd äN rē/) Count de, 1760–1825, French socialist and writer. **2.** Louis de Rouvroy (lwē də rōō vrwä/), 1675–1755, French soldier, diplomat, and author.

Saint Val·en·tine's Day (văl/ən tīnz/), Feb. 14, when tokens of affection or valentines are given.

ăct, āble, dâre, ärt; ĕbb, ēqual; Ĭf, īce; hŏt, ōver, ôrder, oil, bŏŏk, ōōze, out; ŭp, ūse, ûrge; ə = a in alone; ch, chief; g, give; ng, ring; sh, shoe; th, thin; th, that; zh, vision. See the full key on inside cover.

Sai·on·ji (sī'ōn jē',) *n.* **Kimmochi** (kēm'mō chē',) 1849–1940, Japanese statesman.

Sai·pan (sī pän'), *n.* one of the Mariana Islands, in the N Pacific, ab. 1350 mi. S of Japan: taken by U.S. forces, June–July, 1944. 6543 (est. 1955); 71 sq. mi.

Sa·ïs (sā'ĭs), *n.* an ancient city in N Egypt, on the Nile delta: an ancient capital of Lower Egypt.

Sai·shu·to (sī'shōō tō'), *n.* Japanese name of **Cheju.** Also, Korean **Sai·shu** (sī'shōō).

saith (sĕth), *v. Archaic or Poetic.* third pers. sing. pres. of **say.**

Sa·kai (sä'kī'), *n.* a seaport in S Japan, on Honshu island, near Osaka. 213,688 (1950).

sake[1] (sāk), *n.* **1.** cause, account, or interest: *for my sake.* **2.** purpose or end: *for the sake of appearances.* [ME; OE *sacu* lawsuit, cause, c. G *sache*]

sa·ke[2] (sä'kĭ), *n.* a Japanese fermented alcoholic beverage made from rice. [t. Jap.]

sa·ker (sā'kər), *n.* an Old World falcon, *Falco sacer cherrug,* used in falconry. [t. F: m. *sacre,* ult. t. Ar.: m. *çaqr*]

Sa·kha·lin (sä'hä lēn'), *n.* an island off the SE coast of the Soviet Union in Asia, N of Japan: formerly (1905–45) it was divided between the Soviet Union (earlier, Russia) and Japan; under the provisions of the Yalta agreement, **Karafuto** (the southern, Japanese part of the island) now under Soviet Administration. ab. 350,000 pop.; 28,957 sq. mi.

Sa·ki (sä'kĭ), *n.* pen name of **Hector Hugh Munro.**

Sak·ti (sŭk'tĭ'; *Skt.* shŭk'tĭ'), *n.* ——— *nduism.* **1.** the female principle or organ of generative power. **2.** the wife of a Hindu deity, especially of Siva. Also, **Shakti.**

sal (säl), *n. Chiefly Pharm.* salt. [t. L]

sa·laam (sə läm'), *n.* **1.** (in the Orient) a salutation meaning "peace." **2.** a very low bow or obeisance, esp. with the palm of the right hand placed on the forehead. —*v.i.* **3.** to salute with a salaam. **4.** to perform a salaam. —*v.t.* **5.** to salute (someone) with a salaam. [t. Ar.: m. *salām* peace]

sal·a·ble (sā'lə bəl), *adj.* subject to or suitable for sale; readily sold. Also, **saleable.** —**sal'a·bil'i·ty,** *n.* —**sal'a·bly,** *adv.*

sa·la·cious (sə lā'shəs), *adj.* **1.** lustful or lecherous. **2.** (of writings, etc.) obscene. [f. *salaci(ty)* + -OUS. t. L: m.s. *salācitas* lust) + -OUS] —**sa·la'cious·ly,** *adv.* —**sa·la'cious·ness, sa·lac·i·ty** (sə lăs'ə tĭ'), *n.*

sal·ad (säl'əd), *n.* **1.** a dish of lettuce or other vegetables, herbs, or meat or fowl, fish, eggs, fruit, etc., prepared with various seasonings or dressings and usually served cold. **2.** any herb or plant used for such a dish or eaten raw. **3.** *Dial.* lettuce. [ME *salade,* t. OF, t. OPr.: m. *salada,* der. *salar* to salt, der. L *sal* salt]

salad days, days of youthful inexperience.

salad dressing, an appetizing sauce for a salad.

Sal·a·din (săl'ə dĭn), *n.* (*Salāh-ed-Dīn Yūsuf ibn Ayyūb*) 1137–93, sultan of Egypt and Syria, 1175?–1193: capturer of Jerusalem and opponent of the crusaders.

Sa·la·do (sä lä'dō), *n.* **Río** (rē'ō), a river in N Argentina, flowing SE to the Paraná river. ab. 1000 mi.

Sal·a·man·ca (săl'ə mäng'kə; *Sp.* sä'lä mäng'kä), *n.* a city in W Spain: Wellington's defeat of the French here, 1812. 86,062 (est. 1955).

sal·a·man·der (săl'ə măn'dər), *n.* **1.** any of various tailed amphibians, most of which have an aquatic larval stage but are terrestrial as adults, esp. the American spotted and tiger salamander, genus *Ambystoma.* **2.** a mythical lizard or other reptile, or a being supposed to be able to live in fire. [ME *salamandre,* t. OF, t. L: m. *salamandra,* t. Gk.] —**sal·a·man·drine** (săl'ə măn'drĭn), *adj.* —Syn. **2.** See **sylph.**

Tiger salamander.
Ambystoma tigrinum
(8 in. long)

Sa·lam·bri·a (sä'läm brē'ä; *Gk.* -brēä'), *n.* a river flowing through Thessaly, Greece, into the Gulf of Salonika. 125 mi. Ancient, **Peneus.**

sa·la·mi (sä lä'mĭ), *n.* a kind of sausage, originally Italian, often flavored with garlic. [t. It. (pl.), ult. der. L *salāre* to salt]

Sal·a·mis (săl'ə mĭs), *n.* **1.** an island off the SE coast of Greece, in the Gulf of Aegina: the Greeks defeated the Persians near Salamis in a naval battle. 480 B.C. 17,738 pop. (1951); 39 sq. mi. **2.** an ancient city on Cyprus, in the E Mediterranean: the Apostle Paul made his first missionary journey to Salamis. Acts 13:5.

sal ammoniac, ammonium chloride.

sal·a·ried (săl'ə rĭd), *adj.* **1.** receiving a salary. **2.** having a salary attached.

sal·a·ry (săl'ə rĭ), *n., pl.* **-ries.** a fixed compensation periodically paid to a person for regular work or services, esp. work other than that of a manual, mechanical, or menial kind. [ME *salarie,* t. AF, t. L: m. *salārium,* orig., money allowed to soldiers for the purchase of salt]

sale (sāl), *n.* **1.** act of selling. **2.** quantity sold. **3.** opportunity to sell; demand: *slow sale.* **4.** a special disposal of goods, as at reduced prices. **5.** transfer of property for money or credit. **6. for sale** or **on sale,** offered to be sold; offered to purchasers. [ME; late OE *sala,* c. Icel. and OHG *sala.* See SELL]

sale·a·ble (sā'lə bəl), *adj.* salable. —**sale'a·bil'i·ty,** *n.* —**sale'a·bly,** *adv.*

Sa·lem (sā'ləm), *n.* **1.** a seaport in NE Massachusetts: founded, 1626; execution of "witches," 1692; home of Nathaniel Hawthorne. 39,211 (1960). **2.** the capital of Oregon, in the NW part, on the Willamette river. 49,142 (1960). **3.** a city in S India, in Madras state. 202,335 (1951).

sal·ep (săl'ĕp), *n.* a starchy drug or foodstuff consisting of the dried tubers of certain orchids. [t. Turk., t. d. Ar.: m. *sa'leb,* var. of *tha'leb,* short for *khasyu'ith-tha'lab,* lit., fox's testicles]

sal·e·ra·tus (săl'ə rā'təs), *n.* baking soda (sodium bicarbonate), used in cookery, etc. [t. NL: m. *sal āerātus* aerated salt]

Sa·ler·no (sə lûr'nō; *It.* sä-lĕr'nō), *n.* a seaport in SW Italy: taken by U.S. forces, Sept., 1943. 93,000 (est. 1954).

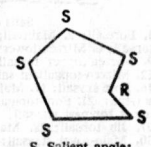

sales·clerk (sālz'klûrk'), *n.* a salesman in a store.

sales·girl (sālz'gûrl'), *n.* a girl engaged in selling goods, esp. in a store.

sales·la·dy (sālz'lā'dĭ), *n., pl.* **-dies.** a saleswoman.

sales·man (sālz'mən), *n., pl.* **-men.** a man engaged in selling. —**sales'man·ship',** *n.*

sales·peo·ple (sālz'pē'pəl), *n.pl.* people engaged in selling.

sales·per·son (sālz'pûr'sən), *n.* one engaged in selling goods, esp. in a store.

sales resistance, a negative buyer attitude or other condition which retards the sale of a commodity.

sales·room (sālz'rōōm', -rŏŏm'), *n.* **1.** a room in which goods are sold or displayed. **2.** an auction room.

sales tax, a tax on sales or on receipts from sales.

sales·wom·an (sālz'wŏŏm'ən), *n., pl.* **-women.** a woman who sells goods, esp. in a store.

Sal·ford (sôl'fərd, sŏl'-, săl'-), *n.* a city in N England, near Manchester. 167,400 (est. 1956).

Sa·li·an (sā'lĭ ən), *adj.* **1.** of or pertaining to the **Salii,** a tribe of Franks who dwelt in the regions of the Rhine near the North Sea. —*n.* **2.** a Salian Frank.

Sal·ic (săl'ĭk, sā'lĭk), *adj.* of or pertaining to the Salian Franks. Also, **Salique.** [t. ML: s. *Salicus*]

sal·i·ca·ceous (săl'ə kā'shəs), *adj.* belonging to the *Salicaceae,* a family of trees and shrubs containing the willows and poplars. [f. s. L *salix* willow + -ACEOUS]

sal·i·cin (săl'ə sĭn), *n.* a colorless, crystalline glucoside, $C_{13}H_{18}O_7$, obtained from the American aspen bark and used as an antipyretic. [t. F: m. *salicine,* f. s. L *salix* willow + -*ine* -INE[2]]

Salic law, 1. a code of laws of the Salian Franks and other Germanic tribes, esp. a provision in this code excluding females from the inheritance of land. **2.** the alleged fundamental law of the French monarchy by which females were excluded from succession to the crown. **3.** any law to the same effect.

sal·i·cyl·ate (săl'ə sĭl'āt, sə lĭs'ə lāt'), *n. Chem.* a salt or ester of salicylic acid. [f. SALAC(IN) + -YL + -ATE[2]]

sal·i·cyl·ic acid (săl'ə sĭl'ĭk), *Chem.* an acid, HOC₆-H₄CO₂H, prepared from salicin or from phenol, and used esp. as a remedy for rheumatic and gouty affections, usually in the form of a salicylate.

sa·li·ence (sā'lĭ əns), *n.* **1.** state or condition of being salient. **2.** a salient or projecting object, part, or feature.

sa·li·en·cy (sā'lĭ ən sĭ), *n., pl.* **-cies.** salience.

sa·li·ent (sā'lĭ ənt), *adj.* **1.** prominent or conspicuous: *salient traits.* **2.** projecting or pointing outward, as an angle. **3.** leaping or jumping. —*n.* **4.** a salient angle or part, as the central outward projecting angle of a bastion or an outward projection in a battle line. See diag. under **bastion.** [t. L: s. *saliens,* ppr., leaping forth] —**sa'li·ent·ly,** *adv.*

S. Salient angle; R. Reentering angle

sa·li·en·ti·an (sā'lĭ ĕn'shĭ ən), *adj.* **1.** of, pertaining to, or included in the salientians. —*n.* **2.** any animal of the amphibian order *Salientia,* of which the toads and frogs are typical.

sal·if·er·ous (sə lĭf'ər əs), *adj.* containing or producing salt: *saliferous strata.* [f. L *sal* salt + -(I)FEROUS]

sal·i·fy (săl'ə fī'), *v.t.* **-fied, -fying. 1.** to form into a salt, as by chemical combination. **2.** to mix or combine with a salt. [t. NL: m. *salificāre,* der. L *sal* salt. See -FY]

sa·li·na (sə lī'nə), *n.* **1.** a saline marsh, spring, or the like. **2.** a saltworks. [t. Sp., g. L (found in pl. only)]

Sa·li·na (sə lī'nə), *n.* a city in central Kansas. 43,202 (1960).

sa·line (sā'līn), *adj.* **1.** salty or saltlike; containing or tasting like common table salt: *a saline solution.* **2.** of or pertaining to a chemical salt, esp. of sodium, potassium, magnesium, etc., as used as a cathartic. —*n.* **3.** a saline medicine. [f. L: m.s. *salīnus* (found only in neut.), der. *sal* salt] —**sa·lin·i·ty** (sə lĭn'ə tĭ), *n.*

Sa·lique (sə lēk', săl'ĭk, sā'lĭk), *adj.* Salic.

Salis·bur·y (sôlz′bĕr′ĭ, -bər′ĭ), *n.* **1.** a city in S England: the county seat of Wiltshire; famous cathedral. 32,910 (1951). **2.** a city in SE Africa: the capital of Rhodesia. 90,024 (est. 1953). **3. Robert Arthur Talbot Gascoyne Cecil** (găs′koin), **3rd Marquis of,** 1830–1903, British statesman.

Salisbury Plain, an extended elevated region in S England, N of Salisbury: the site of Stonehenge.

Salisbury steak, Hamburg steak, usually with cream added and breaded before frying.

Sa·lish (sā′lĭsh), *n.* **1.** (*pl.*) the eponymous tribe of the Salishan speech stock of North American Indians, formerly living in Montana, often called Flatheads by surrounding tribes. **2.** a member of this tribe or the Salishan family of tribes. [t. Amer. Ind. (Salishan): m. *sälst* (Salish) people]

Sa·lish·an (sā′lĭsh ən, săl′ĭsh-), *n.* **1.** an American Indian linguistic stock including Coeur-d'Alène and Flathead and other languages of British Columbia and the northwestern U.S. —*adj.* **2.** of this linguistic family.

sa·li·va (sə li′və), *n.* a fluid consisting of the secretions produced by glands which discharge into the mouth, containing ptyalin in man and certain other animals; spittle. [ME, t. L. Cf. Gk. *sialon*] —**sal·i·var·y** (săl′ə-vĕr′ĭ), *adj.*

sal·i·vate (săl′ə vāt′), *v.,* -vated, -vating. —*v.i.* **1.** *Physiol.* to produce saliva. —*v.t.* **2.** to produce an excessive secretion of saliva in, as by the use of mercury. [t. L: m.s. *salīvātus,* pp., spat out, salivated]

sal·i·va·tion (săl′ə vā′shən), *n.* **1.** act or process of salivating. **2.** an abnormally abundant flow of saliva. **3.** mercurial poisoning.

Salk (sôlk), *n.* **Jonas Edward,** born 1914, U.S. bacteriologist: developed anti-poliomyelitis vaccine (**Salk vaccine**) which proved highly effective in mass field test in 1954.

salle à man·ger (sȧl ä män zhĕ′), *French.* a dining room.

sal·let (săl′ĭt), *n.* a light medieval helmet, usually with a vision slit or a movable visor. [late ME, t. F: m. *salade,* t. It.: m. *celata,* g. L *caelāta,* pp. fem., engraved]

sal·low¹ (săl′ō), *adj.* **1.** of a yellowish, sickly hue or complexion: *sallow cheeks.* —*v.t.* **2.** to make sallow. [ME *salowe,* OE *salo,* c. Icel. *sölr* yellow] —**sal·low·ish,** *adj.* —**sal·low·ness,** *n.*

sal·low² (săl′ō), *n.* a willow, esp. *Salix caprea* (**great sallow**), an Old World shrub or bushy tree used in making charcoal for gunpowder. [ME; OE *sealh,* c. OHG *salaha,* Icel. *selja,* L *salix*]

sal·low·y (săl′ō ĭ), *adj.* full of sallows or willows.

Sal·lust (săl′əst), *n.* (*Caius Sallustius Crispus*) 86–34 B.C., Roman historian.

sal·ly (săl′ĭ), *n., pl.* -lies, *v.,* -lied, -lying. —*n.* **1.** a sortie of troops from a besieged place upon an enemy. **2.** a sudden rushing forth or activity. **3.** an excursion or expedition. **4.** an outburst or flight of passion, fancy, etc.: *sally of anger.* **5.** a sprightly or brilliant utterance or remark. —*v.i.* **6.** to make a sally, as a body of troops from a besieged place. **7.** to set out on an excursion or expedition. **8.** to set out briskly or energetically. **9.** (of things) to issue forth. [t. F: m. *saillie* issuing forth, outrush, der. *saillir* leap, g. L *salīre*]

sally lunn (lŭn), a kind of slightly sweetened teacake served hot with butter. [named after a woman who sold it in Bath, England, at the end of the 18th cent.]

sal·ma·gun·di (săl′mə gŭn′dĭ), *n.* **1.** a mixed dish consisting of chopped meat, anchovies, eggs, onions, oil, etc. **2.** any mixture or miscellany. [t. F: m. *salmigondis,* ult. t. It.: m. *salami conditi* pickled sausages]

Sal·ma·gun·di (săl′mə gŭn′dĭ), *n.* a humorous periodical, 1807–08, issued by Washington Irving and others

sal·mi (săl′mĭ), *n.* a ragout of roasted game, fowl, or the like, stewed in wine. Also, **sal·mis** (săl′mĭ; *Fr.* săl-mē′). [t. F, prob. short for *salmigondis.* See SALMAGUNDI]

salm·on (săm′ən), *n., pl.* -mons, (*esp. collectively*) -mon, *adj.* —*n.* **1.** a marine and fresh-water food fish, *Salmo salar* (family *Salmonidae*), with pink flesh, common in the northern Atlantic Ocean near the mouths of large rivers, which it ascends to spawn. **2.** a variety of this species confined to lakes, etc. (**landlocked salmon**). **3.** any of several important food fishes of the North Pacific salmonoid genus *Oncorhynchus,* as the **chinook, king,** or **quinnat, salmon,** *O. tschawytscha;* the **red, sockeye,** or **blueback, salmon,** *O. nerka;* or the **pink** or **humpback salmon,** *O. gorbuscha.* **4.** light yellowish pink. —*adj.* **5.** of the color salmon. [ME, t. AF: m. *salmun,* g. s. L *salmō*]

salm·on·ber·ry (săm′ən bĕr′ĭ), *n., pl.* -ries. **1.** the salmon-colored edible fruit of *Rubus spectabilis,* a raspberry with large red or purple flowers, of the Pacific coast of North America. **2.** the plant.

sal·mo·noid (săl′mə noid′), *adj.* **1.** resembling a salmon. **2.** belonging or pertaining to the suborder *Salmonoidea,* to which the salmon family belongs. —*n.* **3.** a member of the salmon family, *Salmonidae.* **4.** a salmonoid fish.

salmon pink, salmon (defs. 4, 5).

salmon trout, **1.** a European trout, *Salmo trutta.* **2.** the lake trout, *Cristivomer namaycush.* **3.** the steelhead. **4.** any large trout.

sal·ol (săl′ōl, -ŏl), *n.* a white crystalline substance, C₁₃H₁₀O₃, prepared by the interaction of salicylic acid

and phenol, and used as an antipyretic, antiseptic, etc [f. *sal(icyl)* (see SALICYLATE) + -OL¹]

Sa·lo·me (sə lō′mĭ), *n.* **1.** the daughter of Herodias, whose dancing so pleased Herod that he gave her the head of John the Baptist at her request, as dictated by her mother. **2.** a one-act opera (1905) by Richard Strauss based on a drama by Oscar Wilde. [t. LL, t. Gk., t. Heb.: m. *shālōm* peace]

Sal·o·mon (săl′ə mən), *n.* **Haym** (hīm), 1740?–85, American financier and Revolutionary patriot.

sa·lon (sə lŏn′; *Fr.* sȧ lôN′), *n., pl.* -lons (-lŏnz′; *Fr.* -lôN′). **1.** a drawing room or reception room in a large house. **2.** an assembly of guests in such a room, esp. such an assembly consisting of leaders in fashion, art, politics, etc. (common during the 17th and 18th centuries). **3.** a hall or place used for the exhibition of works of art. **4.** (*cap.*) (in France) a public showing of works of art by living artists. [t. F, t. It.: m. *salone,* aug. of *sala* hall, t. Gmc.; cf. OE *sæl* hall]

Sa·lo·ni·ka (sə lō nē′kä), *n.* a seaport in NE Greece, in Macedonia, on the **Gulf of Salonika,** a NW arm of the Aegean. 217,049 (1951). Also, **Sa·lon·i·ca** (sə-lŏn′ə kə) or **Sa·lo·ni·ki** (sä′lō nē′kē). Official name, **Thessalonike.** Ancient, **Thessalonica.**

sa·loon (sə loon′), *n.* **1.** *U.S.* a place for the sale of intoxicating liquors to be drunk on the premises. **2.** *Brit.* (in public houses) a division of the bar with higher social status than the public bar. **3.** a room or place for general use for a specific purpose: *a dining saloon on a ship.* **4.** a large cabin for the common use of passengers on a passenger vessel. **5.** *Brit.* a sedan. **6.** *Obsolete.* a drawing room or reception room. [t. F: m. *salon* SALON]

saloon carriage, *Brit.* a railroad parlor car.

sa·loop (sə loop′), *n.* a hot drink prepared from salep, or, later, from sassafras, etc., formerly popular in London. [var. of SALEP]

Sal·op (săl′əp), *n.* Shropshire. [var. of *Slop,* var. of SHROP(SHIRE)] —**Sa·lo·pi·an** (sə lō′pĭ′ən), *adj., n.*

sal·pa (săl′pə), *n.* any of the free-swimming oceanic tunicates constituting the genus *Salpa,* common in warm regions, and having a transparent, more or less fusiform body. [NL, special use of L *salpa* stockfish] —**sal·pi·form** (săl′pə fôrm′), *adj.*

sal·pinx (săl′pĭngks), *n., pl.* salpinges (săl pĭn′jēz). *Anat.* a trumpet-shaped tube, as the Fallopian (uterine) and Eustachian (auditory) tubes. [NL, t. Gk: trumpet]

sal·si·fy (săl′sə fĭ), *n.* a purple-flowered plant, *Dragopogon porrifolius,* whose root has an oysterlike flavor and is used as a culinary vegetable; oyster plant. [t. F: m. *salsifis,* t. It.: m. *sassefrica,* g. L *saxifraga* SAXIFRAGE]

sal soda, sodium carbonate.

salt (sôlt), *n.* **1.** a crystalline compound, sodium chloride, NaCl, occurring as a mineral, a constituent of sea water, etc., and used for seasoning food, as a preservative, etc. **2.** *Chem.* a compound which upon dissociation yields cations (positively charged) of a metal, and anions (negatively charged) of an acid radical. **3.** (*pl.*) any of various salts used as purgatives: *Epsom salts.* **4.** that which gives liveliness, piquancy, or pungency to anything: *some salt of youth.* **5.** wit; pungency. **6.** *Colloq.* a sailor, esp. an experienced one. **7. salt of the earth,** the best element of people. **8. with a grain of salt,** with reserve or allowance. —*v.t.* **9.** to season with salt. **10.** to cure, preserve, or treat with salt. **11.** to furnish with salt: *to salt cattle.* **12.** *Chem.* **a.** to treat with common salt or with any chemical salt. **b.** to add common salt to (a solution) in order to separate a dissolved substance (usually with *out*). **13.** to introduce rich ore or other valuable matter fraudulently into (a mine, ground, sample, etc.) to create a false impression of value. **14. salt away** or **down, a.** to preserve by adding quantities of salt. **b.** *Colloq.* to lay or store away in reserve: *to salt a lot of money away.* —*adj.* **15.** containing salt; having the taste of salt: *salt water.* **16.** cured or preserved with salt: *salt cod.* **17.** overflowed with or growing in salt water: *salt marsh.* **18.** pungent or sharp: *salt speech.* [ME; OE *sealt,* c. G *salz,* Icel. and Goth. *salt;* akin to Gk. *háls,* L *sal*] —**salt′like′,** *adj.* —Syn. **6.** See **sailor.**

sal·tant (săl′tənt), *adj.* dancing; leaping; jumping. [t. L: s. *saltans,* ppr.]

sal·ta·rel·lo (săl′tə rĕl′ō; *It.* säl′tä rĕl′lō), *n., pl.* -relli (-rĕl′ĭ; *It.* -rĕl′lē). **1.** a lively Italian dance for one person or a couple. **2.** the music for it. [It., ult. der. L *saltāre* dance]

sal·ta·tion (săl tā′shən), *n.* **1.** dancing; leaping. **2.** an abrupt movement or transition. **3.** *Biol.* a mutation.

sal·ta·to·ri·al (săl′tə tōr′ĭəl), *adj.* **1.** pertaining to saltation. **2.** *Zool.* characterized by or adapted for leaping.

sal·ta·to·ry (săl′tə tōr′ĭ), *adj.* **1.** pertaining to or adapted for saltation. **2.** proceeding by abrupt movements.

salt·cel·lar (sôlt′sĕl′ər), *n.* a shaker or dish for salt. [ME *saltsaler,* f. SALT + (now obs.) -*saler* saltcellar, t. OF: m. *saliere,* der. *sel* salt, g. L *sal*]

salt·ed (sôl′tĭd), *adj.* **1.** seasoned, cured, or otherwise treated with salt. **2.** *Slang.* experienced in some occupation, etc.

salt·er (sôl′tər), *n.* **1.** one who makes or deals in salt. **2.** one who salts meat, fish, etc.

ăct, āble, dâre, ärt; ĕbb, ēqual; ĭf, īce; hŏt, ōver, ôrder, oil, bŏŏk, ōōze, out; ŭp, ūse, ûrge; ə = a in alone; ch, chief; g, give; ng, ring; sh, shoe; th, thin; ŧħ, that; zh, vision. See the full key on inside cover.

salt·ern (sôl′tərn), *n.* **1.** a saltworks. **2.** a plot of land laid out in pools for the evaporation of sea water to produce salt. [OE *sealtern* saltworks, f. *sealt* SALT + *ern* house. Cf. BARN]

sal·ti·grade (săl′tə grād′), *adj.* **1.** moving by leaping. **2.** belonging to the *Saltigradae*, a group of saltatorial spiders. [f. *salti-* (comb. form of L *saltus* leap) + -GRADE]

Sal·til·lo (säl tē′yō), *n.* a city in N Mexico: the capital of Coahuila state. 69,869 (1950).

sal·tire (săl′tīr), *n. Her.* an ordinary in the form of a St. Andrew's cross. Also, **sal′tier.** [ME *sawtire*, t. OF: m. *sautoir*, orig., saddle cord for aid in mounting, der. *sauter* leap, g. L *saltāre*]

salt·ish (sôl′tĭsh), *adj.* somewhat salt; salty.

Salt Lake City, the capital of Utah, in the N part, near Great Salt Lake. 189,454 (1960).

salt lick, a place to which wild animals resort to lick salt occurring naturally there.

salt marsh, a marshy tract, wet with salt water or flooded by the sea.

Sal·ton Sink (sôl′tən), the lowest part of the Imperial Valley, in S California: submerged by the Colorado river in 1906, forming the **Salton Sea.** 282 ft. below sea level.

salt·pe·ter (sôlt′pē′tər), *n.* **1.** niter (nitrate of potassium), KNO₃. **2.** Chile saltpeter. Also, **salt′pe′tre.** [alter. (after SALT) of ME *salpetre*, t. ML: m. *sal petrae* salt of the rock]

salt pit, a pit where salt is obtained.

salt rheum, *U.S.* any of various common cutaneous eruptions, as eczema.

Salt River, a river flowing from E Arizona W to the Gila river near Phoenix: Roosevelt Dam. ab. 200 mi.

salt·wa·ter (sôlt′wô′tər, -wŏt′ər), *adj.* **1.** of or pertaining to salty water. **2.** inhabiting salt water.

salt·works (sôlt′wûrks′), *n. sing. and pl.* a building or place where salt is made.

salt·wort (sôlt′wûrt′), *n.* any of various plants of sea beaches, salt marshes, and alkaline regions, esp. of the chenopodiaceous genus *Salsola*, as *S. Kali*, a bushy plant with prickly leaves, or of the chenopodiaceous genus *Salicornia*. See **glasswort.**

salt·y (sôl′tĭ), *adj.*, **salti·er, salti·est. 1.** containing, or tasting of, salt. **2.** piquant; sharp; witty; racy. **—salt′i·ly,** *adv.* **—salt′i·ness,** *n.*

sa·lu·bri·ous (sə loo′brĭ əs), *adj.* favorable to health; promoting health: now used esp. of air, climate, etc. [f. SALUBRI(TY) (t. L: m.s. *salūbritas* healthfulness) + -OUS] **—sa·lu·bri·ous·ly,** *adv.* **—sa·lu·bri·ous·ness, sa·lu·bri·ty** (sə loo′brə tĭ), *n.*

Sa·lus (sā′ləs), *n.* the Roman goddess of health and prosperity.

sa·lus po·pu·li su·pre·ma lex es·to (sā′ləs pŏp′yə lī′ soo prē′mə lĕks ĕs′tō), *Latin.* let the welfare of the people be the supreme law (one of the two mottoes of Missouri).

sal·u·tar·y (săl′yə tĕr′ĭ), *adj.* **1.** conducive to health; healthful. **2.** promoting or conducive to some beneficial purpose; wholesome. [t. L: m. *salūtāris*] **—sal′u·tar′i·ly,** *adv.* **—sal′u·tar′i·ness,** *n.* **—Syn. 1.** See **healthy.**

sal·u·ta·tion (săl′yə tā′shən), *n.* **1.** act of saluting. **2.** something uttered, written, or done by way of saluting. **3.** the opening of a letter, as "Dear Sir."

sa·lu·ta·to·ri·an (sə loo′tə tôr′ĭ ən), *n.* (in American colleges and schools) the student who delivers the salutatory oration.

sa·lu·ta·to·ry (sə loo′tə tôr′ĭ), *adj., n., pl.* **-ries. —adj. 1.** pertaining to or of the nature of a salutation. **—n. 2.** an address of welcome, esp. (in American colleges and schools) one given by a member of the graduating class to begin the commencement exercises.

sa·lute (sə loot′), *v.,* **-luted, -luting,** *n.* **—v.t. 1.** to address with expressions of good will, respect, etc.; greet. **2.** to make a bow, gesture, or the like to in greeting, farewell, respect, etc. **3.** *Mil., Naval.* to pay respect to or honor by some formal act, as by raising the right hand to the side of the headgear, presenting arms, firing cannon, dipping colors, etc. **—v.i. 4.** to perform a salutation. **5.** *Mil., Naval.* to give a salute. **—n. 6.** an act of saluting; salutation; greeting. **7.** *Mil., Naval.* **a.** the special act of respect paid in saluting. **b.** the position of the hand or rifle in saluting: *at the salute.* [ME, t. L: m. s. *salūtāre* greet] **—sa·lut′er,** *n.*

Salv., Salvador.

Sal·va·dor (săl′və dôr′; *Sp.* säl′vä dôr′), *n.* **1.** El Salvador. **2.** Official name of Sao Salvador. **—Sal′va·do′ran, Sal·va·do·ri·an** (săl′və dôr′ĭ ən), *adj., n.*

sal·vage (săl′vĭj), *n., v.,* **-vaged, -vaging. —n. 1.** act of saving a ship or its cargo from perils of the seas. **2.** the property so saved. **3.** compensation given to those who voluntarily save a ship or its cargo. **4.** the saving of anything from fire, danger, etc., or the property so saved. **5.** the value or proceeds upon sale of goods recovered from a fire. **—v.t. 6.** to save from shipwreck, fire, etc. [t. ML: m.s. *salvāgium*, der. L *salvāre* save] **—sal′vag·er,** *n.*

sal·var·san (săl′vər săn′), *n. Pharm.* **1.** arsphenamine. **2.** (*cap.*) a trademark for it. [f. s. L *salvus* well + ARS(ENIC) + -AN]

sal·va·tion (săl vā′shən), *n.* **1.** act of saving or delivering. **2.** state of being saved or delivered. **3.** a source, cause, or means of deliverance: *to be the salvation of a friend.* **4.** *Theol.* deliverance from the power and penalty of sin; redemption. [ME, t. LL: s. *salvātio*]

Salvation Army, a quasi-military religious organization, founded in England in 1865 by William Booth to revive religion among the masses.

salve[1] (săv, säv), *n., v.,* **salved, salving. —n. 1.** a healing ointment to be applied to wounds and sores for relief or healing. **2.** anything that soothes or mollifies. [ME; OE *sealf*, c. G *salbe*] **—v.t. 3.** to soothe as if with salve: *to salve one's conscience.* **4.** *Obs.* to apply salve to. [ME; OE *sealfian*, c. Goth. *salbōn*]

salve[2] (sălv), *v.i., v.t.,* **salved, salving.** to save from loss or destruction; to salvage. [back formation from SALVAGE]

sal·ve[3] (săl′vĭ), *interj.* Hail! [L: be in good health!]

Sal·ve·mi·ni (säl vĕ′mē nē′), *n.* Gaetano (gä′ĕ tä′nō), 1873–1957, Italian historian, in the U.S.

sal·ver (săl′vər), *n.* a tray. [f. Sp. *salva* foretasting, hence tray (der. *salvar* protect, save, t. L: m. *salvāre*) + *-er*, modeled after *platter* or the like]

sal·vi·a (săl′vĭ ə), *n.* any of the menthaceous herbs or shrubs constituting the genus *Salvia*, as *S. splendens*, the scarlet sage, an ornamental garden plant, and *S. officinalis*, the common sage. [t. L]

Sal·vi·ni (säl vē′nē), *n.* Tommaso (tôm mä′zō), 1829–1916, Italian tragedian.

sal·vo[1] (săl′vō), *n., pl.,* **-vos, -voes. 1.** a discharge of artillery or other firearms, in regular succession, often intended as a salute. **2.** a round of cheers, applause, etc. [earlier *salva*, t. It. See SALVE[3]]

sal·vo[2] (săl′vō), *n., pl.* **-vos.** *Rare.* **1.** an excuse or quibbling evasion. **2.** something to save a person's reputation, feelings, etc. [t. L, abl. of *salvus* safe, used in legal phrases, as *salvo jūre* the right being safe]

sal vo·la·ti·le (săl võ lăt′ə lē′), **1.** ammonium carbonate. **2.** an aromatic alcoholic solution of this salt.

sal·vor (săl′vər), *n.* one who salvages or helps to salvage a ship, cargo, etc.

Sal·ween (săl′wēn′), *n.* a river flowing from SW China, S through E Burma into the Bay of Bengal. ab. 1750 mi.

Salz·burg (sôlz′bûrg; *Ger.* zälts′bŏŏrкн), *n.* a city in W Austria: the birthplace of Mozart. 102,927 (1951).

Sam., *Bible.* Samuel.

S.Am., 1. South America. **2.** South American.

Sa·mar (sä′mär), *n.* one of the Philippine Islands, in the E part of the group. 757,212 pop. (1948); 5050 sq. mi.

sam·a·ra (săm′ə rə, sə mär′ə), *n. Bot.* an indehiscent, usually one-seeded, winged fruit, as of the elm. [t. NL, special use of L *samara* seed of the elm]

Sa·ma·ra (sə mä′rə), *n.* former name of Kuibyshev.

Sa·ma·rang (sə mä′räng), *n.* Semarang.

Sa·mar·i·a (sə mâr′ĭ ə), *n.* **1.** an ancient kingdom in N Palestine between the Jordan river and the Mediterranean: later a province; now in Jordan. See map under **Tyre. 2.** the ancient capital of this kingdom.

Sa·mar·i·tan (sə măr′ə tən), *n.* **1.** an inhabitant of Samaria. **2.** See **good Samaritan. 3.** one who is compassionate and helpful to a fellow being in distress. *—adj.* **4.** pertaining to Samaria, or to Samaritans.

sa·mar·i·um (sə mâr′ĭ əm), *n. Chem.* a rare-earth metallic element discovered in samarskite. *Symbol:* Sm; *at. wt.:* 150.43; *at. no.:* 62. [f. SAMAR(SKITE) + -IUM]

Sam·ar·kand (săm′ər kănd′; *Russ.* sä′mär känt′), *n.* a city in the SW Soviet Union in Asia, N of Afghanistan: taken by Alexander the Great, 329 B.C.; Tamerlane's capital in the 14th century. 170,000 (est. 1956). Also, **Sam′ar·cand′.**

sa·mar·skite (sə mär′skīt), *n.* a velvet-black mineral, a complex columbate-tantalate of uranium, cerium, etc., occurring in masses, a minor source of uranium. [t. G: m. *samarskit*, named after Col. *Samarski*, a Russian. See -ITE[1]]

Sa·ma-Ve·da (sä′mə vä′də, -vē′də), *n.* See **Veda.**

sam·ba (săm′bə), *n.* a ballroom dance of Brazilian (ultimately African) origin.

sam·bar (săm′bər, säm′-), *n.* a medium-to-large deer of the subgenus *Rusa*, having three-pointed antlers, found in southeastern Asia and many of the Indo-Australian islands. [t. Hind.]

sam·bo (săm′bō), *n., pl.* **-bos.** the offspring of Negro and Indian (or mulatto) parents. [prob. t. Sp. m. *zambo*]

Sam·bre (sän′br), *n.* a river flowing NE through N France and S Belgium into the Meuse at Namur: battle, 1918. ab. 100 mi.

Sam Browne belt (săm′ broun′), a military belt having a supporting strap over the right shoulder, worn by officers.

sam·bu·ca (săm bū′kə), *n.* an ancient stringed musical instrument used in Greece and the Near East. [t. L, t. Gk.: m. *sambўkē*. Cf. Aramaic *sabbeka*]

same (sām), *adj.* **1.** identical with what is about to be or has just been mentioned: *the very same man.* **2.** being one or identical, though having different names, aspects, etc.: *these are one and the same thing.* **3.** agreeing in

Samara
(cross sections)
A. White ash,
Fraxinus americana; B. Slippery elm, *Ulmus fulva;* C. Black birch, *Betula lenta*

kind, amount, etc.; corresponding: *two boxes of the same dimensions.* **4.** unchanged in character, condition, etc. —*pron.* **5.** the same person or thing. **6. the same,** with the same manner (used adverbially). **7. all the same, a.** notwithstanding; nevertheless. **b.** without any material difference. **8. just the same, a.** in the same manner. **b.** nevertheless. [ME and OE, c. Icel. *sami, sama, samr;* in OE used only as adv.]
—**Syn. 1.** similar, like, corresponding, interchangeable, equal. SAME, SIMILAR agree in indicating a correspondence between two or more things. SAME means or pretends to mean alike in kind, degree, quality; that is, identical (with): *to eat the same food every day, at the same price.* SIMILAR means like, resembling, having certain qualities in common, somewhat the same as, or nearly of the same kind as: *similar in appearance; don't treat them as if they were the same, when they are only similar.* —**Ant. 1.** different, unlike.

same·ness (sām′nĭs), *n.* **1.** state of being the same; identity; uniformity. **2.** lack of variety; monotony.

S.Amer., 1. South America. **2.** South American.

sam·iel (săm′yĕl), *n.* simoom. [t. Turk.: m. *samyel,* f. *sam* (t. Ar.: m. *samma* to poison) + *yel* wind]

sam·i·sen (săm′ĭ sĕn′), *n.* a Japanese guitarlike musical instrument, having an extremely long neck and three strings, played with a plectrum. [t. Jap.. t. Chinese: m. *san-hsien* three-stringed (instrument)]

sam·ite (săm′īt, sā′mīt), *n.* a heavy silk fabric, sometimes interwoven with gold, worn in the Middle Ages. [ME, t. OF: m. *samit,* t. MGk.: m. *hexámiton,* lit., six-threaded]

sam·let (săm′lĭt), *n.* a young salmon. [syncopated and dissimilated var. of *salmonet,* f. SALMON + -ET]

Sam·ni·um (săm′nĭ əm), *n.* an ancient country in central Italy. —**Sam·nite** (săm′nīt), *adj., n.*

Sa·mo·a (sə mō′ə), *n.* a group of islands in the S Pacific comprising: **Western Samoa** (the former trusteeship of New Zealand) 113,567 pop. (1961); 1131 sq. mi; and **American Samoa,** 20,051 pop. (1960); 76 sq. mi. Formerly, **Navigators Islands.**

Sa·mo·an (sə mō′ən), *adj.* **1.** pertaining to Samoa or its (Polynesian) people. —*n.* **2.** a native or inhabitant of Samoa. **3.** the Polynesian language of Samoa.

Sa·mos (sā′mŏs; Gk. sä′mŏs), *n.* a Greek island in the Aegean, off the W coast of Asia Minor. 59,709 pop. (1951); 194 sq. mi. —**Sa·mi·an** (sā′mĭ ən), *adj., n.*

Sam·o·thrace (săm′ə thrās), *n.* a Greek island in the NE Aegean, the Apostle Paul visited Samothrace on his trip to Macedonia. Acts 16:11. Greek, **Sa·mo·thra·ke** (sä′mō thrä′kē). —**Sam·o·thra·cian** (săm′ə thrā′shən), *adj., n.*

sam·o·var (săm′ə vär′, săm′ə vär′), *n.* a metal urn, commonly of copper, used in the Soviet Union and elsewhere for heating the water for making tea. [t. Russ.: self-boiler]

Sam·o·yed (săm′ə yĕd′), *n.* **1.** a member of a Ural-Altaic people dwelling in northwestern Siberia and along the northeastern coast of the Soviet Union in Europe. **2.** a family of five closely related Uralian languages scattered over a large area of the northwestern Asiatic and northeastern European Soviet Union. **3.** one of a breed of Russian dogs, medium in size, with a coat of long, dense, white hair. [t. Russ.: self-eater]

Sam·o·yed·ic (săm′ə yĕd′ĭk), *adj.* of or pertaining to the Samoyeds.

samp (sămp), *n.* *U.S.* **1.** coarsely ground corn. **2.** a porridge made of it. [t. Algonquian: m. *nasamp,* lit., softened by water]

sam·pan (săm′păn), *n.* any of various small boats of China, etc., as one propelled by a single scull over the stern, and provided with a roofing of mats. [t. Chinese: m. *san-pan,* lit., three boards]

Sampan

sam·phire (săm′fīr), *n.* **1.** a succulent apiaceous herb, *Crithmum maritimum,* of Europe, growing in clefts of rock near the sea. **2.** the glasswort. [earlier *sampere, sampire,* alter. of F (*herbe de*) *Saint Pierre* St. Peter's herb]

sam·ple (săm′pəl, säm′-), *n., adj., v.,* -pled, -pling. —*n.* **1.** a small part of anything or one of a number, intended to show the quality, style, etc., of the whole; a specimen. —*adj.* **2.** serving as a specimen: *a sample copy.* —*v.t.* **3.** to take a sample or samples of; test or judge by a sample. [ME, aphetic var. of *essample,* var. of EXAMPLE] —**Syn. 1.** See **example.**

sam·pler (săm′plər, säm′-), *n.* **1.** one who samples. **2.** a piece of cloth embroidered with various devices, serving to show a beginner's skill in needlework. [ME *samplere,* t. OF: aphetic m. *essamplaire,* g. LL *exemplārium,* der. L *exemplum* EXAMPLE]

sampling inspection. See **acceptance sampling.**

Samp·son (sămp′sən), *n.* **William Thomas,** 1840–1902, U.S. rear admiral: in command of the blockade of Cuba in the Spanish-American war.

Sam·son (săm′sən), *n.* **1.** a performer of Herculean exploits, the fifteenth of the "judges" of Israel. Judges 13–16. **2.** any man of extraordinary strength.

Sam·u·el (săm′yŏŏ əl), *n.* **1.** a Hebrew judge and prophet. I Sam. 1–3, 8–15. **2.** either of the two Old Testament books bearing his name.

sam·u·rai (săm′ŏŏ rī′), *n., pl.* -rai. (in feudal Japan) **1.** a member of the military class. **2.** a retainer of a Japanese feudal noble, holding land or receiving a stipend in rice or money. [t. Jap.]

San (săn), *n.* a river flowing from the Carpathian Mountains in the W Soviet Union through SE Poland into the Vistula: battles, 1914–15. ab. 280 mi.

Sa·n'a (sä nä′), *n.* a city in SW Arabian Peninsula: the capital of Yemen. 80,000 (est. 1950). Also, **Sa·naa′.**

San An·ge·lo (săn ăn′jə lō′), a city in W Texas. 58,815 (1960).

San An·to·ni·o (săn′ ăn tō′nĭ ō′), a city in S Texas: site of the Alamo. 587,718 (1960).

san·a·tive (săn′ə tĭv), *adj.* having the power to heal; curative. [t. ML: m.s. *sānātīvus*]

san·a·to·ri·um (săn′ə tōr′ĭ əm), *n., pl.* -toriums, -to·ri·a (-tōr′ĭ ə). sanitarium (def. 2). [t. NL, prop. neut. of LL *sānātōrius* health-giving, der. L *sānātus,* pp., healed] —**Syn.** See **hospital.**

san·a·to·ry (săn′ə tōr′ĭ), *adj.* favorable for health; curative; healing. [t. LL: m.s. *sānātōrius*]

san·be·ni·to (săn′bə nē′tō), *n., pl.* -tos. (under the Spanish Inquisition) **1.** a yellow garment ornamented with flames, devils, etc., worn by a condemned heretic at an auto-da-fé. **2.** a penitential garment worn by a confessed heretic. [t. Sp., named after *San Benito* St. Benedict, from its resemblance to the scapular introduced by him]

San Ber·nar·di·no (săn′ bûr′nər dē′nō), **1.** a city in S California. 91,922 (1960). **2. Mount,** a peak in the San Bernardino Mountains in S California. 10,630 ft. **3.** a mountain pass in the Alps, in SE Switzerland. 6766 ft. high.

San Bernardino Mountains, a mountain range in S California. Highest peak, San Gorgonio, 11,485 ft.

San Blas (săn bläs′), **1.** Gulf of, a gulf of the Caribbean on the N coast of Panama. **2. Isthmus of,** the narrowest part of the Isthmus of Panama. 31 mi. wide.

San Bue·na·ven·tu·ra (săn bwä′nə vĕn tŏŏr′ə), a city in SW California. 29,114 (1960).

San·cho Pan·za (săng′kō păn′zə; *Sp.* sän′chō pän′thä), the credulous and amusing esquire of Don Quixote.

sanc·ti·fied (săngk′tə fīd′), *adj.* **1.** made holy; consecrated: *sanctified wine.* **2.** sanctimonious.

sanc·ti·fy (săngk′tə fī′), *v.t.,* -fied, -fying. **1.** to make holy; set apart as sacred; consecrate. **2.** to purify or free from sin: *sanctify your hearts.* **3.** to impart religious sanction to; render legitimate or binding: *to sanctify a vow.* **4.** to entitle to reverence or respect. **5.** to make productive of or conducive to spiritual blessing. [t. Eccl. L: m. *sanctificāre* make holy; r. ME *seintefie,* t. OF] —**sanc′ti·fi·ca′tion,** *n.* —**sanc′ti·fi′er,** *n.*

sanc·ti·mo·ni·ous (săngk′tə mō′nĭ əs), *adj.* **1.** making a show of holiness; affecting sanctity. **2.** *Obs.* holy; sacred. [f.SANCTIMONY + -OUS] —**sanc′ti·mo′ni·ous·ly,** *adv.* —**sanc′ti·mo′ni·ous·ness,** *n.*

sanc·ti·mo·ny (săngk′tə mō′nĭ), *n.* **1.** pretended, affected, or hypocritical holiness or devoutness. **2.** *Obs.* sanctity; sacredness. [t. L: m. s. *sanctimōnia*]

sanc·tion (săngk′shən), *n.* **1.** authoritative permission; countenance or support given to an action, etc.; solemn ratification. **2.** something serving to support an action, etc. **3.** binding force given, or something which gives binding force, as to an oath, rule of conduct, etc. **4.** *Law.* **a.** a provision of a law enacting a penalty for disobedience or a reward for obedience. **b.** the penalty or reward. **5.** *Internat. Law.* action by one or more states toward another state calculated to force it to comply with legal obligations. —*v.t.* **6.** to authorize, countenance, or approve: *sanctioned by usage.* **7.** to ratify or confirm: *to sanction a law.* [t. L: s. *sanctio*]

sanc·ti·ty (săngk′tə tĭ), *n., pl.* -ties. **1.** holiness, saintliness, or godliness. **2.** sacred or hallowed character: *inviolable sanctity of the temple.* **3.** a sacred thing. [t. L: m.s. *sanctitas;* r. ME *saintite,* t. OF]

sanc·tu·ar·y (săngk′chŏŏ ĕr′ĭ), *n., pl.* -aries. **1.** a sacred or holy place. **2.** *Jewish Hist.* **a.** the temple at Jerusalem, particularly the most retired part of it (the *holy of holies*) in which the ark of the covenant was kept. **b.** the tabernacle in the wilderness after the exodus from Egypt. **3.** an especially holy place in a temple or church. **4.** the part of a church about the altar; the chancel. **5.** a church or other sacred place where fugitives were formerly entitled to immunity from arrest; asylum. **6.** immunity afforded by refuge in such a place. [ME, t. L: m.s. *sanctuārium*] —**Syn. 1.** church, temple, shrine, altar, sanctum, adytum.

sanc·tum (săngk′təm), *n., pl.* -tums, (*Rare*) -ta (-tə). **1.** a sacred or holy place. **2.** an especially private place or retreat. [t. L: (neut.) holy]

sanc·tum sanc·to·rum (săngk′təm săngk tōr′əm), **1.** the "holy of holies" of the Jewish tabernacle and temple. **2.** any especially private place or retreat. [L (Vulgate), translated from Gk. (Septuagint), itself translating Heb. *qodhesh haqqodhāshīm* holy of holies]

Sanc·tus (săngk′təs), *n.* **1.** *Liturgy.* the hymn beginning "Holy, holy, holy, Lord God of hosts," with which the Eucharistic preface culminates. **2.** a musical setting for this hymn. [L: holy, the first word of the hymn]

Sanctus bell, a bell rung during the celebration of Mass to give notification of the more solemn portions.

sand (sănd), *n.* **1.** the more or less fine debris of rocks, consisting of small, loose grains, often of quartz. **2.** (*usually pl.*) a tract or region composed principally of sand. **3.** the sand in an hourglass, or a grain of this. **4.** (*pl.*) moments of time or of one's life. **5.** *U.S. Colloq.* pluck. **6.** a dull reddish-yellow color. —*v.t.* **7.** to smooth or polish with sand. **8.** to sprinkle with, or as with, sand. **9.** to fill up with sand, as a harbor. **10.** to add sand to: *to sand sugar.* [ME and OE, c. G *sand*]

Sand (sănd; *Fr.* sänd), *n.* George (jôrj; *Fr.* zhôrzh), (*Madame Amandine Lucile Aurore Dudevant*) 1804–76, French novelist.

san·dal[1] (săn′dəl), *n., v.,* **-daled, -daling.** —*n.* **1.** a kind of shoe, consisting of a sole of leather or other material fastened to the foot by thongs or straps. **2.** any of various kinds of low shoes or slippers. **3.** a kind of light, low rubber overshoe. **4.** a band for fastening a low shoe or slipper on, by passing over the instep or round the ankle. —*v.t.* **5.** to furnish with sandals. [t. F.: m. *sandale;* r. ME *sandalie,* t. L: m. *sandalium,* t. Gk.: m. *sandálion,* lit., little sandal] —**san′daled;** *esp. Brit.,* **san′dalled,** *adj.*

san·dal[2] (săn′dəl), *n.* sandalwood.

san·dal·wood (săn′dəl woŏd′), *n.* **1.** the fragrant heartwood of any of certain Asiatic trees of the genus *Santalum* (family *Santalaceae*), used for ornamental carving and burned as incense. **2.** any of these trees, esp. *S. album* (**white sandalwood**), an evergreen of India. **3.** any of various related or similar trees or their woods, esp. an East Indian fabaceous tree, *Pterocarpus santalinus* (**red sandalwood**), or its heavy dark-red wood, which is used as a dyestuff. [f. *sandal* (t. ML: s. *sandalum,* ult. of Skt. orig.) + WOOD]

Sandalwood Island, Sumba.

san·da·rac (săn′də răk′), *n.* **1.** a brittle, usually pale-yellow, more or less transparent, faintly aromatic resin exuding from the bark of the sandarac tree and used chiefly as incense and in making varnish. **2.** the sandarac tree. [t. L: s. *sandaraca,* t. Gk.: m. *sandarákē*]

sandarac tree, a pinaceous tree, *Tetraclinis articulata* (*Callitris quadrivalvis*), native in northwestern Africa, yielding the resin sandarac, and having a fragrant, hard, dark-colored wood much used in building.

sand·bag (sănd′băg′), *n., v.,* **-bagged, -bagging.** —*n.* **1.** a bag filled with sand, used in fortification, as ballast, etc. **2.** such a bag used as a weapon. —*v.t.* **3.** to furnish with sandbags. **4.** to hit or stun with a sandbag.

sand bar, a bar of sand formed in a river or sea by the action of tides or currents.

sand·blast (sănd′blăst′, -bläst′), *n.* **1.** a blast of air or steam laden with sand, used to clean, grind, cut, or decorate hard surfaces, as of glass, stone, or metal. **2.** the apparatus used to apply such a blast. —*v.t., v.i.* **3.** to clean, smooth, etc., with a sandblast.

sand·blind (sănd′blīnd′), *adj. Archaic or Dial.* partially blind; dim-sighted. [ME; for **samblind,* f. OE *săm-* half (c. L *sēmi-*) + BLIND]

sand·box (sănd′bŏks′), *n.* a box or receptacle for holding sand, esp. for dropping from a locomotive or a streetcar to the rails to prevent slipping.

sandbox tree, a euphorbiaceous tree, *Hura crepitans,* of tropical America, bearing a furrowed roundish fruit about the size of an orange which when ripe and dry bursts with a sharp report and scatters the seeds.

sand·bur (sănd′bûr′), *n.* **1.** any of several bur-bearing weeds growing in sandy places, as *Solanum rostratum,* a species of nightshade of the western U.S. **2.** a common weed, *Franseria acanthicarpa,* related to the bristly ragweeds. Also, **sand′burr′.**

Sand·burg (sănd′bûrg, sänd′-), *n.* **Carl,** born 1878, U.S. poet, biographer, and writer.

sand·cast (sănd′kăst′, -käst′), *v.t.* **-cast, -casting.** to produce (a casting) by pouring molten metal into sand molds.

sand crack, a crack or fissure in the hoof of a horse, extending from the coronet downward toward the sole, occurring on any part of the wall of the hoof, caused by a dryness of horn and liable to cause lameness.

sand dab, any of several flatfishes used as food.

sand dollar, any of various flat, disklike sea urchins, esp. *Echinarachnius parma,* which live on sandy bottoms off the coasts of the U.S.

sand eel, a sand launce.

sand·er (săn′dər), *n.* **1.** one who sands or sandpapers. **2.** an apparatus for sanding or sandpapering.

sand·er·ling (săn′dər lĭng), *n.* a widespread small shore bird, *Crocethia alba,* found on sandy beaches.

sand flea, 1. a beach flea. **2.** the chigoe.

sand·fly (sănd′flī′), *n., pl.* **-flies. 1.** a small bloodsucking dipterous fly of the genus *Phlebotomus,* carrier of several human diseases. **2.** a small bloodsucking dipterous fly of the genus *Calicoides.*

sand·glass (sănd′glăs′, -gläs′), *n.* an hourglass.

sand grouse, any of certain birds inhabiting sandy tracts of the Old World, which constitute the family *Pteroclidae,* structurally allied to the pigeons.

san·dhi form (săn′dĭ), the phonetic or phonemic form of a word or phrase occurring in a context of other (preceding and following) forms, when different from the absolute form, e.g., in *Jack's at home* the *'s* is a sandhi form corresponding to the absolute form *is.* [*sandhi,* t. Skt.: putting together]

sand·hog (sănd′hôg′), *n.* **1.** a laborer who digs or works in sand. **2.** one who works, usually in a caisson, in tunneling under water.

sand hopper, a beach flea.

Sand·hurst (sănd′hûrst), *n.* a village in S England, SE of Reading: military college. 5244 (1951).

San Di·e·go (săn′ dĭ ā′gō), a seaport in SW California: naval and marine base. 573,224 (1960).

sand launce, an elongate fish of the family *Ammodytidae,* with oblique cross ridges in the skin of the sides, capable of burrowing in the sand. Also, **sand lance.**

sand lily, a small stemless plant, *Leucocrinum montanum,* of the western U.S., bearing lilylike flowers.

sand lot, *U.S.* a vacant lot in or adjacent to a city, used for games or sports.

sand·man (sănd′măn′), *n.* the man who, in the fairy tale, makes children sleepy by putting sand in their eyes.

sand·pa·per (sănd′pā′pər), *n.* **1.** strong paper coated with a layer of sand, used for smoothing or polishing. —*v.t.* **2.** to smooth or polish with or as with sandpaper.

sand·pip·er (sănd′pī′pər), *n.* any of numerous shore-inhabiting birds of the family *Scolopacidae,* typically having a piping note and a bill shorter than that of a true snipe, as the common European sandpiper, *Actitis hypoleuca,* and the New World spotted sandpiper, *Actitis macularia.*

Spotted sandpiper, *Actitis macularia* (8 in. long)

San·dro·cot·tus (săn′drō kŏt′əs), *n.* Greek name of **Chandragupta.**

sand shoe, *Brit.* a light tennis shoe; sneaker.

sand·stone (sănd′stōn′), *n.* a rock formed by the consolidation of sand, the grains being held together by a cement of silica, lime, gypsum, or clay.

sand·storm (sănd′stôrm′), *n.* a storm of wind that bears along clouds of sand.

San·dus·ky (sən dŭs′kĭ), *n.* a city in N Ohio: a port on Lake Erie. 31,989 (1960).

sand verbena, any of a genus (*Abronia*) of low, mostly trailing nyctaginaceous herbs of the western U.S., having showy verbenalike flowers, esp. either of two Pacific coast species, one yellow (*A. latifolia*) and the other pink (*A. umbellata*).

sand viper, 1. *U.S. Dial.* a hognose (snake). **2.** the horned viper.

sand·wich (sănd′wĭch, -wĭj), *n.* **1.** two slices of bread (or toast), plain or buttered, with a layer of meat, fish, cheese, or the like between them. **2.** something formed by a similar combination. —*v.t.* **3.** to put into a sandwich. **4.** to insert between two other things. [named after the fourth Earl of *Sandwich* (1718–92)]

Sand·wich (sănd′wĭch), *n.* a town in SE England, in Kent: one of the Cinque Ports. 4142 (1951).

Sandwich Islands, former name of the **Hawaiian Islands.**

sandwich man, *Colloq.* a man with advertising boards hung from his shoulders, one before and one behind.

sand·wort (sănd′wûrt′), *n.* any of the plants constituting the caryophyllaceous genus *Arenaria,* many of which grow in sandy soil.

sand·y (săn′dĭ), *adj.,* **sandier, sandiest. 1.** of the nature of or consisting of sand; containing or covered with sand. **2.** of a yellowish-red color: *sandy hair.* **3.** having such hair. **4.** shifting or unstable, like sand. —**sand′i·ness,** *n.*

Sandy Hook, a peninsula in E New Jersey at the entrance to lower New York Bay, partially enclosing **Sandy Hook Bay** on the west: lighthouse. 6 mi. long.

sane (sān), *adj.,* **saner, sanest. 1.** free from mental derangement: *a sane person.* **2.** having or showing reason, sound judgment, or good sense: *sane advice.* **3.** *Rare.* sound; healthy. [t. L: m.s. *sānus* sound, healthy] —**sane′ly,** *adv.* —**sane′ness,** *n.*

San·for·ize (săn′fə rīz′), *v.t.,* **-ized, -izing.** *Trademark.* to shrink (cotton or linen fabrics) mechanically by a patented process before tailoring.

San Fran·cis·co (săn′ frən sĭs′kō), a seaport in W California, on San Francisco Bay: earthquake and fire, 1906; United Nations Conference, 1945. 742,855 (1960).

San Francisco Bay, a large estuary in W California, forming one of the finest land-locked harbors in the world: connected with the Pacific by the Golden Gate. ab. 50 mi. long; 3–12 mi. wide.

San Francisco Mountain, a mountain mass in N Arizona. Highest peak (in the State), Humphrey's Peak, 12,611 ft.

sang (săng), *v.* pt. of **sing.**

san·ga·ree (săng′gə rē′), *n.* a drink composed of wine, diluted, sweetened, and spiced. [t. Sp.: m. *sangría,* lit., bleeding (with reference to color), der. *sangre* blood]

Sang·er (săng′ər), *n.* **Margaret,** 1883–1966, U.S. leader in birth-control movement.

sang-froid (sän frwä/), *n. French.* coolness of mind; calmness; composure. [F: cold blood]

San·graal (säng gräl/), *n.* the Holy Grail. [ME *sangrayle*, t. OF: m. *Saint Graal.* See SAINT, GRAIL]

San·gre de Cris·to (säng/grĕ dĕ krēs/tō), a range of the Rocky Mountains in S Colorado and N New Mexico. Highest point, Blanca Peak, 14,390 ft.

san·guif·er·ous (sång gwĭf/ərəs), *adj.* conveying blood, as a blood vessel. [f. *sangui-* (comb. form repr. L *sanguis* blood) + -FEROUS]

san·gui·nar·i·a (sång/gwĭ när/Yə), *n.* 1. the bloodroot. 2. its medicinal rhizome. [short for L *herba sanguinäria* bloody plant (in NL applied to bloodroot)]

san·gui·nar·y (sång/gwĭ nĕr/Y), *adj.* 1. attended with or characterized by bloodshed; bloody: *a sanguinary struggle.* 2. bloodthirsty: *a sanguinary person.* 3. inflicting the death penalty freely. [t. L: m.s. *sanguinārius*] —**san/gui·nar/i·ly**, *adv.* —**san/gui·nar/i·ness**, *n.*

san·guine (sång/gwĭn). *adj.* 1. naturally cheerful and hopeful: *a sanguine disposition.* 2. hopeful or confident: *sanguine expectations.* 3. ruddy: *a sanguine complexion.* 4. (in the old physiology) having blood as the predominating humor, and hence ruddy-faced, cheerful, etc. 5. sanguinary. 6. blood-red; red. —*n.* 7. a red iron oxide crayon used in making drawings. [ME, t. L: s. *sanguineus*, der. *sanguis* blood (cf. def. 4)] —**san/guine·ly**, *adv.* —**san/guine·ness**, *n.*

san·guin·e·ous (sång gwĭn/Yəs), *adj.* 1. of, pertaining to, or containing blood. 2. of the color of blood. 3. abounding with blood. 4. sanguine; confident.

san·guin·o·lent (sång gwĭn/əlent), *adj.* 1. of or pertaining to blood. 2. containing, or tinged with, blood; bloody. [t. L: s. *sanguinolentus*]

San·he·drin (săn/hĭ drĭn, sång/Y-), *n.* 1. the supreme council and highest ecclesiastical and judicial tribunal of the ancient Jewish nation, with seventy-one members. 2. a similar lower tribunal, with twenty-three members. Also, **San·he·drim** (săn/hĭ drĭm, sång/Y-). [t. LHeb., t. Gk.: m. *synédrion* f. *syn-* SYN- + *hédrion*, der. *hédra* seat]

san·i·cle (săn/Ykəl), *n.* any of the umbelliferous herbs constituting the genus *Sanicula*, as *S. marilandica*, an American species used medicinally. [ME, t. AF or OF, f. ML: m. *sānicula*, dim. of L *sāna* (fem.) healthy]

sa·ni·es (sā/nY ēz/), *n. Pathol.* a thin serous fluid, often greenish, discharged from ulcers, etc. [t. L]

San Il·de·fon·so (săn ēl/dĕ fōn/sō), a town in central Spain, near Segovia: termed the "Spanish Versailles" for its palace (La Granja); treaty, 1800. 3245 (1950).

sa·ni·ous (sā/nYəs), *adj.* characterized by the discharge of a thin fluid, as from an ulcer. [t. L: m.s. *saniōsus* pertaining to or yielding sanies.]

san·i·tar·i·an (săn/ə tår/Yən), *adj.* 1. sanitary. —*n.* 2. one expert or engaged in sanitary work.

san·i·tar·i·um (săn/ə tår/Yəm), *n., pl.* **-tariums, -taria** (-tår/Yə). 1. an establishment for the treatment of invalids, convalescents, etc., esp. in a favorable climate: *a tuberculosis sanitarium.* 2. a health resort. [f. L *sănit(as)* health + -ARIUM] —**Syn.** 1. See hospital.

san·i·tar·y (săn/ə tĕr/Y), *adj., n., pl.* **-taries.** —*adj.* 1. of or pertaining to health or the conditions affecting health, esp. with reference to cleanliness, precautions against disease, etc. 2. favorable to health; free from dirt, germs, etc. —*n.* 3. a public water closet, urinal, or lavatory. [f. L *sănit(as)* health + -ARY¹] —**san/i·tar/i·ly**, *adv.* —**san/i·tar/i·ness**, *n.*

—**Syn.** 1. SANITARY, HYGIENIC agree in being concerned with health. SANITARY refers more especially to conditions affecting health or measures for guarding against infection or disease: *to insure sanitary conditions in preparing food.* HYGIENIC is applied to whatever concerns the care of the body and the promotion of health: *to live in hygienic surroundings with plenty of fresh air.* —**Ant.** 1. unclean, unwholesome.

san·i·ta·tion (săn/ə tā/shən), *n.* the working out and practical application of sanitary measures.

san·i·ty (săn/ə tY), *n.* 1. state of being sane; soundness of mind. 2. soundness of judgment. [t. L: m.s. *sānitas*]

San Ja·cin·to (săn/ jəsĭn/tō), a river in E Texas, flowing SE to Galveston Bay: the Texans decisively defeated the Mexicans near the mouth of this river, 1836.

san·jak (săn/jăk/), *n. Turkey.* one of the administrative districts into which a vilayet is divided. [t. Turk.: m. *sanjāq*, lit., flag, standard]

San Joa·quin (săn/ wŏ kēn/), a river flowing from the Sierra Nevada Mountains NW through central California, joining the Sacramento river as it enters San Francisco Bay. ab. 350 mi.

San Jo·se (săn/ hō zā/), a city in W California. 204,196 (1960).

San Jo·sé (săn hō sĕ/), the capital of Costa Rica, in the central part. 93,229 (est. 1953).

San Jo·se scale (săn/ hō zā/), a scale insect, *Quadraspidiotus perniciosus*, very injurious to many trees and shrubs throughout the United States, first found at San Jose, California.

San Juan (săn hwän/; *Sp.* săn), 1. a seaport in, and the capital of, Puerto Rico, in the N part. 224,767 (1950). 2. a city in W Argentina. 82,410 (1947).

San Juan Hill, a hill in SE Cuba, near Santiago de Cuba: captured by U.S. forces, 1898.

San Juan Islands, a group of islands between NW Washington and SE Vancouver Island, Canada: a part of Washington.

San Juan Mountains, a range of the Rocky Mountains in SW Colorado and N New Mexico. Highest peak, Uncompahgre Peak, 14,306 ft.

sank (sångk), *v.* pt. of **sink.**

San·khya (sång/kyə), *n.* one of the six leading systems of Hindu philosophy, stressing the reality and duality of spirit and matter. [t. Skt., var. of *samkhyā* number]

Sankt Mo·ritz (zängkt mō/rĭts), German name of **St. Moritz.**

San Le·an·dro (săn lY ăn/drō), a city in W California. 65,962 (1960).

San Lu·is Po·to·sí (săn/ lōō-ēs/ pô/tō sē/), 1. a state in central Mexico. 897,054 (est. 1952); 24,415 sq. mi. 2. the capital of this state. 125,640 (1950).

San Ma·ri·no (săn/ mä rē/nō), a small republic in E Italy: the oldest independent country in Europe. 13,500 (est. 1953); 38 sq. mi. *Cap.*: San Marino.

San Mar·tin (săn/ mär tēn/), **José de** (hō sĕ/ dĕ), 1778–1850, South American patriot, general, and statesman, born in Argentina: won independence from Spain for Chile and Peru.

San Ma·te·o (săn/mə tā/ō), a city in W California. 69,870 (1960).

San Mi·guel (săn/ mēgĕl/), a city in E El Salvador. 28,730 (est. 1953).

San Pa·blo Bay (săn pä/blō), the N part of San Francisco Bay, in W California.

San Re·mo (săn rĕ/mō), a seaport in NW Italy, on the Riviera: resort. 37,959 (1951).

sans (sănz; *Fr.* săn), *prep. Archaic or French.* without. [ME, t. OF, ult. g. L *absentiā*, in the absence of, b. with *sine* without]

San Sal·va·dor (săn săl/vədôr/; *Sp.* săn säl/vädōr/). 1. Also, **Watling Island.** an island in the E Bahama Islands: first land in the New World seen by Christopher Columbus, 1492. 994 (1953); 60 sq. mi. 2. the capital of El Salvador. 180,713 (est. 1953).

San·scrit (săn/skrĭt), *n.* Sanskrit.

sans-cu·lotte (sănz/kyōō lŏt/; *Fr.* sänkylŏt/), *n.* 1. (in the French Revolution) a contemptuous designation for a republican of the poorer class, adopted by the revolutionaries as a designation of honor, as if synonymous with "patriot." 2. any extreme republican or revolutionary. [t. F: without (knee) breeches] —**sans-cu·lot·tic** (sănz/kyōō lŏt/Yk), *adj.* —**sans/-cu·lot/tism**, *n.*

sans-cu·lot·tide (sănz/kyōō lŏt/Yd; *Fr.* sänkylōtēd/), *n.* (in the calendar of the first French republic) one of the 5 (in leap year, 6) complementary days added at the end of the month Fructidor.

San Se·bas·tián (săn/ sĕbäs/tyän/), a seaport in N Spain: resort. 120,540 (est. 1955).

San·sei (săn/sā/), *n.* a grandchild of Japanese immigrants to the United States. [t. Jap., t. Chinese: third born, third generation]

san·se·vi·e·ri·a (săn/sĭ vY Yr/Yə), *n.* any plant of a genus, *Sanseveria*, grown as a house plant for its stiff, sword-shaped leaves. [NL, named after the Prince of *Sanseviero* (18th cent.), a learned Neapolitan]

sans gêne (săn zhĕn/), *French.* without constraint or embarrassment; free and easy.

Sansk., Sanskrit.

San·skrit (săn/skrĭt), *n.* an extinct Indic language, the ancient classical literary language of India, with a voluminous literature extending over several centuries. It is one of the oldest recorded Indo-European languages. Also, **Sanscrit.** [t. Skt.: m. *samskrita* prepared, cultivated] —**San·skrit/ic**, *adj.* —**San/skrit·ist**, *n.*

sans pa·reil (săn på rĕ/y), *French.* without equal.

sans peur et sans re·proche (săn pœr/ ĕ săn rəprōsh/), *French.* without fear and without reproach.

sans-ser·if (sănz/sĕr/Yf), *n. Print.* a style of type which does not have any serifs.

sans sou·ci (săn sōō sē/), *French.* carefree.

San Ste·fa·no (săn stĕ/fä nō/), a village in Turkey, near Istanbul: treaty between Russia and Turkey, 1878.

San·ta An·a (săn/tə ăn/ə; *Sp.* săn/tää/nä), 1. a city in NW El Salvador. 56,952 (est. 1953). 2. a city in SW California. 100,350 (1960).

San·ta An·na (săn/tə ä/nä), **Antonio López de** (än tō/nyō lō/pĕs dĕ), 1795–1876, Mexican general and politician: massacred Alamo defenders. Also, **Santa Ana.**

San·ta Bar·ba·ra (săn/tə bär/bərə), a city on the SW coast of California: Spanish mission. 58,768 (1960).

Santa Barbara Islands, a group of islands off the SW coast of California.

San·ta Cat·a·li·na (săn/tə kăt/əlē/nə), island off the SW coast of California, opposite Long Beach: resort. 1630 pop. (1950); 132 sq. mi. Also, **Catalina Island.**

San·ta Cla·ra (săn/tə klä/rä), 1. a city in central Cuba. 85,678 (1953). 2. a city in central California, S of San Francisco 58,880 (1960).

San·ta Claus (săn/tə klôz/), the patron saint of children, dispenser of gifts on Christmas Eve; Saint Nicholas. [t. d. D: m. *Sante Klaas* St. Nicholas]

San·ta Cruz (săn/tə krōōz/; *Sp.* săn/tä krōōs/), 1. one of the Santa Barbara Islands, off the SW coast of California. 2. St. Croix (def. 1).

San·ta Cruz de Ten·er·ife (săn'tə krōōz' də těn'ə-rīf'; Sp. sän'tä krōōs' dĕ tĕ'nĕ rē'fĕ), a seaport in the Canary Islands on Tenerife island. 111,615 (est. 1955).

San·ta Fe (săn'tə fā'), 1 the capital of New Mexico, in the N part: founded c1605. 34,676 (1960).

San·ta Fé (sän'tä fě'), a city in E Argentina. 177,000 (est. 1952).

Santa Fe Trail, an important trade route linking Independence, Missouri, and Santa Fe, New Mexico, which flourished from 1822 until about 1880.

san·tal (săn'təl), n. sandalwood.

san·ta·la·ceous (săn'tə lā'shəs), adj. belonging to the Santalaceae, or sandalwood family of plants. [f. s. NL Santalāceae (der. santalum sandalwood) + -ous]

San·ta Ma·ri·a (sän'tä märē'ä), 1. the flagship of Columbus in his voyage of 1492. 2. an active volcano in W Guatemala. ab. 12,500 ft.

San·ta Mau·ra (sän'tä mou'rä), Italian name of Levkas.

San·ta Mon·i·ca (săn'tə mŏn'ə kə), a city in SW California, near Los Angeles, on **Santa Monica Bay**: resort. 83,249 (1960).

San·tan·der (săn'tän dĕr'), n. a seaport in N Spain: fine harbor; Altamira prehistoric cave drawings nearby. 111,758 (est. 1955).

San·ta Ro·sa de Co·pán (sän'tä rō'sä dĕ kō-pän'), a town in W Honduras: the site of extensive Mayan ruins. 6417 (1950). Also, **Copán.**

San·ta·ya·na (săn'tǐ än'ə; Sp. sän'tä yä'nä), n. George, 1863–1952, U.S. poet, essayist, and philosophical writer, born in Spain.

San·tee (săn tē'), n. a river flowing from central South Carolina SE to the Atlantic. 143 mi.

San·ti·a·go (săn'tē ä'gō), n. 1. the capital of Chile, in the central part. 1,412,940 (est. 1953). 2. Also, **Santiago de Com·po·ste·la** (dĕ kôm'pôstĕ'lä) a city in NW Spain: pilgrimages; cathedral. 49,191 (1950).

Santiago de Cu·ba (dĕ kōō'bä), a seaport in SE Cuba: naval battle, 1898. 163,237 (1953).

san·tir (sän'tǐr), n. a musical instrument somewhat like a dulcimer, used by the Arabs and Persians.

San·to Do·min·go (săn'tō də mǐng'gō; Sp. sän'tô dō-mǐng'gō), 1. the capital of the Dominican Republic on the S coast: the first European settlement in America (1496). 419,477 (est. 1961). 2. Dominican Republic.

san·ton·i·ca (săn tŏn'ə kə), n. 1. a wormwood, Artemisia cina. 2. the dried flower heads of this plant, used as a vermifuge. [t. L, prop. fem. of Santonicus pertaining to the Santoni, a tribe of ancient Gaul]

san·to·nin (săn'tə nǐn), n. Chem. a crystalline compound, $C_{15}H_{18}O_3$, the active principle of santonica.

San·tos (săn'tōōs), n. a seaport in S Brazil: the world's greatest coffee port. 201,739 (est. 1952).

San·tos-Du·mont (săn'tōōz dy mônt'), n. **Alberto** (äl bĕr'tōō), 1873–1932, Brazilian inventor of dirigibles and airplanes, in France.

São Fran·cis·co (souɴ' frän sēs'kōō), a river flowing through E Brazil into the Atlantic. ab. 1800 mi.

São Luiz do Ma·ra·nhão (souɴ lwēs' dōō mä'rə-nyouɴ'), a seaport on an island off the NE coast of Brazil. 81,432 (est. 1952). Also, **Sao Luiz.**

São Mi·guel (souɴ' mē gĕl'), the largest island of the Azores. 177,057 pop. (1950); 288 sq. mi.

Saône (sōn), n. a river flowing from NE France S to the Rhone at Lyons. ab. 300 mi.

São Pau·lo (souɴ pou'lōō), a city in S Brazil: the third largest city in South America. 2,017,025 (1950).

São Paulo de Lo·an·da (də lō än'də), Loanda.

Saor·stat Eir·eann (sâr'stät âr'ən; Gaelic ā'rôn), Gaelic. Irish Free State.

São Sal·va·dor (souɴ' säl'və dôr'), a seaport in E Brazil. 396,000 (est. 1952). Also, **Bahia.** Official name, **Salvador.**

São To·mé (souɴ' tōmě'), Portuguese name of St. Thomas (def. 3). Also, **Sao' Tho·mé'.**

sap¹ (săp), n. 1. the juice or vital circulating fluid, esp. of a woody plant. 2. sapwood. 3. Slang. a fool. [ME; OE sæp, c. D sap, akin to G saft, Icel. safi]

sap² (săp), n., v., **sapped, sapping.** —n. 1. Fort. a deep narrow trench constructed to approach a besieged place or an enemy's position. —v.t. 2. Fort. a. to approach (a besieged place, etc.) with deep narrow trenches protected by gabions or parapets. b. to dig such trenches in (ground). 3. to undermine; weaken or destroy insidiously. —v.i. 4. Fort. to dig a sap. [earlier zappe, t. It.: m. zappa spade, hoe, special use of zappa goat, through similarity of handle to goat's horns]

sap·a·jou (săp'ə jōō'), n. a capuchin monkey. [t. F; f. S. Amer. orig.]

sa·pan·wood (sə păn'wŏŏd'), n. sappanwood.

sap·head (săp'hĕd'), n. Slang. a simpleton; a fool.

sap·head·ed (săp'hĕd'ĭd), adj. Slang. silly; foolish.

sa·phe·na (sə fē'nə), n., pl. **-nae** (-nē). either of two large superficial veins of the leg, one (**long** or **internal saphena**) on the inner side, and the other (**short, external,** or **posterior saphena**) on the outer and posterior sides. [t. ML, t. Ar.: m. çāfin] —**sa·phe'nous,** adj.

sap·id (săp'ĭd), adj. 1. having taste or flavor. 2. palatable. 3. to one's liking; agreeable. [t. L: s. sapidus savory] —**sa·pid'i·ty,** n.

sa·pi·ent (sā'pĭ ənt), adj. wise or sage (often used ironically). [late ME, t. L: s. sapiens, ppr., being wise] —**sa'pi·ence, sa'pi·en·cy,** n. —**sa'pi·ent·ly,** adv.

sa·pi·en·tial (sā'pĭ ĕn'shəl), adj. containing, exhibiting, or affording wisdom; characterized by wisdom. [t. LL: s. sapientiālis] —**sa'pi·en·tial·ly,** adv.

sap·in·da·ceous (săp'ĭn dā'shəs), adj. belonging to the Sapindaceae, or soapberry family of plants. [f. s. NL Sapindāceae (der. sapindas soapberry) + -ous]

sap·less (săp'lĭs), adj. 1. destitute of sap; withered; sapless plants. 2. lacking vitality; insipid.

sap·ling (săp'lĭng), n. 1. a young tree. 2. a young person.

sap·o·dil·la (săp'ə dĭl'ə), n. 1. a large evergreen tree, Achras Zapota, of tropical America, bearing an edible fruit (**sapodilla plum**) and yielding chicle. 2. the fruit. [t. Sp.: m. zapotilla, dim. of zapote sapota]

sap·o·na·ceous (săp'ə nā'shəs), adj. soaplike; soapy. [t. NL: m. sāpōnāceus, der. L sāpo soap]

sap·on·i·fy (sə pŏn'ə fī), v., **-fied, -fying.** Chem. —v.t. 1. to convert (a fat) into soap by treating with an alkali. 2. to decompose (any ester), forming the corresponding alcohol and acid or salt. —v.i. 3. to become converted into soap. [t. NL: m. sāpōnificāre, f. L: s. sāpo soap + -(i)ficāre make] —**sa·pon'i·fi·a·ble,** adj. —**sa·pon'i·fi·ca'tion,** n. —**sa·pon'i·fi'er,** n.

sap·o·nins (săp'ə nĭnz), n.pl. amorphous glucosidal compounds of steroid structure obtainable from many plants. Their aqueous solutions foam like soap on shaking and are used as detergents. [t. F. m. saponine, f. s. L sāpo soap + -ine -INE²]

sa·por (sā'pôr, -pər), n. that quality in a substance which affects the sense of taste; savor; flavor. [t. L] —**sap·o·rous** (săp'ə rəs), adj.

sa·po·ta (sə pō'tə), n. 1. a general term employed in tropical America for widely differing fruits. 2. the fruit and tree of Calocarpum Sapota. 3. the sapodilla. [NL, repr. Sp. and Pg. zapote, t. Mex.: m. zapotl]

sap·o·ta·ceous (săp'ə tā'shəs), adj. belonging to the Sapotaceae, or sapodilla family of plants.

sap·pan·wood (să păn'wŏŏd'), n. 1. a dyewood yielding a red color, produced by a small East Indian caesalpiniaceous tree, Caesalpinia Sappan. 2. the tree itself. Also, **sapanwood.** [f. m. sapan (t. Malay: m. sapang) + woоd¹]

sap·per (săp'ər), n. Brit. a soldier employed in the construction of trenches, fortifications, fieldworks, etc. [f. SAP² + -ER¹]

Sap·phic (săf'ĭk), adj. 1. pertaining to Sappho or to certain meters or a form of strophe or stanza used by or named after her. —n. 2. a Sapphic verse. [t. L: s. sapphicus, t. Gk.: m. sapphikós]

Sapphic ode. See ode (def. 5).

Sap·phi·ra (sə fī'rə), n. a woman who, with her husband, Ananias, was struck dead for lying. Acts 5.

sap·phire (săf'īr), n. 1. a variety of corundum, esp. a transparent blue kind valued as a gem. 2. a gem of this kind. 3. the color of the gem, a deep blue. —adj. 4. resembling sapphire; deep-blue: a sapphire sky. [t. m.s. sapphīrus, t. Gk.: m. sáppheiros; r. ME saphyr, t. OF]

sap·phir·ine (săf'ər ĭn, -ə rēn', -ə rīn'), adj. 1. consisting of sapphire; like sapphire, esp. in color. —n. 2. a pale-blue or greenish, usually granular mineral, a silicate of magnesium and aluminum. 3. a blue variety of spinel.

sap·phism (săf'ĭz əm), n. lesbianism. [f. SAPPHO (accused of this vice) + -ISM]

Sap·pho (săf'ō), n. a Greek lyric poetess of Lesbos, lived about 600 B.C.

Sap·po·ro (sä'pô rō'), n. a city in N Japan, on Hokkaido island. 313,850 (1950).

sap·py (săp'ĭ), adj. 1. abounding in sap, as a plant. 2. full of vitality and energy. 3. Slang. silly or foolish.

sa·pre·mi·a (sə prē'mĭə), n. Pathol. a form of blood poisoning, esp. that due to the toxins produced by certain microorganisms. [f. SAPR- + -(H)EMIA]

sapro-, a word element meaning "rotten," or "saprophytic," as in saprolite. Also, before vowels, **sapr-.** [t. Gk., comb. form of saprós putrid]

sap·ro·gen·ic (săp'rō jĕn'ĭk), adj. 1. producing putrefaction or decay, as certain bacteria. 2. formed by putrefaction. Also, **sa·prog·e·nous** (sə prŏj'ə nəs).

sap·ro·lite (săp'rō līt'), n. Petrog. soft, disintegrated, usually more or less decomposed rock, remaining in its original place.

sap·ro·phyte (săp'rō fīt'), n. any vegetable organism that lives on dead organic matter, as certain fungi, bacteria, etc. —**sap·ro·phyt·ic** (săp'rō fĭt'ĭk), adj.

sap·sa·go (săp'sə gō'), n. a hard, greenish cheese flavored with melilot, made in Switzerland. [t. G: alter. of schabziger, f. s. schaben grate + ziger a kind of cheese]

sap·suck·er (săp'sŭk'ər), n. any of various small American woodpeckers of the genus Sphyrapicus, which drill holes in maple, apple, hemlock, etc., drinking the sap and eating the insects which gather there.

sap·wood (săp'wŏŏd'), n. alburnum.

Sar., Sardinia.

---

b., blend of, blended; c., cognate with; d., dialect, dialectal; der., derived from; f., formed from; g., going back to; m., modification of; r., replacing; s., stem of; t., taken from; ?, perhaps. See the full key on inside cover.

S.A.R., Sons of the American Revolution.

sar·a·band (săr′ə bănd′), *n.* 1. a popular and vigorous Spanish castanet dance. 2. a slow, stately Spanish dance in triple rhythm derived from this. 3. a piece of music for, or in the rhythm of, this dance, usually forming one of the movements in the classical suite, following the courante. [t. F: m. *sarabande*, t. Sp.: m. *zarabanda*; prob. of Oriental orig.]

Sar·a·cen (săr′ə sən), *n.* 1. (among the later Romans and Greeks) a member of the nomadic tribes on the Syrian borders of the Roman Empire. 2. (in later use) an Arab. 3. any Mohammedan or Moslem, esp. with reference to the Crusades. [mod. E and OE, t. LL: s. *Saracēnus*, t. LGk.: m. *Sarakēnós*; r. ME *Sarezin*, t. OF] —**Sar·a·cen·ic** (săr′ə sĕn′ĭk), **Sar′a·cen′i·cal,** *adj.*

Sar·a·gos·sa (săr′ə gŏs′ə), *n.* a city in NE Spain, on the Ebro river. 281,145 (est. 1955). Spanish, **Zaragoza.**

Sar·ah (săr′ə), *n.* the wife of Abraham and mother of Isaac: earlier, **Sar·ai** (săr′ī, -ā ī′). Gen. 17:15–22, etc.

Sa·ra·je·vo (sä′rä′yĕ vô), *n.* a city in central Yugoslavia, in Bosnia: the assassination of the Austrian archduke Francis Ferdinand here, June 28, 1914, was the external event that precipitated World War I. 135,657 (1953). Also, **Serajevo.** See map under **Serbia.**

sa·ran (sə răn′), *n.* a thermoplastic copolymer, used as a fiber and to make acid-resistant piping.

Sar·a·nac (săr′ə năk′), *n.* any of three lakes in NE New York, in the Adirondacks: **Upper Saranac, Middle Saranac, Lower Saranac.**

Saranac Lake, a village in NE New York, near the Saranac Lakes: health resort. 6913 (1950).

Sar·a·to·ga (săr′ə tō′gə), *n.* a village in E New York, on the Hudson: the scene of Burgoyne's defeat and surrender in the Battle of Saratoga, 1777. Now called **Schuylerville.**

Saratoga Springs, a city in E New York: health resort; horse races. 16,630 (1960).

Saratoga trunk, a type of large trunk used by women in the 19th century.

Sa·ra·tov (sä rä′tôf), *n.* a city in the E Soviet Union in Europe, on the Volga. 518,000 (est. 1956).

Sa·ra·wak (sə rä′wäk; *native* -wä), *n.* a former British crown colony in NW Borneo: now part of the federation of Malaysia. 626,600 pop. (est. 1956); ab. 50,000 sq. mi. *Cap.:* Kuching.

sarc-, a word element meaning "flesh," as in *sarcous.* Also, before consonants, **sarco-.** [t. Gk.: m. *sark-,* comb. form of *sárx*]

sar·casm (săr′kăz əm), *n.* 1. harsh or bitter derision or irony. 2. an ironical taunt or gibe; a sneering or cutting remark. [t. LL: s. *sarcasmus,* t. LGk.: m. *sarkasmós* sneer] —**Syn.** 1. See **irony**[1].

sar·cas·tic (săr kăs′tĭk), *adj.* 1. characterized by, of the nature of, or pertaining to sarcasm: *a sarcastic reply.* 2. using, or given to the use of, sarcasm: *he is too sarcastic about her appearance.* —**sar·cas′ti·cal·ly,** *adv.* —**Syn.** 2. See **cynical.**

sarce·net (särs′nĭt), *n.* a very fine, soft, silk fabric, used esp. for linings. [ME, t. AF: m. *sarzinett,* dim. of *Sarzin* Saracen. Cf. OF *drap sarrasinois* Saracen cloth]

sar·co·carp (săr′kō kärp′), *n. Bot.* 1. the fleshy mesocarp of certain fruits, as the peach. 2. any fruit of fleshy consistency.

sar·co·ma (săr kō′mə), *n., pl.* **-mata** (-mə tə), **-mas.** *Pathol.* any of various malignant tumors originating in the connective tissue, attacking esp. the bones. [NL, t. Gk.: m. *sárkōma*] —**sar·co·ma·toid** (săr kō′mə toid′), **sar·co·ma·tous** (săr kō′mə təs, -kōm′ə-), *adj.*

sar·co·ma·to·sis (săr kō′mə tō′sĭs), *n. Pathol.* a condition marked by the production of an overwhelming number of sarcomas throughout the body. [NL, f. m.s. Gk. *sárkōma* SARCOMA + -OSIS]

sar·coph·a·gus (săr kŏf′ə gəs), *n., pl.* **-gi** (-jī′), **-guses.** 1. a stone coffin, esp. one bearing sculpture or inscriptions, etc., often displayed as a monument. 2. (among the ancient Greeks) a kind of stone supposed to consume the flesh of corpses, used for coffins. [t. L, t. Gk.: m. *sarkophágos,* orig. adj., flesh-eating]

sar·cous (săr′kəs), *adj.* consisting of or pertaining to flesh or skeletal muscle. [f. m.s. Gk. *sárx* flesh + -OUS]

sard (särd), *n.* a brownish-red chalcedony, or a piece of it, used in jewelry, etc. [ME *saarde,* t. L: m. *sarda* SARDIUS]

Sar·da·na·pa·lus (săr′də nə pā′ləs), *n.* Ashurbanipal.

sar·dine (săr dēn′), *n., pl.* **-dines,** (*esp. collectively*) **-dine.** 1. the common pilchard, often preserved in oil as a table delicacy. 2. any of various allied or similar fishes used in this way, esp. the **California sardine,** *Sardinops caeruleus.* [ME *sardyn,* t. It.: m.s. *sardina,* g. L *sardina,* der. *sarda* kind of fish]

Sar·din·i·a (săr dĭn′ĭ ə), *n.* 1. a large island in the Mediterranean, W of Italy: with small nearby islands it comprises a department of Italy. 1,343,000 pop. (est. 1954); 9301 sq. mi. 2. a former kingdom (1720–1860), including this island and Savoy, Piedmont, and Genoa (after 1815) in NW Italy; ruled by the House of Savoy. *Cap.:* Turin.

Sar·din·i·an (săr dĭn′ĭ ən), *adj.* 1. of or pertaining to Sardinia. —*n.* 2. a native or inhabitant of Sardinia. 3. a Romance language spoken in Sardinia.

Sar·dis (săr′dĭs), *n.* an ancient city in W Asia Minor: the capital of ancient Lydia.

sar·di·us (săr′dĭ əs), *n.* 1. sard. 2. the precious stone in the breastplate of the Jewish high priest, thought to have been a ruby. [ME, t. L (Vulgate), t. Gk.: m. *sárdios* (stone) of Sardis]

sar·don·ic (săr dŏn′ĭk), *adj.* bitterly ironical; sarcastic; sneering: *a sardonic grin.* [t. F: m. *sardonique,* der. L *Sardonius,* t. Gk.: m. *Sardónios* Sardinian, for earlier *sardánios* bitter, scornful, from the notion of a Sardinian plant said to bring on convulsions resembling laughter] —**sar·don′i·cal·ly,** *adv.*

sar·do·nyx (săr′də nĭks), *n.* a kind of onyx containing layers or bands of sard. [ME, t. L, t. Gk. See SARD, ONYX]

Sar·dou (săr dōō′), *n.* **Viktorien** (vēk tô ryăN′), 1831–1908, French dramatist.

Sarg (särg), *n.* **Tony,** (*Anthony Frederick Sarg*) 1882–1942, U.S. illustrator and producer of marionette shows.

sar·gas·so (săr găs′ō), *n.* the gulfweed. [t. Pg.: m. *sargaço, sargasso,* der. L *sargus* a kind of sea fish]

Sar·gas·so Sea (săr găs′ō), a relatively calm area in the N Atlantic, NE of the West Indies, where there is an abundance of free-floating plants of the alga *Sargassum.*

sar·gas·sum (săr găs′əm), *n.* any seaweed of the genus *Sargassum,* widely distributed in the warmer waters of the globe, as *S. bacciferum,* the common gulfweed. [NL, t. Pg.: m. *sargasso*]

Sar·gent (săr′jənt), *n.* **John Singer,** 1856–1925, U.S. painter.

Sar·gon II (săr′gŏn), died 705 B.C., king of Assyria, 722–705 B.C.

sa·ri (sä′rē), *n., pl.* **-ris.** a long piece of cotton or silk, the principal outer garment of Hindu women, worn round the body with one end over the head. [t. Hind.]

sark (särk), *n. Scot. or Archaic.* a shirt or chemise. [ME, t. Scand.; cf. Icel. *serkr,* c. OE *serc*]

Sar·ma·ti·a (săr mā′shĭ ə), *n.* the ancient name used to designate a region, now in Poland and the W Soviet Union, extending from the Vistula to the Volga. —**Sar·ma′ti·an,** *adj., n.*

sar·men·tose (săr mĕn′tōs), *adj. Bot.* having runners. [t. L: m.s. *sarmentōsus*]

sa·rong (sə rông′), *n.* 1. the principal garment for both sexes in the Malay Archipelago, etc., consisting of a piece of cloth enveloping the lower part of the body like a skirt. 2. a kind of cloth for such garments. [t. Malay: m. *sārung.* Cf. Skt. *sāranga* variegated]

Sa·ros (sä′rōs), *n.* Gulf of, a gulf in the NE part of the Aegean, N of Gallipoli Peninsula.

Sa·roy·an (sə roi′ən), *n.* **William,** born 1908, U.S. author.

Sar·pe·don (săr pē′dən, -dŏn), *n. Gk. Legend.* a Lycian prince, son of Zeus, killed by Patroclus in Trojan War.

sar·ra·ce·ni·a (săr′ə sē′nĭ ə), *n.* any plant of the genus *Sarracenia,* comprising American marsh plants with hollow leaves of a pitcherlike form in which insects are trapped and digested, as *S. purpurea,* a common pitcher plant. [NL; named after D. *Sarrazin* of Quebec, who first sent samples of the plant to Europe]

sar·ra·ce·ni·a·ceous (săr′ə sē′nĭ ā′shəs), *adj.* belonging to the *Sarraceniaceae,* the American pitcher-plant family.

Sarre (săr), *n.* French name of Saar.

sar·sa·pa·ril·la (săr′sə pə rĭl′ə), *n.* 1. any of various climbing or trailing tropical American plants of the genus *Smilax,* having a root which has been much used in medicine as an alterative. 2. the root. 3. an extract or other preparation made of it. 4. a soft drink flavored with it. [t. Sp.: m. *zarzaparilla,* f. *zarza* bramble + -*parilla* (? dim. of *parsa* vine)]

Sar·to (săr′tō), *n.* **Andrea Del** (än drĕ′ä dĕl), 1486–1531, Italian painter.

sar·to·ri·al (săr tōr′ĭ əl), *adj.* 1. of or pertaining to a tailor or his work: *sartorial splendor.* 2. *Anat.* pertaining to the sartorius. [f. s. L *sartōrius* a tailor + -AL[1]]

sar·to·ri·us (săr tōr′ĭ əs), *n. Anat.* a flat, narrow muscle, the longest in the human body, running from the hip to the inner side of the shinbone, and crossing the thigh obliquely in front. [NL: pertaining to a tailor]

Sar·tor Re·sar·tus (săr′tər rĭ săr′təs), a satirical work (1833–34) by Carlyle. [LL: the tailor retailored]

Sar·tre (săr′tr), *n.* **Jean Paul** (zhän pōl), born 1905, French writer and philosopher: exponent of existentialism.

Sar·um use (sâr′əm), the procedure of service or the general liturgy of the late medieval Salisbury (Sarum).

Sa·se·bo (sä′sĕ bô′), *n.* a seaport in SW Japan, on Kyushu island. 194,453 (1950).

Sa·se·no (sä′sĕ nô′), *n.* a fortified island at the entrance to Valona Bay, in Albania. 2 sq. mi.

sash[1] (săsh), *n.* a long band or scarf of silk, etc., worn over one shoulder or round the waist, as by military officers as a part of the costume, or by women and children for ornament. [dissimilated var. of *shash,* t. Ar.: turban]

sash[2] (săsh), *n.* 1. a movable framework in which panes of glass are set, as in a window or the like. 2. the part of a window which moves. 3. such frameworks collectively. —*v.t.* 4. to furnish with sashes or with windows having sashes. [ME; alter. of CHASSIS]

sa·shay (să shā′), *v.i. U.S. Colloq.* 1. to glide, move, or go. 2. to chassé in dancing. [alter. of CHASSE]

sa·sin (sä′sĭn), *n.* the black buck of India. [t. E. Ind.]

Sask., Saskatchewan.

ăct, āble, dâre, ärt; ĕbb, ēqual; ĭf, īce; hŏt, ōver, ôrder, oil, bŏok, ōoze, out; ŭp, ūse, ûrge; ə = a in alone; ch, chief; g, give; ng, ring; sh, shoe; th, thin; ŧħ, that; zh, vision. See the full key on inside cover.

Sas·katch·e·wan (săs·kăch′ə·wŏn′), *n.* **1.** a province in W Canada. 861,000 (est. 1953); 251,700 sq. mi. *Cap.*: Regina. **2.** a river in SW Canada, flowing E to Lake Winnipeg: formed by the junction of the **North Saskatchewan** and **South Saskatchewan.** Length to the source of the South Saskatchewan, ab. 1205 mi.

Sas·ka·toon (săs′kə·tōōn′), *n.* a city in SW Canada, in Saskatchewan. 53,268 (1951).

sas·ka·toon (săs′kə·tōōn′), *n.* **1.** any of several shadbushes, esp. the serviceberry, *Amelanchier canadensis.* **2.** the berry of this bush. [t. Cree: m. *misáskwatomin* serviceberry, fruit of *misáskwat* the tree of much wood]

sas·sa·by (săs′ə·bĭ), *n., pl.* **-bies.** a large, blackish-red South African antelope, *Damaliscus lunatus.* [t. d. Bantu: m. *tsessĕbe*]

sas·sa·fras (săs′ə·frăs′), *n.* **1.** an American lauraceous tree, *Sassafras albidum.* **2.** the aromatic bark of its root, used medicinally and esp. for flavoring beverages, confectionery, etc. [t. Sp.: m. *sasafras,* orig. uncert.]

sassafras oil, a volatile oil derived from the root of the sassafras tree, consisting of camphor, pinene, etc.

Sas·san·i·dae (să·săn′ə·dē′), *n. pl.* the Persian dynasty which ruled about A.D. 226–641. Also, **Sas·sa·nids** (săs′ə·nĭdz), **Sas·sa·ni·ans** (să·să′nĭ·ənz).

Sas·se·nach (săs′ə·nəкн, -năk′), *n.* Englishman: a name applied by the Gaelic inhabitants of the British Isles. [t. Gaelic: m. *Sasunnach* Englishman, f. *Sasunn* Saxon + *-ach* (adj. suffix)]

Sas·soon (să·sōōn′), *n.* **Siegfried (Loraine)** (sēg′frēd lō·răn′), born 1886, British soldier, poet, and writer.

sas·sy[1] (săs′ĭ), *adj.,* **-sier,-siest,** *U.S. Dial.* saucy. [d. var. of SAUCY]

sas·sy[2] (săs′ĭ), *n.* sassy bark. [t. West African; said to be t. E. See SASSY[1]]

sassy bark, **1.** the bark of a large African caesalpinaceous tree, *Erythrophleum guineense,* used by the natives as a poison in ordeals. **2.** Also, **sas·sy·wood** (săs′ĭ·wŏod′), the tree itself. [see SASSY[2]]

sat (săt), *v.* pt. and pp. of **sit.**

Sat., **1.** Saturday. **2.** Saturn.

Sa·tan (sā′tən), *n.* the chief evil spirit; the great adversary of man; the devil. Cf. **Lucifer.** [ME and OE, t. L (Vulgate), t. Gk. (Septuagint and N.T.), t. Heb.: adversary]

sa·tang (sä·tăng′), *n., pl.* **-tang.** a Siamese bronze coin and money of account equivalent to one hundredth of a baht. [t. Siamese: m. *sātăn*]

sa·tan·ic (sā·tăn′ĭk, sə-), *adj.* **1.** of Satan. **2.** characteristic of or befitting Satan; extremely wicked; diabolical. Also, **sa·tan′i·cal.** —**sa·tan′i·cal·ly,** *adv.*

Sa·tan·ism (sā′tə·nĭz′əm), *n.* **1.** the worship of Satan. **2.** a form of such worship which travesties Christian rites. **3.** satanic disposition or practice. —**Sa′tan·ist,** *n.*

satch·el (săch′əl), *n.* a small bag, sometimes with a shoulder strap. [ME, t. OF: m. *sachel,* der. *sac* sack, g. L *saccus.* See SACK[1]]

sate[1] (sāt), *v.t.,* **sated, sating. 1.** to satisfy (any appetite or desire) to the full. **2.** to surfeit; glut. [b. obs. *sade* satiate (OE *sadian*) and L *sat* enough. See SAD]

sate[2] (săt, sāt), *v.* Archaic. pt. and pp. of **sit.**

sa·teen (să·tēn′), *n.* a cotton fabric woven in satin weave and resembling satin in gloss. [var. of SATIN, by assoc. with VELVETEEN]

sat·el·lite (săt′ə·līt′), *n.* **1.** *Astron.* a small body which revolves round a planet; a moon. **2.** an attendant upon a person of importance. **3.** a subservient or obsequious follower. **4.** a country under the domination or influence of another. **5.** a man-made device for launching from the earth into orbit around a planet or the sun. [t. L: m.s. *satelles* attendant, guard]

sa·ti·a·ble (sā′shĭ·ə·bəl), *adj.* that can be satiated. —**sa′ti·a·bil′i·ty, sa′ti·a·ble·ness,** *n.* —**sa′ti·a·bly,** *adv.*

sa·ti·ate (*v.* sā′shĭ·āt′; *adj.* sā′shĭ·ĭt, -āt′), *v.,* **-ated, -ating,** *adj.* —*v.t.* **1.** to supply with anything to excess, so as to disgust or weary; surfeit; cloy. **2.** *Now Rare.* to satisfy to the full. —*adj.* **3.** Archaic or Poetic. satiated. [t. L: m.s. *satiātus,* pp., filled full] —**sa′ti·a′tion,** *n.*

sa·ti·e·ty (sə·tī′ə·tĭ), *n.* state of being satiated; surfeit. [t. L: m.s. *satietas* abundance]

sat·in (săt′ən), *n.* **1.** a weave producing a shiny surface. **2.** a fabric made in a warp-face satin weave, usually rayon or silk, but sometimes cotton or linen. —*adj.* **3.** of or like satin; smooth; glossy. [ME *satine,* t. OF, t. It.: m. *setino,* ult. der. L *sēta* silk] —**sat′in·like′,** *adj.*

sat·i·net (săt′ə·nĕt′), *n.* **1.** an inferior kind of satin containing cotton. **2.** *Obs.* a thin light satin. Also, **sat′i·nette′.** [t. F. See SATIN, -ET]

sat·in·pod (săt′ən·pŏd′), *n.* either of two European cruciferous plants constituting the genus *Lunaria, L. annua* and *L. rediviva,* often cultivated for their shiny flowers and large, round, flat, satiny pods.

sat·in·wood (săt′ən·wŏod′), *n.* **1.** the satiny wood of an East Indian meliaceous tree, *Chloroxylon Swietenia,* used for cabinetwork, etc. **2.** the tree itself.

sat·in·y (săt′ən·ĭ), *adj.* satinlike; smooth; glossy.

sat·ire (săt′īr), *n.* **1.** the use of irony, sarcasm, ridicule, etc., in exposing, denouncing, or deriding vice, folly, etc. **2.** a literary composition, in verse or prose, in which vices, abuses, follies, etc., are held up to scorn, derision, or ridicule. **3.** the species of literature constituted by such composition. [t. L: m.s. *satira,* var. of *satura* medley, prop. fem. of *satur* full, sated] —**Syn. 1.** See **irony**[1].

sa·tir·i·cal (sə·tĭr′ə·kəl), *adj.* **1.** of or pertaining to satire; of the nature of satire: *satirical novels.* **2.** indulging in or given to satire: *a satirical poet.* Also, **sa·tir′ic.** —**sa·tir′i·cal·ly,** *adv.* —**sa·tir′i·cal·ness,** *n.* —**Syn. 1.** See **cynical.**

sat·i·rist (săt′ə·rĭst), *n.* **1.** a writer of satires. **2.** one who indulges in satire.

sat·i·rize (săt′ə·rīz′), *v.t.,* **-rized, -rizing.** to assail with satire; make the object of satire. Also, *esp. Brit.,* **sat′i·rise′.** —**sat′i·riz′er,** *n.*

sat·is·fac·tion (săt′ĭs·făk′shən), *n.* **1.** act of satisfying. **2.** state of being satisfied. **3.** the cause of being satisfied. **4.** reparation, as of a wrong or injury. **5.** the opportunity of repairing a supposed wrong, as by a duel. **6.** payment, as for debt; discharge, as of obligations. **7.** *Eccles.* the performance by a penitent of the penal acts enjoined by Church authority for injury done to another or God. [ME, t. L: s. *satisfactio*] —**Syn. 2.** gratification, enjoyment, pleasure. **4.** expiation, amends.

sat·is·fac·to·ry (săt′ĭs·făk′tə·rĭ), *adj.* **1.** affording satisfaction; fulfilling all demands or requirements: *a satisfactory answer.* **2.** *Theol.* atoning or expiating. —**sat′is·fac′to·ri·ly,** *adv.* —**sat′is·fac′to·ri·ness,** *n.*

sat·is·fy (săt′ĭs·fī′), *v.,* **-fied, -fying.** —*v.t.* **1.** to fulfill the desires, expectations, needs, or demands of, or content (a person, the mind, etc.); supply fully the needs of (a person, etc.). **2.** to fulfill (a desire, expectation, want, etc.). **3.** to give assurance to; convince: *to satisfy oneself by investigation.* **4.** to answer sufficiently (an objection, etc.); solve (a doubt, etc.). **5.** to discharge fully (a debt, etc.). **6.** to make reparation to (a person, etc.) or for (a wrong, etc.). **7.** to pay (a creditor). **8.** to fulfill the requirements or conditions of: *to satisfy an algebraic equation.* —*v.i.* **9.** to give satisfaction. [ME *satisfye,* t. OF: m. *satisfier,* t. L: m. *satisfacere* do enough] —**sat′is·fi′er,** *n.* —**sat′is·fy′ing·ly,** *adv.* —**Syn. 1.** gratify, appease, pacify. SATISFY, CONTENT refer to meeting one's desires or wishes. To SATISFY is to meet to the full one's wants, expectations, etc: *to satisfy a desire to travel.* To CONTENT is to give enough to keep one from being disposed to find fault or complain: *to content oneself with a moderate meal.*

sa·trap (sā′trăp, săt′răp), *n.* **1.** a governor of a province under the ancient Persian monarchy. **2.** a subordinate ruler, often a despotic one. [ME, t. L: s. *satrapa,* t. Gk.: m. *satrápēs,* t. OPers.: lit., country-protector]

sa·trap·y (sā′trə·pĭ, săt′rə·pĭ), *n., pl.* **-trapies.** the province or jurisdiction of a satrap.

Sa·tsu·ma (sä′tsōō·mä′), *n.* a former province in SW Japan, on Kyushu island: famous for its porcelain ware.

sat·u·ra·ble (săch′ər·ə·bəl), *adj.* that may be saturated. —**sat′u·ra·bil′i·ty,** *n.*

sat·u·rate (*v.* săch′ə·rāt′; *adj.* săch′ə·rĭt, -rāt′), *v.,* **-rated, -rating,** *adj.* —*v.t.* **1.** to cause (a substance) to unite with the greatest possible amount of another substance, through solution, chemical combination, or the like. **2.** to charge to the utmost, as with magnetism. **3.** to soak, impregnate, or imbue thoroughly or completely. —*adj.* **4.** *Chiefly Poetic.* saturated. [t. L: m.s. *saturātus,* pp., satisfied, saturated] —**Syn. 3.** See **wet.**

sat·u·rat·ed (săch′ə·rā′tĭd), *adj.* **1.** soaked, impregnated, or imbued thoroughly; charged thoroughly or completely; brought to a state of saturation. **2.** (of colors) of maximum chroma or purity; of the highest intensity of hue; free from admixture of white.

sat·u·ra·tion (săch′ə·rā′shən), *n.* **1.** act or process of saturating. **2.** the resulting state. **3.** *Meteorol.* a condition in the atmosphere corresponding to 100 percent relative humidity. **4.** (of colors) the degree of purity or chroma; degree of freedom from admixture with white.

saturation point, the point at which a substance will receive no more of another substance in solution, chemical combination, etc.

Sat·ur·day (săt′ər·dĭ), *n.* the seventh day of the week, following Friday. [ME; OE *Sæterdæg, Sætern(es)dæg,* c. D *zaterdag,* LG *Saterdag,* half trans., half adoption of L *Sāturnī dies* day of Saturn (the planet)]

Sat·urn (săt′ərn), *n.* **1.** *Astron.* the second largest planet, the sixth in order from the sun. Its period of revolution is 29.5 years, its mean distance from the sun about 886,000,000 miles, and its diameter 72,000 miles. It has 9 satellites and is remarkable for the thin rings surrounding it, said to be made up of ice crystals. **2.** *Rom. Myth.* the god of agriculture and vegetation, whose reign was characterized by happiness and virtue. **3.** *Alchemy.* the metal lead.

Sat·ur·na·li·a (săt′ər·nā′lĭ·ə), *n.pl.* **1.** (in ancient Rome) the festival of Saturn, celebrated in December, and observed as a time of general feasting and unrestrained merrymaking. **2.** (*l.c.*) any period of unrestrained revelry. [t. L] —**Sat′ur·na′li·an,** *adj.*

Sa·tur·ni·an (sə·tûr′nĭ·ən), *adj.* **1.** of or pertaining to the planet Saturn. **2.** of or pertaining to the god Saturn, whose reign is referred to as "the golden age." **3.** prosperous, happy, or peaceful: *Saturnian days.*

sa·tur·ni·id (sə·tûr′nĭ·ĭd), *n.* any of the large moths of the family *Saturniidae,* including many of the most strikingly colored species. [t. NL: s. *Sāturniidae,* der. L *Sāturnius* of Saturn]

sat·ur·nine (săt′ər·nīn′), *adj.* **1.** having or showing a sluggish, gloomy temperament; gloomy; taciturn. **2.** suffering from lead poisoning, as a person. **3.** due to absorption of lead, as disorders. [f. SATURN + -INE[1]; the

---

b., blend of, blended; c., cognate with; d., dialect, dialectal; der., derived from; f., formed from; g., going back to; m., modification of; r., replacing; s., stem of; t., taken from; ?, perhaps. See the full key on inside cover.

planet being supposed to give a gloomy nature to those born under its sign] —**sat′ur·nine′ly**, *adv.*

sat·ur·nism (săt′ər nĭz′əm), *n.* lead poisoning; plumbism.

Sat·ya·gra·ha (sŭt′yə grŭ′hə), *n. India.* a policy of resistance without violence inaugurated by Gandhi in 1919. [t. Hind., t. Skt.: truth-grasping]

sat·yr (săt′ər, sā′tər), *n.* **1.** *Class. Myth.* one of a class of woodland deities, attendant on Bacchus, represented as part human and part goat, and noted for riot and lasciviousness. **2.** a lascivious man. **3.** a man affected with satyriasis. **4.** any of the rather somber butterflies that constitute the family Satyridae. [ME, t. L: s. *satyrus*, t. Gk.: m. *sátyros*] —**sa·tyr·ic** (sə tĭr′ĭk), *adj.*

sat·y·ri·a·sis (săt′ə rī′ə sĭs), *n. Pathol.* morbid and uncontrollable sexual desire in men. [NL, t. Gk.]

sauce (sôs), *n., v.,* **sauced, saucing.** —*n.* **1.** any preparation, usually liquid or soft, eaten as a relish or appetizing accompaniment to food. **2.** something that adds piquance. **3.** *U.S.* stewed fruit: *applesauce.* **4.** *Colloq.* sauciness. **5.** *Dial.* garden vegetables, etc., eaten with meat. —*v.t.* **6.** to dress or prepare with sauce; season: *meat well sauced.* **7.** to give zest to. **8.** to make agreeable or less harsh. **9.** *Colloq.* to speak impertinently to. [ME, t. OF, g. VL *salsa*, fem of *salsus* salted]

sauce·box (sôs′bŏks′), *n. Colloq.* a saucy person.

sauce·pan (sôs′păn′), *n.* a metal container of moderate depth, usually having a long handle and sometimes a cover, for stewing, etc.

sau·cer (sô′sər), *n.* **1.** a small, round, shallow dish to hold a cup. **2.** any similar dish, plate, or the like; any saucerlike thing. [ME, t. OF: m. *saucier(e)* vessel for holding sauce, der. *sauce* SAUCE]

sau·cy (sô′sĭ), *adj.,* **-cier, -ciest. 1.** impertinent; insolent: *a saucy remark or child.* **2.** piquantly pert; smart: *saucy hat.* —**sau′ci·ly,** *adv.* —**sau′ci·ness,** *n.*

Sa·u·di Arabia (sä ōō′dĭ), a kingdom in N and central Arabia, including Hejaz, Nejd, and dependencies. 7,000,000 pop. (est. 1952); ab. 600,000 sq. mi. *Capitals:* Mecca and Riyadh.

sauer·kraut (sour′krout′), *n.* cabbage cut fine, salted, and allowed to ferment until sour. [t. G: f. *sauer* sour + *kraut* vegetable, cabbage]

sau·ger (sô′gər), *n.* a fresh-water North American pike perch, *Stizostedion canadense.*

Sauk (sôk), *n.* Sac.

Saul (sôl), *n.* **1.** the first king of Israel. I Sam. 9. **2.** the original name of the apostle Paul. See Acts 9:1–30. etc.

Sault Ste. Ma·rie (sōō′ sänt′ mə rē′), **1.** the rapids of the St. Marys river, between NE Michigan and Ontario, Canada. **2.** a city in S Canada, in Ontario, near these rapids. 32,452 (1951). **3.** a city opposite it, in NE Michigan. 18,722 1960.

Sault Ste. Marie Canals, two ship canals with locks, N and S of the St. Marys river rapids and connecting Lakes Superior and Huron: one canal is in Canada and the other in Michigan; heaviest canal traffic in the world. 1½ mi. long. Also, **Soo Canals.**

saun·ter (sôn′tər, sän′-), *v.i.* **1.** to walk with a leisurely gait; stroll. —*n.* **2.** a leisurely walk or ramble; a stroll. **3.** a leisurely gait. [late ME; orig. uncert.] —**saun′ter·er,** *n.* —**Syn. 1.** See **stroll.**

-saur, a word element meaning "lizard." [see SAURO-]

sau·rel (sôr′əl), *n.* scad (def 2). [t. F, der. *saur* dried (fish), t. Gmc.; cf. MLG *sōr* SERE]

sau·ri·an (sôr′ĭ ən), *adj.* **1.** belonging or pertaining to the Sauria, a group of reptiles orig. including the lizards, crocodiles, etc., but now technically restricted to the lizards or lacertilians. **2.** lizardlike. —*n.* **3.** a saurian animal, as a dinosaur or lizard. [f. s. NL *sauria* an order of reptiles (der. Gk. *saûros* lizard) + -AN]

sauro-, a word element meaning "lizard." [comb. form of Gk. *saûros*]

sau·ro·pod (sôr′ə pŏd′), *n.* **1.** any of the Sauropoda, a group of herbivorous dinosaurs with small head, long neck and tail, and five-toed limbs, the largest known land animals. —*adj.* **2.** belonging or pertaining to the Sauropoda. —**sau·rop·o·dous** (sô rŏp′ə dəs), *adj.*

-saurus, Latinized var. of -saur.

sau·ry (sôr′ĭ), *n., pl.* **-ries. 1.** a sharp-snouted fish, *Scomberesox saurus,* of the Atlantic. **2.** any of various related fishes, esp. the **Pacific saury,** *Cololabis saira.* [appar. t. Gk.: m. *saûros* sea fish (Aristotle)]

sau·sage (sô′sĭj), *n.* **1.** minced pork, beef, or other meats (often combined), with various added ingredients and seasonings, usually stuffed into linked parts of a prepared intestine. **2.** *Aeron.* a sausage-shaped observation balloon, formerly used in warfare. [ME *sausige,* t. ONF: m. *saussiche,* g. LL *salsīcia,* der. L *salsus* salted]

sau·té (sō tā′; *Fr.* sō tě′), *adj., v.,* **-téed, -téeing,** *n.* —*adj.* **1.** cooked or browned in a pan containing a little

fat. —*v.t.* **2.** to cook in a small amount of fat; pan-fry. —*n.* **3.** a dish of sauté food. [t. F, pp. of *sauter* leap (used in causative sense), g. L *saltāre*]

sau·terne (sō tûrn′; *Fr.* sō těrn′), *n.* a rich sweet white table wine, esp. one produced near Bordeaux, France. [named after the district *Sauterne,* near Bordeaux, where it is made]

sau·toir (sō twär′), *n. French.* a long ribbon, chain, beaded band, or the like, worn about the neck.

sauve qui peut (sōv kē pœ′), *French.* a stampede; a general rout. [F: lit., save himself who can]

Sa·va (sä′vä), *n.* a river flowing from NW Yugoslavia E to the Danube at Belgrade. ab. 450 mi. Also, **Save.**

sav·age (săv′ĭj), *adj.* **1.** wild or rugged, as country or scenery: *savage wilderness.* **2.** uncivilized; barbarous: *savage tribes.* **3.** unpolished; rude: *savage manners.* **4.** fierce, ferocious, or cruel; untamed: *savage beasts.* **5.** enraged, or furiously angry, as a person. **6.** *Obs.* uncultivated (as a plant). —*n.* **7.** an uncivilized human being. **8.** a fierce, brutal, or cruel person. **9.** a rude, boorish person. [ME *sauvage,* t. OF, g. LL *salvāticus,* of the woods, wild, r. L *silvāticus*] —**sav′age·ly,** *adv.* —**sav′age·ness,** *n.* —**Syn. 4.** See **cruel.**

Savage Island, Niue.

sav·age·ry (săv′ĭj rĭ), *n., pl.* **-ries. 1.** uncivilized state or condition; a state of barbarism. **2.** savage nature, disposition, conduct, or act; barbarity.

Sav·age's Station (săv′ĭj ĭz), a locality in E Virginia, near Richmond: battle, 1862.

Sa·vai·i (sä vī′ē), *n.* an island in Western Samoa: the largest of the Samoa group. 31,642 pop. (1961); 703 sq. mi.

sa·van·na (sə văn′ə), *n.* **1.** a plain, characterized by coarse grasses and scattered tree growth, esp. on the margins of the tropics where the rainfall is seasonal, as in the Sudan of Africa. **2.** grassland region with scattered trees, grading into either open plain or woodland, usually in subtropical or tropical regions. Also, **sa·van′-nah.** [t. Sp.: m. *zavana, savana,* t. Carib]

Sa·van·nah (sə văn′ə), *n.* **1.** a seaport in E Georgia, near the mouth of the Savannah river. 149,245 (1960). **2.** a river forming most of the boundary between Georgia and South Carolina, flowing SE to the Atlantic. 314 mi.

sa·vant (să vänt′, săv′ənt; *Fr.* să vän′), *n., pl.* **savants** (să vänts′, săv′ənts; *Fr.* să vän′), a man of learning. [t. F, n. use of (former) ppr. of *savoir,* g. L *sapere* be wise]

save[1] (sāv), *v.,* **saved, saving.** —*v.t.* **1.** to rescue from danger; preserve from harm, injury, or loss: *saved from drowning.* **2.** to keep safe, intact, or unhurt; safeguard: *God save the king.* **3.** to keep from being lost: *to save the game.* **4.** to avoid the spending, consumption, or waste of: *to save fuel with this new stove.* **5.** to set apart, reserve, or lay by: *to save money.* **6.** to treat carefully in order to reduce wear, fatigue, etc.: *to save one's eyes.* **7.** to prevent the occurrence, use, or necessity of; obviate: *a stitch in time saves nine.* **8.** *Theol.* to deliver from the power and consequences of sin. —*v.i.* **9.** to lay up money, etc., as the result of economy. **10.** to be economical in expenditure. **11.** to preserve something from harm, injury, loss, etc. **12.** *Colloq.* to admit of being kept without spoiling, as food. [ME, t. OF: m. *sauver, salver,* g. L *salvāre*] —**sav′a·ble,** *adj.* —**sav′er,** *n.*

save[2] (sāv), *prep.* **1.** except; but. —*conj.* **2.** except; but. **3.** *Archaic.* unless. [ME; var. of SAFE, adj., in obs. sense of reserving, making exception of] —**Syn. 1.** See **except**[1].

Save (säv), *n.* Sava.

save-all (sāv′ôl′), *n.* **1.** a means, contrivance, or receptacle for preventing loss or waste. **2.** overalls.

sav·e·loy (săv′ə loi′), *n. Chiefly Brit.* a highly seasoned, dried sausage. [t. F: alter. of *cervelas* a kind of sausage orig. containing hogs' brains, t. It.: m. *cervellata,* der. *cervello* brain, g. L *cerebellum*]

sav·in (săv′ĭn), *n.* **1.** a juniper, *Juniperus sabina,* whose dried tops are used as a drug. **2.** the drug itself. **3.** the red cedar. Also, **sav′ine.** [ME and OE *savine,* t. VL, g. L (*herba*) *sabīna,* lit., Sabine herb]

sav·ing (sā′vĭng), *adj.* **1.** that saves; rescuing; preserving. **2.** redeeming: *a saving sense of humor.* **3.** economical: *a saving housekeeper.* **4.** making a reservation: *a saving clause.* —*n.* **5.** economy in expenditure, outlay, use, etc. **6.** a reduction or lessening of expenditure or outlay: *a saving of ten percent.* **7.** that which is saved. **8.** (*pl.*) sums of money saved by economy and laid away. **9.** *Law.* a reservation or exception. —*prep.* **10.** except: *none remains saving these ruins.* **11.** with all due respect to or for: *saving your presence.* —*conj.* **12.** save. [f. SAVE[1] + -ING[2], -ING[1]] —**sav′ing·ly,** *adv.*

savings bank (sā′vĭngz), an institution for the secure investment of money saved.

sav·ior (săv′yər), *n.* **1.** one who saves, rescues, or delivers: *the savior of the country.* **2.** (*cap.*) a title of God, esp. of Christ (commonly spelled **Saviour**). Also, *esp. Brit.,* **sav′iour.** [ME *saveour,* t. OF, g. LL *salvātor.* See SAVE[1]]

sa·voir-faire (săv′wär fâr′; *Fr.* să vwár fěr′), *n.* knowledge of just what to do in any situation; tact. [t. F: lit., to know how to act]

sa·voir-vi·vre (săv′wär vē′vrə; *Fr.* să vwár vē′vr), *n. French.* knowledge of the world and the usages of polite society. [F: lit., to know how to live]

ăct, āble, dâre, ärt; ĕbb, ēqual; Yf, Ice; hŏt, ōver, ôrder, oil, bŏŏk, ōōze, out; ŭp, ūse, ûrge; ə = a in alone; ch, chief; g, give; ng, ring; sh, shoe; th, thin; ŧħ, that; zh, vision.   See the full key on inside cover.

Sav·o·na·ro·la (săv′ənərō′lə; *It.* sä′vōnärô′lä), *n.* **Girolamo** (jērō′lämō′), 1452–98, Italian monk, reformer, and martyr.

sa·vor (sā′vər), *n.* **1.** the quality in a substance which affects the sense of taste or of smell. **2.** a particular taste or smell. **3.** distinctive quality or property. **4.** power to excite or interest. **5.** *Archaic.* repute. —*v.i.* **6.** to have savor, taste, or odor. **7.** to exhibit the peculiar characteristics; smack (fol. by *of*). —*v.t.* **8.** to give a savor to; season; flavor. **9.** to perceive by taste or smell, esp. with relish. **10.** to give oneself to the enjoyment of. **11.** to show traces of the presence or influence of. Also, esp. *Brit.*, **sa′vour.** [ME *savour*, t. OF, g. L *sapor* taste, savor] —**sa′vor·er,** *n.* —**sa′vor·less,** *adj.* —**sa′vor·ous,** *adj.* —Syn. 1. See **taste.**

sa·vor·y[1] (sā′vərĭ), *adj.*, **-vorier, -voriest,** *n.*, *pl.* **-vories.** —*adj.* **1.** having savor; agreeable in taste or smell: *a savory smell.* **2.** giving a relish; piquant: *savory jelly.* **3.** pleasing or agreeable. —*n.* **4.** *Brit.* an appetizing dish served at the beginning or end of a dinner. Also, esp. *Brit.*, **sa′vour·y.** [ME *savure*, t. OF: m. *savoure*, pp. See **savor,** v.] —**sa′vor·i·ness,** *n.*

sa·vor·y[2] (sā′vərĭ), *n.*, *pl.* **-vories.** any of the aromatic plants constituting the menthaceous genus *Satureia*, esp. *S. hortensis* (**summer savory**), a European herb used in cookery, or *S. Montana* (**winter savory**). [ME *saverey*, OE *sætheriē*, *saturēge*, t. L: m. *saturēia*]

Sa·voy (səvoi′), *n.* **1.** a region in SE France, adjacent to the Swiss-Italian border: formerly a duchy; later a part of the kingdom of Sardinia; ceded to France, 1860. **2. House of,** the rulers of the former duchy of Savoy, and since 1861 comprising the royal house of Italy: prior to the dissolution of the Italian monarchy (1946) it was the oldest reigning dynasty of Europe.

sa·voy (səvoi′), *n.* a variety of the common cabbage with a compact head and leaves reticulately wrinkled. [named after **Savoy** (def. 1)]

Sa·voy·ard (səvoi′ärd; *Fr.* sá vwá yàr′), *n.* **1.** a native or inhabitant of Savoy. **2.** one enthusiastic about, or connected with, Gilbert and Sullivan operas, so called from the Savoy Theatre in London, where the operas were first given. —*adj.* **3.** of or pertaining to Savoy.

sav·vy (săv′ĭ), *v.*, **-vied, -vying,** *n.* *Slang.* —*v.t.*, *v.i.* **1.** to know; understand. [t. Sp.: alter. of *sabe* (*usted*) do you know] —*n.* **2.** understanding; intelligence; sense. [var. of d. Scot. *savie*, t. F: alter. of *savoir* know, g. L *sapere*]

saw[1] (sô), *n.*, *v.*, **sawed, sawed** or **sawn, sawing.** —*n.* **1.** a tool or device for cutting, typically a thin blade of metal with a series of sharp teeth. **2.** any similar tool or device, as a rotating disk, in which a sharp continuous edge replaces the teeth. —*v.t.* **3.** to cut or divide with a saw. **4.** to form by cutting with a saw. **5.** to cut as if using a saw: *to saw the air with one's hands.* **6.** to work (something) from side to side like a saw. —*v.i.* **7.** to use a saw. **8.** to cut with, or as with, a saw. **9.** to cut as a saw does. [ME *sawe*, OE *saga*, *sagu*, c. D *zaag*; akin to G *säge* saw, L *secāre* cut] —**saw′er,** *n.*

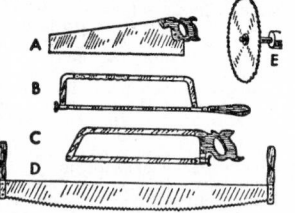

Saws
A. Handsaw; B. Hacksaw;
C. Butcher's saw; D. Lumberman's saw;
E. Circular saw

saw[2] (sô), *v.* pt. of **see**[1].

saw[3] (sô), *n.* a sententious saying; maxim; proverb: *he could muster an old saw for almost every occasion.* [ME; OE *sagu*, c. G *sage*, Icel. *saga* **saga**; akin to **say**]

Sa·watch (səwäch′), *n.* a range of the Rocky Mountains in central Colorado. Highest peak, Elbert Peak, 14,431 ft. Also, **Saguache.**

saw·buck (sô′bŭk), *n.* *U.S.* **1.** a sawhorse. **2.** *Slang.* a ten-dollar bill. [cf. D *zaagbok*]

saw·dust (sô′dŭst), *n.* small particles of wood produced in sawing.

saw·fish (sô′fĭsh), *n.*, *pl.* **-fishes,** (*esp. collectively*) **-fish.** a large, elongate ray (genus *Pristis*) of tropical coasts and lowland rivers, with a bladelike snout bearing strong teeth on each side.

Florida sawfish (side and top view), *Pristis pectinatus* (10 to 20 ft. long)

saw·fly (sô′flī′), *n.*, *pl.* **-flies.** any of the hymenopterous insects constituting the family *Tenthredinidae*, the females of which are characterized by a pair of sawlike organs for cutting slits in plants to hold their eggs.

saw grass, any of various cyperaceous plants, esp. of the genus *Cladium*, with the margins of the leaves toothed like a saw.

saw·horse (sô′hôrs′), *n.* a movable frame for holding wood that is being sawed.

saw log, a log large enough to saw into boards.

saw·mill (sô′mĭl′), *n.* an establishment in which timber is sawed into planks, boards, etc., by machinery.

saw palmetto, **1.** a shrublike palmetto, *Serenoa repens*, of the southern U.S., having the leafstalks set with spiny teeth. **2.** a shrublike palmetto, *Paurotis Wrightii*, of Florida and the West Indies.

saw set, an instrument used to bend the point of each alternate tooth of a saw out slightly so that the kerf made by the saw will be wider than its blade.

saw-toothed (sô′tōōtht′), *adj.* serrate.

saw·yer (sô′yər), *n.* **1.** one who saws, esp. as an occupation. **2.** any wood-boring larva which cuts off twigs and branches, esp. that of the longicorn beetle, *Oncinderes cingulatus.* [ME *sawier*, f. **saw**[1] + **-ier**]

Sax., **1.** Saxon. **2.** Saxony.

sax·a·tile (săk′sətĭl), *adj.* living or growing on or among rocks. [t. L: m.s. *saxātilis*]

Saxe (săks), *n.* **1. Hermann Maurice de** (ĕr mán′ mōrēs′ də), 1696–1750, marshal of France and general. **2.** French name of **Saxony.**

Saxe-Al·ten·burg (săks′äl′tən bûrg′), *n.* a former duchy in Thuringia in central Germany.

Saxe-Co·burg-Go·tha (săks′kō′bûrg gō′thə), *n.* **1.** a former duchy in central Germany. **2. House of,** the name of the British royal family from 1901 until 1917, when it became the house of Windsor. **3. Prince of.** See **Albert** (def. 1).

Saxe-Mei·ning·en (săks′mī′nĬng ən), *n.* a former duchy in Thuringia in central Germany.

Saxe-Wei·mar-Ei·sen·ach (săks′vī′mär ī′zən äкн′), *n.* a former grand duchy in Thuringia in central Germany.

sax·horn (săks′hôrn′), *n.* any of a family of brass instruments close to the cornets and tubas. [named after *Adolphe Sax* (1814–94), a Belgian, who invented the instrument]

sax·i·fra·ga·ceous (săk′sə frə gā′shəs), *adj.* belonging to the *Saxifragaceae*, or saxifrage family of plants.

sax·i·frage (săk′sə frĭj), *n.* any of the plants, mostly perennial herbs, constituting the genus *Saxifraga*, many of which grow wild in the clefts of rocks, others being cultivated for their flowers. [ME. t. L: m. *saxifraga* (*herba*), lit., rock-breaking herb]

Saxhorn

Sax·o Gram·mat·i·cus (săk′sō grə măt′ə kəs), c1150–c1206, Danish historian and poet.

Sax·on (săk′sən), *n.* **1.** a person of the English race or of English descent. **2.** an Anglo-Saxon. **3.** Anglo-Saxon (language). **4.** the Old English dialects of the regions settled by the Saxons. **5.** Continental Saxon. **6.** a native or inhabitant of Saxony in modern Germany. **7.** a member of a Germanic people anciently dwelling near the mouth of the Elbe, a portion of whom invaded and occupied parts of Britain in the 5th and 6th centuries. —*adj.* **8.** English. **9.** of or pertaining to the early Continental Saxons or their language. **10.** of or pertaining to Saxony in modern Germany. [ME, t. L: s. *Saxo*, *Saxonēs* (pl.), t. Gmc.; r. OE *Seaxan*, pl., g. Gmc.]

Sax·on·ism (săk′sə nĬz′əm), *n.* an idiom supposedly peculiarly English and not of foreign (esp. Latin) origin.

Sax·o·ny (săk′sə nĬ), *n.* **1.** a former state in E Germany. 5,231,739 pop. (1939); 5788 sq. mi. *Cap.*: Dresden. **2.** a former province in N Germany. 9857 sq. mi. *Cap.*: Magdeburg. **3.** a medieval division of N Germany with varying boundaries: at its height it extended from the Rhine to E of the Elbe. **4.** a fine woolen yarn for knitting, etc., or cloth made from it. German, **Sachsen;** French, **Saxe** for defs. 1, 2, 3.

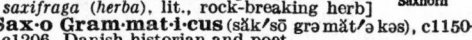

Saxony, 1815–1871

sax·o·phone (săk′sə fōn′), *n.* a musical wind instrument consisting of a conical metal tube (usually brass) with keys or valves, and a clarinet mouthpiece. [see **saxhorn**] —**sax′o·phon′ist,** *n.*

sax·tu·ba (săks′tū′bə, -tōō′bə), *n.* a large (bass) form of saxhorn. [f. *sax* (as in **saxhorn**) + **tuba**]

Man playing a saxophone

say (sā), *v.*, **said, saying,** *n.* —*v.t.* **1.** to utter or pronounce; speak. **2.** to express in words; state; declare. **3.** to state as an opinion, or with assurance: *it is hard to say what is wrong.* **4.** to recite or repeat: *to say one's prayers.* **5.** to assume as a hypothesis or an estimate: *to learn in, say, ten lessons.* **6.** to report or allege; maintain: *people say he will resign.* —*v.i.* **7.** to speak; declare; express an opinion. **8. that is to say,** in other words; otherwise. —*n.* **9.** what a person says or has to say. **10.** *Colloq.* the right or opportunity to say, speak, or decide. **11.** turn to say something: *it is now my say.* **12. have the say,** *U.S.* to have final authority: *The treasurer has the say on a budget of this size.* [ME; OE *secgan*, c. D *zeggen*, G *sagen*, Icel. *segja*] —**say′er,** *n.* —Syn. 1. remark, affirm.

Sa·yan Mountains (sä yän′), a range of mountains in the S Soviet Union in Asia. Highest peak, Munku Sardik, 11,447 ft.

---

b., blend of, blended; *c.,* cognate with; *d.,* dialect, dialectal; *der.,* derived from; *f.,* formed from; *g.,* going back to; *m.,* modification of; *r.,* replacing; *s.,* stem of; *t.,* taken from; *?,* perhaps. See the full key on inside cover.

sayest 1081 scale insect

say·est (sā′ĭst), *v.* *Archaic.* 2d pers. sing. of **say.** Also, **sayst** (sāst).

say·ing (sā′ĭng), *n.* **1.** something said, esp. a proverb or apothegm. **2. go without saying,** to be completely self-evident.

say-so (sā′sō′), *n.* *Colloq.* **1.** one's personal statement or assertion. **2.** final authority. **3.** a command.

say·yid (sī′yĭd), *n.* (in Mohammedan countries) a person supposed to be descended from Mohammed through his daughter Fatima. [t. Ar.: lord. Cf. CID]

Sb, (L *stibium*) antimony.

sb., substantive.

S.B., (L *Scientiae Baccalaureus*) Bachelor of Science. **2.** South Britain (England and Wales).

'sblood (zblŭd), *interj.* *Archaic.* a reduced form of *God's blood,* used as an oath.

Sc, *Chem.* scandium.

Sc., **1.** Scotch. **2.** Scotland. **3.** Scots. **4.** Scottish.

sc., **1.** scale. **2.** scene. **3.** science. **4.** scientific. **5.** scilicet. **6.** screw. **7.** scruple.

S.C., **1.** Sanitary Corps. **2.** Signal Corps. **3.** South Carolina. **4.** Staff Corps. **5.** Supreme Court.

s.c., **1.** small capitals. **2.** supercalendered.

scab (skăb), *n., v.,* **scabbed, scabbing.** —*n.* **1.** the incrustation which forms over a sore during healing. **2.** *Vet. Sci.* a mangy disease in animals, esp. sheep; scabies. **3.** *Plant Pathol.* a hyperplasic plant disease with scablike lesions: *apple scab.* **4.** a workman who refuses to join or act with a labor union, who takes a striker's place, or the like. **5.** *Slang.* a rascal or scoundrel. —*v.i.* **6.** to become covered with a scab. **7.** to act or work as a scab. [ME *scab,* t. Scand.; cf. Sw. *skabb,* c.d. E *shab,* OE *sceabb.* See SHABBY] —**scab′like′,** *adj.*

scab·bard (skăb′ərd), *n.* **1.** a sheath or cover for the blade of a sword, dagger, or the like. —*v.t.* **2.** to put into a scabbard; sheathe. [ME *scauberd,* t. AF: m. *escauberz* (pl.); prob. of Gmc. orig]

scabbard fish, any fish of the family *Trichiuridae,* with daggerlike teeth and thin, whip-shaped body.

scab·ble (skăb′əl), *v.t.,* **-bled, -bling.** to shape or dress (stone) roughly. [var. of scapple, t. F: m. *escapeler* dress timber]

scab·by (skăb′ĭ), *adj.,* **-bier, -biest.** **1.** covered with scabs; blotchy. **2.** consisting of scabs. **3.** affected with the scab. **4.** *Colloq.* mean or contemptible: *that was a scabby trick.*

sca·bies (skā′bĭ ēz′, -bēz), *n.* *Vet. Sci.* any of several infectious skin diseases occurring especially in sheep and cattle (and in man), caused by parasitic mites; itch. [t. L: roughness, the itch (der. *scabere* scratch, scrape, c. SHAVE)] —**sca·bi·et·ic** (skā′bĭ ĕt′ĭk), *adj.*

sca·bi·ous¹ (skā′bĭ əs), *adj.* **1.** scabby. **2.** pertaining to or of the nature of scabies. [t. L: m. *scabiōsus*]

sca·bi·ous² (skā′bĭ əs), *n.* any plant of the composite genus *Scabiosa,* comprising a large number of hairy herbs with flowers in dense heads. **2.** either of two species, the purple-flowered **field scabious,** *S. atropurpurea,* and the **sweet scabious,** *S. arvensis.* Also, **sca·bi·o·sa** (skā′bĭ ō′sə). [ME *scabiose,* t. ML: m. *scabiōsa (herba)* scabies-curing herb]

scab·land (skăb′lănd′), *n.* rough, barren, volcanic topography with thin soils and little vegetation.

sca·brous (skā′brəs), *adj.* **1.** rough with minute points or projections. **2.** harsh; full of difficulties. **3.** somewhat indelicate; risqué: *scabrous books.* [t. LL: m.s. *scabrōsus,* der. L *scaber* rough] —**sca′brous·ly,** *adv.* —**sca′brous·ness,** *n.*

scad (skăd), *n.* (*usually pl.*) *Slang.* a large quantity: *he has scads of money.* **2.** a small marine carangoid fish of the genus *Trachurus;* saurel. [? t. Celtic; cf. OIrish *scatán* herring]

Sca·fell Pike (skô′fĕl′), a mountain peak in NW England, in Cumberland: highest in England. 3210 ft.

scaf·fold (skăf′əld, -ōld), *n.* **1.** a temporary structure for holding workmen and materials during the erection, repair, or decoration of a building. **2.** an elevated platform on which a criminal is executed, usually by hanging. **3.** a raised platform or stage for exhibiting spectacles, seating spectators, etc. **4.** any raised framework. **5.** scaffolding. —*v.t.* **6.** to furnish with a scaffold or scaffolding. **7.** to support by or place on a scaffold. [ME, t. OF: m. *escafaud,* f. *es-* E- + *cafaud,* ult. g. LL *catafalicum,* f. *cata-* CATA- + s. *fala* tower, gallery + *-icum* -IC]

scaf·fold·ing (skăf′əld ĭng), *n.* **1.** a scaffold or system of scaffolds. **2.** materials for scaffolds.

scagl·io·la (skăl yō′lə), *n.* plasterwork imitating marble, granite, or the like. [t. It.: m. *scagliuola,* dim. of *scaglia* chip of marble. t. Gmc.; cf. SCALE¹]

scal·a·ble (skā′lə bəl), *adj.* that may be scaled: *the scalable slope of a mountain.*

sca·lade (skə lād′), *n.* *Obs.* or *Archaic.* escalade.

scal·age (skā′lĭj), *n.* **1.** a percentage deduction granted in dealings with goods that are likely to shrink, leak, or otherwise vary in the amount or weight originally stated. **2.** the amount of lumber estimated to be contained in a log being scaled.

sca·lar (skā′lər), *adj.* **1.** representable by position on a line; having only magnitude: *a scalar variable.* **2.** *Math.* of or pertaining to a scalar. or something utilizing scalars. —*n.* **3.** *Math.* a quantity possessing only magnitude (contrasted with a *vector*). [t. L: s. *scalāris*]

scalar·e (skə lâr′ĭ, -lär′ĭ), *n.* **1.** an angelfish (def. 1). **2.** any of three deep-bodied, bizarre, cichlid fishes, *Pterophyllum scalare, P. altum,* and *P. eimekei,* of northern South American rivers, widely cultivated as home aquarium fishes.

sca·lar·i·form (skə lär′ə fôrm′), *adj.* *Biol.* ladderlike. [t. NL: s. *scalāriformis,* der. L *scalāris* SCALAR. See -FORM]

scal·a·wag (skăl′ə wăg′), *n.* **1.** *Colloq.* scamp; rascal. **2.** a native white Southerner of the Reconstruction period, who acted with the Republican party. Also, *esp. Brit.,* **scallawag.** [orig. uncertain. Cf. WAG (def. 9)]

scald¹ (skôld), *v.t.* **1.** to burn or affect painfully with, or as with, hot liquid or steam. **2.** to subject to the action of boiling or hot liquid. **3.** to heat to a temperature just short of the boiling point: *to scald milk.* —*v.i.* **4.** to be or become scalded. —*n.* **5.** a burn caused by hot liquid or steam. **6.** any similar condition, esp. as the result of too much heat or sunlight. **7.** *Plant Pathol.* one of several nonparasitic diseases, especially of the apple, which resemble the effects of too much heat or sunlight. [ME *skalde(n),* t. ONF: m.s. *escalder* burn, scald, g. LL *excaldāre* wash in hot water]

scald² (skôld, skäld), *n.* skald.

scale¹ (skāl), *n., v.,* **scaled, scaling.** —*n.* **1.** one of the thin, flat, horny or hard plates that form the covering of certain animals, as fishes. **2.** any thin platelike piece, lamina, or flake such as peels off from a surface. **3.** *Bot.* **a.** a small rudimentary body, usually a specialized leaf, covering the leaf buds of deciduous trees in cold climates. **b.** a thin scarious or membranous part of a plant, as a bract of a catkin. **4.** a scale insect, as the San José scale. **5.** a coating or incrustation as on the inside of a boiler, formed by the deposition of salts from the water. **6.** (*pl.* or *sing.*) *Metall.* an oxide, esp. a ferric oxide, forming in blackish scales on iron brought to a high temperature. **7.** (*pl.*) something that causes blindness. See Acts 9:18. —*v.t.* **8.** to remove the scales or scale from: *to scale fish.* **9.** to remove in scales or thin layers. **10.** to cover with an incrustation or scale. **11.** to skip, as a stone over water. —*v.i.* **12.** to come off in scales. **13.** to shed scales. **14.** to become coated with scale, as the inside of a boiler. [ME, t. OF: aphetic m. *escale;* of Gmc. orig.] —**scale′like′,** *adj.*

scale² (skāl), *n., v.,* **scaled, scaling.** —*n.* **1.** the pan, or either of the pans or dishes, of a balance. **2.** (*usually pl.*) a balance, or any of various other more or less complicated devices for weighing. **3.** **Scales,** *Astron.* the zodiacal constellation or sign Libra; the Balance. —*v.t.* **4.** to weigh in or as in scales. **5.** to have a weight of. [ME, t. Scand.; cf. Icel. *skālar* (pl.), c. OE *scealu* scale (of a balance)]

scale³ (skāl), *n., v.,* **scaled, scaling.** —*n.* **1.** a succession or progression of steps or degrees; a graduated series. **2.** a point on such a scale. **3.** a series of marks laid down at determinate distances, as along a line, for purposes of measurement or computation: *the scale of a thermometer.* **4.** a graduated line, as on a map, representing proportionate size. **5.** a graduated table of prices, wages, etc. **6.** an instrument with graduated spaces, for measuring, etc. **7.** the proportion which the representation of an object bears to the object: *a model on a scale of one inch to a foot.* **8.** the ratio of distances (or, less commonly, of areas) on a map to the corresponding values on the earth. **9.** a certain relative or proportionate size or extent: *a residence on a yet more magnificent scale.* **10.** a standard of measurement or estimation. **11.** *Arith.* a system of numerical notation: *the decimal scale.* **12.** *Music.* a succession of tones ascending or descending according to fixed intervals, esp. such a series beginning on a particular note: *the major scale of C.* **13.** *Educ., Psychol.* a graded series of tests or tasks for measuring intelligence, achievement, adjustment, etc. **14.** anything by which one may ascend. **15.** *Obs.* a ladder; a flight of stairs. —*v.t.* **16.** to climb by, or as by, a ladder; climb up or over. **17.** to make according to scale. **18.** to reduce in amount according to a fixed scale or proportion (often fol. by *down*): *to scale down wages.* **19.** to measure by, or as if by, a scale. **20.** *Lumbering.* **a.** to measure (logs). **b.** to estimate the amount of (standing timber). —*v.i.* **21.** to climb; ascend; mount. **22.** to progress in a graduated series. [ME, t. L: m. *scāla* staircase, ladder] —**Syn. 16.** See **climb.**

Scales (def. 12)
A. Major diatonic; B. Minor diatonic; C. Chromatic

scale-board (skāl′bōrd′, skăb′ərd), *n.* **1.** a very thin board, as for the back of a picture. **2.** *Print.* a thin strip of wood used in justifying. **3.** a thin sheet of wood used as veneer, etc. [f. SCALE² + BOARD]

scale insect, any of various small plant-destroying insects of the homopterous family *Coccidae,* the females

ăct, āble, dâre, ärt; ĕbb, ēqual; ĭf, īce; hŏt, ōver, ôrder, oil, bŏŏk, ōōze, out; ŭp, ūse, ûrge; ə = a in alone; ch, chief; g, give; ng, ring; sh, shoe; th, thin; ŧħ, that; zh, vision. See the full key on inside cover.

of which mostly have the body and eggs covered by a large scale or shield formed by secretions.

scale moss, any thalloid liverwort (class *Hepaticae*).

sca·lene (skā̇lēn′), *adj.* **1.** *Anat.* referring to one of a a group of deep muscles in the front and sides of the neck. **2.** *Geom.* a. (of a cone, etc.) having the axis inclined to the base. b. (of a triangle) having three unequal sides. [t. LL: m.s. *scalēnus*, t. Gk.: m. *skalēnós* unequal]

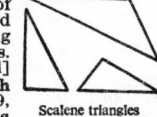

Scalene triangles

Scal·i·ger (skăl′ə jər), *n.* **1.** Joseph Justus (jŏ′zəf jŭs′təs), 1540–1609, French scholar and critic. **2.** Julius Caesar (sō′zər), 1484–1558, Italian scholar, philosopher, and critic, in France.

scal·la·wag (skăl′ə wăg′), *n. Chiefly Brit.* scalawag.

scal·lion (skăl′yən), *n.* **1.** any onion which does not form a large bulb. **2.** shallot. **3.** leek. [ME *scalyon*, t. AF: m. *scal(o)un*, g. L (*caepa*) *Ascalōnia* Ascalonian onion, f. *Ascalon* var. of *Ashkelon* city in Palestine]

scal·lop (skŏl′əp, skăl′-), *n.* **1.** any of various bivalve mollusks of the genus *Pecten* and allied genera, having fluted shell valves that they clap together to accomplish swimming. **2.** the adductor muscle of certain species of such mollusks, esteemed as an article of food. **3.** one of the shells of such a mollusk, usually having radial ribs and a wavy outer edge. **4.** a scallop shell or a dish in which flaked fish or the like is baked and served. **5.** one of a series of rounded projections along the edge of a garment, cloth, etc. —*v.t.* **6.** to finish (an edge) with scallops. **7.** to escallop. Also, **scollop.** [ME *scalop*, t. OF: aphetic m. *escalope* shell; of Gmc. orig. Cf. D *schelp* shell] —**scal′lop·er,** *n.*

scalp (skălp), *n.* **1.** the integument of the upper part of the head, usually including the associated subcutaneous structures. **2.** a part of this integument with the accompanying hair, taken by the North American Indians as a trophy of victory. **3.** any token of victory. **4.** the integument on the top of an animal's head, esp. a canine's. **5.** *Colloq.* a small profit made in quick buying and selling. —*v.t.* **6.** to cut or tear the scalp from. **7.** *Colloq.* to buy and sell so as to make small, quick profits, as stocks. **8.** *Colloq.* to buy (tickets) cheap and sell at other than official rates. —*v.i.* **9.** *Colloq.* to scalp tickets, stocks, etc. [ME (North.), t. Scand.; cf. Icel. *skálpr* leather sheath, d. Dan. *skalp* shell] —**scalp′er,** *n.*

scal·pel (skăl′pəl), *n.* a small, light, usually straight knife used in surgical and anatomical operations and dissections. [t. L: m.s. *scalpellum*, dim. of *scalprum* knife]

scalp lock, a long lock or tuft of hair left on the scalp by North American Indians as an implied challenge to their enemies.

Scalpel

scal·y (skā′lĭ), *adj.,* **scalier, scaliest. 1.** covered with or abounding in scales or scale. **2.** characterized by or consisting of scales; scalelike. **3.** peeling or flaking off in scales. **4.** *Slang.* shabby; despicable. [f. SCALE¹ + -Y¹] —**scal′i·ness,** *n.*

scaly anteater, a pangolin.

Sca·man·der (skə măn′dər), *n.* ancient name of Menderes (def. 2).

scam·mo·ny (skăm′ə nĭ), *n.* **1.** a twining Asiatic species of convolvulus, *Convolvulus Scammonia.* **2.** the cathartic gum resin obtained from its root. [ME and OE *scamonie*, t. L: m. *scammōnia*, t. Gk.: m. *skammōnía*]

scamp (skămp), *n.* **1.** a worthless person; rascal. —*v.t.* **2.** to perform (work, etc.) in a hasty or careless manner. [special uses of obs. *scamp*, v., go (on highway), appar. t. D (obs.): m.s. *schampen* flee, t. It.: m. *scampare* run away] —**scamp′er,** *n.* —**scamp′ish,** *adj.*

scam·per (skăm′pər), *v.i.* **1.** to run or go hastily or quickly. —*n.* **2.** a scampering; a quick run. [f. obs. *scamp,* v., go + -ER⁶. See SCAMP, n.]

scan (skăn), *v.,* **scanned, scanning,** *n.* —*v.t.* **1.** to examine minutely; scrutinize. **2.** to glance at or run through hastily: *to scan a page.* **3.** to analyze (verse) as to its prosodic or metrical structure; read or recite so as to indicate or test the metrical form. **4.** *Television.* to traverse (a surface) with a beam of light or electrons in order to reproduce or transmit a picture. —*v.i.* **5.** to examine the meter of verse. **6.** (of verse) to conform to the rules of meter. **7.** *Television.* to scan a surface. —*n.* **8.** act of scanning; close examination or scrutiny. [ME *scanne,* t. LL: m. *scandere* scan verse, L climb] —**scan′na·ble,** *adj.* —**scan′ner,** *n.*

Scan., Scandinavia.

Scand., **1.** Scandinavia. **2.** Scandinavian.

scan·dal (skăn′dəl), *n., v.,* **-daled, -daling** or (*esp. Brit.*) **-dalled, -dalling.** —*n.* **1.** a disgraceful or discreditable action, circumstance, etc. **2.** offense caused by faults or misdeeds. **3.** damage to reputation; disgrace. **4.** defamatory talk; malicious gossip. **5.** a person whose conduct brings disgrace or offense. —*v.t.* **6.** *Archaic or Dial.* to spread scandal concerning. **7.** *Obs.* to disgrace. **8.** *Obs.* to scandalize. [t. L: s. *scandalum,* orig., trap, t. Gk.: m. *skándalon*; r. ME *scandle,* t. ONF] —**Syn. 3.** discredit, dishonor. **4.** slander, calumny. See **gossip.**

scan·dal·ize (skăn′də līz′), *v.t.,* **-ized, -izing.** to shock or horrify by something considered immoral or im-

proper. Also, *esp. Brit.,* **scan′dal·ise′.** —**scan′dal·iz′er,** *n.*

scan·dal·mon·ger (skăn′dəl mŭng′gər), *n.* one who spreads scandal.

scan·dal·ous (skăn′dəl əs), *adj.* **1.** disgraceful to reputation; shameful or shocking. **2.** defamatory or libelous, as a speech or writing. **3.** addicted to scandal, as a person: *she was a scandalous old monster.* —**scan′-dal·ous·ly,** *adv.*

scan·dent (skăn′dənt), *adj.* climbing, as a plant. [t. L: s. *scandens,* ppr.]

Scan·der·beg (skăn′dər bĕg′), *n.* (*George Castriota*) 1403?–1468, Albanian chief and hero.

scan·di·a (skăn′dĭ ə), *n. Chem.* oxide of scandium, Sc_2O_3, a white infusible powder. [special use of L *Scandia Scandinavia*]

scan·dic (skăn′dĭk), *adj. Chem.* of or pertaining to scandium: *scandic oxide.*

Scan·di·na·vi·a (skăn′də nā′vĭ ə), *n.* **1.** the collective name of Norway, Sweden, Denmark, and sometimes also Iceland and the Faeroe Islands: the former lands of the Norsemen. **2.** the peninsula consisting of Norway and Sweden. [t. L (Pliny), t. Gmc. orig.; cf. OE *Scedenig*]

Scan·di·na·vi·an (skăn′də nā′vĭ ən), *adj.* **1.** of or pertaining to Scandinavia, its inhabitants, or their languages. —*n.* **2.** a native or inhabitant of Scandinavia. **3.** the subgroup of Germanic languages that includes the languages of Scandinavia and Iceland in their historical and modern forms; North Germanic.

scan·di·um (skăn′dĭ əm), *n. Chem.* a rare trivalent metallic element present in euxenite. *Symbol:* Sc; *at. wt.:* 45.10; *at. no.:* 21. [t. NL. See SCANDIA, -IUM]

scan·sion (skăn′shən), *n. Pros.* the metrical analysis of verse. The usual marks for scansion are ˘ for a short or unaccented syllable, – or ′ for a long or accented syllable, ˄ for a rest, | for a foot division, and ‖ for a caesura or pause. [t. L: s. *scansio,* lit., a climbing]

scan·so·ri·al (skăn sōr′ĭ əl), *adj. Zool.* **1.** capable of or adapted for climbing, as the feet of certain birds, lizards, etc. **2.** habitually climbing, as a woodpecker. [f. s. L *scansōrius* used for climbing + -AL¹]

scant (skănt), *adj.* **1.** barely sufficient in amount or quantity; not abundant; inadequate: *to do scant justice.* **2.** limited; not large: *a scant amount.* **3.** barely amounting to as much as indicated: *a scant two hours.* **4.** having an inadequate or limited supply (fol. by *of*): *scant of breath.* —*v.t.* **5.** to make scant; cut down; diminish. **6.** to stint the supply of; withhold. **7.** to treat slightly or inadequately. —*adv.* **8.** *Dial.* scarcely; barely; hardly. [ME, t. Scand.; cf. Icel. *skamt,* neut. of *skammr* short] —**scant′ly,** *adv.* —**scant′ness,** *n.*

scant·ling (skănt′lĭng), *n.* **1.** a timber of comparatively small cross section, as a rafter or a purlin. **2.** such timbers collectively. **3.** the size of a timber in width and thickness, or the dimensions of a stone or other building material. **4.** a small upright timber, esp. in the frame of a building. **5.** a small quantity or amount. [late ME *scantillon,* t. OF, der. *eschanteler* to splinter, der. *chantel* shield boss, ult. der. L *cantus* ring, corner, prob. t. Gk.: m. *kanthós* corner of the eye]

scant·y (skăn′tĭ), *adj.,* **scantier, scantiest. 1.** scant in amount, quantity, etc.; barely sufficient. **2.** meager; not adequate. **3.** lacking amplitude in extent or compass. —**scant′i·ly,** *adv.* —**scant′i·ness,** *n.* —**Syn. 1.** SCANTY, MEAGER, SPARSE refer to insufficiency or deficiency in quantity, number, etc. SCANTY denotes smallness or insufficiency of quantity, number, supply, etc.: *a scanty supply of food.* MEAGER indicates that a person is gaunt and lean (*meager in appearance*) or that something is poor, scanty, stinted, inadequate (*meager fare, a meager income*). SPARSE applies particularly to that which grows thinly or is thinly strewn or sown, often over a wide area: *sparse vegetation, a sparse population.* —**Ant. 1.** plentiful.

Sca·pa Flow (skä′pə, skăp′ə), a sound in the Orkney Islands, N of Scotland: British naval base; German warships scuttled, 1919.

scape¹ (skāp), *n.* **1.** *Bot.* a leafless peduncle rising from the ground. **2.** *Zool.* a stemlike part, as the shaft of a feather. **3.** *Archit.* the shaft of a column. [t. L: m.s. *scāpus,* t. Gk. (Doric): m. *skāpos* staff, sceptre]

scape² (skāp), *n., v.t., v.i.,* **scaped, scaping.** *Archaic.* escape. Also, **'scape.** [ME, aphetic var. of ESCAPE]

S, Scape

scape·goat (skāp′gōt′), *n.* **1.** one who is made to bear the blame for others or to suffer in their place. **2.** (in ancient Jewish ritual) a goat sent into the wilderness after the chief priest on the Day of Atonement had symbolically laid the sins of the people upon it. Lev. 16. [f. SCAPE², v. + GOAT]

scape·grace (skāp′grās′), *n.* a reckless, good-for-nothing person; a ne'er-do-well; a scamp. [short for phrase, '(one who) escapes (divine) grace']

scape wheel, *Horol.* (in the escapement of a time-piece) a toothed wheel which actuates the pendulum or balance. [f. SCAPE² + WHEEL]

scaph·oid (skăf′oid), *adj.* **1.** boat-shaped. **2.** *Anat.* noting esp. a bone of the radial side of the carpus, or a bone on the inner side of the tarsus. —*n.* **3.** *Anat.* a scaphoid bone. [t. NL: s. *scaphoīdēs,* t. Gk.: m. *skaphoeidḗs*]

---

b., blend of, blended; c., cognate with; d., dialect, dialectal; der., derived from; f., formed from; g., going back to; m., modification of; r., replacing; s., stem of; t., taken from; ?, perhaps. See the full key on inside cover.

scap·o·lite (skăp′əlīt′), *n.* any of a group of minerals of variable composition, essentially silicates of aluminum, calcium, and sodium, occurring in crystals and also massive, and usually of a white or grayish-white color. [t. G: m. *skapolith.* See SCAPE¹, -LITE]

sca·pose (skā′pōs), *adj.* **1.** *Bot.* having scapes; consisting of a scape. **2.** resembling a scape. [f. SCAPE¹ + -OSE¹]

s. caps., small capitals.

scap·u·la (skăp′yələ), *n., pl.* -lae (-lē′), -las. **1.** (in man) either of two flat, triangular bones, each forming the back part of a shoulder; a shoulder blade. See diag. under **shoulder. 2.** *Zool.* a dorsal bone of the pectoral arch. [t. NL: shoulder blade (in L only in pl.)]

scap·u·lar (skăp′yələr), *adj.* **1.** of or pertaining to the shoulders or the scapula or scapulae. —*n.* **2.** *Eccles.* a loose, sleeveless monastic garment, hanging from the shoulders. **3.** two small pieces of woolen cloth, joined by strings passing over the shoulders, worn under the ordinary clothing as a badge of affiliation with a religious order, a token of devotion, etc. **4.** *Surg.* a shoulder dressing which keeps the shoulder or another bandage in place. **5.** *Anat., Zool.* scapula. **6.** *Ornith.* a scapular feather. [t. NL: s. *scapulāris*, der. L *scapula* shoulder]

scap·u·lar·y (skăp′yəlĕr′ĭ), *adj., n., pl.* -laries. scapular.

scar¹ (skär), *n., v.,* **scarred, scarring.** —*n.* **1.** the mark left by a healed wound, sore, or burn. **2.** any blemish remaining as a trace or result: *scars upon one's good name.* **3** *Bot.* a mark indicating a former point of attachment, as where a leaf has fallen from a stem. —*v.t.* **4.** to mark with a scar. —*v.i.* **5.** to heal with a resulting scar. [ME, t. OF: aphetic m. *escare,* t. LL: m. *eschara* scab, t. Gk.: lit., hearth]

scar² (skär), *n. Brit.* **1.** a precipitous rocky place; a cliff. **2.** a low or submerged rock in the sea. [ME *skerre,* t. Scand.; cf. Icel. *sker* SKERRY]

scar·ab (skăr′əb), *n.* **1.** any scarabaeid beetle, esp. *Scarabaeus sacer,* regarded as sacred by the ancient Egyptians. **2.** a representation or image of a beetle, much used among the ancient Egyptians as a symbol, seal, amulet, or the like. **3.** a gem (as of emerald, green feldspar, etc.) cut in the form of a beetle. [t. L: m.s. *scarabaeus*; cf. Gk. *kárabos* a kind of beetle]

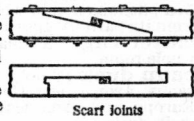

Scarab (def. 2)
A. Top;
B. Bottom

scar·a·bae·id (skăr′əbē′ĭd), *adj.* **1.** belonging or pertaining to the *Scarabaeidae,* a family of lamellicorn beetles, including the scarabs, June beetles, dung beetles, cockchafers, etc. —*n.* **2.** any scarabaeid beetle. [t. NL: s. *scarabaeidae,* der. L *scarabaeus.* See SCARAB, -ID]

scar·a·bae·oid (skăr′əbē′oid), *adj.* Also, **scar·ab·oid** (skăr′əboid′). **1.** resembling a scarab. **2.** of the nature of, or resembling, a scarabaeid. —*n.* **3.** an imitation or counterfeit scarab.

scar·a·bae·us (skăr′əbē′əs), *n., pl.* -baeuses, -baei (-bē′ī). scarab (defs. 2, 3).

Scar·a·mouch (skăr′əmouch′, -mōōsh′), *n.* **1.** a stock character in Italian comedy and farce, a cowardly braggart who is constantly beaten by Harlequin. **2.** (*l.c.*) a rascal or scamp. [t. F: m. *Scaramouche,* t. It.: m. *Scaramuccia,* lit., SKIRMISH]

Scar·bor·ough (skär′bûr′ō, -bərə), *n.* a seaport in NE England, in Yorkshire: resort. 43,920 (est. 1956).

scarce (skârs), *adj.,* **scarcer, scarcest,** *adv.* —*adj.* **1.** insufficient for the need or demand; not abundant: *commodities scarce in wartime.* **2.** seldom met with; rare: *a scarce book.* **3.** **make oneself scarce,** *Colloq.* to go or keep away. —*adv.* **4.** *Literary.* scarcely. [ME *scars,* t. ONF: scant, stingy, ult. der. LL *excarpere,* r. L *excerpere* excerpt, pluck] —**scarce′ness,** *n.* —**Syn.** **1.** See **rare¹.**

scarce·ly (skârs′lĭ), *adv.* **1.** barely; hardly; not quite. **2.** definitely not. **3.** probably not. —**Syn. 1.** See **hardly.**

scarce·ment (skârs′mənt), *n.* a footing or ledge formed by a setoff in a wall.

scar·ci·ty (skâr′sətĭ), *n., pl.* -ties. **1.** insufficiency or smallness of supply; dearth. **2.** rarity; infrequency.

scare (skâr), *v.,* **scared, scaring,** *n.* —*v.t.* **1.** to strike with sudden fear or terror. **2.** to raise; get (fol. by *up*): *to scare up money.* —*v.i.* **3.** to become frightened: *that horse scares easily.* —*n.* **4.** a sudden fright or alarm, esp. with little or no ground. **5.** *Golf.* the part of a club where the head joins the shaft. [unexplained var. of ME *skerre,* t. Scand.; cf. Icel. *skirra,* der. *skjarr* shy, timid, startled] —**scar′er,** *n.* —**scar′ing·ly,** *adv.* —**Syn. 1.** terrify, alarm, startle. See **frighten.**

scare·crow (skâr′krō′), *n.* **1.** an object, usually a figure of a man in old clothes, set up to frighten crows, etc., away from crops. **2.** a person in ragged clothes. **3.** anything terrifying but not really dangerous.

scare·head (skâr′hĕd′), *n. U.S. Colloq.* a newspaper heading in large type.

scare·mon·ger (skâr′mŭng′gər), *n.* one who creates or spreads scares.

scarf¹ (skärf), *n., pl.* **scarfs,** (*esp. Brit.*) **scarves** (skärvz), *v.* —*n.* **1.** a long, broad strip of silk, lace, or other material worn about the neck, shoulders, or head for ornament or protection; a muffler; a necktie or cravat

with hanging ends. **2.** a long cover of cloth for a bureau, table, etc. —*v.t.* **3.** to cover or wrap with, or as with, a scarf. **4.** to use in the manner of a scarf. [? t. ONF: m. *escarpe* sash, sling for arm, prob. var. of OF *escharpe* a pilgrim's scrip hung around the neck. Cf. Icel. *skreppa* scrip]

scarf² (skärf), *n., pl.* **scarfs,** *v.* —*n.* **1.** either of the tapered or specially cut ends of the pieces forming a scarf joint. **2.** *Whaling.* a strip of skin along the body of the whale. —*v.t.* **3.** to join by a scarf or overlapping joint. **4.** to form a scarf, chamfer, or the like on, for a scarf joint. **5.** *Whaling.* to make a groove in and remove (the blubber and skin). [t. Scand.; cf. Sw. *skarf* in like senses] —**scarf′er,** *n.*

scarf joint, a joint by which the ends of two timbers or the like are fitted with long tapers or laps and glued, nailed, or bolted into a continuous piece.

scarf·skin (skärf′skĭn′), *n.* the outermost layer of the skin; the epidermis.

Scarf joints

scar·i·fi·ca·tion (skăr′əfəkā′shən), *n.* **1.** act of scarifying. **2.** result of scarifying; a scratch or scratches.

scar·i·fi·ca·tor (skăr′əfəkā′tər), *n.* **1.** one who scarifies. **2.** a surgical instrument for scarifying. [t. NL, der. LL *scarificāre* SCARIFY]

scar·i·fy (skăr′əfī′), *v.t.,* **-fied, -fying. 1.** to make scratches or superficial incisions in (the skin, a wound, etc.), as in surgery. **2.** to lacerate by severe criticism. **3.** to loosen (the soil) with a type of cultivator. **4.** to hasten the sprouting of (hard-covered seeds) by making incisions in the seed coats. [late ME, t. LL: m. *scarificāre,* t. Gk.: m. *skariphāsthai* scratch an outline] —**scar′i·fi′er,** *n.*

scar·i·ous (skâr′ĭəs), *adj. Bot.* thin, dry, and membranous, as certain bracts. [t. NL: m. *scariōsus,* der. L *scaria* thorny shrub]

scar·la·ti·na (skär′lətē′nə), *n. Pathol.* **1.** scarlet fever. **2.** a mild form of scarlet fever. [t. NL, t. It.: m. *scarlattina* (fem.), dim. of *scarlatto* scarlet]

scar·la·ti·noid (skär′lətē′noid, skär′lăt′ənoid′), *adj.* resembling scarlatina or its eruption.

Scar·lat·ti (skärlät′tē), *n.* **Alessandro** (ä′lĕssän′drō), 1659–1725, Italian composer; considered founder of modern opera.

scar·let (skär′lĭt), *n.* **1.** bright-red color inclining toward orange. **2.** cloth or garments of this color. —*adj.* **3.** of the color scarlet. [ME, t. OF: aphetic m. *escarlate,* ? ult. t. Pers.: m. *saqalāt* a rich cloth]

scarlet fever, a contagious febrile disease, now chiefly of children, caused by streptococci and characterized by a scarlet eruption.

scarlet letter, 1. a scarlet letter "A," formerly worn by one convicted of adultery. **2. The Scarlet Letter,** a novel (1850) by Hawthorne.

scarlet runner, a high-twining South American bean plant, *Phaseolus coccineus,* bearing scarlet flowers.

scarlet tanager, an American tanager, *Piranga olivacea.* The male in breeding plumage is bright-red with black wings and tail.

Scarlet Woman, the woman described in Rev. 17, variously explained as symbolizing pagan Rome or (opprobriously) the Church of Rome.

scarp (skärp), *n.* **1.** a steep slope. **2.** *Fort.* an escarp. —*v.t.* **3.** to slope steeply. [t. It.: m. *scarpa.* See ESCARP]

Scar·ron (skärôN′), *n.* **Paul** (pōl), 1610–60, French novelist, dramatist, and poet.

scarves (skärvz), *n. Chiefly Brit.* pl. of **scarf¹.**

scar·y (skâr′ĭ), *adj.,* **scarier, scariest.** *Colloq.* **1.** causing fright or alarm. **2.** easily frightened; timid.

scat (skăt), *v.,* **scatted, scatting.** *U.S. Colloq.* —*v.i.* **1.** to go off hastily (usually in the imperative). —*v.t.* **2.** to drive off by saying "scat." [? f. a hiss + CAT]

scathe (skāth), *v.,* **scathed, scathing,** *n.* —*v.t.* **1.** to attack with severe criticism. **2.** *Archaic or Dial.* to hurt, harm, or injure; sear. —*n.* **3.** *Archaic or Dial.* hurt, harm, or injury. [ME, t. Scand.; cf. Icel. *skathi* harm, damage, c. OE *sc(e)atha* malefactor, injury, G *schade*] —**scathe′less,** *adj.*

scath·ing (skā′thĭng), *adj.* **1.** bitterly severe, as a remark. **2.** that scathes or sears. —**scath′ing·ly,** *adv.*

sca·tol·o·gy (skətŏl′əjĭ), *n.* **1.** the study of, or preoccupation with, images of physical filth (excrement) in literature. **2.** the science of fossil excrement. [f. m. *skato-* (comb. form of Gk. *skōr* dung) + -LOGY] —**scat·o·log·ic** (skăt′əlŏj′ĭk), **scat·o·log·i·cal,** *adj.*

scat·ter (skăt′ər), *v.t.* **1.** to throw loosely about; distribute at irregular intervals; disperse. **2.** to separate and drive off in various directions; disperse. **3.** *Physics.* **a.** to reflect or refract (light, etc.) so as to diffuse it in many directions. **b.** to deflect irregularly: *scattering alpha particles.* —*v.i.* **4.** to separate and disperse; go in different directions. —*n.* **5.** act of scattering. **6.** that which is scattered. [ME *scatere;* orig. uncert.] —**scat′ter·er,** *n.* —**scat′ter·ing·ly,** *adv.*

—**Syn. 1.** See **sprinkle. 2.** SCATTER, DISPEL, DISPERSE, DISSIPATE imply separating and driving something away so that its original form disappears. To SCATTER is to separate something tangible into parts at random, and drive these in different directions: *the wind scattered leaves all over the lawn.* To DISPEL is to drive away or scatter usually intangible things so that they vanish or cease to exist: *photographs of the race* *dispelled all doubts as to which horse won* To DISPERSE is to cause (usually) a compact or organized tangible body to separate or scatter in different directions, to be reassembled if desired: *tear gas dispersed the mob* To DISSIPATE is usually to scatter by dissolving or reducing to small atoms or parts which cannot be brought together again: *he dissipated his money and his energy in useless activities.*

scat·ter·brain (skăt′ər brān′), *n.* one incapable of serious, connected thought. **—scat′ter·brained′,** *adj.*

scat·ter·good (skăt′ər gŏŏd′), *n.* a spendthrift.

scat·ter·ing (skăt′ər ĭng), *adj.* 1. distributed or occurring here and there at irregular intervals. 2. straggling, as an assemblage of parts. 3. (of votes) cast in small numbers for various candidates. 4. that scatters. **—n.** 5. a phenomenon in which an atomic particle is diverted from its path by another, usually larger, particle.

scatter rug, a small rug, not meant to carpet a whole room.

scaup duck (skôp), any of certain diving ducks of the genus *Aythya,* esp. the **greater scaup,** *A. marila,* of Europe and America; bluebill. [? phonetic var. of *scalp duck*]

scav·enge (skăv′ĭnj), *v.,* **-enged, -enging. —v.t.** 1. to cleanse from filth, as a street. 2. to expel or sweep out burnt gases from (the cylinder of an internal-combustion engine). 3. *Metall.* to clean (molten metal) by the introduction of another substance which will combine chemically with the impurities in it. **—v.i.** 4. to act as a scavenger. 5. to become scavenged of burnt gases. 6. to search for food. [back formation from SCAVENGER]

scav·en·ger (skăv′ĭn jər), *n.* 1. an organism, object, or person that scavenges, esp. any of various animals feeding on dead organic matter. 2. a street cleaner. [alter. of ME *scavager* (cf. *passenger, messenger*), t. AF: m. *scawager,* der. OF *escauver* inspect]

Sc. B., (L *Scientiae Baccalaureus*) Bachelor of Science.

Sc. D., (L *Scientiae Doctor*) Doctor of Science.

sce·nar·i·o (sĭ nâr′ĭ ō′. -när′-), *n., pl.* **-narios.** 1. an outline of the plot of a dramatic work, giving particulars as to the scenes, characters, situations, etc. 2. the outline or manuscript of a motion-picture play, giving the action in the order in which it takes place, the description of scenes and characters, the printed matter to be shown on the screen, etc. [v. It., t. LL: m. *scēnārius* pertaining to stage scenes, der. L *scēna* scene]

sce·nar·ist (sĭ när′ĭst, -när′-), *n.* a writer of scenarios for moving pictures.

scend (sĕnd), *Naut.* **—v.i.** 1. to be heaved upward by a swell. **—n.** 2. this motion. [var. of SEND (def. 11)]

scene (sēn), *n.* 1. the place where any action occurs. 2. any view or picture. 3. an incident or situation in real life. 4. an exhibition or outbreak of excited or violent feeling before others. 5. a division of a play or of an act of a play, now commonly representing what passes between certain of the actors in one place. 6. a unit of dramatic action within a play, in which a single point or effect is made. 7. the place in which the action of a play or part of a play is supposed to occur. 8. scenery (def. 2). 9. an episode, situation, or the like, as described in writing. 10. the setting of a story or the like. 11. *Obs.* or *Rare.* the stage of a theater. [t. L: m. *scēna,* t. Gk.: m. *skēnē* tent, stage] **—Syn.** 2. See view.

scen·er·y (sē′nə rĭ), *n., pl.* **-eries.** 1. the general appearance of a place; the aggregate of features that give character to a landscape. 2. hangings, draperies, structures, etc., on the stage to represent some place or furnish decorative background.

sce·nic (sē′nĭk, sĕn′ĭk), *adj.* 1. of or pertaining to natural scenery; having fine scenery. 2. of or pertaining to the stage or to stage scenery; dramatic; theatrical. 3. representing a scene, action, or the like, as painting or sculpture. Also, **sce′ni·cal. —sce′ni·cal·ly,** *adv.*

sce·nog·ra·phy (sē nŏg′rə fĭ), *n.* 1. the representing of objects, as buildings, according to the rules of perspective. 2. scene painting (used esp. with reference to ancient Greece). [t. L: m. *scēnographia,* t. Gk.: m. *skēnographia* —**sce·no·graph·ic** (sē′nə grăf′ĭk, sĕn′ə-), **sce′no·graph′i·cal,** *adj.*

scent (sĕnt), *n.* 1. distinctive odor, esp. when agreeable. 2. an odor left in passing, by means of which an animal or person may be traced. 3. a track or trail as indicated by such an odor. 4. *Chiefly Brit.* a perfume. 5. the sense of smell. **—v.t.** 6. to perceive or recognize by the sense of smell. 7. to perceive or detect in any way: *to scent trouble.* 8. to fill with an odor; perfume. **—v.i.** 9. to hunt by the sense of smell, as a hound. [ME *sent,* t. F: s. *sentir* feel, perceive, smell, g. L *sentīre*] **—scent′less,** *adj.*

scep·ter (sĕp′tər), *n.* 1. a rod or wand borne in the hand as an emblem of regal or imperial power. 2. royal or imperial power or authority; sovereignty. **—v.t.** 3. to give a scepter to; invest with authority. Also, *esp. Brit.,* **scep′tre.** [ME *sceptre,* t. OF, t. L: m. *scēptrum,* t. Gk.: m. *skēptron*] **—scep′tered,** *adj.*

scep·tic (skĕp′tĭk), *n., adj.* skeptic.

Schaer·beek (sκнär′bāk), *n.* a city in central Belgium, near Brussels. 122,172 (est. 1952).

Schaff·hau·sen (shäf′hou′zən), *n.* a city in N Switzerland, on the Rhine. 25,971 (1950).

Schaum·burg-Lip·pe (shoum′bŏŏrкн lĭp′ə), *n.* a former state in NW Germany.

sched·ule (skĕj′ŏŏl; *Brit.* shĕd′ūl), *n., v.,* **-uled, -uling.**

—n. 1. a written or printed statement of details, often in classified or tabular form, esp. one forming an appendix or explanatory addition to another document. 2. a timetable. 3. *Obs.* a written paper. **—v.t.** 4. to make a schedule of; enter in a schedule. 5. *Colloq.* to plan for a certain date: *to schedule publication for June.* [t. LL: m. *scedula,* dim. of L *sceda* leaf of paper, prob. ult. der. L *scindere* split; r. ME *cedule,* t. OF]

scheel·ite (shē′līt), *n. Mineral.* calcium tungstate, CaWO₄, usually occurring in crystals, an important ore of tungsten. [named after K. W. Scheele (1742–86), Swedish chemist. See -ITE¹]

Sche·her·a·za·de (shə hĕr′ə zä′də. -hîr′-/), *n.* 1. (in the *Arabian Nights' Entertainments*) the wife of the sultan of India, to whom she nightly relates such interesting tales that he spares her life. 2. a symphonic suite (1888) by Rimski-Korsakov.

Scheldt (skĕlt), *n.* a river flowing from N France through W Belgium and SW Netherlands into the North Sea. ab. 250 mi. Flemish, **Schel·de** (sκнĕl′də). French, **Escaut.**

Schel·ling (shĕl′ĭng), *n.* **Friedrich Wilhelm Joseph von** (frē′drĭκн vĭl′hĕlm yō′zĕf fən), 1775–1854, German philosopher.

sche·ma (skē′mə), *n., pl.* **-mata** (-mə tə). a diagram, plan, or scheme. [t. Gk.: form]

sche·mat·ic (skē măt′ĭk), *adj.* pertaining to or of the nature of a schema, diagram, or scheme; diagrammatic. **—sche·mat′i·cal·ly,** *adv.*

sche·ma·tism (skē′mə tĭz′əm), *n.* 1. the particular form or disposition of a thing. 2. a schematic arrangement. [t. NL: s. *schēmatismus,* t. Gk.: m. *schēmatismós* formalization]

sche·ma·tize (skē′mə tīz′), *v.t.,* **-tized, -tizing.** to reduce to or arrange according to a scheme. [t. Gk.: m.s. *schēmatizein*] **—sche′ma·ti·za′tion,** *n.* **—sche′ma·tiz′er,** *n.*

scheme (skēm), *n., v.,* **schemed, scheming. —n.** 1. a plan or design to be followed; a program of action; a project. 2. an underhand plot; intrigue. 3. a visionary or impractical project. 4. a body or system of related doctrines, theories, etc.: *a scheme of philosophy.* 5. any system of correlated things, parts, etc., or the manner of its arrangement. 6. an analytical or tabular statement. 7. a diagram, map, or the like. 8. an astrological diagram of the heavens. **—v.t.** 9. to devise as a scheme; plan; plot; contrive. **—v.i.** 10. to lay schemes; devise plans; plot. [t. ML: m. *schēma,* t. Gk.] **—schem′er,** *n.*

schem·ing (skē′mĭng), *adj.* given to forming plans, esp. underhand ones; crafty.

Sche·nec·ta·dy (skə nĕk′tə dĭ), *n.* a city in E New York, on the Mohawk river. 81,682 (1960).

scher·zan·do (skĕr tsän′dō, -tsän′dō), *adj. Music.* playful; sportive. [It., gerund of *scherzare* play, sport. See SCHERZO]

scher·zo (skĕr′tsō), *n., pl.* **-zos, -zi** (-tsē). *Music.* a movement or passage of light or playful character, esp. as the second or third division of a sonata or a symphony. [t. It.: sport, jest, t. G: m. *scherz*]

Sche·ven·ing·en (sκнā′vən ĭng′ən), *n.* a city in W Netherlands, near The Hague: seaside resort.

Schia·pa·rel·li (skyä′pä rĕl′lē), *n.* **Giovanni** (jô vän′nē), 1835–1910, Italian astronomer.

Schick test (shĭk), *Med.* a diphtheria-immunity test in which diphtheria toxoid is injected cutaneously, nonimmunity being characterized by an inflammation at the injection site. [named after Dr. Bela *Schick* (b. 1877, Vienna)]

Schil·ler (shĭl′ər), *n.* **Johann Christoph Friedrich von** (yō′hän krĭs′tôf frē′drĭκн fən), 1759–1805, German poet, dramatist, and writer.

schil·ler (shĭl′ər), *n.* a peculiar, almost metallic luster, sometimes with iridescence, occurring on certain minerals. [t. G: play of colors]

schil·ler·ize (shĭl′ə rīz′), *v.t.,* **-ized, -izing.** to give a schiller to (a crystal) by developing microscopic inclusions along certain planes. **—schil·ler·i·za·tion** (shĭl′-ər ə zā′shən), *n.*

schil·ling (shĭl′ĭng), *n.* 1. the monetary unit and copper and nickel coin used in Austria since 1925, equal to $0.1407 in the U.S. 2. a minor coin formerly used in Germany. [t. G, c. SHILLING]

schip·per·ke (skĭp′ər kĭ), *n.* one of a breed of small black tailless dogs, orig. used as watchdogs on boats in the Netherlands and Belgium. [t. d. D: little boatman]

schism (sĭz′əm), *n.* 1. division or disunion, esp. into mutually opposed parties. 2. the parties so formed. 3. *Eccles.* a. a formal division within, or separation from, a church or religious body over some doctrinal difference. b. a sect or body formed by such a division. c. the offense of causing or seeking to cause such a division. [t. L: m. *schisma,* t. Gk; r. ME *cisme,* t. OF]

schis·mat·ic (sĭz măt′ĭk), *adj.* 1. Also, **schis·mat′i·cal.** of, pertaining to, or of the nature of schism; guilty of schism. **—n.** 2. one who promotes schism; an adherent of a schismatic body.

schist (shĭst), *n.* any of a class of crystalline rocks whose constituent minerals have a more or less parallel or foliated arrangement, due mostly to metamorphic action. [t. F: m. *schiste,* t. L: m. *schistus* fissile, readily splitting, t. Gk.: m. *schistós*]

schis·tose (shĭs′tōs), *adj.* of, resembling, or in the form of schist.

---

b., blend of, blended; c., cognate with; d., dialect, dialectal; der., derived from; f., formed from; g., going back to; m., modification of; r., replacing; s., stem of; t., taken from; ?, perhaps. See the full key on inside cover.

schis·to·some (shĭs'tə sōm'), *n.* a fluke of long, slender form that inhabits the blood vessels of birds and mammals and is one of the most important and detrimental human parasites in tropical countries.

schizo-, a word element referring to cleavage. Also, before vowels, **schiz-.** [t. Gk.: parted (cf. *schízein* split), as in *schizópodes* with parted toes]

schiz·o·carp (skĭz'ə kärp'), *n. Bot.* a dry fruit which at maturity splits into two or more one-seeded indehiscent carpels. —**schiz·o·car'pous,** *adj.*

schiz·o·gen·e·sis (skĭz'ə jĕn'ə sĭs), *n. Biol.* reproduction by fission. Also, **schi·zog·o·my** (skĭ zŏg'ə mĭ, skī-).

schiz·oid (skĭz'oid, skĭt'soid), *adj.* related to, predisposed to, or afflicted with schizophrenia.

schiz·o·my·cete (skĭz'ō mī sēt'), *n.* any of the *Schizomycetes,* a class or group of plant organisms comprising the bacteria.

schiz·o·my·co·sis (skĭz'ō mī kō'sĭs, skĭt'sō)-, *n. Pathol.* any disease due to schizomycetes.

schiz·o·phre·nia (skĭz'ə frē'nĭ ə, skĭt'sə-), *n. Psychiatry.* a mental disorder characterized by splitting of the personality, dissociation, and emotional deterioration. —**schiz·o·phrene** (skĭz'ə frēn', skĭt'sə-), *n.* —**schiz·o·phren·ic** (skĭz'ə frĕn'ĭk, skit'se-), *adj., n.*

schiz·o·phy·ceous (skĭz'ə fĭ'shəs, -fĭsh'əs), *adj. Bot.* belonging to the *Schizophyceae,* a class or group of unicellular and multicellular green or bluish-green algae, occurring in both salt and fresh water, and often causing pollution of drinking water.

schiz·o·phyte (skĭz'ə fīt'), *n.* any of the *Schizophyta,* a group of plants comprising the schizomycetes and the schizophyceous algae, characterized by a simple structure and by reproduction by simple fission or by spores. [t. NL: m. *Schizophyta* (pl.). See SCHIZO-, -PHYTE] —**schiz·o·phyt·ic** (skĭz'ə fĭt'ĭk), *adj.*

schiz·o·pod (skĭz'ə pŏd'), *n.* 1. any of the *Schizopoda,* an order or division of crustaceans with a soft carapace, comprising the opossum shrimps and their allies. —*adj.* 2. belonging or pertaining to the *Schizopoda.* —**schi·zop·o·dous** (skĭ zŏp'ə dəs, skī-), *adj.*

schiz·o·thy·mi·a (skĭz'ə thī'mĭ ə, skĭt'sə-), *n. Psychiatry.* an emotional state or temperament out of keeping with the individual content. [f. SCHIZO- + Gk. *-thymía,* der. *thymós* mind] —**schiz'o·thy'mic,** *adj.*

Schle·gel (shlā'gəl), *n.* 1. **August Wilhelm von** (ou'gōōst vĭl'hĕlm fən), 1767-1845, German critic, translator, and poet. 2. his brother, **Friedrich von** (frē'drĭKH fən), 1772-1829, German poet, critic, and scholar.

Schlei·er·ma·cher (shlī'ər mä'KHər), *n.* **Friedrich Ernst Daniel** (frē'drĭKH ĕrnst dä'nĭ ĕl), 1768-1834, German theologian and philosopher.

schle·miel (shlə mēl'), *n. Slang.* an awkward and unlucky person for whom things never turn out right. Also, **schle·mihl'.** [f. *Schlemihl* surname of title character of book (1814) by *Adelbert von Chamisso,* 1781-1838; ? surname t. Yiddish, ult. t. Heb.: proper name *Shēlūmīēl* God is my welfare]

Schle·si·en (shlā'zĭ ən), *n.* German name of Silesia.

Schles·wig (slĕs'wĭg; *Ger.* shläs'vĭKH), *n.* 1. a seaport in N West Germany, on the Baltic. 33,800 (est. 1953). 2. a former duchy of Denmark: annexed by Prussia, 1864; the N part was returned to Denmark as the result of a plebiscite, 1920. Also, **Sleswick.** Danish, **Slesvig.**

Schles·wig-Hol·stein (shläs'vĭKH hōl'shtīn), *n.* 1. two duchies of Denmark that were a center of international tension in the 19th century: annexed by Prussia, 1864 (Schleswig) and 1866 (Holstein). 2. a state of N West Germany, including the former duchies of Holstein and Lauenburg and part of Schleswig. 2,271,000 pop. (est. 1955); 6055 sq. mi. *Cap.:* Kiel.

Schleswig-Holstein 1815-1871 (def. 1)

Schley (slī), *n.* **Winfield Scott,** 1839-1911, U.S. rear admiral: won the battle of Santiago, 1898.

Schlie·mann (shlē'män), *n.* **Heinrich** (hīn'rĭKH), 1822-90, American archaeologist, born in Germany.

schlie·ren (shlĭr'ən), *n.pl. Petrog.* streaks or irregularly shaped masses in an igneous rock, which differ in texture or composition from the main mass. [t. G, pl. of *schliere* streak] —**schlie·ric** (shlĭr'ĭk), *adj.*

Schmal·kal·den (shmäl'käl'dən), *n.* a town in what is now East Germany: a league to defend Protestantism was formed here, 1531. 12,663 (1946).

Schmidt optics (shmĭt), optical systems (used in wide field cameras and reflecting telescopes) by means of which spherical aberration and coma are reduced to a minimum by specially-designed objectives. [named after *Bernard Schmidt,* 1879-1935, German inventor]

schmo (shmō), *n. U.S. Slang.* a foolish, boring, or stupid person; a jerk. Also, **shmo.**

schnap·per (shnăp'ər, snăp'-), *n.* 1. *Australia.* snapper (def. 2). 2. a food fish (*Pagrosomus auratus*), abundant off Australia and New Zealand. [alter. of SNAPPER, appar. under German influence]

schnapps (shnăps, snäps), *n.* any spirituous liquor

(a term used by the Dutch and Germans). Also, **schnaps.** [t. G: dram, "nip"; akin to *schnappen* snap]

schnau·zer (shnou'zər; *Ger.* shnou'tsər), *n.* one of a German breed of terrier with a wiry gray coat. [t. G]

Schnitz·ler (shnĭts'lər), *n.* **Arthur** (är'tōōr), 1862-1931, Austrian dramatist and novelist.

schnor·kle (shnôr'kəl), *n.* snorkel.

Scho·field (skō'fēld), *n.* **John McAllister** (mə kăl'ĭs-tər), 1831-1906, U. S. general.

schol·ar (skŏl'ər), *n.* 1. a learned or erudite person. 2. a student; pupil. 3. a student who, because of merit, etc., is granted money or other aid to pursue his studies. [t. LL: s. *scholāris;* r. ME and OE *scolere,* t. LL (as above)] —**Syn.** 2. See **pupil**[1].

schol·arch (skŏl'ärk), *n.* 1. the head of a school. 2. the head of an Athenian school of philosophy. [t. Gk.: s. *scholárchēs,* f. *schol(ḗ)* school + *-archēs* ruler]

schol·ar·ly (skŏl'ərlĭ), *adj.* 1. of, like, or befitting a scholar: *scholarly habits.* 2. having the qualities of a scholar: *a scholarly person.* —*adv.* 3. like a scholar. —**schol'ar·li·ness,** *n.*

schol·ar·ship (skŏl'ərshĭp'), *n.* 1. learning; knowledge acquired by study; the academic attainments of a scholar. 2. the position of a student who, because of merit, etc., is granted money or other aid to pursue his studies. 3. the sum of money or other aid granted to a scholar. 4. a foundation to provide financial assistance to students. —**Syn.** 1. See **learning.**

scho·las·tic (skō läs'tĭk, skə-), *adj.* Also, **scho·las'ti·cal.** 1. of or pertaining to schools, scholars, or education: *scholastic attainments.* 2. of or pertaining to secondary education or schools: *a scholastic meet.* 3. of or pertaining to the medieval schoolmen. 4. pedantic. —*n.* 5. (*sometimes cap.*) a schoolman, a disciple of the schoolmen, or an adherent of scholasticism. 6. a pedantic person. [t. L: s. *scholasticus,* t. Gk.: m. *scholastikós* studious, learned] —**scho·las'ti·cal·ly,** *adv.*

scho·las·ti·cism (skō läs'tə sĭz'əm, skə-), *n.* 1. the doctrines of the schoolmen; the system of theological and philosophical teaching predominant in the Middle Ages, based chiefly upon the authority of the church fathers and of Aristotle and his commentators, and characterized by marked formality in methods. 2. narrow adherence to traditional teachings, doctrines, or methods.

scho·li·ast (skō'lĭ ăst'), *n.* 1. an ancient commentator upon the classics. 2. one who writes scholia. [t. LL: s. *scholiasta,* t. LGk.: m. *scholiastḗs*] —**scho·li·as'tic,** *adj.*

scho·li·um (skō'lĭ əm), *n., pl. -lia* (-lĭ ə). 1. (*often pl.*) a. an explanatory note or comment. b. an ancient annotation upon a passage in a Greek or Latin author. 2. a note added to illustrate or amplify, as in a mathematical work. [t. ML, t. Gk.: m. *schólion* commentary]

Schön·berg (shœn'bĕrKH), *n.* **Arnold** (är'nəld) *Ger.* är'nōlt), 1874-1952, Austrian composer, in the U.S.

school[1] (skōōl), *n.* 1. a place or establishment where instruction is given, esp. one for children. 2. the body of students or pupils attending a school. 3. a regular course of meetings of a teacher or teachers and students for instruction: *a school held during the summer months.* 4. a session of such a course: *no school today.* 5. a building, room, etc., in a university, set apart for the use of one of the faculties or for some particular purpose. 6. (*pl.*) the faculties of a university. 7. a particular faculty or department of a modern university having the right to recommend candidates for degrees, and usually beginning its program of instruction after the student has completed general education: *medical school.* 8. an instructive place, situation, etc. 9. the body of pupils or followers of a master, system, method, etc.: *the Platonic school of philosophy.* 10. any body of persons who agree: *gentlemen of the old school.* 11. *Obs.* the schoolmen. 12. *Mil., Naval.* parts of close-order drill applying to the individual (**school of the soldier**), the squad (**school of the squad**), or the like. —*adj.* 13. of or connected with a school or schools. 14. *Obs.* of the schoolmen. —*v.t.* 15. to educate in, or as in, a school; teach; train. 16. *Archaic.* to reprimand. [ME *scole,* OE *scōl,* t. L: m. *schola,* t. Gk.: m. *scholḗ,* orig., leisure, hence employment of leisure, study]

school[2] (skōōl), *n.* 1. a large number of fish, porpoises, whales, or the like, feeding or migrating together. —*v.i.* 2. to form into, or go in, a school, as fish. [ME *schol(e),* t. D: m. *school* troop, multitude, c. OE *scolu* SHOAL[2]]

school age, *Educ.* 1. the age set by law for children to start school attendance. 2. the period of school attendance required by law.

school board, a local board or committee in charge of public education.

school·book (skōōl'bōōk'), *n.* a book for study in schools.

school·boy (skōōl'boi'), *n.* a boy attending a school.

school·fel·low (skōōl'fĕl'ō), *n.* a schoolmate.

school·girl (skōōl'gûrl'), *n.* a girl attending school.

school·house (skōōl'hous'), *n.* a building in which a school is conducted.

school·ing (skōō'lĭng), *n.* 1. the process of being taught in a school. 2. education received in a school. 3. act of teaching. 4. *Archaic.* reprimand.

school·man (skōōl'mən), *n., pl. -men.* 1. one versed in scholastic learning or engaged in scholastic pursuits. 2. (*sometimes cap.*) a master in one of the schools or universities of the Middle Ages; one of the medieval writers who dealt with theology and philosophy after the methods of scholasticism.

school·mas·ter (skōōl/măs/tər, -mäs/-), *n.* **1.** a man who presides over or teaches in a school. **2.** anything that teaches or directs. **3.** a snapper, *Lutianus apodus*, a food fish found in Florida, the West Indies, etc. —*v.t.*, *v.i.* **4.** to teach or direct as a schoolmaster.

school·mate (skōōl/māt/), *n.* a companion or associate at school.

school·mis·tress (skōōl/mĭs/trĭs), *n.* a woman who presides over or teaches in a school.

school·room (skōōl/rōōm/, -rŏŏm/), *n.* a room in which a school is conducted or pupils are taught.

school·teach·er (skōōl/tē/chər), *n.* a teacher in a school, esp. in one below the college level.

school·yard (skōōl/yärd/), *n.* playground of a school.

school year, *Educ.* the months during a year when a school is open, or attendance is legally required.

schoon·er (skōō/nər), *n.* **1.** a sailing vessel with two or more masts and fore-and-aft rig. **2.** *U.S. Colloq.* a very tall glass, as for beer. [orig. uncert.; said to be der. from New England verb *scoon* skim along (as on water)]

schoon·er-rigged (skōō/nər rĭgd/), *adj.* fore-and-aft-rigged.

Scho·pen·hau·er (shō/pən hou/ər), *n.* **Arthur** (är/tōōr), 1788–1860, German philosopher.

Scho·pen·hau·er·ism (shō/pən hou/ə rĭz/əm), *n.* the pessimistic philosophy of Schopenhauer, who taught that only the cessation of desire could solve the problems arising from the universal impulse of the will to live.

schorl (shôrl), *n.* a black tourmaline. [t. G: m. *schörl*; orig. unknown] —**schor·la·ceous** (shôr lā/shəs), *adj.*

schot·tische (shŏt/ĭsh), *n.* **1.** a round dance resembling the polka. **2.** its music. [t. G: Scottish (dance)]

Schrei·ner (shrī/nər), *n.* **Olive,** ("*Ralph Iron*") c1862–1920, British author and feminist.

Schu·bert (shōō/bərt; *Ger.* -bĕrt), *n.* **Franz** (fränts), 1797–1828, Austrian composer of music.

Schu·mann (shōō/män), *n.* **Robert** (rō/bĕrt), 1810–1856, German composer.

Schu·mann-Heink (shōō/män hīngk/), *n.* **Ernestine,** 1861–1936, U.S. contralto, born in Bohemia.

Schuman Plan, a limited federation of France, West Germany, Belgium, Netherlands, Italy, and Luxembourg (**European Coal and Steel Community**), created in 1952 for pooling coal and steel resources. [proposed by *Robert Schuman,* 1886–1963, French political leader]

Schurz (shōōrts), *n.* **Carl,** 1829–1906, U.S. general, statesman, and publicist, born in Germany.

Schutz·staf·fel (shōōts/shtä/fəl), *n. German.* an elite military unit of the Nazi party which served as Hitler's bodyguard and as a special police force.

Schuy·ler (skī/lər), *n.* **Philip John,** 1733–1804, American general in the Revolutionary War, and statesman.

Schuy·ler·ville (skī/lər vĭl), *n.* a village in E New York, on the Hudson. 1314 (1950). See **Saratoga.**

Schuyl·kill (skōōl/kĭl), *n.* a river from E Pennsylvania SE to the Delaware river at Philadelphia. 131 mi.

schwa (shwä; *Ger.* shvä), *n. Phonet.* **1.** the indeterminate vowel sound, or sounds, of most unstressed syllables of English, however represented; e.g., the sound, or sounds, of *a* in *alone* and *sofa, e* in *system, i* in *easily, o* in *gallop, u* in *circus.* **2.** a mid-central, neutral vowel. **3.** the phonetic symbol ə. [t. G, t. Heb.: m. *sh'wa*]

Schwa·ben (shvä/bən), *n.* German name of **Swabia.**

Schwarz·wald (shvärts/vält/), *n.* German name of the **Black Forest.**

Schwein·furt (shvīn/fŏŏrt), *n.* a city in West Germany, in Bavaria, on the Main river. 51,400 (est. 1953).

Schweit·zer (shvīt/sər), *n.* **Albert,** 1875–1965, born in Alsace; writer, missionary, doctor, musician; active in French Equatorial Africa; Nobel peace prize, 1952.

Schweiz (shvīts), *n.* German name of **Switzerland.**

Schwe·rin (shvä rēn/), *n.* a city in N East Germany; former capital of Mecklenburg. 88,164 (1946).

Schwyz (shvēts), *n.* a canton in central Switzerland, bordering on the Lake of Lucerne. 71,900 pop. (est. 1952); 350 sq. mi. **2.** its capital. 10,040 (1950).

sci., **1.** science. **2.** scientific.

sci·ae·noid (sī ē/noid), *adj.* **1.** belonging or pertaining to the *Sciaenidae,* a family of carnivorous acanthopterygian fishes including the drumfishes, certain king-fishes, etc. —*n.* **2.** a sciaenoid fish. Also, **sci·ae·nid** (sī-ē/nĭd). [f. NL *Sciaen(idae)* (der. L *sciaena,* t. Gk.: m. *sklaina* fish name) + -OID]

sci·am·a·chy (sī ăm/ə kī), *n., pl.* **-chies.** a fighting with a shadow or an imaginary enemy. Also, **sciomachy.** [t. Gk.: m.s. *skiamachia* shadow fighting]

sci·at·ic (sī ăt/ĭk), *adj.* **1.** of the ischium or back of the hip: *sciatic nerve.* **2.** affecting the hip or the sciatic nerves. [t. ML: s. *sciaticus,* alter. of L *ischiadicus*]

sci·at·i·ca (sī ăt/ə kə), *n. Pathol.* **1.** pain and tenderness at some points of the sciatic nerve; sciatic neuralgia. **2.** any painful disorder extending from the hip down the back of the thigh and surrounding area. [late ME, t. ML, prop. fem. of adj. *sciaticus* SCIATIC]

sci·ence (sī/əns), *n.* **1.** a branch of knowledge or study dealing with a body of facts or truths systematically arranged and showing the operation of general laws: *the mathematical sciences.* **2.** systematic knowledge of the physical or material world. **3.** systematized knowledge in general. **4.** knowledge, as of facts or principles;

knowledge gained by systematic study. **5.** a particular branch of knowledge. **6.** skill; proficiency. [ME, t. OF, t. L: m. *scientia* knowledge]

science fiction, a form of fiction which draws imaginatively on scientific knowledge and speculation in its plot, setting, theme, etc.

sci·en·tial (sī ĕn/shəl), *adj.* **1.** having knowledge. **2.** of or pertaining to science or knowledge.

sci·en·tif·ic (sī/ən tĭf/ĭk), *adj.* **1.** of or pertaining to science or the sciences: *scientific studies.* **2.** occupied or concerned with science: *scientific men.* **3.** regulated by or conforming to the principles of exact science: *a scientific method.* **4.** systematic or accurate in the manner of an exact science. [t. LL: s. *scientificus.* See SCIENCE, -FIC] —**sci·en·tif/i·cal·ly,** *adv.*

sci·en·tist (sī/ən tĭst), *n.* one versed in or devoted to science, esp. physical or natural science.

scil·i·cet (sĭl/ə sĕt/), *adv.* to wit; namely. [L, short for *scire licet* it is permitted to know]

scil·la (sĭl/ə), *n.* a plant of the liliaceous genus *Scilla,* bearing bell-shaped flowers in early spring; squill.

Scil·la (sĭl/ə; *It.* shēl/lä), *n.* modern name of **Scylla.**

Scil·ly Isles (sĭl/ĭ), a group of ab. 140 small islands, SW of Land's End, England. 1732 pop. (1951); 6½ sq. mi. *Cap.:* Hugh Town. Also, **Scilly Islands.**

scim·i·tar (sĭm/ə tər), *n.* a curved single-edged sword of Oriental origin. Also, **scim/i·ter, simitar.** [t. It.: m. *scimitarra*]

scin·coid (sĭng/koid), *adj.* **1.** resembling the skinks, as certain lizards. —*n.* **2.** a scincoid lizard. [t. NL: s. *scincoīdes,* der. L *scincus* skink. See -OID]

scin·til·la (sĭn tĭl/ə), *n.* a spark; a minute particle; a trace: *not a scintilla of recognition.* [t. L: spark]

scin·til·lant (sĭn/tə lənt), *adj.* scintillating; sparkling. [t. L: s. *scintillans,* ppr.]

scin·til·late (sĭn/tə lāt/), *v.,* **-lated, -lating.** —*v.i.* **1.** to emit sparks. **2.** to sparkle; flash. **3.** to twinkle, as the stars. —*v.t.* **4.** to emit as sparks; flash forth. [t. L: m.s. *scintillātus,* pp.] —**scin/til·lat/ing,** *adj.*

scin·til·la·tion (sĭn/tə lā/shən), *n.* **1.** act of scintillating; a sparkling. **2.** a spark or flash. **3.** *Astron.* the twinkling or tremulous motion of the light of the stars.

sci·o·lism (sī/ə lĭz/əm), *n.* superficial knowledge. [f. s. LL *sciolus* one having little knowledge + -ISM] —**sci/-o·list,** *n.* —**sci/o·lis/tic,** *adj.*

sci·om·a·chy (sī ŏm/ə kī), *n., pl.* **-chies.** sciamachy.

sci·on (sī/ən), *n.* **1.** a descendant. **2.** a shoot or twig, esp. one cut for grafting or planting; a cutting. Cf. **cion.** [ME, t. OF: m. *cion,* g. s. L *sectio* a cutting. b. with *scier* saw. g. L *secāre* cut]

Scip·i·o (sĭp/ĭ ō/), *n.* **1. Publius Cornelius Scipio Africanus Major** (pŭb/lĭ əs kôr nēl/yəs sĭp/ĭ ō/ af/rĭ kā/nəs mā/jər), ("*Scipio the Elder*") 237 or 234–183 B.C., Roman general: victor over Hannibal. **2.** his adopted grandson, **Publius Cornelius Scipio Aemilianus Africanus Minor** (ē mĭl/ĭ ā/nəs äf/rĭ kā/nəs mī/nər), ("*Scipio the Younger*") c. 185–129 B.C., Roman general: besieger and destroyer of Carthage.

sci·re fa·ci·as (sī/rē fā/shĭ ăs/), *Law.* **1.** a writ requiring the party against whom it is brought to show cause why a judgment, letters patent, etc., should not be executed, vacated, or annulled. **2.** such a judicial proceeding. [L: lit., make (him) to know, after the words in the writ]

scir·rhus (skĭr/əs, sĭr/-), *n., pl.* **scirrhi** (skĭr/ī, sĭr/ī), **scirrhuses.** *Pathol.* a hard, indolent tumor; a hard cancer. [NL, t. Gk.: m. *skirrhos,* var. of *skīros* hard covering] —**scir·rhous** (skĭr/əs, sĭr/-), **scir·rhoid** (skĭr/oid, sĭr/-), *adj.*

scis·sile (sĭs/ĭl), *adj.* capable of being cut or divided; splitting easily. [t. L, neut. of *scissilis*]

scis·sion (sĭzh/ən, sĭsh/-), *n.* a cutting, dividing, or splitting; division; separation. [late ME, t. LL: s. *scissio*]

scis·sor (sĭz/ər), *v.t.* to cut or clip out with scissors.

scis·sors (sĭz/ərz), *n.pl. or sing.* **1.** a cutting instrument consisting of two blades (with handles) so pivoted together that their edges work against each other (often called *a pair of scissors*). **2.** *Gymnastics.* exercises in which the legs execute a scissorlike motion. **3.** *Wrestling.* a hold in which a wrestler encircles the head or body of his opponent with his legs. [ME *sisours, cysoures,* t. OF: m. *cisoires* (fem. pl.), g. LL *cisōria* (found only in sing., *cisōrium* cutting instrument), der. L *caesus,* pp., cut, slain; sp. due to confusion with L *scissor* one who cuts]

scissors kick, *Swimming.* a propelling motion of the legs in which they move somewhat like the blades of a pair of scissors, used in the side stroke.

scis·sor·tail (sĭz/ər tāl/), *n.* a flycatcher, *Muscivora forficata,* of the southern U.S., Mexico, and Central America, with a deeply cleft tail which it opens and closes.

sci·u·rine (sī/yŏŏ rīn/, -rĭn), *adj.* of or pertaining to the squirrels and allied rodents of the family *Sciuridae.* [f. s. L *sciūrus* (t. Gk.: m. *skīouros* squirrel) + -INE¹]

sci·u·roid (sī yŏŏr/oid), *adj.* **1.** sciurine. **2.** *Bot.* resembling a squirrel tail, as the spikes of certain grasses. [f. s. L *sciūrus* (see SCIURINE) + -OID]

sclaff (sklăf), *Golf.* —*v.t., v.i.* **1.** to scrape (the ground) with the club before hitting the ball. —*n.* **2.** a sclaffing stroke. [spec. use of Scot. *sclaf* shuffle] —**sclaff/er,** *n.*

scle·ra (sklĭr/ə), *n. Anat.* a dense, white, fibrous membrane forming with the cornea the external covering of the eyeball. See diag. under **eye**. [t. NL, t. Gk.: m. *sklērā* (fem.) hard]

scle·ren·chy·ma (sklĭ·rĕng/kə·mə), *n. Bot.* supporting or protective tissue composed of thickened and indurated cells from which the protoplasm has usually disappeared. [f. SCLER(O)- + Gk. *énchyma* infusion] —**scle·ren·chym·a·tous** (sklĭr/ĕng·kĭm/ə·təs), *adj.*

scle·rite (sklĭr/īt), *n. Zool.* any chitinous, calcareous, or similar hard part, plate, spicule, or the like. [f. SCLER(O)- +-ITE[1]] —**scle·rit·ic** (sklĭ·rĭt/ĭk), *adj.*

scle·ri·tis (sklĭ·rī/tĭs), *n. Pathol.* inflammation of the sclera.

sclero-, a word element meaning "hard." Also, before vowels, **scler-.** [t. NL, t. Gk.: m. *sklēro-*, comb. form of *sklērós*]

scle·ro·der·ma (sklĭr/ō·dûr/mə, sklēr/ō-), *n. Pathol.* a serious disease in which all the layers of the skin become hardened and rigid. [NL. See SCLERO-, -DERM]

scle·ro·der·ma·tous (sklĭr/ō·dûr/mə·təs, sklēr/ō-), *adj. Zool.* covered with a hardened tissue, as scales.

scle·roid (sklĭr/oid), *adj. Biol.* hard or indurated.

scle·ro·ma (sklĭ·rō/mə), *n., pl.* **-ma·ta** (-mə·tə) *Pathol.* a tumorlike induration of tissue. [NL, t. Gk.: m. *sklē-rōma*]

scle·rom·e·ter (sklĭ·rŏm/ə·tər), *n.* an instrument for determining with precision the degree of hardness of a substance, esp. a mineral.

scle·rosed (sklĭ·rōst/, sklĭr/ōzd), *adj.* hardened or indurated, as by sclerosis.

scle·ro·sis (sklĭ·rō/sĭs), *n., pl.* **-ses** (-sēz). **1.** *Pathol.* a hardening or induration of a tissue or part; increase of connective tissue or the like at the expense of more active tissue. **2.** *Bot.* a hardening of a tissue or cell wall by thickening or lignification. [t. ML, t. Gk.: m. *sklērōsis* hardening] —**scle·ro/sal,** *adj.*

scle·rot·ic (sklĭ·rŏt/ĭk), *adj.* **1.** *Anat.* designating or pertaining to sclera. **2.** *Pathol., Bot.* pertaining to or affected with sclerosis. [t. ML: s. *sclerótica (tunica),* t. LGk.: m. *sklērōtikē,* fem. adj., pertaining to hardening]

scle·ro·ti·tis (sklĭr/ō·tī/tĭs, sklēr/ō-), *n. Pathol.* scleritis. —**scle·ro·tit·ic** (sklĭr/ō·tĭt/ĭk, sklēr/ō-), *adj.*

scle·ro·ti·um (sklĭ·rō/shĭ·əm), *n., pl.* **-tia** (-shĭ·ə). *Bot.* a vegetative, resting, food-storage body in certain higher fungi, composed of a compact mass of indurated mycelia. [NL, f. *sclerot-,* t. Gk.: m.s. *sklērōtēs* hardness) + -*ium* -IUM] —**scle·ro·tial** (sklĭ·rō/shəl), *adj.*

scle·rot·o·my (sklĭ·rŏt/ə·mĭ), *n., pl.* **-mies.** *Surg.* incision into the sclera, as to extract foreign bodies.

scle·rous (sklĭr/əs), *adj.* hard; firm; bony. [t. Gk.: m. *sklērós* hard]

Sc. M., (L *Scientiae Magister*) Master of Science.

scoff (skŏf, skôf), *n.* **1.** an expression of mockery, derision, or derisive scorn; a jeer. **2.** an object of mockery or derision. —*v.i.* **3.** to speak derisively; mock; jeer (often fol. by *at*). —*v.t.* **4.** *Rare.* to deride. [ME *scof,* t. Scand.; cf. obs. Dan. *skof* mockery] —**scoff/er,** *n.* —**scoff/ing·ly,** *adv.*

—**Syn. 3.** SCOFF, JEER, SNEER imply behaving with scornful disapproval toward someone or about something. To SCOFF is to express insolent doubt or derision, openly and emphatically: *to scoff at a new invention.* To JEER is to shout in disapproval and scorn more coarsely and unintelligently than in scoffing: *you may jeer, but can you do any better?* To SNEER is to show by facial expression or tone of voice ill-natured contempt or disparagement: *he sneered unpleasantly in referring to his opponent's misfortunes.* —**Ant. 3.** praise, admire.

scold (skōld), *v.t.* **1.** to find fault with; chide. —*v.i.* **2.** to find fault; reprove. **3.** to use abusive language. —*n.* **4.** a person, esp. a woman, addicted to abusive speech. [ME, var. of *scald,* t. Scand.; cf. Icel. *skāld* poet] —**scold/er,** *n.* —**scold/ing,** *adj., n.* —**scold/ing·ly,** *adv.* —**Syn. 1.** See **reproach.**

scol·e·cite (skŏl/ə·sīt/, skō/lə-), *n.* a zeolite mineral, a hydrous calcium aluminum silicate, CaAl₂Si₃O₁₀·3H₂O, occurring in (usually) acicular crystals and also massive, and commonly white. [f. m.s. Gk. *skōlēx* worm + -ITE[1]]

sco·lex (skō/lĕks), *n., pl.* **scoleces** (skō·lē/sēz), **scolices** (skŏl/ə·sēz/, skō/lə-). *Zool.* the anterior segment or head of a tapeworm, provided with organs of attachment. It develops singularly or in multiples in the larval stage; when it reaches the final host it gives rise to the chain of segments by growth from its posterior end or neck. [NL, t. Gk.: m. *sklōlēx* worm]

sco·li·o·sis (skō/lĭ·ō/sĭs, skŏl/ĭ-), *n. Pathol.* lateral curvature of the spine. [NL, t. Gk.: m. *skoliōsis* a bending]

scol·lop (skŏl/əp), *n., v.t.* scallop.

scol·o·pen·drid (skŏl/ə·pĕn/drĭd), *n. Zool.* any of the *Scolopendrida,* an order of myriapods including many large and poisonous centipedes. [t. NL: s. *Scolopendridae* (pl.), der. *Scolopendra,* t. Gk.: m. *skolópendra* kind of multiped. See -ID[2]] —**scol·o·pen·drine** (skŏl/ə·pĕn/drĭn, -drĭn), *adj.*

scom·broid (skŏm/broid), *adj.* **1.** resembling the mackerel. **2.** belonging or pertaining to the mackerel family (*Scombridae*) or the superfamily (*Scombroidea*) containing the mackerel family. —*n.* **3.** a mackerel or related scombroid fish. Also, **scom·brid** (skŏm/brĭd). [f. m.s. Gk. *skómbros* mackerel + -OID]

sconce[1] (skŏns), *n.* a wall bracket for holding one or more candles or other lights. [ME, t. monastic L: m. *sconsa,* der. *absconsa,* fem. pp., hidden]

sconce[2] (skŏns), *n., v.,* **sconced, sconcing.** —*n.* **1.** *Fort.* a small detached fort or earthwork, as for defense of a pass or ford. **2.** *Obs. or Rare.* a shelter, screen, or protection. —*v.t.* **3.** *Fort.* to protect with a sconce. **4.** *Obs. or Rare.* to fortify; shelter. [t. D: m. *schans*]

sconce[3] (skŏns), *v.,* **sconced, sconcing,** *n.* —*v.t.* **1.** to fine, as among Oxford University undergraduates for a breach of etiquette. —*n.* **2.** such a fine. [orig. obscure]

sconce[4] (skŏns), *n. Colloq.* **1.** the head or skull. **2.** sense or wit. [? special use of SCONCE[1] or SCONCE[2]]

scone (skōn, skŏn), *n.* **1.** a flat, round cake of wheat flour, barley meal, or the like. **2.** one of the four quadrant-shaped pieces into which it is often cut. **3.** Also, **dropped scone.** biscuit (def. 1). [t. MD: m. *schoon(brōt)* fine bread. See SHEEN, BREAD]

Scone (skōōn, skŏn), *n.* **The Stone of,** a famous stone, formerly at Scone, Scotland, upon which the Scottish kings sat at coronation, now beneath the coronation chair in Westminster Abbey.

scoop (skōōp), *n.* **1.** a ladle or ladlelike utensil, esp. a small, deep shovel with a short handle, for taking up flour, sugar, etc. **2.** the bucket of a dredge, steam shovel, etc. **3.** *Surg.* a spoonlike apparatus used to remove substances or foreign objects. **4.** a place scooped out; a hollow. **5.** act of scooping; a movement as of scooping. **6.** the quantity taken up. **7.** *Colloq.* a big haul, as of money. **8.** *Journalism Slang.* a beat. —*v.t.* **9.** to take up or out with, or as with, a scoop. **10.** *Colloq.* to gather or appropriate as if with a scoop (often fol. by *in*). **11.** to empty with a scoop. **12.** to form a hollow or hollows in. **13.** to form with, or as with, a scoop. **14.** *Journalism. Slang.* to get the better of by a scoop or beat, as a rival newspaper. [ME *scope,* t. MLG or MD: vessel used for drawing or bailing water] —**scoop/er,** *n.*

scoot (skōōt), *Colloq.* —*v.i.* **1.** to dart; go swiftly or hastily. —*v.t.* **2.** to send or impel at high speed. —*n.* **3.** a swift, darting movement or course. [of Scand. orig.; akin to SHOOT]

scoot·er (skōō/tər), *n.* **1.** a low vehicle with two wheels, one in front of the other, and a tread or footboard between them, and sometimes with a saddle or seat. It is steered by a handle bar and propelled by pushing against the ground with one foot. **2.** a similar motordriven vehicle for one or two persons. **3.** *U.S.* a sailboat with runners, for use on either water or ice. —*v.i.* **4.** to sail, go, or travel in or on a scooter.

scop (skŏp), *n.* an Old English bard or poet. [OE, c. Icel. *skop* mockery. See SCOFF, SCOLD]

scope (skōp), *n.* **1.** extent or range of view, outlook, application, operation, effectiveness, etc.: *an investigation of wide scope.* **2.** space for movement or activity; opportunity for operation: *to give one's fancy full scope.* **3.** extent in space; a tract or area. **4.** length, or a length. **5.** *Archery.* the length of span within which an arrow carries. **6.** *Rare.* aim; purpose. **7.** short form of *microscope, periscope, radarscope,* etc. [t. It.: m. *scopo,* t. Gk.: m. *skopós* mark, aim] —**Syn. 1.** See **range.**

-scope, a word element referring to instruments of viewing, as in *telescope.* [t. NL: m.s. -*scopium,* t. Gk.: m. -*skopion* or -*skopeion,* der. *skopeîn* look at]

sco·pol·a·mine (skō·pŏl/ə·mēn/, -mĭn, skō/pə·lăm/ēn, -ĭn), *n. Chem., Pharm.* a crystalline alkaloid, C₁₇H₂₁O₄N·HCl·2H₂O, obtained from the rhizome of certain solanaceous plants, used as a depressant and mydriatic, and in producing the so-called twilight sleep. [f. s. NL *Scopola* (genus of plants named for G.A. *Scopoli* of Pavia) + AMINE]

sco·po·line (skō/pə·lēn/, -lĭn), *n. Pharm.* a crystalline glucoside, C₈H₁₃NO₂, a derivative of scopolamine, used as a narcotic.

scop·u·late (skŏp/yə·lāt/), *adj. Zool.* broom-shaped; brushlike.

-scopy, a word element for forming abstract action nouns related to -*scope,* as in *telescopy.* [t. Gk.: m.s. -*skopia,* lit., watching. See -SCOPE]

scor·bu·tic (skôr·bū/tĭk), *adj.* pertaining to, of the nature of, or affected with scurvy. Also, **scor·bu/ti·cal.** [t. NL: s. *scorbúticus,* der. ML *scorbútus* scurvy, appar. t. D: m. *scheurbot* (now *scheurbuik*)]

scorch (skôrch), *v.t.* **1.** to affect in color, taste, etc., by burning slightly. **2.** to parch or shrivel with heat. **3.** to criticize severely. —*v.i.* **4.** to be or become scorched. **5.** *Colloq.* to ride at high speed. —*n.* **6.** a superficial burn. [b. unrecorded *scorp* shrivel (t. Scand.; cf. Icel. *skorpinn* shriveled) and PARCH] —**Syn. 1.** See **burn[1].**

scorched earth, a state in which all things useful to an invading army are destroyed, as by fire.

scorch·er (skôr/chər), *n.* **1.** one who or that which scorches. **2.** *Colloq.* a very hot day. **3.** anything caustic or severe. **4.** *Colloq.* an excessively fast driver.

scorch·ing (skôr/chĭng), *adj.* **1.** burning; very hot. **2.** caustic or scathing. —**scorch/ing·ly,** *adv.*

score (skōr), *n., v.,* **scored, scoring.** —*n.* **1.** the record of points made by the competitors in a game or match. **2.** the aggregate of points made by a side or individual. **3.** the scoring of a point or points. **4.** *Educ., Psychol.* the performance of an individual, or sometimes of a group, on an examination or test, expressed by a letter, number, or other symbol. **5.** a notch or scratch; a stroke or line. **6.** a notch or mark for keeping an account or record. **7.** a reckoning or account so kept. **8.** any account showing indebtedness. **9.** an amount recorded as due. **10.** a line drawn as a boundary, the beginning of a

---

ăct, āble, dâre, ärt; ĕbb, ēqual; ĭf, īce; hŏt, ōver, ôrder, oil, bŏŏk, ōōze, out; ŭp, ūse, ûrge; ə = a in alone; ch, chief; g, give; ng, ring; sh, shoe; th, thin; ᵺ, that; zh, vision. See the full key on inside cover.

race, etc. **11.** a group or set of twenty: *about a score of years ago.* **12.** (*pl.*) a great many. **13.** account, reason, or ground: *to complain on the score of low pay.* **14.** a successful move, remark, etc. **15.** pay off, or **settle, a score, a.** to avenge a wrong. **b.** to fulfill an obligation. **16.** *Music.* a written or printed piece of music with all the vocal and instrumental parts arranged on staves, one under the other. —*v.t.* **17.** to gain for addition to one's score in a game. **18.** to make a score of. **19.** to be worth (as points): *four aces scores one hundred.* **20.** *Educ., Psychol.* to evaluate the responses a person has made on (a test or an examination). **21.** *Music.* **a.** to orchestrate. **b.** to write out in score. **22.** *Cookery.* to cut with shallow slashes, as meat. **23.** to make notches, cuts, or lines in or on. **24.** to record by notches, marks, etc.; to reckon (often fol. by *up*). **25.** to write down as a debt. **26.** to record as a debtor. **27.** to gain or win: *a comedy scoring a great success.* **28.** *U.S.* to censure severely: *newspapers scored him severely for the announcement.* —*v.i.* **29.** to make a point or points in a game or contest. **30.** to keep score, as of a game. **31.** to achieve an advantage or a success. **32.** to make notches, cuts, lines, etc. **33.** to run up a score or debt. [ME; late OE *scoru,* t. Scand.; cf. Icel. *skor* notch] —**scor′er,** *n.*

sco·ri·a (skôr′Yə), *n., pl.* **scoriae** (skôr′Yē′). **1.** the refuse, dross, or slag left after smelting or melting metals. **2.** a clinkerlike cellular lava. [t. L, t. Gk.: m. *skōría* slag] —**sco·ri·a·ceous** (skôr′Yā′shəs), *adj.*

sco·ri·fy (skôr′əfī′), *v.t.,* **-fied, -fying.** to reduce to scoria. [f. SCORI(A) + -FY] —**sco′ri·fi·ca′tion,** *n.*

scorn (skôrn), *n.* **1.** open or unqualified contempt; disdain. **2.** mockery or derision. **3.** an object of derision or contempt. **4.** *Archaic.* a derisive or contemptuous action or speech. —*v.t.* **5.** to treat or regard with scorn. **6.** to reject or refuse with scorn. —*v.i.* **7.** *Obs.* to mock; jeer. [ME; var. of *skarn,* t. OF: aphetic m. *escarn* mockery, derision; of Gmc. orig.] —**scorn′er,** *n.* —Syn. **1.** See **contempt.** —Ant. **2.** praise.

scorn·ful (skôrn′fəl), *adj.* full of scorn; derisive; contemptuous: *he smiled in a scornful way.* —**scorn′ful·ly,** *adv.* —**scorn′ful·ness,** *n.*

scor·pae·nid (skôr pē′nYd), *n.* any of the *Scorpaenidae,* a family of marine fishes.

scor·pae·noid (skôr pē′noid), *Ichthyol.* —*adj.* **1.** of the scorpaenids. —*n.* **2.** scorpaenid. [f. s. L *scorpaena* (t. Gk.: m. *skórpaina* prickly fish) + -OID]

Scor·pi·o (skôr′pYō′), *n.* **1.** *Astron.* the Scorpion, a zodiacal constellation, containing the star Antares. **2.** the eighth sign of the zodiac. Also, **Scorpius.** See diag. under **zodiac.** [ME, t. L. See SCORPION]

scor·pi·oid (skôr′pYoid′), *adj.* **1.** resembling a scorpion. **2.** belonging to the *Scorpionida,* the order of arachnids comprising the scorpions. **3.** curved (at the end) like the tail of a scorpion. [t. Gk.: m.s. *skorpioeidēs*]

scor·pi·on (skôr′pY ən), *n.* **1.** any of numerous arachnids belonging to the order *Scorpiones* (*Scorpionida*) from the warmer parts of the world, having a long narrow tail terminating in a venomous sting. **2.** (*cap.*) *Astron.* Scorpio. **3.** something having the effect of a scorpion (insect). **4.** a (supposed) whip or scourge armed with spikes. I Kings: 12; 11. [ME, t. L: s. *scorpio* (der. *scorpius,* t. Gk.: m. *skorpíos*)]

Scorpion,
Buthus carolinus
(Ab. 3 in. long)

scorpion fish, a rockfish, esp. of the genus *Scorpaena,* which has poisonous dorsal spines.

scorpion fly, any of the harmless insects of the order *Mecoptera,* in which the male has an abdominal structure resembling a scorpion sting.

Scor·pi·us (skôr′pY əs), *n.* *Astron.* Scorpio.

Scot (skôt), *n.* **1.** a native or inhabitant of Scotland; a Scotchman. **2.** one of an ancient Gaelic people who came from northern Ireland about the 6th century and settled in the northwestern part of Great Britain, and after whom Scotland was named. [ME; OE *Scottas* (pl.), t. LL: m. *Scottī* the Irish; of unknown orig.]

scot (skôt), *n.* *Hist.* **1.** a payment or charge; one's share of a payment. **2.** an assessment or tax. [ME, t. Scand.; cf Icel. *skot,* c. OE *gescot* payment]

Scot., **1.** Scotch. **2.** Scotland. **3.** Scottish.

scot and lot, 1. *Brit. Hist.* a municipal tax assessed proportionately upon the members of a community. **2.** pay scot and lot, to pay in full; settle.

Scotch (skŏch), *adj.* **1.** of or pertaining to the Scots, Scotland, or the dialect of English spoken in Scotland. —*n.* **2.** the people of Scotland collectively. **3.** *Colloq.* Scotch whiskey. **4.** Scottish (language). [var. of SCOTS] —Syn. **1.** SCOTCH, SCOTS, SCOTTISH are proper adjectives corresponding to Scot and Scotland. SCOTCH is the form used originally in the dialect of the Midlands and Southern England: *a Scotch terrier.* In Northern England and in Scotland, SCOTS and SCOTTISH (or *Scottis;* cf. *Inglis,* the N form of the word *English*) are preferred: *Scots language; Scottish Church.*

scotch (skŏch), *v.t.* **1.** to injure so as to make harmless. **2.** to cut, gash, or score. **3.** to crush, or stamp out, as something dangerous. **4.** to block or prop with a scotch. —*n.* **5.** a cut, gash, or score. **6.** a block or wedge put

under a wheel, barrel, etc., to prevent slipping. [b. SCORE and NOTCH]

Scotch-Gael·ic (skŏch′gā′lYk), *n.* the Celtic of Scotland.

Scotch-I·rish (skŏch′Ī′rYsh), *adj.* **1.** of or pertaining to descendants of Scotch immigrants to North Ireland. **2.** of mixed Scotch and Irish blood. —*n.* **3.** a person of Scotch and Irish descent.

Scotch·man (skŏch′mən), *n., pl.* **-men.** a native of Scotland. Also, **Scotsman.**

Scotch terrier
10 in. high at the shoulder)

Scotch tape, *Trademark.* a transparent adhesive tape, made of cellulose.

Scotch terrier, a breed of terrier with short legs and shaggy hair, originally from Scotland.

Scotch whiskey, barley-malt whiskey distilled in Scotland.

Scotch woodcock, a dish composed of eggs, milk butter, etc., cooked together, seasoned with anchovy paste, and served on toast.

sco·ter (skō′tər), *n.* any of the large diving ducks constituting the genera *Melanitta* and *Oidemia,* found in northern parts of the Northern Hemisphere.

scot-free (skŏt′frē′), *adj.* **1.** unhurt; clear; safe: *to get off scot-free.* **2.** free from payment of scot.

sco·tia (skō′shə), *n.* *Archit.* a concave molding, as in the base of a column. [t. L, t. Gk.: m. *skotía,* lit., darkness]

Sco·tia (skō′shə), *n.* *Poetic.* Scotland. [t. ML, der. LL *Scōtus* SCOT]

Sco·tism (skō′tYzəm), *n.* the doctrines of Duns Scotus, his fundamental doctrine being that distinctions which the mind inevitably draws, though nonexistent apart from their relations to mind, are to be considered as real. —**Sco′tist,** *n.*

Scot·land (skŏt′lənd), *n.* a division of the United Kingdom in the N part of Great Britain. 4,842,980 pop. (1951); 29,796 sq. mi. *Cap.:* Edinburgh.

Scotland Yard, 1. a short street in London, England, formerly the site of the London police headquarters, now removed to **New Scotland Yard** on the Thames embankment. **2.** the London police, esp. the branch engaged in crime detection.

sco·to·ma (skō tō′mə), *n., pl.* **-mata** (-mə tə). *Pathol.* loss of vision in a part of the visual field; a blind spot. [t. LL, t. Gk.: m. *skótōma* dizziness]

Scots (skŏts), *n.* **1.** the Scottish dialect of English. —*adj.* **2.** Scottish or Scotch. [ME *Scottis,* northern var. of SCOTTISH] —Syn. **2.** See **Scotch.**

Scots·man (skŏts′mən), *n., pl.* **-men.** a Scotchman.

Scott (skŏt), *n.* **1.** Robert Falcon, 1868–1912, British naval officer and antarctic explorer. **2.** Sir Walter, 1771–1832, Scottish novelist and poet. **3.** Winfield, 1786–1866, U.S. general.

Scot·ti·cism (skŏt′ə sYz′əm), *n.* an idiom peculiar to Scottish.

Scot·tish (skŏt′Ysh), *adj.* **1.** of or pertaining to the Scots, their country, the dialect of English spoken there, or their literature. —*n.* **2.** the Scotch people. **3.** the English dialects of Scotland; Scottish English; Scots; Scotch. —Syn. **1.** See **Scotch.**

Scottish terrier, Scotch terrier.

scoun·drel (skoun′drəl), *n.* **1.** an unprincipled, dishonorable man; a villain. —*adj.* **2.** *Rare.* scoundrelly. [orig. uncert.] —Syn. **1.** See **knave.**

scoun·drel·ly (skoun′drəl Y), *adj.* **1.** having the character of a scoundrel. **2.** of or like a scoundrel.

scour¹ (skour), *v.t.* **1.** to cleanse or polish by hard rubbing: *to scour pots and pans.* **2.** to remove dirt, grease, etc., from: *to scour soiled clothing.* **3.** to clear out (a channel, drain, etc.). **4.** to purge thoroughly, as an animal. **5.** to clear or rid of what is undesirable. **6.** to remove by, or as by, cleansing; get rid of. —*v.i.* **7.** to rub a surface in order to cleanse or polish it. **8.** to remove dirt, grease, etc. —*n.* **9.** act of scouring. **10.** the place scoured. **11.** an apparatus or a material used in scouring. **12.** (*pl.*) persistent diarrhea in animals. [ME, prob. t. MD or MLG: m. *schüren,* prob. t. OF: m. *escurer,* g. L ex- EX-¹ and *cūrāre* care for, clean]

scour² (skour), *v.i.* **1.** to move rapidly or energetically. **2.** to range about, as in search of something. —*v.t.* **3.** to run or pass quickly over or along. **4.** to range over, as in search. [ME *scoure.* Cf. Norw. *skura* rush]

scour·er¹ (skour′ər), *n.* **1.** one who scours or cleanses. **2.** an implement or device for scouring. [der. SCOUR¹]

scour·er² (skour′ər), *n.* **1.** one who scours or ranges about. **2.** (in the 17th and 18th centuries) a prankster who roamed the streets at night. [der. SCOUR²]

scourge (skûrj), *n., v.,* **scourged, scourging.** —*n.* **1.** a whip or lash, esp. for the infliction of punishment or torture. **2.** any means of punishment. **3.** a cause of affliction or calamity. —*v.t.* **4.** to whip with a scourge; lash. **5.** to punish or chastise severely; afflict; torment. [ME, t. AF: m. *escorge,* ult. der. LL *excoriāre* strip off the hide] —**scourg′er,** *n.*

scouring rush, any of certain horsetails, esp. *Equisetum hyemale,* used for scouring and polishing.

---

b., blend of, blended; c., cognate with; d., dialect, dialectal; der., derived from; f., formed from; g., going back to; m., modification of; r., replacing; s., stem of; t., taken from; ?, perhaps. See the full key on inside cover.

scour·ings (skour′ĭngz), *n.pl.* **1.** dirt or refuse removed by scouring. **2.** refuse removed from grain.

scouse (skous), *n. Naut.* a baked food served to sailors, as **bread scouse** which contains no meat. See **lobscouse.**

scout[1] (skout), *n.* **1.** a soldier, warship, airplane, or the like, employed in reconnoitering. **2.** a person sent out to obtain information. **3.** *Sports.* a person detailed to observe and report on the techniques, players, etc., of opposing teams. **4.** act of scouting. **5.** a Boy Scout or Girl Scout. **6.** *Slang.* a fellow: *a good old scout.* **7.** a male college servant, as at Oxford, England. —*v.i.* **8.** to act as a scout; reconnoiter. —*v.t.* **9.** to examine, inspect, or observe for the purpose of obtaining information; reconnoiter: *to scout the enemy's defenses.* [ME *scowte,* t. OF: m. *escoute* (fem.) action of listening, der. *escouter* listen, g. L *auscultāre*]

scout[2] (skout), *v.t., v.i.* to reject with scorn; flout. [t. Scand.; cf. Icel. *skūta* scold]

scout·ing (skou′tĭng), *n.* the activities of a scout or scouts.

scout·mas·ter (skout′măs′tər, -mäs′-), *n.* **1.** the leader or officer in charge of a band of scouts. **2.** the adult leader of a troop of Boy Scouts.

scow (skou), *n* a large flat-bottomed unpowered vessel used chiefly for freight, as mud or coal; a low-grade lighter or barge. [t. D: m. *schouw* ferry boat]

scowl (skoul), *v.i.* **1.** to draw down or contract the brows in a sullen or angry manner. **2.** to have a gloomy or threatening look. —*v.t.* **3.** to affect or express with a scowl. —*n.* **4.** a scowling expression, look, or aspect. [ME *skoul,* t. Scand.; cf. Dan. *skule*] —**scowl′er,** *n.* —**scowl′ing·ly,** *adv.*

scr., scruple (defs. 3, 4).

scrab·ble (skrăb′əl), *v.,* **-bled, -bling,** *n.* —*v.t., v.i.* **1.** to scratch or scrape, as with the claws or hands. **2.** to scrawl; scribble. —*n.* **3.** a scrabbling or scramble. **4.** a scrawled character, writing, etc. **5.** (*Cap.*) *Trademark.* a game similar to anagrams and crossword puzzles in which 2 to 4 players use counters of varying point values to form words on a playing board. [t. D: m.s. *schrabbelen,* freq. of *schrabben* scratch]

scrag (skrăg), *n., v.,* **scragged, scragging.** —*n.* **1.** a lean or scrawny person or animal. **2.** the lean end of a neck of mutton, etc. **3.** *Slang.* the neck of a human being. —*v.t.* **4.** *Slang.* to wring the neck of; hang; garrote. [prob. akin to CRAG[2]]

scrag·gly (skrăg′lĭ), *adj.,* **-glier, -gliest.** irregular; ragged; shaggy.

scrag·gy (skrăg′ĭ), *adj.,* **-gier, -giest.** **1.** lean or thin. **2.** meager. **3.** irregular; jagged. —**scrag′gi·ness,** *n.*

scram (skrăm), *v.i.,* **scrammed, scramming.** *U.S. Slang.* to get out or away. [alter. of SCRAMBLE]

scram·ble (skrăm′bəl), *v.,* **-bled, -bling,** *n.* —*v.i.* **1.** to make one's way by a struggling use of the hands and feet, as over rough ground. **2.** to struggle with others for possession; strive rudely with others. —*v.t.* **3.** to collect in a hurried or disorderly manner (fol. by *up,* etc.). **4.** to mix together confusedly. **5.** to cook (eggs) in a pan, mixing whites and yolks with butter, milk, etc. —*n.* **6.** a climb or progression over rough, irregular ground, or the like. **7.** a struggle for possession. **8.** any disorderly struggle or proceeding. [nasalized var. of SCRABBLE] —**scram′bler,** *n.*

scran·nel (skrăn′əl), *adj. Archaic.* **1.** thin or slight. **2.** squeaky or unmelodious. [cf. Norw. *skran* lean]

Scran·ton (skrăn′tən), *n.* a city in NE Pennsylvania. 111,443 (1960).

scrap[1] (skrăp), *n., adj., v.,* **scrapped, scrapping.** —*n.* **1.** a small piece or portion; a fragment: *scraps of paper.* **2.** (*pl.*) a fragment of food. **3.** a detached piece of something written or printed: *scraps of poetry.* **4.** (*pl.*) the remains of animal fat after the oil has been tried out. **5.** (*pl.*) pieces of old metal that can be reworked, esp. scrap iron. —*adj.* **6.** consisting of scraps or fragments: *scrap heap.* **7.** in the form of fragments or remnants of use only for reworking, as metal. —*v.t.* **8.** to make into scraps or scrap; break up. **9.** to discard as useless or worthless. [ME *scrappe,* t. Scand.; cf. Icel. *skrap* scraps, trifles, lit., scrapings]

scrap[2] (skrăp), *n., v.i.,* **scrapped, scrapping.** *Slang.* fight or quarrel. [var. of SCRAPE (cf. defs. 5, 6, 8)]

scrap·book (skrăp′bŏŏk′), *n.* a blank book in which pictures, newspaper clippings, etc., are pasted.

scrape (skrāp), *v.,* **scraped, scraping,** *n.* —*v.t.* **1.** to deprive of or free from an outer layer, adhering matter, etc., by drawing or rubbing something, esp. a sharp or rough instrument, over the surface. **2.** to remove (an outer layer, adhering matter, etc.) in this way. **3.** to scratch; produce as by scratching. **4.** to collect by or as by scraping, or laboriously, or with difficulty (fol. by *up* or *together*). **5.** to rub harshly on or across (something). **6.** to draw or rub (a thing) roughly across something. **7.** to level (an unpaved road) with a grader. —*v.i.* **8.** to scrape something. **9.** to rub against something gratingly. **10.** to produce a grating and unmusical tone from a string instrument. **11.** to draw back the foot in making a bow. **12.** to manage or get by with difficulty. **13.** to practice laborious economy or saving. —*n.* **14.** act of scraping. **15.** a drawing back of the foot in making a bow. **16.** a scraping sound. **17.** a scraped place. **18.** an embarrassing situation. [ME, t. Scand.; cf. Icel. *skrapa*]

scrap·er (skrā′pər), *n.* **1.** one who or that which scrapes. **2.** any of various implements for scraping.

scrap·ing (skrā′pĭng), *n.* **1.** act of one who or that which scrapes. **2.** the sound. **3.** (*usually pl.*) that which is scraped off, up, or together.

scrap iron, old iron used for remelting or reworking.

scrap·ple (skrăp′əl), *n.* a sausagelike preparation of minced pork, herbs, corn, or other meal, etc., fried in slices. [der. SCRAP[1]]

scrap·py (skrăp′ĭ), *adj.,* **-pier, -piest.** **1.** made up of scraps or of odds and ends; fragmentary; disconnected. **2.** *Slang.* given to fighting. —**scrap′pi·ly,** *adv.* —**scrap′pi·ness,** *n.*

scratch (skrăch), *v.t.* **1.** to break or mark slightly by rubbing, scraping, or tearing with something sharp or rough. **2.** to dig, scrape, or to tear (*out, off,* etc.) with the claws, the nails, etc. **3.** to rub or scrape lightly with the fingernails, etc., as to relieve itching. **4.** to rub gratingly, as a match, on something. **5.** to erase or strike out (writing, a name, etc.). **6.** to withdraw (a horse, etc.) from the list of entries in a race or competition. **7.** *U.S.* (of a voter) **a.** to divide (one's vote), though predominately supporting one party. **b.** to strike out or reject a particular name or names on (a party ticket). **c.** to reject (a candidate) on a ticket. —*v.i.* **8.** to use the nails, claws, etc., for tearing, digging, etc. **9.** to relieve itching by rubbing with the nails, etc. **10.** to make a slight grating noise, as a pen. **11.** to manage with difficulty: *scratch along on very little money.* **12.** to withdraw from a contest. **13.** *Billiards and Pool.* to commit a scratch. —*n.* **14.** a mark produced by scratching, such as one on the skin. **15.** a rough mark of a pen, etc.; a scrawl. **16.** an act of scratching. **17.** the sound produced. **18.** the starting place, starting time, or status of a competitor in a handicap who has no allowance and no penalty. **19. from scratch,** from the beginning or from nothing. **20.** the standard in ability, courage, etc.: *to come up to scratch.* **21.** *Billiards and Pool.* **a.** a shot resulting in a penalty. **b.** a fluke. —*adj.* **22.** used for hasty writing, notes, etc.: *scratch paper* or *pad.* **23.** starting from scratch, or without allowance or penalty, as a competitor: *a scratch shot.* **24.** *Colloq.* done by or dependent on chance: *a scratch shot.* **25.** *Colloq.* gathered hastily and indiscriminately: *a scratch crew.* [b. obs. *scrat* and *cratch,* both meaning scratch] —**scratch′er,** *n.*

scratch·es (skrăch′ĭz), *n.pl.* (construed as sing.) *Vet. Sci.* a disease of horses, in which dry rifts or chaps appear on the skin near the fetlock, behind the knee or in front of the hock.

scratch hit, *Baseball.* an accredited hit which ordinarily would have been an out; an accidental hit.

scratch·y (skrăch′ĭ), *adj.,* **scratchier, scratchiest.** **1.** that scratches: *a scratchy pen.* **2.** consisting of mere scratches. **3.** uneven; haphazard. **4.** suffering from scratches. —**scratch′i·ly,** *adv.* —**scratch′i·ness,** *n*

scrawl (skrôl), *v.t.* **1.** to write or draw in a sprawling awkward manner. —*n.* **2.** something scrawled, as a letter or a note. **3.** awkward or careless handwriting: *his letters are always careless scrawls.* [special use of obs. *scrawl* sprawl, influenced by *scribble,* etc.] —**scrawl′er,** *n.* —**scrawl′y,** *adj.*

scraw·ny (skrô′nĭ), *adj.,* **-nier, -niest.** *U.S.* lean; thin; scraggy: *a long scrawny neck.* [var. of *scranny,* var. of SCRANNEL] —**scraw′ni·ness,** *n.* —Ant. robust.

screak (skrēk), *v.i.* **1.** to screech. **2.** to creak. —*n.* **3.** a screech. [t. Scand.; cf. Icel. *skrækja*]

scream (skrēm), *v.i.* **1.** to utter a loud, sharp, piercing cry. **2.** to emit a shrill, piercing sound, as a whistle, etc. **3.** to laugh immoderately. **4.** to make something known by violent, startling words. —*v.t.* **5.** to utter with a scream or screams. **6.** to make by screaming: *to scream oneself hoarse.* —*n.* **7.** a loud, sharp, piercing cry. **8.** shrill, piercing sound. **9.** something funny. [ME *screme;* orig. uncert.] —Syn. **1.** SCREAM, SHRIEK, SCREECH apply to crying out in a loud, piercing way. To SCREAM is to utter a loud, piercing cry, esp. of pain or fear: *to scream with terror.* The word is used also for a shrill, barely audible cry given by one who is startled. SHRIEK usually refers to a sharper and briefer cry than SCREAM; when due to fear or pain, it is indicative of more terror or distress; SHRIEK is also used for the shrill half-suppressed cries of giddy women or girls: *to shriek with laughter.* SCREECH emphasizes the disagreeable shrillness and harshness of an outcry; the connotation is lack of dignity: *to screech like an old crone.*

scream·er (skrē′mər), *n.* **1.** one who or that which screams. **2.** *Slang.* something causing screams of astonishment, mirth, etc. **3.** *Print. Slang.* exclamation point. **4.** *Journalism. Slang.* a sensational headline. **5.** *Ornith.* any of the long-toed South and Central American birds which constitute the family *Anhimidae,* including *Anhima cornuta* (**horned screamer**) and *Chauna chavaria* and *C. torquata* (both known as **crested screamer**).

scream·ing (skrē′mĭng), *adj.* **1.** that screams. **2.** startling in effect: *screaming colors.* **3.** causing screams of mirth: *a screaming farce.* —**scream′ing·ly,** *adv.*

scree (skrē), *n. N. Eng.* a steep mass of detritus on the side of a mountain. [t. Scand.; cf. Icel. *skridha* landslip and OE *scrithan* go, glide]

ăct, āble, dâre, ärt; ĕbb, ēqual; ĭf, īce; hŏt, ōver, ôrder, oil, bŏŏk, ōōze, out; ŭp, ūse, ûrge; ə = a in alone; ch, chief; g, give; ng, ring; sh, shoe; th, thin; *t̶h,* that; zh, vision. See the full key on inside cover.

screech (skrēch), *v.i.* **1.** to utter a harsh, shrill cry. —*v.t.* **2.** to utter with a screech. —*n.* **3.** a harsh, shrill cry. [var. of archaic *scritch*; prob. imit.] —**screech′er**, *n.* —**screech′y**, *adj.* —Syn. 1. See **scream**.

screech owl, **1.** any of various small American owls of the genus *Otus*, having hornlike tufts of feathers, as *Otus asio naevius* of the northeastern U.S. **2.** any owl with a harsh cry, esp. the barn owl.

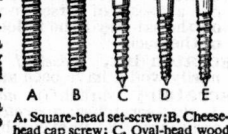

Screech owl. *Otus asio* (8½ to 10 in. long)

screed (skrēd), *n.* **1.** a long piece of writing; harangue. **2.** *Plastering.* a strip of plaster (or wood) of the proper thickness, applied to a wall as a guide or gauge for the rest of the work. [ME *screde*, doublet of *shrede*, OE *scrēade* SHRED]

screen (skrēn), *n.* **1.** a covered frame or the like, movable or fixed, serving as a shelter, partition, etc.: *a fire screen.* **2.** *Chiefly Brit.* an ornamental partition of wood, stone, etc., as in a church. **3.** something affording a surface for displaying motion pictures, slides, etc. **4.** motion pictures collectively. **5.** anything that shelters, protects, or conceals: *a screen of secrecy.* **6.** wire mesh serving as protection: *window screens.* **7.** a sieve or riddle, as for grain, sand, etc. **8.** *Mil.* a body of men sent out to cover the movement of an army. **9.** *Naval.* a protective formation of small vessels, as destroyers. **10.** *Physics.* a shield designed to prevent interference between various effects: *electric screens.* **11.** *Photoengraving.* a transparent plate containing two sets of the fine parallel lines, one crossing the other, used in the half-tone process. —*v.t.* **12.** to shelter, protect, or conceal with, or as with, a screen. **13.** to sift by passing through a screen **14.** to project (pictures, etc.) on a screen. **15.** to photograph with a motion-picture camera; film. **16.** to adapt (a story, play, etc.) for presentation as a motion picture. **17.** to check the loyalty, character, ability, etc., of applicants, employees, or the like. —*v.i.* **18.** to be projected, or suitable for projection, on a screen. [ME *scren(e)*, t. OF: aphetic m. *escren*, var. of *escrime*, t. OHG: m. *skirm* (G *schirm*)] —**screen′a·ble**, *adj.* —**screen′er**, *n.* —Syn. **5.** See **cover**.

screen·ing (skrē′nĭng), *n.* **1.** act or work of one who screens. **2.** (*pl.*) matter separated out with a screen.

screw (skrōō), *n.* **1.** a metal device resembling and serving as a nail, having a slotted head and a tapering spiral thread, and driven into wood, etc., with the aid of a screwdriver (**wood screw**). **2.** a mechanical device consisting of a cylinder having a helical ridge winding round it (**external or male screw**). **3.** a corresponding part into which such a device fits when turned, consisting of a cylindrical socket in whose wall is cut a helical groove (**internal or female screw**). **4.** something having a spiral form. **5.** a propeller. **6.** pressure or coercion: *to put the screws on a debtor.* **7.** *Chiefly Brit.* a little tobacco, salt, etc., in a twisted paper. **8.** a twisting movement; a turn of a screw. **9.** *Chiefly Brit.* a hard bargainer; a miser. **10.** *Chiefly Brit.* a broken-down horse. **11.** *Brit. Colloq.* wages. —*v.t.* **12.** to force, press, hold fast, stretch tight, etc., by or as by means of a screw. **13.** to operate or adjust by a screw, as a press. **14.** to attach with a screw or screws: *to screw a bracket to a wall.* **15.** to work (a screw, etc.) by turning. **16.** to twist; contort; distort. **17.** to force: *screw up one's courage.* **18.** to put compulsion on; force (a seller) to lower a price (often fol. by *down*). **19.** to extract or extort. —*v.i.* **20.** to turn as or like a screw. **21.** to be adapted for being connected or taken apart by means of a screw or screws (fol. by *on, together, off,* etc.). **22.** to turn with a twisting motion. **23.** to practice extortion. [ME; OF *escro(ue)* nut, MD *schrūve* screw]

A. Square-head set-screw; B. Cheese-head cap screw; C. Oval-head wood screw; D. Round-head wood screw; E. Flat-head wood screw

screw·ball (skrōō′bôl), *U.S. Slang.* —*n.* **1.** an erratic, eccentric, or unconventional person. —*adj.* **2.** erratic, eccentric, or unconventional.

screw bean, **1.** a mimosaceous tree, *Strombocarpa odorata* (*Prosopis pubescens*) of the southwestern U.S., bearing twisted pods used as fodder. **2.** the pod itself.

screw·driv·er (skrōō′drī′vər), *n.* **1.** a tool fitting into the slotted head of a screw for driving in or withdrawing it by turning. **2.** a cocktail made from vodka and orange juice. Also, **screw driver**.

screwed (skrōōd), *adj.* **1.** fastened with a screw or screws. **2.** having grooves like a screw. **3.** twisted; awry. **4.** *Chiefly Brit. Slang.* somewhat intoxicated.

screw eye, a screw having a ring-shaped head.

screw jack, jackscrew.

screw pine, a pandanus (plant): so called from its leaves, which have a spiral arrangement.

screw thread, **1.** the helical ridge of a screw. **2.** a full turn of the spiral ridge of a screw.

Scria·bin (skryä′bĭn), *n.* **Aleksandr Nikolaievich** (ä′lĕ ksän′dər nĭ kŏ lä′yə vĭch), 1872–1915, Russian composer and pianist.

scrib·ble (skrĭb′əl), *v.,* -bled, -bling, *n.* —*v.t.* **1.** to write hastily or carelessly: *to scribble a letter.* **2.** to cover with meaningless writing or marks (often fol. by *over*). —*v.i.* **3.** to write literary matter in a hasty, careless way. **4.** to make meaningless marks. —*n.* **5.** a hasty or careless piece of writing. [ME *scribyl, scrible,* t. ML: m.s. *scribillāre.* Cf. L *conscribillāre* scribble]

scrib·bler (skrĭb′lər), *n.* **1.** one who scribbles. **2.** an unimportant writer or author.

scribbling block, *Brit.* a scratch pad.

scribe[1] (skrīb), *n., v.,* scribed, scribing. —*n.* **1.** a penman; a copyist. **2.** any of various officials of ancient or former times who performed clerical duties. **3.** *Jewish Hist.* one of a class of teachers who interpreted the Jewish law to the people. **4.** a writer or author. —*v.t.* **5.** *Rare.* to write or write down. [ME, t. L: m. *scrība* writer] —**scrib′al**, *adj.*

scribe[2] (skrīb), *v.t.,* scribed, scribing. to mark or score (wood, etc.) with a pointed instrument. [? aphetic var. of DESCRIBE]

Scribe (skrēb), *n.* **Augustin Eugène** (ō̄gys tăN′ œ̄ zhĕN′), 1791–1861, French dramatist.

scrib·er (skrī′bər), *n.* a tool for scribing wood, etc.

scrim (skrĭm), *n.* a cotton or linen fabric of open weave, used for curtains, etc. [orig. uncert.]

scrim·mage (skrĭm′ĭj), *n., v.,* -maged, -maging. —*n.* **1.** a rough or vigorous struggle. **2.** *Football.* the action between contesting lines of players when the ball is put in play. —*v.i., v.t.* **3.** to engage in a scrimmage. [var. of *scrimish,* var. of SKIRMISH] —**scrim′mag·er**, *n.*

scrimp (skrĭmp), *v.t.* **1.** to be sparing of or in; stint. **2.** to keep on short allowance, as of food. —*v.i.* **3.** to use severe economy: *they scrimped on butter as best they could.* [orig. obscure; ? akin to SHRIMP]

scrimp·y (skrĭm′pĭ), *adj.,* scrimpier, scrimpiest. scanty; meager. —**scrimp′i·ly**, *adv.* —**scrimp′i·ness**, *n.*

scrim·shaw (skrĭm′shô), *v.i.* **1.** to accomplish a small mechanical task neatly. —*v.t.* **2.** to make (scrimshaw work). —*n.* **3.** carved or scratched work or articles of bone, ivory, steel, wood, etc., made by sailors in leisure time. [orig. obscure]

scrip[1] (skrĭp), *n.* **1.** a writing, esp. a receipt or certificate. **2.** a scrap of paper. **3.** *Finance.* **a.** a certificate representing a fraction of a share of stock. **b.** a certificate to represent a dividend not paid in cash but a promise to pay at a later date. **4.** *Colloq.* a. paper currency in denominations of less than one dollar, formerly issued in the United States. **b.** such currency as a whole. [var. of SCRIPT]

scrip[2] (skrĭp), *n.* *Archaic.* a bag or wallet carried by wayfarers. [ME *scrippe,* t. Scand.; cf. Icel. *skreppa*]

Scripps (skrĭps), *n.* **Edward Wyllis,** 1854–1926, U.S. newspaper publisher.

script (skrĭpt), *n.* **1.** handwriting; the characters used in handwriting. **2.** *Print.* a type imitating handwriting. **3.** *Theat.* the manuscript of a play or role. **4.** *Motion Pictures.* the manuscript of a motion picture containing a synopsis of the plot, the scenario, the cast, etc. [t. L: s. *scriptum,* neut. pp., (something) written; r. ME *scrit,* t. OF: aphetic m. *escrit*]

Script., **1.** Scriptural. **2.** Scripture.

scrip·to·ri·um (skrĭp tōr′ĭ əm), *n., pl.* -toriums, -toria (-tōr′ĭ ə). a room in a monastery set apart for the writing or copying of manuscripts. [t. ML, prop. neut. of L *scriptōrius* of writing]

scrip·tur·al (skrĭp′chər əl), *adj.* of, pertaining to, or in accordance with the Scriptures. Also, **Scriptural.** —**scrip′tur·al·ly**, *adv.*

Scrip·ture (skrĭp′chər), *n.* **1.** the sacred writings of the Old and the New Testament or of either of them (often called **Holy Scripture** and **the Scriptures**); Holy Writ; the Bible. **2.** (*l.c.*) any sacred writing or book. [ME *scriptur,* t. L: s. *scriptūra* writing]

scriv·en·er (skrĭv′nər), *n.* *Archaic.* **1.** a professional or public writer; a clerk. **2.** a notary. [ME, f. obs. *scriveyn* (t. OF) + -ER[1]]

scro·bic·u·late (skrō bĭk′yə lĭt, -lāt′), *adj.* *Bot., Zool.* furrowed or pitted. [f. s. LL *scrobiculus* (dim. of *scrobis* ditch, trench) + -ATE[1]]

scrod (skrŏd), *n.* *U.S.* a young codfish, esp. one that is split for cooking. [? akin to SHRED]

scrof·u·la (skrŏf′yə lə), *n.* *Pathol.* a constitutional disorder of a tuberculous nature, characterized chiefly by swelling and degeneration of the lymphatic glands, esp. of the neck, and by inflammation of the joints, etc. [t. ML, sing. of L *scrōfulae* glandular swelling]

scrof·u·lous (skrŏf′yə ləs), *adj.* **1.** pertaining to, of the nature of, or affected with scrofula. **2.** morally tainted. —**scrof′u·lous·ly**, *adv.* —**scrof′u·lous·ness**, *n.*

scroll (skrōl), *n.* **1.** a roll of parchment or paper, esp. one with writing on it. **2.** something, esp. an ornament, resembling a partly unrolled sheet of paper or having a spiral or coiled form. **3.** a piece of writing; a list or schedule. [ME *scrowle,* var. of *scrowe,* t. AF: m. *escrowe*; of Gmc. orig. and akin to SHRED]

Scroll (def. 1)

scroll saw, **1.** a narrow saw mounted vertically in a frame and operated with an up-and-down motion, used for cutting curved ornamental designs. **2.** such a saw mounted in a power-driven machine.

scroll·work (skrōl′wûrk′), *n.* **1.** decorative work in which scroll forms are important. **2.** ornamental work cut out with a scroll saw.

Scrooge (skrōōj), *n.* **Ebenezer** (ĕb′ə nē′zər), a miserly curmudgeon in Dickens's *Christmas Carol.*

scroop (skrōōp), *v.i.* **1.** to emit a harsh, grating sound: *the gate scrooped as he swung it shut.* —*n.* **2.** a scrooping sound. [imit.]

scroph·u·lar·i·a·ceous (skrŏf′yə lâr′Y ā′shəs), *adj.* belonging to the *Scrophulariaceae*, or figwort family of plants, including the snapdragon, foxglove, toadflax, mullen, eyebright, etc. [f. s. NL *Scrophularia* the typical genus (reputed remedy for scrofula) + -ACEOUS]

scro·tum (skrō′təm), *n., pl.* **-ta** (-tə). *Anat.* the pouch of skin that contains the testicles and their coverings. [t. L] —**scro′tal,** *adj.*

scrouge (skrouj, skrōōj), *v.t., v.i.,* **scrouged, scrouging.** *Colloq. or Dial.* to squeeze; crowd.

scrounge (skrounj), *v.t., v.i.* *Slang.* to pilfer; to take for one's own use. —**scroung′er,** *n.*

scrub[1] (skrŭb), *v.,* **scrubbed, scrubbing,** *n.* —*v.t.* **1.** to rub hard with a brush, cloth, etc., or against a rough surface, in washing. **2.** to cleanse (a gas). —*v.i.* **3.** to cleanse things by hard rubbing. —*n.* **4.** act of scrubbing. [ME *scrobbe,* appar. t. MD: m. *schrubben, schrob-ben* scratch, rub, scrub]

scrub[2] (skrŭb), *n.* **1.** low trees or shrubs, collectively. **2.** a large area covered with scrub, as the Australian "bush," or American sagebrush. **3.** an animal of common or inferior breeding. **4.** a mean, insignificant person. **5.** anything undersized or inferior. **6.** *Sports.* a scrub team, etc., or a member of it. —*adj.* **7.** stunted or undersized; inferior. **8.** *Sports.* composed of substitute or untrained players or members, as a team, etc. **9.** belonging or pertaining to such a team, etc. **10.** participated in by such teams, as a game. [var. of SHRUB[1]]

scrub·ber (skrŭb′ər), *n.* one who or that which scrubs.

scrub·by (skrŭb′Y), *adj.,* **-bier, -biest.** **1.** low or stunted, as trees. **2.** consisting of or covered with stunted trees, etc., or scrub. **3.** undersized or inferior, as animals. **4.** wretched; shabby. —**scrub′bi·ness,** *n.*

scruff (skrŭf), *n.* the nape or back of the neck.

scrum·mage (skrŭm′Yj), *n., v.t., v.i.,* **-maged, -maging.** *Chiefly Brit.* scrimmage (specif. in Rugby football). —**scrum′mag·er,** *n.*

scrump·tious (skrŭmp′shəs), *adj.* *Slang.* superlatively fine or nice; splendid: *to have a scrumptious time.* [orig. d., meaning 'stingy,' ult. der. SCRIMP]

scrunch (skrŭnch), *v.t., v.i.* **1.** to crunch; crush. —*n.* **2.** act or sound of scrunching. [var. of CRUNCH]

scru·ple (skrōō′pəl), *n., v.,* **-pled, -pling.** —*n.* **1.** hesitation or reluctance from conscientious or other restraining reasons. **2.** a very small portion or amount. **3.** a unit of weight equal to 20 grains or $^1/_3$ of a dram, apothecaries' weight. **4.** an ancient Roman unit of weight equivalent to $^1/_{24}$ of an ounce or $^1/_{288}$ of an as or pound. —*v.i.* **5.** to have scruples. —*v.t.* **6.** to have scruples about; hesitate at. [t. L: m.s. *scrūpulus,* lit., small stone, fig., anxiety, doubt, scruple (dim. of *scrūpus* sharp stone)]

scru·pu·lous (skrōō′pyə ləs), *adj.* **1.** having scruples; having or showing a strict regard for what is right. **2.** punctiliously or minutely careful, precise, or exact. —**scru·pu·los·i·ty** (skrōō′pyəlŏs′ətY), **scru′pu·lous·ness,** *n.* —**scru′pu·lous·ly,** *adv.*
—**Syn. 2.** SCRUPULOUS, PUNCTILIOUS imply abiding exactly by rules. SCRUPULOUS implies conscientious carefulness in attending to details: *scrupulous attention to details.* PUNCTILIOUS suggests strictness, preciseness, and rigidity, esp. in observance of social conventions. —**Ant. 2.** careless.

scru·ta·ble (skrōō′tə bəl), *adj.* that may be penetrated or understood by investigation.

scru·ta·tor (skrōōtā′tər), *n.* one who investigates.

scru·ti·neer (skrōō′tə nYr′), *n. Now Rare.* an official examiner, esp. of votes at an election.

scru·ti·nize (skrōō′tə nīz′), *v.t., v.i.,* **-nized, -nizing.** to examine closely or critically. *Also, esp. Brit.,* **scru′ti·nise′.** —**scru′ti·niz′er,** *n.* —**scru′ti·niz′ing·ly,** *adv.*

scru·ti·ny (skrōō′tə nY), *n., pl.* **-nies.** searching examination or investigation; minute inquiry. [t. LL: m.s. *scrūtinium*] —**Syn.** See **examination.**

SCUBA (skōō′bə), *n.* a portable breathing device for free-swimming divers, consisting of a mouthpiece joined by hoses to one or two tanks of compressed air which are strapped on the back. [self-contained underwater breathing apparatus] *Also,* **Scu′ba.**

scud (skŭd), *v.,* **scudded, scudding,** *n.* —*v.i.* **1.** to run or move quickly or hurriedly. **2.** *Naut.* to run before a gale with little or no sail set. —*n.* **3.** act of scudding. **4.** clouds, spray, or the like, driven by the wind; a driving shower; a gust of wind. **5.** low drifting clouds appearing beneath a cloud from which precipitation is actively falling. [t. Scand.; cf. Norw. *skudda* push]

Scu·dé·ry (sky dĕ rē′), *n.* **Magdeleine de** (mȧg də lĕn′də), 1607–1701, French novelist.

scu·do (skōō′dō), *n., pl.* **-di** (-dē). **1.** a former silver coin and money of account of various Italian states, usually equivalent to about 97 U.S. cents. **2.** a former Italian gold coin, usually of the same value. [t. It., g. L *scūtum* shield]

scuff (skŭf), *v.i.* **1.** to walk without raising the feet; shuffle. —*v.t.* **2.** to scrape with the feet. **3.** to mar by scraping or hard use, as shoes, furniture, etc. —*n.*

4. act or sound of scuffing. **5.** a type of slipper that does not have a quarter or a counter. [? short for SCUFFLE]

scuf·fle (skŭf′əl), *v.,* **-fled, -fling,** *n.* —*v.i.* **1.** to struggle or fight in a rough, confused manner. **2.** to go or move in hurried confusion. **3.** to move at a shuffle; scuff. —*n.* **4.** a rough, confused struggle or fight. **5.** a shuffling: *a scuffle of feet.* **6.** a spadelike hoe which is pushed instead of pulled· [? of Scand. orig.; cf. Sw. *skuffa* push] —**scuf′fler,** *n.*

scull (skŭl), *n.* **1.** an oar worked from side to side over the stern of a boat as a means of propulsion. **2.** one of a pair of oars operated, one on each side, by one person. **3.** a boat propelled by a scull or sculls. **4.** a light racing boat propelled by one rower with a pair of oars. —*v.t.* **5.** to propel or convey by means of a scull or sculls. —*v.i.* **6.** to propel a boat with a scull or sculls. [ME; orig. unknown] —**scull′er,** *n.*

Man sculling

scul·ler·y (skŭl′ər Y), *n., pl.* **-leries.** *Chiefly Brit.* a small room where the rough, dirty work of a kitchen is done. **2.** the place in which kitchen utensils are cleaned and kept. [ME *squillerye,* t. OF: m. *escuelerie,* ult. der. *escuele* dish, g. L *scutella* salver]

scul·lion (skŭl′yən), *n. Archaic.* **1.** a kitchen servant who does menial work. **2.** a low or contemptible person. [ME *sculyon,* t. OF: m. *escouillon* dishcloth]

scul·pin (skŭl′pYn), *n.* **1.** a small fresh-water fish of the genus *Cottus* (family *Cottidae*), with a large head armed on each side by one or more spines; bullhead. **2.** any marine fish of the same family. **3.** (in California) a common scorpionfish, *Scorpaena guttata.*

sculp·sit (skŭlp′sYt), *Latin.* (he or she) engraved, carved, or sculptured (it).

sculp·tor (skŭlp′tər), *n.* one who practices the art of sculpture. [t. L] —**sculp·tress** (skŭlp′trYs), *n. fem.*

sculp·ture (skŭlp′chər), *n., v.,* **-tured, -turing.** —*n.* **1.** the fine art of forming figures or designs in relief, in intaglio, or in the round by cutting marble, wood, granite, etc., by fashioning plastic materials, by modeling in clay, or by making molds for casting in bronze or other metal. **2.** sculptured work. **3.** a piece of such work. —*v.t.* **4.** to carve, make, or execute by sculpture, as a figure, design, etc.; represent in sculpture. **5.** *Phys. Geog.* to change the form of (the land surface) by erosion. [ME, t. L: m. *sculptūra*] —**sculp′tur·al,** *adj.* —**sculp′tur·al·ly,** *adv.*

sculp·tur·esque (skŭlp′chə rĕsk′), *adj.* in the manner of, or suggesting, sculpture: *sculpturesque beauty.* —**sculp′tur·esque′ly,** *adv.* —**sculp′tur·esque′ness,** *n.*

scum (skŭm), *n., v.,* **scummed, scumming.** —*n.* **1.** a film of foul or extraneous matter on a liquid. **2.** refuse or offscourings: *scum of the earth.* **3.** low, worthless persons. **4.** the scoria of molten metals. —*v.t.* **5.** to remove the scum from. **6.** to remove as scum. —*v.i.* **7.** to form scum; become covered with scum. [ME, t. MD: m. *schūme,* c. G *schaum* foam]

scum·ble (skŭm′bəl), *v.,* **-bled, -bling,** *n.* —*v.t.* **1.** *Painting and Drawing.* to modify the effect of a painting by overlaying parts of it with a thin application of opaque or semiopaque color. —*n.* **2.** application of such color. **3.** the color used. [der. SCUM]

scum·my (skŭm′Y), *adj.,* **-mier, -miest.** **1.** consisting of or having scum. **2.** worthless; despicable.

scup (skŭp), *n.* a sparoid food fish, *Stenotomus,* of the E coast of the U.S., having a compressed body and high back. [t. Narragansett: m. *scuppang* or *mischup,* f. *mische* great + *kuppe* close together, referring to the scales]

scup·per (skŭp′ər), *n.* **1.** *Naut.* an opening in the side of a ship at or just below the level of the deck, to allow water to run off. —*v.t.* **2.** *Brit. Mil. Slang.* to overwhelm; surprise and massacre. [orig. uncert.]

scup·per·nong (skŭp′ər nŏng′, -nŏng′), *n.* a cultivated fox grape of the southern U.S. [short for *Scuppernong* grape, named after a river in N.C.]

scurf (skûrf), *n.* **1.** the scales or small shreds of epidermis that are continually exfoliated from the skin; esp., in England, dandruff. **2.** any scaly matter or incrustation on the surface. [ME and OE. t. Scand.; cf. Dan. *skurv,* c. OE *sceorf*] —**scurf′y,** *adj.*

scur·rile (skûr′Yl), *adj. Archaic.* scurrilous. [t. L, neut. of *scurrīlis*]

scur·ril·i·ty (skər Yl′ə tY), *n., pl.* **-ties.** **1.** scurrilous quality. **2.** a scurrilous remark or attack.

scur·ril·ous (skûr′ə ləs), *adj.* **1.** grossly or indecently abusive: *a scurrilous speaker.* **2.** characterized by or using low buffoonery; coarsely jocular or derisive: *a scurrilous jest.* [see SCURRILE, -OUS] —**scur′ril·ous·ly,** *adv.* —**scur′ril·ous·ness,** *n.*

scur·ry (skûr′Y), *v.,* **-ried, -rying,** *n., pl.* **-ries.** —*v.i.* **1.** to go or move quickly or in haste. **2.** to send hurrying along. —*n.* **3.** a scurrying rush: *we heard the scurry of little feet down the stairs.* **4.** a fairly short run or race. [abstracted from HURRY-SCURRY]

scur·vy (skûr′vY), *n., adj.,* **-vier, -viest.** —*n.* **1.** *Pathol.* a disease marked by swollen and bleeding gums, livid spots on the skin, prostration, etc., due to a diet lacking in vitamin C. —*adj.* **2.** low, mean, or contemptible: *a scurvy trick.* [orig. adj., f. SCURF + -Y[1]] —**scur′vi·ly,** *adv.* —**scur′vi·ness,** *n.*

scurvy grass, a brassicaceous plant, *Cochlearia officinalis,* purported to be a remedy for scurvy.

scut (skŭt), *n.* a short tail, esp. that of a hare, rabbit, or deer. [t. Scand.; cf. Icel. *skott* tail]

scu·tage (skū′tĭj), *n.* (in the feudal system) a payment exacted in lieu of military service. [late ME, t. ML: m.s. *scūtāgium,* der. L *scūtum* shield]

Scu·ta·ri (skōō′tä rē′). *n.* 1. Also, **Skutari.** Turkish, **Usküdar.** a section of Istanbul, Turkey, on the Asiatic shore of the Bosporus. 69,671 (1950). 2. Albanian, **Shkodër.** a city in NW Albania, on Lake Scutari: a former capital of Albania. 33,852 (1945). 3. Lake, a picturesque lake between NW Albania and Yugoslavia. ab. 135 sq. mi.

scu·tate (skū′tāt), *adj.* 1. *Bot.* formed like a round buckler. 2. *Zool.* having scutes, shields, or large scales. [t. L: m.s. *scūtātus* having a shield]

scutch (skŭch), *v.t.* 1. to dress (flax) by beating. **—n.** Also, **scutch/er.** 2. a device for scutching flax fiber. 3. a flat double-edged cutting head with a handle set perpendicularly to the cutting edges, used in trimming brick. [cf. OF *escousser* shake]

scutch·eon (skŭch′ən), *n.* 1. an escutcheon. 2. *Zool.* a scute.

scute (skūt), *n.* 1. a dermal plate, as on an armadillo, turtle, etc. 2. a large scale. [t. L: m.s. *scūtum* shield]

scu·tel·late (skū těl′ĭt, -āt, skū′tə lāt′), *adj. Zool.* 1. having scutes. 2. formed into a scutellum. Also, **scu/tel·lat/ed.** [t. NL: m.s. *scūtellātus.* See SCUTELLUM, -ATE¹]

scu·tel·la·tion (skū′tə lā′shən), *n.* 1. scutellate state or formation; a scaly covering, as on a bird's leg. 2. arrangement of scutella or scales.

scu·tel·lum (skū těl′əm), *n., pl.* **-tella** (-těl′ə). *Zool., Bot.* a small plate, scutum, or other shieldlike part. [t. NL, irreg. dim. of L *scūtum* shield]

scu·ti·form (skū′tə fôrm′), *adj.* shield-shaped. [t. NL: s. *scūtiformis,* f. L *scūti-* shield + *-formis* -FORM]

scut·ter (skŭt′ər), *v.i., n. Chiefly Brit. Dial. and Scot.* scurry. [var. of SCUTTLE²]

scut·tle¹ (skŭt′əl), *n.* 1. a deep container for coal; a coal hod. 2. *Brit. Dial.* a broad, shallow basket. [ME and OE *scutel,* orig., a dish or platter, t. L: m.s. *scutella*]

scut·tle² (skŭt′əl), *v.,* **-tled, -tling,** *n.* **—v.i.** 1. to run with quick, hasty steps; hurry. **—n.** 2. a quick pace; a short, hurried run. [? var. of *scuddle,* freq. of SCUD]

scut·tle³ (skŭt′əl), *n., v.,* **-tled, -tling.** **—n.** 1. a small rectangular opening in a ship's deck, with a movable lid or cover. 2. a similar opening in a ship's side, or in a roof, wall, etc. **—v.t.** 3. to cut a hole or holes through the bottom, sides, or deck of (a ship or boat) for any purpose, esp. through the bottom or sides for the purpose of sinking it. [late ME *skottell* hatchway lid, appar. der. D *schutten* to shut. Cf. F *écoutille,* Sp. *escotilla* hatchway]

scut·tle·butt (skŭt′əl bŭt′), *n.* 1. *Naut.* a cask having a hole cut in it for the introduction of a cup or dipper, and used to hold drinking water. 2. *Slang.* rumor; gossip.

scu·tum (skū′təm), *n., pl.* **-ta** (-tə). 1. *Zool.* scute (def. 1). 2. *Rom. Hist.* a large, oblong shield, as of heavy-armed legionaries. [t. L: shield]

S.C.V., Sons of Confederate Veterans.

Scyl·la (sĭl′ə), *n.* 1. Modern, **Scilla.** a dangerous rock on the Italian side of the Strait of Messina, facing Charybdis, a whirlpool on the Sicilian side, both personified in classical mythology as female monsters. 2. **between Scylla and Charybdis,** between two evils or dangers, either one of which can be safely avoided only by risking the other.

scy·phi·form (sī′fĭ fôrm′), *adj. Bot.* shaped like a cup or goblet.

Scy·pho·zo·a (sī′fə zō′ə), *n.pl.* a class of coelenterates comprising the larger medusae or jellyfishes. [NL, f. m. Gk. *skypho-,* comb. form of *skýphos* cup, can + *-zoa* -ZOA]

scy·pho·zo·an (sī′fə zō′ən), *n.* one of the *Scyphozoa.*

scy·phus (sī′fəs), *n., pl.* **-phi** (-fī). 1. *Bot.* a cup-shaped part of a flower, etc. 2. a large Greek drinking cup. [NL, special use of L *scyphus* goblet, t. Gk.: m. *skýphos* can, cup]

scythe (sīth), *n., v.,* **scythed, scything.** **—n.** 1. an agricultural implement consisting of a long, curving blade fastened at an angle to a handle, for mowing grass, etc., by hand. **—v.t.** 2. to cut or mow with a scythe. [ME *sith,* OE *sīthe,* c. Icel. *sigdh;* spelling *sc* by pseudo-etymological assoc. with L *scindere* cut]

Scyth·i·a (sĭth′ī ə), *n.* the ancient name of an undefined region in SE Europe and Asia, lying N and E of the Black and Caspian Seas: now part of the Soviet Union.

Scyth·i·an (sĭth′ī ən), *adj.* 1. pertaining to Scythia, its people, or their language. **—n.** 2. a native or inhabitant of Scythia. 3. an extinct Iranian language.

sd., sound.

s.d., sine die.

S. Dak., South Dakota. Also, **S.D.**

'sdeath (zdĕth), *interj. Archaic.* a reduced form of *God's death,* used as an oath.

se-, a prefix applied mainly to stems not used as words, having a general meaning of withdrawal, as in *seclude, seduce.* [t. L]

Se, *Chem.* selenium.

SE, 1. Southeast. 2. Southeastern. Also, **S.E.**

sea (sē), *n.* 1. the salt waters that cover the greater part of the earth's surface. 2. a division of these waters, of considerable extent, more or less definitely marked off by land boundaries: *the North Sea.* 3. one of the seven seas. 4. a large lake or landlocked body of water. 5. the turbulence of the ocean or other body of water as caused by the wind; the waves. 6. a large, heavy wave. 7. a widely extended, copious, or overwhelming quantity: *a sea of faces, a sea of troubles.* 8. **at sea, a.** out on the ocean. **b.** in a state of uncertainty or perplexity. 9. **follow the sea,** to follow a nautical career. 10. **go to sea, a.** to set out upon a voyage. **b.** to take up a nautical career. 11. **put to sea,** to set out on a voyage. [ME *see,* OE *sæ,* c. D *zee,* G *see,* Icel. *sær,* Goth. *saiws*]

sea anchor, a floating anchor used at sea to prevent a ship from drifting or to keep its head to the wind: commonly consisting of a framed cone of canvas dragged along with its large open base toward the ship.

sea anemone, any of the common marine animals of the phylum *Coelenterata,* class *Anthozoa,* of sedentary habits, having a columnar body topped by a disk bearing one to many circles of tentacles.

sea bass (băs), 1. any of a number of marine serranoid fishes, as the **black sea bass** of the northeastern U.S., *Centropristes striatus,* or the **black sea bass** of California, *Stereolepis gigas.* 2. any of a number of related or similar marine food fishes, as the **white sea bass,** *Cynoscion nobilis,* of California.

Sea·bees (sē′bēz′), *n.pl.* the construction battalions of the U.S. Navy, established in Dec. 1941, to build landing facilities, airfields, etc., in combat areas. [alter. of C. B., abbreviation for Construction Battalion]

sea bird, a bird frequenting the sea or coast.

sea biscuit, ship biscuit; hardtack.

sea·board (sē′bôrd′), *n.* 1. the line where land and sea meet; the seashore. **—adj.** 2. bordering on or adjoining the sea.

sea-born (sē′bôrn′), *adj.* born in or of the sea; produced in or by the sea.

sea-borne (sē′bôrn′), *adj.* conveyed by sea; carried on the sea.

sea bread, ship biscuit; hardtack.

sea bream, 1. any of a number of British, South African, or Australian marine sparoid food fishes, as the common sea bream, *Pagellus centrodontus,* of Europe. 2. any sparoid fish.

sea breeze, a thermally produced wind blowing from the cool ocean surface onto the adjoining warm land.

sea calf, the harbor seal.

sea captain, the captain or commanding officer of a ship.

sea·coast (sē′kōst′), *n.* the land immediately adjacent to the sea.

sea cow, 1. any sirenian, as the manatee, dugong, etc. 2. *Obs.* the hippopotamus.

sea cucumber, a holothurian.

sea devil, a manta ray.

sea dog, 1. a sailor, esp. one of long experience. 2. the harbor seal.

sea duck, any diving duck of the subfamily *Aythyinae,* including the scaups, goldeneyes, scoters, eiders, etc., found principally on salt water.

sea eagle, any of various eagles of the genus *Haliaetus* which feed on fish, esp. the **gray sea eagle,** *H. albicilla,* of the Old World and Greenland.

sea fan, any of certain anthozoans, esp. *Gorgonia flabellum* of the West Indies, in which the colony assumes a fanlike form.

sea·far·er (sē′fâr′ər), *n.* 1. a sailor. 2. a traveler on the sea.

sea·far·ing (sē′fâr′ĭng), *adj.* 1. that travels by sea. 2. following the sea as a calling. **—n.** 3. the business or calling of a sailor. 4. traveling by sea.

sea fight, a fight between ships at sea.

sea foam, 1. the foam of the sea. 2. meerschaum.

sea food, any salt-water fish or shellfish which is used for food.

sea-fowl (sē′foul′), *n.* a sea bird.

sea front, the side or edge of land and buildings bordering on the sea.

sea-girt (sē′gûrt′), *adj.* surrounded by the sea.

sea-go·ing (sē′gō′ĭng), *adj.* 1. designed or fit for going to sea, as a vessel. 2. going to sea; seafaring.

sea green, clear, light bluish green (the color of the sea on a clear day).

sea gull, a gull, esp. any of the marine species.

sea hog, a porpoise.

sea holly, the eryngo (plant), *Eryngium maritimum.*

sea horse, 1. a fish (genus *Hippocampus*) of the pipefish family, with a prehensile tail and a beaked head that is turned at right angles to the body. 2. a fabulous marine animal with the foreparts of a horse and the hinder parts of a fish. 3. a walrus.

sea-is·land (sē′ī′lənd), *adj.* 1. of a group of islands (**Sea Islands**) off South Carolina and Georgia. 2. denoting a long-staple variety of cotton grown on these islands and elsewhere, or the plant producing it.

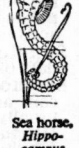

Sea horse, *Hippocampus hudsonius* (5 in. long)

sea kale, a broad-leaved, maritime cruciferous plant, *Crambe maritima,* of Europe, used as a potherb.

sea king, one of the piratical Scandinavian chiefs who ravaged the coasts of medieval Europe. [trans. of Icel. *sækonungr.* Cf. OE *sǣcyning*]

seal¹ (sēl), *n.* **1.** a device impressed on a piece of wax or the like, or an impression, wafer, etc., representing this, affixed to a document as evidence of authenticity or attestation. **2.** a stamp engraved with such a device. **3.** *Law.* a mark or symbol attached to a legal document and imparting a formal quality to it, originally defined as wax with an impression. **4.** a piece of wax or similar substance, affixed to a document, an envelope, a door, etc., which cannot be opened without breaking this. **5.** anything that effectively closes a thing. **6.** something for keeping a thing close or secret. **7.** a decorative stamp: *a Christmas seal.* **8.** a mark or the like serving as visible evidence of something. **9.** *Plumbing.* **a.** a small amount of water left standing in a trap to prevent the escape of foul air from below. **b.** the depth of the water between the dip and the overflow of a trap. **10. the seals,** *Brit.* the tokens or signs of public office. —*v.t.* **11.** to affix a seal to in authorization, confirmation, etc. **12.** to impress a seal upon as an evidence of legal or standard exactness, measure, quality, etc. **13.** to fasten with a seal, mucilage, etc. **14.** to close by any form of fastening that must be broken before access can be had. **15.** to fasten or close as if by a seal. **16.** to decide irrevocably: *to seal someone's fate.* **17.** to grant under one's seal or authority, as a pardon. **18.** *Mormon Ch.* to make forever binding, to give in marriage, or to join in family ties, according to the principle of marriage for eternity. **19.** *Elect.* to bring (a plug and jack or socket, etc.) into locked or fully aligned position. [ME *seel,* t. OF, g. LL *sigellum,* r. L *sigillum*] —**seal′-a-ble,** *adj.*

Seal of the United States

seal² (sēl), *n.,* *pl.* **seals,** (*esp. collectively*) **seal** for 1. **1.** any of the marine carnivores of the suborder *Pinnipedia,* including the eared or fur seals, as the sea lion and fur seal of commerce, and the earless or hair seals, of which the **harbor seal,** *Phoca vitulina,* is best known. **2.** the skin of the seal. **3.** leather made from it. **4.** the fur of the fur seal; sealskin. **5.** a fur used as a substitute for sealskin. —*v.i.* **6.** to hunt or take seals. [ME *sele,* OE *seolh,* c. Icel. *selr*]

sea lavender, 1. an Old World plumbaginaceous plant, *Limonium vulgare,* a seashore perennial bearing one-sided spikes of small lavender-colored flowers. **2.** some similar plant of the same genus, as *Limonium carolinianum* of the eastern coast of North America.

sea lawyer, *Colloq.* an argumentative or querulous sailor.

seal brown, rich, dark brown suggestive of dressed and dyed sealskin.

sea leather, the skin of sharks, porpoises, dogfishes, etc., prepared to be used for the same purposes as ordinary leather.

sealed book, something past understanding.

sealed orders, sealed written orders, not to be opened until after leaving port, given to the commander of a vessel to instruct him where to proceed on a voyage.

sea legs, *Colloq.* ability to walk with steadiness or ease on a rolling ship.

seal-er¹ (sē′lər), *n.* an officer appointed to examine and test weights and measures, and to set a stamp upon such as are true to the standard. [f. SEAL¹ + -ER¹]

seal-er² (sē′lər), *n.* a person or vessel engaged in hunting seals. [f. SEAL² + -ER¹]

seal-er-y (sē′lə rĭ), *n., pl.* **-eries. 1.** the occupation of hunting or taking seals. **2.** a place where seals are caught.

sea lettuce, any seaweed of the genus *Ulva,* a green alga with large leaflike blades.

sea level, the horizontal plane or level corresponding to the surface of the sea when halfway between mean high and low water.

sea lily, a crinoid.

sealing wax, a resinous preparation, soft when heated, used for sealing letters, etc.

sea lion, any of various eared seals of large size, as *Eumetopias jubata* of the northern Pacific, and *Zalophus californianus* of the Pacific coast of North America.

seal ring, a finger ring bearing a seal.

seal-skin (sēl′skĭn′), *n.* **1.** the skin of the seal. **2.** the skin or fur of the fur seal, dressed for use. **3.** a garment or article made of this fur. **4.** the hide of the seal prepared for leather bags, etc.

Northern Pacific sea lion,
Eumetopias jubata
(Adult male, 10 ft. or more long,
female smaller)

sea lungwort, a boraginaceous herb, *Mertensia maritima,* growing on northern seacoasts.

Sea-ly-ham terrier (sē′lĭ hăm′, -lɏ əm), a terrier of Welsh origin having short legs, square jaws, and a shaggy white coat with markings on the head and ears.

Sealyham terrier
(10 in. high at the shoulder)

seam (sēm), *n.* **1.** the line formed by sewing together pieces of cloth, leather, or the like. **2.** any line between abutting edges; a crack or fissure; a groove. **3.** any linear indentation or marks, as a wrinkle or a scar. **4.** *Knitting.* a line of stitches formed by purling. **5.** *Geol.* a comparatively thin stratum; a bed, as of coal. —*v.t.* **6.** to join with a seam; sew the seams of. **7.** to furrow; mark with wrinkles, scars, etc. **8.** *Knitting.* to knit with or in a seam. —*v.i.* **9.** to become cracked, fissured, or furrowed. **10.** *Knitting.* to make a seam. [ME *seme,* OE *sēam,* c. G *saum;* akin to SEW] —**seam′-er,** *n.*

sea-maid (sē′mād′), *n. Poetic.* **1.** a mermaid. **2.** a goddess or nymph of the sea.

sea-man (sē′mən), *n., pl.* **-men. 1.** one whose occupation it is to assist in the navigation of a ship; a sailor; specif. one below the rank of officer. **2.** *U.S. Navy.* an enlisted man assigned to the care of a ship, operation of its guns, etc. —**Syn. 1.** See **sailor.**

sea-man-like (sē′mən līk′), *adj.* like or befitting a seaman; showing good seamanship.

sea-man-ship (sē′mən shĭp′), *n.* the knowledge of and skill in all things pertaining to the operation, management, safety, and maintenance of ships and vessels other than in the engineering department.

sea-mark (sē′märk′), *n.* a conspicuous object on land, visible from the sea, and serving to guide or warn mariners.

sea mew, a sea gull, esp. a common European species, *Larus canus.*

sea moss, *Zool.* a polyzoan.

sea mouse, any of various large marine annelids of the genus *Aphrodite* and allied genera, of a somewhat mouselike appearance, due to a covering of long, fine, hairlike setae.

seam-stress (sēm′strĭs *or, esp. Brit.,* sĕm′-), *n.* a woman whose occupation is sewing. Also, **sempstress.**

seam-y (sē′mĭ), *adj.,* **seamier, seamiest. 1.** least pleasing or favorable; worst: *the seamy side of life.* **2.** having or showing seams; of the nature of a seam. —**seam′i-ness,** *n.*

Sean-ad Eir-eann (săn′äd âr′ən), *Irish.* the Senate of Eire. See **Oireachtas.**

sé-ance (sā′äns; *Fr.* sĕ äns′), *n.* **1.** a meeting of spiritualists seeking to receive communications from spirits. **2.** session. [t. F: a sitting, der. OF *seoir* (g. L *sedēre*) sit]

sea onion, 1. a liliaceous plant, *Urginea maritima,* of Mediterranean regions, yielding medicinal squill. **2.** the little spring squill, *Scilla verna,* of the Isle of Wight.

sea otter, a marine otter, *En-hydra lutris,* of the shores of the northern Pacific, with a very valuable fur.

sea pen, a coelenterate consisting of a central fleshy axis bearing fleshy lateral leaves provided with small polyps, exemplified by *Pennatula* and related forms.

sea-plane (sē′plān′), *n.* a hydroplane for use over the sea, esp. one provided with floats rather than a boatlike underpart.

Sea otter, *Enhydra lutris*
(Total length ab. 4 ft.,
tail ab. 1 ft.)

sea-port (sē′pōrt′), *n.* **1.** a port or harbor providing accommodation for seagoing vessels. **2.** a town or city at such a place.

sea power, 1. a nation having an important navy or great influence on the sea. **2.** naval strength.

sea purse, the horny egg case of certain rays and sharks.

sea-quake (sē′kwāk′), *n.* an agitation of the sea due to a submarine eruption or earthquake.

sear¹ (sĭr), *v.t.* **1.** to burn or char the surface of. **2.** to mark with a branding iron. **3.** to burn or scorch injuriously or painfully. **4.** to harden, or make callous or unfeeling. **5.** to dry up or wither. **6.** to brown the surface of (meat) by a brief application of high heat. —*v.i.* **7.** to become dry or wither, as vegetation. [ME *sere(n),* OE *sēarian,* der. *sēar* dry. See SEAR, adj.] —*n.* **8.** a mark or the like made by searing. [n. use of v.] —*adj.* **9.** *Chiefly Poetic.* dry or withered. [ME *sere,* OE *sēar,* c. D *zoor*] —**Syn. 1.** See **burn¹.**

sear² (sĭr), *n.* a pivoted piece in the firing mechanism of small arms which holds the hammer at full cock or half cock. [t. F: m. *serre* lock, grasp, der. *serrer* to grasp, hold, ult. g. LL *serāre* to bar, bolt (der. L *sera* bar), b. with *serrāre* to saw (der. *serra* saw)]

sea raven, a large marine fish of the genus *Hemitripterus,* as *H. americanus,* common on the northern Atlantic coast of America.

search (sûrch), *v.t.* **1.** to go or look through carefully in seeking to find something; explore. **2.** to examine (a person) for concealed objects by going through his pockets or the like. **3.** to probe (a wound, etc.). **4.** (of wind, cold, gunfire, etc.) to pierce or penetrate. **5.** to bring or find (out) by a search: *to search out all the facts.*

—*v.i.* **6.** to seek; make examination or investigation. —*n.* **7.** act of searching; careful examination or investigation. **8.** the searching of a neutral vessel, or the examining of its papers, cargo, etc., as at sea, by officers of a belligerent state, in order to verify its nationality and ascertain whether it carries contraband, etc. [ME *serch(en)*, t. OF: m. *cerchier*, g. LL *circāre*, der. L *circus* circle] —**search/a·ble,** *adj.* —**search/er,** *n.*

search·ing (sûr/chĭng), *adj.* **1.** examining carefully or thoroughly. **2.** keenly observant; penetrating, as the eyes, gaze, etc. **3.** piercing or sharp, as the wind, etc. —**search/ing·ly,** *adv.*

search·light (sûrch/līt/), *n.* **1.** a device, usually consisting of a light and reflector, for throwing a beam of light in any direction. **2.** a beam of light so thrown.

search warrant, *Law.* a court order authorizing the searching of a house, etc., as for stolen goods.

sea robber, pirate.

sea robin, any of various gurnards (fishes), esp. certain American species of the genus *Prionotus*.

sea room, space at sea free from obstruction in which a ship can be easily maneuvered or navigated.

sea rover, **1.** a pirate. **2.** a pirate ship.

sea·scape (sē/skāp/), *n.* a view or picture of the sea.

sea serpent, an enormous imaginary snakelike or dragonlike marine animal.

sea shell, the shell of any marine mollusk.

sea·shore (sē/shôr/), *n.* **1.** land along the sea or ocean. **2.** *Law.* the ground between the ordinary high-water and low-water marks.

sea·sick (sē/sĭk/), *adj.* affected with seasickness.

sea·sick·ness (sē/sĭk/nĭs), *n.* nausea or other physical derangement caused by the motion of a vessel at sea.

sea·side (sē/sīd/), *n.* **1.** the seashore; the seacoast. —*adj.* **2.** situated at, or pertaining to, the seaside.

sea snake, any of the venomous marine snakes with a finlike tail, constituting the family *Hydrophidae*.

sea·son (sē/zən), *n.* **1.** one of the four periods of the year (spring, summer, autumn, and winter), astronomically beginning each at an equinox or solstice, but geographically at different dates in different climates. **2.** a period of the year characterized by particular conditions of weather, temperature, etc. **3.** the period of the year when something is best or available: *the oyster season.* **4.** a period of the year marked by certain conditions, festivities, activities, etc.: *the baseball season, a dull season in trade.* **5.** any period or time. **6.** a suitable, proper, fitting, or right time. **7. in good season,** sufficiently early. **8. in season, a.** in the time or state for use, eating, hunting, etc. **b.** at the right time; opportunely. **9. out of season, a.** not in the time or state for use, eating, hunting, etc. **b.** not at the right time. —*v.t.* **10.** to heighten or improve the flavor of (food) by adding condiments, spices, herbs, or the like. **11.** to give relish or a certain character to: *conversation seasoned with wit.* **12.** to mature, ripen, or condition by exposure to suitable conditions or treatment. **13.** to dry and harden (timber) by due process. **14.** to accustom or harden: *troops seasoned by battle.* —*v.i.* **15.** to become seasoned, matured, hardened, or the like. [ME *seson(e)*, t. OF: m. *seson*, g. s. L *satio* (time of) sowing] —**sea/son·er,** *n.*

sea·son·a·ble (sē/zən ə bəl), *adj.* **1.** suitable to the season: *seasonable weather.* **2.** timely; opportune. **3.** early. —**sea/son·a·ble·ness,** *n.* —**sea/son·a·bly,** *adv.* —**Syn. 2.** See **opportune.**

sea·son·al (sē/zən əl), *adj.* pertaining to or dependent on the seasons of the year or some particular season; periodical: *seasonal work.* —**sea/son·al·ly,** *adv.*

sea·son·ing (sē/zən ĭng), *n.* something that seasons, esp. salt, spices, herbs, or other condiments.

Sea·sons (sē/zənz), *n.* **The,** an oratorio (1801) by Haydn.

season ticket, a ticket good for a period of time usually at a reduced rate.

sea squirt, an ascidian; tunicate.

seat¹ (sēt), *n.* **1.** something for sitting on, as a chair or bench; the place on or in which one sits. **2.** the part of a chair or the like on which one sits. **3.** the part of the body on which one sits. **4.** the part of the garment covering it. **5.** manner of sitting, as on horseback. **6.** that on which the base of anything rests. **7.** the base itself. **8.** the throne or authority of a king, bishop, etc. **9.** a space for a spectator in a theater or the like. **10.** right of admittance to such a space, esp. as indicated by ticket. **11.** a right to sit as a member in a legislative or similar body. **12.** a right to the privileges of membership in a stock exchange or the like. —*v.t.* **13.** to place on a seat or seats; cause to sit down. **14.** to find seats for; accommodate with seats: *a hall that seats a thousand persons.* **15.** to put a seat (on a chair, into a garment, etc.). **16.** to put in a position of authority or in a legislative body. [ME *sete*, t. Scand.; cf. Icel. *sæti*, c. G *gesäss*] —**seat/er,** *n.*

seat² (sēt), *n.* **1.** a place in which something prevails or is established: *a seat of learning.* **2.** established place or center, as of government. **3.** site, location, or locality. **4.** abode or residence. —*v.t.* **5.** to fix in a particular place. [ME *sete*, OE *sǣte* house, c. OHG *sāza*]

sea tangle, any of various seaweeds, esp. of the genus *Laminaria*.

seat·ing (sē/tĭng), *n.* **1.** act of furnishing with seats. **2.** the arrangement of the seats in a building, etc. **3.** material for seats, esp. upholstery. **4.** seat¹ (def. 5).

SEATO (sē/tō), *n.* Southeast Asia Treaty Organization.

sea trout, **1.** any of various species of trout found in salt water, as the salmon trout, *Salmo trutta.* **2.** any of several fishes of the genus *Cynoscion*.

Se·at·tle (sē ăt/əl), *n.* a seaport in W Washington, on Puget Sound. 557,087 (1960).

sea urchin, any echinoderm of the class *Echinoidea*, comprising marine animals having a more or less globular or discoid form, and a spine-bearing shell composed of many calcareous plates.

sea wall, a strong wall or embankment to prevent the encroachments of the sea, act as a breakwater, etc.

sea·wan (sē/wən), *n.* beads, usually unstrung, made from shells, used by North American Indians as money. Also, **sewan.** [t. Algonquian (Narragansett): m. *siwan* scattered, der. *siwen* he scatters]

sea·ward (sē/wərd), *adv.* **1.** Also, **sea/wards.** toward the sea. —*adj.* **2.** facing or tending toward the sea: *their seaward course.* **3.** coming from the sea, as a wind. —*n.* **4.** the direction toward the sea or away from the land.

sea·ware (sē/wâr/), *n.* seaweed, esp. coarse, large seaweed, used for manure, etc.

sea·way (sē/wā/), *n.* **1.** a way over the sea. **2.** the open sea. **3.** the progress of a ship through the waves. **4.** a rough sea.

sea·weed (sē/wēd/), *n.* **1.** any plant or plants growing in the ocean. **2.** a marine alga.

sea·wor·thy (sē/wûr/t͟hē), *adj.* (of a ship) adequately constructed and equipped to sail at sea. —**sea/wor/thi·ness,** *n.*

sea wrack, seaweed, esp. of the larger kinds cast up on the shore.

se·ba·ceous (sĭ bā/shəs), *adj. Physiol.* **1.** pertaining to, of the nature of, or resembling tallow or fat; fatty; greasy. **2.** secreting a fatty substance. [t. NL: m. *sebāceus*, der. L *sēbum* tallow]

sebaceous glands, any of the cutaneous glands which secrete oily matter for lubricating hair and skin. See diag. under **hair.**

se·bac·ic acid (sĭ băs/ĭk, -bā/sĭk), *Chem.* a white crystalline dibasic acid, $C_{10}H_{18}O_4$. [alteration of earlier SEBACEOUS (*acid*), r. *-eous* with *-ic*]

Se·bas·to·pol (sĭ băs/tə pōl/), *n.* Sevastopol.

se·bif·er·ous (sĭ bĭf/ər əs), *adj. Bot.* producing vegetable wax or tallow. [f. *sebi-* (comb. form repr. L *sēbum* tallow, grease) + -FEROUS]

seb·or·rhe·a (sĕb/ə rē/ə), *n. Pathol.* an excessive and morbid discharge from the sebaceous glands. Also, **seb/or·rhoe/a.** [NL: f. *sebo-* (comb. form repr. L *sēbum* grease) + -*rrhea* -RRHEA]

se·bum (sē/bəm), *n. Physiol.* the fatty secretion of the sebaceous glands. [t. L: tallow, grease]

sec (sĕk), *adj. French.* (of wines) dry; not sweet.

SEC, Securities and Exchange Commission.

sec., 1. secant. **2.** second. **3.** secondary. **4.** secretary. **5.** section. **6.** sector. **7.** secundum.

se·cant (sē/kənt, -kănt), *n.* **1.** *Geom.* an intersecting line. **2.** *Trig.* **a.** (orig.) a line from the center of a circle through one extremity of an arc to the tangent from the other extremity. **b.** the ratio of the length of this line to that of the radius of the circle. —*adj.* **3.** cutting or intersecting, as one line or surface in relation to another. [t. L: s. *secans*, ppr., cutting]

Secant
Ratio of AB
to AD, secant
of angle A;
AB, secant of
arc CD

se·cede (sĭ sēd/), *v.i.,* **-ceded, -ceding.** to withdraw formally from an alliance or association, as from a political or religious organization. [t. L: m.s. *sēcēdere* go back, withdraw] —**se·ced/er,** *n.*

se·cern·ent (sĭ sûr/nənt), *adj. Physiol.* secreting. [t. L: s. *sēcernens*, ppr., separating]

se·ces·sion (sĭ sĕsh/ən), *n.* **1.** act of seceding. **2.** (*often cap.*) the attempted withdrawal from the Union of eleven Southern States in 1860–61, which brought on the Civil War. [t. L: s. *sēcessio*] —**se·ces/sion·al,** *adj.*

se·ces·sion·ist (sĭ sĕsh/ən ĭst), *n.* one who secedes or who favors secession. —**se·ces/sion·ism,** *n.*

Seck·el (sĕk/əl), *n. Hort.* a small, high-quality pear. [named after the grower, a Pennsylvania farmer]

se·clude (sĭ klōōd/), *v.t.,* **-cluded, -cluding.** to shut off or keep apart; place in or withdraw into solitude. [t. L: m.s. *sēclūdere*]

se·clud·ed (sĭ klōō/dĭd), *adj.* shut off or separated from others: *a secluded place.* —**se·clud/ed·ly,** *adv.* —**se·clud/ed·ness,** *n.*

se·clu·sion (sĭ klōō/zhən), *n.* **1.** act of secluding. **2.** state of being secluded; retirement; solitude: *he sought seclusion in a little room in the attic, but to no avail.* **3.** a secluded place.

se·clu·sive (sĭ klōō/sĭv), *adj.* **1.** tending to seclude. **2.** affecting seclusion. —**se·clu/sive·ly,** *adv.* —**se·clu/sive·ness,** *n.*

sec·ond¹ (sĕk/ənd), *adj.* **1.** next after the first in order, place, time, rank, value, quality, etc. (the ordinal of two). **2.** *Music.* the lower of two parts for the same instrument or voice: *second alto, second trombone.* **3.** other or another: *a second Solomon.* —*n.* **4.** one who or that which is second. **5.** one who aids or supports another; an assistant; a backer. **6.** one who acts as aid to a principal in a prize fight. **7.** one who acts as representative of and aid to a principal in a duel. **8.** *Auto.* the second normal forward gear ratio. **9.** *Music.* **a.** a tone on the next degree from a given tone. **b.** the interval between such tones. **c.** the harmonic combination of such tones. **d.** the lower of two parts in a piece of concerted music. **e.** a voice or instrument rendering such a part. **f.** (in popular usage) an alto. **10.** (*pl.*) *Com.* products or goods below the first or perfect quality. —*v.t.* **11.** to support, back up, or assist. **12.** to further or advance, as aims. **13.** to express support of (a motion, etc.) as a necessary preliminary to further discussion of the motion or to a vote on it. **14.** to act as second to (a pugilist, etc.). —*adv.* **15.** in the second place, group, etc. [ME *seconde*, t. F, t. L: m. *secundus*] —**sec'ond·er,** *n.* —**sec'ond·ly,** *adv.*

sec·ond² (sĕk'ənd), *n.* **1.** the sixtieth part of a minute. **2.** *Geom., etc.* the sixtieth part of a minute of a degree (often represented by the sign ''; thus, 12° 10′ 30′′ means 12 degrees, 10 minutes, and 30 seconds). **3.** a moment or instant. [ME *seconde*, t. F, t. ML: m. *secunda* (*minūta*), i.e., the result of the second sexagesimal division of the hour]

Second Advent. See **advent** (def. 4). —**Second Adventist.**

sec·ond·ar·y (sĕk'ən dĕr'Y), *adj., n., pl.* **-aries.** —*adj.* **1.** next after the first in order, place, time, importance, etc. **2.** belonging or pertaining to a second order, division, stage, period, rank, or the like. **3.** derived or derivative; not primary or original. **4.** of minor importance; subordinate; auxiliary. **5.** *Educ.* noting or pertaining to secondary schools. **6.** *Chem.* **a.** involving, or obtained from replacement of, two atoms or radicals. **b.** denoting or containing a carbon atom united to two other carbon atoms in a chain or ring molecule. **7.** *Elect.* noting or pertaining to the induced circuit, coil, or current in an induction coil or the like. **8.** *Geol.* noting or pertaining to a mineral produced from another mineral by decay, alteration, or the like. **9.** *Gram.* **a.** (of derivation) with an underlying element which is itself further analyzable, as *likeably* composed of *likeable* + *ly,* but the first element *likeable* is further analyzable into *like* + *able.* **b.** (of Latin, Greek, Sanskrit tenses) having reference to past time only. **10.** *Ornith.* pertaining to any of a set of flight feathers on the second segment (that corresponding to the forearm in higher vertebrates) of a bird's wing. —*n.* **11.** one who or that which is secondary. **12.** a subordinate; a delegate or deputy. **13.** *Elect.* a secondary circuit or coil. **14.** *Ornith.* a secondary feather. [ME, t. L: m.s. *secundārius*] —**sec'ond·ar'i·ly,** *adv.*

secondary accent, *Phonet.* a stress accent weaker than primary accent but stronger than lack of stress.

secondary group, *Sociol.* a group of people with whom one's contacts are detached and impersonal.

secondary school, a high school or a school of corresponding grade, ranking between the lower schools and the college or university.

secondary seventh chord, *Music.* a chord formed by superposition of three thirds upon any degree of the scale except the dominant.

second childhood, senility; dotage.

sec·ond-class (sĕk'ənd kläs', -kläs'), *adj.* **1.** of or belonging to the second class. **2.** second-rate; inferior.

Second Coming, Second Advent.

se·conde (sĭ kônd'; Fr. səgôⁿd'), *n.* *Fencing.* the second of eight defensive positions. [t. F, fem. of *second* SECOND¹]

second fiddle, a minor or secondary part: *to play second fiddle.*

second growth, the growth that follows the destruction of virgin forest.

sec·ond-hand (sĕk'ənd hănd'), *adj.* **1.** obtained from another; not original: *second-hand knowledge.* **2.** previously used or owned: *second-hand clothes.* **3.** dealing in previously used goods: *a second-hand bookseller.*

second lieutenant. See **lieutenant** (def. 1b).

second mortgage, a mortgage that is next in priority to a first mortgage.

second nature, habit, tendency, etc. so long practiced that it is inalterably fixed in one's character: *correcting the English of others is second nature to him.*

se·con·do (sĕ kŏn'dō), *n., pl.* **-di** (-dē). *Music.* **1.** the second or lower part in a duet, esp. in piano duets. **2.** its performer. [It., g. L *secundus*]

second person, *Gram.* See **person** (def. 13a).

sec·ond-rate (sĕk'ənd rāt'), *adj.* **1.** of the second rate or class, as to size, quality, etc. **2.** inferior; mediocre: *a second-rate person.* —**sec'ond-rat'er,** *n.*

Second Reich. See **Reich** (def. 3).

second sight, a supposed faculty of seeing distant objects and future events; clairvoyance.

se·cre·cy (sē'krə sY), *n., pl.* **-cies.** **1.** state of being secret or concealed: *a meeting in strict secrecy.* **2.** privacy; retirement; seclusion. **3.** ability to keep a secret. **4.** secretive habits; lack of openness. [f. obs. *secre(e)* SECRET + -CY; r. ME *secretee,* f. *secre* secret + -*tee* -TY²]

se·cret (sē'krYt), *adj.* **1.** done, made, or conducted without the knowledge of others: *secret negotiations.* **2.** kept from the knowledge of any but the initiated: *a secret sign.* **3.** faithful or cautious in keeping secrets; close-mouthed; reticent. **4.** designed to escape observation or knowledge: *a secret drawer.* **5.** retired or secluded, as a place. **6.** beyond ordinary human understanding. —*n.* **7.** something secret, hidden, or concealed. **8.** a mystery: *the secrets of nature.* **9.** the reason or explanation, not immediately or generally apparent. **10.** a method or art known only to the initiated or the few: *the secret of happiness.* **11.** (*cap.*) *Liturgy.* a variable prayer in the Roman and other Latin liturgies, said inaudibly by the celebrant after the offertory, etc., and immediately before the preface. **12.** in secret, secretly. [ME *secrete,* t, F, t. L: m. *sēcrētus* (adj.), orig. pp., divided off] —**se'cret·ly,** *adv.*

sec·re·tar·i·at (sĕk'rə târ'Y ət), *n.* **1.** the officials or office entrusted with maintaining records and performing secretarial duties, esp. for an international organization. **2.** a group or department of secretaries. **3.** the place where a secretary transacts business, preserves records, etc. [t. F, t. ML: s. *sēcrētāriātus* the office of a secretary. See SECRETARY]

sec·re·tar·y (sĕk'rə tĕr'Y), *n., pl.* **-taries.** **1.** a person who conducts correspondence, keeps records, etc., for an individual or an organization. **2.** See **private secretary.** **3.** an officer of state charged with the superintendence and management of a particular department of government: *Secretary of State.* **4.** a piece of furniture for use as a writing desk. **5.** a desk with bookshelves on top of it. [t ML: m.s. *sēcrētārius* confidential officer, der. L *sēcrētum* (something) secret. See SECRET] —**sec·re·tar·i·al** (sĕk'-rə târ'Y əl), *adj.* —**sec're·tar'y·ship',** *n.*

secretary bird, a large, long-legged raptorial bird, *Sagittarius serpentarius,* of Africa, which feeds on reptiles (so called from its crest, which suggests pens stuck over the ear).

sec·re·tar·y-gen·er·al (sĕk'rə tĕr'Y jĕn'ər əl), *n., pl.* **secretaries-general,** the head of a secretariat.

Secretary bird,
Sagittarius serpentarius
(Total length 4 ft., 4 ft. high)

se·crete (sĭ krēt'), *v.t.* **-creted, -creting.** **1.** *Biol.* to separate off, prepare, or elaborate from the blood, as in the physiological process of secretion. **2.** to hide or conceal; keep secret. [t. L: m.s. *sēcrētus,* pp., put apart] —**se·cre'tor,** *n.* —**Syn.** **2.** See **hide¹.**

se·cre·tin (sĭ krē'tYn), *n.* *Biochem.* a hormone produced in the small intestine which activates the pancreas to secrete pancreatic juice.

se·cre·tion (sĭ krē'shən), *n.* **1.** the process or function of an animal body, executed in the glands, by which various substances, as bile, milk, etc., are separated and elaborated from the blood. **2.** the product secreted. [t. L: s. *sēcrētio*] —**se·cre·tion·ar·y** (sĭ krē'shə nĕr'Y), *adj.*

se·cre·tive (sĭ krē'tYv), *adj.* **1.** having or showing a disposition to secrecy; reticent: *he seemed secretive about his new job.* **2.** secretory. —**se·cre'tive·ly,** *adv.* —**se·cre'tive·ness,** *n.*

se·cre·to·ry (sĭ krē'tə rY), *adj., n., pl.* **-ries.** —*adj.* **1.** pertaining to secretion. **2.** performing the office of secretion. —*n.* **3.** a secretory organ, vessel, or the like.

secret service, **1.** the branch of governmental service charged with secret investigation, etc., esp. (*caps.*) the branch of the U.S. Treasury Department with the main function of discovering and punishing counterfeiting and of protecting the President. **2.** official service of a secret nature; espionage.

secret society, a society whose members use secret oaths, passwords, rites, etc.

sect (sĕkt), *n.* **1.** a body of persons adhering to a particular religious faith; a religious denomination. **2.** a group regarded as deviating from the general religious tradition or as heretical. **3.** (in the sociology of religion) a Christian denomination characterized by insistence on strict qualifications for membership, as distinguished from the more inclusive groups called churches. [ME *secte,* t. L: m. *secta* following]

-sect, a word element meaning "cut," as in *intersect.* [t. L: s. *sectus,* pp.]

sect., section.

sec·tar·i·an (sĕk târ'Y ən), *adj.* **1.** of or pertaining to sectaries or sects. **2.** confined or devoted to a particular sect. —*n.* **3.** a member of a sect. **4.** a bigoted adherent of a sect. [f. SECTARY + -AN]

sec·tar·i·an·ism (sĕk târ'Y ə nYz'əm), *n.* the spirit or tendencies of sectarians; adherence or excessive devotion to a particular sect, esp. in religion.

sec·tar·i·an·ize (sĕk târ'Y ə nīz'), *v.t.,* **-ized, -izing.** to make sectarian.

sec·ta·ry (sĕk'tə rY), *n., pl.* **-ries.** **1.** a member of a particular sect, esp. an adherent of a religious body regarded as heretical or schismatic. **2.** a Protestant of a nonconformist sect; esp. an Independent. **3.** one zealously devoted to a particular sect. [t. ML: m.s. *sectārius,* der. L *secta* sect]

sec·tile (sĕk′tĭl), *adj.* capable of being cut smoothly by a knife. [t. L, neut. of *sectilis*] —**sec·til/i·ty,** *n.*

sec·tion (sĕk′shən), *n.* **1.** a part cut off or separated. **2.** a distinct portion of a book, writing, or the like; a subdivision, as of a chapter; a division of a legal code. **3.** one of a number of parts that can be fitted together to make a whole: *sections of a fishing rod.* **4.** a distinct part of a country, community, class, or the like. **5.** (in most of the U.S. west of Ohio) one of the 36 numbered sections, each of one mile square, into which each township was divided in the public-land survey. **6.** act of cutting; separation by cutting. **7.** a thin slice of a tissue, mineral, or the like, as for microscopic examination. **8.** a representation of an object as it would appear if cut by a plane, showing the internal structure. **9.** *Mil.* **a.** a small unit, which may consist of two or more squads. **b. staff section,** one of the subdivisions of any staff. **10.** *Railroads.* **a.** a division of a sleeping car containing both an upper and a lower berth. **b.** a length of trackage, roadbed, signal equipment, etc., maintained by one crew. **c.** a train scheduled jointly with another or others. **11.** Also, **section mark.** a mark (§) used to denote a section of a book, chapter, or the like, or as a mark of reference to a footnote or the like. —*v.t.* **12.** to cut or divide into sections. **13.** to cut through so as to present a section. [t. L: s. *sectio* a cutting]

A

B C

Sections of a pipe
A, Longitudinal;
B, Cross or transverse;
C, Oblique

sec·tion·al (sĕk′shən əl), *adj.* **1.** pertaining to a particular section; local: *full of sectional pride.* **2.** composed of several independent sections. —**sec/tion·al·ly,** *adv.*
sec·tion·al·ism (sĕk′shən ə lĭz/əm), *n.* excessive regard for sectional or local interests; sectional spirit, prejudice, etc.
sec·tion·al·ize (sĕk′shən ə līz/), *v.t.,* **-ized, -izing. 1.** to render sectional. **2.** to divide into sections, esp. geographical sections. —**sec/tion·al·i·za/tion,** *n.*
section gang, *U.S.* a group of workmen who take care of a section of railroad track.
sec·tor (sĕk′tər), *n.* **1.** *Geom.* a plane figure bounded by two radii and the included arc of a circle, ellipse, or the like. **2.** a mathematical instrument consisting of two flat rulers hinged together at one end and bearing various scales. **3.** *Mil.* one of the sections of a forward combat area as divided for military operations, etc. —*v.t.* **4.** to divide into sectors. [t. LL, special use of L *sector* cutter]

D
B
C
DCB, Sector
of a circle

sec·u·lar (sĕk′yə lər), *adj.* **1.** of or pertaining to the world, or to things not religious, sacred, or spiritual; temporal; worldly. **2.** not pertaining to or connected with religion, as literature, music, etc. **3.** dealing with nonreligious subjects, or, esp., excluding religious instruction, as education, etc. **4.** (of members of the clergy) not belonging to a religious order (opposed to *regular*). **5.** occurring or celebrated once in an age or century: *the secular games of Rome.* **6.** going on from age to age; continuing through long ages. —*n.* **7.** a layman. **8.** one of the secular clergy. [t. L: m.s. *saeculāris* belonging to an age, LL worldly; r. ME *seculer,* t. OF] —**sec/u·lar·ly,** *adv.*
sec·u·lar·ism (sĕk′yə lə rĭz/əm), *n.* **1.** secular spirit or tendencies, esp. a system of political or social philosophy which rejects all forms of religious faith and worship. **2.** the view that public education and other matters of civil policy should be conducted without the introduction of a religious element. —**sec/u·lar·ist,** *n.* —**sec/u·lar·is/tic,** *adj.*
sec·u·lar·i·ty (sĕk′yə lăr/ə tĭ), *n., pl.* **-ties. 1.** secularism. **2.** worldliness. **3.** a secular matter.
sec·u·lar·ize (sĕk′yə lə rīz/), *v.t.,* **-ized, -izing. 1.** to make secular; separate from religious or spiritual connection or influences; make worldly or unspiritual; imbue with secularism. **2.** to change (clergy) from regular to secular. **3.** to transfer (property) from ecclesiastical to civil possession or use. —**sec/u·lar·i·za/tion,** *n.* —**sec/u·lar·iz/er,** *n.*
se·cund (sē′kŭnd, sĕk′ŭnd), *adj. Bot., Zool.* arranged on one side only; unilateral. [t. L: s. *secundus* following]
Se·cun·der·a·bad (sĭ kŭn/drä bäd/), *n.* a city, and former military cantonment, in central India adjacent to Hyderabad; now a part of that city. Also, **Sikandarabad.**
sec·un·dine (sĕk′ən dīn/, -dĭn), *n. Bot.* the inner integument of an ovule. [t. L: m. *secundīnae* (pl.) afterbirth]
se·cun·dum (sĭ kŭn/dəm), *prep. Latin.* according to.
se·cure (sĭ kyŏŏr′), *adj., v.,* **-cured, -curing.** —*adj.* **1.** free from or not exposed to danger; safe. **2.** not liable to fail, yield, become displaced, etc., as a support or a fastening. **3.** affording safety, as a place. **4.** in safe custody or keeping. **5.** free from care; without anxiety. **6.** sure; certain: *to be secure of victory.* **7.** that can be counted on: *victory is secure.* **8.** *Obs.* or *Rare.* overconfident. —*v.t.* **9.** to get hold or possession of; obtain. **10.** to make secure from danger or harm; make safe. **11.** to make secure or certain; ensure. **12.** to make firm or fast. **13.** to assure a creditor of payment by

the pledge or mortgaging of property. —*v.i.* **14.** to be safe; get security: *to secure against danger.* [t. L: m. s. *sēcūrus* free from care] —**se·cure/ly,** *adv.* —**se·cure/-ness,** *n.* —**se·cur/er,** *n.* —**Syn. 1.** See **safe. 9.** See **get.**
se·cu·ri·ty (sĭ kyŏŏr/ə tĭ), *n., pl.* **-ties. 1.** freedom from danger, risk, etc.; safety. **2.** freedom from care, apprehension, or doubt; confidence. **3.** overconfidence. **4.** something that secures or makes safe; a protection; a defense. **5.** an assurance; guarantee. **6.** *Law.* **a.** something given or deposited as surety for the fulfillment of a promise or an obligation, the payment of a debt, etc. **b.** one who becomes surety for another. **c.** an evidence of debt or of property, as a bond or a certificate of stock. **7.** (*usually pl.*) stocks and bonds. [ME, t. L: m.s. *sēcūritās*]
sec'y., secretary.
Se·da·li·a (sĭ dā′lĭ ə), *n.* a city in central Missouri. 23,874 (1960).
se·dan (sĭ dăn′), *n.* **1.** a closed automobile body seating four or more persons (including the driver) on two full-width seats, both in one compartment. **2.** sedan chair. [orig. uncert.; ? t. It., ult. der. L *sēdes* seat]
Se·dan (sĭ dăn′; *Fr.* sə dän′), *n.* a city in NE France, on the Meuse river: scene of the disastrous defeat of Napoleon III in the Franco–Prussian War, 1870. 17,637 (1954).
sedan chair, a portable wheelless vehicle for one person, borne on poles by two men, one before and one behind, much used during the 17th and 18th centuries.

Sedan chair

se·date (sĭ dāt′), *adj.* calm, quiet, or composed; sober; undisturbed by passion or excitement. [t. L: m.s. *sēdātus,* pp., calmed] —**se·date/ly,** *adv.* —**se·date/ness,** *n.* —**Syn.** See staid. —**Ant.** frivolous.
sed·a·tive (sĕd′ə tĭv), *adj.* **1.** tending to calm or soothe. **2.** *Med.* allaying irritability or excitement; assuaging pain; lowering functional activity. —*n.* **3.** a sedative agent or remedy.
se de·fen·den·do (sē dĕf/ĕn dĕn/dō), *Law.* defending himself (a plea in a homicide trial). [L]
sed·en·tar·y (sĕd′ən tĕr/ĭ), *adj.* **1.** characterized by or requiring a sitting posture: *a sedentary occupation.* **2.** accustomed to sit much or take little exercise. **3.** *Chiefly Zool.* **a.** abiding in one place; not migratory. **b.** referring to animals that move about but little or are permanently attached. [t. L: m. *sedentārius*] —**sed/en·tar/i·ly,** *adv.* —**sed/en·tar/i·ness,** *n.*
sedge (sĕj), *n.* **1.** any of various rushlike or grasslike plants constituting the cyperaceous genus *Carex,* growing in wet places. **2.** any cyperaceous plant. [ME *segge,* OE *secg;* akin to SAW¹; appar. so named because of its sawlike edges]
sedged (sĕjd), *adj.* **1.** made of sedge. **2.** abounding or bordered with sedge: *sedged brooks.*
Sedge·moor (sĕj′mŏŏr/), *n.* a broad plain in SW England: Monmouth's final defeat, 1685.
sedg·y (sĕj′ĭ), *adj.* **1.** abounding, covered, or bordered with sedge. **2.** of or like sedge.
se·di·le (sĭ dī/lē), *n., pl.* **sedilia** (sĭ dĭl/ĭ ə). *Eccles.* one of the seats (usually three) on the south side of the chancel, often recessed, for the use of the officiating clergy. [t. L: seat]
sed·i·ment (sĕd′ə mənt), *n.* **1.** matter which settles to the bottom of a liquid; lees; dregs. **2.** *Geol.* mineral or organic matter deposited by water, air, or ice. [t. F, t. L: s. *sedimentum* a settling]
sed·i·men·ta·ry (sĕd/ə mĕn′tə rĭ), *adj.* **1.** of, pertaining to, or of the nature of sediment. **2.** *Geol.* formed by deposition of sediment, as rocks. Also, **sed/i·men/tal.** —**sed/i·men/ta·ri·ly,** *adv.*
sed·i·men·ta·tion (sĕd/ə mĕn tā′shən), *n.* the deposition or accumulation of sediment.
se·di·tion (sĭ dĭsh′ən), *n.* **1.** incitement of discontent or rebellion against the government; action or language promoting such discontent or rebellion. **2.** *Archaic.* rebellious disorder. [ME *sedicion,* t. L: m.s. *sēditio,* lit., a going apart] —**Syn. 1.** See **treason.**
se·di·tion·ar·y (sĭ dĭsh′ə nĕr′ĭ), *adj., n., pl.* **-aries.** —*adj.* **1.** seditious. —*n.* **2.** one guilty of sedition.
se·di·tious (sĭ dĭsh′əs), *adj.* **1.** of, pertaining to, or of the nature of sedition. **2.** given to or guilty of sedition. —**se·di/tious·ly,** *adv.* —**se·di/tious·ness,** *n.*
se·duce (sĭ dūs′, -dōōs′), *v.t.,* **-duced, -ducing. 1.** to lead astray; entice away from duty or rectitude; corrupt. **2.** to induce (a woman) to surrender her chastity. **3.** to lead or draw away, as from principles, faith, or allegiance. **4.** to win over; entice. [late ME t. L: m.s. *sēdūcere* lead aside] —**se·duc/er,** *n.* —**se·duc/i·ble,** *adj.* —**Syn. 1.** beguile, inveigle. See **tempt.**
se·duc·tion (sĭ dŭk′shən), *n.* **1.** act of seducing. **2.** condition of being seduced. **3.** a means of seducing; an enticement. Also, **se·duce/ment.**
se·duc·tive (sĭ dŭk′tĭv), *adj.* tending to seduce; enticing; captivating: *a seductive smile.* —**se·duc/tive·ly,** *adv.* —**se·duc/tive·ness,** *n.*
se·du·li·ty (sĭ dū/lə tĭ, -dōō/-), *n.* sedulous quality.
sed·u·lous (sĕj′ə ləs), *adj.* **1.** diligent in application or attention; persevering. **2.** persistently or carefully

---

b., blend of, blended; c., cognate with; d., dialect, dialectal; der., derived from; f., formed from; g., going back to; m., modification of; r., replacing; s., stem of; t., taken from; ?, perhaps. See the full key on inside cover.

maintained; *sedulous flattery.* [t. L: m. *sēdulus* busy, careful] **—sed/u·lous·ly,** *adv.* **—sed/u·lous·ness,** *n.*

se·dum (sē/dəm), *n.* any plant of the crassulaceous genus *Sedum,* which comprises fleshy, chiefly perennial, herbs with (usually) yellow, white, or pink flowers. Cf. **stonecrop.** [NL, special use of L *sedum* houseleek]

see¹ (sē), *v.,* **saw, seen, seeing.** —*v.t.* **1.** to perceive with the eyes; look at. **2.** to view; visit or attend as a spectator: *to go to see a show.* **3.** to perceive mentally; discern; understand: *to see the point of an argument.* **4.** to ascertain, learn, or find out: *see who it is.* **5.** to have knowledge or experience of: *to see service.* **6.** to make sure: *see that the work is done.* **7.** to meet and converse with. **8.** to receive as a visitor. **9.** to attend or escort: *to see someone home.* **10.** *Poker, etc.* to meet (a bet), or meet the bet of (a better), by staking an equal sum. —*v.i.* **11.** to have the power of sight. **12.** to understand; discern. **13.** to give attention or care: *see to it that the work is done.* **14.** to find out; make inquiry: *go and see for yourself.* **15.** to consider; think; deliberate. **16.** *Obs. except imperative.* to look. **17. see after,** to attend to; take care of. **18. see through,** to penetrate (a disguise, false appearance, etc.); detect (an imposture, etc.). [ME; OE *sēon,* c. D *zien,* G *sehen,* Icel. *sjā,* Goth. *saihwan*] **—Syn. 1.** See **watch.**

see² (sē), *n. Eccles.* the seat, center of authority, office, or jurisdiction of a bishop. [ME *se,* t. OF, var. (influenced by L) of *sie, sied,* ult. g. L *sēdes*]

see-catch (sē/kăch/), *n.* the adult male of the fur seal, *Callorhinus alascanus,* of Alaska.

seed (sēd), *n., pl.* **seeds, seed,** *v.* —*n.* **1.** the propagative part of a plant, esp. as preserved for growing a new crop, including ovules, tubers, bulbs, etc. **2.** such parts collectively. **3.** any small, seedlike part or fruit, as a grain of wheat. **4.** the germ or beginning of anything: *the seeds of discord.* **5.** offspring; progeny. **6.** birth: *not of mortal seed.* **7.** semen or sperm. **8.** the ovum or ova of certain animals, as the lobster and the silkworm moth. **9.** seed oysters. **10. go to seed, a.** to pass to the stage of yielding seed. **b.** to approach the end of vigor, usefulness, prosperity, etc. —*v.t.* **11.** to sow (land) with seed. **12.** to sow or scatter (seed). **13.** to sow or scatter (clouds) with crystals or particles of silver iodide, solid carbon dioxide, etc., to induce precipitation. **14.** to remove the seeds from (fruit). **15.** to modify (the ordinary drawing of lots for position in a tournament, as at tennis) by distributing ranking players so that they will not meet in the early rounds of play. **16.** to distribute (ranking players) in this manner. —*v.i.* **17.** to sow seed. **18.** to produce or shed seed. [ME; OE *sēd* (Anglian), *sǣd,* c. G *saat*] **—seed/less,** *adj.* **—seed/like/,** *adj.*

Cross section of violet seed
A, Endosperm; B, Cotyledon; C, Testa; D, Hypocotyl; E, Hilum

seed·cake (sēd/kāk/), *n.* a sweet cake containing aromatic seeds.

seed capsule, *Bot.* the ripened walls of the ovary.

seed·case (sēd/kās/), *n.* a seed capsule; pericarp.

seed coat, *Bot.* the outer integument of a seed.

seed corn, ears or kernels of maize set apart as seed.

seed·er (sē/dər), *n.* **1.** one who or that which seeds. **2.** an apparatus for sowing seeds in the ground.

seed leaf, *Bot.* a cotyledon.

seed·ling (sēd/lĭng), *n.* **1.** a plant or tree grown from a seed. **2.** a tree not yet three feet high.

seed oysters, spat of oysters; very young oysters.

seed pearl, a very small pearl (less than ¼ grain).

seed plant, a seed-bearing plant; a spermatophyte.

seeds·man (sēdz/mən), *n., pl.* **-men. 1.** a sower of seed. **2.** a dealer in seed.

seed·time (sēd/tīm/), *n.* the season for sowing seed.

seed vessel, *Bot.* a pericarp.

seed·y (sē/dĭ), *adj.,* **seedier, seediest. 1.** abounding in seed. **2.** gone to seed. **3.** no longer fresh or new; shabby. **4.** wearing shabby clothes. **5.** *Colloq.* out of sorts physically. **—seed/i·ly,** *adv.* **—seed/i·ness,** *n.*

See·ger (sē/gər), *n.* **Alan,** 1888–1916, U.S. poet.

see·ing (sē/ĭng), *conj.* in view of the fact (that); considering; inasmuch as.

Seeing Eye, an organization in Morristown, N. J., that provides dogs (**Seeing Eye dogs**) trained to aid their blind owners in crossing streets, etc.

seek (sēk), *v.,* **sought, seeking.** —*v.t.* **1.** to go in search or quest of: *to seek a new home.* **2.** to find (*out*) by searching or endeavor. **3.** to try to obtain: *to seek fame.* **4.** to try or attempt (fol. by an infinitive): *to seek to convince a person.* **5.** to go to: *to seek a place.* **6.** to ask for; request: *to seek advice.* **7.** *Dial.* to search or explore. —*v.i.* **8.** be **sought after,** to be desired or in demand. **9.** to make search or inquiry. [ME *seke,* OE *sēcan,* c. G *suchen*] **—seek/er,** *n.*

See·land (sē/lǎnd), *n.* Zealand.

seem (sēm), *v.i.* **1.** to appear to be; appear (to be, feel, do, etc.). **2.** to appear to oneself (to be, do, etc.): *I seem to hear someone calling.* **3.** to appear to exist: *there seems no need to go now.* **4.** to appear to be true or the case: *it seems likely to rain.* [ME *seme,* t. Scand.; cf. Icel. *sǣma* (impers.) beseem, befit] **—seem/er,** *n.*
—Syn. 4. SEEM, APPEAR, LOOK refer to an outward aspect which may or may not be contrary to reality. SEEM is ap-

plied to that which has an aspect of truth and probability: *it seems warmer today.* APPEAR suggests the giving of an impression which may be superficial or illusory: *the house appears to be deserted.* LOOK more vividly suggests the use of the eye (literally or figuratively) or the aspect as perceived by the eye: *she looked very much frightened.*

seem·ing (sē/mĭng), *adj.* **1.** apparent; appearing to be such (whether truly or falsely): *a seeming advantage.* —*n.* **2.** appearance, esp. outward or deceptive appearance. **—seem/ing·ly,** *adv.*

seem·ly (sēm/lĭ), *adj.,* **-lier, -liest,** *adv.* —*adj.* **1.** fitting or becoming with respect to propriety or good taste; decent; decorous. **2.** suitable. **3.** *Archaic or Dial.* of pleasing appearance; handsome. —*adv.* **4.** in a seemly manner; fittingly; becomingly. [ME *semeli,* t. Scand.; cf. Icel. *sǣmiligr* becoming] **—seem/li·ness,** *n.*

seen (sēn), *v.* pp. of **see¹.**

seep (sēp), *v.i.* **1.** to pass gradually, as liquid, through a porous substance; ooze. —*n.* **2.** moisture that seeps out. **3.** a small spring, or soakage of ground water at the surface. [? var. of d. *sipe,* OE *sīpian,* c. MLG *sipen*]

seep·age (sē/pĭj), *n.* **1.** act or process of seeping; leakage. **2.** that which seeps or leaks out.

se·er¹ (sē/ər for 1; sĭr for 2, 3), *n.* **1.** one who sees. **2.** a prophet. **3.** a crystal-gazer. [f. SEE¹ + -ER¹] **—seer·ess** (sĭr/ĭs), *n. fem.*

seer² (sĭr), *n.* ser.

seer·suck·er (sĭr/sŭk/ər), *n.* a fabric, usually striped cotton with alternate stripes crinkled in the weaving. [t. East Ind., t. Pers.: alter. of *shīr o shakkar,* lit., milk and sugar]

see·saw (sē/sô/), *n.* **1.** a sport in which two children move alternately up and down when seated at opposite ends of a plank balanced at the middle. **2.** a plank adjusted for this sport. **3.** moving up and down or back and forth. **4.** an up-and-down or a back-and-forth movement or procedure. **5.** *Whist.* a crossruff. —*v.i., v.t.* **6.** to move, or cause to move, in a seesaw manner. [varied reduplication suggested by SAW¹]

seethe (sēth), *v.,* **seethed** or (*Obs.*) **sod; seethed** or (*Obs.*) **sodden** or **sod; seething;** *n.* —*v.t.* **1.** to soak or steep. **2.** *Archaic.* to boil; prepare, cook, or extract the essence of, by boiling. —*v.i.* **3.** to boil. **4.** to surge or foam as if boiling. **5.** to be in a state of agitation or excitement. —*n.* **6.** act of seething. **7.** state of agitation or excitement. [ME; OE *sēothan,* c. G *sieden*] **—seeth/ing·ly,** *adv.* **—Syn. 5.** See **boil¹.**

seg·ment (sĕg/mənt), *n.* **1.** one of the parts into which anything naturally separates or is naturally divided; a division or section. **2.** *Geom.* **a.** a part cut off from a figure (esp. a circular or a spherical one) by a line or a plane, as a part of a circular area contained by an arc and its chord, or by two parallel lines or planes. **b.** a finite section of a line. **3.** *Zool.* any one of the rings that compose the body of an arthropod, or one of the sections of a limb between the joints. —*v.t., v.i.* **4.** to separate or divide into segments. [t. L: s. *segmentum*] **—seg·men·tal** (sĕg·mĕn/təl), **seg·men·tar·y** (sĕg/mən·tĕr/ĭ), *adj.* **—seg·men/tal·ly,** *adv.*

ACB, Segment of a circle

seg·men·ta·tion (sĕg/mən·tā/shən), *n.* **1.** division into segments. **2.** *Biol.* **a.** the subdivision of an organism or of an organ into more or less equivalent parts. **b.** cell division. Cf. **cleavage.**

segmentation cavity, *Embryol.* a blastocoele; the hollow of a blastula.

se·gno (sĕ/nyō), *n., pl.* **-gni** (-nyē). *Music.* **1.** a sign. **2.** a sign or mark at the beginning or end of a repetition. [It., g. L *signum*]

se·go (sē/gō), *n., pl.* **-gos.** sego lily.

sego lily, 1. a showy flowered plant, *Calochortus Nuttallii,* common in the western U. S. (the State flower of Utah). **2.** its edible root. [t. Paiute: m. *pasi'go*]

Se·go·via (sĕ·gō/vyä), *n.* a city in central Spain: well-preserved Roman aqueduct. 30,875 (1950).

seg·re·gate (*v.* sĕg/rə·gāt/; *adj.* sĕg/rə·gĭt, -gāt/), *v.,* **-gated, -gating,** *adj.* —*v.t.* **1.** to separate or set apart from the others or from the rest, esp. by race; isolate. —*v.i.* **2.** to separate or go apart; separate from the main body and collect in one place; become segregated. **3.** *Biol.* (of allelomorphic characters) to separate according to Mendel's laws. —*adj.* **4.** segregated; set apart. [ME, t. L: m.s. *sēgregātus,* pp., separated from the flock] **—seg/re·ga/tive,** *adj.* **—seg/re·ga/tor,** *n.*

seg·re·ga·tion (sĕg/rĭ·gā/shən), *n.* **1.** act of segregating. **2.** state of being segregated. **3.** something segregated. **4.** *Biol.* the separation of genes in paternal chromosomes from those in maternal chromosomes at the reduction division, and the consequent separation of their hereditary characters as observed in the progeny of hybrids.

seg·re·ga·tion·ist (sĕg/rə·gā/shən·ĭst), *n. U.S.* an advocate of racial segregation.

se·gui·dil·la (sĕ/gē·dē/lyä), *n.* **1.** *Pros.* a stanza of four to seven lines with a peculiar rhythm. **2.** a Spanish dance in triple rhythm for two persons. **3.** the music for it. [t. Sp., der. *seguida* following, sequence]

sei·cen·to (sē·chĕn/tō), *n.* the 17th century, with reference to the Italian art or literature of that period. [It., short for *milleseicento* one thousand six hundred]

seiche (sāsh), *n.* an occasional rhythmical movement from side to side of the water of a lake, with fluctuation of the water level. [t. Swiss F, ? a graphic adoption of G *seiche* sinking]

Seid·litz powder (sĕd′lĭts), an aperient consisting of two powders, one tartaric acid and the other a mixture of sodium bicarbonate and Rochelle salt: dissolved separately, mixed, and drunk while effervescing.

sei·gneur (sēn′yûr′; *Fr.* sĕ nyœr′), *n.* a feudal lord. [t. F, g. L *senior.* See SENIOR]

seign·ior (sēn′yər), *n.* **1.** a lord; a ruler. **2.** the lord of a manor; a gentleman (also formerly used as a title of respect). [ME *segnour*, t. AF, g. L *senior.* See SENIOR]

seign·ior·age (sēn′yər ĭj), *n.* **1.** something claimed by a sovereign or superior as a prerogative. **2.** a charge on bullion brought to the mint to be coined. **3.** the difference between the cost of the bullion plus minting expenses and the value as money of the pieces coined.

seign·ior·y (sēn′yər ĭ), *n., pl.* **-iories.** **1.** the power or authority of a seignior. **2.** *Hist.* a lord's domain. Also, **signory.**

sei·gno·ri·al (sēn yōr′ĭ əl), *adj.* of or pertaining to a seignior. Also, **seign·ior·al** (sēn′yər əl).

Seine (sān; *Fr.* sĕn), *n.* a river flowing from E France NW through Paris to the English Channel. ab. 480 mi.

seine (sān), *n., v.,* **seined, seining.** —*n.* **1.** a fishing net which hangs vertically in the water, having floats at the upper edge and sinkers at the lower. —*v.t.* **2.** to catch with a seine. **3.** to use a seine in (water). —*v.i.* **4.** to fish with a seine. [ME *seyn(e)*, OE *segne*, ult. t. L: m. *sagēna*, t. Gk.: m. *sagēnē* fishing net]

seised (sēzd), *adj. Law.* having possession of a freehold estate. [var. of *seized*, pp. of SEIZE]

sei·sin (sē′zĭn), *n. Law.* seizin.

seism (sī′zəm, -səm), *n.* an earthquake. [t. Gk.: s. *seismós*]

seis·mic (sīz′mĭk, sīs′-), *adj.* pertaining to, of the nature of, or caused by an earthquake. Also, **seis′mal, seis′mi·cal.** [f. s. Gk. *seismós* earthquake + -IC]

seis·mism (sīz′mĭz əm, sīs′-), *n.* the phenomena of earthquakes. [f. s. Gk. *seismós* earthquake + -ISM]

seismo-, a word element meaning "seismic," as in *seismology.* [t. Gk., comb. form of *seismós* earthquake]

seis·mo·gram (sīz′mə grăm′, sīs′-), *n.* a record made by a seismograph.

seis·mo·graph (sīz′mə grăf′, -gräf′, sīs′-), *n.* an instrument for recording the phenomena of earthquakes. —**seis′mo·graph′ic,** *adj.*

seis·mog·ra·phy (sīz mŏg′rə fĭ, sīs-), *n.* **1.** the scientific description of earthquake phenomena. **2.** the science of the use of the seismograph.

seis·mol·o·gy (sīz mŏl′ə jĭ, sīs-), *n.* the science or study of earthquakes and their phenomena. —**seis·mo·log·ic** (sīz′mə lŏj′ĭk, sīs′-), **seis′mo·log′i·cal,** *adj.* —**seis′mo·log′i·cal·ly,** *adv.* —**seis·mol′o·gist,** *n.*

seis·mom·e·ter (sīz mŏm′ə tər, sīs-), *n.* an instrument for measuring the direction, intensity, and duration of earthquakes. —**seis·mo·met·ric** (sīz′mə mĕt′rĭk, sīs′-), **seis′mo·met′ri·cal,** *adj.*

seize (sēz), *v.,* **seized, seizing.** —*v.t.* **1.** to lay hold of suddenly or forcibly; grasp: *to seize a weapon.* **2.** to grasp with the mind: *to seize an idea.* **3.** to take possession of by force or at will: *to seize enemy ships.* **4.** to take possession or control of as if by suddenly laying hold: *panic seized the crowd.* **5.** to take possession of by legal authority; confiscate: *to seize smuggled goods.* **6.** to put in seizin or legal possession of. **7.** to capture; take into custody. **8.** to take advantage of promptly: *to seize an opportunity.* **9.** *Naut.* to bind, lash, or fasten together with several turns of light rope, cord, or the like. —*v.i.* **10.** to lay hold suddenly or forcibly: *to seize on a rope.* [ME *sayse,* t. OF: m. *saisir,* g. VL *sacīre* set, put (in possession), t. Gmc.; cf. Goth. *satjan* SET] —**seiz′er;** *Law,* **sei·zor** (sē′zor, -zôr), *n.* —**Syn. 7.** apprehend, arrest. **7, 8.** See **catch.** —**Ant. 7.** release.

sei·zin (sē′zĭn), *n. Law.* **1.** (orig.) possession of either land or chattel. **2.** the kind of possession, or right to possession, characteristic of estates of freehold. Also, **sei·sin.** [ME *saisine,* t. OF, der. *saisir* SEIZE]

seiz·ing (sē′zĭng), *n.* **1.** act of seizing. **2.** *Naut.* a binding or lashing, consisting of several turns of light line, marline, or the like, holding two ropes, etc., together.

sei·zure (sē′zhər), *n.* **1.** act of seizing. **2.** a taking possession, legally or by force. **3.** a sudden attack, as of disease.

se·jant (sē′jənt), *adj. Her.* in a sitting posture. [also *seiant,* t. OF: m. *seant,* ppr. of *seoir* sit, g. L *sedēre*]

Sejm (sām), *n.* (in Poland from 1918–22) the Constituent Assembly, which later became the lower house of the Parliament. [Pol.: assembly]

se·la·chi·an (sĭ lā′kĭ ən), *adj.* **1.** belonging to the *Selachii,* a large group of fishes comprising the sharks, skates, and rays. —*n.* **2.** a selachian fish, as a shark. [f. s. NL *selachiī,* pl. (r. *selachē,* t. Gk.: sharks) + -AN]

sel·a·gi·nel·la (sĕl′ə jĭ′nĕl′ə), *n. Bot.* any of a genus of heterosporous vascular cryptogams, typical of the *Selaginellaceae,* including species cultivated in conservatories. [NL, dim. of L *Selago* a genus of plant]

Nautical seizings

se·lah (sē′lə), *n.* a word occurring frequently in the Psalms, supposed to be a liturgical or musical direction, probably a direction by the leader to raise the voice, or perhaps indicating a pause. [t. Heb.]

se·lam·lik (sĭ läm′lĭk), *n.* the portion of a Turkish palace or house reserved for men. [t. Turk.]

Se·lan·gor (sĕ läng′gôr), *n.* a state in the former Federation of Malaya: now part of the federation of Malaysia. 1,012,929 pop. (1957); 3160 sq. mi. *Cap.:* Kuala Lumpur.

sel·dom (sĕl′dəm), *adv.* **1.** rarely; infrequently; not often. —*adj.* **2.** *Obs.* rare; infrequent. [ME; OE *seldum,* var. of *seldan,* c. G *selten*]

se·lect (sĭ lĕkt′), *v.t.* **1.** to choose in preference to another or others; pick out. —*adj.* **2.** selected; chosen in preference to others. **3.** choice; of special value or excellence. **4.** careful or fastidious in selection; exclusive: *a select party.* [t. L: s. *sēlectus,* pp., chosen] —**se·lect′ness,** *n.* —**se·lec′tor,** *n.* —**Syn. 1.** See **choose.**

se·lect·ee (sĭ lĕk′tē′), *n.* one selected by draft for military or naval service.

se·lec·tion (sĭ lĕk′shən), *n.* **1.** act of selecting or the fact of being selected; choice. **2.** a thing or a number of things selected. **3.** *Biol.* the singling out of certain forms of animal and vegetable life for reproduction and perpetuation, either by the operation of natural causes (cf. **natural selection**) which result in the survival of the fittest, or by man's agency (**artificial selection**) as in breeding animals and in cultivating fruits, vegetables, etc. **4.** *Linguistics.* **a.** the choice of one form instead of another in a position where both can occur, e.g., of *ask* instead of *tell* or *with* in the phrase *ask John.* **b.** the choice of one form class in a construction, to the exclusion of others which do not occur there, e.g., of a noun like *John* as direct object of *ask,* to the exclusion of adjectives and adverbs. **c.** the feature of a construction resulting from such a choice. The phrases *ask John, tell John,* and *with John* differ in selection; no adjective or adverb occurs as direct object of a verb in English. —**Ant. 1.** rejection.

se·lec·tive (sĭ lĕk′tĭv), *adj.* **1.** having the function or power of selecting; making selection. **2.** characterized by selection. **3.** *Radio.* having good selectivity.

selective service, compulsory military service.

selective transmission, *Mach.* an automobile gear box in which the available forward and reverse speeds may be engaged in any order, without passing progressively through the different changes of gear.

se·lec·tiv·i·ty (sĭ lĕk′tĭv′ə tĭ), *n.* **1.** state or quality of being selective. **2.** *Elect.* the property of a circuit, instrument, or the like, by virtue of which it responds to electric oscillations of a particular frequency. **3.** *Radio.* (of a receiving set) the ability to receive any one of a band of frequencies or waves to the exclusion of others.

se·lect·man (sĭ lĕkt′mən), *n., pl.* **-men.** *New England.* one of a board of town officers chosen to manage certain public affairs.

sel·e·nate (sĕl′ə nāt′), *n. Chem.* a salt of selenic acid.

Se·le·ne (sĭ lē′nē), *n. Gk. Myth.* the goddess of the moon. Cf. **Luna.** [t. Gk., personification of *selēnē* moon]

se·len·ic (sĭ lē′nĭk, -lĕn′ĭk), *adj. Chem.* of or containing selenium, esp. in the hexavalent state (Se+⁶).

selenic acid, *Chem.* a strong corrosive dibasic acid, H_2SeO_4, resembling sulfuric acid.

se·le·ni·ous (sĭ lē′nĭ əs), *adj. Chem.* containing tetravalent or divalent selenium.

sel·e·nite (sĕl′ə nīt′, sĭ lē′nīt), *n.* **1.** a variety of gypsum, found in transparent crystals and foliated masses. **2.** *Chem.* a salt of selenious acid. [t. L: m. *selēnītēs,* t. Gk.: lit., (stone) of the moon]

se·le·ni·um (sĭ lē′nĭ əm), *n. Chem.* nonmetallic element chemically resembling sulfur and tellurium, occurring in several allotropic forms (crystalline, amorphous, etc.), and having an electrical resistance which varies under the influence of light. *Symbol:* Se; *at. wt.:* 78.96; *at. no.:* 34; *sp. gr.:* (gray) 4.80 at 25°C., (red) 4.50 at 25°C. [NL, f. s. Gk. *selēnē* moon + -ium -IUM]

sel·e·nog·ra·phy (sĕl′ə nŏg′rə fĭ), *n.* the science dealing with the moon, esp. with reference to its physical features. [See SELENE, -GRAPHY] —**sel′e·nog′ra·pher,** *n.* —**se·le·no·graph·ic** (sĭ lē′nə grăf′ĭk), *adj.*

sel·e·nol·o·gy (sĕl′ə nŏl′ə jĭ), *n.* that branch of astronomy dealing with the moon. —**sel′e·nol′o·gist,** *n.*

Se·leu·ci·a (sĭ lōō′shə), *n.* **1.** an ancient city of Babylonia, on the Tigris, N of Babylon. **2.** an ancient coastal city in NW ancient Syria, near the mouth of the Orontes river: the port of Antioch.

Se·leu·cid (sĭ lōō′sĭd), *n.* one of the Seleucidae.

Se·leu·ci·dae (sĭ lōō′sə dē′), *n.pl.* a dynasty founded in Asia about 312 B.C. by Seleucus. It lasted until about 64 B.C. —**Se·leu·ci·dan** (sĭ lōō′sə dan) *adj.*

Se·leu·cus I (sĭ lōō′kəs), **Nicator** (nĭ kā′tôr), c358–281? B.C., Macedonian general of Alexander the Great, and ruler and conqueror in Babylonia, Syria, etc.

self (sĕlf), *n., pl.* **selves,** *adj., pron., pl.* **selves.** —*n.* **1.** a person or thing referred to with respect to individuality; one's own person: *one's own self.* **2.** one's nature, character, etc.: *one's better self.* **3.** personal interest; selfishness. **4.** *Philos.* the individual consciousness in its relation to itself. —*adj.* **5.** being the same throughout, as a color; uniform. **6.** being of one piece or material with the rest. **7.** *Archaic.* same. —*pron.* **8.** myself, himself, etc.: *to make a check payable to self.* [ME and OE, c. D *zelf*, G *selb*]

self-, prefixal use of *self,* appearing in various parts of speech, expressing principally reflexive action, e.g., subject identical with direct object, as in *self-control, self-government, self-help;* with indirect-object or adverbial-type relations, as in *self-conscious, self-centered, self-evident.*

self-ab·ne·ga·tion (sĕlf'ăb'nĭ gā'shən), *n.* self-denial.

self-a·buse (sĕlf'ə būs'), *n.* **1.** abuse of oneself. **2.** masturbation.

self-act·ing (sĕlf'ăk'tĭng), *adj.* automatic.

self-ad·dressed (sĕlf'ə drĕst'), *adj.* addressed to oneself.

self-ag·gran·dize·ment (sĕlf'ə grăn'dĭz mənt), *n.* increase of one's own power, wealth, etc., usually aggressively.

self-as·ser·tion (sĕlf'ə sûr'shən), *n.* insistence on or expression of one's own importance, claims, wishes, opinions, etc. —**self'-as·ser'tive,** *adj.*

self-as·sur·ance (sĕlf'ə shŏŏr'əns), *n.* self-confidence.

self-as·sured (sĕlf'ə shŏŏrd'), *adj.* self-confident.

self-cen·tered (sĕlf'sĕn'tərd), *adj.* **1.** engrossed in self; selfish. **2.** centered in oneself or itself. **3.** being itself fixed as a center.

self-col·ored (sĕlf'kŭl'ərd), *adj.* **1.** of one uniform color. **2.** of the natural color.

self-com·mand (sĕlf'kə mănd', -mänd'), *n.* self-control.

self-com·pla·cent (sĕlf'kəm plā'sənt), *adj.* pleased with oneself; self-satisfied. —**self'-com·pla'cent·ly,** *adv.*

self-con·ceit (sĕlf'kən sēt'), *n.* overweening opinion of oneself, one's abilities, etc. —**self'-con·ceit'ed,** *adj.*

self-con·fi·dence (sĕlf'kŏn'fə dəns), *n.* confidence in one's own judgment, ability, power, etc., sometimes to an excessive degree. —**self'-con'fi·dent,** *adj.* —**self'-con'fi·dent·ly,** *adv.*

self-con·scious (sĕlf'kŏn'shəs), *adj.* **1.** excessively conscious of oneself as an object of observation to others. **2.** conscious of oneself or one's own thoughts, etc. —**self'-con'scious·ly,** *adv.* —**self'-con'scious·ness,** *n.*

self-con·sist·ent (sĕlf'kən sĭs'tənt), *adj.* consistent with oneself or itself.

self-con·tained (sĕlf'kən tānd'), *adj.* **1.** containing in oneself or itself all that is necessary; independent. **2.** reserved or uncommunicative. **3.** (of a machine) complete in itself.

self-con·tent (sĕlf'kən tĕnt'), *n.* satisfaction with oneself; self-complacency. Also, **self'-con·tent'ment.**

self-con·tra·dic·tion (sĕlf'kŏn'trə dĭk'shən), *n.* **1.** act or fact of contradicting oneself or itself. **2.** a statement containing contradictory elements. —**self'-con'-tra·dic'to·ry,** *adj.*

self-con·trol (sĕlf'kən trōl'), *n.* control of oneself or one's actions, feelings, etc.

self-de·cep·tion (sĕlf'dĭ sĕp'shən), *n.* act or fact of deceiving oneself. Also, **self-de·ceit** (sĕlf'dĭ sēt'). —**self'-de·cep'tive,** *adj.*

self-de·fense (sĕlf'dĭ fĕns'), *n.* act of defending one's own person, reputation, etc. —**self'-de·fen'sive,** *adj.*

self-de·ni·al (sĕlf'dĭ nī'əl), *n.* the sacrifice of one's own desires; unselfishness. —**self'-de·ny'ing,** *adj.* —**self'-de·ny'ing·ly,** *adv.*

self-de·struc·tion (sĕlf'dĭ strŭk'shən), *n.* the destruction of oneself or itself; suicide.

self-de·ter·mi·na·tion (sĕlf'dĭ tûr'mə nā'shən), *n.* **1.** determination by oneself or itself, without outside influence. **2.** the determining by a people or nationality of the form of government it shall have, without reference to the wishes of any other nation. —**self'-de·ter'-mined,** *adj.* —**self'-de·ter'min·ing,** *adj.,* *n.*

self-de·vo·tion (sĕlf'dĭ vō'shən), *n.* devotion of oneself: self-sacrifice. —**self'-de·vo'tion·al,** *adj.*

self-dis·ci·pline (sĕlf'dĭs'ə plĭn), *n.* discipline and training of oneself, usually for improvement.

self-dis·trust (sĕlf'dĭs trŭst'), *n.* lack of confidence in oneself, one's abilities, etc.

self-ed·u·cat·ed (sĕlf'ĕj'ə kā'tĭd), *adj.* educated by one's own efforts, without formal instruction, or without financial assistance. —**self'-ed'u·ca'tion,** *n.*

self-ef·face·ment (sĕlf'ĭ fās'mənt), *n.* act or fact of keeping oneself in the background, as in humility.

self-es·teem (sĕlf'ĕs tēm'), *n.* favorable opinion of oneself; conceit. —**Syn.** See pride. —**Ant.** diffidence.

self-ev·i·dent (sĕlf'ĕv'ə dənt), *adj.* evident in itself without proof; axiomatic. —**self'-ev'i·dence,** *n.* —**self'-ev'i·dent·ly,** *adv.*

self-ex·am·i·na·tion (sĕlf'ĭg zăm'ə nā'shən), *n.* examination into one's own state, conduct, motives, etc.

self-ex·e·cut·ing (sĕlf'ĕk'sə kū'tĭng), *adj.* providing for its own execution, and needing no legislation to enforce it: *a self-executing treaty.*

self-ex·ist·ent (sĕlf'ĭg zĭs'tənt), *adj.* **1.** existing independently of any cause, as God. **2.** having an independent existence. —**self'-ex·ist'ence,** *n.*

self-ex·plan·a·to·ry (sĕlf'ĭk splăn'ə tôr'ĭ), *adj.* needing no explanation; obvious. Also, **self'-ex·plain'ing.**

self-ex·pres·sion (sĕlf'ĭk sprĕsh'ən), *n.* the expression of one's personality by poetry, music, etc.

self-fer·ti·li·za·tion (sĕlf'fûr tə lə zā'shən), *n.* *Bot.* the fertilization of a flower by its own pollen (opposed to *cross-fertilization*).

self-for·get·ful (sĕlf'fər gĕt'fəl), *adj.* forgetful, or not thinking, of one's own advantage, interest, etc.

self-gov·erned (sĕlf'gŭv'ərnd), *adj.* governed by itself, or having self-government, as a state or community; independent. —**self'-gov'ern·ing,** *adj.*

self-gov·ern·ment (sĕlf'gŭv'ərn mənt), *n.* **1.** government of a state, community, or other body or persons by its members jointly; democratic government. **2.** the condition of being self-governed. **3.** self-control.

self-hard·en·ing (sĕlf'här'dən ĭng), *adj.* noting or pertaining to any of certain steels which harden without the usual quenching, etc., necessary for ordinary steel. —**self'-hard'ened,** *adj.*

self-heal (sĕlf'hēl'), *n.* **1.** a menthaceous plant, *Prunella vulgaris,* once accredited with great remedial virtues. **2.** any of various other plants similarly credited.

self-help (sĕlf'hĕlp'), *n.* act of getting along or the ability to get along without assistance from others.

self-hood (sĕlf'hŏŏd), *n.* **1.** state of being an individual person. **2.** one's personality. **3.** selfishness.

self-i·den·ti·ty (sĕlf'ī dĕn'tə tĭ), *n.* the identity, or consciousness of identity, of a thing with itself.

self-im·por·tant (sĕlf'ĭm pôr'tənt), *adj.* having or showing an exaggerated opinion of one's own importance. —**self'-im·por'tance,** *n.* —**self'-im·por'tant·ly,** *adv.*

self-im·posed (sĕlf'ĭm pōzd'), *adj.* imposed on one by oneself: *a self-imposed task.*

self-im·prove·ment (sĕlf'ĭm prŏŏv'mənt), *n.* improvement of one's mind, etc., by one's own efforts.

self-in·duced (sĕlf'ĭn dūst', -dōōst'), *adj.* **1.** induced by oneself or itself. **2.** produced by self-induction.

self-in·duc·tion (sĕlf'ĭn dŭk'shən), *n.* *Elect.* the production of an induced electromotive force in a circuit by a varying current in that circuit.

self-in·dul·gent (sĕlf'ĭn dŭl'jənt), *adj.* **1.** indulging one's own desires, passions, etc. **2.** characterized by such indulgence. —**self'-in·dul'gence,** *n.* —**self'-in·dul'gent·ly,** *adv.*

self-in·flict·ed (sĕlf'ĭn flĭk'tĭd), *adj.* inflicted on one by oneself: *a self-inflicted wound.*

self-in·sur·ance (sĕlf'ĭn shŏŏr'əns), *n.* the insuring of one's property, etc., through oneself, as by setting aside a fund for the purpose.

self-in·ter·est (sĕlf'ĭn'tər ĭst), *n.* **1.** regard for one's own interest or advantage, esp. with disregard of others. **2.** personal interest or advantage.

self·ish (sĕl'fĭsh), *adj.* **1.** devoted to or caring only for oneself. **2.** characterized by caring only for oneself: *selfish motives.* —**self'ish·ly,** *adv.* —**self'ish·ness,** *n.* —**Syn. 1.** self-interested, self-seeking, egoistic.

self-knowl·edge (sĕlf'nŏl'ĭj), *n.* knowledge of oneself, one's character, abilities, etc.

self·less (sĕlf'lĭs), *adj.* unselfish.

self-liq·ui·dat·ing (sĕlf'lĭk'wə dā'tĭng), *adj.* assured of being sold and converted into cash within a short period of time or before the date on which the supplier, etc., must be paid: *a self-liquidating loan.*

self-load·ing (sĕlf'lō'dĭng), *adj.* reloading automatically.

self-love (sĕlf'lŭv'), *n.* the instinct by which man's actions are directed to the promotion of his own welfare. —**self'-lov'ing,** *adj.*

self-made (sĕlf'mād'), *adj.* **1.** having succeeded in life unaided: *a self-made man.* **2.** made by oneself.

self-mas·ter·y (sĕlf'măs'tə rĭ, -măs'-), *n.* self-control.

self-mov·ing (sĕlf'mōō'vĭng), *adj.* moving of itself, without external agency.

self-o·pin·ion (sĕlf'ə pĭn'yən), *n.* **1.** opinion, esp. exaggerated opinion, of oneself. **2.** obstinacy in one's own opinion.

self-o·pin·ion·at·ed (sĕlf'ə pĭn'yə nā'tĭd), *adj.* **1.** conceited. **2.** obstinate in one's own opinion.

self-pit·y (sĕlf'pĭt'ĭ), *n.* pity for oneself.

self-pol·li·nat·ed (sĕlf'pŏl'ə nā'tĭd), *adj.* *Bot.* having the pollen transferred from the anthers to the stigmas of the same flower. —**self'-pol'li·na'tion,** *n.*

self-pos·sessed (sĕlf'pə zĕst'), *adj.* having or showing control of one's feelings, behavior, etc. —**self'-pos·ses'sion,** *n.*

self-pres·er·va·tion (sĕlf'prĕz'ər vā'shən), *n.* preservation of oneself from harm or destruction.

self-pro·duced (sĕlf'prə dūst', -dōōst'), *adj.* produced by oneself or itself.

self-pro·pelled (sĕlf'prə pĕld'), *adj.* **1.** propelled by itself. **2.** (of a vehicle, etc.) propelled by its own engine, motor, or the like, rather than drawn or pushed by a horse, locomotive, etc. —**self'-pro·pel'ling,** *adj.*

self-pro·tec·tion (sĕlf'prə tĕk'shən), *n.* protection of oneself or itself.

self-re·al·i·za·tion (sĕlf'rē'ə lə zā'shən), *n.* the fulfillment of one's potential capacities.

self-re·cord·ing (sĕlf'rĭ kôr'dĭng), *adj.* recording automatically, as an instrument.

self-re·gard (sĕlf'rĭ gärd'), *n.* **1.** consideration for oneself or one's own interests. **2.** self-respect.

self-reg·is·ter·ing (sĕlf'rĕj'ĭs tər ĭng), *adj.* registering automatically, as an instrument; self-recording.

self-re·li·ance (sĕlf'rĭ lī'əns), *n.* reliance on oneself or one's own powers. —**self'-re·li'ant,** *adj.*

self-re·nun·ci·a·tion (sĕlf'rĭ nŭn'sĭ ā'shən, -shĭ-), n. renunciation of one's own will, interests, etc.; self-sacrifice. —**self'-re·nun'ci·a·to'ry,** adj.

self-re·proach (sĕlf'rĭ prōch'), n. blame or censure by one's own conscience.

self-re·spect (sĕlf'rĭ spĕkt'), n. proper esteem or regard for the dignity of one's character.

self-re·spect·ing (sĕlf'rĭ spĕk'tĭng), adj. having or showing self-respect.

self-re·straint (sĕlf'rĭ strānt'), n. restraint imposed on one by oneself; self-control.

self-right·eous (sĕlf'rī'chəs), adj. righteous in one's own esteem; pharisaic. —**self'-right'eous·ly,** adv. —**self'-right'eous·ness,** n.

self-ris·ing (sĕlf'rī'zĭng), adj. that rises without the addition of leaven: self-rising pancake flour.

self-sac·ri·fice (sĕlf'săk'rə fīs'), n. sacrifice of one's interests, desires, etc., as for duty or the good of another. —**self'-sac'ri·fic'ing,** adj.

self·same (sĕlf'sām'), adj. (the) very same; identical. —**self'same'ness,** n.

self-sat·is·fac·tion (sĕlf'săt'ĭs făk'shən), n. satisfaction with oneself, one's achievements, etc.

self-sat·is·fied (sĕlf'săt'ĭs fīd'), adj. feeling or showing satisfaction with oneself; self-complacent.

self-seek·er (sĕlf'sē'kər), n. one who seeks his own interest or selfish ends.

self-seek·ing (sĕlf'sē'kĭng), n. 1. the seeking of one's own interest or selfish ends. —adj. 2. given to or characterized by self-seeking; selfish.

self-serv·ice (sĕlf'sûr'vĭs), n. the serving of oneself in a restaurant, shop, or the like, instead of being served by attendants.

self-sown (sĕlf'sōn'), adj. 1. sown by itself, or without human or animal agency. 2. sown by any agency other than man, as by birds, the wind, etc.

self-start·er (sĕlf'stär'tər), n. a device which starts an internal-combustion engine without cranking by hand, as an electric motor, a spring, gas pressure, etc.

self-styled (sĕlf'stīld'), adj. styled or called by oneself (as specified): a self-stlyed leader.

self-suf·fi·cient (sĕlf'sə fĭsh'ənt), adj. 1. able to supply one's own needs. 2. having undue confidence in one's own resources, powers, etc. Also, **self-suf·fic·ing** (sĕlf'sə fī'sĭng). —**self'-suf·fi'cien·cy,** n.

self-sup·port (sĕlf'sə pōrt'), n. act or fact of supporting or maintaining oneself unaided. t—**self'-sup·port'·ed,** adj. —**self'-sup·port'ing,** adj.

self-sur·ren·der (sĕlf'sə rĕn'dər), n. the surrender or yielding up of oneself, one's will, affections, etc., as to another person, an influence, etc.

self-sus·tain·ing (sĕlf'sə stā'nĭng), adj. self-supporting.

self-taught (sĕlf'tôt'), adj. taught by oneself without aid from others.

self-will (sĕlf'wĭl'), n. 1. one's own will. 2. willfulness; obstinacy.

self-willed (sĕlf'wĭld'), adj. obstinately or perversely insistent on one's own will.

self-wind·ing (sĕlf'wīn'dĭng), adj. (of a clock) winding itself automatically by a motor or the like.

self-wrong (sĕlf'rông', -rŏng'), n. wrong done to oneself.

Sel·juk (sĕl jōōk'), adj. 1. noting or pertaining to certain Turkish dynasties which ruled over large parts of Asia from the 11th to the 13th century. —n. 2. a member of a Seljuk dynasty or of a tribe ruled by them. Also, **Sel·juk·i·an** (sĕl jōō'kĭ ən).

Sel·kirk (sĕl'kûrk), n. 1. Also, **Sel·kirk·shire** (sĕl'kûrk shĭr', -shər). a county in SE Scotland. 21,200 pop. (est. 1956); 268 sq. mi. Co. seat: Selkirk. 2. **Alex·ander,** (orig. Alexander Selcraig) 1676–1721, Scotch sailor marooned on a Pacific island: supposed prototype of Robinson Crusoe.

Selkirk Mountains, a range of mountains in SW Canada, in SE British Columbia. Highest peak, Mt. Sir Donald, 11,123 ft.

sell (sĕl), v., **sold, selling,** n. —v.t. 1. to give up or make over to another for a consideration; dispose of to a purchaser for a price. 2. to deal in; keep for sale. 3. to cause to be accepted: to sell an idea to the public. 4. to cause to accept: to sell the voters on a candidate. 5. to accept a price for or make profit of (something not a proper object for such action); betray, esp. for a price: to sell a cause. 6. Slang. to cheat; hoax. 7. **sell out, a.** to dispose of entirely by selling. **b.** Slang. to betray by a secret bargain. —v.i. 8. to sell something; engage in selling. 9. to be on sale; find purchasers. 10. Colloq. to win acceptance, approval, or adoption. —n. 11. Slang. a cheat; hoax. [ME selle(n), OE sellan, c. LG sellen] —Syn. 1. See trade.

sell·er (sĕl'ər), n. 1. one who sells; a vender. 2. an article, as a book, considered with reference to its sale: one of the best sellers.

seller's market, a market in which the seller is at an advantage because of scarcity of supply.

sell·ing-plat·er (sĕl'ĭng plā'tər), n. a horse that competes in a race (**selling race**) at the end of which it is offered for sale.

sell·out (sĕl'out'), n. 1. U.S. act of selling out. 2. Colloq. a play, show, etc., for which all seats are sold.

Sel·ma (sĕl'mə), n. a city in central Alabama, on the Alabama river. 28,385 (1960).

Selt·zer (sĕlt'sər), n. 1. a natural effervescent mineral water containing common salt and small quantities of sodium, calcium, and magnesium carbonates. 2. (also l.c.) an artificial water of similar composition. Also, **Seltzer water.** [t. G: m. Selterser, der. Selters, a village near Wiesbaden]

sel·vage (sĕl'vĭj), n. 1. the edge of woven fabric finished to prevent raveling, often in a narrow tape effect, different from the body of the fabric. 2. any similar strip or part of surplus material, as at the side of wallpaper. Also, **sel'vedge.** [late ME, f. SELF + EDGE. Cf. D zelfegge]

selves (sĕlvz), n. pl. of **self.**

Sem., 1. Seminary. 2. Semitic.

se·man·tic (sĭ măn'tĭk), adj. 1. pertaining to signification or meaning. 2. Linguistics. concerning the meaning of words and other linguistic forms. [t. Gk.: m. s. sēmantikós significant]

se·man·tics (sĭ măn'tĭks), n. 1. Linguistics. the study of meaning and changes of meaning. 2. that branch of modern logic which studies the relations between signs and what they denote or signify. 3. Also, **general semantics,** a discipline concerning the relationship between symbols and behavior.

sem·a·phore (sĕm'ə fōr'), n., v., **-phored, -phoring.** —n. 1. an apparatus for conveying information by means of signals. —v.t. 2. to signal by semaphore or by some system of flags. [f. Gk. sēma sign + -PHORE] —**sem·a·phor·ic** (sĕm'ə fōr'ĭk, -fôr'-), adj.

Se·ma·rang (sə mä'räng), n. a seaport in Indonesia, in N Java. 334,959 (1953). Also, **Samarang.**

se·ma·si·ol·o·gy (sĭ mā'sĭ ŏl'ə jĭ), n. semantics, esp. the study of semantic change. [f. s. Gk. sēmasía signification + -(o)LOGY] —**se·ma·si·o·log·i·cal** (sĭ mā'sĭ ə lŏj'ə kəl), adj. —**se·ma·si·ol·o·gist,** n.

se·mat·ic (sĭ măt'ĭk), adj. Biol. serving as a sign or warning of danger, as the conspicuous colors or markings of certain poisonous animals. [f. s. Gk. sêma sign + -IC]

sem·bla·ble (sĕm'blə bəl), Archaic. —adj. 1. like or similar. 2. seeming or apparent. —n. 3. likeness; resemblance. [ME, t. OF, der. sembler appear. See SEMBLANCE] —**sem'bla·bly,** adv.

sem·blance (sĕm'bləns), n. 1. outward aspect or appearance. 2. an assumed or unreal appearance; a mere show. 3. a likeness, image, or copy. [ME, t. OF, der. sembler be like, seem, g. L similāre, for simulāre]

Sem·brich (zĕm'brĭкн), n. **Marcella** (mär tsĕl'ä), (Praxede Marcelline Kochanska) 1858–1935, Austrian soprano.

se·me (sə mā'; Fr. -mě'), adj. Her., etc. strewn or covered with small figures of the same kind, as stars or flowers. [t. F, pp. of semer sow, strew, g. L sēmināre]

se·mei·ol·o·gy (sē'mī ŏl'ə jĭ), n. semiology.

se·mei·ot·ic (sē'mī ŏt'ĭk), adj. semiotic. Also, **se'·mei·ot'i·cal.**

Sem·e·le (sĕm'ə lē'), n. Gk. Myth. the daughter of Cadmus, and mother by Zeus of Dionysus. Zeus destroyed her by lightning when she asked to see him in all his glory.

se·men (sē'mən), n. the impregnating fluid produced by male reproductive organs; seed; sperm. [t. L: seed]

se·mes·ter (sĭ mĕs'tər), n. 1. (in many U.S. educational institutions) a major division of the regular annual session; this session commonly falls into either two or three such divisions, of from 15 to 18 weeks each. 2. (in German universities) a session, lasting about six months, inclusive of periods of recess. [t. G, t. L: m. sēme(n)stris, f. sē- (comb. form of sex six) + menstris monthly] —**se·mes'tral,** adj.

semi-, a prefix modifying the latter element of the word, meaning "half" in its precise and less precise meanings, as in semicircle, semiannual, semidetached, semiaquatic. [t. L, c. Gk. hēmi-, OE sām-, sŏm- half]

sem·i·an·nu·al (sĕm'ĭ ăn'yōō əl), adj. 1. occurring every half year. 2. lasting for half a year. —**sem·i·an'nu·al·ly,** adv.

sem·i·a·quat·ic (sĕm'ĭ ə kwăt'ĭk, -kwŏt'-), adj. Bot., Zool. partly aquatic; growing or living close to water, and sometimes found in or entering water.

sem·i·au·to·mat·ic (sĕm'ĭ ô'tə măt'ĭk), adj. 1. partly automatic. 2. (of a firearm) self-loading. —n. 3. a self-loading rifle or other firearm.

sem·i·breve (sĕm'ĭ brēv'), n. Music. a note having half the length of a breve, being the longest note in common use; a whole note. See illus. under **note.**

sem·i·cen·ten·ni·al (sĕm'ĭ sĕn tĕn'ĭ əl), adj. 1. occurring at, or celebrating, the completion of fifty years or half a century. —n. 2. a semicentennial celebration.

sem·i·cir·cle (sĕm'ĭ sûr'kəl), n. 1. the half of a circle. 2. anything having, or arranged in, the form of a half of a circle. —**sem·i·cir·cu·lar** (sĕm'ĭ sûr'kyə lər), adj.

semicircular canal, Anat. any of three curved tubular canals in the labyrinth of the ear, concerned with equilibrium. See diag. under **ear.**

sem·i·civ·i·lized (sĕm′sĭv′ə līzd′), *adj.* half or partly civilized.

sem·i·co·lon (sĕm′kō′lən), *n.* a mark of punctuation (;) used to indicate a more distinct separation between parts of a sentence than that indicated by a comma.

sem·i·con·duc·tor (sĕm′kən dŭk′tər), *n.* a substance whose electronic conductivity at ordinary temperatures is intermediate between that of a metal and an insulator.

sem·i·con·scious (sĕm′kŏn′shəs), *adj.* half-conscious; not fully conscious.

sem·i·de·tached (sĕm′dĭ tăcht′), *adj.* partly detached (used esp. in England of a pair of houses joined by a party wall but detached from other buildings).

sem·i·di·am·e·ter (sĕm′dī ăm′ə tər), *n.* the half of a diameter; a radius.

sem·i·di·ur·nal (sĕm′dī ûr′nəl), *adj.* 1. pertaining to, consisting of, or accomplished in half a day. 2. occurring every twelve hours.

sem·i·di·vine (sĕm′dĭ vīn′), *adj.* partly divine.

sem·i·dome (sĕm′dōm′), *n.* half a dome, esp. as formed by a vertical section, as over a semicircular apse.

sem·i·el·lip·ti·cal (sĕm′ĭ lĭp′tə kəl), *adj.* shaped like the half of an ellipse, esp. one whose base is the major axis of the ellipse.

sem·i·fi·nal (sĕm′fī′nəl), *adj.* 1. designating a round, contest, match, etc., which immediately precedes the final and decisive one. 2. pertaining to such a round, contest, etc. —*n.* 3. a semifinal round, contest, etc.

sem·i·fi·nal·ist (sĕm′fī′nəl ĭst), *n.* *Sport.* any player who competes in the semifinals.

sem·i·flu·id (sĕm′flōō′ĭd), *adj.* 1. imperfectly fluid, i.e., having both fluid and solid characteristics. 2. a semifluid substance. Also, **sem·i·liq·uid** (sĕm′lĭk′wĭd).

sem·i·lu·nar (sĕm′lōō′nər), *adj.* shaped like a half-moon; crescent.

semilunar bone, *Anat.* the second bone from the thumb side of the proximal row of the carpus.

semilunar valve, *Anat.* 1. a crescent-shaped valve consisting of three flaps, in the orifice of the aorta, which prevents blood from flowing back into the left ventricle. 2. a similar valve in the pulmonary artery, which prevents blood from flowing back into the right ventricle.

sem·i·month·ly (sĕm′mŭnth′lĭ), *adj., n., pl.* **-lies,** *adv.* —*adj.* 1. occurring every half month. —*n.* 2. a thing occurring every half month. 3. a semimonthly publication. —*adv.* 4. every half month.

sem·i·nal (sĕm′ə nəl), *adj.* 1. of, pertaining to, or of the nature of semen. 2. *Bot.* of or pertaining to seed. 3. having possibilities of future development: *seminal principles.* [ME, f. s. L *sēmen* seed + -AL¹] —**sem′i·nal·ly,** *adv.*

sem·i·nar (sĕm′ə när′, sĕm′ə när′), *n.* 1. a small group of students, as in a university, engaged in advanced study and original research under a member of the faculty. 2. the gathering place of such a group. 3. a course or subject of study for advanced graduate students. [t. G, t. L: m.s. *sēminārium* (neut.) of or for seed]

sem·i·nar·y (sĕm′ə nĕr′ĭ), *n., pl.* **-naries.** 1. a school, esp. one of higher grade. 2. a school for the education of men for the priesthood or ministry. 3. a school of secondary or higher level for young women. 4. a seminar. 5. a place of origin and development. [late ME, t. L: m.s. *sēminārium* nursery]

sem·i·na·tion (sĕm′ə nā′shən), *n.* dissemination.

sem·i·nif·er·ous (sĕm′ə nĭf′ər əs), *adj.* 1. *Anat.* conveying or containing semen. 2. *Bot.* bearing or producing seed. [f. semini- (t. NL, comb. form. repr. L *sēmen* seed) + -FEROUS]

Sem·i·nole (sĕm′ə nōl′), *n., pl.* **-nole, -noles** (-nōlz). *adj.* —*n.* 1. a member of a Muskogean tribe of American Indians, an offshoot of the Creeks, resident in Florida, and now also in Oklahoma. —*adj.* 2. of or pertaining to this tribe. [t. Creek: m. *Sim-a-nō-le,* or *Isti siminóla* separatist, runaway]

sem·i·of·fi·cial (sĕm′ə fĭsh′əl), *adj.* having some degree of official authority. —**sem′i·of·fi′cial·ly,** *adv.*

se·mi·ol·o·gy (sē′mĭ ŏl′ə jĭ), *n.* 1. the science of signs. 2. sign language. 3. the branch of medical science dealing with symptoms. Also, **semeiology.** [f. m. Gk. *sēmeîo(n)* sign + -LOGY]

se·mi·ot·ic (sē′mĭ ŏt′ĭk), *adj.* 1. pertaining to signs. 2. *Med.* pertaining to symptoms; symptomatic. Also, **se′mi·ot′i·cal, semeiotic, semeiotical.** [f. m.s. Gk. *sēmeîon* sign + -OTIC]

Se·mi·pa·la·tinsk (sĕ′mĭ pə lä′tĭnsk), *n.* a city in the S Soviet Union in Asia, on the Irtish river. 136,000 (est. 1956).

sem·i·pal·mate (sĕm′ĭ păl′māt, -mĭt), *adj.* partially or imperfectly palmate, as a bird's foot; half-webbed. Also, **sem′i·pal′mat·ed.**

sem·i·par·a·sit·ic (sĕm′ĭ păr′ə sĭt′ĭk), *adj.* 1. *Biol.* commonly parasitic but capable of living on dead or decaying animal matter. 2. *Bot.* partly parasitic and partly photosynthetic.

Semipalmate foot

sem·i·per·me·a·ble (sĕm′ĭ pûr′mĭ ə bəl), *adj.* permeable to some substances more than to others: *a semipermeable membrane.*

sem·i·plas·tic (sĕm′ĭ plăs′tĭk), *adj.* imperfectly plastic.

sem·i·por·ce·lain (sĕm′ĭ pôr′sə lĭn, -pôrs′lĭn), *n.* a partly vitrified, somewhat porous and nontranslucent pottery ware, inferior to porcelain.

sem·i·post·al (sĕm′ĭ pōs′təl), *Philately.* —*adj.* 1. of a postage stamp a portion of whose face value goes to charity, government use, etc. —*n.* 2. such a stamp.

sem·i·pre·cious (sĕm′ĭ prĕsh′əs), *adj.* having value, but not strictly precious, as the amethyst, garnet, etc.

sem·i·pub·lic (sĕm′ĭ pŭb′lĭk), *adj.* partly or to some degree public.

sem·i·qua·ver (sĕm′ĭ kwā′vər), *n.* *Chiefly Brit.* (in music) a sixteenth note. See illus. under **note.**

Se·mir·a·mis (sĭ mĭr′ə mĭs), *n.* *Gk. Legend.* an Assyrian queen of surpassing greatness, wisdom, and beauty: the founder of Babylon. See **Ninus.**

sem·i·rig·id (sĕm′ĭ rĭj′id), *adj.* *Aeron.* designating a type of airship whose shape is maintained by means of a rigid keellike structure and by internal gas pressure.

sem·i·skilled (sĕm′ĭ skĭld′), *adj.* partly skilled or trained.

sem·i·sol·id (sĕm′ĭ sŏl′ĭd), *adj.* 1. half-solid; of a somewhat firm consistence. —*n.* 2. a semisolid substance.

Sem·ite (sĕm′īt, sē′mīt), *n.* a member of a speech family comprising the Hebrews, Arabs, Assyrians, etc., supposedly descended from Shem. Gen. 10. [t. NL: m. *Sēmīta,* der. L *Sēm* Shem, t. Gk. See -ITE¹]

Se·mit·ic (sə mĭt′ĭk), *n.* 1. an important family of languages, related to the Hamitic, including Akkadian, Hebrew, Aramaic, Arabic, and Amharic. —*adj.* 2. of or pertaining to the Semites or their languages.

Se·mit·ics (sə mĭt′ĭks), *n.* the study of the Semitic languages, literature, etc.

Sem·i·tism (sĕm′ə tĭz′əm, sē′mə-), *n.* 1. Semitic characteristics, esp. the ways, ideas, influence, etc., of the Jewish people. 2. a Semitic word or idiom.

Sem·i·tist (sĕm′ə tĭst, sē′mə-), *n.* an authority on Semitics.

sem·i·tone (sĕm′ĭ tōn′), *n.* *Music.* the smallest interval used in music; a half tone; a half step.

sem·i·trans·lu·cent (sĕm′ĭ trăns lōō′sənt, -trănz-), *adj.* imperfectly translucent.

sem·i·trans·par·ent (sĕm′ĭ trăns pâr′ənt), *adj.* imperfectly transparent.

sem·i·trop·i·cal (sĕm′ĭ trŏp′ə kəl), *adj.* subtropical.

sem·i·vit·re·ous (sĕm′ĭ vĭt′rĭ əs), *adj.* partially vitreous, as mineral constituents of volcanic rocks.

sem·i·vow·el (sĕm′ĭ vou′əl), *n.* *Phonet.* a speech sound of vowel quality used as a consonant, such as *w* in *wet* or *y* in *yet.*

sem·i·week·ly (sĕm′ĭ wēk′lĭ), *adj., n., pl.* **-lies,** *adv.* —*adj.* 1. occurring or appearing every half week. —*n.* 2. a semiweekly publication. —*adv.* 3. every half week.

sem·i·year·ly (sĕm′ĭ yĭr′lĭ), *adj., n., pl.* **-lies,** *adv.* —*adj.* 1. occurring or appearing twice a year. —*n.* 2. a thing occurring twice a year. —*adv.* 3. twice a year.

sem·o·li·na (sĕm′ə lē′nə), *n.* the large, hard parts of wheat grains retained in the bolting machine after the fine flour has passed through it: used for making puddings, etc. [t. It.: m. *semolino,* dim. of *semola* bran, g. L *simila* fine flour]

Sem·pach (zĕm′päкн), *n.* a village in central Switzerland, in Lucerne canton: the Austrians were defeated here by the Swiss, 1386. 1308 (1950).

sem·per fi·de·lis (sĕm′pər fĭ dē′lĭs), *Latin.* always faithful (motto of the U.S. Marine Corps).

sem·per pa·ra·tus (sĕm′pər pə rā′təs), *Latin.* always ready (motto of the U.S. Coast Guard).

sem·pi·ter·nal (sĕm′pĭ tûr′nəl), *adj.* *Archaic or Literary.* everlasting; eternal. [ME, t. LL: s. *sempiternālis,* der. L *sempiternus* everlasting] —**sem·pi·ter′ni·ty** (sĕm′pĭ tûr′nə tĭ), *n.*

sem·pli·ce (sĕm′plē chĕ′), *adj.* *Music.* plain and simple. [It.]

sem·pre (sĕm′prĕ), *adv.* *Music.* throughout. [It.]

semp·stress (sĕmp′strĭs, sĕm′strĭs), *n.* seamstress.

sen (sĕn), *n.* a Japanese monetary unit and copper or bronze coin, equal to the hundredth part of a yen, or, formerly, about half of a United States cent. [t. Jap.]

Sen., 1. Senate. 2. Senator. 3. Senior.

sen·a·ry (sĕn′ə rĭ), *adj.* of or pertaining to the number six. [t. L: m.s. *sēnārius*]

sen·ate (sĕn′ĭt), *n.* 1. an assembly or council of citizens having the highest deliberative functions in the government; a legislative assembly of a state or nation. 2. (*cap.*) the upper house of the legislature of certain countries, as the United States, France, Italy, Canada, Ireland, Union of South Africa, Australia, and some Latin American countries. 3. the supreme council of state in ancient Rome, whose membership and functions varied at different periods. 4. a governing, advisory, or disciplinary body, as in certain universities. [ME *senat,* t. L: s. *senātus*]

sen·a·tor (sĕn′ə tər), *n.* a member of a senate. [ME *senatour,* t. L: m. *senātor*] —**sen′a·tor·ship′,** *n.*

sen·a·to·ri·al (sĕn′ə tôr′ĭ əl), *adj.* 1. of or pertaining to a senator or senators; characteristic of or befitting a senator. 2. consisting of senators. 3. *U.S.* entitled to elect a senator: *a senatorial district.*

se·na·tus con·sul·tum (sə nā′təs kən sŭl′təm), *pl.* **senatus consulta** (kən sŭl′tə). *Latin.* a decree of the senate of ancient Rome.

ăct, āble, dâre, ärt; ĕbb, ēqual; ĭf, īce; hŏt, ōver, ôrder, oil, bŏŏk, ōōze, out; ŭp, ūse, ûrge; ə = a in alone; ch, chief; g, give; ng, ring; sh, shoe; th, thin; t͟h, that; zh, vision. See the full key on inside cover.

send (sĕnd), *v.*, **sent, sending,** *n.* —*v.t.* **1.** to cause to go; order or direct to go: *to send a messenger.* **2.** to cause to be conveyed or transmitted to a destination: *to send a letter.* **3.** to compel or force to go: *to send the enemy flying.* **4.** to impel; throw: *to send a ball 200 yards.* **5.** to give (fol. by *forth, out,* etc.), as light, odor, or sound. **6.** *Elect.* **a.** to transmit. **b.** to transmit (an electromagnetic wave, etc.) in the form of pulses. **7.** *Swing Music.* to excite or inspire (a jazz performer or listener). **8. be sent down,** *Brit.* to be expelled, esp. from Oxford or Cambridge. —*v.i.* **9.** to despatch a messenger, agent, message, etc. **10.** *Naut.* **a.** to lurch forward from the force of a wave. **b.** to scend. —*n.* **11.** *Naut.* **a.** the driving impulse of a wave or waves upon a ship. **b.** act of sending; a sudden plunge of a vessel. [ME *sende(n)*, OE *sendan,* c. G *senden*]

Sen·dai (sĕn′dī′), *n.* a city in central Japan, on Honshu island. 341,685 (1950).

sen·dal (sĕn′dəl), *n.* a silk fabric in use during the Middle Ages, or a piece or garment of it. [ME, t. OF: m. *cendal,* prob. ult. t. Gk.: m. *sindōn* fine linen]

send·er (sĕn′dər), *n.* **1.** one who or that which sends. **2.** a transmitter of electrical pulses, as in telegraphy.

send-off (sĕnd′ôf′, -ŏf′), *n.* *Colloq.* **1.** a friendly demonstration for a person, etc., setting out on a journey, career, etc. **2.** a start given to a person or thing.

Sen·e·ca (sĕn′ə kə), *n.* **1.** (*pl.*) the largest tribe of the Iroquois Confederacy of North American Indians, in western New York and conspicuous in the wars south and west of Lake Erie. **2.** a member of this tribe. [Anglicization of Dutch pron. of Mohegan rendering of Iroquoian *oneniute' a'ka* Oneida, with different suffix *oneniute' ron' non,* lit., people of the standing or projecting rock or stone]

Sen·e·ca (sĕn′ə kə), *n.* **Lucius Annaeus** (lōō′shəs ə nē′əs), c4 B.C.-A.D. 65, Roman philosopher and writer of tragedies.

Seneca Lake, a lake in W New York: one of the Finger Lakes. ab. 35 mi. long; 1–3 mi. wide.

sen·e·ga (sĕn′ə gə), *n.* **1.** the dried root of a milkwort, *Polygala Senega* (**Seneca snakeroot**), of the eastern U.S., used as an expectorant and diuretic. **2.** the plant itself. [Latinization of SENECA¹]

Sen·e·gal (sĕn′ĭ gôl′), *n.* **1.** a republic in W Africa: independent member of the French Community; formerly part of French West Africa. 2,260,000 pop. (est. 1959); 76,084 sq. mi. *Cap.*: Dakar. **2.** a river in W Africa, rising in E Mali, flowing NW to the Atlantic at St. Louis. ab. 1000 mi. French, **Sé·né·gal** (sĕ nĕ gàl′).

Sen·e·ga·lese (sĕn′ə gō lēz′, -lēs′, -gə-), *adj., n., pl.* **-lese.** —*adj.* **1.** of or pertaining to Senegal (def. 1). —*n.* **2.** a native or inhabitant of Senegal. **3.** their language.

Sen·e·gam·bi·a (sĕn′ə găm′bĭ ə), *n.* a region in W Africa between the Senegal and Gambia rivers, now mostly in Senegal colony.

se·nes·cent (sə nĕs′ənt), *adj.* growing old; aging. [t. L: s. *senescens,* ppr., growing old] —**se·nes′cence,** *n.*

sen·es·chal (sĕn′ə shəl), *n.* an officer in the household of a medieval prince or dignitary, who had full charge of domestic arrangements, ceremonies, the administration of justice, etc.; a steward. [ME, t. OF, t. ML: m. *seniscalh,* t. Gmc.; cf. OHG *siniscalh,* lit., old servant]

se·nile (sē′nīl, -nĭl), *adj.* **1.** of, pertaining to, or characteristic of old age. **2.** *Phys. Geog.* (of topographical features) having advanced in reduction by erosion, etc., to a featureless plain that stands everywhere at base level. [t. L, neut. of *senilis*]

se·nil·i·ty (sə nĭl′ə tĭ), *n.* senile state; old age; the weakness or mental infirmity of old age.

sen·ior (sēn′yər), *adj.* **1.** older or elder (used after the name of the older of two persons bearing the same name). *Abbr.*: Sr. or Sen. **2.** of higher rank or standing, esp. by virtue of longer service. **3.** (in American universities, colleges, and schools) noting or pertaining to the highest class or the last year of the course. —*n.* **4.** a person who is older than another. **5.** one of higher rank or standing, esp. by virtue of longer service. **6.** *U.S.* a member of the senior class in a university, college, or school. **7.** (in English universities) the faculty members and graduates. [ME, t. L, compar. of *senex* old]

senior high school. See **high school** (def. 2).

sen·ior·i·ty (sēn yôr′ə tĭ, -yŏr′-), *n., pl.* **-ties.** **1.** state or fact of being senior; priority of birth; superior age. **2.** priority or precedence in age or service.

Sen·lac (sĕn′lăk), *n.* a hill in SE England, in Sussex: site of the Battle of Hastings, 1066. See **Hastings** (def. 2).

sen·na (sĕn′ə), *n.* **1.** a cathartic drug consisting of the dried leaflets of various plants of the caesalpiniaceous genus *Cassia,* as **Alexandrian senna** from *C. acutifolia,* or **Indian senna** from *C. angustifolia.* **2.** any plant yielding this drug. **3.** any of various similar plants, as *Cassia Marylandica.* [t. NL, t. Ar.: m. *sanā*]

Sen·nach·er·ib (sə năk′ər ĭb), *n.* d. 681 B.C., king of Assyria, 705–681 B.C.

Sen·nar (sĕn när′), *n.* a region in E Sudan between the

White and Blue Nile rivers, S of Khartoum: a former kingdom.

sen·night (sĕn′īt, -ĭt), *n.* *Archaic.* a week. Also, **se'n'night.** [ME *sennyght, sevenyght,* OE *seofan nihta* seven nights. See SEVEN, NIGHT. Cf. FORTNIGHT]

sen·nit (sĕn′ĭt), *n.* a kind of flat braided cordage used on shipboard, formed by plaiting strands of rope yarn or other fiber. [earlier *sinnet*; ? f. SEVEN + KNIT]

se·ñor (sĕ nyôr′), *n., pl.* **-ñores** (-nyô′rĕs). *Spanish.* **1.** a gentleman. **2.** (as a term of address) sir. **3.** (as a title) Mr. [Sp., g. L *senior.* See SENIOR]

se·ño·ra (sĕ nyô′rä), *n.* *Spanish.* **1.** Mrs.; madame. **2.** lady; gentlewoman.

se·ño·ri·ta (sĕ nyô rē′tä), *n.* *Spanish.* **1.** Miss. **2.** young lady.

sen·sate (sĕn′sāt), *adj.* perceived by the senses.

sen·sa·tion (sĕn sā′shən), *n.* **1.** the operation or function of the senses; perception through the senses. **2.** a mental condition produced through an organ of sense or resulting from a particular condition of some part of the body; a physical feeling, as of cold, dizziness, etc. **3.** *Physiol.* the faculty of perception of stimuli. **4.** *Psychol.* an experience arising directly from stimulation of sense organs. **5.** a mental feeling, esp. a state of excited feeling. **6.** a state of excited feeling or interest caused among a number of persons or throughout a community by some occurrence, etc. **7.** a cause of such feeling or interest. [t. ML: s. *sensātio,* der. LL *sensātus* having sense] —**Syn. 2.** See **sense.**

sen·sa·tion·al (sĕn sā′shən əl), *adj.* **1.** such as to produce a startling or thrilling impression: *a sensational novel.* **2.** aiming at startling or thrilling impressions, as a writer, etc. **3.** of or pertaining to sensation or the senses. —**sen·sa′tion·al·ly,** *adv.*

sen·sa·tion·al·ism (sĕn sā′shən ə lĭz′əm), *n.* **1.** matter, language, or style producing or designed to produce startling or thrilling impressions, or to excite and please vulgar taste. **2.** tendency of a writer, artist, etc., to be obsessed with a desire to thrill. **3.** *Ethics.* the doctrine that the good is to be judged only by the gratification of the senses; sensualism. **4.** *Philos.* the doctrine that all ideas are derived from, and are essentially reducible to, sensations; the denial of abstract ideas. —**sen·sa′tion·al·ist,** *n.*

sen·sa·tion·ism (sĕn sā′shə nĭz′əm), *n.* *Psychol.* a school of psychology which holds that mental life is constituted solely of sensations. —**sen·sa′tion·ist,** *n.*

sense (sĕns), *n., v.,* **sensed, sensing.** —*n.* **1.** each of the special faculties connected with bodily organs by which man and other animals perceive external objects and their own bodily changes (commonly reckoned as sight, hearing, smell, taste, and touch). **2.** these faculties collectively. **3.** their operation or function; sensation. **4.** a feeling or perception produced through the organs of touch, taste, etc., or resulting from a particular condition of some part of the body: *to have a sense of cold.* **5.** a faculty or function of the mind or soul analogous to sensation: *the moral sense.* **6.** any special capacity for perception, estimation, appreciation, etc.: *a sense of humor.* **7.** (*usually pl.*) clear or sound mental faculties. **8.** any more or less vague perception or impression: *a sense of security.* **9.** a mental discernment, realization, or recognition: *a just sense of the worth of a thing.* **10.** the recognition of something as incumbent or fitting: *a sense of duty.* **11.** sound practical intelligence: *he has no sense.* **12.** what is sensible or reasonable: *to talk sense.* **13.** the meaning, or one of the meanings, of a word, group of words, or a passage. **14.** an opinion or judgment formed or held, now esp. by an assemblage or body of persons: *the sense of a meeting.* **15.** *Math.* one of two opposite directions in which a vector may point. —*v.t.* **16.** to perceive by or as by the sense; become aware of. **17.** *Colloq.* to comprehend or understand. [ME, t. L: m.s. *sensus*] —**Syn. 4.** SENSE, SENSATION refer to consciousness of stimulus or of a perception with an interpretation as pleasant or unpleasant. A SENSE is an awareness or recognition of something; the stimulus may be subjective, and the entire process may be mental or intellectual: *a sense of failure.* A SENSATION is an impression derived from an objective (external) stimulus through any of the sense organs: *a sensation of heat.* The feeling is also applied to a general, indefinite bodily feeling: *a sensation of weariness.* **13.** See **meaning.**

Sense and Sensibility, a novel (1811) by Jane Austen (written 1797–98).

sense datum, *Psychol.* any experiential factor that results from the action of a stimulus on a sense organ.

sense·less (sĕns′lĭs), *adj.* **1.** destitute or deprived of sensation; unconscious. **2.** destitute of mental perception or appreciation. **3.** stupid or foolish, as persons. **4.** nonsensical or meaningless, as words: *this letter is either ingenious code or senseless.* —**sense′less·ly,** *adv.* —**sense′less·ness,** *n.*

sense organ, a specialized structure which receives impressions, such as one of the taste buds or tactile corpuscles.

sen·si·bil·i·ty (sĕn′sə bĭl′ə tĭ), *n., pl.* **-ties.** **1.** capacity for sensation or feeling; responsiveness to sensory stimuli. **2.** mental susceptibility or responsiveness; quickness and acuteness of apprehension or feeling. **3.** keen consciousness or appreciation. **4.** (*pl.*) emotional capacities. **5.** (*sing.* or *pl.*) liability to feel hurt or offended; sensitive feelings. **6.** capacity for the higher or more refined feelings; delicate sensitiveness of taste.

---

b., blend of, blended; c., cognate with; d., dialect, dialectal; der., derived from; f., formed from; g., going back to; m., modification of; r., replacing; s., stem of; t., taken from; ?, perhaps. See the full key on inside cover.

7. the property, as in plants or instruments, of being readily affected by external influences. —**Syn. 2.** SENSIBILITY, SUSCEPTIBILITY, SENSITIVENESS, SENSITIVITY mean capacity to respond to, or be affected by, something. SUSCEPTIBILITY is the state or quality of being impressionable and responsive, esp. to emotional stimuli; in the plural much the same as SENSIBILITY: *a person of keen susceptibilities.* SENSIBILITY is, particularly, capacity to respond to aesthetic and emotional stimuli; delicacy of emotional or intellectual perception: *the sensibility of the artist.* SENSITIVENESS is the state or quality of being sensitive, having a capacity of sensation and of responding to external stimuli: *sensitiveness to light.* SENSITIVITY is esp. capability of being sensitive to physiological, chemical action: *the sensitivity of a nerve.* —**Ant. 1.** apathy.

sen·si·ble (sĕn′sə bəl), *adj.* **1.** having, using, or showing good sense or sound judgment. **2.** cognizant; keenly aware (usually fol. by *of*): *sensible of his fault.* **3.** appreciable; considerable: *a sensible reduction.* **4.** capable of being perceived by the senses: *the sensible universe.* **5.** capable of feeling or perceiving, as organs or parts of the body. **6.** perceptible to the mind. **7.** conscious: *speechless but still sensible.* **8.** *Now Rare.* sensitive. [ME, t. LL: m. *sensibilis*] —**sen′si·ble·ness,** *n.* —**sen′si·bly,** *adv.* —**Syn. 1.** See **practical.**

sen·si·tive (sĕn′sə tĭv), *adj.* **1.** endowed with sensation. **2.** readily affected by external agencies or influences. **3.** having acute mental or emotional sensibility; easily affected, pained, annoyed, etc. **4.** pertaining to or connected with the senses or sensation. **5.** *Physiol.* having a low threshold of sensation or feeling. **6.** responding to stimulation, as leaves which move when touched. **7.** highly susceptible to certain agents, as photographic plates, films, or paper to light. **8.** constructed to indicate, measure, or be affected by small amounts or changes, as a balance or thermometer. **9.** *Radio.* easily affected by external influences, esp. by radio waves. [ME, t. ML: m. *sensitivus*, der. L *sensus* sense] —**sen′si·tive·ly,** *adv.* —**sen′si·tive·ness,** *n.*

sensitive plant, 1. a tropical American plant, *Mimosa pudica,* cultivated in greenhouses, with bipinnate leaves whose leaflets fold together when touched. **2.** any of various other plants sensitive to touch.

sen·si·tiv·i·ty (sĕn′sə tĭv′ə tĭ), *n., pl.* **-ties. 1.** state or quality of being sensitive. **2.** *Physiol.* **a.** the ability of an organism or part of an organism to react to stimuli; irritability. **b.** degree of susceptibility to stimulation. **3.** *Radio.* the ability to react to incoming radio waves. —**Syn. 1.** See **sensibility.**

sen·si·tize (sĕn′sə tīz′), *v.t.* **-tized, -tizing. 1.** to render sensitive. **2.** *Photog.* to render (a plate, film, etc.) sensitive to light or other forms of radiant energy. **3.** *Immunol.* to render sensitive to a serum by a series of injections. —**sen′si·ti·za′tion,** *n.* —**sen′si·tiz′er,** *n.*

sen·si·tom·e·ter (sĕn′sə tŏm′ə tər), *n. Photog.* an instrument for making a series of accurately known exposures on photographic surfaces, used to determine sensitiveness and other properties.

sen·so·ri·um (sĕn sōr′ĭ əm), *n., pl.* **-soriums, -soria** (-sōr′ĭ ə). *Anat.* the supposed seat of sensation in the brain, usually taken as the cortex or gray matter.[t. LL, der. L *sensus*, pp., felt]

sen·so·ry (sĕn′sə rĭ), *adj.* **1.** pertaining to sensation. **2.** *Physiol.* noting a structure that conveys an impulse that results or tends to result in sensation, as a nerve. Also, **sen·so·ri·al** (sĕn sōr′ĭ əl).

sen·su·al (sĕn′shŏŏ əl), *adj.* **1.** excessively inclined to the gratification of the senses; voluptuous. **2.** lewd or unchaste. **3.** pertaining to or given to the gratification of the senses or the indulgence of appetite. **4.** of or pertaining to the senses or physical sensation. **5.** pertaining to the doctrine of sensationalism. [late ME, t. LL: s. *sensuālis.* See SENSE, -AL¹] —**sen′su·al·ly,** *adv.* —**Syn. 1.** SENSUAL, SENSUOUS, VOLUPTUOUS refer to experience through the senses. SENSUAL refers, usually unfavorably, to the enjoyments derived from the senses, generally implying grossness or lewdness: *a sensual delight in eating, sensual excesses.* SENSUOUS refers, favorably or literally, to what is experienced through the senses: *sensuous impressions, sensuous poetry.* VOLUPTUOUS implies the luxurious gratification of sensuous or sensual desires: *voluptuous joys, voluptuous beauty.* —**Ant. 1.** ascetic.

sen·su·al·ism (sĕn′shŏŏ əl ĭz′əm), *n.* **1.** subjection to sensual appetites; sensuality. **2.** *Ethics.* the theory that the highest good consists in sensual gratification. **3.** *Philos.* the doctrine of sensationalism. **4.** *Aesthetics.* emphasis on objective sensuality, or on the quality of the sensual as the most important in the beautiful.

sen·su·al·ist (sĕn′shŏŏ əl ĭst), *n.* **1.** one given to the indulgence of the senses or appetites. **2.** one who holds the doctrine of sensationalism. —**sen′su·al·is′tic,** *adj.*

sen·su·al·i·ty (sĕn′shŏŏ ăl′ə tĭ), *n., pl.* **-ties. 1.** sensual nature. **2.** excessive indulgence in sensual pleasures. **3.** lewdness; unchastity. Also, **sen′su·al·ness.**

sen·su·al·ize (sĕn′shŏŏ ə līz′), *v.t.* **-ized, -izing.** to render sensual. —**sen′su·al·i·za′tion,** *n.*

sen·su·ous (sĕn′shŏŏ əs), *adj.* **1.** of or pertaining to the senses. **2.** perceived by or affecting the senses: *the sensuous qualities of music.* **3.** readily affected through the senses: *a sensuous temperament.* —**sen′su·ous·ly,** *adv.* —**sen′su·ous·ness,** *n.* —**Syn. 1.** See **sensual.**

sent (sĕnt), *v.* pt. and pp. of **send.**

sen·tence (sĕn′təns), *n., v.,* **-tenced, -tencing.** —*n.* **1.** a linguistic form (a word or a sequence of words arranged in a grammatical construction) which is not part of any larger construction, typically expressing an independent statement, inquiry, command, or the like, e.g., *Fire!* or *Summer is here* or *Who's there?* **2.** an opinion pronounced on some particular question. **3.** *Law.* **a.** an authoritative decision; a judicial judgment or decree, esp. the judicial determination of the punishment to be inflicted on a convicted criminal. **b.** the punishment itself. **4.** *Music.* a period. **5.** *Archaic.* a saying, apothegm, or maxim. —*v.t.* **6.** to pronounce sentence upon; condemn to punishment. [ME, t. F, t. L: m. *sententia* opinion] —**sen′tenc·er,** *n.*

sen·ten·tial (sĕn tĕn′shəl), *adj.* pertaining to or of of the nature of a judicial sentence.

sen·ten·tious (sĕn tĕn′shəs), *adj.* **1.** abounding in pithy sayings or maxims: *sententious style.* **2.** affectedly judicial in utterance; magisterial. **3.** given to or using pithy sayings or maxims. **4.** of the nature of a maxim; pithy. [late ME, t. L: m.s. *sententiōsus*] —**sen·ten′tiously,** *adv.* —**sen·ten′tious·ness,** *n.*

sen·tience (sĕn′shəns), *n.* sentient condition or character; capacity for sensation or feeling. Also, **sen′tien·cy.**

sen·tient (sĕn′shənt), *adj.* **1.** that feels; having the power of perception by the senses. **2.** characterized by sensation. —*n.* **3.** one who or that which is sentient. **4.** the mind. [t. L: s. *sentiens,* ppr., feeling] —**sen′tient·ly,** *adv.*

sen·ti·ment (sĕn′tə mənt), *n.* **1.** mental attitude with regard to something; opinion. **2.** a mental feeling; emotion: *a sentiment of pity.* **3.** refined or tender emotion; manifestation of the higher or more refined feelings. **4.** exhibition or manifestation of feeling or sensibility, or appeal to the tender emotions, in literature, art, or music. **5.** a thought influenced by or proceeding from feeling or emotion. **6.** the thought or feeling intended to be conveyed by words as distinguished from the words themselves. [t. LL: s. *sentimentum,* der. L *sentīre* feel; r. ME *sentement,* t. OF] —**Syn. 1.** See **opinion. 2.** See **feeling. 3.** SENTIMENT, SENTIMENTALITY are terms for sensitiveness to emotional feelings. SENTIMENT is a sincere and refined sensibility, a tendency to be influenced by emotion rather than by reason or fact: *to appeal to sentiment.* SENTIMENTALITY implies affected, excessive, sometimes mawkish sentiment: *weak sentimentality.* —**Ant. 2.** realism, logic.

sen·ti·men·tal (sĕn′tə mĕn′təl), *adj.* **1.** expressive of or appealing to sentiment or the tender emotions: *a sentimental song.* **2.** pertaining to or dependent on sentiment: *sentimental reasons.* **3.** weakly emotional; mawkishly susceptible or tender: *a sentimental schoolgirl.* **4.** characterized by or showing sentiment or refined feeling. —**sen′ti·men′tal·ly,** *adv.*

sen·ti·men·tal·ism (sĕn′tə mĕn′tə lĭz′əm), *n.* **1.** sentimental tendency or character; predominance of sentiment over reason. **2.** weak emotionalism; excessive indulgence in sentiment. **3.** a display of sentimentality.

sen·ti·men·tal·ist (sĕn′tə mĕn′təl ĭst), *n.* one given to sentiment or sentimentality.

sen·ti·men·tal·i·ty (sĕn′tə mĕn tăl′ə tĭ), *n., pl.* **-ties.** sentimental quality, disposition, behavior, etc. —**Syn.** See **sentiment.**

sen·ti·men·tal·ize (sĕn′tə mĕn′tə lĭz′), *v.,* **-ized, -izing.** —*v.i.* **1.** to indulge in sentiment. —*v.t.* **2.** to render sentimental, as a person, etc. **3.** to be sentimental over; turn into an object of sentiment.

sen·ti·nel (sĕn′tə nəl), *n., v.,* **-neled, -neling** or (*esp. Brit.*) **-nelled, -nelling.** —*n.* **1.** one who or that which watches, or stands as if watching. **2.** a soldier stationed as a guard to challenge all comers and prevent a surprise attack: *to stand sentinel.* —*v.t.* **3.** to watch over or guard as a sentinel. [t. F: m. *sentinelle,* t. It.: m. *sentinella,* der. LL *sentīnāre* avoid danger, der. *sentīre* perceive]

sen·try (sĕn′trĭ), *n., pl.* **-tries. 1.** a soldier stationed at a place to keep guard and prevent the passage of unauthorized persons, watch for fires, etc.; a sentinel. **2.** a member of a guard or watch. [? short for obs. *centrinel,* var. of SENTINEL]

sentry box, a small structure for sheltering a sentry from inclement weather.

Se·nu·si (sĕ nōō′sĭ), *n., pl.* **-sis.** a member of a fanatical and belligerent North African Moslem sect. Also, **Se·nus′si.** —**Se·nu′si·an,** *adj.*

Se·oul (sä′ŏŏl′; *Kor.* syœ′ŏŏl′), *n.* the capital of South Korea, in the W part. 715,572 (est. 1952). Japanese, **Keijo.**

Sep., 1. September. **2.** Septuagint.

se·pal (sē′pəl), *n. Bot.* each of the individual leaves or parts of the calyx of a flower. [t. NL: s. *sēpalum,* b. L *sēp(arātus)* separate and L *(pet)alum* petal]

-sepalous, a word element meaning "having sepals," as in *polysepalous.* [f. SEPAL + -OUS]

sep·a·ra·ble (sĕp′ə rə bəl), *adj.* capable of being separated. —**sep′a·ra·bil′i·ty, sep′a·ra·ble·ness,** *n.* —**sep′a·ra·bly,** *adv.*

Sepals
A. Flower and sepal of marsh marigold, *Caltha palustris*
B. Flower and calyx of chickweed, *Stellaria media*

sep·a·rate (v. sĕp′ə rāt′; adj., n. sĕp′ər ĭt), v., **-rated,** **-rating,** adj., n. —v.t. **1.** to keep apart or divide, as by an intervening barrier, space, etc. **2.** to put apart; part: *to separate persons fighting.* **3.** to disconnect; disunite: *to separate church and state.* **4.** to remove from personal association: *separated from his wife.* **5.** to part or divide (an assemblage, mass, compound, etc.) into individuals, components, or elements. **6.** to take (fol. by *from* or *out*) by such parting or dividing: *separate metal from ore.* —v.i. **7.** to part company; withdraw from personal association. **8.** to draw or come apart; become disconnected or disengaged. **9.** to become parted from a mass or compound, as crystals. **10.** to withdraw (fol. by *from*): *to separate from a church.* —adj. **11.** separated, disconnected, or disjoined. **12.** unconnected or distinct: *two separate questions.* **13.** being or standing apart; cut off from access: *separate houses.* **14.** existing or maintained independently: *separate organizations.* **15.** individual or particular: *each separate item.* —n. **16.** something separate. [ME, t. L: m.s. *sēparātus,* pp.] —**sep′a·rate·ly,** adv. —**sep′a·rate·ness,** n.
—Syn. **1.** SEPARATE, DIVIDE imply a putting apart or keeping apart of things from each other. To SEPARATE is to remove from each other things previously associated: *to separate a mother from her children.* To DIVIDE is to split or break up carefully according to measurement, rule, or plan: *to divide a cake into equal parts.* —Ant. **1.** combine, unite.

sep·a·ra·tion (sĕp′ə rā′shən), n. **1.** act of separating. **2.** state of being separated. **3.** a place, line, or point of parting. **4.** *Law.* **a.** a limited divorce. **b.** cessation of conjugal cohabitation, as by mutual consent.

separation center, a place at which army or navy personnel are released from service into civilian life.

sep·a·ra·tist (sĕp′ər ə tĭst), n. **1.** one who separates, withdraws, or secedes, as from an established church. **2.** an advocate of separation, esp. ecclesiastical or political separation. —**sep·a·ra·tism** (sĕp′ər ə tĭz′əm), n.

sep·a·ra·tive (sĕp′ə rā′tĭv), adj. tending to separate; causing separation.

sep·a·ra·tor (sĕp′ə rā′tər), n. **1.** one who or that which separates. **2.** an apparatus for separating one thing from another, as cream from milk, steam from water, or wheat from chaff, dirt, etc. [t. LL]

Se·phar·dim (sĭ fär′dĭm), n.pl. Spanish-Portuguese Jews and their descendants. Cf. **Ashkenazim.** [t. Heb., der. *s′phāradh,* country mentioned in Obad. 20] —**Sephar′dic,** adj.

se·pi·a (sē′pĭ ə), n. **1.** a brown pigment obtained from the inklike secretion of various cuttlefish, and used with brush or pen in drawing. **2.** a drawing made with sepia. **3.** a dark brown. **4.** *Photog.* a brown-colored image, supposed to duplicate sepia ink. **5.** a cuttlefish of the genus *Sepia* or some allied genus. —adj. **6.** of a brown similar to that from sepia ink. [t. L, t. Gk.]

se·pi·o·lite (sē′pĭ ə līt′), n. meerschaum. [t. G: m. *sepiolith,* f. Gk. *sēpio(n)* cuttlebone + *-lith* -LITE]

se·poy (sē′poi), n. (in India) a native soldier in the military service of Europeans, esp. of the British. [t. Pg.: m. *sipae,* t. Hind. and Pers.: m. *sipāhī* horseman, der. *sipāh* army]

Sepoy Rebellion, a revolt of the sepoy troops in British India, 1857–59, resulting in the transfer of the administration of India from the East India Company to the crown. Also, **Sepoy Mutiny.**

sep·sis (sĕp′sĭs), n. *Pathol.* local or generalized bacterial invasion of the body, especially by pyogenic organisms: *dental sepsis, wound sepsis.* [NL, t. Gk.]

sept (sĕpt), n. **1.** a clan (orig. with reference to tribes or families in Ireland). **2.** *Anthropol.* a group believing itself derived from a common ancestor. [special use of *sept* enclosure, fold (t. L: s. *sēptum*), by contam. with obs. *sect* clan (Irish)]

sept-, a prefix meaning "seven," in *septet.* Also, **septem-, septo-, septi-**[1]. [t. L, comb. form of *septem*]

Sept., 1. September. **2.** Septuagint.

sep·ta (sĕp′tə), n. pl. of **septum.**

sep·tal (sĕp′tal), adj. of or pertaining to a septum.

sep·tar·i·um (sĕp târ′ĭ əm), n., pl. **-taria** (-târ′ĭ ə). *Geol.* a concretionary nodule or mass, usually of calcium carbonate or of argillaceous carbonate of iron, traversed within by a network of cracks filled with calcite and other minerals. [NL, der. L *sēptum* enclosure] —**sep·tar′i·an,** adj.

sep·tate (sĕp′tāt), adj. divided by a septum or septa. [t. NL: m.s. *sēptātus.* See SEPTUM, -ATE[1]]

Sep·tem·ber (sĕp tĕm′bər), n. the ninth month of the year, containing 30 days. [OE, t. L, the seventh month in the early Roman calendar]

Sep·tem·brist (sĕp tĕm′brĭst), n. (in the French Revolution) one of those who instigated or took part in the massacre of royalist and other inmates of the prisons of Paris, Sept. 2–6, 1792.

sep·tem·par·tite (sĕp′tĕm pär′tīt), adj. separated into seven sections.

sep·te·nar·y (sĕp′tə nĕr′ĭ), adj., n., pl. **-naries.** —adj. **1.** of or pertaining to the number seven; forming a group of seven. **2.** septennial. —n. **3.** a group or set of seven. **4.** a period of seven years. **5.** the number seven. **6.** *Pros.* a line with seven feet. [t. L: m.s. *septēnārius*]

sep·ten·ni·al (sĕp tĕn′ĭ əl), adj. **1.** occurring every seven years. **2.** of or for seven years. [f. s. L *septennium* seven years + -AL[1]] —**sep·ten′ni·al·ly,** adv.

sep·ten·tri·o·nal (sĕp tĕn′trĭ ə nəl), adj. *Archaic.* northern. [ME, t. L: s. *septentriōnālis*]

sep·tet (sĕp tĕt′), n. **1.** any group of seven persons or things. **2.** a company of seven singers or players. **3.** a musical composition for seven voices or instruments. Also, esp. *Brit.,* **sep·tette′.** [t. G. See SEPT-, -ET]

septi-[1], var. of **sept-,** before most consonants.

septi-[2], a word element representing **septum,** as in *septicidal.*

sep·tic (sĕp′tĭk), adj. **1.** infective, usually with a pus-forming microbe. **2.** pertaining to or of the nature of sepsis; infected. —n. **3.** an agent which causes sepsis. [t. L: s. *sēpticus,* t. Gk.: m. *sēptikós*] —**sep·tic·i·ty** (sĕp tĭs′ə tĭ), n.

sep·ti·ce·mi·a (sĕp′tə sē′mĭ ə), n. *Pathol.* the invasion and persistence of pathogenic bacteria in the blood stream. Also, **sep′ti·cae′mi·a.** [NL, f. Gk. See SEPTIC, -(H)EMIA] —**sep′ti·ce′mic,** adj.

sep·ti·cid·al (sĕp′tə sĭd′əl), adj. *Bot.* characterized by splitting through the septa or dissepiments, as a mode of dehiscence. [f. SEPTI-[2] + s. L -*cīdere* cut + -AL[1]]

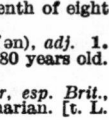

septic sore throat, an acute, toxic, streptococcus infection of the throat producing fever, tonsillitis, and other serious effects.

septic tank, a tank in which solid organic sewage is decomposed and purified by anaerobic bacteria.

sep·tif·ra·gal (sĕp tĭf′rə gəl), adj. *Bot.* characterized by the breaking away of the valves from the septa or dissepiments, in dehiscence. [f. SEPTI-[2] + L *frag-* break + -AL[1]]

Septicidal dehiscence V, Valves; D, Dissepiments; C, Axis

sep·til·lion (sĕp tĭl′yən), n. **1.** (usually with *one* or *a*) a cardinal number represented (in the U.S. and France) by one followed by 24 zeros, and (in Gt. Britain and Germany) by one followed by 42 zeros. —adj. **2.** (usually with *one* or *a*) amounting to one septillion in number. [t. F, f. L *sept(em)* + (m)*illion* MILLION] —**sep·til′lionth,** n., adj.

sep·time (sĕp′tēm), n. *Fencing.* the seventh of eight defensive positions. [t. L: m.s. *septimus*]

sep·tu·a·ge·nar·i·an (sĕp′chŏŏ ə jə nâr′ĭ ən), adj. **1.** of the age of 70 years, or between 70 and 80 years old. —n. **2.** a septuagenarian person.

sep·tu·ag·e·nar·y (sĕp′chŏŏ ăj′ə nĕr′ĭ or, esp. *Brit.,* -ə jē′nə rĭ), adj., n., pl. **-naries.** septuagenarian. [t. L: m.s. *septuāgēnārius*]

Sep·tu·a·ges·i·ma (sĕp′chŏŏ ə jĕs′ə mə), n. the third Sunday before Lent (more fully, **Septuagesima Sunday**). [t. L: *septuāgēsima* (*dies*) seventieth day]

Sep·tu·a·gint (sĕp′chŏŏ ə jĭnt′, -chŏŏ-), n. the Greek version of the Old Testament traditionally said to have been made at the request of Ptolemy II, king of Egypt (309–247? B.C.), by 72 Jewish scholars, in 72 days. [t. L: s. *septuāginta* seventy]

sep·tum (sĕp′təm), n., pl. **-ta** (-tə). **1.** *Biol.* a dividing wall, membrane, or the like in a plant or animal structure; a dissepiment. **2.** an osmotic membrane. [t. L: enclosure]

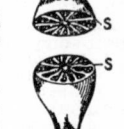

sep·tu·ple (sĕp′tyŏŏ pəl, -tŏŏ-, sĕp tū′pəl, -tŏŏ′-), adj., v., **-pled, -pling.** —adj. **1.** sevenfold; seven times as great. —v.t. **2.** to make seven times as great. [t. LL: m.s. *septuplus*]

sep·ul·cher (sĕp′əl kər), n. **1.** a tomb, grave, or burial place. **2.** *Eccles.* a structure or a recess in some old churches in which the sacred elements, the cross, etc., were deposited with due ceremonies on Good Friday to be taken out at Easter, in commemoration of Christ's entombment and resurrection (often called **Easter sepulcher**). —v.t. **3.** to place in a sepulcher; bury. Also, esp. *Brit.,* **sepulchre.** [ME *sepulcre,* t. OF, t. L: m. *sepulcrum*]

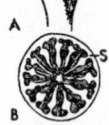

S, Septum A, Transverse section of fruit of poppy; B, Diagram of same

se·pul·chral (sə pŭl′krəl), adj. **1.** of, pertaining to, or serving as a tomb. **2.** of or pertaining to burial. **3.** proper to or suggestive of a tomb; funereal or dismal. **4.** hollow and deep: *sepulchral tone.* —**se·pul′chral·ly,** adv.

sep·ul·chre (sĕp′əl kər), n., v.t., **-chred, -chring.** *Chiefly Brit.* sepulcher.

sep·ul·ture (sĕp′əl chər), n. **1.** act of placing in a sepulcher or tomb; burial. **2.** *Archaic.* sepulcher; tomb. [ME *sepulture,* t. OF, t. L: m. *sepultūra*]

seq., 1. sequel. **2.** (L *sequens*) the following (one).

seqq., (L *sequentia*) the following (ones).

se·qua·cious (sĭ kwā′shəs), adj. *Rare.* **1.** following another person, esp. unreasoningly. **2.** following with smooth regularity, as musical tones, thoughts, etc. [f. SEQUACI(TY) (t. L: m.s. *sequācitas* facility in following) + -OUS] —**se·qua′cious·ly,** adv. —**se·quac·i·ty** (sĭ kwăs′ə tĭ), n.

se·quel (sē′kwəl), n. **1.** a literary work, complete in itself, but continuing a preceding work. **2.** an event or circumstance following something; subsequent course of affairs. **3.** a result, consequence, or inference. [ME *sequele,* t. L: m. *sequēla*]

---

b., blend of, blended; c., cognate with; d., dialect, dialectal; der., derived from; f., formed from; g., going back to; m., modification of; r., replacing; s., stem of; t., taken from; ?, perhaps. See the full key on inside cover.

se·que·la (sĭ kwē′lə), n., pl. **-lae** (-lē). Pathol. a morbid affection resulting from a previous disease. [t. L]

se·quence (sē′kwəns), n. **1.** the following of one thing after another; succession. **2.** order of succession: a list of books in alphabetical sequence. **3.** a continuous or connected series: a sonnet sequence. **4.** something that follows; a subsequent event; result; consequence. **5.** Music. a melodic or harmonic pattern repeated three or more times at different pitches, with or without modulation. **6.** Rom. Cath. Ch. a hymn sometimes sung after the gradual and before the gospel; a prose. **7.** Motion Pictures. a portion of a film story set in the same place and time, and without interruptions or breaks of any sort. **8.** Cards. a set of three or more cards following one another in order of value. [ME, t. LL: m. sequentia, der. L sequens, ppr., following] **—Syn. 1.** See series.

se·quent (sē′kwənt), adj. **1.** following; successive. **2.** following logically or naturally; consequent. **3.** characterized by continuous succession; consecutive. —n. **4.** that which follows in order or as a result. [t. L: s. sequens, ppr., following]

se·quen·tial (sĭ kwĕn′shəl), adj. **1.** characterized by regular sequence of parts. **2.** following; subsequent; consequent. **—se·quen′tial·ly,** adv.

se·ques·ter (sĭ kwĕs′tər), v.t. **1.** to remove or withdraw into solitude or retirement; seclude. **2.** to remove or separate. **3.** Law. to remove (property) temporarily from the possession of the owner; seize and hold, as the property and income of a debtor, until legal claims are satisfied. **4.** Internat. Law. to requisition, hold, and control (enemy property). [ME sequestre, t. LL: m. sequestrāre separate, der. L sequester depositary, trustee]

se·ques·tered (sĭ kwĕs′tərd), adj. secluded or out-of-the-way: a sequestered village.

se·ques·trate (sĭ kwĕs′trāt), v.t., **-trated, -trating. 1.** Law. **a.** to sequester (property). **b.** to confiscate. **2.** Archaic. to separate; seclude. **—se·ques·tra·tor** (sē′kwĕs trā′tər, sĭ kwĕs′trā tər), n.

se·ques·tra·tion (sē′kwĕs trā′shən, sĕk′wĕs-), n. **1.** removal or separation; banishment or exile. **2.** withdrawal, retirement, or seclusion. **3.** Law. **a.** the sequestering of property. **b.** confiscation or seizure.

se·ques·trec·to·my (sē′kwĕs trĕk′tə mĭ), n., pl. **-mies.** Surg. the removal of dead spicules or portions, esp. of bone.

se·ques·trum (sĭ kwĕs′trəm), n., pl. **-tra** (-trə). Pathol. a dead portion of bone separated from the living bone. [NL, special use of NL sequestrum something detached, prop. neut. of L sequester mediating]

se·quin (sē′kwĭn), n. **1.** a small shining disk or spangle used to ornament a dress, etc. **2.** Also, **zecchino, zechin.** a former Italian and Turkish gold coin, worth about $2.25, first minted in Venice about 1280. [t. F, t. It.: m. zecchino, a Venetian coin, der. zecca mint, t. Ar.: m. sikka a die for coins] **—se′quined** adj.

se·quoi·a (sĭ kwoi′ə), n. a generic part of the name of either of two related, extremely large coniferous trees in California (the big tree and redwood), both formerly included in the genus Sequoia. The big tree is now classified in the genus Sequoiadendron, the redwood retaining the name Sequoia. [t. NL, named for Sikwâyi, a Cherokee Indian, inventor of a syllabary for writing Cherokee]

se·quoi·a·den·dron (sĭ kwoi′ə dĕn′drŏn), n. a coniferous big tree of the western slopes of the Sierra Nevada Mts. in California, Sequoiadendron giganteum, or Sequoia gigantea.

Sequoia National Park, a national park in central California: giant sequoia trees. 604 sq. mi.

ser (sĭr), n. a unit of weight in India, varying in value but usually ¹⁄₄₀ of a maund. The government ser is divided into 80 tolas of 180 English grains and equals nearly 2 lbs. 1 oz. avoirdupois. Also, **seer.** [t. Hind.]

ser., **1.** series. **2.** sermon.

sé·rac (sē răk′), n. a large block or pinnaclelike mass of ice on a glacier, formed by melting or movement of the ice. [t. Swiss-F, orig. the name of a white cheese]

se·rag·lio (sĭ răl′yō, -răl′-), n., pl. **-raglios. 1.** the part of a Mohammedan house or palace in which the wives and concubines are secluded; a harem. **2.** a Turkish palace, esp. of the Sultan. [t. It.: m. serraglio (rendering Turk. serāi SERAI), ult. der. L serāre lock up]

se·ra·i (sə rä′ē, -rī′), n., pl. **-rais.** (in Eastern countries) a caravansary. [t. Turk., t. Pers.: lodging, palace]

Se·ra·je·vo (sĕ′rä′yĕ′vō), n. Sarajevo.

se·ra·pe (sē rä′pĕ), n. a kind of shawl or wrap, often of gay colors, worn by Spanish-Americans. [t. Mex. Sp.]

ser·aph (sĕr′əf), n., pl. **-aphs, -aphim** (-ə fĭm) **1.** one of the celestial beings hovering above God's throne in Isaiah's vision. Isa. 6. **2.** a member of the highest order of angels, often represented as a child's head with wings above, below, and on each side. [back formation from seraphim (pl.), ME serafin, t. LL: m. seraphīm, t. Heb.]

se·raph·ic (sĭ răf′ĭk), adj. of, like, or befitting a seraph. Also, **se·raph′i·cal. —se·raph′i·cal·ly,** adv.

ser·a·phim (sĕr′ə fĭm), n. a pl. of seraph.

Se·ra·pis (sĭ rā′pĭs), n. a deity of Egyptian origin who was worshiped as the dead Apis under the attributes of Osiris. His cult was started under the Ptolemies and introduced into Greece and Rome.

Serb (sûrb), n. **1.** a Serbian. **2.** Serbo-Croatian (language). **3.** Serbian (language). —adj. **4.** Serbian. [t. Serbian]

Ser·bi·a (sûr′bĭ ə), n. a former kingdom in S Europe: now (with revised boundaries) a constituent republic of Yugoslavia, in the SE part. 7,335,000 pop. (est. 1956); ab. 35,000 sq. mi. Cap.: Belgrade.

Serbia, 1878–1914

Ser·bi·an (sûr′bĭ ən), adj. **1.** of Serbia, its inhabitants, or their language. —n. **2.** a native or inhabitant of Serbia, esp. one of the Slavic race inhabiting it. **3.** Serbo-Croatian, esp. as spoken in Serbia.

Serbo-, a word element representing Serb.

Ser·bo-Cro·a·tian (sûr′bō-krō ā′shən), n. the principal Slavic language of Yugoslavia, usually written with Cyrillic letters in Serbia but with Roman letters in Croatia.

Ser·bo·ni·an (sûr bō′nĭ ən), adj. of or designating a large marshy tract in ancient northern Egypt, in which entire armies are said to have been swallowed up. [f. Serboni(s) (t. Gk.: name of the marsh) + -AN]

Serbs, Croats, and Slovenes. See Yugoslavia.

sere[1] (sĭr), adj. dry; withered. [var. of SEAR]

sere[2] (sĭr), n. the series of stages in an ecological succession. [back formation from SERIES]

se·rein (sə răN′), n. Meteorol. a very fine rain falling from a clear sky after sunset. [F: evening damp, OF serain nightfall, der. L sērum evening, sērus late]

ser·e·nade (sĕr′ə nād′), n., v., **-naded, -nading.** —n. **1.** a complimentary performance of vocal or instrumental music in the open air at night, as by a lover under the window of his lady. **2.** a piece of music suitable for such performance. —v.t., v.i. **3.** to entertain with or perform a serenade. [t. F, t. It.: m. serenata. See SERENATA] **—ser′e·nad′er,** n.

ser·e·na·ta (sĕr′ə nä′tə), n., pl. **-tas, -te** (-tĕ). Music. **1.** a form of secular cantata, often of a dramatic or imaginative character. **2.** an instrumental composition in several movements, intermediate between the suite and the symphony. [t. It.: an evening song, der. sereno the open air, n. use of adj. sereno serene (g. L serēnus)]

Ser·en·dip (sĕr′ən dĭp′), n. old name for Ceylon.

ser·en·dip·i·ty (sĕr′ən dĭp′ə tĭ), n. the faculty of making desirable but unsought-for discoveries by accident. [f. (The Three Princes of) SERENDIP (who had this faculty) by H. Walpole + -ITY]

se·rene (sə rēn′), adj. **1.** calm; peaceful; tranquil: serene sea, a serene old age. **2.** clear; fair: serene weather. **3.** (often cap.) an epithet used in titles of princes, etc.: his Serene Highness. —n. **4.** Poetic. a clear or tranquil expanse of sky, sea, etc. [t. L: m.s. serēnus] **—se·rene′ly,** adv. **—se·rene′ness,** n. **—Syn. 1.** unruffled, undisturbed. See peaceful. **—Ant. 1.** agitated.

se·ren·i·ty (sə rĕn′ə tĭ), n., pl. **-ties. 1.** calmness; tranquility. **2.** clearness, as of the sky, air, etc. **3.** (usually cap., with his, your, etc.) a title of honor given to certain reigning princes, etc.

Se·reth (zā′rət), n. German name of Siret.

serf (sûrf), n. **1.** a person in a condition of servitude, required to render services to his lord, and commonly attached to the lord's land and transferred with it from one owner to another. **2.** Obs. a slave. [late ME, t. F, g. L servus slave] **—serf·dom** (sûrf′dəm), **serf′hood**, n.

Serg., Sergeant. Also, **Sergt.**

serge (sûrj), n. **1.** a twilled worsted or woolen fabric used esp. for clothing. **2.** cotton, rayon, or silk in a twill weave. [t. F; r. ME sarge, t. OF, g. var. of L sērica silken]

ser·geant (sär′jənt), n. **1.** a noncommissioned army officer of rank above that of corporal. **2.** a police officer of higher rank than a common policeman or constable. **3.** an officer of a court, charged with the arrest of offenders, the summoning of defendants, and with the enforcement of the decrees of the court or of its presiding official. **4.** a sergeant at arms. **5.** Also, **sergeant at law.** Brit. a member of a superior order of barristers, now abolished. **6.** Obs. a tenant by military service, below the rank of knight. Also, esp. Brit., **serjeant.** [ME sergeaunte, t. OF: m. sergent, g. s. L serviens, ppr., serving] **—ser·gean·cy** (sär′jən sĭ), **ser′geant·ship′**, n.

sergeant at arms, an executive officer of a legislative or other body, whose duty it is to enforce the commands of the body, preserve order, etc.

sergeant first class, U.S. Army. a noncommissioned officer ranking below a master sergeant and above a sergeant.

sergeant fish, 1. a large fusiform fish, Rachycentron canadus, found on the eastern coast of temperate and tropical America, in the East Indies, and in Japan. **2.** the large robalo, Centropomus undecimalis.

sergeant major, 1. U.S. the senior noncommissioned officer in charge of the enlisted clerical force in a regimental or similar headquarters. **2.** Brit. the highest noncommissioned military officer. **3.** U.S. Local. the cow pilot (fish).

se·ri·al (sĭr′ĭ əl), n. **1.** anything published, broadcast, etc., in short installments at regular intervals, as a novel appearing in successive issues of a magazine. **2.** a journal or report issued in successive numbers. (In library usage serial does not include newspapers, but does include other periodicals and reports issued annually or less frequently.) —*adj.* **3.** published in installments or successive parts: *a serial story.* **4.** pertaining to such publication. **5.** of, pertaining to, or arranged in a series. [t. NL: s. *seriālis*, der. L *series* series] —**se/ri·al·ly,** *adv.*

se·ri·al·ize (sîr/ĭ ə līz/), *v.t.,* **-ized, -izing.** to publish in serial form.

serial number, an individual number assigned to a particular person, article, etc.

se·ri·ate (sîr/ĭ ĭt, -āt/), *adj.* arranged or occurring in one or more series. —**se/ri·ate·ly,** *adv.*

se·ri·a·tim (sîr/ĭ ā/tĭm, sĕr/ĭ-), *adv.* in a series; one after another. [t. ML, der. L *series* series; modeled on *literatim, verbatim,* etc.]

se·ri·ceous (sĭ rĭsh/əs), *adj.* **1.** silky. **2.** covered with silky down, as a leaf. [t. L: m. *sēriceus*]

ser·i·cin (sĕr/ə sĭn), *n. Chem.* a gelatinous organic compound obtained from silk.

ser·i·cul·ture (sĕr/ə kŭl/chər), *n.* the rearing and keeping of silkworms, for the production of raw silk. [short for *sericiculture.* t. F, f. *sērici-* (repr. L *sēricum* silk) + *culture* CULTURE] —**ser/i·cul/tur·al,** *adj.* —**ser/i·cul/tur·ist,** *n.*

ser·i·e·ma (sĕr/ĭ ē/mə, -ā/mə), *n.* **1.** a large bird, *Cariama cristata,* with long legs and a crested head, native in southern Brazil, etc. **2.** a smaller allied bird, *Chunga burmeisteri,* native to Argentina. [t. NL, t. Tupi: m. *siriema,* said to mean crested]

se·ries (sîr/ĭz), *n., pl.* **-ries. 1.** a number of things, events, etc., ranged or occurring in spatial, temporal, or other succession; a sequence. **2.** a set, as of coins, stamps, etc. **3.** a set of volumes, as of a periodical, or as issued in like form with similarity of subject or purpose. **4.** *Math.* the sum of the terms of a sequence of entities. **5.** *Rhet.* a succession of coördinate sentence elements. **6. in series,** *Elect.* with the positive pole, terminal, or the like, of one, joined to the negative of the next (of batteries, etc.). [t. L] —**Syn. 1.** SERIES, SEQUENCE, SUCCESSION are terms for an orderly following of things one after another. SERIES is applied to a number of things of the same kind, usually related to each other, arranged or happening in order: *a series of baseball games.* SEQUENCE stresses the continuity in time, thought, cause and effect, etc : *the scenes came in a definite sequence.* SUCCESSION implies that one thing is followed by another (or others in turn), usually though not necessarily with a relation or connection between them: *succession to a throne, a succession of calamities.*

se·ries-wound (sîr/ĭz wound/), *adj. Elect.* denoting a commutator motor in which the field circuit and armature circuit are connected in series.

ser·if (sĕr/ĭf), *n. Print.* a smaller line used to finish off a main stroke of a letter, as at the top and bottom of M. See diag. under **type.** [prob. t. D: m. *schreef* stroke, line, der. *schrijven* write]

ser·in (sĕr/ĭn), *n.* a small finch, *Serinus canarius,* of Europe, northwest Africa, etc., from which the common canary has been developed. [t. F; orig. uncert.]

ser·ine (sĕr/ēn, sîr/ēn, -ĭn), *n. Biochem.* an amino acid, $C_3H_7O_3N$, obtained by the hydrolysis of sericin, the protein constituting silk gum. [f. SER(UM) + -INE²]

se·rin·ga (sə rĭng/gə), *n.* any of several Brazilian trees of the genus *Hevea,* yielding rubber. [t. Pg.]

Se·rin·ga·pa·tam (sə rĭng/gə pə täm/), *n.* a town in S India: the former capital of Mysore state; taken by the British, 1799. 7678 (1941).

se·ri·o·com·ic (sîr/ĭ ō kŏm/ĭk), *adj.* partly serious and partly comic. Also, **se/ri·o·com/i·cal.**

se·ri·ous (sîr/ĭ əs), *adj.* **1.** of grave or solemn disposition or character; thoughtful. **2.** of grave aspect: *serious dress.* **3.** being in earnest; not trifling. **4.** demanding earnest thought or application: *serious reading.* **5.** weighty or important: *a serious matter.* **6.** giving cause for apprehension; critical: *a serious illness.* [ME, t. L: s. *sēriōsus,* der. L *sērius*] —**se/ri·ous·ly,** *adv.* —**se/ri·ous·ness,** *n.* —**Syn. 1.** See **earnest.**

ser·jeant (sär/jənt), *n. Chiefly Brit.* sergeant.

ser·mon (sûr/mən), *n.* **1.** a discourse for the purpose of religious instruction or exhortation, esp. one based on a text of Scripture and delivered from a pulpit. **2.** any similar serious discourse or exhortation. **3.** a long, tedious speech. [ME, t. L: s. *sermo* discourse, ML *sermon*]

ser·mon·ic (sər mŏn/ĭk), *adj.* pertaining to, of the nature of, or resembling a sermon. Also, **ser·mon/i·cal.**

ser·mon·ize (sûr/mə nīz/), *v.,* **-ized, -izing.** —*v.i.* **1.** to deliver or compose a sermon; preach. —*v.t.* **2.** to give serious exhortation to ; lecture. —**ser/mon·iz/er,** *n.*

Sermon on the Mount, the discourse delivered by Jesus, recorded in Matt. 5–7 and Luke 6:20–49.

sero-, a word element representing serum, as in *serology.*

se·rol·o·gy (sĭ rŏl/ə jĭ), *n.* the scientific study of the properties and action of the serum of the blood.

ser·o·tine¹ (sĕr/ə tĭn, -tīn/), *adj. Rare.* late. Also, **se·rot·i·nous** (sĭ rŏt/ə nəs). [t. F, t. L: m. *sērōtinus* late]

ser·o·tine² (sĕr/ə tĭn, -tīn/), *n.* a small European bat, *Vespertilio* or *Vesperugo serotinus.* [t. F, t. L: m. *sērōtina* (fem.) late, i.e. flying late in the evening]

ser·o·to·nin (sĕr/ə tō/nĭn), *n.* a hormone which induces muscular contraction: found in the brain, intestines, and platelets. [f. SERO- + TON(E) + -IN²]

se·rous (sîr/əs), *adj.* **1.** of a watery nature, or resembling serum. **2.** containing serum; secreting serum.

3. pertaining to or characterized by serum. [t. L: m. s. *serōsus*] —**se·ros·i·ty** (sĭ rŏs/ə tĭ), *n.*

serous fluid, any of various animal liquids resembling blood serum, as the fluids of the serous membranes.

serous membrane, *Anat., Zool.* any of various thin membranes, as the peritoneum, which line certain cavities of the body and exude a serous fluid.

ser·ow (sĕr/ō), *n.* a goat antelope, genus *Capricornis,* of eastern Asia, related to the goral. [native name]

ser·pent (sûr/pənt), *n.* **1.** a snake. **2.** a wily, treacherous, or malicious person. **3.** Satan. Gen. 3: 1–5. **4.** a kind of firework which burns with serpentine motion or flame. **5.** an old wooden musical wind instrument of serpentine form and deep tone. [ME, t. L: s. *serpens* creeping thing, prop. ppr. of *serpere* creep; c. Gk. *hérpein*]

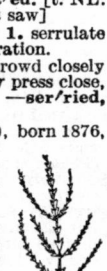

Man playing a serpent, 18th century

ser·pen·tine¹ (sûr/pən tēn/, -tīn/), *adj.* **1.** of or pertaining to a serpent. **2.** moving in a winding course or having a winding form; tortuous; winding. **3.** having the qualities of a serpent; subtle, wily, or cunning. [ME, t. L: m. *serpentīnus*]

ser·pen·tine² (sûr/pən tēn/), *n.* a common mineral, hydrous magnesium silicate, $H_4Mg_3Si_2O_9$, usually oily green and sometimes spotted, occurring in many varieties: used for architectural and decorative purposes. [ME, t. ML: m. *serpentīnum,* prop. neut. of L *serpentīnus*]

ser·pi·go (sər pī/gō), *n. Pathol.* a creeping or spreading skin disease, as ringworm. [ME, t. ML, der. L *serpere* creep] —**ser·pig·i·nous** (sər pĭj/ə nəs), *adj.*

Ser·ra Ju·ní·pe·ro (sĕr/rä hōō nē/pĕ rô/), **Miguel José** (mē gĕl/ hô sĕ/), 1713–1784, Spanish Roman Catholic missionary to the Indians in California and Mexico.

ser·ra·noid (sĕr/ə noid/), *adj.* **1.** belonging to the *Serranidae,* a numerous family of fishes including the sea basses, groupers, jewfishes, etc. —*n.* **2.** a serranoid fish, as the red grouper. [f. s. NL *Serrānus,* genus of fishes (der. L *serra* saw, sawfish) + -OID]

ser·rate (sĕr/ĭt, -āt), *adj. Chiefly Biol.* having sharp teeth. Also, **ser·rat·ed** (sĕr/ā tĭd). [t. L: m.s. *serrātus* saw-shaped]

ser·ra·tion (sĕ rā/shən), *n.* **1.** serrated condition or form. **2.** a serrated edge or formation. **3.** one of the notches or teeth of such an edge or formation. Also, **ser·ra·ture** (sĕr/ə chər).

Serrate leaf

ser·ri·form (sĕr/ə fôrm/), *adj.* resembling a saw; serrate. [f. *serri-* (t. NL, comb. form repr. L *serra* saw) + -FORM]

ser·ru·late (sĕr/yə lĭt, -lāt/, sĕr/ə-), *adj.* finely or minutely serrate, as a leaf. Also, **ser/ru·lat/ed.** [t. NL: m.s. *serrulātus,* der. L *serrula,* dim. of *serra* saw]

ser·ru·la·tion (sĕr/yə lā/shən, sĕr/ə-), *n.* **1.** serrulate condition or form. **2.** a fine or minute serration.

ser·ry (sĕr/ĭ), *v.i., v.t.,* **-ried, -rying.** to crowd closely together. [appar. t. F: m. *serré,* pp. of *serrer* press close, ult. g. L *serāre* bar, bolt, der. L *sera* bar] —**ser/ried,** *adj.*

Sert (sĕrt), *n.* **José María** (hô sĕ/ mä rē/ä), born 1876, Spanish mural painter.

Ser·to·ri·us (sər tōr/ĭ əs), *n.* **Quintus** (kwĭn/təs), died 72 B.C., Roman general and statesman.

ser·tu·lar·i·an (sûr/chŏŏ lâr/ĭ ən), *n. Zool.* a type of hydroid that forms stiff feathery colonies in which the cups holding the zoöids are sessile. [f. s. NL *Sertulāria,* genus name (der. L *sertula,* dim. of *serta* garland) + -AN]

Sertularian

se·rum (sîr/əm), *n., pl.* **serums, sera** (sîr/ə). **1.** the clear, pale-yellow liquid which separates from the clot in the coagulation of blood; blood serum. **2.** a fluid of this kind obtained from the blood of an animal which has been rendered immune to some disease by inoculation, used as an antitoxic or therapeutic agent. **3.** any watery animal fluid. **4.** the thin clear fluid medium in which plant substances are held. **5.** (of milk) **a.** that portion left after butterfat, casein, and albumin have been removed. **b.** that portion left after the manufacture of cheese. [t. L: whey]

ser·val (sûr/vəl), *n.* a long-limbed African cat, *Felis serval,* having a tawny coat spotted with black, and about the size of a bobcat. [t. NL, t. Pg.: m. (*lobo) cerval* lynx, der. L (*lupus) cervus* (wolf) deer]

serv·ant (sûr/vənt), *n.* **1.** a person employed in domestic duties. **2.** a person in the service of another. **3.** a person employed by the government: *a public servant.* [ME, t. OF, prop. ppr. of *servir* SERVE] —**Syn. 1.** SERVANT, EMPLOYEE refer to persons who work for others for pay. SERVANT, with the exception of such traditional expressions as *public servant* or *civil servant,* is now restricted

Serval, *Felis serval*
(Total length ab. 5 ft., tail 1 ft.)

---

b., blend of, blended; c., cognate with; d., dialect, dialectal; der., derived from; f., formed from; g., going back to; m., modification of; r., replacing; s., stem of; t., taken from; ?, perhaps. See the full key on inside cover.

largely to one who works in domestic service: *a faithful old servant.* EMPLOYEE may refer to anyone who is employed, especially by the government or by a business or industrial concern: *federal employees, factory employees.*

serve (sûrv), *v.,* **served, serving,** *n.* —*v.i.* **1.** to act as a servant. **2.** to wait at table; hand food to guests. **3.** to render assistance; help. **4.** to go through a term of service; do duty as a soldier, sailor, congressman, juror, etc. **5.** to have definite use; be of use. **6.** to answer the purpose: *that will serve to explain my actions.* **7.** to be favorable, suitable, or convenient, as weather, time, etc. **8.** *Tennis, etc.* to put the ball in play. **9.** *Eccles.* to act as server. —*v.t.* **10.** to be in the service of; work for. **11.** to render service to; help. **12.** to go through (a term of service, imprisonment, etc.). **13.** to render active service to (a king, commander, etc.). **14.** to render obedience or homage to (God, a sovereign, etc.). **15.** to perform the duties of (an office, etc.): *to serve his mayoralty.* **16.** to be useful or of service to. **17.** to answer the requirements of; suffice. **18.** to contribute to; promote. **19.** to wait upon; set food before. **20.** to set (food) on a table. **21.** to provide with a regular or continuous supply of something. **22.** to treat in a specified manner: *it serves him right.* **23.** to gratify (desire, etc.). **24.** (of a male animal) to mate with. **25.** *Tennis, etc.* to put (the ball) in play. **26.** *Law.* **a.** to make legal delivery of (a process or writ). **b.** to present (a person) with a writ. **27.** to operate or work (a gun, etc.). **28.** *Naut. etc.* to bind or wind (a rope, etc.) with small cord or the like, as to strengthen or protect it. —*n.* **29.** the act, manner, or right of serving, as in tennis. [ME *serven,* t. OF: m. *servir,* g. L *servīre*]

serv·er (sûr′vər), *n.* **1.** one who serves. **2.** that which serves or is used in serving, as a salver. **3.** *Eccles.* an attendant on the priest at Mass, who arranges the altar, makes the responses, etc. **4.** *Tennis, etc.* the player who puts the ball in play.

Ser·ve·tus (sər vē′təs), *n.* **Michael,** 1511–53, Spanish physician and theologian, accused of heresy and burned at stake. Spanish, **Miguel Ser·ve·to** (mē gĕl′ sĕr vĕ′tō).

Ser·vi·a (sûr′vĭ ə), *n.* former name of **Serbia.** —**Ser′·vi·an,** *adj., n.*

serv·ice[1] (sûr′vĭs), *n., adj., v.,* **-viced, -vicing.** —*n.* **1.** an act of helpful activity. **2.** the supplying of any articles, commodities, activities, etc., required or demanded. **3.** the providing of some accommodation required by the public, as messengers, telegraphs, telephones, or conveyance. **4.** the organized system of apparatus, appliances, employees, etc., for supplying some accommodation required by the public. **5.** the supplying of water, gas, or the like to the public. **6.** the performance of duties as a servant; occupation or employment as a servant. **7.** employment in any duties or work for another, a government, etc. **8.** a department of public employment, or the body of public servants in it: *the diplomatic service.* **9.** the duty or work of public servants. **10.** the serving of a sovereign, state, or government in some official capacity. **11.** *Mil.* **a.** the armed forces: *in the service.* **b.** period or duration of active service. **12.** *Ordn.* the actions required in loading and firing a cannon: *service of the piece.* **13.** (*often pl.*) the performance of any duties or work for another; helpful activity: *medical services.* **14.** public religious worship according to prescribed form and order: *divine service.* **15.** a ritual or form prescribed for public worship or for some particular occasion: *the marriage service.* **16.** the serving of God by obedience, piety, etc.: *voluntary service.* **17.** a musical setting of the sung portions of a liturgy. **18.** a set of dishes, utensils, etc., for a particular use: *a tea service.* **19.** *Law.* the serving of a process or writ upon a person. **20.** *Naut., etc.* a small cord or the like wound about a rope, etc., as for strengthening or protection. **21.** *Tennis, etc.* **a.** act or manner of putting the ball in play. **b.** the ball as put in play. **22.** the mating of a female animal by the male. —*adj.* **23.** of service; useful. —*v.t.* **24.** to make fit for service; restore to condition for service: *to service an automobile.* [ME; OE *serfise,* t. OF: m. *servise,* g. L *servitium*]

serv·ice[2] (sûr′vĭs), *n.* **1.** a service tree (def. 1), esp. *Sorbus domestica.* **2.** the shadbush. [orig. *serves,* pl. of obs. *serve,* OE *syrfe,* of L orig.; cf. L *sorbus* service tree]

Ser·vice (sûr′vĭs), *n.* **Robert William,** 1874–1958, Canadian writer, born in England.

serv·ice·a·ble (sûr′vĭs ə bəl), *adj.* **1.** being of service; useful. **2.** capable of doing good service. **3.** wearing well; durable: *serviceable cloth.* **4.** *Archaic.* diligent or attentive in serving. —**serv′ice·a·bil′i·ty, serv′ice·a·ble·ness,** *n.* —**serv′ice·a·bly,** *adv.*

serv·ice·ber·ry (sûr′vĭs bĕr′ĭ), *n., pl.* **-ries. 1.** the fruit of any service tree. **2.** a North American rosaceous shrub or small tree (*Amelanchier canadensis*) with a berrylike fruit; shadbush or Juneberry. **3.** any of various other species of *Amelanchier.*

service club, 1. any of several organizations maintained to contribute to the growth and general welfare of its members and the community. **2.** a recreational center for members of the armed forces.

service flat, *Brit.* an apartment in an apartment hotel, with attendance and (often) meals furnished.

service man, one whose occupation is to maintain or repair something: *a telephone service man.*

serv·ice·man (sûr′vĭs măn′), *n., pl.* **-men.** a member of the army or navy.

service station, 1. a place selling gas, oil, etc., or automobiles. **2.** a place supplying parts for or making repairs on radios, electrical devices, etc.

service tree, 1. either of two European trees, *Sorbus domestica,* bearing a small, acid fruit that is edible when overripe, or *S. torminalis* (**wild service tree**), with similar fruit; checker tree. **2.** serviceberry (defs. 2, 3).

ser·vi·ent tenement (sûr′vĭ ənt). See **dominant** tenement.

ser·vi·ette (sûr′vĭ ĕt′), *n.* a napkin. [t. F, der. *servir.* serve]

ser·vile (sûr′vĭl), *adj.* **1.** slavishly submissive or obsequious: *servile flatterers.* **2.** of or pertaining to slaves; proper to or customary for slaves; characteristic of a slave; abject: *servile obedience.* **3.** yielding slavishly, or truckling (fol. by *to*). **4.** slavishly exact; without originality. **5.** *Archaic.* being in slavery; oppressed. [ME, t. L, neut. of *servilis*] —**ser′vile·ly,** *adv.* —**ser·vil′i·ty, ser′vile·ness,** *n.*

—**Syn. 1, 2.** SERVILE, MENIAL, OBSEQUIOUS, SLAVISH characterize one who behaves like a slave or an inferior. SERVILE means cringing, fawning, abjectly submissive: *servile behavior.* MENIAL applies to that which is considered undesirable kinds of drudgery: *the most menial tasks.* OBSEQUIOUS implies the ostentatious subordination of oneself to the wishes of another, either from fear or from hope of gain: *an obsequious waiter.* SLAVISH stresses the dependence and laborious toil of one who follows or obeys with abject submission: *slavish attentiveness to orders.* —**Ant. 1.** domineering.

ser·vi·tor (sûr′və tər), *n.* one who is in or at the service of another; an attendant. [ME, t. OF, t. LL]

ser·vi·tude (sûr′və tūd′, -tōōd′), *n.* **1.** slavery; bondage: *political or intellectual servitude.* **2.** compulsory service or labor as a punishment for criminals: *penal servitude.* **3.** *Law.* a right possessed by one person with respect to some other property, and consisting either of a right to use such other property, or of a power to prevent certain uses of the other property. [late ME, t. L: m. *servitūdo*] —**Syn. 1.** See **slavery.** —**Ant. 1.** liberty.

ser·vo·mech·an·ism (sûr′vō mĕk′ə nĭz′əm, sûr′vō- mĕk′-), *n.* an electronic device used to maintain constant performance of a machine. Also, **ser′vo.** [f. SERV(E) + -o- + MECHANISM]

ses·a·me (sĕs′ə mĭ), *n.* **1.** a tropical herbaceous plant, *Sesamum indicum,* whose small oval seeds are edible and yield an oil. **2.** the seeds themselves. **3.** See **Open sesame.** [t. Gk.; r. late ME *sysane,* ult. t. Gk.: m. *sēsámē*]

ses·a·moid (sĕs′ə moid′), *adj. Anat.* shaped like a sesame seed, as certain small nodular bones and cartilages. [t. L: s. *sēsamoīdēs,* t. Gk.: m. *sēsamoeidēs*]

sesqui–, 1. a word element meaning "one and a half," as in *sesquicentennial.* **2.** a prefix applied to compounds where the ratio of radicals is 2 : 3 : *iron sesquichloride* (Fe₂Cl₃). [t. L, contr. of *sēmis* a half + *-que* besides]

ses·qui·cen·ten·ni·al (sĕs′kwĭ sĕn tĕn′ĭ əl), *adj.* **1.** pertaining to, or marking the completion of, a period of a century and a half, or 150 years. —*n.* **2.** a 150th anniversary, or its celebration.

ses·qui·ox·ide (sĕs′kwĭ ŏk′sīd, -sĭd), *n. Chem.* an oxide containing three atoms or equivalents of oxygen to two of the other element or of some radical.

ses·qui·pe·da·li·an (sĕs′kwĭ pə dā′lĭ ən), *adj.* **1.** measuring a foot and a half. **2.** given to using long words. **3.** (of words or expressions) very long. —*n.* **4.** a sesquipedalian word. [f. *sesquipeda₁* (t. L: s. *sesquipedālis*) + -IAN]

ses·sile (sĕs′ĭl), *adj. Biol.* **1.** attached by the base, or without any distinct projecting support, as a leaf issuing directly from the stem. **2.** permanently attached. [t. L, neut. of *sessilis* sitting down]

A. Sessile flower; B. Sessile leaves

ses·sion (sĕsh′ən), *n.* **1.** the sitting together of a court, council, legislature, or the like, for conference or the transaction of business: *Congress is now in session.* **2.** a single continuous sitting, or period of sitting, of persons so assembled. **3.** a continuous series of sittings or meetings of a court, legislature, or the like. **4.** the period or term during which such a series is held. **5.** (*pl.*) the sittings or a sitting of justices in court, usually to deal with minor offenses, grant licenses, etc. **6.** a single continuous course or period of lessons, study, etc., in the work of a day at school: *two afternoon sessions a week.* **7.** a portion of the year into which instruction is organized at a college or other educational institution. [ME, t. L: s. *sessio*] —**ses′sion·al,** *adj.*

ses·terce (sĕs′tûrs), *n.* an ancient Roman coin equal to a quarter of a denarius. [t. L: m. *sestertius,* prop. adj. two and a half]

ses·ter·ti·um (sĕs tûr′shĭ əm), *n., pl.* **-tia** (-shĭ ə). an ancient Roman money of account equal to a thousand sesterces. [L]

ses·tet (sĕs tĕt′, sĕs′tĕt), *n.* **1.** the last six lines of a sonnet. **2.** sextet (defs. 2, 3). [t. It.: m. *sestetto,* dim. of *sesto* sixth, g. L *sextus*]

ses·ti·na (sĕs tē′nə), *n. Pros.* a poem of six six-line stanzas and a three-line envoy, orig. without rhyme, in which each stanza repeats the end words of the lines of the first stanza, but in different order, the envoy using the six words again, three in the middle of the lines and three at the end. [t. It., der. *sesto* sixth. See SESTET]

Ses·tos (sĕs′tŏs), *n.* an ancient Thracian town on the Hellespont opposite Abydos: Xerxes crossed the Hellespont here when he began his invasion of Greece.

set (sĕt), *v.,* **set, setting,** *n., adj.* —*v.t.* 1. to put in a particular place or position: *to set a vase on a table.* 2. to put into some condition or relation: *to set a house on fire.* 3. to put (a price or value) upon something. 4. to fix the value of at a certain amount or rate. 5. to put (*much, little store,* etc.) as a measure of esteem: *to set great store by a thing.* 6. to post, station, or appoint for the purpose of performing some duty: *to set spies on a person.* 7. to fix, appoint, or ordain: *to set a limit.* 8. to place in thought or estimation: *to set an early date.* 9. to present or fix for others to follow: *to set an example.* 10. to prescribe or assign, as a task. 11. to put in the proper position, order, or condition for use; adjust or arrange: *to set a table.* 12. to adjust according to a standard: *to set a clock.* 13. to fix or mount (a gem, etc.) in gold or the like; place in a frame or setting. 14. to adorn with, or as with, precious stones. 15. to cause to sit; seat. 16. to put (a hen) on eggs to hatch them; place (eggs) under a hen or in an incubator. 17. to give an account of (fol. by *forth*): *setting forth his theory.* 18. to put into a fixed, rigid, or settled state, as the countenance, the muscles, or the mind. 19. to fix at a given point or calibration: *to set a micrometer.* 20. to cause to take a particular direction. 21. *Surg.* to put (a broken or dislocated bone) back in position. 22. (of a hunting dog) to indicate the position of (game) by standing stiffly and pointing with the muzzle. 23. *Music.* **a.** to fit, as words to music. **b.** to arrange for musical performance. **c.** to arrange (music) for certain voices or instruments. 24. to put on (stage) the scenery and properties for an act or scene. 25. to spread (sails) so as to catch the wind. 26. *Print.* **a.** to arrange (type) in the order required for printing. **b.** to put together types corresponding to (copy): *to set an article.* 27. *Baking.* to put aside (a substance to which yeast has been added) in order that it may rise. 28. to change into a curd. 29. to cause (something, as mortar) to become firm or hard: *to set mortar.* 30. to cause to be hostile or antagonistic (fol. by *against*). —*v.i.* 31. to pass below the horizon; sink: *the setting sun.* 32. to decline; wane. 33. to assume a fixed or rigid state, as the countenance, the muscles, etc. 34. to become firm or solid, as mortar. 35. to sit on eggs, as a hen. 36. to hang or fit, as clothes. 37. to begin to move; start (fol. by *forth, off, out,* etc.). 38. to make an attack. 39. to begin to apply oneself to something. 40. (of the ovary of the flower) to develop into a fruit. 41. (of a hunting dog) to indicate the position of game. 42. to have a certain direction or course, as a wind, current, etc. 43. (of a sail) to fit and take shape. 44. Some verb phrases are:
set about, to begin upon; start.
set aside, 1. to put to one side. 2. to discard from use; dismiss from the mind. 3. to annul or quash: *to set aside a verdict.*
set back, to hinder; stop.
set down, 1. to put down in writing or printing. 2. to consider: *to set someone down as a fool.* 3. to ascribe or attribute.
set in, 1. to begin: *darkness set in.* 2. to blow or flow toward the shore.
set off, 1. to explode. 2. to begin; start. 3. to intensify or improve by contrast.
set to, to begin; start to work, fight, etc.
set up, 1. to start in business, etc. 2. to lay claim. —*n.* 45. a number of things customarily used together or forming a complete assortment, outfit, or collection: *a set of dishes.* 46. a series of volumes by one author, about one subject, or the like. 47. a number or group of persons associating or classed together. 48. the fit: *the set of his coat.* 49. fixed direction or bent, as of the mind, etc. 50. bearing or carriage: *the set of one's shoulders.* 51. the assumption of a fixed, rigid, or hard state, as by mortar, etc. 52. a radio- or television-receiving apparatus. 53. *Philately.* a group of stamps which form a complete series. 54. *Tennis, etc.* a group of games counting as one of the units of a match. 55. *Theat.* a construction representing a place in which action takes place in a motion picture. 56. a number of pieces of stage scenery arranged together. 57. *Mach.* the bending out of the points of alternate teeth of a saw in opposite directions. 58. *Hort.* a young plant, or a slip, tuber, or the like, suitable for setting out or planting. 59. *Dancing, etc.* **a.** the number of couples required to execute a quadrille or the like. **b.** a series of movements or figures that make up a quadrille or the like. 60. *Naut.* **a.** the direction of a wind, current, etc. **b.** the fit and shape of sails. 61. *Psychol.* readiness to respond in a specific way. —*adj.* 62. fixed beforehand: *a set time.* 63. prescribed beforehand: *set rules.* 64. deliberately composed; customary: *set phrases.* 65. fixed; rigid: *a set smile.* 66. resolved or determined; habitually or stubbornly fixed: *to be set in one's opinions.* 67. formed, built, or made (as specified): *thick-set.* [ME *sette*(*n*), OE *settan,* c. G *setzen*]

Set (sĕt), *n. Egypt. Myth.* the god of evil, brother or son and deadly opponent of Osiris, and represented with a beast's head and snout: called by the Greeks Typhon. [t. Gk.: m. *Seth,* t. Egypt.: m. *Setesh*]

se·ta (sē′tə), *n., pl.* **-tae** (-tē). *Zool., Bot.* a stiff hair; a bristle; a bristlelike part. [t. L: bristle]

se·ta·ceous (sĭ·tā′shəs), *adj.* 1. bristlelike; bristle-shaped. 2. furnished with bristles. [t. NL: m. *sētāceus*]

set·back (sĕt′băk′), *n.* 1. a check to progress; reverse. 2. *Archit.* **a.** a flat, plain setoff in a wall. **b.** such a setting back at a particular height in a tall building, or one of a number of such recessions at different heights, for allowing better light and ventilation in the street.

set chisel, a chisel with a wide cutting edge on a gently tapering head, for shearing off nails, rivets, etc.

Seth (sĕth), *n.* the third son of Adam. Gen. 4:25. [t. L (Vulgate), t. Gk. (Septuagint), t. Heb.: m. *Shēth*]

seti-, a word element meaning "bristle." [comb. form repr. L *sēta*]

se·ti·form (sē′tə·fôrm′), *adj.* bristle-shaped; setaceous.

se·tig·er·ous (sĭ·tĭj′ər·əs), *adj.* having setae or bristles. Also, **se·tif·er·ous** (sĭ·tĭf′ər·əs). [f. L *sētiger* having bristles + -OUS]

set·off (sĕt′ôf′, -ŏf′), *n.* 1. anything that counterbalances or makes up for something else. 2. a counterbalancing debt or claim. 3. *Archit.* **a.** a reduction in the thickness of a wall, etc. **b.** a flat or sloping projection on a wall, buttress, or the like, below a thinner part.

se·ton (sē′tən), *n. Surg.* 1. a thread or the like inserted beneath the skin in order to maintain an artificial passage or issue. 2. the issue itself. [t. F, t. It.: m. *setone,* der. *seta* silk]

Se·ton (sē′tən), *n.* **Ernest Thompson,** 1860–1946, British writer and illustrator, born in America.

se·tose (sē′tōs, sĭ·tōs′), *adj.* covered with setae or bristles; bristly. [t. L: m.s. *sētōsus*]

set·screw (sĕt′skrōō′), *n.* a screw holding firmly together two machine parts, one being otherwise subject to movement along the other.

set·te·cen·to (sĕt′tĕ·chĕn′tō), *n.* the 18th century, as a period in Italian cultural history. [It., short for *millesettecento* one thousand seven hundred]

set·tee (sĕ·tē′), *n.* a seat for two or more persons, with a back and usually arms. [? dim. of SEAT¹]

set·ter (sĕt′ər), *n.* 1. one who sets. 2. one of a breed of long-haired hunting dogs which originally had the habit of crouching when game was scented, but which are now trained to stand stiffly and point the muzzle toward the scented game, the breed being made up of three distinct groups: the Irish setters, English setters, and Gordon setters.

set theory, the branch of mathematics that deals with the properties of collections of elements classed together.

set·ting (sĕt′ĭng), *n.* 1. act of one who or that which sets. 2. the surroundings or environment of anything. 3. that in which something, as a jewel, is set or mounted. 4. the scenery, costumes, etc., of a play. 5. *Music.* **a.** a piece of music composed for certain words. **b.** a piece of music composed for a particular medium, or arranged for other than the original medium.

set·tle¹ (sĕt′əl), *v.,* **-tled, -tling.** —*v.t.* 1. to appoint or fix definitely; agree upon (a time, price, conditions, etc.). 2. to place in a desired position or in order. 3. to pay (a bill, etc.). 4. to close (an account) by payment. 5. to take up residence in (a country, place, house, etc.). 6. to cause to take up residence. 7. to furnish (a place) with inhabitants or settlers. 8. to establish in a way of life, a business, etc. 9. to bring to rest; quiet (the nerves, stomach, etc.). 10. *Colloq.* to cause to cease from opposition or annoyance. 11. to make stable; place on a permanent basis. 12. to cause (a liquid) to deposit dregs. 13. to cause (dregs, etc.) to sink. 14. to cause to sink down gradually; make firm or compact. 15. to close up; dispose of finally: *to settle an estate.* 16. *Law.* **a.** to secure (property, title, etc.) on or to a person by formal or legal process. **b.** to terminate (legal proceedings) by mutual consent of the parties. —*v.i.* 17. to decide; arrange: *to settle on a plan of action.* 18. to arrange matters in dispute; come to an agreement: *to settle with a person.* 19. to make a financial arrangement; pay. 20. to take up residence in a new country or place. 21. to come to rest, as from flight: *a bird settled on a bough.* 22. to come to rest in a particular place: *a cold settles in one's head.* 23. to come to rest; become calm or composed (sometimes fol. by *down*). 24. to set oneself to a regular way of life, esp. upon marrying (often fol. by *down*). 25. to sink down gradually; subside. 26. to become clear, by the sinking of particles, as a liquid. 27. to sink to the bottom as sediment. 28. to become firm or compact. [ME; OE *setlan* (c. D *zetelen* place, settle), der. *setl* SETTLE²] —Syn. 24. See staid.

set·tle² (sĕt′əl), *n. Chiefly Brit.* a long seat or bench, usually wooden and with arms and high back. [ME; OE *setl,* c. G *sessel.* See SIT, v.]

set·tle·ment (sĕt′əl·mənt), *n.* 1. act of settling. 2. state of being settled. 3. act of making stable or putting on a permanent basis. 4. the resulting state. 5. arrangement; adjustment. 6. the establishment of a person in an employment, office, or charge. 7. the settling of persons in a new country or place. 8. a colony, esp. in its early stages; a small village or collection of houses. 9. the satisfying of a claim or demand;

a coming to terms. **10.** *Law.* **a.** final disposition of an estate or the like. **b.** the settling of property, title, etc., upon a person. **c.** the property so settled. **11.** *Brit.* legal residence in a particular place, or the right to maintenance, if a pauper. **12.** *Social Work.* a welfare establishment in an underprivileged area providing facilities for the people in the area, including personnel to assist them. **13.** a subsidence or sinking of a structure or part of one.

settlement worker, one who devotes time to a settlement (def. 12).

set·tler (sĕt′lər), *n.* **1.** one who or that which settles. **2.** one who settles in a new country.

set·tling (sĕt′lĭng), *n.* **1.** act of one who or that which settles. **2.** (*usually pl.*) sediment.

set-to (sĕt′tōō′), *n., pl.* **-tos.** *Colloq.* a fight; bout; contest. [f. SET + TO]

set·up (sĕt′ŭp′), *n.* **1.** organization; arrangement. **2.** *U.S.* carriage, as of the body. **3.** ice, soda water, etc. (except the liquor), for mixing drinks. **4.** *U.S. Slang.* an undertaking or contest deliberately made easy. **5.** *U.S. Slang.* a match or game arranged with an opponent who can be defeated without risk or effort.

Seu·rat (sœrä′), *n.* Georges (zhôrzh), 1859–1891, French painter.

Se·vas·to·pol (sĭ′văs′tə-pōl′; *Russ.* sĕ′väs′tô′pôl′y), *n.* a fortified seaport in the SW Soviet Union: famous for its heroic resistance during sieges of 349 days in 1854–1855, and 245 days in 1941–1942. 133,000 (est. 1956). Also, **Sebastopol.**

sev·en (sĕv′ən), *n.* **1.** a cardinal number, six plus one. **2.** a symbol for this number, as 7 or VII. **3.** a set of seven persons or things. **4.** a playing card with seven pips. —*adj.* **5.** amounting to seven in number. [ME; OE *seofon*, c. G *sieben*]

Seven against Thebes, 1. *Gk. Legend.* the seven heroes (Adrastus, Amphiaraus, Capaneus, Hippomedon, Parthenopaeus, Polynices, and Tydeus) who made an expedition against Thebes to seat Polynices on the throne. They were defeated, but ten years later the descendants of the seven (the Epigoni) attacked Thebes successfully. **2.** a tragedy by Aeschylus (exhibited 468 B.C.).

seven deadly sins. See **deadly sins.**

sev·en·fold (sĕv′ən·fōld′), *adj.* **1.** comprising seven parts or members; seven times as great or as much. —*adv.* **2.** in sevenfold measure.

Seven Hills, the seven hills (the Aventine, Caelian, Capitoline, Esquiline, Palatine, Quirinal, and Viminal) on and about which the ancient city of Rome was built.

Seven Pines. See **Fair Oaks.**

seven seas, the navigable waters of the world.

sev·en·teen (sĕv′ən·tēn′), *n.* **1.** a cardinal number, ten plus seven. **2.** a symbol for this number, as 17 or XVII. —*adj.* **3.** amounting to seventeen in number. [ME *seventene*, OE *seofontēne*, c. D *zeventien*]

sev·en·teenth (sĕv′ən·tēnth′), *adj.* **1.** next after the sixteenth. **2.** being one of seventeen equal parts. —*n.* **3.** a seventeenth part, esp. of one (¹/₁₇). **4.** the seventeenth member of a series.

seventeen-year locust, a cicada, *Magicicada septendecim,* of the U.S., remarkable for its length of life (13 to 17 years) in the larval state underground.

sev·enth (sĕv′ənth), *adj.* **1.** next after the sixth. **2.** being one of seven equal parts. —*n.* **3.** a seventh part, esp. of one (¹/₇). **4.** the seventh member of a series. **5.** *Music.* **a.** a tone on the seventh degree from a given tone (counted as the first). **b.** the interval between such tones. **c.** the harmonic combination of such tones.

seventh chord, *Music.* a chord formed by the superposition of three thirds.

sev·enth-day (sĕv′ənth·dā′), *adj.* (*often cap.*) designating certain Christian sects who make Saturday their chief day of rest and religious observance: *Seventh-Day Adventists.*

seventh heaven, 1. (in Talmudic literature) the highest heaven where God and the most exalted angels dwell. **2.** a state of extreme happiness: *she was in seventh heaven with her new washing machine.*

sev·en·ty (sĕv′ən·tĭ), *n., pl.* **-ties,** *adj.* —*n.* **1.** a cardinal number, ten times seven. **2.** a symbol for this number, as 70 or LXX. **3. the Seventy,** the body of (seventy-two) scholars who, according to tradition, made the Septuagint. —*adj.* **4.** amounting to seventy in number. [ME; OE *seofontig,* c. G *siebzig*] —**sev·en·ti·eth** (sĕv′ən·tĭ′ĭth), *adj., n.*

sev·en·ty-five (sĕv′ən·tĭ·fīv′), *n. Mil.* **1.** a gun with a 75 mm. caliber. **2.** the field gun of that caliber used in the French and U.S. armies in World War I.

sev·en-up (sĕv′ən·ŭp′), *n.* a card game played by two or more persons, seven points constituting a game.

Seven Wonders of the World, the seven most remarkable structures of ancient times: the Egyptian pyramids, the Mausoleum erected by Artemisia at Halicarnassus, the Temple of Artemis at Ephesus, the walls and hanging gardens of Babylon, the Colossus of Rhodes, the statue of Zeus by Phidias at Olympia, and the Pharos or lighthouse at Alexandria.

sev·er (sĕv′ər), *v.t.* **1.** to put apart; separate. **2.** to divide into parts, esp. forcibly; cut; cleave. **3.** to break off or dissolve (ties, relations, etc.). —*v.i.* **4.** to separate or part, from each other or one from another; to become divided into parts. **5.** to make a separation or division, as between things. [ME *severe*(*n*), t. AF: m. *severer,* g. LL *sēperāre,* r. L *sēparāre*] —**Ant. 1.** unite.

sev·er·a·ble (sĕv′ər·ə·bəl), *adj.* **1.** capable of being severed. **2.** *Law.* separable or capable of being treated as separate from a whole legal right or obligation: *a severable contract obligation.*

sev·er·al (sĕv′ər·əl), *adj.* **1.** being more than two or three, but not many. **2.** respective; individual: *they went their several ways.* **3.** separate; different: *three several occasions.* **4.** single; particular. **5.** divers; various: *the several steps in a process.* **6.** *Law.* binding two or more persons who may be sued separately on a common obligation. —*n.* **7.** several persons or things; a few; some. [ME, t. AF, g. L *sēpar* distinct + *-ālis* -AL¹]

sev·er·al·ly (sĕv′ər·ə·lĭ), *adv.* **1.** separately; singly. **2.** respectively.

sev·er·al·ty (sĕv′ər·əl·tĭ), *n., pl.* **-ties. 1.** state of being separate. **2.** the condition, as of land, of being held or owned by separate or individual right.

sev·er·ance (sĕv′ər·əns), *n.* **1.** act of severing. **2.** state of being severed. **3.** breaking off, as of relations. [ME, t. AF. See SEVER, -ANCE]

se·vere (sĭ·vǐr′), *adj.,* **-verer, -verest. 1.** harsh; harshly extreme: *severe criticism or laws.* **2.** serious; stern: *a severe face.* **3.** grave: *a severe illness.* **4.** rigidly restrained in style or taste; simple; plain. **5.** causing discomfort or distress by extreme character or conditions, as weather, cold, heat, etc.; unpleasantly violent, as rain or wind, a blow or shock, etc. **6.** hard to endure, perform, fulfill, etc.: *a severe test.* **7.** rigidly exact, accurate, or methodical: *severe conformity to standards.* [t. L: m.s. *sevērus*] —**se·vere′ly,** *adv.* —**se·vere′ness,** *n.* —**Syn. 2.** See **stern¹.** —**Ant. 1.** lenient. **2.** gentle.

se·ver·i·ty (sĭ·vĕr′ə·tĭ), *n., pl.* **-ties. 1.** harshness, sternness, or rigor. **2.** austere simplicity, as of style or taste. **3.** violence or sharpness, as of cold, pain, etc. **4.** grievousness; hard or trying character or effect. **5.** gravity; austerity. **6.** rigid exactness or accuracy.

Sev·ern (sĕv′ərn), *n.* a river flowing from central Wales through W England into the Bristol Channel. ab. 210 mi.

Se·ver·sky (sə·vẽr′skĭ), *n.* **Alexander Procofieff de** (prŏ·kō′fyĕf·də), born 1894, U.S. airplane designer and manufacturer, born in Russia.

Se·ve·rus (sə·vǐr′əs), *n.* **Lucius Septimius** (lōō′shəs sĕp·tĭm′ĭəs), A.D. 146–211, Roman emperor, A.D. 193–211.

Sé·vi·gné (sĕ·vē·nyĕ′), *n.* **Marie de** (mȧ·rē′ də), (*Marie de Rabutin-Chantal*) 1626–96, French letter writer.

Se·ville (sə·vǐl′, sĕv′ǐl), *n.* a city in SW Spain: a port on the Guadalquivir river: site of the Alcazar; cathedral. 404,265 (est. 1955). Spanish, **Se·vil·la** (sĕ·vēl′yä).

Sè·vres (sĕ′vr), *n.* **1.** a suburb of Paris in N France. 17,109 (1954). **2.** a choice and costly kind of porcelain made there.

sew (sō), *v.,* **sewed, sewed** or **sewn, sewing.** —*v.t.* **1.** to join or attach by a thread or the like, as with a needle. **2.** to make, repair, etc., (a garment) by such means. **3.** to fasten or secure with stitches: *flour sewed in bags.* **4.** to close (a hole, wound, etc.) by means of stitches (usually fol. by *up*). —*v.i.* **5.** to work with a needle and thread, or with a sewing machine. [ME *sewe*(*n*), OE *siw*(*i*)*an*; akin to L *suere*]

sew·age (sōō′ĭj), *n.* the waste matter which passes through sewers.

Sew·all (sōō′əl), *n.* **Samuel,** 1652–1730, American jurist, born in England.

se·wan (sē′wən), *n.* seawan.

Sew·ard (sōō′ərd), *n.* **William Henry,** 1801–72, U. S. statesman.

Seward Peninsula, a peninsula in W Alaska, on Bering Strait.

sew·er¹ (sōō′ər), *n.* an artificial conduit, usually underground, for carrying off waste water and refuse, as from a town or city. [ME, t. OF: m. *sewiere* channel from a fishpond, g. L *ex* out of + *aquāria,* fem., of water]

sew·er² (sō′ər), *n.* one who or that which sews. [f. SEW + -ER¹]

sew·er³ (sōō′ər), *n.* (formerly) a household officer or head servant in charge of the service of the table. [ME, t. AF: aphetic m. *asseour* seater, g. L *assidēre* sit at]

sew·er·age (sōō′ər·ĭj), *n.* **1.** the removal of waste water and refuse by means of sewers. **2.** a system of sewers. **3.** sewage.

sew·ing (sō′ĭng), *n.* **1.** act or work of one who sews. **2.** something sewed or to be sewed.

sewing circle, a society of women who meet regularly to sew for the benefit of charity or the like.

sewing machine, a machine for sewing.

sewn (sōn), *v.* a pp. of **sew.**

sex (sĕks), *n.* **1.** the character of being either male or female: *persons of different sexes.* **2.** the sum of the anatomical and physiological differences with reference to which the male and the female are distinguished, or

ăct, āble, dâre, ärt; ĕbb, ēqual; ĭf, īce; hŏt, ōver, ôrder, oil, bŏŏk, ōōze, out; ŭp, ūse, ûrge; ə = a in alone; ch, chief; g, give; ng, ring; sh, shoe; th, thin; ŧħ, that; zh, vision.   See the full key on inside cover.

the phenomena depending on these differences. **3.** the instinct or attraction drawing one sex toward another, or its manifestation in life and conduct. **4.** men collectively or women collectively: *the fair sex.* [ME, t. L: s. *sexus* sex, ? orig., division]

sex-, a word element meaning "six," as in *sexcentenary.* [t. L, comb. form of *sex*]

sex·a·ge·nar·i·an (sĕk'sə jə nâr'Yən), *adj.* **1.** of the age of 60 years, or between 60 and 70 years old. —*n.* **2.** a sexagenarian person.

sex·ag·e·nar·y (sĕks ăj'ə nĕr'Y), *adj., n., pl.* **-naries.** —*adj.* **1.** of or pertaining to the number 60. **2.** composed of or proceeding by sixties. **3.** sexagenarian. —*n.* **4.** a sexagenarian. [t. L: m.s. *sexāgēnārius*]

Sex·a·ges·i·ma (sĕk'sə jĕs'ə mə), *n.* the second Sunday before Lent (more fully, **Sexagesima Sunday**). [t. L: *sexāgēsima (dies)* sixtieth day]

sex·a·ges·i·mal (sĕk'sə jĕs'ə məl), *adj.* **1.** pertaining to or based upon the number sixty. —*n.* **2.** a fraction whose denominator is 60 or a power of sixty. [t. ML: s. *sexāgēsimālis,* der. L *sexāgēsimus* sixtieth]

sex appeal, the quality of attracting the opposite sex.

sex·cen·te·nar·y (sĕks sĕn'tə nĕr'Y, sĕks'sĕn tĕn'ə rY), *adj., n., pl.* **-naries.** —*adj.* **1.** pertaining to six hundred or a period of six hundred years; marking the completion of six hundred years. —*n.* **2.** a six-hundredth anniversary, or its celebration.

sex chromosome, *Biol.* any chromosome carrying sex-determining factors, esp. such chromosomes that differ morphologically from the ordinary "autosomes," called X and Y, W and Z chromosomes.

sex·en·ni·al (sĕks ĕn'Yəl), *adj.* **1.** of or for six years. **2.** occurring every six years. —*n.* **3.** an occurrence every six years. [f. s. L *sexennium* + -AL¹] —**sex·en'ni·al·ly,** *adv.*

sex hygiene, a branch of hygiene which concerns itself with sex and sexual behavior as it relates to the well-being of the individual and the community.

sex·less (sĕks'lYs), *adj.* having or seeming to have no sex. —**sex'less·ly,** *adv.* —**sex'less·ness,** *n.*

sex-link·age (sĕks'lYngk'Yj), *n. Genetics.* inheritance in which both parents do not contribute equally to their progeny because the genes involved are borne on the sex chromosomes in which the parents differ.

sex·par·tite (sĕks pär'tīt), *adj.* divided into or consisting of six parts, as a vault, etc. [f. SEX- + PARTITE]

sext (sĕkst), *n. Eccles.* the fourth of the seven canonical hours, or the service for it, orig. fixed for the sixth hour of the day (or noon). [ME, t. L: s. *sexta (hōra)* sixth (hour)]

sex·tan (sĕks'tən), *adj.* **1.** (of a fever, etc.) characterized by paroxysms which recur every sixth day. —*n.* **2.** a sextan fever or ague. [t. NL: s. *sextāna* (der. L *sextus* sixth), short for *sextāna febris*]

Sex·tans (sĕks'tənz), *n., gen.* **Sextantis** (sĕks tăn'tYs). *Astron.* an equatorial constellation between Hydra and Leo. [t. L. See SEXTANT]

sex·tant (sĕks'tənt), *n.* **1.** an astronomical instrument used in measuring angular distances, esp. the altitudes of sun, moon, and stars at sea in determining latitude and longitude. **2.** (*cap.*) *Astron.* Sextans. [t. L: s. *sextans* sixth part]

Sextant

A, Telescope; B, Mirror; C, Colored glass filters; D, Half mirror, half glass; E, Graduated arc; F, Handle; G, Movable index arm; H, Magnifying glass

sex·tet (sĕks tĕt'), *n.* **1.** any group or set of six. **2.** a company of six singers or players. **3.** a musical composition for six voices or instruments. Also, *esp. Brit.,* **sex·tette'.** [alter. of SESTET, ult. der. L *sex* six]

sex·tile (sĕks'tYl), *Astron.* —*adj.* **1.** noting or pertaining to the aspect or position of two heavenly bodies when 60° distant from each other. —*n.* **2.** a sextile position or aspect. [t. L, neut. of *sextilis* sixth]

sex·til·lion (sĕks tYl'yən), *n.* **1.** (usually with *one* or *a*) a cardinal number represented (in the U.S. and France) by one followed by 21 zeros or (in Gt. Britain and Germany) by one followed by 36 zeros. —*adj.* **2.** (usually with *one* or *a*) amounting to one sextillion in number. [t. F: f. s. L *sextus* sixth (power of) + (*m*)*illion* MILLION] —**sex·til'lionth,** *adj., n.*

sex·to·dec·i·mo (sĕks'tō dĕs'ə mō'), *n., pl.* **-mos,** *adj.* —*n.* **1.** a volume printed from sheets folded to form 16 leaves or 32 pages, approximately 4 x 6 inches. *Abbr.:* 16mo. or 16°. —*adj.* **2.** in sextodecimo. [t. L, abl. sing. of *sextusdecimus* sixteenth]

sex·ton (sĕks'tən), *n.* an official of a church charged with taking care of the edifice and its contents, ringing the bell, etc., and sometimes with burying the dead. [ME *segerstone,* t. AF: m. *segrestaine,* t. ML: m. *sacristānus* sacristan]

sex·tu·ple (sĕks'tyŏŏ pəl, -tŏŏ-, sĕks tū'pəl, -tŏŏ'-), *adj., v.,* **-pled, -pling.** —*adj.* **1.** sixfold; consisting of six parts; six times as great. **2.** *Music.* characterized by six beats or pulses to the measure: *sextuple rhythm.* —*v.t.* **3.** to make or become six times as great. [f. s. L *sextus* sixth + -*uple,* as in QUINTUPLE]

sex·tu·plet (sĕks'tyŏŏ plYt, -tŏŏ-, sĕks tū'plYt, -tŏŏ'-), *n.* **1.** one of the six children born at one birth. **2.** a group or combination of six things.

sex·u·al (sĕk'shŏŏ al), *adj.* **1.** of or pertaining to sex. **2.** occurring between or involving the two sexes. **3.** having sex or sexual organs, or reproducing by processes involving both sexes, as animals or plants. [t. LL: s. *sexuālis*] —**sex'u·al·ly,** *adv.*

sex·u·al·i·ty (sĕk'shŏŏ ăl'ə tY), *n.* **1.** sexual character; possession of sex. **2.** the recognition or emphasizing of sexual matters.

sexual selection, mate selection, esp. in higher animals, leading to the perpetuation of certain characteristics, as strength, combativeness, beauty, etc.

sex·y (sĕk'sY), *adj.,* **sexier, sexiest.** *Slang.* having or involving a predominant or excessive concern with sex: *a sexy novel.*

Sey·chelles (sā shĕl', -shĕlz'), *n.pl.* a group of 92 islands in the Indian Ocean, NE of Madagascar: a British colony. 37,800 pop. (1954); 156 sq. mi. *Cap.:* Victoria.

Sey·mour (sē'môr), *n.* **Jane,** c1510–37, third wife of Henry VIII of England, and mother of Edward VI.

sf, science fiction.

sf., *Music.* sforzando. Also, **sfz.**

Sfax (sfäks), *n.* a seaport in N Africa, in E Tunisia. 65.635 (1956).

Sfor·za (sfôr'tsä), *n.* **1.** Count **Carlo** (kär'lō), 1873–1952, Italian statesman: anti-Fascist leader. **2.** **Francesco** (frän chĕs'kō), 1401–66, Italian condottiere, and duke of Milan 1450–66. **3.** his father, **Giacomuzzo** or **Muzio** (jä'kō mōōt'tsō *or* mōō'tsyō) **Attendolo** (ät·tĕn'dō lō'), 1369–1424, Italian condottiere. **4.** **Lodovico** (lō'dō vē'kō), ("*the Moor*") 1451–1508, duke of Milan, 1494–1500: son of Francesco Sforza.

sfor·zan·do (sfôr tsän'dō), *adj. Music.* forcing (used as a direction, to indicate that a tone or chord is to be rendered with special emphasis). Also, **forzando, sfor·za·to** (sfôr tsä'tō). *Abbr.:* **sf., sfz.** [It., ppr. of *sforzare* force]

s. g., specific gravity.

's Gra·ven·ha·ge (sKHrä'vən hä'KHə), *n.* Dutch name of **The Hague.**

Sgt., Sergeant.

sh., **1.** sheep. **2.** *Bookbinding.* sheet. **3.** shilling.

shab·by (shăb'Y), *adj.,* **-bier, -biest. 1.** having the appearance impaired by wear, use, etc.: *shabby clothes.* **2.** wearing worn clothes; seedy. **3.** making a poor appearance. **4.** meanly ungenerous or unfair; contemptible, as persons, actions, etc. [f. *shab* (ME; OE *sceabb* scab) + -Y¹] —**shab'bi·ly,** *adv.* —**shab'bi·ness,** *n.*

shab·by-gen·teel (shăb'Y jĕn tēl'), *adj.* trying to appear genteel despite shabbiness.

Sha·bu·oth (shä vōō'ōth, shə vōō'əs), *n.pl.* the Jewish holiday Feast of Weeks, or Pentecost.

shack (shăk), *n. U.S. and Canadian Colloq.* a rough cabin; a shanty. [short for *shackle* in same sense, itself short for RAMSHACKLE] —**Syn.** See cottage.

shack·le (shăk'əl), *n., v.,* **-led, -ling.** —*n.* **1.** a ring or fastening of iron or the like for securing the wrist, ankle, etc.; a fetter. **2.** a hobble or fetter for a horse or other animal. **3.** any of various fastening or coupling devices, as the curved bar of a padlock which passes through the staple. **4.** anything that serves to prevent freedom of procedure, thought, etc. —*v.t.* **5.** to put a shackle or shackles on; confine or restrain. **6.** to fasten or couple with a shackle. **7.** to restrain in action, thought, etc. [ME *schackle,* OE *sceacel* fetter, c. LG *schakel* hobble (for a horse)] —**shack'ler,** *n.*

Shack·le·ton (shăk'əl tən), *n.* **Sir Ernest Henry,** 1874–1922, British antarctic explorer.

shad (shăd), *n., pl.* **shad,** (*for different species*) **shads. 1.** a deep-bodied herring, *Alosa sapidissima,* that runs up streams to spawn, and is valued as a food fish. **2.** any other species of *Alosa* or of related genera. **3.** any of several unrelated fishes. [OE *sceadd;* cf. LG *schade*]

shad·ber·ry (shăd'bĕr'Y), *n., pl.* **-ries. 1.** the fruit of the shadbush. **2.** the shadbush itself.

shad·bush (shăd'bŏŏsh'), *n.* **1.** the North American serviceberry, *Amelanchier canadensis,* a shrub or small tree with racemose white flowers and a berrylike fruit, which blossoms about the time when shad appear in the rivers. **2.** any of various other species of *Amelanchier.* Also, **shad·blow** (shăd'blō').

shad·dock (shăd'ək), *n.* **1.** the large roundish or pear-shaped, usually pale-yellow, orangelike fruit of the rutaceous tree, *Citrus grandis,* grown extensively in the Orient. **2.** the tree itself. [named after Captain *Shaddock* who brought the seed from the East Indies]

shade (shād), *n., v.,* **shaded, shading.** —*n.* **1.** the comparative darkness caused by the interception of rays of light. **2.** an area of comparative darkness; a shady place. **3.** (*pl.*) darkness gathering at the close of day. **4.** (*chiefly pl.*) a retired or obscure place. **5.** comparative obscurity. **6.** a specter or ghost. **7.** *Class. Myth.* **a.** an inhabitant of Hades. **b.** (*pl.*) the spirits of the dead collectively. **c.** the world or abode of the dead; Hades. **8.** *Chiefly Poetic.* a shadow. **9.** degree of darkening of a color by adding black or by decreasing the illumination. **10.** comparative darkness as represented pictorially; the dark part, or a dark part, of a picture. **11.** a slight variation, amount, or degree: *there is not a* *shade of difference between them.* **12.** something used for protection against excessive light, heat, etc.: *a window shade.* —*v.t.* **13.** to produce shade in or on. **14.** to obscure, dim, or darken. **15.** to screen or hide from view. **16.** to protect (something) from light, heat, etc., as by a screen; to cover or screen (a light, candle, etc.). **17.** to introduce degrees of darkness into (a drawing or painting) for effects of light and shade or different colors. **18.** to render the values of light and dark in (a painting or drawing). **19.** to change by imperceptible degrees into something else. **20.** *Colloq.* to make a small concession in price. —*v.i.* **21.** to pass or change by slight graduations, as one color or one thing into another. [ME; OE *sceadu.* See SHADOW] —**shade/less,** *adj.* —**Syn. 1.** SHADE, SHADOW imply partial darkness or something less bright than the surroundings. SHADE indicates the lesser brightness and heat of an area where the direct rays of light do not fall: *the shade of a tree.* It differs from SHADOW in that it implies no particular form or definite limit, while a SHADOW often represents in form or outline the object which intercepts the light: *the shadow of a dog.* **12.** See **curtain.** —**Ant. 1.** light, glare.

shade tree, a tree planted or valued for its shade.

shad·ing (shā/dĭng), *n.* **1.** a slight variation or difference of color, character, etc. **2.** act of one who or that which shades. **3.** the representation of the different values in a painting or drawing.

sha·doof (shä dōōf/), *n.* a contrivance used in the East for raising water, esp. for irrigation, consisting of a long suspended rod with a bucket at one end and a weight at the other. [t. Egypt. Ar.: m. *shādūf*]

Shadoofs

shad·ow (shăd/ō), *n.* **1.** a dark figure or image cast on the ground or some surface by a body intercepting light. **2.** shade or comparative darkness; an instance or area of comparative darkness. **3.** (*pl.*) darkness coming after sunset. **4.** shelter; protection. **5.** a slight suggestion, a trace: *not a shadow of a doubt.* **6.** a specter or ghost: *pursued by shadows.* **7.** a shadowy or faint image: *shadows of things to come.* **8.** a mere semblance: *the shadow of power.* **9.** a reflected image. **10.** the dark part, or shade, or a dark part, of a picture. **11.** a cloud, as on friendship or reputation. **12.** an inseparable companion. **13.** one who follows a person in order to keep watch upon him, as a spy or detective. —*v.t.* **14.** to overspread with shadow; shade. **15.** to cast a gloom over; cloud. **16.** to screen or protect from light, heat, etc. **17.** *Obs.* to shade in painting, drawing, etc. **18.** to follow (a person) about secretly, in order to keep watch over his movements. **19.** to represent faintly, prophetically, etc. (often fol. by *forth*). **20.** *Archaic.* to shelter or protect. [ME; OE *scead(u)we,* oblique case of *sceadu* SHADE, c. D *schaduw;* akin to G *schatten*] —**shad/ower,** *n.* —**shad/ow·less,** *adj.* —**Syn. 1.** See **shade.**

shad·ow·box·ing (shăd/ō bŏk/sĭng), *n.* boxing carried on with an imaginary opponent, as for exercise.

shad·ow·graph (shăd/ō grăf/, -gräf/), *n.* **1.** a picture produced by throwing a shadow, as of the hands, on a lighted screen. **2.** a radiograph.

shad·ow·land (shăd/ō lănd/), *n.* a land or region of shadows, phantoms, unrealities, or uncertainties.

shad·ow·y (shăd/ō ĭ), *adj.* **1.** resembling a shadow in faintness, slightness, etc.: *shadowy outlines.* **2.** unsubstantial, unreal, or illusory. **3.** abounding in shadow; shady: *a shadowy path.* **4.** enveloped in shadow. **5.** casting a shadow.

Sha·drach (shā/drăk), *n.* a companion of Daniel: one of the three (Shadrach, Meshach, Abednego) thrown into the fiery furnace of Nebuchadnezzar. Dan. 3:12–30.

Shad·well (shăd/wĕl, -wəl), *n.* **Thomas,** 1642?–92, British dramatist: poet laureate (1688–92).

shad·y (shā/dĭ), *adj.,* **shadier, shadiest. 1.** abounding in shade; shaded: *shady paths.* **2.** giving shade. **3.** shadowy; indistinct; spectral. **4.** *Colloq.* uncertain; questionable; of dubious character or reputation. **5. keep shady,** *Slang.* to keep out of sight, or in hiding. **6. on the shady side of,** *Colloq.* beyond in age: *on the shady side of forty.* —**shad/i·ly,** *adv.* —**shad/i·ness,** *n.*

SHAEF, Supreme Headquarters Allied Expeditionary Forces. Also, **Shaef** (shāf).

shaft (shăft, shäft), *n.* **1.** the long, slender rod forming the body of a spear or lance, or of an arrow. **2.** something directed as in sharp attack: *shafts of sarcasm.* **3.** a ray or beam: *shafts of sunlight.* **4.** the handle of a hammer, ax, golf club, or other long implement. **5.** a revolving bar serving to transmit motion, as from an engine to various machines. **6.** a flagpole. **7.** the body of a column or pillar between the base and the capital; a column. See diag. under **column. 8.** a monument in the form of a column, obelisk, or the like. **9.** either of the parallel bars of wood between which the animal drawing a vehicle is placed. **10.** any well-like passage or vertical enclosed space, as in a building: *an elevator shaft.* **11.** an inclined (sloping) or vertical passageway into a mine. **12.** *Bot.* the trunk of a tree. **13.** *Zool.* the main stem of a feather distal to the superior umbilicus. **14.** that part of a candlestick which supports its branches. [ME; OE *sceaft,* c. G *schaft*]

Shaftes·bur·y (shăfts/bə rĭ, shäfts/-), *n.* **1. Anthony Ashley Cooper, 1st Earl of,** 1621–83, British statesman. **2. Anthony Ashley Cooper, 7th Earl of,** 1801–85, British philanthropist.

shaft·ing (shăf/tĭng, shäf/-), *n. Mach.* **1.** shafts for communicating motion. **2.** a system of such shafts. **3.** material for such shafts.

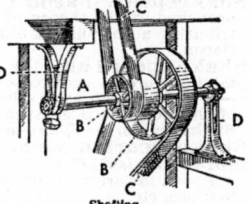

Shafting

A, Shaft; B, Pulley; C, Belt; D, Support

shag (shăg), *n., v.,* **shagged, shagging.** —*n.* **1.** rough, matted hair, wool, or the like. **2.** a mass of this. **3.** a cloth with a nap, at times one of silk but commonly a heavy or rough woolen fabric. **4.** a coarse tobacco cut into fine shreds. —*v.t.* **5.** to make rough or shaggy, esp. with vegetation. **6.** to make rough or sharp. [OE *sceacga* wool, etc., c. Icel. *skegg* beard, der. *skaga* stick out]

shag·bark (shăg/bärk/), *n.* **1.** a species of hickory, *Carya ovata,* with rough bark, yielding light-colored, ellipsoidal, slightly angular nuts, but most valued for its wood. **2.** the wood. **3.** the nut of this tree.

shag·gy (shăg/ĭ), *adj.,* **-gier, -giest. 1.** covered with or having long, rough hair. **2.** unkempt. **3.** rough and matted; forming a bushy mass, as the hair, mane, etc. **4.** having a rough nap, as cloth. —**shag/gi·ness,** *n.*

sha·green (sha grēn/), *n.* **1.** a kind of untanned leather with a granular surface, prepared from the skin of the horse, shark, seal, etc. **2.** the rough skin of certain sharks, used as an abrasive. [formerly *chagrin,* t. F, t. Turk.: m. *çāghrĭ,* lit., the rump of a horse]

shah (shä), *n.* king: esp. used (*usually cap.*) as a title of the ruler of Persia. Cf. **Padishah.** [t. Pers.]

Shah Ja·han (shä/ jə hän/), 1592?–1666, Mogul emperor in India, 1628?–58: built the Taj Mahal.

Shah·ja·han·pur (shä/jə han/pŏŏr/), *n.* a city in N India, in Uttar Pradesh. 98,949 (1951).

Shairp (shârp, shärp), *n.* **John Campbell,** ("*Principal Shairp*") 1819–85, British critic, poet, and educator.

Shai·tan (shī tän/), *n.* **1.** (in Mohammedan usage) Satan; the devil. **2.** (*l.c.*) a person of evil disposition; a vicious animal. [t. Ar., t. Heb.: alter. of *sātān* Satan]

shake (shāk), *v.,* **shook, shaken, shaking,** *n.* —*v.i.* **1.** to move or sway with short, quick, irregular vibratory movements. **2.** to tremble with emotion, cold, etc. **3.** to fall (fol. by *down, off,* etc.) by such motion: *sand shakes off readily.* **4.** to totter; become unsteady. **5.** *Music.* to execute or trill. —*v.t.* **6.** to move to and fro with short, quick, forcible movements. **7.** to brandish or flourish. **8.** to bring, throw, force, rouse, etc., by or as by some vigorous movement to and fro; cause to quiver or tremble: *leaves shaken by the breeze.* **9.** to cause to totter or waver: *to shake the very foundations of society.* **10.** to agitate or disturb profoundly in feeling. **11.** to unsettle; weaken: *to shake one's faith.* **12.** *Music.* to trill (a note, etc.). **13.** *Dice.* to mix (the dice) before they are cast. **14.** *Slang.* to get rid of. **15. shake down, a.** to bring down. **b.** to cause to settle. **c.** to condition: *to shake down a vessel by a first voyage.* **d.** *Slang.* to extort money from. **16. shake hands,** to clasp hands in greeting, congratulation, agreement, etc. **17. shake the dust from one's feet,** to take one's departure, esp. with a determination not to return. **18. shake up, a.** to shake in order to mix, loosen, etc. **b.** to stir up; upset. **c.** to jar mentally or physically. —*n.* **19.** act of shaking. **20.** tremulous motion. **21.** a tremor. **22.** a disturbing blow; shock. **23.** something resulting from shaking. **24.** *Colloq.* an earthquake. **25.** a fissure in the earth. **26.** a crack or fissure in timber, produced during growth by wind, sudden change of temperature, or the like. **27.** *Music.* a trill. **28.** a drink made by shaking ingredients together: *a milk shake.* **29.** *Slang.* an instant. [ME; OE *sceacan,* c. LG *schacken*] —**Syn. 1.** SHAKE, QUIVER, TREMBLE, VIBRATE refer to an agitated movement which, in living things, is often involuntary. To SHAKE is to agitate more or less quickly, abruptly, and often unevenly so as to disturb the poise, stability, or equilibrium of a person or thing: *a pole shaking under his weight.* To QUIVER is to exhibit a slight vibratory motion such as that resulting from disturbed or irregular (surface) tension: *the surface of the pool quivered in the breeze.* To TREMBLE (used more often of a person) is to be agitated by intermittent, involuntary movements of the muscles, much like shivering and caused by fear, cold, weakness, great emotion, etc.: *even stout hearts tremble with dismay.* To VIBRATE is to exhibit a rapid, incessant rhythmical motion: *a violin string vibrates when a bow is drawn across it.*

shake·down (shāk/doun/), *n.* **1.** a bed of straw, blankets, or other bedding spread on the floor. **2.** any makeshift bed. **3.** a process of shaking down.

shak·er (shā/kər), *n.* **1.** one who or that which shakes. **2.** that with which something is shaken. **3.** (*cap.*) one of an American communistic celibate religious sect so called, popularly, from the movements of the body which form part of their ceremonial. —**Shak/er·ism,** *n.*

Shaker Heights, a city in NE Ohio, near Cleveland. 36,460 (1960).

Shake·speare (shāk′spĭr), *n.* **William**, 1564–1616, English poet and dramatist. Also, **Shakspere**, **Shak·speare**.

Shakespeare-Bacon Controversy, a dispute provoked by the theory of Delia Bacon (1811–59) attributing authorship of Shakespeare's plays to Francis Bacon.

Shake·spear·i·an (shāk spĭr′Ĭən), *adj.* **1.** of, pertaining to, or suggestive of Shakespeare or his works. —*n.* **2.** a Shakespearian scholar; a specialist in the study of the works of Shakespeare. Also, **Shake·spear′e·an**, **Shaksperian.** —**Shake·spear′i·an·ism,** *n.*

Shakespearian sonnet, the Elizabethan sonnet.

shake-up (shāk′ŭp′), *n.* a thorough change in a business, department, or the like, as by dismissals, demotions, etc.

Shakh·ty (shäKH′tĬ), *n.* a city in the S Soviet Union in Europe, in the Donets Basin. 180,000 (est. 1956).

shak·ing (shā′kĬng), *n.* **1.** act of one who or that which shakes. **2.** ague, with or without chill and fever.

shaking palsy, a disease of the brain, characterized by tremors, esp. of fingers and hands, rigidity of muscles, slowness of movements and speech, and a masklike, expressionless face; Parkinson's disease.

shak·o (shăk′ō), *n., pl.* -os. a military cap in the form of a cylinder or truncated cone, with a visor and a plume or pompon. [t. Magyar: m. *csákó* peaked (cap)]

Shako

Shak·spere (shāk′spĭr), *n.* **William.** See **Shakespeare.** Also, **Shak′speare** —**Shak·sper′i·an,** *adj., n.*

Shak·ti (shŭk′tĬ), *n. Hinduism.* Sakti. [t. Skt.: m. *sakti* power, force]

shak·y (shā′kĬ), *adj.,* **shakier, shakiest. 1.** shaking. **2.** trembling; tremulous. **3.** liable to break down or give way; insecure; not to be depended upon. **4.** wavering, as in allegiance. —**shak′i·ly,** *adv.* —**shak′i·ness,** *n.*

shale (shāl), *n.* a rock of fissile or laminated structure formed by the consolidation of clay or argillaceous material. [special use of obs. *shale* scale (of a fish, etc.), OE *scealu* shell, husk. See SCALE¹]

shall (shăl; *unstressed* shəl), *aux. v., pres. sing.* 1 **shall**; 2 **shall** or (*Poetic*) **shalt**; 3 **shall**; *pl.* **shall**; *pt.* 1 **should**; 2 **should** or (*Archaic*) **shouldst** or **shouldest**; *pl.* **should**; imperative, inf., and participles lacking. **1.** (used, generally, in the first person to indicate simple future time): *I shall go today.* **2.** (used generally, in the second and third persons, to indicate promise or determination): *you shall do it.* **3.** (used interrogatively, in questions that admit of *shall* in the answer): *Shall he be told? He shall.* **4.** (used conditionally, in all persons to indicate future time): *if he shall come.* [ME *shal,* OE *sceal,* c. Icel. *skal;* akin to G *soll*]
—**Syn.** SHALL, WILL are two distinct and separate verbs but the confusion between them is of such long standing that certain arbitrary rules for usage were established. According to those, SHALL is used in the first person (both singular and plural) to indicate futurity, and simply foretells or declares what is about to take place: *I shall go to town tomorrow.* Used with the second or third persons, SHALL implies authority, command, threat, promise, determination, or inevitability: *thou shalt not steal.* With the first person, WILL denotes consent, promise, determination, or resolution: *we will meet you at noon.* WILL in the second and third persons (sing. or pl.) indicates simple futurity: *they will come by train.* Interrogatively, SHALL is used when SHALL is expected in the answer; WILL when WILL is expected: *Shall I tell him?* (*Yes, you shall*). *Will he go?* (*He will not*). The tendency now is for all forms to level to *will.*

shal·loon (shă lōōn′), *n.* a light, twilled woolen fabric used chiefly for linings. [ME *chalon* coverlet, appar. t. F: m. *chalon,* from *Châlons-sur-Marne*]

shal·lop (shăl′əp), *n. Poetic.* a small, light boat. [F: m. *chaloupe,* t. D: m. *sloepe*]

shal·lot (shə lŏt′), *n.* **1.** a plant of the lily family, *Allium ascalonicum,* whose bulb forms bulblets which are used for flavoring in cookery and as a vegetable. **2.** the bulb or bulblet. [aphetic var. of *eschalot,* t. F: m. *eschalotte,* alter. of OF *eschaloigne.* See SCALLION].

shal·low (shăl′ō), *adj.* **1.** of little depth; not deep: *shallow water, a shallow dish.* **2.** lacking depth; superficial: *shallow mind.* —*n.* **3.** a shallow part of a body of water; a shoal. —*v.t., v.i.* **4.** to make or become shallow. [ME *schalowe.* Cf. OE *sceald* shallow] —**shal′low·ly,** *adv.* —**shal′low·ness,** *n.*

shalt (shălt), *v. Poetic.* 2nd pers. sing of **shall.**

shal·y (shā′lĬ), *adj.* of, like, or containing shale.

sham (shăm), *n., adj., v.,* **shammed, shamming.** —*n.* **1.** something that is not what it purports to be; a spurious imitation. **2.** a cover or the like for giving a thing a different outward appearance: *a pillow sham.* **3.** *Obs.* hoax. [n. use of SHAM, v.] —*adj.* **4.** pretended; counterfeit: *sham attacks.* **5.** that pretends or shams. —*v.t.* **6.** to produce an imitation of; pretend to be. **7.** to assume the appearance of: *to sham illness.* —*v.i.* **8.** to make a false pretense; pretend. [special use of *sham,* northern var. of SHAME] —**Syn.** 4. spurious, make-believe, simulated. See FALSE. —**Ant.** 4. genuine.

sha·man (shä′mən, shā′-, shăm′ən), *n.* a medicine man; a worker with the supernatural. [t. G: m. *schamane,* t. Russ.: m. *shaman,* t. Tungusic: m. *samân*] —**sha·man·ic** (shə măn′Ĭk), *adj.*

sha·man·ism (shä′mə nĬz′əm, shā′-, shăm′ə-), *n.* **1.** the primitive religion of northern Asia embracing a belief in controlling spirits who can be influenced only by shamans. **2.** any similar religion. —**sha′man·ist,** *n., adj.* —**sha′man·is′tic,** *adj.*

Sha·mash (shä′mäsh), *n.* the Assyro-Babylonian sun god worshiped for his beneficence and power to encourage the fertility of earth.

sham·ble¹ (shăm′bəl), *n.* **1.** (*pl. often construed as sing.*) a slaughterhouse. **2.** (*pl. often construed as sing.*) any place of carnage: *to turn cities into shambles.* **3.** *Local in certain Brit. towns.* a table or stall for the sale of meat. [ME *shamel,* OE *sc(e)amel* stool, table, ult. t. L: m.s. *scamellum,* dim. of *scamnum* bench]

sham·ble² (shăm′bəl), *v.,* -**bled, -bling,** *n.* —*v.i.* **1.** to walk or go awkwardly; shuffle. —*n.* **2.** a shambling gait. [v. use of *shamble,* adj., awkward, itself attributive use of SHAMBLE¹]

shame (shām), *n., v.,* **shamed, shaming.** —*n.* **1.** the painful feeling arising from the consciousness of something dishonorable, improper, ridiculous, etc., done by oneself or another. **2.** susceptibility to this feeling: *to be without shame.* **3.** disgrace; ignominy. **4.** a fact or circumstance bringing disgrace or regret. **5.** put to shame, **a.** to disgrace. **b.** to outdo or surpass. **6. for shame!** you should feel shame! —*v.t.* **7.** to cause to feel shame; make ashamed. **8.** to drive, force, etc., through shame. **9.** to cover with ignominy or reproach; disgrace. [ME; OE *sc(e)amu,* c. G *scham*] —**Syn.** 1. SHAME, HUMILIATION imply painful feelings caused by lowering of one's pride or self-respect. SHAME is a painful feeling caused by the consciousness or exposure of unworthy or indecent conduct or circumstances: *one feels shame at being caught in a lie.* HUMILIATION is mortification or chagrin at being humbled in the estimation of others: *being ignored gives one a sense of humiliation.* —**Ant.** 1. pride, self-esteem, self-respect.

shame·faced (shām′fāst′), *adj.* **1.** modest or bashful. **2.** showing shame: *shamefaced apologies.* [SHAME, n., + FACE, n. + -ED³; r. *shamefast,* OE *sceamfæst* (see FAST¹, adj.)] —**shame·fac·ed·ly** (shām′fā′sĬd lĬ, shām′fāst′lĬ), *adv.* —**shame′fac′ed·ness,** *n.*

shame·ful (shām′fəl), *adj.* **1.** that causes or ought to cause shame. **2.** disgraceful or scandalous: *shameful treatment.* —**shame′ful·ly,** *adv.* —**shame′ful·ness,** *n.*

shame·less (shām′lĬs), *adj.* **1.** destitute of shame; immodest; audacious. **2.** insensible to disgrace. **3.** showing no shame: *shameless conduct.* —**shame′less·ly,** *adv.* —**shame′less·ness,** *n.* —**Syn.** 1. unblushing, brazen, indecent.

sham·mer (shăm′ər), *n.* one who shams.

sham·my (shăm′Ĭ), *n., pl.* -mies. chamois. [respelling of CHAMOIS to indicate pronunciation]

Sha·mo (shä′mō′), *n.* Chinese name of the Gobi.

Sha·mo·kin (shə mō′kĬn), *n.* a borough in E Pennsylvania. 16,879 (1950).

sham·poo (shăm pōō′), *v.,* -**pooed, -pooing.** *n.* —*v.t.* **1.** to wash (the head or hair). **2.** to massage. —*n.* **3.** act of shampooing. **4.** a preparation used for shampooing. [t. Hind.: m. *chāmpo,* impv. of *chāmpnā* to shampoo, lit., to press, squeeze] —**sham·poo′er,** *n.*

sham·rock (shăm′rŏk), *n.* a plant with trifoliate leaves (usually a yellow-flowered species of trefoil, *Trifolium dubium or minus*) taken as the national emblem of Ireland. [t. Irish: m. *seamrog,* dim. of *seamar* clover]

Shamrock

Shan (shän, shän), *n.* **1.** a group of Mongoloid tribes in the hills of Burma. **2.** a northern Thai language, spoken in the Shan States.

shan·dy·gaff (shăn′dĬ găf′), *n. Chiefly Brit.* a mixed drink of beer with ginger beer.

Shang·hai (shăng′hī′; *Ch.* shäng′hī′), *n.* **1.** a seaport in E China, near the mouth of the Yangtze. 5,410,000 (est. 1954). **2.** one of a long-legged breed of domestic fowls supposedly introduced from Shanghai.

shang·hai (shăng′hī, shăng hī′), *v.t.,* -**haied, -haiing. 1.** *Naut.* to render insensible, as by drugs, in order to ship forcibly on a vessel needing sailors. **2.** to effect by fraud or compulsion. [appar. short for "to ship to Shanghai"]

Shan·gri-la (shăng′grə lä′), *n.* **1.** a paradise on earth. **2.** a secret airfield or base of operations used by the U.S. Army Air Forces. [named after a hidden paradise in James Hilton's *Lost Horizon*]

Shan·hai·kwan (shän′hī′gwän′), *n.* former name of Linyu.

shank (shăngk), *n.* **1.** that part of the leg in man between the knee and the ankle. **2.** a part in certain animals corresponding or analogous to the human shank. See illus. under HORSE. **3.** the whole leg. **4.** a cut of meat from the top part of the front (**fore shank**) or back (**hind shank**) leg. **5.** that portion of an instrument, tool, etc., connecting the acting part with the handle or any like part. **6.** *Music.* a crook. **7.** *Colloq.* the latter end or part of anything. **8.** the narrow part of a shoe, connecting the broad part of the sole with the heel. **9.** the piece of metal or fiber used to give it form. **10.** *Print.* the body of a type, between the shoulder and the foot. [ME; OE *sc(e)anca,* c. LG *schanke* leg, thigh]

Shan·non (shăn′ən), *n.* **1.** a river flowing from N Ireland SW to the Atlantic: the principal river of Ireland. ab. 240 mi. **2.** international airport in W Ireland, near Limerick.

---

b., blend of, blended; c., cognate with; d., dialect, dialectal; der., derived from; f., formed from; g., going back to; m., modification of; r., replacing; s., stem of; t., taken from; ?, perhaps. See the full key on inside cover.

Shan·si (shän/sē/), n. a province in N China. 14,314,-485 pop. (1953); 60,394 sq. mi. *Cap.*: Taiyüan.

Shan States (shän, shän), two groups of native states (Northern and Southern) in E Burma, along the Salween river. 1,699,000 pop. (1941); ab. 56,000 sq. mi.

shan't (shănt, shänt), *Colloq.* contraction of *shall not.* Also, **sha'n't.**

Shan·tung (shän/tŭng/; *Ch.* shän/dŏŏng/ for 1, 2), n. 1. a maritime province in NE China. 48,876,548 pop. (1953); 56,447 sq. mi. *Cap.*: Tsinan. 2. a peninsula in the E part of this province, extending into the Yellow Sea. 3. (*l.c.*) a silk fabric, a heavy variety of pongee made of rough, spun wild silk. 4. (*l.c.*) a fabric imitating this made of rayon or cotton. Also, **Shan/tung** for 3, 4.

shan·ty¹ (shăn/tĭ), n., pl. **-ties.** a roughly built hut, cabin, or house. [probably t. Canadian F: alter. of *chantier* log hut, F shed, g. L *canthērius* framework] —**Syn.** See **cottage.**

shan·ty² (shăn/tĭ), n., pl. **-ties.** chantey.

Shao·hing·fu (shou/shĭng/fōō/), n. a city in E China, in Chekiang province. 93,000 (est. 1950).

shape (shāp), n., v. **shaped, shaping.** —n. 1. the quality of a thing depending on its outline or external surface. 2. the form of a particular thing, person, or being. 3. an imaginary form; phantom. 4. an assumed appearance; guise. 5. a particular or definite form of nature: *things taking shape.* 6. proper form; orderly arrangement. 7. condition: *affairs in bad shape.* 8. something used to give form, as a mold or a pattern. [ME, n. use of SHAPE, v.; r. ME *shap*, OE (*ge*)*sceap* form, creature, g. Icel. *skap* state, mood] —*v.t.* 9. to give definite form, shape, or character to; fashion or form. 10. to couch or express in words: *to shape a statement.* 11. to adjust; adapt. 12. to direct (one's course). 13. *Obs.* to appoint; decree. —*v.i.* 14. to take shape or form; assume a definite form or character. 15. to come out: *everything was shaping up well.* [ME; r. ME *schippe*, OE *scieppan* create, shape (pp. *scapen*, whence current present form), c. Goth. *gaskapjan* create] —**shap/er,** n. —**Syn.** 1. See **form.**

shape·less (shāp/lĭs), adj. 1. having no definite or regular shape or form. 2. lacking beauty or elegance of form. —**shape/less·ly,** adv. —**shape/less·ness,** n.

shape·ly (shāp/lĭ), adj., **-lier, -liest.** having a pleasing shape; well-formed. —**shape/li·ness,** n.

shard (shärd), n. 1. a fragment, esp. of broken earthenware. 2. *Zool.* a scale, as of an egg or snail. Also, **sherd.** [ME; OE *sceard*, c. LG *schaard*]

share¹ (shâr), n., v. **shared, sharing.** —n. 1. the portion or part allotted or belonging to, or contributed or owed by, an individual or group. 2. one of the equal fractional parts into which the capital stock of a joint-stock company or a corporation is divided. —*v.t.* 3. to divide and distribute in shares; apportion. 4. to use, participate in, enjoy, etc., jointly. —*v.i.* 5. to have a share or part; take part (often fol. by *in*). [ME; OE *scearu* cutting, division, c. G *schar* troop. See SHEAR, v.] —**shar/er,** n. —**Syn.** 5. SHARE, PARTAKE, PARTICIPATE mean to join with others or to receive in common with others. To SHARE is to give or receive a part of something, or to enjoy or assume something in common: *to share in another's experiences.* To PARTAKE is to take for one's own personal use a portion of something: *to partake of food.* To PARTICIPATE is esp. to join with others in some thought, feeling, or, particularly, some action: *to participate in a race, in a conversation.*

share² (shâr), n. a plowshare. [ME; OE *scear*, c. G *schar*; akin to SHARE¹, SHEAR]

share·crop·per (shâr/krŏp/ər), n. a tenant farmer who pays as rent a share of the crop.

share·hold·er (shâr/hōl/dər), n. *Chiefly Brit.* one who holds or owns a share or shares, as in a corporation.

Sha·ri (shä/rē), n. a river in French Equatorial Africa, flowing NW to Lake Chad. ab. 1400 mi.

shark¹ (shärk), n. any of a group of elongate elasmobranch (mostly marine) fishes, certain species of which are large and ferocious, and destructive to other fishes and sometimes dangerous to man. [orig. obscure]

Great white shark.
Carcharodon carcharias
(30 ft. long)

shark² (shärk), n. 1. a person who preys greedily on others. 2. *Slang.* one who has unusual ability in a particular field. —*v.t.* 3. to obtain by trickery or fraud; steal. —*v.i.* 4. to live by shifts and stratagems. [t. G: m. *schork*, var. of *schurke* rascal]

shark·skin (shärk/skĭn/), n. heavy rayon suiting with a dull or chalklike appearance.

Shar·on (shăr/ən), n. 1. a fertile coastal plain in ancient Palestine. 2. a city in W Pennsylvania. 25,267 (1960).

sharp (shärp), adj. 1. having a thin cutting edge or a fine point; well adapted for cutting or piercing. 2. terminating in an edge or point; not blunt or rounded. 3. having sudden change of directions, as a turn. 4. abrupt, as an ascent. 5. composed of hard, angular

grains, as sand. 6. distinct; marked, as a contrast. 7. pungent or biting in taste. 8. piercing or shrill in sound. 9. keenly cold, as weather, etc. 10. intensely painful; distressing: *sharp pain.* 11. harsh; merciless: *sharp words.* 12. fierce or violent: *a sharp struggle.* 13. keen or eager: *sharp desire.* 14. quick or brisk. 15. vigilant: *a sharp watch.* 16. mentally acute: *a sharp lad.* 17. shrewd or astute: *sharp at making a bargain.* 18. shrewd to the point of dishonesty: *sharp practice.* 19. *Music.* a. above an intended pitch, as a note; too high. b. (of a tone) raised a half step in pitch: *F sharp.* 20. *Phonet.* fortis; voiceless. —*v.t.* 21. *Music.* to raise in pitch, esp. one half step. —*v.i.* 22. *Music.* to sound above the true pitch. —*adv.* 23. keenly or acutely. 24. abruptly or suddenly: *to pull a horse up sharp.* 25. punctually: *at one o'clock sharp.* 26. vigilantly: *look sharp!* 27. briskly; quickly. 28. *Music.* above the true pitch. —n. 29. something sharp. 30. a needle with a very sharp point. 31. a sharper. 32. *Colloq.* an expert. 33. *Music.* a. a tone one half step above a given tone. b. (in musical notation) the symbol (♯) indicating this. [ME; OE *scearp*, c. G *scharf*] —**sharp/ly,** adv. —**sharp/ness,** n.
—**Syn.** 1. SHARP, KEEN refer to the edge or point of an instrument, tool, and the like. SHARP applies, in general, to a cutting edge or a point capable of piercing: *a sharp knife, razor.* KEEN is esp. applied to long edges, as of a saber: *a keen sword blade.* 16. SHARP, KEEN, INTELLIGENT, QUICK may be applied figuratively to mental qualities. SHARP implies an acute, sensitive, alert, penetrating quality: *a sharp mind.* KEEN implies observant, incisive, and vigorous: *a keen intellect.* INTELLIGENT means not only acute, alert, and active, but also able to reason and understand: *an intelligent reader.* QUICK suggests lively and rapid comprehension, prompt response to instruction, and the like: *quick at figures.* —**Ant.** 16. dull.

Sharp (shärp), n. **William,** ("Fiona Macleod") 1855?-1905, Scottish poet and critic.

sharp·en (shär/pən), *v.t., v.i.* to make or become sharp or sharper. —**sharp/en·er,** n.

sharp·er (shär/pər), n. 1. a shrewd swindler. 2. a professional gamester: *a card sharper.*

sharp·ie (shär/pĭ), n. *New England.* a kind of long, flat-bottomed boat with one or (commonly) two masts, each rigged with a triangular sail.

Sharps·burg (shärps/bûrg), n. a town in NW Maryland: nearby is the site of the battle of Antietam, 1862.

sharp·set (shärp/sĕt/), adj. 1. very hungry. 2. keen or eager. 3. set to present a sharply angled edge.

sharp·shoot·er (shärp/shōō/tər), n. one skilled in shooting, esp. with the rifle. —**sharp/shoot/ing,** n.

sharp·sight·ed (shärp/sī/tĭd), adj. 1. having keen sight. 2. having or showing mental acuteness. —**sharp/-sight/ed·ness,** n.

sharp·wit·ted (shärp/wĭt/ĭd), adj. having or showing sharp wits; acute. —**sharp/-wit/ted·ness,** n.

Shas·ta (shăs/tə), n. Mount, a volcanic peak in N California, in the Cascade Range. 14,161 ft.

Shasta daisy, a horticultural variety of *Chrysanthemum maximum.* [named after Mt. *Shasta*]

Shatt-al-A·rab (shăt/ əl ä/räb), a river in SE Iraq, formed by the junction of the Tigris and Euphrates rivers, flowing SE to the Persian Gulf. 123 mi.

shat·ter (shăt/ər), *v.t.* 1. to break in pieces, as by a blow. 2. to damage, as by breaking or crushing: *ships shattered by storms.* 3. to impair (health, nerves, etc.). —*v.i.* 4. to break suddenly into fragments. —n. 5. (pl.) *Chiefly Dial.* fragments due to shattering. [ME *schater*(en). Cf. SCATTER] —**Syn.** 1. See **break.**

shave (shāv), v. **shaved, shaved** or **shaven, shaving,** n. —*v.i.* 1. to remove a growth of beard with a razor. —*v.t.* 2. to remove hair from (the face, legs, etc.) by cutting it close to the skin. 3. to cut off (hair, esp. the beard) close to the skin (often fol. by *off* or *away*). 4. to cut or scrape away the surface of with a sharp-edged tool: *to shave hides in preparing leather.* 5. to reduce to shavings or thin slices: *to shave wood.* 6. to cut or trim closely: *to shave a lawn.* 7. to scrape or graze; come very near to: *to shave a corner.* 8. *U.S. Colloq.* to purchase (a note) at the rate of discount greater than is legal or customary. —n. 9. act or process of shaving. 10. a thin slice; a shaving. 11. *Colloq.* a narrow miss or escape: *a close shave.* 12. any of various tools for shaving, scraping, removing thin slices, etc. [ME; OE *sceafan,* c. D, LG, G *schaben*]

shave·ling (shāv/lĭng), n. young fellow; youngster.

shav·er (shā/vər), n. 1. one who or that which shaves. 2. *Colloq.* a small child. 3. a fellow. 4. one who makes close bargains or is extortionate.

shave·tail (shāv/tāl/), n. *U.S. Army Slang.* a second lieutenant.

Sha·vi·an (shā/vĭ ən), adj. 1. of, pertaining to, or characteristic of George Bernard Shaw: *Shavian humor.* —n. 2. an admirer of George Bernard Shaw or of his works.

shav·ing (shā/vĭng), n. 1. (often *pl.*) a very thin piece or slice, esp. of wood. 2. act of one who or that which shaves.

Shaw (shô), n. 1. **George Bernard,** 1856-1950, Irish dramatist, critic, and novelist. 2. **Henry Wheeler,** ("Josh Billings") 1818-85, U.S. humorist. 3. **Irwin,** born 1913, U. S. dramatist and author. 4. **Thomas Edward.** See **Lawrence, Thomas Edward.**

shawl (shôl), *n.* a square or oblong piece of material, worn about the shoulders, head, etc., chiefly by women, in place of coat or hat. [t. Pers.: m. *shāl*]

shawm (shôm), *n.* an early wood wind instrument with a double reed, forerunner of the modern oboe. [ME *schallemelle*, t. OF: m. *chalemel*, g. L *calamellus* little pipe, der. L *calamus* reed]

Shaw·nee (shô nē′), *n.* **1.** (*pl.*) an Algonquian-speaking tribe formerly in the east-central U.S., now in Oklahoma. **2.** a member of this tribe. **3.** a city in central Oklahoma. 24,326 (1960). [t. Fox and other Algonquian dialects; cf. *shawun* south, *shawunoki* southerners]

shay (shā), *n. Colloq.* a chaise. [back formation from CHAISE]

Shays (shāz), *n.* **Daniel,** 1747–1825, leader of a popular insurgent movement (**Shays' Rebellion,** 1786–87) in Massachusetts.

Shcher·ba·kov (shchĭr′bə kôf′), *n.* a city in central Soviet Union in Europe, on the Volga. 162,000 (est. 1956).

she (shē), *pron., sing. nom.* **she,** *poss.* **her** *or* **hers,** *obj.* **her;** *pl. nom.* **they,** *poss.* **their** *or* **theirs,** *obj.* **them;** *n., pl.* **shes.** —*pron.* **1.** the female in question or last mentioned. **2.** the woman: *she who listens learns.* —*n.* **3.** a woman or female. [ME, sandhi var. of ME *ghe*, OE *hēo*. See HE]

she-, prefixal use of **she** to denote the female of a class, as in *she-wolf.*

shea (shē), *n.* an African sapotaceous tree, *Butyrospermum Parkii,* the seeds of which yield a butterlike fat (**shea butter**), used as food, in making soap, etc. [t. Mandingo: m. *sye*]

sheaf (shēf), *n., pl.* **sheaves,** *v.* —*n.* **1.** one of the bundles in which cereal plants, as wheat, rye, etc., are bound after reaping. **2.** any bundle, cluster, or collection: *a sheaf of papers.* —*v.t.* **3.** to bind into a sheaf or sheaves. [ME *shefe,* OE *scēaf,* c. D *schoof,* G *schaub* wisp of straw]

shear (shĭr), *v.,* **sheared** *or* (*Archaic*) **shore; sheared** *or* **shorn; shearing;** *n.* —*v.t.* **1.** to cut with shears or other sharp instrument: *to shear metal.* **2.** to remove by or as by cutting with a sharp instrument: *to shear wool from sheep.* **3.** to cut the hair, fleece, wool, etc., from. **4.** to strip or deprive (fol. by *of*): *shorn of its legislative powers.* **5.** *Dial.* to reap with a sickle. **6.** *Archaic.* to cut with a sharp instrument (fol. by *through*). —*v.i.* **7.** *Mech., etc.* to become fractured by a shear or shears. **8.** *Dial.* to reap grain, etc., with a sickle. —*n.* **9.** act or process of shearing. **10.** one blade of a pair of shears. **11.** a pair of shears. **12.** a shearing of sheep (used in stating the age of sheep): *a sheep of one shear (one year old).* **13.** a quantity of wool, grass, etc., cut off at one shearing. **14.** any machine using an adaption of the shearing principle, esp. to cut metal sheets. **15.** *Mech.* the tendency produced by loads to deform or fracture a member by sliding one section against another. [ME *shere(n),* OE *sceran,* c. D and G *scheren,* Icel. *skera*] —**shear′er,** *n.*

shears (shĭrz), *n.pl.* **1.** scissors of large size (often called a *pair of shears*). **2.** any of various other cutting implements or machines resembling or suggesting scissors. **3.** Also, **shear legs.** an apparatus for hoisting heavy weights, consisting of two or more spars fastened together near the top with their lower ends separated and a tackle suspended from the top and steadying guys.

shear·wa·ter (shĭr′wô′tər, -wŏt′ər), *n.* any of various long-winged sea birds, esp. of the genus *Puffinus,* allied to the petrels, appearing, when flying low, to cleave the water with their wings. [f. SHEAR, v. + WATER, n.]

sheat·fish (shēt′fĭsh′), *n., pl.* **-fishes,** (*esp. collectively*) **-fish.** a large fresh-water fish, *Silurus glanis,* the great catfish of central and eastern Europe, sometimes reaching 400 pounds. [f. *sheat* (OE *sceota* trout) + FISH]

sheath (shēth), *n., pl.* **sheaths** (shēᵺz), *v.* —*n.* **1.** a case or covering for the blade of a sword, dagger, or the like. **2.** any similar covering. **3.** *Biol.* a closely enveloping part or structure, as in an animal or plant organism. See diag. under *neuron.* **4.** *Bot.* the leaf base when it forms a vertical coating surrounding the stem. —*v.t.* **5.** to sheathe. [ME *sheth(e),* OE *scēath,* c. G *scheide*]

sheath·bill (shēth′bĭl′), *n.* either of two sea birds with white plumage, *Chionis alba* and *C. minor,* of the colder parts of the Southern Hemisphere: so called from the horny case which partly sheathes the bill.

sheathe (shēᵺ), *v.t.,* **sheathed, sheathing. 1.** to put (a sword, etc.) into a sheath. **2.** to plunge (a sword, etc.) in something as if in a sheath. **3.** to enclose in or as in a casing or covering. **4.** to cover or provide with a protective layer or sheathing: *to sheathe a roof with copper.* [ME *shethe,* der. SHEATH] —**sheath′er,** *n.*

sheath·ing (shē′ᵺĭng), *n.* **1.** act or one who sheathes. **2.** that which sheathes; a covering or outer layer of metal, wood, or other material, as one of metal plates on a ship's bottom, the first covering of boards on a house, etc. **3.** material for forming any such covering.

sheath knife, a knife carried in a sheath.

sheave¹ (shēv), *v.t.,* **sheaved, sheaving.** to gather, collect, or bind into a sheaf or sheaves. [der. SHEAF]

sheave² (shēv), *n.* **1.** a grooved wheel forming a pulley. **2.** any of various other wheels or disks with a grooved rim. [ME *sheeve;* akin to G *scheibe* disk]

sheaves (shēvz), *n.* **1.** pl. of **sheaf. 2.** pl. of **sheave.**

She·ba (shē′bə), *n.* the Biblical name of an ancient country in S Arabia, noted for its extensive trade in spices, gems, etc. Also, **Saba.**

she·bang (shə băng′), *n. Slang.* **1.** thing; affair. **2.** establishment.

She·bat (shə bät′), *n.* (in the Jewish calendar) the fifth month of the year. [t. Heb.: m. *sh'bhat*]

she·been (shĭ bēn′), *n. Irish and Scot.* a place where liquor is sold illegally. [t. Irish: m. *sibín*]

She·boy·gan (shĭ boi′gən), *n.* a city in E Wisconsin a port on Lake Michigan. 45,747 (1960).

She·chem (shē′kĕm), *n.* a town of ancient Palestine, near city of Samaria; now in Jordan. Modern, **Nablus.**

shed¹ (shĕd), *n.* **1.** a slight or rude structure built for shelter, storage, etc. **2.** a large, strongly built structure, often open at the sides or end. [ME *shadde,* OE *scead, sced* shelter, SHADE]

shed² (shĕd), *v.,* **shed, shedding.** —*v.t.* **1.** to pour forth (water, etc.) as a fountain does. **2.** to emit and let fall (tears). **3.** to let flow or cause to flow (blood). **4.** shed blood, to kill by violence. **5.** to cast; give or send forth (light, sound, fragrance, influence, etc.). **6.** to throw off readily: *cloth that sheds water.* **7.** to cast off or let fall by natural process (leaves, hair, feathers, skin, shell, etc.). —*v.i.* **8.** to fall off, as leaves, etc. **9.** drop out, as seed, grain, etc. **9.** to cast off hair, feathers, skin, or other covering or parts by natural process. [ME; OE *scēadan,* earlier *sc(e)ādan,* c. D and G *scheiden*]

shed·der (shĕd′ər), *n.* **1.** one who or that which sheds. **2.** a lobster, crab, etc., just before it molts.

sheen (shēn), *n.* **1.** luster; brightness; radiance. **2.** *Poetic.* gleaming attire. [der. SHEEN, *adj.,* or SHINE, *v.*] —*adj.* Archaic. **3.** shining. **4.** beautiful. —*v.i.* **5.** *Scot. and Eng. Dial.* to be bright; shine. [ME *sheene,* d. OE *scēne* beautiful, bright, c. G *schön*] —**Syn. 1.** See **polish.**

sheen·y (shē′nĭ), *adj.* shining; lustrous.

sheep (shēp), *n., pl.* **sheep. 1.** any of the ruminant mammals constituting the genus *Ovis* (family *Bovidae*), closely allied to the goats, esp. *O. aries,* which has many domesticated varieties or breeds, valuable for their flesh, fleece, etc. **2.** leather made from the skin of these animals. **3.** a meek, timid, or stupid person. [ME; OE *scēp* (Anglian), *scēap,* c. G *schaf*]

Sheep, Southdown variety, *Ovis aries* (2 ft. high at the shoulder)

sheep·ber·ry (shēp′bĕr′ĭ), *n., pl.* **-ries.** a caprifoliaceous shrub or small tree, *Viburnum Lentago,* of North America, bearing cymes of small white flowers, and edible, berrylike black drupes; black haw.

sheep·cote (shēp′kōt′), *n.* a slight covered structure for sheltering sheep.

sheep dip, *Vet. Sci.* a lotion or wash applied to the fleece or skin of sheep to kill vermin, usually applied by immersing the animals in vats.

sheep dog, a dog trained to watch and tend sheep, esp. a collie, or one of a large, shaggy, bobtailed breed (**old English sheep dog**), usually blue-gray and white.

sheep·fold (shēp′fōld′), *n. Chiefly Brit.* an enclosure for sheep.

sheep·herd·er (shēp′hûr′dər), *n. Western U.S.* a shepherd (def. 1).

sheep·ish (shē′pĭsh), *adj.* **1.** awkwardly bashful or embarrassed. **2.** like sheep, as in meekness, timidity, etc. —**sheep′ish·ly,** *adv.* —**sheep′ish·ness,** *n.*

sheep laurel, a North American ericaceous, low shrub, *Kalmia angustifolia,* reputed to be poisonous to sheep and other animals.

sheep·shank (shēp′shăngk′), *n.* a kind of knot, hitch, or bend made on a rope to shorten it temporarily.

sheeps·head (shēps′hĕd′), *n.* **1.** a deep-bodied, black-banded food fish, *Archosargus probatocephalus,* of the Atlantic coast of the U.S. **2.** the fresh-water drumfish, *Aplodinotus grunniens,* of N North America. **3.** a labroid food fish, *Pimelometopon pulchrum,* common in southern California. **4.** a foolish or stupid person.

sheep·shear·ing (shēp′shĭr′ĭng), *n.* **1.** act of shearing sheep. **2.** the time or season of shearing sheep, or a feast held then. —**sheep′shear′er,** *n.*

sheep·skin (shēp′skĭn′), *n.* **1.** the skin of a sheep, esp. such a skin dressed with the wool on, as for a garment. **2.** leather, parchment, or the like made from the skin of sheep. **3.** *U.S. Colloq.* a diploma.

sheep sorrel, a slender polygonaceous weed, *Rumex Acetosella,* with hastate leaves of an acid taste, abounding in poor, dry soils.

sheep tick, a parasitic, wingless fly, *Melophagus ovinus,* of the dipterous family *Hippoboscidae,* quite injurious to sheep.

sheep·walk (shēp′wôk′), *n. Brit.* a tract of land on which sheep are pastured.

sheer¹ (shĭr), *adj.* **1.** transparently thin; diaphanous, as fabrics, etc. **2.** unmixed with anything else: *sheer rock.* **3.** unqualified; utter: *a sheer waste of time.* **4.** extending down or up very steeply: *a sheer descent of rock.* **5.** *Brit. Obs.* bright; shining. —*adv.* **6.** clear; completely; quite. **7.** down or up very steeply. —*n.* **8.** thin, diaphanous material, as chiffon or voile. [ME *schere,* c. Icel. *skærr* clear, bright, pure; akin to OE *scīr*] —**sheer′ly,** *adv.* —**sheer′ness,** *n.* —**Syn. 3.** absolute, downright. **4.** abrupt, precipitous, perpendicular.

sheer² (shĭr), *v.i.* **1.** to deviate from a course, as a ship; swerve. —*v.t.* **2.** to cause to sheer. —*n.* **3.** a deviation or divergence, as of a ship from her course; a swerve. **4.** the upward longitudinal curve of a ship's deck or bulwarks. **5.** the position in which a ship at anchor is placed to keep her clear of the anchor. [special use of SHEAR, v. Cf. D and G *scheren* depart]

Sheer·ness (shĭr'nĕs/), *n.* a seaport in SE England at the mouth of the Thames: government dockyards. 15,727 (1951).

sheet[1] (shēt), *n.* **1.** a large rectangular piece of linen, cotton, or other material, used as an article of bedding, commonly one of a pair spread immediately above and below the sleeper. **2.** a broad, thin mass, layer, or covering; a broad, relatively thin piece of iron, glass, etc. **3.** an oblong or square piece of paper or parchment, esp. one on which to write or print. **4.** (*pl.*) the pages or leaves of a book, etc. **5.** a newspaper. **6.** *Bookmaking.* a piece of definite size from which book paper is made. **7.** *Philately.* the impression from a plate, etc., on a single piece of paper, before the individual stamps have been separated. **8.** an extent, stretch, or expanse, as of lightning, water, etc.: *sheets of flame.* **9.** *Geol.* a more or less horizontal mass of rock, esp. eruptive rock intruded between strata or spread over a surface. —*v.t.* **10.** to furnish with sheets. **11.** to wrap in a sheet. **12.** to cover with a sheet or layer of something: *sheeted with ice.* [ME *shete*, OE *scēte* (Anglian), *sciete*, der. *scēat* lap, c. D *schoss*, Icel. *skaut* skirt]

sheet[2] (shēt), *Naut.* —*n.* **1.** a rope or chain fastened: **a.** to a lower aftercorner of a sail, or to the boom of a fore-and-aft sail, to control its trim. **b.** to both lower corners of a square sail to extend them to the yardarms below. **2.** (*pl.*) the spaces beyond the thwarts in the forward or the after end of an open boat. —*v.t.* **3.** to trim, extend, or secure by means of a sheet or sheets. **4. to sheet sails home**, to extend them to the utmost by hauling on the sheets. [ME *schete*, OE *scēata* rope tied to lower corner of a sail, c. LG *schote*; in some senses akin to SHOOT]

sheet anchor, 1. a large anchor used only in cases of emergency. **2.** a final reliance or resource. [late ME *shute anker*; orig. uncert.]

sheet bend, *Naut.* a knot used to bend the end of a line onto a bight or eye of another line, used esp. with large lines.

sheet·ing (shē'tĭng), *n.* **1.** act of covering with or forming into sheets. **2.** wide muslin used for sheets, etc.

sheet iron, iron in sheets or thin plates.

sheet lightning, lightning appearing merely as a general illumination over a broad surface, usually due to the reflection of the lightning of a distant thunderstorm.

sheet metal, metal in sheets or thin plates.

sheet music, musical compositions printed on unbound sheets.

Shef·field (shĕf'ēld), *n.* a city in central England, in S Yorkshire. 512,850 (1951).

sheik (shēk; *Brit.* shāk), *n.* **1.** (in Arab and other Mohammedan use) **a.** chief or head; the head man of a village or tribe. **b.** the head of a religious body. **2.** *Slang.* a masterful man of irresistible romantic charm. Also, **sheikh.** [t. Ar.: m. *shaikh* old man]

sheik·dom (shēk'dəm), *n.* the land or territory under the control of a sheik.

shek·el (shĕk'əl), *n.* **1.** an ancient, orig. Babylonian, unit of weight, of varying value (taken as equal to the fiftieth or the sixtieth part of a mina, and to about half an ounce). **2.** a coin of this weight, esp. the chief silver coin of the Hebrews. **3.** (*pl.*) *Slang.* money. [t. Heb.: m. *sheqel*, akin to *shāqal* weigh]

Obverse   Reverse
Hebrew shekel

She·ki·nah (shə kī'nə), *n.* *Jewish Theol.* the divine presence, or a radiance forming the visible manifestation of the divine presence. [t. LHeb.: lit., dwelling]

shel·drake (shĕl'drāk/), *n.*, *pl.* -drakes, (*esp. collectively*) -drake. **1.** any of the Old World ducks constituting the genera *Tadorna* and *Casarca*, certain of which are highly variegated in color. **2.** any of various other ducks, esp. the goosander or merganser. [ME *sheldedrake*; prob. f. *sheld* particolored (now obs.) + DRAKE]

Sheldrake, *Tadorna tadorna* (26 in. long)

shelf (shĕlf), *n.*, *pl.* **shelves. 1.** a thin slab of wood or other material fixed horizontally to a wall, or in a frame, for supporting objects. **2.** the contents of such a shelf. **3.** a shelflike surface or projection; a ledge. **4.** a sand bank or submerged extent of rock in the sea or a river. **5.** *Mining, etc.* bedrock, as under alluvial deposits. **6.** *Archery.* the upper portion of the hand, as it grasps the bow, on which an arrow rests when shooting. **7. on the shelf**, put aside or out of service. [ME. Cf. LG *schelf*] —**shelf′like/**, *adj.*

shell (shĕl), *n.*, *pl.* **shells** or (for 7–10) **shell. 1.** a hard outer covering of an animal, as the hard case of a mollusk, or either half of the case of a bivalve mollusk. **2.** any of various objects resembling a shell, as in shape, or in being more or less concave or hollow. **3.** the material constituting any of various kinds of shells. **4.** the

hard exterior of an egg. **5.** a more or less hard outer covering of a seed, fruit, or the like, as the hard outside portion of a nut, the pod of peas, etc. **6.** an enclosing case or cover suggesting a shell. **7.** a hollow projectile for a cannon, etc., filled with an explosive charge arranged to explode during flight or upon impact or after penetration. **8.** a metallic cartridge used in small arms and small artillery pieces. **9.** a metal or paper cartridge, as for use in a shotgun. **10.** a cartridgelike pyrotechnic device which explodes in the air. **11.** *Cookery.* the lower pastry crust, baked before the filling is added. **12.** *Physics.* a class of electron orbits in an atom, all of which have the same energy. **13.** a light, long, narrow racing boat rowed by means of outriggers. **14.** tortoise shell. **15.** a mollusk. —*v.t.* **16.** to take out of the shell, pod, etc. **17.** to remove the shell of. **18.** to separate (Indian corn) from the ear or cob. **19.** to throw shells or explosive projectiles into, upon, or among; bombard. **20. shell out**, *Slang.* to hand over; pay up. —*v.i.* **21.** to fall or come out of the shell, husk, etc. **22.** to come away or fall off, as a shell or outer coat. [ME; OE *scell* (Anglian), *sciell*, d. D *schel*. See SCALE[1]] —**shell′-like/**, *adj.*

shel·lac (shə lăk/), *n.*, *v.*, **-lacked, -lacking.** —*n.* **1.** lac which has been purified and formed into thin plates, used for making varnish. **2.** a varnish (**shellac varnish**) made by dissolving this material in alcohol or a similar solvent. —*v.t.* **3.** to coat or treat with shellac. [f. SHELL + LAC[1], trans. of F *laque en écailles* lac in thin plates] —**shel·lack′er,** *n.*

shell·back (shĕl'băk/), *n.* **1.** an old sailor. **2.** one who has crossed the equator by boat.

shell·bark (shĕl'bärk/), *n.* shagbark.

shell bean, 1. any of the various kinds of bean (plant) the unripe seeds of which are removed from the pods before cooking. **2.** the seed itself.

Shel·ley (shĕl'ĭ), *n.* **1. Mary Wollstonecraft Godwin** (wōŏl/stən krăft/, -krăft/), 1797–1851, British author: wife of Percy Bysshe Shelley. **2. Percy Bysshe** (bĭsh), 1792–1822, British poet.

shell·fire (shĕl'fīr/), *n.* *Mil.* the firing of explosive shells or projectiles.

shell·fish (shĕl'fĭsh/), *n.*, *pl.* **-fishes**, (*esp. collectively*) **-fish.** an aquatic animal (not a fish in the ordinary sense) having a shell, as the oyster and other mollusks and the lobster and other crustaceans. [ME *shelfish*, OE *scilfisc*, c. Icel. *skelfiskr*. See SHELL, FISH]

shell game, 1. a swindling game resembling thimblerig but employing walnut shells or the like instead of thimblelike cups. **2.** any dishonest swindling.

shell jacket, a semiformal jacket, close-fitting, with a short back, worn in the tropics in place of a tuxedo.

shell·proof (shĕl'prŏŏf/), *adj.* protected against the explosive effect of shells or bombs.

shell shock, *Psychiatry.* nervous or mental disorder in various forms, characterized by loss of self-command, memory, speech, sight, or other powers, at first supposed to be brought on by the explosion of shells in battle, but now explained as the result of the cumulative strain of modern warfare. —**shell′-shocked/**, *adj.*

shell·y (shĕl'ĭ), *adj.*, **shellier, shelliest. 1.** abounding in shells. **2.** consisting of a shell or shells. **3.** like a shell or shells.

shel·ter (shĕl'tər), *n.* **1.** something which affords protection or refuge, as from rain or attack; a place of refuge or safety. **2.** protection afforded; refuge. —*v.t.* **3.** to be a shelter for; afford shelter to. **4.** to provide with a shelter; place under cover. **5.** to protect as by shelter; take under one's protection. —*v.i.* **6.** to take shelter; find a refuge. [orig. uncert.] —**shel′ter·er,** *n.* —**shel′ter·less,** *adj.* —**Syn. 1.** See **cover.**

shelter tent, a small waterproof tent formed by buttoning two shelter halves together.

shelve[1] (shĕlv), *v.t.*, **shelved, shelving. 1.** to place on a shelf or shelves. **2.** to lay or put aside from consideration: *to shelve the question.* **3.** to remove from active service. **4.** to furnish with shelves. [der. *shelves*, pl. of SHELF]

shelve[2] (shĕlv), *v.i.*, **shelved, shelving.** to slope gradually. [cf. OE *sceolh* squinting, awry, Icel. *skelgja* make squint]

shelv·ing (shĕl'vĭng), *n.* **1.** material for shelves. **2.** shelves collectively.

Shem (shĕm), *n.* the eldest of the three sons of Noah. Gen. 10:21.

Shen·an·do·ah (shĕn/ən dō'ə), *n.* **1.** a river flowing through N Virginia NE to the Potomac at Harpers Ferry, West Virginia. ab. 200 mi. **2.** a valley along a part of the course of this river, between the Blue Ridge and the Allegheny Mountains: Civil War campaigns, 1862–1864. **3.** a borough in E Pennsylvania. 15,704 (1950).

she·nan·i·gan (shə năn/ə gən), *n.* (*often pl.*) *Colloq.* nonsense; deceit.

Shen·si (shĕn/sē/; *Ch.* shŭn/shē/), *n.* a province in N China. 15,881,281 (1953); 72,919 sq. mi. *Cap.*: Sian.

Shen·stone (shĕn'stən), *n.* **William,** 1714–63, British poet.

Shen·yang (shŭn/yăng/), *n.* Mukden.

She·ol (shē/ōl), *n.* **1.** the abode of the dead or of departed spirits. **2.** (*l.c.*) hell. [t. Heb.]

ăct, āble, dâre, ärt; ĕbb, ēqual; ĭf, īce; hŏt, ōver, ôrder, oil, bŏŏk, ōōze, out; ŭp, ūse, ûrge; ə = a in alone; ch, chief; g, give; ng, ring; sh, shoe; th, thin; ŧħ, that; zh, vision. See the full key on inside cover

shep·herd (shĕp/ərd), n. **1.** a man who herds, tends, and guards sheep. **2.** one who cares for a group of people. **3.** a clergyman. **4.** the Shepherd, Jesus Christ. —v.t. **5.** to tend or guard as a shepherd. **6.** to watch over carefully. [ME shepherde, OE scēphyrde. See SHEEP, HERD²] —shep·herd·ess (shĕp/ərdĭs), n. fem.

shepherd dog, a sheep dog.

shep·herd's-purse (shĕp/ərdz pûrs/), n. a cruciferous weed, Capsella Bursa-pastoris, with white flowers and purselike pods.

Shep·pard s adjustment (shĕp/ərdz), Statistics. a method of correcting the bias in standard deviations and higher moments of distributions due to grouping values of the variable.

Sher·a·ton (shĕr/ə tən), n. **1.** Thomas, 1751–1806, British cabinetmaker and furniture designer. —adj. **2.** pertaining to, or in the style of, Thomas Sheraton.

sher·bet (shûr/bət), n. **1.** a frozen fruit-flavored mixture, similar to an ice, but with milk, egg white, or gelatin. **2.** Brit. a drink made of fruit juice diluted with water and sweetened, often cooled with snow. [t. Turk. and Pers., der. Ar. sharbah, lit., a drink]

Sher·brooke (shûr/brŏŏk), n. a city in SE Canada, in Quebec province. 50,543 (1951).

sherd (shûrd), n. shard.

Sher·i·dan (shĕr/ə dən), n. **1.** Philip Henry, 1831–88, U.S. general. **2.** Richard Brinsley (brĭnz/lĭ), 1751–1816, Irish dramatist and political leader.

she·rif (shĕ rēf/), n. **1.** a descendant of Mohammed the Prophet who was, or is, governor of Mecca. **2.** a title used by the rulers of Morocco (also called sultans) claiming descent from Hasan, grandson of the Prophet Mohammed. **3.** amir (def. 2). Also, **she·reef/.** [t. Ar.: m. sharīf noble, glorious, der. sharafa be exalted]

sher·iff (shĕr/ĭf), n. **1.** the law enforcement officer of a county or other civil subdivision of a state. **2.** (formerly) an important civil officer in an English shire. [ME sher(r)ef, OE scīrgerēfa. See SHIRE, REEVE¹]

Sher·man (shûr/mən), n. **1.** John, 1823–1900, U.S. statesman (brother of William T.). **2.** Roger, 1721–93, American statesman: helped draw up Declaration of Independence and the Articles of Confederation. **3.** William Tecumseh (tĭ kŭm/sə), 1820–91, U.S. general.

Sher·pa (shĕr/pə, shûr/-), n. one of a tribe of people of Mongolian stock living in the Himalayas: they often serve as guides in mountain climbing.

Sher·ring·ton (shĕr/ĭng tən), n. Sir Charles Scott, 1861–1952, British physiologist: Nobel prize, 1932.

sher·ry (shĕr/ĭ), n., pl. -ries. strong white wine of southern Spain, or a similar wine made elsewhere. [earlier sherris, taken as pl., t. Sp.: m. (vino de) Xeres wine of Xeres, now Jerez, city in southern Spain]

sherry cobbler, a cobbler (drink) made with sherry, sliced fruits, and ice.

's Her·to·gen·bosch (sĕr/tō KHən bôs/), n. a city in S Netherlands. 63,330 (est. 1954). French, Bois-le-Duc.

Sher·wood (shûr/wŏŏd/), n. Robert Emmet, 1896–1955, U.S. dramatist.

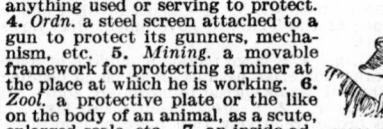

Sherwood Forest, an ancient royal forest in central England, chiefly in Nottinghamshire: the traditional haunt of Robin Hood.

Shet·land Islands (shĕt/lənd), an island group NE of the Orkney Islands, comprising a county of Scotland. 18,600 pop. (est. 1956); 550 sq. mi. Co. seat: Lerwick. Also, **Shetland** or **Zetland.**

Shetland pony, a pony of a small, sturdy, rough-coated breed, orig. from the Shetland Islands.

Shetland wool, thin, loosely twisted, wool yarn for knitting or weaving.

shew (shō), v.t., v.i., shewed, shewn, shewing, n. Chiefly Brit. or Archaic. show.

shew·bread (shō/brĕd/), n. (among the ancient Jews) the bread placed every Sabbath before Jehovah on the table beside the altar of incense, and eaten at the end of the week by the priests alone. Ex. 25:30; Lev. 24:5–9. Also, **showbread.** [trans. of L (Vulgate) pānes prōpositiōnis, Gk. (Septuagint) ártoi enōpioi, rendering Heb. le-chem pānī-m]

Shetland pony
(3 ft. or less high
at the shoulder)

Shi·ah (shē/ə), n. **1.** one of the two great religious divisions of Islam, which regards Ali (the son-in-law of Mohammed) as the latter's legitimate successor and rejects the first three caliphs along with the Sunnite books handed down under their protection. **2.** a Shiite.

shib·bo·leth (shĭb/ə lĕth/), n. **1.** a peculiarity of pronunciation, or a habit, mode of dress, etc., which distinguishes a particular class or set of persons. **2.** a test word or pet phrase of a party, sect, etc. **3.** a Hebrew word used by Jephthah as a test word by which to distinguish the fleeing Ephraimites (who could not pronounce the sh) from his own men, the Gileadites. Judges 12:4–6. [t. Heb.: stream in flood]

shied (shīd), v. pt. and pp. of shy.

shield (shēld), n. **1.** a piece of defensive armor of various shapes, carried on the left arm or in the hand to protect the body in battle. **2.** something shaped like a shield. **3.** anything used or serving to protect. **4.** Ordn. a steel screen attached to a gun to protect its gunners, mechanism, etc. **5.** Mining. a movable framework for protecting a miner at the place at which he is working. **6.** Zool. a protective plate or the like on the body of an animal, as a scute, enlarged scale, etc. **7.** an inside addition to a dress, usually made of some rubberized material and worn under the arms, to protect against soiling by perspiration. **8.** Her. a shield-shaped escutcheon on which armorial bearings are displayed. —v.t. **9.** to protect with or as with a shield. **10.** to serve as a protection for. **11.** Obs. to avert; forbid. —v.i. **12.** to act or serve as a shield. [ME shelde, OE sceld, c. D and G schild] —shield/er, n.

Shield of mounted man-at-arms. 14th century

shift (shĭft), v.i. **1.** to move from one place, position, etc., to another. **2.** to manage to get along or succeed. **3.** to get along by indirect methods; employ shifts or evasions. **4.** to change gears in driving an automobile. **5.** Archaic or Dial. to change one's clothes. —v.t. **6.** to put by and replace by another or others; change. **7.** to transfer from one place, position, person, etc., to another: to shift the blame on someone else. **8.** Auto. to change (gears) from one ratio or arrangement to another. **9.** Linguistics. to change, as in a shift. —n. **10.** a shifting from one place, position, person, etc., to another; a transfer. **11.** the portion of the day scheduled as a day's work when a shop or industry operates continuously during the 24 hours, or works both day and night: night shift. **12.** a group of workmen on such a turn. **13.** Football. a lateral movement generally from one side of the line to the other, just prior to beginning a play. **14.** Mining. a fault, or the dislocation of a seam or stratum. **15.** Music. (in playing the violin or a similar instrument) any position of the left hand except that nearest the nut. **16.** Linguistics. a change, or system of parallel changes, which seriously affects the phonetic or phonemic structure of the language, as the change in English vowels from Middle English to Modern English. **17.** an expedient; ingenious device. **18.** an evasion, artifice, or trick. **19.** Archaic or Dial. a woman's chemise. **20.** change or substitution. **21.** make shift, a. to manage to get along or succeed. b. to manage with effort or difficulty. c. to do one's best (fol. by with). [ME; OE sciftan, c. G schichten arrange in order] —shift/er, n.

shift·less (shĭft/lĭs), adj. **1.** lacking in resource. **2.** inefficient; lazy. **3.** showing inefficiency or laziness. —shift/less·ly, adv. —shift/less·ness, n.

shift·y (shĭf/tĭ), adj., shiftier, shiftiest, **1.** resourceful; fertile in expedients. **2.** given to or full of evasions; tricky. —shift/i·ly, adv. —shift/i·ness, n.

Shi·ite (shē/ĭt), n. a member of the Shiah sect. [f. Shiah (t. Ar.: m. shī'ah sect) + -ITE¹] —Shi/ism, n. —Shi·it·ic (shē ĭt/ĭk), adj.

shi·kar (shĭ kär/), n. (in India) hunting, as of game. [t. Urdū, t. Pers.]

shi·ka·ri (shĭ kä/rē), n., pl. -ris. **1.** (in India) a hunter. **2.** a native hunter, aid, or guide. Also, **shi·ka/ree.** [t. Urdū, der. shikār shikar, t. Pers]

Shi·ko·ku (shē/kō kōō/), n. an island in SW Japan, S of Honshu island: the smallest of the main islands of Japan. 3,879,672 pop. (1946); 7249 sq. mi.

shill (shĭl), n. U.S. Slang. the accomplice of a street peddler, gambler, etc., esp. one who starts the buying, etc., to encourage others.

shil·le·lagh (shə lā/lə, -lǐ), n. (in Ireland) a cudgel of blackthorn or oak. Also, **shil·la/lah, shil·la/la, shil·le/lah.** [from the name of a barony and village in County Wicklow]

shil·ling (shĭl/ĭng), n. **1.** a British money of account and silver coin of the value of 12 pence or one twentieth of a pound sterling, and equivalent to about 14 U.S. cents. **2.** a money of account of changing value, and any of the corresponding coins. This spelling usually refers to the British Isles or colonies. **3.** U.S. Hist. a similar money denomination, with varying value throughout the thirteen colonies. [ME; OE scilling, c. D schelling, G schilling, Icel. skillingr]

Shil·long (shĭl lông/), n. a city in NE India: the capital of Assam state; resort. 53,756 (1951).

shil·ly-shal·ly (shĭl/ĭ shăl/ĭ), v.i., -lied, -lying, n., adj., adv. —v.i. **1.** to be irresolute; vacillate. —n. **2.** irresolution; indecision; vacillation. —adj. **3.** irresolute; undecided; vacillating. —adv. **4.** irresolutely. [earlier (stand) shill I, shall I, OE scyle subj., sceal ind.]

Shi·loh (shī/lō), n. **1.** a national military park in SW Tennessee, including a cemetery and battlefield (1862). **2.** an ancient town in what is now W Jordan.

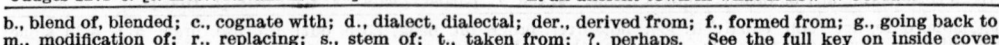

b., blend of, blended; c., cognate with; d., dialect, dialectal; der., derived from; f., formed from; g., going back to; m., modification of; r., replacing; s., stem of; t., taken from; ?, perhaps. See the full key on inside cover.

shi·ly (shī′lĭ), *adv.* shyly.

shim (shĭm), *n.*, *v.*, **shimmed, shimming.** —*n.* 1. a thin strip of metal, wood, or the like, for filling in, as for bringing one part in line with another. —*v.t.* 2. to fill out or bring to a level by inserting a shim or shims. [orig. uncert.]

shim·mer (shĭm′ər), *v.i.* 1. to shine with a subdued, tremulous light; gleam faintly. —*n.* 2. a subdued, tremulous light or gleam. [ME *schimere*, late OE *scimerian*, appar. freq. of *scīmian* shine. Cf. G *schimmern*] —Syn. 1. See glisten.

shim·mer·y (shĭm′ərĭ), *adj.* shimmering; shining softly.

shim·my (shĭm′ĭ), *n.*, *pl.* **-mies,** *v.*, **-mied, -mying.** —*n.* 1. an American ragtime dance, marked by shaking of the hips or shoulders. 2. excessive wobbling in the front wheels of a motor vehicle. 3. *Colloq. or Dial.* a chemise. —*v.i.* 4. to dance the shimmy. 5. to vibrate. [alter. of CHEMISE]

Shi·mo·no·se·ki (shĭm′ə nə säk′ĭ; *Jap.* shē′mô nô sĕ′-kē), *n.* a seaport in SW Japan, on Honshu island: the treaty ending the Chino-Japanese War was signed there, 1895. 193,572 (1950).

shin (shĭn), *n.*, *v.*, **shinned, shinning.** —*n.* 1. the front part of the leg from the knee to the ankle. 2. the lower part of the foreleg in cattle; the metacarpal bone. 3. the shinbone or tibia, esp. its sharp edge or front portion. —*v.t.*, *v.i.* 4. to climb by holding fast with the hands or arms and legs and drawing oneself up. [ME *s(c)hine*, OE *scinu*, c. D *scheen* shin, G *scheine* shin plate]

Shi·nar (shī′när), *n.* the Biblical name of Babylonia, or the southern part known as Sumer.

shin·bone (shĭn′bōn′), *n.* the tibia.

shin·dig (shĭn′dĭg), *n.* *U.S. Slang.* a dance, party, or other festivity. [orig. obscure; ? f. SHIN + DIG a dig on the shin]

shin·dy (shĭn′dĭ), *n.*, *pl.* **-dies.** *Slang.* 1. a row; rumpus. 2. a merrymaking; party. [? for *shinty* SHINNY¹]

shine (shīn), *v.*, **shone** or (*esp. for def. 7*) **shined, shining,** *n.* —*v.i.* 1. to give forth, or glow with, light; shed or cast light. 2. to be bright with reflected light; glisten; sparkle. 3. to be unusually bright, as the eyes or face. 4. to appear with brightness or clearness, as feelings. 5. to excel: *to shine in society.* —*v.t.* 6. to cause to shine. 7. to put a gloss or polish on (shoes, etc.). —*n.* 8. radiance; light. 9. luster; polish. 10. sunshine; fair weather: *come rain or shine.* 11. a polish given to shoes. 12. a giving of such a polish. 13. *U.S. Colloq.* a caper; prank. 14. *U.S. Colloq.* a liking; fancy: *to take a shine to.* [ME; OE *scīnan*, c. G *scheinen*] —Syn. 1. SHINE, BEAM, GLARE refer to the emitting or reflecting of light. SHINE refers to a steady glowing or reflecting of light: *to shine in the sun.* That which BEAMS gives forth a radiant or bright light: *to beam like a star.* GLARE refers to the shining of a light which is not only bright but so strong as to be unpleasant and dazzling: *to glare like a headlight.*

shin·er (shī′nər), *n.* 1. one who or that which shines. 2. *Slang.* a black eye. 3. any of various small American fresh-water fishes, mostly minnows, with glistening scales, as the **golden shiner,** *Notemigonus crysoleucas,* and the numerous species of *Notropis.*

shin·gle¹ (shĭng′gəl), *n.*, *v.*, **-gled, -gling.** —*n.* 1. a thin piece of wood, asbestos, etc., usually oblong and with one end thicker than the other, used in overlapping rows to cover the roofs and sides of houses. 2. a close-cropped haircut. 3. *U.S. Colloq.* a small signboard, esp. that of a professional man. —*v.t.* 4. to cover (a roof, etc.) with shingles. 5. to cut (hair) close to the head. [ME; var. of *shindle,* ult. t. L: m. *scindula*] —**shin′gler,** *n.*

shin·gle² (shĭng′gəl), *n.* *Chiefly Brit.* 1. small, water-worn stones or pebbles such as lie in loose sheets or beds on the seashore. 2. an extent of small, loose stones or pebbles. [earlier *chingle;* ? f. imit. orig.]

shin·gles (shĭng′gəlz), *n. sing. or pl. Pathol.* a cutaneous disease characterized by vesicles which sometimes form a girdle about the body; herpes zoster. [ME *schingles,* t. ML: m. *cingulum* (var. of *cingulum* girdle) used to translate Gk. *zōnē* or *zōstēr,* name of the disease]

shin·gly (shĭng′glĭ), *adj.* consisting of or covered with shingle, or small, loose stones or pebbles.

shin·ing (shī′nĭng), *adj.* 1. radiant; gleaming; bright. 2. resplendent; brilliant: *shining talents.* 3. conspicuously fine: *a shining example.* —**shin′ing·ly,** *adv.* —Syn. 1. See bright.

shin·leaf (shĭn′lēf′), *n.*, *pl.* **-leaves.** 1. a North American herb, *Pyrola elliptica,* whose leaves are said to have been once used for plasters. 2. any plant of the same genus.

shin·ny¹ (shĭn′ĭ), *n.*, *pl.* **-nies,** *v.*, **-nied, -nying.** —*n.* 1. a simple variety of hockey, played with a ball or the like and clubs curved at one end. 2. the club used. —*v.i.* 3. to play shinny. 4. to drive the ball at shinny. [? var. of *shin ye,* cry used in the game]

shin·ny² (shĭn′ĭ), *v.i.* **-nied, -nying.** *U.S. Colloq.* to climb using the shins. [der. SHIN, n.]

shin·plas·ter (shĭn′plăs′tər, -pläs′-), *n.* 1. a plaster for the shin or leg. 2. *U.S.* a. a piece of paper money of low denomination. b. money of little value, as that issued on insufficient security or greatly depreciated.

Shin·to (shĭn′tō), *n.* the native religion of Japan, primarily a system of nature and ancestor worship. Also, **Shin′to·ism.** [t. Jap., t. Chinese: m. *shin tao* way of the gods] —**Shin′to·ist,** *n.*, *adj.*

shin·y (shī′nĭ), *adj.*, **shinier, shiniest.** 1. bright; glossy. 2. worn to a glossy smoothness, as clothes. —**shin′i·ness,** *n.*

ship (shĭp), *n.*, *v.*, **shipped, shipping.** —*n.* 1. any vessel intended or used for navigating the water, esp. one of large size and not propelled by oars, paddles, or the like. 2. *Naut.* a vessel with a bowsprit and three or more masts (foremast, mainmast, and mizzenmast), each consisting of a lower mast, a topmast, and topgallant-mast. 3. the personnel of a vessel. 4. an airship or airplane. 5. fortune: *when my ship comes in.* —*v.t.* 6. to put or take on board a ship or the like, for transportation; to send or transport by ship, rail, etc. 7. *Naut.* to take in (water) over the side, as a vessel does when waves break over it. 8. to bring (an object) into a ship or boat: *to ship oars.* 9. to engage for service on a ship. 10. to fix in a ship or boat in the proper place for use. 11. *Colloq.* to send away or get rid of. —*v.i.* 12. to go on board a ship; embark. 13. to engage to serve on a ship. [ME; OE *scip,* c. D *schip,* G *schiff*]

-ship, a suffix of nouns denoting condition, character, office, skill, etc., as in *clerkship, friendship, statesman-ship.* [ME; OE *-scipe,* c. West Fris. and West Flem. *-schip;* akin to G *-schaft*]

ship biscuit, hardtack.

ship·board (shĭp′bôrd′), *n.* 1. a ship, or its deck or interior. 2. **on shipboard,** on or in a ship.

ship·build·er (shĭp′bĭl′dər), *n.* one whose occupation is the designing and constructing of ships. —**ship′-build′ing,** *n.*, *adj.*

ship canal, a canal navigable by ships.

ship chandler, *Chiefly Brit.* one who deals in cordage, canvas, and other supplies for ships.

Ship·ka Pass (shĭp′kä), a mountain pass over the Balkan Mountains, in central Bulgaria: the site of a Turkish defeat, 1877. 4376 ft. high.

ship·load (shĭp′lōd′), *n.* a full load for a ship.

ship·man (shĭp′mən), *n.*, *pl.* **-men.** *Archaic or Poetic.* 1. a sailor. 2. the master of a ship.

ship·mas·ter (shĭp′măs′tər, -mäs′-), *n.* the master, commander, or captain of a ship.

ship·mate (shĭp′māt′), *n.* one who serves with another on the same vessel.

ship·ment (shĭp′mənt), *n.* 1. act of shipping goods, etc.; the delivery of goods, etc., for transportation. 2. that which is shipped. —Syn. 2. See freight.

ship money, *Early Eng. Law.* a tax levied in time of war on ports, maritime towns, etc., to provide ships.

ship of the line, a ship with heavy enough armor and gunpower to be in the line of battle; a battleship.

ship·own·er (shĭp′ō′nər), *n.* owner of a ship or ships.

ship·per (shĭp′ər), *n.* one who ships goods, or makes shipments.

ship·ping (shĭp′ĭng), *n.* 1. act of one who ships goods, etc. 2. the action or business of sending or transporting goods, etc., by ship, rail, etc. 3. ships collectively, or their aggregate tonnage. 4. *Obs.* a voyage.

shipping clerk, a clerk who attends to shipments.

shipping room, a place in a business concern where goods are packed and shipped.

shipping ton. See ton¹ (def. 5).

ship-rigged (shĭp′rĭgd′), *adj.* *Naut.* rigged with three or more masts, with square sails on all masts.

ship·shape (shĭp′shāp′), *adj.* 1. in good order; well arranged. —*adv.* 2. in a shipshape manner.

ship's papers, necessary papers presented at all legal inspections of a ship, and containing the owner's name, description of cargo, destination, etc.

ship·way (shĭp′wā′), *n.* 1. the structure which supports a ship being built. 2. ship canal.

ship·worm (shĭp′wûrm′), *n.* any of various marine bivalve mollusks which burrow into the timbers of ships, etc. *Teredo* is the most common of these.

ship·wreck (shĭp′rĕk′), *n.* 1. the destruction or loss of a ship, as by sinking. 2. the remains of a ship. 3. destruction or ruin: *the shipwreck of one's hopes.* —*v.t.* 4. to cause to suffer shipwreck. 5. to destroy; ruin. —*v.i.* 6. to suffer shipwreck.

ship·wright (shĭp′rīt′), *n.* one employed in the construction or repair of ships.

ship·yard (shĭp′yärd′), *n.* a yard or enclosure near the water, in which ships are built or repaired.

Shi·raz (shē räz′), *n.* a city in SW Iran. 116,274 (est. 1950).

shire (shīr), *n.* 1. one of the counties of Great Britain. 2. the **Shires,** the counties in the Midlands in which hunting is especially popular. [ME; OE *scīr,* c. OHG *scīra* care, official charge]

Shi·ré (shē′rĕ), *n.* a river in SE Africa, flowing from Lake Nyasa S to the Zambezi river. ab. 370 mi.

shire horse, one of a breed of large, strong draft horses, long cultivated in midland England.

shirk (shûrk), *v.t.* 1. to evade (work, duty, etc.). —*v.i.* 2. to evade work, duty, etc. [v. use of SHIRK, n.] —*n.* 3. Also, **shirk′er.** one who seeks to avoid work, duty, etc. [? t. G: m. *schurke* parasite, sharper]

Shir·ley (shûr′lĭ), *n.* **James,** 1596-1666, British dramatist.

shirr (shûr), *v.t.* 1. to draw up or gather (cloth) on parallel threads. 2. to bake (eggs removed from the shell) in a shallow dish or in individual dishes buttered

---

ăct, āble, dâre, ärt; ĕbb, ēqual; ĭf, īce; hŏt, ōver, ôrder, oil, bŏŏk, ōōze, out; ŭp, ūse, ûrge; ə = a in alone; ch, chief; g, give; ng, ring; sh, shoe; th, thin; ŧħ, that; zh, vision. See the full key on inside cover.

and lined with crumbs. —*n.* 3. Also, **shirr′ing.** a shirred arrangement of cloth, etc. [orig. uncert.]

shirt (shûrt), *n.* 1. a garment for the upper part of a man's body, with or without collar, having long sleeves with cuffs. 2. an undergarment of cotton, or other material, for the upper part of the body. 3. a woman's shirtwaist. 4. a nightshirt. [ME *schirte,* OE *scyrte;* akin to G *schürze* apron]

shirt·ing (shûr′tĭng), *n.* a fabric for men's shirts.

shirt·waist (shûrt′wāst′), *n.* a woman's loosely fitting waist of cotton, linen, silk, flannel, or other material, worn with a separate skirt.

shit·tim wood (shĭt′ĭm), the wood of which the ark of the covenant and various parts of the Jewish tabernacle were made. Ex. 25–27. Also, **shit′tim.**

Shi·va (shē′və), *n. Hinduism.* Siva.

shiv·a·ree (shĭv′ə·rē′), *n., v.,* **-reed, -reeing.** *U.S.* —*n.* 1. a mock serenade with kettles, pans, horns, etc. —*v.t.* 2. to serenade with kettles, etc. [alter. of CHARIVARI]

shiv·er¹ (shĭv′ər), *v.i.* 1. to shake or tremble with cold, fear, excitement, etc. —*v.t.* 2. *Naut.* to cause a sail to luff by coming to. —*n.* 3. a tremulous motion; a tremble or quiver. [ME *shivere(n);* orig. uncert.]
—**Syn.** 1. SHIVER, QUAKE, SHUDDER refer to a vibratory muscular movement, a trembling, usually involuntary. We SHIVER with cold, or a sensation such as that of cold: *to shiver in thin clothing on a frosty day, to shiver with pleasant anticipation* We QUAKE esp. with fear: *to quake with fright.* We SHUDDER with horror or abhorrence; the agitation is more powerful and deep-seated than shivering or trembling: *to shudder at pictures of a concentration camp.*

shiv·er² (shĭv′ər), *v.t., v.i.* 1. to break or split into fragments. —*n.* 2. a fragment; a splinter. [ME *chivere(n);* orig. uncert.]

shiv·er·y¹ (shĭv′ər·ĭ), *adj.* 1. shivering; quivering; tremulous. 2. inclined to shiver or shake. 3. causing shivering. [f. SHIVER¹ + -Y¹]

shiv·er·y² (shĭv′ər·ĭ), *adj.* readily breaking into shivers or fragments; brittle. [f. SHIVER² + -Y¹]

Shi·zu·o·ka (shē′zō̄ō̄′kä), *n.* a seaport in central Japan, on Honshu Island. 238,629 (1950).

Shko·dër (shkō′dər), *n.* Albanian name of **Scutari** (def. 2). Also, **Shko·dra** (shkō′drä).

Sho·a (shō′ä), *n.* a former kingdom in E Africa: now a province of Ethiopia. 1,800,000 pop. (est. 1939); 25,290 sq. mi. *Cap.:* Addis Ababa.

shoal¹ (shōl), *adj.* 1. of little depth, as water; shallow. —*n.* 2. a place where the water is shallow. 3. a sand bank or sand bar in the bed of a body of water, esp. one which shows at low water. —*v.i.* 4. to become shallow or more shallow. —*v.t.* 5. to cause to become shallow. 6. *Naut.* to proceed from a greater to a less depth of (water). [ME *schold, schald,* OE *sceald* shallow]

shoal² (shōl), *n.* 1. any large number of persons or things. 2. a group of fish crowded fairly close together. —*v.i.* 3. to collect in a shoal; throng. [OE *scolu* shoal (of fishes), multitude, troop, c. D *school.* See SCHOOL²]

shoal·y (shōl′ĭ), *adj.* full of shoals or shallows.

shoat (shōt), *n.* a young weaned pig. Also, **shote.** [ME. Cf. Flem. *schote* young pig]

shock¹ (shŏk), *n.* 1. a sudden and violent blow or impact, collision, or encounter. 2. a sudden disturbance or commotion. 3. something that shocks mentally, emotionally, etc. 4. *Pathol.* a sudden collapse of the nervous mechanism caused by violent physical or psychic factors, such as severe injuries or a strong emotional disturbance. 5. *Psychol.* a momentary reaction to an unexpected, strong physical or psychic stimulus. 6. the physiological effect of an electric current upon the human body. —*v.t.* 7. to strike with intense surprise, horror, disgust, etc. 8. to strike against violently. 9. to give an electric shock to. —*v.i.* 10. to come into violent contact; collide. [appar. t. F: m. *choc,* der. *choquer* strike against, shock, t. MD: m. *schokken*]
—**Syn.** 7. SHOCK, STARTLE, PARALYZE, STUN suggest a sudden, sharp surprise which affects one somewhat like a blow. SHOCK suggests a strong blow, as it were, to one's nerves, sentiments, sense of decency, etc.: *the onlookers were shocked by the accident.* STARTLE implies the sharp surprise of sudden fright: *to be startled by a loud noise.* PARALYZE implies such a complete shock as to render one temporarily helpless: *paralyzed with fear.* STUN implies such a shock as bewilders or stupefies: *stunned by the realization of an unpleasant truth.*

shock² (shŏk), *n.* 1. a group of sheaves of grain placed on end and supporting one another in the field. —*v.t.* 2. to make into shocks. [ME; c. LG *schok* shock of grain, group of sixty, G *schock* sixty]

shock³ (shŏk), *n.* 1. a thick, bushy mass, as of hair. 2. a dog with long, shaggy hair, esp. a poodle. —*adj.* 3. shaggy, as hair. [? var. of SHAG]

shock absorber, *Mach.* a device for deadening shock or concussion, esp. one on an automobile for checking sudden or excessive movements of the springs.

shock action, *Mil.* a method of attack by mobile units in which the suddenness, violence, and massed weight of the first impact produce the main effect.

shock·er (shŏk′ər), *n.* 1. one who or that which shocks. 2. *Brit. Colloq.* a sensational work of fiction.

shock·head·ed (shŏk′hĕd′ĭd), *adj.* having a shock or thick mass of hair on the head.

shock·ing (shŏk′ĭng), *adj.* 1. causing intense surprise, disgust, horror, etc. 2. *Colloq.* very bad: *shocking manners.* —**shock′ing·ly,** *adv.*

shock therapy, *Psychiatry.* a recently developed form or method of treating certain psychotic disorders, as schizophrenia, by the use of chemical (e.g., metrazol, insulin, etc.) or electrical means. The drugs are injected subcutaneously; electrical shocks are administered by electrodes: both are followed by coma and often convulsions. Also, **shock treatment.**

shock troops, *Mil.* troops especially selected, trained, and equipped for engaging in assault.

shock wave, a region of abrupt change of pressure and density moving in a gas at or above the velocity of sound.

shod (shŏd), *v.* pt. and pp. of **shoe.**

shod·dy (shŏd′ĭ), *n., pl.* **-dies,** *adj.,* **-dier, -diest.** —*n.* 1. a fibrous material obtained by shredding woolen rags or waste. 2. anything inferior made to resemble what is of superior quality; anything inferior but pretentious. 3. pretense, as in art, manufacture, etc. —*adj.* 4. pretending to a superiority not possessed; sham. 5. made of or containing shoddy. [orig. uncert.] —**shod′di·ly,** *adv.* —**shod′di·ness,** *n.*

shoe (shō̄ō̄), *n., pl.* **shoes,** (*Archaic*) **shoon;** *v.,* **shod, shoeing.** —*n.* 1. an external covering, usually of leather, for the human foot, consisting of a more or less stiff or heavy sole and a lighter upper part. 2. such a covering ending a short distance above the ankle, or at or below the ankle. 3. some thing or part resembling a shoe in form, position, or use. 4. a horseshoe, or a similar plate for the hoof of some other animal. 5. a ferrule or the like, as of iron, for protecting the end of a staff, pole, etc. 6. the part of a brake mechanism fitting into the drum and expanded outwardly to apply the friction lining to the drum rim for stopping or slowing a car, truck, etc. 7. the outer casing of a pneumatic automobile tire. 8. a drag or skid for a wheel of a vehicle. 9. a part having a larger area than the end of an object on which it fits, serving to disperse or apply its thrust. 10. the sliding contact by which an electric car or locomotive takes its current from the third rail. 11. that part of a bridge in contact with its foundation. 12. a band of iron on the bottom of the runner of a sleigh. —*v.t.* 13. to provide or fit with a shoe or shoes. 14. to protect or arm at the point, edge, or face with a ferrule, metal plate, or the like. [ME *shoo,* OE *scōh,* c. G *schuh*]

shoe·bill (shō̄ō̄′bĭl′), *n.* a large African wading bird, *Balaeniceps rex,* with a broad bill shaped somewhat like a shoe, found esp. on the White Nile.

shoe·black (shō̄ō̄′blăk′), *n.* a bootblack.

shoe·horn (shō̄ō̄′hôrn′), *n.* a shaped piece of horn, metal, or the like, inserted in a shoe at the heel to make it slip on more easily.

shoe·lace (shō̄ō̄′lās′), *n.* a string or lace for fastening a shoe.

shoe·mak·er (shō̄ō̄′mā′kər), *n.* one who makes or mends shoes.

sho·er (shō̄ō̄′ər), *n.* one who shoes horses, etc.

shoe·string (shō̄ō̄′strĭng′), *n.* 1. a shoelace. 2. *Colloq.* a very small amount of money or capital used to start or carry on an enterprise or business.

shoe·tree (shō̄ō̄′trē′), *n.* a device, usually of metal or wood, placed in shoes when they are not being worn, to maintain the shape.

sho·far (shō′fär), *n.* shophar.

sho·gun (shō′gŭn′, -gōn′), *n.* (in Japan) 1. a title originating in the 8th century, in the wars against the Ainus, equivalent to commander in chief. 2. (in later history) a member of a quasi-dynasty, holding the real power though parallel to the imperial dynasty, which was theoretically and ceremonially supreme. [t. Jap., t. Chinese: m. *chiang chun* lead army (i.e., general)]

sho·gun·ate (shō′gŭn′ĭt, -gōn′-, -āt), *n.* the office or rule of a shogun.

Sho·la·pur (shō′lə·pŏŏr′), *n.* a city in S India, in Bombay state. 266,050 (1951).

shone (shōn, shŏn), *v.* pt. and pp. of **shine.**

shoo (shō̄ō̄), *interj., v.,* **shooed, shooing.** —*interj.* 1. an exclamation used to scare or drive away poultry, birds, etc. —*v.t.* 2. to drive away by calling "shoo." —*v.i.* 3. to call out "shoo." [cf. G *schu*]

shook¹ (shŏŏk), *n.* 1. a set of staves and headings sufficient for one hogshead, barrel, or the like. 2. a set of the parts of a box, piece of furniture, or the like, ready to be put together. 3. a shock of sheaves or the like. [? var. of SHOCK², n.]

shook² (shŏŏk), *v.* pt. of **shake.**

shoon (shō̄ō̄n), *n. Archaic.* pl. of **shoe.**

shoot (shō̄ō̄t), *v.,* **shot, shooting,** *n.* —*v.t.* 1. to hit, wound, or kill with a missile discharged from a weapon. 2. to put to death with a bullet as a penalty. 3. to send forth (arrows, bullets, etc.) from a bow, firearm, or the like. 4. to discharge (a bow, firearm, etc.): *to shoot off a gun.* 5. to send forth like an arrow or bullet: *to shoot questions at someone.* 6. to send swiftly along. 7. to go over (country) in shooting game. 8. to pass rapidly through, over, down, etc.: *to shoot a rapid.* 9. to emit (rays, etc.) swiftly. 10. to variegate by threads, streaks, etc., of another color. 11. to cause to extend or project. 12. to dump or empty; send down a chute. 13. to kick

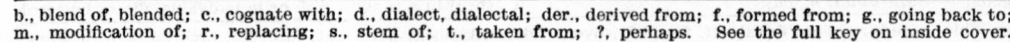

Shoebill.
Balaeniceps rex
(Ab. 5 ft. high,
total length 3¼ ft.)

or drive (the ball, etc.), as at the goal. **14.** to accomplish by kicking or driving the ball, etc.: *to shoot a goal*. **15.** (in games) to propel (a marble) from the thumb and forefinger. **16.** *Dice*. to toss (the dice). **17.** to take a picture of (something) with a camera. **18.** to put forth (buds, branches, etc.), as a plant does. **19.** to slide (a bolt, etc.) into or out of its fastening. **20.** to take the altitude of a heavenly body: *to shoot the sun*. **21.** *Mining*. to detonate.
—*v.i.* **22.** to send forth missiles, from a bow, firearm, or the like. **23.** to send forth missiles, or be discharged, as a firearm. **24.** to move or pass suddenly or swiftly; dart. **25.** to come forth from the ground, a stem, etc. **26.** to put forth buds or shoots, as a plant; germinate. **27.** to grow, esp. rapidly (often fol. by *up*). **28.** to take a picture with a camera. **29.** to begin to film a scene. **30.** to extend; jut: *a cape shooting out into the sea*. **31.** to propel a thing in a particular direction or way, as in games. **32.** to have sharp, darting pains, as a part of the body. **33.** to kill game with a gun for sport.
—*n*. **34.** an act of shooting with a bow, firearm, etc. **35.** *Chiefly Brit*. an expedition for shooting game. **36.** a match or contest at shooting. **37.** a growing or sprouting, as of a plant. **38.** a new or young growth which shoots off from some portion of a plant. **39.** a young branch, stem, twig, or the like. **40.** amount of such growth. **41.** a sprout which is not three feet high. **42.** *Rowing*. the interval between strokes. [ME *shote*, var. of *shete*, OE *scēotan*, c. G *schiessen*, Icel. *skjota*]
shoot·er (shoō′tər), *n*. **1.** one who shoots. **2.** something that shoots; a gun, pistol, or the like.
shooting box, *Brit*. a small house or lodge for the accommodation of a sportsman or sportsmen during the shooting season. Also, **shooting lodge.**
shooting gallery, a place containing targets used to practice shooting.
shooting iron, *U.S. Slang*. a firearm, esp. a pistol or revolver.
shooting star, 1. a falling star; a meteor. **2.** the American cowslip, *Dodecatheon meadia*, having bright nodding flowers and reflexed lobes of the corolla.
shop (shŏp), *n*., *v*., **shopped, shopping.** —*n*. **1.** a place for selling goods; a store. **2.** a place for doing certain work; a workshop: *a carpenter's shop*. **3. talk shop,** to discuss one's trade, profession, or business. —*v.i.* **4.** to visit shops for purchasing or examining goods. [ME *shoppe*, OE *sceoppa* booth, c. G *schopf* lean-to; akin to d. *shippon* cowshed]
shop assistant, *Brit*. a store clerk; a clerk.
shop·girl (shŏp′gûrl′), *n*. *Chiefly Brit*. a salesgirl.
sho·phar (shō′fär), *n*. an ancient Jewish musical instrument of the trumpet kind, usually made of the curved horn of a ram, still used in Jewish religious services, as on Rosh Hashanah. Also, **shofar.** [t. Heb.]
shop·keep·er (shŏp′kē′pər), *n*. *Chiefly Brit*. one who carries on business in a shop or store; a tradesman.
shop·lift·er (shŏp′lĭf′tər), *n*. one who steals goods from a shop, as while ostensibly making purchases. [f. obs. *shoplift* shoplifter (f. SHOP + LIFT) + -ER¹] —**shop′·lift·ing,** *n*.
shop·man (shŏp′mən), *n*., *pl*. **-men. 1.** a salesman in a shop. **2.** *Rare*. a shopkeeper.
shop·per (shŏp′ər), *n*. **1.** one who shops. **2.** *Com*. one employed to compare the goods of competitors. **3.** a retail buyer for another person or concern.
shop·ping (shŏp′ĭng), *n*. act of one who shops.
shopping center, a group of stores within a single architectural plan, supplying most of the basic shopping needs, esp. in suburban areas.
shop·walk·er (shŏp′wô′kər), *n*. *Brit*. a floorwalker.
shop·win·dow (shŏp′wĭn′dō), *n*. a window used for display of merchandise.
shop·worn (shŏp′wôrn′), *adj*. worn or marred, as goods handled and exposed in a store.
shore¹ (shōr), *n*. **1.** land on or near an ocean, lake, etc. **2.** some particular country: *my native shore*. **3.** land: *marines serving on shore*. **4.** *Law*. the space between the ordinary high-water mark and low-water mark. [ME *schore*, prob. t. MLG, c. D *schoor* sea marsh]
—**Syn. 1.** SHORE, BANK, BEACH, COAST refer to an edge of land abutting on an ocean, lake, or other large body of water. SHORE is the general word: *the ship reached shore*. BANK denotes the land along a river or other watercourse, sometimes steep but often not: *the river flows between its banks*. BEACH refers to sandy or pebbly margins along a shore, esp. those made wider at ebb tide: *a private beach for bathers*. COAST applies only to land along an ocean: *the Pacific coast*.
shore² (shōr), *n*., *v*., **shored, shoring.** —*n*. **1.** a supporting post or beam and auxiliary members, esp. one placed obliquely against the side of a building, a ship in dock, or the like; a prop; a strut. —*v.t.* **2.** to support by a shore or shores; prop (usually fol. by *up*). [ME, prob. t. MLG: m. *schore*, c. D *schoor* prop]
shore³ (shōr), *v*. *Archaic*. pt. of **shear.**
Shore (shōr), *n*. **Jane,** 1445?-1527, mistress of Edward IV of England.
shore bird, a limicoline bird, i.e. one which frequents the seashore, estuaries, etc., esp. the snipes, sandpipers, plovers, turnstones, etc., constituting the families *Charadriidae* and *Scolopacidae*.

shore·less (shōr′lĭs), *adj*. **1.** boundless. **2.** without a shore for landing on: *a shoreless island*.
shore·line (shōr′līn′), *n*. the line where shore and water meet.
shor·ing (shōr′ĭng), *n*. **1.** shores or props for supporting a building, a ship, etc. **2.** the act of setting up shores.
shorn (shōrn), *v*. pp. of **shear.**
short (shôrt), *adj*. **1.** having little length; not long. **2.** not tall; low. **3.** extending or reaching only a little way: *short memory*. **4.** brief; not extensive: *a short speech*. **5.** concise, as writing. **6.** rudely brief; hurting. **7.** low in amount; scanty: *short rations*. **8.** not reaching a mark or the like, as a throw or a missile. **9.** below the standard in extent, quantity, duration, etc.: *short measure*. **10.** less than; inferior to (fol. by *of*): *little short of the best*. **11.** having a scanty or insufficient amount of (money, food, etc.). **12. short for,** being a shorter form of: "*phone*" *is short for* "*telephone*." **13. make short work of,** to finish or dispose of quickly. **14.** breaking or crumbling readily, as pastry that contains a large proportion of butter or other shortening. **15.** (of metals) deficient in tenacity; friable; brittle. **16.** (of the head or skull) of less than ordinary length from front to back. **17.** *Com*. **a.** not possessing at the time of sale commodities or stocks that one sells. **b.** noting or pertaining to sales of commodities or stocks which the seller does not possess; depending for profit on a decline in prices. **18.** *Phonet*. **a.** lasting a relatively short time: *bit* has a shorter vowel than *bid* or *bead*. **b.** belonging to a class of sounds considered as usually shorter in duration than another class, such as the vowel of *hot* as compared to *bought*; conventionally, the vowels of *bat*, *bet*, *bit*, *hot*, *good*, and *but*. **19.** (of an alcoholic drink) small: *a short drink*.
—*adv*. **20.** abruptly or suddenly: *to stop short*. **21.** briefly; curtly. **22.** on the hither side of an intended or particular point: *to fall short*. **23.** without going to the length (fol. by *of*): *to stop short of actual crime*. **24.** *Com*. without possessing at the time the stocks, etc., sold: *to sell short*.
—*n*. **25.** something that is short. **26.** what is deficient or lacking. **27.** (*pl*.) **a.** breeches, knickerbockers, or short, loose trousers worn in sports, etc. **b.** short breeches worn by men as an undergarment. **c.** knee breeches or smallclothes, formerly worn by men. **28.** *Mil*. a shot which strikes or bursts short of the target. **29.** *Elect*. a short circuit. **30.** *Com*. one who has sold short. **31.** *Pros*. a short sound or syllable. **32.** *Baseball*. the shortstop. **33. in short,** in few words; briefly; briefly. **34. for short,** by way of abbreviation. —*v.t.*, *v.i.* **35.** to short-circuit. [ME; OE *sc(e)ort*] —**short′ness,** *n*.
—**Syn. 4.** SHORT, BRIEF are opposed to long, and indicate slight extent or duration. SHORT may imply duration but is also applied to physical distance and certain purely spatial relations: *a short journey*. BRIEF refers esp. to duration of time: *brief intervals*. —**Ant. 4.** long.
short account, *Exchanges*. **1.** a short seller's account. **2.** the total short sales in a market, or the total short sales of a particular commodity.
short·age (shôr′tĭj), *n*. **1.** deficiency in quantity. **2.** an amount deficient.
short·bread (shôrt′brĕd′), *n*. a kind of butter cooky, commonly rolled and cut in fancy shapes.
short·cake (shôrt′kāk′), *n*. **1.** a cake made with butter or other shortening. **2.** a food made of shortened (and sometimes sweetened) biscuit dough baked or split in layers, with a filling of strawberries or other fruit.
short-change (shôrt′chānj′), *v.t.*, **-changed, -changing.** *Colloq*. **1.** to give less than proper change to. **2.** to cheat. —**short′-chang′er,** *n*.
short circuit, *Elect*. an abnormal connection of relatively low resistance, whether made accidentally or intentionally, between two points of different potential in a circuit.
short-cir·cuit (shôrt′sûr′kĭt), *Elect*. —*v.t.* **1.** to establish a short circuit in. **2.** to carry (a current) as a short circuit. **3.** to cut off by a short circuit. —*v.i.* **4.** to form a short circuit.
short·com·ing (shôrt′kŭm′ĭng), *n*. a failure or defect in conduct, condition, etc.
short-com·mons (shôrt′kŏm′ənz), *n*. scanty allowance of food.
short covering, *Exchanges*. purchases which close out short sales.
short cut, a shorter or quicker way.
short·en (shôr′tən), *v.t.* **1.** to make shorter; curtail. **2.** to take in; reduce: *to shorten sail*. **3.** to make (pastry, etc.) short, as with butter or other fat. —*v.i.* **4.** to become shorter. **5.** (of odds) to decrease. —**short′en·er,** *n*.
—**Syn. 1.** condense, lessen, limit, restrict. SHORTEN, ABBREVIATE, ABRIDGE, CURTAIL mean to make shorter or briefer. SHORTEN is a general word meaning to make less in extent or duration: *to shorten a dress, a prisoner's sentence*. The other three words suggest methods of shortening. To ABBREVIATE is to make shorter by omission or contraction: *to abbreviate a word*. To ABRIDGE is to reduce in length or size by condensing, summarizing, and the like: *to abridge a document*. CURTAIL suggests deprivation and lack of completeness because of cutting off some part: *to curtail an explanation*. —**Ant. 1.** lengthen.
short·en·ing (shôr′tən ĭng, shôrt′nĭng), *n*. butter, lard, or other fat, used to make pastry, etc., short.

Shorter Catechism, one of the two catechisms established by the Westminster Assembly in 1647, used in the Presbyterian, and, formerly, in Congregational churches.

short·hand (shôrt′hănd′), *n.* **1.** a method of rapid handwriting using extremely simple strokes in place of letters, often with other abbreviating devices. —*adj.* **2.** using shorthand. **3.** written in shorthand.

Shorthand (Gregg system) "This is an example of shorthand"

short-hand·ed (shôrt′hăn′dĭd) *adj.* not having the necessary number of workmen, helpers, etc.

short·head (shôrt′hĕd′), *n.* **1.** a brachycephalic person. **2.** a head with a cephalic index of 81 and over. —**short′-head′ed,** *adj.*

short·horn (shôrt′hôrn′), *n.* one of a breed of beef cattle originating in England, ranging from pure white to pure red, with a high percentage of roan.

shor·ti·a (shôr′tĭ·ə), *n.* any plant of the genus *Shortia,* esp. *S. uniflora* of Japan, and *S. galacifolia* of the mountains of North and South Carolina, with evergreen radical leaves and white nodding flowers. [NL, named after C. W. *Short* (1794–1863), U.S. botanist]

short·ish (shôr′tĭsh), *adj.* rather short.

short-lived (shôrt′līvd′, -lĭvd′), *adj.* living or lasting only a little while.

short·ly (shôrt′lĭ), *adv.* **1.** in a short time; soon. **2.** briefly; concisely. **3.** curtly; rudely.

short shrift, 1. short shriving or time for shriving, or confession and absolution, given to a condemned person before execution. **2.** little mercy or delay in dealing with a person, a matter, etc.

short-sight·ed (shôrt′sī′tĭd), *adj.* **1.** unable to see far; near-sighted; myopic. **2.** lacking in foresight. —**short′-sight′ed·ly,** *adv.* —**short′-sight′ed·ness,** *n.*

short-spo·ken (shôrt′spō′kən), *adj.* speaking in a short, brief, or curt manner.

short·stop (shôrt′stŏp′), *n. Baseball.* a fielder between second and third base.

short story, a piece of prose fiction, usually under 10,000 words.

short-tem·pered (shôrt′tĕm′pərd), *adj.* having a hasty temper.

short-term (shôrt′tûrm′), *adj.* having a maturity within a comparatively short time: *a short-term loan.*

short ton, 2000 pounds.

short wave, *Radio.* electromagnetic waves 60 meters or less in length.

short-wind·ed (shôrt′wĭn′dĭd), *adj.* short of breath; liable to difficulty in breathing.

Sho·sho·ne (shō·shō′nĭ), *n.* **1.** a river in NW Wyoming, flowing into the Big Horn river. 120 mi. **2.** a dam on this river. 328 ft. high. **3.** an American Indian language of the Shoshonean group.

Sho·sho·ne·an (shō·shō′nĭ·ən, shō′shə·nē′ən), *adj.* belonging to or constituting a linguistic group of North American Indians of the western U.S., including the Shoshone, Comanche, Ute, Paiute, Hopi, etc.; a subdivision of the great Uto-Aztecan speech family.

Shoshone Cavern, a large cave in NW Wyoming: a national monument.

Shoshone Falls, falls of the Snake river, in S Idaho. 210 ft. high.

Sho·sta·ko·vich (shō·stä·kô′vĭch), *n.* **Dimitri Dimitrievich** (dĭ mē′trĭ dĭ mē′trĭ ə vĭch), born 1906, Russian composer.

shot[1] (shŏt), *n., pl.* **shots** or (for 6, 8) **shot,** *v.,* **shotted, shotting.** —*n.* **1.** the discharge or a discharge of a firearm, bow, etc. **2.** the range of the discharge, or the distance passed over by the missile in its flight: *a long shot.* **3.** range in general. **4.** an attempt to hit with a projectile discharged from a gun or the like. **5.** act of shooting. **6.** a small ball or pellet of lead, of which a number are used for one charge of a sportsman's gun. **7.** such pellets collectively: *a charge of shot.* **8.** a projectile for discharge from a firearm or cannon. **9.** such projectiles collectively. **10.** a person who shoots: *he was a good shot.* **11.** anything like a shot. **12.** a heavy metal ball which competitors cast as far as possible in shot-putting contests. **13.** an aimed stroke, throw, or the like, as in games, etc. **14.** an attempt or try. **15.** a remark aimed at some person or thing. **16.** a guess at something. **17.** *Slang.* an injection or dose of a drug, as cocaine. **18.** *Slang.* a drink of liquor. **19.** an amount due, esp. at a tavern. **20.** *Photog.* **a.** the making of a photograph. **b.** a photograph. **21.** *Mining, etc.* an explosive charge in place for detonation. —*v.t.* **22.** to load or supply with shot. **23.** to weight with shot. [ME; OE *sc(e)ot, gesceot,* c. G *schoss, geschoss;* akin to SHOOT]

shot[2] (shŏt), *v.* **1.** pt. and pp. of **shoot.** —*adj.* **2.** woven so as to present a play of colors, as silk.

shote (shōt), *n.* shoat.

shot·gun (shŏt′gŭn′), *n.* a smooth-bore gun for firing small shot to kill birds and small quadrupeds, though often used with buckshot to kill larger animals.

shot-put (shŏt′pŏot′), *n.* **1.** the athletic exercise of putting the shot. See **shot** (def. 12). **2.** one throw of the shot in this exercise.

shot·ten (shŏt′ən), *adj.* **1.** (of fish, esp. herring) that has recently spawned. **2.** *Pathol.* dislocated. [old pp. of SHOOT]

should (shŏod), *v.* **1.** pt. of **shall. 2.** (specially used)

a. to denote duty, propriety, or expediency: *you should not do that.* **b.** to make a statement less direct or blunt: *I should hardly say that.* **c.** to emphasize the uncertainty in conditional and hypothetical clauses: *if it should be true.* [ME *sholde,* OE *sc(e)olde.* See **SHALL**] —**Syn. 2a.** See **must.**

shoul·der (shōl′dər), *n.* **1.** either of two corresponding parts of the human body, situated at the top of the trunk and extending respectively from the right side and left side of the neck to the upper joint of the corresponding arm. **2.** (*pl.*) these two parts together with the portion of the back joining them, forming a place where burdens are sometimes carried. **3.** a corresponding part in animals. See illus. under **horse. 4.** the upper foreleg and adjoining parts of a sheep, etc. **5.** the joint connecting the arm or the foreleg with the trunk. **6.** a shoulderlike part or projection. **7.** *Fort.* the angle of a bastion between the face and the flank. **8.** *Print.* the flat surface on a type body extending beyond the base of the letter or character. See diag. under **type. 9.** that part of a garment which covers, or fits over the shoulder. **10.** *Leather Mfg.* that part of the hide anterior to the butt. **11.** the unpaved portion at the edge of a road. **12. shoulder to shoulder,** with united action and support. **13. straight from the shoulder,** without evasion. —*v.t.* **14.** to push, as with the shoulder, esp. roughly. **15.** to take upon or support with the shoulder. **16.** to assume as a burden: *to shoulder the expense.* —*v.i.* **17.** to push with the shoulder. [ME *sholder,* OE *sculdor,* c. G *schulter*]

Diagram of left shoulder (front view)
A. Clavicle;
B. Acromion;
C. Scapula;
D. Humerus;
E. Radius;
F. Ulna
G. Carpus;
H. Metacarpal;
I. Phalanx

shoulder blade, the scapula.

shoulder knot, a knot of ribbon or lace worn on the shoulder, as by men of fashion in the 17th and 18th centuries, by servants in livery, or by women or children.

shoulder strap, 1. a strap worn over the shoulder as to support a garment. **2.** a strip on the shoulder of a uniform to distinguish the rank, etc., of an officer.

should·n't (shŏod′ənt), contraction of *should not.*

shouldst (shŏodst), *v. Archaic.* 2nd pers. sing. of **should.** Also, **should·est** (shŏod′ĭst)

shout (shout), *v.i.* **1.** to call or cry out loudly and vigorously. **2.** to speak or laugh noisily or unrestrainedly. —*v.t.* **3.** to express by a shout or shouts. [ME; c. Icel. *skúta* scold, chide] —*n.* **4.** a loud call or cry. **5.** a loud burst, as of laughter. [ME; c. Icel. *skúti, skúta* a taunt] —**shout′er,** *n.* —**Syn. 1.** See **cry.**

shove (shŭv), *v.,* **shoved, shoving,** *n.* —*v.t.* **1.** to move along by force from behind. **2.** to push roughly or rudely; jostle. —*v.i.* **3.** to push. **4. shove off, a.** to push a boat off. **b.** *Slang.* to leave; start. —*n.* **5.** an act of shoving. [ME *shovve,* OE *scúfan,* c. G *schauben* (obs.)] —**shov′er,** *n.* —**Syn. 1.** See **push.**

shov·el (shŭv′əl), *n., v.,* **-eled, -eling** or (*esp. Brit.*) **-elled, -elling. 1.** an implement consisting of a broad blade or scoop attached to a handle, used for taking up and removing loose matter, as earth, snow, coal, etc. **2.** a contrivance or machine for shoveling, removing matter, etc.: *a steamshovel.* **3.** a shovelful. **4.** *Colloq.* a shovel hat. —*v.t.* **5.** to take up and cast or remove with a shovel. **6.** to gather or put in quantities or carelessly: *to shovel up food.* **7.** to dig or clear with a shovel: *to shovel a path.* —*v.i.* **8.** to work with a shovel. [ME *schovel,* OE *scofl;* akin to G *schaufel*]

shov·el·board (shŭv′əl·bōrd′), *n.* shuffleboard.

shov·el·er (shŭv′əl·ər), *n.* **1.** one who or that which shovels. **2.** Also, **shov·el·bill** (shŭv′əl·bĭl′). a widely distributed fresh-water duck, *Spatula clypeata,* with a broad, flat bill; spoonbill. Also, *esp. Brit.,* **shov′el·ler.**

shovel hat, a hat with a broad brim turned up at the sides and projecting with a shovellike curve in front and behind; worn by some ecclesiastics, chiefly in England.

shov·el·head (shŭv′əl·hĕd′), *n.* **1.** the hackleback. **2.** a shark, *Sphyrna tiburo,* of the hammerhead family, with a kidney-shaped head.

shov·el·nose (shŭv′əl·nōz′), *n.* **1.** any of various animals with a shovellike snout or head, as a shark, *Hexanchus corinus,* of the Pacific, or a guitarfish, *Rhinobatos productus,* of California. **2.** the hackleback. —**shov′el·nosed′,** *adj.*

show (shō), *v.,* **showed, shown** or **showed, showing,** *n.* —*v.t.* **1.** to cause or allow to be seen; exhibit; display. **2.** to point out: *to show the way.* **3.** to guide: *he showed me to my room.* **4.** to make clear; make known; explain. **5.** to prove; demonstrate. **6.** to indicate: *the thermometer showed ten below.* **7.** to allege, as in a legal document; plead, as a reason or cause. **8.** to produce, as facts in an affidavit or at a hearing. **9.** to make evident by appearance, behavior, etc.: *to show one's feelings.* **10.** to accord or grant (favor, etc.). —*v.i.* **11.** to be seen; be or become visible. **12.** to look or appear: *to show to advantage.* **13.** *Colloq.* to give an exhibition or performance. **14.** *Racing Slang.* to finish in first, second, or third place in a race. **15. show off, a.** to display ostentatiously. **b.** to display one's abilities, cleverness, etc. **16. show up, a.** to expose (faults, etc.). **b.** to stand out. **c.** to turn up; appear. —*n.* **17.** a display: *a show of*

freedom. **18.** ostentatious display. **19.** any kind of public exhibition. **20.** act of showing. **21.** appearance: *to make a sorry show.* **22.** an unreal or deceptive appearance. **23.** an indication; trace. **24.** *Colloq.* a theatrical performance or company. **25.** *Colloq.* a chance: *to get a fair show.* **26.** a sight or spectacle. [ME *showen,* var. of *shewan* look at, show, OE *scēawian* look at, c. D *schowen,* G *schauen* look at] **—show′er,** *n.*
—Syn. 17. SHOW, DISPLAY, OSTENTATION, POMP suggest the presentation of a more or less elaborate, often pretentious, appearance, for the public to see. SHOW often indicates an external appearance which may or may not accord with actual facts: *a show of modesty.* DISPLAY applies to an intentionally conspicuous show: *a great display of wealth.* OSTENTATION is vain, ambitious, pretentious, or offensive display: *tasteless and vulgar ostentation.* POMP suggests such a show of dignity and authority as characterizes a ceremony of state: *the coronation was carried out with pomp and ceremonial.*

show bill, an advertising poster or placard.
show·boat (shō′bōt′), *n.* a boat, esp. a paddle-wheel steamer, used as a traveling theater.
show·bread (shō′brĕd′), *n.* shewbread.
show·case (shō′kās′), *n.* a glass case for the display and protection of articles in shops, museums, etc.
show·down (shō′doun′), *n.* **1.** the laying down of one's cards, face upward, in a card game, esp. poker. **2.** a forced disclosure of actual resources, power, etc.
show·er (shou′ər), *n.* **1.** a brief fall of rain, or hail, sleet, or, sometimes, snow. **2.** a similar fall, as of tears, sparks, or bullets. **3.** a large supply or quantity: *a shower of questions.* **4.** a bestowal of presents on a prospective bride: *a linen shower.* **5.** a shower bath. **—v.t. 6.** to wet as with a shower. **7.** to pour down in a shower. **8.** to bestow liberally or lavishly. **—v.i. 9.** to rain in a shower. **10.** to take a shower bath. [ME *shour,* OE *scūr,* c. G *schauer*] **—show′er·y,** *adj.*
shower bath, 1. a bath in which water is showered upon the body from above. **2.** the apparatus for it.
show·ing (shō′ĭng), *n.* **1.** exhibition; show. **2.** a setting forth or presentation, as of facts or conditions.
show·man (shō′mən), *n., pl.* **-men. 1.** one who exhibits a show. **2.** one who presents things well. **—show′·man·ship′,** *n.*
shown (shōn), *v.* pp. of **show.**
show-off (shō′ôf′, -ŏf′), *n.* **1.** pretentious display. **2.** one given to pretentious display.
show·room (shō′rōōm′, -rŏŏm′), *n.* a room used for the display of goods or merchandise.
show window, a display window in a store.
show·y (shō′ĭ), *adj.,* **showier, showiest. 1.** making an imposing display: *showy flowers.* **2.** ostentatious; gaudy. **—show′i·ly,** *adv.* **—show′i·ness,** *n.* **—Syn. 2.** See gaudy[1].
shrank (shrăngk), *v.* pt. of **shrink.**
shrap·nel (shrăp′nəl), *n.* **1.** *Mil.* **a.** a hollow projectile containing bullets or the like and a bursting charge, arranged to explode before reaching the object, and to set free a shower of missiles. **b.** such projectiles collectively. **2.** shell fragments. [named after the inventor, H. *Shrapnel* (1761–1842), officer in the British army]

Cross section of shrapnel
A. Powder charge; B. Shrapnel balls; C. Case; D. Fuse

shred (shrĕd), *n., v.,* **shredded** or **shred, shredding. —n. 1.** a piece cut or torn off, esp. in a narrow strip. **2.** a bit; scrap. **—v.t. 3.** to cut or tear into small pieces, esp. small strips; reduce to shreds. [ME *schrede,* OE *scrēade,* c. G *schrot* chips] **—shred′der,** *n.*
Shreve·port (shrēv′pôrt′), *n.* a city in N W Louisiana, on the Red River. 164,372 (1960).
shrew[1] (shrōō), *n.* a woman of violent temper and speech; a termagant. [special use of SHREW[2]]
shrew[2] (shrōō), *n.* any of various small insectivore mammals of the genus *Sorex* and allied genera, having a long, sharp snout and a mouse-like form, as the **water shrew,** *Sorex palustris,* of North America. [OE *scrēawa;* of unknown origin]
shrewd (shrōōd), *adj.* **1.** astute or sharp in practical matters: *a shrewd politician.* **2.** *Archaic.* keen; piercing. **3.** *Archaic.* malicious. **4.** *Obs.* bad. **5.** *Obs.* shrewish. **6.** *Obs.* artful. [ME *shrewed,* pp. of *shrew* curse (now obs.), v. use of SHREW[1], n.] **—shrewd′ly,** *adv.* **—shrewd′ness,** *n.* **—Syn. 1.** See acute.

Common short-tailed shrew, *Blarina brevicauda* (Total length 5 in., tail 1 in.)

shrew·ish (shrōō′ĭsh), *adj.* having the disposition of a shrew. **—shrew′ish·ly,** *adv.* **—shrew′ish·ness,** *n.*
shrew·mouse (shrōō′mous′), *n., pl.* **-mice.** a shrew, esp. *Sorex vulgaris,* the common shrew of Europe.
Shrews·bur·y (shrōz′bĕr′ĭ, -bə rĭ, shrōōz′-), *n.* a city in W England: county seat of Shropshire. 44,926 (1951).
shriek (shrēk), *n.* **1.** a loud, sharp, shrill cry. **2.** a loud, high sound of laughter. **3.** any loud, shrill sound, as of a whistle. **—v.i. 4.** to utter a loud, sharp, shrill cry, as birds. **5.** to cry out sharply in a high voice: *to shriek with pain.* **6.** to utter loud, high-pitched sounds in laughing. **7.** (of a musical instrument, a whistle, the wind, etc.) to give forth a loud, shrill sound. **—v.t. 8.** to

cry in a shriek: *to shriek defiance.* [earlier *shrick,* northern var. of *shritch* (now d.), ME *schriche*] **—shriek′er,** *n.* **—Syn. 5.** See **scream.**
shrieve (shrēv), *n.* *Obs.* sheriff.
shrift (shrĭft), *n.* *Archaic.* **1.** the imposition of penance by a priest on a penitent after confession. **2.** absolution or remission of sins granted after confession and penance. **3.** confession to a priest. **4.** the act of shriving. [ME; OE *scrift* (c. D and G *schrift* writing), der. SHRIVE]
shrike (shrīk), *n.* any of numerous predacious oscine birds of the family *Laniidae,* with a strong hooked and toothed bill, which feed on insects and sometimes on small birds and other animals, as the butcherbirds of the genus *Lanius,* and the thick-headed shrikes of the genus *Pachycephala,* of the Australian region. [OE *scríc*]
shrill (shrĭl), *adj.* **1.** high-pitched and piercing: *a shrill cry.* **2.** producing such sound. **3.** full of such sound. **4.** *Poetic.* keen; piercing. **—v.t., v.i. 5.** to cry shrilly. **—n. 6.** a shrill sound. **—adv. 7.** shrilly. [ME *shrille,* c. G *schrill* (of LG orig.); akin to OE *scrallettan* sound loudly] **—shrill′ness,** *n.* **—shril′ly,** *adv.*
shrimp (shrĭmp), *n., pl.* **shrimps** or for **1** (*esp.* collectively) **shrimp. 1.** any of various small, long-tailed, chiefly marine, decapod crustaceans of the genus *Crangon* and allied genera (suborder *Macrura*), as the European *C. vulgaris,* esteemed as a table delicacy. **2.** a diminutive or insignificant person. [ME *shrimpe.* Cf. G *shrumpfen* shrink up, and OE *scrimman* shrink]
shrine (shrīn), *n., v.,* **shrined, shrining. —n. 1.** a receptacle for sacred relics; a reliquary. **2.** an erection, often of a stately or sumptuous character, enclosing the remains or relics of a saint and forming an object of religious veneration and pilgrimage. **3.** any structure or place consecrated or devoted to some saint or deity, as an altar, chapel, church, or temple. **4.** any place or object hallowed by its history or associations. **—v.t. 5.** to enshrine. [ME *schrine,* OE *scrín* (c. G *schrein*), t. L: m.s. *scrínium* case for books and papers]

Shrimp, *Crangon vulgaris* (Ab. 2 in. long)

shrink (shrĭngk), *v.,* **shrank** or **shrunk, shrunk** or **shrunken, shrinking,** *n.* **—v.i. 1.** to draw back, as in retreat or avoidance. **2.** to contract with heat, cold, moisture, etc. **3.** to become reduced in extent or compass. **—v.t. 4.** to cause to shrink or contract. **5.** *Textiles.* to cause to shrink in order to prevent future shrinkage. **—n. 6.** a shrinking. **7.** a shrinking movement. [ME *schrinke(n),* OE *scrincan,* c. MD *schrinken;* akin to Sw. *skrynka* wrinkle] **—shrink′a·ble,** *adj.* **—shrink′er,** *n.* **—shrink′ing·ly,** *adv.* **—Syn. 3.** See decrease. **—Ant. 3.** expand.
shrink·age (shrĭngk′ĭj), *n.* **1.** act or fact of shrinking. **2.** the amount or degree of shrinking. **3.** reduction or depreciation in quantity, value, etc. **4.** contraction of a fabric in finishing or washing. **5.** the difference between the original weight of livestock and that after it has been prepared for marketing.
shrive (shrīv), *v.,* **shrove** or **shrived, shriven** or **shrived, shriving. —v.t. 1.** to impose penance on for sin. **2.** to grant absolution to (a penitent). **3.** to confess to a priest, for the purpose of obtaining absolution. **4.** to hear the confession of. **—v.i. 5.** to hear confessions. **6.** to go to or make confession. [ME; OE *scrífan* (c. G *schreiben* write), ult. t. L: m. *scríbere* write]
shriv·el (shrĭv′əl), *v.t., v.i.,* **-eled, -eling** or (*esp. Brit.*) **-elled, -elling. 1.** to contract and wrinkle, as from great heat or cold. **2.** to wither; make or become impotent. [orig. unknown] **—Syn. 1.** See wither.
shroff (shrŏf), *n.* **1.** (in India) a banker or money-changer. **2.** (in China, etc.) a native expert employed to test coins and separate the base from the genuine. **—v.t. 3.** to test (coins) in order to separate the base from the genuine. [earlier *sharoffe,* t. Pg.: m. *xarrafo,* t. Hind.: m. *çairáf* money-changer]
Shrop·shire (shrŏp′shĭr, -shər), *n.* **1.** Also, **Salop.** a county in W England. 289,802 pop. (1951); 1347 sq. mi. *Co. seat:* Shrewsbury. **2.** a hornless English breed of mutton sheep having dark-brown or black face and legs, and fleece of a white wool.
Shropshire Lad, a volume of poetry (1896) by A. E. Housman.
shroud (shroud), *n.* **1.** a white cloth or sheet in which a corpse is wrapped for burial. **2.** something which covers or conceals like a garment: *a shroud of rain.* **3.** (*usually pl.*) *Naut.* one of a set of strong ropes extended from the mastheads to the sides of a ship to help support the masts. See illus. under **ratline.** **—v.t. 4.** to wrap or clothe for burial. **5.** to cover; hide from view. **6.** to veil, as in obscurity or mystery. **7.** *Obs.* to shelter. **—v.i. 8.** *Archaic.* to take shelter. [ME; OE *scrūd,* c. Icel. *skrúdh;* akin to SHRED] **—shroud′less,** *adj.*
shroud-laid (shroud′lād′), *adj.* (of a rope) made with four strands and (usually) a central core or heart.
shrove (shrōv), *v.* pt. of **shrive.**
Shrove Sunday, the Sunday before Ash Wednesday.
Shrove·tide (shrōv′tīd′), *n.* the three days before Ash Wednesday, once a time of confession and absolution.
Shrove Tuesday, the last day of Shrovetide, long observed as a season of merrymaking before Lent.

ăct, āble, dâre, ärt; ĕbb, ēqual; ĭf, īce; hŏt, ōver, ôrder, oil, bŏŏk, ōōze, out; ŭp, ūse, ûrge; ə = a in alone; ch, chief; g, give; ng, ring; sh, shoe; th, thin; ŧħ, that; zh, vision. See the full key on inside cover.

shrub[1] (shrŭb), *n.* a woody perennial plant smaller than a tree, usually having permanent stems branching from or near the ground. [ME *shrubbe*, OE *scrybb* brushwood, c. d. Dan. *skrub*] —**shrub′like′**, *adj.*

shrub[2] (shrŭb), *n.* any of various beverages made from the juice of fruit, sugar, and other ingredients. [t. Ar., metathetic var. of *shurb* drink]

shrub·ber·y (shrŭb′ər̄ĭ), *n., pl.* **-beries.** shrubs collectively.

shrub·by (shrŭb′ĭ), *adj.*, **-bier, -biest. 1.** shrublike. **2.** abounding in shrubs. **3.** consisting of shrubs. —**shrub′bi·ness,** *n.*

shrug (shrŭg), *v.*, **shrugged, shrugging,** *n.* —*v.t., v.i.* **1.** to raise and contract (the shoulders), expressing indifference, disdain, etc. —*n.* **2.** this movement. [ME]

shrunk (shrŭngk), *v.* pp. and a pt. of **shrink.**

shrunk·en (shrŭngk′ən), *v.* a pp. of **shrink.**

shuck (shŭk), *n.* **1.** a husk or pod, as the outer covering of corn, hickory nuts, chestnuts, etc. **2.** (*pl.*) *U.S. Colloq.* something useless: *not worth shucks.* **3.** the shell of an oyster or clam. —*v.t.* **4.** to remove the shucks from: *she sat there placidly shucking the corn.* **5.** to remove as or like shucks. [orig. unknown] —**shuck′er,** *n.*

shucks (shŭks), *interj. Colloq.* an exclamation of disgust or regret.

shud·der (shŭd′ər), *v.i.* **1.** to tremble with a sudden convulsive movement, as from horror, fear, or cold. —*n.* **2.** a convulsive movement of the body, as from horror, fear, or cold. [ME *shodder, shuder* (c. G *schaudern*), freq. of OE *scūdan* move, shake] —**shud′der·ing·ly,** *adv.* —**Syn. 1.** See **shiver**[1].

shuf·fle (shŭf′əl), *v.*, **-fled, -fling,** *n.* —*v.i.* **1.** to walk without lifting the feet or with clumsy steps and a shambling gait. **2.** to scrape the feet over the floor in dancing. **3.** to get (*into*, etc.) in a clumsy manner: *to shuffle into one's clothes.* **4.** to get (*in, out, of,* etc.) in an underhand or evasive manner: *to shuffle out of responsibilities.* **5.** to act in a shifting or evasive manner; employ deceitful pretenses; equivocate. **6.** to mix cards in a pack so as to change their relative position. —*v.t.* **7.** to move (the feet, etc.) along the ground or floor without lifting them. **8.** to perform (a dance, etc.) with such movements. **9.** to move this way and that. **10.** to put, thrust, or bring (*in, out,* etc.) trickily, evasively, or haphazardly. **11.** to mix (cards in a pack) so as to change their relative position. **12.** to jumble together; mix in a disorderly heap. **13.** to shuffle off, to thrust aside or get rid of. —*n.* **14.** a scraping movement; a dragging gait. **15.** an evasive trick; evasion. **16.** act of shuffling. **17.** a shuffling of cards in a pack. **18.** right or turn to shuffle in card playing. **19.** a dance in which the feet are shuffled along the floor. [t. LG: m. *schuffeln* walk clumsily or with dragging feet. See **shove**]

shuf·fle·board (shŭf′əl bōrd′), *n.* **1.** a game in which coins or disks are driven along a smooth board, table, or other surface, toward certain lines, etc., on it. **2.** the board, table, or the like. **3.** a similar game played with large disks pushed with a cue. Also, **shovelboard.**

shuf·fler (shŭf′lər), *n.* **1.** one who shuffles. **2.** one who mixes the cards. **3.** any scaup duck.

Shu·fu (shoo′foo′), *n.* Kashgar.

Shu·lam·ite (shoo′lə mīt′), *n.* epithet of the bride in the Song of Solomon 6:13.

shun (shŭn), *v.t.*, **shunned, shunning.** to keep away from (a place, person, etc.), from dislike, caution, etc.; take pains to avoid. [ME *shunen*, OE *scunian*; orig. obscure] —**shun′ner,** *n.*

shunt (shŭnt), *v.t.* **1.** to shove or turn aside or out of the way. **2.** to sidetrack; get rid of. **3.** *Elect.* to divert (a part of a current) by connecting a circuit element in parallel with another; to place on or furnish with a shunt. **4.** to shift (a train, or part of it) from one line of rails to another or from the main track to a siding. —*v.i.* **5.** to move or turn aside or out of the way. **6.** (of a train) to move from one railroad track to another, or from one point to another; to shift cars about as in a freight yard. —*n.* **7.** act of shunting; a shift. **8.** *Elect.* a conducting element bridged across a circuit or a portion of a circuit, establishing a current path auxiliary to the main circuit. **9.** a railroad switch. [ME; orig. obscure, ? der. **shun**] —**shunt′er,** *n.*

Shu·shan (shoo′shăn), *n.* Biblical name of **Susa.**

shut (shŭt), *v.*, **shut, shutting,** *adj., n.* —*v.t.* **1.** to put (a door, cover, etc.) in position to close or obstruct. **2.** to close the doors of (often fol. by *up*): *shut up the shop.* **3.** to close by bringing together or folding: *to shut one's eyes.* **4.** to confine; enclose: *to shut into a cage.* **5.** to bar; exclude: *to shut out of one's house.* **6.** (in games) to keep from scoring (fol. by *out*). **7.** *Obs.* to bolt; bar. —*v.i.* **8.** to become shut or closed; close. **9. shut down, a.** to settle down so as to cover or envelop. **b.** to close for a time, as a factory. **c.** *Colloq.* to put a stop or check to (fol. by *on* or *upon*). **10. shut up,** *Colloq.* to stop talking. —*adj.* **11.** closed; fastened up. **12.** *Dial.* or *Colloq.* free or rid (fol. by *of*). **13.** *Phonet.* checked. —*n.* **14.** act or time of shutting or closing. **15.** the line where two pieces of welded metal are united. [ME *schutte*, OE *scyttan* bolt (a door); akin to **shoot**] —**Syn. 1.** See **close.**

shut·down (shŭt′doun′), *n.* a shutting down; a closing of a factory or the like for a time.

shut·in (shŭt′ĭn′), *adj.* **1.** confined to the house, hospital, etc. **2.** *Psychiatry.* disposed to desire solitude.

—*n.* **3.** a person confined by infirmity or disease to the house, hospital, etc.

shut·off (shŭt′ôf′, -ŏf′), *n.* something that shuts off: *the automatic shutoff on a heater.*

shut·out (shŭt′out′), *n.* **1.** act of shutting out. **2.** state of being shut out. **3.** *Sports.* **a.** a preventing of the opposite side from scoring, as in the game of baseball. **b.** any game in which one team does not score.

shut·ter (shŭt′ər), *n.* **1.** a hinged or otherwise movable cover for a window. **2.** a movable cover, slide, etc., for an opening. **3.** one who or that which shuts. **4.** *Photog.* a mechanical device for opening and closing the aperture of a camera lens to expose a plate or film. —*v.t.* **5.** to close or provide with shutters. —**Syn. 1.** See **curtain.**

shut·tle (shŭt′əl), *n., v.*, **-tled, -tling.** —*n.* **1.** a device in a loom for passing or shooting the weft thread through the shed from one side of the web to the other, usually consisting of a boat-shaped piece of wood containing a bobbin on which the weft thread is wound. **2.** the sliding container that carries the lower thread in a sewing machine. **3.** *U.S.* a shuttle train. —*v.t., v.i.* **4.** to move quickly to and fro like a shuttle. [ME *schutylle, shittle,* OE *scytel* dart, arrow, c. Icel. *skutill* harpoon; akin to **shut, shoot**]

shut·tle·cock (shŭt′əl kŏk′), *n.* **1.** a piece of cork, or of similar light material, with feathers stuck in one end, intended to be struck into the air with a battledore in play. **2.** Also, **battledore and shuttlecock.** the play or game. —*v.t.* **3.** to send, or bandy to and fro, like a shuttlecock.

shuttle train, a train running for a short distance to and fro, as on a branch line, or in commuter service.

Shver·nik (shvĕr′nĭk), *n.* **Nikolai** (nĭkō lī′), born 1888, president of the Soviet Union, 1946–1953.

shy[1] (shī), *adj.*, **shyer, shyest** or **shier, shiest,** *v.*, **shied, shying,** *n., pl.* **shies.** —*adj.* **1.** bashful; retiring. **2.** easily frightened away; timid. **3.** suspicious; distrustful. **4.** reluctant; wary. **5.** short: *shy of funds.* **6.** *U.S. Slang.* short in amount, degree, etc. **7.** *Colloq.* failing to pay something due, as one's ante in poker. **8.** not bearing or breeding freely, as plants or animals. —*v.i.* **9.** to start back or aside, as in fear, esp. a horse. **10.** to draw back; recoil. —*n.* **11.** a sudden start aside, as in fear. [ME *schey,* OE *scēoh,* c. MHG *schiech*; akin to G *scheu*] —**shy′er,** *n.* —**shy′ly,** *adv.* —**shy′ness,** *n.* —**Syn. 1.** SHY, BASHFUL, DIFFIDENT imply a manner which shows discomfort or lack of confidence in association with others. SHY implies a constitutional shrinking from contact or close association with others, together with a wish to escape notice: *shy and retiring.* BASHFUL suggests timidity about meeting others, and trepidation and awkward behavior when brought into prominence or notice: *a bashful child.* DIFFIDENT emphasizes self-distrust, fear of censure, failure, etc., and a hesitant, tentative manner as a consequence: *a diffident approach to a subject.* —**Ant. 1.** bold, confident.

shy[2] (shī), *v.*, **shied, shying,** *n., pl.* **shies.** —*v.i., v.t.* **1.** to throw with a swift, sudden movement: *to shy a stone.* —*n.* **2.** a quick, sudden throw. **3.** *Colloq.* a gibe or sneer. **4.** *Colloq.* a try. [orig. uncert.]

Shy·lock (shī′lŏk), *n.* **1.** a relentless and revengeful moneylender in Shakespeare's *Merchant of Venice.* **2.** an extortionate usurer.

shy·ster (shī′stər), *n. U.S. Slang.* **1.** a lawyer who uses unprofessional or questionable methods. **2.** one who gets along by petty, sharp practices. [appar. f. SHY in slang sense of shady, disreputable + -STER]

si (sē), *n. Music.* the syllable used for the seventh tone of a scale and sometimes for the tone B. [see GAMUT]

Si (sē), *n.* a river in S China, flowing from Yünnan Province E to the South China Sea near Canton. ab. 1250 mi. Also, **Si-kiang.**

Si, *Chem.* silicon.

S.I., 1. Sandwich Islands. **2.** Staten Island.

si·a·la·gog·ic (sī′ə lə gŏj′ĭk), *Med.* —*adj.* **1.** encouraging salivary flow. —*n.* **2.** sialagogue.

si·al·a·gogue (sī ăl′ə gŏg′, -gōg′), *adj.* **1.** promoting the flow or secretion of saliva. —*n.* **2.** a sialagogue agent or medicine. [t. NL: m.s. *sialagōgus,* f. Gk.: s. *sialon* saliva + m. *agōgós* leading, drawing forth]

Si·al·kot (sē äl′kōt′), *n.* a city in Pakistan, in W Punjab: military station. 167,543 (1951).

si·a·loid (sī′ə loid′), *adj.* resembling saliva. [f. s. Gk. *sialon* saliva + -OID]

Si·am (sīăm′, sī′ăm). *n.* **1.** former name of a kingdom in SE Asia. Official name (1939–1945 and since 1949), **Thailand. 2. Gulf of,** an arm of the South China Sea, S of Siam.

si·a·mang (sē′ə măng′), *n.* a large black gibbon, *Hylobates syndactylus,* of Sumatra and the Malay Peninsula, with very long arms and having the second and third digits united. [t. Malay, der. *āmang* black]

Si·a·mese (sī′ə mēz′, -mēs′), *adj., n., pl.* **-mese.** —*adj.* **1.** of or pertaining to Siam, its people, or their language. **2.** (in allusion to the Siamese twins) twin; closely connected; similar. —*n.* **3.** a native of Siam. **4.** the official language of Thailand, and the most important Thai language.

Siamese twins, 1. two Siamese men, Chang and Eng (1811–74), who were joined to each other by a short tubular cartilaginous band. **2.** any twins who are born joined together in any manner.

Si·an (sē′än′, shē′-), *n.* a city in central China: the capital of Shensi province; ancient capital of the Chinese Empire. 559,000 (est. 1950). Also, **Singan**.

Siang·tan (syäng/tän′, shyäng′-), *n.* a city in S China, in Hunan province. 83,000 (est. 1950).

sib¹ (sĭb), *adj.* **1.** related by blood; akin. —*n.* **2.** a kinsman; relative. **3.** one's kin or kindred. [ME (*i*)*sib*, OE (*ge*)*sibb* related (as n., a relation); cf. Icel. *sifi* kinsman]

sib² (sĭb), *n. Anthropol.* a unilateral descent group. [ME and OE *sib* kinship, c. G *sippe*]

Si·be·li·us (sĭ bā/lǐ əs; *Fin.* -lyŏŏs), *n.* Jean Julius Christian (zhän yŏŏ/lyŏŏs krǐs/tyän), 1865–1957, Finnish composer.

Si·be·ri·a (sī bĭr/ĭ ə), *n.* a part of the Soviet Union, in N Asia, extending from the Ural Mountains to the Pacific. Russian, **Si·bir** (sǐ bēr′). —**Si·be/ri·an,** *adj., n.*

sib·i·lant (sĭb/ə lənt), *adj.* **1.** hissing. **2.** *Phonet.* characterized by a hissing sound; denoting sounds like those spelled with *s* in *this, rose, pressure, pleasure.* —*n.* **3.** *Phonet.* a sibilant sound. [t. L: s. *sībilans*, ppr.] —**sib/·i·lance, sib/i·lan·cy,** *n.* —**sib/i·lant·ly,** *adv.*

sib·i·late (sĭb/ə lāt′), *v.,* -lated, -lating. —*v.i.* **1.** to hiss. —*v.t.* **2.** to utter or pronounce with a hissing sound. —**sib/i·la/tion,** *n.*

sib·ling (sĭb/lǐng), *n.* **1.** a brother or sister. **2.** *Anthropol.* a comember of a sib². [OE]

sib·yl (sĭb/ĭl), *n.* **1.** any of certain women of antiquity reputed to possess powers of prophecy or divination. **2.** a prophetess or witch. [ME *sibil,* t. ML: m.s. *Sibilla,* L *Sibylla,* t. Gk.] —**sib·yl/ic, sib·yl·line** (sĭb/ə lǐn′, -lĭn′, -lǐn), *adj.*

Sibylline Books, *Rom. Hist.* a collection of oracular utterances, in Greek hexameters, concerning religious worship and Roman policy. They were reputedly bought by Tarquinius Superbus from the Cumaean sibyl.

sic¹ (sĭk), *adv. Latin.* so; thus (often used parenthetically to show that something has been copied exactly from the original).

sic² (sĭk), *v.t.,* **sicked, sicking. 1.** to attack (esp. of a dog). **2.** to incite to attack. [var. of SEEK]

Sic., 1. Sicilian. **2.** Sicily.

Si·ca·ni·an (sǐ kā/nǐ ən), *adj.* Sicilian.

sic·ca·tive (sĭk/ə tǐv), *adj.* **1.** causing or promoting absorption of moisture; drying. —*n.* **2.** a siccative substance, esp. in paint. [t. LL: m.s. *siccātīvus,* der. *siccāre* to dry]

Si·cil·i·an Vespers (sǐ sĭl/ĭ ən), a general massacre of the French in Sicily by the natives, begun at the sound of the vesper bell on Easter Monday, 1282.

Sic·i·lies (sĭs/ə lĭz), *n.pl.* **The Two,** a former kingdom in Sicily and S Italy: it existed intermittently from 1130 to 1861.

Sic·i·ly (sĭs/ə lǐ), *n.* the largest island in the Mediterranean, comprising a department of Italy: separated from the SW tip of the Italian mainland by the Strait of Messina. 4,624,000 pop. (est. 1954); 9924 sq. mi. *Cap.:* Palermo. Italian, **Si·ci·lia** (sē chē/lyä). —**Si·cil·i·an** (sǐ sĭl/ĭ ən), *adj., n.*

sick (sĭk), *adj.* **1.** affected with any disorder of health; ill, unwell, or ailing. **2.** of or attended with sickness. **3.** *Prevailing sense in England.* affected with nausea; inclined to vomit, or vomiting. **4.** of or appropriate to sick persons: *on sick leave.* **5.** deeply affected with some feeling comparable to physical disorder, as sorrow, longing, repugnance, weariness, etc.: *sick at heart.* **6.** *Slang.* disgusted; chagrined. **7.** pale; wan. **8.** not in proper condition; impaired. **9.** *Agric.* a. failing to sustain adequate harvests of some crop, usually specified: *an alfalfa-sick soil.* **b.** containing harmful microörganisms: *a sick field.* —*n.* **10.** sick people. **11.** *Brit.* vomit. [ME *sik, sek,* OE *sēoc,* c. G *siech*]
—**Syn. 1.** SICK, AILING, INDISPOSED refer to any departure from a state of health. SICK refers to a condition presumably temporary, however severe. AILING implies a somewhat unhealthy condition, usually extending over some time. INDISPOSED applies to a slight, temporary illness. See also ILL. —**Ant. 1.** well, healthy.

sick bay, (in a ship) a hospital or dispensary.

sick·bed (sĭk/bĕd′), *n.* a bed used by a sick person.

sick·en (sĭk/ən), *v.i., v.t.* to become or make sick.

sick·en·ing (sĭk/ən ĭng), *adj.* making sick; causing nausea, disgust, or loathing: *a sickening display of bad temper.* —**sick/en·ing·ly,** *adv.*

sick headache, headache accompanied by nausea; migraine.

sick·ish (sĭk/ĭsh), *adj.* **1.** somewhat sickening or nauseating. **2.** somewhat sick or ill. —**sick/ish·ly,** *adv.* —**sick/ish·ness,** *n.*

sick·le (sĭk/əl), *n.* **1.** an implement for cutting grain, grass, etc., consisting of a curved, hooklike blade mounted in a short handle. **2.** (*cap.*) *Astron.* a group of stars in the constellation Leo, likened to this implement. [ME *sikel,* OE *sicol* (c. G *sichel*), t. L: m.s. *secula*]

Sickle

sick·le·bill (sĭk/əl bĭl′), *n.* any of various birds with a curved bill, esp. the long-billed curlew, *Numenius longirostus.*

sickle cell, a cell containing a mutant gene which affects the blood of humans, usually Negroes: thought to offer resistance to malaria. It causes **sickle cell anemia,**

a hereditary disease characterized by the crystallization of sickle cells within erythrocytes, distorting them and clogging blood vessels. —**sick/le-cell/,** *adj.*

sickle feather, one of the paired, elongated, sickle-shaped, middle feathers of the tail of the rooster.

sick·ly (sĭk/lǐ), *adj.,* -lier, -liest, *adv.,* -v., -lied, -lying. —*adj.* **1.** not strong; unhealthy; ailing. **2.** of, connected with, or arising from ill health: *a sickly complexion.* **3.** marked by the prevalence of ill health, as a region. **4.** causing sickness. **5.** nauseating. **6.** weak; mawkish: *sickly sentimentality.* **7.** faint or feeble, as light, color, etc. —*adv.* **8.** in a sick or sickly manner. —*v.t.* **9.** to cover with a sickly hue. —**sick/li·ness,** *n.* —**Syn. 1.** unwell, frail, weak, puny.

sick·ness (sĭk/nĭs), *n.* **1.** a particular disease or malady. **2.** state of being sick; illness. **3.** nausea.

sic pas·sim (sĭk pǎs/ĭm), *Latin.* the same wherever found (as in a book or notes).

sic sem·per ty·ran·nis (sĭk sĕm/pər tǐ rǎn/ĭs), *Latin.* thus always to tyrants (motto of Virginia).

sic tran·sit glo·ri·a mun·di (sĭk trǎn/sǐt glôr/ĭ ə mŭn/dǐ), *Latin.* thus passes away the glory of this world (or worldly glory).

Si·cy·on (sǐsh/ǐ ŏn′), *n.* an ancient city in S Greece, near Corinth.

Sid·dhar·tha (sǐ där/tä), *n.* Buddha.

Sid·dons (sǐd/ ənz), *n.* **Sarah,** (nee *Kemble*) 1755–1831, British actress.

sid·dur (sǐd/ŏŏr), *n. Jewish Relig.* the book containing daily, Sabbath, and festival prayers. [t. Heb.: order]

side (sīd), *n., adj., v.,* sided, siding. —*n.* **1.** one of the surfaces or lines bounding a thing. **2.** either of the two surfaces of paper, cloth, etc. **3.** one of the two surfaces of an object other than the front, back, top, and bottom. **4.** either of the two lateral (right and left) parts of a thing. **5.** either lateral half of the body of a person or an animal, esp. of the trunk. **6.** an aspect; phase: *all sides of a question.* **7.** region, direction, or position with reference to a central line, space, or point: *the east side of a city.* **8.** a slope, as of a hill. **9.** one of two or more parties concerned in a case, contest, etc. **10.** the position, course, or part of one person or party opposing another: *to take sides.* **11.** line of descent through either the father or the mother: *his maternal side.* **12.** *Brit. Slang.* pretentious airs: *to put on side.* **13.** either of the two lateral parts of the framework of a ship. **14.** *Chiefly Brit.* english (def. 5). **15.** off side, not within the field or rules of the game. **16.** on side, within the field or rules of the game. —*adj.* **17.** being at or on one side: *the side aisles of a theater.* **18.** coming from one side: *side glance.* **19.** directed toward one side: *side blow.* **20.** subordinate: *a side issue.* —*v.i.* **21.** side with, to place oneself with a side or party; take sides. [ME and OE; c. G *seite*]

side arms, *Mil.* weapons (as pistol, sword, etc.) carried at the side or in the belt.

side·board (sīd/bôrd′), *n.* a piece of furniture, as in a dining room, often with shelves, drawers, etc., for holding articles of table service.

side·burns (sīd/bûrnz′), *n.pl. U.S.* short whiskers extending from the hairline to below the ears and worn with an unbearded chin. [alter. of BURNSIDES]

side·car (sīd/kär′), *n.* a small car attached on one side to a motorcycle and supported on the other by a wheel of its own: used for a passenger, parcels, etc.

side dish, a dish served in addition to the principal dish of a course.

side·hill (sīd/hǐl′), *n. U.S.* hillside.

side·kick (sīd/kǐk′), *n. Slang.* **1.** a close friend; chum. **2.** a confederate.

side light, 1. light coming from the side. **2.** incidental information. **3.** either of two lights carried by a vessel under way at night, a red one on the port side and a green on the starboard. **4.** a window or other aperture for light, in the side of a building, ship, etc. **5.** a window at the side of a door or another window.

side line, 1. a line at the side of something. **2.** an additional or auxiliary line of goods or of business. **3.** *Sports.* **a.** a line or mark defining the limit of play on the side of the field in football, etc. **b.** (*pl.*) the area immediately beyond any of the side lines. **c.** the location of those not playing in the contest.

side·long (sīd/lông′, -lŏng′), *adj.* **1.** directed to one side. —*adv.* **2.** toward the side; obliquely.

side·piece (sīd/pēs′), *n.* a piece forming a side or a part of a side, or fixed by the side, of something.

si·de·re·al (sī dĭr/ĭ al), *adj.* **1.** determined by the stars: *sidereal time.* **2.** of or pertaining to the stars. [f. s. L *sidereus* pertaining to the stars + -AL¹]

sidereal day, the interval between two successive passages of the vernal equinox over the meridian, being about 4 minutes shorter than a mean solar day.

sidereal hour, one 24th part of a sidereal day.

sidereal year. See **year** (def. 6).

sid·er·ite (sǐd/ə rīt′), *n.* **1.** a common mineral, iron carbonate, $FeCO_3$, usually occurring in yellowish to deep-brown cleavable masses: a minor ore of iron. **2.** a meteorite consisting almost entirely of metallic minerals. [t. L: m. *siderītēs,* t. Gk.; in later use f. SIDER- + -ITE²] —**sid·er·it·ic** (sǐd/ə rǐt/ǐk), *adj.*

sidero-, a word element meaning "iron," "steel," as in *siderolite.* Also, before vowels, **sider-.** [t. Gk., comb. form of *sidēros* iron]

sid·er·o·lite (sĭd′ərə līt′), *n.* a meteorite of roughly equal proportions of metallic iron and stony matter.

sid·er·o·sis (sĭd′ə rō′sĭs), *n. Pathol.* a disease of the lungs due to inhaling iron or other metallic particles.

side-sad·dle (sĭd′săd′əl), *n.* a saddle on which the rider sits with both feet on the same (usually the left) side of the horse: used chiefly by women.

side show, 1. a minor show or exhibition in connection with a principal one. **2.** any subordinate event or matter.

side·slip (sĭd′slĭp′), *v.,* **-slipped, -slipping,** *n.* —*v.i.* **1.** to slip to one side. **2.** (of an airplane when banked excessively) to slide sideways in a downward direction, toward the center of the curve executed in turning. —*n.* **3.** act of sideslipping.

side·split·ting (sĭd′splĭt′ĭng), *adj.* convulsively uproarious: *sidesplitting farce.* —**side′split′ting·ly,** *adv.*

side step, a step to one side, as in avoidance.

side-step (sĭd′stĕp′), *v.i., v.t.,* **-stepped, -stepping. 1.** to step, or avoid by stepping, to one side. **2.** to evade, as decisions, problems, etc. —**side′-step′per,** *n.*

side stroke, a swimming stroke in which the body is turned sideways in the water, the hands pull alternately, and the legs perform a scissors kick.

side·swipe (sĭd′swīp′), *v.,* **-swiped, -swiping,** *n. U.S.* —*v.t.* **1.** to strike with a sweeping stroke or blow with or along the side. —*n.* **2.** such a stroke or blow.

side·track (sĭd′trăk′), *v.t., v.i.* **1.** to move to a sidetrack, as a train. **2.** to move or distract from the main subject or course. —*n.* **3.** a railroad siding.

side·walk (sĭd′wôk′), *n.* a walk, esp. a paved one, at the side of a street or road.

side·wall (sĭd′wôl′), *n.* the part of a pneumatic tire between the edge of the tread and the rim of the wheel.

side·ward (sĭd′wərd), *adj.* **1.** directed or moving toward one side. —*adv.* **2.** Also, **side′wards.** toward one side.

side·way (sĭd′wā′), *n.* **1.** a byway. —*adj., adv.* **2.** sideways.

side·ways (sĭd′wāz′), *adv., adj.* **1.** with the side foremost. **2.** facing to the side. **3.** toward or from one side. Also, **side·wise** (sĭd′wīz′).

side-wheel (sĭd′hwēl′), *adj.* having a paddle wheel on each side, as a steamboat. —**side′-wheel′er,** *n.*

side whiskers, hair on the side of a man's face when worn long and with the chin clean-shaven. —**side′-whis′kered,** *adj.*

side·wind·er (sĭd′wīn′dər), *n.* **1.** *Slang.* a disabling swinging blow from the side. **2.** the small species of rattlesnake, *Crotalus cerastes,* that moves in loose sand by throwing loops of the body forward.

sid·ing (sĭ′dĭng), *n.* **1.** a short auxiliary or side track, usually connected by a switch at one or both ends with the main-line track, and used mainly for meeting and passing trains or for loading, unloading, and storing freight cars. **2.** *U.S.* the boarding, metal, or composition forming the sides of a timber building.

si·dle (sĭ′dəl), *v.,* **-dled, -dling,** *n.* —*v.i.* **1.** to move sideways or obliquely. **2.** to edge along furtively. —*n.* **3.** a sidling movement. [back formation from *sideling* SIDELONG]

Sid·ney (sĭd′nĭ), *n.* **Sir Philip,** 1554–86, English poet, writer, statesman, and soldier. Also, **Sidney.**

Si·don (sĭ′dən), *n.* a city of ancient Phoenicia: an early and powerful Mediterranean seaport. Modern, **Saïda.** —**Si·do·ni·an** (sī dō′nĭ ən), *adj., n.*

Sid·ra (sĭd′rä), *n.* **Gulf of,** a large, open gulf of the Mediterranean, on the N coast of Libya.

siè·cle (syĕ′kl), *n. French.* an age; a century; a generation. [F (in OF *secle*), t. L: m. *saeculum* generation]

siege (sēj), *n., v.,* **sieged, sieging.** —*n.* **1.** the operation of reducing and capturing a fortified place by surrounding it, cutting off supplies, undermining, bringing guns to bear, bombing, and other offensive operations. **2.** any prolonged or persistent endeavor to overcome resistance. **3.** *Obs.* a seat. **4.** *Obs.* rank. **5.** *Obs.* a throne. —*v.t.* **6.** to lay siege to; besiege. [ME, t. OF: m. *sege, siege,* ult. der. L *sēdes* seat]
—**Syn. 1.** SIEGE, BLOCKADE are terms for prevention of free movement to or from a place during wartime. SIEGE implies surrounding a city and cutting off its communications, and usually includes direct assaults on its defenses. BLOCKADE is applied more often to operations by ships, which block all commerce and especially thereby cut off food and other supplies from defenders.

Siege Perilous (sēj), *Arthurian Romance.* a vacant seat at the Round Table, which could be filled only by the predestined finder of the Holy Grail, and was fatal to pretenders. [f. SIEGE (def. 3) + PERILOUS]

Sieg·fried (sēg′frēd; *Ger.* zēкн′frēt), *n.* **1.** *German Legend.* the hero of the Nibelungenlied, a prince of a region on the lower Rhine. He captures the treasure of the Nibelungs, slays a dragon, and wins Brünhild for King Gunther. In Wagnerian opera he rescues the Valkyrie Brünnehilde from the sleep into which she was cast by her father. **2.** See **Ring of the Nibelung.**

Siegfried Line, a zone of fortifications in W Germany facing the Maginot Line, constructed in the years preceding the invasion of France, 1940.

Sie·mens (sē′mənz; *Ger.* zē′məns), *n.* **Sir William,** (*Karl Wilhelm Siemens*) 1823–83, British inventor, born in Germany.

Sie·na (syĕ′nä), *n.* a city in central Italy, in Tuscany: cathedral. 53,000 (est. 1954).

Sien·kie·wicz (shĕn kyĕ′vĭch), *n.* **Henryk** (hĕn′rĭk), 1846–1916, Polish novelist: Nobel prize, 1905.

si·en·na (sĭ ĕn′ə), *n.* **1.** a ferruginous earth used **as a** yellowish-brown pigment (**raw sienna**) or, after roasting in a furnace, as a reddish-brown pigment (**burnt sienna**). **2.** the color of such a pigment. [short for It. *terra di Sien(n)a* earth of Siena]

si·er·ra (sĭ ĕr′ə), *n.* **1.** a chain of hills or mountains the peaks of which suggest the teeth of a saw. **2.** the Spanish mackerel. [t. Sp.: lit., saw, g. L *serra*]

Si·er·ra Le·o·ne (sĭ ĕr′ə lĭ ō′nĭ, lĭ ōn′), an independent country in W Africa: member of the Brit. Commonwealth; formerly a British colony and protectorate. 3,000,000 pop. (est. 1958); 27,925 sq. mi. *Cap.:* Freetown.

Si·er·ra Ma·dre (syĕr′rä mä′drĕ), two parallel mountain chains in Mexico, bordering the central plateau on the E and W.

Si·er·ra Ne·vad·a (sĭ ĕr′ə nə väd′ə *for 1;* syĕr′rä nĕ vä′dä *for 2).* **1.** a mountain range in E California. Highest peak, Mt. Whitney, 14,495 ft. **2.** a mountain range in S Spain. Highest peak, Mulhacén, 11,420 ft.

si·es·ta (sĭ ĕs′tə), *n.* a midday or afternoon rest or nap, esp. as taken in Spain and other hot countries. [t. Sp., g. L *sexta* sixth (hour), midday]

sieur (syœr), *n.* an old French title of rank or respect for a man, now chiefly in French legal use.

sieve (sĭv), *n., v.,* **sieved, sieving.** —*n.* **1.** an instrument with a meshed or perforated bottom, used for separating coarse from fine parts of loose matter, for straining liquids, etc., esp. one with a circular frame and fine meshes or perforations. **2.** one who cannot keep a secret. —*v.t.* **3.** to sift. [ME *sive,* OE *sife,* c. G *sieb*]

sieve cells, *Bot.* an elongated cell whose walls contain perforations (**sieve pores**) which are arranged in circumscribed areas (**sieve plates**) and which afford communication with similar adjacent cells.

sieve tube, *Bot.* **1.** a tubelike structure, part of the phloem, composed of sieve cells placed end to end. **2.** a single sieve cell.

sift (sĭft), *v.t.* **1.** to separate the coarse parts of (flour, ashes, etc.) with a sieve. **2.** to scatter by means of a sieve: *to sift sugar onto cake.* **3.** to separate by or as by a sieve. **4.** to examine closely. **5.** to question closely. [ME *siften,* OE *siftan* (der. *sife* SIEVE), c. G *sichten*] —**sift′er,** *n.*

sig., 1. signature. 2. signor.

sigh (sī), *v.i.* **1.** to let out one's breath audibly, as from sorrow, weariness, relief, etc. **2.** to yearn or long. **3.** to make a sound suggesting a sigh: *sighing wind.* —*v.t.* **4.** to express with a sigh. **5.** to lament with sighing. —*n.* **6.** act or sound of sighing. [ME *sighe(n),* back formation from *sihte* sighed, past tense of ME *siken, sichen,* OE *sīcan,* of unknown orig.] —**sigh′er,** *n.*

sight (sīt), *n.* **1.** the power or faculty of seeing; vision. **2.** the act or fact of seeing. **3.** range of vision: *in sight of land.* **4.** a view; glimpse. **5.** mental view or regard. **6.** something seen or to be seen; spectacle: *the sights of the town.* **7.** *Colloq.* something that looks unusual or distressing: *their clothes were a sight.* **8.** *Colloq.* a great display or number. **9.** an observation taken with a surveying or other instrument. **10.** a device on or used with a surveying instrument, a firearm, etc., serving to guide the eye. **11.** *Obs.* insight. **12.** at sight, a. as soon as one sees a thing. **b.** *Com.* on presentment: *a draft payable at sight.* **13.** on or upon sight, at sight. **14.** sight unseen, unseen: *to buy sight unseen.* **15.** know by sight, to know or recognize when seen. —*v.t.* **16.** to get sight of: *to sight a ship.* **17.** to take a sight or observation of, esp. with an instrument. **18.** to direct by a sight or sights, as a firearm. **19.** to provide with sights, or adjust the sights of, as a gun. —*v.i.* **20.** to take a sight, as in shooting. [ME; OE *gesiht* (c. G *gesicht*), *sihth,* der. *sēon* SEE¹]

sight draft, a draft payable upon presentation.

sight·less (sīt′lĭs), *adj.* **1.** blind. **2.** invisible.

sight·ly (sīt′lĭ), *adj.,* **-lier, -liest. 1.** pleasing to the sight. **2.** U.S. affording a fine view. —**sight′li·ness,** *n.*

sight-see·ing (sīt′sē′ĭng), *n.* **1.** act of seeing objects or places of interest. —*adj.* **2.** seeing or showing sights: *a sightseeing bus.* —**sight′se′er,** *n.*

sig·il (sĭj′ĭl), *n.* a seal; signet. [t. LL: m.s. *sigillum,* dim. of *signum* mark] —**sig·il·lar·y** (sĭj′ə lĕr′ĭ), *adj.*

Sig·is·mund (sĭj′ĭs mənd, sĭg′ĭs-; *Ger.* zē′gĭs mŏŏnt′), *n.* 1368–1437, Holy Roman emperor, 1411–37.

sig·ma (sĭg′mə), *n.* the eighteenth letter (Σ, σ, s = English S, s) of the Greek alphabet.

sig·mate (sĭg′mĭt, -māt), *adj.* having the form of the Greek sigma or the letter s.

sig·moid (sĭg′moid), *adj.* pertaining to the sigmoid flexure: *the sigmoid artery* (which supplies this flexure). Also, **sig·moi·dal.** [t. Gk.: m.s. *sigmoeidēs.* See -OID]

sigmoid flexure, 1. *Zool.* an S-shaped curve consisting of several parts. **2.** *Anat.* the last curve of the large intestine before terminating in the rectum.

sign (sīn), *n.* **1.** a token; indication. **2.** a conventional mark, figure, or symbol used technically instead of the word or words which it represents, as an abbreviation. **3.** an arbitrary or conventional symbol used in musical notation to indicate tonality, tempo, etc. **4.** a motion or gesture intended to express or convey an idea. **5.** an inscribed board, space, etc., serving for information, advertisement, etc., on a building, along a street, or the like. **6.** *Med.* the objective indications of a disease. **7.** a trace; vestige. **8.** *U.S.* the trace of wild animals, etc. **9.** an omen; portent. **10.** *Astron.* any of the twelve divisions of the zodiac, each denoted by the name of a constellation or its symbol, and each (because of the precession of the equinoxes) now containing the constellation west of the one from which it took its name. —*v.t.* **11.** to affix a signature to. **12.** to write as a signature: *to sign one's name.* **13.** to dispose of by affixing one's signature to a document (fol. by *away*, etc.). **14.** to engage by written agreement: *to sign a new player.* **15.** to direct by a sign. **16.** to indicate; betoken. **17.** to communicate by a sign. **18.** to mark with a sign, esp. the sign of the cross. —*v.i.* **19.** to write one's signature, as a token of agreement, obligation, receipt, etc. **20.** to make a sign or signal. **21.** to end radio broadcasting (fol. by *off*). **22.** to bind oneself to work by signature (fol. by *on*). [ME, t. OF: m. *signe*, t. L: m. *signum* mark, signal] —**Syn. 9.** indication, hint. SIGN, OMEN, PORTENT name that which gives evidence of a future event. SIGN is a general word for whatever gives evidence of an event, past, present, or future: *dark clouds are a sign of rain or snow.* An OMEN is an augury or warning of things to come; formerly depending upon religious practices or beliefs, it is used only of the future, in general, as good or bad: *birds of evil omen.* PORTENT, limited, like OMEN, to prophecy of the future, may be used of a specific event, usually a misfortune: *portents of war.*

sig·nal (sĭg′nəl), *n., adj., v.,* **-naled, -naling** or (*esp. Brit.*) **-nalled, -nalling.** —*n.* **1.** a gesture, act, light, etc., serving to warn, direct, command, or the like. **2.** anything agreed upon or understood as the occasion for concerted action. **3.** an exciting cause: *the signal for revolt.* **4.** a token; indication. **5.** *Radio, etc.* **a.** the impulses, waves, sounds, etc., transmitted or received. **b.** the wave which modulates the carrier wave. **6.** *Cards.* a play which reveals to one's partner a wish that he continue or discontinue the suit led. —*adj.* **7.** serving as a sign: *a signal flag.* **8.** conspicuous or notable: *a signal exploit.* —*v.t.* **9.** to make a signal to. **10.** to make known by a signal. —*v.i.* **11.** to make communication by a signal or signals. [ME, t. ML: s. *signāle*, prop. neut. adj., der. L *signum* SIGN] —**sig′nal·er**; *esp. Brit.* **sig′nal·ler**, *n.*

sig·nal·ize (sĭg′nə līz′), *v.t.,* **-ized, -izing. 1.** to make notable. **2.** to point out or indicate particularly. Also, *esp. Brit.,* **sig′nal·ise′.**

sig·nal·ly (sĭg′nə lĭ), *adv.* conspicuously; notably.

sig·nal·man (sĭg′nəl mən), *n., pl.* **-men.** a man employed in signaling, as on a railroad or in the army.

sig·nal·ment (sĭg′nəl mənt), *n.* a description of a person, as for police purposes.

sig·na·to·ry (sĭg′nə tôr′ĭ), *adj., n., pl.* **-ries.** —*adj.* **1.** that has signed, or has joined in signing, a document: *the signatory powers to a treaty.* —*n.* **2.** a signer, or one of the signers, of a document, as a treaty.

sig·na·ture (sĭg′nə chər), *n.* **1.** a person's name, or a mark representing it, as signed or written by himself or by deputy, as in subscribing a letter or other document. **2.** act of signing a document. **3.** *Music.* a sign or set of signs at the beginning of a staff to indicate the key or the time of a piece. **4.** *Radio.* a theme; the sound effect (song or musical arrangement) which regularly identifies a program. **5.** *Pharm.* that part of a prescription which gives the directions to be marked on the container of the medicine. **6.** *Bookbinding.* a printed sheet folded to form a section of a book. **7.** *Print.* **a.** a letter or other symbol generally placed by the printer at the foot of the first page of every section to guide the binder in arranging the sections in sequence. **b.** a sheet as thus marked. **c.** a printed sheet in multiples of four pages which, when folded as a unit, forms a section of a book or pamphlet. [t. ML: m.s. *signātūra*]

sign·board (sīn′bôrd′), *n.* a board bearing an inscription, advertisement, or the like.

sign·er (sī′nər), *n.* **1.** one who signs. **2.** one who writes his name, as in token of agreement, etc.

sig·net (sĭg′nĭt), *n.* **1.** a small seal, as in a finger ring. **2.** a small official seal. **3.** an impression made by or as if by a signet. —*v.t.* **4.** to stamp or mark with a signet. [ME, t. ML: s. *signetum,* der. L *signum* SIGN]

signet ring, a finger ring containing a signet.

sig·nif·i·cance (sĭg nĭf′ə kəns), *n.* **1.** importance; consequence. **2.** meaning; import. **3.** the quality of being significant or having a meaning. Also, **sig·nif′i·can·cy.** —**Syn. 2.** See **meaning.**

sig·nif·i·cant (sĭg nĭf′ə kənt), *adj.* **1.** important; of consequence. **2.** expressing a meaning; indicative of. **3.** having a special or covert meaning; suggestive. —*n.* **4.** *Archaic.* something significant; a sign. [t. L: s. *significans,* ppr., signifying] —**sig·nif′i·cant·ly,** *adv.* —**Syn. 2.** See **expressive.**

sig·ni·fi·ca·tion (sĭg′nə fə kā′shən), *n.* **1.** meaning; import; sense. **2.** act or fact of signifying; indication.

sig·nif·i·ca·tive (sĭg nĭf′ə kā′tĭv), *adj.* **1.** serving to signify. **2.** significant; suggestive.

sig·ni·fy (sĭg′nə fī′), *v.,* **-fied, -fying.** —*v.t.* **1.** to make known by signs, speech, or action. **2.** to be a sign of; mean; portend. —*v.i.* **3.** to be of importance or consequence. [ME *signefie(n),* t. L: m. *significāre* show by signs] —**sig′ni·fi′er,** *n.* —**Syn. 2.** represent, indicate, denote.

sign language, a substitute for speech using gestures, as the methods used by deaf-mutes, or by American Indians of the Plains for intertribal communication.

sign manual, an autograph signature, esp. that of a sovereign or official on a public document.

si·gnor (sē′nyôr), *n. Italian.* **1.** Mr.; sir. **2.** a gentleman; an aristocrat.

si·gno·ra (sē nyô′rä), *n., pl.* **-re** (-rĕ). *Italian.* **1.** Mrs.; Madam. **2.** lady; gentlewoman. [It., fem., der. *signore.* See SIGNORE]

si·gno·re (sē nyô′rĕ), *n., pl.* **-ri** (-rĕ). *Italian.* **1.** gentleman. **2.** Mr.; sir. [It., g. L *senior* SENIOR]

si·gno·ri·na (sē′nyô rē′nä), *n., pl.* **-ne** (-nĕ). *Italian.* **1.** Miss. **2.** young lady. [It., dim. of *signora* SIGNORA]

si·gno·ri·no (sē′nyô rē′nô), *n., pl.* **-ni** (-nĕ). *Italian.* young sir or master (used as a title of respect). [It., dim. of *signore* SIGNOR]

si·gno·ry (sē′nyə rĭ), *n., pl.* **-ries.** seigniory.

sign·post (sīn′pōst′), *n.* a post bearing a sign for information or guidance.

Sigs·bee (sĭgz′bĭ), *n.* **Charles Dwight,** 1845–1923, U.S. naval officer: captain of the *Maine* in 1898.

Sig·urd (sĭg′ərd; *Ger.* zē′gŏŏrt), *n.* (in the northern Volsunga Saga) the Siegfried of the Nibelungenlied.

Si·kan·dar·a·bad (sĭ kŭn′drä bäd′), *n.* Secunderabad.

Si·kang (shē′käng′), *n.* a province in W China: formed out of parts of Szechwan and E Tibet. 3,381,064 pop. (1953); 164,891 sq. mi. *Cap.:* Tatsienlu.

Sikh (sēk), *n.* **1.** a member of a religious sect founded near Lahore in NW India by a Hindu reformer. —*adj.* **2.** of or pertaining to the Sikhs. [t. Hind.: lit., disciple]

Sikh·ism (sēk′ĭzəm), *n.* the religious system and practices of the Sikhs. Starting in the 16th century as an attempt to effect a peaceful harmony of Hinduism and Mohammedanism in India, Sikhism has branched off into a new independent religion.

Si·kiang (sē′kyäng′, shē′jyäng′), *n.* Si.

Sik·kim (sĭk′ĭm), *n.* a state in NE India, in the Himalayas between Nepal and Bhutan. 137,158 pop. (1951); 2745 sq. mi. *Cap.:* Gangtok.

Si·kor·sky (sĭ kôr′skĭ), *n.* **Igor** (ē′gôr′y), born 1889, U.S. aeronautical engineer, born in Russia.

si·lage (sī′lĭj), *n.* fodder preserved in a silo; ensilage. [f. SILO + -AGE, modeled on ENSILAGE]

Si·las Mar·ner (sī′ləs mär′nər), a novel (1861) by George Eliot.

si·le·na·ceous (sī′lə nā′shəs), *adj.* caryophyllaceous.

si·lence (sī′ləns), *n., v.,* **-lenced, -lencing,** *interj.* —*n.* **1.** absence of any sound or noise; stillness. **2.** the state or fact of being silent; muteness. **3.** omission of mention: *to pass over a matter in silence.* **4.** oblivion. **5.** secrecy. —*v.t.* **6.** to put or bring to silence; still. **7.** to put to rest (doubts, etc.); quiet. **8.** *Mil.* to still (enemy guns, etc.), as by a more effective fire. —*interj.* **9.** be silent! [ME, t. OF, t. L: m.s. *silentium*]

si·lenc·er (sī′lən sər), *n.* **1.** one who or that which silences. **2.** a device for deadening the report of a firearm. **3.** *Chiefly Brit.* the muffler on an internal-combustion engine.

si·lent (sī′lənt), *adj.* **1.** making no sound; quiet; still. **2.** refraining from speech. **3.** speechless; mute. **4.** taciturn; reticent. **5.** characterized by absence of speech or sound: *a silent prayer.* **6.** tacit: *a silent assent.* **7.** omitting mention of something, as in a narrative. **8.** inactive or quiescent, as a volcano. **9.** not sounded or pronounced: *a silent letter,* such as "b" in "doubt." [t. L: s. *silens,* ppr., being silent] —**si′lent·ly,** *adv.* —**si′lent·ness,** *n.* —**Syn. 1.** See **still¹.** —**Ant. 1.** noisy. **2.** talkative.

silent partner, a partner taking no active part in the conduct of a business, or not openly announced as a partner.

Si·le·nus (sī lē′nəs), *n.* **1.** *Gk. Myth.* the foster father of Bacchus, and leader of the satyrs. **2.** (*l.c.*) a satyr.

Si·le·sia (sī lē′shə, sī-), *n.* a region in central Europe: formerly divided between Germany (the largest portion), Poland, and Czechoslovakia; by provision of the Potsdam agreement (1945) the greater part of German Silesia is now in Poland; rich deposits of coal, iron, and other minerals. German, **Schlesien.** Polish, **Slask.** Czech, **Slezsko.** —**Si·le′sian,** *adj., n.*

si·le·sia (sī lē′shə, sī-), *n.* a light-weight, smooth-finish, twilled, cotton fabric, used for linings, originally made in Silesia.

si·lex (sī′lĕks), *n.* **1.** silica. **2.** heat-resistant glass. **3.** (*cap.*) a trademark for a coffee maker of this material. [t. L: flint]

sil·hou·ette (sĭl′ŏŏĕt′), *n., v.,* **-etted, -etting.** —*n.* **1.** an outline drawing, uniformly filled in with black, like a shadow. **2.** a dark image outlined against a lighter background. —*v.t.* **3.** to show in, or as in, a silhouette. [named after Étienne de *Silhouette* (1709–1767), French author and politician]

Silhouette

silic-, a word element meaning "flint," "silica," "silicon," as in *silicide.* Also, **silici-, silico-.** [comb. form repr. L *silex* flint]

sil·i·ca (sĭl′ə kə), *n.* silicon dioxide, SiO_2, appearing as quartz, sand flint, and agate. [t.NL, der. L *silex* flint]

silica gel, *Chem.* a highly absorbent gelatinous form of silica.

sil·i·cate (sĭl′ə kĭt, -kāt′), *n. Chem.* any salt derived from the silicic acids or from silica.

si·li·ceous (sĭ lĭsh′əs), *adj.* 1. containing, consisting of, or resembling silica. 2. growing in soil rich in silica. Also, **si·li·cious.** [t. L: m. *siliceus* of flint or limestone]

si·lic·ic (sĭ lĭs′ĭk), *adj. Chem.* 1. containing silicon. 2. of or pertaining to silica or acids derived from it.

silicic acid, any of certain acids formed when alkaline silicates are treated with acids. Amorphous gelatinous masses, they dissociate readily into silica and water.

sil·i·cide (sĭl′ə sīd′, -sĭd), *n. Chem.* a compound, usually of two elements only, one of which is silicon.

si·lic·i·fied wood (sĭ lĭs′ə fīd′), wood which has been changed into quartz by a replacement of the cellular structure of the wood by siliceous waters.

si·lic·i·fy (sĭ lĭs′ə fī′), *v.t., v.i.,* -**fied,** -**fying.** to convert or be converted into silica. —**si·lic·i·fi·ca′tion,** *n.*

si·li·ci·um (sĭ lĭsh′Y əm, sĭ lĭs′-), *n.* earlier name for silicon. [NL, f. *silic-* SILIC- + *-ium* -IUM]

sil·i·cle (sĭl′ə kəl), *n. Bot.* a short silique. [t. L: m. *silicula*, dim. of *siliqua* pod]

silico-, var. of **silic-,** before vowels.

sil·i·con (sĭl′ə kən), *n. Chem.* a nonmetallic element, having amorphous and crystalline forms, occurring in the combined state in minerals and rocks and constituting more than one fourth of the earth's crust; used in steelmaking, etc. Symbol: Si; at. wt.: 28.06; at. no.: 14; sp. gr.: 2.4 at 20°C. [f. SILIC- + *-on*, modeled on BORON, CARBON]

sil·i·cone (sĭl′ə kōn′), *n. Chem.* any of a number of compounds made by substituting silicon for carbon in an organic substance, and characterized by greater stability and resistance to extremes of temperature than the parent substance. Among the silicones are oils, greases, resins, and a synthetic rubber.

sil·i·co·sis (sĭl′ə kō′sĭs), *n. Pathol.* a disease of the lungs due to inhaling siliceous particles, as by stonecutters. [f. SILIC- + -OSIS]

sil·ic·u·lose (sĭ lĭk′yə lōs′), *adj. Bot.* 1. bearing silicles. 2. having the form or appearance of a silicle.

si·lique (sĭ lēk′, -lĭk′), *n. Bot.* the long two-valved seed vessel or pod of cruciferous plants. [t. F, or t. L: m. *siliqua* pod]

sil·i·quose (sĭl′ə kwōs′), *adj.* 1. bearing siliques. 2. resembling a silique or silicle. Also, **sil·i·quous** (sĭl′ə kwəs).

Silique
A. Jointed charlock, *Raphanus raphanistrum;* B, Spring cress, *Cardamine bulbosa;* C, Mustard, *Hexiophila crithmifolia*

silk (sĭlk), *n.* 1. the fine, soft, lustrous fiber obtained from the cocoon of the silkworm. 2. thread made of this fiber. 3. cloth made of this fiber. 4. a garment of this cloth. 5. the gown of such material, worn distinctively by a king's or queen's counsel at the English bar. 6. any fiber or filamentous matter resembling silk. 7. the hairlike styles on an ear of maize. —*adj.* 8. made of silk. 9. resembling silk; silky. 10. of or pertaining to silk. —*v.i.* 11. *U.S.* (of corn) to be in the course of forming silk. [ME; OE *sioloc, seoloc* (c. Icel. *silki*), t. Baltic or Slavic. Cf. Prussian *silkas*, Russian *shëlk*]

silk·a·line (sĭl′kə lēn′), *n.* a soft, thin cotton fabric with a smooth finish, used for curtains, etc.

silk cotton, the silky covering of the seeds of certain tropical trees of the family *Bombacaceae*, used for stuffing cushions, etc. See **kapok.**

silk-cotton tree, any of several trees of the family *Bombacaceae*, having seeds surrounded by silk cotton, esp. *Ceiba pentandra*, from which kapok is obtained.

silk·en (sĭl′kən), *adj.* 1. made of silk. 2. like silk. 3. smooth; soft. 4. clad in silk. 5. elegant; luxurious.

silk-screen (sĭlk′skrēn′), *n.* a stencil process using fine cloths that have been painted with an impermeable coating except in areas where color is to be forced through onto paper, etc.

silk-stock·ing (sĭlk′stŏk′ĭng), *adj.* 1. wearing silk stockings; luxurious; aristocratic. —*n.* 2. a person of the luxurious class; an aristocrat.

silk·weed (sĭlk′wēd′), *n.* any milkweed of the family *Asclepiadaceae*, so called from the silky down in the pod.

silk·worm (sĭlk′wûrm′), *n.* the caterpillar of any moth of the family *Bombycidae*, which spins a fine, soft filament (silk) to form a cocoon, in which it is enclosed while in the pupal stage, esp. the Chinese silkworm, *Bombyx mori.* [ME *sylkewyrme*, OE *seolcwyrm.* See SILK, WORM]

Silkworm and cocoon. *Bombyx mori*

silk·y (sĭl′kY), *adj.,* **silkier, silkiest.** 1. of or like silk; lustrous; smooth. 2. *Bot.* covered with fine, soft, closely set hairs, as a leaf. —**silk′i·ly,** *adv.* —**silk′i·ness,** *n.*

sill (sĭl), *n.* 1. a horizontal timber, block, or the like, serving as a foundation of a wall, house, etc. 2. the horizontal piece or member beneath a window, door, or other opening. 3. *Geol.* a tabular body of intrusive igneous rock, ordinarily between beds of sedimentary rocks or layers of volcanic ejecta. [ME *sille*, OE *syl, syll(e)*, c. LG *süll*; akin to G *schwelle*]

sil·la·bub (sĭl′ə bŭb′), *n.* a dish made of milk or cream mixed with wine, cider, or the like, so as to form a curd, and often sweetened and flavored. Also, **syllabub.**

Sil·lan·pää (sĭl′län pâ′), *n.* **Frans Eemil** (fräns ĕ′- mĭl), 1888–1964, Finnish author.

sil·ler (sĭl′ər), *n. Scot.* silver.

sil·ly (sĭl′Y), *adj.,* -**lier,** -**liest,** *n., pl.* -**lies.** —*adj.* 1. lacking good sense; foolish; stupid. 2. absurd or ridiculous. 3. *Colloq.* stunned. 4. *Archaic.* simpleminded. 5. *Obs.* simple; homely. 6. *Obs.* weak; helpless. —*n.* 7. *Colloq.* a silly person. [var. of earlier *seely* happy, helpless, silly, ME *seli*, OE *sēlig* (Anglian), *sǣlig* (c. G *selig*) f. *sēl, sǣl* happiness + *-ig* -Y¹] —**sil′li·ly,** *adv.* —**sil′li·ness,** *n.* —**Syn.** 1. See **foolish.** —**Ant.** 1. sensible.

si·lo (sī′lō), *n., pl.* -**los,** *v.,* -**loed,** -**loing.** —*n.* 1. an airproof tower-like structure, in which fermenting green fodder is preserved for future use as silage. 2. a pit or underground watertight space for storing grain, green feeds, etc. —*v.t.* 3. to put into or preserve in a silo. [t. Sp., g. L *sīrus*, t. Gk.: m. *sīrós* pit to keep grain in]

Si·lo·am (sī lō′əm, sī-), *n. Bible.* a pool at Jerusalem. John 9:7.

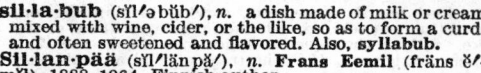

Silo (def. 1)

silt (sĭlt), *n.* 1. earthy matter, fine sand, or the like, carried by moving or running water and deposited as a sediment. —*v.i.* 2. to become filled or choked up with silt. —*v.t.* 3. to fill or choke up with silt. [ME *silte.* Cf. OE *unsylt* unsalted, G *sülze* saltpan] —**silt′y,** *adj.*

si·lun·dum (sĭ lŭn′dəm), *n.* silicon carbide, SiC, a very hard, insoluble, crystalline compound, used as an abrasive and in objects exposed to high temperature, as electrical resistors. [f. SILICON and CARBORUNDUM]

Si·lu·res (sĭl′yə rēz′), *n.pl.* an ancient British people who lived chiefly in southeastern Wales at the time of the Roman conquest and were in active resistance to it about A.D. 48.

Si·lu·ri·an (sĭ lŏŏr′Y ən, sī-), *adj.* 1. of or pertaining to the Silures or their country. 2. *Stratig.* pertaining to an early Paleozoic geological period or system of rocks which corresponds to **Upper Silurian** of usage before 1879. —*n.* 3. *Stratig.* the period or system following Ordovician and preceding Devonian.

si·lu·rid (sĭ lŏŏr′ĭd, sī-), *n.* 1. any of the *Siluridae*, or catfish family, comprising chiefly fresh-water fishes with long barbels and without true scales, and including many species used for food. —*adj.* 2. belonging to or pertaining to the *Siluridae*. Also, **si·lu·roid** (sĭ lŏŏr′oid, sī-). [t. NL: s. *Silūridae*, der. L *silūrus* a river fish, t. Gk.: m. *sílouros*]

sil·va (sĭl′və), *n.* 1. the forest trees of a particular area. 2. a descriptive flora of forest trees. Also, **sylva.** [t. L]

sil·van (sĭl′vən), *adj., n.* sylvan. [t. L: s. *silvānus*, der. *silva* wood. See -AN]

Sil·va·nus (sĭl vā′nəs), *n.* a Roman god of forests and fields.

sil·ver (sĭl′vər), *n.* 1. *Chem.* a white ductile metallic element, used for making mirrors, coins, ornaments, table utensils, etc. Symbol: Ag (for argentum); at. wt.: 107.88; at. no.: 47; sp. gr.: 10.5 at 20°C. 2. coin made of this metal; money. 3. silverware; table articles made of or plated with silver. 4. something resembling this metal in color, luster, etc. 5. a lustrous grayish white or whitish gray; color of metallic silver. 6. *U.S. Photog.* silver nitrate or some other silver salt. —*adj.* 7. consisting or made of silver; plated with silver. 8. of or pertaining to silver. 9. producing or yielding silver. 10. resembling silver: *the silver waves.* 11. clear and soft: *silver sounds.* 12. eloquent; persuasive: *a silver tongue.* 13. urging the use of silver as a currency standard. 14. indicating the 25th event of a series, as a wedding anniversary. —*v.t.* 15. to coat with silver or some silverlike substance. 16. to give a silvery color to. —*v.i.* 17. to become a silvery color. [ME; OE *siolfor*, c. G *silber*] —**sil′ver·er,** *n.* —**sil′ver-like′,** *adj.*

silver age, the second of the mythological ages of mankind, inferior to the first or golden age, and a period of luxury and impiety.

silver bell, any of the handsome North American shrubs or small trees, with white bell-shaped flowers, constituting the styracaceous genus *Halesia*. Also, **sil′ver-bell′** tree.

sil·ver·ber·ry (sĭl′vər bĕr′Y), *n., pl.* -**ries.** a shrub, *Elaeagnus argentea*, of the northern central part of North America, having silvery leaves and flowers and silvery drupelike edible fruits.

silver bromide, a light-sensitive compound, AgBr, which is of basic importance in photography. It is obtained from the reaction of a bromide with a silver salt.

silver certificate. See **certificate** (def. 4).

silver chloride, a light-sensitive compound, AgCl, used in sensitizing photographic paper.

sil·ver·fish (sĭl′vər fĭsh′), *n., pl.* -**fishes,** (esp. collectively) -**fish.** 1. a white or silvery goldfish, *Carassius auratus.* 2. any of various other silvery fishes, as the tarpon, silversides, or shiner. 3. any of certain small wingless thysanuran insects (genus *Lepisma*) damaging to books, wallpaper, etc.

---

silver fox, the common red fox, *Vulpes fulva,* in a melanistic variation, in which the pelage is black, overlaid with silver-gray ends of the longer hairs.

sil·ver·ing (sĭl′vər ĭng), *n.* **1.** the act or process of coating with silver or a substance resembling silver. **2.** the coating thus applied.

sil·ver·ly (sĭl′vər lĭ), *adv.* with a silvery appearance or sound.

sil·vern (sĭl′vərn), *adj. Archaic.* of or like silver.

silver nitrate, *Chem.* a salt, AgNO₃, obtained by treating silver with nitric acid, and appearing in commerce as colorless crystals or white fused or molded masses, used in photography, medicine, etc.

sil·ver·sides (sĭl′vər sīdz′), *n., pl.* **-sides.** any of the small fishes, with a silvery stripe along the sides, which constitute the family *Atherinidae,* as *Menidia menidia,* a species abundant along the Atlantic coast of the U.S.

sil·ver·smith (sĭl′vər smĭth′), *n.* one who makes articles of silver.

silver standard, a monetary system with silver of specified weight and fineness as the unit of value.

Silver Star, *U.S. Army.* a bronze star with a small silver star at the center, awarded to a soldier who has been cited in orders for gallantry in action, when the citation does not warrant the award of a Medal of Honor or the Distinguished Service Cross.

sil·ver-tongued (sĭl′vər tŭngd′), *adj.* eloquent.

sil·ver·ware (sĭl′vər wâr′), *n.* articles, esp. for table use, made of silver.

silver wedding, the 25th anniversary of a wedding.

sil·ver·weed (sĭl′vər wēd′), *n.* **1.** a rosaceous plant, *Potentilla anserina,* with pinnate leaves having on the underside a silvery pubescence. **2.** a short-stemmed potentilla, *P. argentea,* of Europe and North America, having similar leaves.

sil·ver·y (sĭl′və rĭ), *adj.* **1.** resembling silver; of a lustrous grayish-white color. **2.** having a clear, ringing sound like that of silver. **3.** containing or covered with silver. **—sil′ver·i·ness,** *n.*

sil·vi·cul·ture (sĭl′və kŭl′chər), *n.* the cultivation of forest trees; forestry. Also, **sylviculture.** [f. L *silvi-* (comb. form of *silva* wood) + CULTURE] **—sil′vi·cul′tur·al,** *adj.* **—sil′vi·cul′tur·ist,** *n.*

s'il vous plaît (sēl vōō plĕ′), *French.* please.

si·mar (sĭ mär′), *n.* a loose, light jacket or robe worn by women, fashionable in 17th and 18th centuries. Also, **cymar.** [t. F: m. *simarre,* t. It.: m. *zimarra* robe, cassock, ult. t. Ar.: m. *sammūr* Siberian weasel]

sim·a·rou·ba (sĭm′ə rōō′bə), *n.* **1.** any of the trees of the simaroubaceous genus *Simaruba,* of tropical America, with pinnate leaves, a drupaceous fruit, and a root whose bark contains a tonic principle. **2.** the bark. [t. Carib]

sim·a·rou·ba·ceous (sĭm′ə rōō bā′shəs), *adj.* belonging to the *Simarubaceae,* a family of trees and shrubs, mostly tropical, which includes the mountain damson, paradise tree, ailanthus, quassia, etc.

Sim·e·on (sĭm′ĭ ən), *n.* a devout man of Jerusalem who, recognizing the infant Jesus as the Christ, spoke the Nunc Dimittis. Luke 2:25–35.

Sim·fe·ro·pol (sĭm fĕ rô′pôl′y), *n.* a city in the SW Soviet Union. 159,000 (est. 1956).

Sim·hath To·rah (sĭm кнäth′ tô rä′; sĭm′кнäs tôr′ä), the Jewish holiday of Rejoicing over the Law, on the ninth day of Tabernacles. Also, **Sim·chas′ To·rah′.**

sim·i·an (sĭm′ĭ ən), *adj.* **1.** of or pertaining to an ape or monkey. **2.** characteristic of apes or monkeys. **—n.** **3.** an ape or monkey. [f. s. L *simia* ape + -AN]

sim·i·lar (sĭm′ə lər), *adj.* **1.** having likeness or resemblance, esp. in a general way. **2.** *Geom.* (of figures) having the same shape; having corresponding sides proportional and corresponding angles equal. [f. s. L *similis* like + -AR¹] **—sim′i·lar·ly,** *adv.* **—Syn. 1.** See **same.**

sim·i·lar·i·ty (sĭm′ə lǎr′ə tĭ), *n., pl.* **-ties.** **1.** state of being similar; likeness. **2.** a point of resemblance. **—Syn. 1.** See **resemblance.**

sim·i·le (sĭm′ə lē′), *n.* **1.** *Rhet.* a figure of speech directly expressing a resemblance, in one or more points, of one thing to another. **2.** an instance of this figure, or a use of words exemplifying it. [ME, t. L, neut. of *similis* like]

si·mil·i·tude (sĭ mĭl′ə tūd′, -tōōd′), *n.* **1.** likeness; resemblance. **2.** a person or thing that is the like, match, or counterpart of another. **3.** semblance; image. **4.** a likeness or comparison; a parable or allegory. [ME, t. L: m. *similitūdo*]

sim·i·ous (sĭm′ĭ əs), *adj.* simian.

sim·i·tar (sĭm′ə tər), *n.* scimitar.

Sim·la (sĭm′lə), *n.* a city in N India, capital of Himachal Pradesh: the summer capital of India. 46,150 (1951).

sim·mer (sĭm′ər), *v.i.* **1.** to continue in a state approaching boiling. **2.** to make a gentle murmuring sound, as liquids just below the boiling point. **3.** to continue in a state of subdued activity, excitement, etc. **—v.t. 4.** to keep in a state approaching boiling. **—n. 5.** state or process of simmering. [earlier *simber,* ME *simper;* orig. unknown] **—Syn. 3.** See **boil¹.**

Simms (sĭmz), *n.* William Gilmore, 1806–70, U.S. author.

si·mo·le·on (sə mō′lĭ ən), *n. U.S. Slang.* a dollar.

Si·mon (sī′mən), *n.* **1.** Also, **Simon Peter,** the original name of Peter. Mark 3:16. **2.** a brother or relative of Jesus. Mark 6:3. **3.** a tanner of Joppa at whose house St. Peter resided. Acts 10:6. **4.** Simon, surnamed Magus, a sorcerer of Samaria. Acts 8:9–24.

Si·mon (sī′mən), *n.* **Sir John (Allsebrook),** born 1873, British statesman and lawyer.

si·mo·ni·ac (sī mō′nĭ ăk′), *n.* one who practices simony. **—si·mo·ni·a·cal** (sī′mə nī′ə kəl, sĭm′ə-), *adj.* **—si′mo·ni·a·cal·ly,** *adv.*

Si·mon·i·des (sī mŏn′ə dēz′), *n.* 556?–468? B.C., Greek lyric poet. Also, **Simonides of Ce·os** (sē′ŏs).

Si·mon Le·gree (sī′mən lĭ grē′), **1.** the brutal slave dealer in *Uncle Tom's Cabin* by Harriet Beecher Stowe. **2.** any harsh, merciless master.

si·mon-pure (sī′mən pyŏōr′), *adj.* real; genuine. [from *Simon Pure,* a Quaker in Mrs. Centlivre's comedy, "A Bold Stroke for a Wife" (1718), who is impersonated by one of the other characters]

si·mo·ny (sī′mə nĭ, sĭm′ə-), *n.* **1.** making profit out of sacred things. **2.** the sin of buying or selling ecclesiastical preferments, benefices, etc. Also, **si·mo·nism.** [ME *symonie,* t. ML: m. *simōnia,* der. SIMON MAGUS. See Acts 8:18–19] **—si′mon·ist,** *n.*

si·moom (sī mōōm′), *n.* a hot, suffocating sand-laden wind of the deserts of Arabia, Syria, Africa, etc. Also, **si·moon** (sī mōōn′). [t. Ar.: m. *semūm,* der. *samm* poison]

simp (sĭmp), *n. U.S. Slang.* a fool. [for SIMPLETON]

sim·per (sĭm′pər), *v.i.* **1.** to smile in a silly, self-conscious way. **—v.t. 2.** to say with a simper. **—n. 3.** a silly, self-conscious smile. [orig. uncert. Cf. G *zimper* affected] **—sim′per·er,** *n.* **—sim′per·ing·ly,** *adv.*

sim·ple (sĭm′pəl), *adj.,* **-pler, -plest,** *n.* **—adj. 1.** easy to understand, deal with, use, etc.: *a simple matter, simple tools.* **2.** not elaborate or artificial: *a simple style.* **3.** not ornate or luxurious. **4.** unaffected; unassuming. **5.** not complex or complicated: *a simple design.* **6.** occurring or considered alone; mere; bare: *the simple truth or fact.* **7.** sincere; innocent. **8.** common or ordinary: *a simple soldier.* **9.** plain; unpretentious. **10.** humble or lowly (often opposed to *gentle*). **11.** unimportant or insignificant. **12.** unlearned; ignorant. **13.** lacking mental acuteness or sense. **14.** *Chem.* **a.** composed of but one substance or element: *a simple substance.* **b.** not mixed. **15.** *Bot.* not divided into parts: *a simple leaf* (one having only a single blade), *a simple stem* (one that does not branch). **16.** *Zool.* not compound: *a simple ascidian.* **17.** *Music.* single; uncompounded or without overtones: *simple tone.* **—n. 18.** an ignorant or foolish person. **19.** something simple, unmixed, or uncompounded. **20.** *Archaic.* an herb or plant used for medicinal purposes. **21.** *Archaic.* a person of humble condition. [ME, t. OF, t. L: m. *simplus* or *simplex*] **—sim′ple·ness,** *n.*

—Syn. 9. SIMPLE, HOMELY (HOMEY), PLAIN imply absence of adornment or embellishment. That which is SIMPLE is not elaborate or complex: *a simple type of dress* In the United States, HOMELY usually suggests absence of natural beauty: *an unattractive child almost homely enough to be called ugly.* In England, the word suggests a wholesome simplicity without artificial refinement or elegance; since it characterizes that which is comfortable and attractive, it is equivalent to HOMEY: *a homely cottage.* That which is PLAIN has little or no adornment: *expensive but plain clothing.*

simple fraction, a ratio of two whole numbers.

simple fruit, a fruit formed from one pistil.

simple interest, interest which is not compounded, that is, payable only on the principal amount of a debt.

simple machines, the six (sometimes more) elementary mechanisms: the lever, wheel and axle, pulley, screw, inclined plane, and wedge.

sim·ple-mind·ed (sĭm′pəl mīn′dĭd), *adj.* **1.** artless; unsophisticated. **2.** lacking in mental acuteness or sense. **3.** mentally deficient. **—sim′ple-mind′ed·ly,** *adv.* **—sim′ple-mind′ed·ness,** *n.*

simple sentence, a sentence with only one clause.

simple time, *Music.* rhythm characterized by two or three beats or pulses to a measure.

sim·ple·ton (sĭm′pəl tən), *n.* a silly person; fool. [f. SIMPLE + -TON]

sim·plex (sĭm′plĕks), *adj.* simple; consisting of or characterized by a single element, action, or the like: *a simplex circuit* (in which one telephone call and one telegraph message are transmitted simultaneously over a single pair of wires). [t. L]

sim·pli·ci·den·tate (sĭm′plə sĭ dĕn′tāt), *adj.* belonging or pertaining to the *Simplicidentata,* formerly regarded as a suborder or division of rodents (including all except the hares, rabbits, and pikas) in which there is only one pair of upper incisor teeth. [f. *simplici-* (comb. form of L *simplex* simple) + DENTATE]

sim·plic·i·ty (sĭm plĭs′ə tĭ), *n., pl.* **-ties. 1.** state or quality of being simple. **2.** freedom from complexity, intricacy, or division into parts. **3.** absence of luxury, pretentiousness, ornament, etc.; plainness. **4.** naturalness; sincerity; artlessness. **5.** lack of mental acuteness or shrewdness. [ME *symplicite,* t. L: m.s. *simplicitas*]

sim·pli·fy (sĭm′plə fī′), *v.t.,* **-fied, -fying.** to make less complex or complicated; make plainer or easier. [t. F: m.s. *simplifier,* t. ML: m. *simplificāre.* See -FY] **—sim′pli·fi·ca′tion,** *n.* **—sim′pli·fi′er,** *n.*

Sim·plon (sĭm′plŏn; Fr. săn plôn′), *n.* **1.** a mountain pass in S Switzerland, in the Lepontine Alps: crossed by a road constructed by Napoleon. 6592 ft. high. **2.** a tunnel between Switzerland and Italy, NE of Simplon Pass: the longest tunnel in the world. 12¼ mi. long.

sim·ply (sĭm′plĭ), *adv.* **1.** in a simple manner. **2.** plainly; unaffectedly. **3.** artlessly. **4.** merely; only. **5.** unwisely; foolishly. **6.** absolutely: *simply irresistible.* [ME *simpleliche,* f. SIMPLE + *-liche* -LY]

Sims (sĭmz), *n.* **William Sowden** (sou′dən), 1858–1936, U.S. admiral, born in Canada.

sim·u·la·crum (sĭm′yə lā′krəm), *n., pl.* **-cra** (-krə). **1.** a mere, faint, or unreal semblance. **2.** image. [t. L]

sim·u·lar (sĭm′yə lər), *n.* **1.** one who or that which simulates. —*adj.* **2.** simulated; false. **3.** simulative (fol. by *of*). [f. SIMUL(ATE) + -AR³]

sim·u·late (*v.* sĭm′yə lāt′; *adj.* sĭm′yə lĭt, -lāt′), *v.,* **-lated, -lating,** *adj.* —*v.t.* **1.** to make a pretense of. **2.** to assume or have the appearance of. —*adj.* **3.** simulated. [t. L: m.s. *simulātus,* pp., made like] —**sim·u·la′tive,** *adj.* —**sim·u·la′tive·ly,** *adv.* —**sim′u·la·tor,** *n.*

sim·u·la·tion (sĭm′yə lā′shən), *n.* **1.** pretending; feigning. **2.** assumption of a particular appearance or form. **3.** *Psychiatry.* the conscious attempt to imitate some mental or physical disorder to escape punishment or to gain some desirable objective.

si·mul·cast (sī′məl kăst′, -käst′), *n.* a program broadcast simultaneously on radio and TV. [short for SIMUL-(TANEOUS BROAD)CAST] —**si′mul·cast′,** *v.t.*

si·mul·ta·ne·ous (sī′məl tā′nĭ əs, sĭm′əl-), *adj.* existing, occurring, or operating at the same time: *simultaneous movements.* [t. ML: m. *simultāneus* simulated; meaning altered by assoc. with L *momentāneus* and L *simul* at the same time as] —**si′mul·ta·ne·ous·ly,** *adv.* —**si′mul·ta′ne·ous·ness,** **si·mul·ta·ne·i·ty** (sī′məl tə nē′ə tĭ, sĭm′əl-), *n.*

simultaneous equations, *Alg.* equations which must be satisfied simultaneously by the same values of the unknowns.

sin (sĭn), *n., v.,* **sinned, sinning.** —*n.* **1.** transgression of divine law. **2.** an act regarded as such transgression, or any violation, esp. a willful or deliberate one of some religious or moral principle. **3.** any serious transgression or offense. —*v.i.* **4.** to do a sinful act. **5.** to offend against a principle, standard, etc. —*v.t.* **6.** to do or perform sinfully. **7.** to bring, drive, etc., by sinning. [ME; OE *syn(n),* akin to D and G *sünde* sin, L *sons* guilty] —Syn. **2.** See **crime.**

Si·nai (sī′nī, sī′nī ī′), *n.* **1.** a peninsula in NE Egypt at the N end of the Red Sea between the Gulfs of Suez and Aqaba. ab. 230 mi. long. **2. Mount,** the mountain, of uncertain identity, from which the law was given to Moses. Ex. 19. —**Si·na·it·ic** (sī′nī ĭt′ĭk), *adj.*

Si·na·lo·a (sē′nä lō′ä), *n.* a state in W Mexico, bordering on the Gulf of California. 669,117 pop. (est. 1952); 22,582 sq. mi. *Cap.:* Culiacán.

sin·a·pism (sĭn′ə pĭz′əm), *n. Med.* a mustard plaster. [t. L: s. *sināpismus,* t. Gk.: m. *sināpismós*]

Sin·ar·quist (sĭn′är kwĭst), *n.* a member or advocate of a fascist movement organized in Mexico about 1937. —**Sin′ar·quism,** *n.* —**Sin′ar·quis′tic,** *adj.*

Sin·bad (sĭn′băd), *n.* Sindbad.

since (sĭns), *adv.* **1.** from then till now (often preceded by *ever*). **2.** between a particular past time and the present; subsequently: *he at first refused, but has since consented.* **3.** ago; before now: *long since.* —*prep.* **4.** continuously from or counting from: *since noon.* **5.** between (a past time or event) and the present: *changes since the war.* —*conj.* **6.** in the period following the time when: *he has written once since he left.* **7.** continuously from or counting from the time when: *busy since he came.* **8.** because; inasmuch as. [ME *syns,* *synnes,* f. *syn,* *sine* (contracted var. of *sithen,* OE *siththan* then) + adv. suffix *-es*] —Syn. **8.** See **because.**

sin·cere (sĭn sĭr′), *adj.,* **-cerer, -cerest. 1.** free from any element of deceit, dissimulation, or duplicity. **2.** *Archaic.* pure; unmixed. **3.** *Obs.* sound; unimpaired. [t. L: m.s. *sincērus*] —**sin·cere′ly,** *adv.* —**sin·cere′ness,** *n.* —Syn. **1.** candid, honest. See **earnest.**

sin·cer·i·ty (sĭn sĕr′ə tĭ), *n., pl.* **-ties.** freedom from deceit, dissimulation, or duplicity; honesty. [t. L: m.s. *sincēritas*] —Syn. See **honor.**

sin·ci·put (sĭn′sə pŭt′), *n. Anat.* **1.** the forepart of the skull. Cf. *occiput.* **2.** the upper part of the skull. [L: half a head] —**sin·cip·i·tal** (sĭn sĭp′ə təl), *adj.*

Sin·clair (sĭn klâr′), *n.* **Upton Beall** (bĕl), born 1878, U.S. novelist, socialist, and reformer.

Sind (sĭnd), *n.* a province in Pakistan, in the lower Indus valley. 4,608,000 pop. (1951); 48,136 sq. mi. *Cap.:* Karachi.

Sind·bad the Sailor (sĭnd′băd), (in the *Arabian Nights' Entertainments*) a wealthy citizen of Bagdad, who relates the adventures of his seven wonderful voyages. Also, **Sinbad.**

sine¹ (sīn), *n. Math.* **1.** (of an angle) a trigonometric function equal to the ratio of the ordinate of the end point of the arc to the radius vector of this end point, the origin being at the center of the circle on which the arc lies and the initial point of the arc being on the x-axis. **2.** (orig.) a perpendicular line drawn from one extremity of an arc of a circle to the diameter which passes through its other extremity. [t. L: m.s. *sinus* curve, used to translate Ar. *jaib* chord of an arc]

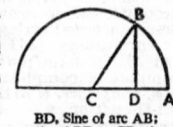

BD, Sine of arc AB;
ratio of BD to CB, sine
of angle ACB

si·ne² (sī′nĭ), *prep. Latin.* without.

si·ne·cure (sī′nĭ kyŏŏr′, sĭn′ĭ-), *n.* **1.** an office requiring little or no work, esp. one yielding profitable returns. **2.** an ecclesiastical benefice without cure of souls. [short for L phrase (*beneficium*) *sine cūrā,* with E *cure* substituted for *cūrā*] —**si′ne·cur′ist,** *n.*

si·ne di·e (sī′nĭ dī′ē), *Latin.* without a day; without fixing a day for future action or meeting.

si·ne qua non (sī′nĭ kwä nŏn′), *Latin.* something essential; an indispensable condition.

sin·ew (sĭn′ū), *n.* **1.** a tendon. **2.** that which supplies strength. **3.** strength; vigor. —*v.t.* **4.** to furnish with sinews; strengthen as by sinews. [ME; OE *sinu* (nom.), *sinuwe* (gen.), c. G *sehne,* Icel. *sin*] —**sin′ew·less,** *adj.*

sin·ew·y (sĭn′ū ĭ), *adj.* **1.** having strong sinews; strong. **2.** vigorous; forcible, as language, style, etc. **3.** like a sinew; tough; stringy. **4.** from or characteristic of strong sinews.

sin·fo·ni·a (sĭn′fō nē′ə; *It.* sēn′fô nē′ä), *n., pl.* **-nie** (-nē′ĕ). *Music.* a symphony. [It.]

sin·ful (sĭn′fəl), *adj.* full of sin; wicked. —**sin′ful·ly,** *adv.* —**sin′ful·ness,** *n.* —Syn. iniquitous, depraved, evil.

sing (sĭng), *v.,* **sang** or **sung, sung, singing,** *n.* —*v.i.* **1.** to utter words or sounds in succession with musical modulations of the voice. **2.** to execute a song or voice composition, as a professional singer. **3.** to produce melodious sounds, as certain birds, insects, etc. **4.** to compose verse; tell of something in verse. **5.** to admit of being sung, as verses. **6.** to give out a continuous ringing, whistling, murmuring, or other sound of musical quality, as a teakettle, a brook, etc. **7.** to have the sensation of a ringing or humming sound, as the ears. —*v.t.* **8.** to utter with musical modulations of the voice, as a song. **9.** to escort or accompany with singing. **10.** to proclaim enthusiastically: *to sing a person's praises.* **11.** to bring, send, put, etc., with or by singing: *to sing a child to sleep.* **12.** to chant or intone. —*n.* **13.** act or performance of singing. **14.** *Colloq.* a meeting of persons for singing. **15.** a singing, ringing, or whistling sound, as of a bullet. [ME; OE *singan,* c. G *singen*] —**sing′a·ble,** *adj.*

sing., singular.

Sin·gan (sē′ngän′), *n.* Sian.

Sin·ga·pore (sĭng′gə pôr′, sĭng′ə-), *n.* **1.** an island in SE Asia, at the S end of the Malay Peninsula: an independent state, formerly part of the federation of Malaysia. 1,700,000 pop. (est. 1961); 220 sq. mi. **2.** a seaport in this state: naval base. 912,343 (1957).

singe (sĭnj), *v.,* **singed, singeing,** *n.* —*v.t.* **1.** to burn superficially. **2.** to burn the ends or projections of (hair, etc.). **3.** to subject to flame in order to remove hair, etc. —*n.* **4.** a superficial burn. **5.** act of singeing. [ME *senge,* OE *sencgan,* c. G *sengen;* akin to Icel. *sangr* singed, burnt] —Syn. **1.** See **burn¹.**

sing·er (sĭng′ər), *n.* **1.** one who sings, esp. a trained or professional vocalist. **2.** a poet. **3.** a singing bird.

Sing·er (sĭng′ər), *n.* **Isaac Merrit,** 1811–1875, American inventor and industrialist.

Sin·gha·lese (sĭng′gə lēz′, -lēs′), *adj., n., pl.* **-lese.** —*adj.* **1.** pertaining to Ceylon, its native people, or their language. —*n.* **2.** a member of the Singhalese people. Also, **Sinhalese.** [f. m. Skt. *Sinhala* Ceylon + -ESE]

sin·gle (sĭng′gəl), *adj., v.,* **-gled, -gling,** *n.* —*adj.* **1.** one only; separate; individual. **2.** of or pertaining to one person, family, etc.: *a single room.* **3.** alone; solitary. **4.** unmarried. **5.** pertaining to the unmarried state. **6.** of one against one, as combat or fight. **7.** consisting of one part, element, or member. **8.** sincere; honest: *single devotion.* **9.** having but one set of petals, as a flower. **10.** *Brit.* of only moderate strength or body, as ale, etc. **11.** (of the eye) seeing rightly. —*v.t.* **12.** to pick or choose out from others (usually fol. by *out*): *to single out a fact for special mention.* —*v.i.* **13.** *Baseball.* to hit the ball so as to reach first base safely. **14.** (of a horse) to go at singlefoot. —*n.* **15.** something single or separate; a single one. **16.** *Brit. Railroad.* a one-way ticket. **17.** *Baseball.* a hit which allows the batter to reach first base only. **18.** (*pl.*) *Tennis, etc.* a game or match played with one person on each side. **19.** *Golf.* a contest between two golfers (as differentiated from a *foursome*). **20.** *Cricket.* a hit for which one run is scored. [ME *sengle,* t. OF, g. L *singulus*] —Syn. **1.** See **only.**

sin·gle-act·ing (sĭng′gəl ăk′tĭng), *adj.* (of any reciprocating machine or implement) acting effectively in only one direction (distinguished from *double-acting*).

sin·gle-ac·tion (sĭng′gəl ăk′shən), *adj.* requiring cocking the hammer by hand before firing: *a single-action rifle.*

sin·gle-breast·ed (sĭng′gəl brĕs′tĭd), *adj.* (of a garment) overlapping across the breast only sufficiently to allow of fastening. See **double-breasted.**

sin·gle-cross (sĭng′gəl krôs′, -krŏs′), *n. Genetics.* the first-generation hybrid between two inbred lines.

---

b., blend of, blended; c., cognate with; d., dialect, dialectal; der., derived from; f., formed from; g., going back to; m., modification of; r., replacing; s., stem of; t., taken from; ?, perhaps.   See the full key on inside cover.

single entry, *Bookkeeping.* **1.** an item noted only once. **2.** a simple accounting system noting only amounts owed by and due to a business. Cf. **double entry.**

single file, a line of persons or things arranged one behind the other; Indian file.

sin·gle-foot (sĭng′gəl fo͝ot′), *n.* **1.** a gait of a horse. See **rack³.** —*v.i.* **2.** (of a horse) to go at such a gait.

sin·gle-hand·ed (sĭng′gəl hăn′dĭd), *adj.* **1.** acting or working alone or unaided. **2.** having, using, or requiring the use of but one hand or one person. **—sin′gle-hand′ed·ly,** *adv.*

sin·gle-heart·ed (sĭng′gəl härt′ĭd), *adj.* sincere in feeling or spirit. **—sin′gle-heart′ed·ly,** *adv.*

sin·gle-mind·ed (sĭng′gəl mīn′dĭd), *adj.* **1.** having or showing undivided purpose. **2.** having or showing a sincere mind. **—sin′gle-mind′ed·ly,** *adv.* **—sin′gle-mind′ed·ness,** *n.*

sin·gle-name paper (sĭng′gəl nām′), *Banking.* commercial paper bearing only the maker's endorsement.

sin·gle·ness (sĭng′gəl nĭs), *n.* state or quality of being single.

sin·gle-phase (sĭng′gəl fāz′), *adj. Elect.* denoting or pertaining to a circuit having an alternating current of one phase.

sin·gle-stick (sĭng′gəl stĭk′), *n.* **1.** a stick requiring the use of but one hand, used in fencing. etc. **2.** fencing, etc., with such a stick. **3.** any short, heavy stick.

sin·gle-stick·er (sĭng′gəl stĭk′ər), *n. Colloq.* a vessel, esp. a sloop, having one mast.

sin·glet (sĭng′glĭt), *n. Chiefly Brit.* a kind of undershirt or jersey worn by men.

single tax, *Econ.* a tax on a single object, particularly land.

sin·gle·ton (sĭng′gəl tən), *n.* **1.** something occurring singly. **2.** *Cards.* a card which is the only one of a suit in a hand. [f. SINGLE + -TON]

sin·gle·tree (sĭng′gəl trē′, -trĭ), *n.* whiffletree. [var. of SWINGLETREE. See SWINGLE]

sin·gly (sĭng′glĭ), *adv.* **1.** apart from others; separately. **2.** one at a time; as single units. **3.** single-handed. [ME *sengely.* See SINGLE, -LY]

Sing Sing (sĭng′ sĭng′), **1.** the state prison at Ossining, New York. **2.** former name of **Ossining.**

sing-song (sĭng′sông′, -sŏng′), *n.* verse, or a piece of verse, of a jingling or monotonous character. **2.** monotonous rhythmical cadence, tone, or sound. **3.** *Brit.* a community sing. **—**_adj._ **4.** monotonous in rhythm.

sin·gu·lar (sĭng′gyə lər), *adj.* **1.** extraordinary; remarkable: *singular success.* **2.** unusual or strange; odd; eccentric. **3.** being the only one of the kind; unique. **4.** separate; individual. **5.** *Gram.* designating the number category that normally implies one person, thing, or collection, as English *man, thing, he, goes.* **6.** *Logic.* of or pertaining to something individual, specific, or not general: *"Socrates was mortal" is a singular proposition.* **7.** *Obs.* pertaining to an individual. **8.** *Obs.* private. **—***n.* **9.** *Gram.* the singular number, or a form therein. [ME, t. L: s. *singulāris*] **—sin′gu·lar·ly,** *adv.* **—sin′gu·lar·ness,** *n.*

sin·gu·lar·i·ty (sĭng′gyə lăr′ə tĭ), *n., pl.* **-ties. 1.** state, fact, or quality of being singular. **2.** something singular; a peculiarity.

sin·gu·lar·ize (sĭng′gyə lə rīz′), *v.t.,* **-ized, -izing.** to make singular.

Sin·ha·lese (sĭn′hə lēz′, -lēs′), *adj., n., pl.* **-lese.** Singhalese.

Sin·i·cism (sĭn′ə sĭz′əm), *n.* Chinese methods or customs; a Chinese usage. [f. *Sinic* Chinese (t. ML: s. *Sinicus,* t. MGk.: m. *Sinikós*) + -ISM]

sin·is·ter (sĭn′ĭs tər), *adj.* **1.** threatening or portending evil; ominous. **2.** bad; evil; base. **3.** unfortunate; disastrous; unfavorable (fol. by *to*). **4.** of or on the left side; left. **5.** *Her.* on the shield at the left of the bearer. See diag. under **escutcheon.** [ME, t. L; orig. referring to omens observed on the left (the unlucky) side] **—sin′is·ter·ly,** *adv.* **—sin′is·ter·ness,** *n.* **—sin′is·ter·wise′,** *adv.*

sin·is·tral (sĭn′ĭs trəl), *adj.* of or pertaining to the left side; left (opposed to *dextral*). **—sin′is·tral·ly,** *adv.*

sin·is·trorse (sĭn′ĭs trôrs′, sĭn′ĭs trôrs′), *adj.* rising spirally from right to left (from a point of view at the center of the spiral), as a stem. [t. L: m.s. *sinistrorsus* toward the left] **—sin′is·tror′sal,** *adj.*

sin·is·trous (sĭn′ĭs trəs), *adj.* **1.** ill-omened; unlucky; disastrous. **2.** sinistral.

sink (sĭngk), *v.,* **sank or sunk, sunk or sunken, sinking,** *n.* —*v.i.* **1.** to descend gradually to a lower level, as water, flames, etc. **2.** to go down toward or below the horizon. **3.** to slope downward, as ground. **4.** to go under or to the bottom; become submerged. **5.** to settle or fall gradually, as a heavy structure. **6.** to fall slowly from weakness, fatigue, etc. **7.** to pass gradually (into slumber, silence, oblivion, etc.). **8.** to pass or fall into some lower state, as of fortune, estimation, etc. **9.** to degenerate; decline. **10.** to fail in physical strength. **11.** to decrease in amount, extent, degree, etc., as value, prices, rates, etc. **12.** to become lower in tone or pitch, as sound. **13.** to enter; permeate (fol. by *in, into,* etc.). **14.** to fall in; become hollow, as the cheeks. —*v.t.* **15.** to cause to fall or descend. **16.** to cause to sink or become submerged. **17.** to depress (a part, area, etc.),

as by excavating. **18.** to put down (a pipe, post, etc.), as into the ground. **19.** to bring to a worse state; lower. **20.** to bring to ruin or perdition. **21.** to reduce in amount, extent, etc., as value or prices. **22.** to lower (the voice, etc.). **23.** to suppress; ignore; omit. **24.** to invest (money), now esp. unprofitably. **25.** to lose (money) in an unfortunate investment, etc. **26.** to make (a hole, shaft, well, etc.) by excavating or boring downward; hollow out (any cavity). —*n.* **27.** a basin or receptacle, esp. in a kitchen, for receiving and carrying off dirty water. **28.** a low-lying area where waters collect or where they disappear by sinking down into the ground or by evaporation. **29.** a place of vice or corruption. **30.** a drain or sewer. **31.** *Rare.* a cesspool. [ME; OE *sincan,* c. G *sinken*] **—sink′a·ble,** *adj.*

sink·er (sĭngk′ər), *n.* **1.** one who or that which sinks. **2.** one employed in sinking, as one who sinks shafts. **3.** a weight of lead, etc., for sinking a fishingline, fishing net, or the like in the water. **4.** *U.S. Slang.* a doughnut, or, sometimes, a biscuit or muffin.

sink·hole (sĭngk′hōl′), *n.* a hole formed in soluble rock by the action of water, serving to conduct surface water to an underground passage.

Sin·kiang (sĭn′kyäng′) *Chin.* shĭn′jyäng′), *n.* the westernmost province of China, bordering Tibet, India, the Soviet Union, and Mongolia. 4,873,608 pop. (1953); 705,961 sq. mi. *Cap.:* Urumchi.

sinking fund, a fund to extinguish an indebtedness, usually a bond issue.

sink·less (sĭnk′ləs), *adj.* unsinkable, as a ship.

sin·less (sĭn′lĭs), *adj.* free from or without sin. **—sin′less·ly,** *adv.* **—sin′less·ness,** *n.*

sin·ner (sĭn′ər), *n.* one who sins; a transgressor.

Sinn Fein (shĭn′ fān′), **1.** a political organization in Ireland, founded about 1905, advocating the advancement of Ireland along national lines and its complete political separation from Great Britain. **2.** a member of this organization. [t. Irish: we ourselves] **—Sinn′ Fein′er,** *n.* **—Sinn′ Fein′ism,** *n.*

Sino-, a word element meaning "Chinese," as in *Sino-Tibetan, Sinology.* [t. NL, comb. form repr. L *Sīnae* the Chinese (t. Gk.: m. *Sīnai*)]

Si·nol·o·gist (sī nŏl′ə jĭst, sĭ-), *n.* one versed in Sinology. Also, **Si·no·logue** (sī′nə lôg′, -lŏg′, sĭn′ə-).

Si·nol·o·gy (sī nŏl′ə jĭ, sĭ-), *n.* the study of the language, literature, history, customs, etc., of China. **—Si·no·log·i·cal** (sī′nə lŏj′ə kəl, sĭn′ə-), *adj.*

Si·no-Ti·bet·an (sī′nō tĭ bĕt′ən, sĭn′ō-), *n.* a linguistic family, including languages spoken from Tibet to the ocean, from North China to Siam: Tibeto-Burman, Chinese, and Thai.

sin·ter (sĭn′tər), *n.* **1.** siliceous or calcareous matter deposited by springs, as that formed around the vent of a geyser. **2.** *Metall.* the product of a sintering operation. —*v.t.* **3.** *Metall.* to bring about agglomeration in by heating. [t. G: dross. See CINDER]

sin·u·ate (sĭn′yo͝o ĭt, -āt′), *adj.* **1.** bent in and out; winding; sinuous. **2.** *Bot.* having the margin strongly or distinctly wavy, as a leaf. Also, **sin′u·at′ed.** [t. L: m.s. *sinuātus,* pp., bent, wound] **—sin′u·ate·ly,** *adv.*

sin·u·a·tion (sĭn′yo͝o ā′shən), *n.* a winding; a sinuosity.

sin·u·os·i·ty (sĭn′yo͝o ŏs′ə tĭ), *n., pl.* **-ties. 1.** (*often pl.*) a curve, bend, or turn. **2.** sinuous form or character.

sin·u·ous (sĭn′yo͝o əs), *adj.* **1.** having many curves, bends, or turns; winding. **2.** indirect; devious. **3.** *Bot.* sinuate, as a leaf. [t. L: m.s. *sinuōsus*] **—sin′u·ous·ness,** *n.* **—sin′u·ous·ly,** *adv.*

si·nus (sī′nəs), *n.* **1.** a curve; bend. **2.** a curving part or recess. **3.** *Anat.* **a.** any of various cavities, recesses, or passages, as a hollow in a bone, or a reservoir or channel for venous blood. **b.** one of the hollow cavities in the skull connecting with the nasal cavities. **c.** an expanded area in a canal or tube. **4.** *Pathol.* a narrow, elongated abscess with a small orifice; a narrow passage leading to an abscess or the like. **5.** *Bot.* a small, rounded depression between two projecting lobes, as of a leaf. [t. L]

Sinuate leaf

si·nus·i·tis (sī′nə sī′tĭs), *n. Pathol.* inflammation of a sinus or sinuses.

Si·on (sī′ən), *n.* Zion.

-sion, a suffix having the same function as **-tion,** as in *compulsion.* [t. L: s. *-sio, f. -s,* final surd in pp. stem + *-io,* noun suffix. Cf. -TION]

Siou·an (so͞o′ən), *n.* a linguistic family formerly widespread from Saskatchewan to the lower Mississippi and in the Virginia and Carolina piedmont, including Iowa, Osage, Dakota, Winnebago, Crow, and Catawba.

Sioux (so͞o), *n., pl.* **Sioux** (so͞o, so͞oz), *adj.* —*n.* **1.** (*pl.*) the Dakota tribe proper of the Siouan linguistic family as distinguished from the Assiniboin tribe of the Dakota division of Siouan-speaking North American Indians. —*adj.* **2.** of or pertaining to this tribe.

Sioux City, a city in W Iowa: a port on the Missouri river. 89,159 (1960).

Sioux Falls, a city in SE South Dakota. 65,466 (1960).

sip (sĭp), *v.,* **sipped, sipping,** *n.* —*v.t.* **1.** to drink a little at a time. **2.** to drink from by sips. **3.** to taste; absorb. —*v.i.* **4.** to drink by sips. —*n.* **5.** an act of

---

ăct, āble, dâre, ärt; ĕbb, ēqual; ĭf, īce; hŏt, ōver, ôrder, oil, bo͝ok, o͞oze, out; ŭp, ūse, ûrge; ə = a in alone; ch, chief; g, give; ng, ring; sh, shoe; th, thin; ŧħ, that; zh, vision. See the full key on inside cover.

sipping. **6.** a small quantity taken by sipping. [ME *sippe*, OE *sypian* drink in] **—Syn. 1.** See **drink.**

si·phon (sī′fən), *n.* **1.** a tube or conduit in the form of an inverted U through which liquid flows over the wall of a tank or reservoir to a lower elevation by atmospheric pressure. **2.** a siphon bottle. **3.** a projecting tubular part of some animals, through which water enters or leaves the body. *—v.t., v.i.* **4.** to convey or pass through a siphon. Also, **syphon.** [t. L: s. *sipho*, t. Gk.: m. *sīphōn* pipe, tube] **—si′phon·ic** (sī fŏn′ĭk), *adj.*

S. Siphon

si·phon·age (sī′fən ĭj), *n.* the action of a siphon.

siphon bottle, a bottle for aerated water, fitted with a bent tube through the neck, the water being forced out, when a valve is opened, by the pressure on its surface of the gas accumulating within the bottle.

siphono-, combining form meaning "siphon," "tube," as in *siphonostele.* [t. Gk., comb. form of *siphōn*]

si·pho·no·phore (sī′fə nə fôr′, sī fŏn′ə fôr′), *n.* any of the *Siphonophora*, an order of pelagic hydrozoans occurring in many diverse forms but consisting typically of a hollow stem or stock, budding into a number of polyps and bells. [t. NL: m. *siphōnophora* (pl.), t. Gk.: m. *siphōnophóros* tube-carrying. See SIPHONO-, -PHORE]

si·pho·no·ste·le (sī′fə nə stē′lĭ, -stēl′), *n. Bot.* a hollow tube or vascular tissue enclosing a pith and embedded in ground tissue.

sip·id (sĭp′ĭd), *adj.* **1.** having a pleasing taste or flavor. **2.** of agreeably distinctive character.

Si·ple (sī′pəl), *n.* **Mount,** a mountain on the Marie Byrd Land coast of Antarctica, S of Amundsen Sea. ab. 15,000 ft.

sip·per (sĭp′ər), *n.* **1.** one who sips. **2.** a paper tube through which to sip; a straw.

sip·pet (sĭp′ĭt), *n.* a small bit; a fragment. [f. SIP + -ET]

si quae·ris pen·in·su·lam a·moe·nam, cir·cum·spi·ce (sī kwĭr′ĭs pĕ nĭn′sŏŏ lăm′ ə mē′năm, sər kŭm′spĭ sē′), *Latin.* if you are seeking a pleasant peninsula, look around you (motto of Michigan).

Si·quei·ros (sē kě′ē rôs′), *n.* **David Alfaro** (äl fä′rô), born 1898, Mexican mural painter.

sir (sûr), *n.* **1.** a respectful or formal term of address used to a man. **2.** (*cap.*) the distinctive title of a knight or baronet: *Sir Walter Scott.* **3.** a title of respect for some notable personage of ancient times: *Sir Pandarus of Troy.* **4.** *Archaic.* a title of respect prefixed to a noun designating profession, rank, etc.: *sir priest.* **5.** an ironic or humorous title of respect: *sir critic.* **6.** *Obs.* a lord; gentleman. [weak var. of SIRE]

Si·ra·cu·sa (sē′rä kōō′zä), *n.* Italian name of **Syracuse** (def. 2).

Si·raj-ud-dau·la (sī′räj′ŏŏd dou′lə), *n.* 1728?–57, the nawab of Bengal who resisted British colonization in India: ordered the Black Hole of Calcutta; defeated by Clive in 1757. Also, **Su·ra·jah Dowlah** (sə rä′jə).

sir·dar (sər där′), *n.* **1.** (in India, etc.) a military chief or leader. **2.** (formerly) the British commander of the Egyptian army. [t. Hind., t. Pers.: m. *sardār*, lit., head-possessing one (i.e. commander)]

sire (sīr), *n., v.,* **sired, siring.** *—n.* **1.** the male parent of a quadruped. **2.** *Poetic.* a father or forefather. **3.** a respectful term of address, now used only to a sovereign. **4.** *Obs.* a lord; person of importance. *—v.t.* **5.** to beget. [ME, t. OF, g. L *senior* SENIOR]

si·ren (sī′rən), *n.* **1.** *Class. Myth.* one of several sea nymphs, part woman and part bird, supposed to lure mariners to destruction by their seductive singing. **2.** any alluring or dangerous woman. **3.** an acoustical instrument for producing musical tones, consisting essentially of a disk pierced with holes arranged equidistantly in a circle, rotated over a jet or stream of compressed air, steam, or the like, so that the stream is alternately allowed to pass and interrupted. **4.** a device of this kind used as a whistle, fog signal, etc. **5.** any of certain eellike salamanders (family *Sirenidae*) with small forelimbs and no hind ones, and external gills persistent throughout life. *—adj.* **6.** of or like a siren. **7.** dangerously alluring. [ME, t. L: t. Gk.: m. *seirēn* (def. 1)]

si·re·ni·an (sī rē′nĭ ən), *n.* any of the *Sirenia*, an order of aquatic herbivorous mammals that includes the manatee, dugong, etc. [f. s. NL *Sirēnia* (der. L *sīren* SIREN) + -AN]

Si·ret (sī rĕt′), *n.* a river flowing from the Carpathian Mountains in the SW Soviet Union SE through E Rumania to the Danube. ab. 270 mi. German, **Sereth.**

Sir·i·us (sĭr′ĭ əs), *n.* the Dog Star, in Canis Major: the brightest star in the heavens. [t. L, t. Gk.: m. *Seírios*]

sir·loin (sûr′loin), *n.* the portion of the loin of beef in front of the rump. [earlier *surloyn*. Cf. OF *surlonge*, f. *sur* over, above + *longe* loin]

si·roc·co (sə rŏk′ō), *n., pl.* **-cos. 1.** a hot, dry, dust-laden wind blowing from northern Africa and affecting parts of southern Europe. **2.** a warm, sultry south or southeast wind accompanied by rain, occurring in the same regions. **3.** any hot, oppressive wind, esp. one in the warm sector of a cyclone. [t. F: m. *siroco*, t. It.: m. *scirocco*, ult. t. Ar.: m. *shoruq*, der. *sharq* east]

sir·rah (sĭr′ə), *n. Archaic.* a term of address used to inferiors in impatience, contempt, etc. [unexplained var. of SIR]

sir-rev·er·ence (sûr′rĕv′ər əns), *n. Obs.* an expression used apologetically, as before unseemly or indelicate words. [mistaken spelling of *sa′reverence*, reduced form of *save reverence* saving (your or his) reverence]

sir·up (sĭr′əp, sûr′-), *n., v.t.* syrup. **—sir′up·y,** *adj.*

si·sal (sī′səl, sĭs′əl), *n.* **1.** a fiber yielded by *Agave sisalana* of Yucatán, used for making ropes, etc. **2.** a plant yielding such fiber. Also, **sisal hemp.** [named after *Sisal*, a port in Yucatán]

sis·kin (sĭs′kĭn), *n.* a small fringilline bird, esp. *Spinus spinces* of Europe and the pine siskin (*S. pinus*) of America. [earlier *syskin*, t. Flem., var. o *sijsken* (now *sijsje*). Cf. MLG *sisek*, appar. t. Pol.: m. *czyzik*]

Sis·mon·di (sĭs mŏn′dĭ; *Fr.* sēs môn dē′), *n.* **Jean Charles Léonard Simonde de** (zhän shärl lā ô när′ sē môNd′ də), 1773–1842, Swiss historian and economist.

sis·sy (sĭs′ĭ), *n., pl.* **-sies. 1.** *Colloq.* an effeminate boy or man. **2.** a little girl. **—sis′sy·ish,** *adj.*

sis·ter (sĭs′tər), *n.* **1.** a daughter of the same parents or parent. **2.** a female friend. **3.** a thing regarded as feminine and associated as if by kinship with something else. **4.** a female fellow member, as of a church. **5.** a female member of a religious community, which observes the simple vows of poverty, chastity and obedience: a *Sister of Charity.* **6.** *Brit.* the nurse in charge of a hospital ward. *—adj.* **7.** being a sister; related by, or as by, sisterhood: *sister ships.* [ME, t. Scand.; cf. Icel. *systir*, c. OE *sweostor*, G *schwester*, Goth. *swistar*; akin to Russ. *sestra*, L *soror*]

sis·ter·hood (sĭs′tər hŏŏd′), *n.* **1.** state of being a sister. **2.** a group of sisters, esp. of women bound by religious vows or similarly devoted.

sis·ter-in-law (sĭs′tər ĭn lô′), *n., pl.* **sisters-in-law. 1.** one's husband's or wife's sister. **2.** one's brother's wife.

sis·ter·ly (sĭs′tər lĭ), *adj.* of, like, or befitting a sister.

Sis·tine (sĭs′tēn, -tĭn), *adj.* of or pertaining to any pope named Sixtus. [t. It.: m. *Sistino*]

Sistine Chapel, the chapel of the Pope in the Vatican at Rome, built for Pope Sixtus IV, and decorated with frescoes by Michelangelo and others.

Sistine Madonna, a famous Madonna painted by Raphael for the Church of St. Sixtus at Piacenza, Italy.

sis·troid (sĭs′troid), *adj. Geom.* included between the convex sides of two intersecting curves (opposed to *cissoid*): *a sistroid angle.*

sis·trum (sĭs′trəm), *n., pl.* **-trums, -tra** (-trə). an ancient musical instrument, a form of metal rattle, used esp. in Egypt in the worship of Isis. [t. L, t. Gk.: m. *seĭstron*]

Sistrum

Sis·y·phe·an (sĭs′ə fē′ən), *adj.* **1.** of or pertaining to Sisyphus. **2.** endless and unavailing, as labor or a task.

Sis·y·phus (sĭs′ə fəs), *n. Gk. Myth.* a king of Corinth, condemned in Hades to roll a heavy stone up a steep hill, only to have it always roll down again when he approached the top.

sit (sĭt), *v.,* **sat** or (*Archaic*) **sate, sitting.** *—v.i.* **1.** to rest on the lower part of the body; be seated. **2.** to be situated; dwell. **3.** to rest or lie. **4.** to place oneself in position for an artist, photographer, etc.: *to sit for a portrait.* **5.** to act as a model. **6.** to remain quiet or inactive. **7.** (of a bird) to perch or roost. **8.** to cover eggs to hatch them. **9.** to fit or be adjusted, as a garment. **10.** to occupy a seat in an official capacity, as a judge or bishop; esp. in England, to have a seat in a legislative assembly, etc. **11.** to be convened or in session, as an assembly. *—v.t.* **12.** to cause to sit; seat (often with *down*). **13.** to sit upon (a horse, etc.). [ME *sitte*(n), OE *sittan*, c. D *zitten*, G *sitzen* Icel. *sitja*; akin to L *sedēre*] **—Syn. 1.** SIT, SET are not synonyms, but they have been confused for centuries. SIT, which has the irregular forms, means "to take a seat" or "to be seated." It is usually intransitive: *one sits in a chair.* SET (with no change in form except for *setting*) originally meant "to cause something to sit;" that is, "to put or place," and should therefore always have an object: *to set a kettle on the stove.* (However, the confusion between these verbs began occurring so long ago that in a few cases the mistaken form has become the accepted usage: *the sun sets, a hen sets, cement sets.*)

sit-down strike (sĭt′doun′), a strike during which workers occupy their place of employment and refuse to work or to allow others to work until the strike is settled. Also, **sit′-down′.**

site (sīt), *n.* **1.** the position of a town, building, etc., esp. as to its environment. **2.** the area on which anything is, has been, or is to be located. [t. L: m. *situs* position]

sith (sĭth), *adv., conj., prep. Archaic.* since.

Sit·ka (sĭt′kə), *n.* a town in SE Alaska, on an island in the Alexander Archipelago: the capital of former Russian America. 3,237 (1960).

sito-, a word element referring to food. [t. Gk., comb. form of *sítos* food made from grain]

si·to·ma·ni·a (sī′tō mā′nĭ ə), *n. Pathol.* insane craving for food.

si·to·pho·bi·a (sī′tō fō′bĭ ə), *n. Pathol.* insane aversion to food.

si·tos·ter·ol (sī tŏs′tə rōl′, -rŏl′), *n. Chem.* a sterol, $C_{29}H_{49}OH$, derived from wheat, corn, Calabar beans, etc. [f. SITO- + (CHOLE)STEROL]

Si·tsang (sē′tsäng′), *n.* Chinese name of Tibet.

sit·ter (sĭt′ər), *n.* **1.** one who sits. **2.** a brooding bird. **3.** one who stays with young children while the parents go out, usually for the evening.

sit·ting (sĭt′ĭng), *n.* **1.** act of one who or that which sits. **2.** a period of remaining seated, as for a portrait. **3.** the space on or in which one sits, as in a church. **4.** a brooding, as of a hen upon eggs, or the number of eggs on which a bird sits during one hatching. **5.** a session, as of a court or legislature.

Sitting Bull, a noted Sioux Indian warrior, tribal leader, and sacred dreamer of Hunkpapa Teton division of the Sioux: born on Grand river, South Dakota, 1834; died 1890.

sitting room, a parlor.

sit·u·ate (*v.* sĭch′ōō āt′; *adj.* sĭch′ōō ĭt, -āt′), *v.,* **-ated, -ating,** *adj.* —*v.t.* **1.** to give a site to; locate. —*adj.* **2.** *Archaic.* located; placed. [t. LL: m.s. situātus, pp., der. L *situs* site]

sit·u·at·ed (sĭch′ōō ā′tĭd), *adj.* **1.** located; placed. **2.** fixed: *well situated financially.*

sit·u·a·tion (sĭch′ōō ā′shən), *n.* **1.** manner of being situated; a location or position with reference to environment. **2.** a place or locality. **3.** condition; case; plight. **4.** the state of affairs; combination of circumstances: *to meet the demands of the situation.* **5.** a position or post of employment. **6.** a state of affairs of special significance in the course of a play, novel, etc. —**Syn.** 4. See **state.** 5. See **position.**

sit·u·a·tion·ism (sĭch′ōō ā′shən ĭz′əm), *n.* *Psychol.* the doctrine that personality traits manifested in a social situation are in direct response to its nature.

si·tus (sī′təs), *n.* **1.** position; situation. **2.** the proper or original position, as of a part or organ. [t. L]

Sit·well (sĭt′wəl), *n.* **1. Edith,** 1887–1964, British poet and critic. **2.** her brother, **Osbert,** born 1892, British poet and novelist. **3.** her brother, **Sacheverell** (sə-shĕv′ər əl), born 1900, British poet and novelist.

sitz bath (sĭts), **1.** a bathtub in which the thighs and trunk of the body to the waistline are immersed in warm water. **2.** the bath so taken. [half adoption, half trans. of G *sitzbad*, f. *sitz* seat + *bad* bath]

Si·va (sē′və, shē′və), *n.* *Hinduism.* one of the three chief divinities, the third member of the Hindu trinity: known also as "the Destroyer." Also, **Shiva.** [t. Hind., t. Skt.: m. *çiva* propitious] —**Si′va·ism,** *n.* —**Si′va·ist,** *n.* —**Si′va·is′tic,** *adj.*

Si·van (sē′vän), *n.* (in the Jewish calendar) the ninth month of the year. [t. Heb.]

Si·vas (sē′väs′), *n.* a city in central Turkey. 66,350 (1955).

six (sĭks), *n.* **1.** a cardinal number, five plus one. **2.** a symbol for this number, as 6 or VI. **3.** a set of this many persons or things. **4.** a playing card, die face, etc., with six pips. **5. at sixes and sevens,** in disorder or confusion. —*adj.* **6.** amounting to six in number. [ME and OE, t. D *zes,* LG *ses,* G *sechs,* Icel. *sex,* L *sex*]

Six Nations, the Five Nations (which see) of the Iroquois confederacy and the Tuscaroras.

six·pence (sĭks′pəns), *n.* **1.** a sum of money of the value of six British pennies, or about 1.2 U.S. cents. **2.** a British silver coin of this value.

six·pen·ny (sĭks′pĕn′ĭ, -pə nĭ), *adj.* **1.** of the amount or value of sixpence; costing sixpence. **2.** of trifling value; cheap; paltry.

six-shoot·er (sĭks′shōō′tər), *n.* *Slang.* a revolver with which six shots can be fired without reloading.

sixte (sĭkst), *n.* *Fencing.* the sixth of eight defensive positions. [F]

six·teen (sĭks′tēn′), *n.* **1.** a cardinal number, ten plus six. **2.** a symbol for this number, as 16 or XVI. —*adj.* **3.** amounting to sixteen in number. [ME *sixtene,* OE *sixtēne,* c. D *zestien,* G *sechzehn,* Icel. *sextān*]

six·teen·mo (sĭks′tēn′mō), *n., pl.* **-mos.** sextodecimo.

six·teenth (sĭks′tēnth′), *adj.* **1.** next after the fifteenth. **2.** being one of sixteen equal parts. —*n.* **3.** a sixteenth part esp. of one (¹⁄₁₆). **4.** the sixteenth member of a series. **5.** *Music.* See **sixteenth note.**

sixteenth note, *Music.* a note having one sixteenth of the time value of a whole note; a semiquaver. See illus. under **note.**

sixth (sĭksth), *adj.* **1.** next after the fifth. **2.** being one of six equal parts. —*n.* **3.** a sixth part, esp. of one (¹⁄₈). **4.** the sixth member of a series. **5.** *Music.* **a.** a tone on the sixth degree from a given tone (counted as the first). **b.** the interval between such tones. **c.** the harmonic combination of such tones. —**sixth′ly,** *adv.*

sixth chord, *Music.* an inversion of a triad in which the second note (next above the root) is in the bass.

sixth sense, a power of perception beyond the five senses; intuition.

six·ti·eth (sĭks′tĭ ĭth), *adj.* **1.** next after the fifty-ninth. **2.** being one of sixty equal parts. —*n.* **3.** a sixtieth part, esp. of one (¹⁄₆₀). **4.** the sixtieth member of a series.

Six·tus (sĭks′təs), *n.* the name of five popes.

six·ty (sĭks′tĭ), *n., pl.* **-ties,** *adj.* —*n.* **1.** a cardinal number, ten times six. **2.** a symbol for this number, as 60 or LX. —*adj.* **3.** amounting to sixty in number. [ME; OE *sixtig,* c. D *zestig,* G *sechzig,* Icel. *sextigir*]

six·ty-fourth note (sĭks′tĭ fôrth′), *Music.* a note having one sixty-fourth of the time value of a whole note; a hemidemisemiquaver. See illus. under **note.**

siz·a·ble (sī′zə bəl), *adj.* **1.** of fair size; fairly large: *he inherited a sizable fortune.* **2.** *Obs.* of convenient size. Also, **sizeable.** —**siz′a·ble·ness,** *n.* —**siz′a·bly,** *adv.*

siz·ar (sī′zər), *n.* (formerly at Cambridge and Dublin) an undergraduate who receives aid from the college for maintenance. [der. SIZE (see def. 6)]

size[1] (sīz), *n., v.,* **sized, sizing.** —*n.* **1.** the dimensions, proportions, or magnitude of anything: *the size of a city.* **2.** considerable or great magnitude: *to seek size rather than quality.* **3.** one of a series of graduated measures for articles of manufacture or trade: *children's sizes of shoes.* **4.** extent; amount; range. **5.** *Colloq.* actual condition, circumstances. etc. **6.** *Obs.* a fixed standard, as for food or drink. —*v.t.* **7.** to separate or sort according to size. **8.** to make of a certain size. **9. to size up, a.** to form an estimate of. **b.** to come up to size, grade, etc. **10.** *Obs.* to regulate according to a standard. [ME *syse,* t. OF: m. *sise,* aphetic var. of *assize* ASSIZE; later meanings arose from def. 10]
—**Syn.** 1. SIZE, VOLUME, MASS, BULK are terms referring to extent or dimensions of that which has magnitude and occupies space. SIZE is the general word: *of great size, small in size.* VOLUME often applies to something which has no fixed shape: *smoke has volume.* MASS, also, does not suggest shape, but suggests the weight of a quantity of matter in a solid body: *a mass of concrete.* BULK suggests weight, and often a recognizable, though perhaps unwieldy, shape: *the huge bulk of an elephant.*

size[2] (sīz), *n., v.,* **sized, sizing.** —*n.* **1.** any of various gelatinous or glutinous preparations made from glue, starch, etc., used for glazing or coating paper, cloth, etc. —*v.t.* **2.** to coat or treat with size. [ME *syse;* ? special use of SIZE[1]]

size·a·ble (sī′zə bəl), *adj.* sizable. —**size′a·ble·ness,** *n.* —**size′a·bly,** *adv.*

sized (sīzd), *adj.* having size as specified: *middle-sized.*

siz·ing (sī′zĭng), *n.* **1.** act or process of applying size or preparing with size. **2.** size, as for glazing paper.

siz·y (sī′zĭ), *adj.* thick; viscous. [f. SIZE[2] + -Y[1]]

siz·zle (sĭz′əl), *v.,* **-zled, -zling,** —*v.i.* **1.** to make a hissing sound, as in frying or burning. **2.** *Colloq.* to be very hot. —*n.* **3.** a sizzling sound. [imit.]

S.J., Society of Jesus (Jesuit).

Sjael·land (shĕl′län), *n.* Danish name of **Zealand.**

S.J.D., (L *Scientiae Juridicae Doctor*) Doctor of Juridical Science.

Ska·gen (skä′gən), *n.* See **Skaw, The.**

Skag·er·rak (skăg′ər răk′), *n.* an arm of the North Sea between Denmark and Norway. ab. 140 mi. long; ab. 75 mi. wide.

Skag·way (skăg′wā′), *n.* a town in SE Alaska, near the famous White and Chilkoot passes to the Klondike gold fields: railway terminus. 659 (1960).

skald (skôld, skäld), *n.* an ancient Scandinavian poet. Also, **scald.** [t. Icel.: poet]

skat (skät), *n.* a card game in which there are three active players, 32 cards being used. [t. G, t. It.: m. *scarto* a discard, der. *scartare* discard]

skate[1] (skāt), *n., v.,* **skated, skating.** —*n.* **1.** a steel runner attached to the bottom of a shoe, enabling a person to glide on ice. **2.** a shoe with such a runner attached. **3.** a roller skate. —*v.i.* **4.** to glide over ice, the ground, etc., on skates. **5.** to glide or slide smoothly along. [t. D: m. *schaats,* MD *schaetse,* t. ONF: m. *escache* stilt]

skate[2] (skāt), *n., pl.* **skates,** (*esp. collectively*) **skate.** any of certain rays (genus *Raja*), usually having a pointed snout and spines down the back, but no serrated spine on the tail. The common large skate of the Pacific coast is *R. binoculata.* [ME *scate,* t. Scand.; cf. Icel. *skata*]

skate[3] (skāt), *n.* *Slang.* a term of contempt for a person, a horse, etc. [? special use of SKATE[2]]

skat·er (skā′tər), *n.* **1.** one who skates. **2.** a water strider.

Skaw (skô), **the,** a cape at the N tip of Denmark. Also, **Skagen.**

Barn-door skate
Raia stabuliforis
(6 ft. long)

skean (shkēn, skēn), *n.* a kind of knife or dagger formerly used in Ireland and among the Scottish Highlanders. [t. Irish and Gaelic: m. *sgian*]

Skeat (skēt), *n.* **Walter William,** 1835–1912, British philologist and lexicographer.

ske·dad·dle (skĭ dăd′əl), *v.,* **-dled, -dling,** *n.* *Slang.* —*v.i.* **1.** to run away; disperse in flight. —*n.* **2.** a hasty flight. [orig. obscure]

skee (skē), *n., pl.* **skees, skee,** *v.i.,* **skeed, skeeing.** ski.

skeet (skēt), *n.* a form of trapshooting in which clay targets are thrown from two traps forty yards apart and the shooter moves to different stations, thus firing from various angles as in real game shooting.

skeg (skĕg), *n.* **1.** the after part of a ship's keel. **2.** a projection abaft a ship's keel for the support of a rudder. [t. D: m. *scheg,* t. Scand.; cf. Icel. *skegg* beard]

skein (skān), *n.* a length of thread or yarn wound in a coil. [ME *skayne,* t. OF: m. *escaigne*]

skel·e·tal (skĕl′ə təl), *adj.* of or pertaining to a skeleton.

ăct, āble, dâre, ärt; ĕbb, ēqual; ĭf, īce; hŏt, ōver, ôrder, oil, bŏŏk, ōōze, out; ŭp, ūse, ûrge; ə = a in alone; ch, chief; g, give; ng, ring; sh, shoe; th, thin; ħ, that; zh, vision. See the full key on inside cover.

skel·e·ton (skĕl′ə tən), *n.* **1.** the bones of a human or other animal body considered together, or assembled or fitted together as a framework; the bony or cartilaginous framework of a vertebrate animal. **2.** a very lean person or animal. **3.** a supporting framework, as of a leaf, building, or ship. **4.** mere lifeless, dry, or meager remains. **5.** an outline, as of a literary work. —*adj.* **6.** of or pertaining to a skeleton. **7.** like a skeleton or mere framework. [t. NL, t. Gk., neut of *skeletós* dried up]

skel·e·ton·ize (skĕl′ə tə nīz′), *v.t.,* **-ized, -izing. 1.** to reduce to a skeleton. **2.** to construct in outline.

skeleton key, a key with nearly the whole substance of the bit filed away, so that it may open various locks.

skel·lum (skĕl′əm), *n. Archaic or Dial.* a rascal. [t. D: m. *schelm*, t. G]

Skel·ton (skĕl′tən), *n.* **John,** c1460–1529, British poet.

skep·tic (skĕp′tĭk), *n.* **1.** one who questions the validity or authenticity of something purporting to be knowledge; one who maintains a doubting attitude. **2.** one who doubts the truth of the Christian religion or of important elements of it. **3.** (*cap.*) *Philos.* **a.** a member of a philosophical school of ancient Greece, the earliest group of which consisted of Pyrrho and his followers, who maintained that real knowledge of things is impossible. **b.** any later thinker who doubts or questions the possibility of real knowledge of any kind. —*adj.* **4.** pertaining to skeptics or skepticism; skeptical. **5.** (*cap.*) pertaining to the Skeptics. Also, *esp. Brit.,* **sceptic.** [t. L: m.s. *scepticus* inquiring, reflective, t. Gk.: m. *skeptikós*] —**Syn. 2.** See **atheist.**

skep·ti·cal (skĕp′tə kəl), *adj.* **1.** inclined to skepticism; having doubt. **2.** showing doubt: *a skeptical smile.* **3.** denying or questioning the tenets of religion. **4.** of or pertaining to skeptics or skepticism. —**skep′ti·cal·ly,** *adv.* —**skep′ti·cal·ness,** *n.* —**Syn. 1.** See **doubtful.**

skep·ti·cism (skĕp′tə sĭz′əm), *n.* **1.** skeptical attitude or temper; doubt. **2.** doubt or unbelief with regard to the Christian religion. **3.** the doctrines or opinions of philosophical skeptics; universal doubt.

sker·ry (skĕr′ĭ), *n., pl.* **-ries.** *Chiefly Scot.* **1.** a small, rocky island. **2.** a coastline with a series of such islands offshore. [Orkney word, t. Scand.; cf. Icel. *sker* reef]

sketch (skĕch), *n.* **1.** a simply or hastily executed drawing or painting, esp a preliminary one, giving the essential features without the details. **2.** a rough design, plan, or draft, as of a literary work. **3.** a brief or hasty outline of facts, occurrences, etc. **4.** a short play or slight dramatic performance, as one forming part of a vaudeville program. —*v.t.* **5.** to make a sketch of. **6.** to set forth in a brief or general account. —*v.i.* **7.** to make a sketch or sketches. [t. D: m. *schets,* t. It.: m. *schizzo,* g. L *schedium* extemporaneous poem, t. Gk.: m. *schédios* extempore] —**sketch′er,** *n.* —**Syn. 5.** See **depict.**

sketch·a·ble (skĕch′ə bəl), *adj.* suitable for being sketched.

sketch·book (skĕch′boŏk′), *n.* **1.** a book for making sketches in. **2.** a book of literary sketches.

sketch·y (skĕch′ĭ), *adj.,* **sketchier, sketchiest. 1.** like a sketch; giving only outlines. **2.** slight; imperfect; superficial: *a sketchy meal.* —**sketch′i·ly,** *adv.* —**sketch′i·ness,** *n.*

skete (skēt), *n.* a settlement of monks or ascetics of the Greek Church.

skew (skū), *v.i.* **1.** to turn aside or swerve; take an oblique course. **2.** to look obliquely; squint. —*v.t.* **3.** to give an oblique direction to; shape or form obliquely. **4.** to distort; depict unfairly. —*adj.* **5.** having an oblique direction or position; slanting. **6.** having a part which deviates from a straight line, right angle, etc.: *skew gearing.* —*n.* **7.** an oblique movement, direction, or position. [ME *skewe,* t. ONF: m.s. *eskiu(w)er* escape. See **eschew**]

skew arch, *Archit.* an arch whose axis is not perpendicular to the faces of its abutments.

skew·back (skū′băk′), *n. Archit.* **1.** a sloping surface against which the end of an arch rests. **2.** a stone, course of masonry, or the like, presenting such a surface.

S, Skewback

skew·bald (skū′bôld′), *adj.* (of horses, etc.) having patches of different colors, esp. of white and brown or red. [cf. obs. E *skewed* skewbald (orig. uncert.)]

skew·er (skū′ər), *n.* **1.** a long pin of wood or metal for putting through meat to hold it together or in place while being cooked. **2.** any similar pin for some other purpose. —*v.t.* **3.** to fasten with, or as with, skewers. [earlier *skiver,* of unknown orig.]

skew·ness (skū′nĭs), *n. Statistics.* the degree of departure of a frequency distribution from symmetry.

ski (skē; *Nor.* shē), *n., pl.* **skis, ski,** *v.,* **skied, skiing.** —*n.* **1.** one of a pair of long, slender pieces of hard wood, one fastened to each shoe, used for traveling or gliding over snow, and often (esp. as a sport) down declivities. —*v.i.* **2.** to travel on or use skis. Also, **skee.** [t. Norw., var. of *skid,* c. Icel. *skídh,* OE *scíd* thin slip of wood, G *scheit* thin board]

ski·a·scope (skī′ə skōp′), *n. Med.* an apparatus which determines the refractive power of the eye by observing the lights and shadows on the pupil when a mirror illumines the retina; retinoscope. [f. Gk. *skia* shadow + -scope] —**ski·as·co·py** (skī ăs′kə pĭ), *n.*

skid (skĭd), *n., v.,* **skidded, skidding.** —*n.* **1.** a plank, bar, log, or the like, esp. one of a pair, on which something heavy may be slid or rolled along. **2.** one of a number of such logs or timbers forming a skidway. **3.** a plank or the like, esp. one of a number, on or by which something is supported. **4.** *Naut.* **a.** (*pl.*) a wooden framework fitted to the outside of a ship to prevent injury while loading, etc. **b.** (*usually pl.*) a framework above the main deck on which ships' boats are carried. **5.** a shoe or some other device for preventing the wheel of a vehicle from rotating, as when descending a hill. **6.** a runner on the under part of some airplanes, enabling the machine to slide along the ground when alighting. **7.** an act of skidding: *the car went into a skid on the icy pavement.* —*v.t.* **8.** to place on or slide along a skid or skids. **9.** to check with a skid, as a wheel. —*v.i.* **10.** to slide along without rotating, as a wheel to which a brake has been applied. **11.** to slip or slide sideways relative to direction of wheel rotation, as an automobile in turning a corner rapidly. **12.** (of an airplane when not banked sufficiently) to slide sideways, away from the center of the curve executed in turning. [cf. OFris. *skidel* spoke]

skid·doo (skĭd′doō′), *interj. Slang.* get out; go away.

skid fin, *Aeron.* an auxiliary airfoil over the upper main wing in some early airplanes.

ski·er (skē′ər), *n.* one who skis.

skiff (skĭf), *n.* any of various types of boats small enough for sailing or rowing by one person. [t. F: m. *esquif,* t. It.: m. *schifo,* t. OHG: m. *scif* SHIP]

ski·ing (skē′ĭng), *n.* gliding on skis.

ski·jor·ing (skē jōr′ĭng), *n.* a sport in which a skier is pulled over snow or ice, generally by a horse. [t. Norw.]

ski jump, 1. a jump made by a skier. **2.** the runway designed for such a jump.

skil·ful (skĭl′fəl), *adj.* skillful. —**skil′ful·ly,** *adv.* —**skil′ful·ness,** *n.*

skill[1] (skĭl), *n.* **1.** the ability that comes from knowledge, practice, aptitude, etc., to do something well. **2.** competent excellence in performance; expertness; dexterity. **3.** *Obs.* understanding. **4.** *Obs.* a reason; cause. [ME, t. Scand.; cf. Icel. *skil* distinction]

skill[2] (skĭl), *v.i. Archaic.* **1.** to matter. **2.** to help. [t. Scand.; cf. Icel. *skilja* distinguish]

skilled (skĭld), *adj.* **1.** having skill; trained or experienced. **2.** showing, involving, or requiring skill, as work. **3.** of or pertaining to workers performing a specific operation requiring apprenticeship or other special training or experience. **4.** (of workmen) having special ability in operating machinery or mechanical devices. —**Syn. 1.** See **skillful.**

skil·let (skĭl′ĭt), *n.* **1.** a frying pan. **2.** a long-handled saucepan or stewpan. [orig. obscure]

skill·ful (skĭl′fəl), *adj.* **1.** having or exercising skill. **2.** showing or involving skill: *a skillful display of fancy diving.* **3.** *Obs.* reasonable. Also, **skilful.** —**skill′ful·ly,** *adv.* —**skill′ful·ness,** *n.* —**Syn. 1.** SKILLFUL, SKILLED, EXPERT refer to readiness and adroitness in an occupation, craft, or art. SKILLFUL suggests esp. adroitness and dexterity: *a skillful watchmaker.* SKILLED implies having had long experience and thus having acquired a high degree of proficiency: *not an amateur but a skilled workman.* EXPERT means having the highest degree of proficiency; it may mean much the same as skillful or skilled, or both: *expert workmanship.* —**Ant. 1.** awkward, clumsy, amateurish.

skil·ling (skĭl′ĭng), *n.* (formerly) in various northern European countries. **1.** a money of account valued below one cent. **2.** the coin. [cf. Dan. *skilling* shilling]

skim (skĭm), *v.,* **skimmed, skimming,** *n.* —*v.t.* **1.** to take up or remove (floating matter) from a liquid with a spoon, ladle, etc.: *to skim cream.* **2.** to clear (liquid) thus: *to skim milk.* **3.** to move or glide lightly over or along the surface of (the ground, water, etc.) . **4.** to cause (a thing) to fly over or near a surface, or in a smooth course: *to skim stones.* **5.** to go over in reading, treatment, etc., in a superficial manner. **6.** to cover (liquid, etc.) with a thin layer. —*v.i.* **7.** to pass or glide lightly along over or near a surface. **8.** to go, pass, glance, etc. over something in a superficial way (usually fol. by *over*). **9.** to become covered with a thin layer. —*n.* **10.** the act of skimming. **11.** that which is skimmed off. **12.** skim milk. **13.** *Obs.* scum. [d. var. of obs. *scum,* v., skim. See **scum**]

A. Cranium; B. Vertebrae; C. Sternum; D. Ribs; E. Ilium; F. Sacrum; G. Coccyx; H. Pubis; I. Ischium; J. Clavicle; K. Humerus; L. Ulna; M. Radius; N. Carpus; O. Metacarpus; P. Phalanx; Q. Femur; R. Patella; S. Tibia; T. Fibula; U. Tarsus; V. Metatarsus

Human Skeleton

---

b., blend of, blended; c., cognate with; d., dialect, dialectal; der., derived from; f., formed from; g., going back to; m., modification of; r., replacing; s., stem of; t., taken from; ?, perhaps. See the full key on inside cover.

skim·ble-scam·ble (skĭm′bəl skăm′bəl, skĭm′əl-skăm′əl), *adj.* rambling; confused; nonsensical.

skim·mer (skĭm′ər), *n.* **1.** one who or that which skims. **2.** a shallow utensil, usually perforated, used in skimming liquids. **3.** any of various gull-like birds of the family *Rynchopidae*, which skim the water with the curiously elongated lower mandible in obtaining food.

skim milk, milk from which the cream has been skimmed.

skim·ming (skĭm′ĭng), *n.* **1.** (*usually pl.*) that which is removed by skimming. **2.** (*pl.*) *Metall.* dross.

skimp (skĭmp), *v.t., v.i.* **1.** to scrimp. **2.** to scamp. —*adj.* **3.** skimpy. [orig. obscure]

skimp·y (skĭm′pĭ), *adj.,* **skimpier, skimpiest. 1.** lacking in size, fullness, etc.; scanty: *a skimpy hem.* **2.** too thrifty; stingy: *a skimpy housewife.* —**skimp′i·ly,** *adv.* —**skimp′i·ness,** *n.*

skin (skĭn), *n., v.,* **skinned, skinning.** —*n.* **1.** the external covering or integument of an animal body, esp. when soft and flexible. **2.** such an integument stripped from the body of an animal; pelt. **3.** any integumentary covering, outer coating, or surface layer, as an investing membrane, the rind or peel of fruit, or a film on liquid. **4.** a single nacreous layer in a pearl, the outermost at any time. **5.** the planking or iron plating which covers the ribs of a ship. **6.** a container made of animal skin, used for holding liquids. **7.** *Slang.* a swindler; cheat. **8.** *Slang.* a skinflint. **9.** **save one's skin,** to escape harm. **10. by the skin of one's teeth,** scarcely; just barely. —*v.t.* **11.** to strip or deprive of skin; flay; peel. **12.** to strip off, as or like skin. **13.** to cover with or as with skin. **14.** *Slang.* to strip of money or belongings; fleece, as in gambling. —*v.i.* **15.** *U.S. Slang.* to slip off hastily; abscond. [ME, t. Scand.; cf. Icel. *skinn,* c. d. G *schind, schinde* skin of fruit]
—**Syn. 2.** SKIN, HIDE, PELT are names for the outer covering of animals, including man. SKIN is the general word: *an abrasion of the skin, the skin of a muskrat.* HIDE applies to the skin of large (esp. domesticated) animals, such as cattle: horses, elephants: *a buffalo hide.* PELT applies to the untanned skin of smaller animals: *a mink pelt.*

skin·bound (skĭn′bound′), *adj.* having the skin drawn tightly over the flesh, as in scleroderma.

skin-deep (skĭn′dēp′), *adj.* **1.** superficial; slight. —*adv.* **2.** slightly; superficially.

skin-div·ing (skĭn′dī′vĭng), *n.* an underwater sport in which the swimmer, equipped with a lightweight mask and air cylinder and foot fins, can move about quickly and easily. —**skin′-dive,** *v.i.* —**skin′-div′er,** *n.*

skin·flint (skĭn′flĭnt′), *n.* a mean, niggardly person.

skin friction drag, aerodynamic resistance due to contact of moving air with the surface of a body.

skin grafting, *Surg.* the transplanting of healthy skin from the patient's or another's body to a wound or burn, to form new skin.

skink (skĭngk), *n.* any of the harmless, generally smooth-scaled, lizards constituting the family *Scincidae,* as *Scincus scincus,* formerly much used (dried) for medicinal purposes. [t. L: m.s. *scincus,* t. Gk.: m. *skínkos*]

Skink. *Eumeces fasciatus* (6 in. long)

skinned (skĭnd), *adj.* having a skin, esp. as specified: *thick-skinned, light-skinned.*

skin·ner (skĭn′ər), *n.* **1.** one who skins. **2.** one who prepares, or deals in, skins.

Skin·ner (skĭn′ər), *n.* **1.** Otis, 1858–1942, U.S. actor. **2.** his daughter, **Cornelia Otis,** born 1901, U.S. actress and author.

skin·ner·y (skĭn′ər ĭ), *n.., pl.* **-neries.** a place where skins are prepared, or kept for the market.

skin·ny (skĭn′ĭ), *adj.,* **-nier, -niest. 1.** lean; emaciated. **2.** of or like skin. —**skin′ni·ness,** *n.*

skin-tight (skĭn′tīt′), *adj.* fitting as tightly as skin.

skip¹ (skĭp), *v.,* **skipped, skipping,** *n.* —*v.i.* **1.** to spring, jump, or leap lightly; gambol. **2.** to pass from one point, thing, subject, etc., to another, disregarding or omitting what intervenes. **3.** *U.S. Colloq.* to go away hastily; abscond. **4.** *Educ.* to be advanced two or more classes or grades. **5.** to ricochet, as a missile passing with rebounds along a surface. —*v.t.* **6.** to jump lightly over. **7.** to pass over without reading, notice, mention, action, etc. **8.** to send (a missile) ricocheting along a surface. **9.** *Colloq.* to leave hastily, or flee from, as a place. —*n.* **10.** a skipping movement; a light jump. **11.** a gait marked by such jumps. **12.** a passing from one point or thing to another, with disregard of what intervenes. **13.** *Music.* a melodic interval greater than a second. [ME. Cf. MSw. *skuppa* skip]
—**Syn. 1.** SKIP, BOUND refer to an elastic, springing movement. To SKIP is to give a series of light, quick leaps alternating the feet: *to skip along.* BOUND suggests a series of long, rather vigorous leaps; it is also applied to a springing or leaping type of walking or running rapidly and actively: *a dog came bounding up to meet him.*

skip² (skĭp), *n.* the captain of a team or side at curling or bowling. [short for SKIPPER¹]

skip·jack (skĭp′jăk′), *n., pl.* **-jacks,** (*esp. collectively*) **-jack. 1.** any of various fishes that leap from the water. **2.** an important tuna, *Katsuwonus pelamis,* of tropical waters. **3.** a North American fresh-water herring, *Pomolobus chrysochloris.* **4.** the fresh-water silversides.

skip·knot (skĭp′nŏt′), *n.* a knot which may be easily slipped or undone.

skip·per¹ (skĭp′ər), *n.* **1.** the master or captain of a ship, esp. of a small trading or fishing vessel. **2.** a captain or leader, as of a team. —*v.t.* **3.** to act as skipper of. [ME. t. MD: m. *schipper,* der. *schip* SHIP]

skip·per² (skĭp′ər), *n.* **1.** one who or that which skips. **2.** any of various insects that hop or fly with jerky motions. **3.** any of the quick-flying lepidopterous insects constituting the family *Hesperiidae,* closely related to the true butterflies. **4.** the saury. [f. SKIP¹ + -ER¹]

skip·pet (skĭp′ĭt), *n.* a small round box for protecting a seal as attached by a ribbon or cord to a document.

skirl (skûrl), *Scot. and Brit. Dial.* —*v.i., v.t.* **1.** to sound loudly and shrilly (used esp. of the bagpipe). **2.** to shriek. —*n.* **3.** the sound of the bagpipe. **4.** a shrill sound. [metathetic var. of ME *scrille,* t. Scand.; cf. d. Norw. *skrylla*]

skir·mish (skûr′mĭsh), *n.* **1.** *Mil.* a fight between small bodies of troops, esp. advanced or outlying detachments of opposing armies. **2.** any brisk encounter. —*v.i.* **3.** to engage in a skirmish. [ME *skirmysshe,* t. OF: m. *eskirmiss-,* s. *eskirmir,* t. OHG: m. *skirman* defend, der. *skirm* shield. See SCREEN] —**skir′mish·er,** *n.*
—**Syn. 1.** See battle¹.

skirr (skûr), *v.i.* **1.** to go rapidly; fly; scurry. **2.** to go rapidly over. —*n.* **3.** a grating or whirring sound.

skir·ret (skĭr′ĭt), *n.* an umbelliferous plant. *Sium sisarum,* cultivated in Europe for its edible tuberous root. [ME *skirwhit(e),* f. *skire* pure (t. Scand.; cf. Icel. *skírr*) + WHITE]

skirt (skûrt), *n.* **1.** the lower part of a gown, coat, or the like, hanging from the waist. **2.** a separate garment (outer or under) worn by women and girls, extending from the waist downward. **3.** some part resembling or suggesting the skirt of a garment. **4.** one of the flaps hanging from the sides of a saddle. **5.** a skirting or bordering finish in building. **6.** (*usually pl.*) the bordering, marginal, or outlying part of a place, group, etc. **7.** *Slang.* a woman or girl. —*v.t.* **8.** to lie on or along the border of. **9.** to border or edge with something. **10.** to pass along or around the border or edge of: *to skirt a town.* —*v.i.* **11.** to be, lie, live, etc., on or along the edge of something. **12.** to pass or go around the border of something. [ME., t. Scand.; cf. Icel. *skyrta* SHIRT]

skit (skĭt), *n.* **1.** a literary trifle of humorous or satirical character. **2.** a short comic play. **3.** *Scot. and Dial.* a good-humored joke. [akin to SKITTER]

skit·ter (skĭt′ər), *v.i.* **1.** to go, run, or glide lightly or rapidly. **2.** to skim along a surface. **3.** *Angling.* to draw a spoon or a baited hook over the water with a skipping motion. —*v.t.* **4.** to cause to skitter. [freq. of *skit* move fast, ? t. Scand.; cf. Icel. *skeyti* dart]

skit·tish (skĭt′ĭsh), *adj.* **1.** apt to start or shy. **2.** restlessly or excessively lively. **3.** fickle; uncertain. **4.** coy. [akin to SKITTER] —**skit′tish·ly,** *adv.* —**skit′-tish·ness,** *n.*

skit·tle (skĭt′əl), *n.* **1.** (*pl.*) *Chiefly Brit.* ninepins. **2.** one of the pins. [t. Scand.; cf. Dan. *skyttel* kind of ball (child's plaything)]

skive (skīv), *v.t.,* **skived, skiving.** to split or cut (leather, etc.) into layers or slices; shave (hides, etc.). [t. Scand.; cf. Icel. *skífa,* v., n., slice, c. ME *schive* slice (of bread)]

skiv·er (skī′vər), *n.* **1.** one who or that which skives. **2.** a thin sheepskin used for bookbinding.

skiv·y (skĭv′ĭ), *n., pl.* **skivies.** *Brit. Slang.* (in contemptuous use) a chambermaid or servant.

skoal (skōl), *n.* a word used in drinking someone's health. [t. Scand.; cf. Dan. *skaal* bowl, toast]

Sko·kie (skō′kĭ), *n.* a city in NE Illinois, near Chicago. 59,364 (1960).

Skop·lje (skôp′lyĕ), *n.* a city in SE Yugoslavia: earthquake 1963; 121,551 (1953). Turkish, **Usküb.**

Skt., Sanskrit. Also, **Skr.**

sku·a (skū′ə), *n.* a predatory gull or jaeger. [t. Faeroese: m. *skúgvur,* c. Icel. *skúfr;* orig. uncert.]

skul·dug·ger·y (skŭl dŭg′ə rĭ), *n.* *U.S.* dishonorable proceedings; mean dishonesty or trickery. [var. of d. *sculduddery;* orig. obscure]

Antarctic skua, *Catharacta skua* (2 ft. long)

skulk (skŭlk), *v.i.* **1.** to lie or keep in hiding, as for some evil reason. **2.** to shirk duty; malinger. **3.** to move or go in a mean, stealthy manner; sneak; slink. —*n.* **4.** one who skulks. **5.** an act of skulking. [ME, t. Scand.; cf. Dan. *skulke*] —**skulk′er,** *n.* —**Syn. 1.** See lurk.

skull (skŭl), *n.* **1.** the bony framework of the head, enclosing the brain and supporting the face; the skeleton of the head. **2.** (usually in disparaging use) the head as the seat of intelligence or knowledge. [ME *scolle,* t. Scand.; cf. d. Norw. *skol, skul* shell (of an egg or a nut)]

skull and crossbones, a representation of a front view of a human skull above two crossed bones, orig. used on pirate's flags, and now designating poisons.

skull·cap (skŭl′kăp′), *n.* **1.** a brimless cap of silk, velvet, or the like, fitting closely to the head. **2.** *Bot.* any of various labiate herbs (genus *Scutellaria*) in which the calyx suggests a helmet.

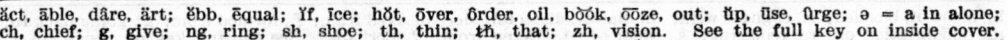

skunk (skŭngk), *n.* **1.** a small, striped, fur-bearing, bushy-tailed, North American mammal, *Mephitis mephitis*, of the weasel family, *Mustelidae*, which ejects a fetid fluid when attacked. **2.** any of various allied or similar animals, as a spotted variety (genus *Spilogale*) or the members of the genus *Cenepatus*. **3.** *Colloq.* a thoroughly contemptible person. —*v.t.* **4.** *U.S. Slang.* (in games) to beat so completely as to keep from scoring. [t. Amer. Ind. (Algonquian dialects): m. *segankw* or *segongw* (Abnaki); c. Cree *sīkāk*, Chippewa *shikag*, etc.]

Common skunk.
Mephitis mephitis
(Total length 2 ft.,
tail 6½ to 7½ in.)

skunk cabbage, 1. a low, fetid, broad-leaved, araceous plant, *Symplocarbus foetidus*, of North America, growing in moist ground. **2.** a similar araceous plant, *Lysichitum americanum*, found on the western coast of North America and in Siberia, Japan, etc. Also, **skunk·weed** (skŭngk′wēd′).

Sku·ta·ri (skōō′tä rē′), *n.* Scutari (def. 1).

sky (skī), *n.*, *pl.* **skies**, *v.*, **skied** or **skyed**, **sky·ing.** —*n.* **1.** (*often pl.*) the region of the clouds or the upper air. **2.** (*often pl.*) the heavens or firmament, appearing as a great arch or vault. **3.** the supernal or celestial heaven. **4.** climate. **5.** *Obs.* a cloud. **6. to the skies,** highly; extravagantly. —*v.t.* **7.** *Colloq.* to raise aloft; strike (a ball) high into the air. **8.** *Colloq.* to hang (a picture, etc.) high on the wall of a gallery. [ME, t. Scand.; cf. Icel. *skȳ* cloud, c. OE *scēo* cloud] —**sky′like′**, *adj.*

sky blue, the color of the unclouded sky in daytime; azure. —**sky′-blue′**, *adj.*

Skye (skī), *n.* an island in the Hebrides, in NW Scotland. 8265 (1951). 670 sq. mi.

Skye terrier, a small, short-legged, very shaggy terrier. [named after the Isle of *Skye*]

Skye terrier
(Ab. 9 in. high at the shoulder)

sky·ey (skī′ī), *adj.* *Chiefly Poetic.* **1.** of or from the sky. **2.** in the sky; lofty. **3.** skylike; sky blue.

sky-high (skī′hī′), *adv.*, *adj.* very high.

sky·lark (skī′lärk′), *n.* **1.** a European lark, *Alauda arvensis*, famous for its singing in flight. —*v.i.* **2.** *Colloq.* to frolic; indulge in rough sport. —**sky′lark′er**, *n.*

Skylark. *Alauda arvensis*
(Ab. 8 in. long)

sky·light (skī′līt′), *n.* **1.** an opening in a roof or ceiling, fitted with glass, for admitting daylight. **2.** the frame set with glass fitted to such an opening.

sky·line (skī′līn′), *n.* **1.** the boundary line between earth and sky; the apparent horizon. **2.** the outline of something seen against the sky.

sky·man (skī′mən), *n.*, *pl.* **-men.** *Colloq.* an aviator.

sky pilot, *Slang.* **1.** clergyman. **2.** an aviator.

sky·rock·et (skī′rŏk′ĭt), *n.* **1.** a rocket (firework) that ascends into the air and explodes at a height. —*v.i.* **2.** *Colloq.* to move like a skyrocket; rise suddenly.

Sky·ros (skē′rŏs), *n.* an island of the Northern Sporades group, E of Greece. 3193 pop. (1951); 81 sq. mi.

sky·sail (skī′sāl′; *Naut.* -səl), *n.* *Naut.* (on a square-rigged vessel) a light square sail next above the royal.

sky·scrap·er (skī′skrā′pər), *n.* a relatively tall building of many stories, esp. one for office or commercial use.

sky·ward (skī′wərd), *adv.*, *adj.* toward the sky.

sky·wards (skī′wərdz), *adv.* skyward.

sky·writ·ing (skī′rī′tĭng), *n.* **1.** the act or practice of writing against the sky with chemically produced smoke released from an airplane. **2.** the words, etc., traced.

s.l., (L *sine loco*) without place.

slab[1] (slăb), *n.*, *v.*, **slabbed, slabbing.** —*n.* **1.** a broad, flat, somewhat thick piece of stone, wood, or other solid material. **2.** a thick slice of anything: *a slab of bread.* **3.** a rough outside piece cut from a log, as in sawing it into boards. **4.** *Baseball Slang.* the pitcher's plate. —*v.t.* **5.** to make into a slab or slabs. **6.** to cover or lay with slabs. **7.** to cut the slabs or outside pieces from (a log, etc.). [ME *slabbe, sclabbe*; orig. uncert.]

slab[2] (slăb), *adj.* *Archaic.* thick in consistence. [cf. Dan. *slab* mire, Icel. *slabb* slush]

slab·ber (slăb′ər), *v.i.*, *v.t.*, *n.* slobber.

slab-sid·ed (slăb′sī′dĭd), *adj.* *Colloq.* **1.** having the sides long and flat, like slabs. **2.** tall and lank.

slack[1] (slăk), *adj.* **1.** not tense or taut; loose: *slack rope.* **2.** indolent; negligent; remiss. **3.** slow; sluggish. **4.** lacking in activity; dull; not brisk: *slack times for business.* **5.** sluggish, as the water, tide, or wind. —*adv.* **6.** in a slack manner; slackly. —*n.* **7.** a slack condition, interval, or part. **8.** part of a rope, sail, or the like, that hangs loose, without strain upon it. **9.** a decrease in activity, as in business, work, etc.; a period of decreased activity. **10.** *Geog.* a cessation in a strong flow, as of a current at its turn. **11.** a depression between hills, in a hillside, or in the surface of ground. **12.** *Scot. and Brit. Dial.* a boggy or wet hollow, or a morass. **13.** *Pros.* (in sprung rhythm) the unaccented syllable or syllables. —*v.t.* **14.** to be remiss in respect to (some matter, duty, right, etc.); shirk; leave undone. **15.** to make or allow to become less active, vigorous, intense, etc.; relax or abate (efforts, labor, speed, etc.). **16.** to moderate. **17.** to make loose, or less tense or taut, as a rope; loosen. **18.** to slake (lime). —*v.i.* **19.** to be remiss; shirk one's duty or part. **20.** to become less active, vigorous, rapid, etc. **21.** to moderate; slacken. **22.** to become less tense or taut, as a rope; to ease off. **23.** to become slaked, as lime. [ME *slac*, OE *sleac, slæc*, c. Icel. *slakr*] —**slack′ly**, *adv.* —**slack′ness**, *n.*

slack[2] (slăk), *n.* the fine screenings of coal; small or refuse coal. [ME *slac*, t. Scand.; cf. Icel. *slakki* dip in the ground]

slack·en (slăk′ən), *v.i.*, *v.t.* **1.** to make or become less active, vigorous, intense, etc. **2.** to make or become looser or less taut.

slack·er (slăk′ər), *n.* **1.** one who evades his duty. **2.** one who evades military service.

slacks (slăks), *n.pl.* loose-fitting trousers worn by both men and women as informal or sports costume.

slag (slăg), *n.*, *v.*, **slagged, slagging.** —*n.* **1.** the more or less completely fused and vitrified matter separated during the reduction of a metal from its ore. **2.** the scoria from a volcano. —*v.t.* **3.** to convert into slag. —*v.i.* **4.** to form slag; become a slaglike mass. [t. MLG: m. *slagge*, c. G *schlacke* dross, slag] —**slag′gy**, *adj.*

slain (slān), *v.* pp. of **slay.**

slake (slāk), *v.*, **slaked, slaking.** —*v.t.* **1.** to allay (thirst, desire, wrath, etc.) by satisfying. **2.** to cool or refresh. **3.** to make less active, vigorous, intense, etc. **4.** to disintegrate or treat (lime) with water or moist air, causing it to change into calcium hydroxide (**slaked lime**). **5.** *Obs.* to make loose or less tense. —*v.i.* **6.** (of lime) to become slaked. **7.** *Rare.* to become less active, vigorous, etc. [ME; OE *slacian*, der. *slæc* slack]

sla·lom (slä′lōm), *n.* a downhill skiing race in a winding course. [t. Norw.]

slam[1] (slăm), *v.*, **slammed, slamming**, *n.* —*v.t.*, *v.i.* **1.** to shut with force and noise. **2.** to dash, strike, etc., with violent and noisy impact. **3.** *U.S. Slang.* to criticize severely. —*n.* **4.** a violent and noisy closing, dashing, or impact. **5.** the noise made. **6.** *U.S. Slang.* a severe criticism. [orig. uncert.]

slam[2] (slăm), *n.* *Cards.* **1.** the winning of all the tricks in one deal, as at whist (in bridge, called **grand slam**), or of all but one (in bridge, called **little slam**). **2.** an old type of card game associated with ruff. [orig. obscure]

slan·der (slăn′dər), *n.* **1.** defamation; calumny. **2.** a malicious, false, and defamatory statement or report. **3.** *Law.* defamation by oral utterance rather than by writing, etc. —*v.t.* **4.** to utter slander concerning; defame. —*v.i.* **5.** to utter or circulate slander. [ME *sclandre*, t. AF: m. *esclaundre*, t. L: m. *scandalum*. See SCANDAL] —**slan′der·er**, *n.* —**slan′der·ous**, *adj.* —**slan′der·ous·ly**, *adv.* —**slan′der·ous·ness**, *n.*

slang (slăng), *n.* **1.** language of a markedly colloquial character, regarded as below the standard of cultivated speech. **2.** the jargon of a particular class, profession, etc. **3.** the special vocabulary of thieves, vagabonds, etc.; argot. —*v.i.* **4.** to use slang or abusive language. —*v.t.* **5.** to assail with abusive language. [orig. uncert.]

slang·y (slăng′ī), *adj.*, **slangier, slangiest. 1.** pertaining to or of the nature of slang. **2.** using much slang. —**slang′i·ly**, *adv.* —**slang′i·ness**, *n.*

slank (slăngk), *v.* *Archaic.* pt. of **slink.**

slant (slănt), *v.i.*, *v.t.* **1.** to slope. [var. of *slent* (t. Scand.; cf. Norw. *slenta*), with vowel of ASLANT] —*n.* **2.** slanting or oblique direction; slope: *the slant of a roof.* **3.** a slanting line, surface, etc. **4.** a mental leaning or tendency; a bias. **5.** *Colloq.* a glance or look. —*adj.* **6.** slanting; oblique. [aphetic var. of ASLANT] —**slant′ing**, *adj.* —**slant′ing·ly, slant′ly,** *adv.* —Syn. **1.** See **slope. 2.** incline, inclination, pitch, obliquity, obliqueness.

slant·wise (slănt′wīz′, slănt′-), *adv.* **1.** aslant; obliquely. —*adj.* **2.** slanting; oblique. Also, **slant·ways** (slănt′wāz′, slănt′-).

slap (slăp), *n.*, *v.*, **slapped, slapping,** *adv.* —*n.* **1.** a smart blow, esp. with the open hand or with something flat. **2.** a sarcastic or censuring hit or rebuke. —*v.t.* **3.** to strike smartly, esp. with the open hand or with something flat. **4.** to bring (the hands, etc.) against with a smart blow. **5.** to dash or cast forcibly. —*adv.* **6.** smartly; suddenly. **7.** *Colloq.* directly; straight. [t. LG: m. *slapp, slappe;* imit.]

slap·dash (slăp′dăsh′), *adv.*, *adj.* **1.** in a hasty, haphazard manner. **2.** carelessly hasty or offhand.

slap·jack (slăp′jăk′), *n.* **1.** a simple card game. **2.** *U.S.* a flapjack or griddlecake.

slap·stick (slăp′stĭk′), *n.* **1.** broad comedy in which rough play and knockabout methods prevail. **2.** a stick or lath used by harlequins, clowns, etc., as in pantomime, for striking other performers, often a combination of laths which make a loud, clapping noise without hurting a person struck. —*adj.* **3.** using or marked by the use of, slapstick: *a slapstick motion picture.*

slash (slăsh), *v.t.* **1.** to cut with a violent sweep or by striking violently and at random. **2.** to lash. **3.** to cut, reduce, or alter. **4.** to make slits in (a garment) to show an underlying fabric. —*v.i.* **5.** to lay about one with sharp strokes; make one's way by cutting. **6.** to make a sweeping, cutting stroke. —*n.* **7.** a sweeping stroke. **8.** a cut or wound made with such a stroke; a gash. **9.** an ornamental slit in a garment showing an underlying fabric. **10.** (in forest land) a. an open area strewn with debris of trees from felling or from wind or fire. **b.** the debris itself. **11.** (*often in pl.*) *U.S.* a tract of wet or swampy ground overgrown with bushes or trees. [ME *slasch(en)*, ? t. OF: m. *esclachier* break] —**slash'-er,** *n.*

slash·ing (slăsh'ĭng), *n.* **1.** slash. —*adj.* **2.** sweeping; cutting. **3.** violent; severe. **4.** dashing; impetuous **5.** *Colloq.* very large or fine: *a slashing fortune.* —**slash'-ing·ly,** *adv.*

slash pine, **1.** a pine, *Pinus caribaea,* with a hard, durable wood, common in slashes and swamps in the southeastern U.S. **2.** the wood of this tree. **3.** the loblolly pine, *Pinus Taeda.*

Slask (shlŏnsk), *n.* Polish name of **Silesia.**

slat¹ (slăt), *n., v.,* **slatted, slatting.** —*n.* **1.** a long, thin, narrow strip of wood, metal, etc., used as a support for a bed, as one of the horizontal laths of a Venetian blind, etc. —*v.t.* **2.** to furnish or make with slats. [ME *slatt,* var. of *sclat,* t. OF: m. *esclat* piece broken or split off, akin to *esclater* burst]

slat² (slăt), *v.,* **slatted, slatting,** *n.* *Dial.* —*v.t.* **1.** to throw or dash with force. —*v.i.* **2.** to flap violently, as sails. —*n.* **3.** a slap; a sharp blow. [orig. obscure]

slate (slāt), *n., v.,* **slated, slating.** —*n.* **1.** a fine-grained rock formed by the compression of clay, shale, etc., that tends to split along parallel cleavage planes, usually at an angle to the planes of stratification. **2.** a thin piece or plate of this rock or a similar material, used esp. for roofing, or (when framed) for writing on. **3.** a dull, dark bluish gray. **4.** *U.S.* a tentative list of candidates, officers, etc., for acceptance by a nominating convention or the like. **5. clean slate,** a good record. —*v.t.* **6.** to cover with or as with slate. **7.** to write or set down for nomination or appointment. [ME *sclate,* t. OF: m. *esclate* (fem.). See **slat¹**]

slat·ing (slā'tĭng), *n.* **1.** the operation of covering with slates. **2.** slates collectively. **3.** the material for slating.

slat·tern (slăt'ərn), *n.* a slovenly, untidy woman or girl.

slat·tern·ly (slăt'ərnlĭ), *adj.* **1.** having the appearance or ways of a slattern. **2.** characteristic or suggestive of a slattern. —*adv.* **3.** in the manner of a slattern.

slat·y (slā'tĭ), *adj.,* **slatier, slatiest.** **1.** consisting of, resembling, or pertaining to slate. **2.** slate-colored.

slaugh·ter (slô'tər), *n.* **1.** the killing or butchering of cattle, sheep, etc., esp. for food. **2.** the brutal or violent killing of a person. **3.** the killing by violence of great numbers of persons; carnage; massacre. —*v.t.* **4.** to kill or butcher (animals), esp. for food. **5.** to kill in a brutal or violent manner. **6.** to slay in great numbers; massacre. [ME *slaghter,* t. Scand.; cf. Icel. *slātr* butcher's meat, *slātra* kill; akin to **slay**] —**slaugh'ter·er,** *n.* —**Syn.** 4-6. SLAUGHTER, BUTCHER, MASSACRE all imply violent and bloody methods of killing. SLAUGHTER and BUTCHER, primarily referring to the killing of animals for food, are used also of the brutal or indiscriminate killing of human beings: *to slaughter cattle, to butcher a hog.* MASSACRE indicates a general slaughtering of helpless or unresisting victims: *to massacre the peasants of a region.*

slaugh·ter·house (slô'tər hous'), *n.* a building or place where animals are butchered for food; an abattoir.

slaugh·ter·ous (slô'tər əs), *adj.* murderous; destructive.

Slav (släv, slăv), *n.* **1.** one of a race of peoples widely spread over eastern, southeastern, and central Europe, including the Russians and Ruthenians (**Eastern Slavs**), the Bulgars, Serbs, Croats, Slavonians, Slovenes, etc. (**Southern Slavs**), and the Poles, Czechs, Moravians, Slovaks, etc. (**Western Slavs**). —*adj.* **2.** of, pertaining to, or characteristic of, the Slavs; Slavic. [t. ML: s. *Slavus;* r. ME *Sclave,* t. ML: m.s. *Sclavus*]

Slav., Slavic.

slave (slāv), *n., v.,* **slaved, slaving.** —*n.* **1.** one who is the property of and wholly subject to, another; a bond servant. **2.** one entirely under the domination of some influence: *a slave to a drug.* **3.** a drudge. —*v.i.* **4.** to work like a slave; drudge. —*v.t.* **5.** to enslave. [ME *sclave,* t. OF: m. *esclave,* t. ML: m. *sclavus* slave, SLAV; from the fact that many Slavs were reduced to slavery]

slave ant, an ant, as *Formica fusca,* held in captivity by any other species, as *Formica sanguinea* (called **slave-making ants**).

Slave Coast, the coast of W equatorial Africa, N of the Gulf of Guinea and between the Benin and Volta rivers: a center of slavery traffic, 16th-19th centuries.

slave driver, **1.** an overseer of slaves. **2.** a hard taskmaster.

slave·hold·er (slāv'hōl'dər), *n.* one who owns slaves.

slav·er¹ (slā'vər), *n.* **1.** a dealer in or an owner of slaves. **2.** a vessel engaged in the traffic in slaves. [f. SLAVE + -ER¹]

slav·er² (slăv'ər), *v.i.* **1.** to let saliva run from the mouth; slobber. **2.** to fawn. —*v.t.* **3.** to wet or smear with saliva. —*n.* **4.** saliva coming from the mouth. **5.** drivel; twaddle. [ME, appar. t. Scand.; cf. Icel. *slafra*]

slav·er·y (slā'vərĭ), *n.* **1.** the condition of a slave; bondage. **2.** the keeping of slaves as a practice or insti-

tution. **3.** a state of subjection like that of a slave. **4.** severe toil; drudgery. —**Syn.** 1. SLAVERY, BONDAGE, SERVITUDE refer to involuntary subjection to another or others. SLAVERY emphasizes the idea of complete ownership and control by a master: *the institution of slavery.* BONDAGE indicates a state of subjugation or captivity often involving burdensome and degrading labor: *in bondage to a cruel master.* SERVITUDE is compulsory service, often such as is required by a legal penalty: *penal servitude.* —**Ant.** 1. liberty.

slav·ey (slā'vĭ), *n., pl.* **-eys.** *Brit. Colloq.* a female domestic servant; maid of all work.

Slav·ic (slăv'ĭk, slä'vĭk), *n.* **1.** one of the principal groups of Indo-European languages, usually divided into West Slavic (Polish, Czech, Slovak, Serbian), East Slavic (Russian, Ukrainian, Ruthenian), and South Slavic (Old Church Slavic, Bulgarian, Serbo-Croatian, and Slovene). —*adj.* **2.** of or pertaining to the Slavs, or their languages.

slav·ish (slā'vĭsh), *adj.* **1.** of or befitting a slave: *slavish submission.* **2.** being or resembling a slave; abjectly submissive. **3.** base; mean; ignoble: *slavish fears.* **4.** imitative; lacking originality: *a slavish reproduction.* —**slav'ish·ly,** *adv.* —**slav'ish·ness,** *n.* —**Syn.** 2. See **servile.** —**Ant.** 2. independent.

Slav·ism (slăv'ĭz əm, slä'-), *n.* the racial character, spirit, or tendencies of the Slavs.

Slavo-, form of **Slav** used in combination, as in *Slavo-Germanic.*

slav·oc·ra·cy (slăv ŏk'rə sĭ), *n., pl.* **-cies.** **1.** the rule or domination of slaveholders. **2.** a dominating body of slaveholders. [f. SLAV(E) + -O- + -CRACY]

Sla·vo·ni·a (slə vō'nĭ ə), *n.* a region in N Yugoslavia.

Sla·vo·ni·an (slə vō'nĭ ən), *adj.* **1.** of or pertaining to Slavonia or its inhabitants. **2.** Slavic. —*n.* **3.** a native or inhabitant of Slavonia. **4.** a Slav.

Sla·von·ic (slə vŏn'ĭk), *adj.* **1.** Slavonian. **2.** Slavic.

Slav·o·phile (slăv'ə fĭl', -fĭl, slăv'-), *n.* **1.** a friend or admirer of the Slavs. —*adj.* **2.** friendly to or admiring the Slavs; favoring the Slavic interests, aims, etc. Also, **Slav·o·phil** (slăv'ə fĭl, slăv'-). —**Sla·voph·i·lism** (slə vŏf'ə lĭz'əm, slăv'ə fĭl'Ĭz'əm, slăv'-), *n.*

Slav·o·phobe (slăv'ə fōb', slăv'-), *n.* one who fears the Slavs, or their influence or ascendancy.

slaw (slô), *n.* **1.** sliced or chopped cabbage served uncooked or cooked (cold or hot) with seasoning or dressing; coleslaw. [t. D: m. *sla,* short for *salade* SALAD]

slay (slā), *v.t.,* **slew, slain, slaying.** **1.** to kill by violence. **2.** to destroy; extinguish. **3.** *Obs.* to strike; smite. [ME; OE *slēan,* c. G *schlagen*] —**slay'er,** *n.*

sleave (slēv), *v.,* **sleaved, sleaving,** *n.* —*v.t.* **1.** to divide or separate into filaments, as silk. —*n.* **2.** anything matted or raveled. **3.** a filament of silk obtained by separating a thicker thread. **4.** a silk in the form of such filaments. [OE *slǣfan,* akin to *slūfan* split]

slea·zy (slā'zĭ, slē'zĭ), *adj.,* **-zier, -ziest.** thin or poor in texture, as a fabric; flimsy. [orig. uncert.] —**slea'zi·ly,** *adv.* —**slea'zi·ness,** *n.*

sled (slĕd), *n., v.,* **sledded, sledding.** —*n.* **1.** a vehicle mounted on runners for conveying loads over snow, ice, rough ground, etc.; a sledge. **2.** a small vehicle of this kind used in coasting, etc. **3.** to ride or be carried on a sled. —*v.t.* **4.** to convey on a sled. [ME *sledde,* t. MFlem. or MLG; akin to G *schlitten* sled]

sled·der (slĕd'ər), *n.* **1.** one who rides on a sled. **2.** a horse or other animal that draws a sled.

sled·ding (slĕd'ĭng), *n.* **1.** the state of the ground permitting use of a sled. **2.** the going, or kind of travel, for sleds, as determined by the ground, etc.: *rough sledding.* **3.** the act of conveying or riding on a sled.

sledge¹ (slĕj), *n., v.,* **sledged, sledging.** —*n.* **1.** a sled for conveying loads over snow, ice, rough ground, etc. **2.** a vehicle mounted on runners, and of various forms, used for traveling over snow and ice, as in northern countries. **3.** *Brit.* a light form of such a sledge used for pleasure driving, etc. —*v.i., v.i.* **4.** to convey or travel by sledge. [t. MD: m. *sleedse*]

sledge² (slĕj), *n., v.,* **sledged, sledging.** —*n.* **1.** Also, **sledge hammer,** a large, heavy hammer, commonly wielded with both hands. —*v.i., v.t.* **2.** to strike or beat with, or as with, a sledge. [ME *slegge,* OE *slecg,* c. D *slegge*]

sledge-ham·mer (slĕj'hăm'ər), *v.t.* **1.** sledge². —*adj.* **2.** like a sledge; powerful; ruthless.

sleek¹ (slēk), *adj.* **1.** smooth; glossy, as hair, an animal, etc. **2.** well fed or well groomed. **3.** smooth of manners, speech, etc. **4.** suave; insinuating. [var. of SLICK¹] —**sleek'ly,** *adv.* —**sleek'ness,** *n.*

sleek² (slēk), *v.t.* to make sleek; smooth. [var. of SLICK²] —**sleek'er,** *n.*

sleek·y (slē'kĭ), *adj.* **1.** sleek; smooth. **2.** artful; sly. Also, *Scot.,* **sleek·it** (slē'kĭt).

sleep (slēp), *v.,* **slept, sleeping,** *n.* —*v.i.* **1.** to take the repose or rest afforded by a suspension of the voluntary exercise of the bodily functions and the natural suspension, complete or partial, of consciousness. **2.** *Bot.* to assume, esp. at night, a state similar to the sleep of animals, marked by closing of petals, leaves, etc. **3.** to be dormant, quiescent, or inactive, as faculties. **4.** to lie in death. **5.** *Brit.* to sleep at the place of one's work (fol. by *in*). —*v.t.* **6.** to take rest in (sleep). **7.** to spend or pass (time, etc.) in sleep (fol. by *away* or *out*). **8.** to get rid of (a headache, etc.) by sleeping (fol. by *off* or *away*). [ME *slepe*, OE *slēpan*, *slāpan*, c. G *schlafen*] —*n.* **9.** the state of a person, animal, or plant that sleeps. **10.** a period of sleeping: *a brief sleep.* **11.** dormancy or inactivity. **12.** the repose of death. [ME; OE *slēp* (Anglian), *slāp*, c. D *slaap*, G *schlaf*]

sleep·er (slē′pər), *n.* **1.** one who or which sleeps. **2.** *Brit.* a timber or beam laid in a railway track, serving as a foundation or support for the rails; a cross tie, bridge tie or switch tie in a railroad track. **3.** a sleeping car.

sleep·ing (slē′pĭng), *n.* **1.** condition of being asleep. —*adj.* **2.** that sleeps. **3.** used for sleeping.

sleeping bag, a large bag made of fur or the like, for sleeping in, esp. out of doors.

sleeping car, a railroad car fitted with berths, compartments, bedrooms, or drawing rooms, for travelers who wish to sleep during the journey.

sleeping partner, *Chiefly Brit.* silent partner.

sleeping sickness, *Pathol.* **1.** African sleeping sickness. **2.** a form of inflammation of the brain marked by extreme weakness, drowsiness, or sleepiness, usually associated with paralysis, of some cerebral nerves.

sleep·less (slēp′lĭs), *adj.* **1.** without sleep: *a sleepless night.* **2.** alert. **3.** always active: *the sleepless ocean.* —**sleep′less·ly,** *adv.* —**sleep′less·ness,** *n.*

sleep·walk·ing (slēp′wô′kĭng), *n.* **1.** state or act of walking while asleep. —*adj.* **2.** of or pertaining to the state of walking while asleep. —**sleep′walk′er,** *n.*

sleep·y (slē′pĭ), *adj.,* **sleepier, sleepiest. 1.** ready or inclined to sleep; drowsy. **2.** of or showing drowsiness. **3.** languid; languorous. **4.** lethargic; sluggish. **5.** quiet: *a sleepy village.* **6.** inducing sleep. —**sleep′i·ly,** *adv.* —**sleep′i·ness,** *n.*

sleet (slēt), *n.* **1.** the frozen coating on trees, wires, and other bodies that sometimes forms when rain or sleet falls at a low temperature. **2.** *U.S. Weather Bureau.* frozen or partly frozen rain. **3.** *Brit. Meteorol. Office.* snow and rain falling together. —*v.i.* **4.** to send down sleet. **5.** to fall as or like sleet. [ME *slete*, akin to LG *slote*, G *schlossen* hail] —**sleet′y,** *adj.*

sleeve (slēv), *n., v.,* **sleeved, sleeving.** —*n.* **1.** the part of a garment that covers the arm, varying in form and length but commonly tubular. **2.** *Mach.* a tubular piece, as of metal, fitting over a rod or the like. **3.** **up one's sleeve,** ready; at hand. —*v.t.* **4.** to furnish with sleeves. **5.** *Mech.* to fit with a sleeve; join or fasten by means of a sleeve. [ME *sleve*, OE *slēfe* (Anglian), c. D *sloof* apron] —**sleeve′less,** *adj.*

sleigh (slā), *n.* **1.** a light, usually open vehicle on runners, generally horse-drawn, used for pleasure driving, etc., in snowy weather. —*v.i.* **2.** to travel or ride in a sleigh. [t. D: m. *slee*, short for *slede* BLED] —**sleigh′er,** *n.*

sleight (slīt), *n.* **1.** skill; dexterity. **2.** *Rare.* an artifice; stratagem. **3.** *Obs.* cunning; craft. [ME, var. of *siegthe*, t. Scand.; cf. Icel. *slǣgdh*, der. *slǣgr* SLY]

sleight of hand, 1. skill in feats of jugglery or legerdemain. **2.** the performance of such feats. **3.** a feat of legerdemain.

slen·der (slĕn′dər), *adj.* **1.** small in circumference in proportion to height or length. **2.** small in size, amount, extent, etc.: *a slender income.* **3.** having little value, force, or justification: *slender prospects.* **4.** thin or weak, as sound. [ME *slendre, sclendre*; orig. uncert.] —**slen′der·ly,** *adv.* —**slen′der·ness,** *n.*
—**Syn. 1.** SLENDER, SLIGHT, SLIM imply a tendency toward thinness. As applied to the human body, SLENDER implies a generally attractive and pleasing thinness: *slender hands.* SLIGHT often adds the idea of frailness to that of thinness: *a slight figure almost fragile in appearance.* SLIM implies a lithe or delicate thinness: *a slim and athletic figure.* —Ant. **1.** fat, stocky.

slen·der·ize (slĕn′də rīz′), *v.t.,* **-ized, -izing. 1.** to make slender or more slender. **2.** to cause to appear slender: *dresses that slenderize the figure.*

slept (slĕpt), *v.* pt. and pp. of **sleep.**

Sles·vig (slĕs′vĭкн), *n.* Danish name of **Schleswig.**

Sles·wick (slĕs′wĭk), *n.* **Schleswig.**

sleuth (slōōth), *n.* **1.** *U.S. Colloq.* a detective. **2.** a sleuthhound or bloodhound. —*v.t., v.i.* **3.** to track or trail as a detective does. [ME *sloth*, t. Scand.; cf. Icel. *slōdh* track, trail]

sleuth·hound (slōōth′hound′), *n.* **1.** a bloodhound. **2.** *U.S. Colloq.* a detective.

slew¹ (slōō), *v.* pt. of **slay.**

slew² (slōō), *n.* **1.** a twist; turn. —*v.t., v.i.* **2.** to twist; swing round; turn. [orig. unknown]

slew³ (slōō), *n.* *U.S. and Canada.* a marshy pool or inlet. [var. of SLOUGH¹]

slew⁴ (slōō), *n.* *Colloq.* a great number. Also, **slue.** [orig. obscure]

Slez·sko (slĕs′kô), *n.* Czech name of **Silesia.**

slice (slīs), *n., v.,* **sliced, slicing.** —*n.* **1.** a thin, broad, flat piece cut from something: *a slice of bread.* **2.** a part; portion. **3.** any of various implements with a thin, broad blade or part, as for turning food in a frying pan, for serving fish at table, for taking up printing ink, etc. **4.** *Golf.* a slicing stroke. —*v.t.* **5.** to cut into slices; divide into parts. **6.** to cut through or cleave like a knife: *the ship sliced the sea.* **7.** to cut (*off, away, from,* etc.) as or like a slice. **8.** to remove by means of a slice (implement), slice bar, or the like. **9.** *Golf.* to hit (the ball) with a glancing stroke that causes it to curve off to

the right (or in the case of a left-handed player, the left). —*v.i.* **10.** *Golf.* to slice the ball. [ME, t. OF: m. *esclice, esclisse* splinter, shiver of wood, ult. t. Gmc.; cf. OHG *slitz* slit] —**slice′a·ble,** *adj.* —**slic′er,** *n.*

slice bar, a long-handled instrument with a blade at the end, for clearing away or breaking up clinkers, etc., in a furnace.

slick¹ (slĭk), *adj.* **1.** sleek; glossy. **2.** smooth of manners, speech, etc. **3.** sly; shrewdly adroit. **4.** ingenious; cleverly devised. **5.** slippery, as though covered with oil. —*n.* **6.** a smooth place or spot, as an oil-covered area on the ocean. **7.** *U.S. Slang.* a magazine in which the paper is finished to have a more or less glossy surface, implying a high-grade content. —*adv.* **8.** smoothly; cleverly. [ME *slike,* adj., c. Flem. *sleek* even, smooth] —**slick′ly,** *adv.* —**slick′ness,** *n.*

slick² (slĭk), *v.t.* **1.** to make sleek or smooth. **2.** *Colloq.* to make smart or fine (fol. by *up*). —*n.* **3.** *Foundry.* a small trowel used for smoothing the surface of the mold. [ME *slike*(n), v., OE *-slician*; akin to Icel. *slīkja* give a gloss to]

slick·en·side (slĭk′ən sīd′), *n.* *Geol.* a rock surface which has become more or less polished and striated from the sliding or grinding motion of an adjacent mass of rock. [f. *slicken* (d. var. of SLICK¹) + SIDE]

slick·er (slĭk′ər), *n.* *U.S.* **1.** a long, loose oilskin or waterproof outer coat. **2.** *Colloq.* a swindler; a sly cheat.

slide (slīd), *v.,* **slid, slid or slidden, sliding,** *n.* —*v.i.* **1.** to move along in continuous contact with a smooth or slippery surface: *to slide down a snow-covered hill.* **2.** to slip, as one losing foothold or as a vehicle skidding. **3.** to glide or pass smoothly onward. **4.** to slip easily, quietly, or unobtrusively (fol. by *in, out, away,* etc.). **5.** to go unregarded: *to let things slide.* **6.** to pass or fall gradually into a specified state, character, practice, etc. —*v.t.* **7.** to cause to slide, as over a surface or with a smooth, gliding motion. **8.** to slip (something) easily or quietly (fol. by *in, into,* etc.). —*n.* **9.** act of sliding. **10.** a smooth surface for sliding on. **11.** *Geol.* **a.** a landslide or the like. **b.** the mass of matter sliding down. **12.** a single image for projection in a projector, as a lantern slide. **13.** a plate of glass or other material on which objects are placed for microscopic examination. **14.** *Music.* **a.** an embellishment or grace consisting of an upward or downward series of three or more tones, the last of which is the principal tone. **b.** a portamento. **c.** (in instruments of the trumpet class, esp. the trombone) a section of the tube, usually U-shaped, which can be pushed in or out to alter the length of the air column and thus the pitch of the tones. [ME; OE *slīdan,* c. MLG *slīden*]
—**Syn. 1.** SLIDE, GLIDE, SLIP suggest movement over a smooth surface. SLIDE suggests a rather brief movement of one surface over another in contact with it: *to slide downhill.* GLIDE suggests a continuous, smooth, easy, and (usually) noiseless motion: *a skater glides over the ice.* To SLIP is to slide smoothly, often in a sudden or accidental way: *to slip on the ice and fall.*

slide fastener, a zipper (def. 1).

slide knot, a knot which forms an eye which may be slipped free.

Slide Mountain, a mountain in SE New York: highest peak of the Catskill Mountains. 4204 ft.

slide rule, a device for rapid calculation, consisting essentially of a rule having a sliding piece moving along it, both marked with graduated logarithmic scales.

slide trombone. See **trombone.**

slide valve, *Mach.* a valve that slides (without lifting) to open or close an aperture, as the valves of the ports in the cylinders of certain steam engines

sliding scale, 1. a variable scale, esp. of industrial costs, as wages, raw materials, etc., which may be adapted to demand. **2.** a wage scale varying with the selling price of goods produced, the cost of living, or profits.

sli·er (slī′ər), *adj.* compar. of **sly.**

sli·est (slī′ĭst), *adj.* superl. of **sly.**

slight (slīt), *adj.* **1.** small in amount, degree, etc.: *a slight increase, a slight odor.* **2.** of little weight or importance; trifling. **3.** slender; slim. **4.** frail; flimsy. **5.** lacking in solid or substantial qualities. —*v.t.* **6.** to treat as of slight importance. **7.** to treat with indifference; ignore. **8.** to do negligently; scamp. —*n.* **9.** slighting indifference or treatment. **10.** an instance of slighting treatment. **11.** a pointed and contemptuous ignoring; an affront. [ME; OE *sliht* smooth (in *eorthslihtes* close to earth), c. Icel. *slēttr* smooth, G *schlecht* bad, Goth. *slaihts* smooth] —**slight′ly,** *adv.* —**slight′ness,** *n.*
—**Syn. 3.** See **slender. 6.** SLIGHT, DISREGARD, NEGLECT, OVERLOOK mean to pay no attention or too little attention to someone or something. To SLIGHT is irresponsibly to give only superficial attention to something important: *to slight one's work.* To DISREGARD is to pay no attention to a person or thing: *to disregard the rules*; in some circumstances, to DISREGARD may be admirable: *to disregard a handicap.* To NEGLECT is to shirk paying sufficient attention to a person or thing: *to neglect one's correspondence.* To OVERLOOK is to fail to see someone or something (possibly because of carelessness): *to overlook a bill which is due.* **11.** See **insult.** —**Ant. 6.** notice.

slight·ing (slī′tĭng), *adj.* derogatory; disparaging. —**slight′ing·ly,** *adv.*

---

b., blend of, blended; **c.,** cognate with; **d.,** dialect, dialectal; **der.,** derived from; **f.,** formed from; **g.,** going back to; **m.,** modification of; **r.,** replacing; **s.,** stem of; **t.,** taken from; **?,** perhaps. See the full key on inside cover.

Sli·go (slī′gō), n. **1.** a county in NW Ireland, in Connaught province. 56,828 pop. (prelim. 1956); 694 sq. mi. **2.** its county seat: a seaport. 13,529 (1951).

sli·ly (slī′lĭ), adv. slyly.

slim (slĭm), adj., **slimmer, slimmest**, v., **slimmed, slimming.** —adj. **1.** slender, as in girth or form; slight in build or structure. **2.** poor: a slim chance, a slim excuse. **3.** small, inconsiderable, or scanty: a slim income. —v.t. **4.** to make slim. —v.i. **5.** to become slim. [t. D or LG; c. G schlimm bad] —**slim′ly**, adv. —**slim′ness**, n. —**Syn. 1.** See slender.

slime (slīm), n., v., **slimed, sliming.** —n. **1.** thin, glutinous mud. **2.** any ropy or viscous liquid matter, esp. of a foul or offensive kind. **3.** a viscous secretion of animal or vegetable origin. —v.t. **4.** to cover or smear with, or as with, slime. **5.** to remove slime from, as fish for canning. [ME slyme, OE slīm, c. G schleim]

slime mold, any of the group Myxomycetes (Mycetozoa), primitive organisms with characters relating them to both the plant and animal worlds.

slim·sy (slĭm′zĭ), adj. U.S. flimsy; frail.

slim·y (slī′mĭ), adj., **slimier, slimiest. 1.** of or like slime. **2.** abounding in or covered with slime. **3.** foul; vile. —**slim′i·ly**, adv. —**slim′i·ness**, n.

sling[1] (slĭng), n., v., **slung, slinging.** —n. **1.** an instrument for hurling stones, etc., by hand, consisting of a strap or piece for holding the missile, with two strings attached, the ends of which are held in the hand (or attached to a staff), the whole being whirled rapidly before discharging the missile. **2.** a slingshot. **3.** a rope or chain used in hoisting cargo in and out of a ship. **4.** (usually pl.) Naut. a rope or chain supporting a yard. **5.** a bandage used to suspend a part, commonly an arm or hand. **6.** a strap, band, or the line forming a loop by which something is suspended or carried, as a strap attached to a rifle and passed over the shoulder. **7.** act of slinging. —v.t. **8.** to throw, cast, or hurl; fling, as from the hand. **9.** to place in or secure with a sling to raise or lower. **10.** to raise, lower, etc., by such means. **11.** to hang in a sling or so as to swing loosely: to sling a rifle over one's shoulder. **12.** to suspend. [ME slynge(n), t. Scand.; cf. Icel. slyngva] —**sling′er**, n.

sling[2] (slĭng), n. U.S. an iced alcoholic drink, containing gin or the like, water, sugar, and lemon or lime juice. [cf. G schlingen swallow]

sling·shot (slĭng′shŏt′), n. a Y-shaped stick with an elastic strip between the prongs for shooting stones, etc.

slink (slĭngk), v., **slunk** or (Archaic) **slank; slunk; slinking;** n., adj. —v.i. **1.** to go in a furtive, abject manner, as from fear, cowardice, or shame. —v.t. **2.** (of cows, etc.) to bring forth (young) prematurely. —n. **3.** a prematurely born calf or other animal. —adj. **4.** born prematurely: a slink calf. [ME slynke, OE slincan creep, crawl, c. LG slinken, G schlinken] —**slink′ing·ly**, adv.

slip[1] (slĭp), v., **slipped** or (Archaic) **slipt; slipped; slipping;** n. —v.i. **1.** to pass or go smoothly or easily; glide; slide (fol. by along, away, down, off, over, through, etc.): water slips off a smooth surface. **2.** to slide suddenly and involuntarily, as on a smooth surface, to lose one's foothold. **3.** to move, slide, or start from place, position, fastenings, the hold, etc. **4.** to get away, escape, or be lost: to let an opportunity slip. **5.** to go, come, get, etc., easily or quickly: to slip into a dress. **6.** to pass insensibly, as from the mind or memory; pass quickly or imperceptibly (fol. by away, by, etc.), as time. **7.** to go quietly; steal. **8.** to pass superficially, carelessly, or without attention, as over a matter. **9.** to make a slip, mistake, or error (often fol. by up). **10.** Colloq. to become somewhat reduced in quantity or quality: the market slipped today. **11. let slip,** to say unintentionally: to let slip the truth. —v.t. **12.** to cause to slip, pass, put, draw, etc., with a smooth, easy, or sliding motion: to slip one's hand into a drawer. **13.** to put or draw quickly or stealthily: to slip a letter into a person's hand. **14.** to put (on) or take (off) easily or quickly, as a garment. **15.** to let slip from fastenings, the hold, etc. **16.** to release from a leash or the like, as a hound or a hawk. **17.** to untie or undo (a knot). **18.** Naut. to let go entirely, as an anchor cable or an anchor. **19.** to let pass unheeded; neglect, or miss. **20.** to pass over or omit, as in speaking or writing. **21.** to slip away from, escape from or elude, as a pursuer. **22.** to escape (one's memory, notice, knowledge, etc.). **23.** (of animals) to bring forth (offspring) prematurely. —n. **24.** act of slipping. **25.** a slipping of the feet, as on slippery ground. **26.** a mishap. **27.** a mistake, often inadvertent, as in speaking or writing: a slip of the tongue. **28.** an error in conduct; an indiscretion. **29.** the slipping away from a pursuer, guard, or other person: to give one the slip. **30.** something easily slipped on or off. **31.** a kind of dog leash. **32.** a woman's underdress. **33.** a pillowcase. **34.** an inclined plane sloping to the water, on which vessels are built or repaired. **35.** Naut. the difference between the speed at which a screw propeller or paddle wheel would move if it were working against a solid and the actual speed at which it advances through the water. **36.** an artificial slope beside navigable water, serving as a landing place. **37.** U.S. a space between two wharves or in a dock, for vessels to lie in. **38.** (in pumps) the difference between the actual volume of water or other liquid delivered by a pump during one complete stroke, and the theoretical

volume as determined by calculation of the displacement. **39.** Cricket. **a.** the position of a fielder who stands behind and to the off side of the wicket keeper. **b.** the fielder himself. **40.** Geol. **a.** the relative displacement of formerly adjacent points on opposite sides of a fault, measured along the fault plane. **b.** a small fault. [ME slyppe, prob. t. MLG: m. slippen, c. d. G schlippen, but cf. OE -slype, slyp- slip (def. 30)] —**Syn. 2.** See slide. **27.** See mistake.

slip[2] (slĭp), n., v., **slipped, slipping.** —n. **1.** a piece suitable for propagation cut from a plant; a scion or cutting. **2.** any long, narrow piece or strip, as of wood, paper, land, etc. **3.** a young person, esp. one of slender form. **4.** a small paper form on which information is noted: a withdrawal slip. **5.** a small whetstone having a wedge-shaped cross section in which one or two sides are rounded. **6.** U.S. a long seat or narrow pew, as in a church. —v.t. **7.** to take slips or cuttings from (a plant); take (a part), as a slip from a plant. [late ME, t. MD or MLG: m. slippe cut, slit, strip, etc.]

slip[3] (slĭp), n. Ceramics. potter's clay made semifluid with water, used for coating or decorating pottery. [ME and OE slype; orig. uncert. Cf. Norw. slip slime]

slip cover, a cloth cover for a piece of furniture, made so as to be easily removable.

slip·knot (slĭp′nŏt′), n. a knot which slips easily along the cord or line round which it is made. See illus. under knot.

slip·noose (slĭp′nōōs′), n. a noose with a knot that slides along the rope, thus forming a noose that tightens as the rope is pulled.

slip·on (slĭp′ŏn′, -ôn′), adj. **1.** designed to be slipped on easily, as a loose blouse. **2.** slipover. —n. **3.** a slip-on garment or article of dress.

slip·o·ver (slĭp′ō′vər), adj. designed for slipping over the head, as a blouse or sweater.

slip·page (slĭp′ĭj), n. **1.** act of slipping. **2.** the amount or extent of slipping. **3.** Mach. the amount of work dissipated by slipping of parts, excess play, etc.

slip·per (slĭp′ər), n. a light shoe into which the foot may be easily slipped, worn chiefly indoors. [f. slip[1], v. + -er[1]] —**slip′pered**, adj. —**slip′per·like′**, adj.

slip·per·ing (slĭp′ər ĭng), n. a beating with a slipper.

slip·per·less (slĭp′ər lĭs), adj. without slippers.

slip·per·y (slĭp′ə rĭ), adj., **-perier, -periest. 1.** tending to cause slipping or sliding, as ground, surfaces, things, etc. **2.** tending to slip from the hold or grasp or from position: a slippery rope. **3.** likely to slip away or escape. **4.** not to be depended on; fickle; shifty, tricky, or deceitful. **5.** unstable or insecure, as conditions, etc. [f. obs. slipper slippery (ME sliper, OE slipor) + -y[1]] —**slip′per·i·ness**, n.

slippery elm, 1. a species of elm, Ulmus fulva, of eastern North America, with a mucilaginous inner bark. **2.** the bark, used as a demulcent.

slip·py (slĭp′ĭ), adj. Now Colloq. or Dial. **1.** slippery. **2.** nimble, quick, or sharp. —**slip′pi·ness**, n.

slip ring, a metal ring, usually of copper or cast iron, mounted so that current may be conducted through stationary brushes into or out of a rotating member.

slip·sheet (slĭp′shēt′), v.t., v.i. to insert (blank sheets) between printed sheets as they come off the press to prevent offset. —n. **2.** a sheet so inserted.

slip·shod (slĭp′shŏd′), adj. **1.** untidy or slovenly. **2.** wearing slippers or loose shoes, esp. ones down at the heel.

slip·slop (slĭp′slŏp′), n. Colloq. **1.** a sloppy food or drink. **2.** loose or trifling talk or writing. [varied redupl. of slop[1]]

slip stream, the air forced back by an airplane propeller at speeds greater than the surrounding air.

slipt (slĭpt), v. Archaic. pt. of slip[1].

slip-up (slĭp′ŭp′), n. Colloq. a mistake or error: several minor slip-ups in spelling.

slit (slĭt), v., **slit, slitting,** n. —v.t. **1.** to cut apart or open along a line; make a long cut, fissure, or opening in. **2.** to cut or rend into strips; split. —n. **3.** a straight, narrow cut, opening, or aperture. [ME slitte, OE -slittan (North.), c. OHG slizzan (G schlitzen) split, slit. See slice] —**slit′ter**, n.

slith·er (slĭth′ər), v.i. **1.** to slide down or along a surface. esp. unsteadily or with more or less friction or noise. **2.** to go or walk with a sliding motion. —v.t. **3.** to cause to slither or slide. —n. **4.** a slithering movement; a slide. [ME; var. of d. slidder (c. LG slidderan), OE slidrian, freq. of slīdan slide]

slit trench, 1. a narrow trench for one or more persons for protection against enemy fire and fragmentation bombs. **2.** a foxhole.

sliv·er (slĭv′ər), n. **1.** a slender piece, as of wood, split, broken, or cut off, usually lengthwise or with the grain; splinter. **2.** a continuous strand or band of loose, untwisted wool, cotton, etc., ready for roving or slubbing. —v.t. **3.** to split or cut off, as a sliver; split or cut into slivers. **4.** to form (wool, cotton, etc.) into slivers. —v.i. **5.** to split. [ME slivere, der. slyve, OE slīfan split]

Sloan (slōn), n. **John,** 1871-1951, U. S. painter.

Sloane (slōn), n. **Sir Hans,** 1660-1753, British physician and naturalist.

slob (slŏb), n. **1.** Irish. mud or ooze, or a stretch of mud, esp. along a shore. **2.** Slang. a stupid, clumsy, or slovenly person. [t. Irish: m. slab mud, t. E. See slab[2]]

slob·ber (slŏb′ər), *v.i.* **1.** to let saliva, etc., run from the mouth; slaver; drivel. **2.** to indulge in mawkish sentimentality. —*v.t.* **3.** to wet or make foul by slobbering. **4.** to utter with slobbering. —*n.* **5.** saliva or liquid dribbling from the mouth; slaver. **6.** mawkishly sentimental speech or actions. Also, **slabber.** [var. of *slabber,* der. SLAB²] —**slob′ber·er,** *n.*

slob·ber·y (slŏb′ər ĭ), *adj.* **1.** characterized by slobbering. **2.** disagreeably wet; sloppy.

sloe (slō), *n.* **1.** the small, sour, blackish fruit (drupe) of the blackthorn, *Prunus spinosa.* **2.** the shrub itself. **3.** any of various other species or plants, as *P. alleghaniensis,* a shrub or small tree with dark-purple fruit. [ME *slo,* OE *slā*(*h*), c. G *schlehe*]

sloe-eyed (slō′īd′), *adj.* having eyes like sloes; dark-eyed.

sloe gin, a cordial or liqueur flavored with sloe.

slog (slŏg), *v.,* **slogged, slogging.** —*v.t.* **1.** to hit hard, as in boxing, cricket, etc. **2.** to drive with blows. —*v.i.* **3.** to deal heavy blows. **4.** to walk or plod heavily. **5.** to toil. [var. of SLUG², v.] —**slog′ger,** *n.*

slo·gan (slō′gən), *n.* **1.** a distinctive cry or phrase of any party, class, body, or person; a catchword. **2.** a war cry or gathering cry, as formerly used among the Scottish clans. [t. Gaelic: m. *sluagh-ghairm* army cry]

sloop (slōōp), *n.* *Naut.* a sailing vessel with a single mast, fitted with a jib and mainsail. [t. D: m. *sloep,* c. G *schlup;* akin to OE *slūpan* glide]

sloop of war, *Brit.* a small sailing or steam vessel, mounting guns on only one deck.

slop¹ (slŏp), *v.,* **slopped, slopping,** *n.* —*v.t.* **1.** to spill or splash (liquid). **2.** to spill liquid upon. —*v.i.* **3.** to spill or splash liquid (sometimes fol. by *about*). **4.** (of liquid) to run (over) in spilling. **5.** *Colloq.* (of persons, etc.) to be unduly effusive; gush (fol. by *over*). **6.** to walk or go through mud, slush, or water. —*n.* **7.** a quantity of liquid carelessly spilled or splashed about. **8.** (*often pl.*) *Chiefly Brit.* weak or unappetizing liquid or semiliquid food. **9.** (*often pl.*) the dirty water, liquid refuse, etc., of a household or the like. **10.** swill, or the refuse of the kitchen, etc., often used as food for pigs or the like. **11.** liquid mud. **12.** (*pl.*) *Distilling.* the mash remaining after distilling. [ME *sloppe* mudhole, OE *-sloppe* (in *cūsloppe* cowslip, lit., cow slime); akin to SLIP³]

slop² (slŏp), *n.* **1.** clothing, bedding, etc., supplied to seamen from the ship's stores. **2.** a loose outer garment, as a jacket, tunic, or smock. **3.** cheap ready-made clothing in general. [ME *sloppe,* OE *-slop* (in *oferslop* overgarment), c. Icel. *sloppr* gown]

slop chest, a store of seamen's clothing, etc., kept on board a ship for sale to the crew during a voyage.

slope (slōp), *v.,* **sloped, sloping,** *n.* —*v.i.* **1.** to take or have an inclined or slanting direction, esp. downward or upward from the horizontal. **2.** to descend or ascend at a slant. —*v.t.* **3.** to direct at a slope or inclination; incline from the horizontal. **4.** to form with a slope or slant. —*n.* **5.** inclination or slant, esp. downward or upward. **6.** deviation from the horizontal. **7.** an inclined surface. [aphetically der. *aslope,* adv., on a slant] —**slop′er,** *n.* —**slop′ing,** *adj.* —**slop′ing·ly,** *adv.* —**slop′ing·ness,** *n.*

—**Syn. 1.** SLOPE, SLANT mean to incline away from some surface or line used as a reference. To SLOPE is to incline in an oblique direction from a perpendicular line: *the ground slopes sharply here* To SLANT is to fall to one side, to lie obliquely to some line whether horizontal or perpendicular: *the road slants off to the right.*

slop·py (slŏp′ĭ), *adj.,* **-pier, -piest. 1.** muddy, slushy, or very wet, as ground, walking, weather, etc. **2.** splashed or soiled with liquid. **3.** of the nature of slops, as food; watery and unappetizing. **4.** *Colloq.* weak, silly, or maudlin: *sloppy sentiment.* **5.** *Colloq.* loose, careless, or slovenly: *to use sloppy English.* **6.** *Colloq.* untidy, as dress. —**slop′pi·ly,** *adv.* —**slop′pi·ness,** *n.*

slop·shop (slŏp′shŏp′), *n.* a cheap clothing shop.

slop·work (slŏp′wûrk′), *n.* **1.** the manufacture of cheap clothing. **2.** clothing of this kind. **3.** any work done cheaply or poorly. —**slop′work′er,** *n.*

slosh (slŏsh), *n.* **1.** slush. **2.** *Colloq.* watery or weak drink. —*v.i.* **3.** to splash in slush, mud, or water. —*v.t.* **4.** to stir in some fluid: *to slosh the mop through the pail.* [b. SLOP¹ and SLUSH] —**slosh′y,** *adj.*

slot¹ (slŏt), *n., v.,* **slotted, slotting.** —*n.* **1.** a narrow, elongated depression or aperture, esp. one to receive or admit something. —*v.t.* **2.** to provide with a slot or slots; make a slot in. [ME, t. OF: m. *esclot* hollow between breasts]

slot² (slŏt), *n.* **1.** the track or trail of a deer or other animal, as shown by the marks of the feet. **2.** the track, trace, or trail of anything. [t. AF and OF: m. *esclot* hoofprint of a horse; prob. akin to SLEUTH]

sloth (slŏth, slōth), *n.* **1.** habitual disinclination to exertion; indolence; laziness. **2.** any of three genera of sluggish arboreal edentates of the family *Bradypodidae* of tropical America: the **two-toed sloth,** *Choloepus,* having two toes on the front foot; and the **three-toed sloth,** *Bradypus,* having three

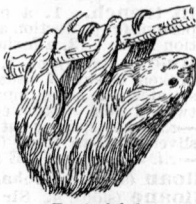

Two-toed sloth,
Choloepus hoffmanni
(2 ft. long)

toes on the front foot; and the **maned sloth,** *Scaeopus,* having a long black mane. [ME *slowth* (f. SLOW + -TH¹), r. OE *slǣwth* (der. *slǣw,* var. of *slǣw* SLOW)]

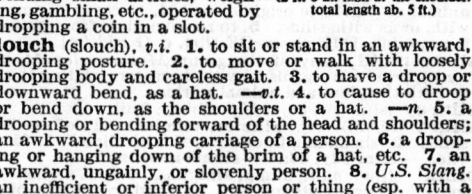

sloth bear, a coarse-haired, long-snouted bear, *Melursus labiatus,* of India and Indo-china.

Sloth bear. *Melursus labiatus*
(2 ft. 8 in. high at the shoulder,
total length ab. 5 ft.)

sloth·ful (slŏth′fəl, slōth′-). *adj.* sluggardly; indolent; lazy. —**sloth′ful·ly,** *adv.* —**sloth′ful·ness,** *n.* —**Syn.** See idle.

slot machine, a machine for vending small articles, weighing, gambling, etc., operated by dropping a coin in a slot.

slouch (slouch), *v.i.* **1.** to sit or stand in an awkward, drooping posture. **2.** to move or walk with loosely drooping body and careless gait. **3.** to have a droop or downward bend, as a hat. —*v.t.* **4.** to cause to droop or bend down, as the shoulders or a hat. —*n.* **5.** a drooping or bending forward of the head and shoulders; an awkward, drooping carriage of a person. **6.** a drooping or hanging down of the brim of a hat, etc. **7.** an awkward, ungainly, or slovenly person. **8.** *U.S. Slang.* an inefficient or inferior person or thing (esp. with a negative). [orig. uncert.; first occurs as n.] —**slouch′y,** *adj.* —**slouch′i·ly,** *adv.* —**slouch′i·ness,** *n.*

slouch hat, a soft hat, esp. one with a broad, flexible brim.

slough¹ (slou *for 1, 3;* slōō *for 2*), *n.* **1.** a piece of soft, muddy ground; a hole full of mire, as in a road. **2.** *U.S. and Canada.* a marshy or reedy pool, pond, inlet, or the like. **3.** a condition of degradation, embarrassment, or helplessness. [ME; OE *slōh,* c. MLG *slōch,* MHG *sluoche* ditch] —**slough′y,** *adj.*

slough² (slŭf), *n.* **1.** the skin of a snake, esp. the outer skin which is shed periodically. **2.** *Pathol.* a mass or layer of dead tissue which separates from the surrounding or underlying tissue. —*v.i.* **3.** to be shed or cast off, as the slough of a snake. **4.** to cast off a slough. **5.** *Pathol.* to separate from the sound flesh, as a slough. —*v.t.* **6.** to cast (fol. by *off*). **7.** to shed as or like a slough. **8.** *Bridge.* to dispose of (a losing card). [ME *slugh*(*e*), *slouh,* c. G *schlauch* skin, bag] —**slough′y,** *adj.*

Slo·vak (slō′văk, slō văk′), *n.* **1.** one of a Slavic people dwelling in Slovakia. **2.** the language of Slovakia, a Slavic language very similar to Czech. —*adj.* **3.** of or pertaining to the Slovaks, their language, etc. [t. Czech, c. Polish *Slowak.* Cf. SLOVENE]

Slo·va·ki·a (slō vä′kĭ a, slō văk′ĭ a), *n.* a province in E Czechoslovakia: an independent republic under German protection, 1939–45. 3,434,369 (1948); 18,921 sq. mi. *Cap.:* Bratislava, Czech. **Slo·ven·sko** (slō′věn-skō′). —**Slo·vak·i·an** (slō văk′ĭ ən), *adj., n.*

slov·en (slŭv′ən), *n.* **1.** one who is habitually negligent of neatness or cleanliness in dress, appearance, etc. **2.** one who works, or does anything, in a negligent, slipshod manner. [ME *sloveyn.* Cf. D *slof* careless, negligent]

Slo·vene (slō vēn′, slō′vēn), *n.* **1.** one of a Slavic people dwelling in Slovenia. **2.** a South Slavic language spoken in Slovenia. —*adj.* **3.** of or pertaining to the Slovenes, their language, etc. [t. G, t. Slovenian, g. OSlavonic *Slověne.* Cf. SLAV, SLOVAK]

Slo·ve·ni·a (slō vē′nĭ ə), *n.* a constituent republic of Yugoslavia, in the NW part: formerly in Austria. 1,516,000 pop. (est. 1956); 6265 sq. mi. *Cap.:* Ljubljana. —**Slo·ve′ni·an,** *adj., n.*

slov·en·ly (slŭv′ən lĭ), *adj.,* **-lier, -liest,** *adv.* —*adj.* **1.** having the habits of a sloven; untidy. **2.** characteristic of a sloven; slipshod. —*adv.* **3.** in a slovenly manner. —**slov′en·li·ness,** *n.* —**Ant. 1.** neat.

slow (slō), *adj.* **1.** taking or requiring a comparatively long time for moving, going, acting, occurring, etc.; not fast, rapid, or swift. **2.** leisurely; gradual, as change, growth, etc. **3.** sluggish in nature, disposition, or function. **4.** dull of perception or understanding, as a person, the mind, etc. **5.** not prompt, readily disposed, or in haste (fol. by *to* or an infinitive): *slow to take offense.* **6.** burning or heating with little speed or intensity, as a fire or an oven. **7.** slack, as trade. **8.** running at less than the proper rate of speed, as a clock. **9.** passing heavily, or dragging, as time. **10.** not progressive; behind the times. **11.** dull, humdrum, uninteresting, or tedious. —*adv.* **12.** in a slow manner; slowly. —*v.t.* **13.** to make slow or slower. **14.** to retard; reduce the speed of. —*v.i.* **15.** to become slow or slower; slacken in speed. [ME; OE *slāw* sluggish, dull, c. D *sleeuw.* Cf. SLOTH] —**slow′ly,** *adv.* —**slow′ness,** *n.*

—**Syn. 1.** SLOW, DELIBERATE, GRADUAL, LEISURELY mean unhurried and not happening rapidly. That which is SLOW acts or moves without haste or rapidity: *a slow procession of cars.* DELIBERATE implies the slowness which marks careful consideration before and while acting: *a deliberate and calculating manner.* GRADUAL suggests the slowness of that which advances one step at a time: *a gradual improvement in service.* That which is LEISURELY moves with the slowness allowed by ample time or the absence of pressure: *an unhurried and leisurely stroll.* **4.** See dull. —**Ant. 1.** fast, hasty, sudden, hurried.

slow·down (slō′doun′), *n.* a delay in progress (of an action, process, etc.); esp. a deliberate slowing of pace by workers to win demands from their employers.

---

b., blend of, blended; c., cognate with; d., dialect, dialectal; der., derived from; f., formed from; g., going back to; m., modification of; r., replacing; s., stem of; t., taken from; ?, perhaps. See the full key on inside cover.

slow match, a slow-burning match or fuse, often consisting of a rope or cord soaked in a solution of saltpeter.

slow-mo·tion (slō′mō′shən), *adj.* noting or pertaining to motion pictures in which the images on the screen move more slowly than the original, the camera taking a relatively greater number of frames per second.

slow-wit·ted (slō′wĭt′ĭd), *adj.* slow of wit or intelligence; dull of understanding.

slow·worm (slō′wûrm′), *n.* a blindworm.

sloyd (sloid), *n.* a system of manual training in woodworking, etc., orig. developed in Sweden. [= Sw.: m. *slöjd* craft, industrial art, woodworking, c. SLEIGHT]

slub (slŭb), *v.,* **slubbed, slubbing,** *n.* —*v.t.* 1. to draw out and twist slightly after carding or slivering, as wool or cotton. —*n.* 2. the partially twisted wool or the like produced by slubbing. 3. yarn made with bunches of untwisted fibers at intervals. [orig. uncert.]

sludge (slŭj), *n.* 1. mud, mire, or ooze; slush. 2. a deposit of ooze at the bottom of bodies of water. 3. any of various more or less mudlike deposits or mixtures. 4. the sediment in a steam boiler or water tank. 5. broken ice, as on the sea. 6. a mixture of some finely powdered substance and water. 7. sediment deposited during the treatment of sewage. 8. a fine, mudlike powder produced by a mining drill. —**sludg′y,** *adj.*

slue[1] (slōō), *v.,* **slued, sluing,** *n.* —*v.t.* 1. to turn (a mast, etc.) round upon its own axis, or without removing it from its place. 2. to swing round. —*v.i.* 3. to turn about; swing round. —*n.* 4. act of sluing. 5. a position slued to. [orig. uncert.]

slue[2] (slōō), *n.* *Colloq.* slew[4].

slug[1] (slŭg), *n.* 1. any of various slimy, elongated terrestrial gastropods related to the terrestrial snails, but having no shell or only a rudimentary one. 2. a slow-moving animal, vehicle, or the like. 3. any heavy piece of crude metal. 4. a piece of lead or other metal for firing from a gun. 5. a metal disk used as a coin, generally counterfeit. 6. *Print.* a. a thick strip of type metal less than type-high. b. such a strip containing a type-high number, etc. for temporary use. c. a line of type in one piece, as produced by a linotype machine. 7. *Mech.* a unit of mass, equal to about 32.2 pounds, which, if acted upon by a force of one pound, will have an acceleration of one foot per second per second. [ME *slugge,* t. Scand.; cf. d. Norw. *sluggje* heavy, slow person]

Common garden slug,
Deroceras agreste
1½ in. long)

slug[2] (slŭg), *v.,* **slugged, slugging,** *n.* *Colloq.* —*v.t.* 1. to strike heavily; hit hard, esp. with the fist. —*n.* 2. a heavy blow, esp. with the fist. [? orig., hit with a slug (piece of lead)]

slug·a·bed (slŭg′ə·bĕd′), *n.* one given to lying long in bed, as from laziness.

slug·gard (slŭg′ərd), *n.* 1. one who is habitually inactive or slothful. —*adj.* 2. sluggardly. [ME *slogard(e),* f. obs. *sluggy* sluggish + -ARD]

slug·gard·ly (slŭg′ərd·lǐ), *adj.* like or befitting a sluggard; slothful; lazy.

slug·ger (slŭg′ər), *n.* *Colloq.* 1. one who strikes hard, esp. with the fists or a baseball bat. 2. a prize fighter.

slug·gish (slŭg′ĭsh), *adj.* 1. indisposed to action or exertion, esp. by nature; inactive, slow, or of little energy or vigor. 2. not acting or working with full vigor, as bodily organs. 3. moving slowly, or having little motion, as a stream. 4. slow, as motion. —**slug′gish·ly,** *adv.* —**slug′gish·ness,** *n.* —Syn. 1. See **inactive.**

sluice (slōōs), *n., v.,* **sluiced, sluicing.** —*n.* 1. an artificial channel for conducting water, fitted with a gate (**sluice gate**) at the upper end for regulating the flow. 2. the body of water held back or controlled by a sluice gate. 3. any contrivance for regulating a flow from or into a receptacle. 4. a channel, esp. one carrying off surplus water; a drain. 5. a stream of surplus water. 6. an artificial channel for moving solid matter on or in: *a lumbering sluice.* 7. *Mining.* a. a long, sloping trough or the like, with grooves in its bottom, into which water is directed to separate gold from gravel or sand. b. a long inclined trough to wash ores. —*v.t.* 8. to let out (water, etc.) or draw off the contents of (a pond, etc.) by, as or by, the opening of a sluice. 9. to open a sluice upon. 10. to flush or cleanse with a rush of water. 11. *Mining.* to wash in a sluice. 12. to send (logs, etc.) down a sluiceway. —*v.i.* 13. to flow or pour through or as through a sluice. [ME *scluse,* t. OF: m. *escluse,* g. LL *exclūsa,* fem. pp., shut out]

sluice·way (slōōs′wā′), *n.* 1. a channel controlled by a sluice gate. 2. any artificial channel for water.

slum (slŭm), *n., v.,* **slummed, slumming.** —*n.* 1. (*often pl.*) a thickly populated, squalid part of a city, inhabited by the poorest people. —*v.i.* 2. to visit slums, esp. from curiosity [first occurs as slang for room; orig. obscure]

slum·ber (slŭm′bər), *v.i.* 1. to sleep, esp. lightly; doze; drowse. 2. to be in a state of inactivity, negligence, quiescence, or calm. —*v.t.* 3. to spend (time) in slumbering (fol. by *away,* etc.). 4. to drive (away) by slumbering. —*n.* 5. sleep, esp. light sleep. 6. a period of sleep, esp. light sleep. 7. a state of inactivity, quiescence, etc. [ME *slumeren,* freq. of *slumen* slumber, doze, der. OE *slūma,* n. Cf. G *schlummern*]

slum·ber·ous (slŭm′bər·əs), *adj.* 1. inclined to slumber; sleepy; heavy with drowsiness, as the eyelids.

2. causing or inducing sleep. 3. pertaining to, characterized by, or suggestive of slumber. 4. inactive or sluggish; calm or quiet. Also, **slum′ber·y, slum′brous.**

slum·lord (slŭm′lôrd′), *n.* a· landlord who refuses to make improvements in the slum buildings he owns, and who charges his tenants exorbitant rents. [b. SLUM, LORD]

slump (slŭmp), *v.i.* 1. to drop heavily. 2. to sink into a bog, muddy place, etc., or through ice or snow. 3. to fall suddenly and markedly, as prices, the market, etc. 4. to have a decided falling off in progress, as an enterprise, a competitor, etc. 5. to sink heavily, as the spirits, etc. —*n.* 6. act of slumping. 7. a decline in prices or sales. 8. a decided falling off in progress, as in an undertaking. [v. use of d. *slump* bog, c. LG *schlump*]

slung (slŭng), *v.* pt. and pp. of **sling.**

slung shot, a piece of metal, a stone, etc., fastened to a short strap, chain, or the like, used as a weapon.

slunk (slŭngk), *v.* pt. and pp. of **slink.**

slur (slûr), *v.,* **slurred, slurring,** *n.* —*v.t.* 1. to pass over lightly, or without due mention or consideration (often fol. by *over*). 2. to pronounce (a syllable, word, etc.) indistinctly, as in hurried or careless utterance. 3. *Music.* a. to sing to a single syllable or play without a break (two or more tones of different pitch). b. to mark with a slur. 4. to calumniate, disparage, or depreciate. 5. *Obs.* to smirch or sully. —*v.i.* 6. to go through anything hurriedly and carelessly. —*n.* 7. a slurred utterance or sound. 8. *Music.* a. the combination of two or more tones of different pitch, sung to a single syllable or played without a break. b. a curved mark indicating this. 9. *Print.* a spot which is blurred or unclear. 10. a disparaging remark; a slight. 11. a blot or stain, as upon reputation. [der. d. *slur* fluid mud, ? akin to Icel. *slor* offal (of fish)]

Slur (def. 8)

slush (slŭsh), *n.* 1. snow in a partly melted state. 2. liquid mud; watery mire. 3. refuse fat, grease, etc., from the galley of a ship. 4. a mixture of grease and other materials for lubricating. 5. silly, or weakly emotional talk, writing, etc. —*v.t.* 6. to splash with slush. 7. to grease, polish, or cover with slush. 8. to fill or cover with mortar or cement. 9. to wash with much water, as by dashing it on. [c. Norw. *slusk* slops]

slush fund, *U.S.* 1. a fund for use in campaign propaganda or the like, esp. secretly or illicitly, as in bribery. 2. a fund from the sale of slush, refuse fat, etc., aboard ship, spent for any small luxuries.

slut (slŭt), *n.* 1. a dirty, slovenly woman. 2. *Chiefly U.S.* an immoral woman. 3. an impudent girl. 4. a female dog. [ME; cf. d. E *slut* mud, d. Norw. *slutr* sleet, impure liquid] —**slut′tish,** *adj.*

sly (slī), *adj.,* **slyer, slyest** or **slier, sliest.** 1. cunning or wily, as persons or animals, or their actions, ways, etc. 2. stealthy, insidious, or secret. 3. playfully artful, mischievous, or roguish: *sly humor.* [ME *sly, sley,* t. Scand.; cf. Icel. *slægr* sly, cunning, Sw. *slög* dexterous] —**sly′ly,** *adv.* —**sly′ness,** *n.* —Syn. 2. surreptitious.

slype (slīp), *n.* *Archit.* a covered passage, esp. one from the transept of a cathedral to the chapter house. [cf. West Flem. *slijpe* secret path]

Sm, *Chem.* samarium.

S.M., (L *Scientiae Magister*) Master of Science.

smack[1] (smăk), *n.* 1. a taste or flavor, esp. a slight flavor distinctive or suggestive of something. 2. a trace, touch, or suggestion of something. 3. a taste, mouthful, or small quantity. —*v.i.* 4. to have a taste, flavor, trace, or suggestion (often fol. by *of*). [ME *smacke,* OE *smæc,* c. MLG *smak,* G *(ge)schmack* taste]

smack[2] (smăk), *v.t.* 1. to separate (the lips) smartly so as to produce a sharp sound, often as a sign of relish, as in eating. 2. to bring, put, throw, send, etc., with a sharp, resounding blow or a smart stroke. 3. to strike smartly, esp. with the open hand or anything flat. —*v.i.* 4. to smack the lips. 5. to come or strike smartly or forcibly, as against something. 6. to make a sharp sound as of striking against something. —*n.* 7. a smacking of the lips, as in relish. 8. a resounding or loud kiss. 9. a smart, resounding blow, esp. with something flat. —*adv.* 10. *Colloq.* with a smack; suddenly and sharply; plump. 11. *Colloq.* directly; straight. [cf. D and LG *smakken,* d. G *schmacken;* of imit. orig.]

smack[3] (smăk), *n.* 1. a sailing vessel, usually sloop-rigged, used esp. in coasting and fishing. 2. a fishing vessel with a well to keep fish alive. [prob. t. D: m. *smak*]

smack·ing (smăk′ĭng), *adj.* 1. smart, brisk, or strong, as a breeze. 2. *Brit. Dial.* unusually big or large.

small (smôl), *adj.* 1. of limited size; of comparatively restricted dimensions; not big; little. 2. slender, thin, or narrow. 3. not large, as compared with other things of the same kind. 4. not great in amount, degree, extent, duration, value, etc. 5. not great numerically. 6. of low numerical value; denoted by a low number. 7. having but little land, capital, etc., or carrying on business on a limited scale: *a small businessman.* 8. of minor importance, moment, weight, or consequence. 9. humble, modest, or unpretentious. 10. characterized by or indicative of littleness of mind or character; mean-spirited; ungenerous. 11. ashamed or mortified: *to feel small.* 12. of little strength or force. 13. (of sound or the voice) gentle, soft, or low. 14. weak; diluted: *small beer.* —*adv.* 15. in a small manner. 16. into small pieces: *to slice small.* 17. in low tones; softly. —*n.* 18.

that which is small. **19.** the small or narrow part, as of the back. **20.** something small. **21.** (*pl.*) commodities of relatively small size. [ME *smal(e)*, OE *smæl*, c. D *smal*, G *schmal*] **—small′ness,** *n.*
—Syn. 1. See **little. 3.** SMALLER, LESS indicate a diminution, or not so large a size or quantity in some respect. SMALLER, as applied to concrete objects, is used with reference to size: *smaller apples.* LESS is used of material in bulk, with reference to amount, and in cases where attributes such as value and degree are in question: *a nickel is less than a dime* (in value), *a sergeant is less than a lieutenant* (in rank). As an abstraction, amount may be either SMALLER OR LESS, though SMALLER is usually used when the idea of size is suggested: *a smaller opportunity.* LESS is used when the idea of quantity is present: *less courage.* **8.** trifling, trivial, petty. **—Ant. 3.** larger, more.

small·age (smô′lĭj), *n.* celery, *Apium graveolens*, esp. in its wild state. [ME *smalege, smalache*, f. *smal* small + *ache* parsley (t. OF, g. L *apium*)]

small beer, 1. weak beer. **2.** *Chiefly Brit.* matters or persons of little or no importance.

small calorie. See **calorie** (def. 1a).

small caps, small capital letters; letters having the form of regular capitals of a particular printing type, but being about one-third smaller in size.

small change, 1. metallic money of small denomination. **2.** *U.S.* an insignificant person or thing.

small circle, a circle on a sphere, whose plane does not pass through the center of the sphere.

small·clothes (smôl′klōz′, -klŏthz′), *n.pl. Archaic.* knee breeches, esp. the close-fitting ones formerly worn.

small fry, 1. small or young fish. **2.** young or unimportant persons or objects.

small hours, the early hours of the morning.

small·ish (smô′lĭsh), *adj.* rather small.

small letter, one of the ordinary written or printed letters (as opposed to a *capital letter*).

small-mind·ed (smôl′mĭn′dĭd), *adj.* selfish or narrow in attitude. **—small′-mind′ed·ness,** *n.*

small·mouth (smôl′mouth′), *n.* a species of black bass, *Micropterus dolomieu*, belonging to the sunfish family. Also, **smallmouth bass, small′-mouthed′ bass.**

small potatoes, (*often construed as sing.*) *U.S. Colloq.* insignificant things or persons.

small·pox (smôl′pŏks′), *n.* an acute, highly contagious, febrile disease characterized by a pustular eruption which often leaves permanent pits or scars.

smalls (smôlz), *n. pl. Colloq.* (at Oxford University) responsion (def. 2).

small stores, *Naval.* personal articles available for issue to the crew and charged to their pay.

small·sword (smôl′sôrd′), *n.* a light, tapering sword for thrusting, used esp. in fencing.

small talk, light, unimportant talk; chitchat.

smalt (smôlt), *n.* a deep-blue pigment prepared by powdering a glass colored with cobalt. [t. F, t. It.: m. *smalto*, t. G: m. *schmalte*; akin to SMELT]

smart (smärt), *v.i.* **1.** to be a source of sharp local and, usually, superficial pain, as a wound. **2.** to cause a sharp pain, as an irritating application, a blow. etc. **3.** to wound the feelings, as with words. **4.** to feel a sharp pain, as in a wounded surface. **5.** to suffer keenly from wounded feelings. **6.** to suffer in punishment or in return for something. **—v.t. 7.** to cause a sharp pain to or in. [ME *smerten*, OE *smeortan*, c. G *schmerzen* smart; prob. akin to L *mordēre* bite]
—adj. 8. sharp or keen, as pain. **9.** sharply severe, as blows, strokes, etc. **10.** sharply brisk, vigorous, or active. **11.** quick or prompt in action, as persons. **12.** having or showing quick intelligence or ready capability; clever. **13.** shrewd or sharp, as a person in dealing with others, or as dealings, bargains, etc. **14.** cleverly ready or effective, as a speaker or a speech, rejoinder, etc. **15.** dashingly or effectively neat or trim in appearance, as persons, dress, etc. **16.** socially elegant, or fashionable. **17.** *Colloq.* or *Dial.* considerable, or fairly large. [ME; OE *smeart*]
—adv. 18. in a smart manner; smartly. [ME *smerte*]
—n. 19. sharp local pain, usually superficial, as from a wound or sting. **20.** keen mental suffering, as from wounded feelings, affliction, grievous loss, etc. [ME *smerte*, c. G *schmerz*] **—smart′ly,** *adv.* **—smart′ness,** *n.* **—Ant. 12.** dull.

smart aleck, an obnoxiously conceited and cocky person.

smart·en (smär′tən), *v.t.* **1.** to make more trim or spruce; improve in appearance. **2.** to make brisker, as a pace.

smart money, *Law.* punitive or exemplary damages.

smart set, sophisticated, fashionable people as a group.

smart·weed (smärt′wēd′), *n.* the plant *Polygonum Hydropiper*, a weed growing in wet places, which causes smarting or inflammation of the skin; water pepper.

smash (smăsh), *v.t.* **1.** to break to pieces with violence and often with a crashing sound, as by striking, letting fall, or dashing against something; shatter; crush. **2.** to defeat utterly, as a person; overthrow or destroy, as a thing. **3.** to ruin financially. **4.** *Tennis.* to strike (the ball) hard and fast with an overhand stroke. **—v.i. 5.** to break to pieces from a violent blow or collision. **6.** to dash with a shattering or crushing force or with great violence; crash (fol. by *against, into, through,* etc.).

7. to become financially ruined or bankrupt (often fol. by *up*). **—n. 8.** a smashing or shattering, or the sound of it. **9.** a destructive collision. **10.** smashed or shattered condition. **11.** a process or state of collapse, ruin, or destruction. **12.** financial failure or ruin. **13.** a drink made of brandy, or other liquor, with sugar, water, mint, and ice. [? b. SMACK² and MASH] **—smash′er,** *n.* **—Syn. 1.** See **break.**

smash-up (smăsh′ŭp′), *n.* a complete smash.

smat·ter (smăt′ər), *v.t.* **1.** to speak (a language, words, etc.) with but superficial knowledge or understanding. **2.** to dabble in. **—n. 3.** slight or superficial knowledge; a smattering. [ME, t. Scand.; cf. Sw. *smattra* patter, rattle] **—smat′ter·er,** *n.*

smat·ter·ing (smăt′ərĭng), *n.* a slight or superficial knowledge of something. **—smat′ter·ing·ly,** *adv.*

smear (smĭr), *v.t.* **1.** to rub or spread with oil, grease, paint, dirt, etc.; daub with anything. **2.** to spread or daub (oil, grease, etc.) on or over something. **3.** to rub or draw (something) over a thing so as to produce a smear. **4.** to soil or sully, as one's reputation. **5.** *U.S. Slang.* to defeat decisively. **—n. 6.** a mark or stain made by, or as by, smearing. **7.** something smeared, or to be smeared, on a thing, as a glaze for pottery. **8.** a small quantity of something smeared on a slide for microscopic examination. [ME *smere*, OE *smeoru*, c. G *schmer* grease]

smear·y (smĭr′ĭ), *adj.,* **smearier, smeariest. 1.** showing smears; smeared; bedaubed. **2.** tending to smear or soil. **—smear′i·ness,** *adj.*

smell (smĕl), *v.,* **smelled** or **smelt, smelling,** *n.* **—v.t. 1.** to perceive through the nose, by means of the olfactory nerves; inhale the odor of. **2.** to test by the sense of smell. **3.** to perceive, detect, or discover by shrewdness or sagacity. **4.** to search or find as if by smell (fol. by *out*). **—v.i. 5.** to use the sense of smell; inhale the odor of a thing (fol. by *at, of*). **6.** to search or investigate (usually fol. by *about*). **7.** to give out an odor, esp. as specified: *to smell sweet.* **8.** to give out an offensive odor. **9.** to have the odor (fol. by *of*). **10.** to have a trace or suggestion (fol. by *of*). **—n. 11.** the faculty or sense of smelling. **12.** that quality of a thing which is or may be smelled; odor. **13.** a trace or suggestion. **14.** act of smelling. [ME *smellen, smullen*; orig. uncert.]

smell·er (smĕl′ər), *n.* **1.** one who smells. **2.** one who tests by smelling. **3.** a tactile hair or process, as one of the whiskers of a cat; a feeler.

smelling salts, a preparation for smelling, consisting essentially of ammonium carbonate with some agreeable scent, used as a restorative in cases of faintness, headache, etc.

smell·y (smĕl′ĭ), *adj.,* **smellier, smelliest.** emitting a strong or offensive smell.

smelt¹ (smĕlt), *v.t.* **1.** to fuse or melt (ore) in order to separate the metal contained. **2.** to obtain or refine (metal) in this way. [prob. t. MD or MLG: s. *smelten*, c. G *schmelzen* melt, smelt. See MELT]

smelt² (smĕlt), *n., pl.* **smelts,** (*esp. collectively*) **smelt. 1.** a small silvery food fish, *Osmerus eperlanus*, of Europe. **2.** any other fish of the family *Osmeridae*, as the American smelt, *Osmerus mordax.* **3.** any of several superficially similar but unrelated fishes, esp. certain silversides (*Atherinidae*) of California. [ME and OE. Cf. Norw. *smelta* whiting]

smelt³ (smĕlt), *v.* pt. and pp. of **smell.**

smelt·er (smĕl′tər), *n.* **1.** one who or that which smelts. **2.** the owner of, or a workman in, a smeltery. **3.** a place or establishment where ores are smelted.

smelt·er·y (smĕl′tərĭ), *n., pl.* **-eries.** smelter (def. 3).

Sme·ta·na (smĕ′tänä), *n.* **Bedrich** (bĕ′dər zhĭ̄KH), 1824–84, Czech composer.

Smeth·wick (smĕth′ĭk), *n.* a city in central England, near Birmingham. 76,379 (1951).

smew (smū), *n.* a small saw-billed duck or merganser, *Mergus albellus*, of northerly parts of the eastern hemisphere, the adult male of which is white, marked with black and gray, and, on the crested head, with green.

smi·la·ca·ceous (smī′ləkā′shəs), *adj.* belonging to the *Smilacaceae*, the smilax or greenbrier family of plants. [f. s. L *smilac* SMILAX + -ACEOUS]

smi·lax (smī′lăks), *n.* **1.** any plant of the genus *Smilax*, of the tropical and temperate zones, consisting mostly of vines with woody stems, esp. the sarsaparilla plant, *Smilax aristolochiifolia.* **2.** a delicate, twining liliaceous plant, *Asparagus asparagoides*, with glossy, bright-green leaves, cultivated by florists. [t. L, t. Gk.]

smile (smīl), *v.,* **smiled, smiling,** *n.* **—v.i. 1.** to assume a facial expression, characterized esp. by a widening of the mouth, indicative of pleasure, favor, kindliness, amusement, derision, scorn, etc. **2.** to look with such an expression, esp. (fol. by *at, on,* or *upon*) in a pleasant or kindly way, or (fol. by *at*) in amusement. **3.** to have a pleasant or agreeable aspect, as natural scenes, objects, etc. **—v.t. 4.** to assume or give (a smile). **5.** to express by a smile: *to smile approval.* **6.** to bring, put, drive, etc., by smiling: *to smile one's tears away.* **—n. 7.** act of smiling; a smiling expression of the face. **8.** favoring look or regard: *fortune's smile.* **9.** pleasant or agreeable look or aspect. [ME, c. OHG *smīlan*, Dan. *smile*] **—smil′er,** *n.* **—smil′ing·ly,** *adv.* **—Syn. 7.** See **laugh. —Ant. 7.** frown.

smirch (smûrch), *v.t.* **1.** to discolor or soil with some substance, as soot, dust, dirt, etc., or as the substance does. **2.** to sully or tarnish, as with disgrace. **—n. 3.** a dirty mark or smear. **4.** a stain or blot, as on reputation. [ME *smorch*; b. SMEAR and SMUTCH]

smirk (smûrk), *v.i.* **1.** to smile in an affected, would-be agreeable, or offensively familiar way. —*v.t.* **2.** to utter with a smirk. —*n.* **3.** the smile or the facial expression of one who smirks. [ME; OE *sme(a)rcian*] —**smirk'er,** *n.* —**smirk'ing·ly,** *adv.*

smite (smīt), *v.,* **smote** or (*Obs.*) **smit; smitten** or **smit; smiting.** —*v.t.* **1.** to strike or hit hard, as with the hand, a stick or weapon, etc., or as the hand or a weapon does. **2.** to deal (a blow, etc.) by striking hard. **3.** to render by, or as by, a blow: *to smite a person dead.* **4.** to strike down or slay. **5.** to afflict, chasten, or punish in a grievous manner. **6.** to fall upon or attack with deadly or disastrous effect, as lightning, blight, pestilence, etc., do. **7.** to affect mentally with a sudden pang: *his conscience smote him.* **8.** to affect suddenly and strongly with a specified feeling: *smitten with terror.* **9.** to impress favorably; charm; enamor: *smitten with a person's charms.* —*v.i.* **10.** to strike; deal a blow or blows. **11.** to come, fall, etc., with or as with the force of a blow. [ME; OE *smītan,* c. G *schmeissen* strike] —**smit'er,** *n.*

smith (smith), *n.* **1.** a worker in metal. **2.** a blacksmith. [ME and OE, c. G *schmied*]

Smith (smith), *n.* **1. Adam,** 1723–90, Scottish political economist. **2. Alfred Emanuel,** 1873–1944, U.S. political leader. **3. Edmund Kirby,** 1824–93, Confederate general. **4. Francis Hopkinson,** 1838–1915, U.S. novelist, painter, and engineer. **5. Captain John,** 1580–1631, British adventurer, colonist in Virginia (1607). **6. Joseph,** 1805–44, U.S. religious leader who founded the Mormon Church. **7. Logan Pearsall** (lō'gən pir'səl), 1865–1946, U.S. essayist, in England. **8. Sydney,** 1771–1845, British clergyman and writer. **9. William,** 1769–1839, British geologist.

smith·er·eens (smith'ə rēnz'), *n. pl. Colloq.* small fragments. [der. *smithers* (orig. unknown), with Irish dim. suffix *-een*]

smith·er·y (smith'ər ĭ), *n., pl.* **-eries. 1.** the work or craft of a smith. **2.** a smithy.

Smith·son (smith'sən), *n.* **James,** (until 1800: *James Lewis Macie*) 1765–1829, British chemist and mineralogist: founded Smithsonian Institution.

Smith·so·ni·an Institution (smith sō'nĬ ən), an institution in Washington, D.C., founded 1846 with a grant left by James Smithson, for the increase and diffusion of knowledge.

smith·son·ite (smith'sə nīt'), *n.* **1.** a native carbonate of zinc, ZnCO₃: an important ore of zinc. **2.** *Obs.* the zinc silicate calamine. [named after James SMITHSON, who distinguished it from calamine. See -ITE¹]

smith·y (smith'ĭ, smith'ĭ), *n., pl.* **smithies. 1.** the workshop of a smith, esp. a blacksmith. **2.** a forge.

smit·ten (smit'ən), *adj.* **1.** struck, as with a hard blow. **2.** stricken with affliction, etc. **3.** *Colloq.* very much in love. —*v.* **4.** pp. of **smite.**

smock (smok), *n.* **1.** any loose overgarment, esp. one worn to protect the clothing while at work: *an artist's smock.* —*v.t.* **2.** to clothe in a smock. **3.** to draw (a fabric) by needlework into a honeycomb pattern with diamond-shaped recesses. [ME; OE *smocc,* c. OHG *smoccho*; orig. name of garment with a hole for the head. Cf. Icel. *smjúga* to put on (a garment) over the head]

smock frock, a loose overgarment of linen or cotton worn by European farm laborers, etc.

smock·ing (smok'ĭng), *n.* **1.** smocked needlework. **2.** embroidery stitches used to hold gathered cloth in even folds.

smog (smog), *n. Colloq.* a mixture of smoke and fog.

smoke (smōk), *n., v.,* **smoked, smoking.** —*n.* **1.** the visible exhalation given off by a burning or smoldering substance, esp. the gray, brown, or blackish mixture of gases and suspended carbon particles resulting from the combustion of wood, peat, coal, or other organic matter. **2.** something resembling this, as vapor or mist, flying particles, etc. **3.** something unsubstantial, evanescent, or without result. **4.** obscuring conditions. **5.** an act or spell of smoking tobacco, or the like. **6.** that which is smoked, as a cigar or cigarette. **7.** *Phys. Chem.* a dispersed system of solid particles in a gaseous medium. —*v.i.* **8.** to give off or emit smoke. **9.** to give out smoke offensively or improperly, as a stove. **10.** to send forth steam or vapor, dust, or the like. **11.** to draw into the mouth and puff out the smoke of tobacco or the like, as from a pipe, cigar, or cigarette. **12.** to ride or travel (along) with great speed. —*v.t.* **13.** to draw into the mouth and puff out the smoke of (tobacco, etc.). **14.** to use (a pipe, etc.) in this process. **15.** to expose to smoke. **16.** to fumigate (rooms, etc.). **17.** to cure (meat, fish, etc.) by exposure to smoke. **18.** to color or darken by smoke. **19.** to drive by means of smoke, as an animal from its hole (fol. by *out,* etc.). **20.** to force into public view or knowledge (fol. by *out*). [ME; OE *smoca*; akin to Scot. *smeek* (OE *smēocan*) emit smoke]

smoke·house (smōk'hous'), *n.* a building or place in which meat, fish, etc., are treated with smoke.

smoke·jack (smōk'jăk'), *n.* an apparatus for turning a roasting spit, set in motion by the current of ascending gases in a chimney.

smoke·less (smōk'lĬs), *adj.* emitting, producing, or having no (or but little) smoke.

smokeless powder, any of various substitutes for

ordinary gunpowder which give off little or no smoke, esp. one composed wholly or mostly of guncotton.

smok·er (smō'kər), *n.* **1.** one who or that which smokes. **2.** Also, **smoking car,** a railroad car, or a compartment in one, for travelers who wish to smoke. **3.** an informal gathering of men for smoking and entertainment.

smoke screen, a mass of dense smoke produced to conceal an area, vessel, or plane from the enemy.

smoke·stack (smōk'stăk'), *n.* a pipe for the escape of the smoke or gases of combustion, as on a steamboat, locomotive, or building.

smoke tree, 1. an anacardiaceous treelike shrub, *Cotinus Coggygria,* native in southern Europe and Asia Minor, bearing small flowers in large panicles, that develop a light, feathery appearance suggestive of smoke. **2.** a related American species, *Cotinus americanus.*

smoking room, a room set apart for smoking, as in a hotel, clubhouse, or the like.

smok·y (smō'kĭ), *adj.,* **smokier, smokiest. 1.** emitting smoke, or much smoke, as a fire, a torch, etc. **2.** hazy; darkened or begrimed with smoke. **3.** having the character or appearance of smoke. **4.** pertaining to or suggestive of smoke. **5.** of a dull or brownish gray; cloudy. —**smok'i·ly,** *adv.* —**smok'i·ness,** *n.*

Smoky Mountains, Great Smoky Mountains.

smol·der (smōl'dər), *v.i.* **1.** to burn or smoke without flame. **2.** to exist or continue in a suppressed state or without outward demonstration. **3.** to display repressed feelings, esp. of indignation: *his eyes smoldered.* —*n.* **4.** dense smoke resulting from slow or suppressed combustion. **5.** a smoldering fire. Also, **smoulder.** [ME *smoulder(en),* der. *smolder* smoky vapor, dissimilated var. of earlier *smorther* SMOTHER, n.]

Smo·lensk (smō lĕnsk'), *n.* a city in the W Soviet Union: Napoleon defeated the Russians here, 1812. 131,000 (est. 1956).

Smol·lett (smŏl'Ĭt), *n.* **Tobias George** (tō bī'əs), 1721–71, British novelist.

smolt (smōlt), *n.* a young, silvery salmon going down to the sea.

smooth (smōōth), *adj.* **1.** free from projections or irregularities of surface such as would be perceived in touching or stroking. **2.** free from hairs or a hairy growth. **3.** free from inequalities of surface, ridges or hollows, obstructions, etc. **4.** generally flat or unruffled, as a calm sea. **5.** of uniform consistence; free from lumps, as a batter, a sauce, etc. **6.** free from or proceeding without breaks, abrupt bends, etc. **7.** smooth from unevenness or roughness: *smooth driving.* **8.** easy and uniform, as motion, the working of a machine, etc. **9.** having projections worn away: *a smooth tire casing.* **10.** free from hindrances or difficulties. **11.** undisturbed, tranquil, or equable, as the feelings, temper, etc. **12.** easy, flowing, elegant, or polished, as speech, a speaker, etc. **13.** pleasant, agreeable, or ingratiatingly polite, as manner, persons, etc. **14.** bland or suave; free from harshness or sharpness of taste, as wine. **15.** not harsh to the ear, as sound. **16.** *Gram.* without aspiration. —*adv.* **17.** in a smooth manner; smoothly. —*v.t.* **18.** to make smooth of surface, as by scraping, planing, pressing, stroking, etc. **19.** to remove (projections, etc.) in making something smooth (often fol. by *away* or *out*). **20.** to make more polished, elegant, agreeable, or plausible, as wording, verse, manners, the person, etc. **21.** to tranquilize, calm, or soothe, as the feelings. **22.** to gloss over or palliate, as something unpleasant or wrong (usually fol. by *over*). —*n.* **23.** act of smoothing. **24.** that which is smooth; a smooth part or place. [ME *smothe,* OE *smōth.* Cf. OE *smēthe* smooth, c. OS *smōthi*] —**smooth'er,** *n.* —**smooth'ly,** *adv.* —**smooth'ness,** *n.* —Syn. **1.** See **level.** —Ant. **1.** rough.

smooth·bore (smōōth'bōr'), *adj.* (of firearms) having a smooth bore; not rifled.

smooth breathing, *Gk. Gram.* a symbol (') indicating nonaspiration of the initial vowel. [trans. of L *spiritus lēnis*]

smooth·en (smōō'thən), *v.t., v.i.* to make or become smooth.

smooth·faced (smōōth'fāst'), *adj.* **1.** beardless or clean-shaven. **2.** having a smooth surface, as cloth. **3.** deceitfully ingratiating.

smör·gås·bord (smœr'gŏs bōrd'), *n.* the hors d'oeuvres at a Scandinavian dinner.

smote (smōt), *v.* pt. of **smite.**

smoth·er (smuth'ər), *v.t.* **1.** to stifle or suffocate, esp. by smoke or by depriving of the air necessary for life. **2.** to extinguish or deaden (fire, etc.) by covering so as to exclude air. **3.** to cover closely or thickly (often fol. by *up*); envelop (in). **4.** to suppress: *to smother a scandal.* **5.** to repress, as feelings, impulses, etc. **6.** *Cookery.* to cook in a closed vessel: *smothered chicken.* —*v.i.* **7.** to become stifled or suffocated; be prevented from breathing freely by smoke or otherwise. **8.** to be stifled; be suppressed or concealed. —*n.* **9.** dense, stifling smoke. **10.** a smoking or smoldering state, as of burning matter; a smoldering fire. **11.** dust, fog, spray, etc., in a dense or enveloping cloud. **12.** an overspreading profusion of anything. [ME *smorther,* der. OE *smorian* suffocate] —**smoth'er·y,** *adj.*

smoul·der (smōl'dər), *v.i., n.* smolder.

smudge (smŭj), *n.*, *v.*, **smudged, smudging.** —*n.* 1. a dirty mark or smear. 2. a smeary state. 3. a stifling smoke. 4. a smoky fire, esp. one made for the purpose of driving away mosquitoes, etc. —*v.t.* 5. to mark with dirty streaks or smears. 6. to fill with smoke from a smudge, as to drive away insects. —*v.i.* 7. to form a smudge on something. 8. to be smudged. [ME *smoge*; orig. uncert.]

smudg·y (smŭj′ĭ), *adj.*, **smudgier, smudgiest.** 1. marked with smudges; smeared; smeary. 2. emitting a stifling smoke; smoky. 3. *Brit. Dial.* close or sultry, as air. —**smudg′i·ly,** *adv.* —**smudg′i·ness,** *n.*

smug (smŭg), *adj.*, **smugger, smuggest.** 1. complacently proper, righteous, clever, etc.; self-satisfied. 2. trim; spruce; smooth; sleek. [? t. D: m. *smuk* neat] —**smug′ly,** *adv.* —**smug′ness,** *n.*

smug·gle (smŭg′əl), *v.*, **-gled, -gling.** —*v.t.* 1. to import or export (goods) secretly, without payment of legal duty or in violation of law. 2. to bring, take, put, etc., surreptitiously: *She smuggled the gun into the jail inside a cake.* —*v.i.* 3. to smuggle goods. [t. LG: m.s. *smuggeln*, c. G *schmuggeln*] —**smug′gler,** *n.*

smut (smŭt), *n.*, *v.*, **smutted, smutting.** —*n.* 1. a particle of soot; sooty matter. 2. a black or dirty mark; a smudge. 3. indecent talk or writing; obscenity. 4. a fungous disease of plants, esp. cereals, in which the affected parts are converted into a black powdery mass of spores, caused by fungi of the order *Ustilaginales.* 5. the fungus itself. —*v.t.* 6. to soil or smudge. —*v.i.* 7. to become affected with smut, as a plant. [alter. of earlier *smit* (OE *smitte*) by association with SMUDGE, SMUTCH]

smutch (smŭch), *v.t.* 1. to smudge or soil. —*n.* 2. a smudge or stain. 3. dirt, grime, or smut. [? t. MHG: m. *smutzen* smear] —**smutch′y,** *adj.*

Smuts (smŭts), *n.* **Jan Christiaan** (yän krĭs′tĭ·än′), 1870–1950, South African statesman and general: prime minister, 1919–24 and 1939–48.

smut·ty (smŭt′ĭ), *adj.*, **-tier, -tiest.** 1. soiled with smut, soot, or the like; grimy; dirty. 2. indecent or obscene, as talk, writing, etc.: *a smutty novel.* 3. given to such talk, etc., as a person. 4. (of plants) affected with the smut disease. —**smut′ti·ly,** *adv.* —**smut′ti·ness,** *n.*

Smyr·na (smûr′nə), *n.* former name of **Izmir.**

Sn, (L *stannum*) *Chem.* tin.

snack (snăk), *n.* 1. a small portion of food or drink; a light meal. 2. a share or portion. [n. use of *snack*, v., snap. Cf. MD *snacken* snap]

snaf·fle (snăf′əl), *n.*, *v.*, **-fled, -fling.** —*n.* 1. a slender, jointed bit used on a bridle. —*v.t.* 2. to put a snaffle on (a horse, etc.); control by or as by a snaffle. [cf. D *snavel*, G *schnabel* beak, mouth]

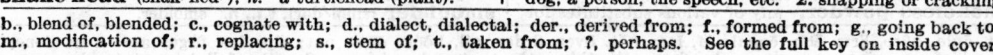

Snaffle

sna·fu (snă′fōō′), *adj.*, *v.*, **-fued, -fuing.** *Orig. Mil. Slang.* —*adj.* 1. in disorder; out of control; chaotic. —*v.t.* 2. to throw into disorder; muddle. [from the initial letters of "Situation normal—all fouled up"]

snag (snăg), *n.*, *v.*, **snagged, snagging.** —*n.* 1. a tree or part of a tree held fast in the bottom of a river or other water and forming an impediment or danger to navigation. 2. a short, projecting stump, as of a branch broken or cut off. 3. any sharp or rough projection. 4. a stump of a tooth; a projecting tooth; snaggletooth. 5. any obstacle or impediment: *to strike a snag in carrying out plans.* —*v.t.* 6. to run or catch upon, or damage by, a snag. 7. to obstruct or impede, as a snag does. 8. to clear of snags. [cf. d. Norw. *snag* stump, etc., Icel. *snagi* clothes peg] —**snag′like′,** *adj.*

snag·gle·tooth (snăg′əl·tōōth′), *n.*, *pl.* **-teeth.** a tooth growing out beyond or apart from others. —**snag·gle-toothed** (snăg′əl·tōōtht′), *adj.*

snag·gy (snăg′ĭ), *adj.*, **-gier, -giest.** 1. having snags or sharp projections, as a tree. 2. abounding in snags or obstructions, as a river. 3. snaglike; projecting sharply or roughly.

snail (snāl), *n.* 1. a mollusk of the class *Gastropoda* having a single, usually spirally coiled shell. 2. a slow or lazy person; a sluggard. [ME; OE *snegel*, c. G *schnägel*]

English garden snail, *Capaea hortensis* (¾ in. long)

snail-paced (snāl′pāst′), *adj.* slow of pace or motion, like a snail; sluggish.

snake (snāk), *n.*, *v.*, **snaked, snaking.** —*n.* 1. a scaly, limbless, usually slender reptile, occurring in venomous and nonvenomous forms, widely distributed in numerous genera and species and constituting the order (or suborder) *Serpentes.* 2. a treacherous person; an insidious enemy. —*v.i.* 3. to move, twist, or wind in the manner of a snake. —*v.t.* 4. *U.S.* to drag or haul, esp. by a chain or rope fastened around one end of the object, as a log. 5. *U.S.* to jerk (fol. by *out*, etc.). [ME; OE *snaca*, c. MLG *snake*. Cf. Icel. *snākr*] —**snake′like′,** *adj.*

snake·bird (snāk′bûrd′), *n.* any of various totipalmate swimming birds of the family *Anhingidae*, having a long, snaky neck.

snake fence, *U.S.* a fence of zigzag outline made of rails laid horizontally with the ends resting one across another at an angle; a worm fence.

snake·head (snāk′hĕd′), *n.* a turtlehead (plant).

snake·mouth (snāk′mouth′), *n.* a swamp orchid, *Pogonia ophioglossoides*, of eastern North America, having pale-rose, nodding flowers on a slender stem.

Snake River, a river flowing from NW Wyoming through S Idaho and N along the Oregon-Idaho boundary into the Columbia river in SE Washington: Shoshone Falls. 1038 mi.

snake·root (snāk′rōōt′, -rŏŏt′), *n.* 1. any of various plants whose roots have been regarded as a remedy for snake bites, as *Aristolochia Serpentaria* (**Virginia snakeroot**), an herb with medicinal rhizome and rootlets, and *Polygala Senega* (**Seneca snakeroot**), a white-flowered plant with a medicinal root. 2. the root or rhizome of such a plant. 3. the North American bugbane. 4. a white eupatorium, *Eupatorium rugosum.* 5. the dogbane, *Rauwolfia serpentina*, with roots that yield drugs.

snake·weed (snāk′wēd′), *n.* bistort (def. 1).

snak·y (snā′kĭ), *adj.*, **snakier, snakiest.** 1. of or pertaining to snakes. 2. abounding in snakes, as a place. 3. snakelike; twisting, winding, or sinuous. 4. venomous; treacherous or insidious. 5. consisting of, entwined with, or bearing snakes or serpents.

snap (snăp), *v.*, **snapped, snapping,** *n.*, *adj.*, *adv.* —*v.i.* 1. to make a sudden, sharp sound; crack, as a whip; crackle. 2. to click, as a mechanism. 3. to move, strike, shut, catch, etc., with a sharp sound, as a door, lid, or lock. 4. to break suddenly, esp. with a sharp, cracking sound, as something slender and brittle. 5. to flash, as the eyes. 6. to act or move with quick, neat motions of the body: *to snap to attention.* 7. *Photog.* to take instantaneous photographs. 8. to make a quick or sudden bite or snatch (often fol. by *at*). 9. to utter a quick, sharp speech, reproof, retort, etc. (often fol. by *at*). —*v.t.* 10. to seize with, or as with, a quick bite or snatch (usually fol. by *up* or *off*). 11. to secure hastily, as a decision, legislation, etc., not subjected to due deliberation. 12. to cause to make a sudden, sharp sound: *to snap one's fingers.* 13. to crack (a whip). 14. to bring, strike, shut, open, operate, etc., with a sharp sound or movement: *to snap a lid down.* 15. to address or interrupt (a person) quickly and sharply (usually fol. by *up*). 16. to utter or say in a quick, sharp manner (sometimes fol. by *out*). 17. to break suddenly, esp. with a crackling sound. 18. *Photog.* to take an instantaneous photograph of. 19. *Football.* to place (the ball) back into play by sending it back with a sharp motion. —*n.* 20. a sharp, crackling or clicking sound, or a movement or action causing such a sound: *a snap of a whip.* 21. a catch or the like operating with such a sound. 22. a sudden breaking, as of something brittle or tense, or a sharp, crackling sound caused by it. 23. a small, thin, brittle or crisp cake. 24. crispness, smartness, or liveliness, as of writings or style. 25. *Colloq.* briskness, vigor, or energy, as of persons or actions. 26. a quick, sharp speech, or manner of speaking. 27. a quick or sudden bite or snatch, as at something. 28. something obtained by or as by biting or snatching. 29. short spell, as of cold weather. 30. *Photog.* a snapshot. 31. *Slang.* an easy and profitable or agreeable position, piece of work, or the like. —*adj.* 32. denoting devices closing by pressure on a spring catch, or articles using such devices. 33. made, done, taken, etc., suddenly or offhand: *a snap judgment.* 34. easy: *a snap course at college.* —*adv.* 35. in a brisk, sudden manner. [t. D or LG: m.s. *snappen*]

snap·back (snăp′băk′), *n. Football.* 1. the snapping or passing back of the ball by the center, which puts it in play. 2. snapper-back.

snap bean, 1. any of various kinds of beans (plant) whose unripe pods are used as foods. 2. the pod itself.

snap·drag·on (snăp′drăg′ən), *n.* 1. a plant of the scrophulariaceous genus *Antirrhinum*, esp. *A. majus*, an herb long cultivated for its spikes of showy flowers, of various colors, with a corolla that has been supposed to look like the mouth of a dragon. 2. the game of flapdragon. 3. the raisins which are snapped in this game.

snap link, a link having a latchlike opening at one side through which another link, or catch, can be fitted.

snap·per (snăp′ər), *n.* 1. any of various large marine fishes of the family *Lutianidae* of warm seas, as the **red snapper,** *Lutianus blackfordii*, a food fish of the Gulf of Mexico. 2. any of various other fishes, as the bluefish, *Pomatomus saltratix.* 3. a snapping turtle.

snap·per-back (snăp′ər-băk′), *n. Football.* the center; snapback.

snapping beetle, a click beetle.

snapping turtle, a large and savage turtle, *Chelydra serpentina*, of American rivers, having powerful jaws with which it lunges and snaps at an enemy.

Common snapping turtle. *Chelydra serpentina* (20 to 30 in. long)

snap·pish (snăp′ĭsh), *adj.* 1. apt to snap or bite, as a dog. 2. disposed to speak or reply quickly and sharply, as a person. 3. impatiently or irritably sharp; curt. —**snap′pish·ly,** *adv.* —**snap′pish·ness,** *n.*

snap·py (snăp′ĭ), *adj.*, **-pier, -piest.** 1. snappish, as a dog, a person, the speech, etc. 2. snapping or crackling in sound, as a fire. **3.** quick or sudden in action or performance. **4.** *Colloq.* crisp, smart, lively, brisk, etc. **—snap′pi·ly,** *adv.* **—snap′pi·ness,** *n.*

snap·shot (snăp′shŏt′), *n.* **1.** an instantaneous photograph. **2.** a quick shot taken without deliberate aim.

snare[1] (snâr), *n., v.,* **snared, snaring.** **—n. 1.** a device, usually consisting of a noose, for capturing birds or small animals. **2.** anything serving to entrap, entangle, or catch unawares; a trap. **3.** *Surg.* a wire noose which removes tumors, etc. by the roots or the base. **—v.t. 4.** to catch with a snare; entrap; entangle. **5.** to catch or involve by trickery or wile. [ME, t. Scand. (cf. Icel. *snara*); r. OE *snearh,* c. OHG *snarahha*] **—snar′er,** *n.* **—Syn. 1.** See **trap**[1].

snare[2] (snâr), *n.* one of the strings of gut stretched across the skin of a snare drum. [t. LG: string]

snare drum, a small double-headed drum carried at the side, having snares across the lower head to produce a rattling or reverberating effect.

Snare drum

snark (snärk), *n.* a mysterious, imaginary animal. [b. SNAKE and SHARK; coined by Lewis Carroll]

snarl[1] (snärl), *v.i.* **1.** to growl angrily or viciously, as a dog. **2.** to speak in a savagely sharp, angry, or quarrelsome manner. **—v.t. 3.** to utter or say with a snarl. **—n. 4.** act of snarling. **5.** a snarling sound or utterance. [freq. of obs. *snar* snarl, c. D and LG *snarren,* G *schnarren*] **—snarl′er,** *n.* **—snarl′ing·ly,** *adv.* **—snarl′y,** *adj.*

snarl[2] (snärl), *n.* **1.** a tangle, as of thread or hair. **2.** a complicated or confused condition or matter. **3.** a knot in wood. **—v.t. 4.** to bring into a tangled condition, as thread, hair, etc.; tangle. **5.** to render complicated or confused. **6.** to raise or emboss, as parts of a thin metal vessel, by hammering on a tool (**snarling iron**) held against the inner surface of the vessel. **—v.i. 7.** to become tangled; get into a tangle. [ME *snarle* snare, t. Scand.; cf. O Swed. *snarel* noose, der. *snara* SNARE[1]] **—snarl′er,** *n.*

snatch (snăch), *v.i.* **1.** to make a sudden effort to seize something, as with the hand (usually fol. by *at*). **—v.t. 2.** to seize by a sudden or hasty grasp (often fol. by *up, from, out of, away,* etc.). **3.** to take, get, secure, etc., suddenly or hastily. **4.** to rescue or save by prompt action. **—n. 5.** act of snatching. **6.** a sudden motion to seize something. **7.** a bit, scrap, or fragment of something: *snatches of conversation.* **8.** a brief spell of effort, activity, or any experience: *to work in snatches.* **9.** a brief period of time. [ME *snacchen,* var. of earlier *snecchen;* orig. uncert.] **—snatch′er,** *n.*

snatch·y (snăch′ĭ), *adj.* consisting of, occurring in, or characterized by snatches; spasmodic; irregular.

snath (snăth), *n.* the shaft or handle of a scythe. Also, **snathe** (snāth). [unexplained var. of *snead,* ME *snede,* OE *snæd;* orig. uncert.]

sneak (snēk), *v.i.* **1.** to go in a stealthy or furtive manner; slink; skulk (fol. by *about, along, in, off, out,* etc.). **2.** to act in a furtive, underhand, or mean way. **3.** *Colloq.* to go away quickly and quietly. **—v.t. 4.** to move, put, pass, etc., in a stealthy or furtive manner. **5.** *Colloq.* to take surreptitiously, or steal. **—n. 6.** one who sneaks; a sneaking, underhand, or contemptible person. **7.** *Colloq.* an act of sneaking; a quiet departure. **8.** (*pl.*) *Colloq.* sneakers. [akin to OE *snīcan* sneak along] **—Syn. 1.** See **lurk.**

sneak·er (snē′kər), *n.* **1.** *U.S. Colloq.* a shoe with a rubber or other soft sole used esp. in gymnasiums. **2.** one who sneaks; a sneak.

sneak·ing (snē′kĭng), *adj.* **1.** acting in a furtive or underhand way. **2.** deceitfully underhand, as actions, etc.; contemptible. **3.** secret; not generally avowed, as a feeling, notion, suspicion, etc. **—sneak′ing·ly,** *adv.*

sneak thief, a burglar who steals by sneaking into houses through open doors, etc.

sneak·y (snē′kĭ), *adj.,* **sneakier, sneakiest.** like or suggestive of a sneak; sneaking. **—sneak′i·ly,** *adv.* **—sneak′i·ness,** *n.*

sneer (snîr), *v.i.* **1.** to smile or curl the lip in a manner that shows scorn, contempt, etc. **2.** to speak or write in a manner expressive of derision, scorn, or contempt. **—v.t. 3.** to utter or say in a sneering manner. **4.** to bring, put, force, etc., by sneering. **—n. 5.** a look or expression suggestive of derision, scorn, or contempt. **6.** a derisive or scornful utterance or remark, esp. one more or less covert or insinuative. **7.** an act of sneering. [ME *snere,* c. N Fris. *sneere* scorn, of unknown orig.] **—sneer′er,** *n.* **—sneer′ing,** *adj.* **—sneer′ing·ly,** *adv.* **—Syn. 2.** See **scoff.**

sneeze (snēz), *v.,* **sneezed, sneezing,** *n.* **—v.i. 1.** to emit air or breath suddenly, forcibly, and audibly through the nose and mouth by involuntary, spasmodic action. **2.** *Colloq.* to show contempt for, or treat with contempt (fol. by *at*). **—n. 3.** an act or course of sneezing. [late ME *snese,* earlier *fnese,* OE *fnēosan,* c. MHG *fnūsen*] **—sneez′er,** *n.* **—sneez′y,** *adj.*

sneeze·weed (snēz′wēd′), *n.* the false sunflower, *Helenium autumnale,* a North American composite plant, the powdered leaves and flowers of which cause sneezing.

sneeze·wort (snēz′wûrt′), *n.* an asteraceous plant, *Achillea Ptarmica,* a native of Europe, the powdered leaves of which cause sneezing.

snell (snĕl), *n.* a short piece of gut or the like by which a fishhook is attached to a longer line. [orig. unknown]

snick (snĭk), *v.t.* **1.** to cut, snip, or nick. **2.** to strike sharply. **3.** to snap (a gun, etc.). **—v.i. 4.** to click. **—n. 5.** a small cut; a nick. **6.** a click. **7.** *Cricket.* a. a glancing blow given to the ball. b. the ball so hit. [orig. uncert. Cf. Scot. *sneck* cut (off), Icel. *snikka* whittle]

snick·er (snĭk′ər), *v.i.* **1.** to laugh in a half-suppressed, often indecorous or disrespectful, manner. **—v.t. 2.** to utter with a snicker. **—n. 3.** a snickering laugh. Also, *esp. Brit.,* **snigger.** [imit.]

snick·er·snee (snĭk′ər·snē′), *n.* a knife, esp. one used as a weapon. [var. (by alliterative assimilation) of earlier *stick or snee* thrust or cut, t. D: m. *steken* stick and *snijen* cut]

snide (snīd), *adj.:* derogatory in a nasty, insinuating manner: *snide remarks about the Mayor.*

sniff (snĭf), *v.t.* **1.** to draw air through the nose in short, audible inhalation. **2.** to clear the nose by so doing; sniffle, as with emotion. **3.** to smell by short inhalations. **4.** to show disdain, contempt, etc., by a sniff (often fol. by *at*). **—v.t. 5.** to draw in or up through the nose by sniffing, as air, odor, liquid, powder, etc.; inhale. **6.** to perceive by, or as if by, smelling. **—n. 7.** an act of sniffing; a single short, audible inhalation. **8.** the sound made. **9.** a scent or odor perceived. [ME; back formation from SNIVEL]

snif·fle (snĭf′əl), *v.,* **-fled, -fling,** *n.* **—v.i. 1.** to sniff repeatedly, as from a cold in the head or in repressing tearful emotion. **—n. 2.** an act or sound of sniffling. **3. the sniffles,** a condition marked by sniffling. [freq. of SNIFF]

sniff·y (snĭf′ĭ), *adj.,* **sniffier, sniffiest.** *Colloq.* inclined to sniff, as in disdain; disdainful; supercilious.

snif·ter (snĭf′tər), *n.* **1.** a pear-shaped glass, narrowing at the top to intensify the aroma of the brandy, liqueur, etc. **2.** *U.S. Slang.* a very small drink of liquor.

snig·ger (snĭg′ər), *v.i., v.t., n. Chiefly Brit.* snicker.

snig·gle (snĭg′əl), *v.,* **-gled, -gling.** **—v.i. 1.** to fish for eels by thrusting a baited hook into their lurking places. **—v.t. 2.** to take by sniggling. [der. *snig* eel, ME *snigge*]

snip (snĭp), *v.,* **snipped, snipping,** *n.* **—v.t. 1.** to cut with a small, quick stroke, or a succession of such strokes, with scissors or the like. **2.** to take off by, or as by, cutting thus. **—v.i. 3.** to cut with small, quick strokes. **—n. 4.** act of snipping, as with scissors. **5.** a small cut made by snipping. **6.** a small piece snipped off. **7.** a small piece, bit, or amount of anything. **8.** *U.S. Colloq.* a small or insignificant person. **9.** (*pl.*) small, stout hand shears for the use of sheet metal workers. [cf. D and LG *snippen* snip, snatch, clip]

snipe (snīp), *n., v.,* **sniped, sniping.** **—n. 1.** any of several long-billed limicoline birds constituting the genera *Capella* and *Lymnocryptes,* frequenting marshes and much sought by gunners, as the American Wilson's snipe (*C. delicata*), the European great snipe (*C. media*), and the European jacksnipe (*Lymnocryptes minima*). **2.** any of several related shore birds, as the **red-breasted snipe** (*Limnodromus griseus*). **3.** a shot usually from a hidden position. **—v.i. 4.** to shoot or hunt snipe. **5.** to shoot at individual soldiers, etc., as opportunity offers from a concealed or long-range position. [ME *snype,* t. Scand.; cf. Icel. *snípa*] **—snip′er,** *n.*

Wilson's snipe. *Capella delicata* (11 in. long)

snip·pet (snĭp′ĭt), *n.* **1.** a small piece snipped off; a small bit, scrap, or fragment. **2.** *U.S. Colloq.* a small or insignificant person.

snip·py (snĭp′ĭ), *adj.,* **-pier, -piest.** **1.** *Colloq.* sharp or curt, esp. in a supercilious way. **2.** scrappy or fragmentary. Also, **snip·pe·ty** (snĭp′ə·tĭ). **—snip′pi·ness,** *n.*

snitch[1] (snĭch), *v.t. Slang.* to snatch or steal. [? var. of SNATCH]

snitch[2] (snĭch), *Slang.* **—v.i. 1.** to turn informer. **—n. 2.** an informer. [orig. uncert.] **—snitch′er,** *n.*

sniv·el (snĭv′əl), *v.,* **-eled, -eling** or (*esp. Brit.*) **-elled, -elling.** **—v.i. 1.** to weep or cry with sniffling. **2.** to affect a tearful state; whine. **3.** to run at the nose. **4.** to draw up mucus audibly through the nose. **—v.t. 5.** to utter with sniveling or sniffing. **—n. 6.** weak or pretended weeping. **7.** a light sniff, as in weeping. **8.** a hypocritical show of feeling. **9.** mucus running from the nose. [ME *snyvele,* c. OE *snyflung,* der. *snofl* mucus] **—sniv′el·er;** *esp. Brit.,* **sniv′el·ler,** *n.*

snob (snŏb), *n.* **1.** one who admires, imitates, or cultivates those with social rank, wealth, etc., and is condescending or overbearing to others. **2.** one who affects social importance and exclusiveness. [orig. nickname for cobbler or cobbler's apprentice; orig. uncert.]

snob·ber·y (snŏb′ər·ĭ), *n., pl.* **-beries.** snobbish character, conduct, trait, or act.

snob·bish (snŏb′ĭsh), *adj.* **1.** of, pertaining to, or characteristic of a snob. **2.** having the character of a snob. **—snob′bish·ly,** *adv.* **—snob′bish·ness,** *n.*

snood (snood), *n.* **1.** the distinctive headband formerly worn by young unmarried women in Scotland and northern England. **2.** a band or fillet for the hair. **3.** a netlike hat or part of a hat. **—v.t. 4.** to bind or confine (the hair) with a snood. [OE *snod;* orig. uncert.]

snook (snook, snŏŏk), *v.i. Chiefly Scot.* to lurk; lie in ambush; pry about. [ME *snoke,* t. Scand.; cf. d. Norw. *snoka* snuff, smell]

snoop (snōōp), *Colloq.* —*v.i.* 1. to prowl or pry; go about in a sneaking, prying way; pry in a mean, sly manner. —*n.* 2. an act or instance of snooping. 3. one who snoops. [t. D: m. *snoepen* take and eat (food or drink) on the sly] —**snoop′er,** *n.* —**snoop′y,** *adj.*

snoot (snōōt), *n. Slang.* 1. the nose. 2. the face, esp. if contorted by emotion. [d. or colloq. var. of SNOUT]

snoot·y (snōō′tĭ), *adj.,* **snootier, snootiest.** *U.S. Colloq.* snobbish.

snooze (snōōz), *v.i.,* **snoozed, snoozing.** *Colloq.* to sleep; slumber; doze; nap. [orig. uncert.]

Sno·qual·mie Falls (snō kwŏl′mĭ), falls of the Snoqualmie river, in W Washington. 270 ft. high.

snore (snōr), *v.,* **snored, snoring,** *n.* —*v.i.* 1. to breathe during sleep with hoarse or harsh sounds. —*v.t.* 2. to spend or pass (time) in snoring (fol. by *away* or *out*). —*n.* 3. an act of snoring, or the sound made. [ME; ? b. SNIFF and ROAR] —**snor′er,** *n.*

snor·kel (snôr′kəl), *n.* a device on a submarine consisting of two vertical tubes for the intake and exhaust of air for Diesel engines and general ventilation, thus permitting cruising at periscope depth for very long periods.

Snor·ri Stur·lu·son (snôr′rĭ stŭr′lə sôn), 1179–1241, Icelandic historian and poet.

snort (snôrt), *v.i.* 1. to force the breath violently through the nostrils with a loud, harsh sound, as a horse, etc. 2. to express contempt, indignation, etc. by such a sound. 3. *Colloq.* to laugh outright or boisterously. —*v.t.* 4. to utter with a snort. 5. to expel by or as by snorting. —*n.* 6. act or sound of snorting. [ME; ? b. SNORE and ME *route* snore (OE *hrūtan*)]—**snort′er,** *n.*

snot (snŏt), *n.* mucus from the nose. [OE *gesnot*] —**snot′ty,** *adj.*

snout (snout), *n.* 1. the part of an animal's head projecting forward and containing the nose and jaws; the muzzle. 2. *Entomol.* a prolongation of the head bearing the feeding organs, as in scorpion flies and snout beetles. 3. anything that resembles or suggests an animal's snout in shape, function, etc. 4. a nozzle or spout. 5. *Humorous or Contemptuous.* a person's nose, esp. when large or prominent. [ME, c. D *snuit,* G *schnauze*]

snout beetle, a weevil (def. 1) having a protruding snout or rostrum.

snow (snō), *n.* 1. the aqueous vapor of the atmosphere precipitated in partially frozen crystalline form and falling to the earth in white flakes. 2. these flakes as forming a layer on the ground, etc. 3. the fall of these flakes. 4. something resembling snow. 5. the white hair of age. 6. *Poetic.* white blossoms. 7. *Poetic.* the white color of snow. 8. *Chem.* carbon dioxide snow. 9. *Slang.* cocaine or heroin. 10. white spots on a television screen caused by a weak signal. —*v.i.* 11. to send down snow; fall as snow. 12. to descend like snow. —*v.t.* 13. to let fall as or like snow. 14. to cover, obstruct, etc., with snow (fol. by *over, under,* etc.). [ME; OE *snāw,* c. D *sneeuw,* G *schnee*] —**snow′like,** *adj.*

snow·ball (snō′bôl′), *n.* 1. a ball of snow pressed or rolled together. 2. any of certain shrubs, varieties of the genus *Viburnum,* with white sterile flowers born in large snowball-like clusters. —*v.t.* 3. to throw snowballs at. —*v.i.* 4. to grow larger at an accelerating rate.

snow·bell (snō′bĕl′), *n.* a white-flowered small tree of the styracaceous genus *Styrax.*

snow·ber·ry (snō′bĕr′ĭ), *n., pl.* **-ries.** 1. a caprifoliaceous shrub, *Symphoricarpos albus,* native in North America, cultivated for its ornamental white berries. 2. any of certain other white-berried plants.

snow·bird (snō′bûrd′), *n.* 1. a junco. 2. the snow bunting. 3. *U.S. Slang.* a cocaine or heroin addict.

snow-blind (snō′blīnd′), *adj.* having the sight dimmed or affected by exposure of the eyes to the glare of snow. —**snow blindness.**

snow·blink (snō′blĭngk′), *n.* the peculiar reflection that arises from fields of snow or ice.

snow·bound (snō′bound′), *adj.* shut in by snow.

snow broth, melting or melted snow.

snow bunting, a fringilline bird, *Plectrophenax nivalis,* inhabiting cold parts of the northern hemisphere.

snow·bush (snō′bŏŏsh′), *n.* any of several ornamental shrubs bearing a profusion of white flowers, as *Ceanothus velutinus,* of western North America.

snow-capped (snō′kăpt′), *adj.* topped with snow.

snow-clad (snō′klăd′), *adj.* covered with snow.

Snow·don (snō′dən), *n.* a mountain in NW Wales: the highest in Wales and England. 3560 ft.

snow·drift (snō′drĭft′), *n.* 1. a mass or bank of snow driven together by wind. 2. snow driven before wind.

snow·drop (snō′drŏp′), *n.* 1. a low spring-blooming herb, *Galanthus nivalis,* bearing drooping white flowers. 2. its bulbous root or flower. 3. the woodland anemone, *Anemone quinquefolia.*

snow·fall (snō′fôl′), *n.* 1. a fall of snow. 2. the amount of snow at a particular place or in a given time.

snow·flake (snō′flāk′), *n.* 1. one of the small feathery masses or flakes in which snow falls. 2. any of certain European amaryllidaceous plants (genus *Leucoium*) resembling the snowdrop. 3. the snow bunting.

snow line, 1. the line, as on mountains, above which there is perpetual snow. 2. the latitudinal line marking the limit of the fall of snow at sea level.

snow·man (snō′măn′), *n., pl.* **-men** (-mĕn′). a figure, resembling that of a man, made out of packed snow.

snow pellets, small, crisp, white, opaque grains of snowlike structure that fall from clouds during showers.

snow plant, a leafless parasitic plant, *Sarcodes sanguinea,* of the pine forests of the Sierra Nevada in California, having numerous erect red flowers, a thickly scaled stem, and a corallike mass of roots.

snow-plow (snō′plou′), *n.* an implement or machine for clearing away snow from highways, railroads, etc.

snow pudding, a light pudding, prepared by folding whipped egg whites into a lemon gelatine mixture.

snow-shed (snō′shĕd′), *n.* a structure, as over an extent of railroad on a mountainside, for protection against snow.

snow·shoe (snō′shōō′), *n., v.,* **-shoed, -shoeing.** —*n.* 1. a contrivance attached to the foot to enable the wearer to walk on deep snow without sinking in, as a ski, or esp., a light racket-shaped frame across which is stretched a network of rawhide. —*v.i.* 2. to walk or travel on snowshoes. —**snow′sho′er,** *n.*

Snowshoes

snow-slide (snō′slīd′), *n.* 1. the sliding down of a mass of snow on a slope. 2. the snow.

snow·storm (snō′stôrm′), *n.* a storm accompanied by a heavy fall of snow.

snow-suit (snō′sōōt′), *n.* a child's one- or two-piece outer garment for cold weather, having pants and long sleeves and fitting snugly at the ankles, wrists, and neck.

snow-white (snō′hwīt′), *adj.* white as snow.

snow·y (snō′ĭ), *adj.,* **snowier, snowiest.** 1. abounding in or covered with snow. 2. characterized by snow, as weather, etc. 3. consisting of snow; pertaining to or resembling snow. 4. snow-white. 5. immaculate; unsullied; stainless. —**snow′i·ly,** *adv.* —**snow′i·ness,** *n.*

snub (snŭb), *v.,* **snubbed, snubbing,** *n., adj.* —*v.t.* 1. to treat with disdain or contempt. 2. to put, force, etc., by doing this: *to snub one into silence.* 3. to check or rebuke sharply. 4. to check or stop suddenly (a rope or cable running out). 5. to check (a boat, an unbroken horse, etc.) by means of a rope or line made fast to a post or other fixed object. 6. to pull (*up*) thus. —*n.* 7. an act of snubbing; a sharp rebuke. 8. a disdainful affront or slight. 9. a sudden check given to a rope or cable running out. a moving boat, or the like. —*adj.* 10. (of the nose) short, and turned up at the tip. [ME, t. Scand.; cf. Icel. *snubba* rebuke] —**snub′ber,** *n.*

snub·by (snŭb′ĭ), *adj.,* **-bier, -biest.** 1. somewhat snub, as the nose. 2. tending to snub people.

snuff[1] (snŭf), *v.t.* 1. to draw in through the nose by inhaling. 2. to perceive by or as by smelling. 3. to examine by smelling, as an animal does. —*v.i.* 4. to draw air, etc., into the nostrils by inhaling, as in order to smell something. 5. to inhale powdered tobacco; take snuff. 6. *Obs.* to express disdain, contempt, displeasure, etc., by sniffing (often fol. by *at*). —*n.* 7. an act of snuffing; an inhalation; a sniff. 8. smell, scent, or odor. 9. a preparation of powdered tobacco, usually taken into the nostrils by inhalation. 10. a pinch of such tobacco. [t. MD: s. *snuffen* snuffle]

snuff[2] (snŭf), *n.* 1. the charred or partly consumed portion of a candlewick or the like. 2. a thing of little or no value, esp. if left over. —*v.t.* 3. to cut off or remove the snuff (of a candle, etc.). 4. to extinguish (fol. by *out*). [ME *snoffe*; orig. uncert.]

snuff-box (snŭf′bŏks′), *n.* a box for holding snuff, esp. one small enough to be carried in the pocket.

snuff·er[1] (snŭf′ər), *n.* 1. one who snuffs or sniffs. 2. one who takes snuff. [f. SNUFF[1] + -ER[1]]

snuff·er[2] (snŭf′ər), *n.* 1. (*usually pl.*) an instrument for snuffing out candles, etc. 2. one who snuffs candles. [f. SNUFF[2] + -ER[1]]

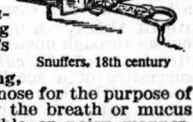

Snuffers. 18th century

snuf·fle (snŭf′əl), *v.,* **-fled, -fling,** *n.* —*v.i.* 1. to draw air into the nose for the purpose of smelling something. 2. to draw the breath or mucus through the nostrils in an audible or noisy manner. 3. to speak through the nose or with a nasal twang (often implying canting or hypocritical speech). —*v.t.* 4. to utter in a snuffling or nasal tone. —*n.* 5. an act of snuffling. 6. the **snuffles,** a condition of the nose, as from a cold, causing snuffling. 7. a nasal tone of voice. [t. D or Flem.: m.s. *snuffelen,* freq. of *snuffen.* See SNUFF[1],v.] —**snuf′fler,** *n.*

snuff·y (snŭf′ĭ), *adj.,* **snuffier, snuffiest.** 1. resembling snuff. 2. soiled with snuff. 3. given to the use of snuff. 4. having an unpleasant appearance. 5. having hurt feelings. 6. easily displeased. —**snuff′i·ness,** *n.*

snug (snŭg), *adj.,* **snugger, snuggest,** *v.,* **snugged, snugging,** *adv.* —*adj.* 1. comfortable or cozy, as a place, accommodations, etc. 2. trim, neat, or compactly arranged, as a ship or its parts. 3. fitting closely, but not too closely, as a garment. 4. more or less compact or limited in size, and sheltered or warm. 5. comfortably circumstanced, as persons, etc. 6. pleasant or agreeable, esp. in a small, exclusive way. 7. enabling one to live in comfort: *a snug fortune.* 8. in hiding: *to lie snug.* 9. secret. —*v.i.* 10. to lie closely or comfortably; nestle. —*v.t.* 11. to make snug. 12. *Naut.* to prepare for a storm by taking in sail, lashing deck gear, etc. (usually fol. by *down*). —*adv.* 13. in a snug manner.

[t. Scand.; cf. Icel. *snöggr* short-haired, etc.] —**snug′ly,** *adv.* —**snug′ness,** *n.*

snug·ger·y (snŭg′ə rĭ), *n.*, *pl.* **-ger·ies. 1.** a snug place or position. **2.** a comfortable or cozy room.

snug·gle (snŭg′əl), *v.*, **-gled, -gling.** —*v.i.* **1.** to lie or press closely, as for comfort or from affection; nestle; cuddle. —*v.t.* **2.** to draw or press closely, as for comfort or from affection. [freq. of SNUG, v.]

so¹ (sō), *adv.* **1.** in the way or manner indicated, described, or implied: *do it so.* **2.** in that or this manner or fashion; thus. **3.** as stated or reported: *is that so?* **4.** in the aforesaid state or condition: *it is broken, and has long been so.* **5.** to that extent; in that degree: *do not walk so fast.* **6.** very or extremely: *you are so kind.* **7.** very greatly: *my head aches so!* **8.** (used as the antecedent in the correlation *so . . . as,* expressing comparison) to such a degree or extent: *so far as I know.* **9.** having the purpose of. **10.** for a given reason; hence; therefore. **11.** because of; for the reason that. **12.** in such manner as to follow or result from. **13.** in the way that follows; in this way. **14.** in such way as to end in. **15.** (equivalent to "is that so?"). **16. and so, a.** (a continuative used to confirm or emphasize a previous statement): *I said I would come, and so I will.* **b.** likewise or correspondingly: *he is going, and so am I.* **c.** consequently or accordingly: *she is ill, and so cannot come.* **d.** thereupon or thereafter: *and so they were married.* **17. or so,** about thus, or about that amount or number: *a day or so ago.* **18. so as, a.** with the result or purpose (followed by an infinitive). **b.** provided that. **19. so called, a.** called or designated thus. **b.** incorrectly called or styled thus. **20. so that, a.** with the effect or result that. **b.** in order that: *he wrote so that they might expect him.* **c.** provided that. **21. so to speak** (or **say**), to use such a manner of speaking. —*conj.* **22.** *Colloq.* consequently; with the result that. **23.** under the condition that (often fol. by *that*). —*pron.* **24.** such as has been stated: *to be good and stay so.* **25.** more or less: *at three o'clock or so.* —*interj.* **26.** how can that be! **27.** that will do! stop! [ME; OE *swā,* c. D *zoo,* G *so*] —Syn. **10.** See therefore.

so² (sō), *n.* *Music.* sol. [see GAMUT]

So., **1.** South. **2.** southern.

soak (sōk), *v.i.* **1.** to lie in and become saturated or permeated with water or some other liquid. **2.** to pass, as a liquid, through pores or interstices (usually fol. by *in, through, out,* etc.). **3.** to be thoroughly wet. **4.** to become known slowly to: *the facts soaked into his mind.* **5.** *Colloq.* to drink immoderately. —*v.t.* **6.** to place and keep in liquid in order to saturate thoroughly; steep. **7.** to wet thoroughly. or drench. **8.** to permeate thoroughly, as liquid or moisture does. **9.** *Slang.* to intoxicate with liquor. **10.** *Colloq.* to drink, esp. to excess. **11.** to take in or up by absorption (often fol. by *up*): *blotting paper soaks up ink.* **12.** to draw (*out*) by or as by soaking. **13.** *U.S. Slang.* **a.** to beat hard; punish severely. **b.** to charge exorbitantly, etc. **14.** *Slang.* to put in pawn. **15.** *Slang.* to compel to pay. —*n.* **16.** act of soaking. **17.** the state of being soaked. **18.** the liquid in which anything is soaked. **19.** *Slang.* a heavy drinker. [ME *soke,* OE *socian;* akin to SUCK, v.] —**soak′er,** *n.* —Syn. **6.** See wet.

soak·age (sō′kĭj), *n.* **1.** act of soaking. **2.** liquid which has oozed out or been absorbed.

so-and-so (sō′ən sō′), *n.*, *pl.* **-sos.** someone or something not definitely named: *Mr. So-and-so.*

soap (sōp), *n.* **1.** a substance used for washing and cleansing purposes, usually made by treating a fat with an alkali (as sodium or potassium hydroxide), and consisting chiefly of the sodium or potassium salts of the acids contained in the fat. **2.** any metallic salt of an acid derived from a fat. **3.** *U. S. Slang.* money, esp. as used for bribery in politics. —*v.t.* **4.** to rub, cover, or treat with soap. [ME *sope,* OE *sāpe,* c. G *seife*]

soap·bark (sōp′bärk′), *n.* **1.** a middle-sized rosaceous Chilean tree, *Quillaja Saponaria,* bearing undivided evergreen leaves and small white flowers: the inner bark is used as a substitute for soap. **2.** the inner bark of this tree, used as a substitute for soap: quillai bark. **3.** any of various other saponaceous barks, as of several tropical American shrubs of the mimosaceous genus *Pithecolobium.* **4.** a plant yielding such bark.

soap·ber·ry (sōp′bĕr′ĭ), *n.*, *pl.* **-ries. 1.** the fruit of any of certain tropical and subtropical trees of the genus *Sapindus,* esp. *S. Saponaria,* used as a substitute for soap. **2.** a tree bearing such fruit, as *S. Drummondii,* of the southwestern U. S., which yields a useful wood.

soap·box (sōp′bŏks′), *n.* **1.** a box, usually wooden, in which soap had been packed, esp. one used as a temporary platform by agitators addressing people on the streets. —*v.i.* **2.** to address a street audience thus.

soap opera, *Colloq.* a radio play presented serially in short week-day programs, dealing usually with domestic problems in a highly emotional manner.

soap·stone (sōp′stōn′), *n.* a massive variety of talc with a soapy or greasy feel, used for hearths, washtubs, table tops, carved ornaments, etc.

soap·suds (sōp′sŭdz′), *n. pl.* suds made with water and soap.

soap·wort (sōp′wûrt′), *n.* an herb of the pink family, *Saponaria officinalis,* whose leaves are used for cleansing.

soap·y (sō′pĭ), *adj.,* **soapier, soapiest. 1.** containing, or impregnated with, soap: *soapy water.* **2.** covered with soap or lather. **3.** of the nature of soap; resembling

soap. **4.** pertaining to or characteristic of soap. —**soap′i·ly,** *adv.* —**soap′i·ness,** *n.*

soar (sōr), *v.i.* **1.** to fly upward, as a bird. **2.** to fly at a great height, without visible movements of the pinions, as a bird. **3.** to glide along at a height, as an airplane. **4.** to rise or ascend to a height, as a mountain. **5.** to rise or aspire to a higher or more exalted level. —*n.* **6.** act of soaring. **7.** the height attained in soaring. [ME *sore,* t. OF: m. *essorer* fly up, soar, g. L *exaurāre,* der. *ex-* out of + *aura* air] —**soar′er,** *n.* —Syn. **1.** See fly¹.

sob (sŏb), *v.,* **sobbed, sobbing,** *n.* —*v.i.* **1.** to weep with a sound caused by a convulsive catching of the breath. **2.** to make a sound resembling this. —*v.t.* **3.** to utter with sobs. **4.** to put, send, etc., by sobbing or with sobs: *to sob oneself to sleep.* —*n.* **5.** act of sobbing; a convulsive catching of the breath in weeping. **6.** any sound suggesting this. [ME *sobbe(n);* appar. imit.] —**sob′bing·ly,** *adv.*

so·be·it (sō bē′ĭt), *conj.* *Archaic.* if it be so that; provided.

so·ber (sō′bər), *adj.* **1.** not intoxicated or drunk. **2.** habitually temperate, esp. in the use of liquor. **3.** quiet or sedate in demeanor, as persons. **4.** marked by seriousness, gravity, solemnity, etc., as demeanor, speech, etc. **5.** subdued in tone, as color; not gay or showy, as clothes. **6.** free from excess, extravagance, or exaggeration: *sober facts.* **7.** showing self-control. **8.** sane or rational. —*v.i.,* *v.t.* **9.** to make or become sober. [ME, t. OF: m. *sobre,* t. L: m.s. *sōbrius*] —**so′ber·ly,** *adv.* —**so′ber·ness,** *n.* —Syn. **4.** See grave². **5.** somber, dull. —Ant. **4.** gay.

so·ber-mind·ed (sō′bər mīn′dĭd), *adj.* self-controlled; sensible. —**so′ber-mind′ed·ness,** *n.*

So·bies·ki (sō byĕs′kĭ), *n.* **John,** 1624–96, Polish general who, as John III, was king of Poland (1674–96).

So·bran·je (sō brän′yə), *n.* the national assembly of Bulgaria, consisting of a single chamber of elected deputies. [t. Bulgarian: assembly]

Soc., society.

soc·age (sŏk′ĭj), *n.* *Medieval Eng. Law.* the system of nonmilitary land tenure, usually free as distinguished from servile, by which land was commonly held in England. [ME, t. AF: f. *soc* SOKE + *-age* -AGE] —**soc′ager,** *n.*

so-called (sō′kôld′), *adj.* **1.** called or designated thus. **2.** incorrectly called or styled thus.

soc·cer (sŏk′ər), *n.* a form of football in which the use of the hands and arms either for playing the ball or for interfering with an opponent is prohibited; association football. [f. (AS)SOC(IATION) + -ER¹]

So·che (sō′chŭ), *n.* a city in W China, in W Sinkiang province: in a large oasis of the Tarim Basin. ab. 60,000. Also, **Yarkand.**

so·cia·bil·i·ty (sō′shə bĭl′ə tĭ), *n.,* *pl.* **-ties.** sociable disposition or tendency; disposition or inclination for the society of others.

so·cia·ble (sō′shə bəl), *adj.* **1.** inclined to associate with or be in the company of others. **2.** friendly or agreeable in company; companionable. **3.** characterized by or pertaining to companionship with others. —*n.* **4.** *U.S.* an informal social gathering, esp. of members of a church. [part. L: m. s. *sociābilis*] —**so′cia·ble·ness,** *n.* —**so′cia·bly,** *adv.* —Syn. **1.** See social.

so·cial (sō′shal), *adj.* **1.** pertaining to, devoted to, or characterized by friendly companionship or relations: *a social club.* **2.** friendly or sociable, as persons or the disposition, spirit, etc. **3.** pertaining to, connected with, or suited to polite or fashionable society: *a social function.* **4.** living, or disposed to live, in companionship with others or in a community, rather than in isolation. **5.** of or pertaining to human society, esp. as a body divided into classes according to worldly status: *social rank.* **6.** of or pertaining to the life and relation of human beings in a community: *social problems.* **7.** noting or pertaining to activities designed to remedy or alleviate certain unfavorable conditions of life in a community, esp. among the poor: *social work.* **8.** venereal: *a social disease.* **9.** pertaining to or advocating socialism. **10.** (of animals) living together in communities, as bees, ants, etc. (opposed to *solitary*). **11.** *Bot.* growing in patches or clumps. **12.** *Hist.* of, pertaining to, or between allies or confederates, as a war. —*n.* **13.** a social gathering or party. [t. L: s. *sociālis*] —**so′cial·ly,** *adv.* —**so′cial·ness,** *n.*

—Syn. **1.** SOCIAL, SOCIABLE agree in being concerned with the mutual relations of mankind living in an organized society. SOCIAL is a general word: *social laws, equals, advancement.* SOCIABLE means fond of company and society, companionable, genial, and affable, good at "mixing": *a friendly and sociable sort of person.* A SOCIAL evening is one spent enjoyably in company with others at a more or less formal event; a SOCIABLE evening is one spent companionably with perhaps only one person or a few. —Ant. **4.** individual, introverted.

social class, *Sociol.* a broad group in society having common economic, cultural, or political status.

social control, *Sociol.* **1.** the enforcement of conformity by society upon its members, either by law or by attitudes. **2.** the influence of any element in social life working to maintain the pattern of such life.

Social Democrat, a member of any of certain political parties with socialistic principles, in Germany, etc.

Social-Democratic party. See **Socialist Labor party.**

Social Democratic Workingmen's party. See Socialist Labor party.

social distance, *Sociol.* the extent to which individuals or groups are removed from or excluded from participating in each other's life.

social environment, *Sociol.* culture factor.

social evolution, *Sociol.* societal development.

social heritage, *Sociol.* the entire inherited pattern of cultural activity present in a society.

social interaction, *Sociol.* the interstimulation and response taking place between individuals and between groups, with particular reference to cultural activity.

so·cial·ise (sō′shə līz′), *v.t.,* **-ised, -ising.** *Chiefly Brit.* socialize.

so·cial·ism (sō′shəl ĭz′əm), *n.* **1.** a theory or system of social organization which advocates the vesting of the ownership and control of the means of production, capital, land, etc. in the community as a whole. **2.** procedure or practice in accordance with this theory.

social isolation, *Sociol.* a state or process in which persons, groups, or cultures lose or do not have communication or coöperation with one another. Social isolation often develops into open conflict.

so·cial·ist (sō′shəl ĭst), *n.* **1.** an advocate or supporter of socialism. **—adj. 2.** socialistic.

so·cial·is·tic (sō′shə lĭs′tĭk), *adj.* **1.** of socialists or socialism. **2.** in accordance with socialism. **3.** advocating or supporting socialism. **—so′cial·is′ti·cal·ly,** *adv.*

Socialist Labor party, the U.S. socialist political party (1874–77 called the Social Democratic Workingmen's party) from 1877 to about 1900 when most of its members formed the Social-Democratic party, developing later into the Socialist party.

Socialist party, the U.S. political party professing adherence to socialism. See **Socialist Labor party.**

so·cial·ite (sō′shə līt′), *n.* *U.S. Colloq.* a member of the social elite.

so·ci·al·i·ty (sō′shĭ ăl′ə tĭ), *n., pl.* **-ties. 1.** social nature or tendencies as shown in the assembling of individuals in communities. **2.** the action on the part of individuals of associating together in communities. **3.** the state or quality of being social.

so·cial·ize (sō′shə līz′), *v.t.,* **-ized, -izing. 1.** to make social; make fit for life in companionship with others. **2.** to make socialistic; establish or regulate according to the theories of socialism. **3.** *Educ.* to turn from an individual activity into one involving all or a group of pupils. Also, *esp. Brit.,* **socialise. —so′cial·i·za′tion,** *n.*

socialized medicine, any of various systems to provide the entire population, especially the lower-income groups, with medical care through federal subsidization of medical and health services, general regulation of these services, etc.

social organization, *Sociol.* the structure of relations inside of a group, usually the relations of subgroups and of institutions.

social process, *Sociol.* the means by which culture and social organization change or are preserved.

social register, a book listing the principal members of polite or fashionable society.

social science, the group of studies seeking to establish a science of the social life of human groups.

social security, an insurance plan, relating to life insurance and old age pensions, offered by the government to specified groups of the population, on either a gratuitous or contributory basis.

social service, organized welfare efforts carried on under professional rules by a trained personnel.

social settlement. See **settlement** (def. 12).

Social War, 1. *Gk. Hist.* the war between Athens and its confederates in 357–355 B.C. **2.** *Rom. Hist.* the war between Rome and its Italian allies in 90–88 B.C.

social work, organized work directed toward the betterment of social conditions in the community, as by seeking to improve the condition of the poor, to promote the welfare of children, etc. **—social worker.**

so·ci·e·tal (sə sī′ə təl), *adj.* noting or pertaining to large social groups, or to their activities, customs, etc.

societal development, *Sociol.* the formation and transformation of social life, customs, institutions, etc.

so·ci·e·ty (sə sī′ə tĭ), *n., pl.* **-ties. 1.** an organization of persons associated together for religious, benevolent, literary, scientific, political, patriotic, or other purposes. **2.** a body of individuals living as members of a community: *a society of human beings.* **3.** the body of human beings generally, associated or viewed as members of a community: *the evolution of human society.* **4.** human beings collectively regarded as a body divided into classes according to worldly status: *the lower classes of society.* **5.** a body of persons associated by their calling, interests, etc.: *diplomatic society.* **6.** those with whom one has companionship. **7.** companionship or company: *to enjoy one's society.* **8.** the social relations, activities, or life of the polite or fashionable world. **9.** the body of those associated in the polite or fashionable world; the

rich upper class. **10.** the condition of those living in companionship with others, or in a community, rather than in isolation. **11.** any community. **12.** *Ecol.* a closely integrated grouping of organisms of the same species held together by mutual dependence and showing division of labor. **13.** *Eccles.* an ecclesiastical society. [t. L: m. *societas*] **—Syn. 1.** See circle.

Society Islands, a group of islands in the S Pacific: a part of French Polynesia; largest island, Tahiti. (Excluding minor islands) 48,287 pop. (1951); 453 sq. mi. *Cap.:* Papeete.

Society of Friends, the proper designation of the sect founded by George Fox about 1650, and opposed to oath taking and all war, commonly called Quakers.

Society of Jesus. See **Jesuit.**

society verse, light, graceful, entertaining poetry, appealing to polite society. [trans. of F *vers de société*]

So·cin·i·an (sō sĭn′ĭ ən), *n.* **1.** a follower of Socinus who denied Christ's divinity, although holding that he was miraculously begotten and entitled to adoration. **—adj. 2.** of or pertaining to the Socinians or their doctrines. **—So·cin′i·an·ism,** *n.*

So·ci·nus (sō sī′nəs), *n.* Faustus (fôs′təs), (*Fausto Sozzini*) 1539–1604, and his uncle, Laelius (lē′lĭ əs), (*Lelio Sozzini*) 1525–62, Italian Protestant theologians and reformers.

socio-, a word element representing "social," "sociological," as in *sociometry.* [comb. form repr. L *socius* companion]

sociol. 1. sociological. **2.** sociology.

so·ci·ol·o·gy (sō′sĭ ŏl′ə jĭ, sō′shĭ-), *n.* the science or study of the origin, development, organization, and functioning of human society; the science of the fundamental laws of social relations, institutions, etc. **—so′ci·o·log′i·cal,** *adj.* **—so′ci·ol′o·gist,** *n.*

so·ci·om·e·try (sō′sĭ ŏm′ə trĭ, sō′shĭ-), *n.* the measurement of attitudes of social acceptance or rejection through expressed preferences among members of a social grouping.

sock¹ (sŏk), *n.* **1.** a short stocking reaching about halfway to the knee, or only above the ankle. **2.** a light shoe worn by ancient Greek and Roman comic actors, sometimes taken as a symbol of comedy. See buskin. [ME *sokke,* OE *socc,* t. L: s. *soccus* (def. 2)]

sock² (sŏk), *Slang.* **—v.t. 1.** to strike or hit hard. **—n. 2.** a hard blow. [orig. uncert.]

sock·dol·a·ger (sŏk dŏl′ə jər), *n.* *U.S. Slang.* **1.** something unusually large, heavy, etc. **2.** a decisive reply, argument, etc. **3.** a heavy, finishing blow. [slang coinage based on SOCK² + DOXOLOGY (in slang sense of finish) + -ER¹]

sock·et (sŏk′ĭt), *n.* **1.** a hollow part or piece for receiving and holding some part or thing. **2.** a device intended to support an electric lamp mechanically and connect it electrically to circuit wires. **3.** *Anat.* **a.** a hollow in one part, which receives another part: *the socket of the eye.* **b.** the concavity of a joint: *the socket of the hip.* **—v.t. 4.** to place in or fit with a socket. [ME *soket,* t. AF, dim. of *soc* plowshare; of Celtic orig.]

S. Socket. (def. 3b) of right scapula (front view)

sock·eye (sŏk′ī′), *n.* the red salmon. *Oncorhynchus nerka,* most highly valued of the Pacific salmons. [t. Amer. Ind. (Salishan dialects): alter. of *sukkegh* Fraser river salmon, blueback, etc.]

sock suspender, *Brit.* a garter.

so·cle (sŏk′əl, sō′kəl), *n.* *Archit.* a low, plain member supporting a wall, pedestal, or the like. [t. F, t. It.: m. *zoccolo,* g. L *socculus,* dim. of *soccus* SOCK¹]

So·co·tra (sō kō′trə, sŏk′ə trə), *n.* an island in the Indian Ocean, S of Arabia: a part of Aden protectorate. ab. 12,000 pop.; 1382 sq. mi. *Cap.:* Tamarida. Also, Sokotra.

Soc·ra·tes (sŏk′rə tēz′), *n.* 469?–399 B.C., Athenian philosopher.

So·crat·ic (sō krăt′ĭk), *adj.* **1.** of or pertaining to Socrates or his philosophy, followers, etc. **—n. 2.** a follower of Socrates. **3.** one of the Greek philosophers stimulated by Socrates. **—So·crat′i·cal·ly,** *adv.*

Socratic irony. See **irony¹** (def. 3).

Socratic method, the use of questions as employed by Socrates to develop a latent idea, as in the mind of a pupil, or to elicit admissions, as from an opponent, tending to establish or to confute some proposition.

sod¹ (sŏd), *n., v.,* **sodded, sodding. —n. 1.** a piece (usually square or oblong) cut or torn from the surface of grassland, containing the roots of grass, etc. **2.** the surface of the ground, esp. when covered with grass; turf; sward. **—v.t. 3.** to cover with sods. [ME, t. MD or MLG: m. *sode* turf]

sod² (sŏd), *v.* *Obs.* pt. and pp. of **seethe.**

so·da (sō′də), *n.* **1.** sodium hydroxide, NaOH; caustic soda. **2.** the oxide of sodium, Na₂O. **3.** sodium (in phrases): *carbonate of soda.* **4.** soda water. **5.** a drink made with soda water, served with fruit or other syrups, ice cream, etc. **6.** (in faro) the turned-up card in the dealing box before one begins to play. [t. ML, t. It., fem. of *sodo,* g. L *solidus* solid]

soda biscuit, 1. a biscuit using soda and sour milk or buttermilk as leavening agents. **2.** a soda cracker.

soda cracker, a thin crisp biscuit prepared from a yeast dough which has been neutralized by baking soda.

---

b., blend of, blended; c., cognate with; d., dialect, dialectal; der., derived from; f., formed from; g., going back to; m., modification of; r., replacing; s., stem of; t., taken from; ?, perhaps.   See the full key on inside cover.

soda fountain, 1. a counter at which sodas, ice cream, light meals, etc., are served. **2.** a container from which soda water is drawn off by faucets.

soda jerk, *U.S Slang.* a soda fountain clerk.

soda lime, a mixture of sodium hydroxide and calcium hydroxide.

so·da·lite (sō′də līt′), *n.* a mineral, sodium aluminum silicate with sodium chloride, 3NaAlSiO₄·NaCl, occurring in crystals and massive, white, gray, or blue in color: found in certain alkali-rich igneous rocks.

so·dal·i·ty (sō dăl′ə tĭ). *n., pl. -ties.* **1.** fellowship. **2.** an association or society. **3.** *Rom. Cath. Ch.* a society with religious or charitable objects. [t. L: m. *sodālitas*]

soda water, 1. an effervescent beverage consisting of water charged with carbon dioxide. **2.** (orig.) a beverage made with sodium bicarbonate.

sod·den (sŏd′ən), *adj.* **1.** soaked with liquid or moisture. **2.** heavy, doughy, or soggy, as food. **3.** having the appearance of having been soaked. **4.** bloated, as the face. **5.** expressionless, dull, or stupid. **6.** *Rare.* boiled. —*v.t., v.i.* **7.** to make or become sodden. [ME *sothen*, pp. of SEETHE] —**sod′den·ly,** *adv.* —**sod′den·ness,** *n.*

so·di·um (sō′dĭ əm), *n. Chem.* a soft, silver-white metallic element which oxidizes rapidly in moist air, occurring in nature only in the combined state. The metal is used in the synthesis of sodium peroxide, sodium cyanide, and ethyl (def. 2). *Symbol:* Na (for *natrium*); *at. wt.:* 22.997; *at. no.:* 11; *sp. gr.:* 0.97 at 20° C. [f. SOD(A) + -IUM]

sodium bicarbonate, a white, crystalline compound, NaHCO₃, used in cooking, medicine, etc.

sodium carbonate, a compound of sodium, Na₂CO₃, occurring in an anhydrous form as a white powder, called soda ash. As a hydrate, Na₂CO₃·10H₂O, known as washing soda.

sodium chlorate, *Chem.* a sodium salt, NaClO₃, used in explosives, as an antiseptic in toothpastes, etc.

sodium chloride, common salt, NaCl.

sodium dichromate, a red water-soluble crystalline salt, Na₂Cr₂O₇·2H₂O.

sodium hydroxide, a white caustic solid, NaOH, used in making soap, etc.

sodium hyposulfite, 1. a colorless crystalline compound, Na₂S₂O₄, used in solution as a bleach. **2.** sodium sulfate.

sodium nitrate, a crystalline water-soluble compound, NaNO₃, which occurs naturally as Chile saltpeter, used in fertilizers, explosives, and glass.

sodium pentothal, a barbiturate, injected intravenously as a general anesthetic. Also, **pentothal sodium, thiopental sodium;** *Brit.,* **thiopentone sodium.**

sodium thiosulfate, a water-soluble crystalline salt, Na₂S₂O₃, sometimes called sodium hyposulfite (the "hypo" of photographers, used as a fixing bath).

so·di·um-va·por lamp (sō′dĭ əm vā′pər), *Elect.* an electric lamp in which sodium vapor is activated by current passing between two electrodes, producing a yellow, glareless light used on streets and highways.

Sod·om (sŏd′əm). *n.* **1.** an ancient city near the Dead Sea, which, according to the Biblical account, was destroyed by fire from heaven because of the wickedness of its inhabitants. Gen. 18–19. **2.** any very wicked place.

So·do·ma, Il (sō′dō mä′, ēl), *n.* Giovanni Antonio de' Bazzi (jō vän′nē än tō′nyō dē bät′tsē), 1477–1549, Italian painter.

Sod·om·ite (sŏd′ə mīt′), *n.* **1.** an inhabitant of Sodom. **2.** (*l.c.*) one who practices sodomy.

sod·om·y (sŏd′əm ĭ), *n.* unnatural sexual intercourse, esp. of one man with another or of a human being with an animal. [ME, t. OF: m. *sodomie*. See SODOM. -Y³]

Soem·ba (sōōm′bä), *n.* Dutch name of **Sumba.**

Soem·ba·wa (sōōm bä′wä), *n.* Dutch name of **Sumbawa.**

Soe·ra·ba·ja (sōō′rä bä′yä), *n.* Dutch name of **Surabaya.**

so·ev·er (sō ĕv′ər), *adv.* at all; in any case; of any kind; in any way (used with generalizing force after *who, what, when, where, how, any, all,* etc., sometimes separated by intervening words, often in composition): *choose what person soever you please.*

-soever, suffix making intensive and generalized forms of interrogatives, as in *whatsoever.*

so·fa (sō′fə), *n.* a long upholstered seat, or couch, with a back and two arms or raised ends. [t. Ar.: m. *soffah* part of floor made higher for use as seat]

sof·fit (sŏf′ĭt), *n. Archit.* the under surface of an architrave, arch, beam, or the like. [earlier *soffita, -o,* t. It., f. so- (g. L *sub*) under + *-fita, -fito,* pp. of *figgere* (g. L *figere*) fix]

So·fi·a (sō′fĭ ə, sō fē′ə; *Bulg.* sô′fĭ yä′), *n.* the capital of Bulgaria, in the W part. 600,000 (est. 1953). Also, **So′fi·ya′.**

soft (sôft, sŏft), *adj.* **1.** yielding readily to touch or pressure; easily penetrated, divided, or altered in shape; not hard or stiff. **2.** relatively deficient in hardness, as metal. **3.** smooth and agreeable to the touch; not rough or coarse. **4.** producing agreeable sensations; pleasant, easeful, or comfortable: *soft slumber.* **5.** low or subdued in sound; gentle and melodious. **6.** not harsh or unpleasant to the eye; not glaring, as light or color. **7.** not hard or sharp, as outlines. **8.** gentle or mild, as wind, rain, etc.; genial or balmy, as climate, air, etc. **9.** gentle, mild, lenient, or compassionate.

10. smooth, soothing, or ingratiating, as words. **11.** not harsh or severe, as terms. **12.** yielding readily to the tender emotions, as persons; impressionable. **13.** sentimental, as language. **14.** not strong or robust; delicate; incapable of great endurance or exertion. **15.** *Colloq.* not hard, trying, or severe; involving little effort: *a soft job.* **16.** *Colloq.* easily influenced or swayed, as a person, the mind, etc.; easily imposed upon. **17.** (of water) relatively free from mineral salts that interfere with the action of soap. **18.** *Photog.* having delicate gradations of tone (opposed to *contrasty*). **19.** *Phonet. a.* (of consonants) lenis, esp. lenis and voiced. **b.** (of *c* and *g*) pronounced as in *cent* and *gem.* **c.** (of consonants in Slavic languages) palatalized. —*n.* **20.** that which is soft or yielding; the soft part; softness. —*adv.* **21.** in a soft manner. —*interj. Archaic.* **22.** be quiet! hush! **23.** not so fast! stop! [ME *softe,* OE *sōfte,* c. G *sanft*] —**soft′ly,** *adv.* —**soft′ness,** *n.*

sof·ta (sŏf′tə), *n. Turkey.* a Mohammedan student of theology and sacred law. [t. Turk., t. Pers.: m. *sūhtah,* lit., fired (by love of learning)]

soft·ball (sôft′bôl′, sŏft′-), *n.* **1.** a form of baseball played with a larger and softer ball. **2.** the ball itself.

soft coal, bituminous coal.

soft drink, a drink which is not alcoholic or intoxicating, as root beer, ginger ale, etc.

sof·ten (sôf′ən, sŏf′ən), *v.t., v.i.* to make or become soft or softer. —**sof′ten·er,** *n.*

softening of the brain, *Pathol.* **1.** a softening of the cerebral tissues, which are transformed into a mushy, fatlike substance. **2.** *Obs.* dementia associated with general paresis.

soft-finned (sôft′fĭnd′, sŏft′-), *adj. Icthyol.* having fins supported by articulated rays rather than by spines, as a malacopterygian (contrasted with *spiny-finned*).

soft-head·ed (sôft′hĕd′ĭd, sŏft′-), *adj.* foolish; stupid. —**soft′-head′ed·ness,** *n.*

soft-heart·ed (sôft′här′tĭd, sŏft′-), *adj.* very generous or sympathetic. —**soft′-heart′ed·ness,** *n.*

soft pedal, a pedal, as in a piano, for softening tones.

soft-ped·al (sôft′pĕd′əl, sŏft′-), *v.,* **-aled, -aling** or (*esp. Brit.*) **-alled, -alling.** —*v.i.* **1.** to use the soft pedal. —*v.t.* **2.** to soften the sound of by means of the soft pedal. **3.** *Colloq.* to tone down; make less strong, uncompromising, noticeable, or the like.

soft sell, a method of advertising or selling which is quietly persuasive, subtle, and indirect. See **hard sell.**

soft-shelled crab (sôft′shĕld′, sŏft′-), the common edible crab, *Callinectes,* recently molted and therefore in a suitable state to be fried or broiled and eaten in its entirety. Also, **soft′shell′.**

soft-shelled turtle, a turtle with a leathery shell overlying the bony carapace and plastron, instead of the usual one of horny plates. The many species constitute the family *Trionychidae.* See **leatherback.**

soft soap, 1. the semifluid soap produced when potassium hydroxide is used in the saponification of a fat or an oil. **2.** *Colloq.* smooth words; flattery.

soft-soap (sôft′sōp′, sŏft′-), *v.t.* **1.** to apply soft soap to. **2.** to ply with smooth words; cajole; flatter. —*v.i.* **3.** to use soft soap in washing. —**soft′-soap′er,** *n.*

soft-spo·ken (sôft′spō′kən, sŏft′-), *adj.* **1.** (of persons) speaking with a soft or gentle voice; mild. **2.** (of words) softly or mildly spoken; persuasive.

soft·wood (sôft′wood′, sŏft′-), *n.* **1.** any wood which is relatively soft or easily cut. **2.** a tree yielding such a wood. **3.** *Forestry.* a coniferous tree or its wood.

soft·y (sôf′tĭ, sŏf′-), *n., pl. -ties. Colloq.* **1.** one who is easily imposed upon. **2.** an effeminate or unmanly person. **3.** a soft, silly, or weak-minded person.

Sog·di·an (sŏg′dĭ ən), *n.* **1.** an individual belonging to the ancient peoples of Iran who lived in Sogdiana. **2.** the extinct Iranian language of Sogdiana.

Sog·di·a·na (sŏg′dĭ ă′nə), *n.* a province of the ancient Persian Empire between the Oxus and Jaxartes rivers: now in the SW Soviet Union in Asia. *Cap.:* Samarkand.

sog·gy (sŏg′ĭ), *adj., -gier, -giest.* **1.** soaked; thoroughly wet. **2.** damp and heavy, as ill-baked bread. **3.** spiritless, dull, or stupid. [der. *sog* bog (now d.). Cf. d. Norw. *soggjast* get soaked] —**sog′gi·ly,** *adv.* —**sog′gi·ness,** *n.*

So·ho (sō′hō′, sō′hō), *n.* a district in London, England, including **Soho Square:** since 1685 it has been predominantly a foreign quarter, noted for its restaurants.

soi-di·sant (swä′dē zän′), *adj. French.* **1.** calling oneself thus; self-styled: *a soi-disant marquis.* **2.** so-called or pretended: *a soi-disant science.*

soi·gné (swä nyē′), *adj. masc. French.* **1.** carefully done. **2.** well groomed. —**soi·gnée′,** *adj. fem.*

soil¹ (soil), *n.* **1.** that portion of the earth's surface in which plants grow; a well-developed system of inorganic and organic material and of living organisms. **2.** a particular kind of earth: *sandy soil.* **3.** the ground as producing vegetation or cultivated for its crops: *fertile soil.* **4.** a country, land, or region: *on foreign soil.* **5.** the ground or earth. [ME *soyle,* t. AF: m. *soyl,* g. L *solium* seat, confused with *solum* ground]

soil² (soil), *v.t.* **1.** to make dirty or foul, esp. on the surface: *to soil one's clothes.* **2.** to smirch, smudge, or stain. **3.** to sully or tarnish, as with disgrace; defile morally, as with sin. —*v.i.* **4.** to become soiled. —*n.* **5.** a soiling. **6.** a being soiled. **7.** a spot, mark, or stain

ăct, āble, dâre, ärt; ĕbb, ēqual; ĭf, īce; hŏt, ōver, ôrder, oil, bŏŏk, ōōze, out; ŭp, ūse, ûrge; ə = a in alone; ch, chief; g, give; ng, ring; sh, shoe; th, thin; ᵺ, that; zh, vision. See the full key on inside cover.

due to soiling. **8.** dirty or foul matter; filth; sewage. **9.** ordure; manure or compost. [ME *soilen*, t. OF: m. *suill(i)er, soill(i)er*, der. *souille* pigsty, ult. der. L *sus* pig]

soil³ (soil), *v.t.* **1.** to feed (cattle, etc.) on freshly cut green fodder, for fattening. **2.** to feed (horses, cattle, etc.) on green food, for purging. [orig. uncert.]

soil·age (soi′lĭj), *n.* grass or leafy plants raised as feed for fenced-in livestock.

soil bank, a plan providing cash payments to farmers who cut production of some surplus crops in favor of soil-enriching ones. **—soil′·bank′,** *adj.*

soil pipe, *Plumbing.* a pipe carrying liquid wastes from all fixtures, including water closets. Cf. **waste pipe.**

soil·ure (soil′yər), *n. Archaic.* a stain.

soi·ree (swä rā′; *Fr.* swȧ rĕ′), *n.* an evening party or social gathering, often for a particular purpose: *a musical soiree.* Also, **soi·rée′.** [t. F, der. *soir* evening, g. L *sērō* late, adv., der. *sērus* late]

Sois·sons (swä sôN′), *n.* a city in N France, on the Aisne river: battles, A.D. 486, 1918, 1944. 20,484 (1954).

so·journ (*v.* sō jûrn′, sō′jûrn; *n.* sō′jûrn), *v.i.* to dwell for a time in a place; make a temporary stay. **—n.** **2.** a temporary stay. [ME *sojurne*, t. OF: m. *so(z)jorner*, der. *soz* (g. L *subtus* under, about) + *jorn* day (g. L *diurnum* daily)] **—so·journ′er,** *n.*

soke (sōk), *n. Early Eng. Law.* **1.** the privilege of holding court, usually connected with the feudal rights of lordship. **2.** a district over which local jurisdiction was exercised. [late ME, t. ML: m. *soca*, t. OE: m. *sōcn* seeking, inquiry, jurisdiction; akin to SEEK]

soke·man (sōk′mən), *n., pl.* **-men.** a feudal tenant or vassal, usually holding in socage.

So·ko·to (sō′kō′tō′), *n.* a sultanate and province in NW Nigeria: in the 19th century it was the center of a Fulah empire. 2,681,000 (est. 1953); 39,940 sq. mi.

So·ko·tra (sō kō′trə, sōk′ə trə), *n.* Socotra.

Sol (sŏl), *n.* **1.** the sun, personified by the Romans as a god. **2.** *Alchemy.* gold. [t. L]

sol¹ (sōl), *n. Music.* the syllable used for the fifth tone of a scale, and sometimes for the tone G. Also, **so.** See **sol-fa.** [t. ME, t. L. See GAMUT]

sol² (sōl), *n.* an old French coin and money of account, equal to the twentieth part of a livre. [t. F, g. L *solidus* (*nummus*) solid (coin)]

sol³ (sōl: *Sp.* sŏl), *n., pl.* **sols,** *Sp.* **soles** (sō′lĕs). **1.** Also, **libra.** a former gold coin of Peru. **2.** since 1930, a silver coin and money of account of Peru stabilized at 28 U.S. cts. [t. Sp.: sun, g. L *sōl*]

sol⁴ (sōl, sŏl), *n. Chem.* a colloidal suspension of a solid in a liquid. [abstracted from (HYDRO)SOL]

Sol., **1.** Solicitor. **2.** Solomon.

sol., **1.** soluble. **2.** solution.

so·la (sō′lə), *adj.* fem. of **solus.**

sol·ace (sŏl′ĭs), *n., v.,* **-aced, -acing. —n. 1.** comfort in sorrow or trouble; alleviation of distress or discomfort. **2.** something that gives comfort, consolation, or relief. **—v.t. 3.** to comfort, console, or cheer (a person, oneself, the heart, etc.). **4.** to alleviate or relieve (sorrow, distress, etc.). [ME *solas*, t. OF, g. L *solācium*] **—sol′ace·ment,** *n.* **—sol′ac·er,** *n.* **—Syn. 1.** consolation, relief, cheer. **4.** soothe.

so·lan (sō′lən), *n.* the gannet. Also, **solan goose.** [ME *soland*, f. Scand.; cf. Icel. *sūla* gannet, Dan. *and* duck]

sol·a·na·ceous (sŏl′ə nā′shəs), *adj.* belonging to the *Solanaceae*, or nightshade family of plants, which includes, besides the many species of *Solanum*, the belladonna, henbane, mandrake, stramonium, tobacco, capsicum pepper, tomato, petunia, etc. [f. s. NL *Solānāceae* (pl.) (der. L *solānum* nightshade) + -ous]

so·la·num (sō lā′nəm), *n.* any plant of the genus *Solanum*, which comprises gamopetalous herbs, shrubs, and small trees, including the nightshades, eggplant, common potato, etc. [t. L: nightshade]

so·lar (sō′lər), *adj.* **1.** of or pertaining to the sun: *solar phenomena.* **2.** determined by the sun: *solar hour.* **3.** proceeding from the sun, as light or heat. **4.** operating by the light or heat of the sun, as a mechanism. **5.** indicating time by means of or with reference to the sun: *a solar chronometer.* **6.** *Astrol.* subject to the influence of the sun. [t. L: s. *sōlāris*]

solar battery, a storage unit for the electricity converted from solar energy by means of photovoltaic cells.

solar furnace, a furnace using sunlight as the direct source of heat.

so·lar·ism (sō′lə rĭz′əm), *n.* the interpretation of myths by reference to the sun, esp. such interpretation carried to an extreme. **—so′lar·ist,** *n.*

so·lar·i·um (sō lâr′Ĭ əm), *n., pl.* **-laria** (-lâr′Ĭ ə). a room, gallery, or the like, exposed to the sun's rays, as at a seaside hotel or for convalescents in a hospital. [t. L]

so·lar·ize (sō′lə rīz′), *v.,* **-ized, -izing. —v.t. 1.** *Photog.* to produce partial reversal in, as from a negative to a positive image, by exposure to light during development. **2.** to affect by sunlight. **—v.i. 3.** *Photog.* to become injured by overexposure. **—so′lar·i·za′tion,** *n.*

solar month. See **month** (def. 1).

solar plexus, 1. *Anat.* a network of nerves situated at the upper part of the abdomen, behind the stomach and in front of the aorta. **2.** *Colloq.* a point on the stomach wall, just below the sternum, where a blow will affect this nerve center.

solar system, the sun together with all the planets, etc., directly or indirectly revolving round it.

solar year. See **year** (def. 5).

sold (sōld), *v.* pt. and pp. of **sell.**

sol·der (sŏd′ər), *n.* **1.** any of various fusible alloys, some (**soft solders**) fusing readily, and others (**hard solders**) fusing only at red heat, applied in a melted state to metal surfaces, joints, etc., to unite them. **2.** anything that joins or unites. **—v.t. 3.** to unite with solder or some other substance or device. **4.** to join closely and intimately. **5.** to mend; repair; patch up. **—v.i. 6.** to unite things with solder. **7.** to become soldered or become united; grow together. [ME *soudur*, t. OF: m. *soldure*, der. *solder* to solder, g. L *solidāre* make firm] **—sol′der·er,** *n.*

sol·dier (sōl′jər), *n.* **1.** one who serves in an army for pay; one engaged in military service. **2.** one of the rank and file in such service, sometimes including noncommissioned officers. **3.** a man of military skill or experience. **4.** one who contends or serves in any cause. **5.** *Zool.* (in certain ants and termites) an individual with powerful jaws or other device for protecting the colony. **—v.i. 6.** to act or serve as a soldier. **7.** *Colloq.* to make a mere show of working; feign illness; malinger. [ME *souldeour*, t. OF, der. *soulde* pay, der. L *solidus.* See SOL²] **—sol′dier·ship′,** *n.*

sol·dier·ly (sōl′jər lǐ), *adj.* of, like, or befitting a soldier.

soldier of fortune, a military adventurer, ready to serve anywhere for pay, etc.

Soldier's Medal, a medal awarded to any member of the Army of the United States (or of any military organization serving with it) who distinguishes himself by heroism not involving conflict with an enemy.

sol·dier·y (sōl′jər Ĭ), *n., pl.* **-dieries. 1.** soldiers collectively. **2.** a body of soldiers. **3.** military training.

sol·do (sōl′dō; *It.* sôl′dō), *n., pl.* **-di** (-dē). an Italian copper coin and money of account, the twentieth part of a lira (or 5 centesimi). [t. It., g. L *solidus.* See SOL²]

sole¹ (sōl), *adj.* **1.** being the only one or ones; only. **2.** being the only one of the kind; unique. **3.** belonging or pertaining to one individual or group to the exclusion of all others; exclusive: *the sole right to a thing.* **4.** functioning automatically or with independent power. **5.** *Chiefly Law.* unmarried. **6.** *Archaic.* alone. [t. L: m.s. *sōlus* alone; r. ME *soul(e)*, t. OF] **—Syn. 1.** See **only.**

sole² (sōl), *n., v.,* **soled, soling. —n. 1.** the bottom or under surface of the foot. **2.** the corresponding under part of a shoe, boot, or the like, or this part exclusive of the heel. **3.** the bottom, under surface, or lower part of anything. **4.** *Golf.* the under surface or part of a golf club, which rests on the ground. **—v.t. 5.** to furnish with a sole, as a shoe. **6.** *Golf.* to place the sole of (a club) on the ground, as in preparation for a stroke. [ME and OE, t. L: s. *solea* sandal, shoe] **—soled,** *adj.*

sole³ (sōl), *n., pl.* **soles,** (*esp. collectively*) **sole. 1.** any flatfish of the families *Soleidae* and *Cynoglossidae*, with a hooklike snout. **2.** any of several other flatfishes used as food, especially when filleted. [ME, t. F, g. L *solea.* See SOLE²]

sol·e·cism (sŏl′ə sĭz′əm), *n.* **1.** a substandard intrusion into standard speech, as "they was." **2.** a breach of good manners or etiquette. **3.** any error, impropriety, or inconsistency. [t. L: m.s. *soloecismus*, t. Gk.: m.s. *soloikismós* incorrectness of speech] **—sol′e·cis′tic,** *adj.*

sole·ly (sōl′lǐ), *adv.* **1.** as the only one or ones: *solely responsible.* **2.** exclusively or only: *plants found solely in the tropics.* **3.** wholly; merely.

sol·emn (sŏl′əm), *adj.* **1.** grave, sober, or mirthless, as a person, the face, speech, tone, mood, etc. **2.** gravely or somberly impressive; such as to cause serious thoughts or a grave mood: *solemn music.* **3.** serious or earnest: *solemn assurances.* **4.** characterized by dignified or serious formality, as proceedings; of a formal or ceremonious character. **5.** made in due legal or other express form, as a declaration, agreement, etc. **6.** marked or observed with religious rites; having a religious character. **7.** made according to religious forms. [ME *solemne*, t. L: m. *sōlempnis*] **—sol′emn·ly,** *adv.* **—sol′emn·ness,** *n.* **—Syn. 1.** See **grave².**

so·lem·ni·ty (sə lĕm′nə tǐ), *n., pl.* **-ties. 1.** state or character of being solemn; earnestness; gravity; impressiveness. **2.** (*often pl.*) a solemn observance, ceremonial proceeding, or special formality. **3.** observance of rites or ceremonies, esp. a formal, solemn, ecclesiastical observance, as of a feast day. **4.** *Law.* a formality which renders an act or document valid. [ME *solempnete*, t. L: m.s. *sōlempnitas*]

sol·em·nize (sŏl′əm nīz′), *v.t.,* **-nized, -nizing. 1.** to observe or commemorate with rites or ceremonies. **2.** to hold or perform (ceremonies, etc.) in due manner. **3.** to perform the ceremony of (marriage). **4.** to go through with ceremony or formality. **5.** to render solemn, serious, or grave. Also, *esp. Brit.,* **sol′em·nise′. —sol′em·ni·za′tion,** *n.* **—sol′em·niz′er,** *n.*

so·le·noid (sō′lə noid′), *n.* an electrical conductor wound as a helix with a small pitch, or as two or more coaxial helices, current through which establishes a magnetic field. [f. Gk. *sōlēn* channel, pipe, shellfish + -OID] **—so′le·noi′dal,** *adj.* **—so′le·noi′dal·ly,** *adv.*

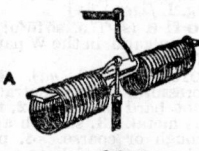

A. Solenoid with both ends returned to the middle.
B. Diagram of A

So·lent (sō′lənt), *n.* **The,** a channel between the Isle of Wight and the mainland of S England. 2–5 mi. wide.
sole trader, *Law.* feme-sole trader.
So·leure (sô lœr′), *n.* French name of **Solothurn.**
sol-fa (sōl′fä′, sŏl′-), *n., v.,* **-faed, -faing.** **—***n.* **1.** *Music.* the set of syllables, *do* or *ut, re, mi, fa, sol, la,* and *si* or *te* (all but *do* and *si* or *te* are attributed to Guido d'Arezzo), sung to the respective tones of the scale. **2.** the system of singing tones to these syllables. **—***v.i.* **3.** to use the sol-fa syllables in singing, or to sing these syllables. **—***v.t.* **4.** to sing to the sol-fa syllables, as a tune. [f. SOL + FA. See GAMUT] **—sol′-fa′ist,** *n.*
sol·fa·ta·ra (sōl′fä tä′rä), *n.* a volcanic vent or area which gives off only sulfurous gases, steam, and the like. [t. It. (Neapolitan), der. *solfo,* g. L *sulfur* SULFUR] **—sol′fa·ta′ric,** *adj.*
sol·feg·gio (sŏl fĕj′ō, -fĕj′ĭ ō′), *n., pl.* **-gi** (-ē), **-gios.** *Music.* **1.** an exercise for the voice in which the sol-fa syllables are used. **2.** the use of the sol-fa syllables to name or represent the tones of a melody or voice part, or the tones of the scale, or of a particular series, as the scale of C; solmization. [t. It., der. *sol, fa.* See SOL-FA]
Sol·fe·ri·no (sŏl′fĕ rē′nō), *n.* **1.** a village in N Italy, in Lombardy: battle, 1859. 2929 (1951). **2.** (*l.c.*) a dye obtained from rosaniline. **3.** (*l.c.*) vivid purplish pink.
soli-[1], a word element meaning "alone," "solitary," as in *solifidian.* [t. L, comb. form of *solus*]
soli-[2], a word element meaning "sun." [t. L, comb. form of *sōl*]
so·lic·it (sə lĭs′ĭt), *v.t.* **1.** to seek for by entreaty, earnest or respectful request, formal application, etc.: *to solicit contributions.* **2.** to entreat or petition (a person, etc.) for something or to do something; urge; importune. **3.** to seek to influence or incite to action, esp. unlawful or wrong action. **4.** to accost a man with immoral intention. **—***v.i.* **5.** to make petition or request, as for something desired. **6.** to solicit orders or trade, as for a business house. **7.** to accost (a man) with immoral intention. [ME, t. L: s. *sōlicitāre* disturb, incite]
so·lic·i·ta·tion (sə lĭs′ə tā′shən), *n.* **1.** act of soliciting. **2.** entreaty, urging, or importunity; a petition or request. **3.** enticement or allurement. **4.** *Law.* the crime of asking another to commit or to aid in a crime.
so·lic·i·tor (sə lĭs′ə tər), *n.* **1.** one who solicits. **2.** one whose business it is to solicit business, trade, etc. **3.** *U.S.* an officer having charge of the legal business of a city, town, etc. **4.** *Eng.* a member of that branch of the legal profession whose services consist of advising clients, representing them before the lower courts, and preparing cases for barristers to try in the higher courts.
solicitor general, *pl.* **solicitors general. 1.** a law officer who maintains the rights of the state in suits affecting the public interest, next in rank to the attorney general. **2.** the chief law officer in some States.
so·lic·it·ous (sə lĭs′ə təs), *adj.* **1.** anxious or concerned over something (fol. by *about, for, etc.,* or a clause): *solicitous about a person's health.* **2.** anxiously desirous: *solicitous of the esteem of others.* **3.** eager (fol. by infinitive): *to be solicitous to please.* **4.** careful or particular. [t. L: m. *sōlicitus*] **—so·lic′it·ous·ly,** *adv.* **—so·lic′it·ous·ness,** *n.*
so·lic·i·tude (sə lĭs′ə tūd′, -tōōd′), *n.* **1.** state of being solicitous; anxiety or concern; anxious desire or care. **2.** (*pl.*) causes of anxiety or care. **3.** excessive anxiety or assistance. [t. L: m. *sōlicitūdo*]
sol·id (sŏl′ĭd), *adj.* **1.** having three dimensions (length, breadth, and thickness), as a geometrical body or figure. **2.** of or pertaining to bodies or figures of three dimensions: *solid geometry.* **3.** having the interior completely filled up, free from cavities, or not hollow: *a solid ball of matter.* **4.** without openings or breaks: *a solid wall.* **5.** firm, hard, or compact in substance: *solid ground.* **6.** having relative firmness, coherence of particles, or persistence of form, as matter that is not liquid or gaseous: *solid particles floating in a liquid.* **7.** pertaining to such matter: *ice is water in a solid state.* **8.** dense, thick, or heavy in nature or appearance: *solid masses of cloud.* **9.** substantial, or not flimsy, slight, or light, as buildings, furniture, fabrics, food, etc. **10.** of a substantial character; not superficial, trifling, or frivolous: *solid learning.* **11.** undivided or continuous: *a solid row of buildings.* **12.** whole or entire: *one solid hour.* **13.** forming the whole; being the only substance or material: *solid gold.* **14.** uniform in tone or shade, as a color. **15.** real or genuine: *solid comfort.* **16.** sound or good, as reasons, arguments, etc. **17.** sober-minded or sensible. **18.** financially sound or strong. **19.** cubic: *a solid foot contains 1,728 solid inches.* **20.** written without a hyphen, as a compound word. **21.** having the lines not separated by leads, or having few open spaces, as type or printing. **22.** thorough, vigorous, great, big, etc. (with emphatic force, often after *good*): *a good solid blow.* **23.** firmly united or consolidated: *a solid combination.* **24.** united in opinion, policy, etc., or unanimous: *the solid South.* **25.** *U.S. Colloq.* (of individuals) firm in opinion, support, etc. **26.** *U.S. Colloq.* on a friendly, favorable, or advantageous footing. **27.** *U.S. Slang.* (of dance music, rhythm, etc.) excellent. **—***n.* **28.** a body or magnitude having three dimensions (length, breadth, and thickness). **29.** a solid substance or body; a substance exhibiting rigidity. [ME, t. L. s. *solidus*] **—sol′id·ly,** *adv.* **—sol′id·ness,** *n.* **—Syn. 5.** See **firm**[1]. **—Ant. 6.** fluid.
sol·i·da·go (sŏl′ə dā′gō), *n., pl.* **-gos.** any plant of the composite genus *Solidago,* mostly native to North America; a goldenrod. [t. NL, special use of ML *solidago* comfrey, der. L *solidus* SOLID]
solid angle, *Geom.* an angle formed by three or more planes intersecting in a common point or at the vertex of a cone.
sol·i·dar·i·ty (sŏl′ə dăr′ə tĭ), *n., pl.* **-ties. 1.** solidary character or relation. **2.** union or fellowship arising from common responsibilities and interests, as between members of a group or between classes, peoples, etc. **3.** community of interests, feelings, purposes, etc. [t. F: m. *solidarité,* der. *solidaire,* ult. der. L *solidus* solid]
sol·i·dar·y (sŏl′ə dĕr′ĭ), *adj.* characterized by or involving community of responsibilities and interests.
solid geometry, the geometry of solid figures; geometry of three dimensions.
so·lid·i·fy (sə lĭd′ə fī′), *v.,* **-fied, -fying.** **—***v.t.* **1.** to make solid; make into a hard or compact mass; change from a liquid or gaseous to a solid form. **2.** to unite firmly or consolidate. **3.** to form into crystals. **—***v.i.* **4.** to become solid. **5.** to form into crystals. [see SOLID, -(I)FY] **—so·lid′i·fi·ca′tion,** *n.*
so·lid·i·ty (sə lĭd′ə tĭ), *n., pl.* **-ties. 1.** the state, property, or quality of being solid. **2.** substantialness. **3.** strength of mind, character, finances, etc. **4.** *Geom.* the amount of space occupied by a solid body; volume.
solid state physics, the branch of physics that deals with the structure and properties of solids.
sol·i·dus (sŏl′ə dəs), *n., pl.* **-di** (-dī′). **1.** a Roman gold coin introduced by Constantine, which continued under the Byzantine Empire and received in Western Europe the name bezant. Cf. **bezant** (def. 1). **2.** (in medieval Europe) a money of account valued at 12 denarii. **3.** the shilling mark, a sloping line (/) representing the old long form of the letter s (abbreviation of solidus), as used to separate shillings from pence (as in 2/6 for 2 shillings, 6 pence), and generally as a dividing line, as in dates, fractions, etc. [t. LL. See SOL[2]]
sol·i·fid·i·an (sŏl′ə fĭd′ĭ ən), *n.* *Theol.* one who maintains that faith alone, without works, is all that is necessary for justification. [f. SOLI-[1] + L *fid(es)* faith + -IAN]
so·lil·o·quize (sə lĭl′ə kwīz′), *v.,* **-quized, -quizing.** **—***v.i.* **1.** to utter a soliloquy; talk to oneself. **—***v.t.* **2.** to utter in a soliloquy; say to oneself. **—so·lil·o·quist** (sə lĭl′ə kwĭst), **so·lil′o·quiz′er,** *n.* **—so·lil′o·quiz′ing·ly,** *adv.*
so·lil·o·quy (sə lĭl′ə kwĭ), *n., pl.* **-quies.** act of talking when alone or as if alone; an utterance or discourse by one who is talking to himself or is regardless of any hearers present. [t. LL: m.s. *sōliloquium*]
So·li·mões (sô′lē mônzh′), *n.* Brazilian name of a part of the Amazon, from its junction with the Río Negro to the Peruvian border.
sol·ip·sism (sŏl′ĭp sĭz′əm), *n.* *Metaphys.* the theory that the self is the only object of verifiable knowledge, or that nothing but the self exists. [f. SOL(I)-[1] + L *ips(e)* self + -ISM] **—sol′ip·sist,** *n.*
sol·i·taire (sŏl′ə târ′), *n.* **1.** a game played by one person alone, as a game played with marbles or pegs on a board having hollows or holes, or any of various card games. **2.** a precious stone, esp. a diamond, set by itself, as in a ring. [t. F, t. L: m. *sōlitārius* alone]
sol·i·tar·y (sŏl′ə tĕr′ĭ), *adj., n., pl.* **-taries.** **—***adj.* **1.** quite alone; without companions; unattended. **2.** living alone; avoiding the society of others. **3.** alone by itself. **4.** characterized by the absence of companions: *solitary confinement.* **5.** done without assistance or accompaniment; done in solitude. **6.** being the only one or ones: *a solitary exception.* **7.** characterized by solitude, as a place; unfrequented, secluded, or lonely. **8.** *Zool.* not social, as certain wasps. **—***n.* **9.** one who lives alone or in solitude, or avoids the society of others. **10.** one who lives in solitude from religious motives. [ME, t. L: m.s. *sōlitārius*] **—sol′i·tar′i·ly,** *adv.* **—sol′i·tar′i·ness,** *n.*
sol·i·tude (sŏl′ə tūd′, -tōōd′), *n.* **1.** the state of being or living alone; seclusion. **2.** remoteness from habitations, as of a place; absence of human life or activity. **3.** a lonely, unfrequented place. [ME, t. L: m. *sōlitūdo*] **—Syn. 1.** SOLITUDE, ISOLATION refer to a state of being or living alone. SOLITUDE emphasizes the quality of being or feeling lonely and deserted: *to live in solitude.* ISOLATION may mean merely a detachment and separation from others: *in isolation because of having an infectious disease.*
sol·ler·et (sŏl′ə rĕt′, sŏl′ə rĕt′), *n.* flexible armor for the foot, made of overlapping plates. [t. OF: m. *soleret,* dim. of *soler* shoe, ult. der. LL *subtel* arch of foot]
sol·mi·za·tion (sŏl′mə zā′shən), *n.* *Music.* act, process, or system of using certain syllables, esp. the sol-fa syllables, to represent the tones of the scale. [t. F: m. *solmisation,* der. *solmiser,* der. *sol* SOL[1] + *mi* MI]
so·lo (sō′lō), *n., pl.,* **-los, -li** (-lē), *adj.* **—***n.* **1.** a musical composition performed by or intended for one singer or player, with or without accompaniment. **2.** any performance, as a dance, by one person. **3.** a flight in an airplane during which the aviator is unaccompanied by an instructor or other person. **4.** *Cards.* any of certain games in which one person plays alone against others. **—***adj.* **5.** *Music.* performing alone, as an instrument or its player. **6.** performed alone; not combined with other parts of equal importance; not concerted. **7.** alone; without a companion or partner: *a solo flight in an airplane.* [t. It., g. L *sōlus* alone]

So·lo (sō′lō), *n.* a city in central Java. 340,455 (est. 1953). Formerly, **Surakarta.**

so·lo·ist (sō′lō ĭst), *n.* one who performs a solo or solos.

Sol·o·mon (sŏl′ə mən), *n.* 1. a 10th century B.C. king of Israel, famous for his wisdom. He was the son of David. 2. an extraordinarily wise man; a sage. [t. L, t. Gk., t. Heb.: m. *Sh'lōmōh*]

Solomon Islands, an archipelago in the S Pacific, E of New Guinea: the larger, SE part forms a British protectorate (103,000 pop., est. 1954; 11,458 sq. mi.): the NW islands (formerly a German colony), principally Bougainville and Buka, are part of the Australian trusteeship Territory of New Guinea (ab. 4100 sq. mi.); important battles of World War II were fought in the Solomon Islands.

Sol·o·mon's-seal (sŏl′ə mənz sēl′), *n.* any of various plants of the liliaceous genus *Polygonatum*, with a thick rootstock bearing seallike scars.

Solomon's seal, a figure resembling a six-pointed star, formed of two triangles interlaced, or placed one upon the other.

Solomon's seal

So·lon (sō′lən), *n.* 1. c638–c558 B.C., Athenian statesman: noted for his political reforms and his wisdom. 2. a wise lawgiver.

so long, *Colloq.* good-by.

So·lo·thurn (zō′lō tŏŏrn′), *n.* a city in NW Switzerland, on the Aar river. 17,500 (est. 1953). French, **Soleure.**

sol·stice (sŏl′stĭs), *n.* 1. *Astron.* either of the two times in the year when the sun is at its greatest distance from the celestial equator and apparently does not move either north or south, about June 21, when it enters the sign of Cancer, and about Dec. 22, when it enters the sign of Capricorn (called respectively, in the Northern Hemisphere, **summer solstice** and **winter solstice**). 2. either of the two points in the ecliptic farthest from the equator. 3. a furthest or culminating point; a turning point. [ME, t. OF, t. L: m. *solstitium*]

sol·sti·tial (sŏl stĭsh′əl), *adj.* 1. of or pertaining to a solstice or the solstices: *a solstitial point.* 2. occurring at or about the time of a solstice. 3. characteristic of the summer solstice. [t. L: s. *solstitiālis*]

sol·u·bil·i·ty (sŏl′yə bĭl′ə tĭ), *n., pl.* **-ties.** the quality or property of being capable of being dissolved; relative capability of being dissolved.

sol·u·ble (sŏl′yə bəl), *adj.* 1. capable of being dissolved or liquefied. 2. capable of being solved or explained. [ME, t. L: m.s. *solūbilis*] —**sol′u·ble·ness,** *n.* —**sol′u·bly,** *adv.*

soluble glass, water glass (def. 5).

so·lus (sō′ləs), *adj. masc.* alone; by oneself: used esp. in stage directions. [t. L] —**so·la** (sō′lə), *adj. fem.*

sol·ute (sŏl′ūt, sŏl′lōōt), *n.* 1. the substance dissolved in a given solution. —*adj.* 2. dissolved; in solution. 3. *Bot.* not adhering; free. [t. L: m.s. *solūtus,* pp.]

so·lu·tion (sə lōō′shən), *n.* 1. the act of solving a problem, etc., or state of being solved. 2. a particular instance or method of solving; an explanation or answer. 3. *Math.* **a.** the act of determining the answer to a problem. **b.** the answer. 4. the act by which a gas, liquid, or solid is dispersed homogeneously in a gas, liquid, or solid without chemical change. 5. the fact of being dissolved; dissolved state: *salt in solution.* 6. a homogeneous molecular mixture of two or more substances. 7. *U.S.* a watery solution of a potent drug. 8. *Med.* **a.** the termination of a disease. **b. solution of continuity,** a breach or break in anything, esp. one in parts of the body normally continuous, as from fracture or laceration. [ME *solucion,* t. L: m.s. *solūtio*]

solv·a·ble (sŏl′və bəl), *adj.* 1. capable of being solved, as a problem. 2. capable of being dissolved. —**solv′a·bil′i·ty, solv′a·ble·ness,** *n.*

Sol·vay Process (sŏl′vā), a process for manufacturing soda from sodium chloride (common salt). It consists essentially of saturating a concentrated solution of sodium chloride with ammonia, and passing carbon dioxide through it; the product of this reaction (sodium bicarbonate) is then calcined, and yields soda.

solve (sŏlv), *v.t.,* **solved, solving.** 1. to clear up or explain; find the answer to. 2. to work out the answer or solution to (a mathematical problem). [ME, t. L: m.s. *solvere* loosen, dissolve] —**solv′er,** *n.*

sol·ven·cy (sŏl′vən sĭ), *n., pl.* **-cies.** solvent condition; ability to pay all just debts.

sol·vent (sŏl′vənt), *adj.* 1. able to pay all just debts. 2. having the power of dissolving; causing solution. —*n.* 3. the component of a solution which dissolves the other component: *water is a solvent for sugar.* 4. something that solves or explains. [t. L: s. *solvens,* ppr., dissolving]

Sol·way Firth (sŏl′wā), an arm of the Irish Sea between SW Scotland and NW England. 38 mi. long.

Sol·y·man (sŏl′ĭ mən), *n.* ("The Magnificent") 1495?–1566, sultan of the Turkish Empire, 1520–66. Also, **Suleiman.**

so·ma (sō′mə), *n., pl.* **-mata** (-mə tə). *Biol.* the body of an organism as contrasted with its germ cells. [NL, t. Gk.: body]

So·ma·li (sō mä′lĭ), *n., pl.* **-lis, -li, -lis.** 1. a member of a Hamitic race showing an admixture of Arab, Negro, and other ancestry, and dwelling in Somaliland and adjacent regions. 2. a modern Cushitic language.

So·ma·li·a (sō mä′lĭ ə, -mäl′yə), *n.* an independent republic on the east coast of Africa, formed from former British Somaliland and the former Italian trust territory of Somalia. 1,950,000 (1959); ab. 256,000 sq. mi. *Cap.:* Mogadiscio.

So·ma·li·land (sō mä′lĭ länd′), *n.* a coastal region in E Africa, including French Somaliland, Somalia, and part of Ethiopia.

so·mat·ic (sō măt′ĭk), *adj.* 1. *Anat., Zool.* pertaining to the cavity of the body of an animal, or, more especially, to its walls. 2. *Biol.* pertaining to the soma. 3. of the body; bodily; physical. [t. Gk.: m.s. *sōmatikós*]

somatic cell, *Biol.* one of the cells which take part in the formation of the body, becoming differentiated into the various tissues, organs, etc.

so·ma·tol·o·gy (sō′mə tŏl′ə jĭ), *n.* that branch of anthropology which deals with man's physical characteristics. [f. somato- (comb. form repr. Gk. *sōma* body) + -LOGY] —**so·ma·to·log·ic** (sō′mə tə lŏj′ĭk), **so·ma·to·log′i·cal,** *adj.* —**so·ma·tol′o·gist,** *n.*

so·ma·to·pleure (sō′mə tə plōōr′), *n. Embryol.* the outer of the two layers into which the mesoderm of vertebrates splits, and which forms the body wall.

som·ber (sŏm′bər), *adj.* 1. gloomily dark, shadowy, or dimly lighted. 2. dark and dull, as color, or as things in respect to color. 3. gloomy, depressing, or dismal. Also, *esp. Brit.,* **som·bre;** *Archaic,* **som·brous** (sŏm′brəs). [t. F, ? ult. der. L *umbra* shade, darkness] —**som′ber·ly,** *adv.* —**som′ber·ness,** *n.*

som·bre·ro (sŏm brâr′ō), *n., pl.* **-ros.** a broad-brimmed hat, usually of felt, worn in Spain, Mexico, the southwestern U.S., etc. [t. Sp., der. *sombra* shade, ? ult. der. L *umbra*]

some (sŭm; *unstressed* səm), *adj.* 1. being an undetermined or unspecified one: *some poor fellow.* 2. certain (with plural nouns): *some friends of mine.* 3. of a certain unspecified number, amount, degree, etc.: *some variation.* 4. unspecified but considerable in number, amount, degree, etc.: *he was here some weeks.* 5. (used with numerals and with words expressing extent, etc., to indicate an approximate amount): *some four or five of us.* 6. *U.S. Slang.* of considerable account or consequence; notable of the kind: *that was some storm.* —*pron.* 7. certain persons, instances, etc., not specified: *some think he is dead.* 8. an unspecified number, amount, etc., as distinguished from the rest. —*adv.* 9. *Slang.* to some degree or extent; somewhat. 10. *U.S. Colloq.* to a great degree or extent; considerably: *that's going some!* [ME; OE *sum,* c. MLG and MHG *sum,* Icel. *sumr,* Goth. *sums*] —**Syn.** 8. SOME, ANY refer to an appreciable amount or number, and often to a portion of a larger amount. SOME suggests that no specified quantity is meant. ANY suggests that no particular amount is being distinguished from any other or from the remainder; it is any at all (or none). Both SOME and ANY may be used in affirmative or negative questions: *Will you (won't you) have some? Do you (don't you) have any?* But SOME must be used in affirmative statements and answers: *You may have some; Yes, I'd like some.* And ANY must be used in negative statements and answers: *I don't care for any; No, I can't take any.*

-some¹, suffix found in some adjectives showing especially a tendency, as in *quarrelsome, burdensome.* [ME; OE *-sum,* akin to G *-sam*]

-some², collective suffix used with numerals, as in *twosome, threesome, foursome.* [special use of SOME]

-some³, a word element meaning "body," as in *chromosome.* [see SOMA]

some·bod·y (sŭm′bŏd′ĭ, -bŭd′ĭ, -bədĭ), *pron., n., pl.* **-bodies.** —*pron.* 1. some person. —*n.* 2. a person of some note or importance.

some·day (sŭm′dā′), *adv.* at an indefinite future time.

some·deal (sŭm′dēl), *adv. Archaic or Dial.* somewhat.

some·how (sŭm′hou′), *adv.* 1. in some way not specified, apparent, or known. 2. **somehow or other,** in a way not as yet determined.

some·one (sŭm′wŭn′, -wən), *pron.* some person; somebody.

som·er·sault (sŭm′ər sôlt′), *n.* 1. an acrobatic movement of the body in which it describes a complete revolution, heels over head. 2. a complete overturn or reversal, as of opinion. —*v.i.* 3. to perform a somersault. Also, **summersault.** [t. OF: m. *sombresaut,* t. Pr.: m. *sobresaut,* f. *sobre* (g. L *suprā*) above + *saut* (g. L *saltus*) leap]

Som·er·set·shire (sŭm′ər sĕt shĭr′, -shər), *n.* a county in SW England. 551,453 pop. (1951); 1616 sq. mi. *Co. seat:* Taunton. Also, **Som′er·set′.**

Som·er·ville (sŭm′ər vĭl), *n.* a city in E Massachusetts, near Boston. 94,697 (1960).

some·thing (sŭm′thĭng), *pron.* 1. some thing; a certain undetermined or unspecified thing. —*n.* 2. a thing or person of some value or consequence. —*adv.* 3. in some degree; to some extent; somewhat.

some·time (sŭm′tīm′), *adv.* 1. at some indefinite or indeterminate point of time: *he will arrive sometime next week.* 2. at an indefinite future time: *come over sometime.* 3. *Rare.* sometimes; on some occasions. 4. *Archaic.* at one time; formerly. 5. *Obs.* on a certain occasion in the past. —*adj.* 6. having been formerly; former: *sometime professor of history at Oxford.*

some·times (sŭm′tīmz′), *adv.* 1. on some occasions; at times; now and then. 2. *Obs.* once; formerly.

Man wearing a sombrero

---

b., blend of, blended; c., cognate with; d., dialect, dialectal; der., derived from; f., formed from; g., going back to; m., modification of; r., replacing; s., stem of; t., taken from; ?, perhaps. See the full key on inside cover.

some·way (sŭm'wā'), *adv.* in some way; somehow.

some·what (sŭm'hwŏt', -hwət), *adv.* **1.** in some measure or degree; to some extent. —*n.* **2.** some part, portion, amount, etc.

some·where (sŭm'hwâr'), *adv.* **1.** in or at some place not specified, determined, or known. **2.** to some place not specified or known. **3.** at or to some point in amount, degree, etc. (fol. by *about*, etc.): *he is somewhere about 60.* **4.** at some point of time (fol. by *about* or *in*): *this happened somewhere about 1580.* —*n.* **5.** an unspecified or uncertain place.

some·while (sŭm'hwīl'), *adv.* *Rare.* **1.** at some former time. **2.** at one time or another; sometime. **3.** at times; sometimes. **4.** for some time.

some·whith·er (sŭm'hwĭth'ər), *adv.* **1.** to some place. **2.** in some direction.

so·mite (sō'mīt), *n.* any of the longitudinal series of segments or parts into which the body of certain animals is divided; a metamere. [f. SOMA + -ITE[1]] —**so·mi·tal** (sō'mə təl), **so·mit·ic** (sō mĭt'ĭk), *adj.*

Somme (sŏm), *n.* a river in N France, flowing NW to the English Channel: battles, 1916, 1918, 1944. ab. 140 mi.

som·nam·bu·late (sŏm năm'byə lāt'), *v.* **-lated, -lating.** —*v.i.* **1.** to walk during sleep, as a somnambulist does. —*v.t.* **2.** to traverse during sleep. [f. s. L *somnus* sleep + *ambulate* (t. L: m.s. *ambulātus*, pp., walked)] —**som·nam·bu·lant** (sŏm năm'byə lənt), *adj.*, *n.* —**som·nam'bu·la'tion**, *n.* —**som·nam'bu·la'tor**, *n.*

som·nam·bu·lism (sŏm năm'byə lĭz'əm), *n.* the fact or habit of walking about, and often of performing various other acts, while asleep; sleepwalking. —**som·nam'bu·list**, *n.* —**som·nam'bu·lis'tic**, *adj.*

som·nif·er·ous (sŏm nĭf'ər əs), *adj.* bringing or inducing sleep, as drugs, influences, etc. [f. L *somnifer* sleep-bearing + -OUS]

som·nif·ic (sŏm nĭf'ĭk), *adj.* causing sleep; soporific; somniferous. [t. L: s. *somnificus*]

som·nil·o·quy (sŏm nĭl'ə kwĭ), *n.* the act or habit of talking while asleep. —**som·nil'o·quist**, *n.*

som·no·lent (sŏm'nə lənt), *adj.* **1.** sleepy; drowsy. **2.** tending to cause sleep. [late ME, t. L: s. *somnolentus*] —**som'no·lence**, *n.* —**som'no·lent·ly**, *adv.*

son (sŭn), *n.* **1.** a male child or person in relation to his parents. **2.** one adopted as a son; one in the legal position of a son. **3.** any male descendant. **4.** a son-in-law. **5.** one related as if by ties of sonship. **6.** a male person looked upon as the product or result of particular agencies, forces, influences, etc.: *sons of liberty.* **7.** a familiar term of address to a man or boy from an older person, an ecclesiastic, etc. **8.** the Son, the second person of the Trinity; Jesus Christ. [ME *sone*, OE *sunu*, c. D *zoon*, G *sohn*, Icel. *sunr*, *sonr*, Goth. *sunus*]

so·nance (sō'nəns), *n.* **1.** the condition or quality of being sonant. **2.** *Obs.* a sound; a tune.

so·nant (sō'nənt), *adj.* **1.** sounding; having sound. **2.** *Phonet.* voiced. —*n.* **3.** *Phonet.* **a.** a speech sound which by itself makes a syllable or subordinates to itself the other sounds in the syllable; a syllabic sound (opposed to *consonant*). **b.** a voiced sound. **c.** (in Indo-European) a sonorant. [t. L: s. *sonans*, ppr., sounding] —**so·nan·tal** (sō năn'təl), *adj.*

so·nar (sō'när), *n.* a device to determine the presence and location of objects under water by measuring the direction and return time of a sound echo.

so·na·ta (sə nä'tə), *n.* *Music.* an extended instrumental composition usually in several (commonly three or four) movements in contrasted moods and keys, each movement being developed with a balanced form in mind. [t. It., fem. pp. of *sonare* sound; orig. a sounded (i.e. instrumental) composition as opposed to one sung]

son·a·ti·na (sŏn'ə tē'nə); *It.* sō'nä tē'nä), *n.*, *pl.* **-nas, -ne** (-nĕ). *Music.* a short or simplified sonata. [t. It., dim. of *sonata* SONATA]

son·der·class (zŏn'dər kläs', -kläs'), *n.* a special class of small racing yachts, restricted as to size, sail area, cost, etc. [half adoption, half trans. of G *sonderklasse* special class]

song (sông, sŏng), *n.* **1.** a short metrical composition intended or adapted for singing, esp. one in rhymed stanzas; a lyric; a ballad. **2.** a piece adapted for singing or simulating a piece to be sung: *Mendelssohn's "Songs without Words."* **3.** poetical composition; poetry. **4.** the act or art of singing; vocal music. **5.** that which is sung. **6.** the musical or tuneful sounds produced by certain birds, insects, etc. **7.** for a song, at a very low price. [ME and OE, c. G *sang*, Icel. *söngr*]

song·bird (sông'bûrd', sŏng'-), *n.* **1.** a bird that sings. **2.** a woman who sings.

song·ful (sông'fəl, sŏng'-), *adj.* abounding in song; melodious.

Song·ka (sông'kä'), *n.* a river flowing from SW China SE through Indochina to the Gulf of Tonkin. ab. 500 mi. Also, **Red River.**

song·less (sông'lĭs, sŏng'-), *adj.* devoid of song; lacking the power of song, as a bird.

Song of Solomon, The, a book of the Old Testament; Canticles.

song sparrow, a small fringilline songbird, *Melospiza melodia*, of North America.

song·ster (sông'stər, sŏng'-), *n.* **1.** one who sings; a singer. **2.** a writer of songs or poems; a poet. **3.** a

songbird. [ME; OE *sangestre*, c. D *zangster*. See SONG, -STER] —**song·stress** (sông'strĭs, sŏng'-), *n.* *fem.*

song thrush, a well-known European song bird, *Turdus philomelus.*

son·hood (sŭn'hŏŏd), *n.* sonship.

son·ic (sŏn'ĭk), *adj.* **1.** of or pertaining to sound. **2.** denoting a speed approximating that of the propagation of sound.

so·nif·er·ous (sō nĭf'ər əs), *adj.* conveying or producing sound. [f. *soni-* (t. L, comb. form of *sonus* sound) + -FEROUS]

son-in-law (sŭn'ĭn lô'), *n.*, *pl.* **sons-in-law.** the husband of one's daughter.

son·net (sŏn'ĭt), *n.* **1.** *Pros.* a poem, properly expressive of a single, complete thought, idea, or sentiment, of 14 lines (usually in 5-foot iambic meter) with rhymes arranged according to one of certain definite schemes, being in the strict or Italian form divided into a major group of 8 lines (the octave) followed by a minor group of 6 lines (the sestet), and in a common English form into 3 quatrains followed by a couplet. —*v.i.* **2.** to compose sonnets. —*v.t.* **3.** to celebrate in a sonnet or sonnets. [t. F, t. It.: m. *sonetto*, t. O Pr.: m. *sonet*, der. *son* sound, g. L *sonus*]

son·net·eer (sŏn'ə tĭr'), *n.* **1.** a composer of sonnets. —*v.i.* **2.** to compose sonnets.

son·ny (sŭn'ĭ), *n.*, *pl.* **-nies.** little son (often used as a familiar term of address to a boy).

So·no·ra (sō nō'rä), *n.* a state in NW Mexico. 546,570 pop. (est. 1952); 70,484 sq. mi. *Cap.:* Hermosillo.

so·no·rant (sō nôr'ənt), *n.* *Phonet.* a voiced sound less sonorous than a vowel but more sonorous than a stop or fricative, as *l, r, m, n, y, w*: such a sound may be now a sonant, now a consonant, as in modern English; thus, *y* is a sonant in *any*, a consonant in *yet.*

so·nor·i·ty (sə nôr'ə tĭ, -nŏr'-), *n.*, *pl.* **-ties.** the condition or quality of being resonant or sonorous.

so·no·rous (sə nôr'əs), *adj.* **1.** giving out, or capable of giving out, a sound, esp. a deep resonant sound, as a thing or a place. **2.** loud, deep, or resonant, as a sound. **3.** rich and full in sound, as language, verse, etc. **4.** highflown; grandiloquent: *a sonorous address.* [t. L: m. *sonōrus*] —**so·no'rous·ly**, *adv.* —**so·no'rous·ness**, *n.*

-sonous, a word element used in adjectives to refer to sounds, as in *unisonous.* [t. L: m. *-sonus*]

son·ship (sŭn'shĭp), *n.* state, fact, or relation of being a son.

son·sy (sŏn'sĭ), *adj.*, **-sier, -siest.** *Scot., Irish,* and *N. Eng.* buxom or comely. [see UNSONSY]

Soo Canals (sōō), Sault Ste. Marie Canals.

Soo·chow (sōō'chou'; *Chin.* sōō'jō'), *n.* former name of Wuhsien.

soon (sōōn), *adv.* **1.** within a short period after this (or that) time, event, etc.: *we shall soon know.* **2.** before long; in the near future; at an early date. **3.** promptly or quickly: *no sooner said than done.* **4.** readily or willingly: *I would as soon walk as ride.* **5.** *Dial.* early in a period of time. **6.** *Obs.* immediately, or at once. [ME; OE *sōna* at once, c. OHG *sān*, akin to Goth. *suns*]

soon·er (sōō'nər), *n.* *U.S.* **1.** one who settles on government land before it is legally opened to settlers in order to gain the choice of location. **2.** one who gains an unfair advantage by getting ahead of others. **3.** (*cap.*) native of Oklahoma.

Soong (sōōng), *n.* a Chinese family distinguished in public affairs. **1. Charles Jones**, died 1927, Chinese merchant, father of the following: **2. Ai-ling** (ī'lĭng'), born 1888, wife of H. H. Kung, Chinese statesman. **3. Ching-ling** (chĭng'lĭng'), born 1890, widow of Sun Yat-sen. **4. Mei-ling** (mā'lĭng'), born 1898, wife of Chiang Kai-shek. **5. Tsè-vèn** (tsōō'wŭn'), (**T. V.**) born 1891, Chinese financier.

soot (sŏŏt, sōōt), *n.* **1.** a black carbonaceous substance produced during the imperfect combustion of coal, wood, oil, etc., rising in fine particles and adhering to the sides of the chimney or pipe conveying the smoke. —*v.t.* **2.** to mark, cover, or treat with soot. [ME; OE *sōt*, c. D *zoet*]

sooth (sōōth), *n.* **1.** *Archaic.* truth, reality, or fact. [ME; OE *sōth*, c. OS *sōth.* See SOOTH, adj.] —*adj.* **2.** *Poetic.* soothing, soft, or delicious. **3.** *Archaic.* true or real. [ME; OE *sōth*, c. OS *sōth*, Icel. *sannr*, akin to Goth. *sunjis* true] —**sooth'ly**, *adv.*

soothe (sōōth), *v.*, **soothed, soothing.** —*v.t.* **1.** to tranquilize or calm, as a person, the feelings, etc.; relieve, comfort, or refresh. **2.** to mitigate, assuage, or allay, as pain, sorrow, doubt, etc. —*v.i.* **3.** to exert a soothing influence; bring tranquility, calm, ease, or comfort. [ME *sothe*, OE *sōthian*, der. *sōth* SOOTH, adj.] —**sooth'er**, *n.* —**sooth'ing**, *adj.* —**sooth'ing·ly**, *adv.* —Syn. **1.** See comfort. **2.** See allay.

sooth·say (sōōth'sā'), *v.i.* **-said, -saying.** to foretell events; predict.

sooth·say·er (sōōth'sā'ər), *n.* one who professes to foretell events. [ME *sothseyere*; f. SOOTH, adj. or n., + SAY, v., + -ER[1]]

sooth·say·ing (sōōth'sā'ĭng), *n.* **1.** the practice or art of foretelling events. **2.** a prediction or prophecy.

soot·y (sŏŏt'ĭ, sōōt'ĭ), *adj.*, **sootier, sootiest.** **1.** covered, blackened, or smirched with soot; consisting of or resembling soot. **2.** of a dark, blackish, or dusky color. —**soot'i·ly**, *adv.* —**soot'i·ness**, *n.*

sop (sŏp), *n.*, *v.*, **sopped, sopping.** —*n.* **1.** a piece of

bread or the like dipped, or for dipping, in liquid food.
2. anything thoroughly soaked. 3. something given to
pacify or quiet, or as a bribe. —*v.t.* 4. to dip or soak
(bread, etc.) in some liquid. 5. to drench. 6. to take
up (water, etc.) by absorption (usually fol. by *up*).
—*v.i.* 7. to become or be soaking wet. 8. (of a liquid) to
soak (*in*, etc.). [ME; OE *sopp*]

sop., soprano.

soph·ism (sŏf'ĭzəm), *n.* 1. a specious but fallacious
argument, used to display ingenuity in reasoning or to
deceive someone. 2. any false argument; a fallacy.
[t. L: m. *sophisma*, t. Gk.: clever device, argument; r.
ME *sophime*, t. OF]

soph·ist (sŏf'ĭst), *n.* 1. (*often cap.*) a. any of a class of
professional teachers in ancient Greece who gave instruction in various fields, as in general culture, rhetoric,
politics, or disputation. b. any member of a portion of
this class at a later period who, while professing to teach
skill in reasoning, concerned himself with ingenuity and
specious effectiveness rather than soundness of argument. 2. one who reasons adroitly and speciously
rather than soundly. 3. a man of learning. [t. L: s.
sophista, t. Gk.: m. *sophistēs*]

soph·ist·er (sŏf'ĭstər), *n. Chiefly Hist.* 1. (in certain
universities) a student after the completion of his first
year, esp. one in his second or third year (**junior or
senior sophister**). 2. a specious but unsound reasoner.
3. *Obs.* an ancient Greek sophist.

so·phis·tic (səfĭs'tĭk), *adj.* 1. of the nature of sophistry; fallacious. 2. characteristic or suggestive of sophistry. 3. given to the use of sophistry. 4. of or pertaining to sophists or sophistry. Also, **so·phis·ti·cal.** —**so-
phis·ti·cal·ly,** *adv.* —**so·phis·ti·cal·ness,** *n.*

so·phis·ti·cate (*v.* səfĭs'təkāt′; *n.* səfĭs'təkāt′, -kĭt),
v., -**cated,** -**cating,** *n.* —*v.t.* 1. to make less natural,
simple, or ingenuous; to make worldly-wise. 2. to mislead or pervert. —*v.i.* 3. to use sophistry; quibble. —*n.*
4. a sophisticated person. [t. ML: m.s. *sophisticātus*, pp.,
der. L *sophisticus* sophistical. See SOPHIST]

so·phis·ti·cat·ed (səfĭs'təkā′tĭd), *adj.* 1. (of a person, the ideas, tastes, manners, etc.) altered by education, worldly experience, etc.; changed from the natural
character or simplicity; artificial. 2. adapted to the
tastes of sophisticates: *sophisticated music.* 3. deceptive; misleading. —**Ant.** 1. naïve.

so·phis·ti·ca·tion (səfĭs′təkā′shən), *n.* 1. sophisticated character, ideas, tastes, or ways as the result of
education, worldly experience, etc. 2. change from the
natural character or simplicity, or the resulting condition. 3. impairment or debasement, as of purity or
genuineness. 4. the use of sophistry; a sophism, quibble,
or fallacious argument.

soph·ist·ry (sŏf'ĭstrĭ), *n., pl.* -**ries.** 1. a subtle,
tricky, beguiling, but generally fallacious method of
reasoning. 2. a false argument; sophism.

Soph·o·cles (sŏf'əklēz′), *n.* 495?–406? B.C., Greek
poet: writer of tragedies. —**Soph·o·cle·an** (sŏf′əklē′ən),
adj.

soph·o·more (sŏf'əmôr′, sŏf'môr′), *n. Chiefly U.S.* a
student in the second year of the course at a university,
college, or school. [f. *sophom* (var. of SOPHISM, def. 1,
with reference to the fact that such arguments were used
as school exercises) + m. -OR²]

soph·o·mor·ic (sŏf′əmôr′ĭk, -mŏr′-), *adj. Chiefly
U.S.* 1. of or pertaining to a sophomore or sophomores.
2. suggestive of or resembling the traditional sophomore,
as in intellectual pretensions, self-assurance, etc. Also,
soph·o·mor·i·cal. —**soph·o·mor·i·cal·ly,** *adv.*

So·phy (sō'fĭ, sŏf'ĭ), *n., pl.* -**phies.** *Hist.* a western
title for one of the Persian Safavi dynasty. [t. Pers.: m.
çafī, surname of the dynasty]

-**sophy,** a word element referring to systems of thought,
as in *theosophy.* [t. Gk.: m.s. -*sophia,* comb. form of
sophia skill, wisdom]

so·por (sō'pər), *n. Pathol.* a deep, unnatural sleep;
lethargy. [t. L]

so·po·rif·er·ous (sō′pərĭf′ərəs, sŏp′ə-), *adj.* bringing
sleep; soporific. [f. L *soporifer* sleep-bringing + -OUS]
—**so·po·rif·er·ous·ly,** *adv.* —**so·po·rif·er·ous·ness,** *n.*

so·po·rif·ic (sō′pərĭf′ĭk, sŏp′ə-), *adj.* 1. causing or
tending to cause sleep. 2. pertaining to or characterized by sleep or sleepiness; sleepy; drowsy. —*n.* 3. something causing sleep, esp. a medicine. [f. SOPOR + -(I)FIC]

sop·ping (sŏp'ĭng), *adj.* soaked; drenched: *sopping
wet.*

sop·py (sŏp'ĭ), *adj.,* -**pier,** -**piest.** 1. soaked, drenched,
or very wet, as ground. 2. rainy, as weather. 3. *Brit.
Slang.* excessively sentimental; mawkish.

so·pran·o (səprăn′ō, -prä′nō), *n., pl.* -**pranos,** -**prani**
(-prä′nē), *adj. Music.* —*n.* 1. the uppermost part or
voice. 2. the highest singing voice in women and boys.
3. a part for such a voice. 4. a singer with such a voice.
—*adj.* 5. of or pertaining to soprano; having the compass
of a soprano. [t. It., der. *sopra* above, g. L *suprā*]

soprano clef, *Music.* a sign locating middle C on
the bottom line of the staff.

so·ra (sōr′ə), *n.* a small, short-billed North American
rail or crake, *Porzana carolina*; the Carolina rail.

So·ra·ta (sō rä′tä), *n.* **Mount,** a mountain in W Bolivia, in the Andes, near Lake Titicaca, with two peaks:
Anchuma, 21,490 ft., and Illampu, 21,276 ft.

Sorb (sôrb), *n.* a Wend. [t. G: m. *Sorbe.* See SERB]

sorb (sôrb), *n.* 1. a European service tree, *Sorbus*

domestica. 2. its fruit (**sorb apple**). [t. L: s. *sorbum*
serviceberry, or *sorbus* service tree]

Sor·bi·an (sôr′bĭ ən), *adj.* 1. of or pertaining to the
Wends or their language. —*n.* 2. a Slavic language
spoken by an isolated group in Prussia and Saxony;
Wendish; Lusatian. 3. a Wend.

Sor·bon·ist (sôr′bən ĭst), *n.* a student or a doctor of
the Sorbonne. [t. NL: s. *Sorbonista*, or t. F: m. *Sor-
boniste.* See SORBONNE]

Sor·bonne (sôr bŏn′; *Fr.* sôr bôn′), *n.* 1. the seat of
the faculties of letters and science of the University of
Paris. 2. a theological college founded in Paris in 1257
by Robert de Sorbon, suppressed in 1792, and ceasing
to exist about 1850. [F, named after Robert de *Sorbon*]

sorb·ose (sôr′bōs), *n.* a ketohexose, C₆H₁₂O₆, derived
from the mountain ash, and obtainable industrially by
bacterial oxidation, used in the synthesis of vitamin C.

sor·cer·er (sôr′sərər), *n.* one supposed to exercise
supernatural powers through evil spirits; a magician
or enchanter. —**sor·cer·ess** (sôr′sər ĭs), *n.fem.*

sor·cer·ous (sôr′sərəs), *adj.* 1. of the nature of or
involving sorcery. 2. using sorcery.

sor·cer·y (sôr′sərĭ), *n., pl.* -**ceries.** the art, practices,
or spells of a sorcerer; magic, esp. black magic, in which
supernatural powers are exercised through the aid of
evil spirits; witchery. [ME, t. ML: m.s. *sorceria,* ult.
der. L *sors* lot] —**Syn.** See **magic.**

sor·did (sôr′dĭd), *adj.* 1. dirty or filthy. 2. morally
mean or ignoble: *sordid gains.* 3. meanly selfish, self-
seeking, or mercenary. [t. L: s. *sordidus* dirty, base]
—**sor·did·ly,** *adv.* —**sor·did·ness,** *n.* —**Syn.** 1. foul,
squalid. 2. degraded, low, base. See **mean².**

sor·di·no (sôr dē′nō), *n., pl.* -**ni** (-nē). *Music.* a mute.
[t. It., ult. der. L *surdus* deaf, mute]

sore (sôr), *adj., sorer, sorest, n., adv.* —*adj.* 1. physically painful or sensitive, as a wound, hurt, diseased part,
etc. 2. suffering bodily pain from wounds, bruises, etc.,
as a person. 3. suffering mental pain; grieved, distressed,
or sorrowful: *to be sore at heart.* 4. causing great mental
pain, distress, or sorrow: *a sore bereavement.* 5. causing
very great suffering, misery, hardship, etc.: *sore need.*
6. *Colloq.* irritated, offended, or feeling aggrieved: *What
are you sore about?* 7. being an occasion of irritation: *a
sore subject.* —*n.* 8. a sore spot or place on the body. 9. a
source or cause of grief, distress, irritation, etc. —*adv.*
10. *Archaic or Poetic.* sorely. [ME; OE *sār,* c. D *zeer*]
—**sore·ly,** *adv.* —**sore·ness,** *n.*

sore·head (sôr′hĕd′), *n. U.S. Slang.* a disgruntled or
vindictive person, esp. an unsportsmanlike loser.

sore mouth, *Vet. Sci.* ecthyma of sheep.

sor·ghum (sôr′gəm), *n.* 1. a cereal grass, *Sorghum
vulgare,* of many varieties, which may be divided into four
groups, the **sweet sorghums** (used especially for making
molasses or syrup and for forage), the **grain sorghums**
(used for forage and as a food for man), the **grass
sorghums** (used principally for producing hay), and
the **broomcorns** (used for making brooms and brushes).
2. the syrup made from the sweet or saccharine sorghums. [t. NL, der. It. *sorgo,* g. L *syricum* Syrian]

sor·go (sôr′gō), *n., pl.* -**gos.** any of the sweet sorghums.
[t. It. See SORGHUM]

sor·i·cine (sôr′əsĭn′, -sĭn), *adj.* of or resembling the shrews. See **shrew².** [t. L: m.s. *sōricīnus*]

so·ri·tes (sō rī′tēz), *n. Logic.* a form of argument having several premises and one conclusion, and resolvable
into a number of syllogisms, the conclusion of each of
which is a premise of the next. [t. L, t. Gk: m. *sōreítēs,*
lit., heaped] —**so·rit·i·cal** (sō rĭt′əkəl), *adj.*

So·rol·la y Bas·ti·da (sō rō′lyä ē bäs tē′dä), **Joaquín** (hwä kēn′), 1863–1923, Spanish painter.

so·ror·ate (sôr′ə rāt′), *n.* marriage with a wife's sister.

so·ror·i·cide¹ (sə rôr′əsīd′, -rôr′-), *n.* one who kills
his or her sister. [t. L: m.s. *sorōricīda*] —**so·ror·i·
cid·al,** *adj.*

so·ror·i·cide² (sə rôr′əsīd′, -rôr′-), *n.* act of killing
one's own sister. [t. LL: m.s. *sorōricīdium*]

so·ror·i·ty (sə rôr′ətĭ, -rŏr′-), *n., pl.* -**ties.** *U.S.* a
society or club of women or girls, as in a college. [t. ML:
m.s. *sorōritas*]

so·ro·sis (sə rō′sĭs), *n., pl.* -**ses** (-sēz). 1. *Bot.* a fleshy
multiple fruit composed of many flowers, seed vessels,
and receptacles consolidated, as in the pineapple and
mulberry. 2. a woman's club. [t. NL, f. s. Gk. *sōrós*
heap + -*ōsis* -OSIS]

sorp·tion (sôrp′shən), *n. Phys. Chem.* the binding of
one substance by another by any mechanism, such as
absorption, adsorption, or persorption.

sor·rel¹ (sôr′əl, sŏr′-), *n.* 1. light reddish brown. 2. a
horse of this color. [ME *sorel,* t. OF, der. *sore* yellowish-
brown, t. Gmc.; cf. MLG *sōr* sere]

sor·rel² (sôr′əl, sŏr′-), *n.* 1. any of various plants of
the genus *Rumex,* having succulent acid leaves used in
salads, sauces, etc. 2. any of various sour-juiced plants
of the genus *Oxalis;* wood sorrel. 3. any of various
similar plants. [ME *sorell,* t. OF: m. *surele,* der. *sur,*
adj., t. Gmc.: sour]

sorrel tree, a North American ericaceous tree,
Oxydendrum arboreum, having leaves with an acid flavor
and racemes of white flowers.

Sor·ren·to (sə rĕn′tō; *It.* sôr rĕn′tō), *n.* a seaport in
SW Italy, on the Bay of Naples: resort; cathedral;
ancient ruins. 10,851 (1951).

b., blend of, blended; c., cognate with; d., dialect, dialectal; der., derived from; f., formed from; g., going back to;
m., modification of; r., replacing; s., stem of; t., taken from; ?, perhaps. See the full key on inside cover.

sor·row (sŏr′ō, sôr′ō), *n.* **1.** distress caused by loss, affliction, disappointment, etc.; grief, sadness, or regret. **2.** a cause or occasion of grief or regret. **3.** an affliction, misfortune, or trouble. —*v.i.* **4.** to feel sorrow; grieve. [ME; OE *sorg,* c. *G sorge*] —**sor′row·er,** *n.*
—Syn. **1.** SORROW, DISTRESS, GRIEF, MISERY, WOE imply bitter suffering, especially as caused by loss or misfortune. SORROW is the most general term. GRIEF is keen suffering, esp. for a particular reason. DISTRESS implies anxiety, anguish, or acute suffering caused by the pressure of trouble or adversity. MISERY suggests such great and unremitting pain or wretchedness of body or mind as crushes the spirit. WOE is deep or inconsolable grief or misery. —Ant. **1.** joy.

sor·row·ful (sŏr′ə fəl, sôr′-), *adj.* **1.** full of or feeling sorrow; grieved; sad. **2.** indicative or expressive of sorrow; mournful; plaintive. **3.** involving or causing sorrow; distressing. —**sor′row·ful·ly,** *adv.* —**sor′row·ful·ness,** *n.*

sor·ry (sŏr′ĭ, sôr′ĭ), *adj.,* **-ri·er, -ri·est.** **1.** feeling regret, compunction, sympathy, pity, etc.: *to be sorry for a remark.* **2.** of a deplorable, pitiable, or miserable kind: *to come to a sorry end.* **3.** sorrowful, grieved, or sad. **4.** associated with sorrow; suggestive of grief or suffering; melancholy; dismal. **5.** wretched, poor, mean, or pitiful: *a sorry horse.* [ME; OE *sārig* (c. LG *sērig,* OHG *sērag*), der. *sār* SORE] —**sor′ri·ly,** *adv.* —**sor′ri·ness,** *n.* —Syn. **5.** See **wretched.**

sort (sôrt), *n.* **1.** a particular kind, species, variety, class, group, or description, as distinguished by the character or nature: *to discover a new sort of mineral.* **2.** character, quality, or nature. **3.** a more or less adequate or inadequate example of something. **4.** manner, fashion, or way. **5.** (*usually pl.*) *Print.* one of the kinds of characters of a font of type. **6. of sorts, a.** of a mediocre or poor kind. **b.** of one sort or another; of an indefinite kind. **7. out of sorts, a.** not in a normal condition of good health, spirits, or temper. **b.** *Print.* short of certain characters of a font of type. —*v.t.* **8.** to arrange according to sort, kind, or class; separate into sorts; classify. **9.** to separate or take (out) from other sorts, or from others. **10.** to assign to a particular class, group, or place (fol. by *with, together,* etc.). —*v.i.* **11.** *Archaic.* to agree; accord. **12.** *Scot. and Brit. Dial.* to associate. [ME, t. OF: m. *sorte,* g. L *sors* lot, condition, LL class, order] —**sort′a·ble,** *adj.* —**sort′er,** *n.*

sor·tie (sôr′tē), *n.* **1.** a sally of troops from a besieged place to attack the besiegers. **2.** a body of troops making such a sally. **3.** the flying of an airplane on a combat mission. [t. F: a going out, der. *sortir* go out, ult. der. s. L *surgere* arise]

sor·ti·lege (sôr′tə lĭj), *n.* **1.** the drawing of lots for divination; divination by lot. **2.** sorcery; magic. [ME, t. ML: m.s. *sortilegium,* der. L *sortilegus* diviner]

so·rus (sôr′əs), *n., pl.* **so·ri** (sôr′ī). *Bot.* one of the clusters of sporangia on the back of the fronds of ferns. [NL, t. Gk.: m. *sōrós* heap]

S O S (ĕs′ō′ĕs′), **1.** the letters represented by the radio telegraphic signal used, as by ships in distress, to call for help. **2.** *Colloq.* any call for help.

Sos·no·wiec (sôs nô′vyĕts), *n.* a city in S Poland. 91,050 (est. 1954).

so-so (sō′sō′), *adj.* **1.** indifferent; neither very good nor very bad. —*adv.* **2.** in an indifferent or passable manner; indifferently; tolerably.

A B C D E
Sori on pinnules of ferns
A. Spleenwort. *Asplenium angustifolium;* B. Chain fern. *Woodwardia angustifolia;* C. Polypody. *Polypodium Californicum;* D. Maidenhair. *Adiantum pedatum;* E. Filmy fern. *Trichomanes radicans*

sos·te·nu·to (sŏs′tĕ nōō′tō), *adj., n., pl.* **-tos, -ti** (-tē). *Music.* —*adj.* **1.** sustained or prolonged in the time value of the tones. —*n.* **2.** a movement or passage played in this manner. [It., pp. of *sostenere* sustain]

sot (sŏt), *n.* a confirmed drunkard. [ME *sotte,* OE *sott,* t. VL: s. *sottus;* orig. uncert.]

so·te·ri·ol·o·gy (sə tĭr′ĭ ŏl′ə jĭ), *n. Theol.* the doctrine of salvation through Jesus Christ. [f. Gk. *sōtério(s)* saving + -LOGY] —**so·te·ri·o·log·ic** (sə tĭr′ĭ ə lŏj′ĭk), **so·te·ri·o·log′i·cal,** *adj.*

Soth·ern (sŭth′ərn), *n.* **Edward Hugh,** 1859–1933, U.S. actor.

So·thic (sō′thĭk, sŏth′ĭk), *adj.* of Sirius, the Dog Star. [f. s. Gk. *Sōthis,* Egyptian name for Sirius + -IC]

Sothic cycle, (in the ancient Egyptian calendar) a period of 1460 Sothic years. Also, **Sothic period.**

Sothic year, the fixed year of the ancient Egyptians, determined by the heliacal rising of Sirius, and equivalent to 365¼ days.

so·tol (sō′tōl, sō tōl′), *n.* any plant of the liliaceous genus *Dasylirion,* of the SW U.S. and N Mexico, resembling the yucca. [t. Mex. Sp., t. Nahuatl: m. *tzotolli*]

sot·tish (sŏt′ĭsh), *adj.* **1.** stupefied, as with drink. **2.** given to excessive drinking. **3.** pertaining to or befitting a sot. —**sot′tish·ly,** *adv.* —**sot′tish·ness,** *n.*

sot·to vo·ce (sŏt′ō vō′chĭ; *It.* sôt′tô vō′chĕ), in a low tone intended not to be overheard. [t. It.: under (normal) voice (level)]

sou (sōō), *n.* **1.** the French bronze 5-centime piece, worth about ¹/₂₀ U.S. cent, or the bronze 10-centime piece.

2. a former French coin, orig. of gold, then of silver, and finally of copper. [t. F; in OF *sol* SOL²]

sou., **1.** south. **2.** southern.

sou·a·ri nut (sōō ä′rĭ), the large, edible, oily nut of a tall tree, *Caryocar nuciferum,* of tropical South America; butternut. [t. Galibi: m. *saouari*]

sou·bise (sōō bēz′), *n.* a strained onion white sauce for meats, etc. [named after Prince Charles *Soubise* (1715–87), marshal of France]

sou·brette (sōō brĕt′), *n.* **1.** a maid servant or lady's maid in a play or opera, esp. one displaying coquetry, pertness, and intrigue. **2.** an actress playing such a rôle. **3.** any lively or pert young woman character. [t. F, t. Pr.: m. *soubreto,* fem. of *soubret* coy, reserved, der. *soubra* to set aside, (earlier) be left over, g. L *superāre* be above] —**sou·bret′tish,** *adj.*

sou·bri·quet (sōō′brə kā′), *n.* sobriquet.

sou·car (sou kär′), *n.* a Hindu banker. Also, **sowcar.** [t. Urdu (Hind.): m. *sāhūkār* great merchant]

sou·chong (sōō′shŏng′, -chŏng′), *n.* a variety of black tea grown in India and Ceylon. [t. Chinese: m. Cantonese *siu-chung* small sort]

Sou·dan (sōō dän′), *n.* French name of **Sudan.**

souf·flé (sōō flā′, sōō′flā), *adj.* **1.** puffed up; made light, as by beating and cooking. —*n.* **2.** a light baked dish made fluffy with beaten egg whites combined with egg yolks, white sauce, and fish, cheese, or other ingredients. **3.** a similar dish of sweetened fruit pulp. [t. F, pp. of *souffler* blow, puff, g. L *sufflāre* blow up]

souf·fle (sōō′fəl), *n. Pathol.* a murmuring or blowing sound. [t. F, der. *souffler* blow. See SOUFFLE]

Sou·frière (sōō fryĕr′), *n.* **a.** a volcano on St. Vincent, in the British West Indies. ab. 3600 ft. **2.** a volcano on Guadeloupe, in the French West Indies, 4869 ft.

sough (sŭf, sou), *v.i.* **1.** to make a rushing, rustling, or murmuring sound. —*n.* **2.** such a sound. [ME *swoghe,* OE *swōgan* make a noise, c. OS *swōgan* and akin to OE *swēgan* make a noise (c. Goth -*swōgjan*)]

sought (sôt), *v.* pt. and pp. of **seek.**

soul (sōl), *n.* **1.** the principle of life, feeling, thought, and action in man, regarded as a distinct entity separate from the body, and commonly held to be separable in existence from the body; the spiritual part of man as distinct from the physical. **2.** the spiritual part of man regarded in its moral aspect, or as believed to survive death and be subject to happiness or misery in a life to come. **3.** the emotional part of man's nature, or the seat of the feelings or sentiments. **4.** high-mindedness; noble warmth of feeling, spirit or courage, etc. **5.** the animating principle or essential element or part of something. **6.** the inspirer or moving spirit of some action, movement, etc. **7.** the embodiment of some quality. **8.** a disembodied spirit of a deceased person. **9.** a human being; person. [ME; OE *sāwl,* c. Goth. *saiwala,* akin to D *ziel,* G *seele,* Icel. *sāl*]

soul·ful (sōl′fəl), *adj.* of, or expressive of, deep feeling or emotion: *soulful eyes.* —**soul′ful·ly,** *adv.* —**soul′ful·ness,** *n.*

soul·less (sōl′lĭs), *adj.* **1.** without a soul. **2.** lacking in nobility of soul, as persons; without spirit or courage. —**soul′less·ly,** *adv.* —**soul′less·ness,** *n.*

Soult (sōolt), *n.* **Nicolas Jean de Dieu** (nē kō lä′ zhän də dyœ), (*Duke of Dalmatia*) 1769–1851, French marshal.

Sou·mak rug (sōō mäk′), Kashmir rug.

sound¹ (sound), *n.* **1.** the sensation produced in the organs of hearing when certain vibrations (**sound waves**) are caused in the surrounding air or other elastic medium, as by a vibrating body. **2.** the vibrations in the air, or vibrational energy, producing this sensation: longitudinal vibrations propagated at about 1100 feet per second. **3.** the particular auditory effect produced by a given cause: *the sound of music.* **4.** any auditory effect, or vibrational disturbance such as to be heard. **5.** a noise, vocal utterance, musical tone, or the like. **6.** *Phonet.* a segment of speech corresponding to a single articulation or to a combination of articulations constantly associated in the language; a phone. **7.** the quality of an event, letter, etc., as it affects a person: *this report has a bad sound.* **8.** the distance within which the noise of something may be heard. **9.** mere noise, without meaning. **10.** *Obs.* a report; news; tidings. [ME *soun,* t. AF: var. of OF *son,* g. L *sonus*]
—*v.i.* **11.** to make or emit a sound. **12.** to give forth a sound as a call or summons. **13.** to be heard, as a sound. **14. sound off,** *U.S. Slang.* **a.** to speak or complain frankly. **b.** to call out one's name, sequence number, etc. **15.** to convey a certain impression when heard or read: *to sound strange.* **16.** to give a specific sound: *to sound loud.* **17.** to give the appearance of being: *to sound true.* **18.** *Law.* to have as its basis or the import of: *his action sounds in contract.* —*v.t.* **19.** to cause (an instrument, etc.) to make or emit a sound. **20.** to give forth (a sound). **21.** to announce, order, or direct by a sound as of a trumpet: *to sound a retreat.* **22.** to utter audibly, pronounce, or express: *to sound each letter.* **23.** to examine by percussion or auscultation. [ME *soune(n),* t. OF: m. *soner,* g. L *sonāre*]
—Syn. **1.** SOUND, NOISE, TONE refer to something heard. SOUND and NOISE are often used interchangeably for anything perceived by means of hearing. SOUND, however, is more general in application, being used for anything within earshot: *the sound of running water.* NOISE, caused by

irregular vibrations, is more properly applied to a loud, discordant, or unpleasant sound: *the noise of shouting.* TONE is applied to a musical sound; one conceived of as possessing a certain quality, resonance, pitch, to express emotion, etc.

sound² (sound), *adj.* **1.** free from injury, damage, decay, defect, disease, etc.; in good condition; healthy; robust: *a sound heart.* **2.** financially strong, secure, or reliable: *sound business house.* **3.** solidly good or reliable: *sound judgment.* **4.** without defect as to truth, justice, or reason: *sound advice.* **5.** of substantial or enduring character: *sound value.* **6.** without logical defect, as reasoning. **7.** without legal defect, as a title. **8.** theologically correct or orthodox, as doctrines or a theologian. **9.** free from moral defect or weakness; upright, honest, or good; honorable; loyal. **10.** unbroken and deep, as sleep. **11.** vigorous, hearty, or thorough, as a beating. [ME *sund*, OE *gesund*, c. D *gezond*, G *gesund*] **—sound/ly,** *adv.* **—sound/ness,** *n.*

sound³ (sound), *v.t.* **1.** to measure or try the depth of (water, a deep hole, etc.) by letting down a lead or plummet at the end of a line, or by some equivalent means. **2.** to measure (depth) in such a manner, as at sea. **3.** to examine or test (the bottom of water, etc.) with a lead that brings up adhering bits of matter. **4.** to examine or investigate; seek to fathom or ascertain: *to sound a person's views.* **5.** to seek to elicit the views or sentiments of (a person) by indirect inquiries, suggestive allusions, etc. **6.** *Surg.* to examine, as the urinary bladder, with a sound (def. 11). **—v.i. 7.** to use the lead and line (or some other device) for measuring depth, etc., as at sea. **8.** to go down or touch bottom, as a lead. **9.** to plunge downward or dive, as a whale. **10.** to make investigation; seek information, esp. by indirect inquiries, etc. **—n. 11.** *Surg.* a long, solid, slender instrument for sounding or exploring body cavities or canals [ME; OE *sund* channel (in *sundgyrd* sounding pole, lit., channel pole), t. Scand.; cf. Icel. *sund* channel, c. OE *sund* sea; akin to SWIM]

sound⁴ (sound), *n.* **1.** a relatively narrow passage of water, not a stream, between larger bodies or between the mainland and an island: *Long Island Sound.* **2.** an inlet, arm, or recessed portion of the sea: *Puget Sound.* **3.** the swimming bladder of a fish. [ME; OE *sund* swimming, channel, sea. See SOUND³]

Sound (sound), *n.* **The,** a strait between SW Sweden and the Danish island of Zealand, connecting the Kattegat and the Baltic. ab. 75 mi. long; 3–30 mi. wide. Swedish and Danish, *Öresund.*

sound barrier, (in popular usage) the phenomena observed when an object approaches and passes the speed of sound in air. Such phenomena (vibration, resonance, etc.) are actually the result of certain parts of the object moving at subsonic, others at sonic, and still others at supersonic velocities. Also, **transonic barrier.**

sound·board (sound/bôrd′), *n.* sounding board.

sound·box (sound/bŏks′), *n.* **1.** a chamber in a musical instrument, as the body of a violin, for increasing the sonority of its tone. **2.** the part of a phonograph pickup in which the mechanical movements of the needle are converted into acoustic impulses, usually based upon a diaphragm vibrated by the needle.

sound·er¹ (soun/dər), *n.* **1.** one who or that which makes a sound or noise, or sounds something. **2.** *Teleg.* a receiving instrument by the sounds of which a telegraphic message may be read. [f. SOUND- + -ER¹]

sound·er² (soun/dər), *n.* one who or that which sounds the depth of water, etc. [f. SOUND³ + -ER¹]

sound·ing¹ (soun/dYng), *adj.* **1.** emitting or producing a sound or sounds. **2.** resounding or sonorous. **3.** having an imposing sound; high-sounding; pompous. [f. SOUND¹ + -ING²] **—sound/ing·ly,** *adv.*

sound·ing² (soun/dYng), *n.* **1.** (*often pl.*) act or process of measuring depth, examining the bottom of water, etc., with or as with a lead and line. **2.** (*pl.*) depths of water ascertained by means of a lead and line, as at sea. **3.** (*pl.*) parts of the water in which the ordinary sounding lead will reach bottom. [f. SOUND³ + -ING¹]

sounding board, **1.** a thin, resonant plate of wood forming part of a musical stringed instrument, and so placed as to enhance the power and quality of the tone. **2.** a structure over, or behind and above, a speaker, orchestra, etc., to reflect the sound towards the audience. **3.** a board used in the deadening of floors, partitions, etc.

sounding line, a line weighted with a lead or plummet (**sounding lead**) and bearing marks to show the length paid out, used for sounding, as at sea.

sound·less¹ (sound/lYs), *adj.* without sound. [f. SOUND¹ + -LESS] **—sound/less·ly,** *adv.*

sound·less² (sound/lYs), *adj.* unfathomable. [f. SOUND³ + -LESS]

sound·proof (sound/prŏof′), *adj.* **1.** impervious to sound. **—v.t. 2.** to cause to be soundproof.

sound ranging, the location of a sound source by microphonic detection of the sound signals.

sound track, sound record on a motion-picture film.

soup (sŏop), *n.* **1.** a liquid food made from meat, fish, or vegetables, with various added ingredients, by boiling. **—v.t. 2.** soup up, *U.S. Slang.* to speed up (a motor or engine) by increasing the richness of the fuel mixture or the efficiency of the fuel. [t. F: m. *soupe* sop, broth, of Gmc. orig.; cf. OE *sūpan* slp, *sopp* SOP]

soup·con (sŏop sôn′), *n.* **1.** a suspicion; a slight trace or flavor. **2.** a very small amount. [t. F, g. LL *suspectio,* r. L *suspicio* suspicion]

sour (sour), *adj.* **1.** having an acid taste, such as that of vinegar, lemon juice, etc.; tart. **2.** rendered acid or affected by fermentation; fermented. **3.** characteristic of what is so affected: *a sour smell.* **4.** distasteful or disagreeable; unpleasant. **5.** harsh in spirit or temper; austere; morose; peevish. **6.** *Agric.* (of soil) having excessive acidity. **7.** (of substances such as gasoline) contaminated by sulfur compounds. **—n. 8.** that which is sour; something sour. **9.** *U.S.* an acid drink, as whiskey with lemon juice, sugar, etc. **—v.i., v.t. 10.** to become or make sour. [ME; OE *sūr,* c. G *sauer*] **—sour/ish,** *adj.* **—sour/ly,** *adv.* **—sour/ness,** *n.*

source (sôrs), *n.* **1.** any thing or place from which something comes, arises, or is obtained; origin. **2.** a spring of water from the earth, etc., or the place of issue; a fountain; the beginning or place of origin of a stream or river. **3.** a book, statement, person, etc., supplying information. **4.** the person or business making interest or dividend payments. [ME, t. OF, n. use of pp. of *sourdre* rise, spring up, g. L *surgere* rise]

source material, original authoritative materials utilized in research, as diaries, manuscripts, records, etc.

sour·dine (sŏor dēn′), *n.* *Music.* **1.** sordino. **2.** kit. **3.** *Hist.* an obsolete member of the oboe family. [t. F, der. *sourd* deaf, g. L *surdus*]

sour·dough (sour/dō′), *n.* **1.** *Western U.S. and Canada, Alaska, Brit. Dial.* leaven, esp. fermented dough kept from one baking to start the next instead of beginning each time with fresh yeast. **2.** *Western U.S. and Canada, Alaska.* a prospector or pioneer (in allusion to his use of sourdough). **—adj. 3.** *Western U.S. and Canada, Alaska.* leavened with sourdough.

sour gourd, **1.** the acid fruit of a bombacaceous tree, *Adansonia Gregorii,* of northern Australia. **2.** the tree. **3.** the fruit of the baobab, *A. digitata,* of Africa.

sour grapes, something that a person pretends to despise, only because he cannot have it.

sour gum, the tupelo, *Nyssa sylvatica.*

sour·sop (sour/sŏp′), *n.* **1.** the large, slightly acid, pulpy fruit of a small tree, *Annona muricata,* native in the West Indies. **2.** the tree.

Sou·sa (sŏo/zə), *n.* **John Philip,** 1854–1932, U.S. band conductor and composer of music.

sou·sa·phone (sŏo/sə fōn′, sŏo/zə-), *n.* a form of bass tuba, similar to the helicon, used in brass bands. [f. SOUSA + -PHONE. Cf. SAXOPHONE]

souse¹ (sous), *v.,* **soused, sousing,** *n.* **—v.t. 1.** to plunge into water or other liquid. **2.** to drench with water, etc. **3.** to dash or pour, as water. **4.** to steep in pickle. **5.** *Slang.* to intoxicate. **—v.i. 6.** to plunge into water, etc.; fall with a splash. **7.** to be soaked or drenched. **8.** to be steeping or soaking in something. **9.** *Slang.* to drink to intoxication. **—n. 10.** an act of sousing. **11.** something kept or steeped in pickle, esp. the head, ears, and feet of a pig. **12.** a liquid used as a pickle. **13.** *Slang.* a drunkard. [ME *sows,* t. OF: m. *souce,* t. OHG: m. *sulza* brine; akin to SALT]

souse² (sous), *v.,* **soused, sousing,** *n.* *Archaic.* **—v.i. 1.** to swoop. **—v.t. 2.** to swoop or pounce on. **—n. 3.** *Falconry.* **a.** a rising while in flight. **b.** a swooping or pouncing. [var. of SOURCE in (now obs.) sense 'rise']

sou·tache (sŏo tāsh′), *n.* a narrow braid, commonly of mohair, silk, or rayon, used for trimming. [t. F, t. Hung.: m. *sujtás* blow, trimming]

sou·tane (sŏo tän′), *n.* *Eccles.* a cassock. [t. F, t. It.: m. *sottana,* der. *sotto* under, g. L *subtus*]

south (south), *n.* **1.** a cardinal point of the compass directly opposite to the north. **2.** the direction in which this point lies. **3.** (*l.c. or cap.*) a quarter or territory situated in this direction. **4.** (*cap.*) the general area south of Pennsylvania and the Ohio river and east of the Mississippi, consisting mainly of those States which formed the Confederacy. **—adj. 5.** lying toward or situated in the south; directed or proceeding toward the south. **6.** coming from the south, as a wind. **—adv. 7.** toward, in, or from the south. [ME; OE *sūth,* c. OHG *sund-;* akin to G *süd*]

South Africa, Republic of, a country in S Africa; former member of the British Commonwealth. 14,418,000 (est. 1958); 472,000 sq. mi. *Capitals:* Pretoria and Cape Town.

South African, **1.** of southern Africa. **2.** of the Union of South Africa. **3.** a native or inhabitant of the Union of South Africa. esp. one of European descent.

South African Dutch, **1.** Afrikaans. **2.** the Boers.

South African Republic, the name of Transvaal when it was an independent Boer state.

South America, a continent in the S part of the Western Hemisphere. 124,000,000 pop. (est. 1955); ab. 6,900,000 sq. mi. **—South American.**

South·amp·ton (south ămp′tən, -hămp′-), *n.* **1.** an administrative county in S England: a part of Hampshire. 1,197,170 pop. (1951); 1503 sq. mi. *Co. seat:* Winchester. **2.** a seaport in this county. 196,400 (est. 1956).

South Australia, a state in S Australia. 797,094 pop. (1954); 380,070 sq. mi. *Cap.:* Adelaide.

South Bend, a city in N Indiana. 132,445 (1960).

south by east, one point or degree east of south on a compass card or dial. See diag. under **compass card.**

south by west, one point or degree west of south on a compass card or dial. See diag. under **compass card.**

b., blend of, blended; c., cognate with; d., dialect, dialectal; der., derived from; f., formed from; g., going back to; m., modification of; r., replacing; s., stem of; t., taken from; ?, perhaps. See the full key on inside cover.

South Carolina, a State in the SE United States, on the Atlantic coast. 2,382,594 pop. (1960); 31,055 sq. mi. *Cap.:* Columbia. *Abbr.:* S.C. —**South Carolinian.**

South Caucasic, a family of languages of southern Caucasia, including Georgian.

South China Sea, a part of the Pacific, partially enclosed by southeastern China, Vietnam, the Malay Peninsula, Borneo, and the Philippine Islands.

South Da·ko·ta (də kō′tə), a State in the N central United States: a part of the Midwest. 680,514 pop. (1960); 77,047 sq. mi. *Cap.:* Pierre. *Abbr.:* S. Dak. —**South Da·ko′tan.**

south·down (south′doun′), *n.* one of a breed of high-quality mutton sheep, orig. reared on the South Downs.

South Downs, a range of low hills in S England.

south·east (south′ēst′; *Naut.* sou′-), *n.* **1.** the point or direction midway between south and east. **2.** a region in this direction. —*adj.* **3.** lying toward, situated in, or directed toward the southeast. **4.** coming from the southeast, as a wind. —*adv.* **5.** in the direction midway between south and east. **6.** from this direction. —**south′east′ern,** *adj.*

Southeast Asia Treaty Organization, the group of nations that signed the **Southeast Asia Collective Defense Treaty** in 1954: Australia, France, Great Britain, New Zealand, Pakistan, The Philippines, Thailand, and the United States.

southeast by east, *Navig., Survey.* 11°15′ (one point) east of southeast; 123°45′ from due north.

southeast by south, *Navig., Survey.* 11°15′ (one point) south of southeast; 146°15′ from due north.

south·east·er (south′ēs′tər; *Naut.* sou′-), *n.* a wind, gale, or storm from the southeast.

south·east·er·ly (south′ēs′tər lǐ; *Naut.* sou′-), *adj., adv.* toward or from the southeast.

south·east·ward (south′ēst′wərd; *Naut.* sou′-), *adj., adv.* **1.** Also, **south′east′ward·ly.** toward the southeast. —*n.* **2.** the southeast.

south·east·wards (south′ēst′wərdz; *Naut.* sou′-), *adv.* southeastward.

South·end-on-Sea (south′ĕnd′ŏn sē′), *n.* a seaport in SE England, on Thames estuary. 155,800 (est. 1956).

south·er (sou′thər), *n.* a wind or storm from the south.

south·er·ly (sŭth′ər lǐ), *adj., adv.* **1.** toward the south: *a southerly course.* **2.** from the south: *a gentle southerly wind.* Also, **south′ern·ly.** —**south′er·li·ness,** *n.*

south·ern (sŭth′ərn), *adj.* **1.** lying toward, situated in, or directed toward the south. **2.** coming from the south, as a wind. **3.** of or pertaining to the south. **4.** (*cap.*) of or pertaining to the South of the United States. **5.** *Astron.* south of the celestial equator or of the zodiac. **6.** one living in a southern region or country. [ME; OE *sūtherne.* See SOUTH, -ERN]

Southern Alps, a mountain range in New Zealand, on South Island. Highest peak, Mt. Cook, 12,349 ft.

Southern Cross, *Astron.* the southern constellation Crux: its four chief stars are in the form of a cross.

Southern Crown, *Astron.* the Corona Australis.

south·ern·er (sŭth′ər nər), *n.* a native or inhabitant of the south, esp. (*cap.*) of the southern United States.

Southern Hemisphere, the half of the earth between the South Pole and the equator.

south·ern·most (sŭth′ərn mōst′), *adj.* farthest south.

Southern Rhodesia, a state in S Africa: formerly a British colony and part of the Federation of Rhodesia and Nyasaland. 4,010,000 pop. (est. 1963); 150,391 sq. mi. *Cap.:* Salisbury. Also called **Rhodesia.**

south·ern·wood (sŭth′ərn wood′), *n.* a woody-stemmed wormwood, *Artemisia Abrotanum,* of southern Europe, having aromatic, finely dissected leaves.

Sou·they (sou′thǐ, sŭth′ĭ), *n.* Robert, 1774–1843, British poet and prose writer: poet laureate (1813–43).

South Gate, a city in SW California, near Los Angeles. 53,831 (1960).

South Georgia, a British island in the S Atlantic, ab. 800 mi. SE of the Falkland Islands. 1400 (1953); ab. 1000 sq. mi.

South Holland, a province in SW Netherlands. 2,506,576 pop. (est. 1954); 1212 sq. mi. *Cap.:* The Hague.

south·ing (sou′thǐng), *n.* **1.** *Astron.* **a.** the transit of a heavenly body across the celestial meridian. **b.** south declination. **2.** movement or deviation toward the south. **3.** distance due south made by a ship.

South Island, the largest island of New Zealand. 568,463 pop. (est. 1953); 58,093 sq. mi.

south·most (south′mōst), *adj.* southernmost.

south·paw (south′pô′), *Sports Slang.* —*n.* **1.** a left-handed pitcher, player, etc. —*adj.* **2.** left-handed.

South Platte, a river flowing from central Colorado NE to the Platte river in W Nebraska. 424 mi.

South Pole, *Geog.* that end of the earth's axis of rotation marking the southernmost point of the earth.

South·port (south′pôrt′), *n.* a seaport in W England, in Lancashire: resort. 82,100 (est. 1956).

south·ron (sŭth′rən, south′rən), *n.* **1.** a southerner. **2.** (*usually cap.*) *Scot.* an Englishman. [ME; alter. of *southren* (var. of SOUTHERN) on model of *Saxon,* etc.]

South San Francisco, a city in central California. 39,418 (1960)

South Sea Islands, the islands in the S Pacific Ocean. See **Oceania.**

South Seas, the seas S of the equator.

South Shields, a seaport in NE England at the mouth of the Tyne river. 108,100 (est. 1951).

south-south·east (south′south′ēst′; *Naut.* sou′sou′-), *n. Navig., Survey.* that point midway between south and southeast; 157°30′ from due north.

south-south·west (south′south′wĕst′; *Naut.* sou′sou′-), *n. Navig., Survey.* that point midway between south and southwest; 202°30′ west of due south.

South Vietnam, that part of Vietnam S of ab. 17° N latitude, provisionally controlled by a non-communist government; formerly a part of French Indochina. ab. 11,000,000 *Cap.:* Saigon.

south·ward (south′wərd; *Naut.* sŭth′ərd), *adj.* **1.** moving, bearing, facing, or situated toward the south. —*adv.* Also, **south′wards. 2.** toward the south; south. —*n.* **3.** the southward part, direction, or point.

south·ward·ly (south′wərd lǐ; *Naut.* sŭth′ərd lǐ), *adj., adv.* **1.** toward the south. **2.** from the south.

South·wark (sŭth′ərk), *n.* a central borough of London, England, S of the Thames. 97,191 (1951).

south·west (south′wĕst′; *Naut.* sou′-), *n.* **1.** the point or direction midway between south and west. **2.** a region in this direction. —*adj.* **3.** lying toward, situated in, or directed toward the southwest. **4.** coming from the southwest, as a wind. —*adv.* **5.** in the direction which is midway between south and west. **6.** from this direction. —**south′west′ern,** *adj.*

South-West Africa, a territory in SW Africa: a mandate of the Union of South Africa. 414,601 pop. (1951); 317,725 sq. mi. *Cap.:* Windhoek. Formerly, **German Southwest Africa.**

southwest by south, *Navig., Survey.* 11°15′ (one point) south of southwest; 213°45′ from due north.

southwest by west, *Navig., Survey.* 11°15′ (one point) west of southwest; 236°15′ from due north.

south·west·er (south′wĕs′tər; *Naut.* sou′-), *n.* **1.** a wind, gale, or storm from the southwest. **2.** a waterproof hat having the brim very broad behind, worn esp. by seamen. Also, **sou′·west·er** (sou′wĕs′tər).

south·west·er·ly (south′wĕs′tər lǐ; *Naut.* sou′-), *adj., adv.* toward or from the southwest.

south·west·ward (south′wĕst′wərd; *Naut.* sou′-), *adj., adv.* **1.** Also, **south′west′ward·ly.** toward the southwest. —*n.* **2.** the southwest.

south·west·wards (south′wĕst′wərdz; *Naut.* sou′-), *adv.* southwestward.

sou·ve·nir (sōō′və nïr′, sōō′və nïr′), *n.* **1.** something given or kept for remembrance; a memento. **2.** a memory. [t. F: n. use of *souvenir* (reflex.) to remember, t. L: m. *subvenīre* come to mind]

sov·er·eign (sŏv′rǐn, sŭv′-), *n.* **1.** a monarch; a king or queen. **2.** one who has sovereign power or authority. **3.** a group or body of persons or a state possessing sovereign authority. **4.** a British gold coin valued at 2 pounds 18 shillings, minted only for use abroad. —*adj.* **5.** belonging to or characteristic of a sovereign or sovereignty. **6.** having supreme rank, power, or authority. **7.** supreme, as power, authority, etc. **8.** greatest in degree; utmost or extreme. **9.** being above all others in character, importance, excellence, etc. **10.** efficacious or potent, as a remedy. [ME, t. OF: m. *soverain,* ult. der. L *super* above] —**sov′er·eignly,** *adv.*

sov·er·eign·ty (sŏv′rǐn tǐ, sŭv′-), *n., pl.* **-ties. 1.** the quality or state of being sovereign. **2.** the status, dominion, power, or authority of a sovereign. **3.** supreme and independent power or authority in government as possessed or claimed by a state or community. **4.** a sovereign state, community, or political unit.

So·vetsk (sə vyĕtsk′), *n.* a city in the W Soviet Union on the Memel river; formerly in East Prussia. 50,000 (est. 1948). Formerly called **Tilsit.**

so·vi·et (sō′vǐ ĕt′, -ĭt, sō′vǐ ĕt′), *n.* **1.** (in the Soviet Union) **a.** (before the revolution) a council of any kind, presumably elected by all. **b.** (after the revolution) a local council, orig. elected only by manual workers, with certain powers of local administration. **c.** (after the revolution) a higher local council elected by a local council, part of a pyramid of soviets, culminating in the **Supreme Soviet,** which is the "parliament" of the Soviet Union. **2.** any similar council or assembly connected with a socialistic governmental system elsewhere. —*adj.* **3.** of a soviet. **4.** (*cap.*) of the Soviet Union: *a Soviet statesman.* [t. Russ.: m. *sovyet* council]

so·vi·et·ism (sō′vǐ ə tǐz′əm), *n.* the soviet system of government. —**so′vi·et·ist,** *n., adj.*

so·vi·et·ize (sō′vǐ ə tīz′), *v.t.,* **-ized, -izing.** to bring under the influence or domination of soviets. —**so·vi·et·i·za·tion** (sō′vǐ ĕt′ə zā′shən), *n.*

Soviet Russia, 1. a conventional name of the Soviet Union. **2.** Russian Socialist Federated Soviet Republic.

Soviet Union, a federal union of fifteen constituent republics, in E Europe and W and N Asia, comprising the larger part of the former Russian Empire. 200,200,000 pop. (est. 1956); ab. 8,350,600 sq. mi. *Cap.:* Moscow. Official name, **Union of Soviet Socialist Republics.**

sov·ran (sŏv′rən, sŭv′-), *n., adj. Poetic.* sovereign.

sow¹ (sō), *v.,* **sowed, sown** or **sowed, sowing.** —*v.t.* **1.** to scatter (seed) over land, earth, etc., for growth; plant (seed, and hence a crop). **2.** to scatter seed over (land, earth, etc.) for the purpose of growth. **3.** to introduce for development; seek to propagate or extend; disseminate: *to sow distrust or dissension.* **4.** to strew or sprinkle with anything. —*v.i.* **5.** to sow seed, as for the production of a crop. [ME *sowen*, OE *sāwan*, c. G *sāen*; akin to L *serere*] —**sow′er,** *n.*

sow² (sou), *n.* **1.** the female of swine; an adult female hog. **2.** *Metall.* **a.** a large oblong mass of iron which has solidified in the common channel through which the molten metal flows to the smaller channels in which the pigs solidify. **b.** the common channel itself. [ME; OE *sū,* c. G *sau*]

so·war (sō wär′, -wôr′), *n. India.* a mounted native soldier. [t. Pers. (Urdū): m. *sawār* horseman]

sow bug (sou), any of various small terrestrial isopods, esp. of the genus *Oniscus;* wood louse.

sow·car (sou kär′), *n.* soucar.

sown (sōn), *v.* pp. of **sow¹.**

sow thistle (sou), any plant of the cichoriaceous genus *Sonchus,* esp. *S. oleraceus,* a common weed having thistlelike leaves, yellow flowers, and a milky juice.

soy (soi), *n.* **1.** a salty, fermented sauce much used on fish and other dishes in the Orient, prepared from soybeans. **2.** the plant, *Glycine Soja,* which yields the soybean. **3.** the soybean. Also, *esp. Brit.,* **soy·a** (soi′ə). [t. Jap., var. of *shoy,* short for *shō-yu,* t. Chinese: m. *shī-yu* (f. *shī* kind of bean + *yu* oil)]

soy·bean (soi′bēn′), *n.* the edible seed of the soy (plant). See **soy** (def. 2).

so·zin (sō′zin), *n. Biochem.* any protein normally present in the animal body and serving as a defense against disease. [f. Gk. *sōz(ein)* save + -IN²]

Soz·zi·ni (sôt tsē′nē), *n.* Italian name of **Socinus.**

Sp., 1. Spain. **2.** Spaniard. **3.** Spanish.

sp., 1. special. **2.** species. **3.** specific. **4.** specimen. **5.** spelling. **6.** spirit.

s.p., (L *sine prole*) without issue.

spa (spä), *n.* a mineral spring, or a locality in which such springs exist. [special use of SPA]

Spa (spä, spô), *n.* a resort town in E Belgium, SE of Liège: famous mineral springs. 8862 (1947).

space (spās), *n., v.,* **spaced, spacing.** —*n.* **1.** the unlimited or indefinitely great general receptacle of things, commonly conceived as an expanse extending in all directions (or having three dimensions), in which, or occupying portions of which, all material objects are located. **2.** the portion or extent of this in a given instance; extent or room in three dimensions: *the space occupied by a body.* **3.** extent or area; a particular extent of surface: *to fill out blank spaces in a document.* **4.** a seat, berth, or room on a train, airplane, etc. **5.** linear distance; a particular distance: *trees set at equal spaces apart.* **6.** extent, or a particular extent, of time: *a space of two hours.* **7.** an interval of time; a while: *after a space he continued his story.* **8.** *Music.* one of the degrees or intervals between the lines of the staff. **9.** *Print.* one of the blank pieces of metal used to separate words, etc. **10.** *Teleg.* a period of time having a fixed relation to dots and dashes, during which no signal is transmitted in Morse or similar systems. **11.** *Obs.* time allowed or available for some purpose. —*v.t.* **12.** to fix the space or spaces of; divide into spaces. **13.** to set some distance apart. **14.** *Print., etc.* **a.** to separate (words, letters, or lines) by spaces. **b.** to extend by inserting more space or spaces (usually fol. by *out*). [ME, t. OF: m. *espace,* t. L: m. *spatium*] —**spac′er,** *n.*

space·less (spās′lis), *adj.* **1.** independent of space; infinite. **2.** occupying no space.

space·ship (spās′ship′), *n.* a projected rocket-propelled plane for interplanetary travel.

space station, a manned artificial satellite in orbit around the earth: proposed esp. for the construction and launching of space ships.

space time, a four-dimensional continuum in which the coördinates are the three spatial coördinates and time. The events and objects of any spatial and temporal region may be conceived as part of this continuum.

space-time (spās′tīm′), *adj.* pertaining to a diagram in which distance moved is plotted as a function of time.

spac·ing (spā′shəs), *n.* **1.** act of one who or that which spaces. **2.** the fixing or arranging of spaces.

spa·cious (spā′shəs), *adj.* **1.** containing much space, as a house, room, court, street, etc.; amply large. **2.** occupying much space; vast. **3.** of a great extent or area; broad; large; great. **4.** broad in scope, range, inclusiveness, etc. [ME, t. L: m.s. *spatiōsus*] —**spa′cious·ly,** *adv.* —**spa′cious·ness,** *n.* —**Syn. 1.** roomy, capacious.

spade¹ (spād), *n., v.,* **spaded, spading.** —*n.* **1.** a tool for digging, having an iron blade adapted for pressing into the ground with the foot, and a long handle commonly with a grip or crosspiece at the top. **2.** some implement, piece, or part resembling this. **3.** the sharp part of a gun trail embedded in the ground to restrict backward movement of the carriage during recoil. **4.** a cutting tool used to strip the blubber or skin, as from a whale. **5.** **call a spade a spade,** to call a thing by its real name; speak plainly or bluntly. —*v.t.* **6.** to dig, cut, or remove with a spade. [ME; OE *spadu,* c. G *spaten*] —**spade′ful** (spād′fool′), *n.*

spade² (spād), *n.* **1.** a black figure shaped like an inverted heart with a short stem at the cusp opposite the point, used on playing cards. **2.** a card of the suit bearing such figures. **3.** (*pl.*) the suit of cards bearing this

figure. [t. It., pl. of *spada,* orig., sword, later mark on cards, g. L *spatha,* t. Gk.: m. *spáthē* wooden blade]

spade·fish (spād′fish′), *n., pl.* **-fishes,** (*esp. collectively*) **-fish. 1.** an acanthopterygian food fish, *Chaetodipterus faber,* abundant on the Atlantic coast of the U.S. **2.** a deep-bodied marine fish of the Atlantic coast of North America, *Chaetodipterus faber.*

spade·work (spād′wûrk′), *n.* preliminary or initial work, such as the gathering of data, on which further activity is to be based.

spa·di·ceous (spā dish′əs), *adj.* **1.** *Bot.* **a.** of the nature of a spadix. **b.** bearing a spadix. **2.** of a bright brown color. [t. NL: m. *spādiceus,* der. L *spādix* SPADIX]

spa·dix (spā′diks), *n., pl.* **spadices** (spā-dī′sēz). *Bot.* an inflorescence consisting of a spike with a fleshy or thickened axis, usually enclosed in a spathe. [t. L, t. Gk.: torn-off palm bough, as adj., brown, palm-colored]

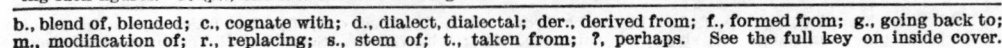
A. Spadix;
B. Spathe

spa·ghet·ti (spə gĕt′ī), *n.* **1.** a kind of food paste of Italian origin in long, slender, solid, cordlike pieces. **2.** *Elect.* an insulating tubing of small diameter into which bare wire can be slipped. [t. It., pl. of *spaghetto,* dim. of *spago* cord]

spa·gyr·ic (spə jīr′īk), *Rare.* —*adj.* **1.** pertaining to alchemy. —*n.* **2.** an alchemist. [t. NL: m.s. *spagiricus,* prob. coined by Paracelsus]

spa·hi (spä′hē), *n., pl.* **-his. 1.** one of a body of native Algerian cavalry in the French service. **2.** (formerly) a cavalryman in the Turkish army. Also, **spa/hee.** [t. Turk.: m. *sipāhī,* t. Pers.]

Spain (spān), *n.* a country in SW Europe: proclaimed a kingdom by Franco, July, 1947. (Including the Balearic and Canary Islands) 29,203,000 pop. (est. 1956); 194,720 sq. mi. *Cap.:* Madrid. Spanish, **España.**

spake (spāk), *v. Archaic.* pt. of **speak.**

Spa·la·to (spä′lä tô′), *n.* Split.

spall (spôl), *n.* **1.** a chip or splinter, as of stone or ore. —*v.t.* **2.** to break into smaller pieces, as ore; split or chip. —*v.i.* **3.** to break or split off in chips or bits. [ME *spalle* chip. Cf. E *spale* chip and *spald,* v., split, c. G *spalten*]

span¹ (spān), *n., v.,* **spanned, spanning.** —*n.* **1.** the distance between the tip of the thumb and the tip of the little finger when the hand is fully extended. **2.** a unit of length corresponding to this distance, commonly taken as 9 inches. **3.** a distance, amount, piece, etc., of this length or of some small extent. **4.** the distance or space between two supports of a bridge. **5.** the full extent, stretch, or reach of anything: *the span of memory.* **6.** *Aeron.* the distance between the wing tips of an airplane. **7.** a short space of time, as the term or period of living. —*v.t.* **8.** to measure by, or as by, the hand with the thumb and little finger extended. **9.** to encircle with the hand or hands, as the waist. **10.** to extend over or across (a space, a river, etc.). **11.** to provide with something that extends over: *to span a river with a bridge.* **12.** to extend, reach, or pass over (space or time). [ME and OE, c. G *spanne*]

span² (spān), *n.* a pair of horses or other animals harnessed and driven together. [t. Flem., D, or LG, der. *spannen* fasten, unite] —**Syn.** See **pair.**

span³ (spān), *v. Archaic.* pt. of **spin.**

Span., Spanish.

Span·dau (spän′dou), *n.* a city in Germany: incorporated into Berlin, 1920. 165,529 (1950).

span·drel (spän′drəl), *n. Archit.* **1.** the triangular space between either half of the extrados of an arch and a rectangular molding or part enclosing the arch. **2.** the space included between the extradoses of two adjacent arches and a horizontal molding or part above. [ME *spaundrell,* appar. dim. of AF *spaundre;* orig. uncert.]

A. Spandrel (def. 1);
B. Spandrel (def. 2)

span·gle (späng′gal), *n., v.,* **-gled, -gling.** —*n.* **1.** a small, thin, often circular piece of glittering material, as metal, for decorating garments, etc. **2.** any small, bright drop, object, spot, or the like. —*v.t.* **3.** to decorate with spangles. **4.** to sprinkle or stud with small, bright pieces, objects, spots, etc. —*v.i.* **5.** to glitter with, or like spangles. [ME *spangele,* f. *spange* spangle (t. MD) + *-le,* dim. suffix]

Span·iard (spän′yərd), *n.* a native or inhabitant of Spain. [ME, t. OF: m. *Espaniard.* See *-ARD*]

span·iel (spän′yəl), *n.* **1.** a dog of any of various breeds of small or medium size, usually with a long, silky coat and drooping ears; used in hunting and as pets. Spaniels are sometimes divided into the **field spaniels,** (more or less for hunting), the **water spaniels,** and the **toy spaniels,** (pets). **2.** a submissive, fawning, or cringing person. [ME *spaynel,* t. OF: m. *espaigneul* Spanish (dog), g. L *Hispaniolus*]

Span·ish (spän′ish), *adj.* **1.** of or pertaining to Spain, its people, or their language. —*n.* **2.** the Spanish people collectively. **3.** a Romance language, the language of Spain, standard also in Latin America (except Brazil) and the Philippine Islands.

Spanish America, the Spanish-speaking countries south of the United States: Mexico, Central America (except British Honduras), South America (except Brazil and the Guianas), and most of the West Indies.

---

b., blend of, blended; **c.,** cognate with; **d.,** dialect, dialectal; **der.,** derived from; **f.,** formed from; **g.,** going back to; **m.,** modification of; **r.,** replacing; **s.,** stem of; **t.,** taken from; **?,** perhaps.   See the full key on inside cover.

Span·ish-A·mer·i·can (spăn′ĭsh ə měr′ə kən), *adj.* **1.** noting or pertaining to the parts of America where Spanish is the prevailing language. **2.** pertaining to Spain and America, sometimes to Spain and the United States: *the Spanish-American War of 1898.* —*n.* **3.** a native or inhabitant of a Spanish-American country, esp. a person of Spanish descent.

Spanish Armada, the fleet sent by Spain against England in 1588, but defeated and later wrecked by storms. See **Armada** (def. 1).

Spanish bayonet, any of certain plants of the liliaceous genus *Yucca,* with narrow, spine-tipped leaves.

Spanish fly, a blister beetle, *Lytta vesicatoria,* which is dried and powdered to yield cantharides, used for raising blisters.

Spanish fly (male), *Lytta vesicatoria* (Ab. ¼ in. long)

Spanish grippe, influenza.

Spanish Guin·ea (gĭn′ĭ), a Spanish colony in W equatorial Africa, consisting of Río Muni on the mainland, and several islands in the Gulf of Guinea. 205,000 (est. 1954); 10,850 sq. mi. *Cap.:* Santa Isabel, on Fernando Po.

Spanish mackerel, any of various scombroid marine food fishes, as *Scomberomorus maculatus* (in the U.S.) or *Pneumatophorus colias* (in England).

Spanish Main, 1. (formerly) the mainland of America adjacent to the Caribbean Sea, esp. between the mouth of the Orinoco river and the Isthmus of Panama. **2.** the Caribbean Sea: the route of the Spanish treasure galleons; a former haunt of pirates.

Spanish Morocco. See **Morocco** (def. 1).

Spanish moss, Florida moss.

Spanish needles, 1. a composite plant, *Bidens bipinnata,* having achenes with downwardly barbed awns. **2.** the achenes of this plant.

Spanish onion, a large-sized, mild, succulent onion, usually sliced and eaten raw.

Spanish paprika, 1. a cultivated, orig. Spanish, pepper, *Capsicum frutescens.* **2.** its pod or condiment.

Spanish Sahara, a territory in NW Africa under Spanish control, comprising Río de Oro, Southern Morocco, and Saguia el Hanra. 37,059 pop. (est. 1951); ab. 103,000 sq. mi. Formerly, **Río de Oro.**

spank (spăngk), *v.t.* **1.** to strike (a person, usually a child) with the open hand, a slipper, etc., esp. on the buttocks, as in punishment. —*n.* **2.** a blow given in spanking; a smart or resounding slap. [imit.]

spank·er (spăngk′ər), *n.* **1.** *Naut.* a. a fore-and-aft sail on the aftermost mast of a ship or barque. See illus. under **sail. b.** (on a schooner-rigged vessel having more than three masts) the fourth mast and sail counting aft from the bow. **2.** *Colloq.* a smartly moving person or animal, esp. a fast horse. [f. *spank* move rapidly (back formation from SPANKING) + -ER¹]

spank·ing (spăngk′ĭng), *adj.* **1.** moving rapidly and smartly. **2.** quick and vigorous, as the pace. **3.** blowing briskly, as a breeze. **4.** *Colloq.* unusually fine, great, large, etc. [cf. Dan. *spanke* strut]

span loading. See loading (def. 4).

span·ner (spăn′ər), *n.* **1.** one who or that which spans. **2.** a tool for clasping and turning a nut or the like. **3.** *Chiefly Brit.* a wrench, esp. one with fixed jaws. [t. G]

spar¹ (spär), *n., v.,* **sparred, sparring.** —*n.* **1.** *Naut.* a stout pole such as those used for masts, etc.; a mast, yard, boom, gaff, or the like. **2.** *Aeron.* a principal lateral member of the framework of a plane of an airplane. —*v.t.* **3.** to provide or make with spars. [ME *sparre,* OE *spearr.* Cf. G *sparren,* Icel. *sperra* rafter]

spar² (spär), *v.,* **sparred, sparring,** *n.* —*v.i.* **1.** to make the motions of attack and defense with the arms and fists; box. **2.** to strike or fight with the feet or spurs, as cocks do. **3.** to bandy words; dispute. —*n.* **4.** a motion of sparring. **5.** a boxing match. **6.** a dispute. [ME; orig. meaning thrust (n. and v.); orig. uncert.]

spar³ (spär), *n.* any of various more or less lustrous crystalline minerals: *fluor spar.* [back formation from *sparstone* spar, OE *spærstān* gypsum. Cf. MLG *spar*]

Spar (spär), *n.* a woman enlisted in the women's reserve of the U.S. Coast Guard. Also, **SPAR.** [from the motto of the Coast Guard, s(EMPER) PAR(ATUS)]

spar·a·ble (spär′ə bəl), *n.* a small, headless nail used by shoemakers. [var. of *sparrow bill*]

spar buoy, *Naut.* a buoy shaped like a log or spar, anchored vertically. See illus. under **buoy.**

spar deck, *Naut.* the upper deck of a vessel, extending from stem to stern. See diag. under **forecastle.**

spare (spär), *v.,* **spared, sparing,** *adj.,* **sparer, sparest,** *n.* —*v.t.* **1.** to refrain from harming or destroying; leave uninjured; forbear to punish: *to spare a fallen adversary.* **2.** to deal gently or leniently with; show consideration for: *to spare a person's feelings.* **3.** to save from strain, discomfort, annoyance, or the like, or from a particular cause of it: *to spare oneself trouble.* **4.** to refrain from, forbear, omit, or withhold, as action or speech. **5.** to refrain from employing, as some instrument, means, aid, etc.: *to spare the rod.* **6.** to set aside for a particular purpose: *to spare land for a garden.* **7.** to part with or let go, as from a supply, esp. without inconvenience or loss: *to spare a sum to a friend.* **8.** to dispense with or do without. **9.** to use economically or frugally; refrain from using up or wasting. —*v.i.* **10.** to use economy; be frugal. **11.** to refrain

from action; forbear. **12.** to refrain from inflicting injury or punishment; exercise lenience or mercy. —*adj.* **13.** kept in reserve, as for possible use: *a spare tire.* **14.** being in excess of present need; free for other use: *spare time.* **15.** frugally restricted; meager, as living, diet, etc. **16.** lean or thin, as a person. **17.** scanty or scant, as in amount, fullness, etc. **18.** sparing, economical, or temperate, as persons. —*n.* **19.** a spare thing, part, etc., as an extra tire for emergency use. **20.** *U.S. Bowling.* a. the knocking down of all the pins with two bowls. b. score so made. [ME; OE *sparian,* c. D and G *sparen*] —**spare′ly,** *adv.* —**spare′ness,** *n.* —**spar′er,** *n.* —Syn. 16. See **thin.**

spare·rib (spär′rĭb′), *n.* a cut of pork containing ribs from the upper or fore end of the row, where there is little meat adhering. [transposed var. of *ribspare,* t. MHG: m. *ribbesper* rib cut. Cf. E *spare,* n., cut, slit]

sparge (spärj), *v.t., v.i.,* **sparged, sparging.** to scatter or sprinkle. [t. L: m.s. *spargere* sprinkle] —**sparg′er,** *n.*

spar·ing (spär′ĭng), *adj.* **1.** that spares. **2.** economical (*in*); chary (*of*). **3.** lenient or merciful. **4.** frugally restricted; limited. —**spar′ing·ly,** *adv.*

spark¹ (spärk), *n.* **1.** an ignited or fiery particle such as is thrown off by burning wood, etc., or produced by one hard body striking against another. **2.** *Elect.* a. the light produced by a sudden discontinuous discharge of electricity through air or another dielectric. b. the discharge itself. c. any electric arc of relatively small energy content. d. such a spark in the spark plug of an internal-combustion engine. e. the arrangement of devices producing and governing this spark. **3.** a small amount or trace of something. **4.** a trace of life or vitality. —*v.i.* **5.** to emit or produce sparks. **6.** to issue as or like sparks. **7.** to send forth gleams or flashes. **8.** (of the ignition in an internal-combustion engine) to function correctly in forming the sparks. —*v.t.* **9.** *Colloq.* to kindle or stimulate (interest, activity, etc.). [ME; OE *spearca,* c. MD and MLG *sparke*]

spark² (spärk), *n.* **1.** a gay, elegant, or showy young man. **2.** a beau, lover, or suitor. —*v.t.* **3.** *Colloq.* to pay attentions to (a woman); court. —*v.i.* **4.** *Colloq.* to engage in courtship; be the beau or suitor. [either fig. use of SPARK¹; or metathetic var. of *sprack* lively, t. Scand.; cf. Icel. *sparkr* sprightly] —**spark′ish,** *adj.*

spark arrester, a device, consisting of wire netting or other material, used to stop or deflect sparks thrown from an open fireplace, a smokestack, or the like.

spark coil, *Elect.* a coil of many turns of insulated wire on an iron core, used for producing sparks.

spark·er (spär′kər), *n.* **1.** something that produces sparks. **2.** an apparatus used to test insulation on wires.

spark gap, *Elect.* a space between two electrodes across which a discharge of electricity may take place.

spark generator, an alternating current power source with a condenser discharging across a spark gap.

spark-kill·er (spärk′kĭl′ər), *n.* *Elect.* a device for preventing injurious sparking in electrical apparatus at points where the circuit is frequently interrupted.

spar·kle (spär′kəl), *v.,* **-kled, -kling,** *n.* —*v.i.* **1.** to issue in or as in little sparks, as fire, light, etc. **2.** to emit little sparks, as burning matter. **3.** to shine with little gleams of light, as a brilliant gem; glisten brightly; glitter. **4.** to effervesce, as wine. **5.** to be brilliant, lively, or vivacious. —*v.t.* **6.** to cause to sparkle. —*n.* **7.** a little spark or fiery particle. **8.** a sparkling appearance, luster, or play of light: *the sparkle of a diamond.* **9.** brilliance; liveliness or vivacity. [freq. of SPARK¹] —Syn. 3. See **glisten.**

spar·kler (spär′klər), *n.* **1.** one who or that which sparkles. **2.** a firework that emits little sparks. **3.** a sparkling gem. **4.** *Colloq.* a bright eye.

spark plug, 1. a device inserted in the cylinder of an internal-combustion engine, containing the two terminals between which passes the electric spark for igniting the explosive gases. **2.** *U.S. Colloq.* a person who leads, inspires, or animates a group.

Sparks (spärks), *n.* **Jared** (jăr′ĭd), 1789–1866, U.S. historian and editor.

spark transmitter, *Radio.* a transmitting set which generates electromagnetic waves because of the characteristic of a spark gap and a tuned circuit through which energy can surge.

spar·ling (spär′lĭng), *n.* the European smelt, *Osmerus eperlanus.* [ME *sperlyng(e),* t. OF: m. *esperlinge,* of Gmc. orig.]

spar·oid (spär′oid, spär′-), *adj.* **1.** resembling a porgy. **2.** belonging or pertaining to the *Sparidae,* a family of deep-bodied fishes including the porgies, the scups, etc. —*n.* **3.** a sparoid fish. [t. NL: s. *Sparoīdēs,* der. L *sparus,* t. Gk.: m. *spáros* kind of fish. See -OID]

spar·row (spär′ō), *n.* **1.** a small, hardy, pugnacious weaverbird, *Passer domesticus,* of Europe, introduced into America, Australia, etc., as a destroyer of insects, but now commonly regarded as a pest; the English sparrow; house sparrow. **2.** any of various weaverbirds (family *Ploceidae*) of the Old World. **3.** any of numerous American finches (family *Fringillidae*), as the **chipping sparrow** (*Spizella passerina*), and **song sparrow** (*Melospiza melodia*). [ME *sparowe,* OE *spearwa,* c. Goth. *sparwa,* Icel. *spörr*]

spar·row·grass (spär′ō grăs′, -gräs′), *n.* *Colloq.* asparagus.

sparrow hawk, 1. a small, short-winged European hawk, *Accipiter nisus,* which preys extensively on birds. **2.** a small American falcon, *Falco sparverius,* which preys especially on grasshoppers, small mammals, etc.

spar·ry (spär/ĭ), *adj.* of or pertaining to mineral spar.

sparse (spärs), *adj.,* **sparser, sparsest. 1.** thinly scattered or distributed: *a sparse population.* **2.** thin; not thick or dense: *sparse hair.* **3.** scanty; meager. [t. L: m.s. *sparsus,* pp., scattered] **—sparse/ly,** *adv.* **—sparse/ness, spar·si·ty** (spär/sə tĭ), *n.* **—Syn. 1.** See **scanty.**

Spar·ta (spär/tə), *n.* an ancient city in S Greece: the capital of Laconia and the chief city of the Peloponnesus; at one time the dominant city of Greece; famous for strict discipline and training of soldiers. Also, **Lacedaemon.**

Spar·ta·cus (spär/tə kəs), *n.* d. 71 B.C., a Thracian who became a slave and gladiator in Italy, and leader of an insurrection of slaves.

Spar·tan (spär/tən), *adj.* **1.** of or pertaining to Sparta or its people. **2.** suggestive of the ancient Spartans; rigorously simple, frugal, or austere; sternly disciplined; brave. **—n. 3.** a native or inhabitant of Sparta. **4.** a person of Spartan characteristics. **—Spar/tan·ism,** *n.*

Spar·tan·burg (spär/tən bûrg/), *n.* a city in NW South Carolina. 44,352 (1960).

Spartan dog, 1. a bloodhound. **2.** a cruel person.

spar·te·ine (spär/tĭ ēn/, -ĭn), *n.* a bitter, poisonous, liquid alkaloid obtained from the common broom, *Cytisus scoparius,* used in medicine. [f. m.s. NL *spartium* genus of broom (der. Gk. *spártos* broom) + -INE²]

spasm (spăz/əm), *n.* **1.** a sudden, abnormal, involuntary muscular contraction; an affection consisting of a continued muscular contraction (**tonic spasm**), or of a series of alternating muscular contractions and relaxations (**clonic spasm**). **2.** any sudden, brief spell of great energy, activity, feeling, etc. [ME *spasme,* t. L: m. *spasmus* or *spasma,* t. Gk.: m. *spasmós* or *spásma*]

spas·mod·ic (spăz mŏd/ĭk), *adj.* **1.** pertaining to or of the nature of a spasm; characterized by spasms. **2.** resembling a spasm or spasms; sudden and violent, but brief; intermittent: *spasmodic efforts.* **3.** given to or characterized by bursts of excitement. Also, **spas·mod/i·cal.** [t. ML: s. *spasmodicus,* der. Gk. *spasmódēs*] **—spas·mod/i·cal·ly,** *adv.*

spastic (spăs/tĭk), *Pathol.* **—adj. 1.** pertaining to, of the nature of, or characterized by spasm, esp. tonic spasm. **—n. 2.** a person exhibiting such spasms, esp. one who has cerebral palsy. [t. L: s. *spasticus,* t. Gk.: m. *spastikós*] **—spas/ti·cal·ly,** *adv.*

spat¹ (spăt), *n., v.* **spatted, spatting. —n. 1.** a petty quarrel. **2.** a light blow; a slap; a smack. **—v.i.** *Colloq.* **3.** to engage in a petty quarrel or dispute. **4.** to slap. **—v.t. 5.** to strike lightly; slap. [prob. imit.]

spat² (spăt), *v.* pt. and pp. of **spit.**

spat³ (spăt), *n.* *(usually pl.)* a short gaiter worn over the instep, usually fastened under the foot with a strap. [short for SPATTERDASH]

spat⁴ (spăt), *n.* **1.** the spawn of an oyster or similar shellfish. **2.** young oysters collectively. **3.** a young oyster. [orig. uncert.; ? akin to SPIT¹, v.]

spate (spāt), *n.* **1.** a sudden, almost overwhelming, outpouring: *a spate of words.* **2.** *Brit.* a flood or inundation; a freshet; a state of flood. **3.** *Brit.* a sudden heavy downpour of rain. [ME; ? OE *spāt-,* as in *spātlian* spit]

spa·tha·ceous (spo thā/shəs), *adj.* *Bot.* **1.** of the nature of or resembling a spathe. **2.** having a spathe.

spathe (spāth), *n.* *Bot.* a bract or pair of bracts, often large and colored, subtending or enclosing a spadix or flower cluster. See **spadix.** [t. Gk.: sword blade] **—spathed,** *adj.* **—spa·those** (spā/thōs, spăth/ōs), *adj.*

spath·ic (spăth/ĭk), *adj.* *Mineral.* like spar. Also, **spath·ose** (spăth/ōs). [f. G *spath* spar + -IC]

spa·tial (spā/shəl), *adj.* **1.** of or pertaining to space. **2.** existing or occurring in space; having extension in space. [f. s. L *spatium* SPACE + -AL] **—spa·ti·al·i·ty** (spā/shĭ ăl/ə tĭ), *n.* **—spa/tial·ly,** *adv.*

spat·ter (spăt/ər), *v.t.* **1.** to scatter or dash in small particles or drops: *to spatter mud.* **2.** to splash with something in small particles: *to spatter the ground with water.* **3.** to sprinkle or spot with something that soils or stains. **—v.i. 4.** to send out small particles or drops, as boiling matter. **5.** to strike as in a shower, as bullets. **—n. 6.** act or the sound of spattering: *the spatter of rain on a roof.* **7.** a splash or spot of something spattered. [appar. a freq. of D and LG *spatten* burst, spout] **—spat/ter·ing·ly,** *adv.*

spat·ter·dash (spăt/ər dăsh/), *n.* *(usually pl.)* a kind of long gaiter worn to protect the trousers or stockings from mud, etc., as in riding. [t. SPATTER + DASH]

spat·ter·dock (spăt/ər dŏk/), *n.* **1.** a coarse yellow-flowered pond lily, *Nymphaea advena,* common in stagnant waters. **2.** any pond lily of genera *Nymphaea* and *Nuphar,* esp. one with yellow flowers.

spat·u·la (spăch/ə lə), *n.* an implement with a broad, flat, flexible blade, used for blending foods, mixing drugs, spreading plasters and paints, etc. [t. L, var. of *spathula,* dim. of *spatha.* See SPADE²] **—spat/u·lar,** *adj.*

spat·u·late (spăch/ə lĭt, -lāt/), *adj.* **1.** shaped like a spatula; rounded more or less like a spoon. **2.** *Bot.* having a broad, rounded end and a narrow, attenuate base, as a leaf.

spav·in (spăv/ĭn), *n.* *Vet. Sci.* **1.** any disease of the hock joint of horses in which enlargements occur, after causing lameness. The enlargement may be due to collection of fluids (**bog spavin**) or to bony growth (**bone spavin**). **2.** an excrescence or enlargement so formed. [ME *spaveyne,* t. OF: m. *espavain;* orig. obscure] **—spav/ined,** *adj.*

Spatulate leaf

spawn (spôn), *n.* **1.** *Zool.* the mass of sex cells of fishes, amphibians, mollusks, crustaceans, etc., after being emitted. **2.** *Bot.* the mycelium of mushrooms, esp. of the species grown for the market. **3.** *Usually Disparaging.* **a.** a swarming brood or numerous progeny. **b.** any person or thing regarded as the offspring of some stock, idea, etc. **—v.i. 4.** to shed the sex cells, esp. as applied to animals that shed eggs and sperm directly into water. **—v.t. 5.** to produce (spawn). **6.** to give birth to; give rise to. **7.** *Usually Disparaging.* to produce in large numbers, or with excessive fecundity. **8.** to plant with mycelium. [ME, t. AF: m. *espaundre* spill, g. L *expandere* expand] **—spawn/er,** *n.*

spay (spā), *v.t.* to remove the ovaries of (a female animal). [ME, t. AF: m.s. *espeier* cut with a sword, der. *espee* sword. See EPEE]

S.P.C.A., Society for the Prevention of Cruelty to Animals.

S.P.C.C., Society for the Prevention of Cruelty to Children.

speak (spēk), *v.,* **spoke** or *(Archaic)* **spake; spoken** or *(Archaic)* **spoke; speaking. —v.i. 1.** to utter words or articulate sounds with the ordinary (talking) voice. **2.** to make oral communication or mention: *to speak to a person of various matters.* **3.** to converse. **4.** to deliver an address, discourse, etc. **5.** to make a plea or recommendation in behalf of somebody or something (fol. by *for*). **6.** to make a statement in written or printed words. **7.** to make communication or disclosure by any means; convey significance. **8.** to emit a sound, as a musical instrument; make a noise or report. **9.** *Chiefly Brit.* (of dogs) to bark when ordered. **10.** to speak of, worth mentioning. **—v.t. 11.** to utter orally and articulately: *to speak words of praise.* **12.** to express or make known with the voice: *to speak the truth.* **13.** to declare in writing or printing, or by any means of communication. **14.** to make known, indicate, or reveal. **15.** to use, or be able to use, in oral utterance, as a language: *to speak French.* **16** to communicate with (a passing vessel, etc.) at sea, as by voice or signal. **17.** to speak to or with. [ME *spek(en),* OE *specan,* unexplained var. of *sprecan,* c. G *sprechen*] **—speak/a·ble,** *adj.* **—Syn. 1.** SPEAK, CONVERSE, TALK mean to make vocal sounds, usually for purposes of communication. To SPEAK is to utter one or more words, not necessarily connected; it usually implies conveying intelligence, and may apply to anything from a few informal words to delivering a formal address before an audience: *to speak sharply.* To CONVERSE is to exchange ideas with someone by speaking: *to converse with a friend.* To TALK is to utter intelligible sounds without regard to content: *the child is learning to talk.*

speak-eas·y (spēk/ē/zĭ), *n., pl.* **-casies.** *U.S. Slang.* a place where intoxicating liquors are illegally sold.

speak·er (spē/kər), *n.* **1.** one who speaks. **2.** one who speaks formally before an audience; an orator. **3.** *(usually cap.)* the presiding officer of the House of Representatives of the U.S., the House of Commons of Great Britain, or some other similar assembly. **4.** *Radio.* a loudspeaker. **5.** a book of selections for practice in declamation. **—speak/er·ship/,** *n.*

speak·ing (spē/kĭng), *n.* **1.** the act, utterance, or discourse of one who speaks. **—adj. 2.** that speaks; giving information as if by speech: *a speaking proof of a thing.* **3.** highly expressive. **4.** lifelike: *a speaking likeness.* **5.** used in, suited to, or involving speaking or talking: *the speaking voice.* **6.** permitting of speaking, as in greeting or conversation: *they are no longer on speaking terms.* **7.** of or pertaining to declamation.

speak·ings (spē/kĭngz), *n.pl.* oral literature.

speaking tube, a tube for conveying the voice to a distance, as from one part of a building to another.

spear¹ (spĭr), *n.* **1.** a weapon for thrusting or throwing, consisting of a long wooden staff to which a sharp head, as of iron or steel, is fixed. **2.** a soldier or other person armed with such a weapon. **3.** some similar weapon or instrument, as one for spearing fish. **4.** act of spearing. **—v.t. 5.** to pierce with or as with a spear. **—v.i. 6.** to go or penetrate like a spear. [ME and OE *spere,* c. D and G *speer*] **—spear/er,** *n.*

spear² (spĭr), *n.* **1.** a sprout or shoot of a plant; an acrospire of grain; a blade of grass, etc. **—v.i. 2.** to sprout; shoot; send up or rise in a spear or spears. [var. of SPIRE¹, ? influenced by SPEAR¹]

spear·fish (spĭr/fĭsh/), *n., pl.* **-fishes,** *(esp. collectively)* **-fish.** a marlin.

spear·head (spĭr/hĕd/), *n.* **1.** the sharp-pointed head which forms the piercing end of a spear. **2.** any person or thing that leads an attack, undertaking, etc. **—v.t. 3.** to act as a spearhead for.

spear·man (spĭr/mən), *n., pl.* **-men.** one who is armed with or uses a spear.

spear·mint (spîr′mĭnt′), *n.* the common mint, *Mentha spicata*, an aromatic herb much used for flavoring. [f. SPEAR¹ + MINT¹]

spear side, the male side, or line of descent, of a family (opposed to *distaff side* or *spindle side*).

spear·wort (spîr′wûrt′), *n.* any of certain crowfoots with long, narrow leaves, as *Ranunculus Flammula* (**lesser spearwort**) and *R. Lingua* (**great spearwort**).

spec., 1. special. 2. specially.

spe·cial (spĕsh′əl), *adj.* 1. of a distinct or particular kind or character: *a special kind of key.* 2. being a particular one; particular, individual, or certain: *a special day.* 3. pertaining or peculiar to a particular person, thing, instance, etc.: *the special features of a plan.* 4. having a particular function, purpose, application, etc.: *a special messenger.* 5. dealing with particulars, or specific, as a statement. 6. distinguished or different from what is ordinary or usual: *a special occasion.* 7. extraordinary; exceptional; exceptional in amount or degree; especial: *special importance.* 8. great; being such in an exceptional degree: *a special friend.* —*n.* 9. a special person or thing. 10. a special train. 11. a special edition of a newspaper. [ME, t. L: s. *speciālis*] —**spe′cial·ly,** *adv.*
—**Syn.** 6. SPECIAL, PARTICULAR, SPECIFIC refer to something pointed out for attention and consideration. SPECIAL means given unusual treatment because of being uncommon: *a special sense of a word.* PARTICULAR implies something selected from the others of its kind and set off from them for attention: *a particular variety of orchid.* SPECIFIC implies plain and unambiguous indication of a particular instance, example, etc.: *a specific instance of cowardice.* —**Ant.** 1. general.

special area. *Brit.* See **distressed area.**

special delivery, an especially fast delivery of mail for an extra fee by a special post-office messenger.

spe·cial·ism (spĕsh′ə lĭz′əm), *n.* devotion or restriction to a special branch of study, etc.

spe·cial·ist (spĕsh′əl ĭst), *n.* 1. one who devotes himself to one subject, or to one particular branch of a subject or pursuit. 2. a medical practitioner who devotes his attention to a particular class of diseases, etc. 3. *U.S. Army.* a soldier of one of four ranks with pay corresponding to that of a noncommissioned officer, but with military position below that of corporal. —**spe′cial·is′tic,** *adj.*

spe·ci·al·i·ty (spĕsh′ĭ ăl′ə tĭ′), *n., pl.* **-ties.** *Preferred in England instead of* **specialty.** 1. special or particular character. 2. a special or distinctive quality or characteristic; a peculiarity. 3. a special point or item; a particular; detail. 4. a specialty, as in study, work, trade, etc. [t. LL: m. *speciālitas.* See SPECIALITY]

spe·cial·ize (spĕsh′ə līz′), *v.,* **-ized, -izing.** —*v.i.* 1. to pursue some special line of study, work, etc.; make a specialty. 2. *Biol.* to become specialized. —*v.t.* 3. to render special or specific; invest with a special character, function, etc. 4. to adapt to special conditions; restrict to specific limits. 5. to restrict payment of (a negotiable instrument) by endorsing over to a specific payee. 6. *Biol.* to modify or differentiate (an organism or one of its organs) to adapt it to a special function or environment. 7. to specify; particularize. Also, *esp. Brit.,* **spe′cial·ise′.** —**spe′cial·i·za′tion,** *n.*

special partner, a partner whose liability for his firm's debts is limited to the amount of his investment.

special pleading, 1. *Law.* pleading that alleges special or new matter in avoidance of the allegations made by the opposite side. 2. pleading or arguing that ignores unfavorable features of a case.

spe·cial·ty (spĕsh′əl tĭ), *n., pl.* **-ties.** 1. a special subject of study, line of work, or the like. 2. an article particularly dealt in, manufactured, etc., or one to which the dealer or manufacturer professes to devote special care. 3. an article of unusual or superior design or quality. 4. a novelty; a new article. 5. an article with such strong consumer demand that it is at least partially removed from price competition. 6. a special or particular point, item, matter, characteristic, or peculiarity. 7. *Law.* a. a special agreement, contract, etc., expressed in an instrument under seal. b. a negotiable instrument not under seal. [ME *specialte,* t. OF: m. *(e)specialte,* t. LL: m.s. *speciālitas*]

spe·cie (spē′shĭ), *n.* 1. coin; coined money. 2. **in specie, a.** in kind. b. (of money) in actual coin. [t. L, abl. sing. of *species* SPECIES]

spe·cies (spē′shĭz; *Lat.* spē′shĭ ēz′), *n., pl.* **-cies.** 1. a class of individuals having some common characteristics or qualities; distinct sort or kind. 2. the basic category of biological classification, intended to designate a single kind of animal or plant, any variations existing among the individuals being regarded as not affecting the essential sameness which distinguishes them from all other organisms. 3. *Logic.* a. a kind or class of things possessing in common certain traits peculiar to them, and included (together with other similar kinds) in a more inclusive kind called the genus: *man and bird are species under the genus animal.* b. the set of things or individuals of the same species. 4. *Eccles.* a. the external form or appearance of the bread or the wine in the Eucharist. b. either of the Eucharistic elements. 5. *Obs.* specie. [t. L: appearance, sort]

specif., 1. specific. 2. specifically.

spec·i·fi·a·ble (spĕs′ə fī′ə bəl), *adj.* that may be specified.

spe·cif·ic (spĭ sĭf′ĭk), *adj.* Also, *Rare,* **spe·cif′i·cal.** 1. having a special application, bearing, or reference; specifying, explicit, or definite: *specific mention.* 2. specified, precise, or particular: *a specific sum of money.* 3. peculiar or proper to something, as qualities, characteristics, effects, etc. 4. of a special or particular kind. 5. *Zool., Bot.* of or pertaining to a species: *specific characters.* 6. *Med.* a. (of a disease) produced by a special cause or infection. b. (of a remedy) having special effect in the prevention or cure of a certain disease. 7. *Com.* denoting customs or duties levied in fixed amounts per unit (number, volume, weight, etc.). —*n.* 8. something specific, as a statement, quality, etc. 9. *Med.* a specific remedy. [t. ML: s. *specificus,* der. L *species*] —**spe·cif′i·cal·ly,** *adv.* —**spec·i·fic·i·ty** (spĕs′ə fĭs′ə tĭ′), *n.* —**Syn.** 1. See special. —**Ant.** 2. vague.

spec·i·fi·ca·tion (spĕs′ə fə kā′shən), *n.* 1. act of specifying. 2. a statement of particulars; a detailed description setting forth the dimensions, materials, etc., for a proposed building, engineering work, or the like. 3. something specified, as in a bill of particulars; a specified particular, item, or article. 4. act of making specific. 5. state of having a specific character.

specific gravity, *Physics.* the ratio of the mass of a given volume of any substance to that of the same volume of some other substance taken as a standard, water being the standard for solids and liquids, and hydrogen or air for gases; relative density.

specific heat, *Physics.* 1. the number of calories required to raise the temperature of 1 gram of a substance 1°C; or the number of BTU's per pound per degree F. 2. (orig.) the ratio of the thermal capacity of a substance to that of some standard material.

spec·i·fy (spĕs′ə fī′), *v.,* **-fied, -fying.** —*v.t.* 1. to mention or name specifically or definitely; state in detail. 2. to give a specific character to. 3. to name or state as a condition. —*v.i.* 4. to make a specific mention or statement. [ME, t. ML: m. *specificāre,* der. *specificus* specific, der. L *species* sort, kind]

spec·i·men (spĕs′ə mən), *n.* 1. a part or an individual taken as exemplifying a whole mass or number; a typical animal, plant, mineral, part, etc. 2. *Colloq.* a person as a specified kind, or in some respect a peculiar kind, of human being. [t. L] —**Syn.** 1. See **example.**

spe·ci·os·i·ty (spē′shĭ ŏs′ə tĭ′), *n., pl.* **-ties.** 1. state of being specious or plausible. 2. something pleasing to the eye but deceptive. 3. *Obs.* state of being beautiful.

spe·cious (spē′shəs), *adj.* 1. fair-seeming, superficially pleasing, or apparently good or right without real merit; plausible: *specious arguments.* 2. pleasing to the eye, but deceptive. 3. *Obs.* pleasing to the eye; fair. [ME, t. L: m.s. *speciōsus* fair, fair-seeming, der. *species* sort, kind] —**spe′cious·ly,** *adv.* —**spe′cious·ness,** *n.* —**Syn.** 1. See **plausible.** —**Ant.** 1. genuine.

speck (spĕk), *n.* 1. a small spot differing in color or substance from that of the surface or material upon which it appears. 2. a very little bit or particle. 3. something appearing small by comparison or by distance. —*v.t.* 4. to mark with, or as with, a speck or specks. [ME *specke,* OE *specca*]

speck·le (spĕk′əl), *n., v.,* **-led, -ling.** —*n.* 1. a small speck, spot, or mark, as on skin. 2. speckled coloring or marking. —*v.t.* 3. to mark with, or as with, speckles. [f. SPECK + -*le,* dim. and freq. suffix]

specs (spĕks), *n.pl. Colloq.* spectacles; eyeglasses.

spec·ta·cle (spĕk′tə kəl), *n.* 1. anything presented to the sight or view, esp. something of a striking kind. 2. a public show or display, esp. on a large scale. 3. (*pl.*) a device to aid defective vision or to protect the eyes from light, dust, etc., consisting usually of two glass lenses set in a frame which rests on the nose and is held in place by pieces passing over or around the ears (often called **a pair of spectacles**). 4. something through which things are viewed or regarded, or by which one's views or opinions are colored or affected. 5. (*often pl.*) something resembling spectacles in shape or function. 6. (*often pl.*) any of various devices suggesting spectacles as one attached to a semaphore to display lights of different colors by colored glass. [ME, t. L: m. *spectāculum*]

spec·ta·cled (spĕk′tə kəld), *adj.* 1. provided with or wearing spectacles. 2. *Zool.* having a marking resembling a pair of spectacles.

spec·tac·u·lar (spĕk tăk′yə lər), *adj.* pertaining to or of the nature of a spectacle; marked by or given to great display; dramatic; thrilling. —**spec·tac′u·lar·ly,** *adv.*

spec·ta·tor (spĕk′tā tər, spĕk tā′-), *n.* 1. one who looks on; an onlooker. 2. one who is present at and views a spectacle or the like. [t. L]

spec·ter (spĕk′tər), *n.* 1. a visible incorporeal spirit, esp. one of a terrifying nature; ghost; phantom; apparition. 2. some object or source of terror or dread. Also, *esp. Brit.,* **spec′tre.** [t. L: m.s. *spectrum* apparition] —**Syn.** 1. See **ghost.**

spec·tra (spĕk′trə), *n.* pl. of **spectrum.**

spec·tral (spĕk′trəl), *adj.* 1. pertaining to or characteristic of a specter; of the nature of a specter. 2. resembling or suggesting a specter. 3. of, pertaining to, or produced by a spectrum or spectra. —**spec·tral·i·ty** (spĕk trăl′ə tĭ′), *n.* —**spec′tral·ly,** *adv.*

spectro-, a word element representing **spectrum.**

spec·tro·bo·lom·e·ter (spĕk′trō bō lŏm′ə tər), *n.* a

combined spectroscope and bolometer, for determining the distribution of radiant heat or energy in a spectrum.

spec·tro·gram (spĕk′trə grăm′), *n.* a representation or photograph of a spectrum.

spec·tro·graph (spĕk′trə grăf′, -gräf′), *n.* **1.** a spectrogram. **2.** an apparatus for making a spectrogram.

spec·tro·he·li·o·gram (spĕk′trō hē′lĭ ə grăm′), *n.* a photograph of the sun made with a spectroheliograph.

spec·tro·he·li·o·graph (spĕk′trō hē′lĭ ə grăf′, -gräf′), *n.* an apparatus for making photographs of the sun with monochromatic light, to show the details of the sun's surface and surroundings as they would appear if only that one kind of light were emitted.

spec·trom·e·ter (spĕk trŏm′ə tər), *n.* any of certain optical instruments for observing a spectrum and measuring the deviation of refracted rays, used for determining wave lengths, angles between faces of a prism, etc.

spec·tro·pho·tom·e·ter (spĕk′trō fō tŏm′ə tər), *n.* an instrument for making photometric comparisons between parts of spectra. —**spec′tro·pho·tom′e·try,** *n.*

spec·tro·scope (spĕk′trə skōp′), *n.* an optical instrument for producing and examining the spectrum of the light or radiation from any source. —**spec·tro·scop·ic** (spĕk′trə skŏp′ĭk), **spec′tro·scop′i·cal,** *adj.* —**spec′tro·scop′i·cal·ly,** *adv.*

spec·tros·co·py (spĕk trŏs′kə pĭ, spĕk′trə skō′pĭ), *n.* the science dealing with the use of the spectroscope and with spectrum analysis. —**spec·tros·co·pist** (spĕk trŏs′kə pĭst, spĕk′trə skō′pĭst), *n.*

spec·trum (spĕk′trəm), *n.*, *pl.* **-tra** (-trə), **-trums.** *Physics.* **1.** the band of colors, or the colored lines or bands, formed when a beam of light from a luminous body or incandescent gas undergoes dispersion by being passed through a prism or reflected from a diffraction grating; the series of colors, passing by insensible degrees from red to violet (ordinarily described as red, orange, yellow, green, blue, indigo, and violet), produced when white light (as sunlight) is passed through a prism, the white light being dispersed into rays of different color and wave length, the rays of longest wave length producing the color red, and the rays of shortest wave length producing the color violet. **2.** this band or series of colors together with extensions at the ends which are not visible to the eye, but which are studied by means of photography, heat effects, etc., and which are produced by the dispersion of radiant energy other than ordinary light rays. [t. L: appearance, form]

spectrum analysis, the determination of the constitution or condition of bodies and substances by means of the spectra they produce.

spec·u·lar (spĕk′yə lər), *adj.* **1.** pertaining to, or having the properties of, a mirror. **2.** pertaining to a speculum. [t. L: s. *speculāris* of or like a mirror]

spec·u·late (spĕk′yə lāt′), *v.*, **-lated, -lating.** —*v.i.* **1.** to engage in thought or reflection, or meditate (often fol. by *on*, *upon*, or a clause). **2.** to indulge in conjectural thought. —*v.t.* **3.** to buy and sell commodities, stocks, etc., in the expectation of profit through a change in their market value; engage in any business transaction involving considerable risk, or the chance of large gains. [t. L: m.s. *speculātus*, pp., observed, examined]

spec·u·la·tion (spĕk′yə lā′shən), *n.* **1.** the contemplation or consideration of some subject. **2.** a single instance or process of consideration. **3.** a conclusion or opinion reached thereby. **4.** conjectural consideration of a matter; conjecture or surmise. **5.** trading in commodities, stocks, etc., in the hope of profit from changes in the market price; engagement in business transactions involving considerable risk but offering the chance of large gains. **6.** a speculative commercial venture or undertaking.

spec·u·la·tive (spĕk′yə lā′tĭv), *adj.* **1.** pertaining to, of the nature of, or characterized by speculation, contemplation, conjecture, or abstract reasoning. **2.** theoretical, rather than practical. **3.** given to speculation, as persons, the mind, etc. **4.** of the nature of or involving commercial or financial speculation. —**spec′u·la′tive·ly,** *adv.* —**spec′u·la′tive·ness,** *n.*

spec·u·la·tor (spĕk′yə lā′tər), *n.* **1.** one engaged in commercial or financial speculation. **2.** a person who purchases in advance tickets for theatrical performances, games, etc., likely to be in demand, in order to sell them later at an increase over the regular price. **3.** one devoted to mental speculation. [t. L: scout, explorer]

spec·u·lum (spĕk′yə ləm), *n.*, *pl.* **-la** (-lə), **-lums.** **1.** a mirror or reflector, esp. one of polished metal, as on a reflecting telescope. **2.** *Surg.* an instrument for rendering a part accessible to observation, as by enlarging an orifice. **3.** *Zool.* a lustrous or specially colored area on the wing of certain birds. [t. L]

sped (spĕd), *v.* pt. and pp. of **speed.**

Spee (shpā), *n.* **Maximilian von** (mäk′sĭ mē′lĭ än′ fən), 1861–1914, German vice-admiral.

speech (spēch), *n.* **1.** the faculty or power of speaking; oral communication; expression of human thought and emotions by speech sounds and gesture. **2.** that which is spoken; an utterance, remark, or declaration: *an eloquent speech.* **3.** a form of communication in spoken language, made by a speaker before an audience for a given purpose. **4.** any single utterance of an actor in the course of the play. **5.** the form of utterance characteristic of a particular people or region; a language or dialect. **6.** manner of speaking, as of a person. **7.** a field of study devoted to the theory and practice of oral communication. **8.** *Archaic.* rumor. [ME *speche*, OE *spǣc,* unexplained var. of *sprǣc,* c. G *sprache*]
—**Syn. 1.** SPEECH, LANGUAGE refer to the means of communication used by people. SPEECH is the expression of ideas and thoughts by means of articulate vocal sounds, or the faculty of thus expressing ideas and thoughts. LANGUAGE is a set of conventional signs, used conventionally and not necessarily articulate or even vocal (any set of signs, signals, or symbols, which convey meaning, including written words, may be called language): *a spoken language.* Thus, LANGUAGE is the set of conventions, and SPEECH is the action of putting these to use: *he couldn't understand the speech of the natives because it was in a foreign language.* **3.** SPEECH, ADDRESS, ORATION, HARANGUE are terms for a communication to an audience. SPEECH is the general word, with no implication of kind or length, or whether planned or not. An ADDRESS is a formal, planned speech, appropriate to a particular subject or occasion. An ORATION is a polished, rhetorical address, given usually on a notable occasion, that employs eloquence and studied methods of delivery. A HARANGUE is a violent, informal speech, often addressed to a casual audience, and intended to arouse strong feeling (sometimes to lead to mob action).

speech clinic, a place at which specialists in speech correction reëducate the speech-handicapped.

speech community, **1.** the aggregate of all the people who use a given language or dialect. **2.** a group of people geographically distributed so that there is no break in intelligibility from place to place.

speech correction, the reëducation of speech habits which deviate from accepted speech standards.

speech·i·fy (spē′chə fī′), *v.i.* **-fied, -fying.** *Depreciatory.* to make a speech or speeches.

speech·less (spēch′lĭs), *adj.* **1.** temporarily deprived of speech by strong emotion, physical weakness, exhaustion, etc.: *speechless with horror.* **2.** characterized by absence or loss of speech: *speechless astonishment.* **3.** lacking the faculty of speech; dumb. **4.** not expressed in speech or words. **5.** refraining from speech. —**speech′less·ly,** *adv.* —**speech′less·ness,** *n.* —**Syn. 1.** See **dumb.**

speech sound, any vocal or articulated sound used in oral communication.

speed (spēd), *n.*, *v.*, **sped** or **speeded, speeding.** —*n.* **1.** rapidity in moving, going, traveling, or any proceeding or performance; swiftness; celerity. **2.** relative rapidity in moving, going, etc.; rate of motion or progress: *full speed ahead.* **3.** *Auto.* a transmission gear ratio. **4.** *Archaic.* success or prosperity. —*v.t.* **5.** to promote the success of (an affair, undertaking, etc.); further, forward, or expedite. **6.** to direct (the steps, course, way, etc.) with speed. **7.** to increase the rate of speed of (usually fol. by *up*): *to speed up industrial production.* **8.** to bring to a particular speed, as a machine. **9.** to cause to move, go, or proceed, with speed. **10.** to expedite the going of: *to speed the parting guest.* **11.** *Archaic.* to cause (a person, etc.) to succeed or prosper. —*v.i.* **12.** to move, go, pass, or proceed with speed or rapidity. **13.** to increase the rate of speed or progress (fol. by *up*). **14.** to get on or fare in a specified or particular manner. **15.** *Archaic.* to succeed or prosper. [ME *spede,* OE *spēd* (c. D *spoed*). Cf. OE *spōwan* prosper, succeed] —**speed′er,** *n.* —**speed′ster,** *n.* —**Syn. 1.** SPEED, VELOCITY agree in meaning rapidity of motion, esp. in relation to time. SPEED (orig. prosperity or success) is now, except in such archaic expressions as *to wish one good speed,* applied to relative rapidity of motion: *the speed of light, a speed of thirty miles an hour.* VELOCITY, the more learned or technical form, is sometimes interchangeable with SPEED *(the velocity of light)*; it is commonly used to refer to high rates of speed, linear or circular: *velocity of a projectile.* **12.** See **rush.** —**Ant. 1.** slowness.

speed·boat (spēd′bōt′), *n.* a motorboat so constructed that it will move rapidly through the water.

speed·om·e·ter (spē dŏm′ə tər), *n.* a device attached to an automobile or the like to record the distance covered in miles and the rate of travel in miles per hour.

speed-up (spēd′ŭp′), *n.* an increasing of speed.

speed·way (spēd′wā′), *n.* a road or course for fast driving, motoring, or the like, or on which more than ordinary speed is allowed.

speed·well (spēd′wĕl), *n.* any of various herbs of the scrophulariaceous genus *Veronica,* as *V. officinalis* (common speedwell) with pale-blue flowers, or *V. Chamaedrys* (germander speedwell) with bright-blue flowers.

speed·y (spē′dĭ), *adj.,* **speedier, speediest.** **1.** characterized by speed; rapid; swift; fast. **2.** coming, given, or arrived at, quickly or soon; prompt; not delayed: *speedy recovery.* —**speed′i·ly,** *adv.* —**speed′i·ness,** *n.*

speiss (spīs), *n.* a product consisting chiefly of one or more metallic arsenides (as of iron, nickel, etc.), obtained in smelting certain ores. [t. G: m. *speise,* lit., food]

spe·lae·an (spĭ lē′ən), *adj.* of, pertaining to, or inhabiting caves. Also, **spe·le′an.** [f. s. NL *spelaeus* (der. L *spēlaeum* cave, t. Gk.: m. *spēlaion*) + -AN]

spe·le·ol·o·gy (spē′lē ŏl′ə jĭ), *n.* the exploration and study of caves. Also, **spe·lae·ol′o·gy.** —**spe′le·o·log′i·cal,** *adj.* —**spe′le·ol′o·gist,** *n.*

spell¹ (spĕl), *v.,* **spelled** or **spelt, spelling.** —*v.t.* **1.** to name, write, or otherwise give (as by signals), in order, the letters of (a word, syllable, etc.). **2.** (of letters) to

---

b., blend of, blended; c., cognate with; d., dialect, dialectal; der., derived from; f., formed from; g., going back to; m., modification of; r., replacing; s., stem of; t., taken from; ?, perhaps. See the full key on inside cover.

form (a word, syllable, etc.). **3.** to read letter by letter or with difficulty (often fol. by *out*). **4.** to discern or find, as if by reading or study (often fol. by *out*). **5.** to signify; amount to: *this delay spells disaster for us.* —*v.i.* **6.** to name, write, or give the letters of words, etc. **7.** to express words by letters, esp. correctly. [ME, t. OF: m.s. *espeller*, of Gmc. orig.; akin to SPELL²]

spell² (spĕl), *n.* a form of words supposed to possess magic power; a charm, incantation, or enchantment. **2.** any dominating or irresistible influence; fascination. [ME and OE *spell* discourse. Cf. SPIEL]

spell³ (spĕl), *n.* **1.** a continuous course or period of work or other activity: *to take a spell at the wheel.* **2.** a turn of work so taken. **3.** a turn, bout, fit, or period of anything experienced or occurring: *a spell of coughing.* **4.** *U.S. Colloq.* a fit of some personal ailment, disturbance of temper, or the like. **5.** *Colloq.* an interval or space of time, usually indefinite or short. **6.** a period of weather of a specified kind: *a hot spell.* **7.** *Australia.* an interval or period of rest. **8.** *Rare.* a person or set of persons taking a turn of work to relieve another. [OE *gespelia*, n., substitute. Cf. *spala* in same sense] —*v.t.* **9.** *Chiefly U.S.* to take the place of or relieve (a person, etc.) for a time. **10.** *Chiefly Australia.* to give an interval of rest to. —*v.i.* **11.** *Australia.* to take an interval of rest. [var. of d. *spele*, OE *spelian* represent]

spell·bind (spĕl′bīnd′), *v.t.* **-bound, -binding.** to render spellbound; bind or hold as by a spell.

spell·bind·er (spĕl′bīn′dər), *n. U.S. Colloq.* a speaker, esp. a politician, who holds his audience spellbound.

spell·bound (spĕl′bound′), *adj.* bound by, or as by, a spell; enchanted, entranced, or fascinated: *a spellbound audience.* [f. SPELL² + BOUND¹]

spell·er (spĕl′ər), *n.* **1.** one who spells words, etc. **2.** an elementary textbook or manual to teach spelling.

spell·ing (spĕl′ĭng), *n.* **1.** the manner in which words are spelled; orthography. **2.** a group of letters representing a word. **3.** the act of a speller.

spelling pronunciation, a pronunciation based on the spelling, usually a variant of the traditional pronunciation.

Spell·man (spĕl′mən), *n.* **Francis Joseph,** born 1889, U.S. Roman Catholic clergyman: cardinal since 1946.

spelt¹ (spĕlt), *v.* pt. and pp. of spell¹.

spelt² (spĕlt), *n.* a kind of wheat, *Triticum spelta* (or a race of *T. sativum*), anciently much cultivated, used in developing improved varieties of wheat. [OE (c. G *spelz, spelt*), t. LL: s. *spelta*]

spel·ter (spĕl′tər), *n.* zinc, esp. in the form of ingots.

spe·lun·ker (spē′lŭngk′ər), *n.* one who explores caves.

Spen·cer (spĕn′sər), *n.* **Herbert,** 1820–1903, British philosopher.

spen·cer¹ (spĕn′sər), *n.* a short coat or jacket, worn by men and women. [named after George John *Spencer*, second Earl of Spencer (1758–1834)]

spen·cer² (spĕn′sər), *n. Naut.* a trysail, usually used as a storm sail. [orig. uncert.]

Spen·ce·ri·an (spĕn sĭr′Ĭ ən), *adj.* **1.** of Herbert Spencer or his philosophy. **2.** of a system of penmanship, characterized by clear, rounded letters slanting to the right. —*n.* **3.** a follower of Herbert Spencer.

Spen·ce·ri·an·ism (spĕn sĭr′Ĭ ən Ĭz′əm), *n.* the philosophy of Herbert Spencer, who attempted to bring the various sciences into a systematic whole.

spend (spĕnd), *v.,* **spent, spending.** —*v.t.* **1.** to pay out, disburse, or expend; dispose of (money, wealth, resources, etc.). **2.** to employ (labor, thought, words, time, etc.) on some object, in some proceeding, etc. **3.** to pass (time) in a particular manner, place, etc. **4.** to use up, consume, or exhaust: *the storm had spent its fury.* **5.** to give (one's blood, life, etc.) for some cause. —*v.i.* **6.** to spend money, etc. **7.** *Obs.* to be consumed or exhausted. [ME *spende*, OE *spendan* (c. G *spenden*), ult. t. L: m. *expendere* EXPEND] —**spend′er,** *n.*
—**Syn. 1.** SPEND, DISBURSE, EXPEND, SQUANDER refer to paying out money. SPEND is the general word: *we spend more for living expenses now.* DISBURSE implies expending from a specific source or sum to meet specific obligations, or paying in definite allotments: *the treasurer has authority to disburse funds.* EXPEND is more formal, and implies spending for some definite and (usually) sensible or worthy object: *to expend most of one's salary on necessities.* SQUANDER suggests lavish, wasteful, or foolish expenditure: *to squander a legacy.* —Ant. **1.** save, keep.

Spen·der (spĕn′dər), *n.* **Stephen,** born 1909, British poet and critic.

spending money, money for small personal expenses.

spend·thrift (spĕnd′thrĭft′), *n.* **1.** one who spends his possessions or money extravagantly or wastefully; a prodigal. —*adj.* **2.** wastefully extravagant; prodigal.

Speng·ler (spĕng′glər; *Ger.* shpĕng′lər), *n.* **Oswald** (ôs′vält), 1880–1936, German philosophical writer.

Spen·ser (spĕn′sər), *n.* **Edmund,** c1552–99, English poet.

Spen·se·ri·an (spĕn sĭr′Ĭ ən), *adj.* **1.** of or characteristic of Spenser or his work. —*n.* **2.** an imitator of Spenser. **3.** a Spenserian stanza. **4.** verse in Spenserian stanzas.

Spenserian stanza, the stanza used by Spenser in his *Faerie Queene* and employed since by other poets, consisting of eight iambic pentameter lines and a final Alexandrine, with a rhyme scheme of ababbcbcc.

spent (spĕnt), *v.* **1.** pt. and pp. of spend. —*adj.* **2.** used up, consumed, or exhausted.

sperm¹ (spûrm), *n.* **1.** spermatic fluid. **2.** a male reproductive cell; a spermatozoön. [ME *sperme*, t. L: m. *sperma*, t. Gk.]

sperm² (spûrm), *n.* **1.** spermaceti. **2.** sperm whale. **3.** sperm oil. [abbr. of defs. above]

sperm-, a word element representing **sperm¹.** Also, **spermo-.**

-sperm, a terminal combining form of **sperm**, as in *angiosperm.*

sper·ma·cet·i (spûr′mə sĕt′Ĭ, -sē′tĬ), *n.* a whitish, waxy substance obtained from the oil in the head of the sperm whale, used in making ointments, cosmetics, etc. [t. ML: orig. phrase *sperma cēti* sperm of whale]

-spermal, a word element used to form adjectives related to **sperm.** [f. -SPERM + -AL¹]

sper·ma·ry (spûr′mə rĬ), *n., pl.* **-ries.** a sperm gland: an organ in which spermatozoa are generated; testis.

sper·mat·ic (spûr măt′Ĭk), *adj.* **1.** of, pertaining to, or of the nature of sperm; seminal; generative. **2.** pertaining to a spermary.

spermatic cord, *Anat.* the solid neck of the spermatic sac by which the testicle is suspended within the scrotum; it contains the vas deferens, the blood vessels and nerves of the testicles, etc.

spermatic fluid, the male generative fluid; semen.

spermatic sac, *Anat.* the hollow portion of the inguinal bursa which contains the testis and is lined by peritoneum.

sper·ma·ti·um (spûr mā′shĬ əm), *n., pl.* **-tia** (-shĬ ə). *Bot.* **1.** the nonmotile male gamete of the red algae. **2.** a minute, colorless cell (conjectured to be a male reproductive body) developed within spermogonia. [NL, t. Gk.: m. *spermation,* dim. of *sperma* SPERM]

spermato-, var. of **sperm-.** Also, **spermat-.** [t. Gk., comb. form of *sperma* SPERM]

sper·ma·to·cyte (spûr′mə tə sīt′), *n. Biol.* a male germ cell at the maturation stage, giving rise to spermatozoids and spermatozoa.

sper·ma·to·gen·e·sis (spûr′mə tə jĕn′ə sĬs), *n. Biol.* the genesis or origin and development of spermatozoa. —**sper·ma·to·ge·net·ic** (spûr′mə tō jə nĕt′Ĭk), *adj.*

sper·ma·to·go·ni·um (spûr′mə tə gō′nĬ əm), *n., pl.* **-nia** (-nĬ ə). *Biol.* one of the primitive germ cells giving rise to spermatocytes. [NL. See SPERMATO-, -GONIUM] —**sper·ma·to·go′ni·al,** *adj.*

sper·ma·toid (spûr′mə toid′), *adj.* resembling sperm.

sper·ma·to·phore (spûr′mə tə fōr′), *n. Zool.* a special case or capsule containing a number of spermatozoa, produced by the male of certain insects, mollusks, annelids, etc., and some vertebrates. —**sper·ma·toph·o·ral** (spûr′mə tŏf′ə rəl), *adj.*

sper·ma·to·phyte (spûr′mə tə fīt′), *n.* any of the *Spermatophyta,* a primary division or group of plants embracing those that bear seeds. —**sper·ma·to·phyt·ic** (spûr′mə tə fĬt′Ĭk), *adj.*

sper·ma·tor·rhe·a (spûr′mə tə rē′ə), *n. Pathol.* abnormally frequent involuntary emission of semen.

sper·ma·to·zo·id (spûr′mə tə zō′Ĭd), *n. Bot.* a motile male gamete produced in an antheridium. [f. SPERMATO-ZO(ON) + -ID]

sper·ma·to·zo·ön (spûr′mə tə zō′ŏn, -ən), *n., pl.* **-zoa** (-zō′ə). *Biol.* one of the minute, usually actively motile, gametes in semen, which serve to fertilize the ovum; a mature male reproductive cell. —**sper·ma·to·zo′al, sper·ma·to·zo′an, sper·ma·to·zo′ic,** *adj.*

sper·mic (spûr′mĬk), *adj.* spermatic.

spermo-, var. of **sperm-,** before consonants.

sper·mo·go·ni·um (spûr′mə gō′nĬ əm), *n., pl.* **-nia** (-nĬ ə). *Bot.* one of the cup-shaped or flask-shaped receptacles in which the spermatia of certain thallophytic plants are produced. [NL. See SPERMO-, -GONIUM]

sperm oil, an oil from the sperm whale.

sper·mo·phile (spûr′mə fĬl′, -fĬl), *n.* any of various burrowing rodents of the squirrel family, esp. of the genus *Citellus* (or *Spermophilus*), sometimes sufficiently numerous to do much damage to crops, as the ground squirrels, susliks, etc.

sper·mo·phyte (spûr′mə fĬt′), *n. Bot.* spermatophyte.

sper·mous (spûr′məs), *adj.* of the nature of, or pertaining to, sperm.

sperm whale, a large, square-headed whale, *Physeter macrocephalus,* valuable for oil and spermaceti; cachalot.

Sperm whale, *Physeter macrocephalus*
(Male 70 to 85 ft. long,
female 23 to 30 ft. long)

sper·ry·lite (spĕr′ə līt′), *n.* a mineral, platinum arsenide, PtAs₂, occurring in minute tin-white crystals, usually cubes: a minor ore of platinum. [named after F. L. *Sperry,* of Sudbury, Ontario, Canada, where it was found. See -LITE]

spew (spū), *v.i.* **1.** to discharge the contents of the stomach through the mouth; vomit. —*v.t.* **2.** to eject from the stomach through the mouth; vomit. —*n.* **3.** that which is spewed; vomit. Also, **spue** (for 1, 2). [ME; OE *spīwan,* c. G *speien.* Cf. L *spuere*] —**spew′er,** *n.*

Spey·er (shpī′ər), *n.* a city in SW West Germany, on the Rhine. 35,000 (est. 1953). Also, **Spires.**

Spe·zia (spē′tsyä), *n.* See **La Spezia.**

sp. gr., specific gravity.

sphac·e·late (sfăs′ə lāt′), *v.t., v.i.,* **-lated, -lating.** *Pathol.* to affect or be affected with sphacelus; mortify. —**sphac′e·la′tion,** *n.*

sphac·e·lus (sfăs′ə ləs), *n. Pathol.* a gangrenous or mortified mass of tissue. [t. L, t. Gk.: m. *sphákelos*]

sphag·nous (sfăg′nəs), *adj.* pertaining to, abounding in, or consisting of sphagnum.

sphag·num (sfăg′nəm), *n.* any of the soft mosses constituting the genus *Sphagnum,* found chiefly on the surface of bogs, used in the mass by gardeners in potting and packing plants, and in surgery for dressing wounds, etc. [NL, t. Gk.: m. *sphágnos* a moss]

sphal·er·ite (sfăl′ə rīt′, sfā′lə-), *n.* a very common mineral, zinc sulfide, ZnS, usually containing some iron and a little cadmium, occurring in yellow, brown, or black crystals or cleavable masses with resinous luster: the principal ore of zinc and cadmium blende; blackjack. [f. s. Gk. *sphalerós* deceptive, uncertain + -ITE[1]]

sphene (sfēn), *n.* the mineral, calcium titanium silicate, CaTiSiO$_5$, occurring in many rocks, usually in wedge-shaped crystals. [t. Gk.: m. *sphēn* wedge; with reference to the shape of its crystals]

sphe·nic (sfē′nĭk), *adj.* wedge-shaped. [f. Gk. *sphēn* wedge + -IC]

sphe·no·gram (sfē′nə grăm′), *n.* a cuneiform character. [f. *spheno-* (t. Gk., comb. form of *sphēn* wedge) + -GRAM]

sphe·noid (sfē′noid), *adj.* Also, **sphe·noi′dal. 1.** wedge-shaped. **2.** *Anat.* noting or pertaining to the compound bone of the base of the skull, at the root of the pharynx. —*n.* **3.** *Anat.* the sphenoid bone. [t. NL: s. *sphēnoïdes,* t. Gk.: m. *sphēnoeides* wedgelike]

spher·al (sfîr′əl), *adj.* **1.** of or pertaining to a sphere. **2.** spherical. **3.** symmetrical; perfect in form.

sphere (sfîr), *n., v.,* **sphered, sphering.** —*n.* **1.** a solid geometrical figure generated by the revolution of a semicircle about its diameter; a round body whose surface is at all points equidistant from the center. **2.** any rounded body approximately of this form; a globular mass, shell, etc. **3.** a heavenly body; a planet or star. **4.** celestial sphere. **5.** *Ancient Astronomy.* any of the transparent, concentric, spherical shells, or "heavens," in which the planets, fixed stars, etc., were supposed to be set. **6.** the place or environment within which a person or thing exists; a field of activity or operation: *to be out of one's sphere.* **7.** a particular social world, stratum of society, or walk of life. **8.** a field of something specified: *a sphere of influence.* —*v.t.* **9.** to enclose in, or as in, a sphere. **10.** to form into a sphere. **11.** to place among the heavenly bodies. [ME, t. LL: m. *sphēra,* t. Gk.: m. *sphaīra*] —**sphere′like′,** *adj.* —**Syn. 2.** See **ball**[1].

-sphere, a word element representing **sphere,** as in *planisphere;* having a special use in the names of the layers of gases, etc., surrounding the earth and other celestial bodies, as in *ionosphere.*

spher·i·cal (sfĕr′ə kəl), *adj.* **1.** having the form of a sphere; globular. **2.** formed in or on a sphere, as a figure. **3.** of or pertaining to a sphere or spheres: *spherical trigonometry.* **4.** pertaining to the heavenly bodies, or to their supposed revolving spheres or shells. **5.** pertaining to the heavenly bodies regarded astrologically as exerting influence on mankind and events. Also, **spher′ic.** —**spher′i·cal′i·ty,** *n.* —**spher′i·cal·ly,** *adv.*

spherical aberration, variation in focal length of a lens from center to edge, due to its spherical shape.

spherical angle, *Geom.* an angle formed by arcs of great circles of a sphere.

spherical sailing, a method of navigation in which the curvature of the earth is taken into consideration.

spherical triangle, *Geom.* a triangle formed by arcs of great circles of a sphere.

sphe·ric·i·ty (sfĭ rĭs′ə tĭ), *n., pl.* **-ties.** spherical state or form.

spher·ics[1] (sfĕr′ĭks), *n. Math.* the geometry and trigonometry of figures formed on the surface of a sphere. [pl. of SPHERIC. See -ICS]

spher·ics[2] (sfĕr′ĭks), *n.* a branch of meteorology in which weather forecasting and atmospheric conditions are studied by means of electronic devices. [f. (ATMO) SPHERIC + -s. See ICS]

sphe·roid (sfĭr′oid), *Geom. n.* **1.** a solid of revolution obtained by rotating an ellipse about one of its two axes. See diag. under **prolate.** —*adj.* **2.** spheroidal.

sphe·roi·dal (sfĭ roi′dəl), *adj.* **1.** pertaining to a spheroid or spheroids. **2.** shaped like a spheroid; approximately spherical. Also, **sphe·roi′dic.** —**sphe·roi′dal·ly,** *adv.*

sphe·roi·dic·i·ty (sfĭr′oi dĭs′ə tĭ), *n.* spheroidal state or form. Also, **sphe·roi·di·ty** (sfĭ roi′də tĭ).

sphe·rom·e·ter (sfĭ rŏm′ə tər), *n.* an instrument for measuring the curvature of spheres and curved surfaces.

spher·ule (sfĕr′ōōl), *n.* a small sphere or spherical body. [t. L: m. *sphaerula,* dim. of *sphaera* SPHERE]

spher·u·lite (sfĕr′ōō līt′), *n.* a rounded aggregate of radiating crystals formed in certain igneous rocks. —**spher·u·lit·ic** (sfĕr′ōō lĭt′ĭk), *adj.*

spher·y (sfĭr′ĭ), *adj. Poetic or Rare.* **1.** having the form of a sphere; spherelike. **2.** pertaining to the heavenly bodies, or to their supposed revolving spheres or shells. **3.** resembling a heavenly body; starlike.

sphinc·ter (sfĭngk′tər), *n. Anat.* a circular band of voluntary or involuntary muscle which encircles an orifice of the body or one of its hollow organs. [t. L, t. Gk.: m. **sphinktēr** band] —**sphinc′ter·al,** *adj.*

sphinx (sfĭngks), *n., pl.* **sphinxes, sphinges** (sfĭn′jēz). **1.** *Egypt. Antiq.* **a.** a figure of an imaginary creature having the head of a man or an animal and the body of a lion. **b.** (*usually cap.*) the colossal recumbent stone figure of this kind near the pyramids of Gizeh. **2.** (*cap.*) *Gk. Myth.* a fabulous monster of Greek mythology, variously represented, commonly with the head and breast of a woman, the body of a lion or a dog, and wings, which proposed a riddle to passers-by near Thebes, killing those unable to guess it. Oedipus solved it and the Sphinx killed herself. **3.** some similar monster. **4.** a sphinxlike person or thing, as one presenting difficult questions or being of an inscrutable nature. [t. L, t. Gk.]

Greek sphinx

sphinx moth, a hawk moth.

sphra·gis·tic (sfrə jĭs′tĭk), *adj.* of or pertaining to seals or signet rings. [t. Gk.: m.s. *sphrāgistikós*]

sphra·gis·tics (sfrə jĭs′tĭks), *n.* the scientific study of seals or signet rings.

sp. ht., specific heat.

sphyg·mic (sfĭg′mĭk), *adj. Physiol., etc.* of or pertaining to the pulse. [t. Gk.: m.s. *sphygmikós*]

sphygmo-, a word element meaning "pulse." Also, before vowels, **sphygm-.** [t. Gk., comb. form of *sphygmós*]

sphyg·mo·gram (sfĭg′mə grăm′), *n.* a tracing or diagram produced by a sphygmograph.

sphyg·mo·graph (sfĭg′mə grăf′, -gräf′), *n.* an instrument for recording the rapidity, strength, and uniformity of the arterial pulse. —**sphyg′mo·graph′ic,** *adj.*

sphyg·moid (sfĭg′moid), *adj. Physiol., etc.* resembling the pulse; pulselike.

sphyg·mo·ma·nom·e·ter (sfĭg′mō mə nŏm′ə tər), *n. Physiol.* an instrument for measuring the pressure of the blood in an artery. [f. SPHYGMO- + MANOMETER]

sphyg·mom·e·ter (sfĭg mŏm′ə tər), *n.* an instrument for measuring the strength of the pulse.

sphyg·mus (sfĭg′məs), *n. Physiol.* the pulse. [NL, t. Gk.: m. *sphygmós* pulsation]

spi·ca (spī′kə), *n., pl.* **-cae** (-sē). **1.** *Archaeol.* an ear of grain. **2.** a type of bandage extending from an extremity to the trunk by means of successive turns and crosses. **3.** (*cap.*) Alpha Virginis, a white star of the first magnitude in the constellation Virgo. [t. L]

spi·cate (spī′kāt), *adj. Bot.* **1.** having spikes, as a plant. **2.** arranged in spikes, as flowers. **3.** in the form of a spike, as in inflorescence. [t. L: m.s. *spīcātus* pp., furnished with spikes]

spic·ca·to (spĕk kä′tô), *adj. Music.* detached; (in violin playing) noting distinct tones produced by short, abrupt, rebounding motions of the bow. [It., pp. of *spiccare* detach, separate]

spice (spīs), *n., v.,* **spiced, spicing.** —*n.* **1.** any of a class of pungent or aromatic substances of vegetable origin, as pepper, cinnamon, cloves, and the like, used as seasoning, preservatives, etc. **2.** such substances as material or collectively. **3.** *Poetic.* a spicy or aromatic odor or fragrance. **4.** something that gives zest. **5.** a piquant element or quality; zest, piquancy, or interest. —*v.t.* **6.** to prepare or season with a spice or spices. **7.** to give zest, piquancy, or interest to by something added. [ME, t. OF: m. *espice,* t. L: m. *species* SPECIES]

spice·ber·ry (spīs′bĕr′ĭ), *n., pl.* **-ries. 1.** the checkerberry or American wintergreen, *Gaultheria procumbens.* **2.** a myrtaceous Caribbean tree, *Eugenia rhombea,* cultivated in Florida for its black or orange fruit.

spice·bush (spīs′bŏŏsh′), *n.* a yellow-flowered lauraceous shrub, *Lindera Benzoin,* of North America whose bark and leaves have a spicy odor.

Spice Islands, Moluccas.

spic·er·y (spī′sər ĭ), *n., pl.* **-eries. 1.** spices. **2.** spicy flavor or fragrance. **3.** *Obs.* a storeroom or place for spices. [ME, t. OF: m. *espicerie,* der. *espice* SPICE]

spick-and-span (spĭk′ən spăn′), *adj.* **1.** neat and clean. **2.** perfectly new; fresh. [short for *spick-and-span-new,* var. of *span-new,* t. Scand.; cf. Icel. *spánnýr,* lit., chip-new]

spic·u·la (spĭk′yə lə), *n., pl.* **-lae** (-lē′). a spicule. [NL, dim. of L *spica* SPIKE[2]. Cf. SPICULUM]

spic·u·late (spĭk′yə lāt′, -lĭt), *adj.* **1.** having the form of a spicule. **2.** covered with or having spicules; consisting of spicules. Also, **spic·u·lar** (spĭk′yə lər). [t. L: m.s. *spīculātus,* pp., pointed]

spic·ule (spĭk′ūl), *n.* **1.** a small or minute, slender, sharp-pointed body or part; a small, needlelike crystal, process, or the like. **2.** *Zool.* one of the small, hard, calcareous or siliceous bodies which serve as the skeletal elements of various animals. [t. L. See SPICULA]

spic·u·lum (spĭk′yə ləm), *n., pl.* **-la** (-lə). *Zool.* a small, needlelike body, part, process, or the like. [t. L, dim. of *spīca* SPIKE[2]]

spic·y (spī′sĭ), *adj.,* **spicier, spiciest. 1.** seasoned with or containing spice. **2.** characteristic or suggestive of spice. **3.** of the nature of or resembling spice. **4.** abounding in or yielding spices. **5.** aromatic or fragrant. **6.** piquant or pungent: *spicy criticism.* **7.** of a somewhat improper nature. **8.** *Slang.* full of spirit. —**spic/i·ly,** *adv.* —**spic/i·ness,** *n.*

spi·der (spī/dər), *n.* **1.** *Zool.* any of the eight-legged, wingless, predaceous, insectlike arachnids which constitute the order *Araneae,* most of which spin webs that serve as nests and as traps for prey. **2.** any of various other arachnids resembling or suggesting these. **3.** any of various things resembling or suggesting a spider. **4.** a frying pan, orig. one with legs or feet. **5.** a trivet or tripod, as for supporting a pot or pan on a hearth. **6.** an evil person who entraps others, or lures them by his wiles. **7.** a pulverizing instrument used with a cultivator. [ME *spithre,* OE *spīthra,* c. Dan. *spinder,* lit., spinner]

Garden spider,
Aranea diadema
(½ in. long)

spider crab, any of various crabs with long, slender legs and comparatively small triangular body.

spider monkey, any of various acrobatic monkeys of tropical America, genera *Ateles,* with a slender body, long slender limbs, and a long prehensile tail.

spider phaeton, a lightly built cart, phaeton, or wagon with a high body and large slender wheels.

spi·der·wort (spī/dər wûrt/), *n.* **1.** any plant of the genus *Tradescantia,* comprising perennial herbs with blue-, purple-, or rose-colored flowers. **2.** any plant of the same family (*Commelinaceae*).

Spider monkey,
Ateles paniscus
(Total length ab. 5 ft.,
tail 3 ft.)

spi·der·y (spī/dər ī), *adj.* **1.** like a spider or a spider's web. **2.** full of spiders.

spie·gel·ei·sen (spē/gəl ī/zən), *n.* a lustrous, crystalline pig iron containing a large amount of manganese, sometimes fifteen percent or more, used in making steel. [t. G: lit. mirror-iron]

spiel (spēl), *U.S. Slang.* —*n.* **1.** a talk or speech. —*v.i.* **2.** to talk or speak; orate. [t. d. G: *gossip, talk*]

spi·er (spī/ər), *n.* one who spies, watches, or discovers.

spiff·y (spīf/ī), *adj.,* **spiffier, spiffiest.** *Slang.* spruce; smart; fine.

spig·ot (spīg/ət), *n.* **1.** a small peg or plug for stopping the vent of a cask, etc. **2.** a small peg which stops the passage in the faucet of a cask, etc. **3.** *U.S.* a faucet or cock for controlling the flow of liquid from a pipe or the like. **4.** the end of a pipe which enters the enlarged end of another pipe to form a joint. [ME, var. of *spicket,* der. SPIKE¹]

spike¹ (spīk), *n., v.,* **spiked, spiking.** —*n.* **1.** a large, strong nail or pin, esp. of iron, as for fastening rails to ties. **2.** a stiff, sharp-pointed piece or part. **3.** a sharp-pointed piece of metal, etc., fastened in something, with the point outward, as for defense. **4.** a sharp metal projection on the sole of a shoe, as of a baseball player, to prevent slipping. **5.** the antler of a young deer, when straight and without branches. **6.** a young mackerel about six inches long. —*v.t.* **7.** to fasten or secure with a spike or spikes. **8.** to provide or set with a spike or spikes. **9.** to pierce with or impale on a spike. **10.** to set or stud with something suggesting spikes. **11.** to injure (another player or a competitor) with the spikes of one's shoe, as in baseball. **12.** to render (a muzzle-loading gun) useless by driving a spike into the touchhole. **13.** to make ineffective, or frustrate the action or purpose of: *to spike a rumor.* **14.** *Slang.* to add alcoholic liquor to (a drink or beverage, in itself usually nonalcoholic). [ME, t. Scand.; cf. Norw. *spik* nail, c. OE *spīc-* in *spīcing* nail] —**spike/like/,** *adj.*

A B C
Spikes (def. 1)
A. Dock spike;
B. Large nail;
C. Railroad
spike

spike² (spīk), *n.* **1.** an ear, as of wheat or other grain. **2.** *Bot.* an inflorescence in which the flowers are sessile (or apparently so) along an elongated, unbranched axis. [ME *spik,* L: m.s. *spica* ear of grain]

spike lavender, a species of lavender, *Lavandula latifolia,* having spikes of pale purple flowers, and yielding an oil (**oil of spike**) used in painting, etc.

spike·let (spīk/lĭt), *n. Bot.* a small or secondary spike in grasses; one of the flower clusters, the unit of inflorescence (consisting of two or more flowers and subtended by one or more glumes variously disposed around a common axis).

A B
Spikes
A. Plantain,
Plantago maior;
B. Barley,
genus *Hordeum*

spike·nard (spīk/nərd, -närd), *n.* **1.** an aromatic East Indian valerianaceous plant, *Nardostachys Jatamansi,* supposedly the same as the ancient nard. **2.** an aromatic substance used by the ancients, supposed to be obtained from this plant. **3.** any of various other plants, esp. an American araliaceous herb, *Aralia racemosa,* with an aromatic root. [ME, t. ML: m. *spīca nardī* spike of nard]

spik·y (spī/kī), *adj.* **1.** having a spike or spikes. **2.** having the form of a spike; spikelike.

spile (spīl), *n., v.,* **spiled, spiling.** —*n.* **1.** a peg or plug of wood, esp. one used as a spigot. **2.** a spout for conducting sap from the sugar maple. **3.** a heavy stake or beam driven into the ground, etc., as a support; a pile. —*v.t.* **4.** to stop up (a hole) with a spile or peg. **5.** to furnish with a spigot or spout, as for drawing off a liquid. **6.** to tap by means of a spile. **7.** to furnish, strengthen, or support with spiles or piles. [t. MD or MLG, c. G *speil*]

spil·i·kin (spīl/ə kĭn), *n. Obs.* spillikin.

spil·ing (spī/lĭng), *n.* piles; spiles.

spill¹ (spīl), *v.,* **spilled** or **spilt, spilling,** *n.* —*v.t.* **1.** to cause or allow (liquid, or any matter in grains or loose pieces) to run or fall from a container, esp. accidentally or wastefully. **2.** to shed (blood), as in killing or wounding. **3.** to scatter. **4.** *Naut.* to let the wind out of (a sail). **5.** *Colloq.* to cause to fall from a horse, vehicle, or the like. **6.** *Slang.* to divulge, disclose, or tell. —*v.i.* **7.** (of a liquid, loose particles, etc.) to run or escape from a container, esp. by accident or in careless handling. —*n.* **8.** a spilling, as of liquid. **9.** a quantity spilled. **10.** the mark made. **11.** *Colloq.* a throw or fall from a horse, vehicle, or the like. [ME; OE *spillan,* c. MLG *spillen*]

spill² (spīl), *n.* **1.** a splinter. **2.** a slender piece of wood or of twisted paper, for lighting candles, lamps, etc. **3.** a peg made of metal. **4.** a small pin for stopping a cask; spile. [ME *spille;* akin to SPILE]

spil·li·kin (spīl/ə kĭn), *n. Obs.* **1.** a jackstraw. **2.** (*pl. construed as sing.*) the game of jackstraws. Also, **spili·kin.** [dim. of SPILL²]

spill·way (spīl/wā/), *n.* a passageway through which surplus water escapes from a reservoir.

spilt (spīlt), *v.* pt. and pp. of **spill¹.**

spin (spīn), *v.,* **spun** or (*Archaic*) **span; spun; spinning;** *n.* —*v.t.* **1.** to make (yarn) by drawing out, twisting, and winding fibers. **2.** to form (any material) into thread. **3.** (of spiders, silkworms, etc.) to produce (a thread, cobweb, gossamer, silk, etc.) by extruding from the body a long, slender filament of a natural viscous matter that hardens in the air. **4.** to cause to turn round rapidly, as on an axis; twirl; whirl: *to spin a coin on a table.* **5.** (in sheet-metal work) to shape into hollow, rounded form, during rotation on a lathe or wheel, by pressure with a suitable tool. **6.** to produce, fabricate, or evolve in a manner suggestive of spinning thread. **7.** to tell (a yarn or story). **8.** to draw out, protract, or prolong (often fol. by *out*): *to spin out a story tediously.* —*v.i.* **9.** to turn round rapidly, as on an axis, as the earth, a top, etc. **10.** to produce a thread from the body, as spiders, silkworms, etc. **11.** to move, go, run, ride, or travel rapidly. **12.** to be affected with a sensation of whirling, as the head. **13.** to fish with a spinning or revolving bait. —*n.* **14.** the act of causing a spinning or whirling motion. **15.** a spinning motion given to a ball or the like when thrown. **16.** a moving or going rapidly along. **17.** a rapid run, ride, drive, or the like, as for exercise or enjoyment. **18.** *Aeron.* a maneuver in which an airplane descends in a vertical direction along a helical path of large pitch and small radius at an angle of attack greater than the stall angle. [ME *spinne(n),* OE *spinnan,* c. D and G *spinnen*] —**Syn. 9.** See **turn.**

spi·na·ceous (spī nā/shəs), *adj.* pertaining to or of the nature of the spinach; belonging to the *Chenopodiaceae,* or spinach or goosefoot family of plants.

spin·ach (spĭn/ĭch, -ĭj), *n.* **1.** an herbaceous annual (*Spinacia oleracea*) cultivated for its succulent leaves, which are eaten boiled. **2.** the leaves. [t. OF: m. (*e*)*spinache, espinage,* t. ML: m. *spinachia,* t. Sp.: m. *espinaca,* t. Ar.: m. *isbānah,* b. with L *spīna* thorn]

spi·nal (spī/nəl), *adj.* of, pertaining, or belonging to any spine or thornlike structure, esp. to the backbone. [t. LL: s. *spīnālis*]

spinal canal, the tube formed by the vertebrae in which the spinal cord and its membranes are located

spinal column, (in a vertebrate animal) the bones of vertebrae forming the axis of the skeleton and protecting the spinal cord; the spine; the backbone.

spinal cord, the cord of nervous tissue extending through the spinal column.

spin·dle (spĭn/dəl), *n., adj., v.,* **-dled, -dling.** —*n.* **1.** a rounded rod, usually of wood, tapering toward each end, used in spinning by hand to twist into thread the fibers drawn from the mass on the distaff, and to wind the thread on as it is spun. **2.** the rod on a spinning wheel by which the thread is twisted and on which it is wound. **3.** one of the rods of a spinning machine which bear the bobbins on which the thread is wound as it is spun. **4.** any rod or pin suggestive of a

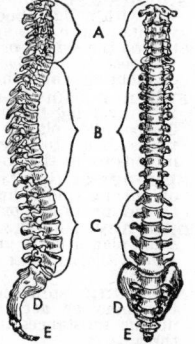

Human spinal column
(Side and front view)
A. Seven cervical vertebrae;
B. Twelve dorsal vertebrae;
C. Five lumbar vertebrae;
D. Five sacral vertebrae;
E. Four caudal or coccygeal
vertebrae, forming a coccyx

spindle used in spinning, as one which turns round or on which something turns; an axle, axis, or shaft. **5.** either of the two shaftlike parts in a lathe which support the work to be turned, one (**live spindle**) rotating and imparting motion to the work, and the other (**dead spindle**) not rotating. **6.** a small axis, arbor, or mandrel. **7.** an iron rod or the like, usually with a ball or cage at the top, fixed to a rock, sunken reef, etc., to serve as a guide in navigation. **8.** a measure of yarn, containing for cotton, 15,120 yards, and for linen 14,400 yards. **9.** a hydrometer. **10.** *Biol.* the fine threads of achromatic material arranged within the cell, during mitosis, in a fusiform manner. **11.** a shaft turned or circular ornament, as in a baluster or stair rail.
—*adj.* **12.** of or resembling spindles. **13.** denoting the maternal line of descent: *spindle side of the house.*
—*v.t.* **14.** to give the form of a spindle to.
—*v.i.* **15.** to shoot up, or grow, into a long, slender stalk or stem, as a plant. **16.** to grow tall and slender, often disproportionately so.
[ME *spindel*, OE *spinel* (c. D and G *spindel*) der. *spinnan* SPIN]

spin·dle·legs (spǐn′dəl·lĕgz′), *n.pl.* **1.** long, thin legs. **2.** (*construed as sing.*) *Colloq.* a tall, thin person with such legs. —**spin·dle·leg·ged** (spǐn′dəl·lĕg′ĭd, -lĕgd′), *adj.*

spin·dle·shanks (spǐn′dəl·shǎngks′), *n.pl.* *Colloq.* spindlelegs. —**spin·dle·shanked** (spǐn′dəl·shǎngkt′), *adj.*

spindle tree, **1.** a European shrub, *Euonymus europaeus*, whose wood was formerly much used for making spindles. **2.** any of various allied plants.

spin·dling (spǐnd′lǐng), *adj.* Also, **spin′dly. 1.** long or tall and slender, often disproportionately so. **2.** growing into a long, slender stalk or stem, often a too slender or weakly one. —*n.* **3.** *Rare.* a spindling person or thing.

spin·drift (spǐn′drǐft′), *n.* spray swept by a violent wind along the surface of the sea. Also, **spoondrift.**

spine (spīn), *n.* **1.** the vertebral or spinal column; the backbone. **2.** any backbonelike part. **3.** a pointed process or projection, as of a bone. **4.** a stiff, pointed process or appendage on an animal, as a quill of a porcupine, or a sharp, bony ray in a fish's fin. **5.** a ridge, as of ground, rock, etc. **6.** a sharp-pointed, hard or woody outgrowth on a plant; a thorn. **7.** *Bookbinding.* the back of a book cover or binding, usually indicating the title and author. [ME, t. L: m. *spina*] —**spined,** *adj.* —**spine′like,** *adj.*

spi·nel (spǐ nĕl′, spǐn′əl), *n.* **1.** any of a group of minerals composed principally of oxides of magnesium, aluminum, iron, manganese, chromium, etc., characterized by their hardness and octahedral crystals. **2.** a mineral of this group, essentially magnesium aluminate, Mg Al₂O₄, and having varieties used as ornamental stones in jewelry. [t. F: m. (*e*)*spinelle*, t. It.: m. *spinella*, dim. of *spina* thorn, g. L]

spine·less (spīn′lǐs), *adj.* **1.** without spines. **2.** having no spine. **3.** having a weak spine; limp. **4.** without moral force, resolution, or courage; feeble. —**spine′less·ly,** *adv.* —**spine′less·ness,** *n.* —**Ant. 4.** resolute.

spi·nes·cent (spī nĕs′ənt), *adj.* **1.** *Bot.* a. becoming spinelike. b. ending in a spine. c. bearing spines. **2.** *Zool.* somewhat spinelike; coarse, as hair. [t. LL: s. *spīnescens,* ppr., growing thorny]

spin·et (spǐn′ĭt), *n.* **1.** a small harpsichord. **2.** an early small square piano. **3.** a commercial name for a modern small upright piano. [t. F: m. *espinette*, ? named after (Giovanni) *Spinetti*, Venetian inventor]

spi·nif·er·ous (spī nǐf′ər əs), *adj.* spiny.

spin·i·fex (spǐn′ə fĕks′), *n.* any of the spiny grasses of the genus *Spinifex*, chiefly of Australia, often useful as binding sand on the seashore. [NL: f. m. *spīna* spine + -*fex* maker]

spin·na·ker (spǐn′ə kər), *n.* *Naut.* a large triangular sail with a light boom (**spinnaker boom**), carried by yachts on the side opposite the mainsail when running before the wind, or with the wind abaft the beam. [supposedly der. *Sphinx* (mispronounced *spinks*), name of yacht on which this sail was first regularly used]

spin·ner (spǐn′ər), *n.* **1.** one who or that which spins. **2.** a revolving bait used in trolling or casting for fish. **3.** *Football.* a play in which the player carrying the ball twirls about, to deceive the other team as to where he intends to hit the line. **4.** *Brit. Colloq.* the nightjar.

spin·ner·et (spǐn′ə rĕt′), *n.* an organ or part by means of which a spider, insect larva, or the like spins a silky thread for its web or cocoon. [dim. of SPINNER]

spin·ney (spǐn′ĭ), *n., pl.* -**neys.** *Brit.* **1.** a thicket. **2.** a small plantation or group of trees. [ME *spenne*, t. OF: m. *espinei* thorny place, der. *espine* SPINE]

spin·ning (spǐn′ĭng), *n.* the technique or act of changing fibrous substances into yarn or thread.

spinning jenny, an early spinning machine having more than one spindle, whereby one person could spin a number of yarns simultaneously.

spinning wheel, an old-fashioned device for spinning wool, flax, etc., into yarn or

Spinning wheel

thread consisting essentially of a single spindle driven by a large wheel operated by hand or foot.

spi·nose (spī′nōs, spī nōs′), *adj.* *Chiefly Biol.* full of spines; spiniferous; spinous. [t. L: m.s. *spīnōsus*] —**spi′nose·ly,** *adv.* —**spi·nos·i·ty** (spī nŏs′ə tĭ), *n.*

spi·nous (spī′nəs), *adj.* **1.** covered with or having spines; thorny, as a plant. **2.** armed with or bearing sharp-pointed processes, as an animal; spiniferous. **3.** spinelike.

Spi·no·za (spǐ nō′zə), *n.* **Baruch** or **Benedict de** (bä′rōōкн *or* bä′nə dǐkt də), 1632–1677, Dutch philosopher.

Spi·no·zism (spǐ nō′zǐzəm), *n.* the pantheistic philosophy of Spinoza. —**Spi·no′zist,** *n.*

spin·ster (spǐn′stər), *n.* **1.** a woman still unmarried beyond the usual age of marrying; an old maid. **2.** a woman still unmarried (in England, a legal designation). **3.** a woman (sometimes, any person) who spins, esp. as a regular occupation. [ME, f. SPIN + -STER] —**spin′ster·hood,** *n.* —**spin′ster·ish,** *adj.*

spin·thar·i·scope (spǐn thăr′ə skōp′), *n.* an apparatus for observing the scintillations produced in a prepared screen, as of zinc sulfide, by the action of radioactive rays. [f. Gk. *spinthari*(*s*) spark + -SCOPE]

spi·nule (spī′nūl, spǐn′ūl), *n.* a small spine. [t. L: m.s. *spīnula*, dim. of *spīna* SPINE] —**spin·u·lose** (spǐn′yə lōs′, spī′nyə lōs′), *adj.*

spin·y (spī′nǐ), *adj.*, **spinier, spiniest. 1.** abounding in or having spines; thorny, as a plant. **2.** covered with or having sharp-pointed processes, as an animal. **3.** in the form of a spine; resembling a spine; spinelike. —**spin′i·ness,** *n.*

spiny anteater, an echidna.

spin·y-finned (spī′nǐ fǐnd′), *adj.* having fins with sharp bony rays, as an acanthopterygian.

spiny lobster, any of the crustaceans of the family *Palinuridae*, lacking the large claws of the American lobster.

spi·ra·cle (spǐ′rə kəl, spī′r ə-), *n.* **1.** a breathing hole; an opening by which a confined space has communication with the outer air; an air hole. **2.** *Zool.* a. an aperture or orifice through which air or water passes in the act of respiration, as the blowhole of a cetacean. b. an opening in the head of sharks and rays through which water is drawn and passed over gills. c. one of the external orifices of a tracheal respiratory system, usually on the sides of the body. [ME, t. L: m.s. *spīrāculum*]

spi·rae·a (spī rē′ə), *n.* any of the herbs or shrubs constituting the rosaceous genus *Spiraea*, with racemes, cymes, panicles, or corymbs of small white or pink flowers, certain species of which are much cultivated for ornament, esp. the meadowsweet, *S. latifolia*, a North American spiraea. Also, **spirea.** [t. L, t. Gk.: m. *speiraía* meadowsweet]

spi·ral (spī′rəl), *n., adj., v.,* -**raled,** -**raling** *or* (*esp. Brit.*) -**ralled,** -**ralling.** —*n.* **1.** a single circle or ring of a spiral or helical curve or object. **2.** a spiral or helical object, formation, or form. **3.** a plane curve traced by a point which runs continuously round and round a fixed point or center while constantly receding from or approaching it. **4.** a helix. **5.** *Aeron.* a maneuver in which an airplane descends in a helix of small pitch and large radius, with the angle of attack within that of the normal flight range. **6.** *Football.* a type of kick or pass in which the ball turns on its longer axis as it flies through the air. —*adj.* **7.** pertaining to or of the nature of a spire or coil; spirelike. **8.** (of a curve) like a spiral. **9.** helical. —*v.i.* **10.** to take a spiral form or course. **11.** *Aeron.* to move an airplane through a spiral course. —*v.t.* **12.** to cause to take a spiral form or course. [t. ML: s. *spīrālis*] —**spi′ral·ly,** *adv.*

Spirals (def 2)

spiral nebula, *Astron.* one of the extragalactic stellar systems which shows spiral structure.

spi·rant (spī′rənt), *n., adj. Phonet.* fricative. [t. L: s. *spīrans,* ppr., breathing]

spire¹ (spīr), *n., v.,* **spired, spiring.** —*n.* **1.** a tall, tapering structure, generally an elongated, upright cone or pyramid, erected on a tower, roof, etc. **2.** such a structure forming the upper part of the steeple, or the whole steeple. See illus. under **steeple. 3.** a tapering, pointed part of something; a tall, sharp-pointed summit, peak, or the like. **4.** the highest point or summit of something. **5.** a sprout or shoot of a plant; an acrospire of grain; a blade or spear of grass, etc. —*v.i.* **6.** to shoot or rise into spirelike form; rise or extend to a height in the manner of a spire. [ME; OE *spīr*, c. D and G *spier*] —**spire′like′,** *adj.*

spire² (spīr), *n.* **1.** a coil or spiral. **2.** one of the series of convolutions of a coil or spiral. **3.** *Zool.* the upper, convoluted part of a spiral shell, above the aperture. [t. L: m. *spīra*, t. Gk.: m. *speíra* coil, winding] —**spire′like′,** *adj.*

spi·re·a (spī rē′ə), *n.* spiraea.

spired (spīrd), *adj.* having a spire.

spi·reme (spī′rēm), *n. Biol.* the chromatin of a cell nucleus, when in a continuous or segmented threadlike form, during mitosis. [t. Gk.: m. *speírēma* coil]

Spires (spīrz), *n.* Speyer.

spi·rif·er·ous (spī rĭf′ər əs), *adj.* **1.** having a spire, or spiral upper part, as a univalve shell. **2.** having spiral appendages, as a brachiopod.

spi·ril·lum (spĭ-rĭl'əm), *n.*, *pl.* **-rilla** (-rĭl'ə). **1.** any of the bacteria constituting the genus *Spirillum*, characterized by spirally twisted, rigid forms and having a bundle of 5 to 20 flagella. See illus. under **bacteria. 2.** any of various similar microörganisms. [NL, dim. of L *spira* SPIRE²]

spir·it (spĭr'ĭt), *n.* **1.** the principle of conscious life, orig. identified with the breath; the vital principle in man, animating the body or mediating between body and soul. **2.** the incorporeal part of man: *present in spirit though absent in body.* **3.** the soul as separable from the body at death. **4.** conscious, incorporeal being, as opposed to matter: *the world of spirit.* **5.** a supernatural, incorporeal being, esp. one inhabiting a place or thing or having a particular character: *evil spirits.* **6.** a fairy, sprite, or elf. **7.** an angel or demon. **8.** an inspiring or animating principle such as pervades and tempers thought, feeling, or action: *a spirit of reform.* **9.** (*cap.*) the divine influence as an agency working in the heart of man. **10.** (in Biblical use) a divine inspiring or animating being or influence. **11.** the third person of the Trinity; Holy Spirit. **12. the Spirit,** God. **13.** the soul or heart as the seat of feelings or sentiments, or as prompting to action: *to break a person's spirit.* **14.** (*pl.*) feelings with respect to exaltation or depression: *in low spirits.* **15.** fine or brave vigor or liveliness; mettle. **16.** temper or disposition: *meek in spirit.* **17.** a person characterized according to character, disposition, action, etc. **18.** the dominant tendency or character of anything: *the spirit of the age.* **19.** vigorous sense of membership in a group: *college spirit.* **20.** the general meaning or intent of a statement, etc. (opposed to *letter*). **21.** *Chem.* the essence or active principle of a substance as extracted in liquid form, esp. by distillation. **22.** (*often pl.*) a strong distilled alcoholic liquor. **23.** (*often pl. in U.S. but sing. in England*) alcohol. **24.** *Pharm.* a solution in alcohol of an essential or volatile principle. **25.** any of certain subtle fluids formerly supposed to permeate the body. —*adj.* **26.** pertaining to something which works by burning alcoholic spirits. **27.** of or pertaining to spiritualist bodies or activities. —*v.t.* **28.** to animate with fresh ardor or courage; inspirit. **29.** to encourage; urge (*on*) or stir (*up*), as to action. **30.** to carry (*away, off,* etc.) mysteriously or secretly: *to spirit away a prisoner.* [ME, t. L: s. *spiritus* breathing] —Syn. 2. life, mind, consciousness. 5. See **ghost.**

spir·it·ed (spĭr'ĭt'ĭd), *adj.* **1.** having a spirit, or having spirits, as specified: *low-spirited.* **2.** having or showing mettle, courage, vigor, liveliness, etc. —**spir'it·ed·ly,** *adv.* —**spir'it·ed·ness,** *n.*

spir·it·ism (spĭr'ĭ·tĭz'əm), *n.* the doctrine or practices of spiritualism. —**spir'it·ist,** *n.* —**spir·it·is'tic,** *adj.*

spir·it·less (spĭr'ĭt·lĭs), *adj.* **1.** without spirit. **2.** without ardor, vigor, animation, etc. —**spir'it·less·ly,** *adv.* —**spir'it·less·ness,** *n.*

spirit level, a device consisting of a glass tube containing alcohol or ether with a movable bubble which when in the center indicates horizontalness.

spi·ri·to·so (spē'rē·tô'sô), *adj. Music.* spirited; lively. [It.]

spir·it·ous (spĭr'ĭtəs), *adj. Archaic.* of the nature of spirit; immaterial, ethereal, or refined.

spirits of hartshorn, an aqueous solution of ammonia. Cf. hartshorn (def. 2).

spirits of turpentine, oil of turpentine.

spirits of wine, alcohol.

spir·it·u·al (spĭr'ĭ·chōō·əl), *adj.* **1.** of, pertaining to, or consisting of spirit or incorporeal being. **2.** of or pertaining to the spirit or soul as distinguished from the physical nature. **3.** characterized by or suggesting predominance of the spirit; ethereal or delicately refined. **4.** of or pertaining to the spirit as the seat of the moral or religious nature. **5.** of or pertaining to sacred things; pertaining or belonging to the church; ecclesiastical; religious; devotional; sacred. **6.** of or relating to the conscious thoughts and emotions. —*n.* **7.** a spiritual or religious song: *Negro spirituals.* **8.** (*pl.*) affairs of the church. **9.** a spiritual thing or matter. [t. L: s. *spirituālis*] —**spir·it·u·al·ly,** *adv.* —**spir·it·u·al·ness,** *n.*

spiritual incest. See incest (def. 2).

spir·it·u·al·ise (spĭr'ĭ·chōō·ə·līz'), *v.t.,* **-ised, -ising.** *Chiefly Brit.* See **spiritualize.**

spir·it·u·al·ism (spĭr'ĭ·chōō·əl·ĭz'əm), *n.* **1.** the belief or doctrine that the spirits of the dead, surviving after the mortal life, can and do communicate with the living, esp. through a person (a medium) particularly susceptible to their influence. **2.** the practices or the phenomena associated with this belief. **3.** the belief that all reality is spiritual. **4.** *Metaphys.* idealism. **5.** spiritual quality or tendency. **6.** insistence on the spiritual side of things, as in philosophy or religion.

spir·it·u·al·ist (spĭr'ĭ·chōō·əl·ĭst), *n.* **1.** an adherent of spiritualism. **2.** one who concerns himself with or insists on the spiritual side of things. —**spir·it·u·al·is'·tic,** *adj.*

spir·it·u·al·i·ty (spĭr'ĭ·chōō·ăl'ə·tĭ), *n., pl.* **-ties. 1.** the quality or fact of being spiritual. **2.** incorporeal or immaterial nature. **3.** predominantly spiritual character, as shown in thought, life, etc.; spiritual tendency or tone. **4.** (*often pl.*) property or revenue of the church or of an ecclesiastic in his official capacity.

spir·it·u·al·ize (spĭr'ĭ·chōō·ə·līz'), *v.t.,* **-ized, -izing. 1.** to make spiritual. **2.** to invest with a spiritual meaning. Also, *esp. Brit.,* **spiritualise.** —**spir·it·u·al·i·za'·tion,** *n.*

spir·it·u·al·ty (spĭr'ĭ·chōō·əl·tĭ), *n., pl.* **-ties. 1.** (*often pl.*) ecclesiastical property or revenue. **2.** the body of ecclesiastics; the clergy.

spi·ri·tu·el (spĭr'ĭ·chōō·ĕl'; *Fr.* spē·rē'ty·ĕl'), *adj.* **1.** showing a refined and graceful mind or wit. **2.** light and airy in movement; ethereal. [t. F. See SPIRITUAL] —**spi·ri·tu·elle',** *adj., fem.*

spir·it·u·ous (spĭr'ĭ·chōō·əs), *adj.* **1.** containing, of the nature of, or pertaining to alcohol; alcoholic. **2.** (of liquors) distilled, as opposed to fermented. —**spir'it·u·ous·ness,** *n.*

spir·i·tus as·per (spĭr'ə·təs ăs'pər), *Gram.* the rough breathing. [L]

spir·i·tus le·nis (spĭr'ə·təs lē'nĭs), *Gram.* the smooth breathing. [L]

spir·ket (spûr'kĭt), *n. Shipbuilding.* a space forward or aft between the floor timbers.

spiro-¹, a word element referring to "respiration," as in *spirograph.* [comb. form repr. L *spīrāre* breathe]

spiro-², a word element meaning "coil," "spiral," as in *spirochete.* [t. Gk.: m. *speiro-*, comb. form of *speira*]

spi·ro·chete (spī'rə·kēt'), *n.* slender, corkscrewlike bacterial microörganisms constituting the genus *Spirochaeta,* and found on man, animals, and plants, and in soil and water. Some cause disease, as the *Spirochaeta pallida* or *Treponema pallidum* (the causative agent of syphilis); most, however, are saprophytic. Also, **spi'ro·chaete'.** [t. NL: m. *Spirochaeta,* f. Gk.: m. *speiro-* SPIRO-² + m. *chaité* hair]

spi·ro·che·to·sis (spī'rə·kē·tō'sĭs), *n. Vet. Sci.* a specific, infectious, usually fatal blood disease of chickens cause by a spirochete, *Borrelia anserina.*

spi·ro·graph (spī'rə·grăf', -gräf'), *n.* an instrument for recording respiratory movements.

spi·ro·gy·ra (spī'rə·jī'rə), *n. Bot.* a widely distributed fresh-water green alga (genus *Spirogyra*) having spiral chlorophyll bands. [NL, f. Gk.: m. *speiro-* SPIRO-² + m. *gÿros* circle, ring]

spi·roid (spī'roid), *adj.* more or less spiral; resembling a spiral. [t. NL: s. *spiroïdes.* See SPIRO-², -OID]

spi·rom·e·ter (spī·rŏm'ə·tər), *n.* an instrument for determining the capacity of the lungs. [f. SPIRO-¹ + -METER]

spirt (spûrt), *v.i., v.t., n.* spurt.

spir·u·la (spĭr'yə·lə, -ōō'lə), *n., pl.* **-lae** (-lē'). any of the small decapod dibranchiate cephalopods of the genus *Spirula,* having in the hinder part of the body, but not completely internal, a shell in the form of a flat spiral with separated whorls, which is divided by partitions into a series of chambers. [NL, dim. of L *spira* SPIRE²]

Spirula. *Spirula spirula* (2 in. long)

spir·y¹ (spĭr'ĭ), *adj.* **1.** having the form of a spire, slender shoot, or tapering pointed body; tapering up to a point like a spire. **2.** abounding in spires or steeples. [f. SPIRE¹ + -Y¹]

spir·y² (spĭr'ĭ), *adj.* spiral; coiled; curling. [f. SPIRE² + -Y¹]

spit¹ (spĭt), *v.,* **spat** or **spit, spitting,** *n.* —*v.i.* **1.** to eject saliva from the mouth; expectorate. **2.** to do this at or on a person, etc., to express hatred, contempt, etc. **3.** to sputter. **4.** to fall in scattered drops or flakes, as rain or snow. —*v.t.* **5.** to eject (saliva, etc.) from the mouth. **6.** to throw out or emit like saliva. **7.** to set a flame to. —*n.* **8.** saliva, esp. when ejected. **9.** act of spitting. **10.** a frothy or spitlike secretion exuded by various insects; spittle (def. 2). **11.** a light fall of rain or snow. **12.** *Colloq.* the image, likeness, or counterpart of a person, etc. [ME; OE *spittan,* c. d. G *spitzen,* akin to OE *spǣtan* spit] —**spit'like',** —**spit'ter,** *n.*

spit² (spĭt), *n., v.,* **spitted, spitting.** —*n.* **1.** a sharply pointed, slender rod or bar for thrusting into or through and holding meat to be roasted at a fire or broiled. **2.** any of various rods, pins, or the like used for particular purposes. **3.** a narrow point of land projecting into the water. **4.** a long, narrow shoal extending from the shore. —*v.t.* **5.** to pierce, stab, or transfix, as with a spit; impale on something sharp. **6.** to thrust a spit into or through. [ME; OE *spitu,* c. D and LG *spil*]

spit·al (spĭt'əl), *n. Obs.* **1.** a hospital, esp. one for lazars. **2.** a shelter on a highway. [short for HOSPITAL; r. earlier *spittle,* ME *spitel,* c. G *spital.* Cf. d. It. *spitale*]

spit·bali (spĭt'bôl'), *n.* **1.** *Colloq.* a small ball or lump of chewed paper used as a missile. **2.** *Baseball.* a variety of curve pitched by moistening one side of the ball with saliva, now outlawed in professional baseball.

spitch·cock (spĭch'kŏk'), *n.* **1.** an eel split, cut into pieces, and broiled or fried. —*v.t.* **2.** to split, cut up, and broil or fry (an eel). **3.** to treat severely. [orig. uncert.]

spite (spīt), *n., v.,* **spited, spiting.** —*n.* **1.** keen, ill-natured desire to humiliate, annoy, or injure another; venomous ill will. **2.** a particular instance of such ill will; a grudge. **3.** *Archaic.* vexation or chagrin. **4. in spite of,** in disregard or defiance of; notwithstanding. —*v.t.* **5.** to wreak one's spite or malice on. **6.** to annoy or thwart, out of spite. **7.** *Archaic.* to fill with spite; vex; offend. [ME; aphetic var. of DESPITE, n.] —Syn. 1. See grudge. 4. See notwithstanding.

spite·ful (spīt′fəl), *adj.* full of spite or malice; showing spite; malicious; malevolent; venomous: *she was a spiteful old woman all her life.* —**spite′ful·ly**, *adv.* —**spite′ful·ness**, *n.*
—**Syn.** SPITEFUL, REVENGEFUL, VINDICTIVE refer to a desire to inflict a wrong or injury on someone, usually in return for one received. SPITEFUL implies a mean or malicious desire for (often petty) revenge: *a spiteful attitude toward a former friend.* REVENGEFUL is a strong word, implying a deep, powerful, and continued intent to repay a wrong: *a fierce and revengeful spirit.* VINDICTIVE does not imply action necessarily, but stresses the unforgiving nature of the avenger: *a vindictive look.*

spit·fire (spīt′fīr′), *n.* a person of fiery temper, easily provoked to outbursts, esp. a girl or woman.

Spit·head (spīt′hĕd′), *n.* a roadstead off the S coast of England between Portsmouth and the Isle of Wight.

Spits·ber·gen (spīts′bûr′gən), *n.* a group of islands in the Arctic Ocean, N of and belonging to Norway. 1200 rotating pop. (est. 1953); 24,-293 sq. mi. Also, **Spitz′ber′gen**. Norwegian, **Svalbard**.

spit·tle (spīt′əl), *n.* **1.** saliva; spit. **2.** the frothy protective secretion exuded by spittle insects. [alter. (conformed to SPIT[1]) of obs. or d. *spattle*, ME *spatel*, OE *spātl*, akin to *spǣtan* spit]

spittle insect, a froghopper.

spit·toon (spī tōōn′), *n.* a cuspidor.

spitz dog (spīts), a kind of small dog with long hair and pointed muzzle and ears, a variety of Pomeranian. [f. *spitz* (t. G: pointed) + DOG]

Spitz dog
(Ab. 14 in high at the shoulder)

spitz·en·burg (spīt′sən bûrg′), *n.* any of several varieties of red or yellow apples of fine flavor, suitable for winter use. Also, **spitz′en·berg′**.

spiv (spīv), *n. Brit. Colloq.* one who lives by his wits, without working. [back formation from d. *spiving* smart. See SPIFFY]

splanch·nic (splăngk′nĭk), *adj.* of or pertaining to the viscera or entrails; visceral. [t. NL: s. *splanchnicus,* t. Gk.: m. *splanchnikós*]

splash (splăsh), *v.t.* **1.** to wet or soil by dashing masses or particles of water, mud, or the like; spatter. **2.** to fall upon (something) in scattered masses or particles, as a liquid does. **3.** to cause to appear spattered. **4.** to dash (water etc.) about in scattered masses or particles. **5.** to make (the way) with splashing. —*v.i.* **6.** to dash a liquid or semiliquid substance about. **7.** to fall, move, or go with a splash or splashes. **8.** (of liquid) to dash with force in scattered masses or particles. —*n.* **9.** act of splashing. **10.** the sound of splashing. **11.** a quantity of some liquid or semiliquid substance splashed upon or in a thing. **12.** a spot caused by something splashed. **13.** a patch, as of color or light. **14.** a striking show, or an ostentatious display. [alter. of PLASH[1]]

splash·board (splăsh′bōrd′), *n.* **1.** a board, guard, or screen to protect from splashing, as a dashboard of a vehicle or a guard placed over a wheel to intercept water, dirt, etc. **2.** a screen to prevent water or spray from coming on the deck of a boat.

splash·er (splăsh′ər), *n.* **1.** one who or that which splashes. **2.** something that protects from splashes.

splash·y (splăsh′ĭ), *adj.,* **splash·i·er, splash·i·est. 1.** making a splash or splashes. **2.** making the sound of splashing. **3.** full of or marked by splashes, or irregular spots; spotty. **4.** *Colloq.* making a show or display.

splat (splăt), *n.* a broad, flat piece of wood, as the central upright part of the back of a chair.

splat·ter (splăt′ər), *v.i., v.t.* to splash.

splay (splā), *v.t.* **1.** to spread out, expand, or extend. **2.** to form with an oblique angle; make slanting; bevel. **3.** to make with a splay or splays. **4.** to A disjoin; dislocate. —*v.i.* **5.** to have an oblique or slanting direction. **6.** to spread or flare. —*n.* **7.** *Archit.* a surface which makes an oblique angle with another, as where the opening through a wall for a window or door widens from the window or door proper toward the face of the wall. —*adj.* **8.** spread out; wide and flat; turned outward. **9.** clumsy or awkward. **10.** oblique or awry. [aphetic var. of DISPLAY]

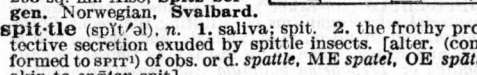

S. Splay
A. Splayed doorway;
B. Plan of A

splay·foot (splā′fŏŏt′), *n.* a broad, flat foot, esp. one turned outward. —**splay′foot′ed,** *adj.*

spleen (splēn), *n.* **1.** a highly vascular, ductless organ, situated in man near the cardiac end of the stomach, in which the blood undergoes certain corpuscular changes. **2.** this organ as supposed (variously) to be the seat of mirth, spirit or courage, ill humor, melancholy, etc. **3.** ill humor; peevish temper, or spite. **4.** *Archaic.* melancholy. **5.** *Obs.* caprice. [ME, t. L: m. *splēn,* t. Gk.] —**spleen′ish, spleen′y,** *adj.*

spleen·ful (splēn′fəl), *adj.* **1.** full of or displaying spleen. **2.** ill-humored; irritable or peevish; spiteful.

spleen·wort (splēn′wûrt′). *n.* any of various ferns of the genus *Asplenium,* having linear or oblong sori on the upper side of an oblique veinlet.

splen·dent (splĕn′dənt), *adj.* **1.** shining or radiant, as the sun; gleaming or lustrous, as metal, marble, etc. **2.** brilliant in appearance, color, etc.; gorgeous; magnificent; splendid. **3.** very conspicuous; illustrious. [late ME, t. L: s. *splendens,* ppr., shining]

splen·did (splĕn′dĭd), *adj.* **1.** gorgeous; magnificent; sumptuous. **2.** grand; superb, as beauty. **3.** glorious, as a name, reputation, victory, etc. **4.** strikingly admirable or fine: *splendid talents.* **5.** *Colloq.* excellent, fine, or very good: *to have a splendid time.* **6.** *Rare.* brilliant in appearance, color, etc. [t. L: s. *splendidus*] —**splen′did·ly,** *adv.* —**splen′did·ness,** *n.* —**Syn. 1.** See magnificent.

splen·dif·er·ous (splĕn dĭf′ər əs), *adj. Colloq.* splendid; magnificent; fine. [f. ML *splendifer* (r. LL *splendōrifer*) splendor-bearing + -OUS]

splen·dor (splĕn′dər), *n.* **1.** brilliant or gorgeous appearance, coloring, etc.; magnificence, grandeur, or pomp, or an instance or display of it: *the splendor and pomp of his coronation.* **2.** brilliant distinction; glory: *the splendor of ancient Roman architecture.* **3.** great brightness; brilliant light or luster. Also, *Brit.,* **splen′dour.** [late ME, t. L] —**splen′dor·ous,** *adj.*

sple·nec·to·my (splĭ nĕk′tə mĭ), *n., pl.* **-mies.** *Surg.* excision or removal of the spleen.

sple·net·ic (splĭ nĕt′ĭk), *adj.* Also, **sple·net′i·cal. 1.** of the spleen; splenic. **2.** irritable, peevish; spiteful. **3.** *Obs.* melancholy. —*n.* **4.** a splenetic person. [t. LL: s. *splēnēticus*] —**sple·net′i·cal·ly,** *adv.*

splen·ic (splĕn′ĭk, splē′nĭk), *adj.* of or pertaining to, connected with, or affecting the spleen: *splenic nerves.* [t. L: s. *splēnicus,* t. Gk.: m. *splēnikós*]

sple·ni·tis (splĭ nī′tĭs), *n. Pathol.* inflammation of the spleen.

splen·i·tive (splĕn′ə tĭv), *adj. Obs.* **1.** impetuous; passionate. **2.** splenetic, ill-humored, or irritable.

sple·ni·us (splē′nĭ əs), *n., pl.* **-nii** (-nĭ′ī). *Anat.* a band-age-shaped muscle which runs obliquely upward on the back and side of the neck. [NL, t. L. *splenion* bandage] —**sple′ni·al,** *adj.*

splice (splīs), *v.,* **spliced, splicing,** *n.* —*v.t.* **1.** to join together or unite, as two ropes or parts of a rope, by the interweaving of strands. **2.** to unite, as two pieces of timber, etc., by overlapping. **3.** to join or unite. —*n.* **4.** a joining of two ropes or parts of a rope by splicing. **5.** the union so effected. **6.** a joining or junction of two pieces of timber, etc., by overlapping and fastening the ends. [t. MD: m. *splissen;* ? akin to SPLIT] —**splic′er,** *n.*

Rope splices
A. Short splice; B. Long splice; C, Eye splice

spline (splīn), *n., v.,* **splined, splining.** —*n.* **1.** a long, narrow, relatively thin strip of wood, metal, etc.; a slat. **2.** a long, flexible strip of wood or the like used in drawing curves. **3.** *Mach.* **a.** a flat, rectangular piece or key fitting into a groove or slot between parts. **b.** the groove. —*v.t. Mach.* **4.** to fit with a spline or key. **5.** to provide with a groove for a spline or key. [? akin to SPLINTER]

Spline (def. 3a)
A. Shaft; B. Pulley; C, Spline

splint (splĭnt), *n.* **1.** a thin piece of wood or other rigid material used to immobilize a fractured or dislocated bone, or to maintain any part of the body in a fixed position. **2.** one of a number of thin strips of wood woven together to make a chair seat, basket, etc. **3.** *Vet. Sci.* an exostosis or bony enlargement of a splint bone of a horse or a related animal. **4.** one of a number of overlapping bands or strips of metal in armor for protecting the body and limbs. **5.** *Brit. Dial.* a splinter. —*v.t.* **6.** to secure, hold in position, or support by means of a splint or splints, as a fractured bone. **7.** to support as if with splints. [ME *splente,* t. MLG: metal plate or pin; akin to SPLINTER] —**splint′like′,** *adj.*

S. Splint (def. 4)

splint bone, one of the rudimentary, splintlike metacarpal or metatarsal bones of the horse or some allied animal, closely applied one on each side of the back of each cannon bone.

splin·ter (splĭn′tər), *n.* **1.** a rough piece of wood, bone, etc., usually comparatively long, thin, and sharp, split or broken off from a main body. **2.** a splint. —*v.t.* **3.** to split or break into splinters. **4.** to break off in splinters. **5.** *Obs.* to secure or support by a splint or splints, as a broken limb. —*v.i.* **6.** to be split or broken into splinters. **7.** to break off in splinters. [ME, t. MD or MLG. See SPLINT] —**splin′ter·y,** *adj.*

split (splĭt), *v.,* **split, splitting,** *n., adj.* —*v.t.* **1.** to rend or cleave lengthwise; separate or part from end to end or between layers, often forcibly or by cutting. **2.** to separate off by rending or cleaving lengthwise: *to split a piece from a block.* **3.** to tear or break asunder; rend or burst. **4.** to divide into distinct parts or portions. **5.** to separate (a part) by such division. **6.** to divide (persons) into different groups, factions, parties, etc., as by discord. **7.** to separate off (a group, etc.) by such division. **8.** to divide between two or more persons, etc.: *to split a bottle of wine.* **9.** to separate into parts by interposing something: *to split an infinitive.* **10.** *Chem.* to divide (molecules or atoms) by cleavage into smaller parts. **11.** split one's votes, vote, or ticket, *U.S.* to vote otherwise than for a straight party ticket. —*v.i.* **12.** to break or part lengthwise, or suffer longitudinal division. **13.** to part, divide, or separate in any way. **14.** to break asunder; part by striking on a rock, by the violence of a storm, etc., as a ship. **15.** to become separated off by such division, as a piece or part from a whole. **16.** to break up or separate through disagreement, etc. **17.** *Colloq.* to divide something with another or others. —*n.* **18.** act of splitting. **19.** a crack, rent, or fissure caused by or as by splitting. **20.** a piece or part separated by or as by splitting. **21.** a strip split from an osier, used in basketmaking. **22.** a breach or rupture in a party, etc., or between persons. **23.** a faction, party, etc., formed by a rupture or schism. **24.** *Colloq.* something combining different elements, as a drink composed of two liquors. **25.** *Colloq.* an ice-cream dish made from sliced fruit (usually banana) and ice cream, and covered with syrup and nuts. **26.** *Colloq.* a drink containing only half the usual quantity. **27.** *Colloq.* a bottle, as of aerated water, half the usual size. **28.** (*often pl.*) the feat of separating the legs while sinking to the floor, until they extend at right angles to the body, as in stage performances. **29.** *Bowling.* the arrangement of the remaining pins after the first bowl so that a spare is practically impossible. **30.** one of the thicknesses of leather into which a skin is cut. **31.** a split vote. —*adj.* **32.** that has undergone splitting; parted lengthwise; cleft. **33.** divided: *a split ticket.* [t. MD.: m.s. *splitten*, akin to G *spleissen*] —**split′ter,** *n.*

Split (splēt), *n.* a seaport in W Yugoslavia: Roman ruins. 75,377 (1953). Also, **Spalato.**

split infinitive, a simple infinitive with a word between the *to* and the verb, as *to readily understand.*

split-lev·el (splĭt′ lĕv′əl), *adj.* describing a home or other building that has less than a full flight of stairs between floors.

split·ting (splĭt′ĭng), *adj.* **1.** that splits. **2.** overpoweringly noisy, as if to split the ears. **3.** violent or severe, as a headache. **4.** very fast or rapid.

splotch (sploch), *n.* **1.** a large, irregular spot; blot; stain. —*v.t.* **2.** to mark with splotches. [? b. OE *splott* spot and PATCH] —**splotch′y,** *adj.*

splurge (splûrj), *n., v.,* **splurged, splurging.** *Colloq.* —*n.* **1.** an ostentatious display; any pretentious affair. —*v.i.* **2.** to make a splurge: *we splurged and bought new hats.* [? b. SPLASH and SURGE]

splut·ter (splŭt′ər), *v.i.* **1.** to talk hastily and confusedly or incoherently, as in excitement or embarrassment. **2.** to make a sputtering sound, or emit particles of something explosively, as an apple in roasting or a pen scattering ink. **3.** to fly or fall in particles or drops; spatter, as a liquid. —*v.t.* **4.** to utter hastily and confusedly or incoherently; sputter. **5.** to spatter (a liquid, etc.). **6.** to bespatter (a person, etc.). —*n.* **7.** spluttering utterance or talk; a dispute; a noise or fuss. **8.** a sputtering or spattering of liquid, etc. [b. SPLASH and SPUTTER] —**splut′ter·er,** *n.*

Spode (spōd), *n.* **1. Josiah,** 1754–1827, British potter. **2.** china or porcelain made by him. —*adj.* **3.** pertaining to, or made or originated by, Josiah Spode.

spod·u·mene (spŏj′oŏ mēn′), *n.* a mineral, lithium aluminum silicate, LiAlSi₂O₆, occurring in prismatic crystals, transparent varieties being used as gems: an ore of lithium. Cf. **kunzite.** [t. Gk.: m. *spodoúmenos*, ppr., burning to ashes]

spoil (spoil), *v.,* **spoiled** or **spoilt, spoiling,** *n.* —*v.t.* **1.** to damage or impair (a thing) irreparably as to excellence, value, usefulness, etc.: *to spoil a sheet of paper.* **2.** to impair in character or disposition by unwise treatment, benefits, etc., esp. by excessive indulgence. **3.** *Archaic* or *Rare.* to strip (persons, places, etc.) of goods, valuables, etc.; plunder, pillage, or rob. **4.** *Archaic.* to take by force, or carry off as booty. —*v.i.* **5.** to become spoiled, bad, or unfit for use, as food or other perishable substances; become tainted or putrid. **6.** to plunder, pillage, or rob. —*n.* **7.** (*often pl.*) booty, loot, or plunder taken in war or robbery. **8.** (*usually pl.*) *Chiefly U.S.* public offices with their emoluments and advantages viewed as won by a victorious political party: *the spoils of office.* **9.** treasures won or accumulated. **10.** waste materials, as those cast up in mining, excavating, quarrying, etc. [ME, t. OF: m.s. *espoillier,* g. L *spoliāre;* ? also an aphetic var. of DESPOIL] —**spoil′er,** *n.* —**Syn. 1.** SPOIL, RUIN, WRECK agree in meaning to impair the value, quality, usefulness, etc., of anything. SPOIL is the general term: *to spoil a delicate fabric.* RUIN implies doing completely destructive or irreparable injury: *to ruin one's health.* WRECK implies a violent breaking up or demolition: *to wreck oneself with drink.*

spoil·age (spoi′lĭj), *n.* **1.** act of spoiling. **2.** that which is spoiled: *spoilage of fruit on the way to market.*

spoil-five (spoil′fīv′), *n.* *Cards.* a game played by from three to ten persons having five cards each.

spoils·man (spoilz′mən), *n., pl.* **-men.** one who seeks or receives a share in political spoils; an advocate of the spoils system in politics.

spoils system, *U.S.* the system or practice in which public offices with their emoluments and advantages are at the disposal of the victorious party for its own purposes and in its own (rather than the public) interest.

spoilt (spoilt), *v.* a pt. and pp. of **spoil.**

Spo·kane (spō kăn′), *n.* a city in E Washington. 181,608 (1960).

spoke¹ (spōk), *v.* pt. and archaic pp. of **speak.**

spoke² (spōk), *n., v.,* **spoked, spoking.** —*n.* **1.** one of the bars, rods, or rungs radiating from the hub or nave of a wheel and supporting the rim or felloe. **2.** one of a number of pins or handles projecting from a cylinder or wheel, or joining hub and rim, esp. on a steering wheel. **3.** a rung of a ladder. —*v.t.* **4.** to fit or furnish with, or as with, spokes. [ME; OE *spāca,* c. D *speek,* G *speiche*]

spo·ken (spō′kən), *v.* **1.** pp. of **speak.** —*adj.* **2.** uttered or expressed by speaking; oral (opposed to *written*). **3.** (in compounds) speaking, or using speech, as specified: *fair-spoken, plain-spoken.*

spoke·shave (spōk′shāv′), *n.* a cutting tool having a blade set between two handles, orig. for shaping spokes, but now in general use for dressing curved edges of wood and in forming round bars and shapes.

spokes·man (spōks′mən), *n., pl.* **-men. 1.** one who speaks for another or others. **2.** a public speaker.

spo·li·a·tion (spō′lĭ ā′shən), *n.* **1.** act of spoiling, plundering, or despoiling. **2.** authorized plundering of neutrals at sea in time of war. **3.** *Law.* the destruction or material alteration of a bill of exchange, will, or the like. [ME *spoliacio(u)n,* t. L: m.s. *spoliātiō*] —**spo′li·a′tive,** *adj.* —**spo′li·a′tor,** *n.*

spon·da·ic (spŏn dā′ĭk), *adj.* **1.** of or pertaining to a spondee. **2.** constituting a spondee. **3.** consisting of spondees; characterized by a spondee or spondees. Also, **spon·da′i·cal.** [t. L: s. *spondaicus*]

spon·dee (spŏn′dē), *n.* *Pros.* a foot consisting of two long syllables or two heavy beats. [ME, t. L: m.s. *spondēus,* t. Gk.: m. *spondeíos*]

spon·dy·li·tis (spŏn′də lī′tĭs), *n.* *Pathol.* a generalized affection of the vertebrae. [NL, f. s. L *spondylus* (t. Gk.: m. *sphóndylos* vertebra) + -*itis* -ITIS]

sponge (spŭnj), *n., v.,* **sponged, sponging.** —*n.* **1.** any of a group of aquatic (mostly marine) animals (phylum *Porifera*) which are characterized by a porous structure and (usually) a horny, siliceous, or calcareous skeleton or framework, and which, except in the larval state, are fixed, occurring in large, complex, often plantlike colonies. **2.** the light, yielding, porous, fibrous skeleton or framework of certain animals or colonies of this group, from which the living matter has been removed, characterized by readily absorbing water, and becoming soft when wet while retaining toughness: used in bathing, in wiping or cleansing surfaces, in removing marks (as from a slate), and for other purposes. **3.** any of various other spongelike substances. **4.** a bath in a small amount of water, esp. with a sponge or washcloth. **5.** one who or that which absorbs something freely, as a sponge does water. **6.** *Colloq.* one who persistently lives at the expense of others; a parasite. **7.** a metal, as platinum, when obtained as a porous or spongy mass consisting of fine, loosely cohering particles. **8.** *Surg.* a sterile surgical dressing of absorbent material, usually cotton gauze, for sponging or wiping to absorb pus, blood, or other fluids during a surgical operation. **9.** *Cookery.* **a.** dough raised with yeast, esp. before kneading, as for bread. **b.** a light sweet pudding of spongy texture, made with gelatin, eggs, fruit juice or other flavoring material, etc. —*v.t.* **10.** to wipe or rub with a wet sponge, as in order to clean or moisten. **11.** to remove with a wet sponge (fol. by *off, away,* etc.). **12.** to wipe out or efface with or as with a sponge (often fol. by *out*). **13.** to take up or absorb with a sponge or the like (often fol. by *up*): *to sponge up water.* **14.** *Colloq.* to get from another or at another's expense by indirect exactions, trading on generosity: *to sponge a dinner.* **15.** *Colloq.* to prey on or fleece (a person) in such a manner. —*v.i.* **16.** to take in liquid by absorption. **17.** to gather sponges. **18.** *Colloq.* to live at the expense of others. [ME and OE, t. L: m. *spongia,* t. Gk.] —**sponge′like′,** *adj.*

sponge cake, a very light kind of sweet cake, made with a comparatively large proportion of eggs but no shortening.

spong·er (spŭn′jər), *n.* **1.** one who or that which sponges. **2.** a person who sponges on others. **3.** a person or a vessel engaged in gathering sponges.

spon·gy (spŭn′jĭ), *adj.,* **-gi·er, -gi·est. 1.** of the nature of or resembling a sponge; light, yielding, and porous; without firmness, and readily compressible, as pith, flesh, etc. **2.** absorbing or holding water or the like, as a sponge does, or yielding it as when pressed. **3.** pertaining to a sponge. **4.** porous but hard, as bone. —**spon′gi·ness,** *n.*

spon·sion (spŏn′shən), *n.* **1.** an engagement or promise, esp. one made on behalf of another. **2.** act of becoming surety for another. [t. L: s. *sponsio*]

spon·son (spŏn′sən), *n.* **1.** a structure projecting from the side of a ship, as a gun platform, or a platform for handling gear. **2.** a buoyant appendage at the gunwale of a canoe to resist capsizing. **3.** a protuberance at the side of a flying-boat hull designed to increase lateral stability in the water. [var. of EXPANSION]

ăct, āble, dâre, ärt; ĕbb, ēqual; ĭf, īce; hŏt, ōver, ôrder, oil, bŏŏk, ōōze, out; ŭp, ūse, ûrge; ə = a in alone; ch, chief; g, give; ng, ring; sh, shoe; th, thin; ŧh, that; zh, vision. See the full key on inside cover.

spon·sor (spŏn'sər), n. 1. one who vouches or is responsible for a person or thing. 2. one who makes an engagement or promise on behalf of another; a surety. 3. one who answers for an infant at baptism, making the required professions and promises; a godfather or godmother. 4. a person, firm, or other organization that finances a radio program in return for advertisement of a commercial product, a political party, etc. —v.t. 5. to act as sponsor for; promise, vouch, or answer for. [t. L] —**spon·so·ri·al** (spŏn sōr'Yal), adj. —**spon'-sor·ship'**, n.

spon·ta·ne·i·ty (spŏn'tənē'ətY), n., pl. -ties. 1. state, quality, or fact of being spontaneous. 2. spontaneous activity. 3. (pl.) spontaneous impulses, movements, or actions.

spon·ta·ne·ous (spŏn tā'nYəs), adj. 1. proceeding from a natural personal impulse, without effort or premeditation; natural and unconstrained: a spontaneous action or remark. 2. (of impulses, motion, activity, natural processes, etc.) arising from internal forces or causes, or independent of external agencies. 3. growing naturally or without cultivation, as plants, fruits, etc. 4. produced by natural process. [t. L: m. spontāneus] —**spon·ta·ne·ous·ly**, adv. —**spon·ta·ne·ous·ness**, n. —Syn. 1. See voluntary.

spontaneous combustion, the ignition of a substance or body from the rapid oxidation of its own constituents, without heat from any external source.

spontaneous generation, Biol. abiogenesis.

spon·toon (spŏn tōōn'), n. Mil. a shafted weapon with broad blade and basal crossbar used in the 18th and 19th centuries. [t. F: m. sponton, t. It.: m. spuntone, der. puntone point, der. punto, g. L punctum]

spoof (spōōf), n., v.t., v.i. Chiefly Brit. Slang. humbug; hoax. [coined by A. Roberts (b. 1852), British comedian]

spook (spōōk), n. Colloq. a ghost; a specter. [t. D. c. G spuk]

spook·y (spōō'kY), adj., spookier, spookiest. Colloq. like or befitting a spook or ghost; suggestive of spooks; eerie. Also, **spook'ish**.

spool (spōōl), n. 1. any cylindrical piece or appliance on which something is wound. 2. a small cylindrical piece of wood or other material on which yarn is wound in spinning, for use in weaving; a bobbin. 3. a small cylinder of wood or other material, now typically expanded at each end and having a hole lengthwise through the center, on which thread is wound. —v.t. 4. to wind on a spool. [ME spole, t. MD or MLG; c. G spule]

spoom (spōōm), v.i. Obs. or Archaic. to run or scud, as a ship before the wind. [var. of obs. spoon in same sense]

spoon (spōōn), n. 1. a utensil consisting of a bowl or concave part and handle, for taking up or stirring liquid or other food, or other matter. 2. any of various implements, objects, or parts resembling or suggesting this. 3. Also, **spoon bait**. Angling. a lure used in casting or trolling for fish, consisting of a bright spoon-shaped piece of metal or the like, swiveled above one or more fishhooks, and revolving as it is drawn through the water. 4. Golf. a club with a wooden head whose face is more lofted than that of the brassie, and with a shorter shaft. 5. a curved piece projecting from the top of a torpedo tube to guide the torpedo in a horizontal direction and prevent it from striking the side of the ship. —v.t. 6. to take up or transfer in or as in a spoon. 7. to hollow out or shape like a spoon. 8. Games. a. to push or shove (the ball) with a lifting motion instead of striking it soundly, as in croquet or golf. b. to hit (the ball) up in the air, as in cricket. 9. Colloq. to make love to, esp. in an openly sentimental manner. —v.i. 10. Games. to spoon the ball. 11. to fish with a spoon. 12. Colloq. to make love, esp. in an openly sentimental manner. [ME and OE spōn, c. LG spon, Icel. spōnn; akin to G span]

spoon·bill (spōōn'bYl'), n. 1. any of the wading birds of the genera Platalea and Ajaia, closely related to the ibises, and having a long, flat bill with spoonlike tip. 2. any of various birds having a similar bill, as the shoveler duck (Spatula clypeata). 3. the paddlefish.

spoon bread, a baked corn-meal mush, often made with meat cracklings, served with a spoon.

spoon·drift (spōōn'drYft'), n. spindrift. [f. spoon scud, run before the wind (orig. uncert.) + DRIFT]

spoon·er·ism (spōō'nərYz'əm), n. a slip of the tongue whereby initial or other sounds of words are accidentally transposed, as in "our queer old dean" for "our dear old queen." [named after Rev. W. A. Spooner (1844–1930) of New College, Oxford, noted for such slips]

spoon·ey (spōō'nY), adj., spoonier, spooniest, n., pl. spoonies. Colloq. spoony.

spoon·fed (spōōn'fĕd'), adj. 1. given food by means of a spoon. 2. treated with excessive solicitude. 3. deprived of a chance to act or think for oneself.

spoon·ful (spōōn'fŏŏl'), n., pl. -fuls. 1. as much as a spoon can hold. 2. a small quantity.

spoon hook, a fishhook with a spoon (lure) attached.

spoon·y (spōō'nY), adj., spoonier, spooniest, n., pl. spoonies. Colloq. —adj. 1. foolishly or sentimentally amorous. 2. Chiefly Brit. foolish; silly. —n. 3. one who is foolishly or sentimentally amorous. 4. Chiefly Brit. a simple or foolish person.

spoor (spōōr, spōr), n. 1. a track or trail, esp. that of a wild animal pursued as game. —v.t., v.i. 2. to track

by or follow a spoor. [t. S Afr. D, c. OE and Icel. spor, akin to G spur]

spor-, var. of sporo-, before vowels, as in sporangium.

Spor·a·des (spŏr'ə dēz'; Gk. spŏ rä'dĕs), n.pl. two groups of Greek islands in the Aegean: the Northern Sporades, off the E coast of Greece, and the Southern Sporades (including the Dodecanese), off the SW coast of Asia Minor.

spo·rad·ic (spŏ răd'Yk), adj. 1. appearing or happening at intervals in time; occasional: sporadic outbreaks. 2. appearing in scattered or isolated instances, as a disease. 3. isolated, as a single instance of something; being or occurring apart from others. 4. occurring singly, or widely apart, in locality: sporadic genera of plants. Also, **spo·rad'i·cal**. [t. ML: s. sporadicus, t. Gk.: m. sporadikós] —**spo·rad'i·cal·ly**, adv. —**spo·rad'i·cal·ness**, n.

spo·ran·gi·um (spŏ răn'jY əm), n., pl. -gia (-jY'ə). Bot. the case or sac within which spores (asexual reproductive cells) are produced. While most evident in cryptogams, the sporangium is also found in phanerogams. In mosses, it is usually the same as capsule. Also, **spore case**. [t. NL, f. spor- SPOR- + m. Gk. angeion vessel] —**spo·ran'gi·al**, adj.

spore (spōr), n., v., spored, sporing. —n. 1. Biol. a walled body that contains or produces one or more uninucleate organisms that develop into an adult individual, esp.: a. a reproductive body (asexual spore) produced asexually and capable of growth into a new individual, such individuals often, as in ferns, etc., being one (a gametophyte) unlike that which produced the spore. b. a reproductive body (sexual spore) produced sexually (by the union of two gametes). 2. a germ, germ cell, seed, or the like. —v.i. 3. to bear or produce spores. [t. NL: m. spora, t. Gk.: seed]

spo·rif·er·ous (spŏ rYf'ər əs), adj. bearing spores.

sporo-, a word element meaning "seed." Also, **spor-**. [comb. form repr. Gk. sporá seed]

spo·ro·carp (spŏr'ə kärp'), n. Bot. (in higher fungi, lichens, and red algae) a pluricellular body developed for the formation of spores.

spo·ro·cyst (spŏr'ə sYst'), n. Zool. 1. a walled body resulting from the multiple division of a sporozoan, which produces one or more sporozoites. 2. a stage in development of trematodes which gives rise, nonsexually, to daughter cercaria.

spo·ro·gen·e·sis (spŏr'ə jĕn'ə sYs), n. Biol. 1. the production of spores; sporogony. 2. reproduction by means of spores. —**spo·rog·e·nous** (spŏ rŏj'ə nəs), adj.

spo·rog·o·ny (spŏ rŏg'ə nY), n. the process of multiplication in the sexual phase of parasitic protozoans of the class Sporozoa, giving rise to sporozoites.

spo·ro·phore (spŏr'ə fōr'), n. Bot. a simple or branched fungus hypha specialized to bear spores.

spo·ro·phyll (spŏr'ə fYl), n. Bot. a more or less modified leaf which bears sporangia. Also, **spo'ro·phyl**.

spo·ro·phyte (spŏr'ə fYt'), n. Bot. the asexual form of a plant in the alternation of generations (opposed to gametophyte).

spo·ro·tri·cho·sis (spŏr'ə trY kō'sYs), n. an infectious fungus disease of horses and man, marked by ulceration of superficial lymph vessels of the skin.

Spo·ro·zo·a (spŏr'ə zō'ə), n.pl. a class of the phylum Protozoa, consisting of parasites that multiply by sporogenesis, i.e., by dividing into reproductive bodies.

spo·ro·zo·an (spŏr'ə zō'ən), n. one of the Sporozoa.

spo·ro·zo·ite (spŏr'ə zō'Yt), n. Zool. one of the minute active bodies into which the spore of certain sporozoa divides, each developing into an adult individual.

spor·ran (spŏr'ən), n. (in Scottish Highland costume) a large purse, commonly of fur, worn hanging from the belt in front. [t. Scot. Gaelic: m. sporan, c. Irish sparán]

sport (spōrt), n. 1. a pastime pursued in the open air or having an athletic character, as hunting, fishing, racing, baseball, tennis, golf, bowling, wrestling, boxing, etc. 2. a particular form of pastime. 3. diversion; recreation; pleasant pastime. 4. playful trifling, jesting, or mirth: to do or say a thing in sport. 5. derisive jesting; ridicule. 6. an object of derision; a laughingstock. 7. something sported with or tossed about like a plaything: to be the sport of circumstances. 8. a sportsman. 9. Slang. a person of sportsmanlike or admirable qualities: be a good sport. 10. Colloq. one who is interested in pursuits involving betting or gambling. 11. Colloq. a flashy person; any person who affects fine clothes, smart manners or pastimes, etc. 12. Biol. an animal or a plant, or a part of a plant, that shows an unusual or singular deviation from the normal or parent type; a mutation. 13. Obs. amorous dalliance. —adj. 14. of or pertaining to sport or sports, esp. of the open-air or athletic kind. 15. suited for outdoor wear. See **sports**. —v.i. 16. to amuse oneself with some pleasant pastime or recreation. 17. to play, frolic, or gambol, as a child or an animal. 18. to engage in some open-air or athletic pastime or sport. 19. to deal lightly; trifle. 20. to ridicule. 21. Bot. to mutate. 22. Archaic. to trifle playfully. —v.t 23. to pass (time) in amusement or sport. 24. to spend or squander lightly or recklessly (often fol. by

Sporran

away).   **25.** *Colloq.* to display freely or with ostentation: *to sport a roll of money.*   **26.** *Obs.* to amuse (esp. oneself). [ME *sporte;* aphetic var. of DISPORT]   —**sport′er,** *n.* —**sport′ful,** *adj.* —**sport′ful·ly,** *adv.* —**sport′fulness,** *n.*

—**Syn. 1.** game. **3.** amusement. See **play. 4.** fun, frolic.

sport·ing (spôr′tĭng), *adj.*   **1.** engaging in, given to, or interested in open-air or athletic sports.   **2.** concerned with or suitable for such sports.   **3.** sportsmanlike.   **4.** interested in or connected with sports or pursuits involving betting or gambling.   **5.** *Colloq.* involving or inducing the taking of risk, as in sport: *a sporting chance.* —**sport′ing·ly,** *adv.*

spor·tive (spôr′tĭv), *adj.*   **1.** playful or frolicsome; jesting, jocose, or merry.   **2.** done in sport, rather than in earnest.   **3.** pertaining to or of the nature of sport or sports.   **4.** *Biol.* mutative.   **5.** *Obs.* amorous.   —**spor′tive·ly,** *adv.* —**spor′tive·ness,** *n.*

sports (spôrts), *adj.* (of garments, etc.) suitable for use in open-air sports, or for outdoor or informal use.

sports car,   a high-powered automobile with low, rakish lines, usually for 2 persons.

sports·man (spôrts′mən), *n., pl.* -**men. 1.** a man who engages in sport, esp. in some open-air sport such as hunting, fishing, racing, etc.   **2.** one who exhibits qualities especially esteemed in those who engage in sports, such as fairness, self-control, etc.   —**sports·man·like′, sports′man·ly,** *adj.* —**sports′wom′an,** *n. fem.*

sports·man·ship (spôrts′mən shĭp′), *n.*   **1.** the character, practice, or skill of a sportsman.   **2.** sportsmanlike conduct.

sport·y (spôr′tĭ), *adj.,* **sportier, sportiest.** *Colloq.* **1.** flashy; vulgarly showy.   **2.** stylish.   **3.** like or befitting a sportsman.   —**sport′i·ness,** *n.*

spor·u·late (spôr′yə lāt′, spôr′-), *v.i.,* -**lated,** -**lating.** *Biol.* to undergo multiple division resulting in the production of spores.   —**spor′u·la′tion,** *n.*

spor·ule (spôr′ŭl, spôr′-), *n.*   *Biol.* a spore, esp. a small spore.

spot (spŏt), *n., v.,* **spotted, spotting,** *adj.*   —*n.* **1.** a mark made by foreign matter, as mud, blood, paint, ink, etc.; a stain, blot, or speck, as on a surface.   **2.** a moral stain, as on character or reputation; blemish or flaw.   **3.** a relatively small, usually roundish, part of a surface differing from the rest in appearance or character: *a sun spot.*   **4.** a place or locality: *a monument marks the spot.*   **5.** *Chiefly Brit.* a small quantity of something: *a spot of tea.*   **6.** a small sciaenoid food fish, *Leiostomus xanthurus,* of the eastern coast of the U.S.   **7. on the spot, a.** at once. **b.** on that very place. **c.** *U.S. Slang.* in difficulty or danger, esp. of death. **d.** *U.S. Slang.* in an embarrassing position.   —*v.t.* **8.** to stain with spots.   **9.** to sully; blemish.   **10.** to mark or diversify with spots, as of color.   **11.** *Colloq.* to detect or recognize.   **12.** to place on a particular spot, as a ball in billiards.   **13.** to scatter in various spots.   **14.** *Mil.* to determine (a location) precisely on either the ground or a map.   —*v.i.* **15.** to make a spot; cause a stain.   **16.** to become spotted, as some fabrics when spattered with water.   —*adj.* **17.** *Radio.* pertaining to the point of origin of a local broadcast.   **18.** made, paid, delivered, etc., at once: *a spot sale.* [ME *spotte,* c. MD and LG *spot* speck, Icel. *spotti* bit, small piece]

spot announcement,   a brief radio announcement, usually an advertisement, made by an individual station during or after a network program.

spot·less (spŏt′lĭs), *adj.*   free from spot, stain, blemish, marks, etc.   —**spot′less·ly,** *adv.* —**spot′less·ness,** *n.*

spot·light (spŏt′līt′), *n.*   **1.** (in theatrical use) a strong light thrown upon a particular spot on the stage in order to render some object, person, or group especially conspicuous.   **2.** an automobile light having a high candle power and a focused beam which the driver can swing in any direction.   **3.** conspicuous public attention.

Spot·syl·va·ni·a (spŏt′sĭl vā′nĭ ə), *n.*   a village in NE Virginia: the scene of battles between the armies of Grant and Lee, May 8–21, 1864.

spot·ted (spŏt′ĭd), *adj.*   **1.** marked with or characterized by a spot or spots.   **2.** sullied; blemished.

spotted adder,   the milk snake.

spotted crake,   a small, short-billed rail, *Porzana porzana,* of Europe; water crake.

spotted crane's-bill,   the common American wild geranium, *Geranium maculatum.*

spotted fever,   *Pathol.* **1.** any of several fevers characterized by spots on the skin, esp. as in cerebrospinal meningitis or typhus fever.   **2.** tick fever.

spot·ter (spŏt′ər), *n.*   **1.** *Colloq.* one employed to keep watch on others, esp. on employees as for evidence of dishonesty.   **2.** *Mil.* the person who determines for the gunner the fall of shots in relation to the target.   **3.** (in civil defense) one who watches for enemy airplanes.

spot·ty (spŏt′ĭ), *adj.,* -**tier,** -**tiest. 1.** full of or having spots; occurring in spots: *spotty coloring.*   **2.** irregular or uneven in quality or character.   —**spot′ti·ly,** *adv.* —**spot′ti·ness,** *n.*

spous·al (spou′zəl), *n.*   **1.** (*often pl.*) the ceremony of marriage; nuptials.   —*adj.* **2.** nuptial; matrimonial.

spouse (spouz, spous), *n., v.,* **spoused, spousing.** —*n.* **1.** either member of a married pair in relation to the

other; one's husband or wife.   —*v.t.* **2.** *Obs.* to join, give, or take in marriage. [ME, t. OF: m. *spus* (masc.), *spuse* (fem.), g. L *sponsus,* pp., betrothed]

spout (spout), *v.t.*   **1.** to discharge or emit (a liquid, etc.) in a stream with some force.   **2.** *Colloq.* to utter or declaim in an oratorical manner.   —*v.i.* **3.** to discharge a liquid, etc., in a jet or continuous stream.   **4.** to issue with force, as liquid through a narrow orifice.   **5.** *Colloq.* to talk or speak at some length or in an oratorical manner.   —*n.* **6.** a pipe or tube, or a tubular or liplike projection, by which a liquid is discharged or poured.   **7.** a trough or shoot for discharging or conveying grain, flour, etc.   **8.** a waterspout.   **9.** a continuous stream of liquid, etc., discharged from, or as if from, a spout.   **10.** a shoot or shaft formerly common in pawnbrokers' shops, up which articles pawned were sent for storage.   **11.** *Slang.* a pawnbroker's shop. [ME *spoute*(n), c. D. *spuiten;* akin to Icel. *spȳta* SPIT[1]]   —**spout′er,** *n.* —**spout′less,** *adj.* —**Syn. 3.** See **flow. 5.** declaim, rant, harangue, speechify.

spp.,   species (pl. of specie).

S.P.Q.R.,   (L *Senatus Populusque Romanus*) the Senate and People of Rome.

sprag (sprăg), *n.*   a chock or pointed steel bar hinged to the rear axle of a vehicle and let down to arrest backward movement on grades. [special use of d. *sprag* twig, OE *spræc* shoot]

sprain (sprān), *v.t.*   **1.** to overstrain or wrench (the ankle, wrist, or other part of the body at a joint) so as to injure without fracture or dislocation.   —*n.* **2.** a violent straining or wrenching of the parts around a joint, without dislocation.   **3.** condition of being sprained. [orig. uncert]   —**Syn. 1.** See **strain**[1].

sprang (sprăng), *v.*   pt. of **spring.**

sprat (sprăt), *n.*   a small, herringlike marine fish, *Clupea sprattus,* of European waters; brisling. [var. of earlier *sprot,* ME and OE *sprott,* c. G *sprott*]

sprawl (sprôl), *v.i.*   **1.** to be stretched out in irregular or ungraceful movements, as the limbs.   **2.** to lie or sit with the limbs stretched out in a careless or ungraceful posture.   **3.** to work one's way awkwardly along with the aid of all the limbs; scramble.   **4.** to spread out in a straggling or irregular manner, as vines, buildings, handwriting, etc.   —*v.t.* **5.** to stretch out (the limbs) as in sprawling.   **6.** to spread out or distribute in a straggling manner.   —*n.* **7.** act of sprawling; a sprawling posture.   **8.** a straggling array of something. [ME *spraule*(n), OE *sprēawlian,* c. North Fris. *spraweli.* See SPRAY[2]]   —**sprawl′er,** *n.*

sprawl·y (sprô′lĭ), *adj.*   tending to sprawl; straggly.

spray[1] (sprā), *n.*   **1.** water or other liquid broken up into small particles and blown or falling through the air.   **2.** a jet of fine particles of liquid discharged from an atomizer or other appliance, as for medicinal treatment, etc.   **3.** a liquid to be discharged in such a jet.   **4.** an appliance for discharging it.   **5.** a quantity of small objects, flying or discharged through the air: *a spray of bullets.* —*v.t.* **6.** to scatter in the form of fine particles. **7.** to apply as a spray: *to spray an insecticide upon plants.* **8.** to sprinkle or treat with a spray: *to spray plants with insecticide.* **9.** to direct a spray of particles, missiles, etc., upon.   —*v.i.* **10.** to scatter spray; discharge a spray. **11.** to issue as spray. [cf. MD *sprayen* sprinkle] —**spray′er,** *n.*

spray[2] (sprā), *n.*   **1.** a single slender shoot, twig, or branch with its leaves, flowers, or berries, growing or detached.   **2.** an ornament, decorative figure, etc. with a similar form. [ME; orig. uncert.]

spread (sprĕd), *v.,* **spread, spreading,** *n.*   —*v.t.* **1.** to draw or stretch out to the full width, as a cloth, a rolled or folded map, folded wings, etc. (often fol. by *out*).   **2.** to extend over a greater or a relatively great area, space, or period (often fol. by *out*): *to spread out handwriting.*   **3.** to force apart, as walls, rails, etc., under pressure.   **4.** to flatten out: *to spread the end of a rivet by hammering.*   **5.** to display in the full extent; set forth in full.   **6.** to dispose or distribute in a sheet or layer: *to spread hay to dry.*   **7.** to apply in a thin layer or coating.   **8.** to extend or distribute over a region, place, etc.   **9.** to overlay, cover, or coat with something.   **10.** to set or prepare (a table, etc.), as for a meal.   **11.** to send out in various directions, as light, sound, mist, etc.   **12.** to shed or scatter abroad; diffuse or disseminate, as knowledge, news, disease, etc.   **13.** *Colloq.* to exert oneself to an unusual extent to produce a good effect or fine impression.   —*v.i.* **14.** to become stretched out or extended, as a flag in the wind; expand, as in growth.   **15.** to extend over a greater or a considerable area or period.   **16.** to be or lie outspread or fully extended or displayed, as a landscape or scene.   **17.** to admit of being spread or applied in a thin layer, as a soft substance.   **18.** to become extended or distributed over a region, as population, animals, plants, etc.   **19.** become shed abroad, diffused, or disseminated, as light, influences, rumors, ideas, infection, etc.   **20.** to be forced apart, as the rails of a car track.   —*n.* **21.** expansion; extension; diffusion.   **22.** the extent of spreading: *to measure the spread of branches.*   **23.** capacity for spreading: *the spread of an elastic material.*   **24.** a stretch, expanse, or extent of something.   **25.** a cloth covering for a bed, table, or the like, esp. a bedspread.   **26.** *Colloq.* a meal set out, esp. a feast.   **27.** *Colloq.* a pretentious display made.   **28.** any food preparation for spreading on bread, etc., as fruit, jam, or peanut

butter. **29.** *Aeron.* the wing span. **30.** advertising covering several columns or a full page of a newspaper, magazine, etc.
[ME *sprede(n)*, OE *sprǣdan*, c. G *spreiten*] —**spread/.er,** *n.* —**Syn. 1.** unfold, unroll, unfurl, open, expand. **12.** disperse, scatter, circulate.

spread eagle, 1. a representation of an eagle with outspread wings (used as an emblem of the U.S.). **2.** a boastful person. **3.** an acrobatic figure in skating.

spread-ea·gle (sprĕd/ē/gəl), *adj., v.,* -**gled,** -**gling.** —*adj.* **1.** having or suggesting the form of a spread eagle. **2.** *U.S. Colloq.* boastful or bombastic, esp. in the display of patriotism or national vanity. —*v.t.* **3.** to stretch out in the manner of a spread eagle.

spread-ea·gle·ism (sprĕd/ē/gəlĭz/əm), *n. U.S. Colloq.* boastfulness or bombast, esp. in the display of patriotism or national vanity.

spree (sprē), *n.* **1.** a lively frolic. **2.** a bout or spell of drinking to intoxication. [orig. uncert.]

Spree (shprā), *n.* a river in East Germany, flowing through Berlin into the Havel river. ab. 220 mi.

sprig (sprĭg), *n., v.,* **sprigged, sprigging.** —*n.* **1.** a small spray of some plant with its leaves, flowers, etc. **2.** a shoot, twig, or small branch. **3.** an ornament or a decorative figure having the form of such a spray. **4.** *Humorous.* a person as a scion or offshoot of a family or class. **5.** a youth or young fellow. **6.** a small wedge-shaped piece of tin for holding glass in a sash. **7.** a headless brad. —*v.t.* **8.** to decorate (fabrics, pottery, etc.) with a design of sprigs. **9.** to fasten with brads. **10.** to remove a sprig or sprigs from (plants or trees). [ME *sprigge*, orig. uncert.] —**sprig/gy,** *adj.*

spright·ly (sprīt/lĭ), *adj.,* -**lier,** -**liest,** *adv.* —*adj.* **1.** animated, vivacious, or gay; lively. —*adv.* **2.** in a sprightly manner. [f. *spright,* var. of SPRITE + -LY] —**spright/li·ness,** *n.*

spring (sprĭng), *v.,* **sprang** or **sprung, sprung, springing,** *n., adj.* —*v.i.* **1.** to rise or move suddenly and lightly as by some inherent power: *to spring into the air, a tiger about to spring.* **2.** to go or come suddenly as if with a leap: *blood springs to the face.* **3.** to fly back or away in escaping from a forced position, as by resilient or elastic force or from the action of a spring: *a trap springs.* **4.** to start or work out of place, as parts of a mechanism, structure, etc. **5.** to issue suddenly, as water, blood, sparks, fire, etc. (often fol. by *forth, out,* or *up*). **6.** to come into being, rise, or arise (often fol. by *up*): *industries spring up.* **7.** to arise by growth, as from a seed or germ, bulb, root, etc.; grow, as plants. **8.** to proceed or originate, as from a source or cause. **9.** to have one's birth, or be descended, as from a family, person, stock, etc. **10.** to rise or extend upward, as a spire. **11.** to take an upward course or curve from a point of support, as an arch. **12.** to start or rise from cover, as partridges. **13.** to become bent or warped, as boards. **14.** to explode, as a mine. **15.** *Archaic.* to begin to appear, as day, light, etc.
—*v.t.* **16.** to cause to spring. **17.** to cause to fly back, move, or act by elastic force, as a spring, etc.: *to spring a lock.* **18.** to cause to start out of place or work loose. **19.** to split or crack. **20.** to come to have by cracking, etc.: *to spring a leak.* **21.** to bend by force, or force (*in*) by bending, as a slat or bar. **22.** to explode (a mine). **23.** to bring out, disclose, produce, make, etc., suddenly: *to spring a joke.* **24.** to leap over. **25.** *Slang.* to remove (someone) from prison, by bail or jailbreak. —*n.* **26.** a leap, jump, or bound. **27.** a springing or starting from place. **28.** a flying back from a forced position. **29.** an elastic or springy movement. **30.** elasticity or springiness. **31.** a split or crack, as in a mast; a bend or warp, as in a board. **32.** an issue of water from the earth, flowing away as a small stream or standing as a pool or small lake, or the place of such an issue: *mineral springs.* **33.** a source of something. **34.** the rise of an arch, or the point or line at which an arch springs from its support. **35.** the first season of the year (in North America taken as comprising March, April, and May; in Great Britain, February, March, and April). **36.** the first and freshest period: *the spring of life.* **37.** an elastic contrivance or body, as a strip or wire of steel coiled spirally, which recovers its shape after being compressed, bent, etc. **38.** *Archaic.* the dawn, as of day, light, etc. —*adj.* **39.** of, pertaining to, characteristic of, or suitable for the season of spring: *spring flowers.* **40.** resting on or containing springs. [ME; OE *springan,* c. D and G *springen,* Icel. *springa*] —**Syn. 1.** leap, jump, bound. **5.** shoot, dart, fly. **8.** emerge, emanate, issue, flow. **30.** resiliency, buoyancy, vigor. **33.** origin.

Springbok,
Antidorcas marsupialis
(2½ ft. high at the shoulder,
total length ab. 5 ft.)

Springer spaniel
(18½ in. high at the shoulder)

Springs (def. 37)
A, Spiral; B, Coil;
C, Volute; D, Leaf

spring·al¹ (sprĭng/əl), *n. Archaic.* an ancient military engine for throwing stones or other missiles. [ME, t. OF: m. *espringale,* der. *espringuer* spring of Gmc. orig.]

spring·al² (sprĭng/əl), *n.* springald¹.

spring·ald¹ (sprĭng/əld), *n. Archaic.* a youth; a young fellow. [ME *springald,* f. SPRING (def. 36) + -ARD (with dissimilation)]

spring·ald² (sprĭng/əld), *n.* springal¹.

spring beauty, an American spring flower of the portulacaceous genus *Claytonia,* esp. *C. virginica,* a low, succulent herb with a raceme of white or pink flowers.

spring·board (sprĭng/bôrd/), *n.* **1.** a projecting semiflexible board from which persons dive. **2.** a flexible board used as a take-off in vaulting, tumbling, etc., to increase the height of leaps.

spring·bok (sprĭng/bŏk/), *n. pl.* **-boks,** (*esp. collectively*) **-bok.** a South African gazelle, *Antidorcas marsupialis,* which has a habit of springing upward in play or when alarmed. Also, **spring·buck** (sprĭng/bŭk/). [t. S Afr. D: f. *spring(en)* SPRING + *bok* goat, antelope]

springe (sprĭnj), *n., v.,* **springed, springing.** —*n.* **1.** a snare for catching small game. —*v.t.* **2.** to catch in a springe. —*v.i.* **3.** to set springes. [ME *sprengen,* akin to obs. *sprenge,* v., cause to spring, OE *sprengan*]

spring·er (sprĭng/ər), *n.* **1.** one who or that which springs. **2.** Also, **springer spaniel.** a spaniel of any of the larger breeds of field spaniels, including the clumber, used to flush game. **3.** *Archit.* the impost of an arch, or the bottom stone of an arch resting upon the impost. See diag. under **arch.**

spring fever, a listless, lazy feeling felt by some people at the beginning of spring weather.

Spring·field (sprĭng/fēld/), *n.* **1.** a city in S Massachusetts, on the Connecticut river. 174,463 (1960). **2.** the capital of Illinois, in the central part. 83,271 (1960). **3.** a city in W Ohio. 82,723 (1960). **4.** a city in SW Missouri. 95,865 (1960).

spring·halt (sprĭng/hôlt/), *n.* stringhalt.

spring·head (sprĭng/hĕd/), *n.* **1.** the spring or fountainhead from which a stream flows. **2.** the source of something.

spring·let (sprĭng/lĭt), *n.* a little spring (of water).

spring·lock (sprĭng/lŏk/), *n.* a lock which fastens automatically by a spring.

spring·tail (sprĭng/tāl/), *n.* any of various wingless insects of the order *Collembola,* having a pair of elastic taillike appendages which are ordinarily folded under the abdomen, but when suddenly extended enable the insect to spring into the air.

spring tide, 1. the large rise and fall of the tide at or soon after the new or the full moon. **2.** any great flood or swelling rush.

spring·time (sprĭng/tīm/), *n.* **1.** the season of spring. **2.** the first or earliest period. Also, **spring/tide/.**

spring·y (sprĭng/ĭ), *adj.,* **springier, springiest. 1.** characterized by spring or elasticity; elastic; resilient: *a springy step.* **2.** abounding in or having springs (of water), as land. —**spring/i·ly,** *adv.* —**spring/i·ness,** *n.*

sprin·kle (sprĭng/kəl), *v.,* -**kled,** -**kling,** *n.* —*v.t.* **1.** to scatter, as a liquid or a powder, in drops or particles. **2.** to disperse or distribute here and there. **3.** to overspread with drops or particles of water, powder, or the like. **4.** to diversify or intersperse with objects scattered here and there. —*v.i.* **5.** to be sprinkled. **6.** to rain slightly. —*n.* **7.** act of sprinkling. **8.** that which is sprinkled. **9.** a light rain. **10.** a small quantity or number. [ME *sprenkle,* c. G *sprenkeln*] —**sprink/ler,** *n.* —**Syn. 1.** SPRINKLE, SCATTER, STREW mean to fling, spread, or disperse. TO SPRINKLE is to fling about small drops or particles: *to sprinkle water on clothes, powder on plants.* TO SCATTER is to disperse or spread widely: *to scatter seeds.* TO STREW is to scatter, esp. in such a way as to cover or partially cover a surface: *to strew flowers on a grave.* —Ant. **1.** concentrate.

sprinkler system, a system of ceiling pipes in a building, with valves which open automatically at certain temperatures, used for extinguishing fires.

sprin·kling (sprĭng/klĭng), *n.* **1.** a small quantity or number scattered here and there. **2.** a small quantity sprinkled or to be sprinkled.

sprint (sprĭnt), *v.i.* **1.** to race at full speed, esp. for a short distance, as in running, rowing, etc. —*n.* **2.** a short race at full speed. **3.** a brief spell of great activity. [t. Scand.; cf. Icel. *spretta* (where *tt* is for early *nt*)] —**sprint/er,** *n.*

sprit (sprĭt), *n. Naut.* a small pole or spar crossing a fore-and-aft sail diagonally from the mast to the upper aftermost corner, thus serving to extend the sail. [ME *spret,* OE *sprēot,* c. D and G *spriet*]

sprite (sprīt), *n.* an elf, fairy, or goblin. [ME, t. OF: m. *esprit,* or similarly reduced from *esperit(e),* AF *spirit(e)* SPIRIT] —**Syn.** See fairy.

S, Sprit

sprit·sail (sprĭt/sāl/; *Naut.* -səl), *n. Naut.* a sail extended by a sprit.

sprock·et (sprŏk′ĭt), *n.* *Mach.* 1. one of a set of projections on the rim of a wheel which engage the links of a chain. 2. a sprocket wheel.

sprocket wheel, *Mach.* a wheel having sprockets.

Sprocket wheel

sprout (sprout), *v.i.* 1. to begin to grow; shoot forth, as a bud from a seed or stock. 2. (of a seed, plant, the earth, etc.) to put forth buds or shoots. 3. to develop or grow quickly. —*v.t.* 4. to cause to sprout. 5. to remove sprouts from. [ME *spruten*, OE *sprūtan*, c. G *spriessen*] —*n.* 6. a shoot of a plant. 7. a new growth from a germinating seed, or from a rootstock, tuber, bud, or the like. 8. something resembling or suggesting a sprout, as in growth. 9. (*pl.*) Brussels sprouts. [ME *sproute*]

spruce¹ (sprōōs), *n.* 1. any member of the coniferous genus *Picea*, consisting of evergreen trees with short angular needle-shaped leaves attached singly around twigs, as *P. Abies* (**Norway spruce**), *P. glauca* (**white spruce**), and *P. mariana* (**black spruce**). 2. any of various allied trees, as the Douglas fir and the hemlock spruce. 3. the wood of any such tree. [ME, sandhi var. of *Pruce* Prussia, t. OF, t. ML: m. *Prussia*]

spruce² (sprōōs), *adj.,* **sprucer, sprucest,** *v.,* **spruced, sprucing.** —*adj.* 1. smart in dress or appearance; trim; neat; dapper. —*v.t.* 2. to make spruce or smart (often fol. by *up*). —*v.i.* 3. to make oneself spruce (usually fol. by *up*). [? special use of SPRUCE¹ through (obs.) *Spruce leather,* a leather from Prussia used in jerkins, etc.] —**spruce′ly,** *adv.* —**spruce′ness,** *n.*

spruce beer, a fermented beverage made with spruce leaves and twigs, or an extract from them.

spruce grouse. See **grouse¹.**

sprue¹ (sprōō), *n.* *Foundry.* 1. an opening through which molten metal is poured into a mold. 2. the waste piece of metal cast in this opening. [orig. obscure]

sprue² (sprōō), *n.* *Pathol.* a chronic disease, occurring chiefly in the tropics, characterized by diarrhea, ulceration of the mucous membrane of the digestive tract, and a smooth, shining tongue; psilosis. [t. D: m. *spruw*]

sprung (sprŭng), *v.* pt. and pp of **spring.**

sprung rhythm, a system of prosody with the accent always on the first syllable of every foot followed by a varying number of unaccented syllables, all feet being given equal time length.

spry (sprī), *adj.,* **spryer, spryest** or **sprier, spriest.** active; nimble; brisk. [orig. obscure] —**spry′ly,** *adv.* —**spry′ness,** *n.*

spt., seaport.

spud (spŭd), *n.,* *v.,* **spudded, spudding.** —*n.* 1. a spadelike instrument, esp. one with a narrow blade, as for digging up or cutting the roots of weeds. 2. a chisel-like tool for removing bark. 3. *Colloq.* a potato. —*v.t.* 4. to remove with a spud. [ME *spudde* kind of knife]

spue (spū), *v.i., v.t.,* **spued, spuing.** spew.

spume (spūm), *n., v.,* **spumed, spuming.** —*n.* 1. foam; froth; scum. —*v.i.* 2. to foam; froth. —*v.t.* 3. to send forth as or like foam or froth. [ME, t. L: m. *spūma*] —**spu′mous, spum′y,** *adj.*

spu·mes·cent (spū mĕs′ənt), *adj.* foamy; foamlike; frothy. —**spu·mes′cence,** *n.*

spu·mo·ne (spə mō′nī; *It.* spōō mō′nĕ), *n.* Italian ice cream of a very fine and smooth texture, usually containing chopped fruit or nuts. Also, **spu·mo′ni.** [t. It.]

spun (spŭn), *v.* 1. pt. and pp. of **spin.** —*adj.* 2. formed by or as by spinning: *spun rayon, spun silk, spun sugar.*

spunk (spŭngk), *n.* 1. *Colloq.* pluck; spirit; mettle. 2. touchwood, tinder, or punk. [b. SPARK¹ and obs. *funk* spark, touchwood (c. D *vonk,* G *funke* spark]

spunk·y (spŭngk′ī), *adj.,* **spunkier, spunkiest.** *Colloq.* plucky; spirited. —**spunk′i·ly,** *adv.* —**spunk′i·ness,** *n.*

spun yarn, *Naut.* cord formed of rope yarns loosely twisted together, for serving ropes, bending sails, etc.

spur (spûr), *n., v.,* **spurred, spurring.** —*n.* 1. a pointed device attached to a horseman's boot heel, for goading a horse onward, etc. 2. anything that goads, impels, or urges to action or speed. 3. a sharp piercing or cutting instrument fastened on the leg of a gamecock, for use in fighting. 4. something projecting, and resembling or suggesting a spur. 5. a short or stunted branch or shoot, as of a tree. 6. a stiff, usually sharp, horny process on the leg of various birds, esp. the domestic rooster. 7. griffe². 8. *Phys. Geog.* a ridge or line of elevation projecting from or subordinate to the main body of a mountain or mountain range. 9. a slender, usually hollow, projection from some part of a flower, as from the calyx of the larkspur or the corolla of the violet. 10. *Archit.* a. a short wooden brace, usually temporary, for strengthening a post or some other part. b. any offset from a wall, etc., as a buttress. 11. spur track. 12. **on the spur of the moment,** offhand; suddenly. 13. **win one's spurs,** to achieve one's first distinction or success. —*v.t.* 14. to prick with, or as with, spurs or a spur, as in order to urge on. 15. to strike or wound with the spur, as a gamecock. 16. to furnish with spurs or a spur. —*v.i.* 17. to prick one's horse with the spur; ride quickly. 18. to proceed hurriedly; press forward. [ME *spura,* c. G *sporn*] —**spur′like′,** *adj.* —**spur′rer,** *n.*

spurge (spûrj), *n.* 1. any plant of the genus *Euphorbia,*

Spur (def. 1)

some species of which have purgative properties. 2. a euphorbia. [ME, t. OF: m. *espurge,* der. *espurgier* purge, g. L *expurgāre*]

spur gear, *Mach.* a gear in which spur wheels are employed. Also, **spur gearing.** See illus. under **gear.**

spurge laurel, a laurellike shrub, *Daphne laureola,* of southern and western Europe and western Asia, with evergreen leaves and green axillary flowers.

Spur·geon (spûr′jən), *n.* **Charles Haddon,** 1834–92, British Baptist preacher.

spu·ri·ous (spyoŏr′ē əs), *adj.* 1. not genuine or true; counterfeit; not from the reputed, pretended, or right source; not authentic. 2. of illegitimate birth; bastard. 3. *Bot.* bearing superficial resemblances but having morphological differences. [t. L: m. *spurius* false] —**spu′ri·ous·ly,** *adv.* —**spu′ri·ous·ness,** *n.*

spurn (spûrn), *v.t.* 1. to reject with disdain; treat with contempt; scorn; despise. 2. *Obs.* to kick. —*v.i.* 3. to show disdain or contempt. —*n.* 4. disdainful rejection; contemptuous treatment. 5. a kick. [ME; OE *spurnan,* akin to OHG *spurnan,* Icel. *spyrna*] —**spurn′er,** *n.* —**Syn.** 1. See **refuse¹.**

spurred (spûrd), *adj.* 1. having spurs or a spur. 2. bearing spurs or spurlike spines.

spur·ri·er (spûr′ī ər), *n.* a maker of spurs.

spur·rey (spûr′ī), *n., pl.* **-reys.** spurry.

spur·ry (spûr′ī), *n., pl.* **-ries.** 1. any of various herbs of the caryophyllaceous genus *Spergula,* esp. a white-flowered species, *S. arvensis,* with numerous whorled linear leaves. 2. any of various allied or similar plants. [t. MD: m. *spurie.* Cf. ML *spergula*]

spurt (spûrt), *v.i.* 1. to gush or issue suddenly in a stream or jet, as a liquid. 2. to show marked activity or energy for a short period. —*v.t.* 3. to throw or force out suddenly in a stream or jet, as a liquid. —*n.* 4. a forcible gush of water, etc., as from a confined place. 5. a sudden outburst, as of feeling. 6. a marked increase of effort for a short period or distance, as in running, rowing, etc. Also, **spirt.** [var. of *spirt,* metathetic var. of *sprit,* ME *sprutten,* OE *spryttan* come forth; akin to SPROUT] —**Syn.** 1. See **flow.**

spur track, *Railroads.* a short branch track leading from the main track, and connected with it at one end only.

spur wheel, *Mach.* a wheel with projecting teeth on the periphery, which are placed radially about and parallel to the axis.

sput·nik (spoŏt′nĭk, spŭt′-; *Russ.* spoŏt′-nĭk), *n.* an artificial satellite, esp. one of those launched by the Soviet Union. [Russ.: companion]

sput·ter (spŭt′ər), *v.i.* 1. to emit particles of anything in an explosive manner, as a candle does in burning. 2. to eject particles of saliva, food, etc., from the mouth in a similar manner. 3. to utter words or sounds in an explosive, incoherent manner. —*v.t.* 4. to emit (anything) in small particles, as if by spitting. 5. to eject (saliva, food, etc.) in small particles explosively and involuntarily, as in excitement. 6. to utter explosively and incoherently. —*n.* 7. act or sound of sputtering. 8. explosive, incoherent utterance. 9. matter ejected in sputtering. [freq. of SPOUT, c. D *sputteren*] —**sput′ter·er,** *n.*

Spur wheel

spu·tum (spū′təm), *n., pl.* **-ta** (-tə). 1. spittle mixed with mucus, purulent matter, or the like. 2. that which is expectorated; spittle. [t. L]

Spuy·ten Duy·vil Creek (spī′tən dī′vəl), a channel in New York City at the N end of Manhattan Island, connecting the Hudson and Harlem rivers.

spy (spī), *n., pl.* **spies,** *v.,* **spied, spying.** —*n.* 1. one who keeps secret watch on the actions of others. 2. one employed by a government to obtain secret information or intelligence, esp. with reference to military or naval affairs of other countries. 3. act of spying; a careful view. —*v.i.* 4. to make secret observations. 5. to be on the lookout; keep watch. 6. to examine or search closely or carefully. —*v.t.* 7. to make secret observations in (a place) with hostile intent (now usually fol. by *out*). 8. to inspect or examine closely or carefully. 9. to find (*out*) by observation or scrutiny. 10. to catch sight of; decry; see. [ME *spien,* t. OF: m. *espier* ESPY]

spy·glass (spī′glás′, -gläs′), *n.* a small telescope.

Sq., Squadron.

sq., 1. sequence. 2. (L *sequens*) the following (one). 3. (L *sequentia*) the following (ones). 4. square.

sq. ft., 1. square foot. 2. square feet.

sq. in., 1. square inch. 2. square inches.

sq. mi., 1. square mile. 2. square miles.

sqq., *pl.* (L *sequentia*) the following ones.

squab (skwŏb), *n.* 1. a nestling pigeon, marketed when fully grown but still unfledged. 2. a short, stout person. 3. a thickly stuffed, soft cushion. —*adj.* 4. short and thick or broad. 5. (of birds) unfledged or lately hatched. [appar. t. Scand.; cf. d. Sw. *sqvabb* loose fat flesh, d. Norw. *skvabb* soft wet mass]

squab·ble (skwŏb′əl), *v.,* **-bled, -bling,** *n.* —*v.i.* 1. to engage in a petty quarrel. —*v.t.* 2. *Print.* to disarrange and mix (composed type). —*n.* 3. a petty quarrel. [? imit.; cf. d. Sw. *sqvabbel*] —**squab′bler,** *n.*

squab·by (skwŏb′ī), *adj.* short and stout; squat.

squad (skwŏd), *n., v.,* **squadded, squadding.** —*n.* 1. a small number of soldiers (commonly ten men, a staff sergeant, and a corporal); the smallest military unit. **2.** any small group or party of persons engaged in a common enterprise, etc. —*v.t.* **3.** to form into squads. **4.** to assign to a squad. [t. F: m. *escouade*, var. of *esquadre* squadron, t. It.: m. *squadra* SQUARE]

squad car, an automobile communicating with police headquarters by short-wave telephone, used by the police for patrolling.

squad·ron (skwŏd′rən), *n.* **1.** a portion of a naval fleet, or a detachment of warships employed on a particular service; a subdivision of a fleet. **2.** an armored cavalry or cavalry unit consisting of two or more troops (companies), a headquarters, and certain supporting units. **3.** *U.S.* the basic administrative and tactical unit of the Air Force, smaller than a group and composed of two or more flights. **4.** a number of persons grouped or united together for some purpose; a group or body in general. —*v.t.* **5.** to form into a squadron or squadrons; marshal or array in or as in squadrons. [t. It.: m. *squadrone*, der. *squadra* SQUARE]

squal·id (skwŏl′ĭd), *adj.* **1.** foul and repulsive, as from the want of care or cleanliness; dirty; filthy. **2.** wretched; miserable; degraded. [t. L: s. *squālidus*] —**squal′id·ly,** *adv.* —**squal′id·ness,** *n.* —Syn. 1. See dirty.

squall[1] (skwôl), *n.* **1.** a sudden, violent gust of wind, often accompanied by rain, snow, or sleet. **2.** *Colloq.* a disturbance or commotion. —*v.i.* **3.** to blow in a squall. [? akin to SQUALL[2]]

squall[2] (skwôl), *v.i.* **1.** to cry out loudly; scream violently. —*v.t.* **2.** to utter in a screaming tone. —*n.* **3.** act or sound of squalling. [imit.] —**squall′er,** *n.*

squall·y (skwô′lĭ), *adj.,* **squallier, squalliest. 1.** characterized by squalls. **2.** *Colloq.* threatening.

squal·or (skwŏl′ər), *n.* filth and misery. [t. L]

squa·ma (skwā′mə), *n., pl.* **-mae** (-mē). a scale or scalelike part, as of epidermis or bone. [t. L]

squa·mate (skwā′māt), *adj.* provided or covered with squamae or scales; scaly. [t. L: m.s. *squāmātus*]

squa·ma·tion (skwā·mā′shən), *n.* **1.** state of being squamate. **2.** the arrangement of the squamae or scales of an animal.

squa·mo·sal (skwā·mō′səl), *adj.* **1.** *Anat.* pertaining to the thin scalelike bone (an element of the temporal bone) in the side of the skull above and behind the ear. **2.** *Zool.* pertaining to a corresponding bone in other vertebrates. **3.** squamous. —*n.* **4.** a squamosal bone.

squa·mose (skwā′mōs, skwə·mōs′), *adj.* squamous. —**squa′mose·ly,** *adv.* —**squa′mose·ness,** *n.*

squa·mous (skwā′məs), *adj.* covered with or formed of squamae or scales; scalelike. [t. L: m.s. *squāmōsus*] —**squa′mous·ly,** *adv.* —**squa′mous·ness,** *n.*

squam·u·lose (skwăm′yə lōs′, skwā′myə-), *adj.* furnished or covered with small scales.

squan·der (skwŏn′dər), *v.t.* **1.** to spend (money, time, etc.) extravagantly or wastefully (often fol. by *away*). **2.** *Dial.* to scatter. —*n.* **3.** extravagant or wasteful expenditure. [orig. obscure] —**squan′der·er,** *n.* —Syn. 1. waste, dissipate. See spend.

square (skwâr), *n., v.,* **squared, squaring,** *adj.,* **squarer, squarest,** *adv.* —*n.* **1.** a four-sided plane figure having all its sides equal and all its angles right angles. **2.** anything having this form or a form approximating it. **3.** a rectangular or quadrilateral area in a city or town, marked off by neighboring and intersecting streets along each side. **4.** the distance along one side of such an area. **5.** an open area in a city or town, as at the intersection of streets, usually planted with grass, trees, etc. **6.** an L-shaped or T-shaped instrument for determining or testing right angles, and for other purposes. **7.** *Arith., Alg.* the second power of a number or quantity: *the square of 4 is 4 x 4, or 16.* **8.** *Slang.* one who is ignorant of or uninterested in the latest fads. **9.** *Mil.* (formerly) a body of troops drawn up in quadrilateral form. **10.** *Rare.* a true standard. [ME, t. OF: m. *esquare*, ult. der. L *quadra*] —*v.t.* **11.** to reduce to square, rectangular, or cubical form. **12.** to mark out in one or more squares or rectangles. **13.** to test with measuring devices for deviation from a right angle, straight line, or plane surface. **14.** *Math.* **a.** to find the equivalent of in square measure. **b.** to multiply (a number or quantity) by itself. **c.** to describe or find a square which is equivalent to: *to square a circle.* **15.** to bring to the form of a right angle or right angles; set at right angles to something else. **16.** *Sports.* to make the score of (a contest) even. **17.** to set (the shoulders, arms, etc.) so as to present a square or rectangular outline. **18.** to make straight, level, or even. **19.** to regulate, as by a standard. **20.** to adjust harmoniously or satisfactorily; balance; settle: *to square a debt.* **21.** *Slang.* to bribe. —*v.i.* **22.** to assume a posture of defense or offense, as in boxing (often fol. by *off*). **23.** to accord or agree (often fol. by *with*): *his theory does not square with the facts.* **24.** *Golf.* to even up the scores. [ME, t. OF: m. *esquarre*, g. LL *exquadrāre*, v., der. L *quadrāre*] —*adj.* **25.** of the form of a right angle; having some part or parts rectangular: *a square corner.* **26.** having four sides and four right angles, but not equilateral; cubical or approximately so; rectangular and of three dimensions: *a square box.* **27.** at right angles, or perpendicular: *one line square to another.* **28.** *Naut.* at right angles to the mast and the keel, as a yard. **29.** designating a unit representing an area in the form of a square: *a*

square mile. **30.** pertaining to such units, or to surface measurement: *square measure.* **31.** *Arith., Alg.* **a.** See **square number. b.** See **square root. 32.** of a specified length on each side of a square: *an area 2 feet square.* **33.** having a square section, or one that is merely rectangular: *a square file.* **34.** having a solid, sturdy form with rectilinear and angular outlines. **35.** straight, level, or even, as a surface or surfaces. **36.** leaving no balance of debt on either side; having all accounts settled: *to make accounts square.* **37.** just, fair, or honest. **38.** straightforward, direct, or unequivocal. **39.** *Colloq.* substantial or satisfying: *a square meal.* —*adv.* **40.** so as to be square; in square or rectangular form. **41.** at right angles. **42.** *Colloq.* fairly, honestly, or uprightly. [ME, t. OF: m. *esquarre,* pp. of *esquarrer* SQUARE, v.] —**square′ly,** *adv.* —**square′ness,** *n.* —**squar′er,** *n.*

square bracket, *Print.* either of two parenthetical marks: [ ].

square dance, a dance, as a quadrille, by a set of couples arranged in a square or in some set form. —**square dancer.** —**square dancing.**

square deal, *Colloq.* **1.** a mutually fair and honest arrangement or attitude. **2.** a distribution of cards according to the rules of a game, without cheating.

squared ring (skwârd), *Colloq.* the boxing ring.

square·head (skwâr′hĕd′), *n. U.S. Slang (unfriendly).* **1.** a German or a Dutchman. **2.** a Scandinavian.

square knot, a common knot in which the ends come out alongside of the standing parts. See **knot.**

square measure, a system of units for the measurement of surfaces or areas.

square number, a number which is the square of some integer number, as 1, 4, 9, 16, 25, etc., with respect to 1, 2, 3, 4, 5, etc.

square piano. See **piano**[1] (def. 3).

square-rigged (skwâr′rĭgd′), *adj. Naut.* having square sails as the principal sails.

square root, the quantity of which a given quantity is the square: 4 *is the square root of* 16.

square sail, *Naut.* See **sail** (def. 1).

square shooter, *Colloq.* an honest, fair person.

square-toed (skwâr′tōd′), *adj.* **1.** having a broad, square toe, as a shoe. **2.** old-fashioned and homely in habits, ideas, etc.

square-toes (skwâr′tōz′), *n.* an old-fashioned person.

squar·ish (skwâr′ĭsh), *adj.* approximately square.

squar·rose (skwăr′ōs, skwô·rōs′), *adj. Biol.* denoting any rough or ragged surface. [t. L: m.s. *squārrōsus*]

squash[1] (skwŏsh), *v.t.* **1.** to press into a flat mass or pulp; crush. **2.** to suppress or put down; quash. **3.** *Colloq.* to silence, as with a crushing retort. —*v.i.* **4.** to be pressed into a flat mass or pulp. **5.** (of a soft, heavy body) to fall heavily. **6.** to make a splashing sound; splash. —*n.* **7.** act or sound of squashing. **8.** the fact of being squashed. **9.** something squashed or crushed. **10.** something soft and easily crushed. **11.** Also, **squash tennis.** a game resembling tennis and rackets, played in a walled court with rackets and a hollow rubber ball. **12.** Also, **squash rackets.** a game like rackets but played with a rubber ball on a smaller court and with a shorter racket. **13.** *Brit.* a beverage based upon a fruit juice: *a lemon squash.* [t. OF: m.s. *esquasser.* See QUASH; ? partly imit.] —**squash′er,** *n.*

squash[2] (skwŏsh), *n.* **1.** the fruit of any of various vinelike, tendril-bearing plants of the genus *Cucurbita,* used as a vegetable, esp. *C. moschata* or *C. maxima.* **2.** any of these plants. [t. Narragansett, Massachusetts, abbr. of *askútasquash,* lit., vegetables eaten green]

squash bug, an ill-smelling, dark-colored heteropterous insect, *Anasa tristis,* of North America, injurious to squashes, pumpkins, melons, etc.

squash·y (skwŏsh′ĭ), *adj.,* **squashier, squashiest. 1.** easily squashed; pulpy. **2.** soft and wet, as ground, etc. **3.** having a squashed appearance. —**squash′i·ly,** *adv.* —**squash′i·ness,** *n.*

squat (skwŏt), *v.,* **squatted** or **squat, squatting,** *adj., n.* —*v.i.* **1.** to sit down in a low or crouching position with the legs drawn up closely beneath or in front of the body. **2.** to crouch or cower down, as an animal. **3.** to settle on land, esp. public or new land, without any title or right. **4.** to settle on public land under government regulation, as to acquire title. —*v.t.* **5.** to cause (a person, oneself, etc.) to squat. —*adj.* **6.** short and thickset or thick, as persons, animals, the body, etc. **7.** low and thick or broad. **8.** seated or being in a squatting position; crouching. —*n.* **9.** act or fact of squatting. **10.** a squatting position or posture. [ME, t. OF: m.s. *esquatir,* f. *es-* (g. L *ex-* EX-[1]) out + *quatir* press down (der. L *coactus,* pp., driven together)]

squat·ter (skwŏt′ər), *n.* **1.** one who or that which squats. **2.** one who settles on land, esp. public or new land, without title or right. **3.** one who settles on land under government regulation, as to acquire title.

squat·ty (skwŏt′ĭ), *adj.,* **-tier, -tiest.** short and thick; low and broad.

squaw (skwô), *n.* a North American Indian woman or wife. [t. Narragansett: m. *eskaw* woman]

squaw·fish (skwô′fĭsh′), *n., pl.* **-fishes,** (*esp. collectively*) **-fish. 1.** a large cyprinoid food fish, *Ptychocheilus*

---

b., blend of, blended; c., cognate with; d., dialect, dialectal; der., derived from; f., formed from; g., going back to; m., modification of; r., replacing; s., stem of; t., taken from; ?, perhaps. See the full key on inside cover.

oregonensis, of rivers of the Pacific coast of the U.S. and Canada. 2. a viviparous perch, *Taenioloca lateralis*, of the Pacific Coast of the U.S.

squawk (skwôk), *v.i.* 1. to utter a loud, harsh cry, as a duck or other fowl when frightened. 2. *Slang.* to complain loudly and vehemently. —*v.t.* 3. to give forth with a squawk. —*n.* 4. a loud, harsh cry or sound. 5. *Slang.* a loud, vehement complaint. 6. the black-crowned night heron (*Nycticorax n. naevius*). [b. SQUALL² and CROAK] —**squawk′er,** *n.*

squaw man, a white or other non-Indian man who has taken (or lives with) an Indian squaw as his wife.

squaw-root (skwô′rŏŏt′, -rŏŏt′), *n.* a fleshy, leafless orobanchaceous plant, *Conopholis americana*, of eastern North America, found in clusters, esp. under oaks.

squeak (skwēk), *n.* 1. a short, sharp, shrill cry; a sharp, high-pitched sound. 2. *Colloq.* a bare chance. 3. *Colloq.* a narrow escape. —*v.i.* 4. to utter or emit a squeak or squeaky sound. 5. *Slang.* to confess or turn informer. —*v.t.* 6. to utter or produce with a squeak or squeaks. [ME *squeke*, appar. t. Scand.; cf. Sw. *sqväka* croak] —**squeak′er,** *n.*

squeak-y (skwē′kĭ), *adj.*, **squeakier, squeakiest.** squeaking; tending to squeak: *his squeaky shoes could be heard across the lobby.* —**squeak′i·ly,** *adv.* —**squeak′-i·ness,** *n.*

squeal (skwēl), *n.* 1. a more or less prolonged, sharp, shrill cry, as of pain, fear, etc. 2. *Slang.* a turning informer. —*v.i.* 3. to utter or emit a squeal or squealing sound. 4. *Slang.* to turn informer. —*v.t.* 5. to reveal or produce with a squeal. 6. *Slang.* to disclose or reveal, as something secret. [imit.] —**squeal′er,** *n.*

squeam-ish (skwē′mĭsh), *adj.* 1. easily shocked by anything slightly immodest; prudish. 2. excessively particular or scrupulous as to the moral aspect of things. 3. fastidious or dainty. 4. easily nauseated. [late ME *squaymysch*, r. ME *squaymous*, earlier *scoymous*, t. AF: m. *escoymous*; orig. unknown] —**squeam′ish·ly,** *adv.* —**squeam′ish·ness,** *n.*

squee-gee (skwē′jē, skwē jē′), *n., v.,* -**geed, -geeing.** —*n.* 1. an implement edged with rubber or the like, for removing water from windows after washing, sweeping water from wet decks, etc. 2. *Photog.* a device for removing surplus water from negatives or prints. —*v.t.* 3. to sweep, scrape, or press with a squeegee. Also, **squilgee.** [? der. *squeege*, var. of SQUEEZE]

squeeze (skwēz), *v.,* **squeezed, squeezing,** *n.* —*v.t.* 1. to press forcibly together; compress. 2. to apply pressure to in order to extract something: *to squeeze a lemon.* 3. to thrust forcibly; force by pressure; cram: *to squeeze three suits into a small suitcase.* 4. to force out, extract, or procure by pressure (usually fol. by *out* or *from*): *to squeeze juice from an orange.* 5. to harass or oppress (a person, etc.) by exactions. 6. *Colloq.* to put pressure upon (a person or persons) to act in a given way, esp. by blackmail. 7. to obtain a facsimile impression of. 8. *Bridge.* to force (an opponent) to dispose of one of two or more winning cards by playing it to a trick he cannot win. —*v.i.* 9. to exert a compressing force. 10. to force a way through some narrow or crowded place (fol. by *through, in, out,* etc.). —*n.* 11. act of squeezing. 12. fact of being squeezed. 13. a tight pressure of another's hand within one's own, as in friendliness. 14. a hug or close embrace. 15. *Colloq.* a situation from which extrication is difficult: *in a tight squeeze.* 16. a small quantity or amount of anything obtained by squeezing. 17. a facsimile impression of an inscription or the like, obtained by pressing some plastic substance over or around it. 18. *Bridge.* the play or circumstances whereby one is squeezed. 19. *Colloq.* act of blackmailing. [akin to obs. *squize* squeeze, OE *cwȳsan* (with *s*- by false division of words in sandhi)] —**squeez′er,** *n.*

squeeze play, 1. *Baseball.* a play executed when there is a runner on third base and usually not more than one man out, in which the runner starts for home as soon as the pitcher makes a motion to pitch, and the batter bunts. 2. *Bridge.* a play in which one forces one's opponent to discard a potentially winning card.

squelch (skwĕlch), *v.t.* 1. to strike or press with crushing force; crush down; squash. 2. *Colloq.* to put down or suppress completely; silence, as with a crushing retort. —*v.i.* 3. to make a splashing sound. 4. to tread heavily in water, mud, wet shoes, etc., with such a sound. —*n.* 5. a squelched or crushed mass of anything. 6. a squelching sound. 7. *Colloq.* a crushing argument or retort. [var. of *quelch* (b. QUELL and CRUSH), with *s*- by false division of words in sandhi] —**squelch′er,** *n.*

sque·teague (skwē tēg′), *n.* 1. an important Atlantic food fish, *Cynoscion regalis*, of the croaker family (*Sciaenidae*). 2. the sea trout (def. 2).

squib (skwĭb), *n., v.,* **squibbed, squibbing.** —*n.* 1. a short witty or sarcastic saying or writing. 2. a firework consisting of a tube or ball filled with powder, which burns with a hissing noise terminated usually by a slight explosion. 3. a firecracker broken in the middle so that when lighted it burns with a hissing noise. 4. *Brit.* any firecracker. 5. *Obs.* a mean or paltry fellow. —*v.i.* 6. to write squibs. 7. to shoot a squib. 8. to go off with a small, sharp sound. 9. to move swiftly and irregularly. —*v.t.* 10. to assail in squibs or lampoons. 11. to toss, shoot, or utilize, as a squib. [orig. uncert.]

squid (skwĭd), *n., pl.* **squids,** (esp. *collectively*) **squid.** any of various decapod dibranchiate cephalopods, esp. any of certain small species (as of *Loligo* and *Ommastrephes*) having slender bodies and caudal fins and much used for bait. [orig. obscure]

squiff-y (skwĭf′ĭ), *adj. Chiefly Brit. Slang.* slightly intoxicated.

squil-gee (skwĭl′jē, skwĭl jē′), *n., v.t.,* -**geed, -geeing.** squeegee.

squill (skwĭl), *n.* 1. the bulb of the sea onion, *Urginea maritima*, cut into thin slices and dried, and used in medicine chiefly as an expectorant. 2. the plant itself. 3. any of the plants of the liliaceous genus *Scilla*. [ME, t. L: s. *squilla*, var. of *scilla*, t. Gk.: m. *skilla*]

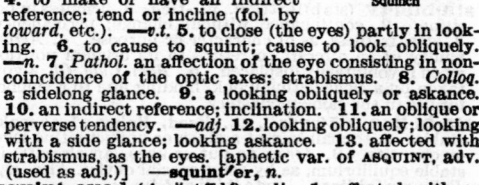
Squid.
Loligo pealei
(6 in. long)

squil-la (skwĭl′ə), *n., pl.* **squillas, squillae** (skwĭl′ē). *Zool.* a mantis crab. [t. L. See SQUILL]

squinch (skwĭnch), *n. Archit.* a small arch, corbeling, or the like, built across the interior angle between two walls, as in a square tower for supporting the side of a superimposed octagonal spire. [var. of obs. or d. *scunch* for *scuncheon*, ME *scochon*, t. OF: m. *escoinson*, appar. der. *es-* (g. L *ex-* EX--) out + *coin* angle (g. L *cuneus* wedge)]

squint (skwĭnt), *v.i.* 1. to look with the eyes partly closed. 2. to be affected with strabismus; be cross-eyed. 3. to look or glance obliquely or sidewise; look askance. 4. to make or have an indirect reference; tend or incline (fol. by *toward*, etc.). —*v.t.* 5. to close (the eyes) partly in looking. 6. to cause to squint; cause to look obliquely. —*n.* 7. *Pathol.* an affection of the eye consisting in non-coincidence of the optic axes; strabismus. 8. *Colloq.* a sidelong glance. 9. a looking obliquely or askance. 10. an indirect reference; inclination. 11. an oblique or perverse tendency. —*adj.* 12. looking obliquely; looking with a side glance; looking askance. 13. affected with strabismus, as the eyes. [aphetic var. of ASQUINT, adv. (used as adj.)] —**squint′er,** *n.*

Squinch

squint-eyed (skwĭnt′īd′), *adj.* 1. affected with or characterized by strabismus. 2. looking obliquely or askance.

squire (skwīr), *n., v.,* **squired, squiring.** —*n.* 1. (in England) a country gentleman, esp. the chief landed proprietor in a district. 2. *U. S.* a justice of the peace, local judge, or other local dignitary (chiefly used as a title) in country districts and small towns. 3. a young man of gentle birth who, as an aspirant to knighthood, attended upon a knight; an esquire. 4. a personal attendant, as of a person of rank. 5. a man who attends or escorts a lady in public. —*v.t.* 6. to attend as or in the manner of a squire. [ME *squier*, t. OF: m. *esquier.* See ESQUIRE]

squire-ar-chy (skwīr′är kĭ), *n., pl.* -**archies.** *Brit.* 1. the class of squires collectively. 2. rule or government by a squire or squires. [f. SQUIRE + -ARCHY]

squire-ling (skwīr′lĭng), *n.* a petty squire.

squirm (skwûrm), *v.i.* 1. to wriggle or writhe. 2. to be sharply or painfully affected, as by reproof or sarcasm. —*n.* 3. a squirming or wriggling movement. [b. SKEW and WORM, v.] —**squirm′y,** *adj.*

squir-rel (skwûr′əl, *or, esp. Brit.,* skwĭr′əl), *n.* 1. any of the arboreal bushy-tailed rodents constituting the genus *Sciurus* (family *Sciuridae*), as the common European squirrel, *S. vulgaris,* and the gray squirrel, *S. carolinensis,* of the United States. 2. any of various other members of the family *Sciuridae,* as the chipmunks, flying squirrels, woodchucks, etc. [ME *squirel,* t. AF: m. *esquirel,* dim. der. LL *sciūrus,* t. Gk.: m. *skiouros,* der. *skiá* shadow + *ourá* tail]

Common gray squirrel,
Sciurus carolinensis
(Total length 18 in., tail 8½ in.)

squirrel corn, an American papaveraceous herb, *Dicentra* (or *Bikukulla*) *canadensis,* with finely dissected leaves and cream-colored flowers.

squirt (skwûrt), *v.i.* 1. to eject liquid in a jet from a narrow orifice. 2. to issue in a jetlike stream. —*v.t.* 3. to cause (liquid) to issue in a jet from a narrow orifice. 4. to wet or bespatter with a liquid so ejected. —*n.* 5. act of squirting. 6. a jet, as of water. 7. an instrument for squirting, as a syringe. 8. a small quantity of liquid squirted. 9. *Colloq.* an insignificant, self-assertive fellow. [orig. obscure] —**squirt′er,** *n.*

squirting cucumber, a cucurbitaceous plant, *Ecballium Elaterium,* native in the Mediterranean region, whose ripened fruit forcibly ejects the seeds and juice.

sq. yd., 1. square yard. 2. square yards.

Sr, *Chem.* strontium.

Sr., 1. Senior. 2. *Spanish.* Señor. 3. Sir.

Sri-na-gar (srē nŭg′ər), *n.* the capital of Kashmir, on the Jhelum river. 207,787 (1941).

S.R.O., standing room only.

SS, 1. (L *Sancti*) Saints. 2. (L *scilicet*) namely.

ss, 1. sections. 2. *Baseball.* shortstop.

S.S., 1. steamship. 2. Sunday School.

SS.D., (L *Sanctissimus Dominus*) Most Holy Lord (a title of the Pope).

SSE, south-southeast. Also, **S.S.E.**

SSR, Socialist Soviet Republic. Also, **S.S.R.**

SS Troops, the Schutzstaffel.

SSW, south-southwest. Also, **S.S.W.**

St., 1. Saint. 2. statute. 3. Strait. 4. Street.

st., 1. stanza. 2. stet. 3. stone (weight). 4. strait. 5. street.

s.t., short ton.

sta., 1. station. 2. stationary.

stab (stăb), *v.,* **stabbed, stabbing,** *n.* —*v.t.* 1. to pierce or wound with, or as with, a pointed weapon. 2. to thrust or plunge (a knife, etc.), as into something. 3. to penetrate sharply, like a knife. —*v.i.* 4. to thrust with or as with a knife or other pointed weapon: *to stab at an adversary.* 5. to deliver a wound, as with a pointed weapon. —*n.* 6. act of stabbing. 7. a thrust or blow with, or as with, a pointed weapon. 8. a wound made by stabbing. [ME, var. of d. *stob* in same sense, ? v. use of ME *stob* stick] —**stab′ber,** *n.*

Sta·bat Ma·ter (stā′băt mā′tər, stä′băt mä′tər), 1. a celebrated 13th century Latin hymn on the Virgin Mary at the Cross. 2. a musical setting for this. [L: the mother was standing]

sta·bile (stā′bῑl, stăb′ῑl), *adj.* 1. fixed in position; stable. 2. *Med.* a. resistant to moderate degrees of heat. b. denoting or pertaining to a mode of application of electricity in which the active electrode is kept stationary over the part to be acted upon (opposed to *labile*). [t. L: m.s. *stabilis* STABLE²]

sta·bil·i·ty (stə·bῑl′ə·tῑ), *n., pl.* **-ties.** 1. firmness in position. 2. continuance without change; permanence. 3. steadfastness, as of character or purpose. 4. *Aeron.* ability of an aircraft to return to its original position when involuntarily displaced. 5. *Rom. Cath. Ch.* a vow taken by a Benedictine monk, binding him to residence for life in the same monastery.

sta·bi·lize (stā′bə·līz), *v.t.,* **-lized, -lizing.** 1. to make stable. 2. to maintain at a given or unfluctuating level or quantity. 3. *Aeron.* to put or keep (an aircraft) in stable equilibrium, as by some special device. Also, *esp. Brit.,* **sta′bi·lise′.** —**sta′bi·li·za′tion,** *n.*

sta·bi·liz·er (stā′bə·lī′zər), *n.* 1. one who or that which stabilizes. 2. *Aeron.* a device for stabilizing an aircraft, as a tail surface on an airplane. 3. any compound which, when included with an explosive, decreases the ability of the latter to decompose spontaneously.

sta·ble¹ (stā′bəl), *n., v.,* **-bled, -bling.** —*n.* 1. a building for the lodging and feeding of horses, cattle, etc. 2. such a building with stalls. 3. a collection of animals belonging in such a building. 4. *Racing.* a. an establishment where race horses are kept and trained. b. the horses belonging to, or the persons connected with, such an establishment. —*v.t.* 5. to put or lodge in or as in a stable. —*v.i.* 6. to live in or as in a stable. [ME, t. OF: m. *estable,* g. L *stabulum*]

sta·ble² (stā′bəl), *adj.* 1. not likely to fall or give way, as a structure, support, foundation, etc.; firm; steady. 2. able or likely to continue or last; enduring or permanent: *a stable government.* 3. steadfast; not wavering or changeable, as a person, the mind, etc. 4. *Physics.* having or showing an ability or tendency to maintain or reestablish position, form, etc.: *stable equilibrium.* 5. *Chem.* not readily decomposing, as a compound; resisting molecular or chemical change. [ME, t. F, g. L *stabilis*] —**sta′ble·ness,** *n.* —**sta′bly,** *adv.*

sta·ble·boy (stā′bəl·boi′), *n.* a boy working in a stable. Also, **sta·ble·man** (stā′bəl·măn′, -mən).

sta·bling (stā′blῑng), *n.* 1. accommodation for horses, etc., in a stable or stables. 2. stables collectively.

stab·lish (stăb′lῑsh), *v.t.* *Archaic.* establish.

stacc., *Music.* staccato.

stac·ca·to (stə·kä′tō; *It.* stäk·kä′tō), *adj. Music.* 1. detached, disconnected, or abrupt. 2. with breaks between the successive tones (opposed to *legato*). [t. It., pp. of *staccare,* short for *distaccare* DETACH]

Written   *Played*

Staccato phrase

stack (stăk), *n.* 1. a large, usually circular or rectangular, pile of hay, straw, or the like. 2. any more or less orderly pile or heap. 3. (*often pl.*) a set of bookshelves ranged one above another, as in a library. 4. a number of chimneys or flues grouped together. 5. a single chimney or funnel for smoke. 6. *Colloq.* a great quantity or number. 7. a number of muskets or rifles hooked together to stand on the ground in a conical group. 8. an English measure for coal and wood, equal to 108 cubic feet. —*v.t.* 9. to pile or arrange in a stack: *to stack hay.* 10. to cover or load with something in stacks or piles. 11. to arrange (playing cards in the pack) in an unfair manner. [ME *siak,* t. Scand.; cf. Icel. *stakkr* haystack; akin to Russ. *stog* haystack] —**stack′er,** *n.*

stac·te (stăk′tē), *n. Bible.* one of the sweet spices which composed the holy incense of the ancient Jews. Ex. 30:34. [t. L, t. Gk.: m. *staktē,* fem. of *staktós* distilling in drops; r. ME *stacten,* t. L, acc. of *staktē*]

stad·hold·er (stăd′hōl′dər), *n.* 1. the chief magistrate of the former republic of the United Provinces of the Netherlands. 2. (formerly, in the Netherlands) the

viceroy or governor of a province. Also, **stadtholder.** [t. D: m. *stadhouder,* f. *stad* place, city + *houder* holder]

sta·di·a¹ (stā′dῑə), *Civ. Eng.* —*n.* 1. a method of surveying in which distances are read by noting the interval on a graduated rod (**stadia rod**) intercepted by two parallel cross hairs (**stadia hairs** or **wires**) mounted in the telescope of a transit, the rod being placed at one end of the distance to be measured and the transit at the other. —*adj.* 2. pertaining to stadia surveying. [orig. uncert.; prob. special use of STADIA²]

sta·di·a² (stā′dῑə), *n. pl.* of **stadium.**

sta·di·om·e·ter (stā′dῑ·ŏm′ə·tər), *n.* an instrument for measuring the lengths of curves, dashed lines, etc., by running a toothed wheel over them. [f. *stadio-* (comb. form of STADIUM) + -METER]

sta·di·um (stā′dῑ·əm), *n., pl.* **-diums, -dia** (-dῑə). 1. an ancient Greek course for foot races, typically semicircular, with tiers of seats for spectators. 2. a similar modern structure for athletic games, etc. 3. an ancient Greek unit of length, equal at Athens to about 607 English feet. [t. L, t. Gk.: m. *stadion*]

stadt·hold·er (stăt′hōl′dər), *n.* stadholder.

Staël-Hols·tein (stäl′ōls·tēn′), *n.* **Anne Louise Germaine Necker** (àn lwēz zhĕr·mĕn′ nĕ·kĕr′), **Baronne de,** (*Madame de Staël*) 1766–1817, French writer.

staff¹ (stăf, stäf), *n., pl.* **staves** (stāvz) or **staffs** for 1–5, 9; **staffs** for 6–8; *adj., v.* —*n.* 1. a stick, pole, rod, or wand for aid in walking or climbing, for use as a weapon, etc. 2. a rod or wand serving as an ensign of office or authority, as a crozier, baton, truncheon, or mace. 3. a pole on which a flag is hung or displayed. 4. something which serves to support or sustain: *bread is the staff of life.* 5. a body of assistants to a manager, superintendent, or executive head. 6. a body of persons charged with carrying out the work of an establishment or executing some undertaking. 7. *Mil., Naval.* a. a body of officers without command authority, appointed to assist a commanding officer. b. the parts of any army concerned with administrative matters, planning, etc., instead of with actual participation in combat. 8. *Music.* a set of horizontal lines, now five in number, with the corresponding four spaces between them, music being written on both the lines [and spaces. 9. *Archaic or Dial.* a stick or pole forming part of something, as the shaft of a spear, a rung of a ladder, etc. —*adj.* 10. of, or being a member of, a military or naval staff or unit: *staff officer.* —*v.t.* 11. to provide with a staff. [ME; OE *stæf,* c. D *staf,* G *stab,* Icel *stafr*]

staff² (stăf, stäf), *n.* a kind of plaster combined with fibrous material, used for temporary ornamental buildings, etc. [orig. unknown]

Staf·fa (stăf′ə), *n.* See **Fingal's Cave.**

Staf·ford (stăf′ərd), *n.* a city in central England: the county seat of Staffordshire. 40,275 (1951).

Staf·ford·shire (stăf′ərd·shῑr′, -shər), *n.* a county in central England. 1,621,034 pop. (1951); 1154 sq. mi. *Co. seat:* Stafford. Also, **Stafford** or **Staffs** (stăfs).

staff sergeant, *U.S.* 1. a noncommissioned officer ranking in the Air Force below a technical sergeant and above an airman first class, in the Marine Corps below a technical sergeant and above a sergeant. 2. in the Army, formerly, a noncommissioned officer below a technical sergeant and above a sergeant (now corresponds to sergeant).

stag (stăg), *n., v.,* **stagged, stagging,** *adj.* —*n.* 1. an adult male deer. 2. the male of various other animals. 3. *Colloq.* a man, esp. a man unaccompanied by a woman at a social gathering. 4. a swine castrated after maturation of the sex organs. —*v.i.* 5. to go to a social function without a woman partner. —*adj.* 6. for or of men only: *a stag dinner.* [ME *stagge,* OE (unrecorded) *stagga,* akin to Icel. *steggr* male fox, tomcat]

Stag of English red deer,
Cervus elephas scoticus
(4 ft. high at the shoulder,
antlers 3 ft. long)

stag beetle, any of the lamellicorn beetles constituting the family *Lucanidae.* The males have mandibles resembling a stag's antlers.

stage (stāj), *n., v.,* **staged, staging.** —*n.* 1. a single step or degree in a process; a particular period in a process of development. 2. a raised platform or floor, as for speakers, performers, etc. 3. *Theat.* a. the platform in a theater on which the actors perform. b. this platform with all the parts of the theater, and all the apparatus back of the proscenium. 4. the theater, the drama, or the dramatic profession. 5. the scene of any action or career. 6. a stagecoach. 7. a place of rest on a journey; a regular stopping place of a stagecoach or the like, for the change of horses, etc. 8. the distance between two places of rest on a journey; each of the portions of a journey. 9. a portion or period of a course of action, of life, etc. 10. **by easy stages,** without rushing; working or traveling with many stops. 11. *Zool.* a. any one of the major time periods in the development of an insect, as the embryonic, larval, pupal, and imaginal stages. b. any one of the periods of larval growth between molts. 12. *Econ., Sociol.* a major phase of the economic or sociological life of man or society: *the matriarchal stage.* **13.** *Geol.* a division of stratified rocks of next lower rank to series, representing deposits formed during the fraction of an epoch that is called an age. **14.** the small platform of a microscope on which the object to be examined is placed. See **microscope. 15.** *Radio.* an element in a complex mechanism, as a tube and its accessory structures in a multiple amplifier. —*v.t.* **16.** to put, represent, or exhibit on or as on a stage. **17.** to furnish with a stage or staging. [ME, t. OF: m. *estage,* ult. der. L *stāre* stand]

Stagecoach

stage-coach (stāj/-kōch/), *n.* a coach that runs regularly over a fixed route with passengers, parcels, etc.

stage-craft (stāj/kraft/, -kräft/), *n.* skill in writing, adapting, or staging plays.

stage fright, nervousness experienced on facing an audience, esp. for the first time.

stage-hand (stāj/hand/), *n.* a person employed to move properties, regulate lighting, etc., in a dramatic production.

stage manager, one who superintends the performance of a play and regulates the stage arrangements.

stag-er (stā/jər), *n.* **1.** a person of experience in some profession, way of life, etc. **2.** *Archaic.* an actor.

stage-struck (stāj/strŭk/), *adj.* obsessed with the desire to become an actor or actress.

stage whisper, 1. a loud whisper on a stage, meant to be heard by the audience. **2.** a whisper meant to be heard by others than the person addressed.

stag-ger (stăg/ər), *v.i.* **1.** to walk, move, or stand unsteadily; sway. **2.** to begin to give way, as troops. **3.** to begin to doubt or waver, as in opinion; hesitate. —*v.t.* **4.** to cause to reel, totter, or become unsteady: *to stagger the mind.* **5.** to shock; render helpless with amazement or the like. **6.** to cause to waver or falter. **7.** to arrange in a zigzag order or manner, as spokes in the hub of a wheel. **8.** *Aeron.* to arrange (the planes of a biplane, etc.) so that the entering edge of an upper plane is either in advance of or behind that of a corresponding lower plane. **9.** to arrange in some other order or manner than the regular, uniform, or usual one, esp. at such intervals that there is a continuous overlapping: *to stagger lunch hours so that the cafeteria is not rushed.* —*n.* **10.** act of staggering; a reeling or tottering movement or motion. **11.** a staggered order or arrangement. **12.** *Aeron.* **a.** a staggered arrangement of planes. **b.** the amount of staggering. **13.** (*pl.* construed as *sing.*) *Vet. Sci.* any of various forms of cerebral and spinal disease in horses, cattle, and other animals, characterized by blindness, a staggering gait, sudden falling, etc. [var. of obs. or prov. *stacker,* ME *staker(en),* t. Scand.; cf. Icel. *stakra*] —**stag/ger-er,** *n.* —**stag/ger-ing-ly,** *adv.*

—**Syn. 1.** STAGGER, REEL, TOTTER suggest an unsteady manner of walking. To STAGGER is successively to lose and regain one's equilibrium and the ability to maintain one's direction: *to stagger with exhaustion, a heavy load, or intoxication.* To REEL is to sway dizzily and be in imminent danger of falling: *to reel when faint with hunger.* TOTTER suggests the immediate likelihood of falling from weakness or feebleness, and is used particularly as of infants or the very aged, who walk with shaky, uncertain, faltering steps: *an old man tottered along with a cane*

stag-ger-bush (stăg/ər boŏsh/), *n.* an American ericaceous shrub, *Pieris mariana,* with a foliage poisonous to animals.

stag-hound (stăg/hound/), *n.* a hound used for hunting stags, etc., resembling the foxhound, but larger.

stag-ing (stā/jing), *n.* **1.** act or process of putting a play on the stage. **2.** a temporary platform or structure of posts and boards for support, as in building; scaffolding. **3.** the business of running stagecoaches. **4.** act of traveling by stages or by stagecoach.

Stag-i-rite (stăj/ə rīt/), *n.* **1.** a native or inhabitant of Stagira, a city of ancient Macedonia. **2. the Stagirite,** Aristotle, who was born there.

stag-nant (stăg/nənt), *adj.* **1.** not running or flowing, as water, air, etc. **2.** foul from standing, as a pool of water. **3.** inactive, sluggish, or dull. [t. L: s. *stagnans,* ppr.] —**stag/nan-cy,** *n.* —**stag/nant-ly,** *adv.*

stag-nate (stăg/nāt), *v.i.* -nated, -nating. **1.** to cease to run or flow, as water, air. etc. **2.** to become foul from standing, as a pool of water. **3.** to become inactive, sluggish, or dull. [t. L: m.s. *stagnātus,* pp.] —**stag-na/-tion,** *n.*

stag-y (stā/jǐ), *adj.,* **stagier, stagiest.** of, pertaining to, or suggestive of the stage; theatrical. —**stag/i-ly,** *adv.* —**stag/i-ness,** *n.*

Stahl-helm (shtäl/hělm/), *n.* a monarchist, nationalist military organization founded by former soldiers in Germany after World War I. [t. G: steel helmet]

staid (stād), *adj.* **1.** of settled or sedate character; not flighty or capricious. **2.** *Rare.* fixed, settled, or permanent. —*v.* **3.** a pt. and pp. of stay[1]. [var. of *stayed,* pp. of STAY[1]] —**staid/ly,** *adv.* —**staid/ness,** *n.*

—**Syn. 1.** STAID, SEDATE, SETTLED indicate a sober and composed type of conduct. STAID indicates an ingrained seriousness and propriety which shows itself in complete

decorum; a colorless kind of correctness is indicated: *a staid and uninteresting old maid.* SEDATE applies to one who is noticeably quiet, composed, and sober in conduct: *a sedate and dignified young man.* One who is SETTLED has become fixed, esp. in a sober or determined way, in his manner, judgments, or mode of life: *he is young to seem so settled in his ways.* —**Ant. 1.** flighty, frivolous, unstable.

stain (stān), *n.* **1.** a discoloration produced by foreign matter; a spot. **2.** a natural spot or patch of different color, as on the body of an animal. **3.** a cause of reproach; blemish: *a stain on one's reputation.* **4.** coloration produced by staining anything. **5.** a dye made into a solution and used to color woods, textiles, tissues, etc. **6.** a reagent or dye used in staining microscopic specimens. —*v.t.* **7.** to discolor with spots or streaks of foreign matter. **8.** to bring reproach upon; blemish. **9.** to sully with guilt or infamy; corrupt. **10.** to color in a particular way. **11.** to color with something which penetrates the substance. **12.** to treat (a microscopic specimen) with some reagent or dye in order to color the whole or parts and so give distinctness, contrast of tissues, etc. —*v.i.* **13.** to produce a stain. **14.** to become stained; take a stain. [ME *steyne,* t. Scand. (cf. Icel. *steina* to paint); in some senses, aphetic var. of DISTAIN] —**stain/a-ble,** *adj.* —**stain/er,** *n.* —**stain/-less,** *adj.* —**stain/less-ly,** *adv.*

stained glass, colored, enameled, or painted glass, usually used in church windows. —**stained/-glass/,** *adj.*

stainless steel, a hard steel alloyed with a high percentage of chromium, from 8 to approximately 25 per cent, proof against rust and many corrosive agents.

stair (stâr), *n.* **1.** a series or flight of steps forming a means of passage from one story or level to another, as in a building. **2.** a single step of such a series. **3.** (*pl.*) such steps collectively, esp. as forming a flight or a series of flights. [ME *steire,* OE *stǣger,* c. D and LG *steiger* landing stage]

stair-case (stâr/kās/), *n.* a flight of stairs with its framework, balusters, etc., or a series of such flights.

stair-head (stâr/hěd/), *n.* the top of a staircase.

stair-way (stâr/wā/), *n.* a way up and down by a series of stairs; a staircase.

stair-well (stâr/wĕl/), *n.* the vertical shaft or opening containing a stairway.

stake[1] (stāk), *n., v.,* **staked, staking.** —*n.* **1.** a stick or post pointed at one end for driving into the ground as a boundary mark, a part of a fence, a support for a plant, etc. **2.** a post, esp. one to which a person is bound for execution, usually by burning. **3. the stake,** the punishment of death by burning. **4.** one of a number of vertical posts fitting into sockets or staples on the edge of the platform of a vehicle, as to retain the load. —*v.t.* **5.** to mark with stakes (often fol. by *off* or *out*). **6.** to protect (*with*), separate (*off*), shut (*in* or *out*), close (*up*), etc., by a barrier of stakes. **7.** to support with a stake or stakes, as a plant. **8.** to tether or secure to a stake, as an animal. **9.** to fasten (*down,* etc.) with a stake or stakes. [ME; OE *staca,* c. D *staak,* G *stake;* akin to STICK[1]]

stake[2] (stāk), *n., v.,* **staked, staking.** —*n.* **1.** that which is wagered in a game, race, or contest. **2.** an interest held in something. **3.** the funds with which a gambler operates. **4.** (*often pl.*) a prize in a race or contest. **5.** state of being staked or at hazard: *to be at stake.* **6.** *U.S. Colloq.* a grubstake. —*v.t.* **7.** to put at hazard upon the result of a game, the event of a contingency, etc.; wager; venture or hazard. **8.** *U.S. Colloq.* to grubstake. **9.** *Slang.* to furnish with necessaries or resources, orig. by way of a business venture with a view to a possible return. [cf. D *staken* fix, place]

Staked Plain (stākt), Llano Estacado.

stake-hold-er (stāk/hōl/dər), *n.* the holder of the stakes of a wager, etc.

Sta-kha-no-vism (stä hä/nō vĭz/əm), *n.* a method developed (1935) in the Soviet Union to increase production by rewarding individual initiative. —**Sta-kha/no-vite/,** *adj., n.*

sta-lac-tite (stə lăk/tīt, stăl/ək tīt/), *n.* a deposit, usually of calcium carbonate, shaped like an icicle, hanging from the roof of a cave or the like, and formed by the dripping of percolating calcareous water. [t. NL: m. *stalactītēs,* f. *stalact-* (t. Gk.: s. *stalaktós* dripping) + *-ītēs* -ITE[1]] —**stal-ac-tit-ic** (stăl/ək tĭt/ĭk), **stal/ac-tit/i-cal,** *adj.*

A. Stalactite; B. Stalagmite

sta-lag-mite (stə lăg/mīt, stăl/əg mīt/), *n.* a deposit, usually of calcium carbonate, more or less resembling an inverted stalactite, formed on the floor of a cave or the like by the dripping of percolating calcareous water. [t. NL: m. *stalagmītēs,* f. *stalagm-* (t. Gk.: m.s. *stalagmós* chopping) + *-ītēs* -ITE[1]] —**stal-ag-mit-ic** (stăl/əg mĭt/ĭk), **stal/ag-mit/i-cal,** *adj.*

St. Al-bans (ôl/bənz), a city in SE England, in Hertfordshire: notable Norman cathedral; site of two battles in the Wars of the Roses, 1455, 1461. 44,106 (1951). Ancient, **Verulamium.**

stale[1] (stāl), *adj.,* **staler, stalest,** *v.,* **staled, staling.** —*adj.* **1.** not fresh; vapid or flat, as beverages; dry or hardened (more or less), as bread. **2.** having lost novelty or interest; hackneyed; trite: *a stale joke.* **3.** having lost fresh vigor, quick intelligence, initiative, or the like, as from overstrain. **4.** *Law.* having lost force or effectiveness through absence of action, as a claim. —*v.t.*, *v.i.* **5.** to make or become stale. [ME; ? akin to STAND] —**stale′ly**, *adv.* —**stale′ness**, *n.*

stale² (stāl), *v.i.*, **staled**, **staling**. (of livestock) to urinate. [ME; special use of STALE¹]

stale-mate (stāl′māt′), *n.*, *v.*, **-mated**, **-mating.** —*n.* **1.** *Chess.* a position of the pieces when no move can be made by a player without putting his own king in check, the result being a draw. **2.** any position in which no action can be taken; a deadlock. —*v.t.* **3.** to subject to a stalemate. **4.** to bring to a standstill. [f. *stale*, n. (? t. AF: m. *estale*, or akin to STALL²) a standstill + MATE²]

Sta-lin (stä′lĭn, -lēn), *n.* **1. Joseph V.,** (*Iosif Vissarionovich Dzugashvili*) 1879–1953, Soviet marshal, statesman, and general secretary of the Soviet Communist party. **2.** Stalino. **3.** Varna. **4.** Brașov.

Sta-lin-a-bad (stä′lĭnäbät′), *n.* a city in the SW Soviet Union in Asia: the capital of the Tadzik Republic. 191,000 (est. 1956). Formerly, **Dyushambe.**

Sta-lin-grad (stä′lĭngräd′; *Russ.* stä′lĭn grät′), *n.* a city in the SE Soviet Union in Europe, on the Volga: the scene of bitter fighting in World War II, Aug., 1942–Feb., 1943. 591,000 (est. 1959); name changed in 1961 to **Volgograd.** Formerly, **Tsaritsyn.**

Sta-li-no (stä′lĭ nô), *n.* former name of Yuzovka.

Sta-linsk (stä′lĭnsk), *n.* a city in the S Soviet Union in Asia: a planned industrial center located here because of coal deposits of the Kuznetsk Basin. 377,000 (est. 1959); name changed in 1961 to **Novokuznetsk.**

stalk¹ (stôk), *n.* **1.** the stem or main axis of a plant. **2.** any slender supporting or connecting part of a plant, as the petiole of a leaf, the peduncle of a flower, or the funicle of an ovule. **3.** a similar structural part of an animal. **4.** a stem, shaft, or slender supporting part of anything. [ME *stalke*, f. OE *stæla* stalk + -*k* suffix] —**stalk′like′,** *adj.*

stalk² (stôk), *v.i.* **1.** to pursue or approach game, etc., stealthily. **2.** to walk with slow, stiff, or haughty strides (said of persons, animals, ghosts, famine, etc.). **3.** *Obs.* to walk or go stealthily along. —*v.t.* **4.** to pursue (game, a person, etc.) stealthily. —*n.* **5.** an act or course of stalking game or the like. **6.** a slow, stiff stride or gait. [ME *stalke*, OE -*stealcian* move stealthily, appar. der. (with -*k* suffix) OE *stalian* go stealthily. See STEAL] —**stalk′er,** *n.*

stalk-ing-horse (stô′kĭng hôrs′), *n.* **1.** a horse, or a figure of a horse, behind which a hunter conceals himself in stalking game. **2.** anything put forward to mask plans or efforts; a pretext. **3.** *Politics.* a candidate used to screen a more important candidate or to draw votes from a rival and hence cause his defeat.

stalk-less (stôk′lĭs), *adj.* **1.** having no stalk. **2.** *Bot.* sessile.

stalk-y (stô′kĭ), *adj.* **1.** abounding in stalks. **2.** stalklike; long and slender.

stall¹ (stôl), *n.* **1.** a compartment in a stable or shed, for the accommodation of one animal. **2.** a stable or shed for horses or cattle. **3.** *Chiefly Brit.* a booth in which merchandise is exposed for sale, or in which some business is carried on: *a bookstall.* **4.** *Chiefly Brit.* one of a number of fixed enclosed seats in the choir or chancel of a church for the use of the clergy. **5.** a chairlike seat in a theater, separated from others by arms or rails, esp. one in the front division of the parquet or in the front of the lower balcony. **6.** a compartment, chamber, sheath, or the like, for any of various purposes: *a fingerstall.* **7.** *Aeron.* the condition of being stalled, when the wing assumes an angle of attack greater than the angle of maximum lift. —*v.t.* **8.** to put or keep in a stall or stalls, as animals. **9.** to confine in a stall for fattening, as cattle. **10.** to bring to a standstill; check the progress or motion of, esp. unintentionally. **11.** to cause to stick fast, as in mire or snow. —*v.i.* **12.** to come to a standstill; be brought to a stop, esp. unintentionally. **13.** to stick fast, as in mire. **14.** *Aeron.* **a.** (of an airplane) to become stalled. **b.** (of an aviator) to stall an airplane. **15.** to occupy a stall, as an animal. [ME; OE *steall,* c. G *stall*]

stall² (stôl), *Slang.* —*n.* **1.** anything used as a pretext, pretense, or trick. —*v.i.* **2.** to act evasively or deceptively. **3.** *Sports.* to play below one's best in order to deceive for any reason. —*v.t.* **4.** to put off, evade, or deceive (often fol. by *off*). [var. of late ME *stale* decoy bird, t. AF: m. *estale,* t. OE: m. *stæl* (in *stælhrān* decoy reindeer), akin to G *stell* (in *stell-vogel* decoy bird)]

stall-feed (stôl′fēd′), *v.t.,* **-fed, -feeding. 1.** to keep and feed (an animal) in a stall. **2.** to fatten by this process, as an animal for killing.

stal-lion (stăl′yən), *n.* a male horse not castrated. [ME *stalun,* t. OF: m. *estalon;* of Gmc. orig.]

stal-wart (stôl′wərt), *adj.* **1.** strongly and stoutly built; well-developed and robust. **2.** strong and brave; valiant. **3.** firm, steadfast, or uncompromising. —*n.* **4.** a physically stalwart person. **5.** a steadfast or uncom-

promising partisan. [ME; Scot. var. of *stalward,* earlier *stalwurthe,* OE *stælwierthe* serviceable, f. *stæl* (contr. of *stathol* foundation) + *wierthe* WORTH] —**stal′wart-ly,** *adv.* —**stal′wart-ness,** *n.* —Syn. **5.** See strong.

Stam-bul (stäm bōōl′), *n.* **1.** the oldest part and principal Turkish residential section of Istanbul, S of the Golden Horn. **2.** an occasional name of Istanbul. Also, **Stam-boul** (stäm bōōl′; *Fr.* stän bōōl′).

sta-men (stā′mən), *n., pl.* **stamens, stamina** (stăm′ə-nə). *Bot.* the pollen-bearing organ of a flower, consisting of the filament and the anther. See diag. under **flower.** [t. L: thread, warp in the upright loom]

Stam-ford (stăm′fərd), *n.* a city in SW Connecticut. 92,713 (1960).

stam-i-na¹ (stăm′ə nə), *n.* strength of physical constitution; power to endure disease, fatigue, privation, etc. [t. L, pl. of *stämen* thread (specifically, those spun by the Fates determining length of life)]

stam-i-na² (stăm′ə nə), *n.* a pl. of **stamen.**

stam-i-nal (stăm′ə nəl), *adv.* **1** of or pertaining to stamina. **2.** *Bot.* of or pertaining to stamens.

stam-i-nate (stăm′ə nĭt, -nāt′), *adj. Bot.* **1.** having a stamen or stamens. **2.** having stamens but no pistils.

stam-i-nif-er-ous (stăm′ə nĭf′ər əs), *adj. Bot.* bearing or having a stamen or stamens.

stam-i-no-di-um (stăm′ə nō′dĭ əm), *n., pl.* **-dia** (-dĭ ə). *Bot.* **1.** a sterile or abortive stamen. **2.** a part resembling such a stamen. [t. NL. See STAMEN, -ODE¹, -IUM]

stam-i-no-dy (stăm′ə nō′dĭ), *n. Bot.* the metamorphosis of any of various flower organs (as a sepal or a petal) into a stamen.

stam-mer (stăm′ər), *v.i.* **1.** to speak with involuntary breaks and pauses, or with spasmodic repetitions of syllables or sounds. —*v.t.* **2.** to say with a stammer (often fol. by *out*). —*n.* **3.** a stammering mode of utterance. **4.** a stammered utterance. [ME; OE *stamerian,* akin to G *stammeln*] —**stam′mer-er,** *n.*

—Syn. **2.** STAMMER, STUTTER agree in referring to a speech difficulty. STAMMER indicates difficulty or a block in uttering a word or syllable, which results in broken or inarticulate sounds that stick in the mouth, and sometimes in complete stoppage of speech; it may be caused by sudden excitement, confusion, embarrassment, or other emotion, or by lack of muscular control: *to stammer one's thanks for a surprise gift.* STUTTER indicates rapid, involuntary spasmodic repetition of an (especially initial) sound or syllable of a word: stuttering, though accentuated by excitement, is more likely than stammering to be an inherent speech defect: *to stutter out an apology.*

stamp (stămp), *v.t.* **1.** to strike or beat with a forcible downward thrust of the foot. **2.** to bring (the foot) down forcibly or smartly on the ground, floor, etc. **3.** to trample, force, drive, etc., by or as by beating down with the foot: *to stamp out a fire or a rebellion.* **4.** to crush or pound with or as with a pestle. **5.** to impress with a particular mark or device, as to indicate genuineness, approval, ownership, etc. **6.** to impress with an official mark. **7.** to mark or impress with any characters, words, designs, etc. **8.** to impress (a design, figure, words, etc.) on something; imprint deeply or permanently on anything. **9.** to affix an adhesive paper stamp to (a letter, etc.). **10.** to characterize, distinguish, or reveal.

—*v.i.* **11.** to bring the foot down forcibly or smartly, as in crushing something, expressing rage, etc. **12.** to walk with forcible or heavy, resounding steps: *to stamp out of a room in anger.*

—*n.* **13.** act of stamping. **14.** a die, engraved block, or the like, for impressing a design, characters, words, or marks. **15.** an impression, design, characters, words, etc., made with or as with a stamp. **16.** an official mark indicating genuineness, validity, etc., or payment of a duty or charge. **17.** the impression of a public seal required for revenue purposes, to be obtained from a government office, for a fee, on the paper or parchment on which deeds, bills, receipts, etc., are written. **18.** a peculiar or distinctive impress or mark: *a story which bears the stamp of truth.* **19.** character, kind, or type. **20.** a small adhesive piece of paper printed with a distinctive design, issued by a government for a fixed sum, for attaching to documents, goods subject to duty, letters, etc., to show that a charge has been paid: *a revenue stamp, a postage stamp.* **21.** a similar piece of paper issued by a private organization to show that the charges for mail carrying have been paid: *a local stamp.* **22.** a similar piece of paper issued privately for various purposes: *a trading stamp.* **23.** an instrument for stamping, crushing, or pounding. **24.** a heavy piece of iron or the like, as in a stamp mill, for dropping on and crushing ore or other material. [early ME *stampen,* c. G *stampfen*] —Syn. **3.** See **abolish.**

Stamp Act, an act of the British Parliament for raising revenue in the American colonies by requiring the use of stamped paper and stamps for legal and official documents, commercial writings, and various articles. It was to go into effect on Nov. 1, 1765, but met with intense opposition and was therefore repealed in March, 1766.

stam-pede (stăm pēd′), *n., v.,* **-peded, -peding.** —*n.* **1.** a sudden scattering or headlong flight of a body of cattle or horses in fright. **2.** any headlong general flight or rush. —*v.i.* **3.** to scatter or flee in a stampede.

---

b., blend of, blended; c., cognate with; d., dialect, dialectal; der., derived from; f., formed from; g., going back to; m., modification of; r., replacing; s., stem of; t., taken from; ?, perhaps. See the full key on inside cover.

4. to make an unconcerted general rush. —v.t. **5.** to cause to stampede. [t. Mex. Sp.: m. *estampida*, der. *estampar* press, of Gmc. orig. See STAMP] —**stam·ped/-er,** n.

stamp·er (stăm/pər), n. **1.** one who or that which stamps. **2.** one who applies postmarks and cancels postage stamps in a post office. **3.** an instrument for stamping. **4.** a pestle, esp. one in a stamp mill.

stamping ground, Colloq. the habitual place of resort of an animal or person.

stamp mill, Metall. a mill or machine in which ore is crushed to powder by means of heavy stamps or pestles.

stance (stăns), n. Golf, etc. the position of a player's feet when making a stroke. [t. F, t. It.: m. *stanza* station, stopping place, room, ult. der. L *stans*, ppr., standing]

stanch[1] (stănch, stänch), v.t. **1.** to stop the flow of (a liquid, esp. blood). **2.** to stop the flow of blood from (a wound). **3.** Archaic or Dial. to check, appease, allay, or assuage. —v.i. **4.** to stop flowing, as blood; be stanched. Also, **staunch.** [ME, t. OF: m.s. *estanchier*] —**stanch/er,** n.

stanch[2] (stänch, stänch), adj. **1.** firm or steadfast in principle, adherence, loyalty, etc., as a person, the heart, etc. **2.** characterized by firmness or steadfastness. **3.** strong; substantial. **4.** impervious to water or liquids; watertight. Also, **staunch.** [late ME, t. OF: m. *estanche*, fem. of *estanc*; akin to STANCH[1]] —**stanch/ly,** adv. —**stanch/-ness,** n. —Syn. **1.** See steadfast.

stan·chion (stăn/shən), n. **1.** an upright bar, beam, post, or support, as in a window, stall, ship, etc. —v.t. **2.** to furnish with stanchions. **3.** to secure by or to a stanchion or stanchions. [ME *stanchon*, t. OF: m. *estanchon*, der. *estance* STANCE]

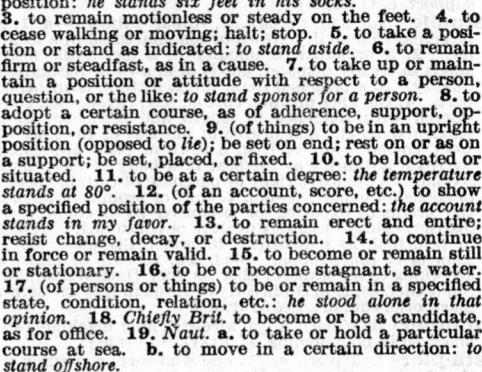

S. Stanchion

stand (stănd), v., **stood, standing,** n. —v.i. **1.** to take or keep an upright position on the feet (opposed to sit, lie, etc.). **2.** to have a specified height when in this position: *he stands six feet in his socks.* **3.** to remain motionless or steady on the feet. **4.** to cease walking or moving; halt; stop. **5.** to take a position or stand as indicated: *to stand aside.* **6.** to remain firm or steadfast, as in a cause. **7.** to take up or maintain a position or attitude with respect to a person, question, or the like: *to stand sponsor for a person.* **8.** to adopt a certain course, as of adherence, support, opposition, or resistance. **9.** (of things) to be in an upright position (opposed to lie); be set on end; rest on or as on a support; be set, placed, or fixed. **10.** to be located or situated. **11.** to be at a certain degree: *the temperature stands at 80°.* **12.** (of an account, score, etc.) to show a specified position of the parties concerned: *the account stands in my favor.* **13.** to remain erect and entire; resist change, decay, or destruction. **14.** to continue in force or remain valid. **15.** to become or remain still or stationary. **16.** to be or become stagnant, as water. **17.** (of persons or things) to be or remain in a specified state, condition, relation, etc.: *he stood alone in that opinion.* **18.** Chiefly Brit. to become or be a candidate, as for office. **19.** Naut. a. to take or hold a particular course at sea. **b.** to move in a certain direction: *to stand offshore.* —v.t. **20.** to cause to stand; set upright; set. **21.** to face or encounter: *to stand an assault.* **22.** to endure, undergo, or submit to: *to stand trial.* **23.** to endure or undergo without hurt or damage, or without giving way: *he cannot stand the sun.* **24.** to tolerate. **25.** Colloq. to bear the expense of. **26.** Some special verb phrases are:

stand a chance, to have a chance or possibility, esp. of winning, surviving, or the like.

stand by, 1. to aid, uphold, or sustain. **2.** to adhere to (an agreement, promise, etc.); abide by.

stand down, Law. to quit the witness stand.

stand off, Colloq. **1.** to keep at a distance. **2.** to put off or evade.

stand on, 1. to rest or depend on. **2.** to be punctilious about (ceremony, etc.); claim respect for (one's rights, dignity, etc.). **3.** Naut. to continue on the same course or tack.

stand out, 1. to project or protrude; be prominent or conspicuous. **2.** to hold aloof. **3.** to persist in opposition or resistance.

stand to reason, to be in accordance with reason.

stand up for, to defend the cause of; support.

—n. **27.** act of standing; an assuming of, or a remaining in, an upright position. **28.** a coming to a position of rest; a halt or stop. **29.** a determined effort against or for something. **30.** the place where a person or thing stands; station. **31.** the place where a witness sits or stands to testify in court. **32.** a raised platform or other structure as for spectators at a race course or an athletic field, or along the route of a parade, or for a band or the like. **33.** a framework on or in which articles are placed for support, exhibition, etc. **34.** a piece of furniture of various forms, on or in which to put articles. **35.** a small, light table. **36.** a stall, booth, table, or the like, where articles are displayed for sale or some business is carried on. **37.** a site or location for business. **38.** a place or station occupied by vehicles available for hire. **39.** the vehicles occupying such a place. **40.** the growing trees, or those of a particular

species or grade, on a given area. **41.** a standing growth, as of grass, wheat, etc. **42.** a halt of a theatrical company on tour, to give a performance or performances: *one-night stands.* **43.** the town at which a theatrical company gives a performance. **44.** a position taken or maintained with respect to others or to some question. **45.** Archaic. the arms and accoutrements for one soldier. [ME; OE *standan*, c. MD *standen*, OHG *stantan*, Icel. *standa*, Goth. *standan*] —Syn. **23.** See bear[1].

stand·ard (stăn/dərd), n. **1.** anything taken by general consent as a basis of comparison; an approved model. **2.** the authorized exemplar of a unit of weight or measure. **3.** a certain commodity in which the basic monetary unit is stated, historically usually either gold or silver (**gold standard, silver standard,** or **single standard**), or both gold and silver in a fixed proportion to each other (**bimetallic standard**). **4.** the legal rate of intrinsic value for coins. **5.** the prescribed degree of fineness for gold or silver. **6.** a grade or level of excellence or advancement: *a high standard of living.* **7.** Com. the lowest of such grades (better grades being called fancy, extra-fine, or the like). **8.** Brit. a class or grade in elementary schools. **9.** a flag, emblematic figure, or other object raised on a pole to indicate the rallying point of an army, fleet, etc. **10.** Mil. a. any of various military or naval flags. **b.** the colors of a mounted unit. **11.** Her. a long tapering flag or ensign, as of a king or a nation. **12.** something which stands or is placed upright. **13.** an upright support or supporting part. **14.** an upright timber, bar, or rod. **15.** Hort. a tree, shrub, or other plant having a tall, erect stem, and not grown in bush form or trained upon a trellis or other support. **16.** Bot. a vexillum. —adj. **17.** a serving as a basis of weight, measure, value, comparison, or judgment. **18.** of recognized excellence or established authority: *a standard author.* **19.** (of a variety of a given language, or of usage in the language) characterized by preferred pronunciations, expressions, grammatical constructions, etc., the use of which is considered essential to social or other prestige, failure to conform to them tending to bring the speaker into disfavor. **20.** Print. (of type) of average height, width, or face weight. [ME, t. OF: aphetic m. *estandard*, t. Gmc. (cf. G *standort* standing-place), conformed to suffix -ard -ARD] —Syn. **1.** STANDARD, CRITERION mean a measure or test. A STANDARD is an authoritative model or measure, a pattern for guidance, by comparison with which the quantity, excellence, correctness, etc., of other things may be determined: *standards of liquid measure.* A CRITERION is a test which is used to judge value, suitability, probability, etc., of something already existing: *wealth is no criterion of a man's worth.*

standard-bearer, n. **1.** an officer or soldier of an army or military unit who bears a standard. **2.** a conspicuous leader of a movement, political party, etc.

stand·ard-bred (stăn/dərd brĕd/), adj. of or pertaining to a breed of trotting and pacing horses used chiefly for harness racing.

standard candle. See candle (def. 3b).

standard deviation, Statistics. the square root of the average of the squares of a set of deviations about an arithmetic mean; the root mean square of the deviations of a set of values.

standard dollar, 1. (since Jan. 31, 1934) a U. S. dollar containing 15⁵/₂₁ grains of gold, 0.900 fine. **2.** (up to 1934) one containing 25.8 grains of gold, 0.900 fine.

standard gauge. See gauge (def. 10).

stand·ard·ize (stăn/dər dīz/), v.t., **-ized, -izing. 1.** to bring to or make of an established standard size, weight, quality, strength, or the like: *to standardize manufactured parts.* **2.** to compare with or test by a standard. Also, esp. Brit., **stand/ard·ise/.** —**stand/ard·i·za/-tion,** n. —**stand/ard·iz/er,** n.

standard of living, a grade or level of subsistence and comforts in everyday life enjoyed by a community, a class in a community, or an individual: *widespread unemployment will depress the nation's standard of living.*

standard time, the civil time officially adopted for a country or region, usually the civil time of some specific meridian lying within the region. The four standard time zones in the U.S., **Eastern, Central, Mountain,** and **Pacific,** use the civil times of the 75th, 90th, 105th and 120th meridians respectively, the difference of time between one zone and the next being exactly one hour. See the illus. under time zone.

stand-by (stănd/bī/), n., pl. **-bys. 1.** a stanch supporter or adherent; one who can be relied upon. **2.** something upon which one can rely; a chief support.

stand·ee (stăn dē/), n. Colloq. one who stands, as at a theatrical performance.

stand-in (stănd/ĭn/), n. **1.** a substitute for a motion-picture star during the preparation of lighting, cameras, etc., or in dangerous scenes. **2.** any substitute. **3.** Slang. inside influence; pull.

stand·ing (stăn/dĭng), n. **1.** position or status, as to rank, credit, reputation, etc.: *men of good standing.* **2.** good position or credit. **3.** length of existence, continuance, residence, membership, experience, etc. **4.** act of one who or that which stands. **5.** the period during which a person or thing stands. **6.** a place where a person or thing stands. —adj. **7.** that stands erect or upright. **8.** performed in or from an erect position: *a standing jump.* **9.** still; not flowing or stagnant, as water; stationary. **10.** continuing without cessation or change; lasting or permanent. **11.** continuing in operation, force, use, etc.: *a standing rule.* **12.** out of use; idle: *a standing engine.* —**Syn. 2.** See **credit.**

standing army, a permanently organized military force kept up by a nation.

standing order, 1. *Mil.* (formerly) a general order that is always in force in a command and that establishes uniform procedures for it; standard operating procedure. **2.** (*pl.*) *Parliamentary Proc.* the rules ensuring continuity of procedure during the meetings of an assembly.

standing rigging, *Naut.* the stays, shrouds, etc., which secure the masts.

standing room, 1. room or space in which to stand. **2.** accommodation only for standing, as in a theater where all the seats have been taken.

standing wave, *Physics.* a distribution of wave displacements, such that the distribution in space is periodic, with fixed maximum and minimum points, with the maxima occurring everywhere at the same time, as in vibrations of strings, electric potentials, acoustic pressures, etc.

Stan·dish (stăn′dĭsh), *n.* **Myles** or **Miles** (mīlz), c1584–1656, British settler at Plymouth, Massachusetts, in 1620: military captain of the colony.

stand·ish (stăn′dĭsh), *n.* *Archaic.* a stand for ink, pens, and other writing materials. [prob. f. STAND + DISH]

stand-off (stănd′ôf′, -ŏf′), *n.* **1.** a standing off or apart; aloofness. **2.** a tie or draw, as in a game. **3.** something that counterbalances. —*adj.* **4.** standing off or apart; aloof; reserved. —**stand′-off′ish,** *adj.*

stand oil, a thick oil used in paints, etc., made by heating linseed oil to temperatures of 600°F. and higher.

stand·out (stănd′out′), *n.* *Colloq.* one who persists in being a minority of one, as on a jury.

stand·pat (stănd′păt′), *Colloq.* —*n.* **1.** Also, **stand′-pat′ter.** one who holds to an existing order of things, policy, etc., refusing to consider proposals of change. —*adj.* **2.** characterized by standing pat.

stand·pipe (stănd′pīp′), *n.* a vertical pipe or tower into which water is pumped to obtain a required head.

stand·point (stănd′point′), *n.* **1.** the point at which one stands to view something. **2.** the mental position from which one views and judges things.

St. An·drews (ăn′drōōz), a seaport in E Scotland, in Fife county: resort; golf courses. 9459 (1951).

stand·still (stănd′stĭl′), *n.* a standing still; a state of cessation of movement or action; a halt; a pause; a stop.

stand-up (stănd′ŭp′), *adj.* **1.** standing erect; upright, as a collar. **2.** performed, taken, etc., while one stands: *a stand-up meal.*

stane (stān), *n., adj., v.* *Scot. and N. Eng.* stone.

stang (stăng), *v.* *Archaic or Obs.* pt. of **sting.**

stan·hope (stăn′hōp, stăn′əp), *n.* a kind of light, two-wheeled, open, one-seated carriage hung on four springs. [named after Fitzroy *Stanhope* (1787–1864)]

Stan·i·slav·sky (stăn′ĭs lăv′skĭ, *Russ.* stă nĭ släf′skĭ), *n.* **Konstantin,** 1863–1938, Russian actor, producer, and director.

Sta·ni·sla·wów (stä′nē slä′vōōf), *n.* a city in the SW Soviet Union, in the Ukrainian Republic: formerly in Poland. 70,000 (est. 1948). German, **Stan·is·lau** (shtän′ĭs lou′). Russian, **Sta·ni·sla·vov** (stä′nĭ slä′vôf).

stank (stăngk), *v.* a pt. of **stink.**

Stan·ley (stăn′lĭ), *n.* **1. Arthur Penrhyn** (pĕn′rĭn), (*Dean Stanley*) 1815–81, British clergyman and author. **2. Sir Henry Morton,** (orig. *John Rowlands*) 1841–1904, British explorer in Africa.

Stan·ley (stăn′lĭ), *n.* **Mount,** a mountain with two summits, in central Africa: highest peak in the Ruwenzori group. 16,790 ft. See **Ruwenzori.**

Stanley Falls, seven cataracts of the Congo river, on the equator in N Belgian Congo.

Stanley Pool, a lake on the boundary between W Belgian Congo and S French Equatorial Africa, formed by the widening of the Congo river ab. 330 mi. from its mouth. ab. 20 mi. long; ab. 15 mi. wide.

stan·na·ry (stăn′ə rĭ), *n., pl.* **-ries. 1.** a tin-mining region or district. **2.** *Brit.* a place where tin is mined or smelted. [t. ML: m.s. *stannāria,* der. LL *stannum* tin]

stan·nic (stăn′ĭk), *adj.* *Chem.* of or containing tin, esp. in the tetravalent state (Sn+4). [f. s. LL *stannum* tin + -IC]

stannic sulfide, a yellowish compound, SnS_2, used in making gilding preparations; mosaic gold.

stan·nite (stăn′ĭt), *n.* a mineral, iron-black to steel-gray in color, with a metallic luster, copper iron tin sulfide, Cu_2FeSnS_4: an ore of tin; tin pyrites.

stan·nous (stăn′əs), *adj.* *Chem.* containing divalent tin (Sn+2).

stan·num (stăn′əm), *n.* tin. [t. LL: tin (in L, alloy of silver and lead)]

Sta·no·voi (stä′nŏ voi′), *n.* a mountain system in the E Soviet Union in Asia: a watershed between the Pacific and Artic oceans. Highest peaks, ab. 8000 ft.

Stan·ton (stăn′tən), *n.* **1. Edwin McMasters,** 1814–1869, U.S. statesman: secretary of war, 1862–67. **2. Mrs. Elizabeth Cady** (kā′dĭ), 1815–1902, U.S. social reformer: advocate of women's rights.

stan·za (stăn′zə), *n.* **1.** *Pros.* a group of lines of verse, commonly four or more in number, arranged and re-

peated according to a fixed plan as regards the number of lines, the meter, and the rhyme, and forming a poem. **2.** a regularly repeated metrical division of a poem. [t. It., ult. der. L *stans,* ppr., standing] —**stan·za·ic** (stăn zā′ĭk), *adj.* —**Syn. 1.** See **verse.**

sta·pe·li·a (stə pē′lĭ ə), *n.* any of the plants constituting the asclepiadaceous genus *Stapelia,* native in South Africa, with short, fleshy, leafless stems, and flowers which are often oddly colored or mottled and in most species emit a fetid, carrionlike odor. [named after J. B. *Stapel,* Dutch botanist]

sta·pes (stā′pēz), *n.* *Anat.* the innermost of three small bones in the middle ear of man and other mammals, having a stirruplike shape. See diag. under **ear.** [t. NL, special use of ML *stapes* stirrup] —**sta·pe·di·al** (stə pē′dĭ əl), *adj.*

staphylo-, 1. a word element referring to **staphylococcus. 2.** a word element referring to the uvula. [comb. form repr. Gk. *staphylē* bunch of grapes]

staph·y·lo·coc·cus (stăf′ə lə kŏk′əs), *n., pl.* **-cocci** (-kŏk′sī). *Bacteriol.* any of certain species of micrococcus in which the individual organisms form irregular clusters, as *Micrococcus* (or *Staphylococcus*) *pyogenes,* which causes pus formation. [f. STAPHYLO- + COCCUS] —**staph·y·lo·coc·cic** (stăf′ə lə kŏk′sĭk), *adj.*

staph·y·lo·ma (stăf′ĭ lō′mə), *n., pl.* **-mata** (-mə tə). *Pathol.* any of various local bulgings of the eyeball.

staph·y·lo·plas·ty (stăf′ə lə plăs′tĭ), *n.* the remedying of defects of the soft palate by plastic surgery.

staph·y·lor·rha·phy (stăf′ə lôr′ə fĭ, -lôr′-), *n.* the uniting of a cleft palate by plastic surgery. Also, **staph′y·lor′a·phy.** [f. STAPHYLO- + -rrhaphy (t. Gk.: m.s. -*rhaphia,* der. *rhaphē* suture)]

sta·ple[1] (stā′pəl), *n., v.,* **-pled, -pling.** —*n.* **1.** a bent piece of wire used to bind papers, sections of a book, etc., together. **2.** a loop of metal with pointed ends for driving into a surface to hold a hasp, hook, pin, bolt, or the like. —*v.t.* **3.** to secure or fasten by a staple or staples: *to staple three sheets together.* [ME; OE *stapol* support, c. G *stapel*]

sta·ple[2] (stā′pəl), *n., adj., v.,* **-pled, -pling.** —*n.* **1.** a principal commodity grown or manufactured in a locality. **2.** a principal commodity in a mercantile field; goods in steady demand; goods of known or recognized quality. **3.** a principal item, thing, feature, element, or part. **4.** the fiber of wool, cotton, flax, rayon, etc., considered with reference to length and fineness. **5.** a particular length and degree of fineness of the fiber of wool, cotton, etc. **6.** *Hist.* a town or place appointed by royal authority as the seat of a body of merchants having the exclusive right of purchase of certain classes of goods for export. —*adj.* **7.** chief or prominent among the products exported or produced by a country or district; chiefly or largely dealt in or consumed. **8.** chief or principal, as industries. **9.** principally used: *staple subjects of conversation.* —*v.t.* **10.** to sort or classify according to the staple or fiber, as wool. [late ME *stapull,* staple (def. 6), t. MD (directly or through AF): m. *stapel* mart, orig. support. See STAPLE[1]]

sta·pler[1] (stā′plər), *n.* a wire-stitching machine, esp. one used in bookbinding. [f. STAPLE[1] + -ER[1]]

sta·pler[2] (stā′plər), *n.* **1.** one who sorts according to the staple or fiber. **2.** *Hist.* a merchant of the staple. [f. STAPLE[2] + -ER[2]]

star (stär), *n., adj., v.,* **starred, starring.** —*n.* **1.** any of the heavenly bodies appearing as apparently fixed luminous points in the sky at night. **2.** *Astron.* any of the self-luminous bodies outside the solar system, as distinguished from planets, comets, and meteors. The sun is classed with the stars and appears to be a typical member of the galaxy. **3.** any heavenly body. **4.** *Astrol.* a heavenly body, esp. a planet that is considered as influencing mankind and events. **5.** *Rare.* destiny or fortune. **6.** a conventional figure having rays (commonly five or six) proceeding from, or angular points disposed in a regular outline about, a central point, and considered as representing a star of the sky. **7.** *Print., etc.* an asterisk. **8.** a person who is preëminent or distinguished in some art, profession, or other field. **9.** a prominent actor, singer, or the like, esp. one who plays the leading role in a performance. —*adj.* **10.** brilliant, prominent, or distinguished; chief. **11.** to set with, or as with, stars; spangle. **12.** to make into a star or stars; place among the stars; present (an actor, etc.) as a star. **13.** to mark with a star or asterisk, as for special notice. —*v.i.* **14.** to shine as a star; be brilliant or prominent. **15.** (of an actor, etc.) to appear as a star: *he starred in several productions of Shaw's plays.* [ME *sterre,* OE *steorra,* c. D *ster,* MHG *sterre,* akin to L *stella,* Gk. *astēr*] —**star′less,** *adj.*

star apple, 1. the edible fruit of a West Indian sapotaceous tree, *Chrysophyllum Cainito,* of the size of an apple, and when cut across presenting a star-shaped figure within. **2.** the tree.

star·board (stär′bôrd′, -bərd), *Naut.* —*n.* **1.** the side of a ship to the right of a person looking toward the bow (opposed to *larboard* and *port*). See illus. under **aft.** —*adj.* **2.** pertaining to the starboard; on the right side. —*adv.* **3.** toward the right side. —*v.t., v.i.* **4.** to turn (the helm) to starboard. [ME *sterbord,* OE *stēorbord,* f. *stēor* steering + *bord* side (of a ship). See STEER[1], v., BOARD, n.]

---

b., blend of, blended; c., cognate with; d., dialect, dialectal; der., derived from; f., formed from; g., going back to; m., modification of; r., replacing; s., stem of; t., taken from; ?, perhaps. See the full key on inside cover.

starch (stärch), *n.* **1.** a white, tasteless solid, chemically a carbohydrate, $(C_8H_{10}O_5)n$, occurring in the form of minute granules in the seeds, tubers, and other parts of plants, and forming an important constituent of rice, corn, wheat, beans, potatoes, and many other vegetable foods. Starch is separable into amylose and amylopectin fractions. **2.** a commercial preparation of this substance used (dissolved in water) to stiffen linen, etc., in laundering, and employed also for many industrial purposes. **3.** *(pl.)* foods rich in starch. **4.** stiffness or formality, as of manner. **5.** *U.S. Slang.* zest; stamina. —*v.t.* **6.** to stiffen or treat with starch. **7.** to make stiff or rigidly formal (sometimes fol. by *up*). [ME *sterce*, v., OE *stercean* make stiff or resolute (in *stercedferhth* made resolute in mind), der. *stearc* STARK[1]]

Starch granules
A. Cells of potato, *Solanum tuberosum*, containing granules; B. Granules (All greatly magnified)

Star Chamber, 1. a former court of inquisitorial and criminal jurisdiction in England, which sat in secret without a jury, and was noted for its arbitrary methods and severe punishments (abolished 1641). **2.** any tribunal, committee, or the like, which proceeds by arbitrary or unfair methods.

starch·y (stär'chĭ), *adj.*, **starchier, starchiest. 1.** pertaining to, or of the nature of, starch. **2.** containing starch. **3.** stiffened with starch. **4.** *Colloq.* stiff and formal, as in manner. —**starch'i·ness**, *n.*

star·dom (stär'dəm), *n.* **1.** the world or class of professional stars, as of the stage. **2.** the status of a star.

star drift, *Astron.* a very slow motion common to a number of fixed stars in the same part of the heavens.

stare (stâr), *v.,* **stared, staring,** *n.* —*v.i.* **1.** to gaze fixedly, esp. with the eyes wide open. **2.** to stand out boldly or obtrusively to view. **3.** (of hair, feathers, etc.) to stand on end; bristle. —*v.t.* **4.** to stare at. **5.** to put, bring, etc., by staring: *to stare one out of countenance.* —*n.* **6.** a staring gaze; a fixed look with the eyes wide open: *the banker greeted him with a glassy stare.* [ME; OE *starian*, c. D *staren*, Icel. *stara*] —Syn. 1. See gaze.

star·fish (stär'fĭsh'), *n., pl.* **-fishes,** *(esp. collectively)* **-fish.** any echinoderm of the class *Asteroidea*, comprising marine animals having the body radially arranged, usually in the form of a star, with five or more rays or arms radiating from a central disk; an asteroid.

star·flow·er (stär'flou'ər), *n.* any of various plants with starlike flowers, as the star-of-Bethlehem or a plant of the primulaceous genus *Trientalis*.

Common starfish, *Asterias rubens* (3½ in. long)

star·gaze (stär'gāz'), *v.i.,* **-gazed, -gazing. 1.** to gaze at or observe the stars. **2.** to daydream. —**star'gaz'-ing,** *n.*

star·gaz·er (stär'gā'zər), *n.* **1.** one who gazes at the stars. **2.** any of the fishes constituting the family *Uranoscopidae*, having eyes directed upward.

star grass, any of various grasslike plants with star-shaped flowers or a stellated arrangement of leaves, as *Hypoxis hirsuta*, an American amaryllidaceous plant.

stark (stärk), *adj.* **1.** sheer, utter, downright, or arrant: *stark madness.* **2.** absolutely naked. **3.** stiff or rigid in substance, muscles, etc. **4.** rigid in death. **5.** harsh, grim, or desolate to the view, as places, etc. **6.** *Archaic.* hard, stern, or severe. —*adv.* **7.** utterly, absolutely, or quite: *stark mad.* **8.** *Dial.* in a stark manner; stoutly or vigorously. [ME; OE *stearc* stiff, c. G *stark* strong] —**stark'ly,** *adv.*

Stark (stärk), *n.* **John,** 1728–1822, American general in the Revolutionary War.

star·let (stär'lĭt), *n.* a small star.

star·light (stär'līt'), *n.* **1.** the light proceeding from the stars. **2.** the time when the stars shine. —*adj.* **3.** of or pertaining to starlight. **4.** starlit.

star·like (stär'līk'), *adj.* **1.** star-shaped. **2.** shining like a star.

star·ling (stär'lĭng), *n.* **1.** any of numerous Old World passerine birds constituting the family *Sturnidae*, esp. the common European species, *Sturnus vulgaris*, which has been introduced into North America. **2.** any of various not closely related passerine birds, esp. the **American starlings** of the family *Icteridae*. [ME; OE *stærling*, der. *stær* starling, c. G *star*. See -LING[1]]

star·lit (stär'lĭt), *adj.* lighted by the stars, or by the stars only.

star·nosed (stär'nōzd'), *adj.* having a starlike ring of small, fleshy radiating processes about the end of the snout, as an American mole, *Condylura cristata*.

Starling, *Sturnus vulgaris* (8½ in. long)

star-of-Beth·le·hem (stär'əv bĕth'lĭ əm, -hĕm'), *n.* an Old World liliaceous plant, *Ornithogalum umbellatum*, with star-shaped flowers.

Star of Bethlehem, the star which guided the three Magi ("wise men") from the East to the manger of the infant Jesus in Bethlehem. Matt. 2:2, 9, 10.

Star of David, Solomon's seal.

starred (stärd), *adj.* **1.** set or studded with, or as with, stars. **2.** presented as a star, as an actor. **3.** decorated with a star, as of an order. **4.** marked with a starlike figure or spot.

star·ry (stär'ĭ), *adj.,* **-rier, -riest. 1.** abounding with or lighted by stars: *a starry sky.* **2.** of, pertaining to, or proceeding from the stars. **3.** of the nature of or consisting of stars: *starry worlds.* **4.** resembling a star; star-shaped or stellate. **5.** shining like stars: *starry eyes.* **6.** studded with starlike figures or markings.

Stars and Bars, the flag adopted by the Confederate States of America, consisting of two broad horizontal bars of red separated by one of white, with a blue union marked with as many white stars, arranged in a circle, as the number of Confederate States.

Stars and Stripes, the national flag of the United States, consisting of thirteen horizontal stripes, alternately red and white, equal to the number of the original States, with a blue union marked with white stars equal in number to the whole number of States.

star sapphire, a sapphire which exhibits by reflected light a star composed of three bright rays, resulting from the crystalline structure of the gem.

star shell, a shell which bursts in the air and produces a bright light: used to illuminate enemy positions.

star-span·gled (stär'spăng'gəld), *adj.* spangled with stars.

Star-Spangled Banner, The, 1. the national flag of the United States. **2.** the American national anthem, composed in 1814 by Francis Scott Key, at the bombardment of Fort McHenry by the British.

start (stärt), *v.i.* **1.** to begin to move, go, or act; set out, as on a journey; begin any course of action or procedure, or one's career, life, etc. (often fol. by *out*). **2.** (of a process or performance) to begin. **3.** to come suddenly into activity, life, view, etc.; come, rise, or issue suddenly. **4.** to spring or move suddenly from a position or place: *to start from one's seat.* **5.** to move with a sudden, involuntary jerk or twitch, as from a shock of surprise, alarm, or pain. **6.** to burst out: *eyes seeming to start from their sockets.* **7.** to spring, slip, or work loose from place or fastenings, as timbers or other structural parts. —*v.t.* **8.** to set moving, going, or acting: *to start an automobile, a fire, etc.* **9.** to set in operation; establish: *to start a newspaper.* **10.** to enter upon or begin: *to start a letter.* **11.** to cause or enable (a person, etc.) to set out on a journey, a course of action, a career, or the like: *to start one's son in business.* **12.** to cause (timbers, structural parts, etc.) to start from place or fastenings. **13.** to rouse (game) from its lair or resting place. **14.** to draw or discharge (liquid or other contents) from a vessel or container, or empty (a container). **15.** *Archaic or Dial.* to cause to start involuntarily; startle. [ME; akin to STARTLE and OE *strytan* start, c. G *stürzen* fall, rush, make fall]
—*n.* **16.** a beginning to move, go, or act; the beginning or outset of anything; a setting in motion. **17.** an impulse to move or proceed; a signal to start, as on a course or in a race. **18.** a sudden, springing movement from a position. **19.** a sudden, involuntary jerking movement of the body: *to awake with a start.* **20.** a lead or advance of specified amount, as over competitors or pursuers. **21.** the position or advantage of one who starts first; the lead: *she has got the start on the rest of us.* **22.** a chance or opportunity given to one of starting on a course or career. **23.** a spurt of activity: *to work by fits and starts.* **24.** a starting of parts from their place or fastenings in a structure. **25.** the resulting condition. **26.** *Archaic.* a burst, outburst, or sally, as of emotion, wit, or fancy. [n. use of START, v.] —Syn. 10. See begin.

start·er (stär'tər), *n.* **1.** one who or that which starts. **2.** a person who gives the signal for starting, as in a race or in the running of a train, elevator, or the like. **3.** a self-starter. **4.** *Sports.* anyone who begins in a race.

star thistle, 1. a low, spreading composite plant, *Centaurea calcitrapa*, a native of Europe, with purple flowerheads and spiny involucres and leaves. **2.** the related but more erect *C. solstitialis*, with yellow flowers.

star·tle (stär'təl), *v.,* **-tled, -tling,** *n.* —*v.t.* **1.** to disturb or agitate suddenly by a shock of surprise, alarm, or the like. **2.** to cause to start involuntarily, as under a sudden shock. —*v.i.* **3.** to start involuntarily, as from a shock of surprise or alarm. —*n.* **4.** a sudden shock of surprise, alarm, or the like. **5.** something that startles. [ME *stertle* rush, caper, OE *steartlian* kick, struggle. See START, v.] —**star'tling,** *adj.* —**star'tling·ly,** *adv.* —Syn. 1. See shock[1].

star·va·tion (stär vā'shən), *n.* **1.** the condition of being starved. **2.** the process of starving.

starve (stärv), *v.,* **starved, starving.** —*v.i.* **1.** to die or perish from hunger. **2.** to be in process of perishing, or to suffer severely, from hunger. **3.** to suffer from extreme poverty and need. **4.** to pine or suffer for lack of something specified (fol. by *for*). **5.** *Dial.* to perish or suffer extremely from cold. **6.** *Obs.* to die. —*v.t.* **7.** to cause to starve; weaken or reduce by lack of food. **8.** to subdue, or force to some condition or action, by hunger: *to starve a besieged garrison into a surrender.* **9.** to cause

---

ăct, āble, dâre, ärt; ĕbb, ēqual; ĭf, īce; hŏt, ōver, ôrder, oil, bŏŏk, ōoze, out; ŭp, ūse, ûrge; ə = a in alone; ch, chief; g, give; ng, ring; sh, shoe; th, thin; ŧh, that; zh, vision. See the full key on inside cover.

to suffer for lack of something needed or craved.
10. *Dial.* to cause to perish, or to suffer extremely, from cold. [ME *sterve(n)*, OE *steorfan* die, c. G *sterben*] **—Syn. 1, 2.** See hungry.

starve-ling (stärv′lǐng), *adj.* **1.** starving; suffering from lack of nourishment; pining with want; poverty-stricken. **2.** poor in condition or quality. **3.** such as to entail or suggest starvation. **—n. 4.** a person, animal, or plant that is starving.

stash (stǎsh), *v.t.*, *v.i. U.S. Slang.* to put away, as for safekeeping or in a prepared place. [b. STOW and CACHE]

sta-sis (stā′sǐs, stǎs′ǐs), *n. Pathol.* stagnation in the flow of any of the fluids of the body, as of the blood in an inflamed area, the intestinal contents proximal to an obstruction, etc. [t. NL, t. Gk.]

-stat, a word element meaning "standing," "stationary," as in *thermostat.* [t. Gk.: m. -*statēs* that stands]

stat., **1.** statuary. **2.** statue. **3.** statute (miles).

state (stāt), *n.*, *adj.*, *v.*, **stated, stating. —n. 1.** the condition of a person or thing, as with respect to circumstances or attributes: *a state of disrepair.* **2.** condition with respect to constitution, structure, form, phase, or the like: *a liquid state, the larval state.* **3.** a mode or form of existence: *the future state.* **4.** a person's condition or position in life, or estate, station, or rank. **5.** the style of living befitting a person of high rank and great wealth; sumptuous, imposing, or ceremonious display of dignity; pomp: *a hall used on occasions of state.* **6.** *Colloq.* a bad condition: *his affairs were in a state.* **7.** a particular condition of mind or feeling: *to be in an excited state.* **8.** *Colloq.* an excited condition: *to be in quite a state over a matter.* **9.** a body of people occupying a definite territory and organized under one government, esp. a sovereign government; the territory, or one of the territories, of a government. **10.** (*usually cap.*) any of the commonwealths or bodies politic, each more or less independent as regards internal affairs, which together make up a federal union, as in the United States of America or the Commonwealth of Australia. **11.** the domain or the authority of a state. **12.** the body politic as organized for supreme civil rule and government (often contrasted with the church). **13.** the operations or activities of supreme civil government, or the sphere of supreme civil authority and administration: *affairs of state.* **14. the States,** *Colloq.* the United States (used outside its borders). **—adj. 15.** of or pertaining to the supreme civil government or authority. **16.** of or pertaining to one of the commonwealths which make up a federal union, as any of the States of the U.S. **17.** characterized by, attended with, or involving ceremony: *a state dinner.* **18.** used on or reserved for occasions of ceremony. **—v.t. 19.** to declare definitely or specifically: *to state one's views.* **20.** to set forth formally in speech or writing: *to state a case.* **21.** to set forth in proper or definite form: *to state a problem.* **22.** to say. **23.** to fix or settle, as by authority. [ME; partly var. of ESTATE; partly t. L: m. *status* condition; in defs. 9–16 a devel. from L *status rērum* state of things, or *status reī publicae* state of the republic] **—Syn. 1.** STATE, CONDITION, SITUATION, STATUS are terms for existing circumstances or surroundings. STATE is the general word, often with no concrete implications or material relationships: *the present state of affairs.* CONDITION carries an implication of a relationship to causes and circumstances: *the conditions made flying impossible.* SITUATION suggests an arrangement of circumstances, related to one another and to the character of a person: *he was master of the situation.* STATUS carries official or legal implications; it suggests a complete picture of interrelated circumstances as having to do with rank, position, standing, a stage reached in progress, etc.: *the status of negotiations.*

state-craft (stāt′kráft′, -kräft′), *n.* **1.** the art of government and diplomacy. **2.** crafty statesmanship.

stat-ed (stā′tǐd), *adj.* **1.** fixed or settled: *for a stated fee.* **2.** explicitly set forth; declared as fact. **3.** recognized or official. **—stat′ed-ly,** *adv.*

State flower, the floral symbol selected by a State or by a group within a State.

state-hood (stāt′hŏŏd), *n.* the condition or status of a state, esp. a State of the U.S.

State-house (stāt′hous′), *n. U.S.* the building in which the legislature of a State sits; the capitol of a State.

state-less (stāt′lǐs), *adj.* without nationality. **—state′less-ness,** *n.*

state-ly (stāt′lǐ), *adj.,* **-lier, -liest,** *adv.* **—adj. 1.** dignified or majestic; imposing in magnificence, elegance, etc.: *a stately palace.* **—adv. 2.** in a stately manner. **—state′li-ness,** *n.*

state-ment (stāt′mənt), *n.* **1.** something stated. **2.** a communication or declaration in speech or writing setting forth facts, particulars, etc. **3.** *Com.* an abstract of an account, as one rendered to show the balance due. **4.** act or manner of stating something.

Stat-en Island (stǎt′ən), an island facing New York Bay, comprising Richmond borough of New York City. 212,020 pop. (1957); 64½ sq. mi.

State prison, a prison maintained by a State for the confinement of felons.

sta-ter (stā′tər), *n.* any of various gold or silver or electrum coin units or coins of the ancient Greek states or cities. [t. L, t. Gk.: standard of weight or money]

State rights, States' rights.

state-room (stāt′rŏŏm′, -rŏŏm′), *n.* a private room

or compartment on a ship, train, etc.

State's attorney, *U.S.* (in judicial proceedings) the legal representative of the State.

state's evidence, *U.S.* **1.** evidence given by an accomplice in a crime who becomes a voluntary witness for the government against the other defendants. **2.** evidence for the State, esp. in criminal trials.

States-Gen-er-al (stāts′jĕn′ər əl), *n.* **1.** the parliament of the present kingdom of the Netherlands. **2.** the legislative body in France before the French Revolution.

state-side (stāt′sīd′), *adj.* **1.** of, in, or toward the United States. **—adv. 2.** in or toward the United States.

states-man (stāts′mən), *n., pl.* **-men. 1.** a man who is versed in the management of affairs of state. **2.** one who exhibits ability of the highest kind in directing the affairs of a government or in dealing with important public issues. [f. *state's,* gen. of STATE + MAN, after F *homme d'état*] **—states′man-like′, states′man-ly,** *adj.* **—Syn. 2.** See politician.

states-man-ship (stāts′mən shǐp′), *n.* the character or procedure of a statesman; skill in the management of public affairs.

state socialism, the theory, doctrine, and movement advocating a planned economy controlled by the state, with state ownership of all industries and natural resources.

States of the Church, Papal States.

States' rights, the rights belonging to the separate States of the United States (used esp. with reference to the strict construction of the Constitution, by which all rights not delegated by the Constitution to the federal government belong to the States). Also, **State rights.**

State university, *U.S.* a university maintained by the government of a State as the highest public educational institution.

stat-ic (stǎt′ǐk), *adj.* Also, **stat′i-cal. 1.** pertaining to or characterized by a fixed or stationary condition. **2.** *Elect.* denoting or pertaining to electricity at rest, as that produced by friction, or the production of such electricity. **3.** denoting or pertaining to atmospheric electricity interfering with the sending and receiving of wireless messages, etc. **4.** *Physics.* acting by mere weight without producing motion: *static pressure.* **5.** *Sociol.* referring to a condition of social life in which no changes are taking place. **6.** *Econ.* pertaining to fixed relations, or different combinations of fixed quantities: *static population.* **—n.** *Elect.* **7.** static or atmospheric electricity. **8.** interference due to such electricity. [t NL: s. *staticus,* t. Gk.: m. *statikós*] **—stat′i-cal-ly,** *adv.*

stat-ics (stǎt′ǐks), *n.* (*pl. construed as sing.*) that branch of mechanics which deals with bodies at rest or forces in equilibrium. [see STATIC, -ICS]

sta-tion (stā′shən), *n.* **1.** a position assigned for standing or remaining in; the place in which anything stands; position. **2.** the place at which something stops; a regular stopping place, as on a railroad. **3.** the building or buildings at a railroad stopping place. **4.** the headquarters of the police force in a municipality or a district thereof. **5.** a place equipped for some particular kind of work, research, or the like: *a postal station.* **6.** standing, as of persons or things, in a scale of estimation, rank, or dignity. **7.** *Mil.* **a.** a military place of duty. **b.** a semipermanent army post. **8.** *Navy.* a place or region to which a government ship or fleet is assigned for duty. **9.** (in India) a place where the British officials of a district or the officers of a garrison reside. **10.** *Radio.* **a.** the location of a transmitting or receiving station. **b.** a radio station: *can't you tune in a better station?* **11.** *Biol.* a particular, or the kind of, place where a given animal or plant is found. **12.** *Australia, New Zealand, etc.* an establishment with its buildings, lands, etc., for raising sheep or cattle. **13.** *Survey.* **a.** a point where an observation is taken. **b.** a length of 100 feet along a survey line. **14.** a position, office, rank, calling, or the like. **15.** *Archaic.* the fact or condition of standing still. **—v.t. 16.** to assign a station to; place or post in a station or position. [ME, t. L: s. *statio*] **—Syn. 3.** STATION, DEPOT are not properly synonyms. A STATION is a stopping place where passengers may get on and off trains or other vehicles: *the Grand Central Station in New York.* A DEPOT is a storehouse or warehouse: *a depot in the wing of the station building.* In the early days in America, the station waiting room and the freight depot were usually in the same building; and, as a result, the names were confused. Since STATION seemed somewhat more dignified, DEPOT was the more commonly used term. STATION has now become the regular word in urban use, and is also widely used in smaller communities. **14.** See appointment.

sta-tion-ar-y (stā′shə nĕr′ǐ), *adj., n., pl.* **-aries. —adj. 1.** standing still; not moving. **2.** having a fixed position; not movable. **3.** established in one place; not itinerant or migratory. **4.** remaining in the same condition or state; not changing. **—n. 5.** one who or that which is stationary. [ME, t. L: m.s. *stationārius*]

stationary engine, a steam engine or other heat engine which remains in a fixed place.

sta-tion-er (stā′shə nər), *n.* **1.** one who sells the materials used in writing, as paper, pens, pencils, ink, etc. **2.** *Obs.* a bookseller. **3.** *Obs.* a publisher. [ME, t. L: m.s. *stationārius* stationary, in ML applied to a tradesman who had a shop, as contrasted with a vendor]

Stationers' Company, a company or guild of the city of London, incorporated in 1556, comprising booksellers, printers, bookbinders, and dealers in writing materials, etc.

sta·tion·er·y (stā'shə nĕr'Ĭ), *n.* **1.** writing paper. **2.** writing materials, as pens, pencils, paper, etc.

station house, a house or building at or serving as a station, esp. a police station.

sta·tion-mas·ter (stā'shən măs'tər, -mäs'-), *n.* a person in charge of a railroad station; a station agent.

stations of the cross, *Eccles.* a series of fourteen representations of successive incidents from the passion of Christ, each with a wooden cross, or a series of wooden crosses alone, set up in a church (or sometimes, in the open air) and visited in order, for prayer and meditation.

station wagon, an automobile having an enclosed wooden body of paneled design with several rows of folding or removable seats behind the driver.

stat·ism (stā'tĭz əm), *n.* **1.** support of or belief in the sovereignty of a state, usually a republic. **2.** the principle or policy of concentrating extensive economic, political, and related controls in the state at the cost of individual liberty. **3.** *Obs.* or *Rare.* statecraft; politics. —stat'ist, *n.*

sta·tis·ti·cal (stə tĬs'tə kəl), *adj.* of or pertaining to statistics; consisting of or based on statistics. Also, **sta·tis'tic.** —**sta·tis'ti·cal·ly,** *adv.*

statistical independence, *Statistics.* a condition on the two-way probability distribution of two variables such that the conditional probability distribution of one variable for a given value of a second variable is identical with that for any other given value of the second variable.

stat·is·ti·cian (stăt'əs tĬsh'ən), *n.* an expert in, or compiler of, statistics. Also, **stat·ist** (stā'tĬst).

sta·tis·tics (stə tĬs'tĬks), *n.* **1.** (*construed as sing.*) the science which deals with the collection, classification, and use of numerical facts or data, bearing on a subject or matter. **2.** (*construed as pl.*) the numerical facts or data themselves. [pl. of *statistic*, t. G: m. *statistik*, t. NL: m.s. *statisticus*, orig., pertaining to a statist]

Sta·ti·us (stā'shĬ əs, -shəs), *n.* **Publius Papinius** (pŭb'-lĬ əs pə pĬn'Ĭ əs), A.D. c45–c96, Roman poet.

stat·o·cyst (stăt'ə sĬst'), *n.* a type of sense organ consisting of a sac enclosing sensory hairs and particles of sand, lime, etc., that has an equilibrating function serving to indicate position in space. [f. Gk. *statŏ*(s) standing) + -CYST]

sta·tor (stā'tər), *n.* *Elect.* the portion of a machine which contains the stationary parts of a dynamo (opposed to *rotor*). [special use of L *stator* attendant]

stat·o·scope (stăt'ə skōp'), *n.* **1.** *Physics.* a form of aneroid barometer for registering minute variations of atmospheric pressure. **2.** *Aeron.* an instrument for detecting a small rate of rise or fall of an aircraft. [f. Gk. *statŏ*(s) standing + -SCOPE]

stat·u·ar·y (stăch'ŏŏ ĕr'Ĭ), *n., pl.* **-aries,** *adj.* —*n.* **1.** statues collectively. [t. L: m.s. *statuāria* statuary art] —*adj.* **2.** of, pertaining to, or suitable for statues. [t. L: m.s. *statuārius* of statues]

stat·ue (stăch'ŏŏ), *n.* a representation of a person or an animal carved in stone or wood, molded in a plastic material, or cast in bronze or the like, esp. one of some size, in the round. [ME, t. F, t. L: m. *statua*]

Statue of Liberty, a giant statue, on Liberty Island, of a woman with a torch in one upraised hand and a tablet in the other, given to the U.S. by France.

stat·u·esque (stăch'ŏŏ ĕsk'), *adj.* like or suggesting a statue, as in formal dignity, grace, or beauty. —**stat'-u·esque'ly,** *adv.* —**stat'u·esque'ness,** *n.*

stat·u·ette (stăch'ŏŏ ĕt'), *n.* a small statue. [t. F, dim. of *statue* STATUE]

stat·ure (stăch'ər), *n.* **1.** the height of an animal body, esp. of man. **2.** the height of any object. **3.** elevation or development attained. [ME, t. OF, t. L: m. *statūra*]

sta·tus (stā'təs, stăt'əs), *n.* **1.** state or condition of affairs. **2.** condition, position, or standing socially, professionally, or otherwise. **3.** *Sociol.* the relative rank or social position of an individual or group. **4.** *Law.* the standing of a person before the law in the class of persons indicated by his or her legal qualities. [t. L] —**Syn. 1.** See state.

status quo (kwō), *Latin.* the state in which anything was or is. Also, **status in quo.** [L: state in which]

status quo an·te bel·lum (ăn'tĬ bĕl'əm), *Latin.* the way things were before the war.

stat·u·ta·ble (stăch'ŏŏ tə bəl), *adj.* **1.** (of an offense) recognized by statute; legally punishable. **2.** prescribed, authorized, or permitted by statute. **3.** conformed or conforming to statutes.

stat·ute (stăch'ŏŏt), *n.* **1.** *Law.* **a.** an enactment made by a legislature and expressed in a formal document. **b.** the document in which such an enactment is expressed. **2.** *Internat. Law.* an instrument annexed or subsidiary to an international agreement, as a treaty. [ME, t. F: m. *statut*, t. LL: s. *statūtum*, prop. neut. of L *statūtus*, pp., decreed, set up]

statute law, law established by legislative enactments.

statute mile. See mile (def. 1a).

statute of limitations, *Law.* a statute defining the period within which a claim may be prosecuted.

stat·u·to·ry (stăch'ŏŏ tŏr'Ĭ), *adj.* **1.** of, pertaining to, or of the nature of a statute. **2.** prescribed or authorized by statute. **3.** conforming to statute. **4.** (of an offense) recognized by statute; legally punishable.

St. Au·gus·tine (ô'gəs tēn'), a seacoast city in NE

Florida: founded by the Spanish, 1565; oldest city in the U.S.; resort. 13,555 (1950).

staunch (stônch, stänch), *v.t., v.i., adj.* stanch.

stau·ro·lite (stôr'ə lĬt'), *n.* a mineral, basic iron aluminum silicate, $HFeAl_5Si_2O_{13}$, occurring in brown to black prismatic crystals, which are often twinned in the form of a cross. [t. F, f. Gk. *staurŏ*(s) cross + -*lite* -LITE] —**stau·ro·lit·ic** (stôr'ə lĬt'Ĭk), *adj.*

stau·ro·scope (stôr'ə skōp'), *n.* an optical instrument for determining the position of the planes of light vibration in sections of crystals.

Sta·vang·er (stä väng'ər), *n.* a seaport in SW Norway. 50,647 (1950).

stave (stāv), *n., v.,* **staved** or **stove, staving.** —*n.* **1.** one of the thin, narrow, shaped pieces of wood which form the sides of a cask, tub, or similar vessel. **2.** a stick, rod, pole, or the like. **3.** a rung of a ladder, chair, etc. **4.** *Pros.* **a.** a verse or stanza of a poem or song. **b.** the alliterating sound in a line of verse; thus, *w* is the stave in *the way of the wind.* **5.** *Music.* a staff. —*v.t.* **6.** to break in a stave or staves of. **7.** to break a hole in; crush inward (often fol. by *in*). **8.** to break (a hole) in a boat, etc. **9.** to break to pieces, splinters, etc. **10.** to furnish with a stave or staves. **11.** to beat with a stave or staff. **12.** to put, ward, or keep (fol. by *off*), as by force or evasion. —*v.i.* **13.** to become stove in, as a boat; break in or up. [ME; back formation from *staves*, pl. of STAFF[1]] —**Syn. 4.** See verse.

staves (stāvz), *n.* **1.** pl. of **staff**[1] (defs. 1–5). **2.** pl. of **stave.**

staves·a·cre (stāvz'ā'kər), *n.* **1.** a larkspur, *Delphinium staphisagria,* native in Europe and Asia Minor, having violently emetic and cathartic poisonous seeds. **2.** the seeds. [ME *staphisagrie,* t. L: m. *staphisagria* wild raisin, t. Gk.]

stay[1] (stā), *v.,* **stayed** or **staid, staying,** *n.* —*v.i.* **1.** to remain in a place, situation, company, etc.; dwell or reside: *we cannot stay home.* **2.** to continue to be (as specified), as to condition, etc.: *to stay clean.* **3.** *Colloq.* to hold out or endure, as in a contest. **4.** *Colloq.* to keep up, as with a competitor in a race. **5.** *Poker.* to continue in a hand by meeting a bet, ante, or raise. **6.** to stop or halt. **7.** to pause or wait, as for a moment, before proceeding or continuing; linger or tarry. **8.** *Archaic.* to cease or desist. **9.** *Archaic.* to stand firm. —*v.t.* **10.** to stop or halt. **11.** to hold back, detain, or restrain, as from going further. **12.** to suspend or delay (proceedings, etc.). **13.** to suppress or quell (violence, strife, etc.). **14.** to appease or satisfy temporarily the cravings of (the stomach, appetite, etc.). **15.** to remain for (a meal, performance, etc.). **16.** to remain through or during (a period of time). **17.** to remain to the end of; remain beyond (fol. by *out*). **18.** *Archaic.* to await. —*n.* **19.** act of stopping. **20.** a stop, halt, or pause; a standstill. **21.** a sojourn or temporary residence. **22.** *Law.* a stoppage or arrest of action; a suspension of a judicial proceeding. **23.** *Colloq.* staying power; endurance. **24.** *Obs.* a cause of stoppage or restraint. [late ME, prob. t. OF: m. *estai-,* s. *ester* stand, g. L *stāre*]

stay[2] (stā), *n., v.,* **stayed, staying.** —*n.* **1.** something used or serving to support or steady a thing; a prop; a brace. **2.** a flat strip of steel, plastic, etc., for stiffening corsets, etc. **3.** (*pl.*) *Chiefly Brit.* a corset. —*v.t.* **4.** to support, prop, or hold up (sometimes fol. by *up*). **5.** to rest for support. **6.** to sustain or strengthen mentally or spiritually. **7.** to fix or rest in dependence or reliance. [appar. same as STAY[3]. Cf. F *étayer,* of Gmc. orig.]

stay[3] (stā), *n., v.,* **stayed, staying.** *Chiefly Naut.* —*n.* **1.** a strong rope, now commonly of wire, used to support a mast. **2.** any rope similarly used; a guy. **3.** in **stays,** heading into the wind while going about from one tack to the other. —*v.t.* **4.** to support or secure with a stay or stays: *to stay a mast.* **5.** to put (a ship) on the other tack. —*v.i.* **6.** (of a ship) to change to the other tack. [ME *stey*(*e*), OE *stæg,* c. D and G *stag*]

stay-in strike (stā'Ĭn'), *Brit.* a sit-down strike.

stay·sail (stā'sāl'; *Naut.* -səl), *n.* *Naut.* any sail hoisted on a stay, as a triangular sail between two masts.

S.T.B., **1.** (L *Sacrae Theologiae Baccalaureus*) Bachelor of Sacred Theology. **2.** (L *Scientiae Theologicae Baccalaureus*) Bachelor of Theology.

St. Ber·nard (sănt bər närd'; *Fr.* săn bĕr når'), **1. Great,** a mountain pass between SW Switzerland and NW Italy, in the Pennine Alps: Napoleon led his army over it, 1800; hospice. 8108 ft. high. **2. Little,** a mountain pass between SE France and NW Italy, in the Alps, S of Mont Blanc. 7177 ft. high. **3.** Saint Bernard (dog).

St. Chris·to·pher (krĬs'tə fər), St. Kitts.

St. Clair (klâr), **1.** a river forming part of the boundary between Michigan and Canada, flowing from Lake Huron S to Lake St. Clair. 41 mi. **2. Lake,** a lake between SE Michigan and Ontario province, Canada. ab. 30 mi. long; ab. 450 sq. mi.

St. Cloud (sănt kloud' *for 1;* săn klōō' *for 2*), **1.** a city in central Minnesota, on the Mississippi. 33,815 (1960). **2.** a suburb of Paris in N France, on the Seine: former royal palace. 20,671 (1954).

St. Croix (sănt kroi'), **1.** Also, **Santa Cruz.** the largest of the Virgin Islands, in the U.S. part of the group. 12,103 pop. (1950); 82 sq. mi. **2.** a river flowing from NW Wisconsin along the Wisconsin-Minnesota boundary into the Mississippi. 164 mi. **3.** a river forming a part of the boundary between Maine and New Brunswick, Canada, flowing into Passamaquoddy Bay. 75 mi.

St. Cyr-l'École (săn sēr lĕ kôl/), a town in N France, W of Versailles: military academy. 4288 (1946).

S.T.D., (L *Sacrae Theologiae Doctor*) Doctor of Sacred Theology.

St. De·nis (săn də nē/). **1.** a suburb of Paris in N France: famous abbey, the burial place of many French kings. 80,705 (1954). **2.** a seaport in and the capital of Réunion island, in the Indian Ocean. 25,332 (1954).

Ste., (F *Sainte*) Saint (female).

stead (stĕd), *n.* **1.** the place of a person or thing as occupied by a successor or substitute: *since he could not come, his brother came in his stead.* **2.** service, advantage, or avail: *to stand one in good stead.* **3.** *Archaic.* a place or locality. —*v.t.* **4.** *Archaic.* to be of service, advantage, or avail to. [ME and OE *stede*, c. G *statt*]

stead·fast (stĕd/făst/, -făst/, -fəst), *adj.* **1.** fixed in direction; steadily directed: *a steadfast gaze.* **2.** firm in purpose, resolution, faith, attachment, etc., as a person. **3.** unwavering, as resolution, faith, adherence, etc. **4.** firmly established, as an institution or a state of affairs. **5.** firmly fixed in place or position. Also, **stedfast.** [ME *stedefast*, OE *stedefæst*, f. *stede* STEAD + *fæst* FAST[1]] —**stead/fast/ly,** *adv.* —**stead/fast/ness,** *n.* —**Syn. 2.** STEADFAST, STANCH, STEADY imply a sureness and continuousness that may be depended upon. STEADFAST literally means fixed in place, but is chiefly used figuratively to indicate undeviating constancy or resolution: *steadfast in one's faith.* STANCH literally means watertight, as of a vessel, and therefore strong and firm; fig., it is used of loyal support that will endure strain: *a stanch advocate of free trade.* Literally, STEADY is applied to that which is relatively firm in position or continuous in movement or duration; fig., it implies sober regularity or persistence: *to run at a steady pace.* —**Ant. 2.** capricious, variable.

stead·y (stĕd/ĭ), *adj.*, **steadier, steadiest,** *interj., n., pl.* **steadies,** *v.,* **steadied, steadying.** —*adj.* **1.** firmly placed or fixed; stable in position or equilibrium; even or regular in movement: *a steady ladder.* **2.** free from change, variation, or interruption; uniform; continuous: *a steady wind.* **3.** constant, regular, or habitual: *steady movie-goers.* **4.** free from excitement or agitation: *steady nerves.* **5.** firm, unwavering, or steadfast, as persons or their principles, policy, etc. **6.** settled, staid, or sober, as a person, habits, etc. **7.** *Naut.* (of a vessel) keeping nearly upright, as in a heavy sea. —*interj.* **8.** be calm! control yourself! **9.** *Naut.* a helm order to steady the vessel on the heading she is on. —*n.* **10.** *Slang.* a person's regular companion and sweetheart. —*v.t.* **11.** to make steady, as in position, movement, action, character, etc. —*v.i.* **12.** to become steady. [f. STEAD + -Y[1]] —**stead/i·er,** *n.* —**stead/i·ly,** *adv.* —**stead/i·ness,** *n.* —**Syn. 2.** undeviating, invariable, regular, constant. **5.** See **steadfast.**

steak (stāk), *n.* **1.** a slice of meat, usually beef or fish, for broiling, frying, etc. **2.** chopped meat prepared in the same manner as a steak: *Salisbury steak.* [ME *steike,* t. Scand.; cf. Icel. *steik*]

steal (stēl), *v.,* **stole, stolen, stealing,** *n.* —*v.t.* **1.** to take, or take away, dishonestly or wrongfully, esp. secretly. **2.** to appropriate (ideas, credit, words, etc.) without right or acknowledgment. **3.** to take, get, or win by insidious, surreptitious, or subtle means: *to steal a nap during a sermon.* **4.** to move, bring, convey, or put secretly or quietly (fol. by *away, from, in, into,* etc.). **5.** *Baseball.* (of a base runner) to advance a base without the help of a hit or an error. **6.** (in various games) to gain (a point, etc.) by strategy, by chance, or by luck. —*v.i.* **7.** to commit or practice theft. **8.** to move, go, or come secretly, quietly, or unobserved. **9.** to pass, come, spread, etc., imperceptibly, gently, or gradually: *the years steal by.* —*n.* **10.** *Colloq.* act of stealing; a theft. **11.** *Colloq.* the thing stolen. **12.** *Colloq.* something acquired at very little cost or effort. [ME *stele(n),* OE *stelan,* c. D *stelen,* G *stehlen,* Icel. *stela*] —**steal/er,** *n.*

steal·ing (stē/lĭng), *n.* **1.** the act of one who steals. **2.** (*chiefly pl.*) something stolen. —*adj.* **3.** that steals.

stealth (stĕlth), *n.* **1.** secret, clandestine, or surreptitious procedure. **2.** *Obs.* a secret departure. **3.** *Obs.* theft. [ME *stelthe.* See STEAL, v., -TH[1]]

stealth·y (stĕl/thĭ), *adj.,* **stealthier, stealthiest.** done, characterized, or acting by stealth; furtive: *stealthy footsteps.* —**stealth/i·ly,** *adv.* —**stealth/i·ness,** *n.*

steam (stēm), *n.* **1.** water in the form of an invisible gas or vapor. **2.** water changed to this form by boiling, extensively used for the generation of mechanical power, for heating purposes, etc. **3.** the mist formed when the gas or vapor from boiling water condenses in the air. **4.** an exhalation. **5.** *Colloq.* power or energy. —*v.i.* **6.** to emit or give off steam or vapor. **7.** to rise or pass off in the form of steam or vapor. **8.** to become covered with condensed steam, as a surface. **9.** to generate or produce steam, as in a boiler. **10.** to move or travel by the agency of steam. —*v.t.* **11.** to expose to or treat with steam, as in order to heat, cook, soften, renovate, or the like. **12.** to emit or exhale (steam or vapor); send out in the form of steam. **13.** to convey by the agency of steam, as in a steamship. —*adj.* **14.** heated by, or heating with, steam: *steam radiator.* **15.** propelled by or propelling with a steam engine: *a steam train.* **16.** operated by steam. **17.** conducting steam: *a steampipe.*

18. bathed with, or affected by, steam. [ME *steme,* OE *stēam,* c. D *stoom*]

steam·boat (stēm/bōt/), *n.* a steamship.

steam boiler, a receptacle in which water is boiled to generate steam.

steam chest, (in a steam engine) the chamber from which the steam enters the cylinder. Also, **steam box.**

steam engine, an engine worked by steam, typically one in which a sliding piston in a cylinder is moved by the expansive action of the steam generated in a boiler.

steam·er (stē/mər), *n.* **1.** something propelled or operated by steam, as a steamship. **2.** one who or that which steams. **3.** a device or container in which something is steamed.

steam fitter, one who installs and repairs steampipes and their accessories.

steam heat, heat obtained by the condensation of steam in pipes, radiators, etc.

steam roller, **1.** a heavy steam locomotive engine having a roller or rollers, for crushing, compacting, or leveling materials in road making. **2.** an agency for crushing opposition, esp. with ruthless disregard of rights.

steam-roll·er (stēm/rō/lər), *v.t.* **1.** to go over or crush as with a steam roller. —*adj.* **2.** suggestive of a steam roller: *steam-roller tactics.*

steam·ship (stēm/shĭp/), *n.* a commercial ship propelled by mechanical power.

steam shovel, a machine for digging or excavating, operated by its own engine and boiler.

steam turbine, See **turbine** (def. 2).

steam·y (stē/mĭ), *adj.,* **steamier, steamiest.** **1.** consisting of or resembling steam. **2.** full of or abounding in steam; emitting steam. **3.** covered with or as if with condensed steam. —**steam/i·ly,** *adv.* —**steam/i·ness,** *n.*

Ste. Anne de Beau·pré (sănt ăn/ də bō prā/; *Fr.* săn tän də bō prĕ/), a village in SE Canada, on the St. Lawrence, NE of Quebec: Roman Catholic shrine.

ste·ap·sin (stĭ ăp/sĭn), *n.* *Biochem.* the lipase of the pancreatic juice. [b. STEA(RIN) and (PEP)SIN]

ste·a·rate (stē/ə rāt/), *n.* *Chem.* a salt or ester of stearic acid.

ste·ar·ic (stĭ ăr/ĭk, stĭr/ĭk), *adj.* of or pertaining to suet or fat.

stearic acid, *Chem.* a monobasic organic acid, $C_{17}H_{35}COOH$, the glycerides of which are the principal components of animal fats. See **stearin.**

ste·a·rin (stē/ə rĭn, stĭr/ĭn), *n.* **1.** *Chem.* any of the three glyceryl esters of stearic acid, esp. $C_3H_5(C_{18}H_{35}O_2)_3$, a soft, white, odorless solid found in many natural fats. **2.** the crude stearic acid of commerce, used in candles, etc. Also, **ste·a·rine** (stē/ə rĭn, -rēn/, stĭr/ĭn, -ēn). [t. F: m. *stéarine,* f. Gk. *stéar* fat + *-ine* -IN[2]]

ste·a·rop·tene (stē/ə rŏp/tēn), *n.* *Chem.* the oxygenated solid part of an essential oil (opposed to *eleoptene,* the liquid part). [f. *stearo-* (repr. Gk. *stéar* tallow, fat, suet) + *-ptene* (t. Gk.: m.s. *ptēnós* winged, volatile)]

ste·a·tite (stē/ə tīt/), *n.* soapstone. [t. L: m. *steatītis,* t. Gk.: doughlike (stone)] —**ste·a·tit·ic** (stē/ə tĭt/ĭk), *adj.*

ste·a·to·py·gi·a (stē/ə tō pĭ/jĭ ə, -pĭj/ĭ ə), *n.* abnormal accumulation of fat on and about the buttocks, as among the Hottentots, Bushmen, and other South African peoples, esp. the women. [NL, f. *steato-* (repr. Gk. *stéar* fat) + *-pȳgia* (der. Gk. *pȳgē* rump)] —**ste·a·to·pyg·ic** (stē/ə tō pĭj/ĭk), **ste·a·to·py·gous** (stē/ə tō pī/gəs), *adj.*

sted·fast (stĕd/făst/, -făst/, -fəst), *adj.* steadfast.

steed (stēd), *n.* **1.** a horse, esp. one for riding. **2.** *Archaic.* a high-spirited horse. [ME *stēde,* OE *stēda* stallion, der. *stōd* STUD[2]; cf. Icel. *stedda* mare]

steel (stēl), *n.* **1.** iron in a modified form, artificially produced, containing a certain amount of carbon (more than in wrought iron and less than in cast iron) and other constituents, and possessing a hardness, elasticity, strength, etc., which vary with the composition and the heat treatment: commonly made by removing a certain amount of the carbon from pig iron, and used in making tools, girders, etc. **2.** **high** or **hard steel,** steel with a comparatively high percentage of carbon. **3.** **low, mild,** or **soft steel,** steel with a comparatively low percentage of carbon. **4.** **medium steel,** a tough-tempering steel having a medium carbon content. **5.** something made of steel. **6.** a sword. **7.** a flat strip of steel for stiffening corsets, etc. **8.** *Exchanges.* **a.** the market quotation of a steel concern. **b.** stocks, bonds, etc., of steel companies. —*adj.* **9.** pertaining to or made of steel. **10.** like steel in color, hardness, or strength. —*v.t.* **11.** to fit with steel, as by pointing, edging, or overlaying. **12.** to cause to resemble steel in some way. **13.** to render insensible, inflexible, unyielding, determined, etc. [ME and d. OE *stēle,* c. D *staal,* G *stahl,* Icel. *stāl*]

steel blue, dark bluish gray.

Steele (stēl), *n.* **Sir Richard,** 1672–1729, British essayist and dramatist.

steel engraving, *Print.* **1.** a method of incising (letters, designs, etc.) on steel. **2.** the imprint, as on paper, from a plate of engraved steel.

steel gray, dark metallic gray with bluish tinge.

steel·head (stēl/hĕd/), *n., pl.* **-heads,** (*esp. collectively*) **-head.** a large, silvery trout, *Salmo gairdnerii,* of the Pacific coast from California northward, now generally

---

b., blend of, blended; c., cognate with; d., dialect, dialectal; der., derived from; f., formed from; g., going back to; m., modification of; r., replacing; s., stem of; t., taken from; ?, perhaps. See the full key on inside cover.

regarded as the sea-run form of the rainbow trout, highly prized as a game fish.

steel·work (stēl′wûrk′), *n.* steel parts or articles.

steel·works (stēl′wûrks′), *n.pl. or sing.* an establishment where steel is made, and often manufactured into girders, rails, etc.

steel·y (stē′lǐ), *adj.*, **steel·ier, steel·iest. 1.** consisting or made of steel. **2.** resembling or suggesting steel; hard or strong like steel. —**steel′i·ness,** *n.*

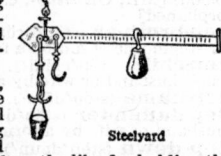

steel·yard (stēl′yärd′, stĭl′yärd), *n.* a portable balance with two unequal arms, the longer one having a movable counterpoise, and the shorter one bearing a hook or the like for holding the object to be weighed. [t. G: mistaken translation of *stahlhof* sample (court)yard]

Steelyard

Steen (stān), *n.* Jan (yän), 1626–79, Dutch painter.

steen·bok (stēn′bŏk′, stān′-), *n.* a small South African antelope, *Raphicerus campestris*, frequenting rocky places, and lacking dewclaws. Also, **steinbok**. [t. S Afr. D: lit., stonebuck]

South African steenbok,
Raphicerus campestris
(Ab. 2 ft. high at the shoulder, ab. 3 ft. long)

steep[1] (stēp), *adj.* **1.** having an almost perpendicular slope or pitch, or a relatively high gradient, as a hill, an ascent, stairs, etc. **2.** *Colloq.* unduly high, or exorbitant, as a price or amount. **3.** *Colloq.* extreme or extravagant, as a statement. **4.** *Obs.* high or lofty. —*n.* **5.** a steep place; a declivity, as of a hill. [ME *stepe*, OE *stēap;* akin to STOOP[1]] —**steep′ly,** *adv.* —**steep′ness,** *n.*

steep[2] (stēp), *v.t.* **1.** to soak in water or other liquid, as for the purpose of softening, cleansing, or the like, or of extracting some constituent: *to steep tea in boiling water.* **2.** to wet thoroughly in or with any liquid, or as a liquid does; drench, saturate, or imbue. **3.** to immerse in some pervading, absorbing, or stupefying influence or agency: *a mind steeped in romance.* —*v.i.* **4.** to lie soaking in a liquid. —*n.* **5.** act or process of steeping. **6.** state of being steeped. **7.** a liquid in which something is steeped. [ME *stepe,* c. Sw. *stöpa*] —**steep′er,** *n.*

steep·en (stē′pən), *v.t., v.i.* to make or become steeper.

stee·ple (stē′pəl), *n.* **1.** a lofty tower attached to a church, temple, or the like, and often containing bells. **2.** such a tower with a spire or other superstructure surmounting it. **3.** a spire on the top of the tower or roof of a church or the like. [ME *stepyl,* OE *stēpel,* der. *stēap* high, steep]

stee·ple·bush (stē′pəl bŏŏsh′), *n.* the hardhack.

stee·ple·chase (stē′pəl chās′), *n.* **1.** a horse race over a course furnished with artificial ditches, hedges, and other obstacles. **2.** a horse race across country. **3.** a race run on foot by persons across country or over a course furnished with ditches, hurdles, etc. —**stee′ple·chas′er,** *n.*

A. Steeple; B. Spire

stee·ple·jack (stē′pəl jăk′), *n.* a man who climbs steeples, tall chimneys, or the like, to make repairs, etc.

steer[1] (stĭr), *v.t.* **1.** to guide the course of (anything in motion) by a rudder, helm, wheel, etc.: *to steer a ship.* **2.** to follow or pursue (a particular course). **3.** *Colloq.* to direct the course of. —*v.i.* **4.** to direct the course of a vessel, vehicle, airplane, or the like by the use of a rudder or other means. **5.** to direct the course, or pursue a course (as specified). **6.** (of a vessel, etc.) to admit of being steered; be steered or guided in a particular direction. **7. steer clear of,** to avoid. —*n.* **8.** *U.S. Slang.* a suggestion on what to do: *a good steer.* [ME *stere,* OE *stēoran,* c. D *sturen,* G *steuern,* Icel. *stȳra*] —**steer′a·ble,** *adj.* —**steer′er,** *n.*

steer[2] (stĭr), *n.* a castrated male bovine, esp. one raised for beef; ox. [ME; OE *stēor,* c. D and G *stier*]

steer·age (stĭr′ĭj), *n.* **1.** a part or division of a ship, orig. that containing the steering apparatus, later varying in use. **2.** (in a passenger ship) the part allotted to the passengers who travel at the cheapest rate.

steer·age·way (stĭr′ĭj wā′), *n.* the degree of forward movement which renders a ship subject to the helm.

steering gear, the apparatus or mechanism for steering a ship, automobile, bicycle, airplane, etc.

steering wheel, a wheel turned by the driver, pilot, etc., in steering an automobile, ship, etc.

steers·man (stĭrz′mən), *n., pl.* **-men. 1.** one who steers a ship; helmsman. **2.** one who drives a machine.

steeve[1] (stēv), *v., steeved, steeving, n.* —*v.t.* **1.** to pack tightly, as cotton or other cargo in a ship's hold. —*n.* **2.** a long derrick or spar, with a block at one end, used in stowing cargo. [late ME, t. F: m. *estiver,* or t. Pr.: m. *estibar,* g. L *stīpāre* pack]

steeve[2] (stēv), *v., steeved, steeving, n. Naut.* —*v.i.* **1.** (of a bowsprit, etc.) to incline upward at an angle instead of extending horizontally. —*v.t.* **2.** to set (a bowsprit, etc.) at an upward inclination. —*n.* **3.** the angle that a bowsprit or the like makes with the horizontal. [cf. OE *stīfig* steep]

Stef·ans·son (stĕf′ən sən; *Icel.* stě′fäns sŏn′), *n.* **Vil·hjalmur** (vĭl′hyoul′mər), 1879–1962, U.S. arctic explorer, born in Canada.

Stef·fens (stĕf′ənz), *n.* **(Joseph) Lincoln,** 1866–1936, U.S. writer, editor, and lecturer.

stego-, a word element meaning "cover," as in *stegosaurus.* [comb. form repr. Gk. *stegos,* var. of *stégē* roof]

steg·o·my·ia (stĕg′ə mī′ə), *n.* former name of the mosquito, *Aëdes aegypti,* which transmits yellow fever.

steg·o·sau·rus (stĕg′ə sôr′əs), *n., pl.* **-sauri** (-sôr′ī). any of the herbivorous dinosaurs constituting the genus *Stegosaurus,* reptiles of great size (sometimes nearly 40 feet long) with a heavy bony armor.

Stei·chen (stī′kən), *n.* **Ed·ward,** born 1879, U.S. photographer, esp. in World Wars I and II.

Stegosaurus. *Stegosaurus stenops*
(18 ft. long)

Stei·er·mark (shtī′ər märk′), *n.* German name of Styria.

stein (stīn), *n.* an earthenware mug, esp. for beer. [t. G: lit., stone]

Stein (stīn), *n.* **Gertrude,** 1874–1946, U.S. author, in France.

Stein, vom und zum (shtīn, fôm ōŏnt tsōŏm), **Heinrich Friedrich Karl** (hīn′rĭКн frē′drĭКн kärl), 1757–1831, German statesman.

Stein·am·ang·er (shtīn′äm äng′ər), *n.* German name of Szombathely.

Stein·beck (stīn′bĕk), *n.* **John Ernst** (ûrnst), born 1902, U.S. novelist.

stein·bok (stīn′bŏk′), *n.* **1.** the steenbok. **2.** an ibex.

Stein·metz (stīn′mĕts), *n.* **Charles Proteus** (prō′tǐ-əs), 1865–1923, U.S. electrical engineer, born in Germany.

ste·le (stē′lē), *n., pl.* **-lae** (-lē), **-les** (-lēz). **1.** *Archaeol.* an upright slab or pillar of stone bearing an inscription, sculptural design, or the like. **2.** *Archit.* a prepared surface on the face of a building, a rock, etc., bearing an inscription or the like. **3.** (in ancient Greece and Rome) a burial stone. **4.** *Bot.* the central cylinder of vascular tissue, etc., in the stem or root of a plant. [t. Gk.: standing block (of stone)]

St. E·li·as (ĭ lī′əs), **Mount,** a mountain between SE Alaska and SW Yukon territory, Canada. 18,008 ft.

stel·lar (stĕl′ər), *adj.* **1.** of or pertaining to the stars; consisting of stars. **2.** starlike. **3.** pertaining to a leading actor, etc. [t. LL: s. *stellāris,* der. L *stella* star]

stel·la·ra·tor (stĕl′ə rā′tər), *n. Physics.* a toroid containing plasma which is magnetically controlled and heated to about 100 million degrees C. (absolute) to sustain a thermonuclear reaction.

stel·late (stĕl′āt, -ǎt), *adj.* being or arranged in the form of a conventional star; star-shaped. Also, **stel′lat·ed.** [t. L: m.s. *stellātus*] —**stel′late·ly,** *adv.*

stel·lif·er·ous (stĕ lĭf′ər əs), *adj. Obs.* having or abounding with stars. [f. L *stellifer* star-bearing + -OUS]

stel·li·form (stĕl′ə fôrm′), *adj.* star-shaped. [t. NL: s. *stelliformis*]

stel·lu·lar (stĕl′yələr), *adj.* **1.** having the form of a small star or small stars. **2.** spotted with star-shaped specks of color. [f. s. LL *stellula* small star + -AR[1]]

St. El·mo's fire (ĕl′mōz), a corposant.

stem[1] (stĕm), *n., v.,* **stemmed, stemming.** —*n.* **1.** the ascending axis of a plant, whether above or below ground, which ordinarily grows in an opposite direction to the root or descending axis. **2.** the stalk which supports a leaf, flower, or fruit. **3.** the main body of that portion of a tree, shrub, or other plant which is above ground; a trunk; a stalk. **4.** a petiole; a peduncle; a pedicel. **5.** a stalk of bananas. **6.** something resembling or suggesting the stem of a plant, flower, etc. **7.** a long, slender part: *the stem of a tobacco pipe.* **8.** the slender, upright part of a goblet, wineglass, etc. **9.** the cylindrical projection on a watch, having a knob at the end for winding. **10.** the circular rod of some locks about which the key fits and rotates. **11.** the stock, or line of descent, of a family; ancestry or pedigree. **12.** *Gram.* the element common to all the forms of an inflectional paradigm, or to some subset thereof, usually more than a root. Thus *ten-* or *tan-* would be the root of Latin *tendere* and *tend-* would be the stem. **13.** *Music.* the vertical line forming part of a note. **14.** the main or relatively thick stroke of a letter in printing, etc. See diag. under **type.** —*v.t.* **15.** to remove the stem from (a leaf, fruit, etc.). —*v.i.* **16.** to arise or originate. [ME; OE *stemn,* akin to G *stamm*] —**stem′less,** *adj.*

stem[2] (stĕm), *v.t.,* **stemmed, stemming. 1.** to stop or check. **2.** to dam up (a stream, etc.). **3.** to tamp, plug, or make tight, as a hole or a joint. **4.** *Scot.* to stanch (bleeding, etc.). [ME, t. Scand.; cf. Icel. *stemma,* c. G *stemmen*] —**stem′ming,** *adj.*

stem[3] (stĕm), *v.t.,* **stemmed, stemming. 1.** to make headway against (a tide, current, gale, etc.). **2.** to make progress against (any opposition). [v. use of STEM[4]]

stem[4] (stĕm), *n. Naut.* **1.** an upright at the bow of a ship into which the side timbers or plates are jointed. **2.** the forward part of a ship: *from stem to stern.* [OE *stefn, stemn* prow, stern (special use of STEM[1])]

stem·mer (stĕm′ər), *n.* **1.** one who stems (tobacco, etc.). **2.** a device for stemming (grapes, etc.). **3.** an implement for stemming or tamping.

stem·son (stĕm′sən), *n. Naut.* a curved timber in the bow, having its lower end scarfed into the keelson. [der. STEM[4], modeled after KEELSON]

stem-wind·er (stĕm′wīn′dər), *n.* a watch wound by turning a knob at the stem.

stem-wind·ing (stĕm′wīn′dĭng), *adj.* wound, as a watch, by turning a knob at the stem.

stench (stĕnch), *n.* **1.** an ill smell or offensive odor. **2.** ill-smelling quality. [ME; OE *stenc,* c. D and G *stank*]

sten·cil (stĕn′səl), *n., v.,* -ciled, -ciling or (*esp. Brit.*) -cilled, -cilling. —*n.* **1.** a thin sheet of cardboard or metal cut through in such a way as to reproduce a design or ornament when color is rubbed through it. **2.** the letters, designs, etc., produced. —*v.t.* **3.** to mark or paint (a surface) or produce (letters, etc.) by means of a stencil. [earlier *stanesile,* appar. der. ME *stansel(en)* adorn with a variety of colors, t. OF: m. *estanceler,* der. *estencele,* g. L. *scintilla* spark]

Sten·dhal (stän dhäl′), *n.* (*Marie Henri Beyle*) 1783–1842, French novelist and critic.

steno-, a word element meaning "little," "narrow," referring especially to shorthand, as in *stenography.* [comb. form repr. Gk. *stenós* narrow, close]

sten·o·graph (stĕn′ə grăf′, -gräf′), *n.* **1.** a writing in shorthand. **2.** any of various keyboard instruments, somewhat resembling a typewriter, used for writing in shorthand, as by means of phonetic or arbitrary symbols. —*v.t.* **3.** to write in shorthand.

ste·nog·ra·pher (stə nŏg′rə fər), *n.* a person who specializes in taking dictation, or in reporting, stenographically. Also, **ste·nog′ra·phist.**

ste·nog·ra·phy (stə nŏg′rə fĭ), *n.* the art of writing in shorthand. —**sten·o·graph·ic** (stĕn′ə grăf′ĭk), **sten′o·graph′i·cal,** *adj.* —**sten′o·graph′i·cal·ly,** *adv.*

sten·o·pet·al·ous (stĕn′ō pĕt′ə ləs), *adj.* having narrow petals.

sten·o·phyl·lous (stĕn′ō fĭl′əs), *adj.* having narrow leaves.

ste·no·sis (stĭ nō′sĭs), *n., pl.* -ses (-sēz). *Pathol.* narrowing of a passage or vessel. [NL, t. Gk.]

sten·o·type (stĕn′ə tīp′), *n.* **1.** a keyboard instrument resembling a typewriter, used in a system of phonetic shorthand. **2.** (*cap.*) a trademark for this machine. **3.** the symbols typed in one stroke on a stenotype machine.

sten·o·typ·y (stĕn′ə tī′pĭ, stə nŏt′ə pĭ), *n.* shorthand in which alphabetic letters or types are used to produce shortened forms of words or groups of words.

Sten·tor (stĕn′tôr), *n.* **1.** (in the *Iliad*) a Greek herald with a loud voice. **2.** (*l.c.*) a person having a very loud or powerful voice.

sten·to·ri·an (stĕn tôr′ĭ ən), *adj.* very loud or powerful in sound: *a stentorian voice.*

step (stĕp), *n., v.,* **stepped, stepping.** —*n.* **1.** a movement made by lifting the foot and setting it down again in a new position, as in walking, running, or dancing. **2.** the space passed over or measured by one movement of the foot in stepping: *to move a step nearer.* **3.** the sound made by the foot in stepping. **4.** a mark or impression made by the foot on the ground; footprint. **5.** the manner of stepping; gait. **6.** pace in marching: *double-quick step.* **7.** pace uniform with that of another or others, or in time with music: *to keep step.* **8.** (*pl.*) movements or course in stepping or walking: *to retrace one's steps.* **9.** a move or proceeding, as toward some end or in the general course of action: *the first step toward peace.* **10.** a measure; a stage in a process. **11.** a support for the foot in ascending or descending: *a step of a ladder, stair, etc.* **12.** a very short distance; a distance easily walked. **13.** a repeated pattern or unit of movement in a dance formed by a combination of foot and body motions. **14.** *Music.* **a.** a degree of the staff or of the scale. **b.** the interval between two adjacent scale degrees; a second (called **half step** if equivalent to one half tone, or **whole step** if equivalent to two half tones). **c.** whole step. **15.** (*pl.*) *Brit.* a stepladder. **16.** *Mech., etc.* a part or offset resembling a step of a stair. **17.** *Naut.* a socket, frame, or platform for supporting the lower end of a mast. **18.** *Quarrying.* a flat-topped ledge on the face of a quarry. **19.** *Radio. Obsolesc.* a stage. [ME; d. OE *steppe,* var. of OE *stepe, stæpe,* c. D and LG *stap*] —*v.i.* **20.** to move, go, etc., by lifting the foot and setting it down again in a new position, or by using the feet alternately in this manner: *to step forward.* **21.** to walk, or go on foot, esp. for a few steps or a short distance: *please step this way.* **22.** to move with measured steps, as in a dance. **23.** to go briskly or fast, as a horse. **24.** to come as if by a step of the foot: *to step into a fortune.* **25.** to put the foot down, as on the ground, a support, etc.; tread (*on* or *upon*), by intention or accident: *to step on a worm.* **26.** to press with the foot, as on a lever, spring, or the like, in order to operate some mechanism. —*v.t.* **27.** to take (a step, pace, stride, etc.). **28.** to go through or perform the steps of (a dance). **29.** to move or set (the foot) in taking a step. **30.** to

measure (a distance, ground, etc.) by steps (sometimes fol. by *off* or *out*). **31.** to make or arrange in the manner of a series of steps. **32.** *Naut.* to fix (a mast) in its step. **33. step down,** to lower or decrease. **34. step up,** to raise or increase. [ME; OE *steppan*] —**step′like,** *adj.*

step-, a prefix indicating connection between members of a family by the remarriage of a parent, and not by blood, [ME; OE *stēop-,* c. G *stief-,* Icel. *stjūp* bereaved, orphaned]

step-broth·er (stĕp′brŭth′ər), *n.* one's stepfathers' or stepmother's son by a former marriage.

step-child (stĕp′chīld′), *n., pl.* -children. a child of one's husband or wife by a former marriage.

step-dame (stĕp′dām′), *n. Archaic.* a stepmother.

step-daugh·ter (stĕp′dô′tər), *n.* a daughter of one's husband or wife by a former marriage.

step-down (stĕp′doun′), *adj. Elect.* converting from a higher to a lower voltage: *a step-down transformer.*

step-fa·ther (stĕp′fä′thər), *n.* a man who occupies one's father's place by marriage to one's mother.

steph·an·ite (stĕf′ə nīt′), *n.* a mineral, silver antimony sulfide, Ag_5SbS_4: an ore of silver.

Ste·phen (stē′vən), *n.* **1.** *Saint,* c975–1038, first king of Hungary, 997–1038. **2.** (*Stephen of Blois*) 1097?–1154, king of England, 1135–54 (successor and nephew of Henry I). **3.** *Sir Leslie,* 1832–1904, British biographer, critic, and editor.

Ste·phens (stē′vənz), *n.* **1. Alexander Hamilton,** 1812–83, U.S. statesman: vice-president of the Confederacy. **2. James,** 1882–1950, Irish author.

Ste·phen·son (stē′vən sən), *n.* **1. George,** 1781–1848, British engineer: improver of steam locomotive. **2.** his son, **Robert,** 1803–59, British engineer and bridge-builder.

step-in (stĕp′ĭn′), *adj.* **1.** (of garments, shoes, etc.) put on by being stepped into. —*n.* **2.** Also, **step-ins.** a step-in garment, etc.

step-lad·der (stĕp′lăd′ər), *n.* a ladder having flat steps or treads in place of rungs.

step-moth·er (stĕp′mŭth′ər), *n.* a woman who occupies one's mother's place by marriage to one's father.

Step·ney (stĕp′nĭ), *n.* an E borough of London, England. 98,581 (1951).

step-par·ent (stĕp′pâr′ənt), *n.* a stepfather or stepmother.

steppe (stĕp), *n.* **1.** an extensive plain, esp. one without trees. **2. The Steppes, a.** the vast Russian grasslands, esp. those in the S and E European and W and SW Asiatic parts of the Soviet Union. **b.** Kırghiz Steppe. [t. Russ.: m. *step*]

step·per (stĕp′ər), *n.* **1.** a person or animal that steps (said esp. of a horse). **2.** *Slang.* a dancer.

stepping stone, 1. a stone, or one of a line of stones, in shallow water, a marshy place, or the like, used for stepping on in crossing. **2.** a stone for use in mounting or ascending. **3.** any means of advancing or rising.

step-sis·ter (stĕp′sĭs′tər), *n.* one's stepfather's or stepmother's daughter by a former marriage.

step-son (stĕp′sŭn′), *n.* a son of one's husband or wife by a former marriage.

step-up (stĕp′ŭp′), *adj. Elect.* converting from a lower to a higher voltage: *a step-up transformer.*

step-wise (stĕp′wīz′), *adv.* in a steplike arrangement.

-ster, a suffix of personal nouns, often derogatory, referring especially to occupation or habit, as in *songster, gamester, trickster,* also having less apparent connotations, as in *youngster, roadster.* [ME; OE *-estre, -istre,* c. D *-ster,* MLG *-(e)ster*]

ster·co·ra·ceous (stûr′kə rā′shəs), *adj. Physiol.* consisting of, resembling, or pertaining to dung or feces. Also, **ster·co·rous** (stûr′kə rəs). [t. L: m. *stercorāceus*]

ster·cu·li·a·ceous (stûr kū′lĭ ā′shəs), *adj.* belonging to the *Sterculiaceae,* a family of trees and shrubs, mostly tropical, including the cacao and kola nut trees. [f. s. NL *Sterculiaceae,* der. *Sterculia,* name of the typical genus (in L *Sterculia* god of manuring) + -ous]

stere (stēr), *n. Fr. stère,* *n.* a cubic meter, equivalent to 35.314 cu. ft. or 1.3079 cu. yds., used to measure cordwood. [t. F, t. Gk.: m. *stereós* solid]

stereo-, a word element referring to hardness, solidity, three-dimensionality, as in *stereogram, stereoscope.* Also, before some vowels, **stere-.** [comb. form repr. Gk. *stereós* solid]

ster·e·o (stĕr′ĭ ō, stĭr′ĭ ō), *n., pl.* **stereos,** *adj. Colloq.* —*n.* **1.** a stereoscopic photograph. —*adj.* **2.** pertaining to stereophonic sound, a stereoscopic photograph, etc.

ster·e·o·bate (stĕr′ĭ ə bāt′, stĭr′-), *n. Archit.* **1.** the foundation or base upon which a building or the like is erected. **2.** the solid platform or structure (including the stylobate) upon which the columns of a classical building rest. [t. L: s. *stereobata,* f. Gk.: *stereo-* STEREO- + m. *-bátēs* stepping, going. Cf. STYLOBATE] —**ster·e·o·bat·ic** (stĕr′ĭ ə băt′ĭk, stĭr′-), *adj.*

ster·e·o·chem·is·try (stĕr′ĭ ō kĕm′ĭs trĭ, stĭr′-), *n.* that branch of chemistry which deals with the relative arrangement in space of the atoms or groups of atoms constituting a molecule.

ster·e·o·chrome (stĕr′ĭ ə krōm′, stĭr′-), *n.* a picture produced by a process in which water glass is used as a vehicle or as a preservative coating. —**ster′e·o·chro′mic,** *adj.* —**ster′e·o·chro′mi·cal·ly,** *adv.*

---

ster·e·o·chro·my (stĕr′Ĭə krō′mĬ, stĬr′-), *n.* the stereochrome process. [t. G: m. *stereochromie.* See STEREO-, CHROME, -Y³]

ster·e·o·gram (stĕr′Ĭə grăm′, stĬr′-), *n.* 1. a diagram or picture representing objects in a way to give the impression of solidity. 2. a stereograph.

ster·e·o·graph (stĕr′Ĭə grăf′, -grăf′, stĬr′-), *n.* a single or double picture for a stereoscope.

ster·e·og·ra·phy (stĕr′Ĭ ŏg′rə fĬ, stĬr′-), *n.* the art of delineating the forms of solid bodies on a plane; a branch of solid geometry dealing with the construction of regularly defined solids. —**ster·e·o·graph·ic** (stĕr′Ĭə grăf′Ĭk, stĬr′-), **ster·e·o·graph′i·cal,** *adj.* —**ster′e·o·graph′i·cal·ly,** *adv.*

ster·e·o·i·som·er·ism (stĕr′Ĭ ō Ĭ sŏm′ər Ĭz′əm, stĬr′-), *n. Chem.* the isomerism ascribed to different relative positions of the atoms or groups of atoms in the molecules of optically active organic compounds.

ster·e·om·e·try (stĕr′Ĭ ŏm′ə trĬ, stĬr′-), *n.* the measurement of volumes. —**ster·e·o·met·ric** (stĕr′Ĭə mĕt′rĬk, stĬr′-), **ster′e·o·met′ri·cal,** *adj.*

ster·e·o·phon·ic (stĕr′Ĭə fŏn′Ĭk), *adj.* of or denoting a system of separately placed microphones or loudspeakers for imparting greater realism of sound, used esp. with wide-screen motion pictures, high-fidelity recordings, etc. [f. STEREO- + PHONIC]

ster·e·op·sis (stĕr′Ĭ ŏp′sĬs, stĬr′-), *n.* stereoscopic vision. [NL. See STEREO-, OPSIS]

ster·e·op·ti·con (stĕr′Ĭ ŏp′tĬ kən, stĬr′-), *n.* an improved form of projector usually consisting of two complete lanterns arranged so that one picture appears to dissolve while another is forming. [t. NL, f. Gk.: *stere-* STERE- + m. Gk. *optikón* OPTIC]

ster·e·o·scope (stĕr′Ĭə skōp′, stĬr′-), *n.* an optical instrument through which two pictures of the same object, taken from slightly different points of view, are viewed, one by each eye, producing the effect of a single picture of the object, with the appearance of depth or relief.

Stereoscope

The light rays from corresponding points of the two pictures P and P′ are refracted in passing through the lenses L. L.′ and their directions changed so that they now seem to the eyes E. E′, to diverge from a common point A beyond the plane of pictures.

ster·e·os·co·py (stĕr′Ĭ ŏs′kə pĬ, stĬr′-), *n.* 1. the study of the stereoscope and its techniques. 2. three-dimensional vision. —**ster·e·o·scop·ic** (stĕr′Ĭ ə skŏp′Ĭk, stĬr′-), **ster′e·o·scop′i·cal,** *adj.* —**ster′e·o·scop′i·cal·ly,** *adv.* —**ster′e·os′co·pist,** *n.*

ster·e·o·tax·is (stĕr′Ĭ ə tăk′sĬs, stĬr′-), *n.* a movement of an organism in response to contact with a solid.

ster·e·ot·ro·pism (stĕr′Ĭ ŏt′rə pĬz′əm, stĬr′-), *n.* a tropism determined by contact with a solid.

ster·e·o·type (stĕr′Ĭə tīp′, stĬr′-), *n., v.* -typed, -typing. —*n.* 1. a process of making metal plates to use in printing by taking a mold of composed type or the like in papier-mâché or other material and then taking from this mold a cast (plate) in type metal. 2. a plate made by this process. 3. a set form; convention. —*v.t.* 4. to make a stereotype of. 5. to give a fixed form to. —**ster′e·o·typ′er,** *n.* —**ster·e·o·typ·ic** (stĕr′Ĭ ə tĬp′Ĭk, stĬr′-), —**ster′e·o·typ′i·cal,** *adj.*

ster·e·o·typed (stĕr′Ĭə tīpt′, stĬr′-), *adj.* 1. reproduced in stereotype plates. 2. fixed or settled in form; hackneyed; conventional. —**Syn.** 2. See **commonplace.**

ster·e·o·typ·y (stĕr′Ĭə tī′pĬ, stĬr′-), *n.* the stereotype process.

ster·ic (stĕr′Ĭk, stĬr′Ĭk), *adj. Chem.* pertaining to the spatial relationship of atoms in the molecule. Also, **ster′i·cal.** [f. STER(EO)- + -IC]

ster·ile (stĕr′Ĭl), *adj.* 1. free from living germs or microörganisms: *sterile bandage.* 2. incapable of producing, or not producing, offspring. 3. barren; unproductive of vegetation, as soil. 4. *Bot.* **a.** denoting a plant in which reproductive structures fail to develop. **b.** bearing no stamens or pistils. 5. unproductive of results; fruitless. [t. L: m.s. *sterilis* barren] —**ster′ile·ly,** *adv.* —**ste·ril·i·ty** (stə rĬl′ə tĬ), *n.* —**Ant.** 2, 3. fertile.

ster·i·li·za·tion (stĕr′ə lə zā′shən), *n.* 1. act of sterilizing. 2. the condition of being sterilized. 3. the destruction of all living microörganisms, as pathogenic or saprophytic bacteria, vegetative forms, and spores.

ster·i·lize (stĕr′ə līz′), *v.t.* -lized, -lizing. 1. to destroy microörganisms in, usually by bringing to a high temperature with steam, dry heat, or boiling liquid. 2. to destroy (one's) ability to reproduce by removing sex organs or inhibiting their functions. Also, *esp. Brit.* **ster′i·lise′.** —**ster′i·liz′er,** *n.*

ster·ling (stûr′lĬng), *adj.* 1. consisting of or pertaining to sterling, or British money. 2. (of silver) **a.** orig., being of the same quality as the silver in the sterling (British coin). **b.** being of standard quality, 92½% pure silver. 3. made of sterling silver: *sterling flatware.* 4. thoroughly excellent: *a man of sterling worth.* —*n.*

5. the standard of fineness of legal coin in Britain: **a.** for silver (**sterling silver**), before 1920, 0.925; now, 0.500. **b.** for gold, at one time 0.995 but now 0.91666. 6. silver having the sterling fineness of .925, used esp. in manufacture. 7. manufactured goods of sterling silver. [ME, name of a silver coin, ? f. *ster* STAR + -LING¹ (with reference to the little star on some of the coins)]

stern¹ (stûrn), *adj.* 1. firm, strict, or uncompromising: *stern discipline.* 2. hard, harsh, or severe: *a stern speech.* 3. rigorous or austere; of an unpleasantly serious character: *stern times.* 4. grim or forbidding in aspect: *a stern face.* [ME; OE *styrne*; akin to G *starr* stiff, Gk. *stereós* hard, solid] —**stern′ly,** *adv.* —**stern′ness,** *n.* —**Syn.** 1, 2. STERN, SEVERE, HARSH agree in referring to methods, aspects, manners, or facial expressions. STERN implies uncompromising, inflexible firmness, and sometimes a hard, forbidding, or "withdrawn" aspect or nature: *a stern parent.* SEVERE implies strictness, lack of sympathy, and a tendency to impose a hard discipline on others: *a severe judge.* HARSH suggests a great severity and roughness, and cruel, unfeeling treatment of others: *a harsh critic.* —**Ant.** 1. mild.

stern² (stûrn), *n.* 1. the hinder part of a ship or boat (often opposed to *stem*). 2. the hinder part of anything. [ME, ? t. Scand.; cf. Icel. *stjörn* steering (see def. of STERNPOST)]

ster·nal (stûr′nəl), *adj.* of or pertaining to the sternum.

stern chase, *Naut.* a chase in which the pursuing vessel follows in the wake of the other or astern of it.

Sterne (stûrn), *n.* **Laurence,** 1713–68, British clergyman and novelist.

stern·most (stûrn′mōst′, -məst), *adj.* 1. farthest astern or in the rear. 2. nearest the stern.

stern·post (stûrn′pōst′), *n. Naut.* the principal piece of timber or iron in the stern of a vessel, having its lower end fastened to the keel, and usually serving as a support for the rudder. See diag. under **transom.**

stern sheets, the after part of an open boat, occupied by the person in command and by passengers.

ster·num (stûr′nəm), *n., pl.* **-na** (-nə), **-nums.** *Anat., Zool.* a bone or series of bones extending along the middle line of the ventral portion of the body of most vertebrates, consisting in man of a flat, narrow bone connected with the clavicles and the true ribs; the breastbone. See diag. under **skeleton.** [NL, t. Gk.: m. *stérnon* chest, breast]

ster·nu·ta·tion (stûr′nyə tā′shən), *n.* act of sneezing. [t. L: s. *sternūtātio*]

ster·nu·ta·tor (stûr′nyə tā′tər), *n. Chem. Warfare.* a chemical agent causing nose irritation, coughing, etc.

ster·nu·ta·to·ry (stər nū′tə tōr′Ĭ, -nōō′-), *adj., n., pl.* **-ries.** —*adj.* 1. Also, **ster·nu′ta·tive.** causing or tending to cause sneezing. —*n.* 2. a sternutatory substance.

stern·ward (stûrn′wərd), *adv.* toward the stern; astern.

stern·way (stûrn′wā′), *n. Naut.* the movement of a ship backward, or stern foremost.

stern-wheel (stûrn′hwēl′), *adj.* propelled by a paddle wheel at the stern. —**stern′-wheel′er,** *n.*

ster·oid (stĕr′oid), *n. Biochem.* any of a large group of certain fat-soluble compounds, most of which have specific physiological action. Among them are the sterols, bile acids, and many hormones.

ster·ol (stĕr′ōl, -ŏl), *n. Biochem.* any of a group of solid, mostly unsaturated, polycyclic alcohols derived from plants or animals, as cholesterol and ergosterol. [abstracted from (CHOLE)STEROL, (ERGO)STEROL]

ster·tor (stûr′tər), *n. Pathol.* a heavy snoring sound accompanying respiration in certain diseases. [NL, der. L *stertere* snore]

ster·to·rous (stûr′tə rəs), *adj.* 1. characterized by stertor or heavy snoring. 2. breathing in this manner. —**ster′to·rous·ly,** *adv.* —**ster′to·rous·ness,** *n.*

stet (stĕt), *v.,* stetted, stetting. —*v.i.* 1. let it stand: a direction on a printer's proof, a manuscript, or the like to retain canceled matter (usually accompanied by a row of dots under or beside the matter). —*v.t.* 2. to mark with the word "stet" or with dots. [t. L: let it stand]

stetho-, a word element meaning "chest." Also, before vowels, **steth-.** [comb. form repr. Gk. *stéthos*]

ste·thom·e·ter (stĕ thŏm′ə tər), *n.* an instrument for measuring the respiratory movements of the walls of the chest and abdomen.

steth·o·scope (stĕth′ə skōp′), *n. Med.* an instrument used in auscultation to convey sounds in the chest or other parts of the body to the ear of the examiner. —**ste·thos·co·py** (stĕ thŏs′kə pĬ), *n.*

Binaural stethoscope

steth·o·scop·ic (stĕth′ə skŏp′Ĭk), *adj.* 1. pertaining to the stethoscope or to stethoscopy. 2. made or obtained by the stethoscope. Also, **steth′o·scop′i·cal.** —**steth′o·scop′i·cal·ly,** *adv.*

St.-É·tienne (săN tĕ tyĕn′), *n.* a city in central France. 181,730 (1954).

Stet·tin (shtĕ tēn′), *n.* a seaport in NW Poland: formerly in Germany. 300,000 (est. 1954). Polish, **Szczecin.**

Steu·ben (stū′bən, stōō′-; *Ger.* shtoi′bən), *n.* **Friedrich Wilhelm Ludolf Gerhard Augustin von** (frē′drĬKH vĬl′hĕlm lōō′dôlf gär′härt ou′gōōs tĕn′ fən), ("*Baron Steuben*") 1730–94, Prussian general who aided Americans in Revolutionary War.

Steu·ben·ville (stū′bən vĭl′, stōō′-), *n.* a city in E Ohio, on the Ohio river. 32,495 (1960).

St. Eu·sta·ti·us (sănt ū stā′shĭ əs, -shəs), an island in the Netherlands Antilles. 1055 (1955); 7 sq. mi.

ste·ve·dore (stē′və dōr′), *n., v.,* **-dored, -doring.** —*n.* 1. a firm or individual engaged in the loading or unloading of a vessel. —*v.t.* 2. to load or unload the cargo of (a ship). —*v.i.* 3. to load or unload a vessel. [t. Sp.: m. *estivador,* der. *estivar* pack, stow, g. L *stīpāre* press]

stevedore's knot, a knot which forms a lump in a line to prevent it from passing through a hole, etc.

Ste·vens (stē′vənz), *n.* **Thaddeus** (thăd′ĭ əs), 1792–1868, U.S. abolitionist and politician.

Ste·ven·son (stē′vən sən), *n.* 1. **Adlai** (ăd′lā), 1900–65, U.S. political leader. 2. **Robert Louis (Balfour)** (băl′tōōr), 1850–94, Scottish novelist, essayist, and poet.

stew (stū, stōō), *v.t.* 1. to cook (food) by simmering or slow boiling. —*v.i.* 2. to undergo cooking by simmering or slow boiling. 3. *Colloq.* to fret, worry, or fuss. —*n.* 4. a preparation of meat, fish, or other food cooked by stewing. 5. *Colloq.* a state of uneasiness, agitation, or worry. 6. *Obs.* a vessel for boiling or stewing. [ME, t. OF: m.s. *estuver,* g. VL *extūfāre* perspire, der. *tūfus* vapor, t. Gk.: m. *typhos*] —**Syn.** 3. See **boil¹.**

stew·ard (stū′ərd, stōō′-), *n.* 1. one who manages another's property or financial affairs; one who administers anything as the agent of another or others. 2. one who has charge of the household of another, providing for the table, directing the servants, etc. 3. an employee who has charge of the table, the servants, etc., in a club or other establishment. 4. a ship's officer who keeps the stores and arranges for the table. 5. any attendant on a ship who waits on passengers. 6. *U.S. Navy.* a petty officer in charge of officers' quarters and mess. —*v.t.* 7. to act as steward of; manage. —*v.i.* 8. to act or serve as steward. [ME; OE *stīweard, stigweard,* f. *stig* hall + *weard* keeper, **WARD²**] —**stew·ard·ess** (stū′ər dĭs, stōō′-), *n. fem.* —**stew·ard·ship′,** *n.*

Stew·art (stū′ərt, stōō′-), *n.* 1. **Dugald** (dū′gəld, dōō′-), 1753–1828, Scottish philosopher. 2. **Henry,** 1545–67, (*Lord Darnley*) second husband of Mary, Queen of Scots, and father of James I, king of England. 3. See **Stuart** (def. 1).

Stewart Island, one of the islands of New Zealand S of South Island. 343 pop. (1945); 670 sq. mi.

stewed (stūd, stōōd), *adj.* 1. cooked by stewing or slow boiling, as food. 2. *Slang.* intoxicated or drunk.

stew·pan (stū′păn′, stōō′-), *n. Chiefly Brit.* a pan for stewing; a saucepan.

St. Gal·len (gä′lən), 1. a canton in NE Switzerland. 313,700 pop. (est. 1952); 777 sq. mi. 2. capital of this canton. 69,700 (est. 1952). French, **St. Gall** (săn gàl′).

St. George's (jôr′jĭz), a seaport in and the capital of Grenada, in the Federation of the West Indies. 20,832 (est. 1950).

St. George's Channel, a channel between Wales and Eire, connecting the Irish Sea and the Atlantic. Least width, 43 mi.

St.-Ger·main-en-Laye (săn zhĕr măn′ än lĕ′), a city in N France, near Paris: royal château and forest; treaties 1570, 1632, 1679, 1919. 29,429 (1954).

St. Got·thard (gŏt′ərd; *Fr.* săn gô tàr′), 1. a range of the Alps in S Switzerland. Highest peak, 10,490 ft. 2. a mountain pass over this range. 6935 ft. high. 3. a railway tunnel under this pass. 9¼ mi. long.

St. He·le·na (hə lē′nə), 1. a British island in the S Atlantic: Napoleon's place of exile, 1815–21. 4878 (est. 1954); 47 sq. mi. 2. a British colony comprising this island, Ascension Island, and the Tristan da Cunha group. 5345 pop. (est. 1954); 126 sq. mi. *Cap.:* Jamestown.

St. Hel·ens (hĕl′ĭnz), a city in W England, near Liverpool. 106,789 (1951).

St. Hel·ier (hĕl′yər; *Fr.* săn tĕ lyĕ′), a seaport on the island of Jersey in the English Channel: resort. 19,398 (1951).

St. Helena (def. 1.)

sthe·ni·a (stha nĭ′ə, sthē′nĭ ə), *n. Pathol.* strength; excessive vital force. Cf. **asthenia.** [NL, abstracted from *asthenia* **ASTHENIA**]

sthen·ic (sthĕn′ĭk), *adj.* sturdy; heavily and strongly built. [abstracted from **ASTHENIC**]

Sthe·no (sthē′nō, sthĕn′ō), *n. Gk. Legend.* one of the three gorgons.

stiac·cia·to (styät chä′tō), *adj. Art.* in very low relief (like a bas-relief pressed flatter). [t. It. pp. of *stiacciare* crush, flatten, by-form of *schiacciare* crack (a nut)]

stib·ine (stĭb′ēn, -ĭn), *n. Chem.* antimonous hydride, SbH₃, a colorless poisonous gas. [f. **STIB**(IUM) + **-INE²**]

stib·i·um (stĭb′ĭ əm), *n.* antimony. [t. L] —**stib·i·al,** *adj.*

stib·nite (stĭb′nīt), *n.* a mineral, antimony sulfide, Sb₂S₃, lead-gray in color with a metallic luster, occurring in crystals, often acicular, or in bladed masses: the most important ore of antimony. [f. **STIB**(I)N(E) + **-ITE¹**]

stich (stĭk), *n.* a verse or line of poetry. [t. Gk.: s. *stichos* row, line, verse]

stich·ic (stĭk′ĭk), *adj.* 1. pertaining to or consisting of stichs. 2. composed of lines of the same metrical form throughout. [t. Gk.: m.s. *stichikós*]

sti·chom·e·try (stĭ kŏm′ə trĭ), *n.* the practice of writing a prose text in lines of lengths corresponding to divisions in the sense and indicating phrasal rhythms. [t. LGk.: m. *stichometría*] —**stich·o·met·ric** (stĭk′ə mĕt′rĭk), **stich′o·met′ri·cal,** *adj.*

stich·o·myth·i·a (stĭk′ə mĭth′ĭ ə), *n.* dramatic practice of dialogue in which each speaker uses exactly one line of the verse. Also, **sti·chom·y·thy** (stĭ kŏm′ə thĭ). [t. Gk.] —**stich·o·myth′ic,** *adj.*

-stichous, *Bot., Zool.* a word element referring to rows, as in *distichous.* [t. Gk.: m. *-stichos* (adj. suffix) having stichs]

stick¹ (stĭk), *n., v.,* **sticked, sticking.** —*n.* 1. a branch or shoot of a tree or shrub cut or broken off. 2. a relatively long and slender piece of wood. 3. an elongated piece of wood for burning, for carpentry, or for any special purpose. 4. a rod or wand; a baton. 5. *Chiefly Brit.* a walking stick or cane. 6. a club or cudgel. 7. an elongated, sticklike piece of some material: *a stick of candy.* 8. *Sports.* **a.** the stick used in hockey or lacrosse. **b.** a hurdle used in racing. 9. *Aeron.* a lever, usually with a handle, by which the longitudinal and lateral motions of an airplane are controlled. 10. *Naut.* a mast, or a part of a mast. 11. *Print.* a composing stick. 12. *Mil.* **a.** a group of bombs so arranged as to be released in a row across a target. **b.** the bomb load. 13. (*pl.*) *U.S. Colloq.* the backwoods, or any region distant from cities or towns. 14. a portion of liquor, as brandy, added to a beverage, etc. —*v.t.* 15. to furnish with a stick or sticks in order to support or prop, as a plant. 16. *Print.* to set (type) in a composing stick. [ME *stikke,* OE *sticca,* akin to G *stecken*]

stick² (stĭk), *v.,* **stuck, sticking,** *n.* —*v.t.* 1. to pierce or puncture with a pointed instrument, as a dagger, spear, or pin; stab. 2. to kill by this means: *to stick a pig.* 3. to thrust (something pointed) in, into, through, etc.: *to stick a pin into a balloon.* 4. to fasten in position by thrusting the point or end into something: *to stick a nail in a wall.* 5. to fasten in position by, or as by, something thrust through: *to stick a badge on one's coat.* 6. to fix or impale upon something pointed: *to stick a potato on a fork.* 7. to set with things piercing the surface: *to stick a cushion full of pins.* 8. to furnish or adorn with things attached or set here and there. 9. to place upon a stick or pin for exhibit: *to stick butterflies.* 10. to thrust or put into a place or position indicated: *to stick one's head out of the window.* 11. to fasten or attach by causing to adhere: *to stick a stamp on a letter.* 12. to bring to a stand; render unable to proceed or go back: *to be stuck in the mud.* 13. *Chiefly Brit. Colloq.* to nonplus or pose. 14. *Slang.* to impose a large bill, an unpleasant task, or the like, on. 15. *Slang.* to cheat. —*v.i.* 16. to have the point piercing, or embedded in something. 17. to remain attached by adhesion: *the mud sticks to one's shoes.* 18. to hold, cleave, or cling: *to stick to a horse's back.* 19. to remain persistently or permanently: *a fact that sticks in the mind.* 20. to remain firm in resolution, opinion, statement, attachment, etc.; hold faithfully, as to a promise or bargain. 21. to keep steadily or unremittingly at a task, undertaking, or the like (fol. by *at* or *to*): *to stick at a job.* 22. *Brit.* to put up with circumstances (fol. by *it*): *England can stick it.* 23. to become fastened, hindered, checked, or stationary by some obstruction; be at a standstill, as from difficulties. 24. to be embarrassed or puzzled; hesitate or scruple (usually fol. by *at*). 25. to be thrust, or extend, project, or protrude (fol. by *through, from, out, up,* etc.). —*n.* 26. a thrust with a pointed instrument; a stab. 27. a stoppage or standstill. 28. something causing delay or difficulty. 29. the quality of adhering or of causing things to adhere. 30. something causing adhesion. [ME *stike*(n), OE *stician,* akin to (M)LG *stikken*] —**Syn.** 17. **STICK, ADHERE, COHERE** mean to cling to or be tightly attached to something. **ADHERE** implies that one kind of material clings tenaciously to another; **COHERE** adds the idea that a thing is attracted to and held by something like itself: *particles of sealing wax cohere and form a mass which will adhere to tin.* **STICK,** more colloquial, often used as the general term, is used particularly when a third kind of material is involved: *a gummed label will stick to a package.*

stick·er (stĭk′ər), *n.* 1. one who or that which sticks. 2. an adhesive label. 3. a persistent, diligent person. 4. *Colloq.* something that nonpluses or puzzles one. 5. a bur, thorn, or the like.

stick·ful (stĭk′fōōl′), *n., pl.* **-fuls.** *Print.* as much set type as a composing stick will hold.

sticking plaster, an adhesive cloth or other material for covering and closing superficial wounds, etc.

stick insect, a walking stick (def. 2).

stick·le (stĭk′əl), *v.i.,* **-led, -ling.** 1. to argue or haggle insistently, esp. on trivial matters. 2. to raise objections; scruple; demur. [ME *stightle* set in order, freq. of obs. *stight,* OE *stihtan,* c. G *stiften*]

stick·le·back (stĭk′əl băk′), *n.* any of the small, pugnacious, spiny-backed fishes of the family *Gasterosteidae,* of northern fresh waters and sea inlets. [ME *stykylbak,* f. OE *sticol* scaly + *bæc* back]

Brook stickleback,
Eucalia inconstans
(2½ in. long)

---

b., blend of, blended; c., cognate with; d., dialect, dialectal; der., derived from; f., formed from; g., going back to; m., modification of; r., replacing; s., stem of; t., taken from; ?, perhaps. See the full key on inside cover.

stick·ler (stĭk′lər), *n.* **1.** a person who insists on something unyieldingly (fol. by *for*): *a stickler for ceremony.* **2.** any puzzling or difficult problem.

stick·pin (stĭk′pĭn′), *n.* a pin, usually with a head of a gem or similar ornament, placed in a necktie.

stick·seed (stĭk′sēd′), *n.* any of the boraginaceous herbs constituting the genus *Lappula*, characterized by prickly seeds which adhere to clothing.

stick·tight (stĭk′tīt′), *n.* a composite herb, *Bidens frondosa*, having flat, barbed achenes which adhere to clothing, etc.

stick-up (stĭk′ŭp′), *n. Slang.* a holdup or robbery.

stick·weed (stĭk′wēd′), *n.* the ragweed.

stick·y (stĭk′ĭ), *adj.*, **stickier, stickiest. 1.** having the property of adhering, as glue; adhesive. **2.** covered with adhesive matter: *sticky hands.* **3.** (of the weather, etc.) humid: *an unbearably sticky day.* —**stick′i·ly,** *adv.* —**stick′i·ness,** *n.*

Stieg·litz (stēg′lĭts), *n.* Alfred, 1864–1946, U.S. photographer and editor.

stiff (stĭf), *adj.* **1.** rigid or firm in substance; not flexible, pliant, or easily bent: *a stiff collar.* **2.** not moving or working easily: *a stiff hinge.* **3.** (of a person, etc.) moving only with difficulty, as from cold, age, exhaustion, etc. **4.** blowing violently, strongly, or with steady force: *stiff winds.* **5.** strong, as liquors or beverages. **6.** firm in purpose or resolution; unyielding; stubborn. **7.** stubbornly maintained, as a struggle, etc. **8.** firm against any lowering action, as prices, etc. **9.** rigidly formal, as persons, manners, proceedings, etc. **10.** lacking ease and grace; awkward: *a stiff style of writing.* **11.** excessively regular, as a design; not graceful in form or arrangement. **12.** *Colloq.* hard to deal with; accomplish, endure, pay, believe, etc. **13.** laborious or difficult, as a task. **14.** severe, as a penalty. **15.** unusually high or great, as a price, demand, etc. **16.** firm from tension; taut: *to keep a stiff rein.* **17.** relatively firm in consistence, as semisolid matter: *a stiff jelly.* **18.** dense, compact, or tenacious: *stiff soil.* **19.** *Naut.* bearing the press of canvas or of wind without careening much: *a stiff vessel.* **20.** *Scot. and Brit. Dial.* sturdy, stout, or strongly built. —*n. Slang.* **21.** a dead body; corpse. **22.** a formal or priggish person. [ME; OE *stif*, c. G *steif*; akin to L *stipare* crowd, pack] —**stiff′ish,** *adj.* —**stiff′ly,** *adv.* —**stiff′ness,** *n.* —**Syn. 1.** See **firm**[1].

stiff·en (stĭf′ən), *v.t.* **1.** to make stiff. —*v.i.* **2.** to become stiff. —**stiff′en·er,** *n.*

stiff-necked (stĭf′nĕkt′), *adj.* **1.** having a stiff neck. **2.** stubborn; perversely obstinate; refractory.

sti·fle[1] (stī′fəl), *v.*, **-fled, -fling.** —*v.t.* **1.** to kill by impeding respiration; smother. **2.** to keep back or repress: *to stifle a yawn.* **3.** to suppress, crush, or stop: *to stifle a revolt.* —*v.i.* **4.** to become stifled or suffocated. **5.** to suffer from difficulty in breathing, as in a close atmosphere. [t. Scand.; cf. Icel. *stīfla* stop up] —**sti′fler,** *n.*

sti·fle[2] (stī′fəl), *n.* the joint of the hind leg of a horse, dog, etc., between the femur and the tibia. Also, **stifle joint.** See illus. under **horse**. [ME; orig. uncert.]

sti·fling (stī′flĭng), *adj.* suffocating; oppressively close: *a stifling atmosphere.* —**sti′fling·ly,** *adv.*

stig·ma (stĭg′mə), *n.*, *pl.* **stigmata** (stĭg′mə tə), **stigmas. 1.** a mark of disgrace or infamy; a stain or reproach, as on one's reputation. **2.** a characteristic mark or sign of defect, degeneration, disease, etc. **3.** *Pathol.* a spot or mark on the skin; esp. a place or point on the skin which bleeds during certain mental states, as in hysteria. **4.** *Zool.* a small mark, spot, pore, or the like, on an animal or organ, as: **a.** the eyespot, usually red, of a protozoan. **b.** (in insects) an entrance into the respiratory system. **5.** *Bot.* that part of a pistil which receives the pollen. See diag. under **flower**. **6.** *Rom. Cath. Ch.* marks said to have been supernaturally impressed upon certain persons in the semblance of the wounds on the crucified body of Christ. **7.** *Archaic.* a mark made by a branding iron on the skin of a criminal or slave. [t. L, t. Gk.]

stig·mat·ic (stĭg măt′ĭk), *adj.* **1.** pertaining to a stigma, mark, spot, or the like. **2.** *Bot.* pertaining to or having the character of a stigma (part of the pistil). **3.** *Optics.* converging to a point; anastigmatic. —*n.* **4.** *Rom. Cath. Ch.* one marked with stigmata.

stig·ma·tism (stĭg′mə tĭz′əm), *n.* **1.** *Optics.* a condition in which there is no astigmatism. **2.** *Pathol.* the condition in which stigmata are present.

stig·ma·tize (stĭg′mə tīz′), *v.t.*, **-tized, -tizing. 1.** to mark with a stigma or brand. **2.** to set some mark of disgrace or infamy upon. **3.** to produce stigmata, marks, spots, or the like on. Also, *esp. Brit.*, **stig′ma·tise′.** —**stig′ma·ti·za′tion,** *n.* —**stig′ma·tiz′er,** *n.*

stil·bes·trol (stĭl bĕs′trōl, -trŏl), *n.* a synthetic hormone, $C_{18}H_{20}O_2$, the parent substance of a group of estrogenic agents, some of which are more active than those of the human body.

stil·bite (stĭl′bīt), *n.* a white to brown or red zeolite mineral, a hydrous silicate of calcium and aluminum, occurring in sheaflike aggregates of crystals and in radiated masses. [f. s. Gk. *stilbein* glitter + -ITE[2]]

stile (stīl), *n.* **1.** a series of steps or the like for ascending and descending in getting over a fence or wall. **2.** a turnstile. **3.** *Carp.* a vertical member in a wainscot, paneled door, or other piece of framing. [ME; OE *stigel*, der. *stīgan*, c. G *steigen* ascend, go]

sti·let·to (stĭ lĕt′ō), *n.*, *pl.* **-tos, -toes,** *v.*, **-toed, -toing.** —*n.* **1.** a dagger having a narrow blade, thick in proportion to its width. **2.** a small sharp-pointed instrument for making eyelet holes in needlework. —*v.t.* **3.** to stab or kill with a stiletto. [t. It., dim. of *stilo* dagger, t. L: m. *stilus* pointed instrument]

Stil·i·cho (stĭl′ə kō′), *n.* **Flavius** (flā′vĭ əs), died A.D. 408, a Vandal who became a Roman general and statesman.

still[1] (stĭl), *adj.* **1.** remaining in place or at rest; motionless; stationary: *to stand still.* **2.** free from sound or noise, as a place, time, etc.; silent: *to keep still about a matter.* **3.** subdued or low in sound; hushed: *a still small voice.* **4.** free from commotion of any kind; quiet; tranquil; calm. **5.** without waves or perceptible current, as water. **6.** not effervescent or sparkling, as wine. **7.** *Photog.* noting or pertaining to a still (photograph). [ME and OE *stille*, c. G *still(e)*] —*n.* **8.** *Poetic.* stillness or silence. **9.** a single photographic picture of a person or other subject. —*adv.* **10.** at this or that time; as previously: *they came for dinner about eight weeks ago and are still here.* **11.** up to this or that time: *points still unsettled.* **12.** in the future as in the past: *objections will still be made.* **13.** even or yet (with comparatives or the like): *still more complaints.* **14.** even then; yet; nevertheless: *to be rich and still crave more.* **15.** *Poetic. or Dial.* steadily; constantly; always. —*conj.* **16.** and yet; but yet; nevertheless: *it was futile, still they fought.* —*v.t.* **17.** to silence or hush (sounds, etc.). **18.** to calm, appease, or allay. **19.** to quiet (waves, winds, commotion, tumult, passion, pain, etc.). —*v.i.* **20.** to become still or quiet. [ME *stille*, OE *stillan*, c. G *stillen*] —**Syn. 2.** STILL, QUIET, HUSHED, NOISELESS, SILENT indicate the absence of noise and of excitement or activity accompanied by sound. STILL indicates the absence of sound or movement: *the house was still.* QUIET implies relative freedom from noise, activity, or excitement: *a quiet engine, a quiet vacation.* HUSHED implies the suppression of sound or noise: *a hushed whisper.* NOISELESS and SILENT characterize that which does not reveal its presence or movement by any sound: *a noiseless footstep,* a *room silent and deserted.* See **but**[1]. —**Ant. 2.** noisy. **4.** moving.

still[2] (stĭl), *n.* **1.** a distilling apparatus, consisting of a vessel in which the substance is heated and vaporized and a cooling device or coil for condensing the vapor. **2.** a distillery. [n. use of v.] —*v.t.*, *v.i.* **3.** *Rare or Obs.* to distill. [aphetic var. of DISTILL]

Still
A, Boiler; B, Head; C, Tube leading to condenser; D, Condenser; E, Tube supplying cold water to condenser; F, Worm; G, Worm outlet; H, Overflow outlet

Still (stĭl), *n.* **Andrew Taylor,** 1828–1917, U.S. scientist: founder of osteopathy.

still alarm, a fire alarm given by other means than the regular system of fire signals, as by telephone.

still·birth (stĭl′bûrth′), *n.* **1.** the birth of a dead child or organism. **2.** a fetus dead at birth.

still·born (stĭl′bôrn′), *adj.* dead when born.

still·er (stĭl′ər), *n. Rare or Obs.* a distiller.

still hunt, 1. a hunt for game carried on stealthily, as by stalking or under cover. **2.** *Colloq.* a quiet or secret pursuit of any object.

still-hunt (stĭl′hŭnt′), *v.t.* **1.** to pursue by a still hunt. —*v.i.* **2.** to carry on a still hunt.

still·li·form (stĭl′ə fôrm′), *adj.* drop-shaped.

still life, *pl.* **still lifes.** a picture representing inanimate objects, such as fruit, flowers, etc. —**still′-life′,** *adj.*

still·ness (stĭl′nĭs), *n.* **1.** absence of motion. **2.** quiet; silence; hush.

Still·son wrench (stĭl′sən), **1.** a monkey wrench with a pivoted adjustable jaw that grips pipes, etc., more tightly when pressure is exerted on the handle. **2.** a trademark for this wrench.

Stillson wrench

stil·ly (*adv.* stĭl′lĭ; *adj.* stĭl′ĭ), *adv.* **1.** quietly; silently. —*adj.* **2.** *Poetic.* still; quiet.

stilt (stĭlt), *n.* **1.** one of two poles, each with a support for the foot at some distance above the ground. **2.** one of several high posts underneath any structure built above land or over water. **3.** any of various limicoline birds, esp. of the genus *Himantopus*, of both hemispheres, with very long legs, long neck, and slender bill, and living esp. in marshes. —*v.t.* **4.** to raise on or as on stilts. [ME *stilte*, c. LG *stilte*, Norw. *stilta* long]

stilt·ed (stĭl′tĭd), *adj.* **1.** stiffly dignified or formal, as speech, literary style, etc.; pompous. **2.** *Archit.* raised on or as on stilts: *a stilted arch.*

Stilted arch

Stil·ton cheese (stĭl′tən), a rich, waxy, white cheese, veined with mold: made principally in England.

Stil·well (stĭl′wĕl, -wəl), n. **Joseph W.**, 1883–1946, U.S. general.

Stim·son (stĭm′sən), n. **Henry Lewis**, 1867–1950, U.S. statesman: secretary of war, 1911–13, 1940–45; secretary of state, 1929–33.

stim·u·lant (stĭm′yələnt), n. 1. Physiol., Med. something that temporarily quickens some vital process or the functional activity of some organ or part. 2. an alcoholic liquor or beverage. 3. Rare. a stimulus or incentive. —adj. 4. Physiol., Med. temporarily quickening some vital process or functional activity. 5. stimulating. [t. L: s. stimulans, ppr., stimulating, inciting]

stim·u·late (stĭm′yəlāt′), v., -lated, -lating. —v.t. 1. to rouse to action or effort, as by pricking or goading; spur on; incite: to stimulate production. 2. Physiol., Med., etc. to excite (an organ, etc.) to its functional activity. 3. to invigorate by an alcoholic stimulant. —v.i. 4. to act as a stimulus or stimulant. [t. L: m.s. stimulātus, pp., goaded on] —stim′u·lat′er, stim′u·la′tor, n. —stim′u·la′tion, n. —Syn. 1. See animate.

stim·u·la·tive (stĭm′yəlā′tĭv), adj. 1. serving to stimulate. —n. 2. a stimulating agency.

stim·u·lus (stĭm′yələs), n., pl. -li (-lī′). 1. something that incites to action or exertion, or quickens action, feeling, thought, etc.; an incentive. 2. Physiol., etc. something that excites an organism or part to functionable activity. [NL, special use of L stimulus goad, sting]

sting (stĭng), v., stung or (Archaic or Obs.) stang; stinging; n. —v.t. 1. to prick or wound with some sharp-pointed, often venom-bearing, organ, with which certain animals are furnished: to be stung by a bee. 2. to affect painfully or irritatingly as a result of contact, as certain plants do: to be stung by nettles. 3. to pain sharply, hurt, or wound: to be stung with remorse. 4. to goad or drive as by sharp irritation. 5. Slang. to impose upon, charge exorbitantly, or the like. —v.i. 6. to use or have a sting, as bees. 7. to cause a sharp, smarting pain, as some plants, an acrid liquid or gas, etc. 8. to cause acute mental pain or irritation, as annoying thoughts, etc. 9. to feel acute mental pain or irritation. 10. to feel a smarting pain, as from the sting of an insect or from a blow. —n. 11. the act of stinging. 12. a wound, pain, or smart caused by stinging. 13. any sharp or smarting wound, hurt, or pain (physical or mental). 14. anything, or an element in anything, that wounds, pains, or irritates: to feel the sting of defeat. 15. capacity to wound or pain. 16. a sharp stimulus or incitement: driven by the sting of jealousy. 17. Bot. a glandular hair on certain plants, as nettles, which emits an irritating fluid. 18. Zool. any of various sharp-pointed, often venom-bearing, organs of insects and other animals, capable of inflicting painful or dangerous wounds. [ME; OE stingan, c. Icel. stinga]

sting·a·ree (stĭng′ərē′, stĭng′ərē′), n. a stingray. [alter. of STING RAY]

sting·er (stĭng′ər), n. 1. one who or that which stings. 2. an animal or plant that stings. 3. the sting of an insect or the like. 4. Colloq. a stinging blow, remark, or the like. 5. U.S. a cocktail of brandy and a liqueur. 6. Brit. Colloq. a highball of whiskey and soda.

stinging hair, Bot. a sting.

sting·ray (stĭng′rā′), n. any of the rays, esp. of the family Dasyatidae, having a long, flexible tail armed near the base with a strong, serrated bony spine, with which they can inflict severe and very painful wounds.

stin·gy¹ (stĭn′jĭ), adj., -gier, -giest. 1. reluctant to give or spend; niggardly; penurious. 2. scanty or meager. [orig. meaning "having a sting," "bad-tempered," der. d. stinge sting, OE steng] —stin′gi·ly, adv. —stin′gi·ness, n.

sting·y² (stĭng′ĭ), adj. having a sting. [f. STING + -Y¹]

stink (stĭngk), v., stank or stunk, stunk, stinking, n. —v.i. 1. to emit a strong offensive smell. 2. to be in extremely bad repute or disfavor. —v.t. 3. to cause to stink. 4. to put, drive, force, etc., by an offensive smell. —n. 5. a strong offensive smell; stench. [ME; OE stincan, c. D and LG stinken. Cf. STENCH] —stink′ing, adj. —stink′ing·ly, adv.

stink·bug (stĭngk′bŭg′), n. 1. any of the broad, flat bugs of the family Pentatomidae, many species of which feed on plant juices. 2. any of various malodorous bugs.

stink·er (stĭngk′ər), n. 1. one who or that which stinks. 2. Slang. a dishonorable, disgusting, or objectionable person. 3. any device emitting a stink, as a bomb, pot, etc. 4. any of several large petrels.

stink·horn (stĭngk′hôrn′), n. any of various ill-smelling fungi of the basidiomycetous genus Phallus, esp. P. impudicus.

stinking smut, a type of smut on wheat; bunt.

stink·pot (stĭngk′pŏt′), n. a jar containing combustibles, etc., which generate offensive and suffocating vapors, formerly used in warfare.

stink·stone (stĭngk′stōn′), n. any of various stones which emit a fetid odor on being struck or rubbed, as from embedded decomposed organic matter.

stink·weed (stĭngk′wēd′), n. any of various ill-smelling plants, as the jimson weed.

stink·wood (stĭngk′wŏŏd′), n. 1. one of several trees with fetid wood. 2. the wood of any of these trees.

stint¹ (stĭnt), v.t. 1. to limit to a certain amount, number, share, or allowance, often unduly; set limits to; restrict. 2. Archaic. to discontinue, cease, or bring to an end. —v.i. 3. to stint oneself; get along on a scanty allowance. 4. Archaic and Dial. to cease action; desist. —n. 5. limitation or restriction, esp. as to amount: to give without stint. 6. a limited or prescribed quantity, share, rate, etc.: to exceed one's stint. 7. an allotted amount or piece of work: to do one's daily stint. 8. Obs. stop. [ME; OE styntan make blunt, dull, c. Icel. stytta shorten. Cf. STUNT, v.] —stint′er, n. —stint′ing·ly, adv.

stint² (stĭnt), n. any of various small shore birds or peeps, esp. the little stint, Erolia minuta, of Europe, and the least sandpiper. [orig. obscure]

stipe (stīp), n. 1. Bot. a stalk or slender support, as the petiole of a fern frond, the stem supporting the pileus of a mushroom, or a stalklike elongation of the receptacle of a flower. 2. Zool. a stemlike part, as a footstalk; a stalk. [t. F, t. L: m. stīpes log, post]

sti·pel (stī′pəl), n. Bot. a secondary stipule situated at the base of a leaflet of a compound leaf. [t. NL: m.s. stipella, dim. of L stipula. See STIPULE] —sti·pel·late (stī pĕl′ĭt, -āt, stī′pəlāt′, -pəlāt′), adj.

S. Stipe
A. Longitudinal section of flower; B. Frond of fern; C. Mushroom

sti·pend (stī′pĕnd), n. 1. fixed or regular pay; salary. 2. any periodic payment, as a pension. [ME stipendy, t. L: m.s. stīpendium]

sti·pen·di·ar·y (stī pĕn′dĭ ĕr′ĭ), adj., n., pl. -aries. —adj. 1. receiving a stipend; performing services for regular pay. 2. paid for by a stipend, as services. 3. pertaining to or of the nature of a stipend. 4. paying taxes or giving services to an overlord or government. —n. 5. one who receives a stipend.

sti·pes (stī′pēz), n., pl. stipites (stĭp′ə tēz′). 1. Zool. the second joint in a maxilla of crustaceans and insects. 2. Bot. a stipe. [t. L: log, post]

stip·i·tate (stĭp′ə tāt′), adj. having, or supported by, a stipe: a stipitate ovary. [t. NL: m.s. stīpitātus, f. s. stīpes STIPE + -ātus -ATE¹]

stip·i·ti·form (stĭp′ə tə fôrm′), adj. having the form of a stipe.

stip·ple (stĭp′əl), v., -pled, -pling, n. —v.t. 1. to paint, engrave, or draw by means of dots or small touches. —n. Also, stip′pling. 2. the method of painting, engraving, etc., by stippling. 3. stippled work; a painting, engraving, or the like, executed by means of dots or small spots. [t. D: m. s. stippelen, freq. of stippen dot, speckle] —stip′pler, n.

stip·u·late¹ (stĭp′yə lāt′), v., -lated, -lating. —v.i. 1. to make an express demand or arrangement (for), as a condition of agreement. —v.t. 2. to arrange expressly or specify in terms of agreement. 3. to require as an essential condition in making an agreement. 4. to promise, in making an agreement. [t. L: m.s. stipulātus, pp.] —stip′u·la′tor, n. —stip·u·la·to·ry (stĭp′yə lə tōr′ĭ), adj.

stip·u·late² (stĭp′yə lĭt, -lāt′), adj. having stipules. [f. STIPULE + -ATE¹]

stip·u·la·tion (stĭp′yə lā′shən), n. 1. act of stipulating. 2. something stipulated; a condition in an agreement or contract.

stip·ule (stĭp′ūl), n. Bot. one of a pair of lateral appendages, often leaflike, at the base of a leaf petiole in many plants. [t. L: m. stipula, dim. of stipes. See STIPE] —stip′u·lar, adj.

stir¹ (stûr), v., stirred, stirring, n. —v.t. 1. to move or agitate (a liquid, or any matter in separate particles or pieces) so as to change the relative position of component parts, as by passing an implement continuously or repeatedly through: to stir one's coffee with a spoon. 2. to move, esp. in some slight way: he would not stir a finger to help them. 3. to set in tremulous, fluttering, or irregular motion; shake: leaves stirred by the wind. 4. to move briskly; bestir: to stir oneself. 5. to rouse from inactivity, quiet, contentment, indifference, etc. (often fol. by up). 6. to incite, instigate, or prompt (often fol. by up): to stir a people to rebellion. 7. to affect strongly; excite: to stir pity, the heart, etc. 8. Rare. to bring up for notice or discussion. 9. Dial. to disturb. —v.i. 10. to

S. Stipule
A. Smilax; B. Dogrose, Rosa canina; C. Field pea, Pisum arvense; D. Locust, Robinia pseudacadia

Common stingray, Dasyatis hastata (Total length 2½ ft.. tail 16 in.)

move, esp. slightly or lightly: *not a leaf stirred.* **11.** to move about, esp. briskly. **12.** to be in circulation, current, or afoot: *is there any news stirring?* **13.** to become active, as from some rousing or quickening impulse. **14.** to be emotionally moved or strongly affected. [ME; OE *styrian*, akin to G *stören*, disturb. Cf. **STORM**] —*n.* **15.** act of stirring or moving, or the sound made. **16.** movement; brisk or busy movement. **17.** a state or occasion of general excitement; a commotion. **18.** a mental impulse, sensation, or feeling. **19.** a jog or thrust. —**Syn. 17.** fuss. See **ado.** —**Ant. 17.** quiet.

stir² (stûr), *n. Slang.* a prison. [orig. unknown]

stir·a·bout (stûr′ə bout′), *n. Brit.* a kind of porridge.

Stir·ling (stûr′lĭng), *n.* **1.** Also, **Stir·ling·shire** (stur′ling shir′, -shər). a county in central Scotland. 190,100 pop. (est. 1956); 451 sq. mi. **2.** its county seat: a port on the Forth river. 26,960 (1951).

stir·pi·cul·ture (stûr′pə kŭl′chər), *n.* the production of special stocks or strains by careful breeding. [f. *stirpi-* (comb. form of **STIRPS**) + **CULTURE**] —**stir′pi·cul′tur·al,** *adj.* —**stir′pi·cul′tur·ist,** *n.*

stirps (stûrps), *n., pl.* **stirpes** (stûr′pēz). **1.** a stock; a family, or a branch of a family; a line of descent. **2.** *Law.* one from whom a family is descended. **3.** *Obs. Bot.* a race or permanent variety. [t. L: stem, root, stock]

stir·rer (stûr′ər), *n.* **1.** one who or that which stirs. **2.** an implement or device for stirring something.

stir·ring (stûr′ĭng), *adj.* **1.** that stirs; moving, active, bustling, or lively. **2.** rousing, exciting, or thrilling: *a stirring speech.* —**stir′ring·ly,** *adv.*

stir·rup (stûr′əp, stĭr′əp), *n.* **1.** a loop, ring, or other contrivance of metal, wood, leather, etc., suspended from the saddle of a horse to support the rider's foot. **2.** any of various similar supports, or any of various clamps, etc., used for special purposes. **3.** *Naut.* a short rope with an eye at the end, hung from a yard to support a footrope, the footrope being rove through the eye. [ME; OE *stigrāp* (f. *stige* ascent + *rāp* **ROPE**), c. G *stegreif*]

Stirrups (def. 1)
A. Metal;
B. Leather

stirrup bone, *Anat.* the stapes.

stirrup cup, *Chiefly Brit.* a farewell drink, esp. one offered to a rider already mounted for departure.

stirrup leather, the strap which holds the stirrup of a saddle.

stirrup pump, *Brit.* a small hand pump for use in fire fighting.

stitch¹ (stĭch), *n.* **1.** one complete movement of a threaded needle through a fabric or material such as to leave behind it a single loop or portion of thread, as in sewing, embroidery, surgical closing of wounds, etc. **2.** a loop or portion of thread disposed in place by one movement in sewing: *to rip out stitches.* **3.** a particular mode of disposing the thread in sewing, or the style of work produced. **4.** one complete movement of the needle or other implement used in knitting, crocheting, netting, tatting, etc. **5.** the portion of work produced. **6.** a particular mode of making such work, or the style of work made. **7.** a thread or bit of any fabric or of clothing, etc.: *every stitch of clothes.* **8.** a sudden, sharp pain, esp. in the intercostal muscles. —*v.t.* **9.** to work upon, join, or fasten with stitches; sew; ornament with stitches. **10.** to put staples through for fastening: *to stitch cartons.* —*v.i.* **11.** to make stitches; sew (by hand or machine). [ME *stiche,* OE *stice,* c. G *stich* prick] —**stitch′er,** *n.*

stitch² (stĭch), *n. Brit. Dial.* a distance, as in walking. [OE *stycce* piece, short time, c. G *stücke*]

stitch·wort (stĭch′wûrt′), *n.* any of certain herbs of the genus *Stellaria* (or *Alsine*), as *S. Holostea,* an Old World white-flowered species. [f. **STITCH¹** + **WORT**]

stith·y (stĭth′ĭ, stĭth′ĭ), *n., pl.* **stithies,** *v.,* **stithied,** **stithying.** —*n.* **1.** an anvil. **2.** a forge or smithy. —*v.t.* **3.** *Archaic.* to forge. [ME *stithie,* var. of *stethie,* t. Scand.; cf. Icel. *stedhja* (acc.)]

sti·ver (stī′vər), *n.* **1.** a Dutch coin worth about 2 U. S. cents. **2.** a small amount or worthless thing. [t. D: m. *stuiver*]

St. James's Palace, 1. a palace in London, England: the royal residence from the time of Henry VIII until the accession of Victoria. **2.** the British royal court. Also, **St. James's.**

St. John, 1. one of the Virgin Islands, in the U.S. part of the group. 749 pop. (1950); ab. 20 sq. mi. **2.** Lake, a lake in SE Canada, in Quebec province, draining into the Saguenay river. 365 sq. mi. **3.** Henry. See **Bolingbroke, 1st Viscount.** See also **Saint John.**

St. Johns, a river flowing through NE Florida into the Atlantic. 276 mi.

St. John's, 1. a seaport in and the capital of Newfoundland, in the SE part of the island. 52,873; with suburbs, 67,749 (1951). **2.** a seaport in and the capital of Antigua in the Federation of the West Indies. 12,000 (est. 1952). Also, **St. John.**

St.-John's-wort (sānt jŏnz′wûrt′), *n.* any of various herbs or shrubs of the genus *Hypericum,* having yellow flowers and pellucid-dotted leaves.

St. Joseph, a city in NW Missouri, on the Missouri river. 79,673 (1960).

St. Kitts (kĭts), one of the Leeward Islands, a British colony. Population, including the dependencies of Nevis

and Anguilla, 56,644 (1960); 68 sq. mi. *Cap.:* Basseterre. Also, **St. Christopher.**

St. Lau·rent (săn lō rän′), **Louis Stephen,** born 1882. prime minister of Canada, 1948–1957.

St. Lawrence, 1. a river in SE Canada, flowing NE from Lake Ontario, draining the five Great Lakes into the Gulf of St. Lawrence. ab. 760 mi. **2.** Gulf of, an arm of the Atlantic between SE Canada and Newfoundland.

St. Lô (săn lō′), a city in N W France: bitter fighting, June-July, 1944. 11,718 (1954).

St. Lou·is (lōō′ĭs, lōō′ĭ for *1;* săn lwē′ *for 2*), **1.** a city in E Missouri: a port on the Mississippi. 750,026 (1960). **2.** a seaport in and the former capital of Senegal, at the mouth of the Senegal river. 39,800 (est. 1957).

St. Louis Park, a city in E Minnesota, near Minneapolis. 43,310 (1960).

St. Lu·ci·a (lōō′shĭ ə, -sY ə), a British colony in the Windward Islands. 94,718 pop. (1960); 233 sq. mi. *Cap.:* Castries.

St. Ma·lo (săn mȧ lō′), a fortified seaport in NW France, in Brittany, on the Gulf of St. Malo, an arm of the English Channel: resort; surrendered by German forces, Aug., 1944. 14,339 (1954).

St. Mar·tin (sănt mär′tĭn, *Fr.* săn mȧr tăn′), an island in the West Indies, belonging to the Netherlands: part of Netherlands Antilles. 1607 (1955); 20 sq mi.; and to France: dependency of Guadeloupe. 3366 (1954); 17 sq. mi.

St. Mar·ys (mâr′Yz), a river forming the boundary between NE Michigan and Ontario, Canada, flowing from Lake Superior into Lake Huron. ab. 40 mi. See **Sault Ste. Marie Canals.**

St.-Mi·hiel (săn mē yĕl′), a town in NE France, on the Meuse river: captured by American forces, 1918. 5035 (1954).

St. Mo·ritz (mōr′Yts), a resort town in SE Switzerland: a popular center for winter sports. 2558 (1950); 6037 ft. high. German, **Sankt Moritz.**

St. Na·zaire (săn nȧ zâr′), a seaport in W France, on the Loire estuary. 39,350 (1954).

sto·a (stō′ə), *n., pl.* **stoae** (stō′ē), **stoas.** *Gk. Archit.* a portico, usually a detached portico of considerable length, that is used as a promenade or meeting place. [t. Gk.]

stoat (stōt), *n.* the ermine, *Mustela erminea,* esp. when in brown summer palage. [ME *stote;* orig. unknown]

sto·chas·tic (stə kăs′tĭk), *adj.* based on one item in the probability distribution of an ordered set of observations; conjectural. [t. Gk.: m.s. *stochastikós,* der. *stóchos* mark, aim]

stock (stŏk), *n.* **1.** an aggregate of goods kept on hand by a merchant or a commercial house for the supply of customers. **2. in stock,** on hand, as for use or sale. **3. out of stock,** lacking, esp. temporarily, from a stock. **4.** a quantity of something accumulated, as for future use: *a stock of provisions.* **5.** livestock; the horses, cattle, sheep, and other useful animals kept or raised on a farm or ranch. **6.** *Hort.* **a.** a stem, tree, or plant that furnishes slips or cuttings; a stock plant. **b.** a stem in which a graft is inserted and which is its support. **7.** the trunk or main stem of a tree or other plant, as distinguished from roots and branches. **8.** a rhizome or rootstock. **9.** the type from which a group of animals or plants has been derived. **10.** a race or other related group of animals or plants. **11.** the person from whom a given line of descent is derived; the original progenitor. **12.** a line of descent; a tribe, race, or ethnic group. **13.** *Ethnol.* a major division of mankind, as Caucasoid, Mongoloid, Negroid. **14.** a group of related families of languages. **15.** any grouping of related languages. **16.** *Zool.* a compound animal organism. **17.** the handle of a whip, etc. **18.** *Firearms.* **a.** the wooden or metal piece to which the barrel and mechanism of a rifle or like firearm are attached. **b.** a part of an automatic weapon, as a machine gun, similar in position or function. **19.** the stump of a tree left standing. **20.** *Dial.* a log or block of wood. **21.** a dull or stupid person. **22.** something lifeless or senseless. **23.** the main upright part of anything, esp. a supporting structure. **24.** (*pl.*) an old instrument of punishment consisting of a framework with holes for the ankles and (sometimes) the wrists of an offender exposed to public derision. **25.** (*pl.*) a frame in which a horse or other animal is secured in a standing position for shoeing or for a veterinary operation. **26.** (*pl.*) the frame on which a boat rests while under construction. **27. on the stocks,** under construction. **28.** an adjustable handle for holding and turning the dies used in cutting screw threads on a rod. **29.** the piece of metal which constitutes the body of a carpenter's plane. **30.** the raw material from which anything is made: *paper stock.* **31.** *Cookery.* the liquor or broth prepared by boiling meat, with or without vegetables, etc., and used as a foundation for soups, sauces, etc. **32.** *Bot.* the gillyflower, or any of various other cruciferous plants. **33.** a collar or a neckcloth fitting like a band about the neck. **34.** *Cards.* that portion of a pack

Stocks (def. 24)

of cards which, in certain games, is not dealt out to the players, but is left on the table, to be drawn from as occasion requires. **35.** *Theat.* the repertoire of pieces produced by a stock company. **36.** *Finance.* **a.** a stick once given in debtor-creditor transactions. **b.** the outstanding capital of a company or corporation. **c.** the shares of a particular company or corporation. **d.** capital stock. **37.** a stocking. **38.** *Obs.* the part of a plow to which the irons, handles, etc., are attached. **39. stock in trade, a.** the goods kept on hand for sale. **b.** one's resources for any purpose. **40. take stock, a.** to make an inventory of stock on hand. **b.** to make an appraisal of resources, prospects, etc. **41. take stock in, a.** to purchase shares of stock in a corporation, etc. **b.** *Colloq.* to take an interest in, attach importance to, or put confidence in. —*adj.* **42.** kept regularly on hand, as for use or sale; staple; standard: *stock articles.* **43.** having as one's job the care of a concern's stock: *a stock clerk.* **44.** of the common or ordinary type; in common use: *a stock argument.* **45.** commonplace: *a stock remark.* **46.** designating or pertaining to livestock raising: *stock farming.* **47.** of or pertaining to stock: *a stock certificate.* **48.** *Theat.* **a.** pertaining to stock plays or pieces, or to a stock company. **b.** appearing together in a repertoire, as a company. **c.** forming part of a repertoire, as a play. —*v.t.* **49.** to furnish with a stock or supply. **50.** to furnish with stock, as a farm with horses, cattle, etc. **51.** to lay up in store, as for future use. **52.** to fasten to or provide with a stock, as a rifle, plow, bell, anchor, etc. **53.** *Obs.* to put in the stocks as a punishment. —*v.i.* **54.** to lay in a stock of something (often fol. by *up*). [ME; OE *stoc(c)*, c. G *stock*]

Stock (stŏk), *n.* **Frederick August,** 1872–1942, U.S. orchestra conductor, born in Germany.

stock·ade (stŏ kād′), *n., v.* **-aded, -ading.** —*n.* **1.** *Fort.* a defensive barrier consisting of strong posts or timbers fixed upright in the ground. **2.** an enclosure or pen made with posts and stakes. —*v.t.* **3.** to protect, fortify, or encompass with a stockade. [t. F: m. *estocade*, ult. der. OPr. *estaca* stake, of Gmc. orig. See STAKE¹]

stock·bro·ker (stŏk′brō′kər), *n.* a broker who, for a commission, buys and sells stocks (and commonly other securities) for customers. —**stock·bro·ker·age** (stŏk′-brō′kər ĭj), **stock′bro′king,** *n.*

stock car, a standard-model car used, with certain motor adjustments, in races. —**stock′-car′,** *adj.*

stock certificate, a certificate evidencing ownership of one or more shares of a corporation's stock.

stock company, 1. *Finance.* a company or corporation whose capital is divided into shares. **2.** *Theat.* a company acting a repertoire of plays, more or less permanently together, usually at its own theater.

stock dove, a wild pigeon of Europe, *Columba oenas.*

stock exchange, 1. a building or place where stocks and other securities are bought and sold. **2.** an association of brokers and dealers in stocks and bonds, who meet together and transact business according to fixed rules.

stock farm, a farm devoted to breeding livestock. —**stock farmer.** —**stock farming.**

stock·fish (stŏk′fĭsh′), *n., pl.* **-fishes,** (*esp. collectively*) **-fish.** fish, as the cod or haddock, cured by splitting and drying in the air without salt.

stock·hold·er (stŏk′hōl′dər), *n.* **1.** *Chiefly U.S.* a holder or owner of stock or shares. Cf. *Brit.* shareholder. **2.** *Australia.* an owner of livestock.

Stock·holm (stŏk′hōm, -hōlm; *Sw.* stŏk′hŏlm), *n.* the capital and chief seaport of Sweden, in the SE part. 769,714 (est. 1953).

stock·i·net (stŏk′ə nĕt′), *n. Chiefly Brit.* an elastic machine-knitted fabric used for making undergarments, etc. [alter. of *stockinet*, f. STOCKING + -ET]

stock·ing (stŏk′ĭng), *n.* **1.** a close-fitting covering, usually knitted (by hand or machine) and of wool, cotton, nylon, silk, etc., for the foot and leg. **2.** something resembling such a covering. [f. STOCK, n. (def. 37) + -ING¹] —**stock′inged,** *adj.* —**stock′ing·less,** *adj.*

stock·ish (stŏk′ĭsh), *adj.* like a block of wood; stupid.

stock·job·ber (stŏk′jŏb′ər), *n.* **1.** *U.S.* a stock salesman (often in contempt). **2.** *Brit.* a stock-exchange operator who acts as an intermediary between brokers but does not do business with the public. —**stock′job′-ber·y, stock′job′bing,** *n.*

stock·man (stŏk′mən), *n., pl.* **-men. 1.** *U.S. and Australia.* a man who raises livestock. **2.** a man employed on a stock farm. **3.** *U.S.* a man in charge of a stock of goods.

stock market, a market where stocks and bonds are bought and sold; a stock exchange.

stock pile, a supply pile of material, as a pile of gravel in road maintenance.

stock-pile (stŏk′pīl′), *v.t.* to put or store in a stock pile.

Stock·port (stŏk′pôrt′), *n.* a city in W England, near Manchester. 141,660 (1951).

stock·pot (stŏk′pŏt′), *n.* a pot in which stock for soup, etc., is made and kept.

stock raising, the breeding and rearing of different kinds of livestock. —**stock raiser.**

stock·room (stŏk′rōōm′, -rŏŏm′), *n.* a room in which a stock of materials or goods is kept for use or sale.

stock-still (stŏk′stĭl′), *adj.* motionless.

Stock·ton (stŏk′tən), *n.* **1. Frank R.,** (*Francis Richard Stockton*) 1834–1902, U. S. writer. **2.** a city in central California, on the San Joaquin river. 86,321 (1960).

Stock·ton-on-Tees (stŏk′tən ŏn tēz′), *n.* a seaport in NE England, near the mouth of the Tees river. 74,024 (1951).

stock·y (stŏk′ĭ), *adj.,* **stockier, stockiest. 1.** of solid and sturdy form or build; thick-set (and often short). **2.** having a strong, stout stem, as a plant. —**stock′i·ly,** *adv.* —**stock′i·ness,** *n.*

stock·yard (stŏk′yärd′), *n.* **1.** an enclosure with pens, sheds, etc., connected with a slaughterhouse, railroad, market, etc., for the temporary keeping of cattle, sheep, swine, or horses. **2.** a yard for livestock.

stodg·y (stŏj′ĭ), *adj.,* **stodgier, stodgiest. 1.** heavy, dull, or uninteresting; tediously commonplace. **2.** of a thick, semisolid consistency; heavy, as food. **3.** *Colloq.* or *Dial.* stocky; thick-set. [f. *stodge,* v., stuff + -Y¹] —**stodg′i·ly,** *adv.* —**stodg′i·ness,** *n.*

stoe·chi·ol·o·gy (stē′kĭ ŏl′ə jĭ), *n.* stoichiology. —**stoe·chi·o·log·i·cal** (stē′kĭ ə lŏj′ə kəl), *adj.*

stoe·chi·om·e·try (stē′kĭ ŏm′ə trĭ), *n.* stoichiometry.

sto·gey (stō′gĭ), *n., pl.* **-gies.** stogy.

sto·gy (stō′gĭ), *n., pl.* **-gies. 1.** a long, slender, roughly made, inexpensive cigar. **2.** a coarse, heavy boot or shoe. Also, **sto′gie.** [earlier *stoga,* short for *Conestoga,* name of a Pennsylvania town]

Sto·ic (stō′ĭk), *adj.* **1.** of or pertaining to the school of philosophy founded by Zeno, who taught that men should be free from passion, unmoved by joy or grief, and submit without complaint to unavoidable necessity. **2.** (*l.c.*) stoical. —*n.* **3.** a member or adherent of the Stoic school of philosophy. **4.** (*l.c.*) one who maintains or affects the mental attitude required by the Stoics. [ME, t. L: s. *stŏicus,* t. Gk.: m. *stōĭkós,* der. *stoá* a porch, specifically the porch in Athens where Zeno lectured]

sto·i·cal (stō′ə kəl), *adj.* **1.** impassive; characterized by calm or austere fortitude. **2.** resembling, suggesting, or befitting the Stoics, as in repression of emotion: *a stoical sufferer.* **3.** (*cap.*) of or pertaining to the Stoics. —**sto′i·cal·ly,** *adv.* —**sto′i·cal·ness,** *n.*

stoi·chei·ol·o·gy (stoi′kĭ ŏl′ə jĭ), *n.* stoichiology. —**stoi·chei·o·log·i·cal** (stoi′kĭ ə lŏj′ə kəl), *adj.*

stoi·chei·om·e·try (stoi′kĭ ŏm′ə trĭ), *n.* stoichiometry.

stoi·chi·ol·o·gy (stoi′kĭ ŏl′ə jĭ), *n.* a physiological study of the cellular components of tissues. Also, **stoechiology.** —**stoi·chi·o·log·i·cal** (stoi′kĭ ə lŏj′ə kəl), *adj.*

stoi·chi·om·e·try (stoi′kĭ ŏm′ə trĭ), *n.* **1.** the calculation of the quantities of chemical elements or compounds involved in chemical reactions. **2.** the branch of chemistry dealing with relationships of combining elements, esp. quantitatively. Also, **stoechiometry.** [f. m. Gk. *stoicheio-* (comb. form of *stoicheion* component) + -METRY] —**stoi·chi·o·met·ric** (stoi′kĭ ə mĕt′rĭk), **stoi·chi·o·met′ri·cal,** *adj.*

Sto·i·cism (stō′ə sĭz′əm), *n.* **1.** the philosophy of the Stoics. **2.** (*l.c.*) conduct conforming to the precepts of the Stoics; repression of emotion; indifference to pleasure or pain. —**Syn. 2.** See **patience.**

stoke (stōk), *v.,* **stoked, stoking.** —*v.t.* **1.** to poke, stir up, and feed (a fire). **2.** to tend the fire of (a furnace, esp. one used with a boiler to generate steam for an engine); supply with fuel. —*v.i.* **3.** to shake up the coals of a fire. **4.** to tend a fire or furnace; act as a stoker: *to make a living by stoking.* [back formation from STOKER]

stoke·hold (stōk′hōld′), *n. Naut.* the space or compartment containing the furnaces, boilers, etc., of a ship.

stoke·hole (stōk′hōl′), *n.* **1.** a compartment where furnace fires are worked, as in a steamship. **2.** a hole through which a furnace is stoked.

Stoke-on-Trent (stōk′ŏn trĕnt′), *n.* a city in W England, on the Trent river: pottery. 275,095 (1951).

Stoke Po·ges (stōk pō′jĭs), a village in S England, in Buckinghamshire, W of London: the churchyard here is probably the scene of Gray's *Elegy.*

stok·er (stō′kər), *n.* **1.** one who or that which stokes. **2.** *Chiefly Brit.* one employed to tend a furnace used in generating steam, as on a locomotive or a steamship. **3.** a mechanical device for supplying solid fuel to a furnace. [t. D, der. *stoken* feed a fire]

Sto·kow·ski (stə kou′skĭ; *Pol.* stŏ kŏf′skĭ), *n.* **Leopold Antoni Stanislaw** (lē′ə pŏld′ än tō′nĭ stä′nē släf′), born 1882, U.S. orchestra conductor, born in England.

stole¹ (stōl), *v.* pt. of **steal.**

stole² (stōl), *n.* **1.** an ecclesiastical vestment, a narrow strip of silk or other material worn over the shoulders (by deacons, over the left shoulder only) and hanging down in front to the knee or below. **2.** a collar of fur, marabou, or the like, extending downward in front in long bands, worn by women. **3.** *Archaic.* a long robe, esp. one worn by Roman matrons. [ME and OE, t. L: m. *stola,* t. Gk.: m. *stolē* clothing, robe]

sto·len (stō′lən), *v.* pp. of **steal.**

stol·id (stŏl′ĭd), *adj.* not easily moved or stirred mentally; impassive, as from dullness or stupidity. [t. L: s. *stolidus*] —**sto·lid·i·ty** (stə lĭd′ə tĭ), **stol′id·ness,** *n.* —**stol′id·ly,** *adv.*

sto·lon (stō′lŏn), *n.* **1.** *Bot.* **a.** a slender branch or shoot, usually a runner or prostrate stem, which takes root at the tip and eventually develops into a new plant. **b.** a rhizome, as of some grasses, used for vegetative reproduction. **2.** *Zool.* a rootlike extension in a compound organism, usually giving rise to new zoöids by budding. [t. L: *s. stolo*]

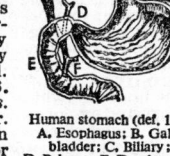

S, Stolon (def. 1a)

sto·ma (stō′ma), *n., pl.* **stomata** (stō′ma ta, stŏm′ə tə). **1.** *Bot.* any of various small apertures, esp. one of the minute orifices or slits in the epidermis of leaves, etc. **2.** *Zool.* a mouth or ingestive opening, esp. when in the form of a small or simple aperture. [NL, t. Gk.: mouth]

stom·ach (stŭm′ək), *n.* **1.** (in man and other vertebrates) **a.** a saclike enlargement of the alimentary canal, forming a part of storage, dilution, and digestion. **b.** such an organ, or an analogous portion of the alimentary canal, when divided into two or more sections or parts, or any one of these sections. **2.** any analogous digestive cavity or tract in invertebrates. **3.** the part of the body containing the stomach; the belly or abdomen. **4.** appetite for food. **5.** desire, inclination, or liking. **6.** *Obs.* spirit or courage. **7.** *Obs.* pride. **8.** *Obs.* resentment or anger. —*v.t.* **9.** to take into or retain in the stomach. **10.** to endure or tolerate. **11.** *Obs.* to be offended at or resent. [ME *stomak*, t. OF: m. *estomac*, t. L: m. *stomachus*, t. Gk.: m. *stómachos* throat, gullet, stomach]

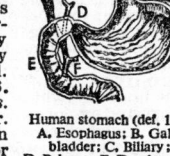

Human stomach (def. 1a)
A. Esophagus; B. Gall bladder; C. Biliary; D. Pylorus; E. Duodenum; F. Pancreatic duct

stomach ache, pain in the stomach or abdomen; gastralgia; colic.

stom·ach·er (stŭm′ək ər), *n.* an article of dress for covering the stomach and chest, formerly worn by both men and women; esp. one worn by women under a bodice.

sto·mach·ic (stō māk′ĭk), *adj.* Also, **sto·mach′i·cal.** **1.** of or pertaining to the stomach; gastric. **2.** beneficial to the stomach; stimulating gastric digestion; sharpening the appetite. —*n.* **3.** a stomachic agent or drug.

Stomacher

stomach tooth, a lower canine milk tooth of infants (so called because there is often gastric disturbance at the time of its appearance).

stomach worm, a nematode worm of the family *Trichostrongylidae, Haemonchus contortus,* parasitic in sheep and related animals; wire worm.

sto·ma·ta (stō′mə tə, stŏm′ə tə), *n.* pl. of **stoma.**

stom·a·tal (stō′ə təl, stō′mə-), *adj.* **1.** of, pertaining to, or of the nature of a stoma. **2.** having stomata.

sto·mat·ic (stō māt′ĭk), *adj.* **1.** pertaining to the mouth. **2.** acting as a remedy for diseases of the mouth, as a drug. **3.** stomatal.

sto·ma·ti·tis (stō′mə tī′tĭs, stŏm′ə-), *n. Pathol.* inflammation of the mouth. [NL, f. Gk.: s. *stóma* mouth + -*itis* -ITIS]

stomato-, a word element referring to the mouth, as in *stomatoplasty.* Also, before vowels, **stomat-.** [t. Gk., comb. form of *stóma* mouth]

sto·ma·tol·o·gy (stō′mə tŏl′ə jĭ), *n.* the science dealing with the mouth and its diseases.

stom·a·to·plas·ty (stŏm′ə tə plăs′tĭ, stō′mə-), *n.* plastic surgery of the mouth.

stom·a·to·pod (stŏm′ə tə pŏd′, stō′mə-), *n.* any of the *Stomatopoda,* an order of crustaceans having some of the legs close to the mouth and having the gills borne on the abdominal segments.

stom·a·tous (stŏm′ə təs, stō′mə-), *adj.* stomatal.

-stome, a word element referring to the mouth, as in *cyclostome.* [comb. form repr. (1) Gk. *stóma* mouth, (2) Gk. *stómion* little mouth]

sto·mo·dae·um (stō′mə dē′əm, stŏm′ə-), *n., pl.* **-daea** (-dē′ə). stomodeum. —**sto·mo·dae′al,** *adj.*

sto·mo·de·um (stō′mə dē′əm, stŏm′ə-), *n., pl.* **-dea** (-dē′ə). *Embryol.* the part of the primary oral cavity which begins as an invagination of the ectoderm. [NL: f. *stom-* (see -STOME) + *odaeum* (t. Gk.: m. *hodaîos* on the way)] —**sto′mo·de′al,** *adj.*

-stomous, an adjectival suffix corresponding to **-stome,** as in *monostomous.*

stomp (stŏmp), *v.t., v.i., n. Chiefly Dial.* stamp.

-stomy, a combining form used in names of surgical operations for making an artificial opening. [t. Gk.: m.s. -*stomia,* der. *stóma* mouth]

stone (stōn), *n., pl.* **stones** (*except* **stone** *for def. 6*), *adj., v.,* **stoned, stoning.** —*n.* **1.** the hard substance of which rocks consist, as distinguished from wood, metal, etc. **2.** a particular kind of rock. **3.** a piece of rock of definite size, shape, etc., for a particular purpose. **4.** a piece of rock of small or moderate size. **5.** precious stone. **6.** a unit of weight of various values, esp. the British stone of 14 lbs. **7.** something resembling a small stone or pebble. **8.** any hard, stonelike seed. **9.** *Bot.* the hard endocarp of a drupe. **10.** *Med.* **a.** a calculous concretion in the body as in the kidney, gall bladder, or urinary bladder. **b.** the disease arising from such a concretion. **11.** a gravestone or tombstone. **12.** a grindstone. **13.** a millstone. **14.** a hailstone. **15.** *Print.* a table with a smooth surface used for composing page forms, formerly made of stone. **16.** a piece in the game of dominoes, checkers, or backgammon. **17.** (*pl.*) testicles. —*adj.* **18.** made of or pertaining to stone. **19.** made of stoneware: *a stone mug or bottle.* —*v.t.* **20.** to throw stones at; drive by pelting with stones. **21.** to put to death by pelting with stones. **22.** to provide or fit with stones, as by paving, lining, facing, etc. **23.** to rub with or on a stone, as to sharpen, polish, smooth, etc. **24.** to free from stones, as fruit. **25.** *Obs.* to turn into stone; petrify. [ME; OE *stān,* c. G *stein*] —**stone′less,** *adj.* —**ston′er,** *n.*

Stone (stōn), *n.* **1. Harlan Fiske** (här′lən), 1872–1946, U.S. jurist: chief justice of the U.S. Supreme Court, 1941–1946. **2. Lucy,** (Mrs. *Henry Broun Blackwell*) 1818–93, U.S. suffragist.

Stone Age, the age in the history of mankind (preceding the bronze and iron ages) marked by the use of stone implements.

stone-blind (stōn′blĭnd′), *adj.* completely blind. —Syn. See **blind.**

stone-broke (stōn′brōk′), *adj. Slang.* having no money whatever.

stone·chat (stōn′chăt′), *n.* any of various small Old World passerine birds, esp. of the genus *Saxicola,* as *S. torquata.* [f. STONE + *chat,* small bird so called because of its chattering cry]

stone·crop (stōn′krŏp′), *n.* **1.** any plant of the genus *Sedum,* esp. a mosslike herb, *Sedum acre,* with small, fleshy leaves and yellow flowers, frequently growing on rocks and walls. **2.** any of various plants of related genera. [ME *stooncroppe,* OE *stāncrop.* See STONE, CROP]

stone·cut·ter (stōn′kŭt′ər), *n.* **1.** one who cuts or carves stone. **2.** a machine for cutting or dressing stone. —**stone′cut′ting,** *n.*

stone-deaf (stōn′dĕf′), *adj.* completely deaf.

stone fly, any of the insects constituting the order *Plecoptera,* whose larvae abound under stones in streams.

stone fruit, a fruit with a stone or hard endocarp, as a peach or a plum; a drupe.

Stone·henge (stōn′hĕnj), *n.* a prehistoric monument in S England, in Wiltshire, N of Salisbury, consisting of a large oval of megalithic posts and lintels.

stone lily, a fossil crinoid.

stone marten, a marten, *Mustela foina,* of Europe and Asia, having a white mark on the throat and breast.

stone·ma·son (stōn′mā′sən), *n.* a dresser of or builder in stone. —**stone′ma′son·ry,** *n.*

Stone Mountain, a granite mountain in N Georgia, near Atlanta: sculptures of Confederate heroes.

Stone River, a river in central Tennessee, flowing NW to the Cumberland river. See **Murfreesboro.**

stone roller, **1.** an American minnow, *Campostoma anomalum,* named from its habit of moving stones in constructing its nest. **2.** any of several other minnows or suckers with similar habits, as *Hypentelium nigricans.*

stone·wall (stōn′wôl′), *v.i. Cricket.* to play a defensive game only (applied to the batsman). —**stone′wall′er,** *n.*

stone·ware (stōn′wâr′), *n.* a more or less vitrified pottery ware, usually made from a single clay.

stone·work (stōn′wûrk′), *n.* **1.** work in stone; stone masonry. **2.** (*usually pl.*) an establishment where stone is prepared for building, etc. —**stone′work′er,** *n.*

stone·wort (stōn′wûrt′), *n.* a green alga of the class *Charophyceae,* having a jointed plant body frequently encrusted with lime and usually growing in fresh water.

ston·y (stō′nĭ), *adj.,* **stonier, stoniest. 1.** full of or abounding in stones or rock. **2.** pertaining to or characteristic of stone. **3.** resembling or suggesting stone, esp. hard like stone. **4.** unfeeling; merciless; obdurate. **5.** motionless or rigid; without expression, as the eyes or look. **6.** petrifying: *stony fear.* **7.** having a stone or stones, as a fruit. **8.** *Colloq.* stone-broke. —**ston′i·ly,** *adv.* —**ston′i·ness,** *n.*

ston·y-broke (stō′nĭ brōk′), *adj. Brit. Slang.* having no money whatever.

stony coral, a true coral or madreporarian consisting of numerous anthozoan polyps imbedded in the calcareous material that they secrete.

ston·y-heart·ed (stō′nĭ här′tĭd), *adj.* hard-hearted.

Stony Point, a village in SE New York, on the Hudson: site of a strategic fort in the Revolutionary War.

stood (stŏŏd), *v.* pt. and pp. of **stand.**

stooge (stŏŏj), *n., v.,* **stooged, stooging.** *U.S.* —*n.* **1.** *Colloq.* an entertainer who feeds lines to a comedian and is often the object of his ridicule. **2.** *Colloq.* (in vaudeville) a person in the audience serving a similar function by heckling. **3.** *Slang.* one who acts on behalf of another, esp. in obsequious or secretive fashion. —*v.i.* 4. *Slang.* to act as a stooge [orig. uncert.]

stool (stōōl), *n.* 1. a wooden seat, either low or high, without arms or a back, and for a single person. 2. a short, low support for resting the feet on, kneeling on, etc. 3. the stump, base, or root of a tree or other plant which has been cut down, from which shoots are produced, as for coppice wood, for saplings, or for layers. 4. the base of plants which annually produce new stems, etc. 5. a cluster of shoots or stems springing up from a stool or from any root, or a single shoot or layer. 6. a bird fastened as a decoy. 7. a decoy duck or similar decoy. 8. a privy. 9. the mass of matter evacuated at each movement of the bowels. 10. the sill of a window. —*v.i.* 11. to throw up shoots from the base or root, as a plant; form a stool. [ME; OE *stōl*, c. G *stuhl*]

stool pigeon, 1. a pigeon used as a decoy. 2. *Chiefly U.S. Slang.* a person employed as a decoy or secret confederate, as by gamblers. 3. *Chiefly U.S. Slang.* one who acts as a spy for the police, employer, etc.

stoop[1] (stōōp), *v.i.* 1. to bend the head and shoulders, or the body generally, forward and downward from an erect position: *to stoop over a desk.* 2. to carry the head and shoulders habitually bowed forward: *to stoop from age.* 3. to bend, bow, or lean (said of trees, precipices, etc.). 4. to descend from one's level of dignity; condescend; deign. 5. to swoop down, as a hawk at prey. 6. *Rare.* to submit; yield. 7. *Obs.* to come down from a height. —*v.t.* 8. to bend (oneself, one's head, etc.) forward and downward. 9. *Archaic.* to abase, humble, or subdue. —*n.* 10. act of stooping; a stooping movement. 11. a stooping position or carriage of body. 12. a descent from dignity or superiority; a condescension. 13. a downward swoop, as of a hawk. [ME *stoupe*, OE *stūpian*; akin to STEEP[1]] —*Syn.* 1. See *bend*[1].

stoop[2] (stōōp), *n.* *U.S.* 1. a raised platform with seats, at the entrance of a house. 2. any raised entrance platform with steps leading up to it; a porch. [t. D: m. *stoep*, akin to STEP]

stop (stŏp), *v.,* **stopped** or (*Poetic*) **stopt; stopping;** *n.* —*v.t.* 1. to cease from, leave off, or discontinue: *to stop running.* 2. to cause to cease; put an end to: *to stop noise in the street.* 3. to interrupt, arrest, or check (a course, proceeding, process, etc.). 4. to cut off, intercept, or withhold: *to stop supplies.* 5. to restrain, hinder, or prevent (fol. by *from*): *to stop a person from doing something.* 6. to prevent from proceeding, acting, operating, continuing, etc.: *to stop a speaker, a car, etc.* 7. to block, obstruct, or close (a passage way, channel, opening, duct, etc.) (often fol. by *up*). 8. to fill the hole or holes in (a wall, a decayed tooth, etc.). 9. to close (a container, tube, etc.) with a cork, plug, bung, or the like. 10. to close the external orifice of (the ears, nose, mouth, etc.). 11. *Fencing, Boxing, etc.* a. to check (a stroke, blow, etc.); parry; ward off. b. to defeat by a knockout or the like. 12. *Banking.* to notify a banker to dishonor (a check) upon presentment. 13. *Bridge.* to have an honor card and a sufficient number of protecting cards to keep an opponent from continuing to win in (a suit). 14. *Music.* a. to close (a fingerhole, etc.) in order to produce a particular note from a wind instrument. b. to press down (a string of a violin, etc.) in order to alter the pitch of the tone produced from it. c. to produce (a particular note) by so doing. 15. **stop down,** *Photog.* to reduce the diaphragm opening of (a camera). —*v.i.* 16. to come to a stand, as in a course or journey; halt. 17. to cease moving, proceeding, speaking, acting, operating, etc.; to pause; desist. 18. to cease; come to an end. 19. to halt for a brief stay at some point in the course of a journey (fol. by *off*). 20. **stop over,** to make a stopover. —*n.* 21. act of stopping. 22. a cessation or arrest of movement, action, operation, etc.; end. 23. a stay or sojourn made at a place, as in the course of a journey. 24. a place where trains or other vehicles halt. 25. a closing or filling up, as of a hole. 26. a blocking or obstructing, as of a passage or way. 27. a plug or other stopper for an opening. 28. an obstacle, impediment, or hindrance. 29. any piece or device that serves to check or control movement or action in a mechanism. 30. *Com.* a. an order to dishonor (a check, etc.). b. stop order. 31. *Music.* a. the act of closing a fingerhole, etc., or of pressing down a string, of an instrument, in order to produce a particular note. b. a device or contrivance, as on an instrument, for accomplishing this. c. (in an organ) a graduated set of pipes of the same kind and giving tones of the same quality. d. a knob or handle which is drawn out or pushed back to permit or prevent the sounding of such a set of pipes or to control some other part of the organ. e. a similar group of reeds on a reed organ. 32. *Naut.* a piece of small line used to lash or fasten something, as a furled sail. 33. *Phonet.* a. an articulation which interrupts the flow of air from the lungs. b. a consonant sound resulting from stop articulation: *p, b, t, d, k,* and *g* are the English stops. 34. *Photog.* the diaphragm opening of a lens, especially as indicated by an F/number. 35. *Chiefly Brit.* a punctuation mark: *a full stop* (*a period*). 36. the word "stop" spelled out, and used instead of a period in telegraphic and cable messages. 37. (*pl.*) a family of games in which a player continues to play cards in a certain sequence until he is stopped, and can no longer play.

[ME *stoppe,* OE *stoppian,* c. D and LG *stoppen,* G *stopfen,* all ult. t. VL. Cf. It. *stoppare* plug (with tow), der. *stoppa,* g. L *stuppa* tow, t. Gk.: m. *stýppē*] —**Syn.** 3. STOP, ARREST, CHECK, HALT imply causing a cessation of movement or progress (literal or figurative). STOP is the general term for the idea: *to stop a clock.* ARREST usually refers to stopping by imposing a sudden and complete restraint: *to arrest development.* CHECK implies bringing about an abrupt, partial, or temporary stop: *to check a trotting horse.* To HALT means to make a temporary stop, esp. one resulting from a command: *to halt a company of soldiers.* 17. STOP, CEASE, PAUSE, QUIT imply bringing movement, action, progress, or conditions to an end. STOP is used in speaking of objects in motion or action: *the clock stopped.* CEASE, a more literary and formal word, suggests the coming to an end of that which has had considerable duration: *a storm ceases.* PAUSE implies the prospect of resumption after a short interval: *one pauses in speaking.* QUIT, in the sense of stop or cease, still very common in the U.S., is not used in England, though it survives in Scottish and Irish English (in England the term used is *leave off*): *make him quit.* —**Ant.** 3, 17. start, begin.

stop·cock (stŏp′kŏk′), *n.* a valve, with a tapered plug operated by a handle, used to control the flow of a liquid or gas from a receptacle or through a pipe.

stope (stōp), *n., v.,* **stoped, stoping.** —*n.* 1. any excavation made in a mine to remove the ore which has been rendered accessible by the shafts and drifts. —*v.t., v.i.* 2. to mine or work by stopes. [appar. akin to STEP, n.]

stop·gap (stŏp′găp′), *n.* 1. something that fills the place of something lacking; a temporary substitute; a makeshift. —*adj.* 2. makeshift.

stop·light (stŏp′līt′), *n.* a taillight coördinated with the brake to light as a car slows or stops.

stop order, an order to the broker to sell out the stock, etc., if the market reaches a designated lower price.

stop·o·ver (stŏp′ō′vər), *n.* any brief stop in the course of a journey, esp. one with the privilege of proceeding later on the ticket originally issued.

stop·page (stŏp′ĭj), *n.* 1. act of stopping; cessation of activity, etc. 2. state of being stopped.

stop payment, an order by the drawer of a check to his bank not to pay a specified check.

stopped (stŏpt), *adj.* 1. halted or checked. 2. closed, filled up, or obstructed. 3. *Music.* a. having the upper end plugged or closed, as an organ pipe. b. acted upon by stopping, as a string. c. produced by the stopping of a string, etc. d. having the bell stopped by the inserted hand, as in a French horn, to lower the pitch or to muffle the sound. 4. *Phonet.* involving stop articulation.

stop·per (stŏp′ər), *n.* 1. one who or that which stops. 2. a plug or piece for closing a bottle, tube, or the like. —*v.t.* 3. to close, secure, or fit with a stopper.

stop·ple (stŏp′əl), *n., v.,* **-pled, -pling.** —*n.* 1. a stopper for a bottle or the like. —*v.t.* 2. to close or fit with a stopple.

stop watch, a watch with a hand or hands that can be stopped or started at any instant, and which is adapted for indicating fractions of a second (used for timing races, etc.).

stor·age (stōr′ĭj), *n.* 1. act of storing. 2. state or fact of being stored. 3. capacity or space for storing. 4. a place where something is stored. 5. the price charged for storing goods.

storage battery, a voltaic battery whose energy is renewed by passing a current through the cells in a direction opposed to the electromotive force.

sto·rax (stōr′ăks), *n.* 1. a solid resin with a vanillalike odor obtained from a small styracaceous tree, *Styrax officinalis,* formerly much used in medicine and perfumery. 2. a liquid balsam (**liquid storax**) obtained from species of liquidambar, esp. from the wood and inner bark of *Liquidambar orientalis* (**Levant storax**), a tree of Asia Minor, etc., and used in medicine, perfumery, etc. [t. L, t. Gk.: m. *stýrax*]

store (stōr), *n., v.,* **stored, storing.** —*n.* 1. *Chiefly U.S.* a place where goods are kept for sale; a shop. 2. a supply or stock (of something), esp. one for future use. 3. (*pl.*) supplies of food, clothing, or other requisites, as for a household or other establishment, a ship, naval or military forces, or the like. 4. the state of being stored up, on hand, or in reserve: *to keep a thing in store.* 5. *Chiefly Brit.* a storehouse or warehouse. 6. measure of esteem or regard: *to set little store by a thing.* 7. quantity, esp. great quantity; abundance, or plenty. —*v.t.* 8. to supply or stock with something, as for future use. 9. to lay up or put away, as a supply for future use (often with *up* or *away*). 10. to deposit in a storehouse, warehouse, or other place, for keeping. [ME, aphetic var. of *astore,* t. OF: m. *estorer* build, furnish, stock, g. L *instaurāre* renew, restore, make]

store·house (stōr′hous′), *n.* 1. a house or building in which things are stored. 2. any repository or source of abundant supplies, as of facts or knowledge.

store·keep·er (stōr′kē′pər), *n.* 1. *Chiefly U.S.* a shopkeeper. 2. one who has charge of a store or stores. 3. *U.S. Navy.* one in charge of naval or military stores.

store·room (stōr′rōōm′, -rŏŏm′), *n.* 1. a room in which stores are kept. 2. room or space for storage.

sto·rey (stōr′ĭ), *n., pl.* **-reys.** *Brit.* story[2].

sto·ried[1] (stōr′ĭd), *adj.* 1. recorded or celebrated in history or story. 2. ornamented with designs representing historical, legendary or similar subjects. [f. STORY[1] + -ED[3]]

sto·ried[2] (stôr′ĭd), *adj.* having stories or floors: *a two-storied house.* Also, *Brit.*, **sto′reyed.** [f. STORY[2] + -ED[3]]

sto·ri·ette (stôr′ĭ·ĕt′), *n.* a very short story. [dim. of STORY[1]. See -ETTE]

stork (stôrk), *n.* one of the long-legged, long-necked, long-billed wading birds, allied to the ibises and herons, which constitute the family *Ciconiidae,* esp. *Ciconia ciconia* (**white stork**) of Europe. [ME; OE *storc,* c. G *storch*]

stork's-bill (stôrks′bĭl′), *n.* any plant of the geraniaceous genus *Pelargonium,* or of the related genus *Erodium,* as *E. cicutarium* (the alfilaria, or **hemlock stork's-bill**): so called from the long-beaked fruit.

White stork.
Ciconia ciconia
(3 ft. or more high,
total length 3 ft.)

storm (stôrm), *n.* **1.** a disturbance of the normal condition of the atmosphere, manifesting itself by winds of unusual force or direction, often accompanied by rain, snow, hail, thunder and lightning, or flying sand or dust. **2.** a heavy fall of rain, snow, or hail, or a violent outbreak of thunder, and lightning, unaccompanied by strong wind. **3.** a wind of Beaufort scale #*11,* i.e., one within the range of 64–75 miles per hour. **4.** a violent assault on a fortified place, strong position, or the like. **5.** a heavy descent or discharge of missiles, blows, or the like. **6.** a violent disturbance of affairs, as a civil, political, social, or domestic commotion. **7.** a violent outburst or outbreak: *a storm of applause.* —*v.i.* **8.** to blow with unusual force, or to rain, snow, hail, etc., esp. with violence (used impersonally): *it stormed all day.* **9.** to rage or complain with violence or fury. **10.** to deliver a violent attack or fire, as with artillery. **11.** to rush to an assault or attack. **12.** to rush with violence: *to storm out of a room.* —*v.t.* **13.** to subject to or as to a storm. **14.** to utter or say with angry vehemence. [ME and OE, c. D *storm,* G *sturm*]

Storm (shtôrm), *n.* **Theodore Woldsen** (tā′ō dōr′ vôlt′-sən), 1817–88, German poet and novelist.

storm·bound (stôrm′bound′), *adj.* confined or detained by storms.

storm cellar, a cellar or underground chamber for refuge during violent storms; a cyclone cellar.

storm center, **1.** the center of a cyclonic storm, the area of lowest pressure and of comparative calm. **2.** a center of disturbance, tumult, trouble, or the like.

storm door, an outer or additional door for protection against inclement weather, as during the winter.

storm·er (stôr′mər), *n.* one who storms.

storm·less (stôrm′lĭs), *adj.* without storms.

storm·proof (stôrm′prōōf′), *adj.* proof against storms.

storm troops, *Mil.* (formerly) German troops specially chosen and equipped for carrying out storming operations. —**storm trooper.**

storm window, a glass covering over a window, providing extra insulation and protection from cold and wind.

storm·y (stôr′mĭ), *adj.,* **stormier, stormiest.** **1.** affected or characterized by, or subject to, storms; tempestuous: *a stormy sea.* **2.** characterized by violent commotion, actions, speech, passions, etc.: *a stormy debate.* —**storm′i·ly,** *adv.* —**storm′i·ness,** *n.*

stormy petrel, **1.** Also, **storm petrel.** a small black-and-white bird, *Hydrobates pelagicus,* of the deep seas. **2.** a person whose coming is supposed to portend trouble or strife.

Stor·thing (stôr′tĭng′), *n.* the parliament of Norway, composed of the Lagthing and the Odelsthing. Also, **Stor′ting′.** [t. Norw.: f. *stor* great + *ting* assembly]

sto·ry[1] (stôr′ĭ), *n., pl.* **-ries,** *v.,* **-ried, -rying.** —*n.* **1.** narrative, either true or fictitious, in prose or verse, designed to interest or amuse the hearer or reader; a tale. **2.** a fictitious tale, shorter and less elaborate than a novel. **3.** such narratives or tales as a branch of literature. **4.** the plot, or succession of incidents, of a novel, poem, drama, etc. **5.** a narration of a series of events, or a series of events that are or may be narrated. **6.** a narration of the events in the life of a person or the existence of a thing, or such events as a subject for narration. **7.** a report or account of a matter; a statement or allegation: *the story goes that he rejected the offer.* **8.** *U.S. Journalism.* an account of some event, situation, etc., in a newspaper. **9.** *Colloq.* a lie. **10.** *Obs.* history. —*v.t.* **11.** to ornament with pictured scenes, as from history or legend. **12.** *Rare.* to tell the history or story of; tell as a story. [ME, t. AF: m. *estorie,* g. L *historia*]

sto·ry[2] (stôr′ĭ), *n., pl.* **-ries.** **1.** a complete horizontal section of a building, having one continuous or approximately continuous floor. **2.** the set of rooms on the same floor or level of a building. **3.** each of the stages, separated by floors, one above another, of which a building consists. Also, *Brit.,* **storey.** [ME. der. OF *estorer* build. See STORE]

Sto·ry (stôr′ĭ), *n.* **1. Joseph,** 1779–1845, U.S. jurist. **2. William Wetmore,** 1819–95, U.S. sculptor and poet.

sto·ry·tell·er (stôr′ĭ tĕl′ər), *n.* one who tells stories. —**sto′ry·tell′ing,** *adj., n.*

stoss (stôs; *Ger.* shtōs), *adj. Geol.* noting the side, as of a hill, etc., that receives, or has received, the thrust of a glacier or other impulse. [t. G: thrust, push]

sto·tin·ka (stō tĭng′kä), *n., pl.* **-ki** (-kĭ). a minor Bulgarian coin equivalent to ¹/₁₀₀ of a lev. [t. Bulg.]

St.-Ouen (săn twän′), *n.* a suburb of Paris in N France. 51,106 (1954).

stoup (stōōp), *n.* **1.** a basin for holy water, as at the entrance of a church. **2.** *Scot.* a pail or bucket. **3.** *Archaic, Scot., and N. Eng.* a. a drinking vessel of various sizes, as a cup or tankard. b. the amount it holds. [ME *stowpe,* t. Scand.; cf. Icel. *staup,* c. OE *stēap*]

Stoup (def. 1)

stout (stout), *adj.* **1.** bulky in figure, solidly built, or thick-set; corpulent or fat. **2.** bold, hardy, or dauntless: *a stout heart.* **3.** firm; stubborn: *stout resistance.* **4.** strong of body, stalwart, or sturdy: *stout fellows.* **5.** having endurance or staying power, as a horse. **6.** strong in substance or construction. **7.** strong and thick or heavy. —*n.* **8.** strong ale or beer. **9.** porter of extra strength. **10.** a stout person. **11.** (*often pl.*) a garment for such a person. [ME, t. OF: m. *estout* brave, proud, t. Gmc.; cf. MLG *stolt*] —**stout′ly,** *adv.* —**stout′ness,** *n.*

—**Syn. 1.** STOUT, FAT, PLUMP imply corpulence of body. STOUT describes a heavily-built but usually strong and healthy body: *a handsome stout lady.* FAT, an informal word with unpleasant connotations, suggests an undesoming fleshy stoutness; it may, however, apply also to a hearty fun-loving type of stout person: *a fat old man, fat and jolly.* PLUMP connotes a pleasing roundness and is often used as a complimentary or euphemistic equivalent for stout, fleshy, etc.: *a plump figure attractively dressed.* —**Ant. 1.** thin, lean.

stout-heart·ed (stout′här′tĭd), *adj.* brave and resolute; dauntless. —**stout′-heart′ed·ly,** *adv.*

stove[1] (stōv), *n.* **1.** an apparatus, portable or fixed, and in many forms, for furnishing heat, as for comfort, cooking, or mechanical purposes, commonly using coal, oil, gas, or electricity. **2.** a heated chamber or box for some special purpose, as a drying room, or a kiln for firing pottery. [ME; OE *stofa* hot air bathroom, c. G *stube* sitting room]

stove[2] (stōv), *v.* a pt. and pp. of **stave.**

stove·pipe (stōv′pīp′), *n.* **1.** a pipe, as of sheet metal, serving as a stove chimney or to connect a stove with a chimney flue. **2.** *U.S. Colloq.* a stovepipe hat.

stovepipe hat, *U.S. Colloq.* a tall silk hat.

sto·ver (stō′vər), *n.* **1.** coarse roughage used as feed for livestock. **2.** *Chiefly U.S.* stalks and leaves, not including grain, of such forages as corn and sorghum. **3.** *Brit. Dial.* fodder minus the grain portion of the plant. [ME, t. OF: m. *estover* necessaries, n. use of *estover, estovoir* to be necessary, der. L *est opus* there is need]

stow (stō), *v.t.* **1.** *Naut.* to place (cargo, etc.) in the hold or some other part of a ship. **2.** to put in a place or receptacle as for storage or reserve; pack. **3.** to fill (a place or receptacle) by packing. **4.** (of a place or receptacle) to afford room for; hold. **5.** *Slang.* to desist from. **6.** *Obs.* to lodge or quarter. **7.** to put away, as in a safe or convenient place (fol. by *away*). —*v.i.* **8. stow away,** to conceal oneself aboard a ship or other conveyance in order to get a free trip. [ME, der. *stowe* place, OE *stōw,* c. Icel. *-stō* in *eldstō* fireplace]

stow·age (stō′ĭj), *n.* **1.** act or operation of stowing. **2.** state or manner of being stowed. **3.** room or accommodation for stowing something. **4.** a place in which something is or may be stowed. **5.** that which is stowed or to be stowed. **6.** a charge for stowing something.

stow·a·way (stō′ə wā′), *n.* one who conceals himself aboard a ship or other conveyance, as to get a free trip.

Stowe (stō), *n.* **Harriet Elizabeth Beecher,** 1811–96, U.S. writer: author of *Uncle Tom's Cabin.*

St. Paul, the capital of Minnesota, in the SE part: a port on the Mississippi. 313,411 (1960).

St. Paul's, a cathedral in London, begun 1675, after the designs of Wren, in place of an older cathedral.

St. Peter's, the great metropolitan church of the see of Rome, one of the finest examples of Renaissance architecture, and especially noted for the structure of its pedimented dome.

St. Pe·ters·burg (pē′tərz bûrg′), **1.** a seaport in W Florida, on Tampa Bay: seaside winter resort. 181,298 (1960). **2.** the capital of Russia under the czars: renamed **Petrograd** in 1914, and **Leningrad** in 1924.

St. Pierre (pyâr′; *Fr.* săn pyĕr′), **1.** a city on Réunion island, in the Indian Ocean. 27,573 (1954). **2.** a former city on Martinique, in the French West Indies: destroyed (with the entire population of 26,000) by an eruption of the volcano Mt. Pelée, 1902.

St. Pierre and Miq·ue·lon (mĭk′ə lŏn′; *Fr.* mē-klôn′), two small groups of islands off the S coast of Newfoundland: France's only colony in North America; important base for fishing. 4606 (1951); 93 sq. mi. *Cap.*: St. Pierre.

St. Quen·tin (kwĕn′tən; *Fr.* săn kän tăn′), a city in N France, on the Somme: retaken from the Germans, 1918. 53,866 (1954).

str., 1. steamer. **2.** strait. **3.** *Music.* a. string. b. strings.

stra·bis·mus (strə bĭz′məs), *n. Pathol.* a disorder of vision due to the turning of one eye or both eyes from the normal position so that both cannot be directed at the same point or object at the same time; squint; cross-eye. [NL, t. Gk.: m. *strabismós*] —**stra·bis′mal, stra·bis′mic, stra·bis′mi·cal,** *adj.*

Stra·bo (strā′bō), *n.* c63 B.C.–A.D. 21?, Greek geographer and historian.

stra·bot·o·my (strə bŏt′ə mĭ), *n., pl.* **-mies.** *Surg.* the operation of dividing one or more of the muscles of the eye for the cure of strabismus.

Stra·chey (strā′chĭ), *n.* (Giles) **Lytton** (jĭlz lĭt′ən), 1880–1932, British writer and biographer.

strad·dle (străd′əl), *v.,* **-dled, -dling,** *n.* —*v.i.* **1.** to walk, stand, or sit with the legs wide apart; stand or sit astride. **2.** to stand wide apart, as the legs. **3.** *Colloq.* to take an equivocal position in regard to something; appear to favor both sides. —*v.t.* **4.** to walk, stand, or sit with one leg on each side of; stand or sit astride of. **5.** to spread (the legs) wide apart. **6.** *Colloq.* to take an equivocal position in regard to; appear to favor both sides of. —*n.* **7.** act of straddling. **8.** the distance straddled over. **9.** *Colloq.* a taking of an equivocal or noncommittal position. **10.** *Finance.* a privilege consisting of a put and a call combined, giving the holder the right, at his option, either of delivering a certain amount of stock, etc., at a specified price, or of buying a certain amount of stock, etc., at another specified price, within a stipulated period. [appar. northern var. of *stroddle,* akin to *striddle,* freq. of **STRIDE**] —**strad′·dler,** *n.* —**strad′dling·ly,** *adv.*

Stra·di·va·ri (strä′dē vä′rē), *n.* **Antonio** (än tō′nyō), (*Antonius Stradivarius*) c1644–1737, Italian violin maker of Cremona.

Strad·i·var·i·us (străd′ə vâr′ĭ əs), *n.* a violin or other instrument made by Stradivari or his family.

strafe (strāf, sträf), *v.t.,* **strafed, strafing. 1.** to attack (ground troops or installations) by airplanes with machine-gun fire. **2.** to bombard heavily. **3.** *Slang.* to punish. [t. G: from the phrase *Gott strafe England* God punish England] —**straf′er,** *n.*

Straf·ford (străf′ərd), *n.* **Thomas Wentworth, 1st Earl of,** 1593–1641, British statesman.

strag·gle (străg′əl), *v.i.,* **-gled, -gling. 1.** to stray from the road, course, or line of march. **2.** to wander about in a scattered fashion; ramble. **3.** to go, come, or spread in a scattered, irregular fashion. [ME; b. **STRAY** and **DRAGGLE**] —**strag′gler,** *n.*

strag·gly (străg′lĭ), *adj.* straggling; rambling.

straight (strāt), *adj.* **1.** without a bend, crook, or curve; not curved; direct: *a straight path.* **2.** (of a line) lying evenly between its points; generated by a point moving constantly in the same direction. **3.** evenly formed or set: *straight shoulders.* **4.** without circumlocution; candid: *straight speaking.* **5.** honest, honorable, or upright, as conduct, dealings, methods, persons, etc. **6.** *Colloq.* reliable, as reports, information, etc. **7.** right or correct, as reasoning, thinking, a thinker, etc. **8.** in the proper order or condition: *to set a room straight.* **9.** continuous or unbroken: *in straight succession.* **10.** *U.S.* thoroughgoing or unreserved: *a straight Republican.* **11.** unmodified or unaltered: *a straight comedy.* **12.** *U.S.* undiluted, as whiskey. **13.** *Theat.* (of acting) straightforward; not striving for effect. **14.** *Card Playing.* made of cards in consecutive denomination, as the two, three, four, five, and six. —*adv.* **15.** in a straight line: *to walk straight.* **16.** in an even form or position: *pictures hung straight.* **17.** directly: *to go straight to a place.* **18.** without circumlocution (often fol by *out*). **19.** honestly, honorably, or virtuously: *to live straight.* **20.** in a continuous course: *to keep straight on.* **21.** without discount regardless of the quantity bought: *candy bars ten cents straight.* —*n.* **22.** the condition of being straight. **23.** a straight form or position. **24.** a straight line. **25.** a straight part, as of a racecourse. **26.** *Games.* a succession of strokes, plays, etc. which gives a perfect score. **27.** *Poker.* a sequence of five cards of various suits. Cf. **sequence.** [ME, orig. pp. of **STRETCH**] —**straight′ly,** *adv.* —**straight′ness,** *n.*

straight angle, an angle of 180°. See diag. under **obtuse angle.**

straight-arm (strāt′ärm′), *v.t.* *Football.* to push (an opponent) away by holding the arm out straight.

straight·a·way (strāt′ə wā′), *adj.* **1.** straight onward, without turn or curve, as a racecourse. —*n.* **2.** a straightaway course or part. —*adv.* **3.** *Brit.* immediately; right away.

straight·edge (strāt′ĕj′), *n.* a bar or strip of wood or metal, of various sizes, having at least one edge of sufficiently reliable straightness, for use in obtaining or testing straight lines, plane surfaces, etc.

straight·en (strā′tən), *v.t., v.i.* to make or become straight in direction, form, position, character, conduct, condition, etc. —**straight′en·er,** *n.*

straight flush, *Poker.* a sequence of five cards of the same suit.

straight·for·ward (strāt′fôr′wərd), *adj.* **1.** going or directed straight forward: *a straightforward glance.* **2.** proceeding without roundaboutness; direct. **3.** free from crookedness or deceit; honest: *straightforward in one's dealings.* —*adv.* **4.** Also, **straight′for′wards.** straight ahead; directly or continuously forward. —**straight′for′ward·ly,** *adv.* —**straight′for′ward·ness,** *n.* —Ant. **1.** devious.

straight-line (strāt′līn′), *adj.* *Mach.* **1.** indicating a lineal arrangement of the working parts of a machine, as in some compressors. **2.** denoting an apparatus copying or initiating motion along a straight line.

straight-line motion, *Mach.* a device, as a linkage, initiating motion in a straight line, or transferring motion from a curved line to a straight.

straight man, an entertainer who plays his part straight, usually as a foil for a comedian.

straight-out (strāt′out′), *adj.* *U.S. Colloq.* **1.** thoroughgoing: *a straight-out Democrat.* **2.** frank; aboveboard.

straight·way (strāt′wā′), *adv.* immediately; at once.

strain¹ (strān), *v.t.* **1.** to draw tight or taut: stretch, esp. to the utmost tension: *to strain a rope.* **2.** to exert to the utmost: *to strain one's ears to catch a sound.* **3.** to impair, injure, or weaken by overexertion or overexertion, as a muscle. **4.** to cause mechanical deformation in (a body or structure) as the result of stress. **5.** to stretch beyond the proper point or limit: *to strain the meaning of a word.* **6.** to make excessive demands upon: *to strain one's resources, credit, etc.* **7.** to pass (liquid matter) through a filter, sieve, or the like, in order to hold back the denser or solid constituents. **8.** to draw off (clear liquid) or hold back (solid particles, etc.) from liquid matter by using a filter, sieve, or the like. **9.** to clasp tightly in the arms, the hand, etc. **10.** *Obs.* to constrain, as to a course of action. —*v.i.* **11.** to pull forcibly: *a dog straining at a leash.* **12.** to stretch one's muscles, nerves, etc., to the utmost. **13.** to make violent physical efforts; strive hard. **14.** to be subjected to tension or stress; suffer strain. **15.** to filter, percolate, or ooze. **16.** to trickle or flow. —*n.* **17.** any force or pressure tending to alter shape, cause fracture, etc. **18.** strong muscular or physical effort; great or excessive effort of any kind. **19.** an injury to a muscle, tendon, etc., due to excessive tension or use; a sprain. **20.** an injury to or deformation of any body or structure resulting from stress. **21.** the condition of being strained or stretched. **22.** extreme or excessive striving after some object or effect. **23.** severe, trying, or wearing pressure or effect: *the strain of hard work.* **24.** a severe demand on resources, feelings, a person, etc.: *a strain on one's hospitality.* **25.** a flow or burst of language, eloquence, etc. **26.** (*sing.* or *pl.* often collective *pl.*) a passage of music or song as rendered or heard: *the strains of the nightingale.* **27.** *Music.* a section of a piece of music more or less complete in itself. **28.** a passage or piece of poetry. **29.** tone, style, or spirit in expression: *a humorous strain.* **30.** *Rare.* a particular degree, height, or pitch attained. [ME *streyne,* t. OF: m. *estrein-,* s. *estreindre* bind tightly, clasp, squeeze, g. L *stringere* draw tight] —**Syn. 3. STRAIN, SPRAIN** imply a wrenching, twisting, and stretching of muscles and tendons. To **STRAIN** is to stretch tightly, make taut, wrench, tear, cause injury to, by long-continued or sudden and too violent effort or movement: *to strain one's heart by over-exertion, one's eyes by reading small print.* To **SPRAIN** is to strain excessively (but without dislocation) by a sudden twist or wrench, the tendons and muscles connected with a joint, esp. those of the ankle or wrist: *to sprain an ankle.*

strain² (strān), *n.* **1.** the body of descendants of a common ancestor, as a family or stock. **2.** any of the different lines of ancestry united in a family or an individual. **3.** a group of plants distinguished from other plants of the variety to which it belongs by some intrinsic quality, such as a tendency to yield heavily. **4.** an artificial variety of a species of domestic animal or cultivated plant. **5.** a variety, esp. of microörganisms. **6.** ancestry or descent. **7.** hereditary or natural character, tendency, or trait: *a strain of insanity in a family.* **8.** a streak or trace. **9.** *Rare.* a kind or sort. **10.** *Obs.* procreation. [ME *straine,* unexplained var. of *strene,* OE *gestrēon* acquisition, c. OHG *gistriuni*]

strained (strānd), *adj.* affected or produced by effort; forced; not natural or spontaneous.

strain·er (strā′nər), *n.* **1.** one who or that which strains. **2.** a filter, sieve, or the like for straining liquids. **3.** a stretcher or tightener.

straining piece, (in a queen-post roof) a horizontal beam uniting the tops of the two queen posts, and resisting the thrust of the roof. Also, **straining beam.** See diag. under **queen post.**

strait (strāt), *n.* **1.** (*often pl. with sing. sense*). a narrow passage of water connecting two large bodies of water. **2.** (*often pl.*) a position of difficulty, distress, or need. **3.** *Archaic.* a narrow passage, space, or area. **4.** *Rare.* an isthmus. —*adj.* **5.** *Archaic.* narrow. **6.** *Archaic or Lit.* affording little room, as a place, bounds, etc. **7.** *Archaic.* strict in requirements, principles, etc. [ME, t. OF: m. *estreit* tight, narrow, g. L *strictus,* pp., bound] —**strait′ly,** *adv.* —**strait′ness,** *n.* —Syn. **2.** See **emergency.**

strait·en (strā′tən), *v.t.* **1.** to put into difficulties, esp. financial ones: *in straitened circumstances.* **2.** to restrict in range, extent, amount, pecuniary means, etc. **3.** *Archaic or Lit.* to make narrow. **4.** *Archaic.* to confine within narrow limits.

strait jacket, a kind of coat for confining the arms of violently insane persons, etc.

strait-laced (strāt′lāst′), *adj.* **1.** excessively strict in conduct or morality; puritanic; prudish. **2.** *Archaic.* tightly laced, or wearing tightly laced garments.

Straits dollar (strāts), a denomination of currency circulating in the Straits Settlements.

Straits Settlements, a former British crown colony in SE Asia, which included the settlements

b., blend of, blended; **c.,** cognate with; **d.,** dialect, dialectal; **der.,** derived from; **f.,** formed from; **g.,** going back to; **m.,** modification of; **r.,** replacing; **s.,** stem of; **t.,** taken from; **?,** perhaps. See the full key on inside cover.

strake of Singapore, Penang, Malacca, and Labuan.

strake (strāk), *n. Naut.* one continuous longitudinal line or breadth of planking or plates on the side or bottom of a vessel. [ME; appar. akin to STRETCH]

Stral·sund (shträl′zŏŏnt), *n.* a seaport in N East Germany: a member of the medieval Hanseatic League; besieged by Wallenstein, 1628. 65,275 (est. 1955).

stra·min·e·ous (strə mĭn′Iəs), *adj.* 1. of straw; strawlike. 2. straw-colored; yellowish. [t. L: m. *strāmineus*]

stra·mo·ni·um (strə mō′nĭəm), *n.* 1. the jimson weed. 2. the dried leaves of this plant, used in medicine as an analgesic, antispasmodic, etc. [NL; orig. uncert.]

strand[1] (stránd), *v.t.* 1. to drive aground on a shore, esp. of the sea, as a ship, a fish, etc. 2. (usually in the passive) to bring into a helpless position. —*v.i.* 3. to be driven or run ashore, as a ship, etc.; run aground. 4. to become halted in difficulties. —*n.* 5. *Poetic.* the land bordering the sea or ocean, or, formerly, a river; the shore. [ME and OE, c. D and G *strand*]

strand[2] (stránd), *n.* 1. a number of yarns or threads which together constitute one of the parts which are twisted together to form a rope, cord, or the like. 2. a similar part of a wire rope. 3. a rope of twisted strands. 4. a fiber or filament, as in animal or plant tissue. 5. a thread of the texture of anything, as cloth. 6. a tress of hair. 7. a string of pearls, beads, etc. —*v.t.* 8. to form (a rope, etc.) by twisting strands. 9. to break one or more strands of (a rope). [ME *strond*; orig. uncert.]

strand line, a shore line, esp. one from which the sea or a lake has receded.

strange (stránj), *adj.,* **stranger, strangest,** *adv.* —*adj.* 1. unusual, extraordinary, or curious; odd; queer: *a strange remark to make.* 2. out of one's natural environment: *to feel strange in a place.* 3. situated, belonging, or coming from outside of one's own or a particular locality: *to move to a strange place.* 4. outside of one's previous experience; hitherto unknown; unfamiliar: *the writing is strange to me.* 5. unacquainted; unaccustomed (*to*) or unexperienced (*at*). 6. distant or reserved. 7. *Archaic.* foreign. —*adv.* 8. *Colloq.* in a strange manner. [ME, t. OF: m. *estrange*, g. L *extrāneus* external, foreign] —**strange′ly,** *adv.* —**strange′ness,** *n.*
—**Syn.** 1. STRANGE, PECULIAR, ODD, QUEER refer to that which is out of the ordinary. STRANGE implies that the thing or its cause is unknown or unexplained; it is unfamiliar and unusual: *a strange expression.* That which is PECULIAR mystifies, or exhibits qualities not shared by others: *peculiar behavior.* That which is ODD is irregular or unconventional, and sometimes approaches the bizarre: *an odd custom.* QUEER sometimes adds to ODD the suggestion of something abnormal and eccentric: *queer in the head.* —**Ant.** 1. familiar.

Strange Interlude, a tragedy by O'Neill (1928).

stran·ger (strān′jər), *n.* 1. a person with whom one has, or has hitherto had, no personal acquaintance. 2. an outsider. 3. a visitor or guest. 4. a newcomer to a place or locality. 5. a person or thing that is unaccustomed or new (fol. by *to*): *he is no stranger to poverty.* 6. *Law.* one not privy or party to an act, proceeding, etc. 7. *Archaic.* a foreigner or alien.
—**Syn.** 1, 2. STRANGER, ALIEN, FOREIGNER all refer to someone regarded as outside of or distinct from a particular group. STRANGER may apply to one who does not belong to some group—social, professional, national, etc.—or may apply to a person with whom one is not acquainted. ALIEN emphasizes a difference in political allegiance and citizenship from that of the country in which one is living. FOREIGNER emphasizes a difference in language, customs, and background.

stran·gle (stráng′gəl), *v.,* **-gled, -gling,** *n.* —*v.t.* 1. to kill by compression of the windpipe, as by a cord around the neck. 2. to kill by stopping the breath in any manner; choke; stifle; suffocate. 3. to prevent the continuance, growth, rise, or action of; suppress. —*v.i.* 4. to be choked, stifled, or suffocated. —*n.* 5. (pl. construed as sing.) an infectious febrile disease of equine animals, characterized by catarrh of the upper air passages and suppuration of the submaxillary and other lymphatic glands; distemper. [ME, t. OF: m. *estrangler*, g. L *strangulāre*, t. Gk.: m. *strangalān*] —**stran′gler,** *n.*

strangle hold, 1. *Wrestling.* a hold by which the adversary's breathing is stopped. 2. anything which prevents motion or development of a person or group.

stran·gu·late (stráng′gyə lāt′), *v.t.,* **-lated, -lating.** 1. *Pathol., Surg.* to compress or constrict (a duct, intestine, vessel, etc.) so as to prevent circulation or suppress function. 2. to strangle. [t. L: m.s. *strangulātus,* pp., strangled] —**stran′gu·la′tion,** *n.*

stran·gu·ry (stráng′gyə rĭ), *n. Pathol.* a condition of the urinary organs in which the urine is painfully emitted, drop by drop. [ME, t. L: m.s. *strangūria,* t. Gk.: m. *strangourĭa*]

strap (stráp), *n., v.,* **strapped, strapping.** —*n.* 1. a narrow strip of flexible material, esp. leather, for fastening or holding things together, etc. 2. a looped band, as one at the top of a boot with which to draw it on, or one on a streetcar to hold onto, etc. 3. a strop for a razor. 4. a long, narrow piece or object; strip; band. 5. a straplike ornament, as a shoulder strap. —*v.t.* 6. to fasten or secure with a strap or straps. 7. to fasten (a thing) around something in the manner of a strap. 8. to sharpen on a strap or strop. 9. to beat or

flog with a strap. [var. of STROP] —**strap′like′,** *adj.*

strap·hang·er (stráp′hăng′ər), *n. Colloq.* a passenger in an overfull streetcar or the like who has to stand holding onto a strap suspended from above.

strap·pa·do (strə pā′dō, -pä′do), *n., pl.* **-does.** 1. a form of punishment or torture in which the victim, tied to a rope, was raised to a height and suddenly let fall almost to the ground. 2. the instrument used for this purpose. [t. It.: m. *strappata,* der. *strappare* drag, pull]

strap·per (stráp′ər), *n.* 1. one who or that which straps. 2. *Colloq.* a tall, robust person.

strap·ping (stráp′Yng), *adj. Colloq.* 1. tall, robust, and strongly built. 2. very large of its kind; whopping.

Stras·bourg (sträs′bûrg, sträz′bŏŏrg; *Fr.* sträz bŏŏr′), *n.* a fortress city in NE France, near the Rhine: cathedral; taken by Allied forces, Nov., 1944. 200,921 (1954). German, **Strass·burg** (shträs′bŏŏrкн).

strass (sträs), *n.* paste (def. 8). [t. G, t. F: m. *stras,* prob. named after Josef *Strasser,* the inventor]

stra·ta (strā′tə, străt′ə), *n.* a pl. of stratum.

strat·a·gem (strát′ə jəm), *n.* 1. a plan, scheme, or trick for deceiving the enemy. 2. any artifice, ruse, or trick. [t. F: m. *stratagème,* t. L: m. *stratēgēma,* t. Gk.]

stra·tal (strā′təl), *adj.* of a stratum or strata.

stra·te·gic (strə tē′jĭk), *adj.* 1. pertaining to, characterized by, or of the nature of strategy: *strategic movements.* 2. important in strategy: *a strategic point.* Also, **stra·te′gi·cal.** —**stra·te′gi·cal·ly,** *adv.*

strat·e·gist (strát′ə jĭst), *n.* one versed in strategy: *a great military strategist.*

strat·e·gy (strát′ə jĭ), *n., pl.* **-gies.** 1. Also, **stra·te·gics** (strə tē′jĭks). generalship; the science or art of combining and employing the means of war in planning and directing large military movements and operations. 2. the use, or a particular use, of this science or art. 3. skillful management in getting the better of an adversary or attaining an end. 4. the method of conducting operations, esp. by the aid of maneuvering or stratagem. [t. Gk.: m.s. *stratēgia* generalship]
—**Syn.** 1. A distinction is made between STRATEGY and TACTICS in military use, STRATEGY dealing with the planning and directing of projects, which involve the movements of forces, etc., and TACTICS rather with the actual processes of moving or handling forces.

Strat·ford (strát′fərd), *n.* a town in SW Connecticut, near Bridgeport. 45,012 (1960).

Stratford de Red·cliffe (də rĕd′klĭf). **Stratford Canning,** Viscount, 1786–1880, British diplomat.

Strat·ford-on-A·von (strát′fərd ŏn ā′vən), *n.* a town in central England, on the Avon river, in Warwickshire: Shakespeare's birthplace and burial place. 14,980 (1951). Also, **Strat′ford-up·on-A′von.**

strath (stráth; *Scot.* sträth), *n. Scot.* a wide valley. [t. Gaelic: m. *srath*]

Stratification

strati-, a word element representing **stratum,** as in *stratify.*

strat·i·fi·ca·tion (strát′ə fə kā′shən), *n.* 1. act of stratifying. 2. stratified state or appearance: *the stratification of medieval society.* 3. *Geol.* a. formation of strata; deposition or occurrence in strata. b. a stratum (def. 3).

strat·i·form (strát′ə fôrm′), *adj.* 1. *Geol.* occurring as a bed or beds; arranged in strata. 2. *Anat.* noting a cartilage occurring in thin layers in bones. 3. *Meteorol.* having the appearance or character of a stratus.

strat·i·fy (strát′ə fī′), *v.,* **-fied, -fying.** —*v.t.* 1. to form in strata or layers. 2. to preserve or germinate (seeds) by placing them between layers of earth. —*v.i.* 3. to form strata. 4. *Geol.* to lie in beds or layers. 5. *Sociol.* to develop horizontal status groups in society. [t. NL: m. *strătificāre.* See STRATI-, FY]

stratig., stratigraphy.

stra·tig·ra·phy (strə tĭg′rə fĭ), *n.* a branch of geology dealing with the classification, nomenclature, correlation, and interpretation of stratified rocks. —**strat·i·graph·ic** (strát′ə gráf′Yk), **strat′i·graph′i·cal,** *adj.*

strato-, a word element meaning "low and horizontal," as in *stratosphere.* [t. NL, comb. form repr. L *strātus,* a spreading out]

strat·o·cruis·er (strát′ə krŏŏ′zər), *n.* 1. a passenger or transport airplane designed to fly at stratospheric altitudes. 2. (*cap.*) a trademark for such an airplane.

stra·to·cu·mu·lus (strā′tō kū′myə ləs), *n., pl.* **-li** (-lī′). *Meteorol.* a low cloud or cloud layer consisting of large, dark, rounded masses, in groups, lines, or waves, the individual masses being larger than in an alto-cumulus.

strat·o·sphere (strát′ə sfĭr′, strā′tə-), *n. Meteorol.* 1. the region of the atmosphere outside the troposphere but within the ionosphere, characterized by relatively uniform temperature over considerable differences in altitude or by a markedly different lapse rate from that of the troposphere below. 2. *Obs.* all of the earth's atmosphere lying outside the troposphere. —**strat·o·spher·ic** (strát′ə sfĕr′Yk, strā′tə-), *adj.*

strat·o·vi·sion (strát′ə vYzh′ən), *n.* the transmission of television and FM programs from airplane, flying in the stratosphere, which extends the area over which broadcasts may be received.

stra·tum (strā′təm, străt′əm), *n.*, *pl.* **strata** (strā′tə, străt′ə), **stratums. 1.** a layer of material, formed either naturally or artificially, often one of a number of parallel layers placed one upon another. **2.** one of a number of portions likened to layers or levels. **3.** *Geol.* a single bed of sedimentary rock, generally consisting of one kind of matter representing continuous deposition. **4.** *Biol.* a layer of tissue; a lamella. **5.** a layer of the ocean or the atmosphere distinguished by natural or arbitrary limits. **6.** *Sociol.* a level or grade of a people or population with reference to social position or education: *the lowest stratum of society.* [NL; in L something spread out]

stra·tus (strā′təs), *n.*, *pl.* **-ti** (-tī). *Meteorol.* a continuous horizontal sheet of cloud, resembling fog but not resting on the ground, usually of uniform thickness and comparatively low altitude.

Straus (strous; *Ger.* shtrous), *n.* **Oscar** (ŏs′kər; *Ger.* ōs′kär) 1870–1954, Austrian composer.

Strauss (strous; *Ger.* shtrous), *n.* **1. David Friedrich** (dä′vĕt frē′drĭKH), 1808–74, German theologian and author. **2. Johann** (yō′hän), 1804–49, Austrian composer. **3.** his son, **Johann,** 1825–99, Austrian composer, esp. of waltzes. **4. Richard** (rĭcH′ərd; *Ger.* rĭ′KHärt), 1864–1949, German composer and conductor.

Stra·vin·ski (strə vĭn′skĭ; *Russ.* strä vēn′-), *n.* **Igor Fëdorovich** (ē′gôr fyô dô rô′vĭch), born 1882, Russian composer now in U.S.

straw (strô), *n.* **1.** a single stalk or stem, esp. of certain species of grain, chiefly wheat, rye, oats, and barley. **2.** a mass of such stalks, esp. after drying and threshing, used as fodder, as material for hats, etc. **3.** a hollow paper tube, plant stem, etc. used in drinking some beverages, etc. **4.** anything of trifling value or consequence: *not to care a straw.* —*adj.* **5.** of, pertaining to, or made of straw. **6.** of little value or consequence; worthless. **7.** sham; fictitious. [ME; OE *strēaw*, c. G *stroh*; akin to STREW]

straw·ber·ry (strô′bĕr′ĭ), *n.*, *pl.* **-ries. 1.** the fruit of any of the stemless herbs constituting the rosaceous genus *Fragaria*, consisting of an enlarged fleshy receptacle bearing achenes on its exterior. **2.** the plant bearing it.

strawberry bush, the wahoo[1] (def. 1).

strawberry shrub, any of various species of the genus *Calycanthus* (or *Butneria*), shrubs with dark-brownish or purplish-red flowers of distinctive fragrance.

strawberry tomato, 1. the small, edible, tomato-like fruit of the solanaceous *Physalis pruinosa.* **2.** the herbaceous plant bearing it.

strawberry tree, an evergreen ericaceous shrub or tree, *Arbutus Unedo*, a native of southern Europe, bearing a scarlet, strawberrylike fruit.

straw·board (strô′bōrd′), *n.* coarse, yellow paper board made of straw pulp, used in packing, and for making boxes, etc.

straw boss, *U.S. Colloq.* a subordinate boss.

straw color, a pale yellow similar to the color of straw. —**straw′-col′ored,** *adj.*

straw man, 1. a puppet made of straw. **2.** a person used by another, esp. a perjured witness. **3.** an unimportant person.

straw vote, *U.S.* an unofficial vote taken, as at a casual gathering or in a particular district, to obtain some indication of the general drift of opinion.

straw wine, wine (usually sweet and rich) from grapes that have been dried in the sun on a bed of straw.

straw·y (strô′ĭ), *adj.* **1.** of, containing, or resembling straw. **2.** strewed or thatched with straw.

stray (strā), *v.i.* **1.** to go from the proper course or place or beyond the proper limits, esp. without settled course or purpose; ramble; roam. **2.** to wander (fol. by *away, off, from, into, to*, etc.). **3.** to deviate, as from the set or right course; go astray. **4.** to digress. —*n.* **5.** a domestic animal found wandering at large or without an owner. **6.** any homeless or friendless creature or person; a person or thing that has strayed. **7.** (*pl.*) *Radio.* static. —*adj.* **8.** straying, or having strayed, as a domestic animal. **9.** found or occurring apart from others, or as an isolated or casual instance. **10.** *Radio.* undesired: *stray capacitance.* [aphetic var. of ME *astray*, t. OF: m.s. *estraier*, ult. g. L *extrā vagārī* wander outside] —**stray′er,** *n.*

streak (strēk), *n.* **1.** a long, narrow mark, smear, band of color, or the like: *streaks of mud, a streak of lightning.* **2.** a portion or layer of something, distinguished by color or nature from the rest; a vein or stratum: *streaks of fat in meat.* **3.** a vein, strain, or admixture of anything: *a streak of humor.* **4.** *U.S. Colloq.* a run (of luck): *to have a streak of bad luck.* **5.** *Mineral.* the line of powder obtained by scratching a mineral or rubbing it upon a hard, rough white surface, often differing in color from the mineral in the mass, and forming an important distinguishing character. **6.** *Bacteriol.* the inoculation of a medium with a loop which contains the material to be inoculated, by passing the loop in a direct or zigzag line over the medium, without scratching the surface. —*v.t.* **7.** to mark with a streak or streaks. **8.** to dispose in the form of a streak or streaks. —*v.i.* **9.** to become streaked. **10.** to flash or go rapidly, like a streak of lightning. [ME *streke,* OE *strica*; akin to STRIKE]

streak·y (strē′kĭ), *adj.,* **streakier, streakiest. 1.** occurring in streaks or a streak. **2.** marked with or char-

acterized by streaks. **3.** *Colloq.* varying or uneven in quality, etc. —**streak′i·ly,** *adv.* —**streak′i·ness,** *n.*

stream (strēm), *n.* **1.** a body of water flowing in a channel or bed, as a river, rivulet, or brook. **2.** a steady current in water, as in a river or the ocean: *to row against the stream.* **3.** any flow of water or other liquid or fluid: *streams of blood.* **4.** a current of air, gas, or the like; a beam or trail of light. **5.** a continuous flow or succession of anything: *a stream of words.* **6.** prevailing direction; drift: *the stream of opinion.* —*v.i.* **7.** to flow, pass, or issue in a stream, as water, tears, blood, etc. **8.** to send forth or throw off a stream; run or flow (fol. by *with*): *eyes streaming with tears.* **9.** to extend in a beam or trail, as light. **10.** to move or proceed continuously like a flowing stream, as a procession. **11.** to wave or float outward, as a flag in the wind. **12.** to hang in a loose, flowing manner, as long hair. —*v.t.* **13.** to send forth or discharge in a stream. **14.** to cause to stream or float outward, as a flag. **15.** to overspread or suffuse with a stream or streams. [ME; OE *strēam,* c. G *strom*] —**Syn. 1.** STREAM, CURRENT refer to a steady flow. In this use they are interchangeable. In the sense of running water, however, a STREAM is a flow which may be as small as a brook or as large as a river: *a number of streams have their sources in mountains.* CURRENT refers to the most rapidly moving part of the stream: *this river has a swift current.*

stream·er (strē′mər), *n.* **1.** something that streams. **2.** a long, narrow flag or pennant. **3.** a long, flowing ribbon, feather, or the like, used for ornament, as in dress. **4.** any long, narrow piece or thing, as a spray of a plant or a strip of cloud. **5.** a stream of light, esp. one appearing in some forms of the aurora borealis. **6.** the headline which extends across the width of the newspaper, usually at the top of the first page.

stream·let (strēm′lĭt), *n.* a small stream; a rivulet.

stream·line (strēm′līn′), *adj., n. v.,* **-lined, -lining.** —*adj.* **1.** denoting, pertaining to, or having a shape designed to offer the least possible resistance in passing through the air, etc., allowing an uninterrupted flow of the fluid about it: *a streamline automobile.* —*n.* **2.** a teardrop line of contour, as of an automobile, belonging to a streamline airfoil shape. **3.** *Physics* a line of motion in a fluid; the actual path of a particle in a flowing fluid mass whose motion is steady. —*v.t.* **4.** to shape with a streamline.

stream of consciousness, *Psychol.* thought regarded as a succession of states constantly moving onward in time.

stream-of-consciousness novel, a novel in which the action is reported through, or along with, the thoughts of one or several characters.

stream·y (strē′mĭ), *adj.* **1.** abounding in streams or watercourses. **2.** flowing in a stream; streaming.

street (strēt), *n.* **1.** a public way or road, paved or unpaved, in a village, town, or city, usually including a sidewalk or sidewalks, and having buildings or lots on one side or both sides. **2.** such a way or road together with the adjacent buildings or lots. **3.** the roadway, or way for vehicles, as distinguished from the sidewalk: *to walk in the street.* **4.** a main way or thoroughfare, in distinction from a lane, alley, or the like. **5.** the inhabitants of or the people in a street. **6.** **the street,** the principal business or financial section of a city. [ME; d. OE *strēt,* OE *strǣt,* c. D *straat,* G *strasse,* all ult. t. L: m. (*via*) *strāta* paved (road)] —**Syn. 1.** STREET, ALLEY, AVENUE, BOULEVARD all refer to public ways or roads in municipal areas. A STREET is a road in a village, town, or city, esp. a road lined with houses. An ALLEY is a narrow street or footway, esp. at the rear of a row of houses or lots. An AVENUE is properly a prominent street, often one bordered by fine residences and impressive buildings, or with a row of trees on each side. A BOULEVARD is a beautiful, broad street, lined with rows of stately trees, esp. used as a promenade. In some cities STREET and AVENUE are used interchangeably, the only difference being that those running one direction (say, North and South) are given one designation and those crossing them are given the other.

street Arab, a child having no home and making his way by begging, stealing, etc.

street·car (strēt′kär′), *n.* *U.S.* a public passenger car running regularly along certain streets, usually on rails.

street·walk·er (strēt′wô′kər), *n.* one who walks the streets, esp. a soliciting prostitute.

strength (strĕngkth, strĕngth), *n.* **1.** the quality or state of being strong; bodily or muscular power; vigor, as in robust health. **2.** mental power, force, or vigor. **3.** moral power, firmness, or courage. **4.** power by reason of influence, authority, resources, numbers, etc. **5.** number, as of men or ships in a force or body: *a regiment of a strength of three thousand.* **6.** effective force, potency, or cogency, as of inducements or arguments. **7.** power of resisting force, strain, wear, etc. **8.** vigor of action, language, feeling, etc. **9.** large proportion of the effective or essential properties of a beverage, chemical, or the like. **10.** a particular proportion of these properties; intensity, as of light, color, sound, flavor, or odor. **11.** something that makes strong; a support or stay. **12.** *Exchanges.* a commodity or price which is either firm or rising. **13. on the strength of,** relying on. [ME; OE *strength(u),* der. STRONG] —**Syn. 4.** STRENGTH, POWER, MIGHT suggest capacity to do something. STRENGTH is inherent capacity to manifest energy, to endure, and to resist. POWER is capacity to do work and to act. FORCE is the exercise of power: *one has the power to do something; he exerts force when he does it; and he* *has sufficient strength to complete it.* MIGHT is power or strength in a great or overwhelming degree: *the might of an army.* —Ant. 4. weakness.

strength·en (strĕngk'thən, strĕng'-), *v.t.* 1. to make stronger; give strength to. —*v.i.* 2. to gain strength; grow stronger. —**strength'en·er,** *n.*

stren·u·ous (strĕn'yoo əs), *adj.* 1. vigorous, energetic, or zealously active, as a person, etc. 2. characterized by vigorous exertion, as action, efforts, life, etc.: *a strenuous opposition.* [t. L: m. *strēnuus;* akin to Gk. *strēnēs* strong] —**stren'u·ous·ly,** *adv.* —**stren'u·ous·ness, stren·u·os·i·ty** (strĕn'yoo ŏs'ə tĭ), *n.* —**Syn.** 1. See **active.**

strep·i·tous (strĕp'ə təs), *adj.* noisy. [f. s. L *strepitus* noise + -ous]

strepto-, a word element meaning "curved," as in *streptococcus.* [t. Gk., comb. form of *streptós*]

strep·to·coc·cus (strĕp'tə kŏk'əs), *n., pl.* -**cocci** (-kŏk'sī). *Bacteriol.* one of a group of organisms (genus *Streptococcus*) which divide in one plane only, and remain attached to one another, forming long, short, or conglomerated chains. Some cause very important diseases such as scarlet fever, erysipelas, puerperal sepsis, sepsis, etc. —**strep·to·coc·cic** (strĕp'tə kŏk'-sĭk), **strep·to·coc·cal** (strĕp'tə kŏk'əl), *adj.*

strep·to·my·cin (strĕp'tō mī'sĭn), *n.* a recently developed antibiotic similar to penicillin, which has proved more effective in combatting certain microbic infections than penicillin.

strep·to·thri·cin (strĕp'tō thrī'sĭn), *n.* an antibacterial substance derived from the soil fungus, *Actinomyces lavendulae.* Also, **strep'to·thry'sin.**

Stre·se·mann (shtrā'zə män'), *n.* **Gustav** (gŏos'täf), 1878–1929, German statesman.

stress (strĕs), *v.t.* 1. to lay stress or emphasis on; emphasize. 2. *Phonet.* to pronounce strongly or with a stress accent. 3. to subject to stress or strain. 4. *Mech.* to subject to mechanical stress. [v. use of STRESS, n.; r. ME *stress,* prob. t. OF: m.s. *estrecier,* ult. der. L *strictus,* pp., drawn tight, compressed] —*n.* 5. importance or significance attached to a thing; emphasis: *to lay stress upon successive incidents.* 6. *Phonet.* relative loudness resulting from special effort or emphasis in utterance. 7. *Pros.* accent or emphasis on syllables in a metrical pattern. 8. emphasis or accent on syllables in speech, as distinct from emphasis placed on a syllable because of the metrical pattern. 9. an accented or stressed syllable. 10. emphasis in music, rhythm, etc. 11. the physical pressure, pull, or other force exerted on one thing by another; strain. 12. *Mech.* **a.** the action on a body of any system of balanced forces whereby strain or deformation results. **b.** the amount of stress, usually measured in number of pounds per square inch. **c.** a load, force, or system of forces producing a strain. **d.** the internal resistance or reaction of an elastic body to the external forces applied to it. 13. *Rare.* strong or straining exertion. [apthetic var. of DISTRESS]

-stress, a feminine equivalent of *-ster,* as in *seamstress, songstress.* [f. *-str* (syncopated var. of *-STER* + -ESS]

stretch (strĕch), *v.t.* 1. to draw out or extend (oneself, the body, limbs, wings, etc.) to the full length or extent (often fol. by *out*): *to stretch oneself out on the ground.* 2. to hold out, reach forth, or extend (the hand or something held, the head, etc.). 3. to extend, spread, or place so as to reach from one point or place to another: *to stretch a rope across a road.* 4. to draw tight or taut: *to stretch the strings of a violin.* 5. to strain (nerves, etc.) to the utmost, as by exertion. 6. to lengthen, widen, distend, or enlarge by tension: *to stretch a rubber band.* 7. to draw out, extend, or enlarge unduly: *clothes stretched at the elbows.* 8. to extend or force beyond the natural or proper limits; strain: *to stretch the facts.* —*v.i.* 9. to recline at full length (usually fol. by *out*): *to stretch out on a couch.* 10. to extend the hand, or reach, as for something. 11. to extend over a distance or area or in a particular direction: *the forest stretches for miles.* 12. to stretch oneself by extending the limbs, straining the muscles, etc. 13. to become stretched, or admit of being stretched, to greater length, width, etc., as any elastic material. —*n.* 14. act of stretching. 15. state of being stretched. 16. a continuous length, distance, tract, or expanse: *a stretch of meadow.* 17. one of the two straight sides of a racecourse, as distinguished from the bend or curve at each end, esp. that part of the course (**home stretch**) between the last turn and the winning post. 18. an extent in time or duration: *a stretch of ten years.* 19. *Slang.* a term of imprisonment. [ME; OE *streccan,* c. G *strecken*] —**stretch'a·ble,** *adj.* —**Syn.** 6. See **lengthen.**

stretch·er (strĕch'ər), *n.* 1. a kind of litter, usually of canvas stretched on a frame, esp. for carrying the sick, wounded, or dead. 2. one who or that which stretches. 3. any of various instruments for extending, widening, distending, etc. 4. a bar, beam, or fabricated material, serving as a tie or brace. 5. a brick or stone laid horizontally with its length in the direction of the face of a wall, usually planned to give added strength to the structure. 6. a simple wooden framework on which the canvas of an oil painting is stretched.

stretch·er·bear·er (strĕch'ər bâr'ər), *n.* a man who helps carry a stretcher, as in removing the wounded from a battlefield. Also, **stretch'er·man** (strĕch'ər mən).

stretch-out (strĕch'out'), *n.* *U.S.* 1. deliberate extension of time for meeting a production quota. 2. a method of mill management by which employees do additional work without commensurate increase in wages.

stretch·y (strĕch'ĭ), *adj.* 1. capable of being stretched; elastic. 2. liable to stretch unduly.

stret·ta (strĕt'tä), *n., pl.* -**te** (-tĕ), -**tas.** *Music.* 1. a concluding passage taken in an accelerated speed. 2. stretto.

stret·to (strĕt'tō), *n., pl.* -**ti** (-tĕ), -**tos.** *Music.* (in a fugue) the close overlapping of voices, each beginning very shortly after the preceding one, often the final section. [t. It.: narrow, g. L *strictus,* pp., drawn tight]

strew (strōō), *v.t.,* **strewed, strewed** or **strewn, strewing.** 1. to let fall in separate pieces or particles over a surface; scatter or sprinkle: *to strew seed in a garden bed.* 2. to cover or overspread (a surface, place, etc.) with something scattered or sprinkled: *to strew a floor with rushes.* 3. to be scattered or sprinkled over (a surface, etc.). [ME *strewe,* OE *strēowian,* c. G *streuen*] —**Syn.** 1. See **sprinkle.**

stri·a (strī'ə), *n., pl.* **striae** (strī'ē). 1. a slight furrow or ridge; a narrow stripe or streak, esp. one of a number in parallel arrangement. 2. (*pl.*) *Geol.* scratches or tiny grooves on the surface of a rock, resulting from the action of moving ice, as of a glacier. 3. (*pl.*) *Mineral.* parallel lines or tiny grooves on the surface of a crystal, or on a cleavage face of a crystal, due to its molecular organization. [t. L: furrow, channel]

stri·ate (*v.* strī'āt; *adj.* strī'ĭt, -āt) *v.,* -**ated, -ating,** *adj.* —*v.t.* 1. to mark with striae; furrow; stripe; streak. —*adj.* 2. Also, **stri'at·ed.** marked with striae; furrowed; striped; streaked.

stri·a·tion (strī ā'shən), *n.* 1. striated condition or appearance. 2. a stria; one of many parallel striae.

strick·en (strĭk'ən), *adj.* 1. struck; hit or wounded by a weapon, missile, or the like. 2. smitten or afflicted, as with disease, trouble, or sorrow. 3. deeply affected, as with horror, fear, or other emotions. 4. characterized by or showing the effects of affliction, trouble, misfortune, a mental blow, etc.

strick·le (strĭk'əl), *n., v.,* -**led, -ling.** —*n.* 1. a straightedge used to sweep off heaped-up grain or the like to a level with the rim of a measure. 2. *Obs.* a piece of wood covered with grease and sand, emery, etc., to sharpen scythes. —*v.t.* 3. to sweep or remove with a strickle. [ME *strikylle,* OE *stricel;* akin to STRIKE]

strict (strĭkt), *adj.* 1. characterized by or acting in close conformity to requirements or principles: *strict observance.* 2. stringent or exacting in requirements, obligations, etc.: *strict laws, a strict judge.* 3. closely or rigorously enforced or maintained. 4. exact or precise: *a strict statement of facts.* 5. narrowly or carefully limited: *a strict construction of the Constitution.* 6. close, careful, or minute: *a strict search.* 7. absolute, perfect, or complete: *told in strict confidence.* 8. *Obs.* drawn tight or close. [t. L: s. *strictus,* pp., drawn together, tight, severe] —**strict'ly,** *adv.* —**strict'ness,** *n.*

—**Syn.** 1. STRICT, RIGID, RIGOROUS, STRINGENT imply inflexibility, severity, and an exacting quality. STRICT "drawn close or tight" implies great exactness, esp. in the observance or enforcement of rules: *strict discipline.* RIGID, literally stiff or unbending, applies to that which is (often unnecessarily or narrowly) inflexible: *rigid economy.* RIGOROUS, with the same literal meaning, applies to that which is severe, exacting, and uncompromising, esp. in action or application: *rigorous self-denial.* STRINGENT applies to that which is vigorously exacting and severe: *stringent measures to suppress disorder.* —Ant. 1. lax.

stric·tion (strĭk'shən), *n.* act of drawing tight, constricting, or straining. [t. L: s. *strictio*]

stric·ture (strĭk'chər), *n.* 1. a remark or comment, esp. an adverse criticism. 2. a morbid contraction of any passage or duct of the body. 3. *Rare.* a drawing or binding tightly, or something that binds tightly. 4. *Obs.* strictness. [ME, t. L: m. *strictūra*]

stride (strīd), *v.,* **strode** or **stridden, striding,** *n.* —*v.i.* 1. to walk with long steps, as with vigor, haste, impatience, or arrogance. 2. to take a long step. 3. to straddle. —*v.t.* 4. to walk with long steps along, on, through, over, etc.: *to stride the deck.* 5. to pass over or across by one stride: *to stride a ditch.* 6. to straddle. —*n.* 7. a striding or a striding gait. 8. a long step in walking. 9. (in animal locomotion) act of progressive movement completed when all the feet are returned to the same relative position as at the beginning. 10. the distance covered by such a movement. 11. a regular or steady course, pace, etc.: *to hit one's stride.* 12. a step forward in development or progress: *rapid strides in mastering algebra.* [ME; OE *strīdan,* c. LG *strīden.* Cf. also G *streiten* quarrel] —**strid'er,** *n.*

stri·dent (strī'dənt), *adj.* making or having a harsh sound; grating; creaking. [t. L: s. *stridens,* ppr., creaking] —**stri'dence, stri'den·cy,** *n.* —**stri'dent·ly,** *adv.*

stri·dor (strī'dôr), *n.* 1. a harsh, grating, or creaking sound. 2. *Pathol.* a harsh respiratory sound due to any of various forms of obstruction. [t. L]

strid·u·late (strĭj'ə lāt'), *v.i.,* -**lated, -lating.** to produce a shrill, grating sound, as a cricket does, by rubbing together certain parts of the body; shrill. —**strid'u·la'tion,** *n.* —**strid·u·la·to·ry** (strĭj'ə lə tôr'ĭ), *adj.*

strid·u·lous (strĭj'ə ləs), *adj.* 1. making or having a harsh or grating sound. 2. *Pathol.* pertaining to or

ăct, āble, dâre, ärt; ĕbb, ēqual; Ĭf, īce; hŏt, ōver, ôrder, oil, bŏŏk, ōōze, out; ŭp, ūse, ûrge; ə = a in alone; ch, chief; g, give; ng, ring; sh, shoe; th, thin; th̶, that; zh, vision. See the full key on inside cover.

characterized by stridor. [t. L: m. *strīdulus*] **—strid′u·lous·ly,** *adv.* **—strid′u·lous·ness,** *n.*

strife (strīf), *n.* **1.** conflict, discord, or variance: *to be at strife.* **2.** a quarrel, struggle, or clash. **3.** *Obs. or Rare.* strenuous effort. **4.** *Obs. or Rare.* competition or rivalry. [ME, t. OF: aphetic m. *estrif.* See STRIVE]

strig·il (strĭj′əl), *n.* **1.** an instrument with a curved blade, used by the ancient Greeks and Romans for scraping the skin at the bath and in the gymnasium. **2.** *Archit.* one of a series of decorative S-shaped flutings, esp. in Roman architecture. [t. L: s. *strigilis*]

stri·gose (strī′gōs, strĭ gōs′), *adj.* **1.** *Bot.* set with stiff bristles or hairs; hispid. **2.** *Zool.* marked with fine, closely set ridges, grooves, or points. [t. NL: m.s. *strigōsus*, der. L *striga* row of bristles]

strike (strīk), *v.*, **struck, struck** or (esp. for 27–30) **stricken, striking,** *n.* **—***v.t.* **1.** to deliver a blow, stroke, or thrust with (the hand, a weapon, etc.). **2.** to deal a blow or stroke to (a person or thing), as with the fist, a weapon, or a hammer; hit. **3.** to deal or inflict (a blow, stroke, etc.). **4.** to drive or thrust forcibly: *to strike the hands together.* **5.** to produce (fire, sparks, light, etc.) by percussion, friction, etc.; cause (a match) to ignite by friction. **6.** to smite or blast with some natural or supernatural agency: *struck by lightning.* **7.** to come into forcible contact or collision with: *the ship struck a rock.* **8.** to fall upon (something), as light or sound does. **9.** to enter the mind of; occur to: *a happy thought struck him.* **10.** to catch or arrest (the eye, etc.): *the first object that strikes one's sight.* **11.** to impress strongly: *a picture which strikes one's fancy.* **12.** to impress in a particular manner: *how does it strike you?* **13.** to come across, meet with, or encounter suddenly or unexpectedly: *to strike the name of a friend in a newspaper.* **14.** to come upon or find (ore, oil, etc.) in prospecting, boring, or the like. **15.** to send down or put forth (a root, etc.), as a plant, cutting, etc. **16.** to balance (a ledger, etc.). **17.** to remove from the stage (the scenery and properties of an act or scene). **18.** *Naut.* **a.** to lower or take down (a sail, mast, etc.). **b.** to lower (a sail, flag, etc.) as a salute or as a sign of surrender. **c.** to lower (something) into the hold of a vessel by means of a rope and tackle. **19.** to hook (a fish) by a jerk or sudden movement of the tackle. **20.** to harpoon (a whale). **21.** to make level or smooth, in various technical uses. **22.** to make level or even, as a measure of grain, salt, etc., by drawing a strickle across the top, or, as potatoes, by making the projections equal to the depressions. **23.** to efface or cancel with, or as with, the stroke of a pen (fol. by *off*, *out*, etc.). **24.** to stamp (a coin, medal, etc.) or impress (a device), by a stroke. **25.** to remove or separate with a cut (usually fol. by *off*). **26.** to indicate (the hour of day) by a stroke or strokes, as a clock: *to strike twelve.* **27.** to afflict suddenly, as with disease, suffering, or death. **28.** to affect deeply or overwhelm, as with terror, fear, etc. **29.** to render (blind, dumb, etc.) suddenly, as if by a blow. **30.** to cause (a feeling) to enter suddenly: *to strike terror into a person.* **31.** to start suddenly into (vigorous movement): *the horse struck a gallop.* **32.** to assume (an attitude or posture). **33.** to cause (chill, warmth, etc.) to pass or penetrate quickly. **34.** to come upon or reach in traveling or in a course of procedure. **35.** to make, conclude, or ratify (an agreement, treaty, etc.). **36.** to enter upon or form (an acquaintance, etc.) (usually fol. by *up*). **37.** to estimate or determine (a mean or average). **38.** to break (camp). **39.** to leave off (work), as a coercive measure, or as at the close of the day. **40.** *Baseball.* (of the pitcher) to cause (a batter) to strike out (fol. by *out*).

—*v.i.* **41.** to deal or aim a blow or stroke, as with the fist, a weapon, or a hammer; make an attack. **42.** to knock, rap, or tap. **43.** to hit or dash on or against something, as a moving body does; come into forcible contact. **44.** to run upon a bank, rock, or other obstacle, as a ship does. **45.** to fall, as light or sound does (fol. by *on* or *upon*). **46.** to make an impression on the mind, senses, etc., as something seen or heard. **47.** to come suddenly or unexpectedly (fol. by *on* or *upon*): *to strike on a new way of doing a thing.* **48.** to sound by percussion: *the clock strikes.* **49.** to be indicated by such sounding: *the hour has struck.* **50.** to be ignited by friction, as a match. **51.** to make a stroke, as with the arms or legs in swimming or with an oar in rowing. **52.** to produce a sound, music, etc., by touching a string or playing upon an instrument. **53.** to take root, as a slip of a plant. **54.** to go, proceed, or advance, esp. in a new direction. **55.** *U.S. Navy.* to train for promotion to third-class petty-officer rank. **56.** (of an employee or employees) to engage in a strike. **57.** *Naut.* **a.** to lower the flag or colors, esp. as a salute or as a sign of surrender. **b.** to run up the white flag of surrender. **58.** *Angling.* to swallow or grasp the bait (applied to fish). **59. strike out,** *Baseball.* (of a batter) to make three strikes and be declared "out."

—*n.* **60.** an act of striking. **61.** a concerted stopping of work or withdrawal of workers' services in order to compel an employer to accede to workers' demands or in protest against terms or conditions imposed by employer. **62.** *Baseball.* an unsuccessful attempt on the part of the batter to hit a pitched ball, or anything ruled to be equivalent to this. **63.** *U.S. Bowling.* **a.** the knocking down of all the pins with the first bowl. **b.** the score made by bowling a strike. **64.** *Brewing.* degree of excellence. **65.** *Angling.* the process of grabbing at the bait. **66.** *Coining.* a quantity or number struck at one time. **67.** *Geol.* **a.** the direction of the line formed by the intersection of the bedding plane of a bed or stratum of sedimentary rock with a horizontal plane. **b.** the direction or trend of a structural feature, as an anticlinal axis or the lineation resulting from metamorphism. **68.** the discovery of a rich vein of ore in mining, of petroleum in boring, etc.

[ME; OE *strīcan*, c. G *streichen.* Cf. STREAK, STROKE[1]]

—Syn. 2. STRIKE, HIT, KNOCK imply suddenly bringing one body in contact with another. STRIKE suggests such an action in a general way: *to strike a child.* HIT is less formal than STRIKE, and often implies giving a single blow, but usually a strong one and definitely aimed: *to hit a baseball.* To KNOCK is to strike, often with a tendency to displace the object struck; it also means to strike repeatedly: *to knock someone down, to knock at a door.* See **beat.** **—Ant. 1.** miss.

strike·break·er (strīk′brā′kər), *n.* one who takes part in breaking up a strike of workers, either by working or by furnishing workers for the employer.

strike·break·ing (strīk′brā′kĭng), *n.* action directed at breaking up a strike of workers.

strike fault, *Geol.* a fault the trend of which is parallel to the strike of the affected rocks.

strik·er (strī′kər), *n.* **1.** one who or that which strikes. **2.** a worker who is on strike. **3.** the clapper in a clock that strikes the hours or rings an alarm. **4.** one who strikes fish, etc., with a spear or harpoon. **5.** *U.S. Army.* a private who acts as a voluntary paid servant to a commissioned officer. **6.** *U.S. Navy.* an enlisted man in training for a specific third-class petty-officer rating. **7.** *Whaling.* the harpoon.

strik·ing (strī′kĭng), *adj.* **1.** that strikes. **2.** attractive; impressive. **3.** being on strike, as workmen. **—strik′ing·ly,** *adv.*

Strind·berg (strĭnd′bûrg; *Swed.* strĭn′băr′y), *n.* **Johan August** (yōō′hän ou′gŭst), 1849–1912, Swedish novelist, dramatist, and essayist.

string (strĭng), *n.*, *v.*, **strung; strung** or (*Rare*) **stringed; stringing.** **—***n.* **1.** a line, cord, or thread, used for tying parcels, etc. **2.** a narrow strip of cloth, leather, etc., for tying parts together: *strings of a bonnet.* **3.** something resembling a string or thread. **4.** a number of objects, as beads or pearls, threaded or strung on a cord. **5.** any series of things arranged or connected in a line or following closely one after another: *a string of islands or of vehicles, to ask a string of questions.* **6.** a set or number, as of animals: *a string of race horses.* **7.** (in musical instruments) a tightly stretched cord or wire which produces a tone when caused to vibrate, as by plucking, striking, or friction of a bow. **8.** (*pl.*) **a.** stringed musical instruments, esp. such as are played with a bow. **b.** players on such instruments in an orchestra or band. **9.** a cord or fiber in a plant. **10.** the tough piece uniting the two parts of a pod: *the strings of beans.* **11.** *Archit.* **a.** a stringcourse. **b.** one of the sloping sides of a stair, supporting the treads and risers. **12.** *Billiards.* **a.** a stroke made by each player from the head of the table to the opposite cushion and back, to determine, by means of the resultant positions of the balls, who shall open the game. **b.** a line from behind which the cue ball is played after being out of play (**string line**). **13.** a series of players listed in accordance with their skill. **14.** *Colloq.* limitations on any proposal: *a proposal with no strings attached.* **15.** *Obs.* a ligament, tendon, nerve, or the like, in an animal body.

—*v.t.* **16.** to furnish with or as with a string or strings. **17.** to extend or stretch (a cord, etc.) from one point to another. **18.** to thread on, or as on, a string: *to string beads.* **19.** to connect in, or as in, a line; arrange in a series or succession. **20.** to adjust the string of (a bow); tighten the strings of (a musical instrument) to the required pitch. **21.** to provide or adorn with something suspended or slung: *a room strung with festoons.* **22.** to deprive of a string or strings; strip the strings from: *to string beans.* **23.** to make tense, as the sinews, nerves, mind, etc. **24.** to kill by hanging (usually fol. by *up*). **25.** *Slang.* to fool or hoax.

—*v.i.* **26.** to form into or move in a string or series. **27.** to form into a string or strings, as a glutinous substance does when pulled.

[ME; OE *streng*, c. D *streng;* akin to G *strang*, L *stringere* bind, Gk. *strangálē* halter] **—string′like′,** *adj.*

string bass, double bass (def. 1).

string bean, **1.** any of various kinds of bean (plant) the unripe pods of which are used as food, usually after stripping off the fibrous thread along the side (usually called *snap bean* by botanists). **2.** the pod itself.

string·board (strĭng′bōrd′), *n.* *Archit.* a board or the like covering the ends of the steps in a staircase.

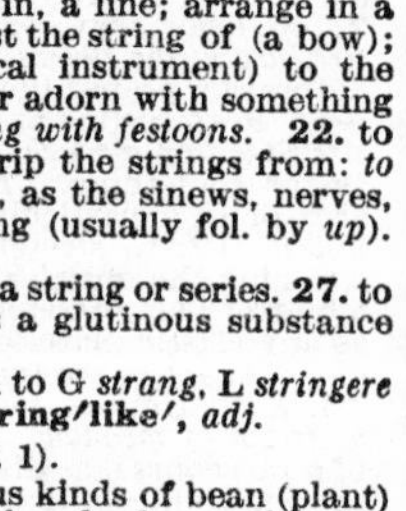

S, Stringcourse

string·course (strĭng′kōrs′), *n.* *Archit.* a horizontal band or course of stone, etc., projecting beyond or flush with the face of a building, often molded and sometimes richly carved.

stringed (strĭngd), *adj.* **1.** (of a musical instrument) having a string or strings. **2.** pertaining to such instruments: *stringed music.*

strin·gen·cy (strĭn′jən sĭ), *n.*, *pl.* **-cies.** **1.** stringent

b., blend of, blended; c., cognate with; d., dialect, dialectal; der., derived from; f., formed from; g., going back to; m., modification of; r., replacing; s., stem of; t., taken from; ?, perhaps. See the full key on inside cover.

character or condition. **2.** strictness; closeness; rigor. **3.** tightness; straitness: *stringency in the money market.*

strin·gen·do (strĕn jĕn′dō), *adj., adv. Music.* progressively quickening the tempo. [It., ppr. of *stringere* compress, draw tight, g. L]

strin·gent (strĭn′jənt), *adj.* **1.** narrowly binding; rigorously exacting; strict; severe: *stringent laws.* **2.** compelling, constraining, or urgent: *stringent necessity.* **3.** convincing or forcible, as arguments, etc. **4.** (of the money market) tight; characterized by a shortage of loan money. [L: s. *stringens,* ppr., drawing tight] —**strin′gent·ly,** *adv.* —**Syn. 1.** See **strict.**

string·er (strĭng′ər), *n.* **1.** one who or that which strings. **2.** *Building, etc.* **a.** a long horizontal timber connecting upright posts, supporting a floor, or the like. **b.** a cross member keeping horizontal timbers in position. **3.** *Archit.* the string of a stair. **4.** *Railroading.* a longitudinal timber spanning a bent of a railway trestle or bridge, and bearing ballast, bridge ties, or both.

string·halt (strĭng′hôlt′), *n.* a nervous disorder in horses, causing exaggerated flexing movements of the hind legs in walking. Also, **springhalt.**

string line, *Billiards, Pool.* string (def. 12b).

string·piece (strĭng′pēs′), *n. Building, etc.* a long piece of timber or the like (esp. a horizontal one) in a framework or structure, as for strengthening the structure or connecting or supporting parts.

string tie, a very narrow necktie.

string·y (strĭng′ĭ), *adj.,* **stringier, stringiest. 1.** resembling a string; consisting of strings or stringlike pieces. **2.** coarsely or toughly fibrous, as meat. **3.** sinewy or wiry, as a person. **4.** ropy, as a glutinous liquid. —**string′i·ness,** *n.*

strip¹ (strĭp), *v.,* **stripped** or (*Rare*) **stript; stripping.** —*v.t.* **1.** to deprive of covering: *to strip a fruit of its rind.* **2.** to deprive of clothing; make bare or naked. **3.** to take away or remove: *to strip pictures from a wall.* **4.** to deprive or divest: *to strip a tree of its fruit.* **5.** to clear out or empty: *to strip a house of its contents.* **6.** to deprive of equipment; dismantle: *to strip a ship of rigging.* **7.** to rob, plunder, or dispossess: *to strip a man of his possessions.* **8.** to separate the leaves from the stalks of (tobacco). **9.** to remove the midrib, etc., from (tobacco leaves). **10.** *Mach.* to tear off the thread of (a screw, bolt, etc.) or the teeth of (a gear, etc.), as by applying too much force. **11.** to draw the last milk from (a cow), esp. by a stroking and compressing movement. **12.** to draw out (milk) thus. —*v.i.* **13.** to strip something; esp., to strip oneself of clothes. **14.** to become stripped. [ME *stripe,* OE *-strȳpan,* c. D *stroopen*]
—**Syn. 7.** STRIP, DEPRIVE, DISPOSSESS, DIVEST imply more or less forcibly taking something away from someone. To STRIP is to take something completely (often violently), from a person or thing so as to leave in a destitute or powerless state: *to strip a man of all his property, the bark from a tree.* To DEPRIVE is to take away forcibly or coercively what one has, or to withhold what one might have: *to deprive one of his income.* To DISPOSSESS is to deprive of the holding or use of something: *to dispossess the renters of a house.* DIVEST usually means depriving of rights, privileges, powers, or the like: *to divest a king of authority.* —**Ant. 4.** supply, furnish.

strip² (strĭp), *n., v.,* **stripped, stripping.** —*n.* **1.** a narrow piece, comparatively long and usually of uniform width: *a strip of cloth, metal, land, etc.* **2.** a continuous series of pictures, as in a newspaper, illustrating incidents, conversation, etc. See **comic strip. 3.** *Philately.* three or more stamps joined together in a horizontal or vertical row. —*v.t.* **4.** to cut into strips. [late ME, ? t. MLG: m. *strippe* strap; akin to STRIPE¹]

stripe¹ (strīp), *n., v.,* **striped, striping.** —*n.* **1.** a relatively long, narrow band of a different color, appearance, weave, material, or nature from the rest of a surface or thing: *the stripes of a zebra.* **2.** a striped fabric or material. **3.** a strip of braid or the like. **4.** (*pl.*) a number or combination of such strips, worn on a military, naval, or other uniform as a badge of rank, service, good conduct, wounds, etc. **5.** a strip, or long, narrow piece of anything. **6.** a streak or layer of a different nature within a substance. **7.** style, variety, sort, or kind: *a man of quite a different stripe.* —*v.t.* **8.** to mark or furnish with a stripe or stripes [t. MD]

stripe² (strīp), *n.,* a stroke with a whip, rod, etc., as in punishment. [late ME; ? special use of STRIPE¹]

striped (strīpt, strī′pĭd), *adj.* having stripes or bands.

striped bass, an American game fish, *Roccus saxatilis,* with blackish stripes along the sides, common on the coasts of the U.S.

striped squirrel, any squirrel with stripes on its back, as a chipmunk.

strip·er (strī′pər), *n. Slang.* **1.** a naval officer who wears stripes on the sleeve of his uniform: *a four-striper* (*a naval captain*). **2.** an enlisted man of any of the armed services, who wears stripes on his sleeve denoting years of service: *a six-striper.*

strip film, film in strips approximately one foot long, forming part of the visual aid materials in a library.

strip·ling (strĭp′lĭng), *n.* a youth just passing from boyhood to manhood. [f. STRIP² + -LING¹]

strip·per (strĭp′ər), *n.* **1.** one who strips. **2.** that which strips, as an appliance or machine for stripping.

strip tease, a burlesque act in which a woman disrobes garment by garment to the accompaniment of music. —**strip-tease** (strĭp′tēz′), *adj.*

strive (strīv), *v.i.,* **strove, striven, striving. 1.** to exert oneself vigorously; try hard. **2.** to make strenuous efforts toward any end: *to strive for success.* **3.** to contend in opposition, battle, or any conflict. **4.** to struggle vigorously, as in opposition or resistance: *to strive against fate.* **5.** *Archaic.* to contend in rivalry; vie. [ME, t. OF: m. *estriver* quarrel, contend; of Gmc. orig.] —**striv′er,** *n.* —**Syn. 1.** See **try.**

strobe (strōb), *n. Colloq., Photog.* a high-intensity flash device used in stroboscopic photography. [short for STROBOSCOPE]

stro·bi·la (strō bī′lə), *n. Zool.* the entire body of a tapeworm. [NL, t. Gk.: m. *strobilē* plug of lint twisted into the shape of a fir cone]

strob·ile (strŏb′ĭl), *n. Bot.* **1.** the more or less conical multiple fruit of the pine, fir, etc. **2.** a conelike mass of sporophylls found in certain club mosses and ferns. [t. Gk. See STROBILA]

strob·o·scope (strŏb′ə skōp′), *n.* an instrument used in studying the motion of a body (esp. one in rapid revolution or vibration) by rendering it visible at frequent intervals, as by illuminating it with an electric spark or the like, or by viewing it through openings in a revolving disk. [f. *strobo-* (comb. form repr. Gk. *strŏbos* a twisting) + SCOPE] —**strob·o·scop·ic** (strŏb′ə skŏp′ĭk), *adj.*

strode (strōd), *v.* pt. of **stride.**

stroke¹ (strōk), *n., v.,* **stroked, stroking.** —*n.* **1.** an act of striking, as with the fist, a weapon, a hammer, etc.; a blow. **2.** a hitting of or upon anything. **3.** a striking of a clapper or hammer, as on a bell, or the sound produced by this. **4.** a throb or pulsation, as of the heart. **5.** something likened to a blow in its effect, as in causing pain, injury, or death; an attack of apoplexy or paralysis. **6.** a destructive discharge of electricity. **7.** a piece of luck, fortune, etc., befalling one: *a stroke of good luck.* **8.** a vigorous movement, as if in dealing a blow. **9.** a single complete movement, esp. one continuously repeated in some process. **10.** *Mech.* **a.** one of a series of alternating continuous movements of something back and forth over or through the same line. **b.** the complete movement of a moving part (esp. a reciprocating part) in one direction. **c.** or the distance traversed. **d.** a half revolution of an engine during which the piston travels from one extreme of its range to the other. **11.** each of the succession of movements of the arms and legs in swimming. **12.** a type or method of swimming: *the crawl is a rapid stroke.* **13.** a vigorous attempt to attain some object: *a bold stroke for liberty.* **14.** a measure adopted for a particular purpose. **15.** a feat or achievement: *a stroke of genius.* **16.** an act, piece, or amount of work, etc.: *not to do a stroke of work.* **17.** a distinctive or effective touch in a literary composition. **18.** a movement of a pen, pencil, brush, graver, or the like. **19.** a mark traced by or as if by a pen, pencil, brush, or the like. **20.** (in some games) a hitting of the ball in a certain manner: *an overhand stroke.* **21.** *Rowing.* **a.** a single pull of the oar. **b.** manner or style of moving the oars. **c.** the oarsman (**stroke oar**) nearest to the stern of the boat, to whose strokes those of the other oarsmen must conform. **d.** the position in the boat occupied by this oarsman. —*v.t.* **22.** to mark with a stroke or strokes, as of a pen; cancel, as by a stroke of a pen. **23.** to row as stroke oarsman of (a boat or crew); row as stroke in (a race). [ME, c. G *streich;* akin to STRIKE] —**Syn. 1.** See **blow¹.**

stroke² (strōk), *v.,* **stroked, stroking.** —*v.t.* **1.** to pass the hand or an instrument over (something) lightly or with little pressure; rub gently, as in soothing or caressing. —*n.* **2.** act of stroking; a stroking movement. [ME; OE *strācian,* c. G *streichen;* akin to STRIKE]

stroll (strōl), *v.i.* **1.** to walk leisurely as inclination directs; ramble; saunter; take a walk. **2.** to wander or rove from place to place; roam: *strolling Gypsies.* —*v.t.* **3.** to saunter along or through. —*n.* **4.** a leisurely walk; a ramble; a saunter: *a short stroll before supper.* [orig. uncert.]
—**Syn. 1.** STROLL, MEANDER, SAUNTER refer to carefree and leisurely walking for pleasure. To STROLL is to walk in a leisurely way as fancy leads, often for the mere pleasure of being out of doors: *to stroll down the street.* To MEANDER is to pursue an indefinite and wandering course: *to meander about the countryside.* To SAUNTER is to go along idly at a slow, easy gait: *to saunter aimlessly.* —**Ant. 1.** hasten.

stroll·er (strō′lər), *n.* **1.** a saunterer. **2.** a wanderer; vagrant. **3.** an itinerant performer. **4.** a light baby carriage, often collapsible, for very small children.

stro·ma (strō′mə), *n., pl.* **-mata** (-mə tə). **1.** the colorless, spongelike framework of a red blood corpuscle or other cell. **2.** the connective tissue forming the framework of an organ (contrasted with *parenchyma*). [NL, in LL bed covering, t. Gk.: a spread] —**stro·mat·ic** (strō măt′ĭk), *adj.*

Strom·bo·li (strŏm′bō lē′), *n.* **1.** an island in the Lipari group, N of Sicily. **2.** an active volcano on this island. 3040 ft.

strong (strông, strŏng), *adj.* **1.** having, showing, or involving great bodily or muscular power; physically vigorous or robust. **2.** mentally powerful or vigorous: *a strong mind.* **3.** especially powerful, able, or competent in a specified field or respect: *strong in mathematics.* **4.** of great moral power, firmness, or courage: *strong under temptation.* **5.** powerful in influence, authority, resources, or means of prevailing or succeeding: *a strong nation.* **6.** clear and firm; loud: *a strong voice.* **7.** well-supplied or rich in something specified: *a strong hand in* trumps. **8.** of great force, effectiveness, potency, or cogency: *strong arguments.* **9.** able to resist force or stand strain, wear, etc.: *strong walls, cloth, etc.* **10.** firm or unfaltering under trial: *strong faith.* **11.** moving or acting with force or vigor: *strong wind.* **12.** containing alcohol, or much alcohol: *strong drink.* **13.** intense, as light or color. **14.** distinct, as marks or impressions; marked, as a resemblance or contrast. **15.** strenuous or energetic; forceful or vigorous: *strong efforts.* **16.** hearty, fervent, or thoroughgoing: *strong prejudice.* **17.** having a large proportion of the effective or essential properties or ingredients: *strong tea.* **18.** having a high degree of flavor or odor: *strong perfume.* **19.** of an unpleasant or offensive flavor or odor: *strong butter.* **20.** *Com.* characterized by steady or advancing prices. **21.** *Gram.* **a.** (of Germanic verbs) indicating differentiation in tense by internal vowel change rather than by the addition of a common inflectional ending, as *sing, sang, sung; ride, rode, ridden.* **b.** (of Germanic nouns and adjectives) inflected with endings generally distinctive of case, number, and gender, as Ger. *alter Mann* "old man." —*adv.* **22.** in a strong manner; powerfully; forcibly; vigorously. [ME and OE, c. MD *stranc;* akin to D and G *streng* severe, strict] —**strong′ly,** *adv.* —**Syn. 1.** STRONG, HALE, ROBUST, STALWART, STURDY imply having health and vitality. STRONG is the general term and denotes the power of enduring strain, resisting disease, or exerting great muscular force: *strong enough to lift a piano.* HALE indicates a condition of sound or vigorous health, esp. in later life: *hale in spite of his age.* ROBUST suggests oaken strength, combining toughness of body with perfect health: *robust enough to meet all the storms of life.* STALWART suggests tallness or largeness combined with great strength or solidity: *he looks stalwart and uncompromising.* STURDY suggests stockiness and solidity, or well-knit strength that is hard to shake or overcome: *not tall but sturdy.* —**Ant.** 1. weak.

strong-arm (strông′ärm′, strông′-), *Colloq.* —*adj.* **1.** having, using, or involving the use of muscular or physical force: *strong-arm methods.* —*v.t.* **2.** to employ violent methods upon. **3.** to steal from by force.

strong·box (strông′bŏks′, strông′-), *n.* a strongly made chest for preserving money, jewels, etc.

strong breeze, *Meteorol.* a wind of Beaufort scale #6 (one within the range of 25–31 miles per hour).

strong gale, *Meteorol.* a wind of Beaufort scale #9 (one within the range of 47–54 miles per hour).

strong·hold (strông′hōld′, strông′-), *n.* a strong or well-fortified place; a fortress.

strong-mind·ed (strông′mīn′dĭd, strông′-), *adj.* **1.** having or showing a strong mind or vigorous mental powers. **2.** (of women) claiming mental and legal equality with men. —**strong′-mind′ed·ly,** *adv.* —**strong′-mind′ed·ness,** *n.*

strong·room (strông′rōōm′, -rŏŏm′, strông′-), *n. Esp. Brit.* a fireproof, burglarproof room for valuables.

strong-willed (strông′wĭld′, strông′-), *adj.* **1.** having a powerful will; resolute. **2.** stubborn.

stron·gyle (strŏn′jĭl), *n.* any of nematode worms constituting the family *Strongylidae,* parasitic as adults in the intestine principally of horses; in the larval stage they burrow into the mucosa, and some enter the circulatory system, giving rise to serious pathological conditions. Also, **stron′gyl.** [t. NL: m. *Strongylus* (name of typical genus), t. Gk.: m. *strongýlos* round]

stron·ti·a (strŏn′shĭ ə), *n. Chem.* **1.** strontium oxide, SrO, a white amorphous powder resembling lime in its general character. **2.** strontium hydroxide, Sr(OH)₂. [NL, der. *Strontian,* parish in Argyll county, Scotland, where the mineral was discovered]

stron·ti·an (strŏn′shĭ ən, strŏn′shən), *n.* **1.** strontianite. **2.** strontia. **3.** strontium.

stron·ti·an·ite (strŏn′shĭ ə nīt′), *n.* a mineral, strontium carbonate, SrCO₃, occurring in radiating, fibrous, or granular aggregates and crystals, varying from white to yellow and pale green: a minor ore of strontium. [f. *Strontian* (see STRONTIA) + -ITE¹]

stron·ti·um (strŏn′shĭ əm, -tĭ əm), *n. Chem.* a bivalent metallic element whose compounds resemble those of calcium: found in nature only in the combined state, as in strontianite. *Symbol:* Sr; *at. wt.:* 87.63; *at. no.:* 38; *sp. gr.:* 2.6. —**stron·tic** (strŏn′tĭk), *adj.*

strontium 90, *Chem.* a harmful radioactive isotope of strontium produced in certain nuclear reactions and present in their fall-out.

strop (strŏp), *n., v.,* **stropped, stropping.** —*n.* **1.** a strip of leather or other flexible material, or a long, narrow piece of wood having its faces covered with leather or an abrasive, or some similar device, used for sharpening razors. —*v.t.* **2.** to sharpen on, or as on, a strop. [ME *stroppe,* OE *strop,* c. D and LG *strop,* prob. t. L: m.s. *stroppus* strap]

stro·phan·thin (strō fǎn′thĭn), *n.* a bitter, poisonous glucoside obtained from the ripe seeds of various species of strophanthus, esp. *Strophanthus Kombe:* used in medicine as a cardiac stimulant. [f. STROPHANTH(US) + -IN²]

stro·phan·thus (strō fǎn′thəs), *n.* **1.** any of the shrubs or small trees of the apocynaceous genus *Strophanthus,* mostly natives of tropical Africa. **2.** the seed. [NL, f. Gk.: s. *stróphos* twisted band + m. *ánthos* flower]

stro·phe (strō′fĭ), *n.* **1.** the part of an ancient Greek choral ode sung by the chorus when moving from right to left. **2.** the first of two metrically corresponding series of lines forming divisions of a lyric poem (the second being the antistrophe), or in a longer poem, the

first section of such a metrical pattern whenever it is repeated. **3.** (in modern poetry) any separate section or extended movement in a poem. The strophe differs from the stanza in that the stanza is a group of lines which necessarily repeats a metrical pattern. [t. Gk.: a turning] —**stroph·ic** (strŏf′ĭk, strō′fĭk), *adj.* —**Syn. 3.** See **verse.**

stroph·u·lus (strŏf′yə ləs), *n. Pathol.* a papular eruption of the skin in infants, occurring in several forms and usually harmless. [NL: alter. of ML *scrophulus* red gum, itself alter. of L.*scrófulae* SCROFULA]

strove (strōv), *v.* pt. of **strive.**

strow (strō), *v.,* **strowed, strown** or **strowed, strowing.** *Archaic.* strew.

struck (strŭk), *v.* **1.** pt. and a pp. of **strike. 2.** —*adj.* shut or otherwise affected by a strike of workers.

struck jury, *Law.* a jury obtained by a special agreement between the opposing attorneys, each striking out 12 members of the impaneled group.

struck measure, a measure, esp. of grain, even with the top of a receptacle.

struc·tur·al (strŭk′chər əl), *adj.* **1.** of or pertaining to structure; pertaining or essential to a structure. **2.** *Biol.* pertaining to organic structure; morphological. **3.** *Geol.* pertaining to the structure of rock, etc. **4.** *Chem.* pertaining to or showing the arrangement or mode of attachment of the atoms which constitute the molecule of a substance. **5.** resulting from, or pertaining to, political or economic structure. —**struc′tur·al·ly,** *adv.*

structural formula. See **formula** (def. 3).

structural iron or **steel,** iron or steel in the various shapes which, singly or in combination, are used for beams, girders, etc. **2.** the kind of iron or steel used.

struc·ture (strŭk′chər), *n.* **1.** mode of building, construction, or organization; arrangement of parts, elements, or constituents. **2.** something built or constructed; a building, bridge, dam, framework, etc. **3.** a complex system considered from the point of view of the whole rather than of any single part: *the structure of modern science.* **4.** anything composed of parts arranged together in some way; an organization. **5.** *Biol.* mode of organization; construction and arrangement of tissues, parts, or organs. **6.** *Geol.* **a.** the attitude of a bed or stratum, or of beds or strata, of sedimentary rocks, as indicated by the dip and strike. **b.** coarser features of rocks as contrasted with their texture. **7.** the manner by which atoms in a molecule are joined to each other, especially in organic chemistry where it is represented by a diagram of the molecular arrangement. [t. L: m. *structūra*] —**Syn. 2.** See **building.**

stru·del (strōō′dəl; *Ger.* shtrōō′dəl), *n.* any of a variety of pastries, usually with fruits, cheeses, etc., rolled in a paper-thin blanket of dough. [G]

strug·gle (strŭg′əl), *v.,* **-gled, -gling,** *n.* —*v.i.* **1.** to contend with an adversary or opposing force. **2.** to contend resolutely with a task, problem, etc.; strive: *to struggle for existence.* **3.** to advance with violent effort: *to struggle through the snow.* —*v.t.* **4.** to bring, put, etc., by struggling. **5.** to make (one's way) with violent effort. —*n.* **6.** act or process of struggling. **7.** a strong effort, or series of efforts, against any adverse agencies or conditions. [ME; b. STRIVE and huggle (freq. of HUG)] —**strug′gler,** *n.* —**Syn. 6.** STRUGGLE, BRUSH, CLASH, refer to a hostile meeting of opposing persons, parties, or forces. STRUGGLE implies vigorous bodily effort or violent exertion: *a hand-to-hand struggle.* A BRUSH is a brief, but smart, and often casual combat: *a brush between patrols.* CLASH implies a direct and sharp collision between opposing parties, efforts, interests, etc.: *a clash of opinions.*

struggle for existence, the adaptations of organisms to changes in environment, pressure of populations, means of subsistence, esp. as factors in evolution.

strum (strŭm), *v.,* **strummed, strumming,** *n.* —*v.t.* **1.** to play on (a stringed musical instrument) unskillfully or carelessly. **2.** to produce (notes, etc.) by such playing: *to strum a tune.* —*v.i.* **3.** to play on a stringed instrument unskillfully or carelessly. —*n.* **4.** act of strumming. [b. STRING and THUMB] —**strum′mer,** *n.*

stru·ma (strōō′mə), *n., pl.* **-mae** (-mē). **1.** *Pathol.* **a.** scrofula. **b.** goiter. **2.** *Bot.* a cushionlike swelling on an organ, as that at one side of the base of the capsule in many mosses. [NL, special use of L: scrofulous tumor]

Stru·ma (strōō′mä), *n.* a river flowing through SW Bulgaria and NE Greece into the Aegean. ab. 225 mi.

stru·mose (strōō′mōs, strōō mōs′), *adj. Bot.* having a struma or strumae.

stru·mous (strōō′məs), *adj. Pathol.* **1.** affected with struma. **2.** characteristic of or of the nature of struma.

strum·pet (strŭm′pĭt), *n.* a prostitute; a harlot. [f. *strump-* (cf. G *strumpf* stump) + -ET]

strung (strŭng), *v.* pt. and pp. of **string.**

strut¹ (strŭt), *v.,* **strutted, strutting,** *n.* —*v.i.* **1.** to walk with a vain, pompous bearing, as with head erect and chest thrown out, as if expecting to impress observers. —*n.* **2.** act of strutting; a strutting walk or gait. [ME *stroute,* OE *strútian* stand stiffly; akin to STRUT²] —**strut′ter,** *n.* —**Syn. 1.** STRUT and SWAGGER refer especially to carriage in walking. STRUT implies swelling pride or pompousness; to walk with a stiff, pompous, affected, self-conscious gait: *a turkey struts about the barnyard.* SWAGGER implies a domineering, sometimes jaunty, superiority or challenge, and a self-important manner: *to swagger down the street.*

---

b., blend of, blended; c., cognate with; d., dialect, dialectal; der., derived from; f., formed from; g., going back to; m., modification of; r., replacing; s., stem of; t., taken from; ?, perhaps. See the full key on inside cover.

strut² (strŭt), *n., v.,* **strutted, strutting.** —*n.* **1.** a piece of wood or iron, or some other member of a structure, designed for the reception of pressure or weight in the direction of its length. —*v.t.* **2.** to brace or support by a strut or struts. [cf. LG *strut* stiff; akin to STRUT¹]

stru·thi·ous (strōō′thĭ əs), *adj.* **1.** related to or resembling the ostrich. **2.** belonging or pertaining to the *Struthioniformes*, an order of birds including, in the restricted sense, the African ostriches only; or, in a wider sense, all the ratite birds (ostriches, cassowaries, emus, etc.). [f. LL *strūthi*(o) ostrich (t. Gk.: m. *strouthíon*) + -ous]

strut·ting (strŭt′ĭng), *adj.* that struts; walking pompously; pompous. —**strut′ting·ly,** *adv.*

strych·nic (strĭk′nĭk), *adj.* of, pertaining to, or obtained from strychnine.

strych·nine (strĭk′nĭn, -nēn, -nĭn), *n.* a colorless crystalline poison, $C_{21}H_{22}N_2O_2$, which can be used in small quantities as a tonic and as an agent to increase the appetite. Also, **strych·nin** (strĭk′nĭn); *Archaic,* **strych·ni·a** (strĭk′nĭ ə). [t. F, f. s. L *strychnos* (t. Gk.: kind of nightshade) + -ine -INE²]

strych·nin·ism (strĭk′nĭ nĭz′əm), *n. Pathol. Obs.* a morbid condition induced by an overdose, or by excessive use, of strychnine.

St. Swithin's Day (swĭth′ənz), July 15; the legend is that if it rains on this day it will rain for 40 days thereafter. [f. *St. Swithin,* 800?–862, bishop of Winchester, England, 852–862]

St. Thomas, 1. one of the Virgin Islands, in the U.S. part of the group. 13,813 pop. (1950): 32 sq. mi. **2.** former name of **Charlotte Amalie. 3.** Portuguese, **São Tomé** or **São Thomé.** a Portuguese island in the Gulf of Guinea, off W coast of Africa. 60,159 (1950): 323 sq. mi.

Stu·art (stū′ərt, stōō′-), *n.* **1.** Also, **Stewart.** the royal house which reigned in Scotland from Robert II to James VI (1371–1603) and in England and Scotland from James I (previously James VI of Scotland) to Anne (1603–1714). **2. Gilbert,** 1755–1828, American portrait painter. **3. James Ewell Brown** (ū′əl), ("Jeb") 1833–64, Confederate general in the Civil War. **4. Mary.** See **Mary Stuart** of Scotland.

stub (stŭb), *n., v.,* **stubbed, stubbing.** —*n.* **1.** a short projecting part. **2.** the end of a fallen tree, shrub, or plant left fixed in the ground; a stump. **3.** a short remaining piece, as of a pencil, a candle, a cigar, etc. **4.** something unusually short, as a short, thick nail or a short-pointed, blunt pen. **5.** a worn horseshoe nail. **6.** (in a checkbook) the inner end of each leaf, on which may be kept a record of the contents of the part torn away. Cf. *Brit.* **counterfoil.** —*v.t.* **7.** *Chiefly U.S.* to strike, as one's toe, against something projecting from a surface. **8.** to clear of stubs, as land. **9.** to dig up by the roots; grub up (roots). [ME and OE, c. MLG and MD *stubbe*]

stub·bed (stŭb′ĭd, stŭbd), *adj.* **1.** reduced to or resembling a stub; short and thick; stumpy. **2.** abounding in or rough with stubs. —**stub′bed·ness,** *n.*

stub·ble (stŭb′əl), *n.* **1.** (*usually pl.*) the stump of a grain stalk or the like, left in the ground when the crop is cut. **2.** such stumps collectively. **3.** any short, rough growth, as of beard. [ME, t. OF: m. *estuble,* g. LL *stupula.* See STIPULE] —**stub′bled, stub′bly,** *adj.*

stub·born (stŭb′ərn), *adj.* **1.** unreasonably obstinate; obstinately perverse. **2.** fixed or set in purpose or opinion; resolute. **3.** obstinately maintained, as a course of action: *a stubborn resistance.* **4.** hard to deal with or manage. **5.** hard, tough, or stiff, as stone or wood. [ME *stiborn*(e), appar. der. OE *stybb* STUB] —**stub′born·ly,** *adv.* —**stub′born·ness,** *n.*

—**Syn. 2.** STUBBORN, DOGGED, OBSTINATE, PERSISTENT imply fixity of purpose or condition, and resistance to change. STUBBORN and OBSTINATE both imply resistance to change, entreaty, remonstrance, or force; but STUBBORN implies more of innate quality and is the more frequently used when referring to inanimate things: *stubborn disposition, stubborn difficulties.* DOGGED implies pertinacity and grimness in doing something, esp. in the face of discouragements: *dogged determination.* PERSISTENT implies having staying or lasting qualities, resoluteness, and perseverance: *persistent questioning.* —**Ant. 2.** complaisant, obedient, manageable.

Stubbs (stŭbz), *n.* **William,** 1825–1901, British bishop and historian.

stub·by (stŭb′ĭ), *adj.,* **-bier, -biest. 1.** of the nature of or resembling a stub. **2.** short and thick or broad; thick-set. **3.** consisting of or abounding in stubs. **4.** bristly, as the hair or beard. —**stub′bi·ness,** *n.*

stub nail, 1. a short, thick nail. **2.** an old or worn horseshoe nail.

stuc·co (stŭk′ō), *n., pl.* **-coes, -cos,** *v.,* **-coed, -coing.** —*n.* **1.** a plaster (as of slaked lime, chalk, and pulverized white marble, or of plaster of Paris and glue) used for cornices and moldings of rooms and for other decorations. **2.** a cement or concrete imitating stone, for coating exterior walls of houses, etc. **3.** any of various plasters, cements, etc. **4.** work made of such materials. —*v.t.* **5.** to cover or ornament with stucco. [t. It., t. Gmc.; cf. OHG *stukki* crust] —**stuc′co·er,** *n.*

stuc·co·work (stŭk′ō wûrk′), *n.* work made of stucco.

stuck (stŭk), *v.* pt. and pp. of **stick².**

stuck-up (stŭk′ŭp′), *adj. Colloq.* conceited; haughty.

stud¹ (stŭd), *n., v.,* **studded, studding.** —*n.* **1.** a boss, knob, nailhead, or other protuberance projecting from a surface or part, esp. as an ornament. **2.** a post or upright prop, as in the wall of a building. **3.** any of various projecting pins, lugs, or the like on machines, etc. **4.** a short rod, threaded on both ends, screwed in and projecting from something, used to fasten parts together or used as a short journal as in the change gears on a screw-cutting lathe. **5.** *Chiefly Brit.* a kind of small button or fastener, commonly of metal, bone, or the like, in the form of a small knob and a disk connected by a stem, used (when passed through small buttonholes or the like) for holding together parts of dress (as shirts) or for ornament. —*v.t.* **6.** to set with or as with studs, bosses, or the like. **7.** to scatter over with things set at intervals. **8.** (of things) to be scattered over the surface of. **9.** to set or scatter (objects) at intervals over a surface. **10.** to furnish with or support by studs or upright props. [ME *stude,* OE *studu,* c. MHG *stud;* akin to G *stütze*]

stud² (stŭd), *n.* **1.** a number of horses, as for racing or hunting, belonging to one owner. **2.** an establishment in which horses are kept for breeding. **3.** a studhorse or stallion. —*adj.* **4.** of, associated with, or pertaining to a studhorse. **5.** retained for breeding purposes. [ME and OE *stōd,* c. Icel. *stōdh*]

stud·book (stŭd′bŏŏk′), *n.* a genealogical register of a stud; a book giving the pedigree of horses.

stud·ding (stŭd′ĭng), *n.* **1.** studs of a wall, partition, or the like, collectively. **2.** material for such studs.

stud·ding·sail (stŭn′sal, stŭd′ĭng sāl′), *n. Naut.* a light sail sometimes set outboard of either of the leeches of a square sail, and extended by booms. See illus. under **sail.**

stu·dent (stū′dənt, stōō′-), *n.* **1.** one who is engaged in or given to study. **2.** one who is engaged in a course of study and instruction, as at a college, university, or professional or technical school. [ME, t. L: s. *studens,* ppr., being eager, studying; r. ME *studiant,* t. OF] —**stu′dent·ship′,** *n.* —**Syn. 1, 2.** See **pupil¹.**

student lamp, an adjustable lamp for reading, etc.

student's t test, *Statistics.* a test for determining whether or not an observed sample mean differs incredibly from a hypothetical normal population mean.

stud·horse (stŭd′hôrs′), *n.* a stallion for breeding.

stud·ied (stŭd′ĭd), *adj.* **1.** marked by or suggestive of effort, rather than spontaneous or natural: *studied simplicity.* **2.** carefully considered. **3.** *Rare.* learned. —**stud′ied·ly,** *adv.* —**stud′ied·ness,** *n.* —**Syn. 1.** See **elaborate.**

stu·di·o (stū′dĭ ō′, stōō′-), *n., pl.* **-dios. 1.** the workroom or atelier of an artist, as a painter or sculptor. **2.** a room or place in which some form of art is pursued: *a music studio.* **3.** a room or set of rooms specially equipped for broadcasting radio programs. [t. It., t. L: m. *studium* zeal, study, LL a place for study]

stu·di·ous (stū′dĭ əs, stōō′-), *adj.* **1.** disposed or given to study: *a studious boy.* **2.** concerned with, characterized by, or pertaining to study: *studious tastes.* **3.** zealous, assiduous, or painstaking: *studious care.* **4.** studied or carefully maintained. **5.** *Poetic.* (of places) used or frequented for purposes of study. [ME, t. L: m.s. *studiōsus*] —**stu′di·ous·ly,** *adv.* —**stu′di·ous·ness,** *n.*

stud·work (stŭd′wûrk′), *n.* **1.** construction with studs or upright scantlings. **2.** work containing or supported by studs.

stud·y (stŭd′ĭ), *n., pl.* **studies,** *v.,* **studied, studying.** —*n.* **1.** application of the mind to the acquisition of knowledge, as by reading, investigation, or reflection. **2.** the cultivation of a particular branch of learning, science, or art: *the study of law.* **3.** a particular course of effort to acquire knowledge: *to pursue special medical studies.* **4.** something studied or to be studied. **5.** zealous endeavor or assiduous effort, or the object of the endeavor or effort. **6.** deep thought, reverie, or a state of abstraction: *to be in a brown study.* **7.** a room in a house or other building, set apart for private study, reading, writing, or the like. **8.** *Music.* a composition, usually instrumental, combining the instructive purpose of an exercise with a certain amount of artistic value; an étude. **9.** (in literature) a composition executed for exercise or as an experiment in a particular method of treatment, or one dealing in detail with a particular subject. **10.** *Art.* something produced as an educational exercise, or as a memorandum or record of observations or effects, or as a guide for a finished production. —*v.i.* **11.** to apply oneself to the acquisition of knowledge, as by reading, investigation, practice, etc. **12.** to apply oneself, or endeavor (to do something). **13.** to think deeply, reflect, or consider. —*v.t.* **14.** to apply oneself to acquiring a knowledge of (a branch of learning, science, or art, or a subject), esp. systematically. **15.** to examine or investigate carefully and in detail: *to study the political situation.* **16.** to observe attentively; scrutinize: *to study a person's face.* **17.** to read (a book, document, etc.) with careful effort. **18.** to seek to learn or memorize, as a part in a play. **19.** to consider, as something to be achieved or devised; think (*out*), as the result of careful consideration or devising. [ME *studie,* t. L: m. *studium* zeal, application, study, LL a place for study]

—**Syn. 15.** STUDY, CONSIDER, REFLECT, WEIGH imply fixing the mind upon something, generally with a view to some decision or action. STUDY implies an attempt to obtain a grasp of something by methodical or exhaustive thought: *to study a problem.* TO CONSIDER is to fix the thought upon something and give it close attention before making a decision concerning it, or beginning an action connected with it: *consider ways and means.* REFLECT implies looking back quietly over past experience and giving it consideration: *reflect on similar cases in the past.* WEIGH implies a deliberate and judicial estimate, as by a balance: *weigh a decision.*

study hall, (in some schools) a room used solely or chiefly for studying.

stuff (stŭf), *n.* **1.** the material of which anything is made. **2.** material to be worked upon, or to be used in making something. **3.** matter or material indefinitely: *cushions filled with some soft stuff.* **4.** *Brit.* woven material or fabric. **5.** *Colloq.* equipments, belongings, baggage, goods, or stock. **6.** something to be swallowed, as food, drink, or medicine. **7.** inward character, qualities, or capabilities: *to have good stuff in one.* **8.** *U.S. Slang.* actions, performances, talk, etc.: *to cut out the rough stuff.* **9.** worthless matter or things. **10.** worthless or foolish ideas, talk, or writing. —*v.t.* **11.** to fill (a receptacle), esp. by packing the contents closely together; cram full. **12.** to fill (an aperture, cavity, etc.) by forcing something into it. **13.** to fill or line with some kind of material as a padding or packing. **14.** to fill or cram (oneself, one's stomach, etc.) with food. **15.** to fill (a chicken, turkey, piece of meat, etc.) with seasoned bread crumbs or other savory matter. **16.** to fill the skin of (a dead animal) with material, preserving the natural form and appearance. **17.** *U.S.* to put fraudulent votes into (a ballot box). **18.** to thrust or cram (something) tightly into a receptacle, cavity, or the like. **19.** to pack tightly in a confined place; crowd together. **20.** to crowd (a vehicle, room, etc.) with persons. **21.** *Leather Mfg.* to treat (a skin, etc.) with a composition of tallow and other ingredients. **22.** to stop up or plug; block or choke (*up*). —*v.i.* **23.** to cram oneself with food; eat gluttonously. [ME, t. OF: m. *estoffe* material, provision, der. *estoffer* provide, ult. t. Gk.: m. *stýphein* pull together, narrow] —**Syn.** 1–3. See **matter.** 9. rubbish, trash. 10. nonsense, twaddle, balderdash. 11. cram, pack, fill.

stuffed shirt (stŭft), *U.S. Slang.* a pompous, pretentious person, usually of little importance.

stuff·ing (stŭf′ĭng), *n.* **1.** the act of one who or that which stuffs. **2.** that with which anything is or may be stuffed. **3.** seasoned bread crumbs or other filling used to stuff a chicken, turkey, etc., before cooking.

stuffing box, *Mach.* a contrivance for securing a steamtight, airtight, or watertight joint at the place or hole where a movable rod (as a piston rod) enters a vessel, consisting typically of a cylindrical box or chamber through the middle of which the rod passes, the rest of the space being filled with packing held in by a cover or adjustable member at one end of the box.

stuffing nut, the nut on a stuffing box that serves to condense the packing and so to tighten the seal.

stuff·y (stŭf′ĭ), *adj.,* **stuffier, stuffiest. 1.** close or ill-ventilated, as a room; oppressive from lack of freshness, as the air, etc. **2.** lacking in interest, as writing or discourse. **3.** affected with a sensation of obstruction in the respiratory passages, as a person. **4.** *U.S. Colloq.* angry or sulky. **5.** dull, self-important, or straightlaced. **6.** *Chiefly Brit.* immune to new ideas. —**stuff′i·ly,** *adv.* —**stuff′i·ness,** *n.*

stull (stŭl), *n. Mining.* **1.** a timber prop. **2.** one piece of timber set for a mine support, usually the top piece. [cf. G *stollen* a prop]

stul·ti·fy (stŭl′tə fī′), *v.t.,* **-fied, -fying. 1.** to make, or cause to appear, foolish or ridiculous. **2.** to render absurdly or wholly futile or ineffectual, as efforts. **3.** *Law.* to allege or prove to be of unsound mind; allege (oneself) to be insane. [t. LL: m.s. *stultificāre,* der. L *stultus* foolish. See -FY] —**stul·ti·fi·ca·tion** (stŭl′tə fə kā′shən), *n.* —**stul′ti·fi′er,** *n.*

stum·ble (stŭm′bəl), *v.,* **-bled, -bling,** *n.* —*v.i.* **1.** to strike the foot against something in walking, running, etc., so as to stagger or fall; trip. **2.** to walk or go unsteadily. **3.** to make a slip, mistake, or blunder, esp. a sinful one. **4.** to proceed in a hesitating or blundering manner, as in action or speech. **5.** to come accidentally or unexpectedly (fol. by *on, upon, across,* etc.). **6.** to falter or hesitate, as at an obstacle to progress or belief. —*v.t.* **7.** to cause to stumble; trip. **8.** to give pause to; puzzle or perplex. —*n.* **9.** act of stumbling. **10.** a moral lapse or error. **11.** a slip or blunder. [ME, c. Norw. *stumla;* akin to STAMMER] —**stum′bler,** *n.* —**stum′bling·ly,** *adv.*

stumbling block, 1. a block, stump, or anything else which causes one to stumble. **2.** an obstacle or hindrance to progress, belief, etc.

stump (stŭmp), *n.* **1.** the lower end of a tree or plant left after the main part falls or is cut off; a standing tree trunk from which the upper part and the branches have been removed. **2.** the part of a limb of the body remaining after the rest has been cut off. **3.** a part of a broken or decayed tooth left in the gum. **4.** a short remnant of a pencil, candle, cigar, etc. **5.** any basal part remaining after the main or more important part has been removed. **6.** a wooden leg. **7.** *Colloq.* a leg. **8.** a short, stumpy person. **9.** a heavy step or gait, as of a wooden-legged or lame person. **10.** the platform or place of political speechmaking: *to go on the stump.* **11.** an instrument consisting of a short, thick, roll of paper or soft leather, or a bar of India rubber or other soft material, usually cut to a blunt point at each end,

used for rubbing the lights and shades in crayon drawing or charcoal drawing, or for otherwise altering the effect. **12.** *Cricket.* each of the three (formerly two) upright sticks which, with the two bails laid on the top of them, form a wicket. —*v.t.* **13.** to reduce to a stump; truncate; lop. **14.** to clear of stumps, as land. **15.** *U.S. Colloq.* to stub, as one's toe. **16.** to nonplus, embarrass, or render completely at a loss. **17.** *U.S. Colloq.* to challenge or dare to do something. **18.** *Colloq.* to make stump speeches in or to. **19.** *Cricket.* (of the wicketkeeper) to put (a batsman) out by knocking down a stump or by dislodging a ball with the ball held in the hand, at a moment when the batsman is off his ground. **20.** to tone or modify (crayon drawings, etc.) by means of a stump. —*v.i.* **21.** to walk heavily or clumsily, as if with a wooden leg: *Cap'n Eli stumped across the room.* **22.** *Colloq.* to make stump speeches. [ME *stomp,* c. G *stumpf*] —**stump′er,** *n.*

stump·age (stŭmp′ĭj), *n.* **1.** standing timber with reference to its value. **2.** the right to cut such timber on the owner's land. **3.** the value of such timber.

stump·y (stŭmp′ĭ), *adj.,* **stumpier, stumpiest. 1.** of the nature of or resembling a stump. **2.** short and thick; stubby; stocky. **3.** abounding in stumps.

stun (stŭn), *v.,* **stunned, stunning,** *n.* —*v.t.* **1.** to deprive of consciousness or strength by or as by a blow, fall, etc. **2.** to strike with astonishment; astound; amaze. **3.** to daze or bewilder by distracting noise. —*n.* **4.** act of stunning. **5.** the condition of being stunned. [ME; OE *stunian* resound, crash. Cf. OF *estoner* resound, stun] —**Syn.** 1. See **shock**[1].

stung (stŭng), *v.* pt. and pp. of **sting.**

stunk (stŭngk), *v.* a pt. and the pp. of **stink.**

stun·ner (stŭn′ər), *n.* **1.** one who or that which stuns. **2.** *Chiefly Brit. Colloq.* a person or thing of striking excellence, beauty, attractiveness, etc.

stun·ning (stŭn′ĭng), *adj.* **1.** that stuns. **2.** *Colloq.* of striking excellence, beauty, etc. —**stun′ning·ly,** *adv.*

stun·sail (stŭn′səl), *n.* studdingsail.

stunt[1] (stŭnt), *v.t.* **1.** to check the growth or development of; dwarf; hinder the increase or progress of. **2.** to check (growth, development, etc.). —*n.* **3.** a check in growth or development. **4.** arrested development. **5.** a creature hindered from attaining its proper growth. [v. use of *stunt,* adj. (now d.), dwarfed, stubborn (in ME and OE foolish), c. MHG *stunz,* Icel. *stuttr* short]

stunt[2] (stŭnt), *Colloq.* —*n.* **1.** a performance serving as a display of strength, activity, skill, or the like, as in athletics, etc.; a feat. **2.** any notable performance. —*v.i.* **3.** to do a stunt or stunts. —*v.t.* **4.** to use in doing stunts: *to stunt an airplane.* [orig. uncert.]

stu·pa (stōō′pa), *n.* a monumental pile of earth or other material, either dome-shaped or pyramidal, in memory of Buddha or a Buddhist saint, and commemorating some event or marking a sacred spot. [t. Skt.]

stupe (stūp, stōōp), *n.* two or more layers of flannel or other cloth soaked in hot water and applied to the skin as a counterirritant. [ME, t. L: m. *stūpa* tow]

stu·pe·fa·cient (stū′pə fā′shənt, stōō′-), *adj.* **1.** stupefying; producing stupor. —*n.* **2.** a drug or agent that produces stupor. [t. L: s. *stupefaciens,* ppr., stupefying]

stu·pe·fac·tion (stū′pə făk′shən, stōō′-), *n.* **1.** act of stupefying. **2.** state of being stupefied; stupor; numbness of the faculties. **3.** overwhelming amazement.

stu·pe·fac·tive (stū′pə făk′tĭv, stōō′-), *adj.* serving to stupefy.

stu·pe·fy (stū′pə fī′, stōō′-), *v.t.,* **-fied, -fying. 1.** to put into a state of stupor; dull the faculties of. **2.** to stun as with a narcotic, a shock, strong emotion, etc. **3.** to overwhelm with amazement; astound. [t. L: m. s. *stupefacere*] —**stu′pe·fi′er,** *n.*

stu·pen·dous (stū pĕn′dəs, stōō′-), *adj.* **1.** such as to cause amazement; astounding; marvelous. **2.** amazingly large or great; immense: *a stupendous mass of information.* [t. L: m. *stupendus,* ger., to be wondered at] —**stu·pen′dous·ly,** *adv.* —**stu·pen′dous·ness,** *n.*

stu·pid (stū′pĭd, stōō′-), *adj.* **1.** lacking ordinary activity and keenness of mind; dull. **2.** characterized by, indicative of, or proceeding from mental dullness: *a stupid act.* **3.** tediously dull or uninteresting: *a stupid book.* **4.** in a state of stupor; stupefied. —*n.* **5.** *Colloq.* a stupid person. [t. L: s. *stupidus*] —**stu′pid·ly,** *adv.* —**stu′pid·ness,** *n.* —**Syn.** 1. See **dull.** 2. See **foolish.**

stu·pid·i·ty (stū pĭd′ə tĭ, stōō′-), *n., pl.* **-ties. 1.** state, quality, or fact of being stupid. **2.** a stupid act, notion, speech, etc.

stu·por (stū′pər, stōō′-), *n.* **1.** suspension or great diminution of sensibility, as in disease or as caused by narcotics, intoxicants, etc. **2.** a state of suspended or deadened sensibility. **3.** mental torpor, or apathy; stupefaction. [ME, t. L] —**stu′por·ous,** *adj.*

stur·dy[1] (stûr′dĭ), *adj.,* **-dier, -diest. 1.** strongly built, stalwart, or robust. **2.** strong, as in substance, construction, texture, etc.: *sturdy walls.* **3.** firm, stout, or indomitable: *sturdy defenders.* **4.** of strong or hardy growth, as a plant. [ME, t. OF: m. *estourdi* dazed, reckless, pp. of *estourdir* stun, LL *exturdīre* deafen (with chatter), der. *turdus* turtledove] —**stur′di·ly,** *adv.* —**stur′di·ness,** *n.* —**Syn.** 1. hardy, muscular, brawny. See **strong.** 3. resolute, vigorous.

---

b., blend of, blended; c., cognate with; d., dialect, dialectal; der., derived from; f., formed from; g., going back to; m., modification of; r., replacing; s., stem of; t., taken from; ?, perhaps. See the full key on inside cover.

stur·dy² (stûr'dĭ), *n. Vet. Sci.* the gid. [ME adj. meaning "giddy," t. OF. See STURDY¹] —**stur'died,** *adj.*

stur·geon (stûr'jən), *n.* any of various large ganoid fishes of the family *Acipenseridae,* found in fresh and salt waters of the North Temperate Zone, and valued for their flesh and as a source of caviar and isinglass. [ME, t. AF, var. of OF sturg(i)un, g. VL *sturio,* t. Gmc.; cf. OHG *sturio*]

Sturm·ab·tei·lung (shtŏŏrm'äp'tī'lŏŏng), *n.* a Nazi party militia, the Brown Shirts, notorious for its violence and terrorism before 1934, and thereafter an instrument of physical training and political education.

Sturm und Drang (shtŏŏrm' ŏŏnt dräng'), a period in German literature (about 1770–90) noted for the impetuosity of thought and style of the younger writers. [G: storm and stress]

stut·ter (stŭt'ər), *v.t., v.i.* **1.** to utter (sounds) in which the rhythm is interrupted by blocks or spasms, repetitions, or prolongation of sounds or syllables, sometimes accompanied by facial contortions. —*n.* **2.** unrhythmical and distorted speech characterized principally by blocks or spasms interrupting the rhythm. [freq. of d. *stut,* ME *stutte(n),* akin to D *stotteren*] —**stut'ter·er,** *n.* —**stut'ter·ing·ly,** *adv.* —**Syn. 1.** See **stammer.**

Stutt·gart (stŭt'gärt; *Ger.* shtŏŏt'gärt), *n.* a city in W West Germany: capital of Baden-Württemberg. 602,928 (est. 1955).

Stuy·ve·sant (stī'və·sənt), *n.* **Peter,** 1592–1672, last governor of the Dutch colony of New Netherlands (1646–64).

St. Vin·cent (vĭn'sənt), **1.** a British colony (including the N part of the Grenadines) in the Windward Islands; in the Federation of the West Indies. 75,190 pop. (est. 1954); 150 sq. mi. *Cap.:* Kingstown. **2. Cape,** the SW tip of Portugal: naval battle, 1797.

St. Vi·tus's dance (vī'təs ĭz), *Pathol.* chorea (def. 1). Also, **St. Vitus dance.**

sty¹ (stī), *n., pl.* **sties,** *v.,* **stied, stying.** —*n.* **1.** *Chiefly Brit.* a pen or enclosure for swine. **2.** any filthy abode. **3.** a place of bestial debauchery. —*v.t.* **4.** to keep or lodge in or as in a sty. —*v.i.* **5.** to live in or as in a sty. [ME; OE *stig,* c. Icel. *stī*; akin to D *stijg*]

sty² (stī), *n., pl.* **sties.** *Pathol.* a circumscribed inflammatory swelling, like a small boil, on the edge of the eyelid. Also, **stye.** [? back formation from ME *styanye,* f. *styan* (OE *stīgend* sty, lit., rising) + *ye* EYE, but taken to mean sty on eye]

styg·i·an (stĭj'ĭ·ən), *adj.* **1.** of or pertaining to the river Styx or the lower world. **2.** dark or gloomy. **3.** infernal; hellish. [f. s. L *Stygius* (t. Gk.: m. *Stýgios*) +-AN]

styl-, var. of **stylo-,** before vowels, as in *stylar.*

sty·lar (stī'lər), *adj.* having the shape of a style (def. 8); resembling a pen, pin, or peg.

style (stīl), *n., v.,* **styled, styling.** —*n.* **1.** a particular kind, sort, or type, as with reference to form, appearance, or character. **2.** a particular, distinctive, or characteristic mode of action. **3.** a mode of living, as with respect to expense or display; elegant or fashionable mode of living. **4.** a mode of fashion, as in dress; esp. good or approved fashion; elegance; smartness. **5.** characteristic mode of writing or speaking, as determined by period, literary form, personality, etc.: *the style of Johnson.* **6.** a particular, distinctive, or characteristic mode or form of construction or execution in any art or work. **7.** a descriptive or distinguishing appellation; esp., a legal, official, or recognized title: *a firm trading under the style of Smith, Jones, & Co.* **8.** an instrument of metal, bone, or the like, used by the ancients for writing on a waxed tablet, having one end pointed for incising the letters, and the other end blunt for rubbing out writing and smoothing the tablet. **9.** something resembling or suggesting such an instrument. **10.** a pointed instrument for drawing, etching, or writing. **11.** the gnomon of a sundial. **12.** a mode of reckoning time. **13. Old Style** or **New Style,** the reckoning of time according to the Julian calendar (which see) or the Gregorian calendar (which see) respectively, the dates in the former calendar being replaced in the latter calendar by dates 10 days later from 1582 to 1700, 11 days later from 1700 to 1800, 12 days later from 1800 to 1900, and 13 days later since 1900, so that now Sept. 3, Old Style, is the same as Sept. 16, New Style. **14.** *Bot.* a narrow, usually cylindrical and more or less filiform extension of the ovary, which, when present, bears the stigma at its apex. **15.** *Zool.* a small, slender, pointed process or part. —*v.t.* **16.** to call by a particular style or appellation (as specified); to denominate; name; call. **17.** to design in accordance with a given or new style: *to style an evening dress.* —*v.i.* **18.** to do decorative work with a style or stylus. [ME, t. OF, t. L: m.s. *stilus* (incorrectly *stylus*); orig. def. 8, whence 6, whence 1, etc. In defs. 11 and 14, confused with derivs. of Gk. *stŷlos* pillar] —**styl'er,** *n.* —**Syn. 4.** See **fashion.**

S. Style (def. 14)

style·book (stīl'bŏŏk'), *n.* **1.** a book containing rules of usage in typography, punctuation, etc., employed by printers, editors, and writers. **2.** a book featuring styles, fashions, or the rules of styles.

sty·let (stī'lĭt), *n.* **1.** a stiletto or dagger. **2.** some similar sharp-pointed instrument. **3.** *Med.* **a.** a probe. **b.** a wire run through the length of a catheter, cannula, or needle to make it rigid or to clear it. **4.** *Zool.* style (def. 15). [t. F, t. It.: m. *stiletto* STILETTO]

sty·li·form (stī'lə·fôrm'), *adj.* having the shape of a style (def. 8); stylar.

styl·ish (stī'lĭsh), *adj.* characterized by style, or conforming to the fashionable standard; fashionably elegant; smart: *several stylish dresses.* —**styl'ish·ly,** *adv.* —**styl'ish·ness,** *n.*

styl·ist (stī'lĭst), *n.* **1.** a writer or speaker who is skilled in or who cultivates a literary style. **2.** one who designs clothing, interior decorations, etc.

sty·lis·tic (stī·lĭs'tĭk), *adj.* of or pertaining to style. —**sty·lis'ti·cal·ly,** *adv.*

sty·lite (stī'līt), *n. Eccles. Hist.* one of a class of solitary ascetics who lived on the top of high pillars or columns. [t. Eccl. Gk.: m. *stylítēs,* der. Gk. *stŷlos* pillar]

styl·ize (stī'līz), *v.t.,* **-ized, -izing.** to conform to a particular style, as of representation or treatment in art; conventionalize. —**styl'i·za'tion,** *n.* —**styl'iz·er,** *n.*

stylo-, a combining form, frequent in scientific terminology, representing (1) **style,** (2) **styloid.**

sty·lo·bate (stī'lə·bāt'), *n. Archit.* a continuous base supporting a row of columns; that part of a stereobate immediately beneath the columns. [t. L: m.s. *stylobata,* t. Gk.: m. *stŷlobátēs*]

sty·lo·graph (stī'lə·grăf', -gräf'), *n.* a fountain pen in which the writing point is a fine, hollow tube instead of a nib. —**sty·lo·graph'ic,** *adj.*

sty·log·ra·phy (stī·lŏg'rə·fĭ), *n.* the art of writing, tracing, drawing, etc., with a stylus. [f. *stylo-* (comb. form repr. STYLUS) + -GRAPHY]

sty·loid (stī'loid), *adj.* **1.** resembling a style; slender and pointed. **2.** denoting several bony processes on the temporal bone, radius, ulna, etc. [t. NL: s. *stŷloīdēs,* t. Gk.: m. *stŷloeidēs*]

sty·lo·lite (stī'lə·līt'), *n. Geol.* a longitudinally streaked, columnar structure occurring in various rocks, esp. limestone, and of the same material as the rock in which it occurs. [f. Gk. *stŷlo*(s) pillar + -LITE]

sty·lo·po·di·um (stī'lə·pō'dĭ·əm), *n., pl.* **-dia** (-dĭ·ə). *Bot.* a glandular disk or expansion surmounting the ovary in umbelliferous plants and supporting the styles.

sty·lus (stī'ləs), *n.* **1.** a pointed instrument for writing on wax or other suitable surfaces. **2.** a cutting tool, often needle-shaped, used to make phonograph records. **3.** a similar device in a phonograph, for reproducing sounds from such a record. [t. L, var. of *stilus*]

sty·mie (stī'mĭ), *n., v.,* **-mied, -mieing.** —*n.* **1.** *Golf.* **a.** an opponent's ball on a putting green when it is directly between the player's ball and the hole for which he is playing, and when the distance between the balls is more than six inches. **b.** the occurrence of a ball in such a position or the position of the ball. —*v.t.* **2.** to hinder or block with or as with a stymie. [orig. uncert.]

sty·my (stī'mĭ), *n., pl.* **-mies,** *v.t.,* **-mied, -mying.** stymie.

styp·sis (stĭp'sĭs), *n.* the employment or application of styptics. [t. L, t. Gk.]

styp·tic (stĭp'tĭk), *adj.* Also, **styp'ti·cal. 1.** contracting organic tissue; astringent; binding. **2.** checking hemorrhage or bleeding, as a drug; hemostatic. —*n.* **3.** a styptic agent or substance. [ME, t. L: s. *stypticus,* t. Gk.: m. *styptikós*] —**styp·tic·i·ty** (stĭp'tĭs'ə·tĭ), *n.*

Styr (stĭr), *n.* a river in the W Soviet Union: formerly in Poland; a battle line in World War I. ab. 300 mi.

sty·ra·ca·ceous (stī'rə·kā'shəs), *adj.* belonging to the *Styracaceae,* or storax family of shrubs and trees. [f. s. L *styrax* STORAX + -ACEOUS]

sty·rene (stī'rēn, stĭr'ēn), *n.* a colorless liquid hydrocarbon, C₆H₅CH:CH₂, with a fragrant, aromatic odor, used in making synthetic rubber. [f. L *styr(ax)* STORAX + -ENE]

styrene resin, the transparent plastic formed by the polymerization of styrene and characterized by its thermoplastic properties.

Styr·i·a (stĭr'ĭ·ə), *n.* a province in SE Austria: formerly a duchy. 1,115,077 pop. (est. 1953); 6327 sq. mi. *Cap.:* Graz. German, **Steiermark.**

Styx (stĭks), *n. Gk. Myth.* a river of the lower world, over which the souls of the dead were ferried by Charon, and by which the gods swore their most solemn oaths.

su-, var. of **sub-** before *sp.*

su·a·ble (sōō'ə·bəl), *adj.* capable of being sued; liable to be sued. —**su'a·bil'i·ty,** *n.*

Sua·kin (swä'kēn), *n.* a seaport in NE Sudan, on the Red Sea. 6900 (est. 1953).

sua·sion (swā'zhən), *n.* **1.** act of advising or urging, or attempting to persuade. **2.** an instance of this; a persuasive effort. [ME, t. L: s. *suāsio*] —**sua·sive** (swā'sĭv), **sua·so·ry** (swā'sə·rĭ), *adj.*

suave (swäv, swāv), *adj.* (of persons or their manner, speech, etc.) smoothly agreeable or polite; agreeably or blandly urbane. [t. L: m. *suāvis* gentle; r. *suaif,* t. F] —**suave'ly,** *adv.* —**Ant.** blunt.

suav·i·ty (swäv'ə·tĭ, swä'və·tĭ), *n., pl.* **-ties. 1.** suave or smoothly agreeable quality (of persons, manner, etc.). **2.** (*pl.*) suave or courteous actions or manners; amenities. Also, **suave'ness.**

sub (sŭb), *n., v.,* **subbed, subbing.** *Colloq.* —*n.* **1.** a shortened form of subaltern, subeditor, sublieutenant, submarine, subordinate, substitute, and other words beginning with this prefix. —*v.i.* **2.** to substitute, or act as a substitute, for another.

sub-, **1.** a prefix meaning "under," freely used like *under* as an attribute (*subway, subarctic, substation*), also attached to stems not used as words with extended meanings, as in *subvert, subtract, succeed.* **2.** *Chem.* **a.** a prefix indicating a basic compound, as in *subacetate, subcarbonate, subnitrate.* **b.** a prefix indicating that the element is present in a relatively small proportion, i.e. in a low oxidation state, as in *subchloride, suboxide.* Also, **su-, suc-, suf-, sug-, sum-, sup-.** [t. L, repr. *sub,* prep., under, close to; akin to HYPO-]

sub., **1.** subscription. **2.** substitute. **3.** suburban. **4.** subway.

sub·ac·id (sŭbăs´ĭd), *adj.* **1.** slightly or moderately acid or sour: *a subacid fruit.* **2.** (of speech, temper, etc., or a person) somewhat tart or sharp.

sub·a·cute (sŭb´əkūt´), *adj.* somewhat or moderately acute.

su·ba·dar (sōō´bädär´), *n. India.* **1.** a provincial governor of the Mogul empire. **2.** the chief native officer of a company of native troops in the British Indian service. Also, **su/bah·dar/.** [t. Urdū (Hind.)]

sub·a·gent (sŭbā´jənt), *n.* **1.** one to whom agency duties are assigned by an agent. **2.** one who works for or under the supervision of an agent.

sub·al·pine (sŭbăl´pīn, -pĭn), *adj.* **1.** pertaining to the regions at the foot of the Alps. **2.** *Bot.* growing on mountains below the limit of tree growth, and above the foothill, or montane, zone.

sub·al·tern (sŭbôl´tərn *or, esp. for 3, 6,* sŭb´əl tûrn´), *adj.* **1.** having an inferior or subordinate position or rank; subordinate. **2.** *Brit. Mil.* of or pertaining to a lieutenant. **3.** *Logic.* denoting the relation of one proposition to another when the first is implied by the second but not conversely. In Aristotelian logic, a particular proposition stands in this relation to the universal proposition having the same subject, predicate, and quality as the particular. —*n.* **4.** one who has a subordinate position. **5.** *Brit. Mil.* a subaltern officer. **6.** *Logic.* a subaltern proposition. [t. LL: s. *subalternus,* f. L *sub* under + *alternus* one after the other, alternate]

sub·al·ter·nate (sŭbôl´tərnĭt, -āl´-), *adj.* **1.** successive. **2.** *Bot.* placed singly along an axis, but tending to become grouped oppositely. —**sub·al·ter·na·tion** (sŭb ôl´tər nā´shən, -āl´-), *n.*

sub·a·que·ous (sŭbā´kwĭəs, -ăk´wĭ-), *adj.* **1.** existing or situated under water. **2.** occurring or performed under water. **3.** used under water.

sub·ar·id (sŭbăr´ĭd), *adj.* moderately arid.

sub·as·trin·gent (sŭb´əstrĭn´jənt), *adj.* slightly astringent.

sub·au·di·tion (sŭb´ôdĭsh´ən), *n.* **1.** act of understanding or mentally supplying something not expressed. **2.** something mentally supplied; understood or implied meaning. [t. L: s. *subauditio*]

sub·au·ric·u·lar (sŭb´ôrĭk´yələr), *adj. Anat.* situated below the ear.

sub·ax·il·la·ry (sŭbăk´səlĕr´ĭ), *adj. Bot.* situated or placed beneath an axil.

sub·base (sŭb´bās´), *n. Archit.* the lowest part of a base (as of a column) which consists of two or more horizontal members.

sub·base·ment (sŭb´bās´mənt), *n.* a basement, or one of a series of basements, below the main basement of a building.

sub·bass (sŭb´bās´), *n. Music.* a pedal stop producing the lowest tones of an organ.

sub·cal·i·ber (sŭbkăl´əbər), *adj. Mil.* **1.** (of a projectile) having a diameter less than the caliber of the gun from which it is fired, the projectile being fitted with a disk large enough to fill the bore, or being fired from a tube attached to the inside or the outside of the gun. **2.** pertaining to such a projectile: *a subcaliber gun.*

sub·car·ti·lag·i·nous (sŭb´kärtĭlăj´ənəs), *adj. Anat., Zool.* **1.** partially or incompletely cartilaginous. **2.** situated below or beneath cartilage.

sub·cat·e·go·ry (sŭbkăt´əgōr´ĭ), *n.* a subordinate category.

sub·ce·les·tial (sŭb´sĭlĕs´chəl), *adj.* **1.** being beneath the heavens; terrestrial. —*n.* **2.** a subcelestial being.

sub·cel·lar (sŭb´sĕl´ər), *n.* a cellar beneath another cellar.

sub·class (sŭb´klăs´, -kläs´), *n.* **1.** a primary division of a class. **2.** a category of related orders, or superorders, within a class. —*v.t.* **3.** to place in a subclass.

sub·cla·vi·an (sŭbklā´vĭən), *Anat.* —*adj.* **1.** situated or extending beneath the clavicle, as certain arteries, veins, etc. **2.** pertaining to such an artery, vein, or the like. —*n.* **3.** a subclavian artery, vein, or the like. [f. s. NL *subclāvius* (der. L *sub-* SUB- + *clāvis* key) + -AN]

subclavian groove, *Anat.* either of two shallow depressions on the first rib, one for the subclavian artery and the other for the subclavian vein.

sub·cli·max (sŭbklī´măks), *n. Ecol.* the imperfect development of a climax community because of some factor (such as repeated fires in a forest) which arrests the normal succession.

sub·com·mit·tee (sŭb´kəmĭt´ĭ), *n.* a secondary committee appointed out of a main committee.

sub·con·scious (sŭbkŏn´shəs), *adj.* **1.** existing or operating beneath or beyond consciousness: *the subconscious self.* **2.** imperfectly or not wholly conscious. —*n.* **3.** the totality of mental processes of which the individual is not aware; unreportable mental activities. —**sub·con/scious·ly,** *adv.* —**sub·con/scious·ness,** *n.*

sub·con·tract (*n.* sŭbkŏn´trăkt; *v.* sŭbkŏn´trăkt/), *Law.* —*n.* **1.** a contract by which one agrees to render services or to provide materials necessary for the performance of another contract. —*v.t.* **2.** to make a subcontract for. —*v.i.* **3.** to make a subcontract.

sub·con·trac·tor (sŭb´kən trăk´tər), *n.* one who contracts to render some performance for another which the latter requires for the performance of his own contract.

sub·cor·tex (sŭb´kôr´tĕks), *n., pl.* **-tices** (-tə sēz´). *Anat.* the portions of the brain situated beneath the cerebral cortex.

sub·cul·ture (sŭb´kŭl´chər), *v.,* **-tured, -turing,** *n. Bacteriol.* —*v.t.* **1.** to cultivate (a bacterial strain) again on a new medium. —*n.* **2.** a culture derived in this way.

sub·cu·ta·ne·ous (sŭb´kūtā´nĭəs), *adj.* **1.** situated or lying under the skin, as tissue. **2.** performed or introduced under the skin, as an injection by a syringe. **3.** living below the several layers of the skin, as certain parasites. —**sub/cu·ta/ne·ous·ly,** *adv.*

sub·dea·con (sŭbdē´kən), *n.* a member of the clerical order next below that of deacon. —**sub·dea·con·ate** (sŭbdē´kən ĭt), *n.*

sub·dean (sŭbdēn´), *n. Chiefly Brit.* an assistant dean.

sub·deb (sŭb´dĕb´), *n. Colloq.* **1.** a girl in her teens who has not yet been formally introduced to society. **2.** any girl of this age.

sub·deb·u·tante (sŭb´dĕb yŏŏ tănt´, -dĕb´yŏŏ tănt´), *n.* a girl preparing for her formal debut. Also, *Colloq.,* **subdeb.**

sub·dis·trict (sŭb´dĭs´trĭkt), *n.* a division of a district.

sub·di·vide (sŭb´dĭ vīd´), *v.,* **-vided, -viding.** —*v.t.* **1.** to divide (a part, or an already divided whole) into smaller parts; divide anew after a first division. **2.** to divide into parts. —*v.i.* **3.** to separate into subdivisions. —**sub·di·vi·sion** (sŭb´dĭ vĭzh´ən), *n.*

sub·dom·i·nant (sŭbdŏm´ənənt), *n. Music.* the fourth tone of a scale, next below the dominant.

sub·du·al (səbdū´əl, -dōō´-), *n.* **1.** act of subduing. **2.** state of being subdued.

sub·duct (səbdŭkt´), *v.t. Rare.* to take away or withdraw; deduct. —**sub·duc/tion,** *n.*

sub·due (səbdū´, -dōō´), *v.t.,* **-dued, -duing.** **1.** to conquer and bring into subjection. **2.** to overpower by superior force; overcome. **3.** to bring into moral subjection, as by persuasion or by inspiring awe or fear; render submissive (to). **4.** to repress (feelings, impulses, etc.). **5.** to bring (land) under cultivation. **6.** to reduce the intensity, force, or vividness of (sound, light, color, etc.); tone down; soften. **7.** to allay (inflammation, etc.). [ME, through AF, t. OF: m. *so(u)duire* seduce, g. L *subdūcere* remove by stealth; sense development in AF affected by L *subdere* subdue] —**sub·du/a·ble,** *adj.* —**sub·dued/,** *adj.* —**sub·du/er,** *n.* —**Syn.** **1.** See defeat. —**Ant.** **4.** awaken, arouse. **6.** intensify.

sub·ed·i·tor (sŭb ĕd´Ĭ tər), *n.* **1.** a subordinate editor. **2.** *Brit.* a copyreader.

su·be·re·ous (sōō bĭr´Ĭ əs), *adj.* of the nature of or resembling cork; suberose. [t. L: m. *sūbereus*]

su·ber·ic (sōō bĕr´Ĭk), *adj.* of or pertaining to cork. [t. F: m. *suberique,* f. L *sūber* cork + -*ique* -IC]

suberic acid, *Chem.* a crystalline dibasic acid, $(CH_2)_6(COOH)_2$, derived from cork.

su·ber·in (sōō´bər Ĭn), *n.* a substance contained in and characteristic of cork tissue.

su·ber·i·za·tion (sōō´bər ə zā´shən), *n. Bot.* the impregnation of cell walls with suberin, causing the formation of cork.

su·ber·ize (sōō´bər īz´), *v.t.,* **-ized, -izing.** *Bot.* to convert into cork tissue. [f. L *sūber* cork + -IZE]

su·ber·ose (sōō´bə rōs´), *adj.* of the nature of cork; corklike; corky. Also, **su·ber·ous** (sōō´bər əs).

sub·fam·i·ly (sŭb făm´Ĭ lĭ, -făm´əl Ĭ), *n., pl.* **-lies.** a category of related genera within a family.

sub·ge·nus (sŭb jē´nəs), *n., pl.* **-genera** (-jĕn´ə rə), **-genuses.** a subordinate genus; a subdivision of a genus. —**sub·ge·ner·ic** (sŭb´jə nĕr´Ĭk), *adj.*

sub·gla·cial (sŭb glā´shəl), *adj.* **1.** beneath a glacier: *a subglacial stream.* **2.** formerly beneath a glacier: *a subglacial deposit.* —**sub·gla/cial·ly,** *adv.*

sub·group (sŭb´grōōp´), *n.* **1.** a subordinate group; a division of a group. **2.** *Chem.* a vertical division of a group in the periodic table; family.

sub·head (sŭb´hĕd´), *n.* **1.** a subordinate head or title, under which is treated one of the divisions of a subject treated under a head. **2.** a subordinate division of a heading or title. **3.** the immediate subordinate of the president or other head of an educational institution.

sub·hu·man (sŭb hū´mən), *adj.* **1.** below the human race or type; less than or not quite human. **2.** almost human.

sub·in·dex (sŭb´Ĭn´dĕks), *n., pl.* **-dices** (-də sēz´). *Math., etc.* a specifying or distinguishing figure or letter following and slightly below a figure, letter, or symbol: *2* is the subindex in b2.

sub·in·feu·date (sŭb′ĭn fū′dāt), *v.t., v.i.,* **-dated, -dating.** to grant subinfeudation (to).

sub·in·feu·da·tion (sŭb′ĭn fyŏŏ dā′shən), *n. Feudal Law.* **1.** secondary infeudation; the granting of a portion of an estate by a feudal tenant to a subtenant, held of the tenant on terms similar to those of the grant to him. **2.** the tenure established. **3.** the estate or fief so created.

sub·in·feu·da·to·ry (sŭb′ĭn fū′də tōr′ĭ), *n., pl.* **-ries.** one who holds by subinfeudation.

sub·ir·ri·gate (sŭb ĭr′ə gāt′), *v.t.,* **-gated, -gating.** to irrigate beneath the surface of the ground, as with water passing through a system of underground pipes or joints mitted through the subsoil from ditches, etc. **—sub′ir·ri·ga′tion,** *n.*

su·bi·to (sōō′bē tō′), *adv. Music.* suddenly; abruptly: *f. subito, p. subito.* [It., t. L, abl. of *subitus* sudden]

subj., 1. subject. **2.** subjective. **3.** subjunctive.

sub·ja·cent (sŭb jā′sənt), *adj.* **1.** situated or occurring underneath or below; underlying. **2.** forming a basis. **3.** being in a lower situation, though not directly beneath. [t. L: s. *subjacens,* ppr., lying under] **—sub·ja′cen·cy,** *n.*

sub·ject (*n., adj.* sŭb′jĭkt; *v.* səb jĕkt′), *n.* **1.** something that forms a matter of thought, discourse, investigation, etc.: *a subject of conversation.* **2.** a ground, motive, or cause: *a subject for complaint.* **3.** the theme of a sermon, book, story, etc. **4.** a theme or melodic phrase on which a musical work or movement is based. **5.** an object, scene, incident, or the like, chosen by an artist for representation, or as represented in art. **6.** one who is under the dominion or rule of a sovereign; one who owes allegiance to a government and lives under its protection: *a Swedish subject.* **7.** the subjects of a realm collectively. **8.** (in English and many other languages) the word or words of a sentence which represent the person or object performing the action expressed in the predicate, e.g., *he* in *he has a hat.* **9.** one who or that which undergoes, or may undergo, some action. **10.** one who or that which is under the control or influence of another. **11.** a person as an object of medical, surgical, or psychological treatment or experiment. **12.** a dead body as used for dissection. **13.** *Logic.* that term of a proposition of which the other is affirmed or denied. **14.** *Philos.* **a.** the substance in which attributes inhere. **b.** substance; external reality as distinguished from its appearance; that which is the object of reference in predication. **c.** the self or ego to which all experiences or mental operations are attributed. **—adj. 15.** being under domination, control, or influence (often fol. by *to*). **16.** being under dominion, rule, or authority, as of a sovereign or a state, or some governing power; owing allegiance or obedience (*to*). **17.** open or exposed (fol. by *to*): *subject to ridicule.* **18.** being dependent or conditional upon something (fol. by *to*): *his consent is subject to your approval.* **19.** being under the necessity of undergoing something (fol. by *to*): *all men are subject to death.* **20.** liable, as to something (esp. something undesirable) that may or often does befall (fol. by *to*): *subject to headaches.* **—v.t. 21.** to bring under domination, control, or influence (usually fol. by *to*). **22.** to bring under dominion, rule, or authority, as of a conqueror or a governing power (usually fol. by *to*). **23.** to cause to undergo or experience something (fol. by *to*): *to subject metal to a white heat.* **24.** to make liable, lay open, or expose (fol. by *to*): *to subject oneself to ridicule.* **25.** *Obs.* to place beneath something or make subjacent. [t. L: s. *subjectus,* pp., placed under; r. ME *suget,* t. OF] **—Syn. 1.** SUBJECT, THEME, TOPIC are often interchangeable to express the material being considered in a speech or written composition. SUBJECT is a broad word for whatever is treated of in writing, speech, art, etc.: *the subject for discussion.* THEME and TOPIC are usually narrower and apply to some limited or specific part of a general subject. A THEME is often the underlying conception of a discourse or composition, perhaps not put into words but easily recognizable: *the theme of a need for reform runs throughout his work.* A TOPIC is the statement of what is to be treated in a section of a composition: *the topic is treated fully in this section.*

subject catalogue, *Library Sci.* a catalogue of subject headings only, to help the library patron to find books and other works on a particular subject or field.

sub·jec·tion (səb jĕk′shən), *n.* **1.** act of subjecting. **2.** state or fact of being subjected.

sub·jec·tive (səb jĕk′tĭv), *adj.* **1.** existing in the mind; belonging to the thinking subject rather than to the object of thought (opposed to *objective*). **2.** pertaining to or characteristic of an individual thinking subject; personal; individual: *subjective poetry.* **3.** *Psychol.* belonging to the thinking subject rather than to the object of thought. **4.** introspective. **5.** relating to or of the nature of a subject as it is known in the mind as distinct from a thing in itself. **6.** relating to properties or specific conditions of the mind as distinct from general or universal experience. **7.** pertaining to the subject or substance in which attributes inhere; essential. **8.** *Gram.* **a.** pertaining to or constituting the subject of a sentence. **b.** (in English and some other languages) denoting a case specialized for that use: in *he hit the ball, he* is in the subjective case. **c.** similar to such a case in meaning. **9.** *Philos. Obs.* of or pertaining to the subject as being nearly synonymous with the real. **10.** *Obs.* pertaining to

or befitting one who is subject to dominion, rule, or control. **—sub·jec′tive·ly,** *adv.* **—sub·jec·tiv·i·ty** (sŭb′jĕk tĭv′ə tĭ), **sub·jec′tive·ness,** *n.*

sub·jec·tiv·ism (səb jĕk′tĭ vĭz′əm), *n.* **1.** the philosophical theory that all knowledge terminates on the experiences of the self, and that transcendent knowledge is impossible. **2.** the ethical theory which finds its end in the attainment of states of thought or feeling. **3.** the doctrine that the good and the right can be distinguished and judged only by the individual feeling. **4.** subjectivity. **—sub·jec′tiv·ist,** *n.* **—sub·jec′ti·vis′tic,** *adj.*

subject matter, 1. the substance of a discourse, book, writing, or the like, as distinguished from its form or style. **2.** the matter which is subject to some operation, or out of which a thing is formed.

sub·join (səb join′), *v.t.* **1.** to add at the end, as of something said or written; append. **2.** to place in sequence or juxtaposition to something else.

sub ju·di·ce (sŭb jŏŏ′də sē′), *Latin.* before the judge.

sub·ju·gate (sŭb′jə gāt′), *v.t.,* **-gated, -gating. 1.** to bring under the yoke or into subjection; subdue; conquer. **2.** to bring under complete control. **3.** to make submissive or subservient. [t. L: m.s. *subjugātus,* pp., brought under the yoke] **—sub′ju·ga′tion,** *n.* **—sub′ju·ga′tor,** *n.*

sub·junc·tion (səb jŭngk′shən), *n.* **1.** act of subjoining. **2.** state of being subjoined. **3.** something subjoined.

sub·junc·tive (səb jŭngk′tĭv), *Gram.* **—adj. 1.** (in many languages) designating or pertaining to a verb mode having among its functions use in various subordinate clauses. **—n. 2.** the subjunctive mode. **3.** a verb in it, as *be* in *if it be true.* [t. LL: m.s. *subjunctivus,* der. L *subjunctus,* pp., subjoined]

sub·king·dom (sŭb kĭng′dəm), *n. Obs.* a phylum.

sub·lap·sar·i·an (sŭb′lăp sâr′ĭ ən), *n., adj.* infralapsarian. [f. s. NL *sublapsārius* (f. L: *sub-* SUB- + s. *lapsus* fall + *-ārius,* adj. suffix) + -AN]

sub·lease (*n.* sŭb′lēs′; *v.* sŭb lēs′), *n., v.,* **-leased, -leasing. —n. 1.** a lease granted by one who is himself a lessee of the property. **—v.t. 2.** to agree to or grant a sublease of; sublet. **3.** to take or hold a sublease of. **—sub·les·see** (sub′lĕ sē′), *n.* **—sub·les·sor** (sŭb′lĕs′ôr, sŭb′lĕ sôr′), *n.*

sub·let (sŭb lĕt′), *v.t.,* **-let, -letting. 1.** to let to another person, the party letting being himself lessee. **2.** to let (work, etc.) under a subcontract.

sub·lieu·ten·ant (sŭb′lŏŏ tĕn′ənt), *n.* **1.** a subordinate lieutenant. **2.** *Brit.* a navy officer ranking next below a lieutenant.

sub·li·mate (*v.* sŭb′lə māt′; *n., adj.* sŭb′lə mĭt, -māt′), *v.,* **-mated, -mating,** *n., adj.* **—v.t. 1.** *Psychol.* to deflect (sexual or other biological energies) into socially constructive or creative channels. **2.** *Chem., etc.* **a.** to sublime (a solid substance); extract by this process. **b.** to refine or purify (a substance). **3.** to make nobler or purer. **—v.i. 4.** to become sublimated; undergo sublimation. **—n. 5.** *Chem.* the crystals, deposit, or material obtained when a substance is sublimated; esp., corrosive sublimate. **—adj. 6.** sublimated. [t. L: m.s. *sublimātus,* pp., elevated] **—sub′li·ma′tion,** *n.*

sub·lime (sə blīm′), *adj., n., v.,* **-limed, -liming. —adj. 1.** elevated or lofty in thought, language, etc.: *sublime poetry.* **2.** impressing the mind with a sense of grandeur or power; inspiring awe, veneration, etc.: *sublime scenery.* **3.** supreme or perfect: *a sublime moment.* **4.** *Poetic.* of lofty bearing. **5.** *Poetic.* haughty or proud. **6.** *Archaic.* raised aloft. **—n. 7.** that which is sublime: *the sublime in art.* **8.** the highest degree or example (fol. by *of*). [t. L: m.s. *sublīmis* lofty] **—v.t. 9.** to make higher, nobler, or purer. **10.** *Chem., etc.* to convert (a solid substance) by heat into a vapor, which on cooling condenses again to solid form, without apparent liquefaction. **11.** *Chem., etc.* to cause to be given off by this or some analogous process. **—v.i. 12.** *Chem., etc.* to volatilize from the solid state to a gas, and then condense again as a solid without passing through the liquid state. [ME, t. L: m.s. *sublīmāre* elevate, der. *sublīmis* SUBLIME, adj.] **—sub·lime′ly,** *adv.* **—sub·lime′ness,** *n.*

Sublime Porte (pôrt). See **Porte.**

sub·lim·i·nal (sŭb lĭm′ə nəl, -lī′mə-), *adj. Psychol.* below the threshold of consciousness; subconscious. **—sub·lim′i·nal·ly,** *adv.*

sub·lim·i·ty (sə blĭm′ə tĭ), *n., pl.* **-ties. 1.** state or quality of being sublime. **2.** a sublime person or thing.

sub·lin·gual (sŭb lĭng′gwəl), *Anat.* **—adj. 1.** situated under the tongue, or on the underside of the tongue. **—n. 2.** a sublingual gland, artery, or the like.

sub·lu·nar·y (sŭb′lŏŏ nĕr′ĭ, sŭb lŏŏ′nə rĭ), *adj.* **1.** situated beneath the moon. **2.** of, on, or being the earth; terrestrial. **3.** mundane or worldly. Also, **sub·lu·nar** (sŭb lŏŏ′nər).

sub·ma·chine gun (sŭb′mə shēn′), a lightweight automatic or semiautomatic gun, fired from the shoulder or hip.

sub·man (sŭb′măn′), *n., pl.* **-men.** a man of very low mental or physical capacity.

sub·mar·gin·al (sŭb mär′jə nəl), *adj.* **1.** *Biol.* near the margin. **2.** below the margin. **3.** not worth cultivating, as land; unproductive. **—sub·mar′gin·al·ly,** *adv.*

sub·ma·rine (*n.* sŭb′mə rēn′; *adj.* sŭb′mə rēn′), *n.* **1.** a type of vessel that can be submerged and navigated

ăct, āble, dâre, ärt; ĕbb, ēqual; Ĭf, īce; hŏt, ōver, ôrder, oil, bŏŏk, ōoze, out; ŭp, ūse, ûrge; ə = a in alone; ch, chief; g, give; ng, ring; sh, shoe; th, thin; ŧħ, that; zh, vision. See the full key on inside cover.

under water, esp. one used in warfare for the discharge of torpedoes, etc. **2.** something submarine, as a plant, animal, etc. —*adj.* **3.** situated, occurring, operating, or living under the surface of the sea. **4.** of, pertaining to, or carried on by submarine boats: *submarine warfare.*

sub·ma·rine chaser, a vessel designed specially for operation against submarines.

sub·max·il·la (sŭb′măk sĭl′ə), *n.,* *pl.* **-maxillae** (-măk sĭl′ē). *Anat., Zool.* the lower jaw or lower jawbone.

sub·max·il·lar·y (sŭb măk′sə lĕr′Y, sŭb′măk sĭl′ə rY), *adj.* of or pertaining to the lower jaw or lower jawbone.

submaxillary gland, either of two saliva-producing glands beneath the lower jaw, one on each side.

sub·me·di·ant (sŭb mē′dY ənt), *n.* *Music.* the sixth tone of a scale, being midway between the subdominant and the upper tonic.

sub·merge (səb mûrj′). *v.,* **-merged, -merging.** —*v.t.* **1.** to put under water; sink below the surface of water or any enveloping medium. **2.** to cover, as water or the like does something beneath it. —*v.i.* **3.** to sink or plunge under water, or beneath the surface of any enveloping medium. [t. L: m.s. *submergere*] —**sub·mer′-gence,** *n.* —**Syn. 1.** See dip.

sub·mer·gi·ble (səb mûr′jə bəl), *adj., n.* submersible. —**sub·mer′gi·bil′i·ty,** *n.*

sub·merse (səb mûrs′), *v.t.,* **-mersed, -mersing.** to submerge. [t. L: m.s. *submersus,* pp., submerged] —**sub·mer·sion** (səb mûr′shən, -zhən), *n.*

sub·mersed (səb mûrst′), *adj.* **1.** submerged. **2.** *Bot.* growing under water.

sub·mers·i·ble (səb mûr′sə bəl), *adj.* **1.** that may be submersed. —*n.* **2.** (formerly) a submarine.

sub·mi·cro·scop·ic (sŭb′mī krə skŏp′Yk), *adj.* smaller than can be seen through a microscope.

sub·mis·sion (səb mĭsh′ən), *n.* **1.** act of submitting. **2.** the condition of having submitted. **3.** submissive conduct or attitude. **4.** *Law.* an agreement to abide by a decision or obey an authority in some matter referred to arbitration. [ME, t. L: s. *submissio*]

sub·mis·sive (səb mĭs′Yv), *adj.* **1.** inclined or ready to submit; unresistingly or humbly obedient. **2.** marked by or indicating submission: *a submissive reply.* —**sub·mis′sive·ly,** *adv.* —**sub·mis′sive·ness,** *n.*

sub·mit (səb mĭt′), *v.,* **-mitted, -mitting.** —*v.t.* **1.** to yield in surrender, compliance, or obedience. **2.** to subject (esp. oneself) to conditions imposed, treatment, etc. **3.** to refer to the decision or judgment of another or others. **4.** to state or urge with deference (with a clause): *I submit that full proof should be required.* —*v.i.* **5.** to yield in surrender, compliance, or obedience: *to submit to a conqueror.* **6.** to allow oneself to be subjected to something imposed or to be subjected: *to submit to punishment.* [ME *submitte,* t. L: m. *submittere* lower, put under] —**sub·mit′tal,** *n.* —**sub·mit′ter,** *n.* —**Syn. 1.** comply, bow. See **yield.** —**Ant. 1.** resist.

sub·mon·tane (sŭb mŏn′tān), *adj.* **1.** under or beneath a mountain or mountains. **2.** at or near the foot of mountains. **3.** pertaining to the lower slopes of mountains. —**sub·mon′tane·ly,** *adv.*

sub·mul·ti·ple (sŭb mŭl′tə pəl), *adj.* **1.** being, or pertaining to, a number or quantity which divides another exactly. —*n.* **2.** a submultiple number or quantity.

sub·nor·mal (sŭb nôr′məl), *adj.* **1.** below the normal; less than or inferior to the normal. **2.** lacking in one or more important psychological traits, as intelligence or some other ability. —*n.* **3.** an individual who is distinctly below average in intelligence, ability, or some other mental trait. **sub′nor·mal′i·ty,** *n.*

sub·o·ce·an·ic (sŭb′ō shY ăn′Yk), *adj.* beneath the ocean.

sub·or·der (sŭb′ôr′dər), *n.* a category of related families within an order.

sub·or·di·nal (sŭb ôr′də nəl), *adj.* of, pertaining to, or ranked as a suborder.

sub·or·di·nate (*adj., n.* sə bôr′də nYt; *v.* sə bôr′də nāt′), *adj., n., v.,* **-nated, -nating.** —*adj.* **1.** placed in or belonging to a lower order or rank. **2.** of inferior importance; secondary. **3.** subject to or under the authority of a superior. **4.** subservient. **5.** dependent. **6.** *Gram.* subordinative. **7.** *Obs.* submissive. —*n.* **8.** a subordinate person or thing. —*v.t.* **9.** to place in a lower order or rank. **10.** to make secondary (fol. by *to*). **11.** to make subject, subservient, or dependent (fol. by *to*). [late ME, t. ML: m.s. *subordinātus,* pp., subordinated] —**sub·or′di·na′tion,** *n.* —**sub·or′di·na′tive,** *adj.*

subordinate clause, (in some languages) a clause whose presence in a sentence depends on the presence of another clause, without which it does not constitute a full sentence, e.g., "*when I came*" in "*They were glad when I came.*"

sub·or·di·nat·ing (sə bôr′də nā′tYng), *adj.* (in some languages) introducing subordinate clauses, as in English "*when,*" called a *subordinating conjunction* in "*They were glad when I came in.*"

sub·or·di·na·tion·ism (sə bôr′də nā′shə nYz′əm), *n.* *Theol.* the doctrine that the first person of the Holy Trinity is superior to the second and the third. —**sub·or′di·na′tion·ist,** *n., adj.*

sub·orn (sə bôrn′), *v.t.* to bribe or procure (a person) unlawfully to commit some act of wickedness, usually perjury. [t. L: s. *subornāre* equip secretly] —**sub·or·na·tion** (sŭb′ôr nā′shən), *n.* —**sub·or·na·tive** (sə bôr′nə tYv), *adj.* —**sub·orn′er,** *n.*

Su·bo·ti·ca (sō̄o′bô′tY tsä), *n.* a city in NE Yugoslavia. 115,402 (1953). Hungarian, **Szabadka.**

sub·ox·ide (sŭb ŏk′sĭd, -sYd), *n.* *Chem.* the oxide of an element containing the smallest proportion of oxygen.

sub·phy·lum (sŭb fī′ləm), *n., pl.* **-la** (-lə). a category ranking below a phylum.

sub·plot (sŭb′plŏt′), *n.* a minor plot in a play, as distinct from the main plot.

sub·poe·na (sə pē′nə, səb-), *n., v.,* **-naed, -naing.** *Law.* —*n.* **1.** the usual writ process for the summoning of witnesses. —*v.t.* **2.** to serve with a subpoena. Also, **sub·pe′na.** [ME, t. L: m. *sub poenā* under penalty, the first words of the writ]

sub·prin·ci·pal (sŭb prYn′sə pəl), *n.* **1.** an assistant or deputy principal. **2.** *Carp.* an auxiliary rafter or additional supporting member. **3.** *Music.* (in an organ) a subbass of the open diapason class.

sub·re·gion (sŭb′rē′jən), *n.* a division or subdivision of a region, esp. a division of a zoögeographical region. —**sub·re′gion·al,** *adj.*

sub·rep·tion (səb rĕp′shən), *n.* **1.** the act of obtaining something, as an ecclesiastical dispensation, by suppression or fraudulent concealment of facts. **2.** a fallacious representation, or an inference from it. [t. L: s. *subreptio* theft] —**sub·rep·ti·tious** (sŭb′rĕp tYsh′əs), *adj.*

sub·ro·gate (sŭb′rō gāt′), *v.t.,* **-gated, -gating. 1.** to put into the place of another; substitute for another. **2.** *Civ. Law.* to substitute a claim against one person for a claim against another person, or transfer a lien originally imposed on one piece of property to another piece of property. [t. L: m.s. *subrogātus,* pp., put in another's place] —**sub′ro·ga′tion,** *n.*

sub ro·sa (sŭb rō′zə), confidentially; privately. [t. L: under the rose; the rose being the symbol of the Egyptian god Horus, identified by the Greeks with Harpocrates, god of silence]

sub·scap·u·lar (sŭb skăp′yə lər), *Anat.* —*adj.* **1.** beneath, or on the deep surface of, the scapula, as a muscle, artery, etc. —*n.* **2.** a subscapular muscle, artery, etc.

sub·scribe (səb skrīb′), *v.,* **-scribed, -scribing.** —*v.t.* **1.** to promise, as by signing an agreement, to give or pay (a sum of money) as a contribution, payment, share, etc. **2.** to give or pay in fulfillment of such a promise. **3.** to express assent or adhesion to (a contract, etc.) by signing one's name; attest by signing, as a statement or a will. **4.** to write or inscribe (something) beneath or at the end of a thing; sign (one's name) to a document, etc. —*v.i.* **5.** to undertake, as by signing an agreement, to give or pay money for some special purpose. **6.** to obtain a subscription to a magazine, newspaper, etc. **7.** to give or pay money as a contribution, payment, etc. **8.** to sign one's name to something. **9.** to assent by, or as by, signing one's name. **10.** to give consent or sanction. [ME, t. L: m.s. *subscrībere*] —**sub·scrib′er,** *n.*

sub·script (sŭb′skrYpt), *adj.* **1.** written below (distinguished from *adscript*). **2.** placed low on the line, as the "2" in "H₂O". —*n.* **3.** something written below. [t. L: s. *subscriptus,* pp.]

sub·scrip·tion (səb skrYp′shən), *n.* **1.** the contribution toward some object or in payment for shares, a book, a periodical, etc. **2.** the right to receive a periodical for a sum subscribed. **3.** *Brit.* dues in a club, society, etc. **4.** a fund raised through sums of money subscribed. **5.** a sum subscribed. **6.** act of subscribing; the signing of one's name, as to a document. **7.** something subscribed, or written beneath or at the end of a thing. **8.** a signature attached to a paper. **9.** assent, agreement, or approval expressed by, or as by, signing one's name. **10.** *Eccles.* assent to or acceptance of a body of principles or doctrines, the purpose of which is to establish uniformity. **11.** *Ch. of Eng.* formal acceptance of the Thirty-nine Articles of 1563 and the Book of Common Prayer. [late ME, t. L: s. *subscriptio*] —**sub·scrip·tive** (səb skrYp′tYv), *adj.* —**sub·scrip′tive·ly,** *adv.*

sub·sec·tion (sŭb sĕk′shən, sŭb′sĕk′shən), *n.* a part or division of a section.

sub·se·quence (sŭb′sə kwəns), *n.* **1.** state or fact of being subsequent. **2.** that which is subsequent; sequel.

sub·se·quen·cy (sŭb′sə kwən sY), *n., pl.* **-cies.** subsequence.

sub·se·quent (sŭb′sə kwənt), *adj.* **1.** coming later or after: *subsequent events.* **2.** following in order or succession: *a subsequent section in a treaty.* **3.** coming or occurring after or later (often with *to*): *on the day subsequent to the event.* [late ME, t. L: s. *subsequens,* ppr.] —**sub′se·quent·ly,** *adv.*

sub·serve (səb sûrv′), *v.t.,* **-served, -serving. 1.** to be useful or instrumental in promoting (a purpose, action, etc.). **2.** *Obs.* to serve under. [t. L: m.s. *subservīre*]

sub·ser·vi·ent (səb sûr′vY ənt), *adj.* **1.** serving or acting in a subservient capacity; subordinate. **2.** (of persons, their conduct, etc.) servile; excessively submissive; obsequious. **3.** of use as a means to promote a purpose or end. [t. L: s. *subserviens,* ppr.] —**sub·ser′vi·ence,** or **sub·ser′vi·en·cy,** *n.* —**sub·ser′vi·ent·ly,** *adv.*

sub·set (sŭb′sĕt′), *n.* a subordinate set.

sub·side (səb sīd′), *v.i.,* **-sided, -siding. 1.** to sink to a low or lower level. **2.** to become quiet, less violent, or less active; abate; *the laughter subsided.* **3.** to sink or fall to the bottom; settle, as lees; precipitate. [t. L: m.s. *subsidere* settle down] —**sub·sid·ence** (səb sĭd′əns, sŭb′sə dəns), *n.*

sub·sid·i·ar·y (səb sĭd′ĭ ĕr′ĭ), *adj.*, *n.*, *pl.* **-ar·ies.** —*adj.* **1.** serving to assist or supplement; auxiliary; supplementary; tributary, as a stream. **2.** subordinate or secondary. **3.** consisting of, pertaining to, or maintained by, a subsidy or subsidies. —*n.* **4.** a subsidiary thing or person. **5.** *Music.* a subordinate theme or subject. [t. L: m.s. *subsidiārius* belonging to a reserve] —**sub·sid′i·ar′i·ly,** *adv.*

subsidiary company, a company the controlling interest in which is owned by another company.

sub·si·dize (sŭb′sə dīz′), *v.t.*, **-dized, -dizing. 1.** to furnish or aid with a subsidy. **2.** to purchase the assistance of by the payment of a subsidy. **3.** to secure the coöperation of by bribery; buy over. Also, *esp. Brit.,* **sub′si·dise′.** [f. SUBSID(Y) + -IZE] —**sub′si·di·za′tion,** *n.* —**sub′si·diz′er,** *n.*

sub·si·dy (sŭb′sə dĭ), *n., pl.* **-dies. 1.** a direct pecuniary aid furnished by a government to a private industrial undertaking, a charity organization, or the like. **2.** a sum paid, often in accordance with a treaty, by one government to another, to secure some service in return. **3.** a grant or contribution of money. **4.** money formerly granted by the English Parliament to the crown for special needs. [ME, t. L: m.s. *subsidium* assistance]
—**Syn. 1.** SUBSIDY, SUBVENTION are both grants of money, especially governmental, to aid private undertakings. A SUBSIDY is usually given to promote commercial enterprise: *a subsidy to manufacturers during a war.* A SUBVENTION is usually a grant to stimulate enterprises connected with science and the arts: *a subvention to a research chemist by one of the major industrial companies.*

sub·sist (səb sĭst′), *v.i.* **1.** to exist, or continue in existence. **2.** to continue alive; live, as on food, resources, etc. **3.** to have existence in, or by reason of, something. **4.** to reside, lie, or consist (fol. by *in*). **5.** *Philos.* to possess the quality of truth and the ability of being construed logically. —*v.t.* **6.** to provide sustenance or support for; maintain. [t. L: s. *subsistere* stand firm, be adequate to]

sub·sist·ence (səb sĭs′təns), *n.* **1.** state or fact of subsisting; continuance. **2.** existence. **3.** the providing of sustenance or support. **4.** means of supporting life; a living or livelihood. **5.** *Philos.* **a.** the process of substance assuming individualization; a single autonomous human being with certain rights. **b.** the rank of something possessing the quality of truth and the ability of being construed logically.

sub·soil (sŭb′soil′), *n.* **1.** the bed or stratum of earth or earthy material immediately under the surface soil. —*v.t.* **2.** to plow so as to break up part of the subsoil.

sub·so·lar (sŭb sō′lər), *adj.* **1.** directly beneath the sun. **2.** between the tropics.

sub·son·ic (sŭb sŏn′ĭk), *adj.* **1.** (of sound frequencies) below the audible limit. **2.** (of velocities) below the velocity of sound in the medium.

sub·spe·cies (sŭb spē′shĭz, sŭb′spē′shĭz), *n., pl.* **-cies.** a subdivision of a species, esp. a geographical or ecological subdivision.

subst., 1. substantive. **2.** substantively. **3.** substitute.

sub·stance (sŭb′stəns), *n.* **1.** that of which a thing consists; matter or material. **2.** a species of matter of definite chemical composition. **3.** the matter with which thought, discourse, study, or the like, is occupied; subject matter. **4.** the actual matter of a thing, as opposed to the appearance or shadow; the reality. **5.** substantial or solid character or quality: *claims lacking in substance.* **6.** body: *soup without much substance.* **7.** the meaning or gist, as of speech or writing. **8.** something that has separate or independent existence. **9.** *Philos.* **a.** that which exists by itself, and in which accidents or attributes inhere; that which receives modifications, and is not itself a mode; that which is causally active; that which is more than an event. **b.** the essential part, or essence, of a thing. **c.** the thing as a continuing whole. **10.** possessions, means, or wealth: *to squander one's substance.* **11. in substance, a.** substantially. **b.** actually; really. [ME, t. OF, g. L *substantia*] —**Syn. 1.** See matter.

sub·stand·ard (sŭb stăn′dərd), *adj.* **1.** below standard. **2.** *U.S. Statute Law.* (without so stating) under the minimum standard established by the legislature. **3.** *Linguistics.* characteristic of a normal, uncultivated variety of a language which has a standard variety, hence tending to reflect prejudicially on the user.

sub·stan·tial (səb stăn′shəl), *adj.* **1.** of a corporeal or material nature; real or actual. **2.** of ample or considerable amount, quantity, size, etc.: *a substantial sum of money.* **3.** of solid character or quality; firm, stout, or strong. **4.** being such with respect to essentials: *two stories in substantial agreement.* **5.** wealthy or influential: *one of the substantial men of the town.* **6.** of real worth or value: *substantial reasons.* **7.** pertaining to the substance, matter, or material of a thing. **8.** of or pertaining to the essence of a thing; essential, material, or important. **9.** being a substance; having independent existence. **10.** *Philos.* pertaining to or of the nature of substance rather than accidents. —*n.* **11.** something substantial. [ME *substancial,* t. LL: m.s. *substantiālis*] —**sub·stan′ti·al′i·ty, sub·stan′tial·ness,** *n.* —**sub·stan′tial·ly,** *adv.* —**Ant. 1.** ethereal.

sub·stan·tial·ism (səb stăn′shə lĭz′əm), *n. Philos.* the doctrine that there are substantial realities back of phenomena. —**sub·stan′tial·ist,** *n.*

sub·stan·ti·ate (səb stăn′shĭ āt′), *v.t.,* **-ated, -ating. 1.** to establish by proof or competent evidence: *to substantiate a charge.* **2.** to give substantial existence to. **3.** to present as having substance. —**sub·stan′ti·a′tion,** *n.* —**sub·stan′ti·a′tive,** *adj.*

sub·stan·tive (sŭb′stən tĭv), *n.* **1.** *Gram.* **a.** a noun. **b.** a noun, pronoun, or other word or phrase having nominal function in sentences or inflected like a noun. **c.** (in Latin and other languages where adjectives are inflected like nouns) a noun or adjective, as Latin *puella* "girl" and *bona* "good" in *puella bona est* "the girl is good." —*adj.* **2.** *Gram.* **a.** pertaining to substantives. **b.** used in a sentence like a noun: *a substantive adjective.* **c.** expressing existence: *"to be" is a substantive verb.* **3.** having independent existence; independent. **4.** belonging to the real nature or essential part of a thing; essential. **5.** real or actual. **6.** of considerable amount or quantity. **7.** *Law.* pertaining to the rules of right which courts are called on to apply, as distinguished from rules of procedure (opposed to *adjective*). **8** *Dyeing.* (of colors) attaching directly to the material without the aid of a mordant or the like (opposed to *adjective*). [ME, t. LL: m.s. *substantīvus* standing by itself. der. L *substantia* substance] —**sub·stan·ti·val** (sŭb′stən tī′vəl), *adj.* —**sub′stan·tive·ly,** *adv.* —**sub′stan·tive·ness,** *n.*

sub·sta·tion (sŭb′stā′shən), *n.* a subsidiary station.

sub·stit·u·ent (səb stĭch′ŏŏ ənt), *n. Chem.* an atom or atomic group which takes the place of another atom or group present in the molecule of the original compound. [t. s. *substituens,* ppr., substituting]

sub·sti·tute (sŭb′stə tūt′, -tŏŏt′), *n., v.,* **-tuted, -tuting.** —*n.* **1.** a person or thing acting or serving in place of another. **2.** (formerly) one who, for a consideration, served in an army or navy in the place of a conscript. **3.** *Gram.* a word which under given conditions replaces any of a class of other words or constructions, as English *do* replacing verbs (I *know* but he *doesn't*). —*v.t.* **4.** to put (one person or thing) in the place of another. **5.** to take the place of; replace. —*v.i.* **6.** to act as substitute. **7.** *Chem.* to replace one or more elements or radicals in a compound by other elements or radicals. [ME, t. L: m.s. *substitūtus,* pp.] —**sub′sti·tu′tion,** *n.* —**sub′sti·tu′tion·al, sub′sti·tu·tion·ar·y** (sŭb′stə tū′shə nĕr′ĭ, -tŏŏ′-), *adj.* —**sub′sti·tu′tion·al·ly,** *adv.*

sub·sti·tu·tive (sŭb′stə tū′tĭv, -tŏŏ′-), *adj.* **1.** serving as, or capable of serving as, a substitute. **2.** pertaining to or involving substitution.

sub·strate (sŭb′strāt), *n.* **1.** a substratum. **2.** *Biochem.* the substance acted upon by an enzyme or ferment.

sub·stra·tum (sŭb strā′təm, -străt′əm), *n., pl.* **-strata** (-strā′tə, -străt′ə). **1.** that which is spread or laid under something else; a stratum or layer lying under another. **2.** something which underlies, or serves as a basis or foundation. **3.** *Agric.* the subsoil. **4.** (of an organism) the base or material on which it lives. **5.** *Metaphys.* that which is regarded as supporting accidents or attributes; substance, as that in which qualities inhere. [NL: (neut. pp.) spread underneath] —**sub·stra′tive,** *adj.*

sub·struc·tion (sŭb strŭk′shən), *n.* a foundation or substructure. [t. L: s. *substructio*] —**sub·struc′tion·al,** *adj.*

sub·struc·ture (sŭb strŭk′chər, sŭb′strŭk′-), *n.* **1.** a structure forming the foundation of a building or the like. **2.** the foundations, piers, abutments, and other parts of a railroad bridge upon which the superstructure rests. —**sub·struc′tur·al,** *adj.*

sub·sume (səb sŏŏm′), *v.t.,* **-sumed, -suming. 1.** to bring (an idea, term, proposition, etc.) under another; bring (a case, instance, etc.) under a rule. **2.** to take up into or include in a larger or higher class or the like. [t. NL: m.s. *subsūmere,* f. L sub- SUB- + *sūmere* take]

sub·sump·tion (səb sŭmp′shən), *n.* **1.** act of subsuming. **2.** state of being subsumed. **3.** that which is subsumed. **4.** a proposition subsumed under another. —**sub·sump′tive** (səb sŭmp′tĭv), *adj.*

sub·tan·gent (sŭb tăn′jənt), *n. Geom.* the part of the x-axis cut off between the ordinate of a given point of a curve and the tangent at the point.

sub·tem·per·ate (sŭb tĕm′pər ĭt), *adj.* pertaining to or occurring in the colder parts of the Temperate Zone.

sub·ten·ant (sŭb tĕn′ənt), *n.* one who rents land, a house, or the like from a tenant. —**sub·ten′an·cy,** *n.*

sub·tend (səb tĕnd′), *v.t.* **1.** *Geom., etc.* to extend under; be opposite to: *a chord subtending an arc.* **2.** *Bot.* (of a leaf, bract, etc.) to enclose or embrace in its axil. [t. L: s. *subtendere* stretch under]

B

A   *C*

Chord AC subtends arc ABC

subter-, a prefix meaning "position underneath," with figurative applications, as in *subterfuge.* [t. L, comb. form of *subter,* prep. and adv.]

sub·ter·fuge (sŭb′tər fūj′), *n.* an artifice or expedient employed to escape the force of an argument, to evade unfavorable consequences, etc. [t. LL: m.s. *subterfugium,* der. L *subterfugere* flee secretly]

sub·ter·nat·u·ral (sŭb′tər năch′ə rəl), *adj.* below what is natural; less than natural.

sub·ter·ra·ne·an (sŭb/tə·rā/nĭ·ən), *adj.* **1.** existing, situated, or operating below the surface of the earth; underground. **2.** existing or operating out of sight or secretly; hidden or secret. Also, **sub/ter·ra/ne·ous.** [f. s. L *subterrāneus* below the earth + -AN]

sub·tile (sŭt/əl, sŭb/tĭl), *adj.* subtle. —**sub/tile·ly,** *adv.* —**sub/tile·ness, sub·til·i·ty** (sŭb·tĭl/ə·tĭ), sub/til·ty, *n.*

sub·til·ize (sŭt/ə·līz/, sŭb/tə·līz/), *v.,* -ized, -izing. —*v.t.* **1.** to elevate in character; sublimate. **2.** to render (the mind, senses, etc.) acute or keen. **3.** to introduce subtleties into; argue subtly upon. **4.** to make thin, rare, or more fluid or volatile; refine. —*v.i.* **5.** to make subtle distinctions; argue subtly. —**sub/til·i·za/tion,** *n.*

sub·ti·tle (sŭb/tī/təl), *n.* **1.** a secondary or subordinate title of a literary work, usually of explanatory character. **2.** a repetition of the leading words in the full title of a book at the head of the first page of text.

sub·tle (sŭt/əl), *adj.* **1.** thin, tenuous, or rarefied, as a fluid. **2.** fine or delicate, often when likely to elude perception or understanding: *subtle irony.* **3.** delicate or faint and mysterious: *a subtle smile.* **4.** requiring mental acuteness, penetration, or discernment: *a subtle point.* **5.** characterized by mental acuteness or penetration: *a subtle understanding.* **6.** cunning, wily, or crafty. **7.** insidious in operation, as poison, etc. **8.** skillful, clever, or ingenious. [ME *sutell,* t. OF: m. *soutil,* g. L *subtīlis* fine, delicate] —**sub/tle·ness,** *n.* —**sub/tly** (sŭt/lĭ), *adv.*

sub·tle·ty (sŭt/əl·tĭ), *n., pl.* -ties. **1.** state or quality of being subtle. **2.** delicacy or nicety of character or meaning; acuteness or penetration of mind; delicacy of discrimination. **3.** the habit of making fine-drawn distinction. **4.** something subtle.

sub·ton·ic (sŭb·tŏn/ĭk), *n. Music.* the seventh tone of a scale, being the next below the upper tonic.

sub·tract (səb·trăkt/), *v.t.* **1.** to withdraw or take away, as a part from a whole. **2.** *Math.* to take (one number or quantity) from another; deduct. —*v.i.* **3.** to take away something or a part, as from a whole. [t. L: s. *subtractus,* pp., carried away] —**sub·tract/er,** *n.* —**Syn. 1, 3.** SUBTRACT, DEDUCT express diminution in sum or quantity. To SUBTRACT suggests taking a part from a whole or a smaller from a larger: *to subtract the tax from one's salary.* To DEDUCT is to take away an amount or quantity from an aggregate or total so as to lessen or lower it: *to deduct a discount.* SUBTRACT is both transitive and intransitive, and has general or figurative uses; DEDUCT is always transitive and usually concrete and practical in application. —**Ant. 1.** add.

sub·trac·tion (səb·trăk/shən), *n.* **1.** act of subtracting. **2.** *Math.* the operation of finding the difference between two numbers or quantities (denoted by the symbol −).

sub·trac·tive (səb·trăk/tĭv), *adj.* **1.** tending to subtract; having power to subtract. **2.** *Math.* (of a quantity) that is to be subtracted; having the minus sign (−).

sub·tra·hend (sŭb/trə·hĕnd/), *n. Math.* the number or quantity to be taken from another (the minuend) in subtraction. [t. L: s. *subtrahendus,* ger., to be subtracted]

sub·treas·ur·y (sŭb·trĕzh/ər·ĭ), *n., pl.* -uries. **1.** a subordinate or branch treasury. **2.** a branch of the U.S. Treasury.

sub·trop·i·cal (sŭb·trŏp/ə·kəl), *adj.* **1.** bordering on the tropics; nearly tropical. **2.** pertaining to or occurring in a region intermediate between tropical and temperate.

sub·trop·ics (sŭb·trŏp/ĭks), *n.pl.* subtropical regions.

sub·type (sŭb/tīp/), *n.* **1.** a subordinate type. **2.** a more special type included in a more general type.

su·bu·late (sōō/byə·lĭt, -lāt/), *adj.* **1.** awl-shaped. **2.** *Bot., Zool., etc.* slender, more or less cylindrical, and tapering to a point. [t. NL: m.s. *sūbulātus,* der. L *sūbula* awl]

Subulate leaves

sub·urb (sŭb/ûrb), *n.* **1.** (*often pl.*) a district lying immediately outside a city or town, esp. a residential section outside of the city boundaries but adjoining them. **2.** (*usually pl.*) an outlying part. [ME *suburbe,* t. L: m.s. *suburbium*]

sub·ur·ban (sə·bûr/bən), *adj.* **1.** pertaining to, inhabiting, or being in a suburb or the suburbs of a city or town. **2.** characteristic of a suburb or suburbs. —*n.* **3.** one who lives in the suburbs of a city or town.

sub·ur·ban·ite (sə·bûr/bə·nīt/), *n.* a suburban resident.

sub·ur·bi·car·i·an (sə·bûr/bə·kâr/ĭ·ən), *adj.* **1.** being near the city (of Rome). **2.** noting or pertaining to the dioceses (now six in number) about Rome under the Pope as metropolitan, whose bishops are cardinals. [f. s. LL *suburbicārius* suburban + -AN]

sub·vene (səb·vēn/), *v.i.,* -vened, -vening. to come under, as an aid or support; arrive or happen, especially so as to prevent something. [t. L: m.s. *subvenīre*]

sub·ven·tion (səb·vĕn/shən), *n.* **1.** a grant of pecuniary aid, esp. by a government or some other authority, in aid or support of some object, institution, or undertaking. **2.** the furnishing of aid or relief. —**sub·ven·tion·ar·y** (səb·vĕn/shə·nĕr/ĭ), *adj.* —**Syn. 1.** See subsidy.

sub ver·bo (sŭb vûr/bō), *Latin.* under the word or

heading (a direction to a reference). Also, **sub vo·ce** (sŭb vō/sĭ).

sub·ver·sion (səb·vûr/shən, -zhən), *n.* **1.** act of subverting; overthrow. **2.** state of being subverted; destruction. **3.** that which subverts or overthrows. Also, **sub·ver·sal** (səb·vûr/səl). [ME, t. LL: s. *subversio*]

sub·ver·sive (səb·vûr/sĭv), *adj.* **1.** tending to subvert; such as to cause subversion. —*n.* **2.** one who adopts subversive principles or policies.

sub·vert (səb·vûrt/), *v.t.* **1.** to overthrow (something established or existing). **2.** to cause the downfall, ruin, or destruction of. **3.** *Rare.* to undermine the principles of; corrupt. [ME, t. L: s. *subvertere*] —**sub·vert/er,** *n.*

sub·way (sŭb/wā/), *n.* **1.** *U.S.* an electric railroad beneath the surface of the streets in a city. **2.** *Chiefly Brit.* an artificial underground way for pedestrians, traffic, etc.

suc-, var. of sub- (by assimilation) before *c.*

suc·ce·da·ne·um (sŭk/sə·dā/nĭ·əm), *n., pl.* -nea (-nĭ·ə). a substitute. [NL, neut. sing. of L *succedāneus* taking the place of something] —**suc/ce·da/ne·ous,** *adj.*

suc·ceed (sək·sēd/), *v.i.* **1.** to turn out or terminate according to desire; turn out successfully; have the desired result. **2.** to have (good or ill) success: *I have succeeded very badly.* **3.** to accomplish what is attempted or intended. **4.** to follow or replace another by descent, election, appointment, etc. (often fol. by *to*). **5.** to come next after something else in an order or series. —*v.t.* **6.** to come after and take the place of, as in an office or estate. **7.** to come next after in an order or series, or in the course of events, or follow. [ME, succeed. t. L: m. *succēdere* go up, be successful] —**suc·ceed/er,** *n.* —**Syn. 1.** SUCCEED, FLOURISH, PROSPER, THRIVE mean to do well. To SUCCEED is to turn out well, to attain a goal: *it is everyone's wish to succeed in life.* To FLOURISH is to give evidence of success or a ripe development of power, reputation, etc.: *culture flourishes among free people.* To PROSPER is to achieve and enjoy material success: *he prospered but was still discontented.* THRIVE suggests vigorous growth and development such as results from natural vitality or favorable conditions: *the children thrived in the sunshine.* **4.** See follow. —**Ant. 1.** fail.

suc·cen·tor (sək·sĕn/tər), *n. Eccles.* a precentor's deputy. [t. LL, der. L *succinere* accompany, sing to]

suc·cès d'es·time (sүk sě/ dĕs tēm/), *French.* a success of esteem (rather than of popularity or profit).

suc·cess (sək·sĕs/), *n.* **1.** the favorable or prosperous termination of attempts or endeavors. **2.** the gaining of wealth, position, or the like. **3.** a successful performance or achievement. **4.** a thing or a person that is successful. **5.** *Obs.* outcome. [t. L: s. *successus*]

suc·cess·ful (sək·sĕs/fəl), *adj.* **1.** achieving or having achieved success. **2.** having succeeded in obtaining wealth, position, or the like. **3.** resulting in or attended with success. —**suc·cess/ful·ly,** *adv.*

suc·ces·sion (sək·sĕsh/ən), *n.* **1.** the coming of one after another in order, sequence, or the course of events; sequence. **2.** a number of persons or things following one another in order or sequence. **3.** the right, act or process, by which one person succeeds to the office, rank, estate or the like, of another. **4.** the order or line of those entitled to succeed. **5.** the descent or transmission, or the principle or mode of transmission, of a throne, dignity, estate, or the like. [ME, t. L: s. *successio*] —**suc·ces/sion·al,** *adj.* —**suc·ces/sion·al·ly,** *adv.* —**Syn. 2.** See series.

suc·ces·sive (sək·sĕs/ĭv), *adj.* **1.** following in order or in uninterrupted course: *three successive days.* **2.** following another in a regular sequence: *the second successive day.* **3.** characterized by or involving succession. —**suc·ces/sive·ly,** *adv.* —**suc·ces/sive·ness,** *n.* —**Syn. 1.** SUCCESSIVE, CONSECUTIVE apply to things which follow one upon another. SUCCESSIVE refers merely to the position of one with reference to another: *discouraged by successive misfortunes.* CONSECUTIVE denotes a close and uninterrupted sequence, sometimes with the implication of an established order: *the army was finally routed by defeats on three consecutive days.*

suc·ces·sor (sək·sĕs/ər), *n.* **1.** one who or that which succeeds or follows. **2.** one who succeeds another in an office, position, or the like. [t. L; r. ME *successour,* t. AF]

suc·cinct (sək·sĭngkt/), *adj.* **1.** expressed in few words; concise; terse. **2.** characterized by conciseness or verbal brevity. **3.** compressed into a small compass. **4.** *Archaic.* encircled, as by a girdle. [ME, t. L: s. *succinctus,* pp., girded up] —**suc·cinct/ly,** *adv.* —**suc·cinct/ness,** *n.*

suc·cin·ic (sək·sĭn/ĭk), *adj.* **1.** pertaining to or obtained from amber. **2.** *Chem.* noting or pertaining to a white crystalline acid, $C_2H_4(COOH)_2$, occurring naturally in amber, but now manufactured synthetically. [t. F: m. *succinique,* f. s. L *succinum* amber + -ique -IC]

suc·cor (sŭk/ər), *n.* **1.** help; relief; aid; assistance. **2.** one who or that which succors; an aid. —*v.t.* **3.** to help or relieve in difficulty, need, or distress; aid; assist. Also, esp. *Brit.,* **suc/cour.** [ME *sucurs,* t. AF, OF, der. *secourir* to help, g. L *succurrere*] —**suc/cor·er,** *n.* —**Syn. 1.** See help.

suc·co·ry (sŭk/ə·rĭ), *n., pl.* -ries. chicory.

suc·co·tash (sŭk/ə·tăsh/), *n.* a dish of North American Indian origin, consisting of corn (removed from the cob) and beans. [t. Narraganset: m. *msiquatash*]

suc·cu·ba (sŭk/yə·bə), *n., pl.* -bae (-bē). a female demon fabled to have sexual intercourse with men in their sleep. Cf. **incubus.** [t. ML, special use of LL *succuba* strumpet]

---

b., blend of, blended; c., cognate with; d., dialect, dialectal; der., derived from; f., formed from; g., going back to; m., modification of; r., replacing; s., stem of; t., taken from; ?, perhaps. See the full key on inside cover.

suc·cu·bus (sŭk′yə bəs), *n., pl.* **-bi** (-bī′). **1.** any demon or evil spirit. **2.** a succuba. [ME; var. of SUCCUBA, with *-us* from INCUBUS]

suc·cu·lent (sŭk′yə lənt), *adj.* **1.** full of juice; juicy. **2.** rich in desirable qualities. **3.** affording mental nourishment; not dry. **4.** (of plants, etc.) having fleshy and juicy tissues. [t. L: s. *succulentus*] —**suc′cu·lence, suc′cu·len·cy,** *n.* —**suc′cu·lent·ly,** *adv.*

suc·cumb (sə kŭm′), *v.i.* **1.** to give way to superior force; yield. **2.** to yield to disease, wounds, old age, etc.; die. [late ME, t. L: s. *succumbere*]

suc·cur·sal (sə kûr′səl), *adj.* subsidiary; esp. noting a religious establishment which is dependent upon a principal one. [t. F, der. L *succursus* SUCCOR]

suc·cuss (sə kŭs′), *v.t.* **1.** to shake up; shake. **2.** *Med.* to shake (a patient) in order to determine if a fluid is present in the thorax or elsewhere. [t. L: s. *succussus*, pp., tossed up]

suc·cus·sa·tion (sŭk′ə sā′shən), *n.* succussion. —**suc·cus·sa·to·ry** (sə kŭs′ə tôr′ĭ), *adj.*

suc·cus·sion (sə kŭsh′ən), *n.* act of succussing. [t. L: s. *succussio*] —**suc·cus·sive** (sə kŭs′ĭv), *adj.*

such (sŭch), *adj.* **1.** of the kind, character, degree, extent, etc., of that or those indicated or implied: *such a man is dangerous*. **2.** of that particular kind or character: *the food, such as it was, was plentiful*. **3.** like or similar: *tea, coffee, and such commodities*. **4.** (preceding an adjective used attributively) so, or in such a manner or degree: *such terrible deeds*. **5.** (with omission of an indication of comparison) so extreme a kind; so great, good, bad, etc.: *he is such a liar*. **6.** being as stated or indicated: *such is the case*. **7.** being the person or thing, or the persons or things, indicated: *if any member be behind in his payments, such member shall be suspended*. **8.** being definite or particular, but not named or specified: *it happened in such and such a town*. —*pron.* **9.** such a person or thing, or such persons or things. **10.** the person or thing, or the persons or things, indicated: *he claims to be a friend but is not such*. **11. as such, a.** as being what is indicated; in that capacity: *the leader, as such, is entitled to respect*. **b.** in itself or themselves: *wealth, as such, does not appeal to him*. [ME; OE *swulc, swylc,* c. G *solch*]

such·like (sŭch′līk′), *adj.* **1.** of any such kind; similar. —*pron.* **2.** persons or things of such a kind.

suck (sŭk), *v.t.* **1.** to draw into the mouth by action of the lips and tongue which produces a partial vacuum: *to suck lemonade through a straw*. **2.** to draw (water, moisture, air, etc.) by any process resembling this: *plants suck up moisture from the earth*. **3.** to apply the lips or mouth to, and draw upon by producing a partial vacuum, esp. for extracting fluid contents: *to suck an orange*. **4.** to apply the mouth to, or take into the mouth, and draw upon similarly, for some other purpose: *to suck one's thumb*. **5.** to take into the mouth and absorb by action of the tongue, etc.: *to suck a piece of candy*. **6.** to render or bring (as specified) by or as by sucking. —*v.i.* **7.** to draw something in by producing a partial vacuum in the mouth, esp. to draw milk from the breast. **8.** to draw or be drawn by, or as by, suction. **9.** (of a pump) to draw air instead of water, as when the water is low or a valve is defective. —*n.* **10.** act of sucking with the mouth or otherwise. **11.** a sucking force. **12.** the sound produced by sucking. **13.** that which is sucked; nourishment drawn from the breast. **14.** *Colloq.* small draft of liquid. [ME *soke, souke(n)*, OE *sūcan*, c. L *sūgere*; akin to OE *sūgan*, G *saugen*]

suck·er (sŭk′ər), *n.* **1.** one who or that which sucks. **2.** an infant or a young animal that is suckled, esp. a suckling pig. **3.** a part or organ of an animal adapted for sucking nourishment, or for adhering to an object as by suction. **4.** any member of the cyprinoid family *Catostomidae*, comprising fresh-water fishes which are mostly North American and often esteemed as food. **5.** the piston of a pump which works by suction, or the valve of such a piston. **6.** a pipe or tube through which anything is drawn. **7.** *Colloq.* a lollipop. **8.** *U.S. Slang.* a person easily imposed upon. **9.** *Bot.* **a.** a shoot rising from a subterranean stem or a root. **b.** an adventitious shoot from the body or a branch of a tree. **c.** a haustorium. —*v.t.* **10.** to strip off suckers or shoots from (a plant); remove superfluous shoots from (tobacco, etc.). —*v.i.* **11.** to send out suckers or shoots, as a plant.

suck·fish (sŭk′fĭsh′), *n., pl.* **-fishes,** (*esp. collectively*) **-fish. 1.** a remora (def. 1). **2.** a clingfish.

suck·le (sŭk′əl), *v.,* **-led, -ling.** —*v.t.* **1.** to nurse at the breast. **2.** to nourish or bring up. **3.** to put to suck. —*v.i.* **4.** to suck at the breast. [freq. of SUCK]

suck·ling (sŭk′lĭng), *n.* an infant or a young animal that is not yet weaned.

Suck·ling (sŭk′lĭng), *n.* **Sir John,** 1609–42, British poet.

Su·cre (sōō′krĕ), *n.* **1. Antonio José de** (än tō′nyō hō·sĕ′ dĕ), 1793–1830, South American general, liberator of Ecuador and Bolivia: first president of Bolivia. **2.** a city in S Bolivia: the nominal capital (La Paz is the seat of the government). 38,400 (1950). **3.** (*l.c.*) the Ecuadorian monetary unit and silver coin equal to 100 centavos and valued at 7 cents in U.S. currency.

su·crose (sōō′krōs), *n. Chem.* a crystalline disaccharide, $C_{12}H_{22}O_{11}$, the sugar obtained from the sugar cane, the sugar beet, and sorghum, and forming the greater part of maple sugar. [f. F *sucr(e)* SUGAR + -OSE²]

suc·tion (sŭk′shən), *n.* **1.** the act, process, or condition of sucking. **2.** the tendency to suck a substance into an interior space when the atmospheric pressure is reduced in the space. **3.** the reduction of pressure in order to cause such a sucking. **4.** the act or process of sucking a gas or liquid by such means. [t. L: s. *suctio*]

suction pump, a pump for raising water or the like by suction, consisting essentially of a vertical cylinder in which a piston works up and down, both with valves.

suction stop, *Phonet.* click (def. 3).

suc·to·ri·al (sŭk tôr′ĭ əl), *adj.* **1.** adapted for sucking or suction, as an organ; functioning as a sucker, whether for imbibing or for adhering. **2.** having sucking organs; imbibing or adhering by suckers. **3.** pertaining to or characterized by suction.

Su·dan (sōō dän′), *n.* **1. a** vast region in N Africa, S of the Sahara and Libyan deserts, extending from the Atlantic to the Red Sea. French, **Soudan. 2.** a country in NE Africa, south of Egypt and bordering the Red Sea. 9,715,905 pop. (est. 1953); 967,500 sq. mi. *Cap.:* Khartoum. Formerly **Anglo-Egyptian Sudan. 3.** See **Mali.**

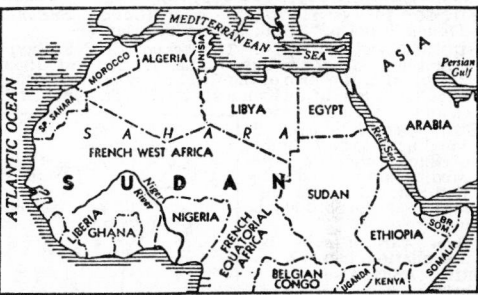

Su·da·nese (sōō′də nēz′, -nēs′), *n., pl.* **-nese,** *adj.* —*n.* **1.** a native of the Sudan. —*adj.* **2.** of or pertaining to the Sudan or its people.

Sudan grass, a sorghum, *Sorghum vulgare* (var. *sudanensis*) introduced into the U.S. in 1909: extensively grown for hay and pasture.

su·dar·i·um (sōō dâr′ĭ əm), *n., pl.* **-daria** (-dâr′ĭə). **1.** a cloth for wiping the face; a handkerchief. **2.** the cloth of St. Veronica, on which, according to a legend, was miraculously impressed a representation of the face of Christ. **3.** any similar cloth venerated as a relic. [t. L]

su·da·to·ri·um (sōō′də tôr′ĭ əm), *n., pl.* **-toria** (-tôr′ĭə). a hot-air bath for inducing sweating. [t. L, prop. neut. of *sūdātōrius* sweat producing]

su·da·to·ry (sōō′də tôr′ĭ), *adj.* **1.** pertaining to or causing sweating. **2.** pertaining to a sudatorium. [see SUDATORIUM]

sudd (sŭd), *n.* floating vegetable matter which often obstructs navigation in the White Nile. [t. Ar.]

sud·den (sŭd′ən), *adj.* **1.** happening, coming, made, or done quickly, without warning or unexpectedly: *a sudden attack*. **2.** quick and unexpected; abrupt: *a sudden turn*. **3.** *Archaic.* unpremeditated, as actions. **4.** *Archaic.* quickly made, prepared, provided, etc. —*adv.* **5.** *Poetic.* suddenly. —*n.* **6.** an unexpected occasion or occurrence. **7. All of a sudden,** suddenly; without warning; quite unexpectedly. [ME *soden,* t. AF: m. *sodein,* g. m. L *subitāneus*] —**sud′den·ly,** *adv.* —**sud′den·ness,** *n.* —**Syn. 2.** SUDDEN, UNEXPECTED, ABRUPT describe acts, events, or conditions for which there has been no preparation or gradual approach. SUDDEN refers to the quickness of an occurrence, though the event may have been expected: *a sudden change in the weather*. UNEXPECTED emphasizes the lack of preparedness for what occurs or appears: *an unexpected crisis*. ABRUPT characterizes something involving a swift adjustment; the effect is often unpleasant, unfavorable, or the cause of dismay: *an abrupt change in manner, the road came to an abrupt end*.

Su·der·mann (zōō′der män′), *n.* **Hermann** (hĕr′män), 1857–1928, German dramatist and novelist.

Su·de·ten (sōō dā′tən; *Ger.* zōō dā′tən), *n.pl.* **1.** Also, **Su·de·tes** (sōō dē′tēz). a mountain range extending along the N boundary of Czechoslovakia between the Oder and Neisse rivers. **2.** (*construed as sing.*) a native or inhabitant of the Sudetenland. **3.** Sudetenland.

Su·de·ten·land (sōō dā′tən länd′; *Ger.* zōō dā′tən länt′), *n.* a mountainous region in N and NW Czechoslovakia, including the Sudeten and the Erz Gebirge: annexed by Germany, 1938; returned to Czechoslovakia, 1945.

su·dor (sōō′dôr), *n.* sweat; perspiration. [t. L] —**su·dor·al** (sōō′dər əl), *adj.*

su·dor·if·er·ous (sōō′də rĭf′ər əs), *adj.* bearing or secreting sweat. [f. LL *sūdōrifer* sweat bringing + -OUS²]

su·dor·if·ic (sōō′də rĭf′ĭk), *adj.* **1.** causing sweat; diaphoretic. **2.** sudoriparous. —*n.* **3.** a sudorific agent. [t. NL: s. *sūdōrificus,* der. L *sūdor* sweat]

su·dor·ip·a·rous (sōō′də rĭp′ə rəs), *adj.* producing or secreting sweat. [t. NL: m. *sūdōriparus*]

suds (sŭdz), *n.pl.* **1.** soapy water. **2.** foam; lather. **3.** *Slang.* beer. [? t. MD: m. *sudse* marsh]

suds·y (sŭd′zĭ), *adj.* consisting of or containing suds; resembling or suggesting suds.

ăct, āble, dâre, ärt; ĕbb, ēqual; Ĭf, īce; hŏt, ōver, ôrder, oil, bŏŏk, ōōze, out; ŭp, ūse, ûrge; ə = a in alone; ch, chief; g, give; ng, ring; sh, shoe; th, thin; ŧh, that; zh, vision. See the full key on inside cover.

sue (sōō), v., **sued, suing.** —v.t. **1.** to institute process in law against, or bring a civil action against. **2.** take court action against (one). **3.** to obtain judicially; to carry through (an action) to decision. **4.** to make application for (a writ, etc.) or apply for and obtain (a writ, etc.), from a court of law (often fol. by *out*). **5.** to make petition or appeal to. **6.** to woo or court. —v.i. **7.** to institute legal proceedings, or bring suit. **8.** to make petition or appeal. **9.** *Archaic.* to be a suitor to a woman. [ME, t. AF: m. *suer*, var. of OF *sivre*, g. VL *sequere*, r. L *sequī* follow] —su·er (sōō′ər), n.

Sue (sōō; *Fr.* sy̆), n. **Eugène** (œ zhĕn′), (*Marie Joseph Sue*) 1804–57, French novelist.

suède (swād; *Fr.* swĕd), n. **1.** kid or other leather finished on the flesh side with a soft, napped surface, or on the outer side after removal of a thin outer layer. **2.** a fabric with a napped surface suggesting this. [t. F: lit., Sweden]

su·et (sōō′ĭt), n. the hard fatty tissue about the loins and kidneys of the ox, sheep, etc., used in cookery, etc., and prepared as tallow. [ME, f. AF *su*(*e*) (g. L *sēbum* tallow, suet) + -ET] —su′et·y, adj.

Sue·to·ni·us (swĭ tō′nĭ əs), n. (*Gaius Suetonius Tranquillus*) A.D. 75–150, Roman historian.

Suez (sōō′ĕz′, sōō′ĕz), n. **1.** a seaport in NE Egypt, near the S end of the Suez Canal. 115,200 (est. 1952). **2.** Gulf of, a NW arm of the Red Sea, W of Sinai Peninsula. **3.** Isthmus of, an isthmus in NE Egypt, joining Africa and Asia. 72 mi. wide.

Suez Canal, a sea-level canal across the Isthmus of Suez, connecting the Mediterranean and the Red Sea: cut by De Lesseps, 1859–69. ab. 100 mi. long.

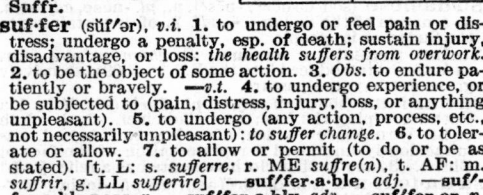

MEDITERRANEAN SEA

suf-, var. of **sub-** (by assimilation) before *f*.

suf., suffix. Also, **suff.**

Suff., Suffragan. Also, **Suffr.**

suf·fer (sŭf′ər), v.i. **1.** to undergo or feel pain or distress; undergo a penalty, esp. of death; sustain injury, disadvantage, or loss: *the health suffers from overwork.* **2.** to be the object of some action. **3.** *Obs.* to endure patiently or bravely. —v.t. **4.** to undergo experience, or be subjected to (pain, distress, injury, loss, or anything unpleasant). **5.** to undergo (any action, process, etc., not necessarily unpleasant): *to suffer change.* **6.** to tolerate or allow. **7.** to allow or permit (to do or be as stated). [t. L: s. *sufferre*; r. ME *suffre*(*n*), t. AF: m. *suffrir*, g. LL *sufferīre*] —suf·fer·a·ble, *adj.* —suf′fer·a·ble·ness, n. —suf′fer·a·bly, adv. —suf′fer·er, n.

suf·fer·ance (sŭf′ər əns, sŭf′rəns), n. **1.** tolerance, as of a person or thing; tacit allowance. **2.** capacity to endure pain, hardship, etc. **3.** *Archaic.* the suffering of pain, distress, injury, etc. **4.** *Archaic.* patient endurance.

suf·fer·ing (sŭf′ər ĭng, sŭf′rĭng), n. **1.** the act of one who suffers. **2.** a particular instance of this.

suf·fice (sə fīs′, -fīz′), v., **-ficed, -ficing.** —v.i. **1.** to be enough or adequate, as for needs, purposes, etc. —v.t. **2.** to be enough or adequate for; satisfy. [t. L: m.s. *sufficere*; r. ME *suffyse*, t. OF] —suf·fic′er, n.

suf·fi·cien·cy (sə fĭsh′ən sĭ), n., pl. **-cies. 1.** the state or fact of being sufficient; adequacy. **2.** a sufficient number or amount; enough. **3.** adequate provision or supply, esp. of wealth.

suf·fi·cient (sə fĭsh′ənt), adj. **1.** that suffices; enough or adequate: *sufficient proof or protection.* **2.** *Archaic.* competent or capable, as a person. [ME, t. L: s. *sufficiens*, ppr., sufficing] —suf·fi′cient·ly, adv.

suf·fix (n. sŭf′ĭks; v. sə fĭks′, sŭf′ĭks), n. **1.** *Gram.* an affix which follows the element to which it is added, as *-ly* in *kindly.* **2.** something suffixed. —v.t. **3.** *Gram.* to add as a suffix. **4.** to affix at the end of something: *to suffix a syllable to a word.* **5.** to fix or put under. —v.i. **6.** *Gram.* (of a linguistic form) to admit a suffix. [t] NL: s. *suffixum*, prop. neut. sp., fastened on] —suf·fix·al (sŭf′ĭk səl), adj. —suf·fix·ion (sə fĭk′shən), n.

suf·flate (sə flāt′), v.t., **-flated, -flating.** *Obs.* to blow up; inflate. [t. L: m.s. *sufflātus*, pp.] —suf·fla′tion, n.

suf·fo·cate (sŭf′ə kāt′), v., **-cated, -cating.** —v.t. **1.** to kill by preventing the access of air to the blood through the lungs or analogous organs, as gills. **2.** to impede the respiration of. **3.** to overcome or extinguish; suppress. —v.i. **4.** to become suffocated; stifle; smother. [t. L: m.s. *suffōcātus*, pp., choked] —suf′fo·cat′ing·ly, adv. —suf′fo·ca′tion, n. —suf′fo·ca′tive, adj.

Suf·folk (sŭf′ək), n. **1.** a county in E England, now divided into the administrative counties of East Suffolk and West Suffolk. **2.** East, 321,652 pop. (1951); 871 sq. mi. *Co. seat:* Ipswich. **3.** West, 120,652 pop. (1951); 611 sq. mi. *Co. seat:* Bury St. Edmunds. **4.** one of a high-quality English mutton sheep with black face and legs. **5.** an English work horse with rather short legs and chestnut color. **6.** a small, black English pig.

suf·fra·gan (sŭf′rə gən), adj. **1.** assisting or assistant: applied: **a.** to any bishop in relation to the archbishop or metropolitan who is his superior. **b.** to an assistant or subsidiary bishop who performs episcopal functions in a diocese, but has no ordinary jurisdiction, as, in the Church of England, a bishop consecrated to assist the ordinary bishop of a see in part of his diocese. **2.** (of a see or diocese) subordinate to an archiepiscopal or metropolitan see. —n. **3.** a suffragan bishop. [ME *suffragane*, t. ML: s. *suffrāgāneus* assistant, der. L *suffrāgor* I support (vote for). See SUFFRAGE]

suf·frage (sŭf′rĭj), n. **1.** the right of voting, as in political affairs. **2.** a vote given in favor of a proposed measure, a candidate, or the like, or more broadly, a vote whether favorable or unfavorable. **3.** *Eccles.* a prayer, esp. a short intercessory prayer or petition. [ME, t. L: m.s. *suffrāgium*]

suf·fra·gette (sŭf′rə jĕt′), n. *Colloq.* a woman who advocates female suffrage. —suf′fra·get′tism, n.

suf·fra·gist (sŭf′rə jĭst), n. an advocate of the grant or extension of political suffrage, esp. to women.

suf·fu·mi·gate (sə fū′mə gāt′), v.t., **-gated, -gating.** to fumigate from below; apply fumes or smoke to. [t. L: m.s. *suffūmigātus*, pp.] —suf·fu′mi·ga′tion, n.

suf·fuse (sə fūz′), v.t., **-fused, -fusing.** to overspread with a liquid, color, etc., or as a liquid does. [t. L: m.s. *suffūsus*, pp., overspread] —suf·fu·sion (sə fū′zhən), n. —suf·fu·sive (sə fū′sĭv), adj.

Su·fi (sōō′fĭ), n., pl. **-fis. 1.** a Mohammedan sect which tends toward asceticism and mysticism. **2.** a member of this sect. **3.** a sovereign of the Safavi dynasty. [t. Ar.: m. *çūfī* man of wool, prob. with reference to the woolen garments worn]

Su·fism (sōō′fĭzəm), n. the ascetic and mystical system of the Sufis. —Su·fis′tic, adj.

sug-, var. of **sub-** (by assimilation) before *g*.

sug·ar (shŏŏg′ər), n. **1.** a sweet crystalline substance, sucrose, cane sugar, or beet sugar, $C_{12}H_{22}O_{11}$, obtained chiefly from the juice of the sugar cane or sugar beet, but present in sorghum, maple sap, etc., and extensively used for food purposes. **2.** a member of the same class of carbohydrates. —v.t. **3.** to cover, sprinkle, mix, or sweeten with sugar. **4.** to revert to sugar crystals, as out of a sugar syrup when candy is cooked or cooled. **5.** to make agreeable. —v.i. **6.** to form sugar. **7.** to make maple sugar. **8.** (in making maple sugar) to complete the boiling down of the syrup in preparation for granulation (fol. by *off*). [ME *sugure*, *zugure*, t. ML: m. *zugurum*, t. Ar.: m. *sukkar*; r. ME *sucure*, *zucur*, t. OF: m. *sukere*, *zuchre*, ult. t. Ar.]

sugar apple, the sweetsop.

sugar beet, a variety of beet, *Beta vulgaris,* with a white root, cultivated for the sugar it yields.

sug·ar·ber·ry (shŏŏg′ər bĕr′ĭ), n., pl. **-ries.** a southern U.S. hackberry, *Celtis laevigata.*

sug·ar·bush (shŏŏg′ər bŏŏsh′), n. *U.S.* a small plantation, orchard, or grove of sugar maples.

sugar cane, a tall grass, *Saccharum officinarum,* of tropical and warm regions, having a stout, jointed stalk, and constituting the chief source of sugar.

sug·ar·coat (shŏŏg′ər kōt′), v.t. **1.** to cover with sugar: *to sugar-coat a pill.* **2.** to make more acceptable or less distasteful in appearance than a thing really is. —sug′ar·coat′ing, n.

sugar corn, sweet corn (def. 1).

sug·ared (shŏŏg′ərd), adj. **1.** covered, mixed, or sweetened with sugar. **2.** sweetened as if with sugar; made agreeable; honeyed, as words, speech, etc.

sugar loaf, 1. a large, approximately conical loaf or mass of hard refined sugar. **2.** anything resembling this in shape. —su′gar-loaf′, adj.

sugar maple, a maple with a sweet sap, esp. *Acer saccharum,* of eastern North America which yields an important timber and is the chief source of maple sugar.

sugar pine, a tall pine, *Pinus Lambertiana,* of California, Oregon, etc., having cones 20 in. long.

sug·ar·plum (shŏŏg′ər plŭm′), n. a small sweetmeat made of sugar with various flavoring and coloring ingredients; a bonbon.

sug·ar·y (shŏŏg′ər ĭ), adj. **1.** of, containing, or resembling sugar. **2.** sweet; excessively sweet. **3.** dulcet; honeyed; cloying; deceitfully agreeable: *her sugary words of greeting sounded insincere.* —sug′ar·i·ness, n.

sug·gest (səg jĕst′), v.t. **1.** to place or bring (an idea, proposition, plan, etc.) before a person's mind for consideration or possible action. **2.** to propose (a person or thing) as suitable or possible. **3.** (of things) to prompt the consideration, making, doing, etc., of. **4.** to bring before a person's mind indirectly or without plain expression. **5.** (of a thing) to call up in the mind (another thing) through association or natural connection of ideas. [t. L: s. *suggestus*, pp., placed under, added, furnished] —sug·gest′er, n. —Syn. 4. See hint.

sug·gest·i·ble (səg jĕs′tə bəl), adj. **1.** capable of being influenced by suggestion. **2.** that may be suggested. —sug·gest′i·bil′i·ty, n.

sug·ges·tion (səg jĕs′chən), n. **1.** act of suggesting. **2.** state of being suggested. **3.** the idea thus called up, or a thing suggested. **4.** a slight trace: *he speaks English with just a suggestion of a foreign accent.* **5.** the calling up in the mind of one idea by another by virtue of some association or of some natural connection between the ideas. **6.** *Psychol.* **a.** the process of accepting a proposition for belief or action in the absence of the intervening and critical thought that would normally occur. **b.** a proposition for belief or action accepted in this way. **c.** the offering of a stimulus in such a way as to produce an uncritical response. [ME, t. L: s. *suggestio*]

---

b., blend of, blended; c., cognate with; d., dialect, dialectal; der., derived from; f., formed from; g., going back to; m., modification of; r., replacing; s., stem of; t., taken from; ?, perhaps.   See the full key on inside cover.

sug·ges·tive (səg jĕs′tĬv), *adj.* **1.** that suggests; tending to suggest thoughts, ideas, etc. **2.** such as to suggest something improper or indecent. —**sug·ges′tive·ly**, *adv.* —**sug·ges′tive·ness**, *n.* —**Syn. 1.** See **expressive**.

su·i·cid·al (sōō′ə sī′dəl), *adj.* pertaining to, involving, or suggesting suicide; tending or leading to suicide. —**su′i·cid·al′ly**, *adv.*

su·i·cide[1] (sōō′ə sīd′), *n.*, *v.*, **-cided, -ciding.** —*n.* **1.** the intentional taking of one's own life. **2.** destruction of one's own interests or prospects. **3. commit suicide,** to kill oneself intentionally. —*v.i.* **4.** *Colloq.* to commit suicide. [t. NL: m.s. *suīcīdium*]

su·i·cide[2] (sōō′ə sīd′), *n.* one who intentionally takes his own life. [t. NL: m. *suīcīda*]

su·i gen·e·ris (sōō′ī jĕn′ər Ĭs), *Latin.* of his, her, its, or their own kind; unique.

sui ju·ris (jōōr′Ĭs), *Law.* one capable of managing his affairs and assuming legal responsibility for his acts, as distinguished from others, as lunatics and infants, whose legal capacity is limited. [L: of one's own right]

su·int (sōō′Ĭnt, swĬnt), *n.* the natural grease of the wool of sheep, consisting of a mixture of fatty matter and potassium salts, used as a source of potash and in the preparation of ointments. [t. F, der. *suer* sweat]

Suisse (swēs), *n.* French name of **Switzerland**.

suit (sōōt), *n.* **1.** a set of garments, vestments, or armor, intended to be worn together; esp., a set of outer garments. **2.** the act or process of suing in a court of law; legal prosecution. **3.** *Cards.* **a.** one of the four sets or classes (spades, clubs, hearts, and diamonds) into which playing cards are divided. **b.** the aggregate of cards belonging to one of these sets held in a player's hand at one time. **4.** a number of things of like kind or purpose forming a series or set. **5.** the wooing or courting of a woman. **6.** the act of making petition or appeal. **7.** a petition, as to a person of exalted station. —*v.t.* **8.** to provide with a suit of clothes; clothe; array. **9.** to make appropriate, adapt, or accommodate, as one thing to another. **10.** to be appropriate or becoming to. **11.** to be or prove satisfactory, agreeable, or acceptable to; satisfy or please. —*v.i.* **12.** to be appropriate or suitable; accord. **13.** to be satisfactory, agreeable, or acceptable. [ME, t. AF: m. *suite*, var. of OF *sieute*, der. *s(u)ivre* follow. See **SUE**]

suit·a·ble (sōō′tə bəl), *adj.* such as to suit; appropriate; fitting; becoming. —**suit′a·bil′i·ty, suit′a·ble·ness**, *n.* —**suit′a·bly**, *adv.*

suit·case (sōōt′kās′), *n.* a flat, oblong valise.

suite (swēt), *n.* **1.** a company of followers or attendants; a train or retinue. **2.** a number of things forming a series or set. **3.** a connected series of rooms to be used together by one person or a number of persons. **4.** a set of furniture. **5.** *Music.* **a.** an ordered series of instrumental dances, in the same or related keys, commonly preceded by a prelude. **b.** an ordered series of instrumental movements of any character. [t. F, der. *suivre*. See **SUIT**]

suit·ing (sōō′tĬng), *n.* a fabric for making suits.

suit·or (sōō′tər), *n.* **1.** one who courts or woos a woman. **2.** *Law.* a petitioner or plaintiff. **3.** one who sues or petitions for anything.

Sui·yüan (soi′ywän′, swä′ yőŏän′; *Chin.* swä′yy′än′), *n.* a former province in N China, now a part of Inner Mongolian Autonomous Area. *Cap.:* Kweihsui. 2,256,000 pop. (est. 1950); 127,413 sq. mi.

su·ki·ya·ki (sōō′kē yä′kē), *n.* a Japanese dish containing fried meat, vegetables, onions, etc. [t. Jap.]

Suk·koth (sŏŏk ōth′), *n.pl.* the Jewish holiday of the Feast of Tabernacles (Lev. 23:34–43), beginning on the eve of the 15th of Tishri and lasting originally eight days and in later Judaism nine days. [t. Heb.]

sul·cate (sŭl′kāt), *adj.* having long, narrow grooves or channels, as a stem; furrowed; cleft, as a hoof. Also, **sul′cat·ed.** [t. L: m.s. *sulcātus*, pp., furrowed] —**sul·ca′tion**, *n.*

Sulcate stem

sul·cus (sŭl′kəs), *n.*, *pl.* **-ci** (-sī). **1.** a furrow or groove. **2.** *Anat.* a fissure between two convolutions of the brain. [t. L]

Su·lei·man (sY′lā män′), *n.* Solyman. See **SOLYMAN**.

sulf-, a word element meaning "sulfur" or "combined with sulfur," as in *sulfarsphenamine*. Also, **sulph-.** Cf. **sulfo-.** [comb. form repr. **SULFUR**]

sul·fa·di·a·zine (sŭl′fə dī′ə zēn′, -zĬn), *n. Pharm.* a sulfanilamide derivative, $C_{10}H_{10}O_2N_4S$, particularly effective against staphylococcal and gonococcal infections.

sul·fa drugs (sŭl′fə), a group of compounds containing the radical SO_2NH_2, used as antibacterials in treatment of various diseases, wounds, burns, etc. Also, **sul·fas** (sŭl′fəz).

sul·fa·nil·a·mide (sŭl′fə nĬl′ə mīd′, -mĬd), *n. Pharm.* a white crystalline amide of sulfanilic acid, $NH_2C_6H_4$-SO_2NH_2, effective against infections caused by hemolytic streptococci, the gonococci, etc. Also, **sulphanil·amide.**

sul·fa·pyr·i·dine (sŭl′fə pĬr′ə dēn′, -dĬn), *n. Pharm.* sulfanilamide derivative, $C_{11}H_{11}N_3O_2S$, more toxic than sulfanilamide but somewhat more effective against infections caused by pneumococci.

sulf·ars·phen·a·mine (sŭlf′ärs fĕn ə mēn′, -fə năm′Ĭn), *n. Pharm.* a compound having the same characteristics as arsphenamine but less efficient and not so irritating to the body.

sul·fate (sŭl′fāt), *n.*, *v.*, **-fated, -fating.** —*n.* **1.** *Chem.* a salt of sulfuric acid. —*v.t.* **2.** to combine, treat, or impregnate with sulfuric acid or with a sulfate or sulfates. **3.** to convert into a sulfate. **4.** *Elect.* to form a deposit of a lead sulfate compound on (the lead plates of a storage battery). —*v.i.* **5.** to become sulfated. Also, **sulphate.** [t. NL: m.s. *sulphātum*, f. L *sulph(ur)* **SULFUR** + *-ātum* -**ATE**[2]]

sul·fa·thi·a·zole (sŭl′fə thī′ə zōl′), *n. Pharm.* a sulfanilamide derivative, $C_9H_9N_3O_2S_2$, effective in the treatment of pneumonia and staphylococcus infections.

sul·fat·ize (sŭl′fə tīz′), *v.t.*, **-ized, -izing.** to convert into a sulfate as by the roasting of ores. Also, **sulphatize.**

sul·fide (sŭl′fīd), *n. Chem.* a compound of sulfur with a more electropositive element or, less often, a radical. Also, **sul·fid** (sŭl′fĬd), **sulphide, sulphid.**

sul·fite (sŭl′fīt), *n. Chem.* a salt of sulfurous acid. Also, **sulphite.**

sulfo-, *Chem.* a prefix indicating a compound in which sulfur has been substituted for oxygen, as *sodium sulfantimonate* (Na_3SbS_4) compared with sodium antimonate (Na_3SbO_4). Thus, formulas such as *sulfantimonite, sulfarsenate*, etc., can be deduced from the formulas of the corresponding antimonite, arsenate, etc. Also, **sulpho-.**

sul·fo·nal (sŭl′fə năl′, sŭl′fə năl′), *n. Pharm.* sulfonmethane.

sul·fo·nate (sŭl′fə nāt′), *n.*, *v.*, **-nated, -nating.** *Chem.* —*n.* **1.** an ester or salt derived from a sulfonic acid. —*v.t.* **2.** to make into a sulfonic acid, as by treating an aromatic hydrocarbon with concentrated sulfuric acid. Also, **sulphonate.**

sul·fo·na·tion (sŭl′fə nā′shən), *n. Chem.* the process of attaching the sulfonic acid radical, -SO_2H, directly to carbon in an organic compound.

sul·fone (sŭl′fōn), *n. Chem.* any of a class of organic compounds containing the bivalent SO_2 group united with two hydrocarbon radicals. Also, **sulphone.**

sul·fon·ic (sŭl fŏn′Ĭk), *adj. Chem.* **1.** noting or pertaining to the group SO_2OH. **2.** *Chem.* noting or pertaining to any of the acids, mostly organic, containing the SO_3H group. Also, **sulphonic.**

sulfonic acid, *Chem.* any of a large group of organic compounds containing the sulfonic radical. They are strong acids, giving neutral sodium salts and used in the synthesis of phenols, dyes, and other substances.

sul·fo·ni·um (sŭl fō′nĬ əm), *n. Chem.* the ion obtained by adding a proton to hydrogen sulfide, as $(H_2S)^+$. Also **sulphonium.**

sul·fon·meth·ane (sŭl′fŏn mĕth′ān, -fŏn-), *n. Pharm.* a crystalline organic compound, $(CH_3)_2C(SO_2C_2H_5)_2$, which is a mild hypnotic or sedative.

sul·fo·nyl (sŭl′fə nĬl, -nēl′), *n.* sulfuryl.

sulfonyl chloride, *Chem.* denoting the radical -SO_2Cl.

sul·fur (sŭl′fər), *n. Chem.* a nonmetallic element which exists in several forms, the ordinary one being a yellow rhombic crystalline solid, and which burns with a blue flame and a suffocating odor: used esp. in making gunpowder and matches, in vulcanizing rubber, in medicine, etc. *Symbol:* S; *at. wt.:* 32.06; *at. no.:* 16; *sp. gr.:* 2.07 at 20° C. Also, **sulphur.** [ME, t. L]

sul·fu·rate (sŭl′fyə rāt′, -fə-), *v.t.*, **-rated, -rating.** to combine, treat, or impregnate with sulfur, the fumes of burning sulfur, or the like. Also, **sulphurate.** —**sul′fu·ra′tion**, *n.* —**sul′fu·ra′tor**, *n.*

sulfur dioxide, *Chem.* a colorless suffocating gas, SO_2, formed when sulfur burns.

sul·fu·re·ous (sŭl fyőŏr′Ĭ əs), *adj.* consisting of, containing, pertaining to, or resembling sulfur; sulfurcolored. Also, **sulphureous.** —**sul·fu′re·ous·ness**, *n.*

sul·fu·ret (*n.* sŭl′fyə rĬt; *v.* sŭl′fyə rĕt′), *n.*, *v.*, **-reted, -reting** or (*esp. Brit.*) **-retted, -retting.** *Chem.* —*n.* **1.** a sulfide. —*v.t.* **2.** to treat or combine with sulfur. Also, **sulphuret.** [t. NL: m.s. *sulphurētum*. See **SULFUR**, **-URET**]

sul·fu·ric (sŭl fyőŏr′Ĭk), *adj.* of, pertaining to, or containing sulfur, esp. in the hexavalent stage (S+6). Also, **sulphuric.**

sulfuric acid. *Chem.* the dibasic acid of sulfur, H_2SO_4, a colorless oily liquid, made from sulfur trioxide and used in many industrial processes: formerly called oil of vitriol.

sul·fu·rize (sŭl′fyə rīz′, -fə-), *v.t.*, **-rized, -rizing. 1.** to combine, treat, or impregnate with sulfur. **2.** to fumigate with sulfur dioxide. Also, **sulphurize.** —**sul′fu·ri·za′tion**, *n.*

sul·fur·ous (sŭl′fər əs, sŭl fyőŏr′əs), *adj.* **1.** relating to sulfur. **2.** of the yellow color of sulfur. **3.** containing tetravalent sulfur (S+4). Also, **sulphurous for 1, 2.**

sulfurous acid, *Chem.* an acid, H_2SO_3, formed by dissolving sulfur dioxide in water, known mainly by its salts (sulfites).

sulfur trioxide, *Chem.* an irritant, corrosive, lowmelting solid, SO_3, prepared by oxidation of sulfur dioxide; an intermediate in the manufacture of sulfuric acid.

sul·fur·yl (sŭl′fər Ĭl, fə rēl′, -fyə rĬl), *n. Chem.* the bivalent radical of sulfuric acid, -SO_2-. Also, **sulphuryl.**

sulfuryl chloride, a colorless fluid, SO₂Cl₂, with a very pungent odor, used as a chlorinating agent, etc.

sulk (sŭlk), *v.i.* **1.** to hold aloof in a sullenly ill-humored or offended mood. —*n.* **2.** a state or fit of sulking. **3.** (*pl.*) ill humor shown by sulking: *to be in the sulks.* **4.** one who sulks. [back formation from SULKY]

sulk·y (sŭl′kĭ), *adj.,* **sulkier, sulkiest,** *n., pl.* **sulkies.** —*adj.* **1.** sullenly ill-humored or resentful; marked by ill-humored aloofness. **2.** (of weather, etc.) gloomy. —*n.* **3.** a light two-wheeled one-horse carriage for one person. [? der. OE *-solcen* slothful, remiss; cf. N Fris. *sulkig* sulky; in def. 3, so called as holding only one person] —**sulk′i·ly,** *adv.* —**sulk′i·ness,** *n.*

Sul·la (sŭl′ə), *n.* **Lucius Cornelius** (lōō′shəs kôr nēl′-yəs), ("*Felix*") 138–78 B.C., Roman general and dictator.

sul·len (sŭl′ən), *adj.* **1.** showing ill humor by a gloomy silence or reserve. **2.** silently and persistently ill-humored; morose. **3.** indicative of gloomy ill humor: *sullen silence.* **4.** gloomy or dismal, as weather, sounds, etc. **5.** sluggish, as a stream. **6.** *Obs.* malignant, as planets, influences, etc. [ME *solein,* t. AF, der. *sol* SOLE¹] —**sul′len·ly,** *adv.* —**sul′len·ness,** *n.* —**Syn. 1.** See **cross.**

Sul·li·van (sŭl′ə vən), *n.* **1. Sir Arthur Seymour,** 1842–1900, British composer. **2. Louis Henri,** U.S. architect, 1856–1924, early advocate of functionalism in architecture.

sul·ly (sŭl′ĭ), *v.,* **-lied, -lying,** *n., pl.* **-lies.** —*v.t.* **1.** to soil, stain, or tarnish. **2.** to mar the purity or luster of; defile. —*v.i.* **3.** to become sullied, soiled, or tarnished. —*n. Obs.* **4.** act of sullying. **5.** a stain. [ME *solien,* OE (ā)*solian* become dirty, der. *sōl* dirty]

Sul·ly (sŭl′ĭ; *Fr.* sy lē′), *n.* **Maximilien de Béthune** (mȧk sē mēl yăṅ′ də bĕ tyn′), **Duc de,** 1560–1641, French statesman.

Sul·ly-Pru·dhomme (sY lē′ prY dôm′), *n.* **René François Armand** (rə nĕ′ frȧṅ swȧ′ ȧr mäṅ′), 1839–1907, French poet.

sulph- var. of **sulf-,** as in *sulphite.* Also, **sulpho-.**

sul·pha·nil·a·mide (sŭl′fə nĭl′ə mĭd′, -mĭd), *n. Pharm.* sulfanilamide.

sul·phate (sŭl′fāt), *v.t.,* **-phated, -phating.** *Elect.* sulfate (def. 4). [t. NL: m.s. *sulphātum,* f. L *sulph(ur)* SULFUR + *-ātum* -ATE²]

sul·phat·ize (sŭl′fə tīz′), *v.t.,* **-ized, -izing.** sulfatize.

sul·phide (sŭl′fīd), *n. Chem.* sulfide.

sul·phite (sŭl′fīt), *n. Chem.* sulfite.

sul·pho·nate (sŭl′fə nāt′), *n., v.,* **-nated, -nating.** *Chem.* sulfonate.

sul·phone (sŭl′fōn), *n. Chem.* sulfone.

sul·phon·ic (sŭl fŏn′ĭk), *adj. Chem.* sulfonic.

sul·pho·ni·um (sŭl fō′nĭ əm), *n. Chem.* sulfonium.

sul·phur (sŭl′fər), *n.* **1.** sulfur. **2.** yellow with greenish tinge; lemon color. **3.** any of various yellow or orange butterflies of the family *Pieridae.* [ME, t. L]

sul·phu·rate (sŭl′fyə rāt′, -fə-), *v.t.,* **-rated, -rating.** sulfurate.

sul·phur-bot·tom (sŭl′fər bŏt′əm), *n.* the blue whale, *Sibbaldus musculus,* of arctic seas, with yellowish underparts: the largest mammal that has ever lived.

sul·phu·re·ous (sŭl fyŏŏr′ē əs), *adj.* sulfureous.

sul·phu·ret (*n.* sŭl′fyə rĭt; *v.* sŭl′fyə rĕt′), *n., v.,* **-reted, -reting** or (*esp. Brit.*) **-retted, -retting.** *Chem.* sulfuret.

sul·phu·ric (sŭl fyŏŏr′ĭk), *adj.* sulfuric.

sul·phu·rize (sŭl′fyə rīz′, -fə-), *v.t.,* **-rized, -rizing.** sulfurize.

sul·phur·ous (sŭl′fər əs, sŭl fyŏŏr′əs), *adj.* **1.** sulfurous (defs. 1, 2). **2.** pertaining to the fires of hell; hellish or satanic. **3.** fiery or heated.

sul·phur·yl (sŭl′fər Yl, -fə rēl′, -fyə rYl), *n. Chem.* sulfuryl.

sul·tan (sŭl′tən), *n.* **1.** the sovereign of a Mohammedan country. **2.** (*cap.*) any of the former sovereigns of Turkey. [t. ML: s. *sultānus,* t. Ar.: m. *sultān* king, ruler, power] —**sul′tan·ship′,** *n.*

sul·tan·a (sŭl tăn′ə, -tä′nə), *n.* **1.** a wife or a concubine of a sultan. **2.** *Chiefly Brit.* a kind of small seedless raisin. [t. It., fem. of *sultano* SULTAN]

sul·tan·ate (sŭl′tə nāt′), *n.* **1.** the office or rule of a sultan. **2.** the territory ruled over by a sultan.

sul·try (sŭl′trĭ), *adj.,* **-trier, -triest. 1.** oppressively hot and close or moist; sweltering. **2.** oppressively hot, as the weather, etc. **3.** characterized by or associated with sweltering heat. **4.** characterized by heat of temper or passion. [f. *sulter* (var. of SWELTER) + -Y¹] —**sul′tri·ly,** *adv.* —**sul′tri·ness,** *n.*

Su·lu (sōō′lōō), *n.* a member of the most numerous and most highly cultivated tribe of Moros, or Mohammedan Malays of the southwestern Philippine Islands, found chiefly in the Sulu Archipelago. [t. Malay]

Sulu Archipelago, an island group in the SW Philippine Islands, separating the Celebes Sea from the Sulu Sea, an arm of the Pacific NE of Borneo. 240,826 pop. (1948); 1086 sq. mi. *Cap.:* Jolo.

sum (sŭm), *n., v.,* **summed, summing.** —*n.* **1.** the aggregate of two or more numbers, magnitudes, quantities, or particulars as determined by mathematical process: *the sum of 5 and 7 is 12.* **2.** a particular aggregate or total, esp. with reference to money: *the expenses came to an enormous sum.* **3.** a quantity or amount, esp. of money: *to lend small sums.* **4.** a series of numbers or quantities to be added up. **5.** an arithmetical problem to be solved, or such a problem worked out and having the various steps shown. **6.** the total amount, or the whole. **7.** the substance or gist of a matter, comprehensively viewed or expressed: *the letter contains the sum and substance of his opinions.* **8.** concise or brief form: *in sum.* **9.** a summary. —*v.t.* **10.** to combine into an aggregate or total (often fol. by *up*). **11.** to ascertain the sum of, as by addition. **12.** to reckon (fol. by *up*): *to sum up advantages and disadvantages.* **13.** to bring into or contain in a small compass (often fol. by *up*). **14.** to bring into or contain in a brief and comprehensive statement (usually fol. by *up*): *the article sums up the work of the year.* **15.** to form a quick estimate of (fol. by *up*): *to sum someone up.* [t. L: m.s. *summa,* prop. fem. of *summus* highest; r. ME *somme,* t. OF] —**Syn. 1.** See **number.**

sum-, occasional var. of **sub-** (by assimilation) before *m.*

su·mac (shōō′măk, sōō′-), *n.* **1.** any of the plants of the anacardiaceous genus *Rhus,* as, in North America, *R. hirta,* a shrub or small tree with long pinnate leaves and pyramidal panicles of crimson drupes, *R. glabra,* a shrub with panicles of small crimson drupes (**smooth sumac**), or *R. Vernix.* See **poison sumac.** **2.** a preparation of the dried and powdered leaves, etc., of certain species of *Rhus,* esp. *R. coriaria* of southern Europe, used in tanning, etc. **3.** the wood of these plants. Also, **su′mach.** [ME, t. OF, t. Ar.: m. *summāq*]

Su·ma·tra (sŏŏ mä′trə), *n.* a large island in the W part of Indonesia. 11,371,233 (est. 1955); 164,147 sq. mi. —**Su·ma′tran,** *adj., n.*

Sum·ba (sŏŏm′bä), *n.* one of the Lesser Sunda Islands, in Indonesia. 182,326 pop. (1930); 4306 sq. mi. Also, **Sandalwood Island.** Dutch, **Soemba.**

Sum·ba·wa (sŏŏm bä′wä), *n.* one of the Lesser Sunda Islands, in Indonesia: destructive eruption of Mt. Tambora, 1815. 314,843 pop. (1930); 5965 sq. mi. Dutch, **Soembawa.**

Su·mer (sŏŏ′mər), *n.* a region in the S part of ancient Babylonia, on the Euphrates. See map under **Chaldea.**

Su·me·ri·an (sŏŏ mĭr′Y ən), *adj.* **1.** noting or pertaining to the primitive inhabitants of Babylonia, believed by most authorities to have been of non-Semitic origin. —*n.* **2.** one of the Sumerian people. **3.** a language of unknown relationship, preserved in very ancient cuneiform inscriptions.

sum·ma cum lau·de (sŭm′ə kŭm lô′dY, sŏŏm′ə kŏŏm lou′dĕ), *Latin.* with the highest honor or praise.

sum·mand (sŭm′ănd′, sŭm′ănd′), *n. Arith.* a part or item of a sum.

sum·ma·rize (sŭm′ə rīz′), *v.t.,* **-rized, -rizing. 1.** to make a summary of; state or express in a concise form. **2.** to constitute a summary of. Also, *esp. Brit.,* **sum′ma·rise′.** —**sum′ma·ri·za′tion,** *n.* —**sum′ma·riz′er,** *n.*

sum·ma·ry (sŭm′ərY), *n., pl.* **-ries,** *adj.* —*n.* **1.** a brief and comprehensive presentation of facts or statements; an abstract, compendium, or epitome. [t. L: m.s. *summārium,* prop. neut. of **summārius* summary, *adj.*] —*adj.* **2.** brief and comprehensive; concise. **3.** direct and prompt; unceremoniously fast. **4.** (of legal proceedings, jurisdiction, etc.) conducted without or exempt from the various steps and delays of a formal trial. [ME, t. ML: m.s. *summārius,* der. L *summa* sum] —**sum·ma·ri·ly** (sŭm′ə rĭ lY; *emphatic* sə mĕr′ə lY), *adv.* —**sum′ma·ri·ness,** *n.* —**Syn. 1.** SUMMARY, BRIEF, DIGEST, SYNOPSIS are terms for a short version of a longer work. A SUMMARY is a brief statement or restatement of main points, esp. as a conclusion to a work: *the summary of a chapter.* A BRIEF is a detailed outline, by heads and subheads, of a discourse (usually legal) to be completed: *a brief for an argument.* A DIGEST is an abridgment of an article, book, etc., or an organized arrangement of material under heads and titles: *a magazine consisting of digests, a digest of Roman law.* A SYNOPSIS is usually a compressed statement of the plot of a novel, play, etc.: *a synopsis of Hamlet.*

sum·ma·tion (sŭm ā′shən), *n.* **1.** the process of summing. **2.** the result of this; an aggregate or total. **3.** *Law.* the final arguments of opposing counsel before a case goes to the jury.

sum·mer¹ (sŭm′ər), *n.* **1.** the second and the warmest season of the year, between spring and autumn (in North America taken as comprising June, July, and August). **2.** the period of finest development, perfection, or beauty previous to any decline: *the summer of life.* —*adj.* **3.** of, pertaining to, or characteristic of summer: *summer resorts.* **4.** having the weather or warmth of summer. —*v.i.* **5.** to spend or pass the summer. —*v.t.* **6.** to keep, feed, or manage during the summer. **7.** to make summerlike. [ME *sumer,* OE *sumor,* c. G *sommer*]

sum·mer² (sŭm′ər), *n.* **1.** a principal timber or beam, as in a floor or any spanning structure. **2.** a stone at the top of a pier, column, or the like, as to support an arch. **3.** a lintel. [ME, t. AF: m. *sumer* beam, pack horse, ult. der. LL *sagma* packsaddle, t. Gk.]

sum·mer·house (sŭm′ər hous′), *n.* a simple, often rustic structure in a park or garden, intended to provide a shady, cool place in the summer.

sum·mer·sault (sŭm′ər sôlt′), *n., v.i.* somersault.

summer squash, any of various squashes, varieties of *Cucurbita Pepo,* used as a summer vegetable.

sum·mer·time (sŭm′ər tīm′), *n.* **1.** the season of summer. **2.** *Brit.* daylight-saving time.

---

b., blend of, blended; c., cognate with; d., dialect, dialectal; der., derived from; f., formed from; g., going back to; m., modification of; r., replacing; s., stem of; t., taken from; ?, perhaps. See the full key on inside cover.

sum·mer·y (sŭm′ər-ĭ), *adj.* of, like, or befitting summer.

sum·mit (sŭm′ĭt), *n.* **1.** the highest point or part, as of a hill, a line of travel, or any object; the top; the apex. **2.** the highest point of attainment or aspiration. **3.** the highest state or degree. —*adj.* **4.** (in diplomacy) between heads of state: *summit conference*. [late ME *sommet*, t. F, der. L *summum*, prop. neut. of *summus* highest]

sum·mon (sŭm′ən), *v.t.* **1.** to call as with authority to some duty, task, or performance; call upon (to do something). **2.** to call for the presence of, as by command, message, or signal; call (fol. by *to, away, from*, etc.). **3.** to call or notify to appear at a specified place, esp. before a court: *to summon a defendant*. **4.** to call together (an assembly, council, or other body) by authority, as for deliberation or action: *to summon a parliament*. **5.** to call into action; rouse; call forth (often fol. by *up*): *to summon up all one's courage*. **6.** to call upon to surrender. [t. L: s. *summonēre* suggest, ML summon; r. ME *somonen*, t. OF] —**sum′mon·er**, *n.* —Syn. **3.** See **call**.

sum·mons (sŭm′ənz), *n., pl.* **-monses**, *v.* —*n.* **1.** an authoritative command, message, or signal by which one is summoned. **2.** a call to do something: *a summons to surrender*. **3.** *Law.* a call or citation by authority to appear before a court or a judicial officer, or the writ by which the call is made. **4.** an authoritative call or notice to appear at a specified place, as for a particular purpose or duty. **5.** a call issued for the meeting of an assembly or parliament. —*v.t.* **6.** to serve with a summons; summon. [ME *somonse*, t. AF, OF, der. *somondre* summon]

sum·mum bo·num (sŭm′əm bō′nəm), *Latin.* the highest or chief good.

Sum·ner (sŭm′nər), *n.* **1. Charles,** 1811–74, U.S. statesman. **2. William Graham,** 1840–1910, U.S. sociologist and economist.

sump (sŭmp), *n.* **1.** a pit, well, or the like in which water or other liquid is collected. **2.** *Mach.* a reservoir situated at the lowest point in a circulating system. **3.** *Mining.* **a.** a space at the bottom of a shaft or below a passageway where water is allowed to collect. **b.** a pilot shaft or tunnel pushed out in front of a main bore. **4.** *Brit. Dial.* a swamp, bog, or muddy pool. [ME *sompe*, t. MLG or MD: m. *sump*, c. G *sumpf*]

sump·ter (sŭmp′tər), *n. Archaic.* a pack horse or any animal for carrying baggage, etc. [ME, t. OF: m. *som(m)etier*, ult. der. L *sagma* packsaddle, t. Gk.]

sump·tu·ar·y (sŭmp′chŏŏ-ĕr′ĭ), *adj.* pertaining to, dealing with, or regulating expense or expenditure. [t. L: m.s. *sumptuārius*]

sumptuary law, a law regulating personal habits which offend the moral or religious conscience of the community.

sump·tu·ous (sŭmp′chŏŏ-əs), *adj.* **1.** entailing great expense, as from fine workmanship, choice materials, etc.; costly: *a sumptuous residence*. **2.** luxuriously fine; splendid or superb. [late ME, t. L: m.s. *sumptuōsus* expensive] —**sump′tu·ous·ly**, *adv.* —**sump′tu·ous·ness**, *n.*

Sum·ter (sŭm′tər, sŭmp′-), *n.* **Fort,** a fort in the harbor of Charleston, South Carolina: its bombardment by the Confederates opened the Civil War, April 12, 1861.

sun (sŭn), *n., v.,* **sunned, sunning.** —*n.* **1.** the star which is the central body of the solar system and around which the planets revolve, and from which they receive light and heat. Its mean distance from the earth is about 93,000,000 miles, its diameter about 866,500 miles, and its mass about 330,000 times that of the earth. Its period of surface rotation is about 25 days at its equator but longer in greater latitudes. **2.** the sun considered with reference to its position in the sky, its visibility, the season of the year, the time at which or the place where it is seen, etc. **3.** a self-luminous heavenly body. **4.** the sunshine: *to be exposed to the sun.* **5.** a figure or representation of the sun, as a heraldic bearing usually surrounded with rays and charged with the features of a human face. **6.** something likened to the sun in brightness, splendor, etc. **7.** *Poetic.* a day. **8.** *Poetic.* a year. **9.** *Archaic.* sunrise or sunset. —*v.t.* **10.** to expose to the sun's rays. **11.** to warm, dry, etc., in the sunshine. **12.** to put, bring, make, etc. (as specified), by exposure to the sun's rays. —*v.i.* **13.** to expose oneself to the sun's rays. [ME and OE *sunne*, c. G *sonne*] —**sun′less**, *adj.*

Sun., Sunday. Also, **Sund.**

sun bath, an exposure of the body to direct sun rays.

sun·beam (sŭn′bēm′), *n.* a beam or ray of sunlight.

sun·bird (sŭn′bûrd′), *n.* any of various small, brilliantly colored, Old World birds of the family *Nectarinidae*.

sun bittern, a South American bird, *Eurypyga helias*, with variegated plumage, allied to the rails.

sun·bon·net (sŭn′bŏn′ĭt), *n.* a large bonnet of cotton or other light material shading the face and projecting down over the neck, worn by women and girls.

sun·bow (sŭn′bō′), *n.* a bow or arc of prismatic colors like a rainbow, appearing in the spray of cataracts, etc.

sun·burn (sŭn′bûrn′), *n., v.,* **-burned** or **-burnt, -burning.** —*n.* **1.** superficial inflammation of the skin, caused by exposure to the sun's rays. **2.** the discoloration or tan so produced. —*v.t., v.i.* **3.** to affect or be affected with sunburn.

sun·burst (sŭn′bûrst′), *n.* **1.** a burst of sunlight; a sudden shining of the sun through rifted clouds. **2.** a firework, a piece of jewelry, an ornament, or the like, resembling the sun with rays issuing in all directions.

sun·dae (sŭn′dĭ), *n.* a portion of ice cream with fruit or other syrup poured over it, and often whipped cream, chopped nuts, or other additions. [orig. uncert.]

Sun·da Islands (sŭn′də; *Du.* sōōn′dä), an island chain in the Malay Archipelago, including Sumatra, Java, and the **Lesser Sunda Islands,** those smaller islands extending from Java E to Timor.

sun dance, a religious ceremony associated with the sun, practiced by North American Indians of the Plains, consisting of dancing attended with various symbolic rites, commonly including self-torture.

Sunda Strait, a strait separating Sumatra from Java. Least width, ab. 16 mi.

Sun·day (sŭn′dĭ), *n.* **1.** the Sabbath of most Christian sects, observed in commemoration of the resurrection of Christ. **2.** the first day of the week. [ME; OE *sunnandæg*, c. G *sonntag*; trans. of L *dies sōlis*, Gk. *hēméra hēlíou*] —Syn. **1.** SUNDAY, SABBATH are not properly synonyms. SUNDAY, kept as a day of special worship and of rest from business, is the first day of the week: *Palm Sunday.* The SABBATH, the day on which the fourth Commandment enjoins abstention from work of all kinds, is the seventh day of the Jewish week; the name has been applied to Sunday by some Protestant religious bodies: *to observe the Sabbath.*

Sun·day-go-to-meet·ing (sŭn′dĭ gō′tə mē′tĭng), *adj. Colloq.* most dressed-up; most presentable; best: *Sunday-go-to-meeting shoes.*

Sunday School, **1.** a school, now usually in connection with a church, for religious (and formerly also secular) instruction on Sunday. **2.** the members of such a school. Also, **Sabbath School.**

sun·der (sŭn′dər), *v.t.* **1.** to separate; part; divide; sever. —*v.i.* **2.** to become separated; part. [ME; late OE *sundrian*, c. G *sondern*]

sun·der·ance (sŭn′dər-əns, -drəns), *n.* separation.

Sun·der·land (sŭn′dər-lənd), *n.* a seaport in NE England, in Durham. 182,800 (est. 1956).

sun·dew (sŭn′dū′, -dōō′), *n.* any of a group of small bog plants, species of the genus *Drosera*, with sticky hairs that capture insects.

sun·di·al (sŭn′dī′əl), *n.* an instrument for indicating the time of day by the position of a shadow (as of a gnomon) cast by the sun on a graduated plate or surface.

sun disk, **1.** the disk of the sun. **2.** a figure or representation of this, esp. in religious symbolism.

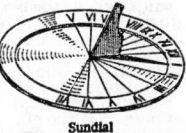

Sundial

sun·dog (sŭn′dôg′, -dŏg′), *n.* **1.** a parhelion. **2.** a small or incomplete rainbow.

sun·down (sŭn′doun′), *n.* sunset; the time of sunset.

sun-dried (sŭn′drĭd′), *adj.* **1.** dried in the sun, as bricks, raisins, etc. **2.** dried up or withered by the sun.

sun·dries (sŭn′drĭz), *n.pl.* sundry things or items.

sun·drops (sŭn′drŏps′), *n., pl.* **-drops.** any of various plants of the onagraceous genus *Oenothera* (*Kneiffa*), related to the evening primrose.

sun·dry (sŭn′drĭ), *adj.* **1.** various or divers: *sundry persons.* **2.** all and sundry, everyone collectively and individually. [ME; OE *syndrig* private, separate, der. *sundor* apart. See -Y¹]

sun·fast (sŭn′făst′, -fäst′), *adj.* not subject to fading in sunlight.

sun·fish (sŭn′fĭsh′), *n., pl.* **-fishes,** (esp. collectively) **-fish.** **1.** a huge fish, the **ocean sunfish,** *Mola mola,* having a deep body abbreviated behind, seeming to consist of little more than the head. **2.** any fish of the same family, *Molidae.* **3.** any of various small fresh-water spiny-rayed fishes of the genus *Lepomis,* of North America, with a deep, compressed body.

sun·flow·er (sŭn′flou′ər), *n.* any plant of the asteraceous genus *Helianthus,* characterized by yellow-rayed flowers, as *H. annuus,* the common species of North America, a tall plant grown for its showy flowers, and for its seeds which are valued as food for poultry and as the source of an oil.

sung (sŭng), *v.* pt. and pp. of **sing.**

Sung (sŏŏng), *n.* a Chinese dynasty, A.D. 960–1280, under which culture, esp. art and Confucian philosophy, flourished in the Yangtze region, until overthrown by the Mongols.

Sun·ga·ri (sŏŏng′gə-rē′), *n.* a river in NE China, flowing through E and central Manchuria into the Amur river on the Siberian boundary. ab. 800 mi.

Sung·kiang (sŏŏng′jyäng′), *n.* a former province in NE China, now a part of Inner Mongolian Autonomous Region. 5,151,000 (est. 1950); 79,151 sq. mi.

sun·glass (sŭn′glăs′, -gläs′), *n.* a burning glass.

sun·glow (sŭn′glō′), *n.* **1.** the glow or warm light of the sun. **2.** a diffused hazy light seen around the sun, due to particles of foreign matter in the atmosphere.

sun god, the sun considered or personified as a deity: a god identified or associated with the sun.

sunk (sŭngk), *v.* a pt. and pp. of **sink.**

sunk·en (sŭngk/ən), *v.* 1. a pp. of **sink.** —*adj.* 2. having sunk or having been sunk beneath the surface; submerged. 3. having settled down to a lower level, as walls. 4. depressed or lying below the general level, as a garden. 5. hollow: *sunken cheeks.*

sunk fence, a wall or other barrier set in a ditch to divide lands without marring the landscape.

sun lamp, 1. a lamp which generates ultraviolet rays, used as a therapeutic device, to induce artificial sunburn, etc. 2. a source of light used in motion-picture photography, consisting essentially of a bright lamp whose light is intensified and directed by an arrangement of parabolic mirrors.

sun·light (sŭn/līt/), *n.* the light of the sun.

sun·lit (sŭn/lĭt/), *adj.* lighted by the sun.

sunn (sŭn), *n.* 1. a tall East Indian fabaceous shrub, *Crotalaria juncea,* with slender branches and yellow flowers, and an inner bark which yields a hemplike fiber used for making ropes, sacking, etc. 2. the fiber. Also, **sunn hemp.** [t. Hind.: m. *san*]

Sun·na (sŏŏn/ə), *n.* the traditional portion of Moslem Law, claimed to be based on the words and acts of Mohammed, although not attributed verbatim to him. [t. Ar.: form, way, path]

Sun·nite (sŏŏn/īt), *n.* one of the so-called orthodox Mohammedans, who accepts the Sunna as of almost equal importance with the Koran. [der. SUNNA]

sun·ny (sŭn/ĭ), *adj.,* **-nier, -niest.** 1. abounding in sunshine: *a sunny day.* 2. exposed to or lighted or warmed by the direct rays of the sun: *a sunny room.* 3. pertaining to or proceeding from the sun; solar. 4. resembling the sun. 5. cheery, cheerful, or joyous: *a sunny disposition.* —**sun/ni·ly,** *adv.* —**sun/ni·ness,** *n.*

Sun·ny·vale (sŭn/ĭ vāl/), *n.* a city in central California, south of San Francisco. 52,898 (1960).

sun parlor, a parlor exposed to sunshine.

sun·rise (sŭn/rīz/), *n.* 1. the rise or ascent of the sun above the horizon in the morning. 2. the atmospheric phenomena accompanying this. 3. the time when the sun rises.

sun·room (sŭn/rŏŏm/, -rŏŏm/), *n.* a room designed to admit a large amount of sunlight.

sun·set (sŭn/sĕt/), *n.* 1. the setting or descent of the sun below the horizon in the evening. 2. the atmospheric phenomena accompanying this. 3. the time when the sun sets. 4. the close or final stage of any period.

sun·shade (sŭn/shād/), *n.* 1. something used as a protection from the rays of the sun. 2. a kind of awning in front of a store. 3. a parasol.

sun·shine (sŭn/shīn/), *n.* 1. the shining of the sun; the direct light of the sun. 2. brightness or radiance; cheerfulness or happiness. 3. a source of cheer or happiness. 4. the effect of the sun in lighting and heating a place. 5. a place where the direct rays of the sun fall. —**sun/shin/y,** *adj.*

sun·spot (sŭn/spŏt/), *n.* one of the relatively dark patches which appear periodically on the surface of the sun, and which have a certain effect on terrestrial magnetism and other terrestrial phenomena.

sun·stroke (sŭn/strōk/), *n. Pathol.* a frequently fatal affection due to exposure to the sun's rays or to excessive heat, marked by sudden prostration, with or without fever, and symptoms resembling those of apoplexy.

sun·struck (sŭn/strŭk/), *adj.* affected with sunstroke.

sun·up (sŭn/ŭp/), *n.* sunrise.

sun·ward (sŭn/wərd), *adv.* 1. Also, **sun/wards.** toward the sun. —*adj.* 2. directed toward the sun.

sun·wise (sŭn/wīz/), *adv.* 1. in the direction of the sun's apparent daily motion. 2. clockwise.

Sun Yat-sen (sŏŏn/yät/sĕn/), 1867–1925, Chinese political leader.

su·o ju·re (sŏŏ/ō jŏŏr/ĭ), *Latin.* in his (her, its, one's) own right.

suo lo·co (lō/kō), *Latin.* in one's own or rightful place.

Su·o·mi (sŏŏ ō/mē), *n.* Finnish name of Finland.

sup¹ (sŭp), *v.,* **supped, supping.** —*v.i.* 1. to eat the evening meal; take supper. —*v.t.* 2. to provide with or entertain at supper. [ME *sope,* t. OE: m. *soper*]

sup² (sŭp), *v.,* **supped, supping,** *n.* —*v.t.* 1. to take (liquid food, or any liquid) into the mouth in small quantities, as from a spoon or a cup. —*v.i.* 2. to take liquid into the mouth in small quantities, as by spoonfuls or sips. —*n.* 3. a mouthful or small portion of liquid food or of drink. [ME *suppe,* OE *suppa,* akin to OE *sūpan,* c. G *saufen* drink. Cf. SIP, SOP, SUP¹, SOUP]

sup-, var. of **sub-** (by assimilation) before *p.*

sup., 1. superior. 2. superlative. 3. supine. 4. supplement. 5. supplementary. 6. supra.

su·per (sŏŏ/pər), *n.* 1. *Colloq.* a shortened form of *superintendent, supernumerary* (esp. in theatrical use), and various other words beginning with the same prefix. 2. *Com.* goods of a superior quality, grade, size, etc. —*adj.* 3. a shortened form of *superficial* and of *superfine.* 4. *Slang.* extremely fine, great, etc.

super-, 1. prefix of superiority, over-, applied variously, as of quality (*superman*), size (*superdreadnought*), degree (*superheat, supersensitive*), space (*superstructure*), and other meanings (*supersede, supernatural*). 2.

chemical prefix like **per-.** [t. L, comb. form of *super,* adv. and prep., above, beyond, in addition]

su·per·a·ble (sŏŏ/pər ə bəl), *adj.* capable of being overcome; surmountable. [t. L: m.s. *superābilis*]

su·per·a·bound (sŏŏ/pər ə bound/), *v.i.* 1. to abound beyond something else. 2. to be very abundant or too abundant (fol. by *in* or *with*).

su·per·a·bun·dant (sŏŏ/pər ə bŭn/dənt), *adj.* exceedingly or excessively abundant; being more than sufficient; excessive. —**su/per·a·bun/dance,** *n.* —**su/per·a·bun/dant·ly,** *adv.*

su·per·add (sŏŏ/pər ăd/), *v.t.* to add over and above; join as a further addition; add besides. [t. L: s. *superaddere*] —**su·per·ad·di·tion** (sŏŏ/pər ə dĭsh/ən), *n.*

su·per·an·nu·ate (sŏŏ/pər ăn/yŏŏ āt/), *v.t.,* **-ated, -ating.** 1. to allow to retire from service or office on a pension, on account of age or infirmity. 2. to set aside as out of date; remove as too old. [t. ML: m.s. *superannnātus* over a year old (said of cattle); for -*u-* see ANNUAL]

su·per·an·nu·at·ed (sŏŏ/pər ăn/yŏŏ ā/tĭd), *adj.* 1. retired on account of age or infirmity. 2. too old for use, work, service, or a position. 3. antiquated or obsolete.

su·per·an·nu·a·tion (sŏŏ/pər ăn/yŏŏ ā/shən), *n.* 1. act of superannuating. 2. state of being superannuated. 3. a pension or allowance to a superannuated person.

su·perb (sŏŏ pûrb/, sə-), *adj.* 1. stately, majestic, or grand: *superb jewels.* 2. admirably fine or excellent: *a superb performance.* 3. of a proudly imposing appearance or kind: *superb beauty.* [t. L: s. *superbus* proud, distinguished] —**su·perb/ly,** *adv.* —**su·perb/ness,** *n.* —Syn. 1. See **magnificent.**

su·per·bomb (sŏŏ/pər bŏm/), *n.* the hydrogen bomb.

su·per·cal·en·dered paper (sŏŏ/pər kăl/ən dərd), paper with a surface glazed by repeated runs through highly polished copper or zinc rollers.

su·per·car·go (sŏŏ/pər kär/gō), *n., pl.* **-goes, -gos.** an officer on a merchant ship who is in charge of the cargo and the commercial concerns of the voyage. [earlier *supra-cargo,* t. Sp.: m. *sobrecargo*]

su·per·charg·er (sŏŏ/pər chär/jər), *n.* a mechanism attached to an internal-combustion engine to deliver to the cylinders a volume of air greater than that from the suction of the pistons alone, used to increase power.

su·per·cil·i·ar·y (sŏŏ/pər sĭl/ĭ ĕr/ĭ), *adj.* 1. situated over the eye. 2. *Anat., Zool.* **a.** of or pertaining to the eyebrow. **b.** having a conspicuous line or marking over the eye, as certain birds. 3. on the frontal bone at the level of the eyebrow. [t. NL: m. *superciliāris,* der. L *supercilium* eyebrow]

su·per·cil·i·ous (sŏŏ/pər sĭl/ĭ əs), *adj.* haughtily disdainful or contemptuous, as persons, their expression, bearing, etc. [t. L: m.s. *superciliōsus*] —**su/per·cil/i·ous·ly,** *adv.* —**su/per·cil/i·ous·ness,** *n.*

su·per·class (sŏŏ/pər klăs/, -kläs/), *n.* 1. a subphylum. 2. a group or category of related classes within a subphylum.

su·per·co·lum·nar (sŏŏ/pər kə lŭm/nər), *adj.* situated above a column or columns; of, pertaining to, or characterized by supercolumniation.

su·per·co·lum·ni·a·tion (sŏŏ/pər kə lŭm/nĭ ā/shən), *n.* the placing of one order of columns above another.

su·per·con·duc·tiv·i·ty (sŏŏ/pər kŏn/dək tĭv/ə tĭ), *n. Physics.* the phenomenon of greatly increased electrical conductivity shown by certain substances at temperatures approaching absolute zero. —**su/per·con·duc/tor** (-kən dŭk/tər), *n.*

su·per·cool (sŏŏ/pər kŏŏl/), *v.t.* 1. to cool (a liquid) below its freezing point without producing solidification. —*v.i.* 2. to become supercooled.

su·per·dread·nought (sŏŏ/pər drĕd/nôt/), *n.* a battleship of the general type of the dreadnought, but much larger and with superior armament.

su·per·e·go (sŏŏ/pər ē/gō, -ĕg/ō), *n. Psychoanal.* that part of the psychic apparatus which mediates between ego drives and social ideals, acting as a conscience which may be partly conscious and partly unconscious.

su·per·el·e·vat·ed (sŏŏ/pər ĕl/ə vā/tĭd), *adj. Brit.* banked (of a curve in a road or race track).

su·per·em·i·nent (sŏŏ/pər ĕm/ə nənt), *adj.* of superior eminence, rank, or dignity; distinguished, conspicuous, or noteworthy above others. [t. L: s. *supereminens*] —**su/per·em/i·nence,** *n.* —**su/per·em/i·nent·ly,** *adv.*

su·per·er·o·gate (sŏŏ/pər ĕr/ə gāt/), *v.i.* **-gated, -gating.** to do more than duty requires. [t. LL: m.s. *supererogātus,* pp., f. L *super* over + *erogātus,* pp., paid out] —**su/per·er/o·ga/tion,** *n.*

su·per·er·o·ga·to·ry (sŏŏ/pər ə rŏg/ə tôr/ĭ), *adj.* 1. going beyond the requirements of duty. 2. superfluous.

su·per·fam·i·ly (sŏŏ/pər făm/lĭ, -əl ĭ), *n., pl.* **-lies.** *Zool., Bot.* a group or category ranking above a family.

su·per·fe·cun·da·tion (sŏŏ/pər fē/kən dā/shən, -fĕk/-ən-), *n. Physiol.* the fertilization of two ova at the same menstruation by two different acts of coition.

su·per·fe·tate (sŏŏ/pər fē/tāt), *v.i.* **-tated, -tating.** *Physiol.* to fertilize an ovum after a prior conception but before the first one has run its course. [t. LL: m.s. *superfētātus,* pp.] —**su/per·fe·ta/tion,** *n.*

su·per·fi·cial (sŏŏ/pər fĭsh/əl), *adj.* 1. of or pertaining to the superficies or surface: *superficial measurement.* 2. being at, on, or near the surface: *a superficial wound.*

---

b., blend of, blended; c., cognate with; d., dialect, dialectal; der., derived from; f., formed from; g., going back to; m., modification of; r., replacing; s., stem of; t., taken from; ?, perhaps.   See the full key on inside cover.

3. external or outward: *a superficial resemblance.* 4. concerned with or comprehending only what is on the surface or obvious: *a superficial observer.* 5. shallow; not profound or thorough: *a superficial writer.* 6. apparent, rather than real: *superficial piety.* [ME, t. LL: s. *superficiālis,* der. L *superficēs* SUPERFICIES] —**su·per·fi·ci·al·i·ty** (sŌŌ/pər fĭsh/ĭ ăl/ə tĭ), su·per·fi·cial·ness, *n.* —**su'per·fi'cial·ly,** *adv.*

su·per·fi·ci·es (sŌŌ/pər fĭsh/ĭ ēz/, -fĭsh/ēz), *n., pl.* -cies. 1. the surface, outer face, or outside of a thing. 2. the outward appearance, esp. as distinguished from the inner nature. [t. L]

su·per·fine (sŌŌ/pər fīn/), *adj.* 1. extra fine; unusually fine. 2. excessively fine, refined, or nice.

su·per·flu·i·ty (sŌŌ/pər flŌŌ/ə tĭ), *n., pl.* -ties. 1. the state of being superfluous; superabundant or excessive amount. 2. something superfluous as a luxury.

su·per·flu·ous (sŌŌ pûr/flŌŌ əs), *adj.* 1. being over and above what is sufficient or required. 2. unnecessary or needless. 3. *Obs.* lavish or extravagant. [ME, t. L: m. *superfluus* overflowing] —**su·per'flu·ous·ly,** *adv.* —**su·per'flu·ous·ness,** *n.*

su·per·for·tress (sŌŌ/pər fôr/trĭs), *n. Mil.* a heavy four-engine bomber, bearing the U.S. Army designation, B-29. Also, **su·per·fort** (sŌŌ/pər fôrt/).

su·per·fuse (sŌŌ/pər fŪz/), *v.,* -fused, -fusing. —*v.t.* 1. to pour (a liquid, etc.) over or on something. 2. to sprinkle or cover (something) with a liquid or the like. —*v.i.* 3. to be poured over or on something. [t. L: m.s. *superfūsus,* pp.] —**su·per·fu·sion** (sŌŌ/pər fŪ/zhən), *n.*

su·per·gla·cial (sŌŌ/pər glā/shəl), *adj.* 1. on the surface of a glacier. 2. believed to have been formerly on the surface of a glacier: *superglacial debris.*

su·per·heat (*n.* sŌŌ/pər hēt/, .pər hēt/), *n.* 1. the state of being superheated. 2. the amount of super-heating. —*v.t.* 3. to heat to an extreme degree or to a very high temperature. 4. to heat (a liquid) above its boiling point without the formation of bubbles of vapor. 5. to heat (a gas, as steam not in contact with water) to such a degree that its temperature may be lowered or its pressure increased without the conversion of any of the gas into liquid. —**su'per·heat'er,** *n.*

su·per·het·er·o·dyne (sŌŌ/pər hĕt/ər ə dīn/), *Radio.* —*adj.* 1. denoting or pertaining to a method of receiving radio signals by which the incoming modulated wave is changed by the heterodyne process to a lower frequency (the intermediate frequency, which is inaudible) and then submitted to stages of radio-frequency amplification with subsequent detection and audio-frequency amplification. —*n.* 2. a superheterodyne receiver.

su·per·high·way (sŌŌ/pər hī/wā/), *n.* a high-speed highway, usually having traffic lanes divided by a raised safety strip, with traffic routed on and off by cloverleaves.

su·per·hu·man (sŌŌ/pər hŪ/mən), *adj.* 1. above or beyond what is human; having a higher nature or greater powers than man has. 2. exceeding ordinary human power, achievement, experience, etc.: *a superhuman effort.* —**su·per·hu·man·i·ty** (sŌŌ/pər hŪ măn/ə tĭ), —**su'per·hu'man·ly,** *adv.*

su·per·im·pose (sŌŌ/pər ĭm pōz/), *v.t.,* -posed, -posing. 1. to impose, place, or set on something else. 2. to put or join as an addition (fol. by *on* or *upon*). —**su·per·im·po·si·tion** (sŌŌ/pər ĭm/pə zĭsh/ən), *n.*

su·per·in·cum·bent (sŌŌ/pər ĭn kŭm/bənt), *adj.* 1. lying or resting on something else. 2. situated above; overhanging. 3. exerted from above, as pressure. —**su'per·in·cum'bence,** **su'per·in·cum'ben·cy,** *n.*

su·per·in·duce (sŌŌ/pər ĭn dŪs/, -dŌŌs/), *v.t.,* -duced, -ducing. to bring in or induce as an added feature, circumstance, etc.; superimpose. [t. LL: m.s. *superindūcere*] —**su·per·in·duc·tion** (sŌŌ/pər ĭn dŭk/shən), *n.*

su·per·in·tend (sŌŌ/pər ĭn tĕnd/, sŌŌ/pər ĭn-), *v.t.* to oversee and direct (work, processes, affairs, etc.); exercise supervision over (an institution, place, etc.). [t. LL: s. *superintendere*] —**su'per·in·tend'ence,** *n.*

su·per·in·tend·en·cy (sŌŌ/pər ĭn tĕn/dən sĭ, sŌŌ/prĭn-), *n., pl.* -cies. 1. a district under a superintendent. 2. the position or work of a superintendent.

su·per·in·tend·ent (sŌŌ/pər ĭn tĕn/dənt, sŌŌ/prĭn-), *n.* 1. one who has the oversight or direction of some work, enterprise, establishment, institution, house, etc. —*adj.* 2. superintending.

su·pe·ri·or (sə pĭr/ĭ ər, sŌŌ-), *adj.* 1. higher in station, rank, degree, or grade: *a superior officer.* 2. above the average in excellence, merit, intelligence, etc. 3. of higher grade or quality. 4. greater in quantity or amount: *superior numbers.* 5. showing a consciousness or feeling of being above others in such respects: *superior airs.* 6. not yielding or susceptible (fol. by *to*): *to be superior to temptation.* 7. *Bot.* a. situated above some other organ. b. (of a calyx) seeming to originate from the top of the ovary. c. (of an ovary) free from the calyx. 8. *Print.* higher than the main line of type, as algebraic exponents, reference figures, etc. 9. *Astron.* a. (of a planet) having an orbit outside that of the earth. b. (of a conjunction of an inferior planet) denoting a conjunction in which the sun is between the earth and the planet. —*n.* 10. one superior to another or others. 11. *Print.* a superior letter or figure. 12. *Eccles.* the head of a monastery, convent, or the like. [ME, t. L, compar. of *superus* above] —**su·pe·ri·or·i·ty** (sə pĭr/ĭ ôr/ə tĭ, -ŏr/-, sŌŌ-), *n.* —**su·pe'ri·or·ly,** *adv.*

Su·pe·ri·or (sə pĭr/ĭ ər, sŌŌ-), *n.* 1. **Lake,** the northernmost of the Great Lakes, between the United States and Canada: the largest body of fresh water in the world. ab. 400 mi. long; ab. 31,810 sq. mi.; greatest depth, 1290 ft.; 602 ft. above sea level. 2. a city in NW Wisconsin: a port on Lake Superior. 33,563 (1960).

superior court, 1. the court of general jurisdiction found in many States of the United States. 2. any court having general jurisdiction above that of inferior courts, as that of a justice of the peace.

su·per·ja·cent (sŌŌ/pər jā/sənt), *adj.* lying above or upon something else. [t. LL: s. *superjacens,* ppr.]

superl., superlative.

su·per·la·tive (sə pûr/lə tĭv, sŌŌ-), *adj.* 1. of the highest kind or order; surpassing all other or others; supreme; extreme: *superlative wisdom.* 2. being more than is proper or normal; exaggerated in language or style. 3. *Gram.* a. denoting the highest degree of the comparison of adjectives and adverbs, as English *smoothest* in contrast to *smooth* and *smoother.* b. having or pertaining to the function or meaning of this degree of comparison. —*n.* 4. something superlative; a superlative example. 5. the utmost degree. 6. *Gram.* the superlative degree, or a form therein. [ME, t. LL: m.s. *superlātīvus,* der. L *superlātus,* pp., carried beyond] —**su·per'la·tive·ly,** *adv.* —**su·per'la·tive·ness,** *n.*

su·per·lu·na·ry (sŌŌ/pər lŌŌ/nə rĭ), *adj.* 1. situated above or beyond the moon. 2. celestial, rather than earthly. Also, **su/per·lu/nar.**

su·per·man (sŌŌ/pər măn/), *n., pl.* -men. 1. a man of more than human powers. 2. an ideal superior being conceived by Nietzsche as the product of human evolution, being in effect a ruthless egoist of superior strength, cunning, and force of will. 3. a man who prevails by virtue of such characteristics. [trans. of G *übermensch*]

su·per·mar·ket (sŌŌ/pər mär/kĭt), *n.* a large market or store, esp. a food store, operated in part on a self-serve, cash-carry basis.

su·per·nal (sŌŌ pûr/nəl), *adj.* 1. being in or belonging to the heaven of divine beings; heavenly, celestial, or divine. 2. lofty; of more than earthly or human excellence, powers, etc. 3. being on high or in the sky or visible heavens. [late ME, f. s. L *supernus* being above, on high + -AL¹] —**su·per'nal·ly,** *adv.*

su·per·na·tant (sŌŌ/pər nā/tənt), *adj.* floating above, or on the surface. [t. L: s. *supernatans,* ppr.]

su·per·nat·u·ral (sŌŌ/pər năch/ə rəl), *adj.* 1. being above or beyond what is natural: *supernatural phenomena.* 2. abnormal or extraordinary. 3. of or pertaining to the supernatural. —*n.* 4. that which is supernatural. 5. the action of the supernatural as it intervenes in the natural order (prec. by *the*). —**su'per·nat'u·ral·ly,** *adv.* —**su'per·nat'u·ral·ness,** *n.* —Syn. 1. superhuman, miraculous, preternatural. See **miraculous.**

su·per·nat·u·ral·ism (sŌŌ/pər năch/ə rəl ĭz/əm), *n.* 1. supernatural character or agency. 2. belief in the doctrine of supernatural (divine) agency as manifested in the world, in human events, religious revelation, etc. —**su'per·nat'u·ral·ist,** *n., adj.* —**su'per·nat'u·ral·is'tic,** *adj.*

su·per·nu·mer·ar·y (sŌŌ/pər nŪ/mə rĕr/ĭ, -nŌŌ/-), *adj., n., pl.* -aries. —*adj.* 1. being in excess of the usual, proper, or prescribed number; additional; extra. 2. associated with a regular body or staff as an assistant or substitute in case of necessity. —*n.* 3. a supernumerary or extra person or thing. 4. a supernumerary official or employee. 5. *Theat.* one not belonging to the regular company, who appears on the stage but has no lines to speak. [t. LL: as. *supernumerārius* in excess, der. L phrase *super numerum* beyond the number]

su·per·or·der (sŌŌ/pər ôr/dər), *n.* a group or category of related orders within a class or subclass.

su·per·or·gan·ic (sŌŌ/pər ôr găn/ĭk), *adj.* above or beyond what is organic.

su·per·phos·phate (sŌŌ/pər fŏs/fāt), *n.* 1. *Chem.* an acid phosphate. 2. any fertilizer containing it.

su·per·phys·i·cal (sŌŌ/pər fĭz/ə kəl), *adj.* above or beyond what is physical; hyperphysical.

su·per·pose (sŌŌ/pər pōz/), *v.t.,* -posed, -posing. 1. to place above or upon something else, or one upon another. 2. *Geom.* to place (one figure) ideally in the space occupied by another, so that the two figures coincide throughout their whole extent. 3. *Aeron.* to arrange in the position of biplane wings, one approximately over the other. [t. F: m.s. *superposer,* f. super- SUPER- + *poser* POSE¹, after L *superpōnere*] —**su·per·po·si·tion** (sŌŌ/pər pə zĭsh/ən), *n.*

su·per·pow·er (sŌŌ/pər pou/ər), *n.* power, esp. mechanical or electric power, on an extraordinary scale secured by the linking together of a number of separate power systems, with a view to more efficient and economical generation and distribution.

su·per·sat·u·rate (sŌŌ/pər săch/ə rāt/), *v.t.,* -rated, -rating. to increase the concentration of (a solution) beyond saturation; saturate abnormally. —**su/per·sat/u·ra/tion,** *n.*

su·per·scribe (sŌŌ/pər skrīb/), *v.t.,* -scribed, -scribing. 1. to write (words, letters, one's name, etc.) above or on something. 2. to inscribe or mark (something) with writing at the top or on the outside or surface; put an inscription above or on. [t. LL: m.s. *superscrībere*]

su·per·script (sōō′pər skrĭpt′), *adj.* **1.** written above, as a diacritical mark or a correction of a word. —*n.* **2.** *Obs.* a superscription, as of a letter.

su·per·scrip·tion (sōō′pər skrĭp′shən), *n.* **1.** the act of superscribing. **2.** that which is superscribed. **3.** an address on a letter or the like. **4.** *Pharm.* the Latin word *recipe* (take), or the symbol ℞ in a prescription.

su·per·sede (sōō′pər sēd′), *v.t.*, **-seded, -seding. 1.** to replace in power, authority, effectiveness, acceptance, use, etc., as by another person or thing. **2.** to set aside, as void, useless, or obsolete, now usually in favor of something mentioned. **3.** to displace in office or promotion by another. **4.** to succeed to the position, function, office, etc., of; supplant. [t. L: m.s. *supersedēre* sit above] —**su′per·sed′er,** *n.* —**Syn. 1.** See **replace.**

su·per·se·dure (sōō′pər sē′jər), *n.* **1.** act of superseding. **2.** state of being superseded. Also, **su·per·ses·sion** (sōō′pər sĕsh′ən).

su·per·sen·si·ble (sōō′pər sĕn′sə bəl), *adj.* beyond the reach of the senses. —**su′per·sen′si·bly,** *adv.*

su·per·sen·so·ry (sōō′pər sĕn′sə rĭ), *adj.* beyond, or independent of, the organs of sense.

su·per·sen·su·al (sōō′pər sĕn′shōō əl), *adj.* **1.** beyond the range of the senses. **2.** spiritual. **3.** very sensual.

su·per·serv·ice·a·ble (sōō′pər sûr′vĭs ə bəl), *adj.* too disposed to be of service; officious.

su·per·son·ic (sōō′pər sŏn′ĭk), *adj.* **1.** greater than the speed of propagation of sound. **2.** ultrasonic.

su·per·state (sōō′pər stāt′), *n.* a state or a governing power presiding over states subordinated to it.

su·per·sti·tion (sōō′pər stĭsh′ən), *n.* **1.** a belief or notion entertained, regardless of reason or knowledge, of the ominous significance of a particular thing, circumstance, occurrence, proceeding, or the like. **2.** any blindly accepted belief or notion. **3.** a system or collection of superstitious beliefs and customs. **4.** irrational fear of what is unknown or mysterious, esp. in connection with religion. [ME, t. L: s. *superstitio,* lit., a standing over, as in wonder or awe]

su·per·sti·tious (sōō′pər stĭsh′əs), *adj.* **1.** of the nature of, characterized by, or proceeding from superstition: *superstitious fears.* **2.** pertaining to or connected with superstition: *superstitious legends.* **3.** full of or addicted to superstition. —**su·per·sti′tious·ly,** *adv.* —**su·per·sti′tious·ness,** *n.*

su·per·stra·tum (sōō′pər strā′təm), *n., pl.* **-ta** (-tə), **-tums.** an overlying stratum or layer.

su·per·struc·ture (sōō′pər strŭk′chər), *n.* **1.** all of an edifice above the basement or foundation. **2.** any structure built on something else. **3.** *Naut.* the parts of a vessel, as a warship, built above the main deck. **4.** that part of a bridge which rests on the piers and abutments. **5.** anything erected on a foundation or basis.

su·per·sub·tle (sōō′pər sŭt′əl), *adj.* extremely or excessively subtle; oversubtle. —**su′per·sub′tle·ty,** *n.*

su·per·tank·er (sōō′pər tăng′kər), *n.* a tanker with a capacity of over 75,000 tons.

su·per·tax (sōō′pər tăks′), *n.* **1.** *Chiefly Brit.* a tax in addition to a normal tax, as one upon income above a certain amount. **2.** *U.S.* a surtax.

su·per·ton·ic (sōō′pər tŏn′ĭk), *n. Music.* the second tone of a scale, being the next above the tonic.

su·per·vene (sōō′pər vēn′), *v.i.*, **-vened, -vening. 1.** to come as something additional or extraneous (sometimes fol. by *on* or *upon*). **2.** to ensue. [t. L: m.s. *supervenīre* follow] —**su·per·ven·ience** (sōō′pər vēn′yəns), **su·per·ven·tion** (sōō′pər vĕn′shən), *n.* —**su·per·ven·ient** (sōō′pər vēn′yənt), *adj.*

su·per·vise (sōō′pər vīz′), *v.t.*, **-vised, -vising.** to oversee (a process, work, workers, etc.) during execution or performance; superintend; have the oversight and direction of. [t. ML: m.s. *supervīsus,* pp.]

su·per·vi·sion (sōō′pər vĭzh′ən), *n.* the act or function of supervising; oversight; superintendence.

su·per·vi·sor (sōō′pər vī′zər), *n.* **1.** one who supervises; a superintendent. **2.** *Educ.* an official responsible for assisting the teachers in the preparation of syllabi, in devising teaching methods, etc., in a department of instruction, esp. in public schools. **3.** *U.S.* an elected administrative officer in some States, often a member of a board governing a county. —**su′per·vi′sor·ship,** *n.*

su·per·vi·so·ry (sōō′pər vī′zə rĭ), *adj.* pertaining to or having supervision.

su·pi·nate (sōō′pə nāt′), *v.*, **-nated, -nating.** *Physiol.* —*v.t.* **1.** to render supine; rotate or place (the hand or forelimb) so that the palmar surface is upward when the limb is stretched forward horizontally. —*v.i.* **2.** to become supinated. [t. L: m.s. *supīnātus,* pp., bent backward, laid on the back]

su·pi·na·tion (sōō′pə nā′shən), *n. Physiol.* **1.** a turning of the hand so that the palm is facing upwards and the bones of the forearm are parallel (opposed to *pronation*). **2.** a comparable motion of the foot, consisting of adduction followed by inversion. **3.** the result of this rotation; the position so assumed.

su·pi·na·tor (sōō′pə nā′tər), *n. Anat.* a muscle which causes supination. [NL. See **SUPINATE,** -OR²]

su·pine (*adj.* sōō pīn′; *n.* sōō′pīn), *adj.* **1.** lying on the back, or with the face or front upward; having the palm upward, as the hand. **2.** inactive; passive; inert; esp., inactive or passive from indolence or indifference. —*n.* **3.** (in Latin) a noun form derived from verbs, appearing

only in the accusative and the dative-ablative, as *dictū* in *mirābile dictū* "wonderful to say." **4.** an analogous form in some other language. [t. L: m.s. *supīnus*] —**su·pine′ly,** *adv.* —**su·pine′ness,** *n.*

supp., supplement. Also, **suppl.**

sup·per (sŭp′ər), *n.* **1.** the evening meal; the last meal of the day, taken in the evening. **2.** any evening repast, often one forming a social entertainment. [ME, t. OF: m. *so(u)per,* n. use of *souper* SUP]

sup·plant (sə plănt′, -plänt′), *v.t.* **1.** to displace or supersede, as one thing does another. **2.** to take the place of (another), as in office or favor, through scheming, strategy, or the like. **3.** to replace (one thing) by something else. [ME *supplante(n),* t. L: m. *supplantāre* trip up, overthrow] —**sup·plan·ta·tion** (sŭp′lăn tā′shən), *n.* —**sup·plant′er,** *n.* —**Syn. 2.** See **replace.**

sup·ple (sŭp′əl), *adj.,* **-pler, -plest,** *v.,* **-pled, -pling.** —*adj.* **1.** bending readily without breaking or deformation; pliant; flexible: *a supple rod.* **2.** characterized by ease in bending; limber; lithe: *supple movements.* **3.** characterized by ease and adaptability in mental action. **4.** compliant or yielding. **5.** obsequious; servile. —*v.t., v.i.* **6.** to make or become supple. [ME, t. OF, g. L *supplex* bending under] —**sup′ple·ly,** *adv.* —**sup′ple·ness,** *n.* —**Ant. 1.** rigid.

sup·ple·jack (sŭp′əl jăk′), *n.* **1.** a strong, pliant cane or walking stick. **2.** any of various climbing shrubs with strong stems suitable for making walking sticks.

sup·ple·ment (*n.* sŭp′lə mənt; *v.* sŭp′lə mĕnt′),   *n.* **1.** something added to complete a thing, supply a deficiency, or reinforce or extend a whole. **2.** a part added to a book, document, or the like to supply deficiencies or correct errors. **3.** a part, usually of special character, issued as an additional feature of a newspaper or other periodical. **4.** *Math.* the quantity by which an angle or an arc falls short of 180° or a semicircle. —*v.t.* **5.** to complete, add to, or extend by a supplement; form a supplement or addition to. **6.** to supply (a deficiency). [ME, t. L: s. *supplēmentum*] —**Syn. 2.** See **appendix. 5.** See **complement.**

Angle BCD, supplement of angle BCA

sup·ple·men·ta·ry (sŭp′lə mĕn′tə rĭ), *adj.* of the nature of or forming a supplement; additional. Also, **sup′ple·men′tal.**

sup·ple·tion (sə plē′shən), *n. Gram.* **a.** the presence of one or more suppletive forms in a paradigm. **b.** the use of suppletive forms, or an instance of such use.

sup·ple·tive (sə plē′tĭv, sŭp′lə tĭv), *adj. Gram.* **a.** (of a linguistic form) serving as an inflected form of a word with a totally different stem, e.g., *went* as the preterit of *go.* **b.** (of a paradigm) including one or more suppletive forms. **c.** (of inflection) characterized by the use of suppletive forms.

sup·ple·to·ry (sŭp′lə tōr′ĭ), *adj.* supplying a deficiency. [t. LL: m.s. *supplētōrius,* der. L *supplētus,* pp., filled up]

sup·pli·ant (sŭp′lĭ ənt), *n.* **1.** one who supplicates; a humble petitioner. —*adj.* **2.** supplicating. **3.** expressive of supplication, as words, actions, etc. [ME, t. F, ppr. of *supplier,* OF *souplier,* g. L *supplicāre* supplicate] —**sup′pli·ant·ly,** *adv.* —**sup′pli·ant·ness, sup′pli·ance,** *n.*

sup·pli·cant (sŭp′lə kənt), *adj.* **1.** supplicating. —*n.* **2.** a suppliant. [t. L: s. *supplicans,* ppr.]

sup·pli·cate (sŭp′lə kāt′), *v.,* **-cated, -cating.** —*v.i.* **1.** to pray humbly; make humble and earnest entreaty or petition. —*v.t.* **2.** to pray humbly to; entreat or petition humbly. **3.** to seek by humble entreaty. [late ME, t. L: m.s. *supplicātus,* pp. begged] —**Syn. 3.** See **appeal.**

sup·pli·ca·tion (sŭp′lə kā′shən), *n.* act of supplicating; humble prayer, entreaty, or petition.

sup·pli·ca·to·ry (sŭp′lə kə tōr′ĭ), *adj.* making or expressing supplication.

sup·ply¹ (sə plī′), *v.,* **-plied, -plying,** *n., pl.* **-plies.** —*v.t.* **1.** to furnish (a person, establishment, place, etc.) with what is lacking or requisite. **2.** to furnish or provide (fol. by *with*): *to supply a person with clothing.* **3.** to furnish or provide (something wanting or requisite): *to supply electricity to a community.* **4.** to make up (a deficiency); make up for (a loss, lack, absence, etc.); satisfy (a need, demand, etc.). **5.** to fill (a place, vacancy, etc.); occupy (a pulpit, etc.) as a substitute. —*v.i.* **6.** to fill the place of another, esp. the minister of a church, as a substitute or temporarily. —*n.* **7.** act of supplying, furnishing, providing, satisfying, etc. **8.** that which is supplied. **9.** a quantity of something provided or on hand, as for use; a stock or store. **10.** (*usually pl.*) a provision, stock, or store of food or other things necessary for maintenance. **11.** *Econ.* the quantity of a commodity, etc., that is in the market and available for purchase, or that is available for purchase at a particular price. **12.** (*pl.*) *Mil.* **a.** articles and materials used by an army or navy of types rapidly used up, such as food, clothing, soap, and fuel. **b.** the furnishing of supplies, and the management of supply units and installations. **13.** one who supplies a vacancy or takes the place of another, esp. temporarily. **14.** *Obs.* reinforcements. **15.** *Obs.* aid. [ME *supplye,* t. OF: m. *so(u)pl(e)ier,* g. L *supplēre* fill up] —**sup·pli′er,** *n.*

sup·ply² (sŭp′lĭ), *adv.* supplely. [f. SUPP(LE) + -LY]

sup·port (sə pōrt′), *v.t.* **1.** to bear or hold up (a load, mass, structure, part, etc.). **2.** to sustain or withstand

(weight, etc.) without giving way. **3.** to undergo or endure, esp. with patience or submission; tolerate. **4.** to sustain (a person, the mind, spirits, courage, etc.) under trial or affliction. **5.** to maintain (a person, family, establishment, institution, etc.) by supplying with things necessary to existence; provide for. **6.** to uphold (a person, cause, policy, etc.) by aid or countenance; back; second (efforts, aims, etc.). **7.** to maintain or advocate (a theory, etc.). **8.** to corroborate (a statement, etc.). **9.** to sustain or act (a part, role, or character). **10.** to act with or second (a leading actor), as on a stage; assist in any performance. —*n.* **11.** act of supporting. **12.** state of being supported. **13.** maintenance, as of a person, family, etc., with necessaries, means, or funds. **14.** a thing or a person that supports. **15.** a thing or a person that gives aid or assistance. **16.** the material, as canvas or wood, on which a picture is painted. [ME, t. OF: s. *supporter* bear, g. L *supportāre* convey]
—**Syn. 1, 6.** SUPPORT, MAINTAIN, SUSTAIN, UPHOLD all mean to hold up and to preserve. To SUPPORT is to hold up or add strength to, literally or figuratively: *the columns support the roof.* To MAINTAIN is to support so as to preserve intact: *to maintain an attitude of defiance.* To SUSTAIN, a rather elevated word, suggests completeness and adequacy in supporting: *the court sustained his claim.* UPHOLD applies esp. to supporting or backing another, as in a statement, opinion, or belief: *to uphold the rights of a minority.* **13.** See **living.**

sup·port·a·ble (sə·pōr′tə·bəl), *adj.* capable of being supported; endurable; maintainable. —**sup·port′a·bil′i·ty, sup·port′a·ble·ness,** *n.* —**sup·port′a·bly,** *adv.*

sup·port·er (sə·pōr′tər), *n.* **1.** one who or that which supports. **2.** a device, usually elastic cotton webbing, for holding up some part of the body. **3.** an upholder, backer, or advocate. **4.** *Her.* a figure as of an animal or a man, holding up an escutcheon or standing beside it.

sup·pose (sə·pōz′), *v.,* **-posed, -posing.** —*v.t.* **1.** to assume (something), without reference to its being true or false, for the sake of argument or for the purpose of tracing the consequences: *suppose the distance to be one mile.* **2.** to consider as a possibility suggested or an idea or plan proposed (used in the imperative): *suppose we wait till tomorrow.* **3.** to assume as true, or believe, in the absence of positive knowledge or of evidence to the contrary: *it is supposed that the occurrence was an accident.* **4.** to take for granted, assume, or presume, without especial thought of possible error: *I supposed that you had gone.* **5.** to think, with reference to mere opinion: *what do you suppose he will do?* **6.** (of a proposition, theory, etc.) to make or involve the assumption of: *this theory supposes the existence of life on Mars.* **7.** (of facts, circumstances, etc.) to require logically; imply; presuppose. **8.** *Obs.* to expect. —*v.i.* **9.** to assume something; presume; think. [ME, t. OF: m. *sup(p)oser,* f. *sup-* SUB- + *poser* POSE[1], after L *supponere*] —**sup·pos′a·ble,** *adj.* —**sup·pos′a·bly,** *adv.* —**Syn. 3.** See **think**[1].

sup·posed (sə·pōzd′), *adj.* **1.** assumed as true, regardless of fact; hypothetical: *a supposed case.* **2.** accepted or received as true, without positive knowledge and perhaps erroneously: *the supposed site of an ancient temple.* **3.** merely thought to be such: *to sacrifice real for supposed gains.* —**sup·pos·ed·ly** (sə·pō′zid·lǐ), *adv.*

sup·po·si·tion (sŭp′ə·zǐsh′ən), *n.* **1.** act of supposing. **2.** that which is supposed; an assumption; a hypothesis. [late ME, t. ML: s. *suppositio* (in L a putting under) used as trans. of Gk. *hypothesis* HYPOTHESIS] —**sup′po·si′tion·al,** *adj.* —**sup′po·si′tion·al·ly,** *adv.*

sup·pos·i·ti·tious (sə·pŏz′ə·tǐsh′əs), *adj.* **1.** fraudulently substituted or pretended; spurious; not genuine. **2.** hypothetical. [t. L: m. *supposittus*] —**sup·pos′i·ti′tious·ly,** *adv.* —**sup·pos′i·ti′tious·ness,** *n.*

sup·pos·i·tive (sə·pŏz′ə·tǐv), *adj.* **1.** of the nature of or involving supposition; suppositional. **2.** supposititious or false. **3.** *Gram.* expressing supposition, as the words *if, granting,* or *provided.* —*n.* **4.** *Gram.* a suppositive word. —**sup·pos′i·tive·ly,** *adv.*

sup·pos·i·to·ry (sə·pŏz′ə·tōr′ǐ), *n., pl.* **-ries.** a solid conical mass of medicinal substance inserted into the rectum or vagina to be dissolved therein. [t. LL: m.s. *suppositōrium* (thing) placed under, der. L *suppositus,* pp., placed under]

sup·press (sə·prĕs′), *v.t.* **1.** to put an end to the activities of (a person, body of persons, etc.). **2.** to do away with by or as by authority; abolish; stop (a practice, etc.). **3.** to keep in or repress (a feeling, smile, groan, etc.). **4.** to withhold from disclosure or publication (truth, evidence, a book, names, etc.). **5.** to arrest (a flow, hemorrhage, etc.). **6.** to quell; crush; vanquish or subdue (a revolt, rebel, etc.). [ME, t. L: s. *suppressus,* pp., put down] —**sup·pres′sor, sup·press′er,** *n.* —**sup·press′i·ble,** *adj.* —**sup·press′ive,** *adj.*

sup·pres·sion (sə·prĕsh′ən), *n.* **1.** act of suppressing or state of being suppressed. **2.** *Psychoanal.* conscious inhibition of an impulse.

sup·pu·rate (sŭp′yə·rāt′), *v.i.,* **-rated, -rating.** to produce or discharge pus, as a wound; maturate. [t. L: m.s. *suppūrātus,* pp., caused to secrete pus]

sup·pu·ra·tion (sŭp′yə·rā′shən), *n.* **1.** the process of suppurating. **2.** the matter produced by suppuration.

sup·pu·ra·tive (sŭp′yə·rā′tǐv), *adj.* **1.** suppurating, or characterized by suppuration. **2.** promoting suppuration. —*n.* **3.** a medicine or application that promotes suppuration.

su·pra (sōō′prə), *adv.* above: esp. used in making reference to parts of a text. [L: above, beyond]

supra-, a prefix meaning "above," equivalent to **super-,** but emphasizing location or position, as in *supraorbital, suprarenal.* [t. L, repr. *suprā,* adv. and prep.]

su·pra·lap·sar·i·an (sōō′prə·lăp·sâr′ǐ·ən), *n.* one who believes in supralapsarianism. [f. s. NL *supralapsārius* (der. L *suprā-* SUPRA- + *lapsus* fall, lapse) + -AN]

su·pra·lap·sar·i·an·ism (sōō′prə·lăp·sâr′ǐ·ən·ǐz′əm), *n. Theol.* the doctrine that the decree of election and reprobation, expressing the ultimate purpose of God, preceded the means by which this purpose was to be accomplished, namely the decree of man's creation and the decree which permitted his fall; high Calvinism (opposed to *infra-* or *sublapsarianism*).

su·pra·lim·i·nal (sōō′prə·lǐm′ə·nəl), *adj. Psychol.* above the limen or threshold of consciousness; of or in consciousness.

su·pra·mo·lec·u·lar (sōō′prə·mə·lĕk′yə·lər), *adj.* **1.** above the molecule; of greater complexity than a molecule. **2.** composed of an aggregation of molecules.

su·pra·or·bit·al (sōō′prə·ôr′bǐt·əl), *adj. Anat.* located above the eye socket.

supra protest, *Law.* upon or after protest (a phrase used with reference to an acceptance or a payment of a bill by a third person for the honor of the drawer after protest for nonacceptance or nonpayment by the drawee). [t. It.: m. *sopra protesto* upon protest]

su·pra·pro·test (sōō′prə·prō′tĕst), *n. Law.* an acceptance or a payment of a bill supra protest.

su·pra·re·nal (sōō′prə·rē′nəl), *Anat.* —*adj.* **1.** situated above or on the kidney. **2.** pertaining to or connected with a suprarenal. —*n.* **3.** a suprarenal body, capsule, or gland. See diag. under **kidney.**

suprarenal gland, *Anat.* a ductless gland situated in man at the upper end, and in most vertebrates at the anterior end, of each kidney, and furnishing at least two important internal secretions.

su·prem·a·cy (sə·prĕm′ə·sǐ, sōō-), *n.* **1.** the state of being supreme. **2.** supreme authority or power.

su·preme (sə·prēm′, sōō-), *adj.* **1.** highest in rank or authority; paramount; sovereign; chief. **2.** of the highest quality, character, importance, etc.: *supreme courage.* **3.** greatest, utmost, or extreme: *supreme disgust.* **4.** last (with reference to the end of life): *the supreme moment.* [t. L: m.s. *suprēmus,* superl. of *superus* that is above] —**su·preme′ly,** *adv.* —**su·preme′ness,** *n.*

Supreme Being, the sovereign of the universe; God.

supreme commander, the military, naval, or air officer commanding all allied forces in a theater of war.

Supreme Court, *U.S.* **1.** the highest court of the nation. **2.** (in most States) the highest court of the State.

supreme sacrifice, the sacrifice of one's own life.

Supreme Soviet, the parliament of the Soviet Union, consisting of two houses, one house representative on the basis of population, the other assuring every nationality, however small, some representation.

Supt., superintendent. Also, **supt.**

sur-[1], a prefix corresponding to **super-** but mainly attached to stems not used as words and having figurative applications (*survive, surname*), used especially in legal terms (*surrebuttal*). [late ME, t. F, g. L *super-* SUPER-]

sur-[2], occasional var. of **sub-** (by assimilation) before *r.*

su·ra (sōōr′ə), *n.* one of the 124 chapters of the Koran. [t. Ar.: m. *surah* row, step, degree]

Su·ra·ba·ya (sōō′rä·bä′yä), *n.* a seaport in NE Java: second largest city in Indonesia: naval base. 925,617 (est. 1953). Dutch, **Soerabaja.**

su·rah (sōōr′ə), *n.* a soft twilled silk or rayon fabric. [appar. named after *Surat,* India]

Su·ra·jah Dow·lah (sə·rä′jə dou′lə). See **Siraj-ud-daula.**

Su·ra·kar·ta (sōō′rä·kär′tä), *n.* former name of **Solo.**

su·ral (sōōr′əl), *adj. Anat.* of or pertaining to the calf of the leg. [t. NL: s. *surālis,* der. L *sura* calf of the leg]

Su·rat (sōō·rät′, sōōr′ət), *n.* a seaport in W India, in Bombay state: the first British settlement in India, 1612. 223,182 (1951).

sur·base (sûr′bās′), *n. Archit.* a molding above a base, as that immediately above a baseboard, the crowning molding of a pedestal, etc.

sur·based (sûr′bāst′), *adj. Archit.* **1.** having a surbase. **2.** depressed; flattened. **3.** (of an arch) having a rise of less than half the span. [Anglicization of F *surbaissé,* f. *sur-* (intensive) + *baisse* lowered. See BASE[2]]

sur·cease (sûr·sēs′), *v.,* **-ceased, -ceasing,** *n. Archaic.* —*v.i.* **1.** to cease from some action; desist. **2.** to come to an end. —*v.t.* **3.** to cease from; leave off. —*n.* **4.** cessation; end. [ME *sursese,* t. OF: m. *sursis,* pp. of *surseoir* refrain, suspend, t. L *supersedēre* desist]

sur·charge (*n.* sûr′chärj′, sûr·chärj′; *v.* sûr·chärj′), *n., v.,* **-charged, -charging.** —*n.* **1.** an additional or excessive charge, load, burden, etc. **2.** an excessive sum or price charged. **3.** *Philately.* an overprint which alters or restates the face value or denomination of a stamp to which it has been applied. **4.** *Law.* act of surcharging. —*v.t.* **5.** to subject to an additional or extra charge (for payment); overcharge. **6.** to show an omission in (an account) of something that operates as a charge against the accounting party. **7.** *Philately.* to print a surcharge on. **8.** to put an additional or excessive burden upon. [ME, t. OF. See SUR-[1], CHARGE, v.] —**sur·charg′er,** *n.*

sur·cin·gle (sûr′sĭng′gəl), *n.* **1.** a girth for a horse or other animal, esp. a large girth passing over and keeping in place a blanket, pack, or the like. **2.** a girdle with which a garment, esp. a cassock, is fastened. [ME *sursengle*, t. OF: m. *surcengle*, f. *sur*-¹ + *cengle* (g. L *cingula* girdle]

sur·coat (sûr′kōt′), *n.* **1.** a garment worn over medieval armor, often embroidered with heraldic arms. **2.** an outer coat or garment. [ME *surcote*, t. OF. See SUR-¹, COAT]

sur·cu·lose (sûr′kyə-lōs′), *adj. Bot.* producing suckers. [t. L: s. *surculōsus*]

surd (sûrd), *adj.* **1.** *Math.* (of a quantity) not capable of being expressed in rational numbers; irrational. **2.** *Phonet.* voiceless. —*n.* **3.** *Math.* a surd quantity. **4.** *Phonet.* a voiceless consonant. [t. L: s. *surdus* deaf, indistinct]

Surcoat. 13th century

sure (shŏŏr), *adj., surer, surest, adv.* —*adj.* **1.** free from apprehension or doubt as to the reliability, character, action, etc., of something (often fol. by *of*): *to be sure of one's data.* **2.** confident, as of something expected: *sure of ultimate success.* **3.** convinced, fully persuaded, or positive, as of something firmly believed: *sure of a person's guilt.* **4.** assured or certain beyond question: *man is sure of death.* **5.** worthy of confidence; reliable: *a sure messenger.* **6.** firm or stable: *to stand on sure ground.* **7.** unfailing; never disappointing expectations: *a sure cure.* **8.** unerring; never missing, slipping, etc.: *a sure aim.* **9.** admitting of no doubt or question: *sure proof.* **10.** inevitable: *death is sure.* **11.** destined; bound inevitably; certain: *he is sure to come.* **12.** *Archaic.* secure or safe. **13. be sure,** be certain or careful (to do or be as specified): *be sure to close the windows.* **14. for sure,** as a certainty; surely. **15. to be sure,** surely; certainly; without doubt. —*adv.* **16.** *Colloq.* surely, undoubtedly, or certainly. **17.** *U.S. Colloq.* inevitably or without fail. [ME, t. OF, g. L *sēcūrus* secure] —**sure′ness,** *n.* —**Syn. 1.** SURE, CERTAIN, CONFIDENT, POSITIVE indicate full belief and trust that something is true. SURE, CERTAIN, and POSITIVE are often used interchangeably. SURE, the simplest and most general, denotes mere absence of doubt. CERTAIN suggests that there are definite reasons which have freed one from doubt. CONFIDENT emphasizes the strength of the belief or the certainty of expectation felt. POSITIVE implies emphatic certainty, which may even become overconfidence or dogmatism. —**Ant. 1.** doubtful.

sure-foot·ed (shŏŏr′fŏŏt′ĭd), *adj.* **1.** not liable to stumble, slip, or fall. **2.** proceeding surely; unerring.

sure·ly (shŏŏr′lĭ), *adv.* **1.** firmly; unerringly; without missing, slipping, etc. **2.** undoubtedly, assuredly, or certainly: *the results are surely encouraging.* **3.** (in emphatic utterances that are not necessarily sustained by fact) assuredly: *surely you are mistaken.* **4.** inevitably or without fail: *slowly but surely the end approached.*

sure·ty (shŏŏr′tĭ, shŏŏr′ə-tĭ), *n., pl.* **-ties.** **1.** security against loss or damage; security for the fulfillment of an obligation, the payment of a debt, etc.; a pledge, guaranty, or bond. **2.** one who has made himself responsible for another. **3.** the state or quality of being sure. **4.** *Archaic.* certainty. **5.** that which makes sure; ground of confidence or safety. **6.** one who has contracted to be answerable for the debt, default, or miscarriage of another. [ME *seurte*, t. OF, g. s. L *sēcūritas*]

sure·ty·ship (shŏŏr′tĭ-shĭp′, shŏŏr′ə-tĭ-), *n. Law.* the relationship between the surety, the principal debtor, and the creditor.

surf (sûrf), *n.* the swell of the sea which breaks upon a shore or upon shoals; the mass or line of foamy water caused by the breaking of the sea upon a shore, etc. [earlier *suff*, ? var. of SOUGH] —**Syn.** See wave.

sur·face (sûr′fĭs), *n., adj., v.* **-faced, -facing.** —*n.* **1.** the outer face, or outside, of a thing. **2.** any face of a body or thing: *the six surfaces of a cube.* **3.** extent or area of outer face; superficial area. **4.** the outward appearance, esp. as distinguished from the inner nature: *to look below the surface of a matter.* **5.** *Geom.* any figure having only two dimensions; part or all of the boundary of a solid. **6.** *Aeron.* an airfoil. —*adj.* **7.** lof, on, or pertaining to the surface; superficial; external; apparent, rather than real. —*v.t.* **8.** to finish as to surface; give a particular kind of surface to; make even or smooth. —*v.i.* **9.** to wash surface deposits of ore; to mine at or near the surface. **10.** to work on or at the surface. [t. F, f. *sur*-¹ + *face* FACE. Cf. SUPERFICIES] —**sur′fac·er,** *n.*

surface plate, *Mach.* a flat plate used by mechanics for testing surfaces which are to be made perfectly flat.

surface tension, *Physics.* a property of liquid or solid matter due to unbalanced molecular forces near a surface, and the measure thereof; an apparent tension in an actually nonexistent surface film associated with capillary phenomena, cohesion, and adhesion.

surf·bird (sûrf′bûrd′), *n.* a shore bird, *Aphriza virgata,* allied to the turnstones, which nests in Alaska and winters along the coast to the southward occasionally as far south as Chile and the Strait of Magellan.

surf·board (sûrf′bôrd′), *n.* a narrow board about five feet in length used as a kind of a float in a sport consisting of riding the crest of a wave towards the shore.

surf·boat (sûrf′bōt′), *n.* a strong, buoyant pulling boat with high ends, adapted for passing through surf.

surf duck, a scoter, esp. the surf scoter.

sur·feit (sûr′fĭt), *n.* **1.** excess; an excessive amount. **2.** excess in eating or drinking. **3.** oppression or disorder of the system due to excessive eating or drinking. **4.** general disgust caused by excess or satiety. —*v.t.* **5.** to bring to a state of surfeit by excess of food or drink. **6.** to supply with anything to excess or satiety; satiate. —*v.i.* **7.** to eat or drink to excess; suffer from the effects of overfeeding. **8.** to indulge to excess in anything. [ME *sorfait,* t. OF: excess, prop. pp. of *sorfaire* overdo, f. *sor-* SUR-¹ + *faire* do (g. L *facere*)] —**sur′feit·er,** *n.*

surf fish, any of the small to medium-sized viviparous fishes constituting the family *Embiotocidae,* inhabiting the shallow waters of the Pacific coast of North America.

surf scoter, a large North American diving duck, *Melanitta perspicillata,* the adult male of which is black except for two white patches on the head.

surf·y (sûr′fĭ), *adj.* abounding with surf; forming or resembling surf.

surg., **1.** surgeon. **2.** surgery. **3.** surgical.

surge (sûrj), *n., v.,* **surged, surging.** —*n.* **1.** a surging movement, rush, or sweep, like that of swelling or rolling waves: *the onward surge of an angry mob.* **2.** a surging, wavelike volume or body of something: *a surge of smoke.* **3.** the rolling swell of the sea. **4.** the swelling and rolling sea: *the surge was seething free.* **5.** a swelling wave; billow. **6.** a large swelling or abrupt wave, the change in depth or pressure generally being maintained after passage. **7.** *Elect.* a sudden rush of current, a violent oscillatory disturbance, or the like. **8.** *Naut.* a surging, or slipping back, as of a rope. —*v.i.* **9.** to rise and fall, or move along, on the waves, as a ship: *to surge at anchor.* **10.** to rise or roll in waves, or like waves: *a crowd surges about a spot.* **11.** to rise as if by a heaving or swelling force: *blood surges to the face.* **12.** *Elect.* to increase suddenly, as a current; oscillate violently. **13.** *Naut.* **a.** to slack off or loosen a rope or cable around a capstan or windlass. **b.** to slip back, as a rope. —*v.t.* **14.** to cause to surge or roll in or as in waves. **15.** to heave or sway with a waving motion. **16.** *Naut.* to slacken (a rope). [orig. uncert. Cf. F *surgeon* spring]

sur·geon (sûr′jən), *n.* one who practices surgery (distinguished from *physician*). [ME *surgien,* t. AF, contr. of OF *serurgien.* See CHIRURGEON]

sur·geon·cy (sûr′jən-sĭ), *n., pl.* **-cies.** the office or position of a surgeon, as in the army or navy.

sur·geon·fish (sûr′jən-fĭsh′), *n., pl.* **-fishes, (***esp. collectively***) -fish.** any tropical coral-reef fish of the family *Acanthuridae,* with one or more spines near the base of the tail fin.

Surgeon General, the chief of medical service in the army or navy, or the chief of public health.

surgeon's knot, a knot resembling a reef knot, used by surgeons for tying ligatures, etc.

sur·ger·y (sûr′jər-ĭ), *n., pl.* **-geries.** **1.** the art, practice, or work of treating diseases, injuries, or deformities by manual operation or instrumental appliances. **2.** the branch of medicine concerned with such treatment. **3.** treatment, operations, etc., performed by a surgeon. **4.** a room or place for surgical operations. **5.** *Brit.* the consulting office and dispensary of a general medical practitioner. [ME, t. OF: m. *surgerie*]

sur·gi·cal (sûr′jə-kəl), *adj.* **1.** pertaining to or involving surgery. **2.** used in surgery. —**sur′gi·cal·ly,** *adv.*

surg·y (sûr′jĭ), *adj.* billowy; surging or swelling.

Su·ri·ba·chi (sŏŏr′ə-bä′chĭ), *n.* a volcano on the island of Iwo Jima: scene of a bloody attack of the U.S. Marines in World War II.

su·ri·cate (sŏŏr′ə-kāt′), *n.* a small, burrowing, South African carnivore, *Suricata suricatta,* of a grayish color with dark bands across the back, related to the mongooses. [earlier *surikate,* t. F, t. D: m. *surikat* macaque]

Su·ri·nam (sŏŏr′ə-näm′), *n.* a possession of the Netherlands on the NE coast of South America, considered an integral part of the Dutch realm. 246,000 (est. 1954); 60,230 sq. mi. *Cap.:* Paramaribo. Also, **Dutch Guiana.**

Suricate, *Suricata suricatta*
(Total length 21 in., tail 9 in.)

sur·ly (sûr′lĭ), *adj.,* **-lier, -liest.** **1.** churlishly rude or ill-humored, as a person or the manner, tone, expression, etc. **2.** (of an animal) ill-tempered and unfriendly. **3.** *Obs.* lordly; arrogant. [var. of obs. *sirly* (f. SIR + -LY) lordly] —**sur′li·ly,** *adv.* —**sur′li·ness,** *n.*

sur·mise (*v.* sər-mīz′; *n.* sər-mīz′, sûr′mīz), *v.,* **-mised, -mising,** *n.* —*v.t.* **1.** to think or infer without certain or strong evidence; conjecture; guess. —*v.i.* **2.** to conjecture or guess. —*n.* **3.** a matter of conjecture. **4.** an idea or thought of something as being possible or likely, although without any certain or strong evidence. **5.** conjecture or surmising. [ME, t. OF. pp. of *surmettre* accuse] —**Syn. 1.** See **guess.**

sur·mount (sər-mount′), *v.t.* **1.** to mount upon; get on the top of; mount upon and cross over: *to surmount a hill.* **2.** to get over or across (barriers, obstacles, etc.). **3.** to prevail over. **4.** to be on top of or above: *a statue surmounting a pillar.* **5.** to furnish with something placed on top or above: *to surmount a tower with a spire.* **6.** *Obs.* to surpass or excel; exceed in amount. [ME *surmounte(n),* t. OF: m. *surmunter.* See SUR-, MOUNT¹] —**sur·mount′a·ble,** *adj.* —**sur·mount′er,** *n.*

sur·mul·let (sər mŭl′ĭt), *n.* a goatfish.

sur·name (*n.* sûr′nām′; *v.* sûr′nām′, sûr nām′), *n.*, *v.*, **-named, -naming.** —*n.* **1.** the name which a person has in common with the other members of his family, as distinguished from his Christian or given name; a family name. **2.** a name added to a person's name or names, as from birth or abode or from some characteristic or achievement. **3.** *Archaic.* an agnomen. —*v.t.* **4.** to give a surname to; call by a surname. [ME; half adoption, half trans. of F *turnom*]

sur·pass (sər păs′, -päs′), *v.t.* **1.** to go beyond in amount, extent, or degree; be greater than; exceed. **2.** to go beyond in excellence or achievement; be superior to; excel. **3.** to be beyond the range or capacity of; transcend: *misery that surpasses description.* [t. F: s. *surpasser*, f. *sur-* (intensive) + *passer* PASS] —**Syn. 2.** See **excel.**

sur·pass·ing (sər păs′ĭng, -päs′-), *adj.* **1.** that surpasses, exceeds, or excels; extraordinary: *structures of surpassing magnificence.* —*adv.* **2.** *Obs. exc. Poetic.* surpassingly. —**sur·pass′ing·ly,** *adv.* —**sur·pass′ing·ness,** *n.*

sur·plice (sûr′plĭs), *n.* **1.** a loose-fitting, broad-sleeved white vestment properly of linen, worn over the cassock by clergymen and choristers. **2.** a garment in which the fronts cross each other diagonally. [ME, t. AF: m. *surpliz*, syncopated var. of OF *sourpeliz* overfur (garment)] —**sur′pliced,** *adj.*

sur·plus (sûr′plŭs, -pləs), *n.* **1.** *Accounting.* the excess of assets over liabilities accumulated throughout the existence of a business, excepting assets against which stock certificates have been issued. **2.** an amount of assets in excess of what is requisite to meet liabilities. **3.** that which remains above what is used or needed. —*adj.* **4.** being a surplus; being in excess of what is required: *the surplus wheat of America.* [ME, t. OF. Cf. ML *superplus.* See PLUS] —**Syn. 3.** See **remainder.**

Anglican surplice

sur·plus·age (sûr′plŭs ĭj), *n.* **1.** surplus; excess. **2.** an excess of words.

sur·print (sûr′prĭnt′), *v.t.* **1.** to print over with additional marks or matter; overprint. **2.** to print (additional marks) over something already printed. —*n.* **3.** something surprinted.

sur·pris·al (sər prī′zəl), *n.* **1.** act of surprising. **2.** state of being surprised. **3.** a surprise.

sur·prise (sər prīz′), *v.*, **-prised, -prising,** *n.* —*v.t.* **1.** to come upon suddenly and unexpectedly; catch (a person, etc.) in the act of doing something; discover (a thing) suddenly. **2.** to assail or attack suddenly or without warning, as an army, fort, or person that is unprepared. **3.** to strike with a sudden feeling of wonder that arrests the thoughts, as at something unexpected or extraordinary. **4.** to bring out, esp. by a surprise: *to surprise the facts from the witness.* **5.** to lead or bring (a person, etc.) unawares, as into doing something not intended. —*n.* **6.** act of surprising; sudden assault or attack; a coming upon unexpectedly or taking unawares. **7.** state or feeling of being surprised as by something unexpected. **8.** something that excites this feeling, as an unexpected or extraordinary occurrence. **9.** take by surprise, **a.** to come upon unawares or without visible preparation. **b.** to catch unprepared. **c.** to amaze; astonish. [late ME, t. F, pp. of *surprendre* surprise, f. *sur-* SUR- + *prendre* take] —**sur·pris′er,** *n.* —**Syn. 3.** SURPRISE, ASTONISH, AMAZE, ASTOUND mean to strike with wonder because of unexpectedness, strangeness, unusualness, etc. To SURPRISE is to take unawares or to affect with wonder: *surprised at receiving a telegram.* To ASTONISH is to strike with wonder by something unlooked for, startling, or seemingly inexplicable: *astonished at someone's behavior.* To AMAZE is to astonish so greatly as to disconcert or bewilder: *amazed at an evidence of stupidity.* To ASTOUND is to overwhelm with surprise that one is unable to think or act: *astounded by a sudden calamity.*

Surprise Symphony, The, Symphony No. 94 (composed 1791) by Haydn.

sur·pris·ing (sər prī′zĭng), *adj.* that surprises. —**sur·pris′ing·ly,** *adv.* —**sur·pris′ing·ness,** *n.*

sur·ra (sŏŏr′ə), *n. Vet. Sci.* a severe infectious disease of horses, camels, elephants, and dogs caused by a blood-infecting protozoan parasite, *Trypanosoma evansi.* [t. Marathi: m. *sūra* air breathed through the nostrils]

sur·re·al·ism (sə rē′ə lĭz′əm), *n.* a recent movement in literature and art (influenced by psychoanalysis), based on the expression of imagination uncontrolled by reason, and seeking to suggest the activities of the subconscious mind whether in dreams or during waking hours. [t. F: m. *surréalisme.* See SUR, REALISM] —**sur·re′al·ist,** *n., adj.* —**sur·re·al·is·tic,** *adj.* —**su·re·al·is′ti·cal·ly,** *adv.*

sur·re·but·tal (sûr′rĭ bŭt′əl), *n. Law.* the giving of evidence to meet a defendant's rebuttal.

sur·re·but·ter (sûr′rĭ bŭt′ər), *n. Law.* a plaintiff's reply to a defendant's rebutter.

sur·re·join·der (sûr′rĭ join′dər), *n. Law.* a plaintiff's reply to a defendant's rejoinder.

sur·ren·der (sə rĕn′dər), *v.t.* **1.** to yield (something) to the possession or power of another; deliver up possession of (something) upon demand or compulsion: *to surrender a fort.* **2.** to give (oneself) up, esp. as a prisoner. **3.** to give up, abandon, or relinquish (comfort,

---

hope, etc.). **4.** to yield or resign (an office, privilege, etc.) in favor of another. **5.** *Obs.* to return: *to surrender thanks.* —*v.i.* **6.** to give oneself up, as into the power of another; submit or yield. —*n.* **7.** act of surrendering. **8.** *Insurance.* the abandonment of a policy by the party insured, for a consideration, the amount receivable (**surrender value**) depending on the number of years elapsed from the commencement of the risk. **9.** the deed by which a legal surrendering is made. [late ME, t. AF, f. *sur-* SUR-¹ + *render* RENDER] —**Syn. 1.** See **yield.** **4.** relinquish, waive, cede, resign, abandon. **6.** capitulate.

sur·rep·ti·tious (sûr′əp tĭsh′əs), *adj.* **1.** obtained, done, made, etc., by stealth; secret and unauthorized; clandestine: *a surreptitious glance.* **2.** acting in a stealthy way. **3.** obtained by subreption; subreptitious. [late ME, t. L: m. *surreptītius,* der. *subreptus,* pp., snatched away secretly] —**sur·rep·ti′tious·ly,** *adv.* —**sur·rep·ti′tious·ness,** *n.*

sur·rey (sûr′ĭ), *n., pl.* **-reys.** a light, four-wheeled, two-seated carriage, with or without a top, for four persons.

Surrey

Sur·rey (sûr′ĭ), *n.* **1.** a county in SE England, bordering S London. 1,602,483 pop. (1951); 722 sq. mi. *Co. seat:* Guilford. **2.** Henry Howard, Earl of, 1517?–47, English poet.

sur·ro·gate (*n.* sûr′ə gāt′, -gĭt; *v.* sûr′ə gāt′), *n., v.,* **-gated, -gating.** —*n.* **1.** one appointed to act for another; a deputy. **2.** *U.S.* a judicial officer having jurisdiction over the probate of wills, the administration of estates, etc. **3.** the deputy of an ecclesiastical judge, esp. of a bishop or his chancellor. **4.** a substitute. —*v.t.* **5.** to put into the place of another as a successor, substitute, or deputy; substitute for another. **6.** to subrogate. [t. L: m.s. *surrogātus,* pp., put in another's place] —**sur′ro·gate·ship′,** *n.*

sur·round (sə round′), *v.t.* **1.** to enclose on all sides, or encompass. **2.** to form an enclosure round; encircle. **3.** to enclose, as a body of troops, so as to cut off communication or retreat. [late ME *suround,* t. AF: s. *surounder,* g. LL *superundāre* overflow]

sur·round·ing (sə roun′dĭng), *n.* **1.** that which surrounds. **2.** (*pl.*) environing circumstances, conditions, etc.; environment. **3.** act of encircling or enclosing. —*adj.* **4.** that encloses, encircles, or environs.

sur·sum cor·da (sûr′sam kôr′də), *Latin.* **1.** lift up (your) hearts (an encouraging exhortation). **2.** the first words of the Preface of the Mass.

sur·tax (*n.* sûr′tăks′; *v.* sûr′tăks′, sûr tăks′), *n.* **1.** an additional or extra tax on something already taxed. **2.** one of a graded series of additional taxes levied on incomes exceeding a certain amount. —*v.t.* **3.** to put an additional or extra tax on; charge with a surtax.

sur·tout (sər tŏŏt′, -tŏŏ′, *Fr.* syr tŏŏ′), *n.* a man's outer coat worn during the Middle Ages. [t. F, f. *sur* SUR- + *tout* (g. L *tōtus*) everything]

surv., **1.** surveying. **2.** surveyor.

sur·veil·lance (sər vā′ləns, -vāl′yəns), *n.* **1.** watch kept over a person, etc., esp. over a suspect, a prisoner, or the like. **2.** supervision or superintendence. [t. F, der. *surveiller.* See SURVEILLANT]

sur·veil·lant (sər vā′lənt, -vāl′yənt), *adj.* **1.** exercising surveillance. —*n.* **2.** one who exercises surveillance. [t. F, prop. ppr. of *surveiller,* f. *sur-* SUR- + *veiller* (g. L *vigilāre*) watch over]

sur·vey (*v.* sər vā′; *n.* sûr′vā, sər vā′), *v., n., pl.* **-veys.** —*v.t.* **1.** to take a general or comprehensive view of. **2.** to view in detail, esp. to inspect or examine formally or officially in order to ascertain condition, value, etc. **3.** to determine the form, boundaries, position, extent, etc., of, as a part of the earth's surface, by linear and angular measurements and the application of the principles of geometry and trigonometry. —*v.i.* **4.** to survey land, etc.; practice surveying. —*n.* **5.** act of surveying; a comprehensive view. **6.** a formal or official examination of the particulars of something, made in order to ascertain condition, character, etc. **7.** a statement or description embodying the result of this. **8.** a determining of form, boundaries, position, extent, etc., as of a part of the earth's surface, by linear and angular measurements, etc. **9.** the plan or description resulting from such an operation. [ME *surveie(n),* t. OF: m. *surveier.* ult. f. L *super-* SUPER- + *vidēre* see] —**sur·vey′a·ble,** *adj.*

survey., surveying.

sur·vey·ing (sər vā′ĭng), *n.* **1.** the process, occupation, or art of making surveys of land, etc. **2.** act of one who surveys.

sur·vey·or (sər vā′ər), *n.* **1.** one whose business it is to survey land, etc. **2.** an overseer or supervisor. **3.** *Chiefly Brit.* one who inspects something officially for the purpose of ascertaining condition, value, etc. **4.** *U.S.* a customs officer whose duty it is to ascertain the quantity and value of imported merchandise. —**sur·vey′or·ship′,** *n.*

surveyor's chain. See **chain** (def. 9).

surveyor's level. See **level** (defs. 8, 9).

surveyor's measure, a system of units of length used in surveying land.

---

sur·viv·al (sər vī'vəl), *n.* **1.** act or fact of surviving. **2.** one who or that which survives, esp. a surviving custom, observance, belief, or the like.

survival of the fittest, *Biol.* the fact or the principle of the survival of the forms of animal and vegetable life best fitted for existing conditions, while related but less fit forms become extinct. See **natural selection.**

sur·vive (sər vīv'), *v.,* **-vived, -viving.** —*v.i* **1.** to remain alive after the death of someone or after the cessation of something or the occurrence of some event; continue to live. **2.** to remain in existence after some person, thing, or event; continue to exist. —*v.t.* **3.** to continue to live or exist after the death, cessation, or occurrence of. [late ME, t. AF: m.s. *survivre,* f. sur- SUR- + *vivre* live, g. L *vivere*] —**sur·viv'ing,** *adj.*

—**Syn. 3.** SURVIVE, OUTLIVE refer to remaining alive longer than someone else or after some event. SURVIVE usually means to succeed in keeping alive against odds, to live after some event which has threatened one: *to survive an automobile accident.* It is also used of living longer than another person (usually a relative), but, today, mainly in the passive, as in the fixed phrase: *the deceased is survived by his wife and children.* OUTLIVE stresses capacity for endurance, the time element, and sometimes a sense of competition: *he outlived all his enemies.* It is also used, however, of one who has lived too long: *he has outlived his usefulness.*

sur·vi·vor (sər vī'vər), *n.* **1.** one who or that which survives. **2.** *Law.* that one of two or more designated persons, as joint tenants or others having a joint interest, who outlives the other or others. —**sur·vi'vor·ship',** *n.*

Su·sa (sōō'sä), *n.* a ruined city in W Iran: the capital of ancient Elam; palaces of Darius and Artaxerxes. Biblical name, **Shushan.**

sus·cep·ti·bil·i·ty (sə sĕp'tə bĭl'ə tĭ), *n., pl.* **-ties. 1.** state or character of being susceptible: *susceptibility to disease.* **2.** capability of being affected, esp. easily; capacity for receiving mental or moral impressions; tendency to be emotionally affected. **3.** (*pl.*) capacities for emotion; sensitive feelings. **4.** *Elect.* the ratio of the magnetization produced in a substance to the magnetizing force. —**Syn. 2.** See **sensibility.**

sus·cep·ti·ble (sə sĕp'tə bəl), *adj.* **1.** capable of receiving, admitting, undergoing, or being affected by, something (fol. by *of* or *to*): *susceptible of a high polish, of various interpretations, etc.* **2.** accessible or especially liable: *susceptible to a disease, flattery.* **3.** capable of being affected, esp. easily; readily impressed; impressionable. [t. ML: m.s. *susceptibilis,* der. L *susceptus,* pp., taken up] —**sus·cep'ti·ble·ness,** *n.* —**sus·cep'ti·bly,** *adv.*

sus·cep·tive (sə sĕp'tĭv), *adj.* **1.** receptive. **2.** susceptible. —**sus·cep·tiv·i·ty** (sŭs'ĕp tĭv'ə tĭ), **sus·cep'tive·ness,** *n.*

sus·lik (sŭs'lĭk), *n.* **1.** a common ground squirrel or spermophile, *Citellus* (or *Spermophilus*) *citellus,* of Europe and Asia. **2.** the fur of this animal. [t. Russ.]

sus·pect (*v.* sə spĕkt'; *n., adj.* sŭs'pĕkt, sə spĕkt'), *v.t.* **1.** to imagine to be guilty, false, counterfeit, undesirable, defective, bad, etc., with insufficient proof or with no proof. **2.** to imagine or believe to be rightly chargeable with something stated, usually something wrong or something considered as undesirable, with little or no evidence: *to suspect a person of murder.* **3.** to imagine to be the case or to be likely; surmise: *I suspect his knowledge did not amount to much.* —*v.i.* **4.** to imagine something, esp. something evil, wrong, or undesirable, to be the case; have suspicion. —*n.* **5.** one suspected; a person suspected of a crime, offense, or the like. —*adj.* **6.** suspected; open to suspicion. [ME, t. L: s. *suspectus,* pp.] —**sus·pect'er,** *n.*

sus·pend (sə spĕnd'), *v.t.* **1.** to hang by attachment to something above; attach so as to allow free movement as on a hinge. **2.** to keep from falling or sinking, as if by hanging: *solid particles suspended in a liquid.* **3.** to hold or keep undetermined; refrain from forming or concluding definitely: *to suspend one's judgment.* **4.** to defer or postpone, as sentence on a convicted person. **5.** to cause to cease, or bring to a stop or stay, usually for a time: *to suspend payment.* **6.** to cause to cease for a time from operation or effect, as a law, rule, privilege, or the like. **7.** to debar, usually for a time, from the exercise of an office or function or the enjoyment of a privilege: *a student is suspended for a breach of discipline.* —*v.i.* **8.** to come to a stop, usually temporarily; cease from operation for a time. **9.** to stop payment; be unable to meet financial obligations. [ME *suspende(n),* t. L: m. *suspendere*] —**Syn. 5.** intermit, discontinue. See **interrupt.**

suspended animation, *Physiol.* temporary cessation of the vital functions, esp. asphyxia.

sus·pend·er (sə spĕn'dər), *n.* **1.** (*pl.*) *Chiefly U.S.* straps or bands worn over the shoulders for holding up the trousers. **2.** *Brit.* a garter. **3.** one who or that which suspends.

sus·pense (sə spĕns'), *n.* **1.** a state of mental uncertainty, as in awaiting a decision or outcome, usually with more or less apprehension or anxiety. **2.** a state of mental indecision. **3.** undecided or doubtful condition, as of affairs: *for a few days matters hung in suspense.* [ME, t. AF: m. *suspens,* in phrase *en suspens* in suspense, g. L *suspensus,* pp., suspended.]

sus·pen·si·ble (sə spĕn'sə bəl), *adj.* capable of being suspended. —**sus·pen'si·bil'i·ty,** *n.*

sus·pen·sion (sə spĕn'shən), *n.* **1.** act of suspending. **2.** state of being suspended. **3.** temporary abrogation, as of a law or privilege. **4.** stoppage of payment of debts or claims because of financial inability, or insolvency. **5.** *Physics.* the state in which particles of a solid are mixed with a fluid but are undissolved. **6.** a substance in such a state. **7.** *Phys. Chem.* a system consisting of small particles kept dispersed by agitation (in **mechanical suspension**) or by the molecular motion in the surrounding medium (in **colloidal suspension**). **8.** something on or by which something else is suspended or hung. **9.** the arrangement of springs, shock absorbers, hangers, etc., in an automobile, railway car, etc., connecting the wheel-suspension units or axles to the chassis frame. **10.** *Elect.* a wire or filament by which the moving part of an instrument or device is suspended. **11.** *Music.* **a.** the prolongation of a tone in one chord into the following chord, usually producing a temporary dissonance. **b.** the tone so prolonged. [t. LL: s. *suspensio*]

S. Suspension (def. 11a)

suspension bridge, a bridge in which the roadway is suspended from cables, usually hung between towers of masonry or steel, and fastened at the extremities.

suspension point, one of a group of dots or periods which indicates the deletion of words, sentences, etc.

sus·pen·sive (sə spĕn'sĭv), *adj.* **1.** pertaining to or characterized by suspension. **2.** undecided in mind. **3.** pertaining to or characterized by suspense. **4.** (of words, phrases, etc.) keeping onein suspense. **5.** having the effect of suspending the operation of something. —**sus·pen'sive·ly,** *adv.* —**sus·pen'sive·ness,** *n.*

sus·pen·sor (sə spĕn'sər), *n.* a suspensory ligament, bandage, etc. [t. ML, der. L *suspensus,* pp. suspended].

sus·pen·so·ry (sə spĕn'sə rĭ), *adj.. n., pl.* **-ries.** —*adj.* **1.** serving or fitted to suspend or hold up, as a ligament, muscle, bandage, etc. **2.** suspending the operation of something. —*n.* **3.** a suspensory bandage, ligament, muscle, or the like.

sus·pi·cion (sə spĭsh'ən), *n.* **1.** act of suspecting; imagination of the existence of guilt, fault, falsity, defect, or the like, on slight evidence or without evidence. **2.** state of mind or feeling of one who suspects. **3.** an instance of suspecting something. **4.** imagination of anything to be the case or to be likely; a vague notion of something. **5.** a slight trace: *a suspicion of a smile.* —*v.t.* **6.** *Colloq.* or *Dial.* to suspect. [late ME, t. L: s. *suspicio;* r. ME *suspecioun,* t. AF, g. L *suspectio*]

—**Syn. 2.** doubt, mistrust, misgiving. SUSPICION, DISTRUST are terms for a feeling that appearances are not reliable. SUSPICION is the positive tendency to doubt the trustworthiness of appearances and therefore to believe that one has detected possibilities of something unreliable, unfavorable, menacing, or the like: *to feel suspicion about the honesty of a prominent man.* DISTRUST is a passive want of trust, faith, or reliance in a person or thing: *to feel distrust of one's own ability.*

sus·pi·cion·al (sə spĭsh'ən əl), *adj.* of or pertaining to suspicion, esp. morbid or insane suspicions.

sus·pi·cious (sə spĭsh'əs), *adj.* **1.** liable to cause or excite suspicion; questionable. **2.** inclined to suspect; esp., inclined to suspect evil; distrustful. **3.** full of or feeling suspicion. **4.** expressing or indicating suspicion. —**sus·pi'cious·ly,** *adv.* —**sus·pi'cious·ness,** *n.*

sus·pi·ra·tion (sŭs'pə rā'shən), *n.* a long, deep sigh.

sus·pire (sə spīr'), *v.i.,* **-pired, -piring.** *Poetic.* to sigh. **2.** to breathe. [t. L: m.s. *suspīrāre* sigh]

Sus·que·han·na (sŭs'kwə hăn'ə), *n.* a river flowing from central New York through E Pennsylvania and NE Maryland into Chesapeake Bay. 444 mi.

Sus·sex (sŭs'ĭks), *n.* **1.** a county in SE England, now divided into the administrative counties of East Sussex and West Sussex. **2. East,** 618,516 pop. (1951); 829 sq. mi. *Co. seat:* Lewes. **3. West,** 318,823 pop. (1951); 628 sq. mi. *Co. seat:* Chichester.

sus·tain (sə stān'), *v.t.* **1.** to hold or bear up from below; bear the weight of; be the support of, as in a structure. **2.** to bear (a burden, charge, etc.). **3.** to undergo, experience, or suffer (injury, loss, etc.); endure without giving way or yielding. **4.** to keep (a person, the mind, the spirits, etc.) from giving way, as under trial or affliction. **5.** to keep up or keep going, as an action or process: *to sustain a conversation.* **6.** to supply with food and drink, or the necessaries of life, as persons; provide for by furnishing means or funds, as an institution; support by aid or countenance, as a person or cause. **7.** to uphold as valid, just, or correct, as a claim or the person making it. **8.** to confirm or corroborate, as a statement. [ME *susteine,* t. OF: m. *sustenir,* g. L *sustinēre*] —**sus·tain'a·ble,** *adj.* —**sus·tain'er,** *n.* —**sus·tain'ment,** *n.* —**Syn. 1.** See **support.**

sustaining program, a radio program without a commercial sponsor.

sus·te·nance (sŭs'tə nəns), *n.* **1.** means of sustaining life; nourishment. **2.** means of livelihood. **3.** process of sustaining. **4.** state of being sustained.

sus·ten·tac·u·lar (sŭs'tĕn tăk'yə lər), *adj. Anat.* supporting. [f. s. L *sustentāculum* a support + -AR[1]]

sus·ten·ta·tion (sŭs'tĕn tā'shən), *n.* **1.** maintenance in being or activity; the sustaining of life through vital processes. **2.** provision with means or funds for upkeep. **3.** means of sustaining life; sustenance. [ME, t. L: s.

sustentātio] —sus·ten·ta·tive (sŭs/tən tā/tĭv, sə stĕn/-tə tĭv), *adj.*

sus·ten·tion (sə stĕn/shən), *n.* **1.** act of sustaining. **2.** state or quality of being sustained. [coinage on model of DETENTION] —**sus·ten·tive** (sə stĕn/tĭv), *adj.*

sus·ti·ne·o a·las (sŭs tĭn/ē ō/ ā/läs), *Latin.* I sustain the wings (motto of the U.S. Air Force).

su·sur·rant (sŏŏ sŭr/ənt), *adj.* softly murmuring; whispering. [t. L: s. *susurrans*, ppr.]

su·sur·ra·tion (sŏŏ/sə rā/shən), *n.* a soft murmur; whisper.

su·sur·rus (sŏŏ sŭr/əs), *n.* a soft murmuring sound. [t. L]

Suth·er·land (sŭth/ər lənd), *n.* a county in N Scotland. 13,670 pop. (1951); 2028 sq. mi. *Co. seat:* Dornoch. Also, **Suth·er·land·shire** (sŭth/ər lənd shĭr/, -shər).

Sutherland Falls, a waterfall in SW South Island, New Zealand. 1904 ft.

Sut·lej (sŭt/lĕj), *n.* a river flowing from SW Tibet through NW India into the Indus river in Pakistan. ab. 900 mi.

sut·ler (sŭt/lər), *n.* a person who follows an army and sells provisions, etc., to the soldiers. [t. early mod. D: m. *soeteler*, der. *soetelen* have a humble occupation]

su·tra (sŏŏ/trə), *n.* **1.** (*also cap.*) Sanskrit Lit. one of a body of aphoristic rules forming a link between the Vedic and the later Sanskrit literature. **2.** concise rules or teachings, chiefly in Hindu or Buddhist literature. Also, **sut·ta** (sŏŏt/ə). [t. Skt.: thread, rule]

sut·tee (sŭ tē/, sŭt/ē), *n.* **1.** a Hindu widow who immolates herself on the funeral pile of her husband. **2.** the self-immolation of a Hindu widow in this manner. [t. Skt.: m. *sati* faithful wife]

Sut·ter (sŭt/ər), *n.* **John Augustus,** 1803–80, U.S. frontiersman in California.

Sut·ter s Mill (sŭt/ərz), the location in central California, NE of Sacramento, near which gold was discovered (1848), precipitating the gold rush of 1849.

su·ture (sŏŏ/chər), *n., v.,* -**tured, -turing.** —*n.* **1.** Surg. **a.** a joining of the lips or edges of a wound or the like by stitching or some similar process. **b.** a particular method of doing this. **c.** one of the stitches or fastenings employed. **2.** Anat. **a.** the line of junction of two bones, esp. of the skull, in an immovable articulation. **b.** the articulation itself. **3.** Zool., Bot. the line of junction, or the junction, of contiguous parts, as the line of closure between the valves of a bivalve shell, a seam where carpels of a pericarp join, etc. **4.** a seam as formed in sewing; a line of junction between two parts. **5.** a sewing together, or a joining as by sewing. —*v.t.* **6.** to unite by or as by a suture. [t. L: m. *sūtūra*] —**su/tur·al,** *adj.* —**su/tur·al·ly,** *adv.*

su·um cui·que (sŏŏ/əm kī/kwē, kwĭ/-), *Latin.* his own to each; to each what rightfully belongs to him.

Su·va (sŏŏ/vä), *n.* a seaport in and the capital of the Fiji Islands, on Viti Levu island. 30,000 pop. (est. 1954).

Su·vo·rov (sŏŏ vô/rôf), *n.* **Aleksandr Vasilevich** (ä/lĕ ksän/dər vä sē/lyə vĭch), (*Count Suvorov Rumnikski, Prince Italiski*) 1729–1800, Russian field marshal.

su·ze·rain (sŏŏ/zə rĭn, -rān/), *n.* **1.** a sovereign or a state exercising political control over a dependent state. **2.** Hist. a feudal overlord. —*adj.* **3.** characteristic of, or being, a suzerain. [t. F, der. *sus* above (g. L *su(r)sum* upwards), modeled on *souverain* sovereign]

su·ze·rain·ty (sŏŏ/zə rĭn/tē, -rān/-), *n., pl.* -**ties.** the position or authority of a suzerain.

S.V., (L *Sancta Virgo*) Holy Virgin.

s.v., **1.** sub verbo. **2.** sub voce.

Sval·bard (sväl/bär), *n.* Norwegian name of **Spitsbergen.**

svelte (svĕlt), *adj.* slender, esp. gracefully slender in figure; lithe. [t. F, t. It.: m. *svelto*, lit., plucked]

Sverd·lovsk (svĕrd lôfsk/), *n.* a city in the W Soviet Union in Asia, on the E slope of the Ural Mountains: execution of Czar Nicholas and his family, 1918. 707,000 (est. 1956). Formerly, **Ekaterinburg.**

Sve·ri·ge (svä/rē yĕ), *n.* Swedish name of **Sweden.**

SW, **1.** southwest. **2.** southwestern.

Sw., **1.** Sweden. **2.** Swedish.

S.W., **1.** South Wales. **2.** southwest. **3.** southwestern.

swab (swŏb), *n., v.,* **swabbed, swabbing.** —*n.* **1.** a large mop used on shipboard for cleaning decks, etc. **2.** a bit of sponge, cloth, or the like, for cleansing the mouth of a sick person, or for applying medicaments, etc. **3.** the material collected with a swab. **4.** a cleaner for the bore of a cannon. **5.** Slang. an awkward or unmannerly fellow. —*v.t.* **6.** to clean with or as with a swab. **7.** to take up, or apply, as moisture, with or as with a swab. **8.** to pass (a swab, etc.) over a surface. Also, **swob.** [back formation from SWABBER]

swab·ber (swŏb/ər), *n.* **1.** one who uses a swab. **2.** Slang. (def. 5). **3.** a swab or mop. [t. D: m. *zwabber*, der. *zwabben* do dirty work]

Swa·bi·a (swā/bĭ ə), *n.* **1.** a medieval duchy in SW Germany: it comprised the area now included in Baden-Württemberg and Bavaria. **2.** a district in SW Bavaria. ab. 3900 sq. mi. *Cap.:* Augsburg. German, **Schwaben.** —**Swa/bi·an,** *adj., n.*

swad·dle (swŏd/əl), *v.,* -**dled, -dling,** *n.* —*v.t.* **1.** to bind (an infant, esp. a new-born infant) with long, narrow strips of cloth to prevent free movement; wrap tightly with clothes. **2.** to wrap (anything) round with bandages. —*n.* **3.** a long, narrow strip of cloth used for swaddling or bandaging. [ME *swathel,* OE *swæthel* swaddling band, akin to SWATHE, v.]

swaddling band, a band for swaddling an infant.

swaddling clothes, **1.** clothes consisting of swaddling bands. **2.** long clothes for an infant.

Swa·de·shi (swə dā/shĭ), *n.* (in India) **1.** the encouragement of domestic production and the boycott of foreign, esp. British, goods as a step towards home rule. —*adj.* **2.** made in India. [t. Bengali: native products]

swag[1] (swăg), *v.,* **swagged, swagging,** *n.* —*v.i.* **1.** to move heavily or unsteadily from side to side or up and down; sway. **2.** to hang loosely and heavily; sink down. —*v.t.* **3.** to cause to sway, sink, or sag. —*n.* **4.** a swagging, swaying, or lurching movement. [prob. t. Scand.; cf. d. Norw. *svagga* sway]

swag[2] (swăg), *n., v.,* **swagged, swagging.** —*n.* **1.** Slang. plundered property; booty. **2.** Australia. a bundle or roll carried across the shoulders or otherwise, and containing the personal belongings of a traveler through the bush, a miner, etc. —*v.i.* **3.** Australia. to travel about carrying one's bundle of personal belongings. [special uses of SWAG[1]]

swage (swāj), *n., v.,* **swaged, swaging.** —*n.* **1.** a tool for bending cold metal to a required shape. **2.** a tool, die, or stamp for giving a particular shape to metal on an anvil, in a stamping press, etc. **3.** swage block. —*v.t.* **4.** to bend or shape by means of a swage. [ME, t. OF: m. *souage*]

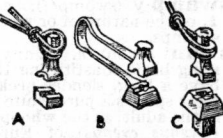

Swages (def. 1)
A. Collar swage; B. Spring swage;
C. Guide swage

swage block, an iron block containing holes and grooves of various sizes, used for heading bolts and shaping objects not easily worked on an anvil.

swag·ger (swăg/ər), *v.i.* **1.** to walk or strut with a defiant or insolent air. **2.** to boast or brag noisily. —*v.t.* **3.** to bring, drive, force, etc., by blustering. —*n.* **4.** swaggering gait, bearing, or air; arrogant show of affected superiority. [freq. of SWAG[1]] —**swag/ger·er,** *n.* —**swag/ger·ing·ly,** *adv.* —Syn. **1.** See strut[1].

swagger stick, a short stick or cane sometimes carried by army officers, soldiers, and others.

Swa·hi·li (swä hē/lē), *n., pl.* -**li, -lis.** **1.** a member of a Bantu (Negroid) people with a large infusion of Arab blood, who inhabit Zanzibar and the neighboring coast. **2.** their language, a lingua franca in central Africa. [t. Ar.: coastal] —**Swa·hi/li·an,** *adj.*

swain (swān), *n.* Chiefly Poetic. **1.** a country lad. **2.** a country gallant. **3.** a lover. [early ME *swein* servant, t. Scand.; cf. Icel. *sveinn* boy] —**swain/ish,** *adj.* —**swain/ish·ness,** *n.*

swale (swāl), *n.* a low place in a tract of land, usually moister and often having a ranker vegetation than the adjacent higher land. [? orig. cool spot. Cf. Icel. *svalr* cool]

swal·low[1] (swŏl/ō), *v.t.* **1.** to take into the stomach through the throat or gullet (esophagus), as food, drink, or other substances. **2.** to take in so as to envelop; withdraw from sight; assimilate; consume (often fol. by *up*). **3.** Colloq. to accept without question or suspicion. **4.** to accept without opposition; put up with: *to swallow an insult.* **5.** to suppress (emotion, a laugh, sob, etc.) as if by drawing it down one's throat. **6.** to take back or retract (one's words, etc.). —*v.i.* **7.** to perform the act of swallowing. —*n.* **8.** act of swallowing. **9.** a quantity swallowed at one time; a mouthful. **10.** capacity for swallowing. **11.** Naut. the space in a block between the groove of the sheave and the shell, through which the rope runs. [ME *swolwe,* var. of *swelwe,* OE *swelgan,* g. *schwelgen*] —**swal/low·a·ble,** *adj.* —**swal/low·er,** *n.*

swal·low[2] (swŏl/ō), *n.* **1.** any of numerous small, long-winged passerine birds constituting the family *Hirundinidae,* notable for their swift, graceful flight and for the extent and regularity of their migrations, as the tree swallow (*Iridoprocne bicolor*) of America; the house martin (*Delichon urbica*) of Europe; and *Hirundo rustica* of both New and Old Worlds (known in America as the barn swallow). **2.** a swallowlike bird not of this family, as, in America, the chimney swift, *Chaetura pelagica,* familiarly known as the **chimney swallow.** [ME *swalwe,* OE *swealwe,* akin to G *schwalbe*] —**swal/low·like/,** *adj.*

swal·low·tail (swŏl/ō tāl/), *n.* **1.** a swallow's tail, or a deeply forked tail like that of a swallow. **2.** any of various butterflies of the family *Papilionidae,* having the hind wings prolonged so as to suggest the tail of a swallow. **3.** Colloq. a swallow-tailed coat.

Tiger swallowtail
Papilio turnus
(Wing expansion ab. 4 in.)

swal·low-tailed (swŏl/ō tāld/), *adj.* 1. having a deeply forked tail like that of a swallow, as various birds. 2. having an end or part suggesting a swallow's tail.

swallow-tailed coat, a dress coat having the lower part cut away over the hips and descending in a pair of tapering skirts behind: worn by men.

swal·low·wort (swŏl/ō wûrt/), *n.* 1. the greater celandine, *Chelidonium majus*. 2. any of various asclepiadaceous plants, esp. a herb, *Vincetoxicum officinale* (or *Cynanchum Vincetoxicum*), of Europe, with an emetic root formerly esteemed as a counterpoison.

swam (swăm), *v.* pt. of **swim**.

swa·mi (swä/mĭ), *n.*, *pl.* **-mis**. a title for a Hindu religious teacher. [t. Hind.: master, t. Skt.: m. *svāmin*]

swamp (swŏmp), *n.* 1. a piece or tract of wet, spongy land; marshy ground. 2. a tract of soft, wet ground having a growth of certain kinds of trees, but unfit for cultivation. —*v.t.* 3. to flood or drench with water or the like. 4. *Naut.* to sink or fill (a boat) with water. 5. to plunge or sink in or as in a swamp. 6. to overwhelm; render helpless. —*v.i.* 7. to fill with water and sink, as a boat. 8. to sink or stick in or as in a swamp. 9. to be plunged into or overwhelmed with difficulties, etc. [akin to **bump**] —**swamp/ish,** *adj.* —**swamp/less,** *adj.*

swamp cypress, bald cypress.

swamp·land (swŏmp/lănd/), *n.* land covered with swamps.

swamp sparrow, a marsh-inhabiting finch, *Melospiza georgiana*, of North America.

swamp·y (swŏmp/ĭ), *adj.*, **swampier, swampiest.** 1. of the nature of or resembling a swamp. 2. found in swamps.

swan¹ (swŏn), *n.* 1. any of several large, stately swimming birds constituting the subfamily *Cygninae*, which have a long, slender neck, and in most species a pure-white plumage in the adult, as the **whooper swan** (*Cygnus cygnus*) of Europe and **whistling swan** (*Cygnus columbianus*) of America. 2. a person or thing of unusual beauty, excellence, purity, or the like. 3. a sweet singer or poet. 4. *Astron.* (*cap.*) the northern constellation Cygnus. [ME and OE, c. G *schwan*] —**swan/like/,** *adj.*

Whooper swan, *Cygnus cygnus* (5 ft. long)

swan² (swŏn), *v.i.* to swear (used chiefly as an exclamation of surprise); *I swan!* [prob. alter. of d. (North.) *Is' wan* I shall warrant]

swan dive, a dive in which the diver while in the air assumes a position with arms outstretched to the side, legs straight and together, and enters the water headforemost.

swang (swăng), *v.* *Archaic and Dial.* pt. of **swing¹**.

swan·herd (swŏn/hûrd/), *n.* one who tends swans.

swank (swăngk), *n.* 1. *Slang.* dashing smartness, as in bearing, appearance, etc.; style. 2. swagger. —*adj.* 3. *Slang.* pretentiously stylish. —*v.i.* 4. to swagger in behavior; show off. [? akin to MLG *swank* supple, MHG *swanken* sway]

swank·y (swăngk/ĭ), *adj.*, **swankier, swankiest.** *Slang.* swank. —**swank/i·ly,** *adv.* —**swank/i·ness,** *n.*

swan maiden, one of a class of fabulous maidens, in many Indo-European and Asiatic tales, capable of transforming themselves into swans, as by a robe or shift of swan's feathers or a magic ring or chain.

swan·ner·y (swŏn/ər ĭ), *n.*, *pl.* **-neries.** a place where swans are kept and reared.

swan's-down (swŏnz/doun/), *n.* 1. the down or under plumage of a swan, used for trimming, powder puffs, etc. 2. a fine, soft, thick woolen cloth. Also, **swans/down/.**

Swan·sea (swŏn/sĭ, -zĭ), *n.* a seaport in S Wales. 161,700 (est. 1956).

swan-skin (swŏn/skĭn/), *n.* 1. the skin of a swan, with the feathers on. 2. a kind of fine twilled flannel.

swan song, 1. fabled song of the dying swan. 2. the last work, utterance, or achievement of a poet, a composer, or other person, before his death or retirement.

swan-up·ping (swŏn/ŭp/ĭng), *n.* *Eng.* 1. the taking up of young swans to mark them with nicks on the beak for the owners. 2. an annual expedition for this purpose on the Thames. [f. **swan¹** + **upping**, der. **up,** v.]

swap (swŏp), *v.*, **swapped, swapping,** *n.* —*v.t.* 1. to exchange, barter, or trade, as one thing for another. —*v.i.* 2. to make an exchange. —*n.* 3. an exchange. Also, **swop.** [ME *swappe* strike, strike hands (in bargaining), c. d. G *schwappen* box (the ear)] —**swap/per,** *n.*

swa·raj (swə räj/), *n.* (in India) 1. self-government. 2. (*cap.*) the political party supporting this principle. [t. Hind.: m. *svarāj*, f. Skt.: *sva* own + *rāj* rule] —**swa·raj/ism,** *n.* —**swa·raj/ist,** *n.*, *adj.*

sward (swôrd), *n.* 1. the grassy surface of land; turf. 2. a stretch of turf; a growth of grass. —*v.t.* 3. to cover with sward or turf. —*v.i.* 4. to become covered with sward. [ME; OE *sweard* skin, c. G *schwarte* rind]

sware (swâr), *v.* *Archaic.* pt. of **swear**.

swarm¹ (swôrm), *n.* 1. a body of honeybees which emigrate from a hive and fly off together, under the direction of a queen, to start a new colony. 2. a body of bees settled together, as in a hive. 3. a great number of things or persons, esp. in motion. 4. *Biol.* a group or aggregation of free-floating or free-swimming cells or organisms. —*v.i.* 5. to fly off together in a body from a hive to start a new colony, as bees. 6. to move about, along, forth, etc., in great numbers, as things or persons. 7. to congregate or occur in swarms or multitudes; be exceedingly numerous, as in a place or area. 8. (of a place) to be thronged or overrun; abound or teem (fol. by *with*). 9. *Biol.* to move or swim about in a swarm. —*v.t.* 10. to swarm about, over, or in; throng; overrun. 11. to produce a swarm of. [ME; OE *swearm*, c. G *schwarm*, Icel. *svarmr* tumult] —**Syn.** 3. multitude, throng. See **crowd.**

swarm² (swôrm), *v.i.*, *v.t.* to climb (a tree, pole, or the like) by clasping it with the hands or arms and legs and drawing oneself up; shin. [special use of **swarm¹**]

swarm·er (swôr/mər), *n.* 1. one of a number that swarm; one of a swarm. 2. *Biol.* a swarm spore.

swarm spore, *Biol.* any minute, motile, naked reproductive body produced in great numbers or occurring in groups or aggregations.

swart (swôrt), *adj.* *Literary or Dial.* swarthy. Also, *Archaic or Dial.,* **swarth.** [ME; OE *sweart*, c. G *schwarz*] —**swart/ness,** *n.*

swarth·y (swôr/thĭ, -thĭ), *adj.*, **swarthier, swarthiest.** dark-colored, now esp. as the skin, complexion, etc., or the person. [var. of obs. *swarfy*, der. *swarf* greasy grit, OE *geswearf* filings] —**swarth/i·ly,** *adv.* —**swarth/i·ness,** *n.* —**Syn.** See **dusky.**

swash (swŏsh), *v.i.* 1. to splash as things in water, or as water does. 2. to dash about, as things in violent motion. 3. to swagger. —*v.t.* 4. to dash or cast violently, esp. to dash (water, etc.) about, down, etc. —*n.* 5. a swashing blow, stroke, or movement, or the sound of it. 6. the dashing of water, waves, etc., or the sound of it. 7. the ground over which water washes. 8. a channel of water through or behind a sandbank. [prob. imit.] —**swash/ing·ly,** *adv.*

swash·buck·ler (swŏsh/bŭk/lər), *n.* a swaggering swordsman or bully. Also, **swash/er.** [f. **swash** (i.e., strike swords against shields) + **buckler**] —**swash/buck/ling,** *adj.*, *n.*

swas·ti·ka (swŏs/tĭ kə, swäs/-), *n.* 1. a figure used as a symbol or an ornament in the Old World and in America since prehistoric times, consisting of a cross with arms of equal length, each arm having a continuation at right angles, and all four continuations turning the same way. 2. this figure with clockwise arms as the official emblem of the Nazi party and the Third Reich. [t. Skt.: m. *svastika*, der. *svasti* well-being]

Swastika

swat (swŏt), *v.*, **swatted, swatting,** *n.* *Colloq.* —*v.t.* 1. to hit with a smart or violent blow. —*n.* 2. a smart or violent blow. Also, **swot.** [orig. var. of **squat**] —**swat/ter,** *n.*

swatch (swŏch), *n.* a sample of cloth or other material.

swath (swŏth, swôth), *n.* 1. the space covered by the stroke of a scythe or the cut of a mowing machine. 2. the piece or strip so cut. 3. a line or ridge of grass, grain, or the like, cut and thrown together by a scythe or mowing machine. 4. a strip, belt, or long and relatively narrow extent of anything. 5. **cut a wide swath,** to make a pretentious display. [ME; OE *swæth*, c. G *schwad*]

swathe¹ (swāth), *v.*, **swathed, swathing,** *n.* —*v.t.* 1. to wrap with swathes of some material; wrap up closely or fully. 2. to enfold or envelop, as wrappings do. 3. to wrap round something as or like a swathe. —*n.* 4. a band of linen or the like in which something is wrapped; a wrapping; a bandage. [ME; late OE *swathian,* der. *swath-* (in *swathum* bandages)] —**swath/er,** *n.*

swathe² (swāth), *n.* swath.

Swa·tow (swä/tou/), *n.* a seaport in SE China, in Kwantung province. 215,000 (est. 1954).

sway (swā), *v.i.* 1. to move to and fro, as something fixed at one end or resting on a support; swing to and fro. 2. to move or incline to one side or in a particular direction. 3. to incline in opinion, sympathy, tendency, etc. 4. to fluctuate or vacillate, as in opinion. 5. to wield power; exercise rule. —*v.t.* 6. to cause to move to and fro; cause to incline from side to side. 7. to cause to move to one side or in a particular direction. 8. *Naut.* to hoist or raise, as a yard or topmast (usually fol. by *up*). 9. to cause to fluctuate or vacillate. 10. to cause (the mind, etc., or the person) to incline or turn in a specified way. 11. to cause to swerve, as from a purpose or a course of action. 12. to dominate; direct. 13. a. *Archaic or Poetic.* to wield (a weapon or instrument, esp. the scepter). b. to exercise rule or sovereignty over. —*n.* 14. act of swaying; swaying movement. 15. rule; dominion. 16. dominating power or influence. [ME, t. Scand.; cf. Icel. *sveigja* sway] —**sway/er,** *n.* —**sway/ing·ly,** *adv.* —**Syn.** 1. See **swing¹**.

sway-back (swā/băk/), *n.* an excessive downward curvature of the spinal column in the dorsal region, esp. of horses.

sway-backed (swā/băkt/), *adj.* having the back sagged to an unusual degree; having a sway-back.

Swa·zi (swä/zĭ), *n.*, *pl.* **-zis.** a member of a Bantu tribe of Zulu descent found in Swaziland, in SE Africa.

---

b., blend of, blended; c., cognate with; d., dialect, dialectal; der., derived from; f., formed from; g., going back to; m., modification of; r., replacing; s., stem of; t., taken from; ?, perhaps. See the full key on inside cover.

Swa·zi·land (swä′zĭ länd′), *n.* a British protectorate in SE Africa between S Mozambique and SE Transvaal in the Union of South Africa. 207,000 (est. 1953); 6704 sq. mi. *Cap.:* Mbabane.

swear (swâr), *v.,* **swore** or (*Archaic*) **sware; sworn; swearing.** —*v.i.* **1.** to make a solemn declaration with an appeal to God or some superhuman being in confirmation of what is declared; make affirmation in a solemn manner by some sacred being or object, as the Deity or the Bible. **2.** to engage or promise on oath or in a solemn manner; vow; bind oneself by oath (fol. by *to*). **3.** to give evidence or make any statement on oath or by solemn declaration (fol. by *to*). **4.** to use profane oaths or language, as in imprecation or anger or for mere emphasis. **5. swear by, a.** to name (some sacred being or thing, etc.) as one's witness or guarantee in swearing. **b.** *Colloq.* to rely on as of highest authority. —*v.t.* **6.** to declare or affirm by swearing by a deity, some sacred object, etc. **7.** to affirm or say with solemn earnestness or great emphasis. **8.** to promise or undertake on oath or in a solemn manner; vow. **9.** to testify or state on oath or by solemn declaration; make oath to (something stated or alleged). **10.** to take (an oath), as in order to give solemnity or force to a declaration, promise, etc. **11.** to bring, get, take, etc., by swearing or oathtaking: *to swear out a warrant for a person's arrest.* **12.** to administer an oath to; bind by an oath (fol. by *to*): *to swear someone to secrecy.* **13.** to admit to office or service by administering an oath (often fol. by *in*). **14. swear off,** *Colloq.* to swear to leave off or give up (something, esp. intoxicating drink). [ME *swere(n),* OE *swerian, c.* G *schwören*] —**swear′er,** *n.* —Syn. 4. See **curse.**

sweat (swĕt), *v.,* **sweat** or **sweated, sweating,** *n.* —*v.i.* **1.** to excrete watery fluid through the pores of the skin, as from heat, exertion, etc.; perspire, esp. freely or profusely. **2.** to exude moisture, as green plants piled in a heap. **3.** to gather moisture from the surrounding air by condensation. **4.** (of tobacco) to ferment. **5.** *Colloq.* to exert oneself strenuously; work hard. **6.** *Colloq.* to suffer severely, as for something one has done. **7.** *Colloq.* to fume, as with impatience or vexation. —*v.t.* **8.** to emit (watery fluid, etc.) through the pores of the skin; exude (moisture, etc.) in drops or small particles. **9.** to send forth or get rid of with or like sweat (often fol. by *out* or *off*). **10.** to wet or stain with sweat. **11.** to cause (a person, a horse, etc.) to sweat. **12.** to cause (substances, etc.) to exude moisture, esp. as a step in some industrial process of treating or preparing. **13.** to cause (persons, etc.) to work hard. **14.** to employ (workers) at low wages, for overlong hours or under other unfavorable conditions. **15.** *Slang.* to deprive (a person) of money, etc., as by exaction. **16.** *Slang.* to subject (a person) to severe questioning in order to extract information, as for police purposes. **17.** *Metall.* **a.** to heat (metal) to partial fusion in order to remove an easily fusible constituent. **b.** to heat (solder or the like) until it melts; join (metal parts) by heating, esp. after applying solder. **18.** to remove part of the metal from (coins, esp. gold) by friction, as by shaking them in a bag. **19.** to cause (tobacco) to ferment. —*n.* **20.** the process of sweating or perspiring, as from heat, exertion, perturbation, disease, etc. **21.** the secretions of sweat glands; the product of sweating. **22.** a process of inducing sweating or perspiration, or of being sweated, as in medical or other special treatment. **23.** moisture or liquid matter exuded from something or gathered on a surface in drops or small particles. **24.** an exuding of moisture by a substance, etc., or an inducing of such exudation, as in some industrial process. **25.** a run given to a horse for exercise, as before a race. **26.** *Colloq.* a state of perturbation, anxiety, or impatience. **27.** *Archaic.* strenuous exertion; hard work. [ME *swete(n),* OE *swǣtan, c.* D *zweeten,* G *schweissen*] —**sweat′less,** *adj.* —**Syn. 21.** See **perspiration.**

sweat·band (swĕt′bănd′), *n.* a band in a hat or cap to protect it against the sweat of the head.

sweat·ed (swĕt′ĭd), *adj.* **1.** made by underpaid workers. **2.** underpaid and overworked. **3.** having poor working conditions.

sweat·er (swĕt′ər), *n.* **1.** a knitted jacket or jersey, worn (orig. to induce sweating and reduce weight) during athletic exercise, or for warmth after it, or otherwise. **2.** one who or that which sweats. **3.** an employer who underpays and overworks employees.

sweat gland, *Anat.* one of the minute, coiled, tubular glands of the skin that secrete sweat; a sudoriferous gland.

sweating sickness, a febrile epidemic disease which appeared in the 15th and 16th centuries, characterized by profuse sweating, and frequently fatal in a few hours.

Section of skin, showing sweat glands
A. Surface opening of sweat gland; B. Epidermis; D. Duct of sweat gland; E. Coiled end of gland; F. Fat cells; C to G, Derma or corium

sweat shirt, a loose pull-over of warm material, worn esp. by athletes to prevent chill.

sweat·shop (swĕt′shŏp′), *n.* a shop employing workers at low wages, during overlong hours, under unsanitary or otherwise unfavorable conditions.

sweat·y (swĕt′ĭ), *adj.,* **sweatier, sweatiest.** **1.** covered, moist, or stained with sweat. **2.** causing sweat. **3.** laborious. —**sweat′i·ly,** *adv.* —**sweat′i·ness,** *n.*

Swed., 1. Sweden. **2.** Swedish.

Swede (swēd), *n.* **1.** a native or inhabitant of Sweden. **2.** (*cap.* or *l.c.*) *Chiefly Brit.* a rutabaga. [t. MLG or MD]

Swe·den (swē′dən), *n.* a kingdom in N Europe, in the E part of the Scandinavian peninsula. 7,316,000 pop. (est. 1956); 173,394 sq. mi. *Cap.:* Stockholm. Swedish, Sverige.

Swe·den·borg (swē′dən bôrg′; *Sw.* svä′dən bôr′y), *n.* **Emanuel** (ĕ mä′nŏŏ əl), (orig. *Emanuel Swedberg*) 1688–1772, Swedish scientist, philosopher, theologian, and mystic.

Swe·den·bor·gi·an (swē′dən bôr′jĭ ən), *adj.* **1.** pertaining to Emanuel Swedenborg, or to his religious doctrines, or to the body of followers adhering to these doctrines and constituting the Church of the New Jerusalem, or New Church. —*n.* **2.** a believer in the religious doctrines of Swedenborg. —**Swe′den·bor′gi·an·ism,** *n.*

Swed·ish (swē′dĭsh), *adj.* **1.** of or pertaining to Sweden, its inhabitants, or their language. —*n.* **2.** a Germanic language, the language of Sweden and parts of Finland, closely related to Danish and Norwegian. **3.** the people of Sweden collectively.

Swedish massage, a massage utilizing Swedish movements.

Swedish movements, a system of muscular exercises for hygienic or therapeutic purposes.

swee·ny (swē′nĭ), *n. Vet. Sci.* atrophy of the shoulder muscles in horses. [cf. d. G *schweine* atrophy]

sweep (swēp), *v.,* **swept, sweeping,** *n.* —*v.t.* **1.** to move, drive, or bring by passing a broom, brush, or the like over the surface occupied, or as the broom or other object does: *to sweep dust away.* **2.** to move, bring, take, etc., by or as by a steady, driving stroke or with continuous, forcible actions: *the wind sweeps the snow into drifts.* **3.** to pass or draw (something) over a surface, or about, along, etc., with a steady, continuous stroke or movement: *to sweep a brush over a table.* **4.** to clear or clean (a floor, room, chimney, etc.) of dirt, litter, etc., by means of a broom or the like. **5.** to make (a path, etc.) by clearing a space with a broom or the like; clear (a surface, place, etc.) of something on or in it: *to sweep the sea of enemy ships, to sweep a harbor for submarine mines.* **6.** to pass over (a surface, region, etc.) with a steady, driving movement or unimpeded course, as winds, floods, etc. **7.** to direct the gaze over (a region, etc.) with the unaided eye or with a telescope or the like; survey with a continuous view over the whole extent. **8.** to pass the fingers or bow over (a musical instrument, its strings or keys, etc.) as in playing, or bring forth (music) thus. —*v.i.* **9.** to sweep a floor, room, etc., as with a broom, or as a broom does: *a new broom sweeps clean.* **10.** to move steadily and strongly or swiftly (fol. by *along, by, down, over,* etc.). **11.** to pass in a stately manner, as a person, a funeral cortege, etc. **12.** to walk in long, trailing garments. **13.** to trail, as garments, etc. **14.** to move or pass in a continuous course, esp. a wide curve or circuit: *his glance swept about the room.* **15.** to extend in a continuous or curving stretch, as a road, a shore, fields, etc. **16.** to conduct an underwater search by towing a drag under the surface of the water, as for submarine mines, a lost anchor, or the like. —*n.* **17.** act of sweeping, esp. a moving, removing, clearing, etc., by or as by the use of a broom: *to abolish all class distinctions at one sweep.* **18.** the steady, driving motion or swift onward course of something moving with force or unimpeded: *the sweep of the wind or waves.* **19.** a trailing movement, as of garments. **20.** a swinging or curving movement or stroke, as of the arm or a weapon, oar, etc. **21.** reach, range, or compass, as of something sweeping about: *the sweep of a road about a marsh.* **22.** a continuous extent or stretch: *a broad sweep of sand.* **23.** a curving, esp. widely or gently curving, line, form, part, or mass. **24.** matter removed or gathered by sweeping. **25.** a leverlike device for raising or lowering a bucket in a well, consisting essentially of a long pole pivoted on an upright post. **26.** a large oar used in small vessels, sometimes to assist the rudder in turning the vessel but usually to propel the craft. **27.** *Chiefly Brit.* one who sweeps, esp. a chimney sweeper. **28.** *Cards.* **a.** (in whist) the winning of all the tricks in a hand. Cf. **slam²** (def. 1). **b.** (in cassino) a pairing or combining, and hence taking, of all the cards on the board. **29.** *Physics.* an irreversible process tending towards thermal equilibrium. **30.** a sweepstakes contest. [ME *swepe;* cf. OE *geswēpa* sweepings, akin to *swāpan* sweep, *c.* G *schweifen*] —**sweep′er,** *n.*

sweep·back (swēp′băk′), *n. Aeron.* the shape of, or the angle formed by, an airplane wing whose leading or trailing edges slope backwards.

sweep·ing (swē′pĭng), *adj.* **1.** of wide range or scope: *a sweeping victory.* **2.** moving or passing about over a wide area: *a sweeping glance.* —*n.* **3.** moving, driving, or passing steadily and forcibly on. **4.** act of one that sweeps. **5.** (*pl.*) matter swept out or up, as dust, refuse, etc.: *put the sweepings in this box.* —**sweep′ing·ly,** *adv.* —**sweep′ing·ness,** *n.*

sweep·stakes (swēp′stāks′), *n. sing.* and *pl.* **1.** a prize in a race or other contest, consisting of the stakes contributed by the various competitors, and taken all by the winner or divided among a certain number of

ăct, āble, dâre, ärt; ĕbb, ēqual; ĭf, īce; hŏt, ōver, ôrder, oil, bŏŏk, ōōze, out; ŭp, ūse, ûrge; ə = a in alone; ch, chief; g, give; ng, ring; sh, shoe; th, thin; ŧħ, that; zh, vision. See the full key on inside cover.

winners. 2. the race or contest itself. 3. a gambling transaction, as on the outcome of a race, in which each of a number of persons contributes a stake, and the stakes are awarded to one or several winners. Also, **sweep/stake/**. [f. SWEEP + STAKE[2]]

sweet (swēt), *adj.* 1. pleasing to the taste, esp., having the pleasant taste or flavor characteristic of sugar, honey, etc. 2. not rancid, or stale; fresh. 3. fresh as opposed to salt, as water. 4. pleasing to the ear; making a pleasant or agreeable sound; musical; 5. pleasing to the smell; fragrant; perfumed. 6. pleasing or agreeable; yielding pleasure or enjoyment; delightful. 7. pleasant in disposition or manners; amiable; kind or gracious, as a person, action, etc. 8. dear; beloved; precious. 9. easily managed; done or effected without effort. 10. (of wine) sweet-tasting (opposed to *dry*). 11. free from sourness or acidity, as soil. 12. *Chem.* a. devoid of corrosive or acidic substances. b. (of substances such as gasoline) containing no sulphur compounds. 13. *Jazz.* in a straight or sentimental style (contrasted with the hot or improvisatory style of performance). —*adv.* 14. in a sweet manner; sweetly. —*n.* 15. sweet taste or flavor; sweet smell; sweetness. 16. that which is sweet. 17. *Chiefly Brit.* candy; a sweetmeat or bonbon. 18. *Brit.* a sweet dish, as a pudding or tart. 19. something pleasant to the mind or feelings. 20. a beloved person; darling; sweetheart. [ME and OE *swēte*, c. D *zoet*, G *süss*, Icel. *sætr*, akin to Goth. *sūts*, L *suāvis*] —**sweet/ly**, *adv.* —**sweet/ness**, *n.* —Syn. 1. sugary, honeyed. 4. melodious, mellifluous, harmonious. 7. winning, lovable, charming.

Sweet (swēt), *n.* Henry, 1845–1912, British philologist and linguist.

sweet alyssum, a cruciferous garden plant, *Lobularia maritima*, with small white or violet flowers.

sweet basil, a plant of the mint family, *Ocimum Basilicum*, whose leaves are used in cookery.

sweet bay, 1. the bay, or European laurel. 2. an American magnolia, *Magnolia virginiana*, with fragrant, white, aromatic flowers, common on the Atlantic coast.

sweet-bread (swēt/brĕd/), *n.* 1. the pancreas (**stomach sweetbread**) of an animal, esp. a calf or a lamb, used for food. 2. the thymus gland (**neck sweetbread** or **throat sweetbread**), likewise so used.

sweet-bri-er (swēt/brī/ər), *n.* a rose, *Rosa Eglanteria*, a native of Europe and central Asia, with a tall stem, stout, hooked prickles often mixed with bristles, and single pink flowers; the eglantine. Also, **sweet/bri/ar.**

sweet cicely, any of several umbelliferous plants nearly allied to chervil, as an English species, *Myrrhis odorata*, sometimes used as a potherb, or some species of the North American genus *Osmorhiza*.

sweet cider, cider which has not fermented.

sweet clover, melilot.

sweet corn, 1. any maize of a sweetish flavor and suitable for eating, esp. a particularly sweet variety, *Zea mays* var. *saccharata*. 2. the unripe and tender ears of corn, esp. when used as a table vegetable; green corn.

sweet-en (swē/tən), *v.t.* 1. to make sweet. 2. to make mild or kind; soften. 3. *Colloq.* to enhance the value of (loan collateral) by including especially valuable or reputable securities. 4. *Slang.* (in poker) to increase (a pot) by adding stakes before opening. —*v.i.* 5. to become sweet. —**sweet/en-er**, *n.*

sweet-en-ing (swē/tən ĭng, swēt/nĭng), *n.* 1. something that sweetens food, etc. 2. the process of causing something to be sweet.

sweet fern, a small North American shrub, *Comptonia peregrina* (*Myrica asplenifolia*), with aromatic fernlike leaves.

sweet flag, an araceous plant, *Acorus Calamus*, with long, sword-shaped leaves and a pungent, aromatic rootstock; calamus.

sweet gale, gale[2].

sweet gum, the American liquidambar, *Liquidambar Styraciflua*, or the balsamic liquid exuded by it.

sweet-heart (swēt/härt/), *n.* 1. one of a pair of lovers with relation to the other, sometimes esp. the girl or woman. 2. a beloved person (often used in affectionate address).

sweet-ie (swē/tĭ), *n.* 1. *Colloq.* a sweetheart (often used as a term of endearment). 2. (*usually pl.*) *Brit.* a sweetmeat, sweet cake, or the like.

sweet-ing (swē/tĭng), *n.* 1. a sweet variety of apple. 2. *Archaic.* a beloved person; darling; sweetheart.

sweet-ish (swē/tĭsh), *adj.* somewhat sweet. —**sweet/ish-ly**, *adv.* —**sweet/ish-ness**, *n.*

sweet marjoram, marjoram.

sweet-meat (swēt/mēt/), *n.* 1. a sweet dainty, prepared with sugar, honey, or the like, as preserves, candy, or formerly cakes or pastry. 2. (*usually pl.*) any sweet dainty of the confectionery or candy kind, as candied fruit, sugar-covered nuts, sugarplums, bonbons, balls or sticks of candy, etc.

sweet oil, olive oil.

sweet pea, an annual climbing plant, *Lathyrus odoratus*, bearing sweet-scented flowers.

sweet pepper, any of the mild flavored peppers, *Capsicum frutescens* var. *grossum*, used for stuffing, pickling, or as a vegetable.

sweet potato, 1. a plant of the morning glory or *Convolvulaceae* family, *Ipomoea Batatas*, grown for its sweet, edible roots. 2. the root.

sweet shop, *Brit.* a candy store.

sweet-sop (swēt/sŏp/), *n.* 1. a sweet, pulpy fruit with a thin, tuberculate rind, borne by an annonaceous tree or shrub, *Annona squamosa*, native in tropical America; sugar apple. 2. the tree or shrub.

sweet spirit of niter, an alcoholic solution of ethyl nitrite, $C_2H_5NO_2$, employed medicinally as a diaphoretic, diuretic, and antispasmodic.

sweet-tem-pered (swēt/tĕm/pərd), *adj.* having a kind and gentle disposition.

sweet tooth, *Colloq.* a strong liking for candy and other sweets.

sweet william, a kind of pink, *Dianthus barbatus*, common in old-fashioned gardens, bearing small flowers of various colors in dense clusters. Also, **sweet William.**

swell (swĕl), *v.*, **swelled, swelled** or **swollen, swelling**, *n.*, *adj.* —*v.i.* 1. to grow in bulk, as by absorption of moisture, by inflation or distention, by addition of material in the process of growth, or the like. 2. to rise in waves, as the sea. 3. to well up, as a spring or as tears. 4. to bulge out or be protuberant, as a sail, a cask in the middle. 5. to grow in amount, degree, force, or the like. 6. to increase gradually in volume or intensity, as sound. 7. to arise and grow within one, as a feeling or emotion. 8. to become puffed up with pride; behave or talk arrogantly or pretentiously. —*v.t.* 9. to cause to grow in bulk. 10. to increase gradually in loudness, as a musical tone. 11. to cause (a thing) to bulge out or be protuberant. 12. to increase in amount, degree, force, etc. 13. to affect with swelling emotion. 14. to puff up with pride. —*n.* 15. act of swelling. 16. condition of being swollen. 17. increase in bulk; inflation or distention. 18. a bulging out, or a protuberant part. 19. a wave, esp. when long and unbroken, or such waves collectively. 20. a gradually rising elevation of the land. 21. increase in amount, degree, force, etc. 22. gradual increase in loudness of sound. 23. *Music.* a. a gradual increase (crescendo) followed by a gradual decrease (diminuendo) in loudness or force of musical sound. b. the sign (< >) for indicating this. c. a contrivance, as in an organ, by which the loudness of tones may be varied. 24. a swelling of emotion within one. 25. *Slang.* a fashionably dressed person; a person of high social standing. —*adj. Slang.* 26. (of things) stylish; elegant; grand: *a swell hotel*. 27. (of persons) fashionably dressed; of high standing, esp. socially. 28. first rate. [ME; OE *swellan*, c. G *schwellen*] —Ant. 1. contract.

swell box, a box or chamber containing a set of pipes in a pipe organ or of reeds in a harmonium, and having movable slats or shutters which can be opened or closed to increase or diminish the loudness of the tones.

swell-fish (swĕl/fĭsh/), *n.*, *pl.* **-fishes**, (*esp. collectively*) **-fish.** puffer. (def. 2).

swell-ing (swĕl/ĭng), *n.* 1. act of one that swells. 2. the condition of being swollen. 3. a swollen part; a protuberance or prominence. 4. *Pathol.* an abnormal enlargement or protuberance. —*adj.* 5. that swells.

swel-ter (swĕl/tər), *v.i.* 1. to suffer or languish with oppressive heat; perspire profusely from heat. —*v.t.* 2. to oppress, or cause to languish, with heat. 3. *Archaic.* to exude like sweat, as venom. —*n.* 4. a sweltering condition. [ME *swelte*, freq. of *swelt* die, swoon, OE *sweltan*, c. Icel. *svelta*]

swel-ter-ing (swĕl/tər ĭng), *adj.* 1. suffering or languishing with oppressive heat. 2. characterized by oppressive heat, as a place, the weather, etc.; sultry. —**swel/ter-ing-ly**, *adv.*

swept (swĕpt), *v.* pt. and pp. of **sweep.**

swerve (swûrv), *v.*, **swerved, swerving**, *n.* —*v.i.* 1. to turn aside in movement or direction; deviate from the straight or direct course. —*v.t.* 2. to cause to turn aside. —*n.* 3. act of swerving; a turning aside; a deviation. 4. that which swerves. [ME; OE *sweorfan* rub, file, c. D *zwerven* rove] —**swerv/er**, *n.* —Syn. 1. See **deviate.**

swift (swĭft), *adj.* 1. moving with great speed or velocity; fleet, rapid: *a swift ship*. 2. coming, happening, or performed quickly or without delay. 3. quick or prompt to act, etc.: *swift to act*. —*adv.* 4. swiftly. —*n.* 5. any of the numerous long-winged birds constituting the family *Micropodidae*, notable for their rapid flight. Though allied to the hummingbirds, they resemble the swallows. 6. any of various small lizards, esp. of the genus *Sceloporus*, which run with great swiftness. 7. an adjustable device upon which a hank of yarn is placed in order to wind off skeins or balls. [ME and OE; akin to SWEEP] —**swift/ly**, *adv.* —**swift/ness**, *n.* —Syn. 1. speedy, fast. See **quick.** —Ant. 1. slow.

Swift (swĭft), *n.* **Jonathan,** (*Dean Swift*) 1667–1745, British satirist and dean of St. Patrick's, in Dublin.

swift-er (swĭf/tər), *n.* *Naut.* 1. a small line joining the outer ends of the bars of a capstan to confine them to their sockets while the capstan is being turned. 2. the forward shroud of the lower rigging on either side of a mast. 3. *Obs.* a rope used to encircle a boat lengthwise in order to strengthen and defend its sides. [der. *swift*, *v.* tie fast; cf. Icel. *svipta* to reef (sails)]

---

b., blend of, blended; c., cognate with; d., dialect, dialectal; der., derived from; f., formed from; g., going back to; m., modification of; r., replacing; s., stem of; t., taken from; ?, perhaps. See the full key on inside cover.

swift-foot·ed (swĭft'fŏŏt'ĭd), *adj.* swift in running.

swig (swĭg), *n., v.,* **swigged, swigging.** *Colloq.* —*n.* 1. a large or deep draft, as of liquor. —*v.t., v.i.* 2. to drink heartily or greedily. —**swig'ger,** *n.*

swill (swĭl), *n.* 1. liquid or partly liquid food for animals, esp. kitchen refuse given to swine; hogwash. 2. kitchen refuse in general; garbage. 3. any liquid matter; slop. 4. a deep draft of liquor. —*v.i.* 5. to drink greedily or excessively. —*v.t.* 6. to drink greedily or to excess; guzzle. 7. *Chiefly Brit. Colloq.* to wash or cleanse by flooding with water. [ME *swile*(n), OE *swilian,* var. of *swillan;* orig. unknown] —**swill'er,** *n.*

swim (swĭm), *v.,* **swam, swum, swimming,** *n.* —*v.i.* 1. to move along or in water by movements of the limbs, fins, tail, etc.; move on or in water or other liquid in any way, esp. on the surface. 2. to float on the surface of water or other liquid. 3. to move, rest, or be suspended in air or the like, as if swimming in water. 4. to move, glide, or go smoothly over a surface. 5. to be immersed or steeped in, or overflowed or flooded with, a liquid. 6. to be dizzy or giddy; have a whirling sensation; seem to whirl. —*v.t.* 7. to move along on or in by swimming; float on or in; cross by swimming, as a stream. 8. to cause to swim; cause to float, as on a stream. 9. to furnish with sufficient water to swim or float. —*n.* 10. an act or period of swimming. 11. a motion as of swimming; a smooth, gliding movement. 12. *Colloq.* the current of affairs (prec. by *the*): *to be in the swim.* [ME *swimme,* OE *swimman,* c. G *schwimmen*] —**swim'mer,** *n.*

swim bladder, an air bladder (def. 2).

swim·mer·et (swĭm'ə rĕt'), *n.* (in many crustaceans) one of a number of abdominal limbs or appendages, usually adapted for swimming, and for carrying eggs, and thus distinguished from other limbs adapted for walking or seizing.

swim·ming·ly (swĭm'ĭng lĭ), *adv.* without difficulty; with great success.

Swin·burne (swĭn'bərn), *n.* **Algernon Charles** (ăl'-jər nən), 1837–1909, British poet and critic.

swin·dle (swĭn'dəl), *v.,* **-dled, -dling,** *n.* —*v.t.* 1. to cheat (a person) as out of money, as a swindler does. 2. to get by swindling. —*v.i.* 3. to put forward plausible schemes or use unscrupulous artifice to defraud others; cheat; defraud. —*n.* 4. act of swindling; a fraudulent transaction or scheme. 5. anything deceptive; a fraud. [back formation from *swindler,* t. G: m. *schwindler,* der. *schwindeln* be giddy, swindle] —**swin'dler,** *n.*

swine (swīn), *n., pl.* **swine.** 1. the domestic hog. 2. any animal of the same family, *Suidae,* of the artiodactyl suborder *Suina,* as the European wild boar, *Sus scrofa,* or of the closely related peccary family of the New World, *Tayassuidae.* 3. *Chiefly Brit.* a coarse, gross, or brutishly sensual person. [ME; OE *swīn,* c. G *schwein;* akin to sow²]

swine·herd (swīn'hûrd'), *n.* *Literary.* one who herds or tends swine.

swine pox, 1. a variety of chicken pox. 2. *Vet. Sci.* a mild pox disease of swine, caused by a virus related to that of cowpox and characterized by the appearance of pustules in the skin, esp. of the abdomen.

swing¹ (swĭng), *v.,* **swung** or (*Archaic and Dial.*) **swang; swung; swinging;** *n.* —*v.t.* 1. to cause to move to and fro, sway, or oscillate, as something suspended from above: *ladies swinging their parasols.* 2. to cause to move in alternate directions, or in either direction, about a fixed point or line of support, as a door on its hinges. 3. to move (something held or grasped) with an oscillating or rotatory movement: *swing a club about one's head.* 4. to cause to move in a curve as if about a central point. 5. to suspend so as to hang freely, as a hammock or a door. 6. *U.S. Colloq.* to sway, influence, or manage as desired: *to swing a district in an election.* —*v.i.* 7. to move to and fro, as something suspended from above, as a pendulum. 8. to move to and fro in a swing, as for sport. 9. to move in alternate directions, or in either direction, about a point or line of support, as a gate on its hinges. 10. to move in a curve as if about a central point, as around a corner. 11. to move with a free, swaying motion, as soldiers on the march. 12. to be suspended so as to hang freely, as a bell, etc. 13. *Colloq.* to suffer death by hanging. —*n.* 14. act or the manner of swinging; movement in alternate directions, or in a particular direction. 15. the amount of such movement. 16. a curving movement or course. 17. a moving of the body with a free, swaying motion, as in walking. 18. a steady, marked rhythm or movement, as of verse or music. 19. *Colloq.* a shift or period of work. 20. freedom of action: *have free swing.* 21. active operation: *to be in full swing.* 22. something that is swung or that swings. 23. a seat suspended from above as in a loop of rope or between ropes or rods, in which one may sit and swing to and fro for sport. [ME; OE *swingan,* c. G *schwingen.* Cf. OE *swinge* blow] —**swing'er,** *n.*

—**Syn.** 7. SWING, SWAY, OSCILLATE, ROCK suggest a movement back and forth. SWING expresses the comparatively regular motion to and fro of a body supported from the end or ends, esp. from above: *a lamp swings from the ceiling.* To SWAY is to swing gently: *the lantern sways in the breeze.* OSCILLATE refers to the smooth, regular, alternating movement of a body within certain limits between two fixed points: *a pendulum oscillates.* ROCK indicates the slow and regular movement back and forth of a body as on curved supports: *a cradle rocks.*

swing² (swĭng), *n., adj., v.,* **swung, swinging.** —*n.* 1. dance music characterized by ingenious modern interpretations and played in a stimulating rhythm, tempo, etc. 2. the rhythmic element that excites dancers and listeners to move in time to jazz music. —*adj.* 3. pertaining to swing. 4. swing music, a modern term for jazz music. —*v.t., v.i.* 5. to play (music) in the manner of jazz. [special use of SWING¹]

swinge (swĭnj), *v.t.,* **swinged, swingeing.** *Archaic.* to whip; punish. [ME *swenge* shake, smite, OE *swengan,* causative of *swingan* SWING] —**swing·er** (swĭn'jər), *n.*

swinge·ing (swĭn'jĭng), *adj.* *Colloq.* 1. very forcible, great, or large: *a swingeing blow.* 2. excellent; top-notch.

swin·gle (swĭng'gəl), *n., v.,* **-gled, -gling.** —*n.* 1. a wooden instrument shaped like a large knife, for beating flax or hemp and scraping from it the woody or coarse portions. —*v.t.* 2. to clean (flax or hemp) by beating and scraping with a swingle. [ME *swengyl,* t. MD: m. *swinghel,* c. OE *swingell* rod]

swin·gle·tree (swĭng'gəl trē'), *n.* whiffletree. Also, **singletree.**

swing shift, *U.S. Colloq.* a work shift in industry, from mid-afternoon (usually 3 p.m.) until 12 midnight.

swin·ish (swī'nĭsh), *adj.* like or befitting swine; hoggish; brutishly gross or sensual. —**swin'ish·ly,** *adv.* —**swin'ish·ness,** *n.*

swink (swĭngk), *v.i.,* **swank** or **swonk, swonken, swinking,** *n.* *Archaic* or *Brit. Dial.* labor; toil. [ME; OE *swincan,* akin to SWING] —**swink'er,** *n.*

Swin·ner·ton (swĭn'ər tən), *n.* **Frank (Arthur),** born 1884, British novelist and critic.

swipe (swīp), *n., v.,* **swiped, swiping.** —*n.* 1. *Colloq.* a sweeping stroke; a stroke with full swing of the arms, as in cricket or golf. 2. a leverlike device for raising or lowering a weight, esp. a bucket in a well; a sweep. 3. *Colloq.* a sideswipe. —*v.t.* 4. *Colloq.* to strike with a sweeping blow. 5. *Slang.* to steal. —*v.i.* 6. *Colloq.* to make a sweeping stroke. [akin to SWEEP]

swipes (swīps), *n.pl.* *Brit. Slang* or *Colloq.* 1. poor, washy beer; small beer. 2. malt liquor in general.

swip·ple (swĭp'əl), *n.* the freely swinging part of a flail, which falls upon the grain in threshing; a swingle. Also, **swi'ple.** [ME *swepelles* broom, OE *swǣpels*(e) robe; akin to SWEEP]

swirl (swûrl), *v.i.* 1. to move about or along with a whirling motion; whirl; eddy. 2. to be dizzy or giddy, or swim, as the head. —*v.t.* 3. to cause to swirl or whirl; twist. —*n.* 4. a swirling movement; a whirl; an eddy. 5. a twist, as of hair about the head or of trimming on a hat. [? imit.; ? akin to d. Norw. *svirla,* D *zwirrelen* whirl, d. G *schwirren* totter]

swirl·y (swûr'lĭ), *adj.* swirling, whirling or twisted.

swish (swĭsh), *v.i.* 1. to move with or make a sibilant sound, as a slender rod cutting sharply through the air, or as small waves washing on the shore. 2. to rustle, as silk. —*v.t.* 3. to flourish, whisk, etc., with a swishing movement or sound: *to swish a cane.* 4. to bring, take, etc., with or as with such a movement or sound: *to swish off the tops of plants with a cane.* 5. to flog or whip. —*n.* 6. a swishing movement or sound. 7. a stock or rod for flogging, or a stroke with this. [imit.]

Swiss (swĭs), *adj.* 1. of or pertaining to Switzerland or the Swiss; derived from or associated with Switzerland. —*n.* 2. a native or inhabitant of Switzerland. 3. a thin crisp fabric, often with woven or printed dots or figures. [t. F: m. *Suisse,* t. MHG: m. *Swiz*]

Swiss chard, chard.

Swiss cheese, a firm, pale-yellow or whitish cheese containing many holes, made usually from cows' milk half skimmed.

Swit., Switzerland. Also, **Switz., Swtz.**

switch (swĭch), *n.* 1. a slender, flexible shoot, rod, etc. used esp. in whipping, beating, etc. 2. act of switching; a stroke, lash, or whisking movement. 3. a slender growing shoot, as of a plant (cf. switch plant). 4. a separate bunch or tress of long hair (or some substitute) fastened together at one end, worn by women to supplement their hair. 5. *Elect.* a device for turning on or off or directing an electric current, or making or breaking a circuit. 6. *Railroads.* a device for shifting moving trains, cars, etc., from one track to another, commonly consisting of a pair of movable rails. 7. a turning, shifting, or changing: *a switch of votes to another candidate.* 8. *Bridge.* a change to a suit other than the one played or bid previously. —*v.t.* 9. to whip or beat with a switch or the like; lash: *he switched the lad with a cane.* 10. to move, swing, or whisk (a cane, a fishing line, etc.) like a switch, or with a swift, lashing stroke. 11. to turn, shift, or divert: *to switch conversation from a painful subject.* 12. *Elect.* to connect, disconnect, or redirect an electric circuit by operating a switch: *he switched on a light.* 13. *Railroads.* **a.** to shift or transfer (a train, car, etc.), esp. in a railway yard or terminal. **b.** to drop or add (cars) or to make up (a train). —*v.i.* 14. to strike with or as with a switch. 15. to change direction or course; turn, shift, or change. 16. to be shifted, turned, etc. by means of a switch. [cf. LG *swutsche*] —**switch'er,** *n.* —**switch'like,** *adj.*

ăct, āble, dâre, ärt; ĕbb, ēqual; ĭf, īce; hŏt, ōver, ôrder, oil, bŏŏk, ōōze, out; ŭp, ūse, ûrge; ə = a in alone; ch, chief; g, give; ng, ring; sh, shoe; th, thin; ŧh, that; zh, vision. See the full key on inside cover.

switch·back (swĭch′băk′), *n.* **1.** a mountain highway having many hairpin curves. **2.** *Railroads.* a zigzag track arrangement for climbing a steep grade. **3.** *Brit.* a roller coaster.

switch·board (swĭch′bôrd′), *n.* a structural unit mounting switches, instruments, and/or meters necessary for the control of electric energy.

switch·man (swĭch′mən), *n., pl.* **-men.** **1.** one who has charge of a switch or switches on a railroad. **2.** one who assists in shifting cars in a railway yard or terminal.

switch·yard (swĭch′yärd′), *n.* a railroad yard in which trains are broken up and made up.

Switz., Switzerland.

Switz·er (swĭt′sər), *n.* a Swiss. [t. MHG]

Switz·er·land (swĭt′sər lənd), *n.* a republic in central Europe. 5,023,000 pop. (est. 1956); 15,944 sq. mi. *Cap.:* Bern. French, **Suisse.** German, **Schweiz.**

swiv·el (swĭv′əl), *n., v.,* **-eled, -eling** or (*esp. Brit.*) **-elled, -elling.** —*n.* **1.** a fastening device which allows the thing fastened to turn round freely upon it. **2.** such a device consisting of two parts, each of which turns round independently, as a compound link of a chain one part of which turns freely in the other by means of a headed pin or the like. **3.** a pivoted support for allowing a gun to turn round in a horizontal plane. **4.** a swivel gun. —*v.t.* **5.** to turn on or as on a swivel. **6.** to fasten by a swivel; furnish with a swivel. —*v.i.* **7.** to turn on a swivel, pivot, or the like. [ME *swyvel,* t. Scand.; cf. Icel. *sveifla* swing, akin to OE *swīfan* revolve] —**swiv′el·like′,** *adj.*

S, Swivel; H, Hook; C, Chain

swivel chair, a chair whose seat turns round horizontally on a swivel.

swivel gun, a gun mounted on a pedestal so that it can be turned from side to side or up and down.

swiz·zle (swĭz′əl), *n.* a drink composed of rum, crushed ice, lemon or lime juice, bitters and sugar. [orig. unknown]

swizzle stick, *Colloq.* a small rod for stirring drinks.

swob (swŏb), *n., v.t.,* **swobbed, swobbing.** swab.

swol·len (swō′lən). *v.* **1.** pp. of **swell.** —*adj.* **2.** Also, *Archaic,* **swoln** (swōln). swelled; enlarged by or as by swelling; puffed up; tumid. **3.** turgid or bombastic.

swoon (swōōn), *v.i.* **1.** to faint; lose consciousness. —*n.* **2.** a faint or fainting fit; syncope. [ME *swo(w)ne,* OE *geswōgen* in a swoon] —**swoon′ing·ly,** *adv.*

swoop (swōōp), *v.i.* **1.** to sweep through the air, as a bird or a bat, esp. down upon prey. **2.** to come down in a sudden, swift attack (often fol. by *down* and *on* or *upon*): *an army swoops down upon a region.* —*v.t.* **3.** to take at one stroke. —*n.* **4.** act of swooping; a sudden, swift descent. [var. of *swope,* OE *swāpan* sweep]

swop (swŏp), *v.t., v.i.,* **swopped, swopping,** *n.* swap.

sword (sôrd), *n.* **1.** a weapon having various forms but consisting typically of a long, straight or slightly curved blade, sharp-edged on one side or both sides, with one end pointed and the other fixed in a hilt or handle. **2.** this weapon as the symbol of military power, punitive justice, authority, etc. **3.** a cause of death or destruction. **4.** war, combat, or slaughter; military force or power. **5. at sword's points,** ready for mutual attack. **6. cross swords, a.** to join in combat. **b.** to argue; disagree violently. [ME; OE *sweord,* c. G *schwert*] —**sword′less,** *adj.* —**sword′like′,** *adj.*

sword bayonet, a kind of short sword for attaching to the muzzle of a gun, to be used as a bayonet.

sword·bill (sôrd′bĭl′), *n.* a hummingbird, *Ensifera ensifera,* of South America whose slender bill is longer than its body.

sword·craft (sôrd′kraft′, -kräft′), *n.* **1.** knowledge of, or skill with, the sword. **2.** military skill or power.

sword·fish (sôrd′fĭsh′), *n., pl.* **-fishes,** (*esp. collectively*) **-fish.** a large marine food fish, *Xiphias gladius,* with the upper jaw elongated into a swordlike weapon; broadbill.

sword grass, any of various grasses or plants with swordlike or sharp leaves, as the sword lily.

sword knot, a looped strap, ribbon, or the like, attached to the hilt of a sword, as a support or ornament.

sword lily, a gladiolus.

sword·play (sôrd′plā′), *n.* the action, practice, or art of wielding a sword; fencing.

swords·man (sôrdz′mən), *n., pl.* **-men.** **1.** one who uses, or is skilled in the use of, a sword. **2.** a fencer. **3.** a soldier. Also, **sword′man.** —**swords′man·ship′,** *n.*

sword·tail (sôrd′tāl′), *n.* any of several small, viviparous, Mexican cyprinodont fishes of the genus *Xiphophorus,* commonly cultivated in home aquariums.

swore (swōr), *v.* pt. of **swear.**

sworn (swōrn), *v.* **1.** pp. of **swear.** —*adj.* **2.** having taken an oath; bound by or as by an oath.

swot[1] (swŏt), *v.t.,* **swotted, swotting,** *n. Colloq.* swat.

swot[2] (swŏt), *v.,* **swotted, swotting,** *n. Brit. Slang.* —*v.i.* **1.** to study or work hard. —*n.* **2.** one who studies hard. **3.** hard study or work. [d. var. of SWEAT]

swound (swound), *n., v.i. Archaic* or *Dial.* swoon. **'swounds** (zwoundz, zoundz), *interj. Obs.* zounds.

swum (swŭm), *v.* pp. of **swim.**

swung (swŭng), *v.* pt. and pp. of **swing.**

---

sy-, var. of **syn-,** before *s* followed by a consonant and before *z,* as in *systaltic.*

Syb·a·ris (sĭb′ə rĭs), *n.* an ancient Greek city in S Italy: noted for its wealth and luxury; destroyed, 510 B.C.

syb·a·rite (sĭb′ə rīt′), *n.* **1.** (*cap.*) an inhabitant of Sybaris. **2.** one devoted to luxury and pleasure; an effeminate voluptuary. —**syb·a·rit·ic** (sĭb′ə rĭt′ĭk), *adj.* —**syb′a·rit′i·cal·ly,** *adv.*

syc·a·mine (sĭk′ə mĭn, -mīn′), *n.* a mulberry (tree), probably the black mulberry. See Luke 17:6. [t. L: m.s. *sycamīnus,* t. Gk.: m. *sȳkámīnos,* t. Aram.: m. *shiqmīn* (pl.)]

syc·a·more (sĭk′ə môr′), *n.* **1.** U.S. a plane tree, the buttonwood, *Platanus occidentalis.* **2.** Eng. a maple, *Acer Pseudoplatanus,* grown as a shady ornamental tree and for its wood. **3.** a tree, *Ficus Sycomorus,* of the Near East, allied to the common fig, which bears a scarcely edible fruit and is useful for shade. [ME *sycomore,* t. LL: m.s. *sȳcomorus,* t. Gk.: m. *sȳkómoros*]

syce (sīs), *n.* (in India) a groom. [t. Hind., t. Ar.: m. *sā′is*]

sy·cee (sī sē′), *n.* fine uncoined silver in lumps of various sizes usually bearing a banker's or assayer's stamp or mark, used in China as a medium of exchange. Also, **sycee silver.** [t. Chinese: m. *sai sz′,* Cantonese var. of Mandarin *si sz′* fine silk, so called because when pure it may be drawn out into fine threads]

sy·co·ni·um (sī kō′nĭ əm), *n., pl.* **-nia** (-nȳə). *Bot.* a multiple fruit developed from a hollow fleshy receptacle containing numerous flowers, as in the fig. [NL, f. m. Gk. *sȳkon* fig + -*ium* -IUM]

syc·o·phan·cy (sĭk′ə fən sĭ), *n., pl.* **-cies.** **1.** self-seeking or servile flattery. **2.** the character or conduct of a sycophant.

syc·o·phant (sĭk′ə fənt), *n.* a self-seeking flatterer. [t. L: s. *sycophanta,* t. Gk.: m. *sȳkophántēs* slanderer, false accuser] —**syc·o·phan·tic** (sĭk′ə fän′tĭk), **syc′o·phan′ti·cal,** *adj.* —**syc′o·phan′ti·cal·ly,** *adv.*

sy·co·sis (sī kō′sĭs), *n. Pathol.* an inflammatory disease of the hair follicles, marked by a pustular eruption. [NL, t. Gk.: m. *sȳkōsis*]

Syd·ney (sĭd′nĭ), *n.* **1.** a seaport in SE Australia: the capital of New South Wales. 193,103 (1954); with suburbs, 1,863,217 (1951). **2.** a seaport in SE Canada, on Cape Breton Island, Nova Scotia. 31,317 (1951). **3.** Sir Philip. See **Sidney.**

Sy·e·ne (sī ē′nē), *n.* ancient name of **Aswan** (def. 1).

sy·e·nite (sī′ə nīt′), *n.* a granular igneous rock consisting typically of feldspar (orthoclase) and hornblende. [t. L: m.s. *Syēnītēs* (*lapis*) (stone) of Syene, modern Aswan, Egypt] —**sy·e·nit·ic** (sī′ə nĭt′ĭk), *adj.*

syl-, variant of **syn-** (by assimilation) before *l,* as in *syllepsis.*

syll., 1. syllable. **2.** syllabus.

syl·la·bar·y (sĭl′ə běr′ĭ), *n., pl.* **-baries. 1.** a list or catalogue of syllables. **2.** a set of graphic symbols, each of which represents a syllable of the language to be written.

syl·la·bi (sĭl′ə bī′), *n.* pl. of **syllabus.**

syl·lab·ic (sĭ lăb′ĭk), *adj.* **1.** of, pertaining to, or consisting of a syllable or syllables. **2.** pronounced with careful distinction of syllables. **3.** of or pertaining to poetry based on the number of syllables as distinct from poetry depending on stresses or quantities. **4.** (of chanting, etc.) having each syllable sung to one note only. **5.** *Phonet.* syllable-forming or -dominating; sonantal. —*n.* **6.** *Phonet.* a syllabic sound (see **sonant,** def. 3a). —**syl·lab′i·cal·ly,** *adv.*

syl·lab·i·cate (sĭ lăb′ə kāt′), *v.t.,* **-cated, -cating.** to form or divide into syllables. —**syl·lab′i·ca′tion,** *n.*

syl·lab·i·fy (sĭ lăb′ə fī′), *v.t.,* **-fied, -fying.** syllabicate. —**syl·lab′i·fi·ca′tion,** *n.*

syl·la·bism (sĭl′ə bĭz′əm), *n.* **1.** the use of syllabic characters, as in writing. **2.** division into syllables.

syl·la·bize (sĭl′ə bīz′), *v.t.,* **-bized, -bizing.** syllabicate.

syl·la·ble (sĭl′ə bəl), *n., v.,* **-bled, -bling.** —*n.* **1.** *Phonet.* a segment of speech uttered with a single impulse of air pressure from the lungs, and consisting of one sound of relatively great sonority (see **sonant,** def. 3a), with or without one or more subordinated sounds of relatively small sonority (see **consonant,** def. 1). **2.** (in writing systems) a character or a set of characters representing (more or less exactly) such an element of speech. **3.** the least portion or amount of speech or writing; the least mention: *do not breathe a syllable of all this.* —*v.t.* **4.** to utter in syllables; articulate. **5.** to represent by syllables. —*v.i.* **6.** to utter syllables; speak. [ME *sillable,* t. AF, var. of OF *sillabre,* t. L: m.s. *syllaba,* t. Gk.: m. *syllabē*]

syl·la·bub (sĭl′ə bŭb′), *n.* sillabub.

syl·la·bus (sĭl′ə bəs), *n., pl.* **-buses, -bi** (-bī′). **1.** a tabular or other brief statement of the main points of a discourse, the subjects of a course of lectures, etc. **2.** *Law.* **a.** a short summary of the legal basis of a court's decision appearing at the beginning of a reported case. **b.** a book containing summaries of the leading cases in a legal field, used esp. by students. [t. NL; mistake for L *sittyba* titleslip on a book, t. Gk.]

syl·lep·sis (sĭ lĕp′sĭs), *n., pl.* **-ses** (-sēz). *Gram., Rhet.* improper use of one word for two syntactical functions, as in "neither he nor we are willing," or in two senses, as in "he fought with desperation and his trusty

---

b., blend of, blended; c., cognate with; d., dialect, dialectal; der., derived from; f., formed from; g., going back to; m., modification of; r., replacing; s., stem of; t., taken from; ?, perhaps. See the full key on inside cover.

sword." [t. LL, t. Gk.: a taking together] **—syl·lep·tic** (sĭ lĕp'tĭk), *adj.*

syl·lo·gism (sĭl'ə jĭz'əm), *n.* **1.** *Logic.* an argument with two premises and a conclusion. Both the premises of a **categorical syllogism** are categorical propositions, containing just three distinct terms between them, e.g. all men are mortal (major premise). Socrates is a man (minor premise), therefore Socrates is mortal (conclusion); at least one premise in a **hypothetical syllogism** is a hypothetical proposition, e.g. if Smith is eligible to vote he is a citizen (major premise), Smith is eligible to vote (minor premise), therefore Smith is a citizen (conclusion); at least one premise in a **disjunctive syllogism** is a disjunctive proposition, e.g. either Smith is out of town or he is ill (major premise). Smith is not ill (minor premise), therefore he is out of town (conclusion). **2.** deductive reasoning. [t. L: s. *syllogismus,* t. Gk.: m. *syllogismós;* r. ME *silogime,* t. F]

syl·lo·gis·tic (sĭl'ə jĭs'tĭk), *n.* **1.** that part of logic which deals with syllogisms. **2.** syllogistic reasoning. **—adj.** Also, **syl'lo·gis'ti·cal. 3.** of or pertaining to a syllogism. **4.** like or consisting of syllogisms. **—syl'-lo·gis'ti·cal·ly,** *adv.*

syl·lo·gize (sĭl'ə jīz'), *v.i., v.t.,* **-gized, -gizing.** to argue or reason by syllogisms. **—syl·lo·gi·za'tion,** *n.* **—syl'lo·giz'er,** *n.*

sylph (sĭlf), *n.* **1.** a slender, graceful, lightly moving woman or girl. **2.** one of a race of imaginary beings supposed (orig. in the system of Paracelsus) to inhabit the air. [t. NL: s. *sylphēs* (pl.), coined by Paracelsus] **—sylph'like', sylph'ish, sylph'y,** *adj.* **—Syn. 2.** SYLPH, SALAMANDER, UNDINE (NYMPH), GNOME were imaginary beings inhabiting the four elements once believed to make up the physical world. All except the GNOMES were feminine. SYLPHS dwelt in the air and were light, dainty, and airy beings. SALAMANDERS dwelt in fire: *"a salamander that ... lives in the midst of flames"* (Addison). UNDINES were water spirits: *by marrying a man, an undine could acquire a mortal soul.* (They were also called NYMPHS, though nymphs were ordinarily minor nature divinities who dwelt in woods, hills, and meadows as well as in waters.) GNOMES were little old men or dwarfs, dwelling in the earth: *"ugly enough to be king of the gnomes."* (Hawthorne).

sylph·id (sĭl'fĭd), *n.* **1.** a little or young sylph. **2.** a female sylph. [t. F: m. *sylphide,* der. *sylphe* SYLPH]

syl·va (sĭl'və), *n., pl.* **-vas, -vae** (-vē). silva.

Syl·va (sĭl'və), *n.* Carmen (kär'mən), 1843–1916, pen name of Elizabeth, Queen of Rumania.

syl·van (sĭl'vən), *adj.* **1.** of, pertaining to, or inhabiting the woods. **2.** consisting of or abounding in woods or trees; wooded; woody. **—n. 3.** a person dwelling in a woodland region. **4.** a fabled deity or spirit of the woods. Also, **silvan.** [t. L: m.s. *silvānus, sylvānus,* der. *silva* forest]

syl·van·ite (sĭl'və nīt'), *n.* a mineral, gold silver telluride, (AuAg)Te₂, silver-white with metallic luster, often occurring in crystals so arranged as to resemble written characters, also bladed, an ore of gold. [f. (*Tran*)*sylvan*(*ia*), where it was first found, + -ITE¹]

syl·vi·cul·ture (sĭl'və kŭl'chər), *n.* silviculture.

syl·vite (sĭl'vīt), *n.* a common mineral, potassium chloride, KCl, colorless to milky-white or red, occurring in crystals, usually cubes, and masses with cubic cleavage, bitter in taste, the most important source of potassium. Also, **syl·vin, syl·vine** (sĭl'vĭn). [f. *Sylv-* in NL *sal Sylvii* salt of *Sylvius*) + -ITE¹]

sym-, var. of **syn-,** before *b, p,* and *m,* as in *symphony.*

sym., **1.** symbol. **2.** *Chem.* symmetrical. **3.** symphony. **4.** symptom.

sym·bi·ont (sĭm'bĭ ŏnt', -bĭ-), *n.* *Biol.* an organism living in a state of symbiosis. [t. Gk.: s. *symbiōn,* ppr., living together]

sym·bi·o·sis (sĭm'bĭ ō'sĭs, -bī-), *n.* *Biol.* the living together of two species of organisms: a term usually restricted to cases in which the union of the two animals or plants is not disadvantageous to either, or is advantageous or necessary to both, as the case of the fungus and alga which together make up the lichen. [t. NL, t. Gk.] **—sym·bi·ot·ic** (sĭm'bĭ ŏt'ĭk, -bī-), **sym·bi·ot'i·cal,** *adj.* **—sym·bi·ot'i·cal·ly,** *adv.*

sym·bol (sĭm'bəl), *n., v.,* **-boled, -boling** or (*esp. Brit.*) **-bolled, -bolling. —n. 1.** something used or regarded as standing for or representing something else; a material object representing something immaterial; an emblem, token, or sign. **2.** a letter, figure, or other character or mark, or a combination of letters or the like, used to represent something: *the algebraic symbol, x; the chemical symbol, Au.* **—v.t. 3.** to symbolize. [t. LL: s. *symbolum,* t. Gk.: m. *sýmbolon* mark, token, ticket]

sym·bol·ic (sĭm bŏl'ĭk), *adj.* **1.** serving as a symbol of something (often fol. by *of*). **2.** of, pertaining to, or expressed by a symbol. **3.** characterized by or involving the use of symbols: *symbolic language.* **4.** (in semantics, esp. formerly) pertaining to a class of words which expressed only relations (contrasted with *presentative*). Also, **sym·bol'i·cal. —sym·bol'i·cal·ly,** *adv.* **—sym·bol'i·cal·ness,** *n.*

symbolical books, *Eccles.* the books of a religion containing the creeds, beliefs, etc.

sym·bol·ise (sĭm'bə līz'), *v.t., v.i.,* **-ised, -ising.** *Chiefly Brit.* symbolize.

sym·bol·ism (sĭm'bə lĭz'əm), *n.* **1.** the practice of representing things by symbols, or of investing things

with a symbolic meaning or character. **2.** a set or system of symbols. **3.** symbolic meaning or character. **4.** the principles and practice of symbolists in art or literature. **5.** a group of symbolist writers or artists.

sym·bol·ist (sĭm'bəl ĭst), *n.* **1.** one who uses symbols or symbolism. **2.** one versed in the study or interpretation of symbols. **3.** *Literature.* **a.** a writer who seeks to express or suggest ideas, emotions, etc., by means of symbols, as by the mention or introduction of things or the use of words and even word-sounds (as vowels) intended to convey a meaning, often with mystical or vague effect. **b.** a member of a group of French and Belgian poets characterized by such procedure (including Verlaine, Mallarmé, and Maeterlinck), which arose during the latter part of the 19th century. **4.** *Art.* an artist who seeks to symbolize or suggest particular ideas by the objects represented, the colors used, etc. **5.** (*often cap.*) *Eccles.* a person who rejects the doctrine of transubstantiation and views the Eucharist symbolically. **6.** a person who favors the use of symbols in religious services. **—sym'bol·is'tic,** *adj.*

sym·bol·ize (sĭm'bə līz'), *v.,* **-ized, -izing. —v.t. 1.** to be a symbol of; stand for, or represent, as a symbol does. **2.** to represent by a symbol or symbols. **3.** to regard or treat as symbolic. **—v.i. 4.** to use symbols. Also, *esp. Brit.,* **symbolise. —sym'bol·i·za'tion,** *n.*

sym·bol·o·gy (sĭm bŏl'ə jĭ), *n.* **1.** the study of symbols. **2.** the use of symbols; symbolism. [t. NL: m. *symbologia,* f. (by haplology) *symbolo-* (see SYMBOL) + *-logia* -LOGY]

sym·met·al·lism (sĭm mĕt'ə lĭz'əm), *n.* the use of two (or more) metals, as gold and silver, combined in assigned proportions as the monetary standard.

sym·met·ri·cal (sĭ mĕt'rə kəl), *adj.* **1.** characterized by or exhibiting symmetry; well-proportioned, as a body or whole; regular in form or arrangement of corresponding parts. **2.** *Logic, Math.* denoting a relation, such that if it is valid between *a* and *b* it is valid between *b* and *a:* as, *a* = *b* implies *b* = *a.* **3.** *Bot.* **a.** divisible into two similar parts by more than one plane passing through the center; actinomorphic. **b.** (of a flower) having the same number of parts in each whorl. **4.** *Chem.* **a.** having a structure which exhibits a regular repeated pattern of the component parts. **b.** denoting a benzene derivative in which three substitutions have occurred at alternate carbon atoms. **5.** *Pathol.* affecting corresponding parts simultaneously, as certain diseases. Also, **sym·met'ric. —sym·met'ri·cal·ly,** *adv.* **—sym·met'ri·cal·ness,** *n.*

sym·me·trize (sĭm'ə trīz'), *v.t.,* **-trized, -trizing.** to reduce to symmetry; make symmetrical. **—sym'me·tri·za'tion,** *n.*

sym·me·try (sĭm'ə trĭ), *n., pl.* **-tries. 1.** the correspondence, in size, form, and arrangement, of parts on opposite sides of a plane, line, or point; regularity of form or arrangement with reference to corresponding parts. **2.** the proper or due proportion of the parts of a body or whole to one another with regard to size and form; excellence of proportion. [t. LL: m.s. *symmetria,* t. Gk.]

Sym·onds (sĭm'ənz), *n.* John Addington, 1840–1893, British critic and poet.

Sy·mons (sī'mənz), *n.* Arthur, 1865–1945, British poet and critic.

sym·pa·thet·ic (sĭm'pə thĕt'ĭk), *adj.* **1.** characterized by, proceeding from, exhibiting, or feeling sympathy; sympathizing; compassionate. **2.** acting or affected by, of the nature of, or pertaining to a special natural sympathy or affinity; congenial. **3.** *Colloq.* looking with favor or liking upon (often fol. by *to* or *toward*): *he is sympathetic to the project.* **4.** *Anat., Physiol.* **a.** pertaining to that portion of the autonomic nervous system which is made up of a system of nerves and ganglia which arise from the thoracic and lumbar regions of the spinal cord, and which supply the walls of the vascular system and the various viscera and glands where they function in opposition to the parasympathetic system, as in dilating the pupil of the eye, etc. **b.** *Obs.* designating the autonomic nervous system in its entirety. **5.** *Physics.* (of vibrations, sounds, etc.) produced by vibrations conveyed through the air (or other medium) from a body already in vibration. Cf. **resonance** (def. 4). **—sym'pa·thet'i·cal·ly,** *adv.*

sympathetic ink, a fluid for producing writing that is invisible until brought out by heat, chemicals, etc.

sympathetic introspection, *Sociol.* See **introspection** (def. 2).

sympathetic strings, thin wire strings used in various obsolete musical instruments, and not played upon, but set into vibration by the plucked or bowed strings, adding to the sound a peculiar silvery timbre. **—sym'pa·thet'i·cal·ly,** *adv.*

sym·pa·thize (sĭm'pə thīz'), *v.i.,* **-thized, -thizing. 1.** to be in sympathy, or agreement of feeling; share in a feeling or feelings (often fol. by *with*). **2.** to feel a compassionate sympathy, as for suffering or trouble (often fol. by *with*). **3.** to express sympathy or condole (often fol. by *with*). **4.** to be in approving accord, as with a person, cause, etc.: *sympathize with a person's aims.* **5.** to agree, correspond, or accord. Also, *esp. Brit.,* **sym'pa·thise'.** [t. F: m. s. *sympathiser,* der. *sympathie* SYMPATHY. See -IZE] **—sym'pa·thiz'er,** *n.* **—sym'pa·thiz'ing·ly,** *adv.*

sym·pa·thy (sĭm′pə thĭ), *n.*, *pl.* **-thies.** 1. community of or agreement in feeling, as between persons or on the part of one person with respect to another. 2. the community of feeling naturally existing between persons of like tastes or opinion or of congenial dispositions. 3. the fact or the power of entering into the feelings of another, esp. in sorrow or trouble; fellow feeling, compassion, or commiseration. 4. (*pl.*) feelings or impulses of compassion. 5. favorable or approving accord: favor or approval. 6. agreement, consonance, or accord. 7. *Psychol.* a relation between persons whereby the condition of one induces a responsive condition in another. 8. *Physiol.*, *Pathol.* the relation between parts or organs whereby a condition, affection, or disorder of one part induces some effect in another. [t. L: m.s. *sympathia*, t. Gk.: m. *sympátheia*, lit., feeling with another]

sympathy strike, a strike by a body of workers, not because of grievances against their own employer, but by way of indorsing and aiding another body of workers who are on strike or have been locked out.

sym·pet·al·ous (sĭm pĕt′əl əs), *adj.* *Bot.* gamopetalous.

sym·phon·ic (sĭm fŏn′ĭk), *adj.* 1. *Music.* of, pertaining to, or having the character of a symphony. 2. of or pertaining to symphony, or harmony of sounds. 3. characterized by similarity of sound, as words.

symphonic poem, *Music.* a form of tone poem scored for a symphony orchestra, originated by Liszt in the mid-nineteenth century and developed esp. by Richard Strauss, in which a literary or pictorial "plot" is treated with considerable program detail.

sym·pho·ni·ous (sĭm fō′nĭ əs), *adj.* harmonious; in harmonious agreement or accord. **—sym·pho′ni·ous·ly,** *adv.*

sym·pho·ny (sĭm′fə nĭ), *n.*, *pl.* **-nies.** 1. *Music.* **a.** an elaborate instrumental composition in three or more movements, similar in form to a sonata but written for an orchestra, and usually of far grander proportions and more varied elements. **b.** an instrumental passage occurring in a vocal composition, or between vocal movements in a composition. **c.** an instrumental piece, often in several movements, forming the overture to an opera or the like. 2. anything characterized by a harmonious combination of elements and esp. an effective combination of colors. 3. *Archaic or Poetic.* harmony of sounds. 4. *Archaic or Poetic.* harmony in general. [ME *symphonie*, t. L: m. *symphōnia*, t. Gk.: lit., a sounding together]

symphony orchestra, a large orchestra composed of wind, string, and percussion instruments and designed to perform symphonic compositions.

sym·phys·i·al (sĭm fĭz′Ɏ əl), *adj.* referring to a symphysis. Also, **sym·phys/e·al.**

sym·phy·sis (sĭm′fə sĭs), *n.*, *pl.* **-ses** (-sēz′). 1. *Anat.*, *Zool.* **a.** the growing together, or the fixed or nearly fixed union, of bones, as that of the two halves of the lower jaw in man, or of the pubic bones in the anterior part of the pelvic girdle. **b.** a line of junction or articulation so formed. 2. *Bot.* a coalescence or growing together of parts. [NL, t. Gk.]

sym·po·di·um (sĭm pō′dɎ əm), *n.*, *pl.* **-dia** (-dɎ ə), *Bot.* an axis or stem which simulates a simple stem but is made up of the bases of a number of axes which arise successively as branches one from another, as in the grapevine; a pseudaxis. Cf. **mono-podium.** [NL. See SYM-, PODIUM]

Sympodium of branch of linden, genus Tilia

sym·po·si·ac (sĭm pō′zɎ ăk′), *adj.* 1. of, pertaining to, or suitable for a symposium. **—n.** 2. a symposium.

sym·po·si·arch (sĭm pō′zɎ ärk′), *n.* 1. the president, director, or master of a symposium. 2. the toastmaster. [t. Gk.: s. *symposíarchos*]

sym·po·si·um (sĭm pō′zɎ əm), *n.*, *pl.* **-siums, -sia** (-zɎ ə). 1. a meeting or conference for discussion of some subject. 2. a collection of opinions expressed, or articles contributed, by several persons on a given subject or topic. 3. an account of such a meeting or of the conversation at it. 4. (among the ancient Greeks) a convivial meeting, usually following a dinner, for drinking, conversation, and intellectual entertainment. [t. L, t. Gk.: m. *sympósion* (def. 4)]

symp·tom (sĭmp′təm), *n.* 1. any phenomenon or circumstance accompanying something and serving as evidence of it; a sign or indication of something. 2. *Pathol.* a phenomenon which arises from and accompanies a particular disease or disorder and serves as an indication of it. [t. LL: m. *symptōma*, t. Gk.; r. ME *synthoma*, t. ML] **—symp′tom·less,** *adj.*

symp·to·mat·ic (sĭmp′tə măt′Ɏk), *adj.* 1. pertaining to a symptom or symptoms. 2. of the nature of or constituting a symptom; indicative (*of*). 3. according to symptoms: *a symptomatic classification of disease.* Also, **symp′to·mat/i·cal.** **—symp′to·mat/i·cal·ly,** *adv.*

symp·tom·a·tol·o·gy (sĭmp′təm ə tŏl′ə jĭ), *n.* that branch of medical science which deals with symptoms. [t. NL: m.s. *symptōmatologia.* See SYMPTOM, -LOGY]

syn-, a prefix in learned words having the same function as co- (def. 1), as in *synthesis, synoptic.* Also, **sy-, syl-, sym-, sys-.** [t. Gk., comb. form of *sýn,* prep., with, and adv., together]

syn., 1. synonym. 2. synonymous. 3. synonymy.

syn·aer·e·sis (sĭ nĕr′ə sĭs), *n. Gram.* 1. the contraction of two syllables or two vowels into one; esp. the contraction of two vowels so as to form a diphthong (opp. to *dieresis*). 2. synizesis. Also, **syneresis.** [t. LL, t. Gk.: m. *synairesis*, lit., a taking together]

syn·aes·the·sia (sĭn′əs thē′zhə, -zhɎ ə), *n.* synesthesia.

syn·a·gogue (sĭn′ə gŏg′, -gôg′), *n.* 1. an assembly or congregation of the Jews for the purposes of religious instruction and worship apart from the service of the temple, constituting, since the destruction of the temple and the dispersion of the Jews, the customary Jewish form of worship. 2. the religious organization of the Jews as typified by this assembly. 3. the building or place of this assembly. [ME *sinagoge*, t. LL: m. *synagōga*, t. Gk.: m. *synagōgē* meeting, assembly] **—syn·a·gog′i·cal** (sĭn′ə gŏj′ə kəl), **syn·a·gog·al** (sĭn′ə gŏg′əl, -gŏg′-əl), *adj.*

syn·a·loe·pha (sĭn′ə lē′fə), *n.* the blending of two successive vowels into one. Also, **syn/a·le/pha, syn·a·le·phe** (sĭn′ə lē′fē). [t. L, t. Gk.: m. *synaloiphē*]

syn·apse (sĭ′năps′), *n. Physiol.* the region of contact between processes of two or more nerve cells, across which an impulse passes. [t. Gk.: m. *sýnapsis* connection]

syn·ap·sis (sĭ năp′sĭs), *n.*, *pl.* **-ses** (-sēz) 1. *Biol.* the conjugation of homologous chromosomes, one from each parent, during early meiosis. 2. *Physiol.* synapse. [NL, t. Gk.] **—syn·ap·tic** (sĭ năp′tĭk), *adj.*

syn·ar·thro·di·a (sĭn′är thrō′dɎ ə), *n.*, *pl.* **-diae** (-dɎ ē′). synarthrosis. [NL] **—syn/ar·thro/di·al,** *adj.*

syn·ar·thro·sis (sĭn′är thrō′sĭs), *n.*, *pl.* **-ses** (-sēz). *Anat.* immovable articulation; a fixed or immovable joint; a suture. [NL, t. Gk.]

syn·carp (sĭn′kärp), *n. Bot.* 1. an aggregate fruit. 2. a collective fruit. [t. NL: m.s. *syncarpium*, f. Gk.: *syn-* SYN- + m. *karpíon*, dim. of *karpós* fruit]

syn·car·pous (sĭn kär′pəs), *adj. Bot.* 1. of the nature of or pertaining to a syncarp. 2. composed of or having united carpels.

syn·chro·mesh (sĭng′krə mĕsh′), *Auto.* **—adj.** 1. of, pertaining to or designating a synchronized shift or shifting. **—n.** 2. a synchronized shift. 3. any gear in such a shift. [f. SYNCHRO(NOUS) + MESH]

syn·chro·nal (sĭng′krə nal), *adj.* synchronous. Also, **syn·chron·ic** (sĭn krŏn′Ɏk, sĭng-), **syn·chron′i·cal.**

syn·chro·nism (sĭng′krə nĭz′əm), *n.* 1. coincidence in time; contemporaneousness; simultaneousness. 2. the arrangement or treatment of synchronous things or events in conjunction, as in a history. 3. a tabular arrangement of historical events or personages, grouped together according to their dates. 4. *Physics.*, *Elect.*, *etc.* state of being synchronous. **—syn′chro·nis/tic, syn/chro·nis/ti·cal,** *adj.* **—syn/chro·nis/ti·cal·ly,** *adv.*

syn·chro·nize (sĭng′krə nĭz′), *v.*, **-nized, -nizing.** **—v.i.** 1. to occur at the same time, or coincide or agree in time. 2. to go on at the same rate and exactly together; recur together. **—v.t.** 3. to cause to indicate the same time, as one timepiece with another. 4. to cause to go on at the same rate and exactly together. 5. to cause to agree in time of occurrence; assign to the same time or period, as in a history. [t. Gk.: m.s. *synchronízein* be contemporary with] **—syn/chro·ni·za/tion,** *n.* **—syn/-chro·niz/er,** *n.*

synchronized shifting, a type of automotive transmission that facilitates gear shifting by automatically bringing gears to be meshed into synchronous (same rate of speed) rotation.

syn·chron·o·scope (sĭn krŏn′ə skōp′), *n. Elect.* an apparatus for indicating synchronism between two alternating-current machines and also for showing their relative speeds.

syn·chro·nous (sĭng′krə nəs), *adj.* 1. occurring at the same time; coinciding in time; contemporaneous; simultaneous. 2. going on at the same rate and exactly together; recurring together. 3. *Physics.*, *Elect.*, *etc.* having the same frequency and no phase difference. [t. LL: m. *synchronus*, t. Gk.: m. *sýnchronos*] **—syn/-chro·nous·ly,** *adv.* **—syn/chro·nous·ness,** *n.*

synchronous converter, *Elect.* a synchronous machine which converts alternating current to direct current, or vice versa. The armature winding is connected to collector rings and commutator.

synchronous machine, *Elect.* an alternating-current machine in which the average speed of normal operation is exactly proportional to the frequency of the system to which it is connected.

synchronous speed, *Elect.* the speed at which an alternating-current machine must operate to generate electromotive force at a given frequency.

syn·chro·tron (sĭng′krə trŏn′), *n. Physics.* a modified cyclotron for the acceleration of electrons, using a magnetic field increasing simultaneously with high-frequency electrical acceleration.

syn·chro unit (sĭng′krō), *Elect.* a type of alternating-current motor designed to maintain continuously, at some remote location, the same rotational angle that may be imposed by force upon the electrically connected rotating element of a similar motor.

syn·clas·tic (sĭn klăs′tĭk), *adj.* noting or pertaining to a point of a surface (such as a sphere) at which the two principal curvatures have the same sign (opp. to *anti-*

clastic. [f. SYN- + m.s. Gk. *klastós* broken + -IC]

syn·cli·nal (sĭn klī′nəl, sĭng′klĭ nəl), *adj.* **1.** sloping downward in opposite directions so as to meet in a common point or line. **2.** *Geol.* **a.** inclining upward on both sides from a median line or axis, as a downward fold of rock strata. **b.** pertaining to such a fold. —*n.* **3.** syncline. [f. m.s. Gk. *synklínein* lean together + -AL[1]]

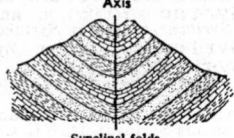

Synclinal folds

syn·cline (sĭng′klīn, sĭn′-), *n. Geol.* a synclinal fold.

syn·co·pate (sĭng′kə pāt′, sĭn′-), *v.t.*, **-pated, -pating. 1.** *Music.* **a.** to place (the accents) on beats which are normally unaccented. **b.** to employ tones so affected in (a passage, piece, etc.). **2.** *Gram.* to contract (a word) by omitting one or more sounds from the middle, as in reducing *Gloucester* to *Gloster.* [t. LL: m.s. *syncopātus,* pp., cut short, der. *syncopē* SYNCOPE] —**syn′co·pa′tor,** *n.*

syn·co·pa·tion (sĭng′kə pā′shən, sĭn′-), *n.* **1.** *Music.* a shifting of the normal accent, usually by stressing normally unaccented beats. **2.** *Gram.* a syncope.

Syncopation

syn·co·pe (sĭng′kə pĭ, -pē′, sĭn′-), *n.* **1.** *Gram.* the contraction of a word by omitting one or more sounds from the middle, as in the reduction of *never* to *ne'er.* **2.** *Pathol.* brief loss of consciousness associated with transient cerebral anemia, as in heart block, sudden lowering of the blood pressure, etc.; fainting. [ME, t. L, t. Gk.: m. *synkopě* a cutting up] —**syn·cop·ic** (sĭn kŏp′ĭk), *adj.*

syn·cre·tism (sĭng′krə tĭz′əm, sĭn′-), *n.* **1.** the attempted reconciliation or union of different or opposing principles, practices, or parties, as in philosophy or religion. **2.** (in linguistic change) the merging into one of two or more former categories, e.g. in substandard English *we, you,* and *they was* is used like *I* or *he was;* in standard English this syncretism does not exist, *were* being used with the second person singular *you.* [t. NL: s. *syncrētismus,* t. Gk.: m. *synkrētismós*] —**syn·cret·ic** (sĭn krĕt′ĭk), **syn·cre·tis·tic** (sĭng′krə tĭs′tĭk, sĭn′-), **syn′cre·tis′ti·cal,** *adj.*

syn·cre·tize (sĭng′krə tīz′, sĭn′-), *v.t., v.i.,* **-tized, -tizing.** to attempt to combine or unite, as different or opposing principles, parties, etc. [t. NL: m.s. *syncretizāre,* t. Gk.: m. *synkrētizein*]

syn·dac·tyl (sĭn dăk′tĭl), *adj.* **1.** Also, **syn·dac·tyle.** having certain digits more or less united, as the kingfisher and the kangaroo, or as a monstrosity of the human species. —*n.* **2.** a syndactyl animal. [f. SYN- + m.s. Gk. *-dáktylos* fingered, toed] —**syn·dac·tyl·ism** (sĭn dăk′tə lĭz′əm), *n.*

Syndactyl foot of kingfisher

syn·des·mo·sis (sĭn′dĕs mō′sĭs), *n., pl.* **-ses** (-sēz). *Anat.* a connection of bones by ligaments, fasciae, or membranes other than in a joint. [NL, f. Gk.: s. *syn-desmos* ligament + -ōsis -OSIS] —**syn·des·mot·ic** (sĭn′dĕs mŏt′ĭk), *adj.*

syn·det·ic (sĭn dĕt′ĭk), *adj.* **1.** serving to unite or connect; connective; copulative. **2.** conjunctive (def. 3c). Also, **syn·det·i·cal.** [t. Gk.: m.s. *syndetikós*] —**syn·det′i·cal·ly,** *adv.*

syn·dic (sĭn′dĭk), *n.* **1.** a person chosen to represent and transact business for a corporation or the like, as a university. **2.** a civil magistrate having different powers in different countries. [t. LL: s. *syndicus* advocate, delegate, t. Gk.: m. *sýndikos* defendant's advocate]

syn·di·cal (sĭn′də kəl), *adj.* **1.** noting or pertaining to a union of persons engaged in a particular trade. **2.** of or pertaining to syndicalism.

syn·di·cal·ism (sĭn′də kə lĭz′əm), *n.* a form or development of trade unionism, originating in France, which aims at the possession of the means of production and distribution, and ultimately at the control of society, by the federated bodies of industrial workers, and which seeks to realize its purposes through general strikes, or terrorism, sabotage, violence, or other criminal means. —**syn′di·cal·ist,** *adj., n.* —**syn′di·cal·ist′ic,** *adj.*

syn·di·cate (*n.* sĭn′də kĭt; *v.* sĭn′dĭ kāt′), *n., v.,* **-cated, -cating.** —*n.* **1.** a combination of bankers or capitalists formed for the purpose of carrying out some project requiring large resources of capital, as the underwriting of an issue of stock or bonds. **2.** any agency which buys and supplies articles, stories, etc., for simultaneous publication in a number of newspapers or other periodicals in different places. **3.** a council or body of syndics. **4.** a local organization of employers or employees in Fascist Italy. —*v.t.* **5.** to combine into a syndicate. **6.** to publish simultaneously, or supply for simultaneous publication, in a number of newspapers or other periodicals in different places. [t. F: m. *syndicat,* der. *syndic* SYNDIC] —**syn′di·ca′tion,** *n.*

syn·drome (sĭn′drōm, sĭn′drə mē′), *n. Pathol., Psychiatry.* the pattern of symptoms in a disease or the like; a number of characteristic symptoms occurring together. [t. NL, t. Gk.: a running together] —**syn·drom·ic** (sĭn drŏm′ĭk), *adj.*

syne (sīn), *adv., prep., conj. Scot.* since.

syn·ec·do·che (sĭ nĕk′də kĭ), *n. Rhet.* a figure of speech by which a part is put for the whole or the whole for a part, the special for the general or the general for the special, as in "a fleet of ten *sail*" (for *ships*), or "a *Croesus*" (for a *rich man*). [t. LL, t. Gk.: m. *synekdochě;* r. ME *synodoche,* t. ML] —**syn·ec·doch·ic** (sĭn′ĕk dŏk′ĭk), **syn′ec·doch/i·cal,** *adj.*

syn·e·cious (sĭ nē′shəs), *adj.* synoicous.

syn·e·col·o·gy (sĭn′ə kŏl′ə jĭ), *n. Ecol.* that branch of autecology which deals with the relation between the species or group and its environment. Cf. **autecology.**

syn·e·re·sis (sĭ nĕr′ə sĭs), *n.* synaeresis.

syn·er·get·ic (sĭn′ər jĕt′ĭk), *adj.* working together; coöperative.

syn·er·gism (sĭn′ər jĭz′əm, sĭ nûr′-), *n. Theol.* the doctrine that the human will coöperates with the divine spirit in the work of regeneration.

syn·er·gist (sĭn′ər jĭst, sĭ nûr′jĭst), *n.* **1.** *Physiol., Med.* a bodily organ, a medicine, etc., that coöperates with another or others; an adjuvant. **2.** *Theol.* one who holds the doctrine of synergism.

syn·er·gis·tic (sĭn′ər jĭs′tĭk), *adj.* working together; synergetic.

syn·er·gy (sĭn′ər jĭ), *n., pl.* **-gies. 1.** combined action. **2.** the coöperative action of two or more bodily organs or the like. **3.** the coöperative action of two or more stimuli or drugs. [t. NL: m.s. *synergia,* t. Gk.] —**syn·er·gic** (sĭ nûr′jĭk), *adj.*

syn·e·sis (sĭn′ə sĭs), *n. Gram.* a construction having a feature which is syntactically extraordinary, e.g., the use of a third-person pronoun with no apparent antecedent, as *it* in *it is going to rain.* [NL, t. Gk.: comprehension]

syn·es·the·sia (sĭn′əs thē′zhə, -zhĭ′ə), *n.* a sensation produced in one modality when a stimulus is applied to another modality, as when the hearing of a certain sound induces the visualization of a certain color. Also, **synaesthesia.**

syn·ga·my (sĭng′gə mĭ), *n. Biol.* union of gametes, as in fertilization or conjugation; sexual reproduction. —**syn·gam·ic** (sĭn găm′ĭk), **syn·ga·mous** (sĭng′gə məs), *adj.*

Synge (sĭng), *n.* **John Millington,** 1871–1909, Irish dramatist.

syn·gen·e·sis (sĭn jĕn′ə sĭs), *n. Biol.* sexual reproduction. —**syn·ge·net·ic** (sĭn′jə nĕt′ĭk), *adj.*

syn·i·ze·sis (sĭn′ə zē′sĭs), *n. Gram.* the combination into one syllable of two vowels (or of a vowel and a diphthong) that do not form a diphthong. [t. L, t. Gk.]

syn·od (sĭn′əd), *n.* **1.** an assembly of ecclesiastics or other church delegates duly convoked, pursuant to the law of the church, for the discussion and decision of ecclesiastical affairs; an ecclesiastical council. **2.** any council. [ME, t. LL: s. *synodus,* t. Gk.: m. *sýnodos* assembly] —**syn′od·al,** *adj.*

syn·od·ic (sĭ nŏd′ĭk), *adj. Astron.* pertaining to a conjunction, or to two successive conjunctions of the same bodies: *synodic month.* Also, **syn·od·i·cal.** —**syn·od′i·cal·ly,** *adv.*

syn·oi·cous (sĭ noi′kəs), *adj. Bot.* having male and female flowers on one head, as in many composite plants. Also, **synecious, syn·oe·cious** (sĭ nē′shəs). [f. m.s. Gk. *synoikía* a living together + -ous]

syn·o·nym (sĭn′ə nĭm), *n.* **1.** a word having the same, or nearly the same, meaning as another in the language, e.g., *joyful, elated, glad.* **2.** a word or expression accepted as another name for something, e.g., *Arcadia* for *pastoral simplicity.* **3.** *Bot., Zool.* a rejected scientific name, other than a homonym. [ME, t. LL: s. *synōnymum,* t. Gk.: m. *synōnymon,* prop. neut. of *synōnymos* synonymous] —**syn′o·nym′ic, syn′o·nym/i·cal,** *adj.* —**syn·o·nym·i·ty** (sĭn′ə nĭm′ĭ tĭ), *n.*

syn·on·y·mize (sĭ nŏn′ə mīz′), *v.t.,* **-mized, -mizing.** to give synonyms for (a word, name, etc.); furnish with synonyms.

syn·on·y·mous (sĭ nŏn′ə məs), *adj.* having the character of synonyms or a synonym; equivalent in meaning; expressing or implying the same idea. [t. ML: m. *synōnymus,* t. Gk.: m. *synōnymos*] —**syn·on′y·mous·ly,** *adv.*

syn·on·y·my (sĭ nŏn′ə mĭ), *n., pl.* **-mies. 1.** the character of being synonymous; equivalence in meaning. **2.** the study of synonyms. **3.** a set, list, or system of synonyms. **4.** *Bot. and Zool.* **a.** a list of the scientific names for a particular species or other group, or for various species, etc., with discriminations or explanatory matter. **b.** these names collectively, whether listed or not. [t. LL: m.s. *synōnymia,* t. Gk.]

synop., synopsis.

syn·op·sis (sĭ nŏp′sĭs), *n., pl.* **-ses** (-sēz). a brief or condensed statement giving a general view of some subject; a compendium of heads or short paragraphs giving a view of the whole. [t. LL, t. Gk.: general view] —**Syn.** See **summary.**

syn·op·tic (sĭ nŏp′tĭk), *adj.* Also, **syn·op′ti·cal. 1.** pertaining to or constituting a synopsis; affording or taking a general view of the whole or of the principal parts of a subject. **2.** (*often cap.*) taking a common view (applied to the first three Gospels, Matthew, Mark, and Luke, from their similarity in contents, order, and statement). **3.** (*often cap.*) pertaining to the synoptic Gospels. —*n.* **4.** one of the synoptic Gospels or their authors. [t. NL: s. *synopticus,* t. Gk.: m. *synoptikós*] —**syn·op′ti·cal·ly,** *adv.*

ăct, āble, dâre, ärt; ĕbb, ēqual; ĭf, īce; hŏt, ōver, ôrder, oil, bŏŏk, ōōze, out; ŭp, ūse, ûrge; ə = a in alone; ch, chief; g, give; ng, ring; sh, shoe; th, thin; ŧħ, that; zh, vision. See the full key on inside cover.

synoptic chart, a chart showing the distribution of meteorological conditions over a wide region at a given moment.

synoptic meteorology, a branch of meteorology analyzing data taken simultaneously over a large area, for the purpose of weather forecasting.

syn·o·vi·a (sǐ nō'vǐ ə), *n. Physiol.* a lubricating liquid resembling the white of an egg, secreted by certain membranes, as those of the joints. [NL; coined by Paracelsus] —**syn·o'vi·al,** *adj.*

syn·o·vi·tis (sǐn'ə vī'tǐs), *n. Pathol.* inflammation of a synovial membrane. [f. SYNOV(IA) + -ITIS]

syn·sep·al·ous (sǐn sěp'əl əs), *adj. Bot.* gamosepalous.

syn·tac·ti·cal (sǐn tǎk'tə kəl), *adj.* of or pertaining to syntax. Also, **syn·tac'tic.** —**syn·tac'ti·cal·ly,** *adv.*

syn·tax (sǐn'tǎks), *n.* 1. *Gram.* **a.** the patterns of formation of sentences and phrases from words in a particular language. **b.** the study and description thereof. See **morphology** (def. 3). 2. *Logic.* **a.** that branch of modern logic which studies the various kinds of signs that occur in a system and the possible arrangements of those signs, complete abstraction being made of the meaning of the signs. **b.** the outcome of such a study when directed upon a specified language. 3. *Obs.* a system. [t. LL: m. *syntaxis,* t. Gk.: arrangement]

syn·the·sis (sǐn'thə sǐs), *n., pl.* **-ses** (-sēz'). 1. the combination of parts or elements, as material substances or objects of thought, into a complex whole (opposed to *analysis*). 2. a complex whole made up of parts or elements combined. 3. *Chem.* the forming or building up of a more complex substance or compound by the union of elements or the combination of simpler compounds or radicals. 4. a process of reasoning which consists in advancing in a direct manner from principles established or assumed, and propositions already provided, to the conclusion. [t. L, t. Gk.:lit., a taking together] —**syn'the·sist,** *n.*

syn·the·size (sǐn'thə sīz'), *v.t.,* **-sized, -sizing.** 1. to make up by combining parts or elements. 2. to combine into a complex whole. 3. to treat synthetically.

syn·thet·ic (sǐn thět'ǐk), *adj.* 1. of, pertaining to, proceeding by, or involving synthesis (opposed to *analytic*). 2. *Chem.* noting or pertaining to compounds formed by chemical reaction in a laboratory, as opposed to those of natural origin. 3. (of languages) characterized by the use of affixes (bound forms) to express relationships between words, e.g., Latin, as opposed to *analytic,* e.g., English. Also, **syn·thet'i·cal.** —*n.* 4. something made by a synthetic (chemical) process. [t. NL: s. *syntheticus,* t. Gk.: m. *synthetikós*] —**syn·thet'i·cal·ly,** *adv.*

synthetic geometry, elementary geometry as distinct from analytic geometry.

synthetic philosophy, the philosophy of Herbert Spencer (1820–1903), as bringing the various sciences into a systematic whole.

syn·the·tize (sǐn'thə tīz'), *v.t.,* **-tized, -tizing.** synthesize.

syn·ton·ic (sǐn tŏn'ǐk), *adj. Elect.* adjusted to oscillations of the same or a particular frequency. Also, **syn·ton'i·cal.** —**syn·ton'i·cal·ly,** *adv.*

syn·to·nize (sǐn'tə nīz'), *v.t.,* **-nized, -nizing.** to render syntonic; to tune to the same frequency. [f. SYNTON(Y) + -IZE] —**syn'to·ni·za'tion,** *n.*

syn·to·ny (sǐn'tə nǐ), *n. Elect.* the state or condition of being syntonic. [t. Gk.: m.s. *syntonía* tension]

syph·i·lis (sǐf'ə lǐs), *n. Pathol.* a chronic, infectious venereal disease, caused by the microörganism *Spirochaeta pallida,* or *Treponema pallidum* (see **spirochete**), and communicated by contact or heredity, usually having three stages, the first (**primary syphilis**), in which a hard chancre forms at the point of inoculation, the second (**secondary syphilis**), characterized by skin affections and constitutional disturbances, and the third (**tertiary syphilis**), characterized by affections of the bones, muscles, viscera, nervous system, etc. [t. NL, der. *Syphilus,* name of shepherd suffering from the disease in L poem of 16th century by Fracastorius]

syph·i·lit·ic (sǐf'ə lǐt'ǐk), *adj.* 1. pertaining to or affected with syphilis. —*n.* 2. one affected with syphilis.

syph·i·loid (sǐf'ə loid'), *adj.* resembling syphilis.

syph·i·lol·o·gy (sǐf'ə lŏl'ə jǐ), *n.* the study or science of syphilis. —**syph'i·lol'o·gist,** *n.*

sy·phon (sī'fən), *n., v.t., v.i.* siphon.

syr., *Pharm.* syrup.

Syr·a·cuse (sǐr'ə kūs'; *for 1 also* sěr'-), *n.* 1. a city in central New York. 216,038 (1960). 2. Italian, **Siracusa.** a seaport in SE Sicily: the ancient city here was founded by the Carthaginians, 734 B.C.; battles, 413 B.C., 212 B.C. 74,000 (est. 1954).

Syr Dar·ya (sǐr där'yä), a river in the SW Soviet Union in Asia, flowing from the Tien Shan Mountains NW to the Aral Sea. ab. 1300 mi. Ancient, **Jaxartes.**

Syr·ette (sǐ rět'), *n. Trademark.* a collapsible tube with an attached hypodermic needle for the subcutaneous administration of medication. [f. SYR(INGE) + -ETTE]

Syr·i·a (sǐr'ǐ ə), *n.* 1. a republic in W Asia at the E end of the Mediterranean. 4,555,267 (1960) 71,227 sq. mi. *Cap.:* Damascus. Official name, **Syrian Arab Republic.** 2. a territory mandated to France in 1922, including the present republics of Syria and Lebanon (Latakia and Djebel Druze were incorporated into Syria, 1942): the French mandatory powers were

nominally terminated as of Jan. 1, 1944. 3. an ancient country in W Asia, including what is now Syria, Lebanon, Israel, and adjacent areas: a part of the Roman Empire, 64 B.C.- A.D. 636. —**Syr·i·an,** *adj., n.*

Syr·i·ac (sǐr'ǐ ǎk'), *n.* an Aramaic language. [t. L: s. *Syriacus,* t. Gk.: m. *Syriakós*]

Syr·i·en (sǐr'ǐ ən), *n.* Zyrian.

sy·rin·ga (sə rǐng'gə), *n.* 1. any of the shrubs constituting the genus *Philadelphus,* including species cultivated for ornament, esp. *P. coronarius,* a familiar cultivated species with fragrant white flowers. 2. a lilac (genus *Syringa*). [t. NL, t. Gk.: m. *sȳrinx* pipe]

syr·inge (sǐr'ǐnj, sǐ rǐnj'), *n., v.,* **-inged, -inging.** —*n.* 1. *Med.* a small device consisting of a glass, metal, or hard rubber tube, narrowed at its outlet, and fitted with either a piston or a rubber bulb for drawing in a quantity of fluid and ejecting it in a stream, used for cleaning wounds, injecting fluids into the body, etc. 2. any similar device for pumping and spraying liquids through a small aperture. —*v.t.* 3. to cleanse, wash, inject, etc., by means of a syringe. [back formation from *syringes,* t. Gk., pl. of *sȳrinx* pipe; r. late ME *siryng,* t. ML]

sy·rin·ge·al (sə rǐn'jǐ əl), *adj. Ornith.* of, pertaining to, or connected with the syrinx.

sy·rin·go·my·e·li·a (sə rǐng'gō mǐ ē'lǐ ə), *n. Med.* a disease of the spinal cord in which the nerve tissue is replaced by a cavity filled with fluid. [NL, f. *syringo-* (comb. form of Gk. *sȳrinx* pipe) + s. Gk. *myelós* marrow (of the spinal cord) + *-ia* -IA]

syr·inx (sǐr'ǐngks), *n., pl.* **syringes** (sə rǐn'jēz), **syrinxes.** 1. *Anat.* the Eustachian tube. 2. *Ornith.* the vocal organ of birds, situated at or near the bifurcation of the trachea into the bronchi. 3. (*cap.*) a nymph who was pursued by Pan and, to escape him, was turned into a reed, of which he made the Panpipe. 4. Panpipe. [t. L, t. Gk.]

syr·phid (sûr'fǐd), *n.* any of the *Syrphidae,* a family of dipterous insects or flies, some of which are beneficial, their larvae feeding on plant lice. Also, **syr·phi·an** (sûr'fǐ ən). [f. s. Gk. *sýrphos* gnat + -ID²]

syr·up (sǐr'əp, sûr'-), *n.* 1. any of various sweet, more or less viscid liquids, as: preparations of water or fruit juices boiled with sugar; the solutions of sugar used in pharmacy; the liquid yielding, or that separated from, crystallized sugar in the process of refining; and various liquids prepared for table use from molasses, glucose, etc. —*v.t.* 2. to bring to the form or consistency of syrup. 3. to cover, fill, or sweeten with syrup. Also, **sirup.** [ME *syrope,* t. OF: m. *sirop,* ult. t. Ar.: m. *sharab* beverage] —**syr'up·like',** *adj.* —**syr'up·y,** *adj.*

Syr·ye·ni·an (sǐr yě'nǐ ən), *n.* Zyrian.

sys-, var. of syn-, before *s,* as in *syssarcosis.*

sys·sar·co·sis (sǐs'är kō'sǐs), *n. Anat.* the union of bones by muscle. [NL, t. Gk.]

Syst., system.

sys·tal·tic (sǐs tǎl'tǐk), *adj. Physiol.* 1. rhythmically contracting; of the nature of contraction. 2. characterized by alternate contraction (systole) and dilatation (diastole), as the action of the heart. [t. LL: s. *systalticus,* t. Gk.: m. *systaltikós* contractile]

sys·tem (sǐs'təm), *n.* 1. an assemblage or combination of things or parts forming a complex or unitary whole: *a mountain system, a railroad system.* 2. any assemblage or set of correlated members: *a system of currency, a system of shorthand characters.* 3. an ordered and comprehensive assemblage of facts, principles, doctrines, or the like in a particular field of knowledge or thought: *a system of philosophy.* 4. a coördinated body of methods, or a complex scheme or plan of procedure: *a system of government, a penal system.* 5. any formulated, regular, or special method or plan of procedure: *a system of marking, numbering, or measuring.* 6. due method, or orderly manner of arrangement or procedure: *have system in one's work.* 7. a number of heavenly bodies associated and acting together according to certain natural laws: *the solar system.* 8. the world or universe. 9. *Astron.* a hypothesis or theory of the disposition and arrangements of the heavenly bodies by which their phenomena, motions, changes, etc., are explained: *the Ptolemaic system, the Copernican system.* 10. *Biol.* **a.** an assemblage of parts of organs of the same or similar tissues, or concerned with the same function: *the nervous system, the digestive system.* **b.** the entire human or animal body: *to expel poison from the system.* 11. a method or scheme of classification: *the Linnean system of plants.* 12. *Geol.* a major division of rocks comprising sedimentary deposits and igneous masses formed during a geological period. 13. *Phys. Chem.* **a.** any substance or group of substances considered apart from the surroundings. **b.** a sample of matter consisting of one or more components in equilibrium in one or more phases. A system is called binary if containing two components, ternary, if containing three, etc. [t. LL: m. *systēma,* t. Gk.: organized whole] —**sys'tem·less,** *adj.*

sys·tem·at·ic (sǐs'tə mǎt'ǐk), *adj.* 1. having, showing, or involving a system, method, or plan: *a systematic course of reading, systematic efforts.* 2. characterized by system or method; methodical: *a systematic person,*

Syrinx of raven

A. Modified tracheal and bronchial rings forming syrinx; B. Trachea; C. Right and left bronchi systematic habits. **3.** arranged in or comprising an ordered system: *systematic theology.* **4.** concerned with classification: *systematic botany.* **5.** pertaining to, based on, or in accordance with a system of classification: *the systematic names of plants.* Also, **sys'tem·at'i·cal.** —**sys'tem·at'i·cal·ly,** *adv.* —**Syn. 2.** See **orderly.**

sys·tem·at·ics (sĭs'tə măt'ĭks), *n.* the study of systems, or of classification.

sys·tem·a·tism (sĭs'təm ə tĭz'əm), *n.* **1.** the practice of systematizing. **2.** adherence to system.

sys·tem·a·tist (sĭs'təm ə tĭst), *n.* **1.** one who constructs a system. **2.** a naturalist engaged in classification. **3.** one who adheres to system.

sys·tem·a·tize (sĭs'təm ə tīz'), *v.t.,* **-tized, -tizing.** to arrange in or according to a system; reduce to a system; make systematic. Also, *esp. Brit.,* **sys'tem·a·tise'.** —**sys'tem·a·ti·za'tion,** *n.* —**sys'tem·a·tiz'er,** *n.*

sys·tem·a·tol·o·gy (sĭs'təm ə tŏl'ə jĭ), *n.* the science of systems or their formation.

sys·tem·ic (sĭs tĕm'ĭk), *adj.* **1.** of or pertaining to a system. **2.** *Physiol. and Pathol.* **a.** pertaining to or affecting the entire bodily system, or the body as a whole. **b.** pertaining to a particular system of parts or organs of the body. —**sys·tem'i·cal·ly,** *adv.*

sys·tem·ize (sĭs'tə mīz'), *v.t.,* **-ized, -izing.** systematize. —**sys'tem·i·za'tion,** *n.* —**sys'tem·iz'er,** *n.*

sys·to·le (sĭs'tə lē', -lĭ), *n.* **1.** *Physiol. etc.* the normal rhythmical contraction of the heart, esp. that of the ventricles, which drives the blood into the aorta and the pulmonary artery. Cf. **diastole. 2.** *Anc. Pros.* the shortening of a syllable regularly long. [t. NL, t. Gk.: contraction] —**sys·tol·ic** (sĭs tŏl'ĭk), *adj.*

syz·y·gy (sĭz'ə jĭ), *n., pl.* **-gies. 1.** *Astron.* the conjunction or opposition of two heavenly bodies; a point in the orbit of a body, as the moon, at which it is in conjunction with or in opposition to the sun. **2.** *Anc. Pros.* a group or combination of two feet (by some restricted to a combination of two feet of different kinds). [t. LL: m.s. *syzygia,* t. Gk.: conjunction] —**sy·zyg·i·al** (sĭ zĭj'ĭ əl), **syz·y·get·ic** (sĭz'ə jĕt'ĭk), *adj.* —**syz'y·get'i·cal·ly,** *adv.*

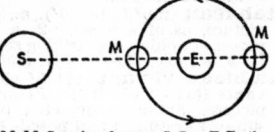
M. M. Syzygies of moon; S. Sun, E. Earth

Sza·bad·ka (sŏ'bŏt kŏ), *n.* Hungarian name of **Subotica.**

Szcze·cin (sh chĕ tsēn'). *n.* Polish name of **Stettin.**

Sze·chwan (sĕ'chwän'; *Chin.* sü'chwän'), *n.* a province in central China. 62,303,999 pop. (1953); 144,996 sq. mi. *Cap.:* Chengtu.

Sze·ged (sĕ'gĕd), *n.* a city in S Hungary, on the Tisza river. 88,590 (est. 1954). German, **Sze·ge·din** (sĕ'gə dĭn).

Szom·bat·hely (sôm'bät hā', -hĕ'y), *n.* a city in W Hungary: founded, A.D. 48. 40,114 (est. 1954). German, **Steinamanger.**

T

T, t (tē), *n., pl.* **T's** or **Ts, t's** or **ts. 1.** a consonant, the 20th letter of the English alphabet. **2.** something shaped like the letter T. **3. to a T,** exactly: *to suit or fit to a T.*

't, a shortened form of *it,* before or after a verb, as in *'twas, 'tis, do't, see't.*

-t, a suffix forming the past tense or past participle of certain verbs; an equivalent of -ed. [(1) pp., ME and OE -t, -(e)d, OE -od; (2) past tense, ME and OE -te. -(e)de, OE -ode]

t, *Statistics.* distribution.

T, 1. absolute temperature. **2.** (surface) tension.

T., 1. Territory. **2.** township. **3.** Tuesday.

t., 1. taken from. **2.** tare. **3.** teaspoon. **4.** temperature. **5.** (*L tempore*) in the time of. **6.** tenor. **7.** *Gram.* tense. **8.** territory. **9.** time. **10.** tome. **11.** ton. **12.** town. **13.** township. **14.** transitive.

Ta, *Chem.* tantalum.

Taal (täl), *n.* a variety of Dutch spoken in the Union of South Africa, esp. around the Cape; South African Dutch. [t. D: speech]

Ta·al (tä äl'), *n.* an active volcano in the Philippine Islands, on SW Luzon, on an island in **Taal Lake:** eruptions, 1749, 1873, 1911. 1050 ft.

tab (tăb), *n., v.,* **tabbed, tabbing. 1.** a small flap, strap, loop, or similar appendage, as on a garment, etc. **2.** a tag or label. —*v.t.* **3.** to furnish or ornament with a tab or tabs. **4. keep tab on,** *Colloq.* to keep account of or a check on: *keep tab on your expenses.* [orig. uncert]

tab·a·nid (tăb'ə nĭd), *n.* a large bloodsucking dipterous fly of the family *Tabanidae;* horsefly or deer fly.

tab·ard (tăb'ərd), *n.* **1.** a loose outer garment, with short sleeves or without sleeves, worn by knights over their armor and generally emblazoned with the arms of the wearer. **2.** an official garment of a herald, emblazoned with the arms of the sovereign. **3.** a coarse, heavy, short coat with or without sleeves, formerly used as an outdoor garment. [ME, t. OF, ult. der. L *tapēte* figured cloth, tapestry]

Herald's tabard, 17th century

tab·a·ret (tăb'ə rĭt), *n.* a durable upholstery fabric made of silk with stripes of satin. [? der. TABBY (def. 6)]

Ta·bas·co (tə băs'kō; *Sp.* tä bäs'kō), *n.* **1.** a state in SE Mexico, on the Gulf of Campeche. 380,595 (est. 1952); 9783 sq. mi. *Cap.:* Villa Hermosa. **2.** (*l.c.*) a pungent condiment sauce prepared from the fruit of a variety of capsicum. **3.** a trademark for this sauce.

tab·by (tăb'ĭ), *n., pl.* **-bies,** *adj., v.,* **-bied, -bying.** —*n.* **1.** a cat with a striped or brindled coat. **2.** a female cat. **3.** an old maid; a spinster. **4.** any spiteful female gossip or tattler. **5.** plain weave. **6.** a watered silk fabric, or any other watered material, as moreen. —*adj.* **7.** striped or brindled. **8.** made of or resembling tabby. —*v.t.* **9.** to give a wavy or watered appearance to (silk,

etc.). [aphetic var. of ME *attaby,* t. OF: m. *atabis,* t. Ar.: m. *attabi* rich watered silk, der. *Attabiya* quarter of Bagdad where first made]

tab·er·nac·le (tăb'ər năk'əl), *n., v.,* **-led, -ling.** —*n.* **1.** a temporary habitation, as a tent or hut. **2.** a dwelling place. **3.** the tent used by the Jews as a portable sanctuary before their final settlement in Palestine. **4.** the Jewish temple. **5.** any place or house of worship, esp. one designed for a large audience. **6.** a canopied niche or recess, as for an image. **7.** *Eccles.* an ornamental receptacle for the reserved Eucharist, now generally found on the altar. **8.** the human body as the temporary abode of the soul. —*v.i., v.t.* **9.** to dwell or place in or as in a tabernacle. [ME, t. L: m. *tabernāculum* tent, booth, der. L *taberna* hut, booth] —**tab·er·nac·u·lar** (tăb'ər năk'yə lər), *adj.*

ta·bes (tā'bēz), *n. Pathol.* **1.** syphilis of the spinal cord and its appendages, characterized by shooting pains and other sensory disturbances, and in the later stages by locomotor ataxia and paralysis. **2.** a gradually progressive emaciation; consumption. [t. L: a decay]

ta·bes·cent (tə bĕs'ənt), *adj.* wasting away. [t. L: s. *tābescens,* ppr.] —**ta·bes'cence,** *n.*

ta·bes dor·sa·lis (tā'bēz dôr sā'lĭs), *Pathol.* locomotor ataxia. [NL: tabes of the back]

ta·bet·ic (tə bĕt'ĭk, tə bē'tĭk), *adj.* **1.** Also, **tab·id** (tăb'ĭd). pertaining to or affected with tabes. —*n.* **2.** one affected with tabes.

tab·la·ture (tăb'lə chər), *n.* a tabular space, surface, or structure. [t. F, t. It.: m. *tavolatura,* der. *tavola,* g. L *tabula* table]

ta·ble (tā'bəl), *n., v.,* **-bled, -bling.** —*n.* **1.** an article of furniture consisting of a flat top resting on legs or on a pillar. **2.** the board at or round which persons sit at meals. **3.** the food placed on a table to be eaten. **4.** a company of persons at a table, as for a meal, game, or business transaction. **5.** a flat or plane surface; a level area. **6.** a tableland or plateau. **7.** a flat and relatively thin piece of wood, stone, metal, or other hard substance, esp. one artificially shaped for a particular purpose. **8.** *Archit.* a flat, vertical, usually rectangular surface forming a distinct feature in a wall, and often ornamental. **9.** a smooth, flat board or slab on which inscriptions, etc., may be put. **10.** (*pl.*) **a.** the tablets on which certain collections of laws were anciently inscribed, used most often of the Twelve Tables. **b.** the laws themselves. **11.** an arrangement of words, numbers, or signs, or combinations of them, as in parallel columns, to exhibit a set of facts or relations in a definite, compact, and comprehensive form; a synopsis or scheme. **12.** *Anat.* the inner or outer hard layer or any of the flat bones of the skull. **13.** *Music.* a sounding board. **14.** *Gem Cutting.* **a.** the upper horizontal surface of a faceted gem. **b.** a gem with such a surface. **15. on the table,** *Parl. Proc.* postponed. See def. 18. —*v.t.* **16.** to place (a card, etc.) on a table. **17.** to enter in or form into a table or list. **18.** *U.S. Parl. Proc.* to place (a proposal, resolution, etc.) on the table of an tableau   1232   tackle

assembly for future discussion, used often as a method of postponing or shelving it. [ME; OE *tablu*, var. of *tabule*, t. L: m. *tabula* board] —**ta′ble·less,** *adj.*

tab·leau (tăb′lō, tă blō′), *n., pl.* **-leaux, -leaus. 1.** a picture, as of a scene. **2.** a picturesque grouping of persons or objects; a striking scene. **3.** a tableau vivant. [t. F: a table, picture, der. *table* TABLE]

ta·bleau vi·vant (tá blō′ vē vän′), *pl.* **tableaux vi·vants** (tá blō′ vē vän′). *French.* a representation of a picture, statue, scene, etc., by one or more persons suitably costumed and posed. [F: living picture]

ta·ble·cloth (tā′bəl klôth′, -klŏth′), *n.* a cloth for covering the top of a table, esp. during a meal.

ta·ble d'hôte (tăb′əl dōt′, tä′bəl; *Fr.* tá blə dōt′), *pl.* **tables d'hôte** (tăb′əlz dōt′, tä′bəlz; *Fr.* tá blə dōt′). meal of prearranged courses served at a fixed time and price, for guests at a hotel or restaurant. Cf. **à la carte.** [t. F: the host's table]

ta·ble·land (tā′bəl lănd′), *n.* an elevated and generally level region of considerable extent; a plateau.

table linen, tablecloths, napkins, etc., used in setting a table.

Table Mountain, a mountain in the Union of South Africa, near Cape Town. 3550 ft.

ta·ble·spoon (tā′bəl spoon′, -spoon′), *n.* **1.** a spoon larger than a teaspoon and a dessertspoon, used in the service of the table and as a standard measuring unit in recipes. **2.** a unit of capacity, equal to ½ fluid ounce, or 3 household teaspoons. **3.** a tablespoonful.

ta·ble·spoon·ful (tā′bəl spoon fool′, -spoon-), *n., pl.* **-fuls.** the quantity a tablespoon holds, about half a fluid ounce.

tab·let (tăb′lĭt), *n.* **1.** a number of sheets of writing paper or the like fastened together at the edge; a pad. **2.** a small, flat slab or surface, esp. one bearing or intended to bear an inscription, carving, or the like. **3.** a leaf or sheet of some inflexible material for writing or marking on, esp. one of a pair or set hinged or otherwise fastened together. **4.** (*pl.*) the set as a whole. **5.** a small, flat or flattish cake or piece of some solid or solidified substance, as a drug, chemical, or the like; esp. (in England) a cake, as of soap. [ME *tablette*, t. F, der. *table* TABLE]

table talk, informal conversation at meals.

table tennis, a miniature tennis game played usually indoors, on a table; ping-pong.

ta·ble·ware (tā′bəl wâr′), *n.* dishes, utensils, etc., used at table or meals.

tab·loid (tăb′loid), *n.* **1.** a newspaper, about one half the ordinary page size, emphasizing pictures and concise writing. **2.** a compressed portion of various drugs, chemicals, etc. —*adj.* **3.** compressed in or as in a tabloid: *a tabloid newspaper.* [f. TABL(ET) + -OID]

ta·boo (tə boo′, tă-), *adj., n., pl.* **-boos,** *v.,* **-booed, -boo·ing.** —*adj.* **1.** (among the Polynesians and other peoples of the southern Pacific) separated or set apart as sacred or unclean; forbidden to general use; placed under a prohibition or ban. —*n.* **2.** a prohibition or interdiction of anything; exclusion from use or practice. **3.** (among the Polynesians, etc.) **a.** the system or practice, or an act, whereby things are set apart as sacred, forbidden to general use, or placed under a prohibition or interdiction. **b.** the fact of being so set apart, forbidden, or placed. **4.** exclusion from social relations; ostracism. —*v.t.* **5.** to put under a taboo; prohibit or forbid. **6.** to ostracize, as a person. Also, **tabu.** [t. Tongan: m. *tabu*] —**Syn. 5.** See **forbid.**

ta·bor (tā′bər), *n.* **1.** a small kind of drum formerly in use, esp. as an accompaniment to a pipe or fife. —*v.i.* **2.** to play upon, or as upon, a tabor; drum. —*v.t.* **3.** to strike or beat as one does a tabor. Also, **ta′bour.** [ME *tabour*, t. OF: of Oriental orig.; cf. Pers. *tabūrāk* drum] —**ta′bor·er,** *n.*

tab·o·ret (tăb′ə rĭt, tăb′ə rĕt′), *n.* **1.** a low seat without back or arms, for one person; a stool. **2.** a small, low stand of similar form. **3.** a frame for embroidery. **4.** a small tabor. Also, **tab′ou·ret.** [ME *taberett*, f. *taber* TABOR + -ett -ET]

Tabor

Ta·briz (tä brēz′), *n.* a city in NW Iran: the capital of Azerbaijan province. 279,168 (est. 1950).

ta·bu (tə boo′, tă-), *adj., n., v.t.* taboo.

tab·u·lar (tăb′yə lər), *adj.* **1.** pertaining to or of the nature of a table or tabulated arrangement. **2.** ascertained from or computed by the use of tables. **3.** having the form of a table, tablet, or tablature. **4.** flat and expansive. [t. L: s. *tabulāris* relating to a board or plate] —**tab′u·lar·ly,** *adv.*

ta·bu·la ra·sa (tăb′yŏŏ lə rā′sə), a mind as yet free from impressions. [t. L: scraped tablet]

tab·u·late (*v.* tăb′yə lāt′, *adj.* tăb′yə lĭt, -lāt′), *v.,* **-lated, -lating,** *adj.* —*v.t.* **1.** to put or form into a table, scheme, or synopsis; formulate tabularly. —*adj.* **2.** shaped like a table or tablet; tabular. **3.** having transverse dissepiments, as certain corals. [t. L: m.s. *tabulātus*, pp., boarded, planked] —**tab′u·la′tion,** *n.*

tab·u·la·tor (tăb′yə lā′tər), *n.* **1.** one who or that which tabulates. **2.** an attachment to a typewriter, for tabulating accounts, etc.

tac·a·ma·hac (tăk′ə mə hăk′), *n.* **1.** any of certain resinous substances used in incenses, ointments, etc.

2. any tree yielding such a product. **3.** (in North America) the balsam poplar, *Populus Tacamahaca.* Also, **tac·a·ma·hac·a** (tăk′ə mə hăk′ə). [t. Sp., t. Mex.]

ta·cet (tā′sĕt), *Music.* an indication that an instrument or voice is to be silent for a time. [L: (it) is silent]

tache (tăch), *n. Archaic.* a buckle; clasp. Also, **tach.** [late ME, t. F. See TACK¹]

tach·i·na fly (tăk′ə nə), any of the dipterous insects of the family *Tachinidae*, the larvae of which are parasitic on other insects such as caterpillars, beetles, etc. [f. NL *tachina* (t. Gk., fem. of *tachinós* swift) + FLY]

ta·chis·to·scope (tə kĭs′tə skōp′), *n.* an apparatus used in experimental psychology which exposes to view an object, group of objects, letters, words, etc., for a selected brief period of time. [f. Gk. *táchisto(s)* swiftest + -SCOPE]

tach·o·gram (tăk′ə grăm′), *n.* the record produced by the action of a tachometer.

tach·o·graph (tăk′ə grăf′, -gräf′), *n.* **1.** a recording tachometer. **2.** a record made by such an instrument. [f. Gk. *tácho(s)* speed + -GRAPH]

ta·chom·e·ter (tə kŏm′ə tər), *n.* **1.** any of various instruments for measuring or indicating velocity or speed, as of a machine, a river, the blood, etc. **2.** an instrument measuring revolutions per minute, as of an engine. [f. Gk. *tácho(s)* speed + -METER] —**ta·chom′e·try,** *n.*

tachy-, a word element meaning "swift," as in *tachygraphy.* [t. Gk, comb. form of *tachýs*]

tach·y·graph (tăk′ə grăf′, -gräf′), *n.* **1.** tachygraphic writing. **2.** a tachygraphic writer.

ta·chyg·ra·phy (tä kĭg′rə fĭ), *n.* the Greek and Roman handwriting used for rapid stenography and writing. —**ta·chyg′ra·pher, ta·chyg′ra·phist,** *n.* —**tach·y·graph·ic** (tăk′ə grăf′ĭk), **tach′i·graph′i·cal,** *adj.*

tach·y·lyte (tăk′ə līt′), *n.* a black, glassy form of basalt, readily fusible and of a high luster. [t. G: m. *tachylit*, f. Gk.: *tachy-* TACHY- + s. *lytós* soluble] —**tach·y·lyt·ic** (tăk′ə lĭt′ĭk), *adj.*

tac·it (tăs′ĭt), *adj.* **1.** silent; saying nothing. **2.** not openly expressed, but implied; understood or inferred. **3.** unspoken: *a tacit prayer.* **4.** *Law.* arising by operation of law, without the intervention of the parties. [t. L: s. *tacitus*, pp.] —**tac′it·ly,** *adv.* —**tac′it·ness,** *n.*

tac·i·turn (tăs′ə tûrn′), *adj.* inclined to silence, or reserved in speech; not inclined to conversation. [t. L: s. *taciturnus*] —**tac·i·tur·ni·ty** (tăs′ə tûr′nə tĭ), *n.* —**tac′i·turn′ly,** *adv.*

Tac·i·tus (tăs′ə təs), *n.* **Publius Cornelius** (pŭb′lĭ əs kôr nēl′yəs), A.D. c55–c120, Roman historian.

tack¹ (tăk), *n.* **1.** a short, sharp-pointed nail or pin, usually with a flat and comparatively large head. **2.** a stitch, esp. a long stitch used in fastening seams, etc., preparatory to a more thorough sewing. **3.** a fastening, esp. in a temporary manner. **4.** *Naut.* **a.** a rope which confines the foremost lower corner of a course on a square-rigged ship. **b.** the part of a sail to which such a rope is fastened. **c.** the lower forward corner of a fore-and-aft sail. **d.** a line secured to the lower outboard corner of a studdingsail to haul it to the end of the boom. **e.** the direction or course of a ship in relation to the position of her sails: *the starboard tack* (when close-hauled with the wind on the starboard side); *the port tack* (when close-hauled with the wind on the port side). **f.** a course obliquely against the wind. **g.** one of the series of straight runs which make up the zigzag course of a ship proceeding to windward. **5.** a course of action or conduct, esp. one differing from some preceding or other course. **6.** one of the movements of a zigzag course on land. —*v.t.* **7.** to fasten by a tack or tacks: *to tack a rug.* **8.** to secure by some slight or temporary fastening. **9.** to join together; unite or combine. **10.** to attach as something supplementary; append or annex. **11.** *Naut.* to change the course of (a ship) to the opposite tack; navigate (a ship) by a series of tacks. —*v.i.* **12.** *Naut.* **a.** to change the course of a ship by bringing her head into the wind and then causing it to fall off on the other side: *he ordered us to tack at once.* **b.** to change its course in this way, as a ship. **c.** to proceed to windward by a series of courses as close to the wind as the vessel will sail, the wind being alternately on one bow and then on the other. **13.** to change one's course of action or conduct. [ME, t. AF: m. *taque* a fastening, clasp, nail, ult. t. Gmc.; cf. G *zacken* prong, D *tak* twig] —**tack′er,** *n.* —**tack′·less,** *adj.*

tack² (tăk), *n.* food; fare. [orig. obscure]

tack·le (tăk′əl), *n., v.,* **-led, -ling.** —*n.* **1.** equipment, apparatus, or gear, esp. for fishing. **2.** a mechanism or apparatus, as a rope and block or a combination of ropes and blocks, for hoisting, lowering, and shifting objects or materials. **3.** any system of leverage using several pulleys. **4.** *Naut.* **a.** gear used in handling a ship. **b.** the rigging of a ship, esp. that used in working the sails, etc. **c.** a purchase consisting of a rope running over two or more sheaves or pulleys. **d.** an arrangement of rope and blocks or sheaves for multiplying power. **5.** an act of tackling, as in football; a seizing or grasping. **6.** either of two players in football, stationed next to the ends in the forward line. —*v.t.* **7.** to undertake to deal with, master, solve, etc. **8.** *Colloq.* to lay hold upon, attack, or encounter. **9.** to harness (a horse). **10.** *Football.* to

seize and stop (an opponent having the ball). [ME *takel* gear, t. MLG, der. *taken* seize, c. TAKE, v.] **—tack′ler**, *n.*

tack·ling (tăk′lĭng), *n.* *Rare.* gear; tackle.

tack·y¹ (tăk′ĭ), *adj.* adhesive; sticky. [f. TACK¹ + -Y¹]

tack·y² (tăk′ĭ), *adj.*, **tackier, tackiest.** *U.S. Colloq.* shabby; dowdy. [orig. obscure]

Tac·na-A·ri·ca (tăk′nä ä rē′kä), *n.* a maritime region in W South America, long in dispute between Chile and Peru: annexed by Chile, 1883; divided as a result of arbitration into Tacna department, Peru, and Arica department, Chile, 1929.

Ta·co·ma (tə kō′mə), *n.* **1.** a seaport in W Washington, on Puget Sound. 147,979 (1960). **2. Mount,** Mount Rainier.

tac·o·nite (tăk′ə nīt), *n.* *Chem.* a low-grade ore of iron found in the region of Lake Superior as a hard rock formation: it contains about 51% silica and 27% iron.

tact (tăkt), *n.* **1.** keen sense of what to say or do to avoid giving offense; skill in dealing with difficult or delicate situations. **2.** touch; the sense of touch. [t. L: s. *tactus* sense of touch]

tact·ful (tăkt′fəl), *adj.* having or manifesting tact: *a tactful person, a tactful reply.* **—tact′ful·ly,** *adv.* **—tact′·ful·ness,** *n.* **—Syn.** See diplomatic.

tac·tic (tăk′tĭk), *n.* **1.** tactics. **2.** a system or a detail of tactics. **—adj.** **3.** of or pertaining to arrangement or order; tactical. [t. NL: s. *tactica,* t. Gk.: m. *taktikē,* fem. of *taktikós,* der. *taktós* ordered]

tac·ti·cal (tăk′tə kəl), *adj.* **1.** of or pertaining to tactics, esp. military or naval tactics. **2.** characterized by skillful tactics or adroit maneuvering or procedure: *tactical movements.* **—tac′ti·cal·ly,** *adv.*

tac·ti·cian (tăk tĭsh′ən), *n.* one versed in tactics.

tac·tics (tăk′tĭks), *n.* **1.** the art or science of disposing military or naval forces for battle and maneuvering them in battle. **2.** (*construed as pl.*) the maneuvers themselves. **3.** (*construed as pl.*) mode of procedure for gaining advantage or success. [pl. of TACTIC. See -ICS] **—Syn. 1.** See strategy.

tac·tile (tăk′tĭl), *adj.* **1.** of or pertaining to the organs or sense of touch; endowed with the sense of touch. **2.** perceptible to the touch; tangible. [t. L: m.s. *tactilis* tangible] **—tac·til′i·ty,** *n.*

tac·tion (tăk′shən), *n.* touch; contact.

tact·less (tăkt′lĭs), *adj.* without tact; showing no tact: *a tactless person.* **—tact′less·ly,** *adv.* **—tact′·less·ness,** *n.*

tac·tu·al (tăk′chŏŏ əl), *adj.* **1.** of or pertaining to touch. **2.** communicating or imparting the sensation of contact; arising from or due to touch. [f. L *tactu(s)* touch + -AL¹] **—tac′tu·al·ly,** *adv.*

Ta·cu·ba·ya (tä′kŏŏ bä′yä), *n.* a former city in the Federal District of Mexico: now a SW district of Mexico City; national observatory.

tad (tăd), *n.* *U.S.* a small child, esp. a boy. [? var. of TOD(DLER)]

Tad·e·ma (tăd′ə mə), *n.* **Lawrence Alma-.** See **Alma-Tadema.**

Tad·mor (tăd′môr), *n.* Biblical name of **Palmyra.**

Ta·djik (tä′jĭk), *n.*, *pl.* **-djik.** Tajik (person).

tad·pole (tăd′pōl′), *n.* the aquatic larva or immature form of frogs, toads, etc., esp. after the enclosure of the gills and before the appearance of the forelimbs and the resorption of the tail. [ME *taddepol,* f. *tadde* TOAD + *pol* POLL (head)]

Tadpole, showing early stages of growth

Ta·dzhik Soviet Socialist Republic (tä jĭk′), a constituent republic of the Soviet Union, in the Asiatic part, N of Afghanistan. 1,800,000 pop. (est. 1956); 54,900 sq. mi. *Cap.:* Stalinabad. Also, **Tajik.**

tae·di·um vi·tae (tē′dĭəm vī′tē), *Latin.* a feeling that life is unbearably wearisome. Also, **tedium vitae.** [L: weariness of life]

tael (tāl), *n.* **1.** liang. **2.** any of various other similar units of weight in the Far East. **3.** a Chinese money of account, being the value of this weight of standard silver. [t. Pg., t. Malay: m. *tahil* weight]

ta′en (tān), *n.* *Poetic.* taken.

tae·ni·a (tē′nĭə), *n.*, *pl.* **-niae** (-nĭ ē′). **1.** *Archaeol.* a headband or fillet. **2.** *Archit.* the fillet or band on the Doric architrave, which separates it from the frieze. See diag. under **column.** **3.** *Anat.* a ribbonlike structure, as certain bands of white nerve fibers in the brain. **4.** *Zool.* tapeworm. Also, **tenia.** [t. L, t. Gk.: m. *tainia*]

tae·ni·a·cide (tē′nĭə sīd′), *n.* *Med.* an agent that destroys tapeworms. Also, **teniacide.** **—tae′ni·a·cid′al,** *adj.*

tae·ni·a·fuge (tē′nĭə fūj′), *Med.* **—adj. 1.** expelling tapeworms, as a medicine. **—n. 2.** an agent or medicine to expel tapeworms from the body.

tae·ni·a·sis (tĭ nī′ə sĭs), *n.* *Pathol.* a diseased condition due to the presence of taeniae or tapeworms.

taf·fa·rel (tăf′ə rəl), *n.* *Obsolete.* taffrail.

taf·fe·ta (tăf′ə tə), *n.* **1.** a lightweight, lustrous, silk or rayon fabric of plain weave. **2.** any of various other fabrics of silk, linen, wool, etc., in use at different periods. **—adj. 3.** of or resembling taffeta. [ME *taffata,* t. ML, ult. t. Pers.: m. *tāftah* silken or linen cloth]

taff·rail (tăf′rāl′), *n.* *Naut.* **1.** the upper part of the stern of a vessel. **2.** the rail across the stern. [earlier *tafferel,* t. D: m. *tafereel* panel (dim. of *tafel* TABLE)]

taf·fy (tăf′ĭ), *n.* **1.** a candy made of sugar or molasses boiled down, often with butter, nuts, etc. **2.** *Colloq.* flattery. Also, *esp. Brit.,* **toffee, toffy.** [var. of TOFFEE]

taf·i·a (tăf′ĭə), *n.* a kind of rum from the lower grades of molasses, refuse sugar, etc., in Haiti. [orig. uncert.]

Ta·fi·lelt (tä fē′lĕlt), *n.* a former oasis region in SE Morocco; ab. 500 sq. mi. Also, **Ta·fi·la·let** (tä′fē lä′lĕt).

Taft (tăft), *n.* **1. Lorado** (lə rä′dō), 1860–1936, U.S. sculptor. **2. William Howard,** 1857–1930, 27th president of United States (1909–13) and chief justice of Supreme Court (1921–30).

tag¹ (tăg), *n., v.,* **tagged, tagging.** **—n. 1.** a piece or strip of strong paper, leather, or the like, for attaching by one end to something as a mark or label. **2.** any small hanging or loosely attached part or piece; tatter. **3.** a loop of material sewn on a garment so that it can be hung up. **4.** a point or binding of metal or other hard substance at the end of a cord, lace or the like. **5.** *Angling.* a small piece made of tinsel or the like, tied to the shank of a hook at the body of an artificial fly. **6.** the tail end or concluding part, as of a proceeding. **7.** the refrain of a song or poem. **8.** the last words of a speech in a play, etc.; an actor's cue. **9.** an addition to a speech or writing, as the moral of a fable. **10.** a quotation added for special effect. **11.** a curlicue in writing. **12.** a lock of hair. **13.** a matted lock of wool on a sheep. **14.** *Obs.* the rabble. **—v.t. 15.** to furnish with a tag or tags; attach a tag to. **16.** to append as a tag to something else. **17.** *Colloq.* to follow closely. **—v.i. 18.** to follow closely; go along or about as a follower. [ME; b. TATTER and RAG¹] **—tag′like′,** *adj.*

tag² (tăg), *n., v.,* **tagged, tagging.** **—n. 1.** a children's game in which one player chases the others till he touches one of them, who then takes his place as pursuer. **—v.t. 2.** to touch in or as in the game of tag. [orig. obscure]

Ta·ga·log (tä gä′lŏg, tăg′ə lŏg′), *n.* **1.** a member of a Malayan people native in the Philippine Islands. **2.** the principal Indonesian language of the Philippine Islands.

Ta·gan·rog (tä′gän rŏk′), *n.* a seaport in the S Soviet Union in Europe, on the **Gulf of Taganrog,** a NE arm of the Sea of Azov. 189,000 (est. 1956).

tag day, *U.S.* a day on which contributions to a fund are solicited, each contributor receiving a tag.

Tag·gard (tăg′ərd), *n.* **Genevieve,** 1894–1948, U.S. poet.

tag·ger (tăg′ər), *n.* **1.** one who or that which tags. **2.** (*pl.*) iron in very thin sheets, either uncoated or coated with tin.

Ta·gore (tə gôr′; *native* tä′gôr), *n.* **Sir Rabindranath** (rə bēn′drə nät′), 1861–1941, Hindu poet.

tag·rag (tăg′răg′), *n.* **1.** riffraff; rabble. **2.** a tatter.

Ta·gus (tā′gəs), *n.* a river flowing westward W through central Spain and Portugal to the Atlantic near Lisbon. 566 mi. Spanish, **Tajo.** Portuguese, **Tejo.**

Ta·hi·ti (tä hē′tē, tĭ′tē), *n.* the principal island of the Society Islands, in the S Pacific. 30,500 pop. (1951); 402 sq. mi. *Cap.:* Papeete.

Ta·hi·ti·an (tä hē′tĭ ən), *adj.* **1.** of or pertaining to Tahiti, its inhabitants, or their language. **—n. 2.** a native or inhabitant of Tahiti. **3.** the language of Tahiti, a Polynesian language.

Ta·hoe (tä′hō, tä′-), *n.* a lake in E California and W Nevada, in the Sierra Nevada Mountains: resort. ab. 200 sq. mi.; 6225 ft. high.

tah·sil·dar (tə sēl′där′), *n.* (in India) a collector for, or official of, the revenue department. Also, **tah·seel′-dar′.** [t. Urdū, f. Pers.: *tahsil* collection + -*dar,* agent suffix]

Tai (tā′ē, tī), *n., adj.* Thai.

tai·ga (tī′gə), *n.* the coniferous, evergreen forests of subarctic lands, covering vast areas of northern North America and Eurasia. [t. Russ.]

Tai·ho·ku (tī hō′kōō), *n.* former name of **Taipeh.**

tail¹ (tāl), *n.* **1.** the hindmost part of an animal, esp. when forming a distinct flexible appendage to the trunk. **2.** something resembling or suggesting this in shape or position: *the tail of a kite.* **3.** the hinder, bottom, or concluding part of anything; the rear. **4.** the inferior or refuse part of anything. **5.** a long braid or tress of hair. **6.** *Astron.* the luminous train extending from the head of a comet. **7.** *Colloq.* (*pl.*) the reverse of a coin. **8.** an arrangement of objects or persons extending as or as if a tail. **9.** a line of persons awaiting their turns. **10.** a retinue. **11.** *Aeron.* the after portion of an airplane or the like. **12.** (*pl.*) *Colloq.* **a.** a swallow-tailed coat. **b.** a long-tailed coat worn as formal attire. **c.** full dress attire. **13.** the lower part of a pool or stream. **14. turn tail, a.** to turn the back, as in aversion or fright. **b.** to run away; flee. **—adj. 15.** coming from behind: *tail wind.* **16.** being in the back or rear: *a tail light.* **—v.t. 17.** to form or furnish with a tail. **18.** to form or constitute the tail or end of (a procession, etc.). **19.** to terminate; follow like a tail. **20.** to join or attach (one thing) at the tail or end of another. **21.** *Bldg. Trades.* to fasten (a beam, etc.) by one of its ends (fol. by *in, into,* etc.). **22.** *Slang.* to follow in order to hinder escape or to observe: *to tail a suspect.* **—v.i. 23.** to form, or move or pass in, a line or continua-

tion suggestive of a tail: *Fido tailed closely behind me.*
24. (of a boat, etc.) to have or take a position with the stern in a particular direction. 25. *Colloq.* to follow close behind. 26. *Building.* (of a beam, etc.) to be fastened by the end (fol. by *in, into*, etc.).
[ME; OE *tægel*, c. Icel. *tagl*] —**tail/less**, *adj.* —**tail/-like/**, *adj.*

tail² (tāl), *n.* 1. *Law.* the limitation of an estate to a person and the heirs of his body, or some particular class of such heirs. 2. *Print., Bookbinding.* the bottom of a page or book. —*adj.* 3. *Law.* limited to a specified line of heirs; being in tail. [ME, t. OF: m. *taille* cutting, tax, der. *taillier*, v., cut] —**tai/lor less**, *adj.*

tail beam, *Bldg. Trades.* tailpiece.

tail-board (tāl/bōrd/), *n.* the board at the back of a wagon, etc., which can be removed or let down for convenience in loading and unloading. Also, **tail/gate/.**

tail·ing (tā/lĭng), *n.* 1. the part of a projecting stone or brick tailed or inserted in a wall. 2. (*pl.*) the residue of any product, as in mining; leavings.

tail·light (tāl/līt/), *n.* a light, usually red, at the rear of an automobile, train, etc. Also, *Brit.*, **tail lamp.**

tai·lor (tā/lər), *n.* 1. one whose business it is to make or mend outer garments. —*v.i.* 2. to do the work of a tailor. —*v.t.* 3. to make by tailor's work. 4. to fit or furnish with clothing. [ME, t. OF: m. *tailleor* cutter, der. *taillier* cut] —**tai/lor·less**, *adj.*

tai·lor·bird (tā/lər bûrd/), *n.* any of various small Asiatic passerine birds of the genus *Orthotomus* and its near relatives, which stitch leaves together to form and hide their nests.

tai·lor·ing (tā/lər ĭng), *n.* the business or work of a tailor.

tai·lor-made (tā/lər mād/), *adj.* made by or as by a tailor (applied esp. to women's garments made of more substantial fabrics or with plainness of cut and finish).

tail·piece (tāl/pēs/), *n.* 1. a piece added at the end; an end piece or appendage. 2. *Print.* a small decorative design at the end of a chapter or at the bottom of a page. 3. (in musical instruments of the viol class) a triangular piece of wood, usually of ebony, to which the lower ends of the strings are fastened. 4. *Bldg. Trades.* a relatively short beam or rafter inserted in a wall by tailing and supported by a header.

tail·race (tāl/rās/), *n.* 1. the race, flume, or channel leading away from a water wheel or the like. 2. *Mining.* the channel for conducting tailings or refuse away in water.

tail skid, *Aeron.* a runner under the tail of an airplane.

tail spin, *Aeron.* a descent of an airplane in a steep spiral course, either as a stunt or by accident.

tail·stock (tāl/stŏk/), *n.* (on a lathe or grinder) the movable or sliding frame supporting the dead spindle.

tail wind, a favorable wind blowing from behind an airplane or ship, thus increasing its speed.

Tai·myr (tī mĭr/), *n.* a large peninsula in the N Soviet Union in Asia between the Kara and Nordenskjöld Seas. Also, **Tai·mir/.**

tain (tān), *n.* 1. a thin tin plate. 2. tin foil for the back of mirrors. [ME *teyne* plate, t. Scand.; cf. Icel. *teina* basket]

Tai·nan (tī/nän/), *n.* a city in SW Formosa. 229,500 (est. 1955).

Taine (tān; *Fr.* tĕn), *n.* **Hippolyte Adolphe** (ē pô-lēt/ à dôlf/), 1828–93, French literary critic and historian.

Tai·no (tī/nō), *n., pl.* **-nos.** 1. (*pl.*) an extinct Arawakan Indian tribe of the West Indies. 2. a member of this tribe.

taint (tānt), *n.* 1. a touch of something offensive or deleterious. 2. a trace of infection, contamination, or the like. 3. a touch of dishonor or discredit. 4. *Obs.* color or tinge. —*v.t.* 5. to modify as by a touch of something offensive or deleterious. 6. to infect, contaminate, or corrupt. 7. to sully or tarnish. 8. *Obs.* to color or tinge. —*v.i.* 9. to become tainted. [ME *taynte*, b. OF *teint* (pp. of *teindre* color, t. L: m. *tingere*) and aphetic var. of ATTAINT] —**taint/less**, *adj.*

Tai·peh (tī/pĕ/), *n.* the capital of Formosa, in the N part of the island. 695,500 (est. 1955). Formerly, **Taihoku.**

Tai·ping (tī/pĭng/), *adj.* 1. designating or pertaining to a dynasty with which Hung Siu-tsuan attempted, as a part of an agrarian revolution, to replace the Manchus by the **Taiping Rebellion** (1850–64). —*n.* 2. a supporter of or participant in the Taiping Rebellion. [t. Chinese, f. *tai* great + *ping* peace]

Tai·sho (tī/shô/), *n.* the reign style (which see) of the Japanese Emperor Yoshihito, 1912–26.

Tai·wan (tī/wän/), *n.* Formosa.

Tai·yüan (tī/yy än/), *n.* a walled city in N China; capital of Shansi province. ab. 220,000. Also, **Yangkü.**

Ta·jik (tä/jĭk), *n., pl.* **-jik.** a person of Iranian descent living in the Tadzhik Republic and vicinity. Also, **Tadjik.**

Ta·jik (tä jĭk/), *n.* Tadzhik Soviet Socialist Republic.

Taj Ma·hal (täj/ mə häl/, täzh/), a white marble mausoleum built at Agra, India, by the Mogul emperor Shah Jahan (fl. 1628–58) for his favorite wife. [t. Pers.: crown of buildings]

Ta·jo (tä/hō), *n.* Spanish name of **Tagus.**

Ta·ka·ma·tsu (tä/kä mä/tsōō), *n.* a seaport in SW Japan, on Shikoku island. 124,557 (1950).

Ta·kao (tä kou/), *n.* Kaohsiung.

---

take (tāk), *v.*, **took, taken, taking,** *n.* —*v.t.* 1. to get into one's hands or possession by force or artifice. 2. to seize, catch, or capture. 3. to grasp, grip, or embrace. 4. to get into one's hold, possession, control etc., by one's own action but without force or artifice. 5. to receive or accept willingly. 6. to receive by way of payment or charge. 7. to get or obtain from a source; derive. 8. to receive into the body or system, as by swallowing or inhaling: *to take food.* 9. to contract (disease, etc.). 10. to pick from a number; select: *take whichever you wish.* 11. to carry off or remove (fol. by *away*, etc.). 12. to remove by death. 13. to subtract or deduct: *to take 2 from 5.* 14. to carry or convey: *take your lunch with you.* 15. to conduct or escort; lead: *where will this road take me?* 16. to attempt to get over, through, round, etc. (something that presents itself), or succeed in doing this: *the horse took the hedge with an easy jump.* 17. to attack or affect, as a disease does: *to be taken with a fit.* 18. to become affected by: *a stone which will take a high polish.* 19. to absorb or become impregnated with (a color, etc.). 20. *Chess, Tennis, etc.* to gain or capture (a piece, point, etc.). 21. *Law.* to acquire property, as on the happening of an event: *they take a fortune under the will.* 22. to receive or adopt (a person) into some specified or implied relation: *to take one in marriage.* 23. to secure regularly by payment: *to take a magazine;* or in England: *to take in a magazine.* 24. to adopt and enter upon (a way, course, etc.); proceed to deal with in some manner: *to take a matter under consideration.* 25. to have recourse to (a vehicle, etc.) as a means of progression or travel: *to take a car to the ferry.* 26. to proceed to occupy: *to take a seat.* 27. to receive in a specified manner: *to take a thing kindly.* 28. to avail oneself of (an opportunity, etc.). 29. to obtain or exact (satisfaction or reparation). 30. to receive, or be the recipient of (something bestowed, administered, etc.): *to take first prize.* 31. to occupy, use up, or consume (space, material, time, etc.). 32. to attract and hold: *a thing takes one's eye.* 33. to captivate or charm: *a thing takes one's fancy.* 34. to assume or adopt (a symbol, badge, or the like): *to take the veil.* 35. to make, put forth, etc.: *to take exception.* 36. to write down (notes, a copy, etc.): *take a record of* (a speech, etc.). 37. to go into or enter: *to take the field.* 38. to make (a reproduction, picture, or photograph of something); make a figure or picture, esp. a photograph, of (a person or thing). 39. to make or perform (a measurement, observation, etc.). 40. to ascertain by inquiry, examination, measurement, scientific observation, etc. 41. to begin to have (a certain feeling or state of mind); experience or feel (delight, pride, etc.). 42. to form and hold in the mind: *to take a gloomy view.* 43. to have effect; act. 44. to understand in a specified way: *how do you take this?* 45. to assume as a fact: *I take it that you will be there.* 46. to regard or consider: *he was taken to be wealthy.* 47. to assume or undertake (a function, duty, responsibility, etc.). 48. to assume the obligation of (a vow, pledge, etc.); perform or discharge (a part, service, etc.); assume or adopt as one's own (a part or side in a contest, etc.); assume or appropriate as if by right: *to take the credit for something, to take a liberty.* 49. to grasp or apprehend mentally, understand, or comprehend. 50. to do, perform, execute, etc.: *to take a walk.* 51. to accept and comply with (advice, etc.). 52. to suffer or undergo. 53. to enter into the enjoyment of (recreation, a holiday, etc.). 54. to employ for some specified or implied purpose: *to take measures to check an evil.* 55. to require: *it takes courage to do that.* 56. to deceive, trick, or cheat (fol. by *in*). 57. *Gram.* to have by usage, either as part of itself or with it in construction (a particular form, accent, etc., or a case, mode, etc.), as a word or the like. —*v.i.* 58. to catch or engage, as a mechanical device. 59. to strike root, or begin to grow, as a plant. 60. to adhere, as ink, etc. 61. to win favor or acceptance, as a play. 62. to have the intended result or effect, as a medicine, inoculation, etc. 63. to enter into possession, as of an estate. 64. to detract (fol. by *from*). 65. to apply or devote oneself. 66. to make one's way; proceed; go. 67. to become (sick or ill). 68. to admit of being photographed (well, badly, etc.). 69. to admit of being taken (out, apart, etc.). 70. Some special verb phrases are:

take after, 1. to follow the example of. 2. to resemble (a parent, etc.).
take down, 1. to pull down. 2. to remove by pulling apart or taking apart. 3. to write down. 4. to lower in power, strength, pride, arrogance, etc.: *I'll take him down a notch or two.*
take off, 1. to remove. 2. to lead off or away. 3. to set off; take one's departure. 4. to leave the ground, as an airplane. 5. to withdraw, as from service. 6. to remove by death. 7. *Colloq.* to imitate or mimic.
take on, 1. to hire. 2. to undertake to handle. 3. *Colloq.* to show great excitement, grief, or other emotion.
take to, 1. to apply, devote, or addict oneself to: *to take to drink.* 2. to be disposed (kindly, etc.) to. 3. to take oneself to: *to take to one's bed.* 4. to resort to; have recourse to: *to take to one's heels.*
—*n.* 71. act of taking. 72. that which is taken. 73. the quantity of fish, etc., taken at one time. 74. *Slang.* the profit or gain. 75. *Journalism.* a portion of copy assigned to a linotype operator or compositor, usually part of a story or article. 76. *Motion Pictures.* a. a scene or a portion of a scene photographed at one time

---

b., blend of, blended; c., cognate with; d., dialect, dialectal; der., derived from; f., formed from; g., going back to; m., modification of; r., replacing; s., stem of; t., taken from; ?, perhaps. See the full key on inside cover.

without any interruption or break. **b.** an instance of such continuous operation of the camera. [ME; late OE *tacan*, t. Scand.; cf. Icel. *taka*, c. MD *taken* grasp, seize; akin to Goth. *tēkan* touch] **—tak′-er**, *n.*

take-down (tāk′doun′), *adj.* **1.** made or constructed so as to be easily taken down or apart. **—n. 2.** act of taking down. **3.** a firearm designed to be swiftly disassembled or assembled. **4.** the point of separation of two or more of the parts of a take-down firearm or other device. **5.** *Colloq.* state of being humbled.

take-home pay (tāk′hōm′), salary remaining after all deductions, esp. tax deductions, have been made.

take-in (tāk′in′), *n.* *Colloq.* a deception, fraud, or imposition.

take-off (tāk′ôf′, -ŏf′), *n.* **1.** a taking or setting off; the leaving of the ground in leaping or in beginning a flight in an airplane. **2.** the place or point at which one takes off. **3.** *Colloq.* an imitating or mimicking, caricature, or burlesque.

take-up (tāk′ŭp′), *n.* **1.** act of taking up. **2.** *Mach.* any device for taking up slack or lost motion.

tak·ing (tā′king), *n.* **1.** act of one who or that which takes. **2.** state of being taken. **3.** that which is taken. **4.** (*pl.*) receipts. **5.** *Colloq.* or *Dial.* state of agitation or distress. **—adj. 6.** captivating, winning, or pleasing. **7.** *Colloq.* infectious or contagious. **—tak′ing·ly**, *adv.* **—tak′ing·ness**, *n.*

Ta·ku (tä′kōō′), *n.* a fortified town in NE China, in Hopeh province, E of Tientsin: battles, 1860, 1900.

tal·a·poin (tăl′ə poin′), *n.* a small, yellowish monkey, *Cercopithecus talapoin*, of West Africa, the smallest of the guenons. [ult. t. Talaing (Old Penguan): m. *tala pòi* my lord]

ta·lar·i·a (tə lâr′ĭ ə), *n. pl.* *Class. Myth.* the winged sandals, or small wings fastened to the ankles, of Hermes (or Mercury) and other divinities.

Ta·la·ve·ra de la Re·i·na (tä′lä vě′rä dě lä rě′ē nä′), a city in central Spain, on the Tagus river: British and Spanish defeat of the French, 1809. 18,631 (1950).

talc (tălk), *n., v.,* **talced, talc·ing** or **talced** (tălkt), **talc·ing** (tăl′king). **—n. 1.** Also, **tal·cum** (tăl′kəm). a soft green-to-gray mineral, hydrous magnesium silicate, $H_2Mg_3(SiO_3)_4$, unctuous to the touch, and occurring usually in foliated masses or compact, used in making lubricants, talcum powder, electrical insulation, etc. **—v.t. 2.** to treat or rub with talc. [t. ML: s. *talcum*, t. Ar.: m. *ṭalq*]

talc·ose (tăl′kōs, tăl kōs′), *adj.* containing, or composed largely of, talc. Also, **talc·ous** (tăl′kəs).

talcum powder, powdered talc or soapstone.

tale (tāl), *n.* **1.** a narrative purporting to relate the facts about some real or imaginary event, incident, or case; a story. **2.** a literary composition having the form of such a narrative: *Chaucer's "Canterbury Tales."* **3.** a falsehood; lie. **4.** a rumor or piece of gossip, esp. when malicious. **5.** *Chiefly Archaic.* the full number or amount. **6.** *Archaic and Poetic.* enumeration, numbering, or counting. **7.** *Obs.* talk or discourse. [ME; OE *talu* reckoning, speech, c. D *taal* speech, language, G *zahl* number]

tale·bear·er (tāl′bâr′ər), *n.* one who carries tales or gossip likely to breed mischief. **—tale′bear′ing**, *adj., n.*

tal·ent (tăl′ənt), *n.* **1.** a special natural ability or aptitude: *a talent for drawing.* **2.** a capacity for achievement or success; natural ability: *young men of talent.* **3.** persons of ability. **4.** a power of mind or body considered as committed to one for use and improvement (from the parable in Matt. 25: 14–30). **5.** an ancient unit of weight, varying with time and place, the later Attic talent being estimated at about 58 pounds avoirdupois, and the Hebrew talent about double this. **6.** this weight of gold, silver, or the like as a monetary unit, the value of the Hebrew gold unit being estimated at about $30,000, that of the Hebrew silver unit at about $2000, and that of the later Attic silver at about $1000 or $1200. **7.** *Obs.* inclination or disposition. [ME and OE *talente*, t. L: m. *talenta*, pl. of *talentum*, t. Gk.: m. *tálanton* (defs. 5, 6); def. 7 from OF *talent*] **—Syn. 1.** See **ability.**

tal·ent·ed (tăl′ən tĭd), *adj.* having talent; gifted.

Tale of Two Cities, A a historical novel (1859) by Dickens.

ta·ler (tä′lər), *n., pl.* **-ler.** thaler.

ta·les (tā′lēz), *n.* *Law.* **1.** (*orig. as pl.*) persons chosen from among the bystanders or those present in court to serve on the jury when the original panel has become deficient in number. **2.** a supply of men, or a man, so chosen. **3.** the order or writ summoning them. [t. ML: *tālēs* (*dē circumstantibus*) such (of the bystanders)]

tales·man (tālz′mən, tā′lēz mən), *n., pl.* **-men.** a person summoned as one of the tales.

tale·tell·er (tāl′těl′ər), *n.* a talebearer. **—tale′-tell′ing**, *n.*

tali-, a word element meaning "ankle," as in *taligrade.* [comb. form repr. L *tālus*]

Ta·lien (dä′lyěn′), *n.* Chinese name of **Dairen.**

Tal·i·es·in (tăl′ĭ ěs′ĭn), *n.* fl. A.D. 6th century, Welsh bard to whom a collection of medieval poetry is ascribed.

tal·i·grade (tăl′ə grād′), *adj.* *Zool.* walking on the outer side of the foot.

tal·i·on (tăl′ĭ ən), *n.* retaliation as authorized by law, esp. when the punishment inflicted corresponds in kind

and degree to the injury, as "eye for eye" (Lev. 24:20). [ME, t. L: s. *tālio*]

tal·i·ped (tăl′ə pĕd′), *adj.* **1.** (of a foot) twisted or distorted out of shape or position. **2.** (of a person) club-footed. **—n. 3.** a taliped person or animal.

tal·i·pes (tăl′ə pēz′), *n.* **1.** clubfoot. **2.** the condition of being clubfooted. [f. TALI- + L *pēs* foot]

tal·i·pot (tăl′ə pŏt′), *n.* a tall palm, *Corypha umbraculifera* of southern India and Ceylon, whose large leaves are much used for making fans and umbrellas, for covering houses, and in place of writing paper. [t. Malayalam: m. *tālipat*, t. Hind.: m. *tālpat*, g. Skt. *tālapattra* leaf of the fan palm]

tal·is·man (tăl′ĭs mən, -ĭz-), *n., pl.* **-mans. 1.** a stone, ring, or other object, engraved with figures or characters under certain superstitious observances of the heavens, which is supposed to possess occult powers, and is worn as an amulet or charm. **2.** any amulet or charm. **3.** anything of almost magi **c power.** [t. Ar.: m. *tilsaman*, pl. of *tilsam*, t. LGk.: m. *télesma* talisman, (earlier) religious rite, performance, completion] **—tal·is·man·ic** (tăl′ĭs măn′ĭk, -ĭz-), **tal′is·man′i·cal**, *adj.*

talk (tôk), *v.i.* **1.** to make known or interchange ideas, information, etc., by means of spoken words; speak or converse. **2.** to consult or confer. **3.** to gossip. **4.** to chatter or prate. **5.** to communicate ideas by other means than speech, as by writing, signs, or signals. **6.** to make sounds imitative or suggestive of speech. **—v.t. 7.** to express in words; utter: *to talk sense.* **8.** to use as a spoken language: *he can talk three languages.* **9.** to discuss: *to talk politics.* **10.** to bring, put, drive, influence, etc., by talk: *to talk a person to sleep.* **—n. 11.** act of talking; speech; conversation, esp. of a familiar or informal kind. **12.** a conference. **13.** report or rumor; gossip. **14.** a subject or occasion of talking, esp. of gossip. **15.** mere empty speech. **16.** a way of talking: *baby talk.* **17.** language, dialect, or lingo. [ME, c. East Fris. *talken*; akin to TALE, n., TELL, v.] **—talk′-er**, *n.* **—Syn. 1.** See **speak.**

talk·a·tive (tô′kə tĭv), *adj.* inclined to talk a great deal. **—talk′a·tive·ly**, *adv.* **—talk′a·tive·ness**, *n.* **—Syn. 1.** TALKATIVE, GARRULOUS, LOQUACIOUS agree in referring to one who talks a great deal. TALKATIVE is a mildly unfavorable word applied to one who is in the habit of talking a great deal and often without significance: *a talkative child.* The GARRULOUS person talks with wearisome persistence about personal and trivial things: *a garrulous old woman.* A LOQUACIOUS person, intending to be sociable, talks continuously and at length: *a loquacious hostess.* **—Ant. 1.** taciturn.

talk·ie (tô′kĭ), *n.* *Colloq.* a talking picture.

talking machine, phonograph.

talking picture, a motion picture with accompanying synchronized speech, singing, etc.

talk·ing-to (tô′kĭng tōō′), *n., pl.* **-tos.** *Colloq.* a scolding.

tall (tôl), *adj.* **1.** having a relatively great stature; of more than average height: *tall grass.* **2.** having stature or height as specified: *a man six feet tall.* **3.** *Colloq.* high, great, or large in amount: *a tall price.* **4.** *Colloq.* extravagant; difficult to believe: *a tall story.* **5.** *Colloq.* high-flown or grandiloquent. **6.** *Obs.* a. brave. **b.** handsome. **c.** excellent. **d.** valiant. [ME *tal*, OE *getæl* prompt; cf. Goth. *untals* disobedient] **—tall′ish**, *adj.* **—tall′ness**, *n.* **—Syn. 1.** See **high. —Ant. 1.** low, short.

tal·lage (tăl′ĭj), *n.* **1.** a tax imposed upon the unfree tenants of a manor by the lord. **2.** a compulsory tax levied by the Norman and early Angevin kings of England upon the demesne lands of the crown and upon all royal towns. [ME, t. OF: m. *taillage*, der. *taillier* cut, limit, tax]

Tal·la·has·see (tăl′ə hăs′ĭ), *n.* the capital of Florida, in the N part. 48,174 (1960).

tall·boy (tôl′boi′), *n.* **1.** *Brit.* a highboy. **2.** a tall chimney pot. **3.** a tall-stemmed glass for wine, etc.

Tal·ley·rand-Pé·ri·gord (tăl′ĭ rănd′; *Fr.* tȧ lē răn′-pě rē gôr′), *n.* **Charles Maurice de** (shȧrl mō rēs′ də), 1754–1838, French statesman, noted for his craftiness.

Tal·linn (tăl′lĭn), *n.* a seaport in the NW Soviet Union, on the Gulf of Finland: capital of the Estonian Republic. 257,000 (est. 1956). Russian, **Revel.** German, **Reval.**

tal·lith (tăl′ĭth, tä′lĭs), *n.* a mantle or a scarflike garment with fringes at the four corners, worn by Jews at prayer. [t. Heb., der. *tālal* cover]

tall oil (tăl), a resinous secondary product resulting from the manufacture of chemical wood pulp: used in making soaps, etc. [t. Sw: m. *talløl* pine beer]

tal·low (tăl′ō), *n.* **1.** the fatty tissue or suet of animals. **2.** the harder fat of sheep, cattle, etc., separated by melting from the fibrous and membranous matter naturally mixed with it, and used to make candles, soap, etc. **3.** any of various similar fatty substances: *vegetable tallow.* **—v.t. 4.** to smear with tallow. [ME *talgh*, c. G *talg*] **—tal′low·like′**, *adj.* **—tal′low·y**, *adj.*

tal·ly (tăl′ĭ), *n., pl.* **-lies, v., -lied, -lying. —n. 1.** a stick of wood with notches cut to indicate the amount of a debt or payment, often split lengthwise across the notches, the debtor retaining one piece and the creditor the other. **2.** anything on which a score or account is kept. **3.** a notch or mark made on or in a tally. **4.** an

ăct, āble, dâre, ärt; ĕbb, ēqual; ĭf, īce; hŏt, ōver, ôrder, oil, bŏok, ōoze, out; ŭp, ūse, ûrge; ə = a in alone; ch, chief; g, give; ng, ring; sh, shoe; th, thin; ᵺ, that; zh, vision. See the full key on inside cover.

account or reckoning; a record of debit and credit, of the score of a game, or the like. **5.** a number or group of objects recorded. **6.** a mark made to register a certain number of objects, in keeping account, as, for instance, a group of five. **7.** a number of objects serving as a unit of computation. **8.** a ticket, label, or mark used as a means of identification, etc. **9.** anything corresponding to another thing as a counterpart or duplicate. —*v.t.* **10.** to mark or enter on a tally; register; record. **11.** to count or reckon up. **12.** to furnish with a tally or identifying label. **13.** *Archaic.* to cause to correspond or agree. —*v.i.* **14.** to correspond, as one part of a tally with the other; accord or agree: *Does his story tally with John's?* [ME *taly*, t. AF: m. *tallie*, ult. t. L: m. *tālea* rod. See TAIL²] —**tal′li·er,** *n.*

tal·ly·ho (*n., v.* tăl′Ȳhō′; *interj.* tăl′Ȳhō′), *n., pl.* **-hos,** *interj., v.,* **-hoed** or **ho′d, -hoing.** *Chiefly Brit.* —*n.* **1.** a mail coach or a four-in-hand pleasure coach. **2.** a cry of "tallyho." —*interj.* **3.** a huntsman's cry on catching sight of the fox. —*v.t.* **4.** to arouse by crying "tallyho," as to hunting dogs. —*v.i.* **5.** to utter a cry of "tallyho." [t. F: m. *taïaut*]

Tallyho

Tal·mud (tăl′mŭd), *n.* **1.** the designation of the two commentaries on the Mishnah, one produced in Palestine (at about A.D. 375) and the other in Babylonia (at about A.D. 500); Gemara. **2.** a designation of both the Mishnah and the commentary on it. [t. Heb.: study, instruction] —**Tal·mud′ic, Tal·mud′i·cal,** *adj.*

Tal·mud·ist (tăl′mŭdĭst), *n.* **1.** one of the writers or compilers of the Talmud. **2.** one who accepts the doctrines of the Talmud. **3.** one versed in the Talmud.

tal·on (tăl′ən), *n.* **1.** a claw, esp. of a bird of prey. **2.** (in a lock) the shoulder on the bolt against which the key presses in shooting the bolt. **3.** *Cards.* the cards left over after the deal; the stock. [ME, t. OF: heel, g. s. LL *tălo* talon, r. L *tālus* ankle, heel] —**tal′oned,** *adj.*

Ta·los (tā′lŏs), *n. Gk. Legend.* **1.** the inventive nephew of Daedalus, by whom he was jealously slain. **2.** a man of brass made by Hephaestus for Minos, to guard Crete.

ta·luk (tă′lŏŏk, tä′lŏŏk′), *n.* (in India) **1.** a hereditary estate belonging to a native proprietor. **2.** a subdivision of a revenue district, placed under a native collector. [t. Hind., of Ar. orig.]

ta·lus¹ (tā′ləs), *n., pl.* **-li** (-lī). *Anat.* the astragalus. [t. L]

ta·lus² (tā′ləs), *n.* **1.** a slope. **2.** *Geol.* a sloping mass of rocky fragments at the base of a cliff. **3.** *Fort.* the sloping side or face of a wall. [t. F, t. L: ankle]

tam (tăm), *n.* tam-o′-shanter.

tam·a·ble (tā′məbəl), *adj.* that may be tamed.

ta·ma·le (təmä′lĬ), *n.* a Mexican dish made of crushed corn and minced meat, seasoned with red peppers, etc., wrapped in corn husks, and steamed. [back formation from *tamales*, t. Mex. Sp.: pl. of *tamal*, t. Aztec: m. *tamalli*]

ta·man·dua (tä′măndwä′), *n.* the four-toed anteater, *Tamandua tetradactyla*, a prehensile-tailed, arboreal edentate of the forests of tropical America. Also, **tam·an·du** (tăm′ən dōō′). [t. Pg., t. Tupi, f. *taa* ant + m. *munden* trap]

tam·a·rack (tăm′ərăk′), *n.* **1.** an American larch, *Larix laricina,* yielding a useful timber; hackmatack. **2.** any of several related, very similar trees. **3.** the wood of these trees. [t. N Amer. Ind.]

ta·ma·rau (tä′mərou′), *n.* a small, sturdy wild buffalo, *Bubalus mindorensis,* of Mindoro, Philippine Islands, having thick brown hair and short, massive horns.

tam·a·rin (tăm′ərĬn), *n.* any of various South American marmosets of the genus *Callithrix* and allied genera. [t. F, t. Carib d. of Cayenne]

tam·a·rind (tăm′ərĬnd), *n.* **1.** the fruit of a large caesalpiniaceous tropical tree, *Tamarindus indica,* a pod containing seeds enclosed in a juicy acid pulp that is used in beverages and food. **2.** the tree, cultivated throughout the tropics for its fruit, fragrant flowers, shade, and timber. [t. ML: s. *tamarindus,* t. Ar.: m. *tamrhindī* date of India]

tam·a·risk (tăm′ərĬsk), *n.* a plant of the Old World tropical genus *Tamarix,* esp. *T. gallica,* native in the Mediterranean region, an ornamental shrub or small tree with slender, feathery branches. [ME *tamariscus,* t. LL. Cf. L *tamarix*]

White-mustached tamarin, *Tamarin imperator* (Total length 22 in., tail 13 in.)

ta·ma·sha (təmä′shə), *n.* (in the East Indies) a spectacle; entertainment. [t. Hind. (Ar., Pers.)]

Ta·ma·tave (tä′mätäv′), *n.* a seaport on the E coast of Madagascar. 36,133 (1951).

Ta·mau·li·pas (tä mä′ŏŏ lē′päs), *n.* a state in NE Mexico, bordering on the Gulf of Mexico. 785,977 pop. (est. 1952); 30,731 sq. mi. *Cap.*: Ciudad Victoria.

Tam·bo·ra (tăm′bō rä′), *n.* a volcano in Indonesia, on Sumbawa island: violent eruption, 1815. 9042 ft.

tam·bour (tăm′bŏŏr), *n.* **1.** a drum. **2.** a drum player. **3.** a circular frame consisting of two hoops, one fitting within the other, in which cloth is stretched for embroidering. **4.** embroidery done on this. —*v.t., v.i.* **5.** to embroider on a tambour. [late ME, t. F. See TABOR]

tam·bou·rine (tăm′bərēn′), *n.* a small drum consisting of a circular wooden frame with a skin stretched over it and several pairs of jingles (metal disks) inserted into the frame, played by striking with the knuckles, shaking, etc. [t. F: m. *tambourin,* dim. of *tambour* TAMBOUR]

Spanish tambourine

Tam·bov (tăm bôf′), *n.* a city in the central Soviet Union in Europe. 150,000 (est. 1956).

tame (tām), *adj.,* **tamer, tamest,** *v.,* **tamed, taming.** —*adj.* **1.** changed from the wild or savage state; domesticated: *a tame bear.* **2.** gentle, fearless, or without shyness, as if domesticated, as an animal. **3.** tractable, docile, or submissive, as a person, the disposition, etc. **4.** lacking in animation; dull; insipid: *a tame existence.* **5.** spiritless or pusillanimous. **6.** cultivated, or improved by cultivation, as a plant, its fruit, etc. —*v.t.* **7.** to make tame; domesticate; make tractable; subdue. **8.** to deprive of courage, ardor, or interest. **9.** to soften; tone down. [ME; OE *tam,* c. G. *zahm;* akin to Goth. *tamjan,* v., L *domāre*] —**tam′a·ble, tame′a·ble,** *adj.* —**tame′ly,** *adv.* —**tame′ness,** *n.*

tame·less (tām′lĬs), *adj.* untamed or untamable. —**tame′less·ness,** *n.*

Tam·er·lane (tăm′ərlān′), *n.* (*Timour* or *Timur*) 1336?–1405, Mongol conqueror of most of southern and western Asia. Also, **Tam·bur·laine** (tăm′bərlān′).

Tam·il (tăm′əl, tŭm′əl), *n.* **1.** a member of a people of Dravidian stock of southern India and Ceylon. **2.** their language, spoken southward from Madras. —*adj.* **3.** of or pertaining to the Tamils or their language.

Taming of the Shrew, a comedy (1603) by Shakespeare.

Tam·ma·ny Hall (tăm′ənĬ), **1.** a powerful Democratic political organization in New York City, founded in 1789 as a fraternal benevolent society (**Tammany Society**). **2.** the building in which the Tammany organization had its headquarters. [t. Amer. Ind: m. *taminy,* var. form of name of an Indian chief in 17th cent. Pa., humorously described as a friend of Washington]

Tam·mer·fors (tăm′mərfôrs′), *n.* Swedish name of Tampere.

Tam·muz (tăm′mōōz; *Bib.* täm′ŭz), *n.* **1.** (in the Jewish calendar) the tenth month of the year. **2.** a Babylonian god of the springtime and of vegetation, whose return to life from the underworld symbolized the rebirth of earth at spring. Also, **Thammuz.** [t. Heb.]

tam-o′-shan·ter (tăm′əshăn′tər), *n.* a cap, of Scottish origin, with a flat crown larger in diameter than the headband; tam. [named after the hero of a poem by Burns]

tamp (tămp), *v.t.* **1.** to force in or down by repeated, somewhat light strokes. **2.** (in blasting) to fill (the hole made by the drill) with earth, etc., after the powder or explosive has been introduced. [appar. akin to TAMPION]

Tam·pa (tăm′pə), *n.* a seaport in W Florida, on Tampa Bay, an inlet of the Gulf of Mexico: fishing resort. 274,970 (1960).

tam·per¹ (tăm′pər), *v.i.* **1.** to meddle, esp. for the purpose of altering, damaging, misusing, etc. (fol. by *with*): *to tamper with a lock.* **2.** to engage secretly or improperly in something. **3.** to undertake underhand or corrupt dealings, as in order to influence improperly (fol. by *with*): *to tamper a witness.* [var. of TEMPER, v.] —**tam′per·er,** *n.*

tamp·er² (tăm′pər), *n.* one who or that which tamps. [f. TAMP + -ER¹]

Tam·pe·re (tăm′pĕ′rĕ), *n.* a city in SW Finland. 97,673 (est. 1951). Swedish, **Tammerfors.**

Tam·pi·co (tăm pē′kō; *Sp.* täm pē′kō), *n.* a seaport in E Mexico, in Tamaulipas state. 114,168 (1956).

tam·pi·on (tăm′pĬən), *n.* a wooden plug or stopper placed in the muzzle of a piece of ordnance when not in use, to keep out dampness and dust. Also, **tompion.** [t. F: m. *tampon,* var. of *tapon,* der. *tape* plug]

tam·pon (tăm′pŏn), *Surg.* —*n.* **1.** a plug of cotton or the like inserted into an orifice, wound, etc., as to stop hemorrhage. —*v.t.* **2.** to fill or plug with a tampon. [t. F. See TAMPION]

tam-tam (tŭm′tŭm′), *n.* **1.** a gong with indefinite pitch. **2.** tom-tom. [var. of TOM-TOM]

tan (tăn), *v.,* **tanned, tanning,** *n., adj.* —*v.t.* **1.** to convert (a hide) into leather, esp. by soaking or steeping in a bath prepared from oak or hemlock bark or synthetically. **2.** to make brown by exposure to the sun. **3.** *Colloq.* to beat or thrash. —*v.i.* **4.** to become tanned. —*n.* **5.** the brown color imparted to the skin by exposure to the sun or open air. **6.** yellowish brown; light brown. **7.** the bark of the oak, hemlock, etc., bruised and broken by a mill, and used for tanning hides. —*adj.* **8.** of the color of tan; yellowish-brown. **9.** used in or relating to tanning processes, materials, etc. [ME *tanne,* blend of OE *tannian,* t. ML: m. *tannāre,* der. *tannum,* n.] —**tan′na·ble,** *adj.*

tan, tangent. Also, **tan.**

Ta·na (tä′nä), *n.* **1.** a river in E Africa, in Kenya, flowing SE to the Indian Ocean. ab. 500 mi. **2. Lake,** Also, **Lake Tsana.** a lake in NW Ethiopia: the source of the Blue Nile. ab. 1150 sq. mi.

tan·a·ger (tăn′ə jər), *n.* any of numerous small, usually brightly colored oscine birds constituting the New World family *Traupidae*, most of which inhabit the warmer parts of South America. Well-known U.S. species are the **summer tanager,** *Piranga rubra,* and the **scarlet tanager,** *P. olivacea.* [t. NL: m. *tanagra,* t. Brazilian (Tupi): m. *tangara*]

Tan·a·gra (tăn′ə grə), *n.* a town in ancient Greece, in Boeotia: terra-cotta figurines; Spartan victory over the Athenians, 457 B.C.

tan·a·grine (tăn′ə grĭn), *adj.* of or pertaining to the tanagers; belonging to the tanager family.

Tan·a·na (tăn′ə nä), *n.* a river flowing from E Alaska NW to the Yukon river. ab. 700 mi. long.

Ta·na·na·rive (tä nä nä rēv′), *n.* the capital of the Malagasy Republic, in the central part. 206,324 (1959). Also, **Antananarivo.**

tan·bark (tăn′bärk′), *n.* bark used in tanning; tan.

Tan·cred (tăng′krĭd), *n.* died 1112, French soldier; a leader of the first Crusade.

tan·dem (tăn′dəm), *adv.* **1.** one behind another; in single file: *to drive horses tandem.* —*adj.* **2.** having animals, seats, parts, etc., arranged tandem, or one behind another: *a tandem bicycle.* —*n.* **3.** a team of horses so harnessed. **4.** a two-wheeled carriage, with a high driver's seat, drawn by two or more horses. **5.** a tandem bicycle or the like. [t. L: at length (in time), prob. at first humorously used]

Tandem

Ta·ney (tô′nĭ), *n.* **Roger Brooke,** 1777–1864, U.S. jurist: chief justice of Supreme Court, 1836–64.

tang[1] (tăng), *n.* **1.** a strong taste or flavor. **2.** the distinctive flavor or quality of a thing. **3.** a pungent or distinctive odor. **4.** a smack, touch, or suggestion of something. **5.** a long and slender projecting strip, tongue, or prong forming part of an object, as a chisel, file, knife, etc., and serving as a means of attachment for another part, as a handle or stock. **6.** surgeonfish. —*v.t.* **7.** to furnish with a tang. [ME *tange,* t. Scand.; cf. Icel. *tangi* pointed object, akin to TONGS]

tang[2] (tăng), *n.,* *v.t.,* *v.i.* ring; clang; twang. [imit.]

Tang (täng), *n.* a Chinese dynasty, A.D. 618–907, noted for territorial expansion (esp. cultural contact with Central Asia), first development of printing, the political as well as religious importance of Buddhism, and the highest development of Chinese poetry. [t. Chinese (Pekingese)]

Tan·gan·yi·ka (tăn′gən yē′kə, tăng′-), *n.* **1. Lake,** a lake in central Africa between Republic of the Congo and Tanganyika: the longest fresh-water lake in the world. ab. 450 mi. long; 30–45 mi. wide; ab. 12,700 sq. mi. **2.** a former independent state in E Africa, now the mainland part of Tanzania. 9,238,000 pop. (est. 1960); 361,800 sq. mi.

Tanganyika and Zanzibar, United Republic of, former name of Tanzania.

Tanganyika Territory, the former name of Tanganyika.

tan·ge·lo (tăn′jə lō), *n., pl.* **-los.** **1.** a hybrid between the tangerine mandarin and the pomelo or grapefruit trees. **2.** its fruit. [b. TANG(ERINE) and (POM)ELO]

tan·gen·cy (tăn′jən sĭ), *n.* state of being tangent.

tan·gent (tăn′jənt), *adj.* **1.** touching. **2.** *Geom.* touching, as a straight line in relation to a curve or surface; passing through two (or more) consecutive points of a curve or surface. **3.** in contact along a single line or element, as a plane with a cylinder. —*n.* **4.** *Geom.* a tangent line or plane. **5.** *Trigon.* **a.** (of an angle) a trigonometric function equal to the ratio of the ordinate of the end point of the arc to the abscissa of this end point, the origin being at the center of the circle on which the arc lies and the initial point of the arc being on the x-axis. *Abbr.:* tan or tgn. **b.** (orig.) a straight line perpendicular to the radius of a circle at one end of an arc and extending from this point to the produced radius which cuts off the arc at its other end. **6.** *Survey.* the straight portion of a survey line between curves, as on railroad or highway alignment. **7.** a sudden divergence from one course, thought, etc., to another: *to fly off on a tangent.* [t. L: s. *tangens,* ppr., touching]

Tangents
A. Ordinary;
B. Inflectional;
C. Cuspidal;
D. Nodal

tan·gen·tial (tăn jĕn′shəl), *adj.* **1.** pertaining to or of the nature of a tangent; being or moving in the direction of a tangent. **2.** merely touching; slightly connected. **3.** divergent or digressive. Also, **tan·gen·tal** (tăn jĕn′təl). —**tan·gen′tial·ly,** *adv.*

tan·ge·rine (tăn′jə rēn′), *n.* **1.** a small, loose-skinned variety of mandarin orange. See **mandarin** (def. 4). **2.** deep orange; reddish orange. [f. TANG(I)ER + -INE[4]]

tan·gi·ble (tăn′jə bəl), *adj.* **1.** capable of being touched; discernible by the touch; material or substantial. **2.** real or actual, rather than imaginary or visionary. **3.** definite; not vague or elusive: *no tangible grounds for suspicion.* [t. L: m.s. *tangibilis*] —**tan′gi·bil′i·ty, tan′gi·ble·ness,** *n.* —**tan′gibly,** *adv.*

tangible assets, resources in the form of real estate or chattels.

Tan·gier (tăn jîr′), *n.* a seaport in N Morocco near the Strait of Gibraltar; formerly capital of the internationalized **Tangier Zone** which became part of Morocco in 1956. 162,110 (est. 1953). See **Morocco.**

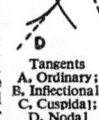

tan·gle (tăng′gəl), *v.,* **-gled, -gling,** *n.* —*v.t.* **1.** to bring together into a mass of confusedly interlaced or intertwisted threads, strands, or other like parts; snarl. **2.** to involve in something that hampers, obstructs, or overgrows: *bushes tangled with vines.* **3.** to catch and hold in, or as in, a net or snare. —*v.i.* **4.** to be or become tangled. —*n.* **5.** a tangled condition. **6.** a tangled or confused mass or assemblage of something. **7.** a confused jumble: *a tangle of contradictory statements.* [ME *tangil,* nasalized var. of *tagil* entangle, t. Scand.; cf. d. Sw. *taggla* disarrange]

tan·gle·ber·ry (tăng′gəl bĕr′ĭ), *n., pl.* **-ries.** a huckleberry, *Gaylussacia frondosa,* of the eastern U.S.

tan·go (tăng′gō), *n., pl.* **-gos,** *v.,* **-goed, -going.** —*n.* **1.** a round dance, of Spanish-American origin, danced by couples, and having many varied steps, figures, and poses. **2.** music for this dance. —*v.i.* **3.** to dance the tango. [t. Sp.]

tan·gram (tăng′grəm), *n.* a Chinese puzzle consisting of a square cut into five triangles, a square, and a rhomboid, which can be combined so as to form a great variety of other figures.

tang·y (tăng′ĭ), *adj.,* **tangier, tangiest.** having a tang.

Ta·nis (tā′nĭs), *n.* an ancient city of Lower Egypt, in Nile delta: ancient capital of Egypt. Biblical, **Zoan.**

tan·ist (tăn′ĭst, thŏn′-), *n. Hist.* the successor apparent to a Celtic chief, usually the oldest or worthiest of his kin, chosen by election among the tribe during the chief's lifetime. [t. Irish, Gaelic: m. *tánaiste* immediate heir to estate]

tan·ist·ry (tăn′ĭs trĭ, thŏn′-), *n.* the system among various Celtic tribes of choosing a tanist.

Tan·jore (tăn jōr′), *n.* a city in SE India, in Madras state. 100,680 (1951).

tank (tăngk), *n.* **1.** a large receptacle or structure for holding water or other liquid **or a gas:** *tanks for storing oil.* **2.** a natural or artificial pool, pond, or lake. **3.** *Mil.* an armored, self-propelled combat vehicle, armed with cannon and machine guns and moving on a caterpillar tread. —*v.t.* **4.** to put or store in a tank. [sandhi var. of ME *stank,* t. OF: m. *estanc* pool. See STANCH] —**tank′less,** *adj.* —**tank′like′,** *adj.*

tank·age (tăngk′ĭj), *n.* **1.** the capacity of a tank or tanks. **2.** act or process of storing liquid in a tank. **3.** the price charged for this. **4.** the residue from tanks in which carcasses and other offal have been steamed and the fat has been rendered, used as a fertilizer.

tank·ard (tăngk′ərd), *n.* a large drinking cup, now usually with a handle and a hinged cover. [ME; cf. MD *tanckaer t*]

Tankard

tank destroyer, a high-speed self-propelled, armored, combat vehicle with antitank cannon.

tank·er (tăngk′ər), *n.* a ship, plane, or truck designed to carry oil or other liquid in bulk.

tank farming, hydroponics.

tan·nate (tăn′āt), *n. Chem.* a salt of tannic acid.

Tan·nen·berg (tän′ən bĕr κH′), *n.* a village in N Poland: formerly in East Prussia; the scene of a decisive German victory over the Russians, 1914.

tan·ner (tăn′ər), *n.* one whose occupation it is to tan hides. [ME and OE *tannere.* See TAN]

tan·ner·y (tăn′ər ĭ), *n., pl.* **-neries.** a place where tanning is carried on.

Tann·häu·ser (tän′hoi′zər; *Ger.* tän′-), *n.* **1.** a Middle High German lyric poet of the 13th century. **2.** an opera (1845) by Wagner.

tan·nic (tăn′ĭk), *adj. Chem.* pertaining to, derived from, or related to tan or its tanning principle.

tan·nin (tăn′ĭn), *n. Chem.* any of a group of astringent vegetable principles or compounds, as the reddish compound which gives the tanning properties to oak bark or the whitish compound (the **common tannin,** or **tannic acid**) which occurs in large quantities in nutgalls. [f. s. ML *tannum* TAN, n., + -IN[2], on model of F *tannin*]

tan·ning (tăn′ĭng), *n.* **1.** the process or art of converting hides or skins into leather. **2.** a making brown, as by exposure to the sun. **3.** *Colloq.* a thrashing.

Tan·nu Tu·va (tän′nōō tōō′vä′), an autonomous region in the S Soviet Union in Asia: formerly an independent republic of Mongolia. ab. 65,000 pop.; ab. 64,000 sq. mi. Capital: Kizil Khoto.

Ta·no·an (tä′nō ən), *n.* an American Indian linguistic stock, which includes five languages spoken in several pueblos in northern New Mexico, including Taos.

ăct, āble, dâre, ärt; ĕbb, ēqual; ĭf, īce; hŏt, ōver, ôrder, oil, bŏŏk, ōōze, out; ŭp, ūse, ûrge; ə = a in alone; ch, chief; g, give; ng, ring; sh, shoe; th, thin; ŧħ, that; zh, vision. See the full key on inside cover.

tan·sy (tăn′zĭ), *n., pl.* **-sies.** any plant of the composite genus *Tanacetum*, esp. *T. vulgare*, a coarse, strong-scented herb with toothed pinnate leaves and corymbs of yellow flowers, a common weed in North America. [ME, t. OF: m. *tanesie*, var. of *athanasie*, t. ML: m. *athanasia*, t. Gk.: immortality]

Tan·ta (tän′tä), *n.* a city in N Egypt, in the Nile delta. 147,800 (est. 1952).

tan·ta·late (tăn′təlāt′), *n. Chem.* a salt of any tantalic acid.

tan·tal·ic (tăn tăl′ĭk), *adj. Chem.* of or pertaining to tantalum, esp. in the pentavalent state (Ta^{+5}).

tantalic acid, *Chem.* an acid, HTaO₃, which forms complex salts (tantalates).

tan·ta·lite (tăn′təlīt′), *n.* a mineral, iron tantalate, FeTa₂O₆, usually containing manganese and columbium, occurring in heavy (sp. gr. 6.0-7.4) black crystals: the principal ore of tantalum.

tan·ta·lize (tăn′təlīz′), *v.t.*, **-lized, -lizing.** to torment with, or as with, the sight of something desired but out of reach; tease by arousing expectations that are repeatedly disappointed. Also, *esp. Brit.*, **tan·ta·lise′.** [f. TANTAL(US) + -IZE] —**tan′ta·li·za′tion,** *n.* —**tan′ta·liz′er,** *n.* —**tan′ta·liz′ing·ly,** *adv.*

tan·ta·lous (tăn′tələs), *adj. Chem.* containing trivalent tantalum (Ta^{+3}).

tan·ta·lum (tăn′tələm), *n. Chem.* a rare element usually associated with columbium. On account of its resistance to single acids, it is used for handling such reactive acids as hydrochloric. *Symbol:* Ta; *at. wt.:* 180.88; *at. no.:* 73; *sp. gr.:* 16.6. [t. NL; der. TANTALUS, from its incapacity to absorb acid]

Tan·ta·lus (tăn′tələs), *n.* **1.** *Gk. Myth.* a son of Zeus and the nymph Pluto: father of Pelops and Niobe. For revealing secrets of the gods, he was condemned to stand, hungry and thirsty, in water up to his chin, under a tree laden with fruit. **2.** *(l.c.)* a stand containing visible decanters, secured by a lock.

tan·ta·mount (tăn′təmount′), *adj.* equivalent, as in value, force, effect, or signification. [appar. f. F *tant* (g L: *tantum* so much) + AMOUNT] —**Syn.** See **equal**

tan·ta·ra (tăn′tərə, tăn tär′ə, -tä′rə), *n.* **1.** a blast of a trumpet or horn. **2.** any similar sound. [imit.]

tan·tiv·y (tăn tĭv′ĭ), *adv., adj., n., pl.* **-tivies, interj.** *Archaic.* —*adv.* **1.** at full gallop or speed: *to ride tantivy.* —*adj.* **2.** swift; rapid. —*n.* **3.** a gallop; a rush. [? imit.]

tant mieux (tän myœ′), *French.* so much the better.

tan·to (tän′tō), *adv. Music.* too much; so much. [t. It., g. L *tantun* so much]

tant pis (tän pē′), *French.* so much the worse.

tan·trum (tăn′trəm), *n.* a sudden burst of ill humor; a fit of ill temper or passion. [orig. uncert.]

Tan·za·ni·a (tăn′zə nē′ə, tän zän′ē·ə; *Swahili* tän zä nē′ä) *n.* a republic in E Africa, comprising the former country Tanganyika, the islands of Zanzibar and Pemba, and adjacent small islands. 9,542,000 pop. (est. 1960); 362,820 sq. mi. *Cap.:* Dar es Salaam.

Tao·ism (dou′ĭzəm, tou′-), *n.* a religious system considered to be founded on the doctrines of Lao-tse and ranked with Confucianism and Buddhism as one of the three religions of China. [f. Chinese *tao* the way + -ISM] —**Tao′ist,** *n., adj.* —**Tao·is′tic,** *adj.*

Taos (tous), *n.* **1.** American Indian language of the Tanoan family. **2.** Indian pueblo in New Mexico.

tap¹ (tăp), *v.,* **tapped, tapping,** *n.* —*v.t.* **1.** to strike lightly but audibly; strike with slight blows. **2.** to make, put, etc., by tapping. **3.** to strike (the hand, foot, etc.) lightly upon or against something. **4.** to add a thickness of leather to the sole or heel of (a boot or shoe), as in repairing. —*v.i.* **5.** to strike lightly but audibly, as to attract attention. **6.** to strike light blows. —*n.* **7.** a light but audible blow. **8.** the sound made by this. **9.** *(pl.) Mil., Naval.* a signal on a drum, bugle, or trumpet, at which all lights in the soldiers' or sailors' quarters must be extinguished. **10.** a thickness of leather added to the sole or heel of a boot or shoe, as in repairing. **11.** a piece of metal attached to the toe or heel of a shoe to make the tapping of a dancer more audible. [ME *tappen*, t. F: m.s. *taper* strike, slap; of Gmc. orig.]

tap² (tăp), *n., v.,* **tapped, tapping.** —*n.* **1.** a cylindrical stick, long plug, or stopper for closing an opening through which liquid is drawn, as in a cask; a spigot. **2.** *Chiefly Brit.* a faucet or cock. **3. on tap, a.** ready to be drawn off and served, as liquor in a cask. **b.** furnished with a tap or cock, as a barrel containing liquor. **c.** ready for immediate use. **4.** a particular kind or quality of drink. **5.** the liquor drawn through a particular tap. **6.** *Brit.* a taphouse or taproom. **7.** an instrument for cutting the thread of an internal screw. **8.** a hole made in tapping, as one in a pipe to furnish connection for a branch pipe. **9.** *Elect.* a connection brought out of a winding at some point between its extremities. —*v.t.* **10.** to draw off (liquid) by drawing out or opening a tap, or by piercing the container; draw liquid from (any vessel or reservoir). **11.** to draw the tap or plug from, or pierce (a cask, etc.). **12.** to penetrate, reach, etc., for the purpose of drawing something off: *to tap telephone wires to hear conversations.* **13.** to furnish (a cask, etc.) with a tap. **14.** to cut a female screw thread in (a hole, etc.). **15.** to open outlets from (power lines, highways, pipes, etc.). [ME; OE *tæppa,* c. G *zapfen*]

ta·pa (tä′pä), *n.* an unwoven cloth of the Pacific islands, made by steeping and beating the inner bark of a tree, *Broussonetia Papyrifera.* [t. Polynesian]

Ta·pa·jós (tä′pə zhôs′), *n.* a river flowing NE through central Brazil to the Amazon. ab. 1100 mi.

tap dance, a dance in which the rhythm or rhythmical variation is audibly tapped out by the toe or heel. —**tap′-dance′,** *v.i.* —**tap′-danc′er,** *n.*

tape (tāp), *n., v.,* **taped, taping.** —*n.* **1.** a long narrow strip of linen, cotton, or the like, used for tying garments, etc. **2.** a long narrow strip of paper, metal, etc. **3.** a tapeline. **4.** a string stretched across the finishing line in a race and broken by the winning contestant. **5.** the ribbon of white paper on which a ticker prints quotations or news. —*v.t.* **6.** to furnish with a tape or tapes. **7.** to tie up or wind with tape. **8.** to measure with, or as if with a tapeline. **9.** *Colloq.* to tape-record. [ME, unexplained var. of ME *tappe,* OE *tæppe* strip (of cloth)] —**tap′er,** *n.* —**tape′less,** *adj.* —**tape′like′,** *adj.*

tape·line (tāp′līn′), *n.* a long strip or ribbon, as of linen or steel, marked with subdivisions of the foot or meter for measuring. Also, **tape measure.**

ta·per (tā′pər), *v.i.* **1.** to become gradually slenderer toward one end. **2.** to grow gradually lean. —*v.t.* **3.** to make gradually smaller toward one end. **4.** to reduce gradually. —*n.* **5.** gradual diminution of width or thickness in an elongated object. **6.** gradual decrease of force, capacity, etc. **7.** a spire or slender pyramid; anything having a tapering form. **8.** a candle, esp. a very slender one. **9.** a long wick coated with wax, tallow, or the like, as for use in lighting candles or gas. [ME *tapere* candle, OE *tapor;* orig. uncert.] —**ta′per·ing·ly,** *adv.*

tape·re·cord (tāp′rĭ kôrd′), *v.t.* to transcribe onto electromagnetic tape.

tape·re·cord·er (tāp′rĭ kôr′dər), *n.* **1.** a device used to record speech, music, etc., on electromagnetic tape. **2.** one who records on tape.

tape·re·cord·ing (tāp′rĭ kôr′dĭng), *n.* **1.** an electromagnetic tape on which speech, music, etc., have been recorded. **2.** the act of recording on electromagnetic tape.

tap·es·try (tăp′ĭs trĭ), *n., pl.* **-tries,** *v.,* **-tried, -trying.** —*n.* **1.** a fabric consisting of a warp upon which colored threads are woven by hand to produce a design, often pictorial, and used for wall hangings, furniture coverings, etc. **2.** a machine-woven reproduction of true tapestry. —*v.t.* **3.** to furnish, cover, or adorn with tapestry. [ME *tapestrye,* t. F: m. *tapisserie,* der. *tapissier* maker of tapestry, der. *tapis* TAPIS] —**tap′es·try·like′,** *adj.*

ta·pe·tum (tə pē′təm), *n., pl.* **-ta** (-tə). **1.** *Bot.* a layer of cells often investing the archespore in a developing sporangium and absorbed as the spores mature. **2.** *Anat., Zool.* any of certain membranous layers or the like, as in the choroid or retina. [t. LL, r. L *tapēte* carpet]

tape·worm (tāp′wûrm′), *n.* any of various flat or tapelike worms of the class *Cestoda,* lacking any alimentary canal, and parasitic when adult in the alimentary canal of man and other vertebrates.

tap·house (tăp′hous′), *n.* **1.** *Brit.* a house where liquor is kept on tap for sale; a drinking house. **2.** a taproom.

tap·i·o·ca (tăp′ĭ ō′kə), *n.* a granular farinaceous food substance prepared from cassava starch by drying while moist on heated plates, used for making puddings, thickening soups, etc. [t. Pg., t. Brazilian (Tupi-Guarani): m. *tipioca,* f. *tipi* residue + *og, ôk* squeeze out]

ta·pir (tā′pər), *n.* **1.** any of various slate-colored, stout-bodied, perissodactyl ungulates (family *Tapiridae*), mostly of tropical America, somewhat resembling swine and having a flexible proboscis. **2.** a Malayan species, closely resembling the New World tapirs but colored white from neck to rump. [t. Brazilian (Tupi): m. *tapira*]

tap·is (tăp′ĭ, tăp′ĭs, tä pē′), *n., pl.* **tapis.** **1.** a carpet, tapestry, or other covering. **2. on the tapis,** under consideration or discussion. [t. F, g. LL *tapētium,* t. Gk.: m. *tapētion,* dim. of *tápes* cloth wrought with figures]

South American tapir.
Tapirus terrestris
(Ab. 2 ft. high at the shoulder, 4 ft. long)

tap·per¹ (tăp′ər), *n.* one who or that which taps or strikes lightly. [f. TAP¹ + -ER¹]

tap·per² (tăp′ər), *n.* one who or what which taps, as trees for the sap or juice. [f. TAP² + -ER¹]

tap·pet (tăp′ĭt), *n. Mach.* a projection, cam, or the like which intermittently comes in contact with another part to which it communicates or from which it receives an intermittent motion. [f. TAP¹ + -ET]

tap·ping¹ (tăp′ĭng), *n.* **1.** the act of one who or that which taps or strikes lightly. **2.** the sound so made. [f. TAP¹ + -ING¹]

tap·ping² (tăp′ĭng), *n.* **1.** act of one who or that which taps casks, etc. **2.** that which is drawn by tapping. [TAP² + -ING¹]

tap·room (tăp′rōōm′, -rŏŏm′), *n. Brit.* a room, as in a tavern, in which liquor is sold; bar; saloon.

tap·root (tăp′rōōt′, -rŏŏt′), *n. Bot.* a main root descending downward from the radicle and giving off small lateral roots.

tap·ster (tăp′stər), *n. Archaic.* a bartender or barmaid. [ME; OE *tæppestre.* See TAP², n., -STER]

Ta·pu·ya (tä·pŏŏ′yə), *n.*, *pl.* **-ya**. a member of a linguistic family (**Tapuyan**) once in central Brazil. [t. Pg., t. Tupi (Brazilian): savage, enemy] —**Ta·pu′yan**, *adj.*

tar[1] (tär), *n.*, *v.*, **tarred, tarring.** —*n.* **1.** any of various dark-colored viscid products obtained by the destructive distillation of certain organic substances, such as coal, wood, etc. **2.** coal-tar pitch. —*v.t.* **3.** to smear or cover with, or as with, tar. [ME *terre*, OE *teru*- (s. *teru*), c. D and G *teer*; akin to TREE[1]]

tar[2] (tär), *n.* *Colloq.* a sailor. [said to be short for TARPAULIN] —**Syn.** See **sailor.**

Tar·a (tär′ə), *n.* a village in Ireland, near Dublin; the Hill of Tara was the home of the ancient Irish kings.

ta·ran·tass (tä′rän täs′), *n.* a large four-wheeled Russian carriage mounted without springs on two parallel longitudinal wooden bars. [t. Russ.: m. *tarantas*]

tar·an·tel·ia (tär′ən tĕl′ə), *n.* **1.** a rapid, whirling southern Italian dance in very quick sextuple (orig. quadruple) rhythm, usually performed by a single couple, and formerly supposed to be a remedy for tarantism. **2.** a popular dance derived from it. **3.** a piece of music for either dance or in its rhythm. [t. It., der. *Taranto*, g. L *Tarentum*]

tar·ant·ism (tär′ən tĭz′əm), *n.* a nervous affection characterized by an uncontrollable impulse to dance; esp. as prevalent in southern Italy from the 15th to the 17th century and popularly attributed to the bite of the tarantula (def. 3). [f. It. *Tarant*(o) name of city + -ISM. See TARANTELLA, TARANTULA]

Ta·ran·to (tä′rän tô′), *n.* a fortified seaport in SE Italy, on the Gulf of Taranto, an arm of the Mediterranean: founded by the Greeks in the 8th century B.C.; naval base. 180,000 (est. 1954). Ancient, **Tarentum.**

ta·ran·tu·la (tərăn′chələ), *n.*, *pl.* **-las, -lae** (-lē′). **1.** any of various large, hairy spiders of the family *Theraphosidae*, as *Eurypelma hentzi*, a common species of the southwestern U.S., whose bite is painful if not dangerous. **2.** any of various related spiders. **3.** a large spider of southern Europe, *Lycosa tarantula*, whose bite was fabled to cause tarantism. [t. ML, t. It: m. *tarantola*, der. *Taranto*]

Ta·ra·wa (tä′rä′wä; *native* tä′rä-wä′), *n.* one of the Gilbert Islands, in the central Pacific: taken by U.S. after severe fighting, Nov., 1943. 3582 (1947); 14 sq. mi.

Texas tarantula.
Eurypelma hentzi
(Body ab. 2 in. long)

ta·rax·a·cum (tərăk′səkəm), *n.* **1.** any of the composite plants, mostly stemless herbs, constituting the genus *Taraxacum*, as the dandelion. **2.** the root of the dandelion, used in medicine as a tonic, diuretic, and aperient. [t. ML, t. Ar.: m. *tarakhshaqōq*, t. Pers.: m. *talkh chakōk* bitter herb]

tar·boosh (tär bŏŏsh′), *n.* a cap of cloth or felt (nearly always red) with a tassel, worn by Mohammedan men either by itself or as the inner part of the turban. [t. Ar.: m. *tarbūsh*]

Tar·dieu (tär dyœ′), *n.* André Pierre Gabriel Amédée (än′ drĕ′ pyĕr′ gȧ brĕ ĕl′ ȧ mĕ dĕ′), 1876–1945, French statesman.

Tarboosh

tar·di·grade (tär′dəgrād′), *adj.* **1.** slow in pace or movement. **2.** of or pertaining to the *Tardigrada*, a class or subclass of minute herbaceous arthropods, lacking well-developed circulatory or respiratory systems. [t. L: m. *tardigradus*]

tar·do (tär′dō), *adj. Music.* slow. [t. It., g. L *tardus*]

tar·dy (tär′dĭ), *adj.*, **-dier, -diest. 1.** late or behindhand. **2.** moving or acting slowly; slow; sluggish. **3.** delaying through reluctance. [ME *tardive*, t. F, g. LL *tardivus*, der. L *tardus* slow] —**tar′di·ly,** *adv.* —**tar′di·ness,** *n.* —**Ant. 1.** prompt.

tare[1] (tär), *n.* **1.** any of various vetches, esp. *Vicia sativa.* **2.** the seed of a vetch. **3.** (in Biblical use) some injurious weed, possibly the darnel. [ME; cf. MD *tarwe* wheat]

tare[2] (tär), *n.*, *v.*, **tared, taring.** —*n.* **1.** the weight of the wrapping, receptacle, or conveyance containing goods. **2.** a deduction from the gross weight to allow for this. **3.** the weight of a vehicle without cargo, passengers, etc. **4.** *Chem.* a counterweight used to balance the weight of a container. —*v.t.* **5.** to ascertain, note, or allow for, the tare of. [late ME, t. ML: m. *tara*, t. Ar.: m. *tarha* deduction]

Ta·ren·tum (tərĕn′təm), *n.* ancient name of **Taranto.**

targe (tärj), *n. Archaic.* a round shield. [ME, t.OF; r. OE *targa*, t. Scand.; cf. Icel. *targa* shield, c. OHG *zarga* frame]

tar·get (tär′gĭt), *n.* **1.** a device, usually marked with concentric circles, to be aimed at in shooting practice or contests. **2.** any object used for this purpose. **3.** anything fired at. **4.** *Brit.* a goal to be reached. **5.** an object of abuse, scorn, derision, etc.; a butt. **6.** a diskshaped signal, as at a railroad switch, indicating the position of a switch. **7.** *Survey.* **a.** the sliding sight on a leveling rod. **b.** any marker on which sights are taken. **8.** *Hist.* a small round shield or buckler. [late ME, t. F: m. *targuete*. See TARGE] —**tar′get·less,** *adj.*

Tar·gum (tär′gŭm; *Heb.* tär gŏŏm′), *n.*, *pl.* **Targums, Targumim** (tär′gŏŏ mēm′). each of a number of translations or paraphrases of the various divisions of the

Hebrew Old Testament in the Aramaic language or dialect. [t. Aram.: interpretation] —**Tar′gum·ist,** *n.*

Tar·heel (tär′hēl′), *n. Colloq.* a native or inhabitant of North Carolina.

tar·iff (tär′ĭf), *n.* **1.** an official list or table showing the duties or customs imposed by a government on exports or, esp., imports. **2.** the system of duties so imposed. **3.** any duty in such a list or system. **4.** any table of charges, as of a railroad. **5.** *Brit.* the bill of fare in a restaurant or hotel. —*v.t.***6.** to subject to a tariff. **7.** to put a valuation on according to a tariff. [t. It.: s. *tariffa*, t. Ar.: m. *tarif* notification, information] —**tar′-iff·less,** *adj.*

Ta·rim (tä′rēm′), *n.* a river in NW China, in Sinkiang province, flowing through the vast **Tarim Basin,** cradled between the Kunlun and Tien Shan mountain systems, and ending in a number of small lakes in a desert region. ab. 1000 mi.

SOVIET UNION / Tarim River / Gobi Desert / AFGHANISTAN / IRAN / TARIM BASIN / W. PAKISTAN / TIBET / INDIA / EAST PAKISTAN / Arabian Sea

Tar·king·ton (tär′kĭng tən), *n.* (**Newton**) **Booth,** 1869–1946, U.S. novelist and playwright.

tar·la·tan (tär′lə tən), *n.* a thin, open, stiff cotton fabric, not washable. [t. F: m. *tarlatane*; orig. uncert.]

tarn (tärn), *n. N. Eng.; Literary in U.S.* a small mountain lake or pool. [ME *terne*, t. Scand.; cf. Icel. *tjörn*]

tar·nish (tär′nĭsh), *v.t.* **1.** to dull or alter the luster of (esp. a metallic surface by oxidation, etc.); discolor. **2.** to diminish or destroy the purity of; stain; sully. —*v.i.* **3.** to grow dull or discolored; lose luster. **4.** to become sullied. —*n.* **5.** a tarnished coating. **6.** tarnished condition; discoloration; alteration of the luster. **7.** stain or blemish. [t. F: m. *terniss*-, *ternir*, der. *terne* dull, dark, prob. of Gmc. orig.; cf. MHG *ternen* darken, OE *derne* obscure] —**tar′nish·a·ble,** *adj.*

Tar·no·pol (*Pol.* tär′nŏ′pŏl; *Russ.* tär′nŏ pŏl′y), *n.* Ternopol.

Tar·nów (tär′nŏŏf), *n.* a city in SE Poland, in Galicia. 58,000 (est. 1955).

ta·ro (tä′rō), *n.*, *pl.* **-ros. 1.** a stemless araceous plant, *Calocasia esculenta,* cultivated in tropical regions, in the Pacific islands and elsewhere, for its tuberous, starchy, edible root. **2.** the root. [t. Polynesian]

tar·pau·lin (tär pô′lĭn), *n.* **1.** a protective covering of canvas or other material waterproofed with tar, paint, or wax. **2.** a hat, esp. a sailor's, made of or covered with such material. **3.** *Rare.* a sailor. [earlier *tarpauling*, f. TAR[1] + PALL + -ING[1]]

Tar·pe·ia (tär pē′ə), *n. Rom. Legend.* a maid slain by Sabine soldiers after she had betrayed the citadel of Rome to them. Having asked for reward, she was killed by the shields they threw on her.

Tar·pe·ian (tär pē′ən), *adj.* of or noting a rock on the Capitoline Hill at Rome from which traitors were hurled.

tar·pon (tär′pŏn), *n.* a large fish, *Tarpon atlanticus,* of the warmer waters of the Atlantic, with compressed body and huge silvery scales, highly prized by anglers for the sport it offers. [orig. uncert.; cf. D. *tarpoen*]

Tar·quin (tär′kwĭn), *n.* **1.** one of a famous family of kings of early Rome. **2.** (*Lucius Tarquinius Superbus,* "the Proud") died after 510 B.C., last Roman king of this family.

tar·ra·gon (tär′ə gŏn′), *n.* **1.** an Old World composite plant, *Artemisia Dracunculus,* whose aromatic leaves are used for flavoring. **2.** the leaves themselves. [t. Sp: m. *taragona,* t. Ar.: m. *tarkhūn,* prob. t. Gk.: m. *drákōn* dragon, or *drakóntion* type of arum]

tar·ry[1] (tär′ĭ), *v.*, **-ried, -rying,** *n.*, *pl.* **-ries.** —*v.i.* **1.** to remain or stay, as in a place; sojourn. **2.** to delay or be tardy in acting, starting, coming, etc.; linger or loiter. **3.** to wait. —*v.t.* **4.** *Archaic.* to wait for. —*n.* **5.** *Archaic.* a stay; sojourn. [ME; orig. uncert.] —**tar′ri·er,** *n.* —**Syn. 3.** See **wait.**

tar·ry[2] (tär′ĭ), *adj.* of or like tar; smeared with tar. [f. TAR[1] + -Y[1]]

Tar·ry·town (tär′ĭ toun′), *n.* a village in SE New York, on the Hudson: Washington Irving's home.

tar·sal (tär′səl), *adj.* **1.** of or pertaining to the tarsus of the foot or leg. **2.** pertaining to the tarsi of the eyelids. —*n.* **3.** a tarsal bone, joint, or the like.

Tar·shish (tär′shĭsh), *n.* an ancient country, said to have been in S Spain: sea trade in silver and gold. I Kings 10:22.

tar·si·er (tär′sĭ′er), *n.* a small arboreal primate, genus *Tarsius,* with enormous eyes, sole representative of a suborder, *Tarsioidea:* found in Indonesia and parts of the Philippine Islands. [t. F. der. *tarse* TARSUS]

tar·so·met·a·tar·sus (tär′sō mĕt′ə tär′səs), *n.*, *pl.* **-si** (-sī). the large bone in the lower leg of a bird with which the toe bones articulate: the third segment from the body in the leg of a bird. [f. *tarso-* (comb. form of TARSUS) + METATARSUS]

tar·sus (tär′səs), *n.*, *pl.* **-si** (-sī). (Total length 14½ in.) *Anat., Zool.* **1.** the proximal segment of the foot; the collection of bones between the tibia and the metatarsus.

Tarsier.
Tarsius carbonarius
(Total length 14½ in.)

entering into the construction of the ankle joint and into the instep of man. See diag. under **skeleton**. **2.** the small plate of connective tissue along the border of an eyelid. **3.** tarsometatarsus. **4.** the fifth segment of an insect's leg. See diag. under **coxa**. [NL, t. Gk.: m. *tarsós* flat of the foot]

Tar·sus (tär/səs), *n.* a city in S Turkey, near the Mediterranean: an important seaport of ancient Cilicia, on the Cydnus river; birthplace of Saint Paul. 39,622 (1955).

tart[1] (tärt), *adj.* **1.** sharp to the taste; sour or acid: *tart apples*. **2.** sharp in character, spirit, or expression; cutting; caustic: *a tart remark*. [ME; OE *teart* sharp, rough. Cf. G *trotz*] —**tart/ly**, *adv.* —**tart/ness**, *n.*

tart[2], *n.* **1.** *U.S.* a small and saucer-shaped shell of pastry, filled with cooked fruit or other sweetened preparation, and having no top crust. **2.** *Brit.* a covered pie containing fruit or the like. **3.** *Chiefly Brit. Slang.* a girl or woman, esp. of low character; a prostitute. [ME *tarte*, t. OF: (m.) *tart(r)e*, g. L *tortula* (der. *torta*, pp., twisted) or ? b. L *tortula* and *tartarum* baked crust]

tar·tan[1] (tär/tən), *n.* **1.** a woolen or worsted cloth woven with stripes of different colors and widths crossing at right angles, worn chiefly by the Scottish Highlanders, each clan having its distinctive pattern. **2.** a design of such a plaid known by name of the clan wearing it. **3.** any plaid. —*adj.* **4.** of, pertaining to, or resembling tartan. **5.** made of tartan. [appar. t. F: m. *tiretaine* linsey-woolsey]

Macpherson tartan

tar·tan[2] (tär/tən), *n.* a single-masted vessel with a lateen sail and a jib, used in the Mediterranean. [t. F: m. *tartane*, t. It.: m. *tartana*, ? t. Ar.: m. *taridah* kind of ship]

tar·tar (tär/tər), *n.* **1.** a hard substance deposited on the teeth by the saliva, consisting of calcium phosphate, mucus, etc. **2.** the deposit from wines, potassium bitartrate. **3.** the partially purified product midway between the crude form (argol) and the further purified form (cream of tartar). [t. ML: s. *tartarum*, t. Gk.: m. *tártaron* (of Ar. orig.); r. ME *tartre*, t. F]

Tar·tar (tär/tər), *n.* **1.** a member of any of a mingled host of Mongolian, Turkish, and other tribes, who, under the leadership of Genghis Khan, overran Asia and eastern Europe during the Middle Ages. **2.** a member of the descendants of this people variously intermingled with other races and tribes, now inhabiting parts of the European and W and central Asiatic Soviet Union. **3.** any of several Turkic languages of W central Asia, particularly Uzbeg. **4.** (*also l.c.*) a savage, intractable person. **5.** (*l.c.*) a shrew or vixen. **6.** one who proves unexpectedly troublesome or powerful (commonly in *to catch a Tartar*). —*adj.* **7.** pertaining to a Tartar or Tartars, or to their language. Also, **Tatar**. [ME, t. ML: s. *Tartarus*, t. Pers.: m. *Tatar*, by association with TARTARUS]

Tar·tar·e·an (tär tär/Yən), *adj.* of or pertaining to Tartarus; infernal.

tartar emetic, potassium antimonyl tartrate, $K(SbO)C_4H_4O_6.½H_2O$, a poisonous salt with a sweetish metallic taste, occurring in white crystals or as a white granular powder, used in medicine, dyeing, etc.

tar·tare sauce (tär/tər), a mayonnaise dressing usually with chopped pickles, onions, olives, capers, and green herbs added. [t. F: m. *sauce tartare*]

tar·tar·ic (tär tär/Yk, -tär/Yk), *adj.* pertaining to or derived from tartar.

tartaric acid, *Chem.* an organic acid, $(CHOH·COOH)_2$, existing in four isomeric modifications, the common or dextrorotatory form being a colorless crystalline compound obtained from grapes, etc.

tar·tar·ize (tär/tə rīz/), *v.t.,* **-ized**, **-izing**. *Chem.* to impregnate, combine, or treat with tartar, or potassium bitartrate. —**tar/tar·i·za/tion,** *n.*

tar·tar·ous (tär/tər əs), *adj.* consisting of or containing tartar.

Tar·ta·rus (tär/tər əs), *n. Gk. Myth.* **1.** a sunless abyss below Hades, in which Zeus imprisoned the Titans. **2.** (later) a place of punishment for the wicked. **3.** Hades, or the lower world in general.

Tar·ta·ry (tär/tə rY), *n.* a historical name used to designate an indefinite region in E Europe and Asia, sometimes extending to the Sea of Japan. Also, **Tatary**.

tart·let (tärt/lYt), *n. Brit.* a small tart.

tar·trate (tär/trāt), *n. Chem.* a salt or ester of tartaric acid. [t. F, der. *tartre* TARTAR]

tar·trat·ed (tär/trā tYd), *adj. Chem.* formed into a tartrate; combined with tartaric acid.

tar·tra·zine (tär/trə zēn/, -zYn), *n. Chem.* a type of yellow dye used in food materials. [f. *tartro-* (comb. form repr. TARTAR) + $AZ(O)$- + -INE[2]]

Tar·tu (tär/tōō), *n.* a city in the W Soviet Union, in the Estonian Republic. 60,000 (est. 1948). German, **Dorpat.** Russian, **Yurev.**

Tar·tuffe (tär tōōf/; *Fr.* tár tyf/), *n.* **1.** a comedy (1667) by Molière. **2.** a hypocritical pretender to piety.

Tash·kent (täsh kĕnt/), *n.* a city in the SW Soviet Union in Asia: the capital of Uzbek Republic. 778,000 (est. 1956).

ta·sim·e·ter (tə sYm/ə tər), *n.* an electrical device for determining minute changes in temperature, etc.,

by means of the changes in pressure caused by expanding or contracting solids. [f. Gk. *tási(s)* tension + -METER] —**tas·i·met·ric** (tăs/ə mĕt/rYk), *adj.* —**ta·sim/e·try,** *n.*

task (tăsk, täsk), *n.* **1.** a definite piece of work assigned or falling to a person; a duty. **2.** any piece of work. **3.** a matter of considerable labor or difficulty. **4. take to task**, to call to account, as for fault; blame or censure. **5.** *Obs.* a tax or impost. —*v.t.* **6.** to subject to severe or excessive labor or exertion; put a strain upon (powers, resources, etc.). **7.** to impose a task on. **8.** *Obs.* to tax. [ME, t. ML: m.s. *tasca*, metathetic var. of *taxa* TAX] —**task/less,** *adj.*

task force, *Naval, Mil.* a temporary grouping of units under one commander, formed for the purpose of carrying out a specific operation or mission.

task·mas·ter (tăsk/măs/tər, täsk/mäs/-), *n.* one whose function it is to assign tasks to others, esp. burdensome tasks.

Tasm., Tasmania.

Tas·man (tăz/mən; *Du.* täs/män), *n.* **Abel Janszoon** (ä/bəl yän/sōn), 1602?–59, Dutch navigator, discoverer of Tasmania, New Zealand, and other islands in the S Pacific.

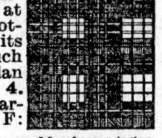

Tas·ma·ni·a (tăz mā/nY ə), *n.* an island S of Australia: one of the states of the Commonwealth of Australia. 308,752 pop. (1954); 26,215 sq. mi. *Cap.*: Hobart. Formerly, **Van Diemen's Land.** —**Tas·ma/ni·an,** *adj., n.*

Tasmanian devil, a ferocious, black-and-white, carnivorous marsupial, *Sarcophilus harrisii,* of Tasmania; ursine dasyure.

Tasmanian wolf, the thylacine. Also, **Tasmanian tiger.**

Tas·man Sea (tăz/mən), a part of the Pacific between SE Australia and New Zealand.

Tasmanian devil, *Sarcophilus harrisii* (Total length 2 ft., tail 9 in.

Tass (tăs, täs), *n.* a news-gathering agency of the Soviet Union.

tas·sel[1] (tăs/əl), *n., v.,* **-seled, -seling** or (*esp. Brit.*) **-selled, -selling.** —*n.* **1.** a pendent ornament, orig. a clasp consisting commonly of a bunch of threads, small cords, or strands hanging from a roundish knob or head. **2.** something resembling this, as the inflorescence of certain plants, esp. that at the summit of a stalk of Indian corn. —*v.t.* **3.** to furnish or adorn with tassels. **4.** to form into a tassel or tassels. **5.** to remove the tassel from (growing Indian corn), e.g. in order to improve the crop. —*v.i.* **6.** (of Indian corn, etc.) to put forth tassels. [ME, t. OF: a fastening for cloak]

tas·sel[2] (tăs/əl), *n. Obs.* tercel.

tas·ses (tăs/Yz), *n.pl.* tassets.

tas·sets (tăs/Yts), *n.pl. Armor.* a pair of defenses for the upper thighs suspended from waist plates by straps.

Tas·so (tăs/ō; *It.* täs/sō), *n.* **Torquato** (tôr kwä/tô), 1544–95, Italian poet.

taste (tāst), *v.,* **tasted, tasting,** *n.* —*v.t.* **1.** to try the flavor or quality of (something) by taking some into the mouth: *to taste food.* **2.** to eat or drink a little of: *he hadn't tasted food for three days.* **3.** to perceive or distinguish the flavor of: *to taste the wine in a sauce.* **4.** to have or get experience, esp. a slight experience. **5.** *Poetic or Dial.* to perceive in any way, esp. by smell. **6.** *Archaic.* to enjoy or appreciate. **7.** *Obs.* to touch, feel, or handle; test or try.
—*v.i.* **8.** to try the flavor or quality of something. **9.** to eat or drink a little (of): *Susan tasted slyly of the cake.* **10.** to perceive or distinguish the flavor of anything. **11.** to have experience, or make trial in experience, of something. **12.** to have a particular flavor: *the milk tastes sour.* **13.** to smack or savor (usually fol. by *of*).
—*n.* **14.** act of tasting food or the like. **15.** the sense by which the flavor or savor of things is perceived when they are brought into contact with special organs of the mouth. **16.** sensation, flavor, or quality as perceived by these organs. **17.** a small quantity tasted; a morsel, bit, or sip. **18.** a relish, liking, or predilection for something: *a taste for music.* **19.** the sense of what is fitting, harmonious, or beautiful; the perception and enjoyment of what constitutes excellence in the fine arts, literature, etc. **20.** manner, style, or general character as showing perception, or lack of perception, of what is fitting or beautiful; characteristic or prevailing style. **21.** a slight experience or a sample of something. **22.** to one's **taste**, agreeable or pleasing to one: *he shopped for hours but found no ties completely to his taste.* **23.** *Obs.* test or trial.
[ME, t. OF: m. *taster* try by touching, ult. g. b. L *tangere* touch and *gustare* taste] —**tast/a·ble,** *adj.*
—**Syn. 16.** TASTE, FLAVOR, SAVOR refer to a quality that is perceived when a substance is placed upon the tongue. TASTE is the general word: *the taste of roast beef.* FLAVOR is a characteristic taste, usually of a pleasing kind, and as of some ingredient put into the food: *lemon flavor.* SAVOR implies pleasing scent as well as taste or flavor, and connotes enjoyment in tasting: *the sauce has an excellent savor.*
—**Ant. 18.** antipathy.

taste bud, any of a number of small, flask-shaped bodies in the epithelium of the tongue, etc., believed to be special organs of taste.

taste·ful (tāst′fəl), *adj.* having, displaying, or in accordance with, good taste. **—taste′ful·ly,** *adv.* **—taste′-ful·ness,** *n.*

taste·less (tāst′lĭs), *adj.* **1.** having no taste or flavor; insipid. **2.** dull; uninteresting. **3.** lacking in good taste; showing lack of good taste. **4.** *Rare.* lacking the sense of taste. **—taste′less·ly,** *adv.* **—taste′less·ness,** *n.*

tast·er (tās′tər), *n.* **1.** one who tastes, esp. one skilled in distinguishing the qualities of liquors, tea, etc., by the taste. **2.** a container for taking samples or tasting. **3.** a wide shallow vessel, usually metal, in which wine is tested. **4.** a pipette.

tast·y (tās′tĭ), *adj.* **tastier, tastiest.** *Colloq.* **1.** pleasing to the taste; savory; appetizing. **2.** having or showing good taste. **—tast′i·ly,** *adv.* **—tast′i·ness,** *n.*

tat[1] (tăt), *v.i., v.t.* **tatted, tatting.** to do, or make by, tatting. [orig. unknown]

tat[2] (tăt), *n.* See **tit for tat.**

Ta·tar (tä′tər), *n., adj.* Tartar. [see *Tartar*] **—Ta·tar·i·an** (tä tär′ĭ ən), **Ta·tar·ic** (tä tär′ĭk), *adj.*

Tatar Republic, an autonomous republic in the E Soviet Union in Europe. 3,067,740 (est. 1941); ab. 25,900 sq. mi. *Cap.:* Kazan.

Ta·ta·ry (tä′tə rĭ), *n.* Tartary.

Tate (tāt), *n.* **(John Orley) Allen,** born 1899, U.S. poet, critic, and editor.

Tat·ler (tăt′lər), *n.* **The,** an English triweekly conducted by Addison and Steele, 1709–11.

tat·ou·ay (tăt′o͞o ā′, tä′to͞o ĭ′), *n.* an armadillo, *Tatoua unicinctus,* of tropical South America. [t. Brazilian]

Ta·tra Mountains (tä′trä), a group of mountains in N Czechoslovakia and S Poland: a part of the central Carpathian system. Highest peak, Gerlachovka, 8737 ft. Also, **High Tatra.**

tat·ter[1] (tăt′ər), *n.* **1.** a torn piece hanging loose from the main part, as of a garment, etc. **2.** a separate torn piece. **3.** (*pl.*) torn or ragged clothing. [ME *tater,* t. Scand.; cf. Icel. *tǫturr* rag] **—v.t. 4.** to tear or wear to tatters. **—v.i. 5.** to become ragged. [back formation from TATTERED]

tat·ter[2] (tăt′ər), *n.* one who makes tatting. [f. TAT[1] + -ER[1]]

tat·ter·de·mal·ion (tăt′ər də mā′lyən, -măl′-), *n.* a person in tattered clothing; a ragged fellow. [f. TATTER[1]; + second element of uncert. orig.]

tat·tered (tăt′ərd), *adj.* **1.** torn to tatters; ragged. **2.** wearing ragged clothing. [f. TATTER[1], n. + -ED[3]]

tat·ter·sall (tăt′ər sôl′), *n.* **1.** a fabric with brightly colored crossbars in a plaid pattern. **—adj. 2.** made of this fabric: *a tattersall vest.* [from Tattersall's, London horse market, where brightly-colored blankets were used]

tat·ting (tăt′ĭng), *n.* **1.** the process or work of making a kind of knotted lace of cotton or linen thread with a shuttle. **2.** such lace. [orig. unknown]

tat·tle (tăt′əl), *v.,* **-tled, -tling,** *n.* **—v.i. 1.** to let out secrets. **2.** to chatter, prate, or gossip. **—v.t. 3.** to utter idly; disclose by tattling. **—n. 4.** act of tattling. **5.** idle talk; chatter; gossip. [ME *tatle,* appar. t. M Flem.: m. *tatelen,* c. LG *tatelen* gabble] **—tat′tling·ly,** *adv.*

tat·tler (tăt′lər), *n.* **1.** one who tattles; a telltale. **2.** a shore bird of the genus *Heteroscelus,* esp. the **wandering tattler** (*H. incanus*) of Alaska, Siberia, etc. **3.** any of various related shore birds having shrill cries, as the **solitary tattler** (*Tringa solitaria*) and the **big tattler** (*Totanus melanoleucus*).

tat·tle·tale (tăt′əl tāl′), *n.* **1.** talebearer. **—adj. 2.** talebearing; revealing: *tattletale gray.*

tat·too[1] (tă to͞o′), *n., pl.* **-toos. 1.** a signal on a drum, bugle, or trumpet at night, for soldiers or sailors to repair to their quarters. **2.** any similar beating or pulsation. **3.** *Brit.* an outdoor military pageant or display. [t. D: m. *taptoe,* lit., the tap (is) to, i.e. the taproom is shut]

tat·too[2] (tă to͞o′), *n., pl.* **-toos,** *v.,* **-tooed, -tooing. —n. 1.** act or practice of marking the skin with indelible patterns, pictures, legends, etc., by making punctures in it and inserting pigments. **2.** a pattern, picture, legend, etc., so made. **—v.t. 3.** to mark (the skin, arms, etc.) with tattoos. **4.** to put (tattoos) on the skin. [earlier *tattow,* t. Polynesian: m. *tatau*] **—tat·too′er,** *n.*

tau (tô, tou), *n.* the nineteenth letter of the Greek alphabet.

tau cross, a T-shaped cross. See illus. under **cross.**

taught (tôt), *v.* pt. and pp. of **teach.**

taunt[1] (tônt, tänt), *v.t.* **1.** to reproach in a sarcastic or insulting manner. **2.** to provoke by taunts; twit. **—n. 3.** an insulting gibe or sarcasm; scornful reproach or challenge. **4.** *Obs.* an object of insulting gibes or scornful reproaches. [orig. uncert] **—taunt′er,** *n.* **—taunt′ing·ly,** *adv.* **—Syn. 2.** See **ridicule.**

taunt[2] (tônt, tänt), *adj. Naut.* unusually high or tall, as a mast. [aphetic var. of *ataunt* fully rigged]

Taun·ton (tän′tən *for 1;* tôn′tən *for 2*), *n.* **1.** a city in SE Massachusetts. 41,132 (1960). **2.** a city in SW England, in Somersetshire. 33,613 (1951).

taupe (tōp), *n.* dark gray usually slightly tinged with brown, purple, yellow or green. [t. F, g. L *talpa* mole]

tau·rine[1] (tôr′īn, tôr′ĭn), *adj.* **1.** of, pertaining to, or

resembling a bull. **2.** pertaining to the zodiacal sign Taurus. [t. L: m. s. *taurinus* pertaining to a bull]

tau·rine[2] (tôr′ēn, tôr′ĭn), *n. Chem.* a neutral crystalline substance, $H_2NCH_2CH_2SO_3H$, obtained from the bile of oxen and other animals, from muscles, lung tissue, etc., and as a decomposition product of taurocholic acid. [f. TAURO(CHOLIC) + -INE[2]]

tau·ro·cho·lic acid (tôr′ə kō′lĭk, -kŏl′ĭk), *Chem.* an acid, $C_{26}H_{45}NO_7S$, occurring as a sodium salt in the bile of oxen, etc., which on hydrolysis yields taurine and cholic acid. [f. *tauro-* (comb. form of Gk. *taûros* bull, ox) + CHOLIC]

Tau·rus (tôr′əs), *n., gen.* **Tauri** (tôr′ī). **1.** the Bull, a zodiacal constellation. **2.** the second sign of the zodiac. See diag. under **zodiac.** [t. L: bull]

Tau·rus (tôr′əs), *n.* a mountain range in S Turkey. Highest peak, ab. 13,000 ft.

taut (tôt), *adj.* **1.** tightly drawn; tense; not slack. **2.** in good order or condition; tidy; neat. [ME *toght,* appar. b. *towen* (OE *togen* drawn) and TIGHT] **—taut′-ly,** *adv.* **—taut′ness,** *n.*

taut·en (tô′tən), *v.t., v.i.* to make or become taut.

tauto-, word element meaning "same," as in *tautonym.* [t. Gk., comb. form of *tautó,* contr. of *tò autó* the same]

tau·tog (tô tôg′, -tŏg′), *n.* a black labroid fish. *Tautoga onitis,* of the N Atlantic coast of the U.S. [t. Narragansett: m. *tautauog* sheepsheads, pl. of *tau, tautau*]

tau·tol·o·gize (tô tŏl′ə jīz′), *v.i.,* **-gized, -gizing.** to use tautology.

tau·tol·o·gy (tô tŏl′ə jĭ), *n., pl.* **-gies. 1.** needless repetition of an idea, esp. in other words in the immediate context, without imparting additional force or clearness, as "to descend down." **2.** *Logic.* **a.** a law that can be shown on the basis of certain rules to exclude no logical possibilities. **b.** an instance of such a law, e.g., *either Smith owns a car or he doesn't own a car.* [t. LL: m.s. *tautologia,* t. Gk.] **—tau·to·log·i·cal** (tô′tə lŏj′ə kəl), *adj.* **—tau′to·log′i·cal·ly,** *adv.* **—tau·tol′o·gist,** *n.*

tau·tom·er·ism (tô tŏm′ər ĭz′əm), *n. Chem.* the ability of certain organic compounds to react in isomeric structures which differ from each other in the position of a hydrogen atom and a double bond. The individual isomers (**tautomers**) are in equilibrium and some pairs of tautomeric isomers have been isolated. [f. TAUTO- + s. Gk. *méros* part + -ISM] **—tau·to·mer·ic** (tô′tə mĕr′ĭk), *adj.*

tau·tom·er·i·za·tion (tô tŏm′ər ə zā′shən), *n.* the conversion into a tautomeric structure.

tau·to·nym (tô′tə nĭm), *n. Bot., Zool.* a scientific name in which the generic and the specific name are the same, as *Chloris chloris* (the greenfinch). [t. Gk.: s. *tautōnymos* of same name] **—tau′to·nym′ic,** *adj.*

tav·ern (tăv′ərn), *n.* **1.** a place where liquors are sold to be drunk on the premises. **2.** a public house for travelers and others; an inn. [ME *taverne,* t. OF, g. L *taberna* hut, booth, inn] **—tav′ern·less,** *adj.* **—Syn. 2.** See **hotel.**

tav·ern·er (tăv′ər nər), *n.* **1.** *Archaic.* the owner of a tavern. **2.** *Obs.* a frequenter of taverns. [ME, t. OF: m. *tavernier*]

taw[1] (tô), *n.* **1.** a choice or fancy playing marble with which to shoot. **2.** a game of marbles. **3.** the line from which the players shoot. [t. Scand.; cf. Icel. *taug* string, rope (whence E line)]

taw[2] (tô), *v.t.* **1.** to prepare or dress (some raw material) for use or further manipulation. **2.** *Obs. exc. Dial.* to beat. [ME *tawe,* OE *tawian,* c. D *touwen*] **—taw′er,** *n.*

taw·dry (tô′drĭ), *adj.,* **-drier, -driest.** (of finery, etc.) gaudy; showy and cheap. [short for (Sain)t Audrey lace, i.e. lace bought at her fair in Ely] **—taw′dri·ly,** *adv.* **—taw′dri·ness,** *n.*

taw·ney (tô′nĭ), *adj.,* **-nier, -niest,** *n.* tawny.

taw·ny (tô′nĭ), *adj.,* **-nier, -niest,** *n.* **—adj. 1.** of a dark yellowish or dull yellowish-brown color. **—n. 2.** a shade of brown tinged with yellow; dull yellowish brown. [ME, t. OF: m. *tane,* pp., TANNED] **—taw′ni·ness,** *n.*

tax (tăks), *n.* **1.** a payment of money or performance of services for the use of the government or for the benefit of the public. **2.** a burdensome charge, obligation, duty, or demand. **3.** *Colloq.* a charge, as for a thing. **—v.t. 4.** to require a payment of money or services for the use of the government or the benefit of the public; impose a tax on. **5.** to estimate or determine the amount or value of (now only in legal use, with reference to assessing costs, etc., judicially). **6.** *Colloq.* to charge (a person). **7.** to lay a burden on; make serious demands. **8.** to take to task; censure; reprove; accuse. [ME, t. L: s. *taxāre* reprove, appraise, ML impose a tax] **—tax′a·ble,** *adj.* **—tax′a·bil′i·ty, tax′a·ble·ness,** *n.* **—tax′a·bly,** *adv.* **—tax′er,** *n.* **—tax′man,** *n.*

tax·a·ceous (tăks ā′shəs), *adj.* belonging to the *Taxaceae,* or yew family of trees and shrubs. [f. s. NL *Taxāceae* (der. L *taxus* yew) + -OUS]

tax·a·tion (tăks ā′shən), *n.* **1.** act of taxing. **2.** fact of being taxed. **3.** a tax imposed. **4.** the revenue raised by taxes.

tax·eme (tăks′ēm), *n. Linguistics.* a feature of the arrangement of elements in a construction, as selection, order, modification, or modulation. [der. TAX(IS) + -EME, modeled after PHONEME]

tax-ex·empt (tăks′ĭg zĕmpt′), *adj.* not subject to taxation.

tax·i (tăk′sĭ), *n., pl.* **taxis,** *v.,* **taxied, taxiing** or **taxy-ing.** —*n.* 1. taxicab. —*v.i.* 2. to ride or travel in a taxicab. 3. (of an airplane) to move over the surface of the ground or water under its own power. —*v.t.* 4. to cause (an airplane) to taxi. [short for TAXICAB]

tax·i·cab (tăk′sĭkăb′), *n.* a public passenger vehicle, esp. an automobile, usually fitted with a taximeter. [short for taximeter cab. See TAXIMETER]

taxi dancer, a professional dance partner in some dance halls, etc.

tax·i·der·my (tăk′sədûr′mĭ), *n.* the art of preparing and preserving the skins of animals, and stuffing and mounting them in lifelike form. [f. *taxi-* (comb. form of Gk. *táxis* arrangement) + *-dermy* (m. s. Gk. *-dermia,* der. *dêrma* skin)] —**tax′i·der′mal, tax′i·der′mic,** *adj.* —**tax′i·der′mist,** *n.*

tax·i·me·ter (tăk′sĭmē′tər, tăksĭm′ətər), *n.* a device fitted to a taxicab or other vehicle, for automatically computing and indicating the fare due. [t. F: m. *taximètre,* der. *taxe* charge. See -METER]

tax·i·plane (tăk′sĭplān′), *n.* an airplane available for chartered or unscheduled trips.

tax·is (tăk′sĭs), *n.* 1. arrangement, order, as in one of the physical sciences. 2. *Biol.* the movement of an organism in a particular direction in response to an external stimulus. 3. *Surg.* the replacing of a displaced part, or the reducing of a hernial tumor or the like, by manipulation without cutting. [t. NL, t. Gk.: arrangement]

-taxis, a word element meaning "arrangement," as in *chemotaxis.* [t. Gk.]

tax·ite (tăk′sīt), *n. Petrog.* a lava appearing to be formed from fragments, because of its parts having different colors, textures, etc. [f. TAX(IS) + -ITE¹] —**tax·it·ic** (tăksĭt′ĭk), *adj.*

tax·on·o·my (tăksŏn′əmĭ), *n.* 1. classification, esp. in relation to its principles or laws. 2. that department of science, or of a particular science, which deals with classification. [t. F: m. *taxonomie,* f. Gk.: m. *táxis* arrangement + m. *nomía* distribution] —**tax·o·nom·ic** (tăk′sə nŏm′ĭk), **tax′o·nom′i·cal,** *adj.* —**tax′o·nom′-i·cal·ly,** *adv.* —**tax·on′o·mist, tax·on′o·mer,** *n.*

tax·pay·er (tăks′pā′ər), *n.* one who pays a tax or is subject to taxation.

tax rate, the percentage of the property value to be paid as a tax.

tax title, *Law.* a title, acquired by the purchaser at a forced sale of property for nonpayment of taxes.

-taxy, var. of **-taxis,** as in *heterotaxy.*

Tay (tā), *n.* a river flowing through central Scotland into the **Firth of Tay** (25 mi. long), an estuary of the North Sea. 118 mi.

Tay·lor (tā′lər), *n.* 1. **Bayard** (bī′ərd, bā′-), 1825–78, U.S. journalist, traveler, and author. 2. **Deems,** 1885–1966, U.S. composer. 3. **Frederick Winslow,** 1856–1915, U.S. engineer. 4. **Jeremy,** 1613–67, British bishop and writer. 5. **Zachary,** 1784–1850, 12th president of the United States, 1849–50: general.

taz·za (tät′tsä), *n.* a shallow, saucerlike ornamental bowl, usually on a high base or foot. [t. It.]

Tb, *Chem.* terbium.

t.b., 1. trial balance. 2. tuberculosis.

T-bar (tē′bär′), *n.* a metal bar having a T-shaped cross section.

Tbi·li·si (tbĭlē̇sē′), *n.* official name of **Tiflis.**

tbs., tablespoon; tablespoons. Also, **tbsp.**

Tchai·kov·sky (chĭkôf′skĭ), *n.* See **Tschaikovsky.**

Tche·khoff (chĕ′hôf), *n.* See **Chekhov.**

Te, *Chem.* tellurium.

tea (tē), *n.* 1. the dried and prepared leaves of the shrub, *Thea sinensis,* from which a somewhat bitter, aromatic beverage is prepared by infusion in hot water. 2. the shrub itself, which is extensively cultivated in China, Japan, India, etc., and has fragrant white flowers. 3. the beverage so prepared, served hot or iced. 4. any kind of leaves, flowers, etc., so used, or any plant yielding them. 5. any of various infusions prepared from the leaves, flowers, etc., of other plants, and used as beverages or medicines. 6. beef tea. 7. *Brit.* a meal (other than dinner) in the late afternoon or the evening. 8. an afternoon reception at which tea is served. [t. Chinese: m. *t'e,* d. var. of Mandarin and Cantonese *ch'a*] —**tea′less,** *adj.*

tea ball, *U.S.* a perforated metal ball or a bag of thin cloth, paper, etc., in which tea leaves are placed to be immersed in hot water to make tea.

tea·ber·ry (tē′bĕr′ĭ), *n., pl.* **-ries.** the spicy red fruit of the American wintergreen, *Gaultheria procumbens.*

tea biscuit, a small, round, soft biscuit, usually shortened and sweetened.

tea caddy, *Chiefly Brit.* a small box or can, for holding tea leaves.

tea·cart (tē′kärt′), *n.* a small wheeled table, used as a server.

teach (tēch), *v.,* **taught, teaching.** —*v.t.* 1. to impart knowledge of or skill in; give instruction in: *he teaches mathematics.* 2. to impart knowledge or skill to; give instruction to: *he teaches a large class.* —*v.i.* 3. to impart knowledge or skill; give instruction. [ME *teche(n),* OE *tǣcan;* akin to TOKEN]

teach·a·ble (tē′chəbəl), *adj.* 1. capable of being instructed, as a person; docile. 2. capable of being taught, as a subject. —**teach′a·bil′i·ty, teach′a·ble·ness,** *n.* —**teach′a·bly,** *adv.*

teach·er (tē′chər), *n.* one who teaches or instructs, esp. as a profession; instructor. —**teach′er·less,** *adj.*

teach·ing (tē′chĭng), *n.* 1. act of one who or that which teaches; the work or profession of a teacher. 2. that which is taught; a doctrine or precept.

tea·cup (tē′kŭp′), *n.* 1. a cup in which tea is served, usually of small or moderate size. 2. a teacupful.

tea·cup·ful (tē′kŭpfo͝ol′), *n., pl.* **-fuls.** as much as a teacup will hold; about four fluid ounces.

teak (tēk), *n.* 1. a large East Indian verbenaceous tree, *Tectona grandis,* with a hard, durable, yellowish-brown, resinous wood valuable for shipbuilding, etc. 2. the wood. 3. any of various similar trees or woods. [earlier *teke,* t. Pg.: m. *teca,* t. Malayalam: m. *tēkka*]

tea·ket·tle (tē′kĕt′əl), *n.* a portable kettle with a cover, a spout, and a handle, in which to boil water for making tea and for other uses.

teal (tēl), *n., pl.* **teals,** (*esp. collectively*) **teal.** any of various small fresh-water ducks, as the European **green-winged teal,** *Anas crecca,* and the American **blue-winged teal,** *A. discors.* [ME *tele.* Cf. D *teling*]

team (tēm), *n.* 1. a number of persons associated in some joint action, esp. one of the sides in a match: *a team of football players.* 2. two or more horses, oxen, or other animals harnessed together to draw a vehicle, plow, or the like. 3. two or more draft animals, or one such animal, together with the harness and the vehicle drawn. 4. *Dial.* a family or brood of young animals. 5. *Obs.* offspring or progeny; race or lineage. —*v.t.* 6. to join together in a team. 7. to convey or transport by means of a team. —*v.i.* 8. to drive a team. [ME *teme,* OE *tēam,* c. G *zaum,* Icel. *taumr* bridle, rein]

team·mate (tēm′māt′), *n.* a member of the same team.

team·ster (tēm′stər), *n.* one who drives a team or a truck for hauling, esp. as an occupation.

team·work (tēm′wûrk′), *n.* 1. the work of a team with reference to coördination of effort and to collective efficiency. 2. work done with a team.

tea·pot (tē′pŏt′), *n.* a container with a lid, spout, and handle, in which tea is made and from which it is poured.

tea·poy (tē′poi), *n.* 1. a small three-legged table or stand. 2. a small table for use in serving tea. [f. *tī* three (t. Hind.: m. *tīn*) + *poy* foot (t. Pers.: m. *pāi*)]

tear¹ (tĭr), *n.* 1. a drop of the limpid fluid secreted by the lachrymal gland, appearing in or flowing from the eye, chiefly as the result of emotion, esp. of grief. 2. something resembling or suggesting a tear, as a drop of a liquid or a tearlike mass of a solid substance. 3. (*pl.*) grief; sorrow. 4. **in tears,** weeping. [ME *tere,* OE *tēar* (c. Icel. *tār*), Vernerian var. of *teagor,* c. Goth. *tagr;* akin to Gk. *dákry,* Cornish *dagr*] —**tear′less,** *adj.*

tear² (târ), *v.,* **tore, torn, tearing,** *n.* —*v.t.* 1. to pull apart or in pieces by force, esp. so as to leave ragged or irregular edges. 2. to pull or pluck violently or with force (fol. by *off, down, up, out,* etc.). 3. to distress greatly: *a heart torn with anguish.* 4. to rend or divide: *a country torn by civil war.* 5. to wound or injure by, or as by, rending; lacerate. 6. to produce or effect by rending: *to tear a hole in one's coat.* 7. to remove by force: *to be unable to tear oneself from a place.* —*v.i.* 8. to become torn. 9. to make a tear or rent. 10. *Colloq.* to move or go with violence or great haste. —*n.* 11. act of tearing. 12. a rent or fissure. 13. a rage or passion; violent flurry or outburst. 14. *Slang.* a spree. [ME *tere,* OE *teran,* c. D *teren,* G *zehren* destroy, consume, Goth. *gatairan* destroy; akin to Gk. *dérein* flay] —**Syn.** 1. TEAR, REND, RIP mean to pull apart. To TEAR is to split the fibers of something by pulling apart, usually so as to leave ragged or irregular edges: *to tear open a letter.* REND implies force or violence in tearing apart or in pieces: *to rend one's clothes in grief.* RIP implies vigorous tearing asunder, esp. along a seam or line: *to rip the sleeves out of a coat.*

tear bomb (tĭr), a bomb or grenade containing tear gas. Also, **tear shell.**

tear·drop (tĭr′drŏp′), *n.* a tear¹.

tear·ful (tĭr′fəl), *adj.* 1. full of tears; weeping. 2. causing tears. —**tear′ful·ly,** *adv.* —**tear′ful·ness,** *n.*

tear gas (tĭr), a gas used in modern warfare or in riots, which makes the eyes smart and water, thus producing a temporary blindness.

tea·room (tē′ro͞om′, -ro͝om′), *n.* a room or shop where tea and other refreshments are served to customers.

tea rose, *Hort.* any of several varieties of cultivated roses having a scent supposed to resemble that of tea.

tear·y (tĭr′ĭ), *adj.* 1. of or like tears. 2. tearful.

Teas·dale (tēz′dāl), *n.* **Sara,** 1884–1933, U.S. poet.

tease (tēz), *v.,* **teased, teasing,** *n.* —*v.t.* 1. to worry or irritate by persistent petty requests, trifling raillery, or other annoyance, often in sport. 2. to pull apart or separate the adhering fibers of, as in combing or carding wool; comb or card (wool, etc.); shred. 3. to raise a nap on (cloth) with teasels; tease. —*v.i.* 4. to worry or disturb a person, etc., by importunity or persistent petty annoyance. —*n.* 5. act of teasing. 6. state of being teased. 7. *Colloq.* one who or that which teases or annoys. [ME *tese,* OE *tǣsan* tear up, c. D *teezen* pull] —**teas′er,** *n.* —**teas′ing·ly,** *adv.* —**Syn.** 1. See **bother.**

tea·sel (tē′zəl), *n.*, *v.*, **-seled, -seling** or (*esp. Brit.*) **-selled, -selling.** —*n.* **1.** any of the herbs with prickly leaves and flower heads constituting the dipsacaceous genus *Dipsacus.* **2.** the dried flower head or bur of *D. fullonum*, used for teasing or teaseling cloth. **3.** any mechanical contrivance used for teaseling. —*v.t.* **4.** to raise a nap on (cloth) with teasels; dress by means of teasels. Also, **teazel, teazle.** ⸤ME *tesel*, OE *tǣsel*; akin to TEASE, v.⸥ —**tea′sel·er,** *esp. Brit.* **tea′sel·ler,** *n.*

tea shop, 1. tearoom. **2.** *Brit.* a lunchroom.

tea·spoon (tē′spōōn, -spōōn′), *n.* **1.** the small spoon commonly used to stir tea, coffee, etc. **2.** a unit of capacity, for household purposes, equal to 1⅓ fluid drams, or ⅓ tablespoon.

tea·spoon·ful (tē′spōōn fōōl′, -spōōn-), *n.*, *pl.* **-fuls.** as much as a teaspoon can hold, about one fluid dram.

teat (tēt), *n.* **1.** the protuberance on the breast or udder in female mammals (except the monotremes), where the milk ducts discharge; a nipple or mammilla. **2.** something resembling a teat. ⸤ME *tete*, t. OF. See TIT⸥

tea wagon, a small table on wheels for carrying articles for use in serving tea.

tea·zel (tē′zəl), *n.*, *v.t.*, **-zeled, -zeling** or (*esp. Brit.*) **-zelled, -zelling.** teasel.

tea·zle (tē′zəl), *n.*, *v.t.*, **-zled, -zling.** teasel.

Te·bet (tā vāth′, tā′vĕs), *n.* (in the Jewish calendar) the fourth month of the year. Also, **Te·beth′.**

tech., **1.** technical. **2.** technology.

tech·ne·ti·um (tĕk nē′shǐ əm, -shəm), *n.* *Chem.* a manganese family element, present in small quantities in columbite, gadolinite, zircon, etc. *Symbol:* Tc; *at. no.:* 43. Originally named **masurium.** [f. s. Gk. *technētos* skilfully made + -IUM]

tech·nic (tĕk′nǐk), *n.* **1.** technique. **2.** a technicality. **3.** technics (def. 2). —*adj.* **4.** technical. [t. Gk.: m.s. *technikós* pertaining to art, skillful, technical]

tech·ni·cal (tĕk′nə kəl), *adj.* **1.** belonging or pertaining to an art or arts: *technical skill.* **2.** peculiar to or characteristic of a particular art, science, profession, trade, etc.: *technical details.* **3.** using technical terms, or treating a subject technically, as a writer or a book. **4.** skilled in, or familiar in a practical way with, a particular art, trade, etc., as a person. **5.** pertaining to or connected with the mechanical or industrial arts and the applied sciences: *a technical school.* **6.** so considered from a technical point of view: *a military engagement ending in a technical defeat.* **7.** *Exchanges.* (of market prices) temporarily distorted by unusual buying or selling. —**tech′ni·cal·ly,** *adv.* —**tech′ni·cal·ness,** *n.*

tech·ni·cal·i·ty (tĕk′nə kăl′ə tǐ), *n.*, *pl.* **-ties. 1.** technical character. **2.** the use of technical methods or terms. **3.** something that is technical; a technical point, detail, or expression.

technical sergeant, *U.S.* **1.** in the Air Force and Marine Corps, a noncommissioned officer ranking below a master sergeant and above a staff sergeant. **2.** in the Army, formerly, a noncommissioned officer below a master sergeant and above a staff sergeant (now corresponds to *sergeant first class*).

tech·ni·cian (tĕk nǐsh′ən), *n.* **1.** one versed in the technicalities of a subject. **2.** one skilled in the technique of an art, as music or painting. **3.** *U.S. Army.* one of several enlisted grades above private, given to specialists.

Tech·ni·col·or (tĕk′nə kŭl′ər), *n.* *Trademark.* a system of making color motion pictures by means of superimposing the three primary colors to produce a final colored print.

tech·nics (tĕk′nǐks), *n.* **1.** technique. **2.** the study or science of an art or of arts in general, esp. of the mechanical or industrial arts.

tech·nique (tĕk nēk′), *n.* **1.** method of performance, esp. in artistic work. **2.** technical skill, esp. in artistic work. [t. F. See TECHNIC]

techno-, a word element referring to "technic," "technology." [t. Gk., comb. form of *téchnē* art, skill]

tech·noc·ra·cy (tĕk nŏk′rə sǐ), *n.* a theory and movement (prominent about 1932) advocating control of industrial resources and reorganization of the social system, based on the findings of technologists and engineers. —**tech·no·crat** (tĕk′nə krăt′), *n.* —**tech′no·crat′ic,** *adj.*

tech·nog·ra·phy (tĕk nŏg′rə fǐ), *n.* description of the arts.

technol., technology.

tech·no·lith·ic (tĕk′nə lǐth′ǐk), *adj.* *Anthropol.* noting or pertaining to stone implements shaped by the operator in accordance with definite designs.

tech·no·log·i·cal (tĕk′nə lŏj′ə kəl), *adj.* **1.** of or pertaining to technology; relating to the arts: *technological schools.* **2.** *Econ.* caused by technical advances in production methods: *technological unemployment.* Also, **tech′no·log′ic.** —**tech′no·log′i·cal·ly,** *adv.*

tech·nol·o·gy (tĕk nŏl′ə jǐ), *n.* **1.** the branch of knowledge that deals with the industrial arts; the sciences of the industrial arts. **2.** the terminology of an art, science, etc.; technical nomenclature. [t. Gk.: m.s. *technologia* systematic treatment] —**tech·nol′o·gist,** *n.*

tech·y (tĕch′ǐ), *adj.*, **techier, techiest.** tetchy. —**tech′i·ly,** *adv.* —**tech′i·ness,** *n.*

tec·ton·ic (tĕk tŏn′ǐk), *adj.* **1.** of or pertaining to building or construction; constructive; architectural.

2. *Geol.* **a.** pertaining to the structure of the earth's crust. **b.** referring to the forces or conditions within the earth that cause movements of the crust such as earthquakes, folds, faults and the like. **c.** designating the results of such movements: *tectonic valleys.* [t. LL: s. *tectonicus,* t. Gk.: m. *tektonikós* (def. 1)]

tec·ton·ics (tĕk tŏn′ǐks), *n.* **1.** the science or art of assembling, shaping, or ornamenting materials in construction; the constructive arts in general. **2.** structural geology.

Te·cum·seh (tǐ kŭm′sə), *n.* 1768?–1813, American Indian chief of the Shawnee tribe. Also, **Te·cum·tha** (tǐ kŭm′thə). [t. Amer. Ind: m. *Tikamthi* he springs]

ted (tĕd), *v.t.*, **tedded, tedding.** to spread out for drying, as newly mown hay. [ME, c. d. G *zetten* scatter]

ted·der (tĕd′ər), *n.* **1.** one who teds. **2.** an implement that spreads and turns newly mown grass or hay from the swath for the purpose of drying.

Te De·um (tē dē′əm), **1.** an ancient Latin hymn of praise, in the form of a psalm, sung regularly at matins in the Roman Catholic Church and (in an English translation) at morning prayer in the Anglican Church, as well as on special occasions as a service of thanksgiving. **2.** a musical setting of the hymn. **3.** a service of thanksgiving in which this hymn forms a prominent part. [L, first two words of the hymn]

te·di·ous (tē′dǐ əs, tē′jəs), *adj.* **1.** marked by tedium; long and tiresome: *tedious tasks, journeys, etc.* **2.** prolix so as to cause weariness, as a speaker. [ME, t. LL: m.s. *taediōsus*] —**te′di·ous·ly,** *adv.* —**te′di·ous·ness,** *n.*

—**Syn. 1.** TEDIOUS, IRKSOME, TIRESOME, WEARISOME characterize that which one finds wearing or exhausting. That is TEDIOUS which tires by reason of its length and slowness: *a tedious assignment of work.* IRKSOME describes that which frets or is wearing, or a task which one is reluctant to undertake: *shopping in crowded stores is irksome.* That which is TIRESOME exhausts either one's patience or physical strength: *monotonous routine is tiresome.* WEARISOME is more emphatic and suggests the necessity of longer endurance: *hard labor is wearisome.* —**Ant. 1.** interesting, absorbing.

te·di·um (tē′dǐ əm), *n.* state of being wearisome; irksomeness; tediousness. [t. L: m. *taedium*]

te·di·um vi·tae (tē′dǐ əm vī′tē), *Latin.* taedium vitae.

tee¹ (tē), *n.* **1.** the letter T, t. **2.** something shaped like a T, as a three-way joint used in fitting pipes together. **3.** a metal beam or bar with a T-shaped section. **4.** the mark aimed at in various games, as curling. —*adj.* **5.** having a crosspiece at the top; shaped like a T.

tee² (tē), *n.*, *v.*, **teed, teeing.** *Golf.* —*n.* **1.** the starting place, usually a hard mound of earth, at the beginning of play for each hole. **2.** a small heap of sand, or a rubber, plastic, or wood object, from which the ball is driven at the beginning of a hole. —*v.t.* **3.** to place (the ball) on a tee. —*v.i.* **4.** to strike the ball from a tee (fol. by *off*). [orig. uncert.]

teem¹ (tēm), *v.i.* **1.** to abound or swarm; be prolific or fertile (fol. by *with*). **2.** to be or become pregnant; bring forth young. —*v.t.* **3.** *Obs.* to produce (offspring). [ME *teme*(n), OE *tēman, tieman* produce (offspring), der. *tēam* child-bearing, offspring] —**teem′er,** *n.*

teem² (tēm), *v.i.*, *v.t.* to empty or pour out; discharge. [ME *teme*(n), t. Scand.; cf. Icel. *tæma*, der. *tōmr*, adj.]

teem·ing (tē′mǐng), *adj.* **1.** abounding or swarming with something, as with people. **2.** prolific or fertile.

-teen, a termination forming the cardinal numerals from thirteen to nineteen. [ME and OE *-tēne*, comb. form of TEN, c. G *-zehn*]

teen age (tēn), the period when the year of a person's age ends in *-teen* (13 through 19). —**teen′-age′,** *adj.* —**teen′-ag′er,** *n.*

teens (tēnz), *n.pl.* the years of one's age (13 through 19) of which the numbers end in *-teen.*

tee·ny (tē′nǐ), *adj.*, **-nier, -niest.** *Colloq.* or *Dial.* tiny.

tee·pee (tē′pē), *n.* tepee.

Tees (tēz), *n.* a river in N England, flowing E along the boundary between Durham and Yorkshire to the North Sea. ab. 70 mi.

tee·ter (tē′tər), *Chiefly U.S. Colloq.* —*v.i.* **1.** to seesaw. **2.** to move unsteadily. —*v.t.* **3.** to move (anything) with a seesaw motion. —*n.* **4.** a seesaw. **5.** a seesaw motion. [var. of *titter,* t. Scand.; cf. Icel. *titra,* c. G *zittern* tremble, quiver]

teeth (tēth), *n.* pl. of **tooth.**

teethe (tēth), *v.i.*, **teethed, teething.** *Dentistry.* to grow teeth; cut one's teeth.

teething ring, a circular disk, usually of plastic, ivory, bone, etc., on which a teething baby may bite.

teeth·ridge (tēth′rǐj′), *n.* *Phonet.* alveolar ridge.

tee·to·tal (tē tō′tal), *adj.* **1.** of or pertaining to, advocating, or pledged to total abstinence from intoxicating drink. **2.** *Colloq.* absolute; complete. [der. TOTAL, with redupl. of initial *t-* for emphasis] —**tee·to′tal·ly,** *adv.*

tee·to·tal·er (tē tō′təl ər), *n.* one who abstains totally from intoxicating drink. Also, **tee·to′tal·ist,** *esp. Brit.* **tee·to′tal·ler.**

tee·to·tal·ism (tē tō′təl ǐz′əm), *n.* the principle or practice of total abstinence from intoxicating drink.

tee·to·tum (tē tō′təm), *n.* **1.** any small top spun with the fingers. **2.** a kind of top having four sides, each marked with a different initial letter, spun with the fingers in an old game of chance. [earlier *T totum*, f. *T.* (abbr. for *tōtum*, used on toy) + *tōtum* (neut. of L *iōtus* all)]

teg·men (tĕg′mĕn), *n.*, *pl.* **-mina** (-mə nə). **1.** a cover, covering, or integument. **2.** *Bot.* the delicate inner integument or coat of a seed. [t. L: covering] **—teg·mi·nal** (tĕg′mə nəl), *adj.*

Te·gu·ci·gal·pa (tĕ gōō′sē gäl′pä), *n.* the capital of Honduras, in the S part. 72,385 (1950).

teg·u·lar (tĕg′yə lər), *adj.* **1.** pertaining to or resembling a tile. **2.** consisting of or arranged like tiles. [f. s. L *tēgula* tile + -AR¹] **—teg′u·lar·ly,** *adv.*

teg·u·ment (tĕg′yə mənt). *n.* a covering or investment; an integument. [t. L: s. *tegumentum*] **—teg·u·men·tal** (tĕg′yə mĕn′təl), **teg·u·men·ta·ry** (tĕg′yə mĕn′tə rĭ), *adj.*

te-hee (tēhē′), *interj., n., v.,* **-heed, -heeing.** *—interj.* **1.** the sound of a tittering laugh. *—n.* **2.** a titter; a snicker. *—v.i.* **3.** titter; snicker. [ME; imit.]

Te·he·ran (tĕ′ə rän′, -răn′; *Pers.* tĕ hrän′), *n.* the capital of Iran, in the N part: wartime conference of Roosevelt, Churchill, and Stalin, 1943. 618,976 (est. 1950). Also, **Te·hran′.**

Te·huan·te·pec (tĕ wän′tə pĕk′), *n.* **Isthmus of,** an isthmus in S Mexico between the Gulf of Tehuantepec, an open bay of the Pacific, and the Gulf of Campeche: often-proposed site of an interoceanic canal. 125 mi. wide.

Te·huel·che (tĕ wĕl′chĕ), *n.* a Patagonian Indian of any of a group of tribes, characterized by tall stature and hunting culture. [t. Patagonian: southeast]

Tei·de (tā′dĕ), *n.* **Pico de** (pē′kô dĕ), a volcanic peak in the Canary Islands, on Tenerife. 12,190 ft. Also, **Pico de Tenerife.**

te ig·i·tur (tĕ′ ĭj′ə tər), *Eccles.* the first paragraph of the canon in the Roman and some other Latin liturgies. [L: thee therefore]

Te·jo (tĕ′zhōō), *n.* Portuguese name of Tagus.

tek·tite (tĕk′tīt), *n.* *Geol.* any of several kinds of small glassy bodies, in various forms, occurring in Australia and elsewhere, whose exact origin is unknown. [f. s. Gk. *tēktós* molten + -ITE¹]

tel-¹, var. of **tele-¹**, as in *telesthesia.* Properly, this form should occur wherever the following word or word element begins with a vowel. However, **teleo-** is more frequently found.

tel-², var. of **tele-²**, as in *telencephalon.* For form, see **tel-¹.**

tel., **1.** telegram. **2.** telegraph. **3.** telephone.

tel·aes·the·sia (tĕl′əs thē′zhə, -zhĭ′ə), *n.* telesthesia.

tel·a·mon (tĕl′ə mŏn′), *n., pl.* **telamones** (tĕl′ə mō′nēz). *Archit.* a figure of a man used like a supporting column; an atlas (def. 6). [t. L, t. Gk.: name of mythological hero]

Tel·a·mon (tĕl′ə mən), *n.* *Gk. Legend.* the father of Ajax and Teucer.

tel·an·gi·ec·ta·sis (tĕl ăn′jĭ′ĕk′tə sĭs), *n., pl.* **-ses** (-sēz′). *Pathol.* chronic dilatation of the capillaries and other small blood vessels, as seen in the faces of alcoholics, those exposed to raw, cold climates, and certain congenital sufferers. [NL, f. Gk.: s. *télos* end + m.s. *angeîon* receptacle + m. *ēktasis* extension]

Tel·au·to·graph (tĕl ô′tə grăf′, -gräf′), *n.* *Trademark.* a form of telegraph for reproducing handwriting, drawings, etc., the movements of a pen or pencil at one end of the line being reproduced in a pen or pencil at the other end by a system of electromagnets.

Tel-A·viv (tĕl′ ə vēv′), *n.* a city in W Israel: one of the centers of Jewish immigration following World War II. 358,500 (with Jaffa; est. 1954).

tele-¹, a word element meaning "distant," especially "transmission over a distance," as in *telegraph.* Also, **tel-¹, telo-¹.** [comb. form repr. Gk. *tēle* far]

tele-², a word element referring to the end, as in *teleological.* Also, **tel-², teleo-, telo-².** [comb. form repr. Gk. *tĕlos* end, *tĕleos* complete]

tel·e·cast (tĕl′ə kăst′, -käst′), *v.,* **-cast** or **-casted, -casting,** *n.* *—v.i., v.t.* **1.** to broadcast by television. *—n.* **2.** a television broadcast.

tel·e·du (tĕl′ə dōō′), *n.* a small mammal, *Mydaus javensis,* of the mountains of Java, Sumatra, and Borneo, which (like the skunk) ejects a fetid secretion, and which is colored like the skunk but has a short tail.

teleg., **1.** telegram. **2.** telegraph. **3.** telegraphy.

te·le·ga (tĕ lĕ′gä), *n.* a Russian cart of rude construction, having four wheels and no springs. [t. Russ.]

te·leg·o·ny (tə lĕg′ə nĭ), *n.* *Genetics.* the supposed influence of a previous sire upon the progeny subsequently borne by the same mother to other sires. **—tel·e·gon·ic** (tĕl′ə gŏn′ĭk), *adj.*

tel·e·gram (tĕl′ə grăm′), *n.* a communication sent by telegraph; a telegraphic message.

tel·e·graph (tĕl′ə grăf′, -gräf′), *n.* **1.** an apparatus, system, or process for transmitting messages or signals to a distance, esp. by means of an electrical device consisting essentially of a transmitting or sending instrument and a distant receiving instrument connected by a conducting wire, or other communications channel, the making and breaking of the circuit at the sending end causing a corresponding effect, as on a sounder, at

the receiving end. **2.** a telegraphic message. *—v.t.* **3.** to transmit or send (a message, etc.) by telegraph. **4.** to send a message to (a person) by telegraph. *—v.i.* **5.** to send a message by telegraph. **—te·leg·ra·pher** (tə lĕg′rə fər; *Brit.* **te·leg′ra·phist,** *n.* **—tel′e·graph·ic,** *adj.* **—tel′e·graph′i·cal·ly,** *adv.*

telegrapher's cramp, *Pathol.* an occupational nerve disorder characterized by spasmodic muscular contractions in some fingers. It occurs in one attempting to send telegraph messages.

tel·e·graph·o·scope (tĕl′ə grăf′ə skōp′), *n.* a telegraphic device by means of which a picture may be reproduced at a distance.

telegraph plant, an East Indian plant, *Desmodium gyrans,* a species of tick trefoil, remarkable for the spontaneous, jerking signal-like motions of its leaflets.

te·leg·ra·phy (tə lĕg′rə fĭ), *n.* the art or practice of constructing or operating telegraphs.

tel·e·kin·e·sis (tĕl′ə kə nē′sĭs), *n.* the production of motion in a body, apparently without the application of material force, a power long claimed by spiritualistic mediums. [f. TELE- + Gk. *kinēsis* movement]

Te·lem·a·chus (tə lĕm′ə kəs), *n.* *Gk. Legend.* the son of Odysseus and Penelope. With his father, he slew the suitors of Penelope.

tel·em·e·ter (tə lĕm′ə tər), *n.* **1.** any of certain devices or attachments for determining distances by measuring the angle subtending a known distance. **2.** *Elect.* the complete measuring, transmitting, and receiving apparatus for indicating, recording, or integrating at a distance, by electrical translating means, the value of a quantity. **—tel·e·met·ric** (tĕl′ə mĕt′rĭk), *adj.* **—te·lem·e·try** (tə lĕm′ə trĭ), *n.*

tel·e·mo·tor (tĕl′ə mō′tər), *n.* a mechanical, electrical, or hydraulic system, by which power is applied at and controlled from a distant point, esp. such a system actuating a ship's rudder.

tel·en·ceph·a·lon (tĕl′ĕn sĕf′ə lŏn′), *n.* the anterior end of the embryonic nervous system which forms the cerebral hemisphere in the adult vertebrate; the end brain. **—tel·en·ce·phal·ic** (tĕl′ĕn sə făl′ĭk), *adj.*

teleo-, var. of **tele-²**, as in *teleology.*

teleological argument, *Metaphys.* the argument for the existence of God based on the assumption that order in the universe implies an orderer and cannot be a natural feature of the universe.

tel·e·ol·o·gy (tĕl′ĭ ŏl′ə jĭ, tē′lĭ-), *n.* **1.** the doctrine of final causes or purposes. **2.** the study of the evidences of design or purpose in nature. **3.** such design or purpose. **4.** the belief that purpose and design are a part of, or are apparent in, nature. **5.** the doctrine in vitalism that phenomena are guided not only by mechanical forces but that they also move toward certain actualities. [t. NL: m. *teleologia,* f. Gk. See TELEO-, -LOGY] **—tel·e·o·log·i·cal** (tĕl′ĭ ə lŏj′ə kəl, tē′lĭ-), *adj.* **—tel′e·o·log′i·cal·ly,** *adv.* **—tel·e·ol·o·gist** (tĕl′ĭ ŏl′ə jĭst, tē′lĭ-), *n.*

tel·e·ost (tĕl′ĭ ŏst′, tē′lĭ-), *adj.* **1.** belonging or pertaining to the *Teleostei,* the group of fishes that have a skeleton composed at least in part of bone rather than of cartilage, including the large majority of living species. *—n.* **2.** a teleost fish. [t. NL: back formation from *teleostei,* pl. (f. Gk.: *tele-* TELE-² + m. *ostéon* bone), by false analysis of pl. form] **—tel·e·os′te·an,** *adj., n.*

tel·e·path·ist (tə lĕp′ə thĭst), *n.* **1.** a student of or believer in telepathy. **2.** one having telepathic power.

tel·e·path·y (tə lĕp′ə thĭ), *n.* communication of one mind with another by some means beyond what is ordinary or normal. **—tel·e·path·ic** (tĕl′ə păth′ĭk), *adj.* **—tel′e·path′i·cal·ly,** *adv.*

teleph., telephony.

tel·e·phone (tĕl′ə fōn′), *n., v.,* **-phoned, -phoning.** *—n.* **1.** an apparatus, system, or process for transmission of sound or speech to a distant point, esp. by an electrical device. *—v.t.* **2.** to speak to or summon (a person) by telephone. **3.** to send (a message, etc.) by telephone. *—v.i.* **4.** to send a message by telephone. **—tel′e·phon′er,** *n.* **—tel·e·phon·ic** (tĕl′ə fŏn′ĭk), *adj.* **—tel′e·phon′i·cal·ly,** *adv.*

te·leph·o·ny (tə lĕf′ə nĭ), *n.* the art or practice of constructing or operating telephones.

tel·e·pho·to (tĕl′ə fō′tō), *adj.* **1.** noting or pertaining to telephotography. **2.** noting or pertaining to a form of photographic lens used in telephotography (def. 1) which produces larger images from a given distance.

tel·e·pho·to·graph (tĕl′ə fō′tə grăf′, -gräf′), *n.* **1.** a picture made with a telephoto lens. **2.** a picture transmitted by wire or radio.

tel·e·pho·tog·ra·phy (tĕl′ə fə tŏg′rə fĭ), *n.* **1.** the art of photographing objects too distant for the ordinary camera, by the use of telephoto lenses. **2.** the art of electrically reproducing photographs or facsimiles over a communications channel. **—tel·e·pho·to·graph·ic** (tĕl′ə fō′tə grăf′ĭk), *adj.*

Tel·e·prompt·er (tĕl′ə prŏmp′tər), *n.* *Trademark.* an electronic prompting device used by actors, speakers, etc., on which the magnified text of the script is unrolled at a pace suitable to the speaker's speed of delivery.

tel·e·ran (tĕl′ə răn′), *n.* *Electronics.* a system of aircraft navigation using radar to map the sky above an airfield, which, together with the map of the airfield itself and other pertinent data, is transmitted by television to the airplane approaching the field. [short for *Tele(vision) R(adar) A(ir) N(avigation)*]

---

b., blend of, blended; c., cognate with; d., dialect, dialectal; der., derived from; f., formed from; g., going back to; m., modification of; r., replacing; s., stem of; t., taken from; ?, perhaps. See the full key on inside cover.

tel·e·scope (těl′ə skōp′), *n., adj., v.,* **-scoped, -scoping.**
—*n.* **1.** an optical instrument for making distant objects appear nearer and larger. There are two principal forms, one (**refracting telescope**) consisting essentially of a lens or object glass for forming an image of the object and an eyepiece or combination of lenses for magnifying this image, and the other (**reflecting telescope**) having a similar arrangement but containing a concave mirror or speculum instead of an object glass. —*adj.* **2.** consisting of parts which fit and slide one within another. —*v.t.* **3.** to force together, one into another, or force into something else, in the manner of the sliding tubes of a jointed telescope. —*v.i.* **4.** to slide together, or into something else, in the manner of the tubes of a jointed telescope. **5.** to be driven one into another, as railroad cars in a collision. [t. NL: m.s. *telescopium*, f. m.s. Gk. *teleskópos* far-seeing + *-ium* -IUM]

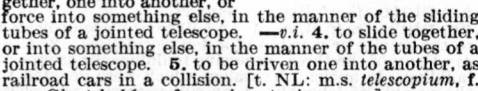

Telescope

tel·e·scop·ic (těl′ə skŏp′ĭk), *adj.* **1.** of, pertaining to, or of the nature of a telescope. **2.** obtained by means of a telescope: *a telescopic view of the moon.* **3.** seen by a telescope; visible only through a telescope. **4.** farseeing: *a telescopic eye.* **5.** consisting of parts which slide one within another like the tubes of a jointed telescope, and thus capable of being extended or shortened. Also, **tel′e·scop′i·cal.** —**tel′e·scop′i·cal·ly,** *adv.*

tel·e·sis (těl′ə sǐs), *n. Sociol.* deliberate, purposeful utilization of the processes of nature and society to obtain particular goals. [t. Gk.: completion]

tel·e·ster·e·o·scope (těl′ə stěr′ĭ ə skōp′, -stǐr′-), *n.* a binocular optical instrument used for stereoscopic viewing of distant objects; a small range finder.

tel·es·the·sia (těl′əs thē′zhə, -zhĭ ə), *n.* sensation or perception received at a distance without the normal operation of the recognized sense organs. Also, **telaesthesia.** [t. NL: m. *telaesthesia.* See TEL-1, ESTHESIA]

tel·e·ther·mom·e·ter (těl′ə thər mŏm′ə tər), *n.* any of various thermometers that indicate or record temperatures at a distance, as by means of an electric current. —**tel′e·ther·mom′e·try,** *n.*

Tel·e·type (těl′ə tīp′), *n., v.,* **-typed, -typing.** *Trademark.* —*n.* **1.** a teletypewriter. **2.** (*l.c.*) a network of teletypewriters with their connecting lines, switchboards, etc. —*v.t.* **3.** (*l.c.*) to send by Teletype. —*v.i.* **4.** (*l.c.*) to operate a Teletype. —**tel′e·typ′er,** *n.*

tel·e·type·writ·er (těl′ə tīp′rī′tər), *n.* a telegraphic apparatus by which signals are sent by striking the letters, etc., of the keyboard of an instrument resembling a typewriter, and are received by a similar instrument which automatically prints them in types corresponding to the keys struck.

tel·e·view (těl′ə vū′), *v.t., v.i.* to view with a television receiver. —**tel′e·view′er,** *n.*

tel·e·vise (těl′ə vīz′), *v.t.,* **-vised, -vising.** to send or receive by television.

tel·e·vi·sion (těl′ə vǐzh′ən), *n.* **1.** the broadcasting of a still or moving image via radiowaves to receivers which project it on a picture tube for viewing at a distance from the point of broadcasting. **2.** the process employed. **3.** the field of broadcasting by television. —**tel·e·vi·sion·al** (těl′ ə vǐzh′ən əl), **tel·e·vi·sion·ar·y** (těl′ə vǐzh′ən ěr′ǐ), *adj.*

tel·fer (těl′fər), *n., adj., v.t.* telpher. —**tel′fer·age,** *n.*

tel·ford pavement (těl′fərd), a form of pavement consisting of large field stones with smaller ones packed tightly between them, the whole mass being rolled after placing. [named after Thomas *Telford*, Scottish engineer (1757–1834)]

tel·har·mo·ni·um (těl′här mō′nǐ əm), *n.* a musical instrument operating by alternating currents of electricity which, on impulse from its keyboard, produces music at a distant point. [t. NL. See TEL-, HARMONIUM]

te·li·al stage (tē′lǐ əl, těl′ǐ-), the phase of the life cycle of the rust fungi in which teliospores are borne.

tel·ic (těl′ĭk), *adj.* **1.** *Gram.* expressing end or purpose, as a clause. **2.** tending to a definite end. [t. Gk.: m.s. *telikós* final]

te·li·o·spore (tē′lǐ ə spōr′, těl′ǐ-), *n. Bot.* a spore of certain rust fungi which carries the fungus through the winter and which, on germination, produces the promycelium.

te·li·um (tē′lǐ əm, těl′ǐ-), *n. Bot.* the sorus of the rust fungi bearing teliospores.

tell (těl), *v.,* **told, telling.** —*v.t.* **1.** to give an account or narrative of; narrate; relate (a story, tale, etc.): *to tell one's experiences.* **2.** to make known by speech or writing (a fact, news, information, etc.); communicate. **3.** to announce or proclaim. **4.** to utter (the truth, a lie, etc.); express in words (thoughts, feelings, etc.). **5.** to reveal or divulge (something secret or private). **6.** to say plainly or positively: *I cannot tell just what was done.* **7.** to discern (a distant person or thing) so as to be able to identify or describe: *can you tell who that is over there?* **8.** to recognize or distinguish: *you could*

hardly tell the difference between them. **9.** to inform or apprise (a person, etc.) of something; to inform a person, etc., of (something): *tell me your name.* **10.** to assure emphatically: *"I won't, I tell you!"* **11.** to bid, order, or command: *tell him to stop.* **12.** to mention one after another, as in enumerating; count or set one by one or in exact amount (fol. by *off, out, down,* etc.): *to tell off five yards in measuring.* **13.** tell off, to scold or rebuke severely.
—*v.i.* **14.** to give an account; make report; give evidence or be an indication (fol. by *of*): *to tell of wonders.* **15.** to disclose something secret or private; play the informer (fol. by *on*). **16.** to have force or effect; operate effectively: *a contest in which every stroke tells.* **17.** to produce a marked or severe effect: *the strain was telling on his health.* **18.** *Brit. Dial.* to talk or chat.
[ME *telle,* OE *tellan,* c. D *tellen* reckon, count, Icel. *telja* tell, count; akin to TALE] —**tell′a·ble,** *adj.*

Tell (těl), *n.* **Wilhelm** (vǐl′hělm). See **William Tell.**

tell·er (těl′ər), *n.* **1.** one who or that which tells, relates, or communicates; a narrator. **2.** one employed in a bank to receive or pay out money over the counter. **3.** one who tells, counts, or enumerates, as one appointed to count votes in a legislative body. —**tell′er·ship′,** *n.*

Tél·lez (těl′yěth), *n.* **Gabriel** (gä′brě ĕl′), ("*Tirso de Molina*") 1571?–1648, Spanish dramatist.

tell·ing (těl′ĭng), *adj.* having force or effect; effective; striking: *a telling blow.* —**tell′ing·ly,** *adv.*

tell·tale (těl′tāl′), *n.* **1.** one who heedlessly or maliciously reveals private or confidential matters; a tattler; a talebearer. **2.** a thing serving to reveal or disclose something. **3.** any of various indicating or registering devices, as a time clock. **4.** *Music.* a gauge on an organ for indicating the air pressure. **5.** an indicator showing the position of a ship's rudder. **6.** a row of strips hung over a track to warn trainmen atop freight trains when they are approaching a low bridge, tunnel, or the like. —*adj.* **7.** that reveals or betrays what is not intended to be known: *a telltale blush.* **8.** giving notice or warning of something, as a mechanical device.

tellur-, *Chem.* a prefix indicating the presence of tellurium, as in *tellurite.*

tel·lu·rate (těl′yə rāt′), *n. Chem.* a salt of telluric acid, of the type H_2TeO_4.

tel·lu·ri·an[1] (tě lŏŏr′ĭ ən), *adj.* **1.** of or characteristic of the earth or an inhabitant of the earth. —*n.* **2.** an inhabitant of the earth. [f. s. L *tellūs* earth + -IAN]

tel·lu·ri·an[2] (tě lŏŏr′ĭ ən), *n.* tellurion.

tel·lu·ric[1] (tě lŏŏr′ĭk), *adj.* **1.** of or pertaining to the earth; terrestrial. **2.** of or proceeding from the earth or soil. [f. s. L *tellūs* earth + -IC]

tel·lu·ric[2] (tě lŏŏr′ĭk), *adj. Chem.* **1.** of or containing tellurium, especially in the hexavalent state (Te+6). **2.** containing tellurium in a higher valence state than the corresponding tellurous compound. [f. TELLUR- + -IC]

tel·lu·ride (těl′yə rīd′, -rǐd), *n. Chem.* a compound of tellurium with an electropositive element or, less often, a radical.

tel·lu·ri·on (tě lŏŏr′ĭ ŏn′), *n.* an apparatus for showing how the diurnal rotation and annual revolution of the earth and the obliquity of its axis produce the alternation of day and night and the changes of the seasons. Also, **tellurian**[2]. [var. of TELLURIUM]

tel·lu·rite (těl′yə rīt′), *n. Chem.* **1.** a salt of tellurous acid, of the type H_2TeO_3. **2.** a mineral, tellurium dioxide, TeO_2.

tel·lu·ri·um (tě lŏŏr′ĭ əm), *n. Chem.* a rare silver-white element resembling sulfur in its chemical properties, and usually occurring in nature combined with gold, silver, or other metals of high atomic weight. It is little used on account of its poisonous nature. *Symbol:* Te; *at. wt.:* 127.61; *at. no.:* 52. [t. NL, f. s. L *tellūs* earth + *-ium* -IUM]

tel·lu·rize (těl′yə rīz′), *v.t.,* **-rized, -rizing.** *Chem.* to mix or cause to combine with tellurium.

tel·lu·rous (těl′yə rəs, tě lŏŏr′əs), *adj. Chem.* containing tetravalent tellurium (Te+4).

Tel·lus (těl′əs), *n. Rom. Myth.* an ancient Italian deity of the Earth, goddess of marriage and fertility.

telo-[1], var. of tele-[1], as in *telodynamic.*

telo-[2], var. of tele-[2], as in *telophase.*

tel·o·dy·nam·ic (těl′ō dī nǎm′ĭk, -dī-), *adj.* pertaining to the transmission of power over considerable distances, as by means of endless wire ropes on pulleys.

tel·o·phase (těl′ə fāz′), *n. Biol.* the final stage of mitotic cell division, in which new nuclei are formed.

tel·pher (těl′fər), *n.* **1.** a traveling unit, car, or carrier in a telpherage. **2.** telpherage. —*adj.* **3.** of or pertaining to a system of telpherage. —*v.t.* **4.** to transport by means of a telpherage. Also, **telher.** [var. of *telephore,* f. TELE- + -PHORE]

tel·pher·age (těl′fər ĭj), *n.* a transportation system in which cars or carriers are suspended from or run on wire cables or the like, esp. one operated by electricity. Also, **telferage.**

tel·son (těl′sən), *n.* the last segment, or an appendage of the last segment, of certain crustaceans and arachnids, as the middle flipper of a lobster's tail. [t. Gk.: boundary, limit]

Tel·u·gu (těl′ŏŏ gōō′), *n., pl.* **-gu, -gus,** *adj.* —*n.* **1.** a Dravidian language spoken in India in the region north of Madras. **2.** one of the people or race speaking this language. —*adj.* **3.** of Telugu or the Telugu.

ăct, āble, dâre, ärt; ĕbb, ēqual; ĭf, īce; hŏt, ōver, ôrder, oil, bŏŏk, ōōze, out; ŭp, ūse, ûrge; ə = a in alone; ch, chief; g, give; ng, ring; sh, shoe; th, thin; ŧh, that; zh, vision. See the full key on inside cover.

tem·blor (těm blôr′), *n.*, *pl.* **-blors, -blores** (-blôr′ěs). *Chiefly U.S.* a tremor; an earthquake. [t. Sp., der. *temblar* tremble, g. Rom. *tremulāre*, der. L *tremulus* trembling]

tem·er·ar·i·ous (těm′ə râr′Ỹ əs), *adj.* reckless; rash. [t. L: m. *temerārius*] —**tem′er·ar′i·ous·ly**, *adv.*

te·mer·i·ty (tə měr′ə tỸ), *n.* reckless boldness; rashness. [late ME *temeryte*, t. L: m.s. *temeritas*]

Tem·es·vár (tě′měsh vär′), *n.* Hungarian name of **Timisoara.**

temp., 1. temperature. 2. temporary. 3. (L *tempore*) in the time of.

Tem·pe (těm′pY), *n.* **Vale of,** a valley of the ancient Peneus river, between Mounts Olympus and Ossa in Thessaly, Greece: sacred to Apollo.

Tem·pel·hof (těm′pəl hŏf), *n.* international airport for Berlin.

tem·per (těm′pər), *n.* 1. the particular state of mind or feelings. 2. habit of mind, esp. with respect to irritability or patience, outbursts of anger, or the like. 3. heat of mind or passion, shown in outbursts of anger, resentment, etc. 4. calm disposition or state of mind: *to lose one's temper.* 5. a substance added to something to modify its properties or qualities. 6. the particular degree of hardness and elasticity imparted to steel, etc., by tempering. 7. *Archaic.* a middle course; compromise. 8. *Obs.* the constitution or character of a substance. [n. use of TEMPER, v.] —*v.t.* 9. to moderate or mitigate. 10. to soften or tone down. 11. to bring to a proper, suitable, or desirable state by, or as by, blending or admixture: *to temper justice with mercy.* 12. to moisten, mix, and work up into proper consistency, as clay or mortar. 13. to heat and cool or quench (metal) to bring the proper degree of hardness, elasticity, etc. 14. to produce internal stresses in (glass) by sudden cooling from low red heat; toughen. 15. to tune (a keyboard instrument, as a piano, organ, etc.) so as to make the tones available in different keys or tonalities. 16. *Archaic.* to combine or blend in due proportions. 17. *Obs.* to pacify. —*v.i.* 18. to be or become tempered. [ME; OE *temprian*, t. L: m. *temperāre* divide or proportion duly, temper] —**tem′per·a·ble,** *adj.* —**tem′per·a·bil′i·ty,** *n.* —**tem′per·er,** *n.* —**Syn.** 2. See **disposition.** 10. See **modify.**

tem·per·a (těm′pər ə), *n.* *Painting.* distemper² (defs. 1, 2). [t. It., in phrase *pingere a tempera* paint in distemper, der. *temp(e)rare* temper, g. L]

tem·per·a·ment (těm′pər ə mənt, -prə mənt), *n.* 1. that individual peculiarity of physical organization by which the manner of thinking, feeling, and acting of every person is permanently affected; natural disposition. 2. unusual personal make-up manifested by peculiarities of feeling, temper, action, etc., with disinclination to submit to ordinary rules or restraints. 3. the combination of the four cardinal humors, the relative proportions of which were supposed to determine physical and mental constitution. 4. *Music.* **a.** the tuning of a keyboard instrument as the piano, organ, etc., so that the tones are available in different keys or tonalities. **b.** a particular system of doing this. 5. *Obs.* act of tempering or moderating. 6. *Obs.* climate. 7. *Obs.* temperature. [late ME, t. L: s. *temperāmentum* due mixture] —**Syn.** 1. See **disposition.**

tem·per·a·men·tal (těm′pər ə měn′təl, -prə měn′-), *adj.* 1. having or exhibiting a strongly marked individual temperament. 2. moody, irritable, or sensitive. 3. of or pertaining to temperament; constitutional. —**tem′-per·a·men′tal·ly,** *adv.*

tem·per·ance (těm′pər əns), *n.* 1. moderation or self-restraint in action, statement, etc.; self-control. 2. habitual moderation in the indulgence of a natural appetite or passion, esp. in the use of alcoholic liquors. 3. total abstinence from alcoholic liquors. [ME, t. AF: m. *temperaunce,* t. L: m. *temperantia* moderation]

tem·per·ate (těm′pər Ỹt), *adj.* 1. moderate or self-restrained; not extreme in opinion, etc. 2. moderate as regards indulgence of appetite or passion, esp. in the use of alcoholic liquors. 3. not excessive in degree, as things, qualities, etc. 4. moderate in respect of temperature. [ME, t. L: m.s. *temperātus,* pp.] —**tem′per·ate·ly,** *adv.* —**tem′per·ate·ness,** *n.*

Temperate Zone, *Geog.* the parts of the earth's surface lying between each of the tropics and the polar circles nearest to it.

tem·per·a·ture (těm′pər ə chər, -prə chər), *n.* 1. the property of a body that determines the sensation of warmth or coldness received from it. By international agreement, its measurement has been based on the constant volume hydrogen thermometer. 2. *Physiol., Pathol.* **a.** the degree of heat of a living body, esp. the human body. **b.** the excess of this above the normal (which, in the adult human being is about 98.6°F., or about 37°C.). 3. *Obs.* mildness, as of the weather. 4. *Obs.* temperament. [t. L: m.s. *temperātūra*]

temperature gradient, *Meteorol.* rate of change of temperature with distance.

tem·pered (těm′pərd), *adj.* 1. having a temper or disposition (as specified): *good-tempered.* 2. *Music.* tuned in accordance with some other temperament than just or pure temperament; specif., tuned in equal temperament. 3. made less intense or violent, esp. by the influence of something added.

tem·pest (těm′pYst), *n.* 1. an extensive current of wind rushing with great velocity and violence, esp. one attended with rain, hail, or snow; a violent storm. 2. a violent commotion, disturbance, or tumult. 3. **The Tempest,** a play (produced 1611) by Shakespeare. —*v.t.* 4. to affect by or as by a tempest; disturb violently. [ME *tempeste,* t. OF, g. Rom. *tempesta* time, storm, der. L *tempestus* seasonable]

tem·pes·tu·ous (těm pěs′chŏŏ əs), *adj.* 1. characterized by or subject to tempests: *the tempestuous ocean.* 2. of the nature of or resembling a tempest: *a tempestuous wind.* 3. tumultuous; turbulent: *a tempestuous period.* [late ME, t. LL: m.s. *tempestuōsus*] —**tem·pes′-tu·ous·ly,** *adv.* —**tem·pes′tu·ous·ness,** *n.*

Tem·plar (těm′plər), *n.* 1. a member of a military order founded at Jerusalem about 1118 among the Crusaders, suppressed in 1312. 2. a member of an order of Freemasons in the U.S., calling themselves **Knights Templars** and claiming descent from the medieval order. [t. ML: apocopated s. *templārius,* der. *templum* TEMPLE¹; r. ME *templer,* t. OF: m. *templier*]

tem·plate (těm′plYt), *n.* templet.

tem·ple¹ (těm′pəl), *n.* 1. an edifice or place dedicated to the service or worship of a deity or deities. 2. (*also cap.*) any of the three successive buildings, or groups of buildings, in ancient Jerusalem which were devoted to the worship of Jehovah. 3. an edifice erected as a place of public worship; a church, esp. a large or imposing one. 4. any place or object regarded as occupied by the Divine Presence, as the body of a Christian (I Cor. 6:19). 5. (in France) a Protestant church. 6. a Mormon church, esp. the main one (built 1853–92 in Salt Lake City, Utah). 7. a building, usually large or pretentious, devoted to some public use: *a temple of music.* 8. (*cap.*) either of two establishments of the medieval Templars, one in London and the other in Paris. 9. (*cap.*) either of two groups of buildings (**Inner Temple** and **Middle Temple**) on the site of the Templars' former establishment in London, occupied by two of the Inns of Court. 10. a building of the order of Freemasons known as Knights Templars. Cf. **templar** (def. 2). [ME *tempel,* OE *templ,* t. L: s. *templum*] —**tem′ple-like′,** *adj.*

tem·ple² (těm′pəl), *n.* 1. the flattened region on either side of the human forehead. 2. a corresponding region in lower animals. 3. either of the sidepieces of a pair of spectacles, extending back above the ears. [ME, t. OF, g. Rom. *tempula,* r. L *tempora,* pl., temples]

tem·ple³ (těm′pəl), *n.* (in a loom) a device for keeping the cloth stretched to the proper width during the weaving. [late ME *tempylle,* t. F: m. *temple* TEMPLET]

Tem·ple (těm′pəl), *n.* 1. **William,** 1628–99, British statesman, diplomat, and author. 2. a city in central Texas. 30,419 (1960).

Temple of Artemis, the large and imposing temple at Ephesus, dedicated to Artemis (Diana). See **Seven Wonders of the World.**

tem·plet (těm′plYt), *n.* 1. a pattern, mold, or the like, usually consisting of a thin plate of wood or metal, serving as a gauge or guide in mechanical work. 2. *Building.* a horizontal piece of timber, stone, or the like, in a wall, to receive and distribute the pressure of a girder, beam, etc. 3. *Shipbuilding.* either of two wedges in each of the temporary blocks forming the support for the keel of a ship while building. Also, **template.** [orig. uncert.; ? F: stretcher, der. L *templum* small timber, purlin]

tem·plon (těm′plŏn), *n.* *Eastern Orth. Ch.* iconostasis.

tem·po (těm′pō), *n., pl.* **-pos, -pi** (-pē). 1. *Music.* relative rapidity or rate of movement (usually indicated by such terms as adagio, allegro, etc., or by reference to the metronome). 2. characteristic rate, rhythm, or pattern of work or activity: *the tempo of city life.* [t. It., g. L *tempus* time]

tem·po·ral¹ (těm′pə rəl), *adj.* 1. of or pertaining to time. 2. pertaining to or concerned with the present life or this world; worldly. 3. enduring for a time only; temporary; transitory. 4. *Gram.* **a.** of, pertaining to, or expressing time: *a temporal adverb.* **b.** of or pertaining to the tenses of a verb. 5. secular, lay, or civil (as opposed to *spiritual* or *ecclesiastical*). —*n.* 6. (*chiefly pl.*) a temporal possession, estate, or the like; a temporality. 7. (*chiefly pl.*) that which is temporal; a temporal matter or affair. [ME, t. L: s. *temporālis* pertaining to or enduring for a time] —**tem′po·ral·ly,** *adv.*

tem·po·ral² (těm′pə rəl), *adj.* *Anat.* 1. noting or pertaining to either of a pair of complex bones which form part of the sides and base of the skull (represented in many vertebrates by several distinct and independent bones). 2. pertaining to the part of the head known as the temple. [t. L: m. *temporālis*]

tem·po·ral·i·ty (těm′pə răl′ə tỸ), *n., pl.* **-ties.** 1. temporal character or nature; temporariness. 2. something temporal. 3. (*chiefly pl.*) a temporal possession, revenue, or the like, as of the church or clergy.

tem·po·rar·y (těm′pə rěr′Ỹ), *adj.* lasting, existing, serving, or effective for a time only; not permanent: *a temporary need.* [t. L: m.s. *temporārius*] —**tem′po·rar′i·ly,** *adv.* —**tem′po·rar′i·ness,** *n.* —**Syn.** TEMPORARY, TRANSIENT, TRANSITORY agree in referring to that which is not lasting or permanent. TEMPORARY implies an arrangement established with no thought of continuance but with the idea of being changed soon: *a temporary structure.* TRANSIENT describes that which is in the process of passing by, and which will therefore last or

---

b., blend of, blended; c., cognate with; d., dialect, dialectal; der., derived from; f., formed from; g., going back to; m., modification of; r., replacing; s., stem of; t., taken from; ?, perhaps.   See the full key on inside cover.

stay only a short time: *a transient condition*. TRANSITORY describes an innate characteristic by which a thing, by its very nature, lasts only a short time: *life is transitory*.

tem·po·rize (tĕm′pə rīz′), *v.i.*, **-rized, -rizing. 1.** to act indecisively or evasively to gain time or delay matters. **2.** to comply with the time or occasion; yield temporarily or ostensibly to the current of opinion or circumstances. **3.** to treat or parley so as to gain time (fol. by *with*). **4.** to come to terms (fol. by *with*); effect a compromise (fol. by *between*). Also, *esp.* Brit., **tem′po·rise′.** [t. ML: m. *temporizāre*, der. *temporāre* delay] **—tem′po·ri·za′tion,** *n.* **—tem′po·riz′er,** *n.* **—tem′po·riz′ing·ly,** *adv.*

tempt (tĕmpt), *v.t.* **1.** to induce or persuade by enticement or allurement. **2.** to allure, appeal strongly to, or invite: *the offer tempts me.* **3.** to render strongly disposed (to do something). **4.** to try to dispose or incite; assail with enticements, esp. to evil. **5.** to put to the test in a venturesome way; risk provoking; provoke: *to tempt one's fate.* **6.** *Obs.* to try or test. [ME, t. L: s. *temptāre* handle, touch, try, test] **—tempt′a·ble,** *adj.* **—Syn. 1.** TEMPT, SEDUCE may both mean to allure or entice to something unwise or wicked. To TEMPT is to attract by holding out the probability of gratification or advantage, often in the direction of that which is wrong or unwise: *to tempt a man with a bribe.* To SEDUCE is literally to lead astray, sometimes from that which absorbs one or demands attention, but oftener, in a moral sense, from rectitude, chastity, etc.: *to seduce a person away from loyalty.* **—Ant. 1.** dissuade.

temp·ta·tion (tĕmp tā′shən), *n.* **1.** act of tempting; enticement or allurement. **2.** something that tempts, entices, or allures. **3.** fact or state of being tempted, esp. to evil. **4.** an instance of it. [ME *temptacion*, t. L: m.s. *temptatio*]

tempt·er (tĕmp′tər), *n.* **1.** one who or that which tempts, esp. to evil. **2.** the Tempter, the devil. **—temptress** (tĕmp′trĭs), *n. fem.*

tempt·ing (tĕmp′tĭng), *adj.* that tempts; enticing or inviting. **—tempt′ing·ly,** *adv.* **—tempt′ing·ness,** *n.*

tem·pus fu·git (tĕm′pəs fū′jĭt), *Latin.* time flies.

ten (tĕn), *n.* **1.** a cardinal number, nine plus one. **2.** a symbol for this number, as 10 or X. **3.** a set of this many persons or things. **4.** a playing card with ten pips. **—adj. 5.** amounting to ten in number. [ME; OE *tĕn,* c. G *zehn,* Goth. *taihun,* L *decem,* Gk. *dĕka*]

ten, 1. tenor. **2.** *Music.* tenuto.

ten·a·ble (tĕn′ə bəl), *adj.* capable of being held, maintained, or defended, as against attack: *a tenable theory.* [t. F, der. *tenir,* g. L *tenēre* hold, keep] **—ten′a·bil′i·ty, ten′a·ble·ness,** *n.* **—ten′a·bly,** *adv.*

ten·ace (tĕn′ās), *n.* *Whist, Bridge.* a combination of the best and third best cards of a suit (**major tenace**), or of the second and fourth best cards (**minor tenace**), esp. when held by the fourth hand. [t. Sp.: m. *tenaza* pincers (referring to cards)]

te·na·cious (tĭ nā′shəs), *adj.* **1.** holding fast; characterized by keeping a firm hold (often fol. by *of*). **2.** highly retentive: *a tenacious memory.* **3.** pertinacious, persistent, stubborn, or obstinate. **4.** adhesive or sticky; viscous or glutinous. **5.** holding together; cohesive; not easily pulled asunder; tough. [f. TENACI(TY) + -OUS] **—te·na′cious·ly,** *adv.* **—te·na′cious·ness,** *n.*

te·nac·i·ty (tĭ năs′ə tĭ), *n.* the quality or property of being tenacious. [t. L: m.s. *tenācitas*] **—Syn.** See perseverance.

te·nac·u·lum (tĭ năk′yə ləm), *n., pl.* **-la (-lə)** *Surg.* a small sharp-pointed hook set in a handle, used for seizing and picking up parts, etc., in operations and dissections. [t. LL: instrument for holding, der. L *tenēre* hold]

te·naille (tĕ nāl′), *n.* *Fort.* an outwork containing one or two reëntering angles, raised in the main ditch immediately in front of a curtain, between two bastions. Also, **te·nail′.** [t. F: forceps, pl. See TENACULUM]

ten·an·cy (tĕn′ən sĭ), *n., pl.* **-cies. 1.** a holding, as of lands, by any kind of title; tenure; occupancy of land, a house, or the like, under a lease or on payment of rent. **2.** the period of a tenant's occupancy. **3.** a holding, or piece of land held by a tenant.

ten·ant (tĕn′ənt), *n.* **1.** one who holds land, a house, or the like, of another (the landlord) for a period of time, as a lessee or occupant for rent. **2.** *Law.* one who holds or possesses lands, tenements, or sometimes personalty, by any kind of title. **3.** an occupant or inhabitant of any place. **—v.t. 4.** to hold or occupy as a tenant; dwell in; inhabit. **—v.i. 5.** to dwell or live (fol. by *in*). [ME *tenaunt,* t. F: m. *tenant,* ppr. of *tenir* hold, g. L *tenēre*] **—ten′ant·a·ble,** *adj.* **—ten′ant·less,** *adj.*

ten·ant·ry (tĕn′ən trĭ), *n., pl.* **-ries. 1.** tenants collectively; the body of tenants on an estate. **2.** state or condition of being a tenant.

tench (tĕnch), *n., pl.* **tenches,** (*esp. collectively*) **tench.** a fresh-water cyprinoid fish, *Tinca tinca,* of Europe. [ME *tenche,* t. OF, g. LL *tinca*]

Ten Commandments, the precepts spoken by God to Israel (Exodus 20, Deut. 10) or delivered to Moses (Exodus 24:12, 34) on Mount Sinai; the Decalogue.

tend[1] (tĕnd), *v.i.* **1.** to be disposed or inclined in action, operation, or effect (to do something): *the particles tend to unite.* **2.** to incline in operation or effect; lead or conduce, as to some result or resulting condition: *measures tending to improved working conditions, governments are tending toward democracy.* **3.** to be directed or lead, as a journey, course, road, etc. (fol. by *to,*

toward, etc.). [ME, t. F: s. *tendre,* g. L *tendere* stretch, go, strive; akin to Gk. *teinein,* Skt. *tan* stretch.]

tend[2] (tĕnd), *v.t.* **1.** to attend to by work or services, care, etc.: *to tend a fire.* **2.** to look after; watch over and care for; minister to or wait on with service. **3.** *Naut.* to handle or watch (a line, etc.). **—v.i. 4.** to attend or wait with ministration or service (fol. by *on* or *upon*). **5.** to attend by action, care, etc. (fol. by *to*). [ME *tende;* aphetic var. of ATTEND]

tend·ance (tĕn′dəns), *n.* **1.** attention; care; ministration, as to the sick. **2.** *Archaic.* attendants collectively.

tend·en·cy (tĕn′dən sĭ), *n., pl.* **-cies. 1.** natural or prevailing disposition to move, proceed, or act in some direction or toward some point, end, or result: *the tendency of falling bodies toward the earth.* **2.** an inclination, bent, or predisposition to something. **3.** special and definite purpose in a novel or other literary work. [t. ML: m. *tendentia,* der. L *tendere* TEND[1]] **—Syn. 1.** TENDENCY, DIRECTION, TREND refer to inclination or line of action. A TENDENCY is an inclination toward a certain line of action (whether or not the action follows), and is often the result of inherent qualities, nature, or habit: *a tendency to procrastinate.* DIRECTION is the line along which an object or course of action moves, often toward some set point or intended goal: *the change is in the direction of improvement.* TREND emphasizes movement in a certain direction, although neither the course nor the goal may be very definite: *there was no evidence of a trend in the stock market.*

ten·den·tious (tĕn dĕn′shəs), *adj.* having or showing a definite tendency, bias, or purpose: *a tendentious novel.* **—ten·den′tious·ly,** *adv.* **—ten·den′tious·ness,** *n.*

ten·der[1] (tĕn′dər), *adj.* **1.** soft or delicate in substance; not hard or tough: *a tender steak.* **2.** weak or delicate in constitution; not strong or hardy. **3.** young or immature: *children of tender age.* **4.** delicate or soft in quality: *tender blue.* **5.** delicate, soft, or gentle: *the tender touch of her hand.* **6.** soft-hearted; easily touched; sympathetic: *a tender person, feelings, etc.* **7.** kind, compassionate, or pitiful. **8.** affectionate or loving; sentimental or amatory. **9.** considerate or careful; chary or reluctant (fol. by *of*). **10.** acutely or painfully sensitive. **11.** readily made uneasy, as the conscience. **12.** yielding readily to force or pressure; easily broken; fragile. **13.** of a delicate or ticklish nature; requiring careful or tactful handling: *a tender subject.* **14.** (of a ship) apt to lean over easily; crank. **—v.t. 15.** to make tender. **16.** *Archaic or Dial.* to regard or treat with tenderness. [ME, t. F: m. *tendre,* g. L *tener* soft, delicate, tender] **—ten′der·ly,** *adv.* **—ten′der·ness,** *n.*

ten·der[2] (tĕn′dər), *v.t.* **1.** to present formally for acceptance; make formal offer of: *to tender one's resignation.* **2.** to offer or proffer. **3.** *Law.* to offer, as money or goods, in payment of a debt or other obligation, esp. in exact accordance with the terms of the law and of the obligation. **—n. 4.** act of tendering; an offer of something for acceptance. **5.** that which is tendered or offered: *legal tender.* **6.** *Com.* an offer made in writing by one party to another to execute certain work, supply certain commodities, etc., at a given cost. **7.** *Law.* an offer, as of money or goods, in payment or satisfaction of a debt or other obligation. [t. AF, g. L *tendere*] **—ten′der·er,** *n.* **—Syn. 1.** See offer.

tend·er[3] (tĕn′dər), *n.* **1.** one who tends; one who attends to or takes charge of something. **2.** an auxiliary vessel employed to attend one or more other vessels, as for supplying provisions. **3.** a small rowboat or motorboat carried or towed by a yacht. **4.** a car attached to a steam locomotive, for carrying coal, water, etc. [late ME; aphetic var. of ATTENDER]

ten·der·foot (tĕn′dər fŏŏt′), *n., pl.* **-foots, -feet (-fēt′).** *Colloq.* **1.** a raw, inexperienced person; a novice. **2.** *U.S.* a newcomer to the ranching and mining regions of the western U.S., unused to hardships.

ten·der·heart·ed (tĕn′dər här′tĭd), *adj.* soft-hearted; sympathetic. **—ten′der·heart′ed·ness,** *n.*

ten·der·loin (tĕn′dər loin′), *n.* **1.** a strip of tender meat forming part of the loin of beef, pork, etc., lying under the short ribs and consisting of the psoas muscle. **2.** a cut of beef lying between the sirloin and ribs. **3.** (*cap.*) a district in a city (orig. New York City) noted for vice and police corruption. [def. 3, so called from its furnishing the "best cut" of graft]

ten·di·nous (tĕn′də nəs), *adj.* **1.** of the nature of or resembling a tendon. **2.** consisting of tendons. [t. ML: m.s. *tendinōsus* full of tendons]

ten·don (tĕn′dən), *n.* *Anat.* a cord or band of dense, tough, inelastic, white fibrous tissue, serving to connect a muscle with a bone or part; a sinew. [t. ML: s. *tendō,* t. Gk.: m. *tĕnōn* sinew (by assoc. with L *tendere* stretch)]

tendon of Achilles, the tendon which connects the muscles of the calf of the leg with the bone of the heel.

ten·dril (tĕn′drĭl), *n.* *Bot.* a filiform leafless organ of climbing plants, often growing in spiral form, which attaches itself to or twines round some other body, so as to support the plant. [t. F.: m. *tendrillon* tender shoot, der. *tendron* tender part, OF *tendrun,* g. L *tenerumen,* der. *tener* tender] **—ten′dril·lar, ten′dril·ous,** *adj.*

Ten·e·brae (tĕn′ə brē′), *n. pl. Rom. Cath. Ch.* the office of matins and lauds for Thursday, Friday, and Saturday of Holy Week, sung

Tendrils of fox grape. *Vitis labrusca*

respectively on the afternoon or evening of Wednesday, Thursday, and Friday of that week, at which candles are gradually extinguished. [t. L: lit., darkness]

ten·e·brif·ic (těn'ə brĭf'ĭk), *adj.* producing darkness. [f. s. L *tenebrae* (*pl.*) darkness + -(I)FIC]

ten·e·brous (těn'ə brəs), *adj.* dark; gloomy; obscure. [late ME, t. L: m.s. *tencbrōsus* dark]

Ten·e·dos (těn'ə dŏs'; *Gk.* -dŏs'), *n.* a small Turkish island in the Aegean, near the entrance to the Dardanelles. Also, **Bozcaada.**

ten·e·ment (těn'ə mənt), *n.* **1.** any house or building to live in; dwelling house. **2.** a portion of a house or building occupied by a tenant as a separate dwelling. **3.** a tenement house. **4.** any habitation, abode, or dwelling place. **5.** any species of permanent property, as lands, houses, rents, an office, a franchise, etc., that may be held of another. **6.** (*pl.*) freehold interests in things immovable considered as subjects of property. [ME, t. OF. der. *tenir* hold, g. L *tenēre*] —**ten·e·men·tal** (těn'ə měn'təl), **ten·e·men·ta·ry** (těn'ə měn'tə rĭ), *adj.*

tenement house, an apartment house, esp. one in the poorer, crowded parts of a large city.

Ten·er·ife (těn'ə rĭf', -rēf'; *Sp.* tě'ně rē'fě), *n.* **1.** the largest of the Canary Islands, off the NW coast of Africa. 321,949 pop. (1950); 794 sq. mi. *Cap.:* Santa Cruz de Tenerife. **2. Pico de** (pē'kô dě). See **Teide, Pico de.** Also, **Ten'er·iffe'.**

te·nes·mus (tə něz'məs, -něs'-), *n. Pathol.* the urgent feeling of need to urinate or defecate, without the ability to do so. [t. ML, g. L *tenesmus*, t. Gk.: straining]

ten·et (těn'ĭt, tē'nĭt), *n.* any opinion, principle, doctrine, dogma, or the like, held as true. [t. L: he holds]

ten·fold (*adj.* těn'fōld'; *adv.* těn'fōld'), *adj., adv.* ten times as great or as much.

Ten·gri Khan (těng'grē кнän'), the highest peak of the Tien Shan mountains, in central Asia. ab. 23,950 ft.

Ten·gri Nor (těng'grē nôr'), a salt lake in E Tibet, NW of Lhasa. ab. 700 sq. mi.; 15,186 ft. high.

te·ni·a (tē'nĭ ə), *n., pl.* **-niae** (-nĭ ē'). taenia.

te·ni·a·cide (tē'nĭ ə sĭd'), *n.* taeniacide.

Ten·iers (těn'yərz; *Flem.* tə nērs'; *Fr.* tě nyě'), *n.* **1. David,** 1610–90, Flemish painter. **2.** his father, **David,** 1582–1649, Flemish painter.

te·nigue (tə nēg'), *n.* mental and physical exhaustion resulting from activities involving considerable nervous tension and physical strain. [b. TENSION and FATIGUE]

Tenn., Tennessee.

ten·nant·ite (těn'ən tīt'), *n.* a mineral, copper arsenic sulfide, approx. Cu₃AsS₃, usually containing some antimony and grading into tetrahedrite: an ore of copper.

Ten·nes·see (těn'ə sē'), *n.* **1.** a State in the SE United States. 3,567,089 pop. (1960); 42,246 sq. mi. *Cap.:* Nashville. *Abbr.:* Tenn. **2.** a river flowing from E Tennessee through N Alabama, W Tennessee, and SW Kentucky into the Ohio near Paducah. 652 mi. —**Ten'nes·se'an,** *adj., n.*

Tennessee Valley Authority, a corporation organized by the U.S. government in 1933, using the Muscle Shoals development as a nucleus, to harness the Tennessee river for cheap electrical power, irrigation, flood control, increased navigation, etc.: numerous large dams and other projects have been built. *Abbr.:* TVA.

Ten·niel (těn'yəl), *n.* **Sir John,** 1820–1914, British caricaturist and illustrator.

ten·nis (těn'ĭs), *n.* **1.** a game in which a ball is driven with a racket (**tennis racket**) back and forth over a net, usually by two players, in a specially constructed enclosed oblong court (**tennis court**); court tennis. **2.** lawn tennis. [ME *tenetz, teneys,* t. AF: m. *tenetz* impv., hold, take]

Ten·ny·son (těn'ə sən), *n.* **Alfred, 1st Baron,** 1809–1892, British poet: poet laureate (1850–92).

teno-, a word element meaning "tendon," as in *tenotomy.* [comb. form repr. Gk. *těnōn*]

ten·on (těn'ən), *n.* **1.** a projection fashioned on an end of a piece of wood, etc., for insertion in a corresponding cavity (mortise) in another piece, so as to form a joint. See diag. under **mortise.** —*v.t.* **2.** to provide with a tenon. **3.** to shape so as to fit into a mortise. **4.** to join securely. [ME, t. OF, der. *tenir* hold, g. L *tenēre*]

ten·o·ni·tis (těn'ə nī'tĭs), *n. Pathol.* inflammation of a tendon.

ten·or (těn'ər), *n.* **1.** continuous course, progress, or movement. **2.** the course of thought or meaning which runs through something written or spoken; purport; drift. **3.** *Music.* **a.** the adult male voice intermediate between the bass and the alto or countertenor. **b.** a part sung by or written for such a voice, esp. the next to the lowest part in four-part texture. **c.** a singer with such a voice. **d.** an instrument corresponding in compass to this voice, specif. the viola. **e.** the lowest-toned bell of a peal. **4.** *Obs.* quality, character, or condition. —*adj.* **5.** *Music.* of, pertaining to, or having the compass of, a tenor. [ME, t. (M)L: course, etc.] —**ten'or·less,** *adj.*

tenor clef, *Music.* a sign locating middle C on the next to the top line of the staff.

te·nor·rha·phy (tə nôr'ə fĭ, -nôr'-), *n., pl.* **-phies.** *Surg.* suture of a tendon. [f. TENO- + m.s. Gk. *-rhaphía*]

te·not·o·my (tə nŏt'ə mĭ), *n., pl.* **-mies.** *Surg.* the cutting or division of a tendon.

ten·pen·ny (těn'pěn'ĭ, těn'pə nĭ), *adj.* **1.** denoting a nail three inches in length. **2.** worth ten pence.

ten·pins (těn'pĭnz'), *n.* **1.** (*construed as sing.*) a game, similar to ninepins, played with ten wooden pins at which a ball is bowled to knock them down. **2.** (*construed as pl.*) the pins used in such a game.

ten·rec (těn'rěk), *n.* any of several insectivorous mammals of Madagascar, which constitute the family *Tenrecidae*, esp. a common tailless species, *Tenrec ecaudatus.* [t. F, t. Malagasy: m. *tàndraka* native name]

Tenrec. Tenrec ecaudatus (12 to 14 in. long)

tense¹ (těns), *adj.,* **tenser, tensest,** *v.,* **tensed, tensing.** —*adj.* **1.** stretched tight, as a cord, fiber, etc.; drawn taut; rigid. **2.** in a state of mental or nervous strain, as a person. **3.** characterized by a strain upon the nerves or feelings: *a tense moment.* **4.** *Phonet.* pronounced with relatively tense muscles. —*v.t., v.i.* **5.** to make or become tense. [t. L: m.s. *tensus,* pp., stretched, taut] —**tense'ly,** *adv.* —**tense'ness,** *n.*

tense² (těns), *n. Gram.* **1.** (in some languages) a category of verb inflection denoting the location of the action or state in past, present, or future time. **2.** a set of such categories or constructions in a particular language. **3.** the meaning of, or typical of, such a category. **4.** such categories or constructions, or their meanings collectively. [ME *tens,* t. OF, g. L *tempus* time]

ten·si·ble (těn'sə bəl), *adj.* capable of being stretched; tensile. —**ten'si·bil'i·ty,** *n.* —**ten'si·bly,** *adv.*

ten·sile (těn'sĭl), *adj.* **1.** of or pertaining to tension: *tensile strain.* **2.** capable of being stretched or drawn out; ductile. [t. NL: m.s. *tensilis,* der. L *tendere* stretch] —**ten·sil'i·ty,** *n.*

tensile strength, *Physics.* the load necessary to rupture a given material when pulled in the direction of length, commonly given in pounds per square inch.

ten·sim·e·ter (těn sĭm'ə tər), *n.* an instrument for determining vapor pressure or tension. [f. TENSI(ON) + -METER]

ten·si·om·e·ter (těn'sĭ ŏm'ə tər), *n.* an apparatus for measuring tensile stress, as in airplane members.

ten·sion (těn'shən), *n.* **1.** act of stretching or straining. **2.** state of being stretched or strained. **3.** mental or emotional strain; strong intellectual effort; intense suppressed excitement. **4.** a strained state of mutual relations. **5.** *Physics.* pressure: *vapor tension.* **6.** *Mech.* **a.** a state in which a body is stretched or increased in size in one direction with a decrease in size in a certain ratio in a perpendicular direction. **b.** a force tending to elongate a body. **7.** *Elect.* **a.** the condition of a dielectric body when its opposite surfaces are oppositely electrified. **b.** electromotive force; potential. **8.** *Mach.* a device for stretching or pulling something. **9.** a device to hold the proper tension on the material being woven in a loom. [t. LL: s. *tensio* act of stretching] —**ten'sion·al,** *adj.* —**ten'sion·less,** *adj.*

ten·si·ty (těn'sə tĭ), *n.* state of being tense.

ten·sive (těn'sĭv), *adj.* stretching or straining. [f. TENSE + -IVE. Cf. F *tensif*]

ten·sor (těn'sər, -sôr), *n. Anat.* a muscle that stretches or tightens some part of the body.

ten-strike (těn'strīk'), *n.* **1.** *Tenpins.* a stroke which knocks down all the pins. **2.** *U.S. Colloq.* any stroke or act which is completely successful.

tent (těnt), *n.* **1.** a portable shelter of skins, coarse cloth, or, esp., canvas, supported by one or more poles and usually extended by ropes fastened to pegs in the ground. **2.** *Surg. Obs.* **a.** a probe. **b.** a roll or pledget, usually of soft absorbent material, as lint or gauze, for dilating an orifice, keeping a wound open, etc. —*v.t.* **3.** to provide with or lodge in tents; cover as with a tent. **4.** *Surg.* to keep open with a tent. —*v.i.* **5.** to live in a tent; encamp. [ME *tente,* t. OF, g. L *tenta,* der. *tentus,* pp., stretched] —**tent'less,** *adj.* —**tent'like',** *adj.*

ten·ta·cle (těn'tə kəl), *n.* **1.** *Zool.* any of various slender, flexible processes or appendages in animals, esp. invertebrates, which serve as organs of touch, prehension, etc.; a feeler. **2.** *Bot.* a sensitive filament or process, as one of the glandular hairs of the sundew. [t. NL: m.s. *tentāculum,* f. L: *tentā*(re) feel, try + -*culum,* dim. suffix] —**ten'ta·cle-like',** *adj.* —**ten·tac·u·lar** (těn tăk'yə lər), *adj.*

tent·age (těn'tĭj), *n.* tents collectively; equipment or supply of tents.

ten·ta·tion (těn tā'shən), *n.* a method of making mechanical adjustments or the like by a succession of trials. [t. L: s. *tentātio,* late var. of *temptātio* attempt]

ten·ta·tive (těn'tə tĭv), *adj.* of the nature of, or made or done as, a trial, experiment, or attempt; experimental. [t. ML: m.s. *tentātivus,* der. L *tentāre* (*temptāre*) try] —**ten'ta·tive·ly,** *adv.* —**ten'ta·tive·ness,** *n.*

tent caterpillar, any of several caterpillars or moths (family *Lasiocampidae*), which spin tentlike, silken webs in which they live gregariously.

ten·ter¹ (těn'tər), *n.* **1.** (in the manufacture of cloth) a framework on which the cloth is stretched so that it may set or dry evenly. **2.** *Obs.* a tenterhook. —*v.t.* **3.** to stretch (cloth) on a tenter or tenters. —*v.i.* **4.** to be capable of being tentered. [ME *tentour,* f. s. L *tentus,* pp., stretched + -*our* -OR²]

ten·ter² (těn'tər), *n. Brit.* one who tends, or has the care of, something, esp. a machine in a factory. [f. *tent tend* + -ER¹]

ten·ter·hook (tĕn′tər hŏŏk′), *n.* **1.** one of the hooks or bent nails which hold cloth stretched on a tenter. **2. on tenterhooks,** in a state of painful suspense.

tenth (tĕnth), *adj.* **1.** next after the ninth. **2.** being one of ten equal parts. —*n.* **3.** a tenth part, esp. of one (1/10). **4.** the tenth member of a series. **5.** *Music.* **a.** a tone distant from another tone by an interval of an octave and a third. **b.** the interval between such tones. **c.** the harmonic combination of such tones. —**tenth′ly,** *adv.*

ten·u·is (tĕn′yŏŏ ĭs), *n., pl.* **tenues** (tĕn′yŏŏ ēz′). *Gram.* a voiceless stop consonant. [t. L: thin, fine, slender]

ten·u·i·ty (tĕn ū′ə tĭ, tĭ nŏŏ′-), *n.* **1.** state of being tenuous. **2.** slenderness. **3.** thinness of consistency; rarefied condition.

ten·u·ous (tĕn′yŏŏ əs), *adj.* **1.** thin or slender in form. **2.** thin in consistency; rare or rarefied. **3.** of slight importance or significance; unsubstantial. [f. s. L *tenuis* slender + -ous] —**ten′u·ous·ly,** *adv.* —**ten′u·ous·ness,** *n.*

ten·ure (tĕn′yər), *n.* **1.** the holding or possessing of anything: *the tenure of an office.* **2.** the holding of property, esp. real property, of a superior in return for services to be rendered. **3.** the period or terms of holding something. [ME, t. OF, der. *tenir*, g. L *tenēre* hold] —**ten·u·ri·al** (tĕn yŏŏr′ĭ əl), *adj.* —**ten·u′ri·al·ly,** *adv.*

te·nu·to (tĕ nŏŏ′tō), *adj., n., pl.* **-tos, -ti** (-tē). *Music.* —*adj.* **1.** held or sustained to its full-time value, as a tone or chord; not staccato. —*n.* **2.** the mark to indicate this. [It.: held]

te·o·cal·li (tē′ə käl′ĭ; *Sp.* tĕ′ō kä′yē), *n., pl.* **-lis.** a ceremonial structure of the Aztecs, consisting of a truncated terraced pyramid supporting a temple. [t. Mex.: f. *teo(tl)* a god + *calli* house]

te·o·sin·te (tē′ə sĭn′tĭ), *n.* a tall annual grass, *Euchlaena mexicana*, native in Mexico and Central America, closely related to corn, and occasionally cultivated as a fodder plant. [t. Mex.: m. *teocintli*, appar. f. *teo(tl)* god + *cintli* dry ear of maize]

te·pee (tē′pē), *n.* a tent or wigwam of the American Indians. Also, **teepee, tipi.** [t. Dakota Ind.: m. *tīpī,* f. *ti* to dwell + *pi* used for]

tep·e·fy (tĕp′ə fī′), *v.t., v.i.,* **-fied, -fying.** to make or become tepid or lukewarm. [t. L: m. *tepefacere* make tepid] —**tep·e·fac·tion** (tĕp′ə făk′shən), *n.*

teph·rite (tĕf′rīt), *n.* *Petrog.* a basaltic rock consisting essentially of pyroxene and plagioclase with nepheline or leucite. [f. s. Gk. *tephrós* ash-colored + -ITE¹] —**teph·rit·ic** (tĕf rĭt′ĭk), *adj.*

tep·id (tĕp′ĭd), *adj.* moderately warm; lukewarm. [ME, t. L: s. *tepidus*] —**te·pid′i·ty, tep′id·ness,** *n.* —**tep′id·ly,** *adv.*

tep·i·dar·i·um (tĕp′ə dâr′ĭ əm), *n., pl.* **-daria** (-dâr′ĭ ə). a tepid room in the ancient Roman thermae. [t. L]

ter., **1.** terrace. **2.** territory.

ter·a·phim (tĕr′ə fĭm), *n. pl., sing.* **teraph** (tĕr′əf), **teraphim.** idols or images reverenced by the ancient Hebrews and kindred peoples, apparently as household gods. [ME *t(h)eraphyn, -ym,* t. L (Vulgate), t. Gk. (Septuagint), t. Heb.: m. *th′rāphīm.* Cf. Aram. *th′rāphīn*]

ter·a·toid (tĕr′ə toid′), *adj.* *Biol.* resembling a monster. [f. *terat-* (t. Gk., comb. form of *téras* monster, marvel) + -OID]

ter·a·tol·o·gy (tĕr′ə tŏl′ə jĭ), *n.* *Biol.* the science or study of monstrosities or abnormal formations in animals or plants. —**ter·a·to·log·i·cal** (tĕr′ə tə lŏj′ə kəl), *adj.* —**ter′a·tol′o·gist,** *n.*

ter·bi·a (tûr′bĭ′ə), *n.* *Chem.* the oxide of terbium, Tb₂O₃, an amorphous white powder. [der. TERBIUM; modeled on ERBIA]

ter·bi·um (tûr′bĭ əm), *n.* *Chem.* a rare-earth, metallic element present in certain minerals, and yielding colorless salts. *Symbol:* Tb; *at. no.:* 65; *at. wt.:* 159.2. [f. (*Yt*)*terb*(y), name of Swedish town where found + -IUM. See YTTERBIUM] —**ter′bic,** *adj.*

terbium metals, *Chem.* See **rare-earth elements.**

Ter Borch (tər bôrKH′), **Gerard** (gā′rärt), 1617–81. Dutch painter.

terce (tûrs), *n.* *Eccles.* tierce (def. 3).

Ter·cei·ra (tĕr sā′rə), *n.* a Portuguese island in the N Atlantic: one of the Azores. 86,443 pop. (1950); 153 sq. mi. *Cap.:* Angra do Heroismo.

ter·cel (tûr′səl), *n.* a male of a hawk trained for falconry, esp. the male peregrine falcon. Also, **terce·let** (tûrs′lĭt). [ME, t. OF, der. *tierz* third, g. L *tertius*]

ter·cen·te·nar·y (tûr sĕn′tə nĕr′ĭ, tûr′sĕn tēn′ə rĭ), *adj., n., pl.* **-naries.** —*adj.* **1.** pertaining to three hundred years or a period of three hundred years; marking the completion of three hundred years. —*n.* **2.** a three hundredth anniversary, or its celebration. Also, **ter·cen·ten′ni·al.** [f. L *ter* thrice + CENTENARY]

ter·cet (tûr′sĭt, tûr sĕt′), *n.* **1.** *Pros.* a group of three lines rhyming together, or connected by rhyme with the adjacent group or groups of three lines. **2.** *Music.* a triplet. [t. F, t. It: m. *terzetto,* dim. of *terzo* third, g. L *tertius*]

te·reb·ic acid (tĕ rĕb′ĭk, -rē′bĭk), *Chem.* an acid, C₇H₁₀O₄, formed by the action of nitric acid on oil of turpentine. [f. TEREB(INTH) + -IC]

ter·e·binth (tĕr′ə bĭnth), *n.* a moderate-sized anacardiaceous tree, *Pistacia Terebinthus,* of the Mediter-

ranean regions, yielding Chian turpentine. [t. L: s. *terebinthus,* t. Gk.: m. *terébinthos*; r. ME *therebynte,* t. OF]

ter·e·bin·thic (tĕr′ə bĭn′thĭk), *adj.* pertaining to or resembling turpentine.

ter·e·bin·thine (tĕr′ə bĭn′thĭn), *adj.* **1.** of, pertaining to, consisting of, or resembling turpentine. **2.** of or pertaining to the terebinth.

te·re·do (tə rē′dō), *n., pl.* **-dos, -dines** (-də nēz′). a shipworm (genus *Teredo*). [t. L, t. Gk.: m. *terēdōn* woodboring worm]

Ter·ence (tĕr′əns), *n.* (*Publius Terentius Afer*) c190–c159 B.C., Roman writer of comedies.

Te·re·sa (tə rē′sə, -zə; *i-p.* tĕ rĕ′sä), *n.* See **Theresa.**

Te·re·si·na (tĕ′rĭ zē′nə), *n.* a city in NE Brazil; a port on the Parnahiba river. 51,418 (1950).

te·rete (tə rēt′, tĕr′ēt), *adj.* **1.** slender and smooth, with a circular transverse section. **2.** cylindrical or slightly tapering. [t. L: m.s. *teres* rounded]

Te·reus (tĭr′ūs, tĭr′ŏŏs), *n.* See **Philomela.**

ter·gal (tûr′gəl), *adj.* of or pertaining to the tergum. [f. s. L *tergum* back + -AL¹]

ter·gi·ver·sate (tûr′jĭ vər sāt′), *v.i.,* **-sated, -sating. 1.** to change one's attitude or opinions with respect to a cause, subject, etc., repeatedly. **2.** to turn renegade. [t. L: m. *tergiversātus,* pp., having turned the back] —**ter′gi·ver·sa′tion,** *n.* —**ter′gi·ver·sa′tor,** *n.*

ter·gum (tûr′gəm), *n., pl.* **-ga** (-gə). **1.** *Zool.* the back or dorsum, esp. of an arthropod. **2.** *Phonet.* the back wall of the pharynx. [t. L: the back]

term (tûrm), *n.* **1.** any word, or group of linguistic forms, naming something, especially as used in some particular field of knowledge, as *atom* in physics, *quietism* in theology, *adze* in carpentry, or *district leader* in politics. **2.** any word or group of linguistic forms considered as a member of a construction or utterance. **3.** the time or period through which something lasts. **4.** a period of time to which limits have been set: *elected for a term of four years.* **5.** each of certain stated periods into which instruction is regularly organized for students or pupils in universities, colleges, and schools. **6.** an appointed or set time or date, as for the payment of rent, interest, wages, etc. **7.** (*pl.*) conditions with regard to payment, price, charge, rates, wages, etc.: *reasonable terms.* **8.** (*pl.*) conditions or stipulations limiting what is proposed to be granted or done: *the terms of a treaty.* **9.** (*pl.*) footing or standing: *on good terms with a person.* **10.** (*pl.*) friendly relations. **11.** (*pl.*) an agreement: *to come to terms with someone.* **12.** *Alg., Arith., etc.* each of the members of which an expression, a series of quantities, or the like, is composed, as one of two or more parts of an algebraic expression. **13.** *Logic.* **a.** the subject or predicate of a categorical proposition. **b.** the word or expression denoting the subject or predicate of a categorical preposition. **14.** *Archit., etc.* a boundary post with a statue or bust on it, esp. a bust of the ancient Roman god Terminus. **15.** *Law.* **a.** an estate or interest in land, etc., to be enjoyed for a fixed period: *a term of years.* **b.** the duration of an estate. **c.** each of the periods during which certain courts of law hold their sessions. **16.** *Archaic.* end, conclusion, or termination. **17.** *Archaic.* a boundary or limit. **18.** (*pl.*) *Obs.* state, situation, or circumstance. —*v.t.* **19.** to apply a particular term or name to; name; call; designate. [ME, t. OF: m. *terme,* g. L *terminus* boundary, limit, end]

term., **1.** terminal. **2.** termination.

ter·ma·gant (tûr′mə gənt), *n.* **1.** a violent, turbulent, or brawling woman. **2.** (*cap.*) *Archaic.* a mythical deity, understood in the Middle Ages to be worshiped by the Mohammedans, represented in some morality plays, etc., as a violent overbearing personage. —*adj.* **3.** violent; turbulent; brawling; shrewish. [ME *Termagaunt, Tervagant,* t. OF: m. *Tervagan* a supposed Mohammedan deity] —**ter′ma·gan·cy,** *n.*

term day, a fixed or appointed day, as for the payment of money due; a quarter day.

term·er (tûr′mər), *n.* one who is serving a term, esp. in prison: *a first termer.*

ter·mi·na·ble (tûr′mə nə bəl), *adj.* **1.** that may be terminated. **2.** (of an annuity) coming to an end after a certain term. —**ter′mi·na·bil′i·ty, ter′mi·na·ble·ness,** *n.* —**ter′mi·na·bly,** *adv.*

ter·mi·nal (tûr′mə nəl), *adj.* **1.** situated at or forming the end or extremity of something. **2.** occurring at or forming the end of a series, succession, or the like; closing; concluding. **3.** pertaining to or lasting for a term or definite period; occurring at fixed terms or in every term. **4.** pertaining to, situated at, or forming the terminus of a railroad. **5.** *Bot.* growing at the end of a branch or stem, as a bud, inflorescence, etc. **6.** *Archit., etc.* designating a figure of the form of a term (def. 14). **7.** pertaining to or placed at a boundary, as a landmark. —*n.* **8.** a terminal part or structure; end or extremity. **9.** *Railroads.* **a.** an originating or terminating point for trains, usually where important stations, yards, and shop facilities are located. **b.** a station, or a city or town, at a terminus. **10.** *Elect.* **a.** the mechanical device by means of which an electrical connection to an apparatus is established. **b.** the point of current entry to, or point of current departure from, any conducting component in an electric circuit. **11.** *Archit., etc.* **a.** a terminal figure. **b.** a carving or the like at the end of something, as a finial. [t. L: s. *terminālis* pertaining to end or boundary] —**ter′mi·nal·ly,** *adv.*

terminal leave, the final leave granted to a member of the armed forces just before his discharge, equal to the total unused leave he has accumulated during active service.

ter·mi·nate (tûr′mə nāt′), v., **-nated, -nating. —v.t. 1.** to bring to an end; put an end to. **2.** to occur at or form the conclusion of. **3.** to bound or limit spatially; form or be situated at the extremity of. —v.i. **4.** to end, conclude, or cease. **5.** to come to an end (often fol. by *at, in,* or *with*). **6.** to issue or result (fol. by *in*). [t. L: m.s. *termin′ātus*, pp., ended, limited, determined] **—ter′mi·na′tive,** adj. **—ter′mi·na′tive·ly,** adv.

ter·mi·na·tion (tûr′mə nā′shən), n. **1.** act of terminating. **2.** fact of being terminated. **3.** the place at which or the part in which anything terminates; bound or limit. **4.** an end or extremity; close or conclusion. **5.** an issue or result. **6.** Gram. a suffix or ending. **—ter′mi·na′tion·al,** adj.

ter·mi·na·tor (tûr′mə nā′tər), n. **1.** one who or that which terminates. **2.** Astron. the dividing line between the illuminated and the unilluminated part of a heavenly body, esp. the moon.

ter·mi·nol·o·gy (tûr′mə nŏl′ə jĭ), n., pl. **-gies. 1.** the system of terms belonging to a science, art, or subject; nomenclature: *the terminology of botany.* **2.** the science of terms, as in particular sciences or arts. [t. G: m. *terminologie,* f. *termino-* (comb. form repr. ML *terminus* term) + *-logie* -LOGY] **—ter·mi·no·log·i·cal** (tûr′mə nə lŏj′ə kəl), adj. **—ter′mi·no·log′i·cal·ly,** adv. **—ter′mi·nol′o·gist,** n.

term insurance, life insurance for a stipulated term of years only, the heirs being paid the face value of the insurance upon death during the term, but nothing being paid upon survival at the completion of the term.

ter·mi·nus (tûr′mə nəs), n., pl. **-ni** (-nī′), **-nuses. 1.** the end or extremity of anything. **2.** either end of a railroad line. **3.** Brit. the station, or the city or town, located there. **4.** the point to which anything tends; goal or end. **5.** a boundary or limit. **6.** a boundary post or stone. **7.** (*cap.*) Roman Myth. the god who presided over boundaries and landmarks. **8.** a figure of this god, representing the upper part of the body and terminating below in a rectangular pillar, which serves as a pedestal. [t. L: boundary, limit, end]

terminus ad quem (ăd kwĕm′), *Latin.* the end to which; later limit.

terminus a quo (ā kwō′), *Latin.* the end from which; earlier limit.

ter·mite (tûr′mīt), n. any of the pale-colored, soft-bodied, mainly tropical, social insects constituting the order *Isoptera,* some of which are very destructive to buildings, furniture, household stores, etc.; a so-called white ant. [t. NL: m.s. *termes* termite (LL wood worm)]

Worker termite. *Termes flavipes* (¼ in. long)

term·less (tûrm′lĭs), adj. **1.** not limited; unconditional. **2.** boundless; endless.

term·or (tûr′mər), n. Law. one who has an estate for a term of years or for life.

tern[1] (tûrn), n. any bird of the subfamily *Sterninae* (family *Laridae*), comprising numerous aquatic species which are allied to the gulls but usually have a slenderer body and bill, smaller feet, a long and deeply forked tail, and a more graceful flight, esp. any of those constituting the genus *Sterna,* as the common sea swallow of Europe and America, *S. hirundo,* a white bird with black crown and gray mantle. [t. Scand.; cf. Dan. *terne*]

Common tern, *Sterna hirundo* (15 in. long)

tern[2] (tûrn), n. **1.** a set of three. **2.** three winning numbers drawn together in a lottery. **3.** a prize won by drawing these. [ME, t. F: m. *terne,* t. It.: m. *terno,* der. L *ternī* three each]

ter·na·ry (tûr′nə rĭ), adj., n., pl. **-ries. —adj. 1.** consisting of or involving three; threefold; triple. **2.** third in order or rank. **3.** based on the number three. **4.** Chem. a. consisting of three different elements or radicals. b. (formerly) consisting of three atoms. **5.** Math. having three variables. **6.** Metall. (of an alloy) having three constituents. **—n. 7.** a group of three. [ME, t. LL: m. s. *ternārius* made up of three]

ter·nate (tûr′nĭt, -nāt), adj. **1.** consisting of three; arranged in threes. **2.** Bot. a. consisting of three leaflets, as a compound leaf. b. having leaves arranged in whorls of three, as a plant. **—ter′nate·ly,** adv.

Ternate leaves
A. Laburnum, *Laburnum laburnum*; B. Rosinweed, *Silphium trifoliatum*

Ter·na·te (tĕr nä′tĕ), n. a small island in Indonesia, W of Halmahera. 53 sq. mi.

terne·plate (tûrn′plāt′), n. an inferior tin plate, in which the tin is alloyed with a large percentage of lead. [f. *terne* (t. F: dull. See TARNISH) + PLATE[1]]

ter·ni·on (tûr′nĭ ən), n. a set or group of three; a triad. [t. L: s. *ternio*]

Ter·no·pol (tĕr′nō pôl′y), n. a city in the SW Soviet Union, in the Ukrainian Republic; formerly in Poland. 40,000 (est. 1948). Also, **Tarnopol.**

ter·pene (tûr′pēn), n. Chem. **1.** any of certain monocyclic hydrocarbons with the formula $C_{10}H_{16}$, occurring in essential or volatile oils. **2.** any of various compounds which contain isoprene structural units for their carbon skeletons. [t. G: m. *terpen,* f. *terp(entin)* TURPENTINE + *-en* -ENE]

ter·pin·e·ol (tûr pĭn′ĭ ōl′, -ŏl′), n. Chem. any of several unsaturated tertiary alcohols, $C_{10}H_{17}OH$, occurring naturally in essential oils or prepared synthetically, used in the manufacture of perfumes. [f. *terpine* (f. TERP(ENE) + -INE[2]) + -OL[1]]

Terp·sich·o·re (tûrp sĭk′ə rĭ), n. Gk. Myth. the Muse of dancing and choral song.

terp·si·cho·re·an (tûrp′sə kə rē′ən), adj. **1.** pertaining to dancing. **2.** (*cap.*) of or pertaining to Terpsichore. **—n. 3.** Colloq. a dancer.

terr., 1. terrace. **2.** territory.

ter·ra (tĕr′ə), n. earth; land. [t. L and It.: earth]

ter·ra al·ba (tĕr′ə ăl′bə), any of various white, earthy or powdery substances, as pipe clay, gypsum, kaolin, or magnesia. [t. L: white earth]

ter·race (tĕr′əs), n., v., **-raced, -racing. —n. 1.** a raised level with a vertical or sloping front or sides faced with masonry, turf, or the like, esp. one of a series of levels rising one above another. **2.** a nearly level strip of land with a more or less abrupt descent along the margin of the sea, a lake, or a river. **3.** the flat roof of a house. **4.** an open (usually paved) area connected with a house and serving as an outdoor living area. **5.** Chiefly Brit. a row of houses running along the face or top of a slope, or a street with such a row or rows. **—v.t. 6.** to form into or furnish with a terrace or terraces. [t. F, der. *terre* earth, g. L *terra*] **—ter′race·less,** adj.

ter·ra cot·ta (tĕr′ə kŏt′ə), **1.** a hard, usually unglazed earthenware of fine quality, used for architectural decorations, statuettes, vases, etc. **2.** something made of this, esp. a work of art. **3.** a brownish-orange color like that of much terra cotta. [t. It.: baked earth, g. L *terra cocta*]

ter·ra-cot·ta (tĕr′ə kŏt′ə), adj. **1.** brownish-orange. **2.** made of terra cotta.

ter·ra fir·ma (tĕr′ə fûr′mə), firm or solid earth; dry land, as opposed to water or air. [t. L: solid earth]

ter·rain (tĕ rān′, tĕr′ān), n. **1.** a tract of land, esp. as considered with reference to its natural features, military advantages, etc. **2.** Geol. terrane. [t. F, der. *terre* earth, g. L *terra*.]

ter·ra in·cog·ni·ta (tĕr′ə ĭn kŏg′nə tə), an unknown or unexplored land. [L: unknown land]

ter·rane (tĕ rān′, tĕr′ān), n. Geol. a geological formation or series of formations. [see TERRAIN]

ter·ra·pin (tĕr′ə pĭn), n. **1.** any of various edible North American fresh-water or tide-water turtles of the family *Emydidae,* esp. any of those constituting the genus *Malaclemmys* (**diamondback terrapins**) of the Atlantic and Gulf coasts of the U.S. **2.** any of various similar turtles. [t. Algonquian (of Va. and Delaware), dim. of *torope, turupe* tortoise]

ter·ra·que·ous (tĕ rā′kwĭ əs), adj. consisting of land and water, as the earth. [f. s. L *terra* earth + AQUEOUS]

ter·rar·i·um (tĕ râr′ĭ əm), n., pl. **-rariums, -raria** (-râr′ĭ ə). a vivarium for land animals (distinguished from *aquarium*). [t. NL, der. *terra* earth; modeled on AQUARIUM]

ter·raz·zo (tĕr rät′tsō), n. a floor material of broken stone and cement polished in place. [t. It: terrace, balcony, der. *terra* earth]

Ter·re Haute (tĕr′ə hōt′, tĕr′ĭ hūt′), a city in W Indiana, on the Wabash. 72,500 (1960).

ter·rene (tĕ rēn′), adj. **1.** earthly; worldly. **2.** earthy. **—n. 3.** the earth. **4.** a land or region. [ME, t. L: m.s. *terrēnus* pertaining to earth]

terre-plein (tĕr′plān′), n. Fort. the top platform or horizontal surface of a rampart, for the cannon. [t. F: f. *terre* earth (g. L *terra*) + *plein* full (g. L *plēnus*)]

ter·res·tri·al (tə rĕs′trĭ əl), adj. **1.** pertaining to, consisting of, or representing the earth: *a terrestrial globe.* **2.** of or pertaining to the land as distinct from the water. **3.** Bot. a. growing on land; not aquatic. b. growing in the ground; not epiphytic or aerial. **4.** Zool. living on the ground; not aquatic, arboreal, or aerial. **5.** of or pertaining to the earth or this world; worldly; mundane. **—n. 6.** an inhabitant of the earth, esp. a human being. [ME, f. L *terrestri(s)* pertaining to earth + -AL[1]] **—Syn. 5.** See earthly.

ter·ret (tĕr′ĭt), n. one of the round loops or rings on the saddle of a harness, through which the driving reins pass. See illus. under **harness.** [var. of ME *toret,* t. OF, dim. of *to(u)r* a round, circumference]

terre-verte (tĕr′vĕrt′), n. an olive-green pigment. [t. F: green earth]

ter·ri·ble (tĕr′ə bəl), adj. **1.** exciting or fitted to excite terror or great fear; dreadful; awful. **2.** distressing; severe: *a terrible winter.* **3.** Colloq. extremely unpleasant or bad: *a terrible performance.* [ME, t. L: m.s. *terribilis*] **—ter′ri·ble·ness,** n. **—ter′ri·bly,** adv. **—Syn. 1.** fearful, frightful, appalling, dire.

ter·ric·o·lous (tĕ rĭk′ə ləs), adj. Bot., Zool. living on or in the ground. [f. s. L *terricola* earth dweller + -OUS]

ter·ri·er[1] (tĕr′ĭ ər), n. one of a variety of dogs, typically small, with a propensity to pursue prey, as the fox, badger, etc., into its burrow, occurring in many breeds including the Airedale, fox terrier, Irish terrier, schnauzer, Scotch terrier, Sealyham terrier, and Skye terrier. [ME *terrere*, t. F: m. (*chien*) *terrier* a hunting dog to start badgers, etc., from their earth or burrow, def. *terre* earth, g. L *terra*]

ter·ri·er² (tĕr′ĭər), *n.* *Law.* a book or document in which are described the site, boundaries, acreage, etc., of lands privately owned by persons or corporations. [ME *terrere*, t. OF: m. *terreoir*, g. L *territōrium* territory]

ter·rif·ic (tərĭf′ĭk), *adj.* 1. causing terror; terrifying. 2. *Colloq.* extraordinarily great, intense, etc.: *terrific speed.* [t. L: s. *terrificus* frightening] **—ter·rif′i·cal·ly,** *adv.*

ter·ri·fy (tĕr′əfī), *v.t.,* -fied, -fying. to fill with terror; make greatly afraid. [t. L: m.s. *terrificāre*] **—ter′ri·fi′er,** *n.* **—Syn.** See **frighten, afraid.**

ter·rig·e·nous (tĕrĭj′ənəs), *adj.* 1. produced by the earth. 2. *Geol.* noting or pertaining to sediments on the sea bottom derived directly from the neighboring land, or to the rocks formed primarily by the consolidation of such sediments. [t. L: m. *terrigenus* earth born]

ter·ri·to·ri·al (tĕr′ətōr′ĭəl), *adj.* 1. of or pertaining to territory or land. 2. of, pertaining to, associated with, or restricted to a particular territory or district; local. 3. pertaining or belonging to the territory of a state or ruler. 4. (*cap.*) of or pertaining to a Territory of the U.S. 5. (*cap.*) *Mil.* organized on a local basis for home defense: *the British Territorial Army.* **—n.** 6. (*cap.*) a member of the British Territorial Army. 7. a soldier in any territorial force. **—ter′ri·to′ri·al·ly,** *adv.*

ter·ri·to·ri·al·ism (tĕr′ətōr′ĭəlĭz′əm), *n.* 1. the principle of the predominance of the landed classes. 2. *Eccles.* Also, **territorial system.** the theory of church policy according to which the supreme ecclesiastical authority is vested in the civil power. **—ter′ri·to′ri·al·ist,** *n.*

ter·ri·to·ri·al·i·ty (tĕr′ətōr′ĭăl′ətĭ), *n.* territorial quality, condition, or status.

ter·ri·to·ri·al·ize (tĕr′ətōr′ĭəlīz), *v.t.,* -ized, -izing. 1. to extend by adding new territory. 2. to reduce to the status of a territory. **—ter′ri·to′ri·al·i·za′tion,** *n.*

ter·ri·to·ry (tĕr′ətōr′ĭ), *n., pl.* -ries. 1. any tract of land; region or district. 2. the land and waters belonging to or under the jurisdiction of a state, sovereign, etc. 3. any separate tract of land belonging to a state. 4. (*cap.*) a. *U.S.* formerly, a region or district not admitted to the Union as a State but having its own legislature, with a governor and other officers appointed by the President and confirmed by the Senate. b. some similar district elsewhere, as in Canada and Australia. 5. the field of action, thought, etc.; domain or province of something 6. the region or district assigned to a representative, agent, or the like, for making sales, etc. [ME, t. L: m.s. *territōrium* land round a town, district]

ter·ror (tĕr′ər), *n.* 1. intense, sharp, overmastering fear: *to be frantic with terror.* 2. a feeling, instance or cause of intense fear: *to be a terror to evildoers.* 3. (*cap.*) a period when a political group uses violence to maintain or achieve supremacy. See **Reign of Terror.** 4. (*cap.*) any terrorist group, program, etc. 5. *Colloq.* a person or thing that is especially annoying or unpleasant. [t. r. ME *terrour*, t. F or L] **—ter′ror·less,** *adj.* **—Syn.** 1. TERROR, HORROR, PANIC, FRIGHT all imply extreme fear in the presence of danger or evil. TERROR implies an intense fear which is somewhat prolonged and may refer to imagined or future dangers: *frozen with terror.* HORROR implies a sense of shock at a danger which is also evil, and the danger may be to others rather than to oneself: *to recoil in horror.* PANIC and FRIGHT both imply a sudden shock of fear. FRIGHT is usually of short duration: *a spasm of fright.* PANIC is uncontrolled and unreasoning fear, often groundless, which may be prolonged: *the mob was in a panic.*

ter·ror·ism (tĕr′ərĭz′əm), *n.* 1. the use of terrorizing methods. 2. state of fear and submission so produced. 3. a method of resisting a government or of governing.

ter·ror·ist (tĕr′ərĭst), *n.* 1. one who uses or favors terrorizing methods. 2. (formerly) a member of a political group in Russia aiming at the demoralization of the government by terror. 3. an agent or partisan of the revolutionary tribunal during the Reign of Terror in France. [t. F: m. *terroriste*, der. L *terror* terror] **—ter′ror·is′tic,** *adj.*

ter·ror·ize (tĕr′ərīz), *v.t.,* -ized, -izing. 1. to fill or overcome with terror. 2. to dominate or coerce by intimidation. **—ter′ror·i·za′tion,** *n.* **—ter′ror·iz′er,** *n.*

ter·ry (tĕr′ĭ), *n., pl.* -ries, *adj.* **—n.** 1. the loop formed by the pile of a fabric when left uncut. 2. Also, **terry cloth.** a pile fabric with loops on both sides, as in a Turkish towel. **—adj.** 3. having the pile loops uncut: *terry velvet.* [? var. of TERRET]

Ter·ry (tĕr′ĭ), *n.* Ellen Alicia, 1848–1928, British actress.

terse (tûrs), *adj.,* **terser, tersest.** neatly or effectively concise; brief and pithy, as language. [t. L: m.s. *tersus,* pp., polished] **—terse′ly,** *adv.* **—terse′ness,** *n.*

ter·tial (tûr′shəl), *Ornith.* **—adj.** 1. pertaining to any of a set of flight feathers situated on the basal segment of a bird's wing. **—n.** 2. a tertial feather. [f. s. L *tertius* third + -AL¹]

ter·tian (tûr′shən), *adj.* 1. (of a fever, ague, etc.) characterized by paroxysms which recur every other day. **—n.** 2. a tertian fever or ague. [ME *tercian,* t. L: m.s. (*febris*) *tertiāna* tertian (fever), der. *tertius* third]

ter·ti·ar·y (tûr′shĭĕr′ĭ, tûr′shərĭ), *adj., n., pl.* -aries. **—adj.** 1. of the third order, rank, formation, etc.; third. 2. *Chem.* a. denoting or containing a carbon atom united to three other carbon atoms. b. formed by replacement of three atoms or radicals. 3. (*cap.*) *Geol.* pertaining to a geological period or a system of rocks which precedes the Quaternary and constitutes the earlier principal division of the Cenozoic era. 4. *Ornith.* tertial. 5. *Eccles.* noting or pertaining to a branch (third order) of certain religious orders which consists of lay members living in community (**regular tertiaries**) or living in the world (**secular tertiaries**). **—n.** 6. (*cap.*) *Geol.* the period or system representing geological time from about 2 to 60 million years ago and comprising Paleocene to Pliocene epochs or series. 7. *Ornith.* a tertial feather. 8. (*also cap.*) *Eccles.* a member of a tertiary branch of a religious order. [t. L: m.s. *tertiārius* of third part or rank]

ter·ti·um quid (tûr′shĭəm kwĭd′), something related in some way to two things, but distinct from both; something intermediate between two things. [t. L, trans. of Gk. *tríton ti* some third thing]

Ter·tul·li·an (tərtŭl′ĭən, -tŭl′yən), *n.* (*Quintus Septimius Florens Tertullianus*) A.D. c150–after 220, Christian theologian of N Africa.

ter·va·lent (tûr·vā′lənt), *adj.* *Chem.* 1. trivalent. 2. possessing three different valences, as cobalt with valences 2, 3, and 4. [f. L *ter* thrice + VALENT]

ter·za ri·ma (tĕr′tsä rē′mä), *Pros.* an Italian form of iambic verse consisting of eleven-syllable lines arranged in tercets, the middle line of each tercet rhyming with the first and third lines of the following tercet. [It.: third rhyme]

Tes·la (tĕs′lä), *n.* Nikola (nē′kô lä′), 1856–1943, U.S. electrician and inventor, born in Croatia.

tes·sel·late (*v.* tĕs′əlāt′; *adj.* tĕs′əlĭt, -lāt′), *v.,* -lated, -lating, *adj.* **—v.t.** 1. to form of small squares or blocks, as floors, pavements, etc,; form or arrange in a checkered or mosaic pattern. **—adj.** 2. tessellated. [t. LL: m.s. *tessellātus,* pp., formed in mosaic]

tes·sel·la·tion (tĕs′əlā′shən), *n.* 1. act or art of tessellating. 2. tessellated form or arrangement. 3. tessellated work.

tes·ser·a (tĕs′ərə), *n., pl.* **tesserae** (tĕs′ərē′). 1. each of the small pieces used in mosaic work. 2. a small square of bone, wood, or the like, anciently used as a token, tally, ticket, due, etc. [t. L, t. d. Gk.: lit., four]

Tesserae, shown separately (above) and combined in mosaic flooring (below)

Tes·sin (tĕ·sēn′), *n.* German name of Ticino.

test¹ (tĕst), *n.* 1. that by which the presence, quality, or genuineness of anything is determined; a means of trial. 2. the trial of the quality of something: *to put to the test.* 3. a particular process or method of doing this. 4. *Educ.* a form of examination for evaluating the performance and capabilities of a student or class. 5. *Psychol.* a standardized procedure for eliciting responses upon which appraisal of the individual can be based: *an intelligence test.* 6. *Chem.* a. the process of detecting the presence of an ingredient in a compound or the like, or of determining the nature of a substance, commonly by the addition of a reagent. b. the reagent used. c. an indication or evidence of the presence of an ingredient, or of the nature of a substance, obtained by such means. 7. a cupel for assaying or refining metals. **—v.t.** 8. to subject to a test of any kind; try. 9. *Chem.* to subject to a chemical test. 10. to assay or refine in a test or cupel. [ME, t. OF: cupel. g. L *testu*(m), var. of *testa* tile, earthen vessel, pot] **—test′a·ble,** *adj.* **—Syn.** 1. See **trial.**

test² (tĕst), *n.* 1. *Zool.* the hard covering of certain invertebrates, as mollusks, arthropods, tunicates, etc.; shell; lorica. 2. *Bot.* testa. [t. L: s. *testa* (see TEST¹)]

Test., Testament.

tes·ta (tĕs′tə), *n., pl.* -tae (-tē). *Bot.* the outer, usually hard, integument or coat of a seed. See diag. under **seed.** [t. L. See TEST²]

tes·ta·ceous (tĕstā′shəs), *adj.* *Bot., Zool.* of a brick-red, brownish-red, or brownish-yellow color. [t. L: m. *testāceus* shell-covered]

tes·ta·cy (tĕs′təsĭ), *n.* state of being testate.

tes·ta·ment (tĕs′təmənt), *n.* 1. *Law.* a. a formal declaration, usually in writing, of a person's wishes as to the disposition of his property after his death. b. a disposition to take effect upon death and relating to personal property (as distinguished from real property disposed of by *will*). 2. a covenant, esp. between God and man. 3. the Mosaic or old covenant or dispensation, or the Christian or new covenant or dispensation. 4. the New Testament, as distinct from the Old Testament. 5. a copy of the New Testament. [ME, t. L: s. *testamentum* will]

tes·ta·men·ta·ry (tĕs′təmĕn′tərĭ), *adj.* 1. of, pertaining to, or of the nature of a testament or will. 2. given, bequeathed, done, or appointed by will. 3. set forth or contained in a will.

tes·tate (tĕs′tāt), *adj.* having made and left a valid will. [late ME, t. L: m.s. *testātus,* pp.]

tes·ta·tor (tĕs′tā′tər, tĕs tā′tər), *n.* 1. one who makes a will. 2. one who has died leaving a valid will. [t. L; r. ME *testatour*, t. AF]

tes·ta·trix (tĕs tā′trĭks), *n., pl.* **-trices** (-trə sēz′). a female testator.

test blank, *Educ., Psychol,* a typed or printed test form containing questions or tasks to be responded to.

test·er[1] (tĕs′tər), *n.* one who or that which tests. [f. TEST[1], v. + -ER[1]]

tes·ter[2] (tĕs′tər), *n.* a canopy, as over a bed, altar, etc. [late ME. Cf. OF *testre* headboard of bed, *testiere* head covering, der. *teste* head, g. L *testa* pot]

tes·ter[3] (tĕs′tər), *n.* 1. the teston of Henry VIII. 2. a sixpence. [appar. alter. of TESTON]

tes·tes (tĕs′tēz), *n.* pl. of **testis**.

tes·ti·cle (tĕs′tə kəl), *n. Anat., Zool.* the male sex gland, either of two oval glands located in the scrotal sac. [t. L: m. *testiculus*, dim. of *testis* TESTIS] **—tes·tic·u·lar** (tĕs tĭk′yə lər), *adj.*

tes·ti·fy (tĕs′tə fī′), *v.,* **-fied, -fying.** —*v.i.* 1. to bear witness; give or afford evidence. 2. to make solemn declaration. 3. *Law.* to give testimony under oath or solemn affirmation, usually in court. —*v.t.* 4. to bear witness to; affirm as fact or truth. 5. to give or afford evidence of in any manner. 6. to declare, profess, or acknowledge openly. 7. *Law.* to state or declare under oath or affirmation, usually in court. [ME, t. L: m.s. *testificārī* bear witness] **—tes′ti·fi′er,** *n.*

tes·ti·mo·ni·al (tĕs′tə mō′nĭ əl), *n.* 1. a writing certifying to a person's character, conduct, or qualifications, or to a thing's value, excellence, etc.; a letter or written statement of recommendation. 2. something given or done as an expression of esteem, admiration, or gratitude. —*adj.* 3. pertaining to or serving as testimony.

tes·ti·mo·ny (tĕs′tə mō′nĭ), *n., pl.* **-nies.** 1. *Law.* the statement or declaration of a witness under oath or affirmation, usually in court. 2. evidence in support of a fact or statement; proof. 3. open declaration or profession, as of faith. 4. (*pl.*) the precepts of God. 5. *Bible.* the Decalogue as inscribed on the two tables of the law, or the ark in which the tables were kept. Ex. 25:16, 16:34. 6. *Archaic.* a declaration of disapproval; protest. [late ME, t. L: m.s. *testimōnium* evidence, attestation] **—Syn. 1. See evidence.**

tes·tis (tĕs′tĭs), *n., pl.* **-tes** (-tēz). testicle. [t. L]

tes·ton (tĕs′tən, tĕs tōn′), *n.* 1. an early silver coin in France, valued between 10 and 14½ sous. 2. any of various silver coins formerly current, with a head or portrait on the obverse; in England, the shilling of Henry VIII, or Edward VI, reduced in value successively to tenpence, ninepence, and sixpence. Also, **tes·toon** (tĕs tōōn′). [t. F, t. It.: m. *testone*, aug. of *testa* head, g. L *testa* potsherd.]

tes·tos·ter·one (tĕs tŏs′tə rōn′), *n. Biochem.* the hormone, $C_{19}H_{28}O_2$, secreted by the testes and obtained by extraction from animal testes and by synthesis. It stimulates the development of masculine characteristics. [f. *testo-* TESTIS + STER(OL) + -ONE]

test paper, 1. *U.S.* the paper bearing answers given in an examination. 2. *Chem.* paper impregnated with a reagent, as litmus, which changes color when acted upon by certain substances.

test tube, *Chem.* a hollow cylinder of thin glass with one end closed, used in chemical tests.

tes·tu·di·nate (tĕs tū′də nĭt, -nāt′, -tōō′-), *adj.* formed like the carapace of a tortoise; arched; vaulted.

tes·tu·do (tĕs tū′dō, -tōō′-), *n., pl.* **-dines** (-də nēz′). 1. *Fort.* **a.** (among the ancient Romans) a movable shelter with a strong and usually fireproof arched roof, used for protection of soldiers in siege operations. **b.** a shelter formed by soldiers overlapping their oblong shields above their heads. 2. *Pathol.* an encysted tumor. [ME, t. L: tortoise]

tes·ty (tĕs′tĭ), *adj.,* **-tier, -tiest.** irritably impatient; touchy. [ME, t. AF: m. *testif* headstrong, der. OF *teste* head, g. L *testa* potsherd] **—tes′ti·ly,** *adv.* **—tes′ti·ness,** *n.*

te·tan·ic (tĭ tăn′ĭk), *adj.* 1. *Pathol.* pertaining to, of the nature of, or characterized by tetanus. 2. *Med.* denoting a remedy which acts on the nerves and through them on the muscles, and which, if taken in overdoses, causes tetanic spasms of the muscles and death. Also, **te·tan′i·cal.**

tet·a·nize (tĕt′ə nīz′), *v.t.,* **-nized, -nizing.** *Physiol.* to induce a condition of tetanus in (a muscle). **—tet′a·ni·za′tion,** *n.*

tet·a·nus (tĕt′ə nəs), *n.* 1. *Pathol.* **a.** an infectious, often fatal disease, due to a specific microorganism, the **tetanus bacillus**, which gains entrance to the body through wounds, characterized by more or less violent tonic spasms and rigidity of many or all the voluntary muscles, esp. those of the neck and lower jaw. Cf. lockjaw. **b.** the microorganism, *Clostridium Tetani*, which causes this disease. 2. *Physiol.* tonic contractions of a skeletal muscle induced by rapid stimulation. [t. L, t. Gk.: m. *tétanos* spasm (of muscles)]

tet·a·ny (tĕt′ə nĭ), *n. Pathol.* a state marked by severe intermittent tonic contractions and muscular pain,

frequently due to a deficiency of calcium salts. [t. NL: m. s. *tetania.* See TETANUS]

te·tar·to·he·dral (tĭ tär′tō hē′drəl), *adj.* (of a crystal) having one fourth the planes or faces required by the maximum symmetry of the system to which it belongs. [f. *tetarto-* (t. Gk., comb. form of *tétartos* fourth) + -HEDR(ON) + -AL[1]]

tetch·y (tĕch′Y), *adj.,* **tetchier, tetchiest.** irritable; touchy. Also, **techy.** [orig. uncert.] **—tetch′i·ly,** *adv.* **—tetch′i·ness,** *n.*

tête-à-tête (tāt′ə tāt′; *Fr.* tĕ tä tĕt′), *adj.* 1. of, between, or for two persons together, without others. —*n.* 2. a private conversation or interview, usually between two people. 3. a sofa shaped like an S so two people are able to converse face to face. —*adv.* 4. (of two persons) together in private: *to sit tête-à-tête.* [t. F: head to head]

tête-bêche (tĕt bĕsh′), *adj. Philately.* (of an unsevered pair of stamps) reversed in relation to each other, either through error or intentionally. [F, f. *tête* head + *bêche*, reduced from *bechenet* double bed head]

tête-de-pont (tĕt də pôN′), *n., pl.* **têtes-de-pont** (tĕt-də pôN′). *Fort.* bridgehead. [F]

teth·er (tĕth′ər), *n.* 1. a rope, chain, or the like, by which an animal is fastened, as to a stake, so that its range of movement is limited. 2. the utmost length to which one can go in action; the utmost extent or limit of ability or resources. 3. **at the end of one's tether,** having exhausted one's possibilities or resources. —*v.t.* 4. to fasten or confine with or as with a tether. [ME *tethir*, appar. t. Scand.; cf. Icel. *tjöthr*]

Te·thys (tē′thĭs), *n. Gk. Myth.* a Titaness and sea goddess, daughter of Uranus and consort of Oceanus.

Te·ton (tē′tən; *orig. Fr.* tĕ tôN′), *n.* a Siouan language.

tet·ra (tĕt′rə), *n.* any of several tropical fish of the family *Characinidae,* kept in home aquariums.

tetra-, a word element meaning "four," as in *tetra·brach.* [t. Gk., comb. form of *téttares*]

tet·ra·bas·ic (tĕt′rə bā′sĭk), *adj. Chem.* 1. (of an acid) having four atoms of hydrogen replaceable by basic atoms or radicals. 2. containing four basic atoms or radicals having a valence of one.

tet·ra·brach (tĕt′rə brăk′), *n. Class. Pros.* a metrical foot or word of four short syllables. [t. Gk.: s. *tetrábrachys* having four short syllables]

tet·ra·bran·chi·ate (tĕt′rə brăng′kĭ Yt, -āt′), *adj.* belonging or pertaining to the *Tetrabranchiata,* a subclass or order of cephalopods with four gills, including the pearly nautilus and numerous fossil forms. [t. NL: m.s. *tetrabranchiātum,* f. Gk. *tetra-* TETRA- + s. Gk. *bránchia* gills + -ātum -ATE[1]]

tet·ra·chord (tĕt′rə kôrd′), *n. Music.* a diatonic series of four tones, the first and last separated by a perfect fourth. [t. Gk: s. *tetráchordos* having four strings] **—tet′ra·chor′dal,** *adj.*

te·trac·id (tĕ trăs′Yd), *n. Chem.* a base or an alcohol containing four hydroxyl (OH) groups.

tet·rad (tĕt′răd), *n.* 1. a group of four. 2. the number four. 3. *Chem.* a tetravalent or quadrivalent element, atom, or radical. [t. Gk.: s. *tetrás* group of four]

te·trad·y·mite (tĕ trăd′ə mīt′), *n.* a mineral, bismuth telluride and sulfide, Bi_2Te_2S, occurring in soft gray to black foliated masses. [f. G: m. *tetradymit,* f. s. Gk. *tetrádymos* fourfold + -it -ITE[1]]

tet·ra·eth·yl lead (tĕt′rə ĕth′əl), *Chem.* an organic compound of lead, $Pb(C_2H_5)_4$, a colorless liquid added to gasoline to promote uniform combustion.

tet·ra·gon (tĕt′rə gŏn′), *n. Geom.* a plane figure having four angles; a quadrangle; a quadrilateral. [t. Gk.: s. *tetrágōnon* quadrangle]

te·trag·o·nal (tĕ trăg′ə nəl), *adj.* 1. pertaining to a tetragon. 2. *Crystall.* noting or pertaining to the tetragonal system.

tetragonal system, *Crystall.* a system of crystallization in which all three axes are at right angles to one another, and the two equal lateral axes differ in length from the vertical axis.

tet·ra·gram (tĕt′rə grăm′), *n.* 1. a word of four letters. 2. (*also cap.*) the Tetragrammaton. [t. Gk.: m.s. *tetrágrammon*]

Tet·ra·gram·ma·ton (tĕt′rə grăm′ə tŏn′), *n.* the Hebrew word written JHVH (or JHWH, YHVH, YH-WH), representing, without vowels, the "ineffable name" of God, pronounced in Hebrew as "Adonai" and commonly transliterated in English as "Jehovah." See **Yahweh.** [ME, t. Gk.: the four-letter (word)]

tet·ra·he·dral (tĕt′rə hē′drəl), *adj.* 1. pertaining to or having the form of a tetrahedron. 2. having four lateral planes in addition to the top and bottom.

tet·ra·he·drite (tĕt′rə hē′drīt), *n.* a steel-gray or blackish mineral with a brilliant metallic luster, essentially copper and antimony sulfide (nearly Cu_8Sb_3), but often containing other elements, as silver, etc. occurring in tetrahedral crystals and massive, and forming an important ore of copper and sometimes of silver.

tet·ra·he·dron (tĕt′rə hē′drən), *n., pl.* **-drons, -dra** (-drə). *Geom.* a solid contained by four plane faces; a triangular pyramid. [t. LGk.: m. *tetráedron,* neut. of *tetráedros* four-sided. See -HEDRON]

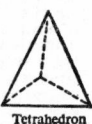

Tetrahedron

te·tral·o·gy (tĕ trăl′ə jY), *n., pl.* **-gies.** 1. a series of four related dramas, operas, etc.

Testudo (def. 1 b) of Roman soldiers

2. a group of four dramas, three tragic and one satiric, exhibited consecutively at the festival of Dionysus in ancient Athens. [t. Gk.: m.s. *tetralogia*]

te·tram·er·ous (tĕ trăm′ər əs), *adj.* 1. consisting of or divided into four parts. 2. *Bot.* (of flowers) having four members in each whorl. [t. NL: m. *tetramerus*, t. Gk.: m. *tetramerēs* four-parted]

te·tram·e·ter (tĕ trăm′ə tər), *Pros.* —*adj.* 1. having four measures. —*n.* 2. a tetrameter line. In ancient poetry, it consisted of four dipodies (eight feet) in trochaic, iambic, or anapestic meter. [t. L: m.s. *tetrametrus*, t. Gk.: m. *tetrámetros*]

Tetramerous flower

tet·ra·pet·al·ous (tĕt′rə pĕt′əl əs), *adj.* *Bot.* having four petals.

te·trap·ter·ous (tĕ trăp′tər əs), *adj.* 1. *Zool.* having four wings or winglike appendages. 2. *Bot.* having four winglike appendages. [t. Gk.: m. *tetrápteros*]

te·trarch (tē′trärk, tĕt′rärk), *n.* 1. any ruler of a fourth part, division, etc. 2. a subordinate ruler generally. 3. one of four joint rulers or chiefs. 4. (in the ancient Roman Empire) the ruler of the fourth part of a country or province. [ME, t. LL: s. *tetrarcha*, var. of L *tetrarchēs*, t. Gk.: ruler of one of four (parts)] —**te·trarch·ate** (tē′trär kāt′, -ĭt, tĕt′rär-), **te·trar·chy** (tē′trär kĭ, tĕt′rär-), *n.*

tet·ra·spo·ran·gi·um (tĕt′rə spō răn′jĭ əm), *n.,pl.* -**gi·a** (-jĭ ə). *Bot.* a sporangium containing four asexual spores (tetraspores).

tet·ra·spore (tĕt′rə spōr′), *n.* *Bot.* one of the four asexual spores produced within a tetrasporangium.

Tetrapterous fruit
A. Silverbell tree. *Halesia Carolina;*
B. Transverse section

te·tras·ti·chous (tĭ trăs′tə kəs), *adj.* *Bot.* 1. arranged in a spike of four vertical rows, as flowers. 2. having four such rows of flowers, as a spike. [t. Gk.: m. *tetrástichos* having four rows]

tet·ra·syl·la·ble (tĕt′rə sĭl′ə bəl), *n.* a word of four syllables. —**tet·ra·syl·lab·ic** (tĕt′rə sĭ lăb′ĭk), **tet′ra·syl·lab′i·cal**, *adj.*

tet·ra·tom·ic (tĕt′rə tŏm′ĭk), *adj.* *Chem.* 1. having four atoms in the molecule. 2. having a valence of four. 3. containing four replaceable atoms or groups.

tet·ra·va·lent (tĕt′rə vā′lənt, tĕ trăv′ə lənt), *adj.* *Chem.* 1. having a valence of 4, as Pt + 4. 2. quadrivalent.

Te·traz·zi·ni (tĕ′trät tsē′nē), *n.* **Luisa** (lōō ē′zä), 1874–1940, Italian operatic soprano.

tet·rode (tĕt′rōd), *n.* *Electronics.* an electron tube containing four elements, usually a plate, two grids, and a cathode.

tet·ro·ploid (tĕt′rə ploid′), *adj.* See **chromosome number**.

te·trox·ide (tĕ trŏk′sīd, -sĭd), *n.* *Chem.* an oxide which contains in its molecule four atoms of oxygen. Also, **te·trox·id** (tĕ trŏk′sĭd).

tet·ryl (tĕt′rĭl), *n.* a military explosive, $C_7H_5N_5O_8$, used as a detonator and as a bursting charge in small-caliber projectiles. [f. TETR(A)- + -YL]

tet·ter (tĕt′ər), *n.* any of various cutaneous diseases, as herpes, eczema, impetigo, etc. [ME; OE *teter*, c. Skt. *dadru* kind of skin disease]

Te·tuán (tĕ twän′), *n.* a seaport in N Morocco, on the Mediterranean: former capital of the Spanish Zone of Morocco. 80,732 (1950).

Tet·zel (tĕt′sal), *n.* **Johann** (yō′hän), 1465?–1519, German monk: seller of papal indulgences. Also, **Tezel.**

Teu·cer (tū′sər, tōō′-), *adj.* *Gk. Legend.* 1. the first king of Troy. 2. a noted archer, son of Telamon.

Teu·cri·an (tū′krĭ ən, tōō′-), *adj.* 1. of or pertaining to the ancient Trojans, or to Teucer, their first king. —*n.* 2. one of the ancient Trojans.

Teut., 1. Teuton. 2. Teutonic.

Teu·to·bur·ger Wald (toi′tō bŏŏr′gər vält′). a chain of wooded hills in N West Germany, in Westphalia: German defeat of the Romans, A.D. 9.

Teu·ton (tū′tən, tōō′tən), *n.* 1. a member of a Germanic people or tribe first mentioned in the 4th century B.C. and supposed to have dwelt in Jutland. 2. a native of Germany or a person of German origin. —*adj.* 3. Teutonic. [t. L: s. *Teutonēs, Teutonī* (pl.) tribal name]

Teu·ton·ic (tū tŏn′ĭk, tōō-), *adj.* 1. of or pertaining to the ancient Teutons. 2. of or pertaining to the Teutons or Germans; German. 3. denoting or pertaining to the northern European stock which includes the German, Dutch, Scandinavian, British, and related peoples. 4. (of languages) Germanic. 5. *Obsolesc.* Nordic.

Teu·ton·i·cism (tū tŏn′ə sĭz′əm, tōō-), *n.* 1. the character or spirit of the Teutons, esp. the Germans. 2. a Teutonic characteristic. 3. a Germanism.

Teutonic Order, a military and religious order founded (c1190) in the Holy Land during the Third Crusade. At first devoted to charitable pursuits, it was later instrumental in the eastward expansion of medieval Germany against the Slavic and Baltic peoples. Also, **Teutonic Knights.**

Teu·ton·ism (tū′tə nĭz′əm, tōō′-), *n.* the culture of the Teutons. —**Teu′ton·ist,** *n.*

Teu·ton·ize (tū′tə nīz′, tōō′-), *v.t., v.i.,* -**ized,** -**izing.** to make or become Teutonic. —**Teu′ton·i·za′tion,** *n.*

Te·ve·re (tĕ′vĕ rĕ), *n.* Italian name of **Tiber.**

Tewkes·bur·y (tūks′bĕr′ĭ, -bə rĭ, tōōks′-), *n.* a town in W England, in Gloucestershire: final defeat of the Lancastrians in the Wars of the Roses, 1471. 5292 (1951).

Tex., 1. Texan. 2. Texas.

Tex·ar·kan·a (tĕk′sär kăn′ə), *n.* two cities on the Texas-Arkansas boundary, forming a single urban area. 30,218 (Texas), 19,788 (Arkansas) in 1960.

Tex·as (tĕk′səs), *n.* 1. a State in the S United States. 9,579,677 pop. (1960); 267,339 sq. mi. *Cap.:* Austin. *Abbr.:* Tex. 2. (*l.c.*) a structure on the hurricane deck of a steamboat, containing officers' cabins, etc., and having the pilothouse in front or on top. —**Tex′an,** *adj., n.*

Texas fever. See **tick fever.**

Texas leaguer, *Baseball.* a batted ball that falls midway between infielders and outfielders. [allusion to the Texas League of baseball clubs]

Texas Rangers, the mounted police force of the State of Texas, originally a semiofficial group of settlers organized to fight the Indians.

Texas sparrow, a fringilline bird, *Arremonops rufivirgatus,* of the lower Rio Grande valley, dull olive-green above with yellow on the wing edgings and dull brown stripes on the head.

text (tĕkst), *n.* 1. the main body of matter in a book or manuscript, as distinguished from notes, appendixes, etc. 2. the original words of an author in distinction from a translation, paraphrase, commentary, or the like. 3. the actual wording of anything written or printed. 4. any of the various forms in which a writing exists. 5. the wording adopted by an editor as representing the original words of an author. 6. any theme or topic. 7. the words of a song or the like. 8. a textbook. 9. a short passage of Scripture, esp. one chosen in proof of a doctrine, as the subject of a sermon, etc. 10. the letter of the Holy Scripture, or the Scriptures themselves. 11. any form of Old English or black-letter type. 12. letterpress, as distinguished from illustrations, margins, etc. [ME, t. ML: m. *textus* wording (of the Gospel), L structure (of a discourse), orig. texture. See TEXTURE] —**text′less,** *adj.*

text·book (tĕkst′bŏŏk′), *n.* a book used by students as a standard work for a particular branch of study.

tex·tile (tĕks′tĭl, -tĭl), *n.* 1. any material that is woven. 2. a material suitable for weaving. —*adj.* 3. woven or capable of being woven: *textile fabrics.* 4. of or pertaining to weaving: *the textile industries.* [t. L: m.s. *textilis* woven]

tex·tu·al (tĕks′chŏŏ əl), *adj.* 1. of or pertaining to the text: *textual errors.* 2. based on or conforming to the text, as of the Scriptures. [ME *textuel,* f. ML *textu(s)* TEXT + -*el* -AL¹] —**tex′tu·al·ly,** *adv.*

tex·tu·al·ism (tĕks′chŏŏ ə lĭz′əm), *n.* strict adherence to the text, esp. of the Scriptures.

tex·tu·al·ist (tĕks′chŏŏ əl ĭst), *n.* 1. one who adheres closely to the text, esp. of the Scriptures. 2. one who is well versed in the text of the Scriptures.

tex·tu·ar·y (tĕks′chŏŏ ĕr′ĭ), *adj., n., pl.* -**aries.** —*adj.* 1. of or pertaining to the text; textual. —*n.* 2. a textualist.

tex·ture (tĕks′chər), *n.* 1. the characteristic disposition of the interwoven or intertwined threads, strands, or the like, which make up a textile fabric: *rough texture.* 2. the characteristic disposition of the constituent parts of any body; general structure or constitution. 3. the structure of the surface of any work of art, or the simulation of the surface structure of the skin, garment, etc., of the object represented in paint, stone, or other medium. 4. anything produced by weaving; woven fabric. [late ME, t. L: m. *textūra* weaving] —**tex′tur·al,** *adj.* —**tex′tur·al·ly,** *adv.*

-th¹, a noun suffix referring to condition, quality, or action, added to words (*warmth*) and to stems related to words (*depth, length*). [OE -*thu, -tho, -th,* c. Icel. -*th*]

-th², the suffix of ordinal numerals (*fourth, tenth, twentieth*), the form -*th* being added in one or two cases to altered stems of the cardinal (*fifth, twelfth*). [OE -*tha, -the,* c. L -*tus,* Gk. -*tos*]

-th³, *Archaic.* See -**eth¹.**

Th, *Chem.* thorium.

Th., Thursday.

T.H., Territory of Hawaii.

Thack·er·ay (thăk′ə rĭ), *n.* **William Makepeace** (māk′pēs′), 1811–63, British novelist, born in India.

Thai (tä′ē, tī), *n.* 1. a group of Sino-Tibetan languages spoken over a wide area of southeastern Asia, including Siamese and Shan. 2. the Siamese language. —*adj.* 3. of, designating, or pertaining to the Thai languages or to the peoples that speak them. 4. Siamese. Also, **Tai.**

Thai·land (tī′lənd), *n.* a kingdom in SE Asia. 20,686,000 pop. (est. 1950); 198,242 sq. mi. *Cap.:* Bangkok. Formerly, **Siam.**

Tha·is (thā′ĭs for 1; tä′ĭs′ for 2, 3), *n.* 1. Athenian courtesan, mistress of Alexander the Great and, after his death, of Ptolemy I. 2. a novel (1890) by Anatole France. 3. an opera (1894) by Massenet, after this novel.

thal·a·men·ceph·a·lon (thăl′ə mĕn sĕf′ə lŏn′), n., pl. **-la** (-lə). Anat. diencephalon. [NL. See THALAMUS, ENCEPHALON]

thal·a·mus (thăl′ə məs). n., pl. **-mi** (-mī′). **1.** Anat. the middle part of the diencephalon through which sensory impulses pass to reach the cerebral cortex; optic thalamus. **2.** Bot. **a.** a receptacle or torus. **b.** thallus. [t. L, t. Gk.: m. thálamos inner room] **—tha·lam·ic** (thə lăm′ĭk), adj.

tha·las·sic (thə lăs′ĭk), adj. **1.** of or pertaining to the seas and oceans (sometimes distinguishing smaller bodies of water from oceanic bodies). **2.** growing, living, or found in the sea; marine. [f. s. Gk. thálassa sea + -IC]

tha·ler (tä′lər), n., pl. **-ler.** any of certain large silver coins of varying value formerly issued in Germany, esp. one of the value of 3 marks, or about 71½ U.S. cents. Also, **taler.** [t. G: dollar]

Tha·les (thā′lēz), n. c640-c546 ʙ.ᴄ., Greek philosopher, born in Miletus.

Tha·li·a (thə lī′ə), n. **1.** the Muse of comedy and idyllic poetry. **2.** Gk. Myth. one of the three Graces. [t. Gk.: m. Tháleia, lit., blooming]

thal·lic (thăl′ĭk), adj. of or containing thallium, esp. in the trivalent state (Tl⁺³).

thal·li·um (thăl′ĭ əm), n. Chem. a soft, malleable, rare, metallic element, used mainly (on account of the poisonous nature of its compounds) in rat poisons. Symbol: Tl; at. wt.: 204.39; at. no.: 81; sp. gr.: 11.85 at 20°C. [t. NL, f. s. Gk. thallós green shoot + -ium -IUM]

thal·loid (thăl′oid), adj. Bot. resembling or consisting of a thallus.

Thal·loph·y·ta (thə lŏf′ə tə), n.pl. Bot. a phylum of plants (including the algae, fungi, and lichens) in which the plant body of larger species is typically a thallus.

thal·lo·phyte (thăl′ə fīt′), n. Bot. any member of the phylum Thallophyta. [t. NL: m. thallophyta (pl.). See THALLUS, -PHYTE] **—thal·lo·phyt·ic** (thăl′ə fĭt′ĭk), adj.

thal·lous (thăl′əs), adj. Chem. containing monovalent thallium (Tl⁺¹). Also, **thal·li·ous** (thăl′ĭ əs).

thal·lus (thăl′əs), n., pl. **thal·li** (thăl′ī). **thalluses.** Bot. a simple vegetative plant body undifferentiated into true leaves, stem, and root: the plant body of typical thallophytes. [t. NL, t. Gk.: m. thallós young shoot, twig]

Thames (tĕmz for 1, 2; thāmz, tāmz, tĕmz for 3), n. **1.** a river flowing from SW England E through London to the North Sea. 209 mi. **2.** a river in SE Canada, in Ontario, flowing SW to Lake St. Clair. 160 mi. **3.** an estuary in SE Connecticut, flowing S past New London to Long Island Sound. ab. 15 mi.

Tham·muz (täm′mŏŏz, täm′ŭz), n. Tammuz.

than (thăn; unstressed thən), conj. a particle used after comparative adjectives and adverbs and certain other words, such as other, otherwise, else, etc., to introduce the second member of a comparison: this train is faster than that one. Than, as a conjunction, has the same case (usually the nominative) after it as before it: he is taller than I am. It is sometimes used as a preposition and followed by a pronoun in the objective case: he is a novelist than whom none is better. [ME and OE; var. of ME and OE thanne than, then, c. G denn. See THEN]

than·age (thā′nĭj), n. **1.** the tenure by which lands were held by a thane. **2.** the lands so held. **3.** the office, rank, or jurisdiction of a thane.

than·a·top·sis (thăn′ə tŏp′sĭs), n. a view or contemplation of death. [f. Gk.: s. thánatos death + ópsis sight, view]

Than·a·tos (thăn′ə tŏs′), n. Gk. Myth. the personification of death. Cf. **Mors.**

thane (thān). n. **1.** Early Eng. Hist. a member of any of several classes of men ranking between earls and ordinary freemen, and holding lands of the king or lord by military service. **2.** Scot. Hist. a person, ranking with an earl's son, holding lands of the king; the chief of a clan, who became one of the king's barons. Also, **thegn.** [late ME, var. of ME thain, OE thegn, c. G degen servant, warrior; akin to Gk. téknon child]

Than·et (thăn′ĭt), n. Isle of, an island forming the NE tip of Kent county, in SE England. ab. 40 sq. mi.

thank (thăngk), v.t. **1.** to give thanks to; express gratitude to. **2. have oneself to thank for,** to be oneself responsible or at fault for. [ME thanke(n), OE thancian (c. D and G danken), der. thanc THANK n.] **—n. 3.** (usually pl.) the expression of grateful feeling, or grateful acknowledgment of a benefit or favor, by words or otherwise: to return a borrowed book with thanks. **4.** (pl.) a common elliptical expression used in acknowledging a favor, service, courtesy, or the like. **5. thanks to, a.** thanks be given to. **b.** as a result or consequence of. [ME; OE thanc gratitude, orig. thoughtfulness, thought. See THINK¹] **—thank′er,** n.

thank·ful (thăngk′fəl), adj. feeling or expressing thanks. **—thank′ful·ly,** adv. **—thank′ful·ness,** n.

thank·less (thăngk′lĭs), adj. **1.** not such as to be rewarded with thanks; not appreciated. **2.** ungrateful. **—thank′less·ly,** adv. **—thank′less·ness,** n.

thanks·giv·er (thăngks′gĭv′ər), n. one who gives thanks.

thanks·giv·ing (thăngks′gĭv′ĭng), n. **1.** act of giving thanks; grateful acknowledgment of benefits or favors, esp. to God. **2.** an expression of thanks, esp. to God. **3.** a day set apart for giving thanks to God. **4.** a public celebration in acknowledgment of divine favor.

Thanksgiving Day, U.S. an annual festival in acknowledgment of divine favor, usually held on the fourth Thursday of November. Also, **Thanksgiving.**

thank·wor·thy (thăngk′wûr′thĭ), adj. deserving gratitude.

Thant (thănt, thŏnt), n. U, b. 1909. Burmese statesman; acting secretary general of United Nations 1961-63, secretary general since 1963. See also U.

Thap·sus (thăp′səs), n. an ancient town on the N coast of Africa (in present-day Tunisia), ab. 100 mi. S of Carthage: decisive victory of Julius Caesar, 46 ʙ.ᴄ.

Tha·sos (thā′sŏs), n. a Greek island in the N Aegean. 15,208 pop. (1951); ab. 170 sq. mi.

that (thăt; unstressed thət), pron., pl. **those,** and adj.; adv.; conj. **—pron. and adj. 1.** a demonstrative pronoun and adjective indicating: **a.** a person, thing, idea, etc., as pointed out or present, as before mentioned, or supposed to be understood, or by way of emphasis. **b.** one of two persons, things, etc., already mentioned, either referring to the one more remote in place, time, or thought, or implying mere contradistinction (opposed to this). **2.** a relative pronoun used: **a.** as the subject or object of a relative clause, esp. one defining or restricting the antecedent (sometimes replaceable by who, whom, or which). **b.** as the object of a preposition, the preposition standing at the end of the relative clause: the man that I spoke of. **c.** in various special or elliptical constructions: fool that he is.
—adv. 3. to that extent; to such a degree; so: **a.** (with adjectives and adverbs of quantity or extent): that much, that far. **b.** Chiefly Colloq. or Dial. (with other adjectives and adverbs): he was that weak he could hardly stand.
—conj. 4. a conjunction used: **a.** to introduce a clause as the subject or object of the principal verb or as the necessary complement to a statement made, or a clause expressing cause or reason, purpose or aim, result or consequence, etc.: that he will come is certain. **b.** elliptically, to introduce a sentence or clause expressing desire, surprise, or indignation.
[ME; OE thæt that, the, c. G das(s), Gk. tó]
—Syn. 1. THAT, WHICH, WHO are all relative pronouns in English. THAT as a relative pronoun originally referred to persons, animals, or things; it is now more frequently used of animals or things, though it can refer to all three: the man that speaks evil of his friends, an animal that eats grass, a plant that likes the shade. WHICH is used only of animals or things, except archaically of persons: animals which bear burdens, plants which grow in the desert, Our Father which art in heaven. WHO is used of persons and occasionally of the higher animals: a man who works hard, a horse who runs successful races. As the object of a preposition, only WHO (in the form of WHOM) or WHICH can be used: the people of whom I was speaking, the city to which I am going. Only WHO and WHICH are found in nonrestrictive clauses (those used parenthetically): the cook, who was very nervous, sent us out of the kitchen; this house, which was just built, burned down last night. Any of the three can be used in a clause which restricts or defines: there is the house that is for sale.

thatch (thăch), n. **1.** a material, as straw, rushes, leaves, or the like, used to cover roofs, grain stacks, etc. **2.** a covering of such a material. **3.** any of various palms, the leaves of which are used for thatching. **4.** the hair covering the head. **—v.t. 5.** to cover with or as with thatch. [ME thacche, var. of thack, OE thæc roof, thatch, c. G dach, L toga covering; akin to Gk. tégos roof] **—thatch′er,** n. **—thatch′less,** adj. **—thatch′y,** adj.

thau·ma·tol·o·gy (thô′mə tŏl′ə jĭ), n. the study or description of miracles. [f. thaumato- (t. Gk., comb. form of thaûma wonder) + -LOGY]

thau·ma·trope (thô′mə trŏp′), n. a card with different pictures on opposite sides (as a horse on one side and a rider on the other), which, when twirled rapidly, causes the pictures to appear as if combined, thus illustrating the persistence of visual impressions. [f. Gk. thaûma wonder + -TROPE]

thau·ma·turge (thô′mə tûrj′), n. a worker of wonders or miracles. Also, **thau′ma·tur′gist,**

thau·ma·tur·gic (thô′mə tûr′jĭk), adj. **1.** pertaining to a thaumaturge or to thaumaturgy. **2.** having the powers of a thaumaturge. Also, **thau′ma·tur′gi·cal.**

thau·ma·tur·gy (thô′mə tûr′jĭ), n. the working of wonders or miracles; magic. [t. Gk.: m. s. thaumatourgía wonderworking, conjuring]

thaw (thô), v.i. **1.** to pass from a frozen to a liquid or semiliquid state; melt. **2.** to be freed from the physical effect of frost or extreme cold. **3.** (of the weather) to become so warm as to melt ice and snow: it will probably thaw today. **4.** to become less cold, formal, or reserved. **—v.t. 5.** to cause to thaw. **6.** to make less cold, formal, or reserved. **—n. 7.** act or process of thawing. **8.** a becoming less cold, formal, or reserved. **9.** a condition of the weather caused by the rise of the temperature above the freezing point. [ME thawe, OE thawian, c. D dooien, Icel. theyja] **—thaw′er,** n. **—Syn. 1.** See melt.

Th.D., (L Theologiae Doctor) Doctor of Theology.

the¹ (stressed thē; unstressed before a consonant thə; unstressed before a vowel thĭ), def. art. a word used, esp. before nouns, with a specifying or particularizing effect, as opposed to the indefinite or generalizing force of the indefinite article a or an: I liked the book that you gave me. Various special uses are: **a.** to mark a noun as indicating something well-known or unique: the Alps. **b.** with, or as part of, a title: the Duke of Wellington, the Reverend John Smith. **c.** to mark a noun as indicating the best-

---

b., blend of, blended; c., cognate with; d., dialect, dialectal; der., derived from; f., formed from; g., going back to; m., modification of; r., replacing; s., stem of; t., taken from; ?, perhaps. See the full key on inside cover.

known, most approved, or most important of its kind: *the skiing center of the U.S.* **d.** to mark a noun as being used generically: *the dog is a quadruped.* **e.** in place of a possessive pronoun, to denote a part of the body or a personal belonging: *to hang the head and weep.* **f.** before adjectives used substantively, and denoting an individual, a class or number of individuals, or an abstract notion: *to visit the sick.* **g.** *Chiefly Brit.* distributively, to denote any one separately, where *a* or *an* is more commonly employed: *at one dollar the pound.* [ME and OE, uninflected var. of demonstrative pronoun. See THAT]

the² (thə, thĭ), *adv.* a word used to modify an adjective or adverb in the comparative degree: **1.** signifying "in or by that," "on that account," "in or by so much," or "in some or any degree": *he is taking more care of himself, and looks the better.* **2.** used correlatively, in one instance with relative force and in the other with demonstrative force, and signifying "by how much . . . by so much" or "in what degree . . . in that degree": *the more the merrier.* [ME and OE; orig. a case form of demon. pronoun. See THAT]

the·a·ceous (thē·ā′shəs), *adj.* belonging to the *Theaceae*, or tea family of plants. [f. s. NL *Theáceae* tea family of plants (der. NL *thea* TEA) + -OUS]

the·an·throp·ic (thē′ăn thrŏp′ĭk), *adj.* of or pertaining to both God and man; both divine and human.

the·an·thro·pism (thē ăn′thrə pĭz′əm), *n.* **1.** the doctrine of the union of the divine and human natures, or of the manifestation of God as man in Christ. **2.** the attribution of human nature to the gods. [f. s. LGk. *theánthrōpos* god-man + -ISM] —**the·an′thro·pist,** *n.*

the·ar·chy (thē′är kĭ), *n., pl.* **-chies.** **1.** the rule or government of God or of a god. **2.** an order or system of deities. [t. Eccl. Gk.: m.s. *thearchía.* See THEO-, -ARCHY] —**the·ar′chic,** *adj.*

theat., theater.

the·a·ter (thē′ə tər), *n.* **1.** a building expressly designed to house dramatic presentations, stage entertainment, or motion-picture shows. **2.** the audience at a performance there. **3.** a room or hall, fitted with tiers of seats rising like steps, used for lectures, anatomical demonstrations, etc. **4.** dramatic performances as a branch of art; the drama. **5.** dramatic works collectively, as of literature, a nation, or an author. **6.** a place of action; field of operations. **7.** a natural formation of land rising by steps or gradations. Also, *esp. Brit.,* **the′a·tre.** [ME, t. L: m.s. *theátrum.* t. Gk.: m. *théātron* seeing place, theater]

the·a·ter-in-the-round (thē′ə tər ĭn thə round′), *n.* a theater with seats arranged around a central stage.

the·at·ri·cal (thĭ ăt′rə kəl), *adj.* Also, **the·at′ric.** **1.** of or pertaining to the theater, or dramatic or scenic representations: *theatrical performances.* **2.** suggestive of the theater or of acting; artificial, pompous, spectacular, or extravagantly histrionic: *a theatrical display of grief.* —*n.* **3.** (*pl.*) dramatic performances, now esp. as given by amateurs. —**the·at′ri·cal·ism,** *n.* —**the·at·ri·cal·i·ty** (thĭ ăt′rə kăl′ə tĭ), *n.* —**the·at′ri·cal·ly,** *adv.*

the·at·rics (thĭ ăt′rĭks), *n.pl.* (construed as *sing.*) the art of staging plays and other stage performances.

The·ba·id (thē′bā̇ĭd, -bǐ-), *n.* **1.** the region around Egyptian or Grecian Thebes. **2.** an epic poem composed about A.D. 80–92 by Statius. [t. L. t. Gk.: s. *Thēbaïs*]

the·ba·ine (thē′bə ĕn′, thĭ bā′ĕn, -ĭn), *n. Chem.* a white crystalline poisonous alkaloid, $C_{19}H_{21}NO_3$, present in opium in small quantities. [f. NL *theba(ia)* + -INE²]

Thebes (thēbz), *n.* **1.** an ancient ruined city in Upper Egypt, on the Nile: a former capital of Egypt. **2.** a city of ancient Greece, in Boeotia: a rival of ancient Athens. —**The·ban** (thē′bən), *adj., n.*

the·ca (thē′kə), *n., pl.* **-cae** (-sē) **1.** a case or receptacle. **2.** *Bot.* **a.** a sac, cell, or capsule. **b.** a spore case. **3.** *Anat., Zool.* a case or sheath enclosing an organ, etc., as the horny covering of an insect pupa. [t. L. t. Gk.: m. *thḗkē* case, cover] —**the·cal,** *adj.*

the·cate (thē′kĭt, -kāt), *adj.* having, or contained in, a theca.

Thebes (def. 1), c1450 B.C.

thé dan·sant (tĕ dän sän′), *pl.* **thés dansants** (tĕ dän sän′). *French.* an afternoon tea party with dancing.

thee (thē), *pron.* **1.** *Archaic.* objective case of thou. **2.** thou. [ME; OE *thē* (orig. dat., later dat. and acc.), c. LG *di,* G *dir*]

thee·lin (thē′lĭn), *n. Biochem.* estrone. [irreg. f. Gk. *thēl(ys)* female + -IN²]

thee·lol (thē′lŏl, -lōl), *n. Biochem.* an estrogenic steroid found in the urine of pregnant females.

theft (thĕft), *n.* **1.** act of stealing; the wrongful taking and carrying away of the personal goods of another; larceny. **2.** an instance of this. **3.** *Now Rare.* something stolen. [ME; OE *thēoft,* earlier *thēofth,* f. *thēof* THIEF + -TH¹, c. Icel. *thȳft,* obs. D *diefte*] —**theft′less,** *adj.*

thegn (thān), *n.* thane.

the·ine (thē′ĭn), *n.* caffeine found in tea. Also, **the·in** (thē′ĭn). [f. s. NL *thea* TEA + -INE²]

their (thâr; *unstressed* thər), *pron.* **1.** the possessive form of *they* used before a noun. **2.** theirs, the form of *their* used predicatively or without a noun following: *it is theirs.* [ME, t. Scand.; cf. Icel. *their(r)a* of those. See THEY]

the·ism (thē′ĭz əm), *n.* **1.** the belief in one God as the creator and ruler of the universe, without rejection of revelation (distinguished from *deism*). **2.** belief in the existence of a God or gods (opposed to *atheism*). [f. s. Gk. *theós* god + -ISM] —**the′ist,** *n., adj.* —**the·is·tic,** (thē ĭs′tĭk), **the·is′ti·cal,** *adj.* —**the·is′ti·cal·ly,** *adv.*

Theiss (tīs), *n.* German name of Tisza.

the·li·tis (thĭ lī′tĭs), *n. Pathol.* inflammation of the nipple. [t. NL, f. Gk.: s. *thēlḗ* nipple + -ítis -ITIS]

them (thĕm; *unstressed* thəm), *pron.* objective case of they. [ME *theym,* t. Scand.; cf. Icel. *theim* to those. See THEY]

the·mat·ic (thĭ măt′ĭk), *adj.* **1.** of or pertaining to a theme. **2.** *Gram.* **a.** of, pertaining to, or producing a theme or themes (def. 4). **b.** pertaining to the theme or stem. The thematic vowel is the vowel that ends the stem and precedes the inflectional ending of a word form, as *i* in Latin *audio I hear.* —**the·mat′i·cal·ly,** *adv.*

theme (thēm), *n.* **1.** a subject of discourse, discussion, meditation, or composition; a topic. **2.** a short, informal essay, esp. a school composition. **3.** *Music.* **a.** a principal subject in a musical composition. **b.** a short subject from which variations are developed. **4.** *Gram.* the element common to all or most of the forms of an inflectional paradigm, often consisting in turn of a root with certain formative elements or modifications. (Cf. stem.) [ME, t. L: m. *thema,* t Gk.] —Syn. 1. See subject.

theme song, 1. a melody in an operetta or musical comedy, so emphasized by repetition as to dominate the presentation. **2.** a melody identifying a radio program, dance band, etc.

The·mis (thē′mĭs), *n. Gk. Myth.* a Greek goddess personifying justice.

The·mis·to·cles (thə mĭs′tə klēz′), *n.* 527?–460? B.C., Athenian statesman.

them·selves (thəm sĕlvz′), *pron. pl.* **1.** an emphatic form of them or they. **2.** a reflexive form of them.

then (thĕn), *adv.* **1.** at that time: *prices were lower then.* **2.** immediately or soon afterward: *he stopped, and then began again.* **3.** next in order of time. **4.** at another time. **5.** in the next place; in addition; besides. **6.** in that case; in those circumstances. **7.** since that is so; therefore; consequently. **8.** but then, but at the same time; but on the other hand. —*adj.* **9.** being; being such; then existing: *the then prime minister.* —*n.* **10.** that time: *till then.* [ME, var. of ME *thenne,* OE *thænne*; orig. var. of THAN.] —Syn. 7. See therefore.

the·nar (thē′när), *n. Anat.* **1.** the fleshy mass of the outer side of the palm of the hand. **2.** the fleshy prominence or ball of muscle at the base of the thumb. —*adj.* **3.** of or pertaining to the thenar. [t. NL, t. Gk.: palm of hand or sole of foot]

the·nard·ite (thə när′dīt, tə-), *n.* a mineral, sodium sulfate, Na_2SO_4, occurring in white crystals and masses, esp. in dried lakes. [named after L. J. *Thénard,* French chemist. See -ITE¹]

thence (thĕns), *adv.* **1.** from that place. **2.** from that time; henceforth. **3.** from that source; for that reason; therefore. [ME *thennes,* f. *thenne* (OE *thanone* thence; c. D *dan,* G *dannen*) + -s, adv. gen. suffix]

thence·forth (thĕns′fôrth′, thĕns′fôrth′), *adv.* from that time or place onward. Also, **thence·for·ward** (thĕns′fôr′wərd), **thence′for′wards.**

theo-, a word element meaning "pertaining to the gods," "divine." [t. Gk., comb. form of *theós* god]

the·o·bro·mine (thē′ə brō′mēn, -mĭn), *n. Chem.* a powder, $C_7H_8N_4O_2$, in the form of microscopic crystals, having alkaline properties, obtained from the seeds and leaves of species of the genus *Theobroma,* and used as a nerve stimulant and a diuretic: the lower homologue of caffeine. [f. NL *theobrom(a)* genus of trees typified by cacao (t. Gk.: lit., god-food) + -INE²]

the·oc·ra·cy (thē ŏk′rə sĭ), *n., pl.* **-cies.** **1.** a form of government in which God or a deity is recognized as the supreme civil ruler, His laws being interpreted by the ecclesiastical authorities. **2.** a system of government by priests claiming a divine commission. **3.** a state or commonwealth under any such form or system of government. [t. Gk.: m.s. *theokratía.* See THEO-, -CRACY]

the·oc·ra·sy (thē ŏk′rə sĭ), *n.* **1.** a mixture of religious forms and deities worshipped. **2.** (in mysticism) the union of the soul and God. [t. Gk.: m.s. *theokrāsía* mingling with god]

the·o·crat (thē′ə krăt′), *n.* **1.** the ruler, or a member of a governing body, in a theocracy. **2.** one who favors theocracy. —**the·o·crat′ic, the·o·crat′i·cal,** *adj.* —**the·o·crat′i·cal·ly,** *adv.*

The·oc·ri·tus (thē ŏk′rə təs), *n.* fl. c270 B.C., Greek pastoral poet.

the·od·i·cy (thē ŏd′ə sĭ), *n., pl.* **-cies.** a vindication of the divine attributes, particularly holiness and justice, in respect to the existence of physical and moral evil. [t. F: m. *théodicée,* title of work by Leibniz, f. Gk.: *theó(s)* god + m. *díkē* justice]

the·od·o·lite (thē ŏd′ə līt′), *n. Survey.* an instrument for measuring horizontal or vertical angles. Cf. transit (def. 5). [coined word; orig. unknown] —**the·od·o·lit·ic** (thē ŏd′ə lĭt′ĭk), *adj.*

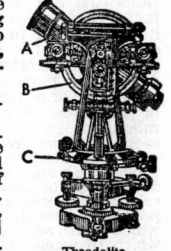

Theodolite
A, Telescope; B, Vertical scale; C, Horizontal scale

The·od·o·ric (thē·ŏd′ə·rĭk), n. ("*the Great*") A.D. c454–526, king of the eastern Goths, who conquered Italy in A.D. 493 and ruled it until his death.

The·o·do·si·us I (thē′ə·dō′shĭ′əs, -shəs), ("*the Great*") A.D. c346–395, Roman emperor of the Eastern Roman Empire, A.D. 379–395.

the·og·o·ny (thē·ŏg′ə·nĭ), n., pl. -nies. 1. the origin of the gods. 2. an account of this; a genealogical account of the gods. [t. Gk.: m.s. *theogonia*] —**the·o·gon·ic** (thē′ə·gŏn′ĭk), adj. —**the·og′o·nist,** n.

theol., 1. theologian. 2. theological. 3. theology.

the·o·lo·gian (thē′ə·lō′jən, -jĭ′ən), n. one versed in theology, esp. Christian theology; divine.

the·o·log·i·cal (thē′ə·lŏj′ə·kəl), adj. 1. of, pertaining to, or connected with theology. 2. based upon the nature and will of God as revealed to man. Also, **the′o·log′ic.** —**the′o·log′i·cal·ly,** adv.

the·ol·o·gize (thē·ŏl′ə·jīz′), v., -gized, -gizing. —v.i. 1. to theorize or speculate upon theological subjects. —v.t. 2. to make theological; treat theologically. —**the·ol′o·gi·za′tion,** n. —**the·ol′o·giz′er,** n.

the·ol·o·gy (thē·ŏl′ə·jĭ), n., pl. -gies. 1. the science which treats of God, His attributes, and His relations to the universe; the science or study of divine things or religious truth; divinity. 2. a particular form, system, or branch of this science or study. [ME *theologie,* t. L: m. *theologia,* t. Gk.]

the·om·a·chy (thē·ŏm′ə·kĭ), n., pl. -chies. a battle with or among the gods. [t. Gk.: m.s. *theomachia*]

the·o·mor·phic (thē′ə·môr′fĭk), adj. having the form or likeness of God. [f. s. Gk. *theómorph(os)* of divine form + -IC]

the·op·a·thy (thē·ŏp′ə·thĭ), n. religious emotion excited by the contemplation of God. [t. Gk.: m.s. *theopátheia* suffering of God] —**the·o·pa·thet·ic** (thē′ə·pə·thĕt′ĭk), **the·o·path·ic** (thē′ə·pǎth′ĭk), adj.

the·oph·a·ny (thē·ŏf′ə·nĭ), n., pl. -nies. a manifestation or appearance of God or a god to man. [t. LL: m.s. *theophania,* t. Gk.]

The·o·phras·tus (thē′ə·frǎs′təs), n. c372–287 B.C., Greek philosopher.

the·o·phyl·line (thē′ə·fĭl′ēn, -ĭn), n. Chem. a white crystalline alkaloid, $C_7H_8N_4O_2$, derived from tea; an isomer of theobromine. [f. *theo-* (irreg. comb. form repr. NL *thea* TEA) + PHYLL(O)- + -INE²]

theor., theorem.

the·or·bo (thē·ôr′bō), n., pl. -bos. an obsolete musical instrument of the lute class, having two necks, one above the other. [t. It.: m. *tiorba*]

the·o·rem (thē′ə·rəm, thĭr′əm), n. 1. Math. a theoretical proposition; a statement embodying something to be proved. 2. a rule or law, esp. one expressed by an equation or formula. 3. Logic. a proposition which can be deduced from the premises or assumptions of a system. [t. LL: m. *theōrēma,* t. Gk.: spectacle, theory, thesis (to be proved)] —**the·o·re·mat·ic** (thē′ə·rə·mǎt′ĭk, thĭr′ə-), adj.

the·o·ret·i·cal (thē′ə·rĕt′ə·kəl), adj. 1. of, pertaining to, or consisting in theory; not practical. 2. existing only in theory; hypothetical. 3. given to forming, or dealing with theories; speculative. Also, **the′o·ret′ic.** —**the′o·ret′i·cal·ly,** adv.

theoretical arithmetic, arithmetic (def. 2).

the·o·re·ti·cian (thē′ə·rə·tĭsh′ən, thĭr′ə-), n. one who deals with or is expert in the theoretical side of a subject.

the·o·ret·ics (thē′ə·rĕt′ĭks), n. the theoretical or speculative part of a science or subject.

the·o·rist (thē′ə·rĭst), n. 1. one who theorizes. 2. one who deals mainly with the theory of a subject: *a theorist in medical research.*

the·o·rize (thē′ə·rīz′), v.i., -rized, -rizing. to form a theory or theories. Also, esp. Brit., **the′o·rise′.** —**the′o·ri·za′tion,** n. —**the′o·riz′er,** n.

the·o·ry (thē′ə·rĭ, thĭr′ĭ), n., pl. -ries. 1. a coherent group of general propositions used as principles of explanation for a class of phenomena: *Newton's theory of gravitation.* 2. a proposed explanation whose status is still conjectural, in contrast to well-established propositions that are regarded as reporting matters of actual fact. 3. Math. a body of principles, theorems, or the like, belonging to one subject: *number theory.* 4. that department of a science or art which deals with its principles or methods, as distinguished from the practice of it. 5. a particular conception or view of something to be done or of the method of doing it; a system of rules or principles. 6. contemplation or mental view. [t. LL: m.s. *theōria,* t. Gk.: contemplation, theory] —**Syn.** 1. THEORY, HYPOTHESIS are both often used colloquially to mean an untested idea or opinion. A THEORY properly is a more or less verified or established explanation accounting for known facts or phenomena: *the theory of relativity.* A HYPOTHESIS is a conjecture put forth as a possible explanation of certain phenomena or relations, which serves as a basis of argument or experimentation by which to reach the truth: *this idea is offered only as an hypothesis.* —**Ant.** 1. principle, axiom, law.

theos., 1. theosophical. 2. theosophy.

the·os·o·phy (thē·ŏs′ə·fĭ), n. 1. any of various forms of philosophical or religious thought in which claim is made to a special insight into the divine nature or to a special divine revelation. 2. the system of belief and doctrine, based largely on Brahmanic and Buddhistic ideas, of the **Theosophical Society** (founded in New York in 1875). [t. ML: m.s. *theosophia,* t. LGk. See THEO-, -SOPHY] —**the·o·soph·ic** (thē′ə·sŏf′ĭk), **the·o·soph′i·cal,** adj. —**the′o·soph′i·cal·ly,** adv. —**the·os′o·phist,** n.

The·o·to·có·pu·li (tĕ′ō·tō·kô′pōō·lē′), n. **Domingo** (dō·mēng′gō). See El Greco.

therapeut., 1. therapeutic. 2. therapeutics. Also, **therap.**

ther·a·peu·tic (thĕr′ə·pū′tĭk), adj. pertaining to the treating or curing of disease; curative. Also, **ther′a·peu′ti·cal.** [t. NL: s. *therapeuticus,* t. Gk.: m. *therapeutikós,* der. *therapeutēs* one who treats medically] —**ther′a·peu′ti·cal·ly,** adv. —**ther′a·peu′tist,** n.

ther·a·peu·tics (thĕr′ə·pū′tĭks), n. the branch of medicine concerned with the remedial treatment of disease. [pl. of *therapeutic,* n., t. NL: s. *therapeutica,* prop. fem. of *therapeuticus* THERAPEUTIC, adj. See -ICS]

ther·a·py (thĕr′ə·pĭ), n., pl. -pies. 1. the treatment of disease, as by some remedial or curative process. 2. a curative power or quality. [t. NI : m. s. *therapia,* t. Gk.: m. *therapeia* healing] —**ther′a·pist,** n.

there (thâr), adv. 1. in or at that place. 2. at that point in an action, speech, etc. 3. in that matter, particular, or respect. 4. into or to that place; thither. 5. often used less definitely, and also unemphatically, as: a. by way of calling the attention to something: *there they go.* b. in interjectional phrases: *there's a good boy!* c. in a sentence or clause in which the verb comes before its subject: *there is no hope.* —n. 6. that place: *he comes from there too.* —interj. 7. an exclamation used to express satisfaction, encouragement, consolation, etc.: *there! it's done!* [ME; OE *thær,* c. D *daar,* G *da*]

there-, a word element meaning "that (place)," "that (time)," etc., used in combination with certain adverbs and prepositions. [special use of THERE, demonstrative adv.]

there·a·bout (thâr′ə·bout′), adv. 1. about or near that place or time. 2. about that number, amount, etc.: Also, **there′a·bouts′.**

there·af·ter (thâr·ǎf′tər, -äf′-), adv. 1. after that in time or sequence; afterwards. 2. Obs. accordingly.

there·a·gainst (thâr′ə·gĕnst′), adv. Archaic. against, or in opposition to, that.

there·at (thâr·ǎt′), adv. Archaic. 1. at that place, time, etc.; there. 2. on that occasion; by reason of that.

there·by (thâr·bī′), adv. 1. by that; by means of that. 2. in that connection or relation: *thereby hangs a tale.* 3. Archaic or Dial. by or near that place. 4. Scot. about that number, quantity, or degree.

there·for (thâr·fôr′), adv. for that or this; for it.

there·fore (thâr′fôr′), adv. in consequence of that; as a result; consequently. [ME *therfore,* f. *ther* THERE + *fore,* var. of *for* FOR] —**Syn.** hence, whence. THEREFORE, WHEREFORE, ACCORDINGLY, CONSEQUENTLY, SO, THEN agree in introducing a statement resulting from, or caused by, what immediately precedes. THEREFORE ("for this or that reason") and WHEREFORE ("for which reason") imply exactness of reasoning; they are esp. used in logic, law, mathematics, etc., and in a formal style of speaking or writing. ACCORDINGLY ("in conformity with the preceding") and CONSEQUENTLY ("as a result, or sequence, or effect of the preceding") are less formal. SO ("because the preceding is true," or "this being the case") and THEN ("since the preceding is true") are conversational in tone.

there·from (thâr·frŏm′, -frŭm′), adv. from that place, thing, etc.

there·in (thâr·ĭn′), adv. 1. in that place or thing. 2. in that matter, circumstance, etc.

there·in·af·ter (thâr′ĭn·ǎf′tər, -äf′-), adv. afterward in that document, statement, etc.

there·in·to (thâr·ĭn′tōō, thâr′ĭn·tōō′), adv. into that place, thing, matter, etc.

ther·e·min (thĕr′ə·mĭn), n. 1. a musical instrument with electronic tone generation, whose pitch and tone volume are controlled by the distance between the player's hands and two metal rods serving as antennas. 2. (cap.) a trademark for this instrument. [named after Léon Thérémin, born 1896, Russian inventor]

there·of (thâr·ŏv′, -ŭv′), adv. 1. of that or it. 2. from or out of that as a source of origin.

there·on (thâr·ŏn′, -ŏn′), adv. 1. on or upon that or it. 2. immediately after that; thereupon.

The·re·sa (tə·rē′sə, -zə; Sp. tě·rě′sä), n. **Saint,** 1515–1582, Spanish nun, mystic, and writer. Also, **Teresa.**

there·to (thâr·tōō′), adv. 1. to that place, thing, matter, etc. 2. Archaic and Poetic. in addition to that. Also, **there·un·to** (thâr′ŭn·tōō′, thâr·ŭn′tōō).

there·to·fore (thâr′tə·fôr′), adv. before that time.

there·un·der (thâr·ŭn′dər), adv. 1. under or beneath that. 2. under the authority of, or in accordance with, that.

there·up·on (thâr′ə·pŏn′, -pôn′), adv. 1. immediately following that. 2. in consequence of that. 3. upon that or it. 4. with reference to that.

there·with (thâr·wĭth′, -wĭth′), adv. 1. with that. 2. in addition to that. 3. following upon that; thereupon.

there·with·al (thâr′wĭth·ôl′,-wĭth-), adv. 1. together with that; in addition to that. 2. following upon that.

Theorbo

b., blend of, blended; c., cognate with; d., dialect, dialectal; der., derived from; f., formed from; g., going back to; m., modification of; r., replacing; s., stem of; t., taken from; ?, perhaps. See the full key on inside cover.

The·re·zi·na (tĕ/rĕ zē/nə), *n.* former name of Tere-sina.

the·ri·an·throp·ic (thĭr/ĭan thrŏp/ĭk), *adj.* **1.** being partly bestial and partly human in form. **2.** of or pertaining to deities conceived or represented in such form. [f. s. Gk. *thēríon* wild beast + s. *ánthrōpos* man + -ɪc] —**the·ri·an·thro·pism** (thĭr/ĭan/thrə pĭz/əm), *n.*

the·ri·o·mor·phic (thĭr/ĭə môr/fĭk), *adj.* (of deities) conceived or represented as having the form of beasts. Also, **the/ri·o·mor/phous.** [f. s. Gk. *theriómorphos* having the shape of a wild beast + -ɪc]

therm (thûrm), *n. Physics.* an indefinite unit of heat: **a.** the small calorie. **b.** the large calorie. **c.** a unit equal to 1000 large calories. **d.** a unit equal to 100,000 British thermal units. Also, **therme.** [t. Gk.: s. *thérmē* heat]

therm-, a word element representing thermal. Also, **thermo-.** [t. Gk., comb. form of *thermós* hot, *thérmē* heat]

ther·mae (thûr/mē), *n. pl.* **1.** hot springs; hot baths. **2.** a public bathing establishment of the ancient Greeks or Romans. [t. L, t. Gk.: m. *thérmai*]

ther·mal (thûr/məl), *adj.* **1.** Also, **ther/mic.** of or pertaining to heat or temperature: *thermal capacity.* **2.** of, pertaining to, or of the nature of thermae. [f. s. Gk. *thérmē* heat + -ᴀʟ¹] —**ther/mal·ly,** *adv.*

thermal barrier, *Astronautics.* the high temperatures produced by the friction between a supersonic object and the earth's atmosphere, esp. in reëntry. Also, **heat barrier.**

therm·an·es·the·sia (thûrm/ăn əs thē/zhə, -zhĭ ə), *n. Pathol.* loss of ability to feel cold or heat; loss of temperature sense.

therm·es·the·sia (thûrm/əs thē/zhə, -zhĭ ə), *n. Physiol.* ability to feel cold or heat; sensitiveness to heat.

Ther·mi·dor (thûr/mə dôr/; *Fr.* tĕr mē dôr/), *n.* (in the calendar of the first French Republic) the eleventh month of the year, extending from July 19 to Aug. 17. [t. F, f. Gk.: m. *thérmē* heat + s. *dōron* gift]

therm·i·on (thûrm/ī/ən, thûr/mī ən), *n. Physics.* any of a class of electrically charged particles such as ions or electrons emitted by incandescent materials.

therm·i·on·ic (thûrm/ī ŏn/ĭk, thûr/mī ŏn/ĭk), *adj.* pertaining to thermionics or thermions: *thermionic emission.*

thermionic current, 1. a flow of thermions. **2.** the electric current so produced.

therm·i·on·ics (thûrm/ī ŏn/ĭks, thûr/mī ŏn/ĭks), *n.* the science of thermionic phenomena.

thermionic valve, *Brit.* electron tube; radio tube.

ther·mis·tor (thər mĭs/tər), *n.* a transistor whose action depends on the change of resistivity of a semiconductor with temperature.

ther·mit (thûr/mĭt), *n.* **1.** Also, **ther·mite** (thûr/mīt). a mixture of finely divided metallic aluminum and one or more oxides, as of iron, producing when ignited an extremely high temperature as the result of the union of the aluminum with the oxygen of the oxide: used in welding, etc. **2.** (*cap.*) a trademark for this substance. [t. G: f. *therm-* ᴛʜᴇʀᴍ- + -*it* -ɪᴛᴇ¹]

thermo-, var. of **therm-,** before consonants, as in *thermochemistry.*

ther·mo·bar·o·graph (thûr/mō băr/ə grăf/, -gräf/), *n.* an apparatus combining a thermograph and a barograph.

ther·mo·ba·rom·e·ter (thûr/mō bə rŏm/ə tər), *n.* **1.** an apparatus in which the change in boiling point indicates the pressure. **2.** a form of barometer so constructed that it may also be used as a thermometer.

ther·mo·chem·is·try (thûr/mō kĕm/ĭs trĭ), *n.* the branch of chemistry that treats of the relations between chemical action and heat. —**ther/mo·chem/i·cal,** *adj.* —**ther/mo·chem/ist,** *n.*

ther·mo·cou·ple (thûr/mō kŭp/əl), *n.* a thermoelectric couple.

thermodynam., thermodynamics.

ther·mo·dy·nam·ics (thûr/mō dī năm/ĭks, -dĭ-), *n.* the science concerned with the relations between heat and mechanical energy or work, and the conversion of one into the other. —**ther/mo·dy·nam/ic,** **ther/mo·dy·nam/i·cal,** *adj.* —**ther/mo·dy·nam/i·cal·ly,** *adv.*

ther·mo·e·lec·tric (thûr/mō ĭ lĕk/trĭk), *adj.* of or pertaining to thermoelectricity. Also, **ther/mo·e·lec/-tri·cal.** —**ther/mo·e·lec/tri·cal·ly,** *adv.*

thermoelectric couple, two conductors of different metals joined at their ends and producing a thermoelectric current when there is a difference in temperature between the ends; thermocouple.

ther·mo·e·lec·tric·i·ty (thûr/mō ĭ lĕk/trĭs/ə tĭ, -ē/-lĕk-), *n.* electricity produced directly from heat, as that generated (in the form of a current) when the ends of two dissimilar metallic conductors are joined to form a closed circuit and one of the junctions is heated.

thermoelectric thermometer, a thermometer based on thermoelectricity containing a thermoelectric couple with an indicator.

ther·mo·e·lec·tro·mo·tive (thûr/mō ĭ lĕk/trə mō/-tĭv), *adj.* noting or pertaining to electromotive force produced by heat, as with a thermoelectric couple.

ther·mo·gen·e·sis (thûr/mō jĕn/ə sĭs), *n.* the production of heat, esp. in an animal body by physiological processes. —**ther/mo·ge·net/ic** (thûr/mō jə nĕt/ĭk), *adj.*

ther·mo·graph (thûr/mə grăf/, -gräf/), *n.* a self-registering thermometer.

ther·mo·la·bile (thûr/mō lā/bĭl), *adj. Biochem.* subject to destruction or loss of characteristic properties through the action of moderate heat, as certain toxins and ferments (opposed to *thermostable*).

ther·mol·y·sis (thər mŏl/ə sĭs), *n.* **1.** *Physiol.* the dispersion of heat from the body. **2.** *Chem.* dissociation by heat. —**ther·mo·lyt·ic** (thûr/mə lĭt/ĭk), *adj.*

ther·mom·e·ter (thər mŏm/ə tər), *n.* an instrument for measuring temperature, as by means of the expansion and contraction of mercury or alcohol in a capillary tube and bulb. —**ther·mo·met·ric** (thûr/mə mĕt/rĭk), **ther/mo·met/-ri·cal,** *adj.* —**ther/mo·met/ri·cal·ly,** *adv.*

ther·mom·e·try (thər mŏm/ə trĭ), *n.* **1.** the measurement of temperature. **2.** the science of the construction and use of thermometers.

ther·mo·mo·tive (thûr/mə mō/-tĭv), *adj.* **1.** pertaining to motion produced by heat. **2.** pertaining to a thermomotor.

Thermometers.
F, Fahrenheit;
C, Centigrade; R, Reaumur

ther·mo·mo·tor (thûr/mə mō/-tər), *n.* an engine operated by heat, esp. one driven by the expansive force of heated air.

ther·mo·nu·cle·ar (thûr/mō nōō/klĭ ər, -nū/klĭ ər), *adj. Chem., Physics.* designating, or capable of producing, those extremely high temperatures resulting from nuclear fusion.

thermonuclear reaction, *Chem., Physics.* a nuclear fusion reaction that takes place between two ions of a gas uniformly heated to a temperature of several million degrees Centigrade.

ther·mo·pile (thûr/mə pīl/), *n. Physics.* a number of thermoelectric couples joined so as to produce a combined effect, used for generating currents or measuring small differences in temperature. [f. ᴛʜᴇʀᴍᴏ- + ᴘɪʟᴇ¹]

ther·mo·plas·tic (thûr/mə plăs/tĭk), *adj.* **1.** soft and pliable whenever heated, as some plastics, without any change of the inherent properties. —*n.* **2.** such a plastic.

Ther·mop·y·lae (thər mŏp/ə lē/), *n.* a narrow pass in E Greece: heroic defense by the Spartans against the Persians, 480 B.C.

ther·mos (thûr/məs), a bottle or the like so made that the interior container is protected by a vacuum which keeps the contents hot or cold. [*thermos,* t. Gk.: hot]

Thermopylae. 480 B.C.

ther·mo·scope (thûr/mə skōp/), *n.* a device for indicating variations in temperature, usually without measuring their amount. —**ther·mo·scop·ic** (thûr/mə-skōp/ĭk), **ther/mo·scop/i·cal,** *adj.*

ther·mo·set·ting (thûr/mō sĕt/ĭng), *adj.* pertaining to a type of plastic which becomes hard and unmoldable when it is heated and is resistant to additional applications of heat once it is set, as the urea resins.

ther·mo·si·phon (thûr/mō sī/fən, -fŏn), *n.* an arrangement of siphon tubes serving to induce circulation of water in a heating apparatus.

ther·mo·sta·ble (thûr/mō stā/bəl), *adj. Biochem.* capable of being subjected to a moderate degree of heat without loss of characteristic properties, as certain toxins and ferments (opposed to *thermolabile*).

ther·mo·stat (thûr/mə stăt/), *n.* a device, including a relay actuated by thermal conduction or convection, which functions to establish and maintain a desired temperature (automatic) or signals a change in temperature for manual adjustment. —**ther/mo·stat/ic,** *adj.* —**ther/mo·stat/i·cal·ly,** *adv.*

ther·mo·stat·ics (thûr/mə stăt/ĭks), *n.* the science concerned with thermal equilibrium.

ther·mo·tax·is (thûr/mə tăk/sĭs), *n.* **1.** *Biol.* the movement of an organism toward or away from a source of heat. **2.** *Physiol.* the regulation of the bodily temperature. —**ther/mo·tax/ic,** *adj.*

ther·mo·ten·sile (thûr/mə tĕn/sĭl), *adj.* pertaining to tensile strength as affected by changes of temperature.

ther·mo·ther·a·py (thûr/mō thĕr/ə pĭ), *n.* treatment of disease by means of heat, either moist or dry.

ther·mot·ics (thər mŏt/ĭks), *n.* the science of heat.

ther·mot·ro·pism (thər mŏt/rə pĭz/əm), *n. Biol.* the property in plants or other organisms of turning or bending (toward or away), as in growth, under the influence of heat. —**ther·mo·trop·ic** (thûr/mə trŏp/ĭk), *adj.*

-thermy, a word element referring to heat. [comb. form repr. Gk. *thérmē*]

the·roid (thĭr/oid), *adj.* having animal propensities or characteristics. [t. Gk.: m.s. *thēroeidḗs*]

Ther·si·tes (thər sī/tēz), *n. Gk. Legend.* the most vindictive, impudent, and foul-mouthed of the Greeks before Troy, railing chiefly at Achilles and Odysseus.

ther·sit·i·cal (thər sĭt/ə kəl), *adj.* scurrilous; foul-mouthed; grossly abusive.

the·sau·rus (thĭ-sôr′əs), *n.*, *pl.* **-sauri** (-sôr′ī). **1.** a storehouse or repository, as of words or knowledge; a dictionary, encyclopedia, or the like. **2.** a treasury. [t. L, t. Gk.: m. *thēsaurós* treasure, treasury]

these (thēz) *pron.*, *adj.* pl. of **this**. [ME; r. OE *thās*]

The·seus (thē′sōōs, -sī′əs), *n. Gk. Legend.* the chief hero of Attica, son of Aegeus, said to have organized a constitutional government and united the separate states at Athens. Among his many exploits he found his way through the Cretan labyrinth (aided by Ariadne, whom he loved but deserted), slew the Minotaur, fought the Amazons, was one of the Argonauts, and took part in the Calydonian hunt. **—The·se·an** (thĭ sē′ən), *adj.*

the·sis (thē′sĭs), *n.*, *pl.* **-ses** (-sēz). **1.** a proposition laid down or stated, esp. one to be discussed and proved or to be maintained against objections. **2.** a subject for a composition or essay. **3.** a dissertation, as one presented by a candidate for a diploma or degree. **4.** *Music.* (in conducting) the downward stroke in a measure (opposed to *arsis*). **5.** *Pros.* **a.** (orig.) the accented syllable of a foot in verse (opposed to *arsis*). **b.** (later) the stressed part of a metrical unit. [ME, t. Gk.: setting down, something set down]

Thes·pi·an (thĕs′pĭ ən), *adj.* **1.** of Thespis. **2.** pertaining to tragedy or to the dramatic art in general; tragic; dramatic. **—n. 3.** a tragedian; an actor or actress.

Thes·pis (thĕs′pĭs), *n.* fl. 6th cent. B.C., Greek poet.

Thess., Thessalonians. Also, **Thes.**

Thes·sa·lo·ni·an (thĕs′ə lō′nĭ ən), *adj.* **1.** of or pertaining to Thessalonica (modern Salonika). **—n. 2.** a native or inhabitant of Thessalonica. **3.** (*pl.*) the two books or epistles of the New Testament addressed by St. Paul to the Thessalonian Christians.

Thes·sa·lo·ni·ke (thĕs′ə lô nē′kē), *n.* official name of **Salonika**. Ancient, **Thes·sa·lo·ni·ca** (thĕs′ə lō nĭ′kə, -lŏ nī′kə).

Thes·sa·ly (thĕs′ə lĭ), *n.* a region in E Greece: a former division of ancient Greece. 628,941 pop. (1951); 5208 sq. mi. **—Thes·sa·li·an** (thĕ sā′lĭ ən), *adj.*, *n.*

the·ta (thā′tə. thē′tə), *n.* the eighth letter (Θ, θ) of the Greek alphabet.

thet·ic (thĕt′ĭk), *adj.* positive; dogmatic. Also, **thet′i·cal.** [t. Gk.: m. s. *thetikós*, der. *thetós* placed] **—thet′i·cal·ly,** *adv.*

The·tis (thē′tĭs), *n. Gk. Myth.* the chief of the Nereids, and mother by Peleus of Achilles.

the·ur·gy (thē′ûr jĭ), *n.*, *pl.* **-gies.** **1.** a system of magic practiced by the Egyptian Platonists and others professing to have communication with and aid from beneficent deities. **2.** the working of some divine or supernatural agency in human affairs; the effects brought about among men by such agency. [t. L: m.s. *theūrgia*, t. Gk: m. *theourgía* sorcery] **—the·ur′gic, the·ur′gi·cal,** *adj.* **—the·ur′gi·cal·ly,** *adv.* **—the′ur·gist,** *n.*

thew (thū), *n.* **1.** (*usually pl.*) muscle or sinew. **2.** (*pl.*) physical strength. [ME; OE *thēaw* custom, usage, c. OHG *dau* discipline] **—thew′y,** *adj.*

thew·less (thū′lĭs), *adj.* without vigor or energy.

they (thā), *pron. pl.*, *poss.* **their** or **theirs**, *obj.* **them.** **1.** nominative plural of **he, she,** and **it.** **2.** (often used to denote persons or a person indefinitely or people in general): *they say he's rich.* [ME, t. Scand.; cf. Icel. *their* those, c. OE *thā,* pl. of *thæt* THAT]

thi-, var. of **thio-,** as in *thiazine.* This is the proper form before a vowel; however, it is not systematically employed (cf. *thioaldehyde*).

thi·a·mine (thī′ə mēn′, -mĭn), *n. Biochem.* a complex organic compound containing a thiazole and a pyrimidine group, $C_{12}H_{17}CIN_4OS$. Its chloride, vitamin B₁, is important in the prevention of beriberi. Also, **thi·a·min** (thī′ə mĭn).

thi·a·zine (thī′ə zēn′, -zĭn), *n. Chem.* any of a class of compounds containing a ring composed of one atom each of sulfur and nitrogen and four atoms of carbon. Also, **thi·a·zin** (thī′ə zĭn). [f. THI- + AZ(O)- + -INE²]

thi·a·zole (thī′ə zōl′), *n. Chem.* **1.** a colorless liquid, C_3H_3NS, with a pungent odor, serving as the parent substance of important dyestuffs. **2.** any of various derivatives of this substance. Also, **thi·a·zol** (thī′ə zŏl′, -zōl′).

Thi·bet (tĭ bĕt′), *n.* Tibet. **—Thi·bet′an,** *adj.*, *n.*

thick (thĭk), *adj.* **1.** having relatively great extent from one surface or side to its opposite; not thin: *a thick slice.* **2.** measuring as specified between opposite surfaces, or in depth, or in a direction perpendicular to that of the length and breadth: *a board one inch thick.* **3.** set close together; compact; dense: *a thick forest.* **4.** numerous, abundant, or plentiful. **5.** filled, covered, or abounding (fol. by *with*): *tables thick with dust.* **6.** having relatively great consistency: *a thick syrup.* **7.** (of darkness, etc.) dense, deep, or profound. **8.** husky, hoarse, muffled, or not clear in sound: *a thick voice.* **9.** containing much solid matter in suspension or solution. **10.** (of mist, smoke, etc.) having the component particles densely aggregated. **11.** (of the weather, etc.) foggy, misty, or hazy. **12.** *Colloq.* close in friendship; intimate. **13.** slow of mental apprehension: *a thick head.* **14.** *Dial.* dull of sense perception. **15.** *Chiefly Brit. Slang.* dis-

agreeably excessive. **—adv. 16.** in a thick manner. **—n. 17.** that which is thick. **18.** the thickest, densest, or most crowded part; the place, time, stage, etc., of greatest activity or intensity: *in the thick of the fight.* **19. through thick and thin,** under all circumstances; unwaveringly. [ME; OE *thicce,* c. G *dick*] **—thick′ish,** *adj.* **—thick′ly,** *adv.*

thick·en (thĭk′ən), *v.t.*, *v.i.* **1.** to make or become thick or thicker. **2.** to make or grow more intense, profound, intricate, or complex. **—thick′en·er,** *n.*

thick·en·ing (thĭk′ən ĭng), *n.* **1.** a making or becoming thick. **2.** a thickened part or area. **3.** something used to thicken.

thick·et (thĭk′ĭt), *n.* a thick or dense growth of shrubs, bushes, or small trees; a thick coppice. [OE *thiccet,* f. *thicce* THICK + *-et,* n. suffix]

thick·head (thĭk′hĕd′), *n.* a stupid person; blockhead. **—thick′-head′ed,** *adj.* **—thick′-head′ed·ness,** *n.*

thick·leaf (thĭk′lēf′), *n.*, *pl.* **-leaves.** any of the succulent herbs or shrubs constituting the genus *Crassula.*

thick·ness (thĭk′nĭs), *n.* **1.** state or quality of being thick. **2.** the third dimension of a solid, distinct from length and breadth. **3.** the thick part or body of something. **4.** a layer.

thick·set (thĭk′sĕt′), *adj.* **1.** set thickly or in close arrangement; dense: *a thick-set hedge.* **2.** set, studded, or furnished thickly: *a sky thick-set with stars.* **3.** of thick form or build; heavily or solidly built. **—n. 4.** a thicket.

thick-skinned (thĭk′skĭnd′), *adj.* **1.** having a thick skin. **2.** not sensitive to criticism, reproach, rebuff, etc.

thick-wit·ted (thĭk′wĭt′ĭd), *adj.* stupid; dull.

thief (thēf), *n.*, *pl.* **thieves.** one who steals, esp. secretly or without open force; one guilty of theft or larceny. [ME; OE *thēof,* c. G *dieb*]

—Syn. THIEF, ROBBER refer to one who steals. A THIEF takes the goods or property of another by stealth without the latter's knowledge: *a horse thief, like a thief in the night.* A ROBBER trespasses upon the house, property, or person of another, and makes away with things of value, even at the cost of violence: *a robber held up two women on the street.*

Thiers (tyĕr), *n.* Louis Adolphe (lwē à dôlf′), 1797–1877, French statesman: president of France, 1871–73.

thieve (thēv), *v.*, **thieved, thieving.** **—v.t. 1.** to take by theft; steal. **—v.i. 2.** to act as a thief; commit theft; steal. [OE *thēofian,* der. *thēof* THIEF]

thiev·er·y (thē′vər ĭ), *n.*, *pl.* **-eries.** **1.** the act or practice of thieving; theft. **2.** something taken by theft.

thiev·ish (thē′vĭsh), *adj.* **1.** given to thieving. **2.** of, pertaining to, or characteristic of a thief; stealthy. **—thiev′ish·ly,** *adv.* **—thiev′ish·ness,** *n.*

thig (thĭg), *v.t.*, *v.i.*, **thigged, thigging.** *Scot.* to beg (alms, food, etc.); solicit (gifts). **—thig′ger,** *n.*

thigh (thī), *n.* **1.** that part of the leg between the hip and the knee in man. **2.** a homologous or apparently corresponding part of the hind limb of other animals; the region of the femur. See illus. under **horse. 3.** (in birds) **a.** the true femoral region, buried in the general integument of the body. **b.** the segment below, containing the fibula and tibia. **4.** *Entomol.* femur. [ME; OE *thēoh,* c. D *dij,* MHG *diech,* Icel. *thjó*]

thigh·bone (thī′bōn′), *n.* femur.

thig·mo·tax·is (thĭg′mə tăk′sĭs), *n. Biol.* the movement of an organism toward or away from any object which provides a mechanical stimulus; stereotaxis. [NL, f. Gk.: m. *thígma* touch + *-taxis* -TAXIS] **—thig·mo·tac·tic** (thĭg′mə tăk′tĭk), *adj.*

thig·mot·ro·pism (thĭg mŏt′rə pĭz′əm), *n. Biol.* the property in plants or other organisms of turning or bending (toward or away), as in growth, under the influence of mechanical contact.

thill (thĭl), *n.* either of the pair of shafts between which a single animal drawing a vehicle is placed. [ME *thylle.* Cf. OE *thille* plank, flooring]

thim·ble (thĭm′bəl), *n.* **1.** a small cap, usually of metal, worn on the finger to push the needle in sewing. **2.** *Mech.* any of various devices or attachments likened to this. **3.** *Naut.* a metal ring with a concave groove on the outside, used to line the outside of a ring of rope forming an eye. [ME *thym(b)yl,* OE *thȳmel.* der. *thūma* thumb] **—thim′ble·like′,** *adj.*

thim·ble·ber·ry (thĭm′bəl bĕr′ĭ), *n.*, *pl.* **-ries.** any of several American raspberries with a thimble-shaped fruit, esp. the black raspberry, *Rubus occidentalis.*

thim·ble·ful (thĭm′bəl fŏŏl′), *n.*, *pl.* **-fuls.** as much as a thimble will hold; a small quantity, esp. of liquor.

thim·ble·rig (thĭm′bəl rĭg′), *n.*, *v.*, **-rigged, -rigging. —n. 1.** a swindling game in which the operator apparently covers a small ball or pea with one of three thimblelike cups, and then, moving the cups about, offers to bet that no one can tell under which cup the ball or pea lies. **—v.t. 2.** to cheat by or as by the thimblerig. **—thim′ble·rig′ger,** *n.*

thim·ble·weed (thĭm′bəl wēd′), *n.* any of various plants with a thimble-shaped fruiting head, as the anemone, *Anemone virginiana,* and the rudbeckia, *Rudbeckia laciniata.*

thin (thĭn), *adj.*, **thinner, thinnest,** *adv.*, *v.*, **thinned, thinning. —adj. 1.** having relatively little extent from one surface or side to its opposite; not thick: *thin ice.* **2.** of small cross section in comparison with the length; slender: *a thin wire.* **3.** having little flesh; spare; lean.

b., blend of, blended; **c.,** cognate with; **d.,** dialect, dialectal; **der.,** derived from; **f.,** formed from; **g.,** going back to; **m.,** modification of; **r.,** replacing; **s.,** stem of; **t.,** taken from; **?,** perhaps. See the full key on inside cover.

4. having the constituent or individual parts relatively few and not close together: *thin vegetation.* **5.** not dense; sparse; scanty. **6.** having relatively slight consistency, as a liquid; fluid; rare or rarefied, as air, etc. **7.** without solidity or substance; unsubstantial. **8.** easily seen through, transparent, or flimsy: *a thin excuse.* **9.** lacking fullness or volume, as sound; weak and shrill. **10.** faint, slight, poor, or feeble. **11.** lacking body, richness, or strength. **12.** lacking in chroma; of light tint. **13.** *Photog.* (of a developed negative) lacking in opaqueness and yielding prints without strong contrasts of light and shade. —*adv.* **14.** in a thin manner. —*v.t.* **15.** to make thin or thinner (often fol. by *down, out,* etc.). —*v.i.* **16.** to become thin or thinner; become reduced or diminished; go, pass, etc. (fol. by *down, off, away,* etc.). [ME and OE *thynne,* c. G *dünn;* akin to L *tenuis*] —**thin′ly,** *adv.* —**thin′ner,** *n.* —**thin′ness,** *n.* —Syn. **3.** THIN, GAUNT, LEAN, SPARE agree in referring to one having little flesh. THIN applies often to one in an unnaturally reduced state, as from sickness, overwork, lack of food, or the like: *a thin, dirty little waif.* GAUNT suggests the angularity of bones prominently displayed in a thin face and body: *to look ill and gaunt.* LEAN usually applies to a person or animal that is naturally thin: *looking lean but healthy after an outdoor vacation.* SPARE implies a muscular leanness with no diminution of vitality: *Lincoln was spare in body.*

thine (ᵺīn), *pron., adj.* *Archaic.* the possessive form of *thou* used predicatively or without a noun following, or before a noun beginning with a vowel or *h.* Cf. **thy.** [ME; OE *thīn,* c. G *dein.* See THOU]

thing[1] (thǐng), *n.* **1.** a material object without life or consciousness; an inanimate object. **2.** some entity, object, or creature which is not or cannot be specifically designated or precisely described: *the stick had a brass thing on it.* **3.** that which is or may become an object of thought, whether material or ideal, animate or inanimate, actual, possible, or imaginary. **4.** a matter or affair: *things are going well now.* **5.** a fact or circumstance: *it is a curious thing.* **6.** an action, deed, or performance: *to do great things.* **7.** a particular or respect: *perfect in all things.* **8.** (*pl.*) clothes or apparel, esp. articles of dress added to ordinary clothing when going outdoors. **9.** (*pl.*) *Colloq.* implements, utensils, or other articles for service: *to help with the breakfast things.* **10.** (*pl.*) *Colloq.* personal possessions or belongings, often such as one carries along on a journey. **11.** *Law.* anything that may be the subject of a property right. **12.** that which is signified or represented, as distinguished from a word, symbol, or idea representing it. **13.** a living being or creature. **14. the thing, a.** that which is proper, correct, or fashionable. **b.** that which is important or necessary. [ME and OE, c. D and G *ding* affair, matter, thing]

thing[2] (thǐng, tǐng), *n.* (in Scandinavian countries) a public meeting or assembly, esp. a legislative assembly or a court of law. [t. Icel.: assembly]

thing-in-it-self (thǐng′ǐn ǐt sělf′), *n. Kantian Philos.* reality as it is apart from experience; what remains to be postulated after space, time, and all the categories of the understanding are assigned to consciousness. See **noumenon.** [trans. of G *Ding an sich*]

thing·um·bob (thǐng′əm bŏb′), *n. Colloq.* an indefinite name for a thing or person which a speaker or person is not able, or does not care, to designate more precisely. Also, **thing·um·a·jig** (thǐng′əm ə jǐg′).

think[1] (thǐngk), *v.,* **thought, thinking.** —*v.t.* **1.** to form or conceive (a thought, etc.) in the mind; have (something) in the mind as an idea, conception, or the like. **2.** to turn over in the mind; meditate; ponder: *he was thinking what it could mean.* **3.** to have the mind full of (a particular subject or the like). **4.** to form or have an idea or conception of (a thing, fact, circumstance, etc.). **5.** to bear in mind, recollect, or remember. **6.** to have in mind, intent, or purpose. **7.** to hold as an opinion; believe; suppose: *they thought that the earth was flat.* **8.** to consider (something) to be (as specified): *he thought the lecture very interesting.* **9.** to anticipate or expect: *I did not think to find you here.* **10.** to bring by thinking. **11.** to give continued thought to, as in order to reach a decision (fol. by *over*): *to think a matter over.* **12. think out** or **through, a.** to finish or complete in thought. **b.** to understand or solve by process of thought. **c.** to devise or contrive by thinking. —*v.i.* **13.** to use the mind, esp. the intellect, actively; cogitate or meditate. **14.** to form or have an idea or mental image (fol. by *of*). **15.** to reflect upon the matter in question: *think carefully before you begin.* **16.** to remember (usually fol. by *of*): *I can't think of his name.* **17.** to have consideration or regard (usually fol. by *of*): *to think of others first.* **18.** to make mental discovery; form or have a plan (usually fol. by *of*): *he thought of it first.* **19.** to have a belief or opinion as indicated. **20.** to have a high, low, or other opinion of a person or thing (fol. by *of*): *to think well of a person.* **21.** to have an anticipation or expectation (fol. by *of*). **22. think fit, good, proper,** or **right,** to deem worthy or worthy of doing. **23. think better of, a.** to think more favorably or highly of (a person, a plan, etc.), as upon further knowledge. **b.** to think more wisely or sensibly of, as by a change of mind or reconsideration. [ME; OE *thencan* (c. D and G *denken*), der. *thanc* thought. See THANK, *n.*] —**think′a·ble,** *adj.* —**think′er,** *n.* —Syn. **4.** conceive, imagine, picture. **6.** intend, mean. **7.** THINK, DEEM, JUDGE, SUPPOSE mean to have an opinion.

THINK is the general word for forming or having a thought, opinion, notion, or idea in the mind: *to think that a hat is becoming.* DEEM, used esp. in formal speech, implies having formed an opinion and holding to it as a standard for measuring, judging, etc.: *to deem it an honor to be invited to speak.* JUDGE suggests a careful balance of reason and evidence: *to judge from previous experience.* SUPPOSE suggests having an opinion that is not certain but appears to be justified: *to suppose that a friend is honest.*

think[2] (thǐngk), *v.i.,* **thought, thinking.** to seem or appear (usually impersonal, with indirect object; now only in *methinks* and *methought*). [ME; OE *thync(e)an,* c. G *dünken*]

think·ing (thǐngk′ǐng), *adj.* **1.** that thinks; reasoning. **2.** thoughtful; reflective. —*n.* **3.** thought; reflection.

thin-skinned (thǐn′skǐnd′), *adj.* **1.** having a thin skin. **2.** sensitive to criticism, reproach, rebuff, or the like; easily offended; touchy.

thio-, a word element used in chemical nomenclature to indicate the replacement of part or all of the oxygen atoms in a compound by sulfur: often used to designate sulfur analogues of oxygen compounds. Also, **thi-.** [comb. form repr. Gk. *theion* sulfur]

thi·o·al·de·hyde (thī′ō ăl′də hīd′), *n. Chem.* any of a class of compounds formed by the action of hydrogen sulfide on aldehydes, and regarded as aldehydes with the oxygen replaced by sulfur.

thi·o·cy·a·nate (thī′ō sī′ə nāt′), *n. Chem.* a salt or ester of thiocyanic acid, characterized by the univalent SCN group, and used in hypertensions to relax and dilate smaller blood vessels.

thi·o·cy·an·ic acid (thī′ō sī ǎn′ǐk), *Chem.* an unstable acid, HSCN, known chiefly in the form of its salts.

thi·on·ic (thī ŏn′ǐk), *adj. Chem.* of or pertaining to sulfur. [f. m. Gk. *theion* sulfur + -IC]

thionic acid, any of four acids of sulfur, of the type $H_2S_xO_6$, where x is a number from 2 to 5.

thi·o·nine (thī′ə nēn′, -nǐn), *n.* **1.** a thiazine derivative occurring in dark crystalline plates, used as a violet dye, as in staining microscopic objects. **2.** any of various related dyes.

thi·o·pen·tal sodium (thī′ə pěn′təl), sodium pentothal. Also, *Brit.* **thi·o·pen·tone sodium** (thī′ə pěn′tōn).

thi·o·phene (thī′ə fēn′), *n. Chem.* a colorless liquid, C_4H_4S, with physical properties resembling benzene, occurring in crude coal-tar benzene and prepared by high-temperature interaction of butane and sulfur. Also, **thi·o·phen** (thī′ə fěn′).

thi·o·sin·am·ine (thī′ə sǐn ăm′ǐn), *n. Chem.* a colorless crystalline compound, $C_4H_8N_2S$, with bitter taste and feeble garliclike odor: obtained by the action of ammonia on a sulfur compound, present in mustard oil.

thi·o·sul·fate (thī′ō sŭl′fāt), *n. Chem.* a salt of thiosulfuric acid.

thi·o·sul·fu·ric acid (thī′ō sŭl fyŏŏr′ǐk), *Chem.* an acid, $H_2S_2O_3$, which may be regarded as sulfuric acid with one oxygen atom replaced by sulfur.

thi·o·u·re·a (thī′ō yŏŏ rē′ə, -yŏŏr′ǐə), *n. Chem.* a colorless, crystalline substance, $CS(NH_2)_2$, with a bitter taste, derived from urea by replacement of the oxygen with sulfur.

third (thûrd), *adj.* **1.** next after the second. **2.** being one of three equal parts. **3.** *Auto.* of or pertaining to third (gear ratio). —*n.* **4.** a third part, esp. of one (¹/₃). **5.** the third gear ratio, usually the highest in passenger cars but not necessarily so in trucks, buses, tractors, etc. **6.** *Auto.* the third forward gear ratio, usually the highest in passenger cars but not necessarily so in trucks, buses, tractors, etc. **7.** (*usually pl.*) *Law.* **a.** the third part of the personal property of a deceased husband, which under certain circumstances goes absolutely to the widow. **b.** a widow's dower. **8.** *Music.* **a.** a tone on the third degree from a given tone (counted as the first). **b.** the interval between such tones. **c.** the harmonic combination of such tones. [ME *thirde,* OE (North.) *thirda,* var. of *thridda,* c. D *derde,* G *dritte;* akin to L *tertius,* Gk. *tritos*] —**third′ly,** *adv.*

third degree, 1. *Chiefly U.S.* the use of severe measures by the police (or others) in examining a person in order to extort information or a confession. **2.** the degree of master mason in Freemasonry.

third estate, the commons. See **estate** (def. 5).

third person, *Gram.* See **person** (def. 13).

third rail, a conductor in the form of a supplementary rail, laid beside the rails of the track of an electric railroad to carry the propulsion current, which is taken off by means of a sliding contact.

third-rate (thûrd′rāt′), *adj.* **1.** of the third rate or class. **2.** distinctly inferior.

thirl (thûrl), *v.t., v.i. Brit. Dial.* **1.** to pierce. **2.** to thrill. [ME; OE *thyrlian,* der. *thyrel* hole. See NOSTRIL]

thirl·age (thûr′lǐj), *n. Scot. Law.* **1.** an obligation imposed on tenants of certain lands, requiring them to bring their grain to a particular mill. **2.** the price paid for such grinding. [var. of obs. *thrillage* bondage]

thirst (thûrst), *n.* **1.** uneasy or painful sensation of dryness in the mouth and throat caused by need of drink. **2.** the physical condition resulting from this need. **3.** strong or eager desire; craving: *a thirst for knowledge.* [n. use of THIRST, *v.;* r. ME and OE *thurst,* c. G *durst*] —*v.i.* **4.** to feel thirst; be thirsty. **5.** to have a strong

desire. [ME; OE *thyrstan*, der. *thurst* THIRST, n.]
—**thirst'er**, n. —**thirst'less**, adj.

thirst·y (thûrs'tĭ), adj., **thirstier, thirstiest.** 1. having thirst; craving drink. 2. needing moisture, as land; dry or arid. 3. eagerly desirous; eager. 4. *Colloq.* causing thirst. —**thirst'i·ly**, adv. —**thirst'i·ness**, n.

thir·teen (thûr'tēn'), n. 1. a cardinal number, ten plus three. 2. a symbol for this number, as 13 or XIII. —adj. 3. amounting to thirteen in number. [ME *thrittene*, OE *thrēotēne*, c. G *dreizehn*. See THREE, -TEEN]

thir·teenth (thûr'tēnth'), adj. 1. next after the twelfth. 2. being one of thirteen equal parts. —n. 3. a thirteenth part, esp. of one (¹/₁₃). 4. the thirteenth member of a series.

thir·ti·eth (thûr'tĭĭth), adj. 1. next after the twenty-ninth. 2. being one of thirty equal parts. —n. 3. a thirtieth part, esp. of one (¹/₃₀). 4. the thirtieth member of a series.

thir·ty (thûr'tĭ), n., pl. **-ties**, adj. —n. 1. a cardinal number, ten times three. 2. a symbol for this number, as 30 or XXX. 3. *Journalism.* the sign 30, often used to mark the end of an article, copy, etc. —adj. 4. amounting to thirty in number. [ME *thritty*, OE *thritig*, f. *thrī* THREE + *-tig* -TY¹, c. G *dreissig*]

thir·ty-sec·ond note (thûr'tĭsĕk'ŏnd), *Music.* a note or rest having ¹/₃₂ of the time value of a whole note or rest; demisemiquaver. See illus. under **note.**

Thirty Years' War, a series of European wars (1618–48) primarily between Protestants and Catholics of the Holy Roman Empire.

this (thĭs), pron. and adj., pl. **these** (thēz), adv. —pron. and adj. 1. a demonstrative term indicating: **a.** a person, thing, idea, etc., as pointed out, present, or near, as before mentioned, or supposed to be understood, as about to be mentioned, or by way of emphasis. **b.** one of two persons, things, etc., already mentioned, either referring to the one nearer in place, time, or thought, or implying mere contradistinction (opposed to *that*). —adv. 2. to this extent or degree (in later use employed chiefly or only to modify adjectives and adverbs of quantity or extent): *this much.* [ME and OE, c. G *dies*]

This·be (thĭz'bĭ), n. *Class. Legend.* a maiden of Babylon, loved by Pyramus. Pyramus killed himself when he saw blood which he mistakenly believed to be Thisbe's, and she killed herself.

this·tle (thĭs'əl), n. 1. any of various prickly composite plants of the genus *Cirsium* and allied genera, as *C. lanceolatum*, a stout herb with handsome purple flower heads, taken as the national emblem of Scotland, or *C. arvense* (the **Canada thistle**). 2. any of various other prickly plants. [ME and OE *thistel*, c. D and G *distel*] —**this'tle·like'**, adj. —**this'tly**, adj.

Thistle.
Cirsium lanceolatun

thith·er (thĭth'ər, thĭth'ər), adv. 1. Also, **thith·er·ward** (thĭth'ər wərd, thĭth'-), **thith·er·wards.** to or toward that place or point. —adj. 2. on the side or in the direction away from the person speaking; farther; more remote. [ME; OE *thider*, earlier *thæder*, c. Icel. *thadhra* there; akin to THAT, THE]

thith·er·to (thĭth'ər tōō', thĭth'-, thĭth'ər tōō', thĭth'-), adv. *Rare.* up to that time; until then.

thix·ot·ro·py (thĭk sŏt'rə pĭ), n. *Chem.* the property exhibited by certain gels of becoming liquid when stirred or shaken. [f. Gk. *thix(is)* a touch + -o- + -TROPY] —**thix·o·trop·ic** (thĭk'sə trŏp'ĭk), adj.

tho (thō), conj., adv. though. Also, **tho'.**

thole¹ (thōl), n. 1. a pin inserted in a boat's gunwale or the like, to act as a fulcrum for the oar. 2. either of two such pins between which the oar works. Also, **thole·pin** (thōl'pĭn'). [ME *tholle*, OE *tholl*, c. LG *dolle*]

Tholes
A. Single; B. Double

thole² (thōl), v.t., **tholed, tholing.** *Dial.* to suffer; bear; endure. [ME; OE *tholian*, c. Icel. *thola*; akin to L *tolerāre*]

thol·o·bate (thŏl'ə bāt'), n. *Archit.* the substructure supporting a dome or cupola.

Thom·as (tŏm'əs), n. 1. *Bible.* an apostle who demanded proof of Christ's resurrection. John 20:24–29. 2. See **doubting Thomas.**

Thom·as (tŏm'əs), n. 1. **George Henry,** 1816–70, Union general in the U.S. Civil War. 2. **Norman Mattoon** (mə tōōn'), born 1884, U.S. socialist leader and writer. 3. **Theodore,** 1835–1905, U.S. orchestra conductor, born in Germany. 4. **Dylan** (dĭl'ən), 1914–53, British poet born in Wales.

Tho·mas (tô mä'), n. **Ambroise** (än brwäz'), 1811–96, French composer.

Thomas of Er·cel·doune (ûr'səl dōōn'), ("Thomas the Rhymer") 1220?–1297?, Scottish poet.

Thomas of Wood·stock (wŏŏd'stŏk'), (*Duke of Gloucester*) 1355–97, English prince (son of Edward III).

Tho·mism (tō'mĭzəm, thō'-), n. a system of philosophy and theology as taught by St. Thomas Aquinas. —**Tho'mist**, n., adj.

Thomp·son (tŏmp'sən, tŏm'-), n. 1. **Benjamin,** (*Count Rumford*) 1753–1814, American-English physi-

cist, and administrator in Bavaria. 2. **Francis,** 1859–1907, British poet.

Thompson seedless, *Hort.* a California grape, of great importance in the raisin industry.

Thompson submachine gun, 1. a type of submachine gun. 2. a trademark for this gun.

Thom·son (tŏm'sən), n. 1. **James,** 1700–1748, British poet, born in Scotland. 2. **James,** ("*B.V.*") 1834–82, British poet: author of *The City of Dreadful Night.* 3. **John Arthur,** 1861–1933, Scottish scientist and author. 4. **Sir Joseph John,** 1856–1940, British physicist. 5. **Sir William,** (*Lord Kelvin*) 1824–1904, British physicist and mathematician.

thong (thông, thŏng), n. 1. a narrow strip of hide or leather, used as a fastening, as the lash of a whip, etc. 2. a similar strip of some other material. [ME; OE *thwong*, akin to Icel. *thvengr*]

Thor (thôr), n. *Scand. Myth.* the ancient Scandinavian god of thunder, represented as wielding a mighty hammer.

tho·rac·ic (thō rǎs'ĭk), adj. of or pertaining to the thorax. Also, **tho·ra·cal** (thôr'ə kəl).

thoracic duct, *Anat.* the main trunk of the lymphatic system, passing along the spinal column in the thoracic cavity, and conveying a large amount of lymph and chyle into the venous circulation.

tho·rac·i·co·lum·bar (thō rǎs'ĭ kō lŭm'bər), adj. pertaining to the thoracic and lumbar areas of the body.

tho·ra·co·plas·ty (thôr'ə kō plǎs'tĭ), n., pl. **-ties.** *Surg.* the operation of removal of selected portions of the bony chest wall (ribs) to compress part of the underlying lung or an abnormal pleural space, usually in the treatment of tuberculosis. [f. *thoraco-* (t. Gk.: m. *thōrako-*, comb. form of *thōrax* THORAX) + -PLASTY]

tho·rax (thôr'ǎks), n., pl. **thoraxes, thoraces** (thôr'ə sēz'). 1. (in man and the higher vertebrates) the part of the trunk between the neck and the abdomen, containing the cavity (enclosed by the ribs, etc.) in which the heart, lungs, etc., are situated; the chest. 2. a corresponding part in other animals. 3. (in insects) the portion of the body between the head and the abdomen. See diag. of **insect.** [ME, t. L, t. Gk.: breastplate, chest]

Tho·reau (thôr'ō, thə rō'), n. **Henry David,** 1817–62, U.S. naturalist and author.

tho·ri·a (thôr'ĭə), n. *Chem.* an oxide of thorium, ThO₂, a white powder, used in making incandescent mantles for gas burners. [f. THORI(UM) + -a; modeled on MAGNESIA]

tho·ri·a·nite (thôr'ĭə nīt'), n. a rare mineral, mainly thorium oxide, ThO₂, but containing also uranium, cerium, etc., occurring in small black cubic crystals, notable for its radioactivity: a minor source of thorium.

tho·ri·um (thôr'ĭəm), n. *Chem.* a radioactive metallic element present in monazite. Thorium oxide (thoria) with 1% cerium oxide (ceria) constitutes Welsbach gas mantles. *Symbol:* Th; *at. wt.:* 232.12; *at. no.:* 90; *sp. gr.:* 11.2. [t. NL: f. *Thor* THOR + -ium -IUM] —**thor·ic** (thôr'ĭk, thôr'-), adj.

thorn (thôrn), n. 1. a sharp excrescence on a plant, esp. a sharp-pointed aborted branch; a spine; a prickle. 2. any of various thorny shrubs or trees, esp. of the genus *Crataegus*, as *C. oxyacantha* (**white thorn,** the common hawthorn), *C. coccinea* (**scarlet thorn,** the scarlet hawthorn), and *C. cordata* (**Washington thorn,** of the southern U.S., planted for hedges or ornament). 3. their wood. 4. something that wounds, or causes discomfort or annoyance. 5. name of the rune for *th* (once used in the English alphabet; still used in Icelandic). —v.t. 6. to prick with a thorn; vex. [ME and OE, c. G *dorn*, Icel. *thorn*] —**thorn'less**, adj. —**thorn'like'**, adj.

Thorn (tôrn), n. German name of Torun.

thorn apple, (thôrn'). 1. any of the poisonous solanaceous plants constituting the genus *Datura*, the species of which bear capsules covered with prickly spines, esp. the jimson weed, *D. Stramonium.* 2. a fruit of some species of thorn tree, genus *Crataegus*; haw.

thorn·back (thôrn'bǎk'), n. *Ichthyol.* 1. a European skate, *Raja clavata*, with short spines on the back and tail. 2. a California ray, *Platyrhinoidis triseriatus*, belonging to the guitarfish group.

Thorn·dike (thôrn'dīk), n. **Edward Lee,** 1874–1949, U.S. psychologist and lexicographer.

thorn·y (thôr'nĭ), adj., **thornier, thorniest.** 1. abounding in or characterized by thorns; spiny; prickly. 2. thornlike. 3. overgrown with thorns or brambles. 4. painful; vexatious. 5. full of points of dispute; difficult: *a thorny question.* —**thorn'i·ness**, n.

tho·ron (thôr'ŏn), n. *Chem.* a radioactive isotope of radon, produced by the disintegration of thorium. *Symbol:* Tn; *at. wt.:* 220; *at. no.:* 86. [der. *thoro-*, comb. form of THORIUM, modeled on NEON]

thor·ough (thûr'ō), adj. 1. carried out through the whole of something; fully executed; complete or perfect: *a thorough search.* 2. being fully or completely (such): *a thorough fool.* 3. thoroughgoing in action or procedure; leaving nothing undone. 4. *Rare.* going, passing, or extending through. —adv., prep. 5. *Archaic.* through. —n. 6. thoroughgoing action, procedure, or policy: applied specif. (*cap.*) to the policy of Strafford and Laud in the reign of Charles I of England. Also, **thor'o** for 1–5. [ME; OE *thuruh*, var. of *thurh* THROUGH] —**thor'ough·ly**, adv. —**thor'ough·ness**, n.

thorough bass (bās), *Music.* 1. a bass part written out in full throughout an entire piece, and accompanied by figures which indicate the successive chords of the harmony. **2.** the science or method of indicating harmonies by such figures. **3.** harmonic composition in general.

thorough brace, either of two strong braces or bands of leather from the front to the back spring and supporting the body of a coach or other vehicle.

thor·ough·bred (thûr′ō̇ brĕd′, thûr′ə-), *adj.* **1.** of pure or unmixed breed, stock, or race, as a horse or other animal; bred from the purest and best blood. **2.** (*cap. or l.c.*) of or pertaining to the Thoroughbred breed of horses. **3.** having qualities characteristic of pure breeding; high-spirited; mettlesome; elegant or graceful. **4.** thoroughly educated or trained. —*n.* **5.** a thoroughbred animal. **6.** (*cap.*) a horse of the English breed of race horses, developed by crossing domestic and Middle Eastern strains. **7.** a well-bred or thoroughly trained person.

thor·ough·fare (thûr′ō̇ fâr′, thûr′ə-), *n.* **1.** a road, street, or the like, open at both ends; esp. a main road or a highway. **2.** a passage or way through: *no thoroughfare.* **3.** a strait, river, or the like, affording passage.

thor·ough·go·ing (thûr′ō̇ gō′ĭng, thûr′ə-), *adj.* **1.** doing things thoroughly. **2.** carried out to the full extent. **3.** complete; unqualified: *a thoroughgoing knave.*

thor·ough·paced (thûr′ō̇ pāst′, thûr′ə-), *adj.* **1.** trained to go through all the possible paces, as a horse. **2.** thoroughgoing, complete, or perfect.

thor·ough·pin (thûr′ō̇ pĭn′, thûr′ə-), *n.* a morbid swelling just above the hock of a horse, usually appearing on both sides of the leg and sometimes causing lameness.

thor·ough·wort (thûr′ō̇ wûrt′, thûr′ə-), *n.* **1.** boneset, a medicinal composite herb (*Eupatorium perfoliatum*). **2.** any of various other eupatoriums.

thorp (thôrp), *n.* *Archaic except in Place Names.* a hamlet, village, or small town. Also, **thorpe.** [ME and OE, c. G *dorf*, Icel. *thorp* village]

Thor·vald·sen (tŏr′väl′sən), *n.* Albert Bertal (äl′bĕrt bär′təl), 1770–1844, Danish sculptor. Also, **Thor·wald·sen** (tŏr′väl′sən).

Thoroughwort.
Eupatorium perfoliatum

those (thōz), *pron., adj.* pl. of **that.** [ME; OE *thās* these; change of meaning variously explained]

Thoth (thōth, tōt), *n.* an Egyptian divinity represented as a human form with the head of an ibis or baboon, whom the Greeks identified with Hermes: the scribe of the gods, the inventor of numbers and letters, and the god of learning, wisdom, and magic. [t. Gk., t. Egyptian: m. *Tehut*]

thou (*th*ou), *pron., sing., nom.* **thou;** *poss.* **thy** or **thine;** *obj.* **thee;** *pl., nom.* **you** or **ye;** *poss.* **your** or **yours;** *obj.* **you** or **ye;** *v.* —*pron.* **1.** the personal pronoun of the second person, in the singular number and nominative case, used to denote the person (or thing) spoken to: formerly in general use, often as indicating: **a.** equality, familiarity, or intimacy. **b.** superiority on the part of the speaker. **c.** contempt or scorn for the person addressed; but now little used (being regularly replaced by *you,* which is plural, and takes a plural verb) except provincially, archaically, in poetry or elevated prose, in addressing the Deity, and by the Friends or Quakers, who, however, usually say not *thou* but *thee,* putting with it a verb in the third person singular (*thee is*). —*v.t.* **2.** to address as "thou." —*v.i.* **3.** to use "thou" in discourse. [ME; OE *thū*, c. G and MD *du*, L *tū*]

though (*th*ō), *conj.* **1.** notwithstanding that; in spite of the fact that (introducing a subordinate clause, which is often marked by ellipsis). **2.** even if; granting that. **3.** yet, still, or nevertheless (introducing an additional statement restricting or modifying a principal one): *I will go though I fear it will be useless.* **4.** if (usually in *as though*). —*adv.* **5.** for all that; however. Also, **tho, tho'.** [ME *thoh*, t. Scand; cf. Icel. *thō*, c. OE *thēah* however]

thought[1] (thôt), *n.* **1.** the product of mental action; that which one thinks. **2.** a single act or product of thinking; an idea or notion: *to collect one's thoughts.* **3.** act or process of thinking; mental activity. **4.** the capacity or faculty of thinking. **5.** a consideration or reflection. **6.** meditation: *lost in thought.* **7.** intention, design, or purpose, esp. a half-formed or imperfect intention: *we had some thought of going.* **8.** anticipation or expectation: *I had no thought of seeing you here.* **9.** consideration, attention, care, or regard: *taking no thought for her appearance.* **10.** a judgment, opinion, or belief. **11.** the intellectual activity or the ideas, opinions, etc., characteristic of a particular place, class, or time: *Greek thought.* **12.** a very small amount; a trifle. [ME *thoght*, OE *thoht* (akin to THINK[1]). Cf. D *gedachte*] —**Syn. 2.** concept, conception, opinion, judgment, belief.

thought[2] (thôt), *v.* pt. and pp. of **think.**

thought·ful (thôt′fəl), *adj.* **1.** occupied with or given to thought; contemplative; meditative; reflective. **2.** characterized by or manifesting thought: *a thoughtful essay.* **3.** careful, heedful, or mindful: *to be thoughtful of one's safety.* **4.** showing consideration for others; considerate. —**thought′ful·ly,** *adv.* —**thought′ful·ness,** *n.* —**Syn. 4.** THOUGHTFUL, CONSIDERATE mean taking thought for the comfort and the good of others. THOUGHTFUL implies providing little attentions, offering services, or in some way

looking out for the comfort or welfare of others: *it was thoughtful of you to send the flowers.* CONSIDERATE implies sparing others annoyance or discomfort, and being careful not to hurt their feelings: *"not considerate, only polite."*

thought·less (thôt′lĭs), *adj.* **1.** not taking thought; unthinking, careless, or heedless. **2.** characterized by or showing lack of thought. **3.** lacking in consideration for others; inconsiderate. **4.** devoid of or lacking capacity for thought. —**thought′less·ly,** *adv.* —**thought′less·ness,** *n.*

thou·sand (thou′zənd), *n.* **1.** a cardinal number, ten times one hundred. **2.** a symbol for this number, as 1000 or M. **3.** a great number or amount. —*adj.* **4.** amounting to one thousand in number. [ME; OE *thūsend*, c. Dan. *tusind.*]

Thousand and One Nights, The, The Arabian Nights' Entertainments.

thou·sand·fold (adj. thou′zənd fōld′; adv. -fōld′), *adj., adv.* a thousand times as great or as much.

Thousand Islands, a group of ab. 1500 islands in the St. Lawrence at the outlet of Lake Ontario: some are in New York, others in Canada: summer resorts.

thou·sandth (thou′zəndth), *adj.* **1.** last in order of a series of a thousand. **2.** being one of a thousand equal parts. —*n.* **3.** a thousandth part, esp. of one (1/1000). **4.** the thousandth member of a series.

Thrace (thrās), *n.* **1.** an ancient region of varying extent in the E part of the Balkan Peninsula: later a Roman province; now in Bulgaria, Turkey, and Greece. **2.** a modern region corresponding to the S part of the Roman province: now divided between Greece (**Western Thrace**) and Turkey (**Eastern Thrace**).

Thrace (def. 2)

thrall (thrôl), *n.* **1.** one who is in bondage; a bondman or slave. **2.** one who is in bondage to some power, influence, or the like. **3.** thralldom. —*v.t.* **4.** *Archaic.* to put or hold in thralldom; enslave. —*adj.* **5.** *Archaic.* in bondage; enslaved. [ME; OE *thrǣl*, t. Scand; cf. Icel. *thrǣll*, c. OHG *dregil* servant]

thrall·dom (thrôl′dəm), *n.* state of being a thrall; bondage; slavery; servitude. Also, **thral′dom.**

thrash (thrăsh), *v.t.* **1.** to beat soundly by way of punishment; administer a beating to. **2.** to beat or defeat thoroughly. **3.** *Naut.* to force (a ship) forward against the wind, etc. **4.** to thresh (wheat, grain, etc.). —*v.i.* **5.** to beat, toss, or plunge wildly or violently about. **6.** *Naut.* to make way against the wind, tide, etc.; beat. —*n.* **7.** act of thrashing; a beating; a blow. **8.** *Swimming.* the upward and downward movement of the legs, as in the crawl. [var. of THRESH] —**Syn. 1.** See beat.

thrash·er (thrăsh′ər), *n.* **1.** one who or that which thrashes or threshes. **2.** any of various long-tailed thrushlike birds, esp. of the genus *Toxostoma,* allied to the mockingbird, as the **brown thrasher. 3.** thresher (def. 4). [cf. OE *thrǣsce* thrush]

thra·son·i·cal (thrā sŏn′ə kəl), *adj.* boastful; vainglorious. [f. s. L *Thraso,* a boastful soldier in Terence's "Eunuch" + -IC + -AL[1]] —**thra·son′i·cal·ly,** *adv.*

Thras·y·bu·lus (thrăs′ə bū′ləs), *n.* died c389 B.C., Athenian patriot and general.

thread (thrĕd), *n.* **1.** a fine cord of flax, cotton, or other fibrous material spun out to considerable length; esp. such a cord composed of two or more filaments twisted together. **2.** twisted fibers of any kind used for sewing (disting. from *yarn,* which is used for knitting and weaving). **3.** one of the lengths of yarn forming the warp and woof of a woven fabric. **4.** a filament or fiber of glass or other ductile substance. **5.** something having the fineness or slenderness of a thread, as a thin continuous stream of liquid, a fine line of color, or a thin seam of ore. **6.** the helical ridge of a screw. **7.** that which runs through the whole course of something, connecting successive parts, as the sequence of events in a narrative. **8.** something conceived as being spun or continuously drawn out, as the course of life fabled to be spun and cut by the Fates. —*v.t.* **9.** to pass the end of a thread through the eye in (a needle). **10.** to fix (beads, etc.) upon a thread that is passed through; string. **11.** to pass continuously through the whole course of (something); pervade. **12.** to make one's way through (a narrow passage, a forest, a crowd, etc.). **13.** to make (one's way, etc.) thus. **14.** to form a thread on or in (a bolt, hole, etc.). —*v.i.* **15.** to thread one's way, as through a passage or between obstacles. **16.** to move in a threadlike course; wind or twine. **17.** *Cookery.* (of boiling syrup) to form a fine thread when dropped from a spoon. [ME *threed,* OE *thrǣd,* c. G *draht.* See THROW] —**thread′er,** *n.* —**thread′less,** *adj.* —**thread′like′,** *adj.*

thread·bare (thrĕd′bâr′), *adj.* **1.** having the nap worn off so as to lay bare the threads of the warp and woof, as a fabric, garment, etc. **2.** meager, scanty, or poor. **3.** hackneyed or trite: *threadbare arguments.* **4.** wearing threadbare clothes; shabby: *a threadbare little old man.*

thread·fin (thrĕd′fĭn′), *n.* any of the spiny-rayed fishes constituting the family *Polynemidae,* the lower part of whose pectoral fin is composed of numerous separate slender filamentous rays.

thread mark, a thin threading in paper currency used to prevent counterfeiting.

thread·worm (thrĕd′wûrm′), *n.* any of various nematode worms, esp. a pinworm.

thread·y (thrĕd′ĭ), *adj.* **1.** consisting of or resembling a thread or threads; fibrous; filamentous. **2.** stringy or viscid, as a liquid. **3.** (of the pulse) thin and feeble. **4.** (of voice, etc.) lacking fullness. —**thread′i·ness,** *n.*

threat (thrĕt), *n.* **1.** a declaration of an intention or determination to inflict punishment, pain, or loss on someone in retaliation for, or conditionally upon, some action or course; a menace. **2.** an indication of probable evil to come; something that gives indication of causing evil or harm. —*v.t., v.i.* **3.** *Archaic or Dial.* to threaten. [ME *threte,* OE *thrēat* throng, threat, distress. Cf. Icel. *thraut* labor, struggle] —**threat′less,** *adj.*

threat·en (thrĕt′ən), *v.t.* **1.** to utter a threat against; menace. **2.** to be a menace or source of danger to. **3.** to offer (a punishment, injury, etc.) by way of a threat. **4.** to give an ominous indication of: *the clouds threaten rain.* —*v.i.* **5.** to utter or use threats. **6.** to indicate impending evil or mischief. [ME *thretne,* OE *thrēatnian,* der. *thrēat* THREAT] —**threat′en·er,** *n.* —**threat′en·ing·ly,** *adv.* —**Syn. 6.** See **imminent.**

three (thrē), *n.* **1.** a cardinal number, two plus one. **2.** a symbol for this number, as 3 or III. **3.** a set of this many persons or things. **4.** a playing card, etc., with three pips. —*adj.* **5.** amounting to three in number. [ME; OE *thrēo,* c. G *drei;* akin to Gk. *treîs,* L *trēs*]

three-base hit (thrē′bās′), *Baseball.* a hit which permits the batter to reach third base without a fielder's error. Also, **three-bag·ger** (thrē′băg′ər).

three-col·or (thrē′kŭl′ər), *adj.* **1.** having or characterized by the use of three colors. **2.** noting or pertaining to a photomechanical process for making reproductions of paintings, etc., usually carried out by making three plates or printing surfaces, each corresponding to a primary color, by the half-tone process, and taking superimposed impressions from these plates in three correspondingly colored inks.

3-D, *adj.* three-dimensional: *3-D movies.*

three-deck·er (thrē′dĕk′ər), *n.* **1.** any vessel, etc., having three decks, tiers, etc. **2.** (formerly) one of a class of sailing warships which carried guns on three decks. **3.** something with three parts.

three-di·men·sion·al (thrē′dĭ mĕn′shən əl), *adj.* having, or seeming to have, the dimension of depth.

three·fold (thrē′fōld′), *adj.* **1.** having three elements or parts. **2.** three times as great or as much; treble. —*adv.* **3.** in threefold manner or measure; trebly.

three-mile limit (thrē′mīl′), *Internat. Law.* the limit of the marine belt which is included within the jurisdiction of the state possessing the coast.

three·pence (thrĭp′əns, thrĕp′əns), *n.* **1.** a sum of money of the value of three English pennies, or about 6 U.S. cents. **2.** a British silver coin worth three pennies.

three-pen·ny (thrĭp′ə nĭ, thrĕp′-, thrē′pĕn′ĭ), *adj.* **1.** of the amount or value of threepence. **2.** of little worth.

three-phase (thrē′fāz′), *adj. Elect.* **1.** denoting or pertaining to a circuit, system, or device which is energized by three electromotive forces which differ in phase by one third of a cycle, i.e., 120 degrees. **2.** having three phases.

three-piece (thrē′pēs′), *adj.* **1.** (of a garment) consisting of a coat, skirt, and blouse. **2.** having three parts.

three-ply (thrē′plī′), *adj.* consisting of three thicknesses, layers, strands, or the like.

three-quar·ter (thrē′kwôr′tər), *adj.* consisting of or involving three quarters of a whole.

three-quarter binding, *Bookbinding.* a binding in which the leather back extends further towards the side covers than in half binding.

Three Rivers, a city in SE Canada, in S Quebec, on the St. Lawrence. with suburbs, 68,306 (1951). French, **Trois-Rivières.**

three R's, reading, 'riting, and 'rithmetic, regarded as the fundamentals of education.

three·score (thrē′skôr′), *adj.* three times twenty; sixty.

three·some (thrē′səm), *adj.* **1.** consisting of three; threefold. **2.** performed or played by three persons. —*n.* **3.** three forming a group. **4.** something in which three persons participate. **5.** *Golf.* a match in which one player, playing his own ball, plays against two opponents with one ball, the latter playing alternate strokes. [ME *thresum.* See THREE, -SOME²]

three-square (thrē′skwâr′), *adj.* having an equilateral triangular cross section, as certain files.

threm·ma·tol·o·gy (thrĕm′ə tŏl′ə jĭ), *n. Biol.* the science of breeding or propagating animals and plants under domestication. [f. Gk. *thremmato-* (comb. form of *thrémma* nursling) + -LOGY]

thre·node (thrē′nōd, thrĕn′ōd), *n.* threnody. —**thre·no·di·al** (thrĭ nō′dĭ əl), **thre·nod·ic** (thrĭ nŏd′ĭk), *adj.* —**thren·o·dist** (thrĕn′ə dĭst), *n.*

thren·o·dy (thrĕn′ə dĭ), *n., pl.* -dies. a song of lamentation, esp. for the dead; a dirge or funeral song. [t. Gk.: m.s. *thrēnōidia*]

thre·o·nine (thrē′ə nēn′, -nĭn), *n. Biochem.* an essential amino acid, CH₃CHOHCH(NH₂)COOH, obtained by the hydrolysis of proteins.

thresh (thrĕsh), *v.t.* **1.** to separate the grain or seeds from (a cereal plant, etc.) by some mechanical means, as by beating with a flail or by the action of a thresher. **2.** to discuss (a matter) exhaustively (usually fol. by *out*). **3.** to beat as if with a flail. —*v.i.* **4.** to thresh wheat, grain, etc. **5.** to deliver blows as if with a flail. —*n.* **6.** act of threshing. [ME *thresshe,* OE *threscan,* c. G *dreschen.* Cf. THRASH]

thresh·er (thrĕsh′ər), *n.* **1.** one who or that which threshes. **2.** one who separates grain or seeds from wheat, etc., by beating with a flail or otherwise. **3.** a device or machine for this purpose. **4.** Also, **thresher shark.** a large shark of the genus *Alopias,* esp. *A. vulpinus,* having a very long tail with which it threshes the water in order to drive together the small fish on which it feeds.

thresh·old (thrĕsh′ōld, thrĕsh′hōld), *n.* **1.** the sill of a doorway. **2.** the entrance to a house or building. **3.** any place or point of entering or beginning. **4.** *Psychol., Physiol.* the limit below which a given stimulus, or the difference between two stimuli, ceases to be perceptible (called in the former case **threshold of consciousness,** and in the latter case **threshold of discrimination);** the limen. [ME *threschold,* OE *threscold, -wold,* c. Icel. *threskjöldr;* appar. der. THRESH, v.]

threw (throō), *v.* pt. of **throw.**

thrice (thrīs), *adv.* **1.** three times, as in succession; on three occasions. **2.** in threefold quantity or degree. **3.** very; greatly; extremely. [ME *thries,* f. obs. *thrie* thrice (OE *thrīga*) + -s, adv. gen. suffix]

thrift (thrĭft), *n.* **1.** economical management; economy; frugality. **2.** an alpine and maritime plumbaginaceous plant, *Statice Armeria,* with pink or white flowers, notable for its vigorous growth. **3.** any of various allied plants. **4.** vigorous growth, as of a plant. **5.** *Obs.* prosperity. [ME, der. THRIVE. Cf. Icel. *thrift* prosperity] —**thrift′less,** *adj.* —**thrift′less·ly,** *adv.* —**thrift′less·ness,** *n.*

thrift·y (thrĭf′tĭ), *adj.,* **thriftier, thriftiest. 1.** using or characterized by thrift or frugality; provident. **2.** thriving, prosperous, or successful. **3.** thriving physically; growing vigorously. —**thrift′i·ly,** *adv.* —**thrift′i·ness,** *n.* —**Syn. 1.** See **economical.**

thrill (thrĭl), *v.t.* **1.** to effect with a sudden wave of keen emotion, so as to produce a tremor or tingling sensation through the body. **2.** to cause to vibrate or quiver; utter or send forth tremulously, as a melody. —*v.i.* **3.** to affect one with a wave of emotion; produce a thrill. **4.** to be stirred by a thrill of emotion. **5.** to move tremulously; vibrate; quiver. —*n.* **6.** a tremor or tingling sensation passing through the body as the result of sudden keen emotion. **7.** thrilling property or quality, as of a story. **8.** a vibration or quivering. **9.** *Pathol.* an abnormal tremor or vibration, as in the respiratory system. [ME; metathetic var. of THIRL, v.] —**thrill′ing·ly,** *adv.* —**thrill′ing·ness,** *n.*

thrill·er (thrĭl′ər), *n.* **1.** one who or that which thrills. **2.** *Colloq.* a sensational play or story.

thrips (thrĭps), *n.* any of numerous small insects of the order *Thysanoptera,* characterized by long, narrow wings fringed with hairs, many species of which are destructive to plants. [t. L, t. Gk.: wood worm]

thrive (thrīv), *v.i.,* **throve** or **thrived, thrived** or **thriven, thriving. 1.** to prosper; be fortunate or successful; increase in property or wealth; grow richer or rich. **2.** to grow or develop vigorously; flourish. [ME, t. Scand; cf. Icel. *thrífask*] —**thriv′er,** *n.* —**thriv′ing·ly,** *adv.* —**Syn. 2.** See **succeed.**

thro' (throō), *prep., adv., adj.* through. Also, **thro.**

throat (thrōt), *n.* **1.** the passage from the mouth to the stomach or to the lungs; the fauces, pharynx, and esophagus; the larynx and trachea. **2.** some analogous or similar narrowed part or passage. **3.** the front of the neck below the chin and above the collarbones. [ME and OE *throte.* Cf. THROTTLE] —**throat′less,** *adj.*

throat·latch (thrōt′lăch′), *n.* a strap which passes under a horse's throat and helps to hold a bridle or halter in place. See illus. under **harness.**

throat·y (thrō′tĭ), *adj.,* **throatier, throatiest.** produced or modified in the throat, as sounds. —**throat′i·ly,** *adv.* —**throat′i·ness,** *n.*

throb (thrŏb), *v.,* **throbbed, throbbing,** *n.* —*v.i.* **1.** to beat with increased force or rapidity, as the heart under the influence of emotion or excitement; palpitate. **2.** to feel or exhibit emotion. **3.** to pulsate; vibrate. —*n.* **4.** act of throbbing. **5.** a violent beat or pulsation, as of the heart. **6.** any pulsation or vibration. [ME (in ppr. *throbbant*); orig. unknown] —**throb′ber,** *n.* —**throb′bing·ly,** *adv.* —**Syn. 3.** See **pulsate.**

throe (thrō), *n.* **1.** a violent spasm or pang; a paroxysm. **2.** a sharp attack of emotion. **3.** (*pl.*) the pains of childbirth. **4.** (*pl.*) the agony of death. **5.** (*pl.*) any violent convulsion or struggle. [ME *throwe;* prob. n. use of THROW, v., in its old sense of torture]

throm·bin (thrŏm′bĭn), *n. Biochem.* the substance or ferment which causes the coagulation of blood. [f. THROMB(US) + -IN²]

throm·bo·sis (thrŏm bō′sĭs), *n. Pathol.* intravascular coagulation of the blood in any part of the circulatory system, as in the heart, arteries, veins, or capillaries. [t. NL, t. Gk.: curdling, clotting] —**throm·bot·ic** (thrŏm bŏt′ĭk), *adj.*

throm·bus (thrŏm′bəs), *n., pl.* -bi (-bī). *Pathol.* a

fibrinous clot which forms in and obstructs a blood vessel, or which forms in one of the heart's chambers. [t. NL, t. Gk.: m. *thrómbos* lump, clot]

throne (thrōn), *n.*, *v.*, **throned, throning.** —*n.* 1. the chair or seat occupied by a sovereign, bishop, or other exalted personage on ceremonial occasions, usually raised on a dais and covered with a canopy. 2. the office or dignity of a sovereign. 3. the occupant of a throne; a sovereign. 4. sovereign power or authority. 5. episcopal office or authority. 6. (*pl.*) an order of angels. —*v.t.*, *v.i.* 7. to set or sit on or as on a throne. [ME, t. L: m. *thronus*, t. Gk.: m. *thrónos* high seat; r. ME *trone*, t. OF] —**throne′less,** *adj.*

throng (thrông, thrŏng), *n.* 1. a multitude of people crowded or assembled together; a crowd. 2. a great number of things crowded or considered together. 3. *Dial.* pressure, as of work. —*v.i.* 4. to assemble, collect, or go in large numbers; crowd. —*v.t.* 5. to crowd or press upon; jostle. 6. to fill or occupy with or as with a crowd. 7. to bring or drive together into a crowd. 8. to fill by crowding or pressing into. [ME; OE *gethrang;* akin to D and G *drang*] —**Syn.** 1. See **crowd.**

thros·tle (thrŏs′əl), *n.* 1. the Old World song thrush, *Turdus philomelus.* 2. a machine for spinning wool, cotton, etc., in which the twisting and winding are simultaneous and continuous. [ME and OE. c. G and D *drossel*, akin to L *turdus* thrush]

throt·tle (thrŏt′əl), *n.*, *v.*, **-tled, -tling.** —*n.* 1. a lever, pedal, or other device to control the amount of fuel being fed to an engine. 2. a throttle valve. 3. *Chiefly Dial.* the throat, gullet, or windpipe. [prob. dim. of ME *throte* THROAT] —*v.t.* 4. to stop the breath of by compressing the throat; strangle. 5. to choke or suffocate in any way. 6. to compress by fastening something tightly about. 7. to silence or check as if by choking. 8. *Mach.* to obstruct the flow of (steam, etc.) by means of a throttle valve or otherwise; check the supply of steam, etc., to (an engine) in this way. [late ME *throtel*, freq. of earlier *throte*, v., strangle (der *throte*, n., THROAT)] —**throt′-tler,** *n.*

throttle lever, a lever, handle, etc., for manipulating a throttle valve.

throttle valve, the valve which regulates the flow of vapor received by the cylinders of an engine.

through (throo), *prep.* 1. in at one end, side, or surface, and out at the other, of: *to pass through a tunnel.* 2. between or among the individual members or parts of: *to swing through the trees.* 3. over the surface or within the limits of: *to travel through a country.* 4. during the whole period of: *to enjoy health through life.* 5. having reached the end of: *to be through one's work.* 6. having finished successfully: *to get through an examination.* 7. by the means or instrumentality of: *it was through him they found out.* 8. by reason of or in consequence of: *to run away through fear.* —*adv.* 9. in at one end, side, or surface and out at the other: *to push a needle through.* 10. all the way; along the whole distance: *this train goes through to Boston.* 11. throughout: *soaking wet through.* 12. from the beginning to the end: *to read a letter through.* 13. to the end: *to carry a matter through.* 14. to a favorable or successful conclusion: *to pull through.* 15. having completed an action, process, etc.: *he is not yet through.* 16. **through and through.** a. through the whole extent or substance; from beginning to end. b. in all respects; thoroughly. 17. **through with.** a. finished or done with. b. at an end of all relations or dealings with. —*adj.* 18. passing or extending from one end, side, or surface to the other. 19. that extends, goes, or conveys through the whole of a long distance with little or no interruption: *a through train.* Also, **thro′, thro, thru.** [ME; metathetic var. of *thourgh*, OE *thurh*, c. G *durch*, akin to Goth. *thairh*] —**Syn.** 7. See **by.**

through·ly (throo′li), *adv. Archaic.* thoroughly.

through·out (throo·out′), *prep.* 1. in or to every part of; everywhere in. 2. from the beginning to the end of. —*adv.* 3. in every part. 4. at every moment or point.

throve (thrōv), *v.* pt. of **thrive.**

throw (thrō), *v.*, **threw, thrown, throwing,** *n.* —*v.t.* 1. to project or propel forcibly through the air by a sudden jerk or straightening of the arm; propel or cast in any way. 2. to hurl or project (a missile), as a gun does. 3. to project or cast (light, a shadow, etc.). 4. to direct (words, a glance, etc.). 5. to cause to go or come into some place, position, condition, etc., as if by throwing: *to throw a man into prison, to throw a bridge across a river, to throw troops into action.* 6. to put hastily: *to throw a shawl over one's shoulders.* 7. *Mach.* a. to move (a lever, etc.) in order to connect or disconnect parts of an apparatus or mechanism. b. to connect, engage, disconnect, or disengage by such a procedure. 8. to shape on a potters' wheel. 9. *Cards.* a. to play (a card). b. to abandon (a hand) (usually fol. by *in*). 10. to cause to fall to the ground; bring to the ground, as an opponent in wrestling. 11. *U.S. Colloq.* to permit an opponent to win (a race, contest, or the like) unnecessarily or in accordance with a previous agreement. 12. to cast (dice). 13. to make (a cast) at dice. 14. (of a horse, etc.) to cause to fall off. 15. (of domestic animals) to bring forth (young). —*v.i.* 16. to cast, fling, or hurl a missile, etc. —*n.* 17. an act of throwing or casting; a cast or fling. 18. the distance to which anything is or may be thrown:

a stone's throw. 19. a venture or chance: *it was his last throw.* 20. *Mach.* a. the movement of a reciprocating part or the like from its central position to its extreme position in either direction, or the distance traversed (equivalent to one half the travel or stroke). b. the arm or the radius of a crank or the like; the eccentricity of an eccentric, or the radius of a crank to which an eccentric is equivalent, being equal to the distance between the center of the disk and the center of the shaft. c. the complete movement of a reciprocating part or the like in one direction, or the distance traversed (equivalent to the travel or stroke). 21. a woman's scarf, boa, or the like. 22. a light blanket, as for use when reclining on a sofa; an afghan. 23. a cast at dice. 24. the number thrown. 25. *Wrestling.* a. a technique whereby the contestant can be thrown. b. an act of throwing. 26. *Geol., Mining.* the amount of vertical displacement produced by fault. [ME; OE *thrāwan* turn, twist, c. G *drehen* twist, twirl] —**throw′er,** *n.*

—**Syn.** 1. THROW, CAST, PITCH, TOSS imply projecting something through the air. THROW is the general word, often used with an adverb which indicates direction, destination, etc.: *throw a rope to him, the paper away.* CAST is a formal word for THROW, archaic except as used in certain idiomatic expressions (*cast a net, black looks, cast down,* the compound *broadcast,* etc.): *to cast off a boat.* PITCH implies throwing with some force and definite aim: *to pitch a baseball.* To TOSS is to throw lightly as with an underhand or sidewise motion, or to move irregularly up and down or back and forth: *to toss a bone to a dog.*

throw·a·way (thrō′ə·wā′), *n.* any advertisement, as a folder or a broadside, passed out on streets, slipped under doors, etc.

throw·back (thrō′băk′), *n.* 1. an act of throwing back. 2. a setback or check. 3. reversion to an ancestral type or character. 4. an example of this.

thrown (thrōn), *v.* 1. pp. of **throw.** —*adj.* 2. (of silk) in filament form (distinguished from *spun*).

thru (throo), *prep., adv., adj.* through.

thrum¹ (thrŭm), *v.*, **thrummed, thrumming,** *n.* —*v.i.* 1. to play on a stringed instrument, as a guitar, by plucking the strings, esp. in an idle, monotonous, or unskillful manner. 2. to sound when thrummed on, as a guitar, etc. 3. to drum or tap idly with the fingers. —*v.t.* 4. to play (a stringed instrument, or a melody on it) by plucking the strings, esp. in an idle, monotonous, or unskillful manner. 5. to drum or tap idly on. 6. to recite or tell in a monotonous way. —*n.* 7. act or sound of thrumming; dull, monotonous sound. [imit.] —**thrum′mer,** *n.*

thrum² (thrŭm), *n.*, *v.*, **thrummed, thrumming.** —*n.* 1. one of the ends of the warp threads in a loom, left unwoven and remaining attached to a loom when the web is cut off. 2. (*pl.*) the row or fringe of such threads. 3. any short piece of waste thread or yarn; a tuft, tassel, or fringe of threads, as at the edge of a piece of cloth. 4. (*pl.* or *sing.*) *Naut.* short bits of rope yarn used for mops, etc. —*v.t.* 5. *Naut.* to insert short pieces of rope yarn through (canvas) and thus give it a rough surface, as in order that it may be wrapped about a part to prevent chafing. 6. *Dial.* to furnish or cover with thrums, ends of thread, or tufts. [ME and OE. c. G *trumm.* Cf. L *terminus* end]

thrush¹ (thrŭsh), *n.* 1. any of numerous passerine birds belonging to the family *Turdidæ*, most of which are moderate in size, migratory, gifted as songsters, and not brightly colored, as the European **song thrush** (*Turdus philomelus*) and American **wood thrush** (*Hylocichla mustelina*). 2. any of various superficially similar birds of other families, as the **water thrushes** of the genus *Seiūrus* (family *Compsothlypidae*). [ME *thrusche*, OE *thrȳsce,* akin to OHG *drōsca*] —**thrush′-like′,** *adj.*

thrush² (thrŭsh), *n.* 1. *Pathol.* a disease, esp. in children, characterized by whitish spots and ulcers on the membranes of the mouth, fauces, etc., due to a parasitic fungus, *Saccharomyces albicans.* 2. *Vet. Sci.* (in horses) a diseased condition of the frog of the foot. [cf. Dan. *troske,* d. Sw. *trosk* (def. 1)]

thrust (thrŭst), *v.*, **thrust, thrusting,** *n.* —*v.t.* 1. to push forcibly; shove; put or drive with force: *he thrust a dagger into her back.* 2. to put forcibly into some position, condition, etc.: *to thrust oneself into danger.* 3. to stab or pierce, as with a sword. —*v.i.* 4. to push against something. 5. to push or force one's way, as against obstacles or through a crowd. 6. to make a thrust, lunge, or stab at something. —*n.* 7. act of thrusting; a forcible push or drive; a lunge or stab. 8. *Engin.* the linear force generated by an engine-driven propeller or by exciting gases (as in jet propulsion). 9. *Geol.* a compressive strain in the crust of the earth, which, in its most characteristic development, produces reversed or thrust faults. 10. *Mech., Archit., etc.* a pushing force or pressure exerted by a thing or a part against a contiguous one. 11. *Archit.* the force exerted in a lateral direction by an arch, and tending to overturn the abutments. [ME *thruste(n),* t. Scand.; cf. Icel. *thrȳsta*] —**thrust′er,** *n.* —**Syn.** 1. See **push.**

thrust fault, *Geol.* a fault along an inclined plane in which the side or hanging wall appears to have moved upward with respect to the lower side or footwall (contrasted with *gravity fault*).

Thu·cyd·i·des (thoo·sĭd′ə·dēz′), *n.* c460–c400 B.C., Greek historian.

ăct, āble, dâre, ärt; ĕbb, ēqual; Yf, īce; hŏt, ōver, ôrder, oil, bŏŏk, ōōze, out; ŭp, ūse, ûrge; ə = a in alone; ch, chief; g, give; ng, ring; sh, shoe; th, thin; ŧħ, that; zh, vision. See the full key on inside cover.

thud (thŭd), n., v., **thudded, thudding.** —n. 1. a dull sound, as of a heavy blow or fall. 2. a blow causing such a sound. —v.i., v.t. 3. to beat or strike with a dull sound of heavy impact. [ME; OE *thyddan*, v.]

thug (thŭg), n. 1. a cutthroat; a ruffian. 2. (sometimes cap.) one of a former body of professional robbers and murderers in India, who strangled their victims. [t. Hind.: m. *thag*] —**thug·ger·y** (thŭg′ə rĭ), n. —**thug′-gish,** adj.

thug·gee (thŭg′ē), n. (sometimes cap.) the system or practices of the thugs in India. [t. Hind.: m. *thagī*]

thu·ja (thōō′jə), n. any of the evergreen pinaceous trees constituting the genus *Thuja*, esp. *T. occidentalis,* the common arborvitae, which yields an aromatic oil. [NL, t. Gk.: m. *thyia* African tree]

Thu·le (thōō′lē), n. 1. the ancient Greek and Latin name for an island or region (variously identified as one of the Shetland Islands, Iceland, Norway, etc.) supposed to be the most northerly region of the world. 2. ultima Thule. [t. L, t. Gk.: m. *Thoulē*; r. ME and OE *Tyle,* t. L: m. *Thȳlē,* t. Gk.]

thu·li·a (thōō′lĭ ə), n. Chem. the oxide of thulium Tm₂O₃. [t. NL, der. L *Thūlē* THULE]

thu·li·um (thōō′lĭ əm), n. Chem. a rare-earth metallic element found in the minerals euxenite, gadolinite, etc. Symbol: Tm; at. wt.: 169.4; at. no.: 69. [t. NL, f. s. L *Thūlē* THULE + -ium -IUM]

thumb (thŭm), n. 1. the short, thick inner digit of the human hand, next to the forefinger. 2. the corresponding digit in other animals; the pollex. 3. that part of a glove, etc., which covers the thumb. 4. Archit. ovolo. 5. under the thumb of, under the power or influence of. —v.t. 6. to soil or wear with the thumbs in handling, as the pages of a book. 7. to run through (the pages of a book, etc.) quickly. 8. to handle, work, etc., awkwardly. 9. to solicit or get (a ride) by pointing the thumb in the direction of one's travel. [ME; OE *thūma,* c. G *daumen*] —**thumb′less,** adj. —**thumb′like′,** adj.

thumb·nail (thŭm′nāl′), n. 1. the nail of the thumb. 2. anything quite small or brief, as a drawing, a short essay, etc. —adj. 3. quite small: *a thumbnail description.*

thumb·screw (thŭm′skrōō′), n. 1. an old instrument of torture by which one or both thumbs were compressed. 2. a screw whose head is so constructed that it may be turned easily with the thumb and a finger.

Thumbscrew (def. 1)

thumb·tack (thŭm′tăk′), n. a tack with a large, flat head, designed to be thrust in by the thumb.

thump (thŭmp), n. 1. a blow with something thick and heavy, producing a dull sound; a heavy knock. 2. the sound made by such a blow. —v.t. 3. to strike or beat with something thick and heavy, so as to produce a dull sound; pound. 4. (of an object) to strike against (something) heavily and noisily. 5. Colloq. to thrash severely. —v.i. 6. to strike or beat heavily, with a dull sound; pound. 7. to walk with heavy, sounding steps. 8. to beat violently, as the heart. [imit.] —**thump′er,** n. —**thump′ing·ly,** adv.

Thun (tōōn), n. 1. a city in central Switzerland, on the Aar river, near the Lake of Thun. 24,157 (1950). 2. Lake of, German, **Thuner See.** a lake in central Switzerland, formed by a widening in the course of the Aar river. ab. 10 mi. long.

thun·der (thŭn′dər), n. 1. the loud noise which accompanies a flash of lightning, due to violent disturbance of the air by a discharge of electricity. 2. Chiefly Poetic. the destructive agent in a thunderstorm. 3. any loud, resounding noise: *thunders of applause.* 4. a threatening or startling utterance, denunciation, or the like. —v.i. 5. to give forth thunder (often with impersonal *it* as subject): *it thundered last night.* 6. to make a loud, resounding noise like thunder. 7. to utter loud or vehement denunciations, threats, or the like. 8. to speak in a very loud tone. —v.t. 9. to strike, drive, inflict, give forth, etc., with loud noise or violent action. [ME; OE *thunor,* c. G *donner,* Icel. *Thōrr* Thor, akin to L *tonitrus* thunder] —**thun′der·less,** adj.

thun·der·bird (thŭn′dər bûrd′), n. (in the folk belief of certain western American Indians) a huge bird capable of producing thunder, lightning, and rain.

thun·der·bolt (thŭn′dər bōlt′), n. 1. a flash of lightning with the accompanying thunder. 2. an imaginary bolt or dart conceived as the material destructive agent cast to earth in a flash of lightning. 3. any of various fossils, stones, or mineral concretions formerly supposed to have been cast to earth with the lightning. 4. something very destructive, terrible, severe, sudden, or startling. 5. one who acts with fury or with sudden and resistless force.

thun·der·clap (thŭn′dər klăp′), n. a crash of thunder.

thun·der·cloud (thŭn′dər kloud′), n. an electrically charged cloud producing lightning and thunder.

thun·der·er (thŭn′dər ər), n. 1. one who thunders. 2. (cap.) Jupiter; Zeus.

thun·der·head (thŭn′dər hĕd′), n. one of the round swelling masses of cumulus clouds appearing above the horizon when conditions are right for thunderstorms, and frequently developing into thunderclouds.

thun·der·ing (thŭn′dər ĭng), adj. 1. that thunders. 2. producing a noise or effect like thunder. 3. Colloq. extraordinary; very great. —**thun′der·ing·ly,** adv.

thun·der·ous (thŭn′dər əs), adj. producing thunder or a loud noise like thunder. Also, **thun′der·y.** —**thun′-der·ous·ly,** adv.

thun·der·peal (thŭn′dər pēl′), n. a crash of thunder.

thun·der·show·er (thŭn′dər shou′ər), n. a shower accompanied by thunder and lightning.

thunder stick, bullroarer.

thun·der·stone (thŭn′dər stōn′), n. one of the fossils, stones, etc., popularly identified as thunderbolts.

thun·der·storm (thŭn′dər stôrm′), n. a storm of thunder and lightning, and usually rain.

thun·der·struck (thŭn′dər strŭk′), adj. 1. struck by a thunderbolt. 2. overcome with consternation, confounded, or astounded: *He was thunderstruck by the news of his promotion.* Also, **thun·der·strick·en** (thŭn′dər-strĭk′ən).

Thu·ner See (tōō′nər zā′). See **Thun, Lake of.**

Thur·ber (thûr′bər), n. **James (Grover),** 1894–1961, U.S. artist and writer.

Thur·gau (tōōr′gou), n. a canton in NE Switzerland. 151,800 pop. (est. 1952); 388 sq. mi. Cap.: Frauenfeld.

thu·ri·ble (thōōr′ə bəl), n. censer. [ME *turrible,* t. L: m. *t(h)uribulum* censer, der. t(h)ūs incense]

thu·ri·fer (thōōr′ə fər), n. one who carries the thurible in religious ceremonies. [t. L: incense-bearing]

Thu·rin·gi·a (thōō rĭn′jĭ ə, -jə), n. a former state in central Germany: formed originally from Thuringian duchies and principalities. German, **Thü·ring·en** (tȳ′-rĭng ən). —**Thu·rin′gi·an,** adj., n.

Thuringian Forest, a forested mountain region in East Germany: a resort region. German, **Thü·ring·er Wald** (tȳ′rĭng ər vält′).

Thurs., Thursday. Also, **Thur.**

Thurs·day (thûrz′dĭ), n. the fifth day of the week, following Wednesday. [ME, t. Scand.; cf. Icel. *Thors-dagr,* c. OE *Thunresdæg,* G *Donnerstag,* day of *Thunor* or *Thor* (trans. of LL *dies Jovis*)]

Thursday Island, a small island in Torres Strait between NE Australia and New Guinea: pearl-fishing center. 2140 pop. (1955). 1¼ sq. mi.

thus (thŭs), adv. 1. in the way just indicated; this way; in the following manner. 2. in accordance with this; accordingly; consequently. 3. to this extent or degree: *thus far.* [ME and OE, c. D *dus*]

thwack (thwăk), v.t. 1. to strike or beat vigorously with something flat; whack. —n. 2. a sharp blow with something flat; whack. [appar. imit.] —**thwack′er,** n.

thwart (thwôrt), v.t. 1. to oppose successfully; prevent from accomplishing a purpose; frustrate (a purpose, etc.); baffle. 2. Archaic. to cross. 3. Archaic. to extend across. —n. 4. a seat across a boat, esp. one used by an oarsman. 5. a transverse member spreading the gunwales of a canoe or the like. See diag. under **gunwale.** —adj. 6. passing or lying crosswise or across; cross; transverse. 7. Archaic. perverse; obstinate. 8. adverse; unfavorable. —prep., adv. 9. across; athwart. [ME *thwert,* adv., t. Scand.; cf. Icel. *thvert* across, neut. of *thverr* transverse, c. OE *thweorh* crooked, cross] —**thwart′er,** n.

—Syn. 1. THWART, FRUSTRATE, BAFFLE imply preventing one, more or less completely, from accomplishing a purpose. THWART and FRUSTRATE apply to purposes, actions, plans, etc.; BAFFLE, to the psychological state of the person himself. THWART suggests stopping one by opposing him, blocking him, or in some way running counter to his efforts. FRUSTRATE implies rendering all attempts or efforts useless or ineffectual, so that nothing ever comes of them. BAFFLE suggests causing defeat by confusing, puzzling, or perplexing, so that a situation seems too hard a problem to understand or solve.

thy (thī), pron., adj. the possessive form corresponding to **thou** and **thee,** used before a noun. Cf. **thine.** [ME, var. of THINE]

Thy·es·tes (thĭ ĕs′tēz), n. Gk. Legend. son of Pelops and brother of Atreus. He seduced his brother's wife, in revenge for which Atreus slew Thyestes' sons and served them to their father at a banquet. —**Thy·es·te·an,** (thĭ ĕs′tĭ ən, thī′ĕs tē′ən). **Thy·es′ti·an,** adj.

thy·la·cine (thī′lə sīn′, -sĭn), n. a carnivorous, wolf-like marsupial, *Thylacinus cynocephalus,* of Tasmania, tan-colored, with black stripes across the back. [t. NL: m.s. *Thylacīnus,* f. s. Gk. *thylakos* pouch + -inus -INE¹]

thyme (tīm), n. any of the plants of the mint family constituting the genus *Thymus,* as *T. vulgaris,* a low sub-shrub with aromatic leaves used for seasoning, or a wild creeping species, *T. Serpyllum* (wild thyme). [ME, t. L: m. *thymum,* t. Gk.: m. *thȳmon*]

thym·e·lae·a·ceous (thĭm′ə lĭ ā′shəs), adj. belonging to the *Thymelaeaceae,* a family of (chiefly) Old World trees, shrubs, and herbs including the mezereon, leatherwood, etc. [f. s. NL *Thymalaeāceae* (der. *Thymelaea* name of species, from Gk.) + -OUS]

thym·ic¹ (tī′mĭk), adj. pertaining to or derived from thyme. [f. THYME + -IC]

thy·mic² (thī′mĭk), adj. of or pertaining to the thymus. [f. THYM(US) + -IC]

thy·mol (thī′mōl, -mŏl), n. Chem. a crystalline phenol, C₁₀H₁₃OH, present in an oil obtained from thyme, used as an antiseptic, etc. [f. THYM(E) + -OL²]

thy·mus (thī′məs), n. Anat. a glandular body or duct-

---

less gland of uncertain function found in vertebrate animals, in man lying in the thorax near the base of the neck and becoming vestigial in the adult. An animal thymus used as food is called *sweetbread*. Also, **thymus gland.** [NL, t. Gk. m. *thýmos*]

thyr-, a combining form of **thyroid,** as in *thyroxine.* Also, before consonants, **thyro-.**

thy·roid (thī′roid), *adj.* **1.** noting or pertaining to the thyroid gland. **2.** noting or pertaining to the principal cartilage of the larynx, forming the projection known in men as "Adam's apple." —*n.* **3.** the thyroid gland. **4.** the thyroid cartilage. **5.** an artery, vein, or the like, of the thyroid region. **6.** a preparation made from the thyroid glands of certain animals, used in treating hypothyroid conditions. [var. of *thyreoid,* t. Gk.: m. *thyreoeídēs* shield shaped] —**thy′roid·less,** *adj.*

thy·roid·ec·to·my (thī′roi děk′tə mǐ), *n., pl.* **-mies.** *Surg.* excision of the whole or a part of the thyroid gland.

thyroid gland, a bilobate ductless gland lying on either side of the windpipe or trachea and connected below the larynx by a thin isthmus of tissue. Its internal secretion is important in regulating the rate of metabolism and, consequently, body growth.

thy·roid·i·tis (thī′roi dī′tǐs), *n. Pathol.* inflammation of the thyroid gland. [NL. See THYROID, -ITIS]

thy·rox·ine (thī rŏk′sēn, -sǐn), *n. Biochem.* the hormone of the thyroid gland (often produced synthetically), C₁₅H₁₁O₄NI₄, used in treating hypothyroidism. Also, **thy·rox·in** (thī rŏk′sǐn). [f. THYR- + OX- + -INE²]

thyr·soid (thûr′soid), *adj. Bot.* having somewhat the form of a thyrsus. Also, **thyr·soi·dal.** [t. Gk.: m.s. *thyrsoeídēs* thyrsuslike]

thyr·sus (thûr′səs), *n., pl.* **-si** (-sī). **1.** *Bot.* Also, **thyrse** (thûrs). a form of mixed inflorescence, as in the lilac, in which the primary ramification is centripetal or indeterminate, and the secondary and successive ramifications are centrifugal or determinate. **2.** *Gk. Myth.* a staff tipped with a pine cone and sometimes twined with ivy and vine branches, borne by Dionysus (Bacchus) and his votaries. [t. L, t. Gk.: m. *thýrsos* Bacchic staff, stem of plant]

thy·sa·nu·ran (thǐ′sə nyŏŏr′ən, -nŏŏr′-, thǐs′ə-), *adj.* **1.** belonging or pertaining to the *Thysanura,* an order of wingless insects with long, filamentous caudal appendages, to which the bristletails belong. —*n.* **2.** a thysanuran insect. [f. s. NL *Thysanūra* (f. Gk.: s. *thýsanos* tassel + m. *ourá* tail) + -AN] —**thy′sa·nu′rous,** *adj.*

thy·self (thǐ sělf′), *pron.* **1.** an emphatic appositive to **thou** or **thee.** **2.** a substitute for reflexive **thee.**

ti¹ (tē), *n. Music.* (in solmization) the syllable corresponding to the seventh note of the diatonic scale; **si.** [substituted for **si** to avoid confusion with the sharp of *sol.* See GAMUT]

ti² (tē), *n., pl.* **tis.** the palmlike plant, *Cordyline australis,* an attractive tropical foliage plant. [t. Polynesian]

Ti, *Chem.* titanium.

Tian Shan (tyän′ shän′), Tien Shan.

ti·ar·a (tī âr′ə, tī är′ə), *n.* **1.** a jeweled ornamental coronet worn by women. **2.** a diadem worn by the Pope, surmounted by the mound (or orb) and cross of sovereignty, and surrounded with three crowns. **3.** the papal position or dignity. **4.** a headdress or turban worn by the ancient Persians and others. [t. L, t. Gk.]

Ti·ber (tī′bər), *n.* a river in central Italy, flowing through Rome into the Mediterranean. 244 mi. Italian, **Tevere.**

Ti·be·ri·as (tī bĭr′ĭ əs), *n.* Sea of. See **Galilee, Sea of.**

Ti·be·ri·us (tī bĭr′ĭ əs), *n.* (*Tiberius Claudius Nero Caesar*) 42 B.C.–A.D. 37, Roman emperor from A.D. 14 to 37.

Ti·bet (tǐ bět′), *n.* a country in S Asia, N of the Himalayas: nominally a dependency of China, it is semi-independent; the highest country in the world. 1,273,969 pop. (1953); ab. 469,400 sq. mi.; average elevation, ab. 16,000 ft. *Cap.:* Lhasa. Also, **Thibet.** Chinese, **Sitsang.**

Ti·bet·an (tǐ bět′ən, tĭb′Yt ən), *adj.* **1.** of or pertaining to Tibet, its inhabitants, or their language. —*n.* **2.** a member of the native Mongolian race of Tibet. **3.** the language of Tibet, a Sino-Tibetan language, esp. its literary standard form. Also, **Thibetan.**

Ti·bet·o-Bur·man (tǐ bět′ō bûr′mən), *n.* a group of Sino-Tibetan languages, including Tibetan and Burmese.

tib·i·a (tǐb′ĭə), *n., pl.* **tibiae** (tǐb′ĭē′), **tibias.** **1.** *Anat.* the shinbone; the inner of the two bones of the lower leg, extending from the knee to the ankle, and articulating with the femur and the astragalus. See diag. under **skeleton. 2.** *Zool.* **a.** a corresponding bone in the hind limb of other animals. **b.** (in insects) the fourth segment of the leg, between the femur and tarsus. See diag. under **coxa.** [t. L: shinbone, flute] —**tib′i·al,** *adj.*

Ti·bul·lus (tǐ bŭl′əs), *n.* **Albius** (ăl′bĭ əs), c54–c19 B.C., Roman poet, noted for his elegies.

Ti·bur (tī′bûr), *n.* ancient name of Tivoli.

tic (tǐk), *n. Pathol.* **1.** tic douloureux. **2.** a sudden, painless, purposeless muscular contraction in the face or extremities, which can be reproduced by the victim of this habit and can be stopped at will. [t. F, t. It.: m. *ticchis;* of Gmc. origin]

ti·cal (tǐ kăl′, -kôl′, tē′kəl), *n., pl.* **-cals, -cal. 1.** a former Siamese unit of weight, equal to 231.5 grains, or about half an ounce. **2.** the monetary unit of Siam until 1928, now supplanted by the baht. **3.** a Siamese silver coin. [t. Siamese, t. Pg., t. Hind.: m. *takā* weight]

tic dou·lou·reux (tǐk′ dōō′lōō rōō′; *Fr.* tĕk′ dōō lōō rœ′), *Pathol.* trifacial or trigeminal neuralgia; paroxysmal darting pain and muscular twitching in the face which may be evoked by rubbing certain points of the face. [t. F: painful tic]

Ti·ci·no (tē chē′nō), *n.* a canton in S Switzerland. 117,700 pop. (est. 1952); 1086 sq. mi. *Cap.:* Bellinzona. German, **Tessin.**

tick¹ (tǐk), *n.* **1.** a slight, sharp recurring click or beat, as of a clock. **2.** *Chiefly Brit. Colloq.* a moment or instant. **3.** a small dot or mark serving as a check or the like. —*v.i.* **4.** to emit or produce a tick, like that of a clock. **5.** to pass as with ticks of a clock: *as the hours ticked by.* —*v.t.* **6.** to sound or announce by a tick or ticks. **7.** *Chiefly Brit.* to mark, note, or check with a tick or ticks. [late ME *tek* little touch, akin to D *tik,* LG *tikk* a touch]

tick² (tǐk), *n.* **1.** any member of a group of large bloodsucking mitelike animals (*Acarina*) of the families *Ixodidae* and *Argasidae,* provided with a barbed proboscis which it buries in the skin of vertebrate animals. **2.** any of the dipterous insects of the family *Hippoboscidae,* often wingless, which are parasitic on certain animals, as sheep, camels, bats, pigeons. [ME *teke, tyke,* OE *ticia* (? mistake for *ticca*). Cf. LG *tieke,* G *zecke*]

Sheep tick.
Melophagus ovinus
(Ab. ¼ in. long)

tick³ (tǐk), *n.* **1.** the cloth case of a mattress, pillow, etc., containing hair, feathers, or the like. **2.** *Colloq.* ticking. [ME *tikke, teke, tyke* (c. D *tijk,* G *zieche*). Cf. L *tēca, thēca,* t. Gk.: m. *thēkē* case]

tick⁴ (tǐk), *n. Colloq.* **1.** a score or account. **2.** *Chiefly Brit.* credit or trust: *to buy on tick.* [short for TICKET]

tick·er (tǐk′ər), *n.* **1.** one who or that which ticks. **2.** a telegraphic instrument which automatically prints stock prices, market reports, etc., on a tape (**ticker tape**). **3.** *Slang.* a watch. **4.** *Slang.* the heart.

tick·et (tǐk′Yt), *n.* **1.** a slip, usually of paper or cardboard, serving as evidence of the holder's title to some service, right, or the like: *a railroad ticket.* **2.** a written or printed slip of paper, cardboard, etc., affixed to something to indicate its nature, price, or the like; a label or tag. **3.** *U.S.* a list of candidates nominated or put forward by a political party, faction, etc., to be voted for. **4.** the license of a ship's officer or of an aviation pilot. **5.** *Banking.* a preliminary recording of transactions prior to their entry in more permanent books of account. **6.** *Colloq.* the correct or proper thing: *that's the ticket.* **7.** *Rare.* a short note, notice, or memorandum. **8.** *Rare.* a placard. —*v.t.* **9.** to attach a ticket to; distinguish by means of a ticket; label. **10.** *U.S.* to furnish with a ticket. [t. F: m. *étiquette* ticket, label. See ETIQUETTE]

ticket of leave, *Brit.* parole for a convict.

ticket-of-leave man, *Brit.* a paroled convict.

tick fever, any fever transmitted by ticks. Some of these fevers, as Rocky Mountain spotted fever, attack man; others, as Texas fever, are confined to some animals, as cattle.

tick·ing (tǐk′Yng), *n.* **1.** a strong cotton fabric, usually twilled, used esp. for ticks. **2.** a similar cloth in satin weave or Jacquard, used esp. for mattress covers. [f. TICK³ + -ING¹]

tick·le (tǐk′əl), *v.,* **-led, -ling,** *n.* —*v.t.* **1.** to touch or stroke lightly with the fingers, a feather, etc., so as to excite a tingling or itching sensation in; titillate. **2.** to poke in some sensitive part of the body so as to excite spasmodic laughter. **3.** to excite agreeably; gratify: *to tickle someone's vanity.* **4.** to excite amusement in. **5.** to get, move, etc., by or as by tickling. —*v.i.* **6.** to be affected with a tingling or itching sensation, as from light touches or strokes. **7.** to produce such a sensation. —*n.* **8.** act of tickling. **9.** a tickling sensation. [ME *tikel(en)*; ? freq. of TICK¹ (in obs. sense) touch lightly]

tick·ler (tǐk′lər), *n.* **1.** one who or that which tickles. **2.** a memorandum book or the like kept to refresh the memory as to appointments, payments due, etc. **3.** *Accounting.* a single-entry account arranged according to the due dates of obligations.

tickler coil, *Radio.* the coil by which the plate circuit of a vacuum tube is inductively coupled with the grid circuit in the process of regeneration.

tick·lish (tǐk′lYsh), *adj.* **1.** sensitive to tickling. **2.** requiring careful handling or action; risky; difficult: *a ticklish situation.* **3.** unstable or easily upset, as a boat; unsteady. —**tick′lish·ly,** *adv.* —**tick′lish·ness,** *n.*

Tick·nor (tǐk′nər, -nôr), *n.* **George,** 1791–1871, U.S. literary historian and educator.

tick·seed (tǐk′sēd′), *n.* **1.** any of various plants having seeds resembling ticks, as a coreopsis or the bugseed. **2.** tick trefoil. [f. TICK² + SEED]

tickseed sunflower, any of various species of bur marigold, esp. *Bidens trichosperma* and *B. coronata,* with conspicuous yellow rays.

tick-tack-toe (tǐk′tăk tō′), *n.* **1.** a commonly played children's game in which two players set down alternately, in the nine compartments of a figure made of crossed lines, the one a cross, and the other a cipher, the object of the game being to be the first to get 3 crosses or 3 ciphers in a row. **2.** a children's game consisting of trying, with the eyes shut, to bring a pencil down upon one of a set of numbers, as on a slate, the number hit being scored. Also, **tick-tack-too** (tĭk/tăk tōō/), **tit-tat-toe**.

tick-tock (tĭk/tŏk/), *n.* **1.** an alternating ticking sound, as that made by a clock. **2.** a device for making a ticking sound, as against a window in playing a practical joke. Also, **tick-tack** (tĭk/tăk). [imit. Cf. TICK[1].]

tick trefoil, any of the plants constituting the leguminous genus *Desmodium,* having trifoliolate leaves and jointed pods with hooked hairs by which they adhere to objects.

Ti·con·der·o·ga (tī/kŏn dər ō/-gə), *n.* a village in NE New York, on Lake Champlain: French fort captured by the English, 1759, and by the Americans under Ethan Allen, 1775. 3,568 (1960).

tid·al (tī/dəl), *adj.* **1.** of, pertaining to, or characterized by tides. **2.** dependent on the state of the tide as to time of departure: *a tidal steamer.*

tidal wave, 1. a large destructive ocean wave produced by an earthquake or the like. **2.** either of the two great wavelike swellings of the ocean surface (due to the attraction of the moon and sun) which move around the earth on opposite sides and give rise to tide. **3.** any widespread or powerful movement, opinion, or the like: *a tidal wave of popular indignation.*

tid·bit (tĭd/bĭt/), *n.* **1.** a delicate bit of food. **2.** a choice or pleasing bit of anything, as news. Also, *esp. Brit.,* **titbit.** [f. TIDE[1] feast day (def. 7) + BIT[2]]

tid·dly·winks (tĭd/lĭ wĭngks/), *n.* a game, the object of which is to snap small disks into a cup placed some distance away. Also, **tid·dle·dy·winks** (tĭd/əl dĭ-wĭngks/).

tide[1] (tīd), *n., v.,* **tided, tiding.** —*n.* **1.** the periodic rise and fall of the waters of the ocean and its inlets, about every 12 hours and 26 minutes, due to the attraction of the moon and sun. **2.** the inflow, outflow, or current of water at any given place resulting from the tidal waves. **3.** the flood tide. **4.** a stream or current. **5.** anything that alternately rises and falls, increases and decreases, etc. **6.** a season or period in the course of the year, day, etc. (now chiefly in compounds): *wintertide.* **7.** *Relig.* a period of time which includes, and follows, an anniversary or festival, etc. **8.** *Archaic.* a suitable time or occasion. **9.** *Obs. or Dial.* an extent of time. —*v.i.* **10.** to flow as the tide; flow to and fro. **11.** to float or drift with the tide. —*v.t.* **12.** to carry, as the tide does. **13.** to get (a person, etc.) over a difficulty, a period of distress, or the like. **14.** to get over (a difficulty, etc.). [ME; OE *tīd,* c. G *zeit* time; akin to TIME] —**tide/less,** *adj.* —**tide/-like/,** *adj.*

tide[2] (tīd), *v.i.,* **tided, tiding.** *Archaic.* to happen or befall. [ME; OE *tīdan, getīdan* happen, der. *tīd* time]

tide·land (tīd/lănd/), *n.* land alternately exposed and covered by the ordinary ebb and flow of the tide.

tide·wait·er (tīd/wā/tər), *n.* (formerly) a customs officer who boarded ships to enforce the customs regulations.

tide·wa·ter (tīd/wô/tər, -wŏt/ər), *n.* **1.** water affected by the flow and ebb of the tide. **2.** the water covering land which is dry at low tide. **3.** seacoast.

tide·way (tīd/wā/), *n.* a channel in which a tidal current runs.

ti·dings (tī/dĭngz), *n.pl.* (sometimes construed as sing.) news, information, or intelligence. [ME; OE *tīdung* (c. G *zeitung* news), der. *tīdan* happen]

ti·dy (tī/dĭ), *adj.,* **-di·er, -di·est,** *v.,* **-died, -dy·ing,** *n., pl.* **-dies.** —*adj.* **1.** neat; trim; orderly: *a tidy room.* **2.** *Colloq.* moderately satisfactory. **3.** *Colloq.* considerable: *a tidy sum.* **4.** *Brit. Colloq.* good of its kind: *that's a tidy question.* —*v.t., v.i.* **5.** to make tidy or neat (often fol. by *up*). —*n.* **6.** any of various articles for keeping things tidy. **7.** *Chiefly U.S.* an ornamental covering for protecting the back of a chair, etc. [ME, der. *tīd* time, c. G *zeitig* timely] —**ti/di·ly,** *adv.* —**ti/di·ness,** *n.* —Syn. **1.** See **neat[1].**

ti·dy·tips (tī/dĭ tĭps/), *n.sing. and pl.* a showy California composite plant, *Layia elegans,* with bright-yellow rays, frequently cultivated as an annual.

tie (tī), *v.,* **tied, tying,** *n.* —*v.t.* **1.** to bind or fasten with a cord, string, or the like, drawn together and knotted. **2.** to draw together the parts of with a knotted string or the like: *to tie a bundle.* **3.** to fasten by tightening and knotting the string or strings of: *to tie one's shoes.* **4.** to draw together into a knot, as a cord. **5.** to form by looping and interlacing, as a knot. **6.** to fasten, join, or connect in any way. **7.** to bind or join closely or firmly. **8.** *Colloq.* to unite in marriage. **9.** to confine, restrict, or limit. **10.** to bind or oblige, as to do something. **11.** to make the same score as; equal in a contest. **12.** *Music.* to connect (notes) by a tie. **13. tie down,**

a. to fasten down by tying. **b.** to hinder; confine. **14. tie up, a.** to fasten securely by tying. **b.** to bind or wrap up. **c.** to hinder. **d.** to bring to a stop or pause. **e.** to invest or place (money) in such a way as to render unavailable. **f.** to place (property) under such conditions or restrictions as to prevent sale or alienation. —*v.i.* **15.** to make a tie, bond, or connection. **16.** to make the same score; be equal in a contest. —*n.* **17.** that with which anything is tied. **18.** a cord, string, or the like, used for tying or fastening something. **19.** a necktie. **20.** a low shoe fastened with a lace. **21.** a knot; an ornamental knot. **22.** anything that fastens, secures, or unites. **23.** a link or connection. **24.** a state of equality in points, votes, etc., as among competitors: *the game ended in a tie.* **25.** a match or contest in which this occurs. **26.** anything, as a beam, rod, etc., connecting or holding together two or more things or parts. **27.** *Music.* a curved line connecting two notes on the same line or space to indicate that the sound is to be sustained for their joint value, not repeated. **28.** *Railroads.* one of the transverse beams, commonly of wood, to which the rails that form a track are fastened; a sleeper. [ME; OE *tīgan* bind, der. *tēag* rope, c. Icel. *taug* rope, *teygja* draw] —Syn. **23.** See **bond.**

Ties (def .27)

tie beam, 1. a timber or piece serving as a tie. **2.** a horizontal beam connecting the lower ends of two opposite principal rafters, forming the base of a roof truss.

tie-in sale (tī/ĭn/), a sale in which the buyer is required to purchase, in addition, some undesired or undesirable item.

Tien Shan (tyœn/ shän/), a mountain system of central Asia, in Sinkiang province, China, and Kirghiz Republic of the Soviet Union. Highest peak, Tengri Khan, ab. 23,950 ft. Also, **Tian Shan.**

Tien·tsin (tĭn/tsĭn/; *Chin.* tyĕn/jĭn/), *n.* a city and port in NE China, in Hopeh. 2,010,000 (est. 1954).

tier[1] (tĭr), *n.* **1.** a row, range, or rank. **2.** one of a series of rows or ranks rising one behind or above another, as of seats in an amphitheater, of boxes in a theater, of guns in a man-of-war, or of oars in an ancient galley. **3.** one of a number of galleries, as in a theater. —*v.t.* **4.** to arrange in tiers. —*v.i.* **5.** to rise in tiers. [t. F: m. *tire* sequence]

ti·er[2] (tī/ər), *n.* **1.** one who or that which ties. **2.** *U.S. Dial.* a child's apron or pinafore. [f. TIE + -ER[1]]

tierce (tĭrs), *n.* **1.** an old measure of capacity equivalent to one third of a pipe, or 42 wine gallons. **2.** a cask or vessel holding this quantity. **3.** Also, **terce.** *Eccles.* the third of the seven canonical hours, or the service for it, orig. fixed for the third hour of the day (or 9 A.M.). **4.** *Fencing.* the third of eight defensive positions. **5.** *Cards.* (esp. in piquet) a sequence of three cards. **6.** *Obs.* a third or third part. [ME *terce,* t. OF, f. L *tertius* third]

Tier·ra del Fue·go (tyĕr/rä dĕl fwē/gō), a group of islands at the S tip of South America, separated from the mainland by the Strait of Magellan, and belonging partly to Argentina (9765 pop. est. 1953; 8074 sq. mi.) and partly to Chile (4071 pop., 1952; 19,402 sq. mi.).

tiers é·tat (tyĕr zĕ tà/), *French.* the third estate.

tie-up (tī/ŭp/), *n.* a stoppage of business, transportation, etc., on account of a strike, storm, accident, etc.

tiff[1] (tĭf), *n.* **1.** a slight or petty quarrel. **2.** a slight fit of ill humor. —*v.i.* **3.** to have a petty quarrel. **4.** to be in a tiff. [orig. uncert.]

tiff[2] (tĭf), *n. Obs.* liquor. [orig. uncert.]

tif·fin (tĭf/ĭn), *n. Brit., from Anglo-Indian use.* **1.** lunch. —*v.i.* **2.** to eat lunch. —*v.t.* **3.** to serve tiffin to. [var. of *tiffing* drinking, der. TIFF[2]]

Tif·lis (tĭf/lĭs; *Russ.* tyĭ flēs/), *n.* a city in the Soviet Union, in Caucasia: capital of the Georgian Republic. 635,000 (est. 1956). Official name, **Tbilisi.**

ti·ger (tī/gər), *n.* **1.** a large, carnivorous feline, *Panthera tigris,* of Asia, tawny-colored, striped with black, ranging in several races from India and the Malay Peninsula to Siberia. **2.** the cougar, jaguar, thylacine, or other animal resembling the tiger. **3.** one who resembles a tiger in fierceness, courage, etc. **4.** one who fights fiercely when aroused. **5.** *U.S.* an additional cheer (often the word *tiger*) at the end of a round of cheering. [ME *tigre,* OE *tīgras* (pl.), t. L: m. *tigris, tigris,* t. Gk.] —**ti/ger·like/,** *adj.*

Tiger. *Panthera tigris*
(Total length ab. 10 ft., tail ab. 3 ft.)

tiger beetle, any beetle of the family *Cicindelidae,* of active, predacious habits.

ti·ger-eye (tī/gər ī/), *n.* **1.** any of various feline quadrupeds smaller than the tiger, but resembling it in markings or ferocity, as the ocelot, etc. **2.** tiger's-eye.

ti·ger·ish (tī/gər ĭsh), *adj.* **1.** tigerlike. **2.** fiercely cruel; bloodthirsty; relentless. Also, **tigrish.**

tiger lily, 1. a lily, *Lilium tigrinum,* with flowers of a dull-orange color spotted with black, and small bulbs or bulbils in the axils of the leaves. **2.** any lily, esp. *L. pardalinum,* of similar coloration.

tiger moth, any of a group of moths (family *Arctiidae*), many of which have conspicuously spotted or striped wings.

ti·ger's-eye (tī/gərz ī/), *n.* a golden-brown chatoyant stone used for ornament, formed by the alteration of crocidolite, and consisting essentially of quartz colored by iron oxide. Also, **tigereye.**

tight (tīt), *adj.* **1.** firmly or closely fixed in place; not easily moved; secure: *a tight knot.* **2.** drawn or stretched so as to be tense; taut. **3.** fitting closely, esp. too closely: *tight trousers.* **4.** difficult to deal with or manage: *to be in a tight place.* **5.** of such close or compacted texture, or fitted together so closely, as to be impervious to water, air, steam, etc. **6.** *Colloq.* close; nearly even: *a tight race.* **7.** *Colloq.* stingy; parsimonious. **8.** *Slang.* drunk; tipsy. **9.** *Com.* (of a commodity) difficult to obtain. **10.** (of the market) characterized by scarcity or eager demand. **11.** *Dial.* competent or skillful. **12.** *Archaic or Dial.* tidy. **13.** *Archaic or Dial.* neatly or well built or made. —*adv.* **14.** in a tight manner; closely; firmly; securely; tensely. [ME, sandhi var. of *thight* dense, solid, c. Icel. *thēttr* tight, D and G *dicht* tight, close, dense] —**tight/ly,** *adv.* —**tight/ness,** *n.*

tight·en (tī/tən), *v.t., v.i.* to make or become tight or tighter. —**tight/en·er,** *n.*

tight-fist·ed (tīt/fĭs/tĭd), *adj.* parsimonious.

tight-lipped (tīt/lĭpt/), *adj.* **1.** having the lips drawn tight. **2.** reluctant to speak.

tight·rope (tīt/rōp/), *n.* a rope stretched tight, on which acrobats perform feats of balancing.

tights (tīts), *n.pl.* a close-fitting garment, usually for the lower part of the body and the legs, worn esp. by dancers, acrobats, gymnasts, etc.

tight·wad (tīt/wŏd/), *n. U.S. Slang.* a close-fisted or stingy person. [f. TIGHT + WAD¹]

Tig·lath-pi·le·ser III (tĭg/lăth pĭ lē/zər, -pī-), died 727 B.C., king of Assyria, 745–727 B.C.

Ti·gré (tē grē/), *n.* a former kingdom in E Africa: now a province in Ethiopia. *Cap.:* Aduwa.

ti·gress (tī/grĭs), *n.* **1.** a female tiger. **2.** a fierce or cruel woman.

Ti·gris (tī/grĭs), *n.* a river flowing from SE Turkey SE through Iraq, joining the Euphrates to empty into the Persian Gulf through the Shatt-al-Arab. ab. 1150 mi.

ti·grish (tī/grĭsh), *adj.* tigerish.

Ti·hwa (dē/hwä/), *n.* Urumchi.

tike (tīk), *n.* tyke.

til (tĭl, tēl), *n.* the plant sesame. [t. Hind.: sesame]

Til·burg (tĭl/bûrg; *Du.* -bœrkH), *n.* a city in S Netherlands, in North Brabant province. 126,939 (est. 1954).

til·bur·y (tĭl/bĕr/ĭ, -bə rĭ), *n., pl.* **-ries.** a light two-wheeled carriage without a top. [named after the inventor]

til·de (tĭl/də), *n.* a diacritical mark (~) placed over a letter, as over the letter *n* in Spanish to indicate a palatal nasal sound (Anglicized as *ny*), as in *cañon.* [t. Sp., ult. t. ML: m. *titulus* TITLE]

Til·den (tĭl/dən), *n.* **Samuel Jones,** 1814–86, U.S. statesman: Democratic candidate for president in the disputed election of 1876.

tile (tīl), *n., v.,* **tiled, tiling.** —*n.* **1.** a thin slab or shaped piece of baked clay, sometimes glazed and ornamented, used for covering roofs, lining walls, paving floors, draining land, in ornamental work, etc. **2.** any of various similar slabs or pieces, as of stone or metal. **3.** tiles collectively. **4.** a pottery tube or pipe used for draining land. **5.** a hollow or cellular block used as a wall unit in masonry construction. **6.** *Colloq.* a stiff hat or a high silk hat. —*v.t.* **7.** to cover with or as with tiles. [ME; OE *tigele,* c. G *ziegel,* both t. L: m. *tēgula*] —**til/er,** *n.* —**tile/like/,** *adj.*

tile·fish (tīl/fĭsh/), *n., pl.* **-fishes,** (*esp. collectively*) **-fish.** a large, brilliantly colored food fish, *Lopholatilus chamaeleonticeps,* of the Atlantic Ocean.

til·i·a·ceous (tĭl/ī ā/shəs), *adj.* belonging to the *Tiliaceae,* or linden family of plants. [t. LL: m. *tiliāceus,* der. L *tilia* lime tree]

til·ing (tī/lĭng), *n.* **1.** the operation of covering with tiles. **2.** tiles collectively. **3.** a tiled surface.

till¹ (tĭl), *prep.* **1.** up to the time of; until: *to fight till death.* **2.** (with a negative) before: *he did not come till today.* **3.** near (a specified time): *till evening.* **4.** *Scot. and N. Eng.* to; unto. —*conj.* **5.** to the time that or when; until. **6.** (with a negative) before. [ME; OE (Northern) *til,* t. Scand.; cf. Icel. *til* to]

till² (tĭl), *v.t.* **1.** to labor, as by plowing, harrowing, etc., upon (land) for the raising of crops; cultivate. **2.** to plow. —*v.i.* **3.** to cultivate the soil. [ME *tille,* OE *tilian* strive, get, c. D *telen* breed, cultivate, G *zielen* aim (at)] —**till/a·ble,** *adj.*

till³ (tĭl), *n.* **1.** a drawer or the like under the back of a counter, as in a shop, in which money is kept. **2.** a drawer, tray, or the like, as in a cabinet or chest, for keeping valuables, etc. [late ME *tylle,* n. use of *tylle,* v., draw (now obs.), OE *tyllan;* akin to L *dolus* trick]

till⁴ (tĭl), *n.* **1.** *Geol.* glacial drift consisting of an unassorted mixture of clay, sand, gravel, and boulders. **2.** a stiff clay. [orig. uncert.]

till·age (tĭl/ĭj), *n.* **1.** the operation, practice, or art of tilling land. **2.** tilled land.

till·land·si·a (tĭl lănd/zĭ ə), *n.* any of the tropical and subtropical American plants constituting the bromeliaceous genus *Tillandsia,* most of which are epiphytic on trees, as Florida moss (*T. usneoides*) which hangs from the branches of trees in long tufts. [t. NL; named after *Tillands,* Swedish botanist]

till·er¹ (tĭl/ər), *n.* one who tills; a farmer. [f. TILL² + -ER¹]

till·er² (tĭl/ər), *n. Naut.* a bar or lever fitted to the head of a rudder, to turn the rudder in steering. [ME *tiler,* t. OF: m. *telier* weaver's beam, der. *teile* cloth, g. L *tēla* web] —**till/er·less,** *adj.*

till·er³ (tĭl/ər), *n.* **1.** a shoot of a plant which springs from the root or bottom of the original stalk. **2.** a sapling. —*v.i.* **3.** (of a plant) to put forth new shoots from the root, or around the bottom of the original stalk. [OE *telgor* twig, shoot]

Til·ly (tĭl/ĭ), *n.* **Count Johan Tserclaes von** (yō/hän tsĕr kläs/ fən), 1559–1632, German general in the Thirty Years' War.

Til·sit (tĭl/zĭt), *n.* a city in the W Soviet Union, on the Memel river: formerly in East Prussia; peace treaty between France, Prussia, and Russia, 1807. Now **Sovetsk.**

tilt¹ (tĭlt), *v.t.* **1.** to cause to lean, incline, slope, or slant. **2.** to hammer or forge with a tilt hammer. **3.** to rush at or charge, as in a joust. **4.** to hold poised for attack, as a lance. —*v.i.* **5.** to move into or assume a sloping position or direction. **6.** to strike, thrust, or charge with a lance or the like (fol. by *at*). **7.** to engage in a joust, tournament, or similar contest. —*n.* **8.** act of tilting. **9.** state of being tilted; a sloping position. **10.** a slope. **11.** a joust or any other contest. **12.** a dispute. **13.** a thrust of a weapon, as at a tilt or joust. **14.** full tilt, with direct and full force. [ME *tylte,* der. OE *tealt* unsteady] —**tilt/er,** *n.*

tilt² (tĭlt), *n.* **1.** a cover of coarse cloth, canvas, etc., as for a wagon. **2.** an awning. —*v.t.* **3.** to furnish with a tilt. [ME, var. of *tild,* OE *teld,* c. G *zelt* tent]

tilth (tĭlth), *n. Brit. and Literary in U.S.* **1.** act or operation of tilling; tillage. **2.** state of being tilled. **3.** the physical condition of soil in relation to plant growth. **4.** tilled .and. [ME and OE, der. OE *tilian* TILL²]

tilt hammer, a drop hammer used in forging, etc., consisting of a heavy head at one end of a pivoted lever.

Tim., Timothy.

tim·bal (tĭm/bəl), *n.* **1.** a kettledrum. **2.** *Entomol.* a vibrating membrane in certain insects, as the cicada. Also, **tymbal.** [t. F: m. *timbale,* aphetic nasalized var. of *attabal,* t. Sp.: m. *atabal* Moorish drum]

tim·bale (tĭm/bəl; *Fr.* tăn bàl/), *n.* **1.** a preparation of minced meat, fish, or vegetables, cooked in a cup-shaped mold. **2.** a small mold of paste, fried and filled with some cooked food. [t. F: kettledrum. See TIMBAL]

tim·ber (tĭm/bər), *n.* **1.** *Chiefly U.S.* the wood of growing trees suitable for structural uses. **2.** *Chiefly U.S.* growing trees themselves. **3.** *Chiefly U.S.* wooded land. **4.** wood, esp. when suitable for building houses, ships, etc., or for use in carpentry, joinery, etc. **5.** a single beam or piece of wood forming, or capable of forming, part of a structure. **6.** *Naut.* (in a ship's frame) one of the curved pieces of wood which spring upward and outward from the keel; a rib. **7.** personal character or quality. —*v.t.* **8.** to furnish with timber. **9.** to support with timber. [ME and OE; orig., building, material for building, c. G *zimmer* room, Icel. *timbr* timber; akin to L *domus* house, Gk. *dómos*] —**tim/ber·less,** *adj.*

tim·bered (tĭm/bərd), *adj.* **1.** made of or furnished with timber. **2.** covered with growing trees; wooded: *timbered acres.*

tim·ber·head (tĭm/bər hĕd/), *n. Naut.* **1.** the top end of a timber, rising above the deck, and serving for belaying ropes, etc. **2.** a bollard resembling this in position and use.

timber hitch, *Naut.* a kind of hitch by which a rope is fastened round a spar.

tim·ber·ing (tĭm/bər ĭng), *n.* **1.** building material of wood. **2.** timberwork.

tim·ber·land (tĭm/bər lănd/), *n. U.S.* land covered with timber-producing forests.

timber line, **1.** the altitude above sea level at which timber ceases to grow. **2.** the arctic or antarctic limit of tree growth.

timber wolf, the large brindled wolf, *Canis lupus lycaon,* of forested Canada and the northern United States.

tim·ber·work (tĭm/bər wûrk/), *n.* work formed of timbers.

Timber wolf,
Canis lupus lycaon
(Total length 4½ to 5½ ft.)

tim·bre (tĭm/bər; *Fr.* tăn/br), *n.* **1.** *Acoustics, Phonet.* that characteristic quality of a sound, independent of pitch and loudness, from which its source or manner of production can be inferred: the saxophone and the clarinet have different timbres, and so do the vowels of *bait* and *boat.* Timbre depends on the relative strengths of the components of different frequencies, which are determined by resonance. **2.** *Music.* the characteristic quality of sound produced by a particular instrument or voice; tone color. [t. F: quality of sound, orig., kind of tambourine, g. L *tympanum,* t. Gk.: m. *týmpanon* timbrel, kettledrum]

tim·brel (tĭm/brəl), *n.* a tambourine or similar instrument. [dim. of ME *timbre.* See TIMBRE]

Tim·buk·tu (tĭm·bŭk′tōō, tĭm′bŭk·tōō′), *n.* **1.** a town in French West Africa, in central French Sudan, near the Niger river. 7000 (1951) French, **Tombouctou.** **2.** any far-away place.

time (tīm), *n., adj., v.,* **timed, timing.** —*n.* **1.** the system of those relations which any event has to any other as past, present, or future; indefinite continuous duration regarded as that in which events succeed one another. **2.** duration regarded as belonging to the present life as distinct from the life to come, or from eternity. **3.** a system or method of measuring or reckoning the passage of time. **4.** a limited extent of time, as between two successive events: *a long time.* **5.** a particular period considered as distinct from other periods: *for the time being.* **6.** (*often pl.*) a period in the history of the world, or contemporary with the life or activities of a notable person: *ancient times.* **7.** (*often pl.*) the period or era now (or then) present. **8.** (*often pl.*) a period considered with reference to its events or prevailing conditions, tendencies, ideas, etc.: *hard times.* **9.** a prescribed or allotted period, as of one's life, for payment of a debt, etc. **10.** a period with reference to personal experience of a specified kind: *to have a good time.* **11.** a period of work of an employee, or the pay for it. **12.** *Colloq.* a term of imprisonment: *to do time.* **13.** the period necessary for or occupied by something: *to ask for time to consider.* **14.** leisure or spare time: *to have no time.* **15.** a particular or definite point in time: *what time is it?* **16.** a particular part of a year, day, etc.: *Christmas time.* **17.** an appointed, fit, due, or proper time: *there is a time for everything.* **18.** the right occasion or opportunity: *to watch one's time.* **19.** each occasion of a recurring action or event: *to do a thing five times.* **20.** (*pl.*) used as a multiplicative word in phrasal combinations expressing how many instances of a quantity or factor are taken together: *four times five.* **21.** *Drama.* one of the three unities. See **unity** (def. 11). **22.** *Pros.* a unit or a group of units in the measurement of meter. **23.** *Music, etc.* **a.** tempo; relative rapidity of movement. **b.** the metrical duration of a note or rest. **c.** proper or characteristic tempo. **d.** the general movement of a particular kind of musical composition with reference to its rhythm, metrical structure, and tempo. **e.** the movement of a dance or the like to music so arranged: *waltz time.* **24.** *Mil.* rate of marching, calculated on the number of paces taken per minute: *double time.* **25.** *Embryol.* **a.** the period of gestation. **b.** the natural termination of that period. **26. at times,** at intervals; occasionally. **27. in time, a.** soon or early enough. **b.** eventually. **c.** following the correct rhythm or tempo. **28. on time, a.** punctually. **b.** for a designated period of time. **c.** involving the extension of credit: *to purchase on time.* **29. time and (time) again,** often; repeatedly: *he warned them time and again to leave before the storm.* —*adj.* **30.** of, pertaining to, or showing the passage of time. **31.** containing a timing device so that it will detonate at the desired moment: *a time bomb.* **32.** *Com.* payable a stated period of time after presentment: *time drafts or notes.* **33.** of or pertaining to purchases with payment postponed. —*v.t.* **34.** to ascertain or record the time, duration, or rate of: *to time a race.* **35.** to fix the duration of. **36.** to regulate as to time, as a train, a clock, etc. **37.** to appoint or choose the moment or occasion for. **38.** to mark the rhythm or measure of, as in music. **39.** *Music.* to classify (notes or syllables) according to meter, accent, rhythm, etc. —*v.i.* **40.** to keep time; sound or move in unison. [ME; OE *tīma,* c. Icel. *tími;* akin to TIDE[1]]

time·card (tīm′kärd′), *n.* a card for recording the time at which an employee arrives and departs.

time clock, a clock with an attachment by which a record may be made of the time of something, as of the arrival and departure of employees.

time deposit, *Banking.* a deposit that can be withdrawn by the depositor only after he has given advance notice or after a period of time agreed upon has elapsed.

time discount, the discount allowed for payment before the invoice or bill is due.

time exposure, *Photog.* any exposure not made automatically by the shutter of the camera.

time-hon·ored (tīm′ŏn′ərd), *adj.* revered or respected because of antiquity and long continuance: *a time-honored custom.*

time immemorial, **1.** a time extending back beyond memory or record. **2.** *Law.* time beyond legal memory, fixed by English statute as prior to the beginning of the reign of Richard I (1189).

time·keep·er (tīm′kē′pər), *n.* **1.** one who or that which keeps time. **2.** one who records time of occurrence or time occupied. **3.** timepiece **4.** a person employed to keep account of the hours of work done by others. **5.** one who beats time in music.

time·less (tīm′lĭs), *adj.* **1.** eternal; unending. **2.** referring to no particular time. —**time′less·ly,** *adv.* —**time′less·ness,** *n.*

time·ly (tīm′lĭ), *adj.,* **-lier, -liest,** *adv.* —*adj.* **1.** occurring at a suitable time; seasonable; opportune; well-timed: *a timely warning.* **2.** *Rare.* early. —*adv.* **3.** seasonably; opportunely. **4.** *Archaic.* early or soon. —**time′li·ness,** *n.* —**Syn.** **1.** See **opportune.**

time·ous (tī′məs), *adj.* *Scot.* **1.** early. **2.** timely.

time out, *Sports.* a short period of rest or deliberation requested by a team during the period of play.

time·piece (tīm′pēs′), *n.* **1.** an apparatus for measuring and recording the progress of time; a chronometer. **2.** a clock or a watch.

tim·er (tī′mər), *n.* **1.** one who or that which times. **2.** one who measures or records time. **3.** a device for indicating or measuring time, as a stop watch. **4.** (in an internal-combustion engine) a set of points actuated by a cam, which causes the spark for igniting the charge at the instant required.

time·sav·ing (tīm′sā′vĭng), *adj.* reducing time required: *timesaving devices or methods.*

time·serv·er (tīm′sûr′vər), *n.* **1.** one who adapts his conduct to conditions. **2.** one who for selfish ends shapes his conduct to conform with the opinions of the time or of persons in power. —**time′serv′ing,** *adj.,n.*

time signature, *Music.* a sign indicating the time of a piece, found after the key signature.

Times Square, a square in central New York City, at Broadway and 42nd Street, around which are many theaters, restaurants, etc.

time·ta·ble (tīm′tā′bəl), *n.* a table or schedule showing the times at or within which certain things occur, esp. one showing the times at which railroad trains, airplanes, etc., arrive and depart.

time·worn (tīm′wôrn′), *adj.* **1.** worn or impaired by time. **2.** showing the ravages or adverse effect of time.

time zone, one of the 24 regions or divisions of the globe approximately coinciding with meridians at successive hours from the observatory at Greenwich, England.

Time zones, United States

tim·id (tĭm′ĭd), *adj.* **1.** subject to fear; easily alarmed; timorous; shy. **2.** characterized by or indicating fear. [t. L: s. *timidus* frightened] —**ti·mid′i·ty,** **tim′id·ness,** *n.* —**tim′id·ly,** *adv.* —**Syn.** **1.** timorous, fearful, faint-hearted. See **cowardly.**

tim·ing (tī′mĭng), *n.* **1.** *Theat.* **a.** a synchronizing of the various parts of a production for theatrical effect. **b.** the result or effect thus achieved. **c.** (in acting) the act of adjusting one's tempo of reading and movement for dramatic effect. **2.** *Sports.* the control of the speed of an action in order that it may reach its height at the proper moment.

Ti·miş·oa·ra (tē′mē·shwä′rä), *n.* a city in W Rumania. 111,987 (1948). Hungarian, **Temesvár.**

ti·moc·ra·cy (tī·mŏk′rə·sĭ), *n., pl.* **-cies.** **1.** a form of government in which love of honor is the dominant motive of the rulers. **2.** a form of government in which a certain amount of property is requisite as a qualification for office. [earlier *timocratie,* t. Gk.: m. *tīmokratia,* der. *tīmē* price, (moral) worth] —**ti·mo·crat·ic** (tī′mə·krăt′ĭk), **ti′mo·crat′i·cal,** *adj.*

Ti·mor (tē′môr), *n.* **1.** an island in the Malay Archipelago: largest and easternmost of Lesser Sunda Islands; divided between Indonesia and Portugal. **2. Dutch,** former name of the W part of this island. 350,064 pop. (1930); 5765 sq. mi. **3. Portuguese,** a Portuguese overseas territory comprising the E part of this island. 475,000 pop. (est. 1956); 7330 sq. mi. *Cap.:* Dili.

tim·or·ous (tĭm′ər·əs), *adj.* **1.** full of fear; fearful. **2.** subject to fear; timid. **3.** characterized by or indicating fear. [late ME, t. ML: m.s. *timōrōsus* fearful, frightened] —**tim′or·ous·ly,** *adv.* —**tim′or·ous·ness,** *n.*

Timor Sea, an arm of the Indian Ocean between Timor and NW Australia.

Ti·mo·shen·ko (tē′mə·shĕng′kô; *Russ.* tē′mō·shĕn′kô), *n.* **Semion Konstantinovich** (sĭ·myōn′ kŏn′stăn·tē′nō·vĭch), born 1895, Soviet general.

Tim·o·thy (tĭm′ə·thĭ), *n.* **1.** a disciple and companion of the apostle Paul, to whom Paul is supposed to have addressed the two New Testament epistles bearing his name. **2.** either of these epistles. [t. L: m.s. *Tīmotheus,* t. Gk.: m. *Tīmotheos,* lit., God-honoring]

tim·o·thy (tĭm′ə·thĭ), *n.* a coarse grass, *Phleum pratense,* with cylindrical spikes, valuable as fodder. Also, **timothy grass.** [named after the man who first cultivated it]

Ti·mour (tĭ·mōōr′), *n.* See **Tamerlane.** Also, **Ti·mur.**

tim·pa·ni (tĭm′pə·nē′), *n. pl., sing.* **-no** (-nō′). kettledrums. [t. It., g. L *tympanum,* t. Gk.: m. *týmpanon*] —**tim′pa·nist,** *n.*

tin (tĭn), *n.*, *adj.*, *v.*, **tinned, tinning.** —*n.* **1.** *Chem.* a low-melting, metallic element nearly approaching silver in color and luster, used in making alloys and in plating. *Symbol:* Sn (for *stannum*); *at. wt.*: 118.70; *at. no.*: 50; *sp. gr.*: 7.31 at 20°C. **2.** tin plate. **3.** *Chiefly Brit.* a pot, pan, can, or box made of tin or tin plate which is hermetically sealed to preserve the contents. **4.** *Slang.* money. —*adj.* **5.** made or consisting of tin or tin plate. **6.** mean; worthless; counterfeit. **7.** indicating the tenth event of a series, as a wedding anniversary. —*v.t.* **8.** to cover or coat with a thin deposit of tin. **9.** *Chiefly Brit.* to put up, pack, or preserve in tins, as foodstuffs; can. [ME and OE, c. G *zinn*] —**tin′like′,** *adj.*

tin·a·mou (tĭn′ə·mōō′), *n.* any of a group of birds (family *Tinemidae*), of South and Central America, superficially resembling the gallinaceous birds but more primitive, and hunted as game. [t. F, t. S Amer. Ind.: m. *tinamu*]

tin·cal (tĭng′kăl, -kôl), *n.* crude native borax (the Oriental name). [t. Malay: m. *tingkal*]

tinct (tĭngkt), *v.t.* **1.** *Obs.* to tinge or tint, as with color. **2.** *Obs.* to imbue. —*adj.* **3.** *Poetic.* tinged; colored; flavored. —*n.* **4.** *Obs.* tint; tinge; coloring. [t. L: s. *tinctus*, pp., colored, tinged]

tinct., tincture.

tinc·to·ri·al (tĭngk·tōr′Yəl), *adj.* pertaining to coloring or dyeing.

tinc·ture (tĭngk′chər), *n.*, *v.*, **-tured, -turing.** —*n.* **1.** *Pharm.* a solution of a medicinal substance in alcohol (or sometimes in a mixture of alcohol and ammonia or ether), prepared by maceration, digestion, or percolation. **2.** a slight infusion, as of some element of quality. **3.** a trace; a smack or smattering. **4.** *Her.* any of the metals, colors, or furs used in coats of arms, etc. **5.** *Obs.* a dye or pigment. —*v.t.* **6.** to impart a tincture or color to; tinge. **7.** to imbue or impregnate with something. [ME, t. L: m. *tinctūra* dyeing, tingeing]

tin·der (tĭn′dər), *n.* **1.** a material or preparation formerly used for catching the spark from a flint and steel struck together for fire or light. **2.** any dry substance that readily takes fire from a spark. [ME; OE *tynder*, c. G *zunder*] —**tin′der·like′,** *adj.*

tin·der·box (tĭn′dər·bŏks′), *n.* **1.** a box for holding tinder, usually fitted with a flint and steel. **2.** a highly inflammable, excitable, etc., person or thing.

tine (tīn), *n.* a sharp projecting point or prong, as in a fork. [ME *tyne*, var. of ME *tind*, c. MHG *zint*]

tin·e·a (tĭn′Yə), *n.* *Pathol.* any of several skin diseases caused by fungi. [NL, in L gnawing worm]

tin·e·id moth (tĭn′Yĭd), any moth of the family *Tineidae*, as the clothes moth.

tin foil, tin, or an alloy of tin and lead, in the form of a thin sheet, much used as a wrapping for drugs, confectionery, tobacco, etc.

ting (tĭng), *v.t.*, *v.i.* **1.** to cause to make, or to make, a high clear, ringing sound. —*n.* **2.** a tinging sound. [imit.]

tinge (tĭnj), *v.*, **tinged, tingeing or tinging,** *n.* —*v.t.* **1.** to impart a trace or slight degree of some color to; tint. **2.** to impart a slight taste or smell to. —*n.* **3.** a slight degree of coloration. **4.** a slight admixture, as of some qualifying property or characteristic. [late ME, t. L: m.s. *tingere* dye, color]

tin·gle (tĭng′gəl), *v.*, **-gled, -gling,** *n.* —*v.i.* **1.** to have a sensation of slight stings or prickly pains, from a sharp blow or from cold. **2.** to cause such a sensation. —*n.* **3.** a tingling sensation. **4.** the tingling action of cold, etc. [ME; appar. var. of TINKLE] —**tin′gler,** *n.* —**tin′gling·ly,** *adv.*

tin hat, *Colloq.* a steel helmet worn by soldiers.

tink·er (tĭngk′ər), *n.* **1.** *Chiefly Brit.* a mender of pots, kettles, pans, etc., usually an itinerant. **2.** an unskillful or clumsy worker; a bungler. **3.** one skilled in various minor kinds of mechanical work; a jack of all trades. **4.** an act or instance of tinkering. **5.** a small species of mackerel, *Pneumatophorus grex*, of the Atlantic coast of the U.S. —*v.i.* **6.** to do the work of a tinker. **7.** to work unskillfully or clumsily at anything. **8.** to busy oneself with a thing without useful results. —*v.t.* **9.** to mend as a tinker. **10.** to repair in an unskillful, clumsy, or makeshift way. [syncopated var. of earlier *tinekere* worker in tin] —**tink′er·er,** *n.*

tinker's damn, *Slang.* something worthless: *not to care a tinker's damn.* Also, **tinker's dam.**

tin·kle (tĭng′kəl), *v.*, **-kled, -kling,** —*v.i.* **1.** to give forth or make a succession of short, light, ringing sounds. —*v.t.* **2.** to cause to tinkle or jingle. **3.** to make known, call attention to, attract, or summon by tinkling. —*n.* **4.** a tinkling sound. **5.** act of tinkling. [ME; freq. of obs. *tink*, v., make a metallic sound; imit.] —**tin′kler,** *n.* —**tin′kling,** *n.*, *adj.*

tin·man (tĭn′mən), *n.*, *pl.* **-men.** tinsmith.

tin·ner (tĭn′ər), *n.* tinsmith.

tin·ni·tus (tĭ·nī′təs), *n.* *Pathol.* a ringing or similar sensation of sound in the ears, due to disease of the auditory nerve, etc. [t. L: a ringing]

tin·ny (tĭn′Y), *adj.*, **-nier, -niest. 1.** of or like tin. **2.** containing tin. **3.** characteristic of tin, as sounds. **4.** not strong or durable. **5.** having the taste of tin. —**tin′ni·ly,** *adv.* —**tin′ni·ness,** *n.*

tin-pan alley (tĭn′păn′), **1.** the district of a city, esp. of New York City, where most of the popular music is published. **2.** the composers of popular music as a group.

tin plate, thin sheet iron or sheet steel coated with tin.

tin-plate (tĭn′plāt′), *v.t.*, **-plated, -plating.** to plate (sheet iron or steel) with tin.

tin·sel (tĭn′səl), *n.*, *adj.*, *v.*, **-seled, -seling or** (*esp. Brit.*) **-selled, -selling.** —*n.* **1.** a glittering metallic substance, as copper, brass, etc., in thin sheets, used in pieces, strips, threads, etc., to produce a sparkling effect without much cost. **2.** a metallic yarn usually wrapped around a core yarn of silk, rayon, or cotton, for weaving brocade or lamé. **3.** anything showy or attractive with little or no real worth; showy pretense. **4.** *Obs.* a fabric of silk or wool interwoven with threads of gold, silver, or (later) copper. —*adj.* **5.** consisting of or containing tinsel. **6.** showy; gaudy; tawdry. —*v.t.* **7.** to adorn with tinsel. **8.** to adorn with anything glittering. **9.** to make showy or gaudy. [t. F: m. *étincelle* spark, flash, g. L *scintilla*] —**tin′sel·like′,** *adj.*

tin·smith (tĭn′smĭth′), *n.* one who works in or with tin; a maker of tinware.

tin·stone (tĭn′stōn′), *n.* cassiterite.

tint (tĭnt), *n.* **1.** a color, or a variety of a color; hue. **2.** a color diluted with white; a color of less than maximum chroma, purity, or saturation (as opposed to a *shade*, which is produced by adding black). **3.** a delicate or pale color. **4.** *Engraving.* a uniform shading, as that produced by series of fine parallel lines. **5.** *Print.* a faintly or lightly colored background upon which an illustration or the like is to be printed. —*v.t.* **6.** to apply a tint or tints to; color slightly or delicately; tinge. [var. of TINCT] —**tint′er,** *n.*

Tin·tag·el Head (tĭn·tăj′əl), a cape in SW England, on the W coast of Cornwall: ruins of **Tintagel Castle,** the legendary birthplace of K'ing Arthur.

tin·tin·nab·u·lar (tĭn′tĭ·năb′yə·lər), *adj.* of or pertaining to bells or bell ringing. Also, **tin·tin·nab·u·lar·y** (tĭn′tĭ·năb′yə·lĕr′Y), **tin·tin·nab′u·lous.** [f. s. L *tin-tinnābulum* bell + -AR¹]

tin·tin·nab·u·la·tion (tĭn′tĭ·năb′yə·lā′shən), *n.* the ringing or sound of bells.

Tin·to·ret·to (tēn′tō·rĕt′tō), *n.* **Il** (ēl), (*Jacopo Robusti*) 1518–94, Venetian painter.

tin·type (tĭn′tīp′), *n.* a photograph (in the form of a positive) taken on a sensitized sheet of enameled tin or iron; a ferrotype.

tin·ware (tĭn′wâr′), *n.* articles made of tin plate.

tin·work (tĭn′wûrk′), *n.* **1.** something made of tin. **2.** (*pl.*, *usually construed as sing.*) an establishment for the mining or manufacture of tin or for the making of tinware.

ti·ny (tī′nY), *adj.*, **-nier, -niest.** very small; minute; wee. [f. obs. *tine* very small (of unknown orig.) + -Y¹]

-tion, a suffix used to form abstract nouns from verbs or stems not identical with verbs, whether as expressing action (*revolution, commendation*), or a state (*contrition, starvation*), or associated meanings (*relation, temptation*). Also, **-ation, -cion, -ion, -sion, -xion.** [t. L: s. *-tio* (f. *-t.* pp. stem ending, + *-io*, noun suffix); also repr. F *-tion*, G *-tion*, etc., from L]

tip¹ (tĭp), *n.*, *v.*, **tipped, tipping.** —*n.* **1.** a slender or pointed extremity, esp. of anything long or tapered: *the tips of the fingers.* **2.** the top, summit, or apex. **3.** a small piece or part, as of metal or leather, forming the extremity of something. —*v.t.* **4.** to furnish with a tip. **5.** to serve as or form the tip of. **6.** to mark or adorn the tip of. [ME *typ*, c. D and LG *tip*] —**tip′less,** *adj.*

tip² (tĭp), *v.*, **tipped, tipping,** *n.* —*v.t.* **1.** to cause to assume a slanting or sloping position; incline; tilt. **2.** to overthrow, overturn, or upset (often fol. by *over*). **3.** to take off (the hat) in salutation. —*v.i.* **4.** to assume a slanting or sloping position; incline. **5.** to tilt up at one end and down at the other. **6.** to be overturned or upset. **7.** to tumble or topple (fol. by *over*). —*n.* **8.** act of tipping. **9.** state of being tipped. [ME *tipe*; orig. uncert.]

tip³ (tĭp), *n.*, *v.*, **tipped, tipping.** —*n.* **1.** a small present of money. **2.** a piece of private or secret information, as for use in betting, speculation, etc. **3.** a useful hint or idea. —*v.t.* **4.** to give a small present of money to. **5.** *Colloq.* to give private or secret information about (something), as for use in betting, speculation, etc. (often fol by *off*). —*v.i.* **6.** to give a gratuity or fee. **7.** *Colloq.* to furnish private or secret information, as for use in betting, speculation, etc. [orig. unknown]

tip⁴ (tĭp), *n.*, *v.*, **tipped, tipping.** —*n.* **1.** a light, smart blow; a tap. —*v.t.* **2.** to strike or hit with a light, smart blow; tap. **3.** *Baseball, etc.* to strike (the ball) obliquely with a slanting bat. [? akin to TAP. Cf. G *tippen* tap]

tip-cart (tĭp′kärt′), *n.* a cart with a body that can be tipped or tilted to discharge the contents.

tip-cat (tĭp′kăt′), *n.* **1.** a short piece of wood tapering at both ends (the cat), used in a game in which it is struck lightly at one end with a stick so as to make it spring up, and while in the air is struck again for the purpose of driving it as far as possible. **2.** the game.

ti·pi (tē′pē), *n.*, *pl.* **-pis.** tepee.

tip-off (tĭp′ôf′, -ŏf′), *n.* **1.** act of tipping off. **2.** state of being tipped off. **3.** a hint or warning: *they got a tip-off on the raid.*

Tip·pe·ca·noe (tĭp/ə·kə·nōō/), n. 1. a river in N Indiana, flowing SW to the Wabash: battle with the Indians, 1811. ab. 200 mi. 2. a nickname of William Henry Harrison, from his victory near the Tippecanoe river.

tip·per (tĭp/ər), n. one who or that which tips.

Tip·per·ar·y (tĭp/ə·râr/ĭ), n. 1. a county in S Ireland, in Munster province. 129,231 (prelim. 1956); 1643 sq. mi. *Co. seat:* Clonmel. 2. a town in this county. 5148 (1951).

tip·pet (tĭp/ĭt), n. 1. a scarf, usually of fur or wool, for covering the neck, or the neck and shoulders, and usually having ends hanging down in front. 2. *Eccles.* a band of silk or the like worn round the neck with the ends pendent in front. 3. *Hist.* a long, narrow, pendent part of a hood, sleeve, etc. [ME; appar. der. TIP¹]

tip·ple¹ (tĭp/əl), v., **-pled, -pling,** n. —v.t. 1. to drink (intoxicating liquor), esp. repeatedly, in small quantities. —v.i. 2. to drink intoxicating liquor, esp. habitually or to some excess. —n. 3. intoxicating liquor. [orig. uncert.; appar. akin to TIP², TIPPLE². Cf. Norw. *tipla* drink little and often] —**tip/pler,** n.

tip·ple² (tĭp/əl), n. *U.S.* 1. a device which tilts or overturns a freight car to dump its contents. 2. a place where loaded cars are emptied by tipping. [der. *tipple,* v., freq. of TIP²]

tip·staff (tĭp/stăf/, -stäf/), n., pl. **-staves** (-stāvz/, -stävz/, -stävz/), **-staffs.** 1. an attendant or crier in a court of law. 2. a staff tipped with metal, formerly carried as a badge of office, as by a constable. 3. any official who carried such a staff.

tip·ster (tĭp/stər), n. *Colloq.* one who makes a business of furnishing tips, as for use in betting, speculation, etc.

tip·sy (tĭp/sĭ), adj., **-sier, -siest.** 1. slightly intoxicated. 2. characterized by or due to intoxication: *a tipsy lurch.* 3. tipping, unsteady, or tilted, as if from intoxication. [appar. der. TIP² in obs. sense of intoxicate] —**tip/si·ly,** adv. —**tip/si·ness,** n.

tip·toe (tĭp/tō/), n., v., **-toed, -toeing,** adj., adv. —n. 1. the tip or end of a toe. 2. **on tiptoe, a.** on the tips of the toes collectively: *to walk on tiptoe.* **b.** eagerly expectant. **c.** cautious; stealthy. —v.i. 3. to move or go on tiptoe, as with caution or stealth. —adj. 4. characterized by standing or walking on tiptoe. 5. straining upward. 6. eagerly expectant. 7. cautious; stealthy. —adv. 8. on tiptoe.

tip·top (tĭp/tŏp/), n. 1. the extreme top or summit. 2. *Colloq.* the highest point or degree, as of excellence. —adj. 3. situated at the very top. 4. *Colloq.* of the highest quality or excellence: *in tiptop condition.* [f. TIP¹ end + TOP highest point; or varied redupl. of TOP]

ti·rade (tī/rād, tə·rād/), n. 1. a prolonged outburst of denunciation. 2. a long, vehement speech. 3. a passage dealing with a single theme or idea, as in poetry. [t. F: draught, shot, t. It.: m. *tirata* volley, der. *tirare* draw]

ti·rail·leur (tē/rä·yœr/), n. French. skirmisher; sharpshooter.

Ti·ra·na (tē·rä/nə), n. the capital of Albania, in the central part. 80,000 (est. 1949). Albanian, **Ti·ra/në.**

tire¹ (tīr), v., **tired, tiring,** n. —v.t. 1. to reduce or exhaust the strength of, as by exertion; make weary; fatigue. 2. to exhaust the interest, patience, etc., of, as by long continuance or by dullness; make weary (fol. by *of*). —v.i. 3. to have the strength reduced or exhausted, as by labor or exertion; become fatigued. 4. to have one's appreciation, interest, patience, etc., exhausted; become or be weary (fol. by *of*). —n. 5. *Dial.* fatigue. [ME *tyre*, OE *tyrian;* of unknown orig.]

tire² (tīr), n., v., **tired, tiring.** —n. 1. a hoop or band of metal, rubber, air-filled rubber tube, or the like, placed around a wheel of a vehicle to form the tread. —v.t. 2. to furnish with a tire or tires. Also, *Brit.,* **tyre.** [late ME *tyre;* special use of TIRE³]

tire³ (tīr), v., **tired, tiring,** n. *Archaic.* —v.t. 1. to attire or array. 2. to dress (the head or hair), esp. with a headdress. —n. 3. attire or dress. 4. a headdress. [ME; aphetic var. of ATTIRE]

tired¹ (tīrd), adj. 1. exhausted, as by exertion; fatigued. 2. weary (fol. by *of*). 3. *Colloq.* impatient or disgusted: *you make me tired!* [f. TIRE¹ + -ED²] —**tired/ly,** adv. —**tired/ness,** n.

—**Syn.** 1. TIRED, EXHAUSTED, FATIGUED, WEARIED, WEARY suggest a condition in which a large part of one's energy and vitality has been consumed. One who is TIRED has used up a considerable part of his bodily or mental resources: *to feel tired at the end of the day.* One who is EXHAUSTED is completely drained of energy and vitality, usually because of arduous or long-sustained effort: *exhausted after a hard run.* One who is FATIGUED has consumed energy to a point where rest and sleep are demanded: *feeling rather pleasantly fatigued.* One who is WEARIED has been under protracted exertion or strain which has gradually worn out his strength: *wearied by a long vigil.* WEARY suggests a more permanent condition than WEARIED: *weary of struggling against misfortunes.* —**Ant.** 1. rested, refreshed.

tire² (tīrd), adj. having a tire or tires. [f. TIRE² + -ED²]

tire·less (tīr/lĭs), adj. untiring; indefatigable: *a tireless worker.* —**tire/less·ly,** adv. —**tire/less·ness,** n.

Ti·re·si·as (tī·rē/sĭ·əs, -shĭ/əs), n. *Gk. Legend.* a Theban seer blinded by Athena, whom he saw bathing. She relented, and gave him prophetic vision.

tire·some (tīr/səm), adj. 1. such as to tire one; wearisome. 2. annoying or vexatious. —**tire/some·ly,** adv. —**tire/some·ness,** n. —**Syn.** See tedious.

tire·wom·an (tīr/wŏm/ən), n., pl. **-women.** *Archaic.* a lady's maid. [see TIRE³]

Ti·rich Mir (tē/rĭch mēr/), a mountain in Pakistan: highest peak of the Hindu Kush Mountains. 25,230 ft.

tir·ing room (tīr/ĭng), *Archaic.* a dressing room, esp. in a theater. [aphetic var. of *attiring room*]

ti·ro (tī/rō), n., pl. **-ros.** tyro.

Tir·ol (tĭr/ŏl; *Ger.* tē·rōl/), n. Tyrol. —**Tir·o·lese** (tĭr/ə·lēz/, -lēs/), **Ti·ro·le·an** (tĭ·rō/lĭ·ən), adj., n.

Tir·pitz (tĭr/pĭts), n. **Alfred von** (äl/frät fən), 1849–1930, German admiral and statesman.

tir·ri·vee (tĭr/ə·vē/), n. *Scot.* a tantrum.

Tir·so de Mo·li·na (tēr/sō dĕ mō·lē/nä), (*Gabriel Téllez*) 1571?–1648, Spanish dramatist.

Tir·u·chi·ra·pal·li (tĭr/ōō·chĭ/rə·pŭl/ĭ), n. a city in S India, in Madras state, on the Cauvery river. 218,921 (1951). Formerly, **Trichinopoly.**

'tis (tĭz), contraction of *it is.*

ti·sane (tĭ·zăn/; *Fr.* tē·zän/), n. *Obs.* a ptisan. [t. F: barley water. See PTISAN]

Tish·ri (tĭsh/rĭ), n. (in the Jewish calendar) the first month of the year. [t. Heb.]

Ti·siph·o·ne (tī·sĭf/ə·nē/), n. *Gk. Myth.* one of the Furies.

Tis·sot (tē·sō/), n. **James Joseph Jacques** (zhám zhō·zĕf/ zhäk), 1836–1902, French painter.

tis·sue (tĭsh/ōō), n., v., **-sued, -suing.** —n. 1. *Biol.* **a.** the substance of which an organism or part is composed. **b.** an aggregate of cells and cell products forming a definite kind of structural material in an animal or plant: *muscular tissue.* 2. a woven fabric, esp. one of light or gauzy texture, orig. woven with gold or silver. 3. an interwoven or interconnected series or mass: *a tissue of falsehoods.* 4. tissue paper. —v.t. *Rare.* 5. to weave, esp. with threads of gold or silver. 6. to clothe or adorn with tissue. [ME, t. OF: m. *tissu* rich kind of cloth, pp. of *tistre* weave, g. L *texere*]

tissue culture, 1. the science of cultivating animal tissue in a prepared medium. 2. the process itself.

tissue paper, a very thin, almost transparent paper used for wrapping delicate articles, covering illustrations in books, copying letters, etc.

Ti·sza (tē/sŏ), n. a river flowing from the Carpathian Mts. through E Hungary and NE Yugoslavia into the Danube N of Belgrade. ab. 800 mi. German, **Theiss.**

tit¹ (tĭt), n. 1. a titmouse. 2. any of various other small birds. 3. *Archaic or Dial.* a girl or young woman. 4. *Chiefly Dial.* a small or poor horse. [ME *tit-,* c. Icel. *tittr* titmouse, d. Norw. *titta* little girl]

tit² (tĭt), n. teat. [ME and OE, c. G. *zitze,* MD, LG *titte*]

Ti·tan (tī/tən), n. 1. *Gk. Myth.* **a.** one of a family of primordial deities, the children of Uranus (heaven) and Gaea (earth), conceived as lawless beings of gigantic size and enormous strength, who overthrew Uranus, the ruler of the world, and raised Cronus, one of their number, to the throne, but were themselves overcome and cast into Tartarus by Zeus, the son of Cronus. **b.** the sun god, Helios (Sol), son of the Titan Hyperion. 2. a person or thing of enormous size, strength, etc. —adj. 3. titanic; gigantic. Also, **titan** for 2, 3. [t. Gk.] —**Ti·tan·ess** (tī/tən·ĭs), n. fem.

ti·tan·ate (tī/tə·nāt/), n. *Chem.* a salt of titanic acid (def. 2).

Ti·tan·esque (tī/tə·nĕsk/), adj. Titanlike; Titanic.

Ti·ta·ni·a (tī·tā/nĭ·ə, tī-), n. (in Shakespeare's *Midsummer Night's Dream*) the wife of Oberon and queen of fairyland.

Ti·tan·ic (tī·tăn/ĭk), adj. 1. of, pertaining to, or characteristic of the Titans. 2. Also, **titanic.** of enormous size, strength, etc.; gigantic. [f. TITAN + -IC]

ti·tan·ic (tī·tăn/ĭk, tī-), adj. *Chem.* of or containing titanium, esp. in the tetravalent state (Ti⁺⁴). [f. TITAN(IUM) + -IC]

titanic acid, *Chem.* 1. titanic oxide. 2. any of various acids derived from it.

titanic oxide, *Chem.* the dioxide of titanium, TiO_2. Also, **titanium dioxide.**

ti·tan·if·er·ous (tī/tə·nĭf/ər·əs), adj. containing or yielding titanium. [f. TITANI(UM) + -FEROUS]

Ti·tan·ism (tī/tə·nĭz/əm), n. the characteristic Titan spirit or quality, esp. of revolt against tradition, convention, and established order.

ti·tan·ite (tī/tə·nīt/), n. sphene. [der. TITANIUM]

ti·ta·ni·um (tī·tā/nĭ·əm, tī-), n. *Chem.* a metallic element occurring combined in various minerals, and isolated as a dark-gray powder with a metallic luster and an ironlike appearance. It is used in metallurgy to remove oxygen and nitrogen from steel and to toughen it. *Symbol:* Ti; *at. wt.:* 47.90; *at. no.:* 22; *sp. gr.:* 4.5 at 20°C. [f. TITAN + -IUM]

Ti·tan·om·a·chy (tī/tə·nŏm/ə·kĭ), n. *Gk. Myth.* the revolt of the Titans.

Ti·tan·o·sau·rus (tī/tə·nə·sôr/əs), n. *Paleontol.* a South American dinosaur (genus *Titanosaurus*) of the Cretaceous era. Also, **ti·tan·o·saur/.** [t. NL: f. *Titano-* (t. Gk., comb. form of *Tītān* Titan) + -saurus -SAURUS]

ti·tan·ous (tī/tən·əs, tī-), adj. *Chem.* containing trivalent titanium (Ti⁺³).

tit·bit (tĭt/bĭt/), n. *Chiefly Brit.* tidbit.

ti·ter (tī/tər, tē/-), n. *Chem.* 1. the amount of a substance by volume or weight, which exactly fulfills certain given requirements in titration. 2. the strength of a standard solution used in titration. Also, *esp. Brit.,* **titre.** [t. F: m. *titre* fineness, strength, t. L: m. *titulus* title]

tit for tat, blow for blow; an equivalent given in retaliation, repartee, etc. [? var. of earlier *tip for tap*]

tith·a·ble (tī′t͟hə bəl), *adj.* liable to be tithed; subject to the payment of tithes.

tithe (tīt͟h), *n., v.,* **tithed, tithing.** —*n.* **1.** (*often pl.*) the tenth part of the annual produce of agriculture, etc., due or paid as a tax for the support of the priesthood, religious institutions, etc. **2.** any tax, levy, or the like, of one tenth. **3.** a tenth part, or any indefinitely small part, of anything. [ME *ti(ghe)the,* OE *teogotha* tenth] —*v.t.* **4.** to give or pay a tithe or tenth of (produce, earnings, etc.). **5.** to pay tithes on. **6.** to exact a tithe from (a person, etc.). **7.** to levy a tithe on (produce, goods, etc.). —*v.i.* **8.** to give or pay a tithe. Also, *Brit.,* **tythe.** [ME *tithen,* OE *te(o)g(o)thian,* v., der. *teogotha* tenth part] —**tithe′less,** *adj.* —**tith′er,** *n.*

tith·ing (tī′t͟hĭng), *n.* **1.** a tithe. **2.** a giving or exacting of tithes. **3.** a company of householders, orig. ten in number, in the old English system of frankpledge. **4.** a rural division in England, orig. regarded as one tenth of a hundred, descended from this system. [ME: OE *tigething,* der. *teogotha* TITHE]

Ti·tho·nus (tī t͟hō′nəs), *n. Gk. Myth.* a son of Laomedon, beloved by Eos (Aurora). He asked and was granted immortality, but finding himself immortally old he asked Eos to take back her gift and was metamorphosed into a grasshopper.

ti·ti[1] (tē tē′), *n., pl.* **-tis.** any of various small reddish or grayish monkeys of the genus *Callicebus* of South America. [native name; orig. uncert.]

ti·ti[2] (tē′tē), *n., pl.* **-tis.** any of the cyrillaceous shrubs or small trees of the southern U.S., esp. *Cliftonia monophylla* (**black titi**) and *Cyrilla racemiflora* (**white titi**), with glossy leaves and racemes of white flowers. [t. S Amer. Sp., t. Aymara]

ti·tian (tĭsh′ən), *n.* a yellowish- or golden-brown color made famous by Titian.

Ti·tian (tĭsh′ən), *n.* (*Tiziano Vecellio*) c1477–1576, Italian painter.

Ti·ti·ca·ca (tē′tē kä′kä), *n.* Lake, a lake in the Andes between S Peru and W Bolivia: the largest in South America, and the highest large lake in the world. ab. 3500 sq. mi.; 12,508 ft. high.

tit·il·late (tĭt′ə lāt′), *v.t.,* **-lated, -lating. 1.** to tickle; excite a tingling or itching sensation in, as by touching or stroking lightly. **2.** to excite agreeably: *to titillate the fancy.* [t. L: m.s. *titillātus* tickled] —**tit·il·la′tion,** *n.* —**tit′il·la′tive,** *adj.*

tit·i·vate (tĭt′ə vāt′), *v.,* **-vated, -vating.** *Colloq.* —*v.t.* **1.** to make smart or spruce. —*v.i.* **2.** to make oneself smart or spruce. Also, **tittivate.** [earlier *tidivate,* ? der. *tidy,* modeled on CULTIVATE] —**tit′i·va′tion,** *n.* —**tit·i·va′tor,** *n.*

tit·lark (tĭt′lärk′), *n.* any of various small larklike birds, esp. of the genus *Anthus,* as *A. spinoletta,* a migratory bird of northern parts of both the New and Old Worlds. [f. TIT[1] + LARK[1]]

ti·tle (tī′təl), *n., v.,* **-tled, -tling.** —*n.* **1.** the distinguishing name of a book, poem, picture, piece of music, or the like. **2.** a descriptive heading or caption, as of a chapter, section, or other part of a book. **3.** a title page. **4.** a descriptive or distinctive appellation, esp. one belonging to a person by right of rank, office, attainment, etc. **5.** *Sports.* the championship: *he lost the title.* **6.** established or recognized right to something. **7.** a ground for a claim. **8.** anything affording ground for a claim. **9.** *Law.* a. legal right to the possession of property, esp. real property. **b.** the ground or evidence of such right. **c.** the instrument constituting evidence of such right. **d.** a unity combining all the requisites to complete legal ownership. **e.** a division of a statute, lawbook, etc., esp. one larger than an article or section. **f.** (in pleading) the designation of one's basis for judicial relief; the cause of action sued upon, as contract, tort, etc. **10.** *Eccles.* **a.** a fixed sphere of work and source of income, required as a condition of ordination. **b.** any of certain Catholic churches in Rome, the nominal incumbents of which are cardinals. —*v.t.* **11.** to furnish with a title; designate by an appellation; entitle. [ME. t. OF, t. L: m. *titulus*; r. OE *titul,* t. L: s. *titulus*] —**Syn. 1, 4.** See **name.**

ti·tled (tī′təld), *adj.* having a title, esp. of nobility.

title deed, a deed or document containing or constituting evidence of ownership.

title page, the page at the beginning of a volume which indicates the title, author's or editor's name, and publication information (usually the publisher, and the place and date of publication).

title role, (in a play, opera, etc.) the role or character from which the title is derived. Also, **title part.**

tit·mouse (tĭt′mous′), *n., pl.* **-mice** (-mīs′). any of various small birds constituting the family *Paridae,* as *Parus atricapillus* of the New and Old Worlds. [ME *titmose,* f. TIT[1] + *mose* (OE *māse*) titmouse]

Tufted titmouse, *Parus bicolor* (6 in. long)

Ti·to (tē′tō), *n.* **Marshal,** (*Josip Broz*) born 1891, president of Yugoslavia since 1953; premier, 1945–53.

Ti·to·ism (tē′tō ĭz′əm), *n.* disaffection from or rebellion against the official line of a dominant political party, used esp. with reference to anti-Soviet policies in a Soviet satellite state, as in Yugoslavia after World War II. [f. TITO + -ISM] —**Ti′to·ist′,** *adj., n.*

ti·trate (tī′trāt, tī′rāt), *v.t., v.i.,* **-trated, -trating.** *Chem., etc.* to ascertain the quantity of a given constituent present in (a compound mixture) by accurately measuring the volume of a liquid reagent of known strength necessary to convert the constituent into another form. [f. s. F *titrer* titrate + -ATE[1]. See TITER] —**ti·tra′tion,** *n.*

ti·tre (tī′tər, tē′-), *n. Chiefly Brit.* titer.

tit-tat-toe (tĭt′tăt tō′), *n.* tick-tack-toe.

tit·ter (tĭt′ər), *v.i.* **1.** to laugh in a low, half-restrained way, as from nervousness or in ill-suppressed amusement. —*n.* **2.** a tittering laugh. [cf. d. Sw. *tittra* giggle] —**tit′ter·er,** *n.* —**tit′ter·ing·ly,** *adv.* —**Syn.** See **laugh.**

tit·tie[1] (tĭt′ĭ), *n. Scot.* sister. Also, **titty.**

tit·tie[2] (tĭt′ĭ), *n.* teat. [OE *tittig*]

tit·ti·vate (tĭt′ə vāt′), *v.t., v.i.,* **-vated, -vating.** titivate.

tit·tle (tĭt′əl), *n.* **1.** a dot or other small mark in writing or printing, used, e.g., as a diacritic. **2.** a very small part or quantity; a particle, jot, or whit. [ME *titel,* t. ML: m.s. *titulus* mark over letter or word. See TITLE]

tit·tle-tat·tle (tĭt′əl tăt′əl), *n., v.,* **-tled, -tling.** gossip. [varied redupl. of TATTLE] —**tit′tle-tat′tler,** *n.*

tit·tup (tĭt′əp), *n., v.,* **-tuped, -tuping** or (*esp. Brit.*) **-tupped, -tupping.** *Chiefly Brit.* —*n.* **1.** a prancing movement; a curvet. —*v.i.* **2.** to go with an up-and-down movement; prance; caper. [f. d. *tit* pull + UP]

tit·ty (tĭt′ĭ), *n., pl.* **-ties.** *Scot.* tittie.

tit·u·ba·tion (tĭch′o͝o bā′shən), *n. Pathol.* a disturbance of body equilibrium in standing or walking, resulting in an uncertain gait and trembling: the result of a disease of the cerebellum. [t. L: s. *titubātio* staggering, stammering]

tit·u·lar (tĭch′ə lər, tĭt′yə-), *adj.* **1.** of, pertaining to, or of the nature of a title. **2.** having a title, esp. of rank. **3.** existing or being such in title only: *a titular prince.* **4.** from whom or which a title or name is taken. **5.** pertaining to the Roman Catholic churches called *titles* (def. 10b). —*n.* **6.** one who bears a title. **7.** one from whom or that from which a title or name is taken. [f. s. L *titulus* TITLE + -AR[1]] —**tit′u·lar·ly,** *adv.*

tit·u·lar·y (tĭch′ə lĕr′ĭ, tĭt′yə-), *adj., n., pl.* **-laries.** titular.

Ti·tus (tī′təs), *n.* **1.** a convert and companion of the apostle Paul, to whom Paul is supposed to have written the short New Testament epistle bearing Titus' name. **2.** this New Testament Epistle. **3.** (*Flavius Sabinus Vespasianus*) A.D. 40?–81, Roman emperor, A.D. 79–81.

Titus An·dron·i·cus (ăn drŏn′ə kəs), a tragedy, probably in part by Shakespeare, produced 1594.

Ti·u (tē′o͞o), *n. Eng. Myth.* a god of the sky and of war, the equivalent of Tyr in Scand. mythology. [var. of OE *Tiw* god of war. See TUESDAY]

Tiv·o·li (tĭv′ə lĭ; *It.* tē′vô lē′), *n.* a town in central Italy, E of Rome: ruins of Roman villas. 23,581 (1951).

tiz·zy (tĭz′ĭ), *n., pl.* **-zies.** *Slang.* **1.** dither. **2.** *Obsolesc. Brit.* a sixpence. [orig. uncert.]

Tl, *Chem.* thallium.

Tlin·git (tlĭng′gĭt), *n.* **1.** (*pl.*) the members of several American Indian tribes of the coastal regions of S Alaska and N British Columbia. **2.** an American Indian linguistic stock of SE Alaska and N British Columbia. Also, **Tlin·kit** (tlĭng′kĭt). [t. d. Tlingit: m. *Lingit* people]

Tm, *Chem.* thulium.

tme·sis (tə mē′sĭs, mē′sĭs), *n. Gram., Rhet.* the separation of words that constitute a compound or construction by the insertion of other elements, as *a great man and good* instead of *a great and good man.* [t. Gk.: a cutting]

Tn, *Chem.* thoron.

tn., ton.

TNT, trinitrotoluene. Also, **T.N.T.**

to (to͞o; *unstressed* to͝o, tə), *prep.* **1.** a particle serving to specify a point approached and reached: *come to the house. To* expresses: **a.** motion or direction toward something: *from north to south.* **b.** limit of movement or extension: *rotten to the core.* **c.** contact or contiguity: *apply varnish to the surface.* **d.** a point or limit in time: *to this day.* **e.** aim, purpose, or intention: *going to the rescue.* **f.** destination; appointed end: *sentenced to death.* **g.** result or consequence: *to his dismay.* **h.** resulting state or condition: *he tore it to pieces.* **i.** the object of inclination or desire: *they drank to his health.* **j.** the object of a right or claim: *claimants to an estate.* **k.** limit in degree or amount: *punctual to the minute, goods to the value of $1000.* **l.** addition or accompaniment: *he added insult to injury, they danced to music.* **m.** attachment or adherence *he held to his opinion.* **n.** comparison or opposition: *quite healthy to his state last year, the score was 9 to 5.* **o.** agreement or accordance: *a position to one's liking.* **p.** reference or relation: *what will he say to this?* **2.** *To* is used to supply the place of the dative in other languages, connecting transitive verbs with their indirect or distant objects, and adjectives, nouns, and intransitive or passive verbs with a following noun which limits their action or application. **3.** *To* is used

as the ordinary sign or accompaniment of the infinitive (expressing orig. motion, direction, purpose, etc., as in the ordinary uses with a substantive object, but now appearing in many cases as a mere meaningless sign). —*adv.* **4.** toward a person, thing, or point implied or understood; to a contact point or closed position: *pull the shutters to.* **5.** to a matter; to action or work: *we turned to with a will.* **6.** to consciousness; to one's senses: *after he came to.* **7. to and fro, a.** to and from some place or thing. **b.** in opposite or different directions alternately. [ME and OE *tō*, c. G *zu*]

to-, an obsolete prefix preceded usually by adverbial *all.* followed by a verb, meaning "asunder," e.g., *all tobreak* "shatter" (Judges 9:53). [ME and OE, var. of *te-*, c. G *zer-*, L *dis-*]

toad (tōd), *n.* **1.** the terrestrial species of tailless (i.e., froglike) amphibians of the genus *Bufo* and allied genera. **2.** any of various tailless amphibians (order *Salientia*). **3.** any of various other animals, as certain lizards. See **horned toad. 4.** a person or thing as an object of disgust or aversion. [ME *tode*, OE *tādige*; orig. unknown] —**toad′like′,** *adj.*

toad·eat·er (tōd′ē′tər), *n.* toady.

toad·fish (tōd′fĭsh′), *n., pl.* **-fishes,** (esp. collectively) **-fish. 1.** any of the thick-headed, wide-mouthed fishes constituting the family *Batrachoididae,* as *Opsanus tau* of the Atlantic coast of the U.S. **2.** a puffer (def. 2).

toad-flax (tōd′flăks′), *n.* **1.** a common European scrophulariaceous plant, *Linaria vulgaris,* having showy yellow-and-orange flowers, naturalized as a weed in the U.S.; butter-and-eggs. **2.** any plant of the same genus.

toad spittle, cuckoo-spit (the secretion).

toad·stone (tōd′stōn′), *n.* any of various stones or stonelike objects, formerly supposed to have been formed in the head or body of a toad, worn as jewels or amulets.

toad·stool (tōd′stool′), *n.* **1.** any of various fleshy fungi having a stalk with an umbrellalike cap, esp. the agarics. **2.** a poisonous agaric, as distinguished from an edible one. **3.** any of various other fleshy fungi, as the puffballs, coral fungi, etc.

toad·y (tō′dĭ), *n., pl.* **toadies,** *v.,* **toadied, toadying.** —*n.* **1.** an obsequious sycophant; a fawning flatterer. —*v.t.* **2.** to be the toady to. —*v.i.* **3.** to be a toady. [TOAD + -Y²] —**toad′y·ish,** *adj.* —**toad′y·ism,** *n.*

to-and-fro (tōō′ən frō′), *adj.* back-and-forth: *to-and-fro motion.*

toast¹ (tōst), *n.* **1.** bread in slices superficially browned by heat. [n. use of v.] —*v.t.* **2.** to brown, as bread or cheese, by exposure to heat. **3.** to heat or warm thoroughly at a fire. —*v.i.* **4.** to become toasted. [ME *tost(en),* t. OF: m. *toster,* der. L *torrēre* dry, parch]

toast² (tōst), *n.* **1.** a person whose health is proposed and drunk; an event, sentiment, or the like, to which one drinks. **2.** a call on another or others to drink to some person or thing. **3.** act of thus drinking. —*v.t.* **4.** to propose as a toast. **5.** to drink to the health of, or in honor of. —*v.i.* **6.** to propose or drink a toast. [fig. use of TOAST¹, n., with reference to a piece of toast being put into a beverage to flavor it]

toast·er¹ (tōs′tər), *n.* **1.** one who toasts something. **2.** an instrument for toasting bread, cheese, etc. [f. TOAST¹, v. + -ER¹]

toast·er² (tōs′tər), *n.* one who proposes, or joins in, a toast or health. [f. TOAST², v. + -ER¹]

toast·mas·ter (tōst′măs′tər, -mäs′-), *n.* **1.** one who presides at a dinner and introduces the after-dinner speakers. **2.** one who proposes or announces toasts.

to·bac·co (tə băk′ō), *n., pl.* **-cos, -coes. 1.** any plant of the solanaceous genus *Nicotiana,* esp. one of those species, as *N. Tabacum,* whose leaves are prepared for smoking or chewing or as snuff. **2.** the leaves so prepared. **3.** any of various similar plants of other genera. [t. Sp.: m. *tabaco,* t. Arawak (from Guarani): pipe for smoking, or roll of leaves smoked, or plant] —**to·bac′co·less,** *adj.*

tobacco heart, *Pathol.* a functional disorder of the heart, characterized by a rapid and often irregular pulse, due to excessive use of tobacco.

to·bac·co·nist (tə băk′ə nĭst), *n. Chiefly Brit.* a dealer in or manufacturer of tobacco.

tobacco worm, the larva of a hawk moth, *Protoparce sexta,* which feeds on the leaves of the growing tobacco plant.

To·ba·go (tə bā′gō), *n.* an island off the NE coast of Venezuela: part of Trinidad and Tobago; formerly a British colony in the Federation of the West Indies. 33,333 pop. (1960); 116 sq. mi.

To·bit (tō′bĭt), *n.* a romance, one of the Old Testament Apocrypha. Also, **To·bi·as** (tō bī′əs).

to·bog·gan (tə bŏg′ən), *n.* **1.** a long, narrow, flat-bottomed sled made of a thin board curved upward and backward at the front end. **2.** a similar light sled with low runners, used in the sport of coasting. —*v.i.* **3.** to use, or coast on, a toboggan. **4.** to fall rapidly, as prices, one's fortune, etc. [t. Canadian F: m. *tabagane,* etc. t. Abnaki: m. *udaba′gan* (what is) used for dragging, der. *uda′be* he drags; cf. *udabauask* sleigh] —**to·bog′gan·er, to·bog′gan·ist,** *n.*

To·bol (tō bŏl′y), *n.* a river in the W Soviet Union in Asia, flowing NE to the Irtish river. ab. 800 mi.

To·bolsk (tō bôlsk′), *n.* a town in the W Soviet Union in Asia, on the Irtish river near the confluence of the Tobol. 40,000 (est. 1948).

to·by (tō′bĭ), *n., pl.* **-bies. 1.** Also, **Toby.** a small jug or mug in the form of a stout old man wearing a three-cornered hat. **2.** *U.S. Slang.* a long, slender, cheap cigar. [short for *Tobias*]

Toby, 18th century

To·can·tins (tō′kän tēns′), *n.* a river in E Brazil, flowing N to the Pará river. ab. 1700 mi.

toc·ca·ta (tə kä′tə; *It.* tôk kä′tä), *n. Music.* a composition in the style of an improvisation, for the piano, organ, or other keyboard instrument, intended to exhibit the player's technique. [It.: (pp. fem.) touched, der. *toccare* TOUCH]

To·char·i·an (tō kär′ĭ ən, -kăr′-), *n.* **1.** a member of a central Asiatic people of high culture, who disappeared about A.D. 1000. **2.** an Indo-European language or languages of central Asia, records of which date from A.D. 600.

to·col·o·gy (tō kŏl′ə jĭ), *n.* obstetrics. Also, **tokology.** [f. m. Gk. *tŏko(s)* child + -LOGY]

to·coph·er·ol (tō kŏf′ə rōl′, -rŏl′), *n. Biochem.* one of several alcohols which comprise the reproductive dietary factor known as vitamin E, occurring in wheat-germ oil, lettuce or spinach leaves, egg yolk, etc. [f. m. Gk. *tŏko(s)* child + s. Gk. *phĕrein* bear + -OL¹]

Tocque·ville (tŏk′vĭl; *Fr.* tôk vēl′), *n.* **Alexis Charles Henri Maurice Clérel de** (à lĕk sē′ shàrl än rē′ mō rēs′ klĕ rĕl′ də), 1805–59, French statesman and author.

toc·sin (tŏk′sĭn), *n.* **1.** a signal, esp. of alarm, sounded on a bell or bells. **2.** a bell used to sound an alarm. [t. F. t. Pr.: m. *tocasenh,* f. *toca(r)* touch, strike + *senh* sign, bell (g. L *signum* sign, ML bell)]

tod¹ (tŏd), *n.* **1.** an English unit of weight, chiefly for wool, commonly equal to 28 pounds but varying locally. **2.** a load. **3.** a bushy mass, esp. of ivy. [ME *todde.* Cf. d. Swed. *todd* mass (of wool), E Fris. *todde* small load]

tod² (tŏd), *n. Scot. and N. Eng.* a fox. [ME, special use of TOD¹ (def. 3), with reference to the fox's bushy tail]

to·day (tə dā′), *n.* **1.** this present day. **2.** this present time or age. —*adv.* **3.** on this present day. **4.** at the present time; in these days. Also, **to-day′.** [ME; OE *tō dæg.* See TO, prep., DAY]

tod·dle (tŏd′əl), *v.,* **-dled, -dling,** *n.* —*v.i.* **1.** to go with short, unsteady steps, as a child or an old person. —*n.* **2.** act of toddling. **3.** an unsteady gait. [b. TOTTER and WADDLE] —**tod′dler,** *n.*

tod·dy (tŏd′ĭ), *n., pl.* **-dies. 1.** a drink made of alcoholic liquor and hot water, sweetened and sometimes spiced with cloves. **2.** the drawn sap, esp. when fermented, of various species of palm (**toddy palms**), used as a drink. [t. Hind.: m. *tārī,* der. *tār* palm tree]

to-do (tə dōō′), *n., pl.* **-dos.** *Colloq.* bustle; fuss. —**Syn.** See ado.

to·dy (tō′dĭ), *n., pl.* **-dies.** any of the small insectivorous West Indian birds constituting the family *Todidae,* related to the motmots and kingfishers, and having a brightly colored green-and-red plumage. [t. F: m. *todier,* der. L *todus,* name of small bird]

toe (tō), *n., v.,* **toed, toeing.** —*n.* **1.** (in man) one of the terminal members or digits of the foot. **2.** an analogous part in other animals. **3.** the forepart of the foot or hoof of a horse or the like. **4.** a part, as of a stocking or shoe, to cover the toes. **5.** a part resembling a toe in shape or position. **6.** *Railroads.* the end of a frog in front of the point and in the direction of the switch. **7.** *Mach.* **a.** a journal or part placed vertically in a bearing, as the lower end of a vertical shaft. **b.** an arm or projecting part on which a cam or the like strikes. **8. on one's toes,** prepared to act; wide-awake. —*v.t.* **9.** to furnish with a toe or toes. **10.** to touch or reach with the toes. **11.** to kick with the toe. **12.** *Golf.* to strike (the ball) with the toe of the club. **13.** *Carpentry.* **a.** to drive (a nail) obliquely. **b.** to toenail. —*v.i.* **14.** to place or move the toes in a manner specified: *to toe in* (in walking). **15.** to tap with the toe, as in dancing. [ME; OE *tā,* c. G *zeh(e),* Icel. *tā*] —**toe′less,** *adj.* —**toe′like′,** *adj.*

toe crack, a sand crack on the front of a horse's hoof.

toed (tōd), *adj.* **1.** having a toe or toes: *five-toed.* **2.** *Carpentry.* **a.** (of a nail) driven at an oblique angle. **b.** fastened by such nails.

toe dance, a dance performed on the ends of the toes, used esp. in ballet. —**toe dancer.**

toe-dance (tō′dăns′, -däns′), *v.i.,* **-danced, -dancing.** to dance on the ends of the toes.

toe hold, **1.** a small ledge or niche, just enough for the toe, in climbing. **2.** any means of support, entry, access, etc. **3.** *Wrestling.* a type of hold whereby the wrestler wrenches the foot of his opponent.

toe-nail (tō′nāl′), *n.* **1.** the nail growing on each of the toes of the human foot. **2.** *Carpentry.* a nail driven obliquely. —*v.t.* **3.** *Carpentry.* to secure with oblique nailing.

toe-shoe (tō′shōō′), *n. Ballet.* a heelless dance slipper fitted with a boxed toe to enable the ballet dancer to toe-dance.

tof·fee (tŏf′ĭ, tôf′ĭ), *n.* taffy. Also, **tof′fy.** [earlier *taffy,* of uncert. orig.]

toft (tôft, tŏft), *n. Dial.* **1.** a homestead or messuage. **2.** a piece of land on which a house, generally with outbuildings, is or has been located, including the yard. [ME and OE, t. Scand.; cf. Icel. *toft* homestead]

tog (tŏg), *n., v.,* **togged, togging.** *Colloq.* —*n.* **1.** a garment. **2.** (*usually pl.*) clothes. —*v.t.* **3.** to clothe; dress (often foll. by *out* or *up*). [appar. short for obs. cant term *togeman(s)* cloak, coat. Cf. D *tuig* trappings]

to·ga (tō'gə), *n., pl.* **-gas, -gae** (-jē). **1.** the loose outer garment of the citizens of ancient Rome when appearing in public in time of peace. **2.** a robe of office, a professional gown, or some other distinctive garment. [t. L] —**to·gaed** (tō'gəd), *adj.*

to·gat·ed (tō'gātĭd), *adj.* **1.** peaceful. **2.** clad in a toga. [f. s. L *togātus* clad in toga + -ED²]

to·ga vi·ri·lis (tō'gə vĭ rī'lĭs), *Latin.* the manly toga assumed by Roman youths at the age of fourteen.

to·geth·er (tŏŏ gĕth'ər), *adv.* **1.** into or in one gathering, company, mass, or body: *to call the people together.* **2.** into or in union, proximity, contact, or collision, as two or more things: *to sew things together.* **3.** into or in relationship, association, business, or friendly relations, etc., as two or more persons: *to bring strangers together.* **4.** taken or considered collectively or conjointly: *this one cost more than all the others together.* **5.** (of a single thing) into or in a condition of unity, compactness, or coherence: *to squeeze a thing together, the argument does not hang together well.* **6.** at the same time; simultaneously: *you cannot have both together.* **7.** without intermission or interruption; continuously; uninterruptedly: *for days together.* **8.** in coöperation; with united action; conjointly: *to undertake a task together.* **9.** with mutual action; mutually; reciprocally: *to confer together, to multiply two numbers together.* [ME *togethir*, OE *to-gædere*, f. TO, prep., + *gædere*, adv., together, c. D *tegader.* Cf. GATHER]

tog·ger·y (tŏg'ərĭ), *n. Colloq.* garments; clothes; togs.

tog·gle (tŏg'əl), *n., v.,* **-gled, -gling.** —*n.* **1.** a transverse pin, bolt, or rod placed through an eye of a rope, link of a chain, or the like, for various purposes. **2.** a toggle joint, or a device furnished with one. —*v.t.* **3.** to furnish with a toggle or toggles. **4.** to secure or fasten with a toggle or toggles. [? akin to TANGLE]

toggle joint, *Mach.* a device consisting of two arms pivoted together at their inner ends and pivoted to other parts at their outer ends, utilized in printing presses, etc., for pressure at the outer ends when the arms are put into a straight line by force applied at the bend between them. *Toggle joint*

toggle switch, *Elect.* a switch in which a projecting knob or arm, moving through a small arc, causes the contacts to open or close the circuit suddenly.

To·go (tō'gō), *n.* **1.** Count Heihachiro (hā'hä chē'rō), 1847–1934, Japanese admiral. **2. Republic of,** an independent country in W Africa; former French trusteeship of Togoland. 1,091,000 (est. 1955); 21,500 sq. mi. *Cap.:* Lomé.

To·go·land (tō'gō lănd'), *n.* **1.** a former German protectorate in W Africa, on the Gulf of Guinea. **2. the E** part of this former protectorate: now a republic. See **Togo** (def. 2). **3.** the W part; formerly a British trusteeship, now part of Ghana.

toil¹ (toil), *n.* **1.** hard and continuous work; exhausting labor or effort. **2.** a laborious task. **3.** *Archaic.* battle; strife; struggle. [ME *toile,* t. AF: m. *toil* dispute, contention, der. *toiler* toil, v.] —*v.i.* **4.** to engage in severe and continuous work; labor arduously. **5.** to move or travel with difficulty, weariness, or pain. —*v.t.* **6.** to bring or effect by toil. [ME *toile(n),* t. AF: m. *toiler* strive, dispute, wrangle, g. L *tudiculāre* stir] —**toil·er,** *n.* —**Syn. 1.** See work.

toil² (toil), *n.* (*usually pl.*) a net or nets set about a space into which game is driven or within which it is known to be. **2.** *Obs.* any snare or trap for wild beasts. [t. F: m. *toile,* g. L *tēla* web]

toile (twäl), *n.* a type of transparent linen. [t. F: linen cloth, canvas. See TOIL²]

toi·let (toi'lĭt), *n.* **1.** *U.S.* a bathroom. **2.** *U.S.* a water closet. **3.** a dressing room, esp. one with a bath. **4.** the act or process of dressing, including bathing, arranging the hair, etc. **5.** the articles used in dressing, etc., as mirror, brush, comb, etc. **6.** a dressing table. **7.** the dress or costume of a person; any particular costume: *toilet of white silk.* **8.** *Surg.* the cleansing of the part or wound after an operation, esp. in the peritoneal cavity. Also, **toi·lette** (toi lĕt'; *Fr.* twä lĕt') for **4, 7.** [t. F: m. *toilette,* dim. of *toile* cloth. See TOIL²]

toi·let·ry (toi'lĭt rĭ), *n., pl.* **-ries.** an article or substance used in dressing or making up.

toilet set, the articles used in dressing, etc., as mirror, brush, comb, etc.

toilet water, a scented liquid used as a light perfume; cologne.

toil·ful (toil'fəl), *adj.* characterized by or involving toil; laborious; toilsome. —**toil·ful·ly,** *adv.*

toil·some (toil'səm), *adj.* characterized by or involving toil; laborious or fatiguing. —**toil·some·ly,** *adv.* —**toil·some·ness,** *n.*

toil·worn (toil'wôrn'), *adj.* **1.** worn by toil. **2.** showing the effects of toil.

To·jo (tō'jō), *n.* **Hideki** (hē'dĕkē'), 1885–1948, Japanese general.

To·kay (tō kā'), *n.* **1.** a rich, sweet, aromatic wine made near Tokay, Hungary. **2.** variety of grape from which it is made. **3.** a similar wine made elsewhere.

to·ken (tō'kən), *n.* **1.** something serving to represent or indicate some fact, event, feeling, etc.; sign: *to wear black as a token of mourning.* **2.** a characteristic mark or indication; symbol. **3.** a memento; a keepsake. **4.** something used to indicate authenticity, authority, etc. **5.** Also, **token coin.** a stamped piece of metal issued as a limited medium of exchange, as for bus fares, at a nominal value much greater than its commodity value. **6.** anything of only nominal value similarly used, as paper currency. **7. in token of,** as a sign or evidence of. [ME; OE *tācen,* c. G *zeichen;* akin to TEACH]

token payment, a small payment binding an agreement or acknowledging a debt.

to·kol·o·gy (tō kŏl'ə jĭ), *n.* tocology.

To·ku·shi·ma (tō'kŏŏ shē'mä), *n.* a seaport in SW Japan, on NE Shikoku island. 121,416 (1950).

To·ky·o (tō'kĭ ō'; *Jap.* tō'kyō'), *n.* a seaport in and the capital of Japan, on Tokyo Bay, an inlet of the Pacific in SE Honshu Island, one of the world's three largest cities: destructive earthquake and fire, 1923; signing of the Japanese surrender document aboard the U.S.S. *Missouri,* Sept. 2, 1945. 6,277,500 (1950). Also, **To'ki·o'.** Formerly, **Yeddo** or **Yedo.**

to·la (tō'lä), *n.* a unit of weight in India. The government tola is 1/80 ser and equals 180 English grains, the weight of a silver rupee. [t. Hind.: a balance, weight]

to·lan (tō'lăn), *n. Chem.* an unsaturated crystalline hydrocarbon, $C_6H_5 \equiv CC_6H_5$. Also, **to·lane** (tō'lān). [f. TOL(U) + -AN(E)]

toll·booth (tōl'bōōth', -bōōth'), *n.* tollbooth.

told (tōld), *v.* **1.** pt. and pp. of **tell. 2. all told,** in all.

tole (tōl), *n.* enameled or lacquered metalware usually with gilt decoration, often used (esp. in the eighteenth century) for trays, lampshades, etc. Also, **tôle.**

To·le·do (tə lē'dō; for *2–4,* also *Sp.* tō lā'dō), *n.* **1.** a city in NW Ohio: a port on Lake Erie. 318,003 (1960). **2.** a city in central Spain, on the Tagus river: the capital of Spain under the Romans. 40,210 (1950). **3.** a sword or sword blade made, or supposed to be made, at Toledo, Spain. **4. Francisco de** (frän thēs'kō dĕ), c1515–84?, Spanish administrator, viceroy of Peru, 1569–81.

tol·er·a·ble (tŏl'ər ə bəl), *adj.* **1.** that may be tolerated; endurable. **2.** fairly good; not bad. **3.** *Colloq.* in fair health. [ME, t. L *tolerābilis* bearable] —**tol'er·a·ble·ness,** *n.* —**tol'er·a·bly,** *adv.* —**Syn. 3.** so-so.

tol·er·ance (tŏl'ər əns), *n.* **1.** the disposition to be patient and fair toward those whose opinions or practices differ from one's own; freedom from bigotry. **2.** *Med.* the power of enduring or resisting the action of a drug, poison, etc. **3.** *Mach.* an allowable variation in the dimensions of a machine or part. Cf. allowance (def. 8). **4.** *Minting.* a permissible deviation in the fineness and weight of coin, owing to the difficulty of securing exact conformity to the standard prescribed by law. —**Syn. 1.** TOLERANCE, TOLERATION agree in allowing the right of something which one does not approve. TOLERANCE suggests a liberal spirit toward the views and actions of others: *tolerance towards religious minorities.* TOLERATION implies the allowance or sufferance of conduct with which one is not in accord: *toleration of graft.*

tolerance limits, *Statistics.* a pair of numbers obtained from a sample such that it can be stated with a given degree of probability that the numbers will include between them at least a specified percentage of values of a variable in the population.

tol·er·ant (tŏl'ər ənt), *adj.* **1.** inclined or disposed to tolerate; showing tolerance; forbearing. **2.** favoring toleration. **3.** *Med.* able to endure or resist the action of a drug, poison, etc. —**tol'er·ant·ly,** *adv.*

tol·er·ate (tŏl'ə rāt'), *v.t.,* **-ated, -ating. 1.** to allow to be, be practiced, or be done without prohibition or hindrance; permit. **2.** to bear without repugnance; put up with. **3.** *Med.* to endure or resist the action of (a drug, poison, etc.). **4.** *Obs.* to endure or sustain, as pain or hardship. [t. L: m.s. *tolerātus* endured] —**tol'er·a'tive,** *adj.* —**tol'er·a'tor,** *n.*

tol·er·a·tion (tŏl'ə rā'shən), *n.* **1.** the tolerating, esp. of what is not actually approved; forbearance. **2.** allowance, by a government, of the exercise of religions other than the religion which is officially established or recognized; recognition of the right of private judgment in matters of faith and worship. —**tol'er·a'tion·ism,** *n.* —**tol'er·a'tion·ist,** *n.* —**Syn. 1.** See tolerance.

tol·i·dine (tŏl'ə dēn', -dĭn), *n. Chem.* any of several isomeric basic derivatives of toluene, one of which is used in making dyes. Also, **tol·i·din** (tŏl'ə dĭn). [f. TOL(U) + -ID(E) + -INE²]

To·li·ma (tō lē'mä), *n.* a volcanic mountain in W Colombia, in the Andes. 18,438 ft.

toll¹ (tōl), *v.t.* **1.** to cause (a large bell) to sound with single strokes slowly and regularly repeated, as for summoning a congregation to church, or esp. for announcing a death. **2.** to sound (a knell, etc.) or strike (the hour), by such strokes. **3.** to announce (a death, etc.) by this means; ring a toll for (a dying or dead person). **4.** to summon or dismiss by tolling. **5.** to lure or decoy (game) by arousing curiosity. **6.** *Obs.* to attract, allure, or entice. —*v.i.* **7.** *U.S.* to sound with single strokes slowly and regularly repeated, as a bell. —*n.* **8.** act of tolling a bell. **9.** a single stroke made in tolling a bell. **10.** the sound made. [ME; akin to OE *-tyllan* in *fortyllan* attract, allure]

toll² (tōl), *n.* **1.** a payment exacted by the state, the local authorities, etc., for some right or privilege, as for passage along a road or over a bridge. **2.** (formerly in England) the right to take such payment. **3.** a compensation for services, as for grinding corn or for transportation or transmission. **4.** *Dial.* grain retained by a miller in payment of his services. **5.** a payment made for a long-distance telephone call. **6.** a tax, duty, or tribute. —*v.t.* **7.** to collect (something) as toll. —*v.i.* **8.** to collect toll; levy toll. [ME and OE (c. G *zoll*), var. of *tohn,* t. LL: m.s. *tolōneum,* var. of L *telōnium,* t. Gk.: m. *telōnion* tollhouse]

toll bar, a barrier, esp. a gate, across a road or bridge, where toll is taken.

toll-booth (tōl′bōōth′, -bōōth′), *n.* **1.** a town hall or guildhall. **2.** *Chiefly Scot.* a town prison; a jail. Also, **tolbooth.** [ME *tolbothe.* See TOLL², BOOTH]

toll bridge, a bridge at which toll is charged.

toll call, any telephone call involving a higher base rate than that fixed for a local message.

Tol·ler (tōl′ər), *n.* **Ernst** (ĕrnst), 1893–1939, German dramatist.

toll-gate (tōl′gāt′), *n.* a gate where toll is taken.

toll-house (tōl′hous′), *n.* a house at a tollgate, occupied by a tollkeeper.

toll-keep·er (tōl′kē′pər), *n.* the collector at a tollgate.

toll line, a telephone line for long-distance calls.

Tol·stoy (tōl′stoi; *Russ.* tōl stoi′), *n.* **Lev** (*Eng.* Leo) **Nikolaevich** (lĕf nĭ kō lī′ə vĭch), 1828–1910, Russian novelist and social reformer. Also, **Tol′stoi.**

Tol·tec (tōl′tĕk), *n.* **1.** (*pl.*) an Indian people who flourished in central Mexico before the advent of the Aztecs, and who laid the foundation, according to tradition, of Aztec culture. —*adj.* **2.** Also, **Tol′tec·an.** of or pertaining to the Toltecs.

to·lu (tō lōō′), *n.* a fragrant yellowish-brown balsam obtained from a South American tree, *Myroxylon Balsamum,* used in medicine as a stomachic and expectorant, and in perfumery. [named after *Tolu* (now Santiago de Tolu) in Colombia where balsam is obtained]

tol·u·ate (tōl′yŏŏ āt′), *n.* *Chem.* a salt or ester of toluic acid.

To·lu·ca (tō lōō′kä), *n.* a city in S central Mexico: the capital of Mexico state. 52,968 (1950).

tol·u·ene (tōl′yŏŏ ēn′), *n.* *Chem.* a colorless, mobile, liquid hydrocarbon, $C_6H_5CH_3$, obtained from tolu, coal tar, etc.: used as a solvent and in the manufacture of coal-tar substances, as TNT. [f. TOLU + -ENE]

tol·u·ic acid (tə lōō′ĭk, tōl′yŏŏ ĭk), *Chem.* any of several isomeric acids, C_7H_7COOH, which are derivatives of toluene.

tol·u·ide (tōl′yŏŏ īd′, -ĭd), *n.* *Chem.* an amide which contains a tolyl radical united to the nitrogen. Also, **tol·u·id** (tōl′yŏŏ ĭd).

tol·u·i·dine (tə lōō′ə dēn′, -dĭn), *n.* *Chem.* any of three isomeric amines, $CH_3C_6H_4NH_2$, derived from toluene, used in dye and drug industries. Also, **to·lu·i·din** (tə lōō′ə dĭn).

tol·u·ol (tōl′yŏŏ ōl′, -ŏl′), *n.* *Chem.* **1.** toluene. **2.** the commercial form of toluene. Also, **tol·u·ole** (tōl′yŏŏ ōl′). [f. TOLU + -OL²]

tol·u·yl group or **radical** (tōl′yŏŏ ĭl), *Chem.* a univalent radical, C_7H_7CO, present in toluic acids. [f. TOLU + -YL]

tol·yl group or **radical** (tōl′ĭl), *Chem.* a univalent hydrocarbon radical, $CH_3C_6H_4$, from toluene. [f. TOL(U) + -YL]

tom (tŏm), *n.* **1.** the male of various animals (often used in composition, as in *tomcat*). **2.** tomcat. [short for *Thomas*]

tom·a·hawk (tŏm′ə hôk′), *n.* **1.** a light ax used by the North American Indians as a weapon and tool, and serving as a token of war. **2.** any of various similar weapons or implements. **3.** (in Australia) a hatchet. —*v.t.* **4.** to strike, cut, or kill with or as with a tomahawk. [t. Algonquian (Va. d.): m. *tommahick,* etc., war club, ceremonial object]

Tom and Jerry, a hot drink composed of rum and water (or milk) with beaten eggs, spiced and sweetened.

to·ma·to (tə mā′tō, -mä′-), *n., pl.* **-toes. 1.** a widely cultivated solanaceous plant, *Lycopersicon esculentum,* bearing a slightly acid, pulpy fruit, commonly red, sometimes yellow, used as a vegetable. **2.** the fruit itself. **3.** any plant of the same genus. **4.** its fruit. [t. Sp.: m. *tomate,* t. Mex.: m. *tomatl*]

tomb (tōōm), *n.* **1.** an excavation in earth or rock for the reception of a dead body. **2.** a grave or mausoleum. **3.** any sepulchral structure. **4.** the state of death. —*v.t.* **5.** to place in or as in a tomb; bury. [ME, t. OF: m. *tombe,* g. LL *tumba,* t. Gk.: m. *týmbos*] —**tomb′less,** *adj.* —**tomb′like′,** *adj.*

Tom·big·bee (tŏm bĭg′bĭ), *n.* a river flowing through NE Mississippi and SW Alabama, joining the Alabama river to form the Mobile river. ab. 450 mi.

Tom·bouc·tou (tôN bōŏk tōō′), *n.* French name of Timbuktu.

tom·boy (tŏm′boi′), *n.* a boisterous, romping girl. —**tom′boy′ish,** *adj.* —**tom′boy′ish·ness,** *n.*

Tombs (tōōmz), *n.* **The,** a prison in New York City.

tomb·stone (tōōm′stōn′), *n.* a stone, usually bearing an inscription, set to mark a tomb or grave.

tom·cat (tŏm′kăt′), *n.* a male cat.

tom·cod (tŏm′kŏd′), *n.* **1.** either of two small cods, *Microgadus tomcod* of the Atlantic, or *M. proximus* of the Pacific. **2.** any of various similar fishes. [f. TOM + COD¹]

Tom Col·lins (kŏl′ĭnz), a tall drink containing gin, lemon or lime juice, and carbonated water, sweetened and served iced.

Tom, Dick, and Harry, common people generally: *they invited every Tom, Dick, and Harry.*

tome (tōm), *n.* **1.** a volume forming a part of a larger work. **2.** any volume, esp. a ponderous one. [t. F, t. L: m. *tomus,* t. Gk.: m. *tómos* volume, section of book]

-tome, a word element referring to cutting, used esp. in scientific terms, as *bronchotome, microtome, osteotome.* [comb. form repr. Gk. *tomḗ* a cutting, section; *tómos* a cut, slice; *-tomos* cutting]

to·men·tose (tə mĕn′tōs, tō′mĕn tōs′), *adj.* **1.** *Anat.* fleecy; flocculent. **2.** *Bot., Entomol.* closely covered with down or matted hair. [t. NL: m.s. *tōmentōsus,* der. L *tōmentum* TOMENTUM]

to·men·tum (tə mĕn′təm), *n., pl.* **-ta** (-tə). *Bot.* pubescence consisting of longish, soft, entangled hairs pressed close to the surface. [NL: special use of L *tōmentum* stuffing (of wool, hair, etc.) for cushions]

tom·fool (tŏm′fōōl′), *n.* **1.** a grossly foolish person; a silly fool. —*adj.* **2.** being, or characteristic of, a tomfool.

tom·fool·er·y (tŏm′fōō′lə rĭ), *n., pl.* **-er·ies. 1.** foolish or silly behavior. **2.** a silly act, matter, or thing.

Tom Jones, a novel (1749) by Henry Fielding.

Tom·lin·son (tŏm′lĭn sən), *n.* **Henry Major,** 1873–1958, British journalist and novelist.

Tom·ma·si·ni (tŏm′mä zē′nē), *n.* **Vicenzo** (vē chĕn′tsō), 1880–1950, Italian composer.

tom·my (tŏm′ĭ), *n., pl.* **-mies.** short for **Tommy Atkins.** Also, **Tommy.**

Tommy At·kins (ăt′kĭnz), **1.** any private of the British army. **2.** the rank and file collectively. [a familiar name for typical British soldier, arising out of the use of the name "Thomas Atkins" in specimen forms given in official regulations from 1815 on]

Tommy gun, *Slang.* a Thompson submachine gun.

tom·my·rot (tŏm′ĭ rŏt′), *n.* *Slang.* nonsense.

to·mog·ra·phy (tə mŏg′rə fĭ), *n.* *Med.* roentgenography of a selected plane in the body.

to·mor·row (tə môr′ō, -mŏr′ō), *n.* **1.** the day after this day: *tomorrow will be fair.* **2.** a day immediately following or succeeding another day. —*adv.* **3.** on the morrow; on the day after this day: *come tomorrow.* Also, **to·mor′row.** [ME *to morowe,* OE *tō morgen* on the morrow, in the morning]

tom·pi·on (tŏm′pĭ ən), *n.* tampion.

Tom Saw·yer (sô′yər), **The Adventures of,** a novel (1876) by Mark Twain.

Tomsk (tômsk), *n.* a city in the central Soviet Union in Asia, E of the Ob river. 224,000 (est. 1956).

Tom Thumb (thŭm), **1.** a diminutive hero of folk tales. **2.** a diminutive man; a dwarf. **3.** a midget, Charles Stratton (1838–83), exhibited in the circus of P. T. Barnum.

tom·tit (tŏm′tĭt′), *n.* **1.** *Brit.* titmouse. **2.** any of various other small birds, as the wren. [f. TOM + TIT¹]

tom-tom (tŏm′tŏm′), *n.* **1.** a native drum of indefinite pitch. **2.** a type of Oriental drum with a handle. **3.** a dully repetitious drumbeat or similar sound. Also, **tam-tam.** [t. Hind. or other East Ind. vernacular: m. *tam-tam.* Cf. Malay *tong-tong;* both imit.]

Tom-toms

-tomy, a noun termination meaning a "cutting," esp. relating to a surgical operation, as in *appendectomy, lithotomy, phlebotomy,* or sometimes a division, as in *dichotomy.* [t. Gk.: m.s. *-tomia*]

ton¹ (tŭn), *n.* **1.** a unit of weight, now usually 20 hundredweight, commonly equivalent to 2,000 pounds avoirdupois (**short ton**) in the U.S. and 2,240 pounds avoirdupois (**long ton**) in Great Britain. **2.** a unit of volume for freight, varying with the different kinds, as 40 cubic feet of oak timber, 20 bushels of wheat, etc. (**freight ton**). **3.** a metric ton. **4.** a unit of displacement of ships, equal to 35 cubic feet of salt water (**displacement ton**). **5.** a unit of volume used in transportation by sea, commonly 40 cubic feet (**shipping ton**). **6.** a unit of internal capacity of ships, equal to 100 cubic feet. [ME; var. of TUN]

ton² (tôN), *n.* fashion; style. [F, g. L *tonus* TONE]

-ton, noun suffix, as in *simpleton, singleton.* [var. of d. *tone* ONE. Cf. TOTHER]

ton·al (tō′nəl), *adj.* *Music.* pertaining to tonality (opposed to *modal*). —**ton′al·ly,** *adv.*

ton·al·ist (tō′nəl ĭst), *n.* *Painting.* one who aims at harmonious effects by subtle use of light and shade, rather than by contrasts of color.

to·nal·i·ty (tō nāl′ə tĭ), *n., pl.* **-ties. 1.** *Music.* **a.** the sum of relations, melodic and harmonic, existing between the tones of a scale or musical system; key. **b.** a particular scale or system of tones; a key. **2.** *Painting, etc.* the system of tones or tints, or the color scheme, of a picture, etc.

to-name (too′nām′), *n. Chiefly Scot.* **1.** a nickname, esp. one to distinguish a person from others of the same name. **2.** a surname. [ME; OE *tōnama*, f. *tō* TO + *nama* NAME]

tone (tōn), *n., v.,* **toned, toning.** —*n.* **1.** any sound considered with reference to its quality, pitch, strength, source, etc.: *shrill tones.* **2.** quality or character of sound. **3.** vocal sound; the sound made by vibrating muscular bands in the larynx. **4.** a particular quality, way of sounding, modulation, or intonation of the voice as expressive of some meaning, feeling, spirit, etc.: *a tone of command.* **5.** an accent peculiar to a person, people, locality, etc., or a characteristic mode of sounding words in speech. **6.** stress of voice on a syllable of a word. **7.** *Phonet.* a musical pitch or melody which may serve to distinguish between words composed of the same sounds, as in Chinese. **8.** *Music.* **a.** a musical sound of definite pitch, consisting of several relatively simple constituents called **partial tones,** the lowest of which is called the **fundamental tone** and the others **harmonics** or **overtones. b.** an interval equivalent to two semitones; a whole tone; a whole step. **c.** any of the nine melodies or tunes in Gregorian music, to which the psalms are sung (called **Gregorian tones**). **9.** a variety of color; a tint; a shade. **10.** hue; that distinctive quality by which colors differ from one another in addition to their differences indicated by chroma, tint, shade; a slight modification of a given color: *green with a yellowish tone, light tone, dull tone, etc.* **11.** *Art.* the prevailing effect of harmony of color and values. **12.** *Physiol.* **a.** the state of tension or firmness proper to the organs or tissues of the body. **b.** that state of the body or of an organ in which all its animal functions are performed with healthy vigor. **c.** healthy sensitivity to stimulation. **13.** normal healthy condition of the mind. **14.** a particular state or temper of the mind; spirit, character, or tenor. **15.** prevailing character or style, as of manners or morals. **16.** style, distinction, or elegance. —*v.t.* **17.** to sound with a particular tone. **18.** to give the proper tone to (a musical instrument). **19.** to modify the tone or general coloring of. **20.** to give the desired tone to (a painting, etc.). **21.** *Photog.* to change the color of (a print), usually by chemical means. **22.** to render (as specified) in tone or coloring. **23.** to modify the tone or character of. **24.** to give physical or mental tone to. **25. tone down, a.** *Painting.* to subdue; make (a color) less intense in hue. **b.** to lower the tone, strength, intensity, etc., of; soften; moderate. **26. tone up,** to give a higher or stronger tone to. —*v.i.* **27.** to take on a particular tone; assume color or tint. **28.** to harmonize in tone or color (fol. by *with* or *in with*). **29. tone down,** to become softened or moderated. **30. tone up,** to gain in tone or strength. [ME; t. ML: m. *tonus,* t. Gk.: m. *tónos* tension, pitch, key] —**tone′less,** *adj.* —**tone′less·ly,** *adv.* —**tone′-less·ness,** *n.* —**ton′er,** *n.* —Syn. **1.** See sound¹.

tone arm, the free-swinging bracket of a phonograph which contains the pickup. Also, **pickup arm.**

tone color, *Music.* quality of tone; timbre.

to·ne·la·da (tō′nĕ·lä′dä), *n.* a unit of weight corresponding to a ton, varying in value, equal in Brazil to nearly 1750 lbs., in Spain to nearly 2030 lbs.

tone poem, *Music.* an instrumental composition intended to suggest a train of poetic images or sentiments.

tong¹ (tông, tŏng), *n.* **1.** (*pl., sometimes construed as sing.*) any of various implements consisting of two arms hinged, pivoted, or otherwise fastened together, for seizing, holding, or lifting something. —*v.t.* **2.** to seize, gather, hold, or handle with tongs, as logs or oysters. —*v.i.* **3.** to use, or work with, tongs. [ME; OE *tang,* c. G *zange*]

tong² (tông, tŏng), *n.* **1.** (in China) an association, society, or political party. **2.** (in the U.S.) a Chinese society or association, usually considered by its members to be a private, closed society, but by Americans often considered a secret society. [t. Chinese: m. *t'ang* meeting place]

Ton·ga (tŏng′gə), *n.* a Polynesian kingdom consisting of three groups of islands in the S Pacific, NE of New Zealand: a British protectorate. 54,300 (est. 1954); ab. 250 sq. mi. *Cap.:* Nukualofa. Also, **Tonga Islands** or **Friendly Islands.**

ton·ga (tŏng′gə), *n.* a light two-wheeled vehicle used in India. [t. Hind.: m. *tangā*]

Tong·king (tŏng′kĭng′), *n.* Tonkin.

tongue (tŭng), *n., v.,* **tongued, tonguing.** —*n.* **1.** an organ in man and most vertebrates occupying the floor of the mouth and often protrusible and freely movable, being the principal organ of taste, and, in man, of articulate speech. See diag. under **mouth. 2.** *Zool.* an organ in the mouth of invertebrates, frequently of a rasping nature. **3.** the tongue of an animal, as an ox, beef, or sheep, as used for food, often prepared by smoking or pickling. **4.** the human tongue as the organ of speech. **5.** the faculty or power of speech: *to find one's tongue.* **6.** speech or talk, esp. mere glib or empty talk. **7.** manner or character of speech: *a flattering tongue.* **8.** the language of a particular people,

country, or locality: *the Hebrew tongue.* **9.** a dialect. **10.** a people as distinguished by its language (a Biblical use): *I will gather all nations and tongues.* **11.** *Chiefly Brit.* the voice of a hound or other dog: *to give tongue.* **12.** something resembling or suggesting an animal's tongue in shape, position, or function. **13.** a strip of leather under the lacing or fastening of a shoe. **14.** a suspended piece inside a bell that produces a sound on striking against the side. **15.** a vibrating reed or the like in a musical instrument. **16.** the pole of a carriage or other vehicle, extending between the animals drawing it. **17.** a projecting strip along the center of the edge or end of a board, for fitting into a groove in another board. **18.** a narrow strip of land extending into a body of water. **19.** *Mach.* a long, narrow projection on a machine. **20.** that part of a railroad switch which is shifted to direct the wheels of a locomotive or car to one or the other track of a railroad. **21.** the pin of a buckle, brooch, etc. **22. on the tip of one's tongue,** on the verge of being uttered. **23. with one's tongue in one's cheek,** mockingly; insincerely. —*v.t.* **24.** to modify (the tones of a flute, cornet, etc.) by strokes of the tongue. **25.** *Carp.* **a.** to cut a tongue on (a board). **b.** to join or fit together by a tongue-and-groove joint. **26.** to touch with the tongue. **27.** to reproach or scold. **28.** *Dial.* to articulate or pronounce. **29.** *Archaic.* to speak or utter. —*v.i.* **30.** to tongue the tones of a flute, etc. **31.** to talk or prate. **32.** to project like a tongue or tongues. [ME and OE *tunge,* c. G *zunge;* akin to L *lingua*] —**tongued** (tŭngd), *adj.* —**tongue′less,** *adj.*

tongue-and-groove joint (tŭng′ən·groov′), *Carp.* a common joint consisting of a tongue (def.17) on the edge of one board and a matching groove on the edge of the next board.

tongue graft, *Hort.* whip graft.

tongue-tie (tŭng′tī′), *n., v.,* **-tied, -tying.** —*n.* **1.** impeded motion of the tongue caused esp. by shortness of the frenum which binds down its underside. —*v.t.* **2.** to make tongue-tied.

tongue-tied (tŭng′tīd′), *adj.* **1.** unable to speak, as from shyness. **2.** affected with tongue-tie.

tongu·ing (tŭng′ĭng), *n. Music.* the manipulation of the tongue in playing a wind instrument to interrupt the tone and produce a staccato effect.

ton·ic (tŏn′ĭk), *n.* **1.** a medicine that invigorates or strengthens. **2.** anything invigorating physically, mentally, or morally. **3.** *Music.* the first degree of the scale; the keynote. —*adj.* **4.** pertaining to, maintaining, increasing, or restoring the tone or healthy condition of the system or organs, as a medicine. **5.** invigorating physically, mentally, or morally. **6.** *Physiol., Pathol.* **a.** pertaining to tension, as of the muscles. **b.** marked by continued muscular tension: *a tonic spasm.* **7.** characterized by distinctions of tone or accent: *a tonic language.* **8.** pertaining to tone or accent in speech. **9.** *Phonet.* **a.** accented, esp. with primary accent. **b.** *Obs.* voiced. **10.** *Music.* **a.** of or pertaining to a tone or tones. **b.** pertaining to or founded on the keynote, or first tone, of a musical scale: *a tonic chord.* [t. Gk.: m.s. *tonikós* pertaining to stretching or tones]

tonic accent, vocal accent, or syllabic stress, in pronunciation or speaking.

to·nic·i·ty (tō·nĭs′ə·tĭ), *n.* **1.** tonic quality or condition. **2.** the state of bodily tone. **3.** *Physiol.* the normal elastic tension of living muscles, arteries, etc., by which the tone of the system is maintained.

tonic sol-fa, a system of singing, in which tonality or key relationship is emphasized, the usual staff notation is discarded, and the tones are indicated by the initial letters of the syllables of the *sol-fa* system.

to·night (tə·nīt′), *n.* **1.** this present or coming night; the night of this present day. **2.** *Dial.* last night. —*adv.* **3.** on this present night; on the night of this present day. Also, **to-night′.** [ME; OE *tō niht.* See TO, prep., NIGHT]

ton·ka bean (tŏng′kə), **1.** the fragrant, black, almond-shaped seed of a tall leguminous tree, *Coumarouna* (or *Dipteryx*) *odorata,* of tropical South America, used in perfumes and snuff. **2.** the tree itself. [t. Guiana Negro: m. *tanka* name of the bean + BEAN]

Ton·kin (tŏn′kĭn′), *n.* **1.** a former state in N French Indochina, now part of North Vietnam. **2.** Gulf of, an arm of the South China Sea, W of Hainan. ab. 300 mi. long. Also, **Tongking** or **Ton·king** (tŏn′kĭng′).

Ton·le Sap (tŏn′lā săp′), a large lake in W Cambodia, draining into the Mekong river: great seasonal variation in area.

tonn., tonnage.

ton·nage (tŭn′ĭj), *n.* **1.** the carrying capacity of a vessel expressed in tons of 100 cubic feet. **2.** ships collectively considered with reference to their carrying capacity or together with their cargoes. **3.** a duty on ships or boats at so much per ton of cargo or freight, or according to the capacity in tons. Also, **tunnage.**

ton·neau (tŭ·nō′), *n., pl.* **tonneaus, tonneaux** (-nōz′). **1.** a rear body or compartment of an automobile, with seats for passengers. **2.** a complete automobile body having such a rear part. **3.** a metric ton; millier. [t. F: cask, dim. of *tonne* TUN]

to·nom·e·ter (tō·nŏm′ə·tər), *n.* **1.** an instrument for measuring the frequencies of tones. **2.** a tuning fork. **3.** a graduated set of tuning forks, whose frequencies have been carefully determined. **4.** any of various physiological instruments, as for measuring the tension within the eyeball, or for determining blood pressure. **5.** *Phys. Chem.* an instrument for measuring strains within a liquid. [f. Gk. *tōno(s)* tension, tone + -METER] **—ton-o-met-ric** (tŏn′ə mĕt′rĭk, tō′nə-), *adj.* **—to-nom′e-try,** *n.*

ton-sil (tŏn′səl), *n. Anat.* either of two prominent oval masses of lymphoid tissue situated one on each side of the fauces. [t. L: m.s. *tonsillae,* pl.] **—ton′sil-lar,** *adj.*

ton-sil-lec-to-my (tŏn′sə lĕk′tə mĭ), *n., pl.* **-mies.** *Surg.* the operation of excising or removing one or both tonsils. [f. s. L *tonsillae* tonsils + -ECTOMY]

ton-sil-li-tis (tŏn′sə lī′tĭs), *n. Pathol.* inflammation of a tonsil or the tonsils. [t. NL, f. s. L *tonsillae* + -*itis* -ITIS] **—ton-sil-lit-ic** (tŏn′sə lĭt′ĭk), *adj.*

ton-so-ri-al (tŏn sōr′əl), *adj.* (often in humorous use) of or pertaining to a barber or his work. [f. s. L *tonsōrius* pertaining to shaving + -AL¹]

ton-sure (tŏn′shər), *n., v.* **-sured, -suring.** **—n.** **1.** act of clipping the hair or shaving the head. **2.** the shaving of the head, or of some part of it, as a religious practice or rite, esp. in preparation for entering the priesthood or a monastic order. **3.** the part of a cleric's head left bare by shaving the hair. **4.** state of being shorn. **—v.t.** **5.** to confer the ecclesiastical tonsure upon. **6.** to subject to tonsure. [ME, t. L: m. *tonsūra* shearing] **—ton′sured,** *adj.*

ton-tine (tŏn′tēn, tŏn tēn′), *n.* **1.** a scheme in which subscribers to a common fund share an annuity with the benefit of survivorship, the shares of the survivors being increased as the subscribers die, until the whole goes to the last survivor. **2.** the annuity shared. **3.** the share of each subscriber. **4.** the number who share. **5.** any of various forms of life insurance in which the chief benefits accrue to participants who are alive and whose policies are in force at the end of a specified period (**tontine period**). [t. F; named after Lorenzo *Tonti,* Neapolitan banker who started the scheme in France about 1653]

to-nus (tō′nəs), *n. Physiol.* a normal state of slight continuous tension in muscle tissue which facilitates its response to stimulation. [NL: special use of L *tonus,* t. Gk.: m. *tónos* tone]

too (tōō), *adv.* **1.** in addition; also; furthermore; moreover: *young, clever, and rich too.* **2.** to an excessive extent or degree; beyond what is desirable, fitting, or right: *too long.* **3.** more (as specified) than should be. **4.** extremely: *only too glad to help you.* [var. of TO, adv.]

took (tōōk), *v.* pt. of **take.**

tool (tōōl), *n.* **1.** an instrument, esp. one held in the hand, for performing or facilitating mechanical operations, as a hammer, saw, file, etc. **2.** any instrument of manual operation. **3.** that part of a lathe, planer, drill, or similar machine, which performs the cutting or machining operation. **4.** the machine itself; a machine tool. **5.** anything used like a tool to do work or effect some result. **6.** a person used by another for his own ends; a cat's-paw. **7.** the design or ornament impressed upon a book cover. **—v.t.** **8.** to work or shape with a tool. **9.** to work decoratively with a hand tool; to ornament with a bookbinders' tool, as on book covers. **10.** *Brit. Colloq.* to drive (a coach, etc.). **—v.i.** **11.** to work with a tool or tools. **12.** *Brit. Colloq.* to drive or ride in a vehicle. [ME; OE *tōl,* c. Icel *tōl,* pl.] **—tool′er,** *n.*
—Syn. 1. TOOL, IMPLEMENT, INSTRUMENT, UTENSIL refer to contrivances for doing work. A TOOL is a contrivance held in and worked by the hand, for assisting the work of (especially) mechanics or laborers: *a carpenter's tools.* An IMPLEMENT is any tool or contrivance designed or used for a particular purpose: *agricultural implements.* An INSTRUMENT is anything used in doing a certain work or producing a certain result, esp. such as requires delicacy, accuracy, or precision: *surgical or musical instruments.* A UTENSIL is especially an article for domestic use: *kitchen utensils.* When used figuratively of human agency, TOOL is generally used in a contemptuous sense; INSTRUMENT, in a neutral or good sense: *a tool of unscrupulous men, an instrument of Providence.*

tool subject, *Educ.* a branch of learning taught to enable students to perform specific or useful tasks, and not for its own sake, as grammar, spelling, calculation.

toon (tōōn), *n.* **1.** a meliaceous tree, *Toona ciliata* (or *Cedrela Toona*), of the East Indies and Australia, yielding a red wood resembling mahogany, but softer, and extensively used for furniture, carving, etc. **2.** the wood. [t. Hind.: m. *tūn*]

toot (tōōt), *v.i.* **1.** (of a horn) to give forth its characteristic sound. **2.** to make a sound resembling that of a horn or the like. **3.** to sound or blow a horn or other wind instrument. **4.** (of grouse) to give forth a characteristic cry or call. **—v.t.** **5.** to cause (a horn, etc.) to sound by blowing it. **6.** to sound (notes, etc.) on a horn or the like. **—n.** **7.** an act or sound of tooting. [late ME, cf. LG and G *tüten,* D *toeten* in same sense] **—toot′er,** *n.*

tooth (tōōth), *n., pl.* **teeth** (tēth), *v.* **—n.** **1.** (in most vertebrates) one of the hard bodies or processes usually attached in a row to each jaw, serving for the prehension and mastication of food, as weapons of attack or defense, etc., and in mammals typically composed chiefly of dentin surrounding a sensitive pulp and covered on the crown with enamel. **2.** (in invertebrates) any of

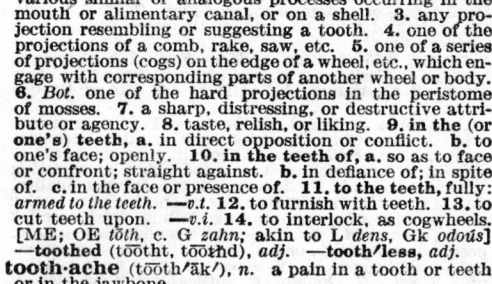

Vertical section of human tooth (enlarged)
A. Enamel;
B. Pulp cavity;
C. Dentin;
D. Cement

various similar or analogous processes occurring in the mouth or alimentary canal, or on a shell. **3.** any projection resembling or suggesting a tooth. **4.** one of the projections of a comb, rake, saw, etc. **5.** one of a series of projections (cogs) on the edge of a wheel, etc., which engage with corresponding parts of another wheel or body. **6.** *Bot.* one of the hard projections in the peristome of mosses. **7.** a sharp, distressing, or destructive attribute or agency. **8.** taste, relish, or liking. **9.** in the (or one's) teeth, a. in direct opposition or conflict. b. to one's face; openly. **10.** in the teeth of, a. so as to face or confront; straight against. b. in defiance of; in spite of. c. in the face or presence of. **11.** to the teeth, fully: *armed to the teeth.* **—v.t.** **12.** to furnish with teeth. **13.** to cut teeth upon. **—v.i.** **14.** to interlock, as cogwheels. [ME; OE *tōth,* c. G *zahn;* akin to L *dens,* Gk *odoús*] **—toothed** (tōōtht, tōōᵺd), *adj.* **—tooth′less,** *adj.*

tooth-ache (tōōth′āk′), *n.* a pain in a tooth or teeth or in the jawbone.

tooth and nail, fiercely; with all one's might: *we fought tooth and nail but lost.*

tooth-brush (tōōth′brŭsh′), *n.* a small brush with a long handle, for cleaning the teeth.

tooth-paste (tōōth′pāst′), *n.* a dentifrice in the form of paste.

tooth-pick (tōōth′pĭk′), *n.* a small pointed piece of wood, etc., for removing substances between the teeth.

tooth-some (tōōth′səm), *adj.* pleasing to the taste; palatable: *a toothsome dish.* **—tooth′some-ly,** *adv.* **—tooth′some-ness,** *n.*

tooth-wort (tōōth′wûrt′), *n.* **1.** a European orobanchaceous plant, *Lathraea Squamaria,* having a rootstock covered with toothlike scales. **2.** any plant of the cruciferous genus *Dentaria,* having toothlike projections upon the creeping rootstock.

too-tle (tōō′təl), *v.,* **-tled, -tling,** *n.* **—v.i.** **1.** to toot gently or repeatedly on a flute or the like. **—n.** **2.** the sound itself. [freq. of TOOT]

top¹ (tŏp), *n., adj., v.,* **topped, topping.** **—n.** **1.** the highest point or part of anything; the apex; the summit. **2.** the uppermost or upper part, surface, etc., of anything. **3.** the higher end of anything on a slope. **4.** *Brit.* a part considered as higher: *the top of a street.* **5.** the part of a plant above ground, as distinguished from the root. **6.** (*usually pl.*) one of the tender tips of the branches or shoots of plants. **7.** that part of anything which is first or foremost; the beginning. **8.** the highest or leading place, position, rank, etc.: *at the top of the class.* **9.** the highest point, pitch, or degree: *to talk at the top of one's voice.* **10.** one who or that which occupies the highest or leading position. **11.** *Poetic.* the most perfect example, type, etc.: *the top of all honors.* **12.** the best or choicest part: *the top of all creation.* **13.** a covering or lid, as of a box, automobile, carriage, etc. **14.** the head. **15.** the crown of the head. **16.** *Naut.* a platform surrounding the head of a lower mast on a ship, and serving as a foothold, a means of extending the upper rigging, etc. **17.** *Chem.* that part of a mixture under distillation which volatilizes first. **18.** *Bridge.* a. the best card of a suit in a player's hand. b. (in duplicate bridge) the best score on a hand. **19.** *Golf, etc.* a. a stroke above the center of the ball, usually failing to give any height, distance, or accuracy. b. the forward spin given to the ball by such a stroke. **20.** on top, successful; victorious; dominant. **21.** on top of, a. upon. b. close upon; following upon. **22.** over the top, *Mil.* over the top of the parapet before a trench, as in issuing to charge against the enemy.
—adj. **23.** pertaining to, situated at, or forming the top; highest; uppermost; upper: *the top shelf.* **24.** highest in degree; greatest: *to pay top prices.* **25.** foremost, chief, or principal: *to win top honors in a competition.*
—v.t. **26.** to furnish with a top; put a top on. **27.** to be at or constitute the top of. **28.** to reach the top of. **29.** to rise above: *the sun had topped the horizon.* **30.** to exceed in height, amount, number, etc. **31.** to surpass, excel, or outdo: *that tops everything!* **32.** to come up to or go beyond the requirements of (a part or character). **33.** to surmount with something specified. **34.** to complete by or as by putting the top on or constituting the top of. **35.** to remove the top of; crop; prune. **36.** to get or leap over the top of (a fence, etc.). **37.** *Chem.* to distill off only the most volatile part of a mixture. **38.** *Golf, etc.* a. to hit (the ball) above the center. b. to make (a stroke, etc.) by hitting the ball in this way. **39.** to top-dress (land).
—v.i. **40.** to rise aloft. **41.** *Golf, etc.* to hit the ball above the center. [ME and OE, c. D *top(p),* G *zopf* top, tuft of hair]

top² (tŏp), *n.* a child's toy, often inversely conical, with a point on which it is made to spin. [ME and OE, c. Flem. *top.* Cf. G *topf*]

top-, var. of topo-, before vowels, as in *toponym.*

to-paz (tō′păz), *n.* **1.** a mineral, a fluosilicate of aluminum, usually occurring in prismatic orthorhombic crystals of various colors, and used as a gem (**true topaz** or **precious topaz**). **2.** a yellow variety of sapphire (**oriental topaz**). **3.** a yellow variety of quartz (**false topaz** or **common topaz**). [t. L: s. *topazus,* t. Gk.: m. *tópazos;* r. ME *topace,* t. OF]

to-paz-o-lite (tō păz′ə līt′), *n.* a yellow or olive-green variety of andradite garnet found in Piedmont. [f. *topazo-* (comb. form repr. Gk. *tópazos* TOPAZ) + -LITE]

top boot, a high boot, esp. one having the upper part of a different material from the rest.

top·coat (tŏp′kōt′), *n.* **1.** a lightweight overcoat. **2.** an outer coat; an overcoat.

top cross, *Genetics.* the progeny of the cross of a variety by one inbred line.

top-dress (tŏp′drĕs′), *v.t.* to manure (land, etc.) on the surface.

top dressing, 1. a dressing of manure on the surface of land. **2.** the action of one who top-dresses. **3.** a top layer of gravel, crushed rock, etc., on a roadway.

tope[1] (tōp), *v.,* **toped, toping.** —*v.i.* **1.** to drink alcoholic liquor habitually and to excess. —*v.t.* **2.** to drink (liquor) habitually and to excess. [var. of obs. *top* drink, appar. special use of *top* tip, tilt, topple; ? akin to TOP[2]]

tope[2] (tōp), *n.* **1.** a small shark, *Galeorhinus galeus*, found along the European coast. **2.** any of various related sharks of small to medium size. [orig. uncert., ? Cornish]

tope[3] (tōp), *n.* (in Buddhist countries) a dome-shaped monument, usually for religious relics. [t. Hind.: m. *tōp*]

East Indian tope

to·pee (tō pē′, tō′pē), *n.* topi.

To·pe·ka (tə pē′kə), *n.* the capital of Kansas, in the NE part, on the Kansas river. 119,484 (1960).

top·er (tō′pər), *n.* a hard drinker; a chronic drunkard. [f. TOPE[1] + -ER[1]]

top-flight (tŏp′flīt′), *adj.* first-rate; superior.

top·gal·lant (tŏp′găl′ənt; *Naut.* tə găl′ənt), *Naut.* —*n.* **1.** the spars and rigging next above the topmast, in a square-rigged vessel. —*adj.* **2.** pertaining to the topgallant. [f. TOP[1] + GALLANT, adj.]

top grafting, *Hort.* grafting in the top, as a tree, in order to replace with a more desired variety or form.

top-ham·per (tŏp′hăm′pər), *n. Naut.* **1.** the light upper sails and their gear and spars, sometimes used to refer to all spars and gear above the deck. **2.** any unnecessary weight, either aloft or about the upper decks.

top hat, a man's tall silk hat.

top-heav·y (tŏp′hĕv′ĭ), *adj.* **1.** having the top disproportionately heavy; liable to fall from too great weight above. **2.** *Finance.* **a.** having a financial structure overburdened with securities which have priority in the payment of dividends. **b.** overcapitalized. —**top′-heav′i·ness,** *n.*

To·phet (tō′fĕt), *n.* **1.** a place in the valley of Hinnom, near Jerusalem, where, contrary to the law, children were offered as sacrifices, esp. to Moloch, later used as a dumping ground for refuse. **2.** the place of punishment for the wicked after death; hell. **3.** some place, condition, etc., likened to hell. Also, **To·pheth** (tō′fĕt). [ME, ult. t. Heb.]

top-hole (tŏp′hōl′), *adj. Brit. Slang.* first-rate.

to·phus (tō′fəs), *n., pl.* **-phi** (-fī). *Pathol.* a calcareous concretion formed in the soft tissue about a joint, in the pinna of the ear, etc.; esp. in gout; a gouty deposit. [t. L, var. of *tōfus* sandstone]

to·pi (tō pē′, tō′pē), *n., pl.* **-pis.** (in India) a helmet of sola pith. Also, **topee.** [t. Hind.: hat]

to·pi·ar·y (tō′pĭ′ĕr′ĭ), *adj., n., pl.* **-aries.** *Gardening.* —*adj.* **1.** clipped or trimmed into (fantastic) shapes. **2.** of or pertaining to such trimming. —*n.* **3.** topiary work; the topiary art. **4.** a garden containing such work. [t. L: m.s. *topiārius* (def. 2)]

top·ic (tŏp′ĭk), *n.* **1.** a subject of conversation or discussion: *to provide a topic for discussion.* **2.** the subject or theme of a discourse or of one of its parts. **3.** *Rhet., Logic.* a general field of considerations from which arguments can be drawn. **4.** a general rule or maxim. [sing. of *topics*, t. L: Anglicization of *topica*, pl., t. Gk.: m. tà *topikă* name of work by Aristotle (lit., things pertaining to commonplaces)] —**Syn. 2.** See **subject.**

top·i·cal (tŏp′ə kəl), *adj.* **1.** pertaining to or dealing with matters of current or local interest. **2.** pertaining to the subject of a discourse, composition, or the like. **3.** of a place; local. **4.** *Med.* pertaining or applied to a particular part of the body. —**top′i·cal·ly,** *adv.*

top kick, *Mil. Slang.* a first sergeant.

top·knot (tŏp′nŏt′), *n.* **1.** a tuft of hair growing on the top of the head. **2.** a knot of hair so worn in some styles of hairdressing. **3.** a knot or bow of ribbon worn on the top of the head. **4.** a tuft or crest of feathers on the head of a bird.

top·loft·y (tŏp′lŏf′tĭ, -lŏf′tĭ), *adj. Colloq.* haughty; pompous; pretentious. —**top′loft′i·ness,** *n.*

top·man (tŏp′mən), *n., pl.* **-men.** *Naut.* a man stationed for duty in a top.

top·mast (tŏp′măst′, -mäst′; *Naut.* -məst), *n. Naut.* the second section of mast above the deck, being that just above the lower mast.

top minnow, any of several small surface-swimming cyprinodont fishes of the egg-laying family *Cyprinodontidae* and the live-bearing family *Poeciliidae.*

top·most (tŏp′mōst′, -məst), *adj.* highest; uppermost.

top·notch (tŏp′nŏch′), *adj. Colloq.* first-rate: *a topnotch job.*

topo-, a word element meaning "place," as in *topography.* Also, **top-,** [t. Gk., comb. form of *tópos*]

topog., 1. topographical. **2.** topography.

to·pog·ra·pher (tə pŏg′rə fər), *n.* **1.** a specialist in topography. **2.** one who describes the surface features of a place or region.

to·pog·ra·phy (tə pŏg′rə fĭ), *n., pl.* **-phies. 1.** the detailed description and analysis of the features of a relatively small area, district, or locality. **2.** the detailed description of particular localities, as cities, towns, estates, etc. **3.** the relief features or surface configuration of an area. [ME, t. LL: m.s. *topographia*, t. Gk.] —**top·o·graph·ic** (tŏp′ə grăf′ĭk), **top′o·graph′i·cal,** *adj.* —**top′o·graph′i·cal·ly,** *adv.*

to·pol·o·gy (tə pŏl′ə jĭ), *n. Math.* the study of those properties of geometric forms that remain invariant under certain transformations, as bending, stretching, etc. [f. TOPO- + -LOGY] —**top·o·log·ic** (tŏp′ə lŏj′ĭk), **top′o·log′i·cal,** *adj.* —**top′o·log′i·cal·ly,** *adv.*

top·o·nym (tŏp′ə nĭm), *n.* **1.** a place name. **2.** a name derived from the name of a place. [f. TOP- + -onym, modeled on SYNONYM]

to·pon·y·my (tə pŏn′ə mĭ), *n., pl.* **-mies. 1.** the study of the place names of a region. **2.** *Anat.* the nomenclature of the regions of the body. —**top·o·nym·ic** (tŏp′ə nĭm′ĭk), **top′o·nym′i·cal,** *adj.*

top·per (tŏp′ər), *n.* **1.** one who or that which tops. **2.** *Slang.* a top hat. **3.** *Brit. Slang.* anything excellent.

top·ping (tŏp′ĭng), *n.* **1.** act of one who or that which tops. **2.** a distinct part forming a top to something. **3.** something put on a thing at the top to complete it. **4.** *(pl.)* that which is removed in topping or cropping plants, as branches. —*adj.* **5.** rising above something else; overtopping. **6.** very high in rank, degree, etc. **7.** *Chiefly Brit. Colloq.* excellent.

top·ple (tŏp′əl), *v.,* **-pled, -pling.** —*v.i.* **1.** to fall forward as having too heavy a top; pitch or tumble down. **2.** to lean over or jut, as if threatening to fall. —*v.t.* **3.** to cause to topple. [freq. of *top* topple. See TOPE[1]]

top·sail (tŏp′sāl′; *Naut.* -səl), *n. Naut.* **1.** a square sail (or either of two square sails) next above the lowest or chief square sail on a mast of a square-rigged vessel, or next above a chief fore-and-aft sail on topsail schooners, etc. See illus. under **sail. 2.** a triangular fore-and-aft sail set above the gaff of a fore-and-aft sail and hoisted to the topmast.

top-se·cret (tŏp′sē′krĭt), *adj. Chiefly Mil.* extremely secret.

top sergeant, *Colloq.* an army officer who holds the position of first sergeant and rank of master sergeant.

top·side (tŏp′sīd′), *n.* **1.** the upper side. **2.** *(usually pl.)* the upper part of a boat's or ship's side, above the main deck.

top·soil (tŏp′soil′), *n.* **1.** the surface or upper part of the soil. —*v.t.* **2.** to remove the topsoil from (land).

top·sy-tur·vy (tŏp′sĭ′tûr′vĭ), *adv., adj., n., pl.* **-vies.** —*adv.* **1.** with the top where the bottom should be; upside down. **2.** in or into a reversed condition or order. **3.** in or into a state of confusion or disorder. —*adj.* **4.** turned upside down; inverted; reversed. **5.** confused or disorderly. —*n.* **6.** inversion of the natural order. **7.** a state of confusion or disorder. [akin to TOP[1] and ME *terve* overturn (cf. OE *tearflian* roll)] —**top′sy-tur′vi·ly,** *adv.* —**top′sy-tur′vi·ness,** *n.*

top·sy-tur·vy·dom (tŏp′sĭ′tûr′vĭ dəm), *n.* a state of affairs or a region in which everything is topsy-turvy.

toque (tōk), *n.* a hat with little or no brim and often with a soft or full crown, worn by women and (formerly) men. [t. F: a hat, bonnet, c. It. *tocca* cap, Sp. *toca* kerchief, Pg. *touca* coif]

tor (tôr), *n. Brit.* a rocky eminence; a hill. [ME; OE *torr,* t. Celtic. Cf. Gael. *torr,* Welsh *tor* protuberance]

To·rah (tôr′ə), *n.* **1.** the five books of Moses; the Pentateuch. **2.** *(also l.c.)* the whole Scripture. **3.** *(also l.c.)* the whole religious literature of Judaism. Also, **To′ra.** [t. Heb.: instruction, law]

Toque

tor·bern·ite (tôr′bər nīt′), *n.* **1.** a mineral, hydrated copper uranium phosphate, $CuU_2P_2O_8·12H_2O$, occurring in square tabular crystals of a bright-green color, a minor ore of uranium. **2.** a cannel coal or very rich oil shale. [named after *Torber* Bergmann, chemist. See -ITE[1]]

torch (tôrch), *n.* **1.** a light to be carried in the hand, consisting of some combustible substance, as resinous wood, or of twisted flax or the like soaked with tallow or other inflammable substance. **2.** something considered as a source of illumination, enlightenment, guidance, etc.: *the torch of learning.* **3.** any of various lamplike devices which produce a hot flame and are used for soldering, burning off paint, etc. **4.** *Brit.* a flashlight. [ME *torche,* t. OF] —**torch-bear·er** (tôrch′bâr′ər), *n.* —**torch′less,** *adj.* —**torch′like′,** *adj.*

torch·light (tôrch′līt′), *n.* the light of a torch or torches.

tor·chon lace (tôr′shŏn; *Fr.* tôr shôN′), **1.** a bobbin-made linen or cotton lace with loosely twisted threads in simple, open patterns. **2.** a machine-made imitation of this, in linen or cotton. [*torchon,* t. F: dishcloth]

torch·wood (tôrch′wŏŏd′), *n.* **1.** any of various resinous woods suitable for making torches, as the wood of the rutaceous tree, *Amyris balsamifera,* of Florida, the West Indies, etc. **2.** any of the trees yielding these woods.

Tor·de·sil·las (tôr'dĕ sē'lyäs), *n.* a town in NW Spain, SW of Valladolid: treaty defining the colonial spheres of Spain and Portugal, 1494. 4515 (1950).

tore[1] (tōr), *v.* pt. of **tear**[2].

tore[2] (tōr), *n.* torus. [t. F, t. L: m. *torus* TORUS]

tor·e·a·dor (tôr'I ə dôr'; *Sp.* tô'rĕ ä dôr'), *n.* a Spanish bullfighter, esp. one who fights on horseback. [t. Sp., der. *torear* fight bulls, der. *toro* bull, g. L *taurus*]

to·re·ro (tô rĕ'rô), *n.*, *pl.* **-ros** (-rôs). a bullfighter who fights on foot. [t. Sp.]

tor·ic (tôr'Ik, tŏr'-), *adj.* 1. denoting or pertaining to a lens with a surface forming a portion of a torus, used for eyeglasses. 2. *Geom.* of or pertaining to a torus. [f. TOR(US) + -IC]

to·ri·i (tôr'I ē'), *n.*, *pl.* **torii.** a form of decorative gateway or portal in Japan, consisting of two upright wooden posts connected at the top by two horizontal crosspieces, and commonly found at the entrance to Shinto temples. [t. Jap.]

To·ri·no (tô rē'nô), *n.* Italian name of **Turin.**

tor·ment (*v.* tôr mĕnt'; *n.* tôr'mĕnt), *v.t.* 1. to afflict with great bodily or mental suffering; pain: *to be tormented with violent headaches.* 2. to worry or annoy excessively: *to torment one with questions.* 3. to throw into commotion; stir up; disturb. —*n.* 4. a state of great bodily or mental suffering; agony; misery. 5. something that causes great bodily or mental pain or suffering. 6. a source of pain, anguish, trouble, worry, or annoyance. 7. *Archaic.* **a.** an instrument of torture, as the rack or the thumbscrew. **b.** the infliction of torture by means of such an instrument. **c.** the torture inflicted. [ME, t. OF: s. *tormenter*, der. *torment* torment, n., g. L *tormentum* something operated by twisting] —**tor·ment'ing·ly,** *adv.*
—**Syn.** 1. TORMENT, RACK, TORTURE suggest causing great physical or mental pain, suffering, or harassment. To TORMENT is to harass as by incessant repetition of vexations or annoyances: *to be tormented with a toothache.* To RACK is to affect with such pain as that suffered by one stretched on a rack; to concentrate with painful effort: *to rack one's brains.* To TORTURE is to afflict with acute and more or less protracted suffering: *to torture one by keeping him in suspense.*

tor·men·til (tôr'mĕn tĬl), *n.* a low rosaceous herb, *Potentilla Tormentilla* (or *erecta*), of Europe, with small bright-yellow flowers, and a strongly astringent root which is used in medicine and in tanning and dyeing. [ME *tormentille*, t. ML: m. *tormentilla*, dim. of *tormentum* TORMENT]

tor·men·tor (tôr mĕn'tər), *n.* 1. one who or that which torments. 2. *Theat.* a curtain or framed structure back of the proscenium at each side of the stage. 3. *Motion Pictures.* a sound-deadening screen used during the taking of scenes to prevent echo and reverberation. Also, **tor·ment'er.**

torn (tôrn), *v.* pp. of **tear**[2].

tor·na·do (tôr nā'dō), *n.*, *pl.* **-does, -dos.** 1. a destructive rotatory storm of the middle United States, usually appearing as a whirling, advancing funnel pendent from a mass of black cloud. 2. a violent squall or whirlwind of small extent, as those occurring during the summer months on the west coast of Africa. 3. a violent outburst, as of emotion or activity. [t. Sp., der. *tornar* to turn, b. with *tronada* thunderstorm, der. *tronar* to thunder, g. L *tonāre*] —**tor·nad'ic** (tôr năd'Ĭk), *adj.* —**tor·na'do·like',** *adj.*

to·roid (tô'roid), *n.* *Geom.* 1. a surface generated by the revolution of any closed plane curve or contour about an axis lying in its plane. 2. the solid enclosed by such a surface. [f. TOR(US) + -OID]

To·ron·to (tə rŏn'tō), *n.* a city in SE Canada, on Lake Ontario: the capital of Ontario. 675,754; with suburbs, 1,117,470 (1951).

to·rose (tôr'ōs, tōrōs'), *adj.* *Bot.* 1. cylindrical, with swellings or constrictions at intervals; knobbed. 2. *Zool.* bulging. Also, **to·rous** (tôr'əs). [t. L: m.s. *torōsus* bulging. See TORUS]

tor·pe·do (tôr pē'dō), *n.*, *pl.* **-does,** *v.*, **-doed, -doing.** —*n.* 1. a self-propelled cigar-shaped missile containing explosives which is launched from a tube in a submarine, torpedo boat, or the like, and explodes upon impact with the ship fired at. 2. any of various submarine explosive devices for destroying hostile ships, as a mine. 3. a cartridge of gunpowder, dynamite, or the like, exploded in an oil well to start or increase the flow of oil, or elsewhere for other purposes. 4. a detonating device which is fastened to the top of a rail and exploded by the pressure of the locomotive or car, to give an audible signal to members of the train crew. 5. any of various other explosive devices, as a firework which consists of an explosive wrapped up with gravel in a piece of tissue paper, and which detonates when thrown forcibly on the ground or against a hard surface. 6. the electric catfish, *Malapterurus*, of the Nile. —*v.t.* 7. to attack, hit, damage, or destroy with a torpedo or torpedoes. 8. to explode a torpedo in (an oil well) to start or increase the flow of oil. —*v.i.* 9. to attack, damage, or sink a ship with torpedoes. [t. L: numbness, torpidity, torpedo fish. Cf. TORPID]

torpedo boat, a warship of small size and high speed used primarily for torpedo attacks.

torpedo-boat destroyer, a vessel somewhat larger than the ordinary torpedo boat, designed for destroying torpedo boats or as a more powerful form of torpedo boat.

torpedo body, a form of automobile body more or less resembling the cigar-shaped submarine torpedo, used esp. for racing and sport cars.

torpedo tube, a tube through which a self-propelled torpedo is launched, usually by the explosion of a charge of powder.

tor·pid[1] (tôr'pĬd), *adj.* 1. inactive or sluggish, as a bodily organ. 2. slow; dull; apathetic; lethargic. 3. dormant, as a hibernating or estivating animal. [t. L: s. *torpidus* numb] —**tor·pid'i·ty, tor'pid·ness,** *n.* —**tor'pid·ly,** *adv.* —**Syn.** 3. See **inactive.**

tor·pid[2] (tôr'pĬd), *n.* (at the University of Oxford) 1. an eight-oared clinker-built boat in which the Lent races are rowed. 2. one of the crew. 3. (*pl.*) the races themselves. [special use of TORPID[1]]

tor·por (tôr'pər), *n.* 1. a state of suspended physical powers and activities. 2. sluggish inactivity or inertia. 3. dormancy, as of a hibernating animal. 4. lethargic dullness or indifference; apathy. [t. L: numbness]

tor·por·if·ic (tôr'pə rĬf'Ĭk), *adj.* causing torpor.

tor·quate (tôr'kwĬt, -kwāt), *adj.* *Zool.* ringed about the neck, as with feathers or a color; collared. [t. L: m.s. *torquātus*, pp., adorned with a necklace]

Tor·quay (tôr kē'), *n.* a city in SW England. in Devonshire; seaside resort. 53,216 (1951).

torque (tôrk), *n.* 1. *Mech.* that which produces or tends to produce torsion or rotation; the moment of a system of forces which tends to cause rotation. 2. *Mach.* the turning power of a shaft. 3. the rotational effect on plane-polarized light passing through certain liquids or crystals. 4. a collar, necklace, or similar ornament consisting of a twisted narrow band, usually of precious metal, worn esp. by the ancient Gauls and Britons. [t. L: m. *torques* twisted metal necklace]

Tor·que·ma·da (tôr'kĕ mä'dä), *n.* **Tomás de** (tô mäs' dĕ), 1420–98, Spanish inquisitor general.

tor·ques (tôr'kwēz), *n.* *Zool.* a ringlike band or formation about the neck, as of feathers, hair, or integument of distinctive color or appearance; a collar. [t. L: twisted neck chain or collar]

Tor·rance (tôr'əns), *n.* a city in SW California, SW of Los Angeles. 100,991 (1960).

tor·re·fy (tôr'ə fī', tŏr'-), *v.t.*, **-fied, -fying.** 1. to dry or parch with heat, as drugs, etc. 2. to roast, as metallic ores. Also, **torrify.** [t. L: m.s. *torrefacere* make dry or hot] —**tor·re·fac·tion** (tôr'ə făk'shən, tŏr'-), *n.*

Tor·rens (tôr'ənz, tŏr'-), *n.* **Lake,** a salt lake in E South Australia. 130 mi. long; 25 ft. below sea level.

tor·rent (tôr'ənt, tŏr'-), *n.* 1. a stream of water flowing with great rapidity and violence. 2. a rushing, violent, or abundant and unceasing stream of anything: *a torrent of lava.* 3. a violent downpour of rain. 4. a violent, tumultuous, or overwhelming flow: *a torrent of abuse.* [t. L: s. *torrens* torrent, lit., boiling; r. ME *torrens*, t. L]

tor·ren·tial (tô rĕn'shəl, tŏ-), *adj.* 1. pertaining to or having the nature of a torrent. 2. resembling a torrent in rapidity or violence. 3. falling in torrents. 4. produced by the action of a torrent. 5. violent, vehement, or impassioned. 6. overwhelming; extraordinarily copious. —**tor·ren'tial·ly,** *adv.*

Tor·res Strait (tôr'Ĭz, tôr'-), a strait between NE Australia and S New Guinea. ab. 80 mi. wide.

Tor·ri·cel·li (tôr'ə chĕl'lē), *n.* **Evangelista** (ĕ'vän jĕ lä'stä), 1608–47, Italian physicist: discovered principle of barometer.

tor·rid (tôr'Ĭd, tŏr'-), *adj.* 1. subject to parching or burning heat, esp. of the sun, as regions, etc. 2. oppressively hot, parching, or burning, as climate, weather, air, etc. 3. ardent; passionate. [t. L: s. *torridus*] —**tor·rid'i·ty, tor'rid·ness,** *n.* —**tor'rid·ly,** *adv.*

Torrid Zone, the part of the earth's surface between the tropics of Cancer and Capricorn.

tor·ri·fy (tôr'ə fī', tŏr'-), *v.t.*, **-fied, -fying.** torrefy.

Tor·ring·ton (tôr'Ĭng tən, tŏr'-), *n.* a city in NW Connecticut. 30,045 (1960).

tor·sade (tôr sād'), *n.* 1. a twisted cord. 2. any ornamental twist, as of velvet. [t. F: twisted fringe, der. *tordre*, g. LL *torcēre*, r. L *torquēre* twist]

tor·si·bil·i·ty (tôr'sə bĬl'ə tĬ), *n.* 1. capability of being twisted. 2. resistance to being twisted. 3. capacity to return to original shape after being twisted.

tor·sion (tôr'shən), *n.* 1. act of twisting. 2. resulting state. 3. *Mech.* **a.** the twisting of a body by two equal and opposite torques. **b.** the internal torque so produced. [ME *torcion*, t. LL: m. *torsio*, der. *torquēre* twist] —**tor'sion·al,** *adj.* —**tor'sion·al·ly,** *adv.*

torsion balance, an instrument for measuring small forces (as electrical attraction or repulsion) by determining the amount of torsion or twisting they cause in a slender wire or filament.

tor·so (tôr'sō), *n.*, *pl.* **-sos, -si** (-sē). 1. the trunk of the human body. 2. a sculptured form representing the trunk of a nude female or male figure. 3. something mutilated or incomplete. [t. It.: trunk, stump, stalk, trunk of statue, g. L *thyrsus* THYRSUS]

tort (tôrt), *n.* *Law.* a civil wrong (other than a breach of contract or trust) such as the law requires compensation for in damages; typically, a willful or negligent injury to a plaintiff's person, property, or reputation. [ME, t. OF, t. LL: s. *tortum* wrong, injustice, L *torquēre* twist]

tor·ti·col·lis (tôr'tə kŏl'Ĭs), *n.* *Pathol.* an affection in which the neck is twisted and the head inclined to one side, by spasmodic contraction of the muscles of the neck. [t. NL: crooked neck. See TORT, COLLAR]

tor·tile (tôr′tĭl), *adj.* twisted; coiled. [t. L: m.s. *tortilis* twisted, winding]

tor·til·la (tôr tē′yä), *n.* (in Mexico, etc.) a thin, round, unleavened cake prepared from corn meal, baked on a flat plate of iron, earthenware, or the like. [t. Sp., dim. of *torta* cake, g. LL *torta* (*pānis*) twisted (bread)]

tor·tious (tôr′shəs), *adj. Law.* of the nature of or pertaining to a tort. [ME *torcious*, t. AF, der. ML *tortio* usé of violence, in L torture] —**tor′tious·ly**, *adv.*

tor·toise (tôr′təs), *n.* 1. a turtle, orig. any turtle other than the marine forms, now esp. a terrestrial turtle as distinguished from the aquatic species. 2. a very slow person or thing. [ME *tortuce*, t. ML: m. *tortuca*, der. L *tortus*, pp., twisted]

tortoise shell, 1. the horny substance, with a mottled or clouded yellow-and-brown coloration, composing the plates or scales that cover the marine tortoise-shell turtle, *Eretmochelys*, formerly used for making combs and other articles, inlaying, etc. 2. any synthetic substance made to appear like natural tortoise shell. 3. any of certain colorful butterflies (family *Nymphalidae*), as *Nymphalis milberti*, with variegated undermarkings.

tor·toise-shell (tôr′təs shĕl′), *adj.* 1. mottled or variegated like tortoise shell, esp. with yellow and black and sometimes other colors. 2. made of tortoise shell.

Tor·tu·ga (tôr tōō′ga), *n.* an island off the N coast of, and belonging to, Haiti: formerly a pirate stronghold. ab. 25 mi. long. French, *La Tor·tue* (lä tôr tv′).

tor·tu·os·i·ty (tôr′chōō ŏs′ə tĭ), *n., pl.* **-ties.** 1. the state of being tortuous; twisted form or course; crookedness. 2. a twist, bend, or crook. 3. a twisting or crooked part, passage, or thing.

tor·tu·ous (tôr′chōō əs), *adj.* 1. full of twists, turns, or bends; twisting, winding, or crooked. 2. not direct or straightforward, as in a course of procedure, thought, speech, or writing. 3. deceitfully indirect or morally crooked, as proceedings, methods, policy, etc. 4. *Geom.* not in one plane, as a curve, such as a helix, which does not lie in a plane. [ME, t. L: m.s. *tortuōsus* full of turns or twists] —**tor′tu·ous·ly**, *adv.* —**tor′tu·ous·ness**, *n.*

tor·ture (tôr′chər), *n., v.,* **-tured, -turing.** —*n.* 1. act of inflicting excruciating pain, esp. from sheer cruelty or in hatred, revenge, or the like. 2. a method of inflicting such pain. 3. (*often pl.*) the pain or suffering caused or undergone. 4. extreme anguish of body or mind; agony. 5. a cause of severe pain or anguish. —*v.t.* 6. to subject to torture. 7. to afflict with severe pain of body or mind. 8. to twist, force, or bring into some unnatural position or form: *trees tortured by storms.* 9. to wrest, distort, or pervert (language, etc.). [t. L: m. *tortūra* twisting, torment, torture] —**tor′tur·er**, *n.* —**tor′tur·ous**, *adj.* —**Syn.** 6. See **torment**.

To·run (tô′rōōn′y), *n.* a city in N Poland, on the Vistula. 77,597 (est. 1954). German, **Thorn.**

to·rus (tôr′əs), *n., pl.* **tori** (tôr′ī). 1. *Archit.* a large convex molding, more or less semicircular in profile, commonly forming the lowest member of the base of a column, or that directly above the plinth (when present), and sometimes occurring as one of a pair separated by a scotia and fillets. See diag. under **column.** 2. *Geom.* **a.** a surface generated by the revolution of a conic (esp. a circle) about an axis lying in its plane. **b.** the solid enclosed by such a surface. 3. *Bot.* the receptacle of a flower. 4. *Anat., etc.* a rounded ridge; a protuberant part. [t. L: bulge, rounded molding]

to·rus pa·la·ti·nus (tôr′əs păl′ə tī′nəs), *Anat.* a rounded ridge on the hard palate. [NL]

To·ry (tôr′ĭ), *n., pl.* **-ries.** 1. a member of a political party in Great Britain, in general favoring conservation of the existing order of things in state and church, more recently known as the Conservative party. Cf. **Whig** (def. 2a). 2. an advocate of conservative principles; one opposed to reform or radicalism. 3. *Amer. Hist.* a member of the British party during the Revolutionary period; a loyalist. 4. (in the 17th century) one of a class of dispossessed Irish, nominally royalists, who became outlaws and were noted for their outrages and cruelties. —*adj.* 5. of or belonging to or characteristic of the Tories. 6. being a Tory. 7. conservative. Also, **tory** for 2, 7. [t. Irish: m. *tóraidhe* pursuer] —**To′ry·ism**, *n.*

Tos·ca·na (tôs′kä nä′), *n.* Italian name of **Tuscany.**

Tos·ca·ni·ni (tŏs′kə nē′nĭ; *It.* tôs′kä nē′nē), *n.* Arturo (är tōō′rô), 1867–1957, U.S. orchestra conductor, born in Italy.

tosh (tŏsh), *n. Brit. Slang.* nonsense.

toss (tôs, tŏs), *v.,* **tossed** or (*Poetic*) **tost; tossing;** *n.* —*v.t.* 1. to throw, pitch, or fling, esp. to throw lightly or carelessly: *to toss a piece of paper into the waste basket.* 2. to throw or send (a ball, etc.) from one to another, as in play. 3. to throw or pitch with irregular or careless motions; fling or jerk about: *a ship tossed by the waves, a tree tosses its branches in the wind.* 4. to agitate, disturb, or disquiet. 5. to throw, raise, or jerk upward suddenly: *she tossed her head disdainfully.* 6. to throw (a coin, etc.) into the air in order to decide something by the side turned up when it falls (often fol. by *up*). —*v.i.* 7. to pitch, rock, sway, or move irregularly, as a ship on a rough sea, or a flag or plumes in the breeze. 8. to fling or jerk oneself or move restlessly about, esp. on a bed or couch: *to toss in one's sleep.* 9. to throw

something. 10. to throw a coin or other object into the air in order to decide something by the way it falls (often fol. by *up*). 11. to go with a fling of the body: *to toss out of a room.* —*n.* 12. act of tossing. 13. a pitching about or up and down. 14. a throw or pitch. 15. a tossing of a coin or the like to decide something, or a tossup. 16. the distance to which something is or may be thrown. 17. a sudden fling or jerk of the body, esp. a quick upward or backward movement of the head. [appar. t. Scand.; cf. d. Sw. *tossa* spread, strew] —**toss′-er**, *n.* —**Syn.** 1. See **throw.**

toss·up (tôs′ŭp′, tŏs′-), *n.* 1. the tossing up of a coin or the like to decide something by its fall. 2. *Colloq.* an even chance.

tost (tôst, tŏst), *v. Poetic.* pt. and pp. of **toss.**

tot[1] (tŏt), *n.* 1. a small child. 2. *Chiefly Brit.* a small portion of drink. 3. a small quantity of anything. [? short for *totterer* child learning to walk]

tot[2] (tŏt), *v.,* **totted, totting;** *n. Chiefly Brit. Colloq.* —*v.t.* 1. to add (often fol. by *up*). —*n.* 2. a total. 3. act of adding. [t. L: so much, so many]

to·tal (tō′təl), *adj., n., v.,* **-taled, -taling** or (*esp. Brit.*) **-talled, -talling.** —*adj.* 1. constituting or comprising the whole; entire; whole: *the total expenditure.* 2. of or pertaining to the whole of something: *a total eclipse.* 3. complete in extent or degree; absolute; unqualified; utter: *a total failure.* —*n.* 4. the total amount; sum; aggregate: *to add the several items to find the total.* 5. the whole; a whole or aggregate: *the costs reached a total of $200.* —*v.t.* 6. to bring to a total; add up. 7. to reach a total of; amount to. —*v.i.* 8. to amount (often fol. by *to*). [ME, t. ML: s. *tōtālis*, der. L *tōtus* entire] —**Syn.** 5. See **whole.**

total depravity, *Theol.* the absolute unfitness of man, due to original sin, for the moral purposes of his being, until born again through the influence of the Spirit of God.

total eclipse, an eclipse in which the whole surface of the eclipsed body is obscured (opposed to *annular eclipse*).

to·tal·i·tar·i·an (tō tăl′ə târ′ĭ ən), *adj.* 1. of or pertaining to a centralized government in which those in control grant neither recognition nor tolerance to parties of differing opinion. —*n.* 2. an adherent of totalitarian principles. —**to·tal′i·tar′i·an·ism,** *n.*

to·tal·i·ty (tō tăl′ə tĭ), *n., pl.* **-ties.** 1. state of being total; entirety. 2. that which is total; the total amount; a whole. 3. *Astron.* total obscuration in an eclipse.

to·tal·i·za·tor (tō′təl ə zā′tər), *n.* 1. an apparatus for registering and indicating the total of operations, measurements, etc. 2. *Chiefly Brit.* an apparatus used at horse races which registers and indicates the number of tickets sold to betters on each horse.

to·tal·ize (tō′tə līz′), *v.t.,* **-ized, -izing.** to make total; combine into a total. —**to′tal·i·za′tion,** *n.*

to·tal·iz·er (tō′tə lī′zər), *n.* 1. totalizator. 2. a machine for adding and subtracting.

to·tal·ly (tō′tə lĭ), *adv.* wholly; entirely; completely.

tote (tōt), *v.,* **toted, toting,** *n. U.S. Colloq. and Dial.* —*v.t.* 1. to carry, as on the back or in the arms, as a burden or load. 2. to carry or have on the person: *to tote a gun.* 3. *Dial.* to transport or convey, as in a vehicle or boat. —*n.* 4. act or course of toting. 5. that which is toted. [orig. uncert.]

to·tem (tō′təm), *n. Anthropol.* 1. an object or thing in nature, often an animal, assumed as the token or emblem of a clan, family, or related group. 2. an object or natural phenomenon with which a primitive family or sib considers itself closely related, usually by blood. 3. a representation of such an object serving as the distinctive mark of the clan or group. [t. Algonquian (Chippewa): m. *ototeman* his brother-sister kin, der. *ote* parents, relations] —**to·tem·ic** (tō těm′ĭk), *adj.*

to·tem·ism (tō′tə mĭz′əm), *n.* 1. the practice of having totems. 2. the system of tribal division according to totems.

to·tem·ist (tō′təm ĭst), *n.* a member of a clan or the like distinguished by a totem. —**to′tem·is′tic,** *adj.*

totem pole, a pole or post carved and painted with totemic figures, erected by Indians of the northwest coast of North America, esp. in front of their houses. Also, **totem post.**

toth·er (tŭth′ər), *adj., pron. Dial.* the other. Also, **t′oth′er.** [ME *the tother*, var. of *thet other* the other]

to·ti·dem ver·bis (tō′tĭ děm vûr′bĭs), *Latin.* with just so many words; in these words.

to·ti·pal·mate (tō′tĭ păl′mĭt, -māt), *adj.* having all four toes fully webbed. [f. L *tōti-* (repr. *tōtus* whole) + PALMATE]

to·ti·pal·ma·tion (tō′tĭ păl mā′shən), *n.* totipalmate condition or formation.

Totipalmate foot

Tot·le·ben (tôt′lĕ běn, tôt lĕ′-), *n.* **Franz Eduard Ivanovich, Count** (fränts ě′dŏŏ ärt′ ĭ vä′nŏ vĭch), 1818–84, Russian military engineer and general.

Tot·ten·ham (tôt′ən əm), *n.* a city in SE England, in Middlesex, near London. 126,929 (1951).

tot·ter (tŏt′ər), *v.i.* 1. to walk or go with faltering steps, as if from extreme weakness. 2. to sway or rock on the base or ground, as if about to fall: *a tottering tower, a tottering government.* 3. to shake or tremble: *a*

tottering load. —*n.* **4.** act of tottering; an unsteady movement or gait. [ME *totre*, t. Scand.; cf. d. Norw. *totra* quiver, shake] —**tot′ter·er,** *n.* —**tot′ter·ing·ly,** *adv.* —**Syn. 1.** See **stagger.**

tot·ter·y (tŏt′ər ĭ), *adj.* tottering; shaky.

tou·can (tōō′kăn, tōō kän′), *n.* any of various fruit-eating birds (family *Ramphastidae*) of tropical America, with an enormous beak and usually a striking coloration. [t. Carib]

Red-billed toucan.
Ramphastos montlis
(22 in. long)

touch (tŭch), *v.t.* **1.** to put the hand, finger, etc., on or into contact with (something) to feel it. **2.** to come into contact with and perceive (something), as the hand or the like does. **3.** to bring (the hand, finger, etc., or something held) into contact with something. **4.** to give a slight tap or pat to with the hand, finger, etc.; strike or hit gently or lightly. **5.** to come into or be in contact with. **6.** *Geom.* (of a line or surface) to be tangent to. **7.** to be adjacent to or border on. **8.** to come up to; reach; attain. **9.** to attain equality with; compare with (usually with a negative). **10.** to mark by strokes of the brush, pencil, or the like. **11.** to modify or improve (a picture, etc.) by adding a stroke here and there (often fol. by *up*). **12.** to mark or relieve slightly, as with color: *a gray dress touched with blue.* **13.** to strike the strings, keys, etc., of (a musical instrument) so as to cause it to sound. **14.** to play or perform, as an air. **15.** to stop at (a place), as a **ship. 16.** to treat or affect in some way by contact. **17.** to affect as if by contact; tinge; imbue. **18.** to affect with some feeling or emotion, esp. tenderness, pity, gratitude, etc.: *his heart was touched by their sufferings.* **19.** to handle, use, or have to do with (something) in any way: *he won't touch another drink.* **20.** to deal with or treat in speech or writing. **21.** to refer or allude to. **22.** to pertain or relate to: *a critic in all affairs touching the kitchen.* **23.** to be a matter of importance to; make a difference to. **24.** to stamp (tested metal) as being of standard purity, etc. **25.** *Slang.* to apply to for money, or succeed in getting money from. —*v.i.* **26.** to place the hand, finger, etc., on or in contact with something. **27.** to come into or be in contact. **28.** to make a stop or a short call at a place, as a ship or those on board (usually fol. by *at*). **29.** to speak or write briefly or casually (fol. by *on* or *upon*) in the course of a discourse, etc.: *he touched briefly on his own travels.* —*n.* **30.** act of touching. **31.** state or fact of being touched. **32.** that sense by which anything material is perceived by means of the contact with it of some part of the body. **33.** the sensation or effect caused by touching something, regarded as a quality of the thing: *an object with a slimy touch.* **34.** a coming into or being in contact. **35.** a close relation of communication, agreement, sympathy, or the like: *to be in touch with public opinion.* **36.** a slight stroke or blow. **37.** a slight attack, as of illness or disease: *a touch of rheumatism.* **38.** a slight added action or effort in doing or completing any piece of work. **39.** manner of execution in artistic work. **40.** act or manner of touching or fingering a musical instrument, esp. a keyboard instrument, so as to bring out its tones. **41.** the mode of action of the keys of an instrument. **42.** *Change Ringing.* a partial series of changes on a peal of bells. **43.** a stroke or dash, as with a brush, pencil, or pen. **44.** a detail in any artistic work. **45.** a slight amount of some quality, attribute, etc.: *a touch of sarcasm in his voice.* **46.** a slight quantity or degree: *a touch of salt.* **47.** a distinguishing characteristic or trait: *the touch of the master.* **48.** quality or kind in general. **49.** act of testing anything. **50.** something that serves as a test. **51.** *Slang.* the act of applying to a person for money, as a gift or a loan. **52.** *Slang.* an obtaining of money thus. **53.** *Slang.* the money obtained. **54.** an official mark or stamp put upon gold, silver, etc., after testing, to indicate standard fineness. **55.** a die, stamp, or the like for impressing such a mark. **56.** *Rugby, etc.* the portion of the land lying outside the field of play, including the touchlines in Rugby. [ME *touche(n)*, t. OF: m. *tochier*; orig. uncert.] —**touch′a·ble,** *adj.* —**touch′er,** *n.*

touch and go, 1. act of touching for an instant and leaving at once. **2.** something done quickly. **3.** a precarious or delicate state of affairs.

touch-and-go (tŭch′ən gō′), *adj.* **1.** hasty, sketchy, or desultory. **2.** risky: *a highly touch-and-go situation.*

touch·back (tŭch′băk′), *n. Football.* act of a player in touching the ball to the ground on or behind his own goal line when it has been driven there by the opposing side.

touch·down (tŭch′doun′), *n. Football.* **1.** act of a player in touching the ball down to the ground behind the opponent's goal line. **2.** the play by which this is done. **3.** the score made by this play, counting 6 points.

tou·ché (tōō shā′), *interj.* **1.** *Fencing.* an expression indicating a touch by the point of a weapon. **2.** Good point! (said in acknowledging a telling remark or rejoinder). [F: past part. of *toucher* to touch]

touched (tŭcht), *adj.* **1.** moved; stirred. **2.** slightly crazy; unbalanced: *touched in the head.*

touch·hole (tŭch′hōl′), *n.* the vent in the breech of an old-time firearm through which fine was communicated to the powder charge. See diag. under **flintlock.**

touch·ing (tŭch′ĭng), *adj.* **1.** affecting; moving; pathetic. **2.** that touches. —*prep.* **3.** in reference or relation to; concerning; about. —**touch′ing·ly,** *adv.* —**touch′ing·ness,** *n.*

touch·line (tŭch′lĭn′), *n. Rugby, etc.* any of the sidelines bordering the play field.

touch-me-not (tŭch′mĭ nŏt′), *n. Bot.* **1.** a yellow-flowered balsaminaceous plant, *Impatiens noli-me-tangere,* whose ripe seed vessels burst open when touched. **2.** any of various other species of the same genus.

touch·stone (tŭch′stōn′), *n.* **1.** a black siliceous stone used to test the purity of gold and silver by the color of the streak produced on it by rubbing it with either metal. **2.** a test or criterion for the qualities of a thing.

touch·wood (tŭch′wŏŏd′), *n.* **1.** wood converted into an easily ignitible substance by the action of certain fungi, and used as tinder; punk. **2.** amadou.

touch·y (tŭch′ĭ), *adj.,* **touchier, touchiest. 1.** apt to take offense on slight provocation; irritable. **2.** precarious, risky, or ticklish, as a subject. **3.** sensitive to touch. **4.** easily ignited, as tinder. [var. of TECHY, by assoc. with TOUCH] —**touch′i·ly,** *adv.* —**touch′i·ness,** *n.*

tough (tŭf), *adj.* **1.** not easily broken or cut. **2.** not brittle or tender. **3.** difficult to masticate, as food. **4.** of viscous consistency, as liquid or semiliquid matter. **5.** capable of great endurance; sturdy; hardy. **6.** not easily influenced, as a person. **7.** hardened; incorrigible. **8.** difficult to perform, accomplish, or deal with; hard, trying, or troublesome. **9.** hard to bear or endure. **10.** vigorous; severe; violent: *a tough struggle.* **11.** *U.S.* rough, disorderly, or rowdyish. —*n.* **12.** *U.S.* a ruffian; a rowdy. [ME; OE *tōh.* Cf. D *taai,* G *zähe, zäh*] —**tough′ly,** *adv.* —**tough′ness,** *n.* —**Ant. 1.** fragile.

tough·en (tŭf′ən), *v.i., v.t.* to make or become tough or tougher. —**tough′en·er,** *n.*

Toul (tōōl), *n.* a fortress town in NE France, on the Moselle: siege, 1870. 12,134 (1954).

Tou·lon (tōō lôn′), *n.* a seaport in SE France: naval base. 141,117 (1954).

Tou·louse (tōō lōōz′), *n.* a city in S France, on the Garonne river. 268,863 (1954).

Tou·louse-Lau·trec (tōō lōōz′lō trĕk′), *n.* **Henri Marie Raymond de** (än rē′ mà rē′ rĕ môn′), 1864–1901, French painter and lithographer.

tou·pee (tōō pā′, -pē′), *n.* **1.** a wig or patch of false hair worn to cover a bald spot. **2.** (formerly) a curl or an artificial lock of hair on the top of the head, esp. as a crowning feature of a periwig. [t. F: m. *toupet,* der. OF *to(u)p* tuft of hair. See TOP[1]]

tour (tōōr), *v.i.* **1.** to travel from place to place. **2.** to travel from city to city with a theatrical company. —*v.t.* **3.** to travel through (a place). **4.** (of a manager) to send or take (a theatrical company, its production, etc.) from city to city. —*n.* **5.** a traveling around from place to place. **6.** a long journey including the visiting of a number of places in sequence. **7.** a journey of a theatrical company from town to town to fulfill engagements: *to go on tour.* **8.** *Chiefly Mil.* a period of duty at one place. [ME, t. F, g. L *tornus,* t. Gk.: m. *tórnos* tool for making a circle] —**Syn. 6.** See **excursion.**

tou·ra·co (tōōr′ə kō′), *n., pl.* **-cos.** any of the large African birds constituting the family *Musophagidae* (genera *Turacus, Musophaga,* etc.), notable for their brilliant plumage and helmetlike crest. [t. West African]

Tou·raine (tōō rĕn′), *n.* a former province in W France. *Cap.:* Tours.

Tour·coing (tōōr kwăn′), *n.* city in N France, near the Belgian border. 83,416 (1954).

tour de force (tōōr də fôrs′), *French.* a feat requiring unusual strength, skill, or ingenuity.

touring car, an open automobile designed for five or more passengers.

tour·ism (tōōr′ĭz əm), *n.* **1.** the practice of touring, esp. for pleasure. **2.** the occupation of providing local transportation, entertainment, lodging, food, etc., for tourists.

tour·ist (tōōr′ĭst), *n.* one who makes a tour, esp. for pleasure.

tourist class, a type of lower-priced fare accommodation for travel, esp. on a ship.

tour·ma·line (tōōr′mə lĭn, -lēn′), *n.* a mineral, essentially a complex silicate containing boron, aluminum, etc., occurring in various colors (black being common), the transparent varieties (red, pink, green, and blue) being used in jewelry. Also, **tour·ma·lin** (tōōr′mə lĭn), **turmaline.** [t. Singhalese: m. *toramalli* carnelian]

Tour·nai (tōōr nĕ′), *n.* a city in W Belgium, on the Scheldt river. 33,300 (est. 1952). Also, **Tour·nay′.**

tour·na·ment (tûr′nə mənt, tōōr′-), *n.* **1.** a meeting for contests in athletic or other sports. **2.** a trial of skill in some game, in which competitors play a series of contests: *a chess tournament.* **3.** *Hist.* **a.** a contest or martial sport in which two opposing parties of mounted and armored combatants fought for a prize, with blunted weapons and in accordance with certain rules. **b.** a meeting at an appointed time and place for the performance of knightly exercises and sports. [ME *tornement,* t. OF: m. *torneiement,* der. *torneier* TOURNEY v.]

Tour·neur (tûr′nər), *n.* **Cyril** (sĭr′ĭl), 1575?–1626, British dramatist.

tour·ney (tûr′nĭ, tŏŏr′nĭ), *n.*, *pl.* **-neys**, *v.*, **-neyed**, **-neying.** —*n.* 1. a tournament. [ME, t. OF: m. *tornei*, *tournay*, der. *torneier* tourney, v.] —*v.t.* 2. to contend or engage in a tournament. [ME, t. OF: m.s. *torneier*, der. *torn* turn, g. L *tornus* lathe]

tour·ni·quet (tŏŏr′nəkĕt′, -kā′, tûr′-). *n.* *Surg.* any device for arresting bleeding by forcibly compressing a blood vessel, as a pad pressed down by a screw, a bandage tightened by twisting, etc. [t. F, der. *tourner* turn]

Tours (tŏŏr), *n.* a city in W France, on the Loire river: Charles Martel defeated the Saracens near here, A.D. 732. 83,618 (1954).

tou·sle (tou′zəl), *v.*, **-sled**, **-sling**, *n.* —*v.t.* 1. to handle roughly. 2. to disorder or dishevel: *his hair was tousled*. —*n.* 3. a tousled mass of hair. 4. a tousled condition; a disordered mass. [ME *tousel*; freq. of *touse* pull]

tous-les-mois (tŏŏ lĕ mwä′), *n.* a large-grained farinaceous food resembling arrowroot, obtained from a South American canna cultivated in the West Indies, *Canna edulis*, and used in baby food and cocoa. [t. F: all the months, prob. alter. of French Antilles *toloman*]

Tous·saint L'Ou·ver·ture (tŏŏ săN′ lŏŏ vĕr tyr′), (Francis Dominique Toussaint) 1743–1803, Negro military and political leader, one of the liberators of Haiti.

tout (tout), *Colloq.* —*v.i.* 1. to solicit business, employment, votes, etc., importunately. 2. to spy on a race horse, etc., to obtain information for betting purposes; act as a tout. —*v.t.* 3. to solicit support for importunately. 4. to describe or proclaim: *a politician touted as a friend of the people.* 5. to praise highly and insistently. 6. to spy on (a race horse, etc.) in order to gain information for betting purposes. 7. to give a tip on (a race horse, etc.), esp. in order to indicate a probable winner. 8. to watch; spy on. —*n.* 9. one who solicits custom, employment, support, etc., importunately. 10. one who spies on race horses, etc., to gain information for betting purposes, or who gives tips on race horses, etc., as a business. [ME *tute*(n); akin to OE *tȳtan* peep out, become visible, shine (said of a star)]

tout à fait (tŏŏ tà fĕ′), *French*. entirely.

tout à vous (tŏŏ tà vŏŏ′), *French.* yours sincerely.

tout de suite (tŏŏt swĕt′), *French.* at once.

tout en·sem·ble (tŏŏ tän säN′bl), *French.* 1. all together. 2. the assemblage of parts or details, as in a work of art, considered as forming a whole; the ensemble.

tout·er (tou′tər), *n.* *Colloq.* one who touts; a tout.

tout le monde (tŏŏ lə mônd′), *French.* all the world; everyone.

to·va·risch (tō vä′rĭsh), *n.* *Russian.* comrade.

tow[1] (tō), *v.t.* 1. to drag or pull (a boat, car, etc.) by means of a rope or chain. —*n.* 2. act of towing. 3. the thing being towed. 4. a rope or chain for towing. 5. **in tow**, **a.** in the condition of being towed. **b.** under guidance; in charge. [ME *towe*(n), OE *togian* pull by force, drag, c. MHG *zogen* draw, tug, drag. Cf. TUG]

tow[2] (tō), *n.* 1. the fiber of flax, hemp, or jute prepared for spinning by scutching. 2. the coarse and broken parts of flax or hemp separated from the finer parts in hackling. —*adj.* 3. made of tow: *a tow rope.* [ME; OE *tōw* in *tōwlīc* pertaining to thread, *tōwhūs* spinning house). Cf. Icel. *tō* wool]

tow·age (tō′ĭj), *n.* 1. act of towing. 2. state of being towed. 3. a charge for towing.

to·ward (*prep.* tōrd, təwôrd′; *adj.* tōrd), *prep.* Also, **to·wards′.** 1. in the direction of (with reference to either motion or position): *to walk toward the north.* 2. with respect to; as regards: *one's attitude toward a proposition.* 3. nearly as late as; shortly before: *toward two o'clock.* 4. as a help or contribution to: *to give money toward a person's expenses.* —*adj.* 5. promising, hopeful, or apt, as a young person. 6. docile; compliant. 7. that is to come; imminent or impending. 8. going on; in progress: *when there is work toward.* [ME, OE *tōweard*, f. *tō-* to + *-weard* -WARD]

to·ward·ly (tōrd′lĭ), *adj.* *Archaic.* 1. promising; apt; tractable or docile. 2. favorable or propitious; seasonable or suitable. —**to′ward·li·ness**, **to′ward·ness**, *n.*

tow·boat (tō′bōt′), *n.* a tugboat.

tow·el (tou′əl), *n.*, *v.*, **-eled**, **-eling** or (*esp. Brit.*) **-elled**, **-elling.** —*n.* 1. a cloth or paper for wiping and drying something wet, esp. one for the hands, face, or body after washing or bathing. —*v.t.* 2. to wipe or dry with a towel. [ME, t. OF: m. *toaille* cloth for washing or wiping, t. Gmc.; cf. MHG *twāhele* towel, OE *thwēal* washbasin]

tow·el·ing (tou′əl ĭng), *n.* a narrow fabric of cotton or linen, in plain, twill, or huck weave, used for hand or dish towels. Also, *esp.* Brit., **tow′el·ling.**

tow·er (tou′ər), *n.* 1. a building or structure high in proportion to its lateral dimensions, either isolated or forming part of any building. 2. such a structure used as or intended for a stronghold, fortress, prison, etc. 3. any of various towerlike structures, contrivances, or objects. 4. a tall, movable structure used in ancient and medieval warfare in storming a fortified place. —*v.i.* 5. to rise or extend far upward like a tower; rise aloft. [ME *tour*, late OE *tūr*, t. OF: r. OE *torr*, t. L: m. *turris*] —**tow′ered**, *adj.* —**tow′er·less**, **tow′er·like′**, *adj.*

tow·er·ing (tou′ər ĭng), *adj.* 1. that towers; very lofty or tall: *a towering oak.* 2. very great. 3. rising to an extreme degree of violence or intensity: *a towering rage.* —**tow′er·ing·ly**, *adv.* —Syn. 1. See high.

Tower of London, a historic fortress in London, England, originally a royal palace, later a prison, now a group of buildings containing an arsenal and museum.

tow·er·y (tou′ər ĭ), *adj.* 1. having towers. 2. lofty.

tow·head (tō′hĕd′), *n.* 1. a head of flaxen or light-colored hair. 2. a person with such hair. —**tow′-head′ed**, *adj.*

tow·hee (tou′hē, tō′hē), *n.* any of several rather long-tailed, ground-inhabiting North American finches of the genus *Pipilo*, esp. the **red-eyed towhee** (*P. erythrophthalmus*) of the eastern U.S. and eastern Canada. Also, **towhee bunting.** [imit. of one of its notes]

tow·line (tō′līn′), *n.* a line, hawser, or the like, by which anything is or may be towed.

town (toun), *n.* 1. a collection of inhabited houses generally larger than a village and having more complete local government. 2. a city or borough. 3. (in some States of the U.S., as in New England) a municipal corporation with less elaborate organization and powers than a city. 4. (in other States of the U.S.) a township. 5. the inhabitants of a town; the townspeople. 6. a particular town under consideration, or that in which the speaker is; the chief town of a district: *to be out of town; to go to town.* 7. Brit. a town which has been granted the right to hold a market at stated times; market town. 8. Brit. Dial. a village or hamlet. 9. **go to town**, Slang. to be successful. [ME; OE *tūn*, c. D *tuin*, G *zaun* hedge. Cf. Irish *dūn* fortified place] —**town′less**, *adj.* —Syn. 1. See community.

town clerk, a clerical official, who keeps the records, issues licenses, calls the town meeting, and acts as secretary of a town.

town crier, a person employed by a town to make public proclamations.

town hall, a hall or building belonging to a town, used for the transaction of the town's business, etc., and often also as a place of public assembly.

town house, a house or mansion in town, as distinguished from a country residence.

town meeting, 1. a general meeting of the inhabitants of a town. 2. a meeting of the qualified voters of a town for the transaction of public business.

town·ship (toun′shĭp), *n.* 1. (in the U.S. and Canada) an administrative division of a county with varying corporate powers. 2. (in U.S. surveys of public land) a region or district 6 miles square, containing 36 sections. 3. *Eng. Hist.* **a.** one of the local divisions or districts of a large parish, each containing a village or small town, usually with a church of its own. **b.** the manor, parish, etc., itself. **c.** its inhabitants. [ME *tounshipe*, OE *tūnscipe*, f. *tūn* TOWN + *-scipe* -SHIP]

towns·man (tounz′mən), *n.*, *pl.* **-men.** 1. an inhabitant of a town. 2. an inhabitant of one's own or the same town. 3. (in New England) a selectman.

towns·peo·ple (tounz′pē′pəl), *n.pl.* the inhabitants collectively of a town. Also, **towns·folk** (tounz′fōk′).

tow·path (tō′păth′, -päth′), *n.* a path along the bank of a canal or river, for use in towing boats.

tow·rope (tō′rōp′), *n.* a rope, hawser, or the like, used in towing boats.

tow·y (tō′ĭ), *adj.* of the nature of or resembling tow[2].

tox-, var. of **toxo-**, before vowels, as in *toxemia.*

tox·al·bu·min (tŏk′săl bū′mĭn), *n.* Biochem. any poisonous protein.

tox·e·mi·a (tŏks ē′mĭ ə), *n.* Pathol. entry into, and persistence in, the blood stream of bacterial toxins absorbed from a local lesion, from which stream these poisons are borne by the circulation to all parts of the body. Also, **tox·ae′mi·a.** [t. NL. See TOX-, -EMIA]

tox·e·mic (tŏks ē′mĭk, -ĕm′ĭk), *adj.* Pathol. 1. pertaining to or of the nature of toxemia. 2. affected with toxemia. Also, **tox·ae′mic.**

tox·ic (tŏk′sĭk), *adj.* 1. of, pertaining to, affected with, or caused by a toxin or poison. 2. poisonous. [t. ML: s. *toxicus*, der. L *toxicum*, poison, t. Gk.: m. *toxikon* (orig. short for *toxikon* (phármakon), lit., (poison) pertaining to the bow, i.e. poison used on arrows)] —**tox′i·cal·ly**, *adv.*

tox·i·cant (tŏk′sə kənt), *adj.* 1. poisonous; toxic. —*n.* 2. a poison.

tox·i·ca·tion (tŏk′sə kā′shən), *n.* poisoning.

tox·ic·i·ty (tŏks ĭs′ə tĭ), *n.*, *pl.* **-ties.** toxic quality; poisonousness.

toxico-, a combining form of **toxic.** Cf. **toxo-.** [comb. form repr. Gk. *toxikón* poison. See TOXIC]

tox·i·co·gen·ic (tŏk′sə kə jĕn′ĭk), *adj.* Physiol., Pathol. 1. generating or producing toxic products or poisons. 2. formed by poisonous matter.

toxicol., toxicology.

tox·i·col·o·gy (tŏk′sə kŏl′ə jĭ), *n.* the science of poisons, their effects, antidotes, detection, etc. —**tox·i·co·log·i·cal** (tŏk′sə kə lŏj′i kəl), *adj.* —**tox·i·co·log′i·cal·ly**, *adv.* —**tox·i·col′o·gist**, *n.*

tox·i·co·sis (tŏk′sə kō′sĭs), *n.*, *pl.* **-ses** (-sēz). Pathol. a morbid condition produced by the action of a poison. [t. NL. See TOXIC, -OSIS]

tox·in (tŏk′sĭn), *n.* 1. any of the specific poisonous products generated by pathogenic microörganisms and constituting the causative agents in various diseases, as tetanus, diphtheria, etc. 2. any of various organic poisons produced in living or dead organisms. 3. their products, as a venom, etc. Also, **tox·ine** (tŏk′sĭn, -sēn). [f. TOX(IC) + -IN(E)[2]] —Syn. 1. See poison.

tox·i·pho·bi·a (tŏk/sə fō/bĭ ə), *n. Psychiatry.* a morbid fear of being poisoned. [f. *toxi-* (var. of TOXO-) + -PHOBIA]

toxo-, a combining form representing **toxin,** or short for **toxico-,** as in *toxoplasmosis.*

tox·oid (tŏk/soid), *n.* a non-toxic toxin produced by treating a toxin with chemical agents or by physical means. [f. TOX(O)- + -OID]

tox·oph·i·lite (tŏks ŏf/ə lĭt/), *n.* a devotee of archery; archer. [f. s. *Toxophilus* (coined Gk. proper name: bow-lover) + -ITE¹] —**tox·oph·i·lit·ic** (tŏks ŏf/ə lĭt/ĭk), *adj.*

tox·o·plas·mo·sis (tŏk/sō plăz mō/sĭs), *n. Vet. Sci., Pathol.* an infection caused by bodies believed to be protozoa which are known as *Toxoplasma gondii,* and occurring in dogs, cats, sheep, and man, the nervous system usually being the part involved.

toy (toi), *n.* 1. an object, often a small imitation of some familiar thing, for children or others to play with; a plaything. 2. a thing or matter of little or no value or importance; a trifle. 3. a small article of little real value, but prized for some reason; a knickknack; a trinket. 4. something diminutive. 5. a close linen or woolen cap, with flaps coming down to the shoulders, formerly worn by women in Scotland. 6. *Obs.* amorous dallying. —*adj.* 7. of or like a toy. 8. made as a toy: *a toy train.* —*v.i.* 9. to play; sport. 10. to act idly or without seriousness; trifle. [ME *toye* dalliance; orig. uncert.] —**toy/er,** *n.* —**toy/less,** *adj.* —**toy/like/,** *adj.*

To·ya·ma (tō/yä mä/), *n.* a city in central Japan, on W Honshu island. 154,484 (1950).

toy dog, 1. any of certain very small breeds of spaniels and terriers. 2. any dog of unusually small size kept as a pet.

Toyn·bee (toin/bĭ), *n.* **Arnold Joseph,** born 1889, British historian.

To·yo·ha·shi (tō/yō hä/shē), *n.* a seaport in central Japan, on Honshu island. 145,855 (1950).

to·yon (tō/yən), *n.* an evergreen rosaceous shrub or small tree, *Heteromeles* (or *Photinia*) *arbutifolia,* of California and Lower California, with white flowers and bright-red berries. [t. Mex. Sp.: m. *tollon,* native name]

tp., township.

Tr, *Chem.* terbium.

tr., 1. transitive. 2. translated. 3. translator. 4. transpose. 5. treasurer. 6. *Music.* trill.

tra·be·at·ed (trā/bǐ ā/tǐd), *adj. Archit.* 1. constructed with horizontal beams, as a flat, unvaulted ceiling, or with a lintel or entablature, as an unarched doorway. 2. pertaining to such construction, as distinct from the vaulted or arched kind. Also, **tra·be·ate** (trā/bǐ ĭt, -āt/). [der. *trabeat(ion)* beam structure, f. L *trabe(m)* beam (acc. of *trabs*) + -ATION] —**tra/be·a/tion,** *n.*

tra·bec·u·la (trə bĕk/yə lə), *n., pl.* **-lae** (-lē/). 1. *Anat., Bot., etc.* a structural part resembling a small beam or crossbar. 2. *Bot.* one of the projections from the cell wall which extend across the cell cavity of the ducts of certain plants, or the plate of cells across the cavity of the sporangium of a moss. [t. L, dim. of *trabs* beam] —**tra·bec/u·lar,** *adj.*

Trab·zon (träb zōn/), *n.* official name of **Trebizond** (def. 2).

trace¹ (trās), *n., v.,* **traced, tracing.** —*n.* 1. a mark, token, or evidence of the former presence, existence, or action of something; a vestige. 2. the track made or left by the passage of a person, animal, or thing. 3. *(esp. in pl.)* a single such mark. 4. a mark, indication, or evidence. 5. a scarcely discernible quantity of something; a very small amount. 6. *Psychol.* the residual effect of an experience in memory; an engram. 7. a line or figure drawn. 8. a record traced by a self-registering instrument. 9. a drawing or sketch of a thing. —*v.t.* 10. to follow the footprints, track, or traces of. 11. to follow or make out the course or line of: *to trace a river to its source.* 12. to follow (footprints, traces, the history of something, the course or line of something, etc.). 13. to follow the course, development, or history of: *to trace a political movement.* 14. to ascertain by investigation; find out; discover. 15. to draw (a line, outline, figure, etc.). 16. to make a plan, diagram, or map of. 17. to copy (a drawing, plan, etc.) by following the lines of the original on a superimposed transparent sheet. 18. to mark or ornament with lines, figures, etc. 19. to make an impression or imprinting of (a design, pattern, etc.). 20. to print in a curved, broken, or wavy-lined manner. 21. to put down in writing. —*v.i.* 22. to trace one's or its history; go back in time. [ME, t. OF: m. *tracer* delineate, trace, pursue, der. L *tractus,* pp., drawn, trailed, or *tractus,* n., a dragging, trailing] —**trace/a·ble,** *adj.* —**trace/a·bil/i·ty, trace/a·ble·ness,** *n.* —**trace/a·bly,** *adv.*

—Syn. 1. TRACE, VESTIGE agree in denoting marks or signs of something usually of the past. TRACE, the broader term, denotes any mark or slight indication of something past or present: *a trace of ammonia in water.* VESTIGE is more limited and refers to some slight, though actual, remains of something that no longer exists: *vestiges of one's former wealth.*

trace² (trās), *n.* 1. each of the two straps, ropes, or chains by which a carriage, wagon, or the like is drawn by a harnessed horse or other draft animal. See illus. under **harness.** 2. *Mach.* a piece in a machine, as a bar, transferring the movement of one part to another part, being hinged to each. [ME *trays,* t. OF: m. *traiz,* pl. of *trait* strap for harness, act of drawing, g. L *tractus,* pp., drawn, or *tractus,* n., draught]

trace element, an element found in plants and animals in minute quantities and believed to be a critical factor in physiological processes.

trac·er (trā/sər), *n.* 1. one who or that which traces. 2. one whose business is the tracing of missing property, parcels, etc. 3. an inquiry form sent from point to point to trace a missing shipment, parcel, or the like, as in a transportation system. 4. any of various devices for tracing drawings, plans, etc. 5. a burning composition placed in ammunition and fired to show the path of the projectile and indicate the target to other firers. 6. a radioactive substance used to study biological, chemical, and industrial processes by following its path on a photographic film, fluoroscope, or other detection device.

tracer bullet, a bullet that leaves a trail of smoke or fire so that aim can be corrected.

trac·er·ied (trā/sər ĭd), *adj.* ornamented with tracery.

trac·er·y (trā/sə rĭ), *n., pl.* **-eries.** 1. ornamental work consisting of ramified ribs, bars, or the like, as in the upper part of a Gothic window, in panels, screens, etc. 2. any delicate interlacing work of lines, threads, etc., as in carving, embroidery, etc.; network.

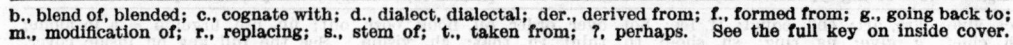

Window tracery

trache-, var. of **tracheo-** before vowels, as in *tracheid.*

tra·che·a (trā/kĭ ə, trə kē/ə), *n., pl.* **tracheae** (trā/kĭ ē/, trə kē/ē). 1. (in air-breathing vertebrates) the tube extending from the larynx to the bronchi, serving as the principal passage for conveying air to and from the lungs; the windpipe. See diag. under **lung.** 2. (in insects and other arthropods) one of the air-conveying tubes of the respiratory system. 3. *Bot.* a duct or vessel formed by a row of cells that have lost their intervening partitions: an element of the xylem. [t. ML, var. of LL *trachīa,* Gk.: m. *trācheia,* short for *artēria trācheia* rough artery (i.e. windpipe)]

tra·che·al (trā/kĭ əl, trə kē/əl), *adj.* 1. *Anat. and Zool.* pertaining to or connected with the trachea or tracheae. 2. *Bot.* of the nature of or composed of tracheae.

tracheal tissue, *Bot.* 1. tissue forming the vessels in the xylem. 2. tissue composed of tracheae or tracheids, or both.

tra·che·id (trā/kĭ ĭd), *n. Bot.* one of the vascular cells with a pitted, lignified wall, in which the end walls are not absorbed, characteristic of the wood of conifers, etc. —**tra·che·i·dal** (trə kē/ə dəl, trā/kĭ ĭ/dəl), *adj.*

tra·che·i·tis (trā/kĭ ī/tĭs), *n. Pathol.* inflammation of the trachea. [t. NL. See TRACHE(A), -ITIS]

tracheo-, a combining form representing **trachea,** as in *tracheoscopy.* Also, **trache-.**

tra·che·os·co·py (trā/kĭ ŏs/kə pĭ), *n. Med.* examination of the interior of the trachea, as with a laryngoscope. —**tra·che·o·scop·ic** (trā/kĭ ə skŏp/ĭk), *adj.* —**tra/che·os/co·pist,** *n.*

tra·che·ot·o·my (trā/kĭ ŏt/ə mĭ), *n., pl.* **-mies.** *Surg.* the operation of cutting into the trachea. —**tra/che·ot/o·mist,** *n.*

tra·cho·ma (trə kō/mə), *n. Pathol.* a contagious inflammation of the conjunctiva of the eyelids, characterized by the formation of granulations or papillary growths. [t. NL, t. Gk.: roughness] —**tra·chom·a·tous** (trə kŏm/ə təs, -kō/mə-), *adj.*

tra·chyte (trā/kĭt, trăk/īt), *n.* a volcanic rock, commonly of porphyritic texture, consisting essentially of alkali feldspar and one or more subordinate minerals, as hornblende, mica, etc. [t. F, t. Gk: m. *trāchȳtēs* roughness]

tra·chyt·ic (trə kĭt/ĭk), *adj. Petrog.* pertaining to the nearly parallel arrangement of feldspar crystals in the groundmass of volcanic rocks.

trac·ing (trā/sĭng), *n.* 1. act of one who or that which traces. 2. that which is produced by tracing. 3. a copy of a drawing, etc., made by tracing. 4. the record traced by a self-registering instrument.

track (trăk), *n.* 1. a structure consisting of a pair of parallel lines of rails with their crossties, etc., to provide a road for railroad trains. 2. a wheel rut. 3. the mark, or series of marks, left by anything that has passed along. 4. *(esp. pl.)* a footprint or other mark left by an animal or a person. 5. a path made or beaten by the feet of men or animals. 6. a line of travel or motion: *the track of a bird.* 7. a course followed. 8. a course of action or conduct; a method of proceeding: *to go on in the same track year after year.* 9. a path or course made or laid out for some particular purpose. 10. *Sports.* a. a course laid out for running or racing. b. the sports which are performed on a track, collectively. c. both track and field sports as a whole. 11. *Auto.* tread; the measured distance in inches, at the ground line, between the centers of both front or rear tires. 12. **keep track of,** to follow the course or progress of; keep sight or knowledge of. 13. **lose track of,** to fail to keep informed on or in view. —*v.t.* 14. to follow up or pursue the track, traces, or footprints of. 15. to follow (a track, course, etc.). 16. to make one's way through; traverse. 17. *U.S.* to make a track of footprints upon (a floor, etc.). 18. *U.S.* to make a track with (dirt, snow, etc., carried on the feet) in walking. 19. to furnish with a track or tracks, as for railroad trains. **20.** *Railroad.* to have (a certain distance) between wheels, runners, rails, etc. —*vi..* **21.** to follow up a track or trail. **22.** to run in the same track, as the wheels of a vehicle. **23.** to be in alignment, as one gearwheel with another. [late ME *trak*, t. F: m. *trac*, ? t. Gmc.; cf. D *trekken* draw, pull] —**track/er,** *n.* —**track/less,** *adj.*

track·age (trăk/ĭj), *n.* **1.** the tracks, collectively, of a railroad. **2.** the right of one railroad company to use the tracks of another. **3.** the money paid for this right.

track·man (trăk/mən), *n., pl.* **-men.** *U.S.* **1.** a man who assists in inspecting, installing, or maintaining railroad tracks. **2.** a trackwalker.

track meet, a series of athletic contests such as running, jumping, etc.

track·walk·er (trăk/wô/kər), *n.* *U.S.* a man employed to walk over and inspect a certain section of railroad track at intervals.

tract¹ (trăkt), *n.* **1.** a stretch or extent of land, water, etc.; region. **2.** *Anat.* **a.** a definite region or area of the body, esp. a group, series, or system of related parts or organs: *the digestive tract.* **b.** a bundle of nerve fibers having a common origin and destination. **3.** a space or extent of time; a period. **4.** *Rom. Cath. Ch.* an anthem consisting of verses of Scripture, sung after the gradual in the Mass from Septuagesima until the day before Easter and on certain other occasions, taking the place of the alleluias and the verse which ordinarily accompany the gradual. [late ME *tracte*, t. L: m. *tractus* drawing, stretch, extent, tract]

tract² (trăkt), *n.* a brief treatise or pamphlet suitable for general distribution, esp. one dealing with some topic of practical religion. [ME *tracte*; appar. short for L *tractātus* TRACTATE]

trac·ta·ble (trăk/tə bəl), *adj.* **1.** easily managed, or docile, as persons, their dispositions, etc. **2.** that may be easily handled or dealt with, as things; malleable. [t. L: m.s. *tractābilis*] —**trac/ta·bil/i·ty, trac/ta·ble·ness,** *n.* —**trac/ta·bly,** *adv.* —**Ant.** 1. stubborn.

Trac·tar·i·an (trăk târ/ĭ ən), *n.* **1.** one of the promoters or adherents of Tractarianism. —*adj.* **2.** pertaining or belonging to the Tractarians.

Trac·tar·i·an·ism (trăk târ/ĭ ə nĭz/əm), *n.* a system of religious opinion and practice promulgated within the Church of England in a series of papers entitled *Tracts for the Times,* published at Oxford between 1833 and 1841. The movement began as a countermovement to the liberalizing tendency in ecclesiasticism and the rationalizing tendency in theology, and was in its inception an endeavor to bring the church back to the principles of primitive and patristic Christianity. The last tract, No. 90, by Dr. (afterwards Cardinal) Newman, evoked bitter criticism, and a part of the Tractarians (incl. Newman in 1845) entered the Roman Catholic Church.

trac·tate (trăk/tāt), *n.* a treatise; a tract. [late ME, t. L: m.s. *tractātus* handling, discussion, treatise]

trac·tile (trăk/tĭl), *adj.* **1.** capable of being drawn. **2.** that may be drawn out in length; ductile. —**trac·til/i·ty,** *n.*

trac·tion (trăk/shən), *n.* **1.** act of drawing or pulling. **2.** state of being drawn. **3.** the drawing of a body, vehicle, train, or the like along a surface, road, track, railway, waterway, etc. **4.** transportation by means of railroads. **5.** the adhesive friction of a body, as of a wheel on a rail. **6.** the pulling or drawing of a muscle, organ, or the like. **7.** attracting power or influence. [t. ML: s. *tractio* act of drawing, der. L *trahere* draw] —**trac/tion·al,** *adj.*

traction engine, a locomotive for drawing heavy loads along an ordinary road, over fields, etc., usually driven by steam or gasoline.

trac·tive (trăk/tĭv), *adj.* serving to draw; drawing.

trac·tor (trăk/tər), *n.* **1.** one who or that which draws or pulls. **2.** something used for drawing or pulling. **3.** a self-propelled vehicle for pulling other vehicles, farm machinery, or the like. **4.** a propeller mounted at the front of an airplane, thus exerting a pull. **5.** Also, **tractor airplane.** an airplane with a propeller so mounted. [f. obs. *tract,* v., draw (t. L: s. *tractus,* pp.) + -OR²]

trade (trād), *n., v.,* **traded, trading.** —*n.* **1.** the buying and selling, or exchanging, of commodities, either by wholesale or by retail, within a country or between countries: *domestic or foreign trade.* **2.** a purchase, sale, or exchange. **3.** a form of occupation pursued as a business or calling, as for a livelihood or profit. **4.** some line of skilled mechanical work: *the trade of a carpenter, plumber, or printer.* **5.** people engaged in a particular line of business: *a lecture of interest only to the trade.* **6.** customers. **7.** (*pl.*) the trade winds. —*v.t.* **8.** to buy and sell; barter; traffic in. **9.** to exchange: *to trade seats with a person.* **10.** to dispose of by sale or barter (fol. by *away*). —*v.i.* **11.** to carry on trade. **12.** to traffic (fol. by *in*): *to trade in wheat.* **13.** to make an exchange. [ME, t. MLG: a track] —**trade/less,** *adj.* —**Syn.** 1. TRADE, COMMERCE, TRAFFIC refer to the exchanging of commodities for other commodities or money. TRADE is the general word: *a brisk trade between the nations.* COMMERCE applies to trade on a large scale and over an extensive area: *international commerce.* TRAFFIC may refer to a particular kind of trade; but it usually suggests the travel, transportation and activity associated with or incident to trade: *the opium traffic; heavy traffic on the railroads.* 3. See occupation. **9.** TRADE, BARGAIN, BARTER, SELL refer to exchange or transfer of ownership for some kind of material considera-

tion. TRADE conveys the general idea, but often means to exchange articles of more or less even value: *to trade with Argentina.* BARGAIN suggests a somewhat extended period of coming to terms: *to bargain about the price of a horse.* BARTER applies esp. to exchanging goods, wares, labor, etc., with no transfer of money for the transaction: *to barter wheat for machinery.* SELL implies transferring ownership usually for a sum of money: *to sell a car.*

trade book, a book published in a form designed for the general public and available through the ordinary book dealer (distinguished from a limited edition, textbook edition, etc., of the same book).

trade discount, a deduction granted a customer from list prices.

trade-in (trād/ĭn/), *n.* **1.** goods given in whole or, usually, part payment of a purchase. —*adj.* **2.** of or pertaining to such goods, or to such a method of payment.

trade·mark (trād/märk/), *n.* **1.** the name, symbol, figure, letter, word, or mark adopted and used by a manufacturer or merchant in order to designate the goods he manufactures or sells, and to distinguish them from those manufactured or sold by others. Any mark entitled to registration under the provisions of a statute is a trademark. —*v.t.* **2.** to stamp or otherwise place a trademark designation upon. **3.** to register the trademark of.

trade name, **1.** a word or phrase used in trade whereby a business or enterprise or a particular class of goods is designated, but which is not technically a trademark, either because it is not susceptible of exclusive appropriation as a trademark or because it is not affixed to goods sold in the market. **2.** the name by which an article or substance is known to the trade. **3.** the name or style under which a firm does business.

trad·er (trā/dər), *n.* **1.** one who trades; a merchant or businessman. **2.** a vessel employed in trade. **3.** *Exchanges.* a member of an exchange trading for his own benefit and not for customers.

trade reference, an individual or company in business to which one is referred for information concerning an applicant's credit standing.

trad·es·can·ti·a (trăd/əs kăn/shĭ ə, -shə), *n.* any plant of the genus *Tradescantia;* a spiderwort (def. 1). [NL; named after John *Tradescant,* gardener to Charles I]

trade school, a school for giving instruction in a trade or trades.

trades·man (trādz/mən), *n., pl.* **-men.** **1.** a man engaged in trade. **2.** *Chiefly Brit.* a shopkeeper. —**trades·wom·an** (trādz/wŏŏm/ən), *n. fem.*

trades·peo·ple (trādz/pē/pəl), *n.pl.* **1.** people engaged in trade. **2.** *Chiefly Brit.* shopkeepers collectively. Also, **trades·folk** (trādz/fōk/).

trade union, **1.** a labor union. **2.** a union of craftsmen or workers in related crafts, as distinguished from general workers, or a union including all workers in an industry. Also, *Brit.,* **trades union.**

trade unionism, **1.** the system, methods, or practice of trade or labor unions. **2.** trade unions collectively.

trade unionist, **1.** a member of a trade union. **2.** one who favors trade unions.

trade wind, **1.** one of the winds prevailing over the oceans from about 30° north latitude to about 30° south latitude, and blowing from northeast to southwest in the Northern Hemisphere, and from southeast to northwest in the Southern Hemisphere toward the equator. **2.** a wind that blows in one regular course, or continually in the same direction.

trading post, a store for carrying on trade in an unsettled or thinly settled region.

trading stamp, a stamp with a certain value given as a premium by a seller to a customer, specified quantities of these stamps being exchangeable for various articles when presented to the issuers of the stamps.

tra·di·tion (trə dĭsh/ən), *n.* **1.** the handing down of statements, beliefs, legends, customs, etc., from generation to generation, esp. by word of mouth or by practice: *a story that has come down to us by popular tradition.* **2.** that which is so handed down: *the traditions of the Eskimos.* **3.** *Theol.* **a.** (among the Jews) an unwritten body of laws and doctrines, or any one of them, held to have been received from Moses and handed down orally from generation to generation. **b.** (among Christians) a body of teachings, or any one of them, held to have been delivered by Christ and His apostles but not committed to writing. **4.** *Law.* act of handing over something to another, esp. in a formal legal manner; delivery; transfer. [ME, t. L: s. *trāditio* delivery, handing down]

tra·di·tion·al (trə dĭsh/ən əl), *adj.* **1.** pertaining to tradition. **2.** handed down by tradition. **3.** in accordance with tradition. Also, **tra·di·tion·ar·y** (trə dĭsh/ə nĕr/ĭ). —**tra·di/tion·al·ly,** *adv.*

tra·di·tion·al·ism (trə dĭsh/ən ə lĭz/əm), *n.* **1.** adherence to tradition as authority, esp. in matters of religion. **2.** a system of philosophy according to which all knowledge of religious truth is derived from divine revelation and received by traditional instruction. —**tra·di/tion·al·ist,** *n., adj.* —**tra·di/tion·al·is/tic,** *adj.*

trad·i·tive (trăd/ə tĭv), *adj.* traditional. [f. TRADIT(ION) + -IVE]

trad·i·tor (trăd/ə tər), *n., pl.* **traditores** (trăd/ə tōr/ēz). an early Christian who betrayed his fellows at the time of the Roman persecutions. [ME, t. L: traitor, betrayer]

tra·duce (trə dūs′, -dōōs′), *v.t.* **-duced, -ducing.** to speak evil or maliciously and falsely of; slander, calumniate, or malign: *to traduce someone's character.* [t. L: m.s. *trādūcere* transport, disgrace] —**tra·duc′er,** *n.* —**traduc′ing·ly,** *adv.*

tra·du·cian·ism (trə dū′shə nĭz′əm, -dōō′-), *n. Theol.* the doctrine that the human soul is propagated along with the body. —**tra·du′cian·ist,** *n., adj.* —**tra·du′cian·is′tic,** *adj.*

Tra·fal·gar (trə făl′gər; *Sp.* trä′ fäl gär′), *n.* **Cape,** a cape on the SW coast of Spain, W of Gibraltar: British naval victory under Nelson over the French and Spanish fleets, 1805.

traf·fic (trăf′ĭk), *n., v.,* **-ficked, -ficking.** —*n.* **1.** the coming and going of persons, vehicles, ships, etc., along a way of passage or travel: *heavy traffic on a street.* **2.** the persons, vehicles, etc., going along such a way. **3.** the transportation of goods for the purpose of trade, by sea or land: *ships of traffic.* **4.** trade; buying and selling; commercial dealings. **5.** trade between different countries or places; commerce. **6.** the business done by a railroad or other carrier in the transportation of freight or passengers. **7.** the aggregate of freight, passengers, telephone or telegraph messages, etc., handled, esp. in a given period. **8.** trade or dealing in some commodity or thing, often trade of an illicit kind. —*v.i.* **9.** to carry on traffic, trade, or commercial dealings. **10.** to carry on dealings of an illicit or improper kind. [t. F: m. *trafique,* t.: m. *traffico,* prob. der. *trafficare* push across, f. *tra-* across (g. L *trans*) + *ficcare* shove, stick, ult. der. L *figere* fix] —**traf′ficker,** *n.* —**traf′fic·less,** *adj.* —Syn. 4. See **trade.**

traffic circle, a circular arrangement at the intersection of two or more roads, so that vehicles may pass from one road to another.

traffic manager, one who supervises the transportation of goods for his employer.

trag·a·canth (trăg′ə kănth′), *n.* **1.** a mucilaginous substance derived from various low, spiny, Asiatic shrubs of the genus *Astragalus,* esp. *A. gummifer,* used to impart firmness to pills and lozenges, stiffen calicoes, etc. **2.** the plants themselves. [t. L: s. *tragacantha* goat's thorn, t. Gk.: m. *tragákantha*]

Traffic circle

tra·ge·di·an (trə jē′dĭ ən), *n.* **1.** an actor of tragedy. **2.** a writer of tragedy.

tra·ge·di·enne (trə jē′dĭ ĕn′), *n.* an actress of tragedy.

trag·e·dy (trăj′ə dĭ), *n., pl.* **-dies. 1.** a dramatic composition of serious or somber character, with an unhappy ending: *Shakespeare's tragedy of "Hamlet."* **2.** that branch of the drama which is concerned with this form of composition. **3.** the art and theory of writing and producing tragedies. **4.** any literary composition, as a novel, dealing with a somber theme carried to a tragic conclusion. **5.** the tragic element of drama, of literature generally, or of life. **6.** a lamentable, dreadful, or fatal event or affair; a disaster or calamity. [ME *tragedie,* t. ML: m. *tragĕdia,* L *tragoedia,* t. Gk: m. *tragōídia,* lit., goat song (reason for name variously explained)]

trag·ic (trăj′ĭk), *adj.* **1.** characteristic or suggestive of tragedy: *tragic solemnity.* **2.** mournful, melancholy, or pathetic in the extreme: *a tragic plight.* **3.** dreadful, calamitous, disastrous, or fatal: *a tragic event.* **4.** pertaining to or having the nature of tragedy: *the tragic drama.* **5.** acting in or composing tragedy. Also, **trag′i·cal.** [t. L: s. *tragicus,* t. Gk: m. *tragikós* of tragedy] —**trag′i·cal·ly,** *adv.* —**trag′i·cal·ness,** *n.*

tragic irony. See **irony**[1] (def. 4).

trag·i·com·e·dy (trăj′ĭ kŏm′ə dĭ), *n., pl.* **-dies. 1.** a dramatic or other literary composition combining elements of both tragedy and comedy. **2.** an incident or series of incidents of mixed tragic and comic character. [t. LL: m.s. *tragicōmoedia,* r. L *tragico-cōmoedia,* f. *tragico-* TRAGIC + *cōmoedia* COMEDY] —**trag·i·com·ic** (trăj′ĭ kŏm′ĭk), **trag·i·com′i·cal,** *adj.* —**trag′i·com′i·cal·ly,** *adv.*

tra·gi·on (trā′gĭ ŏn′), *n., pl.* **tragia** (trā′gĭ ə). *Craniom.* a point in the depth of the notch just over the tragus of the external.

trag·o·pan (trăg′ə păn′), *n.* any of the Asiatic pheasants constituting the genus *Tragopan,* characterized by two fleshy erectile horns on the head, and wattles on the throat. [t. NL, special use of L *tragopān* fabulous Ethiopian bird, t. Gk.]

tra·gus (trā′gəs), *n., pl.* **-gi** (-jī). *Anat.* a fleshy prominence at the front of the external opening of the ear. See diag. under **ear.** [t. LL, t. Gk.: m. *trágos* hairy part of ear (lit., goat)]

trail (trāl), *v.t.* **1.** to drag or let drag along the ground or other surface; to draw or drag along behind. **2.** to bring or have floating after itself: *to trail clouds of dust.*

3. to follow the track or trail of; track. **4.** *U.S. Colloq.* to follow along behind (another or others), as in a race. **5.** to mark out, as a track. **6.** *U.S.* to beat down or make a path or way through (grass, etc.). **7.** to protract. **8.** *Mil.* to carry (a firearm, etc.) in the right hand in an oblique position, with the muzzle forward and the butt near the ground.

—*v.i.* **9.** to be drawn or dragged along the ground or some other surface, as when hanging from something moving: *Her long bridal gown trailed over the church floor.* **10.** to hang down loosely from something. **11.** to stream or float from and after something moving, as dust, smoke, sparks, etc., do. **12.** to follow as if drawn along. **13.** to fish by trailing a line from a moving boat. **14.** to go slowly, lazily, or wearily along. **15.** to pass or extend in a straggling line. **16.** to pass by gradual change, as into silence (fol. by *off*): *her voice trailed off.* **17.** to creep or crawl, as a serpent. **18.** to follow a track or scent, as of game. **19.** (of a plant) to extend itself in growth along the ground and over objects encountered, resting on these for support rather than taking root or clinging by tendrils, etc.

—*n.* **20.** a path or track made across a wild region, over rough country, or the like, by the passage of men or animals: *to follow the trail.* **21.** the track, scent, or the like, left by an animal, person or thing, esp. as followed by a hunter, hound, or other pursuer. **22.** something that is trailed or that trails behind, as the train of a skirt or robe. **23.** a stream of dust, smoke, light, people, vehicles, etc., behind something moving. **24.** *Artillery.* that part of a gun carriage which rests on the ground when the piece is unlimbered. **25.** act of trailing. [ME *traile(n),* t. AF: m. *trailler* trail, OF tow (a boat), der. *traille* towrope, g. L *trāgula* dragnet, der. *trahere* draw, drag] —**trail′less,** *adj.* —Syn. 20. See **path.**

trail·er (trā′lər), *n.* **1.** one who or that which trails. **2.** a vehicle drawn by another vehicle. **3.** such a vehicle in the form of a two- or four-wheel mobile house used mainly by tourists. **4.** a trailing plant.

trailing arbutus, arbutus (def. 2).

trailing edge, *Aeron.* the rear edge of a propeller blade or airfoil.

trail rope, 1. a guide rope on a balloon. **2.** *Mil.* a prolonge.

train (trān), *n.* **1.** a railroad locomotive and a connected series of cars moving together. **2.** a line or procession of persons, vehicles, animals, etc., traveling together. **3.** *Mil.* an aggregation of vehicles, animals, and men accompanying an army to carry supplies, baggage, ammunition, etc. **4.** a series or row of objects or parts. **5.** *Mach.* a series of connected parts, as wheels and pinions, through which motion is transmitted. **6.** order, esp. proper order: *matters were in good train.* **7.** something that is drawn along; a trailing part. **8.** an elongated part of a skirt or robe trailing behind on the ground. **9.** a trail or stream of something from a moving object. **10.** a line or succession of persons or things following after. **11.** a body of followers or attendants; a retinue. **12.** a succession or series of proceedings, events, circumstances, etc. **13.** a succession of connected ideas; a course of reasoning: *to lose one's train of thought.* **14.** *Astron.* the trail of a meteor; the tail of a comet. **15.** a line of combustible material, as gunpowder, for leading fire to an explosive charge. **16.** *Physics.* a succession of wave cycles, pulses, or the like, esp. one caused by a periodic disturbance of short duration.

—*v.t.* **17.** to subject to discipline and instruction; educate: *to train an unruly boy.* **18.** to make proficient by instruction and practice, as in some art, profession, or work: *to train soldiers.* **19.** to make (a person, etc.) fit by proper exercise, diet, etc., as for some athletic feat or contest. **20.** to discipline and instruct (an animal), as in the performance of tasks or tricks. **21.** to treat or manipulate so as to bring into some desired form, position, direction, etc. **22.** *Hort.* to bring (a plant, branch, etc.) into a particular shape or position, by bending, pruning, or the like. **23.** to bring to bear on some object, or point, aim, or direct, as a firearm, a camera, a telescope, the glance, etc.

—*v.i.* **24.** to give the discipline and instruction, drill, practice, etc., designed to impart proficiency or efficiency. **25.** to undergo discipline and instruction, drill, etc. **26.** to get oneself into condition by exercise, etc. [ME, t. OF: m. *tra(h)iner,* v., der. L *trahere* draw] —**train′a·ble,** *adj.* —**train′er,** *n.* —**train′less,** *adj.*

train·band (trān′bănd′), *n. Eng. Hist.* one of the trained bands or forces of citizen soldiery organized in London and elsewhere in the 16th, 17th, and 18th centuries.

train·ee (trā nē′), *n.* **1.** one receiving vocational or military training. **2.** a person or an animal that undergoes training.

train·ing (trā′nĭng), *n.* **1.** act or process of one who or that which trains. **2.** the resulting condition. —Syn. 1. See **education.**

training school, 1. a school for giving training in some art, profession, or line of work. **2.** an institution for the reformation of juvenile delinquents.

training ship, a ship equipped for training men in seamanship, as for naval service.

train·man (trān′mən), *n., pl.* **-men.** a member of the crew that operates a railroad train, usually an assistant to the conductor, such as a brakeman or flagman.

train oil, oil obtained by boiling, from the blubber of whales, or from seals, fishes, etc. [f. *train* (now obs.), earlier *trane* train oil (t. MLG or MD; appar. special use of MLG *träne* tear, drop, c. G *träne*) + OIL]

traipse (trāps), *v.i.*, **traipsed, traipsing.** *Colloq.* to walk aimlessly or idly.

trait (trāt), *n.* **1.** a distinguishing feature or quality; characteristic: *bad traits of character.* **2.** *Rare.* a stroke or touch. [late ME, t. F: draught, g. L *tractus*]

trai·tor (trā′tər), *n.* **1.** one who betrays a person, a cause, or any trust. **2.** one who betrays his country by violating his allegiance; one guilty of treason. [ME, t. OF: m. *traitre*, g. L *trāditor* betrayer] **—trai·tress** (trā′trĭs), *n. fem.*

trai·tor·ous (trā′tər əs), *adj.* **1.** having the character of a traitor; treacherous; perfidious. **2.** characteristic of a traitor. **3.** having the nature of treason: *a traitorous action.* **—trai′tor·ous·ly,** *adv.* **—trai′tor·ous·ness,** *n.*

Tra·jan (trā′jən), *n.* (*Marcus Ulpius Nerva Trajanus*) A.D. 53?–117, Roman emperor, A.D. 98–117.

tra·jec·to·ry (trə jĕk′tə rĭ), *n., pl.* **-ries. 1.** the curve described by a projectile in its flight through the air. **2.** the path described by a body moving under the action of given forces. **3.** *Geom.* a curve or surface which cuts all the curves or surfaces of a given system at a constant angle. [t. ML: m.s. *trājectōrius,* adj., casting over]

Tra·lee (trə lē′), *n.* a seaport in SW Ireland: the county seat of Kerry. 11,045 (1951).

tram¹ (trăm), *n., v.,* **trammed, tramming.** **—n.** **1.** *Brit.* a tramcar. **2.** a tramroad or tramway. **3.** a wheeled truck or car on which loads are transported in mines. **4.** the vehicle or cage of an overhead carrier. **—v.t. 5.** to travel or convey by tram. [t. MLG or MD: m. *trame* beam, rung etc.] **—tram′less,** *adj.*

tram² (trăm), *n., v.,* **trammed, tramming. —n. 1.** a trammel (def. 2). **2.** *Mach.* correct position or adjustment: *the spindle is in tram.* **—v.t. 3.** *Mach.* to adjust (something) correctly. [short for TRAMMEL]

tram·car (trăm′kär′), *n.* **1.** *Brit.* a streetcar. **2.** *Mining.* a car of various design for ore haulage on a mine railroad system, esp. underground.

tram·line (trăm′līn′), *n.* *Brit.* streetcar line or track.

tram·mel (trăm′əl), *n., v.,* **-meled, -meling** or (*esp. Brit.*) **-melled, -melling. —n. 1.** (*usually pl.*) anything that impedes or hinders free action; a restraint: *the trammels of custom.* **2.** an instrument for describing ellipses. **3.** trammel net. **4.** a fowling net. **5.** a contrivance hung in a fireplace to support pots, kettles, etc., over the fire. **6.** a shackle, esp. one for teaching a horse to amble. **—v.t. 7.** to involve or hold in trammels; hamper; restrain. **8.** to catch or entangle in or as in a net. [ME *tramail,* t. OF: net with three layers of meshes, g. LL *tremaculum,* f. L *trē*(s) three + m. *macula* mesh] **—tram′mel·er;** *esp. Brit.,* **tram′mel·ler,** *n.*

trammel net, a three-layered net, the middle layer of which is fine-meshed, the others coarse-meshed, so that fish attempting to pass through the net will become entangled in one or more of the meshes.

tra·mon·tane (trə mŏn′tān, trăm′ən tān′), *adj.* **1.** being or situated beyond the mountains, orig., beyond the Alps as viewed from Italy. **2.** pertaining to the other side of the mountains. **3.** foreign; barbarous. **—n. 4.** one who lives beyond the mountains (orig. applied by the Italians to the peoples beyond the Alps, and by the latter to the Italians). **5.** a foreigner; a barbarian. [ME, t. It.: m. *tramontano,* g. L *transmontānus,* f. *trans* across + s. *mons* mountain + *-ānus* -AN]

tramp (trămp), *v.i.* **1.** to tread or walk with a firm, heavy, resounding step. **2.** to tread heavily or trample (fol. by *on* or *upon*): *to tramp on a person's toes.* **3.** to walk steadily; march; trudge. **4.** to go on a walking excursion or expedition. **5.** to go about as a vagabond or tramp. **6.** to make a voyage on a tramp (def. 18). **—v.t. 7.** to tramp or walk heavily or steadily through or over. **8.** to traverse on foot: *tramp the streets.* **9.** to tread or trample underfoot. **10.** to travel over as a tramp. **11.** to run (a vessel) as a tramp (def. 18). **—n. 12.** act of tramping. **13.** a firm, heavy, resounding tread. **14.** the sound made. **15.** a long, steady walk; trudge. **16.** a walking excursion or expedition. **17.** a person who travels about on foot from place to place, esp. a vagabond living on occasional jobs or gifts of money or food. **18.** a freight vessel which does not run regularly between fixed ports, but takes a cargo wherever shippers desire. **19.** a piece of iron affixed to the sole of a shoe. [ME *trampe*(n), c. LG *trampen* stamp] **—tramp′er,** *n.*

tram·ple (trăm′pəl), *v.,* **-pled, -pling,** *n.* **—v.i. 1.** to tread or step heavily and noisily; stamp. **2.** to tread heavily, roughly, or crushingly (fol. by *on, upon,* etc.), esp. repeatedly. **3.** to act in a harsh, domineering, or cruel way, as if treading roughly (fol. by *on, upon,* etc.): *to trample on an oppressed people.* **—v.t. 4.** to tread heavily, roughly, or carelessly on or over; tread underfoot, etc. **5.** to domineer harshly over; crush: *to trample law and order.* **6.** to put, force, reduce, etc., by trampling: *to trample out a fire.* **—n. 7.** act or sound of trampling. [ME, freq. of TRAMP, c. G *trampeln*] **—tram′pler,** *n.*

tram·po·line (trăm′pə lĭn), *n.* a sheet of canvas attached by resilient cords to a horizontal frame several feet above the floor: used by acrobats and gymnasts as a springboard in tumbling. [It: springboard]

tramp steamer, a tramp (def. 18).

tram·road (trăm′rōd′), *n.* *Mining.* a tracked road within a mine for ore trucks.

tram·way (trăm′wā′), *n.* **1.** a crude road of wooden rails, or wooden rails capped with metal treads. **2.** *Brit.* a streetcar line or track. **3.** *Mining.* **a.** a track (usually elevated) or roadway for mine haulage. **b.** an overhead cable system for transporting ore and mine freight.

trance (trăns, träns), *n., v.,* **tranced, trancing. —n. 1.** a half-conscious state, as between sleeping and waking. **2.** a dazed or bewildered condition. **3.** a fit of complete mental absorption or deep musing. **4.** an unconscious, cataleptic, or hypnotic condition. **5.** *Spiritualism.* a temporary state in which a medium, with suspension of personal consciousness, is controlled by an intelligence from without and used as a means of communication, as from the dead. **—v.t. 6.** to put in a trance. [ME, t. OF: m. *transe* passage, esp. from life to death, deadly suspense or fear, der. *transir* go across, pass over, t. L: m. *transīre*] **—trance′like′,** *adj.*

tran·quil (trăng′kwĭl), *adj.,* **-quiler, -quilest** or (*esp. Brit.*) **-quiller, -quillest. 1.** free from commotion or tumult; peaceful; quiet; calm: *a tranquil country place.* **2.** free from or unaffected by disturbing emotions; unruffled: *a tranquil life.* [earlier *tranquill,* t. L: s. *tranquillus*] **—tran′quil·ly,** *adv.* **—tran′quil·ness,** *n.* **—Syn. 1.** See **peaceful.** **—Ant. 1.** agitated.

tran·quil·ize (trăng′kwə līz′), *v.t., v.i.,* **-ized, -izing.** to make or become tranquil. Also, *esp. Brit.,* **tran′quil·lise′.** **—tran′quil·i·za′tion,** *n.*

tran·quil·iz·er (trăng′kwə līz′ər), *n.* **1.** one who or that which tranquilizes. **2.** a drug that has a sedative or calming effect without inducing sleep. Also, **tran′quil·liz′er.**

tran·quil·li·ty (trăng kwĭl′ə tĭ), *n.* the state of being tranquil; calmness; peacefulness; quiet; serenity; composure. Also, **tran·quil′i·ty.**

trans-, a prefix meaning "across," "beyond," freely applied in geographical terms (*transcontinental, trans-Siberian*), also found attached to stems not used as words, and in figurative meanings, e.g., *transpire, transport, transcend.* [t. L, comb. form of *trans,* prep.]

trans., **1.** transactions. **2.** transferred. **3.** transitive. **4.** translated. **5.** translation. **6.** translator.

trans·act (trăns äkt′, tränz-), *v.t.* **1.** to carry through (affairs, business, etc.) to a conclusion or settlement. **—v.i. 2.** to carry through affairs or negotiations. [t. L: s. *transactus,* pp., carried out, driven through, accomplished] **—trans·ac′tor,** *n.* **—Syn. 1.** See **perform.**

trans·ac·tion (trăns ăk′shən, tränz-), *n.* **1.** act of transacting. **2.** fact of being transacted. **3.** an instance or process of transacting something. **4.** that which is transacted; an affair; a piece of business. **5.** (*pl.*) **a.** records of the doings of a learned society or the like. **b.** reports of papers read, addresses delivered, discussions, etc., at the meetings. [late ME, t. L: s. *transactio* act of carrying out] **—trans·ac′tion·al,** *adj.*

trans·al·pine (trăns ăl′pīn, -pĭn, tränz-), *adj.* **1.** across or beyond the Alps, esp. as viewed from Italy. **—n. 2.** a native or inhabitant of a country beyond the Alps.

trans·An·de·an (trăns′ăn dē′ən, tränz′ăn·dī′ən; tränz′-, tränz-), *adj.* across or beyond the Andes.

trans·at·lan·tic (trăns′ət lăn′tĭk, tränz′-), *adj.* **1.** passing or extending across the Atlantic: *a transatlantic liner.* **2.** beyond, or on the other side of, the Atlantic.

trans·ca·lent (trăns kā′lənt), *adj.* pervious to heat; permitting the passage of heat. [f. TRANS- + s. L *calens,* ppr., being hot] **—trans·ca·len·cy** (trăns kā′lən sĭ), *n.*

Trans·cau·ca·sia (trăns′kô kā′zhə, -shə), *n.* a region in the SW Soviet Union, consisting of that part of Caucasia S of the Caucasus Mountains, formerly comprising (1927–36) the **Transcaucasian Socialist Soviet Republic,** which included the republics of Armenia, Azerbaijan, and Georgia. **—Trans·cau·ca·sian** (trăns′kô kā′shən, -zhən, -kăsh′ən, -kăzh′ən), *adj., n.*

tran·scend (trăn sĕnd′), *v.t.* **1.** to go or be above or beyond (a limit, something with limits, etc.); overpass or exceed. **2.** to go beyond in elevation, excellence, extent, degree, etc.; surpass, excel, or exceed. **3.** *Theol.* (of the Deity) to be above and independent of (the universe). **—v.i. 4.** to be transcendent; excel. [ME, t. L: s. *transcendere* climb over or beyond]

tran·scend·ence (trăn sĕn′dəns), *n.* **1.** state, quality, or fact of being transcendent. **2.** transcedent character. Also, **tran·scend′en·cy.**

tran·scend·ent (trăn sĕn′dənt), *adj.* **1.** transcending; going beyond ordinary limits; surpassing or extraordinary. **2.** superior or supreme. **3.** *Theol.* (of God) transcending the material universe. **4.** *Philos.* **a.** (in scholastic philosophy) above all possible modes of the infinite. **b.** (in the Kantian philosophy) transcending experience; not realizable in human experience. **c.** (in modern realism) referred to, but beyond, direct apprehension; outside consciousness. **—tran·scend′ent·ly,** *adv.* **—tran·scend′ent·ness,** *n.*

tran·scen·den·tal (trăn′sĕn dĕn′təl), *adj.* **1.** transcendent, surpassing, or superior. **2.** transcending ordinary or common experience, thought, or belief; extraordinary; supernatural; abstract or metaphysical. **3.** idealistic, lofty, or extravagant. **4.** *Philos.* **a.** beyond the contingent and accidental in human experience, but not beyond all human knowledge (contrasted with *transcendent*). **b.** pertaining to certain theories, etc., explaining what is objective as the contribution of the mind. **c.** (in the Kantian philosophy) of, pertaining to, based upon, or concerned with a priori elements in experience, which condition human knowledge. **5.** *Math.* not producible by the algebraic operations of addition, subtraction, multiplication, division, and the extraction of roots, each repeated only a finite number of times. —*n.* **6.** *Math.* a transcendental number, such as π or *e*. **7.** (*pl.*) (in the scholastic philosophy) categories which have universal application as being, one, true, good. —**tran′scen·den′tal·ly,** *adv.*

tran·scen·den·tal·ism (trăn′sĕn dĕn′tə lĭz′əm), *n.* **1.** transcendental character, thought, or language. **2.** transcendental philosophy; any philosophy based upon the doctrine that the principles of reality are to be discovered by the study of the processes of thought, or emphasizing the intuitive and spiritual above the empirical (in America, associated with the name of Emerson). —**tran′scen·den′tal·ist,** *n., adj.*

trans·con·ti·nen·tal (trăns′kŏn tə nĕn′təl), *adj.* **1.** passing or extending across a continent: *a transcontinental railroad.* **2.** on the other side of a continent.

tran·scribe (trăn skrīb′), *v.t.,* **-scribed, -scribing. 1.** to make a copy of in writing: *to transcribe a document.* **2.** to reproduce in writing or print as from speech. **3.** to write out in other characters; transliterate: *to transcribe one's shorthand notes.* **4.** *Radio.* to make a recording of (a program, announcement, etc.) for broadcasting. **5.** *Music.* to arrange (a composition) for a medium other than that for which it was originally written. [t. L: m.s. *transcrībere* copy off] —**tran·scrib′er,** *n.*

tran·script (trăn′skrĭpt), *n.* **1.** something transcribed or made by transcribing; a written copy. **2.** a reproduction in writing or print. **3.** a form of something as rendered from one alphabet or language into another. [ME, t. L: s. *transcriptum,* lit., thing copied, pp. (neut.) of *transcrībere* TRANSCRIBE; r. ME *transcrit,* t. OF]

tran·scrip·tion (trăn skrĭp′shən), *n.* **1.** act of transcribing. **2.** a transcript; a copy. **3.** *Music.* **a.** the arrangement of a composition for a medium other than that for which it was originally written. **b.** a composition so arranged. **4.** *Chiefly Radio.* a phonograph record. See **transcribe** (def. 4). —**tran·scrip·tive** (trăn skrĭp′tĭv), *adj.*

trans·cur·rent (trăns kûr′ənt), *adj.* running or extending across or transversely. [t. L: s. *transcurrens,* ppr.]

trans·duc·er (trăns dū′sər, -dōō′-, trănz-), *n. Physics.* a device that transmits energy from one system to another, as an electric transformer. [var. of TRADUCER. See TRADUCE]

tran·sect (trăn sĕkt′), *v.t.* to cut across; dissect transversely. —**tran·sec′tion,** *n.*

tran·sept (trăn′sĕpt), *n. Archit.* **1.** the transverse portion (or, occasionally, portions) of a cruciform church. See diag. under **basilica. 2.** either of the two armlike divisions of this, one on each side of the crossing. [t. Anglo-L: s. *transēptum,* f. L: *trans* across + *sēptum* enclosure] —**tran·sep′tal,** *adj.* —**tran·sep′tal·ly,** *adv.*

trans·e·unt (trăn′sē ənt), *adj. Philos.* passing outward; producing an effect outside itself (contrasted with *immanent*). [t. L: s. *transiens,* ppr., going across]

transf., transferred.

trans·fer (*v.* trăns fûr′; *n.* trăns′fər), *v.* **-ferred, -ferring,** *n.* —*v.t.* **1.** to convey or remove from one place, person, etc., to another. **2.** *Law.* to make over the possession or control of: *to transfer a title to land.* **3.** to convey (a drawing, design, pattern, etc.) from one surface to another. —*r.i.* **4.** to transfer oneself. **5.** to be transferred. **6.** to change from one streetcar, train, or the like, to another, as on a transfer (def. 11). —*n.* **7.** means or system of transferring. **8.** act of transferring. **9.** fact of being transferred. **10.** a point or place for transferring. **11.** a ticket, issued with or without extra charge, entitling a passenger to continue his journey on another streetcar, train, or the like. **12.** that which is transferred, as a drawing, pattern, etc. **13.** *Law.* a conveyance, by sale, gift or otherwise, of real or personal property, to another. **14.** *Finance.* act of having the ownership of a stock or registered bond transferred upon the books of the issuing corporation or its agent. [ME *transferre*(n), t. L: m. *transferre* carry across] —**trans·fer′a·ble,** *adj.* —**trans′fer·a·bil′i·ty,** *n.*

trans·fer·ee (trăns′fə rē′), *n.* **1.** one who is transferred or removed, as from one place to another. **2.** *Law.* one to whom a transfer is made, as of property.

trans·fer·ence (trăns fûr′əns), *n.* **1.** act or process of transferring. **2.** fact of being transferred. **3.** *Psychoanal.* **a.** reproduction of emotions, originally experienced for the most part in childhood, towards a person other than the one towards whom they were initially experienced. **b.** displacement (def. 6).

trans·fer·en·tial (trăns′fə rĕn′shəl), *adj.* pertaining to or involving transference.

trans·fer·or (trăns fûr′ər), *n. Law.* one who makes a transfer, as of property.

trans·fer·rer (trăns fûr′ər), *n.* one who or that which transfers.

trans·fig·u·ra·tion (trăns′fĭg yə rā′shən), *n.* **1.** act of transfiguring. **2.** state of being transfigured. **3.** (*cap.*) the change in the appearance of Christ on the mountain. Mat. 17:1–9. **4.** (*cap.*) the church festival commemorating this, observed on Aug. 6.

trans·fig·ure (trăns fĭg′yər), *v.t.,* **-ured, -uring. 1.** to change in outward form or appearance; transform,

change, or alter. **2.** to change so as to glorify, exalt, or idealize. [ME, t. L: m.s. *transfigūrāre*] —**trans·fig′ure·ment,** *n.*

trans·fix (trăns fĭks′), *v.t.* **1.** to pierce through, as with a pointed weapon, or as the weapon does. **2.** to fix fast with or on something sharp; thrust through. **3.** to make motionless with amazement, terror, etc. [t. L: s. *transfīxus,* pp., pierced, transfixed] —**trans·fix·ion** (trăns fĭk′shən), *n.*

trans·flu·ent (trăns′flōō ənt), *adj.* flowing or running across or through. [t. L: s. *transfluens,* ppr.]

trans·flux (trăns′flŭks), *n.* a flowing across, through, or beyond.

trans·form (trăns fôrm′), *v.t.* **1.** to change in form; change to something of a different form; metamorphose. **2.** to change in appearance, condition, nature, or character. **3.** to change into another substance; transmute. **4.** *Elect.* to change the voltage and current characteristics of a circuit by the use of a transformer. **5.** *Math.* to change the form of (a figure, expression, etc.) without in general changing the value. **6.** *Physics.* to change one form of energy into another. —*v.i.* **7.** to change in form, appearance, or character; become transformed. [ME, t. L: s. *transformāre* change form] —**trans·form′a·ble,** *adj.* —**trans·form·a·tive** (trăns fôr′mə tĭv), *adj.* —**Syn. 1.** TRANSFORM, CONVERT mean to change one thing into another. TRANSFORM suggests changing from one form, appearance, structure, or type to another: *to transform soybeans into oil and meal by pressure.* CONVERT suggests so changing the characteristics as to change the use or purpose: *to convert a barn into a house.*

trans·for·ma·tion (trăns′fôr mā′shən), *n.* **1.** act of transforming. **2.** state of being transformed. **3.** change in form, appearance, nature, or character. **4.** *Theat.* a seemingly miraculous change in the appearance of scenery or actors in view of the audience. **5.** a wig for a woman.

trans·form·er (trăns fôr′mər), *n.* **1.** one who or that which transforms. **2.** *Elect.* an electric device, without continuously moving parts, which by electromagnetic induction transforms electric energy from one or more circuits to one or more circuits at the same frequency, usually with changed values of voltage and current; esp. one for transforming a comparatively small alternating current of higher voltage into a larger current of lower voltage (**step-down transformer**), or, reversely, a current of lower voltage into one of higher voltage (**step-up transformer**).

trans·form·ism (trăns fôr′mĭz əm), *n.* ·*Biol.* **1.** the doctrine of gradual transformation of one species into another by descent with modification through many generations. **2.** such transformation itself. **3.** any doctrine or instance of evolution.

trans·fuse (trăns fūz′), *v.t.,* **-fused, -fusing. 1.** to pour from one container into another. **2.** to transfer or transmit as if by pouring. **3.** to diffuse through something; infuse. **4.** *Med.* **a.** to transfer (blood) from the veins or arteries of one person or animal into those of another. **b.** to inject, as a saline solution, into a blood vessel. [ME, t. L: m.s. *transfūsus,* pp., poured across] —**trans·fus′er,** *n.* —**trans·fus′i·ble,** *adj.* —**trans·fu·sive** (trăns fū′sĭv), *adj.*

trans·fu·sion (trăns fū′zhən), *n.* **1.** act or process of transfusing. **2.** *Med.* **a.** the transferring of blood from one person or animal to another, as in order to renew a depleted blood supply. **b.** the injecting of some other liquid into the veins. [t. L: s. *transfūsio*]

trans·gress (trăns grĕs′, trănz-), *v.t.* **1.** to pass over or go beyond (a limit, etc.): *to transgress the bounds of prudence.* **2.** to go beyond the limits imposed by (a law, command, etc.); violate; infringe; break. —*v.i.* **3.** to violate a law, command, etc.; offend or sin (fol. by *against*). [t. L: s. *transgressus,* pp., having stepped across] —**trans·gres′sive,** *adj.* —**trans·gres′sive·ly,** *adv.* —**trans·gres′sor,** *n.*

trans·gres·sion (trăns grĕsh′ən, trănz-), *n.* act of transgressing; violation of a law, command, etc.; sin.

tran·ship (trăn shĭp′), *v.t., v.i.,* **-shipped, -shipping.** tranship. —**tran·ship′ment,** *n.*

trans·hu·mance (trăns hū′məns), *n.* the seasonal migration of livestock, and the people who tend them, between lowlands and adjacent mountains. [t. F, der. *transhumer,* t. Sp.: m. *trashumar* change ground. See TRANS-, HUMUS]

tran·sience (trăn′shəns), *n.* transient state or quality. Also, **tran′sien·cy.**

tran·sient (trăn′shənt), *adj.* **1.** passing with time; not lasting or enduring; transitory. **2.** lasting but for a time; temporary: *transient authority.* **3.** remaining only for a short time, as a guest at a hotel. **4.** *Philos.* transeunt. —*n.* **5.** one who or that which is transient; a transient guest, boarder, or the like. [m. TRANSEUNT (with *-ie-* from L nom.)] —**tran′sient·ly,** *adv.* —**tran′sient·ness,** *n.* —**Syn. 2.** See **temporary.** —**Ant. 2.** permanent.

transient modulation, *Music.* a modulation of a temporary nature; a passing modulation.

tran·sil·i·ent (trăn sĭl′i ənt), *adj.* leaping or passing from one thing or state to another. [t. L: s. *transiliens,* ppr., leaping across] —**tran·sil′i·ence,** *n.*

trans·il·lu·mi·nate (trăns′ĭ lōō′mə nāt′, trănz′-), *v.t.,* **-nated, -nating. 1.** to cause light to pass through. **2.** *Med.* to throw a strong light through (an organ or part) as a means of diagnosis. —**trans'il·lu/mi·na/-tion**, *n.* —**trans/il·lu/mi·na/tor**, *n.*

trans·isth·mi·an (trăns ĭs/mĬ ən, -Ĭsth/-, trănz-), *adj.* passing or extending across an isthmus.

tran·sis·tor (trăn zĬs/tər), *n. Electronics.* a miniature amplifying device, usually utilizing germanium, that performs nearly all the functions of the electronic vacuum tube.

tran·sis·tor·ize (trăn zĬs/tə rīz/), *v.t.*, **-ized, -izing.** *Electronics.* to equip with or convert to a circuit employing transistors.

trans·it (trăn/sĬt, -zĬt), *n., v.,* **-ited, -iting.** —*n.* **1.** act or fact of passing across or through; passage from one place to another. **2.** conveyance from one place to another, as of persons or goods: *the problem of rapid transit in cities.* **3.** a transition or change. **4.** *Astron.* **a.** the passage of a heavenly body across the meridian of a place or through the field of a telescope. **b.** the passage of an inferior planet (Mercury or Venus) across the disk of the sun, or of a satellite or its shadow across the face of its primary. **c.** a transit instrument. **5.** *Survey.* an instrument for measuring angles; a theodolite. A **plain transit** measures only horizontal angles; an **engineer's** or **surveyor's transit** measures both horizontal and vertical angles and has cross hairs for making stadia measurements. —*v.t.* **6.** to pass across or through. **7.** *Survey.* to turn (the telescope of a surveyor's transit) about its horizontal transverse axis so as to make it point in the opposite direction; reverse, invert, or plunge (the instrument). [late ME, t. L: s. *transitus* act of crossing]

transit instrument, 1. *Astron.* an instrument consisting essentially of a telescope mounted on a horizontal transverse axis which is adjusted so as to be perpendicular to the plane of the meridian of a place, used for observing the passage of a celestial body across the meridian, esp. with respect to the time of transit. **2.** *Survey.* transit (def. 5).

tran·si·tion (trăn zĬsh/ən), *n.* **1.** passage from one position, state, stage, etc., to another. **2.** a passage of this kind. **3.** *Music.* **a.** a passing from one key to another; modulation. **b.** a brief modulation; a modulation used in passing. **c.** a sudden unprepared modulation. [t. L: s. *transitio* act of going across] —**tran·si/tion·al, tran·si·tion·a·ry** (-ə nĕr/Ĭ), *adj.* —**tran·si/tion·al·ly**, *adv.*

tran·si·tive (trăn/sə tĬv), *adj.* **1.** *Gram.* having the nature of a transitive verb. **2.** characterized by or involving transition; transitional; intermediate. **3.** passing over to or affecting something else; transeunt. —*n.* **4.** *Gram.* a transitive verb. [t. LL: m.s. *transitīvus*] —**tran/si·tive·ly**, *adv.* —**tran/si·tive·ness**, *n.*

transitive verb, *Gram.* a verb that is regularly accompanied by a direct object.

tran·si·to·ry (trăn/sə tōr/Ĭ), *adj.* **1.** passing away; not lasting, enduring, permanent, or eternal. **2.** lasting but a short time; brief; transient. —**tran/si·to/ri·ly**, *adv.* —**tran/si·to/ri·ness**, *n.* —**Syn. 2.** See **temporary.**

Trans-Jor·dan (trăns jôr/dən, trănz-), *n.* former name of Jordan.

transl., **1.** translated. **2.** translation.

trans·late (trăns lāt/, trănz-), *v.,* **-lated, -lating.** —*v.t.* **1.** to turn (something written or spoken) from one language into another: *to translate English books into Spanish.* **2.** to change into another form; transform or convert. **3.** to bear, carry, or remove from one place, position, condition, etc., to another; transfer. **4.** *Mech.* to cause (a body) to move without rotation or angular displacement; subject to translation. **5.** *Teleg.* to retransmit or forward (a message), as by a relay. **6.** *Eccles.* **a.** to move (a bishop) from one see to another. **b.** to move (a see) from one place to another. **7.** to exalt in spiritual ecstasy or rapture. **8.** to convey or remove to heaven without death. —*v.i.* **9.** to practice translation. **10.** to admit of translation: *the book translates well.* [ME, t. L: m.s. *translātus*, pp., carried over] —**trans·lat/a·ble**, *adj.* —**trans·lat/a·ble·ness**, *n.* —**trans·la·tor** (trăns lā/tər, trănz-; trăns lā/tər, trănz-), *n.*

trans·la·tion (trăns lā/shən, trănz-), *n.* **1.** the rendering of something into another language. **2.** a version in a different language: *a French translation of Hamlet.* **3.** act of translating. **4.** state of being translated. **5.** *Mech.* motion in which all particles of a body move in straight-line paths. **6.** *Teleg.* the process of forwarding of a message, as by a relay. —**trans·la/tion·al**, *adj.* —**Syn. 2.** TRANSLATION, PARAPHRASE, VERSION refer to a rewording of something. A TRANSLATION is a rendering of the same ideas in a different language from the original: *a translation from Greek into English.* A PARAPHRASE is a free rendering of the sense of a passage in other words, usually in the same language: *a paraphrase of a poem.* A VERSION is a translation, esp. of the Bible, or else an account of something illustrating a particular point of view: *the Douay Version.*

trans·lit·er·ate (trăns lĬt/ə rāt/, trănz-), *v.t.,* **-ated, -ating.** to change (letters, words, etc.) into corresponding characters of another alphabet or language: *to transliterate the Greek X as ch.* [f. TRANS- + m.s. L *līterātus* lettered] —**trans/lit·er·a/tion**, *n.*

trans·lo·cate (trăns lō/kāt), *v.t.,* **-cated, -cating.** to remove from one place to another; cause to change place; displace; dislocate. —**trans/lo·ca/tion**, *n.*

trans·lu·cent (trăns lōō/sənt, trănz-), *adj.* **1.** transmitting light diffusely or imperfectly; semitransparent. **2.** *Now Rare.* clear. [t. L: s. *translūcens,* ppr., shining through] —**trans·lu/cence, trans·lu/cen·cy**, *n.* —**trans·lu/cent·ly**, *adv.* —**Syn. 1.** See **transparent.**

trans·lu·cid (trăns lōō/sĬd), *adj.* translucent.

trans·lu·nar·y (trăns/lōō nĕr/Ĭ), *adj.* **1.** situated beyond or above the moon; superlunary. **2.** celestial, rather than earthly. **3.** ideal; visionary.

trans·ma·rine (trăns/mə rēn/, trănz-), *adj.* overseas.

trans·me·rid·i·o·nal (trăns/mə rĬd/Ĭ ə nəl), *adj.* crossing the meridians; running east and west.

trans·mi·grant (trăns mī/grənt, trănz-; trăns/mə grənt, trănz/-), *n.* **1.** one who or that which transmigrates. **2.** a person passing through a country or place on his way from his own country to a country in which he intends to settle. —*adj.* **3.** transmigrating. [t. L: s. *transmigrans,* ppr.]

trans·mi·grate (trăns mī/grāt, trănz-), *v.,* **-grated, -grating.** —*v.i.* **1.** to remove or pass from one place to another. **2.** to migrate from one country to another in order to settle there. **3.** (of the soul) to be reborn at death in another body. —*v.t.* **4.** to cause to transmigrate, as a soul. [ME, t. L: m.s. *transmigrātus,* pp.] —**trans·mi/gra·tor**, *n.* —**trans·mi·gra·to·ry** (trăns mī/grə tōr/Ĭ, trănz-), *adj.*

trans·mi·gra·tion (trăns/mī grā/shən, trănz-), *n.* **1.** act of transmigrating. **2.** the passage of a soul at death into another body; metempsychosis. [ME, t. LL: s. *transmigrātio*]

trans·mis·si·ble (trăns mĬs/ə bəl, trănz-), *adj.* capable of being transmitted. —**trans·mis/si·bil/i·ty**, *n.*

trans·mis·sion (trăns mĬsh/ən, trănz-), *n.* **1.** act of transmitting. **2.** fact of being transmitted. **3.** that which is transmitted. **4.** *Mach.* **a.** the transmitting or transferring of motive force. **b.** a device for this purpose, esp. the mechanism or gearing for transmitting the power from the revolutions of the engine shaft in an automobile to the driving wheels, at the varying rates of speed and direction of drive as selected in gear changes. **5.** *Radio.* the broadcasting of electromagnetic waves from the transmitting station to the receiving station. [t. L: s. *transmissio*] —**trans·mis/sive**, *adj.*

trans·mit (trăns mĬt/, trănz-), *v.t.,* **-mitted, -mitting. 1.** to send over or along, as to a recipient or destination; forward, dispatch, or convey. **2.** to communicate, as information, news, etc. **3.** to pass on or hand down, as to heirs, successors, or posterity. **4.** *Physics.* **a.** to cause (light, heat, sound, etc.) to pass through a medium. **b.** to convey or pass along (an impulse, force, motion, etc.). **c.** to permit (light, heat, etc.) to pass through: *glass transmits light.* **5.** *Radio.* to emit (electromagnetic waves). [ME, t. L: m.s. *transmittere* send across] —**trans·mit/ti·ble**, *adj.* —**Syn. 1.** See **carry.**

trans·mit·tal (trăns mĬt/əl, trănz-), *n.* act of transmitting (defs. 1–3). Also, **trans·mit/tance.**

trans·mit·ter (trăns mĬt/ər, trănz-), *n.* **1.** one who or that which transmits. **2.** Also, **transmitting set.** *Radio.* a device for sending electromagnetic waves: that part of the broadcasting apparatus which generates and modulates the radiofrequency current and conveys it to the antenna. **3.** that part of a telephonic or telegraphic apparatus converting sound waves or mechanical movements into corresponding electrical waves or impulses.

trans·mog·ri·fy (trăns mŏg/rə fī/, trănz-), *v.t.,* **-fied, -fying.** to change, as by magic; transform. [vulgar or humorous coinage] —**trans·mog/ri·fi·ca/tion**, *n.*

trans·mon·tane (trăns mŏn/tān, trănz-), *adj.* tramontane (def. 1).

trans·mun·dane (trăns mŭn/dān, trănz-), *adj.* beyond the (or this) world.

trans·mu·ta·tion (trăns/mū tā/shən, trănz/-), *n.* **1.** act of transmuting. **2.** fact or state of being transmuted. **3.** change into another nature, substance, form, or condition. **4.** *Biol.* the transformation of one species into another. Cf. **transformism. 5.** *Alchemy.* the (attempted) conversion of base metals into metals of greater value, esp. into gold or silver. —**trans/mu·ta/tion·al, trans·mut·a·tive** (trăns mū/tə tĬv, trănz-), *adj.*

trans·mute (trăns mūt/, trănz-), *v.t.,* **-muted, -muting.** to change from one nature, substance, or form into another; transform. [ME, t. L: m. *transmutāre*] —**trans·mut/a·ble**, *adj.* —**trans·mut/a·bil/i·ty, trans·mut/a·ble·ness**, *n.* —**trans·mut/a·bly**, *adv.* —**trans·mut/er**, *n.*

trans·nep·tu·ni·an (trăns/nĕp tū/nĬ ən, -tōō/-), *adj. Astron.* beyond the planet Neptune.

trans·nor·mal (trăns nôr/məl), *adj.* beyond what is normal; supernormal.

trans·o·ce·an·ic (trăns/ō shĬ ăn/Ĭk, trănz/-), *adj.* across or beyond the ocean.

tran·som (trăn/səm), *n.* **1.** a crosspiece separating a door or the like from a window or fanlight above it. **2.** a window above such a crosspiece. **3.** a crossbar, as of wood or stone, dividing a window horizontally. **4.** a window so divided. **5.** any of several transverse beams or timbers fixed across the stern-post of a ship, to strengthen and give shape to the after part. [ME, t. L: m. *transtrum* (with loss of second *-tr-* by dissimilation)] —**tran/somed**, *adj.*

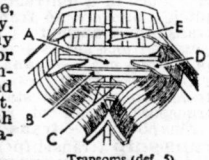

Transoms (def. 5)
A. Main transom; B. Half transom; C. Transom; D. Transom knee; E. Sternpost

tran·son·ic (trăn sŏn/Ĭk), *adj. Chiefly Aeron.* close to the speed of propagation of sound; moving at 700–780 m.p.h. at sea level. Also, **transsonic.**

transonic barrier. See **sound barrier.**

trans·pa·cif·ic (trans/pə sĭf/ĭk), *adj.* 1. passing or extending across the Pacific. 2. beyond or on the other side of, the Pacific.

trans·pa·dane (trăns/pə dān/, trăns pā/dān), *adj.* on the farther (or north) side of the river Po (from Rome). [t. L: m.s. *transpadānus*]

trans·par·en·cy (trăns pâr/ən sĭ, -păr/-), *n., pl.* **-cies.** 1. Also, **trans·par/ence.** the property or quality of being transparent. 2. something which is transparent; a picture, design, or the like on glass or some translucent substance, made visible by light shining through from behind. 3. *Photog.* the fraction of the incident light transmitted by a specific photographic density.

trans·par·ent (trăns pâr/ənt, -păr/-), *adj.* 1. having the property of transmitting rays of light through its substance so that bodies situated beyond or behind can be distinctly seen (opposed to *opaque*, and usually distinguished fron *translucent*). 2. admitting the passage of light through interstices. 3. diaphanous. 4. open, frank, or candid: *the man's transparent earnestness.* 5. easily seen through or understood: *transparent excuses.* 6. manifest or obvious. 7. *Obs.* shining through, as light. [ME, t. ML: s. *transpārens*, f. L: *trans* across + *pārens*, ppr., appearing] —**trans·par/ent·ly,** *adv.* —**trans·par/ent·ness,** *n.*
—**Syn.** 1. TRANSPARENT, TRANSLUCENT agree in describing material that light rays can pass through. That which is TRANSPARENT allows objects to be seen clearly though it: *clear water is transparent.* That which is TRANSLUCENT allows light to pass through, diffusing it, however, so that objects beyond are not distinctly seen: *ground glass is translucent.*

trans·pierce (trăns pîrs/), *v.t.,* **-pierced, -piercing.** to pierce through; penetrate; pass through.

tran·spire (trăn spīr/), *v.,* **-spired, -spiring.** —*v.i.* 1. (*regarded as incorrect or vulgar by many*) to occur, happen, or take place. 2. to emit or give off waste matter, etc., through the surface, as of the body, of leaves, etc. 3. to escape as through pores, as moisture, odor, etc. 4. to escape from secrecy; leak out; become known. —*v.t.* 5. to emit or give off (waste matter, watery vapor, an odor, etc.) through the surface, as of the body, of leaves, etc. [t. ML: m.s. *transpīrāre*, f. L *trans* across + *spīrāre* breathe] —**tran·spi·ra·tion** (trăn/spə rā/shən), *n.* —**tran·spir·a·to·ry** (trăn spīr/ə tôr/ĭ), *adj.*

trans·plant (*v.* trăns plănt/, -plänt/; *n.* trăns/plănt/, -plänt/), *v.t.* 1. to remove (a plant) from one place and plant it in another. 2. *Surg.* to transfer, as an organ or a portion of tissue, from one part of the body to another or from one person or animal to another. 3. to remove from one place to another. 4. to bring (a colony, etc.) from one country to another for settlement. —*n.* 5. a transplanting. 6. something transplanted. 7. a seedling which has been transplanted once or several times. [late ME, t. LL: s. *transplantāre*] —**trans·plant/a·ble,** *adj.* —**trans/plan·ta/tion,** *n.* —**trans·plant/er,** *n.*

trans·po·lar (trăns pō/lər), *adj.* across the (north or south) pole or polar region.

trans·po·ni·ble (trăns pō/nə bəl), *adj.* capable of being transposed. [f. s. L *transpōnere* transpose + -IBLE]

trans·pon·tine (trăns pŏn/tĭn, -tīn), *adj.* 1. across or beyond a bridge. 2. on the southern side of the Thames in London. [f. TRANS- + s. L *pons* bridge + -INE[1]]

trans·port (*v.* trăns pōrt/; *n.* trăns/pōrt), *v.t.* 1. to carry or convey from one place to another. 2. to carry away by strong emotion. 3. to carry into banishment, as a criminal to a penal colony. 4. *Obs.* to kill. —*n.* 5. *Chiefly Brit.* act of transporting or conveying; conveyance. 6. a means of transporting or conveying; a ship employed for transporting soldiers or military stores, or convicts. 7. a convict transported, or sentenced to be transported. 8. an airplane carrying freight or passengers as part of a transportation system. 9. strong emotion; ecstatic joy, bliss, etc. [ME *transporte(n)*, t. L: m. *transportāre* carry across] —**trans·port/a·ble,** *adj.* —**trans·port/a·bil/i·ty,** *n.* —**trans·port/er,** *n.*

trans·por·ta·tion (trăns/pər tā/shən), *n.* 1. act of transporting. 2. state of being transported. 3. means of transport or conveyance. 4. cost of transport or travel by public conveyance. 5. *U.S.* tickets or permits for transport or travel. 6. banishment, as of a criminal to a penal colony; deportation.

trans·pose (trăns pōz/), *v.t.,* **-posed, -posing.** 1. to alter the relative position or order of (a thing in a series, or a series of things). 2. to cause (two or more things) to change places; interchange. 3. to alter the order of (letters in a word, or words in a sentence). 4. *Alg.* to bring (a term) from one side of an equation to the other, with change of the plus or minus sign. 5. *Music.* to reproduce in a different key, by raising or lowering in pitch. 6. *Rare.* to transfer or transport. 7. *Obs.* to transform; transmute. [ME *transpose(n)*, t. F: m. *transposer*, f. *trans-* across + *poser* place. See POSE[1]] —**trans·pos/a·ble,** *adj.* —**trans·pos/er,** *n.*

trans·po·si·tion (trăns/pə zĭsh/ən), *n.* 1. the act of transposing, or the state of being transposed. 2. a transposed form of something. Also, **trans·pos·al** (trăns pō/zəl). —**trans/po·si/tion·al,** *adj.*

trans·ship (trăns shĭp/), *v.,* **-shipped, -shipping.** —*v.t.* 1. to transfer from one ship, car, or other conveyance to another. —*v.i.* 2. to change from one ship or other conveyance to another. Also, **tranship.** —**trans·ship/ment,** *n.*

Trans-Si·be·ri·an Railroad (trăns/sī bîr/ĭ ən), a railroad constructed 1891–99 by the Russian government, traversing Siberia and Manchuria, from Chelyabinsk in the Urals to Vladivostok, over 4000 miles.

trans·son·ic (trăns sŏn/ĭk), *adj.* transonic.

tran·sub·stan·ti·ate (trăn/səb stăn/shĭ āt/), *v.t.,* **-ated, -ating.** 1. to change from one substance into another; transmute. 2. *Theol.* to change (the substance of bread and wine) into the substance of body and blood of Christ, the species (def. 4a) alone remaining of bread and wine. [t. ML: m.s. *transubstantiātus*, pp.]

tran·sub·stan·ti·a·tion (trăn/səb stăn/shĭ ā/shən), *n.* 1. the changing of one substance into another. 2. *Theol.* the conversion, in the Eucharist, of the whole substance of the bread into the body, and of the whole substance of the wine into the blood, of Christ, only the appearance of bread and wine remaining (a doctrine of the Roman Catholic Church). —**tran/sub·stan/ti·a/tion·al·ist,** *n.*

tran·su·da·tion (trăn/sŏŏ dā/shən), *n.* 1. act or process of transuding. 2. a substance which has transuded. Also, **tran·su·date** (trăn/sŏŏ dāt/).

tran·sude (trăn sŏŏd/), *v.i.,* **-suded, -suding.** to pass or ooze through pores or interstices, as a fluid. [t. NL: m.s. *transūdāre,* f. L: *trans* across + *sūdāre* sweat] —**tran·su·da·to·ry** (trăn sŏŏ/də tōr/ĭ), *adj.*

trans·u·ran·ic element (trăns/yŏŏ răn/ĭk, trănz/-), *Chem., Physics.* an element having a higher atomic number than uranium. Neptunium, plutonium, americium, curium, berkelium, californium, einsteinium, fermium, mendelevium, and nobelium (at. nos. 93-102) are the ones known at present.

Trans·vaal (trăns văl/, trănz-), *n.* a NE province in the Union of South Africa. 5,244,000 (est. 1955); 110,450 sq. mi. *Cap.*: Pretoria. Formerly, **South African Republic.** —**Trans·vaal/er,** *n.* —**Trans·vaal/i·an,** *adj.*

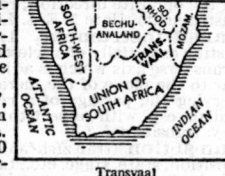

Transvaal

trans·val·ue (trăns văl/ū, trănz-), *v.t.,* **-ued, -uing.** to change the value of. —**trans/val·u·a/tion,** *n.*

trans·ver·sal (trăns vûr/səl, trănz-), *adj.* 1. transverse. —*n.* 2. *Geom.* a line intersecting two or more lines. [late ME, t. ML: s. *transversālis.* See TRANSVERSE, -AL[1]] —**trans·ver/sal·ly,** *adv.*

trans·verse (trăns vûrs/, trănz-), *adj.* 1. lying or being across or in a cross direction; cross; athwart. 2. *Geom.* noting that axis of a hyperbola which passes through the foci. 3. (of a flute) having a mouth hole in the side of the tube, near its end, across which the player's breath is directed. —*n.* 4. something which is transverse. *Geom.* a transverse axis. [t. L: m.s. *transversus,* pp., turned or directed across]

X

Y

XY, Transversal (def. 2)

transverse process, a process which projects from the sides of a vertebra.

transverse vibrations, *Acoustics.* periodic disturbances for which the particle oscillations of the medium are perpendicular to the direction of propagation.

trans·ves·tism (trăns vĕs/tĭz əm, trănz-), *n.* the practice of wearing clothing appropriate to the opposite sex, often as a manifestation of homosexuality. —**trans·ves·tite** (trăns vĕs/tīt, trănz-), *n.*

Tran·syl·va·ni·a (trăn/sĭl vā/nĭ ə), *n.* a province in W and central Rumania: formerly a part of Hungary. 3,402,859 pop. (1948); 24,027 sq. mi. —**Tran/syl·va/ni·an,** *adj., n.*

Transylvanian Alps, a mountain range in S Rumania, forming a SW extension of the Carpathian system: highest peak, Mt. Negoiul, 8345 ft.

trap[1] (trăp), *n., v.,* **trapped, trapping.** —*n.* 1. a contrivance used for taking game or other animals, as a mechanical device that springs shut suddenly, a pitfall, or a snare. 2. any device, stratagem, or the like for catching one unawares. 3. any of various mechanical contrivances for preventing the passage of steam, water, etc. 4. an arrangement in a pipe, as a double curve or a U-shaped section, in which liquid remains and forms a seal, for preventing the passage or escape of air or gases through the pipe from behind or below. 5. (*usually pl.*) *Chiefly Jazz.* a percussion instrument, as a bass drum with a cymbal attached to it, a snare drum, etc. 6. a device for suddenly releasing or tossing into the air objects to be shot at, as pigeons or clay targets. 7. the piece of wood, shaped somewhat like a shoe hollowed at the heel, and moving on a pivot, used in playing the game of trapball. 8. trapball. 9. *Chiefly Brit.* a carriage, esp. a light two-wheeled one. 10. a trap door. —*v.t.* 11. to catch in a trap: *to trap foxes.* 12. to take by stratagem; lead by artifice or wiles. 13. to furnish or set with traps. 14. to provide (a drain, etc.) with a trap. 15. to stop and hold by a trap, as air in a pipe. —*v.i.* 16. to set traps for game: *he was busy trapping.* 17. to engage in catching animals in traps for their

Traps (def. 4)
A, B, Common traps;
C, Ventilating trap

furs. **18.** to work the trap in trapshooting. [ME *trappe,* OE *træppe,* c. MD *trappe.* Cf. ML *trappa*] —trap′like′, *adj.*

—**Syn. 1, 2.** TRAP, PITFALL, SNARE apply to literal or figurative contrivances for deceiving and catching an°mals or people. Literally, a TRAP is a mechanical contrivance for catching animals, the main feature usually being a spring: *a trap baited with cheese for mice.* Figuratively, TRAP suggests the scheme of one person to take another by surprise and gain an advantage from him: *a trap for the unwary.* A PITFALL is (usually) a concealed pit arranged for the capture of large animals or men who may fall into it; figuratively, it is any concealed danger, error, or source of disaster: *to catch elephants in a pitfall.* A SNARE is a device for entangling birds, rabbits, etc., with intent to capture; figuratively, it implies enticement and inveiglement: *a snare for small animals.*

trap² (trăp), *n., v.,* **trapped, trapping.** —*n.* **1.** (*pl.*) *Colloq.* personal belongings; baggage. **2.** *Obs.* a cloth or covering for a horse. —*v.t.* **3.** to furnish with trapping; caparison. [ME *trappe;* orig. uncert.]

trap³ (trăp), *n. Geol.* any of various fine-grained dark-colored igneous rocks having a more or less columnar structure, esp. some form of basalt. [t. Sw.: m. *trapp,* var. of *trappa* stair (so named from their appearance)]

tra·pan (trə păn′), *n., v.t.,* -**panned,** -**panning.** *Archaic.* trepan². —**tra·pan′ner,** *n.*

Tra·pa·ni (trä′pä nē′), *n.* a seaport in NW Sicily. 75,000 (est. 1954).

trap·ball (trăp′bôl′), *n.* **1.** an old game in which a ball placed on the hollowed end of a trap is thrown into the air by striking the other end of the trap with a bat and then driven to a distance with the bat. **2.** the ball used in this game.

trap door, 1. a door or the like, flush, or nearly so, with the surface of a floor, ceiling, roof, etc. **2.** the opening which it covers.

tra·peze (trə pēz′), *n.* **1.** a gymnasium apparatus consisting of a short horizontal bar attached to the ends of two suspended ropes. **2.** *Geom.* trapezium. [t. F, t. L: m. *trapezium* small table, t. Gk.: m. *trapēzion*]

tra·pe·zi·form (trə pē′zə fôrm′), *adj.* formed like a trapezium.

tra·pe·zi·um (trə pē′zĬ əm), *n., pl.* -**ziums,** -**zia** (-zĬ ə). **1.** *Geom.* **a.** (as orig. used by Euclid) any rectilinear quadrilateral plane figure not a parallelogram. **b.** a quadrilateral plane figure of which no two sides are parallel. **c.** *Brit.* a trapezoid (def. 1a). **2.** *Anat.* a bone of the carpus articulating with the metacarpal bone of the thumb. [t. NL. See TRAPEZE]

Trapezium (def. 1b)

trap·e·zoid (trăp′ə zoid′), *n.* **1.** *Geom.* **a.** a quadrilateral plane figure having two parallel and two nonparallel sides. **b.** *Brit.* a trapezium (def. 1b). **2.** *Anat.* a bone of the carpus articulating with the meta-carpal bone of the index finger. [t. NL: s. *trapezoīdēs* tablelike, t. LGk.: m. *trapezoeidēs*] —trap′e·zoid′, **trap′e·zoi′dal,** *adj.*

Trapezoid (def. 1a)

Trappe (trăp), *n.* **La** (lä). See **La Trappe.**

trap·pe·an (trăp′Ĭ ən, trə pē′ən), *adj.* consisting of, pertaining to, or having the nature of trap (rock).

trap·per (trăp′ər), *n.* **1.** one who traps. **2.** one who makes a business of trapping wild animals for their furs.

trap·pings (trăp′Ĭngz), *n.pl.* **1.** articles of equipment or dress, esp. of an ornamental character. **2.** conventional or characteristic articles of dress or adornment. **3.** a covering for a horse, esp. when ornamental in character. [ME. See TRAP², -ING¹]

Trap·pist (trăp′Ĭst), *n.* **1.** a member of a monastic body, a branch of the Cistercian order, observing the extremely austere reformed rule established at the abbey of La Trappe, in Normandy, in 1664. —*adj.* **2.** of or pertaining to the Trappists. [t. F: m. *trappiste*]

trap·rock (trăp′rŏk′), *n. Geol.* trap³.

traps (trăps), *n.pl.* See **trap** (def. 5).

trap·shoot·ing (trăp′shoo′tĬng), *n.* the sport of shooting at live pigeons released from, or clay targets, etc., thrown into the air by, a trap (def. 6). —**trap′-shoot′er,** *n.*

trash (trăsh), *n.* **1.** anything worthless or useless; rubbish. **2.** foolish notions, talk, or writing; nonsense. **3.** a worthless or disreputable person. **4.** such persons collectively. **5.** broken or torn bits, as twigs, splinters, rags, or the like. **6.** that which is broken or lopped off from anything in preparing it for use. **7.** the refuse of sugar cane after the juice has been expressed. —*v.t.* **8.** to free from trash or refuse, as outer leaves from growing sugar cane. **9.** to free from superfluous twigs or branches. [ME *trasche.* Cf. d. Norw. *trask,* Icel. *tros*]

trash·y (trăsh′Ĭ), *adj.,* **trashier, trashiest. 1.** of the nature of trash; rubbishy or worthless: *trashy novels.* **2.** encumbered with trash, as a field. —**trash′i·ly,** *adv.* —**trash′i·ness,** *n.*

Tra·si·me·no (trä′sĕ mĕ′nō), *n.* a lake in central Italy, W of Perugia: the Romans were disastrously defeated here by Hannibal, 217 B.C. Ab. 10 mi. long.

trass (trăs), *n.* a rock common along the Rhine, composed chiefly of comminuted pumice or other volcanic material, used for making hydraulic cement. [t. D: m. *tras,* earlier *tarasse,* var. of *terras,* prob. t. F. See TERRACE]

trau·ma (trô′mə, trou′-), *n., pl.* -**mata** (-mə tə), -**mas. 1.** *Pathol.* **a.** a bodily injury produced by violence, or

any thermal, chemical, etc., extrinsic agent. **b.** the condition produced by this; traumatism. **c.** the injurious agent or mechanism itself. **2.** *Psychiatry.* a startling experience which has a lasting effect on mental life; a shock. [t. Gk: wound]

trau·mat·ic (trô măt′Ĭk), *adj.* **1.** pertaining to or produced by a trauma or wound. **2.** adapted to the cure of wounds. [t. LL: s. *traumaticus,* t. Gk.: m. *traumatikós* pertaining to wound(s)]

trau·ma·tism (trô′mə tĬz′əm), *n. Pathol.* **1.** any morbid condition produced by a trauma. **2.** the trauma or wound itself.

trau·ma·tize (trô′mə tīz′), *v.t.,* -**tized, -tizing.** *Pathol.* to injure (tissues) by force, or by thermal, chemical, electrical, etc., agents.

trav·ail (trăv′āl, trăv′əl), *n.* **1.** physical or mental toil or exertion, esp. when painful. **2.** the labor and pain of childbirth. —*v.i.* **3.** *Archaic.* to toil, or exert oneself. **4.** to suffer the pangs of childbirth; be in labor. [ME, t. OF: suffering, painful effort, trouble, der. *travailler* work (hard), ult. der. LL *trepālium* torture instrument, lit., object made of three stakes]

Trav·an·core (trăv′ən kōr′), *n.* a former state in S India; now Kerala.

trave (trāv), *n.* **1.** *Archit.* **a.** a crossbeam. **b.** a section or bay formed by crossbeams. **2.** a device to inhibit a wild or untrained horse or one being shod. [ME *trave,* t. OF, g. L *trabs* beam]

trav·el (trăv′əl), *v.,* -**eled, -eling** or (*esp. Brit.*) -**elled, -elling,** *n.* —*v.i.* **1.** to go from one place to another; make a journey: *to travel for pleasure.* **2.** to move or go from one place or point to another. **3.** to proceed or advance in any way. **4.** to go from place to place as a representative of a business firm. **5.** *U.S. Colloq.* to move with speed. **6.** to move in a fixed course, as a piece of mechanism. **7.** to pass, or be transmitted, as light, sound, etc. —*v.t.* **8.** to travel, journey, or pass through or over, as a country, district, road, etc. —*n.* **9.** act of traveling; journeying, esp. in distant or foreign places. **10.** (*pl.*) journeys: *to start on one's travels.* **11.** (*pl.*) **a.** journeys as the subject of a written account or literary work. **b.** such an account or work. **12.** the coming and going of persons or conveyances along a way of passage; traffic. **13.** *Mach.* **a.** the complete movement of a moving part (esp. a reciprocating part) in one direction, or the distance traversed; stroke. **b.** length of stroke. **14.** movement or passage in general. [ME; var. of TRAVAIL]

trav·eled (trăv′əld), *adj.* **1.** having traveled, esp. to distant places; experienced in travel. **2.** frequented by travelers, as a road. **3.** *Geol.* moved to a distance from the original site, as a boulder. Also, *esp. Brit.,* **trav·elled.**

trav·el·er (trăv′ələr), *n.* **1.** one who or that which travels. **2.** one who travels or has traveled in distant places or foreign lands. **3.** *Chiefly Brit.* one who travels from place to place as the representative of a business firm. **4.** a piece of mechanism constructed to move in a fixed course. **5.** *Naut.* **a.** metal ring or thimble fitted to move freely on a rope, spar, or rod. **b.** the rope, spar, or rod itself. **c.** a ring attached to the sheet of a fore-and-aft sail and sliding from side to side on a metal rod fastened to the deck. Also, *esp. Brit.,* **trav′el·ler.**

traveler's check, a check issued by a bank, express company, etc., to a traveler, who may cash it by endorsing it in sight of the payer.

Traveler (def. 5) A. Ring; B. Rod; C. Buffer

trav·elled (trăv′əld), *adj. Chiefly Brit.* traveled.

trav·e·logue (trăv′ə lôg′, -lŏg′), *n.* a lecture describing travel, usually illustrated, as with stereopticon views or moving pictures. Also, **trav′e·log′.** [f. TRAVEL + -logue, modeled on DIALOGUE]

trav·erse (trăv′ərs, trə vûrs′), *v.,* -**ersed, -ersing,** *n., adj., adv.* —*v.t.* **1.** to pass across, over, or through. **2.** to go to and fro over or along, as a place. **3.** to cause to move laterally. **4.** to pass in review; survey carefully. **5.** to go counter to; obstruct or thwart. **6.** to contradict or deny. **7.** *Law.* **a.** (in the law of pleading) to deny an allegation of fact set forth in a previous pleading. **b.** to join issue upon. **c.** to deny formally, in pleading at law. **8.** to turn and point (a gun) in any direction. **9.** *Naut.* to brace (a yard) fore and aft. —*v.i.* **10.** to pass or go across; cross; cross over. **11.** to turn freely from side to side, as a gun. **12.** *Fencing.* to glide the blade toward the hilt of the contestant's foil while applying pressure to the blade. [ME *traverse(n),* t. F: m. *traverser* cross, thwart, der. *travers* TRAVERSE, n. or adj.] —*n.* **13.** act of traversing, or passing across, over, or through. **14.** something that crosses, obstructs, or thwarts; obstacle. **15.** a transversal or similar line. **16.** a place where one may traverse or cross; a crossing. **17.** *Archit.* a transverse gallery or loft of communication in a church or other large building. **18.** a member placed or extending across; a crosspiece or crossbar. **19.** a railing, lattice, or screen serving as a barrier. **20.** *Naut.* **a.** the zigzag track of a vessel compelled by contrary winds or currents to sail on different courses. **b.** each of the runs in a single direction made in such sailing.

ăct, āble, dâre, ärt; ĕbb, ēqual, ēqual; Ĭf, īce; hŏt, ōver, ôrder, oil, bŏŏk, ōoze, out; ŭp, ūse, ûrge; ə = a in alone; ch, chief; g, give; ng, ring; sh, shoe; th, thin; ŧh, that; zh, vision. See the full key on inside cover.

21. *Fort.* **a.** a defensive barrier, parapet, or the like placed transversely. **b.** one thrown across the terreplein or the covered way of a fortification to protect it from enfilade fire. **22.** *Gunnery.* the horizontal turning of a gun so as to make it point in any required direction. **23.** *Mach.* **a.** a crosswise or side movement or motion as in the lathe carriage saddle. **b.** a part moving in this way. **24.** *Survey.* a series of distances and angles (or bearings) connecting successive instrument points of a survey. **25.** *Law.* a formal denial of some matter of fact alleged by the other side.
—*adj.* **26.** lying, extending, or passing across; cross; transverse.
—*adv.* **27.** *Obs.* across; crosswise; transversely.
[ME; t. OF: m. *travers* lying athwart, g. LL *trāversus*, L *transversus*, pp.] —**trav′ers·a·ble,** *adj.* —**trav′-ers·er,** *n.*

trav·er·tine (trăv′ər tǐn, -tēn′), *n.* a form of limestone deposited by springs, etc., used in Italy for building purposes. Also, **trav·er·tin** (trăv′ər tǐn). [t. It.: m. *travertino,* b. *tivertino,* g. L *Tīburtīnus* of Tibur (now Tivoli) and *tra-* across (g. L *trans*)]

trav·es·ty (trăv′ĭs tǐ), *n., pl.* **-ties,** *v.,* **-tied, -tying.** **1.** a literary composition characterized by burlesque or ludicrous treatment of a serious work or subject. **2.** literary composition of this kind. **3.** any grotesque or debased likeness or imitation: *a travesty of justice.* —*v.t.* **4.** to make a travesty on; turn (a serious work or subject) to ridicule by burlesque imitation or treatment. **5.** to imitate grotesquely or absurdly. [t. F: m. *travesti,* pp., disguised, t. It.: m. *travestire* disguise, f. *tra* across (g. L *trans*) + *vestire* dress (g. L)]

tra·vois (tră voi′), *n., pl.* **-vois** (-voiz′). a transport device, formerly used by the Plains Indians, consisting of two poles joined by a frame and drawn by an animal. [t. Canadian F: m. *travail* brake]

trawl (trôl), *n.* **1.** Also, **trawl net.** a strong fishing net dragged along the sea bottom in trawling. **2.** Also, **trawl line.** a buoyed line used in sea fishing, having numerous short lines with baited hooks attached at intervals. —*v.i.* **3.** to fish with a net whose edge is dragged along the sea bottom to catch the fish living there. **4.** to fish with a trawl line. **5.** to troll. **6.** to catch with a trawl net or a trawl line. —*v.t.* **7.** to drag (a trawl net). **8.** to troll. [cf. MD *traghel* dragnet]

trawl·er (trô′lər), *n.* **1.** one who trawls. **2.** any of various types of vessels used in fishing with a trawl net.

tray (trā), *n.* **1.** any of various flat, shallow containers or receptacles of wood, metal, etc., with slightly raised edges used for carrying, holding, or exhibiting articles and for various other purposes. **2.** a removable receptacle of this shape in a cabinet, box, trunk, or the like, sometimes forming a drawer. **3.** a tray and what is in it. [ME; OE *trĕg,* c. OSw. *trö* corn measure; akin to TREE]

tray agriculture, hydroponics.

treach·er·ous (trĕch′ərəs), *adj.* **1.** violating faith or betraying trust; disloyal; traitorous. **2.** deceptive, untrustworthy, or unreliable. **3.** unstable or insecure. —**treach′er·ous·ly,** *adv.* —**treach′er·ous·ness,** *n.*

treach·er·y (trĕch′ər ǐ), *n., pl.* **-eries.** **1.** violation of faith; betrayal of trust; treason. **2.** an act of perfidy or faithlessness. [ME *trecherie,* t. OF, der. *tricher* cheat; orig. uncert.] —**Syn. 1.** See **disloyalty.**

trea·cle (trē′kəl), *n.* **1.** *Brit.* molasses, esp. that produced during the refining of sugar. **2.** *Obs.* any of various medicinal compounds formerly in repute as antidotes for poisonous bites or for poisons. **3.** *Obs.* a sovereign remedy. [ME, t. OF: m. *triacle* antidote, g. L *thēriaca,* t. Gk.: m. *thēriakē* (def. 2)] —**trea·cly** (trē′klǐ), *adj.*

tread (trĕd), *v.,* **trod** or (*Archaic*) **trode; trodden** or **trod; treading;** *n.* —*v.t.* **1.** to step or walk on, about, in, or along. **2.** to trample or crush underfoot. **3.** to put into some position or condition by trampling: *to tread a path.* **4.** to domineer harshly over; crush. **5.** to execute by walking or dancing: *to tread a measure.* **6.** (of male birds) to copulate with. **7. tread water,** *Swimming.* to move the arms and legs in such a way as to keep the body in an upright position with the head above water. —*v.i.* **8.** to set down the foot or feet in walking; step; walk. **9.** to step, walk, or trample (fol. by *on* or *upon*). **10.** (of male birds) to copulate. [ME *trede*(n), OE *tredan,* c. G *treten*]
—*n.* **11.** a treading, stepping, or walking, or the sound of this. **12.** manner of treading or walking. **13.** a single step as in walking. **14.** any of various things or parts on which a person or thing treads, stands, or moves. **15.** the sole of the foot or of a shoe that presses on the ground. **16.** the horizontal upper surface of a step in a stair, on which the foot is placed. **17.** the width of this from front to back. **18.** the part of a wheel, tire, or runner which bears on the road, rail, etc. **19.** the part of a rail on which the wheels bear. [ME *trede, tredd.* See TREAD, *v.*] —**tread′er,** *n.*

trea·dle (trĕd′əl), *n., v.,* **-dled, -dling.** —*n.* **1.** a lever or the like worked by the foot to impart motion to a machine. —*v.i.* **2.** to work a treadle. [ME and OE *tredel.* See TREAD, *v.*] —**tread′ler,** *n.*

tread·mill (trĕd′mǐl′), *n.* **1.** an apparatus for producing rotary motion by the weight of men or animals, treading on a succession of moving steps that form a kind of continuous path, as around the periphery of a horizontal cylinder. **2.** a monotonous or wearisome round, as of work or life.

treas., **1.** treasurer. **2.** treasury.

trea·son (trē′zən), *n.* **1. a.** violation by a subject of his allegiance to his sovereign or to the state; high treason. **b.** *U.S.* such a violation directed against the United States, and consisting "only in levying war against them, or in adhering to their enemies, giving them aid and comfort" (*Constitution of the U.S.,* iii. 3. 1). **2.** *Rare.* the betrayal of a trust or confidence; breach of faith; treachery. [ME, t. AF: m. *tre*(y)*soun,* g. L *trāditio* act of betraying]
—**Syn. 2.** See **disloyalty. 1.** TREASON, SEDITION mean disloyalty or treachery to one's country or its government. TREASON is any attempt to overthrow the government or well-being of a state to which one owes allegiance; the crime of giving aid or comfort to the enemies of one's government. SEDITION is any act, writing, speech, etc., directed unlawfully against state authority, the government, or constitution, or calculated to bring it into contempt or to incite others to hostility, ill will or disaffection; it does not amount to treason and therefore is not a capital offense. —**Ant. 2.** loyalty.

trea·son·a·ble (trē′zənə bəl), *adj.* **1.** of the nature of treason. **2.** involving treason; traitorous. —**trea′son·a·ble·ness,** *n.* —**trea′son·a·bly,** *adv.*

trea·son·ous (trē′zən əs), *adj.* treasonable. —**trea′son·ous·ly,** *adv.*

treasr., treasurer.

treas·ure (trĕzh′ər), *n., v.,* **-ured, -uring.** —*n.* **1.** wealth or riches stored or accumulated, esp. in the form of precious metals or money. **2.** wealth, rich materials, or valuable things. **3.** any thing or person greatly valued or highly prized: *this book was his chief treasure.* —*v.t.* **4.** to put away for security or future use, as money; lay up in store. **5.** to retain carefully or keep in store, as in the mind. **6.** to regard as precious; prize; cherish. [ME *tresor,* t. OF, g. L *thēsaurus.* See THESAURUS] —**treas′-ure·less,** *adj.*

Treasure Island, a novel (1883) by R. L. Stevenson.

treas·ur·er (trĕzh′ərər), *n.* **1.** one who is in charge of treasure or a treasury. **2.** one who has charge of the funds of a corporation, private society, or the like. **3.** an officer of a state, city, etc., entrusted with the receipt, care, and disbursement of public money. —**treas′ur·er·ship,** *n.*

treas·ure-trove (trĕzh′ər trōv′), *n.* **1.** *Law.* any money, bullion, or the like, of unknown ownership, found hidden in the earth or in any other place. **2.** anything of the nature of treasure which one finds. [t. AF: m. *tresor-trovē* treasure found]

treas·ur·y (trĕzh′ərǐ), *n., pl.* **-uries. 1.** a place where public revenues, or the funds of a corporation, etc., are deposited, kept, and disbursed. **2.** the funds or revenue of a state or a public or private corporation, etc. **3.** the department of government which has control over the collection, management, and disbursement of the public revenue. **4.** a building, room, chest, or other place for the preservation of treasure or valuable objects. **5.** a repository or a collection of treasures of any kind; a thesaurus.

treasury note, a note or bill issued by the United States Treasury, receivable as legal tender for all debts except as otherwise expressly provided.

treat (trēt), *v.t.* **1.** to act or behave toward in some specified way: *to treat someone with respect.* **2.** to look upon, consider, or regard in a specified aspect, and deal with accordingly: *to treat a matter as unimportant.* **3.** to deal with (a disease, patient, etc.) in order to relieve or cure. **4.** to deal with in speech or writing; discuss. **5.** to deal with, develop, or represent artistically, esp. in some specified manner or style: *to treat a theme realistically.* **6.** to subject to some agent or action in order to bring about a particular result: *to treat a substance with an acid.* **7.** to entertain with food, drink, amusement, etc. **8.** to regale another at one's own expense. —*v.i.* **9.** to deal with a subject in speech or writing, or discourse. **10.** to give, or bear the expense of, a treat. **11.** to carry on negotiations with a view to a settlement, discuss terms of settlement, or negotiate. —*n.* **12.** an entertainment of food, drink, amusement, etc., given by way of compliment or as an expression of friendly regard. **13.** *Colloq.* anything that affords particular pleasure or enjoyment. **14.** act of treating. **15.** one's turn to treat. [ME *treete*(n), t. OF: m. *tretier, traitier,* g. L *tractāre* drag, handle, treat] —**treat′a·ble,** *adj.* —**treat′er,** *n.*

trea·tise (trē′tǐs), *n.* **1.** a book or writing treating of some particular subject. **2.** one containing a formal or methodical exposition of the principles of the subject. [ME *treatis,* t. AF: m. *tretiz,* der. *traitier* TREAT]

treat·ment (trēt′mənt), *n.* **1.** act or manner of treating. **2.** action or behavior toward a person, etc. **3.** management in the application of medicines, surgery, etc. **4.** literary or artistic handling, esp. with reference to style. **5.** subjection to some agent or action.

trea·ty (trē′tǐ), *n., pl.* **-ties. 1.** a formal agreement between two or more states in reference to peace, alliance, commerce, or other international relations. **2.** the formal document embodying such an international agreement. **3.** any agreement or compact. **4.** *Rare.* negotiation with a view to settlement. **5.** *Obs.* entreaty. [ME *tretee,* t. AF: m. *tretē,* pp., handled, treated. See TREAT] —**trea′ty·less,** *adj.*

Treb·bia (trĕb′byä), *n.* a river in N Italy, flowing into the Po near Piacenza: Hannibal decisively defeated the Romans near here, 218 B.C. Ab. 75 mi.

---

b., blend of, blended; **c.,** cognate with; **d.,** dialect, dialectal; **der.,** derived from; **f.,** formed from; **g.,** going back to; **m.,** modification of; **r.,** replacing; **s.,** stem of; **t.,** taken from; **?,** perhaps. See the full key on inside cover.

Treb·i·zond (trĕb′ə zŏnd′), *n.* **1.** a medieval empire (1204–1461) in NE Asia Minor. **2.** Official name, **Trabzon.** a seaport in NE Turkey, on the Black Sea: an ancient Greek colony; capital of the medieval empire of Trebizond. 42,273 (1955).

tre·ble (trĕb′əl), *adj.*, *n.*, *v.*, **-bled, -bling.** —*adj.* **1.** threefold; triple. **2.** *Music.* **a.** of or pertaining to the highest part in harmonized music; soprano. **b.** of the highest pitch or range, as a voice part, voice, singer, or instrument. **c.** high in pitch; shrill. —*n.* **3.** *Music.* **a.** the treble or soprano part. **b.** a treble voice, singer, or instrument. **4.** a high or shrill voice or sound. **5.** the highest-pitched peal of a bell. —*v.t.*, *v.i.* **6.** to make or become three times as much or as many; triple. [ME, t. OF, g. VL *triplus*, L *triplex* triple] —**tre·bly** (trĕb′lĭy), *adv.*

treble clef, *Music.* a sign which locates the G above middle C, placed on the second line of the staff, counting up. See illus. under **clef.**

treb·u·chet (trĕb′yŏŏ shĕt′), *n.* a medieval military engine for hurling stones and making a breach. [ME, t. OF, der. *trebucher* overturn, fall, der. *tre(s)*, across, over (g. L *trāns*) + *buc* trunk of body, t. Gmc.; cf. OE *būc* belly]

tre·cen·to (trĕ chĕn′tō), *n.* the 14th century, with reference to Italy, and esp. to its art or literature. [It., short for *mille trecento* thirteen hundred]

tree (trē), *n.*, *v.*, **treed, treeing.** —*n.* **1.** a perennial plant having a permanent, woody, self-supporting main stem or trunk, ordinarily growing to a considerable height, and usually developing branches at some distance from the ground. **2.** any of various shrubs, bushes, and herbaceous plants, as the banana, resembling a tree in form or size. **3.** a diagram in the outline form of a tree, indicating the source, main stem, and branches of a family (**family tree** or **genealogical tree**). **4.** a pole, post, beam, bar, handle, or the like, as one forming part of some structure. **5.** a boot tree. **6.** a saddletree. **7.** a treelike group of crystals, as one forming in an electrolytic cell. **8.** a gallows or gibbet. **9.** *Archaic or Poetic.* the cross on which Christ was crucified. —*v.t.* **10.** to drive into or up a tree, as a hunted animal, or a man pursued by an animal. **11.** *Colloq.* to put into a difficult position. **12.** to stretch or shape on a tree, as a boot. **13.** to furnish with a tree (def. 4). [ME; OE *trēo(w)*, c. Icel. *trē*, Goth. *triu*; akin to Gk. *drûs* tree, oak] —**tree′less,** *adj.* —**tree′less·ness,** *n.* —**tree′like′,** *adj.*

Tree (trē), *n.* **Sir Herbert Beerbohm** (bĭr′bōm), (*Herbert Beerbohm*) 1853–1917, British actor and theater manager.

tree creeper. See **creeper** (def. 4).

tree fern, any of various ferns, mostly tropical and chiefly of the family *Cyatheaceae*, which attain the size of trees, sending up a straight trunklike stem with foliage at the summit.

tree frog, 1. any of the arboreal frogs of various families, characterized usually by toes with adhesive disks. **2.** a tree toad.

tree heath, a shrubby heath, *Erica arborea,* of Mediterranean regions; brier.

tree kangaroo, any kangaroo of the highly arboreal genus *Dendrolagus,* found in New Guinea and Queensland, Australia.

tree·nail (trē′nāl′, trĕn′əl, trŭn′əl), *n.* a cylindrical pin of hard wood for fastening together timbers in ships, etc. Also, **trenail, trunnel.** [ME *trenayl.* See TREE, NAIL.]

tree of heaven, an Asiatic simarubaceous tree, *Ailanthus altissima,* with ill-scented flowers, frequently planted as a shade tree; ailanthus.

tree of knowledge of good and evil, *Bible.* a tree in the midst of the garden of Eden, bearing the forbidden fruit, the eating of which destroyed the primal innocence of Adam and Eve. Gen. 2:9, etc.

tree of life, *Bible.* **1.** a tree in the midst of the garden of Eden which yielded food giving everlasting life. Gen. 2:9; 3:22. **2.** a tree in the heavenly Jerusalem with leaves for the healing of the nations. Rev. 22:2. **3.** arbor vitae.

tree shrew, any mammal of the insectivorous family *Tupaiadae,* being long-snouted, squirrellike animals of southern Asia and adjoining islands.

tree sparrow, 1. a European weaverbird, *Passer montanus,* related to the English sparrow. **2.** a North American finch, *Spizella arborea,* common in winter in the northern U.S.

tree surgery, the repair of damaged trees, as by the removal of diseased parts, filling of cavities, and prevention of further decay, and by strengthening branches with braces.

tree toad, any of various arboreal salientians, mostly of the family *Hylidae,* and usually having adhesive disks on the ends of the toes.

tree·top (trē′tŏp′), *n.* the top part of a tree.

tre·foil (trē′foil), *n.* **1.** any of the herbs constituting the leguminous genus *Trifolium,* usually having digitate leaves of three leaflets, and reddish, purple, yellow, or white flower heads, and including the common clovers. **2.** any of various similar plants, as the black medic. **3.** an ornamental figure or structure resembling a

Trefoils (def. 3)

trifoliolate leaf. [ME *treyfoyle,* t. AF: m. *trifoil,* g. L *trifolium* triple leaf]

tre·ha·la (trĭ hä′lə), *n.* an edible, sugarlike secretion of the larvae of certain beetles of the genus *Larinus,* found in Asia Minor and neighboring countries, forming a cocoon. [t. Turk: m. *tīqālah*]

tre·ha·lose (trē′hə lōs′), *n.* *Chem.* a white crystalline disaccharide, $C_{12}H_{22}O_{11}$, found in yeast, certain fungi, etc., and used to identify certain bacteria.

treil·lage (trā′lĭj), *n.* latticework; a lattice or trellis. [t. F, der. *treille* arbor, trellis, g. L *trichila* arbor]

Treitsch·ke (trīch′kə), *n.* **Heinrich von** (hĭn′rĭKH fən), 1834–1896, German historian.

trek (trĕk), *v.*, **trekked, trekking,** *n.* —*v.i.* **1.** to travel; migrate. **2.** *South Africa.* to travel by ox wagon. —*v.t.* **3.** *South Africa.* (of a draft animal) to draw (a vehicle or load). —*n.* **4.** the act of trekking. **5.** *South Africa.* a migration or expedition, as by ox wagon. **6.** *South Africa.* a stage of a journey by ox wagon or otherwise, between one stopping place and the next. [t. D: m.s. *trekken* draw, travel] —**trek′ker,** *n.*

trel·lis (trĕl′ĭs), *n.* **1.** a frame or structure of latticework; a lattice. **2.** a framework of this kind used for the support of growing vines, etc. —*v.t.* **3.** to furnish with a trellis. **4.** to enclose in a trellis. **5.** to train or support on a trellis: *trellised vines.* **6.** to form into or like trelliswork. [ME *trelis,* t. OF, orig. adj., g. LL *trīlīcius,* r. L *trilix* woven with three threads] —**trel′·lis-like′,** *adj.*

trel·lis·work (trĕl′ĭs wûrk′), *n.* latticework.

Trellis

trem·a·tode (trĕm′ə tōd′, trē′mə-), *n.* any of the *Trematoda,* a class or group of platyhelminths or flatworms, having one or more suckers, and living as ectoparasites or endoparasites on or in various animals (commonly known as flukes). [t. NL: m. *Trēmatōda,* t. Gk.: m. *trēmatōdēs* having holes]

trem·ble (trĕm′bəl), *v.*, **-bled, -bling,** *n.* —*v.i.* **1.** (of persons, the body, etc.) to shake involuntarily with quick, short movements, as from fear, excitement, weakness, cold, etc.; quake; quiver; shiver. **2.** to be agitated with fear, apprehension, or the like. **3.** (of things) to be affected with vibratory motion. **4.** to be tremulous, as light, sound, etc.: *his voice trembled as he spoke.* —*n.* **5.** act of trembling. **6.** a state or fit of trembling. **7.** (*pl.*) any condition or disease characterized by continued trembling or shaking, as ague. **8.** (*pl.*) *Vet. Sci.* a poison condition of cattle contracted by eating white snakeroot (Eupatorium), and marked by muscular tremors. **9.** (*pl.*) milk sickness. [ME, t. F: m. *trembler,* g. LL *tremulāre,* ult. der. L *tremere*] —**trem′bler,** *n.* —**trem′bling·ly,** *adv.* —**Syn. 1.** See **shake.**

trem·bly (trĕm′blĭy), *adj.* trembling; tremulous.

tre·men·dous (trĭ mĕn′dəs), *adj.* **1.** *Colloq.* extraordinarily great in size, amount, degree, etc. **2.** dreadful or awful, as in character or effect. **3.** *Colloq.* extraordinary; unusual. [t. L: m. *tremendus* dreadful] —**tre·men′dous·ly,** *adv.* —**tre·men′dous·ness,** *n.* —**Syn. 1.** See **huge.**

trem·o·lant (trĕm′ə lənt), *adj.* **1.** having a tremulous or vibrating tone, as certain pipes of an organ. —*n.* **2.** an organ pipe producing a tremolant tone. [t. G, t. It.: m. *tremolante* tremulant]

trem·o·lite (trĕm′ə līt′), *n.* a white or grayish variety of amphibole, $Ca_2Mg_5Si_8O_{22}(OH)_2$, occurring usually in bladed crystals. [f. *Tremol(a)* valley in Switzerland + -ITE[1]]

trem·o·lo (trĕm′ə lō′), *n.*, *pl.* **-los.** *Music.* **1.** a tremulous or vibrating effect produced on certain instruments and in the human voice, as to express emotion. **2.** a mechanical device in an organ by which such an effect is produced. [t. It.: trembling, g. L *tremulus*]

trem·or (trĕm′ər, trē′mər), *n.* **1.** involuntary shaking of the body or limbs, as from fear, weakness, etc.; a fit of trembling. **2.** any tremulous or vibratory movement; a vibration. **3.** a trembling or quivering effect, as of light, etc. **4.** a tremulous sound or note. [ME, t. L: trembling, terror] —**trem′or·less,** *adj.*

trem·u·lant (trĕm′yə lənt), *adj.* trembling; tremulous. Also, **trem′u·lent.**

trem·u·lous (trĕm′yə ləs), *adj.* **1.** (of persons, the body, etc.) characterized by trembling, as from fear, nervousness, weakness, etc. **2.** fearful; timorous. **3.** (of things) vibratory or quivering. **4.** (of writing, etc.) done with a trembling hand. [t. L: m. *tremulus*] —**trem′u·lous·ly,** *adv.* —**trem′u·lous·ness,** *n.*

tre·nail (trē′nāl, trĕn′əl, trŭn′əl), *n.* treenail.

trench (trĕnch), *n.* **1.** *Fort.* a long, narrow excavation in the ground, the earth from which is thrown up in front to serve as a shelter from the enemy's fire, etc. **2.** (*pl.*) a system of such excavations, with their embankments, etc. **3.** a deep furrow, ditch, or cut. —*v.t.* **4.** to surround or fortify with a trench or trenches; entrench. **5.** to cut a trench or trenches in. **6.** to set or place in a trench. **7.** to form (a furrow, ditch, etc.) by cutting into or through something. **8.** to divide or sever by cutting. **9.** to cut. —*v.i.* **10.** to dig a trench or trenches. **11.** to cut. **12.** to encroach or infringe (fol. by *on* or *upon*). **13.** to come close or verge (fol. by *on* or *upon*). **14.** *Obs.* to enter or penetrate so as to affect intimately (fol. by *into* or *unto*). [ME *trenche,* t. OF: act of cutting, slice, der. *trenchier,* v., g. L *truncāre* cut off]

trench·ant (trĕn′chənt), *adj.* **1.** incisive or keen, as language or a person: *trenchant wit.* **2.** thoroughgoing, vigorous, or effective: *a trenchant policy.* **3.** clearly or sharply defined, as an outline. **4.** *Chiefly Poetic.* sharp; keen-edged: *a trenchant blade.* [ME, t. OF, ppr. of *trenchier* cut] —**trench′an·cy,** *n.* —**trench′ant·ly,** *adv.*

trench coat, a waterproof belted overcoat such as is used by Army officers.

trench·er (trĕn′chər), *n.* **1.** one who trenches; one who makes trenches. **2.** *Archaic.* **a.** a rectangular or circular flat piece of wood on which meat, or other food, was formerly served or carved. **b.** such a piece of wood with that which it bears. **3.** *Archaic.* a supply of food. [ME, t. AF: m. *trenchour* a cutting place, trencher, der. *trenchier* cut. See TRENCH]

trench·er·man (trĕn′chər mən), *n., pl.* **-men. 1.** an eater or feeder. **2.** one who has a hearty appetite. **3.** a parasite or hanger-on.

trench fever, *Pathol.* a lice-spread recurrent fever, often suffered by soldiers in trenches in World War I, caused by a Rickettsia transmitted by lice.

trench foot, *Pathol.* a disease of the feet due to exposure to cold and wet, common among soldiers serving in trenches.

trench knife, a long-pointed knife used in modern warfare for stabbing and usually equipped with a guard which may serve as a bludgeon.

trench mouth, *Pathol.* Vincent's angina. [so called because of its prevalence among soldiers]

trend (trĕnd), *n.* **1.** the general course, drift, or tendency: *the trend of events.* **2.** the general direction which a road, river, coastline, or the like, tends to take. —*v.i.* **3.** to have a general tendency, as events, etc. **4.** to tend to take a particular direction; extend in some direction indicated. [ME *trende(n),* OE *trendan;* akin to OE *trinde* ball, D *trent* circumference, Sw. *trind* round. Cf. TRINDLE, TRUNDLE] —**Syn. 1.** See **tendency.**

Treng·ga·nu (trĕng gä′nōō), *n.* a state in the former Federation of Malaya: now part of the federation of Malaysia. 278,269 pop. (1957); 5050 sq. mi. *Cap.:* Kuala Trengganu.

Trent (trĕnt), *n.* **1.** Italian, **Trento.** a city in N Italy, on the Adige river. **2. Council of,** the council of the Roman Catholic Church which met at Trent intermittently from 1545 to 1563, condemning the Reformation and defining church doctrines. **3.** a river in central England, flowing from Staffordshire into the Humber. ab. 170 mi.

trente et qua·rante (trän tĕ kȧ ränt′), the gambling game of rouge et noir, so called because thirty and forty are respectively winning and losing numbers. [F: thirty and forty]

Tren·ti·no-Al·to Adige (trĕn tē′nô äl′tô), a region in NE Italy, formerly Venezia Tridentina. 750,000 (est. 1954); 5256 sq. mi.

Tren·to (trĕn′tô), *n.* Italian name of **Trent** (def. 1).

Tren·ton (trĕn′tən), *n.* the capital of New Jersey, in the W part, on the Delaware river: Washington defeated the Hessians here, 1776. 114,167 (1960).

tre·pan¹ (trĭ păn′), *n., v.,* **-panned, -panning.** —*n.* **1.** a boring tool for sinking shafts or the like. **2.** *Surg.* an obsolete form of the trephine resembling a carpenter's bit and brace. —*v.t.* **3.** *Mach.* **a.** to cut circular disks out of plate stock using a rotating cutter. **b.** to cut a concentric groove around a bored or drilled hole. **4.** to operate upon with a trepan; perforate by a trepan. [ME, t. ML: s. *trepanum* crown saw, t. Gk.: m. *trýpanon* borer] —**trep·a·na·tion** (trĕp′ə nā′shən), *n.*

tre·pan² (trĭ păn′), *n., v.,* **-panned, -panning.** *Archaic.* —*n.* **1.** one who ensnares or entraps others. **2.** a stratagem; a trap. —*v.t.* **3.** to ensnare or entrap. **4.** to entice. **5.** to cheat or swindle. Also, **trapan.** [orig. *trapan,* der. TRAP¹ and confused with TREPAN¹] —**tre·pan′ner,** *n.*

tre·pang (trĭ păng′), *n.* any of various wormlike holothurians or sea cucumbers, as *Holothuria edulis,* used as food in China. [t. Malay: m. *trĭpang*]

tre·phine (trĭ fīn′, -fēn′), *n., v.,* **-phined, -phining.** —*n.* **1.** *Surg.* a small circular saw with a center pin mounted on a strong hollow metal shaft to which is attached a transverse handle: used in surgery to remove circular disks of bone from the skull. —*v.t.* **2.** to operate upon with a trephine. [orig. *trafine,* explained by inventor as m. L *très fīnēs* three ends]

Trephine
A. Center pin for guiding crown saw; B. Crown saw; C. Screw for attaching pin to handle

trep·i·da·tion (trĕp′ə dā′shən), *n.* **1.** tremulous alarm or agitation; perturbation. **2.** vibratory movement; a vibration. **3.** *Pathol.* rapid, repeated, muscular flexion and extension of muscles of the extremities or lower jaw; clonus. [t. L: s. *trepidātio* act of hurrying, or of being alarmed]

tres·pass (trĕs′pəs), *n.* **1.** *Law.* **a.** an unlawful act causing injury to the person, property, or rights of another, committed with force or violence, actual or implied. **b.** a wrongful entry upon the lands of another. **c.** the action to recover damages for such an injury. **2.** an encroachment or intrusion. **3.** an offense, sin, or wrong. —*v.i.* **4.** *Law.* to commit a trespass. **5.** to make an improper inroad on a person's presence, time, etc.; encroach or infringe (fol. by *on* or *upon*). **6.** to commit a

transgression or offense; transgress; offend; sin. [ME *tres-pas(en),* t. OF: m. *trespasser,* v., f. *tres* across (g. L *trans*) + *passer* (g. L *passāre* PASS)] —*tres′pass·er,* n. —**Syn. 2.** TRESPASS, ENCROACH, INFRINGE, INTRUDE imply overstepping boundaries and assuming possession of others' property or crowding onto the rights of others. To TRESPASS is to pass unlawfully within the boundaries of another's property: *hunters trespass on a farmer's fields.* To ENCROACH is to creep, as it were, gradually and often stealthily, upon territory, rights, or privileges, so that a footing is imperceptibly established: *the sea slowly encroached upon the land.* To INFRINGE is to break in upon or invade rights, customs, or the like, by violating or disregarding them: *to infringe upon a patent.* To INTRUDE is to thrust oneself into the presence of a person or into places or circumstances where one is not welcome: *to intrude into a private conversation.*

tress (trĕs), *n.* **1.** a plait or braid of the hair of the head. **2.** (*usually pl.*) any long lock or curl of hair, esp. of a woman, not plaited or braided. [ME *tresse,* t. F: plait or braid of hair; orig. uncert.] —**tressed** (trĕst), *adj.*

-tress, a suffix forming some feminine agent-nouns, corresponding to masculine nouns in *-ter, -tor,* as *actor, actress,* etc. See **-ess.**

tres·sure (trĕsh′ər), *n. Her.* a bearing resembling the orle, consisting of a narrow band, generally considered as being of half the width of an orle, on an escutcheon inside the edge, usually enriched with fleurs-de-lis, and often doubled. [ME, t. OF: m. *tresseur* braid of hair, der. *tresser* braid, plait. See TRESS]

tres·tle (trĕs′əl), *n.* **1.** a frame used as a support, consisting typically of a horizontal beam or bar fixed at each end to a pair of spreading legs. **2.** *Civ. Eng.* **a.** a supporting framework composed chiefly of vertical or inclined pieces with or without diagonal braces, etc., used for various purposes, as for carrying tracks across a gap. **b.** a bridge or the like of such structure. [ME, t. OF: m. *trestel* transom, beam, g. dim. of L *transtrum*]

tres·tle·tree (trĕs′əl trē′), *n. Naut.* either of two horizontal fore-and-aft timbers or bars secured to a masthead, one on each side, to support the crosstrees.

tres·tle·work (trĕs′əl wûrk′), *n.* structural work consisting of a trestle or trestles.

tret (trĕt), *n. Com.* an allowance for waste, after deduction for tare.

Tre·vel·yan (trĭ vĕl′yən, -yĭl′-), *n.* **1.** George Macaulay, 1876–1962, British historian. **2.** his father Sir George Otto, 1838–1928, British biographer, historian, and statesman.

Treves (trēvz), *n.* Trier. French, **Trèves** (trĕv).

trews (trōōz), *n. pl.* close-fitting tartan trousers, worn esp. by certain Scottish regiments. [var. of *trouse* TROUSERS]

trey (trā), *n. Cards or Dice.* three; a card, or the side of a die, having three pips. [ME, t. OF: m. *trei(s),* g. L *très* three]

tri-, a word element meaning "three," as in *triacid.* [t. L, comb. form of *très, tria* three; or t. Gk., comb. form of *trets, tria* three and *tris* thrice]

tri·a·ble (trī′ə bəl), *adj.* **1.** that may be tried. **2.** subject or liable to judicial trial. [late ME, t. AF. See TRY, -ABLE] —**tri′a·ble·ness,** *n.*

tri·ac·id (trī ăs′ĭd), *adj. Chem.* **1.** capable of combining with three molecules of a monobasic acid: *a triacid base.* **2.** denoting acid salts containing three replaceable hydrogen atoms.

tri·ad (trī′ăd), *n.* **1.** a group of three, esp. of three closely related or associated persons or things. **2.** *Chem.* an element, atom, or radical having a valence of three. **3.** *Music.* a chord of three tones, esp. one consisting of a given tone with its major or minor third and its perfect, augmented, or diminished fifth. [t. L: s. *trias,* t. Gk.: group of three] —**tri·ad′ic,** *adj.*

tri·a junc·ta in u·no (trī′ə jŭngk′tə ĭn ū′nō), *Latin.* three united in one (motto of the Order of the Bath).

tri·al (trī′əl, trīl), *n.* **1.** *Law.* **a.** the examination before a judicial tribunal of the facts put in issue in a cause (often including issues of law as well as of fact). **b.** the determination of a person's guilt or innocence by due process of law. **2.** act of trying or testing, or putting to the proof. **3.** test; proof. **4.** an attempt or effort to do something. **5.** tentative or experimental action in order to ascertain results; an experiment. **6.** state or position of a person or thing being tried or tested; probation. **7.** subjection to suffering or grievous experiences; affliction: *comfort in the hour of trial.* **8.** an affliction or trouble. **9.** a trying, distressing, or annoying thing or person. **10.** *Ceramics.* a piece of ceramic material used to try the heat of the kiln and the progress of the firing of its contents. —*adj.* **11.** pertaining to trial or a trial. **12.** done or used by way of trial, test, proof, or experiment. [t. AF, der. *trier* TRY] —**Syn. 2.** TRIAL, EXPERIMENT, TEST imply an attempt to find out something or to find out about something. TRIAL is the general word for a trying of anything: *articles sent for ten days' free trial.* EXPERIMENT looks to the future, and is a trial conducted to prove or illustrate the truth or validity of something, or an attempt to discover something new: *an experiment in chemistry.* TEST is a stronger and more specific word, referring to a trial under approved and fixed conditions, or a final and decisive trial as a conclusion of past experiments: *a test of a new type of airplane.* **8.** See **affliction.**

trial balance, *Bookkeeping.* a statement of all the open debit and credit items, made preliminary to balancing a double-entry ledger.

trial balloon, 1. a statement made to the public to check its reaction on something planned for later release. **2.** a pilot balloon.

trial jury, petty jury.

tri·an·gle (trī′ăng′gəl), *n.* **1.** a geometrical plane figure formed by three (usually) straight lines which meet two by two in three points, thus forming three angles. **2.** a flat triangular piece of wood, vulcanite, or the like, with straight edges, used in connection with a T square for drawing perpendicular lines, etc. **3.** any three-cornered or three-sided figure, object, or piece: *a triangle of land.* **4.** *Music.* an instrument of percussion, made of a steel rod bent into the form of a triangle open at one of the corners, and sounded by being struck with a small, straight steel rod. **5.** a group of three, as three characters (two men and one woman, or two women and one man) in a novel or the like, involved in a love entanglement. [ME, t. L: m. *triangulum*, lit. three-cornered object. See ANGLE[1]]

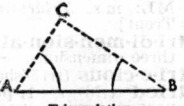

Triangles
A. Right angle; B. Isosceles;
C. Equilateral; D. Obtuse;
E. Acute; F. Scalene

tri·an·gu·lar (trīăng′gyələr), *adj.* **1.** pertaining to or having the form of a triangle; three-cornered. **2.** having a triangle as base or cross section: *a triangular prism.* **3.** comprising three parts or elements; triple. **4.** pertaining to or involving a group of three, as three persons, parties, or things. —**tri·an′gu·lar′i·ty,** *n.* —**tri·an′gu·lar·ly,** *adv.*

tri·an·gu·late (*adj.* trīăng′gyəlĭt, -lāt′; *v.* trīăng′gyəlāt′), *adj., v.,* **-lated, -lating.** —*adj.* **1.** triangular. **2.** composed of or marked with triangles. —*v.t.* **3.** to make triangular. **4.** to divide into triangles. **5.** *Survey.* **a.** to survey (a region, etc.) by establishing dividing points into triangles and measuring the angles of these triangles. **b.** to determine trigonometrically.

tri·an·gu·la·tion (trī′ăng gyəlā′shən), *n. Survey.* **1.** the operation and immediate result of measuring, ordinarily with a theodolite, the angles of a network of triangles laid out on the earth's surface by marking their vertices. **2.** the triangles thus marked.

Triangulation
A, B, Points known; C, Point visible from both A and B, the position of which is plotted by measuring angles A and B

tri·ar·chy (trī′är kĭ), *n., pl.* **-chies. 1.** government by three persons. **2.** a set of three joint rulers; a triumvirate. [t. Gk.: m.s. *triarchía* triumvirate] **3.** a country divided into three governments. **4.** a group of three countries or districts each under its own ruler. [f. TRI- + -ARCHY]

Tri·as·sic (trīăs′ĭk), *Stratig.* —*adj.* **1.** pertaining to the geological period or system that constitutes the earliest principal division of the Mesozoic era. —*n.* **2.** the period or system characterized by widespread land deposits following Permian and preceding Jurassic. [f. LL *trias* the number three (t. Gk.) + -IC; so called because deposits (cf. def. 2) were divided into groups]

tri·at·ic stay (trīăt′ĭk), *Naut.* a device consisting usually of two hanging ropes each lashed to one of two adjacent masts, used for attaching tackles for hoisting boats or other heavy weights in or out. **2.** the stay from the foretopmast head of a schooner back to the main crosstrees. [orig. obscure]

tri·a·tom·ic (trī′ətŏm′ĭk), *adj. Chem.* **1.** having three atoms in the molecule. **2.** containing three replaceable atoms or groups. **3.** having a valence of three.

tri·ax·i·al (trīăk′sĭəl), *adj.* having three axes.

tri·a·zine (trī′əzēn′, -zĭn, trīăz′ēn, -ĭn), *n. Chem.* **1.** any of a group of three compounds, C₃H₃N₃, containing three nitrogen and three carbon atoms arranged in a six-membered ring. **2.** any of a number of their derivatives. Also, **tri·a·zin** (trī′əzĭn, trīăz′ĭn). [f. TRI- + AZ(OTE) + -INE²]

tri·a·zo·ic (trī′əzō′ĭk), *adj.* hydrazoic.

tri·a·zole (trī′əzōl′, trīăz′ōl), *n. Chem.* any of a group of four compounds, C₂H₃N₃, containing three nitrogen and two carbon atoms arranged in a five-membered ring.

trib·ade (trĭb′əd), *n.* a woman who practices tribadism, esp. a female homosexual who assumes the male role. [t. L: m.s. *tribas* rubbing, t. Gk.]

trib·a·dism (trĭb′ə dĭz′əm), *n.* Lesbianism.

trib·al (trī′bəl), *adj.* pertaining to or characteristic of, a tribe or tribes: *tribal customs.* —**trib′al·ly,** *adv.*

tri·bas·ic (trībā′sĭk), *adj. Chem.* **1.** (of an acid) having three atoms of hydrogen replaceable by basic atoms or radicals. **2.** containing three basic atoms or radicals, each having a valence of one, as *tribasic sodium phosphate,* Na₃PO₄.

tribe (trīb), *n.* **1.** any aggregate of people united by ties of descent from a common ancestor, community of customs and traditions, adherence to the same leaders, etc. **2.** a local division of a primitive or barbarous people. **3.** a division of some other people. **4.** a class, kind, or sort of animals, plants, articles, or other things. **5.** *Bot., Zool.* **a.** a classificatory group of animals or plants, ranking variously, as between an order and a family, or between a family and a genus. **b.** any group of plants or animals. **6.** a company, troop, or number of persons or animals. **7.** (in humorous or contemptuous use) **a.** a class or set or persons. **b.** a family. **8.** any of the twelve divisions of ancient Israel, claiming descent from the twelve sons of Jacob. **9.** *Roman Hist.* **a.** any one of three divisions of the people representing the Latin, Sabine, and Etruscan settlements. **b.** (later) one of 30, afterward 35, political divisions of the Roman people. **10.** *Anc. Greece.* a phyle. [t. L: m. *tribus;* r. ME *tribu,* t. OF] —**tribe′less,** *adj.*

tribes·man (trībz′mən), *n., pl.* **-men.** a man belonging to a tribe; a member of a tribe.

tri·brach (trī′brăk, trĭb′răk), *n. Pros.* a foot of three short syllables. [t. L: s. *tribrachys,* t. Gk.]

tri·bro·mo·eth·a·nol (trī brō′mōĕth′ənŏl′, -nŏl′), *n. Chem.* a colorless crystalline compound, CBr₃CH₂OH₁, used as an anesthetic; avertin.

trib·u·la·tion (trĭb′yəlā′shən), *n.* **1.** grievous trouble; severe trial or experience. **2.** an instance of this, or an affliction, trouble, or trial. [ME, t. L: s. *tribulātio,* der. L *tribulāre* afflict, der. *tribulum* threshing sledge]

tri·bu·nal (trībū′nəl, trĭ-), *n.* **1.** a court of justice. **2.** a place or seat of judgment. **3.** a raised platform for the seats of magistrates, orig. in a Roman basilica or hall of justice. [t. L: judgment seat, der. *tribūnus* tribune]

trib·u·nate (trĭb′yənĭt, -nāt′), *n. Hist.* **1.** the office of tribune. **2.** a body of tribunes. [t. L: m.s. *tribūnātus*]

trib·une¹ (trĭb′ūn *or,* esp. *Brit.,* trĭ′būn), *n.* **1.** a person who upholds or defends popular rights. **2.** *Rom. Hist.* **a.** any of various administrative officers, esp. one of ten officers elected to protect the interests and rights of the plebeians from the patricians. **b.** a military officer, six of whom were assigned to a Roman legion. [ME, t. L: m. *tribūnus*] —**trib′une·ship,** *n.*

trib·une² (trĭb′ūn), *n.* **1.** a raised platform, or dais; a rostrum or pulpit. **2.** a raised part, or gallery, with seats, as in a church. **3.** (in a Christian basilica) the bishop's throne in a corresponding recess, or apse. **4.** the apse itself. **5.** tribunal (def. 3). [t. It.: m. *tribuna* tribunal]

trib·u·tar·y (trĭb′yə tĕr′ĭ), *n., pl.* **-taries,** *adj.* —*n.* **1.** a stream contributing its flow to a larger stream or other body of water. **2.** one who pays tribute. —*adj.* **3.** (of a stream) flowing into a larger stream or other body of water. **4.** furnishing subsidiary aid; contributory; auxiliary. **5.** paying or required to pay tribute. **6.** paid as tribute. —**trib′u·tar′i·ly,** *adv.*

trib·ute (trĭb′ūt), *n.* **1.** a personal offering, testimonial, compliment, or the like given as if due, or in acknowledgment of gratitude, esteem, or regard. **2.** a stated sum or other valuable consideration paid by one sovereign or state to another in acknowledgment of submission or as the price of peace, security, protection, or the like. **3.** a rent, tax, or the like, as that paid by a subject to a sovereign. **4.** anything paid as under exaction or by enforced contribution. **5.** the state of being liable to any such payment; the obligation of making such payment. [ME *tribut,* t. L: s. *tribūtum*]

tri·car·pel·lar·y (trīkär′pə lĕr′ĭ), *adj. Bot.* having three carpels.

trice¹ (trīs), *n.* a very short time; a moment; an instant: *to come back in a trice.* [ME *tryse,* special use of TRICE² (*at a trice* at one tug)]

trice² (trīs), *v.t.,* **triced, tricing.** *Naut.* **1.** to pull or haul with a rope. **2.** to haul up and fasten with a rope (usually fol. by *up*). [ME, t. MD: m.s. *trīsen* hoist, appar. der. *trīse* pulley]

tri·cen·ten·ni·al (trī′sĕntĕn′ĭəl), *adj., n.* tercentenary.

tri·ceps (trī′sĕps), *n. Anat.* a muscle having three heads, or points of origin, esp. the extensor muscle at the back of the upper arm. [t. L: three-headed]

trich-, var. of tricho-, before vowels, as in *trichite.*

tri·chi·a·sis (trĭkī′əsĭs), *n. Pathol.* a state in which the eyelashes grow inwardly. [t. Gk., der. *trichiān* be hairy]

tri·chi·na (trĭkī′nə), *n., pl.* **-nae** (-nē). the nematode worm, *Trichinella spiralis,* the adults of which live in the intestine and produce embryos which encyst in the muscle tissue, esp. in pigs, rats, and man. [t. NL, t. Gk, n. use of fem. of *trichinos* of hair]

trich·i·nize (trĭk′ənīz′), *v.t.,* **-nized, -nizing.** to infect with trichinae. —**trich′i·ni·za′tion,** *n.*

Trich·i·nop·o·ly (trĭch′ə nŏp′ə lĭ), *n.* former name of Tiruchirapalli.

trich·i·no·sis (trĭk′ənō′sĭs), *n. Pathol.* a disease due to the presence of the trichina in the intestines and muscular tissues. [t. NL. See TRICHINA, -OSIS]

trich·i·nous (trĭk′ənəs), *adj.* **1.** pertaining to or of the nature of trichinosis. **2.** infected with trichinae.

trich·ite (trĭk′īt), *n. Petrog.* any of various minute hairlike mineral bodies occurring in certain vitreous igneous rocks, esp. obsidian. [TRICH- + -ITE¹]

tri·chlo·ride (trīklōr′ĭd, -ĭd), *n. Chem.* a chloride having three atoms of chlorine, as FeCl₃. Also, **tri·chlo·rid** (trīklōr′ĭd).

tricho-, a word element referring to hair, as in *trichocyst.* [t. Gk., comb. form of *thrix*]

trich·o·cyst (trĭk′ə sĭst′), *n. Zool.* an organ of offense and defense embedded in the outer protoplasm of many infusorians, consisting of a small elongated sac containing a fine, hairlike filament capable of being ejected. —**trich′o·cys′tic,** *adj.*

---

trich·o·gyne (trĭk′ə jīn′, -jĭn), n. Bot. a hairlike prolongation of a carpogonium, serving as a receptive organ for the spermatium. [f. TRICHO- + Gk. gynē woman]

trich·oid (trĭk′oid), adj. hairlike.

tri·chol·o·gy (trĭ kŏl′ə jĭ), n. the science of the hair and its diseases. —**tri·chol′o·gist,** n.

tri·chome (trī′kōm, trĭk′ōm), n. Bot. an outgrowth from the epidermis of plants, as a hair. [t. Gk.: m. trĭchōma growth of hair] —**tri·chom·ic** (trī kŏm′ĭk), adj.

trich·o·mon·ad (trĭk′ō mŏn′ăd), n. any flagellated protozoan of the genus Trichomonas, parasitic in man or animals.

tri·cho·sis (trĭ kō′sĭs), n. Pathol. any disease of the hair.

tri·chot·o·my (trĭ kŏt′ə mĭ), n. 1. division into three parts. 2. arrangement in three divisions. 3. the three-part division of man into body, spirit, and soul. [f. tricho- (repr. Gk. trícha triply) + -TOMY] —**trich·o·tom·ic** (trĭk′ə tŏm′ĭk), **tri·chot′o·mous,** adj.

tri·chro·ic (trī krō′ĭk), adj. 1. having or exhibiting three colors. 2. pleochroic.

tri·chro·mat·ic (trī′krō măt′ĭk), adj. 1. pertaining to the use or combination of three different colors, as in printing or in photography in natural colors. 2. pertaining to, characterized by, or involving three colors. Also, **tri·chro·mic** (trī krō′mĭk).

tri·chro·ma·tism (trī krō′mə tĭz′əm), n. 1. trichromatic condition. 2. the use or combination of three different colors.

trick (trĭk), n. 1. a crafty or fraudulent device, expedient, or proceeding; an artifice, stratagem, ruse, or wile. 2. a deceptive or illusory appearance; mere semblance. 3. a roguish or mischievous performance; prank: to play a trick on someone. 4. a foolish, disgraceful, or mean performance or action. 5. a clever device or expedient, ingenious shift, or dodge: a rhetorical trick. 6. the art or knack of doing something. 7. a clever or dexterous feat, as for exhibition or entertainment: tricks in horsemanship. 8. a feat of jugglery or legerdemain. 9. a peculiar habit, practice, or way of acting. 10. Cards. the cards collectively which are played and won in one round. 11. U.S. Colloq. a child or young girl. 12. a spell or turn of duty. —adj. 13. pertaining to or having the nature of tricks. 14. made for tricks. —v.t. 15. to deceive by trickery. 16. to cheat or swindle (fol. by out of). 17. to beguile by trickery (fol. by into). 18. to dress, array, or deck (often fol. by out or up). —v.i. 19. to practice trickery or deception; cheat. 20. to play tricks, trifle, or play (fol. by with). [ME trik, t. OF: m. trique deceit, der. trichier deceive; orig. uncert.] —**trick′er,** n. —**trick′less,** adj.

—**Syn. 1.** TRICK, DECEPTION, FRAUD, TRICKERY imply cheating or creating a false impression. A TRICK is usually an underhanded act designed to cheat someone. The word emphasizes the ingenuity, cleverness, or dexterity of the agent, and sometimes refers merely to a pleasurable deceiving of the senses: to win by a trick. DECEPTION is an intentional or unintentional act by means of which a false impression is created: to practice the art of deception. A FRAUD is an act or series of acts of subtle deceit or duplicity by which one tries to benefit himself at another's expense: an advertiser convicted of fraud. TRICKERY, the use of tricks and habitual deception, has esp. opprobrious connotations: notorious for trickery in his business deals. **15.** See cheat.

trick·er·y (trĭk′ər ĭ), n., pl. **-er·ies.** 1. the use or practice of tricks; artifice. 2. a trick. —**Syn. 1.** See trick.

trick·ish (trĭk′ĭsh), adj. tricky. —**trick′ish·ly,** adv. —**trick′ish·ness,** n.

trick·le (trĭk′əl), v., **-led, -ling,** n. —v.t. 1. to flow or fall by drops, or in a small, broken, or gentle stream: tears trickled down her cheeks. 2. to come, go, pass, or proceed bit by bit, slowly, irregularly, etc.: subscriptions are trickling in. —v.i. 3. to cause to trickle. —n. 4. a trickling flow or stream. 5. a small, slow, or irregular quantity of anything coming, going, or proceeding: a trickle of visitors. [sandhi var. of obs. strickle, freq. of STRIKE]

trick·ster (trĭk′stər), n. 1. a deceiver; a cheat. 2. one who practices tricks.

trick·sy (trĭk′sĭ), adj. 1. tricky, crafty, or wily. 2. mischievous, frolicsome, or playful. 3. deceptive; uncertain. 4. trim, spruce, or fine. —**trick′si·ly,** adv. —**trick′si·ness,** n.

trick·track (trĭk′trăk′), n. a variety of backgammon. Also, **trictrac.**

trick·y (trĭk′ĭ), adj., **trickier, trickiest.** 1. given to or characterized by deceitful tricks; crafty; wily. 2. skilled in clever tricks or dodges. 3. deceptive, uncertain, or ticklish to deal with or handle. —**trick′i·ly,** adv. —**trick′i·ness,** n.

tri·clin·ic (trī klĭn′ĭk), adj. Crystall. noting or pertaining to a system of crystallization in which the three axes are unequal and intersect at oblique angles. [f. TRI- + m.s. Gk. klīnein lean, slope + -IC]

tri·clin·i·um (trī klĭn′ĭ əm), n., pl. **-clinia** (-klĭn′ĭ ə). Rom. Hist. 1. a couch extending along three sides of a table, for reclining on at meals. 2. a room containing such a couch, i.e., a dining room. [t. L, t. Gk.: m. triklīnion three-couch dining room]

tri·col·or (trī′kŭl′ər), adj. 1. Also, **tri′col′ored.** having three colors. —n. 2. a tricolor flag or the like. 3. the national flag of France, adopted during the

Revolution, consisting of three equal vertical stripes of blue, white, and red. [t. F: m. tricolore, t. LL: m. tricolor, adj., f. tri- TRI- + -color colored]

tri·corn (trī′kôrn), adj. 1. having three horns or hornlike projections, as a hat with the brim turned up on three sides. —n. 2. a tricorn hat.

tri·cos·tate (trī kŏs′tāt), adj. Bot., Zool. having three ribs, costae, or raised lines.

tri·cot (trē′kō; Fr. trēkō′), n. 1. a warp-knit fabric, usually of rayon, with the right and wrong sides different. 2. a kind of woolen cloth. [t. F, der. tricoter knit, ult. of Gmc. orig.]

tric·trac (trĭk′trăk′), n. tricktrack.

tri·cus·pid (trī kŭs′pĭd), adj. Also, **tri·cus′pi·dal.** 1. having three cusps or points, as a tooth. Cf. **bicuspid.** 2. Anat. noting or pertaining to a valve of three segments, guarding the opening from the right auricle into the right ventricle of the heart. —n. 3. Anat. a tricuspid valve. [t. L: s. tricuspis having three points]

tri·cus·pi·date (trī kŭs′pə dāt′), adj. Anat. having three cusps or flaps.

tri·cy·cle (trī′sĭk əl), n. 1. a velocipede with three wheels (usually one in front and one on each side behind) propelled by pedals or hand levers. 2. a three-wheeled motorcycle. [t. F, f. tri- TRI- + cycle (see CYCLE)]

tri·cy·clic (trī sī′klĭk, -sĭk′lĭk), adj. pertaining to or embodying three cycles.

tri·dent (trī′dənt), n. 1. a three-pronged instrument or weapon. 2. Rom. Hist. a three-pronged spear used by the retiarius in gladiatorial combats. 3. Class. Myth. the three-pronged spear forming a characteristic attribute of the sea god Poseidon, or Neptune. 4. a fish spear having three prongs. —adj. 5. having three prongs or tines. [t. L: s. tridens having three teeth]

Tri·den·tine (trī dĕn′tĭn, -tīn, trī-), adj. pertaining to the Council of Trent, or conforming to its decrees and doctrines. [t. ML: m.s. Tridentīnus, der. Tridentum Trent]

Neptune with trident

tri·di·men·sion·al (trī′dĭ mĕn′shən əl), adj. having three dimensions. —**tri·di·men′sion·al·i·ty,** n.

tri·e·cious (trī ē′shəs), adj. Bot. trioecious.

tried (trīd), v. 1. pt. and pp. of try. —adj. 2. tested; proved; having sustained the tests of experience.

tri·en·ni·al (trī ĕn′ĭ əl), adj. 1. lasting three years. 2. occurring every three years. —n. 3. a period of three years. 4. a third anniversary. [f. s. L triennium period of three years + -AL¹] —**tri·en′ni·al·ly,** adv.

tri·en·ni·um (trī ĕn′ĭ əm), n., pl. **-enniums, -ennia** (-ĕn′ĭ ə). a period of three years.

Trier (trēr), n. a city in W West Germany, on the Moselle river: extensive Roman ruins; cathedral. 83,700 (est. 1953). Also, **Treves.** French, **Trèves.**

tri·er·arch (trī′ər ärk′), n. Gk. Hist. 1. the commander of a trireme. 2. (in Athens) a citizen who, singly, or jointly with other citizens, was required to fit out a trireme for the public service. [t. Gk.: s. triērarchos]

tri·er·ar·chy (trī′ər är′kĭ), n., pl. **-chies.** Gk. Hist. 1. the office of a trierarch. 2. trierarchs collectively. 3. (in Athens) the duty of fitting out or furnishing triremes for the public service. [t. Gk: m.s. triērarchía]

Tri·este (trī ĕst′; It. trē ĕs′tĕ), n. 1. a seaport on the Gulf of Trieste, at the N end of the Adriatic, in NE Italy. 250,167 (1951). 2. an area divided in 1954, the N part (86 sq. mi.; 302,200), incl. the city of Trieste, taken over by Italy; the S zone (199 sq. mi.; 73,500) by Yugoslavia.

tri·fa·cial (trī fā′shəl), adj. trigeminal.

tri·fid (trī′fĭd), adj. cleft into three parts or lobes. [t. L: s. trifidus split in three. See -FID]

tri·fle (trī′fəl), n., v., **-fled, -fling.** —n. 1. an article or thing of small value. 2. a matter of slight importance; a trivial or insignificant affair or circumstance. 3. a small, inconsiderable, or trifling sum of money. 4. a small quantity or amount of anything; a little: he's still a trifle angry. 5. a kind of pewter of medium hardness. 6. (pl.) articles made of this. 7. Brit. a dish consisting of whipped cream or some substitute, and usually containing cake soaked in wine or liqueur, and jam, fruit, or the like. [ME trufle idle talk, t. OF] —v.i. 8. to deal lightly or without due seriousness or respect (fol. by with): he was in no mood to be trifled with. 9. to amuse oneself or dally (fol. by with). 10. to play or toy by handling or fingering (fol. by with): he sat trifling with a pen. 11. to act or talk in an idle or frivolous way. 12. to pass time idly or frivolously; waste time; idle. —v.t. 13. to pass (time, etc.) idly or frivolously (usually fol. by away). 14. to utter lightly or idly. [ME treoflen, t. OF: m. truifler make sport of, deceive; orig. uncert.] —**tri′fler,** n.

tri·fling (trī′flĭng), adj. 1. of slight importance; trivial; insignificant: a trifling matter. 2. of small value, cost, or amount: a trifling sum. 3. that trifles; frivolous, shallow, or light. **4.** *U.S. Dial.* mean; worthless. —tri′fling·ly, *adv.* —**Syn. 1.** See **petty.**

tri·fo·li·ate (trīfō′lĭ ĭt, -āt′), *adj.* **1.** having three leaves, leaflike parts or lobes, or three foils. **2.** *Bot.* trifoliolate. Also, **tri·fo′li·at′ed.** [f. TRI- + m.s. L *foliātus* leaved]

tri·fo·li·o·late (trīfō′lĭ ə lāt′), *adj.* *Bot.* **1.** having three leaflets, as a compound leaf. **2.** having leaves with three leaflets, as a plant.

tri·fo·li·um (trīfō′lĭ əm), *n.* the plant trefoil. [t. L: triple leaf]

tri·fo·ri·um (trīfōr′ĭ əm), *n.*, *pl.* **-fo·ria** (-fōr′ĭə). *Archit.* (in a church) the wall at the side of the nave, choir or transept, corresponding to the space between the vaulting or ceiling and the roof of an aisle, often having a blind arcade or an opening in a gallery. [t. AL; of unknown orig.]

Triforium

tri·form (trī′fôrm′), *adj.* **1.** formed of three parts, or in three divisions. **2.** existing or appearing in three different forms. **3.** combining three different forms. Also, **tri′·formed′.** [t. L: s. *triformis*]

tri·fur·cate (*v.* trī′fûr′kāt; *adj.* trī′fûr′kĭt, -kāt), *v.*, **-cated, -cating,** *adj.* —*v.t.*, *v.i.* **1.** to divide into three forks or branches. —*adj.* Also, **tri·fur′cat·ed. 2.** divided into three forks or branches. [f. s. L *trifurcus* three forked + -ATE¹] —**tri·fur·ca′tion,** *n.*

trig¹ (trĭg), *adj.*, *v.*, **trigged, trigging.** —*adj.* **1.** neat, trim, smart, or spruce. **2.** in good physical condition; sound; well. —*v.t.* **3.** to make trig, trim, or smart (often with *up* or *out*). [ME, t. Scand; cf. Icel. *tryggr* safe, c. Goth. *triggus* true, faithful. Cf. TRUE]

trig² (trĭg), *v.*, **trigged, trigging,** *n.* —*v.t.* **1.** to support or prop, as with a wedge. —*v.i.* **2.** to act as a check on the moving of wheels, vehicles, etc. —*n.* **3.** a wedge or block used to prevent a wheel, cask, or the like from rolling. [? t. Scand.; cf. Icel. *tryggja* make fast]

trig., 1. trigonometric. **2.** trigonometry.

tri·gem·i·nal (trījĕm′ə nəl), *Anat.* —*adj.* **1.** noting or pertaining to either of a pair of double-rooted cranial nerves, each dividing into three main branches to supply the face, etc. —*n.* **2.** a trigeminal nerve. [f. s. L *trigeminus* threefold + -AL¹]

trig·ger (trĭg′ər), *n.* **1.** (in firearms) a small projecting tongue which when pressed by the finger liberates the mechanism and discharges the weapon. **2.** a device, as a lever, the pulling or pressing of which releases a detent or spring. —*v.t.* **3.** to start or precipitate something, as a chain of events or a scientific reaction. [earlier *tricker*, t. D: m. *trekker*, der. *trekken* pull] —**trig′ger-less,** *adj.*

trig·ger·fish (trĭg′ər fĭsh′), *n.*, *pl.* **-fishes,** (*esp.* collectively) **-fish.** any of various compressed, deep-bodied fishes of the genus *Balistes*, and allied genera, chiefly of tropical seas, having an anterior dorsal fin with three stout spines.

tri·glyph (trī′glĭf′), *n.* *Archit.* a structural member of a Doric frieze, separating two consecutive metopes, and consisting typically of a rectangular block with two vertical grooves or glyphs, and two chamfers or half grooves at the sides, together counting as a third glyph, and leaving three flat vertical bands on the face of the block. See illus. under **metope.** [t. L: s. *triglyphus*, t. Gk: m. *tríglyphos* thrice-grooved] —**tri·glyph′ic,** *adj.*

tri·go (trē′gō), *n.* wheat; field of wheat. [t. Sp., g. L *trīticum* wheat]

tri·gon (trī′gŏn), *n.* **1.** *Astrol.* the position or aspect of two planets distant 120° from each other. **2.** an ancient Greek harp or lyre triangular in shape. **3.** *Obs.* a triangle. [t. L: s. *trigōnum* triangle, t. Gk: m. *trígōnon*, prop. neut. adj., three-cornered]

trigon., 1. trigonometric. **2.** trigonometry.

trig·o·nal (trĭg′ə nəl), *adj.* **1.** triangular. **2.** *Crystall.* having threefold symmetry.

trig·o·nom·e·ter (trĭg′ə nŏm′ə tər), *n.* an instrument for solving plane right-angled triangles by inspection. [back formation from TRIGONOMETRY]

trig·o·nom·e·try (trĭg′ə nŏm′ə trĭ), *n.* the branch of mathematics that deals with the relations between the sides and angles of triangles (plane or spherical), and the calculations, etc., based on these. [t. NL: m.s. *trigonometria*, f. Gk: *trigōno(n)* triangle + -*metria* -METRY] —**trig·o·no·met·ric** (trĭg′ə nə mĕt′rĭk) **trig·o·no·met′·ri·cal,** *adj.* —**trig·o·no·met′ri·cal·ly,** *adv.*

trig·o·nous (trĭg′ə nəs), *adj.* having three angles or corners; triangular, as stems, seeds, etc. [t. L: m. *trigōnus* triangular, t. Gk: m. *trígonos*]

tri·graph (trī′grăf, -gräf), *n.* a group of three letters representing a single speech sound, as *eau* in *beau.* —**tri·graph′ic,** *adj.*

tri·he·dral (trīhē′drəl), *adj.* *Geom.* having, or formed by, three planes meeting in a point: *a trihedral angle.*

tri·he·dron (trīhē′drən), *n.*, *pl.* **-drons, -dra** (-drə). *Geom.* the figure determined by three planes meeting in a point.

tri·ju·gate (trī′jŏŏ gāt′, trī jŏŏ′gĭt, -gāt), *adj.* *Bot.* having three pairs of leaflets alone. Also, **tri·ju·gous** (trī′jŏŏ gəs, trī jŏŏ′-). [f. TRI- + m.s. L *jugātus* joined]

tri·lat·er·al (trīlăt′ər əl), *adj.* having three sides. [f. s. L *trilaterus* three sided + -AL¹] —**tri·lat′er·al·ly,** *adv.*

tri·lin·e·ar (trīlĭn′ĭ ər), *adj.* pertaining to or involving three lines.

tri·lin·gual (trīlĭng′gwəl), *adj.* using or involving three languages.

tri·lit·er·al (trīlĭt′ər əl), *adj.* **1.** consisting of three letters, as a word. —*n.* **2.** a triliteral word or root.

tri·lit·er·al·ism (trīlĭt′ər əlĭz′əm), *n.* *Gram.* the characteristic presence of triliteral roots in a language, as in the Semitic languages.

trill (trĭl), *v.t.* **1.** to sing with a vibratory effect of voice, esp. in the manner of a shake or trill. **2.** to play with like effect on an instrument. **3.** *Phonet.* to pronounce with vibrating articulation: *Spanish "rr" is trilled with the tip of the tongue.* **4.** (of birds, etc.) to sing or give forth in a succession of rapidly alternating or changing sounds. —*v.i.* **5.** to resound vibrantly, or with a rapid succession of sounds, as the voice, song, laughter, etc. **6.** to utter, give forth, or make a sound or a succession of sounds more or less resembling such singing, as a bird, a frog, a grasshopper, a person laughing, etc. **7.** to execute a shake or trill with the voice or on a musical instrument. —*n.* **8.** the act or sound of trilling. **9.** *Music.* a trilled sound, or a rapid alternation of two consecutive tones, in singing or in instrumental music; a shake. **10.** a similar sound, or succession of sounds, uttered or made

Written   *Played*

Trill (def. 9)

by a bird, an insect, a person laughing, etc. **11.** *Phonet.* **a.** a trilled articulation. **b.** a trilled consonant, as Spanish *rr.* [t. It.: m. *trillo*, n., quaver or warble in singing; of Gmc. orig.]

tril·lion (trĭl′yən), *n.* **1.** a cardinal number represented by one followed (in the U.S. and France) by 12 zeros and (in Gt. Britain and Germany) by 18 zeros. —*adj.* **2.** amounting to one trillion in number. [t. F, f. tri- TRI- + (*m*)*illion* MILLION] —**tril′lionth,** *n.*, *adj.*

tril·li·um (trĭl′ĭ əm), *n.* any of the herbs constituting the liliaceous genus *Trillium*, characterized by a whorl of three leaves from the center of which rises a solitary flower. [NL, appar. f. Sw. *trilling* triplet + L -*ium* -IUM]

tri·lo·bate (trīlō′bāt, trī′lə bāt′), *adj.* having three lobes.

tri·lo·bite (trī′lə bīt′), *n.* any of the *Trilobita*, a group of extinct arthropods, variously classed with the crustaceans or the arachnidans or as intermediate between these, with a flattened oval body varying in length from an inch or less to two feet, their remains being found widely distributed in strata of the Paleozoic era, and important as being among the earliest known fossils. [t. NL: m. *Trilobītēs*, f. tri- TRI- + s. Gk. *lobós* lobe (of ear, etc.) + -*ītēs* -ITE¹] —**tri·lo·bit·ic** (trī′lə bĭt′ĭk), *adj.*

Trilobate leaf

tri·loc·u·lar (trīlŏk′yə lər), *adj.* having three loculi, chambers, or cells. [f. TRI- + s. L *loculus* small receptacle (dim. of *locus* place) + -AR¹]

tril·o·gy (trĭl′ə jĭ), *n.*, *pl.* **-gies. 1.** a series or group of three related dramas, operas, novels, etc. **2.** a series of three complete and usually related tragedies performed in ancient Athens at the festival of Dionysus. **3.** a group of three related things. [t. Gk.: m.s. *trilogia.* See TRI-, -LOGY]

trim (trĭm), *v.*, **trimmed, trimming,** *n.*, *adj.*, **trimmer, trimmest,** *adv.* —*v.t.* **1.** to reduce to a neat or orderly state by clipping, paring, pruning, etc.: *to trim a hedge.* **2.** to remove by clipping, paring, pruning, or the like: (often fol. by *off*) *to trim off loose threads from a ragged edge.* **3.** to modify (opinions, etc.) according to expediency. **4.** *Carp.* to bring (a piece of timber, etc.) to the required smoothness or shape. **5.** *Aeron.* to level off an airship or airplane in flight. **6.** *Naut.* **a.** to distribute the load of (a vessel) so that she sits well on the water. **b.** to stow or arrange, as cargo. **c.** to adjust (the sails or yards) with reference to the direction of the wind and the course of the ship. **7.** to dress or array (often fol. by *up*). **8.** to deck with ornaments, etc.: *to trim a Christmas tree.* **9.** *Colloq.* to rebuke or reprove. **10.** *Colloq.* to beat or thrash. **11.** *Colloq.* to defeat. **12.** *Obs.* to equip. —*v.i.* **13.** *Naut.* **a.** to assume a particular position or trim in the water, as a vessel. **b.** to adjust the sails or yards with reference to the direction of the wind and the course of the ship. **14.** to pursue a neutral, cautious, or time-serving course or policy between parties. —*n.* **15.** proper condition or order: *to find everything out of trim.* **16.** condition or order of any kind. **17.** *Naut.* **a.** the set of a ship in the water, esp. the most advantageous one. **b.** the balance of a ship. **c.** the difference between the draft at the bow of a vessel and that at the stern. **d.** the condition of a ship with reference to her fitness for sailing. **e.** the adjustment of the sails, etc., with reference to the direction of the wind and the course of the ship. **f.** the condition of a submarine as regards buoyancy. **18.** dress, array, or equipment. **19.** decorative trimming. **20.** decoration of a store window. **21.** a trimming by cutting, clipping, or the like. **22.** that which is eliminated and omitted as from a motion picture in editing. **23.** *Aeron.* the attitude of an airplane with respect to the wind axes at which balance occurs in forward flight with free controls. **24.** *Carp.* the visible woodwork of the interior of a building. **25.** *Auto.* **a.** the

upholstery, knobs, handles, and other equipment inside a motor car. **b.** ornamentation on the exterior of an automobile, esp. in chromium or a contrasting color. —*adj.* **26.** pleasingly neat or smart in appearance: *trim lawns.* **27.** in good condition or order. **28.** properly prepared or equipped. **29.** *Obs.* good, excellent, or fine. —*adv.* **30.** Also, **trim′ly.** in a trim manner.
[OE *trymman, trymian* strengthen, prepare, der. *trum* adj., firm, active] —**trim′ness,** *n.* —**Syn. 26.** See **neat**[1].

trim·er·ous (trĭm′ər əs), *adj.* **1.** consisting of or divided into three parts. **2.** *Bot.* (of flowers) having three members in each whorl. **3.** *Entomol.* having three segments or parts. [t. NL: m. *trimerus,* t. Gk.: m. *trimerēs* made up of three parts]

tri·mes·ter (trī mĕs′tər), *n.* a term or period of three months. [t. F: m. *trimestre,* t. L: m.s. *trimestris* of three months] —**tri·mes′tral, tri·mes′tri·al,** *adj.*

trim·e·ter (trĭm′ə tər), *Pros.* —*n.* **1.** a verse of three measures or feet. —*adj.* **2.** consisting of three measures or feet. **3.** *Class. Pros.* composed of six feet or three dipodies. [t. L: m.s. *trimetrus* having three measures, t. Gk.: m. *trimetros*]

tri·met·ric (trī mĕt′rĭk), *adj.* **1.** pertaining to or consisting of a trimeter or trimeters. **2.** *Crystall.* orthorhombic. Also, **tri·met′ri·cal.**

trimetric projection, *Geom.* three-dimensional projection with three different linear scales at arbitrary angles.

trim·mer (trĭm′ər), *n.* **1.** one who or that which trims. **2.** a tool or machine for trimming, clipping, paring, or pruning. **3.** a machine for trimming lumber. **4.** *Bldg. Trades.* a timber or beam into which one of the ends of a header is fitted in the framing about an opening, a chimney, etc. **5.** an apparatus for stowing, arranging, or shifting cargo, coal, or the like. **6.** *Chiefly Brit.* a person who pursues a cautious policy between parties, accommodating himself to one side or another as expediency may dictate.

trim·ming (trĭm′ĭng), *n.* **1.** anything used or serving to trim or decorate: *the trimmings of a Christmas tree.* **2.** a decorative fitting or finish; a garnish. **3.** (*pl.*) *Colloq.* agreeable accompaniments or additions to plain or simple dishes or food. **4.** (*pl.*) pieces cut off in trimming, clipping, paring, or pruning. **5.** act of one who or that which trims. **6.** a rebuking or reproving. **7.** a beating or thrashing. **8.** *Colloq.* a defeat: *our team took another trimming yesterday.*

tri·mo·lec·u·lar (trī′mə lĕk′yə lər), *adj. Chem.* relating to or having three molecules.

tri·month·ly (trī mŭnth′lĭ), *adj.* taking place once each three months.

tri·morph (trī′môrf), *n. Crystall.* **1.** a substance existing in three structurally distinct forms; a trimorphous substance. **2.** any one of the three forms.

tri·mor·phism (trī môr′fĭz əm), *n.* **1.** *Zool.* the occurrence of three forms distinct in structure, coloration, etc., among animals of the same species. **2.** *Bot.* the occurrence of three different forms of flowers, leaves, etc., on the same plant or on distinct plants of the same species. **3.** *Crystall.* the property of some substances of crystallizing in three structurally distinct forms. **4.** the property or condition of occurring in three distinct forms. [f. s. Gk. *trimorphos* having three forms +-ISM] —**tri·mor′-phic, tri·mor′phous,** *adj.*

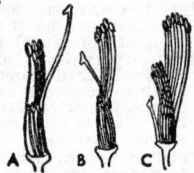

Trimorphism
A. Long style;
B. Intermediate style;
C. Short style

Tri·mur·ti (trī mŏŏr′tĭ), *n.* a Hindu trinity, consisting of Brahma the Creator, Vishnu the Preserver, and Siva the Destroyer, represented symbolically by one body with three heads. [t. Skt., f. *tri* three + *mūrti* shape]

Tri·na·cri·an (trī nā′krĭ ən, trī-), *adj. Poetic or Literary.* Sicilian. [f. s. L *Trinacria* Sicily (t. Gk.: m. *Trinakria*) + -AN]

tri·nal (trī′nəl), *adj.* threefold; triple; trine. [t. LL: s. *trinālis,* f. L: s. *trinus* threefold + -*ālis* -AL[1]]

tri·na·ry (trī′nə rĭ), *adj.* consisting of three parts, or proceeding by three; ternary.

trine (trīn), *adj.* **1.** threefold; triple. **2.** *Astrol.* denoting or pertaining to the trigon aspect of two planets distant from each other 120°, or the third part of the zodiac. —*n.* **3.** a set or group of three; a triad. **4.** (*cap.*) the Trinity. **5.** *Astrol.* the trine aspect of two planets. [ME, t. L: m.s. *trinus* threefold]

Trin·i·dad (trĭn′ə dăd′; *Sp.* trē′nē däd′), *n.* an island in the West Indies, off the NE coast of Venezuela: part of Trinidad and Tobago; formerly a British colony in the Federation of the West Indies. 792,624 pop. (1960); 1864 sq. mi.

Trinidad and Tobago, an independent state in the West Indies comprising the islands of Trinidad and Tobago; formerly a British colony in the Federation of the West Indies. 827,957 pop. (1960); 1980 sq. mi. *Cap.:* Port-of-Spain.

Trin·i·tar·i·an (trĭn′ə târ′ĭ ən), *adj.* **1.** believing in the doctrine of the Trinity. **2.** pertaining to Trinitarians, or believers in the doctrine of the Trinity. **3.** belonging or pertaining to the religious order of Trinitarians. **4.** pertaining to the Trinity. **5.** (*l.c.*) forming a trinity; threefold; triple. —*n.* **6.** one who believes in

the doctrine of the Trinity. **7.** a member of a religious order (**Order of the Holy Trinity**) founded in 1198 to redeem Christian captives from Mohammedans.

Trin·i·tar·i·an·ism (trĭn′ə târ′ĭ ə nĭz′əm), *n.* the belief in, or doctrine of, the Trinity.

trinitro-, a combining form meaning "of three nitro groups," as in *trinitrobenzene.*

tri·ni·tro·ben·zene (trī nī′trō bĕn′zēn, -bĕn zēn′), *n. Chem.* any of three yellow crystalline compounds, $C_6H_3(NO_2)_3$, none of which is produced commercially.

tri·ni·tro·cre·sol (trī nī′trō krĕ′sŏl, -sōl), *n. Chem.* a yellow crystalline compound, $CH_3C_6H(OH)(NO_2)_3$, used in high explosives.

tri·ni·tro·tol·u·ene (trī nī′trō tŏl′yŏŏ ēn′), *n. Chem.* a high explosive, $CH_3C_6H_2(NO_2)_3$, used in modern warfare, etc., exploded by detonators but unaffected by ordinary friction or shock. *Abbr.:* TNT, T.N.T. Also, **tri·ni·tro·tol·u·ol** (trī nī′trō tŏl′yŏŏ ōl′, -ŏl′).

Trin·i·ty (trĭn′ə tĭ), *n., pl.* -**ties. 1.** the union of three persons (Father, Son, and Holy Ghost) in one Godhead, or the threefold personality of the one Divine Being (**the Holy Trinity or Blessed Trinity**). **2.** Trinity Sunday. **3.** (*l.c.*) a group of three; a triad. **4.** (*l.c.*) the state of being threefold or triple; threeness. [ME *trinite,* t. OF, t. L: m. *trīnitas* triad, trio, trinity]

Trinity Sunday, the Sunday next after Pentecost or Whitsunday, observed as a festival in honor of the Trinity.

trin·ket (trĭng′kĭt), *n.* **1.** any small fancy article, bit of jewelry, or the like. **2.** anything trifling. [orig. uncert.]

tri·nod·al (trī nō′dəl), *adj. Bot., etc.* having three nodes or joints. [f. s. L *trinodis* having three knots + -AL[1]]

tri·no·mi·al (trī nō′mĭ əl), *adj.* **1.** *Alg.* consisting of or pertaining to three terms connected by the sign +, the sign -, or both of these. **2.** *Zool., Bot.* **a.** denoting a name comprising three terms, as of genus, species, and subspecies or variety. **b.** characterized by the use of such names. —*n.* **3.** *Alg.* a trinomial expression, as $a + b$ -*c.* **4.** *Bot., Zool.* a trinomial name, as *Rosa gallica pumila.* [f. TRI- + (BI)NOMIAL]

tri·o (trē′ō; *for 4 also* trī′ō), *n., pl.* **trios. 1.** a musical composition for three voices or instruments. **2.** a company of three singers or players. **3.** a subordinate division of a minuet, scherzo, march, etc., usually in a contrasted key and style (perhaps orig. written for three instruments or in three parts). **4.** any group of three persons or things. [t. It., der. *tre* three, modeled after *duo*]

tri·ode (trī′ōd), *n. Electronics.* an electron tube containing three elements, usually plate, grid, and cathode.

tri·oe·cious (trī ē′shəs), *adj. Bot.* having male, female, and hermaphrodite flowers on different plants. Also, **triecious.** [f. s. NL *trioecia* (f. tri- TRI- + m. Gk. *oikíon* house) + -OUS] —**tri·oe′cious·ly,** *adv.*

tri·o·let (trī′ə lĭt), *n.* a short poem of fixed form, consisting of eight lines using two rhymes: ab aa abab. The first line is repeated as the fourth and seventh lines, and the second line is repeated as the eighth. [t. F; orig. uncert.]

tri·ox·ide (trī ŏk′sĭd, -sĭd), *n. Chem.* an oxide containing three oxygen atoms, as As_2O_3. Also, **tri·ox·id** (trī ŏk′sĭd).

trip (trĭp), *n., v.,* **tripped, tripping.** —*n.* **1.** a journey or voyage. **2.** a journey, voyage, or run made by a boat, train, or the like, between two points, or from one point to another and back again (round trip). **3.** a stumble. **4.** a sudden impeding or catching of a person's foot so as to throw him down, esp. in wrestling. **5.** a slip, mistake, or blunder. **6.** a wrong step in conduct. **7.** act of tripping or stepping lightly; a light or nimble movement of the feet. **8.** *Mach.* **a.** a projecting part, catch, or the like for starting or checking some movement. **b.** a sudden starting or releasing.
—*v.i.* **9.** to stumble: *to trip over a child's toy.* **10.** to make a slip or mistake, as in a statement; make a wrong step in conduct. **11.** to step lightly or nimbly; skip; dance. **12.** to go with a light, quick tread. **13.** to tip or tilt. **14.** *Naut.* (of a boom) to roll under water in a seaway. **15.** *Horol.* to move over and beyond the pallet, as a tooth on an escapement wheel. **16.** *Rare.* to make a journey or excursion.
—*v.t.* **17.** to cause to stumble (often fol. by *up*): *the rug tripped him up.* **18.** to overthrow; bring to confusion. **19.** to cause to make a slip or error: *to trip up a witness by artful questions.* **20.** to catch in a slip or error. **21.** to perform with a light or tripping step, as a dance. **22.** to dance upon (ground, etc.). **23.** to tip or tilt. **24.** *Naut.* **a.** to break out (an anchor) by turning it over or lifting it from the bottom by a line (**tripping line**) attached to its crown. **b.** to tip or turn (a yard) from a horizontal to a vertical position. **c.** to lift (an upper mast) before lowering. **25.** to operate, start, or set free (a mechanism, weight, etc.) by suddenly releasing a catch, clutch, or the like. **26.** *Mach.* to release or operate suddenly (a catch, clutch, etc.).
[ME *trippe,* t. OF: m. *tripper* strike with the feet, t. Gmc.; cf. MD *trippen*]
—**Syn. 1.** TRIP, EXPEDITION, JOURNEY, PILGRIMAGE, VOYAGE are terms for a course of travel made to a particular place, usually for some specific purpose. TRIP is the general word, indicating going any distance and returning, by walking or any means of locomotion, for either business or pleasure, and in either a hurried or a leisurely manner: *a trip to Europe, a vacation trip, a bus trip.* An EXPEDITION, made often by an

---

b., blend of, blended; **c.,** cognate with; **d.,** dialect, dialectal; **der.,** derived from; **f.,** formed from; **g.,** going back to; **m.,** modification of; **r.,** replacing; **s.,** stem of; **t.,** taken from; **?,** perhaps. See the full key on inside cover.

organized company, is designed to accomplish a specific purpose: *an archaeological expedition.* JOURNEY indicates a trip of considerable length, wholly or mainly by land, for business or pleasure or other reasons, and is now applied to travel which is more leisurely or more fatiguing than a trip; a return is not necessarily indicated: *the long journey to Siam.* A PILGRIMAGE is made as to a shrine, from motives of piety or veneration: *a pilgrimage to Lourdes.* A VOYAGE is travel by water or air, usually for a long distance and for business or pleasure; if by water, leisure is indicated: *a voyage around the world.*

tri·part·ed (trī pär′tĭd), *adj.* divided into three parts.

tri·par·tite (trī pär′tīt, trĭp′ər tīt′), *adj.* **1.** divided into or consisting of three parts. **2.** *Bot.* divided into three parts by incisions which extend nearly to the base, as a leaf. **3.** participated in by three parties, as a treaty. [ME, t. L: m.s. *tripartītus* divided into three parts] —**tri·par′tite·ly,** *adv.*

tri·par·ti·tion (trī′pär tĭsh′ən, trĭp′ər tĭsh′ən), *n.* division into three parts.

tripe (trīp), *n.* **1.** the first and second divisions of the stomach of a ruminant, esp. of the ox kind, prepared for use as food. **2.** *Slang.* anything poor or worthless. [ME, t. OF, ult. t. Ar.: m. *tarb* folds of peritoneum]

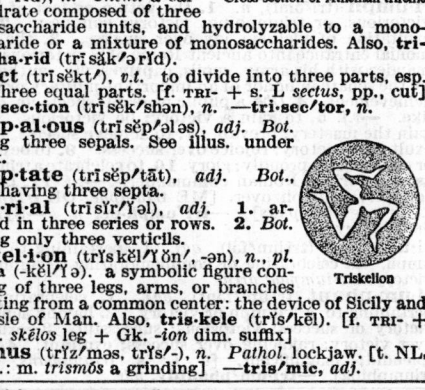

Tripartite leaf

tri·pe·dal (trī′pə dəl, trī pē′dəl, trĭp′ə dəl), *adj.* having three feet. [t. L: s. *tripedālis*]

tri·per·son·al (trī pûr′sən əl), *adj.* consisting of or existing in three persons, as the Godhead.

tri·pet·al·ous (trī pĕt′əl əs), *adj. Bot.* having three petals.

trip·ham·mer (trĭp′hăm′ər), *n. Mach.* a heavy hammer raised and then let fall by means of some tripping device, as a cam. Also, **trip hammer.**

tri·phen·yl·meth·ane (trī′fĕn′ĭl mĕth′ān, -fē′nĭl-), *n. Chem.* a colorless, crystalline organic compound, (C₆H₅)₃CH, from which many dyes (the **triphenyl-methane dyes**) are derived.

triph·thong (trĭf′thŏng, -thŏng, trĭp′-), *n.* **1.** a union of three vowel sounds pronounced in one syllable. **2.** incorrectly, a trigraph. [t. NL: s. *triphthongus*, t. MGk.: m. *triphthongos* with 3 vowels] —**triph·thong′al,** *adj.*

triph·y·lite (trĭf′ə līt′), *n.* a mineral, a phosphate of lithium, iron, and manganese, usually occurring in masses of a bluish or greenish color.

tri·phyl·lous (trī fĭl′əs), *adj. Bot.* having three leaves.

tri·pin·nate (trī pĭn′āt), *adj. Bot.* bipinnate, as a leaf, with the divisions also pinnate. Also, **tri·pin′nat·ed.** —**tri·pin′nate·ly,** *adv.*

tri·plane (trī′plān′), *n.* an airplane with three supporting planes, one above another.

tri·ple (trĭp′əl), *adj., n., v., -pled, -pling.* —*adj.* **1.** threefold; consisting of three parts: *a triple knot.* **2.** of three kinds. **3.** three times as great. **4.** *Internat. Law.* tripartite. —*n.* **5.** an amount, number, etc., three times as great as another. **6.** something triple or threefold; a triad. **7.** *Baseball.* a three-base hit. —*v.t.* **8.** to make triple. —*v.i.* **9.** to become triple. **10.** *Baseball.* to hit a three-base hit. [ME, t. L: m. *triplus*, t. Gk.: m. *triploûs* threefold] —**tri·ply** (trĭp′lĭ), *adv.*

Triple Alliance, 1. the alliance (1882–1915) between Germany, Austria-Hungary, and Italy. **2.** a league (1717) of France, Great Britain, and the Netherlands against Spain. **3.** a league (1668) of England, Sweden, and the Netherlands against France.

triple crown, the tiara worn by the pope.

Triple Entente, 1. an informal understanding among Great Britain, France, and Russia based on (a) a Franco-Russian military alliance, 1894; (b) an Anglo-French entente, 1904; (c) an Anglo-Russian understanding, 1907: considered as a counterbalance to the Dreibund and terminating when the Bolsheviks came into control in Russia in 1917. **2.** the member nations of this entente.

tri·ple-ex·pan·sion (trĭp′əl ĭk spăn′shən), *adj.* noting or pertaining to a steam engine in which the steam is expanded in three cylinders in succession, the exhaust steam from the first cylinder being the driving steam for the second, and so on.

triple measure, *Music.* triple time.

tri·ple-nerved (trĭp′əl nûrvd′), *adj. Bot.* noting a leaf in which two prominent nerves emerge from the middle nerve a little above its base.

triple play, *Baseball.* a play in which three men are retired before the ball again is put into play.

triple point, *Physics.* the condition under which a substance can exist in equilibrium in its three phases, gas, liquid, and solid.

tri·plet (trĭp′lĭt), *n.* **1.** one of three children born at one birth. **2.** (*pl.*) three offspring born at one birth. **3.** any group or combination of three. **4.** *Pros.* three successive verses or lines, esp. when rhyming and of the same length; a stanza of three lines. **5.** *Music.* a group of three notes to be performed in the time of two ordinary notes of the same kind. **6.** an assembled imitation gem with three parts, the center one giving the color, the top and bottom supplying the wearing qualities. **7.** (*pl.*) three cards of the same denomination in some card games. [der. TRIPLE, modeled after DOUBLET. Cf. F *triplet*]

tri·ple·tail (trĭp′əl tāl′), *n.* a large food fish, *Lobotes surinamensis,* of the warmer waters of the Atlantic Ocean and the Mediterranean Sea, with the lobes of its dorsal and anal fins extending backward and with the caudal fin suggesting a three-lobed tail.

triple time, *Music.* time or rhythm characterized by three beats to the measure with an accent on the first beat. Also, **triple measure.**

tri·plex (trī′plĕks, trĭp′lĕks), *adj.* **1.** threefold; triple. —*n.* **2.** something triple. **3.** *Music.* triple time. [t. L: threefold]

trip·li·cate (*v.* trĭp′lə kāt′; *adj., n.* trĭp′lə kĭt, -kāt′), *v., -cated, -cating, adj., n.* —*v.t.* **1.** to make threefold; triple. **2.** to make or produce a third time or in a third instance. —*adj.* **3.** threefold; triple; tripartite. —*n.* **4.** one of three things. [t. L: m.s. *triplicātus,* pp., tripled] —**trip′li·ca′tion,** *n.*

tri·plic·i·ty (trī plĭs′ə tĭ), *n., pl. -ties.* **1.** state of being triple; triple character. **2.** a group or combination of three; triad. **3.** *Astrol.* a set of three signs of the zodiac.

trip·loid (trĭp′loid), *adj.* See **chromosome number.**

tri·pod (trī′pŏd), *n.* **1.** a stool, pedestal, or the like with three legs. **2.** a three-legged stand, as for a camera. [t. L: s. *tripūs,* t. Gk.: m. *trípous* three-footed]

trip·o·dal (trĭp′ə dəl), *adj.* **1.** pertaining to or having the form of a tripod. **2.** having three feet or legs.

tri·pod·ic (trī pŏd′ĭk), *adj.* having or using three feet or legs.

trip·o·dy (trĭp′ə dĭ), *n., pl. -dies. Pros.* a group or verse of three feet. [t. Gk.: m.s. *tripodía*]

Trip·o·li (trĭp′ə lĭ; *It.* trē′pô lē′), *n.* **1.** Also, **Tripoli·tania.** one of the former Barbary States of N Africa: later a province of Turkey; now a part of Libya. **2.** a seaport in and the capital of Libya, in the NW part. 144,616 (est. 1950). **3.** a city in Lebanon, ab. 2 mi. inland from its port on the Mediterranean. 140,000 (est. 1953). **4.** (*l.c.*) any of several siliceous substances, as rottenstone and infusorial earth, used in polishing, etc. —**Trip·o·li·tan** (trī pŏl′ə tən), *adj., n.*

Trip·o·li·ta·ni·a (trĭp′ə lĭ tā′nĭ ə; *It.* trē′pô lē tä′nyä), *n.* Tripoli (def. 1).

Tri·poo·ra (trī poo′rä), *n.* a centrally-administered territory in E India. 639,029 (est. 1956); 4116 sq. mi.

tri·pos (trī′pŏs), *n., pl. triposes.* (at Cambridge University in England) any of various final honors examinations. [t. L: pseudo-Hellenization of *tripūs* tripod]

trip·per (trĭp′ər), *n.* **1.** one who or that which trips. **2.** *Mach.* **a.** a tripping device; a trip. **b.** an apparatus causing a signal, or other operating mechanism, to be tripped or activated. **3.** *Brit. Colloq.* one who goes on a pleasure trip or excursion; an excursionist.

trip·pet (trĭp′ĭt), *n. Mach.* a projection, cam, or the like, for striking some other part at regular intervals.

trip·ping (trĭp′ĭng), *adj.* **1.** light and quick, as the step, pace, etc. **2.** proceeding with a light, easy movement or rhythm. —**trip′ping·ly,** *adv.*

tripping line, *Naut.* See **trip** (def. 24a).

trip·ter·ous (trĭp′tər əs), *adj. Bot.* having three wings or winglike expansions. [f. TRI- + s. Gk. *pterón* wing + -OUS]

Trip·tol·e·mus (trĭp tŏl′ə məs), *n. Gk. Myth.* a favorite of Demeter: the inventor of the plow and patron of agriculture, and connected with the Eleusinian mysteries. Also, **Trip·tol′e·mos.**

trip·tych (trĭp′tĭk), *n.* **1.** *Art.* a set of three panels or compartments side by side, bearing pictures, carvings, or the like. **2.** a hinged or folding three-leaved writing tablet. [t. Gk.: m.s. *tríptychos* of three plates]

tri·que·trous (trī kwē′trəs, -kwĕt′rəs), *adj.* **1.** three-sided; triangular. **2.** having a triangular cross section. [t. L: m. *triquetrus* three-cornered]

tri·ra·di·ate (trī rā′dĭ āt′), *adj.* having, or consisting of, three rays or raylike processes. Also, **tri·ra′di·at′ed.** —**tri·ra′di·ate′ly,** *adv.*

tri·reme (trī′rēm), *n. Class. Hist.* a galley with three rows or tiers of oars on each side, one above another, used chiefly as a warship. [t. L: m.s. *trirēmis*]

Cross-section of Athenian trireme

tri·sac·cha·ride (trī săk′ə rīd′, -rĭd), *n. Chem.* a carbohydrate composed of three monosaccharide units, and hydrolyzable to a monosaccharide or a mixture of monosaccharides. Also, **tri·sac·cha·rid** (trī săk′ə rĭd).

tri·sect (trī sĕkt′), *v.t.* to divide into three parts, esp. into three equal parts. [f. TRI- + L *sectus,* pp., cut] —**tri·sec·tion** (trī sĕk′shən), *n.* —**tri·sec′tor,** *n.*

tri·sep·al·ous (trī sĕp′əl əs), *adj. Bot.* having three sepals. See illus. under **calyx.**

tri·sep·tate (trī sĕp′tāt), *adj. Bot., Zool.* having three septa.

tri·se·ri·al (trī sĭr′ĭ əl), *adj.* **1.** arranged in three series or rows. **2.** *Bot.* having only three verticils.

tris·kel·i·on (trĭs kĕl′ĭ ŏn′, -ən), *n., pl. -kelia* (-kĕl′ĭ ə). a symbolic figure consisting of three legs, arms, or branches radiating from a common center: the device of Sicily and the Isle of Man. Also, **tris·kele** (trĭs′kēl). [f. TRI- + s. Gk. *skélos* leg + Gk. *-ion* dim. suffix]

Triskelion

tris·mus (trĭz′məs, trĭs′-), *n. Pathol.* lockjaw. [t. NL, t. Gk.: m. *trismós* a grinding] —**tris′mic,** *adj.*

tris·oc·ta·he·dron (trĭs″ŏk′tə·hē′drən), n., pl. **-drons, -dra** (-drə). a solid bounded by twenty-four equal faces, three corresponding to each face of an octahedron, called (esp. in *Crystall.*) **trigonal trisoctahedron** when the faces are triangles, and **tetragonal trisoctahedron** when the faces are quadrilaterals. [f. Gk. *trís* thrice + OCTAHEDRON] —**tris·oc·ta·he′dral**, adj.

tri·some (trī′sōm), n. *Genetics.* the triploid condition of one of the chromosomes of a species, the remaining chromosomes being normally diploid.

Trisoctahedron

tri·sper·mous (trī·spûr′məs), adj. *Bot.* three-seeded. [f. TRI- + m. Gk. -*spermos* having seed]

Tris·tan da Cu·nha (trĭs′tän′ dä koon′yä), a group of three volcanic islands in the S Atlantic, belonging to Great Britain. ab. 50 sq. mi.

Tris·tan und I·sol·de (trĭs′tän oont ē·zōl′da), a music drama (composed, 1857–59; première, 1865) by Wagner.

triste (trēst), adj. *French.* sad; sorrowful; melancholy. [OF, t. L: m. *tristis*]

tris·tesse (trēs·tĕs′), n. *French.* sadness; sorrow; gloom. [ME *tristesce*, t. OF, g. L *tristitia*]

tris·tich·ous (trĭs′tĭ·kəs), adj. **1.** arranged in three rows. **2.** *Bot.* arranged in or characterized by three vertical rows. [t. Gk.: m. *tristichos* of three rows]

Tris·tram (trĭs′trəm), n. one of the most famous knights of the Round Table. His love for Iseult, wife of King Mark, is the subject of many romances. Also, **Tris·tan** (trĭs′tən).

Tristram Shan·dy (shăn′dĭ), a novel (1759–67) by Lawrence Sterne.

tri·sty·lous (trī·stī′ləs), adj. *Bot.* having three styles. [f. TRI- + m. Gk. -*stylos* columned]

tri·sul·fide (trī·sŭl′fīd, -fĭd), n. *Chem.* a sulfide containing three sulfur atoms. Also, **tri·sul·fid** (trī·sŭl′fĭd).

tri·syl·la·ble (trī·sĭl′ə·bəl, trī-), n. a word of three syllables, as *telephone.* —**tris·yl·lab·ic** (trĭs′ĭ·lăb′ĭk, trī′sĭ-), **tris′yl·lab′i·cal**, adj. —**tris′yl·lab′i·cal·ly**, adv.

trite (trīt), adj., **triter, tritest. 1.** hackneyed by constant use or repetition; commonplace: *a trite saying.* **2.** *Archaic.* rubbed or worn by use. [t. L: m.s. *tritus*, pp., rubbed, worn] —**trite′ly**, adv. —**trite′ness**, n. —**Syn. 1.** See **commonplace.** —**Ant. 1.** fresh.

tri·the·ism (trī′thē·ĭz′əm), n. *Theol.* belief in three Gods, esp. in the doctrine that the three persons of the Trinity (Father, Son, and Holy Ghost) are three distinct Gods, each an independent center of self-consciousness and self-determination. —**tri′the·ist**, n., adj. —**tri′the·is′tic, tri′the·is′ti·cal**, adj.

trit·i·um (trĭt′ĭ·əm, trĭsh′əm), n. *Chem.* an isotope of hydrogen having an atomic weight of 3.

Tri·ton (trī′tən), n. **1.** *Class. Myth.* **a.** a sea god, son of Poseidon and Amphitrite, represented as having the head and trunk of a man and the tail of a fish, and bearing a conch-shell trumpet. **b.** (later) one of a race of subordinate sea deities similarly represented, attendants on the greater sea gods. **2.** (*l.c.*) any of various marine gastropods constituting the family *Tritonidae* (esp. of the genus *Triton*), having a large, spiral, often beautifully colored shell. **3.** (*l.c.*) the shell of a triton.

tri·tone (trī′tōn′), n. *Music.* an interval consisting of three whole tones. [t. ML: m.s. *tritonus*, t. Gk.: m. *tritonos* having three tones]

trit·u·ra·ble (trĭch′ər·ə·bəl), adj. that may be triturated.

trit·u·rate (trĭch′ə·rāt′), v., **-rated, -rating**, n. —v.t. **1.** to reduce to fine particles or powder by rubbing, grinding, bruising, or the like; pulverize. —n. **2.** a triturated substance. **3.** a trituration. [t. LL: m.s. *trīturātus*, pp., threshed] —**trit′u·ra′tor**, n.

trit·u·ra·tion (trĭch′ə·rā′shən), n. **1.** act of triturating. **2.** state of being triturated. **3.** *Pharm.* **a.** a mixture of a medicinal substance with sugar of milk, triturated to an impalpable powder. **b.** any triturated substance.

tri·umph (trī′əmf), n. **1.** the action or fact of being victorious, or triumphing; victory; conquest. **2.** the exultation of victory; joy over success. **3.** the ceremonial entrance into ancient Rome of a victorious commander with his army, spoils, captives, etc., authorized by the senate in honor of an important military or naval achievement. **4.** *Obs.* a public pageant, spectacle, or the like. —v.i. **5.** to gain a victory; be victorious. **6.** to gain the mastery; prevail. **7.** to achieve success. **8.** to exult over victory; rejoice over success. **9.** to be elated or glad; rejoice proudly; glory. **10.** to celebrate a triumph, as a victorious Roman commander. —v.t. **11.** *Obs.* to conquer; triumph over. [ME *triumphe*, OE *triumpha*, t. L: m. *triumphus*] —**tri′umph·er**, n. —**Syn. 1.** See **victory.**

tri·um·phal (trī·ŭm′fəl), adj. **1.** pertaining to a triumph. **2.** celebrating or commemorating a triumph or victory: *a triumphal arch.*

tri·um·phant (trī·ŭm′fənt), adj. **1.** celebrating, or pertaining to, a triumph or victory. **2.** having achieved victory or success; victorious; successful. **3.** exulting over victory; rejoicing over success; exultant. **4.** *Obs.* splendid; magnificent. [t. L: s. *triumphans*, ppr., triumphing] —**tri·um′phant·ly**, adv.

tri·um·vir (trī·ŭm′vər), n., pl. **-virs, -viri** (-və·rī′). **1.** *Rom. Hist.* one of three officers or magistrates mutually exercising the same public function. **2.** one of three persons associated in any office. [t. L: s. *triumvirī*, pl., back formation from *trium virōrum* of three men] —**tri·um′vi·ral**, adj.

tri·um·vi·rate (trī·ŭm′vər·ĭt, -rāt′), n. **1.** *Rom. Hist.* the office or magistracy of a triumvir. **2.** the government of three joint officers or magistrates. **3.** a coalition of three magistrates or rulers for joint administration. **4.** any association of three in office or authority. **5.** any group or set of three. [t. L: m.s. *triumvirātus*]

tri·une (trī′ūn), adj. **1.** three in one; constituting a trinity in unity, as the Godhead. —n. **2.** (*cap.*) the Trinity. [f. TRI- + m.s. L *ūnus* one]

tri·u·ni·tar·i·an (trī′ū·nə·târ′ĭ·ən), n. Trinitarian.

tri·u·ni·ty (trī·ū′nə·tĭ), n., pl. **-ties.** trinity.

tri·va·lent (trī·vā′lənt, trĭv′ə·lənt), adj. *Chem.* having a valence of three. —**tri·va′lence, tri·va′len·cy**, n.

trivalent carbon, *Chem.* a carbon atom which utilizes only three of its four valences. Most free radicals (which see) contain a trivalent carbon atom.

tri·valve (trī′vălv′), adj. having three valves, as a shell.

Tri·van·drum (trĭ·văn′drəm), n. a city in S India: the capital of Kerala; pilgrimages. 186,931 (1951).

triv·et (trĭv′ĭt), n. **1.** a small metal plate with short legs put under a hot platter or dish at the table. **2.** a three-footed or three-legged stand or support, esp. one of iron placed over a fire to hold cooking vessels or the like. [ME *trevet*, OE *trefet*, appar. b. L *tripēs* and OE *thrifēte* three-footed (with VL -e- for L -i-)]

triv·i·a (trĭv′ĭ·ə), n. pl. inessential or inconsequential things; trifles; trivialities. [appar. back formation from TRIVIAL]

triv·i·al (trĭv′ĭ·əl), adj. **1.** of little importance; trifling; insignificant. **2.** *Biol.* (of names of animals and plants) specific, as distinguished from *generic*. **3.** *Rare.* common, commonplace, or ordinary. [ME, t. L: s. *triviālis* belonging to the crossroads, (hence) common] —**triv′i·al·ly**, adv. —**Syn. 1.** See **petty.** —**Ant. 1.** important.

triv·i·al·ism (trĭv′ĭ·əl·ĭz′əm), n. **1.** trivial character. **2.** something trivial.

triv·i·al·i·ty (trĭv′ĭ·ăl′ə·tĭ), n., pl. **-ties. 1.** something trivial; a trivial matter, affair, remark, etc. **2.** trivial quality or character. Also, **triv′i·al·ness.**

triv·i·um (trĭv′ĭ·əm), n. (during the Middle Ages) the lower division of the seven liberal arts, comprising grammar, rhetoric, and logic. Cf. **quadrivium.** [t. ML, special use of L *trivium* public place (lit. place where three roads meet)]

tri·week·ly (trī·wēk′lĭ), adv., adj., n., pl. **-lies.** —adv. **1.** every three weeks. **2.** three times a week. —adj. **3.** occurring or appearing three times a week. **4.** occurring or appearing every three weeks. —n. **5.** a triweekly publication.

-trix, a suffix of feminine agent-nouns, as in *aviatrix.* Cf. -or². [t. L]

Tro·as (trō′ăs), n. a region in NW Asia Minor around ancient Troy. Also, **The Tro·ad** (trō′ăd).

tro·car (trō′kär), n. *Surg.* a sharp-pointed instrument enclosed in a cannula, used for withdrawing fluid from a cavity, as the abdominal cavity, etc. [earlier *trocart*, t. F, var. of trois-quarts, lit., three-faced]

tro·cha·ic (trō·kā′ĭk), *Pros.* —adj. **1.** pertaining to the trochee. **2.** consisting of or employing a trochee or trochees. —n. **3.** a trochee. **4.** (*usually pl.*) a verse or poem consisting of trochees. [t. L: s. *trochaicus*, t. Gk.: m. *trochaïkós*]

tro·chal (trō′kəl), adj. *Zool.* resembling a wheel. [f. s. Gk. *trochós* wheel + -AL¹]

tro·chan·ter (trō·kăn′tər), n. *Anat., Zool.* (in many vertebrates) a prominence or process on the upper part of the femur. [t. F, t. Gk.]

tro·che (trō′kĭ), n. *Pharm.* a small tablet, esp. a circular one, made of some medicinal substance worked into a paste with sugar and mucilage or the like, and dried. [back formation from obs. *trochisk* troche, t. L: m.s. *trochiscus*, t. Gk.: m.s. *trochískos*]

tro·chee (trō′kē), n. *Pros.* a metrical foot of two syllables, a long followed by a short, or an accented followed by an unaccented. [t. L: m.s. *trochaeus*, t. Gk.: m. *trochaîos* running]

troch·i·lus (trŏk′ə·ləs), n., pl. **-li** (-lī′). **1.** crocodile bird. **2.** any of several small Old World warblers, as the willow warbler (*Phylloscopus trochilus*). **3.** hummingbird. [t. L, t. Gk.: m. *trochílos*]

troch·le·a (trŏk′lĭ·ə), n., pl. **-leae** (-lĭ·ē′). *Anat.* a pulleylike structure or arrangement of parts affording a smooth surface upon which another part glides, as a tendon or bone. [t. L, t. Gk.: m. *trochîla* pulley]

troch·le·ar (trŏk′lĭ·ər), adj. **1.** *Anat.* belonging to or connected with a trochlea. **2.** *Physiol., Anat.* pulleylike. **3.** *Bot.* circular and contracted in the middle so as to resemble a pulley. Also, **troch·le·ar·i·form** (trŏk′lĭ′ăr·ə·fôrm′).

tro·choid (trō′koid), n. **1.** *Geom.* a curve traced by a point rigidly connected with, but not generally on the circumference of, a circle which rolls, without slipping, upon a right line. —adj. **2.** wheellike; rotating like a

---

b., blend of, blended; c., cognate with; d., dialect, dialectal; der., derived from; f., formed from; g., going back to; m., modification of; r., replacing; s., stem of; t., taken from; ?, perhaps. See the full key on inside cover.

wheel, as a joint. [t. Gk.: m. *trochoeidḗs* round like a wheel] —**tro·choi′dal**, *adj.* —**tro·choi′dal·ly**, *adv.*

troch·o·phore (trŏk′ə·fōr′), *n. Zool.* a ciliated free-swimming larva common to several invertebrate groups and important in evolutionary speculations.

trod (trŏd), *v.* pt. and a pp. of **tread.**

trod·den (trŏd′ən), *v.* a pp. of **tread.**

trode (trōd), *v. Archaic.* pt. of **tread.**

trog·lo·dyte (trŏg′lə·dīt′), *n.* 1. a cave man or cave dweller. 2. a person living in seclusion. 3. one unacquainted with affairs of the world. [t. L: m.s. *trōglodyta*, t. Gk.: m. *trōglodýtēs* one who creeps into holes] —**trog·lo·dyt·ic** (trŏg′lə·dĭt′ĭk), **trog′lo·dyt′i·cal**, *adj.*

tro·gon (trō′gŏn), *n.* any bird of the family *Trogonidae*, esp. of the genus *Trogon*, of tropical and subtropical regions, notable for brilliant plumage. See **quetzal** (def. 1). [t. NL, t. Gk.: gnawing]

troi·ka (troi′kə), *n.* (in Russia) 1. a team of three horses abreast. 2. the vehicle drawn by them. 3. the vehicle and horses together. [t. Russ.]

Troi·lus (troi′ləs, trō′ĭl·əs), *n. Class. and Med. Legend.* the warrior son of King Priam of Troy, mentioned by Homer and Vergil, and greatly developed in medieval redactions of the Troy story as the lover of Cressida.

Trois-Ri·vières (trwȧ·rē·vyĕr′), *n.* French name of **Three Rivers.**

Tro·jan (trō′jən), *adj.* 1. of or pertaining to ancient Troy or its inhabitants. —*n.* 2. a native or inhabitant of Troy. 3. *Colloq.* one who shows pluck, determination, or energy: *to work like Trojans.* [ME, t. L: s. *Trōjānus*]

Trojan Horse, *Class. Legend.* the gigantic, hollow, wooden figure of a horse, filled with armed Greeks, and brought into Troy, thus ensuring the destruction of the city (see Vergil's *Aeneid*).

Trojan War, *Class. Legend.* a ten-years' war waged by the confederated Greeks, under the Greek king Agamemnon, against the Trojans, to avenge the abduction of Helen, wife of the Greek king Menelaus, by Paris, son of the Trojan king Priam, and ending in the sack and burning of Troy.

troll¹ (trōl), *v.t.* 1. to sing or utter in a full, rolling voice. 2. to sing in the manner of a round or catch. 3. to fish by trolling. 4. to move (the line or bait) in doing this. 5. to turn round and round. 6. to move by or as by rolling; roll. 7. *Obs.* to pass from one to another, as a bowl of liquor at table. —*v.i.* 8. to sing with a full, rolling voice; give forth full, rolling tones. 9. to be uttered or sound in such tones. 10. to fish with a moving line, as one worked up and down in fishing for pike with a rod, or one trailed behind a boat. 11. to roll; turn round and round. 12. *Obs.* to move nimbly, as the tongue in speaking. —*n.* 13. a song whose parts are sung in succession; a round. 14. act of trolling. 15. the method of trolling for fish. 16. a lure used in trolling for fish. 17. the fishing line containing the lure and hook for use in trolling. [ME *trollen* roll, stroll, t. OF: m. *troller*, t. MHG: m. *trollen*] —**troll′er**, *n.*

troll² (trōl), *n.* (in Scandinavian folklore) one of a race of supernatural beings, sometimes conceived as giants and sometimes as dwarfs, inhabiting caves or subterranean dwellings. [t. Scand.; cf. Icel. *troll*]

trol·ley (trŏl′ĭ), *n.*, *pl.* **-leys**, *v.* —*n.* 1. a trolley car. 2. a pulley or truck traveling on an overhead track, and serving to support and move a suspended object. 3. a grooved metallic wheel or pulley carried on the end of a pole (**trolley pole**) by an electric car or locomotive, and held in contact with an overhead conductor, usually a suspended wire (**trolley wire**), from which it collects the current for the propulsion of the car or locomotive. 4. any of various devices for collecting current for such a purpose, as a bowlike structure (**bow trolley**) sliding along an overhead wire, or a device (**underground trolley**) for taking current from the underground wire or conductor employed by some electric railways. 5. a small truck operated on a track, especially one whose body can be tilted for dumping. 6. *Brit.* any of various kinds of low carts or vehicles. —*v.t.*, *v.i.* 7. to convey or go by trolley. [prob. der. TROLL¹] —**trol′ley·less**, *adj.*

trolley bus, a passenger bus not operating on rails, its electric motor drawing power from overhead wires.

trolley car, a streetcar propelled electrically by current taken from a conductor by means of a trolley.

trol·lop (trŏl′əp), *n.* 1. an untidy or slovenly woman; a slattern. 2. prostitute. [prob. der. TROLL¹, v.]

Trol·lope (trŏl′əp), *n.* Anthony, 1815–82, British novelist.

trom·bi·di·a·sis (trŏm′bə·dī′ə·sĭs), *n. Vet. Sci.* the condition of being infested with chiggers. [NL, f. s. L *trombidium* red mite + *-īāsis* -IASIS]

trom·bone (trŏm′bōn, trŏm·bōn′), *n.* a musical wind instrument consisting of a cylindrical metal tube expanding into a bell and bent twice in U shape, usually equipped with a slide (in which case, called **slide trombone**). [t. It.; der. *tromba* trumpet, t. OHG: m. *trumba*] —**trom·bon·ist** (trŏm′bōn·ĭst, trŏm·bō′nĭst), *n.*

Slide trombone

trom·mel (trŏm′əl), *n. Metall.* a revolving cylindrical or conical screen. [t. G: drum]

Tromp (trŏmp), *n.* 1. Cornelis (kôr·nā′lĭs), 1629–1691, Dutch admiral. 2. his father, **Maarten Harperts-**

zoon (mär′tən här′pərt·sōn′), 1597–1653, Dutch admiral.

trompe (trŏmp), *n. Metall.* the apparatus by which the blast is produced in one type of forge. The principle is that water can be made to fall through a pipe in such a way that it will draw in through side openings a considerable amount of air which by a simple and ingenious arrangement can be utilized as a constant current or blast. [t. F: lit., trump]

tro·na (trō′nə), *n.* a mineral, grayish or yellowish hydrous sodium carbonate and bicarbonate, Na₂CO₃·NaHCO₃·2H₂O, occurring in dried or partly evaporated lake basins. [t. Sw., appar. t. Ar.: m. *trōn.* Cf. NATRON]

Trond·heim (trôn′hām), *n.* a seaport on **Trondheim Fiord** (ab. 80 mi. long), in central Norway. 56,669 (1950). Formerly, **Nidaros** or **Trond·hjem** (trôn′yĕm).

troop (trōōp), *n.* 1. an assemblage of persons or things; a company or band. 2. a great number or multitude. 3. *Mil.* an armored cavalry or cavalry unit consisting of two or more platoons and a headquarters group. 4. (*pl.*) a body of soldiers, police, etc. 5. a unit of 32 boy scouts, equal to four patrols. 6. a herd, flock, or swarm. 7. *Rare.* a band or troupe of actors. —*v.i.* 8. to gather in a company; flock together. 9. to go or come in great numbers. 10. to walk, go, or go away. 11. to go or pass in a troop or troops. 12. to go or pass in rank or order. 13. to associate or consort (fol. by *with*). —*v.t.* 14. to assemble in, form into, or unite with a troop or troops. 15. *Brit. Mil.* to carry the flag or colors in a ceremonial way before troops: *the trooping of the colors.* [t. F: m. *troupe*, g. LL *troppus* flock, from Gmc.] —**Syn.** 1. TROOP, TROUPE both mean a band, company, or group. TROOP has various meanings as indicated in the definitions above. With the spelling TROUPE the word has the specialized meaning of a company of actors, singers, or acrobats. See **company.**

troop·er (trōō′pər), *n.* 1. a horse-cavalry soldier. 2. a mounted policeman. 3. Also, **State trooper.** a State policeman. 4. a cavalry horse. 5. *Chiefly Brit.* a troopship. [der. TROOP. Cf. F *troupier*]

troop·ship (trōōp′shĭp′), *n.* a ship for the conveyance of military troops; a transport.

trop (trō), *adv. French.* too; too many; very much.

tro·pae·o·lin (trō·pē′ə·lĭn), *n. Chem.* any of a number of orange or yellow azo dyes of complex composition.

tro·pae·o·lum (trō·pē′ə·ləm), *n.*, *pl.* **-lums**, **-la** (-lə). any of the pungent herbs constituting the genus *Tropaeolum*, native in tropical America, species of which are well known in cultivation under the name of *nasturtium*. [NL, dim. of L *tropaeum* TROPHY]

-tropal, an adjective combining form identical in meaning with **-tropic.**

trope (trōp), *n.* 1. *Rhet.* a. a figure of speech. b. a word or phrase so used. 2. a phrase, sentence, or verse formerly interpolated in a liturgical text to amplify or embellish. 3. a division or heading of subject matter. [t. L: m.s. *tropus* figure in rhetoric, t. Gk.: m. *trópos* turn]

-trope, a combining form referring to turning, as in *heliotrope.* [t. Gk.: m.s. *-trópos*]

troph·ic (trŏf′ĭk), *adj. Physiol.* of or pertaining to nutrition; concerned in nutritive processes. [t. Gk.: m.s. *trophikós* pertaining to food] —**troph′i·cal·ly**, *adv.*

tro·phied (trō′fĭd), *adj.* adorned with trophies.

tropho-, a word element referring to nourishment, as in *trophoplasm.* [t. Gk., comb. form of *trophḗ*]

troph·o·blast (trŏf′ə·blăst′), *n. Embryol.* the extra-embryonic part of a blastocyst, with mainly trophic or nutritive functions, or developing into fetal membranes with trophic functions.

troph·o·plasm (trŏf′ə·plăz′əm), *n. Biol.* that kind of protoplasm which is regarded as forming the nutritive part of a cell.

tro·phy (trō′fĭ), *n.*, *pl.* **-phies**. 1. anything taken in war, hunting, etc., esp. when preserved as a memento; a spoil or prize. 2. anything serving as a token or evidence of victory, valor, skill, etc. 3. a carved, painted, or other representation of objects associated with or symbolical of victory or achievement. 4. any memento or memorial. 5. a memorial erected by the ancient Greeks, Romans, and others in commemoration of a victory in war, consisting of arms or other spoils taken from the enemy and hung upon a tree, pillar, or the like. [t. F: m. *trophée*, t. L: m. *trop(h)aeum*, t. Gk.: m. *trópaion*, der. *tropḗ* putting to flight, defeat] —**tro′phy·less**, *adj.*

-trophy, a word element denoting nourishment, as in *hypertrophy.* [t. Gk.: m.s. *-trophia* nutrition]

trop·ic (trŏp′ĭk), *n.* 1. *Geog.* a. either of two corresponding parallels of latitude on the terrestrial globe, one (**tropic of Cancer**) about 23½° north, and the other (**tropic of Capricorn**) about 23½° south of the equator, being the boundaries of the Torrid Zone. See diag. under **zone.** b. the tropics, the regions lying between and near these parallels of latitude; the Torrid Zone and neighboring regions. 2. *Astron.* a. (now) either of two circles on the celestial sphere, parallel to the celestial equator, one (**tropic of Cancer**) about 23½° north of it, and the other (**tropic of Capricorn**) about 23½° south of it. b. (formerly) either of the two solstitial points, at which the sun reaches its greatest distance north and south of the celestial equator. —*adj.* 3. pertaining to the tropics; tropical. [ME, t. L: s. *tropicus*, t. Gk.: m. *tropikós* pertaining to a turn]

ăct, āble, dâre, ärt; ĕbb, ēqual; ĭf, īce; hŏt, ōver, ôrder, oil, bŏŏk, ōōze, out; ŭp, ūse, ûrge; ə = a in alone; ch, chief; g, give; ng, ring; sh, shoe; th, thin; th, that; zh, vision. See the full key on inside cover.

-tropic, an adjective combining form corresponding to *-trope, -tropism,* as in *geotropic.*

trop·i·cal (trŏp′ə kəl), *adj.* **1.** pertaining to, characteristic of, occurring in, or inhabiting the tropics, especially the humid tropics: *tropical flowers.* **2.** of or pertaining to the astronomical tropics, or either one of them. **3.** pertaining to, characterized by, or of the nature of a trope or tropes; metaphorical. —**trop′i·cal·ly,** *adv.*

tropical year, *Astron.* See **year** (def. 5).

tropic bird, any of the totipalmate sea birds constituting the family *Phaethontidae,* graceful in flight, of pale coloration, and having a pair of greatly elongated central tail feathers: found chiefly in tropical regions.

tro·pine (trō′pēn, -pĭn), *n.* a white crystalline, hygroscopic basic compound, $C_8H_{15}NO$, formed by the hydrolysis of atropine. Also, **tro·pin** (trō′pĭn). [aphetic var. of ATROPINE]

tro·pism (trō′pĭz əm), *n. Biol.* the response, usually an orientation, of a plant or animal, as in growth, to the influences of external stimuli. The response may be positive as in turning of leaves toward the sun, or negative, as the growth of a stem away from gravitational force. [separate use of -TROPISM] —**tro·pis·tic** (trō pĭs′-tĭk), *adj.*

-tropism, a word element referring to tropism, as in *heliotropism.* [f. -TROP(E) + -ISM]

tropo-, a word element referring to turning or change. [t. Gk., comb. form of *tropos, tropē*]

tro·pol·o·gy (trō pŏl′ə jĭ), *n., pl.* -**gies. 1.** the use of tropes or a trope in speech or writing. **2.** figurative interpretation. **3.** the use of a Scripture text so as to give it a moral interpretation or significance apart from its direct meaning. [t. LL: m.s. *tropologia,* t. Gk. See TROPE] —**trop·o·log·ic** (trŏp′ə lŏj′ĭk), **trop′o·log′i·cal,** *adj.* —**trop′o·log′i·cal·ly,** *adv.*

trop·o·pause (trŏp′ə pôz′), *n. Meteorol.* the boundary, or transition layer, between the troposphere and the stratosphere.

tro·poph·i·lous (trō pŏf′ə ləs), *adj. Ecol.* adapted to a climate with alternate growing and rest periods, as a plant. [f. TROPO- + m. Gk. -*philos* loving]

trop·o·phyte (trŏp′ə fīt′), *n. Ecol.* a plant adapted to a climate alternately favorable or unfavorable to growth. —**trop·o·phyt·ic** (trŏp′ə fĭt′ĭk), *adj.*

trop·o·sphere (trŏp′ə sfĭr′), *n. Meteorol.* the inner layer of the atmosphere, varying in height between about 6 miles and 12 miles, within which there is a steady fall of temperature with increasing altitude. It is the region within which nearly all cloud formations occur and weather conditions manifest themselves.

-tropous, a word element synonymous with *-tropal,* as in *heterotropous.* [f. Gk.: m. *-tropos* pertaining to a turn]

trop·po (trŏp′ō; *It.* trôp′pō), *adv. Music.* too much: used esp. in directions. [t. It.; cf Gmc. orig. See TROOP]

-tropy, a word element synonymous with *-tropism.* [t. Gk.: m. *tropē* turning]

Tros·sachs (trŏs′əks), *n.* a valley in central Scotland, in Perth county, near Loch Katrine.

trot¹ (trŏt), *v.,* **trotted, trotting,** *n.* —*v.i.* **1.** (of a horse, etc.) to go at a gait between a walk and a run, in which the legs move in diagonal pairs, but not quite simultaneously, so that when the movement is slow one foot at least is always on the ground, and when fast all four feet are momentarily off the ground at once. **2.** to go at a similar gait; go at a quick, steady gait; move briskly, bustle, or hurry. —*v.t.* **3.** to cause to trot. **4.** to ride at a trot. **5.** to lead at a trot. **6.** to execute by trotting. **7.** *Colloq.* to bring forward for or as for inspection (fol. by *out*). —*n.* **8.** the gait of a horse, etc., when trotting. **9.** the sound made. **10.** a jogging gait between a walk and a run. **11.** (in harness racing) a race for trotters. **12.** quick, continuous movement: *to be on the trot.* **13.** *U.S. School Slang.* a crib, translation, or other illicit aid. **14.** *Rare.* a toddling child. **15.** (usually in contempt) an old woman. [ME *trotten,* t. OF: m. *trotter,* t. MHG: m. *trotten* run, orig. tread]

trot² (trŏt), *n.* **1.** a trotline. **2.** a short line with hooks, attached to the trotline. [var. of *trat;* orig. obscure]

troth (trôth, trŏth), *n. Archaic.* **1.** faithfulness, fidelity, or loyalty: *by my troth.* **2.** truth or verity: *in troth.* **3.** one's word or promise, esp. in engaging oneself to marry. [ME *trowthe, trouthe,* OE *trēowth.* See TRUTH]

trot·line (trŏt′lĭn′), *n. Fishing.* a strong fishing line strung across a stream, or deep into a river, having individual hooks attached by smaller lines at intervals.

Trot·sky (trŏt′skĭ; *Russ.* trôt′-), *n.* **Leon** (lē′ən), *(Lev,* or *Leiba, Davidovich Bronstein)* 1879–1940, Russian revolutionary leader and writer: minister of war, 1918–25; later exiled. Also, **Trot′ski.** —**Trot′sky·ist, Trot′sky·ite,** *adj., n.*

trot·ter (trŏt′ər), *n.* **1.** an animal which trots; a horse bred and trained to trot. **2.** one who goes at a similar gait, or who moves about briskly and constantly. **3.** the foot of an animal, esp. of a sheep or pig, used as food.

trou·ba·dour (trōō′bə dōr′, -dŏŏr′), *n.* one of a class of lyric poets who flourished in southern France, eastern Spain, and northern Italy from the 11th century to the 13th century, and wrote in Provençal, chiefly on chivalric love and gallantry. [t. F, t. Pr.: m. *trobador,* der. *trobar,* ? g. *tropāre,* der. *tropus* song, orig. figure of speech. See TROPE]

trou·ble (trŭb′əl), *v.,* **-bled, -bling,** *n.* —*v.t.* **1.** to disturb in mind; distress; worry. **2.** to put to inconven-

ience, exertion, pains, or the like: *may I trouble you to shut the door?* **3.** to cause bodily pain or inconvenience to, as a disease or ailment does. **4.** to annoy, vex, or bother. **5.** to disturb or agitate, or stir up so as to make turbid, as water, etc.: *troubled waters.* —*v.i.* **6.** to put oneself to inconvenience. **7.** to worry. —*n.* **8.** molestation, harassment, annoyance, or difficulty: *to make trouble for someone.* **9.** unfortunate position or circumstances. **10.** an instance of this: *a long succession of business troubles.* **11.** disturbance or disorder. **12.** an instance of this: *political troubles.* **13.** physical derangement or disorder, or an instance or form of this: *heart trouble.* **14.** disturbance of mind, distress, or worry, or an instance of this. **15.** inconvenience endured, or exertion or pains taken, in some cause or in order to accomplish something. **16.** something that troubles; a cause or source of annoyance, difficulty, distress, or the like. [ME *troublen,* t. OF: m. *troubler,* g. LL *turbulāre,* r. L *turbidāre,* influenced by *turbulentus* turbulent] —**trou′bler,** *n.* —**Syn. 15.** See **care.**

trou·ble·mak·er (trŭb′əl mā′kər), *n.* one who causes trouble for others.

trou·ble·shoot·er (trŭb′əl shōō′tər), *n.* an expert in discovering and eliminating the cause of trouble in the operation of something.

trou·ble·some (trŭb′əl səm), *adj.* **1.** causing trouble or annoyance; vexatious. **2.** laborious; difficult. **3.** *Archaic.* full of distress or affliction. —**trou′ble·some·ly,** *adv.* —**trou′ble·some·ness,** *n.*

trou·blous (trŭb′ləs), *adj. Archaic.* **1.** characterized by trouble; disturbed; unsettled. **2.** turbulent; restless. **3.** causing annoyance; troublesome.

trou-de-loup (trōō′də lōō′), *n., pl.* **trous-de-loup** (trōō′ də lōō′). *Mil.* a conical or pyramidal pit with a pointed stake fixed vertically in the center, rows of which are dug in front of a work to hinder an enemy's approach, formerly esp. used against cavalry. [F: wolfhole]

trough (trôf, trŏf; *dial.* trôth, trŏth), *n.* **1.** an open, boxlike, usually long and narrow receptacle, as for containing water or food for animals, or for any of various other purposes. **2.** any receptacle of similar shape. **3.** a channel or conduit for conveying water, as under the eaves of a building. **4.** any long depression or hollow, as between two ridges or waves. **5.** *Meteorol.* an elongated area of relatively low pressure. [ME; OE *trōh,* c. D, G, Icel. *trog*] —**trough′like′,** *adj.*

trounce (trouns), *v.t.,* **trounced, trouncing. 1.** to beat or thrash severely. **2.** to punish. **3.** *Colloq.* to defeat. [orig. uncert.]

troupe (trōōp), *n., v.,* **trouped, trouping.** —*n.* **1.** a troupe, company, or band, esp. of players, singers, or the like. —*v.i.* **2.** *Theat.* to travel as a member of a theatrical company; barnstorm. [t. F] —**Syn. 1.** See **troop.**

troup·er (trōō′pər), *n.* **1.** an actor in a theatrical company. **2.** a veteran actor.

troup·i·al (trōō′pĭ əl), *n.* any of the birds of the American family *Icteridae,* including the American blackbirds, American orioles, etc., esp. one with brilliant plumage, as *I. Icterus.* [t. F: m. *troupiale,* der. *troupe* TROOP]

trou·sers (trou′zərz), *n. pl.* **1.** a loose-fitting outer garment for men, covering the lower part of the trunk and each leg separately, and extending to the ankles. **2.** a shorter garment of this kind, reaching to the knees, esp. as worn by boys. [extended form of *trouse,* t. Irish: m. *triubhas*] —**trou′ser·less,** *adj.*

trousse (trōōs), *n.* **1.** a number of small implements carried together, as in a receptacle or case. **2.** a receptacle containing such implements.

trous·seau (trōō sō′, trōō′sō), *n., pl.* **-seaux, -seaus.** a bride's outfit of clothes, linen, etc., which she brings with her at marriage. [t. F: lit., bundle, ult. der. LL *torca,* r. L *torquis* something twisted, der. *torquēre* twist]

trout (trout), *n., pl.* **trouts,** (*esp. collectively*) **trout. 1.** any fish of the genus *Salmo* other than the Atlantic salmon (*S. salar*), including the trout of Europe (*S. trutta*), and the American **rainbow trout** (*S. gairdnerii*) and **cutthroat trout** (*S. Clarkii*). **2.** any of various fishes of the salmon family of the genera *Salvelinus* and *Cristivomer,* also known as chars and noted for their gameness and prized as food, and including several American species, as the **brook trout. 3.** any of several unrelated fishes, such as a bass (*Micropterus salmoides*), a drum of the genus *Cynoscion,* or a greenling of the genus *Hexagrammos.* [ME *troute,* OE *truht,* t. L: m. *tructa,* t. Gk.: m. *trōktēs* gnawer, a sea fish] —**trout′-like′,** *adj.*

trout perch, a peculiar North American fresh-water fish, *Percopsis omiscomaycas,* combining characters of the trouts and the perchlike fishes.

trou·vaille (trōō vä′yə), *n. French.* thing found by chance; unexpected good luck.

trou·vère (trōō vĕr′), *n.* one of a class of poets who flourished in northern France during the 12th and 13th centuries. Also, **trou·veur** (trōō vœr′). [t. F, der. *trouver.* See TROUBADOUR]

Trou·ville-sur-Mer (trōō vēl′syr mĕr′), *n.* a seaport in NW France, on the English Channel: resort. 7040 (1954).

tro·ver (trō′vər), *n. Law.* a common-law action for the recovery of the value of personal property wrongfully converted by another to his own use (orig. brought

---

b., blend of, blended; c., cognate with; d., dialect, dialectal; der., derived from; f., formed from; g., going back to; m., modification of; r., replacing; s., stem of; t., taken from; ?, perhaps. See the full key on inside cover.

against a finder of such goods). [t. OF: find, v., g. LL *tropāre* compose, invent]

trow (trō), *v.i.* *Archaic.* to believe, think, or suppose. [ME *trowen*, OE *truwian* believe, trust, c. G *trauen*]

trow·el (trou′əl), *n.*, *v.*, **-eled, -eling** or (*esp. Brit.*) **-elled, -elling.** —*n.* **1.** any of various tools consisting of a plate of metal or other material, usually flat, fitted into a short handle, used for spreading, shaping, or smoothing plaster or the like. **2.** a similar tool with a curved, scooplike blade, used in gardening for taking up plants, etc. —*v.t.* **3.** to apply, shape, or smooth with or as with a trowel. [ME *truel*, t. OF: m. *truelle*, g. LL *truella*, r. L *trulla* small ladle] —**trow′el·er;** *esp. Brit.,* **trow′el·ler,** *n.*

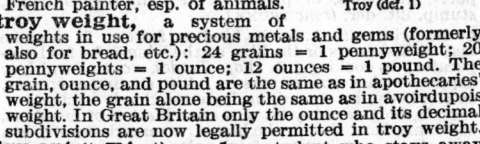

Trowels
A. Plasterer's trowel (def. 1); B. Gardener's trowel (def. 2)

Troy (troi), *n.* **1.** Latin, *Ilium.* Greek, *Ilion.* an ancient ruined city in NW Asia Minor: the sixth of nine settlements on the same site; besieged by the Greeks for ten years. **2.** a city in E New York, on the Hudson. 67,492 (1960).

troy (troi), *adj.* in or by troy weight. [named after TROYES]

Troyes (trwä), *n.* a city in NE France, on the Seine: treaty, 1420. 58,819 (1954).

Tro·yon (trwà yôn′), *n.* **Con·stant** (kôn stän′), 1813-65, French painter, esp. of animals.

Troy (def. 1)

troy weight, a system of weights in use for precious metals and gems (formerly also for bread, etc.): 24 grains = 1 pennyweight; 20 pennyweights = 1 ounce; 12 ounces = 1 pound. The grain, ounce, and pound are the same as in apothecaries' weight, the grain alone being the same as in avoirdupois weight. In Great Britain only the ounce and its decimal subdivisions are now legally permitted in troy weight.

tru·ant (trōō′ənt), *n.* **1.** a student who stays away from school without leave. **2.** one who shirks or neglects his duty. —*adj.* **3.** staying away from school without leave. **4.** pertaining to or characteristic of a truant. —*v.i.* **5.** to play truant. [ME, t. OF, prob. of Celtic orig.] —**tru′an·cy,** *n.*

truce (trōōs), *n.* **1.** a suspension of hostilities, as between armies, by agreement, for a specified period; an armistice. **2.** an agreement or treaty establishing this. **3.** respite or freedom, as from trouble, pain, etc. [ME, var. of *trewes*, pl. of *trewe*, OE *trēow* treaty, good faith. Cf. TRUE] —**truce′less,** *adj.*

Tru·cial O·man (trōō′shəl ō män′), a group of six Arab sheikdoms, on the S coast of the Persian Gulf, in treaty relations with Great Britain.

truck[1] (trük), *n.* **1.** an automotive vehicle designed for carrying loads, having a powerful motor, a transmission geared for heavy pulling, and various types of bodies, as vans, dump trucks, etc. **2.** any of various wheeled frames for moving heavy articles, as a barrow with two very low front wheels (**hand truck**), on which trunks, etc., are tilted. **3.** a low rectangular frame on which heavy boxes, etc., are moved. **4.** a group of two or more pairs of wheels in one frame, for supporting one end of a railroad car, locomotive, etc. **5.** *Brit.* a freight car having no top. **6.** a small (wooden) wheel, cylinder, or roller, as on certain old-style gun carriages. **7.** a circular or square piece of wood fixed on the head of a mast or the top of a flagstaff, and usually containing small holes for signal halyards. —*v.t.* **8.** to transport by a truck or trucks. **9.** to put on a truck. —*v.i.* **10.** to convey articles or goods on a truck. **11.** to drive a truck. [back formation from *truckle* wheel. See TRUCKLE[2]]

truck[2] (trük), *n.* **1.** *U.S.* vegetables, etc., raised for the market. **2.** miscellaneous articles; odds and ends. **3.** *Colloq.* trash or rubbish. **4.** *Colloq.* dealings: *to have no truck with a person.* **5.** barter. **6.** a bargain or deal. **7.** the payment of wages in goods, etc., instead of money. **8.** the system of such payment; truck system. —*v.t.* **9.** to exchange; trade; barter; peddle. —*v.i.* **10.** to exchange commodities; barter; bargain or negotiate. **11.** to traffic; have dealings. [ME *truk(i)e* t. OF: m. *troquer*; orig. uncert.]

truck·age (trük′ij), *n.* **1.** conveyance by a truck or trucks. **2.** the charge for this.

truck·er[1] (trük′ər), *n.* **1.** the driver of a truck. **2.** one whose business is trucking[1]. [f. TRUCK[1] + -ER[1]]

truck·er[2] (trük′ər), *n.* *U.S.* one who grows vegetables, etc., for the market. [f. TRUCK[2] + -ER[1]]

truck farm, *U.S.* a farm devoted to the growing of vegetables, etc., for the market. Also, **truck garden.**

truck·ing[1] (trük′ing), *n.* **1.** the act or business of conveying articles or goods on trucks. **2.** moving goods by truck, esp. by motor trucks. [f. TRUCK[1], v. + -ING[1]]

truck·ing[2] (trük′ing), *n.* *U.S.* the growing of vegetables, etc., for the market. **2.** commercial bartering. [f. TRUCK[2], v. + -ING[1]]

truck·le[1] (trük′əl), *v.*, **-led, -ling.** —*v.i.* **1.** to submit or yield obsequiously or tamely (fol. by *to*). **2.** to be moved on rollers or casters. —*v.t.* **3.** to move on rollers or casters. [special use of obs. *truckle*, v., sleep on truckle bed] —**truck′ler,** *n.* —**truck′ling·ly,** *adv.*

truck·le[2] (trük′əl), *n.* **1.** a pulley. **2.** a truckle bed. [late ME *trocle*, t. L: m. s. *trochlea*, t. Gk.: m. *trochilia* pulley]

truckle bed, a low bed moving on casters, usually pushed under another bed when not in use; trundle bed.

truck·man (trük′mən), *n.*, *pl.* **-men. 1.** a truck driver. **2.** one who is in the trucking business.

truck system, truck[2] (def. 8).

truc·u·lent (trük′yə lənt, trōō′kyə-), *adj.* fierce and cruel; brutally harsh; savagely threatening or bullying. [t. L: s. *truculentus*] —**truc′u·lence, truc′u·len·cy,** *n.* —**truc′u·lent·ly,** *adv.* —**Syn.** See fierce.

trudge (trüj), *v.*, **trudged, trudging,** *n.* —*v.i.* **1.** to walk. **2.** to walk laboriously or wearily. —*n.* **3.** an act of trudging. **4.** a laborious walk. **5.** one who trudges. [orig. uncert.] —**trudg′er,** *n.* —**Syn. 2.** See pace[1].

trudg·en (trüj′ən), *n.* *Swimming.* a stroke in which a double overarm motion and a scissors kick are used. Also, **trudgen stroke.** [named after John *Trudgen,* 1852-1902, British swimmer]

true (trōō), *adj.*, **truer, truest,** *n.*, *adv.*, *v.*, **trued, truing** or **trueing.** —*adj.* **1.** being in accordance with the actual state of things; conforming to fact; not false: *a true story.* **2.** real or genuine: *true gold.* **3.** free from deceit; sincere: *a true interest in someone's welfare.* **4.** firm in allegiance; loyal; faithful; trusty. **5.** steadfast in adherence, as to a friend, cause, or promise. **6.** agreeing with a standard, pattern, rule, or the like: *a true copy.* **7.** exact, correct, or accurate: *a true balance.* **8.** of the right kind; such as it should be; proper: *to arrange things in their true order.* **9.** properly so called; rightly answering to a description: *true statesmanship.* **10.** legitimate or rightful: *the true heir.* **11.** reliable, unfailing, or sure: *a true sign.* **12.** exactly or accurately shaped, formed, fitted, or placed, as a surface, instrument, or part of a mechanism. **13.** *Stockbreeding.* purebred. **14.** truthful. **15.** *Archaic.* honest; honorable; upright. —*n.* **16. the true,** that which is true. **17.** exact or accurate formation, position, or adjustment: *to be out of true.* —*adv.* **18.** in a true manner; truly or truthfully. **19.** exactly or accurately. **20.** in agreement with the ancestral type: *to breed true.* —*v.t.* **21.** to make true; shape, adjust, place, etc., exactly or accurately. [ME; OE *trēowe,* c. G *treu*] —**true′ness,** *n.* —**Syn. 1.** See real[1].

true bill, *Law.* a bill of indictment endorsed by a grand jury, after investigation, as being sufficiently supported by evidence to justify a hearing of the case.

true blue, 1. a nonfading blue dye or pigment. **2.** one who is true-blue. **3.** the color adopted by the 17th century Covenanters in contradistinction to the royal red.

true-blue (trōō′blōō′), *adj.* unchanging; unwavering; stanch; true.

true-heart·ed (trōō′här′tid), *adj.* **1.** faithful or loyal. **2.** honest or sincere.

true level, an imaginary surface everywhere perpendicular to the plumb line, or line of gravity, so that it might be the free surface of a liquid at rest.

true·love (trōō′lüv′), *n.* **1.** a sweetheart; one truly loving or loved. **2.** the herb Paris, *Paris quadrifolia,* having a whorl of four leaves suggesting a truelove knot.

truelove knot, an ornamental knot, esp. a kind of bowknot, used as an emblem of true love or interwoven affections. Also, **true′-lov′er's knot.**

true-pen·ny (trōō′pĕn′i), *n.* *Archaic.* a trusty person; an honest fellow.

true ribs, *Anat.* those ribs which are attached to the sternum by costal cartilages (the first seven pairs in man).

true time, apparent solar time; the time as shown by a sundial.

truf·fle (trüf′əl, trōō′fəl), *n.* **1.** any of various subterranean edible fungi of the ascomycetous genus *Tuber.* **2.** any of various similar fungi of other genera. [t. F: m. *truffe,* t. Pr.: m. *trufa,* or t. It.: m. *truffa,* g. LL *tūfera,* t. Osco-Umbrian: m. *tūfer,* c. LL *tūber* esculent root]

tru·ism (trōō′izm), *n.* a self-evident, obvious truth.

Truk Islands, a group of the Caroline Islands, in the N Pacific: an important Japanese naval base in World War II. ab. 17,000 pop.; ab. 50 sq. mi.

trull (trül), *n.* a prostitute; a strumpet. [t. G: s. *trulle,* var. of *trudel* loose woman]

tru·ly (trōō′li), *adv.* **1.** in a true manner; faithfully. **2.** in accordance with fact or truth. **3.** exactly or accurately. **4.** rightly or duly. **5.** legitimately. **6.** really or genuinely. **7.** *Archaic.* or *Lit.* indeed; really.

Tru·man (trōō′mən), *n.* **Harry S,** born 1884, 33rd president of the United States, 1945-1953 (from death of F. D. Roosevelt; elected to full term in 1948).

Trum·bull (trüm′bəl), *n.* **1. John,** 1750-1831, American poet. **2. John,** 1756-1843, American painter (son of Jonathan Trumbull). **3. Jonathan,** 1710-85, American patriot.

trump[1] (trümp), *n.* **1.** *Cards.* **a.** any playing card of a suit that for the time outranks the other suits, such a card being able to take any card of another suit. **b.** (*often pl.*) the suit itself. **2.** *Colloq.* a person of great excellence. —*v.t.* **3.** *Cards.* to take with a trump. **4.** to excel; surpass; be better than; beat. —*v.i. Cards.* **5.** to play a trump. **6.** to take a trick with a trump. [unexplained var. of TRIUMPH] —**trump′less,** *adj.*

trump² (trŭmp), *v.t.* to devise deceitfully or unfairly, as a charge, etc.; fabricate (fol. by *up*): *trumped up charges.* [special use of TRUMP¹]

trump³ (trŭmp), *Archaic or Poetic.* —*n.* 1. a trumpet. 2. its sound. 3. some similar sound. —*v.i.* 4. to blow a trumpet. 5. to make a trumpetlike sound. —*v.t.* 6. to proclaim, etc., by or as by a trumpet. [ME *trompe*, t. F; of Gmc. orig.]

trump·er·y (trŭm′pər̄), *n., pl.* **-eries,** *adj.* —*n.* 1. something showy but of little intrinsic value; worthless finery. 2. useless stuff; rubbish; nonsense. —*adj.* 3. showy but unsubstantial or useless; of little or no value; trifling; rubbishy. [t. F: m. *tromperie,* der. *tromper* TRUMP², v.]

trum·pet (trŭm′pĭt), *n.* 1. *Music.* **a.** any of a family of musical wind instruments with a penetrating, powerful tone, consisting of a tube, now usually metallic, and commonly once or twice curved round upon itself, having a cup-shaped mouthpiece at one end and a flaring bell at the other. **b.** an organ stop having a tone resembling that of a trumpet.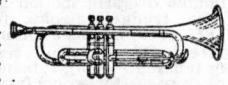

Piston trumpet

c. a trumpeter. 2. a sound like that of a trumpet. 3. the loud cry of the elephant or some other animal. 4. an ear trumpet. 5. (*pl.*) any of several pitcher plants. —*v.i.* 6. to blow a trumpet. 7. to emit a sound like that of a trumpet, as an elephant. —*v.t.* 8. to sound on a trumpet. 9. to utter with a sound like that of a trumpet. 10. to proclaim loudly or widely. [ME, t. OF: m. *trompette,* dim. of *trompe.* See TRUMP³] —**trum′pet·less,** *adj.* —**trum′pet·like′,** *adj.*

trumpet creeper, any of the climbing plants of the bignoniaceous genus *Campsis,* esp. *C. radicans,* a native of the southern U.S. with large red trumpet-shaped flowers.

trum·pet·er (trŭm′pĭt·ər), *n.* 1. one who sounds or plays a trumpet. 2. one who proclaims or announces something with a trumpet. 3. a soldier whose regular duty is to sound trumpet calls at stated hours. 4. one who proclaims or announces something loudly or widely. 5. any of the large South American birds constituting the family *Psophiidae,* esp. the agami, *P. crepitans* (**common trumpeter**), related to the rails. 6. Also, **trumpeter swan.** a large North American wild swan (*Cygnus buccinator*) having a sonorous cry. 7. one of a breed of domestic pigeons.

trumpet flower, 1. any of various plants with pendent flowers shaped like a trumpet. 2. trumpet creeper. 3. trumpet honeysuckle. 4. the flower of any of these plants.

trumpet honeysuckle, an American honeysuckle, *Lonicera sempervirens,* with large tubular flowers, deepred outside and yellow within.

trum·pets (trŭm′pĭts), *n. sing. and pl.* a pitcher plant, *Sarracenia flava.*

trumpet vine, trumpet creeper.

trum·pet·weed (trŭm′pĭt·wēd′), *n.* any of several eupatoriums, as the boneset (*Eupatorium perfoliatum*) and the joe-pye weeds (*E. maculatum* and *E. purpureum*).

trun·cate (trŭng′kāt), *v.,* **-cated, -cating,** *adj.* —*v.t.* 1. to shorten by cutting off a part; cut short; mutilate. —*adj.* 2. truncated. 3. *Biol.* **a.** square or broad at the end, as if cut off transversely. **b.** lacking the apex, as certain spiral shells. [t. L: m.s. *truncātus,* pp., cut] —**trun·ca′tion,** *n.*

Truncate lea

trun·cat·ed (trŭng′kā·tĭd), *adj.* 1. shortened by the cutting off of a part, or appearing as if so shortened. 2. (of a geometrical figure or solid) having the apex, vertex, or end cut off by a plane: *a truncated cone or pyramid.* 3. *Crystall.* **a.** (of a crystal, etc.) having angles or edges cut off or replaced by a single plane. **b.** (of one of the edges or corners) cut off or replaced by a modifying plane which makes equal angles with the adjacent similar planes. 4. *Biol.* truncate.

trun·cheon (trŭn′chən), *n.* 1. *Chiefly Brit.* a club carried by a policeman. 2. a baton, or staff of office or authority. 3. *Archaic.* a club or cudgel. 4. *Archaic.* the shaft of a spear. —*v.t.* 5. to beat with a club. [ME *trunchon,* t. OF: m. *tronçon* piece cut off, ult. der. L *truncus* stump]

Truncated cone

trun·dle (trŭn′dəl), *v.,* **-dled, -dling,** *n.* —*v.t.* 1. to cause (a ball, hoop, etc.) to roll along; roll. 2. to cause to rotate; twirl; whirl. —*v.i.* 3. to roll along. 4. to move or run on a wheel or wheels. —*n.* 5. act of trundling or rolling. 6. a small wheel, roller, or the like. 7. a small wheel adapted to support a heavy weight, as the wheel of a caster. 8. a lantern wheel. 9. each of the bars of a lantern wheel. 10. the impulse which causes something to roll. 11. *Now Rare.* a truck or carriage on low wheels. [OE *tryndel* wheel; cf. LG *tründeln* roll] —**trun′dler,** *n.*

trundle bed, truckle bed.

trunk (trŭngk), *n.* 1. the main stem of a tree, as distinct from the branches and roots. 2. a box or chest for holding clothes and other articles, as for use on a journey. 3. the body of a human being or of an animal, without the head and limbs. 4. *Archit.* **a.** the shaft of a column. **b.** the dado or die of a pedestal. 5. the main line of a river, railroad, canal, or the like. 6. *Teleph.* **a.** a telephone line or channel between two central offices or

switching devices, which is used in providing telephone connections between subscribers generally. **b.** (*pl.*) *Brit.* long distance: *give me trunks.* 7. *Anat.* the main body of an artery, nerve, or the like, as distinct from its branches. 8. (*pl.*) short, tight-fitting breeches, as worn over tights in theatrical use, or worn by athletes, swimmers, etc. 9. the long, flexible, cylindrical nasal appendage of the elephant. 10. *Naut.* **a.** a large enclosed passage through the decks or bulkheads of a vessel, for coaling, ventilation, or the like. **b.** any of various watertight casings in a vessel, as the vertical one above the slot for a centerboard in the bottom of a boat. 11. a shaft or chute. 12. (*pl.*) trunk hose. 13. *Obs.* any of various pipes or tubes, as a speaking tube, a blowgun, or a telescope. —*adj.* 14. noting or pertaining to the main line, as of a railroad. [late ME *trunke,* t. L: m.s. *truncus*] —**trunk′less,** *adj.*

trunk-fish (trŭngk′fĭsh′), *n., pl.* **-fishes,** (*esp. collectively*) **-fish.** any of the plectognath fishes constituting the family *Ostraciontidae,* which inhabit warm seas, and have a boxlike body incased in bony polygonal plates.

trunk hose, full, baglike breeches covering the person from the waist to the middle of the thigh or lower, worn in the 16th and 17th centuries.

trunk piston, *Mach.* a piston with a long skirt to take the sidethrust, as in an automobile engine.

trun·nel (trŭn′əl), *n.* treenail.

trun·nion (trŭn′yən), *n.* 1. either of the two cylindrical projections on a cannon, one on each side, which support it on its carriage. 2. any of various similar supports, gudgeons, or pivots. [t. F: m. *trognon* trunk, stump, ult. der. *tronc* TRUNK]

truss (trŭs), *v.t.* 1. to tie, bind, or fasten. 2. to make fast with skewers or the like, as the wings of a fowl preparatory to cooking. 3. *Bldg. Trades, etc.* to furnish or support with a truss or trusses. 4. to confine or enclose, as the body, by something fastened closely around. —*n.* 5. *Bldg. Trades, etc.* **a.** a combination of members, as beams, bars, ties, or the like, so arranged, usually in a triangle or a collection of triangles, as to form a rigid framework, and used in bridges (**bridge truss**), roofs (**roof truss**), etc., to give support and rigidity to the whole or a part of the structure. **b.** any framework consisting of a number of members connected together and loaded principally at the joints so that the stresses in the members are essentially simple tensions or compressions. 6. *Med.* an apparatus for maintaining a hernia in a reduced state. 7. *Hort.* a compact terminal cluster or head of flowers growing upon one stalk. 8. *Naut.* an iron fitting by which a lower yard is secured to the mast. 9. a collection of things tied together or packed in a receptacle; a bundle; a pack. 10. a bundle of hay or straw, now usually, in England, one containing about 56 pounds of old hay, 60 pounds of new hay, or 36 pounds of straw. [ME *trussen,* t. OF: m. *trusser,* ult. der. L *torca* bundle, r. *torques* necklace, something twisted] —**truss′er,** *n.*

truss bridge, *Civ. Eng.* a bridge in which the greatest strain is taken by trusses.

truss·ing (trŭs′ĭng), *n.* *Bldg. Trades, etc.* 1. the members which form a truss. 2. a structure consisting of trusses. 3. trusses collectively.

trust (trŭst), *n.* 1. reliance on the integrity, justice, etc., of a person, or on some quality or attribute of a thing; confidence. 2. confident expectation of something; hope. 3. confidence in the ability or intention of a person to pay at some future time for goods, etc.; credit: *to sell a factory on trust.* 4. that on which one relies. 5. the state of being relied on, or the state of one to whom something is entrusted. 6. the obligation or responsibility imposed on one in whom confidence or authority is placed: *a position of trust.* 7. the condition of being confided to another's care or guard: *to leave something in trust with a person.* 8. something committed or entrusted to one, as an office, duty, etc. 9. *Law.* a fiduciary relationship in which one person (the trustee) holds the title to property (the trust estate or trust property) for the benefit of another (the beneficiary). 10. *Com.* **a.** a combination of industrial or commercial companies having a central committee or board of trustees, controlling a majority or the whole of the stock of each of the constituent companies, thus making it possible to manage the concerns so as to economize expenses, regulate production, defeat competition, etc. **b.** a monopolistic organization or combination in restraint of trade whether in the form of a trust (def. 10a), contract, association or otherwise. 11. *Rare.* reliability. —*adj.* 12. *Law.* of or pertaining to trusts or a trust. —*v.i.* 13. to have or place trust, reliance, or confidence (usually fol. by *in*). 14. to look or hope (fol. by *for*). 15. to sell goods on trust or credit. 16. **trust to, to** depend on. —*v.t.* 17. to have trust or confidence in; rely on. 18. to believe. 19. to expect confidently, hope (with a clause or an infinitive). 20. to commit or consign with trust or confidence. 21. to permit to be in some place, position, etc., or to do something, without fear of consequences: *he will not trust it out of his sight.* 22. to invest with a trust; entrust with something. 23. to give credit to (a person) for goods, etc., supplied. [ME, t. Scand.; cf. Icel. *traust* trust, c. G *trost* comfort] —**trust′er,** *n.*

—**Syn. 1.** TRUST, ASSURANCE, CONFIDENCE imply a feeling of security. TRUST implies instinctive unquestioning belief in and reliance upon something: *to have trust in the loyalty of* *friends.* CONFIDENCE implies conscious trust because of good reasons, definite evidence, or past experience: *to feel confidence in the outcome of events.* ASSURANCE implies absolute confidence and certainty: *to feel an assurance of victory.*

rust company, a company or corporation organized to exercise the functions of a trustee, but usually occupied also with banking and other financial activities.

trus·tee (trŭs·tē'), *Law.* —*n.* **1.** a person, usually one of a body of persons, appointed to administer the affairs of a company, institution, etc. **2.** a person who holds the title to property for the benefit of another. **3.** (in New England) garnishee. —*v.t.* **4.** to place in the hands of a trustee or trustees. **5.** (in New England) to garnish.

trustee process, *Law.* (in New Eng.) garnishment.

trus·tee·ship (trŭs·tē'shĭp), *n.* **1.** the office or function of a trustee. **2.** the administrative control of a territory granted to a country by the United Nations. **3.** a territory so controlled.

trust·ful (trŭst'fəl), *adj.* full of trust; trusting; confiding. —**trust'ful·ly,** *adv.* —**trust'ful·ness,** *n.*

trust·ing (trŭs'tĭng), *adj.* that trusts; confiding; trustful. —**trust'ing·ly,** *adv.* —**trust'ing·ness,** *n.*

trust·wor·thy (trŭst'wûr'thĭ), *adj.* worthy of trust or confidence; reliable. —**trust'wor'thi·ly,** *adv.* —**trust'wor'thi·ness,** *n.* —Syn. See **reliable.**

trust·y (trŭs'tĭ), *adj.*, **trustier, trustiest,** *n.*, *pl.* **trusties.** —*adj.* **1.** that may be trusted or relied on; trustworthy; reliable. **2.** *Rare.* trustful. —*n.* **3.** one who or that which is trusted. **4.** *Penol.* a well-behaved and trustworthy convict to whom special privileges are granted. —**trust'i·ly,** *adv.* —**trust'i·ness,** *n.*

truth (trōōth), *n.* **1.** that which is true; the true or actual facts of a case: *to tell the truth.* **2.** conformity with fact or reality; verity: *the truth of a statement.* **3.** a verified or indisputable fact, proposition, principle, or the like: *mathematical truths.* **4.** the state or character of being true. **5.** genuineness, reality, or actual existence. **6.** agreement with a standard, rule, or the like. **7.** honesty, uprightness, or integrity. **8.** accuracy, as of position or adjustment. **9. in truth,** in fact; in reality; truly. **10.** *Archaic.* fidelity or constancy. [ME *treuthe,* OE *trēowth,* c. Icel. *tryggdh* faith] —**truth'less,** *adj.*

truth·ful (trōōth'fəl), *adj.* **1.** telling the truth, esp. habitually, as a person. **2.** conforming to truth, as a statement. **3.** corresponding with reality, as a representation. —**truth'ful·ly,** *adv.* —**truth'ful·ness,** *n.*

try (trī), *v.,* **tried, trying,** *n.,* *pl.* **tries.** —*v.t.* **1.** to attempt to do or accomplish: *it seems easy until you try it.* **2.** to test the effect or result of: *to try a new method.* **3.** to endeavor to ascertain by experiment: *to try one's luck.* **4.** to experiment upon, as with something. **5.** to test the quality, value, fitness, accuracy, etc., of: *to try a new invention.* **6.** to attempt to open (a door, window, etc.) in order to find out whether it is locked. **7.** *Law.* to examine and determine judicially, as a cause; determine judicially the guilt or innocence of (a person). **8.** to put to a severe test; strain the endurance, patience, etc., of: *to try one's patience.* **9.** to subject to grievous experiences, affliction, or trouble. **10.** to melt (fat, etc.) to obtain the oil; render (usually fol. by *out*). **11.** to extract or refine by heat, as oil from blubber, metal from ore, etc. (usually with *out*). **12.** *Rare.* to ascertain the truth or right of (a matter, etc.) by test (sometimes fol. by *out*). **13.** *Obs.* to show or prove by test or experience. —*v.i.* **14.** to make an attempt or effort: *try harder next time.* **15.** to make trial or experiment. —*n.* **16.** *Colloq.* an attempt, endeavor, or effort: *to have a try at something.* **17.** *Rugby.* a score of three points earned by advancing the ball to or beyond the opponents' goal line. [ME *tryen,* t. OF: m. *trier* pick, cull] —**tri'er,** *n.* —Syn. **1.** TRY, ATTEMPT, ENDEAVOR, STRIVE imply putting forth effort toward a specific end. TRY is the verb in most general use: *try to do your best.* ATTEMPT is more formal and often carries the idea of more effort: *he attempted to deceive me.* ENDEAVOR suggests resolve and continuous effort, esp. in the face of difficulties: *endeavor to effect a compromise.* STRIVE implies hard and earnest exertion to accomplish something difficult or laborious: *to strive mightily at a task.*

try·ing (trī'ĭng), *adj.* annoying; distressing. —**try'ing·ly,** *adv.* —**try'ing·ness,** *n.*

try·ma (trī'mə), *n.,* *pl.* **-mata** (-mə·tə). *Bot.* a drupaceous nut having a fibrous or fleshy epicarp which is ultimately dehiscent, as in the walnut and hickory. [t. NL, t. Gk.: hole]

try·out (trī'out'), *n.* *U.S. Colloq.* a trial or test to ascertain fitness for some purpose.

tryp·a·fla·vine (trĭp'ə·flā'vĭn, -vēn), *n.* acriflavine.

tryp·a·no·some (trĭp'ə·nə·sōm'), *n.* **1.** any of the minute flagellate protozoans constituting the genus *Trypanosoma,* parasitic in the blood or tissues of man and other vertebrates, usually transmitted by insects, often causing serious diseases, as African sleeping sickness in man, and many diseases in domestic animals. **2.** a protozoan having the form of a trypanosome. Also, **tryp·a·no·so·ma** (trĭp'ə·nə·sō'mə). [f. *trypano-* (comb. form of Gk. *trypanon* borer) + -SOME[3]]

tryp·sin (trĭp'sĭn), *n.* *Biochem.* **1.** a proteolytic enzyme of the pancreatic juice, capable of converting proteins into peptone. **2.** any of several proteolytic enzymes. [var. of *tripsin,* f. s. Gk. *tripsis* friction + -IN[2]] —**tryp·tic** (trĭp'tĭk), *adj.*

tryp·to·phan (trĭp'tə·făn'), *n.* *Biochem.* a colorless, solid, aromatic, essential amino acid, $C_{11}H_{12}N_2O_2$, found in the seeds of some leguminous plants: necessary to animal life. It is released from proteins by tryptic

digestion. Also, **tryp·to·phane** (trĭp'tə·fān'). [f. *trypto-* (comb. form repr. Gk. *triptós* rubbed) + -PHAN(E)]

try·sail (trī'sāl'; *Naut.* -səl), *n.* *Naut.* a small fore-and-aft sail set with or without a gaff, usually loose-footed, on the foremast or mainmast of a vessel, and used esp. in heavy weather.

try square, two straight edges fastened at right angles to each other, used for testing the squareness of work or for laying out right angles.

Carpenter's try square

tryst (trĭst, trīst), *n.* **1.** an appointment to meet at a certain time and place. **2.** an appointed meeting. **3.** an appointed place of meeting. —*v.t.* *Chiefly Scot.* **4.** to make an engagement with (a person) for a meeting. **5.** to appoint (a time, etc.). **6.** to arrange for or order (a thing) in advance. —*v.i.* *Chiefly Scot.* **7.** to make an appointment or agreement. [ME *triste,* t. OF; orig. uncert.] —**tryst'er,** *n.*

trysting place, a place where a tryst is kept or is to be kept.

Tsa·na (tsä'nä), *n.* Lake. See **Tana, Lake.**

tsar (tsär), *n.* czar.

tsar·e·vitch (tsär'ə·vĭch), *n.* czarevitch.

tsa·rev·na (tsä·rĕv'nə), *n.* czarevna.

tsa·ri·na (tsä·rē'nä), *n.* czarina.

tsar·ism (tsär'ĭzəm), *n.* czarism.

Tsa·rit·syn (tsä·rĭt'sĭn), *n.* former name of **Stalingrad.**

tsa·rit·za (tsä·rĭt'sä), *n.* czaritza.

Tschai·kov·sky (chĭ·kôf'skĭ), *n.* **Pëtr Ilich** (pyŏ'tər ĭl'ĕch'), (Eng. *Peter Ilych*) 1840–93, Russian composer. Also, **Tschai·kow·sky, Tchaikovsky.**

tset·se fly (tsĕt'sĭ), any of the blood-sucking flies of the African genus *Glossina,* some of which transmit protozoans (trypanosomes) which cause African sleeping sickness and other serious diseases. Also, **tsetse, tzetze fly.** [native name]

T-shirt (tē'shûrt), *n.* a lightweight, close-fitting pull-over, usually of cotton knit and with short sleeves. Also, **tee'shirt.**

Tsi·nan (jē'nän'), *n.* a city in NE China: the capital of Shantung province. 575,000 (est. 1950).

Tsing·hai (chĭng'hī'), *n.* Chinghai.

Tsing·tao (tsĭng'tou'; *Chin.* chĭng'dou'), *n.* a seaport in E China, on Kiaochow Bay, in Shantung province. Municipal district, 851,000 (est. 1950). See **Kiaochow.**

Tsing·yuan (chĭng'yýän'), *n.* a city in NE China, in Hopeh Province. 130,000 (est. 1948). Formerly, **Paoting.**

Tsin·ling Shan (jē'lĭng' shän'), a mountain range in central China. Highest peak, ab. 13,000 ft.

tsp., teaspoon.

T square, a T-shaped ruler used in mechanical drawing to make parallel lines, etc., the short crosspiece sliding along the edge of the drawing board as a guide.

tsu·na·mi (tsŏō·nä'mē), *n.* a large, often destructive sea wave caused by an underwater earthquake. [t. Jap. tidal wave]

Tsetse fly, *Glossina morsitans* (Ab. ¼ in. long)

Tsu·shi·ma (tsŏō'shē·mä'), *n.* two adjacent Japanese islands between Korea and Kyushu island, Japan: the Japanese fleet decisively defeated the Russian fleet near here, 1905. 57,482 pop. (1947); 271 sq. mi.

Tu, *Chem.* thulium.

Tu., Tuesday.

Tu·a·mo·tu Archipelago (tŏō'ä·mō'tŏō), a group of French islands in the S Pacific. 5617 pop. (1951); 332 sq. mi. Also, **Low** or **Paumotu Archipelago.**

Tua·reg (twä'rĕg), *n.* **1.** a Berber or Hamitic-speaking member of the Moslem nomads of the Sahara. **2.** the language of the Tuaregs, a Berber dialect. [native name]

tub (tŭb), *n.,* *v.,* **tubbed, tubbing.** —*n.* **1.** a vessel or receptacle for bathing in; a bathtub. **2.** *Brit. Colloq.* a bath in a tub. **3.** a broad, round, open, wooden vessel, usually made of staves held together by hoops and fitted around a flat bottom. **4.** any of various vessels resembling or suggesting a tub: *a tub for butter.* **5.** as much as a tub will hold. **6.** *Colloq.* a slow, clumsy ship or boat. **7.** *Mining.* **a.** an ore car in a mine. **b.** a bucket, box, or the like, in which material is brought from or conveyed in a mine. **c.** installation of lining in an excavation (shaft) to prevent inflow of water or caving. —*v.t.* **8.** to put or set in a tub. **9.** *Brit. Colloq.* to wash or bathe in a tub. —*v.i.* **10.** *Brit. Colloq.* to wash oneself in a tub. **11.** *Colloq.* to undergo washing, esp. without damage, as a fabric. [ME *tubbe,* c. LG *tubbe;* orig. unknown] —**tub'ba·ble,** *adj.* —**tub'ber,** *n.* —**tub'like',** *adj.*

tu·ba (tū'bə, tŏō'bə), *n.,* *pl.* **-bas, -bae** (-bē). **1.** a brass wind instrument of low pitch equipped with valves. **2.** an organ reed stop of large scale with tones of exceptional power. **3.** an ancient Roman trumpet. [t. L: trumpet; akin to TUBE]

tub·al (tū'bəl, tŏō'-), *adj.* **1.** of or pertaining to a tube or tubes; tubular. **2.** *Anat.* pertaining to a tube, as the Fallopian tube.

Tuba (def. 1)

Tu·bal-cain (tū'bəl kān', too'-), *n.* *Bible.* a maker of brass and iron articles. Gen. 4:22.

tu·bate (tū'bāt, too'-), *adj.* forming or having a tube or tubes.

tub·by (tŭb'ĭ), *adj.*, **-bier, -biest.** 1. short and fat: *a tubby man.* 2. having a dull sound; without resonance. **—tub'bi·ness,** *n.*

tube (tūb, toob), *n., v.,* **tubed, tubing.** **—***n.* 1. a hollow, usually cylindrical body of metal, glass, rubber, or other material, used for conveying or containing fluids, and for other purposes. 2. a small, collapsible, metal cylinder closed at one end and having the open end provided with a cap, for holding paint, toothpaste, or other semi-liquid substance to be squeezed out by pressure. 3. *Anat. Zool.* any hollow, cylindrical vessel or organ: *the bronchial tubes.* 4. *Bot.* **a.** any hollow, elongated body or part. **b.** the united lower portion of a gamopetalous corolla or a gamosepalous calyx. 5. the tubular tunnel in which an underground railroad runs. 6. *Colloq.* the railroad itself. 7. *Electronics.* an electron tube. 8. *Archaic.* a telescope. **—***v.t.* 9. to furnish with a tube or tubes. 10. to convey or enclose in a tube. 11. to form in the shape of a tube; make like a tube. [t. L: m.s. *tubus* pipe] **—tube'less,** *adj.* **—tube'like',** *adj.*

tube of force, *Elect., Magnetism.* a tubular space bounded by lines of force or induction.

tu·ber[1] (tū'bər, too'-), *n.* 1. *Bot.* a fleshy, usually oblong or rounded thickening or outgrowth (as the potato) of a subterranean stem or shoot, bearing minute scale-like leaves with buds or eyes in their axils, from which new plants may arise. 2. *Anat., etc.* a rounded swelling or protuberance; a tuberosity; a tubercle. [t. L: bump, swelling]

tub·er[2] (tū'bər, too'-), *n.* one who or that which tubes. [f. TUBE + -ER[1]]

tu·ber·cle (tū'bər kəl, too'-), *n.* 1. a small rounded projection or excrescence, as on a bone, on the surface of the body in various animals, or on a plant. 2. *Pathol.* **a.** a small, firm, rounded nodule or swelling. **b.** such a swelling as the characteristic lesion of tuberculosis. [t. L: m.s. *tūberculum* small swelling]

tubercle bacillus, a slender thread-like organism, *Mycobacterium tuberculosis,* very difficult to stain, but retaining stain with great tenacity. It causes tuberculosis in all its forms and was first discovered by Robert Koch in 1882.

tu·ber·cu·lar (tū'bûr'kyə lər, too'-), *adj.* 1. pertaining to tuberculosis; tuberculous. 2. pertaining to or having the nature of a tubercle or tubercles. 3. characterized by tubercles. **—***n.* 4. a tuberculous person. **—tu·ber'cu·lar·ly,** *adv.*

Tubercle bacillus, *Mycobacterium tuberculosis* (Highly magnified)

tu·ber·cu·late (tū'bûr'kyə lĭt, -lāt', too'-), *adj.* 1. tubercular. 2. having tubercles. [t. NL: m.s. *tūberculātus,* der. L *tūberculum* tubercle] **—tu·ber'cu·la'tion,** *n.*

tu·ber·cule (tū'bər kūl', too'-), *n.* *Bot.* a nodule, esp. on the roots of certain legumes.

tu·ber·cu·lin (tū'bûr'kyə lĭn, too'-), *n.* *Med.* a sterile liquid prepared from cultures of the tubercle bacillus, used in the diagnosis and treatment of tuberculosis.

tuberculo-, a word element representing **tuberculous, tuberculosis,** or **tubercle bacillus.** [comb. form repr. L *tūberculum* tubercle]

tu·ber·cu·loid (tū'bûr'kyə loid', too'-), *adj.* resembling a tubercle.

tu·ber·cu·lo·sis (tū'bûr'kyə lō'sĭs, too'-), *n.* *Pathol.* 1. an infectious disease affecting any of various tissues of the body, due to the tubercle bacillus, and characterized by the production of tubercles. 2. this disease when affecting the lungs; pulmonary phthisis; consumption. [t. NL, der. L *tūberculum* TUBERCLE]

tu·ber·cu·lous (tū'bûr'kyə ləs, too'-), *adj.* 1. tubercular. 2. affected with tuberculosis: *several tuberculous patients.*

tube·rose (tūb'rōz', toob'-, tū'bə rōs', too'-), *n.* a bulbous amaryllidaceous plant, *Polianthes tuberosa,* cultivated for its spike of fragrant, creamy-white, lilylike flowers. [t. L: m. *tūberōsa,* fem. of *tūberōsus* tuberous, popularly confused with TUBE + ROSE]

tu·ber·os·i·ty (tū'bə rŏs'ə tĭ, too'-), *n., pl.* **-ties.** 1. a swelling or prominence. 2. a rough projection or protuberance of a bone, as for the attachment of a muscle. 3. state of being tuberous.

tu·ber·ous (tū'bər əs, too'-), *adj.* 1. covered with or characterized by rounded or wartlike prominences or tubers. 2. of the nature of such a prominence. 3. *Bot.* bearing tubers. 4. having the nature of or resembling a tuber. [t. L: m.s. *tūberōsus*]

tuberous root, a true root so thickened as to resemble a tuber, but bearing no buds or eyes.

tub·ing (tū'bĭng, too'-), *n.* 1. material in the form of a tube: *copper tubing.* 2. tubes collectively. 3. a piece of tube.

tu·bu·lar (tū'byə lər, too'-), *adj.* 1. of or pertaining to a tube or tubes. 2. characterized by or consisting of tubes. 3. Also, **tu·bi·form** (tū'bə fôrm', too'-). having the nature or form of a tube; tube-shaped. 4. *Physiol., Pathol.* noting a respiratory sound resembling that produced by a current of air passing through a tube. [t. NL: s. *tubulāris,* der. L *tubulus* little tube]

tu·bu·late (*adj.* tū'byə lĭt, -lāt', too'-; *v.* tū'byə lāt', too'-), *adj., v.,* **-lated, -lating.** **—***adj.* 1. formed into or like a tube; tubular. **—***v.t.* 2. to form into a tube. 3. to furnish with a tube. **—tu'bu·la'tion,** *n.* **—tu'bu·la'tor,** *n.*

tu·bule (tū'būl, too'-), *n.* a small tube; a minute tubular structure. [t. L: m.s. *tubulus* small pipe]

tu·bu·li·flo·rous (tū'byə lə flôr'əs, too'-), *adj.* *Bot.* having the corolla tubular in all the perfect flowers of a head, as certain composite plants.

tu·bu·lous (tū'byə ləs, too'-), *adj.* 1. containing or composed of tubes. 2. having the form of a tube; tubular. 3. *Bot.* having tubular flowers. [t. NL: m.s. *tubulōsus*]

tu·bu·lure (tū'byə lər, too'-), *n.* a short tubular opening, as in a glass jar or at the top of a retort. [t. F, der. L *tubulus* little pipe]

tu·chun (doo'jyn'), *n.* (in China, from 1916–23) the title of a military ruler of a province. [t. Chinese, lit., overseer of troops]

tuck[1] (tŭk), *v.t.* 1. to thrust into some narrow space or close or retired place: *tuck this in your pocket.* 2. to thrust the edge or end of (a garment, covering, etc.) closely into place between retaining parts or things (usually fol. by *in, up,* etc.): *with his napkin tucked under his chin.* 3. to cover snugly in or as in this manner: *to tuck one up in bed.* 4. to draw up in folds or a folded arrangement: *to tuck one's legs under a chair.* 5. *Needlework.* to sew tucks in. 6. *Brit. Slang.* to eat or drink (fol. by *in, away,* etc.). **—***v.i.* 7. to draw together; contract; pucker. 8. *Needlework.* to make tucks. 9. *Brit. Slang.* to eat or drink heartily or greedily (fol. by *in, away,* etc.). **—***n.* 10. a tucked piece or part. 11. *Needlework.* a fold, or one of a series of folds, made by doubling cloth upon itself, and stitching parallel with the edge of the fold. 12. *Naut.* that part of a vessel where the after ends of the outside planking or plating unite at the sternpost. 13. *Brit. Slang.* food. [ME *t*(o)uke stretch (cloth), torment, OE *tūcian* torment. Cf. MLG *tucken,* G *zucken* tug]

tuck[2] (tŭk), *n.* *Archaic.* a rapier with a stiff blade. [? sandhi var. of obs. *stock* sword. Cf. G *stock,* F *estoc*]

Tuck (tŭk), *n.* **Friar,** the jolly priest of Robin Hood's band.

tuck-a-hoe (tŭk'ə hō'), *n.* 1. the edible underground sclerotium of the fungus *Poria cocos,* found on the roots of trees in the southern United States. 2. a poor white. [t. Algonquian (Va. d.): m. *tockawhonge* it is globular]

tuck·er (tŭk'ər), *n.* 1. one who or that which tucks. 2. a piece of linen, muslin, or the like, worn by women about the neck and shoulders. 3. a chemisette. **—***v.t.* 4. *U.S. Colloq.* to weary; tire; exhaust (often fol. by *out*). [f. TUCK[1] + -ER[1]]

Tuc·son (too sŏn', too'sŏn), *n.* a city in S Arizona: health resort. 212,892. (1960).

Tu·cu·mán (too'koo män'), *n.* a city in NW Argentina. 255,038 (est. 1953).

-tude, a suffix forming abstract nouns (generally from Latin adjectives or participles) in words of Latin origin, as in *latitude, fortitude;* but sometimes used directly as an English formative element. [t. L: m. *-tūdo.* Cf. F *-tude*]

Tu·dor (tū'dər, too'-), *adj.* 1. of or pertaining to the line of English sovereigns (Henry VII, Henry VIII, Edward VI, Mary, and Elizabeth) which reigned from 1485 to 1603, and which was descended from **Sir Owen Tudor,** a Welshman who married the widow of Henry V. 2. of or pertaining to the periods of their reigns: *Tudor style of architecture.* 3. one who lived in the Tudor period, as a writer or statesman.

tu·e·bor (tū e'bôr, too'-), *v.* *Latin.* I will defend (motto on the coat of arms of Michigan).

Tues., Tuesday.

Tues·day (tūz'dĭ, tooz'-), *n.* the third day of the week, following Monday. [ME *Tewesday,* OE *Tiwesdæg* Tiw's day (trans. of L *Martis dies* day of Mars)]

tu·fa (tū'fə, too'fə), *n.* *Geol.* 1. Also, **calcareous tufa.** a form of porous limestone deposited by springs, etc. 2. tuff. [t. It.: m. *tufo,* g. L *tōfus* loose porous stone] **—tu·fa·ceous** (tū fā'shəs, too-), *adj.*

tuff (tŭf), *n.* *Geol.* a fragmental rock consisting of the smaller kinds of volcanic detritus, usually more or less stratified. Also, **volcanic tuff.** [t. F: m. *tuf,* t. It.: m. *tufo* TUFA] **—tuff·a·ceous** (tŭf ā'shəs), *adj.*

tuft (tŭft), *n.* 1. a bunch of small, usually soft and flexible things, as feathers, hairs, etc., fixed at the base with the upper part loose. 2. a small clump of bushes, trees, etc. 3. a cluster of short-stalked flowers, leaves, etc., growing from a common point. 4. any of the bunches of threads sewn through a mattress, quilt, etc., in order to strengthen the padding. 5. a button through which a tuft is sewn. 6. a gold tassel on the cap formerly worn at English universities by titled undergraduates. 7. one who wore such a tassel. **—***v.t.* 8. to furnish with a tuft or tufts. 9. to arrange in a tuft or tufts. 10. *Upholstery.* to draw together (a cushion, etc.) by passing a thread through at regular intervals, the depressions thus produced being usually ornamented with tufts or buttons. **—***v.i.* 11. to form a tuft or tufts. [ME *toft;* orig. uncert.]

tuft·ed (tŭf'tĭd), *adj.* 1. furnished with a tuft or tufts. 2. formed into a tuft or tufts.

---

tuft·hunt·er (tŭft′hŭn′tər), *n. Archaic.* **1.** one who seeks the acquaintance of titled persons. **2.** a toady; sycophant. [f. TUFT (defs. 6, 7) + HUNTER] —**tuft′-hunt′ing,** *adj.*

tuft·y (tŭf′tĬ), *adj.* **1.** abounding in tufts. **2.** covered or adorned with tufts. **3.** forming a tuft or tufts.

tug (tŭg), *v.,* **tugged, tugging,** *n.* —*v.t.* **1.** to pull at with force or effort. **2.** to move by pulling forcibly; drag; haul. **3.** to tow (a vessel, etc.) by means of a tugboat. —*v.i.* **4.** to pull with force or effort: *to tug at an oar.* **5.** to strive hard, labor, or toil. —*n.* **6.** act of tugging; a strong pull. **7.** a struggle; a strenuous contest. **8.** a tugboat. **9.** that by which something is tugged. **10.** a trace of a harness; any of various pulling or supporting parts of a harness. [ME *toggen,* appar. intensive var. of TOW[1]] —**tug′ger,** *n.* —**tug′less,** *adj.*

tug·boat (tŭg′bōt′), *n.* a strongly built, heavily powered vessel for towing other vessels.

tug of war, **1.** an athletic contest between two teams at opposite ends of a rope, each team trying to drag the other over a line. **2.** a severe or critical struggle.

Tui·ler·ies (twē′lər Ĭz; *Fr.* twēl rē′), *n.* a former royal residence in Paris, France, begun by Catherine de' Medici, 1564: the seat of the Convention, 1792; burned by the Commune, 1871.

tu·i·tion (tū′Ĭsh′ən, tōō′-), *n.* **1.** teaching or instruction, as of pupils. **2.** the charge or fee for instructions. **3.** *Archaic.* guardianship or custody. [late ME *tuicion,* t. L: m.s. *tuitio* guardianship] —**tu·i′tion·al, tu·i·tion·ar·y** (tū′Ĭsh′ə něr′Ĭ, tōō′-), *adj.* —**tu·i′tion·less,** *adj.*

Tu·la (tōō′lä), *n.* a city in the central Soviet Union in Europe, S of Moscow. 320,000 (est. 1956).

tu·la·re·mi·a (tōō′lə rē′mĬ ə), *n.* a disease of rabbits, squirrels, etc., caused by a bacterium, *Pasturella tularensis* (or *Bacterium tularense*), transmitted to man by insects or by the handling of infected animals, resembling the plague and taking the form in man of an irregular fever lasting several weeks. Also, **tu′la·rae′-mi·a.** [f. *Tulare,* county in California + -EMIA]

tu·le (tōō′lē), *n.* either of two large bulrushes, *Scirpus lacustris* and *S. californicus,* which in California and adjacent regions occupy overflowed land and marshes. [t. Sp., t. Aztec: m. *tullin*]

tu·lip (tū′lĬp, tōō′-), *n.* **1.** any of the liliaceous plants constituting the genus *Tulipa,* cultivated in many varieties, and having large, showy, usually erect, cup-shaped or bell-shaped flowers of various colors. **2.** a flower or bulb of such a plant. [earlier *tulipa(n),* t. Turk.: m. *tulipant* TURBAN] —**tu′lip-like′,** *adj.*

tulip tree, a North American magnoliaceous tree, *Liriodendron Tulipifera,* with tuliplike flowers and a wood that is used in cabinetwork, etc.

tu·lip·wood (tū′lĬp wŏŏd′, tōō′-), *n.* **1.** the wood of the tulip tree. **2.** any of various striped or variegated woods of other trees. **3.** any of these trees.

tulle (tōōl; *Fr.* tẏl), *n.* a thin, fine, silk or rayon net, used in millinery, dressmaking, etc. [t. F, named after *Tulle,* town in France]

tul·li·bee (tŭl′ə bē′), *n.* a deep-bodied cisco, of the whitefish genus *Leucichthys,* found in North American lakes. [t. Canadian F: m. *toulibi,* t. Algonquian (Chippewa-Cree): m. *otonabi* mouth water, f. *oton* its mouth + *abi* water, liquid]

Tul·ly (tŭl′Ĭ), *n.* See **Cicero** (def. 1).

Tul·sa (tŭl′sə), *n.* a city in NE Oklahoma: center of a rich oil-producing region. 261,685 (1960).

tum·ble (tŭm′bəl), *v.,* **-bled, -bling,** *n.* —*v.i.* **1.** to roll or fall over or down as by losing footing, support, or equilibrium: *to tumble down the stairs.* **2.** to fall rapidly, as market prices. **3.** to perform leaps, springs, somersaults, or other feats of bodily agility, as for exhibition or sport. **4.** to roll about by turning one way and another; pitch about; toss. **5.** to stumble or fall (fol. by *over*). **6.** to go, come, get, etc., in a precipitate or hasty way. **7.** *Slang.* to become suddenly alive to some fact, circumstance, or the like (often fol. by *to*). —*v.t.* **8.** to send tumbling or falling; throw over or down; overthrow. **9.** to move or toss about, or turn over, as in handling, searching, etc. **10.** to disorder by or as by tossing about. **11.** to throw, cast, put, send, etc., in a precipitate, hasty, or rough manner. **12.** to subject to the action of a tumbling box. —*n.* **13.** an act of tumbling; a fall; a downfall. **14.** tumbled condition; disorder or confusion. **15.** a confused heap. [ME *tum(b)le* (freq. of *tumben,* OE *tumbian* dance), c. G *tummeln*]

tum·ble·bug (tŭm′bəl bŭg′), *n.* any of various scarabaeid dung beetles which roll up globular masses of dung in which they deposit their eggs and in which the larvae develop.

tum·ble-down (tŭm′bəl doun′), *adj.* dilapidated; ruinous.

tum·bler (tŭm′blər), *n.* **1.** a drinking cup with flat bottom, without handle or stem, and usually of glass. **2.** one who or that which tumbles; one who performs leaps, somersaults, and other bodily feats. **3.** (in a lock) any locking or checking part which, when lifted or released by the action of a key or the like, allows the bolt to move. **4.** (in a gunlock) a leverlike piece which by the action of a spring forces the hammer forward when released by the trigger. **5.** *Mach.* **a.** a part moving a gear into place in a selective transmission. **b.** a single cog or cam on a rotating shaft, transmitting motion to a

part with which it engages. **6.** a tumbling box. **7.** a person who operates a tumbling box. **8.** one of a breed of dogs resembling small greyhounds, formerly used in hunting rabbits. **9.** one of a breed of domestic pigeons having the habit of turning over and over backward in their flight. **10.** a toy, usually representing a fat, squatting figure, with a heavy or weighted and rounded base, so as to rock when touched.

tumbler gear, *Mach.* a transmission having gears actuated by a tumbler.

tum·ble·weed (tŭm′bəl wēd′), *n. U.S.* any of various plants (as an amaranth, *Amaranthus graecizans*) whose branching upper part becomes detached from the roots in autumn and is driven about by the wind.

tumbling box, an apparatus consisting of a box or cylindrical vessel pivoted at each end or at two corners, so that it can be made to revolve, used for polishing objects by allowing them to tumble about with an abrasive substance, for mixing materials, etc.

tum·brel (tŭm′brəl), *n.* **1.** a dumpcart, esp. one for carrying dung. **2.** one of the carts used during the French Revolution to convey victims to the guillotine. **3.** *Obs.* a two-wheeled covered cart accompanying artillery in order to carry tools, ammunition, etc. Also, **tum′bril.** [ME *tumberell,* t. ML: s. *tumberellus,* ult. der. OLG *tumben* fall, c. OE *tumbian* dance. Cf. TUMBLE]

tu·me·fa·cient (tū′mə fā′shənt, tōō′-), *adj.* tumefying; swelling. [t. L: s. *tumefaciens,* ppr., tumefying]

tu·me·fac·tion (tū′mə făk′shən, tōō′-), *n.* act of making or becoming swollen or tumid. [t. L: m.s. *tumefacere*]

tu·me·fy (tū′mə fī′, tōō′-), *v.t., v.i.,* **-fied, -fying.** to make or become swollen or tumid. [t. L: m.s. *tumefacere*]

tu·mes·cent (tū měs′ənt, tōō′-), *adj.* swelling; slightly tumid. [t. L: s. *tumescens* beginning to swell] —**tu·mes′cence,** *n.*

tu·mid (tū′mĬd, tōō′-), *adj.* **1.** swollen, or affected with swelling, as a part of the body. **2.** pompous, turgid, or bombastic, as language, literary style, etc. [t. L: s. *tumidus* swollen] —**tu·mid′i·ty, tu′mid·ness,** *n.* —**tu′mid·ly,** *adv.*

tu·mor (tū′mər, tōō′-), *n.* **1.** a swollen part; a swelling or protuberance. **2.** *Pathol.* an abnormal or morbid swelling in any part of the body, esp. a more or less circumscribed morbid overgrowth of new tissue which is autonomous, differs more or less in structure from the part in which it grows, and serves no useful purpose. **3.** *Obs.* inflated or bombastic character. Also, *esp. Brit.,* **tu′mour.** [t. L: swollen state] —**tu′mor·ous,** *adj.*

tu·mu·lar (tū′myə lər, tōō′-), *adj.* of or like a tumulus or mound. [f. s. L *tumulus* mound + -AR[1]]

tu·mult (tū′mŭlt, tōō′-), *n.* **1.** the commotion or disturbance of a multitude, usually with noise; an uproar. **2.** a popular outbreak or uprising; commotion, disturbance, or violent disorder. **3.** agitation of mind; a mental or emotional disturbance: *trying to keep the schedule was only one cause of his tumult.* [ME, t. L: s. *tumultus*] —Syn. 1. See **ado.**

tu·mul·tu·ar·y (tū mŭl′chōō ĕr′Ĭ, tōō-), *adj.* **1.** tumultuous. **2.** confused; irregular.

tu·mul·tu·ous (tū mŭl′chōō əs, tōō-), *adj.* **1.** full of or marked by tumult or uproar. **2.** making a tumult; disorderly or noisy, as persons, etc. **3.** disturbed or agitated, as the mind, feelings, etc. [t. L: m.s. *tumultuōsus*] —**tu·mul′tu·ous·ly,** *adv.* —**tu·mul′tu·ous·ness,** *n.* —Ant. 3. tranquil.

tu·mu·lus (tū′myə ləs, tōō′-), *n., pl.* **-luses, -li** (-lī′). **1.** a mound or elevation of earth, etc., esp. of artificial origin and more or less antiquity. **2.** such a mound over a tomb; a barrow. [t. L: mound]

tun (tŭn), *n., v.,* **tunned, tunning.** —*n.* **1.** a large cask for holding liquids, etc., esp. wine, ale, or beer. **2.** a measure of capacity for wine, etc., usually equivalent to 252 wine gallons. —*v.t.* **3.** to put into or store in a tun or tuns. [ME and OE *tunne,* c. G *tonne*]

tu·na[1] (tōō′nə), *n.* **1.** any of various species and genera of large oceanic food and game fishes closely related to the tunny. **2.** the tunny. Also, **tuna fish.** [t. Amer. Sp., var. of Sp. *atun* (t. Ar.: m. *tun*) b. with d. *tun* tunny (g. L *thunnus,* t. Gk.: m. *thýnnos*)]

tu·na[2] (tōō′nə), *n.* **1.** any of various prickly pears, esp. the erect, treelike species, *Opuntia Tuna* and others, native in Mexico, bearing a sweet, edible fruit. **2.** the fruit. [t. Sp., t. Haitian]

tun·a·ble (tū′nə bəl, tōō′-), *adj.* **1.** capable of being tuned. **2.** in tune; harmonious; tuneful. Also, **tune-able.** —**tun′a·ble·ness,** *n.* —**tun′a·bly,** *adv.*

Tun·bridge Wells (tŭn′brĬj′), a city in SE England, in Kent: mineral springs; resort. 38,379 (1951).

tun·dra (tŭn′drə, tŏŏn′-), *n.* one of the vast, nearly level, treeless plains of the arctic regions of Europe, Asia, and North America. [t. Russ.: marshy plain]

tune (tūn, tōōn), *n., v.,* **tuned, tuning.** —*n.* **1.** a succession of musical sounds forming an air or melody, with or without the harmony accompanying it. **2.** a musical setting of a hymn or psalm, usually in four-part harmony. **3.** state of being in the proper pitch: *to be in tune.* **4.** agreement in pitch; unison; harmony. **5.** due agreement, as of radio instruments or circuits with respect to frequency. **6.** frame of mind; mood. **7.** accord. **8.** due or good condition. **9.** *Obs.* a tone or sound. —*v.t.* **10.** to adjust (a musical instrument) to a correct or given standard of pitch (often fol. by *up*). **11.** to adapt (the voice, song, etc.) to a particular tone or to the expression of a particular feeling or the like. **12.** to bring into harmony. **13.** *Poetic.* to utter, sound, or express musically. **14.** *Poetic.* to play upon (a lyre, etc.). **15.** to adapt or adjust (mechanisms, etc.) in due agreement. **16.** *Radio.* **a.** to adjust (a circuit, etc.) so as to bring it into resonance with another circuit, a given frequency, or the like. **b.** to adjust (a receiving apparatus) so as to make it in accord in frequency with a sending apparatus whose signals are to be received. **c.** to adjust a receiving apparatus so as to receive (the signals of a sending station). **17.** to put into a proper or a particular condition, mood, etc. —*v.i.* **18.** to put a musical instrument, etc., in tune (often fol. by *up*). **19.** to give forth a musical sound. **20.** to sound or be in harmony. **21. tune in,** to adjust a radio so as to receive signals. **22. tune out,** to adjust a radio so as to avoid the signals of a sending station. [ME; unexplained var. of TONE]

tune·a·ble (tū′nə bəl), *adj.* tunable.

tune·ful (tūn′fəl, tōōn′-), *adj.* **1.** full of melody; melodious: *tuneful compositions.* **2.** producing musical sounds or melody. —**tune′ful·ly,** *adv.* —**tune′ful·ness,** *n.*

tune·less (tūn′lĭs, tōōn′-), *adj.* **1.** unmelodious; unmusical. **2.** making or giving no music; silent: *in the corner stood a tuneless old piano.* —**tune′less·ly,** *adv.*

tun·er (tū′nər, tōō′-), *n.* **1.** one who or that which tunes. **2.** a radio receiver producing an output suitable for feeding into an amplifier instead of a loudspeaker.

tune-up (tūn′ŭp′, tōōn′-), *n.* a routine check or adjustment of working order or condition: *a motor tune-up.*

tung oil (tŭng), a drying oil, a valuable ingredient of varnishes, originally obtained from the seeds of a euphorbiaceous tree, *Aleurites Fordii*, grown in China but now produced extensively in southern U.S. [t. Chinese: m. *t′ung*]

tung·state (tŭng′stāt), *n.* a salt of any tungstic acid.

tung·sten (tŭng′stən), *n.* *Chem.* a rare metallic element having a bright-gray color, a metallic luster, and a high melting point (3370°): found in wolframite, tungstite, and other minerals, and used to make high-speed steel cutting tools, for making electric-lamp filaments, etc. *Symbol:* W (for *wolframium*); *at. wt.:* 183.92; *at. no.:* 74; *sp. gr.:* 19.3. [t. Sw.: heavy stone] —**tung·sten·ic** (tŭng stĕn′ĭk), *adj.*

tungsten lamp, an incandescent electric lamp in which the filament is made of tungsten.

tungsten steel, a hard special steel containing tungsten.

tung·stic (tŭng′stĭk), *adj.* of or containing tungsten, esp. in the pentavalent state (W+⁵) or in the hexavalent state (W+⁶).

tungstic acid, *Chem.* **1.** a hydrate of tungsten trioxide, $H_2WO_4 \cdot H_2O$, used in the manufacture of tungsten-lamp filaments. **2.** any of a group of acids derived from tungsten by polymerization of tungsten trioxide.

tung·stite (tŭng′stīt), *n.* native tungsten trioxide, WO_3, a yellow or yellowish-green mineral occurring usually in a pulverulent form.

Tung·ting (dŏŏng′tĭng′), *n.* a shallow lake in S China, in Hunan province. ab. 2000 sq. mi.

Tun·gus (tŏŏn gŏŏz′), *n., pl.* -**guses,** -**gus.** **1.** a member of the Tunguses. **2.** a language of Siberia and Manchuria of the Tungusic family.

Tun·gus·es (tŏŏn gŏŏz′ĭz), *n. pl.* a group of tribes, of whom the Manchus became most important, Mongolian in descent and Tungusic in speech, living in Siberia east of the Yenisei and in the Amur basin, formerly also in Manchuria.

Tun·gus·ic (tŏŏn gŏŏz′ĭk), *n.* **1.** a family of languages spoken in central and eastern Siberia and Manchuria, including Tungus and Manchu, and perhaps related to the Turkic and Mongolian families. —*adj.* **2.** belonging to or pertaining to the Tunguses or to Tungusic.

Tun·gus·ka (tŏŏn gŏŏs′kä), *n.* any of three tributaries of the Yenisei river in the central Soviet Union in Asia, the **Lower, Upper,** and **Stony Tunguska** rivers.

tu·nic (tū′nĭk, tōō′-), *n.* **1.** *Chiefly Brit.* a coat worn as part of a military or other uniform, called in the U.S. a *blouse.* **2.** a garment like a shirt or gown, worn by both sexes among the ancient Greeks and Romans. **3.** a woman's garment, either loose or close-fitting, extending more or less below the waist and over the skirt. **4.** *Eccles.* a tunicle. **5.** *Anat., Zool.* **a.** any covering or investing membrane or part, as of an organ. **b.** any loose membranous skin not formed from the epidermis. **6.** *Bot.* a natural integument. [OE *tunice*, t. L: m. *tunica*]

tu·ni·ca (tū′nə kə), *n., pl.* -**cae** (-sē′). *Anat., Zool., Bot.* a tunic. [t. NL, special use of L *tunica* tunic]

Tu·ni·ca·ta (tū′nə kā′tə, tōō′-), *n. pl.* a group of marine animals related to the vertebrates, having a saclike body enclosed in a thick membrane (tunic) from which protrude two openings or siphons for the ingress and egress of water; sea squirts.

tu·ni·cate (tū′nə kĭt, -kāt′, tōō′-), *adj.* Also, **tu′ni·cat′ed. 1.** invested with or having a tunic or covering: used esp. in reference to the tunicates. **2.** *Bot.* having, or consisting of, a series of concentric layers, as a bulb. —*n.* **3.** *Zool.* one of any of the *Tunicata*, or *Ascidia*. [t. L: m.s. *tunicātus*, pp., clothed with a tunic]

tu·ni·cle (tū′nə kəl, tōō′-), *n.* *Eccles.* a vestment worn over the alb by subdeacons, as at the celebration of the Mass, and by bishops. [ME, t. L: m. *tunicula*, dim. of *tunica* tunic]

tuning fork, a small steel instrument consisting of two prongs on a stem, designed to produce, when struck, a pure musical tone of a definite, constant pitch, and thus serving as a standard for tuning musical instruments, in acoustical investigation, etc.

Tu·nis (tū′nĭs, tōō′-), *n.* **1.** the capital of Tunisia, in the NE part. 410,000 (prelim. 1956). **2.** one of the former Barbary States in N Africa, notorious for its pirates: modern Tunisia.

Tuning fork

Tu·ni·sia (tū nĭsh′ə, tōō-), *n.* a republic in N Africa on the Mediterranean; a French protectorate until 1956. 3,782,480 pop. (prelim. 1956); 48,330 sq. mi. *Cap.:* Tunis. Also, **Tunis.** —**Tu·ni′sian,** *adj., n.*

tun·nage (tŭn′ĭj), *n.* tonnage.

tun·nel (tŭn′əl), *n., v.,* -**neled, -neling,** or (*esp. Brit.*) -**nelled, -nelling.** —*n.* **1.** a subterranean passage. **2.** a roadway, as for a railroad, etc., beneath the streets of a city, through a hill or mountain, or under a harbor, bay, river, or stream. **3.** any of various underground passages, such as an approximately horizontal passage in a mine. **4.** the burrow of an animal. **5.** *Dial.* a funnel. **6.** *Obs.* the flue of a chimney. —*v.t.* **7.** to make or form a tunnel through or under. **8.** to make or form as or like a tunnel: *to tunnel a passage under a river.* **9.** to perforate as with tunnels. —*v.i.* **10.** to make a tunnel or tunnels: *to tunnel through the Alps.* [late ME *tonel* funnel-shaped net. Cf. OF *tonel* cask, der. *tonne* TON] —**tun′nel·er;** *esp. Brit.,* **tun′nel·ler,** *n.*

tun·ny (tŭn′ĭ), *n., pl.* -**nies,** (*esp. collectively*) -**ny. 1.** any of a number of widely distributed, important, marine food fishes, genus *Thunnus*, of the mackerel family, esp. *T. thynnus*, occurring in the warmer parts of the Atlantic and Pacific oceans, sometimes reaching a weight of 750 pounds or more. **2.** any of various related scombroid fishes, as the albacore, *Germo alalunga* (the **long-finned tunny**). [t. F: m. *thon*, t. Pr.: m. *ton*, g. L *thunnus*, t. Gk.: m. *thŷnnos*]

tu·pe·lo (tōō′pə lō′), *n., pl.* -**los. 1.** any of several trees of the cornaceous genus *Nyssa*, esp. **a.** the black gum, *N. sylvatica*, a large North American tree. **b.** a large tree, *N. aquatica*, of deep swamps and river bottoms of the southern U.S. **2.** the strong, tough wood of any of these trees, esp. in commercial use. [t. Amer. Ind.]

Tu·pi (tōō pē′), *n., pl.* -**pis.** a member of a tribe, or of a widespread group of tribes, of South American Indians, forming a distinct linguistic stock, living along the lower Amazon, along the Brazilian coast, and through Brazil into Paraguay. —**Tu·pi′an,** *adj.*

tup·pence (tŭp′əns), *n.* *Brit.* twopence.

Tu·pun·ga·to (tōō′pŏŏng gä′tô), *n.* a mountain in the Andes, between Argentina and Chile. ab. 22,000 ft.

tuque (tūk, tōōk), *n.* a kind of knitted cap worn in Canada. [t. Canadian F, var. of F *toque* cap]

tu quo·que (tū kwō′kwĭ, tōō), *Latin.* thou, too; you're another: a retort accusing of a similar crime an opponent who has brought charges against one.

Tu·ra·ni·an (tyŏŏ rā′nĭ ən, tōō-), *adj.* **1.** belonging or pertaining to a group of Asiatic peoples or languages comprising all or nearly all those which are neither Indo-European nor Semitic. **2.** *Obs.* Ural-Altaic. —*n.* **3.** a member of any of the races speaking a Turanian (esp. a Ural-Altaic) language. **4.** a member of any of the Ural-Altaic races. [f. Pers. *Turān*, name of district beyond the Oxus + -IAN]

tur·ban (tûr′bən), *n.* **1.** a form of headdress of Mohammedan origin worn by men of Eastern nations, consisting of a scarf of silk, linen, cotton, or the like, wound directly around the head or around a cap. **2.** some headdress resembling this. **3.** a small hat, either brimless or with the brim turned up close against the crown, worn by women and children. [earlier *turband*, t. Turk.: m. *tülbend*, t. Ar.: m. *dulband*, t. Pers., Hind.] —**tur′baned,** *adj.* —**tur′ban·less,** *adj.* —**tur′ban·like′,** *adj.*

tur·ba·ry (tûr′bə rĭ), *n., pl.* -**ries. 1.** land, or a piece of land, where turf or peat may be dug or cut. **2.** *Law.* the right to cut turf or peat on a common or another person's land. [ME *turbarye*, t. ML: m. *turbaria*, der. *turba* TURF]

Oriental turban

tur·bel·lar·i·an (tûr′bə lâr′ĭ ən), *adj.* **1.** belonging to the Turbellaria, a class of platyhelminths or flatworms, mostly aquatic, and characterized by cilia whose motions produce small currents or vortexes in water. —*n.* **2.** a turbellarian platyhelminth. [der. NL *Turbellāria*, f. s. L *turbella* little crowd + -*āria*, neut. pl. of -*ārius*-ARY¹]

tur·bid (tûr′bĭd), *adj.* **1.** (of liquids) opaque or muddy with particles of extraneous matter. **2.** not clear or transparent; thick, as smoke or clouds; dense. **3.** disturbed; confused; muddled. [t. L: s. *turbidus* disturbed] —**tur·bid′i·ty, tur′bid·ness,** *n.* —**tur′bid·ly,** *adv.*

tur·bi·dim·e·ter (tûr′bĭ dĭm′ə tər), a device for measuring the turbidity of water or other liquids.

tur·bi·nal (tûr′bə nəl), *adj.* **1.** turbinate. —*n.* **2.** *Anat.* a turbinate bone. [f. s. L *turbo* top + -AL¹]

tur·bi·nate (tûr'bə nĭt, -nāt'), *adj.* Also, **tur'bi·nat'ed. 1.** scroll-like; whorled; spiral. **2.** *Anat.* noting or pertaining to certain scroll-like spongy bones of the nasal passages in the higher vertebrates. See diag. under **mouth. 3.** inversely conical. —*n.* **4.** a turbinate shell. **5.** *Anat.* a turbinate bone. [t. L: m.s. *turbinātus* shaped like a top]

tur·bi·na·tion (tûr'bə nā'shən), *n.* a turbinate formation.

tur·bine (tûr'bĭn, -bīn), *n.* **1.** any of a class of hydraulic motors in which a vaned wheel or runner is made to revolve by the impingement of a free jet of fluid (**impulse turbine** or **action turbine**) or by the passage of fluid which completely fills the motor (**pressure turbine** or **reaction turbine**). **2.** any of certain analogous motors using other fluids, as steam (**steam turbine**), products of combustion (**gas turbine**), or air (**air turbine**). [t. F, t. L: m.s. *turbo* anything that spins]

tur·bit (tûr'bĭt), *n.* one of a breed of domestic pigeons with a stout, roundish body, a short head and beak, and a ruffled breast and neck. [appar. der. L *turbo* a top; so called because of its figure]

tur·bo·jet (tûr'bə jĕt'), *n.* a jet-propulsion engine in which air is compressed by a turbine-driven compressor.

tur·bo·prop (tûr'bə prŏp'), *n.* **1.** a propellor driven by a turbojet. **2.** a turbojet with such a propellor.

tur·bot (tûr'bət), *n., pl.* **-bot, -bots. 1.** a European flatfish, *Psetta maxima*, with diamond-shaped body. **2.** any of several other flatfishes. **3.** a triggerfish. [ME, t. MD (cf. OF *torbout*); orig. uncert.]

tur·bu·lence (tûr'byə ləns), *n.* **1.** a turbulent state. **2.** *Hydraulics.* the haphazard secondary motion due to eddies within a moving fluid. **3.** *Meteorol.* irregular motion of the atmosphere, as that indicated by gusts and lulls in the wind. Also, **tur'bu·len·cy.**

tur·bu·lent (tûr'byə lənt), *adj.* **1.** disposed or given to disturbances, disorder, or insubordination. **2.** marked by or showing a spirit of disorder or insubordination: *a turbulent period.* **3.** disturbed; tumultuous. [t. L: s. *turbulentus* restless] —**tur'bu·lent·ly,** *adv.*

Tur·co (tûr'kō), *n., pl.* **-cos.** a native of Algeria serving in the light infantry of the French army.

Turco-, a word element meaning "Turkish." [t. F, t. It.]

Tur·co·man (tûr'kə mən), *n., pl.* **-mans.** Turkoman.

tur·di·form (tûr'də fôrm'), *adj.* having the form of a thrush. [t. NL: s. *turdiformis*, f. s. L *turdus* thrush + -(i)*formis*-(I)FORM]

tur·dine (tûr'dĭn, -dĭn), *adj.* belonging or pertaining to the thrushes, birds of the family *Turdidae*. [f. s. L *turdus* thrush + -INE¹]

tu·reen (tŏŏ rēn', tyŏŏ-), *n.* a large deep dish with a cover, for holding soup, etc., at table. [earlier *terrine*, t. F: earthenware dish, ult. der. L *terra* earth]

Tu·renne (ty rĕn'), *n.* Henri de la Tour d'Auvergne de (än rē' də lä tŏŏr' dō vĕrn'y də), 1611–75, French general and marshal.

turf (tûrf), *n., pl.* **turfs,** (*Archaic*) **turves** (tûrvz); *v.* —*n.* **1.** the covering of grass, etc., with its matted roots, forming the surface of grassland. **2.** *Chiefly Brit.* a piece cut or torn from the surface of grassland, with the grass, etc., growing on it; a sod. **3. the turf, a.** the grassy course or other track over which horse races are run. **b.** the practice or institution of racing horses. **4.** a block or piece of peat dug for fuel. **5.** peat as a substance for fuel. —*v.t.* **6.** to cover with turf or sod. [ME and OE, c. G *torf* peat; Latinized, *turba*] —**turf'less,** *adj.* —**turf'like',** *adj.*

turf·man (tûrf'mən), *n., pl.* **-men.** a man interested in horse racing.

turf·y (tûr'fĭ), *adj.,* **turfier, turfiest. 1.** covered with or consisting of grassy turf. **2.** turflike. **3.** abounding in, or of the nature of, turf or peat. **4.** pertaining to or characteristic of horse racing. —**turf'i·ness,** *n.*

Tur·ge·nev (tŏŏr gā'nyĕf), *n.* **Ivan Sergeevich** (Ĭ vän' sĕr gā'ə vĭch), 1818–83, Russian novelist.

tur·gent (tûr'jənt), *adj. Obs.* swelling; swollen; turgid. [t. L: s. *turgens*, ppr., swelling] —**tur'gent·ly,** *adv.*

tur·ges·cent (tûr jĕs'ənt), *adj.* becoming swollen; swelling. [t. L: s. *turgescens*, ppr.] —**tur·ges'cence, tur·ges'cen·cy,** *n.*

tur·gid (tûr'jĭd), *adj.* **1.** swollen; distended; tumid. **2.** pompous or bombastic, as language, style, etc. [t. L: s. *turgidus*] —**tur·gid'i·ty, tur'gid·ness,** *n.* —**tur'gid·ly,** *adv.*

tur·gite (tûr'jīt), *n.* an iron ore, a hydrated ferric oxide, related to limonite but containing less water. [named after *Turginak* mine in Soviet Union. See -ITE¹]

tur·gor (tûr'gər), *n.* **1.** state of being swelled or filled out. **2.** *Plant Physiol.* the normal distention or rigidity of plant cells, resulting from the pressure exerted from within against the cell walls by the cell contents. [t. L, der. *turgēre* swell]

Tur·got (tyr gō'), *n.* **Anne Robert Jacques** (än rô bĕr' zhäk), 1727–81, French statesman, financier, and economist.

Tu·rin (tyŏŏr'ĭn, tyŏŏ rĭn'), *n.* a city in NW Italy, on the Po: capital of the Kingdom of Italy, 1860–65. 783,000 (est. 1954). Italian, **Torino.**

Turk (tûrk), *n.* **1.** a native or inhabitant of Turkey, esp. a Mohammedan. **2.** a member of the dominant race in Turkey. **3.** Turkish. **4.** Turkic. **5.** one of a

breed of horses allied to the Arabian. **6.** any Turkish horse. [ME, ult. t. Pers.]

Turk., 1. Turkey. **2.** Turkish.

Tur·ke·stan (tûr'kĭ stän', -stän'), *n.* a vast region in W and central Asia, E of the Caspian Sea, including **Eastern** or **Chinese Turkestan** (the S and central part of Sinkiang province, China), **Russian Turkestan** (now the Kazak, Kirghiz, Tadzhik, Turkmen, and Uzbek republics of the Soviet Union), and a N strip of Afghanistan. Also, **Turkistan.**

tur·key (tûr'kĭ), *n., pl.* **-keys. 1.** either of two large American gallinaceous birds constituting the genus *Meleagris*, esp. *M. gallopavo*, which is domesticated in most parts of the world, and esteemed for eating. **2.** any of various more or less similar birds. **3.** *Obs.* a guinea fowl. [short for *Turkey cock* and *Turkey hen* cock and hen of Turkey, first applied to guinea fowl, later (by confusion) to the American bird]

Tur·key (tûr'kĭ), *n.* a republic in W Asia and SE Europe. 24,111,778 (prelim. 1955); 296,184 sq. mi. (286,-928 sq. mi. in Asia; 9257 sq. mi. in Europe). *Cap.*: Ankara. See **Ottoman Empire.**

turkey buzzard, a vulture, *Cathartes aura*, common in South and Central America and the southern U.S., having a bare reddish head and a dark plumage.

turkey cock, 1. the male of the turkey. **2.** a strutting, pompous, conceited person.

Turkey red, 1. a bright red produced in fabrics by madder or alizarin. **2.** cotton cloth of this color.

turkey trot, a round dance, danced by couples, properly to ragtime, the step being a springy walk with little or no bending of the knees, and accompanied by a swinging motion of the body with shoulder movements up and down.

Tur·ki (tŏŏr'kē), *n.* **1.** Turkic. —*adj.* **2.** pertaining or belonging to the peoples speaking Turkic. [t. Pers.]

Tur·kic (tûr'kĭk), *n.* a family of languages that includes Turkish, Azerbaijanian, Turkmen, Uzbeg, Kirghiz, and Yakut, perhaps related to the Tungusic and Mongolian families.

Turk·ish (tûr'kĭsh), *adj.* **1.** pertaining or belonging to or derived from the Turks or Turkey. **2.** of or pertaining to the language of the Turks. —*n.* **3.** the language of Turkey; Ottoman Turkish. **4.** Turkic.

Turkish bath, a kind of bath introduced from the East, in which, after copious perspiration in a heated room, the body is soaped, washed, massaged, etc.

Turkish delight, a cubed, gelatin-stiffened candy covered with sugar. Also, **Turkish paste.**

Turkish Empire, Ottoman Empire.

Turkish pound, the Turkish lira, a gold coin which has the symbol £T.

Turkish towel, a thick cotton towel with a long nap usually composed of uncut loops. Also, **turkish towel.**

Turk·ism (tûrk'ĭzəm), *n.* the culture, beliefs, principles, etc., of the Turks.

Tur·ki·stan (tûr'kĭ stän', -stän'), *n.* Turkestan.

Turk·man (tûrk'mən), *n., pl.* **-men.** one of the peoples of the Turkmen Soviet Socialist Republic. —**Turk·me·ni·an** (tûrk mē'nĭ ən), *adj.*

Turk·men (tûrk'mĕn), *n.* a Turkic language spoken east of the Caspian Sea.

Turk·men Soviet Socialist Republic (tûrk'mĕn; *Russ.* tŏŏrk mĕn'), a constituent republic of the Soviet Union, bordering the Caspian Sea, Iran, and Afghanistan. 1,400,000 (est. 1956); 187,100 sq. mi. *Cap.*: Ashkhabad. Also, **Turk·o·men** (tûrk'ə mĕn) or **Turk·men·i·stan** (tûrk'mĕn I stän'; *Russ.* tŏŏrk mĕn I stän').

Turko-, var. of Turco-.

Tur·ko·man (tûr'kə mən), *n., pl.* **-mans. 1.** a member of a Turkish people consisting of a group of tribes which inhabit the region about the Aral Sea and parts of Iran and Afghanistan. **2.** Turkmen. Also, **Turcoman.** [t. Pers.: m. *Turkumān* one resembling a Turk]

Turks and Cai·cos Islands (tûrks; kī'kōs), two groups of islands in the SE part of the Bahama Islands: a dependency of Jamaica. 7000 (est. 1953); ab. 166 sq. mi. *Cap.*: Grand Turk.

Turk's-cap lily (tûrks'kăp'), either of two lilies, *Lilium Martagon* and *L. superbum*, having nodding flowers with the perianth segments strongly revolute.

Turk's-head (tûrks'hĕd'), *n. Naut.* a form of knot made by weaving turns of small cord round a larger rope.

Tur·ku (tŏŏr'kŏŏ), *n.* a seaport in SW Finland. 106,755 (est. 1953). Swedish, **Abo.**

tur·ma·line (tûr'mə lēn'), *m.* tourmaline.

tur·mer·ic (tûr'mər ĭk), *n.* **1.** the aromatic rhizome of *Curcuma longa*, an East Indian zingiberaceous plant. **2.** a powder prepared from it, used as a condiment (esp. in curry powder), a yellow dye, a medicine, etc. **3.** the plant itself. **4.** any of various similar substances or plants. [earlier *tarmaret*, t. ML: m. *terra merita*, lit., deserving earth]

turmeric paper, paper treated with turmeric: used to indicate the presence of alkalis, which turn it brown, or of boric acid, which turns it reddish-brown.

tur·moil (tûr′moil), *n.* **1.** a state of commotion or disturbance; tumult; agitation; disquiet. **2.** *Obs.* harassing labor. [appar. f. TURN + MOIL] —**Syn. 1.** See *agitation.*

turn (tûrn), *v.t.* **1.** to cause to move round on an axis or about a center; rotate: *to turn a wheel.* **2.** to cause to move round or partly round, as for the purpose of opening, closing, tightening, etc.: *to turn a key.* **3.** to reverse the position or posture of: *to turn a page.* **4.** to bring the under parts of (sod, soil, etc.) to the surface, as in plowing. **5.** to change the position of, by or as by rotating; to move into a different position. **6.** to change or reverse the course of; to divert; deflect. **7.** to change or alter the nature, character, or appearance of. **8.** to change or convert (fol. by *into* or *to*): *to turn water into ice.* **9.** to render or make by some change. **10.** to change the color of (leaves, etc.). **11.** to cause to become sour, ferment, or the like: *warm weather turns milk.* **12.** to cause (the stomach) to reject food or anything swallowed. **13.** to change from one language or form of expression to another. **14.** to put or apply to some use or purpose: *to turn a thing to good use.* **15.** to go or pass round or to the other side of: *to turn a street corner.* **16.** to get beyond or pass (a certain age, time, amount, etc.): *a man just turning thirty-three.* **17.** to direct, aim, or set going toward or away from a specified person or thing, or in a specified direction: *to turn toward the north.* **18.** to direct (the eyes, face, etc.) another way; to avert (the eyes, face, etc.). **19.** to shape (a piece of metal, etc.) into rounded form with a cutting instrument while rotating in a lathe. **20.** to bring into a rounded or curved form in any way. **21.** to shape artistically or gracefully, esp. in rounded form. **22.** to form or express gracefully: *to turn a sentence.* **23.** to direct (thought, desire, etc.) toward or away from something. **24.** to cause to go; send; drive: *to turn a person from one's door.* **25.** to revolve in the mind (often with *over*). **26.** to maintain a steady flow or circulation of (money or articles of commerce). **27.** to reverse (a garment, etc.) so that the inner side becomes the outer. **28.** to remake (a garment) by putting the inner side outward. **29.** to curve, bend, or twist. **30.** to bend back or blunt (the edge of a knife, etc.). **31.** to execute, as a somersault, by rotating or revolving. **32.** to disturb the mental balance of, or make mad, distract, or infatuate. **33.** *Obs.* to convert. **34.** *Obs.* to pervert.

—*v.i.* **35.** to move round on an axis or about a center; rotate. **36.** to move partly round in this manner, as a door on a hinge. **37.** to direct the face or gaze, or the course, toward or away from something, or in a particular direction. **38.** to direct one's thought, attention, desire, etc., toward or away from something. **39.** to hinge or depend (fol. by *on* or *upon*): *the question turns on this point.* **40.** to change or reverse the course so as to go in a different or the opposite direction: *to turn to the right.* **41.** to change position so as to face in a different or the opposite direction. **42.** to change or reverse position or posture as by a rotary motion. **43.** to shift the body about as if on an axis: *to turn on one's side in sleeping.* **44.** to assume a curved form; bend. **45.** to be affected with nausea, as the stomach. **46.** to have a sensation as of whirling, or be affected with giddiness, as the head. **47.** to adopt a different religion, manner of life, etc. **48.** to change one's position in order to resist or attack: *the worm will turn.* **49.** to take up an attitude or policy of hostility or opposition: *to turn against a person.* **50.** to change or alter, as in nature, character, or appearance. **51.** to become sour, fermented, or the like, as milk, etc. **52.** to become of a different color, as leaves, etc. **53.** to be changed, transformed, or converted (fol. by *into* or *to*). **54.** to change so as to be; become: *to turn pale.* **55.** to put about or tack, as a ship. **56.** *Archaic.* go over or desert, as to another side or party. **57.** Some special verb phrases are:

turn down, *Slang.* **1.** to refuse the request, offer, etc., of (a person, etc.). **2.** to refuse or reject (a request, etc.).

turn in, *Colloq.* to go to bed.

turn off, **1.** to stop the flow of (water, gas, etc.), as by closing a stopcock. **2.** to put out (a light). **3.** to deflect or divert.

turn on, **1.** to bring on the flow of (water, gas, etc.), as by opening a stopcock. **2.** to put on (a light).

turn one's hand to, to turn one's energies to; set to work at.

turn out, **1.** to extinguish or put out (a light, etc.). **2.** to produce as the result of labor, etc. **3.** to drive out; send away, dismiss, or discharge. **4.** to equip; fit out. **5.** to result or issue. **6.** to come to be; become ultimately. **7.** to be found or known; prove.

turn over, *Com.* **1.** to invest or get back again (capital) in some transaction or in the course of business. **2.** to purchase and then sell (goods or commodities) in some transaction or in the course of business. **3.** to do business, or sell goods, to the amount (a sum specified).

turn up, **1.** to fold up or over, esp. so as to shorten, as a garment. **2.** to make one's or its appearance.

—*n.* **58.** a movement of rotation, whether total or partial: *a slight turn of the handle.* **59.** act of changing or reversing position or posture as by a rotary movement: *a turn of the dice.* **60.** the time for action or proceeding which comes in due rotation or order to each of a num-

ber of persons, etc.: *it's my turn to pay.* **61.** act of changing or reversing the course: *to make a turn to the right.* **62.** a place or point at which such a change occurs. **63.** a place where a road, river, or the like turns. **64.** a single revolution, as of a wheel. **65.** act of turning so as to face or go in a different direction. **66.** direction, drift, or trend: *the conversation took an interesting turn.* **67.** change or a change in nature, character, condition, circumstances, etc. **68.** the point or time of change. **69.** the time during which a workman or a set of workmen is at work in alternation with others. **70.** that which is done by each of a number of persons acting in rotation or succession. **71.** rounded or curved form in general. **72.** shape, form, or mold. **73.** a passing or twisting of one thing round another, as of a rope round a mast. **74.** the condition or manner of being twisted. **75.** a single round, as of a wound or coiled rope. **76.** style, as of expression or language. **77.** a distinctive form or style imparted: *a happy turn of expression.* **78.** a short walk, ride, or the like which includes a going and a returning, esp. by different routes. **79.** natural inclination, bent, tendency, or aptitude. **80.** a spell or piece of work. **81.** a spell or bout of action. **82.** an attack of illness or the like. **83.** an act of service or disservice (with *good, bad, kind,* etc.). **84.** requirement, exigency, or need: *this will serve your turn.* **85.** *Colloq.* a nervous shock, as from fright or astonishment. **86.** *Exchanges.* a completed securities transaction which includes both a purchase and sale. **87.** *Music.* a melodic embellishment or grace, commonly consisting of a principal tone with two auxiliary tones, one above and the other below it. **88.** *Chiefly Brit.* an individual performance, as in a variety entertainment. **89.** *Mil.* a drill movement by which a formation changes fronts. **90.** *Obs.* a contest or round; a bout. **91. by turns,** one after another, alternately or in rotation. **92. in turn,** in due order of succession. **93. to a turn,** to just the proper degree.
[ME; OE *turnian,* t. L: m. *tornāre* turn (in a lathe)]
—**Syn. 35.** TURN, REVOLVE, ROTATE, SPIN indicate moving in a more or less rotary, circular fashion. TURN is the general and popular word for motion on an axis or around a center, but it is used also of motion less than a complete circle: *a gate turns on its hinges.* REVOLVE refers esp. to movement in an orbit around a center, but is sometimes exchangeable with ROTATE, which refers only to the motion of a body round its own center or axis: *the moon revolves about the earth, the earth revolves (or rotates) on its axis.* To SPIN is to rotate very rapidly: *the blades of an electric fan spin.* **79.** TURN, CAST, TWIST are colloquial in use and imply a bent, inclination, or habit. TURN means a tendency or inclination for something: *a turn for art.* CAST means an established habit of thought, a mold, a style: *a melancholy cast.* TWIST means a bias: *a twist for conservatism, against liquor.*

turn·a·bout (tûrn′ə·bout′), *n.* **1.** act of turning in a different or opposite direction. **2.** a change of opinion, loyalty, etc. **3.** *U.S.* a merry-go-round.

turn·buck·le (tûrn′bŭk′əl), *n.* a link or sleeve with a swivel at one end and an internal screw thread at the other, or with an internal screw thread at each end, used as a means of uniting or coupling, and of tightening, two parts, as the ends of two rods.

Open turnbuckle

turn·coat (tûrn′kōt′), *n.* one who changes his party or principles; a renegade.

turn·down (tûrn′doun′), *adj.* that is or may be turned down; folded or doubled down: *a turndown collar.*

turned comma, *Print.* inverted comma.

turn·er¹ (tûr′nər), *n.* **1.** one who or that which turns. **2.** one who fashions objects on a lathe. [ME, f. TURN + -ER¹]

turn·er² (tûr′nər, tŏŏr′-), *n.* **1.** a tumbler; gymnast. **2.** a member of any of the gymnastic societies common among the Germans. [t. G: gymnast, der. *turnen* to exercise, t. F: m. *tourner* turn]

Tur·ner (tûr′nər), *n.* **1.** Frederick Jackson, 1861–1932, U.S. historian. **2.** Joseph Mallord (or Mallad) William (măl′ərd or măl′əd), 1775–1851, British painter.

turn·er·y (tûr′nə·rĭ), *n.* **1.** the art or work of a turner; the forming of objects on a lathe. **2.** articles fashioned on a lathe.

turn·hall (tûrn′hôl′), *n.* a hall or building in which turners or gymnasts practice or perform. [t. G: m. *turnhalle,* f. *turn(en)* practice gymnastics + *halle* hall]

turn·ing (tûr′nĭng), *n.* **1.** act of one who or that which turns (in any sense). **2.** a place or point where anything turns. **3.** the forming of objects on a lathe. **4.** shaping or forming: *the turning of verses.*

turning point, 1. a point at which something turns. **2.** a point at which a decisive change takes place; a critical point; a crisis. **3.** *Survey.* a point on which a foresight and a backsight are taken in direct leveling.

tur·nip (tûr′nəp), *n.* **1.** the thick, fleshy edible root of the cruciferous plant *Brassica Rapa,* the common white turnip, or of *Brassica Napoprassica,* the Swedish turnip or rutabaga. **2.** the plant itself. **3.** the root of this plant used as a vegetable. [earlier *turnepe,* f. TURN (with reference to its neatly rounded shape) + ME *nepe* NEEP] —**tur′nip·like′,** *adj.*

tur·nix (tûr′nĭks), *n.* any of the small, three-toed, quaillike birds constituting the genus *Turnix,* inhabiting the warmer parts of the Old World. [t. NL, aphetic var. of L *coturnix* quail]

turn·key (tûrn'kē'), *n.*, *pl.* **-keys.** one who has charge of the keys of a prison; a prison keeper.

turn·out (tûrn'out'), *n.* **1.** the body of persons who come to an assemblage, muster, spectacle, or the like. **2.** the quantity produced; output. **3.** act of turning out. **4.** the manner or style in which anything is turned out or equipped; getup. **5.** an equipment or outfit. **6.** a short side track or passage which enables vehicles, etc., to pass one another. **7.** *Brit.* **a.** a strike (def. 60). **b.** a striker (def. 2).

turn·o·ver (tûrn'ō'vər), *n.* **1.** act of turning over; upset. **2.** its result. **3.** the conversion of something to a different use. **4.** change from one position, tenancy, or the like to another. **5.** the aggregate of worker replacements in a given period in a given business or industry. **6.** the ratio of the labor turnover to the average number of employees in a given period. **7.** the number of times that capital is invested and reinvested in a line of merchandise during a specified period of time. **8.** the turning over of the capital or stock of goods involved in a particular transaction or course of business (see **turn over** under **turn**, def. 57). **9.** the total amount of business done in a given time. **10.** a small semicircular pie made by folding one half the crust upon the other. —*adj.* **11.** turned over; that may be turned over. **12.** having a part that turns over, as a collar.

turn·pike (tûrn'pīk'), *n.* a barrier set across a road (**turnpike road**) to stop passage until toll is paid; a tollgate.

turn·plate (tûrn'plāt'), *n.* *Brit.* a railroad turntable.

turn·spit (tûrn'spĭt'), *n.* **1.** a person or dog that turns a roasting spit. **2.** a dog of a breed with long body and short legs and resembling the dachshund.

turn·stile (tûrn'stīl'), *n.* **1.** a structure of two horizontal crossed bars on a post, set in a gateway or opening to prevent the passage of cattle, horses, etc., but permitting that of persons. **2.** some similar device set up in an entrance to bar passage until a charge is paid, to record the number of persons passing through, etc.

turn·stone (tûrn'stōn'), *n.* any of the small, migratory, limicoline shore birds constituting the genus *Arenaria*, notable for their habit of turning over stones in search of food, esp. *A. interpres*, common in both Old and New Worlds.

turn·ta·ble (tûrn'tā'bəl), *n.* **1.** *Railroads.* a rotating, track-bearing platform pivoted in the center, used for turning locomotives and cars around. **2.** the rotating disk bearing the record in a phonograph.

turn·up (tûrn'ŭp'), *n.* **1.** that which is turned up or which turns up. **2.** *Brit.* a cuff (on trousers). **3.** *Colloq.* a fight, row, or disturbance. —*adj.* **4.** that is or may be turned up.

Turn·ver·ein (tŏŏrn'fĕr ĭn'), *n.* *German.* a club of turners or gymnasts. [G: f. *turn(en)* practice gymnastics + *verein* union]

tur·pen·tine (tûr'pən tīn'), *n.*, *v.*, **-tined, -tining.** —*n.* **1.** an oleoresin exuding from the terebinth, *Pistacia Terebinthus*. **2.** any of various oleoresins derived from coniferous trees, esp. the longleaf pine, *Pinus palustris*, and yielding a volatile oil and a resin when distilled. **3.** oil of turpentine. —*v.t.* **4.** to treat with turpentine; apply turpentine to. **5.** to gather or take crude turpentine from (trees). [ME *ter(e)bentyn(e)*, t. L: m. *terebinthina*, t. Gk.: m. *terebinthinē*]

tur·peth (tûr'pĭth), *n.* **1.** a drug obtained from the roots of a convolvulaceous plant, *Operculina turpethum*, of the East Indies, formerly used as a purgative. **2.** the plant itself. **3.** its root. [t. ML: s. *turpethum*; r. ME *turbit*, t. ML: m. *turbith(um)*, t. Ar.: m. *turbid*]

tur·pi·tude (tûr'pə tūd', -tōōd'), *n.* **1.** shameful depravity. **2.** a depraved or shameful act. [t. L: m. *turpitūdo* baseness]

tur·quoise (tûr'koiz, -kwoiz), *n.* **1.** a sky-blue or greenish-blue compact opaque mineral, essentially a hydrous phosphate of aluminum containing a little copper and iron, much used in jewelry. **2.** Also, **turquoise blue.** blue-green; bluish green. [t. F: Turkish (stone), der. *Turc* Turk; r. ME *turkeis*, t. OF]

tur·ret (tûr'ĭt), *n.* **1.** a small tower, usually one forming part of a larger structure. **2.** a small tower at an angle of a building, frequently beginning some distance above the ground. **3.** Also, **tur'ret·head'.** a pivoted attachment on a lathe, etc., for holding a number of tools, each of which can be presented to the work in rapid succession by a simple rotating movement. **4.** *Naval, Mil.* a low, towerlike, heavily armored structure, usually revolving horizontally, within which guns are mounted. **5.** *Fort.* a tall structure, usually moved on wheels, formerly employed in breaching or scaling a fortified place, a wall, or the like. [ME *turet*, t. OF: m. *touret* dim. of *tour* TOWER] —**tur'ret·less,** *adj.*

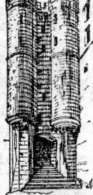

Turrets (def. 2), 13th century

tur·ret·ed (tûr'ĭt ĭd), *adj.* **1.** furnished with a turret or turrets. **2.** having a turretlike part or parts. **3.** *Zool.* having whorls in the form of a long or towering spiral, as certain shells.

Turreted shell

tur·ret lathe, a lathe fitted with a turret (def. 3).

turri-, a word element meaning "tower." [t. L, comb form of *turris*]

tur·ri·cal (tûr'ə kəl), *adj.* pertaining to or resembling a turret or turrets.

tur·ric·u·late (tə rĭk'yə lĭt, -lāt'), *adj.* furnished with or resembling a turret or turrets. [f. s. L *turricula* little tower + -ATE¹]

tur·tle¹ (tûr'təl), *n.*, *v.*, **-tled, -tling.** —*n.* **1.** any of the *Chelonia*, an order or group of reptiles having the body enclosed in a shell consisting of a carapace and a plastron, from between which the head, tail, and four legs protrude. **2.** a marine species of turtle, as distinguished from fresh-water and terrestrial tortoises. —*v.i.* **3.** to catch turtles, esp. as a business. [t. Sp.: m. *tortuga* (g. LL *tortūca*, der. *tortus* twisted), influenced by TURTLE²]

tur·tle² (tûr'təl), *n.* *Archaic.* a turtledove. [ME and OE, var. of *turtur*, t. L]

tur·tle·back (tûr'təl băk'), *n.* **1.** Also, **tur'tle·deck'.** an arched protection erected over the deck of a steamer at the bow, and often at the stern also, to guard against damage from heavy seas. **2.** *Archaeol.* a rude stone implement having one or both faces slightly convex.

tur·tle·dove (tûr'təl dŭv'), *n.* **1.** a small, slender Old World dove, *Streptopelia turtur*, having a long, graduated tail which is conspicuous in flight. **2.** *U.S. Dial.* the mourning dove.

tur·tle·head (tûr'təl hĕd'), *n.* any of the North American herbs constituting the scrophulariaceous genus *Chelone*.

turves (tûrvz), *n.* *Archaic.* pl. of **turf.**

Tus·ca·loo·sa (tŭs'kə lōō'sə), *n.* a city in W Alabama. 63,370 (1960).

Tus·can (tŭs'kən), *adj.* **1.** of or pertaining to Tuscany. **2.** *Archit.* noting or pertaining to a classical (Roman or Renaissance) order of architecture distinguished by a plain (not fluted) column, ring-shaped capital, and a frieze resembling the Doric. —*n.* **3.** the standard literary Italian. **4.** any Italian dialect of Tuscany. **5.** a native of Tuscany.

Tus·ca·ny (tŭs'kə nĭ), *n.* a department in W central Italy: formerly a grand duchy. 3,209,000 pop. (est. 1954); 8879 sq. mi. Italian, **Toscana.**

Tus·ca·ro·ra (tŭs'kə rôr'ə), *n.*, *pl.* **-ra, -ras.** **1.** (*pl.*) a tribe of Indians once living in North Carolina, but, on admission to the Iroquois confederacy, living mainly in New York. **2.** a member of this tribe.

Tus·cu·lum (tŭs'kyə ləm), *n.* an ancient city of Latium, SE of Rome: Roman villas.

tush¹ (tŭsh), *interj.* **1.** an exclamation expressing impatience, contempt, etc. —*n.* **2.** an exclamation of "tush."

tush² (tŭsh), *n.* **1.** one of the four canine teeth of the horse. **2.** tusk. [ME; OE *tusc.* See TUSK]

tusk (tŭsk), *n.* **1.** (in certain animals) a tooth developed to great length, usually as one of a pair, as in the elephant, walrus, wild boar, etc., but singly in the narwhal. **2.** a long, pointed, or protruding tooth. **3.** a projecting part resembling the tusk of an animal. —*v.t.*, *v.i.* **4.** to dig, tear, or gore with the tusks or tusk. [ME *tuske*, metathetic var. of ME and OE *tux*, metathetic var. of OE *tusc*; prob. akin to TOOTH] —**tusked** (tŭskt), *adj.* —**tusk'-less,** *adj.* —**tusk'like',** *adj.*

Tusks of Atlantic walrus

Tus·ke·gee (tŭs kē'gĭ), *n.* a city in E Alabama: Tuskegee Institute here. 1,750 (1960).

tusk·er (tŭs'kər), *n.* an animal with tusks, as an elephant or a wild boar.

tus·sah (tŭs'ə), *n.* a silk from India (called shantung in China) of a tan color, obtained from the cocoon of various undomesticated Asiatic silkworms (*Antheraea mylitta*, etc.). [earlier *tusser*, t. Hind.: m. *tasar* shuttle]

tus·sal (tŭs'əl), *adj.* pertaining to tussis or cough. [f. s. L *tussis* cough + -AL¹]

tus·sis (tŭs'ĭs), *n.* *Pathol.* a cough. [t: L]

tus·sive (tŭs'ĭv), *adj.* of or pertaining to a cough.

tus·sle (tŭs'əl), *v.*, **-sled, -sling,** *n.* —*v.i.* **1.** to struggle or fight roughly or vigorously; wrestle; scuffle. —*n.* **2.** a rough struggle as in fighting or wrestling; a scuffle. **3.** any vigorous conflict or contest. [var. of TOUSLE]

tus·sock (tŭs'ək), *n.* *Chiefly Brit.; Literary in U.S.* a tuft or clump of growing grass or the like. [appar. akin to MHG *zūsach* thicket, *zūse* lock (of hair), brushwood. See TOUSLE, -OCK]

tussock moth, any of various dull-colored moths (family *Lymantriidae*), whose larvae are notorious pests of broad-leaved trees, as the gypsy moth and brown-tail moth.

tus·sock·y (tŭs'ək ĭ), *adj.* *Chiefly Brit.; Literary in U.S.* **1.** abounding in tussocks. **2.** forming tussocks.

tut (tŭt; *or clicked* t'), *interj.* **1.** an exclamation expressing impatience, contempt, etc. —*n.* **2.** an exclamation of "tut!"

Tut·ankh·a·men (to͞ot′ängk ä′mĭn), n. 14th century B.C., king of Egypt, of 18th dynasty (tomb discovered in 1922).

tu·te·lage (tū′tə lĭj, to͞o′-), n. 1. the office or function of a guardian; guardianship. 2. instruction. 3. state of being under a guardian or a tutor. [f. s. L *tūtēla* watching + -AGE]

tu·te·lar·y (tū′tə lĕr′ĭ, to͞o′-), adj. 1. having the position of guardian or protector of a person, place, or thing: *tutelary saint.* 2. of guardianship or a guardian. Also, **tu·te·lar** (tū′tə lər, to͞o′-). [t. L: m.s. *tūtēlārius* guardian]

tu·tor (tū′tər, to͞o′-), n. 1. one employed to instruct another in some branch or branches of learning, esp. a private instructor. 2. a teacher of academic rank lower than instructor in some American universities and colleges. 3. a teacher without institutional connection who assists students to prepare for examinations. 4. one of a class of officers in a university or college, esp. at Oxford and Cambridge, having immediate supervision, in studies or otherwise, of undergraduates assigned to them. 5. *Civil, Roman, and Scot. Law.* the guardian of a boy or girl below age of puberty or majority. —*v.t.* 6. to act as a tutor to; teach or instruct, esp. privately. 7. to train, school, or discipline. 8. to admonish or reprove. 9. to have the guardianship or care of. —*v.i.* 10. to act as a tutor or private instructor. 11. to study under a tutor. [ME, t. L: protector] —**tu′tor·less,** adj. —**tu′tor·ship′,** n.

tu·tor·age (tū′tər ĭj, to͞o′-), n. 1. the office, authority, or care of a tutor; instruction. 2. the charge for instruction by a tutor.

tu·to·ri·al (tū tôr′ĭ əl, to͞o-), adj. pertaining to or exercised by a tutor: *tutorial functions or authority.*

tutorial system, a system of education, esp. in some colleges, in which instruction is given personally by tutors, who also act as general supervisors of a small group of students in their charge.

tut·ti (to͞o′tĭ; It. to͞ot′tē), adj., n., pl. -tis. *Music.* —*adj.* 1. all; all the voices or instruments together (used as a direction). 2. intended for or performed by all (or most of) the voices or instruments together, as a passage or movement in concerted music (opposed to *solo*). —*n.* 3. a tutti passage or movement. 4. the tonal product or effect of tutti performance. [It., pl. of *tutto* TUTTO]

tut·ti-frut·ti (to͞o′tĭ fro͞o′tĭ), n. 1. a preserve of chopped mixed fruits, often with brandy syrup. 2. a variety of fruits (usually candied and minced), used in ice cream, confections, etc. [t. It., lit., all fruits]

tut·to (to͞ot′tō), adj. *Music.* all; entire; the whole (used as a direction in music). [It., t. OF: m. *tout*]

tut·ty (tŭt′ĭ), n. an impure oxide of zinc obtained from the flues of smelting furnaces, or a similar substance occurring as a native mineral, used chiefly as a polishing powder. [ME *tutie*, t, ML: m. *tūtia*, t. Ar.: m. *tūtiyā* oxide of zinc, ? t. Pers.]

tu·tu (ty ty′), n. *French.* a short, full, ballet skirt, usually made of several layers of tarlatan.

Tu·tu·i·la (to͞o′to͞o ē′lä), n. the largest of the islands of American Samoa: excellent harbor at Pago Pago. 15,000 pop. (1950); 53 sq. mi.

tu-whit (to͞o hwĭt′), n., v., -whitted. -whitting. —*n.* 1. a word imitative of the cry of the owl. —*v.i.* 2. to cry or hoot as an owl.

tux·e·do (tŭk sē′dō), n., pl. -dos. U.S. 1. a tailless coat, usually dark, for semiformal wear by men. 2. the complete suit, including the coat. Also, **Tuxedo.** [short for *Tuxedo coat*, named after country club at *Tuxedo* Park, N.Y.]

tu·yère (twē yâr′, twĭr; Fr. tr yĕr′), n. *Metall.* an opening through which the blast of air enters a blast furnace, cupola forge, or the like, to facilitate combustion. [t. F, der. *tuyau* pipe, of Gmc. orig.]

TV, television.

TVA, Tennessee Valley Authority.

Tver (tvĕr), n. former name of **Kalinin** (def. 2).

twad·dle (twŏd′əl), v., -dled, -dling, n. —*v.i.* 1. to talk in a trivial, feeble, silly, or tedious manner; prate. —*v.t.* 2. to utter as twaddle. —*n.* 3. trivial, feeble, silly, or tedious talk or writing. [var. of *twattle*, b. TWIDDLE and TATTLE] —**twad′dler,** n.

twain (twān), adj., n. *Archaic.* two. [ME *twayn*, OE *twēgen*, c. G (obs.) *zween*]

Twain (twān), n. **Mark,** (*Samuel Langhorne Clemens*) 1835-1910, U.S. author and humorist.

twang (twăng), v.i. 1. to give out a sharp, ringing sound, as the string of a musical instrument when plucked. 2. to have a sharp, nasal tone, as the human voice. —*v.t.* 3. to cause to make a sharp, ringing sound, as a string of a musical instrument. 4. to utter or pronounce with a sharp, nasal tone. 5. to sound forth with a twang. —*n.* 6. the sharp, ringing sound produced by plucking or suddenly releasing a tense string. 7. a sound resembling this. 8. a sharp, nasal tone, as of the human voice. [imit.] —**twang′y,** adj.

'twas (twŏz, twŭz; *unstressed* twəz), contr. of *it was.*

tway·blade (twā′blād′), n. any of various orchidaceous plants, esp. of the genera *Listera, Ophrys,* or *Liparis,* characterized by two nearly opposite broad leaves. [f. *tway* (ME *twey,* OE *twēge* TWO) + BLADE]

tweak (twēk), v.t. 1. to seize and pull with a sharp jerk and twist: *to tweak someone's ear.* —*n.* 2. an act of tweaking; a sharp pull and twist. [OE *twiccian* (inferred

from *twiccere,* n.), var. of *twiccian* catch hold of, pluck, gather. See TWITCH] —**tweak′y,** adj.

tweed (twēd), n. 1. a coarse wool cloth in a variety of weaves and colors, either hand-spun and hand-woven in Scotland, or reproduced, often by machine elsewhere. 2. (pl.) garments that are made of this fabric. [appar. back formation from Scot. *tweedling* twilling (now obs.), of unexplained orig.]

Tweed (twēd), n. **William Marcy,** ("*Boss Tweed*") 1823-78, U.S. politician: headed the **Tweed Ring,** a group of Tammany politicians who got control of the financial affairs of New York City about 1870 and misappropriated millions of dollars.

Tweed (twēd), n. a river flowing from S Scotland along a part of the NE boundary of England into the North Sea. 97 mi.

Tweed·dale (twēd′dāl′), n. Peebles.

Twee·dle·dum and Twee·dle·dee (twē′dəl dŭm′, twē′dəl dē′), any two persons, things, etc., nominally different but practically the same. [humorous imit. coinage, appar. first applied as nicknames to Handel and Bononcini, with reference to their musical rivalry]

'tween (twēn), prep. *Poetic.* between.

tweet (twēt), n. 1. the weak chirp of a young or small bird. —*v.i.* 2. to utter a tweet or tweets. [imit.]

tweet·er (twē′tər), n. a small loudspeaker designed for the reproduction of high-frequency sounds.

tweet·er-woof·er (twē′tər wo͞of′ər), n. a loudspeaker, usually coaxial, in which the tweeter is mounted in and in front of the cone of the woofer.

tweez·ers (twē′zərz), n.pl. small pincers or nippers for plucking out hairs, taking up small objects, etc. [pl. of *tweezer,* f. *tweeze* case, receptacle (see ETUI) + -ER[1]]

twelfth (twĕlfth), adj. 1. next after the eleventh. 2. being one of twelve equal parts. —*n.* 3. a twelfth part, esp. of one (¹/₁₂). 4. the twelfth one of a series. [ME; OE *twelfth,* c. G *zwölf*]

Twelfth-day (twĕlfth′dā′), n. the twelfth day after Christmas, Jan. 6, on which the festival of the Epiphany is celebrated, formerly observed as the last day of the Christmas festivities.

Twelfth-night (twĕlfth′nīt′), n. 1. the evening before Twelfth-day, formerly observed with various festivities. 2. the evening of Twelfth-day itself.

Twelfth Night, a comedy (1602) by Shakespeare.

Twelfth·tide (twĕlfth′tīd′), n. the season of Twelfth-night and Twelfth-day.

twelve (twĕlv), n. 1. a cardinal number, ten plus two. 2. a symbol for this number, as 12 or XII. 3. a set of this many persons or things. 4. **the Twelve,** the twelve apostles chosen by Christ. —*adj.* 5. amounting to twelve in number. [ME; OE *twelf,* c. G *zwölf*]

twelve·mo (twĕlv′mō), n., pl. -mos, adj. duodecimo.

twelve·month (twĕlv′mŭnth′), n. *Chiefly Brit.* a year.

Twelve Tables, the, the tablets on which were engraved short statements of Roman law most important in the affairs of daily life, drawn up by the decemvirs in 451 and 450 B.C.

twelve-tone system (twĕlv′tōn′), *Music.* a modern system of tone relationships in which the twelve tones of an octave are not centered around any one tone, but are unified by a selected order of tones for a given composition.

twen·ti·eth (twĕn′tĭ ĭth), adj. 1. next after the nineteenth. 2. being one of twenty equal parts. —*n.* 3. a twentieth part, esp. of one (¹/₂₀). 4. the twentieth member of a series.

twen·ty (twĕn′tĭ), n., pl. -ties, adj. —*n.* 1. a cardinal number, ten times two. 2. a symbol for this number, as 20 or XX. 3. a set of this many persons or things. —*adj.* 4. amounting to twenty in number. [ME; OE *twēntig,* akin to G *zwanzig*]

twen·ty-one (twĕn′tĭ wŭn′), n. a gambling game at cards, in which the object is to obtain from the dealer cards whose pips add up to (or close to) twenty-one without exceeding it.

'twere (twûr; *unstressed* twər), contraction of *it were.*

twi-, a word element meaning "two" or "twice," as in *twibill.* [ME and OE, c. G *zwei-,* L *bi-.* See TWO]

twi-bill (twī′bĭl′), n. 1. a mattock with one arm like that of an adz and the other like that of an ax. 2. *Archaic.* a double-bladed battle-ax. [ME and OE. See TWI-, BILL[3]]

twice (twīs), adv. 1. two times, as in succession: *write twice a week.* 2. on two occasions; in two instances. 3. in twofold quantity or degree; doubly: *twice as much.* [ME *twies,* f. *twie* twice (OE *twiga*) + -s, adv. gen. suffix]

twice-laid (twīs′lād′), adj. 1. made from strands of used rope. 2. made from makeshift or used material.

twice-told (twīs′tōld′), adj. told twice; told before.

Twick·en·ham (twĭk′ən əm), n. a city in SE England, on the Thames, near London. 105,645 (1951).

twid·dle (twĭd′əl), v., -dled, -dling, n. —*v.t.* 1. to turn round and round, esp. with the fingers. 2. **twiddle one's thumbs** or **fingers, a.** to keep turning one's thumbs or fingers idly about each other. **b.** to do nothing; be idle. —*v.i.* 3. to play with something idly, as by touching or handling. 4. to turn round and round; twirl. —*n.* 5. act of twiddling; a twirl. [b. TWITCH and FIDDLE] —**twid′dler,** n.

twig[1] (twĭg), *n.* **1.** a slender shoot of a tree or other plant. **2.** a small offshoot from a branch or stem. **3.** a small dry, woody piece fallen from a branch: *a fire of twigs.* **4.** *Anat.* one of the minute branches of a blood vessel or nerve. [ME and OE *twigge,* akin to G *zweig* branch] —**twig′less,** *adj.* —**twig′like′,** *adj.*

twig[2] (twĭg), *v.,* **twigged, twigging.** *Brit. Slang.* —*v.t.* **1.** to look at; observe. **2.** to catch sight of; perceive. **3.** to understand. —*v.i.* **4.** to understand. [orig. uncert.]

twig·gy (twĭg′ĭ), *adj.* **1.** abounding in twigs. **2.** consisting of twigs. **3.** twiglike.

twi·light (twī′līt′), *n.* **1.** the light from the sky when the sun is below the horizon, esp. in the evening. **2.** the time during which this light prevails. **3.** a condition or period preceding or succeeding full development, glory, etc. —*adj.* **4.** pertaining to or resembling twilight: *the twilight hour.* **5.** crepuscular, as a bat or moth. [ME, TWI- + LIGHT[1]; c. G *zwielicht*] —**twi′light′less,** *adj.*

Twilight of the Gods, Ragnarok.

twilight sleep, *Med.* a state of semiconsciousness usually produced by hypodermic injections of scopolamine and morphine, in order to effect relatively painless childbirth. [trans. of G *dämmerschlaf*]

twill (twĭl), *n.* **1.** a fabric woven with the weft threads so crossing the warp as to produce an effect of parallel diagonal lines, as in serge. **2.** the characteristic weave of such fabrics. —*v.t.* **3.** to weave in the manner of a twill. **4.** to weave in twill construction. [Scot. and North. E var. of *twilly,* ME *twyle,* OE *twili(c),* half trans. half adoption of L *bilīc(em)* having double thread (acc. sing. of unrecorded *bilix*). See TWI-]

'twill (twĭl), contraction of *it will.*

twin (twĭn), *n., adj., v.,* **twinned, twinning.** —*n.* **1.** (*pl.*) two children or animals brought forth at a birth. **2.** one of two such children or animals. **3.** (*pl.*) two persons or things closely related or connected or closely resembling each other. **4.** either of two such persons or things. **5.** *Crystall.* a compound crystal, consisting of two or more parts or crystals definitely oriented each to the other. **6. Twins,** *Astron.* the zodiacal constellation or sign Gemini. —*adj.* **7.** being two, or one of two, children or animals born at the same birth: *twin sisters.* **8.** being two persons or things closely related or associated or much alike; forming a pair or couple. **9.** being one of two such persons or things; forming one of a couple or pair: *a twin peak.* **10.** consisting of two similar parts or elements joined or connected: *a twin vase.* **11.** *Bot., Zool.* occurring in pairs; didymous. **12.** *Crystall.* of the nature of a twin (def. 5). **13.** *Obs.* twofold or double. —*v.t.* **14.** to conceive or bring forth as twins. **15.** to pair or couple. **16.** to furnish a counterpart to. **17.** *Crystall.* to form into a twin. —*v.i.* **18.** to bring forth twins. **19.** to be twinborn. **20.** to be paired or coupled. [ME; OE (ge)*twinn,* c. Icel. *twinnr* double]

twin·ber·ry (twĭn′bĕr′ĭ), *n., pl.* **-ries.** **1.** the partridgeberry, *Mitchella repens.* **2.** a North American honeysuckle shrub, *Lonicera involucrata,* with involucrate flowers of various colors.

twin·born (twĭn′bôrn′), *adj.* born at the same birth.

Twin Cities, Minneapolis and St. Paul (situated on opposite sides of the Mississippi river in Minnesota).

twine (twīn), *n., v.,* **twined, twining.** —*n.* **1.** a strong thread or string composed of two or more strands twisted together. **2.** act of twining. **3.** state of being twined. **4.** a twined or twisted thing or part; a fold, convolution, or coil. **5.** a twist or turn. **6.** a knot or tangle. —*v.t.* **7.** to twist together; interwind; intertwine. **8.** to form by or as by twisting strands: *to twine a wreath.* **9.** to twist (one strand, thread, or thing) with another. **10.** to bring by or as by twisting or winding (fol. by *in, into,* etc.). **11.** to put or dispose by or as by winding (fol. by *about, around,* etc.). **12.** to encircle or wreathe with something wound about. **13.** to enfold. —*v.i.* **14.** to become twined or twisted together, as two things, or as one thing with another. **15.** to wind itself (fol. by *about, around,* etc.). **16.** to wind in a sinuous or meandering course. **17.** (of plants, stems, etc.) to grow in convolutions about a support. [ME; OE, c. D *twijn*] —**twin′er,** *n.*

twin·flow·er (twĭn′flou′ər), *n.* a slender, creeping, evergreen caprifoliaceous plant, *Linnaea borealis,* of Europe, or the American variety or species, *L. americana,* with pink or purplish nodding flowers borne in pairs on threadlike peduncles.

twinge (twĭnj), *n., v.,* **twinged, twinging.** —*n.* **1.** a sudden, sharp pain (in body or mind): *a twinge of rheumatism, a twinge of remorse.* —*v.t.* **2.** to affect with sudden, sharp pain or pains (in body or mind). **3.** to give (a person, etc.) a twinge or twinges. —*v.i.* **4.** to have or feel a twinge or twinges. [ME *twenge,* OE *twengan* pinch]

twi-night (twī′nīt′), *adj.* (of a baseball doubleheader) continuing from the late afternoon into the evening.

twink (twĭngk), *n., v.i.* **1.** wink. **2.** twinkle. [ME *twinken,* c. G *zwinken* wink; akin to TWINKLE]

twin·kle (twĭng′kəl), *v.,* **-kled, -kling,** *n.* —*v.i.* **1.** to shine with slight, quick gleams of light, as stars, distant lights, etc. **2.** to sparkle in the light. **3.** (of the eyes) to be bright with amusement, pleasure, etc. **4.** to appear or move as if with little flashes of light. **5.** *Archaic.* to wink; blink. —*v.t.* **6.** to emit (light) in little gleams or flashes. **7.** *Archaic.* to wink (the eyes, etc.). —*n.* **8.** a twinkling with light. **9.** a twinkling brightness in the eyes. **10.** the time required for a wink; twinkling. **11.** a wink of the eye. [ME; OE *twinclian*] —**twin′kler,** *n.*

twin·kling (twĭng′klĭng), *n.* **1.** act of shining with little gleams of light. **2.** the time required for a wink; an instant. **3.** *Archaic.* winking; a wink.

twin-leaf (twĭn′lēf′), *n., pl.* **-leaves.** a berberidaceous plant, *Jeffersonia diphylla,* of the eastern U.S., with solitary white flowers, and leaves divided into pairs.

twinned (twĭnd), *adj.* **1.** born as twins or as a twin. **2.** paired or coupled. **3.** united or combined. **4.** having the nature of a twin.

twin·ning (twĭn′ĭng), *n.* **1.** the bearing of twins. **2.** coupling; union. **3.** *Crystall.* the union of crystals to form a twin (def. 5).

twin-screw (twĭn′skrōō′), *adj.* *Naut.* (of a vessel) having two screw propellers, which usually revolve in opposite directions.

twirl (twûrl), *v.t.* **1.** to cause to rotate rapidly; spin; whirl; swing circularly. **2.** to twiddle: *to twirl my thumbs.* **3.** to wind idly, as about something. **4.** *Baseball.* to pitch (a game, etc.). —*v.i.* **5.** to rotate rapidly; whirl. **6.** to turn quickly so as to face or point another way. **7.** *Baseball.* to pitch. —*n.* **8.** a twirling or a being twirled; a spin; a whirl; a twist. **9.** something twirled; curl; convolution. [b. TWIST and WHIRL]

twirl·er (twûr′lər), *n.* **1.** one who or that which twirls. **2.** *Colloq.* a baseball pitcher.

twist (twĭst), *v.t.* **1.** to combine, as two or more strands or threads, by winding together; intertwine. **2.** to combine or associate intimately. **3.** to form by or as by winding strands together. **4.** to entwine (one thing) with or in another; wind or twine (something) about a thing. **5.** to encircle (a thing) with something wound about. **6.** to alter in shape, as by turning the ends in opposite directions, so that parts previously in the same straight line and plane are located in a spiral curve. **7.** to wring out of shape or place; contort or distort. **8.** to wrest from the proper form or meaning; pervert. **9.** to form into a coil, knot, or the like by winding, rolling, etc.: *to twist the hair into a knot.* **10.** to bend tortuously. **11.** to cause to move with a rotary motion, as a ball pitched in a curve. **12.** to turn in another direction. —*v.i.* **13.** to twist something. **14.** to make movements serving to twist something. **15.** to be or become intertwined. **16.** to wind or twine about something. **17.** to writhe or squirm. **18.** to take a spiral form or course; wind, curve, or bend. **19.** to turn or rotate, as on an axis; revolve, as about something. **20.** to turn so as to face in another direction. **21.** to change shape with a spiral or screwing movement of parts. **22.** to move with a progressive rotary motion, as a ball pitched in a curve. —*n.* **23.** a curve, bend, or turn. **24.** a turning or rotating as on an axis; rotary motion; spin. **25.** anything formed by or as by twisting or twining parts together. **26.** act or the manner of twisting strands together, as in thread, yarn, or rope. **27.** a wrench. **28.** a twisting awry. **29.** a wresting or perverting, as of meaning. **30.** spiral disposition, arrangement, or form. **31.** spiral movement or course. **32.** an irregular bend; a crook or kink. **33.** a peculiar turn, bent, bias, or the like, as in the mind or nature. **34.** the altering of the shape of anything by or as by turning the ends in opposite directions. **35.** the stress causing this alteration. **36.** the resulting state. **37.** *Baseball, Cricket, etc.,* **a.** a spin given to a ball in pitching, etc. **b.** a ball having such a spin. **38.** a twisting or torsional action, force, or stress. **39.** a kind of strong twisted silk thread, heavier than ordinary sewing silk, used for working buttonholes and for other purposes. **40.** a direction of twisting in weaving yarns, as S twist (left-hand twist), Z twist (right-hand twist). **41.** a loaf or roll of dough twisted and baked. **42.** a kind of tobacco manufactured in the form of a rope or thick cord. **43.** the degree of spiral formed by the grooves in a rifled firearm or cannon. **44.** a vigorous dance performed by couples and characterized by strongly rhythmic gyrations of the torso and flailings of the arms and legs in time to heavily accented music. [ME *twiste* divide, *twist* divided object, rope, OE *-twist,* c. D *twisten* quarrel. See TWI-]

twist drill, *Mach.* a drill with one or more deep spiral grooves in the body.

twist·er (twĭs′tər), *n.* **1.** one who or that which twists. **2.** a ball pitched or moving with a spinning motion. **3.** *U.S.* a whirlwind or tornado.

twit (twĭt), *v.,* **twitted, twitting,** *n.* —*v.t.* **1.** to taunt, gibe at, or banter by references to anything embarrassing. **2.** to reproach or upbraid. —*n.* **3.** act of twitting. **4.** a derisive reproach; taunt; gibe. [aphetic var. of obs. *atwite,* ME *atwiten,* OE *ætwītan* taunt, f. *æt-* AT + *wītan* blame] —**twit′ter,** *n.*

twitch (twĭch), *v.t.* **1.** to give a short, sudden pull or tug at; jerk. **2.** to pull or draw with a hasty jerk. **3.** to move (a part of the body) with a jerk. **4.** to pinch and pull sharply; nip. —*v.i.* **5.** to move or be moved in a quick, jerky way. **6.** to give a short, sudden pull or tug; tug (fol. by *at*). —*n.* **7.** a quick, jerky movement of the body, or of some part of it. **8.** a short, sudden pull or tug; a jerk. **9.** a twinge (of body or mind). **10.** a loop or noose, attached to a handle, for drawing tightly about the muzzle of a horse to bring him under control. [ME *twicchen,* akin to OE *twiccian* pluck]

twitch grass, couch grass; quitch.

twit·ter (twĭt′ər), *v.i.* **1.** to utter a succession of small, tremulous sounds, as a bird. **2.** to titter; giggle. **3.** to tremble with excitement and the like; be in a flutter. —*v.t.* **4.** to express or utter by twittering. —*n.* **5.** act of twittering. **6.** a twittering sound. **7.** a state of tremulous excitement. [ME *twiter,* akin to G *zwitschern*] —**twit′ter·ing·ly,** *adv.*

twit·ter·er (twĭt′ərər), *n.* **1.** a bird that twitters. **2.** a person who twitters.

twit·ter·y (twĭt′ə rĭ), *adj.* **1.** given to or characterized by twittering. **2.** tremulous; shaky.

'twixt (twĭkst), *prep. Archaic.* betwixt.

two (tōō), *n.* **1.** a cardinal number, one plus one. **2.** a symbol for this number, as 2 or II. **3.** a set of this many persons or things. **4.** a playing card, die face, etc., with two pips. **5. put two and two together,** to draw a conclusion from certain circumstances. —*adj.* **6.** amounting to two in number. [ME; OE *twā,* c. G *zwei.* Cf. L *duo,* Gk. *dýo*]

two-base hit (tōō′bās′), *Baseball.* a hit which enables a batter to reach second base without a fielder's error. Also, **two-bag·ger** (tōō′băg′ər).

two-by-four (tōō′bī fôr′), *adj.* **1.** two units thick and four units wide, esp. in inches. **2.** *U.S. Slang.* unimportant; insignificant. —*n.* **3.** a timber measuring two inches by four inches.

two-cy·cle engine (tōō′sī′kəl), an internal-combustion engine in which there is a power stroke every revolution for each cylinder.

two-edged (tōō′ějd′), *adj.* **1.** having two edges, as a sword. **2.** cutting or effective both ways.

two-faced (tōō′fāst′), *adj.* **1.** having two faces. **2.** deceitful; hypocritical. —**two-fac·ed·ly** (tōō′fā′sĭd lĭ, -fāst′lĭ), *adv.* —**two′·fac′ed·ness,** *n.*

two-fist·ed (tōō′fĭs′tĭd), *adj.* **1.** having two fists and able to use them. **2.** *U.S. Slang.* strong and vigorous.

two·fold (tōō′fōld′), *adj.* **1.** having two elements or parts. **2.** twice as great or as much; double. —*adv.* **3.** in twofold measure; doubly.

two-four (tōō′fôr′), *adj. Music.* (of a meter) characterized by two quarter notes to each measure.

Two Gentlemen of Verona, The, a comedy (before 1595) by Shakespeare.

two-hand·ed (tōō′hăn′dĭd), *adj.* **1.** having two hands. **2.** using both hands equally well; ambidextrous. **3.** involving or requiring both hands: *a two-handed sword.* **4.** requiring the hands of two persons to operate: *a two-handed saw.* **5.** engaged in by two persons: *a two-handed game.*

two-mast·er (tōō′măs′tər, -mäs′-), *n. Naut.* a vessel rigged with two masts.

two-name paper (tōō′nām′), *Banking.* commercial paper having more than one obligor, usually a maker as primary obligor and an endorser who is secondarily liable.

two-par·ty system (tōō′pär′tĭ), *Govt.* the situation of having two major political parties, more or less equal in strength.

two·pence (tŭp′əns), *n.* **1.** a sum of money of the value of two British pennies, or about 4 U.S. cents. **2.** a British copper coin of this value, issued in the reign of George III. **3.** a British silver coin of this value (since 1662 coined only as maundy money). **4.** a trifle. Also, **tuppence.**

two·pen·ny (tŭp′ən ĭ), *adj.* **1.** of the amount or value of twopence. **2.** involving an outlay of twopence. **3.** of very little value; trifling; worthless.

two-phase (tōō′fāz′), *adj. Elect.* diphase.

two-ply (tōō′plī′), *adj.* consisting of two thicknesses, layers, strands, or the like.

Two Sicilies, The. See **Sicilies, The Two.**

two·some (tōō′səm), *adj.* **1.** consisting of two. **2.** *Golf, etc.* performed or played by two persons. —*n.* **3.** two together or in company. **4.** *Golf, etc.* a match, as in golf, between two persons. [f. TWO + -SOME²]

two-step (tōō′stĕp′), *n.* **1.** a round dance in duple rhythm, characterized by sliding steps. **2.** a piece of music for, or in the rhythm of, this dance.

two-thirds rule (tōō′thûrdz′), *U.S.* a former rule in the Democratic party requiring a vote of at least two thirds of its national convention delegates to nominate a presidential candidate.

'twould (twŏŏd), contraction of *it would.*

two-way (tōō′wā′), *adj.* **1.** letting persons or vehicles go either way. **2.** having two ways or passages. **3.** *Math.* having a double mode of variation.

twp., township.

-ty¹, a suffix of numerals denoting multiples of ten, as *twenty.* [OE *-tig,* c. G *-zig*]

-ty², a suffix of nouns denoting quality, state, etc., as *unity, enmity.* [ME *-te(e),* t. OF: m. *-te, -iet,* g. s. L *-tas*]

Ty., Territory.

Ty·burn (tī′bərn), *n.* a former place of public execution in London, England.

Ty·che (tī′kĭ), *n. Gk. Mythol.* the goddess of fortune, the counterpart of the Roman Fortuna.

ty·coon (tī kōōn′), *n.* **1.** a title used to describe the shogun of Japan to foreigners from 1603 to 1867. **2.** *U.S. Colloq.* a businessman having great wealth and power. [t. Jap.: m. *taikun,* f. Chinese: *tai* great (d. var. of *ta*) + *kiun* prince]

Ty·deus (tī′dūs, tĭd′Yəs), *n. Gk. Legend.* the brother of Meleager and one of the Seven against Thebes (which see).

tyke (tīk), *n.* **1.** a cur. **2.** *Chiefly Scot.* a low contemptible fellow; a boor. **3.** *Colloq.* a mischievous or troublesome child. **4.** any small child. Also, **tike.** [ME, t. Scand.; cf. Icel. *tīk* bitch]

Ty·ler (tī′lər), *n.* **1. John,** 1790–1862, 10th president of the United States, 1841–45. **2. Moses Coit** (koit), 1835–1900, U.S. historian and educator. **3. Wat** (wŏt), (or **Walter**) died 1381, English rebel: leader of a peasant revolt. **4.** a city in E Texas. 51,230 (1960).

tym·bal (tĭm′bəl), *n.* timbal.

tym·pan (tĭm′pən), *n.* **1.** a sheet or plate of some thin material, in an apparatus. **2.** *Print.* a padlike device interposed between the platen or its equivalent and the sheet to be printed, in order to soften and equalize the pressure. **3.** *Archit.* a tympanum. [t. L: s. *tympanum,* t. Gk.: m. *týmpanon* drum]

tym·pan·ic (tĭm păn′Ĭk), *adj.* pertaining or belonging to a tympanum, esp. the tympanum of the ear.

tympanic bone, *Anat., Zool.* (in mammals) a bone of the skull, supporting the tympanic membrane and enclosing part of the tympanum or middle ear.

tympanic membrane, *Anat., Zool.* a membrane separating the tympanum or middle ear from the passage of the external ear; the eardrum. See diag. under **ear.**

tym·pa·nist (tĭm′pə nĭst), *n.* a person who plays the drums or other percussion instruments in an orchestra.

tym·pa·ni·tes (tĭm′pə nī′tēz), *n. Pathol.* distention of the abdomen caused by the presence of air or gas, as in the intestine. [t. NL, t. Gk.: pertaining to a drum] —**tym·pa·nit·ic** (tĭm′pə nĭt′Ĭk), *adj.*

tym·pa·ni·tis (tĭm′pə nī′tĭs), *n. Pathol.* inflammation of the lining membrane of the tympanum or middle ear. [f. TYMPAN(UM) + -ITIS]

tym·pa·num (tĭm′pə nəm), *n., pl.* **-nums, -na** (-nə). **1.** *Anat., Zool.* the middle ear, comprising that part of the ear situated in a recess of the temporal bone. See diag. under **ear.** **2.** the tympanic membrane. **3.** *Archit.* **a.** the recessed, usually triangular space enclosed between the horizontal and sloping cornices of a pediment, often adorned with sculpture. **b.** a similar space between an arch and the horizontal head of a door or window below. **4.** *Elect.* the diaphragm of a telephone. **5.** a drum or similar instrument. **6.** the stretched membrane forming a drumhead. [t. L, t. Gk.: m. *týmpanon* drum]

Tympanums (defs. 3a and 3b)

Tyn·dale (tĭn′dəl), *n.* **William,** c1492–1536, English religious reformer, translator of the Bible, and martyr.

Tyn·dall (tĭn′dəl), *n.* **John,** 1820–93, British physicist.

Tyn·dar·e·us (tĭn dâr′Yəs), *n. Gk. Myth.* the husband of Leda and father of Clytemnestra.

Tyne (tīn), *n.* a river in NE England, in Northumberland, flowing into the North Sea. ab. 80 mi.

Tyne·mouth (tīn′məth, tīn′-), *n.* a seaport in NE England at the mouth of the Tyne river. 67,700 (est. 1956).

typ·al (tī′pəl), *adj.* pertaining to or forming a type.

type (tīp), *n., v.,* **typed, typing.** —*n.* **1.** a kind, class, or group as distinguished by a particular character. **2.** a person or thing embodying the characteristic qualities of a kind, class, or group; a representative specimen. **3.** the general form, style, or character distinguishing a particular kind, class or group. **4.** *Biol.* **a.** the general form or plan of structure common to a group of animals, plants, etc. **b.** a genus or species which most nearly exemplifies the essential characteristics of a higher group and frequently gives the latter its name. **5.** *Agric.* **a.** the inherited features of an animal or breed favorable for any given purpose: *dairy type.* **b.** a strain, breed, or variety of animals, or a single animal, belonging to a specific kind. **6.** the pattern or model from which something is made. **7.** *Print.* **a.** a rectangular piece or block, now usually of metal, having on its upper surface a letter or character in relief. **b.** such pieces or blocks collectively. **c.** a similar piece in a typewriter or the like. **d.** such pieces collectively. **e.** a printed character or printed characters: *a headline in large type.* **8.** an image or figure produced by impressing or stamping, as the principal figure or device on either side of a coin or medal. **9.** a prefiguring symbol, as an Old Testament event prefiguring an event in the New Testament. —*v.t.* **10.** to typewrite. **11.** to reproduce in type or in print. **12.** *Med.* to ascertain the type of (a blood sample). **13.** to be a type or symbol of. **14.** to represent by a symbol; symbolize. —*v.i.* **15.** to typewrite. [late ME, t. L: m.s. *typus,* t. Gk.: m. *týpos* blow, impression]

Type (def. 7a)
A. Stem; B. Face; C. Serif; D. Hairline; E. Beard or neck; F. Shoulder; G. Body; H. Nicks; I. Pin mark; J. Groove; K. Feet

-type, a word element representing **type,** as in *prototype;* especially used of photographic processes, as in *ferrotype.*

Ty·pee (tī pē′), *n.* an account of adventures in the South Sea islands (1846) by Melville.

type founder, one engaged in the making of metallic types for printers.

type genus, *Biol.* that genus which is formally taken and held to be typical of the family or other higher group to which it belongs.

type-high (tīp′hī′), *adj. Print.* of the same height as type.

type metal, an alloy for making printing types, etc., consisting chiefly of lead and antimony, and sometimes small quantities of tin, copper, etc.

type·script (tīp′skrĭpt′), *n.* **1.** a typewritten copy of a literary composition, a document, or the like. **2.** typewritten material, as distinguished from hand-writing or print.

type·set·ter (tīp′sĕt′ər), *n.* **1.** one who sets or composes type; a compositor. **2.** a typesetting machine.

type·set·ting (tīp′sĕt′ĭng), *n.* **1.** the process or action of setting type. —*adj.* **2.** used or intended for setting type.

type species, *Biol.* that species of a genus which is regarded as the best example of the generic characters, i.e., the species from which a genus is named.

type specimen, *Biol.* an individual animal or plant from which the description of a species has been prepared.

type·write (tīp′rīt′), *v.t., v.i.,* **-wrote, -written, -writing.** to write by means of a typewriter; type.

type·writ·er (tīp′rī′tər), *n.* **1.** a machine for writing mechanically in letters and characters like those produced by printers' types. **2.** *Print.* a type style which gives the appearance of typewritten copy. **3.** a typist.

type·writ·ing (tīp′rī′tĭng), *n.* **1.** act or art of using a typewriter. **2.** work done on a typewriter.

typh·li·tis (tĭf lī′tĭs), *n. Pathol.* inflammation of the caecum. [f. Gk. *typhl(ón)* caecum + -ITIS] —**typh·lit·ic** (tĭf lĭt′ĭk), *adj.*

typh·lol·o·gy (tĭf lŏl′ə jĭ), *n.* the sum of scientific knowledge concerning blindness.

typho-, a word element representing **typhus** and **typhoid,** as in *typhogenic.*

Ty·phoe·us (tī fē′əs), *n. Gk. Myth.* a monster with a hundred serpents' heads, fiery eyes, and a terrifying voice. Zeus set him on fire with thunderbolts and flung him down into Tartarus under Mt. Etna. Cf. **Typhon.**

ty·pho·gen·ic (tī′fə jĕn′ĭk), *adj. Pathol.* producing typhus or typhoid fever.

ty·phoid (tī′foid), *n.* typhoid fever. [f. TYPH(US) + -OID] —**ty·phoi′dal,** *adj.*

typhoid bacillus, a microörganism found in the intestinal ulcers and elsewhere in the bodies of sufferers from typhoid fever.

typhoid fever, *Pathol.* an infectious, often fatal, febrile disease, usually of the summer months, characterized by intestinal inflammation and ulceration, due to the typhoid bacillus which is usually introduced with food or drink.

ty·phoi·din (tī foi′dĭn), *n. Med.* a culture of dead typhoid bacillus used by cutaneous inoculation to detect the presence of a typhoid infection.

ty·pho·ma·lar·i·al (tī′fō məlâr′ĭəl), *adj.* having the character of both typhoid fever and malaria, as a fever.

Ty·phon (tī′fŏn), *n. Class. Myth.* a monster and a son of Typhoeus: later confused with Typhoeus.

ty·phoon (tī foon′), *n.* **1.** a tropical cyclone or hurricane of the western Pacific area and the China seas. **2.** a violent storm or tempest of India. [t. Chinese: m. *tai fung* great wind; influenced by Gk. *typhôn* violent wind] —**ty·phon·ic** (tī fŏn′ĭk), *adj.*

ty·phus (tī′fəs), *n. Pathol.* an acute infectious disease characterized by great prostration, severe nervous symptoms, and a peculiar eruption of reddish spots on the body, now regarded as due to a specific microörganism transmitted by lice and fleas. Also, **typhus fever.** [t. NL, t. Gk.: m. *typhos* vapor] —**ty′phous,** *adj.*

typ·i·cal (tĭp′ə kəl), *adj.* **1.** pertaining to, of the nature of, or serving as a type or emblem; symbolic. **2.** of the nature of or serving as a type or representative specimen. **3.** conforming to the type. **4.** *Biol.* exemplifying most nearly the essential characteristics of a higher group in natural history, and forming the type: *the typical genus of a family.* **5.** pertaining or belonging to a representative specimen; characteristic or distinctive. Also, **typ′ic.** —**typ′i·cal·ly,** *adv.* —**typ′i·cal·ness,** *n.*

typ·i·fy (tĭp′ə fī′), *v.t.,* **-fied, -fying. 1.** to serve as the typical specimen of; exemplify. **2.** to serve as a symbol or emblem of; symbolize; prefigure. **3.** to represent by a type or symbol. [f. s. L *typus* TYPE + -IFY] —**typ′·i·fi·ca′tion,** *n.* —**typ′i·fi′er,** *n.*

typ·ist (tīp′ĭst), *n.* one who operates a typewriter.

typog., **1.** typographer. **2.** typography.

ty·pog·ra·pher (tī pŏg′rəfər), *n.* one skilled or engaged in typography.

ty·po·graph·i·cal (tī′pə grăf′ə kəl), *adj.* pertaining to typography: *typographical errors.* Also, **ty′po·graph′ic.** —**ty′po·graph′i·cal·ly,** *adv.*

ty·pog·ra·phy (tī pŏg′rəfĭ), *n.* **1.** the art or process of printing with types. **2.** the work of setting and arranging types and of printing from them. **3.** the general

character or appearance of printed matter. [t. NL: m.s. *typographia,* f. Gk.: *typo(s)* type + *graphia* writing]

ty·pol·o·gy (tī pŏl′ə jĭ), *n.* **1.** the doctrine or study of types or symbols, esp. those of Scripture. **2.** symbolic significance or representation.

ty·poth·e·tae (tī pŏth′ə tē′, tī′pə thē′tē), *n.pl.* printers, esp. master printers (used in the names of associations). [f. Gk. *typo(s)* type + *-thetae,* Latinized pl. of Gk. *thétēs* one who places]

Tyr (tyr), *n. Scand. Myth.* the god of war and victory, son of Odin. He is represented with one hand, the other having been bitten off by the wolf Fenrir. [Icel.]

ty·ran·ni·cal (tĭ răn′ə kəl, tī-), *adj.* arbitrary or despotic; despotically cruel or harsh; severely oppressive. Also, **ty·ran′nic.** [f. s. L *tyrannicus* (t. Gk.: m. *tyrannikós*) + -AL[1]] —**ty·ran′ni·cal·ly,** *adv.* —**ty·ran′ni·cal·ness,** *n.*

ty·ran·ni·cide[1] (tĭ răn′ə sīd′, tī-), *n.* one who kills a tyrant. [t. L: m. *tyrannicīda.* See -CIDE[1]]

ty·ran·ni·cide[2] (tĭ răn′ə sīd′, tī-), *n.* act of killing a tyrant. [t. L: m. *tyrannicīdium.* See TYRANT, -CIDE[2]]

tyr·an·nize (tĭr′ə nīz′), *v.,* **-nized, -nizing.** —*v.i.* **1.** to exercise power cruelly or oppressively. **2.** to reign as a tyrant. **3.** to rule despotically or cruelly. —*v.t.* **4.** to rule tyrannically. **5.** to act the tyrant or to govern over. Also, *esp. Brit.,* **tyr′an·nise′.** —**tyr′an·niz′er,** *n.* —**tyr′an·niz′ing·ly,** *adv.*

ty·ran·no·sau·rus (tĭ răn′ō sôr′əs), *n.* a great carnivorous dinosaur, of the genus *Tyrannosaurus,* of the later Cretaceous period in North America, which walked erect on its powerful hind limbs.

tyr·an·nous (tĭr′ə nəs), *adj.* tyrannical. —**tyr′an·nous·ly,** *adv.* —**tyr′an·nous·ness,** *n.*

tyr·an·ny (tĭr′ə nĭ), *n., pl.* **-nies. 1.** arbitrary or unrestrained exercise of power; despotic abuse of authority. **2.** the government or rule of a tyrant or absolute ruler. **3.** a state ruled by a tyrant or absolute ruler. **4.** oppressive or unjustly severe government on the part of any ruler. **5.** undue severity or harshness. **6.** a tyrannical act or proceeding. [ME *tirannie,* t. ML: m. *tyrannia,* der. *tyrannus* TYRANT]

ty·rant (tī′rənt), *n.* **1.** a king or ruler who uses his power oppressively or unjustly. **2.** an absolute ruler, as in ancient Greece, owing his office to usurpation. **3.** any person who exercises power despotically. **4.** a tyrannical or compulsory influence. [ME *tirant,* t. OF, t. L: m. *tyrannus,* t. Gk.: m. *tyrannos*]

Tyre (tīr), *n.* an ancient seaport of Phoenicia: one of the great cities of antiquity, famous for its navigators and traders.

tyre (tīr), *n., v.t.,* **tyred, tyring.** *Brit.* tire[2].

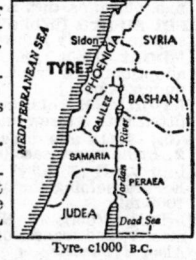
Tyre, c1000 B.C.

Tyr·i·an (tĭr′ĭ ən), *adj.* **1.** pertaining or belonging to ancient Tyre. **2.** of the color of the dye called Tyrian purple. [f. s. L *Tyrius* (t. Gk.: m. *Tyrios*) + -AN]

Tyrian purple, a highly prized purple dye of classical antiquity, orig. obtained at great expense from a certain shellfish. It was later shown to be an indigo derivative and synthesized, and it has been displaced by other synthetic dyes. Cf. **murex.** Also, **Tyrian dye.**

ty·ro (tī′rō), *n., pl.* **-ros.** a beginner in learning anything; a novice. Also, **tiro.** [t. L: m. *tiro* recruit]

Tyr·ol (tĭr′ōl; *Ger.* tē rōl′), *n.* **1.** an alpine region in W Austria and N Italy: a former Austrian crown land. **2.** a province in W Austria. 432,618 (est. 1953); 4883 sq. mi. *Cap.:* Innsbruck. Also, **Tirol.**

Tyr·o·lese (tĭr′ə lēz′, -lēs′), *adj., n., pl.* **-ese.** —*adj.* **1.** of or pertaining to the Tyrol or its inhabitants. —*n.* **2.** a native of Tyrol. Also, **Ty·ro·le·an** (tĭ rō′lĭ ən).

Ty·ro·lienne (tē rō lyĕn′), *n.* **1.** a dance of the Tyrolese peasants. **2.** a song or melody, characteristically a yodel, suitable for such a dance. [t. F, fem. of *tyrolien* pertaining to Tyrol]

Ty·rone (tĭ rōn′), *n.* a county in Northern Ireland. 132,082 (1951); 1218 sq. mi. *Co. Seat:* Omagh.

ty·ro·sin·ase (tī′rō sĭ nās′, tĭr′ō-), *n. Biochem.* an oxidizing enzyme found in plant and animal tissues which changes tyrosine into melanin and other pigments.

ty·ro·sine (tī′rə sĕn′, -sĭn, tĭr′ə-), *n. Biochem.* an amino acid, $C_9H_{11}NO_3$, resulting from the hydrolysis of proteins. [f. Gk. *tyrós* cheese + -INE[2]]

Tyr·rhe·ni·an Sea (tĭ rē′nĭ ən), a part of the Mediterranean, partially enclosed by W Italy, Corsica, Sardinia, and Sicily.

tythe (tĭth), *n., v.,* **tythed, tything.** *Brit.* tithe.

tzar (tsär), *n.* czar.

tzar·e·vich (tsär′ə vĭch), *n.* czarevitch.

tza·rev·na (zä rĕv′nə), *n.* czarevna.

tza·ri·na (tsä rē′nä), *n.* czarina.

tzar·ism (tsär′ĭzəm), *n.* czarism.

tza·rit·za (tsä rĭt′sä), *n.* a czaritza.

tzet·ze fly (tsĕt′sĭ), tsetse fly.

Tzi·ga·ny (tsĭ′gänĭ), *adj.* **1.** pertaining to the Hungarian Gypsies. —*n.* **2.** a Hungarian Gypsy. [t. Hung.]

ăct, āble, dâre, ärt; ĕbb, ēqual; ĭf, īce; hŏt, ōver, ôrder, oil, bŏŏk, ōōze, out; ŭp, ūse, ûrge; ə = a in alone; ch, chief; g, give; ng, ring; sh, shoe; th, thin; th̸, that; zh, vision. See the full key on inside cover.

U

U, u (ū), *n.*, *pl.* **U's** or **Us, u's** or **us.** the 21st letter of the English alphabet.

U (ū, ōō), *n.* a Burmese title of respect for a man (used before the proper name). [t. Burm. *u*, uncle]

U, *Chem.* uranium.

u., 1. uncle. 2. (Ger. *und*) and. 3. university. 4. upper. Also, **U.** for 1, 3.

u·a ma·u ke e·a o ka a·i·na i ka po·no (ōō'ä mä'ōō kä ā'ä ō kä ä'ē'nä' ē kä pō'nō), *Hawaiian.* the life of the land is founded in righteousness (motto of Hawaii).

UAW, United Automobile Workers.

U·ban·gi (ōō bäng'gĭ), *n.* a river forming a part of the boundary between Republic of the Congo and Republic of Congo flowing into the Congo river. ab. 700 mi. (with the Uele, ab. 1400 mi.).

U·ban·gi-Sha·ri (ōō bäng'gĭ shä'rĭ), *n.* a former overseas territory of French Equatorial Africa: now independent within the French Community. See **Central African Republic.**

u·bi·e·ty (ū bī'ĭ tĭ), *n.* the state of being in a definite place; condition with respect to place; local relation. [t. NL: m.s. *ubietas*, der. L *ubi* where]

u·biq·ui·tous (ū bĭk'wə təs), *adj.* characterized by ubiquity; being everywhere at the same time; present everywhere; omnipresent. Also, **u·biq·ui·tar·y** (ū bĭk'-wə tĕr'ĭ). [f. UBIQUIT(Y) + -OUS] —**u·biq'ui·tous·ly,** *adv.* —**u·biq'ui·tous·ness,** *n.* —Syn. See **omnipresent.**

u·biq·ui·ty (ū bĭk'wə tĭ), *n.* state or capacity of being everywhere at the same time; omnipresence. [t. NL: m.s. *ubiquitas*, der. L *ubique* everywhere]

u·bi su·pra (ū'bī sōō'prə), *Latin.* in the page or passage previously referred to. [L: where above]

U-boat (ū'bōt'), *n.* a German submarine. [t. G: half adoption, half trans. of *U-boot*, short for *unterseeboot* undersea boat]

U bolt, a bar of iron bent into the form of the letter U, fitted with a screw and nut at each end.

u.c., 1. (It. *una corda*) *Music.* "one string"; soft pedal. 2. *Print.* upper case (capital letter or letters).

U·ca·ya·li (ōō'kä yä'lĭ), *n.* a river flowing N through E Peru, joining the Marañón to form the Amazon. ab. 1000 mi.

U·dall (ū'dəl), *n.* **Nicholas,** 1505–56, English schoolmaster, and translator, wrote the first English comedy. Also, **Uvedale.**

ud·der (ŭd'ər), *n.* a mamma or mammary gland, esp. when baggy and with more than one teat, as in cows. [ME *uddre*, OE *ūder*, c. G *euter*, akin to L *ūber*] —**ud'der·less,** *adj.*

U·di·ne (ōō'dē nĕ), *n.* a city in NE Italy. 76,000 (est. 1954).

u·do (ōō'dō), *n.* a plant, *Aralia cordata,* cultivated esp. in Japan and China for its edible shoots. [t. Jap.]

u·dom·e·ter (ū dŏm'ə tər), *n.* a rain gauge; a pluviometer. [t. F: m. *udomètre,* f. s. L *ūdus* wet, damp + *-o-* (see *-o-*) + *-mètre* -METER] —**u·do·met·ric** (ū'də mĕt'rĭk), *adj.* —**u·dom'e·try,** *n.*

Ue·le (wā'lə), *n.* a river flowing from the NE Republic of the Congo W to the Ubangi river. ab. 700 mi.

U·fa (ōō fä'), *n.* a city in the E Soviet Union in Europe: the capital of Bashkir Republic. 265,000 (est. 1956).

U·gan·da (ū gän'də; ōō gän'də), *n.* an independent state in E Africa between the NE Republic of the Congo and Kenya: member of the Brit. Commonwealth; formerly a British protectorate. 6,845,000 pop. (est. 1961); 93,981 sq. mi. *Cap.*: Kampala.

ugh (ōōкн, ŭкн, ōō), *interj.* an exclamation expressing disgust, aversion, horror, or the like.

ug·li·fy (ŭg'lə fī'), *v.t.,* -**fied,** -**fying.** to make ugly. [f. UGLY + -FY] —**ug'li·fi·ca'tion,** *n.*

ug·ly (ŭg'lĭ), *adj.,* -**lier,** -**liest.** 1. repulsive or displeasing in appearance; offensive to the sense of beauty: *ugly furniture.* 2. morally revolting: *ugly sin.* 3. disagreeable; unpleasant; objectionable: *ugly tricks.* 4. of a troublesome nature; threatening disadvantage or danger: *ugly symptoms.* 5. unpleasantly or dangerously rough: *ugly weather.* 6. *U.S.* ill-natured; quarrelsome; vicious: *an ugly disposition.* [ME, t. Scand.; cf. Icel. *uggligr* fearful, dreadful] —**ug'li·ly,** *adv.* —**ug'li·ness,** *n.* —Syn. 1. ill-favored, hard-featured, uncomely, unsightly. 2. base, heinous, vile. 6. surly, spiteful.

ugly duckling, an unattractive or unpromising child who becomes a beautiful or much-admired adult.

U·gri·an (ōō'grĭ ən, ū'-), *adj.* 1. denoting or pertaining to a race or ethnological group including the Magyars and related peoples of western Siberia and the northeastern Soviet Union in Europe. —*n.* 2. a member of any of the Ugrian peoples. 3. Ugric.

U·gric (ōō'grĭk, ū'-), *n.* 1. the group of Finno-Ugric languages that consists of Hungarian and two languages spoken in western Siberia (Ostyak and Vogul). —*adj.* 2. Ugrian.

U·gro-Fin·nic (ōō'grō fĭn'ĭk, ū'grō-), *n.* Finno-Ugric.

Uh·de (ōō'də), *n.* **Fritz Karl Hermann von** (frĭtz kärl hĕr'män fən), 1848–1911, German painter.

uhf, ultra high frequency.

uh·lan (ōō'län, ū'lən), *n.* 1. one of a body of mounted soldiers first known in Europe in Poland, usually carrying lances. 2. one of such a body in the former German army, classed as heavy cavalry. Also, **ulan.** [t. G, t. Pol.: m. *ulan,* t. Turk.: m. *oghlān* boy, lad]

Uh·land (ōō'länt), *n.* **Johann Ludwig** (yō'hän lōōt'-vĭкн, lōōd'-), 1787–1862, German poet and writer.

Ui·gur (wē'gŏŏr), *n.* 1. a member of the Turkish race dominant in Mongolia and Eastern Turkestan from the 8th to the 12th century A.D. 2. a Turkic language of northwestern Mongolia. —**Ui·gu·ri·an** (wē gŏŏr'ĭ-ən), **Ui·gu'ric,** *adj.*

u·in·ta·ite (ū ĭn'tə īt'), *n.* gilsonite. Also, **u·in'tah·ite'.** [named after the UINTA Mountains. See -ITE[1]]

U·in·ta Mountains (ū ĭn'tə), a range of the Rocky Mountains in NE Utah. Highest peak (in Utah), Kings Peak, 13,498.

uit·land·er (īt'län'dər, oit'-; *Du.* œYt'län'dər), *n. South Africa.* an outlander; foreigner. [S Afr. D: outlander]

U·ji·ji (ōō jē'jĭ), *n.* a town in W Tanganyika, Africa, on Lake Tanganyika: Stanley found Livingstone here, 1871. ab. 25,000.

Uj·pest (ōō'ĭ pĕsht'), *n.* a city in N Hungary, on the Danube, part of Budapest. 68,530 (est. 1954).

U.K., United Kingdom.

u·kase (ū'kās, ū kāz'), *n.* (in Russia under the Czar) 1. an edict or order of the emperor, having the force of law. 2. any official proclamation. [t. Russ.: m. *ukaz*]

Ukr., Ukraine.

U·kraine (ū'krān, ū krān', ū krīn'), *n.* a constituent republic of the Soviet Union, in the SW part: a rich agricultural region. 40,600,000 (est. 1956); ab. 223,000 sq. mi. *Cap.*: Kiev. Official name, **Ukrainian Soviet Socialist Republic.**

U·krain·i·an (ū krā'nĭ ən, ū krī'-), *adj.* 1. of or pertaining to the Ukraine. —*n.* 2. a native or inhabitant of the Ukraine. 3. a Slavic language closely related to Russian.

u·ku·le·le (ū'kə lā'lĭ; *Hawaiian* ōō'kŏŏ lā'-lā), *n.* a small musical instrument of the guitar kind with a long neck, much used in the Hawaiian Islands. [t. Hawaiian: lit., flea]

u·lan (ōō'län, ū'lən), *n.* uhlan.

U·lan Ba·tor (ōō'län bä'tôr), the capital of the Mongolian People's Republic in E central Asia: former holy city of the Mongols. 100,000 (est. 1954). Formerly, **Urga.**

U·lan U·de (ōō'län ōō'dĕ), a city in the S Soviet Union in Asia, near Lake Baikal. 157,000 est. 1956).

ul·cer (ŭl'sər), *n.* 1. *Pathol.* a sore open either to the surface of the body or to a natural cavity, and accompanied by the disintegration of tissue and the formation of pus, etc. 2. a moral blemish. 3. a corrupting influence. [ME, t. L: s. *ulcus,* akin to Gk. *hélkos*]

Ukulele

ul·cer·ate (ŭl'sə rāt'), *v.t., v.i.,* -**ated,** -**ating.** to affect or be affected with an ulcer; make or become ulcerous. [ME, t. L: m.s. *ulcerātus,* pp.] —**ul'cer·a'tion,** *n.*

ul·cer·a·tive (ŭl'sə rā'tĭv), *adj.* 1. causing ulceration. 2. of the nature of or characterized by ulceration.

ul·cer·ous (ŭl'sər əs), *adj.* 1. of the nature of an ulcer or ulcers; characterized by the formation of ulcers. 2. affected with an ulcer or ulcers. —**ul'cer·ous·ly,** *adv.* —**ul'cer·ous·ness,** *n.*

-ule, a diminutive suffix of nouns, as in *globule.* [t. L: m. *-ulus, -ula, -ulum*]

u·le·ma (ōō'lə mä'), *n.pl.* the doctors of Moslem religion and law, esp. in Turkey. [t. Ar.: learned (men)]

-ulent, an adjective suffix meaning "abounding in," as in *fraudulent.* [t. L: s. *-ulentus* full of]

Ul·fi·las (ül'fĭ ləs), *n.* A.D. c311–c382. Christian bishop among the Goths, and translator of the Bible into the Gothic language. Also, **Ul·fi·la** (ül'fĭ lə), **Wulfilá**.

ul·lage (ül'Yj), *n.* 1. the loss of wine or spirit from its container caused by leakage or evaporation. 2. the amount of goods lost by passing through the sides of a bag. [late ME, t. AF: m. *ulliage*, filling up (of a cask), der. *aouiller*, fill up (a cask), ult. der. L *dōlium* cask]

Ulm (ŏŏlm), *n.* a city in S West Germany, in Baden-Württemberg: a port on the Danube. 82,400 (est. 1953).

ul·ma·ceous (ŭl'mā'shəs), *adj.* belonging to the *Ulmaceae*, or elm family of dicotyledonous trees and shrubs, characterized by erect anthers, two stigmatic branches, flower buds produced on leafless yearly branches, and a compressed fruit with oblique apex, commonly a dry samara. [f. s. NL *Ulmāceae*, pl., genus name (der. L *ulmus* elm) + -OUS]

ul·na (ŭl'nə), *n., pl.* **-nae** (-nē), **-nas.** 1. *Anat.* that one of the two bones of the forearm which is on the side opposite to the thumb. See diag. under **shoulder.** 2. a corresponding bone in the forelimb of other vertebrates. [NL, special use of L *ulna* elbow, arm] —**ul'nar**, *adj.*

-ulose, var. of **-ulous** in scientific terms, as in *granulose, ramulose*. [t. L: m.s. -*ulōsus*. See -ULE, -OSE[1]]

u·lot·ri·chous (ŭ lŏt'rə kəs), *adj.* having woolly hair. [f. Gk.: m. *oûlo(s)* curly + m. *-trichos* -haired]

-ulous, a suffix forming adjectives meaning "tending to," as in *credulous, populous*. [t. L: m.s. -*ulōsus*, or m. -*ulus*]

Ul·pi·an (ül'pĭ ən), *n.* (*Domitius Ulpianus*) died A.D. 228?, Roman jurist.

Ul·ster (ül'stər), *n.* 1. a former province in Ireland, now comprising Northern Ireland and a part of the republic of Ireland. 2. a province in N Ireland. 235,797 (prelim. 1956). 3123 sq. mi. 3. *Colloq.* Northern Ireland. 4. (*l.c.*) a long, loose, heavy overcoat, worn by both men and women, orig. made of Irish frieze.

Ulster (def. 1)

ult., 1. ultimate. 2. ultimately. 3. Also, **ulto.** ultimo.

ul·te·ri·or (ŭl tĭr'ĭ ər), *adj.* 1. being beyond what is seen or avowed; intentionally kept concealed: *ulterior motives.* 2. coming at a subsequent time or stage: *ulterior action.* 3. being or situated beyond, or on the farther side: *ulterior regions.* [t. L: farther, compar. adj. akin to *ultrā*, adv., beyond] —**ul·te/ri·or·ly,** *adv.*

ul·ti·ma (ŭl'tə mə), *n.* the last syllable of a word. [t. L, fem. of *ultimus* farthest, last]

ul·ti·ma ra·ti·o re·gum (ŭl'tə mə rā'shĭ ō' rē'gəm), *Latin.* the last (or final) argument of kings; resort to arms (motto engraved by Louis XIV on his cannon).

ul·ti·mate (ŭl'tə mĭt), *adj.* 1. forming the final aim or object: *his ultimate goal.* 2. coming at the end, as of a course of action, a process, etc.; final; decisive: *ultimate lot in life.* 3. beyond which it is impossible to proceed, as by investigation or analysis; fundamental; elemental: *ultimate principles.* 4. last, as in a series. —*n.* 5. the final point; final result. 6. a fundamental fact or principle. [t. L: m.s. *ultimātus*, pp., ended, der. L *ultimus* last] —**ul'ti·mate·ly,** *adv.* —**ul'ti·mate·ness,** *n.* —**Syn.** 2. See **last[1].**

ul·ti·ma Thu·le (ŭl'tə mə thōō'lĭ), 1. the uttermost degree attainable. 2. the farthest limit or point possible. 3. the farthest north.

ul·ti·ma·tum (ŭl'tə mā'təm), *n., pl.* **-tums, -ta** (-tə). 1. the final terms of one of the parties in a diplomatic relationship, the rejection of which by the other party may involve a rupture of relations or lead to a declaration of war. 2. a final proposal or statement of conditions. [t. NL, prop. neut. of LL *ultimātus* ULTIMATE]

ul·ti·mo (ŭl'tə mō'), *adv.* in or of the month preceding the present: *on the 12th ultimo.* Abbr.: ult. Cf. **proximo.** [t. L: short for *ultimō mense* in the last month]

ul·ti·mo·gen·i·ture (ŭl'tə mō jĕn'ə chər), *n.* the principle of undivided inheritance or succession by the youngest son (opposed to *primogeniture*). [f. *ultimo-* (comb. form repr. L *ultimus* last) + GENITURE]

ulto., ultimo.

ul·tra (ŭl'trə), *adj.* 1. going beyond what is usual or ordinary; excessive; extreme. —*n.* 2. one who goes to extremes, as of fashion, etc. [t. L: beyond, adv., prep.]

ultra-, a prefix meaning: 1. beyond (in space or time) as in *ultraplanetary.* 2. excessive; excessively, as in *ultraconventional.* [t. L, comb. form of *ultrā*, adv., prep., beyond] See the list following:

ul'tra·am·bi'tious	ul'tra·lib'er·al
ul'tra·con'fi·dent	ul'tra·loy'al
ul'tra·con·serv'a·tive	ul'tra·mod'ern
ul'tra·cred'u·lous	ul'tra·mod'est
ul'tra·crit'i·cal	ul'tra·na'tion·al·ism
ul'tra·ex·clu'sive	ul'tra·rad'i·cal
ul'tra·fash'ion·a·ble	ul'tra·re·li'gious

ultra high frequency, designed for the production or reproduction of frequencies ranging from 300 to 3000 megacycles.

ul·tra·ism (ŭl'trə Yz'əm), *n.* 1. extremism. 2. an extreme view or act. —**ul'tra·ist,** *n., adj.* —**ul'tra·is'tic,** *adj.*

ul·tra·ma·rine (ŭl'trə mə rēn'), *adj.* 1. beyond the sea. —*n.* 2. a blue pigment consisting of powdered lapis lazuli. 3. a similar artificial blue pigment. 4. any of various other pigments. 5. a deep-blue color. [t. ML: m.s. *ultrāmarīnus.* See ULTRA-, MARINE]

ul·tra·mi·crom·e·ter (ŭl'trə mī krŏm'ə tər), *n.* a micrometer calibrated to a very fine scale.

ul·tra·mi·cro·scope (ŭl'trə mī'krə skōp'), *n.* an instrument for detecting, by means of diffractive effects, objects too small to be seen by the ordinary microscope. —**ul·tra·mi·cro·scop·ic** (ŭl'trə mī'krə skŏp'Yk), **ul'tra·mi/cro·scop/i·cal,** *adj.*

ul·tra·mi·cros·co·py (ŭl'trə mī krŏs'kə pY, -mī'krə skō'pY), *n.* the use of the ultramicroscope.

ul·tra·mon·tane (ŭl'trə mŏn'tān), *adj.* 1. beyond the mountains. Cf. 2. south of the Alps; Italian. 3. pertaining to or supporting the Roman Catholic belief that the Pope is the spiritual head of the Church in all countries. 4. (formerly) north of the Alps; tramontane. —*n.* 5. one who lives beyond the mountains. 6. one living south of the Alps. 7. a member of the ultramontane party in the Roman Catholic Church. 8. (formerly) one living to the north of the Alps. [t. ML: m.s. *ultrāmontānus.* See ULTRA-, MONTANE] —**ul·tra·mon·ta·nism** (ŭl'trə mŏn'tə nYz'əm), *n.*

ul·tra·mun·dane (ŭl'trə mŭn'dān), *adj.* 1. beyond the limits of the known universe. 2. beyond the present life. [t. LL: m.s. *ultrāmundānus.* See ULTRA-, MUNDANE]

ul·tra·son·ic (ŭl'trə sŏn'Yk), *adj.* referring to periodic disturbances in a medium above the audible limit, i.e. above 20,000 cycles per second.

ul·tra·trop·i·cal (ŭl'trə trŏp'ə kəl), *adj.* 1. outside of the tropics. 2. warmer than the tropics.

ul·tra·vi·o·let (ŭl'trə vī'ə lYt), *adj.* 1. beyond the violet, as the invisible rays of the spectrum lying outside the violet end of the visible spectrum. 2. pertaining to these rays. Cf. **infrared.**

ul·tra vi·res (ŭl'trə vī'rēz), going beyond the legal power or authority of an agent, corporation, or tribunal. [L: beyond the power]

ul·tra·vi·rus (ŭl'trə vī'rəs), *n.* an ultramicroscopic agent which passes through the finest bacterial filters.

u·lu (ōō'lōō), *n.* a type of knife used by Eskimos.

u·lu·lant (ŭl'yə lənt, ül'-), *adj.* ululating; howling. [t. L: s. *ululans*, ppr.; imit.]

u·lu·late (ŭl'yə lāt', ül'-), *v.i.,* **-lated, -lating.** 1. to howl, as a dog or a wolf. 2. to utter some similar sound. 3. to lament loudly. [t. L: m.s. *ululātus*, pp.; imit.] —**u/u·la/tion,** *n.*

Ul·ya·novsk (ōō lyä'nŏfsk), *n.* a city in the E Soviet Union in Europe: birthplace of Lenin. 183,000 (est. 1956).

U·lys·ses (ū lYs'ēz), *n.* 1. Latin name for **Odysseus.** 2. a psychological novel (1922) by James Joyce. —**U·lys·se·an** (ū lYs'Yən), *adj.*

um·bel (ŭm'bəl), *n. Bot.* an inflorescence in which a number of flower stalks or pedicels, nearly equal in length, spread from a common center: called a **simple umbel** when each pedicel is terminated by a single flower, and a **compound umbel** when each pedicel bears a secondary umbel. [t. L: m.s. *umbella* sun shade, parasol, dim. of *umbra* shadow]

Compound umbel

um·bel·late (ŭm'bə lYt, -lāt'), *adj.* having or forming an umbel or umbels. Also, **um'bel·lar, um'bel·lat'ed.** —**um'bel·late·ly,** *adv.*

um·bel·let (ŭm'bə lYt), *n.* an umbellule.

um·bel·lif·er·ous (ŭm'bə lYf'ər əs), *adj.* 1. bearing an umbel or umbels. 2. belonging or pertaining to the *Umbelliferae* (or *Ammiaceae*), a family of plants containing many important umbel-bearing herbs, as the parsley, carrot, etc.; apiaceous. [f. NL *umbellifer* (see UMBEL, -(I)FER) + -OUS]

um·bel·lule (ŭm'bə lūl', ŭmbĕl'ūl), *n.* one of the secondary umbels in a compound umbel. [t. NL: m. *umbellula*, dim. of *umbella* UMBEL] —**um·bel·lu·late** (ŭmbĕl'yə lYt, -lāt'), *adj.*

um·ber (ŭm'bər), *n.* 1. an earth consisting chiefly of a hydrated oxide of iron and some oxide of manganese, used in its natural state (**raw umber**) as a brown pigment, or after heating (**burnt umber**) as a reddish-brown pigment. 2. the color of such a pigment; dark dusky brown or dark reddish brown. —*v.i.* 3. to color with or as with umber. [t. It.: m. (*terra di*) *ombra*, lit., (earth of) shade (see UMBRA); ? prop. Umbrian earth]

umber bird, umbrette.

Um·ber·to (ōōmbĕr'tō), *n.* See **Humbert I.**

um·bil·i·cal (ŭmbYl'ə kəl), *adj.* 1. of the umbilicus or umbilical cord. 2. formed or placed like a navel; central. —*n.* 3. the last cable to be detached from a rocket before launching. [t. ML: s. *umbilīcālis*, der. L *umbilīcus* navel]

umbilical cord, *Anat.* a cord or funicle connecting the embryo or fetus with the placenta of the mother, and transmitting nourishment from the mother.

um·bil·i·cate (ŭmbYl'ə kāt', -kət), *adj.* 1. having the form of an umbilicus or navel. 2. having an umbilicus.

um·bil·i·ca·tion (ŭmbYl'ə kā'shən), *n.* 1. a central navellike depression. 2. umbilicate state or formation.

um·bil·i·cus (ŭmbYl'ə kəs, ŭm'bə lī'kəs), *n., pl.* **-bilici** (-bYl'ə sī', -bə lī'sī). 1. *Anat.* the navel, or depression on the middle of the abdomen indicating the point of attachment of the umbilical cord. 2. *Bot., Zool., etc.* a navellike formation, as the hilum of a seed. [t. L; akin to Gk. *omphalós* and NAVEL]

um·bil·i·form (ŭm bĭl'ə fôrm'), *adj.* having the form of an umbilicus or navel. [f. UMBILI(CUS) + -FORM]

um·ble pie (ŭm'bəl), humble pie. [orig. spelling of HUMBLE PIE. See UMBLES]

um·bles (ŭm'bəlz), *n. pl. Archaic.* numbles. [var. of NUMBLES]

um·bo (ŭm'bō), *n., pl.* umbones (ŭm bō'nēz), umbos. 1. the boss, knob, or projection at or near the center of a shield. 2. any similar boss or protuberance. 3. *Zool.* the beak of a bivalve shell; the protuberance of each valve above the hinge. [t. L] —**um·bon·ic** (ŭm bŏn'ĭk), *adj.*

um·bo·nal (ŭm'bə nəl), *adj.* 1. bosslike. 2. having an umbo or boss. Also, **um·bo·nate** (ŭm'bə nĭt, -nāt'), *adj.*

um·bra (ŭm'brə), *n., pl.* **-brae** (-brē) 1. shade; shadow. 2. *Astron.* **a.** the complete or perfect shadow of an opaque body, as a planet, where the direct light from the source of illumination is wholly cut off. Cf. penumbra. **b.** the dark central portion of a sunspot. 3. ghost. [t. L]

um·brage (ŭm'brĭj), *n.* 1. offense given or taken; resentful displeasure. 2. the foliage of trees, etc., affording shade. 3. *Poetic.* shade or shadows, as that cast by trees, etc. 4. *Rare.* a shadowy appearance or semblance of something. [late ME, t. F: m. *ombrage,* g. L *umbrāticum,* neut. adj., of or in the shade; def. 1 through obs. meanings "suspicion," "disfavor"]

um·bra·geous (ŭm brā'jəs), *adj.* 1. forming or affording shade; shady; shaded. 2. *Rare.* apt or disposed to take umbrage or offense, as a person. —**um·bra'·geous·ly,** *adv.* —**um·bra'·geous·ness,** *n.*

um·brel·la (ŭm brĕl'ə), *n.* 1. a portable shade or screen for protection from sunlight, rain, etc., in its modern form consisting of a light circular canopy of silk, cotton, or other material on a folding frame of bars or strips of steel, cane, etc. 2. the saucer- or bowl-shaped gelatinous body of a medusa; the bell. [t. It.: m. *ombrella,* der. *ombra* shade, g. L *umbra*] —**um·brel'·la·less,** *adj.* —**um·brel'la·like',** *adj.*

umbrella bird, 1. a South American bird, *Cephalopterus ornatus,* with an umbrellalike crest above the head. 2. another bird of this genus, *C. penduliger.*

umbrella leaf, a North American berberidaceous herb, *Diphylleia cymosa,* bearing either a large peltate, umbrellalike, lobed, basal leaf, or two smaller similar leaves on a flowering stem.

umbrella tree, 1. an American magnolia, *Magnolia tripetala,* a tree with large leaves in umbrellalike clusters. 2. any of various other trees suggesting an umbrella, as the tropical African moraceous tree, *Musanga Smithii.*

um·brette (ŭm brĕt'), *n.* a dusky-brown African wading bird, *Scopus umbretta,* allied to the storks and herons; umber bird. [t. F: m. *ombrette* UMBER]

Um·bri·a (ŭm'brĭ·ə; *It.* ōōm'brē ä'), *n.* 1. an ancient district in central and N Italy. 2. a department in central Italy. 814,000 pop. (est. 1954); 3270 sq. mi.

Um·bri·an (ŭm'brĭ·ən), *adj.* 1. of or pertaining to Umbria, or its inhabitants. —*n.* 2. a native or inhabitant of Umbria. 3. an Italic language, which became extinct in ancient times.

um·brif·er·ous (ŭm brĭf'ər əs), *adj.* casting or making shade. [f. L *umbrifer* shade-bearing + -OUS] —**um·brif'er·ous·ly,** *adv.*

u·mi·ak (ōō'mĭ äk'), *n.* an open Eskimo boat consisting of a wooden frame covered with skins and provided with several thwarts, for transport of goods and passengers. Also, **u/mi·ack/, oomisak.** [t. Eskimo (Eastern d.): large skin boat, or woman's boat]

Umiak

um·laut (ōōm'lout), *Gram.* —*n.* 1. (of vowels in Germanic languages) assimilation in which a vowel is influenced by a following vowel or semivowel. 2. a vowel which has resulted from such assimilation, esp. when written *ä, ö,* or *ü* in German. 3. two dots as a diacritic over a vowel to indicate a different vowel sound from that of the letter without the diacritic, esp. as so used in German. —*v.t.* 4. to modify by umlaut. 5. to write the umlaut over. [t. G, f. *um* about + *laut* sound]

umph (əm, əmf), *interj.* humph.

um·pir·age (ŭm'pīr'ĭj, -pə rĭj), *n.* 1. the office or authority of an umpire. 2. the decision of an umpire; arbitrament.

um·pire (ŭm'pīr), *n., v.,* **-pired, -piring.** —*n.* 1. a person selected to rule on the plays in a game. 2. a person to whose decision a controversy between parties is referred; an arbiter or referee. —*v.t.* 3. to act as umpire in (a game). 4. to decide or settle (a controversy, etc.) as umpire; arbitrate. —*v.i.* 5. to act as umpire. [ME *oumpere,* r. *noumpere* (a *noumpere* taken as an *oumpere*), t. OF: m. *nonper* uneven, odd, f. *non* not (g. L *nōn*) + *per* (see PEER, n.)] —**um'pire·ship',** *n.* —**Syn.** 1. referee, arbiter, arbitrator. 2. See judge.

UMW, United Mine Workers.

un-[1], a prefix meaning "not," freely used as an English formative, giving a negative or opposite force, in adjectives (including participial adjectives) and their derivative adverbs and nouns, as in *unfair, unfairly, unfairness, unfelt, unseen, unfitting, unformed, unheard-of, un-get-at-able,* and less freely in certain other nouns, as in *unfaith, unrest, unemployment.* Note: Of the words in **un--,** only a selected number are separately entered below, since in most formations of this class, the meaning, spelling, and pronunciation may readily be determined by reference to the simple word from which each is formed. [ME and OE, c. D *on-,* G and Goth. *un-,* Icel. *ū-, ō-;* akin to L *in-,* Gk. *an-, a-* (alpha privative)] —**Syn.** See in-[3].

un-[2], a prefix freely used in English to form verbs expressing a reversal of some action or state, or removal, deprivation, release, etc., as in *unbend, uncork, unfasten,* etc., or to intensify the force of a verb already having such a meaning, as in *unloose.* [ME and OE *un-, on-,* c. D *ont-,* G *ent-,* Goth. *and-;* akin to L *ante* before, Gk. *anti* opposite to, against]

U.N., United Nations.

un·a·ble (ŭn ā'bəl), *adj.* not able; lacking ability or power (to). —**Syn.** See incapable.

un·a·bridged (ŭn'ə brĭjd'), *adj.* not abridged or shortened, as a book.

un·ac·cent·ed (ŭn ăk'sĕn tĭd, ŭn'ăk sĕn'tĭd), *adj.* not accented.

un·ac·com·mo·dat·ed (ŭn'ə kŏm'ə dā'tĭd), *adj.* 1. not accommodated; not adapted. 2. not having accommodations.

un·ac·com·pa·nied (ŭn'ə kŭm'pə nĭd), *adj.* 1. not accompanied. 2. *Music.* without an accompaniment.

un·ac·com·plished (ŭn'ə kŏmp'lĭsht), *adj.* 1. not accomplished; incomplete. 2. without accomplishments.

un·ac·count·a·ble (ŭn'ə koun'tə bəl), *adj.* 1. not accountable or answerable. 2. not to be accounted for or explained. —**un'ac·count'a·ble·ness,** *n.* —**un'ac·count'a·bly,** *adv.* —**Syn.** 1. unanswerable, irresponsible. 2. inexplicable, inscrutable, strange.

un·ac·cus·tomed (ŭn'ə kŭs'təmd), *adj.* 1. unusual; unfamiliar. 2. not habituated: *to be unaccustomed to hardships.* —**un'ac·cus'tomed·ness,** *n.*

un·ad·vised (ŭn'əd vīzd'), *adj.* 1. not advised; without advice. 2. indiscreet; rash. —**un·ad·vis·ed·ly** (ŭn'əd vī'zĭd lĭ), *adv.* —**un'ad·vis'ed·ness,** *n.*

un·af·fect·ed[1] (ŭn'ə fĕk'tĭd), *adj.* free from affectation; sincere; genuine. [f. UN-[1] + AFFECTED[2]] —**un'af·fect'ed·ly,** *adv.* —**un'af·fect'ed·ness,** *n.* —**Syn.** plain, natural, simple, naïve.

un·af·fect·ed[2] (ŭn'ə fĕk'tĭd), *adj.* not affected, acted upon, or influenced. [f. UN-[1] + AFFECTED[1]] —**Syn.** unmoved, untouched, unimpressed.

U·na·las·ka (ōō'nə läs'kə, ŭn'ə-), *n.* one of the Aleutian Islands, off the SW mainland of Alaska: site of the Dutch Harbor naval base. ab. 75 mi. long.

un·A·mer·i·can (ŭn'ə mĕr'ə kən), *adj.* not American; not characteristic of or proper to America; foreign or opposed to American character, usages, standards, etc.

U·na·mu·no (ōō'nä mōō'nō), *n.* **Miguel de** (mē gēl' dĕ), 1864–1936, Spanish philosopher, poet, novelist, and essayist.

un·a·neled (ŭn'ə nēld'), *adj. Archaic.* not having received extreme unction.

u·na·nim·i·ty (ū'nə nĭm'ə tĭ), *n.* complete accord or agreement.

u·nan·i·mous (ū năn'ə məs), *adj.* 1. of one mind; in complete accord; agreed. 2. characterized by or showing complete accord: *a unanimous vote.* [t. L: m. *ūnanimus*] —**u·nan'i·mous·ly,** *adv.* —**u·nan'i·mous·ness,** *n.*

un·ap·peal·a·ble (ŭn'ə pē'lə bəl), *adj.* 1. not appealable; that cannot be carried to a higher court by appeal, as a cause. 2. not to be appealed from, as a judgment or a judge. —**un'ap·peal'a·ble·ness,** *n.*

un·ap·proach·a·ble (ŭn'ə prō'chə bəl), *adj.* 1. not to be approached; inaccessible. 2. unrivaled. —**un'ap·proach'a·ble·ness,** *n.* —**un'ap·proach'a·bly,** *adv.*

un'a·bashed'	un'ac·quaint'ed	un'al·lied'	un'an·i·mat'ed
un'a·bat'ed	un'ac·quit'ted	un'al·low'a·ble	un'an·nealed'
un'a·bat'ing	un'a·dapt'a·ble	un'al·loyed'	un'an·nounced'
un'a·bet'ted	un'ad·just'a·ble	un'al·ter·a·ble	un'an·swer·a·ble
un'ab·solved'	un'a·dorned'	un'al·tered	un'an·swer·a·bly
un'ac·a·dem'ic	un'a·dul'ter·at·ed	un'al·ter·ing	un'an·swered
un'ac·cept'a·ble	un'ad·vis'a·ble	un'am·big'u·ous	un'a·pol'o·get'ic
un'ac·cept'ed	un'ad·vis'a·bly	un'am·big'u·ous·ly	un'ap·palled'
un'ac·cli'mat·ed	un'aes·thet'ic	un'am·bi'tious	un'ap·par'ent
un'ac·cli'ma·tized'	un'a·fraid'	un·a'mi·a·ble	un'ap·peas'a·ble
un'ac·com'mo·dat'ing	un'ag·i·tat'ed	un'am·pli·fied'	un'ap·peased'
un'ac·count'ed	un'aid'ed	un'a·mus'ing	un'ap·pe·tiz'ing
un'ac·cred'it·ed	un·aimed'	un'a·na·lyt'ic	un'ap·pre'ci·at·ed
un'ac·knowl'edged	un'al·le·vi·at'ed	un·an'a·lyz'a·ble	un'ap·pre'ci·a·tive

---

b., blend of, blended; c., cognate with; d., dialect, dialectal; der., derived from; f., formed from; g., going back to; m., modification of; r., replacing; s., stem of; t., taken from; ?, perhaps. See the full key on inside cover.

un·ap·pro·pri·at·ed (ŭn′ə·prō′prĭ ā′tĭd), adj. 1. not taken possession of. 2. not assigned or allotted.

un·apt (ŭn·ăpt′), adj. 1. unfitted; unsuited. 2. not disposed, likely, or liable. 3. not quick to learn; inapt. —un·apt′ly, adv. —un·apt′ness, n.

un·arm (ŭn·ärm′), v.t. 1. to deprive of weapons. 2. Archaic. to divest or relieve of armor. —v.i. 3. to lay down one's arms. 4. Archaic. to take off one's armor. [ME unarme. See UN-², ARM²]

un·armed (ŭn·ärmd′), adj. 1. without arms or armor. 2. not furnished with claws, prickles, scales, or other armature, as animals and plants.

un·as·sum·ing (ŭn′ə·soō′mĭng), adj. unpretending; modest. —un·as·sum′ing·ly, adv.

un·at·tached (ŭn′ə·tăcht′), adj. 1. not attached. 2. not connected or associated with any particular body, group, organization, or the like; independent. 3. not engaged or married.

un·at·tend·ed (ŭn′ə·tĕn′dĭd), adj. 1. unaccompanied. 2. not attended (often fol. by to).

u·nau (ū nô′, oō nou′), n. a two-toed sloth, Choloepus didactylus. [t. Brazilian (Island of Maranhão)]

un·a·vail·ing (ŭn′ə·vā′lĭng), adj. ineffectual; useless. —un·a·vail′ing·ly, adv.

un·a·void·a·ble (ŭn′ə·voi′də·bəl), adj. 1. not to be avoided; inevitable. 2. incapable of being made null or void. —un·a·void·a·ble·ness, un·a·void·a·bil·i·ty, n. —un·a·void′a·bly, adv.

un·a·ware (ŭn′ə·wâr′), adj. 1. not aware; unconscious, as of something: to be unaware of any change. —adv. 2. unawares.

un·a·wares (ŭn′ə·wârz′), adv. 1. while not aware or conscious of a thing oneself; unknowingly or inadvertently. 2. while another is not aware; unexpectedly: to come upon someone unawares.

un·backed (ŭn·băkt′), adj. 1. without backing or support. 2. not supported by bets. 3. not endorsed. 4. never having been mounted by a rider, as a horse.

un·baked (ŭn·bākt′), adj. 1. not baked. 2. crude; immature.

un·bal·ance (ŭn·băl′əns), v., -anced, -ancing. —v.t. 1. to throw out of balance. 2. to disorder or derange, as the mind. —n. 3. unbalanced condition.

un·bal·anced (ŭn·băl′ənst), adj. 1. not balanced, or not properly balanced. 2. lacking steadiness and soundness of judgment. 3. mentally disordered or deranged. 4. (of an account) not adjusted; not brought to an equality of debits and credits.

un·bal·last·ed (ŭn·băl′əs·tĭd), adj. 1. not ballasted. 2. not properly steadied or regulated.

un·bar (ŭn·bär′), v.t., v.i., -barred, -barring. 1. to remove a bar or bars from. 2. to open; unlock.

un·bat·ed (ŭn·bā′tĭd), adj. not bated or lessened.

un·bear·a·ble (ŭn·bâr′ə·bəl), adj. not bearable; unendurable; intolerable. —un·bear′a·ble·ness, n. —un·bear′a·bly, adv.

un·beat·en (ŭn·bē′tən), adj. 1. not struck or pounded. 2. not defeated. 3. untrodden: unbeaten paths.

un·be·com·ing (ŭn′bĭ·kŭm′ĭng), adj. 1. not becoming; not appropriate; unsuited. 2. improper; unseemly. —un·be·com′ing·ly, adv. —un·be·com′ing·ness, n. —Syn. 2. See improper.

un·be·known (ŭn′bĭ·nōn′), adj. Colloq. unknown; unperceived; without a person's knowledge (often fol. by to, and often used adverbially). Also, un·be·knownst (ŭn′bĭ·nōnst′).

un·be·lief (ŭn′bĭ·lēf′), n. lack of belief; disbelief, esp. in divine revelation or in the truth of the gospel.

un·be·liev·er (ŭn′bĭ·lē′vər), n. 1. one who does not believe. 2. one who does not accept any, or some particular, religious belief.

un·be·liev·ing (ŭn′bĭ·lē′vĭng), adj. 1. not believing; skeptical. 2. not accepting any, or some particular, religious belief. —un·be·liev′ing·ly, adv. —un·be·liev′ing·ness, n.

un·belt (ŭn·bĕlt′), v.t. 1. to remove the belt from. 2. to remove by undoing a supporting belt, as a sword.

un·bend (ŭn·bĕnd′), v., -bent or -bended, -bending. —v.t. 1. to release from the strain of effort or close application; relax by laying aside formality. 2. to release from tension, as a bow. 3. to straighten from a bent form or position. 4. Naut. a. to loose or untie, as a sail, rope, etc. b. to unfasten from spars or stays, as sails. —v.i. 5. to relax the strictness of formality or ceremony; act in an easy, genial manner. 6. to become unbent.

un·bend·ing (ŭn·bĕn′dĭng), adj. not bending; rigid; unyielding; inflexible. —un·bend′ing·ly, adv. —un·bend′ing·ness, n.

un·bent (ŭn·bĕnt′), v. 1. pt. and pp. of unbend. —adj. 2. not bent; unbowed. 3. not forced to yield or submit.

un·be·seem·ing (ŭn′bĭ·sē′mĭng), adj. not beseeming; unbecoming. —un·be·seem′ing·ly, adv. —un·be·seem′ing·ness, n.

un·bi·ased (ŭn·bī′əst), adj. not biased; unprejudiced; impartial. Also, un·bi′assed.

un·bid·den (ŭn·bĭd′ən), adj. 1. not commanded. 2. uninvited. Also, un·bid′.

un·bind (ŭn·bīnd′), v.t., -bound, -binding. 1. to release from bands or restraint, as a prisoner; free. 2. to unfasten or loose, as a band or tie. [ME; OE unbindan, c. G entbinden. See UN-², BIND, v.]

un·bit·ted (ŭn·bĭt′ĭd), adj. 1. not bitted or bridled. 2. uncontrolled.

un·blenched (ŭn·blĕncht′), adj. Obs. undaunted.

un·blessed (ŭn·blĕst′), adj. 1. excluded from a blessing. 2. unhallowed; unholy. 3. unhappy; wretched. Also, un·blest′.

un·blush·ing (ŭn·blŭsh′ĭng), adj. 1. shameless. 2. not blushing. —un·blush′ing·ly, adv.

un·bod·ied (ŭn·bŏd′ĭd), adj. 1. incorporeal. 2. disembodied.

un·bolt (ŭn·bōlt′), v.t. to open the bolt of (a door, etc.).

un·bolt·ed[1] (ŭn·bōl′tĭd), adj. not fastened, as a door. [f. UNBOLT + -ED²; or f. UN-¹ + BOLT¹ + -ED²]

un·bolt·ed[2] (ŭn·bōl′tĭd), adj. not sifted, as grain. [f. UN-¹ + BOLT² + -ED²]

un·boned (ŭn·bōnd′), adj. 1. boneless. 2. not having the bones removed.

un·bon·net (ŭn·bŏn′ĭt), v.i. 1. to uncover the head, as in respect. —v.t. 2. to take off the bonnet from.

un·bon·net·ed (ŭn·bŏn′ĭt·ĭd), adj. bareheaded.

un·born (ŭn·bôrn′), adj. 1. not yet born; yet to come; future: ages unborn. 2. not born.

un·bos·om (ŭn·booz′əm, -boō′zəm), v.t. 1. to disclose (one's thoughts, feelings, etc.) esp. in confidence. —v.i. 2. to disclose one's thoughts, feelings, secrets, etc. [f. UN-² + BOSOM, v.] —un·bos′om·er, n.

un·bound (ŭn·bound′), v. 1. pt. and pp. of unbind. —adj. 2. not bound, as a book.

un·bound·ed (ŭn·boun′dĭd), adj. 1. unlimited; boundless. 2. unrestrained; uncontrolled.

un·bowed (ŭn·boud′), adj. 1. not bowed or bent. 2. not forced to yield or submit.

un·brace (ŭn·brās′), v.t., -braced, -bracing. 1. to remove the braces of. 2. to free from tension; relax. 3. to weaken.

un·braid (ŭn·brād′), v.t. to separate (anything braided, as hair) into the several strands.

un·bred (ŭn·brĕd′), adj. 1. ill-bred. 2. not taught or trained.

un·bri·dle (ŭn·brī′dəl), v.t., -dled, -dling. 1. to remove the bridle from (a horse, etc.). 2. to free from restraint.

un·bri·dled (ŭn·brī′dəld), adj. 1. not having a bridle on, as a horse. 2. unrestrained or uncontrolled.

un·bro·ken (ŭn·brō′kən), adj. 1. whole; intact. 2. uninterrupted; continuous. 3. not tamed. 4. undisturbed; unimpaired. Also, Obs., un·broke′. —un·bro′ken·ly, adv. —un·bro′ken·ness, n.

un·buck·le (ŭn·bŭk′əl), v.t., -led, -ling. to unfasten the buckle or buckles of.

un·build (ŭn·bĭld′), v.t., -built, -building. to demolish (something built); raze.

un·bur·den (ŭn·bûr′dən), v.t. 1. to free from a burden. 2. to relieve (one's mind, conscience, etc., or oneself) by disclosure or confession of something. 3. to cast off or get rid of, as a burden or something burdensome; disclose; reveal.

un·but·ton (ŭn·bŭt′ən), v.t. 1. to unfasten the button or buttons of (a garment, etc., or a person). 2. to unfasten (a button).

un·cage (ŭn·kāj′), v.t., -caged, -caging. to release from or as from a cage.

un·called-for (ŭn·kôld′fôr′), adj. unnecessary and improper; unwarranted.

un·ap·proved′	un·at·taint′ed	un·a·wak′ened	un·blem′ished
un·arched′	un·at·tempt′ed	un·awed′	un·book′ish
un·ar′mored	un·at·test′ed	un·bap·tized′	un·bor′rowed
un·ar·rest′ed	un·at·tract′ed	un·barbed′	un·bought′
un·art′ful	un·at·trac′tive	un·be·fit′ting	un·branched′
un·ar·tis′tic	un·aus·pi′cious	un·be·liev′a·ble	un·brand′ed
un·a·shamed′	un·au·then′tic	un·be·liev′a·bly	un·break′a·ble
un·asked′	un·au·then′ti·cal	un·be·loved′	un·brib′a·ble
un·as′pi·rat·ed	un·au·then′ti·cat·ed	un·ben′e·ficed	un·bridge′a·ble
un·as·pir′ing	un·au·thor·ized′	un·be·sought′	un·bridged′
un·as·sail′a·ble	un·a·vail′a·bil′i·ty	un·be·trayed′	un·broth′er·ly
un·as·sail′a·bly	un·a·vail′a·ble	un·be·trothed′	un·bruised′
un·as·sailed′	un·a·vail′a·bly	un·be·wailed′	un·brushed′
un·as·sign′a·ble	un·a·venged′	un·blam′a·ble	un·bur′ied
un·as·sist′ed	un·a·vowed′	un·blam′a·bly	un·burned′
un·as·sumed′	un·a·vow′ed·ly	un·blamed′	un·burnt′
un·at·tain′a·ble	un·a·waked′	un·bleached′	un·but′toned

ăct, āble, dâre, ärt; ĕbb, ēqual; ĭf, īce; hŏt, ōver, ôrder, oil, boŏk, oōze, out; ŭp, ūse, ûrge; ə = a in alone; ch, chief; g, give; ng, ring; sh, shoe; th, thin; th, that; zh, vision. See the full key on inside cover.

un·can·ny (ŭn kăn′Y), *adj.* **1.** preternaturally good: *uncanny judgment.* **2.** such as to arouse superstitious uneasiness; unnaturally strange. —**un·can′ni·ly,** *adv.* —**un·can′ni·ness,** *n.* —**Syn. 2.** See **weird.**

un·ca·non·i·cal (ŭn′kə nŏn′ə kəl), *adj.* **1.** not in accordance with canons or rules. **2.** not belonging to the canon of Scripture. —**un′ca·non′i·cal·ly,** *adv.*

un·cap (ŭn kăp′), *v.,* **-capped, -capping.** —*v.t.* **1.** to remove the cap from (the head of a person). **2.** to remove a cap or cover from. —*v.i.* **3.** to remove the cap from the head, as in respect.

un·ca·pa·ble (ŭn kā′pə bəl), *adj. Obs.* incapable.

un·caused (ŭn kôzd′), *adj.* not caused; self-existent.

un·cer·e·mo·ni·ous (ŭn′sĕr ə mō′nY əs), *adj.* not ceremonious; informal; abrupt. —**un′cer·e·mo′ni·ous·ly,** *adv.* —**un′cer·e·mo′ni·ous·ness,** *n.*

uncert., uncertain.

un·cer·tain (ŭn sûr′tən), *adj.* **1.** not definitely or surely known; doubtful. **2.** not confident, assured, or decided. **3.** not fixed or determined. **4.** doubtful; vague; indistinct. **5.** not to be depended on. **6.** subject to change; variable; capricious. **7.** dependent on chance. **8.** unsteady or fitful, as light. —**un·cer′tain·ly,** *adv.* —**un·cer′tain·ness,** *n.* —**Syn. 1.** UNCERTAIN, INSECURE, PRECARIOUS imply lacking in predictability. That which is UNCERTAIN is doubtful or problematical; it often involves danger through an inability to predict or to place confidence in the unknown: *the time of his arrival is uncertain.* That which is INSECURE is not firm, stable, reliable, or safe; and hence is likely to give way, fail, or be overcome: *an insecure foundation, footing, protection.* PRECARIOUS suggests great liability to failure, or exposure to imminent danger: *precarious means of existence.* —**Ant. 1.** definite, sure.

un·cer·tain·ty (ŭn sûr′tən tY), *n., pl.* **-ties. 1.** uncertain state. **2.** something uncertain.

un·chain (ŭn chān′), *v.t.* to free from chains; set free.

un·chan·cy (ŭn chăn′sY, -chän′-), *adj. Chiefly Scot.* **1.** unlucky. **2.** dangerous. [f. UN-¹ + CHANCY (def. 2)]

un·charge (ŭn chärj′), *v.t.,* **-charged, -charging. 1.** *Now Rare.* to free from load; unload. **2.** *Obs.* to acquit.

un·char·i·ta·ble (ŭn chăr′ə tə bəl), *adj.* unforgiving; harsh; censorious. —**un·char′i·ta·ble·ness,** *n.* —**un·char′i·ta·bly,** *adv.*

un·char·tered (ŭn chär′tərd), *adj.* **1.** without a charter. **2.** without regulation; lawless.

un·chaste (ŭn chāst′), *adj.* **1.** not chaste or virtuous. **2.** not marked by purity of taste. —**un·chaste′ly,** *adv.* —**un·chaste′ness, un·chas·ti·ty** (ŭn chăs′tə tY), *n.*

un·chris·tian (ŭn krĭs′chən), *adj.* **1.** not Christian. **2.** unworthy of Christians. **3.** unseemly; improper.

un·church (ŭn chûrch′), *v.t.* **1.** to expel (individuals) from a church; excommunicate. **2.** to deprive of the character and rights of a church. [f. UN-² + CHURCH]

un·ci·al (ŭn′shY əl, -shəl), *adj.* **1.** designating, written in, or pertaining to ancient majuscule letters distinguished from capital majuscules by relatively great roundness, inclination, and inequality in height. —*n.* **2.** an uncial letter. **3.** uncial writing. **4.** a manuscript in uncials. [t. L: s. *unciālis* pertaining to an inch] —**un′ci·al·ly,** *adv.*

INSCREN DUMIDQUEAR CENDUMBELLUNINCDU

Latin uncials. 8th century

un·ci·form (ŭn′sə fôrm′), *adj.* **1.** hook-shaped. —*n.* **2.** *Anat.* a bone of the carpus with a hooklike process projecting from the palmar surface. [t. NL: s. *unciformis,* f. *unci* (gen. sing. of L *uncus* hook) + *-formis* -FORM]

un·ci·na·ri·a·sis (ŭn′sə nə rī′ə sĭs), *n.* hookworm disease. [t. NL: f. *Uncinār(ia)* genus of hookworms (der. L *uncīnus* hook) + *-iāsis* -IASIS]

un·ci·nate (ŭn′sə nĭt, -nāt′), *adj. Biol.* hooked; bent at the end like a hook. Also, **un·ci·nal** (ŭn′sə nəl), **un′ci·nat′ed.** [t. L: m.s. *uncīnātus*]

Uncinate prickles

un·cir·cum·cised (ŭn sûr′kəm sīzd′), *adj.* **1.** not circumcised. **2.** not Jewish; Gentile. **3.** heathen; unregenerate.

un·cir·cum·ci·sion (ŭn′sûr kəm sĭzh′ən), *n.* **1.** condition of being uncircumcised. **2.** *Bible.* the Gentiles.

un·civ·il (ŭn sĭv′əl), *adj.* **1.** without good manners; unmannerly; rude; impolite; discourteous. **2.** uncivilized. —**un·ci·vil·i·ty** (ŭn′sə vĭl′ə tY), **un·civ′il·ness,** *n.* —**un·civ′il·ly,** *adv.*

un·civ·i·lized (ŭn sĭv′ə līzd′), *adj.* barbarous; unenlightened.

un·clad¹ (ŭn klăd′), *v.* pt. and pp. of **unclothe.**

un·clad² (ŭn klăd′), *adj.* not clad; unclothed. [f. UN-¹ + CLAD]

un·clasp (ŭn klăsp′, -kläsp′), *v.t.* **1.** to undo the clasp or clasps of; unfasten. **2.** to release from the grasp, as something held. —*v.i.* **3.** to become unclasped, as the hands, etc. **4.** to release or relax the grasp.

un·cle (ŭng′kəl), *n.* **1.** a brother of one's father or mother. **2.** an aunt's husband. **3.** a familiar title applied to any elderly man. **4.** *Slang.* a pawnbroker. [ME, t. AF, g. L *avunculus* mother's brother] —**un′cle·less,** *adj.*

un·clean (ŭn klēn′), *adj.* **1.** not clean; dirty. **2.** morally impure; evil; vile. **3.** ceremonially impure. —**un·clean′ness,** *n.*

un·clean·ly¹ (ŭn klēn′lY), *adv.* in an unclean manner. [f. UNCLEAN + -LY]

un·clean·ly² (ŭn klĕn′lY), *adj.* not cleanly; unclean. [f. UN-¹ + CLEANLY] —**un·clean′li·ness,** *n.*

un·clench (ŭn klĕnch′), *v.t., v.i.* to open or become opened from a clenched state.

Uncle Re·mus (rē′məs), an old plantation Negro in two books by Joel Chandler Harris.

Uncle Sam (săm), the government or people of the United States. [extension of the initials U.S.]

Uncle Tom's Cabin, a novel about slavery (1852) by Harriet Beecher Stowe, extremely popular in the northern States.

un·cloak (ŭn klōk′), *v.t.* **1.** to remove the cloak from. **2.** to reveal; expose. —*v.i.* **3.** to take off the cloak, or the outer garments generally.

un·clog (ŭn klŏg′), *v.t.,* **-clogged, -clogging.** to free from a clog or from anything that clogs.

un·close (ŭn klōz′), *v.t., v.i.,* **-closed, -closing.** to bring or come out of a closed state; open.

un·clothe (ŭn klōth′), *v.t.,* **-clothed** or **-clad, -clothing. 1.** to strip of clothes. **2.** to strip of anything; divest; uncover.

un·co (ŭng′kō), *adj., adv., n., pl.* **-cos.** *Scot. and N. Eng.* —*adj.* **1.** remarkable; extraordinary. **2.** unknown; strange. **3.** uncanny. —*adv.* **4.** remarkably; extremely. —*n.* **5.** something extraordinary. **6.** (*pl.*) news. **7.** *Obs.* a stranger. [var. of UNCOUTH]

un·coil (ŭn koil′), *v.t.* **1.** to unwind. —*v.i.* **2.** to unwind itself.

un·com·fort·a·ble (ŭn kŭm′fər tə bəl, -kŭmf′tə bəl), *adj.* **1.** causing discomfort; disquieting. **2.** in a state of discomfort; uneasy; ill at ease. —**un·com′fort·a·ble·ness,** *n.* —**un·com′fort·a·bly,** *adv.*

un·com·mer·cial (ŭn′kə mûr′shəl), *adj.* **1.** not engaged in commerce or trade. **2.** not in accordance with commercial principles or practices.

un·com·mit·ted (ŭn′kə mĭt′Yd), *adj.* not committed, esp. not bound by pledge or assurance, as to a course.

un·com·mon (ŭn kŏm′ən), *adj.* **1.** not common; unusual or rare. **2.** unusual in amount or degree; above the ordinary. **3.** exceptional. —**un·com′mon·ness,** *n.* —**Syn.** scarce, infrequent.

un·com·mon·ly (ŭn kŏm′ən lY), *adv.* **1.** in an uncommon or unusual degree; remarkably. **2.** rarely; infrequently.

un·com·mu·ni·ca·tive (ŭn′kə mū′nə kā′tĭv), *adj.* not disposed to impart information, opinions, etc.; reserved; taciturn. —**un′com·mu′ni·ca′tive·ly,** *adv.* —**un′com·mu′ni·ca′tive·ness,** *n.*

un·com·pro·mis·ing (ŭn kŏm′prə mī′zYng), *adj.* not admitting of compromise; unyielding; inflexible. —**un·com′pro·mis′ing·ly,** *adv.*

un·con·cern (ŭn′kən sûrn′), *n.* lack of concern; freedom from solicitude or anxiety; indifference. —**Syn.** See **indifference.**

un·con·cerned (ŭn′kən sûrnd′), *adj.* not concerned; disinterested; free from solicitude or anxiety. —**un′con·cern·ed·ly** (ŭn′kən sûr′nYd lY), *adv.* —**un′con·cern′ed·ness,** *n.*

un·can′celed′	un·chap′er·oned′	un·cleav′a·ble	un′com·mis′sioned
un·can′did	un·chart′ed	un·clipped′	un′com·pan′ion·a·ble
un·can′did·ly	un·char′y	un·cloud′ed	un′com·plain′ing
un′ca·non′ic	un·chas′tened	un·cloyed′	un′com·plai′sant
un·car′bu·ret′ed	un·chas·tised′	un′co·ag′u·la′ted	un′com·plai′sant·ly
un·cared′-for′	un·checked′	un·coat′ed	un′com·plet′ed
un·car′ing	un·cheer′ful	un·cocked′	un′com·pli′a·ble
un·car′pet·ed	un·cher′ished	un′co·erced′	un′com·pli′ant
un·cas′trat·ed	un·chewed′	un′col·lect′a·ble	un′com·pli·cat′ed
un·caught′	un·chilled′	un′col·lect′ed	un′com·pli·men′ta·ry
un·ceas′ing	un·chiv′al·rous	un′col·lect′i·ble	un′com·ply′ing
un·cel′e·brat′ed	un·chol′er·ic	un·col′o·nized′	un′com·pound′ed
un·cen′sored	un·cho′sen	un·col′ored	un′com·pre·hend′ed
un·cen′sured	un·chris′tened	un·combed′	un′com·pre·hend′ing
un·cer′ti·fied′	un·claimed′	un′com·bin′a·ble	un′com·pre·hen′si·ble
un·chained′	un·clar′i·fied′	un′com·bin′a·bly	un′com·pressed′
un·chal′lenged	un·clas′si·fi′a·ble	un′com·bined′	un′com·pro·mised′
un·change′a·ble	un·clas′si·fied′	un·come′ly	un′com·put′ed
un·changed′	un·cleaned′	un′com·fort·ed	un′con·ceal′a·ble
un·chang′ing	un·cleansed′	un′com·fort·ing	un′con·cealed′
un·chang′ing·ly	un·cleared′	un′com·mand′ed	un′con·ced′ed

un·con·di·tion·al (ŭn/kən dĬsh/ən əl), *adj.* not limited by conditions; absolute: *an unconditional promise.* —un/con·di/tion·al·ly, *adv.* —un/con·di/tion·al·ness, *n.*

un·con·di·tioned (ŭn/kən dĬsh/ənd), *adj.* 1. not subject to conditions; absolute. 2. *Psychol.* unlearned; natural. Cf. **conditioned response or reflex.**

un·con·form·a·ble (ŭn/kən fôr/mə bəl), *adj.* 1. not conformable; not conforming. 2. *Geol.* denoting discontinuity of any type in stratigraphic sequence. —un/con·form/a·bly, *adv.*

un·con·form·i·ty (ŭn/kən fôr/mə tĬ), *n., pl.* -ties. 1. lack of conformity; incongruity; inconsistency. 2. *Geol.* **a.** a discontinuity in rock sequence denoting interruption of sedimentation, commonly accompanied by erosion of rocks below the break. **b.** the fault plane separating such strata.

un·con·nect·ed (ŭn/kə něk/tĬd), *adj.* 1. not connected; separate; distinct. 2. disconnected; incoherent: *an unconnected report of the accident.*

un·con·scion·a·ble (ŭn kŏn/shən ə bəl), *adj.* 1. not guided by conscience; unscrupulous. 2. not in accordance with what is just or reasonable: *unconscionable behavior.* 3. unreasonably excessive. —un·con/scion·a·ble·ness, *n.* —un·con/scion·a·bly, *adv.*

un·con·scious (ŭn kŏn/shəs), *adj.* 1. not conscious; not aware of something. 2. temporarily devoid of consciousness. 3. not endowed with knowledge of one's own existence, etc. 4. not known to or perceived by oneself: *an unconscious mistake.* 5. unintentional: *an unconscious slight.* 6. *Psychol.* pertaining to mental processes which the individual cannot bring into consciousness. —*n.* 7. **the unconscious,** *Psychoanal.* an organization of the mind containing all psychic material not available in the immediate field of awareness. —un·con/scious·ly, *adv.* —un·con/scious·ness, *n.*

un·con·sti·tu·tion·al (ŭn/kŏn stə tū/shən əl, -tōō/-), *adj.* not constitutional; unauthorized by or inconsistent with the constitution, as of a country. —un/con·sti·tu/tion·al/i·ty, *n.* —un/con·sti·tu/tion·al·ly, *adv.*

un·con·ven·tion·al (ŭn/kən věn/shən əl), *adj.* not conventional; not bound by or conforming to convention, rule, or precedent; free from conventionality. —un/con·ven/tion·al·ly, *adv.*

un·con·ven·tion·al·i·ty (ŭn/kən věn/shə năl/ə tĬ), *n., pl.* -ties. 1. freedom from rules and precedents; originality. 2. something unconventional, as an act.

un·cork (ŭn kôrk/), *v.t.* to draw the cork from.

un·count·ed (ŭn koun/tĬd), *adj.* 1. not counted. 2. innumerable.

un·cou·ple (ŭn kŭp/əl), *v.t.*, -pled, -pling. to undo the coupling of; disconnect.

un·cour·te·ous (ŭn kûr/tĬ əs), *adj.* uncivil; discourteous. —un·cour/te·ous·ly, *adv.*

un·court·ly (ŭn kôrt/lĬ), *adj.* not courtly; rude. —un·court/li·ness, *n.*

un·couth (ŭn kōōth/), *adj.* 1. awkward, clumsy, or unmannerly, as persons, behavior, actions, etc. 2. strange and ungraceful in appearance or form. 3. unusual or strange. [ME; OE *uncūth* (f. *un-* UN-[1] + *cūth*, pp., known), c. D *onkond*] —un·couth/ly, *adv.* —un·couth/ness, *n.*

un·cov·e·nant·ed (ŭn kŭv/ə nən tĬd), *adj.* 1. not agreed to or promised by covenant. 2. not having joined in a covenant.

un·cov·er (ŭn kŭv/ər), *v.t.* 1. to lay bare; disclose; reveal. 2. to remove the cover or covering from. 3. to remove (the hat, or other head covering). —*v.i.* 4. to remove a cover or covering. 5. to take off one's hat or other headcovering, as in respect.

un·cov·ered (ŭn kŭv/ərd), *adj.* 1. having no cover or covering. 2. having the head bare. 3. not protected by security, as a note.

un·crit·i·cal (ŭn krĬt/ə kəl), *adj.* 1. lacking in acuteness of judgment or critical analysis: *an uncritical reader.* 2. not in accordance with the rules of just criticism: *an uncritical estimate.* —un·crit/i·cal·ly, *adv.*

un·crown (ŭn kroun/), *v.t.* 1. to deprive or divest of a crown. 2. to reduce from dignity or preëminence.

un·crowned (ŭn kround/), *adj.* 1. not crowned; not having yet assumed the crown. 2. having royal rank or power without occupying the royal office.

unc·tion (ŭngk/shən), *n.* 1. act of anointing, esp. for the medical purposes or as a religious rite. 2. *Relig.* **a.** the oil used in religious rites, as in anointing the sick or dying. **b.** the shedding of a divine or spiritual influence upon a person. **c.** the influence shed. **d.** extreme unction. 3. something soothing or comforting. 4. a soothing, sympathetic, and persuasive quality in discourse, esp. on religious subjects. 5. a professional, conventional, or affected earnestness or fervor in utterance. [ME, t. L: s. *unctio*] —unc/tion·less, *adj.*

unc·tu·ous (ŭngk/chōō əs), *adj.* 1. of the nature of or characteristic of an unguent or ointment; oily; greasy. 2. characterized by religious unction or fervor, esp. of an affected kind; excessively smooth, suave, or bland. 3. having an oily or soapy feel, as certain minerals. [ME, t. ML: m.s. *unctuōsus*, der. L *unctum* ointment] —unc·tu·os·i·ty (ŭngk/chōō ŏs/ə tĬ), unc/tu·ous·ness, *n.*

un·curl (ŭn kûrl/), *v.t., v.i.* to straighten out, as something curled.

un·daunt·ed (ŭn dôn/tĬd, -dän/-), *adj.* not discouraged; fearless; undismayed. —un·daunt/ed·ly, *adv.* —un·daunt/ed·ness, *n.*

un·dé (ŭn/dā), *adj. Her.* wavy. Also, **un/dée.** [t. OF, f. *unde* wave (g. L *unda*) + *-e(e)*, adj. suffix (see -ATE[1])]

un·dec·a·gon (ŭn děk/ə gŏn/), *n.* a polygon having eleven angles and eleven sides. [f. L *undec(im)* eleven + (DEC)AGON]

un·de·ceive (ŭn/dĬ sēv/), *v.t.*, -ceived, -ceiving. to free from deception, fallacy, or mistake.

un·de·cid·ed (ŭn/dĬ sī/dĬd), *adj.* 1. not decided or determined. 2. not having one's mind made up; irresolute. —un/de·cid/ed·ly, *adv.* —un/de·cid/ed·ness, *n.*

un·de·fined (ŭn/dĬ fīnd/), *adj.* 1. not definitely limited; indefinite. 2. not described by definition or explanation; not explained.

un·de·ni·a·ble (ŭn/dĬ nī/ə bəl), *adj.* 1. not to be refuted; indisputable. 2. that cannot be refused. 3. unquestionably good; unexceptionable. —un/de·ni·a·bly, *adv.*

un·der (ŭn/dər), *prep.* 1. beneath and covered by: *under a table or a tree.* 2. below the surface of: *under water.* 3. at a point or position lower than or further down than: *to hit a man under the belt.* 4. in the position or state of bearing, supporting, sustaining, undergoing, etc.: *to sink under a load, a matter under consideration.* 5. beneath (a head, heading, or the like), as in classification. 6. as designated, indicated, or represented by: *under a new name.* 7. below in degree, amount, price, etc.; less than: *under age.* 8. below in rank, dignity, or the like. 9. subject to the rule, direction, guidance, etc., of: *under supervision.* 10. subject to the influence, conditioning force, etc., of: *under these circumstances.* 11. with the favor or aid of: *under protection.* 12. authorized, warranted, or attested by: *under one's hand or seal.* 13. in accordance with: *under the provisions of the law.* —*adv.* 14. under or beneath something. 15. beneath the surface. 16. in a lower place. 17. in a lower degree, amount, etc. 18. in a subordinate position or

un·con·cert/ed	un·con·tem·plat/ed	un·crowd/ed	un·de·clared/
un·con·cil/i·at/ed	un·con·tend/ing	un·crys/tal·line	un·de·clin/a·ble
un·con·clud/ed	un·con·test/ed	un·crys/tal·liz/a·ble	un·de·clined/
un·con·demned/	un·con·tra·dict/a·ble	un·crys/tal·lized/	un·de·com·pos/a·ble
un·con·densed/	un·con·tra·dict/ed	un·cul/ti·va·ble	un·de·com·posed/
un·con·fined/	un·con·trite/	un·cul/ti·vat·ed	un·dec/o·rat/ed
un·con·firmed/	un·con·trol/la·ble	un·cul/tured	un·de·face/a·ble
un·con·fused/	un·con·trolled/	un·cum/bered	un·de·faced/
un·con·fut/ed	un·con·trol/led·ly	un·cur/a·ble	un·de·fac/ed·ness
un·con·geal/	un·con·vers/a·ble	un·curbed/	un·de·feat/a·ble
un·con·geal/a·ble	un·con·vert/ed	un·cur/dled	un·de·feat/ed
un·con·gealed/	un·con·vert/i·ble	un·cured/	un·de·fend/ed
un·con·gen/ial	un·con·vert/i·bly	un·cu/ri·ous	un·de·fen/si·ble
un·con·ge/ni·al/i·ty	un·con·vinced/	un·curled/	un·de·filed/
un·con·gen/ial·ly	un·con·vinc/ing	un·cur/rent	un·de·fin/a·ble
un·con·nect/ed·ly	un·cooked/	un·cursed/	un·de·formed/
un·con/quer·a·ble	un·co·ör/di·nat·ed	un·cur/tained	un·de·lay/a·ble
un·con/quer·a·bly	un·cor/dial	un·cush/ioned	un·de·layed/
un·con/quered	un·corked/	un·cus/tom·ar/y	un·de·lin/e·at/ed
un·con·sci·en/tious	un·cor·rect/ed	un·cut/	un·de·liv/er·a·ble
un·con·se/crat/ed	un·cor·rob/o·rat/ed	un·dam/aged	un·de·liv/ered
un·con·sent/ing	un·cor·rupt/	un·dan/gered	un·dem·o·crat/ic
un·con·sid/ered	un·cor·rupt/ed	un·dat/ed	un·de·mon/stra·ble
un·con·sid/er·ing	un·cor·rupt/ly	un·daugh/ter·ly	un·de·mon/stra·bly
un·con·soled/	un·cor·rupt/ness	un·daz/zled	un·de·mon/stra·tive
un·con·sol/i·dat/ed	un·count/a·ble	un·de·bat/a·ble	un·de·nied/
un·con/so·nant	un·cre·at/ed	un·de·cayed/	un·de·nom/i·na/tion·al
un·con/stant	un·cred/it·ed	un·de·cay/ing	un·de·pend/a·ble
un·con·sti·tut/ed	un·crip/pled	un·de·ceiv/a·ble	un·de·plored/
un·con·strained/	un·crit/i·ciz/a·ble	un·de·ci/pher·a·ble	un·de·posed/
un·con·strict/ed	un·cropped/	un·de·ci/pher·a·bly	un·de·pre/ci·at/ed
un·con·sumed/	un·crossed/	un·de·ci/phered	un·de·pressed/
un·con·tam/i·nat/ed			un·de·put/ed

condition. 19. in or into subjection or submission. —*adj.* **20.** beneath. **21.** lower in position. **22.** lower in degree, amount, etc. **23.** lower in rank or condition. [ME and OE; c. D *onder*, G *unter*, Icel. *undir*, akin to L *infrā* below] —**Syn. 2.** See **below.**

under-, a prefixal attributive use of *under*, as to indicate place or situation below or beneath, as in *underbrush, undertow*; lower in grade or dignity, as in *undersheriff, understudy*; of lesser degree, extent, or amount, as in *undersized*; or insufficiency, as in *underfeed*.

un·der·act (ŭn/dər ăkt/), *v.t.* to underplay.

un·der·age (ŭn/dər āj/), *adj.* lacking the required age, esp. that of legal maturity.

un·der·arm (ŭn/dər ärm/), *adj.* **1.** under the arm: *an underarm seam.* **2.** *Cricket, etc.* executed with the hand below the shoulder; using underhand bowling.

un·der·armed (ŭn/dər ärmd/), *adj.* not having sufficient weapons.

un·der·bid (ŭn/dər bĭd/), *v.t., -bid, -bidding.* to make a lower bid than (another), as in seeking a contract to be awarded to the lowest bidder. —**un/der·bid/der,** *n.*

un·der·bod·ice (ŭn/dər bŏd/ĭs), *n.* a bodice worn under an outer bodice.

un·der·bred (ŭn/dər brĕd/), *adj.* **1.** of inferior breeding or manners; vulgar. **2.** not of pure breed, as a horse.

un·der·brush (ŭn/dər brŭsh/), *n.* shrubs, small trees, etc., growing under large trees in a wood or forest.

un·der·buy (ŭn/dər bī/), *v.t., -bought, -buying.* **1.** to buy more cheaply than (another). **2.** to buy at less than the actual value.

un·der·car·riage (ŭn/dər kăr/ĭj), *n.* **1.** the supporting framework beneath the body of a carriage, etc. **2.** the portions of an airplane beneath the body, serving as a support when on the ground or water or when alighting.

un·der·charge (*v.* ŭn/dər chärj/; *n.* ŭn/dər chärj/), *v.,* -**charged, -charging,** *n.* —*v.t.* **1.** to charge (a person, etc.) less than the proper or fair price. **2.** to charge (so much) less than a fair price. **3.** to put an insufficient charge or load into. —*n.* **4.** a charge or price less than is proper or fair. **5.** an insufficient charge or load.

un·der·class·man (ŭn/dər klăs/mən, -kläs/-), *n., pl.* **-men.** *U.S.* a freshman or sophomore.

un·der·clothes (ŭn/dər klōz/, -klōthz/), *n. pl.* clothes worn under outer clothes, esp. those worn next to the skin. Also, **un/der·cloth/ing.**

un·der·coat·ing (ŭn/dər kō/tĭng), *n.* a protective seal applied to the underside of an automobile to reduce corrosion and vibration.

un·der·cov·er (ŭn/dər kŭv/ər), *adj.* working or done out of public sight; secret: *an undercover agent.*

un·der·croft (ŭn/dər krŏft/, -krôft/), *n.* a vault or chamber under the ground, esp. in a church. [f. UNDER- + obs. *croft* vault (ult. t. L: m. *crypta* CRYPT)]

un·der·cur·rent (ŭn/dər kûr/ənt), *n.* **1.** a current below the upper currents or below the surface. **2.** an underlying tendency.

un·der·cut (*v.* ŭn/dər kŭt/; *n., adj.* ŭn/dər kŭt/), *v.,* -**cut, -cutting,** *n., adj.* —*v.t.* **1.** to cut under or beneath. **2.** to cut away material from so as to leave a portion overhanging, as in carving or sculpture. **3.** to sell or work at a lower price than. **4.** *Golf.* to hit (the ball) so as to cause a backspin. **5.** *Tennis.* to slice (the ball) using an underhand motion. —*v.i.* **6.** to undercut material, a competitor, a ball, etc. —*n.* **7.** a cut, or a cutting away, underneath. **8.** a notch cut in a tree to determine the direction in which the tree is to fall and to prevent splitting. **9.** *Golf.* a backspin. **10.** *Tennis.* a slice or cut made with an underhand motion. **11.** *Chiefly Brit.* the tenderloin or fillet of beef. —*adj.* **12.** cut away underneath.

un·der·de·vel·op (ŭn/dər dĭ vĕl/əp), *v.t.* to develop short of the required amount: *to underdevelop film.*

un·der·do (ŭn/dər dōō/), *v.i., v.t.,* -**did, -done, -doing.** to do less than is usual or requisite.

un·der·dog (ŭn/dər dôg/, -dŏg/), *n. Colloq.* **1.** the dog that gets the worst of it in a dog fight. **2.** a person who gets the worst of it in the struggle for survival.

un·der·done (ŭn/dər dŭn/), *adj. Chiefly Brit.* (of food) not thoroughly cooked.

un·der·drain·age (ŭn/dər drā/nĭj), *n.* drainage of agricultural lands and removal of excess water and of alkali by drains buried beneath the surface.

un·der·es·ti·mate (*v.* ŭn/dər ĕs/tə māt/; *n.* ŭn/dər ĕs/tə mĭt, -māt/), *v.,* -**mated, -mating,** *n.* —*v.t.* **1.** to estimate at too low a value, rate, or the like. —*n.* **2.** an estimate that is too low. —**un/der·es/ti·ma/tion,** *n.*

un·der·ex·pose (ŭn/dər ĭk spōz/), *v.t.,* -**posed, -posing.** to expose to light too little, as in photography.

un·der·ex·po·sure (ŭn/dər ĭk spō/zhər), *n.* inadequate exposing to light rays.

un·der·feed (ŭn/dər fēd/), *v.t.,* -**fed, -feeding. 1.** to feed insufficiently. **2.** to feed with fuel from beneath.

un·der·foot (ŭn/dər fŏŏt/), *adv.* **1.** under the foot or feet; on the ground; underneath or below. —*adj.* **2.** lying under the foot or feet. **3.** abject; downtrodden.

un·der·fur (ŭn/dər fûr/), *n.* the fur, or fine, soft, thick, hairy coat, under the longer and coarser outer hair in certain animals, as seals, otters, and beavers.

un·der·gar·ment (ŭn/dər gär/mənt), *n.* a garment worn under another garment, esp. next to the skin.

un·der·glaze (ŭn/dər glāz/), *adj. Ceram.* applied before the glaze is put on, as decoration or colors in porcelain painting.

un·der·go (ŭn/dər gō/), *v.t.,* -**went, -gone, -going. 1.** to be subjected to; experience; pass through. **2.** to endure; sustain; suffer. —**Syn. 2.** See **experience.**

un·der·grad·u·ate (ŭn/dər grăj/ŏŏ ĭt), *n.* **1.** a student in a university or college who has not taken his first degree. —*adj.* **2.** having the standing of an undergraduate. **3.** pertaining to, characteristic of, or consisting of undergraduates.

un·der·ground (*adv., adj.* ŭn/dər ground/; *n.* ŭn/dərground/), *adv.* **1.** beneath the surface of the ground. **2.** in concealment or secrecy; not openly. —*adj.* **3.** existing, situated, operating, or taking place beneath the surface of the ground. **4.** used, or for use, underground. **5.** hidden or secret; not open. —*n.* **6.** the place or region beneath the surface of the ground. **7.** an underground space or passage. **8.** a secret organization fighting the established government or occupation forces, esp. one in the fascist-overrun nations of Europe before and during World War II. **9.** *Chiefly Brit.* underground railroad.

underground railroad, 1. Also, **underground railway.** a railroad running through a continuous tunnel, as under city streets; a subway. **2.** *U.S. Hist.* (before the abolition of slavery) an arrangement among opponents of slavery for helping fugitive slaves to escape into Canada or some other place of safety.

un·der·growth (ŭn/dər grōth/), *n.* **1.** shrubs or small trees growing beneath or among large trees. **2.** condition of being undergrown or undersized. **3.** short, fine hair underlying longer outer hair on a skin.

un·der·hand (ŭn/dər hănd/), *adj.* **1.** not open and aboveboard; secret and crafty or dishonorable. **2.** done or delivered underhand. —*adv.* **3.** with the hand below the shoulder, as in pitching or bowling a ball. **4.** with the hand under the object. **5.** secretly; stealthily; slyly.

un·der·hand·ed (ŭn/dər hăn/dĭd), *adj.* **1.** underhand. **2.** shorthanded. —**un/der·hand/ed·ly,** *adv.* —**un/der·hand/ed·ness,** *n.*

un·der·hung (ŭn/dər hŭng/), *adj.* **1.** *Anat.* **a.** (of the under jaw) projecting beyond the upper jaw. **b.** having the under jaw so projecting. **2.** resting on a track beneath, instead of being overhung, as a sliding door.

un·der·laid (ŭn/dər lād/), *adj.* **1.** put beneath. **2.** having an underlay. —*v.* **3.** pt. and pp. of **underlay.**

un·der·lap (ŭn/dər lăp/), *v.t.,* -**lapped, -lapping.** to extend partly under.

un·der·lay (*v.* ŭn/dər lā/; *n.* ŭn/dər lā/), *v.,* -**laid, -laying,** *n.* —*v.t.* **1.** to lay (one thing) under or beneath another. **2.** to provide with something laid underneath; raise or support with something laid underneath. **3.** to extend beneath. —*n.* **4.** something underlaid. **5.** *Printing.* a piece or pieces of paper put under types, etc., to bring them to the proper height for printing.

un·der·let (ŭn/dər lĕt/), *v.t.,* -**let, -letting. 1.** to let below the true value. **2.** to sublet.

un·der·lie (ŭn/dər lī/), *v.t.,* -**lay, -lain, -lying. 1.** to lie under or beneath; be situated under. **2.** to be at the basis of; form the foundation of. **3.** *Gram.* (of a morpheme, word, or other form) to be the primitive of (a form derived by the addition of affixes or by other alteration), e.g., *boy* underlies the complex word *boyish*. **4.** *Finance.* to be primary to another right or security. [ME *underly*, OE *underlicgan* (see UNDER-, LIE²)]

un·der·line (ŭn/dər līn/, ŭn/dər līn/), *v.t.,* -**lined, -lining.** to mark with a line or lines underneath; underscore.

un·der·ling (ŭn/dər lĭng), *n.* a subordinate (esp. in disparagement). [ME and OE; f. UNDER, adv. + -LING¹]

un·der·mine (ŭn/dər mīn/, ŭn/dər mīn/), *v.t.,* -**mined, -mining. 1.** to form a mine or passage under, as in military operations; make an excavation under. **2.** to render unstable by digging into or wearing away the foundations. **3.** to affect injuriously or weaken by secret or underhand means. **4.** to weaken insidiously; destroy gradually. —**un/der·min/er,** *n.*

un·der·most (ŭn/dər mōst/), *adj., adv.* lowest.

un·der·neath (ŭn/dər nēth/, -nēth/), *prep.* **1.** under; beneath. **2.** under the power of: *to live underneath a good king.* —*adv.* **3.** beneath; below. —*adj.* **4.** lower. [ME *undernethe,* OE *underneothan.* See UNDER, BENEATH]

un·der·nour·ish (ŭn/dər nûr/ĭsh), *v.t.* to feed inadequately to maintain normal health. —**un/der·nour/ished,** *adj.* —**un/der·nour/ish·ment,** *n.*

un·der·of·fi·cer (ŭn/dər ôf/ə sər, -ŏf/-), *v.t.* to furnish inadequately with officers.

un·de·rog·a·to·ry (ŭn/də rŏg/ə tō/rĭ), *adj.* not derogatory.

un·der·pass (ŭn/dər păs/, -päs/), *n.* a passage running underneath, esp. a passage for pedestrians or vehicles, or both, crossing under a railway, road, etc.

un·der·pay (ŭn/dər pā/), *v.t.,* -**paid, -paying.** to pay insufficiently.

un·der·pin (ŭn/dər pĭn/), *v.t.,* -**pinned, -pinning. 1.** to pin or support underneath; place something under for support or foundation. **2.** to support with masonry, stones, etc., as a building. **3.** to support; prop.

un·der·pin·ning (ŭn/dər pĭn/ĭng), *n. Archit.* supports or latticework placed under a completed wall.

un·der·play (ŭn/dər plā/), *v.t.* **1.** to act (a part) sketchily. **2.** to act subtly and restrainedly. —*v.i.* **3.** to leave out of one's acting all subtlety and enriching detail. **4.** to achieve an effect in acting with a minimum of emphasis.

un·der·plot (ŭn/dər plŏt/), *n.* a plot subordinate to another plot, as in a play or novel.

---

un·der·priv·i·leged (ŭn′dər prĭv′ə lĭjd), *adj.* denied the enjoyment of the normal privileges or rights of a society because of low economic and social status.

un·der·pro·duc·tion (ŭn′dər prə dŭk′shən), *n.* production that is less than normal, or than the demand.

un·der·proof (ŭn′dər prōōf′), *adj.* containing a smaller proportion of alcohol than proof spirit does.

un·der·prop (ŭn′dər prŏp′), *v.t.,* **-propped, -propping.** to prop underneath; support; uphold.

un·der·quote (ŭn′dər kwōt′), *v.t.,* **-quoted, -quoting.** 1. to quote at a price below another price or the market price. 2. to quote lower prices than (another).

un·der·rate (ŭn′dər rāt′), *v.t.,* **-rated, -rating.** to rate too low; underestimate.

un·der·run (ŭn′dər rŭn′), *v.,* **-ran, -run, -running,** *n.* —*v.t.* 1. to run, pass, or go under. —*n.* 2. that which runs or passes underneath, as a current.

un·der·score (*v.* ŭn′dər skôr′; *n.* ŭn′dər skôr′), *v.,* **-scored, -scoring,** *n.* —*v.t.* 1. to mark with a line or lines underneath; underline. —*n.* 2. a line drawn beneath something written or printed, as for emphasis.

un·der·sea (ŭn′dər sē′), *adj.* 1. submarine. —*adv.* 2. underseas.

un·der·seas (ŭn′dər sēz′), *adv.* beneath the surface of the sea.

un·der·sec·re·tar·y (ŭn′dər sĕk′rə tĕr′ĭ), *n., pl.* **-taries.** a secretary subordinate to a principal secretary.

un·der·sell (ŭn′dər sĕl′), *v.t.,* **-sold, -selling.** 1. to sell things at a lower price than (a competitor). 2. *Rare.* to sell for less than the actual value. —**un′der·sell′er,** *n.*

un·der·serv·ant (ŭn′dər sûr′vənt), *n.* an inferior or subordinate servant.

un·der·set (ŭn′dər sĕt′), *n.* an ocean undercurrent. —Syn. See **undertow.**

un·der·sher·iff (ŭn′dər shĕr′ĭf), *n.* a sheriff's deputy, esp. a deputy on whom the sheriff's duties devolve when the sheriff is incapacitated or when the office is vacant.

un·der·shirt (ŭn′dər shûrt′), *n.* an inner shirt, worn next to the skin.

un·der·shot (ŭn′dər shŏt′), *adj.* underhung; driven by water passing beneath, as a kind of vertical water wheel.

un·der·shrub (ŭn′dər shrŭb′), *n.* a low shrub.

un·der·side (ŭn′dər sīd′), *n.* the under or lower side.

Undershot water wheel

un·der·sign (ŭn′dər sīn′, ŭn′dər sīn′), *v.t.* to sign one's name under, or at the end of (a letter or document); affix one's signature to.

un·der·signed (ŭn′dər sīnd′), *adj.* 1. having signed, as a person, at the end of a letter or document. 2. signed, as a name. —*n.* 3. **the undersigned,** the person or persons undersigning a letter or document.

un·der·sized (ŭn′dər sīzd′), *adj.* below the usual size. Also, **un′der·size′.**

un·der·skirt (ŭn′dər skûrt′), *n.* a skirt worn under an outer skirt or under an overskirt or drapery.

un·der·sleeve (ŭn′dər slēv′), *n.* 1. a sleeve worn under an outer sleeve. 2. an ornamental inner sleeve extending below the outer sleeve.

un·der·slung (ŭn′dər slŭng′), *adj.* attached to the axles from below, as the chassis frame of an automobile.

un·der·soil (ŭn′dər soil′), *n.* subsoil.

un·der·song (ŭn′dər sŏng′, -sông′), *n.* the accompaniment of a song; a subordinate strain.

un·der·sparred (ŭn′dər spärd′), *adj. Naut.* having spars too small to carry enough sail.

un·der·stand (ŭn′dər stănd′), *v.,* **-stood, -standing.** —*v.t.* 1. to perceive the meaning of; grasp the idea of; comprehend. 2. to be thoroughly familiar with; apprehend clearly the character or nature of. 3. to comprehend by knowing the meaning of the words employed, as a language. 4. to grasp clearly as a fact, or realize. 5. to take as a fact, or as settled. 6. to get knowledge of; learn or hear. 7. to accept as a fact; believe. 8. to conceive the meaning of in a particular way: *you are to understand the phrase literally.* 9. to supply mentally, as a word necessary to complete sense. —*v.i.* 10. to perceive what is meant. 11. to have the use of the intellectual faculties. 12. to have information or knowledge about something: *to understand about a matter.* 13. to be informed; believe. [ME; OE *understondan,* c. D *onderstaan,* G *unterstehen*] —Syn. 1. See **know.**

un·der·stand·a·ble (ŭn′dər stăn′də bəl), *adj.* that may be understood. —**un′der·stand′a·ble·ness,** *n.* —**un′der·stand′a·bly,** *adv.*

un·der·stand·ing (ŭn′dər stăn′dĭng), *n.* 1. act of one who understands; comprehension; personal interpretation. 2. intelligence; wit. 3. superior intelligence; superior power of recognizing the truth: *men of understanding.* 4. a mutual comprehension of each other's meaning, thoughts, etc. 5. a state of (good or friendly) relations between persons. 6. a mutual agreement of a private or unannounced kind. 7. *Philos.* the power of abstract thought; the logical power. —*adj.* 8. that understands; possessing or showing intelligence or understanding. —**un′der·stand′ing·ly,** *adv.*

un·der·state (ŭn′dər stāt′), *v.t.,* **-stated, -stating.** to state or represent less strongly than the truth will admit; state too low. —**un′der·state′ment,** *n.*

un·der·stock (*v.* ŭn′dər stŏk′; *n.* ŭn′dər stŏk′), *v.t.* 1. to supply insufficiently with stock. —*n.* 2. *Hort.* (in grafting) the rooted plant which receives the scion.

un·der·stood (ŭn′dər stŏŏd′), *v.* 1. pt. and pp. of **understand.** —*adj.* 2. agreed upon by all concerned. 3. implied; assumed.

un·der·strap·per (ŭn′dər străp′ər), *n.* an underling.

un·der·stra·tum (ŭn′dər strā′təm, -străt′əm), *n., pl.* **-strata** (-strā′tə, -străt′ə), **-stratums.** a substratum.

un·der·stud·y (ŭn′dər stŭd′ĭ), *v.,* **-studied, -studying,** *n., pl.* **-studies.** —*v.t.* 1. to study (a part) in order to replace the regular actor or actress when necessary. 2. to act as understudy to (an actor or actress): *understudy the lead.* —*n.* 3. a person trained and retained to act as substitute for an actor or actress.

un·der·take (ŭn′dər tāk′), *v.,* **-took, -taken, -taking.** —*v.t.* 1. to take on oneself (some task, performance, etc.); take in hand; essay; attempt. 2. to take on oneself by formal promise or agreement; lay oneself under obligation to perform or execute. 3. to warrant or guarantee (fol. by a clause). 4. to take in charge; assume the duty of attending to (a person). 5. *Obs.* to engage with, as in a duel. —*v.i.* 6. to take on oneself any task of responsibility. 7. *Archaic.* to engage oneself by promise (*for*); give a guarantee, or become surety (*for*). 8. *Colloq.* to act as an undertaker or funeral director.

un·der·tak·er (ŭn′dər tā′kər *for 1*; ŭn′dər tā′kər *for 2*), *n.* 1. one who undertakes something. 2. one whose business it is to prepare the dead for burial and to take charge of funerals.

un·der·tak·ing (ŭn′dər tā′kĭng *for 1–3*; ŭn′dər tā′kĭng *for 4*), *n.* 1. act of one who undertakes any task or responsibility. 2. a task, enterprise, etc., undertaken. 3. a promise; pledge; guarantee. 4. the business of an undertaker or funeral director.

un·der·ten·ant (ŭn′dər tĕn′ənt), *n.* a subtenant.

un·der·tint (ŭn′dər tĭnt′), *n.* a subdued tint.

un·der·tone (ŭn′dər tōn′), *n.* 1. a low or subdued tone, as of utterance. 2. an underlying quality or element, or an undercurrent. 3. a subdued color; a color modified by an underlying color.

un·der·took (ŭn′dər tŏŏk′), *v.* pt. of **undertake.**

un·der·tow (ŭn′dər tō′), *n.* 1. the backward flow or draft of the water, below the surface, from waves breaking on a beach. 2. any strong current below the surface of a body of water, moving in a direction different from that of the surface current. —Syn. 2. UNDERTOW, UNDERSET, RIPTIDE are terms for a (usually) strong undercurrent or flow of water in the ocean, contrary to the direction of surface water. UNDERTOW and another "sailors' word" UNDERSET (a set or current contrary to the general set of the water, or contrary to the wind) came into notice early in the 19th century. The former is still in general use along the Atlantic coast; the latter now less well-known. RIP, in use in the U.S. by the late 18th century, properly means a place in the ocean violently disturbed, usually by the meeting of opposing tides. Of recent years, in the form RIPTIDE, it has also been used, esp. on the Pacific coast, to mean much the same as UNDERTOW, dangerous to bathers where heavy surf prevails.

un·der·trump (ŭn′dər trŭmp′), *v.t. Cards.* 1. to trump with a lower trump than has already been played. 2. to play a lower trump than.

un·der·val·ue (ŭn′dər văl′ū), *v.t.,* **-ued, -uing.** 1. to value below the real worth; put too low a value on. 2. to diminish in value; make of less value. 3. to esteem too low; esteem lightly; hold in mean estimation. —**un′der·val′u·a′tion,** *n.*

un·der·vest (ŭn′dər vĕst′), *n. Brit.* an undershirt.

un·der·waist (ŭn′dər wāst′), *n.* a waist worn under another waist.

un·der·wa·ter (ŭn′dər wô′tər, -wŏt′ər), *adj.* 1. being or occurring under water. 2. designed to be used under water. 3. situated below the water line of a ship.

un·der·wear (ŭn′dər wâr′), *n.* underclothes.

un·der·weight (ŭn′dər wāt′; *adj.* ŭn′dər wāt′), *n.* 1. weight short of some norm. —*adj.* 2. lacking usual or required weight.

un·der·went (ŭn′dər wĕnt′), *v.* pt. of **undergo.**

un·der·wing (ŭn′dər wĭng′), *n.* a hind wing of an insect.

un·der·wood (ŭn′dər wŏŏd′), *n.* 1. shrubs or small trees growing under larger trees; underbrush. 2. a growth of underbrush.

un·der·world (ŭn′dər wûrld′), *n.* 1. the lower, degraded, or criminal part of human society. 2. the lower or nether world; Hades. 3. the place or region below the surface of the earth. 4. the opposite side of the earth; the antipodes. 5. the world below the skies; the earth.

un·der·write (ŭn′dər rīt′), *v.,* **-wrote, -written, -writing.** —*v.t.* 1. to write (something) under a thing, esp. under other written matter. 2. to sign one's name to (a document, etc.). 3. to subscribe to (a statement, etc.). 4. to agree to give or pay (a certain sum of money) by signing one's name. 5. to agree to meet the expense of; undertake to finance. 6. to guarantee the sale of (shares or bonds to be offered to the public for subscription). 7. *Insurance.* **a.** to write one's name at the end of (a policy of insurance), thereby becoming liable in case of certain losses specified therein. **b.** to insure. **c.** to assume liability to the extent of (a certain sum) by way of insurance. —*v.i.* 8. to underwrite something. 9. to carry on the business of an underwriter. [ME; OE *underwrītan* (trans. of L *subscrībere*)]

ăct, āble, dâre, ärt; ĕbb, ēqual; ĭf, īce; hŏt, ōver, ôrder, oil, bŏŏk, ōōze, out; ŭp, ūse, ûrge; ə = a in alone; ch, chief; g, give; ng, ring; sh, shoe; th, thin; ŧħ, that; zh, vision. See the full key on inside cover.

un·der·writ·er (ŭn′dər rī′tər), *n.* **1.** one who underwrites policies of insurance, or carries on insurance as a business. **2.** one who underwrites shares or bonds.

un·der·writ·ten (ŭn′dər rĭt′ən), *v.* pp. of **underwrite**.

un·der·wrote (ŭn′dər rōt′), *v.* pt. of **underwrite**.

un·de·sign·ing (ŭn′dĭ zī′nĭng), *adj.* without underhand or selfish designs.

un·de·sir·a·ble (ŭn′dĭ zīr′ə bəl), *adj.* **1.** objectionable. —*n.* **2.** an undesirable person or thing.

un·de·vel·oped (ŭn′dĭ vĕl′əpt), *adj.* not developed. —**Syn.** See **imperfect**.

un·did (ŭn dĭd′), *v.* pt. of **undo**.

un·di·gest·i·ble (ŭn′dĭ jĕs′tə bəl, -dī-), *adj.* indigestible.

un·di·lu·tion (ŭn′dĭ lōō′shən, -dī-), *n.* undiluted state.

un·dine (ŭn dēn′, ŭn′dēn, -dĭn), *n.* one of a class of fabled water spirits of the female sex. According to Paracelsus, when an undine married a mortal and bore a child, she received a soul. [t. NL (Paracelsus): m. *Undina*, der. L *unda* wave] —**Syn.** See **sylph**.

un·di·rect·ed (ŭn′dĭ rĕk′tĭd, -dī-), *adj.* **1.** not directed; not guided. **2.** bearing no address, as a letter.

un·dis·posed (ŭn′dĭs pōzd′), *adj.* not disposed (of).

un·do (ŭn dōō′), *v.t.*, **-did, -done, -doing. 1.** to reverse the doing of; cause to be as if never done. **2.** to do away with; remove. **3.** to bring to ruin or disaster; destroy. **4.** to unfasten and open (something locked, barred, etc.). **5.** to untie or loose (strings, etc.). **6.** to open (a package, a sealed letter, etc.). **7.** *Obs.* to explain; interpret. [ME; OE *undōn*, c. D *ontdoen*; f. UN-² + DO¹] —**un·do′er,** *n.*

un·do·ing (ŭn dōō′ĭng), *n.* **1.** the reversing of what has been done; annulling. **2.** a bringing to destruction, ruin, or disaster. **3.** a cause of destruction or ruin.

un·done¹ (ŭn dŭn′), *adj.* **1.** not done; not accomplished or completed, or finished. **2.** neglected or omitted. [f. UN-¹ + DONE]

un·done² (ŭn dŭn′), *v.* **1.** pp. of **undo**. —*adj.* **2.** brought to destruction or ruin. [see UNDO]

un·dou·ble (ŭn dŭb′əl), *v.t.*, **-bled, -bling.** to unfold; render single.

un·doubt·ed (ŭn dou′tĭd), *adj.* not called in question; accepted as beyond doubt; undisputed. —**un·doubt′ed·ly,** *adv.*

un·drape (ŭn drāp′), *v.t.*, **-draped, -draping.** to strip of drapery; bare.

un·draw (ŭn drô′), *v.*, **-drew, -drawn, -drawing.** —*v.t.* **1.** to draw back or away. —*v.i.* **2.** to be drawn back or withdrawn.

un·dress (ŭn drĕs′), *v.t.* **1.** to take off the clothes of; disrobe. **2.** to strip of whatever adorns. **3.** to remove the dressing from (a wound, etc.). —*v.i.* **4.** to take off one's clothes. —*n.* **5.** ordinary dress, as opposed to full dress. **6.** informal dress; négligé. —*adj.* **7.** of or pertaining to ordinary dress. **8.** informal as to dress.

un·dressed (ŭn drĕst′), *adj.* **1.** not dressed; not specially prepared. **2.** (of leather) having a napped finish on the flesh side.

Und·set (ōōn′sĕt), *n.* **Sigrid** (sĭg′rĭd), 1882–1949, Norwegian novelist.

und so wei·ter (ōōnt zō vī′tər), and so forth. [G]

un·due (ŭn dū′, -dōō′), *adj.* **1.** not requisite or necessary; esp. excessive; too great: *undue haste.* **2.** not proper, fitting, or right: *to exert undue influence.* **3.** not yet owing or payable.

un·du·lant (ŭn′dyə lənt, -də-), *adj.* undulating; waving; wavy. [t. L: s. *undulans*, ppr.]

undulant fever, an irregular, relapsing fever, with swelling of joints, spleen, and rheumatic pains, caused by *Brucella melitensis* ingested in raw milk of diseased cows and goats; Malta fever; Mediterranean fever.

un·du·late (ŭn′dyə lĭt, -lāt′, -də-), *v.*, **-lated, -lating,** *adj.* —*v.i.* **1.** to have a wavy motion; rise and fall in waves. **2.** to have a wavy form or surface; bend with successive curves in alternate directions. —*v.t.* **3.** to cause to move in waves. **4.** to give a wavy form to. —*adj.* Also **un′du·lat′ed. 5.** wavy; bending with successive curves in alternate directions; having a waved form, surface, margin, etc. [t. L: m.s. *undulātus* wavy, der. *unda* wave]

un·du·la·tion (ŭn′dyə lā′shən, -də-), *n.* **1.** act of undulating; a waving motion. **2.** wavy form or outline. **3.** one of a series of wavelike bends, curves, or elevations. **4.** *Physics.* the motion of waves; a wave; a vibration.

un·du·la·to·ry (ŭn′dyə lə tōr′ĭ, -də-), *adj.* **1.** moving in undulations. **2.** having the form or appearance of waves. Also, **un·du·la·tive** (ŭn′dyə lā′tĭv, -də-).

un·du·ly (ŭn dū′lĭ, -dōō′-), *adv.* **1.** excessively. **2.** without proper right.

un·dy·ing (ŭn dī′ĭng), *adj.* deathless; immortal; unending. —**un·dy′ing·ly,** *adv.*

un·earned (ŭn ûrnd′), *adj.* not earned; not gained by labor or service, or as a due return.

unearned increment, the increase in the value of land, etc., due to natural causes, as growth of population, rather than to any labor or expenditure by the owner.

un·earth (ŭn ûrth′), *v.t.* **1.** to dig or get out of the earth; dig up. **2.** to uncover or bring to light by digging, searching, or discovery.

un·earth·ly (ŭn ûrth′lĭ), *adj.* **1.** not of this earth or world. **2.** supernatural; ghostly; unnaturally strange; weird: *an unearthly scream.* **3.** *Colloq.* extraordinary: *to get up at an unearthly hour.* —**un·earth′li·ness,** *n.* —**Syn. 2.** See **weird**.

un·eas·y (ŭn ē′zĭ), *adj.*, **-easier, -easiest. 1.** not easy in body or mind; uncomfortable; restless; disturbed; perturbed. **2.** not easy in manner; constrained. **3.** not conducive to ease; causing bodily discomfort. —**un·eas′i·ly,** *adv.* —**un·eas′i·ness,** *n.*

un·ed·u·cat·ed (ŭn ĕj′ōō kā′tĭd), *adj.* not educated. —**Syn.** See **ignorant**.

un·em·ploy·a·ble (ŭn′ĕm ploi′ə bəl), *adj.* unable to hold a job. —**un′em·ploy·a·bil′i·ty,** *n.*

un·em·ployed (ŭn′ĕm ploid′), *adj.* **1.** out of work; without work or employment. **2.** not employed; not in use; not kept busy or at work. **3.** not in productive or profitable use. —*n.* **4.** one who does not have a job. **5. the unemployed,** those who do not have jobs.

un·em·ploy·ment (ŭn′ĕm ploi′mənt), *n.* lack of employment; unemployed condition.

un·e·qual (ŭn ē′kwəl), *adj.* **1.** not equal; not of the same quantity, value, rank, ability, merit, etc.: *unequal size.* **2.** not adequate, as in amount, power, ability, etc. (fol. by *to*): *strength unequal to the task.* **3.** not evenly proportioned or balanced; not having the parts alike or symmetrical: *an unequal leaf.* **4.** not even or regular, as motion. **5.** inequitable; unfair; unjust. **6.** uneven or variable in character, quality, etc. —*n.* **7.** one who or that which is unequal. —**un·e′qual·ly,** *adv.* —**un·e′qual·ness,** *n.*

un′de·scrib′a·ble	un′dis·cern′i·ble	un′dis·tin′guish·ing	un′e·man′ci·pat′ed
un′de·scried′	un′dis·cern′i·bly	un′dis·tract′ed	un′em·bar′rassed
un′de·served′	un′dis·cern′ing	un′dis·traught′	un′em·bel′lished
un′de·serv′ed·ly	un′dis·cern′ing·ly	un′dis·tressed′	un′e·mo′tion·al
un′de·serv′ing	un′dis·charged′	un′dis·trib′ut·ed	un′em·phat′ic
un′de·serv′ing·ly	un′dis·ci′plined	un′dis·turbed′	un·emp′tied
un·des′ig·nat′ed	un′dis·closed′	un′di·ver′si·fied′	un′en·closed′
un′de·signed′	un′dis·con·cert′ed	un′di·vert′ed	un′en·cum′bered
un′de·sign′ed·ly	un′dis·cour′aged	un′di·vest′ed	un′en·dan′gered
un′de·sir′a·bil′i·ty	un′dis·cov′er·a·ble	un·di′vid′ed	un·end′ed
un′de·sir′a·bly	un′dis·cov′er·a·bly	un′di·vorced′	un·end′ing
un′de·sired′	un′dis·cov′ered	un′di·vulged′	un·end′ing·ly
un′de·sir′ous	un′dis·cred′it·ed	un′do·mes′tic	un′en·dorsed′
un′de·spair′ing	un′dis·crim′i·nat′ing	un′do·mes′ti·cat′ed	un′en·dowed′
un′de·stroyed′	un′dis·crim′i·nat′ing·ly	un′doubt′ing	un′en·dur′a·ble
un′de·tach′a·ble	un′dis·cussed′	un·drained′	un′en·dur′ing
un′de·tached′	un′dis·guised′	un′dra·mat′ic	un′en·force′a·ble
un′de·tect′ed	un′dis·guis′ed·ly	un′dra·mat′i·cal	un′en·forced′
un′de·ter′mi·na·ble	un′dis·heart′ened	un·dram′a·tized′	un′en·gaged′
un′de·ter′mined	un′dis·il·lu′sioned	un·dreamed′	un′en·joy′a·ble
un′de·terred′	un′dis·man′tled	un·dreamt′	un′en·joyed′
un′de·vi′at·ing	un′dis·mayed′	un·dried′	un′en·light′ened
un′de·voured′	un′dis·mem′bered	un·drilled′	un′en·liv′ened
un′de·vout′	un′dis·missed′	un·drink′a·ble	un′en·riched′
un′dif·fer·en′ti·at′ed	un′dis·patched′	un·du′ti·ful	un′en·rolled′
un′dif·fused′	un′dis·pelled′	un·dyed′	un′en·slaved′
un′di·gest′ed	un′dis·pensed′	un·eat′a·ble	un′en·tan′gled
un·dig′ni·fied′	un′dis·put′a·ble	un·eat′en	un·en′tered
un′di·lat′ed	un′dis·put′ed	un′ec·cle′si·as′tic	un′en·ter·pris′ing
un′di·lut′ed	un′dis·sect′ed	un′e·clipsed′	un′en·ter·tain′ing
un′di·min′ish·a·ble	un′dis·sem′bling	un′e·co·nom′ic	un′en·thralled′
un′di·min′ished	un′dis·sem′i·nat′ed	un′e·co·nom′i·cal	un′en·thu′si·as′tic
un·dimmed′	un′dis·solved′	un·ed′i·ble	un′en·ti′tled
un′dip·lo·mat′ic	un′dis·tilled′	un·ed′i·fy′ing	un·en′vi·a·ble
un′dis·cerned′	un′dis·tin′guish·a·ble	un·ed′u·ca·ble	un·en′vied
un′dis·cern′ed·ly	un′dis·tin′guished	un′ef·faced′	un·en′vi·ous
		un′e·lim′i·nat′ed	un·en′vy·ing

---

b., blend of, blended; c., cognate with; d., dialect, dialectal; der., derived from; f., formed from; g., going back to; m., modification of; r., replacing; s., stem of; t., taken from; ?, perhaps.   See the full key on inside cover.

un·e·qualed (ŭn ē′kwəld), *adj.* not equaled; unparalleled; matchless. Also, *esp. Brit.*, **un·e′qualled.**

un·e·quiv·o·cal (ŭn′ĭ kwĭv′ə kəl), *adj.* not equivocal; not ambiguous; clear; plain: *an unequivocal reply.* **—un′e·quiv′o·cal·ly,** *adv.* **—un′e·quiv′o·cal·ness,** *n.*

un·err·ing (ŭn ûr′ĭng, -ĕr′-), *adj.* **1.** not erring; not going astray or missing the mark; without error or mistake. **2.** unfailingly right, exact, or sure. **—un·err′ing·ly,** *adv.* **—un·err′ing·ness,** *n.*

UNESCO (ū nĕs′kō), *n.* the United Nations Educational, Scientific, and Cultural Organization.

un·es·sen·tial (ŭn′ə sĕn′shəl), *adj.* **1.** not of prime importance; not indispensable. **—n. 2.** an unessential thing; a nonessential. **—un′es·sen′tial·ly,** *adv.*

un·e·ven (ŭn ē′vən), *adj.* **1.** not level or flat; rough; rugged. **2.** irregular; varying; not uniform. **3.** not equitable or fair. **4.** not equally balanced; not equal. **5.** (of a number) odd; not divisible into two equal integers: *3, 5, and 7 are uneven numbers.* [ME; OE *unefen,* c. G *uneben.* See UN-[1], EVEN[1]] **—un·e′ven·ly,** *adv.* **—un·e′ven·ness,** *n.*

un·e·vent·ful (ŭn′ĭ vĕnt′fəl), *adj.* not eventful; lacking in important or striking occurrences: *an uneventful day at the office.* **—un′e·vent′ful·ly,** *adv.* **—un′e·vent′ful·ness,** *n.*

un·ex·act·ing (un′ĭg zăk′tĭng), *adj.* not exacting; requiring little; easy.

un·ex·am·pled (ŭn′ĭg zăm′pəld, -zäm′-), *adj.* having no example or similar case; unprecedented: *unexampled kindness, unexampled lawlessness.*

un·ex·cep·tion·a·ble (ŭn′ĭk sĕp′shən ə bəl), *adj.* not open or liable to any exception or objection; beyond criticism. **—un′ex·cep′tion·a·ble·ness,** *n.* **—un′ex·cep′tion·a·bly,** *adv.*

un·ex·cep·tion·al (ŭn′ĭk sĕp′shən əl), *adj.* **1.** not exceptional; not unusual or extraordinary. **2.** admitting of no exception. **3.** unexceptionable.

un·ex·pect·ed (ŭn′ĭk spĕk′tĭd), *adj.* unforeseen; sudden. **—un′ex·pect′ed·ly,** *adv.* **—un′ex·pect′ed·ness,** *n.* **—Syn.** See sudden.

un·ex·pres·sive (ŭn′ĭk sprĕs′ĭv), *adj.* **1.** not expressive; lacking in expression of meaning, feeling, etc. **2.** *Obs.* inexpressible. **—un′ex·pres′sive·ly,** *adv.* **—un′ex·pres′sive·ness,** *n.*

un·fail·ing (ŭn fā′lĭng), *adj.* **1.** incapable of being exhausted: *unfailing sources of supply.* **2.** not or never failing; not giving way: *unfailing friend, hope, etc.* **—un·fail′ing·ly,** *adv.* **—un·fail′ing·ness,** *n.*

un·fair (ŭn fâr′), *adj.* **1.** not fair; biased or partial; not just or equitable; unjust. **2.** using unethical business practices, as deception of customers, payment of illegally low wages, simulation of another's product, etc. [ME; OE *unfæger,* c. Icel. *ūfagr.* See UN-[1], FAIR[1]] **—un·fair′ly,** *adv.* **—un·fair′ness,** *n.*

un·faith·ful (ŭn fāth′fəl), *adj.* **1.** false to duty or promises; disloyal; perfidious; faithless. **2.** not upright; dishonest. **3.** not faithfully accurate or exact. **4.** guilty of adultery. **5.** *Obs.* unbelieving; infidel. **—un·faith′ful·ly,** *adv.* **—un·faith′ful·ness,** *n.*

un·fa·mil·iar (ŭn′fə mĭl′yər), *adj.* **1.** not familiar; not acquainted or conversant: *be unfamiliar with a subject.* **2.** not well-known; unaccustomed; unusual; strange: *a subject unfamiliar to me.* **—un·fa·mil·i·ar·i·ty** (ŭn′-fə mĭl′ĭ ăr′ə tĭ), *n.* **—un′fa·mil′iar·ly,** *adv.*

un·fas·ten (ŭn făs′ən, -fäs′-), *v.t.* **1.** to loose from, or as from, fastenings. **2.** to undo or open (a fastening). **—v.i. 3.** to become unfastened.

un·fa·thered (ŭn fä′thərd), *adj.* **1.** having no father; fatherless. **2.** of unknown paternity; bastard. **3.** not ascribable to a particular author or responsible person.

un·fath·om·a·ble (ŭn făth′əm ə bəl), *adj.* **1.** not fathomable; incapable of being fathomed. **2.** impenetrable by the mind; inscrutable; incomprehensible.

un·fa·vor·a·ble (ŭn fā′vər ə bəl, -fā′vrə-), *adj.* not favorable; not propitious; disadvantageous; adverse. Also, *esp. Brit.*, **un·fa′vour·a·ble.** **—un·fa′vor·a·ble·ness,** *n.* **—un·fa′vor·a·bly,** *adv.*

Un·fed·er·at·ed Malay States (ŭn fĕd′ə rā′tĭd), formerly, a group of five native states in the Malay Peninsula, under indirect British control and a part of the former Federation of Malaya: now part of the federation of Malaysia.

un·feel·ing (ŭn fē′lĭng), *adj.* **1.** not feeling; devoid of feeling; insensible or insensate. **2.** unsympathetic; callous; hard-hearted. **—un·feel′ing·ly,** *adv.* **—un·feel′ing·ness,** *n.* **—Syn. 2.** See hard.

un·feigned (ŭn fānd′), *adj.* not feigned; sincere. **—un·feign·ed·ly** (ŭn fā′nĭd lĭ), *adv.* **—un·feign′ed·ness,** *n.*

un·fet·ter (ŭn fĕt′ər), *v.t.* to free from fetters.

un·fil·i·al (ŭn fĭl′ĭ əl, -fĭl′yəl), *adj.* not filial; unbecoming from a child to a parent; not observing the obligations of a child to a parent. **—un·fil′i·al·ly,** *adv.*

un·fin·ished (ŭn fĭn′ĭsht), *adj.* **1.** not finished; incomplete. **2.** lacking some special finish. **3.** not sheared, as cloth.

"Unfinished" Symphony, Symphony No. 8 in B Minor (composed, 1822; first performed, 1865) by Schubert.

unfinished worsted, men's suiting made of worsted yarns and given a slight nap.

un·fit (ŭn fĭt′), *adj., v.,* **-fitted, -fitting.** **—adj. 1.** not fit; not adapted or suited; unsuitable; not deserving or good enough. **2.** unqualified or incompetent. **3.** not physically fit or in due condition. **—v.t. 4.** to render unfit or unsuitable; disqualify. **—un·fit′ly,** *adv.* **—un·fit′ness,** *n.*

un·fix (ŭn fĭks′), *v.t.* **1.** to render no longer fixed; unfasten; detach; loosen. **2.** to unsettle.

un·fledged (ŭn flĕjd′), *adj.* **1.** not fledged; without feathers sufficiently developed for flight, as a young bird. **2.** immature; undeveloped; callow.

un·flesh·ly (ŭn flĕsh′lĭ), *adj.* not fleshly; not carnal or corporeal; spiritual.

un·flinch·ing (ŭn flĭn′chĭng), *adj.* not flinching; unshrinking: *he faced dangers with unflinching courage.* **—un·flinch′ing·ly,** *adv.*

un·fold (ŭn fōld′), *v.t.* **1.** to bring out of a folded state; spread or open out: *unfold your arms.* **2.** to develop. **3.** to spread out or lay open to view. **4.** to reveal or display. **5.** to reveal or disclose in words; set forth; explain. **—v.i. 6.** to become unfolded; open out. [ME; OE *unfealdan,* c. G *entfalten.* See UN-[2], FOLD[1]] **—un·fold′er,** *n.* **—un·fold′ment,** *n.*

un·for·get·ta·ble (ŭn′fər gĕt′ə bəl), *adj.* not forgettable; never to be forgotten: *scenes of unforgettable beauty.* **—un′for·get′ta·bly,** *adv.*

un·formed (ŭn fôrmd′), *adj.* **1.** not formed; not definitely shaped; shapeless or formless. **2.** undeveloped; crude. **3.** not made or created.

un·for·tu·nate (ŭn fôr′chə nĭt), *adj.* **1.** not fortunate; not having good fortune; unlucky or unhappy. **—n. 2.** an unfortunate person. **—un·for′tu·nate·ly,** *adv.* **—un·for′tu·nate·ness,** *n.*

un·found·ed (ŭn foun′dĭd), *adj.* without foundation; baseless: *unfounded objections.* **—un·found′ed·ly,** *adv.* **—un·found′ed·ness,** *n.*

un·fre·quent·ed (ŭn′frĭ kwĕn′tĭd), *adj.* not frequented, as places; little resorted to or visited; solitary. **—un′fre·quent′ed·ness,** *n.*

un·friend·ed (ŭn frĕn′dĭd), *adj.* without friends; friendless. **—un·friend′ed·ness,** *n.*

un·friend·ly (ŭn frĕnd′lĭ), *adj.* **1.** not friendly; hostile; inimical; unkindly. **—adv. 2.** in an unfriendly manner. **—un·friend′li·ness,** *n.*

un·frock (ŭn frŏk′), *v.t.* **1.** to divest or strip of a frock. **2.** to deprive of the priestly or clerical robe.

un′e·quipped′	un′ex·plained′	un′fed·er·at′ed	un′fore·bod′ing
un′e·rased′	un′ex·plic′it	un·feign′ing·ly	un′fore·known′
un′es·cap′a·ble	un′ex·plod′ed	un·felt′	un′fore·see′a·ble
un′es·sayed′	un′ex·ploit′ed	un·fem′i·nine	un′fore·see′ing
un′es·tab′lished	un′ex·plored′	un·fenced′	un′fore·seen′
un′es·thet′ic	un′ex·port′ed	un·fer·ment′ed	un′for·est·ed
un′es·ti·mat′ed	un′ex·posed′	un·fer′tile	un′fore·told′
un·eth′i·cal	un′ex·pressed′	un·fer′ti·lized′	un′for·feit·ed
un′ex·ag′ger·at′ed	un′ex·punged′	un·fet′tered	un·forged′
un·ex·alt′ed	un·ex′pur·gat′ed	un·filled′	un′for·get′ful
un′ex·am′ined	un′ex·tend′ed	un·filmed′	un′for·get′ting
un′ex·ca·vat′ed	un′ex·ter′mi·nat′ed	un·fil′tered	un′for·giv′a·ble
un·ex·celled′	un′ex·tin′guish·a·ble	un·fired′	un′for·giv′en
un′ex·change′a·ble	un′ex·tin′guished	un·fit′ted	un′for·giv′ing
un·ex·cit′ed	un·fad′a·ble	un·fit′ting	un′for·got′ten
un·ex·cit′ing	un·fad′ed	un·fit′ting·ly	un·for′mu·lat′ed
un′ex·clud′ed	un·fad′ing	un·fixed′	un′for·sak′en
un·ex·cused′	un·fall′en	un·flag′ging	un·for′ti·fied′
un·ex·e·cut′ed	un·fal′ter·ing	un·flag′ging·ly	un·fought′
un′ex·er·cised′	un·fash′ion·a·ble	un·flat′tered	un·found′
un′ex·haust′ed	un·fas′tened	un·flat′ter·ing	un·framed′
un′ex·pand′ed	un·fa′ther·ly	un·fla′vored	un′fran·chised′
un′ex·pend′ed	un·fath′omed	un·flick′er·ing	un·fra·ter′nal
un′ex·pend′i·ble	un·fa·tigued′	un·foiled′	un·fraught′
un′ex·pe′ri·enced	un·fa′vored	un′for·bear′ing	un·free′
un·ex·pert′	un·feared′	un′for·bid′den	un·freez′a·ble
un·ex′pi·at′ed	un·fear′ing	un·forced′	un·fre′quent
un′ex·pired′	un·fea′si·ble	un·forc′ed·ly	un·fre′quent·ly
un′ex·plain′a·ble	un·fed′	un·ford′a·ble	un·fro′zen

un·fruit·ful (ŭn·frōōt′fəl), *adj.* not fruitful; unproductive; barren; fruitless. —**un·fruit′ful·ly**, *adv.* —**un·fruit′ful·ness**, *n.*

un·furl (ŭn·fûrl′), *v.t.* **1.** to spread or shake out from a furled state, as a sail or a flag; unfold. —*v.i.* **2.** to become unfurled.

un·gain·ly (ŭn·gān′lĭ), *adj.* **1.** not gainly; not graceful or shapely; awkward; clumsy; uncouth. —*adv.* **2.** in an awkward manner. [ME *ungaynly*, adv. See UN-[1], GAINLY, adj.] —**un·gain′li·ness**, *n.*

Un·ga·va (ŭng·gä′və, -gä′və), *n.* former name of a region in NE Canada comprising the larger part of the peninsula of Labrador: incorporated into Quebec province, 1912.

un·gen·er·ous (ŭn·jĕn′ər·əs), *adj.* not generous; ignoble; illiberal; mean. —**un·gen′er·ous·ly**, *adv.*

un·gird (ŭn·gûrd′), *v.t.* **1.** to unfasten or take off the girdle or belt of. **2.** to loosen, or take off, by unfastening a girdle. [UN-[2] + GIRD[1]. Cf. G *entgürten*]

un·girt (ŭn·gûrt′), *adj.* **1.** having a girdle loosened or removed. **2.** not taut or tightened for use; loose.

un·glue (ŭn·glōō′), *v.t.*, **-glued, -gluing.** to separate or open (something fastened with, or as with, glue).

un·god·ly (ŭn·gŏd′lĭ), *adj.* **1.** not godly; not conforming to God's laws; irreligious; impious; sinful; wicked. **2.** *Colloq.* outrageous. —**un·god′li·ly**, *adv.* —**un·god′li·ness**, *n.*

un·got·ten (ŭn·gŏt′ən), *adj.* **1.** not obtained or gained. **2.** *Obs.* not begotten.

un·gov·ern·a·ble (ŭn·gŭv′ər·nə·bəl), *adj.* that cannot be governed, ruled, or restrained; uncontrollable. —**un·gov′ern·a·ble·ness**, *n.* —**un·gov′ern·a·bly**, *adv.*

un·grace·ful (ŭn·grās′fəl), *adj.* not graceful; lacking grace or elegance; clumsy; awkward. —**un·grace′ful·ly**, *adv.* —**un·grace′ful·ness**, *n.*

un·gra·cious (ŭn·grā′shəs), *adj.* **1.** not gracious; lacking in gracious courtesy or affability. **2.** unacceptable; unwelcome. **3.** *Obs.* ungraceful; unpleasing. —**un·gra′cious·ly**, *adv.* —**un·gra′cious·ness**, *n.*

un·gram·mat·i·cal (ŭn′grə·măt′ə·kəl), *adj.* **1.** substandard. **2.** not according to native usage, as the language of a foreigner. —**un′gram·mat′i·cal·ly**, *adv.*

un·grate·ful (ŭn·grāt′fəl), *adj.* **1.** unpleasing; disagreeable. **2.** not grateful; not feeling or displaying gratitude; giving no return or recompense. —**un·grate′ful·ly**, *adv.* —**un·grate′ful·ness**, *n.*

un·grudg·ing (ŭn·grŭj′ĭng), *adj.* not grudging; willing; hearty; liberal. —**un·grudg′ing·ly**, *adv.*

un·gual (ŭng′gwəl), *adj.* of or pertaining to, bearing, or shaped like a nail, claw, or hoof. [f. s. L *unguis* nail, claw + -AL[1]]

un·guard·ed (ŭn·gär′dĭd), *adj.* **1.** not guarded; unprotected; undefended. **2.** incautious; imprudent. **3.** having no guard, screen, or the like. —**un·guard′ed·ly**, *adv.* —**un·guard′ed·ness**, *n.*

un·guent (ŭng′gwənt), *n.* any soft preparation or salve, usually of butterlike consistence, applied to sores, etc.; an ointment. [ME, t. L: s. *unguentum*] —**un·guen·tar·y** (ŭng′gwən·tĕr′ĭ), *adj.*

un·guic·u·late (ŭng·gwĭk′yə·lĭt, -lāt′), *adj.* Also, **un·guic′u·lat·ed. 1.** bearing or resembling a nail or claw. **2.** *Zool.* having nails or claws, as distinguished from hoofs. **3.** *Bot.* having a clawlike base, as certain petals. See illus. under **corolla.** —*n.* **4.** an unguiculate animal. [t. NL: m.s. *unguiculātus*, der. L *unguiculus* fingernail, dim. of *unguis* claw]

un·gui·nous (ŭng′gwĭ·nəs), *adj.* consisting of or resembling fat or oil; oily. [t. L: m.s. *unguinōsus* oily]

un·guis (ŭng′gwĭs), *n.*, *pl.* **-gues** (-gwēz). **1.** a nail, claw, or hoof. **2.** *Bot.* the clawlike base of certain petals. [t. L]

un·gu·la (ŭng′gyə·lə), *n.*, *pl.* **-lae** (-lē′). **1.** *Geom.* a part cut off from a cylinder, cone, or the like, by a plane oblique to the base. **2.** *Bot.* an unguis. [t. L]

un·gu·lar (ŭng′gyə·lər), *adj.* pertaining to or of the nature of an ungula; ungual.

un·gu·late (ŭng′gyə·lĭt, -lāt′), *adj.* **1.** having hoofs. **2.** belonging or pertaining to the *Ungulata*, a group sometimes set up, though without phylogenetic justification, in order to classify all hoofed mammals together in one category.

Ungula

3. hooflike. —*n.* **4.** a hoofed mammal. [t. L: m.s. *ungulātus* having claws]

un·hair (ŭn·hâr′), *v.t.* **1.** to free from hair. —*v.i.* **2.** to become free of hair.

un·hal·low (ŭn·hăl′ō), *v.t.* to desecrate; profane.

un·hal·lowed (ŭn·hăl′ōd), *adj.* **1.** not hallowed or consecrated. **2.** profane; impious or wicked.

un·hand (ŭn·hănd′), *v.t.* to take the hand or hands from; release from a grasp; let go.

un·hand·some (ŭn·hăn′səm), *adj.* **1.** not good-looking or comely; plain or ugly. **2.** ungracious; discourteous; unseemly; mean. **3.** ungenerous; illiberal. —**un·hand′some·ly**, *adv.* —**un·hand′some·ness**, *n.*

un·hand·y (ŭn·hăn′dĭ), *adj.* **1.** not handy; not easy to handle or manage, as things. **2.** not skillful in using the hands, as persons. —**un·hand′i·ly**, *adv.* —**un·hand′i·ness**, *n.*

un·hap·py (ŭn·hăp′ĭ), *adj.*, **-pier, -piest. 1.** sad, miserable, or wretched. **2.** unfortunate; unlucky. **3.** unfavorable; inauspicious. **4.** infelicitous: *an unhappy remark.* **5.** *Obs.* of wretched character; reprehensible. —**un·hap′pi·ly**, *adv.* —**un·hap′pi·ness**, *n.* —Syn. **1.** sorrowful, downcast, cheerless, disconsolate. **4.** inappropriate, inapt.

un·harm·ful (ŭn·härm′fəl), *adj.* not harmful; harmless. —**un·harm′ful·ly**, *adv.*

un·har·ness (ŭn·här′nĭs), *v.t.* **1.** to strip of harness; free (a horse, etc.) from harness or gear. **2.** to divest of armor.

un·hasp (ŭn·hăsp′, -häsp′), *v.t.* to loose the hasp of.

un·hat (ŭn·hăt′), *v.*, **-hatted, -hatting.** —*v.t.* **1.** to remove the hat from. —*v.i.* **2.** to take off one's hat, as in respect.

un·health·ful (ŭn·hĕlth′fəl), *adj.* **1.** injurious to health; insalubrious; unwholesome. **2.** not healthful; not possessing health. **3.** not characteristic of health. —**un·health′ful·ly**, *adv.* —**un·health′ful·ness**, *n.*

un·health·i·ness (ŭn·hĕl′thĭ·nĭs), *n.* **1.** state or character of being unhealthy. **2.** that which brings about ill health.

un·health·y (ŭn·hĕl′thĭ), *adj.*, **-healthier, -healthiest. 1.** not healthy; not possessing health; not in a healthy or sound condition. **2.** characteristic of or resulting from bad health. **3.** hurtful to health; unwholesome. **4.** morally harmful; noxious. —**un·health′i·ly**, *adv.* —Syn. **1.** sickly, delicate, frail, weak, ill, diseased. **3.** unhealthful, unsanitary, unhygienic, insalubrious.

un·heard (ŭn·hûrd′), *adj.* **1.** not heard; not perceived by the ear. **2.** not given a hearing or audience. **3.** not heard of; unknown.

un·heard-of (ŭn·hûrd′ŏv′, -ŭv′), *adj.* **1.** that was never heard of; unknown. **2.** such as was never known before; unprecedented.

un·helm (ŭn·hĕlm′), *v.t.* *Archaic.* to deprive of the helm or helmet.

un·hinge (ŭn·hĭnj′), *v.t.*, **-hinged, -hinging. 1.** to take (a door, etc.) off the hinges. **2.** to remove the hinges from. **3.** to detach or separate from something. **4.** to deprive of fixity or stability; throw into confusion or disorder. **5.** to unbalance (the mind, etc.). **6.** to upset or discompose (a person). **7.** to unsettle (opinions, etc.).

un·hitch (ŭn·hĭch′), *v.t.* to free from being hitched or fastened; unfasten.

un·ho·ly (ŭn·hō′lĭ), *adj.*, **-lier, -liest. 1.** not holy; not sacred or hallowed. **2.** impious; sinful; wicked. **3.** *Colloq.* unseemly; reprehensible. [ME; OE *unhālig*, c. D *onheilig*, Icel. *ūheilagr*. See UN-[1], HOLY] —**un·ho′li·ly**, *adv.* —**un·ho′li·ness**, *n.*

un·hood (ŭn·hood′), *v.t.* **1.** to divest of a hood. **2.** to remove from (a hawk) the hood used to blind it.

un·hook (ŭn·hook′), *v.t.* **1.** to loose from a hook. **2.** to open or undo by loosening a hook or hooks. —*v.i.* **3.** to become unhooked.

un·hoped (ŭn·hōpt′), *adj.* not hoped or looked for.

un·horse (ŭn·hôrs′), *v.t.*, **-horsed, -horsing. 1.** to throw from a horse, as in battle. **2.** to cause to fall from the saddle. **3.** to deprive of a horse or horses; dislodge; overthrow.

un·house (ŭn·houz′), *v.t.*, **-housed, -housing.** to drive from a house or habitation; deprive of shelter.

un·husk (ŭn·hŭsk′), *v.t.* to free from, or as from, a husk.

un′ful·filled′	un·got′	un·har′dened	un·he·ro′ic
un·fund′ed	un·gov′erned	un·harmed′	un·hes′i·tat′ing
un·fur′nished	un·gowned′	un·harm′ful	un·hes′i·tat′ing·ly
un·fur′rowed	un·graced′	un·harm′ing	un·hewn′
un·gal′lant	un·grad′ed	un·har·mo′ni·ous	un·hin′dered
un·galled′	un·graft′ed	un·har′nessed	un·hired′
un·gar′nished	un·grained′	un·har′rowed	un·his·tor′ic
un·gar′tered	un·grat′i·fied′	un·har′vest·ed	un·ho·mo·ge′ne·ous
un·gath′ered	un·ground′ed	un·hast′y	un·hoped′-for′
un·gen′ial	un·guid′ed	un·hatched′	un·hos′tile
un′gen·teel′	un·hack′neyed	un·healed′	un·housed′
un·gen′tle	un·hailed′	un·heat′ed	un·hu′man
un·gen′tle·man·ly	un·halved′	un·heed′ed	un·hu′man·ize
un·gen′tly	un·ham′mered	un·heed′ful	un·hung′
un·gift′ed	un·ham′pered	un·heed′ing	un·hurt′
un·glad′dened	un·han′di·capped′	un·heed′ing·ly	un·hurt′ful
un·glazed′	un·han′dled	un·helped′	un·hy·gi·en′ic
un·glossed′	un·hanged′	un·help′ful	un·hy′phen·at′ed
un·gloved′	un·har′assed	un·her′ald·ed	un·hy′phened

uni-, a word element meaning "one," "single," as in *unisexual*. [t. L, comb. form of *ūnus* one]

U·ni·at (ū′nĭ ăt′), *n.* a member of any of various communities of Greek and other Eastern Christians which acknowledge the supremacy of the Pope and are in communion with the Church of Rome, but retain their own liturgy, rites, discipline, etc., to a certain extent. Also, **U·ni·ate** (ū′nĭ Yt, -āt′). [t. Russ.]

u·ni·ax·i·al (ū′nĭ ăk′sĭ əl), *adj.* **1.** having one axis. **2.** *Crystall.* (of a crystal) having one direction in which no double refraction occurs. **3.** *Bot.* (of a plant) having a primary stem which does not branch and which terminates in a flower.

u·ni·cam·er·al (ū′nə kăm′ər əl), *adj.* consisting of a single chamber, as a legislative assembly.

u·ni·cel·lu·lar (ū′nə sĕl′yə lər), *adj.* pertaining to or consisting of a single cell.

unicellular animals, the Protozoa.

u·ni·col·or (ū′nə kŭl′ər), *adj.* of but one color.

u·ni·corn (ū′nə kôrn′), *n.* **1.** a fabulous animal with a single long horn, said to elude every captor save a virgin, and seldom caught. **2.** a heraldic representation of this animal, in the form of a horse with a lion's tail and with a long, straight, and spirally twisted horn. **3.** (in the Authorized Version of the Bible, Deut. 33:17, and elsewhere) a two-horned animal now usually identified with the urus. [ME, t. L: s. *ūnicornis* having one horn]

Unicorn

u·ni·cos·tate (ū′nə kŏs′tāt, -kŏs′-), *adj.* **1.** having only one costa, rib, or ridge. **2.** *Bot.* (of a leaf) having only one primary or prominent rib, the midrib.

u·ni·cy·cle (ū′nə sī′kəl), *n.* a vehicle with only one wheel.

u·ni·di·rec·tion·al (ū′nə dĭ rĕk′shən əl, -dī-), *adj.* having, or moving in, only one direction.

u·ni·fi·a·ble (ū′nə fī′ə bəl), *adj.* that may be unified.

u·nif·ic (ū nĭf′ĭk), *adj.* making one; forming unity; unifying.

u·ni·fi·ca·tion (ū′nə fə kā′shən), *n.* **1.** act of unifying. **2.** state of being unified.

u·ni·fi·lar (ū′nə fī′lər), *adj.* having or involving only one thread, wire, or the like.

u·ni·flo·rous (ū′nə flōr′əs), *adj. Bot.* having or bearing one flower only.

u·ni·fo·li·ate (ū′nə fō′lĭ Yt, -āt′), *adj.* **1.** one-leafed. **2.** unifoliolate.

u·ni·fo·li·o·late (ū′nə fō′lĭ ə lāt′), *adj. Bot.* **1.** compound in structure yet having but one leaflet, as the leaf of the orange. **2.** bearing such leaves, as a plant.

Unifoliolate leaf

u·ni·form (ū′nə fôrm′), *adj.* **1.** having but one form; having always the same form or character; unvarying. **2.** without diversity in appearance, color, etc. **3.** of the same style, materials, and color, as a distinctive dress worn by a body of persons. **4.** regular; even: *a uniform pace.* **5.** consistent in action, opinion, etc., as a person, or as action, etc.; being the same in all places or in all parts of a country: *a uniform divorce law.* **6.** agreeing with one another in form, character, etc.; alike; of the same form, character, etc., with another or others. **—n. 7.** a distinctive dress of uniform style, materials, and color worn by all the members of a military, naval, or other body, and by which they may be recognized as belonging to that body. **8.** a single suit of such dress. **—v.t. 9.** to make uniform. **10.** to clothe or furnish with or as with a uniform. [t. L: s. *ūniformis*] **—u′ni·form′ly,** *adv.* **—u′ni·form′ness,** *n.* **—Syn.** invariable, unchanging. **4.** See **even.**

u·ni·for·mal·ize (ū′nə fôr′mə līz′), *v.t.*, **-ized, -izing,** to bring into uniformity.

u·ni·formed (ū′nə fôrmd′), *adj.* wearing a uniform.

u·ni·form·i·tar·i·an (ū′nə fôr′mə târ′Yən), *adj.* **1.** pertaining to uniformity or a doctrine of uniformity. **2.** *Geol.* pertaining to the thesis that early geological processes are not different from those observed now. **—n. 3.** one who adheres to a doctrine of uniformity. **—u′ni·form′i·tar′i·an·ism,** *n.*

u·ni·form·i·ty (ū′nə fôr′mə tĭ), *n.*, *pl.* **-ties. 1.** state or character of being uniform; sameness of form or character throughout; absence of variation or diversity.

2. regularity or evenness; agreement in form, character, etc. **3.** wearisome sameness; monotony. **4.** something uniform; an extent or expanse of a uniform character.

u·ni·fy (ū′nə fī′), *v.t.*, **-fied, -fying.** to form into one; make a unit of; reduce to unity. [t. ML: m. *ūnificāre*, f. L: *ūni-* UNI- + *-ficāre* -FY] **—u′ni·fi′er,** *n.*

u·nij·u·gate (ū′nij′ōō git, -gāt), *adj. Bot.* (of a pinnate leaf) having but a single pair of leaflets. [f. s. L *ūnijugus* having one yoke + -ATE[1]]

u·ni·lat·er·al (ū′nə lăt′ər əl), *adj.* **1.** pertaining to, occurring on, or affecting one side only. **2.** one-sided. **3.** leaning or turned to one side. **4.** affecting one side, party, or person only. **5.** undertaken or performed by one side only. **6.** concerned with or considering but one side of a matter or question. **7.** *Law.* (of contracts and obligations) binding one party only; more generally, affecting one party only. **8.** *Bot.* having all the parts disposed on one side of an axis, as an inflorescence. **9.** *Sociol.* indicating line of descent through parents of one sex only. **10.** *Phonet.* produced on one side of the tongue, as *unilateral l.* **—u′ni·lat′er·al·ly,** *adv.*

Unilugate leaf

u·ni·lobed (ū′nə lōbd′), *adj.* having, or consisting of, a single lobe.

u·ni·loc·u·lar (ū′nə lŏk′yə lər), *adj.* having, or consisting of, but one loculus, chamber, or cell.

un·im·peach·a·ble (ŭn′Ym pē′chə bəl), *adj.* not impeachable; irreproachable; blameless. **—un′im·peach′a·bly,** *adv.*

un·im·por·tance (un′Ym pôr′təns), *n.* lack of importance; insignificance.

un·im·proved (ŭn′Ym prōōvd′), *adj.* **1.** not turned to account. **2.** not cultivated. **3.** not increased in value by betterments or improvements, as real property. **4.** not bettered, as health.

un·in·flect·ed (ŭn′Yn flĕk′tĭd), *adj.* **1.** not inflected. **2.** not subject to inflection.

un·in·tel·li·gent (ŭn′Yn tĕl′ə jənt), *adj.* **1.** deficient in intelligence; dull, or stupid. **2.** not endowed with intelligence. **—un′in·tel′li·gence,** *n.* **—un′in·tel′li·gent·ly,** *adv.*

un·in·tel·li·gi·ble (ŭn′Yn tĕl′ə jə bəl), *adj.* not intelligible; not capable of being understood. **—un′in·tel′li·gi·bil′i·ty, un′in·tel′li·gi·ble·ness,** *n.* **—un′·in·tel′li·gi·bly,** *adv.*

un·in·ten·tion·al (ŭn′Yn tĕn′shən əl), *adj.* not intentional; not acting with intention; not done purposely, or not designed. **—un′in·ten′tion·al·ly,** *adv.*

un·in·ter·est·ed (ŭn′Yn′tər Ys tĭd, -trĭs tĭd), *adj.* **1.** having or showing no feeling of interest; indifferent. **2.** not personally concerned in something. **—un·in′·ter·est·ed·ly,** *adv.* **—un·in′ter·est·ed·ness,** *n.* **—Syn. 1.** See **disinterested.**

un·ion (ūn′yən), *n.* **1.** act of uniting two or more things into one. **2.** state of being so united; junction; combination. **3.** something formed by uniting two or more things; a combination. **4.** a number of persons, societies, states, or the like, joined or associated together for some common purpose. **5.** the uniting of persons, parties, etc., in general agreement. **6.** a uniting of states or nations into one political body, as that of the American colonies at the time of the Revolution, that of England and Scotland in 1707, or that of Great Britain and Ireland in 1801. **7. the Union,** the United States of America. **8.** a device emblematic of union, used in a flag or ensign, sometimes occupying the upper corner next to the staff, or sometimes occupying the entire field. **9.** a uniting or being united in matrimony, or a marriage. **10.** a trade or labor union, or organization of workmen. **11.** *Eng.* a number of parishes united for the administration of the poor laws, etc. **12.** a workhouse erected and maintained by such a union. **13.** any of various contrivances for connecting parts of machinery, etc., esp.a fitting composed of three parts used to connect the ends of two pipes, neither of which can be turned. **14.** a fabric made of two kinds of yarns. [late ME, t. L: s. *ūnio*]

—Syn. 2. UNION, UNITY agree in referring to a oneness, either created by putting together, or by being undivided. A UNION is a state of being united, a combination, as the result of joining two or more things into one: *to promote the union between two families, the Union of England and Scotland.* UNITY is the state or inherent quality of being one,

un′i·de′al	un′im·pos′ing	un′in·flu·en′tial	un′in·ter·mit′ted
un′i·den′ti·fied′	un′im·preg′nat·ed	un′in·formed′	un′in·ter·mit′tent
un′id·i·o·mat′ic	un′im·pressed′	un′in·fringed′	un′in·ter·mit′ting
un′il·lu′mi·nat′ed	un′im·press′i·ble	un′in·hab′it·a·ble	un′in·ter·po·lat′ed
un′il·lu′mined	un′im·pres′sion·a·ble	un′in·hab′it·ed	un′in·ter·pret′ed
un′il·lus·trat′ed	un′im·pres′sive	un′in·hib′it·ed	un′in·ter·rupt′ed
un′im·ag′i·na·ble	un′im·au′gu·rat′ed	un′i·ni′ti·at′ed	un′in·tim′i·dat′ed
un′im·ag′i·na·bly	un′in·closed′	un′in·jured′	un′in·tox′i·cat′ed
un′im·ag′i·na′tive	un′in·cor′po·rat′ed	un′in·spir′ing	un′in·tox′i·ca′ting
un′im·ag′ined	un′in·cu′bat·ed	un′in·struct′ed	un′in·vad′ed
un′im·bued′	un′in·cum′bered	un′in·struc′tive	un′in·vent′ed
un′im·i·tat′ed	un′in·dem′ni·fied′	un′in·sur′a·ble	un′in·ven′tive
un′im·paired′	un′in·di·cat′ed	un′in·sured′	un′in·vert′ed
un′im·pas′sioned	un′in·dorsed′	un′in·tel·lec′tu·al	un′in·vest′ed
un′im·peached′	un′in·fect′ed	un′in·tend′ed	un′in·vit′ed
un′im·ped′ed	un′in·flam′ma·ble	un′in·ter·est′ing	un′in·vit′ing
un′im·plored′	un′in·flu·enced	un′in·ter·est·ing·ly	un′in·voked′
un′im·por′tant			un′in·volved′

single, individual, and indivisible (often as consequence of union): *to find unity in diversity, to give unity to a work of art.* **4.** See **alliance.** —Ant. **2.** division.

union card, a card identifying one as a member of a particular labor union.

Union City, a city in NE New Jersey. 52,180 (1960).

un·ion·ism (ūn′yə nĭz′əm), *n.* **1.** the principle of union, esp. trade unionism. **2.** attachment to a union. **3.** (*cap.*) loyalty to the federal union of the United States of America, esp. at the time of the Civil War.

un·ion·ist (ūn′yən ĭst), *n.* **1.** one who promotes or advocates union. **2.** a member of a trade union. **3.** (*cap.*) an adherent of the federal union of the United States of America, esp. during the Civil War. **4.** (formerly, in British politics) an upholder of the legislative union of Great Britain and Ireland; an opponent of home rule in Ireland. —**un′ion·is′tic,** *adj.*

un·ion·ize (ūn′yən īz′), *v.,* -ized, -izing. —*v.t.* **1.** to form into a union. **2.** to organize into a trade union; bring into or incorporate in a trade union. **3.** to subject to the rules of a trade union. —*v.i.* **4.** to form a union. **5.** to join in a trade union. —**un′ion·i·za′tion,** *n.*

union jack, 1. a jack consisting of the union of a national flag or ensign. **2.** any flag consisting of a union only. See **union** (def. 8). **3.** (*often caps.*) the British national flag.

Union of South Africa, former name of the Republic of South Africa. See **South Africa.**

Union of Soviet Socialist Republics, official name of the Soviet Union. *Abbr.:* U.S.S.R.

union shop, 1. a shop, business establishment, or portion thereof, in which terms and conditions of employment for all employees are fixed by agreement between the employer and a labor union. **2.** a shop, business, etc., in which membership in a union is made a condition of employment, but in which the employer may hire nonunion workers who must become members after a stated period (commonly 30 days).

Un·ion·town (ūn′yən toun′), *n.* a city n SW Pennsylvania. 17,942 (1960).

u·nip·a·rous (ū nĭp′ə rəs), *adj.* **1.** producing but one at a birth. **2.** *Bot.* (of a cyme) producing but one axis at each branching. [t. NL: m. *ūniparus.* See UNI-, -PAROUS]

u·ni·per·son·al (ū′nə pûr′sən əl), *adj.* **1.** consisting of or existing as but one person. **2.** *Gram.* used in only one person, esp. the third person singular, as certain verbs.

u·ni·pet·al·ous (ū′nə pĕt′əl əs), *adj. Bot.* having only one petal.

u·ni·pla·nar (ū′nə plā′nər), *adj.* lying or taking place in one plane: *uniplanar motion.*

u·ni·po·lar (ū′nə pō′lər), *adj.* **1.** *Physics.* having or pertaining to one pole only. **2.** *Anat.* denoting a nerve cell in spinal and cranial ganglia in which the incoming and outgoing processes fuse outside the cell body. —**u·ni·po·lar·i·ty** (ū′nə pō lăr′ə tĭ), *n.*

u·nique (ū nēk′), *adj.* **1.** of which there is but one; sole; only. **2.** having no like or equal; standing alone in comparison with others; unequaled. **3.** rare or unusual: *a unique experience.* [t. F, t. L: m. *ūnicus;* r. earlier *unic,* t. L: s. *ūnicus*] —**u·nique′ly,** *adv.* —**u·nique′ness,** *n.* —Syn. **1.** See **only.**

u·ni·sep·tate (ū′nə sĕp′tāt), *adj.* having only one septum or partition, as a silicle.

u·ni·sex·u·al (ū′nə sĕk′shōō əl), *adj.* **1.** of or pertaining to one sex only. **2.** having only male or female organs in one individual, as an animal or a flower.

u·ni·son (ū′nə sən, -zən), *n.* **1.** coincidence in pitch of two or more tones, voices, etc. **2.** the theoretical interval between any tone and a tone of exactly the same pitch; a prime. **3.** a sounding together at the same pitch, as of different voices or instruments performing the same part. **4.** a sounding together in octaves, esp. of male and female voices or of higher and lower instruments of the same class. **5.** accord or agreement. [t. LL: s. *ūnisonus* having one sound, f. L *ūni-* UNI- + *-sonus* sounding]

u·nis·o·nous (ū nĭs′ə nəs), *adj.* according in sound or pitch; being in unison. Also, **u·nis′o·nal, u·nis·o·nant** (ū nĭs′ə nənt). [t. LL: m. *ūnisonus*]

un·is·sued (ŭn ĭsh′ōōd), *adj.* not issued.

u·nit (ū′nĭt), *n.* **1.** a single thing or person; any group of things or persons regarded as an individual. **2.** one of the individuals or groups making up a whole, or into which a whole may be analyzed. **3.** any magnitude regarded as an independent whole; a single, undivided entity. **4.** any specified amount of a quantity, as of length, volume, force, momentum, time, by comparison with which any other quantity of the same kind is measured or estimated. **5.** *Math.* the lowest positive integer; one. **6.** *Educ.* the quantity of educational instruction, determined usually by a number of hours of classroom and, sometimes, laboratory work. **7.** *Mil.* an organized body of soldiers of any size, which is a subdivision of a larger body. **8.** *Immunol., Pharm.* **a.** the measured amount of a substance necessary to cause a certain effect; a clinical unit used when substance cannot readily be isolated in pure form and its activity determined directly. **b.** the amount necessary to cause a specific effect upon a specific animal or upon animal tissues. [appar. back formation from UNITY]

Unit., Unitarian.

u·ni·tar·i·an (ū′nə târ′ĭ ən), *n.* **1.** one who maintains

that God is one being, rejecting the doctrine of the Trinity, and emphasizing freedom in religious belief, tolerance of difference in religious opinion, character as the fundamental principle in religion, and the use of all religious history and experience interpreted by reason as a guide to conduct. **2.** (*cap.*) a member of a Christian denomination founded upon the doctrine that God is one being, and giving each congregation complete control over its affairs. **3.** an advocate of unity or centralization, as in government. —*adj.* **4.** (*cap.*) pertaining to the Unitarians or their doctrines; accepting Unitarianism; belonging to the Unitarians. **5.** pertaining to a unit or unity; unitary. —**u′ni·tar′i·an·ism,** *n.*

u·ni·tar·y (ū′nə tĕr′ĭ), *adj.* **1.** of or pertaining to a unit or units. **2.** pertaining to, characterized by, or based on unity. **3.** of the nature of a unit; having the individual character of a unit. **4.** serving as a unit, as of measurement or estimation.

unit character, *Biol.* a characteristic transmitted according to Mendel's laws.

u·nite¹ (ū nīt′), *v.,* united, uniting. —*v.t.* **1.** to join so as to form one connected whole; join, combine, or incorporate in one; cause to be one. **2.** to cause to hold together or adhere. **3.** to join in marriage. **4.** to associate (persons, etc.) by some bond or tie; join in action, interest, opinion, feeling, etc. **5.** to have or exhibit in union or combination. —*v.i.* **6.** to join together so as to form one connected whole; become one; combine. **7.** to join in marriage. **8.** to enter into alliance or association; join in action; act in concert or agreement; become one in opinion or feeling. [ME, t. L: m. *ūnitus,* pp., joined together, made one] —**u·nit′er,** *n.* —Syn. **1.** connect, conjoin, join, couple, link, yoke. See **join. 2.** blend, fuse, weld. —Ant. **1.** divide. **2.** separate.

u·nite² (ū′nīt, ū nīt′), *n.* (during the reign of James I) a gold coin worth 20 shillings. [der. UNITE¹; named with reference to the union of England and Scotland]

u·nit·ed (ū nī′tĭd), *adj.* **1.** joined together; combined **2.** of or produced by two or more persons, etc., in combination. **3.** formed by the union of two or more things, bodies, etc. —**u·nit′ed·ly,** *adv.* —**u·nit′ed·ness,** *n.*

United Arab Republic, a former republic formed by the union of Egypt and Syria, 1958–61; now Egypt only.

United Arab States, the federation (in 1958) of the United Arab Republic and the kingdom of Yemen; dissolved in 1961.

United Brethren, an American Protestant denomination which arose early in the 19th century and sought to unite members of various confessions.

United Kingdom, a kingdom in NW Europe, consisting of Great Britain and Northern Ireland: formerly (1801–1922) it comprised Great Britain and Ireland. 51,208,000 pop. (est. 1956); 93, 377 sq. mi. *Cap.:* London. *Abbr.:* U.K. Official name, **United Kingdom of Great Britain and Northern Ireland.**

United Nations, 1. the nations that signed the joint declaration in Washington, D.C., Jan. 2, 1942, pledging to employ full resources against the Axis powers, not to make a separate peace, etc. **2.** the fifty nations (with subsequent additions) who signed the charter written by the United Nations Conference on International Organization at San Francisco, 1945.

United Press International, a private agency for the gathering and distributing of news; formed in 1958, when **United Press** merged with **International News Service.**

United Provinces, a former province in N India, part of British India. Official name was, **United Provinces of Agra and Oudh.** Now Utta ı Pradesh.

United States, a republic in North America, consisting of 50 States and the District of Columbia. 179,-323,175 pop. (1960); Continental United States, 3,608,-787 sq. mi; United States and possessions, 3,680,114 sq. mi. *Cap.:* Washington, D.C. *Abbr.:* U.S. Also, **United States of America** (*abbr.:* U.S.A.), **America, the States.**

United States Army, the permanent military force of the United States. The term is generally used to refer to the Regular Army, though it includes also the other normal, peacetime components. *Abbr.:* U.S.A. *or* USA Cf. **Army of the United States.**

unit factor, *Biol.* a gene; a substance which functions as the hereditary unit for a single character.

u·ni·tive (ū′nə tĭv), *adv.* serving or tending to unite. [t. LL: m.s. *ūnītivus,* der. L *ūnitus,* pp., made one]

unit rule, (in Democratic national conventions) a rule whereby some States vote as a unit, not recognizing minority votes within the delegation.

u·ni·ty (ū′nə tĭ), *n., pl.* -ties. **1.** state or fact of being one; oneness. **2.** one single thing; something complete in itself, or regarded as such. **3.** the oneness of a complex or organic whole or of an interconnected series; a whole or totality as combining all its parts into one. **4.** the fact or state of being united or combined into one, as of the parts of a whole. **5.** a body formed by union. **6.** freedom from diversity or variety. **7.** unvaried or uniform character, as of a plan. **8.** oneness of mind, feeling, etc., as among a number of persons; concord, harmony, or agreement. **9.** *Math.* the number one; a quantity regarded as one. **10.** (in literature and art) a relation of all the parts or elements of a work consti-

b., blend of, blended; **c.,** cognate with; **d.,** dialect, dialectal; **der.,** derived from; **f.,** formed from; **g.,** going back to; **m.,** modification of; **r.,** replacing; **s.,** stem of; **t.,** taken from; **?,** perhaps. See the full key on inside cover.

tuting a harmonious whole and producing a single general effect. **11.** one of the three principles of plot construction of drama, esp. neoclassic drama: **unity of time** (action taking place during one day); **unity of place** (no extensive shifts in setting); **unity of action** (a single plot). [ME *unite*, t. L: m. *ūnitas*] —**Syn. 1.** See **union. 8.** unison, concert. —**Ant. 1.** diversity.

Unity of Brethren. See **Moravian** (def. 4).

Univ., 1. Universalist. **2.** University.

univ., 1. universal. **2.** universally. **3.** university.

u·ni·va·lence (ū′nə vā′ləns, ū nĭv′ə-), *n.* *Chem.* the quality of being univalent. Also, **u/ni·va/len·cy.**

u·ni·va·lent (ū′nə vā′lənt, ū nĭv′ə-), *adj.* **1.** *Chem.* having a valence of one. **2.** *Biol.* one only; applied to a chromosome which does not possess, or does not join, its homologous chromosome in synapsis. [f. UNI- + -VALENT]

u·ni·valve (ū′nə vălv′), *adj.* Also, **u·ni·valved′, u·ni·val·vu·lar** (ū′nə văl′vyə lər). **1.** having one valve. **2.** (of a shell) composed of a single valve or piece. —*n.* **3.** a univalve mollusk or its shell.

u·ni·ver·sal (ū′nə vûr′səl), *adj.* **1.** of, pertaining to, or characteristic of all or the whole: *universal experience of mankind.* **2.** applicable to many individuals or single cases; general. **3.** affecting, concerning, or involving all: *universal military training.* **4.** used or understood by all: *a universal language.* **5.** existing or prevailing in all parts; everywhere: *universal calm of southern seas.* **6.** versed in or embracing all subjects, fields, etc.: *Leonardo da Vinci was a universal genius.* **7.** given or extended to all: *universal revelation.* **8.** of or pertaining to the universe, all nature, or all existing things: *universal cause.* **9.** *Logic.* relating or applicable to all the members of a class or genus. **10.** *Mach., etc.* adapted or adaptable for all or various uses, angles, sizes, etc. **11.** (of a joint or the like) allowing free movement in all directions within certain limits. **12.** *Archaic.* comprising all; whole; entire. —*n.* **13.** that which may be applied throughout the universe to many things, usually thought of as an entity which can be in many places at the same time (distinguished from *particular*). **14.** a trait or characteristic, as distinguished from a particular individual or event, which can be possessed in common by many distinct things, e.g. *mortality.* **15.** *Logic.* a universal proposition. **16.** *Philos.* **a.** a general term or concept, or the generic nature which such a term signifies; a Platonic idea or Aristotelian form. **b.** a metaphysical entity which is repeatable and remains unchanged in character in a series of changes or changing relations. Cf. **particular** (def. 12). **c.** (in Hegelian terminology) a concrete universal. [ME, t. L: s. *ūniversālis*] —**u/ni·ver′sal·ness,** *n.* —**Syn. 1.** See **general.** —**Ant. 9.** particular.

universal class, *Logic.* (in the logical theory of classes) that class which includes all other classes, and has for its members the individuals who are members of any of these subordinate classes.

universal coupling, universal joint.

u·ni·ver·sal·ism (ū′nə vûr′sə lĭz′əm), *n.* **1.** universal character; universality. **2.** universal range of knowledge, interests, or activities. **3.** (*cap.*) the doctrine or belief of Universalists.

u·ni·ver·sal·ist (ū′nə vûr′səl ĭst), *n.* **1.** one characterized by universalism, as in knowledge, interests, or activities. **2.** (*cap.*) one who believes in the doctrine that all men will finally be saved, or brought back to holiness and God; a member of a Christian denomination which holds this doctrine as its distinctive belief.

u·ni·ver·sal·i·ty (ū′nə vûr′săl′ə tĭ), *n.,* *pl.* -ties. **1.** the character or state of being universal; existence or prevalence everywhere. **2.** relation, extension, or applicability to all. **3.** universal character or range of knowledge, interests, etc.

u·ni·ver·sal·ize (ū′nə vûr′sə līz′), *v.t.,* -ized, -izing. to make universal. —**u/ni·ver/sal·i·za/tion,** *n.*

universal joint, *Mach.* a joint allowing free movement in all directions within certain limits. Also, **universal coupling.**

Single universal joint

u·ni·ver·sal·ly (ū′nə vûr′sə lĭ), *adv.* in a universal manner; in every instance, part, or place; without exception; generally.

u·ni·verse (ū′nə vûrs′), *n.* **1.** the totality of existing or created things, including the earth (with all on or in it), the heavenly bodies, and all else throughout space; the cosmos or macrocosm; all creation. **2.** the whole world; mankind generally: *the whole universe knows it.* **3.** a world or sphere in which something exists or prevails. **4.** *Logic.* the collection of all the objects to which any discourse refers. [t. L: m.s. *ūniversum*]

universe of discourse, *Logic.* the aggregate of objects, ideas, or facts assumed or implied in discourse.

u·ni·ver·si·ty (ū′nə vûr′sə tĭ), *n.,* *pl.* -ties. an institution of learning of the highest grade, having a college of liberal arts and a program of graduate studies, to-

gether with several professional schools and faculties (as of theology, law, medicine, engineering, etc.), and authorized to confer degrees. Continental European universities usually have only graduate and/or professional schools. [ME, t. ML: m.s. *ūniversitas* (*magistrōrum et scholārium*) guild (of teachers and students)]

University City, a city in E Missouri, near St. Louis. 51,249 (1960).

University Park, a city in N Texas. 23,202 (1960).

un·joint (ŭn joint′), *v.t.* to take apart the joints of; disjoint.

un·just (ŭn jŭst′), *adj.* **1.** not just; not acting justly or fairly, as persons. **2.** not in accordance with justice or fairness, as actions. **3.** *Archaic.* unfaithful or dishonest. —**un·just′ly,** *adv.* —**un·just/ness,** *n.* —**Syn. 1.** inequitable, partial, unfair. **2.** undeserved, unmerited, unjustifiable.

un·kempt (ŭn kĕmpt′), *adj.* **1.** not combed, as the hair. **2.** having the hair not combed or cared for. **3.** in an uncared-for, neglected, or untidy state; rough. [var. of *unkembed*, f. UN-² + *kembed*, pp. of obs. *kemb* (ME *kembe*, OE *cemban*) comb] —**un·kempt/ness,** *n.*

un·kenned (ŭn kĕnd′; *Scot.* -kĕnt′), *adj.* *Obs.* or *Dial.* unknown.

un·ken·nel (ŭn kĕn′əl), *v.t.,* -neled, -neling or (*esp. Brit.*) -nelled, -nelling. **1.** to drive or release from, or as from, a kennel; dislodge. **2.** to bring to light.

un·kind (ŭn kīnd′), *adj.* not kind; harsh; cruel; unmerciful; unfeeling and distressing. —**un·kind/ly,** *adv.* —**un·kind/ness,** *n.*

un·kind·ly (ŭn kīnd′lĭ), *adj.* **1.** not kindly; ill-natured; unkind. **2.** inclement or bleak, as weather, climate, etc.; unfavorable for crops, as soil. —**un·kind/li·ness,** *n.*

un·knight·ly (ŭn nīt′lĭ), *adj.* **1.** unworthy of a knight. **2.** not like a knight. —*adv.* **3.** in a manner unworthy of a knight. —**un·knight/li·ness,** *n.*

un·knit (ŭn nĭt′), *v.t.,* -knitted or -knit, -knitting. **1.** to untie or unfasten (a knot, etc.); ravel out (something knitted). **2.** to smooth out (something wrinkled). [ME *unknytte*(*n*), OE *uncnyttan.* See UN-², KNIT, v.]

un·know·a·ble (ŭn nō′ə bəl), *adj.* **1.** not knowable; incapable of being known; transcending human knowledge. —*n.* **2.** something unknowable. **3.** Also, **the Unknowable.** *Philos.* the (postulated) reality lying behind all phenomena but not cognizable by any of the processes by which the mind cognizes phenomenal objects. —**un·know/a·ble·ness,** *n.*

un·know·ing (ŭn nō′ĭng), *adj.* not knowing; ignorant. —**un·know/ing·ly,** *adv.* —**un·know/ing·ness,** *n.*

un·known (ŭn nōn′), *adj.* **1.** not known; not within the range of one's knowledge, cognizance, or acquaintance; unfamiliar; strange. **2.** not ascertained, discovered, or identified. —*n.* **3.** one who or that which is unknown; an unknown person. **4.** *Math.* a symbol representing an unknown quantity.

Unknown Soldier, an unidentified soldier belonging to the army of one of the countries engaged in World War I killed in the war and buried with honors, his tomb serving as a memorial to all the unidentified dead of the army. Also, *Brit.,* **Unknown Warrior.**

un·lace (ŭn lās′), *v.t.,* -laced, -lacing. **1.** to undo the lacing of (a garment, etc.). **2.** to loosen or remove the garments, etc., of by undoing lacing.

un·lade (ŭn lād′), *v.t.,* -laded, -lading. **1.** to take the lading, load, or cargo from; unload. **2.** to discharge (the load or cargo). —*v.i.* **3.** to discharge the load or cargo.

un·laid (ŭn lād′), *adj.* untwisted, as a rope.

un·lash (ŭn lăsh′), *v.t.* to loosen or unfasten, as something lashed or tied fast.

un·latch (ŭn lăch′), *v.t.* **1.** to unfasten or open (a door, etc.) by lifting the latch. —*v.i.* **2.** to become unlatched; open through the lifting of a latch.

un·law·ful (ŭn lô′fəl), *adj.* **1.** not lawful; contrary to law; illegal: not sanctioned by law. **2.** born out of wedlock; illegitimate. —**un·law/ful·ly,** *adv.* —**un·law/ful·ness,** *n.*

un·lay (ŭn lā′), *v.t.,* -laid, -laying. to untwist, as a rope.

un·lead·ed (ŭn lĕd′ĭd), *adj.* not separated or spaced with leads, as lines of type or printed matter.

un·learn (ŭn lûrn′), *v.t.* to put aside from knowledge or memory (something learned); discard or lose knowledge of; forget.

un·learn·ed (ŭn lûr′nĭd *for* 1, 4, ŭn lûrnd′ *for* 2, 3), *adj.* **1.** not learned; not scholarly or erudite; uneducated; ignorant. **2.** not acquired by learning; never learned. **3.** known without being learned. **4.** of or pertaining to unlearned persons. —**un·learn/ed·ly,** *adv.*

un·leash (ŭn lēsh′), *v.t.* to release from or as from a leash; set free to pursue or run at will; let loose.

un·less (ŭn lĕs′), *conj.* **1.** if it be (or were) not that, or if . . . not. —*prep.* **2.** except. [ME *onlesse*, f. ON prep. + *lesse* LESS, orig. meaning on a lower condition (than)]

un·let·tered (ŭn lĕt′ərd), *adj.* not educated; without knowledge of books. —**Syn.** See **ignorant.**

un/jack/et·ed	un·jus/ti·fi/a·ble	un·knot/	un/la·ment/ed
un·jad/ed	un·jus/ti·fi/a·bly	un·knot/ted	un·lashed/
un·joined/	un·kept/	un·la/beled	un·laun/dered
un·joint/ed	un·kin/dled	un·la/bored	un·leased/
un·judged/	un·king/ly	un·la/den	un·leav/ened
un·ju·di/cial	un·kissed/	un·la/dy·like/	un·less/ened

un·li·censed (ŭn·lī'sənst), *adj.* 1. having no license. 2. done or undertaken without license; unauthorized.

un·like (ŭn·līk'), *adj.* 1. not like; different or dissimilar; having no resemblance. —*prep.* 2. otherwise than like; differently from. —**un·like'ness,** *n.* —Syn. 1. diverse, variant, heterogeneous.

un·like·li·hood (ŭn·līk'lĭ·hŏŏd'), *n.* state of being unlikely; improbability.

un·like·ly (ŭn·līk'lĭ), *adj.* 1. not likely; improbable; probably not going (to do, be, etc.). 2. holding out little prospect of success; unpromising. —*adv.* 3. improbably. —**un·like'li·ness,** *n.*

un·lim·ber (ŭn·lĭm'bər), *v.t.* 1. to detach (a gun) from its limber or prime mover. —*n.* 2. act of changing a gun from traveling to firing position.

un·lim·it·ed (ŭn·lĭm'ĭt·ĭd), *adj.* 1. not limited; unrestricted. 2. boundless; limitless. —**un·lim'it·ed·ly,** *adv.* —**un·lim'it·ed·ness,** *n.*

unlimited policy, *Insurance.* a policy which covers, without exceptions, all types of losses within a given area of risk. See **limited policy.**

un·link (ŭn·lĭngk'), *v.t.* 1. to separate the links of (a chain, etc.). 2. to separate or detach by, or as by, undoing a connecting link.

un·list·ed (ŭn·lĭs'tĭd), *adj.* 1. not listed; not entered in a list. 2. (of stock exchange securities) not entered in the regular list of those admitted for dealings.

un·live (ŭn·lĭv'), *v.t.,* **-lived, -living.** 1. to undo or annul (past life, etc.). 2. to live so as to undo the consequences of.

un·load (ŭn·lōd'), *v.t.* 1. to take the load from; remove the burden, cargo, or freight from. 2. to relieve of anything burdensome. 3. to withdraw the charge from (a firearm). 4. to remove or discharge (a load, etc.). 5. *Colloq.* to get rid of or dispose of (stock, etc.) by sale in large quantities. —*v.i.* 6. to unload something; remove or discharge a load. —**un·load'er,** *n.*

un·lock (ŭn·lŏk'), *v.t.* 1. to undo the lock of. 2. to open or release by, or as by, undoing a lock. 3. to open (anything firmly closed or joined): *to unlock the jaws.* 4. to lay open; disclose. —*v.i.* 5. to become unlocked.

un·looked-for (ŭn·lŏŏkt'fôr'), *adj.* not looked for; unexpected; unforeseen.

un·loose (ŭn·lōōs'), *v.t.,* **-loosed, -loosing.** 1. to set or let loose; release from bonds, fastenings, etc.; set free from restraint. 2. to loose or undo (a bond, fastening, knot, etc.). 3. to loosen or relax (the grasp, hold, fingers, etc.).

un·loos·en (ŭn·lōō'sən), *v.t.* to unloose; loosen.

un·love·ly ((ŭn·lŭv'lĭ), *adj.* 1. not lovely; without beauty or charm of appearance; unpleasing to the eye. 2. unattractive, repellent, or disagreeable in character; unpleasant; objectionable. —**un·love'li·ness,** *n.*

un·luck·y (ŭn·lŭk'ĭ), *adj.* not lucky; not having good luck; unfortunate or ill-fated; not attended with good luck. —**un·luck'i·ly,** *adv.* —**un·luck'i·ness,** *n.*

un·make (ŭn·māk'), *v.t.,* **-made, -making.** 1. to cause to be as if never made; reduce to the original matter, elements, or state. 2. to take to pieces; destroy; ruin or undo. 3. to depose from office or authority. —**un·mak'er,** *n.*

un·man (ŭn·măn'), *v.t.,* **-manned, -manning.** 1. to deprive of the character or qualities of a man or human being. 2. to deprive of virility; emasculate. 3. to deprive of manly courage or fortitude; break down the manly spirit of. 4. to deprive of men: *to unman a ship.*

un·man·ly (ŭn·măn'lĭ), *adj.* not manly; not like or befitting a man; womanish or childish; weak; cowardly. —**un·man'li·ness,** *n.*

un·manned (ŭn·mănd'), *adj.* 1. deprived of men: *an unmanned ship.* 2. desolate; having no population. 3. castrated.

un·man·nered (ŭn·măn'ərd), *adj.* without manners; unmannerly.

un·man·ner·ly (ŭn·măn'ər·lĭ), *adj.* 1. not mannerly; ill-bred; rude; churlish. —*adv.* 2. *Obs.* with ill manners. —**un·man'ner·li·ness,** *n.*

un·mask (ŭn·măsk', -mäsk'), *v.t.* 1. to strip of a mask or disguise. 2. to lay open (anything concealed); expose in the true character. 3. *Mil.* to reveal the presence of (guns, etc.) by firing. —*v.i.* 4. to put off a mask or disguise.

un·mean·ing (ŭn·mē'nĭng), *adj.* 1. not meaning anything; without meaning or significance, as words or actions; meaningless. 2. expressionless, vacant, or unintelligent, as the face, etc. —**un·mean'ing·ly,** *adv.* —**un·mean'ing·ness,** *n.*

un·meas·ured (ŭn·mĕzh'ərd), *adj.* 1. of undetermined or indefinitely great extent or amount; unlimited; measureless. 2. unrestrained; intemperate. —**un·meas'ur·a·ble,** *adj.*

un·meet (ŭn·mēt'), *adj.* not meet; unfitting; unbecoming; unseemly. [ME *unmete,* OE *unmǣte.* See UN-[1], MEET[2]] —**un·meet'ly,** *adv.* —**un·meet'ness,** *n.*

un·men·tion·a·ble (ŭn·mĕn'shən·ə·bəl), *adj.* not mentionable; unworthy or unfit to be mentioned. —**un·men'tion·a·ble·ness,** *n.*

un·men·tion·a·bles (ŭn·mĕn'shən·ə·bəlz), *n. pl.* 1. trousers or breeches. 2. *Humorous.* undergarments.

un·mer·ci·ful (ŭn·mûr'sĭ·fəl), *adj.* 1. not merciful; merciless; pitiless; relentless; unsparing. 2. unsparingly great; unconscionable. —**un·mer'ci·ful·ly,** *adv.* —**un·mer'ci·ful·ness,** *n.*

un·mer·it·ing (ŭn·mĕr'ĭt·ĭng), *adj.* not meriting; undeserving.

un·mew (ŭn·mū'), *v.t.* to set free (something mewed up); release, as from confinement. [f. UN-[2] + MEW[3]]

un·mind·ful (ŭn·mīnd'fəl), *adj.* not mindful; regardless; heedless; careless. —**un·mind'ful·ly,** *adv.* —**un·mind'ful·ness,** *n.*

un·mis·tak·a·ble (ŭn'mĭs·tā'kə·bəl), *adj.* not mistakable; admitting of no mistake; clear; plain; evident. —**un'mis·tak'a·ble·ness,** *n.* —**un'mis·tak'a·bly,** *adv.*

un·mi·ter (ŭn·mī'tər), *v.t.* to deprive of a miter; depose from the rank of a bishop.

un·mit·i·gat·ed (ŭn·mĭt'ə·gā'tĭd), *adj.* 1. not mitigated; not softened or lessened. 2. unqualified or absolute. —**un·mit'i·gat·ed·ly,** *adv.*

un·mi·tre (ŭn·mī'tər), *v.t.,* **-tred, -tring.** *Chiefly Brit.* unmiter.

un·mixed (ŭn·mĭkst'), *adj.* not mixed; unmingled; pure; unalloyed. Also, **un·mixt'.**

un·moor (ŭn·mŏŏr'), *v.t.* 1. to loose (a ship, etc.) from moorings or anchorage. 2. to bring to the state of riding with a single anchor after being moored by two or more. —*v.i.* 3. (of a ship, etc.) to become unmoored.

un·mor·al (ŭn·môr'əl, -mŏr'-), *adj.* nonmoral; having no moral aspect; neither moral nor immoral. —**un·mo·ral·i·ty** (ŭn'mə·răl'ə·tĭ), *n.* —**un·mor'al·ly,** *adv.*

un·mor·tise (ŭn·môr'tĭs), *v.t.,* **-tised, -tising.** to unfasten or separate (something mortised).

un·mov·ing (ŭn·mōō'vĭng), *adj.* not moving; motionless.

un·muf·fle (ŭn·mŭf'əl), *v.,* **-fled, -fling.** —*v.t.* 1. to strip of or free from that which muffles. —*v.i.* 2. to throw off that which muffles.

un·mu·si·cal (ŭn·mū'zə·kəl), *adj.* 1. not musical; not melodious or harmonious. 2. harsh or discordant in sound. 3. not fond of or skilled in music. —**un·mu'si·cal·ly,** *adv.* —**un·mu'si·cal·ness,** *n.*

un·muz·zle (ŭn·mŭz'əl), *v.t.,* **-zled, -zling.** 1. to remove a muzzle from (a dog, etc.). 2. to free from restraint, as upon speech or expression.

un·nail (ŭn·nāl'), *v.t.* to take out the nails from.

un·named (ŭn·nāmd'), *adj.* 1. having no name; nameless. 2. not specified or mentioned by name.

un·nat·u·ral (ŭn·năch'ə·rəl), *adj.* 1. not natural; not proper to the natural constitution or character. 2. having or showing a lack of natural or proper instincts, feelings, etc. 3. contrary to the nature of things. 4. at variance with the ordinary course of nature; unusual, strange, or abnormal. 5. artificial or affected; forced or strained. 6. more than usually cruel or evil. —**un·nat'u·ral·ly,** *adv.* —**un·nat'u·ral·ness,** *n.*

un·lev'el	un·maid'en·li·ness	un·ma·tured'	un/mis·tak'en
un·lev'ied	un·maid'en·ly	un·meant'	un·mit'i·ga·ble
un/li·bid'i·nous	un·mail'a·ble	un/me·chan'i·cal	un·mod'i·fied'
un·life'like'	un·mal'le·a·ble	un·med'i·cat·ed	un·mod'ish
un/lift'a·ble	un·man'age·a·ble	un·med'i·tat'ed	un·mois'tened
un·light'ed	un·man'ful	un/me·lo'di·ous	un·mold'
un·lik'a·ble	un·man'i·fest'ed	un·melt'ed	un·mo·lest'ed
un·like'a·ble	un·man'ish	un·men'aced	un·mol'li·fied'
un·lined'	un·man'nish·ly	un·mend'a·ble	un·mol'ten
un·liq'ue·fi'a·ble	un/man·u·fac'tur·a·ble	un·mend'ed	un·mort'gaged
un·liq'ui·dat'ed	un/man·u·fac'tured	un·men'sur·a·ble	un·mo'ti·vat'ed
un·lit'	un·marked'	un·men'tion·a·bil'i·ty	un·mount'ed
un·live'li·ness	un·mar'ket·a·ble	un·men'tion·a·bly	un·mourned'
un·live'ly	un·marred'	un·men'tioned	un·mov'a·ble
un·lo'cat·ed	un·mar'ringe·a·ble	un·mer'ce·nar'y	un·moved'
un·locked'	un·mar'ried	un·mer'chant·a·ble	un·mov'ed·ly
un·lov'a·ble	un·mas'tered	un·mer'it·ed	un·mown'
un·loved'	un·matched'	un/me·thod'i·cal	un·mur'mur·ing
un·lov'ing	un/mat'ed	un·mil'i·tar'y	un·mys'ti·fied'
un·lu'bri·cat'ed	un/ma·ter'nal	un·milled'	un·nam'a·ble
un·mag'ni·fied'	un/mat'ted	un·min'gled	un·name'a·ble
		un·mirth'ful	un·nat'u·ral·ized'

---

b., blend of, blended; c., cognate with; d., dialect, dialectal; der., derived from; f., formed from; g., going back to; m., modification of; r., replacing; s., stem of; t., taken from; ?, perhaps. See the full key on inside cover.

un·nec·es·sary (ŭn něs'ə sĕr'Y), *adj.* not necessary: needless. —**un·nec'es·sar'i·ly,** *adv.* —**un·nec'es·sar'i·ness,** *n.*

un·nerve (ŭn nûrv'), *v.t.* **-nerved, -nerving.** to deprive of nerve, strength, or physical or mental firmness; break down the self-control or courage of.

un·num·bered (ŭn nŭm'bərd), *adj.* **1.** not numbered; uncounted. **2.** countless; innumerable.

un·oc·cu·pied (ŭn ŏk'yə pīd'), *adj.* **1.** not occupied; not possessed or held; vacant. **2.** not employed; idle.

un·or·gan·ized (ŭn ôr'gə nīzd'), *adj.* **1.** not organized; without organic structure. **2.** not formed into an organized or systematized whole. **3.** not having membership in a labor union.

unorganized ferment, an enzyme.

un·pack (ŭn păk'), *v.t.* **1.** to undo or take out (something packed). **2.** to remove the contents packed in (a box, trunk, etc.). **3.** to remove a pack or load from (a horse, etc.); unload (a vehicle, etc.). —*v.i.* **4.** to unpack articles, goods, etc. —**un·pack'er,** *n.*

un·paged (ŭn pājd'), *adj.* (of a publication) having unnumbered pages.

un·paid-for (ŭn pād'fôr'), *adj.* not paid for.

un·par·al·leled (ŭn păr'ə lĕld'), *adj.* not paralleled; having no parallel; unequaled; unmatched.

un·par·lia·men·ta·ry (ŭn'pär lə mĕn'tə rY), *adj.* not parliamentary; not in accordance with parliamentary practice. —**un·par'lia·men'ta·ri·ly,** *adv.* —**un·par'lia·men'ta·ri·ness,** *n.*

un·peg (ŭn pĕg'), *v.t.,* **-pegged, -pegging. 1.** to remove the peg or pegs from. **2.** to open, unfasten, or unfix by removing a peg or pegs.

un·pen (ŭn pĕn'), *v.t.,* **-penned, -penning.** to release from, or as from, a pen.

un·peo·ple (ŭn pē'pəl), *v.t.,* **-pled, -pling.** to deprive of people; depopulate.

un·pile (ŭn pīl'), *v.,* **-piled, -piling.** —*v.t.* **1.** to remove from a pile. —*v.i.* **2.** to be removed from a pile.

un·pin (ŭn pYn'), *v.t.,* **-pinned, -pinning. 1.** to remove the pin or pins from. **2.** to unfasten by removing a pin or pins.

un·plait (ŭn plāt'), *v.t.* to bring out of a plaited state; unbraid, as hair.

un·pleas·ant (ŭn plĕz'ənt), *adj.* not pleasant; unpleasing; disagreeable. —**un·pleas'ant·ly,** *adv.*

un·pleas·ant·ness (ŭn plĕz'ənt nYs), *n.* **1.** the quality or state of being unpleasant. **2.** something unpleasant; an unpleasant state of affairs; a disagreement or quarrel.

un·plug (ŭn plŭg'), *v.t.,* **-plugged, -plugging.** to remove the plug from.

un·plumbed (ŭn plŭmd'), *adj.* **1.** not plumbed; unfathomed; of unknown depth. **2.** having no plumbing installations.

un·pol·i·tic (ŭn pŏl'ə tYk), *adj.* impolitic.

un·polled (ŭn pōld'), *adj.* **1.** not polled. **2.** not voting or not cast at the polls.

un·pop·u·lar (ŭn pŏp'yə lər), *adj.* not popular; not liked by the public or by persons generally. —**un·pop·u·lar·i·ty** (ŭn'pŏp yə lăr'ə tY), *n.* —**un·pop'u·lar·ly,** *adv.*

un·prac·ti·cal (ŭn prăk'tə kəl), *adj.* not practical; impractical; lacking practical usefulness or wisdom; visionary. —**un·prac·ti·cal·i·ty, un·prac'ti·cal·ness,** *n.* —**un·prac'ti·cal·ly,** *adv.*

un·prac·ticed (ŭn prăk'tYst), *adj.* **1.** not practiced; not done habitually or as a practice. **2.** not trained or skilled; inexpert. Also, **un·prac'tised.**

un·prec·e·dent·ed (ŭn prĕs'ə dĕn'tYd), *adj.* having no precedent or preceding instance; never known before; unexampled. —**un·prec'e·dent·ed·ly,** *adv.*

un·prej·u·diced (ŭn prĕj'ə dYst), *adj.* **1.** not prejudiced; unbiased; impartial. **2.** not impaired. —**Syn. 1.** See fair[1].

un·pre·tend·ing (ŭn'prY tĕn'dYng), *adj.* not pretending; unassuming; modest. —**un'pre·tend'ing·ly,** *adv.*

un·priced (ŭn prīst'), *adj.* **1.** not priced; having no price set or indicated. **2.** beyond price; priceless.

un·prin·ci·pled (ŭn prYn'sə pəld), *adj.* **1.** lacking sound moral principles, as a person. **2.** showing want of principle, as conduct, etc. **3.** not instructed in the principles of something (fol. by *in*). —**un·prin'ci·pled·ness,** *n.* —**Syn. 1.** See unscrupulous.

un·print·a·ble (ŭn prYn'tə bəl), *adj.* not printable; unfit to be printed.

un·priz·a·ble (ŭn prī'zə bəl), *adj.* not worthy to be prized; of little worth.

un·pro·fes·sion·al (ŭn'prə fĕsh'ən əl), *adj.* **1.** not professional; not pertaining to or connected with a profession. **2.** contrary to professional ethics; unbecoming in members of a profession. **3.** not belonging to a profession. —**un'pro·fes'sion·al·ly,** *adv.*

un·pub·lished work (ŭn pŭb'lYsht), *Copyright Law.* a literary work which, at the time of registration, has not been reproduced for sale or been publicly distributed.

un·qual·i·fied (ŭn kwŏl'ə fīd'), *adj.* **1.** not qualified; not fitted; not having the requisite qualifications. **2.** not modified, limited, or restricted in any way: *unqualified praise.* **3.** absolute; out-and-out. —**un·qual'i·fied'ly,** *adv.* —**un·qual'i·fied'ness,** *n.* —**Syn. 3.** See absolute.

un·ques·tion·a·ble (ŭn kwĕs'chən ə bəl), *adj.* **1.** not questionable; not open to question; beyond dispute or doubt; indisputable; indubitable. **2.** beyond criticism; unexceptionable. —**un·ques'tion·a·ble·ness,** *n.* —**un·ques'tion·a·bly,** *adv.*

un·ques·tioned (ŭn kwĕs'chənd), *adj.* **1.** not questioned; not interrogated. **2.** not inquired into. **3.** not called in question; undisputed.

un·qui·et (ŭn kwī'ət), *adj.* **1.** not quiet; restless; turbulent; tumultuous. **2.** uneasy; perturbed. **3.** agitated or in commotion; not silent or still. —**un·qui'et·ly,** *adv.* —**un·qui'et·ness,** *n.*

un·quote (ŭn kwōt'), *v.i.,* **-quoted, -quoting.** to close a quotation.

un·nav'i·ga·ble	un·os·ten·ta'tious	un·pit'y·ing	un·prized'
un·nav'i·gat'ed	un·owned'	un·placed'	un·probed'
un·need'ed	un·ox'i·dized'	un·plagued'	un·proc'essed
un·need'ful	un·pac'i·fied'	un·planned'	un·pro·cur'a·ble
un·ne·go'ti·a·ble	un·paid'	un·plant'ed	un·pro·duc'tive
un·neigh'bor·li·ness	un·pain'ful	un·played'	un·pro·faned'
un·neigh'bor·ly	un·paired'	un·pleased'	un·prof'it·able
un·not'ed	un·pal'at·a·ble	un·pleas'ing	un·prof'it·a·ble·ness
un·no'tice·a·ble	un·pal'at·a·bly	un·pledged'	un·prof'it·ed
un·no'tice·a·ble·ness	un·par'a·graphed	un·pli'a·ble	un·pro·gres'sive
un·no'tice·a·bly	un·par'don·a·ble	un·pli'ant	un·pro·hib'it·ed
un·no'ticed	un·par'don·a·bly	un·plight'ed	un·prom'is·ing
un·nur'tured	un·par'doned	un·ploughed'	un·prompt'ed
un·ob·jec'tion·a·ble	un·pa·ren'tal	un·plowed'	un·pro·nounce'a·ble
un·o·bliged'	un·part'ed	un·plucked'	un·pro·nounced'
un·o·blig'ing	un·par'ti·san	un·po·et'ic	un·pro·pi'ti·a·ble
un·ob·nox'ious	un·pas'teur·ized'	un·po·et'i·cal	un·pro·pi'ti·at'ed
un·ob·scured'	un·patched'	un·point'ed	un·pro·por'tion·ate
un·ob·serv'ant	un·pat'ent·ed	un·poised'	un·pro·posed'
un·ob·served'	un·pa·tri·ot'ic	un·po·lar·ized'	un·pros'per·ous
un·ob·serv'ing	un·paved'	un·pol'ished	un·pro·tect'ed
un·ob·struct'ed	un·peace'a·ble	un·po·lit'i·cal	un·proved'
un·ob·tain'a·ble	un·peace'ful	un·pol'lut·ed	un·prov'en
un·ob·tained'	un·ped'i·greed	un·pon'dered	un·pro·vid'ed
un·ob·trud'ing	un·pen'e·trat'ed	un·pop'u·lat'ed	un·pro·voked'
un·ob·tru'sive	un·pen'sioned	un·posed'	un·pro·vok'ing
un·ob·tru'sive·ness	un·per·ceiv'a·ble	un·post'ed	un·pruned'
un·oc·ca'sioned	un·per·ceived'	un·pre·dict'a·ble	un·pub'lished
un·of·fend'ed	un·per·fect'ed	un·pre·med'i·tat'ed	un·punc'tu·al
un·of·fend'ing	un·per·formed'	un·pre·oc'cu·pied'	un·pun'ish·a·ble
un·of·fen'sive	un·per·plexed'	un·pre·pared'	un·pun'ished
un·of'fered	un·per·suad'a·ble	un·pre·par'ed·ness	un·pur'chas·a·ble
un·of·fi'cial	un·per·suad'ed	un·pre·pos·sess'ing	un·pure'
un·of·fi'cious	un·per·sua'sive	un·pre·scribed'	un·purged'
un·oiled'	un·per·turbed'	un·pre·sent'a·ble	un·pu'ri·fied'
un·o'pen	un·pe·rused'	un·pre·served'	un·pur'posed
un·o'pened	un·phil·an·throp'ic	un·pressed'	un·pur·su'ing
un·op·posed'	un·phil·o·log'i·cal	un·pre·sump'tu·ous	un·quaffed'
un·op·pressed'	un·phil·o·soph'ic	un·pre·ten'tious	un·quail'ing
un·or·dained'	un·phil·o·soph'i·cal	un·pre·vail'ing	un·quak'ing
un·or·ig'i·nal	un·pho·net'ic	un·pre·vent'ed	un·quelled'
un·or·na·men'tal	un·picked'	un·primed'	un·quench'a·ble
un·or'tho·dox'	un·pic·tur·esque'	un·prince'ly	un·quenched'
un·or'tho·dox'y	un·pierced'	un·print'ed	un·ques'tion·ing
	un·pit'ied	un·priv'i·leged	un·quot'able

un·rav·el (ŭn·răv′əl), v., **-eled, -eling** or (esp. Brit.) **-elled, -elling. —v.t. 1.** to free from a raveled or tangled state; disentangle; disengage the threads or fibers of (a woven or knitted fabric, a rope, etc.). **2.** to separate by unweaving or the like, as threads. **3.** to free from complication or difficulty; make plain or clear; solve. **—v.i. 4.** to become unraveled. **—un·rav′el·ment**, n.

un·read (ŭn·rĕd′), adj. **1.** not read or perused, as a book. **2.** not having gained knowledge by reading.

un·read·a·ble (ŭn·rē′də·bəl), adj. **1.** not readable; illegible. **2.** not suitable for reading. **3.** not interesting to read.

un·read·y (ŭn·rĕd′ĭ), adj. **1.** not ready; not made ready, as for action or use. **2.** not in a state of readiness or preparation, as a person. **3.** Brit. Dial. not dressed, or not fully dressed. **4.** not prompt or quick: in the historical surname of King Ethelred II ('the Unready'). **—un·read′i·ly**, adv. **—un·read′i·ness**, n.

un·re·al (ŭn·rē′əl, -rēl′), adj. not real; not substantial; imaginary; artificial; unpractical or visionary. **—un·re′al·ly**, adv. **—Syn.** sham, spurious, fictitious, illusive, theoretical, impractical.

un·re·al·i·ty (ŭn′rĭ·ăl′ə·tĭ), n., pl. **-ties. 1.** lack of reality; quality of being unreal. **2.** unpractical or visionary character. **3.** something unreal or without reality.

un·rea·son (ŭn·rē′zən), n. **1.** lack of reason; inability or unwillingness to think or act rationally, reasonably, or sensibly. **2.** that which is devoid of or contrary to reason.

un·rea·son·a·ble (ŭn·rē′zən·ə·bəl, -rēz′nə-), adj. **1.** not reasonable; not endowed with reason. **2.** not guided by reason or good sense. **3.** not based on or in accordance with reason or sound judgment. **4.** exceeding the bounds of reason; immoderate; exorbitant. **—un·rea′son·a·ble·ness**, n. **—un·rea′son·a·bly**, adv. **—Syn. 1, 2.** irrational, senseless, foolish, silly. **4.** excessive, immoderate, exorbitant.

un·rea·son·ing (ŭn·rē′zən·ĭng), adj. not reasoning or exercising reason; reasonless: an unreasoning maniac. **—un·rea′son·ing·ly**, adv.

un·reel (ŭn·rēl′), v.t., v.i. to unwind from a reel. **—un·reel′a·ble**, adj.

un·reeve (ŭn·rēv′), v., **-rove** or **-reeved, -reeving. —v.t. 1.** Naut. to withdraw (a rope, etc.) from a block, thimble, etc. **—v.i. 2.** to unreeve a rope. **3.** (of a rope, etc.) to become unreeved.

un·re·fined (ŭn′rĭ·fīnd′), adj. **1.** not refined; not purified, as substances. **2.** not free from coarseness or vulgarity; lacking nice feeling, taste, etc. **—Syn. 1.** unpurified, crude, coarse. **2.** unpolished, uncultured, ill-bred, rude, boorish, vulgar, gross.

un·re·flec·tive (ŭn′rĭ·flĕk′tĭv), adj. not reflective; acting without deliberation. **—un·re·flec′tive·ly**, adv.

un·re·gen·er·ate (ŭn′rĭ·jĕn′ər·ĭt), adj. **1.** not regenerate; not born again spiritually. **2.** remaining at enmity with God. Also, **un·re·gen·er·at·ed** (ŭn′rĭ·jĕn′ər·ā′tĭd). **—un·re·gen·er·a·cy** (ŭn′rĭ·jĕn′ər·ə·sĭ), n. **—un·re·gen′er·ate·ly**, adv.

un·re·lent·ing (ŭn′rĭ·lĕn′tĭng), adj. **1.** not relenting; not yielding to feelings of kindness or compassion. **2.** not slackening in severity or determination. **3.** maintaining speed or rate of advance. **—un·re·lent′ing·ly**, adv. **—un·re·lent′ing·ness**, n.

un·re·li·a·ble (ŭn′rĭ·lī′ə·bəl), adj. not reliable; not to be relied or depended on. **—un·re·li·a·bil′i·ty, un·re·li′a·ble·ness**, n. **—un·re·li′a·bly**, adv.

un·re·li·gious (ŭn′rĭ·lĭj′əs), adj. **1.** irreligious. **2.** having no connection with or relation to religion; neither religious nor irreligious.

un·re·mit·ting (ŭn′rĭ·mĭt′ĭng), adj. not remitting or slackening; not abating for a time; incessant. **—un·re·mit′ting·ly**, adv. **—un·re·mit′ting·ness**, n.

un·re·pair (ŭn′rĭ·pâr′), n. lack of repair; disrepair; dilapidation. **—un·re·paired′**, adj.

un·re·serve (ŭn′rĭ·zûrv′), n. absence of reserve; frankness.

un·re·served (ŭn′rĭ·zûrvd′), adj. **1.** not reserved; without reservation; full; entire. **2.** free from reserve; frank; open. **—un·re·serv·ed·ly** (ŭn′rĭ·zûr′vĭd·lĭ), adv. **—un·re·serv′ed·ness**, n.

un·rest (ŭn·rĕst′), n. **1.** lack of rest; restless or uneasy state; inquietude. **2.** strong, almost rebellious, dissatisfaction and agitation.

un·re·straint (ŭn′rĭ·strānt′), n. absence of or freedom from restraint.

un·rid·dle (ŭn·rĭd′əl), v.t., **-dled, -dling.** to solve (a riddle, etc.).

un·rid·dled (ŭn·rĭd′əld), adj. not solved, as a riddle.

un·rig (ŭn·rĭg′), v.t., **-rigged, -rigging. 1.** to strip of rigging, as a ship. **2.** to strip of equipment. **3.** Colloq. to undress.

un·right·eous (ŭn·rī′chəs), adj. **1.** not righteous; not upright or virtuous; wicked. **2.** not in accordance with right; unjust. [ME unrightwyse, OE unrihtwís] **—un·right′eous·ly**, adv. **—un·right′eous·ness**, n.

un·rip (ŭn·rĭp′), v.t., **-ripped, -ripping.** to undo by ripping; cut or tear open; rip.

un·ripe (ŭn·rīp′), adj. **1.** not ripe; immature; not fully developed. **2.** Obs. too early; premature. **—un·ripe′ness**, n.

un·ri·valed (ŭn·rī′vəld), adj. having no rival or competitor; having no equal; peerless. Also, esp. Brit., **un·ri′valled**.

un·robe (ŭn·rōb′), v.t., v.i., **-robed, -robing.** to disrobe; undress.

un·roll (ŭn·rōl′), v.t. **1.** to open or spread out (something rolled, coiled, or folded). **2.** to lay open; display; reveal. **3.** Rare. to strike from a roll or register. **—v.i. 4.** to become unrolled.

un·roof (ŭn·rŏŏf′, -rōōf′), v.t. to take the roof off.

un·root (ŭn·rŏŏt′, -rōōt′), v.t. to uproot.

un·round (ŭn·round′), v.t. Phonet. to pronounce without rounding the lips: the vowel of bit is normally unrounded, the vowel of put is often unrounded. **—un·round′ed**, adj.

un·rove (ŭn·rōv′), Naut. **—v.** 1. pt. and pp. of **unreeve. —adj. 2.** withdrawn from a block, thimble, etc.

UNRRA (ŭn′rə), United Nations Relief and Rehabilitation Administration.

un·ruf·fled (ŭn·rŭf′əld), adj. not ruffled; smooth; calm.

un·ru·ly (ŭn·rōō′lĭ), adj. not submissive or conforming to rule; ungovernable; turbulent; refractory; lawless. **—un·ru′li·ness**, n.

un·sad·dle (ŭn·săd′əl), v., **-dled, -dling. —v.t. 1.** to take the saddle from. **2.** to cause to fall or dismount from a saddle; unhorse. **—v.i. 3.** to take the saddle from a horse.

un·safe·ty (ŭn·sāf′tĭ), n. state of being unsafe; exposure to danger or risk; insecurity.

un·said (ŭn·sĕd′), v. pt. and pp. of **unsay.**

un·raised′	un·re·freshed′	un·re·pin′ing	un·re·turned′
un·ran′somed	un·re·fresh′ing	un·re·placed′	un·re·vealed′
un·rat′i·fied′	un·re·gard′ed	un·re·plen′ished	un·re·venged′
un·rav′aged	un·reg′is·tered	un·re·port′ed	un·re·versed′
un·reach′a·ble	un·re·gret′ted	un·rep·re·sent′a·tive	un·re·vised′
un·reached′	un·reg′u·lat′ed	having no representative	un·re·voked′
un·re·al′iz·a·ble	un·re·hearsed′	un·rep·re·sent′ed	un·re·ward′ed
un·re′al·ized′	un·re·lat′ed	un·re·pressed′	un·rhe·tor′i·cal
un·rea′soned	un·re·lat′ed·ness	un·re·priev′a·ble	un·rhymed′
un·re·buk′a·ble	un·re·laxed′	un·re·prieved′	un·rhyth′mic
un·re·buked′	un·re·lax′ing	un·re·prov′a·ble	un·rhyth′mi·cal
un·re·ceipt′ed	un·re·liev′a·ble	un·re·proved′	un·right′ed
un·re·ceiv′a·ble	un·re·lieved′	un·re·quest′ed	un·right′ful
un·re·ceived′	un·rel′ished	un·re·quit′ed	un·rimed′
un·re·cep′tive	un·re·marked′	un·re·sent′ed	un·rip′ened
un·re·cip′ro·cat′ed	un·re·med′ied	un·re·sent′ful	un·roast′ed
un·re·claim′a·ble	un·re·mem′bered	un·re·signed′	un·ro·man′tic
un·re·claimed′	un·re·mit′ta·ble	un·re·sist′ant	un·ro·man′ti·cal·ly
un·rec·og·niz′a·ble	un·re·mit′ted	un·re·sist′ed	un·rough′
un·rec·og·nized′	un·re·morse′ful	un·re·sist′ing	un·ruled′
un·rec·om·mend′ed	un·re·mov′a·ble	un·re·sist′ing·ly	un·safe′
un·rec·om·pensed′	un·re·moved′	un·re·solved′	un·safe′ly
un·rec·on·cil′a·ble	un·re·mu′ner·at′ed	un·re·spect′a·ble	un·saint′ly
un·rec·on·ciled′	un·re·mu′ner·a′tive	un·re·spect′ful	un·sal′a·bil′i·ty
un·re·cord′ed	un·ren′dered	un·res·pit′ed	un·sal′a·ble
un·re·count′ed	un·re·newed′	un·re·spon′sive	un·sale′a·bil′i·ty
un·re·cov′er·a·ble	un·re·nounced′	un·re·spon′sive·ly	un·sale′a·ble
un·re·cruit′ed	un·re·nowned′	un·re·spon′sive·ness	un·sal′a·ried
un·rec′ti·fied′	un·rent′	un·rest′ed	un·salt′ed
un·re·deemed′	un·rent′ed	un·re·strain′a·ble	un·sanc′ti·fied′
un·re·dressed′	un·re·paid′	un·re·strained′	un·sanc′tioned
un·re·flect′ed	un·re·pair′a·ble	un·re·strain′ed·ly	un·san′i·tar′y
un·re·flect′ing	un·re·pealed′	un·re·strict′ed	un·sat′ed
un·re·flect′ing·ly	un·re·pent′ant	un·re·tard′ed	un·sa′ti·a·ble
un·re·form′a·ble	un·re·pent′ed	un·re·ten′tive	un·sa′ti·at′ed
un·re·formed′	un·re·pent′ing	un·re·tract′ed	un·sa′ti·at′ing
		un·re·trieved′	

---

b., blend of, blended; **c.**, cognate with; **d.**, dialect, dialectal; **der.**, derived from; **f.**, formed from; **g.**, going back to; **m.**, modification of; **r.**, replacing; **s.**, stem of; **t.**, taken from; **?**, perhaps.   See the full key on inside cover.

un·sat·is·fac·to·ry (ŭn′săt ĭs făk′tə rĭ, -trĭ), *adj.* not satisfactory; not satisfying the desires or requirements; inadequate. **—un′sat·is·fac′to·ri·ly,** *adv.* **—un′sat·is·fac′to·ri·ness,** *n.*

un·sat·u·rat·ed (ŭn săch′ə rā′tĭd), *adj.* 1. not saturated; having the power to dissolve still more of a substance. 2. *Chem.* capable of taking on an element, etc., by direct chemical combination without the liberation of other elements or compounds.

unsaturated radical, *Chem.* an organic radical with a double or triple bond linking two carbon atoms.

un·sa·vor·y (ŭn sā′və rĭ), *adj.* 1. not savory; tasteless or insipid. 2. unpleasant in taste or smell. 3. morally unpleasant or offensive. Also, *esp. Brit.,* **un·sa′vour·y.** **—un·sa′vor·i·ly,** *adv.* **—un·sa′vor·i·ness,** *n.*

un·say (ŭn sā′), *v.t.,* **-said, -saying.** to retract (something said).

un·scathed (ŭn skāt͡hd′), *adj.* not scathed; unharmed; uninjured.

un·sci·en·tif·ic (ŭn′sī ən tĭf′ĭk), *adj.* 1. not scientific; not in accordance with the requirements of science. 2. not conforming to the principles or methods of science. **—un′sci·en·tif′i·cal·ly,** *adv.*

un·scram·ble (ŭn skrăm′bəl), *v.t.,* **-bled, -bling.** *Colloq.* to bring out of a scrambled condition; reduce to order.

un·screw (ŭn skrōō′), *v.t.* 1. to draw the screw or screws from. 2. to unfasten by withdrawing screws. 3. to loosen or withdraw a screw, screwlike plug, etc.). **—v.i.** 4. to permit of being unscrewed.

un·scru·pu·lous (ŭn skrōō′pyə ləs), *adj.* not scrupulous; unrestrained by scruples; conscienceless; unprincipled. **—un·scru′pu·lous·ly,** *adv.* **—un·scru′pu·lous·ness,** *n.*
—Syn. UNSCRUPULOUS, UNPRINCIPLED refer to lack of moral standards or conscience to guide one's conduct. The UNSCRUPULOUS man is without scruples of conscience, and disregards, or has contempt for, laws of right or justice with which he is perfectly well acquainted, and which should restrain him in his actions: *unscrupulous in methods of making money, in taking advantage of the unfortunate.* The UNPRINCIPLED man is without moral principles or ethical standards in his conduct or actions: *an unprincipled rogue, unprincipled conduct.*

un·seal (ŭn sēl′), *v.t.* 1. to break or remove the seal of. 2. to open, as something sealed or firmly closed.

un·seam (ŭn sēm′), *v.t.* to open the seam or seams of; rip apart.

un·search·a·ble (ŭn sûr′chə bəl), *adj.* not searchable; not to be searched into or understood by searching; inscrutable; unfathomable. **—un·search′a·ble·ness,** *n.* **—un·search′a·bly,** *adv.*

un·sea·son·a·ble (ŭn sē′zən ə bəl, -sēz′nə-), *adj.* 1. not seasonable; out of season. 2. untimely; ill-timed; inopportune. **—un·sea′son·a·ble·ness,** *n.* **—un·sea′son·a·bly,** *adv.*

un·sea·soned (ŭn sē′zənd), *adj.* 1. (of things) not seasoned; not matured, dried, etc., by due seasoning. 2. (of persons) not inured to a climate, work, etc.; inexperienced. 3. (of food) not flavored with seasoning.

un·seat (ŭn sēt′), *v.t.* 1. to displace from a seat. 2. to throw from a saddle, as a rider. 3. to depose from an official seat or from office.

un·se·cured (ŭn′sĭ kyoŏrd′), *adj.* 1. not secured. 2. not insured against loss, as by a bond, pledge, etc.

un·seem·ly (ŭn sēm′lĭ), *adj.* 1. not seemly; unfitting; unbecoming; improper; indecorous. **—adv.** 2. in an unseemly manner. **—un·seem′li·ness,** *n.* **—Syn.** 1. See **improper.**

un·seen (ŭn sēn′), *adj.* not seen; unperceived; unobserved; invisible.

un·self·ish (ŭn sĕl′fĭsh), *adj.* not selfish; disinterested; altruistic. **—un·self′ish·ly,** *adv.* **—un·self′ish·ness,** *n.*

un·set (ŭn sĕt′), *adj.* 1. not set. 2. (of gems) unmounted.

un·set·tle (ŭn sĕt′əl), *v.,* **-tled, -tling.** **—v.t.** 1. to bring out of a settled state; cause to be no longer firmly fixed or established; render unstable; disturb; disorder. 2. to shake or weaken (beliefs, feelings, etc.); derange (the

mind, etc.). **—v.i.** 3. to become unfixed or disordered.

un·set·tled (ŭn sĕt′əld), *adj.* 1. not settled; not fixed in a place or abode. 2. not populated, as a region. 3. not fixed or stable, as conditions; without established order, as times. 4. liable to change, as weather. 5. wavering or uncertain, as the mind, opinions, etc., or the person. 6. undetermined, as a point at issue. 7. not adjusted, closed, or disposed of finally, as an account or an estate. **—un·set′tled·ness,** *n.*
—Syn. 3, 4. UNSETTLED, UNSTABLE, UNSTEADY imply a lack of fixity, firmness, and dependability. That which is UNSETTLED is not fixed or determined: *unsettled weather, unsettled claims.* That which is UNSTABLE is wavering, changeable; easily moved, shaken, or overthrown: *unstable equilibrium, an unstable decision.* That which is UNSTEADY is infirm or shaky in position or movement: *unsteady on one's feet, unsteady of purpose.* **—Ant.** 3. stable.

un·sew (ŭn sō′), *v.t.,* **-sewed, -sewed** or **-sewn, -sewing.** to undo (something) sewed; rip.

un·sex (ŭn sĕks′), *v.t.* 1. to change from the actual sex, esp. of women; render (oneself) no longer of the proper sex, as by unnatural conduct. 2. (of the conduct, life, etc.) to deprive (a woman) of womanly character.

un·shack·le (ŭn shăk′əl), *v.t.* to free from shackles; unfetter.

un·shad·owed (ŭn shăd′ōd), *adj.* not shadowed; not darkened or obscured; free from gloom.

un·shaped (ŭn shāpt′), *adj.* not shaped or definitely formed.

un·shap·en (ŭn shā′pən), *adj.* 1. not shaped or definitely formed; shapeless; formless; indefinite. 2. not shapely; unpleasing in shape; ill-formed. 3. misshapen or deformed.

un·sheathe (ŭn shēt͡h′), *v.t.,* **-sheathed, -sheathing.** 1. to draw from a sheath, as a sword, knife, or the like. 2. to bring or put forth from a covering, threateningly or otherwise.

un·shell (ŭn shĕl′), *v.t.* to take out of the shell; remove or release, as from a shell.

un·ship (ŭn shĭp′), *v.t.,* **-shipped, -shipping.** 1. to put or take off from a ship, as persons or goods. 2. *Colloq.* to put or take away, or get rid of. 3. to remove from the proper place for use, as an oar, tiller, etc.

un·shroud (ŭn shroud′), *v.t.* to remove the shroud from; divest of something that shrouds; uncover; unveil.

un·sight (ŭn sīt′), *adj.* without inspection or examination (used in the phrase *unsight, unseen*): *to buy a thing unsight, unseen* (that is, without seeing it).

un·sight·ly (ŭn sīt′lĭ), *adj.* not pleasing to the sight; forming an unpleasing sight. **—un·sight′li·ness,** *n.*

un·skilled (ŭn skĭld′), *adj.* 1. of or pertaining to workers lacking training or experience for a specific kind of work. **—n.** 2. **the unskilled,** untrained labor.

un·skill·ful (ŭn skĭl′fəl), *adj.* not skillful; inexpert; awkward; bungling. Also, **un·skil′ful. —un·skill′ful·ly,** *adv.* **—un·skill′ful·ness,** *n.*

un·slaked lime (ŭn slākt′). See **lime** (def. 1).

un·sling (ŭn slĭng′), *v.t.* **-slung, -slinging.** 1. to remove (something) from a position in which it is slung. 2. *Naut.* to take off the slings of; release from slings.

un·snap (ŭn snăp′), *v.t.,* **-snapped, -snapping.** to release by opening a snap fastener.

un·snarl (ŭn snärl′), *v.t.* to bring out of a snarled condition; disentangle.

un·so·cia·ble (ŭn sō′shə bəl), *adj.* not sociable; having, showing, or marked by a disinclination to friendly social relations. **—un′so·cia·bil′i·ty, un·so′cia·ble·ness,** *n.* **—un·so′cia·bly,** *adv.*

un·sof·tened (ŭn sôf′ənd, -sôf′-), *adj.* not softened.

un·sol·der (ŭn sŏd′ər), *v.t.* 1. to separate (something soldered). 2. to disunite; dissolve.

un·son·sy (ŭn sŏn′sĭ), *adj.* *Scot.* or *Brit. Dial.* bringing or boding ill luck. [f. UN-² + *sonsy,* der. *sonse* prosperity (t. Gaelic: m. *sonas*)]

un·so·phis·ti·cat·ed (ŭn′sə fĭs′tə kā′tĭd), *adj.* 1. not sophisticated; simple; artless. 2. unadulterated; pure; genuine. **—un′so·phis′ti·cat′ed·ly,** *adv.* **—un′so·phis′ti·cat′ed·ness, un′so·phis′ti·ca′tion,** *n.*

un·sat′is·fied′	un·scrip′tur·al	un·shake′a·ble	un·sim′i·lar
un·sat′is·fy′ing	un·sculp′tured	un·shak′en	un·sing′a·ble
un·saved′	un·sealed′	un·shamed′	un·sink′a·ble
un·sawn′	un·seat′ed	un·shape′ly	un·sis′ter·ly
un·say′a·ble	un·sea′wor′thi·ness	un·shared′	un·sized′
un·scab′bard·ed	un·sea′wor′thy	un·shav′en	un·slacked′
un·scaled′	un·sec′ond·ed	un·shaved′	un·slaked′
un·scanned′	un′sec·tar′i·an	un·sheathed′	un·smil′ing
un·scared′	un·seed′ed	un·shed′	un·smirched′
un′scar′i·fied	un·see′ing	un·shelled′	un·smoked′
un·scarred′	un·seg′ment·ed	un·shel′tered	un·soaked′
un·scent′ed	un·seized′	un·shod′	un·so′ber
un·scep′ti·cal	un′se·lect′ed	un·shorn′	un·so′cial
un·sched′uled	un·se·lec′tive	un·shrink′a·ble	un·soiled′
un·schol′ar·like′	un·sen′si·tive	un·shrink′ing	un·sold′
un·schol′ar·ly	un·sent′	un·shroud′ed	un·sol′dier·like′
un·schooled′	un′sen·ti·men′tal	un·shrunk′	un·sol′dier·ly
un·scorched′	un·served′	un·shunned′	un′so·lic′it·ed
un·scorned′	un·serv′ice·a·ble	un·shut′	un′so·lic′it·ous
un·scoured′	un·serv′ice·a·bly	un·sift′ed	un·sol′id
un·scourged′	un·sev′ered	un·sight′ed	un·sol′u·ble
un·scraped′	un·sex′u·al	un·sight′ed·ly	un·solv′a·ble
un·scratched′	un·shad′ed	un·signed′	un·solved′
un·screened′	un·shak′a·ble	un·si′lenced′	un·soothed′

un·sound (ŭn′sound′), *adj.* **1.** not sound; diseased, as the body or mind. **2.** decayed, as timber or fruit; impaired or defective, as goods. **3.** not solid or firm, as foundations. **4.** not well-founded or valid; fallacious. **5.** easily broken; light: *unsound slumber.* **6.** not financially strong; unreliable. —**un·sound′ly,** *adv.* —**un·sound′ness,** *n.*

un·spar·ing (ŭn·spâr′ĭng), *adj.* **1.** not sparing; liberal or profuse. **2.** unmerciful. —**un·spar′ing·ly,** *adv.* —**un·spar′ing·ness,** *n.*

un·speak (ŭn·spēk′), *v.t.,* **-spoke, -spoken, -speaking.** to retract (something spoken); unsay.

un·speak·a·ble (ŭn·spē′kə·bəl), *adj.* **1.** not speakable; that may not be spoken. **2.** exceeding the power of speech; unutterable; inexpressible. **3.** inexpressibly bad or objectionable. —**un·speak′a·bly,** *adv.*

un·sphere (ŭn·sfîr′), *v.t.,* **-sphered, -sphering.** to remove from its or one's sphere.

un·sta·ble (ŭn·stā′bəl), *adj.* **1.** not stable; not firm or firmly fixed; unsteady. **2.** liable to fall, change, or cease. **3.** unsteadfast; inconstant; wavering. **4.** *Chem.* denoting compounds which readily decompose or change into other compounds. —**un·sta′ble·ness,** *n.* —**un·sta′bly,** *adv.* —**Syn. 2, 3. See unsettled.**

un·stalked (ŭn·stôkt′), *adj.* without a stalk or stalks.

un·stead·y (ŭn·stĕd′ĭ), *adj.* **1.** not steady; not firmly fixed; faltering. **2.** fluctuating or wavering; unsteadfast. **3.** irregular in habits. —**un·stead′i·ly,** *adv.* —**un·stead′i·ness,** *n.* —**Syn. 1, 2. See unsettled.**

un·steel (ŭn·stēl′), *v.t.* to bring out of a steeled condition; soften.

un·step (ŭn·stĕp′), *v.t.,* **-stepped, -stepping.** to remove (a mast, etc.) from its step.

un·stick (ŭn·stĭk′), *v.t.,* **-stuck, -sticking.** to free, as one thing stuck to another.

un·stop (ŭn·stŏp′), *v.t.,* **-stopped, -stopping. 1.** to remove the stopper from. **2.** to free from any obstruction; open. **3.** to draw out the stops of (an organ).

un·strained (ŭn·strānd′), *adj.* **1.** not under strain or tension. **2.** not separated or cleared by straining.

un·strap (ŭn·străp′), *v.t.,* **-strapped, -strapping.** to take off or slacken the strap of.

un·strat·i·fied (ŭn·străt′ə·fīd′), *adj.* not stratified; not arranged in strata or layers: *unstratified rocks* (such as the igneous rocks granite, prophyry, etc.).

un·stressed (ŭn·strĕst′), *adj.* not stressed; unaccented.

un·string (ŭn·strĭng′), *v.t.,* **-strung, -stringing. 1.** to deprive of a string or strings. **2.** to take from a string. **3.** to loosen the strings of. **4.** to relax the tension of. **5.** to relax unduly, or weaken (the nerves). **6.** to weaken the nerves of.

un·striped (ŭn·strīpt′, -strī′pĭd), *adj.* not striped; nonstriated, as muscular tissue.

un·strung (ŭn·strŭng′), *v.* **1.** pt. and pp. of **unstring.** —*adj.* **2.** having the string or strings loosened or removed, as a bow or harp. **3.** having the nerves weakened or in bad condition, as a person.

un·stud·ied (ŭn·stŭd′ĭd), *adj.* **1.** not studied; not premeditated or labored; natural; unaffected. **2.** not having studied; unversed.

un·sub·stan·tial (ŭn′sŏb·stăn′shəl), *adj.* not substantial; not solid, firm, or strong; flimsy; slight; unreal; insubstantial. —**un′sub·stan′ti·al′i·ty,** *n.* —**un′sub·stan′tial·ly,** *adv.*

un·suc·cess (ŭn′sŏk·sĕs′), *n.* lack of success; failure.

un·suc·cess·ful (ŭn′sŏk·sĕs′fəl), *adj.* not successful; without success; unfortunate. —**un′suc·cess′ful·ly,** *adv.* —**un′suc·cess′ful·ness,** *n.*

un·suit·a·ble (ŭn·sōō′tə·bəl), *adj.* not suitable; inappropriate; unfitting; unbecoming. —**un′suit·a·bil′i·ty, un·suit′a·ble·ness,** *n.* —**un·suit′a·bly,** *adv.*

un·sung (ŭn·sŭng′), *adj.* **1.** not sung; not uttered or rendered by singing. **2.** not framed or told in verse. **3.** not celebrated in song or verse.

un·sus·pect·ed (ŭn′sə·spĕk′tĭd), *adj.* **1.** clear of or not under suspicion. **2.** not imagined to exist. —**un′sus·pect′ed·ly,** *adv.*

un·sus·tain·a·ble (ŭn′sə·stā′nə·bəl), *adj.* not sustainable; not to be supported, maintained, upheld, or corroborated.

un·swathe (ŭn·swāth′), *v.t.* **-swathed, -swathing.** to free from that which swathes; take wrappings from.

un·swear (ŭn·swâr′), *v.t.,* **-swore, -sworn, -swearing.** to retract (something sworn, or sworn to); recant by a subsequent oath; abjure.

un·sym·me·try (ŭn·sĭm′ə·trĭ), *n.* lack of symmetry.

un·tack (ŭn·tăk′), *v.t.* **1.** to unfasten (something tacked). **2.** to loose or detach by removing a tack or tacks.

un·tan·gle (ŭn·tăng′gəl), *v.t.,* **-gled, -gling. 1.** to bring out of a tangled state; disentangle; unsnarl. **2.** to straighten out or clear up (anything confused or perplexing).

un·taught (ŭn·tôt′), *v.* **1.** pt. and pp. of **unteach.** —*adj.* **2.** not taught; not acquired by teaching. **3.** not instructed or educated; ignorant.

un·teach (ŭn·tēch′), *v.t.,* **-taught, -teaching. 1.** to cause to be forgotten or disbelieved, as by contrary teaching. **2.** to cause to forget or disbelieve something previously taught.

Un·ter·mey·er (ŭn′tər·mī′ər), *n.* Louis, born 1885, U.S. poet, critic, and editor of poetry anthologies.

Un·ter·wal·den (ŏͦn′tər·väl′dən), *n.* a canton in central Switzerland. 41,900 pop. (est. 1952); 296 sq. mi.

un·teth·er (ŭn·tĕth′ər), *v.t.* to loose from a tether.

un·thank·ful (ŭn·thăng′fəl), *adj.* **1.** not thankful; ungrateful. **2.** not repaid with thanks; thankless. —**un·thank′ful·ly,** *adv.* —**un·thank′ful·ness,** *n.*

un·thatch (ŭn·thăch′), *v.t.* to throw off the thatch from.

un·think (ŭn·thĭngk′), *v.t.,* **-thought, -thinking.** to retract in thought; change one's mind about.

un·think·a·ble (ŭn·thĭngk′ə·bəl), *adj.* **1.** inconceivable. **2.** not to be considered.

un·think·ing (ŭn·thĭngk′ĭng), *adj.* **1.** not thinking; thoughtless; heedless. **2.** indicating lack of thought or reflection. —**un·think′ing·ly,** *adv.*

un·thread (ŭn·thrĕd′), *v.t.* **1.** to draw out or take out the thread from. **2.** to thread one's way out of.

un·throne (ŭn·thrōn′), *v.t.,* **-throned, -throning.** to dethrone.

un·ti·dy (ŭn·tī′dĭ), *adj.* not tidy or neat; slovenly; disordered. —**un·ti′di·ly,** *adv.* —**un·ti′di·ness,** *n.*

un·tie (ŭn·tī′), *v.,* **-tied, -tying.** —*v.t.* **1.** to loose or unfasten (anything tied); let or set loose by undoing a knot. **2.** to undo the string or cords of. **3.** to undo, as a cord or a knot; unknot. **4.** to free from restraint. **5.** to resolve, as perplexities. —*v.i.* **6.** to become untied.

un·til (ŭn·tĭl′), *conj.* **1.** up to the time that or when; till. **2.** (with negatives) before: *he did not come until the meeting was half over.* —*prep.* **3.** onward to, or till (a specified time); up to the time of (some occurrence). **4.** (with negatives) before: *he did not go until night.* **5.** *Scot.* and *N. Eng.* to; unto. [ME *untill,* f. *un-* (t. Scand.; cf. Icel. *unz* up to, as far as) + TILL]

un·time·ly (ŭn·tīm′lĭ), *adj.* Also, *Scot.,* **un·time·ous** (ŭn·tī′məs). **1.** not timely; not occurring at a suitable time or season; ill-timed or inopportune. **2.** premature. —*adv.* **3.** unseasonably. —**un·time′li·ness,** *n.*

un·ti·tled (ŭn·tī′təld), *adj.* **1.** not titled; without a title, as of nobility. **2.** having no right or claim.

un·to (ŭn′tŏͦ; *unstressed* ŭn′tŏͦ *or, before consonant,* ŭn′tə), *prep. Archaic.* **1.** to (in its various uses, except as the accompaniment of the infinitive). **2.** until; till. [ME; f. *un-* (see UNTIL) + TO]

un·sort′ed	un·stand′ard·ized′	un·sure′	un·tapped′
un·sought′	un·starched′	un·sur·mount′a·ble	un·tar′nished
un·sound′ed	un·starred′	un·sur·pass′a·ble	un·tast′ed
un·soured′	un·stat′ed	un·sur·prised′	un·tax′a·ble
un·sowed′	un·states′man·like′	un·sus·cep′ti·ble	un·taxed′
un·sown′	un·stead′fast′	un·sus·pi′cious	un·teach′a·ble
un·spe′cial·ized′	un·stemmed′	un·sus·tained′	un·tech′ni·cal
un·spec′i·fied′	un·ster′i·lized′	un·swayed′	un·tem′pered
un·spec′u·la′tive	un·stig′ma·tized′	un·sweet′ened	un·ten′a·ble
un·spelled′	un·stint′ed	un·swept′	un·ten′ant·ed
un·spent′	un·stitched′	un·swerv′ing	un·tend′ed
un·spilled′	un·stri′at·ed	un·sworn′	un·ter′ri·fied′
un·spilt′	un·stripped′		un·test′ed
un·spir′it·u·al	un·stuffed′	un·sym·met′ri·cal	un·teth′ered
un·spir′it·u·al′i·ty	un·stung′	un·sym·pa·thet′ic	un·thanked′
un·spir′it·u·al·ly	un·sub·dued′	un·sym·pa·thiz′ing	un·thatched′
un·spir′it·u·al·ness	un·sub·mis′sive	un·sys·tem·at′ic	un′the·at′ri·cal
un·spoiled′	un·sub·scribed′	un·sys·tem·a·tized′	un·thought′
un·spoilt′	un·sub·si·dized′	un·tact′ful	un·thought′ful
un·spo′ken	un·sub·stan′ti·at′ed	un·taint′ed	un·thought′-of′
un·sports′man·like′	un·sug·ges′tive	un·tak′en	un·thrift′i·ness
un·sprin′kled	un·suit′ed	un·tal′ent·ed	un·thrift′y
un·sprung′	un·sul′lied	un·talked′-of′	un·till′a·ble
un·squan′dered	un·sunk′	un·tame′	un·tilled′
un·squared′	un·sup·port′a·ble	un·tam′a·ble	un·tilt′ed
un·stain′a·ble	un·sup·port′ed	un·tame′a·ble	un·tinged′
un·stained′	un·sup·port′ed·ly	un·tamed′	un·tired′
un·stamped′	un·sup·pressed′	un·tanned′	un·tir′ing

b., blend of, blended; c., cognate with; d., dialect, dialectal; der., derived from; f., formed from; g., going back to; m., modification of; r., replacing; s., stem of; t., taken from; ?, perhaps. See the full key on inside cover.

un·told (ŭn tōld′), *adj.* **1.** not told; not related; not revealed. **2.** not numbered or enumerated; uncounted. **3.** countless; incalculable.

un·touch·a·bil·i·ty (ŭn′tŭch ə bĭl′ə tĭ′), *n.* the defiling character ascribed to low-caste Indians or non-Hindus by high-caste Hindus or Brahmans.

un·touch·a·ble (ŭn tŭch′ə bəl), *adj., n.* **1.** that may not be touched; of a nature such that it cannot be touched; not palpable; intangible. **2.** too distant to be touched. **3.** vile or loathsome to the touch. —*n.* **4.** a member of the lower classes in India whose touch is believed to defile a high-caste Hindu.

un·to·ward (ŭn tōrd′), *adj.* **1.** unfavorable or unfortunate. **2.** *Archaic.* froward or perverse. [f. UN-¹ + TOWARD] —**un·to′ward·ly,** *adv.* —**un·to′ward·ness,** *n.*

un·trav·eled (ŭn trăv′əld), *adj.* **1.** not having traveled, esp. to distant places; not having gained experience by travel. **2.** not traveled through or over; not frequented by travelers.

un·tread (ŭn trĕd′), *v.t.,* **-trod, -trodden** or **-trod, -treading.** to go back through in the same steps.

un·tried (ŭn trīd′), *adj.* **1.** not tried; not tested or put to the proof; not attempted. **2.** not yet tried at law.

un·true (ŭn trōō′), *adj.* **1.** not true, as to a person or a cause; to fact, or to a standard. **2.** unfaithful; false. **3.** incorrect or inaccurate. —**un·true′ness,** *n.* —**un·tru′ly,** *adv.*

un·truss (ŭn trŭs′), *v.t.* to loose from or as from a truss; unfasten or untie; undress.

un·truth (ŭn trōōth′), *n.* **1.** state or character of being untrue. **2.** want of veracity; divergence from truth. **3.** something untrue; a falsehood or lie. **4.** *Obs.* unfaithfulness or disloyalty. —**Syn. 3.** See **falsehood.**

un·truth·ful (ŭn trōōth′fəl), *adj.* not truthful; wanting in veracity; diverging from or contrary to the truth; not corresponding with fact or reality. —**un·truth′ful·ly,** *adv.* —**un·truth′ful·ness,** *n.*

un·tuck (ŭn tŭk′), *v.t.* to release from or bring out of a tucked condition.

un·tu·tored (ŭn tū′tərd, -tōō′-), *adj.* not tutored; untaught; uninstructed.

un·twine (ŭn twīn′), *v.t., v.i.,* **-twined, -twining.** to bring or come out of a twined condition.

un·twist (ŭn twĭst′), *v.t., v.i.* to bring or come out of a twisted condition.

un·used (ŭn ūzd′), *adj.* **1.** not used; not put to use. **2.** never having been used. **3.** not accustomed.

un·u·su·al (ŭn ū′zhŏŏ əl), *adj.* not usual, common, or ordinary; uncommon; uncommon in amount or degree; of an exceptional kind. —**un·u′su·al·ly,** *adv.* —**un·u′su·al·ness,** *n.*

un·ut·ter·a·ble (ŭn ŭt′ər ə bəl), *adj.* **1.** not utterable; incapable of being uttered or expressed. **2.** inexpressible; unspeakable. —**un·ut′ter·a·bly,** *adv.*

un·var·nished (ŭn vär′nĭsht), *adj.* **1.** not varnished. **2.** not embellished; plain.

un·veil (ŭn vāl′), *v.t.* **1.** to remove a veil from; disclose to view; reveal. —*v.i.* **2.** to remove a veil; reveal oneself; become unveiled.

un·vo·cal (ŭn vō′kəl), *adj.* **1.** lacking a voice. **2.** tending to restrain expression of feelings.

un·voice (ŭn vois′), *v.t.,* **-voiced, -voicing.** *Phonet.* to deprive of tonal vibration in pronouncing: before a pause, the end of a voiced fricative is *unvoiced* in English, as in *If you please,* where the final *z* sound ends like *s.*

un·voiced (ŭn voist′), *adj.* **1.** not voiced; not uttered. **2.** *Phonet.* surd; without voice.

un·warped (ŭn wôrpt′), *adj.* **1.** not warped. **2.** unbiased; impartial.

un·war·y (ŭn wâr′ĭ), *adj.* not wary; not cautious; unguarded. —**un·war′i·ly,** *adv.* —**un·war′i·ness,** *n.*

un·wea·ried (ŭn wĭr′ĭd), *adj.* **1.** not wearied; not fatigued. **2.** indefatigable.

un·weave (ŭn wēv′), *v.t.,* **-wove, -woven, -weaving.** to undo, take apart, or separate (something woven); ravel.

un·well (ŭn wĕl′), *adj.* not well; ailing; ill.

un·wept (ŭn wĕpt′), *adj.* **1.** not wept, or wept for; unmourned. **2.** not wept or shed, as tears.

un·whole·some (ŭn hōl′səm), *adj.* **1.** not wholesome; unhealthful; deleterious to health or well-being, physically or morally. **2.** not sound in health; unhealthy, esp. in appearance; suggestive of disease. —**un·whole′some·ly,** *adv.* —**un·whole′some·ness,** *n.*

un·wield·y (ŭn wēl′dĭ), *adj.* not wieldy; wielded with difficulty; not readily handled or managed in use or action, as from size, shape, or weight. —**un·wield′i·ly,** *adv.* —**un·wield′i·ness,** *n.*

un·willed (ŭn wĭld′), *adj.* not willed; involuntary.

un·will·ing (ŭn wĭl′ĭng), *adj.* not willing; loath; reluctant. —**un·will′ing·ly,** *adv.* —**un·will′ing·ness,** *n.*

un·winc·ing (ŭn wĭn′sĭng), *adj.* that does not wince.

un·wind (ŭn wīnd′), *v.* **-wound, -winding.** —*v.t.* **1.** to undo (something wound); loose or separate, as what is wound. **2.** to disentangle. —*v.i.* **3.** to become unwound.

un·wis·dom (ŭn wĭz′dəm), *n.* **1.** lack of wisdom. **2.** unwise action; folly.

un·wise (ŭn wīz′), *adj.* not wise; foolish; imprudent; injudicious. —**un·wise′ly,** *adv.*

un·wish (ŭn wĭsh′), *v.t.* **1.** to cease to wish. **2.** *Obs.* to wish away.

un·wished (ŭn wĭsht′), *adj.* not wished; undesired; unwelcome.

un·wit·ting (ŭn wĭt′ĭng), *adj.* not witting or knowing; ignorant; unaware; unconscious. —**un·wit′ting·ly,** *adv.*

un·wont·ed (ŭn wŭn′tĭd, -wŏn′-), *adj.* **1.** unaccustomed or unused. **2.** not customary, habitual, or usual. —**un·wont′ed·ly,** *adv.* —**un·wont′ed·ness,** *n.*

un·world·ly (ŭn wûrld′lĭ), *adj.* **1.** not worldly; not seeking material advantage or gain; spiritually minded. **2.** not terrestrial; unearthly. —**un·world′li·ness,** *n.*

un·wor·thy (ŭn wûr′ᵺĭ), *adj.* **1.** not worthy; lacking worth or excellence. **2.** not commendable or creditable. **3.** not of adequate merit or character. **4.** of a kind not worthy (with *of,* expressed or understood). **5.** beneath the dignity (*of*). **6.** undeserving. —**un·wor′thi·ly,** *adv.* —**un·wor′thi·ness,** *n.*

un·wound (ŭn wound′), *v.* pt. and pp. of **unwind.**

un·wrap (ŭn răp′), *v.,* **-wrapped, -wrapping.** —*v.t.* **1.** to bring out of a wrapped condition; unfold or open, as something wrapped. —*v.i.* **2.** to become unwrapped.

un·wreathe (ŭn rēᵺ′), *v.t.,* **-wreathed, -wreathing.** to bring out of a wreathed condition; untwist; untwine.

un·wrin·kle (ŭn rĭng′kəl), *v.t.,* **-kled, -kling.** to smoothe the wrinkles from.

un·writ·ten (ŭn rĭt′ən), *adj.* **1.** not written; not reduced to writing. **2.** not actually formulated or expressed; customary. **3.** containing no writing; blank. [ME and OE *unwriten;* f. UN-¹ + *written,* pp. of WRITE]

unwritten law, 1. law which rests for its authority on custom, judicial decision, etc., as distinguished from law originating in written command, statute, or decree. **2. the unwritten law,** the supposed principle of the right of the individual to avenge wrongs against personal or family honor, esp. in cases involving relations between the sexes (sometimes urged in justification of persons guilty of criminal acts of vengeance).

un·yoke (ŭn yōk′), *v.,* **-yoked, -yoking.** —*v.t.* **1.** to free from or as from a yoke. **2.** to part or disjoin, as by removing a yoke. —*v.i.* **3.** to remove a yoke. **4.** to cease work.

U. of S. Afr., Union of South Africa.

up (ŭp), *adv., prep., adj., n., v.* **upped, upping.** —*adv.* **1.** to, toward, or in a more elevated position: *to climb up to the top of a ladder.* **2.** to or in an erect position: *to stand up.* **3.** out of bed: *to get up.* **4.** above the horizon: *the moon is up.* **5.** to or at any point that is considered higher: *up north.* **6.** to or at a source, origin, center, or the like: *to follow a stream up to its source.* **7.** to or at a higher point or degree in a scale, as of rank, size, value, pitch, etc. **8.** to or at a point of equal advance, extent,

un·touched′	un·tune′ful	un·vol′a·til·ized′	un·whet′ted
un·tow′ered	un·turned′	un·vul′can·ized′	un·whipped′
un·trace′a·ble	un·twilled′	un·wak′ened	un·wife′like′
un·traced′	un·twist′ed	un·walled′	un·wife′ly
un·tracked′	un·typ′i·cal	un·want′ed	un·wink′ing
un·tract′a·ble	un·urged′	un·war′like′	un·with′er·a·ble
un·trade′a·ble	un·us′a·ble	un·warmed′	un·with′ered
un·trained′	un·u′ti·liz′a·ble	un·warned′	un·with′er·ing
un·tram′meled	un·u′ti·lized′	un·war′rant·ed	un·wit′nessed
un·tram′melled	un·ut′tered	un·washed′	un·wom′an·like′
un·trans·fer′a·ble	un·vac′ci·nat′ed	un·wast′ed	un·wom′an·ly
un·trans·ferred′	un·vac′il·lat′ing	un·wast′ing	un·won′
un·trans·lat′a·ble	un·val′i·dat′ed	un·watched′	un·wood′ed
un·trans·lat′ed	un·val′ued	un·wa′ver·ing	un·wooed′
un·trans·mit′ted	un·van′quished	un·weak′ened	un·work′a·ble
un·trapped′	un·var′ied	un·weaned′	un·worked′
un·trav′ers·a·ble	un·var′y·ing	un·wear′a·ble	un·work′man·like′
un·trav′ersed	un·veiled′	un·wea′ry	un·worn′
un·treas′ured	un·ven′ti·lat′ed	un·wea′ry·ing	un·wor′shiped
un·trimmed′	un·ve′ra′cious	un·weath′ered	un·wound′ed
un·trou′bled	un·ver′i·fi′a·ble	un·wed′	un·wov′en
un·trust′wor′thy	un·ver′i·fied′	un·wed′ded	un·wrought′
un·trust′i·ness	un·versed′	un·weed′ed	un·wrung′
un·tuft′ed	un·vexed′	un·wel′come	un·yield′ing
un·tun′a·ble	un·vis′it·ed	un·weld′ed	un·youth′ful
un·tuned′	un·vit′ri·fied′	un·welt′ted	un·zeal′ous

etc.: *to catch up in a race.* **9.** having adequate power or ability, or equal: *to be up to the needs of an emergency, to be up to a task.* **10.** well advanced or versed, as in a subject: *to be up in mathematics.* **11.** into or in activity, operation, etc.: *to set up vibrations, to be up in arms.* **12.** in process of going on or happening: *what's up over there?* **13.** into view, prominence, or consideration: *the lost papers have turned up.* **14.** into or in a place of safekeeping, storage, retirement, etc.: *to lay up riches, to put up preserves.* **15.** into or in a state of union, contraction, etc.: *to add up a column of figures, to fold up.* **16.** to the required or final point: *to pay up one's debts, burned up.* **17.** to or at an end: *his hour is up.* **18.** *Baseball.* at bat. **19.** (sometimes used as an imperative; see def. 35): *up with my tent there.* **20. all up with,** all over with. **21. be up to,** *Colloq.* to be before as a duty; be incumbent on: *it is up to him to make the next move.* **22.** *Colloq.* confronting or facing, as something to be dealt with (fol. by *against*). **23.** *Colloq.* about to do; doing; engaged in (fol. by *to*): *to be up to mischief.* **24.** *Golf.* ahead of an opponent a specified number of holes (opposed to *down*). **25.** *Colloq.* (in tennis, handball, etc.) each; apiece. **26.** *Naut.* toward the wind.
—*prep.* **27.** to, toward, or at a higher place on or in: *up the stairs, up a tree.* **28.** to, toward, near, or at the top of. **29.** to, toward, or at a point of, considered as higher: *up the street.* **30.** toward the source, origin, etc., of: *up the stream.* **31.** toward or in the interior of (a region, etc.): *the explorers went up country.* —*adj.* **32.** going or directed up; tending upward. —*n.* **33.** an upward movement; an ascent. **34.** a rise of fortune, mood, etc.: *to have one's ups and downs.* —*v.t.* *Colloq.* **35.** to put or take up. **36.** to make larger; step up: *to up output.* **37.** to raise; go better than (a preceding wager). —*v.i.* **38.** *Colloq.* to get or start up. [ME and OE, c. LG *up*, and akin to G *auf*]

up-, a prefixal, attributive use of **up,** in its various meanings, as in *upland, upshot, upheaval.* [ME and OE]

UP, United Press. See **United Press International.**

U·pan·i·shad (ōō păn′ə shăd′, -păn′ə shäd′), *n.* the chief theological documents of ancient Hinduism, expounding more elaborately the mystical knowledge contained in the earlier Vedas, esp. the pantheistic doctrine that, in all things, but preëminently in each human soul, there may be seen manifested the supreme, impersonal Brahma or Atman, the World Soul.

u·pas (ū′pəs), *n.* **1.** the poisonous milky sap of *Antiaris toxicaria,* a large moraceous tree of Java, used for arrow poison. **2.** the tree. [t. Malay: poison]

up·bear (ŭp bâr′), *v.t.,* **-bore, -borne, -bearing.** to bear up; raise aloft; support; sustain. —**up·bear′er,** *n.*

up·borne (ŭp bōrn′), *v.* **1.** pp. of **upbear.** —*adj.* **2.** raised on high; sustained; held up.

up·bow (ŭp′bō′), *n.* (in bowing on a stringed instrument) a stroke toward the handle of the bow: indicated in scores by the symbol V (opposed to *down-bow*).

up·braid (ŭp brād′), *v.t.* **1.** to reproach for some fault or offense; reprove severely; chide. **2.** (of things) to bring reproach on; be a reproach to. —*v.i.* **3.** to utter reproaches. [ME; OE *upbregdan.* See **UP-, BRAID,** v.] —**up·braid′er,** *n.*

up·braid·ing (ŭp brā′dĭng), *n.* **1.** act or language of one who upbraids. —*adj.* **2.** reproachful; chiding. —**up·braid′ing·ly,** *adv.*

up·bring·ing (ŭp′brĭng′ĭng), *n.* the bringing up or rearing of a person from childhood; care and training devoted to the young while growing up.

up·build (ŭp bĭld′), *v.t.,* **-built, -building.** to build up; establish. —**up·build′er,** *n.*

up·burst (ŭp′bûrst′), *n.* a burst upward.

up·cast (ŭp′kăst′, -käst′), *n.* **1.** act or an act of casting upward. **2.** state of being cast upward. **3.** something that is cast up. **4.** a shaft or passage up which air passes, as from a mine (opp. to *downcast*). —*adj.* **5.** cast up; directed upward.

up·coun·try (ŭp′kŭn′trĭ), *adj.* **1.** being or living remote from the coast or border; interior: *an upcountry village.* **2.** *Derogatory.* unsophisticated. —*n.* **3.** the interior of the country. —*adv.* **4.** toward or in the interior of a country.

up·date (ŭp′dāt′), *v.t.,* **-dated, -dating.** to bring up to date.

up·end (ŭp ĕnd′), *v.t.* **1.** to set on end, as a barrel. —*v.i.* **2.** to stand on end.

up·grade (*n.* ŭp′grād′; *adj., adv.* ŭp′grād′), *n.* **1.** an incline going up in the direction of movement. —*adj.* **2.** being or pertaining to an upgrade. —*adv.* **3.** up a slope.

up·growth (ŭp′grōth′), *n.* **1.** the process of growing up; development. **2.** something that grows up.

up·heav·al (ŭp hē′vəl), *n.* **1.** act of upheaving. **2.** state of being upheaved. **3.** *Geol.* an upward warping of a part of the earth's crust, forcing certain areas into a relatively higher position than before.

up·heave (ŭp hēv′), *v.,* **-heaved** *or* **-hove, -heaving.** —*v.t.* **1.** to heave or lift up; raise up or aloft. —*v.i.* **2.** to be lifted up; rise as if thrust up.

up·held (ŭp hĕld′), *v.* pt. and pp. of **uphold.**

up·hill (ŭp′hĭl′), *adv.* **1.** up, or as if up, the slope of a hill; upward. —*adj.* **2.** going or tending upward on or as on a hill. **3.** at a high place or point. **4.** laboriously fatiguing or difficult.

up·hold (ŭp hōld′), *v.t.,* **-held, -holding. 1.** to hold up; raise. **2.** to keep up, or keep from sinking; support. **3.** to sustain; maintain; countenance. **4.** *Brit.* to upholster. —**up·hold′er,** *n.* —**Syn. 3.** See **support.**

up·hol·ster (ŭp hōl′stər), *v.t.* **1.** to provide (chairs, sofas, etc.) with coverings, cushions, stuffing, springs, etc. **2.** to furnish (rooms, etc.) with hangings, curtains, carpets, or the like. [back formation from **UPHOLSTERER**]

up·hol·ster·er (ŭp hōl′stər ər), *n.* one whose business it is to furnish and put in place hangings, curtains, carpets, or the like, and to cushion and cover furniture, etc. [f. earlier *upholster* (f. **UPHOLD,** v. + **-STER**) + **-ER¹**]

up·hol·ster·y (ŭp hōl′stərĭ, -strĭ), *n.,* *pl.* **-steries. 1.** the fittings or decorations supplied by an upholsterer, as hangings, draperies, cushions, furniture coverings, and the like; material used to cushion and cover furniture. **2.** the business of an upholsterer.

u·phroe (ū′frō, ū′vrō), *n.* *Naut.* euphroe.

UPI, United Press International.

up·keep (ŭp′kēp′), *n.* **1.** the process of keeping up or maintaining; the maintenance, or keeping in operation, due condition, and repair, of an establishment, a machine, etc. **2.** the cost of this, including operating expenses, cost of renewal or repair, etc.

up·land (ŭp′lənd, -lănd′), *n.* **1.** land elevated above other land. **2.** the higher ground of a region or district; an elevated region. —*adj.* **3.** of or pertaining to uplands or elevated regions.

upland plover, a large field-inhabiting American shore bird, *Bartramia longicauda,* resembling a plover and valued as a game bird.

up·lift (*v.* ŭp lĭft′; *n.* ŭp′lĭft′), *v.t.* **1.** to lift up; raise; elevate. **2.** to raise socially or morally. **3.** to exalt emotionally or spiritually. —*n.* **4.** act of lifting up or raising; elevation. **5.** the process or work of raising socially or morally. **6.** emotional or spiritual exaltation. **7.** *Geol.* an upheaval. —**up·lift′ment,** *n.*

up·lift·er ŭp lĭf′tər), *n.* **1.** one who or that which uplifts. **2.** a person engaged in or devoted to social or moral uplift.

U·po·lu (ōō pō′lōō), *n.* an island in Western Samoa, in the S Pacific: the home of Robert Louis Stevenson for the last five years of his life. 81,925 (1961); 430 sq. mi.

up·on (əpŏn′, əpôn′), *prep.* **1.** up and on; upward so as to get or be on. **2.** in an elevated position on. **3.** on, in any of various senses (used as an equivalent of *on* with no added idea of ascent or elevation, and preferred in certain cases only for euphonic or metrical reasons). [ME. See **UP,** adv., **ON,** prep.]

up·per (ŭp′ər), *adj.* **1.** higher, as in place or position, or in a scale. **2.** superior, as in rank, dignity, or station. **3.** (of places) situated at a higher level, or farther from the sea level or the sea. **4.** (*often cap.*) *Stratig.* denoting a later division of a period, system, or the like: *the upper Devonian.* —*n.* **5.** the upper part of a shoe or boot, above the sole, comprising the vamp and the quarters. **6. be on one's uppers,** *Colloq.* **a.** to have worn out the soles of one's shoes. **b.** to be reduced to extreme shabbiness or poverty. **7.** (*pl.*) cloth gaiters. **8.** *Colloq.* the higher of two bunks or berths.

Upper Austria, a province in N Austria. 1,111,123 pop. (est. 1953); 4631 sq. mi. *Cap.:* Linz.

Upper Canada, a former British province (1791–1840) in Canada: now the S part of Ontario province.

up·per·case (ŭp′ər kās′), *adj., v.,* **-cased, -casing.** —*adj.* **1.** (of a letter) capital (as opposed to *small*). **2.** *Print.* pertaining to or belonging in the upper case. See **case²** (def. 7). —*v.t.* **3.** to print or write with an upper-case letter or letters.

up·per·class (ŭp′ər klăs′, -kläs′), *adj.* relating to or typical of a high-ranking class in society.

up·per·class·man (ŭp′ər klăs′mən, -kläs′-), *n., pl.* **-men.** a member of either the junior or senior class in a high school or college.

up·per·cut (ŭp′ər kŭt′), *n., v.,* **-cut, -cutting.** —*n.* **1.** a swinging blow directed upward, as to an adversary's chin. —*v.t., v.i.* **2.** to strike with an uppercut.

Upper Egypt. See **Egypt.**

upper hand, the dominating or controlling position; the advantage.

Upper House, (*often l.c.*) one of two branches of a legislature generally smaller and less representative than the lower branch.

up·per·most (ŭp′ər mōst′), *adj.* **1.** highest in place, order, rank, power, etc. **2.** topmost; predominant. —*adv.* **3.** in the highest or first place.

Upper Silesia, a highly industrialized region divided between Germany and Poland after World War I.

Upper Tun·gus·ka (tŏŏn gŏŏs′kä). See **Angara.**

Upper Volta, Republic of, an independent member of the French Community in W Africa; formerly part of French West Africa. 3,472,000 pop. (1959); 106,011 sq. mi. *Cap.:* Ouagadougou.

upper works, *Naut.* the parts of a ship above the surface of the water when she is loaded for a voyage.

up·pish (ŭp′ĭsh), *adj.* *Colloq.* proud; arrogant; self-assertive; assuming. Also, **up·pi·ty** (ŭp′ə tĭ). [f. **UP,** adv. + **-ISH¹**] —**up′pish·ly,** *adv.* —**up′pish·ness,** *n.*

Upp·sa·la (ŭp′sä′lə; *Swed.* ōōp′sä′lä), *n.* a city in SE Sweden. 67,087 (est. 1953). Also, **Upsala.**

up·raise (ŭp rāz′), *v.t.,* **-raised, -raising.** to raise up.

up·rear (ŭp rîr′), *v.t.* to rear up; raise.

up·right (ŭp′rīt′, ŭp rīt′), *adj.* **1.** erect or vertical, as in position or posture. **2.** raised or directed vertically or upward. **3.** adhering to rectitude; righteous, honest, or just. **4.** in accord with what is right. —*n.* **5.** state

of being upright or vertical. **6.** something standing erect or vertical, as a piece of timber. **7.** an upright piano. **8.** (*pl.*) *Football.* the goal posts. —*adv.* **9.** in an upright position or direction; vertically. [ME; OE *uppriht,* c. G *aufrecht*] —**up′right′ly,** *adv.* —**up′right′-ness,** *n.*
—**Syn. 1.** plumb. UPRIGHT, ERECT, VERTICAL, PERPENDICULAR imply that something is in the posture of being straight upward, not leaning. That which is UPRIGHT is in a position corresponding to that of a man standing up: *a tree which has fallen is no longer upright, an upright piano.* ERECT emphasizes the straightness of position or posture: *proud and erect, a flagpole stands erect.* VERTICAL esp. suggests upward direction along the shortest line from the earth to a level above it: *the vertical edge of a door, ornamented by vertical lines.* PERPENDICULAR, a term frequently interchangeable with VERTICAL, is esp. used in mathematics: *the perpendicular side of a right triangle, to erect a perpendicular line from the base of a figure.* —**Ant. 1.** leaning, bent, horizontal.

upright piano. See **piano** (def. 4).

up·rise (*v.* ŭp·rīz′, *n.* ŭp′rīz′), *v.,* -**rose, -risen, -rising,** *n.* —*v.i.* **1.** to rise up; get up, as from a lying or sitting posture. **2.** to rise in revolt. **3.** to come into being or action. **4.** to move upward; mount up; ascend. **5.** to come above the horizon. **6.** to slope upward. **7.** to increase in height; swell up. —*n.* **8.** act of rising up.

up·ris·ing (ŭp′rī′zĭng, ŭp·rī′zĭng), *n.* **1.** act of rising up. **2.** an insurrection or revolt. **3.** an ascent or acclivity.

up·roar (ŭp′rôr′), *n.* **1.** violent and noisy disturbance, as of a multitude. **2.** an instance or state of this. **3.** tumultuous or confused noise or din. **4.** an instance of it. [t. D: m. *oproer* tumult; sense affected by ROAR] —**Syn. 1.** See **disorder.**

up·roar·i·ous (ŭp·rôr′Yəs), *adj.* **1.** characterized by or in a state of uproar; tumultuous. **2.** making an uproar, or disorderly and noisy, as an assembly, persons, etc. **3.** confused and loud, as sounds, utterances, etc. **4.** expressed by or producing uproar. —**up·roar′i·ous-ly,** *adv.* —**up·roar′i·ous·ness,** *n.*

up·root (ŭp·rōōt′, -rŏŏt′), *v.t.* **1.** to root up; tear up by the roots. **2.** to eradicate; remove utterly. —**up-root′al,** *n.* —**up·root′er,** *n.*

up·rose (ŭp·rōz′), *v.* pt. of **uprise.**

up·rouse (ŭp·rouz′), *v.t.,* -**roused, -rousing.** to rouse up; arouse; awake.

Up·sa·la (ŭp′sä′lə; *Swed.* ōōp′sä′lä), *n.* Uppsala.

up·set (*v., adj.* ŭp·sĕt′; *n.* ŭp′sĕt′), *v.,* -**set, -setting,** *n., adj.* —*v.t.* **1.** to overturn. **2.** to overthrow or defeat. **3.** to disturb or derange completely; put out of order; throw into disorder. **4.** to disturb mentally; perturb. **5.** to shorten and thicken by hammering on the end, as a heated piece of iron. **6.** to shorten (a tire, etc.) in resetting it. —*v.i.* **7.** to become upset or overturned. —*n.* **8.** an upsetting or being upset; overturn; overthrow. **9.** *Colloq.* a defeat of a contestant favored to win. **10.** a nervous, irritable state of mind. **11.** a disordered arrangement. **12.** *Mach.* **a.** a tool for upsetting. **b.** that which is upset, as a bar end. —*adj.* **13.** overturned; capsized. **14.** put in disorder. **15.** in an irritable state of mind; worried. **16.** raised up. —**up·set′ter,** *n.*
—**Syn. 1.** UPSET, CAPSIZE, OVERTURN imply a change from an upright or other stable position to a prostrate one. UPSET is a familiar word, applied to simple, everyday actions: *to upset a table, a glass of water.* CAPSIZE is applied especially to the upsetting of a boat or vessel: *to capsize a canoe.* OVERTURN usually suggests violence in upsetting something supposedly stable: *the earthquake overturned houses.* All three are used figuratively, also: *to upset the stock market, to capsize a plan, to overturn a government.*

upset price, the lowest price at which a person is willing that his property shall be sold at auction.

up·shot (ŭp′shŏt′), *n.* **1.** the final issue, the conclusion, or the result. **2.** the gist, or sum and substance. [f. UP- (in sense of termination) + SHOT[1]]

up·side (ŭp′sīd′), *n.* the upper side or part.

upside down, 1. with the upper part undermost. **2.** in complete disorder; topsy-turvy. [alter. of ME *up so down*]

up·si·lon (ŭp′sə·lŏn′; *Brit.* ūp·sī′lən), *n.* the twentieth letter (Υ, υ = English U, u, or Y, y) of the Greek alphabet. [t. Gk.: m. *ŷ psilon* simple or slender *u* or *y*]

up·spring (ŭp·sprĭng′), *v.i.,* -**sprang** or -**sprung, -sprung, -springing.** to spring up.

up·stage (ŭp′stāj′), *adv.* **1.** on or to the back of the stage, which was at one time higher in elevation than the front. —*adj.* **2.** of or pertaining to the back of the stage. **3.** *Slang.* haughtily aloof; haughty; supercilious.

up·stairs (ŭp′stârz′), *adv.* **1.** up the stairs; to or on an upper floor. **2. kick upstairs,** to promote (someone) in order to get him out of the way. —*adj.* **3.** on or pertaining to an upper floor. —*n.* **4.** an upper story or stories. **5.** an upper story; that part of a building above the ground floor.

up·stand·ing (ŭp·stăn′dĭng), *adj.* **1.** standing erect; erect and tall, esp. of persons erect, well-grown, and vigorous in body or form. **2.** of a fine, vigorous type. **3.** upright; honorable.

up·start (*n., adj.* ŭp′stärt′; *v.* ŭp·stärt′), *n.* **1.** one who has risen suddenly from a humble position to wealth or power, or to assumed consequence. **2.** a pretentious and objectionable parvenu. —*adj.* **3.** being or resembling an upstart. **4.** characteristic of an upstart. —*v.i.* **5.** to start up. —*v.t.* **6.** to cause to start up.

up·state (ŭp′stāt′), *n.* *U.S.* **1.** the part of a State farther north or away from the coast, esp. the more northerly part of New York State. —*adj.* **2.** of or coming from the parts of a State farther north or away from the coast. —**up′stat′er,** *n.*

up·stream (ŭp′strēm′), *adv.* toward or in the higher part of a stream; against the current.

up·stroke (ŭp′strōk′), *n.* an upward stroke, esp. of a pen or pencil, or of a piston in a vertical cylinder.

up·surge (ŭp·sûrj′), *v.i.,* -**surged, -surging.** to surge up.

up·sweep (*v.* ŭp·swēp′; *n.* ŭp′swēp′), *v.,* -**swept, -sweeping,** *n.* —*v.t.* **1.** to sweep upward. —*v.i.* **2.** to be arranged in an upsweep. —*n.* **3.** a sweeping upward. **4.** a curved shape of the lower jaw of some animals.

up·swell (ŭp·swĕl′), *v.i.,* -**swelled, -swelled** or -**swollen, -swelling.** to swell up.

up·swing (*n.* ŭp′swĭng′; *v.* ŭp·swĭng′), *n., v.,* -**swung, -swinging.** —*n.* **1.** an upward swing or swinging movement, as of a pendulum. **2.** marked advance. —*v.i.* **3.** to make an upward swing.

up·take (ŭp′tāk′), *n.* **1.** act of taking up; a lifting. **2.** apprehension or understanding. **3.** a pipe or passage leading upward from below, as for conducting smoke, a current of air, or the like.

up·throw (ŭp′thrō′), *n.* **1.** an upheaval. **2.** *Geol.* an upward displacement of rock on one side of a fault.

up·thrust (ŭp′thrŭst′), *n.* **1.** a thrust in an upward direction. **2.** *Geol.* an upheaval or uplift.

up·tilt (ŭp·tĭlt′), *v.t.* to tilt up.

up-to-date (ŭp′tə·dāt′), *adj.* **1.** extending to the present time; including the latest facts: *an up-to-date record.* **2.** in accordance with the latest or newest standards, ideas, or style; modern. **3.** (of persons, etc.) keeping up with the times, as in information, ideas, methods, style, etc. —**up′-to-date′ness,** *n.*

up·town (ŭp′toun′), *adv.* **1.** to or in the upper part of a town. —*adj.* **2.** moving toward, situated in, or pertaining to the upper part of a town.

up·turn (*v.* ŭp·tûrn′; *n.* ŭp′tûrn′), *v.t.* **1.** to turn up or over. **2.** to point up. —*v.i.* **3.** to turn up. —*n.* **4.** an upward turn, or a changing and rising movement, as in prices, business, etc.

up·turned (ŭp·tûrnd′), *adj.* **1.** turned upward. **2.** turned over; upside down. **3.** having a turned-up end.

up·ward (ŭp′wərd), *adv.* Also, **up′wards. 1.** toward a higher place or position. **2.** toward a higher or greater rank, degree, age, etc.: *ten years upward.* **3.** more: *fourscore and upward.* **4.** toward the source or origin: *trace a stream upward.* **5.** in the upper parts; above. —*adj.* **6.** moving or tending upward; directed upward: *an upward course.* [ME; OE *upweard,* c. D *opwaart;* f. UP- + -WARD] —**up′ward·ly,** *adv.*

upward of, more than; above. Also, **upwards of.**

up·whirl (ŭp·hwûrl′), *v.i., v.t.* to whirl upward.

Ur (ûr), *n.* an ancient Sumerian city and district in S Babylonia, on the Euphrates: the home of Abraham.

Ur, *Chem.* uranium.

u·rae·mi·a (yŏŏ·rē′mYə), *n.* *Pathol.* uremia. —**u·rae′mic,** *adj.*

u·rae·us (yŏŏ·rē′əs), *n.* the sacred asp (a cobra, *Naja haje*) as represented upon the headdress of divinities and royal personages of ancient Egypt, usually directly over the forehead, as an emblem of supreme power. [NL, t. Gk.: m. *ouraios,* repr. Egyptian name of cobra]

U·ral (yŏŏr′əl), *n.* **1.** a mountain system in the Soviet Union, extending N and S from the Arctic Ocean to near the Caspian Sea, forming a natural boundary between Europe and Asia. Highest peak, Mt. Telpos, 5540 ft. **2.** a river flowing from the Ural Mountains into the Caspian Sea. ab. 1400 mi. **3.** a former administrative division comprising a region in the Ural Mountains and its slopes. —*adj.* **4.** of or pertaining to these mountains or this river.

U·ral-Al·ta·ic (yŏŏr′əl·ăl·tā′Yk), *adj.* **1.** of or pertaining to the Ural Mountains, on the border between the Soviet Union in Europe and Siberia, and the Altai Mountains, in southern Siberia and northwestern Mongolia, or the country or peoples around them. **2.** pertaining to the peoples using Ural-Altaic (def. 3). —*n.* **3.** a supposed, but unproved, linguistic phylum combining the Uralian, Turkic, Tungusic, and Mongolian families of languages.

U·ra·li·an (yŏŏ·rā′lYən), *n.* a linguistic stock or family comprising the Finno-Ugric and Samoyed languages.

U·ra·ni·a (yŏŏ·rā′nYə), *n.* **1.** *Gk. Myth.* the Muse of astronomy. **2.** a name of Aphrodite, as representing spiritual love. [t. L, t. Gk.: m. *Ourania* heavenly one]

U·ra·ni·an (yŏŏ·rā′nYən), *adj.* pertaining to the planet Uranus.

u·ran·ic[1] (yŏŏ·răn′Yk), *adj.* *Chem.* **1.** of or containing uranium, esp. in the tetravalent state (U +4). **2.** containing uranium in a valence state higher than the corresponding uranous compound. [f. URAN(IUM) + -IC]

u·ran·ic[2] (yŏŏ·răn′Yk), *adj.* of or pertaining to the heavens; celestial; astronomical. [f. s. Gk. *ouranós* heaven + -IC]

u·ran·i·nite (yŏŏ·răn′ə·nīt′), *n.* a mineral, probably originally uranium dioxide (UO₂), but altered by radioactive decay, and usually containing more or less uranium trioxide, lead, radium, and helium, occurring in several varieties, including pitchblende: the most important ore of uranium. [f. URAN(IUM) + -IN² + -ITE¹]

u·ra·nite (yŏŏr′ə nīt′), *n.* either of two minerals, autunite (lime uranite) or torbernite (copper uranite). [t. G: m. *uranit*. See URANIUM, -ITE¹] —**u·ra·nit·ic** (yŏŏr′ə nĭt′ĭk), *adj.*

u·ra·ni·um (yŏŏ rā′nĭ əm), *n. Chem.* a white, lustrous, radioactive, metallic element, having compounds which are used in photography and in coloring glass. The isotope U²³⁵ is capable of continuous fission and is used in the atomic bomb. *Symbol:* U; *at. wt.:* 238.07; *at. no.:* 92; *sp. gr.:* 18.7. [NL; see URAN(US) (def. 1), -IUM]

urano-, a word element meaning "heaven," as in *uranography*. [t. Gk., comb. form of *ouranós*]

u·ra·nog·ra·phy (yŏŏr′ə nŏg′rə fĭ), *n.* the branch of astronomy concerned with the description and mapping of the heavens, and esp. of the fixed stars. [t. Gk.: m.s. *ouranographía*. See URANO-, -GRAPHY] —**u·ra·nog′ra·pher**, **u·ra·nog′ra·phist**, *n.* —**u·ra·no·graph′ic** (yŏŏr′-ə nə grăf′ĭk), **u·ra·no·graph′i·cal**, *adj.*

u·ra·nous (yŏŏr′ə nəs), *adj. Chem.* containing trivalent uranium (U⁺³).

U·ra·nus (yŏŏr′ə nəs), *n.* **1.** *Astron.* the seventh major planet in order from the sun. Its period of revolution is 84.02 years, its mean distance from the sun about 1783 million miles, and its diameter 30,880 miles. It has 5 satellites. *Symbol:* ♅. **2.** *Gk. Myth.* the personification of Heaven, and ruler of the world, son and husband of Gaea (Earth) and father of the Titans, the Cyclopes, etc., who confined his children in Tartarus and was dethroned by his son Cronus, youngest of the Titans, at the instigation of Gaea. [t. L, t. Gk.: m. *Ouranós* (def. 2)]

u·ra·nyl (yŏŏr′ə nĭl), *n. Chem.* the divalent radical UO₂⁺², which forms salts with acids. [f. URAN(IUM) + -YL] —**u·ra·nyl′ic**, *adj.*

u·rate (yŏŏr′āt), *n. Chem.* a salt of uric acid. [f. UR(O)-¹ + -ATE²]

ur·ban (ûr′bən), *adj.* **1.** of, pertaining to, or comprising a city or town. **2.** living in a city or cities. **3.** characteristic of or accustomed to cities; citified. [t. L: s. *urbānus*]

Ur·ban (ûr′bən), *n.* name of eight popes.

Urban II, (*Odo* or *Otho*) c1042–99, French ecclesiastic; pope, 1088–99.

Ur·ban·a (ûr băn′ə), *n.* a city in E Illinois. 27,294 (1960).

urban district, a minor administrative division in England, Wales, and Northern Ireland, with local self-government by a district council, but lacking the charter of a borough.

ur·bane (ûr bān′), *adj.* **1.** courteous or polite, esp. in a refined or elegant way. **2.** smoothly polite; suave. [t. L: m.s. *urbānus*] —**ur·bane′ly**, *adv.* —**ur·bane′ness**, *n.*

ur·ban·i·ty (ûr băn′ə tĭ), *n., pl.* -ties. **1.** the quality of being urbane; refined or elegant courtesy or politeness; suavity. **2.** (*pl.*) civilities or amenities. [t. L: m. *urbānitas*]

ur·ban·ize (ûr′bə nīz′), *v.t.*, -ized, -izing. to render urban, as in character. —**ur′ban·i·za′tion**, *n.*

ur·bi et or·bi (ûr′bī ĕt ôr′bī), *Latin.* to the city (Rome) and the world. Papal bulls are so addressed.

ur·ce·o·late (ûr′sĭ ə lĭt, -lāt′), *adj.* shaped like a pitcher; swelling out like the body of a pitcher and contracted at the orifice, as a corolla. [t. NL: m.s. *urceolātus*, der. L *urceolus*, dim. of *urceus* pitcher]

ur·chin (ûr′chĭn), *n.* **1.** a mischievous boy, or any small boy, or youngster. **2.** a sea urchin. **3.** *Archaic.* a kind of elf or mischievous sprite. **4.** *Archaic or Dial.* a hedgehog. [ME *urchone*, t. d. OF: m. *hirechon*, ult. der. L *ericius* hedgehog]

Ur·du (ŏŏr′dŏŏ, ôŏr dŏŏ′, ûr-), *n.* **1.** a language derived from Hindustani, used by Moslems and written with Arabic letters. **2.** Hindustani. [t. Hind.: camp (speech), t. Turki: m. *ordu* camp. See HORDE]

-ure, an abstract-noun suffix of action, result, and instrument, as in *legislature*, *pressure*. [repr. F -*ure* and L -*ūra*]

u·re·a (yŏŏ rē′ə, yŏŏr′ə), *n.* a colorless, crystalline substance, CO(NH₂)₂, used in fertilizers and in making plastics and adhesives. [NL, f. m. Gk. *oūrê(sis)* urination + -*a*, noun ending] —**u·re′al**, *adj.*

urea resins, a group of resins formed by the interaction of urea and formaldehyde.

u·re·ase (yŏŏr′ĭ ās′, -āz′), *n. Biochem.* an enzyme found in bacteria, fungi, etc., which changes urea into ammonium carbonate. [f. URE(A) + -ASE]

u·re·di·um (yŏŏ rē′dĭ əm), *n. Bot.* the fructification of the rust-fungi-bearing uredospores. Also, **u·re·din·i·um** (yŏŏr′ə dĭn′ĭ əm), **u·re·do·so·rus** (yŏŏr′ĭ də sōr′əs).

u·re·do (yŏŏ rē′dō), *n.* a skin irritation; hives; urticaria. [t. L: rust fungus, itch]

u·re·do·spore (yŏŏr′ĭ də spōr′), *n. Bot.* the spore of the rust fungi which appears between the aeciospore and the teliospore, commonly the summer spore.

u·re·do·stage (yŏŏr′ĭ də stāj′), *n. Bot.* the phase in the life cycle of a rust fungus when the uredospores are formed. Also, **u·re·di·al stage** (yŏŏ rē′dĭ əl).

u·re·ide (yŏŏr′ĭd′, -ĭd), *n. Chem.* any of several derivations of urea.

u·re·mi·a (yŏŏ rē′mĭ ə), *n. Pathol.* the morbid condition resulting from the retention of urinary constituents. Also, **uraemia**. [t. NL. See URO-¹, -EMIA]

u·re·mic (yŏŏ rē′mĭk), *adj.* **1.** pertaining to uremia. **2.** afflicted with uremia. Also, **uraemic**.

-uret, a suffix having the same force as -ide, as in *arseniuret*. [t. NL: s. -*urētum*]

u·re·ter (yŏŏ rē′tər), *n. Anat.* a muscular duct or tube conveying the urine from a kidney to the bladder or cloaca. See diag. under **kidney**. [t. L, t. Gk.] —**u·re′ter·al**, **u·re·ter·ic** (yŏŏr′ə tĕr′ĭk), *adj.*

u·re·thane (yŏŏr′ə thān′, yŏŏ rĕth′ān), *n. Chem.* **1.** any derivative of carbamic acid with the type formula, NH₂COOR. **2.** a colorless, crystalline compound, the ethyl ester of carbamic acid, NH₂COOC₂H₅, used to induce hypnosis and in the synthesis of organic compounds. [f. UR(EA) + ETHANE]

urethr-, var. of urethro- before vowels, as in *urethritis*.

u·re·thra (yŏŏ rē′thrə), *n., pl.* -thrae (-thrē), -thras. *Anat.* the membranous tube which extends from the bladder to the exterior. In the male it conveys semen as well as urine. [t. LL, t. Gk.] —**u·re′thral**, *adj.*

u·re·thri·tis (yŏŏr′ə thrī′tĭs), *n. Pathol.* inflammation of the urethra. —**u·re·thrit·ic** (yŏŏr′ə thrĭt′ĭk), *adj.*

urethro-, a word element representing urethra, as in *urethroscope*. Also, **urethr-**.

u·re·thro·scope (yŏŏ rē′thrə skōp′), *n. Med.* an apparatus for observing the urethra.

u·re·thros·co·py (yŏŏr′ə thrŏs′kə pĭ), *n. Med.* observation of the urethra by a urethroscope.

U·rey (yŏŏr′ĭ), *n.* Harold Clayton, born 1893, U.S. chemist: discovered heavy hydrogen.

Ur·fa (ŏŏr fä′), *n.* a city in SE Turkey, E of the Euphrates river. 48,013 (1955). See Edessa.

Ur·ga (ŏŏr′gä), *n.* former name of Ulan Bator Khoto.

urge (ûrj), *v.*, urged, urging, *n.* —*v.t.* **1.** to push or force along; impel with force or vigor: *urge the cause along.* **2.** to drive with incitement to speed or effort: *urge dogs on with shouts.* **3.** to press, push, or hasten (the course, activities, etc.): *urge one's flight.* **4.** to impel, constrain, or move to some action: *urged by necessity.* **5.** to endeavor to induce or persuade, as by entreaties or earnest recommendations; entreat or exhort earnestly: *urge a person to greater caution.* **6.** to press (something) upon the attention: *urge a claim.* **7.** to insist on, allege, or assert with earnestness: *urge the need of haste.* **8.** to press by persuasion or recommendation, as for acceptance, performance, or use; recommend or advocate earnestly: *urge a plan of action.* —*v.i.* **9.** to exert a driving or impelling force; to give an impulse to haste or action: *hunger urges.* **10.** to make entreaties or earnest recommendations. **11.** to press arguments or allegations, as against a person. —*n.* **12.** act of urging; impelling action, influence, or force; impulse. **13.** an involuntary, natural, or instinctive impulse. [t. L: m.s. *urgēre* press, drive] —**urg′er**, *n.*

ur·gen·cy (ûr′jən sĭ), *n., pl.* -cies. **1.** urgent character; imperativeness; insistence; importunateness. **2.** (*pl.*) urgent requirements or needs.

ur·gent (ûr′jənt), *adj.* **1.** pressing; compelling or requiring immediate action or attention; imperative. **2.** insistent or earnest in solicitation; importunate, as a person. **3.** expressed with insistence, as requests or appeals. [t. L: s. *urgens*, ppr.] —**ur′gent·ly**, *adv.*

-urgy, a word element meaning "a technology," as in *metallurgy*. [t. Gk.: m.s. -*ourgia*, der. -*ourgos* working]

U·ri (ŏŏ′rē), *n.* a canton in central Switzerland. 29,000 pop. (est. 1952); 415 sq. mi. *Cap.:* Altdorf.

-uria, a word element meaning "urine." [NL, t. Gk.: m. -*ouría*, der. *oūron* urine]

U·ri·ah (yŏŏ rī′ə), *n.* a Hittite officer, husband of Bathsheba. David contrived his death in battle. II Sam. 11. [t. Heb.: m. *Uriyāh*]

u·ric (yŏŏr′ĭk), *adj.* pertaining to or obtained from urine. [f. UR(O)-¹ + -IC]

uric acid, a colorless, scaly compound, C₅H₄N₄O₃, found in the joints in gout: the principal nitrogenous component of the excrement of reptiles or birds.

U·ri·el (yŏŏr′ĭ əl), *n.* one of the archangels in Jewish angelology. [t. Heb.: m. *Ūrī′el*]

Urim and Thum·mim (yŏŏr′ĭm; thŭm′ĭm), objects (or parts of one object) worn upon the breastplate of the high priests of Israel, evidently used to discover the will of Yahweh. (Exodus 28:30)

u·ri·nal (yŏŏr′ə nəl), *n.* **1.** a glass or metallic receptacle to receive urine. **2.** a place for urinating. [ME, t. L]

u·ri·nal·y·sis (yŏŏr′ə năl′ə sĭs), *n., pl.* -ses (-sēz′). urine analysis. [f. URIN(E) + (AN)ALYSIS]

u·ri·nar·y (yŏŏr′ə nĕr′ĭ), *adj., n., pl.* -naries. —*adj.* **1.** of or pertaining to urine. **2.** pertaining to the organs secreting and discharging urine. —*n.* **3.** a reservoir for the reception of urine, etc., for manure. **4.** a urinal.

urinary calculus, *Pathol.* a calcareous concretion in the urinary tract.

u·ri·nate (yŏŏr′ə nāt′), *v.i.*, -nated, -nating. to pass or discharge urine. —**u·ri·na′tion**, *n.* —**u·ri·na′tive**, *adj.*

u·rine (yŏŏr′ĭn), *n.* the secretion of the kidneys (in mammals, a fluid), which in most mammals is conducted to the bladder by the ureter, and from there to the exterior by the urethra. [ME, t. L: m. *ūrīna*, akin to Gk. *oūron*]

urine analysis, analysis of urine chemically or microscopically.

u·ri·nif·er·ous (yŏŏr′ə nĭf′ər əs), *adj.* conveying urine.

---

b., blend of, blended; c., cognate with; d., dialect, dialectal; der., derived from; f., formed from; g., going back to; m., modification of; r., replacing; s., stem of; t., taken from; ?, perhaps. See the full key on inside cover.

u·ri·no·gen·i·tal (yŏŏr′ə nō jĕn′ə təl), *adj.* urogenital.

u·ri·nous (yŏŏr′ə nəs), *adj.* pertaining to, resembling, or containing urine. Also, **u·ri·nose** (yŏŏr′ə nōs′).

Ur·mi·a (ŏŏr′mĭ ə), *n.* **Lake,** a salt lake in NW Iran. ab. 2000 sq. mi. (large seasonal variation).

urn (ûrn), *n.* **1.** a kind of vase, of various forms, esp. one with a foot or pedestal. **2.** such a vase for holding the ashes of the dead after cremation. **3.** a vessel or apparatus with a faucet or cock, used at table for making tea, coffee, etc. **4.** *Bot.* the spore-bearing part of the capsule of a moss, between lid and seta. [ME *urne*, t. L: m. *urna*] —**urn′like′,** *adj.*

uro-[1], a word element referring to urine and the urinary tract, as in *urochrome.* [t. Gk., comb. form of *oûron* urine]

uro-[2], a word element meaning "tail," as in *urochord.* [comb. form repr. Gk. *ourá*]

u·ro·chord (yŏŏr′ə kôrd′), *n.* *Zool.* the notochord of an ascidian or tunicate, found mostly in the larva, or more conspicuous in the larva than in the adult, confined chiefly to the caudal region. [f. URO-[2] + CHORD[1]] —**u′ro·chor′dal,** *adj.*

u·ro·chrome (yŏŏr′ə krōm′), *n.* a yellow-colored pigment which gives the color to urine. [f. URO-[1] + CHROME]

u·ro·gen·i·tal (yŏŏr′ō jĕn′ə təl), *adj.* genitourinary. [f. URO-[1] + GENITAL]

u·rog·e·nous (yŏŏ rŏj′ə nəs), *adj. Physiol.* **1.** secreting or producing urine. **2.** contained in urine.

u·ro·lith (yŏŏr′ə lĭth), *n. Pathol.* a urinary calculus. [f. URO-[1] + -LITH] —**u′ro·lith′ic,** *adj.*

u·rol·o·gy (yŏŏ rŏl′ə jĭ), *n.* the scientific study of the urine and genitourinary tract, with special reference to the diagnostic significance of changes in its anatomy and physiology. [f. URO-[1] + -LOGY] —**u·ro·log·ic** (yŏŏr′ə lŏj′ĭk), **u·ro·log′i·cal,** *adj.* —**u·rol′o·gist,** *n.*

u·ro·pod (yŏŏr′ə pŏd′), *n.* an abdominal limb of an arthropod, esp. one of those on either side of the telson, as in a lobster. [f. URO-[2] + -POD]

u·ro·pyg·i·al (yŏŏr′ə pĭj′ĭ əl), *adj.* *Ornith.* of or pertaining to the uropygium. [f. UROPYGI(UM) + -AL[1]]

uropygial gland, *Ornith.* a gland opening on the uropygium at the root of the tail in most birds, and secreting an oily fluid used by the bird in preening its feathers.

u·ro·pyg·i·um (yŏŏr′ə pĭj′ĭ əm), *n.* *Ornith.* the projecting terminal portion of a bird's body, from which the tail feathers spring. [t. ML, t. Gk.: m. *ouropýgion*]

Top of uropygium of a jaeger

u·ros·co·py (yŏŏ rŏs′kə pĭ), *n. Med.* inspection of the urine as a means of diagnosis, etc. [f. URO-[1] + -SCOPY] —**u·ro·scop·ic** (yŏŏr′ə skōp′ĭk), *adj.* —**u·ros′co·pist,** *n.*

u·ro·xan·thin (yŏŏr′ə zăn′thĭn), *n.* indican (def. 2). [t. G. See URO-[1], -XANTHIN]

Ur·quhart (ûr′kərt), *n.* **Sir Thomas,** 1611–60, Scottish author and translator.

Ur·sa Ma·jor (ûr′sə mā′jər), *gen.* **Ursae Majoris** (ûr′sē mə jôr′ĭs). *Astron.* the Great Bear, the most prominent constellation in the northern heavens, containing the seven stars that form the Dipper. [L: greater bear]

Ur·sa Mi·nor (ûr′sə mī′nər), *gen.* **Ursae Minoris** (ûr′sē mĭ nôr′ĭs). *Astron.* the Little Bear, a northern constellation containing the stars forming the Little Dipper, the outermost of which (at the end of the tail of the Little Bear) is Polaris, the polestar. [L: lesser bear]

ur·si·form (ûr′sə fôrm′), *adj.* having the form of a bear; bearlike. [f. *ursi-* (comb. form of L *ursus* bear) + -FORM]

ur·sine (ûr′sīn, -sĭn), *adj.* **1.** of or pertaining to a bear or bears. **2.** bearlike. [t. L: m.s. *ursinus*]

ursine dasyure, Tasmanian devil.

ursine howler, the red howling monkey, *Alouatta seniculus,* of northern South America.

Ur·spra·che (ŏŏr′shprä′кнə), *n.* a hypothetically reconstructed parent language, e.g., the primitive Germanic (reconstructed by comparative linguistics) from which the Germanic languages have developed. [G: f. *ur-* primitive, original + *sprache* language]

Ur·su·la (ûr′syŏŏ lə, -sə lə), *n.* **Saint,** a legendary British Christian princess said to have been put to death, with 11,000 attendant virgins, by the Huns, at Cologne, in the 3d (or 5th) century.

Ur·su·line (ûr′syŏŏ lĭn, -lĭn′, -sə-), *n.* **1.** one of a religious order of Roman Catholic women founded by St. Angela Merici at Brescia, Italy, in 1535, and devoted to the teaching of girls. —*adj.* **2.** of or pertaining to the Ursulines. [f. URSULA + -INE[1]]

ur·ti·ca·ceous (ûr′tə kā′shəs), *adj.* belonging to Urticaceae, or nettle family of plants. [f. s. NL *Urticáceae,* pl. (der. L *urtíca* nettle) genus of nettles + -OUS]

ur·ti·car·i·a (ûr′tə kâr′ĭ ə), *n.* *Pathol.* a skin disease characterized by transient eruptions of itching wheals caused chiefly by gastric derangement; nettle rash; hives. [NL, der. L *urtíca* nettle] —**ur′ti·car′i·al,** *adj.*

ur·ti·cate (ûr′tə kāt′), *v.,* **-cated, -cating.** —*v.t.* **1.** to sting with, as with, or like nettles. **2.** to whip (a benumbed or paralytic limb) with nettles in order to restore sensation. —*v.i.* **3.** to sting as or like a nettle; use urtication in treating paralysis, etc. [t. ML: m.s. *urtícātus,* pp., der. L *urtíca* nettle]

ur·ti·ca·tion (ûr′tə kā′shən), *n.* the action or result of urticating or stinging.

Uru., Uruguay.

U·ru·guay (yŏŏr′ə gwā′; *Sp.* ōō′rōō gwī′), *n.* **1.** a republic in SE South America. 2,615,000 pop. (est. 1955); 72,172 sq. mi. *Cap.:* Montevideo. **2.** a river flowing from S Brazil along the E boundary of Argentina into the Río de la Plata. 981 mi. —**U·ru·guay·an** (yŏŏr′ə gwā′ən, -gwī′ən), *adj., n.*

U·rum·chi (ōō rōōm′chē), *n.* a city in NW China: the capital of Sinkiang province. 70,000 (est. 1950). Also, **U·rum·tsi** (ōō rōōm′chē) or **Tihwa.**

U·run·di (ōō rōōn′dĭ), *n.* See **Ruanda-Urundi.**

u·rus (yŏŏr′əs), *n.* the aurochs. [t. L; of Gmc. orig.]

u·ru·shi·ol (ōōr′ōō shĭ ōl′, -ŏl′), *n.* a toxic, liquid, catechol derivative, the active irritant principle in several species of the plant genus *Rhus,* as poison ivy. [f. Jap. *urushi* lacquer + -OL[2]]

us (ŭs), *pron.* objective case of **we.** [ME and OE, c. G and Goth. *uns*]

U.S., United States.

u.s., **1.** ubi supra. **2.** ut supra.

U.S.A., **1.** United States of America. **2.** Also, **USA** United States Army. **3.** Union of South Africa.

U.S.A.F., United States Air Force.

us·a·ble (ū′zə bəl), *adj.* **1.** that is available for use. **2.** that is in condition to be used. Also, **useable.** —**us′a·bil′i·ty, us′a·ble·ness,** *n.*

us·age (ū′sĭj, ū′zĭj), *n.* **1.** customary way of doing; a custom or practice: *the usages of the last fifty years.* **2.** customary manner of using a language or any of its forms, esp. standard practice in a given language: *English usage.* **3.** a particular instance of this: *a usage borrowed from the French.* **4.** way of using or treating, or treatment: *hard or rough usage.* **5.** habitual or customary use; long-continued practice: *immemorial usage.* **6.** act of using or employing; use. [ME, t. OF, der. *us* use, g. L *ūsus*]

us·ance (ū′zəns), *n.* **1.** *Com.* the length of time, exclusive of days of grace, allowed by custom or usage for the payment of foreign bills of exchange (it varies between different places). **2.** *Econ.* the income of benefits of every kind derived from the ownership of wealth. **3.** *Obs.* use. **4.** *Obs.* custom. **5.** *Obs.* usury. [ME, t. OF, der. *user* USE, v.]

Us·beg (ŭs′bĕg), *n.* Uzbek.

U.S.C.G., United States Coast Guard.

use (*v.* ūz; *n.* ūs), *v.,* **used, using,** *n.* —*v.t.* **1.** to employ for some purpose; put into service; make use of: *use a knife.* **2.** to avail oneself of; apply to one's own purposes. **3.** to expend or consume in use: *we have used the money provided.* **4.** to practice habitually or customarily; make a practice of. **5.** to act or behave toward, or treat, in some manner. **6.** to habituate or accustom (except in dial., now only in **used,** pp.): *used to hardships.* —*v.i.* **7.** to be accustomed, wont, or customarily found (with an infinitive expressed or understood, and, except in archaic use, now only in the past): *he used to go every day.* **8.** *Archaic* or *Dial.* to resort, stay, or dwell customarily. —*n.* **9.** act of employing or using, or putting into service: *the use of tools.* **10.** state of being employed or used: *this book is in use.* **11.** an instance or way of employing or using something: *each successive use of the tool.* **12.** a way of being employed or used; a purpose for which something is used: *the instrument has different uses.* **13.** the power, right, or privilege of employing or using something: *to lose the use of the right eye.* **14.** service or advantage in or for being employed or used; utility or usefulness: *of no practical use.* **15.** help; profit; resulting good: *what's the use.* **16.** occasion or need, as for something to be employed or used: *have you any use for another calendar?* **17.** continued, habitual, or customary employment or practice; custom; practice: *follow the prevailing use of such occasions.* **18.** way of using or treating; treatment. **19.** *Law.* **a.** the enjoyment of property, as by the employment, occupation, or exercise of it. **b.** the benefit or profit of property (lands and tenements) in the possession of another who simply holds them for the beneficiary. **c.** the equitable ownership of land the legal title to which is in another; a passive trust. **20.** *Liturgy.* the distinctive form of ritual or of any liturgical observance used in a particular church, diocese, community, etc. **21.** *Obs.* usual experience. **22.** Some special noun phrases are: **have no use for, 1.** to have no occasion or need for. **2.** *Colloq.* to have no liking or tolerance for. **in use,** occupied; employed to some purpose. **make use of,** to employ; put to use; use for one's own purposes or advantages. **of no use,** or (elliptically) **no use,** of no service, advantage, or help. **put to use,** to employ. [ME, t. OF: m. *user,* der. L *ūsus,* pp.] —**Syn. 1.** USE, UTILIZE mean to make something serve one's purpose. USE is the general word: *to use a telephone, to use a saw and other tools, to use one's eyes, to use coal, eggs in cooking.* (What is USED often has depreciated or been diminished, sometimes completely consumed: *a used automobile, all the butter has been used.*) As applied to persons, USE implies some selfish or sinister purpose: *to use another to advance oneself.* UTILIZE implies practical or profitable use: *to utilize the means at hand, a modern system of lighting.*

ăct, āble, dâre, ärt; ĕbb, ēqual; ĭf, īce; hŏt, ōver, ôrder, oil, bŏŏk, ōōze, out; ŭp, ūse, ûrge; ə = a in alone; ch, chief; g, give; ng, ring; sh, shoe; th, thin; ŧh, that; zh, vision. See the full key on inside cover.

use·a·ble (ū′zə bəl), *adj.* usable. **—use′a·bil′i·ty, use′a·ble·ness,** *n.*

use·ful (ūs′fəl), *adj.* **1.** being of use or service; serving some purpose; serviceable, advantageous, helpful, or of good effect. **2.** of practical use, as for doing work; producing material results; supplying common needs: *the useful arts.* **—use′ful·ly,** *adv.* **—use′ful·ness,** *n.*

use·less (ūs′lĭs), *adj.* **1.** of no use; not serving the purpose or any purpose; unavailing or futile. **2.** without useful qualities; of no practical good. **—use′less·ly,** *adv.* **—use′less·ness,** *n.*

—Syn. 1. inutile, fruitless, profitless, valueless, worthless. USELESS, FUTILE, INEFFECTUAL, VAIN refer to that which is unavailing. That is USELESS which is unavailing because of the circumstances of the case or some inherent defect: *it is useless to cry over spilt milk.* FUTILE suggests wasted effort and complete failure to attain a desired end: *all attempts were futile.* That is INEFFECTUAL which weakly applies energy in an ill-advised way and does not produce a desired effect: *an ineffectual effort.* That which is VAIN is fruitless or hopeless even after all possible effort: *it is vain to keep on hoping.* **2.** unserviceable, unusable. **—Ant. 1.** effective.

us·er (ū′zər), *n.* **1.** one who or that which uses. **2.** *Law.* **a.** the right to the enjoyment of property. **b.** the exercise of a right to the enjoyment of property.

USES, United States Employment Service.

USHA, United States Housing Authority.

Ush·ant (ŭsh′ənt), *n.* an island off the NW coast of France: naval battles, 1778, 1794. 2071 pop. (1954); 4½ mi. long. French, **Ouessant.**

U-shaped (ū′shāpt′), *adj.* being in the form of a U.

U·shas (ŏŏ′shəs, ŏŏ shäs′), *n.* Dawn, a Vedic deity, daughter of Sky, and sister of Night. [t. Skt.: m. *Usas*]

ush·er (ŭsh′ər), *n.* **1.** one who escorts persons to seats in a church, theater, etc. **2.** an officer or servant having charge of an entrance door; a doorkeeper. **3.** an officer whose business it is to introduce strangers or to walk before a person of rank. **4.** *Brit. Obsolesc.* a subordinate teacher or an assistant in a school. **—***v.t.* **5.** to act as an usher to; conduct or show (fol. by *in, into, out,* etc.). **6.** to attend or bring at the coming or beginning. [ME, t. AF: m. *usser,* g. LL *ustiārius* doorkeeper, r. L *ostiārius*] **—ush·er·ette** (ŭsh′ə rĕt′), *n. fem.* **—ush′er·less,** *adj.*

Usk (ŭsk), *n.* a river in SE Wales and SW England, flowing into the Severn estuary. ab. 70 mi.

Us·küb (ʏskyp′), *n.* Turkish name of **Skoplje.** Also, **Us·küp.**

Us·kü·dar (ʏskʏ′där), *n.* Turkish name of **Scutari** (def. 1).

U.S.M., 1. United States Mail. **2.** United States Marine(s). **3.** United States Mint.

U.S.M.A., United States Military Academy.

U.S.M.C., United States Marine Corps. Also, **USMC**

USN, United States Navy. Also, **U.S.N.**

U.S.N.A., 1. United States National Army. **2.** United States Naval Academy.

Us·nach (ŏŏsh′nəкʜ), *n.* See **Deirdre.**

U.S.N.G., United States National Guard.

U.S.N.R., United States Naval Reserve. Also, **USNR**

U.S.P., United States Pharmacopoeia.

Us·pal·la·ta Pass (ŏŏs′pä yä′tä), a mountain pass in the Andes, linking Mendoza, Argentina, and Santiago, Chile: "Christ of the Andes" statue nearby. ab. 12,800 ft. high.

U.S.P.H.S., United States Public Health Service.

us·que·baugh (ŭs′kwĭ bô′, -bä′), *n.* (in Scotland and Ireland) whiskey. [t. Irish and Scot. Gaelic: m. *uisge beatha* water of life]

U.S.S., 1. United States Senate. **2.** United States Service. **3.** United States Ship. **4.** United States Steamer. **5.** United States Steamship.

U.S.S.B., United States Shipping Board.

U.S.S.R., Union of Soviet Socialist Republics. Also, **USSR**

Us·su·ri (ŏŏs sŏŏ′rē), *n.* a river forming a part of the boundary between E Manchuria and the SE Soviet Union, flowing N to the Amur river. ab. 500 mi.

us·tu·late (ŭs′chə lĭt, -lāt′), *adj.* colored or blackened as if scorched. [t. L: m.s. *ūstulātus,* pp., burned]

us·tu·la·tion (ŭs′chə lā′shən), *n.* **1.** act of scorching or burning. **2.** *Pharm.* the roasting or drying of moist substances so as to prepare them for pulverizing.

usu., 1. usual. **2.** usually.

u·su·al (ū′zhŏŏ əl), *adj.* **1.** habitual or customary: *his usual skill.* **2.** such as is commonly met with or observed in experience; ordinary: *the usual January weather.* **3.** in common use; common: *say the usual things.* **4.** as usual, as is (or was) usual; in the customary or ordinary manner: *he will come as usual.* [ME, t. L: s. *ūsuālis*] **—u′su·al·ly,** *adv.* **—u′su·al·ness,** *n.*

—Syn. 1. USUAL, CUSTOMARY, HABITUAL refer to a settled and constant practice. USUAL indicates that which is to be expected by reason of previous experience, which shows it to occur more often than not: *there were the usual crowds at the celebration.* That which is CUSTOMARY is in accordance with prevailing usage or individual practice: *it is customary to finish up with a bonfire.* That which is HABITUAL has become settled or constant as the result of habit on the part of

the individual: *the merchants wore habitual smiles throughout the season.* **2.** general, prevailing, prevalent, everyday. **—Ant. 1.** unexpected, extraordinary.

u·su·fruct (ū′zyŏŏ frŭkt′, ū′syŏŏ-), *n. Rom. and Civ. Law.* the right of enjoying all the advantages derivable from the use of something which belongs to another, so far as is compatible with the substance of the thing not being destroyed or injured. [t. LL: s. *ūsūfructus,* L *ūsusfructus,* for *ūsus et fructus* use and fruit]

u·su·fruc·tu·ar·y (ū′zyŏŏ frŭk′chŏŏ ĕr′ī, ū′syŏŏ-), *adj., n., pl. -aries.* **—***adj.* **1.** of, pertaining to, or of the nature of a usufruct. **—***n.* **2.** a person who has a usufruct property. [t. LL: m.s. *ūsūfructuārius,* der. *ūsūfructus* USUFRUCT]

u·su·rer (ū′zhə rər), *n.* **1.** one who lends money at an exorbitant rate of interest. **2.** *Obs.* one who lends money at interest. [ME, t. AF, der. *usure* USURY]

u·su·ri·ous (ū zhŏŏr′ī əs), *adj.* **1.** practicing usury; taking exorbitant interest for the use of money. **2.** pertaining to or of the nature of usury: *usurious interest.* **—u·su′ri·ous·ly,** *adv.* **—u·su′ri·ous·ness,** *n.*

u·surp (ū zûrp′, -sûrp′), *v.t.* **1.** to seize and hold (an office or position, power, etc.) by force or without right. **—***v.i.* **2.** to commit forcible or illegal seizure of an office, power, etc.; encroach. [ME *usurpe,* t. L: m. *ūsurpāre*] **—u·surp′er,** *n.* **—u·surp′ing·ly,** *adv.*

u·sur·pa·tion (ū′zər pā′shən, ū′sər-), *n.* **1.** act of usurping; the seizing and holding of the place, power, or the like, of another without right. **2.** the wrongful seizure and occupation of a throne.

u·su·ry (ū′zhə rī), *n., pl. -ries.* **1.** an exorbitant amount or rate of interest, esp. in excess of the legal rate. **2.** the lending, or practice of lending, money at an exorbitant rate of interest. **3.** *Obs.* interest paid for the use of money. [ME *usurie,* t. ML: m. *ūsūria* interest]

usw, *German.* und so weiter. Also, **u.s.w.**

ut (ŭt, ŏŏt), *n. Music.* the syllable once generally used for the first tone or keynote of a scale and sometimes for the tone C: now commonly superseded by *do.* See **sol-fa.** [t. L. See GAMUT]

Ut., Utah.

u.t., universal time.

U·tah (ū′tô, ū′tä), *n.* a State in the W United States. 890,627 pop. (1960); 84,916 sq. mi. *Cap.:* Salt Lake City. *Abbr.:* Ut. **—U′tah·an,** *adj., n.*

ut dict., (L *ut dictum*) as directed.

Ute (ūt, ū′tī), *n.* **1.** (*pl.*) an important tribe of the Shoshonean stock of North American Indians, now on reservations in Utah and Colorado. **2.** a member of this tribe. **3.** their language, of the Uto-Aztecan stock.

u·ten·sil (ū tĕn′səl), *n.* **1.** any of the instruments or vessels commonly used in a kitchen, dairy, or the like. **2.** an instrument or implement. [ME *utensyl(e),* t. ML: m. *ūtensile* prop. neut. of L *ūtensilis* useful] **—Syn. 2.** See **tool.**

u·ter·ine (ū′tər ĭn, -ə rīn′), *adj.* **1.** of or pertaining to the uterus or womb. **2.** related through having had the same mother. [ME, t. LL: m.s. *uterīnus,* der. L *uterus* uterus]

u·ter·us (ū′tər əs), *n., pl.* uteri (ū′tə rī′). *Anat., Zool.* that portion of the oviduct in which the fertilized ovum implants itself and develops or rests during prenatal development; the womb of mammals. See **oviduct.** [t. L]

Ut·gard (ŏŏt′gärd), *n.* Jotunheim.

U Thant. See **Thant.**

U·ther (ū′thər), *n. Arthurian Romance.* king of Britain and father of Arthur. Also, **Uther Pendragon.**

U·ti·ca (ū′tə kə), *n.* **1.** a city in central New York, on the Mohawk river. 100,410 (1960). **2.** an ancient city on the N coast of Africa, NW of Carthage.

u·tile (ū′tĭl), *adj. Obs.* useful. [t. L: m.s. *ūtilis*]

u·ti·le dul·ci (ū′tə lĭ dŭl′sī), *Latin.* the profitable with the pleasant.

u·ti·lise (ū′tə līz′), *v.t., -lised, -lising. Chiefly Brit.* utilize.

u·til·i·tar·i·an (ū tĭl′ə târ′ĭən), *adj.* **1.** pertaining to or consisting in utility. **2.** having regard to utility or usefulness rather than beauty, ornamentality, etc. **3.** of, pertaining to, or adhering to the doctrine of utilitarianism. **—***n.* **4.** an adherent of utilitarianism.

u·til·i·tar·i·an·ism (ū tĭl′ə târ′ĭ ə nĭz′əm), *n.* the ethical doctrine that virtue is based on utility, and that conduct should be directed toward promoting the greatest happiness of the greatest number of persons.

u·til·i·ty (ū tĭl′ə tī), *n., pl. -ties.* **1.** state or character of being useful. **2.** something useful; a useful thing. **3.** a public service, as a streetcar or railroad line, a gaslight or electric-light system, or the like. Cf. **public utility. 4.** *Econ.* the capacity of an object for satisfying a human want. **5.** well-being or happiness; that which is conducive to the happiness and well-being of the greatest number: the principle and purpose of utilitarianism. **6.** *Exchanges.* public-utility stocks. [ME *utilite,* t. L: m.s. *ūtilitas*]

utility man, 1. a worker expected to serve in any capacity when called on. **2.** an actor of miscellaneous small parts.

u·ti·lize (ū′tə līz′), *v.t., -lized, -lizing.* to put to use; turn to profitable account: *to utilize a stream for driving machinery.* Also, *esp. Brit.,* utilise. **—u′ti·liz′a·ble,** *adj.* **—u′ti·li·za′tion,** *n.* **—u′ti·liz′er,** *n.* **—Syn.** See **use.**

ut in·fra (ŭt ĭn′frə), *Latin.* as below.

u·ti pos·si·de·tis (ū′tī pŏs′ə dē′tĭs). *Internat. Law.* the principle which vests in either of the belligerents at the end of a war all territory actually occupied and controlled by them. [L: lit., as you possess]

ut·most (ŭt′mōst, -məst), *adj.* **1.** of the greatest or highest degree, quantity, or the like; greatest: *of the utmost importance.* **2.** being at the furthest point or extremity; furthest: *the utmost boundary of the East.* —*n.* **3.** the greatest degree or amount: *the utmost that can be said.* **4.** the most possible: *do your utmost.* **5.** the extreme limit or extent. [ME *utmest*, OE *ūtemest*, double superl., f. *ūte* OUT + -*mest* -MOST]

U·to-Az·tec·an (ū′tō ăz′tĕk ən), *n.* an American Indian linguistic stock, widespread from Idaho to the Isthmus of Tehuantepec, and from the Rocky Mountains to the Pacific; this stock includes Hopi, Ute, Shoshone, Comanche, Nahuatl (Aztec), Piman, and other languages.

U·to·pi·a (ū tō′pĭ ə), *n.* **1.** an imaginary island described in Sir Thomas More's *Utopia* (1516) as enjoying the utmost perfection in law, politics, etc. **2.** (*often l.c.*) a place or state of ideal perfection. **3.** (*often l.c.*) any visionary system of political or social perfection. [NL, f. Gk.: m. *ou* not + -*topia*, der. *tópos* place]

U·to·pi·an (ū tō′pĭ ən), *adj.* **1.** of, pertaining to, or resembling Utopia. **2.** (*often l.c.*) founded upon or involving imaginary or ideal perfection. **3.** given to dreams or schemes of such perfection. —*n.* **4.** an inhabitant of Utopia. **5.** (*often l.c.*) an ardent but unpractical political or social reformer; a visionary; an idealist.

u·to·pi·an·ism (ū tō′pĭ ə nĭz′əm), *n.* the views or habit of mind of a Utopian; impracticable schemes of political or social reform.

U·trecht (ū′trĕkt; *Du.* Y′trĕKHt), *n.* a city in central Netherlands: treaties ending the War of the Spanish Succession were signed here, 1714. 241,723 (est. 1954).

u·tri·cle (ū′trə kəl), *n.* **1.** a small sac or baglike body, as an air-filled cavity in a seaweed. **2.** *Bot.* a thin bladderlike pericarp or seed vessel. **3.** *Anat.* the larger of two sacs in the membranous labyrinth of the internal ear and concerned with equilibrium. Cf. **saccule.** [t. L: m.s. *ūtriculus*, dim. of *uter* bag]

u·tric·u·lar (ū trĭk′yə lər), *adj.* **1.** pertaining to or of the nature of a utricle; baglike. **2.** having a utricle or utricles.

u·tric·u·late (ū trĭk′yə lĭt, -lāt′), *adj.* having a utricle; utricular; baglike.

u·tric·u·li·tis (ū trĭk′yə lī′tĭs), *n.* *Pathol.* inflammation of the utricle bone of the middle ear. [f. UTRICUL- (US) + -ITIS]

u·tric·u·lus (ū trĭk′yə ləs), *n., pl.* -li (-lī′). utricle.

U·tril·lo (yōō trĭl′ō, *Fr.* Y trē lō′), *n.* [**Maurice** (mô rēs′), 1883-1955, French painter.

ut su·pra (ŭt sōō′prə), *Latin.* as above (a formula in judicial acts, directing that what precedes be reviewed).

Ut·tar Pra·desh (ŏŏt′ər prə dāsh′), a state in N India, formerly United Provinces. 63,215,742 pop. (1951); 113,409 sq. mi. *Cap.:* Lucknow.

ut·ter[1] (ŭt′ər), *v.t.* **1.** to give audible expression to; speak or pronounce: *unable to utter her feelings, the words were uttered in my hearing.* **2.** to give forth (cries, notes, etc.) with the voice: *utter a sigh.* **3.** to express or make known in any manner. **4.** to give forth (a sound) otherwise than with the voice: *the engine uttered a shriek.* **5.** to express by written or printed words. **6.** to make publicly known; publish: *utter a libel.* **7.** to put into circulation, as coins, notes, etc., and esp. counterfeit money, forged checks, etc. **8.** *Rare.* to expel; emit. **9.** *Obs.* to publish, as a book. **10.** *Obs.* to sell. [ME *outre* (freq. of OUT, v.), c. G *äussern* declare] —**ut′ter·a·ble,** *adj.*

ut·ter[2] (ŭt′ər), *adj.* **1.** complete; total; absolute: *her utter abandonment to grief.* **2.** unconditional; unqualified: *an utter denial.* [ME; OE *ūtera* (compar. of *ūt* OUT), c. G *äusser*] —**Syn. 1.** See **absolute.**

ut·ter·ance[1] (ŭt′ərəns), *n.* **1.** act of uttering; vocal expression. **2.** manner of speaking; power of speaking. **3.** something uttered; a word or words uttered; a cry, animal's call, or the like. **4.** a putting into circulation. [ME; f. UTTER, v., + -ANCE]

ut·ter·ance[2] (ŭt′ərəns), *n.* *Obs.* the utmost extremity; death. [ME, t. OF: m. *oultrance,* der. *oultrer* pass beyond, der. L *ultrā* beyond]

ut·ter·er (ŭt′ərər), *n.* one who utters; one who puts into circulation, publishes, or expresses audibly.

ut·ter·ing (ŭt′ər ĭng), *n.* *Crim. Law.* the crime of knowingly tendering or showing a forged instrument or counterfeit coin to another with intent to defraud.

ut·ter·ly (ŭt′ərlĭ), *adv.* in an utter manner; completely; absolutely.

ut·ter·most (ŭt′ər mōst′, -məst), *adj.* **1.** utmost; furthest; extreme. **2.** of the greatest degree, etc.: *uttermost distress.* —*n.* **3.** the extreme limit or extent; the utmost. [ME; f. UTTER[2] + -MOST]

U-235, the uranium isotope with an atomic weight of 235.

U-238, the uranium isotope with an atomic weight of 238; it comprises about 99 percent of natural uranium.

U-239, the uranium isotope with an atomic weight of 239. It is artificially produced by the neutron bombardment of U-238, and undergoes radioactive decay.

u·va·rov·ite (ōō vä′rŏf ĭt′), *n.* an emerald-green variety of garnet containing chromium, to which its color is due. [named after Count S.S. *Uvarov* (1785-1855), President of St. Petersburg Academy. See -ITE[1]]

u·ve·a (ū′vĭ ə), *n.* *Anat.* the middle tunic of the eye (iris, choroid, and ciliary body, taken collectively). [t. ML, der. L *ūva* grape] —**u′ve·al, u′ve·ous,** *adj.*

Uve·dale (ū′dəl, ūv′dāl), *n.* **Nicholas.** See **Udall.**

u·ve·i·tis (ū′vĭ ī′tĭs), *n.* *Pathol.* inflammation of the uvea. [NL, f. s. ML *ūvea* UVEA + -*itis* -ITIS] —**u·ve·it·ic** (ū′vĭ ĭt′ĭk), *adj.*

u·vu·la (ū′vyə lə), *n., pl.* -las, -lae (-lē′). *Anat.* the small, fleshy, conical body projecting downward from the middle of the soft palate. See diag. under **mouth.** [ME, t. ML, dim. of L *ūva* grape]

u·vu·lar (ū′vyə lər), *adj.* **1.** of or pertaining to the uvula. **2.** *Phonet.* pronounced with the back of the tongue held close to or touching the uvula: *Parisian French uses uvular "r."* —*n.* **3.** *Phonet.* a uvular sound.

u·vu·li·tis (ū′vyə lī′tĭs), *n.* *Pathol.* inflammation of the uvula. [NL, f. s. ML *ūvula* UVULA + -*itis* -ITIS]

ux., (L *uxor*) wife.

Ux·mal (ōōsh mäl′), *n.* an ancient ruined city in SE Mexico, in Yucatán: a center of later Mayan civilization.

ux·o·ri·al (ŭk sōr′ĭ əl, ŭg zōr′-), *adj.* of or pertaining to a wife; typical of or befitting a wife.

ux·o·ri·cide[1] (ŭk sōr′ə sĭd′, ŭg zōr′-), *n.* one who kills his wife. [f. L *uxori-* wife + -CIDE[1]] —**ux·o′ri·cid′al,** *adj.*

ux·o·ri·cide[2] (ŭk sōr′ə sĭd′, ŭg zōr′-), *n.* act of killing one's wife. [f. L: m.s. *uxōricīdium* wife-slaying]

ux·o·ri·ous (ŭk sōr′ĭ əs, ŭg zōr′-), *adj.* excessively or foolishly fond of one's wife; doting on a wife. [t. L: m. *uxōrius*] —**ux·o′ri·ous·ly,** *adv.* —**ux·o′ri·ous·ness,** *n.*

Uz·beg (ŭz′bĕg), *n.* **1.** a member of a Turkish people of mixed origin and high culture, resident in W central Asia, where they form an influential class, largely urban. **2.** a Turkic language spoken in Turkestan. Also, **Usbeg.**

Uz·bek Soviet Socialist Republic (ŭz′bĕk; *Russ.* ŏŏz bĕk′), *n.* a constituent republic of the Soviet Union, in the S part, N of Afghanistan. 7,300,000 (est. 1956); 158,500 sq. mi. *Cap.:* Tashkent. Also, **Uz·bek·i·stan** (ŏŏz′bĕ kĭ stän′).

V

V, v, (vē), *n., pl.* **V's** or **Vs, v's** or **vs. 1.** a consonant, the 22d letter of the English alphabet. **2.** See **Roman numerals. 3.** something shaped like the letter V. **4.** a form or outline like that of the letter V. **5.** *U.S. Colloq.* (from the Roman numeral V, meaning "five," on some issues) a five-dollar bill. **6.** the symbol of Allied victory in World War II.

V, 1. *Chem.* vanadium. **2.** *Math.* vector. **3.** velocity. **4.** volt.

v, volt.

V., 1. Venerable. **2.** Viscount.

v., 1. valve. **2.** vector. **3.** verb. **4.** verse. **5.** version. **6.** versus. **7.** vice-. **8.** vide. **9.** vocative. **10.** voice. **11.** volt. **12.** voltage. **13.** volume. **14.** von.

Va., Virginia.

VA, Veterans' Administration.

V.A., 1. Veterans' Administration. **2.** Vicar Apostolic. **3.** Vice-Admiral. **4.** (Order of) Victoria and Albert.

v.a., verb active.

Vaal (väl), *n.* a river in the Union of South Africa, flowing from Transvaal SW to the Orange river. ab. 700 mi.

va·can·cy (vā′kən sĭ), *n., pl.* -cies. **1.** state of being vacant; emptiness; unoccupied state. **2.** something vacant; vacant space. **3.** a gap or opening. **4.** an unoccupied office or position: *to fill vacancies by election.* **5.** lack of thought or intelligence; vacuity. **6.** *Rare.*

absence of occupation; idleness or inactivity. **7.** *Obs.* unoccupied or leisure time.

va·cant (vā/kənt), *adj.* **1.** having no contents; empty; void. **2.** devoid or destitute (*of*). **3.** destitute of an occupant: *vacant chairs.* **4.** untenanted, as a house, etc. **5.** not in use, as a room. **6.** free from work, business, etc., as time. **7.** characterized by or proceeding from absence of occupation: *a vacant life.* **8.** unoccupied with thought or reflection, as the mind. **9.** characterized by, showing, or proceeding from lack of thought or intelligence. **10.** not occupied by an incumbent, official, or the like, as a benefice, office, etc. **11.** *Law.* **a.** idle or unutilized; open to any claimant, as land. **b.** without an incumbent; abandoned: *a vacant estate* (one having no heir or claimant). [ME, t. L: s. *vacans*, ppr.] —**va/cant·ly,** *adv.* —**Syn. 1.** See empty. **9.** blank, vacuous, inane.

va·cate (vā/kāt), *v.*, **-cated, -cating.** —*v.t.* **1.** to make vacant; cause to be empty or unoccupied. **2.** to quit the occupancy of. **3.** to give up or relinquish (an office, position, etc.). **4.** to render inoperative; deprive of validity; annul: *to vacate a legal judgment.* —*v.i.* **5.** to withdraw from occupancy or possession; leave; quit. [t. L: m.s. *vacātus,* pp., freed, emptied]

va·ca·tion (vā kā/shən), *n.* **1.** freedom or release from duty, business, or activity. **2.** a period of suspension of work or activity; a holiday period. **3.** a part of the year when the activities of law courts are suspended. **4.** act of vacating. —*v.i.* **5.** to take or have a vacation. [ME, t. L: s. *vacātio*] —**va·ca/tion·less,** *adj.*

va·ca·tion·ist (vā kā/shən ĭst), *n.* one who is taking a vacation or holiday. Also, **va·ca/tion·er.**

vac·ci·nal (văk/sə nəl), *adj. Med.* pertaining or due to vaccine or vaccination.

vac·ci·nate (văk/sə nāt/), *v.*, **-nated, -nating.** *Med.* —*v.t.* **1.** to inoculate with the vaccine of cowpox, so as to render the subject immune to smallpox. **2.** to inoculate with the modified virus of any of various other diseases, as a preventive measure. —*v.i.* **3.** to perform or practice vaccination. [der. VACCINE, adj.]

vac·ci·na·tion (văk/sə nā/shən), *n.* act or practice of vaccinating; inoculation with vaccine.

vac·ci·na·tion·ist (văk/sə nā/shən ĭst), *n. Med.* an advocate of vaccination.

vac·ci·na·tor (văk/sə nā/tər), *n. Med.* **1.** one who vaccinates. **2.** an instrument used in vaccination.

vac·cine (văk/sēn, -sĭn), *n.* **1.** the virus of cowpox, obtained from the vesicles of an affected cow or person, and used in vaccination. **2.** the modified virus of any of various other diseases, used for preventive inoculation. —*adj.* **3.** pertaining to vaccinia or to vaccination. **4.** of, pertaining to, or derived from cows. [t. L: m.s. *vaccīnus* pertaining to cows]

vaccine point, *Med.* a thin, pointed, vaccine-coated piece of bone or the like, for use in vaccinating.

vac·cin·i·a (văk sĭn/ĭ ə), *n. Pathol.* cowpox. [NL, der. L *vaccinus* VACCINE (def. 4)]

vac·cin·i·a·ceous (văk sĭn/ĭ ā/shəs), *adj.* belonging to the *Vacciniaceae,* a family of plants usually included in the *Ericaceae,* containing the blueberry, whortleberry, huckleberry, cranberry, etc. [f. s. NL *Vacciniăceae,* pl., genus of plants (der. L *vaccinium* blueberry) + -OUS]

vac·ci·ni·za·tion (văk/sə nə zā/shən), *n. Med.* a vaccination produced by a series of virus inoculations.

vac·il·late (văs/ə lāt/), *v.i.*, **-lated, -lating. 1.** to sway unsteadily; waver; stagger. **2.** to fluctuate. **3.** to waver in mind or opinion; be irresolute or inconstant. [t. L: m.s. *vacillātus,* pp.] —**Syn. 1.** See **waver.**

vac·il·lat·ing (văs/ə lā/tĭng), *adj.* **1.** that vacillates; wavering. **2.** characterized by vacillation. Also, **vac·il·la·to·ry** (văs/ə lə tōr/ĭ). —**vac/il·lat/ing·ly,** *adv.*

vac·il·la·tion (văs/ə lā/shən), *n.* **1.** act of vacillating; wavering in mind or opinion; irresolution. **2.** an instance of this. **3.** unsteady movements.

vac·u·a (văk/yōō ə), *n.* pl. of **vacuum.**

va·cu·i·ty (vă kū/ə tĭ), *n.*, pl. **-ties. 1.** state of being vacuous or empty; absence of contents; emptiness. **2.** an empty space; a vacuum. **3.** absence or lack of something specified. **4.** vacancy of mind, thought, etc. **5.** absence of ideas or intelligence; inanity. **6.** something inane or senselessly stupid. [t. L: m. *vacuitas*]

vac·u·o·late (văk/yōō ə lĭt, -lāt/), *adj.* provided with or containing a vacuole or vacuoles. Also, **vac/u·o·lat/ed.**

vac·u·o·la·tion (văk/yōō ə lā/shən), *n.* **1.** the formation of vacuoles. **2.** state of being vacuolate. **3.** a system of vacuoles.

vac·u·ole (văk/yōō ōl/), *n.* **1.** a cavity within a cell, often containing a watery liquid or secretion. See diag. under **cell. 2.** a minute cavity or vesicle in organic tissue. [t. NL: m.s. *vacuolum,* dim. of *vacuum* VACUUM]

vac·u·ous (văk/yōō əs), *adj.* **1.** empty; without contents. **2.** empty of ideas or intelligence; stupidly vacant. **3.** showing mental vacancy: *a vacuous look.* **4.** purposeless; idle. [t. L: m. *vacuus*] —**vac/u·ous·ly,** *adv.* —**vac/u·ous·ness,** *n.*

vac·u·um (văk/yōō əm), *n.*, pl. **vacuums, vacua** (văk/-yōō ə), *adj., v.* —*n.* **1.** a space entirely void of matter (**perfect** or **complete vacuum**). **2.** an enclosed space from which air (or other gas) has been removed, as by an air pump (**partial vacuum**). **3.** the state or degree of

exhaustion in such an enclosed space. **4.** empty space. —*adj.* **5.** pertaining to, employing, or producing a vacuum. **6.** (of a hollow container) partly exhausted of gas. **7.** pertaining to apparatuses or processes which utilize gas pressures below atmospheric pressure. —*v.t.* **8.** *Colloq.* to clean with a vacuum cleaner or treat with any vacuum device. [t. L, prop. neut. of *vacuus* empty]

vacuum bottle, a bottle or flask protected by a vacuum jacket which prevents the escape of heat from hot contents or the entrance of heat to cold contents.

vacuum cleaner, an apparatus for cleaning carpets, floors, etc., by suction.

vacuum fan, a fan which ventilates a room or the like by drawing out the vitiated air by suction.

vacuum gauge, a device for measuring pressures below atmospheric pressure in the receiver of an air pump, in steam condensers, and the like.

vacuum pump, a pump or device by which a partial vacuum can be produced.

vacuum tube, *Electronics.* **1.** a sealed glass bulb used in radio and electronics to detect or rectify alternating currents, to generate electric oscillations, etc. In its typical form, as a triode, its elements are a heated cathode or filament (emitting electrons), the electron receiving plate (a metal plate at a positive potential), and the grid (a wire mesh or coil between cathode and plate) which by its potential controls the flow of electrons from cathode to plate. **2.** a sealed glass tube containing a partial vacuum or a highly rarefied gas, in which may be observed the effects of a discharge of electricity passed through the tube between electrodes leading into it. Also, *Brit.,* **vacuum valve.**

vacuum valve, *Brit.* a vacuum tube.

va·de me·cum (vā/dĭ mē/kəm), *Latin.* **1.** anything that a person carries about with him as being of service. **2.** a book for ready reference; a manual or handbook. [L: go with me]

vae vic·tis (vē vĭk/tĭs), *Latin.* woe to the vanquished. Livy V, 48 (words of Brennus, Gallic invader of Italy, 4th century B.C.).

vag·a·bond (văg/ə bŏnd/), *adj.* **1.** wandering from place to place without settled habitation; nomadic. **2.** leading an irregular or disreputable life. **3.** good-for-nothing; worthless. **4.** of or pertaining to a vagabond or vagrant: *vagabond habits.* **5.** moving about without certain direction. —*n.* **6.** one who is without a fixed abode and wanders from place to place. **7.** an idle wanderer without visible means of support; a tramp or vagrant. **8.** an idle, worthless fellow; a scamp; a rascal. [ME, t. L: m.s. *vagābundus* strolling about] —**Syn. 7.** See **vagrant.**

vag·a·bond·age (văg/ə bŏn/dĭj), *n.* **1.** state or habits of a vagabond; idle wandering. **2.** the class of vagabonds. Also, **vag/a·bond/ism.**

va·gar·y (və gâr/ĭ), *n.*, pl. **-garies. 1.** an extravagant idea or notion. **2.** a wild, capricious, or fantastic action; a freak. [appar. t. L: m. *vagārī* wander]

va·gi·na (və jī/nə), *n.*, pl. **-nas, -nae** (-nē). **1.** *Anat.* **a.** the passage leading from the uterus to the vulva in a female mammal. Cf. **oviduct. b.** a sheathlike part or organ. **2.** *Bot.* the sheath formed by the basal part of certain leaves where they embrace the stem. [t. L: sheath]

vag·i·nal (văj/ə nəl, və jī/nəl), *adj.* **1.** *Anat., etc.* pertaining to the vagina of a female mammal. **2.** pertaining to or resembling a sheath.

vag·i·nate (văj/ə nĭt, -nāt/), *adj.* furnished with a vagina or sheath; sheathed.

vag·i·ni·tis (văj/ə nī/tĭs), *n. Pathol.* inflammation of the vagina; colpitis. [NL. See VAGINA, -ITIS]

va·gran·cy (vā/grən sĭ), *n.*, pl. **-cies. 1.** the condition, conduct, or practice of a vagrant, idle vagabond, or idle and disorderly person. **2.** vagrant condition or life. **3.** an instance of it.

va·grant (vā/grənt), *n.* **1.** one who wanders from place to place; wanderer; rover. **2.** an idle wanderer; vagabond; tramp. **3.** *Law.* an idle or disorderly person, as a tramp, beggar, unlicensed peddler, prostitute, etc., whose habits of life are inconsistent with the good order of society, and who is liable to arrest and imprisonment. —*adj.* **4.** wandering or roaming from place to place; nomadic. **5.** living in idle vagabondage. **6.** characteristic of a vagrant: *a vagrant life.* **7.** (of plants) straggling in growth. **8.** (of things) not fixed or settled; moving hither and thither. [late ME *vag(a)raunt* wandering (person), der. freq. of ME *vague,* v., wander, t. L: m.s. *vagārī*] —**va/grant·ly,** *adv.* —**va/grant·ness,** *n.*

—**Syn. 2.** VAGRANT, VAGABOND describe an idle, disreputable person who lacks a fixed abode. VAGRANT suggests the idea of a tramp, a person with no settled abode or livelihood, an idle and disorderly person: *picked up by police as a vagrant.* VAGABOND especially emphasizes the idea of worthless living, often by trickery, thieving, or other disreputable means: *actors were once classed with rogues and vagabonds.*

va·grom (vā/grəm), *adj. Archaic.* vagrant.

vague (vāg), *adj.*, **vaguer, vaguest. 1.** not definite in statement or meaning; not explicit or precise: *vague promises.* **2.** of an indefinite or indistinct character, as ideas, feelings, etc. **3.** indistinct to the sight or other sense, or perceptible or recognizable only in an indefinite way: *vague forms seen through mist,* vague

A

B

A. Vaginate culm; B. Vaginate leaf

---

murmurs. **4.** not definitely fixed, determined, or known; uncertain. **5.** (of persons, etc.) indefinite in statement; not clear in thought or understanding. **6.** (of the eyes; expression, etc.) showing absence of clear perception or understanding. [t. L: m. *vagus* wandering] **—vague·ly**, *adv.* **—vague·ness**, *n.*

va·gus (vā′gǝs), *n.*, *pl.* **-gi** (-jī). *Anat.* either of two cranial nerves extending through the neck into the thorax and the upper part of the abdomen; a pneumogastric nerve. Also, **vagus nerve.** [t. L: wandering]

vail (vāl), *v.t.* *Archaic.* **1.** to cause or allow to descend or sink; lower. **2.** to take off or doff (a hat, etc.), as in respect or submission. [ME *vale*, aphetic var. of obs. *avale*, t. OF: m. *avaler* descend, der. phrase *à val* down, g. L *ad vallem* to the valley]

vain (vān), *adj.* **1.** without real value or importance; hollow, idle, or worthless; without force or efficacy; producing no good result; unavailing, futile, or useless: *vain entreaties, efforts, or regrets.* **2. in vain**, without effect or avail; to no purpose: *to strive or plead in vain.* **3.** having an excessive pride in one's own appearance, qualities, gifts, achievements, etc.; conceited. **4.** excessively proud (*of*). **5.** proceeding from or showing personal vanity: *vain boasts.* **6.** *Archaic.* senseless or foolish. [ME, t. OF, g. L *vānus* empty, idle] **—vain′ly**, *adv.* **—vain′ness**, *n.* **—Syn. 1.** See **useless. 3.** egotistical, self-complacent, vainglorious, proud, arrogant, overweening. **—Ant. 2.** effective. **3.** modest.

vain·glo·ri·ous (vān·glōr′ī·ǝs), *adj.* **1.** filled with or given to vainglory. **2.** characterized by, showing, or proceeding from vainglory. **—vain·glo′ri·ous·ly**, *adv.* **—vain·glo′ri·ous·ness**, *n.*

vain·glo·ry (vān·glōr′ī), *n.* **1.** inordinate elation or pride over one's achievements, abilities, etc. **2.** vain pomp or show. [ME; trans. of ML *vāna glōria*]

vair (vâr), *n.* a kind of fur much used for lining and trimming garments during the 13th and 14th centuries, and generally assumed to have been the skin of a variety of squirrel with a gray back and white belly. Cf. **miniver.** [ME, t. OF, g. L *varius* parti-colored]

Va·lais (và·lě′), *n.* a canton in SW Switzerland. 160,600 pop. (est. 1953); 2021 sq. mi. *Cap.:* Sion.

val·ance (văl′ǝns), *n.* **1.** a short curtain or piece of dependent drapery, as at the edge of a canopy, from the frame of a bed to the floor, etc. **2.** a short ornamental piece of drapery placed across the top of a window. [late ME; ? der. OF *avaler* descend. See **VAIL**] **—val′anced**, *adj.*

Val·dai Hills (văl·dī′), a region of hills and plateaus in the W Soviet Union at the source of the Volga river. Highest point, ab. 1150 ft.

Val·de·mar I (văl′dǝ·mär′). See **Waldemar I.**

vale[1] (vāl), *n.* *Chiefly Poetic.* a valley. [ME, t. OF: m. *val*, g. L *vallis*]

va·le[2] (vā′lī), *interj.*, *n.* *Latin.* good-by; farewell.

val·e·dic·tion (văl′ǝ·dĭk′shǝn), *n.* a bidding farewell; a leave-taking. [f. s. L *valedictus*, pp., bidden good-by + **-ION**]

val·e·dic·to·ri·an (văl′ǝ·dĭk·tōr′ī·ǝn), *n.* (in colleges and schools) the student (usually the one who ranks highest in scholarship) who pronounces the valedictory or farewell oration at the graduating exercises of his or her class.

val·e·dic·to·ry (văl′ǝ·dĭk′tǝ·rī), *adj.*, *n.*, *pl.* **-ries.** **—adj. 1.** bidding farewell; farewell. **2.** pertaining to an occasion of leave-taking. **—n. 3.** a valedictory address or oration. **4.** (in colleges and schools) the oration delivered by the valedictorian.

va·lence (vā′lǝns), *n.* *Chem.* **1.** the quality which determines the number of atoms or radicals with which any single atom or radical will unite chemically. **2.** the relative combining capacity of an atom or radical compared with the standard hydrogen atom: *a valence of one* (the capacity to unite with one atom of hydrogen or its equivalent). Also, **va′len·cy.** [t. L: m.s. *valentia* strength]

Va·len·ci·a (vǝ·lĕn′shĭ·ǝ, -chǝ; *Sp.* vä·lĕn′thyä), *n.* **1.** a region in E Spain: formerly a Moorish kingdom. 1,416,384 (est. 1955); 9085 sq. mi. **2.** a seaport in E Spain. 543,666 (est. 1956). **3.** a city in N Venezuela. 105,315 (est. 1953).

Va·len·ci·ennes (vǝ·lĕn′sĭ′ĕnz′; *Fr.* và·län·syĕn′), *n.* **1.** a city in N France. 43,434 (1954). **2.** a fine bobbin-made lace of which the pattern and the net ground are made together, of the same threads. **3.** a machine-made imitation of it. Also, **Valenciennes lace for 2, 3.**

Va·lens (vā′lĕnz), *n.* *Flavius.* (flā′vĭ·ǝs), *A.D.* c328–378, emperor of the Eastern Roman Empire, *A.D.* 364–378.

-valent, a word element meaning "having worth or value," used esp. in scientific terminology to refer to valence, as in *quadrivalent.* [t. L: s. *valens*]

val·en·tine (văl′ǝn·tīn′), *n.* **1.** an amatory or sentimental (sometimes satirical or burlesque) card or the like, or some token or gift, sent by one person to another on St. Valentine's Day. **2.** a sweetheart chosen on St. Valentine's Day. **3.** the object of one's affection.

Val·en·tine (văl′ǝn·tīn′), *n.* **Saint,** died *A.D.* c270, Christian martyr at Rome.

Val·en·tin·i·an (văl′ǝn·tĭn′ĭ·ǝn), *n.* name of three Roman emperors: **Valentinian I** (*A.D.* 321?–375), **Valentinian II** (*A.D.* c371–392), and **Valentinian III** (*A.D.* 419?–455). Also, **Val·en·tin·i·a·nus** (văl′ǝn·tĭn′ī·ā′nǝs).

Va·le·ra (vǝ·lâr′ǝ, -lĭr′ǝ; *Irish* vä·lā′rǝ), *n.* **Eamon De** (ā′mǝn). See **De Valera.**

Va·le·ra y Al·ca·lá Ga·lia·no (vä·lě′rä ē äl′kä·lä′ gä·lyä′nō), **Juan** (hwän), 1824–1905, Spanish novelist, critic, diplomat, and statesman.

va·le·ri·an (vǝ·lĭr′ĭ·ǝn), *n.* **1.** any of the perennial herbs constituting the genus *Valeriana*, as *V. officinalis,* a plant with white or pink flowers and a medicinal root. **2.** a drug consisting of or made from the root, used as a nerve sedative and antispasmodic. [ME, t. ML: s. *valeriāna,* fem. adj., der. *Valerius,* personal name]

Va·le·ri·an (vǝ·lĭr′ĭ·ǝn), *n.* (*Publius Licinius Valeri-anus*) died after *A.D.* 260, Roman emperor, *A.D.* 253–260.

va·le·ri·a·na·ceous (vǝ·lĭr′ĭ·ǝ·nā′shǝs), *adj.* belonging to the *Valerianaceae,* a family of plants containing valerian, spikenard, etc. [f. s. NL *Valeriānāceae* (see **VALERIAN**) + **-OUS**]

va·ler·ic (vǝ·lĕr′ĭk, -lĭr′-), *adj.* pertaining to or derived from valerian. Also, **va·le·ri·an·ic** (vǝ·lĭr′ī·ăn′ĭk). [f. **VALER**(**IAN**) + **-IC**]

valeric acid, *Chem.* any of several isomeric organic acids, C_4H_9COOH, the common one being a liquid of pungent odor obtained from valerian roots.

Va·lé·ry (vȧ·lě·rē′), *n.* **Paul** (pōl), 1871–1945, French poet and philosopher.

val·et (văl′ĭt, văl′ā; *Fr.* và·lě′), *n.*, *v.*, **-eted, -eting. —n. 1.** a manservant who is his employer's personal attendant, assisting in his toilet, caring for clothing, etc. **2.** one who performs similar services for patrons of a hotel, etc. **—v.t.**, *v.i.* **3.** to attend or act as valet. [t. F, var. of *varlet* **VARLET**] **—val′et·less**, *adj.*

va·let de cham·bre (và·lě′ dǝ shăn′br), *pl.* **valets de chambre** (và·lě′ dǝ shăn′br). *French.* valet (def. 1). [F, lit., chamber valet]

val·e·tu·di·nar·i·an (văl′ǝ·tū·dǝ·nâr′ĭ·ǝn, -tŏŏ′-), *n.* **1.** an invalid. **2.** one who affects invalidism or the condition or habits of an invalid. **—adj. 3.** in poor health; sickly; invalid. **4.** affecting invalidism. **5.** characterized by or pertaining to invalidism: *valetudinarian habits.* [f. s. L *valetūdinārius* in poor health + **-AN**]

val·e·tu·di·nar·i·an·ism (văl′ǝ·tū′dǝ·nâr′ĭ·ǝn·ĭz′ǝm, -tŏŏ′-), *n.* valetudinarian condition or habits.

val·e·tu·di·nar·y (văl′ǝ·tū′dǝ·nĕr′ĭ, -tŏŏ′-), *n.*, *pl.* **-naries**, *adj.* valetudinarian.

val·gus (văl′gǝs), *adj.* *Pathol.* of or pertaining to an abnormal position of a part of the human body, as **genu valgum**, knock-kneed, etc. [t. L: bowlegged]

Val·hal·la (văl·hăl′ǝ), *n.* *Scand. Myth.* the hall of immortality into which the souls of heroes slain in battle are received. Also, **Val·hall** (văl·hăl′), **Walhalla.** [t. NL, t. Icel.: m. *valhöll* hall of the slain]

val·ian·cy (văl′yǝn·sĭ), *n.* quality of being valiant; valor; bravery; courage. Also, **val′iance.** [var. of late ME *valiance,* t. AF, var. of OF *vaillance,* der. *vaillant* **VALIANT**]

val·iant (văl′yǝnt), *adj.* **1.** brave, courageous, or stout-hearted, as persons. **2.** marked by or showing bravery or valor, as deeds, attempts, etc. [ME, t. OF: m. *vaillant,* der. *valeir* be strong, g. L *valēre*] **—val′iant·ly,** *adv.* **—val′iant·ness**, *n.*

val·id (văl′ĭd), *adj.* **1.** sound, just, or well-founded: *a valid reason, a valid objection.* **2.** having force, weight, or cogency; authoritative. **3.** legally sound, effective, or binding; having legal force; sustainable in law. **4.** *Logic.* denoting arguments in which the premises imply the conclusion (opposed to *invalid*). **5.** *Archaic.* robust or well. [t. L: s. *validus* strong] **—val′id·ly,** *adv.* **—val′id·ness**, *n.*

val·i·date (văl′ǝ·dāt′), *v.t.*, **-dated, -dating. 1.** to make valid; confirm. **2.** to give legal force to; legalize. **—val′i·da′tion,** *n.*

va·lid·i·ty (vǝ·lĭd′ǝ·tĭ), *n.*, *pl.* **-ties. 1.** soundness, as of arguments, conclusions, etc. **2.** legal soundness or force.

va·lise (vǝ·lēs′), *n.* a traveler's case for holding clothes, toilet articles, etc., now esp. one of leather, of moderate size, for carrying by hand; a traveling bag. [t. F, t. It.: m. *valigia;* orig. uncert.]

Val·kyr·ie (văl·kĭr′ĭ, -kĭr′ĭ, văl′kĭr′ĭ), *n.* *Scand. Myth.* one of the handmaids of Odin who ride through the air to battle and choose the heroes who are to be slain and taken to Valhalla. Also, **Val·kyr** (văl′kĭr), **Wal·kyrie.** [t. Icel.: m. *valkyrja* chooser of the slain] **—Val·kyr′i·an,** *adj.*

Val·la·do·lid (vä′lyä·dō·lēd′), *n.* a city in N Spain: Columbus died here, 1506. 133,409 (est. 1955).

val·la·tion (vǝ·lā′shǝn), *n.* *Fort.* **1.** a rampart or entrenchment. **2.** the process or technique of constructing ramparts. [t. LL: s. *vallātio,* der. L *vallum* rampart]

val·lec·u·la (vǝ·lĕk′yǝ·lǝ), *n.*, *pl.* **-lae** (-lē′). *Anat., Bot.* a furrow or depression. [t. LL, dim. of L *valles* valley] **—val·lec′u·lar,** *adj.*

val·lec·u·late (vǝ·lĕk′yǝ·lāt′), *adj.* having a vallecula or valleculae.

Va·le·jo (vǝ·lā′hō), *n.* a city in W California, on San Pablo Bay, NE of San Francisco. 60,877 (1960).

Val·let·ta (vǝ·lĕt′ǝ), *n.* a seaport in and the capital of Malta, on the NE coast: naval station. 19,145 (est. 1953).

val·ley (văl′ĭ), *n.*, *pl.* **-leys. 1.** an elongated depression, usually with an outlet, between uplands, hills, or mountains, esp. one following the course of a stream. **2.** the extensive, more or less flat, and relatively low region drained by a great river system. **3.** any hollow or structure likened to a valley. **4.** *Archit.* a depression or angle formed by the meeting of two inclined sides of a roof. **5.** the lower phase of a horizontal wave motion. [ME *valey*, t. OF: m. *valee*, der. *val*, g. L *vallis*] —**val′-ley-like′**, *adj.*

Valley Forge, a village in SE Pennsylvania: winter quarters of George Washington and his army, 1777–78.

Valley of Ten Thousand Smokes, a volcanic area in SW Alaska, in the Katmai National Monument, including numerous small smoke and steam vents.

Valley Stream, a village in SE New York, on Long Island. 38,629 (1960).

Val·lom·bro·sa (väl′lôm brō′sä), *n.* a resort in central Italy, near Florence: famous abbey.

Va·lois (vȧ lwȧ′), *n.* **1.** a duchy of Ile de France in the Middle Ages. **2.** House of, a French dynasty, 1328–1589: a branch of the Capetian family.

Va·lo·na (vȧ lō′nä), *n.* a seaport in SW Albania, on Valona Bay, an inlet of the Adriatic. 14,640 (1945). Also, **Avlona**.

va·lo·ni·a (vȧ lō′nĬ ȧ), *n.* acorn cups of the **valonia oak**, *Quercus Aegilops*, used in tanning, dyeing, and making ink. [t. It.: m. *vallonia*, t. mod. Gk.: m. *balánia* acorns]

val·or (văl′ər), *n.* boldness or firmness in braving danger; bravery or heroic courage, esp. in battle. Also, *Brit.*, **val′our**. [t. LL (der. L *valēre* be strong, be worth); r. ME *valour*, t. OF] —**Syn.** See **courage**.

val·or·ize (văl′ə rīz′), *v.t.*, **-ized**, **-izing**. **1.** to assign a value to. **2.** (of a government) to fix the value or price of (a commercial commodity) and provide for maintaining it against a decline (as to a price below the cost of production), by purchase of the commodity at the fixed price or by other means (esp. with reference to the action of Brazil in fixing the price of coffee). [f. obs. *valor* worth (see VALOR) + -IZE] —**val′or·i·za′tion**, *n.*

val·or·ous (văl′ər əs), *adj.* **1.** having or displaying valor; valiant or brave, as persons. **2.** characterized by valor, as actions, etc. [late ME, t. ML: m.s. *valorōsus*] —**val′or·ous·ly**, *adv.* —**val′or·ous·ness**, *n.*

Val·pa·rai·so (văl′pə rī′sō, -zō), *n.* a seaport in central Chile. 222,238 (est. 1954). Spanish, **Val·pa·ra·í·so** (väl′pä rä ē′sō).

valse (väls), *n.* *French*. waltz.

val·u·a·ble (văl′yŏŏ ə bəl, văl′yə bəl), *adj.* **1.** of monetary worth. **2.** representing a large market value: *valuable paintings*. **3.** of considerable use, service, or importance: *valuable information*, *valuable aid*. **4.** capable of having the value estimated. —*n.* **5.** (usually pl.) a valuable article, as of personal property or of merchandise, esp. one of comparatively small size. —**val′u·a·ble·ness**, *n.* —**val′u·a·bly**, *adv.*
—**Syn.** **2.** costly, expensive, rare. VALUABLE, PRECIOUS refer to that which has pecuniary or other value. VALUABLE applies to whatever has value, but esp. to what has considerable value either in money or because of its usefulness, rarity, etc: *a valuable watch*. That which is PRECIOUS has a very high intrinsic value, or is very dear for its own sake, associations, or the like: *a precious jewel, friendship*. —**Ant.** **1.** worthless.

val·u·a·tion (văl′yŏŏ ā′shən), *n.* **1.** an estimating or fixing of the value of a thing. **2.** a value estimated or fixed; estimated worth. —**val′u·a′tion·al**, *adj.*

val·u·a·tor (văl′yŏŏ ā′tər), *n.* an appraiser.

val·ue (văl′ū), *n., v.,* **-ued**, **-uing**. —*n.* **1.** that property of a thing because of which it is esteemed, desirable, or useful, or the degree of this property possessed; worth, merit, or importance: *the value of education*. **2.** material or monetary worth, as in traffic or sale: *even the waste has value*. **3.** the worth of a thing as measured by the amount of other things for which it can be exchanged, or as estimated in terms of a medium of exchange. **4.** equivalent worth or equivalent return: *for value received*. **5.** estimated or assigned worth; valuation. **6.** force, import, or significance: *the value of a word or phrase*. **7.** (pl.) *Sociol.* the things of social life (ideals, customs, institutions, etc.) toward which the people of the group have an affective regard. These values may be positive, as cleanliness, freedom, education, etc., or negative, as cruelty, crime, or blasphemy. **8.** *Ethics*. any object or quality desirable as a means or as an end in itself. **9.** *Painting*. degree of lightness or darkness in a color. **10.** *Music*. the relative length or duration of a tone signified by a note. **11.** *Phonet.* **a.** quality. **b.** the phonetic equivalent of a letter: *one value of the letter "a" is the vowel sound in "hat," "sang," etc.*
—*v.t.* **12.** to estimate the value of; rate at a certain value or price; appraise. **13.** to consider with respect to worth, excellence, usefulness, or importance. **14.** to regard or esteem highly.
[ME, t. OF, pp. of *valeir* be worth, g. L *valēre*]
—**Syn.** **1.** VALUE, WORTH imply intrinsic excellence or desirability. VALUE is that quality of anything which renders it desirable or useful: *the value of sunlight or good books*. WORTH implies esp. spiritual qualities of mind and character, or moral excellence: *few knew his true worth*. **14.** See **appreciate**.

val·ued (văl′ūd), *adj.* **1.** highly regarded or esteemed. **2.** estimated or appraised. **3.** having the value specified.

val·ue·less (văl′yŏŏ lĬs), *adj.* without value; worthless. —**val′ue·less·ness**, *n.*

val·u·er (văl′yŏŏ ər), *n.* *Brit.* an appraiser.

val·vate (văl′vāt), *adj.* **1.** furnished with or opening by a valve or valves. **2.** serving as or resembling a valve. **3.** *Bot.* **a.** opening by valves, as certain capsules and

anthers. **b.** meeting without overlapping, as the parts of certain buds. **c.** composed of or characterized by such parts. [t. L: m.s. *valvātus* having folding doors]

valve (vălv), *n., v.,* **valved**, **valving**. —*n.* **1.** any device for closing or modifying the passage through a pipe, outlet, inlet, or the like, in order to control the flow of liquids, gases, etc. **2.** a hinged lid or other movable part in such a device, which closes or modifies the passage. **3.** *Anat.* a membranous fold or other structure which controls the flow of a fluid, as one which permits blood to flow in one direction only. **4.** (in musical wind instruments of the trumpet class) a device for changing the length of the air column to alter the pitch of a tone. **5.** *Zool.* **a.** one of the two or more separable pieces composing certain shells. **b.** either half of the silicified shell of a diatom. **6.** *Bot.* **a.** one of the segments into which a capsule dehisces. See diag. under **septicidal**. **b.** a flap or lidlike part of certain anthers. **7.** *Electronics. Brit.* an electron tube. **8.** *Archaic.* one of the halves or leaves of a double or folding door. —*v.t.* **9.** to provide with a means of control of fluid flow, as gas from a balloon, by inserting a valve. [ME, t. L: m. *valva* leaf of a door (pl. folding doors)] —**valve′less**, *adj.* —**valve′like′**, *adj.*

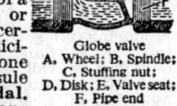

Globe valve
A. Wheel; B. Spindle; C. Stuffing nut; D, Disk; E. Valve seat; F, Pipe end

valve-in-head engine (vălv′ĭn hĕd′), an internal-combustion engine in which the cylinder head contains the inlet and exhaust valves.

valve·let (vălv′lĬt), *n.* a small valve; a valvule.

val·vu·lar (văl′vyə lər), *adj.* **1.** having the form of a valve. **2.** furnished with or operating by a valve or valves. **3.** of a valve or valves, esp. of the heart.

val·vule (văl′vūl), *n.* a small valve or valvelike part. [t. L: m. *valvula*, dim. of *valva*. See VALVE]

val·vu·li·tis (văl′vyə lī′tĬs), *n.* *Pathol.* inflammation of the cardiac valve leaflets, caused by an acute infectious process, usually rheumatic fever or syphilis. [f. s. NL *valvula* valvule + -ITIS]

val·vu·lot·o·my (văl′ vyə lŏt′ə mĬ′), *n., pl.* **-mies**. *Surg.* the opening, slitting, or fracturing of a heart valve along natural lines of cleavage. [NL, f. VALVUL(E) + -O- + -TOMY]

va·moose (vă mōōs′), *v.,* **-moosed**, **-moosing**. *U.S. Slang.* —*v.i.* **1.** to make off; decamp. —*v.t.* **2.** to decamp from; quit hurriedly. Also, **va·mose** (vă mōs′). [t. Sp.: m. *vamos* let us go]

vamp[1] (vămp), *n.* **1.** the front part of the upper of a shoe or boot, being the part between the sole and the top and in front of a line drawn downward from the ankle-bone or thereabout. **2.** a piece or patch added to an old thing to give it a new appearance. **3.** anything patched up or pieced together. **4.** *Music.* an accompaniment, usually improvised, consisting of a succession of simple chords. —*v.t.* **5.** to furnish with a vamp; esp., to repair with a new vamp, as a shoe or boot. **6.** to patch up or repair. **7.** to give an appearance of newness to. **8.** *Music.* to improvise (an accompaniment or the like). —*v.i.* **9.** *Music.* to improvise an accompaniment, tune, etc. [ME *vampe*, t. OF: alter. of *avanpie* forepart of the foot, f. *avant* before (g. L *ab ante* from in front) + *pie* foot, g. s. L *pēs*] —**vamp′er**, *n.*

vamp[2] (vămp), *Slang.* —*n.* **1.** a self-seeking or unscrupulous flirt. —*v.i.* **2.** to act as a vamp. —*v.t.* **3.** to use one's feminine charms or arts upon (a man). [short for VAMPIRE] —**vamp′er**, *n.*

vam·pire (văm′pīr), *n.* **1.** a preternatural being, in the common belief a reanimated corpse of a person improperly buried, supposed to suck the blood of sleeping persons at night. **2.** one who preys ruthlessly on others; an extortionist. **3.** a woman who uses her feminine charms or seductions to extract profit from male victims, or to feed her vanity at their expense. **4.** a self-seeking or unscrupulous flirt. **5.** an actress known for roles as a vampire. **6.** *Zool.* Also, **vampire bat. a.** any of various South and Central American bats including *Desmodus rotundus, Diphylla ecaudata,* and *Diaemus youngi*, the **true vampires**, which feed on the blood of animals including man. **b.** any large South American bat of the genera *Phyllostomus* and *Vampyrus*, erroneously reputed to suck blood. **c.** any of the false vampires of Asia and Australia. See **false vampire**. [t. F, t. G: m. *vampir*, ? ult. t. Turk.: m. *uber* witch] —**vam·pir·ic** (văm pĬr′Ĭk), **vam·pir·ish** (văm′pĬr′Ĭsh), *adj.*

Vampire.
Desmodus rufus
(3½ in. long)

vam·pir·ism (văm′pĬr Ĭz′əm, văm′pə rĬz′əm), *n.* **1.** the belief in the existence of preternatural vampires. **2.** acts or practices of vampires.

van[1] (văn), *n.* **1.** (formerly) the foremost division or the front part of an army, a fleet, or any body of individuals advancing, or in order for advancing. **2.** the forefront in any movement, course of progress, or the like. **3.** those who are in the forefront of a movement or the like. [short for VANGUARD]

van[2] (văn), *n.* **1.** a covered vehicle, usually of considerable size, for moving furniture, household effects,

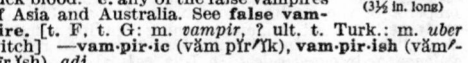

b., blend of, blended; c., cognate with; d., dialect, dialectal; der., derived from; f., formed from; g., going back to; m., modification of; r., replacing; s., stem of; t., taken from; ?, perhaps. See the full key on inside cover.

etc. **2.** *Brit.* a kind of vehicle, either covered or open, used by tradesmen for carrying light goods, etc. **3.** *Brit.* a covered railroad car for baggage, for accommodation of guards, etc. [short for CARAVAN]

van³ (văn; *Du.* vän; *Ger.* fän), *prep.* (in personal names) of; from: written with a small or capital *v* according to the preference of the person bearing the name. (In foreign languages it is commonly written with a small *v*.) [t. D]

van⁴ (văn), *n.* *Poetic.* a wing. [var. of FAN]

Van (văn), *n.* **1. Lake,** a salt lake in E Turkey. ab. 1450 sq. mi. **2.** a town on this lake. 13,471 (prelim. 1955).

vanad-, a word element indicating the presence of vanadium, as in *vanadate.*

van·a·date (văn'ə dāt'), *n.* *Chem.* a salt of a vanadic acid. Also, **va·na·di·ate** (və nā'dĭ āt').

va·nad·ic (və năd'ĭk, -nā'dĭk), *adj.* *Chem.* of or containing vanadium, esp. in the trivalent or pentavalent state.

vanadic acid, any of certain acids containing vanadium, esp. one with the formula H_3VO_4.

va·nad·i·nite (və năd'ə nīt'), *n.* a mineral, lead chlorovanadate, $Pb_5(VO_4)_3Cl$, occurring in yellow, brown, or greenish crystals: an ore of lead and vanadium.

va·na·di·um (və nā'dĭ əm), *n.* *Chem.* a rare element occurring in certain minerals, and obtained as a light-gray powder with a silvery luster: used as an ingredient of steel to toughen it and increase shock resistance. *Symbol:* V; *at. wt.:* 50.95; *at. no.:* 23; *sp. gr.:* 5.96. [f. Icel. *Vanad*(īs) epithet of goddess FREYA + -IUM; so called because discovered in Sweden]

vanadium steel, a special steel containing approx. 0.10–0.20 percent vanadium to increase elasticity, etc.

van·a·dous (văn'ə dəs), *adj.* *Chem.* containing divalent or trivalent vanadium. Also, **va·na·di·ous** (və nā'dĭ əs).

Van·brugh (văn brōō' or, esp. *Brit.,* văn'brə), *n.* **John** 1664–1726, British dramatist and architect.

Van Bu·ren (văn byŏŏr'ən), **Martin,** 1782–1862, 8th president of the U.S., 1837–41.

Van·cou·ver (văn kōō'vər), *n.* **1.** a large island in SW Canada, off the SW coast of British Columbia. 215,003 pop. (1951); 12,-408 sq. mi. **2.** a seaport in SW British Columbia, on Georgia Strait opposite SE Vancouver Island. 344,833; with suburbs, 530,728 (1951). **3.** a city in SW Washington. 32,464 (1960).

Van·dal (văn'dəl), *n.* **1.** a member of a Germanic people which in the 5th century A.D. ravaged Gaul and Spain, settled in Africa, and in 455 sacked Rome. **2.** (*l.c.*) one who willfully or ignorantly attacks or mars anything beautiful or valuable. —*adj.* **3.** of or pertaining to the Vandals. **4.** (*often l.c.*) imbued with or characterized by vandalism. [t. LL: s. *Vandalus,* Latinizat.on of native tribal name] —**Van·dal·ic** (văn dăl'ĭk), *adj.*

van·dal·ism (văn'də lĭz'əm), *n.* **1.** conduct or spirit characteristic of the Vandals. **2.** willful or ignorant destruction of artistic or literary treasures. **3.** hostility to what is beautiful or venerable. **4.** a vandalic act.

Van·den·berg (văn'dən bûrg'), *n.* **1. Arthur Hendrick** 1884–1951, U.S. statesman. **2. Hoyt Sanford,** 1899–1954, U.S. general: Chief of Staff of Air Force, 1948–1953.

Van·der·bilt (văn'dər bĭlt), *n.* **Cornelius,** 1794–1877, U.S. capitalist.

van der Waals' forces (văn dər wälz', vän dər väls), *Chem.* weak, non-specific forces between molecules. [named after J. D. *van der Waals,* 1837–1923, Dutch physicist]

Van Die·men's Land (văn dē'mənz), former name of Tasmania.

Van Do·ren (văn dōr'ən), **1. Carl,** 1885–1950, U.S. writer. **2.** his brother, **Mark,** born 1894, U.S. writer.

Van Dyck (văn dĭk'; *Flem.* vän), **Sir Anthony,** 1599–1641, Flemish painter who lived for some years in England. Also, **Vandyke.**

Van·dyke (văn dīk'), *adj.* **1.** of or pertaining to Sir Anthony Van Dyck, or the style of dress, etc., characteristic of his portraits. —*n.* (*usually l.c.*) **2.** a Vandyke beard. **3.** a Vandyke collar.

Vandyke beard, a short, pointed beard.

Vandyke brown, any of several dark-brown pigments consisting of iron oxide admixed with lampblack or similar materials.

Vandyke collar, a wide collar of lace or the like with the edge formed into deep points.

vane (văn), *n.* **1.** a flat piece of metal, or some other device, fixed upon a spire or other elevated object in such a way as to move with the wind and indicate its direction; a weathercock. **2.** a similar piece, or sail, in the wheel of a windmill, to be moved by the air. **3.** any plate, blade, or the like, attached to an axis, and moved by or in air or a liquid: *a vane of a screw propeller.* **4.** *Ornith.* the web of a feather. [ME; OE *fana* flag, c. G *fahne*] —**vaned,** *adj.* —**vane'less,** *adj.*

Vane (văn), *n.* **Sir Henry,** (*Sir Harry Vane*) 1613–1662, British statesman and author.

Vä·ner (vĕ'nər), *n.* a lake in SW Sweden. ab. 2150 sq. mi. Also, **Vä·nern** (vĕ'nərn) or **Vener.**

vang (văng), *n.* *Naut.* a rope extending from the peak of a gaff to the ship's rail, or to a mast, and used to steady the gaff. [t. D: catch]

Van Gogh (văn gō', gôkh'; *Du.* vän кнōкн'), **Vincent** (vĭn sĕnt'). See **Gogh.**

van·guard (văn'gärd'), *n.* **1.** the foremost division or the front part of an army; the van. **2.** the leading position in any field. **3.** the leaders of any intellectual or political movement. [late ME *vandgard,* t. OF: aphetic m. *avan*(t)-*garde,* f. *avant* before + *garde* guard]

va·nil·la (və nĭl'ə), *n.* **1.** any of the tropical climbing orchids constituting the genus *Vanilla,* esp. *V. planifolia,* whose podlike fruit (**vanilla bean**) yields an extract used in flavoring food, in perfumery, etc. **2.** the fruit or bean. **3.** the extract. [t. NL, t. Sp.: m. *vainilla* little pod, der. *vaina* sheath, g. L *vagina*]

Vanilla, *Vanilla planifolia* A. Flowering branch; B. Fruit

va·nil·lic (və nĭl'ĭk), *adj.* pertaining to, derived from, or resembling vanilla or vanillin.

van·il·lin (văn'ə lĭn, və nĭl'ĭn), *n.* a white crystalline compound, $C_8H_8O_3$, the active principle of vanilla, now prepared artificially and used as a flavoring agent and a substitute for vanilla. Also, **van·il·line** (văn'ə lĭn, -lēn', və nĭl'ĭn, -ēn).

Va·nir (vä'nĭr), *n.pl.* *Scand. Myth.* a race of gods originally at war with the Aesir, but later received into Asgard. Frey and Freya were of the Vanir. [t. Icel.]

van·ish (văn'ĭsh), *v.i.* **1.** to disappear from sight, or become invisible, esp. quickly. **2.** to disappear by ceasing to exist; come to an end; cease. **3.** *Math.* (of a number or quantity) to become zero. —*n.* **4.** *Phonet.* the last part of a vowel sound when it differs noticeably in quality from the main sound. [ME *vanisshen,* t. OF: aphetic m. *evaniss-,* s. *evanir.* See EVANESCE.] —**van'-ish·er,** *n.* —Syn. **1.** See **disappear.**

vanishing point, 1. a point of disappearance. **2.** *Perspective.* that point toward which receding parallel lines appear to converge.

van·i·ty (văn'ə tĭ), *n., pl.* **-ties. 1.** the quality of being personally vain; excessive pride in one's own appearance, qualities, gifts, achievements, etc. **2.** an instance or display of this quality or feeling. **3.** something about which one is vain. **4.** vain or worthless character; want of real value; hollowness or worthlessness. **5.** something vain or worthless. **6.** a vanity case. **7.** a dressing table. [ME *vanite,* t. OF, t. L: m.s. *vānitas* emptiness] —Syn. **1.** conceit, self-esteem, egotism. See **pride. 4.** emptiness, unreality, sham, folly.

vanity case, a small case fitted with a mirror, a powder puff, etc., carried by a woman. Also, **vanity box, vanity bag.**

Vanity Fair, 1. (in Bunyan's *Pilgrim's Progress*) a fair which goes on perpetually in the town of Vanity. It symbolizes worldly ostentation and frivolity. **2.** any place or scene, as the world, a great city, or the world of fashion, regarded as given over to vain pleasure or empty show. **3.** a novel (1847–48) by Thackeray.

Van Loon (văn lōn'), **Hendrik Willem** (hĕn'drĭk vĭl'əm), 1882–1944, U.S. author, born in Netherlands.

van·quish (văng'kwĭsh, văn'-), *v.t.* **1.** to conquer or defeat in battle or conflict; reduce to subjection by superior force. **2.** to defeat in any contest. **3.** to overcome or overpower. [ME *vencusche,* t. OF: m. *vencus,* pp. of *veintre,* g. L *vincere*] —**van'quish·a·ble,** *adj.* —**van'quish·er,** *n.*

Van Rens·se·laer (văn rĕn'sə lər, -lĭr'), **Stephen,** ("*the Patroon*") 1765–1839, U.S. political leader and major general.

van·tage (văn'tĭj, vän'-), *n.* **1.** position or condition affording superiority, as for action. **2.** opportunity likely to give superiority. **3.** *Tennis.* advantage. [ME, aphetic m. *avantage* ADVANTAGE.]

vantage ground, a position which gives one an advantage, as for action or defense; favorable position.

Va·nu·a Le·vu (vä nōō'ä lĕ'vōō), one of the Fiji Islands, in the S Pacific. 39,958 (1946); 2137 sq. mi.

Van Vech·ten (văn vĕk'tən), **Carl,** born 1880, U.S. author.

van·ward (văn'wərd), *adj.* toward or in the van or front (opposed to *rearward*).

Van·zet·ti (văn zĕt'ĭ; *It.* vän dzĕt'tē), *n.* **Bartolomeo** (bär'tô lô mĕ'ô), 1888–1927, Italian political radical, in the U.S. See **Sacco, Nikola.**

vap·id (văp'ĭd), *adj.* **1.** having lost life, sharpness, or flavor; insipid; flat. **2.** without animation or spirit; dull, uninteresting, or tedious, as talk, writings, persons, etc. [t. L: s. *vapidus*] —**va·pid'i·ty, vap'id·ness,** *n.* —**vap'id·ly,** *adv.* —Ant. **1.** pungent. **2.** stimulating.

va·por (vā'pər), *n.* **1.** a visible exhalation, as fog, mist, condensed steam coming from a teakettle, smoke, atomized medicinal liquid, etc. **2.** a substance in the gaseous state (sometimes restricted to substances in the gaseous state when below their critical points); a gas. **3.** matter converted into vapor for technical or medicinal uses, etc. **4.** a combination of vaporized matter and air: *the vapor in an automobile cylinder.* **5.** gaseous particles of drugs that can be inhaled as a therapeutic agent. **6.** an invisible exhalation, as of moisture.

noxious gases, etc. **7.** something unsubstantial or transitory. **8.** (*pl.*) *Archaic.* hypochondria, low spirits, or the blues. **9.** (*pl.*) *Obs.* injurious exhalations formerly supposed to be produced within the body, esp. the stomach. —*v.t.* **10.** to cause to rise or pass off in, or as in, vapor. **11.** *Archaic.* to affect with vapors or the blues. —*v.i.* **12.** to rise or pass off in the form of vapor. **13.** to emit vapor or exhalations. **14.** to talk or act grandiloquently or boastfully; bluster. Also, *Brit.*, **vapour.** [t. L: steam; r. ME *vapour*, t. AF] —**va′por·er,** *n.* —**va′por·less,** *adj.* —**va′por·like′,** *adj.*

va·por·es·cence (vā′pə rĕs′əns), *n.* a changing into vapor. [f. VAPOR + -ESCENCE] —**va′por·es′cent,** *adj.*

va·por·if·ic (vā′pə rĭf′ĭk), *adj.* **1.** producing vapor, or connected with the production of vapor; tending towards vapor. **2.** pertaining to or of the nature of vapor. [t. NL: s. *vaporificus*]

va·por·im·e·ter (vā′pə rĭm′ə tər), *n.* an instrument for measuring vapor pressure or volume.

va·por·ing (vā′pər ĭng), *adj.* **1.** that vapors. **2.** foolishly boastful. —*n.* **3.** act of bragging or blustering; ostentatious or windy talk. —**va′por·ing·ly,** *adv.*

va·por·ish (vā′pər ĭsh), *adj.* **1.** of the nature of vapor. **2.** abounding in vapor. **3.** inclined to or affected by the vapors or low spirits; depressed.

va·por·i·za·tion (vā′pər ə zā′shən), *n.* **1.** the process by which a liquid is converted into vapor. **2.** the rapid change of water into steam, esp. in a boiler. **3.** *Med.* a vapor therapy.

va·por·ize (vā′pə rīz′), *v.*, **-ized, -izing.** —*v.t.* **1.** to cause to pass into the gaseous state. —*v.i.* **2.** to become converted into vapor. Also, esp. *Brit.*, **va′por·ise′.** —**va′por·iz′a·ble,** *adj.*

va·por·iz·er (vā′pə rī′zər), *n.* **1.** one who or that which vaporizes. **2.** a form of atomizer.

va·por·ous (vā′pər əs), *adj.* **1.** full of or abounding in vapor; foggy or misty. **2.** dimmed or obscured with vapor. **3.** of the form of vapor; unsubstantial. **4.** given to fanciful or foolish ideas or discourse. —**va′por·ous·ly,** *adv.* —**va′por·ous·ness,** **va·por·os·i·ty** (vā′pə rŏs′ə tĭ), *n.*

vapor tension, vapor pressure; the elastic pressure of a vapor, esp. that of the water vapor in the atmosphere.

va·por·y (vā′pə rĭ), *adj.* **1.** vaporous. **2.** vaporish.

va·pour (vā′pər), *n.*, *v.t.*, *v.i.* *Brit.* vapor.

va·que·ro (vä kĕ′rō), *n.*, *pl.* **-ros** (-rōs). *Spanish America and Southwestern U.S.* a herdsman or cowboy. [t. Sp., der. *vaca* cow, g. L *vacca*]

var., **1.** variant. **2.** variation. **3.** variety. **4.** various.

va·ra (vä′rä), *n.* **1.** a unit of length in Spanish and Portuguese speaking countries varying from about 32 in. to about 43 in. **2.** the square vara, as a unit of area. [t. Sp., Pg.: rod, pole, g. L *vāra* forked pole]

Va·ran·gi·an (və răn′jĭ ən), *n.* one of the Northmen who under Rurik established a dynasty in Russia in the 9th century. [der. ML *Varangus*, ult. t. Scand.; cf. Icel. *Væringi*]

Var·dar (vär′där), *n.* a river flowing from SE Yugoslavia through N Greece into the Gulf of Salonika. ab. 200 mi.

Var·gas (vär′gəs), *n.* **Getulio Dornelles** (zhə too̅′lyo̅o̅ do̅o̅r nĕ′lĭs), 1883–1954, Brazilian statesman.

var·i·a·ble (vâr′ĭ ə bəl), *adj.* **1.** apt or liable to vary or change; changeable. **2.** capable of being varied or changed; alterable. **3.** inconstant or fickle, as a person. **4.** *Biol.* deviating from the usual type, as a species or a specific character. **5.** *Astron.* (of a star) changing in brightness. **6.** *Meteorol.* (of wind) tending to change in direction. —*n.* **7.** something variable. **8.** *Math.* a symbol which may represent any one of a given set of objects. **9.** *Astron.* a star whose light varies in intensity. **10.** *Meteorol.* a shifting wind, esp. as opposed to a tradewind. **11.** (*pl.*) a region where such winds occur. —**var′i·a·bil′i·ty,** **var′i·a·ble·ness,** *n.* —**var′i·a·bly,** *adv.* —**Ant.** **1.** constant.

Variable Zones, *Geog.* Temperate Zones.

va·ri·a lec·ti·o (vâr′ĭ ə lĕk′shĭ ō′), *pl.* **variae lectiones** (vâr′ĭ ē′ lĕk′shĭ ō′nēz), *Latin.* a variant reading.

var·i·ance (vâr′ĭ əns), *n.* **1.** state or fact of varying; divergence or discrepancy. **2.** an instance of this; difference. **3.** *Statistics.* the square of the standard deviation. **4.** *Phys. Chem.* the maximum number of conditions which can be varied without altering the number of phases in a phase-rule system. **5.** *Law.* **a.** a difference or discrepancy, as between two statements or documents in law which should agree. **b.** a departure from the cause of action originally stated in the complaint. **6.** a disagreement, dispute, or quarrel. **7. at variance, a.** in a state of difference, discrepancy, or disagreement, as things. **b.** in a state of controversy or of dissension as persons. [ME, t. OF]

var·i·ant (vâr′ĭ ənt), *adj.* **1.** exhibiting diversity; varying; tending to change or alter. **2.** being an altered or different form of something: *a variant spelling of a word.* —*n.* **3.** a variant form. **4.** a different form or spelling of the same word: *"lanthorn" is an old variant of "lantern."* **5.** a different reading of a passage. **6.** *Statistics.* the numerical value of an attribute belonging to a statistical item. [ME, t. L: s. *varians*, ppr., varying]

var·i·ate (vâr′ĭ ĭt), *n.* *Statistics.* the numerical value of an attribute belonging to a statistical item.

var·i·a·tion (vâr′ĭ ā′shən), *n.* **1.** act or process of varying; change in condition, character, degree, etc. **2.** an instance of this, or a point of difference. **3.** amount or rate of change. **4.** a different form of something; a variant. **5.** *Music.* **a.** the transformation of a melody or theme with changes or elaborations in harmony, rhythm, and melody. **b.** a varied form of a melody or theme, esp., one of a series of such forms developing the capacities of the subject. **6.** *Astron.* **a.** any deviation from the mean orbit of a heavenly body, esp. of a planetary or satellite orbit. **b.** an inequality in the moon's motion having a period of one-half synodic month. **7.** *Biol.* **a.** a deviation in the structure or character of an organism from that of others of the same species or group, or that of the parents. **b.** an organism exhibiting such deviation; variety. [ME *variacio(u)n*, t. L: m.s. *variātio*] —**var′i·a′tion·al,** *adj.*

var·i·cel·la (vâr′ə sĕl′ə), *n.* *Pathol.* chicken pox. [t. NL: f. *vari(ola)* VARIOLA + -*cella*, dim. suffix]

var·i·cel·late (vâr′ə sĕl′ĭt, -āt), *adj.* having small varices, as certain shells. [f. s. NL *varicella* (alter. of L *varicula*, dim. of *varix* varicose vein) + -ATE¹]

var·i·cel·loid (vâr′ə sĕl′oid), *adj.* resembling varicella.

var·i·ces (vâr′ə sēz′), *n.* pl. of **varix.**

varico-, a word element meaning "varicose veins," as in *varicocele.* Also, before vowels, **varic-.** [comb. form repr. L *varix* VARIX]

var·i·co·cele (vâr′ə kō sēl′), *n.* *Pathol.* a varicose condition of the spermatic veins of the scrotum. [t. NL, f. *varico-* VARICO- + -*cele* (t. Gk.: m. *kēlē* tumor)]

var·i·col·ored (vâr′ĭ kŭl′ərd), *adj.* **1.** having various colors; variegated in color; motley. **2.** varied; assorted. Also, *Brit.*, **var′i·col′oured.**

var·i·cose (vâr′ə kōs′, vâr′-), *adj.* **1.** permanently lengthened, dilated, and usually tortuous, as a vein. **2.** pertaining to, affected with, varices or varicose veins, which often affect the superficial portions of the lower limbs. [t. L: m.s. *varicōsus.* See VARIX]

var·i·co·sis (vâr′ə kō′sĭs), *n.* *Pathol.* **1.** the formation of varices. **2.** varicosity. [f. VARIC(O)- + -OSIS]

var·i·cos·i·ty (vâr′ə kŏs′ə tĭ), *n.*, *pl.* **-ties.** *Pathol.* **1.** state or condition of being varicose. **2.** varix.

var·ied (vâr′ĭd), *adj.* **1.** made various, diversified; characterized by variety: *a varied assortment.* **2.** changed or altered: *a varied form of a word.* **3.** variegated, as in color, as an animal. —**var′ied·ly,** *adv.* —**var′ied·ness,** *n.*

varied thrush, a plump, robinlike thrush, *Ixoreus naevius*, of western North America, having black and gray upper parts and orange-tan under parts, with a dark band across the chest. Also, **varied robin.**

var·i·e·gate (vâr′ĭ ə gāt′, -ĭ gāt′), *v.t.*, **-gated, -gating.** **1.** to make varied in appearance; mark with different colors, tints, etc. **2.** to give variety to; diversify. [t. LL: m.s. *variegātus*, pp. (def. 1)]

var·i·e·gat·ed (vâr′ĭ ə gā′tĭd, -ĭ gā′tĭd), *adj.* **1.** varied in appearance or color; marked with patches or spots of different colors. **2.** varied; diversified; diverse.

var·i·e·ga·tion (vâr′ĭ ə gā′shən, -ĭ gā′shən), *n.* **1.** act of variegating. **2.** state or condition of being variegated; varied coloration.

va·ri·e·tal (və rī′ə təl), *adj.* **1.** of, pertaining to, or characteristic of a variety. **2.** constituting a variety. —**va·ri·e·tal·ly,** *adv.*

va·ri·e·ty (və rī′ə tĭ), *n.*, *pl.* **-ties.** **1.** state or character of being various or varied; diversity, or absence of uniformity or monotony. **2.** difference or discrepancy. **3.** a number of things of different kinds. **4.** a kind or sort. **5.** a different form, condition, or phase of something. **6.** a category within a species, based on some hereditary difference not considered great enough to distinguish species. **7.** a group or type of animals or plants produced by artificial selection. **8.** *Chiefly Brit. Theat.* entertainment of mixed character, consisting of a number of individual performances or "acts," as of singing, dancing, acrobatic exhibitions, playlets, etc. (often used attributively as *variety show, theater, actor*). Cf. vaudeville. **9.** difference or discrepancy. [t. L: m.s. *varietas*] —**Syn.** **3.** diversity, multiplicity. **6.** assortment, collection, group. **7.** kind, sort, class, species.

var·i·form (vâr′ĭ fôrm), *adj.* varied in form; having various forms. [f. s. L *varius* various + -FORM]

va·ri·o·la (və rī′ə lə), *n.* *Pathol.* smallpox. [t. ML, der. L *varius* various, spotted)

va·ri·o·lar (və rī′ə lər), *adj.* variolous.

va·ri·o·late (vâr′ĭ ə lāt′), *v.t.*, **-lated, -lating.** to inoculate with virus of variola. —**var′i·o·la′tion,** *n.*

var·i·ole (vâr′ĭ ōl′), *n.* **1.** a shallow pit or depression like the mark left by a smallpox pustule; a foveola. **2.** *Petrog.* one of the spherules of variolite.

var·i·o·lite (vâr′ĭ ə līt′), *n.* *Petrog.* any of certain fine-grained, basic igneous rocks containing light-colored spherules, which, esp. on weathered surfaces, give them a pock-marked appearance. [f. VARIOL(A) + -ITE¹]

var·i·o·lit·ic (vâr′ĭ ə lĭt′ĭk), *adj.* *Petrog.* **1.** of or resembling variolite, esp. in texture. **2.** spotted; speckled.

var·i·o·loid (vâr′ĭ ə loid′), *adj.* **1.** resembling variola or smallpox. **2.** pertaining to varioloid. —*n.* **3.** a mild smallpox, esp. as occurring in persons who have been vaccinated or have previously had smallpox.

va·ri·o·lous (və rī′ə ləs), *adj.* **1.** pertaining to variola

---

b., blend of, blended; c., cognate with; d., dialect, dialectal; der., derived from; f., formed from; g., going back to; m., modification of; r., replacing; s., stem of; t., taken from; ?, perhaps. See the full key on inside cover.

or smallpox. **2.** affected with smallpox. **3.** having pits like those left by smallpox. Also, **variolar.**

var·i·om·e·ter (vâr′Y̆ŏm′ə tər), *n.* *Elect.* **1.** an instrument for comparing the intensity of magnetic forces, esp. the magnetic force of the earth, at different points. **2.** an instrument for varying inductance, consisting of a fixed coil and a movable coil connected in series (used as a tuning device). [f. *vario-* (comb. form repr. L *varius* various) + -METER]

var·i·o·rum (vâr′Y̆ ōr′əm), *adj.* **1.** (of an edition, etc.) characterized by various versions of the text or commentaries by various editors: *a variorum edition of Shakespeare.* —*n.* **2.** a variorum edition, text, etc. [short for L *ēditio cum notis variōrum* edition with notes of various persons]

var·i·ous (vâr′Y̆ əs), *adj.* **1.** differing one from another, or of different kinds, as two or more things. **2.** divers, several, or many: *in various parts of the world.* **3.** exhibiting or marked by variety or diversity. **4.** differing in different parts, or presenting differing aspects. [t. L: m. *varius*] —**var′i·ous·ly,** *adv.* —**var′i·ous·ness,** *n.* —**Syn. 1.** VARIOUS, DIFFERENT, DISTINCT, DIVERSE refer to things which are sufficiently unlike to be perceivably of more than one kind. VARIOUS implies that there are several kinds of the same general thing: *various types of seaweed.* DIFFERENT is applied either to a single thing differing in identity or character from another, or to two or more things differing thus from one another: *two different stories concerning an event.* DISTINCT implies want of connection between things, which, however, may possibly be alike or similar: *two distinct accounts which coincide.* DIVERSE commonly implies a number or assortment of things or parts differing one from another: *three completely diverse proposals for preventing inflation.* —**Ant. 1.** identical, same, similar, uniform.

var·ix (vâr′Y̆ks), *n.*, *pl.* **varices** (vâr′ə sēz′). **1.** *Pathol.* a permanent abnormal dilation and lengthening of a vein, usually accompanied by some tortuosity; a varicose vein. **2.** *Zool.* a mark or scar on the surface of a shell at a former position of the lip of the aperture. [ME, t. L: dilated vein]

var·let (vär′lY̆t), *n.* *Archaic.* **1.** an attendant. **2.** a page attached to a knight. **3.** a low fellow or a rascal. [ME, t. OF, var. of *va(s)let* VALET. See VASSAL]

var·let·ry (vär′lY̆ trY̆), *n.* *Archaic.* **1.** varlets collectively. **2.** the mob or rabble.

var·mint (vär′mənt), *n.* *Dial.* vermin. Also, **var′ment.**

Var·na (vär′nä), *n.* a seaport in NE Bulgaria, on the Black Sea. 77,792 (1946). Also, **Stalin.**

var·nish (vär′nY̆sh), *n.* **1.** a preparation which consists of resinous matter (as copal, lac, etc.) dissolved in an oil (**oil varnish**) or in alcohol (**spirit varnish**) or other volatile liquid, and which, when applied to the surface of wood, metal, etc., dries and leaves a hard, more or less glossy, usually transparent coating. **2.** the sap of certain trees, used for the same purpose (**natural varnish**). **3.** any of various other preparations similarly used, as one having India rubber, pyroxylin, or asphalt for the chief constituent. **4.** a coating or surface of varnish. **5.** something resembling a coating of varnish; a gloss. **6.** a merely external show, or a veneer. —*v.t.* **7.** to lay varnish on. **8.** to invest with a glossy appearance. **9.** to give an improved appearance to; embellish; adorn. **10.** to cover with a specious or deceptive appearance. [ME *vernisshe(n)*, t. OF: m. *vernisser*, der. *vernis* varnish, n., t. ML: m. *vernicium* sandarac, sweet-smelling resin, t. MGk.: m. *berníkē*, Gk. *Beroníkē*, a city in Cyrenaica] —**var′nish·er,** *n.*

varnish tree, any of various trees yielding sap or other substances used for varnish, as *Rhus verniciflua* of Japan. See **lacquer.**

Var·ro (vär′ō), *n.* **Marcus Terentius** (mär′kəs tə rĕn′shY̆ əs), c116–27? B.C., Roman scholar and author.

var·si·ty (vär′sə tY̆), *n.*, *pl.* **-ties. 1.** colloquial reduction of *university*, used esp. with reference to sports. **2.** the first-string team, in any activity, which will represent a school, college, university, or the like.

Var·u·na (vär′ŏŏ na, vŭr′-), *n.* (in the Hindu Rig-Veda) the god of the sky or heaven, all-encompassing and all-seeing. [t. Skt.: deity]

var·us (vâr′əs), *n.* *Pathol.* abnormal angulation of bone or joint, with the angle pointing away from midline. [t. L: bandy-legged]

var·y (vâr′Y̆), *v.*, **varied, varying.** —*v.t.* **1.** to change or alter, as in form, appearance, character, substance, degree, etc. **2.** to cause to be different, one from another. **3.** to diversify (something); relieve from uniformity or monotony. **4.** *Music.* to alter (a melody or theme) by modification or embellishments, without changing its identity. —*v.i.* **5.** to be different, or show diversity, in different parts, specimens, etc., as a thing. **6.** to undergo change in form, appearance, character, substance, degree, etc. **7.** *Math.* to be subject to change. **8.** to change in succession, follow alternately, or alternate. **9.** *Biol.* to exhibit variation. [ME, t. L: m.s. *variāre,* der. *varius* various] —**var′i·er,** *n.* —**var′y·ing·ly,** *adv.*

vas (văs), *n.*, *pl.* **vasa** (vā′sə). *Anat., Zool., Bot.* a vessel or duct. [t. L: vessel]

Va·sa·ri (vä zä′rē), *n.* **Giorgio** (jôr′jō), 1511–74, Italian painter, architect, and art historian.

vas·cu·lar (văs′kyə lər), *adj.* *Zool., Bot.* pertaining to, composed of, or provided with vessels or ducts which convey fluids, as blood, lymph, or sap. Also, **vas·cu-**

lose (văs′kyə lōs′), **vas·cu·lous** (văs′kyə ləs). [t. NL: s. *vāsculāris,* der. L *vāsculum* little vessel] —**vas·cu·lar·i·ty,** *n.* —**vas′cu·lar·ly,** *adv.*

vascular bundle, bundle (def. 4).

vascular tissue, *Bot.* plant tissue consisting of ducts or vessels which, in highly developed plants, form the system by which sap is conveyed through the plant.

vas·cu·lum (văs′kyə ləm), *n.*, *pl.* **-la** (-lə), **-lums.** a kind of case or box used by botanists for carrying specimens as they are collected. [t. L, dim. of *vās* vessel]

vas de·fe·rens (văs dĕf′ə rĕnz′), *pl.* **vasa deferentia** (vā′sə dĕf′ə rĕn′shY̆ ə). the deferent duct of the testicle which transports the sperm from the epididymus to the penis. [L: vessel carrying down]

vase (vās, vāz *or, esp. Brit.,* väz), *n.* a hollow vessel, generally higher than wide, now chiefly used as a flower container or for decoration. [t. F, t. L: m. *vās* vessel] —**vase′like′,** *adj.*

vas·ec·to·my (vă sĕk′tə mY̆), *n.*, *pl.* **-mies.** *Surg.* excision of the vas deferens, or of a portion of it.

Vas·e·line (văs′ə lēn′, -lY̆n), *n.* *Trademark.* a translucent, yellow or whitish, semisolid petroleum product (a form of petrolatum), used as a remedial ointment and internal remedy, and in various medicinal and other preparations. [f. *vas* (t. G: m. *wasser* water) + *-el-* (t. Gk.: m. *élaion* oil) + -INE²]

vaso-, a word element meaning "vessel," as in *vaso-constrictor.* [comb. form repr. L *vās* vessel]

vas·o·con·stric·tor (văs′ō kən strY̆k′tər), *adj.* *Physiol.* serving to constrict blood vessels, as certain nerves or chemical substances.

vas·o·di·la·tor (văs′ō dî lā′tər, -dY̆-), *adj.* *Physiol.* serving to dilate or relax blood vessels, as certain nerves or chemical substances.

vas·o·mo·tor (văs′ō mō′tər), *adj.* *Physiol.* serving to regulate the caliber of blood vessels, as certain nerves.

vas·sal (văs′əl), *n.* **1.** (in the feudal system) a person holding lands by the obligation to render military service or its equivalent to his superior. **2.** a feudatory tenant. **3.** a person holding some similar relation to a superior; a subject, follower, or retainer. **4.** *Archaic.* a servant or slave. —*adj.* **5.** pertaining to or characteristic of a vassal. **6.** being a vassal or in vassalage. [ME, t. OF, g. LL *vassallus,* der. *vassus* servant; of Celtic orig.] —**vas′sal·less,** *adj.*

vas·sal·age (văs′əl Y̆j), *n.* **1.** state of being a vassal; the status of a vassal. **2.** homage or service due from a vassal. **3.** a territory held by a vassal. **4.** *Hist.* a body of vassals. **5.** dependence, subjection, or servitude.

vast (văst, väst), *adj.* **1.** of very great extent or area; very extensive, or immense. **2.** of very great size or proportions; huge; enormous. **3.** very great in number, quantity, or amount, or as number, quantity, etc.: *a vast army, a vast sum.* **4.** very great in degree, intensity, etc.: *in vast haste, vast importance.* —*n.* **5.** *Chiefly Poetic.* a vast expanse or space. [t. L: s. *vastus*] —**vast′ly,** *adv.* —**vast′ness,** *n.*

vas·ti·tude (văs′tY̆ tūd′, -tōōd′, väs′-), *n.* **1.** vastness or immensity. **2.** a vast expanse or space.

vast·y (văs′tY̆, väs′tY̆), *adj.* *Poetic.* vast; immense.

vat (văt), *n.*, *v.*, **vatted, vatting.** —*n.* **1.** a large container for liquids. —*v.t.* **2.** to put into or treat in a vat. [ME; OE *fæt*, c. G *fass* keg]

Vat., Vatican.

vat·ic (văt′Y̆k), *adj.* prophetic. Also, **vat′i·cal.** [appar. back formation from VATICINAL]

Vat·i·can (văt′ə kən), *n.* **1.** Also, **Vatican Palace.** the palace of the popes in Rome: a mass of buildings containing a library, museums of art, etc., immediately to the north of St. Peter's Church (the chief residence of the popes since 1377). **2.** the papal power or government, as distinguished from the Quirinal (representing the Italian government). [t. L: s. *Vāticānus (mons)* Vatican (hill)]

Vatican City, an independent state within the city of Rome, on the right bank of the Tiber: established in 1929, it is ruled by the Pope and includes St. Peter's Church and the Vatican. ab. 1000 (est. 1954); 109 acres.

va·tic·i·nal (və tY̆s′ə nəl), *adj.* prophetic. [f. s. L *Vāticinus* prophetic + -AL¹]

va·tic·i·nate (və tY̆s′ə nāt′), *v.t.*, *v.i.*, **-nated, -nating.** to prophesy. [t. L: m.s. *vāticinātus,* pp.] —**va·tic′i·na′tor,** *n.*

va·tic·i·na·tion (văt′ə sə nā′shən), *n.* **1.** prophesying. **2.** a prophecy.

Vät·ter (vĕt′tər), *n.* a lake in S Sweden. ab. 80 mi. long; 733 sq. mi. Also, **Vät′tern** (vĕt′tərn) or **Vetter.**

Vau·ban (vō bäN′), *n.* **Sébastien le Prestre de** (sĕ bäs tyäN′ lə prĕ′tr də), 1633–1707, French military engineer and marshal.

Vaud (vō), *n.* a canton in W Switzerland. 382,700 pop. (est. 1952); 1239 sq. mi. *Cap.*: Lausanne. German, **Waadt.**

vaude·ville (vōd′vY̆l, vô′də vY̆l), *n.* **1.** *Chiefly U.S.* theatrical entertainment consisting of a number of individual performances, acts, or mixed numbers, as of singing, dancing, gymnastic exhibitions, etc. (often used attributively, as in *vaudeville performance, sketch*). **2.** a theatrical piece of light or amusing character, interspersed with songs and dances. [t. F, alter. of *chanson du Vau de Vire* song of the Valley of Vire (in Normandy)]

Vau·dois (vō·dwä′), *n., pl.* **-dois.** **1.** a native or inhabitant of Vaud (a Swiss canton). **2.** the dialect spoken there.

Vau·dois (vō·dwä′), *n.pl.* the Waldenses.

Vaughan (vôn), *n.* **Henry,** 1622–95, British poet and mystic.

Vaughan Wil·liams (vôn wĭl′yəmz), **Ralph,** 1872–1958, British composer.

vault[1] (vôlt), *n.* **1.** an arched structure, commonly made of stones, concrete, or bricks, forming a ceiling or roof over a hall, room, sewer, or other wholly or partially enclosed construction. **2.** an arched space, chamber, or passage, esp. one underground. **3.** an underground chamber, as a cellar or a division of a cellar. **4.** *Anat.* an arched roof of a cavity. **5.** something resembling an arched roof: *the vault of heaven.* —*v.t.* **6.** to construct or cover with a vault. **7.** to make in the form of a vault; arch. [ME *vaute,* t. OF: m. *voute,* g. Rom. *volta,* der. *vol(vi)tus,* r. L *volūtus,* pp., turned, rolled] —**vault′like′,** *adj.*

Vaults (def. 1)
A. Barrel; B. Intersecting

vault[2] (vôlt), *v.i.* **1.** to leap or spring, as to or from a position or over something. **2.** to leap with the aid of the hands supported on something, sometimes on a pole: *to vault over a fence or a bar.* —*v.t.* **3.** to vault over: *to vault a fence.* —*n.* **4.** act of vaulting. [ME *voute,* t. OF: m. *vouter*] —**vault′er,** *n.* —**Syn. 1.** See **jump.**

vault·ed (vôl′tĭd), *adj.* **1.** constructed or covered with a vault, as a building, chamber, etc. **2.** provided with a vault or vaults, as below the surface of the grounds.

vault·ing[1] (vôl′tĭng), *n.* **1.** act or process of constructing vaults. **2.** the structure forming a vault or vaults. **3.** a vault, vaulted ceiling, or the like, or such structures collectively. [f. VAULT[1] + -ING[1]]

vault·ing[2] (vôl′tĭng), *adj.* **1.** that vaults. **2.** used in vaulting: *a vaulting pole.* **3.** exaggerated: *vaulting conceit.* [f. VAULT[2] + -ING[2]]

vaunt (vônt, vänt), *v.t.* **1.** to speak vaingloriously or boastfully of. —*v.i.* **2.** *Archaic or Literary.* to talk vaingloriously or boastfully; boast; brag. —*n.* **3.** vainglorious or boastful utterance. [ME *vaunt(en),* t. F: m. *vanter,* g. LL *vānitāre,* der. L *vānus* vain] —**vaunt′er,** *n.* —**vaunt′ing·ly,** *adv.*

vaunt-cour·i·er (vänt′kŏor′ĭ ər, vônt′-), *n.* *Archaic.* one who goes in advance, as a herald.

vaunt·y (vôn′tĭ), *adj.* *Scot.* boastful; vainly ostentatious.

vav·a·sor (văv′ə sôr′), *n.* (in the feudal system) a vassal, or feudal tenant, holding of a great lord (but not of the sovereign). Also, **vav·a·sour** (văv′ə sŏor′). [ME, t. OF, g. ML *vassus vassōrum* vassal of vassals]

vb., **1.** verb. **2.** verbal.

V.C., 1. Veterinary Corps. **2.** Vice-Chairman. **3.** Vice-Chamberlain. **4.** Vice-Chancellor. **5.** Vice-Consul. **6.** Victoria Cross.

Vd, *Chem.* vanadium.

V.D., venereal disease.

v.d., various dates.

V-Day (vē′dā′), *n.* the day proclaimed in the United States by President Truman as marking the final victory for the Allies in World War II (Dec. 31, 1946).

Ve·a·dar (vē′ä där′, vä′-), *n.* (in the Jewish calendar) an intercalary month of 29 days inserted, when required, after Adar. [t. Heb.: and (yet another) Adar]

veal (vēl), *n.* **1.** a calf, esp. as intended or used for food. **2.** the flesh of the calf as used for food. [ME *veel,* t. OF, g. L *vitellus* little calf]

Veb·len (vĕb′lən), *n.* **Thorstein** (thôr′stĭn), 1857–1929, U.S. economist.

vec·tor (vĕk′tər), *n.* **1.** *Math.* a complex quantity possessing both magnitude and direction and represented by any of a system of equal and parallel (and similarly directed) line segments. **2.** *Biol.* an insect or other organism transmitting germs or other agents of disease. [t. L: carrier] —**vec·to·ri·al** (vĕk tōr′ĭ əl), *adj.*

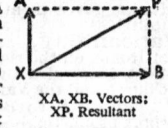

XA, XB, Vectors;
XP, Resultant

vector field, a region, each point of which is characterized by a definite value of some vector quantity; a field of force.

Ved., Vedic.

Ve·da (vā′də, vē′də), *n.* (*sometimes pl.*) the entire sacred scriptures of Hinduism, esp. as comprising the four Books of Wisdom which have the word 'Veda' in their titles: **Rig-Veda** or **The Veda** of Psalms or Verses, the **Yajur-Veda** or **The Veda** of Sacred Formulas, **Sama-Veda** or **The Veda Chants,** and the **Atharva-Veda** or **The Veda** of Charms. [t. Skt.:lit.,knowledge] —**Ve·da·ic** (vĭ dā′ĭk), *adj.* —**Ve·da·ism** (vā′də ĭz′əm, vē′-), *n.*

Ve·dan·ta (vĭ dän′tə, -dăn′-), *n.* the chief philosophy among the Hindus, a system of idealistic monism, chiefly as expounded by the philosopher S(h)ankara about 800 A.D., with some varieties occurring later. It is concerned with the end of the Vedas, both chronologically and teleologically. [t. Skt., f. *Veda* VEDA + *anta* end] —**Ve·dan′tic,** *adj.* —**Ve·dan′tism,** *n.* —**Ve·dan′tist,** *n.*

V-E Day, the day of victory in Europe for the Allies in World War II (May 8, 1945).

Ved·da (vĕd′ə), *n.* a Ceylon aborigine. Also, **Ved′-dah.** [t. Sinhalese: hunter]

ve·dette (və dĕt′), *n.* **1.** Also, **vedette boat.** a small naval launch used for scouting. **2.** a mounted sentry in advance of the outposts of an army. Also, **vidette.** [t. F, t. It.: m. *vedetta,* der. *vedere* see, g. L *vidēre*]

Ve·dic (vā′dĭk, vē′dĭk), *adj.* **1.** of or pertaining to the Veda or Vedas. —*n.* **2.** the language of the Veda, closely related to classical Sanskrit.

vee (vē), *n.* **1.** *Colloq.* *U.S.* a five-dollar bill. —*adj.* **2.** in the shape of a V.

veep (vēp), *n.* *Colloq.* a vice-president, esp. (*cap.*) of the United States. [for V.P.(Vice-President), modeled on JEEP.]

veer[1] (vĭr), *v.i.* **1.** to turn or shift to another direction, or point of the compass, as the wind or anything moving with the wind. **2.** to change direction, or turn about or aside; shift, change, or vary. **3.** (of the wind) **a.** to change direction by moving round the points of the compass in the usual manner. See **back**[1] (def. 21). **b.** *Naut.* to shift more aft in relation to the vessel's course (opp. to *haul*). —*n.* **4.** a change of direction. [t. F: m. *virer,* g. LL *gīrāre* turn (der. *gȳrus* a turn, t. Gk.: m. *gȳros*) b. with *vertere* turn] —**veer′ing·ly,** *adv.*

veer[2] (vĭr), *v.t.* *Naut.* to slacken or let out: *to veer chain.* [late ME *vere,* t. MD: m.s. *vieren* let out]

veer·y (vĭr′ĭ), *n., pl.* **veeries.** a thrush, *Hylocichla fuscescens,* common in the eastern U.S., of retiring habits and noted for its song; the Wilson's thrush. [prob. imit.]

Ve·ga (vē′gə), *n.* *Astron.* a brilliant white star of the first magnitude, in the constellation Lyra. [t. Sp. or t. ML, t. Ar.: m. *wāqi* the falling (vulture)]

Ve·ga (vā′gä), Lope de. See **de Vega.**

Ve·ga Car·pio (vā′gä kär′pyō). See **de Vega.**

veg·e·ta·ble (vĕj′tə bəl, vĕj′ə-), *n.* **1.** any herbaceous plant, annual, biennial, or perennial, whose fruits, seeds, roots, tubers, bulbs, stems, leaves, or flower parts are used as food, mainly with the entree, as tomato, bean, beet, potato, asparagus, cabbage, etc. **2.** the edible part of such plants, as the fruit of the tomato or the tuber of the potato. **3.** any member of the vegetable kingdom; a plant. —*adj.* **4.** of, consisting of, or made from edible vegetables: *a vegetable diet, a vegetable dinner.* **5.** pertaining to or characteristic of plants: *vegetable life or processes.* **6.** derived from plants or some part of plants: *vegetable fiber, vegetable oils.* **7.** consisting of or containing the substance or remains of plants: *vegetable matter.* **8.** of the nature of a plant; consisting of or comprising plants: *a vegetable organism, the vegetable kingdom.* [ME, t. LL: m. *vegetābilis* vivifying]

vegetable butter, any of various concrete, fixed, vegetable fats which are solid at ordinary temperatures, but usually melt at or below body temperature.

vegetable ivory, See **ivory** (def. 8).

vegetable kingdom, the plants of the world collectively (distinguished from *animal kingdom*).

vegetable marrow, a kind of squash of oblong form, the fruit of a variety of *Cucurbita Pepo,* used as a vegetable, esp. in England.

vegetable silk, a fine and glossy fiber, kindred to silk cotton, borne on the seeds of *Chorisia speciosa* of Brazil, a member of the *Bombacaceae.*

vegetable tallow, any of several tallowlike substances of vegetable origin, used in making candles, soap, etc., and as lubricants.

vegetable wax, a wax or waxlike substance obtained from various plants, as the wax palm.

veg·e·tal (vĕj′ə təl), *adj.* **1.** pertaining to or of the nature of plants or vegetables; vegetable. **2.** characterized by or pertaining to the series of vital phenomena common to plants and animals (esp. as distinguished from *rational* and *volitional*). **3.** vegetative (def. 3).

veg·e·tant (vĕj′ə tənt), *adj.* **1.** encouraging vigorous, healthy development. **2.** of vegetative life as it differs from animal life. [t. L: s. *vegetans,* ppr., enlivening]

veg·e·tar·i·an (vĕj′ə tär′ĭ ən), *n.* **1.** one who on principle lives on vegetable food (refusing meat, etc.), or maintains that vegetables and farinaceous substances constitute the only proper food for man. —*adj.* **2.** of or pertaining to the practice or principle of living solely or chiefly on vegetable food. **3.** devoted to or advocating this practice. **4.** consisting of vegetables.

veg·e·tar·i·an·ism (vĕj′ə tär′ĭ ə nĭz′əm), *n.* the belief in or practice of eating only fruits and vegetables.

veg·e·tate (vĕj′ə tāt′), *v.i.,* **-tated, -tating.** **1.** to grow in the manner of plants; increase as if by vegetable growth. **2.** to live like vegetables, in an inactive, passive, or unthinking way. **3.** *Pathol.* to grow, or increase by growth, as an excrescence. [t. L: m.s. *vegetātus,* pp., enlivened]

veg·e·ta·tion (vĕj′ə tā′shən), *n.* **1.** plants collectively; the communities of plants in a region, as distinct from the flora or census of kinds: *mountains bare of vegetation.* **2.** act or process of vegetating. **3.** *Pathol.* a morbid growth or excrescence. —**veg′e·ta′tion·al,** *adj.*

veg·e·ta·tive (vĕj′ə tā′tĭv), *adj.* **1.** vegetating; growing or developing as or like plants. **2.** pertaining to or connected with vegetation or vegetable growth. **3.** denoting the parts of a plant not specialized for reproduction. **4.** (of reproduction) asexual. **5.** denoting or pertaining to those bodily functions which, being performed unconsciously or involuntarily, are likened to the processes of vegetable growth; inactive; quiescent.

6. having the power to produce or support growth in plants: *vegetative mold.* Also, **veg·e·tive** (vĕj′ə tĭv). —**veg′e·ta′tive·ly,** *adv.* —**veg′e·ta′tive·ness,** *n.*

ve·he·mence (vē′ə məns), *n.* **1.** the quality of being vehement; violent ardor; fervor; fire. **2.** impetuosity; violence; fury. Also, **ve′he·men·cy.**

ve·he·ment (vē′ə mənt), *adj.* **1.** eager, impetuous, or impassioned, in feeling, action, or speech, as persons. **2.** characterized by violence of feeling or endeavor: *vehement opposition.* **3.** passionate, as feeling: *vehement desire, vehement dislike.* [late ME, t. L: s. *vehemens*] —**ve′he·ment·ly,** *adv.*

ve·hi·cle (vē′ə kəl), *n.* **1.** any receptacle, or means of transport, in which something is carried or conveyed, or travels. **2.** a carriage or conveyance moving on wheels or runners. **3.** a means of conveyance, transmission, or communication: *air is the vehicle of sound.* **4.** a medium by which ideas or effects are communicated: *language was with him a mere vehicle for thought.* **5.** *Phar.* a substance, usually fluid, possessing little or no medicinal action, used as a medium for active remedies. **6.** *Painting.* a liquid, as oil, in which a pigment is mixed before being applied to a surface. [t. L: m.s. *vehiculum* conveyance]

ve·hic·u·lar (vē hĭk′yə lər), *adj.* **1.** of or pertaining to a vehicle or vehicles. **2.** serving as a vehicle.

Vehm·ge·richt (fām′gə rĭ̄кнт′), *n.,* *pl.* **-richte** (-rĭ̄кн′-tə). *German.* any of a class of irregular tribunals in medieval Germany, esp. in Westphalia, often meeting in secret, and exercising broad powers, including the power of life and death in case of serious crimes. [G: punishment tribunal]

Ve·ii (vē′yī), *n.* an ancient Etruscan city in central Italy, near Rome: often at war with ancient Rome.

veil (vāl), *n.* **1.** a piece of material, usually light and more or less transparent, worn, esp. by women, over the head or face, as to conceal the face or to protect it from the sun or wind. **2.** a piece of material worn so as to fall over the head and shoulders on each side of the face, forming a part of the headdress of a nun. **3.** the life accepted or the vows made by a woman, when she makes either her novice's vows and takes the white veil, or her irrevocable vows and takes the black veil of a nun. **4. take the veil,** to enter a convent; become a nun. **5.** something that covers, screens, or conceals: *a veil of smoke or mist.* **6.** a mask, disguise, or pretense. *Bot., Anat., Zool.* a velum. **8.** *Dial.* a caul. —*v.t.* **9.** to cover or conceal with or as with a veil. **10.** to hide the real nature of; mask; disguise. [ME, t. AF, g. L *vēlum* sail, covering] —**veiled,** *adj.* —**veil′less,** *adj.* —**veil′like′,** *adj.*

veil·ing (vā′lĭng), *n.* **1.** a veil. **2.** a thin net for veils.

vein (vān), *n.* **1.** one of the system of branching vessels or tubes conveying blood from various parts of the body to the heart. **2.** (loosely) any blood vessel. **3.** one of the tubular riblike thickenings that ramify in an insect's wing. **4.** one of the strands or bundles of vascular tissue forming the principal framework of a leaf. **5.** any body or stratum of ore, coal, etc. clearly separated or defined. **6.** a body or mass of igneous rock, deposited mineral, or the like, occupying a crevice or fissure in rock; a lode. **7.** a small natural channel or watercourse within the earth, or the water running through it. **8.** a streak or marking, as of a different shade or color, running through marble, wood, etc. **9.** some line, course, or the like suggestive of a vein. **10.** a strain or intermixture of some quality traceable in character or conduct, writing, etc.: *a vein of stubbornness, to write in a poetic vein.* —*v.t.* **11.** to furnish with veins. **12.** to mark with lines or streaks suggesting veins. **13.** to extend over or through (something) in the manner of veins. [ME *veine,* t. OF, g. L *vēna*] —**veined,** *adj.* —**vein′less,** *adj.* —**vein′like′,** *adj.*

vein·ing (vā′nĭng), *n.* a process of forming or arrangement of veins or veinlike markings.

vein·let (vān′lĭt), *n.* a small vein.

vein·stone (vān′stōn′), *n.* gangue.

vein·ule (vān′ūl), *n.* a venule. [t. F, t. L: m. *vēnula* little vein]

vein·y (vā′nĭ), *adj.,* **veinier, veiniest.** full of veins; veined.

vel., vellum.

ve·la (vē′lə), *n.* pl. of **velum.**

ve·la·men (və lā′mĭn), *n.,* *pl.* **-lamina** (-lăm′ə nə). **1.** *Anat.* a membranous covering; a velum. **2.** *Bot.* the thick, spongy integument or epidermis covering the aerial roots of epiphytic orchids. [t. L: covering]

ve·lar (vē′lər), *adj.* **1.** of or pertaining to a velum or veil, esp. that of the palate. **2.** *Phonet.* with the back of the tongue held close to or touching the soft palate. —*n.* **3.** a velar sound. [t. L: s. *vēlāris,* der. *vēlum* curtain]

ve·lar·i·um (və lâr′ī əm), *n.,* *pl.* **-laria** (-lâr′ī ə). *Rom. Antiq.* an awning drawn over a theater or amphitheater as a protection from rain or the sun. [t. L]

ve·lar·ize (vē′lə rīz′), *v.t.,* **-ized, -izing.** *Phonet.* to pronounce with velar articulation.

ve·late (vē′lĭt, -lāt), *adj.* **1.** veiled. **2.** *Bot., Zool.* having a velum. —*v.t.* **3.** *Phonet.* to velarize. [t. L: m.s. *vēlātus* veiled]

ve·la·tion (vē lā′shən), *n.* *Phonet.* pronunciation with velar articulation. [t. LL: s. *vēlātiō*]

Ve·láz·quez (vē läth′kĕth), *n.* **Diego Rodríguez de Silva y** (dyĕ′gō rô drē′gĕth dĕ sēl′vä ē), 1599–1660, Spanish painter. Also, **Ve·lás·quez** (vē läs′kĕth).

veld (vĕlt, fĕlt), *n.* the open country, bearing grass, bushes, or shrubs, or thinly forested, characteristic of parts of southern Africa. Also, **veldt.** [t. S Afr. D: field]

ve·li·tes (vē′lə tēz′), *n.pl.* light-armed ancient Roman soldiers. [t. L]

vel·le·i·ty (və lē′ə tĭ), *n.,* *pl.* **-ties. 1.** volition in its weakest form. **2.** a mere wish, unaccompanied by an effort to obtain it. [t. ML: m.s. *velleitas,* der. L *velle* wish]

vel·li·cate (vĕl′ə kāt′), *v.t., v.i.,* **-cated, -cating.** to pluck or twitch. [t. L: m.s. *vellicātus,* pp., der. *vellere*] —**vel′li·ca′tion,** *n.* —**vel′li·ca′tive,** *adj.*

vel·lum (vĕl′əm), *n.* **1.** a sheet of calfskin prepared as parchment for writing or bookbinding. **2.** a manuscript or the like on such parchment. **3.** a texture of paper or cloth resembling that of such parchment. —*adj.* **4.** made of or resembling vellum. **5.** bound in vellum. [ME *velym,* t. OF: m. *velin,* der. *veel* VEAL]

ve·lo·ce (vĕlō′chĕ), *adj.* *Music.* with velocity and spirit in tempo. [It., quick, g. s. L *vēloz*]

ve·loc·i·pede (və lŏs′ə pēd′), *n.* **1.** a bicyclelike vehicle, usually with two wheels or three wheels, impelled by the rider. **2.** an early kind of bicycle or tricycle. **3.** a kind of handcar used on railroads. [t. F: m. *vēlocipède,* f. L: *vēlōci-* swift + m.s. *pēs* foot]

ve·loc·i·ty (və lŏs′ə tĭ), *n.,* *pl.* **-ties. 1.** rapidity of motion or operation; swiftness; quickness. **2.** *Physics.* a time rate of change of displacement. **3.** *Mech.* **a.** a time rate of change of position. **b.** a rate of motion in which direction as well as speed is considered. [t. L: m.s. *vēlōcitas* swiftness] —**Syn. 1.** See **speed.**

ve·lours (və lo͝or′; *Fr.* -loŏr′), *n. sing. and pl.* a French term for velvet. Also, **ve·lour′.** [t. F: velvet, earlier *velous,* t. Pr.: m. *velos,* ult. der. L *villus* hair]

ve·lou·té (və lo͞o tĕ′), *n.* *French.* a smooth white sauce made with chicken or veal stock. Also, **velouté sauce.** [F, der. *velours* velvet]

ve·lum (vē′ləm), *n.,* *pl.* **-la** (-lə). **1.** *Biol.* any of various veillike or curtainlike membranous partitions. **2.** *Anat.* the soft palate. [t. L: sail, covering]

ve·lure (və lo͝or′), *n., v.,* **-lured, -luring.** —*n.* **1.** velvet or a substance resembling it. **2.** a hatters' pad of velvet, plush, or the like, for smoothing or dressing silk hats. —*v.t.* **3.** to smooth or dress (a hat) with a velure. [var. of *velour* VELOURS]

ve·lu·ti·nous (və lo͞o′tə nəs), *adj.* having a soft, velvety surface, as certain plants. [t. NL: m. *velutinus,* der. ML *velutum* velvet]

vel·vet (vĕl′vĭt), *n.* **1.** a fabric of silk, silk and cotton, cotton, etc. with a thick, soft pile formed of loops of the warp thread either cut at the outer end (as in ordinary velvet) or left uncut (as in uncut or terry velvet). **2.** something likened to the fabric velvet in softness, etc. **3.** the soft, deciduous covering of a growing antler. **4.** *Slang.* money gained through gambling or speculation. **5.** *Slang.* clear gain or profit. —*adj.* **6.** made of velvet or covered with velvet. **7.** resembling velvet; velvety; smooth and soft. [ME, t. ML: s. *velvetum,* ult. der. L *villus* shaggy hair] —**vel′vet·like′,** *adj.*

velvet carpet, a carpet or rug of pile weave resembling Wilton.

vel·vet·een (vĕl′və tēn′), *n.* **1.** a cotton pile fabric with short pile. **2.** (*pl.*) trousers or knickerbockers made of velveteen. —*adj.* **3.** Also, **vel′vet·eened′.** made of velveteen. [der. VELVET]

vel·vet·y (vĕl′vĭ tĭ), *adj.* **1.** like or suggestive of velvet; smooth and soft. **2.** (of liquor, etc.) having no harshness; smooth. **3.** gentle and smooth in contact.

Ven., 1. Venerable. **2.** Venice.

ve·na (vē′nə), *n., pl.* **-nae** (-nē). *Anat.* a vein. [L]

ve·na ca·va (vē′nə kā′və), *pl.* **venae cavae** (vē′-nē kā′vē). *Anat.* either of two large veins discharging into the right auricle of the heart. See diag. under **heart.** [L: hollow vein]

ve·nal (vē′nəl), *adj.* **1.** ready to sell one's services or influence unscrupulously; accessible to bribery; corruptly mercenary. **2.** purchasable like mere merchandise, as things not properly bought and sold. **3.** characterized by venality: *a venal period, a venal agreement.* [t. L: s. *vēnālis* for sale] —**ve′nal·ly,** *adv.* —**Syn. 1.** See **corrupt.**

ve·nal·i·ty (vē nǎl′ə tĭ), *n., pl.* **-ties.** the quality of being venal; prostitution of talents or principles for money or reward.

ve·nat·ic (vē năt′ĭk), *adj.* of or pertaining to hunting. Also, **ve·nat′i·cal.** [t. L: s. *vēnāticus*] —**ve·nat′i·cal·ly,** *adv.*

ve·na·tion (vē nā′shən), *n.* **1.** the arrangement of veins, as in a leaf or an insect's wing. **2.** these veins collectively. [t. NL: s. *vēnātio,* der. L *vēna* vein] —**ve·na′tion·al,** *adj.*

Leaf venations
A. Pinnate; B. Palmate; C. Parallel

vend (vĕnd), *v.t.* **1.** to dispose of by sale; sell. **2.** to give utterance to (an opinion, etc.). —*v.i.* **3.** to vend something. **4.** to be disposed of by sale. [t. L: s. *vendere* sell]

vend·ee (vĕn dē′), *n.* *Chiefly Legal.* the person to whom a thing is vended or sold.

Ven·dée (vän dā′), *n.* a department in W France, on the Atlantic: royalist revolt, 1793–95. 395,641 pop. (1954); 2709 sq. mi. *Cap.:* La Roche-sur-Yon.

Ven·dé·miaire (vän dě myēr′), *n. French.* (in the calendar of the first French republic) the first month of the year, extending from Sept. 22 to Oct. 21. [F, der. L *vindēmia* grape gathering]

vend·er (věn′dər), *n.* 1. one who vends or sells, esp. in the streets. 2. a vending machine.

ven·det·ta (věn dět′ə), *n.* a state of private war in which a murdered man s relatives execute vengeance on the slayer or his relatives; a blood feud, esp. as existing in Corsica and parts of Italy. [t. It., g. L *vindicta* vengeance] —**ven·det′tist,** *n.*

vend·i·ble (věn′də bəl), *adj.* 1. capable of being vended or sold; salable. 2. mercenary; venal. —*n.* 3. a vendible article. —**vend′i·bil′i·ty, vend′i·ble·ness,** *n.* —**vend′i·bly,** *adv.*

vending machine, a coin-operated machine for selling small articles.

ven·di·tion (věn dǐsh′ən), *n.* act of vending; sale.

Ven·dôme (vän dōm′), *n.* **Louis Joseph de** (lwē zhô-zěf′ də), 1654–1712, French general and marshal.

ven·dor (věn′dər, věn dôr′), *n.* 1. *Chiefly Legal.* one who vends, or disposes of a thing by sale. 2. vending machine. [f. VEND + -OR²]

ven·due (věn dū′, -dōō′), *n.* a public auction. [t. D: m. *vendu,* t. OF: m. *vendue* sale, der. *vendre* sell]

ve·neer (və nēr′), *v.t.* 1. to overlay or face (wood) with thin sheets of some material such as fine woods, ivory, tortoise shell, etc. 2. to cover (an object) with a thin layer of costly material, to give an appearance of superior quality. 3. to cement (layers of wood veneer) to form plywood. 4. to give a merely superficially fair appearance to. —*n.* 5. a thin layer of wood of a superior kind, or other fine material, used in veneering. 6. one of the several layers of plywood. 7. a merely superficial fair appearance or show: *a veneer of good manners.* [t. G: m. *furnir,* t. F: m. *fournir.* See FURNISH] —**ve·neer′er,** *n.*

ve·neer·ing (və nēr′ǐng), *n.* 1. the process, work, or craft of applying veneers. 2. material applied as a veneer. 3. the surface thus formed. 4. a merely superficial show or outward display: *a veneering of civilization.*

ven·e·nose (věn′ə nōs′), *adj. Now Rare.* poisonous.

Ve·ner (vě′nər), *n.* Väner.

ven·er·a·ble (věn′ər ə bəl), *adj.* 1. worthy of veneration or reverence, as on account of high character or office. 2. commanding respect by reason of age and dignity of appearance. 3. (of places, buildings, etc.) hallowed by religious, historic, or other lofty associations. 4. impressive or interesting from age, antique appearance, etc. 5. ancient: *a venerable error.* [ME, t. L: m. *venerābilis*] —**ven′er·a·bil′i·ty, ven′er·a·ble·ness,** *n.* —**ven′er·a·bly,** *adv.*

ven·er·ate (věn′ə rāt′), *v.t.* **-ated, -ating.** to regard with reverence, or revere. [t. L: m.s. *venerātus,* pp., having reverenced] —**ven′er·a′tor,** *n.*

ven·er·a·tion (věn′ə rā′shən), *n.* 1. act of venerating. 2. state of being venerated. 3. the feeling of one who venerates; reverence: *filled with veneration for the traditions of one's country.* 4. the outward expression of reverent feeling. —**Syn.** 3. See **respect.**

ve·ne·re·al (və nēr′ē əl), *adj.* 1. arising from or connected with sexual intercourse with an infected person: *venereal disease.* 2. pertaining to diseases so arising. 3. infected with or suffering from venereal disease. 4. adapted to the cure of such disease: *a venereal remedy.* 5. of or pertaining to sexual desire or intercourse. [ME; f. s. L *venereus* pertaining to Venus + -AL¹]

ven·er·er (věn′ər ər), *n. Pseudoarchaic.* a huntsman.

ven·er·y¹ (věn′ər ĭ), *n. Archaic.* the gratification of sexual desire. [f. s. L *Venus* goddess of love + -Y³]

ven·er·y² (věn′ər ĭ), *n. Archaic.* the practice or sport of hunting; the chase. [ME *venerye,* t. OF: m. *venerie,* der. *vener* hunt, g. L *vēnāri*]

ven·e·sec·tion (věn′ə sěk′shən, vě′nə-), *n. Med.* phlebotomy. [f. ML *vēnē* (gen. sing. of *vēna* vein) + s. L *sectio* a cutting]

Ve·ne·ti·a (və nē′shǐ ə, -shə), *n.* 1. an ancient Roman province in N Italy between the Po river and the Alps. 2. Venezia.

Ve·ne·tian (və nē′shən), *adj.* 1. of or pertaining to Venice, in Italy. —*n.* 2. a native or inhabitant of Venice. 3. (*l.c.*) *Colloq.* a Venetian blind. 4. (*l.c., pl.*) a tape or braid for holding the slats of Venetian blinds in place.

Venetian blind, a blind, as for a window, having overlapping horizontal slats that may be opened or closed, esp. one in which the slats may be raised and drawn together above the window by pulling a cord.

Venetian glass, ornamental glassware made at or near Venice, Italy.

Venetian red, 1. a red pigment, orig. prepared from a natural oxide of iron, but now usually made by calcining a mixture of lime and iron sulfate. 2. a dark shade of orangeish red.

Ve·ne·to (vě′ně tô′), *n.* Venezia (def. 1).

Venez., Venezuela.

Ve·ne·zia (vě ně′tsyä), *n.* 1. Also, **Veneto** or **Venetia.** a department in NE Italy. 3,911,000 pop. (est. 1954); 7095 sq. mi. 2. Italian name of **Venice.**

Venezia Giu·lia (jōō′lyä), a former region at the N end of the Adriatic: formerly entirely in NE Italy; the larger part, including the area surrounding the Free Territory of Trieste, was ceded to Yugoslavia, 1947: now part of Friuli-Venezia Giulia.

Venezia Tri·den·ti·na (trē′-děn tē′nä), a department in N Italy, including the Trentino region. Now called **Trentino-Alto Adige.**

Ven·e·zue·la (věn′ə zwä′lə; *Sp.* vě/ně swě′lä), *n.* a republic in N South America. 6,006,000 pop. (est. 1956); 352,143 sq. mi. *Cap.:* Caracas. —**Ven′e·zue′lan,** *adj., n.*

venge (věnj), *v.t.* **venged, venging.** *Archaic.* to avenge. [ME, t. OF: m. *venger,* g. L *vindicāre*]

venge·ance (věn′jəns), *n.* 1. the avenging of wrong, injury, or the like, or retributive punishment. 2. infliction of injury or suffering in requital for wrong done or other cause of bitter resentment. 3. **with a vengeance. a.** with force or violence. **b.** extremely. **c.** with surprising or disconcerting force, thoroughness, etc. [ME, t. OF, der. *venger* VENGE] —**Syn.** 1. See **revenge.**

venge·ful (věnj′fəl), *adj.* 1. desiring or seeking vengeance, as persons; vindictive. 2. characterized by or showing a vindictive spirit: *a vengeful sort of person.* 3. taking or executing vengeance. —**venge′ful·ly,** *adv.* —**venge′ful·ness,** *n.*

ve·ni, vi·di, vi·ci (vē′nī, vī′dī, vī′sī; wā′nē, wē′dē, wē′kē), *Latin.* I came, I saw, I conquered (words used by Julius Caesar in reporting one of his victories).

ve·ni·al (vē′nĭ əl), *adj.* 1. that may be forgiven or pardoned; not seriously wrong, as a sin (in *theol.* opposed to *deadly* or *mortal*). 2. excusable, as an error or slip. [ME, t. L: s. *veniālis,* der. *venia* pardon] —**ve′ni·al′i·ty, ve′ni·al·ness,** *n.* —**ve′ni·al·ly,** *adv.*

venial sin, *Rom. Cath. Ch.* a voluntary transgression of God's law, which without destroying charity or union with God retards man in attaining final union with Him.

Ven·ice (věn′ĭs), *n.* 1. a seaport in NE Italy, built on numerous small islands in the Lagoon of Venice, an inlet of the Adriatic. 328,000 (est. 1954). 2. Gulf of, the N part of the Adriatic Sea. Italian, **Venezia.**

ven·i·punc·ture (věn′ə-pungk′chər, vē′nə-), *n. Med.* the puncture of a vein for surgical or therapeutic purposes. [f. *veni-* (comb. form repr. L *vēna* vein) + PUNCTURE]

ve·ni·re fa·ci·as (vĭ nī′rē fā′shĭ əs), *Law.* a writ or precept directed to the sheriff, requiring him to summon qualified citizens to act as jurors in the trial of cases. Also, **ve·ni′re.** [L: lit., cause to come]

ve·ni·re·man (vĭ nī′rē mən), *n., pl.* **-men.** *Law.* a man summoned under a *venire facias.*

ven·i·son (věn′ə zən *or, esp. Brit.,* věn′zən), *n.* the flesh of a deer or similar animal. [ME, t. OF: m. *veneson,* g. s. L *vēnātio* hunting]

Ve·ni·te (vĭ nī′tē), *n.* 1. the 95th Psalm (94th in the Vulgate and Douay), used as a canticle at matins or morning prayers. 2. a musical setting of this psalm. [L: come ye; so called from first word of L version]

Ve·ni·ze·los (vě′ně zě′lôs), *n.* **Eleutherios** (ě′lěf-thě′ryôs), 1864–1936, prime minister of Greece for many years.

ven·om (věn′əm), *n.* 1. the poisonous fluid which some animals, as certain snakes, spiders, etc., secrete, and introduce into the bodies of their victims by biting, stinging, etc. 2. something resembling or suggesting poison in its effect; spite or malice. 3. *Rare.* poison in general. —*v.t.* 4. to infect with venom; make venomous; envenom. [ME *venim,* t. OF, var. of *venin,* g. L *venēnum* poison] —**ven′om·er,** *n.* —**ven′om·less,** *adj.* —**Syn.** 1. See **poison.**

ven·om·ous (věn′əm əs), *adj.* 1. (of an animal) having a gland or glands for secreting venom; inflicting a poisoned bite, sting, or wound. 2. full of venom; poisonous. 3. spiteful or malignant: *a venomous disposition, a venomous attack.* —**ven′om·ous·ly,** *adv.* —**ven′om·ous·ness,** *n.*

ve·nose (vē′nōs), *adj.* 1. having many or prominent veins. 2. venous. [t. L: m.s. *vēnōsus*]

ve·nos·i·ty (vĭ nŏs′ə tĭ), *n. Physiol.* venous or venose state, quality, or characteristic.

ve·nous (vē′nəs), *adj.* 1. of, pertaining to, or of the nature of a vein or veins. 2. pertaining to the blood of the veins which has given up oxygen and become charged with carbon dioxide, and, in the higher animals, is dark-red in color. [t. L: m.s. *vēnōsus*] —**ve′nous·ly,** *dv.* —**ve′nous·ness,** *n.*

vent¹ (věnt), *n.* 1. an opening or aperture serving for outlet, as of a fluid: *the vent of the kitchen chimney.* the small opening at the breech of a gun by which fire is communicated to the charge. 3. *Zool.* the anal or excretory opening of animals, esp. of those below mammals, as birds and reptiles. 4. a means of escaping or passing out; an outlet, as from confinement. [appar. coalescence of VENT² and VENT³] —**vent′less,** *adj.*

vent[2] (vĕnt), *n.* **1.** expression or utterance: *to give vent to emotions, to complaints.* **2.** act or fact of venting; emission or discharge; issue. —*v.t.* **3.** to give free course or expression to (an emotion, passion, etc.): *glad of any excuse to vent her pique.* **4.** to give utterance to; publish or spread abroad. **5.** to relieve by giving vent to something: *Adams vented his soul with gifts to charity.* **6.** to let out or discharge (liquid, smoke, etc.). **7.** to furnish (a cask, etc.) with an outlet to the air. [t. F: aphetic m. *évent* a breaking forth, *éventer* break forth, der. *vent* (g. L *ventus* wind] —**vent′er,** *n.*

vent[3] (vĕnt), *n.* the slit in the back of a coat. [ME, var. of *fente,* t. OF: slit]

vent·age (vĕn′tĭj), *n.* a small hole or vent, as one of the fingerholes of a flute.

ven·tail (vĕn′tāl), *n.* *Armor.* the pivoted middle element of a face defense of a close helmet. [ME, t. OF: m. *ventaille,* der. *vent* wind]

ven·ter (vĕn′tər), *n.* **1.** *Anat., Zool.* the abdomen or belly. **2.** a bellylike cavity or concavity. **3.** a bellylike protuberance. **4.** *Law.* the womb, or a wife or mother, as a source of offspring. [t. L: belly, womb]

ven·ti·duct (vĕn′tə dŭkt′), *n.* a duct, pipe, or passage for wind or air, as for ventilating apartments. [f. *venti*- (comb. form repr. L *ventus* wind) + DUCT]

ven·ti·late (vĕn′tə lāt′), *v.t.,* **-lated, -lating. 1.** to provide (a room, mine, etc.) with fresh air in place of air which is vitiated. **2.** to introduce fresh air: *the lungs ventilate the blood.* **3.** (of air, wind, etc.) to circulate through, blow on, etc., so as to freshen. **4.** to expose (substances, etc.) to the action of air or wind. **5.** to submit (a question, etc.) to free examination and discussion. **6.** to give utterance or expression to (an opinion, etc.). **7.** to furnish with a vent or opening, as for the escape of air or gas. [t. L: m.s. *ventilātus,* pp., fanned]

ven·ti·la·tion (vĕn′tə lā′shən), *n.* **1.** act of ventilating. **2.** state of being ventilated. **3.** means of ventilating.

ven·ti·la·tive (vĕn′tə lā′tĭv), *adj.* **1.** promoting or producing ventilation. **2.** pertaining to ventilation.

ven·ti·la·tor (vĕn′tə lā′tər), *n.* **1.** one who or that which ventilates. **2.** any contrivance for replacing foul or stagnant air by fresh air.

Ven·tôse (väɴ tōz′), *n. French.* (in the calendar of the first French republic) the sixth month of the year, from Feb. 19 to March 20. [F, t. L: m. *ventōsus* windy]

ven·tral (vĕn′trəl), *adj.* **1.** of or pertaining to the venter or belly; abdominal. **2.** situated on the abdominal side of the body. **3.** of, pertaining to, or situated on the anterior or lower side or surface, as of an organ or part. **4.** *Bot.* of or designating the lower or inner surface, as of a petal, etc. —*n.* **5.** a ventral fin. [t. L: s. *ventrālis*] —**ven′tral·ly,** *adv.*

ventral fin, (in fishes) either of a pair of fins on the lower surface of the body, and corresponding to the hind limbs of higher vertebrates.

Fish with ventral fin behind pectoral fin

ven·tri·cle (vĕn′trə kəl), *n.* **1.** any of various hollow organs or parts in an animal body. **2.** one of the two main cavities of the heart which receive the blood from the auricles and propel it into the arteries. See diag. under **heart. 3.** one of a series of connecting cavities of the brain. [ME, t. L: m. *ventriculus,* dim. of *venter* belly]

ven·tri·cous (vĕn′trə kəs), *adj.* **1.** swelling out, esp. on one side or unequally; protuberant. **2.** having a large abdomen. [t. NL: m.s. *ventricōsus,* der. L *venter* belly] —**ven·tri·cos·i·ty** (vĕn′trə kŏs′ə tĭ′), *n.*

ven·tric·u·lar (vĕn trĭk′yə lər), *adj.* **1.** of, pertaining to, or of the nature of a ventricle. **2.** swelling out; distended.

ven·tric·u·lus (vĕn trĭk′yə ləs), *n.* **1.** the stomach of an insect: the part of the food tract where digestion and absorption take place. **2.** the muscular portion of a bird's stomach. [t. L, dim. of *venter* belly]

ven·tri·lo·qui·al (vĕn′trə lō′kwĭ əl), *adj.* of, pertaining to, or using ventriloquism. Also, **ven·tri·lo·qual** (vĕn trĭl′ə kwəl). —**ven′tri·lo′qui·al·ly,** *adv.*

ven·tril·o·quism (vĕn trĭl′ə kwĭz′əm), *n.* the art or practice of speaking or of uttering sounds in such a manner that the voice appears to come, not from the speaker, but from some other source. Also, **ven·tril·o·quy.** [f. s. LL *ventriloquus* one who apparently speaks from the belly + -ISM] —**ven·tril′o·quist,** *n.* —**ven·tril′o·quis′tic,** *adj.*

ven·tril·o·quize (vĕn trĭl′ə kwīz′), *v.i.,* **-quized, -quizing.** to speak or produce sounds in the manner of a ventriloquist.

ven·ture (vĕn′chər), *n., v.,* **-tured, -turing.** —*n.* **1.** a hazardous or daring undertaking; any undertaking or proceeding involving uncertainty as to the outcome. **2.** a business enterprise or proceeding in which loss is risked in the hope of profit; a commercial or other speculation. **3.** that on which risk is taken in a business enterprise or speculation, as a ship, cargo, merchandise, etc. **4.** at a venture, according to mere chance; at random. **5.** *Archaic.* hazard or risk. —*v.t.* **6.** to put to hazard, or risk. **7.** to take the risk of; brave the dangers of. **8.** to undertake to utter or express, as if with a sense of daring. **9.** *Archaic.* to take the risk of sending. —*v.i.* **10.** to make a venture; risk oneself. **11.** to take a risk; dare or

presume (often fol. by *on* or *upon* or an infinitive): *venture on an ambitious project, never venture to oppose him.* [ME, aphetic var. of *aventure,* earlier form of ADVENTURE] —**ven′tur·er,** *n.* —Syn. **11.** See **dare.**

ven·ture·some (vĕn′chər səm), *adj.* **1.** having or showing a disposition to venture or take risks, often rashly; daring. **2.** attended with risk; hazardous. —**ven′ture·some·ly,** *adv.* —**ven′ture·some·ness,** *n.*

ven·tur·ous (vĕn′chər əs), *adj.* **1.** disposed to venture; bold; daring; adventurous. **2.** hazardous; risky. —**ven′tur·ous·ly,** *adv.* —**ven′tur·ous·ness,** *n.* —Ant. **1.** timid.

ven·ue (vĕn′ū, vĕn′ōō), *n.* **1.** *Law.* **a.** the place of a crime or cause of action. **b.** the county or place where the jury is gathered and the cause tried. **c.** the designation, in the pleading, of the jurisdiction where trial will be held. **d.** the statement naming the place and person before whom an affidavit was sworn. **2.** the scene of any action or event. [ME, t. OF: coming]

ven·ule (vĕn′ūl), *n.* **1.** a small vein. **2.** one of the branches of the veins in an insect's wing. Also, **veinule.** [t. L: m. *vēnula,* dim. of *vēna* vein] —**ven′u·lar,** *adj.*

ven·u·lose (vĕn′yə lōs′), *adj.* having veinlets. Also, **ven·u·lous** (vĕn′yə ləs).

Ve·nus (vē′nəs), *n.* **1.** an ancient Italian goddess of gardens and spring, identified by the Romans with Aphrodite as the goddess of love and beauty. **2.** a beautiful woman. **3.** *Astron.* the most brilliant planet, having an orbit next inside the earth's and second from the sun. Its period of revolution is 225 days, its mean distance from the sun about 67,000,000 miles, and its diameter 7700 miles. It has no satellites. Symbol: ♀ **4.** *Old Chem.* copper.

Venus and Adonis, a narrative poem (1593) by Shakespeare.

Ve·nus·berg (vē′nəs bûrg′; *Ger.* vā′nŏŏs bĕrкн′), *n.* a mountain in central Germany, between Eisenach and Gotha. According to medieval legend, Venus held her pagan court in the caverns of this mountain.

Venus of Mi·lo (mē′lō), the most famous extant Greek statue of antiquity, found 1820 in Milo or Melos, and now in the Louvre, Paris. It represents Venus naked above the thighs; the arms are missing. Also, **Venus of Melos.**

Ve·nus's-fly·trap (vē′nəs ĭz flī′trăp′), *n.* a plant, *Dionæa muscipula,* native to North and South Carolina, whose leaves have two lobes which close like a trap when certain delicate hairs on them are irritated, as by a fly.

Ve·nus's-hair (vē′nəs ĭz hâr′), *n.* a delicate maidenhair fern, *Adiantum Capillus-Veneris.*

Venus's-flytrap. *Dionæa muscipula*

ver., **1.** verse; verses. **2.** version.

ve·ra·cious (və rā′shəs), *adj.* **1.** speaking truly; truthful or habitually observant of truth: *a veracious witness.* **2.** characterized by truthfulness; true: *a veracious statement or account.* [f. VERACI(TY) + -OUS] —**ve·ra′cious·ly,** *adv.* —**ve·ra′cious·ness,** *n.*

ve·rac·i·ty (və răs′ə tĭ′), *n., pl.* **-ties. 1.** truthfulness in speaking or statement; habitual observance of truth. **2.** conformity to truth or fact, as of statements. **3.** correctness or accuracy, as of the senses, a scientific instrument, etc. **4.** something veracious; a truthful statement; a truth. [t. ML: m.s. *vērācitas,* ult. der. L *vērus* true]

Ve·ra·cruz (vĕr′ə krōōz′; *Sp.* vĕ′rä krōōs′), *n.* **1.** a state in E Mexico, on the Gulf of Mexico. 2,137,567 (est. 1952); 27,759 sq. mi. *Cap.:* Jalapa. **2.** a seaport in this state: the chief port of Mexico. 113,803 (est. 1951). Formerly, **Ver′a Cruz′.**

ve·ran·da (və răn′də), *n.* an open portico or gallery, usually roofed and sometimes partly enclosed, attached to the exterior of a house or other building; a piazza, porch, or gallery. Also, **ve·ran′dah.** [orig. from India, in several native languages, appar. m. Pg. and OSp. *varanda* railing, der. L *vāra* rod] —**ve·ran′da·less,** *adj.*

ve·rat·ric acid (və răt′rĭk), *Chem.* a white crystalline acid, (CH₃O)₂C₆H₃CO₂H, obtained by the decomposition of veratrine and in other ways. [*veratric,* f. s. L *verātrum* hellebore + -IC]

ve·rat·ri·dine (və răt′rə dēn′, -dĭn), *n. Chem.* an amorphous alkaloid occurring with veratrine in the seeds of the sabadilla. Also, **ve·rat·ri·din** (və răt′rə dĭn).

ver·a·trine (vĕr′ə trēn′, -trĭn), *n. Chem.* a poisonous alkaloid, or mixture of alkaloids, obtained from the seeds of the sabadilla, formerly used in medicine, chiefly in the local treatment of rheumatism, neuralgia, etc., and causing prolonged contraction of voluntary muscle. Also, **ve·ra·tri·a** (və rā′trĭ ə), **ver·a·trin** (vĕr′ə trĭn), **ver·a·tri·na** (vĕr′ə trī′nə).

ver·a·trize (vĕr′ə trīz′), *v.t.,* **-trized, -trizing.** to treat, drug, or poison with veratrine, as animals.

verb (vûrb), *n. Gram.* **1.** (in most languages) one of the major form classes, or "parts of speech," comprising words which express the occurrence of an action, existence of a state, and the like, and such other words as show similar grammatical behavior, as English *discover, remember, write, be.* **2.** any such word. **3.** any word or construction of similar function or meaning. [ME, t. L: s. *verbum* word, verb] —**verb′less,** *adj.*

ver·bal (vûr′bəl), *adj.* **1.** of or pertaining to words: *verbal symbols.* **2.** consisting of or in the form of words:

a verbal picture of a scene. **3.** expressed in spoken words; oral rather than written: *verbal tradition, a verbal message.* **4.** pertaining to or concerned with words only, rather than ideas, facts, or realities: *verbal changes in an article.* **5.** corresponding word for word: *a verbal copy or quotation.* **6.** *Gram.* **a.** of, pertaining to, or derived from a verb. **b.** used in a sentence as or like a verb, as participles and infinitives. —*n.* **7.** *Gram.* a word, particularly a noun or adjective, derived from a verb. [late ME, t. L: s. *verbālis,* der. *verbum* word] —ver′bal·ly, *adv.* —Syn. **3.** See oral.

ver·bal·ism (vûr′bəlĭz′əm), *n.* **1.** a verbal expression; a word or phrase. **2.** a formal phrase or sentence, with little or no meaning. **3.** predominance of mere words, as over ideas or realities.

ver·bal·ist (vûr′bəlĭst), *n.* **1.** one skilled in words. **2.** one who deals with words merely, rather than ideas or realities.

ver·bal·ize (vûr′bəlīz′), *v.,* -ized, -izing. —*v.t.* **1.** to express in words. **2.** *Gram.* to convert into a verb: *to verbalize "butter" into "to butter."* —*v.i.* **3.** to use many words; be verbose. —ver′bal·i·za′tion, *n.* —ver′bal·iz′er, *n.*

verbal noun, *Gram.* a noun derived from a verb, esp. in a language where nouns are derived by the same or similar means from all or nearly all verbs.

ver·ba·tim (vərbā′tĭm), *adv.* word for word, or in exactly the same words. [t. ML, der. L *verbum* word]

ver·ba·tim et lit·te·ra·tim (vərbā′tĭm ĕt lĭt′ərā′-tĭm), *Latin.* word for word and letter for letter; in exactly the same words.

ver·be·na (vərbē′nə), *n.* any plant of the genus *Verbena,* comprising species characterized by elongated or flattened spikes of sessile flowers, some of which are much cultivated as garden plants. [t. L: foliage]

ver·be·na·ceous (vûr′bənā′shəs), *adj.* belonging to the *Verbenaceae,* or verbena family of plants, which includes also the lantana, teak, etc.

ver·bi·age (vûr′bĭ′ĭj), *n.* abundance of useless words, as in writing or speech; wordiness. [t. F, der. *verbier* gabble, ult. der. L *verbum* word. See -AGE]

ver·bid (vûr′bĭd), *n. Gram.* a nonfinite verb form; an infinitive or participle.

ver·bose (vərbōs′), *adj.* expressed in, characterized by the use of, or using many or too many words; wordy. [t. L: m.s. *verbōsus* full of words] —ver·bose′ly, *adv.* —ver·bose′ness, *n.* —Ant. laconic.

ver·bos·i·ty (vərbŏs′ətĭ), *n.* quality of being verbose; wordiness; superfluity of words. —Ant. reticence.

ver·bo·ten (fĕr′bō′tən), *adj.* forbidden, as by law; prohibited. [t. G, pp.]

verbum sap., *verbum sapienti sat est.*

ver·bum sa·pi·en·ti sat est (vûr′bəm săp′Ĭ·ĕn′-tĭ săt′ ĕst′), *Latin.* a word to the wise is sufficient.

Ver·cin·get·o·rix (vûr′sĭn·jĕt′ə·rĭks, -gĕt′-), *n.* died 45? B.C., Gallic chieftain conquered by Caesar.

ver·dant (vûr′dənt), *adj.* **1.** green with vegetation; covered with growing plants or grass: *a verdant valley.* **2.** of a green color. **3.** inexperienced; unsophisticated. [f. VERD(URE) + -ANT] —ver′dan·cy, *n.* —ver′dant·ly, *adv.*

verd an·tique (vûrd′ ăn·tēk′), **1.** any of various greenish stones. **2.** a green mottled or veined impure serpentine, much used by the ancient Romans for interior decoration. [t. OF: antique green]

Verde (vûrd), *n.* Cape, a cape in Senegal, near Dakar: the westernmost point of Africa.

ver·der·er (vûr′dərər), *n. Eng. Forest Law.* a judicial officer in the royal forests having charge esp. of the vert, or trees and undergrowth. Also, ver′der·or. [t. AF, ult. g. LL *viridārius* forester, der. *viridis* green]

Ver·di (vĕr′dē), *n.* **Giuseppe** (jōō·zĕp′pĕ), 1813–1901, Italian composer.

ver·dict (vûr′dĭkt), *n.* **1.** *Law.* the finding or answer of a jury given to the court concerning a matter submitted to their judgment. **2.** a judgment or decision: *the verdict of the public.* [b. ML *vērēdictum* verdict (lit., truly said) and ME *verdit* (t. OF: lit., true saying)]

ver·di·gris (vûr′də·grēs′, -grĭs), *n.* a green or bluish patina formed on copper, brass, or bronze surfaces exposed to the atmosphere for long periods of time, consisting principally of basic copper sulfate. [ME *verde-gres(e),* t. AF: m. *vert de Grece,* lit., green of Greece]

ver·din (vûr′dĭn), *n.* a small yellow-headed titmouse, *Quriparus flaviceps,* inhabiting arid parts of the southwestern U.S. and Mexico, and building a compact, spherical nest of thorny twigs. [t. F: yellowhammer]

ver·di·ter (vûr′də·tər), *n.* **1.** either of two pigments, consisting usually of carbonate of copper prepared by grinding either azurite (**blue verditer**) or malachite (**green verditer**). **2.** *Obs.* verdigris. [t. F: m. *vert de terre,* lit., green of earth]

Ver·dun (vâr·dŭn′; *Fr.* vĕr·dœN′), *n.* a fortress city in NE France, on the Meuse river: a German offensive was stopped here in the bloodiest fighting of World War I, 1916. 18,831 (1954).

ver·dure (vûr′jər), *n.* **1.** greenness, esp. of fresh, flourishing vegetation. **2.** green vegetation, esp. grass or herbage. **3.** freshness in general; flourishing condition. [ME, t. OF, f. *verd* green (g. L *viridis*) + -ure -URE] —ver′dure·less, *adj.*

ver·dur·ous (vûr′jər əs), *adj.* **1.** rich in verdure or fresh greenness, as vegetation. **2.** covered with verdure or green vegetation, as places. **3.** consisting of verdure. **4.** pertaining to or characteristic of verdure. —ver′-dur·ous·ness, *n.*

ver·e·cund (vĕr′ə·kŭnd′), *adj. Rare.* bashful; modest. [t. L: s. *verēcundus*]

Ver·ein (fĕr·īn′), *n. German.* a union, association, or society.

Ve·resh·cha·gin (vĕ·rĕsh·chä′gĭn), *n.* **Vasili Vasilie·vich** (vä·sē′lĭĭ vä·sēl′yə·vĭch), 1842–1904, Russian painter, esp. of military subjects.

verge[1] (vûrj), *n., v.,* **verged, verging.** —*n.* **1.** the edge, rim, or margin of something. **2.** the limit or point beyond which something begins or occurs: *to be on the verge of tears.* **3.** a limiting belt, strip, or border of something, esp. when circular. **4.** space within boundaries; room or scope. **5.** an area or district subject to a particular jurisdiction. **6.** *Hist.* such an area or district in England, being the jurisdiction of the Marshalsea Court, and embracing the royal palace. **7.** *Archit.* the edge of the tiling projecting over the gable of a roof. **8.** the shaft of a column; a small ornamental shaft. **9.** a rod, wand, or staff, esp. one carried as an emblem of authority or ensign of office of bishop, dean, and the like. **10.** *Print.* a triggerlike device for releasing the matrices of a linotype machine. **11.** *Watchmaking.* a lever with lips or projections, in a clock, which intermittently lock the escape wheel and transmit impulses from the escape wheel to the pendulum. **12.** *Obs.* a stick or wand held in the hand by a person swearing fealty to the lord on being admitted as a tenant. —*v.i.* **13.** to be on the verge or border, or touch at the border. [ME, t. F, g. L *virga* rod]

verge[2] (vûrj), *v.i.,* **verged, verging.** to incline or tend (usually fol. by *on* or *upon*): *to verge on nonsense, insanity,* etc. [t. L: m.s. *vergere* turn, incline]

ver·ger (vûr′jər), *n.* **1.** *Chiefly Brit.* an official who takes care of the interior of a church and acts as attendant. **2.** an official who carries the verge or other symbol of office before a bishop, dean, or other dignitary. [late ME, t. F(obs.), der. *verge* rod. See VERGE[1]]

Ver·gil (vûr′jĭl), *n.* (*Publius Vergilius Maro*) 70–19 B.C., Roman poet: author of *The Aeneid.* Also, **Virgil.** —Ver·gil′i·an, *adj.*

ve·rid·i·cal (və·rĭd′ə·kəl), *adj.* truth-telling; truthful; veracious. Also, **ve·rid′ic.** [f. s. L *vēridicus* truth-telling + -AL[1]] —ve·rid′i·cal′i·ty, *n.* —ve·rid′i·cal·ly, *adv.*

ver·i·est (vĕr′ĭ·ĭst), *adj.* utmost; thoroughgoing: *the veriest stupidity.*

ver·i·fi·ca·tion (vĕr′ə·fə·kā′shən), *n.* **1.** act of verifying. **2.** state of being verified. **3.** formal assertion of the truth of something. **4.** *Law.* a short confirmatory affidavit at the end of a pleading or petition. —ver′i·fi·ca′tive, *adj.*

ver·i·fy (vĕr′ə·fī′), *v.t.,* -fied, -fying. **1.** to prove (something) to be true, as by evidence or testimony; confirm or substantiate. **2.** to ascertain the truth or correctness of, esp. by examination or comparison: *to verify dates, spelling, or a quotation.* **3.** to state to be true, esp., in legal use, formally or upon oath. **4.** *Law.* to allege proof of one's allegations. [ME *verifie,* t. OF: m. *verifier,* t. LL: m. *vērificāre,* der. L *vērus* true] —ver′i·fi′a·ble, *adj.* —ver′i·fi′er, *n.*

ver·i·ly (vĕr′ə·lĭ), *adv. Archaic.* in very truth; truly; really; indeed. [ME; f. VERY + -LY]

ver·i·sim·i·lar (vĕr′ə·sĭm′ə·lər), *adj.* having the appearance of truth; likely or probable. [m. L *vērisimilis* to agree with SIMILAR] —ver′i·sim′i·lar·ly, *adv.*

ver·i·si·mil·i·tude (vĕr′ə·sĭ·mĭl′ə·tōd′, -tōod′), *n.* **1.** appearance or semblance of truth; probability. **2.** something having merely the appearance of truth. [t. L: m. *vērī similitūdo* likeness of truth]

ver·ism (vĭr′ĭz·əm), *n.* the theory that rigid representation of truth and reality is essential to art and literature and therefore the ugly and vulgar must be included. [f. s. L *vērus* true + -ISM] —ver′ist, *n., adj.* —ve·ris′-tic, *adj.*

ver·i·ta·ble (vĕr′ə·tə·bəl), *adj.* **1.** being truly such; genuine or real: *a veritable triumph.* **2.** *Rare.* true, as statements, etc. [late ME, t. AF, der. *verite,* t. L: m.s. *vēritas* truth] —ver′i·ta·ble·ness, *n.* —ver′i·ta·bly, *adv.*

Ve·ri·tas (vĕr′ə·tăs′), *n. Latin.* truth (motto of Harvard College and of University of South Dakota).

ve·ri·tas vos li·be·ra·bit (vĕr′ə·tăs′ vōs lĭb′ə·rä′-bĭt), *Latin.* truth will liberate you (motto of Johns Hopkins University).

vé·ri·té sans peur (vĕ·rē·tĕ′ säN pœr′), *French.* truth without fear.

ver·i·ty (vĕr′ə·tĭ), *n., pl.* -ties. **1.** quality of being true, or in accordance with fact or reality. **2.** a truth, or true statement, principle, belief, idea, or the like. [ME *verite,* t. L: m.s. *vēritas*]

ver·juice (vûr′jōōs), *n.* **1.** an acid liquor made from the sour juice of crab apples, unripe grapes, etc., formerly much used for culinary and other purposes. **2.** sourness, as of temper or expression. —*adj.* Also, ver′juiced′. **3.** of or pertaining to verjuice. **4.** sour in temper, expression, etc. [ME *verjous,* t. OF: m. *vertjus,* f. *vert* green + *jus* juice]

Ver·laine (vĕr·lĕn′), *n.* **Paul** (pōl), 1844–96, French symbolist poet.

---

b., blend of, blended; c., cognate with; d., dialect, dialectal; der., derived from; f., formed from; g., going back to; m., modification of; r., replacing; s., stem of; t., taken from; ?, perhaps. See the full key on inside cover.

Ver·meer (vər mȳr′; *Du.* -mār′), *n.* **Jan** (yän), (*Jan van der Meer of Delft*) 1632–75, Dutch painter.

ver·meil (vûr′mȳl), *n.* **1.** *Poetic.* vermilion red. **2.** metal, as silver or bronze, coated with gilt. —*adj.* **3.** of the color vermilion. [ME *vermaile*, t. OF: m. *vermail* bright red, g. L *vermiculus* little worm, applied to cochineal]

vermi-, a word element meaning "worm," as in *vermiform.* [t. L, comb. form of *vermis*]

ver·mi·cel·li (vûr′mə sĕl′ĭ, -chĕl′ĭ), *n.* a kind of paste of Italian origin in the form of long, slender, solid threads (thinner than spaghetti), to be cooked for food. Cf. **macaroni** (def. 1). [t. It., pl. of *vermicello* little worm, der. *verme* worm, g. L *vermis*]

ver·mi·cide (vûr′mə sĭd′), *n.* any agent that kills worms, esp. a drug used to kill parasitic intestinal worms. —**ver′mi·cid′al**, *adj.*

ver·mic·u·lar (vər mĭk′yə lər), *adj.* consisting of or characterized by sinuous or wavy outlines or markings, resembling the tracks of worms. [t. ML: s. *vermiculāris*, der. L *vermiculus* little worm] —**ver·mic′u·lar·ly**, *adv.*

ver·mic·u·late (*v.* vər mĭk′yə lāt′; *adj.* vər mĭk′yə lĭt, -lāt′), *v.*, **-lated, -lating**, *adj.* —*v.t.* **1.** to work or ornament with winding or wavy outlines or markings, resembling the tracks of worms. —*adj.* **2.** worm-eaten, or appearing as if worm-eaten; vermiculated; vermicular. **3.** (of thought processes) subtly sinuous. [t. L: m.s. *vermiculātus*, pp., worm-eaten] —**ver·mic′u·la′tion**, *n.*

ver·mic·u·lite (vər mĭk′yə lĭt′), *n.* any of various micaceous minerals, usually formed by alteration of the common micas, occurring in yellow to brown foliated masses with inelastic laminae, and used for heat-insulating material, etc. [f. s. L *vermiculus* little worm + -ITE¹]

ver·mi·form (vûr′mə fôrm′), *adj.* like a worm in form; long and slender. [t. ML: s. *vermiformis.* See VERMI-, -FORM]

vermiform appendix, *Anat.* a narrow blind tube protruding from the caecum: in man, situated in the lower right-hand part of the abdomen, and having no known useful function, its diameter being about that of a pencil and its length 3 to 4 inches. See diag. under **intestine.**

vermiform process, *Anat.* **1.** the median lobe or division of the cerebellum. **2.** the vermiform appendix

ver·mi·fuge (vûr′mə fūj′), *adj.* **1.** serving to expel worms or other animal parasites from the intestines, as a medicine. —*n.* **2.** a vermifuge medicine or agent.

ver·mil·ion (vər mĭl′yən), *n.* **1.** brilliant scarlet red. **2.** a bright-red pigment consisting of mercuric sulfide; cinnabar. —*adj.* **3.** of the color of vermilion. —*v.t.* **4.** to color with or as with vermilion. [ME *vermilioun*, t. OF: m. *vermillon* bright red, der. *vermeil* VERMEIL]

ver·min (vûr′mĭn), *n. pl. or sing.* **1.** noxious, troublesome, or objectionable animals collectively, esp. troublesome or disgusting insects or other minute animals, more particularly creeping ones parasitic on living animals or plants. **2.** *Obs. or Rare.* a single animal of this kind. **3.** objectionable or obnoxious persons collectively. **4.** a single person of this kind. [ME *vermyne*, t. OF: m. *vermin*, der. *verm* worm, g. L *vermis*]

ver·mi·na·tion (vûr′mə nā′shən), *n.* **1.** the breeding of vermin. **2.** the fact of being infested with vermin, esp. parasitic vermin.

ver·min·ous (vûr′mĭn əs), *adj.* **1.** of the nature of or resembling vermin. **2.** pertaining or due to vermin. **3.** infested with vermin, esp. parasitic vermin. —**ver′min·ous·ly**, *adv.* —**ver′min·ous·ness**, *n.*

Ver·mont (vər mŏnt′), *n.* a State of the NE United States: a part of New England. 389,881 pop. (1960); 9609 sq. mi. *Cap.*: Montpelier. *Abbr.*: Vt.

Ver·mont·er (vər mŏn′tər), *n.* a native or inhabitant of Vermont.

ver·mouth (vûr′mōōth, vər mōōth′; *Fr.* vĕr mōōt′), *n.* an aromatized white wine in which herbs, roots, barks, bitters, and other flavorings have been steeped. [t. F: m. *vermout*, t. G: m. *wermuth* wormwood]

ver·nac·u·lar (vər năk′yə lər), *adj.* **1.** native or originating in the place of its occurrence or use, as language or words (often as opposed to *literary* or *learned* language). **2.** expressed or written in the native language of a place, as literary works. **3.** using such a language, as a speaker or a writer. **4.** pertaining to such a language. **5.** native or peculiar to popular taste, as a style of architecture. **6.** endemic, as a disease. **7.** of or pertaining to the common name for a plant or animal. —*n.* **8.** the native speech or language of a place. **9.** the language or phraseology peculiar to a class or profession. **10.** a vernacular word or expression. **11.** the common name for a plant or animal rather than the scientific term which gives genus and species. [f. s. L *vernăculus* native + -AR¹] —**ver·nac′u·lar·ly**, *adv.* —**Syn. 8.** See **language.**

ver·nac·u·lar·ism (vər năk′yə lə rĭz′əm), *n.* **1.** a vernacular word or expression. **2.** the use of the vernacular.

ver·nal (vûr′nəl), *adj.* **1.** of or pertaining to spring. **2.** appearing or occurring in spring. **3.** appropriate to or resembling spring. **4.** belonging to youth. [t. L: s. *vernālis*] —**ver′nal·ly**, *adv.*

vernal equinox. See **equinox.** Also, **vernal point.**

ver·nal·ize (vûr′nə līz′), *v.t.*, **-ized, -izing.** *Chiefly Agric.* to shorten the growth period before blossoming and fruit or seed bearing of (a plant) by chilling its seed or bulb. —**ver′nal·i·za′tion**, *n.*

ver·na·tion (vər nā′shən), *n.* *Bot.* the disposition of the foliage leaves within the bud. [t. L: s. *vernātio* shedding of the skin of snakes, ult. der. *ver* spring]

Verne (vûrn; *Fr.* vĕrn), *n.* **Jules** (jōōlz; *Fr.* zhȳl), 1828–1905, French novelist.

Ver·ner (vûr′nər; *Dan.* vĕr′-), *n.* **Karl Adolph** (kärl ä′dŏlf), 1846–96, Danish linguist.

Verner's law, (in the history of Indo-European languages) the statement by Verner of some hitherto unexplained features in the system formulated by Grimm's law, showing the continuance into later languages of the effects of the primitive Indo-European word accent. —**Ver·ner·i·an** (vûr nĕr′ĭ ən), *adj.*

ver·ni·er (vûr′nĭ ər), *n.* **1.** Also, **vernier scale.** a small, movable, graduated scale running parallel with the fixed graduated scale of a sextant, theodolite, barometer, or other graduated instrument, and used for measuring a fractional part of one of the divisions of the fixed scale. **2.** *Mach.* an auxiliary device for giving a piece of apparatus a higher adjustment accuracy. —*adj.* **3.** equipped with a vernier: *a vernier barometer.* [t. F; named after Pierre Vernier, 1580–1637, mathematician]

Ver·no·le·ninsk (vĕr′nŏ lĕ nĕnsk′), *n.* former name of Nikolaev.

Ver·non (vûr′nən), *n.* **Edward,** ("Old Grog") 1684–1757, British admiral.

Ve·ro·na (və rō′nə; *It.* vĕ rô′nä), *n.* a city in N Italy, on the Adige river. 187,000 (est. 1954).

Ver·o·nal (vĕr′ə nəl), *n.* **1.** barbital. **2.** a trade name for barbital. [t. G]

Ve·ro·ne·se (vĕ′rô nĕ′sĕ), *n.* **Paolo** (pä′ô lô′). See **Cagliari, Paolo.**

ve·ron·i·ca (və rŏn′ə kə), *n.* **1.** any plant of the scrophulariaceous genus *Veronica*, as the speedwell. **2.** the representation of the face of Christ which, according to a legend, was miraculously impressed on a cloth which St. Veronica offered to Him to wipe His brow as He carried His cross to Calvary. **3.** the cloth itself. Cf. **sudarium.** **4.** any similar picture of Christ's face, as on a garment. [t. ML, appar. named after St. *Veronica*]

Ver·ra·za·no (vĕr′rä tsä′nô), *n.* **Giovanni da** (jō·vän′nĕ dä), c1480–1527?, Italian navigator who explored along the coast of North America for France. Also, **Ver′raz·za·no** or **Ver·ra·za·ni** (vĕr′rä tsä′nĕ).

Ver·roc·chio (vĕr rŏk′kyô), *n.* **Andrea del** (än drĕ′ä dĕl), 1435–88, Italian goldsmith, sculptor, and painter.

ver·ru·ca (vĕ rōō′kə), *n., pl.* **-cae** (-sē). **1.** *Med.* a wart. **2.** *Zool.* a small, flattish, wartlike prominence. [t. L]

ver·ru·cose (vĕr′ə kōs′), *adj.* studded with wartlike excrescences or elevations. —**ver·ru·cos·i·ty** (vĕr′ə kŏs′ə tĭ), *n.*

vers, *Trig.* versed sine.

Ver·sailles (vər sālz′; *Fr.* vĕr sä′y), *n.* a city in N France, ab. 12 mi. SW of Paris: palace of Louis XIV; treaty of peace between the Allies and Germany, 1919. 84,445 (1954).

ver·sant (vûr′sənt), *n.* **1.** a slope of a mountain or mountain chain. **2.** the general slope of a country or region. [t. F, ppr. of *verser* turn, g. L *versāre*, der. *vertere*]

ver·sa·tile (vûr′sə tĭl), *adj.* **1.** capable of or adapted for turning with ease from one to another of various tasks, subjects, etc.; many-sided in abilities. **2.** *Bot.* attached at or near the middle so as to swing freely, as an anther. **3.** *Zool.* turning either forward or backward: *a versatile toe.* **4.** variable or changeable, esp. in feeling, purpose, policy, etc. [t. L: m.s. *versātilis* turning about] —**ver′sa·tile·ly**, *adv.* —**ver′sa·til′i·ty**, *n.* **ver′sa·tile·ness**, *n.*

vers de so·ci·é·té (vĕr də sô syĕ tĕ′), *French.* humorous light verse dealing with fashions and foibles of the time.

A. Versatile anthers

verse (vûrs), *n.* **1.** a succession of metrical feet written or printed or orally composed as one line; one of the lines of a poem. **2.** a particular type of metrical line: *a hexameter verse.* **3.** a poem, or piece of poetry. **4.** metrical composition; poetry, esp. as involving metrical form. **5.** a particular type of metrical composition: *iambic verse, elegiac verse.* **6.** a line of prose, esp. a sentence, or part of a sentence, written as one line; a stich. **7.** a subdivision in any literary work (usually more properly termed a stanza, strophe, or section): *the first verse of a hymn.* **8.** a short division of a chapter in the Bible, usually one sentence, or part of a long sentence. [ME and OE *vers*, t. L: s. *versus* line, row]

—**Syn. 4.** See **poetry. 7.** VERSE, STANZA, STROPHE, STAVE are terms for a metrical grouping in poetic composition. VERSE is often substituted for STANZA, but is properly only a single metrical line. A STANZA is a succession of lines (verses) commonly bound together by a rhyme scheme, and usually forming one of a series of similar groups which constitute a poem: *the four-line stanza is the one most frequently used in English.* STROPHE (originally the section of a Greek choral ode sung while the chorus was moving from right to left) is in English poetry practically equivalent to "section"; ASTROPHE may be unrhymed or without strict form, but may be a stanza: *strophes are divisions of odes.* STAVE is a word (now seldom used) which meant a stanza set to music or intended to be sung: *a stave of a hymn, of a drinking song.*

versed (vûrst), *adj.* experienced; practiced; skilled (fol. by *in*): *well versed in a subject.* [half adoption, half trans. of L *versātus*, pp., busied, engaged]

versed sine, *Trig.* one minus the cosine (of a given angle or arc). *Abbr.:* vers

ver·si·cle (vûr′sə kəl), *n.* 1. a little verse. 2. *Eccles.* one of a series of short sentences, or parts of sentences, usually from the Psalms, said or sung by the officiant, as distinguished from the response of the choir or congregation. Cf. **response** (def. 3a). [ME, t. L: m.s. *versiculus* little verse]

ver·si·col·or (vûr′sə kül′ər), *adj.* 1. changeable in color. 2. of various colors; parti-colored. Also, *esp. Brit.,* **ver′si·col′our.** [t. L]

ver·sic·u·lar (vər sĭk′yə lər), *adj.* of or consisting of versicles or verses. [f. s. L *versiculus* little verse + -AR¹]

ver·si·fi·ca·tion (vûr′sə fə kā′shən), *n.* 1. act of versifying. 2. form or style of verse; metrical structure. 3. a metrical version of something. 4. the rules or customs of versemaking.

ver·si·fy (vûr′sə fī′), *v.i.,* **-fied, -fying.** 1. to relate or describe in verse; treat as the subject of verse. 2. to turn into terse or metrical form. 3. to compose verses. [ME *versifie*, t. L: m. *versificāre* put into verse] —**ver′si·fi′er,** *n.*

ver·sion (vûr′zhən, -shən), *n.* 1. a translation. 2. (*often cap.*) a translation of the Bible or a part of it: *the King James Version.* 3. a particular account of some matter, as from one person or source, as contrasted with some other account or accounts. 4. a particular form or variant of anything. 5. *Med.* act of turning a child in the uterus so as to bring it into a more favorable position for delivery. 6. *Pathol.* an abnormal direction of the axis of the uterus. [t. L: s. *versio* turning] —**ver′sion·al,** *adj.* —Syn. 1. See **translation.**

vers li·bre (vĕr lē′br), *French.* free verse. —**vers li·brist** (vĕr lē′brĭst)

ver·so (vûr′sō), *n., pl.* **-sos.** 1. *Print.* the left-hand page of a book or manuscript. 2. the reverse, back, or other side of some object. [t. L: short for *versō foliō,* lit., on the turned leaf]

ver·sus (vûr′səs), *prep.* against (used esp. in *Law* to indicate an action brought by one party against another, and in *Sports* to denote a contest between two teams or players). *Abbr.:* v. or vs. [t. L]

vert (vûrt), *n.* 1. *Eng. Forest Law.* a. vegetation bearing green leaves in a forest and capable of serving as a cover for deer. b. the right to cut such green trees or shrubs. 2. *Her.* green. [late ME, t. AF: green]

ver·te·bra (vûr′tə brə), *n., pl.* **-brae** (-brē′). **-bras.** *Anat., Zool.* any of the bones or segments composing the spinal column: in man and the higher animals consisting typically of a more or less cylindrical body (centrum) and an arch (neural arch) with various processes, forming a foramen through which the spinal cord passes. [t. L]

ver·te·bral (vûr′tə brəl), *adj.* 1. of or pertaining to a vertebra or the vertebrae; spinal. 2. of the nature of a vertebra. 3. composed of vertebrae. 4. having vertebrae.

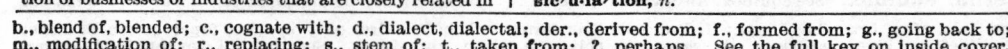

Vertebra
A, Spine; B, Facet of rib; C, Pedicel; D, Body; E, Lamina; F, Transverse process; G, Articular process; H, Spinal canal

vertebral column, the spinal column.

ver·te·brate (vûr′tə brāt′,-brĭt), *n.* 1. a vertebrate animal. —*adj.* 2. having vertebrae; having a back bone or spinal column. 3. belonging or pertaining to the *Vertebrata,* a comprehensive division of animals, including all those that have a segmented spinal column, now generally classified as a chordate subphylum. [t. L: m.s. *vertebrātus* jointed]

ver·te·brat·ed (vûr′tə brā′tĭd), *adj.* 1. having vertebrae; vertebrate. 2. consisting of vertebrae.

ver·te·bra·tion (vûr′tə brā′shən), *n.* vertebrate formation.

ver·tex (vûr′tĕks), *n., pl.* **-texes, -tices** (-tə sēz′). 1. the highest point of something; the apex; the top; the summit. 2. *Anat., Zool.* the crown or top of the head. 3. *Craniom.* the highest point on the mid-sagittal plane of skull or head viewed from the left side when the skull or head is in the Frankfurt Horizontal. 4. *Astron., etc.* a point in the celestial sphere toward which or from which the common motion of a group of stars is directed. 5. *Math.* a. the point farthest from the base. b. (of a geometrical figure) (1) a point in a plane figure common to two or more sides. (2) a point in a solid common to three or more sides. c. the point of intersection of the tangents extended from each end of a circular curve. [t. L: whirl, crown of the head, summit]

ver·ti·cal (vûr′tə kəl), *adj.* 1. being in a position or direction perpendicular to the plane of the horizon; upright; plumb. 2. of, pertaining to, or situated at the vertex. 3. *Bot.* a. (of a leaf) having the blade in a perpendicular plane, so that neither of the surfaces can be called upper or under. b. in the same direction as the axis; lengthwise. 4. of or pertaining to the consolidation of businesses or industries that are closely related in

the manufacture or sale of a certain commodity. —*n.* 5. a vertical line, plane, or the like. 6. vertical or upright position. 7. (in a truss) a vertical member. [t. LL: s. *verticālis,* der. *vertex* VERTEX] —**ver′ti·cal′i·ty, ver′ti·cal·ness,** *n.* —**ver′ti·cal·ly,** *adv.* —Syn. 1. See **upright.** —Ant. 1. horizontal.

vertical circle, *Astron.* (in the celestial sphere) any great circle passing through the zenith and the nadir.

vertical union, a labor union which attempts to organize workers according to industry rather than skill or craft.

ver·ti·ces (vûr′tə sēz′), *n.* a pl. of **vertex.**

ver·ti·cil (vûr′tə sĭl), *n. Bot., Zool.* a whorl or circle, as of leaves, hairs, etc., arranged round a point on an axis. [t. L: m.s. *verticillus,* dim. of *vertex* whorl (of a spindle)]

ver·ti·cil·las·ter (vûr′tə sĭ lăs′tər), *n. Bot.* an inflorescence in which the flowers are arranged in a seeming whorl, consisting in fact of a pair of opposite axillary, usually sessile, cymes, as in many mints. [t. NL: f. s. L *verticillus* whorl + -aster -ASTER]

ver·tic·il·late (vər tĭs′ə lĭt, -lāt′, vûr′tə sĭl′āt), *adj.* 1. disposed in or forming verticils or whorls, as flowers, etc. 2. (of plants) having flowers, etc., so arranged or disposed. Also, **ver·tic′il·lat′ed.** —**ver·tic′il·late·ly,** *adv.* —**ver·tic′il·la′tion,** *n.*

Verticils

ver·tig·i·nous (vər tĭj′ə nəs), *adj.* 1. whirling or rotary. 2. affected with vertigo. 3. liable to cause vertigo. 4. apt to change quickly; unstable. [t. L: m.s. *vertīginōsus* suffering from giddiness] —**ver·tig′i·nous·ly,** *adv.* —**ver·tig′i·nous·ness,** *n.*

ver·ti·go (vûr′tə gō′), *n., pl.* **vertigoes, vertigines** (vər tĭj′ə nēz′). *Pathol.* a disordered condition in which an individual, or whatever is around him, seems to be whirling about; dizziness. [t. L: lit., whirling around]

ver·tu (vər tōō′, vûr′tōō), *n.* virtu.

Ver·tum·nus (vər tŭm′nəs), *n.* the Roman divinity of gardens and orchards, worshiped as the god of the changing seasons. Also, **Vortumnus.** [t. L, der. *vertere* turn, change]

Ver·u·la·mi·um (vĕr′yŏŏ lā′mĭ əm), *n.* ancient name of St. Albans.

ver·vain (vûr′vān), *n.* any plant of the genus *Verbena* (see **verbena**), esp. one of the species with small spicate flowers, as *V. officinalis,* a common European species. [ME *verveine,* t. OF, g. L *verbēna* green bough]

verve (vûrv), *n.* 1. enthusiasm or energy, as in literary or artistic work; spirit, liveliness, or vigor: *her novel lacks verve.* 2. *Rare.* talent. [t. F: enthusiasm, fancy; orig. uncert.]

ver·vet (vûr′vĭt), *n.* an African monkey, *Cercopithecus æthiops pygerythrus,* allied to the green monkey and the grivet, but distinguished by a rusty patch at the root of the tail. [t. F, b. *ver(t)* green and *(gri)vet* grivet]

ver·y (vĕr′ĭ), *adv., adj.,* **verier, veriest.** —*adv.* 1. in a high degree, extremely, or exceedingly. 2. (a mere intensive emphasizing superlatives or stressing identity or oppositeness): *the very best thing to be done, in the very same place.* —*adj.* 3. precise or identical: *the very thing you should not have done.* 4. even (what is specified): *they grew to dread his very name.* 5. mere: *the very thought is distressing.* 6. sheer: *to weep for very joy.* 7. actual: *caught in the very act.* 8. (with emphatic or intensive force) being such in the true or full sense of the term: *the very heart of the matter.* 9. true, genuine, or real: *the very God.* 10. *Archaic.* rightful or legitimate. [ME, t. OF: m. *verai,* der. L *vērus* true]

very high frequency, designed for the production or reproduction of frequencies ranging from 30 to 300 megacycles. *Abbr.:* vhf

ve·si·ca (vĭ sī′kə), *n., pl.* **-cae** (-sē). 1. a bladder; a sac. 2. the urinary bladder, *Vesica urinaria,* or gall bladder, *V. fellea.* [L: bladder, blister]

ves·i·cal (vĕs′ə kəl), *adj.* of or pertaining to a vesica or bladder, esp. the urinary bladder.

ves·i·cant (vĕs′ə kənt), *adj.* 1. vesicating; producing a blister or blisters, as a medicinal substance. —*n.* 2. a vesicant agent or substance. 3. *Chem. War.* a chemical agent that causes burns and destruction of tissue both internally and externally. [t. NL: s. *vēsicans* blistering]

ves·i·cate (vĕs′ə kāt′), *v.t.,* **-cated, -cating.** to raise vesicles or blisters on; blister. —**ves′i·ca′tion,** *n.*

ves·i·ca·to·ry (vĕs′ə kə tōr′ĭ, və sĭk′ə tōr′ĭ), *adj., n., pl.* **-ries.** vesicant.

ves·i·cle (vĕs′ə kəl), *n.* 1. a little sac or cyst. 2. *Anat., Zool.* a small bladderlike cavity, esp. one filled with fluid. 3. *Pathol.* a circumscribed elevation of the epidermis containing serous fluid. 4. *Bot.* a small bladder, or bladderlike air cavity. 5. *Geol.* a small, usually spherical cavity in a rock or mineral, due to gas or vapor. [t. L: m.s. *vēsicula,* dim. of *vēsica* bladder, blister]

ve·sic·u·lar (və sĭk′yə lər), *adj.* 1. of or pertaining to vesicles. 2. having the form of a vesicle. 3. characterized by or consisting of vesicles. —**ve·sic′u·lar·ly,** *adv.*

vesicular exanthema, a specific infectious disease of swine, closely resembling foot-and-mouth disease.

ve·sic·u·late (*adj.* və sĭk′yə lĭt, -lāt′; *v.* və sĭk′yə lāt′), *adj., v.,* **-lated, -lating.** —*adj.* 1. characterized by or covered with vesicles. 2. of the nature of a vesicle. —*v.t., v.i.* 3. to make or become vesiculate or vesicular. —**ve·sic′u·la′tion,** *n.*

Ves·pa·si·an (věs·pā′zhĭ ən, -zhən), *n*. (*Titus Flavius Sabinus Vespasianus*) A.D. 9–79, Roman emperor from A.D. 70 to 79.

ves·per (věs′pər), *n*. **1.** evening. **2.** (*cap*.) the evening star, esp. Venus; Hesper. **3.** an evening prayer, service, song, etc. **4.** a vesper bell. **5.** (*pl*.) vespers. —*adj*. **6.** of, pertaining to, appearing in, or proper to the evening. **7.** of or pertaining to vespers. [ME, t. L]

ves·per·al (věs′pər əl), *n. Eccles*. **1.** that part of the antiphonarium which contains the chants for vespers. **2.** a cloth used between offices to cover the altar cloth.

ves·pers (věs′pərz), *n.pl*. (*sometimes cap*.) **1.** a religious service held in the late afternoon or the evening. **2.** the sixth of the seven canonical hours, or the service for it, occurring in the late afternoon or evening. **3.** *Rom. Cath. Ch*. a part of the office to be said in the evening by those in major orders, frequently made a public ceremony in the afternoon or evenings of Sundays and holy days. **4.** evensong. [t. ML: m. *vesperae*, pl., vespers, special use of L *vespera* evening]

vesper sparrow, the common bay-winged bunting, *Pooecetes gramineus*, of North America.

ves·per·til·i·o·nine (věs′pər tĭl′Y ə nīn′, -nYn), *adj*. of or pertaining to the bats of the subfamily *Vespertilioninae*, common in temperate regions and including many well-known species. [f. s. L *vespertilio* bat + -INE[1]] —*ves·per·til·i·o·nid* (věs′pər tĭl′Y ə nYd), *n*., *adj*.

ves·per·tine (věs′pər tYn, -tīn′), *adj*. **1.** of, pertaining to, or occurring in the evening. **2.** *Bot*. opening or expanding in the evening, as certain flowers. **3.** *Zool*. appearing or flying in the early evening; crepuscular. Also, **ves·per·ti·nal** (věs′pər tī′nəl). [t. L: m.s. *vespertīnus* of the evening]

ves·pi·ar·y (věs′pĭ ĕr′Y), *n*., *pl*. **-aries**. a wasp's nest. [f. s. L *vespa* wasp + -*iary* as in APIARY]

ves·pid (věs′pYd), *n*. **1.** any member of the *Vespidae*, a widely distributed family of social wasps, including the hornets, which live in communities composed of males (drones), females (queens), and workers. —*adj*. **2.** belonging or pertaining to the *Vespidae*. [t. NL: s. *Vespidae*, der. L *vespa* wasp]

ves·pine (věs′pīn, -pYn), *adj*. **1.** of or pertaining to wasps. **2.** wasplike.

Ves·puc·ci (věs pōōt′chē), *n*. **Amerigo** (ä′mĕ rē′gô), (*Americus Vespucius*) 1451–1512, Italian merchant, adventurer, and explorer after whom America was named.

ves·sel (věs′əl), *n*. **1.** a craft for traveling on water, now esp. one larger than an ordinary rowboat; a ship or boat. **2.** an airship. **3.** a hollow or concave article, as a cup, bowl, pot, pitcher, vase, bottle, etc., for holding liquid or other contents. **4.** *Anat., Zool*. a tube or duct, as an artery, vein, or the like, containing or conveying blood or some other body fluid. **5.** *Bot*. a duct formed of connected cells which have lost their intervening partitions, containing or conveying sap, etc. **6.** a person regarded as a receptacle or container (chiefly in or after Biblical expressions). [ME, t. OF, g. L *vascellum* small vase. See VASE]

vest (věst), *n*. **1.** a short sleeveless garment worn by men under the coat. **2.** a similar garment, or a part or trimming simulating the front of such a garment, worn by women. **3.** *Brit*. an undervest or undershirt. **4.** a long garment resembling a cassock, worn by men in the time of Charles II. **5.** *Poetic*. dress, apparel, or vesture. **6.** *Archaic*. an outer garment, robe, or gown. **7.** *Rare*. an ecclesiastical vestment. [t. It.: m. *veste*, g. L *vestis* garment] —*v.t*. **8.** to clothe, dress, or robe. **9.** to dress in ecclesiastical vestments. **10.** to cover or drape (an altar). **11.** to place or settle (something, esp. property, rights, powers, etc.) in the possession or control of a person or persons (usually fol. by *in*): *to vest an estate or a title in a person*. **12.** to invest or endow (a person, etc.) with something, esp. with powers, functions, etc. —*v.i*. **13.** to put on vestments. **14.** to become vested in a person or persons, as a right. **15.** to pass into possession; to devolve upon a person as possessor. [ME, t. OF: m. *vestir*, g. L *vestīre* clothe] —*vest′less*, *adj*.

Ves·ta (věs′tə), *n*. **1.** *Rom. Myth*. the goddess of the hearth and hearth fire, worshiped in a temple containing an altar on which a sacred fire was kept burning under the care of vestal virgins. **2.** (*l.c.*) *Brit*. a short friction match of wax. **3.** (*l.c.*) *Brit*. a similar match of wood.

ves·tal (věs′təl), *adj*. **1.** of or pertaining to Vesta. **2.** pertaining to, characteristic of, or resembling a vestal virgin; virgin; chaste. —*n*. **3.** a vestal virgin. **4.** a virgin; a chaste unmarried woman. **5.** a nun.

vestal virgin, (among the ancient Romans) one of four, later six, virgins consecrated to Vesta and to the service of watching the sacred fire kept burning perpetually on her altar.

vest·ed (věs′tYd), *adj*. **1.** settled or secured in the possession of a person or persons, as a complete or fixed right, an interest sometimes possessory, sometimes future, which has substance because of its relative certainty. **2.** clothed or robed, esp. in ecclesiastical vestments: *a vested choir*.

vest·ee (věs tē′), *n*. a decorative front piece worn under a woman's jacket or blouse and visible between its open edges. [f. VEST + -*ee*, dim. suffix]

ves·ti·ar·y (věs′tĭ ĕr′Y), *adj*. of or pertaining to garments or dress. [t. L: m.s. *vestiārius*]

ves·tib·u·lar (věs tĭb′yə lər), *adj*. of, pertaining to, or resembling a vestibule.

ves·ti·bule (věs′tə būl′), *n*., *v*., **-buled**, **-buling**. —*n*. **1.** a passage, hall, or antechamber between the outer door and the interior parts of a house or building. **2.** a covered and enclosed space at the end of a railroad passenger car, having side and trap doors for entering and leaving the train, and itself affording protected passage to the next car. **3.** *Anat., Zool*. any of various cavities or hollows regarded as forming an approach or entrance to another cavity or space: *the vestibule of the ear*. See diag. under ear. —*v.t*. **4.** to provide with a vestibule or vestibules, as a railroad car. **5.** to unite by means of vestibules, as a railroad train. [t. L: m.s. *vestibulum*]

vestibule school, a department of an industrial establishment in which new employees are trained for the work they are to perform.

ves·tige (věs′tYj), *n*. **1.** a mark, trace, or visible evidence of something which is no longer present or in existence. **2.** a surviving evidence or memorial of some condition, practice, etc. **3.** a very slight trace or amount of something. **4.** *Biol*. a degenerate or imperfectly developed organ or structure having little or no utility, but which in an earlier stage of the individual or in preceding generations performed a useful function. **5.** *Rare*. a footprint or track. [t. F, t. L: m. *vestīgium* footprint] —**Syn. 1.** See trace[1].

ves·tig·i·al (věs tĭj′Yəl), *adj*. pertaining to or of the nature of a vestige. —**ves·tig′i·al·ly**, *adv*.

ves·tig·i·um (věs tĭj′Yəm), *n*., *pl*. **-tigia** (-tĭj′Yə). *Anat*. a vestige; a vestigial structure of any kind.

vest·ing (věs′tYng), *n*. cloth for making vests.

vest·ment (věst′mənt), *n*. **1.** a garment, esp. an outer garment, robe, or gown. **2.** an official or ceremonial robe. **3.** *Eccles*. **a.** one of the garments worn by the clergy and their assistants, choristers, etc., during divine service and on other occasions. **b.** one of the garments worn by the celebrant, deacon, and subdeacon during the celebration of the Eucharist. **4.** something that clothes or covers like a garment. [ME *vestement*, t. OF, der. *vestir* clothe, on model of L *vestimentum* clothing] —*vest′ment·al*, *adj*.

vest-pock·et (věst′pŏk′Yt), *adj*. miniature; designed to be carried in a pocket of the vest.

ves·try (věs′trY), *n*., *pl*. **-tries**. **1.** a room in or a building attached to a church, in which the vestments, and sometimes also the sacred vessels, etc., are kept; a sacristy. **2.** (in some churches) a room in or a building attached to a church, used as a chapel, for prayer meetings, for the Sunday school, etc. **3.** (in the Protestant Episcopal Church in the U.S.) a committee, chosen by the members of a congregation, who, in conjunction with the churchwardens, manage the temporal affairs of a church. **4.** (in parishes of the Church of England) a meeting of all, or of a committee of, the parishioners held in the vestry for the despatch of the official business of the parish. [ME, f. VEST, v. + -RY]

ves·try·man (věs′trY mən), *n*., *pl*. **-men**. a member of a church vestry.

ves·ture (věs′chər), *n*., *v*., **-tured**, **-turing**. —*n*. **1.** *Archaic* or *Literary*. clothing; garments. **2.** *Archaic* or *Literary*. something that covers like a garment; a covering. **3.** *Law*. **a.** everything growing on and covering the land, with the exception of trees. **b.** any such product, as grass or wheat. —*v.t*. **4.** *Archaic* or *Literary*. to clothe, as with vesture. [ME, t. OF, der. *vestir* clothe, influenced by ML *vestitūra* clothing]

Ve·su·vi·an (və sōō′vY ən), *adj*. **1.** of, pertaining to, or resembling Mount Vesuvius; volcanic. —*n*. (*l.c.*) **2.** a kind of match used for lighting cigars, etc.; a fusee. **3.** vesuvianite.

ve·su·vi·an·ite (və sōō′vY ə nīt′), *n*. a mineral, a hydrous silicate of calcium and aluminum chiefly, commonly in prismatic crystals and usually of a brown to green color; idocrase.

Ve·su·vi·us (və sōō′vY əs), *n*. **Mount**, an active volcano in SW Italy, near Naples: many severe eruptions; the ancient cities of Pompeii and Herculaneum were buried by an eruption, A.D. 79. ab. 4000 ft.

vet[1] (vět), *n*., *v*., **vetted**, **vetting**. *Colloq*. —*n*. **1.** veterinarian. —*v.t*. **2.** to examine or treat as a veterinarian or (humorously) a doctor does. —*v.i*. **3.** to work as a veterinary surgeon. [short for VETERINARY]

vet[2] (vět), *n*. *Colloq*. a veteran.

vet., **1.** veteran. **2.** veterinarian; veterinary.

vetch (věch), *n*. **1.** any of various leguminous plants, mostly climbing herbs, of the genus *Vicia*, as *V. sativa*, the common vetch, cultivated for forage and soil improvement. **2.** any of various allied plants, as *Lathyrus sativus*, of Europe, cultivated for its edible seeds and as a forage plant. **3.** the beanlike seed or fruit of any such plant. [ME *veche*, t. d. OF, g. L *vicia*] —*vetch′like*, *adj*.

vetch·ling (věch′lYng), *n*. any of the plants constituting the leguminous genus *Lathyrus*, as *L. pratensis* which is common in meadows.

veter., veterinary.

vet·er·an (vět′ər ən, vět′rən), *n*. **1.** one who has seen long service in any occupation or office. **2.** one who has had experience in some field, esp. a soldier. —*adj*. **3.** (of soldiers) having had service or experience in warfare:

veteran troops. **4.** experienced through long servce or practice; having served for a long period; grown old in service. **5.** of, pertaining to, or characteristic of veterans. [t. L: s. *veterānus*, der. *vetus* old]

vet·er·i·nar·i·an (vĕt/ərə när/Ĭ ən, vĕt/rə-), *n.* one who practices veterinary medicine or surgery.

vet·er·i·nar·y (vĕt/ər ə nĕr/Ĭ, vĕt/rə-), *n., pl.* **-naries**, *adj.* —*n.* **1.** a veterinarian. —*adj.* **2.** of the medical and surgical treatment of domesticated animals. [t. L: m.s. *veterīnārius*, der. *veterīnus* pertaining to cattle]

Veterans' Day, See **Armistice Day.**

veterinary medicine, that branch of medicine that concerns itself with the study, prevention, and treatment of animal diseases.

vet·i·ver (vĕt/ə vər), *n.* **1.** the long fibrous aromatic roots of an East Indian grass, *Vetiveria zizanoides*, used for making hangings and screens, and yielding **vetiver** oil which is used in perfumery. **2.** the grass itself. [t. Tamil: m. *vettĭvēru*]

ve·to (vē/tō), *n., pl.* **-toes**, *v.,* **-toed**, **-toing.** —*n.* **1.** the power or right vested in one branch of a government to negative the determinations of another branch; esp., the right of a chief executive, as a president or governor, to reject bills passed by the legislature. **2.** the exercise of this right. **3.** a document or message by which this right is exercised, in which the executive officially communicates his reasons for rejecting a legislative bill. **4.** a prohibition directed against some proposed or intended act. **5.** the power or right of preventing action by a prohibition. —*v.t.* **6.** to reject, as a legislative bill, by exercising the right of veto. **7.** to refuse to consent to. [t. L: I forbid] —**ve/to·er**, *n.* —**ve/to·less**, *adj.*

vet. sci., veterinary science.

Vet·ter (vĕt/ər), *n.* Vätter.

vex (vĕks), *v.t.* **1.** to irritate; annoy; provoke; make angry: *enough to vex a saint.* **2.** to torment; plague; worry: *want of money vexes many.* **3.** to agitate, discuss, or debate (a subject, etc.) with vigor: *a vexed question.* **4.** *Archaic or Poetic.* to disturb by motion; stir up; toss about. **5.** *Archaic.* to trouble or afflict physically. [ME *veze*(n), t. L: m. *vexāre* agitate] —**vex/er**, *n.* —**vex/-ing·ly**, *adv.*

vex·a·tion (vĕks ā/shən), *n.* **1.** act of vexing. **2.** state of being vexed. **3.** something that vexes.

vex·a·tious (vĕks ā/shəs), *adj.* **1.** causing vexation; vexing; annoying. **2.** *Law.* (of legal actions) instituted without sufficient grounds, and serving only to cause annoyance to the defendant. —**vex·a/tious·ly**, *adv.* —**vex·a/tious·ness**, *n.*

vexed (vĕkst), *adj.* **1.** disturbed; troubled; annoyed. **2.** much discussed or disputed. **3.** tossed about, as waves. —**vex·ed·ly** (vĕk/sĭd lĭ), *adv.* —**vex/ed·ness**, *n.*

vex·il·lar·y (vĕk/sə lĕr/Ĭ), *n., pl.* **-laries**, *adj.* —*n.* **1.** one of the oldest class of ancient Roman veteran soldiers, who served under a special standard. —*adj.* **2.** Also, **vex/il·lar.** of or pertaining to a vexillum. [t. L: m.s. *vexillārius*]

vex·il·late (vĕk/sə lĭt, -lāt/), *adj.* having a vexillum or vexilla.

vex·il·lum (vĕk sĭl/əm), *n., pl.* **vexilla** (vĕk sĭl/ə). **1.** a military standard or flag carried by ancient Roman troops. **2.** a body of men serving under such a standard. **3.** Also, **vex·il** (vĕk/sĭl). *Bot.* the large upper petal of a papilionaceous flower. See illus. under **papilionaceous. 4.** *Ornith.* the web or vane of a feather. [t. L: standard]

V.F.W., Veterans of Foreign Wars.

V.G., Vicar-General.

v.g., (L *verbi gratia*) for example.

vhf, very high frequency.

Vi, *Chem.* virginium.

V.I., **1.** Vancouver Island. **2.** Virgin Islands.

v.i., **1.** verb intransitive. **2.** vide infra.

vi·a (vī/ə), *prep.* by way of; by a route that passes through: *go to Reno via Akron.* [t. L, abl. of *via* way]

vi·a·ble (vī/ə bəl), *adj.* **1.** capable of living. **2.** *Physiol.* **a.** physically fitted to live. **b.** (of a fetus) having reached such a stage of development as to permit continued existence, under normal conditions, outside of the womb. **3.** *Bot.* able to live and grow. [t. F, der. *vie* life, g. L *vīta*] —**vi/a·bil/i·ty**, *n.*

vi·a·duct (vī/ə dŭkt/), *n.* **1.** a bridge consisting of a series of narrow masonry arches with high supporting piers, for carrying a road, railroad, etc., over a valley, ravine, or the like. **2.** a similar bridge of steel girders. [f. L *via* way + *-duct* as in AQUEDUCT]

Viaduct (def. 1)

vi·al (vī/əl, vīl), *n., v.,* **-aled**, **-aling** or (*esp. Brit.*) **-alled**, **-alling.** —*n.* **1.** a small vessel, as of glass, for liquids; phial. **2.** (*pl. or sing.*) a store or accumulation (of wrath, indignation, etc.) poured upon an offender, victim, etc. (Rev. 15:7; 16:1–17). —*v.t.* **3.** to put into or keep in a vial. [OF *fiole*, Pr. *fiola*, t. LL *fiola*, L *phiala*, der. Gk. *phialē* saucer-like drinking vessel]

vi·a me·di·a (vī/ə mē/dĭ ə), *Latin.* a middle way; a mean between two extremes.

vi·and (vī/ənd), *n.* **1.** an article of food. **2.** (*pl.*) articles or dishes of food, now usually of a choice or delicate kind. [ME *vyaunde*, t. OF: m. *viande*, g. L. *vivenda* things to be lived on]

vi·at·ic (vī ăt/Ĭk), *adj.* pertaining to a way or road, a journey, or traveling. Also, **vi·at·i·cal.** [t. L: s. *viāticus*]

vi·at·i·cum (vī ăt/ə kəm), *n., pl.* **-ca** (-kə), **-cums.** **1.** *Eccles.* the Eucharist or Communion as given to a person dying or in danger of death. **2.** (among the ancient Romans) a provision or allowance for traveling, orig. of transportation and supplies, later of money, made to officials on public missions. **3.** money or necessaries for any journey. [t. L]

vi·a·tor (vī ā/tôr), *n., pl.* **viatores** (vī/ə-tôr/ēz). a traveler; a wayfaring person. [t. L]

Vi·borg (vē/bôr/y), *n.* Swedish name of **Vyborg.**

vi·brac·u·lum (vī brăk/yə ləm), *n., pl.* **-la** (-lə). one of the long, tapering, whiplike, movable appendages possessed by certain polyzoans. [NL, der. L *vibrāre* shake] —**vi·brac/u·lar**, *adj.*

Vibracula (magnified)

vi·brant (vī/brənt), *adj.* **1.** moving to and fro rapidly; vibrating. **2.** vibrating so as to produce sound, as a string. **3.** (of sounds) characterized by perceptible vibration, or resonant. **4.** pulsating with energy. **5.** full of vigor; energetic; powerful. **6.** exciting; producing a thrill. **7.** *Phonet.* made with tonal vibration of the vocal cords; voiced. —*n.* **8.** *Phonet.* a vibrant sound (opposed to *surd*). [t. L: s. *vibrans*, ppr.] —**vi/bran·cy**, *n.* —**vi/brant·ly**, *adv.*

vi·brate (vī/brāt), *v.,* **-brated**, **-brating.** —*v.i.* **1.** to move to and fro, as a pendulum does; oscillate. **2.** to move to and fro or up and down quickly and repeatedly; quiver; tremble. **3.** (of sounds) to produce or have a quivering or vibratory effect; resound. **4.** to thrill, as in emotional response. **5.** to move between extremes; fluctuate; vacillate. —*v.t.* **6.** to cause to move to and fro, swing, or oscillate. **7.** to cause to move to and fro or up and down quickly and repeatedly; cause to quiver or tremble. **8.** to give forth or emit (sound, etc.) by or as by vibratory motion. **9.** to measure or indicate by vibration or oscillation: *a pendulum vibrating seconds.* [t. L: m.s. *vibrātus*, pp., shaken] —**Syn. 2.** See **shake.**

vi·bra·tile (vī/brə tĭl, -tĭl/), *adj.* **1.** capable of vibrating, or susceptible of being vibrated. **2.** having a vibratory motion. **3.** pertaining to or of the nature of vibration. —**vi·bra·til·i·ty** (vī/brə tĭl/ə tĭ), *n.*

vi·bra·tion (vī brā/shən), *n.* **1.** act of vibrating; oscillation. **2.** state of vibrating; tremulous effect. **3.** *Physics.* **a.** the oscillating, reciprocating, or other periodic motion of a rigid or elastic body forced from a position or state of equilibrium. **b.** the analogous motion of the particles of a mass of air, etc., whose state of equilibrium has been disturbed, as in transmitting sound, etc. **c.** the vibratory motion of a string or other sonorous body, producing musical sound. **4.** a single vibrating motion; an oscillation; a quiver or tremor. —**vi·bra/tion·al**, *adj.* —**vi·bra/tion·less**, *adj.*

vi·bra·tion-proof (vī brā/shən proof/), *adj.* not subject to vibration.

vi·bra·tive (vī/brə tĭv), *adj.* vibratory.

vi·bra·to (vē brä/tō), *n., pl.* **-tos.** *Music.* a pulsating effect, produced in singing by the rapid reiteration of emphasis on a tone, and on bowed instruments by a rapid change of pitch corresponding to the vocal tremolo. [It., pp. of *vibrare* vibrate, t. L]

vi·bra·tor (vī/brā tər), *n.* **1.** one who or that which vibrates. **2.** any of various instruments or devices causing a vibratory motion or action. **3.** an appliance with a rubber or other tip of variable shape, made to oscillate very rapidly, used in vibratory massage. **4.** *Elect.* a device in which, by continually repeated impulse, an appropriately designed component is set in continuous vibration. **5.** a device for producing electrical oscillations.

vi·bra·to·ry (vī/brə tôr/Ĭ), *adj.* **1.** producing vibration. **2.** vibrating, or admitting of vibration. **3.** of the nature of or consisting in vibration. **4.** pertaining to vibration. Also, **vibrative.**

vib·ri·o (vĭb/rĭ ō/), *n., pl.* **-rios.** *Bacteriol.* any bacterium of the genus *Vibrio*, made up of comma-shaped organisms, the most important of which is V. *comma*, the causative agent of Asiatic cholera. [NL der. L *vibrāre* shake] —**vib·ri·oid** (vĭb/rĭ oid/), *adj.*

vi·bris·sa (vī brĭs/ə), *n., pl.* **-brissae** (-brĭs/ē). **1.** one of the stiff, bristly hairs growing about the mouth of certain animals, as a whisker of a cat. **2.** one of the long, slender, bristlelike feathers growing along the side of the mouth in many birds. [t. L: hair in the nostrils]

vi·bur·num (vī bûr/nəm), *n.* **1.** any of the shrubs or small trees constituting the caprifoliaceous genus *Viburnum*, species of which, as the cranberry bush, V. *Opulus*, or snowball, are cultivated for ornament. **2.** the dried bark of various species of *Viburnum*, used in medicine. [t. L: the wayfaring tree or hobblebush]

vic·ar (vĭk/ər), *n.* **1.** *Ch. of Eng.* **a.** a person acting as priest of a parish in place of the rector, or as representative of a religious community to which the tithes belong. **b.** the priest of a parish the tithes of which are impropriated, and who receives only the smaller tithes or a salary. **2.** *Prot. Episc. Ch.* **a.** a clergyman whose sole or chief charge is a chapel dependent on the church of a parish. **b.** a bishop's assistant in charge of a church or mission. **3.** *Rom. Cath. Ch.* **a.** an ecclesiastic representing the

Pope or a bishop. **b.** the Pope as the representative on earth of God or Christ. **4.** one acting in place of another. **5.** a person authorized to perform the functions of another; a deputy. [ME *vicare*, t. AF, t. L: m.s. *vicārius* substitute] —**vic′ar·ship′,** *n.*

vic·ar·age (vĭk′ər ĭj), *n.* **1.** residence of a vicar. **2.** the benefice of a vicar. **3.** the office or duties of a vicar.

vicar apostolic, *Rom. Cath. Ch.* **1.** a missionary or titular bishop stationed either in a country where no episcopal see has yet been established, or in one where the succession of bishops has been interrupted. **2.** (formerly) an archbishop, bishop, or other ecclesiastic to whom the Pope delegated a portion of his jurisdiction.

vic·ar·ate (vĭk′ər ĭt, -ə rāt′), *n.* vicariate.

vicar fo·rane (fō rān′), *Rom. Cath. Ch.* an ecclesiastical dignitary appointed by the bishop to exercise a limited jurisdiction in a particular town or district of his diocese. [f. VICAR + s. L *forāneus* living outside]

vic·ar-gen·er·al (vĭk′ər gĕn′ər əl), *n.*, *pl.* **vicars-general. 1.** *Rom. Cath. Ch.* a priest deputized by a bishop to assist him in the administration of a diocese. **2.** *Ch. of Eng.* an ecclesiastical officer, usually a layman, who assists a bishop or an archbishop in the discharge of his judicial or administrative duties. **3.** a deputy with extensive power or jurisdiction (a title given to Thomas Cromwell).

vi·car·i·al (vī kâr′ĭ əl, vĭ-), *adj.* **1.** of or pertaining to a vicar or vicars. **2.** acting as or holding the office of a vicar. **3.** delegated or vicarious, as powers.

vi·car·i·ate (vī kâr′ĭ ĭt, -āt′, vĭ-), *n.* **1.** the office or authority of a vicar. **2.** a district under a vicar. Also, **vicarate.**

vi·car·i·ous (vī kâr′ĭ əs, vĭ-), *adj.* **1.** performed, exercised, received, or suffered in place of another: *vicarious punishment.* **2.** taking the place of another person or thing; acting or serving as a substitute. **3.** pertaining to or involving the substitution of one for another. **4.** *Physiol.* pertaining to or denoting the performance by one organ of part of the functions normally performed by another. [t. L: m. *vicārius* substituted] —**vi·car′i·ous·ly,** *adv.* —**vi·car′i·ous·ness,** *n.*

vic·ar·ly (vĭk′ər lĭ), *adj.* pertaining to, resembling, or suggesting a vicar in manner, function, dress, etc.

Vicar of (Jesus) Christ, *Rom. Cath. Ch.* the pope, with reference to his claim to stand in the place of Jesus Christ and possess His authority in the church.

Vicar of Wakefield, The, a novel (1766) by Goldsmith.

vice[1] (vīs), *n.* **1.** an immoral or evil habit or practice; a grave moral fault. **2.** immoral conduct or life; indulgence in impure or degrading practices. **3.** a particular form of depravity. **4.** a fault, defect, or imperfection: *a vice of literary style.* **5.** a physical defect or infirmity: *a constitutional vice.* **6.** a bad habit, as in a horse. **7.** (*cap.*) a character in the English morality plays, a personification of general vice or of a particular vice, serving as the buffoon. [ME, t. OF, g. L *vitium* fault] —**Syn. 1.** See **fault.**

vice[2] (vīs), *n.*, *v.t.*, **viced, vicing.** vise.

vi·ce[3] (vī′sĭ), *prep.* instead of; in the place of. [t. L, abl. of *vicis* turn]

vice-, a prefix denoting a substitute, deputy, or subordinate: *vice-chairman, viceroy, vicegerent.* [see VICE[3]]

vice-ad·mi·ral (vīs′ ăd′mə rəl), *n.* a naval officer next in rank below an admiral.

vice-chan·cel·lor (vīs′chăn′sə lər, -chän′-), *n.* **1.** a substitute, deputy, or subordinate chancellor. **2.** a chancery judge acting as assistant to the chancellor.

vice-con·sul (vīs′ kŏn′səl), *n.* a consular officer of a grade below that of consul.

vice·ge·ral (vīs jĭr′əl), *adj.* of a vicegerent or his position.

vice·ge·ren·cy (vīs jĭr′ən sĭ), *n.*, *pl.* **-cies. 1.** the position, government, or office of a vicegerent. **2.** the territory or district under a vicegerent.

vice·ge·rent (vīs jĭr′ənt), *n.* **1.** an officer deputed by a ruler or supreme head to exercise the powers of the ruler or head. **2.** any deputy. —*adj.* **3.** exercising delegated powers. **4.** characterized by delegation of powers. [t. ML: s. *vicegerens,* ppr., place-holding, substituting]

vice·less (vīs′lĭs), *adj.* free from vices or vice.

vic·e·nar·y (vīs′ə ner′ĭ), *adj.* pertaining to or consisting of twenty. [t. L: m.s. *vicēnārius*]

vi·cen·ni·al (vī sĕn′ĭ əl), *adj.* **1.** of or for twenty years. **2.** occurring every twenty years. [f. s. L *vicennium* period of twenty years + -AL[1]]

Vi·cen·za (vē chĕn′tsä), *n.* a city in NE Italy, in Venezia. 83,000 (est. 1954).

Vice-Pres., Vice-President.

vice-pres·i·dent (vīs′prĕz′ə dənt), *n.* an officer next in rank to a president and taking his place under certain conditions (as the **Vice-President of the United States,** who is elected at the same time as the President, and succeeds to the presidential office on the resignation, removal, death, or disability of the President). —**vice′-pres′i·den·cy,** *n.* —**vice′-pres·i·den′tial,** *adj.*

vice·re·gal (vīs rē′gəl), *adj.* of or pertaining to a viceroy. —**vice·re′gal·ly,** *adv.*

vice-re·gent (vīs′rē′jənt), *n.* **1.** a deputy regent; one who acts in the place of a ruler, governor, or sovereign. —*adj.* **2.** of, pertaining to, or occupying the position of a vice-regent. —**vice′-re′gen·cy,** *n.*

vice·roy (vīs′roi), *n.* **1.** one appointed to rule a country or province as the deputy of the sovereign: *the viceroy of India.* **2.** an American butterfly, *Basilarchia archippus,* having an orange-red color with black markings, whose larvae feed on willow and other trees. [t. F, f. *vice* VICE[3] + *roi* king] —**vice′roy·ship′,** *n.*

vice·roy·al·ty (vīs roi′əl tĭ), *n.*, *pl.* **-ties. 1.** the dignity, office, or period of office of a viceroy. **2.** a country or province ruled by a viceroy.

vi·ce ver·sa (vī′sĭ vûr′sə), conversely; the order being changed (from that of a preceding statement): *A distrusts B, and vice versa.* [t. L]

Vi·chy (vĭsh′ĭ; *Fr.* vē shē′), *n.* a city in central France: the capital of unoccupied France, 1940–44; hot springs. 30,403 (1954).

vi·chy·ssoise (vĭsh′ĭ-swäz′), *n. French.* a creamy potato and onion soup, usually served cold.

vichy water (vĭsh′ĭ), **1.** a natural mineral water from springs at Vichy, containing sodium bicarbonate, other alkaline salts, etc., used in the treatment of digestive disturbances, gout, etc. **2.** some water of similar composition, natural or artificial. Also, **Vi′chy, vichy.**

vic·i·nage (vĭs′ə nĭj), *n.* **1.** the vicinity; the region near or about a place. **2.** a particular neighborhood or district, or the people belonging to it. **3.** proximity. [ME, t. OF, der. L *vīcīnus* near]

vic·i·nal (vĭs′ə nəl), *adj.* **1.** belonging to a neighborhood or district. **2.** neighboring; adjacent. **3.** *Crystall.* denoting planes whose position varies very little from planes of much simpler indices which they replace. [t. L: s. *vīcīnālis* neighboring]

vi·cin·i·ty (vĭ sĭn′ə tĭ), *n.*, *pl.* **-ties. 1.** the region near or about a place; the neighborhood or vicinage. **2.** the state or fact of being near in place; proximity; propinquity. [t. L: m.s. *vīcīnitas*]

vi·cious (vĭsh′əs), *adj.* **1.** addicted to or characterized by vice or immorality; depraved; profligate. **2.** given or disposed to evil or bad. **3.** reprehensible, blameworthy, or wrong, as an action, practice, etc. **4.** spiteful or malignant: *a vicious attack.* **5.** *Colloq.* unpleasantly severe: *a vicious headache.* **6.** characterized or marred by faults or defects; faulty; defective: *vicious reasoning.* **7.** (of a horse, etc.) having bad habits or an ugly disposition. **8.** *Obs.* morbid, foul, or noxious. [ME, t. L: m.s. *vitiōsus* faulty] —**vi′cious·ly,** *adv.* —**vi′cious·ness,** *n.*

vicious circle, 1. a situation in which solution of one problem creates problems whose solution is incompatible with the original circumstances. **2.** *Logic.* **a.** (in demonstration) the use of one proposition to establish a second, when the second proposition is in turn used to establish the first. **b.** (in definition) the use of one term in defining a second, the second in turn being used to define the first. **3.** *Med.* a series of unhealthy changes in which the first change produces the second which in turn affects the first.

vi·cis·si·tude (vĭ sĭs′ə tūd′, -tŏod′), *n.* **1.** a change or variation, or something different, occurring in the course of a thing. **2.** interchange or alternation, as of states or things. **3.** (*pl.*) changes, variations, successive or alternating phases or conditions, etc., in the course of anything. **4.** regular change or succession of one state or thing to another. **5.** change, mutation, or mutability. [t. L: m. *vicissitūdo* change] —**vi·cis·si·tu·di·nar·y** (vĭ sĭs′ə tū′də nĕr′ĭ, -tŏod′-), **vi·cis′si·tu′di·nous,** *adj.*

Vicks·burg (vĭks′bûrg), *n.* a city in W Mississippi, on the Mississippi river: important siege and Confederate surrender, 1863. 29,130 (1960).

vi·comte (vē kôNt′), *n. French.* viscount. —**vi·com·tesse** (vē kôN tĕs′), *n. fem.*

vi·con·ti·el (vī kŏn′tĭ əl), *adj. Early Eng. Law.* pertaining to the sheriff or viscount. [t. AF, der. *viconte* sheriff, viscount]

vic·tim (vĭk′tĭm), *n.* **1.** a sufferer from any destructive, injurious, or adverse action or agency: *victims of disease or oppression.* **2.** a dupe, as of a swindler. **3.** a person or animal sacrificed, or regarded as sacrificed: *war victims.* **4.** a living creature sacrificed in religious rites. [t. L: s. *victima* beast for sacrifice]

vic·tim·ize (vĭk′tə mīz′), *v.t.*, **-ized, -izing. 1.** to make a victim of. **2.** to dupe, swindle, or cheat: *to victimize poor widows.* **3.** to slay as or like a sacrificial victim. —**vic′tim·i·za′tion,** *n.* —**vic′tim·iz′er,** *n.* —**Syn. 2.** See **cheat.**

vic·tor (vĭk′tər), *n.* **1.** one who has vanquished or defeated an adversary; a conqueror. **2.** a winner in any struggle or contest. [ME, t. L]

Victor Em·man·u·el I (ĭ măn′yŏŏ əl), (It. *Vittorio Emanuele*) 1759–1824, king of Sardinia, 1802–21.

Victor Emmanuel II, 1820–78, king of Sardinia (1849–78) and first king of Italy (1861–78).

Victor Emmanuel III, 1869–1947, king of Italy, 1900–46. In June, 1944 his royal powers were given to Crown Prince Humbert but he kept his title of king and his position as head of the House of Savoy until the dissolution of the monarchy.

Vic·to·ri·a (vĭk tôr′Ĭ ə), *n.* **1.** 1819–1901, queen of Great Britain and Ireland (1837–1901), and empress of India (1876–1901). **2.** a state in SE Australia. 2,452,341 pop. (1954); 87,884 sq. mi. *Cap.:* Melbourne. **3.** Also, **Hong Kong.** a seaport in and the capital of Hong Kong colony, on the SE coast of China. 767,000 (est. 1955). **4.** a seaport in SW Canada, on Vancouver Island: the capital of British Columbia. with suburbs, 104,303 (1951). **5.** Lake. Also, **Victoria Nyanza.** a lake in E Africa: the second largest fresh-water lake in the world: principal head waters of the Nile. 26,828 sq. mi. **6. Mount,** a mountain of the Owen Stanley Range, in SE New Guinea. 13,030 ft. **7.** (*l.c.*) a low, light, four-wheeled carriage with a calash top, a seat for two passengers, and a perch in front for the driver. **8.** (*l.c.*) a touring car with a folding top, commonly covering only the rear seat. **9.** a water lily, *Victoria regia* (or *amazonica*), a native of still waters from Paraguay to Venezuela, with leaves often over 6 feet in diameter, and white to rose nocturnal flowers 12 to 18 inches across.

Victoria (def. 7)

Victoria Cross, a British decoration awarded to soldiers and sailors for acts of conspicuous bravery in the presence of the enemy.

Victoria Falls, 1. falls of the Zambezi river in S Africa between Zambia and Rhodesia near Livingstone. ab. 400 ft. high; over a mile wide. **2.** Iguassú Falls.

Victoria Land, a region in Antarctica, bordering on the Ross Sea: largely in Ross Dependency.

Vic·to·ri·an (vĭk tôr′Ĭ ən), *adj.* **1.** of or pertaining to Queen Victoria or her reign or period: *the Victorian age.* **2.** having the characteristics usually attributed to the Victorians, as bigotry and prudishness. —*n.* **3.** a person belonging to the Victorian period.

Vic·to·ri·an·ism (vĭk tôr′Ĭ ə nĭz′əm), *n.* **1.** the distinctive character, thought, tendencies, etc., of the Victorian period. **2.** a Victorian characteristic.

Victoria Ny·an·za (nĬ ăn′zə, nyän′zä). See **Victoria.**

vic·to·ri·ous (vĭk tôr′Ĭ əs), *adj.* **1.** having achieved a victory. **2.** characterized by or pertaining to victory. **3.** conquering; triumphant. —**vic·to′ri·ous·ly,** *adv.* —**vic·to′ri·ous·ness,** *n.*

vic·to·ry (vĭk′tə rĬ), *n., pl.* **-ries. 1.** the ultimate and decisive superiority in a battle or any contest. **2.** a success or triumph won over the enemy in battle or war, or an engagement ending in such a triumph: *naval victories.* **3.** any success or successful performance achieved over an adversary or opponent, opposition, difficulties, etc. [ME *victorie*, t. L: m. *victōria*] —**Syn. 1.** VICTORY, CONQUEST, TRIUMPH refer to a successful outcome of a struggle. VICTORY suggests the decisive defeat of an opponent in a contest of any kind: *victory in battle, a football victory.* CONQUEST implies the taking over of control by the victor, and the obedience of the conquered: *a war of conquest, the conquest of Peru.* TRIUMPH implies a particularly outstanding victory: *the triumph of a righteous cause, of justice.* —**Ant. 1.** defeat.

Victory Medal, a round bronze medal awarded to all men who served in the armed forces of the United States during World War I.

victory ribbon, a service ribbon worn on the left breast by men entitled to wear the Victory Medal.

vic·tress (vĭk′trĬs), *n.* a female victor.

Vic·tro·la (vĭk trō′lə), *n. Trademark.* a phonograph.

vict·ual (vĭt′əl), *n., v.,* **-ualed, -ualing** or (*esp. Brit.*) **-ualled, -ualling.** —*n.* **1.** (*pl.*) *Chiefly Dial. or Colloq.* articles of food prepared for use. **2.** *Archaic or Dial.* food or provisions, usually for human beings. —*v.t.* **3.** to supply with victuals. —*v.i.* **4.** to take or obtain victuals. **5.** *Archaic.* to eat or feed. [ME *vitaile,* t. OF, g. LL *victuālia* provisions] —**vict′ual·less,** *adj.*

vict·ual·age (vĭt′əl Ĭj), *n.* food; provisions; victuals.

vict·ual·er (vĭt′əl ər, vĭt′lər), *n.* **1.** one who furnishes victuals or provisions; a sutler. **2.** a supply ship. **3.** *Brit.* a keeper of an inn or tavern. Also, *esp. Brit.,* **vict′ual·ler.**

vi·cu·ña (vĬ kōōn′yə, vĬ kōōn′nə), *n.* **1.** a wild South American ruminant, *Lama vicugna,* of the Andes, related to the guanaco but smaller, and having a soft, delicate wool. **2.** a fabric made of this wool, or of some substitute, usually twilled and finished with a soft nap. [t. Sp., t. Kechua: m. *vicunna*]

Vicuna, *Lama vicugna* (2½ ft. or more high at the shoulder)

vid., vide.

Vi·dar (vē′där), *n. Scand. Myth.* a taciturn god of great strength, son of Odin and the giantess Grid.

vi·de (vī′dĬ), *v. Latin.* see (used esp. in making reference to parts of a text).

vi·de an·te (vī′dĬ ăn′tĬ), *Latin.* see before.

vi·de in·fra (vī′dĬ Ĭn′frə), *Latin.* see below.

vi·de·li·cet (vĬ dĕl′ə sĬt), *adv.* namely; that is to say (used to introduce examples, details, lists, etc.). *Abbr.:* viz. [t. L, for *vidēre licet* it is permitted to see]

vid·e·o (vĬd′Ĭ ō′), *adj. Television.* pertaining to or employed in the transmission or reception of a televised image. [t. L: I see]

vi·de post (vī′dĬ pōst′), *Latin.* see after or afterwards; refer to later material.

vi·de su·pra (vī′dĬ sōō′prə), *Latin.* see above.

vi·dette (vĬ dĕt′), *n.* vedette.

vi·de ut su·pra (vī′dĬ ŭt sōō′prə), *Latin.* see as above; refer as directed previously.

vie (vī), *v.,* **vied, vying.** —*v.i.* **1.** to strive in competition or rivalry with another; to contend for superiority. —*v.t.* **2.** *Archaic.* to put forward or offer in competition or rivalry. **3.** *Obs.* to stake in card playing. [t. F: aphetic m. *envier* challenge, t. L: m. *invitāre* invite]

Vi·en·na (vĬ ĕn′ə), *n.* the capital of Austria, in the NE part: a port on the Danube. 1,766,102 (1951). German, **Wien.** See **Congress of Vienna.**

Vienne (vyĕn′), *n.* a city in SE France, on the Rhone river, S of Lyons: Roman ruins. 25,669 (1954).

Vi·en·nese (vē′ə nēz′, -nēs′), *adj., n., pl.* **-nese.** —*adj.* **1.** of Vienna. —*n.* **2.** a native or inhabitant of Vienna.

vi et ar·mis (vī′ ĕt är′mĬs), *Latin.* by force of arms.

Vi·et·minh (vē′ĕt mĬn′), *n.* the Communist movement in Vietnam, now the government of North Vietnam.

Vi·et·nam (vē′ĕt näm′), *n.* a republic in SE Asia, comprising Annam, Tonkin, and Cochin-China: formerly part of French Indochina. 25,880,000 pop. (est. 1953); ab. 125,000 sq. mi. Provisionally divided into **South Vietnam** (ab. 11,000,000; *Cap.:* Saigon) and **North Vietnam** (ab. 14,500,000; *Cap.:* Hanoi).—**Vi·et·nam·ese** (vĬ ĕt′nä mēz′, -ēs′), *adj., n.*

Vi·ë·tor (fē′ä tôr′), *n.* **Wilhelm** (vĬl′hĕlm), 1850–1918, German philologist and phonetician.

view (vū), *n.* **1.** a seeing or beholding; an examination by the eye. **2.** sight or vision: *exposed to view.* **3.** range of sight or vision: *objects in view.* **4.** a sight or prospect of some landscape, scene, etc. **5.** a picture of a scene. **6.** the aspect, or a particular aspect, of something. **7.** mental contemplation or examination; a mental survey. **8.** contemplation or consideration of a matter with reference to action: *a project in view.* **9.** aim, intention, or purpose. **10.** prospect or expectation: *with no view of success.* **11.** consideration or regard: *in view of the risks.* **12.** a general account or description of a subject. **13.** a particular way of regarding something. **14.** a conception, notion, or idea of a thing; an opinion or theory. **15.** a survey or inspection. **16. in view, a.** within range of vision. **b.** under consideration. **c.** before one as an end sought. **17. in view of, a.** in sight of. **b.** in prospect or anticipation of. **c.** in consideration of. **d.** on account of. **18. on view,** in a place for public inspection; on exhibition. **19. with a view to, a.** with an aim or intention directed to. **b.** with an expectation or hope of. **c.** in consideration of. **d.** with regard to. —*v.t.* **20.** to see or behold. **21.** to look at, survey, or inspect. **22.** to contemplate mentally; consider. **23.** to regard in a particular light or as specified. [ME *vewe,* t. AF, var. of *veue,* pp. of *veoir* see, g. L *vidēre*] —**Syn. 4.** VIEW, PROSPECT, SCENE, VISTA refer to a landscape or perspective. VIEW is a general word, referring to whatever lies open to sight: *a fine view of the surrounding country.* PROSPECT suggests a sweeping and often distant view, as from a place of vantage: *a beautiful prospect to the south.* SCENE suggests an organic unity in the details such as is to be found in a picture: *a woodland scene.* VISTA suggests a long narrow view, as along an avenue between rows of trees: *a pleasant vista.* **14.** See **opinion.**

view halloa, the shout uttered by a huntsman on seeing a fox break cover.

view·less (vū′lĬs), *adj.* **1.** that cannot be viewed or seen; invisible. **2.** without views or opinions. —**view′less·ly,** *adv.*

view·point (vū′point′), *n.* **1.** a place affording a view of something. **2.** a point of view; an attitude of mind: *the viewpoint of an artist.*

view·y (vū′Ĭ), *adj. Colloq.* theorizing; visionary.

vi·ges·i·mal (vī jĕs′ə məl), *adj.* **1.** pertaining to or based upon twenty. **2.** twentieth. **3.** proceeding by twenties. [f. s. L *vigēsimus* twentieth + -AL¹]

vig·il (vĬj′əl), *n.* **1.** a keeping awake for any purpose during the natural hours of sleep. **2.** a watch kept by night or at other times; a course or period of watchful attention. **3.** a period of wakefulness from inability to sleep. **4.** *Eccles.* **a.** a devotional watching, or keeping awake, during the customary hours of sleep. **b.** (*often pl.*) a nocturnal devotional exercise or service, esp. on the eve before a church festival. **c.** the eve, or day and night, before a church festival, an eve which is a fast. [ME *vigile,* t. AF, g. L *vigilia* watch]

vig·i·lance (vĬj′ə ləns), *n.* **1.** the quality or fact of being vigilant; watchfulness. **2.** *Pathol.* insomnia.

vigilance committee, *U.S.* **1.** an unauthorized committee of citizens organized for the maintenance of order and the summary punishment of crime in the absence of regular or efficient courts. 2. *Hist.* (in the South) an organization of citizens using extralegal means to control or intimidate Negroes and abolitionists, and, during the Civil War, to suppress loyalty to the Union.

vig·i·lant (vĭj′ə lənt), *adj.* 1. keenly attentive to detect danger; wary: *a vigilant sentry.* 2. ever awake and alert; sleeplessly watchful. [late ME, t. L: s. *vigilans* watching] **—vig′i·lant·ly,** *adv.* **—vig′i·lant·ness,** *n.* **—Syn.** 1. See **alert.** **—Ant.** 1. careless.

vig·i·lan·te (vĭj′ə lăn′tĭ), *n. U.S.* a member of a vigilance committee. [t. Sp.: vigilant]

vi·gnette (vĭn yĕt′), *n., v.,* **-gnetted, -gnetting. —n.** 1. a decorative design or small illustration used on the title page of a book, or at the beginning or end of a chapter. 2. an engraving, drawing, photograph, or the like, shading off gradually at the edges; a design without a border line. 3. decorative work representing meandering branches, as in architecture or in manuscripts. 4. any small, pleasing picture or view. 5. a small, graceful literary sketch. **—v.t.** 6. to finish (a picture, photograph, etc.) in the manner of a vignette. [t. F, dim. of *vigne* vine] **—vi·gnett′ist,** *n.*

vi·gnett·er (vĭn yĕt′ər), *n. Photog.* a device for vignetting.

Vi·gno·la (vē nyô′lä), *n.* **Giacomo da** (jä kô′mô dä), (*Giacomo Barocchio*) 1507–73, Italian architect.

Vi·gny (vē nyē′), *n.* **Alfred Victor de** (àl frĕd′ vĕk tôr′ də), 1797–1863, French poet, novelist, and dramatist.

Vi·go (vē′gô), *n.* a seaport in NW Spain, on the **Bay of Vigo,** an inlet of the Atlantic (19 mi. long): naval battle, 1702. 55,319 (est. 1955).

vig·or (vĭg′ər), *n.* 1. active strength or force, as of body or mind. 2. healthy physical or mental energy or power. 3. energy; energetic activity. 4. force of healthy growth in any living matter or organism, as a plant. 5. active or effective force. Also, *esp. Brit.,* **vig′our** [t. L: liveliness; r. ME *vigour,* t. AF]

vi·go·ro·so (vē′gô rō′sô), *adj. Music.* vigorous or spirited in manner. [t. It.]

vig·or·ous (vĭg′ərəs), *adj.* 1. full of or characterized by vigor. 2. strong and active; robust. 3. energetic or forcible. 4. powerful in action or effect. 5. growing well, as a plant. [ME, t. ML: m.s. *vigorōsus*] **—vig′or·ous·ly,** *adv.* **—vig′or·ous·ness,** *n.* **—Syn.** 2. See **active.** **—Ant.** 2. lethargic.

Vii·pu·ri (vē′pŏŏ rē′), *n.* former name of **Vyborg.**

Vi·king (vī′kĭng), *n.* a Scandinavian rover or sea robber of the type that infested the seas about northern and western Europe during the 8th, 9th, and 10th centuries, making raids upon the coasts. Also, **viking.** [t. Icel.: s. *vīkingr* freebooter, pirate, c. OE *wīcing*]

vil., village.

vi·la·yet (vē′lä yĕt′), *n.* a province, or main administrative division of Turkey. Also, **eyalet.** [t. Turk., t. Ar.: m. *welâyet* district]

vile (vīl), *adj.,* **viler, vilest.** 1. wretchedly bad: *vile weather.* 2. highly offensive, obnoxious, or objectionable. 3. repulsive or disgusting, as to the senses or feelings; despicably or revoltingly bad. 4. morally base, depraved, or despicable, as persons or the mind, character, actions, etc.: *vile thoughts.* 5. foul, as language. 6. poor or wretched, as in quality or state. 7. of mean or low condition, as a person. 8. mean or menial, as tasks, etc. 9. low, degraded, or ignominious, as a condition, etc.: *vile servitude.* 10. of little value or account; paltry. [ME, t. AF, g. L *vīlis* cheap, base] **—Syn.** 3. See **mean².** 4. iniquitous, vicious, villainous. **—vile′ly,** *adv.* **—vile′ness,** *n.*

vil·i·fy (vĭl′ə fī′), *v.t.,* **-fied, -fying.** 1. to speak evil of; defame; traduce. 2. *Obs. or Rare.* to make vile. [late ME, t. LL: m.s. *vīlificāre*] **—vil′i·fi·ca′tion,** *n.* **—vil′i·fi′er,** *n.* **—Syn.** 1. depreciate, disparage, slander, calumniate, malign. **—Ant.** 1. praise.

vil·i·pend (vĭl′ə pĕnd′), *v.t.* 1. to regard or treat as of little value or account. 2. to vilify. [late ME, t. L: s. *vīlipendere,* f. *vīli(s)* vile + *pendere* consider] **—vil′i·pend′er,** *n.*

vil·la (vĭl′ə), *n.* 1. a country residence, usually of some size and pretensions. 2. a mansion in the suburbs or at the seashore. 3. *Brit.* a detached or semidetached dwelling house, usually suburban. 4. a country seat. [t. L or It.: country house] **—vil′la·like′,** *adj.*

Vil·la (vē′yä), *n.* **Francisco** (frän sēs′kô), (*Doroteo Arango,* "*Pancho Villa*") 1877–1923, Mexican general and revolutionist.

vil·la·dom (vĭl′ə dəm), *n. Brit.* 1. villas collectively. 2. the narrow and dull section of society regarded as villa occupants. [f. VILLA + -DOM]

vil·lage (vĭl′ĭj), *n.* 1. a small assemblage of houses in a country district, larger than a hamlet and generally smaller than a town, and sometimes (as in parts of the U.S.) incorporated as a municipality. 2. the inhabitants collectively. 3. an assemblage of animal dwellings, resembling a village. **—adj.** 4. of, belonging to, or characteristic of, a village; rustic. [ME, t. OF, der. *ville,* g. L *villa* villa] **—vil′lage·less,** *adj.* **—Syn.** 1. See **community.**

village community, an early form of organization, in which the land belonged to the village, the arable land being allotted by it to the members or households of

the community, by more or less permanent arrangements, the waste or common land remaining undivided.

vil·lag·er (vĭl′ĭjər), *n.* an inhabitant of a village.

vil·lain (vĭl′ən), *n.* 1. a wicked person; scoundrel. 2. a character in a play, novel, or the like, who constitutes an important evil agency in the plot. 3. villein. [ME, t. OF, g. L *villānus* farm servant] **—vil·lain·ess** (vĭl′ən ĭs), *n. fem.*

vil·lain·age (vĭl′ə nĭj), *n.* villeinage. Also, **vil′lan·age.**

vil·lain·ous (vĭl′ən əs), *adj.* 1. having the character of a villain. 2. pertaining to or befitting a villain. 3. base; wicked; vile. 4. very bad or unpleasant; wretched: *villainous weather.* **—vil′lain·ous·ly,** *adv.* **—vil′lain·ous·ness,** *n.*

vil·lain·y (vĭl′ə nĭ), *n., pl.* **-lainies.** 1. the action or conduct of a villain or scoundrel. 2. a villainous act or deed. 3. *Obs.* villeinage.

Vil·la-Lo·bos (vē′lyä lô′bŏŏsh, -bŏŏs), *n.* **Heitor** (ā′tŏŏr), 1881–1959, Brazilian composer.

vil·la·nel·la (vĭl′ə nĕl′ə; *It.* vēl′lä nĕl′lä), *n., pl.* **-nelle** (-nĕl′ĭ; *It.* -nĕl′lĕ), **-nellas.** an Italian rustic part song without accompaniment. [t. It.: rustic, dim. of *villano* peasant, der. *villa* villa]

vil·la·nelle (vĭl′ə nĕl′), *n. Pros.* a short poem of fixed form, written in tercets (usually five) with a final quatrain, on two rhymes. [t. F, t. It. See VILLANELLA]

Vil·lard (vĭ lär′, vĭ lärd′), *n.* **Oswald Garrison,** 1872–1949, U.S. journalist and author.

Vil·lars (vē lär′), *n.* **Claude Louis Hector de** (klôd lwē ĕk tôr′ də), 1653–1734, marshal of France.

vil·lat·ic (vĭ lăt′ĭk), *adj.* of or pertaining to a farm; rural. [t. L: s. *villāticus,* der. *villa* villa]

vil·lein (vĭl′ən), *n.* a member of a class of half-free persons under the feudal system who were serfs with respect to their lord but had the rights and privileges of freemen with respect to others. Also, **villain.** [var. of VILLAIN]

vil·lein·age (vĭl′ən ĭj), *n.* 1. the tenure by which a villein held land and tenements from his lord. 2. the condition or status of a villein. Also, **villainage, villanage, vil′len·age.** [ME, t. OF. See VILLAIN, -AGE]

Ville·neuve (vēl nœv′), *n.* **Pierre Charles Jean Baptiste Silvestre de** (pyĕr shärl zhän bä tēst′ sēl vĕs′tr də), 1763–1806, French admiral.

Ville·ur·banne (vēl yr bàn′), *n.* a city in E France, near Lyons. 81,769 (1954).

Vil·liers (vĭl′ərz, vĭl′yərz), *n.* **George.** See **Buckingham** (defs. 1, 2).

vil·li·form (vĭl′ə fôrm′), *adj.* 1. having the form of a villus. 2. so shaped and closely set as to resemble the pile of velvet, as the teeth of certain fishes. [t. NL: s. *villiformis.* See VILLUS, -FORM]

Vil·lon (vē yôn′), *n.* **François** (frän swà′), 1431–after 1463, French poet.

vil·los·i·ty (vĭ lŏs′ə tĭ), *n., pl.* **-ties.** 1. a villous surface or coating. 2. a number of villi together. 3. a villus.

vil·lous (vĭl′əs), *adj.* 1. covered with or of the nature of villi. 2. abounding in villiform processes. 3. *Bot.* pubescent with long and soft hairs which are not interwoven. [t. L: m.s. *villōsus* hairy] **—vil′lous·ly,** *adv.*

vil·lus (vĭl′əs), *n., pl.* **villi** (vĭl′ī). 1. *Anat.* one of the minute, wormlike, vascular processes on certain animal membranes, esp. on the mucous membrane of the small intestine, where they serve in absorbing nutriment. 2. *Bot.* one of the long, soft, straight hairs covering the fruit, flowers, and other parts of certain plants. [t. L: tuft of hair, shaggy hair]

Vil·na (vĭl′nə; *Russ.* vēl′nä), *n.* a city in the W Soviet Union: capital of the Lithuanian Republic; formerly in Poland. 200,000 (est. 1956) Polish, **Wilno.** Lithuanian, **Vil·ni·us** (vĭl′nĭ ŏŏs).

vim (vĭm), *n.* force; energy; vigor in action. [t. L, acc. of *vis*]

vi·men (vī′mĕn), *n., pl.* **vimina** (vĭm′ə nə). *Bot.* a long, flexible shoot of a plant. [t. L: twig] **—vim·i·nal** (vĭm′ə nəl), *adj.*

Vim·i·nal (vĭm′ə nəl), *n.* the northeasternmost of the seven hills of ancient Rome, north of the Esquiline.

vi·min·e·ous (vĭ mĭn′ĭəs), *adj. Bot.* 1. of, like, or producing long, flexible shoots. 2. of, or made of, twigs. [t. L: m. *vīmineus* made of twigs]

v. imp., verb impersonal.

Vi·my (vē′mē), *n.* a town in N France, N of Arras: battle of Vimy Ridge, 1917. 2623 (1946).

vi·na (vē′nä), *n.* a Hindu musical instrument with numerous strings stretched over a long sticklike fingerboard with movable frets, which rests on gourds.

Vina

vi·na·ceous (vī nā′shəs), *adj.* 1. relating to, or resembling, wine or grapes. 2. wine-colored. [t. L: m. *vīnāceus*]

vin·ai·grette (vĭn′ə grĕt′), *n.* a small ornamental bottle or box for holding aromatic vinegar, smelling salts, or the like. Also, **vinegarette.** [t. F, dim. of *vinaigre* vinegar]

vinaigrette sauce, a cold, tart sauce of oil, vinegar, chopped pickle, seasonings, and herbs.

vi·nasse (vĭ näs′), *n. Distilling.* the residuum in a still after distillation. Cf. **slop**¹ (def. 12). [t. F, t. Pr.: m. *vinassa*, g. L *vīnācea* grapeskin]

Vin·cennes (vĭn sĕnz′; *for 2 also Fr.* văɴ sĕn′), *n.* **1.** a city in SW Indiana, on the Wabash: the first permanent settlement in Indiana, 1702. 18,046 (1960). **2.** a city in N France, near Paris: castle; park. 50,434 (1954).

Vin·cent de Paul (vĭn′sənt də pôl′; *Fr.* văɴ săɴ′ də pōl′), Saint, 1576–1660, French Roman Catholic priest and reformer.

Vin·cent's angina (vĭn′sənts; *Fr.* văɴ săɴz′), *Pathol.* a disease characterized by ulceration of the mucosa of the tonsils, pharynx, and mouth and the development of a membrane, caused by a bacillus and a spirillum; trench mouth. Also, **Vincent's infection.** [named after H. *Vincent*, French physician]

Vin·ci (vēn′chē), *n.* **Leonardo da** (lĕ′ô när′dō dä), 1452–1519, Italian painter, sculptor, architect, musician, engineer, mathematician, and scientist.

vin·ci·ble (vĭn′sə bəl), *adj.* capable of being conquered or overcome. [t. L: m.s. *vincibilis*] —**vin′ci·bil′i·ty, vin′ci·ble·ness,** *n.*

vin·cit om·ni·a ve·ri·tas (vĭn′sĭt ŏm′nĭ ə vĕr′ĭ tăs′), *Latin.* truth conquers all things.

vin·cu·lum (vĭng′kyə ləm), *n., pl.* **-la** (-lə). **1.** a bond of union; a tie. **2.** *Math.* a stroke or brace drawn over a quantity consisting of several members or terms, as *a* + *b*, in order to connect them and show that they are to be considered together. [t. L: fetter]

Vind·hya Hills (vĭnd′yä), a mountain range in central India, N of the Narbada river.

vin·di·ca·ble (vĭn′də kə bəl), *adj.* that may be vindicated.

vin·di·cate (vĭn′də kāt′), *v.t.* **-cated, -cating. 1.** to clear, as from a charge, imputation, suspicion, or the like. **2.** to afford justification for: *subsequent events vindicated his policy.* **3.** to uphold or justify by argument or evidence. **4.** to assert, maintain, or defend (a right, cause, etc.) against opposition. **5.** to lay claim to, for oneself or another. **6.** *Rom. and Civ. Law.* to regain possession, under claim of title of property through legal procedure or to assert one's right to its possession. **7.** *Obs.* to deliver from something. **8.** *Obs.* to avenge, revenge, or punish. [t. L: m.s. *vindicātus*, pp., set free, punished] —**vin′di·ca′tor,** *n.*

vin·di·ca·tion (vĭn′də kā′shən), *n.* **1.** the act of vindicating. **2.** the state of being vindicated. **3.** defense or justification. **4.** something that vindicates: *the success of his plan was the real vindication.*

vin·di·ca·to·ry (vĭn′də kə tôr′ĭ), *adj.* **1.** serving to vindicate. **2.** justificatory. **3.** punitive; retributive. Also, **vin·dic·a·tive** (vĭn dĭk′ə tĭv, vĭn′də kā′-).

vin·dic·tive (vĭn dĭk′tĭv), *adj.* **1.** disposed or inclined to revenge; revengeful: *a vindictive person.* **2.** proceeding from or showing a revengeful spirit. [f. s. L *vindicta* vengeance + -IVE] —**vin·dic′tive·ly,** *adv.* —**vin·dic′tive·ness,** *n.* —**Syn. 1.** See spiteful.

vine (vīn), *n.* **1.** any plant with a long, slender stem that trails or creeps on the ground or climbs by winding itself about a support or holding fast with tendrils or claspers. **2.** the stem of any such plant. **3.** any of the climbing plants constituting the genus *Vitis*, having a woody stem and bearing grapes, esp. *V. vinifera*, the common European species; a grapevine. [ME, t. OF, g. L *vīnea*] —**vine′less,** *adj.* —**vine′like′,** *adj.*

vine·dress·er (vīn′drĕs′ər), *n.* one who dresses, trims, or cultivates vines, esp. grapevines.

vin·e·gar (vĭn′ə gər), *n.* **1.** a sour liquid consisting of dilute and impure acetic acid, obtained by acetous fermentation from wine, cider, beer, ale, or the like, and used as a condiment, preservative, etc. **2.** *Pharm.* a solution of a medicinal substance in dilute acetic acid, or vinegar. **3.** sour or crabbed speech, temper, or countenance. [ME *vinegre*, t. OF, f. *vin* wine + *egre* sour] —**vin′e·gar·like′,** *adj.*

vinegar eel, a minute nematode worm, *Anguillula aceti*, found in vinegar, etc. Also, **vinegar worm.**

vin·e·gar·ette (vĭn′ə gə rĕt′), *n.* vinaigrette.

vinegar fly, any fly of the genus *Drosophila*, esp. *D. melanogaster*; fruit fly.

vin·e·gar·ish (vĭn′ə gər ĭsh), *adj.* slightly sour; resembling vinegar.

vin·e·gar·roon (vĭn′ə gə rōōn′), *n.* a large whip scorpion, *Thelyphonus giganteus*, of the southern U.S., etc., which emits a vinegarlike odor when alarmed. [t. Sp.: m. *vinagrón*, der. *vinagre* vinegar]

vin·e·gar·y (vĭn′ə gər ĭ), *adj.* of the nature of or resembling vinegar; sour.

vin·er·y (vī′nər ĭ), *n., pl.* **-eries. 1.** a grapery; vineyard. **2.** vines collectively.

vine·yard (vĭn′yərd), *n.* **1.** a plantation of grapevines, for producing grapes for winemaking, etc. **2.** a sphere of activity, esp. on a high spiritual plane. [ME; f. VINE + YARD²] —**vine′yard·ist,** *n.*

vingt-et-un (văn tĕ œn′), *n. Cards.* twenty-one. [F]

vi·nic (vī′nĭk, vĭn′ĭk), *adj.* of, pertaining to, found in, or extracted from wine. [f. s. L *vīnum* wine + -IC]

vin·i·cul·ture (vĭn′ə kŭl′chər), *n.* the study or science of winemaking. [f. *vini-* (comb. form of L *vīnum* wine) + CULTURE] —**vin′i·cul′tur·al,** *adj.* —**vin′i·cul′tur·ist,** *n.*

vin·i·fi·ca·tor (vĭn′ə fə kā′tər), *n.* a condenser for alcohol vapors escaping from fermenting wine. [f. *vini-* (comb. form of L *vīnum* wine) + L *-ficator* maker]

vin·om·e·ter (vī nŏm′ə tər, vĭ-), *n.* a hydrometer for measuring the percentage of alcohol in wine. [f. *vino-* (comb. form repr. L *vīnum* wine) + -METER]

vin or·di·naire (văn ôr dē nĕr′), *French.* a cheap wine of popular consumption. [F: common wine]

vi·nous (vī′nəs), *adj.* **1.** having the nature of or resembling wine. **2.** pertaining to or characteristic of wine. **3.** produced by, indicative of, or given to indulgence in wine. **4.** wine-colored. [t. L: m.s. *vīnōsus*] —**vi·nos·i·ty** (vī nŏs′ə tĭ), *n.*

Vin·son (vĭn′sən), *n.* **Frederick Moore,** 1890–1953, chief justice of the U. S. Supreme Court 1946–1953.

vin·tage (vĭn′tĭj), *n.* **1.** the wine from a particular harvest or crop. **2.** the annual produce of the grape harvest, esp. with reference to the wine obtained: *a luxuriant vintage.* **3.** an exceptionally fine wine from the crop of a good year, designated and sold as the produce of that year. **4.** act of gathering ripe grapes. **5.** the season of gathering grapes, or of winemaking. **6.** winemaking. **7.** *Colloq.* the crop or output of anything: *a hat of last year's vintage.* **8.** *Poetic.* wine, esp. good wine. [late ME, t. AF, b. *vinter* VINTNER and *vendage*, OF *vendange* (g. L *vindēmia* grape gathering)]

vin·tag·er (vĭn′tĭjər), *n.* one who gathers grapes at the harvest season.

vint·ner (vĭnt′nər), *n.* Brit., Archaic in U.S. a dealer in wine; a wine merchant. [late ME *vyntenere,* alter. of ME *viniter,* t. AF. Cf. ML *vīnetārius* wine seller]

vi·num (vī′nəm), *n. Pharm.* a solution of a medicinal substance in wine. [special use of L *vīnum* wine]

vin·y (vī′nĭ), *adj.* **1.** pertaining to, of the nature of, or resembling vines. **2.** abounding in or producing vines.

vi·nyl (vī′nĭl, vĭn′ĭl), *n. Chem.* the univalent radical CH₂:CH, derived from ethylene, compounds of which undergo polymerization to form high-molecular-weight plastics and resins. [f. s. L *vīnum* wine + -YL]

vinyl acetate, a colorless, easily polymerized fluid, CH₃COOCH = CH₂, used in the plastics industry.

vinyl chloride, a colorless liquid, CH₂CHCl, widely used in the plastics industry.

vi·nyl·ite (vī′nə līt′, vĭn′ə līt′), *n.* **1.** a synthetic, thermoplastic substance used in the manufacture of molded plastic ware, esp. phonograph records. **2.** (*cap.*) a trademark for this substance.

vinyl polymers, a group of compounds derived from vinyl compounds such as vinyl acetate, styrene, etc., by polymerization.

vi·ol (vī′əl), *n.* a bowed musical instrument, differing from the violin in having deeper ribs, sloping shoulders, a greater number of strings (usually 6) and frets: common in the 16th and 17th centuries in various sizes from the **treble viol** to the **bass viol.** [earlier *viole,* t. F; r. late ME *vyell,* t. F: m. *vielle;* ? both g. ML *vitula, vidula*]

vi·o·la¹ (vĭ ō′lə, vĭ-; *It.* vyō′lä), *n.* **1.** a four-stringed musical instrument of the violin class, slightly larger than the violin; a tenor or alto violin. **2.** a labial organ stop of 8-foot or 4-foot pitch, giving tones of a penetrating stringlike quality. [t. It. See VIOL]

vi·o·la² (vī′ələ, vī ō′lə), *n.* **1.** any of a genus of plants, *Viola,* including the violet and the pansy, bearing irregular flowers on axillary peduncles. **2.** a pansy, *V. cornuta,* cultivated as a garden plant. [t. L: violet]

vi·o·la·ble (vī′ə lə bəl), *adj.* that may be violated. [t. L: m.s. *violābilis*] —**vi′o·la·bil′i·ty, vi′o·la·ble·ness,** *n.* —**vi′o·la·bly,** *adv.*

vi·o·la·ceous (vī′ə lā′shəs), *adj.* **1.** belonging to the *Violaceae,* or violet family of plants. **2.** of a violet color; bluish-purple. [t. L: m.s. *violāceus* violet-colored]

vio·la da brac·cio (vyō′lä dä brät′chō), an old musical instrument of the viol family, held against the shoulder like a violin: superseded by the modern viola. [It.: lit., viol for the arm]

vio·la da gam·ba (vyō′lä dä gäm′bä), **1.** an old musical instrument of the viol family, held on or between the knees: superseded by the modern violoncello; bass viol. **2.** an organ stop of 8-foot pitch giving a stringlike tone. [It.: it., viol for the leg]

vio·la d'a·mo·re (vyō′lä dä mô′rĕ), a viol with numerous sympathetic strings (in addition to several gut strings), producing a characteristic silvery tone. [It.: lit., viol of love]

vi·o·late (vī′ə lāt′), *v.t.* **-lated, -lating. 1.** to break, infringe, or transgress (a law, rule, agreement, promise, instructions, etc.). **2.** to break in upon or disturb rudely: *to violate privacy, peace, or a peaceful spot.* **3.** to break through or pass by force or without right: *to violate a frontier.* **4.** to do violence to. **5.** to deal with or treat in a violent or improper way; desecrate or profane: *to violate a temple or an altar.* **6.** to outrage or ravish (a woman). [late ME, t. AF: L: m.s. *violātus,* pp.] —**vi′o·la·tive,** *adj.* —**vi′o·la′tor,** *n.*

vi·o·la·tion (vī′ə lā′shən), *n.* **1.** act of violating. **2.** state of being violated. **3.** breach, infringement, or

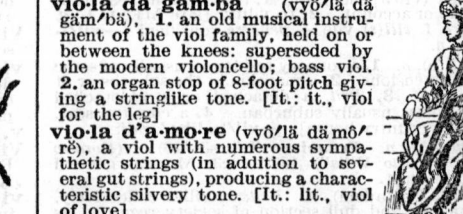

Vinegarroon,
Thelyphonus giganteus

Viola da gamba

transgression, as of a law, promise, etc. 4. desecration. 5. ravishment or rape. 6. *Obs.* act of treating with violence. [ME, t. L: s. *violātio*]

vi·o·lence (vī′ə ləns), *n.* 1. rough force in action: *the violence of the wind.* 2. rough or injurious action or treatment: *to die by violence.* 3. any unjust or unwarranted exertion of force or power, as against rights, laws, etc.; injury; wrong; outrage. 4. a violent act or proceeding. 5. rough or immoderate vehemence, as of feeling or language; fury; intensity; severity. 6. a distortion of meaning or fact. [ME, t. OF, t. L: m. *violentia* vehemence]

vi·o·lent (vī′ə lənt), *adj.* 1. acting with or characterized by uncontrolled, strong, rough force: *a violent blow, explosion, tempest, etc.* 2. acting with, characterized by, or due to injurious or destructive force: *violent measures, a violent death.* 3. intense in force, effect, etc.; severe; extreme: *violent heat, pain, contrast, etc.* 4. roughly or immoderately vehement, ardent, or passionate: *violent feeling.* 5. furious in impetuosity, energy, etc.: *violent haste.* [ME, t. L: s. *violentus*] —**vi′o·lent·ly,** *adv.*

vi·o·les·cent (vī′ə lĕs′ənt), *adj.* tending to a violet color. [f. s. L *viola* violet + -ESCENT]

vi·o·let (vī′ə lĭt), *n.* 1. any plant of the genus *Viola,* comprising chiefly low, stemless or leafy-stemmed herbs with purple, blue, yellow, white, or variegated flowers, as *V. cucullata,* a species common in wet woods, *V. odorata* (**English violet** or **sweet violet**), a fragrant species much cultivated, and *V. tricolor,* the pansy, whose flowers often bear petals differing in coloring. 2. any such plant except the pansy and the viola. 3. any of various similar plants of other genera. 4. a bluish-purple color. —*adj.* 5. of the color called violet; bluish-purple. [ME, t. OF: m. *violete,* der. L *viola*] —**vi′o·let-like′,** *adj.*

violet ray, light of the shortest visible wave length.

violet wood, kingwood.

vi·o·lin (vī′ə lĭn′), *n.* 1. the treble of the family of modern bowed instruments, which is held nearly horizontal by the player's arm, with the lower part supported against the collarbone or shoulder; a fiddle. 2. any modern instrument of the same general class, as a viola or a violoncello. 3. a violinist. [t. It.: m. *violino,* dim. of *viola* viol] —**vi′o·lin·less,** *adj.*

vi·o·lin·ist (vī′ə lĭn′ĭst), *n.* a player on the violin.

vi·ol·ist (vī′ə lĭst), *n.* a player on the viol.

vi·o·lon·cel·list (vē′ə lən chĕl′ĭst), *n.* a cellist.

vi·o·lon·cel·lo (vē′ə lən chĕl′ō), *n., pl.* **-los.** a cello. [t. It., dim. of *violone* bass viol]

vi·o·lo·ne (vyô lō′nā), *n.* 1. the double-bass viol, or contrabass. 2. a sixteen-foot organ pedal stop, resembling the violoncello. [t. It., aug. of *viola* viol]

vi·os·ter·ol (vī ŏs′tə rōl′, -rŏl′), *n. Pharm.* a vitamin D preparation produced by the irradiation of ergosterol. [f. *vi-* (in ULTRAVIOLET) + (ERG)OSTEROL]

VIP, *Colloq.* very important person.

vi·per (vī′pər), *n.* 1. any of the Old World venomous snakes of the genus *Vipera,* esp. *V. berus,* a small European species. 2. any snake of the highly venomous family *Viperidae,* confined to the Old World and including the common vipers, the puff adder, and various other types, all characterized by erectile venom-conducting fangs. 3. any adder. 4. any of various venomous or supposedly venomous snakes of allied or other genera, as the **horned viper,** *Cerastes cornutus,* a venomous species of Egypt, Palestine, etc., with a horny process above each eye. 5. a venomous, malignant, or spiteful person. 6. a false or treacherous person. [t. L: s. *vipera,* for *vivipera,* f. *vivi-* alive and *-pera* bringing forth] —**vi′per·like′,** *adj.*

vi·per·ine (vī′pər īn, -pər ĭn), *adj.* of or like a viper.

vi·per·ish (vī′pər ĭsh), *adj.* viperlike; viperous.

vi·per·ous (vī′pər əs), *adj.* 1. of the nature of a viper or vipers; viperlike. 2. pertaining to vipers. 3. characteristic of vipers. 4. venomous or malignant. —**vi′per·ous·ly,** *adv.*

viper's bugloss, blueweed.

vi·ra·go (vi rā′gō, vĭ-), *n., pl.* **-goes, -gos.** 1. a turbulent, violent, or ill-tempered, scolding woman; a shrew. 2. *Archaic.* a woman of masculine strength or spirit. [ME and OE, t. L: manlike woman]

Vir·chow (fĭr′khō), *n.* **Rudolf** (rōō′dôlf), 1821–1902, German physicist, anthropologist, and political leader.

vir·e·lay (vĭr′ə lā′), *n.* 1. an old French form of short poem, with short lines running on two rhymes, and having two opening lines recurring at intervals. 2. any of various similar or other forms of poem, as one consisting of stanzas made up of longer and shorter lines, the lines of each kind rhyming together in each stanza, and having the rhyme of the shorter lines of one stanza forming the rhyme of the longer lines of the next stanza. Also, French, *vire-lai* (vēr lĕ′). [ME, t. OF, f. *virel(i)* dance + *lai* song]

vir·e·o (vĭr′ē ō′), *n., pl.* **vireos.** any of several small American insectivorous birds constituting the family *Vireonidae,* having the plumage olive-green or gray above, and white or yellow below; a greenlet. [t. L: some small bird, ? the greenfinch]

vi·res·cence (vī rĕs′əns), *n. Bot.* state of becoming green, though usually not green, due to the abnormal presence of chlorophyll.

vi·res·cent (vī rĕs′ənt), *adj.* 1. turning green. 2. tending to a green color; slightly greenish. [t. L: s. *virescens,* ppr.]

vir·ga (vûr′gə), *n. Meteorol.* rain or snow that is dissipated in falling and does not reach the ground, commonly appearing in trails descending from a cloud layer. [t. L: twig, streak]

vir·gate[1] (vûr′gĭt, -gāt), *adj.* shaped like a rod or wand; long, slender, and straight. [t. L: m.s. *virgātus*]

vir·gate[2] (vûr′gĭt, -gāt), *n.* an early English measure of land of varying extent, generally regarded as having been equivalent to a quarter of a hide, or about thirty acres. [t. ML: m.s. *virgāta,* short for *virgāta terrae* (trans. of OE *geard landes,* lit., yard of land)]

Vir·gil (vûr′jĭl), *n.* Vergil. [t. L: m.s. *Virgilius,* misspelling of L *Vergilius*] —**Vir·gil′i·an,** *adj.*

vir·gin (vûr′jĭn), *n.* 1. a woman, esp. a young woman, who has had no sexual intercourse. 2. a girl, young woman, or unmarried woman. 3. *Eccles.* (usually of saints) an unmarried religious woman. 4. the Virgin, Mary, the mother of Christ (often called **the Blessed Virgin**). 5. any female animal which has not copulated. 6. a youth or man who has not had sexual intercourse. 7. an unfertilized insect. 8. (*cap.*) the zodiacal constellation or sign Virgo. —*adj.* 9. being a virgin: *Virgin Mother, the Virgin Queen* (Queen Elizabeth I of England). 10. consisting of virgins. 11. pertaining to, characteristic of, or befitting a virgin. 12. resembling or suggesting a virgin; pure; unsullied; undefiled: *virgin snow.* 13. without admixture, alloy, or modification: *virgin gold.* 14. untouched, untried, or unused: *virgin soil.* 15. *Zool.* unfertilized. 16. *Metall.* made directly from ore or from first smelting. 17. denoting the oil obtained, as from olives, etc., by the first pressing without the application of heat. [ME *virgine,* t. OF, t. L: s. *virgo* maiden]

vir·gin·al[1] (vûr′jə nəl), *adj.* 1. of, pertaining to, characteristic of, or befitting a virgin. 2. continuing in a state of virginity. 3. pure or unsullied; untouched; fresh. 4. *Zool.* unfertilized. [t. L: s. *virginālis* maidenly] —**vir′gin·al·ly,** *adv.*

vir·gin·al[2] (vûr′jə nəl), *n.* 1. a small harpsichord of rectangular shape, with the strings stretched parallel to the keyboard, the earlier types placed on a table: common in the 16th and 17th centuries; also used in the plural, and sometimes called *a pair of virginals.* 2. any harpsichord. [appar. special use of VIRGINAL[1]]

virgin birth, 1. *Theol.* the doctrine or dogma that the birth of Christ did not, by the miraculous agency of God, impair or prejudice the virginity of Mary. Cf. **Immaculate Conception.** 2. *Zool.* parthenogenesis; a birth resulting from a female who has not copulated.

Vir·gin·ia (vər jĭn′yə), *n.* a State in the E United States, on the Atlantic coast: part of the historical South. 3,966,949 pop. (1960); 40,815 sq. mi. *Cap.:* Richmond. *Abbr.:* Va. —**Vir·gin′ian,** *adj., n.*

Virginia City, a mining town in W Nevada: famous for the discovery of the rich Comstock silver lode, 1859.

Virginia cowslip, a boraginaceous wild herb, *Mertensia virginica,* of the eastern U.S., grown as a garden perennial for its handsome clustered blue flowers.

Virginia creeper, a vitaceous climbing plant, *Parthenocissus quinquefolia,* of North America, having palmate leaves, usually with five leaflets, and bluish-black berries; woodbine.

Virginia deer, 1. the common white-tailed deer, *Odocoileus virginianus,* of eastern North America. 2. any related variety of white-tailed deer.

Virginia fence, a snake fence. Also, **Virginia rail fence.**

Virginia reel, an American country dance in which the partners start by facing each other in two lines.

Virginia trumpet flower, the trumpet creeper.

vir·gin·i·bus pu·er·is·que (vər jĭn′ə bəs pū′ə rĭs′kwĭ), *Latin.* for girls and boys.

Virgin Islands, a group of islands in the West Indies, E of Puerto Rico, divided into the **Virgin Islands of the United States** (formerly, **Danish West Indies**), including the islands of St. Thomas, St. John, and St. Croix, purchased from Denmark, 1917; 22,000 (est. 1954); 133 sq. mi. (*cap.*: Charlotte Amalie), and the **British Virgin Islands,** a colony in the Leeward Islands. 7760 pop. (est. 1955); 67 sq. mi. (*cap.*: Road Town). *Abbr.:* V.I.

vir·gin·i·ty (vər jĭn′ə tĭ), *n.* the condition of being a virgin; virginal chastity; maidenhood.

vir·gin·i·um (vər jĭn′ĭ əm), *n. Chem.* former name of francium. [t. NL; named after the state *Virginia*]

Virgin Mary, Mary, the mother of Jesus.

Virgin Queen, Queen Elizabeth I of England.

vir·gin's-bow·er (vûr′jĭnz bou′ər), *n.* any of several climbing varieties of clematis with small white flowers in large panicles, as *Clematis Vitalba* of Europe, or *C. virginiana* of the U.S.

virgin wool, wool which has never gone through the manufacturing process.

Vir·go (vûr′gō), *n., gen.* **Virginis** (vûr′jə nĭs). 1. an equatorial constellation south of Ursa Major, containing the bright star Spica; the Virgin. **2.** the sixth sign of the zodiac. See diag. under **zodiac.** [t. L: maiden]

vir·gu·late (vûr′gyə lĭt, -lāt′), *adj.* rod-shaped; virgate.

vir·gule (vûr′gūl), *n.* *Print.* a short oblique stroke (/) between two words designating that the interpretation may be made in either sense. Example: *and/or.* [t. L: m. *virgula* little rod]

vir·i·des·cent (vĭr′ə dĕs′ənt), *adj.* slightly green or greenish. [t. LL: s. *viridescens* becoming green] —**vir′i·des′cence,** *n.*

vir·id·i·an (və rĭd′ĭ ən), *n.* a bluish-green pigment of great permanency, consisting of a hydrated oxide of chromium. [f. L *viridi*(s) green + -AN]

vir·id·i·ty (və rĭd′ə tĭ), *n.* **1.** greenness; verdancy; verdure. **2.** inexperience or simplicity. [late ME, t. L: m.s. *viriditas* greenness]

vir·ile (vĭr′əl, vī′rəl), *adj.* **1.** of, pertaining to, or characteristic of a man, as opposed to a woman or a child; masculine or manly; natural to or befitting a man. **2.** having or exhibiting in a marked degree masculine strength, vigor, or forcefulness. **3.** characterized by a vigorous masculine spirit: *a virile literary style.* **4.** pertaining to or capable of procreation. [t. L: m.s. *virīlis,* der. *vir* man] —**Syn. 2.** See **male.**

vir·i·lism (vĭr′ə lĭz′əm), *n.* hermaphroditism in which a female has certain minor sexual characteristics resembling those of a male, as a low voice, etc.

vi·ril·i·ty (və rĭl′ə tĭ), *n., pl.* **-ties. 1.** state or quality of being virile; manhood; masculine or manly character, vigor, or spirit. **2.** the power of procreation.

vi·rol·o·gy (vī rŏl′ə jĭ, vĭ-), *n.* the study of viruses and the diseases caused by them. [f. *viro-* comb. form of VIRUS + -LOGY]

vir·tu (vər tōō′, vûr′tōō), *n.* **1.** excellence or merit in objects of art, curios, and the like. **2.** (*construed as pl.*) such objects or articles collectively. **3.** a taste for or knowledge of such objects. Also, **vertu.** [t. It., t. L: m. *virtūs* VIRTUE]

vir·tu·al (vûr′chōō əl), *adj.* **1.** being such in power, force, or effect, although not actually or expressly such: *the regent is a virtual king.* **2.** *Optics.* **a.** denoting an image formed by the apparent convergence of rays geometrically (but not actually) prolonged, as the image in a mirror (opposed to *real*). **b.** denoting a focus of a corresponding nature. **3.** *Rare.* having virtue or inherent power to produce effects. [ME *vertual,* t. ML: m.s. *virtuālis*] —**vir′tu·al′i·ty,** *n.* —**vir′tu·al·ly,** *adv.*

vir·tue (vûr′chōō), *n.* **1.** moral excellence or goodness. **2.** conformity of life and conduct to moral laws; uprightness; rectitude. **3.** chastity, esp. in women. **4.** a particular moral excellence: *the cardinal virtues* (justice, prudence, temperance, and fortitude); *the theological virtues* (faith, hope, and charity). **5.** an excellence, merit, or good quality: *brevity is often a virtue.* **6.** effective force: *there is no virtue in such measures.* **7.** a power or property of producing a particular effect. **8.** inherent power to produce effects; potency or efficacy: *a medicine of sovereign virtue.* **9.** (*pl.*) an order of angels. See **angel** (def. 1). **10.** *Obs.* manly excellence, spirit, or valor. **11. by** or **in virtue of,** by reason of: *to act by virtue of authority conferred.* [ME *virtu,* t. L: m. *virtus* manliness (der. *vir* man); r. ME *vertu,* t. OF] —**Syn. 1.** See **goodness.** —**Ant.** 1. vice.

vir·tu·os·i·ty (vûr′chōō ŏs′ə tĭ), *n., pl.* **-ties. 1.** the character or skill of a virtuoso. **2.** lovers of the elegant arts collectively. **3.** a fondness for or interest in virtu.

vir·tu·o·so (vûr′chōō ō′sō), *n., pl.* **-sos, -si** (-sē). **1.** one who has special knowledge or skill in any field, as in music. **2.** one who excels in musical technique or execution. **3.** one who has a cultivated appreciation of artistic excellence; a connoisseur of works or objects of art; a student or collector of objects of art, curios, antiquities, etc. **4.** *Obs.* one who has special interest or knowledge in art and science. [t. It.: learned, skillful]

vir·tu·ous (vûr′chōō əs), *adj.* **1.** morally excellent or good; conforming or conformed to moral laws; upright; righteous; moral; chaste. **2.** *Archaic.* having effective virtue, potent, or efficacious. [ME, t. LL: m.s. *virtuōsus;* r. ME *vertuous,* t. OF, der. *vertu* VIRTUE] —**vir′tu·ous·ly,** *adv.* —**vir′tu·ous·ness,** *n.* —**Ant.** 1. vicious.

vir·tu·te et ar·mis (vər tū′tĭ ĕt är′mĭs, vər tōō′tĭ), *Latin.* by valor and arms (motto of Mississippi).

vir·u·lence (vĭr′yə ləns, vĭr′ə-), *n.* **1.** the quality of being virulent; actively poisonous or malignant quality. **2.** venomous hostility. **3.** intense acrimony. Also, **vir′u·len·cy.**

vir·u·lent (vĭr′yə lənt, vĭr′ə-), *adj.* **1.** actively poisonous, malignant, or deadly: *a virulent poison, a virulent form of a disease.* **2.** *Med.* highly infective; malignant or deadly. **3.** *Bacteriol.* of the nature of an organism causing specific or general clinical symptoms. **4.** violently or venomously hostile. **5.** intensely bitter, spiteful, or acrimonious. [ME, t. L: s. *vīrulentus* poisonous. See VIRUS] —**vir′u·lent·ly,** *adv.*

vi·rus (vī′rəs), *n.* **1.** an infective agent; in a restricted sense, an infective agent smaller than a common microörganism, and requiring living cells for multiplication. Cf. **filterable** (def. 2). **2.** the liquid excretions from the cowpox blisters, used in smallpox vaccinations. **3.** the venom of a poisonous animal. **4.** a moral or intellectual poison; a corrupting influence. [t. L: slimy liquid, poison] —**Syn. 1.** See **poison.**

vis (vĭs), *n., pl.* **vires** (vī′rēz), *Latin.* force.

Vis., 1. Viscount. **2.** Viscountess.

vi·sa (vē′zə), *n., v.* **-saed, -saing.** —*n.* **1.** *Govt.* an endorsement made, by an authorized representative of a country, upon a passport of another country, testifying that the passport has been examined and found in order, and permitting passage to the country making the endorsement. —*v.t.* **2.** to put a visa on; examine and endorse, as a passport. Also, **visé.** [t. L, short for *carta vīsa* paper (has been) seen]

vis·age (vĭz′ĭj), *n.* **1.** the face, esp. of a human being, and commonly with reference to shape, features, expression, etc.; the countenance. **2.** aspect; appearance. [ME, t. AF and OF, der. *vis* (g. L *vīsus*). See -AGE] —**vis′aged,** *adj.* —**Syn. 1.** See **face.**

vis·ard (vĭz′ərd), *n.* vizard.

vis-à-vis (vē′zə vē′; *Fr.* -zā-), *adv., adj.* **1.** face to face. —*prep.* **2.** regarding; with relation to: *they conferred with the treasurer vis-à-vis the proposed budget.* —*n.* **3.** one face to face with, or situated opposite to, another. **4.** a carriage in which the occupants sit face to face. **5.** a sofa in the shape of the letter S, with seats for two persons thus enabled to face each other. [F: face to face]

Vi·sa·yan (vē sä′yən), *n.* **1.** one of a Malay people, the most numerous native race of the Philippine Islands. **2.** the language of this people. Also, **Bisayan.**

Visayan Islands, an island group in the central Philippine Islands, including Panay, Negros, Cebú, Bohol, Leyte, Samar, Masbate, and smaller islands. Also, **Bisayas.**

Vis·by (vēs′bY), *n.* a seaport on the Swedish island of Gotland, in the Baltic: an important member of the Hanseatic League. 14,962 (1950). German, **Wisby.**

Visc., 1. Viscount. **2.** Viscountess.

vis·ca·cha (vĭs kä′chə), *n.* **1.** a burrowing rodent, *Lagostomus trichodactylus,* about the size of a ground hog, inhabiting the pampas of Paraguay and Argentina, allied to the chinchilla. **2.** a related genus, *Lagidium,* of the Andes (**alpine** or **mountain viscacha**), about the size of a gray squirrel, having long rabbitlike ears and a squirrellike tail. [t. Sp., t. Kechua]

vis·cer·a (vĭs′ər ə), *n. pl., sing.* **viscus** (vĭs′kəs). **1.** the soft interior organs in the cavities of the body, including the brain, lungs, heart, stomach, intestines, etc., esp. such of these as are confined to the abdomen. **2.** (in popular use) the intestines or bowels. [t. L]

vis·cer·al (vĭs′ər əl), *adj.* **1.** of the viscera. **2.** affecting the viscera. **3.** having the character of viscera.

vis·cid (vĭs′ĭd), *adj.* **1.** sticky, adhesive, or glutinous; of a glutinous consistency; viscous. **2.** *Bot.* covered by a sticky substance, as a leaf. [t. LL: s. *viscidus,* der. L *viscum* birdlime] —**vis·cid′i·ty, vis′cid·ness,** *n.* —**vis′cid·ly,** *adv.*

vis·coid (vĭs′koid), *adj.* somewhat viscous. Also, **vis·coi′dal.** [f. VISC(OUS) + -OID]

Vis·con·ti (vēs kôn′tē), *n.* an Italian family that ruled Milan and Lombardy from 1277 to 1447.

vis·cose (vĭs′kōs), *n.* **1.** a viscous solution prepared by treating cellulose with caustic soda and carbon bisulfide: used in manufacturing regenerated cellulose fibers, sheets, or tubes, as rayon or cellophane. —*adj.* **2.** relating to, or made from, viscose. [t. L: m. s. *viscōsus.* See VISCOUS]

vis·co·sim·e·ter (vĭs′kō sĭm′ə tər), *n.* apparatus for determining the viscosity of liquids, either through rate of flow through an orifice or resistance to movement of a submerged object.

vis·cos·i·ty (vĭs kŏs′ə tĭ), *n., pl.* **-ties. 1.** state or quality of being viscous. **2.** *Physics.* a property of a fluid which resists change in the shape or arrangement of its elements during flow, and the measure thereof.

vis·count (vī′kount), *n.* **1.** a nobleman next below an earl or count and next above a baron. **2.** (formerly) a deputy of a count or earl. **3.** a sheriff. [ME, t. AF: m. *viscounte,* f. *vis* VICE³ + *counte* COUNT²]

vis·count·cy (vī′kount sĭ), *n., pl.* **-cies.** the rank or dignity of a viscount. Also, **vis′count·ship′.**

vis·count·ess (vī′koun tĭs), *n.* **1.** the wife or widow of a viscount. **2.** a woman holding in her own right a rank equivalent to that of a viscount.

vis·count·y (vī′koun tĭ), *n., pl.* **-counties. 1.** viscountcy. **2.** the jurisdiction of a historical viscount, or the territory under his authority.

vis·cous (vĭs′kəs), *adj.* **1.** sticky, adhesive, or glutinous; of a glutinous character or consistency; ropy; thick. **2.** having the property of viscosity. [ME *viscouse,* t. L: m. *viscōsus,* der. *viscum* birdlime] —**vis′cous·ly,** *adv.* —**vis′cous·ness,** *n.*

Visct., 1. Viscount. **2.** Viscountess.

vise (vīs), *n., v.,* **vised, vising.** —*n.* **1.** any of various devices, usually having two jaws, which may be brought together or separated by means of a screw, lever, or the like, used to hold an object firmly while work is being done upon it. —*v.t.* **2.** to hold, press, or squeeze with or as with a vise. Also, **vice.** [ME *vyse,* t. OF: m. *vis* screw, g. L *vītis* vine] —**vise′like′,** *adj.*

Vise

---

vi·sé (vē′zā, vĕzā′), *n., v.t.*, viséed, viséing. visa. [t. F. See VISA]

Vish·nu (vĭsh′nōō), *n.* **1.** "the Pervader," one of a half dozen solar deities in the Rig-Veda, daily traversing the sky in three strides, morning, noon, and night. **2.** (in popular Hinduism) a deity believed to have descended from heaven to earth in several incarnations, or avatars, varying in number from nine to twenty-two, but always including animals. His most important human incarnation is the Krishna of the Bhagavad Gita. **3.** (in later Hinduism) "the Preserver"; the second member of an important trinity, along with Brahma the Creator and Siva the Destroyer. [t. Skt.]

vis·i·bil·i·ty (vĭz′əbĭl′ətĭ), *n., pl.* **-ties.** **1.** state or fact of being visible; capability of being seen. **2.** the relative capability of being seen under given conditions of distance, light, atmosphere, etc.: *low or high visibility.* **3.** something visible; a visible thing.

vis·i·ble (vĭz′əbəl), *adj.* **1.** capable of being seen; perceptible by the eye; open to sight or view. **2.** perceptible by the mind. **3.** apparent; manifest; obvious. **4.** represented visually; prepared or converted for visual presentation: *visible sound* (an oscillograph of a sound wave). [ME, t. L: m.s. *visibilis*] —**vis′i·ble·ness,** *n.* —**vis′i·bly,** *adv.*

Vis·i·goth (vĭz′ĭgŏth′), *n.* a member of the westerly division of the Goths, which formed a monarchy about A.D. 418, maintaining it in southern France until A.D. 507 and in Spain until A.D. 711. [t. LL: s. *Visigothī* (pl.), Latinization of Gmc. tribal name] —**Vis′i·goth′ic,** *adj.*

vi·sion (vĭzh′ən), *n.* **1.** act of seeing with the eye; the power, faculty, or sense of sight. **2.** act or power of perceiving what is not actually present to the eye, whether by some supernatural endowment or by natural intellectual acuteness: *to lack vision in dealing with great problems.* **3.** something seen or presented to the mind otherwise than by natural, ordinary sight in the normal waking state. **4.** a mental view or image, whether of supernatural origin or merely imaginative, of what is not actually present in place or time: *visions of the past or the future.* **5.** a vivid imaginative conception or anticipation: *visions of wealth or glory.* **6.** something seen; an object of sight. **7.** a sight seen in a dream, ecstasy, trance, or the like. **8.** a sight such as might be seen in a vision, dream, etc.: *a vision of loveliness.* **9.** a scene, person, etc., of extraordinary beauty. —*v.t.* **10.** to show, or to see, in or as in a vision. [ME, t. L: s. *visio* sight] —**vi′sion·less,** *adj.*

vi·sion·al (vĭzh′ənəl), *adj.* **1.** of or pertaining to visions. **2.** belonging to or seen in a vision. —**vi′sion·al·ly,** *adv.*

vi·sion·ar·y (vĭzh′ənĕr′ĭ), *adj., n., pl.* **-aries.** —*adj.* **1.** given to or characterized by fanciful or unpractical ideas, views, or schemes: *a visionary enthusiast.* **2.** given to or concerned with seeing visions. **3.** belonging to or seen in a vision. **4.** unreal or imaginary: *visionary evils.* **5.** purely ideal or speculative; unpractical. **6.** proper only to a vision. —*n.* **7.** one who sees visions. **8.** one given to unpractical ideas or schemes; an unpractical theorist or enthusiast. —**vi′sion·ar′i·ness,** *n.*

vis·it (vĭz′ĭt), *v.t.* **1.** to go to see (a person, place, etc.) in the way of friendship, ceremony, duty, business, curiosity, or the like. **2.** to call upon (a person, family, etc.) for social or other purposes. **3.** to make a stay or sojourn with, as a guest. **4.** (in general) to come or go to. **5.** to go to for the purpose of official inspection or examination; inspect or examine. **6.** to come to in order to comfort or aid. **7.** to come upon or assail: *the plague visited London in 1665.* **8.** to afflict with suffering, trouble, etc. **9.** to inflict punishment for. —*v.i.* **10.** to make a visit or visits. **11.** to inflict punishment. —*n.* **12.** an act of visiting. **13.** a going to see a person, place, etc. **14.** a call paid to a person, family, etc. **15.** a stay or sojourn as a guest. **16.** a going to a place to make an official inspection or examination. **17.** the visiting of a vessel, as at sea, by an officer of a belligerent state, to ascertain its nationality, the nature of its cargo (whether contraband), etc.: *the right of visit and search.* [ME, t. L: s. *visitāre* to go to see]

vis·it·a·ble (vĭz′ĭtəbəl), *adj.* **1.** capable of or suitable for being visited. **2.** liable or subject to official visitation.

vis·it·ant (vĭz′ətənt), *n.* **1.** a visitor; a guest; a temporary resident. **2.** a migratory bird or other animal, at a temporary feeding place, etc., or on its nesting-ground (**summer visitant**) or wintering ground (**winter visitant**). —*adj.* **3.** visiting; paying a visit. —Syn. **1.** See **visitor**.

vis·it·a·tion (vĭz′ətā′shən), *n.* **1.** act of visiting; a visit. **2.** visiting or a visit for the purpose of making an official inspection or examination. **3.** (*cap. or l.c.*) the visit of the Virgin Mary to her cousin Elizabeth. (See Luke 1: 39–56.) **4.** (*cap.*) a church festival, held on July 2, in commemoration of this visit. **5.** a visiting with comfort or aid, or with affliction or punishment, as by God. **6.** a special dispensation from heaven, whether of favor or of affliction. **7.** any experience or event, esp. an unpleasant one, regarded as occurring by divine dispensation. **8.** an affliction or punishment from God. **9.** a judgment. —**vis·it·a·tion·al,** *adj.*

vis·it·a·to·ri·al (vĭz′ətətōr′ĭəl), *adj.* **1.** pertaining to an official visitor or to official visitation. **2.** having the power of visitation.

visiting card, a calling card.

vis·i·tor (vĭz′ətər), *n.* one who visits, or makes a visit, as for friendly, business, official, or other purposes. —**vis·i·tress** (vĭz′ətrĭs), *n. fem.*

—Syn. VISITOR, CALLER, GUEST, VISITANT are terms for one who comes to spend time with or stay with others, or in a place. A VISITOR often stays some time, for social pleasure, for business, sightseeing, etc.: *a visitor at our neighbor's house, in San Francisco.* A CALLER comes for a brief (usually) formal visit: *the caller merely left her card.* A GUEST is anyone receiving hospitality, and the word has been extended to include anyone who pays for meals and lodging: *a welcome guest, a paying guest.* VISITANT applies to a migratory bird or to a supernatural being: *a warbler as a visitant.*

vis·i·to·ri·al (vĭz′ətōr′ĭəl), *adj.* of or pertaining to a visitor; visitatorial.

vis ma·jor (vĭs mā′jər), *Law.* force majeure. [L: lit., greater force]

vi·sor (vī′zər, vĭz′ər), *n.* **1.** the movable front elements of a helmet, covering the face, esp. the uppermost element which protects the eyes. **2.** the projecting forepiece of a cap, for protecting the eyes. **3.** any disguise or means of concealment. —*v.t.* **4.** to protect or mask with a visor; shield. Also, **vizor.** [ME *viser,* t. AF, der. *vis* face] —**vi′sored,** *adj.* —**vi′sor·less,** *adj.*

Spanish helmet with.
V. visor, 16th century

vis·ta (vĭs′tə), *n.* **1.** a view or prospect, esp. one seen through a long, narrow avenue or passage, as between rows of trees, houses, or the like. **2.** such an avenue or passage. **3.** a mental view of a far-reaching kind: *vistas of thought.* **4.** a mental view extending over a long time or a stretch of remembered, imagined, or anticipated experiences, etc.: *dim vistas of the past or the future.* [t. It.: sight, view, fem. of *visto,* pp. of *vedere* see, g. L *videre*] —**vis·taed** (vĭs′təd), *adj.* —**vis′ta·less,** *adj.* —Syn. **1.** See **view.**

Vis·tu·la (vĭs′chōōlə), *n.* a river in Poland, flowing from the Carpathian Mountains past Warsaw into the Baltic near Danzig. ab. 650 mi. Polish, **Wisla.** German, **Weichsel.**

vis·u·al (vĭzh′ōōəl), *adj.* **1.** of or pertaining to sight. **2.** used in sight: *the visual nerve.* **3.** *Optics.* optical. **4.** perceptible by the sight; visible. **5.** perceptible by the mind; of the nature of a mental vision. [ME, t. LL: s. *visuālis* belonging to sight]

visual aid, *Educ.* a device, technique, or the like, which uses the student's sense of sight in carrying on or assisting the learning process: *motion pictures and photographs are good visual aids.*

vis·u·al·ize (vĭzh′ōōəlīz′), *v.,* -ized, -izing. —*v.i.* **1.** to call up or form mental images or pictures. —*v.t.* **2.** to make visual or visible. **3.** to form a mental image of. **4.** to make perceptible to the mind or imagination. Also, *esp. Brit.,* **vis′u·al·ise′.** —**vis′u·al·i·za′tion,** *n.* —**vis′u·al·iz′er,** *n.*

vis·u·al·ly (vĭzh′ōōəlĭ), *adv.* in a visual manner or respect; by sight.

visual purple, the substance in the rod cells of the retina of the eye which is photosensitive to dim light.

vi·ta·ceous (vī tā′shəs), *adj.* belonging to the *Vitaceae,* or grape family of plants, which includes the ampelopsis, Japanese ivy, Virginia creeper, etc. [f. s. NL *Vitāceae* the grape genus (der. L *vītis* vine) + -OUS]

vi·tal (vī′təl), *adj.* **1.** of or pertaining to life: *vital functions or processes.* **2.** having life, or living. **3.** being the seat or source of life: *the vital parts or organs.* **4.** necessary to life. **5.** necessary to the existence, continuance, or well-being of something; indispensable; essential: *a vital necessity.* **6.** affecting the existence, well-being, truth, etc., of something: *a vital error.* **7.** of critical importance: *vital problems.* **8.** imparting life or vigor; vitalizing, or invigorating. **9.** affecting life; destructive to life: *a vital wound.* —*n., pl.* **10.** those bodily organs which are essential to life, as the brain, heart, lungs, and stomach. **11.** the essential parts of anything. [ME, t. L: s. *vitālis*] —**vi′tal·ly,** *adv.* —**vi′tal·ness,** *n.*

vital force, the animating force in animals and plants. Also, **vital principle.**

vi·tal·ism (vī′təlĭz′əm), *n.* **1.** the doctrine that phenomena are only partly controlled by mechanical forces and that they are in some measure self-determining (opposed to *mechanism*). **2.** *Biol.* the doctrine that ascribes the functions of a living organism to a vital principle distinct from chemical and other forces. —**vi′tal·ist,** *n., adj.* —**vi′tal·is′tic,** *adj.*

vi·tal·i·ty (vī tăl′ətĭ), *n., pl.* **-ties.** **1.** vital force. **2.** the principle of life. **3.** power to live, or physical strength as a condition of life. **4.** exuberant physical vigor: *of terrific vitality.* **5.** power of continued existence, as of an institution, a book, etc. **6.** something having vital force. **7.** (*pl.*) vital powers or energies.

vi·tal·ize (vī′təlīz′), *v.t.,* -ized, -izing. **1.** to make vital or living, or give life to. **2.** to give vitality or vigor to; animate. —**vi′tal·i·za′tion,** *n.* —**vi′tal·iz′er,** *n.*

vital statistics, statistics concerning human life or the conditions affecting human life and the maintenance of population.

vi·tam im·pen·de·re ve·ro (vī′täm ĭm pĕn′dərē′ vĭr′ō), *Latin.* to consecrate (one's) life to truth. Juvenal, *Satires* IV, 91. Motto chosen by J. J. Rousseau.

vi·ta·min (vī'tə mĭn), *n.* any of a group of food factors essential in small quantities to maintain life but not themselves supplying energy. The absence of any one of them results in a characteristic deficiency disease. They were named in 1912 by Casimir Funk. Also, **vi·ta·mine** (vī'tə mĭn, -mēn). [f. L *vīt(a)* life + AMIN(E)] —**vi·ta·min'ic,** *adj.*

vitamin A, a yellow, fat-soluble, solid terpene alcohol, obtained from carotene and found in green and yellow vegetables, egg yolk, etc.; essential to growth, the protection of epithelial tissue, and the prevention of night blindness.

vitamin A₂, a vitamin similar to vitamin A, derived from liver oils of fresh-water fish.

vitamin B₁, thiamine.

vitamin B₂, riboflavin.

vitamin B₆, pyridoxine.

vitamin B complex, an important group of water-soluble vitamins containing vitamin B₁, vitamin B₂, etc.

vitamin C, ascorbic acid.

vitamin D, any of the several fat-soluble antirachitic vitamins D₁, D₂, D₃, found in milk and fish-liver oils, esp. cod and halibut, or obtained by irradiating provitamin D with ultraviolet light.

vitamin D₁, a mixture of lumisterol and calciferol, obtained by ultraviolet irradiation of ergosterol.

vitamin D₂, calciferol.

vitamin D₃, the naturally occurring D-vitamin, found in fish-liver oils, differing from vitamin D₂ by slight structural differences in the molecule.

vitamin E, a pale-yellow viscous fluid, found in wheat-germ oil, which promotes fertility in mammals and prevents human abortions. See **tocopherol.**

vitamin G, riboflavin.

vitamin H, biotin.

vitamin K₁, a vitamin found in leafy vegetables, rice bran, hog liver, etc., and obtained from alfalfa oil or putrefied sardine meat, which promotes blood clotting by increasing the prothrombin content of the blood.

vitamin K₂, a compound similar in activity to vitamin K₁, with the formula $C_{40}H_{54}O_2$.

vitamin P, a water-soluble vitamin, present in citrus fruits, rose hips, and paprika, which maintains the resistance of cell and capillary walls to permeation and change of pressure; citrin.

vi·ta·scope (vī'tə skōp'), *n.* a cinematograph. [f. L *vīta* life + -SCOPE]

Vi·tebsk (vē'tĕpsk), *n.* a city in the W Soviet Union, on the Dvina river. 128,000 (est. 1956).

vi·tel·lin (vī tĕl'ĭn, vī-), *n. Biochem.* a phosphoprotein in the yolk of eggs. [f. VITELL(US) + -IN²]

vi·tel·line (vī tĕl'ĭn, vī-), *adj.* **1.** pertaining to the egg yolk. **2.** having a yellow color.

vitelline membrane, the membrane surrounding the egg yolk.

vi·tel·lus (vī tĕl'əs, vī-), *n.* the yolk of an egg. [t. L]

vi·ti·a·ble (vĭsh'ĭ ə bəl), *adj.* subject to being vitiated.

vi·ti·ate (vĭsh'ĭ āt'), *v.t.* -ated, -ating. **1.** to impair the quality of; make faulty; mar. **2.** to contaminate; corrupt; spoil. **3.** to make legally defective or invalid; invalidate. [t. L: m.s. *vitiātus,* pp., spoiled] —**vi'ti·a'tion,** *n.* —**vi'ti·a'tor,** *n.*

vi·ti·at·ed (vĭsh'ĭ ā'tĭd), *adj.* spoiled; corrupted; rendered invalid.

vit·i·cul·ture (vĭt'ə kŭl'chər, vī'tə-), *n.* **1.** the culture or cultivation of the grapevine; grape growing. **2.** the study or science of grapes and their culture. [f. viti- (t. L, comb. form of *vītis* vine) + CULTURE] —**vit'i·cul'tur·al,** *adj.* —**vit'i·cul'tur·er, vit'i·cul'tur·ist,** *n.*

Vi·ti Le·vu (vē'tē lĕ'vōō), the largest of the Fiji Islands, in the S Pacific. 176,822 pop. (1946); 4053 sq. mi. *Cap.:* Suva.

vit·i·li·go (vĭt'ə lī'gō), *n. Pathol.* a disease in which smooth white patches are formed on various parts of the body, owing to loss of the natural pigment. [t. L: tetter]

Vi·to·ria (vē tō'ryä), *n.* a city in N Spain: decisive defeat of the French forces in Spain, 1813. 56,601 (est. 1956).

vit·re·ous (vĭt'rĭ əs), *adj.* **1.** of the nature of glass; resembling glass, as in transparency, brittleness, hardness, etc.; glassy. **2.** of or pertaining to glass. **3.** obtained from glass. [t. L: m. *vitreus,* der. *vitrum* glass] —**vit're·ous·ly,** *adv.* —**vit're·ous·ness, vit·re·os·i·ty** (vĭt'rĭ ŏs'ə tĭ), *n.*

vitreous electricity, positive electricity; electricity produced on glass by rubbing with silk.

vitreous humor, *Anat.* the transparent gelatinous substance filling the eyeball behind the crystalline lens. See diag. under **eye.**

vi·tres·cent (vĭ trĕs'ənt), *adj.* **1.** turning into glass. **2.** tending to become glass. **3.** capable of being formed into glass. [f. s. L *vitrum* glass + -ESCENT] —**vi·tres'cence,** *n.*

vitri-, a word element meaning "glass," as in *vitriform.* [comb. form repr. L *vitrum*]

vit·ric (vĭt'rĭk), *adj.* **1.** of or pertaining to glass. **2.** of the nature of glass; glasslike. [f. s. L *vitrum* glass + -IC]

vit·ri·fi·ca·tion (vĭt'rə fə kā'shən), *n.* **1.** act or process of vitrifying. **2.** state of being vitrified. **3.** something vitrified. Also, **vit·ri·fac·tion** (vĭt'rə făk'shən).

vit·ri·form (vĭt'rə fôrm'), *adj.* having the form or appearance of glass.

vit·ri·fy (vĭt'rə fī'), *v.t., v.i.,* -fied, -fying. **1.** to convert or be converted into glass. **2.** to make or become vitreous. —**vit'ri·fi'a·ble,** *adj.* —**vit'ri·fi'a·bil'i·ty,** *n.*

vit·ri·ol (vĭt'rĭ əl), *n., v.,* -oled, -oling or (*esp. Brit.*) -olled, -olling. —*n.* **1.** *Chem.* any of certain metallic sulfates of glassy appearance, as of copper (blue vitriol), or iron (green vitriol), of zinc (white vitriol), etc. **2.** oil of vitriol; sulfuric acid. **3.** something highly caustic, or severe in its effects, as criticism. —*v.t.* **4.** to injure or burn with vitriol or sulfuric acid; vitriolize. [ME, t. ML: s. *vitriolum,* der. L *vitrum* glass]

vit·ri·ol·ic (vĭt'rĭ ŏl'ĭk), *adj.* **1.** of or pertaining to vitriol. **2.** obtained from vitriol; resembling vitriol. **3.** severely caustic or scathing: *vitriolic criticism.*

vit·ri·ol·ize (vĭt'rĭ ə līz'), *v.t.,* -ized, -izing. **1.** to treat with or change into vitriol. **2.** to injure or burn with vitriol or sulfuric acid, as by throwing it on one's face. —**vit'ri·ol·i·za'tion,** *n.*

Vi·tru·vi·us Pol·li·o (vĭ trōō'vĭ əs pŏl'ĭ ō'), **Marcus** (mär'kəs). lived in the first century B.C., Roman architect, engineer, and author. —**Vi·tru'vi·an,** *adj.*

vit·ta (vĭt'ə), *n., pl.* **vittae** (vĭt'ē). **1.** *Bot.* a tube or receptacle for oil, found in the fruits of most umbelliferous plants. **2.** *Zool., Bot.* a streak or stripe, as of color. **3.** a headband or fillet. [t. L: ribbon, fillet]

vit·tate (vĭt'āt), *adj.* **1.** provided with or having a vitta or vittae. **2.** striped longitudinally.

vit·u·line (vĭch'ə lĭn', -lĭn), *adj.* of, pertaining to, or resembling a calf or veal. [t. L: m.s. *vitulīnus*]

Vitta (def. 1)
The black spots indicate the vittae in the transverse section of the fruits of A, spotted cowbane, B, celery, and C, parsley.

vi·tu·per·ate (vī tū'/pə rāt', -tōō'-, vī-), *v.t.,* -ated, -ating. **1.** to find fault with abusively. **2.** to address abusive language to; revile; objurgate. [t. L: m.s. *vituperātus,* pp.] —**vi·tu'per·a'tor,** *n.*

vi·tu·per·a·tion (vī tū'/pə rā'shən, -tōō'-, vī-), *n.* **1.** act of vituperating. **2.** verbal abuse. —Ant. **1.** praise.

vi·tu·per·a·tive (vī tū'/pə rā'tĭv, -tōō'-, vī-), *adj.* characterized by or of the nature of vituperation; abusive. —**vi·tu'per·a'tive·ly,** *adv.*

vi·va (vē'vä), *interj.* **1.** *Italian.* "(long) live (the person named)!"—used in phrases of acclamation. —*n.* **2.** a shout of "viva!" [t. It.: lit., may he live, subj. of *vivere* live]

vi·va·ce (vē vä'chĕ), *adj. Music.* vivacious; lively. [It., g. L *vīvax*]

vi·va·cious (vī vā'shəs, vī-), *adj.* **1.** lively, animated, or sprightly: *a vivacious manner or style, vivacious conversation.* **2.** *Archaic.* long-lived, or tenacious of life. [f. VIVACI(TY) + -OUS] —**vi·va'cious·ly,** *adv.* —**vi·va'cious·ness,** *n.* —Ant. **1.** languid.

vi·vac·i·ty (vī văs'ə tĭ, vī-), *n., pl.* -ties. **1.** the quality of being vivacious. **2.** liveliness; animation; sprightliness. **3.** a vivacious act or speech; a lively sally. [late ME, t. L: m.s. *vīvācitas*]

vi·van·dière (vē vän dyêr'), *n.* a woman accompanying a French or other Continental regiment to sell provisions and liquor to the soldiers. [t. F, fem. of *vivandier* sutler, der. ML *vivenda* victuals]

vi·var·i·um (vī vâr'ĭ əm), *n., pl.* -variums, -varia (-vâr'ĭ ə). a place, such as a laboratory, where animals are kept alive in conditions simulating their natural state. Cf. **terrarium** and **aquarium.** [t. L: enclosure for live game]

vi·va vo·ce (vī'və vō'sĭ), by word of mouth; orally. [t. ML: lit., with the living voice] —**vi·va-vo'ce,** *adj.*

vive (vēv), *interj. French.* (long) live (the person named)! —used in phrases of acclamation.

vive la ba·ga·telle (vēv là bà gà tĕl'), *French.* long live frivolity!

vive le roi (vēv lə rwà'), *French.* long live the king!

vi·ver·rine (vī vĕr'īn, -ĭn, vī-), *adj.* **1.** of or pertaining to the *Viverridae,* a family of small carnivorous mammals including the civets, genets, palm cats, etc. —*n.* **2.** a viverrine animal. [t. NL: m.s. *viverrīnus,* der. L *viverra* ferret]

vi·ve va·le·que (vī'vĭ vä lē'kwĭ), *Latin.* live and keep well, or thrive (used at the end of letters). Horace, *Satires* II, 5, 110.

Viv·i·an (vĭv'ĭ ən), *n. Arthurian Romance.* an enchantress, the mistress of Merlin; known as "the Lady of the Lake." Also, **Viv'i·en.**

Vi·vi·a·ni (vē vyä nē'), *n.* **René** (rə nĕ'). 1863-1925, French statesman, premier of France 1914-15.

viv·id (vĭv'ĭd), *adj.* **1.** strikingly bright, as color, light, objects, etc.: *a vivid green.* **2.** strikingly alive; full of life: *a vivid personality.* **3.** lively or intense, as feelings, etc. **4.** vigorous, as activities, etc. **5.** lively, or presenting the appearance, freshness, spirit, etc., of life, as a picture. **6.** clearly perceptible to the eye or mind. **7.** strong and distinct, as an impression or recollection. **8.** forming distinct and striking mental images, as the imagination. **9.** lively in operation. [t. L: s. *vīvidus* animated] —**viv'id·ly,** *adv.* —**viv'id·ness,** *n.* —Syn. **1.** bright, brilliant, intense. **2.** animated, spirited, lively. **5.** See **picturesque.**

viv·i·fy (vĭv'ə fī'), *v.t.,* -fied, -fying. **1.** to give life to; quicken. **2.** to enliven; render lively or animated;

brighten. [t. L: m.s. *vivificāre*] —viv·i·fi·ca'tion, *n.*
—viv/i·fi/er, *n.*

vi·vip·a·ra (vī vĭp'ə rə), *n. pl.* viviparous animals.

vi·vip·a·rous (vī vĭp'ə rəs), *adj.* 1. *Zool.* bringing forth living young (rather than eggs), as most mammals and some reptiles and fishes. 2. *Bot.* producing seeds that germinate on the plant. [t. L: m. *viviparus* bringing forth living young] —viv·i·par·i·ty (vĭv'ə păr/ə tĭ'), vi·vip'a·rous·ness, *n.* —vi·vip'a·rous·ly, *adv.*

viv·i·sect (vĭv'ə sĕkt', vĭv'ə sĕkt'), *v.t.* 1. to dissect the living body of. —*v.i.* 2. to practice vivisection. [f. *vivi-* (t. L, comb. form of *vivus* alive) + -SECT] —viv/i·sec/tor, *n.*

viv·i·sec·tion (vĭv'ə sĕk/shən), *n.* 1. the action of cutting into or dissecting a living body. 2. the practice of subjecting living animals to cutting operations, esp. in order to advance physiological and pathological knowledge. —viv'i·sec/tion·al, *adj.*

viv·i·sec·tion·ist (vĭv'ə sĕk/shən ĭst), *n.* 1. a vivisector. 2. one who favors or defends the practice of vivisection.

vix·en (vĭk/sən), *n.* 1. an ill-tempered or quarrelsome woman; a spitfire. 2. a female fox. [(South.) d. var. of ME *fixen* she-fox, f. OE *fyxe* she-fox + -*en*, obs. fem. suffix] —vix/en·ish, vix/en·ly, *adj.*

viz., videlicet.

viz·ard (vĭz/ərd), *n.* 1. a visor. 2. a mask. Also, **vis·ard.** [alter. of VISOR] —viz/ard·ed, *adj.*

vi·zier (vĭ zĭr', vĭz/yər), *n.* 1. a principal helper of a Mohammedan sovereign. The Abbassides had only one; the Ottoman sultans had several with the Grand Vizier as chairman. 2. a minister of state. Also, **vi·zir'.** [t. Turk.: m. *vezīr*, t. Ar.: m. *wazīr* bearer of burdens] —vi·zier·ate (vĭ zĭr/ĭt, -āt, vĭz/yər'ĭt, -yə rāt'), **vi·zier/i·al,** *adj.* —vi·zier/ship, *n.* —vi·zier/i·al, *adj.*

vi·zor (vĭ/zər, vĭz/ər), *n., v.t.* visor. —vi/zored, *adj.* —vi/zor·less, *adj.*

V-J Day, the day of victory over Japan for the Allies in World War II (Sept. 2, 1945).

VL, Vulgar Latin.

v.l., varia lectio.

Vla·di·kav·kaz (vlä/dĭ käf käs'), *n.* former name of Ordzhonikidze.

Vlad·i·mir (vlăd/ə mĭr'; *Russ.* vlä dē'mĭr), *n.* A.D. c956–1015, grand prince of Russia, A. D. 980–1015; first Christian Russian ruler of Russia. Also, **Wladimir.**

Vla·di·vos·tok (vlăd/ə vŏs'tŏk; *Russ.* vlä/dĭ vŏs tŏk'), *n.* a seaport in the SE Soviet Union in Asia, on the Sea of Japan: eastern terminus of the Trans-Siberian Railroad. 265,000 (est. 1956).

Vla·minck (vlä mănk'), *n.* **Maurice de** (mô rēs'), 1876–1958, French artist.

Vlis·sing·en (vlĭs/ĭng ən), *n.* Dutch name of **Flushing.**

Vl·ta·va (vŭl/tä·vä), *n.* Czech name of the Moldau.

V-mail (vē/māl'), *n.* a service during World War II for dispatching letters to U.S. armed forces outside the continental U.S., esp. by miniature films.

V.M.D., (L *Veterinariae Medicinae Doctor*) Doctor of Veterinary Medicine.

v.n., verb neuter.

vo., verso.

voc., vocative.

vocab., vocabulary.

vo·ca·ble (vō/kə bəl), *n.* 1. a word; a term. 2. a word considered merely as composed of certain sounds or letters, without regard to meaning. —*adj.* 3. that may be spoken. [t. L: m.s. *vocābulum* name, term]

vo·cab·u·lar·y (vō kăb/yə lĕr'ĭ), *n., pl.* -laries. 1. the stock of words used by a people, or by a particular class or person. 2. a list or collection of the words of a language, book, author, branch of science, or the like, usually in alphabetical order and defined; a wordbook, glossary, dictionary, or lexicon. 3. the words of a language. [t. ML: m.s. *vocābulārius*, der. L *vocābulum* vocable]

vocabulary entry, 1. a word entered in a vocabulary. 2. (in dictionaries) a word or phrase listed with its definition, etc., in alphabetical order or listed for identification after the word from which it is derived or to which it is related.

vo·cal (vō/kəl), *adj.* 1. of or pertaining to the voice; uttered with the voice; oral: *the vocal organs.* 2. rendered by or intended for singing, as music. 3. having a voice: *a vocal being.* 4. giving forth sound with or as with a voice. 5. inclined to express oneself in speech; stridently insistent. 6. *Phonet.* **a.** vocalic (def. 1). **b.** voiced. —*n.* 7. a vocal sound. [ME, t. L: s. *vōcālis*, der. *vox* voice] —vo·cal·i·ty (vō kăl/ə tĭ), vo/cal·ness, *n.* —vo/cal·ly, *adv.*

vocal cords, *Anat.* folds of mucous membrane projecting into the cavity of the larynx, the edges of which can be drawn tense and made to vibrate by the passage of air from the lungs, thus producing vocal sound.

vo·cal·ic (vō kăl/ĭk), *adj.* 1. of or pertaining to a vowel or vowels; vowellike. 2. containing many vowels.

vo·cal·ism (vō/kə lĭz'əm), *n.* 1. *Phonet.* **a.** the system of vowels of a particular language. **b.** the nature of one or more given vowels. 2. the use of the voice, as in speech or song. 3. the act, principles, or art of singing.

vo·cal·ist (vō/kəl ĭst), *n.* a singer.

vo·cal·ize (vō/kə līz'), *v.,* -ized, -izing. —*v.t.* 1. to make vocal; form into voice; utter or articulate; sing. 2. to endow with voice or utterance. 3. *Phonet.* **a.** to use as a vowel, as the *l* of *bottle.* **b.** to change into a vowel. **c.** to voice. 4. (of Hebrew, Arabic, and similar systems of writing) to furnish with vowels or vowel points. —*v.i.* 5. to use the voice, as in speech or song. 6. *Phonet.* to become changed into a vowel. —vo/cal·i·za/tion, *n.* —vo/cal·iz/er, *n.*

vocat., vocative.

vo·ca·tion (vō kā/shən), *n.* 1. a particular occupation, business, or profession; a trade or calling. 2. a calling or summons, as to a particular activity or career. 3. a divine call to God's service or to the Christian life. 4. a function or station to which one is called by God. [late ME *vocacion*, t. L: m. s. *vocātio* calling]

vo·ca·tion·al (vō kā/shən əl), *adj.* of or pertaining to a vocation or occupation: *vocational schools* (schools that train persons for various occupations). —vo·ca/tion·al·ly, *adv.*

voc·a·tive (vŏk/ə tĭv), *adj.* 1. *Gram.* **a.** (in some languages) designating a case that indicates the person or thing addressed. **b.** similar to such a case form in function or meaning. 2. pertaining to or used in calling. —*n.* 3. *Gram.* **a.** the vocative case. **b.** any other formation of vocative meaning. **c.** a word therein, as Latin *Paule*, "Paul" (nominative *Paulus*). [late ME, t. L: m.s. *vocātivus*, der. *vocāre* call] —voc/a·tive·ly, *adv.*

vo·ces (vō/sēz), *n.* pl. of **vox.**

vo·cif·er·ance (vō sĭf/ər əns), *n.* vociferant utterance; vociferation.

vo·cif·er·ant (vō sĭf/ər ənt), *adj.* 1. vociferating. —*n.* 2. one who vociferates.

vo·cif·er·ate (vō sĭf/ə rāt'), *v.i., v.t.,* -ated, -ating. to cry out loudly or noisily; shout; bawl. [t. LL: m. s. *vōciferātus*, pp.] —vo·cif/er·a/tor, *n.*

vo·cif·er·a·tion (vō sĭf/ə rā/shən), *n.* noisy outcry; a clamor.

vo·cif·er·ous (vō sĭf/ər əs), *adj.* 1. crying out noisily; clamorous. 2. of the nature of vociferation; uttered with clamor. [f. VOCIFER(ATE) + -OUS] —vo·cif/er·ous·ly, *adv.* —vo·cif/er·ous·ness, *n.*

vod·ka (vŏd/kə), *n.* a Russian alcoholic liquor, distilled orig. from wheat, but now from corn, other cereals, and potatoes. [t. Russ., dim. of *voda* water]

vogue (vōg), *n.* 1. the fashion, as at a particular time: *a style in vogue fifty years ago.* 2. popular currency, acceptance, or favor: *the book had a great vogue in its day.* [t. F, der. *voguer* row, t. It.: m. *vogare*, ? g. L *vocāre* call (through use in sailors' chanties)] —Syn. 1. See **fashion.**

Vo·gul (vō/gool), *n.* a Finno-Ugric language of the Ugric group, spoken east of the Ural Mountains.

voice (vois), *n., v.,* voiced, voicing. —*n.* 1. the sound or sounds uttered through the mouth of living creatures, esp. of human beings in speaking, shouting, singing, etc. 2. the sounds naturally uttered by a single person in speech or vocal utterance, often as characteristic of the utterer. 3. such sounds considered with reference to their character or quality: *a manly voice, a sweet voice.* 4. the condition of the voice for speaking or singing, esp. effective condition: *she was in poor voice.* 5. any sound likened to vocal utterance: *the voice of the wind.* 6. anything likened to speech as conveying impressions to the mind: *the voice of nature.* 7. the faculty of uttering sounds through the mouth, esp. articulate sounds; utterance; speech. 8. expression in spoken or written words, or by other means: *to give voice to one's disapproval by a letter.* 9. expressed opinion or choice: *his voice was for compromise.* 10. the right to express an opinion or choice; vote; suffrage: *have no voice in a matter.* 11. expressed wish or injunction: *obedient to the voice of God.* 12. the person or other agency by which something is expressed or revealed. 13. musical tone created by the vibration of the vocal cords and amplified by oral and other throat cavities; tone produced in singing. 14. *Phonet.* the sound produced by tonal vibration of the vocal cords, as air from the lungs is forced through between them. 15. *Gram.* **a.** (in some languages) a category of verb inflection denoting the relation between the action expressed by the verb and the subject of the sentence (e.g., as acting or as acted upon). Compare: *John eats the bread. The bread was eaten.* **b.** (in some other languages) one of several contrasting constructions with similar meanings. **c.** a set of such categories or constructions in a particular language, e.g., the *active* and *passive* voices in Latin. **d.** the meaning of, or typical of, such a category or construction. **e.** such categories or constructions, or their meanings, collectively. 16. the finer regulation, as of intensity and color, in tuning, esp. of a piano or organ. 17. a singer. 18. a voice part. 19. *Obs.* rumor. 20. *Obs.* reputation. —*v.t.* 21. to give voice, utterance, or expression to (an emotion, opinion, etc.); express; declare; proclaim: *to voice one's discontent.* 22. *Music.* **a.** to regulate the tone of, as the pipes of an organ. **b.** to write the voice parts for (music). 23. to utter with the voice. [ME, t. AF, g. L *vox*] —voic/er, *n.*

voiced (voist), *adj.* **1.** having a voice: *low-voiced.* **2.** expressed vocally. **3.** *Phonet.* having voice (def. 14).

voice·ful (vois′fəl), *adj.* having a voice, esp. a loud voice; sounding; sonorous.

voice·less (vois′lĭs), *adj.* **1.** having no voice; mute; dumb. **2.** uttering no speech or words; silent. **3.** having an unmusical voice. **4.** unspoken or unuttered. **5.** *Phonet.* surd; uttered without tonal vibration of the vocal cords: *p, f,* and *s* are *voiceless.* **6.** having no voice or vote. —**voice′less·ly**, *adv.* —**voice′less·ness**, *n.* —Syn. 1. See **dumb.**

voice part, *Music.* the melody or succession of tones for one of the voices or instruments in a harmonic or concerted composition.

void (void), *adj.* **1.** *Law.* without legal force or effect; not legally binding or enforceable. **2.** useless; ineffectual; vain. **3.** empty; devoid; destitute (fol. by *of*). **4.** without contents. **5.** without an incumbent, as an office. —*n.* **6.** an empty space: *the void of heaven.* **7.** a place without the usual or desired occupant: *his death left a void among us.* **8.** a gap or opening, as in a wall. **9.** emptiness; vacancy. —*v.t.* **10.** to make void or of no effect; invalidate; nullify. **11.** to empty or discharge (contents); evacuate (excrement, etc.). **12.** *Archaic.* to make empty or vacant. **13.** *Archaic.* to clear or rid (fol. by *of*). **14.** *Archaic.* to leave, as a place. [ME, t. OF: m. *voide,* g. LL *vocitus,* ult. der. *vocuus,* r. L *vacuus* empty] —**void′er,** *n.* —**void′ness,** *n.*

void·a·ble (voi′də bəl), *adj.* **1.** capable of being voided. **2.** *Law.* capable of being made or adjudged void. —**void′a·ble·ness,** *n.*

void·ance (voi′dəns), *n.* **1.** act of voiding. **2.** annulment, as of a contract. **3.** ejection from a benefice. **4.** vacancy, as of a benefice.

void·ed (voi′dĭd), *adj.* **1.** having a void or opening. **2.** having been made void. **3.** *Her.* cut out (with a narrow rim left) so as to show the field.

voi·là tout (vwá lá tōō′), *French.* that's all.

voile (voil; *Fr.* vwàl), *n.* a dress fabric of wool, silk rayon, or cotton, with an open, canvaslike weave. [t. F: veil. See **VEIL**]

voir dire (vwår dēr′), *Law.* **1.** an oath administered to a proposed witness or juror by which he is sworn to speak the truth in an examination to ascertain his competence. **2.** the examination itself, i.e., the preliminary examination of a prospective witness or juror touching his competence. [t. AF, f. *voir* true, truly + *dire* say]

voi·ture (vwä tyr′), *n. French.* a carriage, wagon, or wheeled vehicle.

voix cé·leste (vwä sĕ lĕst′), an organ stop having two pipes for each note tuned to very slightly different pitches and producing a wavering, gentle tone. [F: heavenly voice]

vol., **1.** volcano. **2.** volume. **3.** volunteer.

vo·lant (vō′lənt), *adj.* **1.** flying; having the power of flight. **2.** *Poetic.* moving lightly; nimble. **3.** *Her.* represented as flying. [t. L: s. *volans,* ppr. of *volāre* fly]

Vo·la·pük (vō′lə pyk′), *n.* one of the earliest of the artificially constructed international auxiliary languages, invented about 1879. Also, **Vol·a·puk** (vŏl′ə pŏŏk′). [f. *vol* (repr. E *world*) + *pük* (repr. E *speak, speech*)] —**Vo′la·pük′ist,** *n.*

Bird volant

vo·lar (vō′lər), *adj.* of or pertaining to the palm of the hand or the sole of the foot. [f. s. L *vola* hollow of the hand or foot + -AR[1]]

vol·a·tile (vŏl′ə tĭl), *adj.* **1.** evaporating rapidly; passing off readily in the form of vapor: *a volatile oil.* **2.** light and changeable of mind; frivolous; flighty. **3.** fleeting; transient. **4.** *Archaic.* able or accustomed to fly, as winged creatures. [ME *volatil,* t. L: s. *volātilis* flying] —**vol′a·til′i·ty, vol′a·tile·ness,** *n.*

volatile oil, a distilled oil, esp. an essential oil distilled from plant tissue. Such oils are distinguished from glyceride oils by their volatility and failure to saponify.

volatile salt, sal volatile.

vol·a·til·ize (vŏl′ə tə līz′), *v.,* -ized, -izing. —*v.i.* **1.** to become volatile; pass off as vapor. —*v.t.* **2.** to make volatile; cause to pass off in the form of vapor. —**vol′a·til·iz′a·ble,** *adj.* —**vol′a·til·i·za′tion,** *n.* —**vol′a·til·iz′er,** *n.*

vo·la·tion (və lā′shən), *n.* flying, as of birds.

vol·can·ic (vŏl kăn′ĭk), *adj.* **1.** of or pertaining to a volcano or volcanoes: *a volcanic eruption.* **2.** discharged from or produced by volcanoes: *volcanic mud.* **3.** characterized by the presence of volcanoes. **4.** suggestive of a volcano, or its eruptive violence, etc. —**vol·can′i·cal·ly,** *adv.* —**vol·can·ic·i·ty** (vŏl′kə nĭs′ə tĭ), *n.*

volcanic glass, a natural glass produced when molten lava cools very rapidly; obsidian.

vol·can·ism (vŏl′kə nĭz′əm), *n.* the phenomena connected with volcanoes and volcanic activity.

vol·ca·no (vŏl kā′nō), *n., pl.* -noes, -nos. **1.** a vent in the earth's crust through which molten rock (lava), steam, ashes, etc., are expelled from within, either continuously or at irregular intervals, gradually forming a conical heap (or in time a mountain), commonly with a cup-shaped hollow (crater) about the vent. Cf. **active**

(def. 8), **dormant** (def. 3), **extinct** (def. 1). **2.** the mountain or hill having such a vent and formed in whole or in part of its own lava. [t. It., g. L *Volcānus* Vulcan, god of fire]

Volcano Islands, three small Japanese islands in the N Pacific, ab. 750 mi. S of Tokyo. See **Iwo Jima.**

vol·can·ol·o·gy (vŏl′kə nŏl′ə jĭ). *n.* the scientific study of volcanoes and volcanic phenomena. Also, **vulcanology.** —**vol·can·o·log·i·cal** (vŏl′kən ə lŏj′ə kəl), *adj.* —**vol′can·ol′o·gist,** *n.*

vole (vōl), *n.* any of the rodents of the genus *Microtus* and allied genera, resembling and belonging to the same family as the common rats and mice, and usually of heavy build and having short limbs and tail. [short for *volemouse* field mouse; *vole,* t. Scand.; cf. Norw. *voll* field, c. OE *weald* forested area]

Vole. *Microtus pennsylvanicus*
7 in. long, tail ab. 2 in.)

Vol·ga (vŏl′gə; *Russ.* vôl′gä), *n.* a river flowing from the Valdai Hills in the W Soviet Union E and then S to the Caspian Sea: the longest river in Europe. 2325 mi.

Vol·go·grad (vŏl′gə gräd′). See **Stalingrad.**

vol·i·tant (vŏl′ə tənt), *adj.* **1.** flying; having the power of flight; volant. **2.** active; moving. [t. L: s. *volitans,* ppr., flying to and fro]

vol·i·ta·tion (vŏl′ə tā′shən), *n.* action or the power of flying; flight. [t. ML: s. *volitātio,* der. *volitāre,* freq. of *volāre* fly] —**vol′i·ta′tion·al,** *adj.*

vo·li·tion (vō lĭsh′ən), *n.* **1.** act of willing exercise of choice to determine action. **2.** a determination by the will. **3.** the power of willing; will. [t. ML: s. *volitio,* der. L *volo* I wish] —**vo·li′tion·al, vo·li·tion·ar·y** (vō lĭsh′ə-nĕr′ĭ), *adj.* —**vo·li′tion·al·ly,** *adv.* —Syn. 1. See **will**[2].

vol·i·tive (vŏl′ə tĭv), *adj.* **1.** characterized by or pertaining to volition. **2.** *Gram.* expressing a wish or permission: *a volitive construction.* [f. VOLIT(ION) + -IVE]

Volks·lied (fôlks′lēt′), *n., pl.* -lieder (-lē′dər). *German.* a folksong.

vol·ley (vŏl′ĭ), *n., pl.* -leys, *v.,* -leyed, -leying. —*n.* **1.** the flight of a number of missiles together. **2.** the discharge of a number of missiles or firearms simultaneously. **3.** a burst or outpouring of many things at once or in quick succession. **4.** *Tennis.* **a.** a flight of a ball in play before striking the ground. **b.** a return of the ball by the racket before it touches the ground. **5.** *Soccer.* a kick of the football before it bounces back. **6.** *Cricket.* a ball so bowled that it hits the wicket before it touches the ground. **7.** *Mining.* the explosion of several blasts in the rock at one time. —*v.t.* **8.** to discharge in or as in a volley. **9.** *Tennis.* to return (the ball) before it strikes the ground. **10.** *Soccer.* to kick (the ball) before it bounces back. **11.** *Cricket.* to bowl (a ball) in such a manner that it is pitched near the top of the wicket. —*v.i.* **12.** to fly or be discharged together, as missiles. **13.** to move or proceed with great rapidity, as in a volley. **14.** to fire a volley or sound together, as firearms. **15.** to emit or produce loud sounds simultaneously or continuously. [t. F: m. *volée* flight, der. *voler* fly, g. L *volāre*] —**vol′ley·er,** *n.*

vol·ley·ball (vŏl′ĭ bôl′), *n.* a game, usually played in a gymnasium, the object of which is to keep a large ball in motion, from side to side over a high net, by striking it with the hands before it touches the ground.

Vo·log·da (vō′lŏg dä), *n.* a city in the N Soviet Union in Europe. 127,000 (est. 1956).

vo·lost (vō′lŏst), *n.* **1.** (formerly) a small administrative peasant division in Russia. **2.** a rural soviet. [t. Russ.]

vol·plane (vŏl′plān′), *v.i.,* -planed, -planing. to glide toward the earth in an airplane, with no motor power or with the power shut off.

vols., volumes.

Vol·sci (vŏl′sī), *n.pl.* an Italian people in southern Latium, subdued by Rome late in the 4th century B.C.

Vol·scian (vŏl′shən), *adj.* **1.** of or pertaining to the Volsci or to their language. —*n.* **2.** one of the Volsci.

Vol·stead (vŏl′stĕd), *n.* **Andrew Joseph,** 1860–1946, U.S. legislator.

Vol·stead·ism (vŏl′stĕd ĭz′əm), *n.* **1.** the policy of prohibiting the sale of liquor to be used as or for a beverage. **2.** the enforcement of this policy, so called after Congressman A. J. Volstead, author of such a prohibition bill passed in 1919 and repealed in 1933.

Vol·sun·ga Sa·ga (vŏl′sŏŏng gə sä′gə). (in Icelandic literature) the mythical history of the Nibelungs and of the Volsungs, a heroic race. The central hero is Sigurd (the Siegfried of the Nibelungenlied). It is the principal source of Wagner's "Ring of the Nibelung." [t. Icel.: m. *Völsungasaga*]

volt[1] (vōlt), *n. Elect.* the unit of electromotive force, or potential difference, being the difference of potential or potential difference which will cause a current of one ampere to flow through a resistance of one ohm. Approximately 10[8] CGS electromagnetic units. *Abbr.:* **v.** or **V.** [named after Alessandro VOLTA]

volt² (vōlt), *n.* **1.** *Fencing.* a sudden movement or leap to avoid a thrust. **2.** *Manège.* **a.** a circular or turning movement of a horse. **b.** a gait in which a horse going sidewise turns around a center, with the head turned outward. [t. F: m. *volte*, t. It.: m. *volta* turn, ult. der. L *volvere* turn]

vol·ta (vōl′tə; *It.* vôl′tä), *n., pl.* **-te** (-tĕ). *Music.* turn; time: used in phrases: *una volta, once; duo volte, twice; prima volta, first time, etc.* [It.: turn]

Vol·ta (vōl′tä *for 1;* vōl′tä *for 2),* *n.* **1. Count Ales·sandro** (ä′lĕs·sän′drô), 1745–1827, Italian physicist. **2.** a river in W Africa, in Ghana, flowing into the Bight of Benin, ab. 200 mi. (with its main upper branch, the **Black Volta**, ab. 790 mi.).

volta-, combining form of voltaic, as in *voltameter.*

volt·age (vōl′tĭj), *n. Elect.* electromotive force reckoned or expressed in volts.

vol·ta·ic (vōl′tä′Ĭk), *adj.* **1.** denoting or pertaining to the electricity or electric currents produced by chemical action, or, more broadly, to any electric current; galvanic. **2.** (*cap.*) of or pertaining to Alessandro Volta.

voltaic battery, a source of electric current consisting of one or more voltaic cells; an electric battery.

voltaic cell. See cell (def. 9).

voltaic couple, (in a voltaic cell) the substances (commonly two metallic plates) in the dilute acid or other electrolyte, giving rise to the electric current.

voltaic electricity, electric current; moving electric charges.

Vol·taire (vōl·târ′; *Fr.* vôl′tĕr′), *n.* **François Marie Arouet de** (frän·swä′ mä·rē′ ä·rwĕ′ də), 1694–1778, French philosopher, historian, dramatist, and essayist.

vol·ta·ism (vōl′tə·Ĭz′əm), *n.* the branch of electrical science that deals with the production of electricity or electric currents by chemical action.

vol·tam·e·ter (vōl·tăm′ə·tər), *n.* a device for measuring the quantity of electricity passing through a conductor by the amount of electrolytic decomposition it produces, or for measuring the strength of a current by the amount of such decomposition in a given time. —**vol·ta·met·ric** (vōl′tə·mĕt′rĬk), *adj.*

volt·am·me·ter (vōlt′ăm′mē′tər), *n.* an instrument which can be used for measuring either volts or amperes.

volt·am·pere (vōlt′ăm′pĭr), *n.* an electrical unit equal to the product of one volt and one ampere, which with continuous currents is equivalent to one watt.

volte-face (vōlt·fäs′; *Fr.* vôl·tə·fäs′), *n.* a turning so as to face in the opposite direction; a reversal of opinion or policy. [F, t. It.: m. *volta faccia* turn the face, f. *volta* (der. *voltare* turn) + *faccia* face (g. L *facies*)]

vol·ti (vōl′tē), *impv. Music.* turn; turn over (a direction to turn the page). [It.]

volt·me·ter (vōlt′mē′tər), *n.* an instrument for measuring the voltage between two points.

Vol·tur·no (vōl·tōōr′nô), *n.* a river flowing from the Apennines in C Italy into the Tyrrhenian Sea. ab. 110 mi.

vol·u·ble (vōl′yə·bəl), *adj.* characterized by a ready and continuous flow of words, as a speaker or his tongue or speech; glibly fluent: *a voluble talker.* [t. L: m. s. *volūbilis,* der. *volvere* roll, turn] —**vol′u·bil′i·ty, vol′u·ble·ness,** *n.* —**vol′u·bly,** *adv.* —**Syn.** See fluent.

vol·ume (vōl′ūm, -yəm), *n.* **1.** a collection of written or printed sheets bound together and constituting a book. **2.** a book forming one of a related set or series. **3.** *Hist.* a roll of papyrus, parchment, or the like, or of manuscript. **4.** the size, measure, or amount of anything in three dimensions; cubic magnitude: *gases expanding to a greater volume.* **5.** a mass or quantity, esp. a large quantity, of anything: *a volume of sound, to pour out volumes of abuse.* **6.** amount: *the volume of travel on a railroad for a given period.* **7.** loudness or softness. **8.** fullness or quantity of tone or sound. [ME *volym,* t. OF: m. *volum,* t. L: m. *volūmen* roll (of papyrus or parchment); def. 4, etc., developed from meaning "dimensions of a book"] —**Syn. 4.** See size¹.

vol·umed (vōl′ūmd, -yəmd), *adj.* **1.** consisting of a volume or volumes (usually with a qualifying adverb): *a many-volumed work.* **2.** in volumes of rolling or rounded masses, as smoke.

vo·lu·me·ter (və·lōō′mə·tər), *n.* any of various instruments or devices for measuring volume, as of gases, liquids, or solids.

vol·u·met·ric (vōl′yə·mĕt′rĬk), *adj. Chem., Physics.* denoting, pertaining to, or depending upon measurement by volume. Also, **vol′u·met′ri·cal.** —**vol·u·met′ri·cal·ly,** *adv.* —**vo·lu·me·try** (və·lōō′mə·trē), *n.*

volumetric analysis, **1.** chemical analysis by volume, esp. by titration. **2.** determination of the volume of gases or changes in their volume during combination.

vo·lu·mi·nous (və·lōō′mə·nəs), *adj.* **1.** forming, filling, or writing a large volume or book, or many volumes: *a voluminous author.* **2.** sufficient to fill a volume or volumes: *a voluminous correspondence.* **3.** of great volume, size, or extent; in great volumes: *a voluminous flow of lava.* **4.** of ample size, extent, or fullness, as garments, draperies, etc. **5.** *Obs.* having many coils, convolutions, or windings. [t. LL: m. s. *volūminōsus* full of folds. See VOLUME] —**vo·lu′mi·nous·ly,** *adv.* —**vo·lu′mi·nous·ness, vo·lu·mi·nos·i·ty** (və·lōō′mə·nŏs′ə·tĬ), *n.*

vol·un·ta·rism (vōl′ən·tə·rĬz′əm), *n. Philos.* any theory that regards the will rather than the intellect as the fundamental agency or principle. —**vol′un·ta·rist,** *n.,* *adj.* —**vol′un·ta·ris′tic,** *adj.*

vol·un·tar·y (vōl′ən·tĕr′Ĭ), *adj., n., pl.* **-taries.** —*adj.* **1.** done, made, brought about, undertaken, etc., of one's own accord or by free choice: *a voluntary contribution.* **2.** acting of one's own will or choice: *a voluntary substitute.* **3.** pertaining to or depending on voluntary action: *voluntary schools* (in England and Wales, schools supported by voluntary contributions). **4.** *Law.* **a.** acting or done without compulsion or obligation. **b.** done by intention, and not by accident: *voluntary manslaughter.* **c.** made without valuable consideration: *a voluntary conveyance or settlement.* **5.** *Physiol.* subject to or controlled by the will: *voluntary muscles.* **6.** having the power of willing or choosing: *a voluntary agent.* **7.** proceeding from a natural impulse; spontaneous: *voluntary faith.* —*n.* **8.** something done voluntarily. **9.** a piece of music, frequently spontaneous and improvised, performed as a prelude to a larger work, esp., a piece of organ music performed before, during, or after an office of the church. [ME, t. L: m. s. *voluntarius*] —**vol′un·tar′i·ly,** *adv.* —**vol′un·tar′i·ness,** *n.*
—**Syn. 1.** See deliberate. **7.** VOLUNTARY, SPONTANEOUS agree in applying to something which is a natural outgrowth or natural expression arising from circumstances and conditions. VOLUNTARY implies having given previous consideration, or having exercised judgment: *a voluntary confession, a voluntary movement, the offer was a voluntary one.* That which is SPONTANEOUS arises as if by itself from the nature of the circumstances or condition: *spontaneous applause, combustion, expression of admiration.* —**Ant. 7.** forced.

vol·un·tar·y·ism (vōl′ən·tĕr′Ĭ·yəm), *n.* the principle or system of supporting churches, schools, etc., by voluntary contributions or aid, independently of the state. —**vol′un·tar′y·ist,** *n.*

vol·un·teer (vōl′ən·tĬr′), *n.* **1.** one who enters into any service of his own free will, or who offers himself for any service or undertaking. **2.** *Mil.* one who enters the service voluntarily (rather than through conscription or draft), specif. for special or temporary service (rather than as a member of the regular or permanent army). **3.** *Law.* **a.** a person whose actions are not founded on any legal obligation to so act. **b.** one to whom a conveyance is made or promise given without valuable consideration. **4.** *Agric.* a volunteer plant. —*adj.* **5.** entering voluntarily into any service; being a volunteer; consisting of volunteers. **6.** *Agric.* springing up spontaneously, or without being planted. —*v.i.* **7.** to offer oneself for some service or undertaking. **8.** to enter service or enlist as a volunteer. **9.** to make an offer or attempt to do something. —*v.t.* **10.** to offer (one's services, etc., or oneself) for some duty or purpose. **11.** to offer to undertake or undergo: *volunteer a dangerous duty.* **12.** to offer to give, or to give, bestow, show, etc., voluntarily: *volunteer a song* (without being asked). **13.** to offer in speech; communicate, tell, or say voluntarily: *to volunteer an explanation.* [t. F: m. *volontaire,* t. L: m. *voluntārius* VOLUNTARY]

Volunteers of America, a religious reform and relief organization, similar to the Salvation Army, founded in New York City in 1896, by Ballington Booth, son of William Booth, the founder of the Salvation Army.

vo·lup·tu·ar·y (və·lŭp′chŏō·ĕr′Ĭ), *n., pl.* **-aries,** *adj.* —*n.* **1.** one given up to luxurious or sensuous pleasures. —*adj.* **2.** pertaining to or characterized by luxurious or sensuous pleasures: *voluptuary habits.* [t. L: m. s. *voluptuārius,* var. of *voluptārius,* der. *voluptas* pleasure]

vo·lup·tu·ous (və·lŭp′chŏō·əs), *adj.* **1.** full of, characterized by, or ministering to pleasure or luxurious or sensuous enjoyment: *a voluptuous life.* **2.** derived from luxurious or full gratification of the senses: *voluptuous pleasure.* **3.** directed toward luxurious or sensuous enjoyment: *voluptuous desires.* **4.** given or inclined to luxurious enjoyment of the pleasures of the senses: *a voluptuous woman.* **5.** suggestive of an inclination to sensuous pleasure: *a voluptuous mouth.* **6.** sensuously pleasing or delightful: *voluptuous beauty.* [ME, t. L: m. s. *voluptuōsus,* der. *voluptas* pleasure] —**vo·lup′tu·ous·ly,** *adv.* —**vo·lup′tu·ous·ness,** *n.* —**Syn. 1.** See sensual.

vo·lute (və·lōōt′), *n.* **1.** a spiral or twisted formation or object. **2.** *Archit.* a spiral scroll-like ornament, esp. one forming the distinctive feature of the Ionic capital or a more or less important part of the Corinthian and Composite capitals. **3.** *Zool.* **a.** a turn or whorl of a spiral shell. **b.** any of the *Volutidae,* a family of tropical marine gastropods, many species of which have shells prized for their beauty. —*adj.* **4.** in the form of a volute; rolled up. **5.** *Mach.* **a.** spirally shaped or having a part so shaped. **b.** moving in a circular way, esp. if combined with a lateral motion. [t. L: m.s. *volūta* scroll] —**vo·lu′tion,** *n.*

Volute of an Ionic capital

vol·va (vōl′və), *n. Bot.* the membranous envelope which encloses various immature or button mushrooms. [t. L: covering]

vol·vu·lus (vōl′vyə·ləs), *n. Pathol.* a torsion or twisting of the intestine causing intestinal obstruction. [t. NL, der. L *volvere* turn]

vo·mer (vō′mər), *n. Anat.* a bone of the skull in most vertebrates, in man being shaped like a plowshare, and forming a large part of the nasal septum, or partition between the right and left nasal cavities. [t. L: plowshare] —**vo·mer·ine** (vō′mər ĭn, vŏm′ər-), *adj.*

vom·i·ca (vŏm′ə kə), *n.*, *pl.* **-cae** (-sē′). *Pathol.* **1.** a cavity, usually in the lungs, containing pus. **2.** the pus content of such a cavity. [t. L: ulcer]

vom·it (vŏm′ĭt), *v.i.* **1.** to eject the contents of the stomach by the mouth; spew. **2.** to be ejected or come out with force or violence. —*v.t.* **3.** to throw up or eject from the stomach through the mouth; spew. **4.** to cast out or eject as if in vomiting; to send out with force or copiously. **5.** to cause (a person) to vomit. —*n.* **6.** act of vomiting. **7.** matter ejected in vomiting. [late ME *vomyte*, t. L: m. *vomitāre*] —**vom′it·er**, *n.* —**vom′i·tive**, *adj.*

vom·i·to (vŏm′ə tō′; *Sp.* vŏ′mē tô′), *n.* *Pathol.* the black vomit of yellow fever. [t. Sp., t. L: m.s. *vomitus*]

vom·i·to·ry (vŏm′ə tōr′ĭ), *adj., n., pl.* **-ries.** —*adj.* **1.** inducing vomiting; emetic. **2.** pertaining to vomiting. —*n.* **3.** an emetic. **4.** an opening through which something is ejected or discharged.

vom·i·tu·ri·tion (vŏm′ə chŏŏ rĭsh′ən), *n.* *Pathol.* **1.** ineffectual efforts to vomit. **2.** the vomiting of but little matter. **3.** *Obs.* vomiting with little effort.

von (vŏn; *Ger.* fôn, *unstressed* fən), *prep.* German. from; of: much used in German personal names, orig. before names of places or estates, and later before family names as an indication of nobility or rank.

voo·doo (vōō′dōō), *n., pl.* **-doos**, *adj., v.,* **-dooed, -dooing.** —*n.* **1.** a class of mysterious rites or practices, of the nature of sorcery, witchcraft, or conjuration, prevalent among the Negroes of the West Indies and the southern U.S., and probably of African origin. **2.** one who practices such rites. **3.** a fetish or other object of voodoo worship. —*adj.* **4.** pertaining to, associated with, or practicing voodoo or voodooism. —*v.t.* **5.** to affect by voodoo sorcery or conjuration. [t. Haitian Creole: m. *vodum*, t. African: m. *vodu*. See HOODOO]

voo·doo·ism (vōō′dōō ĭz′əm), *n.* the voodoo rites or practices; voodoo sorcery; the voodoo superstition. —**voo′doo·ist**, *n.* —**voo′doo·is′tic**, *adj.*

vo·ra·cious (vō rā′shəs), *adj.* **1.** devouring or craving food in large quanties: *a voracious appetite.* **2.** greedy in eating; ravenous. [f. *voraci*(*ty*) (t. L: m.s. *vorācitas* greediness) + -ous] —**vo·ra′cious·ly**, *adv.* —**vo·rac·i·ty** (vō răs′ə tĭ), **vo·ra′cious·ness**, *n.* —**Syn. 1.** See **ravenous.**

Vor·la·ge (fōr′lä′gə), *n.* German. (in skiing) a position in which the skier leans forward but keeps his heels in contact with the skis. [G: forward position]

Vo·ro·nezh (vŏ rô′nĕsh), *n.* a city in central Soviet Union in Europe, near the Don river. 400,000 (est. 1956).

Vo·ro·noff (vŏ rô′nôf, vô′rô-), *n.* Serge (sĕrzh), 1866–1951. Russian physician.

Vo·ro·shi·lov (vŏ rŏ shē′lôf), *n.* Kliment Efremovich (klē′mĕnt ĕ frĕ′mô vĭch), born 1881, Soviet general, president of the Soviet Union 1953–1960.

Vo·ro·shi·lov·grad (vŏ′rŏ shē′lôf grät′), *n.* a city in the S Soviet Union in Europe. 251,000 (est. 1956). Formerly, **Lugansk.**

-vorous, a word element meaning "eating," as in *carnivorous, herbivorous, omnivorous.* [t. L: m. *-vorus* devouring]

vor·tex (vōr′tĕks), *n., pl.* **-texes**, **-tices** (-tə sēz′). **1.** a whirling movement or mass of water, as a whirlpool. **2.** a whirling movement or mass of air, as a whirlwind. **3.** a whirling mass of fire, flame, etc. **4.** a state of affairs likened to a whirlpool for violent activity, irresistible force, etc. **5.** something looked upon as drawing into its powerful whirl or current everything that is near it. **6.** (in old theories, as in the Cartesian philosophy) a rapid rotatory movement of cosmic matter about a center, regarded as accounting for the origin or phenomena of bodies or systems of bodies in space. [t. L, var. of *vertex* VERTEX]

vor·ti·cal (vōr′tə kəl), *adj.* **1.** of or pertaining to a vortex. **2.** resembling a vortex. **3.** moving in a vortex. —**vor′ti·cal·ly**, *adv.*

vor·ti·cel·la (vōr′tə sĕl′ə), *n., pl.* **-cellae** (-sĕl′ē). a transparent, bell-shaped animalcule on a fine elastic stem.

vor·ti·ces (vōr′tə sēz′), *n.* a pl. of **vortex.**

vor·ti·cose (vōr′tə kōs′), *adj.* vortical; whirling. [t. L: m.s. *vorticōsus*, der. *vortex* VERTEX]

vor·tig·i·nous (vōr tĭj′ə nəs), *adj.* whirling; vortical. [var. of VERTIGINOUS]

Vor·tum·nus (vōr tŭm′nəs), *n.* Vertumnus.

Vosges (vōzh), *n.* a range of low mountains in NE France. Highest peak, 4668 ft.

vot·a·ble (vō′tə bəl), *adj.* subject to a vote.

vo·ta·ry (vō′tə rĭ), *n., pl.* **-ries.** —*n.* Also, **vo′ta·rist. 1.** one who is bound by a vow, esp. one bound by vows to a religious life; a monk or a nun. **2.** a devotee of some form of religious worship; a devoted worshiper, as of God, a saint, etc. **3.** one devoted to some pursuit, study, etc. **4.** a devoted follower or admirer. —*adj.* **5.** consecrated by a vow. **6.** votive. [f. s. L *vōtum* vow + -ARY] —**vo·ta·ress** (vō′tə rĭs), **vo·tress** (vō′trĭs), *n. fem.*

vote (vōt), *n., v.,* **voted, voting.** —*n.* **1.** a formal expression of will, wish, or choice in some matter, whether of a single individual, as one of a number interested in common, or of a body of individuals, signified by voice, by holding up the hand, by standing up, by ballot, etc. **2.** the means by which such expression is made, as a ballot, ticket, etc. **3.** the right to such expression. **4.** the decision reached by voting, as by a majority of ballots cast. **5.** a number of votes (or expression of will) collectively: *the labor vote, a light vote was polled.* **6.** an award, grant, or the like, voted: *a vote of $1,000,000 for a new building.* **7.** *Obs.* a vow. **8.** *Obs.* an ardent wish or prayer. [late ME, t. L: m.s. *vōtum* vow, wish] —*v.i.* **9.** to express or signify the will or choice in a matter undergoing decision, as by a voice, ballot, or otherwise; give or cast a vote or votes: *for whom will you vote for president?* —*v.t.* **10.** to enact, establish, or determine by vote; bring or put (*in, out, down,* etc.) by vote; grant by vote: *to vote an appropriation for a new school.* **11.** to support by one's vote: *to vote the Republican ticket.* **12.** to advocate by or as by one's vote: *to vote that the report be accepted.* **13.** to declare by general consent: *they voted the trip a success.* [t. L: m.s. *vōtus*, pp., vowed]

vot·er (vō′tər), *n.* **1.** one who votes. **2.** one who has a right to vote; an elector.

voting machine, a mechanical substitute for the paper ballot, which automatically registers and counts votes.

voting paper, *Brit.* a ballot.

vo·tive (vō′tĭv), *adj.* **1.** offered, given, dedicated, etc., in accordance with a vow: *a votive offering.* **2.** performed, undertaken, etc., in consequence of a vow. **3.** of the nature of or expressive of a wish or desire. **4.** *Rom. Cath. Ch.* optional; not prescribed: *a votive Mass* (a Mass which does not correspond with the office of the day, but is said at the choice of the priest). [t. L: m.s. *vōtivus* pertaining to a vow] —**vo′tive·ly**, *adv.* —**vo′tive·ness**, *n.*

Vo·ty·ak (vō′tĭ ăk′), *n.* a Finno-Ugric language of the Permian group.

vouch (vouch), *v.i.* **1.** to answer (*for*) as being true, certain, reliable, justly asserted, etc. **2.** to give warrant or attestation; give one's own assurance, as surety or sponsor (fol. by *for*): *I can vouch for him.* —*v.t.* **3.** to warrant; attest; confirm. **4.** to sustain or uphold by some practical proof or demonstration, or as such proof does. **5.** to affirm or declare as with warrant; vouch for. **6.** to adduce or quote in support, as extracts from a book or author; cite in warrant or justification, as authority, instances, facts, etc. **7.** to support or authenticate with vouchers. **8.** *Obs., or Hist. in legal use.* to call or summon (a person) into court to make good a warranty of title. **9.** *Archaic.* to call or take to witness, as a person. —*n. Obs.* **10.** a vouching. **11.** a supporting warrant or attestation. [ME *vouche*, t. AF: m. *voucher*, akin to L *vocāre* call]

vouch·er (vou′chər), *n.* **1.** one who or that which vouches, as for something. **2.** a document, receipt, stamp, or the like, which proves the truth of a claimed expenditure. **3.** (in early English law) **a.** one called into court to warrant another's title. **b.** the act of vouching another person to make good a warranty.

vouch·safe (vouch sāf′), *v.,* **-safed, -safing.** —*v.t.* **1.** to grant or give, by favor, graciousness, or condescension: *to vouchsafe a reply.* **2.** to allow or permit, by favor or graciousness. —*v.i.* **3.** to condescend; deign; have the graciousness (to do something). [ME *vouche safe,* lit., guarantee as safe. See VOUCH] —**vouch·safe′ment,** *n.*

vouge (vōōzh), *n.* a long-handled weapon with a kind of ax blade prolonged to a point at the top, used by foot soldiers in the 14th century and later.

vous·soir (vōō swär′), *n. Archit.* any of the pieces, in the shape of a truncated wedge, which form an arch or vault. See diag. under **arch.** [ME, t. F, ult. der. L *volvere* turn]

vow (vou), *n.* **1.** a solemn promise, pledge, or personal engagement: *marriage vows, a vow of secrecy.* **2.** a solemn, religiously binding promise made to God or to any deity or saint, as to perform some act, make some offering or gift, or enter some service or condition. **3.** take vows, to enter a religious order or house. **4.** a solemn or earnest declaration. —*v.t.* **5.** to make a vow of; promise by a vow, as to God or a saint: *to vow a crusade or a pilgrimage.* **6.** to pledge oneself to do, make, give, observe, etc.; make a solemn threat or resolution of: *I vowed revenge.* **7.** to declare solemnly or earnestly; assert emphatically, or asseverate (often with a clause as object): *she vowed she would go to law.* **8.** to make (a vow). **9.** to dedicate or devote by a vow: *to vow oneself to the service of God.* —*v.i.* **10.** to make a vow or solemn promise: *he vowed never to drink liquor again.* **11.** to make a solemn or earnest declaration. [ME *vou,* t. AF, g. L *vōtum*] —**vow′er,** *n.* —**vow′less,** *adj.*

vow·el (vou′əl), *n.* **1.** *Phonet.* a speech sound articulated so that there is a clear channel for the voice through the middle of the mouth: *law ends with a vowel.* **2.** *Gram.* a letter which usually represents a vowel, as in, English, *a, e, i, o,* and *u,* and sometimes *w* and *y.* —*adj.* **3.** pertaining to a vowel. [ME, t. OF: m. *vouel,* g. L *vōcālis* (*littera*) vocal (letter)] —**vow′el·less,** *adj.*

vow·el·ize (vou′ə līz′), *v.t.,* **-ized, -izing.** to provide (a Hebrew, Arabic, etc., text) with vowel points. —**vow′el·i·za′tion,** *n.*

---

b., blend of, blended; c., cognate with; d., dialect, dialectal; der., derived from; f., formed from; g., going back to; m., modification of; r., replacing; s., stem of; t., taken from; ?, perhaps. See the full key on inside cover.

vowel point, (in Hebrew and Arabic writing and systems derived from them) any of certain marks placed above or below consonant letters to indicate vowels.

vox (vŏks), *n., pl.* **voces** (vō′sēz). **1.** voice; sound. **2.** word; expression. [L]

vox an·ge·li·ca (ăn jĕl′a ka), *Music.* an organ stop producing delicate tones, and having two pipes for each digital, one of which is tuned slightly sharp, so that by their dissonance a wavy effect is produced. Also, **vox cae·les·tis** (sĭ lĕs′tĭs). [L: angelic voice]

vox bar·ba·ra (băr′ba ra), *Latin.* a barbarous word or term (applied esp. to Neo-Latin terms in botany, zoölogy, etc., that are formed from elements that are neither Latin nor Greek).

vox hu·ma·na (hū mā′na), *Music.* an organ stop designed to produce tones resembling those of the human voice. [L: human voice]

vox pop., vox populi.

vox po·pu·li (pŏp′yŏo lī′), *Latin.* the voice or opinion of the people.

vox populi, vox De·i (dē′ī), the voice of the people (is) the voice of God. Alcuin, *Epistles*, c800.

voy·age (voi′ĭj), *n., v.,* **-aged, -aging.** —*n.* **1.** a passage, or course of travel, by sea or water, esp. to a distant place. **2.** a flight through air or space, as a journey in an airplane. **3.** (formerly) a journey or passage from one place to another, by land or by water. **4.** (*often pl.*) a voyage as the subject of a written account, or the account itself. **5.** *Obs.* an enterprise or undertaking. —*v.i.* **6.** to make or take a voyage; travel by sea or water. —*v.t.* **7.** to traverse by a voyage. [t. F; r. ME *viage*, t. OF, g. L *viāticum* provision for a journey] —**voy′ag·er,** *n.* —Syn. 1. See **trip.**

vo·ya·geur (vwà yà zhœr′), *n., pl.* **-geurs** (-zhœr′). *French.* a French Canadian or half-breed who is an expert woodsman and boatman, esp. one hired as a guide by a fur company whose stations are in remote and unsettled regions. [F, der. *voyager* travel]

vo·yeur (vwà yœr′), *n.* a pervert who attains sexual gratification by looking at sexual objects or situations. [t. F, der. *voir* see]

vo·yeur·ism (vwà yœr′ĭz əm), *n.* a perversion in which sexual gratification is obtained by looking at nude or partly nude bodies.

V.P., Vice-President. Also, **V. Pres.**

v.p., verb passive.

V.R., (L *Victoria Regina*) Queen Victoria.

V.r., verb reflexive.

vrai·sem·blance (vrĕ săn blăns′), *n. French.* appearance of truth; verisimilitude. [F, f. *vrai* true + *semblance* appearance]

V. Rev., Very Reverend.

Vries (vrēs), *n.* **Hugo de** (hy′gō də). See **De Vries.**

vrouw (vrou; *S. Afr. D.* frou), *n. Dutch.* **1.** a woman; a wife; a lady. **2.** Mrs. Cf. **Frau.**

vs., **1.** verse. **2.** versus.

V.S., Veterinary Surgeon.

v.s., vide supra.

V-shaped (vē′shăpt′), *adj.* in the shape of the letter V.

Vt., Vermont.

v.t., verb transitive.

Vte., Vicomte.

Vtesse., Vicomtesse.

Vuel·ta A·ba·jo (vwĕl′tä ä bä′hô), a region in W Cuba: famous for its tobacco.

vug (vŭg, vŏog), *n. Mining.* a small cavity in a rock or lode, often lined with crystals. Also, **vugg, vugh.** [t. Cornish: m. *vooga* cave] —**vug′gy,** *adj.*

Vul., Vulgate.

Vul·can (vŭl′kən), *n.* the Roman god of fire and metalworking. Cf. **Hephaestus.** [t. L: s. *Vulcānus*.]

Vul·ca·ni·an (vəl kā′nĭ ən), *adj.* **1.** of or associated with Vulcan. **2.** (*l.c.*) volcanic. **3.** (*l.c.*) of metalworking.

vul·can·ism (vŭl′kə nĭz′əm), *n. Geol.* the phenomena connected with the genesis and movement of molten rock material within and at the surface of the earth (including those phenomena connected with plutonic rocks as well as volcanism).

vul·can·ite (vŭl′kə nīt′), *n.* a hard rubber, readily cut and polished, used for making combs, buttons, etc., and for electric insulation, and obtained by vulcanizing India rubber with a large amount of sulfur; ebonite.

vul·can·ize (vŭl′kə nīz′), *v.t.,* **-ized, -izing. 1.** to treat (India rubber) with sulfur or some compound of sulfur, and subject to a moderate heat (110°–140°C.), in order to render it nonplastic and give greater elasticity, durability, etc.; or, when a large amount of sulfur and a more extensive heat treatment are employed, in order to make it very hard, as in the case of vulcanite. **2.** to treat (India rubber) similarly with sulfur or sulfur compounds, but without heat, in which case the effects are only superficial. **3.** to subject (substances other than India rubber) to some analogous process, as to harden. Also, *esp. Brit.,* **vul′can·ise′.** —**vul′can·iz′a·ble,** *adj.* —**vul′can·iz·a′tion,** *n.* —**vul′can·iz′er,** *n.*

vul·can·ol·o·gy (vŭl′kə nŏl′ə jĭ), *n.* volcanology. —**vul·can·o·log·i·cal** (vŭl′kə nə lŏj′ə kəl), *adj.* —**vul′can·ol′o·gist,** *n.*

vulg., **1.** vulgar. **2.** vulgarly.

vul·gar (vŭl′gər), *adj.* **1.** marked by ignorance of or want of good breeding or taste, as manners, actions, language, dress, display, etc.: *a vulgar costume, vulgar language.* **2.** underbred or crudely unrefined, as persons. **3.** belonging to or constituting the common people of society: *the vulgar herd.* **4.** of, pertaining to, or current among the multitude or general mass of the people: *vulgar errors or superstitions.* **5.** spoken by, or being in the language spoken by, the people generally; vernacular: *a vulgar translation of the Greek text of the New Testament.* **6.** common or ordinary: *a vulgar fraction.* —*n.* **7.** *Archaic.* the common people. **8.** *Obs.* the vernacular. [ME. t. L: s. *vulgāris* pertaining to the common people] —**vul′gar·ly,** *adv.* —**vul′gar·ness,** *n.* —Syn. 1. unrefined, inelegant, low, coarse, ribald. See **common.** 2. crude; boorish.

vulgar fraction, common fraction.

vul·gar·i·an (vəl gâr′ĭ ən), *n.* a vulgar person, esp. one whose vulgarity is the more conspicuous for his wealth, prominence, or pretensions to good breeding.

vul·gar·ism (vŭl′gə rĭz′əm), *n.* **1.** vulgar character or action; vulgarity. **2.** a vulgar expression; a word or phrase used only in common colloquial, and esp. in coarse, speech.

vul·gar·i·ty (vəl găr′ə tĭ), *n., pl.* **-ties. 1.** state or quality of being vulgar; commonness; plebeian character; want of good breeding, manners, or taste; coarseness. **2.** something vulgar; a vulgar act or speech; a vulgar expression; vulgarism.

vul·gar·ize (vŭl′gə rīz′), *v.t.,* **-ized, -izing.** to make vulgar, common, or commonplace; to lower; debase: *to vulgarize manners or taste.* Also, *esp. Brit.,* **vul′gar·ise′.** —**vul′gar·i·za′tion,** *n.* —**vul′gar·iz′er,** *n.*

Vulgar Latin, popular Latin, as opposed to literary or standard Latin; esp. those forms of popular Latin speech from which sprang the Romance languages of later times.

Vul·gate (vŭl′gāt, -gĭt), *n.* **1.** the Latin version of the Scriptures, accepted as the authorized version of the Roman Catholic Church. It was prepared by Jerome near the end of the 4th century, and was the first book printed (about 1455). **2.** (*l.c.*) any vulgate text or version. —*adj.* **3.** of or pertaining to the Vulgate. **4.** (*l.c.*) common, or in common use. [t. L: m.s. *vulgāta,* short for *vulgāta ēditio* popular edition]

vul·ner·a·ble (vŭl′nər ə bəl), *adj.* **1.** susceptible of being wounded; liable to physical hurt. **2.** not proof against moral attacks, as of criticism or calumny, or against temptations, influences, etc. **3.** (of a place, fortress, etc.) open to attack or assault; weak in the matter of defense. **4.** *Contract Bridge.* exposed to greater than usual penalties (applied to the partners who have won one of the games having made a rubber). [t. LL: m.s. *vulnerābilis* wounding] —**vul′ner·a·bil′i·ty, vul′ner·a·ble·ness,** *n.* —**vul′ner·a·bly,** *adv.*

vul·ne·rant om·nes, ul·ti·ma ne·cat (vŭl′nə rănt′ ŏm′nēz, ŭl′tə mə nē′kăt), *Latin.* all (hours) wound, the last (one) kills: inscription used on dials of clocks in churches or on public monuments.

vul·ner·ar·y (vŭl′nə rĕr′ĭ), *adj., n., pl.* **-aries.** —*adj.* **1.** used or useful for healing wounds, as plants or remedies. —*n.* **2.** a remedy for wounds.

Vul·pec·u·la (vŭl pĕk′yə lə), *n. Astron.* the little Fox, a northern constellation lying between Cygnus and Aquila. [t. L, dim. of *vulpes* fox]

vul·pec·u·lar (vŭl pĕk′yə lər), *adj.* pertaining to or of the nature of a young fox or any fox; vulpine.

vul·pine (vŭl′pīn, -pĭn), *adj.* pertaining to, like, or characteristic of a fox. [t. L: m.s. *vulpīnus*]

vul·ture (vŭl′chər), *n.* **1.** any of various large, carrion-eating birds related to the eagles, kites, hawks, falcons, etc., but having less powerful toes and straighter claws and usually having a naked head, esp. the species of the Old World family *Vulturidae,* as the Egyptian vulture (*Neophron percnopterus*), and those of the New World family *Cathartidae,* as the turkey vulture (*Cathartes aura*). **2.** a person or thing that preys ravenously and ruthlessly. [ME *vultur,* t. L] —**vul′ture-like′,** *adj.*

vul·tur·ine (vŭl′chə rīn′, -chər ĭn), *adj.* **1.** pertaining to or characteristic of vultures. **2.** resembling a vulture. Also, **vul·tur·ous** (vŭl′chər əs). [t. L: m.s. *vulturīnus*]

Vulture, *Gyps indicus* (3 ft. long)

vul·va (vŭl′və), *n., pl.* **-vae** (-vē), **-vas.** *Anat.* the external female genitalia, specif. the two pairs of labia and the cleft between them. [t. L: wrapper] —**vul′val, vul′var,** *adj.* —**vul·vi·form** (vŭl′və fôrm′), *adj.*

vv., **1.** verses. **2.** violins.

v.v., vice versa.

vv. ll., variae lectiones.

Vyat·ka (vyät′kä), *n.* former name of **Kirov.**

Vy·borg (vē′bôrg), *n.* a seaport in the NW Soviet Union, on the Gulf of Finland; formerly in Finland. 40,000 (est. 1948). Formerly, **Viipuri;** Swedish, **Viborg.**

Vyer·nyi (vyĕr′nĭ), *n.* former name of **Alma-Ata.**

vy·ing (vī′ĭng), *adj.* that vies; competing: *women busily vying with one another for attention from the only man at the party.* —**vy′ing·ly,** *adv.*

W

W, w (dŭb′əl yōō), *n.*, *pl.* **W's** or **Ws, w's** or **ws.**
1. the 23rd letter of the English alphabet. 2. the twenty-third in order or of a series.

W, 1. watt. 2. west. 3. western. 4. *Chem.* a. wolfram. b. wolframium.

W., 1. Wales. 2. Wednesday. 3. Welsh. 4. west. 5. western.

w., 1. watt. 2. week; weeks. 3. weight. 4. west. 5. western. 6. wide. 7. width. 8. wife. 9. with. 10. won. 11. *Physics.* work.

W.A., 1. West Africa. 2. Western Australia.

W.A.A.C., 1. *Brit.* Women's Army Auxiliary Corps. 2. *U.S.* former name of the **WAC.**

Waadt (vät), *n.* German name of Vaud.

Waal (wäl), *n.* See **Rhine.**

Wa·bash (wô′băsh), *n.* a river flowing from W Ohio through Indiana and S along part of the boundary between Indiana and Illinois into the Ohio river. 475 mi.

wab·ble (wŏb′əl), *v.i.*, *v.t.*, **-bled, -bling,** *n.* wobble. —**wab′bler,** *n.* —**wab′bling,** *adj.* —**wab′bling·ly,** *adv.* —**wab′bly,** *adj.*, *adv.*

WAC (wăk), *U.S.* 1. Women's Army Corps. —*n.* 2. a member of the Women's Army Corps.

Wace (wās, wäs; *Fr.* wås), *n.* **Robert** (rŏb′ərt; *Fr.* rô-bĕr′), fl. 1170, Anglo-Norman writer of chronicles in verse.

wack (wăk), *n.* *Slang.* an erratic, irrational, or unconventional person.

wack·e (wăk′ə), *n.* a soft rock of fine texture, derived from disintegrated basaltic rocks. [t. G: kind of stone]

wack·y (wăk′ĭ), *adj.* **wackier, wackiest.** *Slang.* erratic, irrational, or unconventional. Also, **whacky.**

Wa·co (wā′kō), *n.* a city in central Texas, on the Brazos river. 97,808 (1960).

wad¹ (wŏd), *n.*, *v.*, **wadded, wadding.** —*n.* 1. a small mass or lump of anything soft. 2. a small mass of cotton, wool, or other fibrous or soft material, used for stuffing, padding, packing, etc. 3. a ball or mass of something squeezed together: *a wad of folded paper.* 4. a roll, as of paper money. 5. *Slang.* one's stock of money: *have a good fat wad salted away.* 6. a plug of cloth, tow, paper, or the like, used to hold the powder or shot, or both, in place in a gun or cartridge. 7. *Brit. Dial.* a bundle, esp. a small one, of hay, straw, etc. —*v.t.* 8. to form into a wad. 9. *U.S.* to roll tightly (often fol. by *up*): *wadding his cap into his pocket.* 10. to hold in place by a wad, as powder or shot. 11. to put a wad into (a gun, etc.). 12. to fill out with or as with wadding; stuff; pad. [orig. uncert.; akin to Sw. *wadd,* G *watte* wadding] —**wad′der,** *n.*

wad² (wŏd), *n.* a soft, earthy, black to dark-brown mass of manganese oxide minerals. [orig. uncert.]

wad³ (wäd, wəd), *v.* *Scot.* would.

Wa·dai (wä dī′), *n.* a former independent sultanate of the Sudan: now the E part of Chad Colony, in French Equatorial Africa. ab. 170,000 sq. mi.

wad·ding (wŏd′ĭng), *n.* 1. any fibrous or soft material for stuffing, padding, packing, etc., esp. carded cotton in specially prepared sheets. 2. material for wads for guns, etc. 3. a wad or lump.

wad·dle (wŏd′əl), *v.*, **-dled, -dling,** *n.* —*v.i.* 1. to walk with short steps and swaying or rocking from side to side, as a duck. 2. to move with a similar movement. —*n.* 3. act of waddling; a waddling gait. [freq. of WADE] —**wad′dler,** *n.* —**wad′dling·ly,** *adv.*

wad·dy (wŏd′ĭ), *n.*, *pl.* **-dies,** *v.*, **-died, -dying.** *Australia.* —*n.* 1. a heavy wooden war club of the Australian aborigines. —*v.t.* 2. to beat or strike with a waddy.

wade (wād), *v.*, **waded, wading,** *n.* —*v.i.* 1. to walk through any substance, as water, snow, sand, etc., that impedes free motion: *wading in mud, wading through high grass.* 2. to make one's way with labor or difficulty: *to wade through a dull book.* 3. *Colloq.* to make a sharp attack or energetic beginning (fol. by *in* or *into*): *to wade into a berry patch.* 4. *Obs.* to go or proceed. —*v.t.* 5. to pass through or cross by wading; ford: *to wade a stream.* —*n.* 6. act of wading. [ME; OE *wadan* go, c. G *waten,* L *vādāre*]

wad·er (wā′dər), *n.* 1. one who or that which wades. 2. any of various long-legged birds, as cranes, herons, storks, sandpipers, plovers, etc., that wade in water in search of food. 3. (*pl.*) high waterproof boots used for wading.

wa·di (wä′dĭ), *n.*, *pl.* **-dis.** (in Arabia, Syria, northern Africa, etc.) 1. the channel of a watercourse which is dry except during periods of rainfall. 2. the stream or watercourse itself. [t. Ar.]

Wa·di Hal·fa (wä′dĭ hăl′fə), a town in the N Sudan, on the Nile. 12,700 (est. 1953).

wading bird, wader (def. 2).

wad·set (wŏd′sĕt′), *n.*, *v.t.*, **-setted, -setting.** *Scot. Law.* mortgage. [ME *wedset,* OE *tō wedde settan* set for pledge]

wa·dy (wä′dĭ), *n.*, *pl.* **-dies.** wadi.

wae (wā), *n.* *Scot. and N. Eng.* woe.

wae·sucks (wā′sŭks), *interj.* *Scotch.* alas! [Scot., f. *wae* WOE + *sucks,* var. of SAKE(s)]

waf (wăf, wäf), *adj.* *Scot.* waff².

WAF (wăf), *U.S.* 1. Women in the Air Force. —*n.* 2. a member of Women in the Air Force.

Wafd (wŏft), *n.* the nationalist party in modern Egypt. [t. Ar.: deputation] —**Wafd′ist,** *n.*, *adj.*

wa·fer (wā′fər), *n.* 1. a thin cake or biscuit, variously made, and often sweetened and flavored. 2. a thin disk of unleavened bread, used in the Eucharist, as in the Roman Catholic Church. 3. any of various other thin, flat cakes, sheets, or the like. 4. a thin disk of dried paste, gelatin, adhesive paper, or the like, used for sealing letters, attaching papers, etc. 5. *Med.* a thin, circular sheet of dry paste or the like, or a pair of such sheets, used upon moistening to wrap about or enclose a powder to be swallowed. —*v.t.* 6. to seal, close, or attach by means of a wafer or wafers: *to wafer a letter.* [ME *wafre,* t. OF: m. *waufre,* t. MLG: m. *wafel* honeycomb. Cf. WAFFLE] —**wa′fer·like′, wa′fer·y,** *adj.*

waff¹ (wăf, wäf), *n.* *Scot. and N. Eng.* 1. a puff or blast of air, wind, etc. 2. a brief view. [var. of WAVE]

waff² (wăf, wäf), *adj.* *Scot.* worthless. Also, **waf.**

waf·fle (wŏf′əl), *n.* a batter cake with a grid of deep indentations formed by baking it in a metal appliance having two hinged parts (**waffle iron**). [t. D: m. *wafel.* Cf. WAFER]

waft¹ (wăft, wäft), *v.t.* 1. to bear or carry through the air or over water: *the gentle breeze wafted the sound of voices, icebergs wafted by the wind.* 2. to bear or convey lightly as if in flight: *wafted away to town.* 3. *Obs.* to signal to, summon, or direct by waving. —*v.i.* 4. to float or be carried, esp. through the air. —*n.* 5. a sound, odor, etc. carried through the air: *a waft of bells.* 6. a wafting movement; current or gust: *a waft of wind.* 7. act of wafting. 8. *Naut.* waif (def. 4). [back formation from obs. *wafter,* late ME *waughter* armed escort vessel, t. D or LG: m. *wachter* guard; in some senses confused with *waff* WAVE] —**waft′er,** *n.*

waft² (wăft, wäft), *n.* *Scot.* weft.

waft·age (wăf′tĭj, wäf′-), *n.* *Archaic.* 1. act of wafting. 2. state of being wafted.

waf·ture (wăf′chər, wäf′-), *n.* 1. act of wafting. 2. something wafted: *waftures of incense.*

wag (wăg), *v.*, **wagged, wagging,** *n.* —*v.t.* 1. to move from side to side, forward and backward, or up and down, esp. rapidly and repeatedly: *a dog wagging his tail.* 2. to move (the tongue) in talking. —*v.i.* 3. to be moved from side to side or one way and the other, esp. rapidly and repeatedly, as the head or the tail. 4. (of the tongue) to move busily, esp. in idle or indiscreet talk. 5. to get along; travel; proceed: *how the world wags.* 6. to totter or sway. 7. *Brit. Slang.* to play truant; play hooky. —*n.* 8. act of wagging. 9. a humorous person; joker. [ME *wagge,* t. Scand.; cf. Icel. *vagga* to rock]

wage (wāj), *n.*, *v.*, **waged, waging.** —*n.* 1. (*usually pl., sometimes construed as sing.*) that which is paid for work or services, as by the day or week; hire; pay. 2. (*pl.*) *Econ.* the share of the products of industry received by labor for its work, as distinct from the share going to capital. 3. (*usually pl., sometimes construed as sing.*) recompense or return: *the wages of sin is death.* 4. *Obs.* a pledge or security. —*v.t.* 5. to carry on (a battle, war, conflict, etc.): *to wage war against a nation.* 6. *Obs.* or *Brit. Dial.* to hire. 7. *Obs.* a. to stake or wager. b. to pledge. —*v.i.* 8. *Obs.* to contend; battle. [ME, t. OF: m. *wagier,* der. *wage* pledge. See GAGE¹] —**wage′less.** —**Syn.** 1. compensation, emolument, earnings.

wage earner, one who works for wages (sometimes distinguished from salaried employees).

wa·ger (wā′jər), *n.* 1. something staked or hazarded on an uncertain event; a bet. 2. act of betting. 3. the subject of a bet. 4. *Early Eng. Law.* a pledge to make good one's cause: *wager of battle.* —*v.t.* 5. to hazard (something) on the issue of a contest or any uncertain event or matter; stake; bet. 6. *Hist.* to pledge oneself to (battle) for the decision of a case. —*v.i.* 7. to make or offer a wager; bet. [ME, t. AF: m. *wageure.* See WAGE] —**wa′ger·er,** *n.* —**Syn.** 1. stake, hazard, risk, venture.

wage scale, 1. a schedule of wages paid workers performing connected operations in an industry or shop. 2. a particular employer's wage schedule.

wage·work·er (wāj′wûr′kər), n. a member of the laboring class; a worker for wages; wage earner.

wag·ger·y (wăg′ərĭ), n., pl. **-geries.** 1. the action, spirit, or language of a wag. 2. a waggish act; a jest.

wag·gish (wăg′ĭsh), adj. 1. like a wag; roguish in merriment and good humor; jocular. 2. characteristic of or befitting a wag: *waggish humor.* —**wag′gish·ly,** adv. —**wag′gish·ness,** n. —Syn. 1. See **humorous.**

wag·gle (wăg′əl), v. **-gled, -gling,** n. —v.t., v.i. 1. to wag with short, quick movements. —n. 2. a waggling motion. [freq. of WAG. Cf. G *wackeln* stagger] —**wag′gling·ly,** adv.

wag·gly (wăg′lĭ), adj. waggling; unsteady.

wag·gon (wăg′ən), n. Brit. wagon. —**wag′gon·age,** n. —**wag′gon·er,** n. —**wag′gon·ette,** n.

wag·gon-head·ed (wăg′ən hĕd′ĭd), adj. Brit. wagon-headed.

Wag·ner (väg′nər), n. **Richard** (rĭch′ərd; Ger. rĭĸн′ärt), 1813–83, German composer.

Wag·ne·ri·an (väg nĭr′ĭ ən), adj. 1. of, pertaining to, or like Richard Wagner or his works. —n. 2. Also, **Wag·ner·ite** (väg′nə rīt′). a follower or admirer of the music or theories of Richard Wagner.

Wag·ner·ism (väg′nər ĭz′əm), n. 1. Wagner's theory or method as exemplified in his music dramas, which, departing from the conventional methods of earlier (esp. Italian) opera, shows constant attention to dramatic and emotional effect, and the abundant use of the leitmotif. 2. the study, imitation, or influence of the music of Richard Wagner. —**Wag′ner·ist,** n.

wag·on (wăg′ən), n. 1. any of various kinds of four-wheeled vehicles, esp. one designed for the transport of heavy loads, delivery, etc. 2. Brit. a railroad freight car. 3. (cap.) Astron. Charles's Wain, or the Big Dipper. 4. a police van for transporting prisoners. 5. Obs. a chariot. 6. **on the wagon,** Slang. abstaining from alcoholic drink. —v.t. 7. to transport or convey by wagon. Also, Brit., **waggon.** [t. D: m. *wagen,* c. OE *wægn* WAIN] —**wag′on·less,** adj. —Syn. 1. cart, van, wain, truck, dray, lorry.

wag·on·age (wăg′ən ĭj), n. 1. transport or convey-ance by wagon. 2. money paid for this. 3. a collection of wagons; wagons collectively. Also, Brit., **waggonage.**

wag·on·er (wăg′ən ər), n. 1. one who drives a wagon. 2. (cap.) Astron. the northern constellation Auriga. 3. Obs. a charioteer. Also, Brit., **waggoner.**

wag·on·ette (wăg′ə nĕt′), n. a four-wheeled pleasure vehicle, with or without a top, having a crosswise seat in front and two lengthwise seats facing each other at the back. Also, Brit., **waggonette.**

wag·on-head·ed (wăg′ən hĕd′ĭd), adj. Archit. of the form of a round arch or a semicylinder, like the cover of a wagon when stretched over the bows, as a ceiling, roof, etc. Also, Brit., **waggon-headed.**

wag·on-lit (và gôN lē′), n. (in French and other Continental use) a railroad sleeping car. [F, f. *wagon* railway coach, WAGON + *lit* bed]

wag·on·load (wăg′ən lōd′), n. the load carried by a wagon.

wagon soldier, Mil. Slang. a field artillery soldier.

wagon train, a train of wagons and horses, esp. one carrying military supplies.

Wa·gram (vä′gräm), n. a village in NE Austria: Napoleon defeated the Austrians here, 1809.

wag·tail (wăg′tāl′), n. 1. any of numerous small, chiefly Old World birds of the family *Motacillidae,* hav-ing a slender body with a long, narrow tail which is habitually wagged up and down. 2. any of various similar birds, as the water thrushes (genus *Seiurus*) of the American wood-warbler family *Compsothlypidae.*

Wa·ha·bi (wä hä′bē), n., pl. **-bis.** one of the followers of Abd al-Wahhab (1691?–1787?), a Mohammedan re-former who opposed all practices which are not sanc-tioned by the Koran. They are today the most con-servative Mohammedans, located mostly in central Arabia. Also, **Wa·ha·bee, Wa·ha·bite** (wä hä′bīt), **Wah-ha·bi.** [t. Ar.] —**Wa·ha′bi·ism, Wa·ha′bism,** n.

wa·hoo¹ (wä hōō′, wä′hōō), n., pl. **-hoos.** 1. a shrub or small tree, *Euonymus atropurpureus,* native to North America, with pendulous capsules which in dehiscing reveal the bright-scarlet arils of the seeds; burning-bush. 2. any of various other American shrubs or small trees, as an elm, *Ulmus alata,* or a linden, *Tilia heterophylla.* [t. Dakota (Siouan): m. *wanku* arrowwood; or t. Creek (Muskhogean): m. *uhawha* cork or winged elm]

wa·hoo² (wä hōō′, wä′hōō), n., pl. **-hoos.** a large, swift game fish, *Acanthocybium solandri,* of the high seas. [t. Amer. Ind.]

Wai·chow (wī′jō′), n. a city in SE China, in Kwang-tung province, E of Canton. ab. 35,000.

waif (wāf), n. 1. a person without home or friends, esp. a child. 2. a stray thing or article: *old waifs of rhyme.* 3. something found, of which the owner is not known, as an animal. 4. Naut. a signaling, or a signal given, by a flag rolled and stopped or fastened. [ME, t. AF, prob. t. Scand.; cf. Icel. *veif* oscillation]

Wai·ki·ki (wī′kē kē′, wī′kē kē′), n. a famous bathing beach in the Hawaiian Islands, in Honolulu harbor.

wail (wāl), v.i. 1. to utter a prolonged, inarticulate, mournful cry, usually high-pitched or clear-sounding, as in grief or suffering: *to wail with pain, a wailing baby.* 2. to sound mournfully, as music, the wind, etc. 3. to lament or mourn bitterly. —v.t. 4. to wail over; bewail; lament: *to wail the dead.* 5. to cry or say in lamentation. —n. 6. act of wailing. 7. a wailing cry, as of grief, pain, etc. 8. any similar mournful sound: *the wail of an old tune.* [ME *weile,* t. Scand.; cf. Icel. *væla* wail, der. *væ.* var. of *vei* woe] —**wail′er,** n. —**wail′ing·ly,** adv.

wail·ful (wāl′fəl), adj. mournful; plaintive. —**wail′-ful·ly,** adv.

Wailing Wall of the Jews, an enclosure in Jerusalem where, traditionally, Jews hold prayers and lamentation each Friday. One wall reputedly is built of stones from the temple of Solomon. Also, **Wailing Wall.**

wail·some (wāl′səm), adj. wailing.

wain (wān), n. 1. **the Wain,** Charles's Wain; the Big Dipper. 2. Chiefly Poetic. a wagon or cart. [ME; OE *wægn,* c. D and G *wagen.* Cf. OE *wegan* carry]

wain·scot (wān′skət, -skŏt), n., v., **-scoted, -scoting** or (esp. Brit.) **-scotted, -scotting.** —n. 1. oak or other wood, usually in panels, serving to line the walls of a room, etc.: *a room paneled with varnished wainscot.* 2. a dado, or a facing of any material on interior walls, etc. 3. the lower portion of a wall surfaced in a different manner or material from the upper portion. 4. (orig.) a superior quality of oak imported into England for fine paneled work and the like. —v.t. 5. to line (a room, walls, etc.) with wainscot or wood: *a room wainscoted in oak.* [ME *waynscot,* half trans., half adoption of MLG *wagenschot,* f. *wagen* WAIN + *schot,* of doubtful meaning]

wain·scot·ing (wān′skət ĭng, -skŏt-), n. 1. paneling or woodwork with which walls, etc., are wainscoted. 2. wainscots collectively. Also, esp. Brit., **wain′-scot·ting.**

wain·wright (wān′rīt′), n. a wagon maker.

Wain·wright (wān′rīt′), n. **Jonathan Mayhew** (mā′-hū), 1883–1953, U.S. general.

waist (wāst), n. 1. the part of the human body be-tween the ribs and the hips. 2. the contraction marking this. 3. the part of a garment covering the waist. 4. a garment or a part of a garment covering the body from the neck or shoulders to the waistline, esp. in women's or children's dress. 5. a child's undergarment to which other articles of apparel may be attached. 6. that part of an object, esp. a central or middle part, which bears some analogy to the human waist: *the waist of a violin.* 7. Naut. the central part of a ship; that part of the deck between the forecastle and the quarter-deck. 8. the narrow part or petiole of the abdomen of certain insects, as the wasp. [ME *wast,* c. Icel. *vöxtr,* OHG *wahst* growth. See WAX², v., grow] —**waist′less,** adj.

waist·band (wāst′bănd′, -bənd), n. a band encircling the waist, esp. as a part of a skirt, trousers, etc.

waist·cloth (wāst′klôth′, -klŏth′), n. a loincloth.

waist·coat (wāst′kōt′, wĕs′kət), n. 1. Chiefly Brit. a man's vest. 2. a similar garment sometimes worn by women. 3. a body garment for men, formerly worn under the doublet. —**waist′coat·ed,** adj.

waist·line (wāst′līn′), n. 1. the line of the waist, be-tween the chest and hips. 2. the juncture point between the skirt and waist of a dress.

wait (wāt), v.i. 1. to stay or rest in expectation; re-main in a state of quiescence or inaction, as until some-thing expected shall happen (often fol. by *for, till,* or *until*): *waiting for him to go.* 2. (of things) to be in readiness: *a letter waiting for you.* 3. to remain neglected for a time: *a matter that can wait.* 4. **wait on** or **upon,** a. to perform the duties of an attendant or servant for. b. to supply the wants of (a person) at table. c. to call upon or visit (a person, esp. a superior): *to wait on the Emperor in his palace.* d. to attend as an accompani-ment or consequence. —v.t. 5. to continue stationary or inactive in expectation of; await: *to wait one's turn at a telephone booth.* 6. (of things) to be in readiness for; be reserved for: *glory waits thee.* 7. Colloq. to defer or postpone in expecta-tion of the arrival of someone: *to wait dinner for someone.* 8. Obs. to attend upon or escort, esp. as a sign of honor. 9. **wait table,** to wait on a table; serve. —n. 10. act of waiting or awaiting; delay; halt. 11. a period or interval of waiting. 12. Theat. the time between two acts or the like. 13. ambushment or an ambush: *to lie in wait.* 14. (usually pl.) Brit. one of a band of singers and musicians who go about the streets by night at Christmas and New Year's singing and playing carols, etc., in order to obtain gratuities. 15. Obs. one of a body of musicians in the employ of a city or town. 16. Obs. a watchman. [ME *waite(n),* t. OF: m. *waitier,* t. OHG: m. *wahtēn* watch; akin to WATCH] —Syn. 1. await, linger, remain, abide. WAIT, TARRY imply pausing to linger and thereby putting off further activity until later. WAIT usually implies staying for a limited time and for a definite purpose, that is, for something expected: *to wait for a train.* TARRY is a somewhat archaic word for WAIT but it suggests lingering, perhaps aimlessly delaying, or pausing (briefly) in a journey: *to tarry on the way home, to tarry overnight at an inn.* 10. waiting, tarrying, lingering, pause, stop.

wait-a-bit (wāt′ə bĭt′), n. any of various plants bearing thorns or prickly appendages, as a procumbent herb, *Harpagophytum procumbens*, of southern Africa, or the greenbrier. [trans. of S Afr. D *wacht-een-beetje*]

wait·er (wā′tər), *n.* **1.** a man who waits on table, esp. in a hotel or restaurant. **2.** a tray on which dishes, etc., are carried. **3.** one who waits or awaits. **4.** *Obs.* an attendant. —wait′er·less, *adj.*

wait·ing (wā′tĭng), *n.* **1.** a period of waiting. **2. in waiting, a.** in attendance, as upon a king, queen, prince, etc. **b.** *Brit. Mil.*, *Nav.* being next due for some obligation or privilege. —*adj.* **3.** that serves or attends: *a waiting man, a waiting maid.*

waiting room, a room for the use of persons waiting, as in a railroad station, a physician's office, etc.

wait·ress (wā′trĭs), *n.* a woman who waits on table. —wait′ress·less, *adj.*

waive (wāv), *v.t.*, **waived, waiving. 1.** to forbear to insist on; relinquish; forgo: *to waive one's rank, to waive honors.* **2.** *Law.* to relinquish (a known right, etc.) intentionally. **3.** to put aside for the time; defer. **4.** to put aside or dismiss from consideration or discussion: *waiving my attempts to explain.* [ME *weyven*, t. AF: m. *weyver* abandon. See WAIF]

waiv·er (wā′vər), *n.* *Law.* **1.** an intentional relinquishment of some right, interest, or the like. **2.** an express or written statement of such relinquishment. [t. AF: m. *weyver.* See WAIVE]

Wa·kash·an (wäkäsh′ən, wô′kəshän′), *n.* an American Indian linguistic stock including languages spoken in British Columbia and Washington, e.g., Nootka and Kwakiutl.

Wa·ka·ya·ma (wä′käyä′mä), *n.* a seaport in S Japan, on S Honshu island. 191,337 (1950).

wake[1] (wāk), *v.*, **waked** or **woke; waked** or (*Archaic and Dial.*) **woken; waking;** *n.* —*v.i.* **1.** to become roused from sleep; awake (often fol. by *up*). **2.** to be or continue awake: *waking or sleeping.* **3.** to remain awake for some purpose, duty, etc. **4.** to become roused from a quiescent or inactive state. **5.** to become alive, as to something perceived. **6.** *Dial.* to hold a wake over a corpse. **7.** *Archaic or Dial.* to keep watch or vigil. —*v.t.* **8.** to rouse from sleep; awake (often fol. by *up*). **9.** to rouse from quiescence, inactivity, lethargy, unconsciousness, etc.: *to wake controversy, to wake ambition.* **10.** *Dial.* to hold a wake over, as a corpse. **11.** *Archaic or Dial.* to keep watch or vigil over. —*n.* **12.** a watching, or a watch kept, esp. for some solemn or ceremonial purpose. **13.** an all-night watch by the body of a dead person before burial, now chiefly among the Irish. **14.** an annual festival held formerly, or now locally, in England in commemoration of the dedication of a parish church. **15.** state of being awake: *between sleep and wake.* [ME *wake(n)*, OE *wacian*, c. D *waken*, G *wachen*, Icel. *vaka* wake, watch; ME *woke*, OE *wōc* (past tense)] —wak′er, *n.* —**Syn. 8.** waken, arouse.

wake[2] (wāk), *n.* **1.** the track left by a ship or other object moving in the water. **2.** the path or course of anything that has passed or preceded. [t. Scand.; cf. Icel. *vök* hole in the ice]

Wake·field (wāk′fēld), *n.* **1.** a city in central England, in S Yorkshire: battle, 1460. 60,380 (1951). **2.** See **Bridges Creek.**

wake·ful (wāk′fəl), *adj.* **1.** indisposed or unable to sleep, as a person. **2.** characterized by absence of sleep: *a wakeful night.* **3.** watchful or vigilant: *a wakeful foe.* —wake′ful·ly, *adv.* —wake′ful·ness, *n.* —**Syn. 1.** sleepless, insomnious, restless.

Wake Island, a small island in the N Pacific, belonging to the U.S.: trans-Pacific and naval air base; taken by Japan, 1941. 3 sq. mi.

wak·en (wā′kən), *v.t.* **1.** to rouse from sleep; awake. **2.** to rouse from inactivity; stir up or excite; arouse. —*v.i.* **3.** to wake, or become awake. [ME; OE *wæcnan*, c. Icel. *vakna.* See WAKE[1]] —wak′en·er, *n.*

wake·rife (wāk′rīf′), *adj.* *Scot. and N. Eng.* wakeful. —wake′rife′ness, *n.*

wake-rob·in (wāk′rŏb′ĭn), *n.* **1.** the cuckoopint. **2.** any of various other arums or araceous plants, as the jack-in-the-pulpit. **3.** *U.S.* any of various plants of the liliaceous genus *Trillium,* as *T. erectum,* a species with ill-scented purple, pink, or white flowers.

wake-up (wāk′ŭp′), *n.* *U.S. Colloq.* flicker[1].

Wal., **1.** Wallachian. **2.** Walloon.

Wa·la·chi·a (wŏlā′kĭə), *n.* a former principality in SE Europe: it united with Moldavia to form Rumania, 1861. 29,569 sq. mi. *Cap.:* Bucharest. Also, **Wallachia.** —**Wa·la′chi·an,** *adj.*, *n.*

Wal·che·ren (wäl′кнərən), *n.* an island in SW Netherlands, in Zeeland province. 77,839 (est. 1956); 82 sq. mi.

Wald (wôld), *n.* **Lillian,** 1867–1940, U.S. social worker.

Wal·de·mar I (väl′dəmär′), ("*the Great*") 1131–82, king of Denmark, 1157–82. Also, **Valdemar I.**

Wal·den, or Life in the Woods (wôl′dən), a book (1854) by Thoreau.

Wal·den·ses (wŏldĕn′sēz), *n.pl.* a Christian sect which arose after 1170 in southern France under the leadership of Pierre Waldo, a merchant of Lyons, and in the 16th century joined the Reformation movement. [t. ML, pl. of *Waldensis,* der. *Waldo*] —**Wal·den·si·an** (wŏldĕn′sĭən, -shən), *adj.*, *n.*

wald·grave (wôld′grāv), *n.* (in the old German Empire) an officer having jurisdiction over a royal forest. [t. G: m. *waldgraf,* f. *wald* forest + *graf* count]

Wal·dorf salad (wôl′dôrf), a salad of celery, diced apples, nuts, and mayonnaise dressing. [so called by assoc. with Waldorf-Astoria Hotel in New York City]

Wald·stein (vält′shtīn), *n.* See **Wallenstein.**

wale[1] (wāl), *n.*, *v.*, **waled, waling.** —*n.* **1.** a streak, stripe, or ridge produced on the skin by the stroke of a rod or whip; a welt. **2.** a ridge or raised line formed in the weave of cloth. **3.** the texture of a fabric; the kind of weave. **4.** *Naut.* **a.** any of certain strakes of thick outside planking on the sides of a wooden ship. **b.** (sometimes) the gunwale. —*v.t.* **5.** to mark with wales. **6.** to weave with wales. [ME; OE *walu* weal, ridge, prob. akin to Icel. *völr,* Goth *walus* rod, wand]

wale[2] (wāl), *n.*, *v.*, **waled, waling.** *Scot. and N. Eng.* —*n.* **1.** the choicest or best specimen, part, etc. —*v.t.* **2.** to choose; select; pick out. [ME *wal(e),* t. Scand.; cf. Icel. *val* choice, c. G *wahl*]

Wa·ler (wā′lər), *n.* (in Anglo-Indian use) a horse imported from Australia.

Wales (wālz), *n.* a division of the United Kingdom: the SW part of Great Britain. 2,172,339 pop. (1951); 8016 sq. mi.

Wal·hal·la (wälhăl′ə, wălhä′lə), *n.* *Scand. Myth.* Valhalla.

walk (wôk), *v.i.* **1.** to go or travel on foot at a moderate pace; to proceed by steps, or by advancing the feet in turn, at a moderate pace (in bipedal locomotion, so that there is always one foot on the ground, and in quadrupedal locomotion, so that there are always two or more feet on the ground). **2.** to go about or travel on foot for exercise or pleasure. **3.** to go about on the earth, or appear to living persons, as a ghost. **4.** (of things) to move in a manner suggestive of walking, as through repeated vibrations or the effect of alternate expansion and contraction. **5.** to conduct oneself in a particular manner, or pursue a particular course of life: *to walk humbly with thy God.* **6.** *Baseball.* to take first base as a base on balls. **7.** *Basketball.* to take more than two steps while in possession of the ball without a bounce or pass. **8.** *Colloq.* to go out from work on a strike (fol. by *out*). **9.** **walk off with,** to obtain by winning, taking, stealing, etc. **10.** *Obs.* to be in motion or action. —*v.t.* **11.** to proceed through, over, or upon by walking: *walking London streets by night.* **12.** to make, put, drive, etc., by walking: *to walk off a headache.* **13.** to cause to walk; lead, drive, or ride at a walk, as an animal: *walking their horses toward us.* **14.** to force or help to walk, as a person. **15.** to conduct on a walk: *he walked them about the park.* **16.** to move (an object, as a box or a trunk) in a manner suggestive of walking, as by a rocking motion. **17.** *Baseball.* to pitch a base on balls to. **18.** *Basketball.* to advance (the ball) by taking more than two steps without dribbling or passing. **19.** to examine, measure, etc., by traversing on foot: *to walk a track.* **20.** **walk the plank, a.** to walk along and off a plank extending from a ship's side over the water, under compulsion. **b.** to quit an office or position under compulsion. —*n.* **21.** act or course of walking, or going on foot. **22.** a spell of walking for exercise or pleasure: *to take a walk.* **23.** a distance walked or to be walked, often in terms of the time required: *a ten minutes' walk from town.* **24.** the gait or pace of a person or animal that walks. **25.** manner of walking: *impossible to mistake her walk.* **26.** manner of behavior, or course of life. **27.** a department or branch of activity, or a particular line of work: *they found every walk of life closed against them.* **28.** *Baseball.* a base achieved by having four balls pitched to the batter. See **ball**[1] (def. 4). **29.** *Athletics.* a walking race. **30.** a way for foot passengers at the side of a street or road; a sidewalk. **31.** a place prepared or set apart for walking. **32.** a path in a garden or the like. **33.** a passage between rows of trees. **34.** an enclosure in which poultry may run about freely. **35.** a sheepwalk. **36.** a ropewalk. **37.** a plantation of coffee or other trees, as in the West Indies. **38.** *Brit.* **a.** the route of a tradesman, hawker, or the like. **b.** the district traversed. **39.** *Eng.* a division of a forest under the charge of a forester or keeper. **40.** *Obs.* a haunt or resort. [ME; OE *wealcan* roll, toss, *gewealcan* go, c. D and G *walken* full (cloth), Icel. *válka* toss] —walk′er, *n.* —**Syn. 1.** step, stride, stroll, saunter, ambulate, promenade, pace, march, tramp, hike, tread. **22.** stroll, promenade, march, tramp, hike, constitutional.

walk·a·way (wôk′əwā′), *n.* an easy victory or conquest.

walk·ie-talk·ie (wô′kĭ tô′kĭ), *n.* *Radio.* a combined transmitter and receiver light enough to be carried by one man: developed for military use in World War II.

walk·ing (wô′kĭng), *adj.* **1.** that walks. **2.** of or pertaining to an animal-drawn instrument operated by a erson on foot: *a walking plow.* **3.** of or pertaining to a echanical part that moves back and forth. —*n.* **4.** act f one who or that which walks: *walking was the best cercise for him.* **5.** manner or style of walking. **6.** state f that on which one walks: *dry walking in the garden.*

alking bass, *Jazz.* a figure or motive, usually in h notes, which is commonly used in the bass part of oogie-woogie compositions.

alking delegate, (formerly) an official appointed y a trade union to go from place to place in the interests f the union.

alking fern, a fern of the family *Polypodiaceae, amptosorus rhizophyllus,* with simple fronds tapering ¹to a prolongation which often takes root at the apex.

alking leaf, any orthopterous insect of the family ʰyllidae of the Old World tropics, noted for earing a remarkable resemblance to leaves.

alking papers, *Colloq.* dismissal.

alking stick, **1.** *Chiefly Brit.* a stick used ¹ walking; a cane. **2.** any of certain orthopter-us insects of the family *Phasmidae,* with long, ¹ender, twiglike bodies; a stick insect.

alk·out (wôk′out′), *n.* *Colloq.* a strike of ¹borers or workers.

alk·o·ver (wôk′ō′vər), *n.* *Colloq.* **1.** *Rac-ng.* a going over the course at a walk or other-ʲise by a contestant who is the only starter. ². an unopposed or easy victory.

alk-up (wôk′ŭp′), *U.S. Colloq.* —*n.* **1.** a ¹uilding, esp. an apartment, that has no eleva-or. —*adj.* **2.** having no elevator.

al·kü·re (välky′rə), *n.* See **Ring f the Nibelung.** [G, t. Icel. See VALKYRIE]

al·kyr·ie (wäl′kĭr′Y, väl-), *n. Scand. Myth.* ʸalkyrie.

Walking stick, *Diapher-omera femorata*

all (wôl), *n.* **1.** an upright work or struc-ure of stone, brick, or similar material, serving ʲor enclosure, division, support, protection, etc.: ¹s one of the upright enclosing sides of a building or a ʲoom, or a solid fence of masonry. **2.** (*usually pl.*) ¹ rampart raised for defensive purposes. **3.** anything which resembles or suggests a wall: *a wall of prej-udice.* **4.** a wall-like enclosing part, thing, mass, etc.: *a wall of fire, a wall of troops.* **5.** an embankment to pre-vent flooding. **6.** *drive* (*push,* etc.) **to the wall,** to drive ¹to the last extremity; make helpless. **7. go to the wall, a.** to give way or suffer defeat in a conflict or competi-tion. **b.** to fail in business, or become bankrupt. —*adj.* **8.** of or pertaining to a wall. **9.** growing against or on a wall. —*v.t.* **10.** to enclose, shut off, divide, protect, etc., with or as with a wall. **11.** to fill up (a doorway, etc.) with a wall. [ME and OE, t. L: m.s. *vallum*] —**walled,** *adj.* —**wall′·less,** *adj.* —**wall′·like′,** *adj.* —**Syn.** **2.** battlement, breastwork, bulwark.

val·la (wä′lä), *n.* wallah.

val·la·by (wŏl′əbĭ), *n., pl.* **-bies,** (*esp. collectively*) **-by,** any of various small and medium-sized kangaroos of the genera *Macropus, Thylogale, Petro-gale,* etc., some of which are no larger than rabbits. [t. native Australian]

Val·lace (wŏl′Ys, wô′lYs), *n.* **1.** Al-fred Russel, 1823–1913, British natu-ralist and traveler. **2. Henry Agard,** 1888–1965, U.S. statesman: secretary of agriculture, 1933–40; vice-president of the U.S., 1941–45; and secretary of commerce, 1945–46. **3.** Lewis (or Lew), 1827–1905, U.S. general and novelist. **4. Sir William,** c1272–1305, Scottish military leader and hero in the struggle against Edward I of England.

Agile wallaby, *Wallabia axilis* Total length 5 ft., tail ab. 2¼ ft.

Val·la·chi·a (wŏlā′kĭ′ə), *n.* Walachia.

Val·la·chi·an (wŏlā′kĭ′ən), *n.* **1. a.** the Rumanian of Walachia. **b.** *Obs.* Rumanian in general. **2.** Wala-chian. —*adj.* **3.** Walachian.

val·lah (wä′lä), *n.* (in Anglo-Indian use) a person employed at or concerned with a particular thing (used esp. in compounds). Also, **walla.** [t. Hind.: m. *-wālā*]

val·la·roo (wŏl′ərōō′), *n.* any of several large kangaroos, subgenus *Osphranter,* of the grassy plains of Australia.

Val·la·sey (wŏl′əsĭ), *n.* a city in W England, on the Mersey estuary, near Liverpool. 102,300 (est. 1956).

Val·la Wal·la (wŏl′ə wŏl′ə), a city in SE Washing-ton. 24,536 (1960).

vall·board (wôl′bōrd′), *n.* an artificial sheet material for use in making or covering walls, ceilings, etc., as a substitute for wooden boards or plaster.

vall creeper, a small gray and crimson Old World bird, *Tichodroma muraria,* which makes its home among precipitous rocks.

Val·len·stein (wŏl′ənstīn′; *Ger.* väl′ənshtīn′), *n.* Albrecht Wenzel Eusebius von (äl′brĕкHт vĕn′tsəl oi-zā′bĭ′ōōs′ fən), (*Duke of Friedland*) 1583–1634, Austrian imperial general in the Thirty Years' War, born in Bohemia. Also, **Waldstein.**

Val·ler (wŏl′ər, wô′lər), *n.* **Edmund,** 1607–87, British poet.

wal·let (wŏl′Yt, wô′lYt), *n.* **1.** a pocketbook, esp. one large enough for holding papers, paper money laid flat,

etc. **2.** a bag for personal necessaries, food, or the like, as for use on a journey. [ME *walet;* orig. uncert.]

wall·eye (wôl′ī′), *n.* **1.** any of various fishes with large, staring eyes, including: **a.** Also, **walleyed pike.** a pike perch, *Stizostedion vitreum.* **b.** Also, **walleyed perch, walleyed surf fish.** a viviparous surf fish, *Hy-perprosopon argenteum,* of California of the family *Em-bistocidae.* **c.** Also, **walleyed herring.** the alewife, *Pomolobus pseudo-harengus.* **d.** Also, **walleyed pollack.** a North Pacific cod, *Theragra chalcogramma.* **2.** an eye such as is seen in a walleyed person or animal.

wall·eyed (wôl′īd′), *adj.* **1.** having eyes in which there is an abnormal amount of the white showing, be-cause of divergent strabismus. **2.** having an eye or the eyes presenting little or no color, as the result of a light-colored or white iris or of white opacity of the cornea. **3.** having large, staring eyes, as some fishes. [ME *wawil-eghed,* t. Scand.: cf. Icel. *vagl-eygr,* f. *vagl* film over eye + *-eygr -eyed*]

wall·flow·er (wôl′flou′ər), *n.* **1. a** European perennial, *Cheiranthus Cheiri,* growing wild on old walls, cliffs, etc., and also cultivated in gardens, with sweet-scented flowers, commonly yellow or orange but in cultivation varying from pale-yellow to brown, red, or purple. **2.** any plant of the brassicaceous genera *Cheiranthus* and *Erys-imum.* **3.** *Colloq.* a person, esp. a woman, who looks on at a dance, esp. from failure to obtain a partner.

Wal·loon (wŏlōōn′), *n.* **1.** one of a people inhabiting chiefly the southern and southeastern parts of Belgium and adjacent regions in France. **2.** the French dialect of Belgium, esp. of the southeast. —*adj.* **3.** of or per-taining to the Walloons or their language. [t. F: m. *Wallon,* g. ML *Wallo,* t. Gmc.; cf. OHG *walh* foreigner]

wal·lop (wŏl′əp), *v.t.* *Colloq.* **1.** to beat soundly; thrash. **2.** to strike with a vigorous blow. **3.** to defeat thoroughly, as in a game. —*v.i.* *Prov.* or *Colloq.* **4.** to gallop. **5.** to move heavily and clumsily about. —*n.* **6.** *Colloq.* a vigorous blow. **7.** *Colloq.* (in boxing, etc.) an ability to deliver such blows. **8.** *Prov.* or *Colloq.* a gallop. **9.** *Prov.* or *Colloq.* a heavy, clumsy movement; a lurch. [ME *walop,* t. OF, akin to F *galoper* gallop]

wal·lop·er (wŏl′əp ər), *n.* *Colloq.* **1.** one who or that which wallops. **2.** something big, huge, or inordinately exaggerated.

wal·lop·ing (wŏl′əpYng), *Colloq.* —*n.* **1.** a sound beat-ing or thrashing. **2.** a thorough defeat. —*adj.* **3.** big.

wal·low (wŏl′ō), *v.i.* **1.** to roll the body about, or lie, in water, snow, mud, dust, or the like, as for refresh-ment: *goats wallowing in the dust.* **2.** to live or continue contentedly or self-indulgently or luxuriously: *to wallow in wealth, to wallow in sensuality.* **3.** to flounder about or along clumsily or with difficulty: *the gunboat wallowing on the water.* **4.** to surge up, as smoke, heat, etc. —*n.* **5.** act of wallowing. **6.** a place to which animals, as buffaloes, resort to wallow. **7.** the indentation pro-duced by their wallowing. [ME *walwe,* OE *wealwian* roll, akin to Goth. *walwjan,* L *volvere* roll] —**wal′low·er,** *n.* —**Syn.** **1.** welter, flounder.

wall·pa·per (wôl′pā′pər), *n.* **1.** paper, commonly with printed decorative patterns in color, for pasting on and covering the walls or ceilings of rooms, etc. —*v.t.* **2.** to put wallpaper on; furnish with wallpaper.

wall pellitory, a small, bushy, Old World urtica-ceous plant, *Parietaria officinalis,* growing on walls, and said to be a diuretic and refrigerant.

wall plate, **1.** *Building.* a plate or timber placed horizontally in or on a wall, under the ends of girders, joists, or other timbers, in order to distribute pressure. **2.** *Mach.* a vertical metal plate secured against a wall or the like, as to attach a bracket.

wall rock, *Mining.* the rock forming the walls of a vein.

wall rocket, a European cruciferous plant, *Diplo-taxis tenuifolia,* growing along old walls, etc.

wall rue, a small delicate fern, *Asplenium ruta-muraria,* growing on walls and cliffs.

Walls·end (wôlz′ĕnd′), *n.* **1.** a city in NE England, on the Tyne, near Newcastle. 48,645 (1951). **2.** *Brit.* a size or type used in classifying coal.

Wall Street, **1.** a street in the S part of the borough of Manhattan, in New York City: famous as the chief financial center of the U.S. **2.** the money market or the financiers of the U.S.

wal·ly (wā′lY), *adj., n., pl.* **-lies.** *Scot.* —*adj.* **1.** fine. **2.** ample; strong; big. —*n.* **3.** a toy; gewgaw. [? akin to WALE²]

wal·ly·drag (wā′lY drăg′, -drăg′, wŏl′Y-), *n. Scot.* a feeble, ill-grown creature. Also, **wal·ly·drai·gle** (wā′lY-drā′gəl, wŏl′Y-).

wal·nut (wôl′nŭt′, -nət), *n.* **1.** the edible nut of trees of the genus *Juglans,* of the North Temperate zone. **2.** a tree bearing this nut, as *J. regia* (English or Persian walnut), or *J. nigra* (black walnut), which yields both a valuable timber and a distinctively flavored nut. **3.** the wood of such a tree. **4.** any of various fruits or trees resembling the walnut. **5.** a shade of brown, as that of the heartwood of the black walnut tree. [ME *walnotte,* OE *walhhnutu,* lit., foreign nut]

Wal·pole (wôl′pōl, wôl′-), *n.* **1. Horace,** (*4th Earl of Orford*) 1717–97, British author. **2. Sir Hugh Seymour,** 1884–1941, British novelist, born in New Zealand. **3. Sir Robert,** (*1st Earl of Orford*) 1676–1745, prime minister of England, 1721–42.

Wal·pur·gis Night (väl pŏŏr′gĭs), the eve of (before) May 1, the feast day of St. **Walpurgis** (an English missionary and abbess in Germany, who died about A.D. 780), on which, according to German popular superstition, witches ride to some appointed rendezvous, esp. the Brocken, the highest of the Harz Mountains. Also, German, **Wal·pur·gis·nacht** (väl pŏŏr′gĭs näкнt′).

wal·rus (wôl′rəs, wŏl′-), n., pl. **-ruses,** (esp. collectively) **-rus.** either of two large marine mammals of the genus Odobenus, of arctic seas, related to the seals, and having flippers, a pair of large tusks, and a thick, tough skin. [t. D: lit., whalehorse. Cf. G walross, Dan. hvalros; also OE horshwæl horse-whale]

walrus mustache, a mustache hanging down loosely at both ends.

Atlantic walrus. Odobenus rosmarus (Male 10 ft. to 11 ft. long. female ⅓ smaller)

Wal·sall (wôl′sôl), n. a city in central England, in Staffordshire, near Birmingham. 114,700 (est. 1956).

Wal·sing·ham (wôl′sĭng-əm), n. Sir Francis, 1530?–1590, British statesman: secretary of state, 1573–90.

Wal·ter (väl′tər), n. **Bruno** (brōō′nō), (Bruno Schlesinger) 1876–1962 German orchestra conductor, in U.S.

Wal·tham (wôl′thəm), n. a city in E Massachusetts. 55,413 (1960).

Wal·tham·stow (wôl′təm stō′, -thəm-), n. a city in SE England, in Essex, near London. 116,700 (est. 1956).

Wal·ton (wôl′tən), n. Izaak (ī′zək), 1593–1683, British writer and famous fisherman.

waltz (wôlts), n. 1. a round dance in triple rhythm, danced by couples. 2. a piece of music for, or in the rhythm of, this dance. —adj. 3. of, pertaining to, or characteristic of the waltz, as music, rhythm, or dance. —v.i., v.t. 4. to dance or move in the movement or step of a waltz. 5. Slang. to move nimbly or quickly. [t. G: m. walzer, der. walzen roll, dance a waltz] **—waltz′er,** n. **—waltz′like′,** adj.

Wal·vis Bay (wôl′vĭs), 1. a bay on the coast of South-West Africa. 2. a seaport on this bay. 3. an exclave of the Union of South Africa around this bay, administered by South-West Africa. 2421 pop. (1951); 374 sq. mi.

wam·ble (wŏm′əl, wăm′-), v., **-bled, -bling,** n. Chiefly Dial. —v.i. 1. to move with an uncertain motion. 2. to twist; roll the body. —n. 3. act or movement of that which wambles. [ME wamle. Cf. Norw. vamla stagger] **—wam′bling·ly,** adv. **—wam′bly,** adj.

wame (wām), n. Scot. and N. Eng. belly. [var. of WOMB]

wamp·ish (wăm′pĭsh, wäm′-), v.i. Scot. to toss about.

wam·pum (wŏm′pəm, wôm′-), n. 1. cylindrical beads made from shells, pierced and strung, used by North American Indians as money and for ornament: properly denoting a white variety but applied also to a black or dark-purple variety commonly considered twice as valuable as the white; peag. 2. Slang. money. [short for wompanpeag, t. Algonquian (New England area): m. wanpanpiak string of shell beads, der. wap white + anpi string of shell beads + ak, animate pl. suffix]

wam·pum·peag (wŏm′pəm pēg′, wôm′-), n. wampum (def. 1). [see WAMPUM]

wa·mus (wō′məs, wŏm′əs), n. U.S. 1. a type of cardigan. 2. Also, **wam·mus** (wŏm′əs), **wam·pus** (wŏm′pəs). a durable, coarse, outer jacket. [t. D: m. wammes, earlier wambuis, t. OF: m. wambois leather doublet, der. OHG wamba belly. See WOMB]

wan (wŏn), adj., **wanner, wannest,** v., **wanned, wanning.** —adj. 1. of an unnatural or sickly pallor; pallid: his wan face flushed. 2. pale in color or hue: cowslips wan. 3. showing or suggesting ill health, worn condition, unhappiness, etc.: a wan look, a wan smile. 4. Archaic or Scot. dark or gloomy. —v.i., v.t. 5. Poetic. to become or make wan. [ME; OE wann dark, gloomy] **—wan′ly,** adv. **—wan′ness,** n. **—Syn.** 1. See pale[1].

Wan·a·ma·ker (wŏn′ə mā′kər), n. John, 1838–1922, U.S. merchant.

Wan·chu·an (wän′chy än′), n. a city in NE China; formerly capital of Chahar province. 151,000 (est. 1950). Formerly, **Kalgan.**

wand (wŏnd), n. 1. a slender stick, or rod, esp. one used by a conjurer or diviner. 2. a rod or staff borne as an ensign of office or authority. 3. a slender shoot, stem, or branch of a shrub or tree: lissome as a hazel wand. 4. Archery, U.S. a slat 6 feet by 2 inches placed at a distance of 100 yards for men and 60 yards for women, and used as a mark. [ME, t. Scand.; cf. Icel. vöndr, c. Goth. vandus] **—wand′like′,** adj.

wan·der (wŏn′dər), v.i. 1. to ramble without any certain course or object in view; roam, rove, or stray: to wander over the earth. 2. to go aimlessly or casually: wandering into the adjoining room. 3. to pass or extend in an irregular course or direction: off to the south wandered the purple hills. 4. to move, pass, or turn idly, as the hand, the pen, the eyes, etc. 5. (of the mind, thoughts, desires, etc.) to take one direction or another without intention or control. 6. to stray from a path, place, companions, etc. 7. to deviate in conduct,

belief, etc.; err; go astray: let me not wander from thy commandments. 8. to think or speak confusedly or incoherently. —v.t. 9. Poetic. to wander over or through. [ME wandre(n), OE wandrian, c. MD wanderen, G wandern] **—wan′der·er,** n. **—wan′der·ing·ly,** adv. **—Syn.** 1. range, stroll, meander, saunter.

wandering albatross, a large albatross, Diomedea exulans, of southern waters, having the plumage mostly white with dark markings on the upper parts.

Wandering Jew, 1. a legendary character condemned to roam without rest because he struck Christ on the day of Crucifixion. 2. Also, **wandering Jew, Wandering jew.** any of various trailing or creeping plants, as Zebrina pendula or Tradescantia fluminensis.

Wan·der·jahr (vän′dər yär′), n. German. travel year; a journeyman's year of travel before settling to work.

wan·der·lust (wŏn′dər lŭst′; Ger. vän′dər lŏŏst′), n. instinctive impulse to rove or travel about. [t. G]

wan·der·oo (wŏn′də rōō′), n. 1. any of several langurs, of Ceylon. 2. a macaque, Macacus silenus, of southern India. [t. Singhalese: m. wanderu monkey]

wan·dle (wän′dəl, -əl), adj. Scot. supple.

Wands·worth (wŏnz′wərth), n. a SW borough of London, England. 330,328 (1951).

wane (wān), v., **waned, waning,** n. —v.i. 1. (of the moon) to decrease periodically in the extent of its illuminated portion after the full moon (opposed to wax). 2. to decline in power, importance, prosperity, etc. 3. to decrease in strength, intensity, etc.: daylight waned, and night came on. 4. to draw to a close, or approach an end. —n. 5. gradual decrease or decline in strength, intensity, power, etc.: his favor was on the wane. 6. the drawing to a close of life, a time, etc.: the wane of life. 7. the waning of the moon. 8. a period of waning. 9. a beveled edge of a plank or board as sawed from an unsquared log, due to the curvature of the log. [ME; OE wanian lessen, c. MD and MHG wanen] **—Ant.** 1. wax.

wan·gle (wăng′gəl), v., **-gled, -gling,** n. Colloq. —v.t. 1. to bring about, accomplish, or obtain by contrivance, scheming, or, often, indirect or insidious methods. 2. to manage, as under difficulties; adjust in a makeshift way. —v.i. 3. to use contrivance, scheming, or indirect methods to accomplish some end. 4. to adjust things in a makeshift manner. —n. 5. an act of chicanery. [b. WAG and DANGLE] **—wan′gler,** n.

Wan·hsien (wän′shyĕn′), n. a city in central China, on the Yangtze. 110,000 (est. 1950).

waning moon. See moon (def. 2f).

wan·ion (wŏn′yən), n. Archaic. ill luck; vengeance (used esp. in with a wanion). [ME waniand, ppr. of wanien WANE]

wan·nish (wŏn′ĭsh), adj. somewhat wan.

want (wŏnt, wônt), v.t. 1. to feel a need or a desire for; wish for: to want one's dinner, always wanting something new. 2. to wish or desire (often fol. by infinitive): I want to see you, he wants to be notified. 3. to be without or be deficient in: to want judgment or knowledge. 4. to fall short by: the sum collected wants but a few dollars of the desired amount. 5. Chiefly Brit. to require or need: her pens wanted fixing. —v.i. 6. to be lacking or absent, as a part or thing necessary to completeness: two yards long, wanting an inch. 7. to be deficient by the absence of some part or thing, or fall short (sometimes fol. by for): he did not want for abilities. 8. to have need: if you want for anything, let him know. 9. to be in a state of destitution or poverty. —n. 10. something lacking, but desired or needed; a necessity. 11. a need or requirement: the wants of mankind. 12. absence or deficiency of something desirable or requisite; lack: plants dying for want of rain. 13. state of being without something desired or needed; need: to be in want of an assistant. 14. state of being without the necessaries of life; destitution; poverty. 15. a sense of lack or need of something: to feel a vague want. [ME wante, t. Scand.; cf. Icel. vanta lack] **—want′er,** n. **—want′less,** adj. **—Syn.** 1. See wish. 3. lack, need. 10. desideratum. 12. dearth, scarcity, scarceness, inadequacy, insufficiency, scantiness, paucity. 14. privation. See poverty.

want ad, Colloq. a one-column-wide notice. usually of a few lines, to advertise opportunities for employment, real estate, etc., needed or for sale; classified ad.

want·age (wŏn′tĭj, wôn′-), n. that which is wanting or lacking; an amount lacking.

want·ing (wŏn′tĭng, wôn′-), adj. 1. lacking or absent: an apparatus with some of the parts wanting. 2. deficient in some part, thing, or respect: to be wanting in courtesy. —prep. 3. lacking; without. 4. less; minus: a century, wanting three years.

wan·ton (wŏn′tən), adj. 1. done, shown, used, etc., maliciously or unjustifiably: a wanton attack, injury, or affront, wanton cruelty. 2. deliberate and uncalled for: Why break up your life in this wanton way? 3. reckless or disregardful of right, justice, humanity, etc., as persons: a wanton disturber of men's religious convictions. 4. lawless or unbridled with respect to sexual morality; loose, lascivious, or lewd. 5. Now Poetic. sportive or frolicsome, as children, young animals, gambols, etc. 6. Chiefly Poetic. having free play: wanton breezes, a wanton brook. 7. luxurious, as persons, living, dress, etc. 8. Poetic. luxuriant, as vegetation. —n. 9. a wanton or lascivious person, esp. a woman. —v.i. 10. to act, grow, etc. in a wanton manner. —v.t. 11. to squander (away), as in pleasure. [ME wantowen, lit., undisciplined, f.

b., blend of, blended; c., cognate with; d., dialect, dialectal; der., derived from; f., formed from; g., going back to; m., modification of; r., replacing; s., stem of; t., taken from; ?, perhaps.   See the full key on inside cover.

wan·ton·ly *wan-* not + OE *togen* disciplined] —**wan'ton·ly,** *adv.* —**wan'ton·ness,** *n.* —Syn. 1. reckless, malicious. 3. unruly, wild. 4. dissolute, licentious, immoral.

wap (wŏp, wăp), *v.t., v.i.,* **wapped, wapping,** *n. Colloq.* or *Dial.* whop.

wap·en·take (wŏp'ən·tāk', wăp'-), *n.* (formerly or locally, in certain counties of northern and midland England) a division of the county corresponding to the historical hundred of other counties. [ME; OE *wapentac,* t. Scand.; cf. Icel. *vāpnatak,* lit. taking of weapons, i.e. show of weapons at public voting]

wap·i·ti (wŏp'ə·tĭ), *n., pl.* **-tis,** (*esp. collectively*) **-ti.** a North American species of deer, *Cervus canadensis,* with long, slender antlers: usually called *elk.* [t. Shawnee (Algonquian): white rump]

wap·pen·shaw (wăp'ən·shô', wä'pən-), *n.* a muster or review of persons under arms, formerly held at certain times in the districts of Scotland, to satisfy the military chiefs that their men were properly armed. [short for *wappenshawing* (Scot.) weapon-showing]

wap·per·jaw (wŏp'ər·jô'), *n. U.S. Colloq.* a projecting underjaw. —**wap'per·jawed',** *adj.*

war[1] (wôr), *n., v.,* **warred, warring,** *adj.* —*n.* 1. conflict carried on by force of arms, as between nations or states (**international war** or **public war**), or between parties within a state (**civil war**); warfare (by land, by sea, or in the air). 2. a contest carried on by force of arms, as in a series of battles or campaigns: *the war of 1812.* 3. active hostility or contention; conflict; contest: *a war of words.* 4. armed fighting, as a department of activity, a profession, or an art: *war is our business.* 5. *Obs., Poetic.* a battle; engagement. 6. **at war,** in a state of hostility or active military operations. —*v.i.* 7. to make or carry on war; fight. 8. to carry on active hostility or contention: *to war with evil.* 9. to be in a state of strong opposition: *warring principles.* —*adj.* 10. of, belonging to, used in, or due to war. [ME *werre,* t. OF, t. OHG: m. *werra* strife] —**war'less,** *adj.*

war[2] (wâr), *adv., adj. Scot.* worse.

War and Peace, a long novel (1865–72) by Tolstoy.

War·beck (wôr'bĕk), *n.* **Perkin,** 1474–99, British commoner, pretender to the throne as the would-be son of Edward IV.

War between the States, *Amer. Hist.* the Civil War (used esp. in the former Confederate States).

war·ble[1] (wôr'bəl), *v.,* **-bled, -bling,** *n.* —*v.i.* 1. (of persons, also of birds) to sing with trills, quavers, or melodic embellishments. 2. *U.S.* to yodel. —*v.t.* 3. to sing with trills, quavers, or melodious turns; carol. 4. to express or celebrate in song. —*n.* 5. a warbled song. 6. act of warbling. [ME *werblen,* t. OF: m. *werbler* quaver, t. Gmc.; cf. OHG *werbel* something that revolves]

war·ble[2] (wôr'bəl), *n.* 1. a small, hard tumor on a horse's back, produced by the galling of the saddle. 2. a lump in the skin of an animal's back, containing the larva of a warble fly. [orig. uncert. Cf. obs. Sw. *varbulde* boil] —**war'bled,** *adj.*

warble fly, any of various flies of the family *Hypodermatidae,* whose larva produce warbles.

war·bler (wôr'blər), *n.* 1. one who or that which warbles. 2. any of numerous small, insectivorous New World birds constituting the family *Compsothlypidae,* many of which are brightly colored, as the American redstart, *Setophaga ruticilla.* As a group they are often referred to as the **wood warblers.** 3. any of the small, chiefly Old World, singing birds constituting the family *Sylviidae,* including the reed warbler, blackcap, etc.

war cry, 1. a cry or a word or phrase, shouted in charging or in rallying to attack; a battle cry. 2. a party cry or slogan in any contest.

ward (wôrd), *n.* 1. a division or district of a city or town, as for administrative or representative purposes. 2. one of the districts into which certain English and Scottish boroughs are divided. 3. a division of a hospital or the like, as for a particular class of patients: *a convalescent ward.* 4. each of the separate divisions of a prison. 5. *Fort.* an open space within walls, or between lines of walls, of a castle or fortified place: *the castle's lower ward.* 6. *Law.* a. a person, esp. a minor, who has been legally placed under the care of a guardian or a court. b. state of being under the care or control of a legal guardian. c. guardianship over a minor or some other person legally incapable of managing his own affairs. 7. state of being under restraining guard or in custody. 8. one who is under the protection or control of another. 9. a movement or posture of defense, as in fencing. 10. a curved ridge of metal inside a lock, forming an obstacle to the passage of a key which has not a corresponding notch. 11. the notch or slot in the bit of a key, into which such a ridge fits. 12. act of keeping guard or protective watch (*archaic,* except in *watch and ward*). [ME *warde,* OE *weard.* See WARD, v.] —*v.t.* 13. to avert, repel, or turn aside, as danger, an attack, assailant, etc. (usually fol. by *off*): *to ward off a blow.* 14. to place in a ward, as of a hospital. 15. *Archaic.* to guard. [ME; OE *weardian,* c. MD *waerden,* G *warten.* See GUARD, v.] —**ward'less,** *adj.*

Ward (wôrd), *n.* 1. **Artemas** (är'tə·məs), 1727–1800, American general in the Revolutionary War. 2. **Artemus,** (*Charles Farrar Browne*) 1834–67, U.S. humorist. 3. **Mrs. Humphry,** (*Mary Augusta Arnold*) 1851–1920, British novelist.

-ward, a word element of a small set of words, indicating direction, as in *onward, seaward, backward.* Also, **-wards.** [ME; OE *-weard* towards]

war dance, (among primitive people) a dance preliminary to a warlike excursion or in celebration of a victory.

ward·ed (wôr'dĭd), *adj.* having notches, slots, or wards, as in locks and keys.

ward·en[1] (wôr'dən), *n.* 1. one charged with the care or custody of something; a keeper. 2. the chief administrative officer in charge of a prison. 3. any of various public officials charged with superintendence, as over a port, etc. 4. (in Connecticut) the chief executive officer of a borough. 5. *Hist.* the principal official in a region, town, etc. 6. *Chiefly Brit.* the head of certain colleges, schools, etc., esp. in England. 7. a member of the governing body of a guild. 8. a churchwarden. 9. *Now Rare.* a gatekeeper. [ME *wardein,* t. OF. See GUARDIAN] —**ward'en·ship',** *n.* —Syn. 1. warder, guardian, guard, custodian.

ward·en[2] (wôr'dən), *n. Eng.* one of a group of cooking pears distinguished for crisp, firm flesh. [orig. uncert.]

ward·en·ry (wôr'dən·rĭ), *n., pl.* **-ries.** the office, jurisdiction, or district of a warden.

ward·er[1] (wôr'dər), *n.* 1. one who wards or guards something. 2. a soldier or other person set to guard an entrance. 3. *Chiefly Brit.* an official having charge of prisoners in a jail. [ME, der. WARD, v.] —**ward'er·ship',** *n.*

ward·er[2] (wôr'dər), *n.* a truncheon or staff of office or authority, used in giving signals. [late ME; orig. uncert.]

ward heeler, *U.S.* a minor hanger-on of a political machine who canvasses voters and does party chores.

ward·ress (wôr'drĭs), *n. Chiefly Brit.* a female warder.

ward·robe (wôrd'rōb'), *n.* 1. a stock of clothes or costumes, as of a person or of a theatrical company. 2. a piece of furniture for holding clothes, now usually a tall, upright case fitted with hooks, shelves, etc. 3. a room or place for keeping clothes or costumes in. 4. the department of a royal or other great household charged with the care of wearing apparel. [ME *warderobe,* t. OF. See WARD, ROBE]

ward·room (wôrd'room', -rŏŏm'), *n.* (in a warship) 1. the apartment constituting the living quarters of commissioned officers other than the commanding officer. 2. the dining saloon and lounge for these officers. 3. these officers collectively.

-wards, var. of **-ward.**

ward·ship (wôrd'shĭp), *n.* 1. guardianship; custody. 2. *Law.* the guardianship over a minor or ward.

ware[1] (wâr), *n.* 1. (*usually pl.*) articles of merchandise or manufacture, or goods: *a peddler selling his wares.* 2. a particular kind or class of articles of merchandise or manufacture (now chiefly in composition): *tinware, silverware.* 3. pottery, or a particular kind of pottery: *Delft ware.* [ME; OE *waru,* c. G *ware*]

ware[2] (wâr), *adj., v.,* **wared, waring.** —*adj. Archaic.* 1. watchful, wary, or cautious. 2. aware or conscious. [ME; OE *wær,* c. Icel. *varr,* Goth. *wars*] —*v.t.* 3. to beware of: *ware the dog!* [ME *waren,* OE *warian*]

ware[3] (wâr), *v.t.,* **wared, waring.** *Scot. and N. Eng.* to spend (money, time, care, etc.). [ME, t. Scand.; cf. Icel. *verja* spend, invest (also wrap), c. OE *werian* WEAR]

ware·house (*n.* wâr'hous'; *v.* wâr'houz', -hous'), *n., v.,* **-housed, -housing.** —*n.* 1. a storehouse for wares or goods. 2. *Chiefly Brit.* a wholesale store, or a large retail store. —*v.t.* 3. to deposit or store in a warehouse. 4. to place in a government or bonded warehouse, to be kept until duties are paid.

ware·house·man (wâr'hous'mən), *n., pl.* **-men.** 1. one who stores goods for others for pay; a bailee of goods placed in his custody, usually issuing a warehouse receipt which may be negotiable or nonnegotiable. 2. one who is employed in a warehouse.

warehouse receipt, a receipt for goods placed in a warehouse, either negotiable or nonnegotiable.

ware·room (wâr'room', -rŏŏm'), *n.* a room in which goods are stored or are displayed for sale.

war·fare (wôr'fâr'), *n.* operations against an enemy; the making of war; war.

war game, *Mil.* a training exercise that imitates war, in which commanders, staffs, and assistants perform war duties, but no troops are used.

war·head (wôr'hĕd'), *n.* the forward, explosive-containing section of a self-propelled missile, bomb, torpedo, etc.

war horse, 1. a horse used in war; a charger. 2. *Colloq.* a person who has taken part in many conflicts, controversies, etc.

war·i·ly (wâr'ə·lĭ), *adv.* in a wary manner.

war·i·ness (wâr'ĭ·nĭs), *n.* quality of being wary.

war·i·son (wăr'ə·sən), *n.* (erroneously) a note sounded as a signal for assault. [ME, t. OF: protection. Cf. GARRISON]

wark (wärk), *n., v.i. Eng. Dial.* and *Scot.* pain; ache. [var. of WORK]

war·like (wôr'līk'), *adj.* 1. fit, qualified, or ready for war; martial: *warlike fleet, warlike tribes.* 2. threatening or betokening war: *a warlike tone.* 3. of or pertaining to war: *a warlike expedition, warlike deeds.* —**war'like·ness,** *n.* —Syn. 2. bellicose, belligerent, hostile.

ăct, āble, dâre, ärt; ĕbb, ēqual; ĭf, īce; hŏt, ōver, ôrder, oil, bŏŏk, ōoze, out; ŭp, ūse, ûrge; ə = a in alone; ch, chief; g, give; ng, ring; sh, shoe; th, thin; t͟h, that; zh, vision. See the full key on inside cover.

war·lock (wôr′lŏk′), *n.* *Scot. and Archaic.* **1.** one who practices magic arts by the aid of the devil; a sorcerer or wizard. **2.** a fortuneteller, conjurer, or the like. [ME *warloghe*, OE *wǣrloga* oathbreaker, devil]

warm (wôrm), *adj.* **1.** having or communicating a moderate degree of sensible heat. **2.** of or at a moderately high temperature; characterized by comparatively high temperature: *a warm climate.* **3.** having a sensation of bodily heat: *to be warm from fast walking.* **4.** producing such a sensation: *warm clothes.* **5.** (of color, effects of color, etc.) suggestive of warmth; inclining toward red or orange, as yellow (rather than toward green or blue). **6.** characterized by or showing lively feelings, passions, emotions, sympathies, etc.: *a warm heart, warm interest.* **7.** strongly attached, or intimate: *warm friends.* **8.** cordial or hearty: *a warm welcome.* **9.** heated, irritated, or angry: *to become warm when contradicted.* **10.** animated, lively, brisk, or vigorous: *a warm debate.* **11.** strong or fresh: *a warm scent.* **12.** *Colloq.* relatively close to something sought, as in a game. **13.** *Colloq.* uncomfortable or unpleasant. **14.** *Colloq.* well off; in easy circumstances. —*v.t.* **15.** to make warm; heat (often fol. by *up*): *to warm, or warm up, a room.* **16.** to excite ardor, enthusiasm, or animation in. **17.** to inspire with kindly feeling; affect with lively pleasure: *it warms my soul.* —*v.i.* **18.** to become warm (often fol. by *up*). **19.** to become ardent, enthusiastic, animated, etc. (often fol. by *up* or *to*). **20.** to grow kindly, friendly, or sympathetically disposed (often fol. by *to, toward,* or *towards*): *my heart warms towards him.* **21.** to prepare for play by practice and calisthenics (fol. by *up*). —*n.* **22.** *Colloq.* a warming or heating: *sit at the fire and have a warm.* [ME; OE *wearm,* c. D, G *warm*] —**warm′er,** *n.* —**warm′ish,** *adj.* —**warm′ly,** *adv.* —**warm′ness,** *n.* —**Syn. 1.** lukewarm, tepid, heated. **6.** hearty, enthusiastic, zealous, fervent, fervid.

warm-blood·ed (wôrm′blŭd′ĭd), *adj.* **1.** denoting or pertaining to animals, as mammals and birds, whose blood ranges in temperature from about 98° to 112° F., and remains relatively constant, irrespective of the temperature of the surrounding medium. **2.** ardent, impetuous, or passionate: *young and warm-blooded valor.*

warm front, *Meteorol.* **1.** the contact surface between two air masses where the warmer mass is advancing against and over the cooler mass. **2.** the line of intersection of this surface with the surface of the earth.

warm-heart·ed (wôrm′här′tĭd), *adj.* having or showing sympathy, cordiality, etc. —**warm′-heart′ed·ly,** *adv.* —**warm′-heart′ed·ness,** *n.*

warming pan, a long-handled, covered, flat vessel, as of brass, for holding hot coals or the like, formerly in common use for warming beds before they were to be occupied.

war·mon·ger (wôr′mŭng′gŏr), *n.* one who advocates war or seeks to bring it about.

warm sector, *Meteorol.* the region bounded by the cold and warm fronts of a cyclone.

Warm Springs, a city in W Georgia: site of foundation for treatment of poliomyelitis. 557 (1950).

warmth (wôrmth), *n.* **1.** state of being warm; moderate or gentle heat. **2.** the sensation of moderate heat. **3.** liveliness of feelings, emotions, or sympathies; ardor or fervor; enthusiasm or zeal. **4.** slight irritation: *his denial betrayed some warmth.*

warn (wôrn), *v.t.* **1.** to give notice or intimation to (a person, etc.) of danger, impending evil, possible harm, or anything unfavorable: *to warn a person of a plot against him, warned that he was in danger.* **2.** to urge or advise to be on one's guard; caution: *to warn a foolhardy person.* **3.** to admonish or exhort as to action or conduct: *to warn a person to be on time.* **4.** to notify, apprise, or inform: *to warn a person of an intended visit.* **5.** to give notice to (a person, etc.) to go, stay, or keep (away, off, etc.): *to warn trespassers off private grounds.* **6.** to give authoritative or formal notice to, order, or summon: *to warn a person to appear in court.* [ME; OE *warnian,* c. G *warnen.* Cf. WARE²] —**warn′er,** *n.* —**Syn. 1.** WARN, CAUTION, ADMONISH imply attempting to prevent another from running into danger or getting into unpleasant or undesirable circumstances. To WARN is to speak plainly and usually in strong terms: *to warn him about danger and possible penalties.* To CAUTION is to advise about necessary precautions, to put one on his guard about or against some circumstance or condition, (usually less serious): *caution him against trying to go,* thus emphasizing avoidance of penalties. ADMONISH suggests giving earnest, authoritative advice, exhortation, with only tacit references to danger or penalty: *to admonish one for neglecting duties.*

War·ner (wôr′nŏr), *n.* **Charles Dudley,** 1829–1900, U.S. editor and author.

warn·ing (wôr′nĭng), *n.* **1.** act of warning, giving notice, or cautioning. **2.** something serving to warn, give notice, or caution. —*adj.* **3.** that warns. —**warn′ing·ly,** *adv.* —**Syn. 2.** caution, admonition, advice.

war nose, a device in the front end of a projectile, as a torpedo, for detonating the explosive charge.

War of American Independence, *Brit.* American Revolution.

War of 1812, a war between the United States and Great Britain, 1812–15.

War of Independence, *Amer. Hist.* the American Revolution.

War of Secession, *Amer. Hist.* the Civil War.

War of the Nations, World War (def. 1).

War of the Spanish Succession, a war (1701–1714) fought by Austria, England, the Netherlands, and Prussia, against France and Spain, arising out of disputes about the succession in Spain after the death of Charles II of Spain.

warp (wôrp), *v.t.* **1.** to bend or twist out of shape, esp. from a straight or flat form, as timbers, flooring, etc. **2.** to bend or turn from the natural or true direction or course. **3.** to distort from the truth, fact, true meaning, etc.; bias or pervert: *prejudice warps the mind, warped in his political principles.* **4.** *Aeron.* to bend (a wing, plane, or airfoil) at the end or ends, to promote equilibrium or to secure lateral control. **5.** *Naut.* to move (a ship, etc.) into some desired place or position by hauling on a rope or warp which has been fastened to something fixed, as a buoy, anchor, or the like. **6.** *Agric.* to treat (land) by inundation with water that deposits alluvial warp. —*v.i.* **7.** to become bent or twisted out of shape, esp. out of a straight or flat form: *the wood has warped in drying.* **8.** to turn or change from the natural or proper course, state, etc. **9.** *Naut.* **a.** to warp a ship or the like along. **b.** to move by being warped, as a ship. [ME *werpe,* OE *weorpan* throw, c. D *werpen,* G *werfen*] —*n.* **10.** a bend or twist in something, as in wood that has dried unevenly. **11.** a mental twist or bias. **12.** yarns placed lengthwise in the loom, across the weft or woof, and interlaced. See diag. under **weave.** **13.** *Naut.* a rope for warping or hauling a ship or the like along or into a position. **14.** alluvial matter deposited by water, esp. water let in to inundate low land so as to enrich it. [ME *warpe,* OE *wearp,* c. G *warf*] —**warp′er,** *n.* —**Syn. 1.** turn, contort, distort.

war paint, **1.** paint applied to the face and body by savages upon going to war. **2.** *Colloq.* full dress; finery.

war·path (wôr′păth′, -päth′), *n.* **1.** the path or course taken by American Indians on a warlike expedition. **2. on the warpath. a.** engaging in, seeking, or preparing for war. **b.** in state of wrath; bellicose.

warp knit, a fabric or garment so constructed that runs do not occur.

war·plane (wôr′plān′), *n.* an airplane for warfare.

war·rant (wôr′ənt, wŏr′-), *n.* **1.** authorization, sanction, or justification. **2.** that which serves to give reliable or formal assurance of something; a guarantee. **3.** something having the force of a guarantee or positive assurance of a thing: *the cavalry and artillery were reckoned sure warrants of success.* **4.** a writing or document certifying or authorizing something, as a certificate, receipt, license, or commission. **5.** *Law.* an instrument, issued by a magistrate, authorizing an officer to make an arrest, seize property, make a search, or carry a judgment into execution. **6.** (in the army and navy) the certificate of authority or appointment issued to an officer below the rank of a commissioned officer. **7.** a warehouse receipt. **8.** a writing authorizing the payment or receipt of money: *a treasury warrant.* —*v.t.* **9.** to give authority to; authorize. **10.** to afford warrant or sanction for, or justify: *the circumstances warrant such measures.* **11.** to give one's word for; vouch for (often used with a clause in mere emphatic assertion): *I'll warrant he did!* **12.** to give a formal assurance, or a guarantee or promise, to or for; guarantee: *I warrant you honorable treatment, to warrant payment or safe delivery.* **13.** to guarantee the quantity, quality, and other representations made to a purchaser of goods. **14.** to guarantee or secure title to (the purchaser of goods); assure indemnification against loss to. **15.** *Law.* to guarantee title of an estate or other granted property (to a grantee). [ME *warant,* t. OF. var. of *guarant* defender, t. Gmc.; cf. MHG *warend* warranty] —**war′rant·a·ble,** *adj.* —**war′rant·a·bly,** *adv.* —**Syn. 12.** WARRANT, GUARANTEE are etymologically the same and frequently interchangeable to indicate pledging that something is safe or genuine. To WARRANT is to give such a pledge: *to warrant the soundness of a horse, warranted silverware.* To GUARANTEE is to make something sure or certain by binding oneself to replace it or refund its price if it is not as represented: *to guarantee a watch.*

war·ran·tee (wôr′ən tē′, wŏr′-), *n.* *Law.* one to whom a warranty is made.

war·rant·er (wôr′ən tər, wŏr′-), *n.* one who warrants.

warrant officer, **1.** (in the U.S. Armed Forces) an officer of one of four grades ranking above enlisted men and below commissioned officers. **2.** a similar officer in other countries.

war·ran·tor (wôr′ən tôr′, wŏr′-), *n.* *Law.* one who warrants, or makes a warranty.

war·ran·ty (wôr′ən tĭ, wŏr′-), *n.,* *pl.* **-ties. 1.** act of warranting; warrant; assurance. **2.** *Law.* **a.** an engagement, express or implied, in assurance of some particular in connection with a contract, as of sale: *an express warranty of the quality of goods.* **b.** a covenant in a deed to land by which the party conveying assures the grantee that he will enjoy the premises free from interference by any person claiming under a superior title. A **warranty deed** is a deed containing such a covenant, as distinguished from a *quitclaim* deed, which conveys without any assurances only such title as the grantor may have. **c.** (in the law of insurance) a statement or promise, made by the party insured, and included as an essential part of the contract, falsity or nonfulfillment of which renders the policy void. **d.** a judicial document, as a warrant or writ. [ME *warantie,* t. OF. Cf. GUARANTEE, WARRANT]

war·ren (wôr′ən, wor′ən), *n.* **1.** a place where rabbits breed or abound. **2.** a building or buildings containing many tenants in limited quarters. [ME, t. AF: m. *warenne* game park; akin to GUARD, WARD]

War·ren (wôr′ən, wor′-), *n.* **1.** a city in NE Ohio, N of Youngstown. 59,648 (1960). **2. Earl,** born 1891, chief justice of the U.S. Supreme Court since 1953. **3. Robert Penn,** born 1905, U.S. author.

war·ren·er (wôr′ənər, wor′-), *n.* the keeper of a warren (def. 1).

War·ring·ton (wôr′Ing tən, wor′-), *n.* a city in W England, on the Mersey river. 79,620 (est. 1956).

war·ri·or (wôr′Iər, wor′-, -yər), *n.* a man engaged or experienced in warfare; soldier. [ME *werreour*, t. ONF: m. *werreieor*. See WAR] —**war′ri·or·like′,** *adj.*

war risk insurance, government insurance for members of the armed forces.

war·saw (wôr′sô), *n.* **1.** a jewfish, *Promicrops itaiara,* of both coasts of tropical America. **2.** a large grouper, *Epinephelus nigrita,* of the southern Atlantic and Gulf coasts of the U.S., etc. [t. Sp.: alter. of *guasa*]

War·saw (wôr′sô), *n.* the capital of Poland, in the E central part, on the Vistula river. 950,000 (est. 1954). Polish, **War·sza·wa** (vär shä′vä).

war·ship (wôr′shIp), *n.* a ship built or armed for combat purposes.

war·sle (wär′səl), *v.i., v.t.,* **-sled, -sling,** *n. Dial.* wrestle. Also, **war′stle.**

Wars of the Roses, *Hist.* See **rose** (def. 9c).

wart (wôrt), *n.* **1.** a small, usually hard, abnormal elevation on the skin, caused by a filterable virus. **2.** a small protuberance. [ME; OE *wearte,* c. G *warze*] —**wart′like′,** *adj.*

War·ta (vär′tä), *n.* a river flowing through W Poland into the Oder. 445 mi. German, **War·the** (vär′tə).

Wart·burg (värt′bŏŏrкн), *n.* a castle in East Germany, in Thuringia, near Eisenach: Luther translated the New Testament here, 1521–22.

wart hog, an African wild swine, *Phacochoerus aethiopicus,* having large tusks, and warty excrescences on the face.

war·time (wôr′tIm), *n.* **1.** a time or season of war. —*adj.* **2.** of or occurring during war: *wartime conferences.*

wart·y (wôr′tY), *adj.,* **wartier, wartiest. 1.** having warts; covered with or as with warts. **2.** like a wart.

Wart hog,
Phacochoerus aethiopicus
(2½ ft. high at the shoulder,
total length ab. 5½ ft.)

war whoop, a yell uttered by American Indians, or others, in attacking, etc.

War·wick (wôr′Ik, wor′- *for 1, 3;* wôr′wYk *for 2*). **1. Richard Neville, Earl of,** (*"the Kingmaker"*) 1428–1471, English soldier and statesman. **2.** a city in E Rhode Island. 68,504 (1960). **3.** a town in central England: castle. 15,350 (1951).

War·wick·shire (wôr′Ik shYr′, -shər, wor′-), *n.* a county in central England. 1,861,670 pop. (1951); 983 sq. mi. *Co. seat:* Warwick. Also, **Warwick.**

war·y (wâr′Y), *adj.,* **warier, wariest. 1.** watchful, or on one's guard, esp. habitually; on the alert; cautious; careful. **2.** characterized by caution: *wary walking.* [f. WARE², adj. + -Y¹] —**war′i·ly,** *adv.* —**war′i·ness,** *n.* —**Syn. 1.** alert, vigilant, circumspect. See **careful.**

was (wŏz, wŭz; *unstressed* wəz), *v.* first and third pers. sing., pt. indicative of **be.** [ME; OE *wæs,* c. G *war*]

Wa·satch Range (wô′säch), a mountain range in N Utah and SE Idaho. Highest peak, Mt. Timpanogos, 12,008 ft.

wash (wŏsh, wôsh), *v.t.* **1.** to apply a liquid, esp. water, to for the purpose of cleansing; cleanse by dipping, rubbing, or scrubbing in water, etc. **2.** to remove (dirt, stains, paint, or any matter) by or as by the action of water, or as water does (fol. by *out, off,* etc.). **3.** to free from ceremonial defilement, or from sin, guilt, etc. **4.** to wet with water or other liquid, or as water does: *the rose wash'd with morning dew.* **5.** to flow over or against: *a shore or cliff washed by waves.* **6.** to carry or bring (along, up, down, etc.) with water or any liquid, or as the water or liquid does. **7.** to wear, as water does by flowing over or against a surface (often fol. by *out* or *away*). **8.** to form (a channel, etc.), as flowing water does. **9.** *Mining, etc.* **a.** to subject (earth, etc.) to the action of water in order to separate valuable material. **b.** to separate (valuable material, as gold) thus. **10.** to purify (a gas or gaseous mixture) by passage through or over a liquid. **11.** to cover with a watery or thin coat of color. **12.** to overlay with a thin coat or deposit of metal: *to wash brass with gold.* —*v.i.* **13.** to wash oneself: *time to wash for supper.* **14.** to wash clothes. **15.** to cleanse anything with or in water or the like. **16.** to undergo washing, esp. without injury. **17.** *Chiefly Brit. Colloq.* to stand being put to the proof: *his patriotism will not wash.* **18.** to be carried or driven (along, ashore, etc.) by water. **19.** to flow or beat with a lapping sound, as waves on a shore. **20.** to move along in or as in waves, or with a rushing movement, as water. **21.** to be eroded, as by a stream, rainfall, etc.: *a hillside that washes frequently.* **22.** to be worn by the action of water, as a hill (often fol. by *away*). —*n.* **23.** act of washing with water or other liquid. **24.** a quantity of clothes, etc., washed, or to be washed, at one time. **25.** a liquid with which something is washed, wetted, colored, overspread, etc. **26.** the flow, sweep, dash, or breaking of water. **27.** the sound made by this: *listening to the wash of the Atlantic.* **28.** water moving along in waves or with a rushing movement. **29.** the rough or broken water left behind a moving ship, etc. **30.** *Aeron.* the disturbance in the air left behind by a moving airplane or any of its parts. **31.** any of various liquids for toilet purposes: *a hair wash.* **32.** a medicinal lotion. **33.** earth, etc., from which gold or the like can be extracted by washing. **34.** the wearing away of the shore by breaking waves. **35.** a tract of land washed by the action of the sea or a river, and sometimes overflowed and sometimes left dry. **36.** a fen, marsh, or a bog. **37.** a small stream or shallow pool. **38.** a shallow arm of the sea or a shallow part of a river. **39.** a depression or channel formed by flowing water. **40.** alluvial matter transferred and deposited by flowing water. **41.** *Western U.S.* the dry bed of an intermittent stream; dry wash. **42.** a broad, thin layer of color applied by a continuous movement of the brush, as in water-color painting. **43.** a thin coat of metal applied in liquid form. **44.** waste liquid matter, refuse food, etc., from the kitchen, as for hogs; hogwash. **45.** washy or weak liquor or liquid food. **46.** the fermented wort from which the spirit is extracted in distilling. —*adj.* **47.** capable of being washed without injury; washable: *a wash dress.* [ME; OE *wascan,* c. D *wasschen,* G *waschen,* Icel. *vaska*] —**Syn. 1.** clean, lave, rinse, launder, scrub, mop, swab.

Wash (wŏsh, wôsh), *n.* **The,** a shallow bay of the North Sea, on the E coast of England. ab. 22 mi. long; ab. 15 mi. wide.

Wash., Washington.

wash·a·ble (wŏsh′ə bəl, wôsh′-), *adj.* capable of being washed, esp. without injury: *a washable fabric.*

wash·board (wŏsh′bôrd′, wôsh′-), *n.* **1.** a board or frame with a corrugated metallic or other surface, on which clothes are rubbed in the process of washing. **2.** a baseboard around the walls of a room. **3.** *Naut.* **a.** a thin broad plank fastened to and projecting above the gunwhale or side of a boat to keep out the spray and sea. **b.** a similar board on the sill of a port.

wash·bowl (wŏsh′bōl′, wôsh′-), *n.* a bowl or basin for use in washing the person. Also, *esp. Brit.,* **wash·ba·sin** (wŏsh′bā′sən, wôsh′-).

wash·cloth (wŏsh′klôth′, -klŏth′, wôsh′-), *n.* a small cloth for washing the body.

wash·day (wŏsh′dā′, wôsh′-), *n.* the day set apart in a household for washing clothes.

washed-out (wŏsht′out′, wôsht′-), *adj.* **1.** faded, esp. during washing. **2.** *Colloq.* utterly fatigued; exhausted.

washed-up (wŏsht′ŭp′, wôsht′-), *adj.* **1.** *Colloq.* utterly fatigued. **2.** *Slang.* having failed, esp. abjectly.

wash·er (wŏsh′ər, wôsh′-), *n.* **1.** one who or that which washes. **2.** a machine or apparatus for washing something. **3.** a flat ring or perforated piece of leather, rubber, metal, etc., used to give tightness to a joint, to prevent leakage, and to distribute pressure (as under the head of a bolt, under a nut, etc.).

wash·er·man (wŏsh′ər mən, wôsh′-), *n., pl.* **-men.** a man who washes clothes, etc. for hire.

wash·er·wom·an (wŏsh′ər wŏŏm′ən, wôsh′-), *n., pl.* **-women.** a woman who washes clothes, etc. for hire.

wash goods, textiles not faded or weakened by washing.

wash·ing (wŏsh′Ing, wôsh′-), *n.* **1.** act of one who or that which washes; ablution. **2.** clothes, etc., washed or to be washed, esp. those washed at one time. **3.** (*sing. or pl.*) liquid that has been used to wash something. **4.** matter removed in washing something. **5.** material, as gold dust, obtained by washing earth, etc. **6.** a placer or other superficial deposit so washed. **7.** a thin coating or covering applied in liquid form.

washing machine, an apparatus for washing clothing or other material.

washing soda, crystalline sodium carbonate, or sal soda, used as a cleansing agent.

Wash·ing·ton (wŏsh′Ing tən, wôsh′-), *n.* **1. Booker Taliaferro** (bŏŏk′ər tŏl′ə vər), 1856–1915, U.S. Negro writer and educator. **2. George,** 1732–99, American general and 1st president of U.S. 1789–97. **3. Mrs.,** (*Martha Dandridge, Mrs. Custis*) 1732–1802, wife of George. **4.** the capital of the United States, on the Potomac between Maryland and Virginia: coextensive with the District of Columbia. 763,956 (1960). **5.** a State in the NW United States, on the Pacific coast. 2,853,214 pop. (1960); 68,192 sq. mi. *Cap.:* Olympia. *Abbr.:* Wash. **6.** a city in SW Pennsylvania. 23,545 (1960). **7. Mount,** a peak of the White Mountains, in N New Hampshire: the highest peak in the NE United States. 6293 ft. **8. Lake,** a lake in W Washington, near Seattle. 20 mi. long.

Wash·ing·to·ni·an (wŏsh′Ing tō′nY ən, wôsh′-), *adj.* **1.** of Washington (D.C. or State). —*n.* **2.** a native or inhabitant of Washington (D.C. or State).

Washington palm, either of the fan palms, *Washingtonia filifera* and *W. gracilis* (*robusta*), native in southern California and adjoining regions.

Washington pie, a layer cake with a cream, chocolate, jelly, or other filling.

Wash·i·ta (wŏsh′ə tô′, wôsh′-), *n.* Ouachita.

wash·out (wŏsh′out′, wôsh′-), *n.* **1.** a washing out of earth, etc., by water, as from an embankment or a roadway by heavy rain or a freshet. **2.** the hole or break produced. **3.** *Slang.* a failure or fiasco.

wash·rag (wŏsh′răg′, wôsh′-), *n.* washcloth.

wash·room (wŏsh′rŏŏm′, -rŏŏm′, wôsh′-), *n.* a room having washstands and other toilet facilities.

wash sale, an illegal and fictitious sale on the stock exchange, effected by simultaneous purchases and sales, designed to give the appearance of market activity.

wash·stand (wŏsh′stănd′, wôsh′-), *n.* **1.** a piece of furniture for holding a basin, a pitcher, etc., for use in washing the person. **2.** a stationary fixture having faucets with running water, for the same purpose.

wash·tub (wŏsh′tŭb′, wôsh′-), *n.* a tub for use in washing something, esp. clothes, etc. Also, *Brit.*, **washing tub.**

wash·wom·an (wŏsh′wŏŏm′ən, wôsh′-), *n.*, *pl.* **-wom·en.** washerwoman.

wash·y (wŏsh′ĭ, wôsh′ĭ), *adj.*, **washier, washiest.** **1.** too much diluted; weak: *washy coffee.* **2.** weak, thin, or poor, as if from excessive dilution: *washy coloring.*

was·n't (wŏz′nt, wŭz′nt), contraction of *was not.*

wasp (wŏsp), *n.* **1.** any of numerous hymenopterous, stinging insects, included for the most part in two superfamilies, *Sphecoidea* and *Vespoidea.* Their habits vary from a solitary life to colonial organization. **2.** a waspish person. [ME *waspe,* OE *wæsp,* akin to D *wesp,* G *wespe,* L *vespa*] **—wasp′like′, wasp′y,** *adj.*

Solitary wasp. *Eumenes fraternus* (⅓ in. long)

wasp·ish (wŏs′pĭsh), *adj.* **1.** like or suggesting a wasp. **2.** quick to resent a trifling affront or injury; snappish. **3.** showing irascibility or petulance: *waspish writing.* **4.** having a slender waist, like a wasp. **—wasp′ish·ly,** *adv.* **—wasp′ish·ness,** *n.*

wasp waist, a slender, or tightly laced, waist. **—wasp′-waist′ed,** *adj.*

was·sail (wŏs′əl, wăs′-), *n.* **1.** a salutation wishing health to a person, used in England in early times when presenting a cup of drink or when drinking to the person. **2.** a festivity or revel with drinking of healths. **3.** liquor for drinking healths on festive occasions, esp. spiced ale, as on Christmas Eve and Twelfth-night. **4.** *Obs.* or *Prov. Eng.* a song sung in wassailing. **—v.i. 5.** to drink healths; revel with drinking. **—v.t. 6.** to drink to the health or success of. [early ME *wes hail,* t. Scand.; cf. early Icel. *ves heill,* c. OE *wes hāl* be hale or whole] **—was′sail·er,** *n.*

Was·ser·mann (väs′ər män′), *n.* **1. August von** (ou′gŏōst fən), 1866–1925, German physician and bacteriologist. **2. Jakob** (yä′kôp), 1873–1934, German novelist.

Was·ser·mann reaction (wäs′ər mən; *Ger.* väs′ər män′), a diagnostic test for syphilis using the fixation of a complement by the serum of a syphilitic individual. Also, **Wassermann test.** [named after A. von *Wassermann,* German bacteriologist]

wast (wŏst), *unstressed* wəst), *v.* 2nd pers. sing. pt. indic. of *be* (now only in solemn or poetic use).

wast·age (wās′tĭj), *n.* loss by use, wear, decay, etc.

waste (wāst), *v.*, **wasted, wasting,** *n.*, *adj.* **—v.t. 1.** to consume, spend, or employ uselessly or without adequate return; use to no avail; squander: *to waste money, time, efforts, or words.* **2.** to fail or neglect to use, or let go to waste: *to waste an opportunity.* **3.** to destroy or consume gradually, or wear away. **4.** to wear down or reduce in bodily substance, health, or strength; emaciate; enfeeble: *to be wasted by disease or hunger.* **5.** to lay waste, devastate, or ruin: *a country wasted with fire and sword.* **—v.i. 6.** to go to waste, as something not put to use. **7.** to become gradually consumed, used up, or worn away: *a candle wastes in burning.* **8.** to become physically wasted, lose flesh or strength, or become emaciated or enfeebled. **9.** to diminish gradually, or dwindle, as wealth, power, etc. **10.** to pass gradually, as time. **—n. 11.** useless consumption or expenditure, or use without adequate return: *waste of material, money, or time.* **12.** neglect, instead of use: *waste of opportunity.* **13.** gradual destruction, impairment, or decay: *the waste and repair of bodily tissue.* **14.** devastation or ruin, as from war, fire, etc. **15.** a region or place laid waste or in ruins. **16.** anything unused, unproductive, or not properly utilized. **17.** an uncultivated tract of land. **18.** a tract of wild land, desolate country, or desert. **19.** an empty, desolate, or dreary tract or extent: *a waste of snow.* **20.** anything left over or superfluous, as excess material, by-products, etc., not of use for the work in hand. **21.** remnants from the working of cotton, etc., used for wiping machinery, absorbing oil, etc. **22.** *Phys. Geog.* material derived by mechanical and chemical disintegration of rock, as the detritus transported by streams, etc. **—adj. 23.** not used or in use: *waste energy.* **24.** (of land, regions, etc.) uninhabited and wild, desolate and barren, or desert. **25.** (of regions, towns, etc.) in a state of desolation and ruin, as from devastation or decay. **26.** left over or superfluous: *to utilize waste products of manufacture.* **27.** having served a purpose and no longer of use. **28.** rejected as useless or worthless, or refuse: *waste paper.* **29.** *Physiol.* pertaining to material unused by or unusable to the organism. [ME, t. OF: m. *wast,* g. b. L *vastus* desert and OHG *wuosti* desert] **—Syn. 1.** misspend, dissipate, fritter away. **13.** diminution, decline, emaciation, consumption. **18.** See desert[1]. **20.** refuse, rubbish, trash.

waste·bas·ket (wāst′băs′kĭt, -bäs′-), *n.* a basket for wastepaper, or papers, scraps of paper, etc., to be disposed of as refuse. Also, **wastepaper basket.**

waste·ful (wāst′fəl), *adj.* **1.** given to or characterized by useless consumption or expenditure: *wasteful methods or living.* **2.** squandering, or grossly extravagant. **3.** devastating or destructive: *wasteful war.* **—waste′ful·ly,** *adv.* **—waste′ful·ness,** *n.*

Waste Land, The, a poem (1922) by T. S. Eliot.

waste·ness (wāst′nĭs), *n.* state of being waste or desolate.

waste·pa·per (wāst′pā′pər), *n.* paper thrown away as useless.

waste pipe, 1. a pipe for conveying away water, etc. **2.** *Plumbing.* a pipe carrying liquid wastes from all fixtures except water closets. Cf. **soil pipe.**

wast·er (wās′tər), *n.* **1.** one who or that which wastes. **2.** a spendthrift. **3.** *Chiefly Eng.* an idler or good-for-nothing.

wast·ing (wās′tĭng), *adj.* **1.** gradually reducing the fullness and strength of the body: *a wasting disease.* **2.** laying waste; devastating; despoiling.

wast·rel (wās′trəl), *n.* **1.** a wasteful person; spendthrift. **2.** *Chiefly Eng.* an idler, or good-for-nothing. [f. WASTE + -REL]

watch (wŏch), *v.i.* **1.** to be on the lookout, look attentively, or be closely observant, as to see what comes, is done, happens, etc.: *to watch while an experiment is performed.* **2.** to look or wait attentively and expectantly (fol. by *for*): *to watch for a signal, an opportunity.* **3.** to be careful or cautious (fol. by *out*). **4.** to keep awake, esp. for a purpose; keep a vigilant watch (*over*) as for protection or safekeeping. **5.** to keep vigil, as for devotional purposes. **6.** to keep guard. [ME *wacche,* OE *wæcca* (Northern), var. of *wacian* WAKE] **—v.t. 7.** to keep under attentive view or observation, as in order to see or learn something; view attentively or with interest: *to watch a play or a game.* **8.** to contemplate or regard mentally: *to watch his progress.* **9.** to look or wait attentively and expectantly for: *to watch one's chance or opportunity.* **10.** to watch over or guard for protection or safekeeping. **—n. 11.** close, constant observation for the purpose of seeing or discovering something. **12.** a lookout, as for something expected: *to be on the watch.* **13.** vigilant guard, as for protection, restraint, etc. **14.** a keeping awake for some special purpose: *a watch beside a sickbed.* **15.** a period of time for watching or keeping guard. **16.** *Naut.* **a.** a period of time (usually four hours) during which one part of a ship's crew is on duty, taking turns with another part. **b.** a certain part (usually a half) of the officers and crew of a vessel who together attend to working it for an allotted period of time. **17.** one of the periods (in Jewish use three or four) into which the night was anciently divided: *the fourth watch of the night.* **18.** something that measures and indicates the progress of time. **19.** a small, portable, timepiece with a spring-driven mechanism. **20.** a watchman, or a body of watchmen. [ME *wacche,* OE *wæcca* (North.), var. of *wacian* WAKE] **—watch′er,** *n.* **—Syn. 1.** WATCH, LOOK, SEE imply being aware of things around one by perceiving them through the eyes. To WATCH is to be a spectator, to look on or observe, or to fix the attention upon during passage of time: *to watch while a procession passes.* To LOOK is to direct the gaze with the intention of seeing, to use the eyesight with attention: *to look for violets in the spring, to look at articles displayed for sale.* To SEE is to perceive with the eyes, to obtain a visual impression, with or without fixing the attention: *animals able to see in the dark.*

watch·case (wŏch′kās′), *n.* the case or outer covering for the works of a watch.

watch·dog (wŏch′dôg′, -dŏg′), *n.* **1.** a dog kept to guard property. **2.** a watchful guardian.

watch fire, a fire maintained during the night as a signal and for a watching party.

watch·ful (wŏch′fəl), *adj.* **1.** vigilant or alert; closely observant. **2.** characterized by vigilance or alertness. **3.** *Archaic.* wakeful or sleepless. **—watch′ful·ly,** *adv.* **—watch′ful·ness,** *n.* **—Syn. 1.** attentive, heedful, careful, circumspect. See **alert.**

watch guard, a chain, cord, or ribbon for securing a watch when worn on the person.

watch·less (wŏch′lĭs), *adj.* **1.** that does not watch, or is not watched. **2.** having no watch.

watch·mak·er (wŏch′mā′kər), *n.* one whose occupation it is to make and repair watches. **—watch′mak′ing,** *n.*

watch·man (wŏch′mən), *n.*, *pl.* **-men.** **1.** one who keeps guard over a building at night, to protect it from fire or thieves. **2.** (formerly) one who guarded or patrolled the streets at night.

watch meeting, a religious meeting or service held at night, usually on the last night of the year, and terminated on the arrival of the new year.

watch night, 1. the last night of the year, observed in a watch meeting. 2. a watch meeting.

watch·tow·er (wŏch/tou/ər), *n.* a tower on which a sentinel watches for enemies, etc.

watch·word (wŏch/wûrd/), *n.* 1. a word or short phrase to be communicated, on challenge, to a sentinel or guard; a password; a countersign. 2. a word or phrase expressive of a principle or rule of action. 3. a rallying cry of a party, etc.; a slogan.

wa·ter (wô/tər, wŏt/ər), *n.* 1. the liquid which in a more or less impure state constitutes rain, oceans, lakes, rivers, etc., and which in a pure state is a transparent, odorless, tasteless liquid, a compound of hydrogen and oxygen, H_2O, freezing at 32° F. or 0° C., and boiling at 212° F. or 100° C. It contains 11.188 percent hydrogen and 88.812 percent oxygen, by weight. 2. a special form or variety of this liquid, as rain. 3. (*often pl.*) the liquid obtained from a mineral spring. 4. the water of a river, etc., with reference to its relative height, esp. as dependent on tide: *high or low water.* 5. that which enters a vessel through leaks: *the ship is making water.* 6. the surface of water: *above, below, or on the water.* 7. (*pl.*) flowing water, or water moving in waves: *the mighty waters rolling evermore.* 8. a liquid solution or preparation: *toilet water.* 9. any of various solutions of volatile or gaseous substances in water: *ammonia water.* 10. any liquid or aqueous organic secretion, exudation, humor, or the like, as tears, perspiration, the amniotic fluids, etc. 11. *Finance.* fictitious values behind shares of stock of a corporation (see def. 23). 12. a wavy, lustrous pattern or marking, as on silk fabrics, metal surfaces, etc. 13. the degree of transparency and brilliancy of a diamond or other precious stone. 14. **above water,** out of embarrassment or trouble, esp. of a financial nature. 15. **by water,** by ship or boat. 16. **like water,** abundantly; freely: *to spend money like water.* 17. **of the first water,** of the finest quality or rank: *a literary critic of the first water.*
—*v.t.* 18. to sprinkle, moisten, or drench with water: *to water a road or street.* 19. to supply (animals) with water for drinking. 20. to furnish with a supply of water, as a ship. 21. to furnish water to (a region, etc.), as by streams; supply (land, etc.) with water, as by irrigation. 22. to dilute or adulterate with water (often fol. by *down*): *to water soup.* 23. *Finance.* to issue (shares of stock) without receiving a corresponding amount of cash or property. 24. to produce a wavy lustrous pattern, marking, or finish on (fabrics, metals, etc.).
—*v.i.* 25. to discharge, fill with, or secrete water or liquid, as the eyes, or as the mouth at the sight or thought of tempting food. 26. to drink water, as an animal. 27. to take in a supply of water, as a ship: *our ship watered at Islip.*
—*adj.* 28. of or pertaining to water in any way. 29. holding water: *a water jug.* 30. worked or powered by, or treating, water: *a water wheel.* 31. used in or on water: *water wings.* 32. prepared with water for hardening, dilution, etc.: *water mortar.* 33. located or occurring on, in, or by water: *water music, water frontage.* 34. residing by or in, or ruling over, water: *water people, water deity.*
[ME; OE *wæter,* c. D *water,* G *wasser;* akin to Icel. *vatn,* Goth. *watō*] —**wa′ter·er,** *n.* —**wa′ter·less,** *adj.* —**wa′ter·like′,** *adj.*

wa·ter·age (wô/tər Yj, wŏt/ər-), *n. Eng.* 1. delivery of goods over water routes. 2. the cost of this.

water back, a reservoir, set of pipes, or the like, at the back of a stove or fireplace, providing a supply of hot water.

Water Bearer, Aquarius.

water beetle, any of the aquatic beetles of the family *Dytiscidae* (diving beetles) or *Hydrophilidae.*

Water beetle, *Notonecta undulata* (Ab. ¾ in. long)

water bird, an aquatic bird, or bird that frequents the water; a swimming or wading bird.

water biscuit, a crackerlike biscuit prepared from flour and water.

water blister, a blister which contains a clear, serous fluid, as distinguished from a blood blister in which the fluid is sanguineous.

wa·ter·borne (wô/tər-bôrn/, wŏt/ər-), *adj.* 1. supported by the water; carried by the water. 2. conveyed by ship or boat.

water bottle, *Chiefly Brit.* a canteen.

wa·ter·brain (wô/tər-brān/, wŏt/ər-), *n.* gid, in sheep.

water brash, *Pathol.* pyrosis.

wa·ter·buck (wô/tər-bŭk/, wŏt/ər-), *n., pl.* -**bucks,** (*esp. collectively*) -**buck.** any of various African antelopes of the genus *Kobus,* frequenting marshes and reedy places, esp.

Common waterbuck, *Kobus ellipsiprymnus* (4 to 4½ ft. high at the shoulder)

K. ellipsiprymnus, a large species of southern and central Africa. The males bear long, forward-curving ringed horns. [t. D: m. *waterbok*]

water buffalo, the common flat-horned buffalo, *Bubalus bubalus,* of the Old World tropics; water ox.

water bug, 1. any of various aquatic heteropterous insects, as the **giant water bugs** (*Belostomatidae*), or water scorpions (*Nepidae*). 2. a cockroach.

Wa·ter·bur·y (wô/tər-bĕr/Y), *n.* a city in W Connecticut. 107,130 (1960).

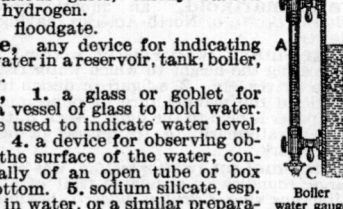

Water buffalo, *Bubalus bubalus* (5 to 6 ft. high at the shoulder)

water chestnut, 1. any of the aquatic plants constituting the genus *Trapa,* bearing an edible, nutlike fruit, esp. *T. natans,* a native of the Old World. 2. the fruit. Also, **water caltrop.**

water chinquapin, 1. an American water lily, *Nelumbium pentapetalum,* with an edible nutlike seed resembling that of the chinquapin. 2. the seed.

water clock, a device, as a clepsydra, for measuring time by the flow of water.

water closet, 1. a privy having some contrivance for carrying off the discharges through a waste pipe below by the agency of water. 2. the contrivance.

water color, *Painting.* 1. a pigment for which water and not oil is used as a vehicle. 2. the art or method of painting with such pigments. 3. a painting or design executed by this method. —**wa′ter·col/or,** *adj.*

wa·ter·cool (wô/tər-kool/, wŏt/ər-), *v.t.* to cool by means of water, esp. by water circulating in pipes or a jacket. —**wa′ter·cooled/,** *adj.*

water cooler, a vessel for holding drinking water which is cooled and drawn off for use by a faucet.

wa·ter·course (wô/tər-kôrs/, wŏt/ər-), *n.* 1. a stream of water, as a river or brook. 2. the bed of such a stream. 3. a natural channel conveying water. 4. a channel or canal made for the conveyance of water.

wa·ter·craft (wô/tər-kräft/, -kräft/, wŏt/ər-), *n.* 1. skill in boating and water sports. 2. any boat or ship. 3. boats and ships collectively.

water crake, 1. the spotted crake. 2. the Old World water ouzel (*Cinclus aquaticus*).

water cress, 1. a perennial cress, *Rorippa Nasturtium-aquaticum,* usually growing in clear, running water, and bearing pungent leaves. 2. the leaves, used for salads, soups, and as a garnish. —**wa′ter·cress/,** *adj.*

water cure, 1. hydropathy or hydrotherapy. 2. *Colloq.* torture by means of forcing water in great quantities into the victim's stomach.

water dog, 1. a dog accustomed to or delighting in the water, or trained to go into the water to retrieve game. 2. *Colloq.* a person who is at home on or in the water.

Wa·ter·ee (wô/tər-ē/), *n.* a river flowing from W North Carolina into South Carolina, where it joins the Congaree river to form the Santee river. Also, **Catawba** (in North Carolina).

wa·ter·fall (wô/tər-fôl/, wŏt/ər-), *n.* 1. a steep fall or flow of water from a height; a cascade. 2. a chignon.

wa·ter·find·er (wô/tər-fīn/dər, wŏt/ər-), *n.* one who uses a divining rod to discover water in the ground.

water flea, any of various small crustaceans which move about in the water like fleas, as *Daphnia.*

Wa·ter·ford (wô/tər-fərd), *n.* 1. a county in S Ireland, in Munster. 74,002 (prelim. 1956); 710 sq. mi. 2. its county seat: a seaport. 28,858 (prelim. 1956).

wa·ter·fowl (wô/tər-foul/, wŏt/ər-), *n.* 1. a water bird, esp. a swimming bird. 2. such birds collectively, esp. swimming game birds.

water front, 1. land abutting on a body of water. 2. a part of a city or town so abutting. 3. a vessel placed before a stove to heat water.

water gap, a transverse gap in a mountain ridge, cut by and giving passage to a stream.

water gas, a poisonous gas used for illuminating purposes, etc., made by passing steam over incandescent coal or other carbon fuel, and consisting of a mixture of various gases, chiefly carbon monoxide and hydrogen.

water gate, floodgate.

water gauge, any device for indicating the height of water in a reservoir, tank, boiler, or other vessel.

water glass, 1. a glass or goblet for drinking. 2. a vessel of glass to hold water. 3. a glass tube used to indicate water level, as in a boiler. 4. a device for observing objects beneath the surface of the water, consisting essentially of an open tube or box with a glass bottom. 5. sodium silicate, esp. a solution of it in water, or a similar preparation of potassium silicate, used to produce a transparent coating on objects in order to protect, preserve, or fireproof them; soluble glass; liquid glass. Also, **wa′ter·glass/.**

Boiler water gauge A. Water level; B. Upper cock; C. Lower cock

water gum, 1. (in the U.S.) a tupelo, *Nyssa sylvatica,* var. *biflora,* of the southern States. 2. (in Australia) any of several myrtaceous trees growing near water.

water hammer, the concussion which results when a moving volume of water in a pipe is suddenly arrested.

water hemlock, any of the poisonous plants constituting the umbelliferous genus *Cicuta,* as *C. virosa* of Europe, and *C. maculata* of North America, growing in swamps and marshy places.

water hen, 1. the moor hen or gallinule, *Gallinula chloropus,* of Europe. **2.** the coot, *Fulica americana.*

water ice, 1. ice formed by direct freezing of fresh or salt water, and not by compacting of snow. **2.** *Chiefly Brit.* sherbet.

wa·ter-inch (wô′tər ỹnch′, wŏt′ər-), *n. Hydraulics.* the quantity of water (very nearly 500 cubic feet) discharged in 24 hours through a circular opening of 1 inch diameter leading from a reservoir in which the water is constantly only high enough to cover the orifice.

wa·ter·i·ness (wô′tər ĭ nĭs, wŏt′ər-), *n.* watery state.

wa·ter·ing (wô′tər ĭng, wŏt′ər-), *n.* **1.** act of one who or that which waters. **2.** a watered appearance on silk, etc. —*adj.* **3.** that waters. **4.** pertaining to medicinal springs or a sea-bathing resort.

watering place, 1. *Chiefly Brit.* a place of resort for its mineral waters; a spa. **2.** *Chiefly Brit.* a resort by the sea or other body of water for bathing, boating, etc. **3.** a place where water may be obtained.

watering pot, a vessel, esp. with a spout having a perforated nozzle, for watering or sprinkling plants, etc.

wa·ter·ish (wô′tər ĭsh, wŏt′ər-), *adj.* watery.

water jacket, a casing or compartment containing water, placed about something to keep it cool or otherwise regulate its temperature, as around the cylinder or cylinders of an internal-combustion engine.

wa·ter-jack·et (wô′tər jăk′ĭt, wŏt′ər-), *v.t.* to surround or fit with a water jacket.

water jump, any small body of water which a horse must jump over, as in a steeplechase.

water level, 1. the surface level of any body of water. **2.** *Naut.* water line.

water lily, 1. any of the aquatic plants constituting the genus *Nymphaea (Castalia)* family *Nymphaeaceae),* the species of which have large, disklike, floating leaves and showy, fragrant flowers, esp. *N. odorata* of America or *N. alba* of Europe. **2.** any plant of the genus *Nuphar* of the same family (**yellow water lily** or **yellow pond lily**). **3.** a nymphaeaceous plant. **4.** the flower of any such plant.

American water lily,
Nymphaea odorata

water line, 1. *Naut.* **a.** that part of the outside of the hull of a ship that is just at the water level. **b.** any of several lines marked on the hull of a ship, showing the depth to which it sinks when unloaded and when partially or fully loaded. **2.** water level. **3.** the line in which water at its surface borders upon a floating body. Also, **wa′ter·line′.**

wa·ter-logged (wô′tər lôgd′, -lŏgd′, wŏt′ər-), *adj.* **1.** so filled with water, by leakage or overflow, as to be heavy or unmanageable, as a ship, etc. **2.** excessively saturated with water: *waterlogged ground.*

Wa·ter·loo (wô′tər lōō′, wô′tər lōō′; *for 1 also Flem.* vä′tər lō′), *n.* **1. a.** a village in central Belgium, S of Brussels: scene of Napoleon's decisive defeat, June 18, 1815. **2.** a decisive or crushing defeat. **3.** a city in E Iowa. 71,755 (1960).

water main, a main or principal pipe or conduit in a system for conveying water.

wa·ter·man (wô′tər mən, wŏt′ər-), *n., pl.* **-men. 1.** a man who manages, or works on, a boat; boatman. **2.** a person with reference to his skill in rowing, etc.: *a good waterman.*

wa·ter·man·ship (wô′tər mən shĭp′, wŏt′ər-), *n.* **1.** the function of a waterman. **2.** skill in rowing, etc.

water marigold, an aquatic composite plant, *Bidens Beckii,* of North America, having golden-yellow flowers.

wa·ter·mark (wô′tər märk′, wŏt′ər-), *n.* **1.** a mark indicating the height to which water rises or has risen, as in a river, etc. **2.** a figure or design impressed in the fabric in the manufacture of paper and visible when the paper is held to the light. —*v.t.* **3.** to mark (paper) with a watermark. **4.** to impress (a design, etc.) as a watermark.

wa·ter·mel·on (wô′tər mĕl′ən, wŏt′ər-), *n.* **1.** the large, roundish or elongated fruit of a trailing cucurbitaceous vine, *Citrullus vulgaris,* having a hard, green rind and a (usually) pink or red pulp which abounds in a sweetish, watery juice. **2.** the plant or vine.

water meter, a device for measuring and registering the quantity of water that passes through a pipe, etc.

water milfoil, any of various aquatic plants, chiefly of the genus *Myriophyllum,* the submersed leaves of which are very finely divided.

water mill, a mill with machinery driven by water.

water moccasin, 1. the venomous moccasin, *Ancistrodon piscivorus.* **2.** any of various similar, but harmless, water snakes, usually thought to be venomous.

water motor, any form of prime mover, or motor, that is operated by the kinetic energy, pressure, or weight of water, esp. a small turbine or water wheel fitted to a pipe supplying water.

water nymph, 1. a nymph of the water, as a naiad, a Nereid, or an Oceanid. **2.** a water lily. **3.** any of the aquatic plants constituting the genus *Naias.*

water oak, 1. an oak, *Quercus nigra,* of the southern U.S., growing chiefly along streams and swamps. **2.** any of several other American oaks.

water of crystallization, *Chem.* water of hydration: formerly thought necessary to crystallization, but now usually regarded as affecting crystallization only as it forms new molecular combinations.

water of hydration, *Chem.* that portion of a hydrate which is represented as, or can be driven off as, water: now usually regarded as being in true molecular combination with the other atoms of the compound, and not existing in the compound as water.

water ou·zel (ōō′zəl), any of several plump, thick-plumaged, aquatic birds of the family *Cinclidae,* allied to the thrushes, esp. *Cinclus aquaticus* of Europe, and *C. mexicanus* of western North America, having the habit of jerking the body or "dipping" as they perch, walk, etc.; a dipper.

water ox, water buffalo.

water parting, a watershed or divide.

water pepper, any of various plants of the polygonaceous genus *Polygonum,* growing in wet places, esp. the smartweed, *P. Hydropiper.*

water pimpernel, 1. the brookweed. **2.** the ordinary pimpernel, *Anagallis arvensis.*

water pipit, pipit.

water plantain, any of the aquatic herbs of the genus *Alisma,* esp. *A. Plantago-aquatica,* a species growing in shallow water and having leaves suggesting those of the common plantain (*Plantago*).

water polo, a water game played by two teams, each having six swimmers, with a semi-inflated ball, in which the object is to carry or pass the ball over the goal line.

water power, 1. the power of water used, or capable of being used, to drive machinery, etc. **2.** a fall or descent in a stream, capable of being so used. **3.** a water right possessed by a mill.

water pox, *Pathol.* chicken pox.

wa·ter·proof (wô′tər prōōf′, wŏt′ər-), *adj.* **1.** impervious to water. **2.** rendered impervious to water by some special process, as coating or treating with rubber or the like (contrasted with *water-repellent*). —*n.* **3.** any of several coated or rubberized fabrics which will hold water. **4.** *Chiefly Brit.* an outer garment of waterproof material. —*v.t.* **5.** to make waterproof.

water purslane, any of various marsh plants somewhat resembling purslane, as a lythraceous plant, *Didiplis diandra,* of North America.

water rat, 1. any of several different rodents of aquatic habits, as the European vole, *Arvicola amphibius.* **2.** the muskrat, *Fiber zibethicus.* **3.** (in Australia and New Guinea) any of the aquatic rats of the subfamily *Hydromyinae,* esp. of the genus *Hydromys.* **4.** *Slang.* vagrant or thief who frequents a water front.

wa·ter-re·pel·lent (wô′tər rĭ pĕl′ənt, wŏt′ər-), *adj.* finished to decrease the absorption of water (contrasted with *waterproof*).

water right, the right to make use of the water from a particular stream, lake, or irrigation canal.

water sapphire, a transparent variety of cordierite, found in Ceylon, Madagascar, and elsewhere, sometimes used as a gem. [trans. of F *saphir d'eau*]

wa·ter·scape (wô′tər skāp′, wŏt′ər-), *n.* a picture or view of the sea or other body of water. [f. WATER + -scape, modeled on LANDSCAPE]

water scorpion, any of the aquatic hemipterous insects constituting the family *Nepidae* (genera *Nepa, Ranatra,* etc.), having a taillike process through which respiration is effected.

wa·ter·shed (wô′tər shĕd′, wŏt′ər-), *n.* **1.** *Chiefly Brit.* the ridge or crest line dividing two drainage areas; a water parting; a divide. **2.** the region or area drained by a river, etc.; a drainage area. [f. WATER + SHED²]

water shield, any of the aquatic plants of the nymphaeaceous genera *Brasenia* and *Cabomba,* with peltate floating leaves.

wa·ter·sick (wô′tər sĭk′, wŏt′ər-), *adj. Agric.* excessively watered, esp. by irrigation, so that tilling and planting cannot be done.

wa·ter·side (wô′tər sīd′, wŏt′ər-), *n.* **1.** the margin, bank, or shore of the sea, a river, a lake, etc. **2.** of, relating to, or situated at the waterside: *waterside insects.* **3.** working by the waterside: *waterside police.*

water snake, 1. any of the harmless colubrine snakes of the genus *Natrix,* found in or near fresh water. **2.** any of various other snakes living in or frequenting water.

wa·ter-soak (wô′tər sōk′, wŏt′ər-), *v.t.* to soak with water.

wa·ter-sol·u·ble (wô′tər sŏl′yə bəl, wŏt′ər-), adj. Biochem. (of certain vitamins) able to dissolve in water: water-soluble B and C.

water spaniel, a curly-haired spaniel of either of two varieties, taking to water and readily trained for hunting.

water speedwell, a speedwell, Veronica Anagallis-aquatica, found esp. in marshes.

Irish water spaniel
(Ab. 2 ft. high at the shoulder)

wa·ter·spout (wô′tər spout′, wŏt′ər-), n. 1. a pipe running down the side of a house to take away water from the gutter of the roof. 2. a spout, nozzle, or orifice from which water is discharged. 3. Meteorol. a. a tornadolike storm or whirlwind over the ocean or other body of water, which takes the form of a progressive gyrating mass of air laden with mist and spray, presenting the appearance of a solid column of water reaching upward to the clouds. b. a sudden and violent downpour of rain; cloudburst.

water sprite, a sprite or spirit inhabiting the water.

water starwort, any plant of the genus, Callitriche, of aquatic herbs.

water strider, any of the hemipterous insects constituting the family Hydrobatidae, having long, slender legs, and darting about on the surface of water.

water system, 1. a river and all its branches. 2. a system of supplying water.

water table, 1. Civ. Eng., etc. the depth below which the ground is saturated with water. 2. Archit. a projecting stringcourse or similar member placed to throw off water.

water thrush, 1. either of two American tail-wagging warblers, Seiurus noveboracensis, and S. motacilla, usually found near water. 2. the European water ouzel.

wa·ter·tight (wô′tər tīt′, wŏt′ər-), adj. 1. impervious to water. 2. without fault; capable of only one interpretation: a watertight argument or alibi.

water tower, 1. a vertical pipe or tower into which water is pumped to obtain a required head; a standpipe. 2. a fire-extinguishing apparatus throwing a stream of water on the upper parts of a tall burning building.

Wa·ter·town (wô′tər toun′), n. 1. a town in E Massachusetts, on the Charles river, near Boston: U.S. arsenal. 39,092 (1960). 2. a city in N New York. 33,306 (1960).

water turkey, the snakebird or anhinga (Anhinga anhinga).

water vapor, gaseous water, esp. when diffused and below the boiling point: distinguished from steam.

Wa·ter·ville (wô′tər vĭl), n. a city in SW Maine. 18,695 (1960).

Wa·ter·vliet (wô′tər vlēt′), n. a city in E New York, on the Hudson: oldest U.S. arsenal. 15,197 (1960).

water wave, 1. a wave of water. 2. a wave set into lotioned hair with combs and then allowed to dry by the application of the heat from a drier.

wa·ter-wave (wô′tər wāv′, wŏt′ər-), v.t., -waved, -waving. to set (hair) in a water wave.

wa·ter·way (wô′tər wā′, wŏt′ər-), n. 1. a river, canal, or other body of water as a route or way of travel or transport. 2. a channel for vessels, esp. a fairway in a harbor, etc.

wa·ter·weed (wô′tər wēd′, wŏt′ər-), n. 1. an aquatic plant without special use or beauty. 2. a plant, Anacharis (Elodea) canadensis, of North America, common in fresh-water streams and ponds.

water wheel, 1. a wheel turned by water and used to perform mechanical work; a water turbine. 2. a wheel with buckets for raising water, as a noria.

water wings, a fabric contrivance shaped like a pair of wings and inflated with air, usually worn under the arms to keep the body afloat while one learns to swim.

water witching, the supposed discovering of subterranean streams by means of a divining rod. Also, **water witch.**

wa·ter·works (wô′tər wûrks′, wŏt′ər-), n.pl. 1. (often construed as sing.) an aggregate of apparatus and structures by which water is collected, preserved, and distributed for domestic and other purposes, as for a city. 2. Slang. tears, or the source of tears. 3. a marine scene or pageant. 4. Obs. an ornamental fountain.

wa·ter·worn (wô′tər wôrn′, wŏt′ər-), adj. worn by the action of water; smoothed by water in motion.

wa·ter·y (wô′tər ĭ, wŏt′ər ĭ), adj. 1. pertaining to or connected with water: watery Neptune. 2. full of or abounding in water, as soil, a region, etc. 3. containing much or too much water, as food. 4. insipid and soft or flabby: a watery fish. 5. tearful, as the eyes. 6. of the nature of water: watery vapor. 7. resembling water in appearance or color: watery sunlight. 8. resembling water in consistency: a watery fluid. 9. weak, thin, washy, vapid, or poor: watery writing. 10. consisting of water: a watery grave. 11. discharging, filled with, or secreting a waterlike morbid discharge.

Wat·kins Glen (wŏt′kĭnz), a village in W New York, on Seneca Lake: gorge and cascades. 2,813 (1960).

Wat·ling Island (wŏt′lĭng), San Salvado (def. 1).

Wat·son (wŏt′sən), n. 1. John, (Ian Maclaren) 1850-1907, Scottish clergyman and novelist. 2. John Broadus,

1878-1958, U.S. psychologist. 3. Sir William, 1858-1935, British poet.

watt (wŏt), n. a unit of power equal to one joule per second; the power of a current of one ampere flowing across a potential difference of one volt. [named after James Watt]

Watt (wŏt), n. James, 1736-1819, British engineer and inventor (of the steam engine).

watt·age (wŏt′ĭj), n. 1. Elect. power, in watts. 2. the watts required to operate an electrical device.

Wat·teau (wŏ tō′; Fr. và tō′; adj. also wŏt′ō), n. 1. Jean Antoine (zhän än twän′), 1684-1721, French painter. —adj. 2. pertaining to or in the style of Watteau: a Watteau shepherdess.

Watteau back, a long, loose, full back of a woman's gown, held in, in folds, at the neck and slightly below.

Wat·ter·son (wŏt′ərsən), n. Henry, 1840-1921, U.S. journalist and politician.

watt-hour (wŏt′our′), n. Elect. the product of average power in watts and the time in hours during which such power is maintained: the commonly used unit of electrical energy.

wat·tle (wŏt′əl), n., v., -tled, -tling, adj. —n. 1. (pl. or sing.) Chiefly Brit. rods or stakes interwoven with twigs or branches of trees, used for making fences, walls, roofs, etc. 2. (pl.) the poles forming the framework of a thatched roof. 3. (in Australia, etc.) any of various acacias whose shoots and branches were much used by the early colonists for wattles, now valued esp. for their bark, which is used in tanning. 4. Prov. Eng. and Scot. a twig, wand, stick, or rod. 5. Prov. Eng. a hurdle. 6. a fleshy lobe or appendage hanging down from the throat or chin of certain birds, as the domestic fowl, the turkey, etc. —v.t. 7. to bind, wall, fence, or otherwise fit with wattles. 8. to roof or frame with wattles or in similar fashion. 9. to form into a basketwork; interweave; interlace. 10. to form by interweaving twigs or branches: to wattle a fence. —adj. 11. built or roofed with wattles. [ME wattel, OE watul covering, var. of wætla bandage] —wat′tled, adj.

wattle and daub, wattle (def. 1).

wat·tle·bird (wŏt′əl bûrd′), n. an Australian bird of the honey eater family (Meliphagidae), Anthochaera paradoxa, having a pendulous wattle on each side of the throat.

watt·less (wŏt′lĭs), adj. Elect. without watts or power: a wattless alternating current (one differing in phase by 90 degrees from the associated emf); a wattless electromotive force (one differing in phase by 90 degrees from the current).

watt·me·ter (wŏt′mē′tər), n. Elect. an instrument for measuring electric power in watts.

Watts (wŏts), n. 1. George Frederick, 1817-1904, British painter and sculptor. 2. Isaac, 1674-1748, British theologian and hymnist.

Watts-Dun·ton (wŏts′dŭn′tən), n. Walter Theodore, 1832-1914, British critic, poet, and novelist.

waucht (Scot. wäkнt, wôkнt; Eng. Dial. wäft), Scot. and N. Eng. —n. 1. a copious draft. —v.t., v.i. 2. to drink fully. Also, **waught.**

Waugh (wô), n. Evelyn Arthur St. John, 1903-1966, British novelist.

Wau·ke·gan (wô kē′gən), n. a city in NE Illinois, on Lake Michigan, N of Chicago. 55,719 (1960).

waul (wôl), v.i. to cry as a cat; squall. Also, **wawl.**

Wau·sau (wô′sô), n. a city in central Wisconsin. 56,923 (1960).

Wau·wa·to·sa (wô′wə tō′sə), n. a city in SE Wisconsin, near Milwaukee. 33,324 (1950).

wave (wāv), n., v., waved, waving. —n. 1. a disturbance of the surface of a liquid body, as the sea or a lake, in the form of a ridge or swell. 2. Poetic. water, a body of water, or the sea. 3. any progressive movement or any progressing part resembling a wave of the sea: a wave of the pulse. 4. a swell, surge, or rush, as of feeling, excitement, prosperity, etc.: a great wave of enthusiasm among the public. 5. an outward curve, or one of a series of such curves, in a surface or line; an undulation. 6. Physics. a progressive vibrational disturbance propagated through a medium, as air, without corresponding progress or advance of the parts or particles themselves, as in the transmission of sound, light, and an electromagnetic field. 7. act of waving, as a flag or the hand. 8. a sign made with a wave of the hand, a flag, etc. —v.i. 9. to move with advancing swells and depressions of surface, as the sea, a flag, etc. 10. to curve alternately in opposite directions; have an undulating form. 11. to bend or sway up and down or to and fro, as branches or plants in the wind. 12. to be moved, esp. alternately in opposite directions: the lady's handkerchief waved in token of encouragement. 13. to give a signal by waving something: she waved to me with her hand. —v.t. 14. to cause to wave; cause to move with advancing swells and depressions: the night wind waved the tattered banners. 15. to cause to bend or sway up and down or to and fro. 16. to give an undulating form to; cause to curve up and down or in and out. 17. to give a wavy appearance or pattern to; water, as silk. 18. to move, esp. alternately in opposite directions: to wave the hand. 19. to signal to by waving a flag or the like; direct by a waving movement: to wave a train to a halt. 20. to signify or express by a waving movement: to wave a last good-by.

[ME; OE *wafian*, akin to Icel. *vāfa* swing] —**wav′er**, *n.* —**wave′less**, *adj.* —**wave′like′**, *adj.*
—**Syn. 1.** WAVE, RIPPLE, BREAKER, SURF refer to a ridge or swell on the surface of water. WAVE is the general word: *waves in a high wind* A RIPPLE is the smallest kind of wave, such as is caused by a stone thrown into a pool: *ripples in a brook.* A BREAKER is a wave breaking, or about to break, upon the shore or upon rocks: *the roar of breakers.* SURF is the collective name for breakers: *heavy surf makes bathing dangerous.* **11.** undulate, fluctuate, flutter, float, sway, rock.
Wave (wāv), *n.* an enlisted member of the Waves.
wave front, *Physics.* an imaginary surface that is the locus of all adjacent points at which the phase of vibration is the same.
wave guide, *Electronics.* a piece of hollow, conducting tubing, usually rectangular or circular in cross section, used as a conductor or directional transmitter for microwaves which are propagated through its interior.
wave length, *Physics.* the distance, measured in the direction of propagation of a wave, between two successive points that are characterized by the same phase of vibration.
wave·let (wāv′lĭt), *n.* a small wave; ripple.
wa·vell·ite (wā′vǝ līt′), *n.* a white to yellowish-green or brown mineral, a hydrous aluminum fluophosphate. [named after Dr. Wm. *Wavell*, its discoverer]
wa·ver (wā′vǝr), *v.i.* **1.** to sway to and fro; flutter: *the foliage of some wavering thicket.* **2.** to flicker or quiver, as light, etc.: *wavering tongues of flame.* **3.** to become unsteady, or begin to fail or give way: *her wavering senses.* **4.** to shake or tremble, as the hands, etc.: *the voice wavered.* **5.** to feel or show doubt or indecision, or vacillate: *wavered in my determination.* **6.** (of things) to fluctuate or vary. **7.** to totter. [ME, freq. of OE *wafian* WAVE; c. d. G *wabern* move about, Icel. *vafra* toddle] —**wa′ver·er**, *n.* —**wa′ver·ing·ly**, *adv.*
—**Syn. 5.** WAVER, FLUCTUATE, VACILLATE refer to an alternation or hesitation between one direction and another. WAVER means to hesitate between choices: *to waver as to what course to pursue.* FLUCTUATE suggests irregular change from one side to the other or up and down: *the prices of stocks fluctuate when there is bad news followed by good.* VACILLATE is to make up one's mind and change it again suddenly; to be undecided as to what to do: *we must not vacillate but must set a day.*
Wa·ver·ley Novels (wā′vǝr lĭ), a group of novels written by Sir Walter Scott.
Waves (wāvz), Women's Reserve, U. S. Naval Reserve. [from the initial letters of W(OMEN'S) A(PPOINTED) V(OLUNTEER) E(MERGENCY) S(ERVICE)]
wave train, *Physics.* a group or series of successive waves sent out along the same path or course by a vibrating body, a wireless antenna, or the like.
wav·y (wā′vĭ), *adj.,* **wavier, waviest. 1.** curving alternately, in opposite directions in movement or form: *a wavy course, wavy hair.* **2.** abounding in or characterized by waves: *the wavy sea.* **3.** resembling or suggesting waves. **4.** *Bot.* **a.** bending with successive curves in opposite directions, as a margin. **b.** having such a margin, as a leaf. **5.** vibrating or tremulous; unsteady; wavering. —**wav′i·ly**, *adv.* —**wav′i·ness**, *n.*
wawl (wôl), *v.i.* waul.
wax[1] (wăks), *n.* **1.** a solid yellowish substance secreted by bees, plastic when warm and melting at about 145° F., and allied to the fats and oils though containing no glycerin, which is used by bees in constructing their honeycomb, and which is variously employed otherwise, as in making candles, models, casts, ointments, etc.; beeswax. **2.** any of various similar substances, as spermaceti, the secretions of certain insects (wax insects), and the secretions (vegetable wax) of certain plants. **3.** one of a group of substances composed of esters, hydrocarbons, high-atomic alcohols, and fatty acids. **4.** *Physiol.* cerumen. **5.** a resinous substance used by shoemakers for rubbing their thread. **6.** sealing wax. **7.** something suggesting wax as being readily molded, worked upon, handled, managed, etc.: *helpless wax in their hands.* —*v.t.* **8.** to rub, smear, stiffen, polish, etc., with wax; treat with wax: *waxed mustaches, a waxed floor.* [ME; OE *weax*, c. D *was*, G *wachs*, Icel. *vax*] —**wax′er**, *n.* —**wax′like′**, *adj.*
wax[2] (wăks), *v.i.,* **waxed; waxed** or (*Poetic*) **waxen; waxing. 1.** to increase in extent, quantity, intensity, power, etc.: *discord waxed daily.* **2.** (of the moon) to increase in the extent of its illuminated portion before the full moon (opposed to *wane*). **3.** to grow or become (as stated): *my bones waxed old.* [ME; OE *weaxan*, c. G *wachsen*]
wax[3] (wăks), *n. Chiefly Brit. Colloq.* a fit of anger. [orig. uncert.; ? from phrase to wax angry (see WAX[2], def. 3)]
wax bean, any variety of snap bean with a yellowish color and waxy appearance.
wax·ber·ry (wăks′bĕr′ĭ), *n., pl.* **-ries. 1.** the wax myrtle, or the bayberry. **2.** the snowberry.
wax·bill (wăks′bĭl′), *n.* any of various weaver birds, esp. of the genus *Estrilda,* having white, pink, or red bills of waxlike appearance, and including many well-known cage birds, as an African species, *Estrilda astrild,* the amadavat, and the Java sparrow.
wax·en (wăk′sǝn), *adj.* **1.** made of or covered with wax. **2.** resembling or suggesting wax: *the deathly waxen appearance of his face.* **3.** soft, plastic, or impressible, as a person or his characteristics. —*v.* **4.** *Poetic.* pp. of wax[2].

waxing moon. See **moon** (def. 2e).
wax insect, any of various homopterous insects, as a Chinese scale insect, *Ericerus pela,* which secrete a wax or waxlike substance.
wax myrtle, a shrub or tree of the genus *Myrica,* as *M. cerifera,* which bears small berries coated with wax (sometimes used in making candles, etc.), or *M. pensylvanica.* Cf. **bayberry.**
wax palm, 1. a tall pinnate-leaved palm, *Ceroxylon andicola,* of the Andes, whose stem and leaves yield a resinous wax. **2.** a palmate-leaved palm, *Copernicia cerifera,* of Brazil, the carnauba, whose young leaves are coated with a hard wax.
wax paper, paper made moistureproof by coating with paraffin.
wax·plant (wăks′plănt′, -plänt′), *n.* any of the climbing or trailing plants of the asclepiadaceous genus *Hoya,* natives of tropical Asia and Australia, having glossy leaves and umbels of pink, white, or yellowish waxy flowers.
wax·weed (wăks′wēd′), *n.* an American lythraceous herb, *Cuphea* (or *Parsonsia*) *petiolata,* with a viscid pubescence and purple flowers.
wax·wing (wăks′wĭng′), *n.* any bird of the passerine family *Bombycillidae,* having a showy crest and small red appendages like bits of sealing wax at the tips of the secondary wing feathers and sometimes the tail feathers, as *Bombycilla garrula* of the northern hemisphere, or *B. cedrorum,* the cedar bird of North America.
wax·work (wăks′wûrk′), *n.* **1.** figures, ornaments, etc., made of wax, or one such figure. **2.** (*pl. construed as sing.*) an exhibition of wax figures, ornaments, etc.
wax·y (wăk′sĭ), *adj.,* **waxier, waxiest. 1.** resembling wax, as in substance or appearance. **2.** abounding in, covered with, or made of wax. **3.** *Pathol.* pertaining to or suffering from a degeneration caused by deposits of a waxlike insoluble material in an organ. **4.** pliable, yielding, or impressible. —**wax′i·ness**, *n.*
way (wā), *n.* **1.** manner, mode, or fashion: *a new way of looking at a matter, to reply in a polite way.* **2.** characteristic or habitual manner: *that is only his way.* **3.** a course, plan, or means for attaining an end: *to find a way to reduce friction.* **4.** respect or particular: *a plan defective in several ways.* **5.** direction: *look this way.* **6.** passage or progress on a course: *to make one's way on foot, to lead the way.* **7.** distance: *a long way off.* **8. a.** a path or course leading from one place to another. **b.** *Brit.* an old Roman road: *Icknield Way.* **c.** *Brit.* a minor street in a town: *he lives in Stepney Way.* **9.** a road, route, passage, or channel: *a highway, waterway, doorway.* **10.** *Law.* a right of way. **11.** any line of passage or travel used or available: *blaze a way through dense woods.* **12.** space for passing or advancing: *make way, give way.* **13.** (*often pl.*) a habit or custom: *I don't like his ways at all.* **14.** one's preferred course or mode of procedure: *to have one's own way.* **15.** *Colloq.* condition, as to health, prosperity, etc.: *to be in a bad way.* **16.** range of experience or notice: *the best device that ever came in my way.* **17.** course of life, action, or experience: *the way of transgressors is hard.* **18.** *Colloq.* calling or business: *in the grocery way.* **19.** (*pl.*) (in shipbuilding) the timbers on which a ship is launched. **20.** *Mach.* a longitudinal strip, as in a planer, guiding a moving part along a surface. **21.** *Naut.* movement or passage through the water. **22. by the way, a.** incidentally; in the course of one's remarks: *by the way, have you received that letter yet?* **b.** on the way: *they will faint by the way.* **23. by way of, a.** by the route of; via; through. **b.** as a way, method, or means of: *to number articles by way of distinguishing them.* **c.** as or for: *to wear a wig by way of disguise.* **d.** *Brit.* in the position of, or ostensibly (being, doing, etc.): *he is by way of being an authority on the subject.* **24. make one's way, a.** to proceed. **b.** to achieve advancement. **25. out of the way, a.** so as not to obstruct or hinder. **b.** off one's hands. **c.** out of existence: *to put a person or an animal out of the way.* **d.** out of the frequented way or beaten track. **e.** unusual, improper, or amiss. **f.** mislaid or lost. **26. under way, a.** in motion, or moving along, as a ship that has weighed anchor. **b.** in progress, as an enterprise. [ME; OE *weg,* c. D and G *weg,* Icel. *vegr,* Goth. *wigs*] —**Syn. 3.** See **method. 7.** space, interval.
way·bill (wā′bĭl′), *n.* a list of goods sent by a common carrier, as a railroad, with shipping directions.
way·far·er (wā′fâr′ǝr), *n.* a traveler, esp. on foot.
way·far·ing (wā′fâr′ĭng), *adj., n.* traveling, esp. on foot.
way·go·ing (wā′gō′ĭng), *adj.* **1.** going away; departing: *a waygoing tenant.* **2.** of or pertaining to one who goes away.
way·laid (wā′lād′), *v.* pt. and pp. of **waylay.**
Way·land the Smith (wā′lǎnd), (in English folklore) an invisible, marvelously skilled smith. Also, **Wayland.**
way·lay (wā′lā′), *v.t.,* **-laid, -laying. 1.** to fall upon or assail from ambush, as in order to rob, seize, or slay. **2.** to await and accost unexpectedly. [f. WAY + LAY[1]. Cf. G *wegelagern*] —**way′lay′er**, *n.*
way·leave (wā′lēv′), *n. Brit.* right of way.
Wayne (wān), *n.* Anthony, ("Mad Anthony") 1745–1796, American Revolutionary general.
Way of All Flesh, The, a novel (1903) by Samuel Butler.

ways, a suffix of manner creating adverbs, as in *sideways*, *lengthways*. See **-wise.** [orig. gen. of WAY]

ways and means, 1. legislation, methods, and means of raising revenue for the use of the government. 2. methods and means of accomplishing something.

way·side (wā′sīd′), *n.* 1. the side of the way; the border or edge of the road or highway. —*adj.* 2. being, situated, or found at or along the wayside: *a wayside inn.*

way station, *U.S.* a station intermediate between principal stations, as on a railroad.

way train, a local train.

way·ward (wā′wərd), *adj.* 1. turned or turning away from what is right or proper; perverse: *a wayward son.* 2. swayed or prompted by caprice, or capricious: *a wayward fancy or impulse.* 3. turning or changing irregularly; irregular: *a wayward stream or breeze.* [ME; aphetic var. of *awayward*] —**way′ward·ly,** *adv.* —**way′ward·ness,** *n.* —Syn. 1. contrary, headstrong, stubborn, obstinate, disobedient, unruly, refractory, intractable. See **willful.**

way·worn (wā′wôrn′), *adj.* worn or wearied by travel.

Wa·zir·i·stan (wä zĭr′ĭ stän′), *n.* a mountainous district in Pakistan, in North-West Frontier Province.

W/B, waybill. Also, **W.B.**

w.b., 1. warehouse book. 2. waybill. 3. westbound.

W.C., West Central (postal district, London).

w.c., 1. *Chiefly Brit.* water closet. 2. without charge.

W.C.T.U., Woman's Christian Temperance Union.

wd., 1. ward. 2. word.

W.D., War Department.

we (wē; *unstressed* wĭ), *pron., pl.; poss.* **our** or **ours;** *obj.* **us.** nominative pl. of **I** (specially used by a speaker or writer to denote people in general, including himself, or by a sovereign when alluding to himself in formal speech, or by an editor or other writer to avoid any appearance of egotism from the use of *I*). [ME and OE, c. D *wij*, G *wir*, Icel. *vēr*, Goth. *weis*]

weak (wēk), *adj.* 1. liable to yield, break, or collapse under pressure or strain; fragile; frail; not strong: *a weak fortress, a weak spot in armor.* 2. deficient in bodily strength or healthy vigor, as from age, sickness, etc.; feeble; infirm: *a weak old man; weak eyes.* 3. deficient in political strength, governing power, or authority: *a weak nation or ruler.* 4. lacking in force, potency, or efficacy; impotent, ineffectual, or inadequate: *weak prayers.* 5. lacking in rhetorical force or effectiveness: *a weak style.* 6. lacking in logical or legal force or soundness: *a weak argument.* 7. deficient in mental power, intelligence, or judgment: *a weak mind.* 8. deficient in moral strength or firmness, resolution, or force of character: *prove weak under temptation, weak compliance.* 9. deficient in amount, volume, loudness, intensity, etc.; faint; slight: *weak vibrations, a weak current of electricity.* 10. deficient, wanting, or poor in something specified: *a hand weak in trumps, weak in spelling.* 11. deficient in the essential or desirable properties or ingredients: *weak tea, a weak infusion.* 12. unstressed. 13. (of Germanic verbs) inflected with suffixes, without inherited change of the root vowel, as English *work, worked,* or *keep, kept* (in which the vowel change is not inherited). 14. (of Germanic nouns and adjectives) inflected with endings originally appropriate to stems terminating in *-n. "Alte"* in German *der alte Mann* "the old man" is a weak adjective. 15. pertaining to a flour or wheat which has a low gluten content. 16. *Photog.* thin; not dense. 17. *Com.* tending downward in price. [ME *weik,* t. Scand.; cf. Icel. *veikr,* c. OE *wāc,* G *weich*] —Syn. 2. WEAK, DECREPIT, FEEBLE, WEAKLY imply a lack of strength or of good health. WEAK means not physically strong, because of extreme youth, old age, illness, etc.: *weak after an attack of fever.* DECREPIT means old and broken in health to a marked degree: *decrepit and barely able to walk.* FEEBLE denotes much the same as WEAK, but connotes being pitiable or inferior: *feeble and almost senile.* WEAKLY suggests a longstanding sickly condition, a state of chronic bad health: *a weakly child may become a strong man.* 6. unsound, ineffective, inadequate, illogical, inconclusive, unsustained, unsatisfactory, lame. 8. vacillating, wavering, unstable, irresolute, weak-kneed. —Ant. 2. strong, robust.

weak·en (wē′kən), *v.t., v.i.* to become or make weak or weaker. —**weak′en·er,** *n.* —Syn. enfeeble, debilitate, enervate, undermine, sap, exhaust, deplete, lessen, diminish, lower, reduce, impair, minimize, invalidate.

weak ending, *Pros.* a verse ending in which the metrical stress falls on a word or syllable which would not be stressed in natural utterance, as a preposition whose object is carried over to the next line.

weak·fish (wēk′fĭsh′), *n., pl.* **-fishes,** (*esp. collectively*) **-fish.** any of the sciaenoid food fishes constituting the genus *Cynoscion,* as *C. regalis* (the common weakfish, or squeteague) of the Atlantic and Gulf coasts of the U.S.

weak-kneed (wēk′nēd′), *adj.* yielding readily to opposition, intimidation, etc.

weak·ling (wēk′lĭng), *n.* 1. a weak or feeble creature (physically or morally). —*adj.* 2. weak; not strong.

weak·ly (wēk′lĭ), *adj.,* **-lier, -liest,** *adv.* —*adj.* 1. weak or feeble in constitution; not robust; sickly. —*adv.* 2. in a weak manner. —**weak′li·ness,** *n.* —Syn. 1. See **weak.**

weak-mind·ed (wēk′mīn′dĭd), *adj.* 1. having or showing a want of firmness of mind. 2. having or showing a weak or feeble mind. —**weak′-mind′ed·ness,** *n.*

weak·ness (wēk′nĭs), *n.* 1. state or quality of being weak; feebleness. 2. a weak point, as in a person's character; slight fault or defect. 3. a self-indulgent inclination or liking; tenderness. —Syn. 2. See **fault.**

weal[1] (wēl), *n.* 1. *Archaic.* well-being, prosperity, or happiness: *in weal or woe, zealous only for the public weal.* 2. *Obs.* wealth or riches. [ME *wele,* OE *wela.* See WELL[1]]

weal[2] (wēl), *n.* a wale or welt. [var. of WALE[1]]

weald (wēld), *n. Poetic.* an open country. [ME *weeld,* OE *weald* forest, var. of *wald* WOLD]

Weald (wēld), *n.* **The,** a former wooded district of SE England, in Kent, Surrey, and Essex counties: now primarily an agricultural region.

wealth (wĕlth), *n.* 1. a great store of valuable possessions, property, or riches: *the wealth of a city.* 2. a rich abundance or profusion of anything: *a wealth of imagery.* 3. *Econ.* **a.** all things having a value in money, in exchange, or in use. **b.** anything having utility and capable of being appropriated or exchanged. 4. rich or valuable contents or produce: *the wealth of the soil.* 5. state of being rich; affluence: *persons of wealth and standing.* 6. *Obs.* or *Archaic.* well-being or prosperity. [ME *welth,* f. *wel* WELL[1] + -TH[1]] —Syn. 3. **a.** possessions, assets, goods, property. 5. opulence, fortune.

wealth·y (wĕl′thĭ), *adj.,* **wealthier, wealthiest.** 1. possessed of wealth; rich: *a wealthy person or nation.* 2. characterized by, pertaining to, or suggestive of wealth: *a wealthy appearance.* 3. rich in character, quality, or amount; abundant or ample. —**wealth′i·ly,** *adv.* —**wealth′i·ness,** *n.* —Syn. 1. affluent, opulent, prosperous, well-to-do, moneyed. See **rich.**

Wealth·y (wĕl′thĭ), *n.* a variety of red apple, grown in the U.S., maturing in early autumn.

wean[1] (wēn), *v.t.* 1. to accustom (a child or animal) to food other than its mother's milk. 2. to withdraw from any object or form of habit or enjoyment (usually fol. by *from*). [ME *wene,* OE *wenian,* c. D *wennen* accustom, G *gewöhnen,* Icel. *venja*] —**wean′er,** *n.*

wean[2] (wēn), *n. Scot.* a child. [contraction of *wee ane* little one]

wean·ling (wēn′lĭng), *n.* 1. a child or animal newly weaned. —*adj.* 2. newly weaned.

weap·on (wĕp′ən), *n.* 1. any instrument for use in attack or defense in combat, fighting, or war, as a sword, rifle, cannon, etc. 2. anything serving as an instrument for making or repelling an attack: *the deadly weapon of meekness.* 3. *Zool.* any part or organ serving for attack or defense, as claws, horns, teeth, stings, etc. [ME *wepen,* OE *wǣpen,* c. G *waffe*] —**weap′oned,** *adj.* —**weap′on·less,** *adj.*

wear (wâr), *v.,* **wore, worn, wearing,** *n.* —*v.t.* 1. to carry or have on the body or about the person as a covering, equipment, ornament, or the like: *wear a coat, a watch, wear a disguise.* 2. to have or use on the person habitually: *to wear a beard.* 3. to bear or have in the aspect or appearance: *to wear a smile, or an air of triumph.* 4. to impair (garments, etc.) by wear: *gloves worn at the fingertips.* 5. to impair, deteriorate, or consume gradually by use or any continued process: *a well-worn volume.* 6. to waste or diminish gradually by rubbing, scraping, washing, etc.: *rocks worn by the waves.* 7. to make (a hole, channel, way, etc.) by such action. 8. to bring, reduce, make, take, etc. (as specified), by wear or any gradual change: *to wear clothes to rags or a person to a shadow.* 9. to weary or exhaust: *worn with toil or care.* 10. to pass (time, etc.) gradually or tediously (commonly fol. by *away* or *out*). 11. *Naut.* to bring (a vessel) on another tack by turning her head away from the wind until the wind is on her stern, and then bringing her head up towards the wind on the other side. 12. **wear out, a.** to wear or use until no longer fit for use: *to wear out clothes or tools.* **b.** to use up. **c.** to exhaust by continued use, strain, or any gradual process: *to wear out patience.* —*v.i.* 13. to undergo gradual impairment, diminution, reduction, etc., from wear, use, attrition, or other causes (often fol. by *away, down, out,* or *off*). 14. to hold out or last under wear, use, or any continued strain: *materials or colors that will wear, or wear well.* 15. to become; grow gradually: *my patience is wearing thin.* 16. to pass, as time, etc., esp. slowly or tediously (often fol. by *away* or *on*). 17. *Naut.* (of a vessel) to come round on another tack by turning away from the wind. 18. *Obs.* to be commonly worn or used. —*n.* 19. act of wearing; use, as of a garment: *articles for winter wear.* 20. state of being worn, as on the person. 21. clothing, garments, or other articles for wearing. 22. style of dress, adornment, etc., esp. when proper or fashionable. 23. gradual impairment, wasting, diminution, etc., as from use: *the carpet shows wear.* 24. *Naut.* a tactical maneuver by which a sailing vessel is changed from one tack to another. [ME *were,* OE *werian,* c. Icel. *verja,* Goth. *wasjan clothe*] —**wear′er,** *n.*

wear·a·ble (wâr′ə bəl), *adj.* 1. that may be worn. —*n.* 2. (*chiefly pl.*) that which may be worn, esp. clothing.

wear and tear, loss by wearing; diminution, decay or injury sustained by ordinary use.

wea·ri·ful (wēr′ĭ fəl), *adj.* wearisome; tedious. —**wea′ri·ful·ly,** *adv.* —**wea′ri·ful·ness,** *n.*

wea·ri·less (wēr′ĭ lĭs), *adj.* unwearying; tireless.

wear·ing (wâr′ĭng), *adj.* 1. relating to or made for wear. 2. gradually impairing or wasting. 3. wearying or exhausting. —**wear′ing·ly,** *adv.*

wearing apparel, dress in general; garments.

wea·ri·some (wĭr′ĭ səm), *adj.* **1.** causing weariness; fatiguing: *a difficult and wearisome march.* **2.** tiresome or tedious: *a wearisome person, day, or book.* —**wea′ri·some·ly,** *adv.* —**wea′ri·some·ness,** *n.* —**Syn.** 2. irksome, monotonous, humdrum, dull, prosy. See **tedious.**

wea·ry (wĭr′ĭ), *adj.*, **-ri·er, -ri·est,** *v.*, **-ried, -ry·ing.** —*adj.* **1.** exhausted physically or mentally by labor, exertion, strain, etc.; fatigued; tired: *weary eyes, feet, or brain.* **2.** characterized by or causing fatigue: *a weary journey.* **3.** impatient or dissatisfied at excess or over-long continuance (often fol. by *of*): *weary of excuses.* **4.** characterized by or causing such impatience or dissatisfaction; tedious; irksome: *a weary wait.* —*v.t., v.i.* **5.** to make or become weary; fatigue or tire. **6.** to make or grow impatient or dissatisfied at having too much of something (often fol. by *of*). [ME *wery,* OE *wērig*] —**wea′ri·ly,** *adv.* —**wea′ri·ness,** *n.* —**Syn.** 1. wearied, spent. See **tired[1].**

wea·sand (wē′zənd), *n. Archaic.* the windpipe or trachea. [ME *wesand,* OE *wǣsend,* var. of *wāsend* gullet]

wea·sel (wē′zəl), *n.* **1.** any of certain small carnivores of the genus *Mustela* (family *Mustelidae,* esp. *M. frenata,* a common American species having a long, slender body, and feeding largely on small rodents. **2.** any of various similar animals of the *Mustelidae.* **3.** a cunning, sneaking fellow. **4.** a tracked vehicle used in snow; a kind of tractor. —*v.i.* **5.** to renege (def. 2); evade, as an obligation. [ME *wesel,* OE *weosul,* c. G *wiesel*]

Weasel, *Mustela frenata* (Total length 13 to 16 in.)

weasel words, intentionally ambiguous statements.

weath·er (wĕ*th*′ər), *n.* **1.** state of the atmosphere with respect to wind, temperature, cloudiness, moisture, pressure, etc. **2.** windy or stormy weather. **3. under the weather,** *Colloq.* **a.** indisposed; ill; ailing. **b.** drunk. **4. keep one's weather eye open,** *Colloq.* to be on one's guard. —*v.t.* **5.** to expose to the weather; to dry, season, or otherwise affect by exposure to the air or atmosphere. **6.** to discolor, disintegrate, or affect injuriously, as by atmospheric agencies. **7.** to bear up against and come safely through (a storm, danger, trouble, etc.). **8.** *Naut.* (of a ship, mariner, etc.) to pass or sail to the windward of: *to weather a cape.* **9.** *Archit.* to cause to slope, so as to shed water. —*v.i.* **10.** to undergo change, as discoloration or disintegration, as the result of exposure to atmospheric conditions. **11.** to endure or resist exposure to the weather. **12.** to go or come safely through a storm, danger, trouble, etc. (fol. by *through*). **13.** of or pertaining to the side or part, as of a ship, that is exposed to the wind: *the weather bow.* [ME and OE *weder,* c. D *weder,* G *wetter,* Icel. *vedhr*]

weath·er-beat·en (wĕ*th*′ər bē′tən), *adj.* **1.** bearing evidences of exposure to the weather. **2.** seasoned or hardened by exposure to weather: *a weather-beaten face.*

weath·er·board (wĕ*th*′ər bôrd′), *n.* **1.** *Chiefly Brit.* one of a series of thin boards, usually thicker along one edge than along the other, nailed on an outside wall or a roof in overlapping fashion to form a protective covering which will shed water. **2.** *Naut.* the side of a vessel toward the wind. —*v.t.* **3.** *Chiefly Brit.* to cover or furnish with weatherboards.

weath·er·board·ing (wĕ*th*′ər bôr′dĭng), *n. Chiefly Brit.* **1.** a covering or facing of weatherboards or the like. **2.** weatherboards collectively.

weath·er-bound (wĕ*th*′ər bound′), *adj.* delayed by bad weather.

Weather Bureau, a bureau of the U. S. Department of Commerce, having charge of the gathering of the meteorological reports in order to forecast the weather, issue warnings of storms, floods, etc.

weath·er·cock (wĕ*th*′ər kŏk′), *n.* **1.** a weather vane in the shape of a cock. **2.** any weather vane. **3.** a fickle or inconstant person or thing.

weath·ered (wĕ*th*′ərd), *adj.* **1.** seasoned or otherwise affected by exposure to the weather or elements. **2.** (of wood) discolored or stained by the action of air, rain, etc., or by artificial means. **3.** (of rocks) worn, disintegrated, or changed in color or composition, by the action of the elements. **4.** *Archit.* made sloping or inclined, as a window sill, to prevent the lodgment of water.

weather gauge, **1.** the (advantageous) position of a ship when it is to windward of another ship. **2.** the position of advantage; the upper hand.

weath·er·glass (wĕ*th*′ər glăs′, -gläs′), *n.* any of various instruments, as a barometer or a hygroscope, designed to indicate the state of the atmosphere.

weath·er·ly (wĕ*th*′ər lĭ), *adj. Naut.* (of a boat) making very little leeway when close-hauled. —**weath′er·li·ness,** *n.*

weath·er·man (wĕ*th*′ər măn′), *n., pl.* **-men.** *Colloq.* **1.** one who foretells weather. **2.** an employee or officer of the U.S. Weather Bureau.

weather map, a map or chart showing weather conditions over a wide area at a particular time, compiled from simultaneous observations at different places.

weath·er·proof (wĕ*th*′ər prōōf′), *adj.* **1.** proof against the weather; able to withstand exposure to all kinds of weather. —*v.t.* **2.** to make proof against the weather.

---

weather station, an installation equipped and used for the making of meteorological observations.

weather strip, a narrow strip, as of India rubber covering the joint between a door, window sash, or the like, and the jamb, casing, etc., to exclude wind, rain, etc.

weath·er-strip (wĕ*th*′ər strĭp′), *v.t.,* **-stripped, -stripping.** to fit with weather strips.

weather stripping, **1.** weather strip. **2.** weather strips collectively.

weather vane, a vane for indicating the direction of the wind; a weathercock.

weath·er-wise (wĕ*th*′ər wĭz′), *adj.* **1.** skillful in predicting weather. **2.** skillful in predicting reactions, opinions, etc.

weath·er-worn (wĕ*th*′ər wôrn′), *adj.* weather-beaten.

weave (wēv), *v.,* **wove** or (*Rare*) **weaved; woven** or **wove; weaving;** *n.* —*v.t.* **1.** to interlace (threads, yarns, strips, fibrous material, etc.) so as to form a fabric or texture. **2.** to form by interlacing threads, yarns, strands, or strips of some material: *to weave a basket, to weave cloth.* **3.** to form by combining various elements or details into a connected whole: *to weave a tale or a plot.* **4.** to introduce as an element or detail into a connected whole: *to weave a melody into a musical composition.* **5.** to follow in a winding course; to move from side to side: *to weave one's way through traffic.* —*v.i.* **6.** to weave cloth, etc. **7.** to compose any connected whole. **8.** to become woven or interwoven. **9.** to move from side to side. —*n.* **10.** a manner of interlacing yarns; plain, twill, or satin weave. [ME *weve,* OE *wefan,* c. G *weben*] —**Syn.** 3. contrive, fabricate, construct.

Weave
A. Warp; B. Weft

weav·er (wē′vər), *n.* **1.** one who weaves. **2.** a weaverbird.

weav·er·bird (wē′vər bûrd′), *n.* any of numerous (chiefly African and Asiatic) passerine birds of the family *Ploceidae,* related to the finches and building elaborately woven nests.

weaver's hitch, sheet bend. Also, **weaver's knot.**

web (wĕb), *n., v.,* **webbed, webbing.** —*n.* **1.** something formed as by weaving or interweaving. **2.** a thin silken fabric spun by spiders, and also by the larvae of some insects, as the webworms, tent caterpillars, etc.; cobweb. **3.** a woven fabric, esp. a whole piece of cloth in the course of being woven or after it comes from the loom. **4.** *Zool.* **a.** a membrane which connects the digits of an animal. **b.** that which connects the toes of aquatic birds and aquatic mammals. **5.** *Ornith.* **a.** the series of barbs on each side of the shaft of a feather. **b.** the series on both sides, collectively. **6.** a solid or open system connecting the chords or flanges of structural members, such as a steel plate connecting the top and bottom chords of a plate girder. **7.** *Archit.* the part of a ribbed vault enclosed by ribs. **8.** the flat woven strip, without pile, often found at one or both ends of Oriental rugs. —*v.t.* **9.** to cover with or as with a web; envelop. [ME and OE *webbe,* Icel. *vefr;* akin to **weave**] —**web′less,** *adj.* —**web′like′,** *adj.*

Weaverbird, *Ploceus cucullatus* (Ab. 7 in. long)

Webb (wĕb), *n.* **1. Beatrice Potter,** 1858–1943, British writer on economic and social problems. **2.** her husband, **Sidney James,** (*Lord Passfield*) 1859–1947, British economist, sociologist, and statesman.

webbed (wĕbd), *adj.* **1.** having the digits connected by a web, as the foot of a duck or a beaver. **2.** (of the digits) connected thus. **3.** formed like or with a web.

web·bing (wĕb′ĭng), *n.* **1.** woven material of hemp, cotton, or jute, in bands of various widths, for use where strength is required. **2.** such woven bands nailed on furniture under springs or upholstery, for support. **3.** *Zool.* the membrane forming a web or webs.

web·by (wĕb′ĭ), *adj.* **1.** pertaining to, of the nature of, or resembling a web. **2.** webbed.

We·ber (vā′bər), *n.* **1. Baron Karl Maria von** (kärl mä′rē·ä fon), 1786–1826, German composer of music. **2. Ernest Heinrich** (ĕrnst hīn′rĭхн), 1795–1878, German physiologist. **3.** his brother, **Wilhelm Eduard** (vĭl′hĕlm ā′dōō·ärt′), 1804–91, German physicist.

we·ber (vā′bər, wē′bər), *n.* (formerly) **1.** coulomb. **2.** ampere. [named after Wilhelm *Weber*]

web-foot (wĕb′fŏŏt′), *n., pl.* **-feet. 1.** a foot with the toes joined by a web. **2.** an animal with webfeet. —**web′-foot′ed,** *adj.*

Web·ster (wĕb′stər), *n.* **1. Daniel,** 1782–1852, U.S. statesman and orator. **2. John,** 1580?–1625?, British dramatist. **3. Noah,** 1758–1843, U.S. lexicographer and writer.

web·ster (wĕb′stər), *n. Obs.* or *Dial.* a weaver.

web-toed (wĕb′tōd′), *adj.* web-footed.

web·worm (wĕb′wûrm′), *n.* any of various more or less gregarious caterpillars which spin webs, as the **garden webworm,** *Phlyctaenodes similalis.*

wed (wĕd), *v.,* **wedded, wedded** or **wed, wedding.** —*v.t.* **1.** to bind oneself to (a person) in marriage; take

---

r husband or wife. **2.** to unite (a couple) or join one person to another) in marriage or wedlock; marry. . to bind by close or lasting ties; attach firmly: *to be edded to a theory.* —*v.i.* **4.** to contract marriage; marry. . to become united as if in wedlock. [ME; OE *weddian* ledge, c. G *wetten* bet, Icel. *vedhja* pledge]

e'd (wēd; *unstressed* wĭd), contraction of *we had, we hould,* or *we would.*

ed., Wednesday.

ed·ded (wĕd/ĭd), *adj.* **1.** united in matrimony; married. **2.** joined. **3.** joined by devotion: *he was wedded*) *the cause.*

ed·dell Sea (wĕd/əl), a wide arm of the S Atlantic, n Antarctica, E of Palmer Peninsula.

ed·ding (wĕd/ĭng), *n.* **1.** act or ceremony of marrying; marriage; nuptials. **2.** a celebration of an anniversary of a marriage, as a silver wedding, celebrated on the 25th anniversary of a marriage. [ME; OE *weddung.* ee WED] —**Syn. 1.** See **marriage.**

e·de·kind (vā/dəkĭnt), *n.* **Frank** (fränk), 1864–918, German poet and dramatist.

edge (wĕj), *n., v.* wedged, wedging. —*n.* **1.** a device (one of the so-called simple machines) consisting of a iece of hard material with two principle faces meeting in a sharply acute angle. **2.** a piece of nything of like shape: *a wedge of pie or cheese.* **3.** *Meteorol.* an elongated area of relatively high ressure. **4.** a wedge-shaped cuneiform character or stroke. **5.** something that serves to art, divide, etc.: *an entering wedge to disrupt the* arty. **6.** *Mil.* (formerly) a tactical formation enerally in the form of a V with the point toward the nemy. —*v.t.* **7.** to cleave or split with or as with a vedge. **8.** to pack or fix tightly by driving in a wedge r wedges. **9.** to thrust, drive, or fix (in, between, etc.) ke a wedge: *to wedge oneself through a narrow opening.* —*v.i.* **10.** to force a way (in, etc.) like a wedge. [ME;)E *wecg,* c. d. G *weck*] —**wedge/like/, wedg/y,** *adj.*   *Wedge*

edg·wood (wĕj/wŏŏd/), *n.* **1. Josiah,** 1730–95, British potter. **2.** Wedgwood ware. —*adj.* **3.** pertaining to, or made or originated by Josiah Wedgwood.

edgwood ware, a type of artistic pottery with inted ground and white decoration in relief in designs atterned after Greek and Roman models.

ed·lock (wĕd/lŏk), *n.* state of marriage; matrimony. ME *wedlok,* OE *wedlāc,* f. *wed* pledge + *-lāc,* suffix naking neut. nouns]

ednes·day (wĕnz/dĭ), *n.* the fourth day of the veek, following Tuesday. [ME *Wednesdai,* OE *Wōdnes æg* Woden's day, c. D *Woensdag,* Dan. *Onsdag;* trans. f L *Mercurĭ dies*]

ee (wē), *adj.,* **weer, weest,** *n.* —*adj.* **1.** little; very mall. —*n.* **2.** *Scot. and Prov. Eng.* a short space of ime. [ME *we,* var. of *wei* (small) quantity, OE *wēg* veight, amount]

eed[1] (wēd), *n.* **1.** a plant occurring obtrusively in ultivated ground to the exclusion or injury of the esired crop. **2.** any useless, troublesome, or noxious lant, esp. one that grows profusely. **3. the weed,** *olloq.* tobacco. **4.** *Colloq.* a cigar, or cigarette. **5.** a hin, ungainly person or animal. **6.** a sorry animal, esp. horse unfit for racing or breeding purposes. —*v.t.* **7.** to free from weeds or troublesome plants: *to weed a* arden. **8.** to root out or remove (a weed) (often fol. y *out*). **9.** to remove as being undesirable or superluous (often fol. by *out*): *to weed out undesirable members.* **10.** to rid of what is undesirable or superfluous. —*v.i.* **11.** to remove weeds or the like. [ME *wede,* OE *wēod*] —**weed/er,** *n.* —**weed/less,** *adj.* —**weed/like/,** *adj.*

eed[2] (wēd), *n.* **1.** (*pl.*) mourning garments: *widow's eeds.* **2.** a mourning band of black crepe or cloth, as on man's hat or coat sleeve. **3.** *Archaic or Prov.* a garnent or clothing or dress: *clad in rustic weeds.* [ME *wede,*)E *wēd,* var. of *wǣd* garment, c. Icel. *vādh* cloth]

eed (wēd), *n.* **Thurlow** (thûr/lō), 1797–1882, U.S. ournalist and politician.

eed·y (wē/dĭ), *adj.,* **weedier, weediest. 1.** abounding in weeds. **2.** consisting of or pertaining to weeds. **3.** of a poor, straggling growth, as a plant. **4.** thin and ngainly, as a person or animal. —**weed/i·ness,** *n.*

eek (wēk), *n.* **1.** a period of seven successive days, ommonly understood as beginning (unless otherwise pecified or implied) with Sunday, followed by Monday, Tuesday, Wednesday, Thursday, Friday, and Saturday. **2.** the working days or working portion of the seven-day eriod: *a working week of 44 hours.* **3.** *Brit.* seven days fter a specified day: *I shall come Tuesday week.* [ME *eke,* OE *wice,* c. D *week,* akin to G *woche*]

eek·day (wēk/dā/), *n.* **1.** any day of the week except Sunday. —*adj.* **2.** of or on a weekday: *weekday ccupations.*

eek end, 1. the period from Friday night or Saturlay to Monday, as a time for recreation, visiting, etc. **2.** an overnight social gathering during the week end.

eek-end (wēk/ĕnd/), *adj.* **1.** of, for, or on a week nd. —*v.i.* **2.** to pass the week end, as at a place. —**week/-end/er,** *n.*

eek·ly (wēk/lĭ), *adj., adv., n., pl.* **-lies.** —*adj.* **1.** peraining to a week, or to each week. **2.** done, happening, ppearing, etc., once a week, or every week. **3.** continuing for a week. —*adv.* **4.** once a week. **5.** by the veek. —*n.* **6.** a periodical appearing once a week.

Weems (wēmz), *n.* **Mason Locke,** 1759–1825, U.S. clergyman and biographer.

ween (wēn), *v.i., v.t.* *Archaic.* to think or suppose. [ME *wene,* OE *wēnan* expect, c. G *wähnen* imagine]

weep[1] (wēp), *v.,* **wept, weeping,** *n.* —*v.i.* **1.** to manifest grief or anguish, orig. by outcry, now by tears; shed tears, as from sorrow, unhappiness, or any overpowering emotion; cry: *to weep for joy or rage.* **2.** to let fall drops of water or liquid; drip. **3.** to exude water or liquid, as soil, rock, a plant stem, a sore, etc. —*v.t.* **4.** to weep for; mourn with tears or other expression of sorrow: *he wept his dead brother.* **5.** to shed (tears, etc.). **6.** to let fall or give forth in drops: *trees weeping odorous gums.* **7.** to pass, bring, put, etc., with the shedding of tears (fol. by *away, out,* etc.): *to weep one's eyes out.* —*n.* **8.** *Colloq.* weeping, or a fit of weeping. **9.** exudation of water or liquid. [ME *wepe,* OE *wēpan* wail, c. Goth. *wōpjan* call] —**Syn. 1.** sob, bewail, lament.

weep[2] (wēp), *n.* the lapwing, *Vanellus vanellus,* of Europe, so called from its cries. [special use of WEEP[1]]

weep·er (wē/pər), *n.* **1.** one who weeps. **2.** a hired mourner at a funeral. **3.** thing worn as a badge of mourning.

weep·ing (wē/pĭng), *adj.* **1.** that weeps. **2.** (of trees, etc.) having slender, drooping branches.

wee·ver (wē/vər), *n.* **1.** either of two small marine fishes of the genus *Trachinus, T. draco* (**greater weever**), and *T. vipera* (**lesser weever**), common in British waters, notable for their sharp dorsal and other spines. **2.** any fish of the same family (*Trachinidae*). [? OE *wifer* dart (c. Icel. *vifr* sword); modern meaning by association with obs. *wyver* WIVERN]

wee·vil (wē/vəl), *n.* **1.** any of the numerous beetles of the family *Curculionidae,* many of which are economically important, being destructive to nuts, grain, fruit, the stems of leaves, the pith of trees, etc.; a snout beetle. **2.** any of the beetles of the family *Lariidae,* known as **seed weevils** or **bean weevils.** [ME *wevel,* OE *wifel;* akin to WAVE or WEAVE]

wee·vil·y (wē/vəlĭ), *adj.* infested with weevils. Also, **wee/vil·ly, wee·viled, wee·villed** (wē/vəld).

weft (wĕft), *n.* **1.** woof or filling yarns which interlace with warp running from selvage to selvage. See diag. under **weave. 2.** a woven piece. [ME and OE. See WEAVE]

Weich·sel (vīk/səl), *n.* German name of the **Vistula.**

wei·ge·la (wīgē/lə, -jē/-, wī/gə lə), *n.* any of various shrubby caprifoliaceous plants of the genus *Weigela,* native in E Asia, including species or varieties familiar in cultivation, with funnel-shaped white, pink, or crimson flowers. [t. NL, after C.E. *Weigel,* German physician]

weigh[1] (wā), *v.t.* **1.** to ascertain the weight of by means of a balance, scale, or other mechanical device: *to weigh gold, gases, persons, etc.* **2.** to hold up or balance, as in the hand, in order to estimate the weight. **3.** to measure (a certain quantity of something) according to weight (usually fol. by *out*): *to weigh out five pounds of sugar.* **4.** to bear (down) by weight, heaviness, oppression, etc.: *weighed down with care, a bough weighed down by fruit.* **5.** to balance in the mind; consider carefully in order to reach an opinion, decision, or choice: *to weigh facts or a proposal.* **6. weigh one's words,** to consider and choose one's words carefully in speaking or writing. **7.** to raise or lift (now chiefly in the phrase *to weigh anchor*). **8.** *Obs.* to regard or esteem. —*v.i.* **9.** to have weight or heaviness: *to weigh little or less, to weigh a ton.* **10.** *Boxing, Wrestling, etc.* to determine a contestant's weight immediately prior to a match. **11.** to have importance, moment, or consequence: *wealth weighs little in this case.* **12.** to bear down as a weight or burden: *such responsibility weighed upon him.* **13.** to consider carefully or judicially: *weigh well before deciding.* [ME *weghe,* OE *wegan* carry, weigh, c. D *wegen,* G *wägen,* Icel. *vega*] —**weigh/er,** *n.* —**Syn. 5.** See **study.**

weigh[2] (wā), *n.* *Naut.* **under weigh,** in motion, as a ship that has weighed anchor.

weight (wāt), *n.* **1.** amount of heaviness; amount a thing weighs. **2.** the force which gravitation exerts upon a material body. It varies with altitude and latitude. It is often taken as a measure of the mass, which does not vary, and is equal to the mass times the acceleration due to gravity. **3.** a system of units for expressing weight or mass: *avoirdupois weight.* **4.** a unit of weight or mass. **5.** a body of determinate mass, as of metal, for using on a balance or scale in measuring the weight or mass of (or weighing) objects, substances, etc. **6.** a quantity of a substance determined by weighing: *a half-ounce weight of gold dust.* **7.** any heavy mass or object, esp. an object used because of its heaviness: *the weights of a clock.* **8.** pressure or oppressive force, as of something burdensome: *the weight of cares, sorrows.* **9.** a burden, as of care or responsibility: *to remove a weight from my mind.* **10.** importance, moment, consequence, or effective influence: *an opinion of great weight, men of weight.* **11.** a measure of the relative importance of an item in a statistical population. **12.** (of clothing) the relative thickness as determined by the weather. **13.** by **weight,** according to weight measurement. —*v.t.* **14.** to add weight to; load with additional weight. **15.** to load (fabrics, threads, etc.) with mineral or other matter to increase the weight or bulk. **16.** to burden with or as with weight: *to be weighted with years.* **17.** *Stat.* to give a (statistical) weight to. [ME; OE *wiht,* c. D *wicht,* G *wucht.* See WEIGH]

---

weight density, the weight per unit volume.

weight·less·ness (wāt′lĭs nĭs), *n.* lack of weight, occurring when the gravitational forces acting on an object equal its mass.

weight·y (wā′tĭ), *adj.,* **weightier, weightiest. 1.** having considerable weight; heavy; ponderous. **2.** burdensome or onerous: *the weightier cares of sovereignty.* **3.** important or momentous: *weighty negotiations.* **4.** influential: *a weighty merchant of Boston.* —**weight′i·ly,** *adv.* —**weight′i·ness,** *n.* —Syn. 3. See **heavy.**

Wei·hai·wei (wā′hī′wā′), *n.* a seaport and district in NE China, in Shantung province: leased to Great Britain, 1898–1930. 175,000 pop. (est. 1950); 285 sq. mi.

Wei·mar (vī′mär), *n.* a city in East Germany. 66,675 (est. 1955).

Weimar Republic, the name of the German Republic from 1919 to 1933: founded at Weimar.

weir (wĭr), *n.* **1.** *Chiefly Brit.* a dam in a river or stream to stop and raise the water, as for conducting it to a mill, for purposes of irrigation, etc. **2.** an obstruction placed across a stream thereby causing the water to pass through a particular opening or notch, thus measuring the quantity flowing. **3.** a fence, as of brush, narrow boards, or a net, set in a stream, channel, etc., for catching fish. [ME and OE *wer,* c. G *wehr*]

weird (wĭrd), *adj.* **1.** involving or suggesting the supernatural; unearthly or uncanny: *a weird scene, light, or sound.* **2.** *Colloq.* startlingly or extraordinarily singular, odd, or queer: *a weird getup.* **3.** concerned with fate or destiny. [adj. use of *weird,* n.] —*n.* **4.** *Archaic* or *Scot.* fate or destiny. **5.** *(cap.) Obs.* or *Archaic.* fate personified, or one of the Fates. [ME *werd,* OE *wyrd;* akin to **WORTH,** v.] —**weird′ly,** *adv.* —**weird′ness,** *n.*

—Syn. 1. WEIRD, EERIE, UNEARTHLY, UNCANNY refer to that which is mysterious and apparently outside natural law. That is WEIRD which is suggestive of the fateful intervention of supernatural influences in human affairs: *the weird adventures of a group lost in the jungle.* That is EERIE which, by suggesting the ghostly, makes one's flesh creep: *an eerie moaning from a deserted house.* That is UNEARTHLY which seems by its nature to belong to another world: *an unearthly light which preceded the storm.* That is UNCANNY which is mysterious because of its apparent defiance of the laws established by experience: *an uncanny ability to recall numbers.*

weird sisters, the Fates.

Weis·mann (vīs′män), *n.* **August** (ou′gŏŏst), 1834–1914, German biologist.

Weis·mann·ism (vīs′män ĭz′əm), *n.* the theories and teachings of the German biologist August Weismann, esp. his theory respecting the continuity of the germ plasm and its isolation from the body plasm, with the accompanying doctrine that acquired characters in the latter are not and cannot be inherited.

weiss beer (vīs), a light-colored, highly effervescent beer prepared largely from malted wheat. [half adoption, half trans. of G *weissbier* white beer]

Weiss·horn (vīs′hôrn), *n.* a mountain of the Alps in S Switzerland, in Valais canton. 14,804 ft.

Weiz·mann (wīz′mən, vīts′män), *n.* **Chaim** (kī′ĭm), 1874–1952, Russian-born chemist and Zionist leader; first president of Israel, 1948–52.

we·ka (wā′kä, wē′kə), *n.* any of several large flightless New Zealand rails constituting the genus *Ocydromus.* [t. Maori]

Welch (wĕlch, wĕlsh), *adj., n.* Welsh.

welch (wĕlch, wĕlsh), *v.t., v.i. Slang.* welsh. —**welch′er,** *n.*

Welch·man (wĕlch′mən, wĕlsh′-), *n., pl.* -**men.** Welshman.

wel·come (wĕl′kəm), *interj., n., v.,* -**comed,** -**coming,** *adj.* —*interj.* **1.** a word of kindly greeting as to one whose coming gives pleasure: *welcome, stranger!* —*n.* **2.** a kindly greeting or reception, as of one whose coming gives pleasure: *to give one a warm welcome.* —*v.t.* **3.** to greet the coming of (a person, etc.) with pleasure or kindly courtesy. **4.** to receive or regard as welcome: *to welcome a change.* —*adj.* **5.** gladly received, as one whose coming gives pleasure: *a welcome visitor.* **6.** agreeable, as something coming, occurring, or experienced: *a welcome letter, a welcome rest.* **7.** given full right by the cordial consent of others: *welcome to anything he can find.* **8.** free to enjoy courtesies, etc., without being under obligation (used in conventional response to thanks): *you are quite welcome.* [ME; OE *wilcuma,* f. *wil-* pleasure + *cuma* guest] —**wel′come·less,** *adj.* —**wel′come·ly,** *adv.* —**wel′come·ness,** *n.* —**wel′com·er,** *n.*

weld¹ (wĕld), *v.t.* **1.** to unite or fuse (pieces of metal, etc.) by hammering, compression, or the like, esp. after rendering soft or pasty by heat, and sometimes with the addition of fusible material like or unlike the pieces to be united. **2.** to bring into complete union. —*v.i.* **3.** to undergo welding; be capable of being welded. —*n.* **4.** a welded junction or joint. **5.** act of welding. [var. of WELL², v.] —**weld′a·ble,** *adj.* —**weld′er,** *n.*

weld² (wĕld), *n.* **1.** a mignonette, *Reseda Luteola,* a native of southern Europe, yielding a yellow dye. **2.** the dye. Also, **wold, woald.** [ME *welde,* c. MLG *walde*]

Welf (wĕlf), *n.* Guelph.

wel·fare (wĕl′fâr), *n.* **1.** state of faring well; wellbeing: *one's welfare, the physical or moral welfare of society.* **2.** welfare work. [ME; see WELL¹, FARE] —Syn. 1. prosperity, success, happiness, weal.

Welfare Island, an island in the East River, in New York City: city prison, hospitals, and other municipal institutions. Formerly, **Blackwells Island.**

welfare state, a state (def. 9) in which the welfare of the people in such matters as social security, health and education, housing, and working conditions is the responsibility of the government.

welfare work, work devoted to the welfare of persons in a community, employees of an industrial or business establishment, or the like.

wel·kin (wĕl′kĭn), *n. Archaic.* the sky; the vault of heaven. [ME *welken(e),* OE *wolcen* cloud, c. G *wolke*]

well¹ (wĕl), *adv., adj., compar.* **better,** *super.* **best,** *interj.* —*adv.* **1.** in a satisfactory, favorable, or advantageous manner; fortunately or happily: *affairs are going well to be well supplied, well situated.* **2.** in a good manner. **3.** commendably, meritoriously, or excellently: *to act, write, or reason well, a good work well done.* **4.** with propriety, justice, or reason: *I could not well refuse.* **5.** in satisfactory or good measure; adequately or sufficiently: *think well before you act.* **6.** thoroughly or soundly: *shake well before using, beat well.* **7.** to a considerable extent or degree: *a sum well over the amount fixed, dilute the acid well.* **8.** personally; to a great degree of intimacy: *to know a person well.* —*adj.* **9.** in good health or sound in body and mind: *I am well, a well man.* **10.** satisfactory or good: *all is well with us.* **11.** proper or fitting. **12.** in a satisfactory position; well-off: *I am very well as I am.* —*interj.* **13.** (used to express surprise, agreement, or merely as a preliminary to further speech): *well, so you have come! well, who would have thought it.* [ME and OE *wel(l),* c. D *wel,* G *wohl,* Icel. *vel,* Goth *waila*] —Syn. 9. healthy, hale, sound, hearty.

well² (wĕl), *n.* **1.** a hole drilled into the earth, generally by boring, for the production of water, petroleum, natural gas, brine, or sulfur. **2.** a spring or natural source of water. **3.** a fountain, fountainhead, or source: *Chaucer, well of English undefiled.* **4.** a vessel, receptacle, or reservoir for a liquid: *an inkwell.* **5.** any sunken or deep, enclosed space, as a shaft for air or light, or for stairs, an elevator, or the like, extending vertically through the floors of a building. **6.** a compartment or enclosure around a ship's pumps to render them easy of access and protect them from being injured by the cargo. [ME and OE, c. G *welle* wave] —*v.i.* **7.** to rise, spring, or gush, as water, from the earth or some source (often fol. by *up, out,* or *forth): tears well up in the eyes.* —*v.t.* **8.** to send welling up or forth: *fountain welling its pure water.* [ME *welle,* OE *wellan* (c. D *wellen,* Icel. *vella*), var. of *wiellan,* causative of *weallan* boil]

we′ll (wĕl; *unstressed* wĭl), cont. of *we will* or *we shall.*

Wel·land Canal (wĕl′ənd), a ship canal in S Canada in Ontario, connecting lakes Erie and Ontario: 8 locks raise or lower ships 325 ft. 25 mi. long; 25 ft. deep.

well·a·way (wĕl′ə wā′), *interj. Archaic.* an exclamation of sorrow. Also, **well·a·day** (wĕl′ə dā′). [ME *welawei,* r. ME and OE *weilawei (wei* t. Scand.; cf. Icel *vei* woe), r. OE *wā lā wā* woe! la! woe!]

well·bal·anced (wĕl′băl′ənst), *adj.* **1.** rightly balanced, adjusted, or regulated. **2.** sensible; sane.

well·be·haved (wĕl′bĭ hāvd′), *adj.* characterized by good behavior or conduct.

well·be·ing (wĕl′bē′ĭng), *n.* good or satisfactory condition of existence; welfare.

well·born (wĕl′bôrn′), *adj.* of good birth or family.

well·bred (wĕl′brĕd′), *adj.* **1.** well brought up, as persons. **2.** showing good breeding, as behavior, manners, etc. **3.** of good breed, as a domestic animal.

well·con·tent (wĕl′kən tĕnt′), *adj.* satisfied.

well·dis·posed (wĕl′dĭs pōzd′), *adj.* **1.** rightly or properly disposed; well-meaning. **2.** favorably or kindly disposed: *well-disposed hearts.*

well·do·er (wĕl′dōō′ər), *n.* **1.** one who does well or acts rightly. **2.** a doer of good deeds.

well·do·ing (wĕl′dō′ĭng), *n.* good conduct or action.

Welles·ley (wĕlz′lĭ), *n.* **1. Arthur.** See **Wellington, 1st Duke of. 2.** his brother, **Richard Colley, Marquis,** 1760–1842, British statesman and administrator: governor general of India, 1797–1805.

well·fa·vored (wĕl′fā′vərd), *adj.* of pleasing appearance; good-looking. Also, *Brit.,* **well′-fa′voured.**

well·fed (wĕl′fĕd′), *adj.* fat; plump.

well·found (wĕl′found′), *adj.* well furnished with supplies, necessaries, etc.

well·found·ed (wĕl′foun′dĭd), *adj.* rightly or justly founded, as on good grounds: *well-founded suspicions.*

well·groomed (wĕl′grōōmd′), *adj.* **1.** well cared for as in matters of the toilet. **2.** tended, cleaned, curried, etc., with great care, as a horse.

well·ground·ed (wĕl′groun′dĭd), *adj.* **1.** based on good grounds or reasons; well-founded. **2.** well or thoroughly instructed in the first principles of a subject.

well·head (wĕl′hĕd′), *n.* a fountainhead; source.

well·in·formed (wĕl′ĭn fôrmd′), *adj.* **1.** having reliable or full information on a subject. **2.** having information on a variety of subjects: *a well-informed man.*

Wel·ling·ton (wĕl′ĭng tən), *n.* **1. Arthur Wellesley, 1st Duke of,** 1769–1852, British general and statesman. **2.** a seaport and the capital of New Zealand, in the S part of North Island. 138,297 (1956).

well·known (wĕl′nōn′), *adj.* **1.** clearly or fully known: *for reasons well-known to you.* **2.** familiarly

---

b., blend of, blended; **c.,** cognate with; **d.,** dialect, dialectal; **der.,** derived from; **f.,** formed from; **g.,** going back to; **m.,** modification of; **r.,** replacing; **s.,** stem of; **t.,** taken from; **?,** perhaps. See the full key on inside cover known, or familiar: *his well-known face.* **3.** generally or widely known: *the well-known sculptor.*

well-man·nered (wĕl'măn'ərd), *adj.* polite; courteous.

well-mean·ing (wĕl'mē'nĭng), *adj.* **1.** meaning or intending well: *a well-meaning but tactless person.* **2.** Also, **well-meant** (wĕl'mĕnt'). proceeding from good intentions.

well-nigh (wĕl'nī'), *adv.* very nearly; almost. —**Syn.** See **almost.**

well-off (wĕl'ôf', -ŏf'), *adj.* **1.** in a satisfactory, favorable, or good position or condition: *to know when one is well-off.* **2.** in good or easy circumstances as to money or means; moderately rich.

well-point (wĕl'point'), *n.* one of a series of pipes with perforated tips, driven into the ground around an excavation site in order to pump the ground-water level below that of the excavation.

well-pre·served (wĕl'prĭ zûrvd'), *adj.* preserving a young or new appearance.

well-read (wĕl'rĕd'), *adj.* **1.** having read much: *well-read in science.* **2.** having an extensive and intelligent knowledge of books or literature.

Wells (wĕlz), *n.* **1. Herbert George,** 1866–1946, British novelist and writer on social and political problems. **2.** a historic town in SW England, in Somersetshire: famous cathedral. 7298 (1951).

well-spo·ken (wĕl'spō'kən), *adj.* **1.** speaking well, fittingly, or pleasingly. **2.** polite in speech. **3.** spoken well.

well-spring (wĕl'sprĭng'), *n.* **1.** a fountainhead. **2.** a source of anything.

well sweep, sweep (def. 25).

well-thought-of (wĕl'thôt'ŏv', -ŭv'), *adj.* having a high reputation.

well-timed (wĕl'tīmd'), *adj.* fittingly timed; opportune; timely: *a well-timed demand for action on housing.*

well-to-do (wĕl'tə dōō'), *adj.* **1.** having a sufficiency of means for comfortable living, well-off, or prosperous. **2.** characterized by or showing a comfortable sufficiency of means, or prosperity: *well-to-do circumstances.*

well-wish·er (wĕl'wĭsh'ər), *n.* one who wishes well to a person, a cause, etc. —**well'-wish'ing,** *adj.*, *n.*

well-worn (wĕl'wôrn'), *adj.* **1.** much worn or affected by use: *well-worn garments or carpets, a well-worn volume.* **2.** trite, hackneyed, or stale: *a well-worn saying or theme.* **3.** fittingly or becomingly worn or borne: *well-worn reserve.*

Wels·bach burner (wĕlz'băk, -bäk; *Ger.* vĕls'bäкн), a gas burner devised by the Austrian chemist Karl Auer von Welsbach, 1858–1929, consisting essentially of a Bunsen burner about the flame of which is placed an incombustible mantle (**Welsbach mantle**) composed of thoria and some ceria, which becomes brilliantly incandescent.

Welsh (wĕlsh, wĕlch), *adj.* **1.** of or pertaining to Wales, its people, or their language. —*n.* **2.** the people of Wales. **3.** the Celtic language of Wales. Also, **Welch.** [ME *Welische,* OE *Welisc,* der. *Walh* Briton, foreigner]

welsh (wĕlsh, wĕlch), *v.t., v.i. Slang.* to cheat by evading payment (sometimes fol. by *on*). Also, **welch.** [orig. obscure] —**welsh'er,** *n.*

Welsh Cor·gi (kôr'gĭ), a dog of either of two ancient Welsh breeds, resembling the dachshund, but having erect ears, the **Cardigan** variety having a long tail and the **Pembroke** a short tail.

Welsh·man (wĕlsh'mən, wĕlch'-), *n., pl.* **-men.** a native or inhabitant of Wales. Also, **Welchman.**

Welsh rabbit, melted cheese, usually mixed with ale or beer, milk, etc., eaten on toast. Also, **Welsh rarebit.** [prob. of jocular origin]

Welsh terrier, a black-and-tan terrier of a breed developed in Wales as a hunting dog.

welt (wĕlt), *n.* **1.** *Colloq.* a ridge or wale on the surface of the body, as from the stroke of a stick or whip. **2.** *Colloq.* a stroke of this kind. **3.** a strip of leather set in between the edges of the inner sole and upper and the outer sole of a shoe. **4.** a strengthening or ornamental finish along a seam, the edge of a garment, etc. **5.** a type of seam in which one edge is cut close to the stitching line and covered by the other edge which is stitched over it. —*v.t.* **6.** *Colloq.* to beat soundly, as with a stick or whip. **7.** to furnish with a welt or welts. [ME *welte, walt;* cf. OE *wæltan, weltan* roll]

Welt·an·schau·ung (vĕlt'än'shou'ŏŏng), *n. German.* the philosophy of an individual or a group (esp. a race) with an interpretation of world history or civilization.

Welt·an·sicht (vĕlt'än'zĭкнt), *n. German.* a world view; an attitude toward, or interpretation of, reality.

wel·ter (wĕl'tər), *v.i.* **1.** to roll, toss, or heave, as waves, the sea, etc. **2.** to roll or tumble about, or wallow, as animals. **3.** to lie bathed or be drenched in something, esp. blood. —*n.* **4.** a rolling or tumbling about: *in the welter of the sea.* **5.** commotion or turmoil: *the welter of our mutable world.* [ME, freq. of obs. *welt* roll, OE *weltan.* Cf. MD *welteren,* LG *weltern* roll]

wel·ter·weight (wĕl'tər wāt'), *n.* a boxer or wrestler with a maximum weight of 147 pounds, intermediate in weight between a middleweight and lightweight. [f. *welter* heavyweight rider or boxer (lit. beater, der. WELT, v.) + WEIGHT]

Welt·po·li·tik (vĕlt'pō lĭ tēk'), *n. German.* the policy of a nation with respect to the world. [G: world politics]

Welt·schmerz (vĕlt'shmĕrts'), *n. German.* sorrow felt and accepted as the necessary portion of the world; sentimental pessimism. [G: world-pain]

Wem·bley (wĕm'blĭ), *n.* a city in SE England, in Middlesex, near London. 131,369 (1951).

Wemyss (wēmz), *n.* a parish in E Scotland, in Fife county, on the Firth of Forth: castle. 28,465 (1951).

wen[1] (wĕn), *n. Pathol.* a benign encysted tumor of the skin, esp. on the scalp, containing sebaceous matter; a sebaceous cyst. [ME and OE *wenn,* c. D *wen*]

wen[2] (wĕn), *n.* the name of the rune for *w.* [ME and OE; var. of obs. *win,* OE *wynn* joy]

Wen·ces·laus (wĕn'səs lôs'), *n.* 1361–1419, emperor of the Holy Roman Empire, 1378–1400, and king of Bohemia as Wenceslaus IV, 1378–1419. Also, **Wenzel.**

wench (wĕnch), *n.* **1.** a girl, or young woman. **2.** a rustic or working girl. **3.** *Archaic or Prov.* a strumpet. —*v.i.* **4.** to consort with strumpets. [ME, var. of *wenchel,* OE *wencel* child. Cf. OE *wancol* weak] —**wench'er,** *n.*

Wen·chow (wĕn'chou'; *Chin.* wŭn'jō'), *n.* former name of **Yungkia.**

wend (wĕnd), *v.,* **wended** or (*Archaic*) **went; wending.** —*v.t.* **1.** *Poetic or Literary.* to direct or pursue (one's way, etc.): *he wended his way to the riverside.* —*v.i.* **2.** *Archaic.* to proceed or go. [ME; OE *wendan,* c. D and G *wenden*]

Wend (wĕnd), *n.* a member of a Slavic people in Saxony and adjoining parts of Prussia; Sorb. [t. G. m. *Wende*]

Wend·ish (wĕn'dĭsh), *adj.* **1.** of or pertaining to the Wends; Sorbian. —*n.* **2.** Sorbian. Also, **Wend'ic.**

wen·ny (wĕn'ĭ), *adj.* **1.** like a wen. **2.** having a wen.

went (wĕnt), *v.* **1.** pt. of **go.** **2.** archaic pt. and pp. of **wend.**

wen·tle·trap (wĕn'təl trăp'), *n.* any of the handsome, usually white, spiral-shelled marine gastropods constituting the genus *Scalaria* or the family *Scalariidae.* [t. D: m. *wenteltrap* winding stair, spiral shell]

Went·worth (wĕnt'wûrth), *n.* **Thomas,** (*1st Earl of Strafford*) 1593–1641, British statesman; chief adviser of Charles I; impeached and executed.

Wen·zel (vĕn'tsəl), *n.* Wenceslaus.

wept (wĕpt), *v.* pt. and pp. of **weep**[1].

were (wûr *or, esp. Brit.,* wâr; *unstressed* wər), *v.* pt. ind. pl. and subj. sing. and pl. of **be.** [ME; OE *wæron, wǣre(n),* c. G *waren.* See WAS]

we're (wĭr), contraction of *we are.*

were·n't (wûrnt), contraction of *were not.*

were·wolf (wĭr'wŏŏlf', wûr'-), *n., pl.* **-wolves** (-wŏŏlvz'). (in old superstition) a human being turned preternaturally into a wolf, or capable of assuming the form of a wolf, while retaining human intelligence. Also, **wer·wolf** (wûr'wŏŏlf', wûr'-). [ME *werwolf,* OE *wer(e)wulf.* f. *wer* man (c. L *vir*) + WOLF]

Wer·fel (vĕr'fəl), *n.* **Franz** (fränts), 1890–1945, German novelist, dramatist, and poet, born in Prague.

wer·gild (wûr'gĭld', wĕr'-), *n. Early Eng. Law.* a fine for manslaughter and other crimes against the person, by paying which to the relatives of the deceased, or to the injured person, the offender freed himself from every further obligation or punishment. Also, **were·gild** (wĭr'-gĭld', wĕr'-). [ME (Scot.) *weregylt,* OE *wer(e)gild,* f. *wer* man + *gild* compensation (see YIELD)]

wer·ner·ite (wûr'nə rīt'), *n.* a variety of scapolite.

wert (wûrt; *unstressed* wərt), *v.* 2nd pers. sing. pt. indic. and subj. of **be** (now only in solemn or poetic use).

We·ser (vā'zər), *n.* a river flowing through N West Germany into the North Sea. ab. 300 mi.

We·ser·mün·de (vā'zər mɣn'də), *n.* former name of Bremerhaven.

Wes·ley (wĕs'lĭ *or, esp. Brit.,* wĕz'-), *n.* **1. Charles,** 1707–88, British Methodist preacher and hymn writer. **2.** his brother, **John,** 1703–91, British preacher, founder of Methodism.

Wes·ley·an (wĕs'lĭ ən *or, esp. Brit.,* wĕz'-), *adj.* **1.** of or pertaining to John Wesley, founder of Methodism. **2.** pertaining to Methodism. —*n.* **3.** a follower of John Wesley. **4.** *Chiefly Brit.* a member of the denomination founded by him; a Methodist. —**Wes'ley·an·ism,** *n.*

Wes·sex (wĕs'ĭks), *n.* **1.** (in the Middle Ages) a kingdom, later an earldom, in S England. *Cap.:* Winchester. See map under **Mercia.** **2.** (in modern times) a region principally in Dorsetshire, described in Hardy's novels.

west (wĕst), *n.* **1.** a cardinal point of the compass, 90° to the left of North. **2.** the direction in which this point lies. **3.** (*l.c. or cap.*) a quarter or territory situated in this direction, as the western part of the U.S. in distinction from the East. **4.** (*cap.*) the western part of the world, as distinguished from the East or Orient; the Occident. **5.** *Ancient and Medieval Hist.* the Western Empire. —*adj.* **6.** directed or proceeding toward the west. **7.** coming from the west, as wind. **8.** lying toward or situated in the west. **9.** *Eccles.* designating, lying toward, or in that part of a church opposite to and furthest from the altar. —*adv.* **10.** in the direction of the sunset; toward or in the west (as of wind). **11.** from the west (as of wind). [ME and OE, c. D and G *west,* Icel. *vestr*]

West (wĕst), *n.* **1. Benjamin,** 1738–1820, American painter in England. **2. Rebecca,** (*Cecily Fairfield*) born 1892, British novelist and critic.

West Al·lis (ăl′ĭs), a city in SE Wisconsin, near Milwaukee. 68,159 (1960).

West Bengal, a state in E India; formerly part of the province of Bengal. 26,250,000 pop. (est. 1956); 33,805 sq.mi. *Cap.*: Calcutta. See **Bengal.**

West Brom·wich (brŭm′ĭj, -ĭch, brŏm′-), a city in central England, near Birmingham. 90,720 (est. 1956).

west by north, one point or degree north of west on a compass card or dial. See diag. under **compass card.**

west by south, one point or degree south of west on a compass card or dial. See diag. under **compass card.**

West Covina (kō vē′nə), a city in SW California, E of Los Angeles. 50,645 (1960).

West End, the aristocratic residential section of London, England.

west·er (wĕs′tər), *v.i.* to move or tend westward.

west·er·ly (wĕs′tər lĭ), *adj., adv., n., pl.* **-lies.** —*adj.* 1. moving, directed, or situated toward the west. 2. coming from the west: *a westerly gale.* —*adv.* 3. toward the west. 4. from the west. —*n.* 5. a westerly wind.

Wes·ter·marck (wĕs′tər märk′; *Fin.* vĕs′tər-), *n.* Edward Alexander, 1862–1939, Finnish sociologist.

west·ern (wĕs′tərn), *adj.* 1. lying toward or situated in the west. 2. directed or proceeding toward the west. 3. coming from the west, as a wind. 4. (*l.c. or cap.*) of or pertaining to the west: *a Western ranch or cowboy.* 5. (*usually cap.*) Occidental. —*n.* 6. one living in a western region or country. 7. *Colloq.* a story or moving picture about the U.S. West. [ME and OE *westerne*]

Western Australia, a state in W Australia. 639,771 pop. (1954); 975,920 sq. mi. *Cap.*: Perth.

Western Church, 1. the Roman Catholic Church, sometimes with the Anglican Church, or, more broadly, the Christian churches of western Europe and those churches elsewhere which are connected with or have sprung from them. 2. the Christian church in the countries once comprised in the Western Empire and in countries evangelized from these countries, or that part of the Christian church which acknowledged the popes after the split between Greek and Latin Christianity.

Western Empire, the western portion of the Roman Empire A.D. 395–476.

west·ern·er (wĕs′tər nər), *n.* a person of or from the western U.S.

Western Hemisphere, 1. a hemisphere of the earth cut along a meridian so chosen as to include all of North and South America, but no part of any other continent. 2. that half of the earth traversed in passing westward from the prime meridian to 180° longitude.

west·ern·ism (wĕs′tər nĭz′əm), *n.* a word, idiom, or practice peculiar to western people, esp. those of the western U.S.

Western Islands, Hebrides.

west·ern·ize (wĕs′tər nīz′), *v.t.*, **-ized, -izing.** to make western in ideas, character, ways, etc.

west·ern·most (wĕs′tərn mōst′), *adj.* farthest west.

Western Samoa, an independent state comprising the western part of the Samoan islands: formerly a trust territory of New Zealand. 113,567 pop. (1961); 1133 sq. mi. *Cap.*: Apia.

West·fa·len (vĕst fä′lən), *n. German.* **Westphalia.**

West Germany. See under **Germany.**

West Ham, a city in SE England, in Essex, near London. 167,000 (est. 1956).

West Hartford, a town in central Connecticut. 62,382 (1960).

West Har·tle·pool (här′təl pōōl′), a seaport in NE England at the mouth of the Tees. 73,200 (est. 1956).

West Haven, a town in S Connecticut, near New Haven. 43,002 (1960).

West Indies, 1. an archipelago in the N Atlantic between North and South America, enclosing the Caribbean Sea and the Gulf of Mexico: divided into the Greater Antilles, the Lesser Antilles, and the Bahama Islands. 2. Federation of the, a federation, 1958–1962, of British islands in the Caribbean, comprising Barbados, Jamaica, Trinidad and Tobago, and the Windward and Leeward Island colonies. —**West Indian.**

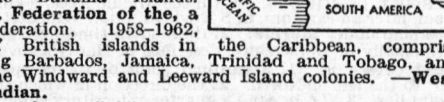

west·ing (wĕs′tĭng), *n.* the distance due west made by a ship on any course tending westward; westerly departure; distance westward.

West·ing·house (wĕs′tĭng hous′), *n.* **George,** 1846–1914, U.S. inventor.

West Ir·i·an (ĭr′ĭən), **the** W part of the island of New Guinea: formerly the Dutch territory of Netherlands New Guinea; since 1963 a province of Indonesia. 750,000 (est. 1961); ab. 159,000 sq. mi. Also formerly called **Dutch New Guinea.**

West Lo·thi·an (lō′t̸hĭ′ən), a county in S Scotland. 91,200 pop. (est. 1956); 120 sq. mi. *Co. seat*: Linlithgow.

Westm., Westminster.

West·min·ster (wĕst′mĭn′stər), *n.* a central borough

(officially a city) of London, England: Westminster Abbey; Houses of Parliament; Buckingham Palace. 98,895 (1951).

Westminster Abbey, a large Gothic church in London, England, rebuilt since 1245 by Henry III and Edward I: burial place of many great Englishmen.

Westminster Assembly, a convocation, mostly of divines, which met at Westminster from 1643 to 1649, whose decisions on matters of faith and discipline have become the standard of orthodoxy in most English-speaking Presbyterian churches.

West·more·land (wĕst′môr lənd; *Brit.* -mər lənd), *n.* a county in NW England, partially in the Lake District. 67,383 (1951); 789 sq. mi. *Co. seat*: Appleby.

West New York, a town in NE New Jersey, across the Hudson from New York City. 35,547 (1960).

West Orange, a town in NE New Jersey, near Newark. 28,605 (1960).

West Pakistan, a part of Pakistan, NW of India and N of the Arabian Sea. 33,779,000 (1951); 310,236 sq. mi. *Cap.*: Lahore.

West Palm Beach, a city in SE Florida: winter resort. 56,208 (1960).

West·pha·li·a (wĕst fā′lĭ ə), *n.* a former province in NW Germany: treaty ending the Thirty Years' War, 1648. Now part of North Rhine-Westphalia. German, **Westfalen.** —**West·pha′li·an,** *adj., n.*

West Point, a military reservation in SE New York, on the Hudson: seat of the U.S. Military Academy.

West Prussia, a former province of Prussia, now in Poland. German, **West·preus·sen** (vĕst′proi′sən).

West Punjab, a state in N Pakistan. 18,828,000 pop. (1951); 62,245 sq. mi.

West Rid·ing (rī′dĭng), an administrative county in Yorkshire, England. 3,586,274 pop. (1951); 2790 sq. mi. *Co. seat*: Wakefield.

West Virginia, a State in the E United States. 1,860,421 pop. (1960); 24,181 sq. mi. *Cap.*: Charleston. *Abbr.*: W.Va. —**West Virginian.**

west·ward (wĕst′wərd), *adj.* 1. moving, bearing, facing, or situated toward the west. —*adv.* 2. Also, **west′wards.** toward the west; west. —*n.* 3. the westward part, direction, or point.

west·ward·ly (wĕst′wərd lĭ), *adj.* 1. having a westward direction or situation. 2. coming from the west, as a wind. —*adv.* 3. toward the west. 4. from the west.

wet (wĕt), *adj.*, **wetter, wettest,** *n., v.,* **wet** or **wetted, wetting.** —*adj.* 1. covered or soaked, wholly or in part, with water or some other liquid: *wet hands, a wet sponge.* 2. moist, damp, or not dry: *wet ink or paint.* 3. characterized by the presence or use of water or other liquid: *the wet way of chemical analysis.* 4. rainy. 5. *U.S.* characterized by or favoring allowance of the manufacture and sale of alcoholic liquors for use as beverages. —*n.* 6. that which makes wet, as water or other liquid; moisture. 7. rain. 8. *U.S.* one who favors allowance of the manufacture and sale of alcoholic liquors for use as beverages. —*v.t.* 9. to make wet. 10. **wet one's whistle,** *Colloq.* to take a drink. —*v.i.* 11. to become wet. [ME *wett,* prop. pp. of *wete,* OE *wǣtan* to wet; r. ME *weet,* OE *wǣt,* c. Icel. *vātr*] —**wet′ly,** *adv.* —**wet′ness,** *n.* —**wet′ter,** *n.* —**wet′tish,** *adj.*

—**Syn.** 1. dampened, drenched. 4. humid, misty, drizzling. 9. WET, DRENCH, SATURATE, SOAK imply moistening something thoroughly. To WET is to moisten in any manner with water or other liquid: *to wet or dampen a cloth.* DRENCH suggests wetting completely as by a downpour: *a heavy rain drenched the fields.* SATURATE implies wetting to the limit of absorption: *to saturate a sponge.* To SOAK is to keep covered or partially covered by a liquid for a time: *to soak beans.*

wet·back (wĕt′băk′), *n.* a Mexican laborer who enters the U.S. illegally, as by wading the Rio Grande.

wet blanket, a person or thing that dampens ardor or has a discouraging or depressing effect.

wet-blan·ket (wĕt′blăng′kĭt), *v.t.* to dampen the ardor of.

wet bulb, the thermometer bulb which is kept moistened when humidity determinations are being made with a psychrometer.

wet cell, *Elect.* a cell whose electrolyte is in liquid form and free to flow.

weth·er (wĕt̸h′ər), *n.* a castrated male sheep. [ME and OE, c. G *widder*; akin to L *vitulus* calf]

wet nurse, a woman hired to suckle another's infant.

wet-nurse (wĕt′nûrs′), *v.t.*, **-nursed, -nursing.** to act as wet nurse to.

wet pack, *Med.* a type of bath in which wet sheets are applied to the patient.

Wet·ter·horn (vĕt′ər hôrn′), *n.* a mountain in S Switzerland, in the Bernese Alps. 12,149 ft.

we've (wēv; *unstressed* wĭv), contraction of *we have.*

Wex·ford (wĕks′fərd), *n.* 1. a county in SE Ireland, in Leinster province. 87,236 pop. (prelim. 1956); 908 sq. mi. 2. its county seat: a seaport. 11,979 (1951).

Wey·gand (vĕgän′), *n.* **Maxime** (måk sēm′), born 1867, French general.

wf, *Print.* wrong font. Also, **w.f.**

W. Ger., West Germanic.

wh., watt-hour.

whack (hwăk), *v.t.* 1. *Colloq.* to strike with a smart, resounding blow or blows. 2. *Slang.* to divide into or take in shares. —*v.i.* 3. *Colloq.* to strike a smart,

esounding blow or blows. **4.** *Slang.* to divide or share
rofits, spoils, etc. (often fol. by *up*). —*n.* **5.** *Colloq.* a
mart, resounding blow: *a whack with his hand.* **6.**
lang. a trial or attempt: *to take a whack at a job.*
7. *Slang.* a portion or share. **8.** *Slang.* condition: good
ondition. [? imit.; ? var. of THWACK] —**whack′er,** *n.*

hack·ing (hwăk′Yng), *adj.* *Chiefly Brit. Colloq.* large.

hack·y (wăk′Y), *adj.,* **whackier, whackiest.** wacky.

hale[1] (hwāl), *n.,* *pl.* **whales,** (*esp. collectively*) **whale,**
, whaled, whaling. —*n.* **1.** *Zool.* any of the larger
marine mammals of the order *Cetacea,* which in-
ludes the large sperm
ad whalebone whales,
nd the smaller dolphins
nd porpoises. All have
shlike bodies, modified
reflippers, and a hori-
ontally flattened tail.
2. *Slang.* something
xtraordinarily big, great,
r fine of its kind: *a whale of a lot, a whale of a scholar.*
—*v.i.* **3.** to carry on the work of taking whales. [ME; OE
wǣl, c. MHG *wal,* Icel. *hvalr*]

Bowhead whale. *Balaena mysticetus*
(50 to 65 ft. long)

hale[2] (hwāl), *v.t.,* **whaled, whaling.** *Colloq.* to whip,
hrash, or beat soundly. [orig. uncert.; ? var. of WALE]

hale·back (hwāl′băk′), *n.* a vessel having a rounded
eck which meets the sides in a continuous curve, some-
imes with upper works, much used on the Great Lakes.

hale·boat (hwāl′bōt′), *n.* a type of very handy boat
esigned for quick turning and use in rough sea; formerly
sed in whaling, now mainly for sea rescue.

hale·bone (hwāl′bōn′), *n.* **1.** an elastic horny sub-
tance growing in place of teeth in the upper jaw of
ertain whales, and forming a series of thin, parallel
lates on each side of the palate; baleen. **2.** a thin
trip of this material, used for stiffening corsets.

hale·man (hwāl′mən), *n.,* *pl.* **-men.** a man engaged
n whaling.

hal·er (hwā′lər), *n.* a person or vessel engaged in
whaling.

hales (hwālz), *n.* **Bay of,** an inlet of the Ross Sea, in
antarctica: Little America is located here.

hal·ing (hwā′lYng), *n.* the work or industry of taking
whales; whale fishing.

hang (hwăng), *Colloq.* —*n.* **1.** a resounding blow, or
ang. —*v.t.* **2.** to strike with such a blow, or bang.
partly imit., partly var. of *thwang* THONG]

hang·ee (hwăng·ē′), *n.* one of the species of the
amboo genus *Phyllostachys,* native to China. [t.
hinese: alter. of *hwang* hard bamboo]

hap (hwŏp), *v.t., v.i.,* **whapped, whapping,** *n.* *Colloq.*
r *Dial.* whop.

hap·per (hwŏp′ər), *n.* *Colloq.* whopper.

hap·ping (hwŏp′Yng), *adj.* *Colloq.* whopping.

harf (hwôrf), *n.,* *pl.* **wharves** (hwôrvz, hwôrfs),
wharfs, *v.* —*n.* **1.** a structure built on the shore of, or
rojecting out into, a harbor, stream, etc., so that vessels
nay be moored alongside to load or unload or to lie at
est; a quay; a pier. **2.** *Obs.* a bank or shore. —*v.t.* **3.**
o provide with a wharf or wharves. **4.** to place or
tore on a wharf. [ME; OE *hwearf* dam, akin to G *werf*
der] —**wharf′less,** *adj.*

harf·age (hwôr′fYj), *n.* **1.** the use of a wharf.
. storage of goods at a wharf. **3.** the charge or payment
or the use of a wharf. **4.** wharves collectively.

harf·in·ger (hwôr′fYn·jer), *n.* one who owns, or has
harge of, a wharf. [f. WHARFAGE + -ER, with n-infix as
n *passenger,* etc.]

har·ton (hwôr′tən), *n.* **Edith,** (*Mrs. Edith Newbold
ones Wharton*) 1862–1937, U.S. novelist.

harve (hwôrv), *n.* *Spinning.* a wheel or round piece
f wood on a spindle, serving as a flywheel or as a pulley.
ME *wherve,* OE *hweorfa*]

harves (hwôrvz), *n.* **1.** pl. of **wharf. 2.** pl. of
harve.

hat (hwŏt, hwŭt; *unstressed* hwət), *pron., pl.* **what,**
dv., *conj.* —*pron.* **1.** interrog. pron. **a.** asking for
he specifying of some thing (not person): *what is your
ame? what did he do?* **b.** inquiring as to the nature,
haracter, class, origin, etc., of a thing or person: *what is
hat animal?* **c.** inquiring as to the worth, usefulness,
orce, or importance of something: *what is wealth without
ealth?* **d.** asking, often elliptically, for repetition or ex-
lanation of some word or words used, as by a previous
peaker: *you need five what? you claim to be what?* **e.** *Brit.
Colloq.* used with a general or vague interrogative force,
sp. at the end of a sentence: *a sort of anarchical fellow,
what?* **f.** used adjectively, before a noun (whether thing
r person): *what news? what men?* **g.** often used inter-
ectionally to express surprise, disbelief, indignation, etc.
. often used with intensive force in exclamatory phrases
preceding an indefinite article, if one is used): *what luck!
hat an idea!* **i.** used in various phrases, often elllipti-
al: *what of it?* (what about it? what does it matter?);
hat for? (for what reason or purpose? why?); *toys,
ictures, and what not* (and anything whatever; and
nything else that there may be; et cetera). **2.** rel. pron.
a. (as a compound relative) that which: *this is what he
ays, I will send what was promised.* **b.** the kind of thing
r person that, or such: *the book is just what it professes
o be, the old man is not what he was.* **c.** anything that,
r whatever: *say what you please, come what may.* **d.**

(in parenthetic clauses) something that: *but he went, and,
what is more surprising, gained a hearing.* **e.** (as a simple
relative) that, which, or who: now regarded as non-
standard English except in the possessive **whose** (see
whose) and the phrase **but what:** *there is no one but what
is pleased,* that is, who is not pleased. **f.** (used adjectively) that or any . . . which; such . . . as: *take what
time and what assistants you need.*
—*adv.* **3.** to what extent or degree, or how much?:
what does it matter? **4.** (in certain expressions) in what
or some manner or measure, or partly: *what with storms,
his return was delayed.* **5.** *Obs.* in what respect or
how?: *what are men better than sheep?* **6.** *Obs.* for what
reason or purpose or why?.
—*conj.* **7.** *Prov.* or *Colloq.* to the extent that, as much
as, or so far as: *he helps me what he can.* **8. but what,**
Colloq. but that, but who; who or that . . . not.
[ME; OE *hwæt,* c. D *wat,* G *was,* Icel. *hvat,* Goth. *hwa*]

what·ev·er (hwŏt·ĕv′ər), *pron.* **1.** indef. rel. pron.
a. anything that: *do whatever you like.* **b.** any amount
or measure (of something) that: *whatever of time or
energy may be mine.* **c.** no matter what: *do it, whatever
happens.* **2.** *Brit.* interrog. *Colloq.* what ever? what?
(used emphatically): *whatever do you mean?* —*adj.*
3. any . . . that: *whatever merit the work has.* **4.** no matter
what: *whatever rebuffs he might receive.* **5.** being what
or who it may be: *for whatever reason, he is unwilling,
any person whatever.* Also, *Poetic,* **what·e′er** (hwŏt·âr′).

what·not (hwŏt′nŏt′), *n.* **1.** a stand with shelves for
bric-a-brac, books, etc. **2.** *Colloq.* anything; no matter
what; what you please: *a chronicler of whatnots.*

what's (hwŏts, hwŭts; *unstressed* hwəts), contraction of
what is.

what·so·ev·er (hwŏt′sō·ĕv′ər), *pron., adj.* intensive
form of **whatever:** *whatsoever it be, in any place whatsoever.* Also, *Poetic,* **what·so·e′er** (hwŏt′sō·âr′).

whaup (hwäp, hwôp), *n.* the large common curlew,
Numenius arquata, of Europe. [cf. OE *hwilpe* plover]

wheal (hwēl), *n.* **1.** a small, burning or itching swelling
on the skin, as from a mosquito bite or from urticaria.
2. a wale or welt. [ME *whale;* akin to obs. *wheal* v., OE
hwelian suppurate]

wheat (hwēt), *n.* **1.** the grain of a widely distributed
cereal grass, genus *Triticum,* esp. *T. aestivum* (*T.
sativum*), used extensively in the form of flour for white
bread, cakes, pastry, etc. **2.** the plant, which bears the
edible grain in dense spikes that sometimes have awns
(**bearded wheat**) and sometimes do not (**beardless
wheat** or **bald wheat**). [ME *whete,* OE *hwǣte,* c. D *weit,*
G *weizen*] —**wheat′less,** *adj.*

wheat·ear (hwēt′Yr′), *n.* a small oscine passerine
bird, *Oenanthe oenanthe,* found principally in the Old
World, notable for its boldly marked tail.

wheat·en (hwē′tən), *adj.* **1.** made of the grain or flour
of wheat: *wheaten bread.* **2.** of or pertaining to wheat.

Wheat·stone (hwēt′stōn′ *or,* esp. *Brit.,* hwēt′stən), *n.*
Sir Charles, 1802–75, British physicist and inventor.

Wheatstone bridge, *Elect.* an instrument designed
for measuring the electrical resistance of a circuit or a
circuit component. Also, **Wheatstone's bridge.**

wheat·worm (hwēt′wûrm′), *n.* a small nematode
worm, *Tylenchus tritici,* causing earcockle in wheat.

whee·dle (hwē′dəl), *v.,* **-dled, -dling.** —*v.t.* **1.** to endeavor to influence (a person) by smooth, flattering, or
beguiling words. **2.** to get by artful persuasions: *wheedling my money from me.* —*v.i.* **3.** to use beguiling or artful persuasions. [orig. obscure. Cf. OE *wǣdlian* beg]
—**whee′dler,** *n.* —**whee′dling·ly,** *adv.*

wheel (hwēl), *n.* **1.** a circular frame or solid disk arranged to turn on an axis, as in vehicles, machinery, etc.
2. any instrument, machine, apparatus, etc., shaped like
this, or having such a frame or disk as an essential feature: *a potter's wheel.* **3.** a circular frame with or without
projecting handles and an axle connecting with the rudder, for steering a ship. **4.** *Colloq.* a bicycle or a tricycle.
5. an old instrument of torture in the form of a circular
frame on which the victim was stretched while his limbs
were broken with an iron bar. **6.** anything resembling
or suggesting a wheel (in first sense) in shape, movement,
etc., as a decoration, or the trochal disk of a rotifer.
7. a circular firework which revolves while burning. **8.** a
rotating instrument which Fortune is represented as
turning in order to bring about changes or reverses in
human affairs. **9.** (*pl.*) moving, propelling, or animating
agencies: *the wheels of trade or of thought.* **10.** a wheeling
or circular movement: *merrily whirled the wheels of the
dizzying dances.* **11.** (formerly) a movement of troops,
ships, etc., drawn up in line, as if turning on a pivot.
—*v.t.* **12.** to cause to turn, rotate, or revolve, as on an
axis. **13.** to perform in a circular or curving direction.
14. to move, roll, or convey on wheels, casters, etc.: *the
servants wheel out the card tables.* **15.** to provide (a vehicle, etc.) with a wheel or wheels.
—*v.i.* **16.** to turn on or as on an axis or about a center;
rotate; revolve. **17.** *Brit. Mil.* to turn: *right wheel!*
18. to move in a circular or curving course: *pigeons
wheeling above.* **19.** to turn or change in procedure or
opinion: (often fol. by *about* or *around*). **20.** to roll
along on, or as on, wheels; to travel along smoothly.
[ME; OE *hwēol, hweogol,* c. D *wiel,* Icel. *hjōl*] —**wheeled**
(hwēld), *adj.* —**wheel′less,** *adj.*

wheel and axle, a device (one of the so-called simple machines) consisting, in its typical form, of a cy-

lindrical drum to which a wheel concentric with the drum is firmly fastened. Ropes are so applied that as one unwinds from the wheel, the other is wound on to the drum.

wheel animalcule, a rotifer.

wheel·bar·row (hwēl/băr/ō), *n.* **1.** a frame or box for conveying a load, usually supported at one end by a wheel and at the other by two vertical legs above which are two horizontal shafts used in lifting the legs from the ground when the vehicle is pushed or pulled. **2.** a similar vehicle with more than one wheel. —*v.t.* **3.** to move or convey in a wheelbarrow.

wheel·base (hwēl/bās/), *n.* *Auto.* the distance measured in inches from the center of the front-wheel spindle to the center of the rear-wheel axle.

wheel bug, a large, predacious heteropterous insect, *Arilus cristatus,* of North America, which destroys other insects. It has a toothed thoracic crest like half a wheel.

wheel chair, a chair mounted on large wheels, and used by invalids.

wheel·er (hwē/lər), *n.* **1.** one who or that which wheels. **2.** something provided with a wheel or wheels: *a side-wheeler, a stern-wheeler.* **3.** a wheel horse (def. 1).

Wheel·er (hwē/lər), *n.* **Joseph,** 1836–1906, Confederate general in the U.S. Civil War and major general in the Spanish-American War.

wheel horse, **1.** a horse, or one of the horses, harnessed behind others and next to the fore wheels of a vehicle. **2.** a plodding, steady, and obedient worker.

wheel·house (hwēl/hous/), *n.* pilothouse.

Wheel·ing (hwē/lĭng), *n.* a city in N West Virginia, on the Ohio river. 53,400 (1960).

wheel lock, an old type of gunlock in which sparks are produced by the friction of a small steel wheel against a piece of iron pyrites.

wheel·man (hwēl/mən), *n., pl.* **-men.** **1.** the man at the steering wheel of a vessel; a steersman. **2.** a rider of a bicycle, tricycle, or the like.

wheels·man (hwēlz/mən), *n., pl.* **-men.** wheelman (def. 1).

wheel static, noise in an automobile radio induced by wheel rotation.

wheel·work (hwēl/wûrk/), *n.* *Mach.* an apparatus consisting of a train of gears.

wheel·wright (hwēl/rīt/), *n.* one whose trade it is to make or repair wheels, wheeled carriages, etc.

wheen (hwēn), *n.* *Scot. and N. Eng.* a few. [ME *quheyn,* OE *hwēne,* instrumental case of *hwōn* few, a few]

wheeze (hwēz), *v.,* **wheezed, wheezing,** *n.* —*v.i.* **1.** to breathe with difficulty and with a whistling sound: *wheezing with corpulency and terror.* —*n.* **2.** a wheezing breath or sound. **3.** a theatrical gag. **4.** a trite saying, story, etc. [ME *whese,* prob. t. Scand.; cf. Icel. *hvǣsa* hiss] —**wheez′er,** *n.* —**wheez′ing·ly,** *adv.*

wheez·y (hwē/zī), *adj.,* **wheezier, wheeziest.** affected with or characterized by wheezing. —**wheez′i·ly,** *adv.* —**wheez′i·ness,** *n.*

whelk¹ (hwĕlk, wĭlk), *n.* any of various large spiral-shelled marine gastropods of the family *Buccinidae,* esp. *Buccinum undatum,* which is used for food in Europe. [ME *welke,* OE *weoloc;* orig. uncert.]

whelk² (hwĕlk), *n.* a pimple or pustule. [ME *whelke,* OE *hwylca.* See WHEAL.]

Common whelk. *Buccinum undatum*

whelm (hwĕlm), *v.t.* **1.** to submerge; engulf. **2.** to overcome utterly, or overwhelm: *sorrow whelmed him.* [ME, appar. b. obs. *whelve* (OE *gehwelfan* bend over) and *helm* (OE *helmian* cover)]

whelp (hwĕlp), *n.* **1.** the young of the dog, or of the wolf, bear, lion, tiger, seal, etc. **2.** (in contemptuous use) a youth. **3.** *Mach.* **a.** any of a series of longitudinal projections or ridges of iron or the like on the barrel of a capstan, windlass, etc. **b.** one of the teeth of a sprocket wheel. —*v.t., v.i.* **4.** (of a bitch, lioness, etc.) to bring forth (young). [ME; OE *hwelp,* c. G *welf*]

when (hwĕn), *adv.* **1.** at what time: *when are you coming?* —*conj.* **2.** at what time: *to know when to be silent.* **3.** at the time that: *when we were young, when the noise stopped.* **4.** at any time, or whenever: *he is impatient when he is kept waiting.* **5.** upon or after which; and then. **6.** while on the contrary, or whereas: *you rub the sore when you should bring the plaster.* —*n.* **7.** what time: *since when have you known this?* **8.** which time: *they left on Monday, since when we have heard nothing.* **9.** the time of anything: *the when and the where of an act.* [ME *when(ne),* OE *hwenne,* c. G *wann* when, *wenn* if, Goth. *hwan* when, how; akin to WHO, WHAT]

when·as (hwĕn/ăz/), *conj.* *Archaic.* when; whereas.

whence (hwĕns), *adv.* **1.** from what place?: *whence comest thou?* **2.** from what source, origin or cause?: *whence hath he wisdom?* —*conj.* **3.** from what place, source, cause, etc.: *he told whence he came.* [ME *whennes,* f. *whenne* (OE *hwanone* whence) + -*s,* adv. gen. suffix]

whence·so·ev·er (hwĕns/sō ĕv/ər), *adv., conj.* from whatsoever place, source, or cause.

when·ev·er (hwĕn ĕv/ər), *conj.* **1.** at whatever time; at any time when: *come whenever you like.* —*adv.* **2.** *Colloq.* when ever? when? (used emphatically): *whenever did he say that?* Also, *Poetic,* **when·e′er** (hwĕn âr/).

when·so·ev·er (hwĕn/sō ĕv/ər), *adv., conj.* at whatsoever time.

where (hwâr), *adv.* **1.** in or at what place?: *where i he? where do you live?* **2.** in what position or circum stances?: *where do you stand on this question? withou money where are you?* **3.** in what particular, respect, way etc.?: *where does this affect us?* **4.** to what place, point or end, or whither?: *where are you going?* **5.** from wha source, or whence: *where did you get such a notion* —*conj.* **6.** in or at what place, part, point, etc.: *fine where he is, or where the trouble is.* **7.** in or at the place part, point, etc., in or at which: *the book is where you lef it.* **8.** in a position, case, or condition, in which: *where ignorance is bliss, 'tis folly to be wise.* **9.** in any place, position, case etc., in which, or wherever: *use the lotion where pain i felt.* **10.** to what or whatever place, or to the or any place to which: *go where you will, I will go where you go* **11.** in or at which place; and there: *they came to th town, where they lodged for the night.* —*n.* **12.** wha place: *from where, where from?* **13.** a place: *the wheres an hows of job hunting.* [ME *wher,* OE *hwâr,* c. D *waar;* akin to Icel. *hvar,* Goth. *hwar*]

where-, a word element meaning "what" or "which." [special use of WHERE]

-where, suffixal use of "where," as in *somewhere* Also, **-wheres.**

where·a·bouts (hwâr/ə bouts/), *adv.* **1.** Also, *Rare* **where′a·bout′.** about where? where? —*conj.* **2.** near or in what place: *seeing whereabouts in the world we were* —*n.* **3.** the place where a person or thing is; the locality of a person or thing: *no clue as to his whereabouts.*

where·as (hwâr ăz/), *conj., n., pl.* **whereases.** —*conj* **1.** while on the contrary: *one came promptly, whereas the others hung back.* **2.** it being the case that, or considering that (esp. used in formal preambles). —*n.* **3.** a statement having "whereas" as the first word: *to read the whereases in the will.*

where·at (hwâr ăt/), *adv., conj.* at what or at which

where·by (hwâr bī/), *adv., conj.* **1.** by what or by which. **2.** by what? how?

wher·e'er (hwâr âr/), *conj., adv.* *Poetic.* wherever.

where·fore (hwâr/fōr/), *adv.* **1.** for what? why? **2.** *Archaic.* as a result of; for the reason that. —*conj* **3.** for what or which cause or reason. —*n.* **4.** the cause or reason. [ME; f. WHERE + *fore* because of, FOR] —Syn. **1.** See **therefore.**

where·from (hwâr frŏm/), *adv.* from which; whence

where·in (hwâr ĭn/), *adv.* in what or in which.

where·in·to (hwâr ĭn/tōō, hwâr ĭn tōō/), *adv., conj.* into what or into which.

where·of (hwâr ŏv/, -ŭv/), *adv., conj.* of what, which or whom.

where·on (hwâr ŏn/, -ôn/), *adv., conj.* on what or on which.

-wheres, var. of **-where.**

where·so·ev·er (hwâr/sō ĕv/ər), *adv., conj.* in or to whatsoever place; wherever. Also, *Poetic,* **where·so·e′er** (hwâr/sō âr/)

where·through (hwâr thrōō/), *adv.* through which.

where·to (hwâr tōō/), *adv., conj.* to what or to which. Also, *Archaic,* **where·un·to** (hwâr ŭn/tōō, hwâr/ŭn tōō/).

where·up·on (hwâr/ə pŏn/, -pôn/), *adv.* **1.** upon what? whereon? —*conj.* **2.** upon what or upon which. **3.** at or after which.

wher·ev·er (hwâr ĕv/ər), *conj.* **1.** in, at, or to whatever place. **2.** in any case or condition: *wherever it is heard of.* —*adv.* **3.** *Colloq.* where ever? where? (used emphatically): *wherever did you find that?* Also, *Poetic* **where′er.**

where·with (hwâr wĭth/, -wĭth/), *adv.* **1.** with what? —*conj.* **2.** with what or which. **3.** (by ellipsis) that with which: *I shall have wherewith to answer him.* —*n.* **4.** wherewithal.

where·with·al (*n.* hwâr/wĭth ôl/; *adv., conj.* hwâr/ wĭth ôl/), *n.* **1.** that wherewith to do something; means or supplies for the purpose or need, esp. money: *the wherewithal to pay my rent.* —*adv., conj.* **2.** *Archaic.* wherewith.

wher·ry (hwĕr/ī), *n., pl.* **-ries,** *v.,* **-ried, -rying.** —*n.* **1.** a kind of light rowboat for one person; skiff. **2.** any of certain larger boats (fishing vessels, barges, etc.) used locally in Great Britain. **3.** a kind of light rowboat used chiefly in England for carrying passengers and goods on rivers. —*v.t., v.i.* **4.** to use, or transport in, a wherry. [late ME; orig. uncert.] —**wher′ry·man,** *n.*

whet (hwĕt), *v.,* **whetted, whetting,** *n.* —*v.t.* **1.** to sharpen (a knife, tool, etc.) by grinding or friction. **2.** to make keen or eager: *to whet the appetite or the curiosity.* —*n.* **3.** act of whetting. **4.** something that whets; an appetizer. [ME *whette,* OE *hwettan,* c. G *wetzen*] —**whet′ter,** *n.*

wheth·er (hwĕth/ər), *conj.* **1.** a word introducing, in dependent clauses or the like, the first of two or more alternatives, and sometimes repeated before the second or later alternative (used in correlation with *or*): *it matters little whether we go or stay; whether we go go on whether we stay, the result is the same.* **2.** used to introduce a single alternative (the other being implied or understood), and hence some clause or element not involving alternatives: *see whether he has come (or not), I doubt whether we can do any better.* **3.** **whether or no,** whether or not; under whatever circumstances: *h threatens to go, whether or no.* —*pron. Archaic.* **4.** which

---

b., blend of, blended; **c.,** cognate with; **d.,** dialect, dialectal; **der.,** derived from; **f.,** formed from; **g.,** going back to **m.,** modification of; **r.,** replacing; **s.,** stem of; **t.,** taken from; **?,** perhaps. See the full key on inside cover (of two)? **5.** a word introducing a question presenting alternatives (usually with the correlative *or*). [ME; OE *hwether, hwæther*, c. Icel. *hvadharr*, Goth. *hwathar*]

whet·stone (hwĕt′stōn′), *n.* **1.** a stone for sharpening cutlery or tools by friction. **2.** anything that sharpens: *a whetstone for dull wits.*

whew (hwū), *interj.* **1.** a whistling exclamation or sound expressing astonishment, dismay, etc. —*n.* **2.** an utterance of "whew."

whey (hwā), *n.* milk serum, separating as a watery liquid from the curd after coagulation, as in cheesemaking. [ME *wheye*, OE *hwæg*, c. D and LG *wei*] —**whey′ish, whey′like′,** *adj.*

whey·ey (hwā′Y), *adj.* of, like, or containing whey.

whey·face (hwā′fās′), *n.* a face or a person that is pallid, as from fear. —**whey′faced′,** *adj.*

whf., wharf.

which (hwYch), *interrog. pron.* **1.** what one (of a certain number mentioned or implied)?: *which of these, or which, do you want?* **2.** used adjectively: *which way shall we go?* —*pron.* **3.** as a simple relative, with antecedent (thing, body of persons, formerly a single person) expressed: **a.** in clauses conveying an additional idea: *I read the book, which was short; five sons, of which he was the eldest.* **b.** used in clauses defining or restricting the antecedent, regularly after *that* (*that which must be will be*), or after a preposition (*the horse on which I rode*), or otherwise in place of the restrictive *that* (*the book which, or that, I gave you*). **c.** used adjectively: *be careful which way you turn.* **4.** as a compound relative, representing both antecedent and consequent (either thing or person), what particular one, or the or any one that: *choose which you like; any one of these men, be it which it may.* **5.** in parenthetic clauses) a thing that: *and, which is worse, all you have done is wrong.* —*adj.* **6.** what one of (a certain number mentioned or implied): *which book do you want?* **7.** no matter what; any that: *go which way you please, you'll end up here.* **8.** being previously mentioned: *it stormed all day, during which time the ship broke up.* [ME; OE *hwilc*, c. D *welk*, G *welch*, Goth. *hwileiks*, lit., of what form, like whom or what. See WHO, WHAT, LIKE] —**Syn. 3.** See **that.**

which·ev·er (hwYch·ĕv′ər), *pron.* **1.** any one (of those in question) that: *take whichever you like.* **2.** no matter which: *whichever you choose, the others will be offended.* **3.** used adjectively: *whichever day, whichever person.*

which·so·ev·er (hwYch′sō·ĕv′ər), *pron.* intensive form of whichever.

whid (hwYd, hwŭd), *v.i.,* **whidded, whidding.** *Scot.* to move briskly and quietly.

whid·ah bird (hwYd′ə), **1.** any of the small African birds which constitute the subfamily *Viduinae*, comprising species of weaver birds the males of which have elongated drooping tail feathers. **2.** any of the birds of the genera *Coliuspasser, Drepanoplectes*, and *Diatropura.* Also, **whid′ah, whydah, widow bird.** [alter. of WIDOW BIRD to agree with name of town in Dahomey, western Africa, one of its haunts]

whiff (hwYf), *n.* **1.** a slight blast or puff of wind or air: *a whiff of fresh air.* **2.** a puff or waft of odor or smell: *a whiff of honeysuckle.* **3.** a puff of vapor, smoke, etc. **4.** a single inhalation or exhalation of air, tobacco smoke, or the like. **5.** a slight outburst: *a little whiff of temper.* —*v.i.* **6.** to blow or come in whiffs or puffs, as wind, smoke, etc. **7.** to inhale or exhale whiffs, as in smoking tobacco. —*v.t.* **8.** to blow or drive with a whiff or puff, as the wind does. **9.** to inhale or exhale (air, tobacco smoke, etc.) in whiffs. **10.** to smoke (a pipe, cigar, etc.). [? b. WHIP and PUFF] —**whiff′er,** *n.*

whif·fet (hwYf′Yt), *n.* **1.** a small dog. **2.** *U.S. Colloq.* an insignificant person; whippersnapper. **3.** a little whiff.

whif·fle (hwYf′əl), *v.,* **-fled, -fling.** —*v.i.* **1.** to blow in light or shifting gusts or puffs, as the wind; veer irregularly (about). **2.** to shift about in; vacillate. —*v.t.* **3.** to blow with light, shifting gusts. [freq. of WHIFF, v.] —**whif′fler,** *n.*

whif·fle·tree (hwYf′əl·trē′, -trY), *n.* a crossbar, pivoted at the middle, to which the traces of the harness are fastened in a cart, carriage, plow, etc.; singletree. Also, **whippletree.** [var. of *whippletree*, ? der. WHIP]

A. Whiffletree; B. Double tree; C. Plow beam; D. Trace

Whig (hwYg), *n.* **1.** *Amer. Hist.* **a.** a member of the patriotic party during the Revolutionary period; a supporter of the Revolution. **b.** a member of a political party (c 1834–1855) which was formed in opposition to the Democratic party, and favored a loose construction of the Constitution and a high protective tariff. **2.** *Brit. Pol.* **a.** a member of a great political party in Great Britain, in general holding liberal principles and favoring various reforms, and more recently known as the "Liberal party." Cf. **Tory** (def. 1). **b.** (in later use) one of the more conservative members of the Liberal party. —*adj.* **3.** being a Whig. **4.** of, pertaining to, or characteristic of the Whigs. [prob. short for *whiggamore*, one of a body of rebels who marched on Edinburgh, 1648]

whig (hwYg), *v.i.,* **whigged, whigging.** to move at an easy, steady pace; jog along.

Whig·ger·y (hwYg′ər′Y), *n., pl.* **-geries.** the principles or practices of Whigs.

Whig·gish (hwYg′Ysh), *adj.* **1.** of, pertaining to, or characteristic of Whigs. **2.** inclined to Whiggism. —**Whig′gish·ly,** *adv.* —**Whig′gish·ness,** *n.*

Whig·gism (hwYg′Yzəm), *n.* the principles of Whigs.

while (hwīl), *n., conj., v.,* **whiled, whiling.** —*n.* **1.** a space of time: *a long while, a while ago.* **2. the while,** during this time. **3. worth one's while,** worth time, pains, or expense. **4.** *Archaic.* or *Dial.* a particular time or occasion. —*conj.* **5.** during or in the time that. **6.** throughout the time that, or as long as. **7.** at the same time that (implying opposition or contrast): *while he appreciated the honor, he could not accept the position.* **8.** *Dial.* until. —*v.t.* **9.** to cause (time) to pass, esp. in some easy or pleasant manner (usually fol. by *away*). [ME; OE *hwīl*, c. D *wijl*, G *weile*, Goth. *hweila*]

whiles (hwīlz), *Archaic* or *Dial.* —*adv.* **1.** at times. **2.** in the meantime. —*conj.* **3.** while.

whi·lom (hwī′ləm), *Archaic.* —*adv.* **1.** at one time; formerly. —*adj.* **2.** former. [ME; OE *hwīlum* at times, dat. pl. of *hwīl* WHILE, n.]

whilst (hwīlst), *conj. Chiefly Brit.* while. [earlier *whilest.* f. WHILES + inorganic *-t*, as in AMONGST]

whim (hwYm), *n.* **1.** an odd or fanciful notion; a freakish or capricious fancy or desire. **2.** capricious humor: *to be swayed by whim.* **3.** *Mining.* a vertical drum on which a hoisting rope winds, usually operated by a horse or horses. [prob. t. Scand.; cf. Icel. *hvim* unsteady look. In some senses short for *whim-wham*, itself der. *whim*, modeled on *trim-tram gewgaw*] —**Syn. 1.** whimsy, humor, caprice, vagary, quirk, notion, crotchet, chimera.

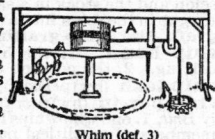

Whim (def. 3)
A. Drum; B. Hoisting rope and pulley

whim·brel (hwYm′brəl), *n.* a small European curlew, *Numenius phaeopus.*

whim·per (hwYm′pər), *v.i.* **1.** to cry with low, plaintive, broken sounds, as a child, a grown person, or a dog. —*v.t.* **2.** to utter in a whimper. —*n.* **3.** a whimpering cry or sound. [freq. of *whimp* (now d.) whine, orig. uncert.; cf. Icel. *hvimpinn* shy (said of horse)] —**whim′-per·er,** *n.* —**whim′per·ing·ly,** *adv.*

whim·sey (hwYm′zY), *n., pl.* **-seys.** whimsy.

whim·si·cal (hwYm′zə·kəl), *adj.* **1.** given to whimsies or odd notions. **2.** of the nature of or proceeding from a whimsy, as thoughts, actions, etc. **3.** of an odd, quaint, or comical kind. —**whim′si·cal·ly,** *adv.* —**whim′si·cal·ness,** *n.* —**Syn. 1.** capricious, notional, changeable, crotchety, freakish, fanciful.

whim·si·cal·i·ty (hwYm′zə·kăl′ə·tY), *n., pl.* **-ties.** **1.** whimsical character. **2.** a whimsical notion, speech, or act.

whim·sy (hwYm′zY), *n., pl.* **-sies.** **1.** an odd or fanciful notion. **2.** anything odd or fanciful; a product of playful fancy, as a literary trifle.

whim·wham (hwYm′hwăm′), *n.* any odd or fanciful object or thing; a gimcrack.

whin[1] (hwYn), *n. Brit.* furze. [late ME *whynne*, appar. t. Scand.; cf. Icel. *hvingras* bent grass]

whin[2] (hwYn), *n.* **1.** whinstone. **2.** any of various other hard dark-colored rocks. [orig. uncert.]

whin·chat (hwYn′chăt′), *n.* a small Old World oscine passerine bird, *Saxicola rubetra*, having buff-colored breast and white at the base of the tail, and closely related to the stonechat. [f. WHIN[2] + CHAT warbler]

whine (hwYn), *v.,* **whined, whining,** *n.* —*v.i.* **1.** to utter a low, complaining cry or sound, as from uneasiness, discontent, peevishness, etc. **2.** to complain in a feeble, unbecoming way. —*v.t.* **3.** to utter with a whine. —*n.* **4.** a whining utterance, sound, or tone. **5.** a feeble, peevish complaint. [ME; OE *hwīnan*, c. Icel. *hvīna* whiz] —**whin′er,** *n.* —**whin′ing·ly,** *adv.* —**whin′y,** *adj.* —**Syn. 2.** See **complain.**

whin·ny (hwYn′Y), *v.,* **-nied, -nying,** *n., pl.* **-nies.** —*v.i.* **1.** (of a horse) to utter its characteristic cry; neigh. —*v.t.* **2.** to express by whinnying. —*n.* **3.** a neigh. [alter. of WHINE in (now obs.) sense "whinny"]

whin·stone (hwYn′stōn′), *n.* any of the dark-colored fine-grained rocks such as dolerite and basalt trap[3].

whip (hwYp), *v.,* **whipped** or **whipt, whipping,** *n.* —*v.t.* **1.** to strike with quick, repeated strokes of something slender and flexible; lash. **2.** to beat with a whip or the like, esp. by way of punishment or chastisement; flog; thrash. **3.** to lash or castigate with words. **4.** to drive (*on, out, in,* etc.) by strokes or lashes. **5.** to bring (*in, into line, together,* etc.) as a party whip does. **6.** *Colloq.* to beat, outdo, or defeat, as in a contest. **7.** *Naut.* to hoist or purchase by means of a whip. **8.** to move quickly and suddenly; pull, jerk, snatch, seize, put, etc., with a sudden movement (fol. by *away, off, out, up, into,* etc.). **9.** to fish (a stream, etc.) with a rod and line. **10.** to overlay or cover (cord, etc.) with cord, thread, or the like wound about it. **11.** to wind (cord, twine, thread, etc.) about something. **12.** to gather, or form into pleats by overcasting the turned edge with small stitches and then drawing up the thread. **13.** to beat (eggs, cream, etc.) to a froth with a whisk, fork, or other implement in order to incorporate air and produce expansion. —*v.i.* **14.** to move or go quickly and suddenly (*away, off, out, in,* etc.); dart; whisk. **15.** to beat or lash about, as a pennant in the wind. **16.** to fish with a rod and line.

17. whip in, *Hunting.* to prevent from wandering, as hounds. —*n.* **18.** an instrument to strike with, as in driving animals or in punishing, typically consisting of a lash or other flexible part with a more rigid handle. **19.** a whipping or lashing stroke or motion. **20.** a windmill vane. **21.** *Chiefly Brit.* one who handles a whip; a driver of horses, **a** coach, etc. **22.** one who has charge of the hounds in hunting. **23.** *Pol.* **a.** a party manager in a legislative body, who secures attendance for voting, and directs other members. **b.** *Eng.* a written call made on members of a party to be in attendance for voting, etc. **24.** a contrivance for hoisting, consisting essentially of a rope and pulley. **25.** a dish made of cream or egg whites whipped to a froth with flavoring, etc., often with fruit pulp or the like: *prune whip.* [ME *whippe,* earlier (*h*)*wippen,* c. D *wippen* swing, oscillate] —**whip′like′,** *adj.* —**whip′per,** *n.* —**Syn. 2.** scourge, lash, flagellate, beat, switch, punish, chastise. **6.** overcome, conquer. **18.** switch, rattan.

whip·cord (hwĭp′kôrd′), *n.* **1.** a worsted fabric with a diagonally ribbed surface. **2.** a kind of strong, hard-twisted cord, sometimes used for the lashes of whips. **3.** a cord made from the intestines of animals; catgut.

whip graft, a graft prepared by cutting both the scion and the stock in a sloping direction and inserting a tongue in the scion into a slit in the stock. See illus. under **graft.** Also, **whip grafting, whip graftage.**

whip hand, 1. the hand that holds the whip, in driving. **2.** the position of control, or the advantage.

whip·lash (hwĭp′lăsh′), *n.* the lash of a whip.

whip·per-in (hwĭp′ər ĭn′), *n., pl.* **whippers-in.** *Chiefly Brit.* **1.** one who whips in hounds. **2.** one who whips in members of a political party for united action; a party whip.

whip·per·snap·per (hwĭp′ər snăp′ər), *n.* a petty or insignificant person, often young, who affects importance.

whip·pet (hwĭp′ĭt), *n.* a dog of an English breed, probably a cross between the greyhound and the terrier, used especially in rabbit coursing and racing. [n. use of obs. *v.,* to frisk, orig. the phrase *whip it* move briskly]

Whippet
(18 to 20 in. high at the shoulder)

whip·ping (hwĭp′ĭng), *n.* **1.** a beating administered with a whip or the like, as for punishment; a flogging. **2.** an arrangement of cord, twine, or the like, whipped or wound about a thing, as to bind parts together.

whipping boy, 1. a scapegoat (def. 1). **2.** (formerly) a boy educated along with and taking punishment in place of a young prince or nobleman.

whipping post, a post to which persons are fastened to undergo whipping as a legal penalty.

whip·ple·tree (hwĭp′əl trē′, -trĭ), *n.* whiffletree.

whip·poor·will (hwĭp′ər wĭl′), *n.* a nocturnal North American goatsucker (bird), *Caprimulgus vociferus,* having a variegated plumage of gray, black, white, and tawny. [imit., from its cry]

whip·saw (hwĭp′sô′), *n.* **1.** a saw used for cutting curved kerfs, consisting essentially of a narrow blade stretched in a frame. —*v.t.* **2.** to cut with a whipsaw. **3.** to win two bets from (a person) at one turn or play, as in faro. **4.** to defeat or worst in two ways at once.

whip scorpion, any of various arachnids of the genus *Thelyphonus* and allied genera, resembling the true scorpions, but having (in the typical members) an abdomen ending in a slender whiplike part.

whip snake, any of various slender snakes in which the scaling of the tail is suggestive of a braided whip.

whip·stitch (hwĭp′stĭch′), *v.t.* **1.** to sew with stitches passing over an edge, in joining, finishing, or gathering. —*n.* **2.** one such stitch. **3.** *U.S. Colloq.* an instant.

whip·stock (hwĭp′stŏk′), *n.* the handle of a whip.

whip·worm (hwĭp′wûrm′), *n.* any of certain parasitic nematode worms of the genus *Trichuris,* having a long, slender anterior end, giving a whiplike shape.

whir (hwûr), *v.,* **whirred, whirring,** *n.* —*v.i., v.t.* **1.** to go, fly, dart, revolve, or otherwise move quickly with a vibratory or buzzing sound. —*n.* **2.** act or sound of whirring: *the whir of wings.* Also, **whirr.** [ME, t. Scand.; cf. Dan. *hvirre;* akin to WHIRL]

whirl (hwûrl), *v.i.* **1.** to turn round, spin, or rotate rapidly. **2.** to turn about or aside quickly. **3.** to move, travel, or be carried rapidly along on wheels or otherwise. **4.** to have the sensation of turning round rapidly. —*v.t.* **5.** to cause to turn round, spin, or rotate rapidly. **6.** to send, drive, or carry in a circular or curving course. **7.** to drive, send, or carry along with great or dizzying rapidity. **8.** *Obs.* to hurl. —*n.* **9.** act of whirling; rapid rotation or gyration. **10.** a whirling movement; a quick turn or swing. **11.** a short drive, run, walk, or the like, or a spin. **12.** something that whirls; a whirling current or mass. **13.** a rapid round of events, affairs, etc. **14.** a state marked by a dizzying succession or mingling of feelings, thoughts, etc. [ME *whirle,* t. Scand.; cf. Icel. *hvirfla*] —**whirl′er,** *n.* —**Syn. 1.** gyrate, pirouette. **5.** revolve, twirl.

whirl·a·bout (hwûrl′ə bout′), *n.* **1.** a whirling about. **2.** a whirligig. —*adj.* **3.** whirling about.

whirl·i·gig (hwûr′lĭ gĭg′), *n.* **1.** something that whirls, revolves, or goes round; a revolving agency or course. **2.** a continuous round or succession. **3.** a giddy or flighty person. **4.** a merry-go-round or carrousel. **5.** a toy for whirling or spinning, as a top. [der. WHIRL. See GIG-]

whirligig beetle, any of the aquatic beetles of the family *Gyrinidae,* commonly seen circling rapidly about in large numbers on the surface of the water.

whirl·pool (hwûrl′pōōl′), *n.* a whirling eddy or current, as in a river or the sea, produced by irregularity in the channel or stream banks, by the meeting of opposing currents, by the interaction of winds and tides, etc.; a vortex of water.

whirl·wind (hwûrl′wĭnd′), *n.* **1.** a mass of air rotating rapidly round and toward a more or less vertical axis, and having at the same time a progressive motion over the surface of the land or sea. **2.** anything resembling a whirlwind, as in violent activity. **3.** any circling rush or violent onward course. [ME, t. Scand.; cf. Icel. *hvirfilvindr.* See WHIRL, WIND[1]]

whirl·y·bird (hwûr′lĭ bûrd′), *n. Slang.* a helicopter.

whirr (hwûr), *v.i., v.t., n.* whir.

whish (hwĭsh), *v.i.* **1.** to make, or move with, a whiz or swish. —*n.* **2.** a whishing sound.

whisht (hwĭst), *interj., adj., Obs. or Dial.* whist[1].

whisk[1] (hwĭsk), *v.t.* **1.** to sweep (dust, crumbs, etc., or a surface) with a whisk broom, brush, or the like. **2.** to move with a rapid, sweeping stroke. **3.** to draw, snatch, carry, etc., lightly and rapidly. —*v.i.* **4.** to sweep, pass, or go lightly and rapidly. —*n.* **5.** act of whisking. **6.** a rapid, sweeping stroke; light, rapid movement. [late ME, t. Scand.; cf. Dan. *viske* wipe]

whisk[2] (hwĭsk), *v.t.* **1.** *Chiefly Brit.* to whip (eggs, cream, etc.) to a froth with a whisk or beating implement. —*n.* **2.** a small bunch of grass, straw, hair, or the like, esp. for use in brushing. **3.** a whisk broom. **4.** *Chiefly Brit.* an implement, in one form a bunch of loops of wire held together in a handle, for beating or whipping eggs, cream, etc. [ME *visk,* t. Scand.; cf. Icel. *visk* wisp, c. G *wisch* wisp of straw]

whisk broom, a small broom to brush clothes, etc.

whisk·er (hwĭs′kər), *n.* **1.** (*usually pl.*) the hair growing on the side of a man's face, esp. when worn long and with the chin clean-shaven. **2.** (*pl.*) the beard generally. **3.** a single hair of the beard. **4.** *Colloq. or Dial.* the mustache. **5.** one of the long, stiff, bristly hairs growing about the mouth of certain animals, as the cat, rat, etc.; a vibrissa. **6.** Also, **whisker boom.** *Naut.* either of two bars of wood or iron projecting laterally one from each side of the bowsprit, to give more spread to the guys which support the jib boom. **7.** one who or that which whisks. [ME; der. WHISK[2]. Cf. LG *wisker* duster] —**whisk′ered,** *adj.* —**whisk′er·less,** *adj.*

whis·key (hwĭs′kĭ), *n., pl.* **-keys.** —*n.* **1.** a distilled alcoholic liquor made from grain, as barley, rye, corn, etc., containing commonly from 43 to 50 percent by weight of alcohol. **2.** a drink of whiskey. —*adj.* **3.** made of, relating to, or resembling, whiskey. [short for *whiskybae,* t. Gaelic: m. *uisgebeatha* water of life]

whis·ky (hwĭs′kĭ), *n., pl.* **-kies,** *adj.* whiskey.

whis·per (hwĭs′pər), *v.i.* **1.** to speak with soft, low sounds, using the breath, lips, etc., without vibration of the vocal cords. **2.** to talk softly and privately (often with implication of gossip, slander, or plotting). **3.** (of trees, water, breezes, etc.) to make a soft, rustling sound. —*v.t.* **4.** to utter with soft, low sounds, using the breath, lips, etc. **5.** to say or tell in a whisper; to tell privately. **6.** to speak to or tell (a person) in a whisper, or privately. —*n.* **7.** the mode of utterance, or the voice, of one who whispers: *to speak in a whisper.* **8.** a sound, word, remark, or the like, uttered by whispering; something said or repeated privately: *low whispers.* **9.** a soft, rustling sound, as of leaves moving in the wind. [ME *whysper,* OE *hwisprian,* c. G *wispern*] —**whis′per·er,** *n.*

whis·per·ing (hwĭs′pər ĭng), *n.* **1.** whispered talk or conversation; a whisper or whispers. —*adj.* **2.** that whispers; making a sound like a whisper. **3.** like a whisper. —**whis′per·ing·ly,** *adv.*

whist[1] (hwĭst), *interj.* **1.** hush! silence! be still! —*adj.* **2.** *Archaic or Dial.* hushed; silent; still. Also, **whisht.** [cf. SHH, etc.]

whist[2] (hwĭst), *n.* a card game played by four players, two against two, with 52 cards. [earlier *whisk,* ? special use of WHISK[1], altered by confusion with WHIST[1]]

whis·tle (hwĭs′əl), *v.,* **-tled, -tling,** —*v.i.* **1.** to make a kind of clear musical sound, or a series of such sounds, by the forcible expulsion of the breath through a small orifice formed by contracting the lips, or through the teeth, together with the aid of the tongue. **2.** to make such a sound or series of sounds otherwise, as by blowing on a particular device. **3.** to produce a more or less similar sound by an instrument operated by steam or the like, or as such an instrument does. **4.** to emit somewhat similar sounds from the mouth, as birds do. **5.** to move, go, pass, etc., with a whizzing sound, as a bullet. —*v.t.* **6.** to produce by whistling. **7.** to call, direct, or signal by or as by whistling. **8.** to send with a whistling or whizzing sound. —*n.* **9.** an instrument for producing whistling sounds, as by the breath, steam, etc., as a small wooden or tin tube or a small pipe. **10.** a sound produced by or as by whistling: *a long-drawn whistle of astonishment.* **11.** fipple flute. **12.** *Slang.* the mouth and throat: *to wet one's whistle.* [ME; OE *hwistlian*]

whis·tler (hwĭs'lər), *n.* **1.** one who or that which whistles. **2.** something that sounds like a whistle. **3.** any of various birds whose wings whistle in flight, esp. the goldeneye and European widgeon. **4.** a large marmot, *Marmota caligata*, of mountainous northwestern North America, closely related to the woodchuck. **5.** *Vet. Sci.* a horse afflicted with whistling.

Whis·tler (hwĭs'lər), *n.* **James Abbott McNeill,** 1834–1903, U.S. painter and etcher: lived in England. —**Whis·tle·ri·an** (hwĭs lîr'ĭ on), *adj.*

whistle stop, a small, unimportant town along a railroad line.

whis·tle-stop (hwĭs'əl stŏp′), *v.i.* to campaign for political office by traveling around the country, originally by train, stopping at small communities to reach voters in small groups. —**whis'tle-stop′,** *adj.* —**whis′tle-stop′ping,** *n.*

whis·tling (hwĭs'lĭng), *n.* **1.** act of one who or that which whistles. **2.** the sound produced. **3.** *Vet. Sci.* a form of roaring characterized by a peculiarly shrill sound. [ME; OE *hwistlung*, der. *hwistlian* WHISTLE, v.]

whistling swan, a large North American swan, *Cygnus columbianus.* The adult is pure white with black bill and feet, and a small yellow spot on the bill in front of the eye.

whit (hwĭt), *n.* a particle; bit; jot (used esp. in negative phrases): *not a whit better.* [unexplained alter. of WIGHT[1]]

Whit·by (hwĭt'bĭ), *n.* a seaport in NE England, in Yorkshire: ruins of an abbey; church council, A.D. 664. 11,668 (1951).

white (hwīt), *adj.,* **whiter, whitest,** *n., v.,* **whited, whiting.** —*adj.* **1.** of the color of pure snow; reflecting sunlight or a similar light without absorbing any of the rays composing it. **2.** light or comparatively light in color. **3.** having a light-colored skin. **4.** noting or pertaining to the Caucasian race. **5.** dominated by or including only members of the white race. **6.** pallid or pale, as from fear or other strong emotion. **7.** silvery, gray, or hoary, as hair. **8.** royalist or reactionary (as opposed to *red* or revolutionary). **9.** *Poetic.* blond or fair. **10.** blank, as an unoccupied space in printed matter. **11.** (of silverware) not burnished. **12.** wearing white clothing: *a white friar.* **13.** *Colloq.* honorable, trustworthy, or square. **14.** benevolent, beneficent, or good: *white magic.* **15.** auspicious or fortunate. **16.** free from spot or stain, or pure or innocent. **17.** (of wines) light-colored or yellowish, as opposed to red. **18.** *Brit.* (of coffee) with milk. —*n.* **19.** a color without hue at one extreme end of the scale of grays, opposite to black. A white surface reflects light of all hues completely and diffusely. Most so-called whites are very light grays: fresh snow, for example, reflects about 80 percent of the incident light, but to be strictly white, snow would have to reflect 100 percent of the incident light. It is the ultimate limit of a series of tints of any color, as black is the ultimate limit of a series of shades of any color. **20.** a hue completely desaturated by admixture with white, the highest value possible. **21.** quality or state of being white. **22.** lightness of skin pigment. **23.** a member of the white or Caucasian race. **24.** something white, or a white part of something. **25.** *Biol.* a pellucid viscous fluid which surrounds the yolk of an egg: albumen. **26.** *Anat., Zool.* the white part of the eyeball. **27.** *(pl.) Pathol.* leucorrhea. **28.** white wine. **29.** a type or breed which is white in color. **30.** *(usually pl.)* a blank space in printing. **31.** *(cap.)* a swine of a white-haired breed, such as Chester White. **32.** *(pl.)* white or near-white clothing. **33.** white fabric. **34.** *Archery.* **a.** the outermost ring of the butt. **b.** an arrow that hits this portion of the butt. **c.** the central part of the butt (target) formerly painted white, but now painted gold or yellow. **d.** *Archaic.* a target painted white. **35.** *Chess, Checkers.* the men or pieces which are light-colored. **36.** a member of a royalist or reactionary party. **37.** *(pl.)* top-grade white flour. —*v.t.* **38.** *Print.* to make white by leaving blank spaces (often fol. by *out*). **39.** *Rare.* to make white; whiten. [ME; OE *hwīt*, c. G *weiss*, Icel. *hvītr*, Goth. *hweits*]

White (hwīt), *n.* **1. Edward Douglass,** 1845–1921, U.S. jurist: chief justice of the Supreme Court, 1910–21. **2. Gilbert,** 1720–1793, British clergyman and writer on natural history. **3. Stanford,** 1853–1906, U.S. architect. **4. William Allen,** 1868–1944, U.S. journalist.

white alkali, *Agric.* a whitish layer of mineral salts, esp. sodium sulfate, sodium chloride, and magnesium sulfate, often found on top of soils under low rainfall.

white ant, a termite.

white·bait (hwīt'bāt′), *n., pl.* **-bait.** any small delicate fish cooked whole without being cleaned. In Europe, the sprat constitutes much of the whitebait.

white bear, the polar bear.

white·beard (hwīt'bîrd′), *n.* a man having a white or gray beard; old man.

white birch, **1.** the European birch, *Betula pendula,* having a hard wood of many uses. **2.** paper birch.

white book, an official document, bound in white.

white bryony, a European bryony, *Bryonia alba.*

white·cap (hwīt'kăp′), *n.* **1.** a wave with a broken white crest. **2.** *(cap.) U.S.* a member of a self-constituted committee in a community, who, in undertaking to deal with persons deemed harmful to the community, commits various outrages and lawless acts.

white cedar, **1.** a coniferous tree, *Chamaecyparis thyoides,* of the swamps of the eastern U.S. **2.** its wood, from which wooden utensils and building articles are often made. **3.** the arbor vitae, *Thuja occidentalis.*

White·chap·el (hwīt'chăp′əl), *n.* an E district of London, England.

white clover, a clover, *Trifolium repens,* with white flowers, common in pastures and meadows.

white coal, water, as of a stream, used for power.

white-col·lar (hwīt'kŏl′ər), *adj. U.S.* belonging or pertaining to workers, professional men, etc., who may wear conventional dress at work: *white-collar jobs.*

white damp, carbon monoxide.

whited sepulcher, a specious hypocrite. Matt. 23:27.

white dwarf, *Astron.* a star of average mass and very small volume in which the density may be a ton per cubic inch, as the companion of Sirius.

white elephant, **1.** an abnormally whitish or pale elephant, found usually in Siam; an albino elephant. **2.** a possession of great value but entailing even greater expense. **3.** an annoyingly useless possession.

white-eye (hwīt'ī′), *n.* any of the numerous small, Old World, chiefly tropical, singing birds constituting the family *Zosteropidae,* most species of which have a ring of white feathers around the eye.

white-faced (hwīt'fāst′), *adj.* **1.** having a white or pale face. **2.** marked with white on the front of the head, as a horse. **3.** having a white front or surface.

white feather, a symbol of cowardice: orig. from a white feather in a gamecock's tail taken as a sign of inferior breeding and hence of poor fighting qualities.

White·field (hwīt'fēld′), *n.* **George,** 1714–70, British Methodist preacher.

white-fish (hwīt'fĭsh′), *n., pl.* **-fishes,** *(esp. collectively)* **-fish. 1.** any fish of the family *Coregonidae,* similar to the trout but with smaller mouths and larger scales, esp. *Coregonus clupeaformis,* the common whitefish, an important and highly valued food fish of the Great Lakes. **2.** a marine food fish of California, *Caulolatilus princeps.* **3.** any of several silvery species of the minnow or carp family (applied esp. to European kinds). **4.** the beluga, *Delphinapterus leucas.*

white flag, an all-white flag, used as a symbol of surrender, etc.

white flax, the plant, gold-of-pleasure.

White Friar, a Carmelite friar: from the white cloak.

White·fri·ars (hwīt'frī′ərz), *n.* a district (a sanctuary until 1697) in central London, England: named from a Carmelite monastery in Fleet Street, founded in 1241.

white frost, frost (def. 3).

white gerfalcon, a beautiful white color phase (not a distinct species) of the black gerfalcon, *Falco rusticolus obsoletus,* highly prized in falconry. The whiteness of the bird increases the regality of its status.

white gold, any of several gold alloys possessing a white color due to the presence of nickel or platinum. Commercial alloys contain gold, nickel, copper, and zinc.

white gum, any of various Australian eucalyptuses with a whitish bark.

White·hall (hwīt'hôl′), *n.* **1.** Also, **Whitehall Palace.** a former palace in central London, England, originally built in the reign of Henry III: execution of Charles I, 1649. **2.** the main London thoroughfare between Trafalgar Square and the Houses of Parliament, flanked by government offices. **3.** the imperial government, or the policies of, the British Empire.

White·head (hwīt'hĕd′), *n.* **Alfred North,** 1861–1947, British mathematician and philosopher, in the U.S.

white-head·ed (hwīt'hĕd′ĭd), *adj.* **1.** having white hair. **2.** having fair or flaxen hair. **3.** *Colloq.* favorite: *white-headed boy.*

white heat, **1.** a stage of intense activity, excitement, feeling, etc.: *to work at a white heat.* **2.** an intense heat at which a substance glows with white light.

White·horse (hwīt'hôrs′), *n.* a town in NW Canada; the capital of Yukon Territory. 2570 pop. (1955).

white horse, a white-topped wave; a whitecap.

white-hot (hwīt'hŏt′), *adj.* **1.** very hot. **2.** showing white heat.

White House, The, 1. the official residence ("Executive Mansion") of the President of the United States, at Washington, D.C.: a large two-story freestone building painted white. **2.** *Colloq.* the President's office; the executive branch of the Federal government.

white lead, 1. basic lead carbonate, $2PbCO_3 \cdot Pb(OH)_2$, a white, heavy powder used as a pigment, in putty, and in medicinal ointments for burns. **2.** the putty made from this substance in oil.

white lead ore, cerussite.

white lie, a lie uttered from polite, amiable, or pardonable motives; a polite or harmless fib.

white line, 1. any blank or white part or margin. **2.** a white layer in a horse's hoof.

white-liv·ered (hwīt'lĭv′ərd), *adj.* **1.** pale or unhealthy. **2.** cowardly.

white·ly (hwīt'lĭ), *adv.* with a white hue or color.

white man's burden, the alleged duty of the white race to care for and educate ignorant or uncivilized peoples, esp. subject peoples, of other races.

white matter, *Anat.* nervous tissue, esp. of the brain and spinal cord, containing fibers only, and nearly white in color.

white meat, any light-colored flesh meat, as veal, the breast of chicken, etc.

white metal, any of various light-colored alloys, as Babbitt metal, Britannia metal, etc.

White Mountains, a mountain range in N New Hampshire: a part of the Appalachian system. Highest peak (in the NE U.S.), Mt. Washington, 6293 ft.

whit·en (hwī'tən), *v.t., v.i.* to make or become white. —**whit'en·er,** *n.*
—Syn. WHITEN, BLANCH, BLEACH mean to make or become white. To WHITEN implies giving a white color or appearance by putting a substance of some kind on the outside: *to whiten shoes.* To BLANCH implies taking away original color throughout: *to blanch celery by keeping it in the dark* To BLEACH implies making white by placing in (sun) light or by using chemicals: *to bleach linen, hair.* —Ant. blacken.

white·ness (hwīt'nĭs), *n.* 1. quality or state of being white. 2. paleness. 3. purity. 4. a white substance.

White Nile, See Nile, White.

whit·en·ing (hwī'tən ĭng), *n.* 1. act or process of making or turning white. 2. a preparation for making something white; whiting.

white oak, 1. an oak, *Quercus alba,* of eastern North America, having a light-gray to white bark and a hard, durable wood. 2. an oak, *Quercus petraea,* of England. 3. any of several other species of oak, as *Q. Garryana* or *Q. lobata* of western North America, or *Q. Robur* of Great Britain. 4. the wood of any of these trees.

white paper, 1. paper bleached white. 2. an official report of a government. 3. *Brit.* a publication of the House of Commons on a specific subject.

White Pass, a mountain pass in SE Alaska, near Skagway. ab. 2800 ft. high.

white pepper, a condiment prepared from the husked dried berries of the pepper plant, used either whole or ground. See **pepper.**

white perch, a percoid fish, *Morone americana,* of the streams and river mouths of the eastern and southern U.S.

white pine, 1. a pine, *Pinus Strobus,* of eastern North America, yielding a light-colored, soft, light wood of great commercial importance. 2. the wood itself. 3. any of various other similar species of pine.

white plague, tuberculosis, esp. pulmonary tuberculosis.

White Plains, a city in SE New York, near New York City: battle, 1776. 50,485 (1960).

white poplar, 1. an Old World poplar, *Populus alba,* widely cultivated in the U.S., having the under side of the leaves covered with a dense silvery-white down. 2. the soft, straight-grained wood of the tulip tree.

white potato. See **potato** (def. 1).

white primary, *U.S.* a direct primary of the Democratic party in southern states in which only white persons may vote.

white race, the Caucasian race.

white rat, an albino variety of the Norway rat, *Rattus norvegicus,* used in biological experiments.

White River, a river flowing from NW Arkansas generally SE to the Mississippi river. ab. 690 mi.

White Rock, a variety of Plymouth Rock (poultry).

white rose. *Hist.* See **rose** (def. 9b).

White Russia, 1. Official name, **White Russian Soviet Socialist Republic.** Also, **Byelorussian Soviet Socialist Republic.** a constituent republic of the Soviet Union, in the W part. 8,000,000 pop. (est. 1956); 86,100 sq. mi. *Cap.:* Minsk. 2. a region in the W part of czarist Russia, inhabited by the White Russians.

White Russian, a member of a division of the Russian people dwelling in White Russia and adjoining parts.

white sauce, a sauce made of butter, flour, seasonings, and milk or sometimes chicken or veal stock.

White Sea, an arm of the Arctic Ocean, in the NW Soviet Union. ab. 36,000 sq. mi.

white slave, 1. a white woman who is sold or forced to serve as a prostitute. 2. a white person held as a slave or in some condition resembling slavery.

white slaver, a person engaged in the traffic in white slaves.

white slavery, the condition of or the traffic in white slaves.

white-slav·ing (hwīt'slā'vĭng), *n.* traffic in white slaves.

white·smith (hwīt'smĭth'), *n.* a tinsmith.

white spruce. See **spruce** (def. 1).

white squall, *Naut.* a whirlwind or violent disturbance of small radius, which is not accompanied by the usual clouds, but is indicated merely by the white-caps and turbulent water beneath it.

white-tailed deer (hwīt'tāld'), a common deer of North America, *Odocoileus virginianus,* and related species, whose tail is white on the underside. Also, **white'-tail'.**

white·throat (hwīt'thrōt'), *n.* 1. a small Old World songbird, *Sylvia communis,* reddish brown above, with white throat, and distinguishable from its closest allies by the white marks on its outer tail feathers. 2. any of several other Old World birds of the same genus.

white-throated sparrow, a well-known North American finch, *Zonotrichia albicollis;* Peabody bird.

white turnip. See **turnip** (def. 1).

white vitriol, zinc sulfate heptahydrate, $ZnSO_4\cdot 7H_2O$, a white crystalline compound, used as an antiseptic, mordant, preservative, etc.

white·wash (hwīt'wŏsh', -wôsh'), *n.* 1. a composition, as of lime and water or of whiting, size, and water, used for whitening walls, woodwork, etc. 2. anything used to cover up defects, gloss over faults or errors, or give a specious semblance of respectability, honesty, etc. 3. *Colloq.* (in various games) a defeat in which the loser fails to score. —*v.t.* 4. to whiten with whitewash. 5. to cover up or gloss over the defects, faults, errors, etc., of by some means. 6. *Colloq.* (in various games) to subject to a whitewash. —**white'wash'er,** *n.*

white wax, *Brit.* paraffin.

white whale, the beluga, *Delphinapterus leucas.*

white·wing (hwīt'wĭng'), *n.* a public street cleaner, as in New York City, wearing a white uniform.

white-winged dove, a common dove, *Zenaida asiatica,* of the southwestern U.S. and Mexico.

white·wood (hwīt'wŏŏd'), *n.* 1. any of numerous trees, as the tulip tree or the linden, having a white or light-colored wood. 2. the wood. 3. the cottonwood of the genus *Populus.*

whith·er (hwĭth'ər), *Archaic and Literary; now replaced* by *where.* —*adv.* 1. to what place? 2. to what point, end, course, etc., or to what? —*conj.* 3. to what, whatever, or which place, point, end, etc. [ME and OE *hwider,* alter. of *hwæder* (c. Goth. *hwadrē*) on model of *hider* HITHER]

whith·er·so·ev·er (hwĭth'ər sō ĕv'ər), *adv.* to whatsoever place.

whith·er·ward (hwĭth'ər wərd), *adv. Archaic.* toward what place; in what direction. Also, **whith'er·wards.**

whit·ing[1] (hwī'tĭng), *n.* 1. a slender Atlantic shore fish of the genus *Menticirrhus,* of the croaker family (*Sciaenidae*). 2. the American Atlantic hake (*Merluccius bilinearis*): 3. any of several European species of the cod family, esp. *Merlangus merlangus.* [late ME *whytynge,* ? alter. of OE *hwitling* kind of fish. Cf. F. *witing*]

whit·ing[2] (hwī'tĭng), *n.* pure-white chalk (calcium carbonate) which has been ground and washed, used in making putty, whitewash, etc., and for cleaning silver, etc. [f. WHITE + -ING[1]]

whit·ish (hwī'tĭsh), *adj.* somewhat white; tending to white. —**whit'ish·ness,** *n.*

whit·low (hwĭt'lō), *n. Pathol.* an inflammation of the deeper tissues of a finger or toe, esp. of the terminal phalanx, usually terminating in sup puration. [ME *whitflawe, whitflowe,* f. WHITE + FLAW[1]]

Whit·man (hwĭt'mən), *n.* **Walt** (orig. **Walter**), 1819–1892, U.S. poet.

Whit·mon·day (hwĭt'mŭn'dĭ), *n.* the Monday following Whitsunday.

Whit·ney (hwĭt'nĭ), *n.* 1. **Eli,** 1765–1825, American inventor (of the cotton gin). 2. **William Dwight,** 1827–1894, U.S. philologist and lexicographer. 3. **Mount,** a mountain in E California, in the Sierra Nevada Mountains: the second highest peak in the United States. 14,495 ft.

Whit·sun (hwĭt'sən), *adj.* of or pertaining to Whitsunday or Whitsuntide.

Whit·sun·day (hwĭt'sŭn'dĭ, hwĭt'sən dā'), *n.* the seventh Sunday after Easter, celebrated as a festival in commemoration of the descent of the Holy Spirit on the day of Pentecost. [ME *whytsonenday,* OE *Hwita Sunnandæg,* lit., white Sunday, from the white (baptismal) robes worn on that day]

Whit·sun·tide (hwĭt'sən tīd'), *n.* the week beginning with Whitsunday, esp. the first three days of this week.

Whit·ti·er (hwĭt'ĭ ər), *n.* 1. **John Greenleaf,** 1807–92, U.S. poet. 2. a city in SW California, E of Los Angeles. 33,663 (1960).

Whit·ting·ton (hwĭt'ĭng tən), *n.* **Dick,** d. 1423, lord mayor of London about whom many legends survive.

whit·tle (hwĭt'əl), *v., -tled, -tling, n.* —*v.t.* 1. to cut, trim, or shape (a stick, piece of wood, etc.) by taking off bits with a knife. 2. to cut off (a bit or bits). 3. to cut by way of reducing amount (esp. fol. by *down*): *to whittle down expenses.* —*v.i.* 4. to cut bits or chips from wood or the like with a knife, as in shaping something or as a mere aimless diversion. [v. use of n.] —*n.* 5. *Archaic or Dial. Scot. or Brit.* a knife. [alter. of *thwittle,* ME *thwitel* knife, der. OE *thwitan* whittle] —**whit'tler,** *n.*

whit·tling (hwĭt'lĭng), *n.* 1. act of one who whittles. 2. (*usually pl.*) a bit or chip whittled off.

whit·y (hwī'tĭ), *adj.* whitish.

whiz (hwĭz), *v.,* **whizzed, whizzing,** *n.* —*v.i.* 1. to make a humming or hissing sound, as an object passing rapidly through the air. 2. to move or rush with such a sound. —*v.t.* 3. to cause to whiz. 4. to treat with a whizzer. —*n.* 5. the sound of a whizzing object. 6. a swift movement producing such a sound. Also, **whizz.** [imit.]

---

b., blend of, blended; c., cognate with; d., dialect, dialectal; der., derived from; f., formed from; g., going back to; m., modification of; r., replacing; s., stem of; t., taken from; ?, perhaps.   See the full key on inside cover.

whiz-bang (hwĭz'băng'), n. 1. Mil. a small, high-speed shell whose sound as it flies through the air arrives almost at the same instant as its explosion. 2. a firecracker with a similar effect. Also, **whizz'-bang'**.

whiz·zer (hwĭz'ər), n. 1. something that whizzes. 2. a centrifugal machine for drying sugar, grain, clothes, etc.

who (hōō), pron.; possessive whose; objective whom. —interrog. pron. 1. what person? who told you so? whose book is this? of whom are you speaking? 2. (of a person) what as to character, origin, position, importance, etc.: who is the man in uniform? —rel. pron. 3. as a compound relative. a. the or any person that; any person, be it who it may. b. Archaic. one that (after as). 4. as a simple relative, with antecedent (a person, or sometimes an animal or a personified thing) expressed. a. in clauses conveying an additional idea: we saw men who were at work. b. used in clauses defining or restricting the antecedent: one on whose word we rely, the man to whom it was told. [ME; OE hwā, c. D wie, G wer, Goth. hwas] —Syn. 4. See that.

whoa (hwō), interj. Stop! (used esp. to horses).

who·dun·it (hōō'dŭn'ĭt), n. Slang. a short novel dealing with a murder or a series of murders and the detection of the criminal.

who·ev·er (hōōĕv'ər), pron. —indef. rel. pron. 1. whatever person, or anyone that: whoever wants it may have it. 2. no matter who. —interrog. pron. 3. Colloq. who ever? who? (used emphatically): whoever is that? Also, Poetic, **who·e'er** (hōō âr').

whole (hōl), adj. 1. comprising the full quantity, amount, extent, number, etc., without diminution or exception; entire, full, or total. 2. containing all the elements properly belonging; complete: a whole set or assortment. 3. undivided, or in one piece: to swallow a thing whole. 4. Math. integral, or not fractional: a whole number. 5. uninjured, undamaged, or unbroken; sound; intact: to get off with a whole skin. 6. being fully or entirely such: whole brother. (brother by both parents). 7. out of whole cloth, without foundation in fact: a story made out of whole cloth. —n. 8. the whole assemblage of parts or elements belonging to a th·ng; the entire quantity, account, extent, or number. 9. a thing complete in itself, or comprising all its parts or elements. 10. an assemblage of parts associated or viewed together as one thing; a unitary system. 11. **as a whole**, all things included or considered. 12. **on** or **upon the whole**. a. on consideration of the whole matter, or in view of all the circumstances. b. as a whole or in general, without regard to exceptions. [ME hole, OE hāl, c. D heel, G heil, Icel. heill. Cf. HALE, HEAL] —**whole'ness,** n. —Syn. 8. WHOLE, TOTAL mean the entire or complete sum or amount. The WHOLE is all there is; every part, member, aspect; the complete sum, amount, quantity of anything, not divided; the entirety: the whole of one's property, family. TOTAL also means whole, complete amount, or number, but conveys the idea of something added together or added up: the total of his gains amounted to millions. —**Ant. 8.** part.

whole-heart·ed (hōl'här'tĭd), adj. 1. hearty; cordial; earnest; sincere. 2. single-hearted. —**whole'-heart'ed·ly,** adv. —**whole'-heart'ed·ness,** n.

whole hog, n. Slang. 1. entireness; completeness. 2. **to go** (the) **whole hog,** to involve oneself to the fullest extent.

whole-life insurance (hōl'līf'), life insurance for the whole of life, the face of the policy being paid upon death at any time, or upon the attainment of specified age.

whole milk, milk containing all its constituents as received from the cow, or other milk-giving animal.

whole note, Music. a semibreve. See illus. under note.

whole number, an integer: 0, 1, 2, 3, 4, 5 . . .

whole·sale (hōl'sāl'), n., adj., adv., v., -saled, -saling. —n. 1. the sale of commodities in large quantities, as to retailers or jobbers rather than to consumers directly (opposed to retail). 2. by wholesale, in large quantities, as in the sale of commodities. b. on a large scale and without discrimination: slaughter by wholesale. —adj. 3. of, pertaining to, or engaged in sale by wholesale. 4. extensive and indiscriminate: wholesale discharge of workers. —adv. 5. in a wholesale way; on wholesale terms. —v.t., v.i. 6. to sell by wholesale. —**whole'sal'er,** n.

whole-seas (hōl'sēz'), adj. completely under the influence of liquor. Also, **whole-seas over.**

whole·some (hōl'səm), adj. 1. conducive to moral or general well-being; salutary; beneficial: wholesome advice. 2. conducive to bodily health; healthful; salubrious: wholesome food, air, or exercise. 3. suggestive of health (physical or moral), esp. in appearance. 4. Rare. healthy or sound. [ME holsum, f. hol WHOLE + -sum -SOME¹] —**whole'some·ly,** adv. —**whole'some·ness,** n. —Syn. 2. nourishing, nutritious. 3. See healthy.

whole-souled (hōl'sōld'), adj. whole-hearted; hearty.

whole step, Music. an interval of two semitones, as A–B or B–C♯; a major second. Also, **whole tone.**

whole-wheat (hōl'hwēt'), adj. prepared with the complete wheat kernel.

who'll (hōōl), contraction of who will or who shall.

whol·ly (hō'lĭ, hōl'lĭ), adv. 1. entirely; totally; altogether; quite. 2. to the whole amount, extent, etc. 3. so as to comprise or involve all.

whom (hōōm), pron. objective case of who. [ME; OE hwām, dat. of whā WHO]

whoop (hōōp, hwōōp), n. 1. the cry or shout uttered by one who whoops. 2. the whooping sound characteristic of whooping cough. 3. **not worth a whoop,** Colloq. not worth a thing. —v.i. 4. to utter a loud cry or shout (orig. the syllable whoop, or hoop), as a call, or in enthusiasm, excitement, frenzy, etc. 5. to cry as an owl, crane, or certain other birds. 6. to make the characteristic sound accompanying the deep inspiration after a series of coughs in whooping cough. —v.t. 7. to utter with or as with a whoop or whoops. 8. to whoop to or at. 9. to call, urge, pursue, or drive with whoops: to whoop dogs on. 10. **whoop it** or **her** or **things up,** Slang. to raise an outcry or disturbance. —interj. 11. a cry to attract attention from afar, or to show excitement, encouragement, enthusiasm, etc. [ME whope, OE hwōpan threaten, c. Goth. hwōpan boast]

whoop·ee (hwōō'pē, hwŏŏp'ē), U.S. Slang. —n. 1. uproarious festivity. —interj. 2. a shout of "whoopee." [extended var. of WHOOP]

whoop·er (hōō'pər, hwōō'-), n. 1. one who or that which whoops. 2. a common Old World swan, Cygnus cygnus, notable for its whooping cry.

whoop·ing cough (hōō'pĭng, hwōōp'ĭng), an infectious disease of the respiratory mucous membrane, esp. of children, characterized by a series of short, convulsive coughs followed by a deep inspiration accompanied by a whooping sound; pertussis.

whop (hwŏp), v., whopped, whopping, n. Colloq. or Dial. —v.t. 1. to throw with force, pitch, or dash. 2. to strike forcibly. 3. to defeat soundly, as in a contest. —v.i. 4. to plump suddenly down; flop. —n. 5. a forcible blow or impact. 6. the sound made by it. 7. a bump; a heavy fall. Also, **whap, wap.** [orig. uncert.]

whop·per (hwŏp'ər), n. Colloq. 1. something uncommonly large of its kind. 2. a big lie. Also, **whapper,** [f. WHOP + -ER¹]

whop·ping (hwŏp'ĭng), adj. Colloq. very large of its kind; thumping; huge. Also, **whapping.**

whore (hōr), n., v., whored, whoring. —n. 1. a prostitute. —v.i. 2. to act as a whore. 3. to consort with whores. —v.t. 4. to make a whore of; debauch. [ME and OE hōre, c. G hure; akin to L cārus dear]

whore·dom (hōr'dəm), n. Rare. 1. prostitution. 2. (in Biblical use) idolatry.

whore·mon·ger (hōr'mŭng'gər), n. Rare. one who consorts with whores. Also, Rare, **whore·mas·ter** (hōr'-măs'tər, -mäs'-).

whore·son (hōr'sən), Obs. —n. 1. a bastard. 2. (in contemptuous or abusive use) a person. —adj. 3. being a bastard. 4. mean; scurvy. [f. WHORE + SON]

whor·ish (hōr'ĭsh), adj. Rare. being or having the character of a whore; lewd; unchaste. —**whor'ish·ly,** adv. —**whor'ish·ness,** n.

whorl (hwûrl, hwôrl), n. 1. a circular arrangement of like parts, as leaves, flowers, etc., round a point on an axis; a verticil. 2. one of the turns or volutions of a spiral shell. 3. Anat. one of the turns in the cochlea of the ear. 4. anything shaped like a coil. [ME whor-vil, f. whorve (OE hweorfa whorl) + -l, suffix]

whorled (hwûrld, hwôrld), adj. 1. having a whorl or whorls. 2. disposed in the form of a whorl, as leaves.

whor·tle·ber·ry (hwûr'təl·bĕr'ĭ), n., pl. -ries. 1. the edible, black berry of the ericaceous shrub, Vaccinium Myrtillus, of Europe and Siberia. 2. the shrub itself. [d. var. of hurtleberry, f. hurtle (der. hurt, OE horta whortleberry) + BERRY]

Whorls of ammonite

who's (hōōz), contraction of who is.

whose (hōōz), pron. possessive case of who, and historically also of what, and hence still used also (as a relative) with a neuter antecedent, although the nominative and the objective what in such constructions are now replaced by which: whose itself becoming interchangeable with of which: a pen whose point is broken, or of which the point is broken. [ME whos, OE hwæs, gen. of hwā who]

who·so (hōō'sō), pron. whosoever; whoever.

who·so·ev·er (hōō'sōĕv'ər), pron. whoever; whatever person.

whr., watt-hour.

why (hwī), adv., n., pl. whys, interj. —adv. 1. for what? for what cause, reason, or purpose? 2. for what cause or reason. 3. for which, or on account of which (after reason, etc.): the reason why he refused. 4. the reason for which: that is why I raised this question again. —n. 5. the cause or reason. —interj. 6. an expression of surprise, hesitation, etc., or sometimes a mere expletive: Why, it is all gone! [ME; OE hwī, hwȳ, instrumental case of hwæt WHAT]

whyd·ah (hwĭd'ə), n. whidah bird.

W.I., 1. West Indian. 2. West Indies.

w.i., when issued; denoting a transaction to be completed when the security is to be issued at a later date.

Wich·i·ta (wĭch'ə·tô), n. a city in S Kansas, on the Arkansas river. 254,698 (1960).

Wichita Falls, a city in N Texas. 101,724 (1960).

wick¹ (wĭk), n. a bundle or loose twist or braid of soft threads, or a woven strip or tube, as of cotton, which in a candle, lamp, oil stove, or the like serves to draw up the melted tallow or wax or the oil or other inflammable liquid to be burned gradually at its own top or end. [ME *wicke, weke,* OE *wice, wēoc(e),* c. G *wieke* lint] **—wick′-less,** *adj.*

wick[2] (wĭk), *n.* *Curling.* a narrow opening in the field, bounded by other players' stones. [n. use of v., to drive a stone through an opening]

wick·ed (wĭk′ĭd), *adj.* **1.** evil or morally bad in principle or practice; iniquitous; sinful. **2.** mischievous or playfully malicious. **3.** *Colloq.* distressingly severe, as cold, pain, wounds, etc. **4.** *Colloq.* or *Dial.* ill-natured, savage, or vicious: *a wicked horse.* **5.** *Colloq.* extremely trying, unpleasant, or troublesome. [ME, f. *wick(e)* wicked (now d.) + -ED[2]. Cf. OE *wicca* wizard] **—wick′ed·ly,** *adv.* **—Syn. 1.** unrighteous, ungodly, godless, impious, profane; unprincipled; immoral, profligate, corrupt, depraved; heinous; infamous, vicious, vile. See **bad**[1].

wick·ed·ness (wĭk′ĭd nĭs), *n.* **1.** quality or state of being wicked. **2.** wicked conduct or practices. **3.** a wicked act or thing.

wick·er (wĭk′ər), *n.* **1.** a slender, pliant twig; an osier; a withe. **2.** plaited or woven twigs or osiers as the material of baskets, chairs, etc.; wickerwork. **3.** something made of wickerwork, as a basket. **—adj. 4.** consisting or made of wicker: *a wicker basket.* **5.** covered with wicker. [ME, t. Scand.; cf. d. Sw. *vikker* willow]

wick·er·work (wĭk′ər wûrk′), *n.* work consisting of plaited or woven twigs or osiers; articles made of wicker.

wick·et (wĭk′ĭt), *n.* **1.** a small door or gate, esp. one beside, or forming part of, a larger one. **2.** a window or opening, often closed by a grating or the like, as in a door, or forming a place of communication in a ticket office, a teller's cage in a bank, etc. **3.** a small gate by which a canal lock is emptied. **4.** a gate by which a flow of water is regulated, as to a water wheel. **5.** *Cricket.* **a.** either of the two frameworks, each consisting of three stumps with two bails in grooves across their tops, at which the bowler aims the ball. **b.** the area between the wickets; the playing field. **c.** one batsman's turn at the wicket. **d.** the period during which two men bat together. **e.** a batsman's inning that is not completed or not begun. **6.** *Croquet.* a hoop or arch. **7.** a turnstile in an entrance. [ME, t. AF, ult. der. Scand.; cf. Icel. *vīkja* move]

wick·et·keep·er (wĭk′ĭt kē′pər), *n.* *Cricket.* the player on the fielding side who stands immediately behind the wicket to stop balls that pass it.

wick·ing (wĭk′ĭng), *n.* material for wicks.

wick·i·up (wĭk′ĭ ŭp′), *n.* **1.** (in Nevada, Arizona, etc.) an American Indian hut made of brushwood or covered with mats. **2.** *Western U.S.* any rude hut. Also, **wiki·up.** [prob. t. Algonquian (Sac-Fox-Kickapoo): m. *wikiyapi* lodge, dwelling]

Wick·liffe (wĭk′lĭf), *n.* **John.** See **Wycliffe.** Also, **Wic′lif.**

Wick·low (wĭk′lō), *n.* a county in E Ireland, in Leinster. 59,818 (prelim. 1956); 782 sq. mi. *Co. seat:* Wicklow.

wic·o·py (wĭk′ə pī), *n., pl.* **-pies. 1.** the leatherwood, *Dirca palustris.* **2.** any of various willow herbs, as *Chamaenerion angustifolium.* **3.** basswood. [t. d. Algonquian: m. *wik′pi, wighebi,* etc., inner bark]

wide (wīd), *adj., wider, widest, adv., n.* **—adj. 1.** having considerable or great extent from side to side; broad; not narrow. **2.** having a certain or specified extent from side to side: *3 feet wide.* **3.** of great horizontal extent; extensive; vast; spacious. **4.** of great range or scope; embracing a great number or variety of subjects, cases, etc.: *wide reading, experience, etc.* **5.** open to the full or a great extent; expanded; distended: *to stare with wide eyes, or a wide mouth.* **6.** full, ample, or roomy, as clothing. **7.** apart or remote from a specified point or object: *a guess wide of the truth.* **8.** *Phonet.* lax. **9.** too far or too much to one side: *a wide ball in baseball.* **—adv. 10.** to a great, or relatively great, extent from side to side. **11.** over an extensive space or region, or far abroad: *scattered far and wide.* **12.** to the full extent of opening: *to open the eyes or the mouth wide.* **13.** to the utmost, or fully: *to be wide awake.* **14.** away from or to one side of a point, mark, purpose, or the like; aside; astray: *the shot went wide.* **—n. 15.** that which goes wide. **16.** *Cricket.* a bowled ball that goes wide of the wicket, and counts as a run for the side batting. **17.** *Poetic.* a wide space or expanse. [ME; OE *wīd,* c. D *wijd,* G *weit*] **—wide′ness,** *n.* **—wid′ish,** *adj.* **—Syn. 1.** WIDE, BROAD refer to dimensions. They are often interchangeable, but WIDE especially applies to things of which the length is much greater than the width: *a wide road, piece of ribbon.* BROAD is more emphatic, and applies to things of considerable or great width, esp. to surfaces extending laterally: *a broad valley.* **4.** extensive, ample, comprehensive. **—Ant. 1.** narrow.

wide-an·gle (wīd′ăng′gəl), *adj.* noting or pertaining to lenses taking pictures including a wider angle, i.e. including more of the subject from a given position.

wide-a·wake (wīd′ə wāk′), *adj.* **1.** fully awake; with the eyes wide open. **2.** alert, keen, or knowing. **—n. 3.** Also, **wide-awake hat.** a soft, low-crowned felt hat.

wide·ly (wīd′lĭ), *adv.* **1.** to a wide extent. **2.** over a wide space or area: *a widely distributed plant.* **3.** throughout a large number of persons: *a man who is widely*

known. **4.** in many or various subjects, cases, etc.: *to be widely read.* **5.** greatly, very much, or very: *two widely different accounts of an affair.*

wid·en (wī′dən), *v.t., v.i.* to make or become wide or wider; broaden; expand. **—wid′en·er,** *n.*

wide-o·pen (wīd′ō′pən), *adj.* **1.** opened to the full extent. **2.** denoting the loose or irregular enforcement or the nonenforcement of laws concerning liquor, vice, gambling, etc.

wide·spread (wīd′sprĕd′), *adj.* **1.** spread over or occupying a wide space. **2.** distributed over a wide region, or occurring in many places or among many persons or individuals. Also, **wide′-spread′ing.**

widg·eon (wĭj′ən), *n.* **1.** any of several fresh-water ducks between the mallard and teal in size, esp. the European widgeon (*Anas penelope*) and the American widgeon or baldpate (*A. americana*). **2.** *Obs.* a fool. Also, **wigeon.** [orig. obscure]

wid·ow (wĭd′ō), *n.* **1.** a woman who has lost her husband by death and has not married again. **2.** *Cards.* an additional hand or part of a hand, as one dealt to the table. **—v.t. 3.** to make (one) a widow (chiefly in pp.). **4.** to deprive of anything valued, or bereave. **5.** *Obs.* **a.** to endow with a widow's right. **b.** to survive as the widow of. [ME; OE *widuwe,* c. G *wittwe;* akin to L *vidua* widow (fem. of *viduus* deprived of)]

widow bird, whidah bird.

wid·ow·er (wĭd′ō ər), *n.* a man who has lost his wife by death and has not married again.

wid·ow·hood (wĭd′ō hŏŏd′), *n.* state or period of being a widow (or, sometimes, a widower).

widow's cruse, the pot of oil of the widow of Zarephath which, at the word of Elijah, yielded an unfailing supply until the coming of rain on the earth. (I Kings 17:10–16. Cf. II Kings 4:1–7).

widow's mite, a small gift of money given in good spirit by one who can ill afford it.

widow's peak, *Colloq.* a point formed by the hair growing down in the middle of the forehead.

width (wĭdth), *n.* **1.** extent from side to side; breadth; wideness. **2.** a piece of the full wideness, as of cloth.

width·wise (wĭdth′wīz′), *adv.* in the direction of the width. Also, **width·ways** (wĭdth′wāz′).

Wi·du·kind (vē′dŏŏ kĭnt), *n.* Wittekind.

wie geht′s? (vē gāts′), *German.* how goes it with you? how do you do? (short for *wie geht es Ihnen*).

Wie·land (vē′länt), *n.* **Christoph Martin** (krĭs′tôf mär′tēn), 1733–1813, German poet, novelist, and critic.

wield (wēld), *v.t.* **1.** to exercise (power, authority, influence, etc.), as in ruling or dominating. **2.** to manage (a weapon, instrument, etc.) in use; handle or employ in action. **3.** *Archaic.* to guide or direct. [ME *welde(n),* OE *wieldan* control, der. *wealdan* rule, govern, c. G *walten*] **—wield′a·ble,** *adj.* **—wield′er,** *n.*

wield·y (wēl′dĭ), *adj.* readily wielded or managed, as in use or action.

Wien (vēn), *n.* German name of **Vienna.**

wie·ner (wē′nər), *n.* *U.S.* a sausage containing beef and pork whose link is usually shorter and more slender than that of a frankfurter. Also, **wie·ner·wurst** (wē′nər wûrst′). [t. G: Viennese sausage]

Wie·ner schnit·zel (vē′nər shnĭt′səl), a breaded veal cutlet, variously seasoned or garnished.

Wies·ba·den (vēs′bä′dən), *n.* a city in W West Germany: health resort; mineral springs. 250,178 (est. 1955).

wife (wīf), *n., pl.* **wives** (wīvz). **1.** a woman joined in marriage to a man as husband. **2.** a woman (*archaic* or *dial.,* except in compounds): *housewife, midwife.* [ME; OE *wīf* woman, wife, c. D *wijf,* G *weib,* Icel. *vīf*] **—wife′dom,** *n.* **—wife′less,** *adj.* **—wife′less·ness,** *n.*

wife·hood (wīf′hŏŏd), *n.* **1.** the position or relation of a wife. **2.** wifely character.

wife·ly (wīf′lĭ), *adj.,* **-lier, -liest.** of, like, or befitting a wife.

wig (wĭg), *n., v.,* **wigged, wigging. —n. 1.** an artificial covering of hair for the head, worn to conceal baldness, for disguise, etc., or formerly as an ordinary head covering. **2.** *Brit. Colloq.* a wigging. **—v.t. 3.** to furnish with a wig or wigs. **4.** *Brit. Colloq.* to reprimand or reprove severely. **—v.i. 5.** *Brit. Colloq.* to scold. [short for PERIWIG] **—wigged,** *adj.* **—wig′less,** *adj.* **—wig′like′,** *adj.*

Wig·an (wĭg′ən), *n.* **1.** a city in W England, in Lancashire. 82,130 (est. 1956). **2.** (*l.c.*) a stiff, canvaslike fabric used for stiffening parts of garments.

wig·eon (wĭj′ən), *n.* widgeon.

wig·ger·y (wĭg′ər ĭ), *n., pl.* **-geries. 1.** wigs or a wig; false hair. **2.** the wearing of wigs.

Wig·gin (wĭg′ĭn), *n.* **Kate Douglas,** 1856–1923, U.S. author of children's books.

wig·ging (wĭg′ĭng), *n.* *Brit. Colloq.* a scolding or reproof.

wig·gle (wĭg′əl), *v.,* **-gled, -gling,** *n.* **—v.i. 1.** to move or go with short, quick, irregular movements from side to side; wriggle. **—v.t. 2.** to cause to wiggle; move quickly and irregularly from side to side. **—n. 3.** a wiggling movement or course. **4.** a wiggly line. [ME *wigle(n),* freq. of *wig* (now d.) wag. Cf. Norw. *vigla* totter, freq. of *vigga* rock oneself, and D and LG *wiggelen*]

wig·gler (wĭg′lər), *n.* **1.** one who or that which wiggles. **2.** wriggler.

Wig·gles·worth (wĭg′əlz wûrth′), n. **Michael**, 1631–1705, American theologian and author, born in England.

wig·gly (wĭg′lĭ), adj. **1.** wiggling: a wiggly child. **2.** undulating; wavy: a wiggly line.

wight[1] (wīt), n. **1.** Archaic or Dial. a human being or person. **2.** Obs. a living being or creature. [ME; OE wiht, c. G wicht]

wight[2] (wīt), adj. Scot. or Archaic. **1.** strong and brave, or valiant. **2.** active; nimble or swift. [ME, t. Scand.; cf. Icel. vīgt, neut. of vīgr able to fight]

Wight (wīt), n. **Isle of,** an island off the S coast of England, forming an administrative county in Hampshire. 96,625 (1951); 147 sq. mi. Co. Seat: Newport.

Wig·town (wĭg′tən, -toun′), n. a county in SW Scotland. 30,500 pop. (est. 1956); 487 sq. mi. Also, **Wigtown·shire** (wĭg′tən shĭr′, -shər, -toun-).

wig·wag (wĭg′wăg′), v. **-wagged, -wagging,** n. —v.t., v.i. **1.** to move to and fro. **2.** Naval, etc. to signal by movements of two flags or the like waved according to a code. —n. Naval, etc. **3.** wigwagging, or signaling by movements of flags or the like. **4.** a message so signaled. [contraction of phrase wig and wag. See WIGGLE, WAG] —**wig′wag′ger,** n.

wig·wam (wĭg′wŏm, -wôm), n. **1.** an American Indian hut or lodge, usually of rounded or oval shape, formed of poles overlaid with bark, mats, or skins. **2.** U.S. Slang. (formerly) a structure, esp. of large size, used for political conventions, etc. **3. the Wigwam,** Tammany Hall. [t. Abnaki (Algonquian): dwelling]

wik·i·up (wĭk′ĭ ŭp′), n. wickiup.

Wil·ber·force (wĭl′bər fôrs′), n. **William,** 1759–1833, British statesman, philanthropist, and religious writer.

Wil·cox (wĭl′kŏks), n. **Ella Wheeler,** 1850–1919, U.S. poet.

wild (wīld), adj. **1.** living in a state of nature, as animals that have not been tamed or domesticated. **2.** growing or produced without cultivation or the care of man, as plants, flowers, fruit, honey, etc. **3.** uncultivated, uninhabited, or waste, as land. **4.** uncivilized or barbarous, as tribes or savages. **5.** of unrestrained violence, fury, intensity, etc.; violent; furious: wild strife, wild storms. **6.** characterized by or indicating violent excitement, as actions, the appearance, etc. **7.** frantic; distracted, crazy, or mad: to drive someone wild. **8.** violently excited: wild with rage, fear, or pain. **9.** undisciplined, unruly, lawless, or turbulent: wild boys, a wild crew. **10.** unrestrained, untrammeled, or unbridled: wild gaiety, wild orgies. **11.** disregardful of moral restraints as to pleasurable indulgence. **12.** unrestrained by reason or prudence: wild schemes. **13.** extravagant or fantastic: wild fancies. **14.** disorderly or disheveled: wild locks. **15.** wide of the mark: a wild throw. **16.** Colloq. intensely eager or enthusiastic. **17.** Cards. (of a card) having its value decided by the wishes of the players. —adv. **18.** in a wild manner; wildly. —n. **19.** an uncultivated, uninhabited, or desolate region or tract; a waste; a wilderness; a desert. [ME and OE wilde, c. D and G wild] —**wild′ly,** adv. —**wild′ness,** n. —Syn. **1.** undomesticated, untamed, feral, ferine, savage. **5.** boisterous, stormy, tempestuous. **6.** enthusiastic, eager. **9.** self-willed, ungoverned, unrestrained, riotous, wayward. **12.** reckless, rash, extravagant, impracticable. **13.** queer, grotesque, bizarre. —Ant. **1.** tame.

wild allspice, spicebush.

wild boar, a wild Old World swine, Sus scrofa, the supposed original of most of the domestic hogs.

wild brier, 1. dog rose. **2.** sweetbrier, Rosa Eglanteria. **3.** any other brier growing wild.

Wild boar, Sus scrofa
(4 ft. long, ab. 3 ft. high at the shoulder)

wild carrot, an umbelliferous weed, Daucus carota, having a thin and woody root, common in fields and waste places: the original of the cultivated carrot.

wild·cat (wīld′kăt′), n., adj., v., **-catted, -catting.** —n. **1.** any of several North American felines of the genus Lynx, esp. L. rufus and L. canadensis, the former widely distributed, the latter largely restricted to Canada. **2.** a forest-dwelling European feline, Felis sylvestris, somewhat larger than, but very much like, the domestic cat, to which it is closely related and with which it interbreeds freely. **3.** a similar North African species, Felis libyca, probably the main source of the domesticated cat. **4.** any of several other of the smaller felines, as the serval, ocelot, etc. **5.** a quick-tempered or savage person. **6.** U.S. Colloq. a single locomotive, with its tender, operating alone, as for shifting cars. **7.** an exploratory well drilled in an effort to discover deposits of oil or gas; a prospect well. **8.** a reckless or unsound enterprise, business, etc. —adj. **9.** characterized by or proceeding from reckless or unsafe business methods: wildcat companies or stocks. **10.** of or pertaining to an illicit enterprise or product. **11.** running without control or regulation, as a locomotive, or apart from the regular schedule, as a train. —v.i., v.t. **12.** to search for oil, ore, or the like, as an independent prospector. —**wild′cat′ting,** n., adj.

wildcat bank, U.S. Colloq. a bank which issued

notes without adequate security, in the period before the establishment of the national banking system in 1864.

wildcat strike, a labor strike which has not been sanctioned by the officials of the union.

wild·cat·ter (wīld′kăt′ər), n. U.S. Colloq. one who prospects for oil or ores or takes other ventures; a prospector.

Wilde (wīld), n. **Oscar Fingal O'Flahertie Wills** (fĭng′gəl ō flä′hər tĭ), 1856–1900, British dramatist, poet, novelist, essayist, and critic.

wil·de·beest (wĭl′də bēst′; Du. vĭl′də bāst′), n. gnu. [t. S Afr. D: lit., wild b·ast]

wil·der (wĭl′dər), Archaic or Poetic. —v.t. **1.** to cause to lose one's way. **2.** tc bewilder. —v.i. **3.** to lose one's way. **4.** to be bewildered. —**wil′der·ment,** n.

Wil·der (wīl′dər), n **Thornton (Niven),** born 1897, U.S. novelist and playwright.

wil·der·ness (wĭl′dər nĭs), n. **1.** a wild region, as of forest or desert; a waste; a tract of land inhabited only by wild animals. **2.** any desolate tract, as of water. **3.** a part of a garden set apart for plants growing with unchecked luxuriance. **4.** a bewildering mass or collection. [ME, f. wilder(n) wild (OE wildēoren) + -NESS] —Syn. **1.** See desert[1].

Wil·der·ness (wĭl′dər nĭs), n. a wooded area in NE Virginia: battle between Grant and Lee, 1864.

wild-eyed (wīld′īd′), adj. glaring in an angry or wild manner.

wild-fire (wīld′fīr′), n. **1.** a highly inflammable composition, as Greek fire, difficult to extinguish when ignited, formerly used in warfare (now referred to chiefly as a type of something that runs or spreads with extraordinary rapidity): the news spread like wildfire. **2.** sheet lightning, unaccompanied by thunder. **3.** the will-o'-the-wisp or ignis fatuus. **4.** Obs. Pathol. erysipelas or some similar disease. **5.** Obs. Vet. Sci. an inflammatory disease of the skin of sheep; scabies.

wild flax, 1. gold-of-pleasure. **2.** the common toadflax, Linaria vulgaris.

wild flower, 1. the flower of a plant not anywhere in cultivation. **2.** such a plant. Also, **wild′flow′er.**

wild fowl, the birds ordinarily sought as game, esp. ducks, geese, and the like. Also, **wild′fowl′.** —**wild′-fowl′er,** n. —**wild′-fowl′ing,** n., adj.

wild goose, any undomesticated goose, esp. the European graylag and the Canada goose or honker.

wild-goose chase, 1. a wild or absurd chase, as after something as erratic in its course as a wild goose. **2.** any senseless pursuit of an object or end.

Wild Huntsman, a spectral hunter of folklore, esp. in Germany.

wild hyacinth, 1. a camass, Camassia Scilloides, of eastern North America. **2.** the harebell, Scilla non-scripta, of Europe.

wild indigo, any of the American leguminous plants constituting the genus Baptisia, esp. B. tinctoria, a species with yellow flowers.

wild·ing (wīl′dĭng), n. **1.** a wild apple tree or apple. **2.** its fruit. **3.** any plant that grows wild. **4.** an escape (plant). **5.** a wild animal. —adj. **6.** Poetic. not cultivated or domesticated; wild.

wild lettuce, any of various uncultivated species of lettuce (genus Lactuca), growing as weeds in fields and waste places, esp. an English species (L. scariola) or a North American species (L. canadensis).

wild·ling (wīld′lĭng), n. a wild plant, flower, or animal.

wild madder, 1. madder (defs. 1, 2). **2.** either of two bedstraws, Galium Mollugo or G. tinctorium.

wild mandrake, the May apple.

wild mustard, the charlock.

wild oat, 1. any uncultivated species of Avena, esp. A. fatua, a common grass or weed resembling the cultivated oat. **2.** (pl.) dissolute life in one's youth. **3. sow one's wild oats,** to live a hectic, dissolute youth.

wild olive, any tree resembling the olive in structure or fruit.

wild pansy, the common pansy, Viola tricolor, in a wild state, varying between inconspicuous field weeds and showy varieties.

wild parsley, one of many umbelliferous plants resembling the parsley in shape and structure.

wild parsnip, an umbelliferous weed, Pastinaca sativa, having an inedible acrid root, common in fields and waste places: the original of the cultivated parsnip.

wild pink, an American catchfly, Silene pennsylvanica.

wild rose, any native species of rose, usually having a single flower with the corolla consisting of one circle of roundish spreading petals.

wild rubber, caoutchouc from trees growing wild.

wild rye, any of the grasses of the genus Elymus, somewhat resembling rye.

wild spinach, any of various plants of the genus Chenopodium, sometimes used in place of spinach.

wild vanilla, a composite plant, Trilisa odoratissima, of the southeastern U.S., bearing leaves with a persistent vanillalike fragrance.

wild West, the western frontier region of the U.S., before the establishment of stable government.

wild·wood (wīld′wŏŏd′), n. a wood growing in the wild or natural state; a forest.

ăct, āble, dâre, ärt; ĕbb, ēqual; ĭf, īce; hŏt, ōver, ôrder, oil, bŏŏk, ōoze, out; ŭp, ūse, ûrge; ə = a in alone; ch, chief; g, give; ng, ring; sh, shoe; th, thin; ŧh, that; zh, vision. See the full key on inside cover.

wile (wīl), *n., v.,* **wiled, wiling.** —*n.* **1.** a trick, artifice, or stratagem. **2.** an artful or beguiling procedure. **3.** deceitful cunning; trickery. —*v.t.* **4.** to pass (time) (fol. by *away*). **5.** to beguile, entice, or lure (*away, from, into,* etc.). [ME *wil(e),* prob. t. Scand.; cf. Icel. *vēl* craft, fraud, *vēla* defraud; in def. 4 confused with *while*]

wil·ful (wĭl′fəl), *adj.* willful. —**wil′ful·ly,** *adv.* —**wil′ful·ness,** *n.*

Wil·helm I (vĭl′hĕlm), William I (def. 3).

Wil·hel·mi·na I (wĭl′ə mē′nə; *Du.* vĭl′hĕl mē′nä), 1880–1962, Queen of the Netherlands from 1890 till her abdication in 1948 (daughter of William III).

Wil·helms·ha·ven (vĭl′hĕlms hä′fən), *n.* a seaport on the North Sea in NW Germany. 99,800 (est. 1955).

Wil·helm·stras·se (vĭl′hĕlm shträ′sə), *n.* **1.** a street in the center of Berlin, Germany, on which are many government and foreign office buildings. **2.** the foreign office or policies of the German government.

Wilkes (wĭlks), *n.* **1. Charles,** 1798–1877, U.S. rear admiral and explorer. **2. John,** 1727–97, British politician, journalist, and writer.

Wilkes-Bar·re (wĭlks′băr′ĭ), *n.* a city in E Pennsylvania, on the Susquehanna river. 63,551 (1960).

Wilkes Land, a coastal area of Antarctica, south of Australia.

Wil·kins (wĭl′kĭnz), *n.* **1. Sir George Hubert,** 1888–1958, Australian antarctic explorer, aviator, and aerial navigator. **2. Mary Eleanor.** See **Freeman, Mary.**

Wil·kins·burg (wĭl′kĭnz bûrg′), *n.* a borough in SW Pennsylvania, near Pittsburgh. 30,066 (1960).

will¹ (wĭl), *v.t.* auxiliary; *pres. indic. sing., 1st and 3d pers.* **will,** *2d* **will** or (*Archaic*) **wilt,** *3d* **will,** *pl.* **will;** *pt. 1st* **would,** *2d* **would** or (*Archaic*) **wouldst,** *3d* **would,** *pl.* **would;** *pp.* (*Obs.*) **would** or **would;** imperative and infinitive lacking. —*auxiliary.* **1.** am about or going to (in future constructions, denoting in the first person promise or determination, in the second and third persons mere futurity). **2.** am (is, are, etc.) disposed or willing to. **3.** am expected or required to. **4.** may be expected or supposed to: *you will not have forgotten him, this will be right.* **5.** am (etc.) determined or sure to (used emphatically): *you would do it, people will talk.* **6.** am accustomed to, or do usually or often: *he would write for hours at a time.* —*v.t.* **7.** to wish; desire; like: *as you will, would it were true.* [ME; OE *wyllan,* c. D *willen,* Icel. *vilja,* Goth. *wiljan;* akin to G *wollen,* L *velle* wish] —**Syn. 1.** See **shall.**

will² (wĭl), *n., v.,* **willed, willing.** —*n.* **1.** the faculty of conscious and esp. of deliberate action: *the freedom of the will.* **2.** power of choosing one's own actions: *to have a strong or a weak will.* **3.** the process of willing, or volition. **4.** wish or desire: *to submit against one's will.* **5.** purpose or determination, often hearty determination: *to have the will to succeed.* **6.** the wish or purpose as carried out, or to be carried out: *to work one's will.* **7.** discretionary pleasure: *to wander at will.* **8.** disposition (good or ill) toward another. **9.** *Law.* **a.** a legal declaration of a person's wishes as to the disposition of his (real) property, etc., after his death, usually in writing, and either signed by the testator and attested by witnesses or holographic. **b.** the document containing such a declaration. —*v.t.* **10.** to decide by act of will. **11.** to purpose, determine on, or elect, by act of will. **12.** to give by will or testament; to bequeath or devise. **13.** to influence by exerting will power. **14.** *Rare.* to wish or desire. —*v.i.* **15.** to exercise the will. **16.** to determine, decide, or ordain, as by act of will. [ME and OE (also ME *wille,* OE *willa*); c. D *wil,* G *wille,* Icel. *vili,* Goth. *wilja*] —**will′er,** *n.*

—**Syn. 5.** WILL, VOLITION refer to conscious choice as to action or thought. WILL denotes fixed and persistent intent or purpose: *where there's a will there's a way.* VOLITION is the power of forming an intention or the incentive for using the will: *to exercise one's volition in making a decision.*

will·a·ble (wĭl′ə bəl), *adj.* capable of being willed, or fixed by will.

Wil·lam·ette (wĭ lăm′ĭt), *n.* a river flowing N through NW Oregon into the Columbia river at Portland. ab. 250 mi.

Wil·lard (wĭl′ərd), *n.* **1. Emma,** 1787–1870, U.S. educator. **2. Frances Elizabeth,** 1839–98, U.S. educator, writer, and temperance advocate.

will contest, legal proceedings to contest the authenticity or validity of a will.

willed (wĭld), *adj.* having a will: *strong-willed.*

wil·lem·ite (wĭl′ə mīt′), *n.* a mineral, a zinc silicate, Zn₂SiO₄, sometimes containing manganese, occurring in prismatic crystals or granular masses, usually greenish, sometimes white, brown, or red: a minor ore of zinc. [t. D: m. *Willemit,* named after King *Willem* I of the Netherlands]

Wil·lem·stad (wĭl′əm stät′), *n.* a seaport on the island of Curaçao in the West Indies: the capital of Netherlands Antilles. 44,062 (est. 1953).

Willes·den (wĭlz′dən), *n.* a city in SE England, in Middlesex, near London. 174,900 (est. 1956).

wil·let (wĭl′ĭt), *n.* a large North American semipalmate shore bird, *Catoptrophorus semipalmatus,* with striking black-and-white wing pattern. [short for *pill-will-willet,* imit. of cry of bird]

will·ful (wĭl′fəl), *adj.* **1.** willed, voluntary, or intentional: *willful murder.* **2.** self-willed or headstrong; perversely obstinate or intractable. Also, **wilful.** [ME;

OE *wilful-* willing (in *wilful-lice* willingly). See WILL, -FUL] —**will′ful·ly,** *adv.* —**will′ful·ness,** *n.*

—**Syn. 2.** WILLFUL, HEADSTRONG, PERVERSE, WAYWARD refer to one who stubbornly insists upon doing as he pleases. WILLFUL suggests a stubborn persistence in doing what one wishes, esp. in opposition to those whose wishes or commands ought to be respected or obeyed: *a willful child who disregarded his parents' advice.* One who is HEADSTRONG is often foolishly, and sometimes violently, self-willed: *reckless and headstrong youths.* The PERVERSE person is unreasonably or obstinately intractable or contrary, often with the express intention of being disagreeable: *perverse out of sheer spite.* WAYWARD in this sense has the connotation of rash wrongheadedness which gets one into trouble: *a reform school for wayward girls.* —**Ant. 2.** obedient.

Wil·liam I (wĭl′yəm), **1.** (*William the Conqueror*) Duke of Normandy, 1027 or 1028–87; king of England, 1066–87, first king of Norman line. **2.** (*Prince of Orange and Count of Nassau; William the Silent*) 1533–84, Dutch statesman and soldier, born in Germany, leader of the revolt of the Netherlands against Spain. **3.** Also, **Wilhelm,** 1797–1888, king of Prussia, 1861–88, and German emperor, 1871–88, brother of Frederick William IV.

William II, 1. (*William Rufus, William the Red*) 1056?–1100, king of England, 1087–1100 (son of William I). **2.** 1859–1941, German emperor from 1888 until he abdicated in 1918.

William III, (*Prince of Orange*) 1650–1702, king of Great Britain and Ireland, 1689–1702 (successor and nephew of James II, and husband of Mary II). Also, **William of Orange.**

William IV, 1765–1837, king of Great Britain and Ireland, 1830–37 (brother of George IV).

William of Malmes·bur·y (mämz′bĕr′ĭ, -brĭ), c1090–c1143, English historian.

Wil·liams (wĭl′yəmz), *n.* **1. Roger,** c1603–83, British clergyman: founder of the colony of Rhode Island. **2. Tennessee,** (*Thomas Lanier Williams*) born 1914, U.S. dramatist. **3. William Carlos** (kär′lōs), 1883–1963, U.S. poet, novelist, and physician.

Wil·liams·burg (wĭl′yəmz bûrg′), *n.* a city in SE Virginia: its colonial capital; now restored as it was in pre-Revolutionary times. 6,832 (1960).

Wil·liams·port (wĭl′yəmz pôrt′), *n.* a city in central Pennsylvania, on the Susquehanna river. 41,967 (1960).

William Tell (tĕl), a legendary Swiss patriot who is supposed to have been forced by the Austrian governor to shoot an apple off his son's head with bow and arrow. Also, *German,* **Wil·helm Tell** (vĭl′hĕlm tĕl′).

will·ing (wĭl′ĭng), *adj.* **1.** disposed or consenting (without being particularly desirous): *willing to take what one can get.* **2.** cheerfully consenting or ready: *a willing worker.* **3.** done, given, borne, used, etc., with cheerful readiness. —**will′ing·ly,** *adv.* —**will′ing·ness,** *n.* —**Syn. 1.** inclined, minded.

Will·kie (wĭl′kĭ), *n.* **Wendell Lewis** (wĕn′dəl), 1892–1944, U.S. executive, lawyer, and political leader.

will-o′-the-wisp (wĭl′ə *th*ə wĭsp′), *n.* **1.** ignis fatuus. **2.** anything that deludes or misleads by luring on.

wil·low (wĭl′ō), *n.* **1.** any of the trees or shrubs constituting the genus *Salix,* many species of which have tough, pliable twigs or branches which are used for wickerwork, etc. **2.** the wood of the willow. **3.** *Colloq.* something made of this, as a cricket bat. **4.** a machine consisting essentially of a cylinder armed with spikes revolving within a spiked casing, for opening and cleaning cotton or other fiber. —*v.t.* **5.** to treat (cotton, etc.) with a willow. [ME *wilwe,* var. of *wilghe,* OE *welig,* c. D *wilg,* LG *wilge*] —**wil′low·like′,** *adj.*

wil·low·er (wĭl′ō ər), *n.* **1.** a person or a thing that willows. **2.** willow (def. 4).

willow herb, 1. an onagraceous plant, *Epilobium* (*Chamaenerion*) *angustifolium,* with narrow willowlike leaves and racemes of purple flowers. **2.** any plant of this genus. **3.** the purple loosestrife, *Lythrum Salicaria.*

willow pattern, a pattern used in china, employing the design of the willow tree, and originated in approximately 1780 by Thomas Turner in England.

Willow Run, airport for Detroit, near Ypsilanti.

wil·low·ware (wĭl′ō wâr′), *n.* china using the willow pattern.

wil·low·y (wĭl′ō ĭ), *adj.* **1.** pliant; lithe. **2.** gracefully slender and supple. **3.** abounding with willows.

will power, control of one's impulses and actions.

wil·ly-nil·ly (wĭl′ĭ nĭl′ĭ), *adv.* **1.** willingly or unwillingly. —*adj.* **2.** shilly-shallying; vacillating. [from phrase *will I* (*he, ye*), *nill I* (*he, ye*); *nill* be unwilling]

Wil·ming·ton (wĭl′mĭng tən), *n.* **1.** a seaport in N Delaware, on the Delaware river. 95,827 (1960). **2.** a seaport in SE North Carolina, on the Cape Fear river. 44,013 (1960).

Wil·no (vĭl′nə; *Pol.* vēl′nô), *n.* Polish name of **Vilna.**

Wil·son (wĭl′sən), *n.* **1. John** ("*Christopher North*"), 1785–1854, Scottish author. **2.** (**Thomas**) **Woodrow,** 1856–1924, the 28th president of the U.S., 1913–21: received Nobel peace prize in 1918. **3. Mount,** a mountain in SW California, near Pasadena: observatory. 5710 ft.

Wilson Dam, a power dam on the Tennessee river, in NW Alabama, at Muscle Shoals: a part of the Tennessee Valley Authority. ab. 4600 ft. long; 137 ft. high.

Wilson's petrel, a small petrel or Mother Carey's chicken, *Oceanites oceanicus,* black with white rump, known to inhabit all oceans except the North Pacific.

Wilson's phalarope, a swimming shore bird, *Steganopus tricolor*, which nests in prairie districts of North America and winters southward to Argentina and Chile.

Wilson's snipe. See *snipe* (def. 1).

Wilson's thrush, the veery.

wilt[1] (wĭlt), *v.i.* **1.** to become limp and drooping, as a fading flower; wither. **2.** to lose strength, vigor, assurance, etc. —*v.t.* **3.** to cause to wilt. —*n.* **4.** act of wilting. **5.** state of being wilted. **6.** a spell of depression, lassitude, or dizziness. [d. var. of *welt* wither, itself var. of *welk*, ME *welken*. Cf. D and G *welken*]

wilt[2] (wĭlt), *Archaic.* second pers. sing. pres. ind. of **will**[1].

wilt[3] (wĭlt), *n.* **1.** *Bot.* any of various plant diseases in which the leaves droop, become flaccid and then dry, usually because water cannot pass through the plant. **2.** a highly infectious disease in certain caterpillars, which causes their bodies to liquefy. Also, **wilt disease**. [special use of **wilt**[1]]

Wil·ton carpet (wĭl′tən), a kind of carpet, woven on a Jacquard loom like Brussels carpet, but having the loops cut to form a velvet pile. Also, **Wilton**. [named after town in Wiltshire, England]

Wilt·shire (wĭlt′shĭr, -shər), *n.* **1.** Also, **Wilts.** a county in S England. 386,692 pop. (1951); 1345 sq. mi. *Co. seat:* Salisbury. **2.** one of an English breed of pure-white sheep with long spiral horns.

wil·y (wī′lĭ), *adj.*, **wilier, wiliest.** full of, marked by, or proceeding from wiles; crafty; cunning. [ME, f. **WIL(E)** + -Y[1]] —**wil′i·ly**, *adv.* —**wil′i·ness**, *n.* —**Syn.** artful, sly, designing, intriguing, tricky, foxy.

wim·ble (wĭm′bəl), *n.*, *v.*, **-bled, -bling.** —*n.* **1.** a device used in mining, etc., for extracting the rubbish from a bored hole. **2.** a marbleworker's brace for drilling. **3.** any of various other instruments for boring, etc. —*v.t.* **4.** to bore or perforate with or as with a wimble. [ME, t. AF. Cf. GIMLET.]

Wim·ble·don (wĭm′bəl dən), *n.* a city in SE England, near London: international tennis meets. 58,158 (1951).

wim·ple (wĭm′pəl), *n.*, *v.*, **-pled, -pling.** —*n.* **1.** a woman's headcloth drawn in folds about the chin, formerly worn out of doors, and still in use by nuns. —*v.t.* **2.** to cover or muffle with or as with a wimple. **3.** to cause to ripple or undulate, as water. **4.** *Archaic.* to lay in folds, as a veil. —*v.i.* **5.** to ripple, as water. **6.** *Archaic.* to lie in folds, as a veil. [ME; var. of ME and OE *wimpel*, c. D and LG *wimpel*]

Wimple

Wims·hurst machine (wĭmz′hûrst), a device for the production of electric charges by electrostatic action; a static machine.

win (wĭn), *v.*, **won** or (*Obs.*) **wan; won; winning;** *n.* —*v.i.* **1.** to succeed by striving or effort (sometimes fol. colloquially by *out*). **2.** to gain the victory. **3.** to get (*in, out, through,* to, etc., *free,* loose, etc.). —*v.t.* **4.** to get by effort, as through labor, competition, or conquest. **5.** to gain (a prize, fame, etc.). **6.** to be successful in (a game, battle, etc.). **7.** to make (one's way), as by effort, ability, etc. **8.** to attain or reach (a point, goal, etc.). **9.** to gain (favor, love, consent, etc.) as by qualities or influence. **10.** to gain the favor, regard, or adherence of. **11.** to bring (over) to favor, consent, etc.; persuade. **12.** to persuade to love or marriage, or gain in marriage. **13.** *Brit. Mining.* **a.** to obtain (ore, coal, etc.). **b.** to prepare (a vein, bed, mine, etc.) for working, by means of shafts, etc. —*n.* **14.** *Colloq.* an act of winning; a success; a victory. [ME *winne(n)*, OE *winnan* work, fight, bear, c. G *gewinnen*] —**Syn.** **4.** obtain, secure, acquire, earn, achieve, attain, reach. See *gain*[1].

wince (wĭns), *v.*, **winced, wincing,** *n.* —*v.i.* **1.** to shrink, as in pain or from a blow; start; flinch. —*n.* **2.** a wincing or shrinking movement; a slight start. [ME *wynse*. Cf. OF *guenchir* turn aside] —**winc′er**, *n.*

winch (wĭnch), *n.* **1.** the crank or handle of a revolving machine. **2.** a windlass turned by a crank, for hoisting, etc. **3.** any one of a number of contrivances to crank objects by. —*v.t.* **4.** to hoist or haul by means of a winch. [ME *wynch*, OE *wince*] —**winch′er**, *n.*

Winch

Win·ches·ter (wĭn′chĕs′tər, wĭn′chĭs tər), *n.* **1.** a city in S England: cathedral; capital of the early Wessex kingdom and of medieval England. 25,710 (1951). **2.** a city in N Virginia: Civil War battles, 1862, 1864. 13,841 (1950). **3.** Winchester rifle.

Winchester rifle, a type of magazine rifle, first made in about 1866. [named after Oliver F. *Winchester* (1810–80), American manufacturer]

Winck·el·mann (vĭng′kəl män′), *n.* **Johann Joachim** (yō′hän yō′ä kнīm), 1717–68, German archaeologist and historian of ancient art.

wind[1] (*n.* wĭnd, *Poetic* wīnd; *v.* wĭnd), *n.* **1.** air in natural motion, as along the earth's surface. **2.** a gale; storm; hurricane. **3.** any stream of air, as that produced by a bellow, a fan, etc. **4.** gas generated in the stomach and bowels. **5.** a wind instrument or wind instruments collectively. **6.** air impregnated with animal odor or scent. **7.** breath or breathing; power of breathing freely, as during continued exertion. **8.** a hint or intimation: *get wind of the scandal.* **9.** empty talk; mere words. **10.** vanity; conceitedness. **11.** *Naut.* the point or direction from which the wind blows. **12.** a point of the compass, esp. a cardinal point. **13.** **in the wind,** stirring; circulating. —*v.t.* **14.** to expose to wind or air. **15.** to follow by the scent. **16.** to make short of wind or breath, as by vigorous exercise. **17.** to let recover breath, as by resting after exertion. [ME and OE, c. D and G *wind*, Icel. *vindr*, Goth. *winds*, L *ventus*] —**Syn.** **1.** WIND, AIR, BLAST, BREEZE, GUST refer to a quantity of air set in motion naturally. WIND applies to any such air in motion, blowing with whatever degree of gentleness or violence. AIR, usually poetical, applies to a very gentle motion of the air. A BREEZE is usually a cool, light wind. BLAST and GUST apply to quick, forceful winds of short duration; BLAST implies a violent rush of air, often a cold one, whereas a GUST is little more than a flurry.

wind[2] (wīnd), *v.*, **wound** or (*Rare*) **winded; winding;** *n.* —*v.i.* **1.** to change direction; bend; turn; take a frequently bending course; meander. **2.** to have a circular or spiral course or direction. **3.** to coil or twine about something. **4.** to be twisted or warped, as a board. **5.** to proceed circuitously or indirectly. **6.** to undergo winding, or winding up. **7. wind up,** *Colloq.* **a.** to conclude action, speech, etc. **b.** to end: *wind up in the poorhouse.* —*v.t.* **8.** to encircle or wreathe, as with something twined, wrapped, or placed about. **9.** to roll or coil (thread, etc.) into a ball or on a spool or the like (often fol. by *up*). **10.** to twine, fold, wrap, or place about something. **11.** to adjust (a mechanism, etc.) for operation by some turning or coiling process (often fol. by *up*): *to wind a clock.* **12.** to haul or hoist by means of a winch, windlass, or the like (often fol. by *up*). **13.** to make (one's or its way) in a winding or frequently bending course. **14.** to make (the way) by indirect or insidious procedure. **15. wind up, a.** to bring to a state of great tension; key up; excite. **b.** to conclude (action, affairs, etc.). —*n.* **16.** a winding; a bend or turn. **17.** a twist producing an uneven surface. [ME; OE *windan*, c. D and G *winden*, Icel. *vinda*, Goth. *-windan*]

wind[3] (wĭnd, wīnd), *v.t.*, **winded** or **wound, winding.** **1.** to blow (a horn, a blast, etc.). **2.** to sound by blowing. **3.** to signal or direct by blasts of the horn or the like. [special use of **WIND**[1]]

wind·a·ble (wīn′də bəl), *adj.* that can be wound.

wind·age (wĭn′dĭj), *n.* **1.** the influence of the wind in deflecting a missile. **2.** the amount of such deflection. **3.** the amount of movement of the sight which compensates for this deflection. **4.** a difference between the diameter of a projectile and that of the gun bore, for the escape of gas and the preventing of friction. **5.** *Naut.* that portion of a vessel's surface upon which the wind acts.

wind·bag (wĭnd′băg′), *n.* *Slang.* an empty, voluble, pretentious talker.

wind-blown (wĭnd′blōn′), *adj.* **1.** blown by the wind. **2.** (of trees) growing in a certain shape because of strong prevailing winds. **3.** bobbed short, with the ends of the hair combed towards the forehead.

wind-borne (wĭnd′bôrn′), *adj.* carried by the wind, as pollen or seed.

wind-break (wĭnd′brāk′), *n.* a growth of trees, a structure of boards, or the like, serving as a shelter from the wind.

wind·break·er (wĭnd′brā′kər), *n.* **1.** a kind of short jacket of suede or chamois leather or the like, with close-fitting elastic hip band, cuffs, and (often) collar, for sports or other outdoor wear. **2.** (*cap.*) a trade name for such a jacket.

wind-bro·ken (wĭnd′brō′kən), *adj.* (of horses, etc.) having the breathing impaired; affected with heaves.

wind·ed[1] (wĭn′dĭd), *adj.* **1.** having wind or breath: *short-winded.* **2.** out of breath. —**wind′ed·ness,** *n.*

wind·ed[2] (wĭn′dĭd, wīn′dĭd), *v.* pt. and pp. of **wind**[3].

wind·er (wĭn′dər), *n.* **1.** one who or that which winds (bends, turns, etc.) or is wound. **2.** a single one of a winding flight of steps. **3.** a plant that coils or twines itself about something. **4.** an instrument or a machine for winding thread, etc.

Win·der·mere (wĭn′dər mĭr′), *n.* **Lake,** a lake in NW England between Westmoreland and Lancashire: the largest lake in England. 10½ mi. long; 5¾ sq. mi.

wind·fall (wĭnd′fôl′), *n.* **1.** something blown down by the wind, as fruit. **2.** an unexpected piece of good fortune.

wind-flow·er (wĭnd′flou′ər), *n.* any plant of the genus *Anemone.* [trans. of Gk. *anemōnē* ANEMONE]

wind-gall (wĭnd′gôl′), *n.* *Vet. Sci.* a puffy distention of the synovial bursa at the fetlock joint. —**wind′-galled′,** *adj.*

wind gap, a cut that indents only the upper part of a mountain ridge.

wind harp, aeolian harp.

Wind·hoek (vĭnt′hŏŏk′), *n.* the capital of South-West Africa, in the central part. 20,490 (1951).

wind·hov·er (wĭnd′hŭv′ər), *n.* the European kestrel (bird), *Falco tinnunculus.* [f. WIND[1], n. + HOVER]

wind·ing (wīn′dĭng), *n.* **1.** act of one who or that which winds. **2.** a bend, turn, or flexure. **3.** a coiling, folding, or wrapping, as of one thing about another.

ăct, āble, dâre, ärt; ĕbb, ēqual; ĭf, īce; hŏt, ōver, ôrder, oil, bŏŏk, ōōze, out; ŭp, ūse, ûrge; ə = a in alone; ch, chief; g, give; ng, ring; sh, shoe; th, thin; ŧh, that; zh, vision. See the full key on inside cover.

4. something that is wound or coiled, or a single round of it. **5.** *Elect.* **a.** a symmetrically laid, electrically conducting current path in any device. **b.** the manner of such coiling: *a series winding.* —*adj.* **6.** bending or turning; sinuous. **7.** spiral, as stairs. —**wind′ing·ly,** *adv.*

winding sheet, 1. a sheet in which a corpse is wrapped for burial. **2.** a mass of tallow or wax that has run down and hardened on the side of a candle.

wind instrument (wĭnd), a musical instrument sounded by the player's breath or by artificial wind.

wind·jam·mer (wĭnd′jăm′ər), *n. Colloq.* **1.** any vessel propelled wholly by sails. **2.** a member of its crew.

wind·lass (wĭnd′ləs), *n.* **1.** a device for raising weights, etc., usually consisting of a horizontal cylinder or barrel turned by a crank, lever, or the like, upon which a cable or the like winds, the outer end of the cable being attached directly or indirectly to the weight to be raised or the thing to be hauled or pulled. —*v.t.* **2.** to raise, haul, or move by means of a windlass. [ME *windelas,* f. *windel* to wind (freq. of WIND[2]) + -*as* pole (t. Scand.; cf. Icel. *āss*)]

Hand-operated windlass

wind·less (wĭnd′lĭs), *adj.* **1.** free from wind; calm. **2.** out of breath.

win·dle·straw (wĭn′dəl strô′), *n. Scot.* or *Dial.* **1.** dry stalk of various grasses. **2.** anything weak or slender.

wind·mill (wĭnd′mĭl′, wĭn′-), *n.* **1.** a mill or machine, as for grinding or pumping, operated by the wind, usually by the wind acting on a set of arms, vanes, sails, or slats attached to a horizontal axis so as to form a vertical revolving wheel. **2.** the wheel itself. **3.** *Aeron.* a small air turbine with blades, like those of an airplane propeller, exposed on a moving aircraft and driven by the air, used to operate gasoline pumps, radio apparatus, etc. **4.** an imaginary opponent, wrong, etc. (in allusion to Cervantes' *Don Quixote*): *to fight windmills.*

win·dow (wĭn′dō), *n.* **1.** an opening in the wall or roof of a building, the cabin of a boat, etc., for the admission of air or light, or both, commonly fitted with a frame in which are set movable sashes containing panes of glass. **2.** such an opening with the frame, sashes, and panes of glass, or any other device, by which it is closed. **3.** the frame, sashes, and panes of glass, or the like, intended to fit such an opening. **4.** a windowpane. **5.** anything likened to a window in appearance or function, as a transparent section in an envelope, displaying the address. —*v.t.* **6.** to furnish with a window or windows. [ME, t. Scand.; cf. Icel. *vindauga,* f. *vind*(r) wind + *auga* eye] —**win′dow·less,** *adj.*

window box, 1. one of the vertical hollows at the sides of the frame of a window, for the weights counterbalancing a sliding sash. **2.** a box for growing plants, placed at or in a window.

window dresser, a person employed to dress the windows of a store, or arrange in them attractive displays of goods for sale. —**window dressing.**

win·dow·pane (wĭn′dō pān′), *n.* a plate of glass used in a window.

window sash, the frame holding the pane or panes of a window.

window seat, a seat built beneath the sill of a recessed or other window.

window shade, a shade or blind for a window.

win·dow·shop (wĭn′dō shŏp′), *v.i.* **-shopped, -shopping.** to look at articles in the windows of stores instead of actually buying. —**win′dow-shop′per,** *n.* —**win′dow-shop′ping,** *adj., n.*

window sill, the sill under a window.

wind·pipe (wĭnd′pīp′), *n.* the trachea of an airbreathing vertebrate.

wind-pol·li·nat·ed (wĭnd′pŏl′ə nā′tĭd), *adj. Bot.* pollinated by air-borne pollen. —**wind′-pol′li·na′tion,** *n.*

Wind River Range, a range of the Rocky Mountains in W Wyoming. Highest peak, Gannett Peak, 13,785 ft.

wind rose, *Meteorol.* a diagram which shows for a given locality or area the frequency and strength of the wind from various directions.

wind·row (wĭnd′rō′, wĭn′-), *n.* **1.** a row or line of hay raked together to dry before being made into cocks or heaps. **2.** any similar row, as of sheaves of grain, made for the purpose of drying. **3.** a row of dry leaves, dust, etc., swept together by the wind. **4.** a deep, narrow trench, esp. in fields of sugar cane, in which cut stalks are placed and buried beneath a layer of soil. —*v.t.* **5.** to arrange in a windrow or windrows. [f. WIND[1] + ROW[2]] —**wind′row′er,** *n.*

wind scale, a numerical scale, like the Beaufort scale, for designating relative wind intensities.

wind shake, 1. a flaw in wood supposed to be caused by the action of strong winds upon the trunk of the tree. **2.** such flaws collectively.

wind-shak·en (wĭnd′shā′kən), *adj.* **1.** affected by windshake. **2.** shaken by the wind.

wind·shield (wĭnd′shēld′), *n.* a framed shield of glass, in one or more sections, projecting above and across the dashboard of an automobile. Also, *Brit.,* **wind·screen** (wĭnd′skrēn′).

Wind·sor (wĭn′zər), *n.* **1.** the royal house of England since 1917. It comprises the Kings George V, Edward VIII and George VI. **2.** Duke of. See **Edward VIII. 3.** Also, **New Windsor.** a city in S England, in Berkshire, on the Thames: the site of **Windsor Castle,** a residence of English sovereigns since William the Conqueror. 23,181 (1951). **4.** a city in SE Canada, in Ontario, opposite Detroit, Michigan. 120,049 (1951).

Windsor chair, a wooden chair of many varieties, having a spindle back and legs slanting outward: common in eighteenth century England and in the American colonies.

Windsor tie, a wide, soft, silk necktie in a loose bow.

wind·storm (wĭnd′stôrm′), *n.* a storm with heavy wind, but little or no precipitation.

wind·suck·er (wĭnd′sŭk′ər), *n.* a horse afflicted with crib-biting.

wind-suck·ing (wĭnd′sŭk′Yng), *adj.* cribbing (def. 1).

wind-swept (wĭnd′swĕpt′), *adj.* open or exposed to the wind.

wind·tight (wĭnd′tīt′), *adj.* so tight as to prevent passage of wind or air.

wind tunnel, *Aerodynamics.* a tube in which a steady current of air can be maintained at high velocity together with devices for measuring forces and moments of models under observation.

wind-up (wĭnd′ŭp′), *n.* **1.** the conclusion of any action, etc.; the end or close. **2.** a final act or part. **3.** *Baseball.* the preparatory movements of the arm before delivering a pitched ball.

wind vane, a device using a pivoted arm with a vertical vane to indicate the direction of the wind.

wind·ward (wĭnd′wərd; *Naut.* wĭn′dərd), *adv.* **1.** toward the wind; toward the point from which the wind blows. —*adj.* **2.** pertaining to, situated in, or moving toward the quarter from which the wind blows (opposed to *leeward*). —*n.* **3.** the point or quarter from which the wind blows. **4.** the side toward the wind. **5. get to the windward of,** to get the advantage of.

Windward Islands, 1. an island group in the West Indies, comprising the S part of the Lesser Antilles. **2.** four British colonies in this island group, Dominica, Grenada, St. Lucia, and St. Vincent and their dependencies; now part of the Federation of the West Indies. 292,105 pop. (est. 1952); 821 sq. mi.

Windward Passage, a strait in the West Indies between Cuba and Hispaniola. ab. 50 mi. wide.

wind·way (wĭnd′wā′), *n.* **1.** a passage for air. **2.** *Music.* flue.

wind·y (wĭn′dĭ), *adj.,* **windier, windiest. 1.** accompanied or characterized by wind: *windy weather.* **2.** exposed to or swept by the wind: *a windy hill.* **3.** consisting of or resembling wind: *the windy tempest of my heart.* **4.** toward the wind, or windward. **5.** unsubstantial or empty. **6.** of the nature of, characterized by, or given to prolonged, empty talk; voluble. **7.** characterized by or causing flatulence. **8.** *Scot.* and *Brit. Dial.* boastful. [ME; OE *windig,* f. *wind* WIND[1] + -*ig* -Y[1]] —**wind′i·ly,** *adv.* —**wind′i·ness,** *n.*

wine (wīn), *n., v.,* **wined, wining.** —*n.* **1.** the fermented juice of the grape, in many varieties (red, white, sweet, dry, still, sparkling, etc.), used as a beverage and in cookery, religious rites, etc. **2.** a particular variety of such fermented grape juice: *port and sherry wines.* **3.** the juice, fermented or unfermented, of various other fruits or plants, used as a beverage, etc.: *gooseberry wine, currant wine.* **4.** a dark reddish color, as of red wines. **5.** *Pharm.* vinum. **6.** something that invigorates, cheers, or intoxicates like wine. **7.** intoxication due to the drinking of wine. **8.** *Brit.* a party for wine drinking. —*v.t.* **9.** to entertain with wine. **10.** to supply with wine. —*v.i.* **11.** to drink wine. [ME; OE *wīn,* c. D *wijn,* G *wein,* Icel. *vín,* Goth. *wein,* all g. to a prehistoric Gmc. word t. L: m. *vinum*] —**wine′less,** *adj.*

wine·bib·ber (wīn′bĭb′ər), *n.* one who drinks much wine. —**wine′bib′bing,** *n., adj.*

wine cellar, 1. a cellar for the storage of wine. **2.** the wine stored there; a store or stock of wines.

wine color, color of (red) wine; dark purplish red; deep carmine. —**wine′-col′ored,** *adj.*

wine gallon, *Brit.* a former gallon of 231 cu. in., equal to the present U.S. standard gallon.

wine·glass (wīn′glăs′, -gläs′), *n.* a small drinking glass for wine.

wine·glass·ful (wīn′glăs fōŏl′, -gläs-), *n., pl.* **-fuls.** the capacity of a wineglass, commonly considered as equal to 2 fluid ounces or ¼ cup.

wine·grow·er (wīn′grō′ər), *n.* one who owns or works in a vineyard and winery.

wine·grow·ing (wīn′grō′Yng), *n.* act or business of a winegrower.

wine measure, an old English system of measures for wine, etc., in which the gallon (wine gallon) was equal to 231 cu. in., and hence smaller than the gallon for beer, etc. The U.S. gallon is equal to this old wine gallon.

wine palm, any of various palms yielding toddy (def. 2).

wine press, a machine in which the juice is pressed from grapes for wine. Also, **wine presser.**

win·er·y (wī′nər Y), *n., pl.* **-eries.** an establishment for making wine.

b., blend of, blended; **c.,** cognate with; **d.,** dialect, dialectal; **der.,** derived from; **f.,** formed from; **g.,** going back to; **m.,** modification of; **r.,** replacing; **s.,** stem of; **t.,** taken from; **?,** perhaps. See the full key on inside cover.

Wine·sap (wīn′săp′), *n.* a long-keeping, red, winter apple of the U.S.

wine·shop (wīn′shŏp′), *n.* a shop where wine is sold.

wine·skin (wīn′skĭn′), *n.* **1.** a vessel made of the nearly complete skin of a goat, or the like, used, esp. in the East, for holding wine. **2.** one who drinks great or excessive quantities of wine.

wing (wĭng), *n.* **1.** either of the two anterior extremities, or appendages of the scapular arch or shoulder girdle, of most birds and of bats, which constitute the forelimbs and correspond to the human arms, but are adapted for flight or aerial locomotion. **2.** either of two corresponding but rudimentary or functionless parts in certain other birds, as ostriches and penguins. **3.** any of certain other winglike structures of other animals, as the patagium of a flying squirrel. **4.** (in insects) one of the thin, flat, movable, lateral extensions from the back of the mesothorax and the metathorax by means of which the insects fly. See diag. under **coleopteron. 5.** a similar structure with which gods, angels, demons, etc., are conceived to be provided for the purpose of flying. **6.** (in humorous use) an arm of a human being. **7.** a means or instrument of flight, travel, or progress. **8.** protection, care, or patronage: *to take a person under one's wing.* **9.** act or manner of flying. **10.** flight; departure: *to take wing.* **11. on the wing, a.** in flight, or flying. **b.** in motion; traveling; active. **12.** something resembling or likened to a wing, as a vane or sail of a windmill. **13.** *Aeron.* **a.** that portion of a main supporting surface confined to one side of an airplane. **b.** a winglike structure; plane. **14.** *Archit.* a part of a building projecting on one side of, or subordinate to, a central or main part. **15.** *Furniture.* an extension on the side of the back of an armchair. **16.** *Mil., Naval.* either of the two side portions of an army or fleet (usually called right wing and left wing, and distinguished from the center); flank units. **17.** *U.S.* an administrative and tactical Air Force unit consisting of two or more groups, a headquarters, and certain supporting and service units. **18.** (pl.) *Mil., Colloq.* the insignia or emblem worn by a flier. **19.** *Fort.* either of the longer sides of a crownwork, uniting it to the main work. **20.** *Sports.* **a.** (in some team games) any one of the positions, or a player in such a position, on the far side of the center position, known as the left and right wings respectively, with reference to the direction of the opposite goal. **b.** such a position or player in the first line of a team. **21.** *Theat.* **a.** the platform or space on the right or left of the stage proper. **b.** one of the long, narrow side pieces of scenery. **22.** *Anat.* an ala: *the wings of the sphenoid.* **23.** *Bot.* **a.** any leaflike expansion, as of a samara. **b.** one of the two side petals of a papilionaceous flower. See illus. under **papilionaceous. 24.** *Brit.* a mudguard shaped to fit around the wheel; fender. **25.** either of the parts of a double door, etc. **26.** the feather of an arrow. **27.** a group within a political party: *right wing, left wing.* —*v.t.* **28.** to equip with wings. **29.** to enable to fly, move rapidly, etc.; lend speed or celerity to. **30.** to supply with a winglike part, a side structure, etc. **31.** to transport on or as on wings. **32.** to perform or accomplish by wings. **33.** to traverse in flight. **34.** to wound or disable (a bird, etc.) in the wing. **35.** *Colloq.* to wound (a person) in an arm or other nonvital part. **36.** *Colloq.* to bring down (an airplane, etc.) by a shot. **37.** to brush or clean with a wing. **38.** *Theat.* to perform (a part, etc.) relying on prompters in the wings. —*v.i.* **39.** to travel on or as on wings; fly; soar. [ME *wenge,* pl., t. Scand.; cf. Icel. *vængir,* pl.] —**wing′-like′,** *adj.*

wing and wing, *Naut.* with a sail extended on each side by a boom, as a schooner sailing with the foresail out on one side and the mainsail out on the other.

wing back formation, *Am. Football.* **1. single wing back formation,** an offensive arrangement in which one of the backfield is put outside of and behind the end. **2. double wing back formation,** an arrangement with two backs behind each end.

wing case, elytron. Also, **wing cover.**

wing chair, a large upholstered chair, with winglike parts projecting from the back above the arms.

wing coverts, *Ornith.* the feathers which cover the bases of the quill feathers of the wing in birds, divided into greater, middle, lesser, and primary coverts.

winged (wĭngd or, *esp. Poetic.,* wĭng′ĭd), *adj.* **1.** having wings. **2.** having a winglike part or parts: *a winged bone, a winged seed.* **3.** abounding with wings or winged creatures. **4.** moving or passing on or as if on wings: *winged words.* **5.** rapid or swift. **6.** elevated or lofty: *winged sentiments.* **7.** disabled in the wing, as a bird. **8.** *Colloq.* wounded in an arm or other nonvital part.

wing-foot·ed (wĭng′fŏŏt′ĭd), *adj. Poetic.* having winged feet; rapid; swift.

wing·less (wĭng′lĭs), *adj.* **1.** having no wings. **2.** having only rudimentary wings, as an apteryx.

wing·let (wĭng′lĭt), *n.* **1.** a little wing. **2.** *Zool.* alula.

wing loading, *Aeron.* See **loading** (def. 4).

wing·spread (wĭng′sprĕd′), *n.* (of a winged creature or object) the distance between the most outward tips of the wings when they are as extended as possible.

wing·y (wĭng′ĭ), *adj.* **1.** having wings. **2.** rapid; swift.

wink (wĭngk), *v.i.* **1.** to close and open the eyes quickly. **2.** (of the eyes) to close and open thus; blink. **3.** to

close and open one eye quickly as a hint or signal or with some sly meaning (often fol. by *at*). **4.** to be purposely blind to a thing, as if to avoid the necessity of taking action (commonly fol. by *at*): *to wink at petty offenses.* **5.** to shine with little flashes of light, or twinkle. —*v.t.* **6.** to close and open (the eyes or an eye) quickly; execute or give (a wink). **7.** to drive or force (away, back, etc.) by winking. **8.** to signal or convey by a wink. —*n.* **9.** the act of winking. **10.** a winking movement, esp. of one eye as in giving a hint or signal. **11.** a hint or signal given by winking. **12.** the time required for winking once; an instant or twinkling. **13.** *Colloq.* **a.** a moment of sleep: *I didn't sleep a wink.* **b. forty winks,** a short nap. **14.** a little flash of light; a twinkle. **15.** *Colloq.* a bit. [ME; OE *wincian,* c. G *winken*]
—**Syn. 1. WINK, BLINK** refer to rapid motions of the eyelid. To **WINK** is to close and open either one or both eyelids with a rapid motion. To **BLINK** suggests a sleepy, dazed, or dazzled condition in which it is difficult to focus the eyes or see clearly: *bright sun makes one blink.*

Win·kel·ried (vĭng′kəl rēt′), *n.* See **Arnold von Winkelried.**

wink·er (wĭngk′ər), *n.* **1.** one who or that which winks. **2.** a blinker or blinder for a horse. **3.** *Colloq.* an eyelash or an eye.

win·kle (wĭng′kəl), *n., v.,* **-kled, -kling.** —*n.* **1.** *Brit.* any of various marine gastropods; a periwinkle. —*v.t.* **2.** *Brit. Colloq.* to pry (something) out of a place, as winkle meat is dug out of its shell with a pin (fol. by *out*). [short for **PERIWINKLE**]

Win·ne·ba·go (wĭn′ə bā′gō), *n.* **1. Lake,** a lake in E Wisconsin. ab. 30 mi. long. **2.** (pl.) a North American Indian tribe speaking a Siouan language closely related to Assiniboin, Teton, and Mandan, located on Green Bay, Wisconsin, in early times: now living at Green Bay and also NE Nebraska.

Win·ne·pe·sau·kee (wĭn′ə pə sô′kĭ), *n.* **Lake,** a lake in central New Hampshire: summer resort. 25 mi. long.

win·ner (wĭn′ər), *n.* one who or that which wins.

win·ning (wĭn′ĭng), *n.* **1.** act of one who or that which wins. **2.** (usually pl.) that which is won. **3.** *Mining.* **a.** an opening of any kind by which coal is being, or has been, won. **b.** a bed of coal ready for mining. —*adj.* **4.** that wins; successful or victorious, as in a contest. **5.** taking, engaging, or charming, as a person or the manner, qualities, ways, etc. —**win′ning·ly,** *adv.* —**Syn. 5.** captivating, attractive, winsome.

winning gallery, *Court Tennis.* the opening that is farthest from the spectator's gallery (so named because any ball struck into it is called a winning ball).

winning opening, *Court Tennis.* the dedans, winning gallery, or the grille (so named because it is a winning stroke to hit a ball into any of them).

winning post, a post on a racetrack, forming the goal of a race.

Win·ni·peg (wĭn′ə pĕg), *n.* **1.** a city in S Canada, on the Red river: the capital of Manitoba. 235,710 (1951). **2. Lake,** a lake in S Canada, in Manitoba. ab. 260 mi. long; ab. 9000 sq. mi. **3.** a river in S Canada, flowing from the Lake of the Woods NW to Lake Winnipeg. ab. 175 mi.

Win·ni·pe·go·sis (wĭn′ə pə gō′sĭs), *n.* **Lake,** a lake in S Canada, in W Manitoba, W of Lake Winnipeg. ab. 2000 sq. mi.

win·now (wĭn′ō), *v.t.* **1.** to free (grain, etc.) from chaff, refuse particles, etc., by means of wind or driven air; fan. **2.** to blow upon, as the wind does upon grain in this process. **3.** to drive or blow (chaff, etc.) away by fanning. **4.** to subject to some process of separating or distinguishing; analyze critically; sift: *to winnow a mass of statements.* **5.** to separate or distinguish: *to winnow truth from falsehood.* **6.** to pursue (a course) with flapping wings in flying. **7.** *Poetic.* to fan or stir (the air) as with the wings in flying. —*v.i.* **8.** to free grain from chaff by wind or driven air. **9.** to fly with flapping wings; flutter. —*n.* **10.** a device or contrivance for winnowing grain, etc. **11.** act of winnowing. [ME *win(d)we,* OE *windwian* (der. *wind*¹, n.). Cf. L *ventilāre*] —**win′now·er,** *n.*

Wi·no·na (wĭ nō′nə), *n.* a city in SE Minnesota, on the Mississippi. 24,895 (1960).

Wins·low (wĭnz′lō), *n.* **Edward,** 1595–1655, British colonist and governor of the Plymouth colony.

win·some (wĭn′səm), *adj.* winning, engaging, or charming: *a winsome smile.* [ME *winsom,* OE *wynsum,* f. *wyn* joy + -*sum*-**SOME**¹] —**win′some·ly,** *adv.* —**win′some·ness,** *n.*

Win·sor (wĭn′zər), *n.* **Justin,** 1831–97, U.S. librarian and historian.

Win·ston-Sa·lem (wĭn′stən sā′ləm), *n.* a city in N North Carolina. 111,135 (1960).

win·ter (wĭn′tər), *n.* **1.** the last and the coldest season of the year, in North America taken as comprising December, January, and February, in Great Britain November, December, and January. **2.** a whole year as represented by this season: *a man of sixty winters.* **3.** a period like winter, as the last or final period of life, a period of decline, decay, inertia, dreariness, or adversity. —*adj.* **4.** of, pertaining to, or characteristic of winter. **5.** (of fruit and vegetables) of a kind that may be kept for use during the winter. **6.** *Agric.* designating varieties of grain, esp. wheat, oats, and barley, which are sown before winter to be harvested the following spring or summer. —*v.i.* **7.** to spend or pass the winter: *planning*

winter aconite

to *winter* in Italy. **8.** to keep, feed, or manage during the winter, as plants or cattle. [ME and OE, c. D and G *winter*, Icel. *vetr*, Goth. *wintrus*] —**win′ter·er,** *n.* —**win′ter·less,** *adj.*

winter aconite, a small ranunculaceous herb, *Eranthis hyemalis,* a native of the Old World, often cultivated for its bright-yellow flowers, which appear very early in the spring.

win·ter·ber·ry (wĭn′tər bĕr′ĭ), *n., pl.* **-ries.** any of several North American species of holly (genus *Ilex*) with red berries that are persistent through the winter.

win·ter·bourne (wĭn′tər bôrn′, -bōrn′), *n.* a channel filled only at a time of excessive rainfall.

win·ter·feed (wĭn′tər fēd′), *v.t.,* **-fed, -feeding.** to feed in the winter, as cattle.

win·ter·green (wĭn′tər grēn′), *n.* **1.** a small, creeping evergreen ericaceous shrub, *Gaultheria procumbens,* common in eastern North America, with white bell-shaped flowers, a bright-red berrylike fruit, and aromatic leaves which yield a volatile oil. **2.** this oil (**oil of wintergreen**). **3.** the flavor of oil of wintergreen or something flavored with it. **4.** any of various other plants of the same genus. **5.** any of various small evergreen herbs of the genera *Pyrola* and *Chimaphila.*

win·ter·ize (wĭn′tə rīz′), *v.t.,* **-ized, -izing.** to prepare (an automobile, house, etc.) for cold weather by (in automobiles) adding antifreeze and changing weight of oil, (in houses) adding insulation, heating units, etc.

win·ter·kill (wĭn′tər kĭl′), *v.t., v.i. U.S.* to kill by or die from exposure to the cold of winter, as wheat. —**win′ter·kill′ing,** *adj., n.*

winter lambs, well-fed lambs born in the fall or early winter and sold prior to May 20.

winter melon, a variety of late-keeping muskmelon (*Cucumis Melo* var. *inodorus*).

win·ter·time (wĭn′tər tīm′), *n.* the season of winter. Also, *Poetic,* **win·ter·tide** (wĭn′tər tīd′).

Win·throp (wĭn′thrəp), *n.* **1. John,** 1588–1649, governor of the colony of Massachusetts. **2.** his son, **John,** 1606–76, governor of the colony of Connecticut.

win·try (wĭn′trĭ), *adj.,* **-trier, -triest. 1.** of or characteristic of winter. **2.** having the season or cold of winter. **3.** suggestive of winter, as in lack of warmth or cheer. Also, **win·ter·y** (wĭn′tər ĭ, -trĭ), **win·ter·ly** (wĭn′tər lĭ). —**win′tri·ly,** *adv.* —**win′tri·ness,** *n.*

win·y (wī′nĭ), *adj.* **1.** of, like, or characteristic of wine. **2.** affected by wine.

winze (wĭnz), *n. Mining.* a small underground shaft, esp. one sunk from one level to another, as for ventilation, etc. [earlier *winds,* appar. der. **WIND¹,** n.]

wipe (wīp), *v.,* **wiped, wiping,** *n.* —*v.t.* **1.** to rub lightly with or on a cloth, towel, paper, the hand, etc., in order to clean or dry. **2.** to take (*away, off, out,* etc.) by rubbing with or on something. **3.** to remove as if by rubbing (fol. by *away, off,* etc.). **4.** to blot (*out*), as from existence or memory. **5.** to rub or draw (something) over a surface, as in cleaning or drying. **6.** *Plumbing.* **a.** to apply (solder in a semifluid state) by spreading with leather or cloth over the part to be soldered. **b.** to form (a joint) in this manner. —*n.* **7.** act of wiping. **8.** a rub, as of one thing over another. **9.** *Colloq. or Dial.* a sweeping stroke or blow. **10.** *Colloq. or Dial.* a gibe. **11.** *Mach.* a wiper. **12.** *Slang.* a handkerchief. [ME; OE *wīpian,* c. OHG *wīfan* wind round, Goth. *weipan* crown; akin to VIBRATE]

wip·er (wī′pər), *n.* **1.** one who or that which wipes. **2.** that with which anything is wiped, as a towel or a handkerchief. **3.** *Elect.* that portion of the moving member of a selector, or other similar device, which makes contact with the terminals of a bank; a type of brush (def. 7a). **4.** *Mach.* a projecting piece, as on a rotating axis, acting on another part, as a stamper, esp. to raise it so that it may fall by its own weight.

wire (wīr), *n., adj., v.,* **wired, wiring.** —*n.* **1.** a piece of slender, flexible metal, ranging from a thickness that can be bent by the hand only with some difficulty down to a fine thread, and usually circular in section. **2.** such pieces as a material. **3.** a cross wire or cross hair. **4.** a barbed wire fence. **5.** a long wire or cable used in a telegraph, telephone, or cable system. **6.** *Colloq.* a telegram. **7.** *Colloq.* the telegraphic system: *to send a message by wire.* **8.** (*pl.*) a system of wires by which puppets are moved. **9.** *Pol.* secret means of directing or controlling the action of others, as in carrying out schemes: *to pull wires to win a nomination.* **10.** a metallic string of a musical instrument. **11.** *Horse Racing.* the imaginary finish line. **12.** *Ornith.* one of the extremely long, slender, wirelike filaments or shafts of the plumage of various birds. **13.** a metal device used to snare rabbits, etc. —*adj.* **14.** made of wire; consisting of or constructed with wires. **15.** wirelike. —*v.t.* **16.** to furnish with a wire or wires. **17.** to install an electric system of wiring, as for lighting, etc. **18.** to fasten or bind with wire. **19.** to put on a wire, as beads. **20.** *Colloq.* to send by telegraph, as a message. **21.** *Colloq.* to send a telegraphic message to. **22.** to snare by means of a wire or wires. **23.** *Croquet.* to arrange (a ball) in such a manner that it will rest behind an arch and thus prevent a shot which would be successful. —*v.i.* **24.** *Colloq.* to send a telegraphic message; telegraph. [ME and OE *wīr,* c. LG *wīr,* Icel. *vīrr*] —**wire′like′,** *adj.*

wire cloth, a texture of wires of moderate fineness, used for strainers, or in the manufacture of paper, etc.

wire cutter, a device designed to cut wire.

wire·danc·er (wīr′dăn′sər, -dän′-), *n.* one who dances or performs other feats upon a high wire. —**wire′danc′ing,** *n.*

wire·draw (wīr′drô′), *v.t.,* **-drew, -drawn, -drawing. 1.** to draw (metal) out into wire, esp. by pulling forcibly through a series of holes gradually decreasing in diameter. **2.** to draw out to great length, in quantity or time; stretch out to excess. **3.** to strain unwarrantably, as in meaning. —**wire′draw′er,** *n.* —**wire′draw′ing,** *n.*

wire entanglement, *Fort.* heavy barbed wire placed either on supports or on the ground to prevent the advance of the enemy.

wire gauge, a gauge calibrated for standard wire diameters.

wire gauze, a gauzelike texture woven of very fine wires.

Wire gauge

wire glass, glass having wire netting embedded within it, as to increase its strength.

wire grass, 1. *U.S.* a widely distributed southern grass, *Cynodon dactylon,* used for pasture and turf. **2.** any of various similar grasses with spreading habit, that may be a pest in cultivated fields.

wire·hair (wīr′hâr′), *n.* a fox terrier having a wiry coat. Also, **wire-haired terrier.**

wire-haired (wīr′hârd′), *adj.* having coarse, stiff, wirelike hair.

wire·less (wīr′lĭs), *adj.* **1.** having no wire. **2.** denoting or pertaining to any of various devices which are operated with or set in action by electromagnetic waves. **3.** *Chiefly Brit.* radio. —*n.* **4.** wireless telegraphy or telephony.

Wirehair
(15½ in. high at the shoulder)

5. a wireless telegraph or telephone, or the like. **6.** a wireless message. **7.** *Chiefly Brit.* radio. —*v.t., v.i.* **8.** to telegraph or telephone by wireless.

wireless telegraphy, telegraphy in which there are no connecting wires, the signals being transmitted by the radiated energy of electromagnetic waves.

wireless telephone, a telephone in which the signal is transmitted by wireless telegraphy.

wireless telephony, a system of transmitting and exchanging voice messages by means of radio.

wire·man (wīr′mən), *n., pl.* **-men.** one who installs and maintains electric wiring.

wire·pho·to (wīr′fō′tō), *n.* a method of sending photographs by wire: a trade name designating a service by the Associated Press.

wire·pull·er (wīr′pŏŏl′ər), *n.* **1.** one who pulls the wires, as of puppets. **2.** one who manipulates secret means of directing or controlling the action of others.

wire·pull·ing (wīr′pŏŏl′ĭng), *n.* **1.** act of pulling the wires, as of puppets. **2.** *Colloq.* the guiding and controlling of any body of persons, esp. a political party, by underhand influence or management. —*adj.* **3.** *Colloq.* using secret and unethical influence on a public official.

wir·er (wīr′ər), *n.* **1.** one who wires. **2.** one who uses wire to snare game.

wire recorder, *Electronics.* a device to record sound on a steel wire by magnetizing the wire as it passes an electromagnet, the sound being reproduced by the motion of the wire past a receiver.

wire rope, a rope with strands of wire.

wire·spun (wīr′spŭn′), *adj.* **1.** drawn out as wire is. **2.** oversubtle. **3.** having too little substance.

wire tapper, 1. one who illicitly taps wires to learn the nature of messages passing over them. **2.** *Colloq.* a swindler who professes to secure by this or some similar means advance information for betting or the like. —**wire′tap′,** *n.* —**wire tapping.**

wire·work (wīr′wûrk′), *n.* **1.** work consisting of wire. **2.** fabrics or articles made of wire.

wire·works (wīr′wûrks′), *n. pl. or sing.* an establishment where wire is made, or is put to some industrial use. —**wire′work′er,** *n.*

wire·worm (wīr′wûrm′), *n.* **1.** any of the slender, hard-bodied larvae of click beetles, which in many species live underground and feed on the roots of plants. **2.** any of various small myriapods. **3.** a stomach worm.

wire-wove (wīr′wōv′), *adj.* **1.** made of woven wire. **2.** denoting fine glazed paper used esp. for letter paper.

wir·ing (wīr′ĭng), *n.* **1.** act of one who wires. **2.** *Elect.* the aggregate of wires, in a lighting system, switchboard, radio, etc. —*adj.* **3.** that installs, or is used in, wiring.

wir·ra (wĭr′ə), *interj. Irish.* an exclamation of sorrow or lament. [in full, *O wirra,* half trans., half adoption of Irish *a Muire* O Mary]

wir·y (wīr′ĭ), *adj.,* **wirier, wiriest. 1.** made of wire. **2.** in the form of wire. **3.** resembling wire, as in form, stiffness, etc.: *wiry grass.* **4.** lean and sinewy. **5.** produced by or resembling the sound of a vibrating wire: *wiry tones.* —**wir′i·ly,** *adv.* —**wir′i·ness,** *n.*

wis (wĭs), *v.t., v.i. Archaic.* to know. [abstracted from *iwis* certainly (OE *gewiss*), misread as *I wis I know*]

Wis., Wisconsin. Also, **Wisc.**

Wis·by (wĭz′bĭ; *Ger.* vĭz′bĭ), *n.* German name of Visby.

Wis·con·sin (wĭs·kŏn′sən), *n.* **1.** a State in the N central United States: a part of the Midwest. 3,951,777 pop. (1960); 56,154 sq. mi. *Cap.*: Madison. *Abbr.*: Wis. or Wisc. **2.** a river flowing from N Wisconsin SW to the Mississippi. ab. 430 mi.

Wisd., Wisdom of Solomon (Apocrypha).

wis·dom (wĭz′dəm), *n.* **1.** the quality or state of being wise; knowledge of what is true or right coupled with just judgment as to action; sagacity, prudence, or common sense. **2.** scholarly knowledge, or learning: *the wisdom of the schools.* **3.** wise sayings or teachings. **4.** a wise act or saying. [ME and OE, c. Icel. *vísdōmr.* See WISE, -DOM] **—wis·dom·less,** *adj.* **—Syn. 1.** discretion, judgment. See **information. 2.** learning, sapience, erudition.

Wisdom of Jesus, Son of Si·rach (sī′răk), Ecclesiasticus.

Wisdom of Solomon, a book of the Apocrypha, on wisdom and its relation to righteousness.

wisdom tooth, the third molar tooth; the last tooth in each quadrant of the jaw; the last tooth to erupt (between the ages of 17–25).

wise[1] (wīz), *adj.*, **wiser, wisest. 1.** having the power of discerning and judging properly as to what is true or right. **2.** characterized by or showing such power; judicious or prudent. **3.** possessed of or characterized by scholarly knowledge or learning; learned; erudite: *wise in the law.* **4.** having knowledge or information as to facts, circumstances, etc.: *we are wiser for his explanations.* **5.** *Slang.* aware or cognizant: *to be wise to a thing* (to be aware of it). **6.** *Archaic* or *Dial.* having knowledge of occult or supernatural things. [ME and OE *wis,* c. D *wijs,* G *weise*] **—wise′ly,** *adv.* **—Ant. 2.** foolish.

wise[2] (wīz), *n.* **1.** way of proceeding; manner; fashion. **2.** respect; degree (now usually in composition or in certain phrases): *in any wise* (in any way, respect, or degree). [ME and OE; c. D *wijze,* G *weise* manner, tune]

Wise (wīz), *n.* **Stephen Samuel,** 1874–1949, U.S. rabbi, Jewish leader, and writer, born in Hungary.

-wise, a suffixal use of **wise**[2] in adverbs denoting manner, direction, position, etc., as in *anywise, edgewise, sidewise.* Cf. **-ways.**

wise·a·cre (wīz′ā′kər, wī′zə kər), *n.* (esp. in ironical or humorous use) one who possesses or affects to possess great wisdom. [t. MD: m. *wijsseggher* soothsayer]

wise·crack (wīz′krăk′), *Slang.* **—n. 1.** a smart or facetious remark. **—v.i. 2.** to make wisecracks. **—wise′crack′er,** *n.*

Wise·man (wīz′mən), *n.* **Nicholas Patrick Stephen,** 1802–65, British cardinal and writer.

wish (wĭsh), *v.t.* **1.** to want; desire; long for (often with an infinitive or a clause as object): *I wish to see him, I wish that he would come.* **2.** to desire (a person or thing) to be (as specified): *to wish oneself elsewhere.* **3.** to entertain wishes, favorably or otherwise, for: *to wish one well or ill.* **4.** to bid, as in greeting or leave-taking: *to wish one a good morning.* **5.** to command: *I wish him to come.* **6.** to force or impose (fol. by on): *to wish a hard job on someone.* **—v.i. 7.** to have a distinct mental inclination toward doing, obtaining, etc. (followed by *for*): *to wish for a book, for news, or for aid.* **8.** to entertain wishes, favorably or otherwise (fol. by *to*): *to wish well to a person or a cause.* **—n. 9.** a distinct mental inclination toward the doing, obtaining, attaining, etc., of something; a desire, felt or expressed: *disregard the wishes of others.* **10.** an expression of a wish, often one of a kindly or courteous nature: *send one's best wishes.* **11.** that which is wished: *get one's wish.* [ME *wisshe,* OE *wyscan,* c. G *wünschen,* Icel. *æskja*] **—wish′er,** *n.* **—wish′less,** *adj.*
—Syn. 1. WISH, DESIRE, WANT indicate a longing for something. To WISH is to feel an impulse toward attainment or possession of something; the strength of the feeling may be of greater or less intensity: *I wish I could go home.* DESIRE, a more formal word, suggests a strong wish: *they desire a new regime.* WANT, usually colloquial in use, suggests a feeling of lack or need which imperatively demands fulfillment: *people all over the world want peace.*

wish·bone (wĭsh′bōn′), *n.* the forked bone (a united pair of clavicles) in front of the breastbone in most birds; the furcula.

wish·ful (wĭsh′fəl), *adj.* having or showing a wish; desirous; longing. **—wish′ful·ly,** *adv.* **—wish′ful·ness,** *n.*

wish·y-wash·y (wĭsh′ĭ wŏsh′ĭ, -wôsh′ĭ), *adj.* **1.** washy or watery, as a liquid; thin and weak. **2.** lacking in substantial qualities; without strength or force; weak, feeble, or poor. [reduplication of WASHY]

Wi·sla (vē′slä), *n.* Polish name of the **Vistula.**

Wis·mar (vĭs′mär), *n.* a Baltic seaport in N East Germany. 54,834 (est. 1955).

wisp (wĭsp), *n.* **1.** a handful or small bundle of straw, hay, or the like. **2.** any small or thin tuft, lock, mass, etc.: *wisps of hair.* **3.** a whisk broom. **4.** *Dial.* a twisted or folded bit of paper, or the like, used for kindling, as a torch, etc. **5.** a will-o'-the-wisp, or ignis fatuus. **—v.t. 6.** to twist into a wisp. [ME *wisp, wips;* akin to WIPE] **—wisp′like′,** *adj.*

wisp·y (wĭs′pĭ), *adj.*, **wispier, wispiest.** being a wisp or in wisps; wisplike: *a wispy plant.* Also, **wisp′ish.**

Wiss·ler (wĭs′lər), *n.* **Clark,** 1870–1947, U.S. anthropologist.

wist (wĭst), *v.* pt. and pp. of **wit**[2].

Wis·ter (wĭs′tər), *n.* **Owen,** 1860–1938, U.S. author.

wis·te·ri·a (wĭs·tĭr′ĭ ə), *n.* any of the climbing shrubs, with handsome pendent racemes of purple flowers, which constitute the leguminous genus *Wisteria* (*Kraunhia*), as *W. chinensis* (**Chinese wisteria**), much used to cover verandas and walls. Also, **wis·tar·i·a** (wĭs·târ′ĭ ə). [after Caspar *Wistar* (1761–1818), American anatomist]

wist·ful (wĭst′fəl), *adj.* **1.** pensive or melancholy. **2.** showing longing tinged with melancholy. [f. obs. *wist* attentive (back formation from *wistly* attentively, var. of *whistly;* see WHIST[1]) + -FUL] **—wist′ful·ly,** *adv.* **—wist′ful·ness,** *n.*

wit[1] (wĭt), *n.* **1.** the keen perception and cleverly apt expression of those connections between ideas which awaken pleasure and especially amusement. **2.** speech or writing showing such perception and expression. **3.** a person endowed with or noted for such wit. **4.** understanding, intelligence, or sagacity: *wit enough to come in out of the rain.* **5.** (*pl.*) mental abilities, or powers of intelligent observation, keen perception, ingenious contrivance, etc.: *to have one's wits about one.* **6.** (*pl.*) mental faculties, or senses: *to lose or regain one's wits.* **7. at one's wits'** (or **wit's**) **end,** at the end of one's powers of knowing, thinking, etc.; utterly at a loss or perplexed. [ME and OE, c. G *witz,* Icel. *vit*] **—Syn. 1.** drollery, facetiousness, repartee. See **humor. 4.** wisdom.

wit[2] (wĭt), *v.t., v.i., pres. 1st pers.* **wot,** *2d pers.* **wost,** *3d pers.* **wot,** *pl.* **wit;** *pt.* and *pp.* **wist;** *pres. p.* **witting. —v.t., v.i.** *Archaic.* **1.** to know. **2. to wit,** that is to say; namely. [ME; OE *witan,* c. D *wetan,* G *wissen*]

wit·an (wĭt′ən), *n.pl. Early English Hist.* **1.** the members of the national council or witenagemot. **2.** (*construed as sing.*) the witenagemot. [OE, pl. of *wita* man of knowledge, councilor]

witch (wĭch), *n.* **1.** a person, now esp. a woman, who professes or is supposed to practice magic, esp. black magic or the black art; a sorceress. **2.** an ugly or malignant old woman; a hag. **—v.t. 3.** to affect by or as by witchcraft; bewitch; charm. **4.** to bring by or as by witchcraft (fol. by *into,* or *to,* etc.). [ME *wiche,* OE *wicce,* der. *wiccian* practice sorcery] **—witch′like′,** *adj.*

witch·craft (wĭch′krăft′, -kräft′), *n.* **1.** the art or practices of a witch; sorcery; magic. **2.** magical influence; witchery. **—Syn. 1.** See **magic.**

witch doctor, a medicine man, esp. among the Kaffirs and other African peoples.

witch-elm (wĭch′ĕlm′), *n.* wych-elm.

witch·er·y (wĭch′ə rĭ), *n., pl.* **-eries. 1.** witchcraft; magic. **2.** magical influence; fascination; charm: *the witchery of her beauty.*

witch·es′-broom (wĭch′ĭz brŏŏm′, -brŏŏm′), *n.* a dense mass of small thin branches frequently emerging from a swelling on a tree branch, as on cherry (caused by *Taphrina*) and on conifers (caused by various mistletoes). Also, **witch·es′-be·som** (wĭch′ĭz bē′zəm).

witch grass, a panic grass, *Panicum capillare,* with a brushlike compound panicle, common as a weed in North America. [see QUITCH GRASS]

witch hazel, 1. a shrub, *Hamamelis virginiana,* of eastern North America, whose bark and leaves afford medicinal preparations used for inflammation, bruises, etc. **2.** a liquid medicinal preparation used externally for inflammations and bruises. Also, **wych-hazel.**

witch hunt, an intensive effort to discover and expose disloyalty, subversion, dishonesty, or the like, usually based on slight, doubtful, or irrelevant evidence. Also, **witch-hunt** (wĭch′hŭnt′). **—witch hunter. —witch hunting.**

witch·ing (wĭch′ĭng), *n.* **1.** the use of witchcraft. **2.** fascination. **—adj. 3.** magical. **4.** enchanting. **—witch′ing·ly,** *adv.*

witch moth, a large, variously colored, noctuid moth, genus *Erebus,* common to the U.S., the West Indies, and South America.

wite (wīt), *n. Scot.* blame; reproach. [ME; OE *wītan*]

wit·e·na·ge·mot (wĭt′ə nə gə mōt′), *n. Early English Hist.* the assembly of the witan; the national council attended by the king, aldermen, bishops, and nobles. [OE: councilors' assembly. See WITAN, MOOT]

with (wĭth, wĭth), *prep.* **1.** accompanied by or accompanying: *I will go with you.* **2.** in some particular relation to (esp. implying interaction, company, association, conjunction, or connection): *to deal, talk, sit, side, or rank with; to mix, compare, or agree with.* **3.** characterized by or having: *a man with initiative.* **4.** (of means or instrument) by the use of: *to line a coat with silk, to cut with a knife.* **5.** (of manner) using or showing: *to work with diligence.* **6.** in correspondence or proportion to: *their power increased with their number.* **7.** in regard to: *to be pleased with a thing.* **8.** (of cause) owing to: *to die with pneumonia, or with thirst.* **9.** in the region, sphere, or view of: *it is day with us while it is night with the Chinese.* **10.** (of separation, etc.) from: *to part with a thing.* **11.** against, as in opposition or competition: *to fight or vie with.* **12.** in the keeping or service of: *leave it with me.* [ME and OE, c. Icel. *vidh*] **—Syn. 4.** See **by.**

with-, limited prefixal use of *with,* separative or opposing, as in *withdraw, withstand.* [ME and OE. See WITH]

with·al (wĭth ôl′, wĭth-), *Archaic.* —*adv.* **1.** with it all; also; as well; besides. —*prep.* **2.** with (used after its object). [f. WITH + AL(L)]

with·draw (wĭth drô′, wĭth-), *v.*, **-drew, -drawn, -drawing.** —*v.t.* **1.** to draw back or away; take back; remove. **2.** to retract or recall: *to withdraw a charge.* —*v.i.* **3.** to retire; retreat; go apart or away. **4.** *Parl. Proc.* to remove an amendment, motion, etc., from consideration. —**Syn. 3.** See **depart.**

with·draw·al (wĭth drô′əl, wĭth-), *n.* act of withdrawing. Also, **with·draw/ment.**

withdrawing room, *Archaic.* a room for withdrawing or retiring to; a drawing room.

with·drawn (wĭth drôn′, wĭth-), *v.* pp. of **withdraw.**

with·drew (wĭth drōō′, wĭth-), *v.* pt. of **withdraw.**

withe (wĭth, wĭth, wĭth), *n.*, *v.*, **withed, withing.** —*n.* **1.** a willow twig or osier. **2.** any tough, flexible twig or stem suitable for binding things together. **3.** an elastic handle for a tool, to lessen shock in using. —*v.t.* **4.** to bind with withes. [ME and OE *withthe*, c. LG *wedde*]

with·er (wĭth′ər), *v.i.* **1.** to shrivel; fade; decay. —*v.t.* **2.** to make flaccid, shrunken, or dry, as from loss of moisture; cause to lose freshness, bloom, vigor, etc. **3.** to affect harmfully: *reputations withered by scandal.* **4.** to abash, as by a scathing glance. [ME; ? var. of WEATHER, v.] —**with/er·ing·ly,** *adv.* —**Syn. 1.** wrinkle, shrink, dry, decline, languish. WITHER, SHRIVEL imply a shrinking, wilting, and wrinkling. WITHER (of plants and flowers) is to dry up, shrink, wilt, fade, whether as a natural process or as the result of exposure to excessive heat or drought: *plants withered in the hot sun.* SHRIVEL, used of thin, flat objects and substances, such as leaves, the skin, etc., means to curl, roll up, become wrinkled: *the leaves shrivel in cold weather, paper shrivels in fire.* —**Ant. 1.** expand.

With·er (wĭth′ər), *n.* **George,** 1588–1667, British poet. Also, **With·ers** (wĭth′ərz).

with·er·ite (wĭth′ə rīt′), *n.* a white to grayish mineral, barium carbonate (BaCO₃), occurring in crystals and masses: a minor ore of barium. [named after W. *Withering* (1741–99), English physician]

withe rod, either of two North American species of *Viburnum*, *V. cassinoides* and *V. nudum*, having tough, osierlike shoots.

With·er·spoon (wĭth′ər spōōn′), *n.* **John,** 1723–94, American theologian, born in Scotland: signer of the Declaration of Independence.

with·ers (wĭth′ərz), *n.pl.* the highest part of a horse's or other animal's back, behind the neck. See illus. under **horse.** [orig. uncert.]

with·er·shins (wĭth′ər shĭnz), *adv. Scot. and Brit. Dial.* in a direction contrary to the apparent course of the sun. [t. MLG: m. *weddersins* in an opposite direction]

with·hold (wĭth hōld′, wĭth-), *v.*, **-held, -holding.** —*v.t.* **1.** to hold back; restrain or check. **2.** to refrain from giving or granting: *to withhold payment.* —*v.i.* **3.** to hold back; refrain. [ME *withholde(n)*. See WITH-HOLD, v.] —**with·hold/er,** *n.* —**Syn. 2.** See **keep.**

withholding tax, that part of one's tax liability withheld by the employer from wages or salary and paid directly to the government.

with·in (wĭth ĭn′, wĭth-), *adv.* **1.** in or into the interior or inner part, or inside. **2.** in or into a house, building, etc., or indoors. **3.** on, or as regards, the inside, or internally. **4.** in the mind, heart, or soul; inwardly. —*prep.* **5.** in or into the interior of or the parts or space enclosed by: *within a city or its walls.* **6.** inside of; in. **7.** in the compass or limits of; not beyond: *within view, to live within one's income.* **8.** at or some point not beyond, as in length or distance; not farther than: *within a radius of a mile.* **9.** at or to some amount or degree not exceeding: *within two degrees of freezing.* **10.** in the course or period of, as in time: *within one's lifetime or memory.* **11.** inside of the limits fixed or required by; not transgressing: *within the law, within reason.* **12.** in the field, sphere, or scope of: *within the family, within one's power.* [ME; OE *withinnan*]

with·in·doors (wĭth ĭn′dôrz′, wĭth-), *adv.* into or inside the house.

with·in·named (wĭth ĭn′nāmd′, wĭth-), *adj.* that is named herein.

with·out (wĭth out′, wĭth-), *prep.* **1.** not with; with no; with absence, omission, or avoidance of; lacking (as opposed to *with*). **2.** free from; excluding. **3.** at, on, or to the outside of; outside of: *both within and without the house or the city.* **4.** beyond the compass, limits, range, or scope of (now used chiefly in opposition to *within*): *whether within or without the law.* —*adv.* **5.** in or into space without, or outside. **6.** outside a house, building, etc. **7.** without, or lacking, something implied or understood: *we must take this or go without.* **8.** as regards the outside, or externally. **9.** as regards external acts, or outwardly. **10.** *Colloq.* unless. [ME; OE *withūtan*]

with·out·doors (wĭth out′dôrz′, wĭth-), *adv. Obs.* out of doors.

with·stand (wĭth stănd′, wĭth-), *v.*, **-stood, -standing.** —*v.t.* **1.** to stand or hold out against; resist or oppose, esp. successfully. —*v.i.* **2.** to stand in opposition. [ME *withstande*, OE *withstandan*, c. Icel. *vidhstanda.* See WITH-STAND] —**Syn. 1.** See **oppose.**

with·y (wĭth′ē, wĭth′ē), *n.*, pl. **withies,** *adj. Chiefly Brit.* —*n.* **1.** a flexible twig, or withe. **2.** a band or halter made of slender twigs. —*adj.* **3.** made of withes.

4. withelike, as in slenderness, flexibility, etc. [ME *withie*, OE *withig.* See WITHE]

wit·less (wĭt′lĭs), *adj.* lacking wit or intelligence; stupid; foolish. —**wit/less·ly,** *adv.* —**wit/less·ness,** *n.*

wit·ling (wĭt′lĭng), *n.* a petty or would-be wit.

wit·ness (wĭt′nĭs), *v.t.* **1.** to see or know by personal presence and perception. **2.** to be present at (an occurrence) as a formal witness or otherwise. **3.** to bear witness to; testify to; give or afford evidence of. **4.** to attest by one's signature. —*v.i.* **5.** to bear witness; testify; give or afford evidence. —*n.* **6.** one who, being present, personally sees or perceives a thing; a beholder, spectator, or eyewitness. **7.** a person or thing that affords evidence. **8.** one who gives testimony, as in a court of law. **9.** one who signs a document in attestation of the genuineness of its execution. **10.** testimony or evidence: *to bear witness to the truth of a statement.* [ME and OE *witnes.* See WIT, n., -NESS] —**wit/ness·er,** *n.* —**Syn. 2.** See **observe.**

witness mark, a mark or stake set to identify a property corner or a survey point.

witness stand, the place occupied by one giving testimony in a court.

Wit·te (vĭt′tə), *n.* **Sergei Yulievich** (sĕr gā′ yōōl′yə vĭch), 1849–1915, Russian statesman.

wit·ted (wĭt′ĭd), *adj.* having wit or wits: *quick-witted, slow-witted.*

Wit·te·kind (vĭt′ə kĭnt), *n.* died A.D. c807, Saxon warrior against Charlemagne. Also, **Widukind.**

Wit·ten·berg (wĭt′ən bûrg′; *Ger.* vĭt′ən bĕr KH′), *n.* a city in East Germany, on the Elbe: Luther taught in the university here; beginnings of the Reformation, 1517. 48,132 (est. 1955).

wit·ti·cism (wĭt′ə sĭz′əm), *n.* a witty remark or sentence. [der. WITTY; modeled on CRITICISM]

wit·ting (wĭt′ĭng), *adj.* knowing; aware; conscious. —**wit/ting·ly,** *adv.*

wit·tol (wĭt′əl), *n. Obs.* a man who knows and tolerates his wife's infidelity. [ME *wetewold*, f. *wete* WIT, v. + *-wold*, modeled on *cokewold* CUCKOLD]

wit·ty (wĭt′ē), *adj.*, **-tier, -tiest. 1.** possessing wit in speech or writing; amusingly clever in perception and expression. **2.** characterized by wit: *a witty remark.* **3.** *Scot. and Brit. Dial.* wise; intelligent. [ME; OE *wittig*, f. *witt* WIT + *-ig* -Y¹] —**wit/ti·ly,** *adv.* —**wit/ti·ness,** *n.* —**Syn. 1.** facetious, droll, clever, original, sparkling, brilliant. See **humorous.**

Wit·wa·ters·rand (wĭt wä′tərs rănt′, -ränd′), *n.* a rocky ridge in the Union of South Africa, near Johannesburg: richest gold fields in world. Also, **The Rand.**

wive (wīv), *v.*, **wived, wiving.** —*v.i.* **1.** to take a wife; marry. —*v.t.* **2.** to take as wife; marry. **3.** to provide with a wife. [ME; OE *wīfian.* See WIFE]

wi·vern (wī′vərn), *n. Her.* a two-legged, winged dragon having the hinder part of a serpent with a barbed tail. Also, **wy·vern.** [f. obs. *wiver* viper (t. OF) + *-n*, of obscure orig. and sense]

Wivern

wives (wīvz), *n.* pl. of **wife.**

wiz·ard (wĭz′ərd), *n.* **1.** one who professes to practice magic; a magician or sorcerer. **2.** a conjurer or juggler. **3.** *Colloq.* a person of high professional skill or knowledge. —*adj.* **4.** of or pertaining to a wizard. **5.** magic. [ME *wysard*, f. *wys* wise + -ARD] —**wiz/ard·like/,** *adj.* —**Syn. 1.** enchanter, necromancer.

wiz·ard·ly (wĭz′ərd lē), *adj.* of, like, or befitting a wizard.

wiz·ard·ry (wĭz′ər drē), *n.* the art or practices of a wizard; sorcery; magic.

wiz·en (wĭz′ən; *Dial.* wē′zən), *Scot. and Brit. Dial.* —*v.i., v.t.* **1.** to wither; shrivel; dry up. —*adj.* **2.** wizened. [ME *wisen*, OE *wisnian*, c. Icel. *visna* wither]

wiz·ened (wĭz′ənd; *Dial.* wē′zənd), *adj.* withered; shriveled.

wk., *pl.* **wks. 1.** week. **2.** work.

wkly., weekly.

w.l., wave length.

Wla·di·mir (vlăd′ə mĭr′; *Russ.* vlä dē′mĭr), *n.* See **Vladimir.**

WLB, War Labor Board.

Wm., William.

WMC, War Manpower Commission.

wmk., watermark.

WNW, west-northwest. Also, **W.N.W.**

wo (wō), *n., interj.* woe.

W.O., warrant officer.

woad (wōd), *n.* **1.** a European brassicaceous plant, *Isatis tinctoria*, formerly much cultivated for a blue dye extracted from its leaves. **2.** the dye. [ME *wode*, OE *wād*, c. G *waid*]

woad·ed (wō′dəd), *adj.* dyed or colored blue with woad.

woad·wax·en (wōd′wăk′sən), *n.* a leguminous shrub, *Genista tinctoria*, whose flowers yield a yellow dye formerly used with woad to make a permanent green dye: now cultivated for ornament. Also, **woodwaxen.** [ME *wodewexen*, OE *wuduweaxan*, pl.]

woald (wōld), *n.* weld².

wob·ble (wŏb′əl), *v.*, **-bled, -bling.** *n.* —*v.i.* **1.** to incline to one side and to the other alternately, as a wheel, top, or other rotating body, when not properly balanced. **2.** to move unsteadily from side to side: *the table wobbled.* **3.** to show unsteadiness; tremble; quaver: *his voice wobbled.* **4.** *Colloq.* to vacillate; waver. —*v.t.* **5.** *Colloq.* to cause to wobble. —*n.* **6.** *Colloq.* act or fact of wobbling; a wobbling motion. Also, **wabble.** [t. LG: m. *wabbeln*, c. Icel. *vafla* toddle] —**wob′bler,** *n.*

wob·bling (wŏb′lĭng), *adj.* that wobbles, or causes to wobble. Also, **wabbling.** —**wob′bling·ly,** *adv.*

wob·bly (wŏb′lĭ), *adj., pl.* **-blies.** —*adj.* **1.** Also, **wabbly.** shaky; unsteady. —*n.* **2.** *Slang.* a member of the Industrial Workers of the World.

Wo·burn (wō′bərn, wōō′bərn), *n.* a city in E Massachusetts, N of Boston. 20,492 (1950).

Wode·house (wŏŏd′hous), *n.* **Pelham Grenville** (pĕl′əm), born 1881, British author, now living in U.S.

Wo·den (wō′dən), *n.* the chief English heathen god, identical with the Scandinavian Odin. Also, **Wo′dan.** [ME and OE, akin to woon²]

woe (wō), *n.* **1.** grievous distress, affliction, or trouble. **2.** an affliction. —*interj.* **3.** an exclamation of grief, distress, or lamentation. Also, *obs.* [ME *wo*, OE *wā*, interj.; c. D *wee*, G *weh*, L *vae*] —Syn. **1.** See **sorrow.**

woe·be·gone (wō′bĭ gôn′, -gŏn′), *adj.* **1.** beset with woe; affected by woe, esp. in appearance. **2.** showing or indicating woe: *he had a perpetual woebegone look on his face.* Also, **wo′be·gone′.**

woe·ful (wō′fəl), *adj.* **1.** full of woe; wretched; unhappy. **2.** affected with, characterized by, or indicating woe: *her poetry is a conglomeration of woeful ditties.* **3.** of wretched quality; sorry; poor. Also, **wo′ful.** —**woe′ful·ly,** *adv.* —**woe′ful·ness,** *n.*

Wof·fing·ton (wŏf′ĭng tən), *n.* **Margaret,** ("*Peg Woffington*") 1714–60, Irish actress in England.

woke (wōk), *v.* a pt. of **wake.**

wok·en (wō′kən), *v.* *Brit.* or *Archaic and Dial. in U.S.* pp. of **wake.**

wold¹ (wōld), *n.* an open, elevated tract of country: esp. applied (in *pl.*) to districts in parts of England (as Yorkshire and Lincolnshire) resembling the downs of the southern counties. [ME; OE *wald* forest, c. G *wald.* Cf. Icel. *völlr* plain]

wold² (wōld), *n.* **weld².**

wolf (wŏŏlf), *n., pl.* **wolves** (wŏŏlvz), *v.* —*n.* **1.** a large, wild carnivore, *Canis lupus,* of Europe, Asia, and North America, belonging to the dog family, a swift-footed, crafty, rapacious animal, destructive to game, sheep, etc. **2.** the fur of such an animal. **3.** some wolflike animal not of the dog family, as the thylacine (Tasmanian wolf). **4.** *Entomol.* the larva of any of various small insects infesting granaries. **5.** a cruelly rapacious person. **6.** *Slang.* a man who is boldly flirtatious or amorous toward many women. **7.** *Music.* **a.** the harsh discord heard in certain chords of keyboard instruments, esp. the organ, when tuned on some system of unequal temperament. **b.** a chord or interval in which such a discord appears. **c.** (in bowed instruments) a discordant or false vibration in a string due to a defect in structure or adjustment of the instrument. —*v.t.* **8.** *Colloq.* to devour or swallow ravenously. —*v.i.* **9.** to hunt for wolves. [ME; OE *wulf,* c. D and G *wolf,* Icel. *ulfr*] —**wolf′like′,** *adj.*

Wolf (vôlf), *n.* **Friedrich August** (frē′drĭкн ou′gŏŏst), 1759–1824, German classical scholar.

wolf·ber·ry (wŏŏlf′bĕr′ĭ), *n., pl.* **-ries.** a caprifoliaceous shrub, *Symphoricarpos Occidentalis,* of northern North America, with white berries.

wolf cub, *Brit.* a member of the junior division (8–11) of the Boy Scouts.

wolf dog, **1.** any of various dogs of different breeds used for hunting wolves. See **wolfhound. 2.** a cross between a wolf and a domestic dog. **3.** an Eskimo dog.

Wolfe (wŏŏlf), *n.* **1. Charles,** 1791–1823, Irish poet. **2. James,** 1727–59, British general, killed at the Battle of Quebec. **3. Thomas,** 1900–1938, U.S. novelist.

wolf eel, a large eellike fish, *Anarhichthyo ocellatus,* of the Pacific coast of North America, like the wolf fish but with the tail drawn out to a point.

Wolff (vôlf), *n.* **1.** Also, **Wolf. Christian von** (krĭs′tĭ-än′ fən), 1679–1754, German philosopher and mathematician. **2. Kaspar Friedrich** (käs′pär frē′drĭкн), 1733–94, German anatomist and physiologist.

Wolf-Fer·ra·ri (vôlf′fĕr rä′rē), *n.* **Ermanno** (ĕr män′nō), 1876–1948, Italian composer.

Wolff·i·an (wŏŏlf′ĭ ən, vôl′-), *adj.* first described by Kaspar Friedrich Wolff.

Wolffian body, *Embryol.* mesonephros.

wolf fish, 1. a large acanthopterygian fish of the genus *Anarrhichas,* as *A. lupus* of the northern Atlantic, allied to the blenny, and noted for its ferocious aspect and habits. **2.** lancet fish.

wolf·hound (wŏŏlf′hound′), *n.* a hound of various breeds used in hunting wolves, as the Russian wolfhound.

wolf·ish (wŏŏlf′ĭsh), *adj.* **1.** resembling a wolf, as in form or characteristics. **2.** characteristic of or befitting a wolf. —**wolf′ish·ly,** *adv.* —**wolf′ish·ness,** *n.*

wolf note, wolf (def. 7c).

wolf·ram (wŏŏl′frəm), *n.* *Chem.* tungsten. [t. G *wolfram*]

wolf·ram·ite (wŏŏl′frə mīt′, vôl′-), *n.* a mineral, iron manganese tungstate, (Fe,Mn)WO₄, occurring in gray-

ish- to brownish-black tabular or bladed crystals, heavy (*sp. gr.*: 7.0–7.5): an important ore of tungsten. Also, **wolfram.** [t. G: m. *wolframit,* f. *wolfram* + *-it* -ITE¹]

wolf·ra·mi·um (wŏŏl frä′mĭ əm, vôl′-), *n.* tungsten.

Wol·fram von Esch·en·bach (vôl′främ fən ĕsh′ən-bäкн′), died 1220?, German epic poet.

wolf′s·bane (wŏŏlfs′bān′), *n.* a plant of the genus *Aconitum,* esp. a yellow-flowered species, *A. lycoctonum.* See **aconite** (def. 1). Also, **wolfs′bane′.**

wol·las·ton·ite (wŏŏl′əs tə nīt′), *n.* a mineral, calcium silicate, CaSiO₃, occurring usually in fibrous white masses. [named after W. H. *Wollaston* (1766–1828), British chemist]

Wo·lof (wō′lŏf), *n.* a language spoken about Dakar, related to Ful.

Wolse·ley (wŏŏlz′lĭ), *n.* **Garnet Joseph,** 1833–1913, British field marshal.

Wol·sey (wŏŏl′zĭ), *n.* **Thomas,** 1475?–1530, British cardinal and statesman.

wolv·er (wŏŏl′vər), *n.* one who hunts for wolves.

Wol·ver·hamp·ton (wŏŏl′vər hămp′tən), *n.* a city in central England, in Staffordshire. 153,100 (est. 1956).

wol·ver·ine (wŏŏl′və rēn′), *n.*
1. the glutton, *Gulo luscus,* of America. **2.** (*cap.*) *U.S.* one born or residing in the State of Michigan. Also, **wol′ver·ene′.** [earlier *wolvering,* f. *wolver* wolflike creature + -ING¹]

Wolverine, Gulo luscus
(Total length 3 to 3½ ft., tail 7 to 8½ in.)

wolves (wŏŏlvz), *n.* pl. of **wolf.**

wom·an (wŏŏm′ən), *n., pl.* **women** (wĭm′ĭn), *v.,* *adj.* —*n.* **1.** the female human being (distinguished from *man*). **2.** an adult female person. **3.** a female attendant on a lady of rank. **4.** a wife. **5.** feminine nature, characteristics, or feelings. —*v.t.* **6.** to call (one) "woman," esp. rudely or condescendingly. **7.** to put into the company of a woman. **8.** *Obs.* to cause to act or yield like a woman. —*adj.* **9.** of women; female. [ME; OE *wīfman,* f. *wīf* female + *man* human being] —**wom′an·less,** *adj.* —Syn. **2.** WOMAN, FEMALE, LADY apply to the adult of the human race correlative with man. WOMAN is the general term: *a woman nearing middle age.* FEMALE refers esp. to sex. It was formerly used interchangeably with WOMAN, but now sometimes has a contemptuous implication: *a strong-minded female.* LADY formerly implied family or social position, but is now used conventionally for any woman (esp. as a courteous term for one engaged in menial tasks: *a scrub lady*): *a highborn lady, the appearance of a lady.*

wom·an·hood (wŏŏm′ən hŏŏd′), *n.* **1.** state of being a woman; womanly character or qualities. **2.** women collectively.

wom·an·ish (wŏŏm′ən ĭsh), *adj.* **1.** womanlike or feminine. **2.** weakly feminine; effeminate. —**wom′an·ish·ly,** *adv.* —**wom′an·ish·ness,** *n.*

wom·an·kind (wŏŏm′ən kīnd′), *n.* women, as distinguished from men; the female sex.

wom·an·like (wŏŏm′ən līk′), *adj.* like a woman; womanly.

wom·an·ly (wŏŏm′ən lĭ), *adj.* **1.** like or befitting a woman; feminine; not masculine or girlish. —*adv.* **2.** in the manner of, or befitting, a woman. —**wom′an·li·ness,** *n.*

woman of the world, a woman versed in the ways and usages of the world, esp. the world of society.

woman's rights, the rights claimed for woman, equal to those of man, with respect to suffrage, property, the professional fields, etc.

woman suffrage, the right of woman to vote; female suffrage. —**wom′an·suf′frage,** *adj.* —**wom′-an·suf′fra·gist,** *n.*

womb (wŏŏm), *n.* **1.** the uterus of the human female and some of the higher mammalian quadrupeds. **2.** *Obs.* the belly. **3.** the place in which anything is formed or produced: *the womb of time.* **4.** the interior of anything. [ME and OE, c. D *wam,* G *wamme,* Goth. *wamba* belly]

wom·bat (wŏm′băt), *n.* any of three species of burrowing marsupials of Australia, constituting the family *Vombatidae,* somewhat resembling ground hogs. [native Australian name]

Common wombat, Vombatus hirsutus (3 ft. long)

wom·en (wĭm′ĭn), *n.* pl. of **woman.**

wom·en·folk (wĭm′ĭn fōk′), *n. pl.* **1.** women in general; all women. **2.** a particular group of women. Also, **wom′en·folks′.**

wom·er·a (wŏm′ər ə), *n.* a weapon devised by Australian aborigines to throw spears. Also, **woomera.** [native Australian name]

won¹ (wŭn), *v.* pt. and pp. of **win.**

won² (wŭn, wŏŏn, wŏn), *v.i.,* **wonned, wonning.** *Archaic or Scot. and N. Eng.* to dwell, abide, or stay. [ME *wone,* OE *wunian,* c. G *wohnen*]

won·der (wŭn′dər), *v.i.* **1.** to think or speculate curiously: *to wonder about a thing.* **2.** to be affected with wonder; marvel. —*v.t.* **3.** to speculate curiously or be curious about; be curious to know (fol. by a clause): *to wonder what happened.* **4.** to feel wonder at (now only

fol. by a clause as object): *I wonder that you went.* —*n.* **5.** something strange and surprising; a cause of surprise, astonishment, or admiration: *it is a wonder he declined such an offer.* **6.** the emotion excited by what is strange and surprising; a feeling of surprised or puzzled interest, sometimes tinged with admiration. **7.** a miracle, or miraculous deed or event. **8. nine days' wonder,** a subject of general surprise and interest for a short time. [ME; OE *wundor,* c. D *wonder,* G *wunder*] —**won′der·er,** *n.* —**Syn. 6.** surprise, astonishment, amazement, bewilderment, awe.

won·der·ful (wŭn′dər fəl), *adj.* of a kind to excite wonder; marvelous; extraordinary; remarkable. [OE *wunderfull.* See WONDER, -FUL] —**won′der·ful·ly,** *adv.* —**won′der·ful·ness,** *n.* —**Syn.** wondrous, miraculous, prodigious, astonishing, amazing, phenomenal, unique, curious, strange.

won·der·ing (wŭn′dər Ĭng), *adj.* expressing admiration or amazement; marveling. —**won′der·ing·ly,** *adv.*

won·der·land (wŭn′dər lănd′), *n.* **1.** a land of wonders or marvels. **2.** a wonderful country or region: *a wonderland of snow, a winter wonderland.*

won·der·ment (wŭn′dər mənt), *n.* **1.** wondering or wonder. **2.** a cause or occasion of wonder.

won·der·strick·en (wŭn′dər strĭk′ən), *adj.* struck or affected with wonder. Also, **won·der·struck** (wŭn′dər strŭk′).

won·der·work (wŭn′dər wûrk′), *n.* a wonderful work; a marvel; a miracle. [ME *wonderworc,* OE *wundorweorc.* See WONDER, WORK] —**won′der·work′ing,** *adj.*

won·der·work·er (wŭn′dər wûr′kər), *n.* a worker or performer of wonders or marvels.

won·drous (wŭn′drəs), *adj.* **1.** *Literary.* wonderful; marvelous. —*adv.* *Archaic or Literary.* in a wonderful or surprising degree; remarkably. [metathetic var. of ME *wonders* (gen. of WONDER) wonderful; sp. conformed to -OUS] —**won′drous·ly,** *adv.* —**won′drous·ness,** *n.*

won·ky (wŏng′kĭ), *adj.* *Brit. Slang.* shaky; unsound. [var. of d. *wanky,* itself alter. of *wankle,* ME *wankel,* OE *wancol* shaky, unsteady]

won·na (wŭn′nə), *Scot.* will not; won't.

won·ner (wŭn′ər), *v.i., v.t., n.* *Scot. and Brit. Dial.* wonder.

Wŏn·san (wœn′sän′), *n.* Japanese name of Gensan.

wont (wŭnt, wŏnt), *adj., n., v.,* **wont, wont** or **wonted, wonting.** —*adj.* **1.** accustomed; used (commonly followed by an infinitive). —*n.* **2.** custom; habit; practice. —*v.t.* **3.** to accustom (a person), as to a thing. **4.** to render (a thing) customary or usual (commonly in the passive). —*v.i.* **5.** *Poetic.* to be wont or accustomed. [ME *woned,* OE *gewunod,* pp. of *gewunian* be accustomed]

won't (wŏnt, wŭnt), contraction of *will not.*

wont·ed (wŭn′tĭd, wŏn′-), *adj.* **1.** accustomed; habituated; used. **2.** rendered customary; habitual or usual: *the old man was in his wonted place.* —**wont′ed·ly,** *adv.* —**wont′ed·ness,** *n.*

woo (wōō), *v.t.* **1.** to seek the favor, affection, or love of, esp. with a view to marriage. **2.** to seek to win: *to woo fame.* **3.** to invite (consequences, good or bad) by one's own action: *to woo one's own destruction.* **4.** to seek to persuade (a person, etc.), as to do something; solicit; importune. [ME *wowe,* OE *wōgian*] —**woo′er,** *n.*

wood[1] (wōōd), *n.* **1.** the hard, fibrous substance composing most of the stem and branches of a tree or shrub, and lying beneath the bark; the xylem. **2.** the trunks or main stems of trees as suitable for architectural and other purposes; timber or lumber. **3.** firewood. **4.** the cask, barrel, or keg, as distinguished from the bottle: *aged in the wood.* **5.** *Print.* a wood block (def. 1). **6.** *Music.* **a.** a wooden wind instrument. **b.** such instruments collectively in a band or orchestra. **7.** (*often pl.*) a large and thick collection of growing trees; a grove or forest. —*adj.* **8.** made of wood; wooden. **9.** used to store, carve, or carry wood: *a woodbox.* **10.** dwelling or growing in woods: *wood bird.* —*v.t.* **11.** to cover or plant with trees. **12.** to supply with wood; get supplies of wood for. —*v.i.* **13.** to take in or get supplies of wood. [ME; OE *wudu,* earlier *widu,* c. Icel. *vidhr,* OHG *witu,* OIrish *fid*] —**wood′less,** *adj.* —**Syn. 7.** See forest.

wood[2] (wōōd), *adj.* *Obs. except Dial.* mad or wild, as with rage or excitement. [ME; OE *wōd,* c. Icel. *ōdhr;* akin to G *wut* rage, OE *wōth* song, L *vātes* seer]

Wood (wōōd), *n.* **1.** Grant, 1892–1942, U.S. painter. **2. Leonard,** 1860–1927, U.S. military doctor and political administrator.

wood alcohol, methyl alcohol.

wood anemone, any of certain species of anemone, esp. *Anemone nemorosa* of the Old World or *A. quinquefolia* of the U.S.

wood betony, **1.** the betony. **2.** a scrophulariaceous herb, *Pedicularis canadensis,* of eastern North America; lousewort.

wood·bin (wōōd′bĭn′), *n.* a box for wood fuel. Also, **wood′box′.**

wood·bine (wōōd′bīn′), *n.* **1.** the common European honeysuckle, *Lonicera Periclymenum,* which is cultivated in the U.S. **2.** any of various other honeysuckles, as *L. Caprifolium* (**American woodbine**). **3.** *U.S.* the Virginia creeper, *Parthenocissus quinquefolia.* [ME *wodebinde,* OE *wudubind,* f. *wudu* WOOD[1] + *-bind* binding]

wood block, **1.** a block of wood engraved in relief, for printing from; a woodcut. **2.** a print or impression from such a block.

wood·chat (wōōd′chăt′), *n.* **1.** Also, **woodchat shrike.** a shrike or butcherbird, *Lanius senator,* of Europe and North Africa, having black forehead and chestnut crown, nape, and upper mantle. **2.** any of various Asiatic thrushes, esp. of the genus *Larvivora.*

wood·chuck (wōōd′chŭk′), *n.* a common North American marmot, *Marmota monax,* of stout, heavy form, that burrows in the ground and hibernates in the winter; the ground hog. [alter. of Algonquian (Cree or Chippewa) *otchek, otchig, odjik* fisher, weasel]

Woodchuck, *Marmota monax* (Total length ab. 2 ft., tail 6 in.)

wood coal, lignite.

wood·cock (wōōd′kŏk′), *n., pl.* **-cocks,** (*esp. collectively*) **-cock.** **1.** an Old World snipelike game bird, *Scolopax rusticula,* with long bill, short legs, and large eyes placed far back in the head. **2.** a similar and closely related but smaller bird, *Philohela minor,* of eastern North America. **3.** *Obs.* a simpleton. [ME *wodecok,* OE *wuducoc.* See WOOD[1], *n.,* COCK[1], *n.*]

wood·craft (wōōd′krăft′, -kräft′), *n.* **1.** skill in anything which pertains to the woods or forest, esp. in making one's way through the woods, or in hunting, trapping, etc. **2.** forestry. **3.** the art of making or carving wooden objects. —**wood′crafts′man,** *n.*

wood·cut (wōōd′kŭt′), *n.* **1.** a carved or engraved block of wood for printing from. **2.** a print or impression from such a block.

wood·cut·ter (wōōd′kŭt′ər), *n.* one who cuts wood. —**wood′cut′ting,** *n.*

wood·ed (wōōd′ĭd), *adj.* **1.** covered with or abounding in woods or trees. **2.** having wood: *a hard-wooded tree.*

wood·en (wōōd′ən), *adj.* **1.** consisting or made of wood. **2.** stiff, ungainly, or awkward. **3.** without spirit or animation: *a wooden stare.* **4.** dull or stupid: *wooden wits.* **5.** indicating the fifth event of a series, as a wedding anniversary. —**wood′en·ly,** *adv.* —**wood′en·ness,** *n.*

wood engraving, **1.** the art or process of engraving designs in relief with a burin on the end grain of wood, for printing. **2.** a block of wood so engraved. **3.** a print or impression from it. —**wood engraver.**

wood·en·head (wōōd′ən hĕd′), *n.* *Colloq.* a blockhead; a dull or stupid person.

wood·en·head·ed (wōōd′ən hĕd′ĭd), *adj.* *Colloq.* thick-headed; dull; stupid. —**wood′en·head′ed·ness,** *n.*

wooden horse. See **Trojan Horse.**

wood·en·ware (wōōd′ən wâr′), *n.* vessels, utensils, etc., made of wood.

wood grouse, capercaillie.

wood·house (wōōd′hous′), *n.* a house or shed in which wood is stored.

wood hyacinth, a beautiful Old World squill, *Scilla nonscripta,* with drooping flowers.

wood ibis, a large naked-headed wading bird, *Mycteria americana,* of the stork family, of the wooded swamps of the southern U.S. and regions southward.

wood·land (*n.* wōōd′lănd′, -lənd; *adj.* wōōd′lənd), *n.* **1.** land covered with woods or trees. —*adj.* **2.** of, pertaining to, or inhabiting the woods; sylvan.

wood·land·er (wōōd′lən dər), *n.* an inhabitant of the woods.

wood·lark (wōōd′lärk′), *n.* a small European songbird, *Lullula arborea,* less famous than the skylark but equally gifted as an aerial songster.

wood lot, a tract, esp. on a farm, set aside for trees.

wood louse, *Zool.* any of certain small terrestrial isopod crustaceans of the genera *Oniscus, Armadillo,* etc., having a flattened elliptical body sometimes capable of being rolled up into a ball.

wood·man (wōōd′mən), *n., pl.* **-men.** **1.** one who dwells in the woods. **2.** one who fells timber. **3.** *Eng.* an officer having charge of the king's woods. **4.** *Obs.* a hunter of forest game.

wood note, a wild or natural musical tone, as that of a forest bird.

wood nymph, **1.** a nymph of the woods, or a dryad. **2.** any of several noctuid moths of the genus *Euthysanotia,* some of which are injurious to the grapevine. **3.** any of several Central and South American hummingbirds, esp. of the genus *Thalurania.*

wood·peck·er (wōōd′pĕk′ər), *n.* any of numerous scansorial birds constituting the family *Picidae,* having a hard, chisellike bill for boring into wood after insects, stiff tail feathers to assist in climbing, and usually a more or less boldly patterned plumage.

wood pe·wee (pē′wē), a small American flycatcher, *Myiochanes virens,* so called in imitation of its cry.

wood pigeon, **1.** a large wild pigeon, *Columba palumbus,* of Europe; the ringdove. **2.** (locally) a large wild pigeon, *Columba fasciata,* of western North America.

wood·pile (wōōd′pīl′), *n.* a pile or stack of wood, esp. wood for fuel.

wood pitch. See **wood tar.**

wood·print (wōōd′prĭnt′), *n.* woodcut.

wood pulp, wood reduced to pulp through mechanical and chemical treatment and used in the manufacture of newsprint and book paper.

wood rat, a pack rat.

wood·ruff (wŏŏd′rŭf′), *n.* a low, aromatic rubiaceous herb, *Asperula odorata*, of the Old World, having small, sweet-scented, white flowers. [ME *woderove*, OE *wudurōfe*, f. *wudu* woon[1] + *rōfe* (c. MLG *rōve* carrot)]

Woods (wŏŏdz), *n.* **Lake of the.** See **Lake of the Woods.**

wood·shed (wŏŏd′shĕd′), *n.* a shed for keeping wood for fuel.

wood·si·a (wŏŏd′zǐ ə), *n.* any fern of the genus *Woodsia*, comprising small and medium-sized species in temperate and cold regions. [named after Joseph *Woods*, British botanist]

woods·man (wŏŏdz′mən), *n., pl.* **-men. 1.** one accustomed to life in the woods and skilled in the arts of the woods, as hunting, trapping, etc. **2.** a lumberman.

wood sorrel, 1. an oxalis. **2.** a low, stemless species, *Oxalis Acetosella*, with single pink-streaked white flowers.

wood spirit, methyl alcohol.

woods·y (wŏŏd′zǐ), *adj. U.S.* of, like, suggestive of, or associated with the woods: *a woodsy fragrance.*

wood tar, a dark viscid product obtained from wood by distillation or burning slowly without flame, used in its natural state to preserve timber, etc., or subjected to further distillation, when it yields creosote, oils, and a final residuum called **wood pitch.**

wood thrush, a songbird, *Hylocichla mustelina*, common in parks and well-shaded woodlands in eastern North America.

wood turning, the forming of wood articles upon a lathe. —**wood turner.**

wood vinegar, 1. an impure acetic acid obtained by the distillation of wood. **2.** pyroligneous acid.

wood·wax·en (wŏŏd′wăk′sən), *n.* woadwaxen. Also, **wood·wax** (wŏŏd′wăks′).

wood wind (wĭnd), **1.** (*pl.*) the group of wind instruments which comprises the flutes, clarinets, oboes, and bassoons. **2.** an instrument of this group. —*adj.* **3.** of, or pertaining to, wind instruments of wood.

wood wool, *Brit.* excelsior (def. 1).

wood·work (wŏŏd′wûrk′), *n.* **1.** objects or parts made of wood. **2.** the interior wooden fittings of a house or the like.

wood·work·er (wŏŏd′wûr′kər), *n.* a worker in wood, as a carpenter, joiner, or cabinetmaker.

wood·work·ing (wŏŏd′wûr′kĭng), *n.* **1.** the act or art of one who works in wood. —*adj.* **2.** pertaining to or used for shaping wood: *woodworking tools.*

wood·worm (wŏŏd′wûrm′), *n.* a worm or larva that is bred in or bores in wood.

wood·y (wŏŏd′ĭ), *adj.*, **woodier, woodiest. 1.** abounding with woods; wooded. **2.** belonging or pertaining to the woods; sylvan. **3.** consisting of or containing wood; ligneous. **4.** resembling wood. —**wood′i·ness,** *n.*

woof (wŏŏf), *n.* **1.** yarns which travel from selvage to selvage in a loom, interlacing with the warp; weft; filling. **2.** texture; fabric. [ME *oof*, OE *ōwef*. See **WEB**, **WEAVE**]

woof·er (wŏŏf′ər), *n.* a loudspeaker designed for the reproduction of low-frequency sounds.

wool (wŏŏl), *n.* **1.** the fine, soft, curly hair, characterized by minute, overlapping surface scales, to which its felting property is mainly due, that forms the fleece of sheep and certain other animals, that of sheep constituting one of the most important materials of clothing. **2.** fabrics and garments made from sheeps' wool. **3.** woolen yarn used for knitting, crocheting, ornamental needlework, etc.; worsted. **4.** any of various substances used commercially as substitutes for the wool of sheep, etc. **5.** a kind of woollike yarn or material made from cellulose by a process similar to that used in manufacturing rayon or artificial silk. **6.** any of certain vegetable fibers, such as cotton, flax, etc., so used, esp. after preparation by special process (**vegetable wool**). **7.** any finely fibrous or filamentous matter suggestive of the wool of sheep: *glass wool.* **8.** any coating of short, fine hairs or hairlike processes, as on a caterpillar or a plant; pubescence. **9.** *Colloq.* the human hair, esp. when short, thick, and curly or kinky. **10. pull the wool over one's eyes,** to deceive or delude one. [ME *wole*, OE *wull*, c. D *wol*, G *wolle*, Icel. *ull*, Goth. *wulla*]

wool·en (wŏŏl′ən), *n.* **1.** yarn from carded or short wool fibers, differing from worsted. **2.** (*pl.*) wool cloth or clothing. —*adj.* **3.** made or consisting of wool: *woolen cloth.* **4.** of or pertaining to wool or woolen fabrics. Also, *esp. Brit.*, **wool′len.**

Woolf (wŏŏlf), *n.* **Virginia,** (Virginia Stephen, Mrs. *Leonard Woolf*) 1882–1941, British novelist and critic.

wool fat, lanolin.

wool·fell (wŏŏl′fĕl′), *n.* the skin of a wool-bearing animal with the fleece still on it. [f. **WOOL** + **FELL**[4]]

wool·gath·er·ing (wŏŏl′găth′ər ĭng), *n.* **1.** gathering of the tufts of wool left caught here and there on bushes, etc., by passing sheep. **2.** indulgence in desultory fancies or a fit of abstraction. —*adj.* **3.** inattentive; abstracted. —**wool′gath′er·er,** *n.*

wool·grow·er (wŏŏl′grō′ər), *n.* one who raises sheep or other wool-bearing animals for the production of wool. —**wool′grow′ing,** *n.*

Wool·cott (wŏŏl′kət), *n.* **Alexander,** 1887–1943, U.S. author and journalist.

Wool·ley (wŏŏl′ĭ), *n.* **(Charles) Leonard,** 1880–1960, British archaeologist and explorer.

wool·ly (wŏŏl′ĭ), *adj.*, **-lier, -liest,** *n., pl.* **-lies.** —*adj.* **1.** consisting of wool. **2.** resembling wool. **3.** clothed or covered with wool or something resembling it. **4.** *Bot.* covered with a pubescence of soft hairs resembling wool. **5.** *U.S. Colloq.* like the rough atmosphere of the early West. —*n.* **6.** *Western U.S.* a wool-bearing animal; sheep. **7.** *Colloq.* an article of clothing made of wool. Also, **wooly.** —**wool′li·ness,** *n.*

woolly bear, the caterpillar of any of various moths, as tiger moths, covered with a dense coat of woolly hairs.

wool·pack (wŏŏl′păk′), *n.* **1.** the package in which wool was formerly done up, as for transportation. **2.** *Chiefly Brit.* a bundle or bale weighing 240 pounds. **3.** *Meteorol.* a cumulus cloud of fleecy appearance.

wool·sack (wŏŏl′săk′), *n.* **1.** a sack or bag of wool. **2.** (in the British House of Lords) one of a number of cloth-covered seats or divans stuffed with wool, for the use of judges, esp. one for the Lord Chancellor. **3.** the Lord Chancellor's office.

wool·sort·ers' disease (wŏŏl′sôr′tərz), pulmonary anthrax in man caused by inhaling the spores of *Bacillus anthracis*.

wool stapler, 1. a dealer in wool. **2.** one who sorts wool, according to the staple or fiber. —**wool′·sta′·pling,** *adj.*

Wool·wich (wŏŏl′ĭj, -ĭch), *n.* an E borough of London, England: royal military academy and arsenal. 147,824 (1951).

Wool·worth (wŏŏl′wûrth), *n.* **Frank Winfield,** 1852–1919, U.S. merchant.

wool·y (wŏŏl′ĭ), *adj.*, **woolier, wooliest.** **woolly.** —**wool′i·ness,** *n.*

woo·mer·a (wŏŏ′mər ə), *n.* womera.

Woon·sock·et (wŏŏn sŏk′ĭt), *n.* a city in NE Rhode Island. 47,080 (1960).

Woo·sung (wŏŏ′sŏŏng′), *n.* a seaport in E China at the mouth of the Yangtze, near Shanghai.

wooz·y (wŏŏ′zĭ, wŏŏz′ĭ), *adj. Slang.* **1.** muddled, or stupidly confused. **2.** out of sorts physically. [? der. *wooze*, var. of **OOZE**] —**wooz′i·ly,** *adv.* —**wooz′i·ness,** *n.*

Worces·ter (wŏŏs′tər), *n.* **1.** a city in central Massachusetts. 186,587 (1960). **2.** a city in W England, on the Severn: cathedral; Cromwell's defeat of the Scots, 1651. 63,400 (est. 1956).

Worces·ter (wŏŏs′tər), *n.* **Joseph Emerson,** 1784–1865, U.S. lexicographer.

Worcester china, a soft-paste porcelain containing little or no clay, made at Worcester, England, from 1751: also called "Royal" since 1788. Also, **Worcester porcelain.**

Worces·ter·shire (wŏŏs′tər shĭr′, -shər), *n.* a county in W central England. 522,846 pop. (1951); 699 sq. mi. *Co. seat:* Worcester. Also, **Worcester.**

Worcestershire sauce, a sharp sauce made with soy, vinegar, spices, etc., orig. from Worcester, England.

word (wûrd), *n.* **1.** a sound or a combination of sounds, or its written or printed representation, used in any language as the sign of a conception. **2.** *Gram.* an element which can stand alone as an utterance, not divisible into two or more parts similarly characterized; thus *boy* and *boyish*, but not *-ish* or *boy scout*, the former being less than a word, the latter more. **3.** (*often pl.*) speech or talk. **4.** a short talk or conversation: *to have a word with a person.* **5.** an expression or utterance: *a word of praise* or *of warning.* **6.** (*pl.*) the text or lyrics of a song as distinguished from the music. **7.** (*pl.*) contentious or angry speech. **8.** warrant, assurance, or promise: *to give* or *keep one's word.* **9.** intelligence or tidings: *to get word of an occurrence.* **10.** a verbal signal, as a password, watchword, or countersign. **11.** an authoritative utterance, or command: *his word was law.* **12.** (*cap.*) *Theol.* **a.** the Scriptures, or Bible (often, **the Word of God**). **b.** the Logos. **13.** *Obs.* a proverb; motto. **14. the last word, a.** the closing remark, as in argument. **b.** the last or latest thing or example in a class or field. —*v.t.* **15.** to express in words, or phrase. —*interj.* **16.** *Chiefly Brit.* an exclamation of astonishment: *my word!* [ME and OE, c. D *woord*, G *wort*, Icel. *ordh*, Goth. *waurd*] —**Syn. 9.** news, report.

word·age (wûr′dĭj), *n.* words collectively.

word-blind (wûrd′blĭnd′), *adj.* suffering from alexia.

word blindness, alexia.

word·book (wûrd′bŏŏk′), *n.* **1.** a book of words, usually with explanations, etc.; a dictionary. **2.** the libretto of an opera.

word·ing (wûr′dĭng), *n.* **1.** the act or manner of expressing in words; phrasing. **2.** the form of words in which a thing is expressed. —**Syn.** See **diction.**

word·less (wûrd′lĭs), *adj.* **1.** speechless, silent, or mute. **2.** not put into words; unexpressed.

word order, the arrangement in a sequence of the words of a sentence or smaller construction, usually to show meaning, as *Jack ate the beef* vs. *the beef Jack ate.*

word square, a set of words such that when arranged one beneath another in the form of a square they read alike horizontally and vertically.

```
s a t e d
a t o n e
t o a s t
e n s u e
d e t e r
```

Words·worth (wûrdz′wûrth), *n.* **William,** 1770–1850, British poet: poet laureate, 1843–50.

word·y (wûr′dĭ), *adj.,* **wordier, wordiest. 1.** characterized by or given to the use of many, or too many, words; verbose. **2.** pertaining to or consisting of words; verbal. **—word′i·ly,** *adv.* **—word′i·ness,** *n.*

wore (wōr), *v.* pt. of **wear.**

work (wûrk), *n., adj., v.,* **worked** or **wrought, working. —n. 1.** exertion directed to produce or accomplish something; labor; toil. **2.** that on which exertion or labor is expended; something to be made or done; a task or undertaking. **3.** productive or operative activity. **4.** *Physics, a, Mech.* the product of the force acting upon a body and the distance through which the point of application of force moves. Cf. **erg; kilogrammeter. b.** the transference of energy from one body or system to another. **5.** employment, as in some form of industry: *out of work, look for work.* **6.** materials, things, etc., on which one is working, or is to work. **7.** the result of exertion, labor, or activity; a deed or performance. **8.** a product of exertion, labor, or activity: *a work of art, literary or musical works.* **9.** an engineering structure, as a building, bridge, dock, or the like. **10.** a building, wall, trench, or the like, constructed or made as a means of fortification. **11.** (*pl.* often construed as *sing.*) a place or establishment for carrying on some form of labor or industry: *iron works.* **12.** (*pl.*) the working parts of a mechanical contrivance. **13.** the piece being cut, formed, ground, or otherwise processed in a machine tool, grinder, punch press, etc. **14.** (*pl.*) *Theol.* acts performed in obedience to the law of God, or righteous deeds. **—adj. 15.** of, for, or concerning work: *work clothes.* [ME *worke,* n., OE *worc* (r. ME *werk,* OE *weorc*), c. D and G *werk,* Icel. *verk,* Gk. *érgon*] **—v.i. 16.** to do work, or labor. **17.** to be employed, as in some industry, as a person. **18.** to be in operation, as a machine. **19.** to act or operate effectively: *the pump will not work, the plan works.* **20.** to get (*up, round, loose,* etc.), as if by continuous effort. **21.** to have an effect or influence, as on a person or on the mind or feelings. **22.** to move in agitation, as the features under strong feeling. **23.** to make way with effort or difficulty: *a ship works to windward.* **24.** *Naut.* to give slightly at the joints, as a vessel under strain at sea. **25.** *Mach.* to move improperly, as from defective fitting of parts or from wear. **26.** to undergo treatment by labor in a given way: *this dough works slowly.* **27.** to ferment, as a liquid. **—v.t. 28.** to use or manage (an apparatus, contrivance, etc.) in operation. **29.** to bring, put, get, render, etc., by work, effort, or action (fol. by *in, off, out,* or other completive words): *to work off a debt, to work up a case.* **30.** to bring about (any result) by or as by work or effort: *to work a change.* **31.** to effect, accomplish, cause, or do. **32.** to expend work on; manipulate or treat by labor: *to work butter.* **33.** to put into effective operation. **34.** to operate (a mine, farm, etc.) for productive purposes. **35.** to carry on operations in (a district or region). **36.** to make, fashion, or execute by work. **37.** to achieve or win by work or effort: *to work one's passage.* **38.** to keep (a person, a horse, etc.) at work. **39.** to solve (often fol. by *out*): *to work, or work out, a problem.* **40.** to find (out) by or as by calculation: *to work out a result.* **41.** to influence or persuade, esp. insidiously: *to work men to one's will.* **42.** to move, stir, or excite in feeling, etc. (often fol. by *up*). **43.** *Slang.* to use arts upon (a person) in order to obtain some profit or favor. **44.** *Slang.* to put into operation or use insidiously or guilefully. **45.** to make or decorate by needlework or embroidery. **46.** to cause (a liquid, etc.) to ferment. [ME *worke* (v. use of *worke,* n.), r. ME *wyrcke,* OE *wyrcean,* c. G *wirken,* Icel. *verkja,* Goth. *waurkjan*] **—work′less,** *adj.*

—Syn. 1. WORK, DRUDGERY, LABOR, TOIL refer to exertion of body or mind in performing or accomplishing something. WORK is the general word, and may apply to exertion which is either easy or hard: *heavy work, part-time work, outdoor work.* DRUDGERY suggests continuous, dreary, and dispiriting work, esp. of a menial or servile kind: *drudgery at household tasks.* LABOR particularly denotes hard manual work: *labor on a farm, in a steel mill.* TOIL suggests wearying or exhausting labor: *toil which breaks down the worker's health.* **2.** enterprise, project, job. **7.** product, achievement, feat. **28.** operate, manipulate, manage, handle. **30.** perform, execute, produce. **36.** form, shape. **—Ant. 1.** play, rest.

work·a·ble (wûr′kə bəl), *adj.* **1.** practicable or feasible. **2.** capable of or suitable for being worked. **—work′a·bil′i·ty, work′a·ble·ness,** *n.*

work·a·day (wûr′kə dā′), *adj.* of or befitting working days; working; practical; everyday.

work·bag (wûrk′băg′), *n.* a bag for holding implements and materials for work, esp. needlework.

work·bench (wûrk′běnch′), *n.* a bench at which an artisan works.

work·book (wûrk′boŏk′), *n.* **1.** a manual of operating instructions. **2.** a book designed to guide the work of a student by inclusion of some instructional material, and usually providing questions, etc. **3.** a book in which a record is kept of work completed or planned.

work·box (wûrk′bŏks′), *n.* a box to hold instruments and materials for work, esp. needlework.

work·day (wûrk′dā′), *n.* **1.** working day. **—adj. 2.** workaday.

worked (wûrkt), *adj.* that has undergone working. **—Syn.** WORKED, WROUGHT both apply to something on

which effort has been applied. WORKED implies expended effort of almost any kind: *a worked silver mine.* WROUGHT implies fashioning, molding, or making, esp., by hand: *a wrought iron railing.*

work·er (wûr′kər), *n.* **1.** one who or that which works. **2.** (in the Soviet Union) a citizen, excluding the peasants and members of the army or navy. **3.** *Entomol.* the sterile or infertile female of bees, wasps, ants, or termites, which does the work of the colony. **4.** *Print.* one of a set of electrotyped plates used to print from, as contrasted with a set of molders. **—work′er·less,** *adj.*

work·folk (wûrk′fōk′), *n.pl.* workpeople. Also, **work′folks′.**

work·house (wûrk′hous′), *n.* **1.** *U.S.* a house of correction. **2.** *Brit.* a house in which paupers are lodged and set to work; a poorhouse. **3.** *Obs.* a workshop.

work·ing (wûr′kĭng), *n.* **1.** act of a person or thing that works. **2.** operation; action. **3.** the process of skillful working of something into a shape. **4.** act of manufacturing or building a thing. **5.** (of a problem) act of solving. **6.** (*commonly pl.*) a part of a mine, quarry, or the like, in which work is being or has been carried on. **7.** the process of fermenting, as of yeasts. **8.** a slow advance involving exertion. **9.** disturbed or twisting motions. **—adj. 10.** that works. **11.** doing some form of work or labor, esp. manual, mechanical, or industrial work, as for a living. **12.** operating, or producing effects. **13.** pertaining to, connected with, or used in operating or working. **14.** serving for the purposes of working. **15.** large enough for working, or being worked: *a working sample.* **16.** that moves with sudden jerks, esp. from deep emotion.

working assets, *Accounting.* invested capital which is comparatively liquid.

working capital, 1. the amount of capital needed to carry on a business. **2.** *Accounting.* current assets minus current liabilities. **3.** *Finance.* liquid as distinguished from fixed capital assets.

working day, 1. the amount of time that a worker must work for an agreed daily wage. **2.** a day ordinarily given to working (opposed to *holiday*). **3.** the daily period of hours for working.

work·ing-day (wûr′kĭng dā′), *adj.* workaday; everyday.

working drawing, a drawing, as of the whole or part of a structure or machine, made to scale and in such detail with regard to dimensions, etc., as to form a guide for the workmen in the construction of the object.

work·ing·man (wûr′kĭng măn′), *n., pl.* **-men,** a man of the working class; a man (skilled or unskilled) who earns his living at some manual or industrial work.

working papers, legal papers giving information often required for employment.

working substance, *Mech.* the substance, as a working fluid, which operates a prime mover.

work·man (wûrk′mən), *n., pl.* **-men. 1.** a man employed or skilled in some form of manual, mechanical, or industrial work. **2.** a male worker. **—work′man·less,** *adj.*

work·man·like (wûrk′mən līk′), *adj.* **1.** like or befitting a workman. **2.** skillful; well executed. Also, **work′man·ly.**

work·man·ship (wûrk′mən shĭp′), *n.* **1.** the art or skill of a workman; skill in working or execution. **2.** quality or mode of execution, as of a thing made. **3.** the product or result of the labor and skill of a workman; work executed.

workmen's compensation insurance, insurance required by law from employers for the protection of employees while engaged in the employer's business. The amount of the claim is stipulated by law (**workmen's compensation law**).

work of art, a piece of creative work in the arts, esp. a painting or a piece of sculpture.

work·out (wûrk′out′), *n. Colloq.* **1.** a trial at running, boxing, a game, or the like, usually preliminary to and in preparation for a contest, exhibition, etc. **2.** any performance for practice or training or as a trial or test.

work·peo·ple (wûrk′pē′pəl), *n.pl. Chiefly Brit.* people employed at work or labor.

work·room (wûrk′room′, -room′), *n.* a room in which work is carried on.

works council, *Brit.* **1.** an elected body of employee representatives which deals with management regarding grievances, working conditions, wages, etc., and which is consulted by management in regard to labor matters. **2.** a joint council or committee representing employer and employees which discusses working conditions, wages, etc. within a plant or business.

work·shop (wûrk′shŏp′), *n.* a shop or building in which work, esp. mechanical work, is carried on.

work·ta·ble (wûrk′tā′bəl), *n.* a table for working at; often with drawers or receptacles for materials, etc., as for sewing.

work·up (wûrk′ŭp′), *n. Print.* a defect caused by spacing material rising up during the press run.

work·wom·an (wûrk′woŏm′ən), *n., pl.* **-women. 1.** a female worker. **2.** a woman employed or skilled in some manual, mechanical, or industrial work.

world (wûrld), *n.* **1.** the earth or globe. **2.** a particular division of the earth: *the New World.* **3.** the earth, with its inhabitants, affairs, etc., during a particular period:

the ancient world. **4.** mankind; humanity. **5.** the public generally: *the whole world knows it.* **6.** the class of persons devoted to the affairs, interests, or pursuits of this life: *the world worships success.* **7.** society; secular, social, or fashionable life, with its ways and interests: *to withdraw from the world.* **8.** a particular class of mankind, with common interests, aims, etc.: *the fashionable world.* **9.** any sphere, realm, or domain, with all that pertains to it: *woman's world, the world of dreams, the insect world.* **10.** the entire system of created things; the universe; the macrocosm. **11.** any complex whole conceived as resembling the universe (cf. **microcosm**). **12.** one of the three general groupings of physical nature, as the **animal world, mineral world, vegetable world.** **13.** any period, state, or sphere of existence: *this world, the world to come.* **14.** a very great quantity or extent: *to do a world of good.* **15.** any indefinitely great expanse. **16.** any heavenly body: *the starry worlds.* **17. for all the world, a.** for any consideration, no matter how great. **b.** in every respect, or precisely. **18. in the world, a.** in the universe, or on earth; anywhere. **b.** at all; ever. **19. world without end,** through all eternity; forever. [ME and OE, var. of OE *weorold,* c. D *wereld,* G *welt,* Icel. *veröld,* all g. Gmc. *wer-ald,* lit., man-age] —**Syn. 1.** See **earth.**

World Court, an international tribunal, sitting at The Hague, Netherlands, provided for in the Covenant of the League of Nations, and established in September, 1921, by action of the assembly of that body, and empowered to render decisions or advisory opinions in disputes threatening future war. Official name, **International Court of Justice.**

world·ling (wûrld′lĭng), *n.* one devoted to the interests and pleasures of this world; a worldly person.

world·ly (wûrld′lĭ), *adj.,* **-lier, -liest,** *adv.* —*adj.* **1.** secular (as opposed to *ecclesiastical, religious,* etc.). **2.** earthly or mundane (as opposed to *heavenly, spiritual,* etc.). **3.** devoted to, directed toward, or connected with the affairs, interests, or pleasures of this world. **4.** of or pertaining to this world. —*adv.* **5.** in a worldly manner. —**world′li·ness,** *n.* —**Syn. 2.** See **earthly.**

world·ly-mind·ed (wûrld′lĭ mīn′dĭd), *adj.* having or showing a worldly mind, or devotion to the affairs and interests of this world. —**world′ly-mind′ed·ly,** *adv.* —**world′ly-mind′ed·ness,** *n.*

world·ly-wise (wûrld′lĭ wīz′), *adj.* wise as to the affairs of this world.

world power, a nation, organization, or institution so powerful that it is capable of influencing or changing the course of world events.

World Series, *Baseball.* a group of games played each fall between the winning teams of the two major leagues to determine the professional champions of the U.S. Also, **World′s Series.**

world soul, a (supposed) soul of the world or universe.

world spirit, God; the moving force in the universe.

World War, 1. Also, **World War I, Great War, War of the Nations.** the war in Europe, Asia, Africa, and elsewhere, extending from July 28, 1914, to Nov. 11, 1918, between the powers of the Triple Entente (Great Britain, France, and Russia), with their allies and associates (Belgium, Serbia, Japan, Italy, the United States, etc.), on the one side, and Germany and Austria-Hungary, with their allies Turkey and Bulgaria, on the other side, which ended with the collapse of the latter group. **2.** Also, **World War II.** the world-wide conflict (1939–45), which arose from the undeclared wars of Japan and China (1931–41) and the threats to peace by Italy and Germany in Ethiopia, Spain, and central Europe (1935–39), began with the German attack on Poland, Sept. 1, 1939, when France and Great Britain declared war. The early German triumphs in Europe encouraged Italian entry in June, 1940, but the superiority of resources and industrial production, best visualized in air power and the atom bomb, esp. after the entry of the Soviet Union and the U. S. (1941), enabled the United Nations to defeat Italy in September, 1943, Germany in May, 1945, and Japan in August, 1945.

world-wea·ry (wûrld′wēr′ĭ), *adj.* weary of the world or of existence.

world-wide (wûrld′wīd′), *adj.* extending or spread throughout the world.

worm (wûrm), *n.* **1.** *Zool.* any of the long, slender, soft-bodied bilateral invertebrates that are comprised by the flatworms, roundworms, acanthocephalans, nemerteans, gordiaceans, and annelids. **2.** (in popular language) any of numerous small creeping animals with more or less slender, elongated bodies, and without limbs or with very short ones, including individuals of widely differing kinds, as earthworms, tapeworms, insect larvae, adult forms of some insects, etc. **3.** something resembling or suggesting a worm in appearance, movement, etc. **4.** the spiral pipe in a still, in which the vapor is condensed. See diag. under **still. 5.** a screw or screw thread. **6.** an endless screw, or a device in which this is the principal feature. **7.** the endless screw (shaft on which a spiral groove is cut) which engages with a worm wheel or worm gear. **8.** a groveling, abject, or contemptible creature. **9.** a downtrodden or miserable person. **10.** something that penetrates, injures, or consumes slowly or insidiously, like a gnawing worm. **11.** (*pl.*) *Pathol.* any disease or

disorder arising from the presence of parasitic worms in the intestines or other tissues. **12.** the lytta of a dog, etc. —*v.i.* **13.** to move or act like a worm; creep, crawl, or advance slowly or stealthily. **14.** to get by insidious procedure (fol. by *into,* etc.). —*v.t.* **15.** to make, cause, bring, etc., along by creeping or crawling, or by stealthy or devious advances. **16.** to get by persistent, insidious efforts (esp. fol. by *out* or *from*): *to worm a secret out of a person.* **17.** to free from worms. **18.** *Naut.* to wind yarn or the like spirally round (a rope) so as to fill the spaces between the strands and render the surface smooth. [ME; OE *wyrm* worm, serpent, c. D *worm,* G *wurm,* Icel. *ormr,* akin to L *vermis*] —**worm′er,** *n.* —**worm′less,** *adj.* —**worm′like′,** *adj.*

worm-eat·en (wûrm′ē′tən), *adj.* **1.** eaten into or gnawed by worms. **2.** impaired by time, decayed, or antiquated.

worm fence, snake fence.

worm gear, *Mach.* **1.** a worm wheel. **2.** such a worm wheel together with the endless screw forming a device by which the rotary motion of one shaft can be transmitted to another shaft at right angles to it.

worm·hole (wûrm′hōl′), *n.* a hole made by a burrowing or gnawing worm, as in timber, nuts, etc.

Worms (wûrmz; *Ger.* vôrms), *n.* **1.** a city in SW West Germany, in Hesse, on the Rhine. 57,200 (est. 1953). **2. Diet of,** an assemblage held here, 1521, at which Luther was condemned as a heretic.

worm·seed (wûrm′sēd′), *n.* **1.** the dried, unexpanded flower heads of santonica, *Artemisia cina* (**Levant wormseed**), or the fruit of certain goosefoots, esp. *Chenopodium anthelminticum* (**American wormseed**), used as an anthelmintic drug. **2.** any of these plants.

worm wheel, *Mach.* a toothed wheel which engages with a revolving worm, or endless screw, in order to receive or impart motion. Cf. **worm gear.**

worm·wood (wûrm′wŏŏd′), *n.* **1.** any plant of the composite genus *Artemisia,* as *A. cina* (*santonica*), *A. moxa* (*moxa*), etc. **2.** a bitter, aromatic herb, *Artemisia Absinthium,* a native of the Old World, formerly much used as a vermifuge and a tonic, but now chiefly in making absinthe. **3.** something bitter, grievous, or extremely unpleasant; bitterness. [f. WORM + WOOD[1]; r. ME *wermode,* OE *wermōd,* c. G *wermut.* See VERMOUTH]

W. Worm wheel

worm·y (wûr′mĭ), *adj.,* **wormier, wormiest. 1.** containing a worm or worms; infested with worms. **2.** worm-eaten. **3.** wormlike; groveling; low. —**worm′i·ness,** *n.*

worn (wôrn), *v.* **1.** pp. of **wear.** —*adj.* **2.** impaired by wear or use: *worn clothing.* **3.** wearied or exhausted.

worn-out (wôrn′out′), *adj.* **1.** worn or used until no longer fit for use. **2.** exhausted by use, strain, etc.

wor·ri·ment (wûr′ĭ mənt), *n. Colloq.* **1.** worrying; harassing annoyance. **2.** worry; anxiety.

wor·ri·some (wûr′ĭ səm), *adj.* **1.** worrying, annoying, or disturbing; causing worry. **2.** inclined to worry. —**wor′ri·some·ly,** *adv.*

wor·ry (wûr′ĭ), *v.,* **-ried, -rying,** *n., pl.* **-ries.** —*v.i.* **1.** to feel uneasy or anxious; fret; torment oneself with or suffer from disturbing thoughts. **2.** *Colloq.* to get (*along* or *through*) by constant effort, in spite of difficulties or troubles. **3.** to worry an animal, prey, or the like, by seizing with the teeth and shaking, mangling, etc. —*v.t.* **4.** to cause to feel uneasy or anxious; trouble; torment with annoyances, cares, anxieties, etc.; plague, pester, or bother. **5.** to, seize (orig. by the throat) with the teeth and shake or mangle, as one animal does another. **6.** to harass by repeated biting, snapping, etc. —*n.* **7.** worried condition or feeling; uneasiness or anxiety. **8.** a cause of uneasiness or anxiety, or a trouble. **9.** act of worrying. [ME *wory,* var. of *wiry,* OE *wyrgan* strangle, c. G *würgen*] —**wor′ri·er,** *n.* —**Syn. 4.** WORRY, ANNOY, HARASS all mean to disturb or interfere with someone's comfort or peace of mind. To WORRY is to cause anxiety, apprehension, or care: *to worry one's parents.* **7.** apprehension, solicitude. See **concern.**

worse (wûrs), *adj., used as compar. of* **bad. 1.** bad or ill in a greater or higher degree; inferior in excellence, quality, or character. **2.** more unfavorable or injurious. **3.** in less good condition; in poorer health. —*n.* **4.** that which is worse. —*adv.* **5.** in a more evil, wicked, severe, or disadvantageous manner. **6.** with more severity, intensity, etc.; in a greater degree. Also, *Dial.,* **wors′er** for 1–3, 5, 6. [ME; OE *wyrsa,* c. Icel. *verri,* Goth. *wairsiza*]

wors·en (wûr′sən), *v.t., v.i.* to make or become worse.

wor·ship (wûr′shĭp), *n., v.,* **-shiped, -shiping** or (*esp. Brit.*) **-shipped, -shipping.** —*n.* **1.** reverent honor and homage paid to God or a sacred personage, or to any object regarded as sacred. **2.** formal or ceremonious rendering of such honor and homage. **3.** adoring reverence or regard: *hero worship.* **4.** the object of adoring reverence or regard. **5.** *Chiefly Brit.* (with *your, his,* etc.) a title of honor used in addressing or mentioning certain magistrates and others of rank or station. **6.** *Archaic.* honorable character or standing:

men of worship. —*v.t.* 7. to render religious reverence and homage to. 8. to feel an adoring reverence or regard for (any person or thing). —*v.i.* 9. to render religious reverence and homage, as to a deity. 10. to attend services of divine worship. 11. to feel an adoring reverence or regard. [ME; OE *worthscip*, northern var. of *weorthscipe*, f. *weorth* WORTH + *-scipe* -SHIP] —wor'ship·er; *esp. Brit.*, wor'ship·per, *n.* —Syn. 1. See reverence. 3. honor, homage, adoration, idolizing, idolatry. 8. honor, venerate, revere, glorify, idolize.

wor·ship·ful (wûr'ship fəl), *adj.* 1. given to the worship of something. 2. *Chiefly Brit.* honorable, or worthy of or regarded with honor (now used chiefly as a respectful epithet). —wor'ship·ful·ly, *adv.* —wor'ship·ful·ness, *n.*

worst (wûrst), *adj., used as superl. of* bad. . bad or ill in the greatest or highest degree; most faulty, unsatisfactory, or objectionable. 2. most unfavorable or injurious. 3. in the poorest condition. —*n.* 4. that which is worst. 5. if (the) worst comes to (the) worst, if the very worst happens. —*adv.* 6. in the most evil, wicked, severe, or disadvantageous manner. 7. with the most severity, intensity, etc.; in the greatest degree. —*v.t.* 8. to give (one) the worst of a contest or struggle; defeat; beat. [ME; OE *wurresta*, northern var. of *wyr(re)sta, wer(re)sta*, c. Icel. *verstr*]

wor·sted (wŏŏs'tĭd), *n.* 1. firmly twisted yarn or thread spun from combed long-staple wool, used for weaving, etc. 2. wool cloth woven from such yarns, having a hard, smooth surface, and no nap. —*adj.* 3. consisting or made of worsted. [named after ME *Worsted*, parish in Norfolk, England (now Worstead)]

wort¹ (wûrt), *n.* the unfermented or fermenting infusion of malt which after fermentation becomes beer or mash. [ME; OE *wyrt*, c. G *würze* spice. See WORT²]

wort² (wûrt), *n.* a plant; herb; vegetable (now used chiefly in composition, as in *liverwort, figwort, colewort*, etc.) [ME; OE *wyrt* root, plant, c. G *wurz*; akin to ROOT]

worth¹ (wûrth), *adj.* 1. good or important enough to justify (what is specified): *advice worth taking, a place worth visiting.* 2. having a value of, or equal in value to, as in money. 3. having property to the value or amount of. —*n.* 4. excellence of character or quality as commanding esteem: *men of worth.* 5. usefulness or importance, as to the world, to a person, or for a purpose. 6. value, as in money. 7. a quantity of something, of a specified value. [ME and OE; c. G *wert*] —Syn. 4. See value. 5. See merit.

worth² (wûrth), *v.i. Archaic.* to happen or betide: *woe worth the day.* [ME; OE *weorthan*, c. G *werden*]

worth·less (wûrth'lĭs), *adj.* without worth; of no use, importance, or value; good-for-nothing; useless; valueless. —worth'less·ly, *adv.* —worth'less·ness, *n.*

worth·while (wûrth'hwīl'), *adj.* such as to repay one's time, attention, interest, work, trouble, etc.: *a worth-while book.*

wor·thy (wûr'thĭ), *adj.*, -thier, -thiest, *n., pl.* -thies. —*adj.* 1. of adequate merit or character. 2. of commendable excellence or merit; deserving (often fol. by *of*, an infinitive, or occasionally a clause). —*n.* 3. a person of eminent worth or merit. 4. (in humorous use) a personage. —wor'thi·ly, *adv.* —wor'thi·ness, *n.* —Syn. 2. meritorious, estimable, excellent, exemplary.

wot (wŏt), *Archaic exc. Dial.* first and third pers. sing. pres. of wit². [ME *woot*, OE *wāt*, c. G *weiss*]

Wot·ton (wŏt'ən), *n.* Henry, 1568–1639, English poet and diplomat.

would (wŏŏd; *unstressed* wəd), *v.* pt. of will¹ used: 1. specially in expressing a wish: *I would it were true.* 2. often in place of *will*, to make a statement or question less direct or blunt: *that would scarcely be fair, would you be so kind?* [ME and OE *wolde*. See WILL¹]

would-be (wŏŏd'bē'), *adj.* 1. wishing or pretending to be: *a would-be wit.* 2. intended to be: *a would-be kindness.*

would·n't (wŏŏd'nt), contraction of *would not.*

wouldst (wŏŏdst), *v. Archaic and Poetic.* second pers. sing. pt. of will¹.

wound¹ (wŏŏnd; *Archaic and Poetic* wound), *n.* 1. an injury to an organism, usually one involving division of tissue or rupture of the integument or mucous membrane, due to external violence or some mechanical agency rather than disease. 2. a similar injury to the tissue of a plant. 3. an injury or hurt to feelings, sensibilities, reputation, etc. —*v.t.* 4. to inflict a wound upon; injure; hurt. —*v.i.* 5. to inflict a wound or wounds. [ME; OE *wund*, c. G *wunde*] —wound'less, *adj.* —Syn. 1. hurt, cut, stab, laceration, lesion. See injury.

wound² (wound), *v.* pt. and pp. of wind² and wind³.

wove (wōv), *v.* pt. and occasional pp. of weave.

wo·ven (wō'vən), *v.* pp. of weave.

wove paper, paper with plain surface (in contrast with laid paper, having wire mark).

wow (wou), *n.* 1. *Slang.* something that proves an extraordinary success. 2. a slow variation in pitch fidelity resulting from fluctuations in the speed of a recording. —*interj.* 3. *Colloq. or Dial.* an exclamation of surprise, wonder, pleasure, dismay, etc.

wow·ser (wou'zər), *n. Australia.* an excessively puritanical person.

WPA, Work Projects Administration.

WPB, War Production Board.

WRA, War Relocation Authority.

wrack (răk), *n.* 1. wreck or wreckage. 2. ruin or destruction. 3. seaweed or other marine vegetation cast ashore. [ME *wrak* wreck, t. MD or MLG]

wraith (rāth), *n.* 1. an apparition of a living person, or one supposed to be living, reputed to portend or indicate his death. 2. a visible spirit. [orig. uncert.] —wraith'like', *adj.*

Wran·gel (răng'gəl; *Russ.* vrän'gĕl'y), *n.* a Russian island in the Arctic Ocean, off the coast of the NE Soviet Union in Asia: meteorological station. ab. 2000 sq. mi.

Wran·gell (răng'gəl), *n.* 1. Mount, a volcano in SE Alaska, in the Wrangell Mountains. 14,005 ft. 2. a town in SE Alaska. 1,315 (1960).

Wrangell Mountains, a mountain range in SE Alaska. Highest peak, Mt. Bona, 16,420 ft.

wran·gle (răng'gəl), *v.*, -gled, -gling, *n.* —*v.i.* 1. to argue or dispute, esp. in a noisy or angry manner. —*v.t.* 2. to argue or dispute. 3. *Western U.S.* to tend (horses). —*n.* 4. a noisy or angry dispute; altercation. [appar. t. LG: m. *wrangeln*, freq. of *wrangen* struggle, make uproar. Cf. WRING]

wran·gler (răng'glər), *n.* 1. one who wrangles or disputes. 2. (formerly, at Cambridge University, England) one of those in the first grade of honors in mathematics. 3. *Western U.S.* a horse wrangler.

wrap (răp), *v.*, wrapped or wrapt, wrapping, *n.* —*v.t.* 1. to enclose, envelop, or muffle in something wound or folded about (often fol. by *up*). 2. to enclose and make fast (an article, bundle, etc.) within a covering of paper or the like (often fol. by *up*). 3. to wind, fold, or bind (something) about as a covering. 4. to protect with coverings, outer garments, etc. (usually fol. by *up*). 5. to surround, envelop, shroud, or hide. 6. to fold or roll up. —*v.i.* 7. to wrap oneself (*up*). 8. to become wrapped, as about something; fold. —*n.* 9. something to be wrapped about the person, esp. in addition to the usual indoor clothing, as a shawl, scarf, or mantle. 10. (*pl.*) outdoor garments, or coverings, furs, etc. [b. obs. *wry*, v., cover and LAP²]

wrap·per (răp'ər), *n.* 1. one who or that which wraps. 2. that in which something is wrapped; a covering or cover. 3. a long, loose outer garment. 4. a woman's loose house gown, or negligee. 5. *Chiefly Brit.* a book jacket. 6. the tobacco leaf used for covering a cigar.

wrap·ping (răp'ĭng), *n.* (*usually pl.*) that in which something is wrapped.

wrapt (răpt), *v.* a pt. and pp. of wrap.

wrasse (răs), *n.* any of various marine fishes of the family Labridae, esp. of the genus *Labrus*, having thick, fleshy lips, powerful teeth, and usually a brilliant color, certain species being valued as food fishes. [t. Cornish: m. *wrach*, var. of *gwrach*]

wrath (răth, räth; *Brit.* rôth), *n.* 1. strong, stern, or fierce anger; deeply resentful indignation; ire. 2. vengeance or punishment, as the consequence of anger. —*adj.* 3. *Archaic.* wroth. [ME; OE *wrǣththo*, der. *wrāth* WROTH. See -TH¹] —wrath'less, *adj.* —Syn. 1. rage, resentment, indignation, dudgeon.

wrath·ful (răth'fəl, räth'-), *adj.* 1. full of wrath, very angry, or ireful. 2. characterized by or showing wrath: *wrathful words.* —wrath'ful·ly, *adv.* —wrath'ful·ness, *n.* —Syn. 1. angry, irate, furious, raging, incensed, resentful, indignant.

wrath·y (răth'ĭ, räth'ĭ), *adj. Colloq.* wrathful; angry. —wrath'i·ly, *adv.* —wrath'i·ness, *n.*

wreak (rēk), *v.t.* 1. to inflict or execute (vengeance, etc.). 2. to carry out the promptings of (one's rage, ill humor, will, desire, etc.), as on a victim or object. [ME *wreke(n)*, OE *wrecan*, c. G *rächen*] —wreak'er, *n.*

wreath (rēth), *n., pl.* wreaths (rēthz). 1. something twisted or bent into a circular form; a circular band of flowers, foliage, or any ornamental work, for adorning the head or for any decorative purpose; a garland or chaplet. 2. any ringlike, curving, or curling mass or formation. [ME *wrethe*, OE *wrǣth*; akin to WRITHE] —wreath'less, *adj.* —wreath'like', *adj.*

wreathe (rēth), *v.*, wreathed; wreathed or (*Archaic*) wreathen; wreathing. —*v.t.* 1. to encircle or adorn with or as with a wreath or wreaths. 2. to form as a wreath, by twisting, twining, or otherwise. 3. to surround in curving or curling masses or form. 4. to envelop: *a face wreathed in smiles.* —*v.i.* 5. to take the form of a wreath or wreaths. 6. to move in curving or curling masses, as smoke.

wreck (rĕk), *n.* 1. any building, structure, or thing reduced to a state of ruin. 2. that which is cast ashore by the sea, as the remains of a ruined vessel or of its cargo; shipwrecked property, or wreckage, cast ashore or (less strictly) floating on the sea. 3. the ruin or destruction of a vessel in the course of navigation; shipwreck. 4. a vessel in a state of ruin from disaster at sea, on rocks, etc. 5. the ruin or destruction of anything: *the wreck of one's hopes.* —*v.t.* 6. to cause the wreck of (a vessel), as in navigation; shipwreck. 7. to involve in a wreck. 8. to cause the ruin or destruction of. —*v.i.* 9. to suffer wreck. 10. to act as a wrecker; engage in wrecking. [ME *wrek*, t. Scand.; cf. Icel. *rek*; akin to WREAK, WRACK] —Syn. 8. See spoil.

wreck·age (rĕk'ĭj), *n.* 1. act of wrecking. 2. state of being wrecked. 3. remains or fragments of something that has been wrecked.

wreck·er (rĕk'ər), n. **1.** one who or that which wrecks. **2.** a person, car, or train employed in removing wreckage, etc., as from railroad tracks. **3.** one whose business it is to tear down buildings, as in clearing sites for other use. **4.** a person or a vessel employed in recovering wrecked or disabled vessels or their cargoes, etc., as for the owners or underwriters. **5.** one who causes shipwrecks, as by false lights on shore, to secure wreckage, or who makes a business of plundering wrecks.

wreck·ful (rĕk'fəl), adj. Archaic. causing wreckage.

wrecking car, a car equipped as a wrecker (def. 2).

wren (rĕn), n. **1.** any of numerous small, active, oscine passerine birds constituting the family Troglodytidae, esp. the Troglodytes troglodytes, known as the wren in England and as the **winter wren** in America; and the common **house wren** (T. aedon) of North America. **2.** any of various similar birds of other families, as the **golden-crested wren** (Regulus regulus). [ME wrenne, OE wrenna. Cf. Icel. rindill]

Wren (rĕn), n. **Sir Christopher**, 1632–1723, British architect.

wrench (rĕnch), v.t. **1.** to twist suddenly and forcibly; pull, jerk, or force by a violent twist. **2.** to overstrain or injure (the ankle, etc.) by a sudden, violent twist. **3.** to affect distressingly as if by a wrench. **4.** to wrest, as from the right use or meaning: to wrench facts or statements. —v.i. **5.** to twist, turn, or move suddenly aside. **6.** to give a wrench or twist at something. —n. **7.** a wrenching movement; a sudden, violent twist. **8.** a painful, straining twist, as of the ankle or wrist. **9.** a sharp, distressing strain, as to the feelings. **10.** a wresting, as of meaning. **11.** a tool for catching upon or gripping and turning or twisting the head of a bolt, a nut, a pipe, or the like, commonly consisting of a bar of metal with fixed or adjustable jaws. [ME wrenche (N.), OE wrencan twist, turn, c. G renken]

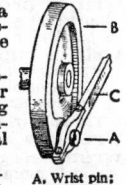

A   B
Wrenches
(def. 11)
A. Single end;
B, S wrench

Wrens (rĕnz), n. Brit. Colloq. Women's Royal Naval Service.

wrest (rĕst), v.t. **1.** to twist or turn; pull, jerk, or force by a violent twist. **2.** to take away by force. **3.** to get by effort: to wrest a living from the soil. **4.** to twist or turn from the proper course, application, use, meaning, or the like. —n. **5.** a wresting; a twist or wrench. **6.** a key or small wrench for tuning stringed musical instruments, as the harp or piano, by turning the pins to which the strings are fastened. [ME wreste(n), OE wrǣstan, c. Icel. reista; akin to WRIST] —**wrest'er**, n. —**Syn. 3.** See **extract**.

wres·tle (rĕs'əl), v., -tled, -tling, n. —v.i. **1.** to engage in wrestling. **2.** to contend, as in a struggle for mastery; grapple. —v.t. **3.** to contend with in wrestling. **4.** to force by or as if by wrestling. **5.** Western U.S. to throw (an animal) for the purpose of branding. —n. **6.** an act of or a bout at wrestling. **7.** a struggle. [ME, freq. of WREST] —**wres'tler**, n.

wres·tling (rĕs'lǐng), n. **1.** an exercise or sport, subject to special rules, in which two persons struggle hand to hand, each striving to throw or force the other to the ground. **2.** act of one who wrestles.

wretch (rĕch), n. **1.** a deplorably unfortunate or unhappy person. **2.** a person of despicable or base character. [ME wretche, OE wrecca exile, adventurer, c. G recke warrior, hero, Icel. rekkr man]

wretch·ed (rĕch'ĭd), adj. **1.** very unfortunate in condition or circumstances; miserable; pitiable. **2.** characterized by or attended with misery. **3.** despicable, contemptible, or mean. **4.** poor, sorry, or pitiful; worthless: a wretched blunderer, wretched little daubs. —**wretch'ed·ly**, adv. —**wretch'ed·ness**, n.

—**Syn. 1.** dejected, distressed, afflicted, woeful, woebegone, forlorn, unhappy. **2.** WRETCHED, MISERABLE, SORRY refer to that which is unhappy, afflicted, or distressed. WRETCHED refers to a condition of extreme affliction or distress, esp. as outwardly apparent: wretched hovels. MISERABLE refers more to the inward feeling of unhappiness or distress: a miserable life. SORRY applies to distressed, often poverty-stricken outward circumstances; but it has connotations of unworthiness, incongruousness, or the like, so that the beholder feels more contempt than pity: in a sorry plight. **3.** base, vile, worthless, bad. —**Ant. 1.** comfortable, happy, admirable.

wrick (rĭk), v.t., v.i., n. wrench or strain.

wri·er (rī'ər), adj. compar. of wry.

wri·est (rī'ĭst), adj. superl. of wry.

wrig·gle (rĭg'əl), v., -gled, -gling, n. —v.i. **1.** to twist to and fro, writhe, or squirm. **2.** to move along by twisting and turning the body, as a worm or snake. **3.** to make one's way by shifts or expedients: to wriggle out of a difficulty. —v.t. **4.** to cause to wriggle. **5.** to bring, get, make, etc., by wriggling. —n. **6.** act of wriggling; a wriggling movement. [t. MLG: m. wriggeln, c. D wriggelen] —**wrig'gly**, adj.

wrig·gler (rĭg'lər), n. **1.** one who or that which wriggles. **2.** the larva of a mosquito.

wright (rīt), n. a workman, esp. a constructive workman (now chiefly in wheelwright, playwright, etc.) [ME; OE wryhta, metathetic var. of wyrhta worker. See WORK]

Wright (rīt), n. **1. Frances**, 1795–1852, U.S. reformer, born in Scotland. **2. Frank Lloyd**, 1869–1959, U.S. architect. **3. Joseph**, 1855–1930, British linguist and

lexicographer. **4. Orville**, 1871–1948, and his brother, **Wilbur**, 1867–1912, U.S. aeronautical inventors.

wring (rĭng), v., **wrung** or (Rare) **wringed**; **wringing**; n. —v.t. **1.** to twist forcibly, as something flexible. **2.** to twist and compress, or compress without twisting, in order to force out water, etc. (often fol. by out): to wring clothes. **3.** to extract or expel by twisting or compression (usually fol. by out or from). **4.** to affect painfully by or as if by some contorting or compressing action; pain, distress, or torment. **5.** to clasp tightly with or without twisting: to wring the hands in pain. **6.** to force (off, etc.) by twisting. **7.** to extract or extort as if by twisting. —v.i. **8.** to perform the action of wringing something. **9.** to writhe, as in anguish. —n. **10.** a wringing; forcible twist or squeeze. [ME; OE wringan, c. G ringen]

wring·er (rĭng'ər), n. **1.** one who or that which wrings. **2.** an apparatus or machine which by pressure forces water or the like out of anything wet.

wrin·kle[1] (rĭng'kəl), n., v., -kled, -kling. —n. **1.** a ridge or furrow on a surface, due to contraction, folding, rumpling, or the like; corrugation; slight fold; crease. —v.t. **2.** to form a wrinkle or wrinkles in; corrugate; crease. —v.i. **3.** to become contracted into wrinkles; become wrinkled. [late ME wrynkle; back formation from wrinkled, OE gewrinclod serrate] —**wrin'kle·less**, adj. —**wrin'kly**, adj.

wrin·kle[2] (rĭng'kəl), n. Colloq. an ingenious indirect or artful procedure or method; a novel or clever trick or device. [der. ME wrink, OE wrenc trick]

wrist (rĭst), n. **1.** the part of the arm between the forearm and the hand; technically, the carpus. **2.** the joint between the radius and the carpus (**wrist joint**). **3.** that part of an article of clothing which fits around the wrist. **4.** Mach. a wrist pin. [ME and OE, c. G rist, back of hand, Icel. rist instep; akin to WRITHE]

wrist·band (rĭst'bănd', rĭz'bənd), n. the band or part of a sleeve, as of a shirt, which covers the wrist.

wrist drop, Pathol. paralysis of the extensor muscles of the hand causing it to droop, due to injuries or some poisons, as lead or arsenic. Also, **wrist'-drop'**.

wrist·let (rĭst'lĭt), n. **1.** a band worn around the wrist, esp. to protect it from cold. **2.** a bracelet. **3.** Humorous or Slang. a handcuff.

wrist·lock (rĭst'lŏk'), n. Wrestling. a hold whereby the opponent is made defenseless by a wrenching grasp on the wrist.

wrist pin, Mach. **1.** a stud or pin projecting from the side of a crank, wheel, or the like, and attaching it to a connecting rod leading to some other part of the mechanism. **2.** a pin in the piston of an internal combustion engine.

wrist watch, a watch (timepiece) attached to a strap or band worn about the wrist.

A. Wrist pin;
B. Wheel;
C. Connecting rod

writ[1] (rĭt), n. **1.** Law. **a.** a formal order under seal, issued in the name of a sovereign, government, court, or other competent authority, enjoining the officer or other person to whom it is. addressed to do or refrain from some specified act. **b.** (in early English law) any formal document in letter form, under seal, and in the king's name. **2.** something written: Holy Writ (the Bible). [ME and OE, c. Icel. rit writing. See WRITE]

writ[2] (rĭt), v. Archaic. pt. and pp. of **write**.

write (rīt), v., **wrote** or (Archaic) **writ**; **written** or (Archaic) **writ**; **writing**. —v.t. **1.** to trace or form (characters, letters, words, etc.) on the surface of some material, as with a pen, pencil, or other instrument or means; inscribe. **2.** to express or communicate in writing; give a written account of. **3.** to fill in the blank spaces of (a form, etc.) with writing: to write a check. **4.** to execute or produce by setting down words, etc.: to write two copies of a letter. **5.** to compose and produce in words or characters duly set down: to write a letter to a friend. **6.** to produce as author or composer. **7.** to trace significant characters on, or mark or cover with writing. **8.** to impress the marks or indications of: honesty is written in his face. —v.i. **9.** to trace or form characters, words, etc., with a pen, pencil, or other instrument or means, or as a pen or the like does. **10.** to act as a clerk, amanuensis, or the like. **11.** to express ideas in writing. **12.** to write a letter or letters, or communicate by letter. **13.** to compose or work as a writer or author. **14.** Some special verb phrases are:

write down, 1. to set down in writing. **2.** to write in depreciation of; injure by writing against.

write off, to cancel, as an entry in an account, as by an offsetting entry.

write out, 1. to put into writing. **2.** to write in full form. **3.** to exhaust the capacity or resources of by excessive writing: a author who has written himself out.

write up, 1. to write out in full or in detail. **2.** to bring up to date or to the latest fact or transaction in writing. **3.** to present to public notice in a written description or account. **4.** to commend to the public by a favorable written description or account. **5.** Accounting. to make an excessive valuation of (an asset). [ME; OE writan, c G reissen tear, draw, akin to Icel. rita write]

write-in (rīt'ĭn'), adj. Colloq. filled in by hand, instead of being printed (esp. referring to a vote cast for a name, etc., not on the regular ballot but added by the individual voter). —**write′-in′**, *n.*

writ·er (rī′tər), *n.* **1.** one who expresses ideas in writing. **2.** one engaged in literary work. **3.** one who writes; a penman. **4.** one whose occupation is writing, as a clerk or amanuensis. **5.** a manual for teaching how to write: *a letterwriter.* **6.** *Scot.* a lawyer or solicitor.

writer's cramp, *Pathol.* spasmodic contractions of the muscles of the thumb and forefinger during writing, sometimes associated with pain.

write-up (rīt′ŭp′), *n. Colloq.* **1.** a written description or account, as in a newspaper or magazine. **2.** *Finance, U.S.* an illegally excessive statement of corporate assets.

writhe (rīᵺ), *v.,* **writhed; writhed** or *(Obs. except Poetic)* **writhen; writhing;** *n.* —*v.t.* **1.** to twist the body about, or squirm, as in pain, violent effort, etc. **2.** to shrink mentally, as in acute discomfort. —*v.t.* **3.** to twist or bend out of shape or position; distort; contort. **4.** to twist (oneself, the body, etc.) about, as in pain. —*n.* **5.** a writhing movement; a twisting of the body, as in pain. [ME; OE *wrīthan* twist, wind, c. Icel. *rīdha* knit, twist] —**with′er,** *n.*

writh·en (rīᵺ′ən), *adj. Obs. exc. Poetic.* twisted.

writ·ing (rī′tYng), *n.* **1.** act of one who or that which writes. **2.** state of being written; written form: *to commit one's thoughts to writing.* **3.** that which is written; characters or matter written with a pen or the like. **4.** such characters or matter with respect to style, kind, quality, etc. **5.** an inscription. **6.** a letter. **7.** any written (or, sometimes, as in law, any printed) paper, document, or the like. **8.** literary matter or work, esp. with respect to style, kind, quality, etc. **9.** a literary composition or production.

writing desk, 1. a piece of furniture with a surface for writing upon, usually with drawers and pigeonholes to hold writing materials, etc. **2.** a portable case for holding writing materials and affording, when opened, a surface for writing upon.

writ of assistance, *Amer. Hist.* a writ issued by a superior colonial court authorizing officers of the crown to summon aid and enter and search any premises.

writ of execution, writ¹ (def. 1).

writ of prohibition, *Law.* a command by a higher court that a lower court shall not exercise jurisdiction in a particular case.

writ of right, 1. *Eng. Law.* one of two writs issued by a manorial court in a dispute between feudal tenants as to ownership or extent of a freehold. **2.** *U.S.* a similar writ, now supplanted by ejectment actions.

writ·ten (rĭt′ən), *v.* pp. of **write.**

Wroc·law (vrôts′läf), *n.* Polish name of **Breslau.**

wrong (rông, rŏng), *adj.* **1.** not in accordance with what is morally right or good. **2.** deviating from truth or fact; erroneous. **3.** not correct in action, judgment, opinion, method, etc., as a person; in error. **4.** not proper, or not in accordance with requirements: *the wrong way to hold a golf club.* **5.** out of order, awry, or amiss: *something is wrong with the machine.* **6.** not suitable or appropriate: *to say the wrong thing.* **7.** that should be worn or kept inward or under. —*n.* **8.** that which is wrong, or not in accordance with morality, goodness, justice, truth, or the like; evil. **9.** state of being wrong, as in action, judgment, or opinion. **10.** *Law.* **a.** an invasion of right, to the damage of another person. **b.** a tort. —*adv.* **11.** in a wrong manner; not rightly; awry or amiss. —*v.t.* **12.** to do wrong to; treat unfairly or unjustly; injure or harm. **13.** to impute evil to unjustly. [ME; OE *wrang,* t. Scand.; cf. Icel. *rangr* awry, c. D *wrang* acid, tart; akin to WRING] —**wrong′er,** *n.* —**wrong′ly,** *adv.* —**wrong′ness,** *n.* —**Syn. 1.** bad, evil, wicked, sinful, immoral, iniquitous, reprehensible, unjust, crooked. **2.** inaccurate, incorrect, false, untrue, mistaken. **6.** improper, unsuitable. **8.** misdoing, wickedness, sin, vice. **12.** maltreat, abuse, oppress, cheat, defraud, dishonor.

wrong·do·er (rông′do͞o′ər, rŏng′-), *n.* one who does wrong.

wrong·do·ing (rông′do͞o′Yng, rŏng′-), *n.* blameworthy action; evil behavior.

wrong font, *Printing.* the improper font, or size and style, for its place. *Abbr.:* w.f. or wf

wrong·ful (rông′fəl, rŏng′-), *adj.* **1.** full of or characterized by wrong. **2.** having no legal right; unlawful. —**wrong′ful·ly,** *adv.* —**wrong′ful·ness,** *n.*

wrong-head·ed (rông′hĕd′Yd, rŏng′-), *adj.* wrong in judgment or opinion; misguided and stubborn; perverse. —**wrong′-head′ed·ly,** *adv.* —**wrong′-head′ed·ness,** *n.*

wrote (rōt), *v.* pt. of **write.**

wroth (rôth, rŏth *or, esp. Brit.,* rōth), *adj.* angry; wrathful (used predicatively). Also, *Archaic,* **wrath.** [ME; OE *wrāth,* c. D *wreed* cruel, Icel. *reidhr* angry. See WRITHE]

wrought (rôt), *v.* **1.** a pt. and pp. of **work.** —*adj.* **2.** worked. **3.** elaborated. **4.** not rough or crude. **5.** produced or shaped by beating with a hammer, as iron or silver articles. —**Syn. 2.** See **worked.**

wrought iron, a comparatively pure form of iron (as that produced by puddling pig iron) which contains practically no carbon, and which is easily forged, welded, etc., and does not harden when suddenly cooled.

wrought-iron casting, 1. casting with mitis metal. **2.** a casting made from mitis metal.

wrought-up (rôt′ŭp′), *adj.* excited; perturbed.

wrung (rŭng), *v.* pt. and pp. of **wring.**

wry (rī), *adj.,* **wrier, wriest. 1.** produced by the distortion of the facial features: *a wry grin.* **2.** abnormally bent or turned to one side; twisted or crooked: *a wry nose.* **3.** devious in course or purpose; misdirected. **4.** distorted or perverted, as in meaning. [adj. use of v., ME *wrye(n),* OE *wrīgian* go forward, swerve] —**wry′ly,** *adv.* —**wry′ness,** *n.*

wry·neck (rī′nĕk′), *n.* **1.** *Colloq.* torticollis. **2.** *Colloq.* a person having torticollis. **3.** any of several small Old World scansorial birds constituting the subfamily *Jynginae,* allied to the woodpeckers, and notable for their peculiar manner of twisting the neck and head.

wry-necked (rī′nĕkt′), *adj.* afflicted with wryneck.

WSA, War Shipping Administration.

WSW, west-southwest. Also, **W.S.W.**

wt., weight.

Wu·chang (wo͞o′chäng′), *n.* a city in E China at the junction of the Han and Yangtze rivers: part of Wuhan. 205,000 (est. 1950).

Wu·han (wo͞o′hän′), *n.* the three cities of Hankow, Hanyang, and Wuchang in E China at the junction of the Han and Yangtze rivers, actually forming one extensive metropolitan area. 1,090,000 (1953). Also, **Han Cities.**

Wu·hsi·en (wo͞o′shY ĕn′), *n.* a city in E China, in Kiangsu province. 381,000 (est. 1950). Formerly, **Soochow.**

Wu·hu (wo͞o′ho͞o′), *n.* a city in E China, in Anhwei province: a port on the Yangtze river. 204,000 (est. 1950).

wul·fen·ite (wo͝ol′fə nīt′), *n.* a mineral consisting of lead molybdate, occurring usually in tabular crystals, and varying in color from grayish to bright-yellow or red.

Wul·fi·la (wo͝ol′fə lə), *n.* See **Ulfilas.**

Wundt (vo͝ont), *n.* **Wilhelm Max** (vYl′hĕlm mäks), 1832–1920, German physiologist and psychologist.

Wup·per·tal (vo͝op′ər täl′), *n.* a city in W West Germany, in the Ruhr: formed by the union of Barmen, Elberfeld, and smaller communities, 1929. 405,359 (est. 1955).

Würt·tem·berg (wûr′təm bûrg′; *Ger.* vyr′təm bĕrkн), *n.* a former state in SW West Germany: now a part of Baden-Württemberg.

Würz·burg (wûrts′bûrg; *Ger.* vyrts′bŏŏrkн), *n.* a city in West Germany, in NW Bavaria, on the Main river. 101,725 (est. 1955).

Wu·sih (wo͞o′sē′, -shē′), *n.* a city in eastern China, in Kiangsu province. ab. 200,000.

Wuth·er·ing Heights (wŭᵺ′ər Yng), a novel (1846) by Emily Brontë.

W.Va., West Virginia.

Wy., Wyoming.

Wy·an·dot (wī′ən dŏt′), *n.* **1.** an Indian of the former Huron tribe or confederacy. A few mixed-blood survivors now live in Oklahoma but the Huron language is extinct. **2.** an Iroquoian language.

Wy·an·dotte (wī′ən dŏt′), *n.* **1.** a city in SE Michigan, on the Detroit river. 43,519 (1960). **2.** one of an American breed of medium-sized domestic fowls, valuable for eggs and for the table. **3.** Wyandot.

Wy·att (wī′ət), *n.* **Thomas,** 1503?–42, English diplomatist and poet. Also, **Wyat.**

wych-elm (wYch′ĕlm′), *n.* an elm, *Ulmus glabra,* of northern and western Europe. Also, **witch-elm.** [f. *wych* (ME *wyche,* OE *wice* wych-elm) + ELM]

Wych·er·ley (wYch′ər lY), *n.* **William,** c1640–1716, British dramatist.

wych-ha·zel (wYch′hā′zəl), *n.* witch hazel.

Wyc·liffe (wYk′lYf), *n.* **John,** 1320?–1384, English religious reformer, and translator of the Bible. Also, **Wyc′lif, Wickliffe, Wiclif.**

Wyc·lif·fite (wYk′lYfīt′), *adj.* **1.** of or pertaining to Wycliffe or the Wycliffites. —*n.* **2.** a follower of John Wycliffe; a Lollard. Also, **Wyc′lif·ite′.**

wyd·ah (wYd′ə), *n.* whidah bird.

wye (wī), *n., pl.* **wyes. 1.** the letter Y, or something having a similar shape. **2.** *Elect.* a form of three-phase circuit arrangement in which 3 line conductors are connected to terminals of 3 circuit elements, as represented by the 3 arms of a Y, the center connection becoming the so-called "neutral."

Wye (wī), *n.* a river flowing from central Wales through SW England into the Severn estuary. ab. 130 mi.

wye level, *Surrey.* an instrument consisting of a spirit level mounted under and parallel to a telescope which can be rotated in its supports (Y's) for adjustment.

Wyld (wīld), *n.* **Henry Cecil Kennedy,** 1870–1945, British lexicographer and linguist.

Wy·lie (wī′lY), *n.* **Elinor,** (Mrs. William Rose Benét) 1885–1928, U.S. poet and novelist.

Wyo., Wyoming.

Wy·o·ming (wī ō′mYng), *n.* a State in the NW United States. 330,066 pop. (1960); 97,914 sq. mi. *Cap.:* Cheyenne. *Abbr.:* Wyo. or Wy. —**Wy·o·ming·ite** (wī ō′mYng ī′t′), *n.*

Wyoming Valley, a valley of the Susquehanna river, in NE Pennsylvania: Indian massacre, 1778.

wy·vern (wī′vərn), *n. Her.* wivern.

X

X, x (ĕks), *n.*, *pl.* **X's** or **Xs, x's** or **xs. 1.** the 24th letter of the English alphabet. **2.** *Math.* a symbol for an unknown quantity or a variable. **3.** a term often used to designate a person, thing, agency, factor, or the like, whose true name is unknown or withheld. **4.** See **Roman numerals. 5.** *U.S.* a ten-dollar bill.

X, 1. Christ. **2.** Christian.

x, 1. abscissa. **2.** ex[1].

xanth-, var. of **xantho-,** before vowels, as in *xanthine.*

xan·thate (zăn′thāt), *n. Chem.* a salt or ester of xanthic acid. [f. XANTH- + -ATE[2]]

xan·the·in (zăn′thĭ ĭn), *n.* that part of the yellow coloring matter in yellow flowers which is soluble in water. Cf. **xanthin** (def. 1). [t. F: m. *xanthéine,* f. *xanth-* yellow + *-éine,* to distinguish it from *xanthine* XANTHIN]

xan·thic acid (zăn′thĭk), *Chem.* an unstable organic acid with the type formula ROCSSH, the methyl and ethyl esters of which are colorless, oily liquids with a penetrating smell. Its copper salts are bright yellow. [t. F: m. *xanthique.* See XANTH-, -IC]

xan·thin (zăn′thĭn), *n.* **1.** that part of the yellow coloring matter in yellow flowers which is insoluble. **2.** a yellow coloring matter in madder. [t. G. See XANTH-, -IN[2]]

xan·thine (zăn′thēn, -thĭn), *n. Chem.* a crystalline nitrogenous compound, $C_5H_4N_4O_2$, related to uric acid, found in urine, blood, and certain animal and vegetable tissues. [t. F. See XANTHO-, -INE[2]]

Xan·thip·pe (zăn tĭp′Y). *n.* **1.** the wife of Socrates, proverbial as a scold. **2.** a scolding or ill-tempered wife; a shrewish woman. Also, **Xan·tip·pe.**

xantho-, a word element meaning "yellow," as in *xanthochroid.* Also, **xanth-.** [t. Gk., comb. form of *xanthós*]

xan·tho·chroid (zăn′tho kroid′), *Ethnol.* —*adj.* **1.** belonging or pertaining to the light-complexioned or light-haired peoples of the white race. —*n.* **2.** one having xanthochroid characteristics. [der. *xanthochroi* yellow-pale ones, f. Gk.: *xanth-* XANTH- + *ōchroí* (pl. of *ōchrós* pale)]

xan·tho·phyll (zăn′tho fĭl), *n. Biochem.* a yellow vegetable pigment, $C_{40}H_{56}O_2$, occurring in grain or leaves; oxygenated derivatives of carotene hydrocarbons. Also, **xan′tho·phyl.** [t. F: m. *xanthophylle,* f. *xantho-* XANTHO- + m.s. Gk. *phýllon* leaf]

xan·tho·pro·te·ic acid (zăn′thō prō tē′Yk), *Chem.* a yellow substance of unknown structure formed by the action of nitric acid on proteins. [f. XANTHO- + PROTE(IN) + -IC]

xan·thous (zăn′thəs), *adj.* **1.** yellow. **2.** denoting or pertaining to the peoples with a yellow complexion (the Mongolians). [t. Gk: m. *zanthós* yellow]

Xan·thus (zăn′thəs), *n.* an ancient city of Lycia, in SW Asia Minor, near the mouth of the Xanthus river: valuable archaeological remains have been found in the ruins.

Xa·vi·er (zā′vY ər, zăv′Y-), *n.* St. Francis, (*Francisco Javier, "the Apostle of the Indies"*) 1506–52, Spanish Jesuit missionary, esp. in India and Japan. Also, **Zavier.**

X chromosome, *Biol.* the sex chromosome having major control in sex determination, often paired with an unlike or Y chromosome. In humans and most mammals the XX condition controls femaleness and XY maleness; in poultry and some insects the reverse is true, the female being the heterozygous sex. See **sex chromosome.**

x-cp., ex coupon.

x-div., ex dividend.

Xe, *Chem.* xenon.

xe·bec (zē′bĕk), *n.* a small three-masted vessel of the Mediterranean, formerly much used by corsairs, and now employed to some extent in commerce. Also, **zebec, zebeck.** [alter. of *chebec,* t. F, influenced by Sp. *xabeque,* now *jabeque,* t. It.: m. *sciabecco,* ult. t. Ar.: m. *sabbāk*]

Xebec

xe·ni·a (zē′nĭ′ə), *n. Bot.* the immediate influence or effect on the seed or fruit by the pollen other than on the embryo. [t. NL, t. Gk., der. *xénos* guest]

xeno-, a word element meaning "alien," "strange," "foreign," as in *xenogenesis.* [t. Gk., comb. form of *xénos,* n., stranger, guest and *xénos,* adj., foreign, alien]

Xe·noc·ra·tes (zə nŏk′rə tēz′), *n.* 396–314 B.C., Greek philosopher.

xen·o·di·ag·no·sis (zĕn′ə dĭ′əg nō′sĭs), *n. Med.* a method of diagnosing certain diseases having insects, ticks, etc., as vectors, by feeding uninfected vectors on the patient and later examining them for infection.

xen·o·gen·e·sis (zĕn′ə jĕn′ə sĭs), *n. Biol.* **1.** heterogenesis. **2.** the supposed generation of offspring completely and permanently different from the parent. Also, **xe·nog·e·ny** (zə nŏj′ə nY). —**xen·o·ge·net·ic** (zĕn′-ō jə nĕt′Yk), **xen·o·gen′ic,** *adj.*

xen·o·lith (zĕn′ə lĭth), *n. Petrog.* a rock fragment foreign to the igneous rock in which it is embedded.

xen·o·mor·phic (zĕn′ə môr′fYk), *adj. Petrog.* denoting or pertaining to a mineral constituent of a rock, which does not have its characteristic crystalline form, but one forced upon it by other constituents of the rock. —**xen′o·mor′phi·cal·ly,** *adv.*

xe·non (zē′nŏn, zĕn′ŏn), *n. Chem.* a heavy, colorless, chemically inactive, monatomic gaseous element present in the atmosphere, one volume in 170,000,000 volumes of air. *Symbol:* Xe; *at. wt.:* 131.3; *at. no.:* 54. [t. Gk., neut. of *xénos* strange]

Xe·noph·a·nes (zə nŏf′ə nēz′), *n.* c570–c480 B.C., Greek philosopher and poet.

xen·o·pho·bi·a (zĕn′ə fō′bY ə), *n.* fear or hatred of foreigners.

Xen·o·phon (zĕn′ə fən), c434–c355 B.C., Greek historian and writer.

Xe·res (shĕ′rĕs), *n.* former name of **Jerez.**

xero-, a word element meaning "dry," as in *xeroderma.* [comb. form repr. Gk. *xērós*]

xe·ro·der·ma (zYr′ō dûr′mə), *n. Pathol.* a disease in which the skin becomes dry and hard, and usually scaly.

xe·roph·i·lous (zY rŏf′ə ləs), *adj.* **1.** *Bot.* growing in or adapted to dry, esp. dry and hot, regions. **2.** *Zool.* living in dry situations. —**xe·roph′i·ly,** *n.*

xe·roph·thal·mi·a (zYr′ŏf thăl′mY ə), *n. Pathol.* abnormal dryness of the eyeball, usually due to long-continued conjunctivitis.

xe·ro·phyte (zY′rə fīt′), *n.* a plant adapted for growth under dry conditions. —**xe·ro·phyt·ic** (zY′rə fĭt′Yk), *adj.*

Xerx·es I (zûrk′sēz), *n.* c519–465 B.C., king of Persia, 486?–465 B.C., son of Darius I and Atossa.

xi (zī, sī; *Gk.* ksē), *n.* the fourteenth letter (Ξ, ξ, = English X, x) of the Greek alphabet.

Xin·gú (shYng goo′), *n.* a river flowing N through central Brazil into the Amazon. ab. 1300 mi.

x-int., ex interess.

-xion, a rare var. of **-tion,** as in *inflexion, flexion.*

xiph·i·ster·num (zYf′ə stûr′nəm), *n.*, *pl.* **-na** (-nə). *Anat., Zool.* the hindmost (or, in man, the lowermost) segment or division of the sternum. [f. *xiphi-* (comb. form repr. Gk. *xíphos* sword) + STERNUM]

xiph·oid (zYf′oid), *Anat., Zool.* —*adj.* **1.** sword-shaped; ensiform. —*n.* **2.** the xiphisternum. [t. Gk.: m. *xiphoīdēs,* t. Gk.: m. *xiphoeidēs* swordlike]

xiph·o·su·ran (zYf′ə soor′ən), *adj.* **1.** of or pertaining to the horseshoe crabs (order *Xiphosura*), in recent treatments not considered arachnids. —*n.* **2.** a member of the order *Xiphosura.* [f. NL *Xiphosūra* (irreg. f. Gk.: *xíphos* sword + *ourá* tail) + -AN]

Xmas, Christmas.

Xn., Christian. Also, **Xtian.**

Xnty., Christianity. Also, **Xty.**

XP (kī′rō′, kē′rō′), *n.* the Christian monogram made from the first two letters of the Greek word for Christ. [t. Gk., repr. chi and rho]

x-ray (ĕks′rā′), *n.* **1.** (*pl.*) electromagnetic radiation of extremely short wave length, approximately 1 angstrom, generated by sudden changes in the velocity of an electric charge, as in atomic transitions or when rapid cathode rays hit a target made of a heavy metal. These rays act on photographic plates, penetrate through solids, and ionize gases. **2.** one of the x-rays. **3.** a radiograph made by means of x-rays. See **roentgenogram.** —*v.t.* **4.** to examine by means of x-rays. **5.** to make an x-ray radiograph of. See **roentgenize. 6.** to treat with x-rays. Also, **X-ray.** [t. G: trans. of *x-strahlen,* so called because their nature was not known]

x-ray photograph, a radiograph made with x-rays.

x-ray therapy, *Med.* treatment of a disease, such as cancer, using controlled quantities of x-rays.

X-rts., ex rights.

Xt., Christ.

xyl-, var. of **xylo-,** before vowels, as in *xylem.*

xy·lan (zī′lăn), *n. Chem.* the pentosan occurring in

ăct, āble, dâre, ärt; ĕbb, ēqual; Yf, īce; hŏt, ōver, ôrder, oil, bŏŏk, ōōze, out; ŭp, ūse, ûrge; ə = a in alone; ch, chief; g, give; ng, ring; sh, shoe; th, thin; ŧh, that; zh, vision. See the full key on inside cover.

woody tissue which hydrolyzes to xylose, used as the source of furfural. [f. XYL- + -AN]

xy·lem (zī′lĕm), *n.* *Bot.* that part of a vascular bundle which consists of tracheids and immediately associated cells, forming the woody portion; woody tissue. See **phloem.** [f. XYL- + -em (t. Gk.: -*ēma* noun suffix)]

xy·lene (zī′lēn), *n.* *Chem.* any of three isomeric hydrocarbons, $C_6H_4(CH_3)_2$, of the benzene series, occurring as oily, colorless liquids obtained chiefly from coal tar, and used in making dyes, etc. Also, **xylol.**

xy·li·dine (zī′lə dēn′, -dǐn, zǐl′ə-), *n.* *Chem.* 1. any of six isomeric compounds, $C_8H_{11}N$, derivatives of xylene, which resemble aniline, used in dye manufacture. 2. an oily liquid consisting of a mixture of certain of these compounds, used commercially in making dyes. Also, **xy·li·din** (zī′lə dǐn, zǐl′ə-). [f. XYL(ENE) or XYL(IC) + -ID³ + -INE²]

xylo-, a word element meaning "wood," as in *xylograph.* Also, **xyl-.** [t. Gk., comb. form of *xýlon*]

xy·lo·graph (zī′lə grăf′, -gräf′), *n.* an engraving on wood. —**xy·log·ra·pher** (zī lŏg′rə fər), *n.*

xy·log·ra·phy (zī lŏg′rə fǐ), *n.* the art of engraving on wood, or of printing from such engravings. [t. F: m. *xylographie.* See XYLO-, GRAPHY] —**xy·lo·graph·ic** (zī′lə grăf′ĭk), **xy·lo·graph·i·cal,** *adj.*

xy·loid (zī′loid), *adj.* resembling wood; ligneous. [t. Gk.: m.s. *xyloeidēs,* f. *xylo-* XYLO- + -*eidēs* -oid]

xy·lol (zī′lŏl, -lŏl), *n.* xylene.

xy·lo·phage (zī′lə făj′), *n.* *Now Rare.* a wood-eating insect.

xy·loph·a·gous (zī lŏf′ə gəs), *adj.* 1. eating wood, as the larvae of certain insects. 2. perforating or destroying timber, as certain mollusks and crustaceans.

xy·lo·phone (zī′lə fōn′, zǐl′ə-), *n.* a musical instrument consisting of a graduated series of wooden bars, usually sounded by striking with small wooden hammers. —**xy·loph·o·nist** (zī lŏf′ə nǐst, zǐl′-), *n.*

Xylophone

xy·lose (zī′lōs), *n.* *Chem.* a colorless crystalline aldopentose, $C_5H_{10}O_5$, derived from xylan, straw, corn cobs, etc., by treating with heated dilute sulfuric acid, and dehydrating to furfural if stronger acid is used.

xy·lot·o·mous (zī lŏt′ə məs), *adj.* boring into or cutting wood, as certain insects.

xy·lot·o·my (zī lŏt′ə mǐ), *n.* the art of cutting sections of wood, as with a microtome, for microscopic examination. —**xy·lot·o·mist,** *n.*

xys·ter (zǐs′tər), *n.* a surgical instrument for scraping bones. [t. Gk.: scraping tool]

Y

Y, y (wī), *n., pl.* **Y's** or **Ys, y's** or **ys.** 1. the 25th letter of the English alphabet. 2. something resembling the letter Y in shape, as a forked clamp for holding drills, a forked support for the telescope, or a surveyor's level, etc. 3. (in medieval Roman numerals) 150.

y-, *Obs.* an inflective prefix used in past participles, as in *y-clept* "named."

-y¹, a suffix of adjectives meaning "characterized by or inclined to" the substance or action of the word or stem to which the suffix is attached, as in *juicy, dreamy, chilly.* Also, **-ey¹.** [OE -*ig.* Cf. G -*ig*]

-y², a diminutive suffix, often affectionate, common in names, as in *Billy, pussy, Whitey.* Also, **-ey², -ie.** [ME; often through Scot. influence]

-y³, a suffix forming action nouns from verbs, as in *inquiry,* also found in other abstract nouns, as *carpentry, infamy.* [repr. L -*ia,* -*ium,* Gk. -*ia,* -*eia,* -*ion,* F -*ie,* G -*ie*]

Y, *Chem.* yttrium.

y, *Math.* 1. an ordinate. (See **abscissa.**) 2. an unknown quantity.

Y., Young Men's Christian Association.

y., 1. yard; yards. 2. year; years.

yab·ber (yăb′ər), *n.* *Australia.* jabber. [t. native d. Australian: m. *yabba* language]

Ya·blo·noi Mountains (yä′blŏ noi′), a mountain range in the SE Soviet Union in Asia, E of Lake Baikal. Also, **Ya·blo·no·voi** (yä′blŏ nŏ voi′).

yacht (yŏt), *n.* 1. a vessel used for private cruising, racing, or other like noncommercial purposes. —*v.i.* 2. to sail, voyage, or race in a yacht. [earlier *yaught,* t. early mod. D: m. *jaght,* short for *jaghtschip* ship for chasing. Cf. G *jacht* hunting]

yacht·ing (yŏt′ǐng), *n.* the practice or sport of sailing or voyaging in a yacht.

yachts·man (yŏts′mən), *n., pl.* -men. one who owns or sails a yacht. —**yachts′man·ship′, yacht′man·ship′,** *n.* —**yachts′wom·an,** *n. fem.*

yack·e·ty-yack (yăk′ə tǐ yăk′), *n.* *U.S. Slang.* empty conversation. [imit.]

Yad·kin (yăd′kǐn), *n.* the name of that part of the Pee Dee river which is in North Carolina.

ya·ger (yä′gər), *n.* jaeger.

yah (yä, yâ), *interj.* an exclamation of impatience or derision.

Ya·ha·ta (yä′hä tä′), *n.* Yawata.

Ya·hoo (yä′hōo, yä′-, yä hōo′), *n.* 1. (in Swift's *Gulliver's Travels*) one of a race of brutes having the form of man and all his degrading passions, who are subject to the Houyhnhnms. 2. (*l.c.*) a rough, coarse, or uncouth person. [a coined name. See YAH]

Yah·weh (yä′wĕ), *n.* a name of God in the Hebrew text of the Old Testament, commonly transliterated Jehovah. See **Tetragrammaton.** Also, **Yah·ve, Yah·veh** (yä′vĕ), **Jahveh, Jahve.**

Yah·wism (yä′wǐz əm), *n.* 1. the religion of the ancient Hebrews, as based on the worship of Yahweh as the national deity. 2. the use of Yahweh as the name of God. Also, **Yah·vism** (yä′vǐz əm).

Yah·wist (yä′wǐst), *n.* the writer (or writers) of one of the major strands or sources of the Hexateuch, in which God is characteristically spoken of as Yahweh (or, erroneously, Jehovah) instead of Elohim. See **Elohist.** Also, **Yah·vist** (yä′vǐst).

Yah·wis·tic (yä wǐs′tǐk), *adj.* 1. of or pertaining to the Yahwist. 2. characterized by the use of Yahweh (Jehovah) instead of Elohim. Also, **Yah·vis·tic** (yä vǐs′tǐk).

Yaj·ur-Ve·da (yŭj′ŏor vä′də, -vē′də). See **Veda.**

yak (yăk), *n.* 1. the long-haired wild ox, *Poephagus grunniens,* of the Tibetan highlands. 2. a domesticated variety of the same species. [t. Tibetan: m. *gyag*]

Tibetan domesticated yak,
Poephagus grunniens
(5 ft. high at the shoulder)

Yak·i·ma (yăk′ə mə), *n.* a city in S Washington. 43,284 (1960).

Ya·kut (yä kōot′), *n.* a Turkic language of northeastern Siberia.

Ya·kutsk (yä kōotsk′), *n.* 1. Also, **Yakut.** an autonomous republic in the E Soviet Union in Asia. 400,544 pop. (1939); 1,170,200 sq. mi. 2. the capital of this republic, on the Lena river. 60,000 (est. 1948).

Yale (yāl), *n.* Elihu (ĕl′ə hū′), 1648–1721, British colonial official and patron of Yale college.

Yal·ta (yäl′tä), *n.* a seaport in the SW Soviet Union, on the Black Sea. 40,000 (est. 1948).

Yalta Conference, a meeting of Roosevelt, Churchill, and Stalin in Yalta (Feb. 4–12, 1945) to continue war and peace planning and esp. to agree upon voting procedure (**Yalta Formula**) in the proposed Security Council of the U.N.

Ya·lu (yä′l/Y′), *n.* a river forming part of the boundary between Manchuria and Korea, flowing SW to the Yellow Sea. ab. 300 mi.

yam (yăm), *n.* 1. the starchy, tuberous root of any of various climbing vines of the genus *Dioscorea,* much cultivated for food in the warmer regions of both hemispheres. 2. any of these plants. 3. *Southern U.S.* the sweet potato. 4. *Scot.* the common white potato. [t. Sp.: m. (*i*)*ñame;* ult. of African orig., t. Senegal: m. *nyami* eat]

Ya·ma·ga·ta (yä′mä gä′tä), *n.* Prince Aritomo (ä′rē tō′mō), 1838–1922, Japanese field marshal and statesman.

Ya·ma·shi·ta (yä′mä shē′tä), *n.* Tomoyuki (tō′mō yōo′kē), ("*the Tiger of Malaya*") 1885–1946, Japanese general.

ya·men (yä′mən), *n.* (in China, under the imperial system prior to 1912) the residence or office (often combined) of any official. [var. of *yamun,* t. Chinese, f. *ya* office + *mun* gate]

yam·mer (yăm′ər), *Colloq.* or *Dial.* —*v.i.* 1. to whine or complain. 2. to make an outcry or clamor; talk loudly and persistently. —*v.t.* 3. to utter or say in complaint.

—*n.* **4.** act of yammering. [ME *yamur,* var. of *yomer,* OE *gėōmrian* complain, akin to G *jammer* lamentation] —**yam′mer·er,** *n.*

Yang-kü (yäng′kü′), *n.* Tai-yüan.

Yang-tze (yäng′sē′; *Chin.* yäng′tsĕ′), *n.* a river flowing from the Tibetan plateau generally E through central China to the East China Sea. ab. 3200 mi. Also, **Yangtze-Kiang** (yäng′sē′kyäng′; *Chin.* yäng′tsĕ′jyäng′).

Ya·ni·na (yä′nēnä′), *n.* Serbian name of **Ioannina.** Also, **Yan′ni·na′.**

yank (yăngk), *Colloq.* —*v.t., v.i.* **1.** to pull with a sudden jerking motion; jerk. —*n.* **2.** a jerk. [orig. uncert.]

Yank (yăngk), *n., adj. Slang.* Yankee.

Yan·kee (yăng′kĭ), *n.* **1.** a native or inhabitant of New England. **2.** a native or inhabitant of a Northern State. **3.** a native or inhabitant of the U.S. **4.** a Federal soldier in the American Civil War. —*adj.* **5.** of, pertaining to, or characteristic of the Yankees. [? back formation from D *Jan Kees* John Cheese, nickname (mistaken for plural)]

Yan·kee·dom (yăng′kĭ dəm), *n.* **1.** the region inhabited by the Yankees. **2.** Yankees collectively.

Yankee Doo·dle (dōō′dəl), a British song (about 1755), taken over by the American troops during the Revolutionary War.

Yan·kee·ism (yăng′kĭ ĭz′əm), *n.* **1.** Yankee character or characteristics. **2.** a Yankee peculiarity, as of speech.

Ya·oun·dé (yä ŏōn′dā′), *n.* the capital of Cameroun in W Africa. 53,833 (1957). Also **Yaunde.**

yap (yăp), *v.,* **yapped, yapping,** *n. Chiefly Slang or Dial.* —*v.i.* **1.** to yelp; bark snappishly. **2.** to talk snappishly, noisily, or foolishly. —*v.t.* **3.** to utter by yapping. —*n.* **4.** a yelp; a snappish bark. **5.** snappish, noisy, or foolish talk. **6.** a peevish or noisy person. [imit.]

Yap (yăp, yäp), *n.* one of the Caroline Islands, in the W Pacific: U.S. cable station. 5108 pop. including adjacent islands (est. 1955); 83 sq. mi.

ya·pok (yə pŏk′), *n.* a small South and Central American aquatic opposum, *Chironectes variegatus* (or *minimus*), with webbed hind feet and variegated fur.

yapp (yăp), *adj.* **1.** designating or pertaining to a style of bookbinding in limp leather or the like with projecting flaps overlapping the edges of the pages, used esp. on Bibles. —*n.* **2.** yapp binding.

Ya·pu·rá (yä′pōō rä′), *n.* Japurá.

Ya·qui (yä′kē), *n.* **1.** (*pl.*) an important division of the Cahita (Piman) Indians, in Sonora, Mexico, named for the river on which they formerly lived. **2.** a member of this tribe. **3.** a river in NW Mexico, flowing into the Gulf of California.

yar·bor·ough (yär′bŭr′ō *or, esp. Brit.,* -bərə), *n. Whist, Bridge.* a hand none of the cards of which are higher than a nine.

yard[1] (yärd), *n.* **1.** a common unit of linear measure in English speaking countries, equal to 3 ft. or 36 in., and equivalent to 0.9144 meter. **2.** *Naut.* a long cylindrical spar with a taper toward each end, slung crosswise to a mast and suspending a square sail, lateen sail, etc. [ME *yerd(e),* OE *gerd* (Anglian), c. D *gard,* G *gerte* rod]

yard[2] (yärd), *n.* **1.** a piece of enclosed ground of small or moderate size adjoining or surrounding a house or other building, or surrounded by it. **2.** a piece of enclosed ground for use as a garden, for animals, or for some other purpose. **3.** an enclosure within which any work or business is carried on: *a brickyard, a navy yard.* **4.** *Railroads.* a system of parallel tracks, crossovers, switches, etc., where cars are switched and made up into trains, and where cars, locomotives, and other rolling stock are kept when not in use or awaiting repairs. **5.** the winter pasture or browsing ground of moose and deer. **6.** the **Yard,** *Brit.* Scotland Yard. —*v.t.* **7.** to put into or enclose in a yard. [ME *yerd,* OE *geard* enclosure, c. D *gaard* garden, Icel. *gardhr* yard, Goth. *gards* house]

yard·age[1] (yär′dĭj), *n.* measurement, or the amount measured, in yards. [f. YARD[1] + -AGE]

yard·age[2] (yär′dĭj), *n.* **1.** the use of a yard or enclosure, as in lading or unlading cattle, etc., at a railroad station. **2.** the charge for such use. [f. YARD[2] + -AGE]

yard·arm (yärd′ärm′), *n. Naut.* either end of a yard of a square sail.

yard grass, a coarse annual grass, *Eleusine indica,* of the Old World, common in dooryards and fields.

yard·mas·ter (yärd′măs′tər, -mäs′-), *n.* a man employed to superintend a terminal yard of a railway.

yard·stick (yärd′stĭk′), *n.* **1.** a stick a yard long, commonly marked with subdivisions, used to measure with. **2.** any standard of measurement.

yare (yâr), *adj. Archaic or Dial.* **1.** ready or prepared. **2.** prompt; brisk or quick. [ME; OE *gearu, gearo,* c. D *gaar,* G *gar* done, dressed (as meat)] —**yare′ly,** *adv.*

Yar·kand (yär′känd′), *n.* former name for **Soche.**

Yar·mouth (yär′məth), *n.* **1.** a seaport in southeast-

---

ern Canada, in southwestern Nova Scotia: summer resort. 8106 (1951). **2. Great. See Great Yarmouth.**

yarn (yärn), *n.* **1.** thread made by twisting fibers, as cotton or wool, and used for knitting and weaving. **2.** thread made from manufactured filaments, as rayon and nylon, where spinning is unnecessary. **3.** the thread, in the form of a loosely twisted aggregate of fibers, as of hemp, of which rope is made (**rope yarn**). **4.** *Colloq.* a story or tale of adventure, esp. one fabricated by the teller as he relates it. —*v.i.* **5.** *Colloq.* to spin a yarn; tell stories. [ME; OE *gearn,* c. G *garn;* akin to Icel. *görn* gut]

yarn-dyed (yärn′dīd′), *adj.* (of fabrics) woven from yarns previously dyed.

Ya·ro·slavl (yä rŏ släv′l), *n.* a city in the central Soviet Union in Europe, on the Volga. 374,000 (est. 1956).

Yar·row (yăr′ō), *n.* a river in SE Scotland, flowing into the Tweed: eulogized in Wordsworth's poetry. 14 mi.

yar·row (yăr′ō), *n.* **1.** an asteraceous plant, *Achillea millefolium,* of Europe and America, with finely divided leaves and whitish flowers, sometimes used in medicine as a tonic and astringent; milfoil. **2.** any of various other plants of the genus *Achillea.* Cf. **sneezewort.** [ME *yarowe, yarwe,* OE *gearwe,* c. G *garbe*]

yash·mak (yäsh mäk′, yäsh′mäk), *n.* the veil worn by Moslem women in public. Also, **yash·mac′.** [t. Ar.]

yat·a·ghan (yăt′əgän′, -gən; *Turk.* yä′tä gän′), *n.* a Turkish saber with recurved blade, peculiar in having an eared pommel and in lacking a guard. Also, **ataghan, yat′a·gan′.** [t. Turk.]

ya·ta·ta (yä′tə tä′), *n. U.S. Slang.* empty conversation. [imit.]

yauld (yôd, yäd, yäld), *adj. Scot.* supple; active.

Yaun·de (youn′dĕ), *n.* Yaoundé.

yaup (yôp, yäp), *v.i., n. Colloq. or Dial.* yawp. —**yaup′-er,** *n.*

yau·pon (yô′pən), *n.* a shrub or small tree, *Ilex vomitoria,* a species of holly, of the southern U.S., with leaves which are sometimes used as a substitute for tea.

yaw (yô), *v.i.* **1.** to deviate temporarily from the straight course, as a vessel. **2.** (of an aircraft) to have a motion about its vertical axis. —*v.t.* **3.** to cause to yaw. —*n.* **4.** a movement of deviation from the direct course, as of a vessel. **5.** a motion of an aircraft about its vertical axis. **6.** an angle (to the right or left) between the direction of progress of an aircraft and its (vertical and longitudinal) plane of symmetry. [orig. uncert.]

Ya·wa·ta (yä′wä tä′), *n.* a city in SW Japan, on Kyushu island. 210,051 (1951). Also, **Yahata.**

yawl[1] (yôl), *n.* **1.** a ship's small boat, manned by four or six oarsmen. **2.** a fore-and-aft-rigged vessel with a large mainmast forward and a much smaller mast set far aft, usually abaft the rudder post. Cf. **ketch.** [t. D: m. *jol* kind of boat; orig. unknown]

yawl[2] (yôl), *n., v.i. Colloq. or Dial.* yowl; howl. [akin to YOWL]

Yawl (def. 2)

yawn (yôn), *v.i.* **1.** to open the mouth involuntarily with a prolonged, deep inspiration, as from drowsiness or weariness. **2.** to open wide like a mouth. **3.** to extend or stretch wide, as an open (and usually deep) space. —*v.t.* **4.** to say with a yawn. **5.** *Poetic.* to open wide, or lay open, as if by yawning. —*n.* **6.** act of yawning. **7.** an opening, open space, or chasm. [ME *yane, yone,* OE *geonian,* akin to OE *gānian, ginan,* G *gähnen*] —**yawn′er,** *n.* —**yawn′ing·ly,** *adv.*

yawp (yôp, yäp), *Colloq. or Dial.* —*v.i.* **1.** to utter a loud, harsh cry or sound; bawl. **2.** to talk noisily and foolishly. —*n.* **3.** a yawping cry. **4.** any harsh or raucous sound. **5.** a noisy, foolish utterance. Also, **yaup.** [imit.] —**yawp′er,** *n.*

yaws (yôz), *n. pl. Pathol.* frambesia.

Yaz·oo (yăz′ōō), *n.* a river flowing from N Mississippi into the Mississippi river at Vicksburg. ab. 300 mi.

Yb, *Chem.* ytterbium.

Y.B., yearbook.

Y chromosome, *Biol.* the mate of the X chromosome in one sex of species having differentiated sex chromosomes.

y-clad (ĭ klăd′), *v. Archaic.* pp. of clothe.

y-clept (ĭ klĕpt′), *pp. Archaic.* called; named; styled. Also, **y-cleped.** [ME; OE *geclypod,* pp. See CLEPE]

yd., yard; yards.

yds., yards.

ye[1] (yē; *unstressed* yĭ), *pron.* **1.** *Archaic.* plural of **thou: a.** used nominatively. **b.** used for the objective **you. c.** used for the nominative singular. **2.** a colloquial or provincial reduction of **you:** *how d'ye do?* [ME; OE *gē,* c. D *gij,* G *ihr,* Icel. *ēr,* Goth. *jus*]

ye[2] (t͟hē), *def. art.* an archaic spelling of **the**[1].

---

yea (yā), *adv.* **1.** yes (used in affirmation or assent). **2.** indeed or truly (used to introduce a sentence or clause). **3.** *Archaic.* not only so, but also (used in adding something which intensifies and amplifies). —*n.* **4.** an affirmation; an affirmative reply or vote. **5.** one who votes in the affirmative. [ME *ye, ya*, OE *gēa*, c. D, G, Icel. and Goth. *ja*]

yean (yēn), *v.t., v.i.* (of a sheep or goat) to bring forth (young). [ME *yene*, OE *geēanian* bring forth (young)]

yean·ling (yēn'lǐng), *n.* **1.** the young of a sheep or a goat; a lamb or a kid. —*adj.* **2.** just born; infant.

year (yĭr), *n.* **1.** a period of 365 or 366 days, divided into 12 calendar months, now reckoned as beginning Jan. 1 and ending Dec. 31 (**calendar year**). **2.** a period of approximately the same length in other calendars. **3.** a space of 12 calendar months reckoned from any point: *he left May 15, to be gone a year.* **4.** a period consisting of 12 lunar months (**lunar year**). **5.** (in scientific use) the time interval between one vernal equinox and the next, or the period of one complete apparent circuit of the ecliptic by the sun, being equal to about 365 days, 5 hours, 48 minutes, 46 seconds (**tropical year, solar year, astronomical year**). **6.** the true period of the earth's revolution round the sun; the time it takes for the apparent traveling of the sun from a given star back to it again, being about 20 minutes longer than the tropical year, which is affected by the precession of the equinoxes (**sidereal year**). **7.** the time in which any planet completes a revolution round the sun. **8.** a full round of the seasons. **9.** a period out of every 12 months, devoted to a certain pursuit, activity, or the like: *the college year.* **10.** *(pl.)* age. **11.** *(pl.)* old age: *a man of years.* **12.** *(pl.)* time, esp. a long time. **13. a year and a day,** a period specified as the limit of time in various legal matters, as in determining a right or a liability, to allow for a full year by any way of counting. [ME *yeer*, OE *gēar*, c. D *jaar*, G *jahr*, Icel. *ār*, Goth. *jēr*]

year·book (yĭr'bŏŏk'), *n.* a book published annually, containing information, statistics, etc., about the year.

year·ling (yĭr'lǐng, yûr'-), *n.* **1.** an animal one year old or in the second year of its age. **2.** *Horse Racing.* a horse one year old, dating from Jan. 1 of the year of foaling. —*adj.* **3.** a year old. **4.** of a year's duration. [f. YEAR + -LING¹. Cf. G *jährling*]

year·long (yĭr'lông', -lŏng'), *adj.* lasting for a year.

year·ly (yĭr'lĭ, yûr'-), *adj., adv., n., pl.* **-lies.** —*adj.* **1.** pertaining to a year, or to each year. **2.** done, made, happening, appearing, coming, etc., once a year, or every year. **3.** continuing for a year. **4.** lasting but a year. —*adv.* **5.** once a year; annually. —*n.* **6.** a publication appearing once a year.

yearn (yûrn), *v.i.* **1.** to have an earnest or strong desire; long. **2.** to be moved or attracted tenderly. [ME *yerne*, OE *giernan*, c. Icel. *girna*]

yearn·ing (yûr'nǐng), *n.* **1.** deep longing; esp. when tinged with tenderness or sadness. **2.** an instance of it. —**yearn'ing·ly,** *adv.* —Syn. 1. See desire.

yeast (yēst), *n.* **1.** a yellowish, somewhat viscid, semifluid substance consisting of the aggregated cells of certain minute fungi, which appears in saccharine liquids (fruit juices, malt worts, etc.), rising to the top as a froth (**top yeast** or **surface yeast**) or falling to the bottom as a sediment (**bottom yeast** or **sediment yeast**), employed to induce fermentation in the manufacture of alcoholic liquors, esp. beer, and as a leaven to render bread, etc., light and spongy, and also used in medicine. **2.** a commercial substance made of living yeast cells and some meallike material, used in raising dough for bread, etc. **3.** a yeast plant. **4.** spume or foam. **5.** ferment or agitation. —*v.i.* **6.** to ferment. **7.** to be covered with froth. [ME *yeest*, OE *gist*, c. G *gäscht, gischt*] —**yeast'-less,** *adj.* —**yeast'like',** *adj.*

yeast cake, living yeast cells compressed with a little starch into a small cake. In **dried yeast cake,** yeasts are inactive; in a **compressed yeast cake** they are active and the product is perishable.

yeast plant, any of the minute, unicellular ascomycetous fungi constituting the genus *Saccharomyces*, and related genera.

yeast·y (yēs'tǐ), *adj.* **1.** of, containing, or resembling yeast. **2.** frothy or foamy. **3.** trifling or frivolous.

Yeats (yāts), *n.* **William Butler,** 1865–1939, Irish poet, dramatist, and essayist: Nobel prize, 1923.

Yed·do (yĕd'dō'), *n.* former name of **Tokyo.** Also, **Ye'do'.**

yegg (yĕg), *n.* *U.S. Slang.* a criminal, esp. one who robs houses, safes, etc. Also, **yeggman.** [orig. obscure; ? var. of *yekk* beggar, a term once popular in California Chinatowns]

yegg·man (yĕg'mən), *n., pl.* **-men.** yegg.

Yeisk (ǎsk), *n.* Eisk.

yeld (yĕld), *adj.* *Scot.* (of a cow, etc.) **1.** barren. **2.** not giving milk. [ME; OE *gelde*, c. G *gelt*. Cf. GELD]

yelk (yĕlk), *n.* *Archaic or Dial.* yolk.

yell (yĕl), *v.i.* **1.** to cry out with a strong, loud, clear sound. **2.** to scream with pain, fright, etc. —*v.t.* **3.** to utter or tell by yelling. —*n.* **4.** a cry uttered by yelling. **5.** *U.S.* a cry or shout of fixed sounds or words, adopted and used by a particular college, etc. [ME *yelle*, OE *gellan, giellan*, c. G *gellen* resound] —**yell'er,** *n.*

yel·low (yĕl'ō), *adj.* **1.** of a bright color like that of butter, lemons, etc.; between green and orange in the spectrum. **2.** having the yellowish skin characteristic of Mongolians. **3.** denoting or pertaining to the Mongolian race. **4.** *U.S. Colloq.* having the yellowish skin characteristic of mulattoes or dark-skinned quadroons. **5.** of yellow or sallow complexion. **6.** *Slang.* cowardly; mean or contemptible. **7.** *Colloq.* (of newspapers, etc.) sensational, esp. morbidly or offensively sensational. **8.** jealous; envious. —*n.* **9.** a hue between green and orange in the spectrum. **10.** the yolk of an egg. **11.** a yellow pigment or dye. —*v.t., v.i.* **12.** to make or become yellow. [ME *yelou*, OE *geolu*, c. G *gelb*, L *helvus*] —**yel'low·ish,** *adj.* —**yel'low·ness,** *n.*

yellow avens, herb bennet.

yel·low·bird (yĕl'ō bûrd'), *n.* **1.** any of various yellow or golden birds, as the golden oriole of Europe. **2.** the American goldfinch. **3.** the yellow warbler.

yellow daisy, the common rudbeckia, *Rudbeckia hirta.*

yellow fever, *Pathol.* a dangerous, often fatal, infectious febrile disease of warm climates, due to a filterable virus transmitted by a mosquito, *Aëdes* (or *Stegomyia*) *calopus*, and characterized by jaundice, vomiting, hemorrhages, etc. Temporary immunization is possible.

yel·low-fin tuna (yĕl'ō fǐn'), an important Pacific food fish, *Neothunnus macropterus.*

yel·low-green (yĕl'ō grēn'), *n.* **1.** color about midway between green and yellow in the spectrum. —*adj.* **2.** of the color yellow-green.

yel·low-ham·mer (yĕl'ō hăm'ər), *n.* **1.** the common yellow bunting, *Emberiza citrinella*, of Europe, the male of which is marked with bright yellow. **2.** *Local, U.S.* the flicker, *Colaptes auratus.* [earlier *yelambre*, f. OE *geolu* YELLOW + *omer* kind of bird (? bunting); -h-? from obs. *yellow-ham*, repr. OE *geolu* YELLOW + *hama* covering (i.e. yellow-feathered bird)]

yellow jack, 1. the (yellow) flag of quarantine. **2.** yellow fever. **3.** any carangoid fish, esp. a Caribbean food fish, *Caranx bartholomaei.*

yellow jacket, any of several social wasps of the family *Vespidae*, having the body marked with bright yellow.

yellow jasmine. See jasmine. Also, **yellow jessamine.**

yellow journalism, the use of sensational reporting and conspicuous displays as a means of attracting readers to a newspaper or journal. —**yellow journal.**

yel·low·legs (yĕl'ō lĕgz'), *n. sing. and pl.* either of two American shorebirds, the **greater yellowlegs** or big tattler (*Totanus melanoleucus*) and the **lesser yellowlegs** or little tattler (*T. flavipes*).

yellow metal, 1. a yellow alloy consisting of approximately three parts of copper and two of zinc. **2.** gold.

yellow peril, 1. the alleged danger of a predominance of the yellow race, with its enormous numbers, over the white race and Western civilization generally. **2.** the yellow race, regarded as presenting such a danger.

yellow pine, 1. any common American pine with a notably strong yellowish wood, usually with needles in clusters of three. **2.** the wood of any such tree. **3.** the tulip tree, *Liriodendron tulipifera.*

yellow poplar, the tulip tree, *Liriodendron tulipifera.*

yellow race, the Mongolian or Mongoloid race.

Yellow River, Hwang Ho.

yel·lows (yĕl'ōz), *n.* **1.** *Bot.* one of various plant diseases such as **peach yellows, cabbage yellows,** and **aster yellows,** whose most prominent symptom is a loss of green pigment in the leaves. **2.** jaundice, esp. in animals. **3.** *Obs.* jealousy.

yellow sapphire, a transparent yellow variety of sapphire.

Yellow Sea, an arm of the Pacific N of the East China Sea, between China and Korea. Chinese, **Hwang Hai.**

yellow spot, *Anat.* a small, circular, yellowish area on the retina, opposite the pupil. See diag. under eye.

Yel·low·stone (yĕl'ō stōn'), *n.* a river flowing from NW Wyoming through Yellowstone Lake (20 mi. long; ab. 140 sq. mi.) in Yellowstone National Park, and NE through Montana into the Missouri river in W North Dakota: two falls; deep canyon. 671 mi.

Yellowstone National Park, a park in NW Wyoming and adjacent parts of Montana and Idaho: geysers, hot springs, falls, canyon. 3458 sq. mi.

yel·low·tail (yĕl'ō tāl'), *n., pl.* **-tails,** (*esp. collectively*) **-tail. 1.** a famous California game fish, *Seriola dorsalis.* **2.** a small West Indian snapper, *Ocyurus chrysurus.* **3.** any of several other fishes with a yellow caudal fin.

yel·low·throat (yĕl'ō thrōt'), *n.* any of several American ground-inhabiting warblers of the genus *Geothlypis*, having a yellow throat, esp. the so-called Maryland yellowthroat (*G. trichas*).

yellow warbler, a small American warbler, *Dendroica petechia*, the male of which has a bright-yellow plumage streaked with brown on the under parts.

yel·low·weed (yĕl'ō wēd'), *n.* **1.** *Local U.S.* any of certain coarse species of goldenrod. **2.** the European ragwort, *Senecio Jacobaea.*

yel·low·wood (yĕl'ō wŏŏd'), *n.* **1.** the hard, yellow wood of *Cladrastis lutea*, a fabaceous tree found locally in the southern U.S., which bears showy white flowers and yields a yellow dye. **2.** the tree. **3.** any of various other yellow woods, as that of *Schaefferia frutescens,*

---

b., blend of, blended; c., cognate with; d., dialect, dialectal; der., derived from; f., formed from; g., going back to; m., modification of; r., replacing; s., stem of; t., taken from; ?, perhaps. See the full key on inside cover.

a small tree of southern Florida and neighboring regions. 4. any of the trees yielding these woods.

yel·low·y (yĕl′ō ĭ), *adj.* somewhat yellow.

yelp (yĕlp), *v.i.* 1. to give a quick, sharp, shrill cry, as dogs, foxes, etc. 2. to call or cry out sharply. —*v.t.* 3. to utter or express by, or as by, yelps. —*n.* 4. a quick, sharp bark or cry. [ME *yelpe*, OE *gelpan* boast; akin to LG *galpen* croak] —**yelp′er**, *n.*

Yem·en (yĕm′ən), *n.* a republic in SW Arabia; formerly a member of United Arab States. 5,000,000 (est. 1960). ab. 75,000 sq. mi. *Cap.:* San'a.

yen[1] (yĕn), *n., pl.* **yen.** 1. the gold monetary unit of Japan, equal to 100 sen, or about 2⁷/₁₀ U.S. cents. 2. a silver coin of this value, formerly current. [t. Jap., t. Chinese: m. *yüan* a round thing, a dollar]

yen[2] (yĕn), *n., v.,* **yenned, yenning.** *Colloq.* —*n.* 1. desire; longing. —*v.i.* 2. to desire. [? alter. of YEARN]

Yen·an (yĕn′än′), *n.* a city in N China, in Shensi province: the capital of Communist China prior to the capture of the city by Nationalist forces, 1947.

Ye·ni·se·i (yĕ′nĭ sĕ′ĭ, -sā′), *n.* a river flowing from Tannu Tuva, in the S Soviet Union in Asia, N to the Arctic Ocean. ab. 2800 mi.

yeo·man (yō′mən), *n., pl.* **-men.** 1. a petty officer in the navy (in the U.S. navy, having chiefly clerical duties). 2. *Archaic or Hist.* a servant, attendant, or subordinate official in a royal or other great household. 3. *Archaic or Hist.* a subordinate or assistant, as of a sheriff or other official or in a craft or trade. 4. *Archaic or Hist.* one of a class of lesser freeholders (below the gentry) who cultivated their own land, early admitted in England to political rights. 5. *Brit.* an independent farmer, often praised for sturdiness and loyalty. [ME *yeman, yoman,* f. *ye, yo* (of uncert. orig.) + MAN]

yeo·man·ly (yō′mən lĭ), *adj.* 1. of the condition or rank of a yeoman. 2. pertaining to or befitting a yeoman. —*adv.* 3. like or as befits a yeoman.

yeoman of the (royal) guard, a member of the bodyguard of the English sovereign, instituted in 1485, which now consists of 100 men (with their officers), having purely ceremonial duties.

yeo·man·ry (yō′mən rĭ), *n.* 1. a British volunteer cavalry force, orig. composed largely of yeomen, which became part of the British Territorial Army. 2. yeomen collectively.

yeoman's service, good, useful, or substantial service. Also, **yeoman service.**

Yer·ba Bue·na (yâr′bə bwā′nə), an island in San Francisco Bay between Oakland and San Francisco, California: a 500-ft. two-story tunnel across this island connects the two spans of the San Francisco-Oakland bridge.

yes (yĕs), *adv., n., pl.* **yeses.** —*adv.* 1. a word used to express affirmation or assent or to mark the addition of something emphasizing and amplifying a previous statement. —*n.* 2. an affirmative reply. [ME; OE *gēse; appar.* f. *gēa* yes + *sī* be it]

yes man, *Colloq.* one who registers unequivocal agreement with his superior, without consideration.

yester-, 1. being, or belonging to, the day next before the present: *yesterevening, yesternight, yestermorning.* 2. being that preceding the present: *yesterweek.* Note: Also used occasionally in poetry as a separate word (quasi adjective): *yester sun.* [back formation from YESTERDAY]

yes·ter·day (yĕs′tər dĭ, -dā′), *adv.* 1. on the day preceding this day. 2. a short time ago. —*n.* 3. the day preceding this day. 4. time in the immediate past. —*adj.* 5. belonging or pertaining to the day before or to a time in the immediate past. [ME; OE *geostrandæg,* f. *geostran* (c. G *gestern* yesterday) + *dæg* day]

yes·tern (yĕs′tərn), *adj. Archaic.* yester.

yes·ter·year (yĕs′tər yĭr′), *adv., n. Chiefly Poetic.* last year.

yes·treen (yĕs trēn′), *n., adv. Scot. and Poetic.* contraction of *yesterevening.*

yet (yĕt), *adv.* 1. as soon as the present time: *don't go yet.* 2. up to a particular time, or thus far: *he had not yet come.* 3. in the time still remaining, or before all is done: *there is yet time.* 4. at this or that time, as previously: *he is here yet.* 5. in addition, or again: *yet once more.* 6. moreover: *he won't do it for you nor yet for me.* 7. even or still (with comparatives): *a yet milder tone.* 8. though the case be such, or nevertheless: *strange and yet true.* 9. as yet, up to the present time. —*conj.* 10. and yet, but yet, or nevertheless: *it is good, yet it could be improved.* [ME; OE *gīet(a),* c. MHG *ieze* yet, now (whence G *jetzt*)] —**Syn.** See **but**[1].

yew (ū), *n.* 1. an evergreen coniferous tree, of the genus *Taxus,* of moderate height, native of the Old World, western North America, and Japan, having a thick, dark foliage and a fine-grained elastic wood. 2. the wood of such a tree. 3. a bow for shooting, made of this wood. [ME *ew.* OE *īw, ēow,* c. G *eibe,* Icel. *ȳr*]

Yezd (yĕzd), *n.* city in central Iran. 50,000 (est. 1949).

Ye·zo (yĕ′zō), *n.* former name of Hokkaido.

Y·gerne (ĭ gârn′) *n.* Arthurian Romance. Igraine.

Ygg·dra·sil (ĭg′drə sĭl′, ȳg′-), *n. Scand. Myth.* the ash tree which binds earth, heaven, and hell. Also, **Igdrasil.**

YHVH. See **Tetragrammaton.** Also, **YHWH.**

Yid·dish (yĭd′ĭsh), *n.* 1. a language consisting of a group of closely similar High German dialects, with

vocabulary admixture from Hebrew and Slavic, written in Hebrew letters, spoken mainly by Jews in countries east of Germany and by Jewish emigrants from these regions, and now the official language of Biro-Bidjan, an autonomous Jewish region in the SE Soviet Union in Asia. —*adj.* 2. Jewish. [t. G: m. *jüdisch* Jewish]

yield (yēld), *v.t.* 1. to give forth or produce by a natural process or in return for cultivation. 2. to give as due or required; furnish or afford: *to yield obedience or thanks.* 3. to produce or furnish as payment, profit, or interest. 4. to give up, as to superior power or authority. 5. to give up or surrender (oneself) (often fol. by *up*). 6. to give up or over, relinquish, or resign. —*v.i.* 7. to give a return, as for labor expended; produce or bear. 8. to surrender or submit, as to superior power. 9. to give way to influence, entreaty, argument, or the like. 10. to give place or precedence (fol. by *to*). 11. to give way to force, pressure, etc., so as to move, bend, collapse, or the like. —*n.* 12. the action of yielding or producing. 13. that which is yielded. 14. the quantity or amount yielded. [ME *yelde(n),* OE *g(i)eldan* pay, c. G *gelten* be worth, apply to] —**yield′er**, *n.*

—**Syn.** 1. furnish, supply, render. 4. YIELD, SUBMIT, SURRENDER mean to give way or give up to someone or something. To YIELD is to concede under some degree of pressure, if not absolute compulsion, but not to cease opposition: *to yield ground to an enemy.* To SUBMIT is to give up more completely to authority, superior force, etc., and to cease opposition: *to submit to control.* To SURRENDER is to yield complete possession of, relinquish, and cease claim to: *to surrender a fortress, one's freedom, rights.* 13. produce, harvest, fruit. See **crop.** —**Ant.** 4. resist.

yield·ing (yēl′dĭng), *adj.* submissive or compliant. —**yield′ing·ly**, *adv.* —**yield′ing·ness**, *n.*

yill (yĭl), *n. Scot.* ale.

yin (yĭn), *adj., n., pron. Scot.* one.

Ying·kow (yĭng′kou′), *n.* a city in NE China, near the Gulf of Liaotung: the seaport of Newchwang, Manchuria. 159,000 (est. 1950). Often called New-chwang.

yip (yĭp), *v.i.,* **yipped, yipping.** *Colloq.* to bark sharply, as a small dog. [imit.]

yird (yûrd), *n., v.i. Scot.* earth.

-yl, a word element used in names of chemical radicals, as in *ethyl.* [comb. form repr. Gk. *hȳlē* wood, matter]

y·lang-y·lang (ē′läng ē′läng), *n.* 1. an aromatic tree, *Canangium odoratum* (or *Cananga odorata*), of the Philippines, Java, etc., bearing fragrant drooping flowers which yield a volatile oil used in perfumery. 2. the oil or perfume. Also, **ilang-ilang.**

Y.M.C.A., Young Men's Christian Association.

Y.M.H.A., Young Men's Hebrew Association.

Y·mir (ē′mĭr, ȳ′mĭr), *n. Scand. Myth.* a giant, the first created being, progenitor of the race.

yo·del (yō′dəl), *n., v.,* **-deled, -deling** or (*esp. Brit.*) **-delled, -delling,** *n.* —*v.t., v.i.* 1. to sing with frequent changes from the ordinary voice to falsetto and back again, in the manner of the Swiss and Tyrolean mountaineers. —*n.* 2. a song, refrain, etc., so sung. Also, **yodle.** [t. G: m.s. *jodeln*] —**yo′del·er;** *esp. Brit.,* **yo′del·ler,** *n.*

yo·dle (yō′dəl), *v.t., v.i.,* **-dled, -dling,** *n.* yodel. —**yo′dler,** *n.*

Yo·ga (yō′gə), *n.* (*also l.c.*) (in Hindu religious philosophy) the union of the human soul with the Universal Spirit; ascetic practice aiming to effect such union through the withdrawal of the senses from all external objects, concentration of the mind on some central truth, etc. [t. Hind., t. Skt.: lit., union; akin to YOKE]

yogh (yōкн), *n.* the name of the Middle English letter (ȝ), used to represent a voiced or voiceless fricative made against the roof of the mouth; the voiced fricative eventually became *y* or *w* according to whether it was palatal or velar; the voiceless fricative finally came to be written *gh* and this is kept in current spelling, though the old fricative has been lost (as in *light*) or has become an *f* (as in *tough*).

yo·gi (yō′gē), *n., pl.* **-gis** (-gēz). 1. one who practices the Yoga system. 2. the doctrine or practice of the yogis. [t. Hind., der. *yoga* YOGA]

yo·gurt (yō′gŏort), *n.* a prepared food of custardlike consistency, sometimes sweetened or flavored, made from milk that has been curdled by the action of cultures. Cf. **kumiss.** [t. Turk.: m. *yŏghurt*]

yo-heave-ho (yō′hēv′hō′), *interj.* a chant formerly shouted by sailors when heaving together.

yo-ho (yō hō′), *interj., v.,* **-hoed, -hoing.** —*interj.* 1. a call or shout to attract attention, accompany effort, etc. —*v.i.* 2. to shout "yo-ho!"

yoicks (yoiks), *interj. Chiefly Brit.* a cry used to urge on the hounds in fox hunting. [cf. HOICKS]

yoke (yōk), *n., v.,* **yoked, yoking.** —*n.* 1. a contrivance for joining together a pair of draft animals, esp. oxen, usually consisting of a crosspiece with two bow-shaped pieces (oxbow) beneath, one at each end, each bow enclosing the head of an animal. 2. a pair of draft animals fastened together by a yoke (*pl.,* after a numeral, **yokes** or **yoke**): *five yoke of oxen.* 3. something resembling a yoke or a bow of a yoke in form or use. 4. a frame fitting the neck and shoulders of a person, for carrying a pair of buckets or the like, one at each end. 5. *Mach.* a viselike

Yoke (def. 1)

piece gripping two parts firmly together. **6.** a crosshead attached to the upper piston of an opposed piston engine with rods to transmit power to the crankshaft. **7.** a crossbar on the head of a boat's rudder. **8.** a neck yoke for suspending the tongue of a vehicle. **9.** a shaped piece in a garment, fitted about or below the neck, shoulders, or about the hips, from which the rest of the garment hangs. **10.** an emblem or token of subjection, servitude, slavery, etc., as one under which prisoners of war were compelled to pass by the ancient Romans and others. **11.** something that couples or binds together, or a bond or tie. **12.** *Scot. and N. Eng.* the time during which a plowman and his team work at one stretch; a period of steady work. **13.** *Scot. and N. Eng.* a part of the working day. —*v.t.* **14.** to put a yoke on; join or couple by means of a yoke. **15.** to attach (a draft animal) to a plow or vehicle; harness a draft animal to (a plow or vehicle). **16.** to join, couple, link, or unite. **17.** *Rare.* to bring into subjection or servitude. —*v.i.* **18.** to be or become joined, linked, or united. [ME *yok*, OE *geoc*, c. D *juk*, G *joch*, Icel. *ok*, L *jugum*] —**yoke′less**, *adj.* —**Syn.** 2. See **pair**.

yoke·fel·low (yōk′fĕl′ō), *n.* **1.** an intimate associate; a partner. **2.** a spouse. Also, **yoke·mate** (yōk′māt′).

yo·kel (yō′kəl), *n.* **1.** a countryman or rustic; a country bumpkin. **2.** *N. Eng.* a plowboy. [orig. uncert.]

Yo·ko·ha·ma (yō′kə hä′mə; *Jap.* yô′kô hä′mä), *n.* a seaport in central Japan, on Tokyo Bay, Honshu island: destructive earthquake, 1923. 951,189 (1950).

Yo·ko·su·ka (yō′kə sōō′kə; *Jap.* yô′kô sōō′kä), *n.* a seaport in central Japan, on Tokyo Bay, Honshu island: naval base. 250,533 (1950).

Yo·kuts (yō′kŭts), *n., pl.* **-kuts.** **1.** a North American Indian linguistic stock, tentatively assigned to the larger Penutian family. **2.** (*pl.*) a North American Indian aggregation of small tribes speaking related dialects, and occupying the southern half of the Great Valley of California and the adjoining eastern foothill regions. Nearly all the Valley Yokuts tribes are extinct; some foothill groups remain.

yolk (yōk, yōlk), *n.* **1.** the yellow and principal substance of an egg, as distinguished from the white. **2.** *Biol.* that part of the contents of the egg of an animal which enters directly into the formation of the embryo (**formative yolk**, or **archiblast**), together with any material which nourishes the embryo during its formation (**nutritive yolk**, deutoplasm, or parablast): distinguished from a mass of albumen (the white of the egg) which may surround it, and from the membrane or shell enclosing the whole. **3.** the essential part; the inner core. **4.** a natural grease exuded from the skin of sheep. [ME *yolke, yelke,* OE *geolca,* der. *geolu* yellow] —**yolk′less,** *adj.* —**yolk′y,** *adj.*

Yom Kip·pur (yŏm kĭp′ər; *Heb.* yōm kĭp′ŏŏr), the Day of Atonement, an annual Jewish fast day observed on the tenth day of the month Tishri. See Lev. 16:29-34. [t. Heb: Day of Atonement]

yon (yŏn), *Archaic or Dial.* —*adj., adv.* **1.** yonder. —*pron.* **2.** that or those yonder. [ME; OE *geon,* akin to G *jener* that]

yond (yŏnd), *adv., adj. Archaic or Dial.* yonder. [ME; OE *geond,* c. D *ginds.* Cf. YON, YONDER]

yon·der (yŏn′dər), *adj.* **1.** being the more distant, or farther. **2.** being in that place or over there, or being that or those over there. —*adv.* **3.** at, in, or to that place (specified or more or less distant); over there. [ME; cf. Goth. *jaindre* there]

Yon·kers (yŏng′kərz), *n.* a city in SE New York, on the Hudson, near New York City. 190,634 (1960).

yore (yōr), *adv., adj. Archaic.* of old; years ago; long ago: now only in the phrase of *yore: the knights-errant of yore.* [ME; OE *geāra,* appar. der. *gēar* YEAR]

York (yôrk), *n.* **1.** English royal house, 1461-85. It comprised three kings: Edward IV, Edward V, and Richard III. **2. Edmund of Langley, 1st Duke of,** 1341-1402, son of Edward III of England. **3.** Yorkshire. **4.** Ancient, **Eboracum,** a city in NE England: the capital of Roman Britain; cathedral. 106,200 (est. 1956). **5.** a city in SE Pennsylvania: meeting place of the Continental Congress, 1777-78. 54,504 (1960). **6.** an estuary in E Virginia, emptying into Chesapeake bay. ab. 40 mi. **7. Cape,** a cape at the NE extremity of Australia.

york·er (yôr′kər), *n. Cricket.* a ball so bowled that it hits the ground immediately before the bat.

York·ist (yôr′kĭst), *n.* **1.** an adherent or member of the house of York, esp. in the Wars of the Roses. —*adj.* **2.** belonging or pertaining to the English royal house of York. **3.** of or pertaining to the Yorkists.

York·shire (yôrk′shĭr, -shər), *n.* a county in N England, including the administrative counties of East Riding, West Riding, and North Riding. 4,728,030 (1951); 6089 sq. mi. Also, **York** or **Yorks.**

Yorkshire pudding, a pudding made of batter (unsweetened), baked under meat, so as to catch the drippings.

Yorkshire terrier, a short-legged, long-bodied terrier with silky hair, golden-tan on the head and bluish or silver on the body.

Yorkshire terrier
(8 in. high at the shoulder)

York·town (yôrk′toun′), *n.* a town in SE Virginia: surrender of Cornwallis, 1781.

Yo·ru·ba (yō′rōō bä′), *n.* a member of a numerous West African coastal Negro nationality and linguistic stock. —**Yo′ru·ban,** *adj.*

Yo·ru·ba·land (yō′rōō bä land′), *n.* a former kingdom in W Africa, in the E part of the Slave Coast: now a region in SW Nigeria.

Yo·sem·i·te (yō sĕm′ə tĭ), *n.* a deep valley in E California, in the Sierra Nevada Mountains: a part of Yosemite National Park. ab. 7 mi. long.

Yosemite Falls, a series of falls in Yosemite National Park. Upper fall, 1436 ft. high; Middle Fall, 626 ft. high; Lower Fall, 320 ft. high. Total height (including rapids) 2526 ft.

Yosemite National Park, a national park in E California: waterfalls, sequoia trees, etc. 1162 sq. mi.

Yo·shi·hi·to (yō′shē hē′tô), *n.* 1879-1926, emperor of Japan, 1912-26 (son of Emperor Mutsuhito).

you (ū), *pron.; poss.* **your** or **yours,** *dat. and obj.* **you.** the ordinary pronoun of the second person, orig. the objective (plural) of *ye,* but now used regularly as either objective or nominative, and with either plural or singular meaning, but always, when used as subject, taking a plural verb. [ME; OE *ēow,* c. D *u*]

you'd (ūd), contraction of *you had* or *you would.*

you'll (ūl), contraction of *you will* or *you shall.*

young (yŭng), *adj.* **1.** being in the first or early stage of life, or growth; youthful; not old. **2.** having the appearance, freshness, vigor, or other qualities of youth. **3.** of or pertaining to youth: *in one's young days.* **4.** inexperienced. **5.** not far advanced in years in comparison with another or others. **6.** junior (applied to the younger of two persons of the same name). **7.** being in an early stage generally, as of existence, progress, operation, etc.; new; early. **8.** representing or advocating recent or progressive tendencies, policies, or the like. —*n.* **9.** young offspring. **10. with young,** pregnant. [ME *yong,* OE *geong,* c. G *jung*] —**young′ish,** *adj.* —**Syn.** 1. YOUNG, YOUTHFUL both refer to lack of years and to disabilities. YOUNG is the general word for that which is undeveloped, immature, and in process of growth: *a young colt, child, shoots of wheat.* YOUTHFUL has connotations suggesting the favorable characteristics of youth, such as vigor, enthusiasm, and hopefulness: *youthful sports, energy.* —**Ant.** 1. mature, old.

Young (yŭng), *n.* **1. Arthur Henry,** (*Art Young*) 1866-1943, U.S. cartoonist. **2. Brigham,** 1801-77, U.S. Mormon leader. **3. Edward,** 1683-1765, British poet. **4. Owen D.,** 1874-1962, U.S. industrialist and financier.

young·ber·ry (yŭng′bĕr′ĭ), *n., pl.* **-ries.** *Hort.* the large, dark-purple, sweet fruit of a trailing blackberry in the southwest U.S., a cross between several blackberries.

young blood, youthful people, ideas, practices, etc.

young-eyed (yŭng′īd′), *adj.* **1.** clear-eyed; brighteyed. **2.** having a youthful outlook; enthusiastic; fresh.

Young Italy, an important secret society in Italy, founded by Mazzini in 1831 to replace the Carbonari.

young·ling (yŭng′lĭng), *Archaic or Poetic.* —*n.* **1.** a young person. **2.** anything young, as a plant, etc. **3.** a novice; a beginner. —*adj.* **4.** young; youthful. [ME *yongling,* OE *geongling,* c. G *jüngling.* See YOUNG, -LING[1]]

Young Pretender, Charles Edward Stuart, grandson of James II of England, and son of James, the Old Pretender, whose landing in Scotland precipitated the rebellion of 1745. Also, **Young Chevalier.**

young·ster (yŭng′stər), *n.* **1.** a child. **2.** a young person. **3.** a young horse or other animal. **4.** (in the British navy) a midshipman of less than four years' standing. **5.** (in the U.S. Naval Academy) a midshipman in his second year.

Youngs·town (yŭngz′toun′), *n.* a city in NE Ohio. 166,689 (1960).

Young Turks, 1. a reforming group in Turkey, about 1856 to 1880. **2.** the controlling party in Turkey, 1908 to 1918.

youn·ker (yŭng′kər), *n.* **1.** *Archaic.* a youngster. **2.** *Obs.* a young gentleman or knight. [t. MD: m. *jonchere* (f. *jonc* young + *here* master), c. G *junker*]

your (yōor), *pron., adj.* the possessive form of you, ye, used before a noun. Cf. **yours.** [ME; OE *ēower* (gen. of *gē* YE), c. G *euer*]

you're (yōor), contraction of *you are.*

yours (yōorz), *pron.* form of *your* used predicatively or without a noun following.

your·self (yōor sĕlf′), *pron., pl.* **-selves** (-sĕlvz′). **1.** an emphatic appositive of *you* or *ye.* **2.** a substitute for reflexive *you.*

yours truly, 1. a conventional phrase used at the end of a letter. **2.** *Colloq.* I, myself, or me.

youth (ūth), *n., pl.* **youths** (ūths, ūthz), (*collectively*) **youth.** **1.** the condition of being young, or youngness. **2.** the appearance, freshness, vigor, spirit, etc. characteristic of one that is young. **3.** the time of being young; early life. **4.** the period of life from puberty to the attainment of full growth; adolescence. **5.** the first or early period of anything. **6.** young persons collectively. **7.** a young person, esp. a young man. [ME *youthe,* OE *geoguth,* c. G *jugend*] —**youth′less,** *adj.*

youth·ful (ūth′fəl), *adj.* **1.** characterized by youth; young. **2.** of, pertaining to, or befitting youth. **3.** having the appearance, freshness, vigor, etc., of youth. **4.** early in time. **5.** *Phys. Geog.* (of topographical features) having advanced in reduction of the land surface by erosion, etc., to a slight extent only. —**youth′ful·ly**, *adv.* —**youth′ful·ness**, *n.* —**Syn. 3.** See **young.**

you've (ūv), contraction of *you have.*

yow (you), *interj., n.* a shout of pain, dismay, etc.

yowl (youl), *v.i.* **1.** to utter a long distressful or dismal cry, as an animal or a person; howl. —*n.* **2.** a yowling cry; a howl. [ME *yowle*, earlier *yuhele*, appar. der. OE *gēoh-* in *gēohthu* care, sorrow]

yo·yo (yō′yō), *n., pl.* **-yos.** a toy, consisting of a round, flat-sided block of wood with a groove around the edge, in which a string is wound. The yoyo is spun out and reeled in by the string, one end of which remains attached to the child's finger.

Y·pres (ē′pr), *n.* a town in W Belgium: the scene of four battles, 1914–1918. 17,682 pop. Flemish, **Ieper.**

Y.P.S.C.E., Young People's Society of Christian Endeavor.

Yp·si·lan·ti (Yp′səlän′tY; *Gk.* ē′psē län′tē), *n.* **1.** Prince **Alexander,** 1792–1828, Greek patriot and revolutionary leader. **2.** his brother, **Demetrios** (dē mē′trē-ōs′), 1793–1832, Greek patriot and revolutionary leader. Also, **Yp·si·lan·tis, Yp·se·lan·tes** (ē′psē län′dēs)

Y·quem (ē kěm′), *n.* a fine, very rich, sweet white wine.

yr., **1.** year; years. **2.** your.

yrs., **1.** years. **2.** yours.

Y·ser (ē zěr′), *n.* a river flowing from N France through NW Belgium into the North Sea: battles, 1914–18. 55 mi.

Y·seult (Y sōōlt′), *n.* *Arthurian Romance.* Iseult.

Yt, *Chem.* yttrium.

Y.T., Yukon Territory.

yt·ter·bi·a (Y tûr′bY ə), *n.* *Chem.* ytterbium oxide, Yb₂O₃, which is white and forms colorless salts. [t. NL, f. *Ytterb*(y) in Sweden, where found + **-IA.** Cf. **ERBIUM, TERBIUM, TERBIA, YTTRIA**]

yt·ter·bite (Y tûr′bīt), *n.* gadolinite.

yt·ter·bi·um (Y tûr′bY əm), *n.* *Chem.* a rare metallic element found in the mineral gadolinite, and forming compounds resembling those of yttrium. *Symbol:* Yb; *at. wt.:* 173.04; *at. no.:* 70. [t. NL; f. **YTTERB(ITE)** + **-IUM**] —**yt·ter′bic,** *adj.*

yt·tri·a (Yt′rY ə), *n.* *Chem.* the sesquioxide of yttrium, Y₂O₃, a white powder. [NL, der. *Ytter*(by) in Sweden]

yt·trif·er·ous (Y trYf′ər əs), *adj.* yielding or containing yttrium.

yt·tri·um (Yt′rY əm), *n.* *Chem.* a rare trivalent metallic element, found in gadolinite and other minerals. *Symbol:* Y or Yt; *at.wt.:* 88.92; *at. no.:* 39; *sp. gr.:* 5.5. See **rare-earth elements.** [t. NL; f. **YTTR(IA)** + **-IUM**] —**yt′tric,** *adj.*

yttrium metals, *Chem.* See **rare-earth elements.**

yu·an (ū än′; *Chin.* yɣ än′), *n., pl.* **-an. 1.** the Chinese monetary unit, valued at $0.4611 in U.S. money. **2.** a silver coin having 23.9025 grams of silver, used in China. **3.** (in China) a department of government, or a council.

Yüan Shih-kai (yɣ än′ shē′kī′), 1859–1916, president of China, 1912–16.

Yu·ca·tán (ū′kə tän′; *Sp.* ū′kä tän′), *n.* **1.** a peninsula comprising parts of SE Mexico, N Guatemala, and British Honduras. **2.** a state in SE Mexico, in N Yucatán Peninsula. 539,440 (est. 1952); 14,868 sq. mi. *Cap.:* Mérida.

yuc·ca (yŭk′ə), *n.* any of the plants of the liliaceous genus *Yucca,* natives of warmer America, having pointed, usually rigid leaves, and whitish flowers in terminal central racemes. [t. NL, t. Sp.: m. *yuca,* t. Arawak]

Yü·en (ū ěn′; *Chin.* yɣ ěn′), *n.* a river in S China flowing NE to Tungting. ab. 1000 mi.

Yu·ga (yŏŏg′ə), *n.* (in Hindu use) **1.** an age of time. **2.** one of four ages distinguished in a period of the world's existence, the first being a golden age, with deterioration in those following. [t. Skt.: age, orig. yoke.]

Yucca.
Yucca gloriosa

Yugo., Yugoslavia.

Yu·go·slav (ū′gō släv′, -släv′), *n.* **1.** a southern Slav; a member of the southern group of Slavic peoples (the Serbs, Croats, Slavonians, Slovenes, etc., with or without the Bulgars), as distinguished from the western group (the Poles, Czechs, Slovaks, etc.) and the eastern (the Russians, with the Ruthenians). —*adj.* **2.** of the Yugoslavs. Also, **Jugoslav, Jugo-Slav.**

Yu·go·sla·vi·a (ū′gō slä′vY ə), *n.* a republic in S Europe: formed in 1918 as the **Kingdom of the Serbs, Croats, and Slovenes** from the kingdoms of Serbia and Montenegro and part of Austria-Hungary; renamed Yugoslavia, 1929. 17,799,000 pop. (est. 1956); 95,558 sq. mi. (1945). *Cap.:* Belgrade. Also, **Jugoslavia.** —**Yu′go·sla′vi·an,** *adj., n.* —**Yu′go·slav′ic,** *adj.*

Yu·kon (ū′kŏn), *n.* **1.** a river flowing from NW Canada generally W through central Alaska to the Bering Sea. ab. 2300 mi. **2.** a territory in NW Canada. 9000 (est. 1953); 207,076 sq. mi. *Cap.:* Whitehorse.

yule (ūl), *n.* Christmas, or the Christmas season. [ME *yole,* OE *gēol*(a) Christmastide, c. Icel. *jōl*]

yule log, a large log of wood which in olden times formed the backlog of the fire at Christmas. Also, **yule block, yule clog.**

yule·tide (ūl′tīd′), *n.* the Christmas season.

Yu·man (ū′mən), *n.* **1.** a North American Indian linguistic stock of the southwestern United States and northern Lower California. The stock includes Yuma (a specific tribe on the lower Colorado river), Mohave, etc. —*adj.* **2.** of or pertaining to the Yumas.

Yung·kia (yŏŏng′kiä′), *n.* a seaport in E China, in Chekiang province. 157,000 (1950). Formerly, **Wenchow.**

Yung·ning (yŏŏng′nYng′), *n.* a city in S China, on the Si river: the capital of Kwangsi province. 203,000 (est. 1950).

Yün·nan (yŏō′nän′; *Chin.* yɣn′nän′), *n.* **1.** a province in SW China. 17,472,737 pop. (1953); 162,342 sq. mi. *Cap.:* Kunming. **2.** Kunming.

Yur·ev (yŏŏr′yěf), *n.* Russian name of Tartu.

Yu·zov·ka (yŏŏ′zôf kä′), *n.* former name of **Donetsk.**

Y.W.C.A., Young Women's Christian Association.

Y.W.H.A., Young Women's Hebrew Association.

y·wis (Y wYs′), *adv.* *Obs.* iwis.

Z

Z, z (zē *or, esp. Brit.,* zěd; *old fash.* Yz′ərd), *n., pl.* **Z's or Zs, z's or zs. 1.** a consonant, the 26th letter of the English alphabet. See **izzard, zed** (def. 1). **2.** (in medieval Roman numerals) 2000.

Z, 1. *Chem.* atomic number. **2.** *Astron.* zenith distance. **3.** Also, **z.** Zone.

z, an unknown quantity.

Zab·rze (zäb′zhě), *n.* a city in SW Poland: formerly in Germany. 127,577 (est. 1954). German, **Hindenburg.**

Za·ca·te·cas (sä′kä tě′käs), *n.* **1.** a state in central Mexico. 687,730 (est. 1952); 28,125 sq. mi. **2.** the capital of this state. 24,254 (1950).

za·ca·tón (sä′kä tōn′), *n.* a grass, *Epicampes* (*Muhlenbergia*) *macroura,* used for papermaking. [t. Sp.: m. *zacatón,* der. *zacate* grass, hay, t. Mex.: *zacatl*]

Za·cyn·thos (zä′kěn thōs′), *n.* ancient name of **Zante** (def. 1).

Za·dar (zä′där), *n.* a seaport in W Yugoslavia, on the Dalmatian coast: formerly, with surrounding territory, it constituted an exclave of Italy. 14,847 (1953). Formerly, **Zara.**

zaf·fer (zăf′ər), *n.* an artificial mixture containing cobalt oxide and usually silica, used to produce a blue color in glass and other ceramic products (related to smalt). Also, **zaf′fre.** [t. F: m. *zafre,* ult. t. Ar.: m. *sufr* yellow copper, influenced by *za′farän* saffron. Cf. **SAPPHIRE**]

Zagh·lul Pa·sha (zäg′lōōl pä′shä), **Saad** (säd), 1860?–1927, prime minister of Egypt, 1924–27.

Za·greb (zä′grěb), *n.* a city in NW Yugoslavia: the capital of Croatia. 350,452 (1953). German, **Agram.**

zai·bat·su (zī′bät sōō′), *n. pl. or sing.* *Japanese.* the great industrial families of Japan.

Za·ma (zä′mə, zä′mä), *n.* an ancient town in N Africa, SW of Carthage: the Romans defeated Hannibal near here in the final battle of the second Punic War, 202 B.C.

Zam·be·zi (zäm bē′zY), *n.* a river in S Africa, flowing through W Angola, Rhodesia, and Mozambique into the Indian Ocean: Victoria Falls. ab. 2200 mi.

Zam·bi·a (zăm′bē ə, zäm′-), *n.* an independent state in S Africa: member of the Brit. Commonwealth; formerly a British protectorate and part of the Federation of Rhodesia and Nyasaland. 2,360,000 pop. (est. 1950); 288,130 sq. mi. *Cap.*: Lusaka.

Zam·bo·an·ga (säm/bō äng/gä), *n.* a seaport in the Philippine Islands, on SW Mindanao island. 124,710 (est. 1952).

za·mi·a (zā/mĭ ə), *n.* any of the plants constituting the cycadaceous genus *Zamia*, chiefly natives of tropical and subtropical America, having a short, tuberous stem and a crown of palmlike pinnate leaves. [NL, misreading of L *azānia* pine-nut (Pliny)]

za·min·dar (zə mēn/där/), *n.* 1. (in India) a native landlord, or a person possessing some property in the soil, responsible to the British government for the land tax on the soil under his jurisdiction. 2. (under Mogul rule) a farmer of revenue, required to pay a fixed sum on the district assigned to him. Also, **zemindar**. [t. Hind., t. Pers.]

Za·mo·ra y Tor·res (thä mô/rä ē tôr/rĕs). **Niceto Alcalá** (nē/thē/tō äl/kä lä/), 1877–1949, Spanish statesman: first president of Spanish Republic, 1931–1936.

Zanes·ville (zānz/vĭl), *n.* city in SE Ohio. 39,077(1960).

Zang·will (zăng/wĭl), *n.* **Israel** (ĭz/rī əl), 1864–1926, British novelist and dramatist.

Zan·te (zăn/tē), *n.* 1. Ancient, **Zacynthos.** one of the Ionian Islands, off the W coast of Greece. 38,062 pop. (1951); 157 sq. mi. 2. the capital of this island: a seaport. 11,209 (1951).

zan·thox·y·lum (zăn thŏk/sə ləm), *n.* the barks of various species of *Zanthoxylum*, esp. *Z. Americanum* and *Z. Clavaherculis*, used in medicine.

za·ny (zā/nĭ), *adj.*, **-nier, -niest,** *n., pl.* **-nies.** *—adj.* 1. extremely comical; clownish. *—n.* 2. an apish buffoon; clown. 3. a silly person; simpleton. [t. F: m. *zani*, t. d. It. (Venetian): m. *zanni* clown, lit., Johnny, c. It. *Giovanni* John]

Zan·zi·bar (zăn/zə bär/, zăn/zə bär/), *n.* 1. an island off the E coast of Africa, opposite Tanganyika. 165,253 pop. (1958); 640 sq. mi. 2. a former independent state comprising the islands of Zanzibar and Pemba and adjacent smaller islands, now part of Tanzania, formerly a British protectorate. 3. a seaport on Zanzibar island: the capital of Zanzibar. 57,923 (1958).

Za·pa·ta (sä pä/tä), *n.* **Emiliano** (ĕ/mē lyä/nō), 1877?–1919, Mexican political leader: revolutionist, 1911–16.

Za·po·rozh·e (zä/pō rôzh/ye), *n.* a city in the SW Soviet Union, on the Dnieper river. 381,000 (est. 1956). Formerly, **Aleksandrovsk.**

zap·ti·ah (zŭp tē/ä), *n.* a Turkish policeman. Also, **zap·ti·eh** (zŭp tē/ĕ). [t. Turk.: m. *ḍabtiyeh*]

Za·ra (zä/rä; *It.* dzä/rä), *n.* former name of **Zadar.**

Zar·a·thus·tra (zăr/ə thōōs/trə), *n.* Zoroaster. **—Zar·a·thus·tri·an** (zăr/ə thōōs/trĭ ən), *adj., n.*

za·re·ba (zə rē/bə), *n.* (in the Sudan and adjoining regions) a protective enclosure, as of thorn bushes. Also, **za·ree/ba.** [t. Ar.]

zarf (zärf), *n.* a cuplike holder, usually of ornamental metal, for a coffee cup without a handle, as used in the Levant. [t. Ar.: vessel]

Za·vi·er (zä/vĭ ər, zăv/ĭ-), *n.* See **Xavier,** St. Francis.

zax (zăks), *n.* an axlike tool for cutting roofing slate. [d. var. of *sax*, ME *sex*, OE *seax* knife]

Zarf

Ze·a (zē/ä), *n.* Keos.

zeal (zēl), *n.* ardor for a person, cause, or object; eager desire or endeavor; enthusiastic diligence. [ME *zele*, t. L: m. *zēlus*, t. Gk.: m. *zēlos*, der. *zéein* boil]

Zea·land (zē/lənd), *n.* the largest island of Denmark: Copenhagen is located here. 1,855,102 (est. 1954); 2709 sq. mi. Also, **Seeland.** Danish, **Sjaelland.**

zeal·ot (zĕl/ət), *n.* 1. one who displays zeal. 2. one carried away by excess of zeal. [t. LL: m.s. *zēlōtēs*, t. Gk., der. *zēlos* zeal]

zeal·ot·ry (zĕl/ətrĭ), *n.* undue or excessive zeal.

zeal·ous (zĕl/əs), *adj.* full of, characterized by, or due to zeal; ardently active, devoted, or diligent. **—zeal/ous·ly,** *adv.* **—zeal/ous·ness,** *n.*

ze·bec (zē/bĕk), *n.* xebec. Also, **ze/beck.**

Zeb·e·dee (zĕb/ə dē/), *n.* father of the apostles James and John (Matt. 4:21).

ze·bra (zē/brə), *n.* a wild, horselike animal, fully and regularly striped with dark bands on a light ground, or with alternating dark and light bands, occurring in three species, each with its own characteristic pattern of markings: the mountain zebra, *Equus zebra*, of southern Africa; the **common zebra,** *E. burchelli*, of southern, central, and eastern Africa; and **Grevy's zebra,** *E. grevyi*, of northeastern Africa. [t. Congolese] **—ze·brine** (zē/brĭn, -brĭn), *adj.*

Common zebra, *Equus burchelli* (4 ft. high at the shoulder)

zebra fish, a popular egg-laying aquarium fish, *Brachydanio rerio*, with zebralike stripes.

ze·bra·wood (zē/brə wŏŏd/), *n.* 1. the striped hardwood of a tropical American tree, *Connarus guianensis*, used for cabinetwork, etc. 2. the tree itself. 3. any of various similar woods or trees.

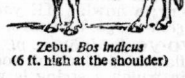

ze·bu (zē/bū), *n.* a bovine animal, *Bos indicus*, varying greatly in size and color in different breeds, but having a characteristic large hump (sometimes double) over the shoulders and a very large dewlap: widely domesticated in India, China, eastern Africa, etc. [t. F; orig. uncert.]

Zebu, *Bos indicus* (6 ft. high at the shoulder)

zec·chi·no (tsĕk kē/nō), *n., pl.* **-ni** (-nē). a sequin (def. 2). Also, **zech·in** (zĕk/ĭn).

Zech., Zechariah.

Zech·a·ri·ah (zĕk/ə rī/ə), *n.* 1. Hebrew prophet of the sixth century (fl. 520 B.C.), author of a book of the Old Testament. 2. the book itself.

zed (zĕd), *n.* 1. *Chiefly Brit.* a name for the letter z. 2. a Z-shaped bar. [ME, t. F: m. *zède*, t. L: m. *zēta*, t. Gk.]

zed·o·a·ry (zĕd/ō ĕr/ĭ), *n.* an East Indian drug consisting of the rhizome of either of two species of curcuma, *Curcuma zedoaria* or *C. aromatica*, used as a stimulant.

zee (zē), *n.* *Chiefly U.S.* a name for the letter z.

Zee·brug·ge (zē/brŏŏg/ə; *Flem.* zā/brœkh/ə), *n.* a seaport in NW Belgium, connected with Bruges by a ship canal: German submarine base in World War I. 3000 (1948).

Zee·land (zē/lənd; *Du.* zā/länt), *n.* a province in SW Netherlands, consisting almost entirely of islands. 274,244 pop. (est. 1954); 1041 sq. mi. *Cap.*: Middelburg.

Zee·man effect (zā/män). *Spectroscopy.* the splitting of spectral lines into components when the light source is operated in a magnetic field.

ze·in (zē/ĭn), *n. Biochem.* a protein found in corn, yielding on hydrolysis mainly glutamic acid and bucine. [f. NL *zē(a)* maize (in L, spelt) + -IN²]

Zeit·geist (tsīt/gīst/), *n. German.* the spirit of the time; general drift of thought or feeling characteristic of a particular period of time. [G: time-spirit]

Zem·strom (zĕm/strəm), *n. U.S.S.R.* an elective assembly of a local district or of a province, having the supervision and regulation of affairs within its territory.

zem·stvo (zĕm/stvō; *Russ.* zyĕm/stfô), *n., pl.* **-stvos** (-stvōz; *Russ.* -stfôz). *Russian Hist.* a county council founded by Alexander II in 1864? to replace the abolished authority of the squires; the core of the liberal movement from 1905–17.

Zen (zĕn), *n. Relig.* a Buddhist sect, popular in Japan (where it was introduced from China in the 12th century), advocating self-contemplation as the key to the understanding of the universe. [Jap., t. Chinese: m. *ch'an*, t. Pali: m. *jhāna*, Skt. *dhyāna* religious meditation]

ze·na·na (zĕ nä/nə), *n.* (in India) 1. that part of the house in which the women and girls of a family are secluded. 2. its occupants collectively. [t. Hind., t. Pers.: m. *zanāna*, der. *zan* woman]

Zend (zĕnd), *n.* 1. the translation and exposition, in a later form of Persian (Pahlavi), of the Zoroastrian Avesta. 2. *Rare.* Avestan. **—Zend·ic** (zĕn/dĭk), *adj.*

Zend-A·ves·ta (zĕnd/ə vĕs/tə), *n.* the Avesta, including the traditional exposition, the Zend. [t. Parsee: alter. of *Avesta -va-Zend* AVESTA with commentary]

Zeng·er (zĕng/ər; *Ger.* tsĕng/ər), *n.* **John Peter,** 1697–1746, American journalist, born in Germany.

ze·nith (zē/nĭth *or*, *esp. Brit.*, zĕn/ĭth), *n.* 1. the point of the celestial sphere vertically above any place or observer, and diametrically opposite to the nadir. 2. highest point or state; culmination. [ME *senyth*, t. ML: m. *cenit*, ult. t. Ar.: m. *semt ar-rās*, lit., way over the head]

zenith tube, *Astron.* a telescope mounted to point only at the zenith, used at the U.S. Naval and other modern observatories for taking time from the stars.

Ze·no of Ci·ti·um (zē/nō; sĭsh/ĭ əm), c336–c264 B.C., Greek philosopher and founder of the Stoic school.

Zeno of Elea, fl. c475 B.C., Greek philosopher.

Ze·no·bi·a (zə nō/bĭə), *n.* **Septimia** (sĕp tĭm/ĭə), died after A.D. 272, queen of Palmyra in Syria, A.D. 267–272.

ze·o·lite (zē/ə līt/), *n.* any of a group of hydrated silicates of aluminum with alkali metals, commonly occurring as secondary minerals in cavities in igneous rocks. [f. *zeo-* (comb. form repr. Gk. *zeein* boil) + -LITE] **—ze·o·lit·ic** (zē/ə lĭt/ĭk), *adj.*

Zeph·a·ni·ah (zĕf/ə nī/ə), *n.* 1. Hebrew prophet of the seventh century B.C. and author of an Old Testament book. 2. the book itself. *Abbr.*: Zeph.

zeph·yr (zĕf/ər), *n.* 1. a soft, mild breeze. 2. (*cap.*) *Poetic.* the west wind personified. 3. any of various things of fine, light quality, as a fabric, yarn, etc. [t. L: s. *zephyrus*, t. Gk.: m. *zéphyros*]

zephyr cloth, a light type of cassimere used for women's clothing.

Zeph·y·rus (zĕf/ə rəs), *n.* the west wind personified.

zephyr yarn, a soft worsted yarn used in embroidery and knitting. Also, **zephyr worsted.**

Zep·pe·lin (zĕp/əlĭn; *Ger.* tsĕp/ə lēn/), *n.* (*often l.c.*) a large dirigible balloon consisting of a long, cylindrical, covered framework containing compartments or cells filled with gas, and of various structures for holding the engines, passengers, etc. [named after F. von *Zeppelin*]

Zep·pe·lin (tsĕp'ə lēn'), *n.* **Ferdinand von** (fĕr'dY̆nänt' fən), **Count**, 1838–1917, German general and airship builder.

Zer·matt (tsĕr mät'), *n.* a village in S Switzerland, near the Matterhorn: resort. 5315 ft. high.

ze·ro (zY̆r'ō), *n., pl.* **-ros, -roes,** *v.,* **-roed, -roing.** —*n.* **1.** the figure or symbol 0, which stands for the absence of quantity in the Arabic notation for numbers; a cipher. **2.** the origin of any kind of measurement; line or point from which all divisions of a scale (as a thermometer) are measured in either a positive or a negative direction. **3.** naught or nothing. **4.** the lowest point or degree. **5.** *Gram.* a hypothetical affix or other alteration of an underlying form to derive a complex word, not present in the phonemic shape of the word but functioning in the same way as other affixes or alterations in the language; e.g., the plural of *deer* is formed by adding a zero ending (that is, by not adding anything). **6.** *Ordn.* a sight setting for both elevation and windage for any given range. —*v.t.* **7.** to adjust (any instrument or apparatus) to a zero point or to an arbitrary reading from which all other readings are to be measured. **8. zero in,** to adjust the sight settings of (a rifle) by calibrated firing on a standard range with no wind blowing. [t. It., t. Ar.: m. çifr CIPHER]

zero hour, 1. *Mil.* (esp. in World War I) the time set for the beginning of an attack. **2.** *Colloq.* the time at which any contemplated move is to begin.

zest (zĕst), *n.* **1.** anything added to impart flavor or cause relish. **2.** an agreeable or piquant flavor imparted. **3.** piquancy, interest, or charm. **4.** keen relish, hearty enjoyment, or gusto. —*v.t.* **5.** to give zest, relish, or piquancy to. [t. F: m. *zeste* orange or lemon peel (used for flavoring); orig. unknown] —**zest'less,** *adj.*

zest·ful (zĕst'fəl), *adj.* **1.** full of zest. **2.** characterized by keen relish or hearty enjoyment. —**zest'ful·ly,** *adv.* —**zest'ful·ness,** *n.*

ze·ta (zā'tə, zē'tə), *n.* the sixth letter (Z, ζ, = English Z, z) of the Greek alphabet.

Ze·thus (zē'thəs), *n.* *Gk. Legend.* See **Amphion.**

Zet·land (zĕt'lənd) *n.* Shetland Islands.

zeug·ma (zōōg'mə), *n.* *Gram., Rhet.* a figure in which a verb is associated with two subjects or objects, or an adjective with two nouns, although appropriate to but one of the two, as in "to wage war and peace." [t. NL, t. Gk.: yoking] —**zeug·mat·ic** (zōōg mat'Yk), *adj.*

Zeus (zōōs), *n.* chief god of the ancient Greeks, ruler of the heavens, identified by the Romans with Jupiter.

Zeux·is (zōōk'sY̆s), *n.* fl. c430–c400 B.C., Greek painter.

Zhda·nov (zhdä'nəf), *n.* a seaport in the SW Soviet Union, on the Sea of Azov. 273,000 (est. 1956).

Zhi·to·mir (zhY̆ tô'mY̆r), *n.* a city in the SW Soviet Union, in the Ukrainian Republic. 110,000 (est. 1948).

Zhu·kov (zhōō'kôf), *n.* **Grigori Konstantinovich** (grY̆ gô'rY̆ kôn'stän tē'nô vY̆ch), born 1895?, Russian general.

zib·el·ine (zY̆b'ə lĭn', -lY̆n), *adj.* **1.** of or pertaining to the sable. —*n.* **2.** the fur of the sable. **3.** a thick woolen cloth with a flattened hairy nap. Also, **zib'el·line'.** [t. F, t. It.: m. *zibellino*, t. ML: m. *sabellīnus*, der. *sabellum* sable, t. Slav.: m. *sobol.* Cf. SABLE]

zib·et (zY̆b'Y̆t), *n.* a civet, *Viverra zibetha*, of India, the Malay Peninsula, etc. [t. ML: m.s. *zibethum*. See CIVET]

Zieg·feld (zY̆g'fĕld), *n.* **Florenz** (flôr'ənz, flôr'-), 1867–1932, U.S. theatrical producer.

zig·gu·rat (zY̆g'ōō rät'), *n.* (among the ancient Babylonians and Assyrians) a temple (of Sumerian origin) in the form of a pyramidal tower consisting of a number of stories, and having about the outside a broad ascent winding round the structure and presenting the appearance of a series of terraces. Also, **zik·ku·rat, zik·u·rat** (zY̆k'ōō rät'). [t. Assyrian: m. *zigguratu* pinnacle]

zig·zag (zY̆g'zäg'), *n., adj., adv., v.,* **-zagged, -zagging.** —*n.* **1.** a line, course, or progression characterized by sharp turns first to one side and then to the other. **2.** one of a series of such turns, as in a line or path. —*adj.* **3.** proceeding or formed in a zigzag. —*adv.* **4.** with frequent sharp turns from side to side. —*v.t.* **5.** to make zigzag, as in form or course; move in a zigzag direction. —*v.i.* **6.** to proceed in a zigzag line or course. [t. F, t. G: m. *zickzack*, reduplication of *zacke* point, tooth]

Zigzag molding

Zil·pah (zY̆l'pə), *n.* *Bible.* mother of Gad and Asher by Jacob. Gen. 30:10–13.

Zim·ba·list (zY̆m'bə lY̆st; *Russ.* zY̆m bä lēst'), *n.* **Efrem** (ĕf'rəm; *Russ.* Y̆frĕm'), born 1889, Russian violinist, in U.S.

zinc (zY̆ngk), *n., v.,* **zincked, zincking** or **zinced** (zY̆ngkt), **zincing** (zY̆ngk'Y̆ng). —*n.* **1.** *Chem.* a bluish-white metallic element occurring combined as the sulfide, oxide, carbonate, silicate, etc., resembling magnesium in its chemical relations, and used in making galvanized iron, alloys such as brass and die-casting metal, etc., as an element in voltaic cells, and, when rolled out into sheets, as a protective covering for roofs, etc. *Symbol.:*

Zn; *at. wt.:* 65.38; *at. no.:* 30; *sp.gr.:* 7.14 at 20° C. **2.** a piece of this metal used as an element in a voltaic cell. —*v.t.* **3.** to coat or cover with zinc. [t. G: m. *zink*, orig. uncert.] —**zinc·ic** (zY̆ngk'Y̆k), **zinck'y,** *adj.*

zinc·ate (zY̆ngk'āt), *n.* *Chem.* a salt derived from H_2ZnO_2, the acid form of amphoteric zinc hydroxide.

zinc blende, sphalerite.

zinc·if·er·ous (zY̆ngk Y̆f'ər əs, zY̆n sY̆f'-), *adj.* yielding or containing zinc.

zinc·i·fy (zY̆ngk'ə fī'), *v.t.,* **-fied, -fying.** to cover or impregnate with zinc. —**zinc'i·fi·ca'tion,** *n.*

zinc·ite (zY̆ngk'īt), *n.* native zinc oxide, ZnO, a brittle deep-red to orange-yellow mineral, usually massive or granular, and an important ore of zinc.

zinck·en·ite (zY̆ng'kə nīt'), *n.* zinkenite.

zin·co·graph (zY̆ng'kə gräf', -gräf'), *n.* **1.** a zinc plate produced by zincography. **2.** a print from such a plate.

zin·cog·ra·phy (zY̆ng kŏg'rə fY̆), *n.* the art or process of producing a printing surface on a zinc plate, esp. of producing one in relief by etching away unprotected parts with acid. —**zin·cog'ra·pher,** *n.* —**zin·co·graph·ic** (zY̆ng'kə gräf'Y̆k), **zin'co·graph'i·cal,** *adj.*

zinc ointment, *Pharm.* an ointment composed of paraffin, white petroleum, and 20 percent of zinc oxide, employed to treat skin conditions.

zinc·ous (zY̆ngk'əs), *adj.* pertaining to zinc.

zinc oxide, *Chem.* a compound of zinc and oxygen, ZnO, having a mild antiseptic and astringent action, and used for the treatment of certain skin diseases.

zinc white, a white pigment consisting of zinc oxide, used in paints.

zing (zY̆ng), *n., v.i., interj.* a sharp singing sound. [imit.]

zin·ga·ra (tsēng'gä rä'), *n., pl.* **-re** (-rē'). *Italian.* a female Gypsy.

zin·ga·ro (tsēng'gä rō'), *n., pl.* **-ri** (-rē'). *Italian.* a Gypsy.

zin·gi·ber·a·ceous (zY̆n'jə bə rā'shəs), *adj.* belonging to the *Zingiberaceae*, or ginger family of plants. Also, **zin·zi·ber·a·ceous** (zY̆n'zə bə rā'shəs). [f. s. NL *zingiberāceae* (see GINGER) + -OUS]

zin·ken·ite (zY̆ng'kə nīt'), *n.* a steel-gray mineral with metallic luster, lead antimony sulfide ($PbSb_2S_4$). Also, **zinckenite.** [t. G: m. *zinkenit,* named after J.K.L. Zincken, Anhalt mining director]

zin·ni·a (zY̆n'Y̆ə), *n.* **1.** any of the plants constituting the composite genus Zinnia (*Crassina*), natives of Mexico and the southwestern U.S. **2.** one variety of zinnia, *Z. elegans,* the floral emblem of Indiana. [t. NL, named after J. G. Zinn, German botanist]

Zi·nov·iev (zY̆ nôf'yĕf), *n.* **Grigori Evseevich** (grY̆ gô'rY̆ ĕf sā'ə vY̆ch), 1883–1936, Russian Communist leader.

Zi·no·vievsk (zY̆ nô'vyĕfsk), *n.* former name of **Kirovograd.**

Zins·ser (zY̆n'sər), *n.* **Hans,** 1878–1940, U.S. bacteriologist.

Zi·on (zī'ən), *n.* **1.** a hill or mount of Jerusalem, the site of the Temple. **2.** the Israelites. **3.** the theocracy, or church of God. **4.** heaven as the final gathering place of true believers. Also, **Sion.** [ME and OE *Sion,* t. LL (Vulgate), t. Gk. (Septuagint), t. Heb.: m. *tsiyōn*]

Zi·on·ism (zī'ə nY̆z'əm), *n.* a modern plan or movement to colonize Hebrews in Palestine. See **Balfour Declaration.** —**Zi'on·ist,** *n., adj.* —**Zi'on·is'tic,** *adj.*

Zion National Park, a park in SW Utah, including a canyon (1500–2500 ft. deep) with beautiful coloring and unusual rock formations. 148 sq. mi.

zip (zY̆p), *n., v.,* **zipped, zipping.** *Colloq.* —*n.* **1.** a sudden, brief hissing sound, as of a bullet. **2.** energy or vim. —*v.i.* **3.** to make or move with a zip. **4.** to proceed with energy. —*v.t.* **5.** to fasten with a zipper. [imit.]

Zi·pan·gu (zY̆ päng'gōō), *n.* Marco Polo's name for Japan.

zip·per (zY̆p'ər), *n.* **1.** a fastener consisting of an interlocking device set along two edges to unite them (or separate them) when an attached piece sliding between them is pulled, and used in place of buttons, hooks, or the like, on clothing, bags, etc. **2.** a kind of rubber and fabric boot or overshoe fastened up the leg by a slide-fastening device. **3.** (*cap.*) a trademark for this boot.

zip·py (zY̆p'Y̆), *adj.,* **-pier, -piest.** *Colloq.* lively; smart.

zir·con (zûr'kŏn), *n.* a common mineral, zirconium silicate, ZrSiO4, occurring in square prismatic crystals or grains of various colors, usually opaque: used as a refractory when opaque and as a gem when transparent. [earlier *cicon,* var. of *jargon,* ? t. Pers.: m. *zargūn* gold-colored]

zir·con·ate (zûr'kə nāt'), *n.* a salt of the acid form of zirconium hydroxide.

zir·co·ni·a (zər kō'nY̆ə), *n.* *Chem.* an oxide of zirconium, ZrO2, of great value for its infusibility, and used in making glowers for Nernst lamps. [NL. See ZIRCON]

zir·co·ni·um (zər kō'nY̆ əm), *n.* *Chem.* a metallic element found combined in zircon, etc., resembling titanium chemically, used in steel metallurgy, as a scavenger, as a refractory, and as an opacifier in vitreous enamels. *Symbol:* Zr; *at. wt.:* 91.22; *at. no.:* 40; *sp. gr.:* 6.4 at 20°C. [NL. See ZIRCON] —**zir·con·ic** (zər kŏn'Y̆k), *adj.*

zir·co·nyl (zûr'kə nY̆l), *n.* *Chem.* containing the radical ZrO^{+2}.

Zis·ka (zY̆s'kə), *n.* **Jan** (yän), c1370–1424, Bohemian general, and leader of the followers of John Huss.

zith·er (zĭth′ər), *n.* a musical folk instrument consisting of a flat sounding box with numerous strings stretched over it, which is placed on a horizontal surface and played with a plectrum and the fingertips. [t. G, t. L: m. *cithara*. See CITHARA] —**zith′er·ist**, *n.*

zith·ern (zĭth′ərn), *n.* 1. cittern. 2. zither.

zit·tern (zĭt′ərn), *n.* cittern.

zi·zith (tsē tsēt′, tsĭ′tsĭs), *n.pl.* the fringes or tassels of entwined blue and white threads at the four corners of the tallith. See **tallith**. [t. Heb.]

Zither

zlo·ty (zlô′tĭ), *n., pl.* **-tys,** (*collectively*) **-ty.** the gold monetary unit of Poland (introduced in 1924); and a nickel coin,e quivalent at present to approx. 1 U.S. cent. [t. Pol.: lit., golden]

Zn, *Chem.* zinc.

-zoa, plural combining form naming zoölogical groups, as in *Protozoa*. [NL, pl. See ZOON]

Zo·an (zō′ăn), *n.* Biblical name of **Tanis.**

zod., zodiac.

zo·di·ac (zō′dĭ ăk′), *n.* 1. an imaginary belt of the heavens, extending about 8° on each side of the ecliptic, within which are the apparent paths of the sun, moon, and principal planets. It contains twelve constellations and hence twelve divisions (called *signs*), each division, however, because of the precession of the equinoxes, now containing the constellation west of the one from which it took its name. 2. a circular or elliptical diagram representing this belt, and usually containing pictures of the animals, etc., which are associated with the constellations and signs. 3. *Rare.* a circuit or round. [ME, t. L: s. *zōdiacus*, t. Gk.: m. *zōidiakós* (*kýklos*) circle of the signs, der. *zōion* animal] —**zo·di·a·cal** (zō dī′ə kəl), *adj.*

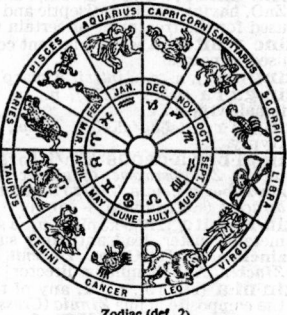

Zodiac (def. 2)

zodiacal light, a luminous tract in the sky, seen in the west after sunset or in the east before sunrise and supposed to be the light reflected from a cloud of meteoric matter revolving round the sun.

Zo·la (zō′lə; *Fr.* zô lä′), *n.* **Émile** (ĕ mēl′), 1840–1902, French novelist.

Zoll·ver·ein (tsôl′fĕr īn′), *n.* *German.* 1. a union of German states for the maintenance of a uniform tariff on imports from other countries, and of free trading among themselves. 2. any similar union or arrangement between a number of states; a customs union.

Zom·ba (zŏm′bə), *n.* a city in and the **capital** of Malawi. 6600 (est. 1956).

zom·bi (zŏm′bĭ), *n., pl.* **-bis.** 1. the python god among certain West Africans. 2. the snake god worshiped in the voodoo ceremonies in the West Indies and certain parts of the southern United States. 3. a supernatural force which brings a corpse to physical life. 4. a dead body brought to life in this way. Also, **zom′bie.** [t. West Afr.] —**zom′bi·ism,** *n.*

zon·al (zō′nəl), *adj.* 1. pertaining to a zone or zones. 2. of the nature of a zone. Also, **zon·a·ry** (zō′nə rĭ). —**zon′al·ly,** *adv.*

zon·ate (zō′nāt), *adj.* 1. marked with a zone or zones, as of color, texture, or the like. 2. arranged in a zone or zones. Also, **zon′at·ed.**

zo·na·tion (zō nā′shən), *n.* 1. zonate state or condition. 2. arrangement or distribution in zones.

zone (zōn), *n., v.,* **zoned, zoning.** —*n.* 1. any continuous tract or area, usually circular, which differs in some respect, or is distinguished for some purpose, from adjoining tracts or areas, or within which certain distinguishing circumstances exist or are established. 2. *Geog.* any of five great divisions of the earth's surface, bounded by lines parallel to the equator, and named according to the prevailing temperature (as, the Torrid Zone, extending from the tropic of Cancer to the tropic of Capricorn; the North Temperate Zone, extending from the tropic of Cancer to the Arctic Circle; the South Temperate Zone, extending from the tropic of Capricorn to the Antarctic Circle; the North Frigid Zone, extending from the Arctic Circle to the North Pole; the South Frigid Zone, extending from the Antarctic Circle to the South Pole). 3. *Phytogeog., Zoögeog.* an area characterized by a particular set of organisms, which are determined by a particular set of

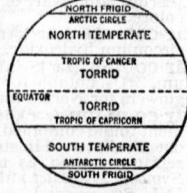

Terrestrial zones

environmental conditions, as an altitudinal belt on a mountain such as the alpine zone. 4. *Geol.* a geological horizon. 5. *Geom.* a part of the surface of a sphere included between two parallel planes. 6. a ringlike or surrounding area, or one of a series of such areas, about a particular place, to all points within which a uniform charge is made for transportation or some similar service. 7. the total number of available railroad terminals within a given circumference around a given shipping center. 8. an area or district in a city or town under special restrictions as to buildings. 9. *Chiefly Poetic.* a girdle, belt, or cincture. —*v.t.* 10. to encircle with or surround like a zone, girdle, or belt. 11. to mark with zones or bands. 12. to divide into zones, tracts, or areas, as according to existing characteristics, or as distinguished for some purpose. 13. to divide (a city or town) into areas subject to special restrictions as to buildings. —*v.i.* 14. to be divided into a zone or zones. [t. L: m. *zōna*, t. Gk.: m. *zōnē* girdle] —Syn. 1. See belt.

zoned (zōnd), *adj.* 1. divided into zones. 2. *Poetic.* wearing a zone or girdle.

zone melting, a process of purifying solids whereby a small portion is heated for a short time by moving it through a heated zone or by moving the zone along the solid. The process is employed to obtain very pure metals for use in transistors.

zon·ule (zōn′ūl), *n.* a little zone, belt, or band. [t. NL: m. *zōnula,* dim. of L *zōna* girdle]

ZOO (zōō), *n.* a zoölogical garden.

zoö-, a word element meaning "living being," as in *zoöchemistry.* Also, **zoo-.** [t. Gk.: m. *zôio-*, comb. form of *zôion* animal]

zo·ö·chem·is·try (zō′ə kĕm′ĭs trĭ), *n.* the chemistry of the constituents of the animal body; animal chemistry. —**zo·ö·chem·i·cal** (zō′ə kĕm′ə kəl), *adj.*

zoögeog., zoögeography.

zo·ö·ge·og·ra·phy (zō′ə jĭ ŏg′rə fĭ), *n.* 1. the science treating of the geographical distribution of animals. 2. the study of the causes, effects, and other relations involved in such distributions. —**zo·ö·ge·og′ra·pher,** *n.* —**zo·ö·ge·o·graph′ic** (zō′ə jē ə grăf′ĭk), **zo·ö·ge·o·graph′i·cal,** *adj.* —**zo·ö·ge·o·graph′i·cal·ly,** *adv.*

zo·ö·gloe·a (zō′ə glē′ə), *n. Bacteriol.* a jellylike mass or aggregate of bacteria formed when the cell walls swell through absorption of water and become contiguous. [f. zoö- + *gloea* (Latinization of Gk. *gloîa* glue)]

zo·ög·ra·phy (zō ŏg′rə fĭ), *n.* that branch of zoölogy which deals with the description of animals. —**zo·o·graph·ic** (zō′ə grăf′ĭk), **zo·ö·graph′i·cal,** *adj.*

zo·öid (zō′oid), *n.* 1. *Biol.* any organic body or cell, whether of animal, vegetable, or equivocal character (as, a protozoan, a spermatozoid, a spermatozoön, etc.) which is capable of spontaneous movement and of an existence more or less apart from or independent of the parent organism. 2. *Zool.* **a.** any animal organism or individual capable of separate existence, and produced by fission, gemination, or some method other than direct sexual reproduction. **b.** one of the individuals, as certain free-swimming medusas, which intervene in the alternation of generations between the products of proper sexual reproduction. **c.** any one of the recognizably distinct individuals or elements of a compound or colonial animal, whether detached or detachable or not. —*adj.* 3. Also, **zo·öi′dal.** resembling, or of the nature of, an animal. [f. zo(o-) + -OID]

zool., 1. zoölogical. 2. zoölogist. 3. zoölogy. Also, **zoöl.**

zo·ö·log·i·cal (zō′ə lŏj′ə kəl), *adj.* 1. of or pertaining to zoölogy. 2. relating to or concerned with animals. Also, **zo·ö·log′ic.** —**zo·ö·log′i·cal·ly,** *adv.*

zoölogical garden, a park or other large enclosure in which live animals are kept for public exhibition.

zo·öl·o·gist (zō ŏl′ə jĭst), *n.* one versed in zoölogy.

zo·öl·o·gy (zō ŏl′ə jĭ), *n., pl.* **-gies.** 1. the science that treats of animals or the animal kingdom. 2. a treatise on this subject. 3. the animals existing in a particular region. [t. NGk.: m.s. *zōiología.* See zoö-, -LOGY]

zoom (zōōm), *v.i.* 1. to make a continuous humming sound. 2. to drive an airplane suddenly and sharply upward at great speed for a short distance, as in regaining altitude, clearing an obstacle, signalling, etc. —*v.t.* 3. to cause (an airplane) to zoom. 4. to fly over (an obstacle) by zooming. —*n.* 5. act of zooming. [imit.]

zo·öm·e·try (zō ŏm′ə trĭ), *n.* measurement of the proportionate lengths or sizes of the parts of animals. —**zo·ö·met·ric** (zō′ə mĕt′rĭk), *adj.*

zo·ö·mor·phic (zō′ə môr′fĭk), *adj.* 1. ascribing animal form or attributes to beings or things not animal; representing a deity under the form of an animal. 2. characterized by or involving such ascription or representation. 3. representing or using animal forms.

zo·ö·mor·phism (zō′ə môr′fĭz əm), *n.* 1. zoömorphic representation, as in ornament. 2. zoömorphic conception, as of a deity.

zo·ön (zō′ŏn), *n., pl.* **zoa** (zō′ə). *Zool.* any of the individuals of a compound organism. [NL, t. Gk.: m. *zôion* animal]

-zoön, a combining form of **zoön.**

zo·öph·i·lous (zō ŏf′ə ləs), *adj.* 1. *Bot.* adapted to pollination by the agency of animals. 2. loving animals.

zo·ö·pho·bi·a (zō′ə fō′bĭ ə), *n.* morbid fear of animals.

zo·o·phyte (zō′ə fīt′), *n.* any of various animals resembling a plant, as a coral, a sea anemone, etc. [t. NL: m. *zōophyton*, t. Gk. See ZOO-, -PHYTE] —**zo·o·phyt·ic** (zō′ə fĭt′ĭk), **zo′o·phyt′i·cal**, *adj.*

zo·o·plas·ty (zō′ə plăs′tĭ), *n. Surg.* the transplantation of living tissue from a lower animal to the human body. —**zo′o·plas′tic**, *adj.*

zo·o·sperm (zō′ə spûrm′), *n. Bot. Obs.* a zoöspore. —**zo·ö·sper·mat·ic** (zō′ə spər măt′ĭk), *adj.*

zo·ö·spo·ran·gi·um (zō′ə spə răn′jĭ əm), *n., pl.* **-gia** (-jĭ ə). *Bot.* a sporangium or spore case in which zoöspores are produced. —**zo′o·spo·ran′gi·al**, *adj.*

zo·o·spore (zō′ə spōr′), *n.* **1.** *Bot.* an asexual spore produced by certain algae and some fungi, capable of moving about by means of flagella. **2.** *Zool.* any of the minute motile flageliform or amoeboid bodies which issue from the sporocyst of certain protozoans. —**zo·o·spor·ic** (zō′ə spôr′ĭk, -spŏr′ĭk), **zo·ös·po·rous** (zō ŏs′pə rəs, zō′ə spōr′əs), *adj.*

zo·öt·o·my (zō ŏt′ə mĭ), *n.* the dissection or the anatomy of animals. [t. NL: m.s. *zōotomia*. See -TOMY] —**zo·o·tom·ic** (zō′ə tŏm′ĭk), **zo′o·tom′i·cal**, *adj.* —**zo′o·öt′om·i·cal·ly**, *adv.* —**zo·öt′o·mist**, *n.*

zoot suit (zoot), *Slang.* an extreme suit with baggy tight-cuffed pants and an oversized coat.

zor·il (zôr′ĭl, zŏr′ĭl), *n.* a South African weasellike animal, *Ictonyx striatus*, resembling a skunk, and capable of emitting a fetid odor. Also, **zo·ril·la** (zō rĭl′ə). [t. F: m. *zorille*, t. Sp.: m. *zorilla*, dim. of *zorra* fox]

Zorn (sôrn), *n.* **Anders Leonhard** (än′dərs lā′ō närd′), 1860–1920, Swedish painter, etcher, and sculptor.

Zo·ro·as·ter (zōr′ō ăs′tər), *n.* fl. c1000? B.C., Persian religious teacher. Also, **Zarathustra**.

Zo·ro·as·tri·an (zōr′ō ăs′trĭ ən), *adj.* **1.** pertaining to Zoroaster, or to the ancient Persian religion founded by him. —*n.* **2.** one of the followers of Zoroaster, now represented by the Guebers and the Parsees.

Zo·ro·as·tri·an·ism (zōr′ō ăs′trĭ ə nĭz′əm), *n.* the strongly ethical dualism, started in ancient Persia (Iran), which teaches a continuous struggle between the Good Spirit of the cosmos, Ahura Mazda, against the Evil Spirit, Angra Mainyu. Also, **Zo′ro·as′trism**.

Zor·ril·la y Mo·ral (thôr rē′lyä ē mō räl′), **José** (hō-sĕ′), 1817–93, Spanish poet and dramatist.

zos·ter (zŏs′tər), *n.* **1.** *Pathol.* herpes zoster. **2.** *Gk. Antiq.* a belt or girdle. [t. L, t. Gk.: girdle]

Zou·ave (zōō äv′, zwäv), *n.* **1.** (*also l.c.*) one of a body of infantry in the French army, composed orig. of Algerians, distinguished for their dash and hardiness, and wearing a picturesque Oriental uniform. **2.** a member of any body of soldiers wearing a similar dress. **3.** a soldier of volunteer regiments (1861–65) in the U.S. Army whose dress resembled the French Zouave uniform. [f. F, from the name of an Algerian tribe]

zounds (zoundz), *interj. Archaic.* a minced oath, often used as a mere emphatic exclamation, as of surprise, indignation, or anger. [short for *by God's wounds*]

Zr, *Chem.* zirconium.

zuc·chet·to (tsōōk kĕt′tō), *n., pl.* **-tos.** a small, round skullcap worn by Roman Catholic ecclesiastics, a priest's being black, a bishop's violet, a cardinal's red, and the Pope's white. [incorrect var. of It. *zucchetta* cap, dim. of *zucca* gourd, head]

Zug (tsōōKH), *n.* **1.** a canton in central Switzerland. 43,800 (est. 1952); 92 sq. mi. **2.** a city in this canton. 15,700 (est. 1952).

Zui·der Zee (zī′dər zē′; *Du.* zœY′dər zā′), a former shallow inlet of the North Sea, in central Netherlands; now IJssel Lake. Also, **Zuyder Zee**.

Zu·lo·a·ga (thōō′lō ä′gä), *n.* **Ignacio** (ĕg nä′thyô), 1870–1945, Spanish painter.

Zu·lu (zōō′lōō), *n., pl.* **-lus, -lu,** *adj.* —*n.* **1.** a great Bantu nation of southeastern Africa, occupying the coastal region between Natal and Lourenço Marques. **2.** a member of the Zulu nation. **3.** their language. —*adj.* **4.** of or pertaining to the Zulus or their language.

Zu·lu·land (zōō′lōō lănd′), *n.* a territory in the Republic of South Africa, in NE Natal province.

Zu·ñi (zōō′nyē, sōō′-), *n., pl.* **-ñis.** **1.** (*pl.*) a tribe of North American Indians, of a linguistic stock related to Penutian, inhabiting the largest of the Indian pueblos, in western New Mexico. **2.** a member of this tribe. [t. Sp., t. Keresan: m. *Súnyitsa*] —**Zu′ñi·an**, *adj., n.*

Zu·rich (zōōr′ĭk), *n.* **1.** a canton in N Switzerland. 802,500 pop. (est. 1952); 668 sq. mi. **2.** the capital of this canton, on the **Lake of Zurich** (25 mi. long; 34 sq. mi.). 400,300 (est. 1952). German, **Zü·rich** (tsY′rĭKH).

Zuy·der Zee (zī′dər zē′; *Du.* zœY′dər zā′), **Zuider Zee**.

Zweig (tsvīKH), *n.* **1.** **Arnold** (är′nôlt), born 1887, German novelist, essayist, and dramatist. **2.** **Stefan** (shtĕ′fän), 1881–1942, Austrian dramatist, critic, biographer, and novelist.

Zwick·au (tsvĭk′ou), *n.* a city in East Germany, in Saxony. 135,751 (est. 1955).

zwie·back (tswē′băk′, swē′-, swī′băk′; *Ger.* tsvē′-bäk′), *n.* a kind of bread cut into slices and dried in the oven. [t. G: twice-baked. Cf. BISCUIT]

Zwing·li (tsvĭng′lē), *n.* **Ulrich** (ōōl′rĭKH) or **Huldreich** (hōōl′drīKH), 1484–1531, Swiss Protestant reformer.

Zwing·li·an (zwĭng′glĭ ən, tsvĭng′lY-), *adj.* **1.** of or pertaining to Ulrich Zwingli or his doctrines, which were largely in agreement with those of Luther and offered a distinctive, spiritualist interpretation of the Lord's Supper. —*n.* **2.** a follower of Zwingli. —**Zwing′li·an·ism,** *n.* —**Zwing′li·an·ist,** *n., adj.*

zwit·ter·i·on (tsvĭt′ər ī′ən), *n. Phys. Chem.* an ion carrying both a positive and a negative charge. Also, **zwit′ter·i′on.** [f. G *zwitter* half-breed + ION] —**zwit·ter·i·on·ic** (tsvĭt′ər ī ŏn′ĭk), *adj.*

zyg·a·poph·y·sis (zĭg′ə pŏf′ə sĭs, zī′gə-), *n., pl.* **-ses** (-sēz′). *Anat., Zool.* one of the articular processes upon the neural arch of a vertebra, usually occurring in two pairs, one anterior and the other posterior, and serving to interlock each vertebra with the one above and below. [f. ZYG- + APOPHYSIS] —**zyg·ap·o·phys·e·al** (zĭg′-ăp ə fĭz′ĭ əl), **zyg′ap·o·phys′i·al**, *adj.*

zygo-, a word element meaning "yoke," especially referring to shape, as in *zygodactyl*. Also, before vowels, **zyg-**. [t. Gk., comb. form of *zygón*]

zy·go·dac·tyl (zī′gə dăk′tYl, zĭg′ə-), *adj.* **1.** (of a bird or bird's foot) having the toes disposed in pairs, one pair before and one pair behind on each foot. —*n.* **2.** a zygodactyl bird.

Zygodactyl foot

zy·go·ma (zī gō′mə, zY-), *n., pl.* **-mata** (-mə tə). *Anat.* **1.** the bony arch below the orbit of the skull, which is formed by the maxillary, jugal, and temporal bones. **2.** Also, **zygomatic process.** a process of the temporal bone forming part of this arch. **3.** the jugal bone. [t. NL, t. Gk., der. *zygón* yoke] —**zy·go·mat·ic** (zī′gə măt′Yk, zY′ə-), *adj.*

zygomatic bone, *Anat.* the malar bone.

zy·go·mor·phic (zī′gə môr′fYk, zY′ə-), *adj. Bot.* (of flowers, etc.) divisible into similar or symmetrical halves by one plane only. Cf. **actinomorphic.** Also, **zy′go·mor′phous.** —**zy·go·mor′phism,** *n.*

zy·go·phyl·la·ceous (zī′gō fə lā′shəs, zY′gō-), *adj.* belonging to the *Zygophyllaceae*, or bean caper family of plants. See **bean caper, guaiacum.** [f. s. NL *zygophyllāceae* (der. *Zygophyllum*; see ZYGO-, PHYLLO-) + -OUS]

zy·go·phyte (zī′gə fYt′, zY′gə-), *n. Bot.* a plant which is reproduced by means of zygospores.

zy·go·spore (zī′gə spōr′, zY′gə-), *n. Bot.* a cell formed by fusion of two similar gametes, as in certain algae and fungi.

zy·gote (zī′gōt, zY′gōt), *n. Biol.* **1.** the cell produced by the union of two gametes. **2.** the individual developing from such a cell. [t. Gk.: m.s. *zygōtós* yoked]

zy·mase (zī′mās), *n. Biochem.* an enzyme in yeast which causes the decomposition of sugar into alcohol and carbon dioxide, obtainable in the form of an extract. [t. F, der. Gk. *zýmē* leaven; modeled on DIASTASE]

zyme (zīm), *n. Pathol.* the specific principle regarded as the cause of a zymotic disease. Cf. **zymosis.** [t. Gk.: leaven]

zymo-, a word element meaning "leaven," as in *zymogen*. Also, before vowels, **zym-**. [comb. form repr. Gk. *zýmē*]

zy·mo·gen (zī′mə jən), *n.* **1.** *Biochem.* any of various substances which by some internal change may give rise to an enzyme. **2.** *Biol.* any of various bacterial organisms which produce enzymes. Also, **zy·mo·gene** (zī′-mə jēn′). [f. G. See ZYMO-, -GEN]

zy·mo·gen·e·sis (zī′mə jĕn′ə sĭs), *n. Biochem.* the change of a zymogen into an enzyme.

zy·mo·gen·ic (zī′mə jĕn′Yk), *adj.* of or pertaining to a zymogen or zymogene.

zymogenic organism, any microörganism producing an enzyme which causes fermentation.

zy·mol·o·gy (zī mŏl′ə jĭ), *n.* the science that treats of fermentation and the action of enzymes. —**zy·mo·log·ic** (zī′mə lŏj′Yk), *adj.* —**zy·mol′o·gist,** *n.*

zy·mol·y·sis (zī mŏl′ə sĭs), *n.* **1.** *Biochem.* the digestive and fermentative action of enzymes. **2.** fermentation or other hydrolytic reactions produced by an enzyme. —**zy·mo·lyt·ic** (zī′mə lĭt′Yk), *adj.*

zy·mom·e·ter (zī mŏm′ə tər), *n.* an instrument for ascertaining the degree of fermentation.

zy·mo·sis (zī mō′sYs), *n., pl.* **-ses** (-sēz). **1.** an infectious or contagious disease. **2.** *Med.* a process analogous to fermentation, by which (according to a theory now obsolete) certain infectious and contagious diseases were supposed to be produced. [t. NL, t. Gk.: fermentation]

zy·mot·ic (zī mŏt′Yk), *adj.* **1.** pertaining to or caused by, or as if by, fermentation. Cf. **zymosis. 2.** pertaining to a zymotic disease. [t. Gk.: m.s. *zymōtikós* causing fermentation]

zymotic disease, an obsolete term for infectious diseases, as smallpox, typhoid fever, etc., which were regarded as due to the presence in the body of a morbific principle acting in a manner analogous to fermentation.

zy·mur·gy (zī′mûr jY), *n.* that branch of chemistry which deals with fermentation, as in winemaking, brewing, distilling, the preparation of yeast, etc. [f. ZYM(O)-+ -URGY]

Zyr·i·an (zYr′Y ən), *n.* a Finno-Ugric language of the Permian group, having written documents from the 13th century. Also, **Syrien, Syryenian.**

SIGNS AND SYMBOLS

ASTRONOMY

1. Astronomical Bodies

☉ **a.** the sun. **b.** Sunday.
⊖ center of sun.
upper limb of sun.
lower limb of sun.
☿ **a.** Mercury. **b.** Wednesday.
♀ **a.** Venus. **b.** Friday.
⊕, ♁, ⊖ the earth.
☾, ☽ **a.** the moon. **b.** Monday.
● new moon.
☽, ☽, ◑, ☽ the moon, first quarter.
○ full moon.
☾, ☾, ◐, ☾ the moon, last quarter.
upper limb of moon.
lower limb of moon.
♂ **a.** Mars. **b.** Tuesday.
①, ③, ⑧, etc. asteroids. Each of the known asteroids is designated by a number within a circle, as ① for Ceres, ② for Pallas, etc.
♃ **a.** Jupiter. **b.** Thursday.
♄ **a.** Saturn. **b.** Saturday.
♅, ♅ Uranus.
♆ Neptune.
P Pluto.
☄ comet.
✳, ∗ star.
α, β, etc. the first, second, etc., brightest star in a specified constellation (fol. by the Latin name of the constellation in the genitive).

2. Signs of Position

☌ in conjunction; having the same longitude or right ascension. Thus, ☌ ♀ ☉ signifies the conjunction of Venus and the sun.
✳ sextile; 60° apart in longitude or right ascension.
□ quadrature; 90° apart in longitude or right ascension.
△ trine; 120° apart in longitude or right ascension.
☍ in opposition; 180° apart in longitude or right ascension. Thus, ☍ ♂ ☉ signifies the opposition of Mars and the sun.
☊ ascending node. See **node.**
☋ descending node. See **node.**
♈ vernal equinox.
♎ autumnal equinox.
α, RA, AR right ascension.
β celestial latitude.
δ, Decl. declination.
θ sidereal time.
λ celestial (or geographical) longitude.

3. Signs of the Zodiac

A. SPRING SIGNS

♈ Aries, the Ram.
♉ Taurus, the Bull.
♊, II Gemini, the Twins.

B. SUMMER SIGNS

♋, ♋ Cancer, the Crab.
♌ Leo, the Lion.
♍ Virgo, the Virgin.

C. AUTUMN SIGNS

♎ Libra, the Balance.
♏ Scorpio, the Scorpion.
♐ Sagittarius, the Archer.

D. WINTER SIGNS

♑ ♑ Capricorn, the Goat.
♒ Aquarius, the Water Bearer.
♓ Pisces, the Fishes.

BIOLOGY

♂, ♁ a male organism, organ, cell, etc.
♀ a female organism, organ, cell, etc.
○ an individual organism, esp. a female.
□ an individual organism, esp. a male.
× (of a hybrid organism) crossed with.
P parent or parental generation; the first generation in a specified line of descent.
F filial generation; any generation following a parental generation.
F_1, F_2, F_3, etc. the first, second, third, etc., filial generations.
+ denoting the presence of a specified trait or characteristic.
− denoting the absence of a specified trait or characteristic.
○, ⊙, ① annual plant.
②, ♂, ⊙⊙ biennial plant.
♃ a perennial herb or plant.
△ an evergreen.
✳ northern hemisphere.
✳ southern hemisphere.
|✳ Old World.
✳| New World.

BOOKS

f° folio.
4 mo, 4° quarto.
8 vo, 8° octavo.
12 mo, 12° duodecimo.
16 mo, 16° sextodecimo.
18 mo, 18° octodecimo.

NOTE: The fold symbols and names above designate the most common types of book manufacture. Each indicates the number of leaves into which a single sheet is folded, and thus the number of pages to a sheet and (usually) the approximate size of the book itself. For full definitions, see the entries under the words. Other, less commonly used, symbols and names (not defined in the text) are:

24 mo, 24° twenty-fourmo: consisting of twenty-four leaves, or forty-eight pages, to a sheet.
32 mo, 32° thirty-twomo: consisting of thirty-two leaves, or sixty-four pages, to a sheet.
48 mo, 48° forty-eightmo: consisting of forty-eight leaves, or ninety-six pages, to a sheet.

CHEMISTRY

1. Elements

Each of the chemical elements is represented by a letter or combination of letters, consisting of the initial or an abbreviation of the English or Latin name of the element, as H (hydrogen), O (oxygen), Na (sodium, for L *natrium*), Cl (chlorine), etc.

2. Compounds

Compounds are represented by combinations of the symbols of their constituent elements, with an inferior numeral to the right of each symbol indicating the number of atoms of the element entering into the compound (number 1 is, however, omitted). Thus, in some simple cases, NaCl (sodium chloride, or common salt) is a compound containing one atom of sodium and one of chlorine, H_2O (water) contains two atoms of hydrogen and one of oxygen, H_2O_2 (hydrogen peroxide, or common peroxide) contains two atoms apiece of hydrogen and oxygen. A molecule may also consist entirely of atoms of a single element, as O_3 (ozone), which consists of three atoms of oxygen. Other symbols used in the formulas of molecules and compounds are:

· **a.** denoting radicals, as in CH_3·COOH. **b.** denoting water of crystallization (or hydration) as in Na_2CO_3·$10H_2O$ (washing soda).
( ) denoting a radical within a compound, as $(C_2H_5)_2O$ (ether).
1, 2, 3, etc. (before a symbol or formula) denoting a multiplication of the symbol or formula. Thus 3H = three atoms of hydrogen; $6H_2O$ = six molecules of water, etc.
1-, 2-, 3-, etc. (in names of compounds) denoting one of several possible positions of substituted atoms or groups.
α, β, etc. (in names of compounds) denoting one of several possible positions of substituted atoms or groups.
+ denoting dextrorotation, as +120°.
− denoting levorotation, as −120°.

3. Valence and Electric Charge

−, =, ≡, etc. **a.** denoting a negative charge of one, two, three, etc., as $(OH)^-$, $(SO_4)^{=}$. **b.** denoting a single, double, triple, etc., bond, as H−O−H.
$^{-1}$, $^{-2}$, $^{-3}$, etc. Same as −, =, ≡, etc. (def. a); as $(OH)^{-1}$; $(SO_4)^{-2}$.
+, ++, +++, etc. denoting a positive charge of one, two, three, etc., as K^+, Ca^{++}.
$^{+1}$, $^{+2}$, $^{+3}$, etc. Same as +, ++, +++, etc., as K^{+1}, Ca^{+2}.
′, ′′, ′′′, etc. **a.** denoting a valence of one, two, three, etc. **b.** denoting a charge, esp. a negative charge, of one, two, three, etc.
·, :, ⁝, etc. denoting a single, double, triple, etc., bond.

4. Chemical Reactions

+ added to; together with.
= form; are equal to; as H + H + O = H_2O.
→, ← denoting a reaction in the direction specified.

⇌ denoting a reversible reaction, i.e. a reaction which proceeds simultaneously in both directions.

↓ (after a symbol or formula) denoting the precipitation of a specified substance.

↑ (after a symbol or formula) denoting the appearance of a specified substance as a gas.

⇌, ⇋ (in a quantitative equation) denoting the quantities of specified substances which will enter completely into a reaction, without leaving excess material.

COMMERCE

@ 1. at: *eggs @ 80c per dz.* 2. to: *woolen cloth per yd. $5.00 @ $8.50.*

a/c account.

B/E bill of exchange.

B/L bill of lading.

B/S bill of sale.

c/d, C/D *Bookkeeping.* carried down.

c/f, C/F *Bookkeeping.* carried forward.

c. & f. cost and freight.

C/L car-load lot.

c/o 1. care of. 2. *Bookkeeping.* carried over.

c/s cases.

L/C letter of credit.

P & L 1. profit and loss. 2. *Bookkeeping.* a summary account to which are transferred the balances of accounts showing either a profit or loss.

S/D sight draft.

1. (before a figure or figures) number; numbered: *#40 thread.* 2. (after a figure or figures) pounds: *20#.*

% 1. percent. 2. order of.

LANGUAGE

~ tilde; as in *cañon.*

^ circumflex accent; as in *fête.*

↵ (with c) cedilla; as in *Alençon.*

′ acute accent; as in *passé.*

` grave accent; as in *à la mode.*

¨ dieresis; as in *zoölogy.*

‾ macron.

˅ breve.

› smooth breathing.

‹ rough breathing.

* denoting a hypothetical or reconstructed form: used esp. in etymologies.

MATHEMATICS

1. Arithmetic and Algebra

+ a. plus. b. positive. c. denoting approximate accuracy, with some figures omitted at the end; as in $\pi = 3.141592+$.

− a. minus. b. negative. c. denoting approximate accuracy, with some figures omitted at the end. Cf. + (def. c).

±, ∓, ±, ∓ a. plus or minus: $4 \pm 2 = 6$ or 2. b. positive or negative: $\pm a = +a$ or $-a$. c. denoting the probable error associated with a figure derived by experiment and observation, approximate calculation, etc.

×, · times; multiplied by. NOTE: multiplication may also be indicated by writing the algebraic symbols for multiplicand(s) and multiplier(s) in a horizontal line; as in: xy; $a(a + b) = a^2 + ab$.

÷, /, −, : divided by; denoting the ratio of; as in: $8 \div 2 = 8/2 = \frac{8}{2} = 8:2 = 4$.

= equals; is equal to.

≡ is identical with.

≠, ≠ is not equal to.

~, ∽ a. is equivalent to. b. is similar to.

> is greater than.

< is less than.

≥, ≧ is equal to or greater than.

≤, ≦ is equal to or less than.

¹, ², ³, etc. (at the right of a symbol, figure, etc.) exponents, indicating the raising of a power to the first, second, third, etc., power: $(ab)^2 = a^2b^2$; $4^3 = 64$.

√, √ the radical sign, indicating the square root of, as in: $\sqrt{81} = 9$.

∛, ∜, ∜, etc. the radical sign used with indices, indicating the third, fourth, etc. root of; as in: $\sqrt[3]{125} = 5$.

½, ⅓, ¼, etc. fractional exponents used to indicate roots, and equal to √, ∛, ∜, etc.; as in: $9^{\frac{1}{2}} = \sqrt{9} = 3$; $a^{\frac{3}{4}} = (a^{\frac{1}{4}})^3 = (a^3)^{\frac{1}{4}} = \sqrt[4]{a^3}$.

$^{-1}$, $^{-2}$, $^{-3}$, etc. negative exponents, used to indicate the reciprocal of the same quantity with a positive exponent; as in: $9^{-2} = \frac{1}{9^2} = \frac{1}{81}$; $a^{-\frac{1}{2}} = \frac{1}{\sqrt{a}}$.

( ) parentheses; as in: $2(a + b)$.

[ ] brackets; as in: $4 + [3(a - b)]$.

{ } braces; as in: $5 + \{6[2 - (a + 2) + 4]\}$.

‾ vinculum; as in: $\overline{a + b}$.

NOTE: Parentheses, brackets, braces, and vinculum are usually applied to quantities consisting of more than one member or term, to connect them and show that they are to be considered together.

∝ varies directly as; is directly proportional to: $x \propto y$.

!, ∟ factorial of: $4! = |4 = 1 \times 2 \times 3 \times 4 = 24$.

f, F, ϕ, etc. function of; as in: $f(x) = a$ function of x. NOTE: In addition to ϕ, other symbols (esp. letters from the Greek alphabet) may be used to indicate functions, as ψ, γ, etc.

′, ″, ‴, etc. prime, double prime, triple prime, etc., used to indicate: a. first, second, third, etc., derivatives of a function, as in: $f'(x)$; $f''(x)$; etc. b. constants, as distinguished from the variable denoted by a letter alone. c. different variables using the same letters, as in y', y'', y''', etc.

σ standard deviation.

r correlation coefficient.

e, ϵ Same as e (def. 1), p. 377.

∞ infinity.

2. Geometry

∠, *pl.* ∠s angle; as in: ∠ACB.

⊥ a. a perpendicular (*pl.* ⊥s). b. is perpendicular to; as in: AB ⊥ CD.

‖ a. a parallel (*pl.* ‖s). b. is parallel to; as in: AB ‖ CD.

△, *pl.* △ triangle, as in: △ ABC.

▱ parallelogram, as in: ▱ ABCD.

□ square, as in: □ ABCD.

○, *pl.* ⊙ circle.

π the Greek letter pi, representing the ratio (3.141592+) of the circumference of a circle to its diameter.

⌒ arc.

° degree; degrees, esp. of arc or (in physics, etc.) of temperature; as in: 60°.

′ minute; minutes; as in: 60°20′.

″ second; seconds; as in: 60°20′5″.

≅, ≡ is congruent to.

∴ therefore; hence.

∵ since; because.

3. Calculus

$\frac{d}{d}$ derivative; as in: $\frac{dy}{dx}$ = the derivative of y with respect to x.

Δ an increment; as Δy = an increment of y.

d differential, as dy = differential y.

$\sum\limits^{n}$ sum of n terms.

$\sum$ sum of an infinite number of terms.

$\prod\limits^{n}$ product of n terms.

$\prod$ product of an infinite number of terms.

lim limit. An example of the use of this abbreviation is: $\lim\limits_{y \to b} (x) = a$; i.e. the limit of x as y approaches b is a.

$\int$ integral. An example of the use of this symbol is: $\int f(x)dx$; i.e. the integral of $f(x)$ with respect to x.

$\int_a^b$ definite integral, giving limits. Thus, $\int_a^b f(x)dx$ is the definite integral of $f(x)$ between limits a and b.

MEDICINE AND PHARMACY

APOTHECARIES' MEASURE. See p. 59.

APOTHECARIES' WEIGHT. See p. 59.

℞ take (L. *recipe*): presumably based on ♃, the sign of Jupiter, and used to propitiate the god in writing a prescription.

℥ mix.

ĀĀ, Ā, āā of each.

S, Sig. write: indicating directions to be written on a package or label for the use of the patient.

+ 1. acid reaction. 2. positive reaction (to a clinical or diagnostic test). 3. excess of.

− 1. alkaline reaction. 2. negative reaction (to a clinical or diagnostic test). 3. deficiency of.

MISCELLANEOUS

&, &, ℴ the ampersand, meaning *and.* Cf. ampersand (p. 42).

&c. et cetera; and others; and so forth; and so on. Cf. et cetera (p. 412).

© copyright; copyrighted.

′ foot; feet; as in: 6′ = six feet.

″ inch; inches; as in: 6′2″ = six feet, two inches.

× 1. by: used in stating dimensions, as in: *a vat that is 2′ × 4′ × 1′*; *a 2″ × 4″ board.* 2. a sign (the cross) made in place of a signature by a person who cannot write; as in:

John × Jones
mark.

♠ *Cards.* spade.
♥ *Cards.* heart.
♦ *Cards.* diamond.
♣ *Cards.* club.
7ber September.
8ber October.
9ber November.
10ber December.
† died: used esp. in genealogical tables.

MONEY

$, $ **1.** dollar; dollars; as in: $1; $10. **2.** (in certain countries, as Mexico, Argentina, etc.) peso; pesos. **3.** (in Portugal) escudo. **4.** (in Brazil) milreis. **5.** (in Honduras) lempira.

¢ cent; cents; as in: 1¢; 25¢.
₱ (in the Philippines) peso; pesos.
£ (in Great Britain) pound; pounds; as in: £3.
/, s. (in Great Britain) shilling; shillings; as in: 5/.
d (in Great Britain) penny; pence; as in: 6d.
£E, £T, £P, etc. (in Egypt, Turkey, Palestine, etc.) pound; pounds.
R, *pl.* Rs rupee.
¥, Y yen.

PHYSICS, ENGINEERING, ETC.

1. Electricity and Magnetism

a. General Concepts

R resistance.
X reactance.
L inductance.
X_L inductive reactance.
C capacitance.
X_C capacitive reactance.
Z impedance.
φ conductivity.
G conductance.
Υ admittance.
E, e, V, v voltage.
I current.
ℜ reluctance.

K, ε dielectric constant.
Ψ electrostatic flux.
Φ magnetic flux.
μ **1.** magnetic permeability. **2.** amplification factor.
℘ permeance.
H magnetic field intensity.
D electrostatic flux density.
B magnetic flux density.
θ, φ phase difference in degrees.
ω **1.** angular frequency. **2.** angular velocity.

b. Some Important Units

Ω ohm; ohms: used to denote resistance or reactance.
H, h henry; henries.
F, f, Φ farad; farads: usually expressed in microfarads (μf) or micromicrofarads (μμf). Cf. **measurement**, below.
A, amp. ampere; amperes.
V, v volt; volts.
VA, va volt-ampere.
W watt; watts.
∿ cycle; cycles (of alternating voltage or current).
γ .00001 gauss (a unit of magnetic intensity).

2. General Signs and Symbols

Å.U., Å angstrom unit. Also, λ.
α **a.** angular acceleration. **b.** angle of optical rotation.
$α_m$ molecular rotation.
β the ratio of any velocity to the velocity of light.
γ **a.** dihedral angle. **b.** surface tension.
δ constant angle of control airfoils in an airplane.
θ **a.** angular distance. **b.** temperature above 0°C; as in: 20θ.
λ **a.** wave length. **b.** angstrom unit. **c.** radioactive constant.
π osmotic pressure.
Π pressure.
ρ **a.** radius of curvature. **b.** refractive power.

3. Measurement

NOTE: The use of prefixes from the metric system, and their symbols, is extremely common in physics. In some cases, they appear more often than the basic unit name itself, as in farads, which are almost always reckoned in microfarads or micromicrofarads; in others, they are at least as common as the unit name, as in kilowatts (for thousands of watts). The most common prefixes in everyday use are:

m- milli-; one thousandth of; as in: 1 mH (1/1000 henry).
μ micro-; one millionth of; as in: 1 μÅ (1/1000000 angstrom unit).
mμ- millimicro-; one thousand millionth of.
μμ- micromicro-; one million millionth of; as in: 1 μμf (one micromicrofarad).
k, K kilo; one thousand; as in: 1 kw (1 kilowatt, or one thousand watts); 10KVA (10 kilovolt-amperes, or ten thousand volt-amperes).
M mega-; one million; as in 1 MΩ (one megohm, or 1,000,000 ohms).

RELIGION

† the cross, a symbol or emblem for Christianity or its tenets, for a crucifix, etc. For various modifications, see illus. under **cross**.
✠, + **1.** *Rom. Cath. Ch.* a modification of the cross used by the pope and by archbishops and bishops before their names. **2.** (in certain service and prayer-books) an indication inserted at those points in the service at which the sign of the cross is to be made. See **cross** (def. 6).
℞ response (def. 3a): used in prayer books, esp. of the *Rom. Cath. Ch.*
✻ *Rom. Cath. Ch.* an indication used in service books to separate the verses of a psalm into two parts, showing where the response begins.
℣, V', V an indication used in service books to show the point at which a versicle (def. 2) begins.
P, P, ₱ a monogram for the first two letters (XP) of the Greek form of the name of Christ, inscribed on a labarum (def. 2).
卍, 卐 gammadion.

GUIDE TO USAGE:
HARRISON PLATT, JR.

WHAT IS GOOD USAGE?

People who lack confidence in their knowledge of good English would like to have each spelling, pronunciation, meaning, and grammatical usage decided for them, once and for all, so that they could know that one is right and another wrong. They feel uncertain where choices are clearly permissible. Partly because they would like to have a fixed standard to settle all questions of usage, they come to believe that one exists and operates, and constantly repeat judgments and rules without examining the basis for them.

But if a fixed standard does exist, it must have a basis. Let us examine some of the possible bases for a rigid standard of good English.

The appeal to immemorial custom and history will not support a fixed standard. The whole history of the language has been one of change. No one would want to outlaw all innovations since *Beowulf*, and it is more than questionable that the language of Chaucer would suit today's needs as well as the speech we use. A word or a construction has no special virtue merely because it is old.

Only in a police state, rigidly controlled, could a fixed standard of correctness rest on a "supreme authority." In the United States we would want to know who is to pick the authority. Moreover, if the judgments of an authority ran counter to the speech habits of many people, its rulings would be ignored. This is indicated by the experience of some countries in which a single central authority to "reform" or control the language has been tried. When the French Academy was set up in the time of Cardinal Richelieu, one of its functions was supervision of the language. The Academy issued dictionaries and from time to time ruled on questions of grammar, spelling, and the like which were submitted to its judgment. Although the Academy has no doubt had some influence on the French language, dialects have continued to flourish in the provinces, a rich and varied slang has never ceased being born in Paris and throughout the country, and even the literary language has evolved very largely without reference to the fiats of the Academy.

In spelling, pronunciation, meaning, and grammar, then, one looks in vain for a fixed standard or for an ultimate authority. Does this mean that there is no standard of good English and that one way of using the language is no better and no worse than any other? Not at all. There are two standards which can be safely followed.

(1) The purpose of language is communication—not communication in a void but communication between the writer or speaker and his audience. The personality and background of the writer or speaker must be taken into account. The way he expresses himself should be in keeping with his nature and background. It should be natural to him, to his habits of speech and thought. It should be as far as possible suitable to his audience. It should take into account their probable knowledge of what he is speaking about, their acquaintance with the concepts and vocabulary of his subject, their ability to follow abstract discussion or their need for illustration, example and explanation. Finally, the way he expresses himself should be adapted to his subject matter. An incident at a ball game requires a different sort of exposition from an explanation of atomic fission. A doctor discussing a problem of nutrition would properly use a different vocabulary, a different sentence structure, and a different approach to his subject if he were addressing, respectively, a convention of doctors, a parent-teacher association, and a class of fourth-grade pupils. That English is good English which communicates well the thought of a given speaker to a given audience. Change the thought, the speaker, or the audience, and the same mode of expression might be extremely bad. The measure of English is the effectiveness of its communication, and this in turn depends on its appropriateness to the subject, the speaker, and the audience.

(2) The second measure of language is social, not functional. People are accustomed to make judgments on the basis of language, just as they do on the basis of clothes and manners. A tuxedo is not better than slacks and sport shirt, it is simply more formal. One is suitable for certain occasions, the others for other occasions. In both formal and informal dress a reasonable degree of neatness and care is expected. It is the same with language.

Writing *thier* for *their* or *her's* for *hers* or saying *it ain't* for *it isn't* does not seriously interfere with communication, but it makes the writer or speaker look ignorant. Noticeably inappropriate mixtures of formal, polysyllabic vocabulary with slang or casual, informal phrases permit the same sort of adverse judgments that wearing a violently colored shirt with otherwise formal dress would. This principle is easy to apply to many language situations.

English has many levels. Communication on any level may be adequate, yet the speaker or writer may be unwilling to let others place him on a particular level because of his use of language. The test here, as before, is appropriateness.

In sum, we may say that English usage is never just good. It is good in respect to a particular situation, speaker, and audience. If it is appropriate to all three, and if it is effective in communication, it is good.

What, in the light of these remarks, is the rôle of a dictionary in settling questions of pronunciation or meaning or grammar? It is *not* a legislating authority on good English. It attempts to record what usage is at any time actually is. Insofar as possible, it points out divided usage. It indicates regional variations of pronunciation or meaning wherever practical. It points out meanings and uses peculiar to a trade, profession, or special activity. It suggests the levels on which certain words or usages are appropriate. A dictionary such as this, based on a realistic sampling of usage, furnishes the information necessary for a sound judgment of what is good English in a given situation. To this extent the dictionary is an authority, and beyond this authority should not go.

SECTION I. WRITTEN ENGLISH

PUNCTUATION

Since English no longer uses more than a handful of inflectional endings (such as are still found in German nouns or French verbs), the relation between the words of a sentence is indicated by their order. Yet there is a great flexibility in word order. In spoken English the rise and fall of the voice, the natural pauses in speaking group the words in their proper relation to one another. In written English this grouping must be indicated by the various marks of punctuation.

In the nineteenth century, writers tended to write long, somewhat formal sentences. In order to guide the reader through the intricate patterns of these long sentences, they ordinarily used much more punctuation than is common today. Modern writers tend toward short sentences, approximating the informality of everyday speech.

The amount of punctuation should vary with the length and complexity of the writer's sentences. Excessive punctuation interferes with ready reading just as much as too little punctuation. Words and punctuation should combine to bring meaning. Any system of punctuation that calls for a particular mark of punctuation regardless of the length and difficulty of the sentence is mechanical and unlikely to produce in practice an easily read or "good" style. The proper punctuation is an integral part of writing a sentence just as the proper arrangement of the words is.

Here is the place for a useful bit of advice. If a sentence is very difficult to punctuate so as to make the meaning clear, the chances are that the arrangement of words and ideas is at fault. The writer will do better if he rearranges his wor order instead of wrestling with his punctuation.

1425

A badly worded sentence cannot be made clear by any punctuation.

Grammars and handbooks of English give many rules of punctuation. These are useful for certain arbitrary customs, such as the use of apostrophes, quotation marks, and hyphens. For all the marks indicating pauses they are not very helpful. The difficulty is not so much in deciding what mark to use in a recognized and well understood situation (as the rulemakers seem to think) but in recognizing a situation that will benefit by punctuation. In the great variety of English sentences, long and short, complicated or simple, these situations are not always clear-cut and require judgment on the writer's part.

On the other hand, there are only a few kinds of punctuation situations. To learn them and learn what to do with them is within the reach of anyone.

ENDING SENTENCES

The sentence is the common unit of thought and language. At the end of a spoken sentence the voice usually drops and always makes a complete pause. In the written language this full stop has to be indicated by punctuation.

STATEMENTS. Most sentences are statements. They may be a single statement like the one just before this, or they may consist of two or more *very closely related in thought*, like this one. The full stop at the end of a statement is commonly indicated by a period (.). Any sentence in this paragraph will serve as an example.

QUESTIONS. If the sentence consists of a question instead of a statement, the full stop at the end is commonly indicated by a question mark (?):

Who owns this book?

Polite orders or requests are often put in question form. Sometimes no question is intended, as in the following:

Will you pass the bread, please.

The writer can use either a period or a question mark, depending on whether he feels there is a real question intended.

EXCLAMATIONS. An exclamation, whether long or short, even a single word, is closed by an exclamation point (!): Single words or characteristic phrasings offer no problem.

Gosh! What a beautiful day!

The degree of feeling or excitement will determine the proper close of sentences like the following:

Get out of here! (or) Get out of here.

An excessive number of exclamatory sentences often bothers readers. They should be used with caution for this reason.

INTERRUPTED THOUGHT. Especially in narrative, a writer sometimes has to deal with a sentence not entirely completed. A sentence broken off abruptly by an interruption may be closed off with a long (2-em) dash:

"Oh, the train doesn't leave for five——"
"All aboard," shouted the conductor.

If a thought is allowed to trail off unfinished, many writers close the sentence with an ellipsis (. . .).

If a writer knows when he has finished a sentence, the best choice of punctuation is not much of a problem. The knowledge that he has finished it is sometimes less simple than it seems.

PUNCTUATION TO SEPARATE

Within the sentence it is necessary to separate, with punctuation, groups of words which might otherwise run together and cause confusion.

MAIN CLAUSES. One of the major categories of sentence elements that should be kept distinct is that of main clauses in compound or in compound complex sentences. Main clauses are grammatically exactly like sentences. Where two or more are very closely related in thought, they are frequently joined together in a single sentence, sometimes with a conjunction between, sometimes with none. Although they are joined, they are not merged.

The old rule taught in most schools called for a semicolon between main clauses if there was no conjunction or if there was interior punctuation within either clause. If there was a conjunction between the clauses, it and a comma were sufficient to separate the clauses. To use a comma when a semicolon was called for, or no punctuation when the rule prescribed a comma, was regarded as a high crime against good English and branded the transgressor, to quote more than one textbook, as "deficient in sentence sense." The offense was called a comma fault, comma blunder, or, among the relatively charitable, a run-on sentence.

A close examination of the actual practice of publishers in current books and magazines will show that these rules are not observed with any regularity. In some magazines there will not be a single semicolon on a close-packed page. If a writer habitually uses a maximum of punctuation, if he writes long, involved clauses, he very frequently does use semicolons to separate them. But if he normally employs a minimum of punctuation and if his clauses are rather short and easily followed, he is likely to separate his clauses with a comma or, if a conjunction is present, by no punctuation at all.

The punctuation to be used depends on the writer's usual method of punctuation and on the length and difficulty of the particular sentence under consideration. Examples follow:

HEAVY OR FORMAL PUNCTUATION

With the abundance of the sea and the lush growth all around, poverty is no spur; and the native will work, if he will work at all, only at tasks which amuse him.
Battleships without air cover were proved fatally vulnerable; their preëminence was gone.

LIGHT OR INFORMAL PUNCTUATION

He could forgive, he could not forget.
She stumbled against him and his arms went around her.

Compound verbs within the same clause are sometimes separated but need not be if the sentence is clearly written and easily followed:

He swung the car into the side road and gradually eased down the accelerator.

COORDINATE ELEMENTS. Many sentences contain series of coördinate (equal and similar) elements. They may be nouns, verbs, adjectives, adverbs, phrases, or clauses. If conjunctions (*and*, *or*, or the like) are used between them, no punctuation is ordinarily used to separate them. If, however, conjunctions are omitted entirely or used only between the last two elements, they are commonly separated by punctuation. If the elements in the series are simple and contain no internal punctuation, commas are ordinarily used. If commas lead to confusion because of internal punctuation, semicolons are used.

When a conjunction appears between the last two elements of a series, usage is divided on whether there should also be punctuation here. As in compound sentences, the answer is in the general system of punctuation being used. If heavy punctuation is the established system, the last two elements of a series should be separated by punctuation, regardless of the presence of the conjunction. If light punctuation is used elsewhere, the punctuation is omitted between the last two elements of a series:

The flag is red, white (,) and blue.
The group consisted of Charles White, the pianist; Willis Twyford, the trap drummer; Elmer Smith, on trumpet (;) and Bill Stone, guitar.
(In the last example, without the semicolons the quartet might be thought of as a sextet.)
Running, blocking, kicking (,) and passing with deadly precision, Young did as he pleased in the second half.
During the long, hot afternoons we splashed in the cool, green, sun-speckled water of the lake.

SUBORDINATE PHRASES OR CLAUSES. Usage is divided as to separating a phrase or a clause preceding a main clause. Again the question of heavy or light punctuation enters in. If the phrase or clause is short and closely related to the main clause, many writers prefer to omit a comma. If the phrase or clause is long or not very closely related to the main clause, as this one is, it is commonly separated from the main clause by a comma. This is a question of judgment, and the writer can decide whether punctuation would make his sentence clearer.

When words are brought together so as to form an apparent phrase not called for by the meaning, they should always be separated by punctuation, usually a comma:

Inside, Norah was weeping as she washed the dishes.
(A reader not guided by the comma might read: *Inside Norah.*)
To Frances, North seemed an old man.
(A reader not guided by the comma might read: *To Frances North.*)

QUOTATIONS. A quotation is separated from its introductory clause by a colon or a comma. If the quotation is long or formally introduced, most writers use a colon:

The President spoke as follows:

In informal quotation, such as dialogue in a story, a comma is the common mark:

Becky answered, "I'm staying right here."

PUNCTUATION TO SET OFF

A child beginning to form sentences frequently succeeds in getting only a single, uncomplicated idea into each one. The result is the primer sentence: I see the dog. The dog is black. It has a curly tail. The next step is to join the three sentences together with *and's* between. The adult mind combines, producing a simple sentence: I see the black dog with a curly tail.

NONRESTRICTIVE PHRASES OR CLAUSES. Frequently a writer wants to add extra information not essential to the central meaning of the sentence. For example, the clause *who is six* does not affect the central meaning of the following sentence:

My niece, *who is six*, almost never cries.

Any word, phrase, or clause thus added to a sentence should be set off by a mark of punctuation *at beginning and end*. If the added information is very loosely related to the sentence, parentheses might be used to set it off. Obviously two marks are required, one at the beginning and one at the close of the added material:

Leningrad (*formerly called Petrograd*) was under siege for months.

Slightly more closely related information would be set off by paired dashes or commas, more commonly by commas. Again the punctuation requires two marks unless one would fall at the beginning or end of the sentence:

Lester Eaker—*a full-blooded Indian*—was the fastest man on the squad.
The radio, *which was playing softly*, filled in the pause.

RESTRICTIVE PHRASES OR CLAUSES. The sense is the best test of whether information is essential to the main meaning of the sentence. If a writer is in doubt, he can read the sentence with the questionable phrase or clause omitted:

People *who mutilate books* should not be allowed library privileges.
People . . . should not be allowed library privileges.

Obviously the writer of the original sentence did not mean that all people should be forbidden the use of the library, but only those few who mutilate books. The omission of the clause changes the main meaning of the sentence. It is therefore essential and should not be set off.

The third baseman, *who was left-handed*, came to bat.
The third baseman . . . came to bat.

The information that the batter was left-handed is not essential. Its omission does not change the main meaning. It should therefore be set off.

Look for additional, nonessential information in situations like the following:

Mary, I want you to clean your room. And you, *Tom*, should cut the grass.
Mr. Elkins, *the football coach*, was very popular with the boys.
The common automobile, *not the airplane*, is the most dangerous form of transportation.
Most of the climbers—*all but three*—turned back when the fog closed down.
It might be added, *incidentally*, that the rumor had no foundation.
Isak Dinesen's *Seven Gothic Tales (published by Random House)* is a remarkable book of short stories.

Although parentheses, paired dashes, or commas serve the same purpose and may be used to set off added but nonessential information, parentheses and dashes often make a break or pause too strong to suit the situation. Commas are by far the most widely used and the most satisfactory for this purpose. There is a prejudice against the use of many dashes held by publishers because they believe a page speckled with dashes is unsightly, and held by teachers because students unable to decide whether to use a comma or a semicolon compromise on a dash, again and again.

STYLES OF PUNCTUATION

Throughout the whole discussion of punctuation a conclusion has been emerging more and more clearly. Usage is almost everywhere divided, but this fact does not mean that there is no standard. In philosophical writing, thoughtful political or economic analysis, and the like, authors are aiming at fine distinctions, carefully weighed judgments. Their sentences are frequently long and much qualified. They tend, therefore, to punctuate heavily to help the reader through their complex thought. The norm in this sort of writing is rather heavy, rather ormal punctuation. It should be consistently maintained. On the other hand, the aim of the mystery story, the news magazine, the light novel is rapid, effortless reading. Sentences are usually rather simple in structure, short and informal. They need little punctuation and would merely be slowed down if more were put in. Publishers

offering this sort of fare try to keep punctuation to its minimum essentials.

The aims of writers and publishers of all sorts are clarity and suitability to the general style. If these two aims are achieved, consistently, the punctuation is good.

The use of the apostrophe, the hyphen, and quotation marks is to a great extent formalized, not subject to judgment, although divided usage will be found here too. The principal uses of these marks are discussed below.

THE APOSTROPHE

POSSESSIVE FORMS. The most common use of the apostrophe is in spelling the possessive forms of nouns and some pronouns. If the word ends with any sound except that of *s* (or sometimes *sh* or *z*), the possessive is formed by the addition of *'s*. If the word ends with the sound of *s* (or sometimes *sh* or *z*), the possessive is formed by the addition of *'* alone:

Ending not in *s*	Ending in *s*
girl's	companies'
nobody's	conscience'
men's	several horses'

Because most singulars do not end in *s* and form the possessive by adding *'s*, many writers feel uncomfortable when they form the possessive of a singular ending in *s* merely by the addition of *'*. There is a growing tendency to add an extra *s* to such words, especially when they consist of a single syllable. The extra *s* then provides an extra syllable and differentiates the sound of the possessive from the simple form:

Tom *Jones's* house instead of Tom *Jones'* house.
The *moss's* color instead of the *moss'* color.

Possessives of the personal pronouns do *not* take the apostrophe:

my, mine	our, ours
your, yours	your, yours
her, hers	their, theirs
his	whose
its	

The possessive is used not only in its obvious function but in such phrases as: two *hours'* work, a *week's* trip.

OMISSION. The apostrophe is also used to show the omission of one or more letters in contractions: *he'll, I'm, it's* [*it is*], *can't*. In quoted dialogue or speech, an apostrophe indicates a speaker's omission of sounds represented by the conventional spelling of the word, for instance: the state of *No'th* Carolina.

PLURAL OF NUMBERS, ETC. An apostrophe is generally used in forming the plural of numbers, letters, or words thought of as words:

two *e's*	the *1890's*
four *6's*	the last two *the's*

PLURAL OF ABBREVIATIONS. Initials used as abbreviations are often treated the same way:

two GI's

THE HYPHEN

The hyphen is regularly used when a word has to be broken at the end of a line to show that the remainder of the word is to follow on the next line. A word should be broken only between syllables: *port-able, run-ning, dis-pense.*

It is bad printing or typing practice to carry over a syllable of only two letters and virtually forbidden to carry over a single letter. It is equally forbidden to leave a single letter at the end of a line. Never break: *e-lapse, read-y, e-rase.* Avoid breaking: *real-ly, el-bow, du-ly.*

The hyphen is also used in a variety of compounds. Here usage is divided violently. A *half-finished* building stands beside a *half finished* building. *Slow-moving* traffic flows along with *slow moving* traffic. A *drug-store* clerk works in a *drug store* called The Evans *Drugstore.* Some publishers prefer to bring compounds into single words without space or hyphen. A wag once said of *Time Magazine,* "*Time* abhors the hyphen." Other publishers simply follow the usage of a given dictionary. Others prefer wherever possible to break compounds into two words. Choose a system and try to be consistent.

The hyphen is sometimes used between a prefix ending with a vowel and a root beginning with the same vowel (*re-enter, co-operate*). Many writers prefer to write *reënter* and *coöperate* or *reenter* and *cooperate.* Again, usage is violently divided.

A hyphen is used when a prefix added would make confusion with another word:

Re-cover a chair but *recover* from an illness.
He decided to *re-turn* the bacon but *return* postage guaranteed.

A hyphen is used between a prefix and a proper name:

pro-Republican	anti-Russian

Compound numerals between twenty-one and ninety-nine and fractions are usually hyphenated:

one hundred and thirty-one   three-quarters

Some writers now omit this hyphen.

QUOTATIONS

In a piece of writing, words spoken by someone other than the author, directly quoted, are usually marked as quotation. Indirectly quoted words are not so marked:

DIRECT: President Coolidge said, "I do not choose to run."

INDIRECT: President Coolidge said that he did not choose to run.

Material is quoted or it is not; there can be no compromise between direct and indirect quotation.

The indication of quotation follows no logic but custom, and the system is arbitrary. Short quotations are usually marked off by quotation marks placed at the beginning and end of the actual quotation. If the quotation is interrupted (for example, by *he said*), the interruption makes a new end and beginning which should be marked off by quotation marks:

"Won't you come to dinner?" he asked. "Come straight from the office."

In the United States quotations are usually indicated by double quotes (like those used above) and quotations within quotations are marked off by single quotes. ('These are single quotes.') In England the opposite system is used. Some publishers of American books and magazines use the English system. Either method is clear, and many book designers claim that the single quotes give a less speckled appearance.

The position of quotation marks in relation to other punctuation is ruled by a rather rigid custom in the United States, although the usage in England, equally fixed, is different. In the United States final quotes follow a period or a comma:

". . . the greatest of these is charity."
The better class of pickers are "blanket stiffs," men who own their own bedding.

Final quotes precede semicolons or colons:

"Divided we fall"; this truth illustrates itself day by day.

These two rules were built up in deference to the esthetic feelings of a generation or two of typesetters.

The position of final quotes in relation to exclamation points, question marks, or dashes is determined by meaning. The test is the same for all three. If a question mark, for example, belongs with the quotation but not with the whole sentence, it goes inside final quotes:

The sentry called, "Who goes there?"

If it goes with the whole sentence, it should be placed outside the final quotes:

Who can say without vanity, "I am an honest man"?

Dashes usually come inside final quotes, but the meaning is the test.

Long quotations are often printed in a different type or with wider margins or with the lines closer together than the main text, to indicate quotation. If this method is followed, no quotation marks are used. It is much used where a number of rather long passages must be quoted, particularly in serious nonfiction.

If a quotation of two or more paragraphs is marked off by quotation marks, beginning quotes are usually placed at the beginning of each paragraph but no final quotes are written until the end of the quotation is reached.

Long or formal quotations are often marked off from their introductory sentences by colons. Short, informal quotations, such as the dialogue in a story, are usually marked off by a comma. Very short quotations, one or two words, require no punctuation:

FORMAL: The Secretary of State spoke as follows: " . . .
INFORMAL: "Hollywood," he said, "always reminds me of a stage set."
VERY SHORT: He said "No." (or) He said *No* (or) *no*.

Titles of songs, stories, chapters of a book, poems, magazines, plays, motion pictures, operas, and so forth are usually written in quotes. Titles of books are sometimes put in quotes although they are more commonly put in italics.

CAPITALIZATION

Although there is considerable variation in the use of capital letters in many situations, copyreaders and compositors have worked out rules for their own use, and for the most part capitalization follows well defined con-

ventions. Some of the commoner conventions are as follows:

1. Capitalize the first word of each sentence; also the beginning of a word or phrase standing independently, like a sentence.

2. Capitalize the beginning of each line of poetry or conventional verse:

The steed bit his master;
How came this to pass?
He heard the good pastor
Cry, "All flesh is grass."
    —ANON.

Exception: Some modern poetry is written without capitals or only with such capitals as prose would have.

3. Capitalize proper nouns and adjectives:

George Washington	French
the United States	Germanic
Elizabeth	New England

4. The German *von* and Dutch *van* in proper names are commonly not printed with a capital when part of a name, but usage varies:

Paul von Hindenburg   Vincent van Gogh

5. The French particles *de* and *du* and the Italian *di* and *da* are commonly written in lower case when they are preceded by a first name or title. Without title or first name, the particle is sometimes dropped, sometimes capitalized. One American newspaper's style book adds: "Except De Gaulle, which is always capped."

Marquis de Lafayette	Count de Mirabeau
[De] Lafayette	[De] Mirabeau

In English or American names these particles are commonly capitalized in all positions:

William De Morgan	Lee De Forest
De Morgan	De Forest

6. Do not capitalize words made from proper nouns now having a special meaning distinct from the proper name:

antimacassar	china
pasteurize	macadam

7. Capitalize recognized geographical names:

Ohio River	Strait of Juan de Fuca
Cascade Mountains	Gulf of Mexico

8. Capitalize the following when they follow a single proper name and are written in the singular:

Butte	Gap	Peninsula
Canyon	Glacier	Plateau
County (in U.S.)	Harbor	Range
Creek	Head	River
Delta	Ocean	Valley

For example, the *Sacramento River*, but the *Tennessee and Cumberland rivers*.

9. Capitalize the following in the singular and plural when they follow a proper name:

Hill	Mountain
Island	Narrows

10. Capitalize in the singular whether placed before or after the name. Capitalize in the plural when they come before the name and sometimes following a single name:

Bay	Military Camp	Shoal
Cape	Lake	Point
Desert	Mount	Strait
Gulf	Peak	Sea
Isle	Plain	Zone

For example, *Lakes George and Champlain* but *Malheur and Goose lakes*. Contrast *Muscle Shoals*.

11. Capitalize compass directions when they designate particular regions, also the nicknames or special names for regions or districts:

East Tennessee	the South
Middle Atlantic States	the Near East
the Hub	Upper Michigan

Exceptions: Do not capitalize merely directional parts of states or countries:

eastern Washington   southern Indiana

12. Capitalize the names of streets, parks, buildings, etc.:

Forty-second Street	Central Park
Merchandise Mart	Palmolive Building

Exceptions: Do not capitalize such categories of buildings as *library*, *post office*, or *museum*, written without a proper name, unless local custom makes the classification equivalent to a proper name.

13. Capitalize the names of political parties, alliances, movements, classes, religious groups, etc.:

Democratic party	Royalist Spain
Labor party	Axis powers
Republicans	Soviet Russia
Protestants	Negroes

14. Capitalize divisions, departments, and offices of

government, when the official name is used. Do not capitalize incomplete or roundabout designations:

> Department of Commerce
> Circuit Court of Marion County
> Bureau of Labor Statistics
> Congress (United States)
> Senate (United States)
> House of Burgesses
> United States Army (but army doctor)
> Board of Aldermen
> the council
> the lower house (of Congress)
> the bureau
> the legislature

15. Capitalize the names of wars, battles, treaties, and important events:

> Revolutionary War   Black Death
> Congress of Vienna   War of 1812

Do not capitalize *war* or *treaty* when used without the distinguishing name.

16. Capitalize the numeral used with kings, dynasties, or organizations. Numerals preceding the name are ordinarily spelled out; those following the name are commonly put in Roman numerals:

> Nineteenth Amendment   Third Army
> Forty-eighth Congress   Henry IV

17. Capitalize titles of rank or honor, military or civil, academic degrees, decorations, etc., when written with the name, and all titles of honor or rank when used for specific persons in place of the name:

> General Bradley
> the Senator from Ohio (but a senator)
> Nicholas Murray Butler, Doctor of Letters
> the Earl of Rochester
> King George
> the Archbishop of Canterbury

18. Capitalization of the titles of books, plays, articles, pieces of music, and so forth is handled in two ways. The commoner method is to capitalize all main words (the nouns, verbs, adjectives, and adverbs) as well as the first word. The Library of Congress style, however, until recently called for the capitalization of only the first word and any proper nouns or adjectives appearing in the title.

> The Gem of the Prairie
> Mourning Becomes Electra

Titles of chapters in a book, and references to parts of a specific book, such as *Bibliography*, *Index*, or *Table of Contents*, are commonly capitalized.

In references to the names of newspapers and periodicals, an initial article need not be capitalized or treated as part of the title:

> The story was reprinted in the *Reader's Digest*.

19. Capitalize the first word of a direct quotation:

> An aide reported, "The left wing is being driven back in confusion."

20. Capitalize the first person singular pronoun in the nominative: I. None of the other pronouns are capitalized.

21. Capitalize personifications:

> Darwin drew a picture of Nature red in tooth and claw.
> The Senator talked grandly of Industry as a mother holding twin children, Labor and Capital, on her capacious lap.

22. Capitalize the various names of God or of the Christian Trinity, both nouns and adjectives, and also pronouns clearly referring to the Deity:

the Savior	the Word	Jehovah
the Messiah	the Son	Yahweh
the Almighty	the Virgin Mary	Holy Ghost

23. In expressions of time, A.M. and P.M. are usually set in small capitals without space between them:

9:40 A.M.	12:00 M. (noon)	6:10 P.M.
12:00 P.M. (midnight)	A.D. 1491	42 B.C.

SECTION II. CORRESPONDENCE

Every business letter performs a double function. The original carries a message to its recipient. The carbon copy, retained in the sender's files, serves as an automatic record. Since either the original or the carbon may be referred to long afterward, both must contain all the information that will then be required.

In addition to the material in the letter proper, the letter must contain the name and address of the recipient (necessary for the file copy) and the name and address of the sender (necessary for reply to the original) as well as the date of writing and often other information.

Certain more or less standardized forms have been worked out for furnishing this information briefly and with a minimum of typing effort, clearly and with an attractive appearance. Within these broad conventions each company or organization works out and employs its own preferred style for all correspondence. A newcomer can familiarize himself with an organization's house style by a few minutes' study of the correspondence files.

Most letters today are variations of the block style because it permits a stenographer to get out a maximum of work in a minimum of time. Brief descriptions of the principal variations will follow a discussion of the standard block style.

HEADING

On plain paper the heading consists of the sender's address and the date of writing. It is commonly placed so as to align with the right margin of the body of the letter, at least two inches below the top of the sheet. Each line should be started directly below the line above so as to form a block:

> 8096 Whiteside Drive
> Detroit 16, Michigan
> November 23, 1947

No punctuation is required at the end of a line.

On a letterhead the sender's address is printed and only the date need be typed in. It is placed so as to end in alignment with the right margin of the letter proper, usually about four spaces below the head but lower down if the letter is short. Sometimes the date is centered below the head.

INSIDE ADDRESS

The inside address should contain the recipient's name and full address. The state is commonly written on the same line as the city. Each line is aligned with the left margin of the letter proper. It is usually placed four spaces below the heading but a little lower if the letter is short.

In letters addressed to an individual some business organizations prefer to have the inside address appear at the end of the letter, two to four spaces below the signature. This position is also useful for personal typewritten correspondence of which a carbon is to be kept. It gets the formal information into the carbon but it avoids a formal look at the opening.

In addressing an individual with a long title the following forms are convenient:

> Mr. John Jackson, Chairman
> Committee on International
>   Commerce
> Mr. John Jackson
> Chairman of the Committee on
>   International Commerce

Frequently people are proud of a military rank, an honorary title, or a doctor's degree. They will appreciate the accurate use of rank or title. Dr. and Mr. are regular abbreviations. Abbreviations of other titles may be used, but it is more courteous to write them out in full. However, some college professors and nonmedical doctors prefer not to use the title. When the recipient's preference is known it should always be followed.

SALUTATION

Beginning at the left margin, usually two spaces below the inside address, in a letter to a single individual write Dear Sir: Dear Madam: Dear Mr. (or Mrs. or Miss) ————:. A woman whose marital status is unknown should always be addressed as Miss. In a letter to an organization, corporation, company, or group of any kind begin Gentlemen: . . . . After any of these it is conventional to use a colon.

Some letters addressed to an organization or company may be directed to the attention of a particular individual or official. This may be done as follows:

> Attention of the Sales Manager (or)
>   Attention: Sales Manager
> Attention of Mr. Wilbur M. Schwartz (or)
>   Attention: Mr. Wilbur M. Schwartz

The line is usually placed between the inside address and the salutation, with two spaces above and below. It is sometimes written on the same line with the salutation placed so as to end in alignment with the right-hand margin. To bring it to the immediate notice of the recipient, it is sometimes underlined. Even though the letter is directed to the attention of a single person, since it is addressed to an organization the proper salutation remains Gentlemen:.

The proper arrangement of inside address, direction of attention, and salutation is as follows:

Stamford Brass Co., Inc.
516 Little Street
Stamford 4, Connecticut
Attention: Advertising Manager
Gentlemen:

Some companies and organizations regularly indicate the subject of the letter to follow. A special place for a brief statement of the subject is provided on some letterheads. On plain paper it is usually centered on the same line as the salutation or two spaces below it:

Nonpareil Woolens
Woonsocket 2, R. I.
Gentlemen: Subject: *Insurance*

The body of the letter follows, typed in single space with double space between paragraphs. Each line begins at the left margin without indentation.

COMPLIMENTARY CLOSE

In formal business correspondence the complimentary close is limited to *Yours truly*, or variations of it such as *Very truly yours*, or, if the letter is addressed to a person of high reputation or office, *Respectfully yours*. Any of these phrases is followed by a comma.

A few conservative writers cling to the old form, now rapidly dropping out of use, in which the final sentence of the body of the letter is run into the complimentary close in the following manner:

Hoping to hear from you soon, I remain
                    Very truly yours,

The complimentary close should be set two spaces below the body of the letter. It is usually begun at the center or very slightly to the right of center.

SIGNATURE

The signature of a letter is handled in a variety of ways. If the firm name is used, it should be typed in full, two spaces below the complimentary close. Below it, or below the complimentary close if no firm name is used, space is left for the longhand signature of the writer. Below the space is typed the writer's position, often preceded by his typewritten name. It may be arranged in block or in an oblique form as the writer prefers:

(1) Yours truly,   (2) Yours truly,
Richard Smith   Richard Smith
Sales Manager   Sales Manager

(3) Yours truly,
ACME MANUFACTURING COMPANY

Richard Smith
Sales Manager

(4) Yours truly,
ACME MANUFACTURING COMPANY

Richard Smith
Sales Manager

When the writer has a personal friendship with the recipient of the letter, he need not restrict himself to the formal phrase. He is free to avail himself of any of the closing phrases of personal correspondence.

In order to identify the writer of the letter and the stenographer, it is customary to put the initials of the writer, followed by those of the stenographer, in the lower left-hand corner: RLS/J or RLS/AJ. If any enclosures are to be made, *Encl.* or *Enclosures* (3) is added directly below these initials as a reminder to the person who puts the letter in its envelope.

ADDRESS ON ENVELOPE

The address should start at or near the center. Double spacing is preferred. Arrangement may be either block or oblique. Where zone numbers are provided, they should be written after the name of the city. The Post Office prefers to have the state written on a separate line. If the address requires more than four lines, the least essential information, such as the room number in a building, should be written separately in the left-hand corner of the envelope.

SPECIAL LETTERS

Occasionally it is necessary to write to an official of the city, state, or national government, to a college president, a dignitary of the Roman Catholic Church, or the like. If the writer happens to be intimately acquainted with the recipient, he can write as he likes. Here is a list:

U. S. SENATOR

Name: The Hon. Horace Dana
Address: United States Senate, Washington, D. C.
Salutation: My dear Senator: (or, less formal)
                    Dear Mr. Dana:
Close: Yours very truly,

CONGRESSMAN

Name: The Hon. Horace Dana
Address: United States House of Representatives, Washington, D. C.
Salutation: Dear Sir: (or, less formal) Dear Mr. Dana:
Close: Yours very truly,

CABINET MEMBER

Name: The Secretary of the Interior
Address: Washington, D. C.
Salutation: Dear Mr. Secretary:
Close: Yours very truly,

PRESIDENT OF THE UNITED STATES

Name: The President
Address: Washington, D. C.
Salutation: Sir: (or, less formal) Dear Mr. President:
Close: Yours very truly,

GOVERNOR OF A STATE

Name: The Hon. Warren Dewey
Address: Governor's Office (or State House or Executive Mansion), state capital, state
Salutation: Dear Sir:
Close: Yours very truly,

MAYOR

Name: The Hon. Richard Farley
Address: Mayor's Office, city, state
Salutation: Dear Sir: (or, less formal) Dear Mr. Mayor:
Close: Yours very truly,

JUDGE

Name: The Hon. Frank Murphy
Address: United States Supreme Court, Washington, D. C.
Salutation: Dear Sir:
Close: Yours very truly,

FOREIGN AMBASSADOR

Name: His Excellency the Brazilian Ambassador
Address: Washington, D. C.
Salutation: Dear Mr. Ambassador:
Close: Yours very truly,

FOREIGN CONSUL

Name: The British Consul
Address: street, city, state
Salutation: Dear Mr. Consul:
Close: Yours very truly,

BISHOP

Name: The Rt. Rev. James Trenton, D. D.
Address: Bishop of Portland, Portland, Oregon
Salutation: Sir: (or) Right Reverend Bishop:
Close: Yours sincerely, or Very truly yours,
Sincerely yours in Christ, should be used by a Catholic writer.

PARISH PRIEST

Name: The Rev. John Kelly
Address: Rector of St. ———'s Church, street and number, city, state.
Salutation: Dear Reverend Father: (or) Reverend and dear Father:
Close: Sincerely yours,   Very truly yours,

VARIATIONS IN STYLE

There are many variations of style. Stenographers should remember that no single style has any special claim to correctness and that a style different from that which they were taught in business school or which they used in a preceding job is not therefore to be condemned. Within limits, each part of the letter may be arranged to suit the preference of the writer.

Block Indented is about as much used as block. It is the same as block except that the first line of each paragraph is indented five spaces or more.

Extreme Block is an ultra-modern arrangement. Heading, inside address, salutation, complimentary close, and signature are all aligned with the left margin of the letter proper. Because the carriage of the typewriter is always thrown clear over, it is quick and easy for the typist. The extreme block is, however, open to the objection that its balance is likely to be too heavy on the left.

Oblique is a legacy of the handwritten letter. In this style the heading, the inside address, and the signature are arranged with each successive line several spaces to the right of the line above. Because this style puts a heavy burden on the stenographer and mistakes in spacing are likely to occur, the use of it has almost disappeared.

SECTION III. PREPARATION OF COPY FOR THE TYPESETTER OR PUBLISHER

GENERAL NOTES

In the event that a piece of writing is to be printed, the writer wants his manuscript in proper form before he sends it in. To prepare a manuscript so as to cause a minimum of resetting and correction, the writer must begin at a point before the final typing of the manuscript is made.

If the manuscript is to go directly to the typesetter, it will have no editing after it leaves the hands of the author. The writer should study similar publications and note details of punctuation, capitalization, the use of italics or quotes for titles, a useful arrangement of footnote material, if any, and so forth. Before the final draft is typed, he should put his manuscript in the form he has decided to adopt.

If the manuscript is to be published in a magazine or book put out by a regular publisher, he should study the publisher's preferred style and, as far as he can, make his own manuscript conform to it. He should also expect that the publisher will have his copy gone over and altered where it fails to conform to the publisher's regular style.

With the rough draft of the manuscript corrected, the final typing is the next step. *It is simple common sense always to make at least one carbon, usually two.* Many a manuscript has gone astray in the mail, or been lost or burned up in a fire. Frequently, too, the publisher or typesetter has a question that requires reference to the text, and if the writer has no text handy he is in an embarrassing position.

The final typing should be double-spaced on one side of regular 8½" x 11" typewriter paper. Margins should be ample, at least an inch and a half at the top and left, at least an inch at the right and bottom. A black typewriter ribbon and fresh carbon paper help to make both original and carbons easily read. Everyone who has to read and handle manuscript appreciates the use of opaque paper.

If corrections are necessary, they should be made neatly and clearly. If an addition is too long to be written clearly between the typed lines, it may be written in the margin and a guide line drawn to the point of insertion. If the corrections on any page destroy legibility, or even impair it, the page should be retyped.

FOOTNOTES AND BIBLIOGRAPHY

A writer often has to make use of the work of other men in the field. Although his combination of ideas may be new and his conclusions original, he is obliged to these earlier men for part of his material. It is no more than courtesy for him to acknowledge the obligation. It is also fair dealing with the reader to let him know the path by which the writer has come to the position he takes in his article. For both reasons the writer should acknowledge his sources.

In formal papers, theses, monographs, dissertations, articles in the learned journals, it is necessary to cite the sources for each important fact or idea in a footnote. The style of footnote varies somewhat in different fields of study and in different journals. A writer knowing that his work is to be published in a certain journal should study its style and prepare his footnotes in accordance with its practices.

In informal papers, popular books, or magazine articles, the source of an idea may be worked into the text:

Bob Casey in *Battle Below* makes you realize that the plumbing on a submarine is not simple to handle and the beginner needs an operational chart.

In an informal article, the source may be indicated in a parenthesis in the text:

Gertrude Stein makes Edmund Wilson uneasy (see *Axel's Castle*) because she always carries an idea to its logical—or illogical—extremity.

The writer will have little difficulty in determining what needs to be footnoted, whether the footnotes are inserted informally in the text or arranged at the bottom of the page or at the end of a chapter. Any direct quotation is the most obvious. If the quotation is from material in copyright, permission of the copyright owner must be shown. If the copyright owner prescribes a form of credit, it must be followed word for word. If not, the usual footnote form may be employed. If a summary of another writer's facts or ideas is presented, it should be acknowledged. Figures, dates, opinions, and interpretations should also be credited to their source.

In scholarly work employing a good many notes each footnote is numbered, often for a chapter, occasionally for each page. In books very lightly footnoted, a footnote may be indicated by an asterisk, a dagger, or other symbols. The reference number or symbol is placed slightly above the line at the exact spot where acknowledgment should be made.

For a book, a citation should include the author, title, place of publication, the publisher (sometimes omitted), the date of publication, the volume number (if any), and the pages cited. For an article, a citation should include the author, the title, the publication, the date, volume, and pages cited:

[1] Otto Eisenschiml and Ralph Newman, *The American Iliad* (Indianapolis: The Bobbs-Merrill Co., 1947), 472–474.
[9] W. L. Jenks, "Patrick Sinclair, Builder of Fort Mackinac," *Michigan Historical Collections*, XXXIX (Lansing, 1915), 61–85.

FOOTNOTE FORM

Footnotes are so stylized and so varied that no short summary will include all the problems that the writer may face. The most important features of the footnote can, however, be indicated. The author, not the title, comes first. The title of a book follows in italics if printed, underlined if in typescript. The title of an article in a periodical or a chapter in a book is put in quotation marks, and the title of the periodical or book is put in italics in type or underlined in typescript.

The first time a book is mentioned the facts of publication are given, the city and year (and the publisher between the city and year, if the writer prefers). The first time an article in a periodical is cited, the year is given, the volume number in Roman numerals, and the pages in Arabic numbers.

For later references to the same sources, short forms can be used. When not more than one work by the same author is being used, the author's last name and a page reference are enough:

[6] Eisenschiml and Newman, 613.

If several works by the same author are cited, the author's name and a shortened title and page reference suffice:

[3] Chateaubriand, *Atala*, 123.

When two references to the same work follow in sequence, the second may use *ibid.* (meaning *in the same place*) instead of author and shortened title.

Quoted passages are commonly quoted exactly, letter for letter and punctuation mark for punctuation mark, even down to errors and misprints. If the writer wants to disclaim responsibility for errors in the original, he can insert in brackets the Latin word *sic* (meaning *thus in the original*). If he is quoting a quotation, he can indicate the fact in a footnote and put off responsibility for the accuracy of his quotation on his actual source:

[2] John Dryden, *Mac Flecknoe*, quoted in W. H. Auden, *The Oxford Book of Light Verse* (Oxford, 1938), 195.

ABBREVIATIONS

Abbreviations in footnotes are conventional. In old books most of the abbreviations represent Latin words. Many of these are being replaced by English words.

cf. (meaning *compare*) sometimes used instead of *see.*

infra (meaning *below*) referring to something discussed later.

op. cit. (*opere citato* meaning *the work cited*).

passim (meaning *here and there, in various passages*) used for scattered references.

supra (meaning *above*) referring to something previously discussed.

vide (meaning *see*) now largely replaced by *see.*

In recent books the following abbreviations are likely to occur:

c. or *ca.* (*circa* meaning *about*) used with dates not exactly ascertainable.

ed. meaning *edited by* or *edition* (4th ed.)

f. meaning *one following page* (47 f.)

ff. meaning *following pages* (287 ff.)

n.d. meaning *no date.* This is used when the date of publication cannot be found.

n.p. meaning *no place.* This is used when the place of publication cannot be found.

p. meaning *page.*

pp. meaning *pages.* If page references are consistently indicated in Arabic numbers and volumes in Roman numerals, the words *volume* and *page* or their abbreviations can be safely omitted.

tr. meaning *translator* or *translated by.*

vol. meaning *volume* or *volumes.* See note under *pp.* above.

Several styles of punctuation are used in footnotes. No one is necessarily better than another. It is important to choose a style which can be followed consistently.

BIBLIOGRAPHY

A bibliography following a piece of writing is a convenient record for the reader of the books, articles, and other items drawn on by the writer for material. Bibliographies vary from formal listings to informal notes written in ordinary sentence form, mentioning and commenting on books and articles that might be of interest to the reader. Such notes are suitable for a popular work with a minimum of footnoting in its body. For a scholarly work a formal bibliography is required. This will supply compactly a complete list of the items drawn on for material, arranged for ready reference but not for reading.

For the informal bibliographical note, no style is prescribed. The only requirement is that each work referred to be adequately identified.

In the formal bibliography the following information should be included: author (last name first, followed by first name or initials), exact title in full, and the facts of publication, sometimes followed by a very brief criticism or characterization. As in footnotes, book titles are put in italics when printed, underlined in typescript. Titles of magazine articles, chapters of books, and the like are put in quotation marks; titles of magazines or newspapers in italics or underlined.

Styles of punctuation within each entry vary. Sometimes the three main parts are punctuated by periods, sometimes by commas. The important point is to use consistent punctuation throughout the bibliography. The name of the publisher may be left out or included between the place of publication and the date. Some typical entries follow:

Howe, Will D. *Charles Lamb and His Friends.* Indianapolis: The Bobbs-Merrill Company, 1944.
Asquith, Henry Herbert, *The Genesis of the War*, New York, 1923.

Cousins, Norman, "Bystanders Are Not Innocent," *The Saturday Review of Literature*, Aug. 2, 1947, Vol. XXX, No. 31, pp. 7–9.
Palmer, Mary B. "Experiment in Health," *Harper's Magazine*, Vol. 194 (May, 1947), 427–32.

The items of the bibliography are commonly arranged alphabetically by authors. If a book or article has no author, it may be alphabetized according to the first main word of its title. If two or more books by the same author are listed, for all those after the first a long dash can be substituted for the author's name.

PROOFREADER'S MARKS AND PROOFREADING

The common marks used by proofreaders and typesetters are listed and illustrated here. If the writer feels the slightest doubt of his ability to make clear his intention with them, he can write on the margin a brief note to the typesetter, explaining precisely what he wants done.

After a piece of writing is set in type, proofs are pulled and sent to the author for correction or approval. Usually the proofs are galleys, long sheets equal to a little more than three pages of an ordinary book. Each galley represents a heavy tray of metal at the typesetter's, and any change in the proof must be duplicated in the type itself.

When the original manuscript was set in type, the typesetter read each line of the manuscript, word for word, and transcribed it. When the corrected galleys go back to the typesetter so that the type can be made to correspond with the amended galleys, the typesetter does not read them. He looks only at the margins. Any correction not clearly marked outside the type area will be ignored. All corrections should be made in the margins and leader lines drawn to the precise spot.

PROOFREADER'S MARKS

⅄	Insert comma	⌄	Superscript (number specified)
⌄	Insert apostrophe		
⌄⌄	Insert quotation marks	⌃	Subscript (number specified)
⊙	Insert period		
⊙	Insert colon	#	Insert space
;/	Insert semicolon	hr#	Hair space between letters
?/	Insert question mark	⌄	Push down space
=/	Insert hyphen	⊏	Move to left
⅟M̄	One-em dash	⊐	Move to right
2/M̄	Two-em dash	⊔	Lower
en	En dash	⊓	Elevate
|.|.|.|	Ellipsis (If preceded by a period there will be 4 dots.)	X	Broken letter
		⌒	Ligature (ÆSsop)
⅌	Delete	sp	Spell out (U.S.)
⌒	Close up	stet	Let it stand (some-day)
⅌	Delete and close up	wf	Wrong font
9	Reverse; upside-down	bf	Set in boldface type
⋀	Insert (caret)	rom	Set in roman type
¶	Paragraph	ital	Set in italic type
no¶	No paragraph; run in	sc	Small capitals
tr	Transpose (their only is)	caps	Capitals
=	Align	lc	Set in lower case
		ld>	Insert lead between lines

COLLEGES AND UNIVERSITIES

Information below is given in the following sequence: the official name of the institution; its location; its control (private, state, etc.), including the denomination when under religious control; its kind of student body (men, women, or coeducational), including its status as a junior college when such; and its date of founding. Abbreviations used are:

A. & M. C., Agricultural & Mechanical College
AC, Advent Christian
Ag, Agricultural
AG, Assemblies of God
AL, American Lutheran
AMA, American Missionary Association
AME, African Methodist Episcopal
AMEZ, African Methodist Episcopal Zion
Bapt, Baptist
Br, Brethren
C., College
CBr, Church of the Brethren
CC, Church of Christ
CG, Church of God
ChristRef, Christian Reformed
CMA, Christian & Missionary Alliance
CNJ, Church of New Jerusalem
cnty, county

Cong, Congregational
DC, Disciples of Christ
dist, district
ELuth, Evangelical Lutheran
Episc, Episcopal
ER, Evangelical Reformed
EUB, Evangelical United Brethren
FMeth, Free Methodist
Fr, Friends
Inst., Institute
Inter, Interdenominational
jr, junior
LDS, Latter-day Saints
Luth, Lutheran
MCA, Missionary Church Association
ME, Methodist Episcopal
Men, Mennonite
Meth, Methodist
Mor, Moravian
mun, municipal

nat, national
Naz, Nazarene
PentHol, Pentacostal Holiness
Presb, Presbyterian
pvt, private
RC, Roman Catholic
Ref, Reformed
RussOrth, Russian Orthodox
Schl., School
Sem., Seminary
SDA, Seventh Day Adventists
SDBapt, Seventh Day Baptists
st, state
T.C., Teachers College
terr, territorial
Theol., Theological
twp, township
U., University
UL, United Lutheran
Unit, Unitarian
YMCA, Young Men's Christian Assn.

Abilene Christian C., Abilene, Tex.; pvt (CC); coed; 1906.
Abraham Baldwin Ag. C., Tifton, Ga.; st (jr); coed; 1933.
Adams State C., Alamosa, Colo.; st; coed; 1921.
Adelphi C., Garden City, NY; pvt; coed; 1896.
Adrian C., Adrian, Mich.; pvt (Meth); coed; 1845.
Agnes Scott C., Decatur, Ga.; pvt; women; 1889.
Akron, U. of, Akron, O.; mun; coed; 1870.
Alabama, U. of, University, Ala.; st; coed; 1831.
Alabama A. & M. C., Normal, Ala.; st; coed; 1875.
Alabama C., Montevallo, Ala.; st; women; 1896.
Alabama Polytech. Inst., Auburn, Ala.; st; coed; 1872.
Alabama State C., Montgomery, Ala.; st; coed; 1874.
Alabama State T. C., Florence, Ala.; st; coed; 1873.
Alabama State T. C., Jacksonville, Ala.; st; coed, 1883.
Alabama State T. C., Livingston, Ala.; st; coed; 1840.
Alabama State T. C., Troy, Ala.; st; coed; 1887.
Alaska, U. of, College, Alaska; st; coed; 1915.
Albany State C., Albany, Ga.; st; coed; 1903.
Albertus Magnus C., New Haven, Conn.; pvt (RC); women; 1925.
Albion C., Albion, Mich.; pvt (Meth); coed; 1835.
Albright C., Reading Pa.; pvt (EUB); coed; 1856.
Alcorn A. & M. C., Lorman, Miss.; st; coed; 1871.
Alderson-Broaddus C., Philippi, W. Va.; pvt (Bapt); coed; 1931.
Alfred U., Alfred, NY; st & pvt; coed; 1836.
Allan Hancock C., Santa Maria, Cal.; dist (jr); coed; 1920.
Allegheny C., Meadville, Pa.; pvt (Meth); coed; 1815.
Allen U., Columbia, S. C.; pvt (AME); coed; 1870.
Alliance C., Cambridge Springs, Pa.; pvt; women; 1912.
Alma C., Alma, Mich.; pvt (Presb); coed; 1886.
Alpena Community C., Alpena, Mich.; mun (jr); coed; 1952.
Alverno C., Milwaukee, Wisc.; pvt (RC); women; 1936.
Alvin Jr. C., Alvin, Tex.; dist (jr); coed; 1949.
Amarillo C., Amarillo, Tex.; mun (jr); coed; 1929.
American Acad. of Art, Chicago, Ill.; pvt (jr); coed; 1923.
American Conserv. of Music, Chicago, Ill.; pvt; coed; 1886.
American Intl. C., Springfield, Mass.; pvt; coed; 1885.
American River Jr. C., Del Paso Heights, Cal.; dist (jr); coed; 1955.
American U., The, Washington, D. C.; pvt; coed; 1893.
Amherst C., Amherst, Mass.; pvt; men; 1821.
Anderson C., Anderson, S. C.; pvt (Bapt, jr); women; 1911.
Anna Maria C. for Women, Paxton, Mass.; pvt (RC); women; 1946.
Annhurst C., South Woodstock, Conn.; pvt (RC) women; 1941.
Antelope Valley Jr. C., Lancaster, Cal.; mun (jr); coed; 1929.
Antioch C., Yellow Springs, O.; pvt; coed; 1852.
Appalachian State T. C., Boone, N. C.; st; coed; 1903.
Aquinas C., Grand Rapids, Mich.; pvt (RC); coed; 1923.
Arizona, U. of, Tucson, Ariz.; st; coed; 1885.
Arizona State C., Flagstaff, Ariz.; st; coed; 1899.
Arizona State U., Tempe, Ariz.; st; coed; 1885.
Arkansas, U. of, Fayetteville, Ark.; st; coed; 1872.

Arkansas A. & M. C., College Heights, Ark.; st; coed; 1909.
Arkansas A. M. & Normal C., Pine Bluff, Ark.; st; coed; 1875.
Arkansas C., Batesville, Ark.; pvt (Presb); coed; 1872.
Arkansas City Jr. C., Arkansas City, Kans.; mun (jr); coed; 1922.
Arkansas Polytech. C., Russellville, Ark.; st; coed; 1909.
Arkansas State C., State College, Ark.; st; coed; 1910.
Arkansas State T. C., Conway, Ark.; st; coed; 1907.
Arlington State C., Arlington, Tex.; st (jr); coed; 1917.
Armstrong C. of Savannah, Savannah, Ga.; mun (jr); coed; 1935.
Aroostook State T. C., Presque Isle, Me.; st; coed; 1902.
Art Center Schl., The, Los Angeles, Cal.; pvt; coed; 1930.
Art Inst. of Chicago, Schl. of the, Chicago, Ill.; pvt; coed; 1869.
Asbury C., Wilmore, Ky.; pvt; coed; 1890.
Asheville-Biltmore C., Asheville, N. C.; mun & cnty (jr); coed; 1927.
Ashland C., Ashland, O.; pvt (Br); coed; 1878.
Ashland Jr. C., Ashland, Ky.; mun (jr); coed; 1938.
Assumption C., Worcester, Mass.; pvt (RC); men; 1904.
Athens C., Athens, Ala.; pvt (Meth); coed; 1822.
Atlanta U., Atlanta, Ga.; pvt; coed; 1867.
Atlantic Christian C., Wilson, N. C.; pvt (DC); coed; 1902.
Atlantic Union C., South Lancaster, Mass.; pvt (SDA); coed; 1882.
Auburn Community C., Auburn, NY; mun (jr); coed; 1953.
Auburn Theol. Sem., NYC; pvt (Inter); coed; 1818.
Augsburg C. & Theol. Sem., Minneapolis, Minn.; pvt (Luth); coed; 1869.
Augusta, Jr. C. of, Augusta, Ga.; cnty (jr); coed; 1925.
Augustana C., Rock Island, Ill.; pvt (Luth); coed; 1860.
Augustana C., Sioux Falls, S. D.; pvt (ELuth); coed; 1860.
Aurora C., Aurora, Ill.; pvt (AC); coed; 1893.
Austin C., Sherman, Tex.; pvt (Presb); coed; 1849.
Austin Jr. C., Austin, Minn.; dist (jr); coed; 1940.
Austin Peay State C., Clarksville, Tenn.; st; coed; 1929.
Averett C., Danville, Va.; pvt (Bapt, jr); women; 1859.
Babson Inst. of Bus. Admin., Babson Park, Mass.; pvt; men; 1919.
Bacone C., Bacone, Okla.; pvt (Bapt, jr); coed; 1880.
Baker U., Baldwin City, Kans.; pvt (Meth); coed; 1858.
Bakersfield C., Bakersfield, Cal.; dist (jr); coed; 1913.
Baldwin-Wallace C., Berea, O.; pvt (Meth); coed; 1845.
Ball State T. C., Muncie, Ind.; st; coed; 1918.
Baltimore, U. of, Baltimore, Md.; pvt; coed; 1925.
Baltimore C. of Commerce, Baltimore, Md.; pvt (YMCA); coed; 1909.
Baltimore Jr. C., Baltimore, Md.; mun (jr); coed; 1947.
Bank Street C. of Ed., NYC; pvt; coed; 1916.
Baptist Bible Sem., Johnson City, NY; pvt (Bapt); coed; 1932.

Barat C. of the Sacred Heart, Lake Forest, Ill.; pvt (RC); women; 1918.
Barber-Scotia C., Concord, N. C., pvt (Presb); coed; 1867.
Bard C., Annandale-on-Hudson, NY; pvt; coed; 1860.
Barnard C., NYC; pvt; women; 1889.
Barry C., Miami, Fla.; pvt (RC); women; 1940.
Bates C., Lewiston, Me.; pvt; coed; 1864.
Bay City Jr. C., Bay City, Mich.; mun (jr); coed; 1922.
Baylor U., Waco, Tex.; pvt (Bapt); coed; 1845.
Beaver C., Jenkintown, Pa.; pvt (Presb); women; 1853.
Beckley C., Beckley, W. Va.; pvt (jr); coed; 1933.
Belhaven C., Jackson, Miss.; pvt (Presb); coed; 1894.
Bellarmine C., Louisville, Ky.; pvt (RC); men; 1950.
Belleville Twp. Jr. C., Belleville, Ill.; dist (jr); coed; 1946.
Belmont Abbey C., Belmont, N. C.; pvt (RC); men; 1878.
Belmont C., Nashville, Tenn.; pvt (Bapt); coed; 1951.
Beloit C., Beloit, Wisc.; pvt; coed; 1846.
Bemidji State C., Bemidji, Minn.; st; coed; 1919.
Benedict C., Columbia, S. C.; pvt; coed; 1870.
Benedictine Heights C., Tulsa, Okla., pvt; coed; 1917.
Benjamin Franklin U., Washington, D. C.; pvt; coed; 1925.
Bennett C., Greensboro, N. C.; pvt (Meth); women; 1873.
Bennett Jr. C., Millbrook, NY; pvt; women; 1891.
Bennington C., Bennington, Vt.; pvt; women; 1932.
Berea C., Berea, Ky.; pvt; coed; 1855.
Berry C., Mt. Berry, Ga.; pvt; coed; 1902.
Bessie Tift C., Forsyth, Ga.; pvt (Bapt); women; 1849.
Bethany C., Lindsborg, Kans.; pvt (Luth); coed; 1881.
Bethany C., Bethany, W. Va.; pvt (DC); coed; 1840.
Bethany-Nazarene C., Bethany, Okla.; pvt (Naz); coed; 1899.
Bethel C., North Newton, Kans.; pvt (Men); coed; 1887.
Bethel C., Hopkinsville, Ky.; pvt (Bapt, jr); coed; 1854.
Bethel C., McKenzie, Tenn.; pvt (Presb); coed; 1842.
Bethel C. & Sem., St. Paul, Minn.; pvt (Bapt); coed; 1871.
Bethune-Cookman C., Daytona Beach, Fla.; pvt (Meth); coed; 1904.
Bible, C. of the, Lexington, Ky.; pvt (DC); men; 1865.
Bible Baptist Sem., Ft. Worth, Tex.; pvt (Bapt); coed; 1939.
Bible Inst. of Los Angeles, Los Angeles, Cal.; pvt; coed; 1908.
Biblical Sem. in NY, NYC; pvt; coed; 1900.
Birmingham-Southern C., Birmingham, Ala.; pvt (Meth); coed; 1856.
Bishop C., Marshall, Tex.; pvt (Bapt); coed; 1880.
Bismarck Jr. C., Bismarck, N. D.; dist (jr); coed; 1939.
Blackburn C., Carlinville, Ill.; pvt (Presb); coed; 1857.
Black Hills T. C., Spearfish, S. D.; st; coed; 1883.
Blinn C., Brenham, Tex.; dist (jr); coed; 1883.
Bloomfield C. & Theol. Sem., Bloomfield, N. J.; pvt (Presb); coed; 1868.
Bluefield C., Bluefield, Va.; pvt (Bapt, jr); coed; 1922.
Bluefield State C., Bluefield, W. Va.; st; coed; 1895.
Blue Mountain C., Blue Mountain, Miss.; pvt (Bapt); women; 1873.
Bluffton C., Bluffton, O.; pvt (Men); coed; 1900.
Bob Jones U., Greenville, S. C.; pvt; coed; 1927.
Boise Jr. C., Boise, Ida.; dist (jr); coed; 1932.
Boone Jr. C., Boone, Ia.; dist; coed; 1927.
Boston C., Chestnut Hill, Mass.; pvt (RC); coed; 1863.
Boston Conserv. of Music, Boston, Mass.; pvt; coed; 1867.
Boston U., Boston, Mass.; pvt; coed; 1839.
Bouvé-Boston Schl., Medford, Mass.; pvt; women; 1913.
Bowdoin C., Brunswick, Me.; pvt; men; 1794.
Bowling Green C. of Commerce, Bowling Green, Ky.; pvt; coed; 1922.
Bowling Green State U., Bowling Green, O.; st; coed; 1910.
Bradford Durfee Tech. Inst., Fall River, Mass.; st; coed; 1898.
Bradford Jr. C., Bradford, Mass.; pvt (jr); women; 1803.
Bradley U., Peoria, Ill.; pvt; coed; 1897.
Brainerd Jr. C., Brainerd, Minn.; dist (jr); coed; 1938.
Brandeis U., Waltham, Mass.; pvt; coed; 1947.
Brenau C., Gainesville, Ga.; pvt; women; 1878.
Brescia C., Owensboro, Ky.; pvt (RC); coed; 1925.
Brevard C., Brevard, N. C.; pvt (Meth, jr); coed; 1883.
Brewton-Parker Jr. C., Mt. Vernon, Ga.; pvt (Bapt, jr); coed; 1904.
Briar Cliff C., Sioux City, Ia.; pvt (RC); women; 1930.
Briarcliff Jr. C., Briarcliff Manor, NY; pvt (jr); women; 1933.
Bridgeport, U. of, Bridgeport, Conn.; pvt; coed; 1927.
Bridgewater C., Bridgewater, Va.; pvt (Br); coed; 1880.
Brigham Young U., Provo, Utah; pvt (LDS); coed; 1875.
Brite C. of the Bible, Ft. Worth, Tex.; pvt (DC); coed; 1906.
Bronx Community C. of the City U. of NY, Brooklyn, NY; (jr); 1957.
Brooklyn C. of the City U. of NY, Brooklyn, NY; 1930.
Brooklyn Law Schl., Brooklyn, NY; pvt; coed; 1901.
Broome Tech. Community C., Binghamton, NY; cnty (jr); coed; 1947.

Brown U., Providence, R. I.; pvt; coed; 1764.
Bryant C., Providence, R. I.; pvt; coed; 1863.
Bryn Mawr C., Bryn Mawr, Pa.; pvt; women; 1885.
Bucknell U., Lewisburg, Pa.; pvt (Bapt); coed; 1846.
Buena Vista C., Storm Lake, Ia.; pvt (Presb); coed; 1891.
Buffalo, U. of, Buffalo, NY; pvt; coed; 1846.
Burlington C., Burlington, Ia.; mun (jr); coed; 1920.
Butler C., Tyler, Tex.; pvt (Bapt); coed; 1905.
Butler U., Indianapolis, Ind.; pvt; coed; 1855.
Caldwell C. for Women, Caldwell, N. J.; pvt (RC); women; 1939.
California, U. of, Berkeley, Cal.; st; coed; 1868.
California, U. of, Davis, Cal.; st; coed; 1908.
California, U. of, Los Angeles, Cal.; st; coed; 1881.
California, U. of, Riverside, Cal.; st; coed; 1954.
California, U. of, San Francisco, Cal.; st; coed; 1873.
California Baptist Theol. Sem., Covina, Cal.; pvt (Bapt); coed; 1944.
California C. of Arts & Crafts, Oakland, Cal.; pvt; coed; 1906.
California Inst. of Tech., Pasadena, Cal.; pvt; men; 1891.
California Schl. of Fine Arts, San Francisco, Cal.; pvt; coed; 1874.
California State Polytech. C., San Luis Obispo, Cal.; st; coed; 1901.
California Western U., San Diego, Cal.; pvt; coed; 1952.
Calvin C., Grand Rapids, Mich.; pvt (Ref); coed; 1876.
Cameron State Ag. C., Lawton, Okla.; st (jr); coed; 1909.
Campbell C., Buies Creek, N. C.; pvt (Bapt, jr); coed; 1887.
Campbellsville C., Campbellsville, Ky.; pvt (Bapt, jr); coed; 1907.
Canal Zone Jr. C., Balboa Heights, Canal Zone; nat (jr); coed; 1933.
Caney Jr. C., Pippapass, Ky.; pvt (jr); coed; 1923.
Canisius C., Buffalo, NY; pvt (RC); coed; 1870.
Capital U., Columbus, O.; pvt (AL); coed; 1850.
Carbon C., Price, Utah; st (jr); coed; 1938.
Cardinal Stritch C., Milwaukee, Wisc.; pvt (RC); women; 1933.
Carleton C., Northfield, Minn.; pvt; coed; 1866.
Carnegie Inst. of Tech., Pittsburgh, Pa.; pvt; coed; 1900.
Carroll C., Helena, Mont.; pvt (RC); coed; 1910.
Carroll C., Waukesha, Wisc.; pvt (Presb); coed; 1846.
Carson-Newman C., Jefferson City, Tenn.; pvt (Bapt); coed; 1851.
Carthage C., Carthage, Ill.; pvt (UL); coed; 1870.
Carver C., Charlotte, N. C.; mun; coed; 1949.
Cascade C., Portland, Ore.; pvt; coed; 1918.
Case Inst. of Tech., Cleveland, O.; pvt; men; 1880.
Casper Jr. C., Casper, Wyo.; cnty (jr); coed; 1945.
Catawba C., Salisbury, N. C.; pvt (ER); coed; 1851.
Cathedral C. of Immaculate Conception, Brooklyn, NY; pvt (RC); men; 1914.
Catholic T. C., Providence, R. I.; pvt (RC); women; 1929.
Catholic U. of America, Washington, D. C.; pvt (RC); coed; 1887.
Catholic U. of Puerto Rico, Ponce, P. R.; pvt (RC); coed; 1948.
Cazenovia Jr. C., Cazenovia, NY; pvt (jr); women; 1824.
Cedar Crest C., Allentown, Pa.; pvt (ER); women; 1867.
Centenary C., Shreveport, La.; pvt (Meth); coed; 1825.
Centenary C. for Women, Hackettstown, N. J.; pvt (jr); women; 1867.
Centerville Community C., Centerville, Ia.; dist (jr); coed; 1930.
Central Bible Inst., Springfield, Mo.; pvt (AG); coed; 1922.
Central C., Pella, Ia.; pvt (Ref); coed; 1853.
Central C., Fayette, Mo.; pvt (Meth); coed; 1855.
Central Christian C., Bartlesville, Okla.; pvt (jr); coed; 1950.
Central Michigan U., Mt. Pleasant, Mich.; st; coed; 1892.
Central Missouri State C., Warrensburg, Mo.; st; coed; 1871.
Central State C., Wilberforce, O.; st; coed; 1887.
Central State C., Edmond, Okla.; st; coed; 1891.
Central Tech. Inst., Kansas City, Mo.; pvt (jr); coed; 1931.
Central Washington C. of Ed., Ellensburg, Wash.; st; coed; 1891.
Centralia Jr. C., Centralia, Wash.; dist; coed; 1925.
Centralia Twp. Jr. C., Centralia, Ill.; dist (jr); coed; 1940.
Centre C. of Kentucky, Danville, Ky.; pvt (Presb); coed; 1819.
Chaffey Jr. C., Ontario, Cal.; dist (jr); coed; 1883.
Chanute Jr. C., Chanute, Kans.; dist (jr); coed; 1936.
Chapman C., Orange, Cal.; pvt (DC); coed; 1861.
Charleston, C. of, Charleston, S. C.; pvt; coed; 1770.
Charlotte C., Charlotte, N. C.; mun (jr); coed; 1946.
Chase (Salmon P.) C., Cincinnati, O.; pvt (YMCA); coed; 1885.
Chatham C., Pittsburgh, Pa.; pvt; women; 1869.
Chattanooga, U. of, Chatt. Tenn.; pvt; coed; 1886.
Chestnut Hill C., Phila. Pa.; pvt (RC); women; 1871.

Chicago, U. of, Chicago, Ill.; pvt; coed; 1892.
Chicago Acad. of Fine Arts, Chicago, Ill.; pvt (jr); coed; 1902.
Chicago City Jr. C., Chicago, Ill.; mun (jr); coed; 1934.
Chicago Conservatory, Chicago, Ill.; pvt; coed; 1857.
Chicago T. C., Chicago. Ill.; mun; coed; 1869.
Chicago Tech. C., Chicago, Ill.; pvt; coed; 1904.
Chico State C., Chico, Cal.; st; coed; 1889.
Chipola Jr. C., Marianna, Fla.; st & cnty (jr); coed; 1947.
Chowan C., Murfreesboro, N. C., pvt (Bapt, jr); coed; 1848.
Christian Brothers C., Memphis, Tenn.; pvt (RC, jr); men; 1871.
Christian C., Columbia, Mo.; pvt (DC, jr); women; 1851.
Cincinnati, C.,-Conserv. of Music of, Cincinnati, O.; pvt; coed; 1867.
Cincinnati, U. of, Cincinnati, O.; mun; coed; 1819.
Cisco Jr. C., Cisco, Tex.; mun (jr); coed; 1940.
Citadel, The, Charleston, S. C.; st; men; 1842.
Citrus Jr. C., Azusa, Cal.; dist (jr); coed; 1915.
City C. of the City U. of NY, NYC; 1847.
City U. of NY, mun; coed; 1847.
Claflin C., Orangeburg. S. C., pvt (Meth); coed; 1869.
Claremont Grad. Schl., Claremont, Cal.; pvt; coed; 1925.
Claremont Men's C., Claremont, Cal.; pvt; men; 1946.
Clarendon Jr. C., Clarendon, Tex.; dist (jr); coed; 1927.
Clarinda Jr. C., Clarinda, Ia.; mun (jr); coed; 1923.
Clark C., Atlanta, Ga.; pvt (ME); coed; 1869.
Clark C., Vancouver, Wash.; dist (jr); coed; 1933.
Clark U., Worcester, Mass.; pvt; coed; 1887.
Clarke C., Dubuque, Ia.; pvt (RC); women; 1843.
Clarke Memorial C., Newton, Miss.; pvt (Bapt, jr); coed; 1908.
Clarkson C. of Tech., Potsdam, NY; pvt; men; 1896.
Cleary C., Ypsilanti, Mich.; pvt; coed; 1883.
Clemson Ag. C., Clemson, S. C.; st; coed; 1893.
Coahoma Jr. C., Clarksdale, Miss.; st (jr); coed; 1949.
Coalinga C., Coalinga, Cal.; dist (jr); coed; 1932.
Coe C., Cedar Rapids, Ia.; pvt (Presb); coed; 1847.
Coffeyville C. of Arts, Sci., & Vocations, Coffeyville, Kans.; mun (jr); coed; 1923.
Coker C., Hartsville, S. C.; pvt; women; 1908.
Colby C., Waterville, Me.; pvt; coed; 1813.
Colby Jr. C. for Women, New London, N. H.; pvt (jr); women; 1837.
Colgate U., Hamilton, NY; pvt; men; 1819.
Colorado, U. of, Boulder, Colo.; st; coed; 1877.
Colorado A. & M. C., Ft. Collins, Colo.; st; coed; 1876.
Colorado C., Colorado Springs, Colo.; pvt; coed; 1874.
Colorado Schl. of Mines, Golden, Colo.; st; coed; 1874.
Colorado State C. of Ed., Greeley, Colo.; st; coed; 1890.
Colorado Woman's C., Denver, Colo.; pvt (jr); women; 1888.
Columbia Basin C., Pasco, Wash.; dist (jr); coed; 1955.
Columbia Bible C., Columbia, S. C.; pvt; coed; 1923.
Columbia C., Chicago, Ill.; pvt; coed; 1890.
Columbia C., Columbia, S. C.; pvt (Meth); women; 1854.
Columbia Theol. Sem., Decatur, Ga.; pvt (Presb); men; 1828.
Columbia U., NYC; pvt; coed; 1754.
Columbian C., Washington, D. C.; pvt; coed; 1821.
Community C. & Tech. Inst., Benton Harbor, Mich.; mun (jr); coed; 1946.
Compton District Jr. C., Compton, Cal.; dist (jr); coed; 1927.
Concord C., Athens, W. Va.; st; coed; 1875.
Concordia C., Moorhead, Minn.; pvt (ELuth); coed; 1891.
Concordia C., St. Paul, Minn.; pvt (Luth, jr); coed; 1893.
Concordia Collegiate Inst., Bronxville, NY; pvt (Luth); coed; 1881.
Concordia Sem., St. Louis. Mo.; pvt (Luth); men; 1839:
Concordia T. C., River Forest, Ill.; pvt (Luth); coed; 1864.
Concordia T. C., Seward, Nebr.; pvt (Luth); coed; 1894.
Connecticut, T. C. of, New Britain, Conn.; st; coed; 1849.
Connecticut, U. of, Storrs, Conn.; st; coed; 1881.
Connecticut C., New London, Conn.; pvt; women; 1911.
Connecticut State Tech. Inst., Hartford, Conn.; st (jr); coed; 1946.
Connors State Ag. C., Warner, Okla.; st (jr); coed; 1908.
Converse C., Spartanburg, S. C.; pvt; women; 1890.
Cooper Union, NYC; pvt; coed; 1859.
Copiah-Lincoln Jr. C., Wesson, Miss.; cnty (jr); coed; 1928.
Coppin State T. C., Baltimore, Md.; st; coed; 1900.
Cornell C., Mt. Vernon, Ia.; pvt (Meth); coed; 1853.
Cornell U., Ithaca, NY; st & pvt; coed; 1865.
Corpus Christi, U. of, Corpus Christi, Tex.; pvt (Bapt.); coed; 1947.
Cottey C., Nevada, Mo.; pvt (jr); women; 1884.
Crane Theol. Schl., Medford, Mass.; pvt (Universalist); coed; 1869.
Creighton U., Omaha, Nebr.; pvt (RC); coed; 1878.
Creston Jr. C., Creston, Ia.; mun (jr); coed; 1926.
Culver-Stockton C., Canton, Mo.; pvt (DC); coed; 1853.

Cumberland C., Williamsburg, Ky.; pvt (Bapt, jr); coed; 1917.
Curry C., Milton, Mass.; pvt; coed; 1879.
Custer County Jr. C., Miles City, Mont.; mun (jr); coed; 1939.
Dakota Wesleyan U., Mitchell, S. D.; pvt (Meth); coed; 1885.
Dallas Theol. Sem. & Grad. Schl. of Theol., Dallas, Tex.; pvt; men; 1924.
Dana C., Blair, Nebr.; pvt (Luth); coed; 1884.
Danbury State T. C., Danbury, Conn.; st; coed; 1904.
Danville Jr. C., Danville, Ill.; mun (jr); coed; 1946.
Dartmouth C., Hanover, N. H.; pvt; men; 1769.
David Lipscomb C., Nashville, Tenn.; pvt; coed; 1891.
Davidson C., Davidson, N. C.; pvt (Presb); men; 1836.
Davis & Elkins C., Elkins, W. Va.; pvt (Presb); coed; 1904.
Dawson County Jr. C., Glendive, Mont.; dist (jr); coed; 1940.
Dayton, U. of, Dayton, O.; pvt (RC); coed; 1850.
Decatur Baptist C., Decatur, Tex.; pvt (Bapt, jr); coed; 1897.
Defiance C., Defiance, O.; pvt (Cong); coed; 1850.
Delaware, U. of, Newark, Del.; st; coed; 1833.
Delaware State C., Dover, Del.; st; coed; 1891.
Del Mar C., Corpus Christi, Tex.; mun (jr); coed; 1935.
Delta State C., Cleveland, Miss.; st; coed; 1924.
Denison U., Granville, O.; pvt; coed; 1831.
Denver, U. of, Denver, Colo.; pvt (Meth); coed; 1864.
DePaul U., Chicago, Ill.; pvt (RC); coed; 1898.
DePauw U., Greencastle, Ind.; pvt (Meth); coed; 1837.
Detroit, U. of, Detroit. Mich.; pvt (RC); coed; 1877.
Detroit Bible Inst., Detroit, Mich.; pvt; coed; 1945.
Detroit C. of Law, Detroit, Mich.; pvt; coed; 1945.
Detroit Inst. of Tech., Detroit, Mich.; pvt; coed; 1891.
Dickinson C., Carlisle, Pa.; pvt (Meth); coed; 1773.
Dillard U., New Orleans, La.; pvt; coed; 1935.
District of Columbia T. C., Washington, D. C.; mun; coed; 1873.
Dixie Jr. C., St. George, Utah; st (jr); coed; 1917.
Doane C., Crete, Nebr.; pvt (Cong); coed; 1872.
Dodge City C., Dodge City, Kans.; dist (jr); coed; 1935.
Dominican C., Racine, Wisc.; pvt (RC); coed; 1935.
Dominican C. of San Rafael, San Rafael, Cal.; pvt (RC); women; 1890.
Donnelly C., Kansas City, Kans.; pvt (RC, jr); coed; 1949.
Douglass C., New Brunswick, N. J.; pvt; women; 1918.
Drake U., Des Moines, Ia.; pvt; coed; 1881.
Drew U., Madison, N. J.; pvt (Meth); coed; 1867.
Drexel Inst. of Tech., Philadelphia, Pa.; pvt; coed; 1891.
Dropsie C., Philadelphia, Pa.; pvt (Jewish); coed; 1907.
Drury, C., Springfield, Mo.; pvt; coed; 1873.
Dubuque, U. of, Dubuque, Ia.; pvt (Presb); coed; 1852.
Duchesne C., Omaha, Nebr.; pvt (RC); women; 1881.
Duke U., Durham, N. C.; pvt (Meth); coed; 1838.
Dumbarton C. of Holy Cross, Washington, D. C.; pvt (RC); women; 1935.
Duquesne U., Pittsburgh, Pa.; pvt (RC); coed; 1878.
D'Youville C., Buffalo, NY; pvt (RC); women; 1908.
Eagle Grove Jr. C., Eagle Grove, Ia.; mun (jr); coed; 1928.
Earlham C., Richmond, Ind.; pvt (Fr); coed; 1847.
East Carolina C., Greenville, N. C.; st; coed; 1907.
East Central Jr. C., Decatur, Miss.; st (jr); coed; 1928.
East Central State C., Ada, Okla.; st; coed; 1909.
East Contra Costa C., Concord, Cal.; dist; coed; 1950.
East Los Angeles Jr. C., Los Angeles, Cal.; st (jr); coed; 1945.
East Mississippi Jr. C., Scooba, Miss.; dist (jr); coed; 1927.
East Tennessee State C., Johnson City, Tenn.; st; coed; 1909.
East Texas Baptist C., Marshall, Tex.; pvt (Bapt); coed; 1914.
East Texas State T. C., Commerce, Tex.; st; coed; 1889.
Eastern Arizona Jr. C., Thatcher, Ariz.; dist (jr); coed; 1891.
Eastern Baptist Theol. Sem., Philadelphia, Pa.; pvt (Bapt); coed; 1925.
Eastern Illinois U., Charleston, Ill.; st; coed; 1899.
Eastern Kentucky State C., Richmond, Ky.; st; coed; 1906.
Eastern Mennonite C., Harrisonburg, Va.; pvt (Men); coed; 1917.
Eastern Michigan U., Ypsilanti, Mich.; st; coed; 1849.
Eastern Montana C. of Ed., Billings, Mont.; st; coed; 1925.
Eastern Nazarene C., Wollaston, Mass.; pvt (Naz); coed; 1918.
Eastern New Mexico U., Portales, N. M.; st; coed; 1934.
Eastern Oklahoma A. & M. C., Wilburton, Okla.; st (jr); coed; 1909.
Eastern Oregon C. of Ed., La Grande, Ore.; st; coed; 1929.
Eastern Washington C. of Ed., Cheney, Wash.; st; coed; 1890.
Edgewood C. of the Sacred Heart, Madison, Wisc.; pvt (RC); women; 1927.
Edward Waters C., Jacksonville, Fla.; pvt (jr); coed; 1886.
El Camino C., El Camino C., Cal.; dist (jr); coed; 1947.

El Dorado Jr. C., El Dorado, Kans.; mun (jr); coed; 1927.

Elgin Community C., Elgin, Ill.; mun (jr); coed; 1949.

Elizabethtown C., Elizabethtown, Pa.; pvt (CBr); coed; 1899.

Ellsworth Jr. C., Iowa Falls, Ia.; mun (jr); coed; 1929.

Elmhurst C., Elmhurst, Ill.; pvt (ER); coed; 1871.

Elmira C., Elmira, NY; pvt; women; 1855.

Elon C., Elon College, N. C., pvt (Cong); coed; 1889.

Ely Jr. C., Ely, Minn.; mun (jr); coed; 1922.

Emerson C., Boston, Mass.; pvt; coed; 1880.

Emmanuel C., Franklin Springs, Ga.; pvt (PentHol, jr); coed; 1938.

Emmanuel C., Boston, Mass.; pvt (RC); women; 1919.

Emmanuel Missionary C., Berrien Springs, Mich.; pvt (SDA); coed; 1874.

Emory & Henry C., Emory, Va.; pvt (Meth); coed; 1836.

Emory U., Atlanta, Ga.; pvt (Meth); coed; 1836.

Emporia, C. of, Emporia, Kans.; pvt (Presb); coed; 1882.

Endicott Jr. C., Beverly, Mass.; pvt (jr); women; 1939.

Erie County Tech. Inst., Buffalo, NY; dist & st (jr); coed; 1946.

Erskine C., Due West, S. C.; pvt (Presb); coed; 1839.

Estherville Jr. C., Estherville, Ia.; dist (jr); coed; 1924.

Eureka C., Eureka, Ill.; pvt (DC); coed; 1855.

Evansville C., Evansville, Ind.; pvt (Meth); coed; 1854.

Everett Jr. C., Everett, Wash.; st (jr); coed; 1941.

Fairbury Jr. C., Fairbury, Nebr.; mun (jr); coed; 1941.

Fairfield U., Fairfield, Conn.; pvt (RC); men; 1942.

Fairleigh Dickinson U., Rutherford & Teaneck, N. J.; pvt; coed; 1941.

Fairmont State C., Fairmont, W. Va.; st; coed; 1867.

Farmington State T. C., Farmington, Me.; st; coed; 1864.

Fashion Inst. of Tech., NYC; st (jr); coed; 1944.

Fayetteville State T. C., Fayetteville, N. C.; st; coed; 1877.

Fenn C., Cleveland, O.; pvt; coed; 1881.

Ferris Inst., Big Rapids, Mich.; st; coed; 1884.

Ferrum Jr. C., Ferrum, Va.; pvt (Meth, jr); coed; 1936.

Finch C., NYC; pvt; women; 1900.

Findlay C., Findlay, O.; pvt (CG); coed; 1882.

Fisk U., Nashville, Tenn.; pvt (Cong); coed; 1865.

Flat River, Jr. C. of, Flat River, Mo.; mun (jr); coed; 1922.

Fletcher Schl. of Law & Diplomacy, Medford, Mass.; pvt; coed; 1933.

Flint Jr. C., Flint, Mich.; mun (jr); coed; 1923.

Flora Macdonald C., Red Springs, N. C.; pvt (Presb); women; 1896.

Flora Stone Mather C., Cleveland, O.; pvt; women; 1888.

Florida, U. of, Gainesville, Fla.; st; coed; 1853.

Florida A. & M. U., Tallahassee, Fla.; st; coed; 1887.

Florida Christian C., Tampa, Fla.; pvt (jr); coed; 1944.

Florida Normal & Indus. Memorial C., St. Augustine, Fla.; pvt (Bapt); coed; 1892.

Florida Southern C., Lakeland, Fla.; pvt (Meth); coed; 1885.

Florida State U., Tallahassee, Fla.; st; coed; 1857.

Fontbonne C., St. Louis, Mo.; pvt (RC); women; 1923.

Fordham U., NYC; pvt (RC); men; 1841.

Fort Dodge Jr. C., Ft. Dodge, Ia.; mun (jr); coed; 1921.

Fort Hays Kansas State C., Hays, Kans.; st; coed; 1902.

Fort Lewis A. & M. C., Durango, Colo.; st (jr); coed; 1927.

Fort Scott Jr. C., Ft. Scott, Kans.; mun (jr); coed; 1919.

Fort Smith Jr. C., Ft. Smith, Ark.; pvt (jr); coed; 1928.

Fort Valley State C., Ft. Valley, Ga.; st; coed; 1895.

Fort Wayne Bible C., Ft. Wayne, Ind.; pvt (MCA); coed; 1904.

Francis T. Nicholls Jr. C., Baton Rouge, La.; st (jr); coed; 1948.

Frank Phillips C., Borger, Tex.; mun (jr); coed; 1948.

Franklin and Marshall C., Lancaster, Pa.; pvt (ER); men; 1787.

Franklin C., Franklin, Ind.; pvt (Bapt); coed; 1834.

Franklin Tech. Inst., Boston, Mass.; pvt (jr); coed; 1908.

Franklin U., Columbus, O.; pvt (YMCA); coed; 1902.

Freed-Hardeman C., Henderson, Tenn.; pvt (CC, jr); coed; 1908.

Fresno Jr. C., Fresno, Cal.; mun (jr); coed; 1910.

Fresno State C., Fresno, Cal.; st; coed; 1911.

Friends U., Wichita, Kans.; pvt (Fr); coed; 1898.

Friendship Jr. C., Rock Hill, S. C.; pvt (Bapt, jr); coed; 1933.

Fullerton Jr. C., Fullerton, Cal.; dist (jr); coed; 1913.

Furman U., Greenville, S. C.; pvt (Bapt); coed; 1826.

Gainesville Jr. C., Gainesville, Tex.; mun (jr); coed; 1924.

Gallaudet C., Washington, D. C.; nat & pvt; coed; 1864.

Gannon C., Erie, Pa.; pvt (RC); men; 1944.

Garden City Jr. C., Garden City, Kans.; mun (jr); coed; 1919.

Gardner-Webb Jr. C., Boiling Springs, N. C.; pvt (Bapt, jr); coed; 1905.

Garland Schl., The, Boston, Mass.; pvt (jr); women; 1872.

General Beadle State T. C., Madison, S. D.; st; coed; 1881.

General Motors Inst., Flint, Mich.; pvt; men; 1919.

General Theol. Sem., NYC; pvt (Episc); men; 1817.

Geneva C., Beaver Falls, Pa.; pvt (Presb); coed; 1848.

George Fox C., Newberg, Ore.; pvt (Fr); coed; 1891.

George Peabody C. for Teachers, Nashville, Tenn.; pvt; coed; 1785.

George Washington U., Washington, D. C.; pvt; coed; 1821.

George Williams C., Chicago, Ill.; pvt; coed; 1890.

Georgetown C., Georgetown, Ky.; pvt (Bapt); coed; 1829.

Georgetown U., Washington, D. C.; pvt (RC); coed; 1789.

Georgetown Visitation Jr. C., Washington, D. C.; pvt (RC, jr); women; 1799.

Georgia, Med. C. of, Augusta, Ga.; st; coed; 1828.

Georgia, U. of, Athens, Ga.; st; coed; 1785.

Georgia Inst. of Tech., Atlanta, Ga.; st; coed; 1885.

Georgia Military C., Milledgeville, Ga.; mun (jr); men; 1879.

Georgia Southwestern C., Americus, Ga.; st (jr); coed; 1926.

Georgia State C. of Bus. Admin., Atlanta, Ga.; st; coed; 1914.

Georgia State C. for Women, Milledgeville, Ga.; st; women; 1889.

Georgia T. C., Collegeboro, Ga.; st; coed; 1924.

Georgian Court C., Lakewood, N. J.; pvt (RC); women; 1908.

Gettysburg C., Gettysburg, Pa.; pvt (Luth); coed; 1832.

Glendale C., Glendale, Cal.; dist (jr); coed; 1927.

Glenville State C., Glenville, W. Va.; st; coed; 1872.

Gogebic Community C., Ironwood, Mich.; mun (jr); coed; 1932.

Golden Gate C., San Francisco, Cal.; pvt (YMCA); coed; 1901.

Goldey Beacom Schl. of Bus., Wilmington, Del.; pvt; coed; 1886.

Gonzaga U., Spokane, Wash.; pvt (RC); coed; 1887.

Good Counsel C., White Plains, NY; pvt (RC); women; 1923.

Gordon C., Beverly Farms, Mass.; pvt; coed; 1889.

Gordon Military C., Barnesville, Ga.; mun (jr); men; 1852.

Gorham State T. C., Gorham, Me.; st; coed; 1878.

Goshen C., Goshen, Ind.; pvt (Men); coed; 1894.

Goucher C., Baltimore, Md.; pvt; women; 1885.

Grace Bible Inst., Omaha, Nebr.; pvt (Men); coed; 1943.

Grace Theol. Sem. & Grace C., Winona Lake, Ind.; pvt (CBr); coed; 1937.

Graceland C., Lamoni, Ia.; pvt (RLDS); coed; 1895.

Grambling C., Grambling, La.; st; coed; 1901.

Grand Canyon C., Phoenix, Ariz.; pvt (Bapt); coed; 1949.

Grand Rapids Baptist Theol. Sem. & Bible Inst., Grand Rapids, Mich.; pvt (Bapt); coed;1941.

Grand Rapids Jr. C., Grand Rapids, Mich.; mun (jr); coed; 1914.

Grand View C., Des Moines, Ia.; pvt (ELuth, jr); coed; 1896.

Grays Harbor C., Aberdeen, Wash.; dist (jr); coed; 1930.

Great Falls, C. of, Great Falls, Mont.; pvt (RC); coed; 1932.

Green Mountain Jr. C., Poultney, Vt.; pvt (Meth, jr); women; 1834.

Greensboro C., Greensboro, N. C.; pvt (Meth); coed; 1838.

Greenville C., Greenville, Ill.; pvt (Meth); coed; 1892.

Grinnell C., Grinnell, Ia.; pvt; coed; 1846.

Grove City C., Grove City, Pa.; pvt; coed; 1876.

Guam, Terr. C. of, Agana, Guam; terr (jr); coed; 1952.

Guilford C., Guilford College, N. C.; pvt (Fr); coed; 1837.

Gulf Park C., Gulfport, Miss.; pvt (jr); women; 1921.

Gustavus Adolphus C., St. Peter, Minn.; pvt (Luth); coed; 1862.

Gwynedd-Mercy Jr. C., Gwynedd Valley, Pa.; pvt (RC, jr); women; 1948.

Hagerstown Jr. C., Hagerstown, Md.; cnty (jr); coed; 1946.

Hahnemann Med. C. & Hosp., Philadelphia, Pa.; pvt; coed; 1848.

Hamilton C., Clinton, NY; pvt; men; 1812.

Hamline U., St. Paul, Minn.; pvt (Meth); coed; 1854.

Hampden-Sydney C., Hampden-Sydney, Va.; pvt (Presb); men; 1776.

Hampton Inst., Hampton, Va.; pvt; coed; 1868.

Hannibal-La Grange C., Hannibal, Mo.; pvt (Bapt, jr); coed; 1858.

Hanover C., Hanover, Ind.; pvt (Presb); coed; 1827.

Harcum Jr. C., Bryn Mawr, Pa.; pvt (jr); women; 1915.

Harding C., Searcy, Ark.; pvt (CC); coed; 1924.

Hardin-Simmons U., Abilene, Tex.; pvt (Bapt); coed; 1891.

Harpur C. (See New York, State U. of)

Harris T. C., St. Louis, Mo.; mun; coed; 1857.

Hartford Sem. Founda., Hartford, Conn.; pvt; coed; 1834.

Hartnell C., Salinas, Cal.; dist (jr); coed; 1924.

Hartt C. of Music, Hartford, Conn.; pvt; coed; 1920.

Hartwick C., Oneonta, NY; pvt (Luth); coed; 1928.
Harvard U., Cambridge, Mass.; pvt; men; 1636.
Hastings C., Hastings, Nebr.; pvt (Presb); coed; 1882.
Haverford C., Haverford, Pa.; pvt (Fr); men; 1833.
Hawaii, U. of, Honolulu, Hawaii; terr; coed; 1907.
Hebrew Union C.,-Jewish Inst. of Rel.,
    Cincinnati, O.; pvt (Jewish); men; 1875.
Heidelberg C., Tiffin, O.; pvt (ER); coed; 1850.
Henderson County Jr. C., Athens, Tex.; st (jr); coed;
    1946.
Henderson State T. C., Arkadelphia, Ark.; st; coed;
    1929.
Hendrix C., Conway, Ark.; pvt (Meth); coed; 1884.
Henry Ford Community C., Dearborn, Mich.; mun
    (jr); coed; 1938.
Hershey Jr. C., Hershey, Pa.; twp (jr); coed; 1938.
Hesston C., Hesston, Kans.; pvt (Men, jr); coed; 1915.
Hibbing Jr. C., Hibbing, Minn.; dist (jr); coed; 1916.
Highland Jr. C., Highland, Kans.; dist (jr); coed; 1858.
Highland Park Jr. C., Highland Park, Mich.; mun
    (jr); coed; 1918.
High Point C., High Point, N. C.; pvt (Meth); coed;
    1924.
Hillsdale C., Hillsdale, Mich.; pvt; coed; 1844.
Hillyer C., Hartford, Conn.; pvt; coed; 1879.
Hinds Jr. C. Raymond, Miss.; dist (jr); coed; 1926.
Hiram C., Hiram, O.; pvt; coed; 1850.
Hiwassee C., Madisonville, Tenn.; pvt (Meth, jr);
    coed; 1849.
Hobart & William Smith Colleges, Geneva, NY; pvt;
    men, women; 1822, 1908.
Hofstra C., Hempstead, NY; pvt; coed; 1935.
Hollins C., Hollins College, Va.; pvt; women; 1842.
Holmes Jr. C., Goodman, Miss.; dist (jr); coed; 1925.
Holy Cross, C. of the, Worcester, Mass.; pvt (RC);
    men; 1843.
Holy Family C., Manitowoc, Wisc.; pvt; women; 1869.
Holy Names, C. of the, Oakland, Cal.; pvt (RC);
    women; 1868.
Holy Names C., Spokane, Wash.; pvt (RC); women;
    1907.
Holyoke Jr. C., Holyoke, Mass.; mun (jr); coed; 1946.
Hood C., Frederick, Md.; pvt (ER); women; 1893.
Hope C., Holland, Mich.; pvt (Ref); coed; 1852.
Houghton C., Houghton, NY; pvt (Meth); coed; 1883.
Houston, U. of, Houston, Tex.; mun; coed; 1934.
Howard C., Birmingham, Ala.; pvt (Bapt); coed; 1842.
Howard County Jr. C., Big Spring, Tex.; dist (jr);
    coed; 1946.
Howard Payne C., Brownwood, Tex.; pvt (Bapt);
    coed; 1889.
Howard U., Washington, D. C.; nat & pvt; coed; 1867.
Hudson Valley Tech. Inst., Troy, NY; dist (jr); men;
    1953.
Humboldt State C., Arcata, Cal.; st; coed; 1913.
Hunter C., NYC; mun; women; 1870.
Huntingdon C., Montgomery, Ala.; pvt (Meth); coed;
    1854.
Huntington C., Huntington, Ind.; pvt; coed; 1897.
Huron C., Huron, S. D.; pvt (Presb); coed; 1883.
Huston-Tillotson C., Austin, Tex.; pvt (Meth); coed;
    1952.
Hutchinson Jr. C., Hutchinson, Kans.; mun (jr); coed;
    1928.
Idaho, C. of, Caldwell, Ida.; pvt (Presb); coed; 1891.
Idaho, U. of, Moscow, Ida.; st; coed; 1889.
Idaho State C., Pocatello, Ida.; st; coed; 1947.
Illinois, U. of, Urbana, Ill.; st; coed; 1869.
Illinois C., Jacksonville, Ill.; pvt; coed; 1829.
Illinois C. of Optometry, Chicago, Ill.; pvt; coed; 1872.
Illinois Inst. of Tech., Chicago, Ill.; pvt; coed; 1892.
Illinois State Normal U., Normal, Ill.; st; coed; 1857.
Illinois Wesleyan U., Bloomington, Ill.; pvt (Meth);
    coed; 1850.
Immaculata C., Immaculata, Pa.; pvt (RC); women;
    1920.
Immaculata Jr. C., Washington, D. C.; pvt (RC, jr);
    women; 1922.
Immaculate Conception Sem., Darlington, N. J.; pvt
    (RC); men; 1856.
Immaculate Heart C., Los Angeles, Cal.; pvt (RC);
    women; 1916.
Imperial Valley C., El Centro, Cal.; pvt (jr); coed;
    1922.
Incarnate Word C., San Antonio, Tex.; pvt (RC);
    women; 1881.
Independence Community C., Independence, Kans.;
    pvt (jr); coed; 1925.
Indiana Central C., Indianapolis, Ind.; pvt (EUB);
    coed; 1902.
Indiana State T. C., Terre Haute, Ind.; st; coed; 1865.
Indiana Tech. C., Ft. Wayne, Ind.; pvt; men; 1930.
Indiana U., Bloomington, Ind.; st; coed; 1820.
Inst. for Advanced Study, Princeton, N. J.; pvt;
    coed; 1930.
Iola Jr. C., Iola, Kans.; pvt (jr); coed; 1923.
Iona C., New Rochelle, NY; pvt (RC); men; 1940.
Iowa, State U. of, Iowa City, Ia.; st; coed; 1847.
Iowa State C. of A. & M. A., Ames, Ia.; st; coed; 1858.
Iowa State T. C., Cedar Falls, Ia.; st; coed; 1876.
Iowa Wesleyan C., Mt. Pleasant, Ia.; pvt (Meth);
    coed; 1842.
Itasca Jr. C., Coleraine, Minn.; dist (jr); coed; 1922.
Itawamba Jr. C., Fulton, Miss.; st & dist (jr); coed;
    1948.
Ithaca C., Ithaca, NY; pvt; coed; 1892.

Jackson C., Medford, Mass.; pvt; women; 1910.
Jackson Jr. C., Jackson, Mich.; mun (jr); coed; 1928.
Jackson State C., Jackson, Miss.; st; coed; 1877.
Jacksonville C., Jacksonville, Fla.; pvt; coed; 1934.
Jamestown C., Jamestown, N. D.; pvt (Presb); coed;
    1884.
Jamestown Community C., Jamestown, NY; st & mun
    (jr); coed; 1950.
Jarvis Christian C., Hawkins, Tex.; pvt (DC); coed;
    1912.
Jefferson City Jr. C., Jefferson City, Mo.; dist (jr);
    coed; 1926.
Jefferson Medical C., Philadelphia, Pa.; st & pvt;
    men; 1825.
Jersey City Jr. C., Jersey City, N. J.; mun (jr); coed;
    1946.
Jewish Theol. Sem. of America, NYC; pvt (Jewish);
    coed; 1887.
John Brown U., Siloam Springs, Ark.; pvt; coed; 1919.
John Carroll U., Cleveland, O.; pvt (RC); men; 1886.
John Herron Art Schl., Indianapolis, Ind.; pvt; coed;
    1902.
Johns Hopkins U., Baltimore, Md.; pvt; men; 1876.
Johnson Bible C., Kimberlin Heights, Tenn.; pvt (CC);
    coed; 1893.
Johnson C. Smith U., Charlotte, N. C.; pvt (Presb);
    coed; 1867.
Joliet Jr. C., Joliet, Ill.; dist (jr); coed; 1901.
Jones County Jr. C., Ellisville, Miss.; dist & st (jr);
    coed; 1927.
Joplin Jr. C., Joplin, Mo.; mun (jr); coed; 1938.
Judson C., Marion, Ala.; pvt (Bapt); women; 1838.
Juilliard Schl. of Music, NYC; pvt; coed; 1905.
Juniata C., Huntingdon, Pa.; pvt (Br); coed; 1876.
Kalamazoo C., Kalamazoo, Mich.; pvt (Bapt); coed;
    1833.
Kansas, U. of, Lawrence, Kans.; st; coed; 1865.
Kansas City, Conserv. of Music of, Kansas City,
    Mo.; mun; coed; 1907.
Kansas City, Jr. C. of, Kansas City, Mo.; dist (jr);
    coed; 1915.
Kansas City, U. of, Kansas City, Mo.; pvt; coed; 1929.
Kansas City Art Inst. & Schl. of Design, Kansas
    City, Mo.; pvt; coed; 1887.
Kansas City Bible C., Kansas City, Mo.; pvt; coed;
    1932.
Kansas City Kansas Jr. C., Kansas City, Kans.; mun
    (jr); coed; 1923.
Kansas State C. of Ag. & Applied Sci., Manhattan,
    Kans.; st; coed; 1863.
Kansas State T. C., Emporia, Kans.; st; coed; 1863.
Kansas State T. C., Pittsburg, Kans.; st; coed; 1903.
Kansas Wesleyan U., Salina, Kans.; pvt (Meth);
    coed; 1886.
Keene T. C., Keene, N. H.; st; coed; 1909.
Kendall C., Evanston, Ill.; pvt (Meth, jr); coed; 1940.
Kent State U., Kent, O.; st; coed; 1910.
Kentucky, U. of, Lexington, Ky.; st; coed; 1865.
Kentucky State C., Frankfort, Ky.; st; coed; 1886.
Kentucky Wesleyan C., Owensboro, Ky.; pvt (Meth);
    coed; 1860.
Kenyon C., Gambier, O.; pvt (Episc); men; 1824.
Keokuk Community C., Keokuk, Ia.; dist (jr); coed;
    1953.
Keuka C., Keuka Park, NY; pvt (Bapt); women; 1890.
Keystone Jr. C., La Plume, Pa.; pvt (jr); coed; 1934.
Kilgore C., Kilgore, Tex.; dist (jr); coed; 1935.
King C., Bristol, Tenn.; pvt (Presb); coed; 1867.
King's C., Briarcliff Manor, NY; pvt; coed; 1938.
King's C., Wilkes-Barre, Pa.; pvt (RC); men; 1946.
Knox C., Galesburg, Ill.; pvt; coed; 1837.
Knoxville C., Knoxville, Tenn.; pvt (Presb); coed;
    1875.
Ladycliff C., Highland Falls, NY; pvt (RC); women;
    1933.
Lafayette C., Easton, Pa.; pvt (Presb); men; 1826.
La Grange C., La Grange, Ga.; pvt (Meth); coed; 1831.
Lain Drafting C., Indianapolis, Ind.; pvt (jr); coed;
    1941.
Lake Erie C., Painesville, O.; pvt; women; 1856.
Lake Forest C., Lake Forest, Ill.; pvt (Presb); coed;
    1857.
Lakeland C., Sheboygan, Wisc.; pvt (ER); coed; 1862.
Lamar Jr. C., Lamar, Colo.; dist (jr); coed; 1937.
Lamar State C. of Tech., Beaumont, Tex.; st; coed;
    1923.
Lambuth C., Jackson, Tenn.; pvt (Meth); coed; 1843.
Lander C., Greenwood, S. C.; pvt; coed; 1872.
Lane C., Jackson, Tenn.; pvt (ME); coed; 1882.
Langston U., Langston, Okla.; st; coed; 1897.
Laredo Jr. C., Laredo, Tex.; st (jr); coed; 1947.
LaSalle C., Philadelphia, Pa.; pvt (RC); men; 1863.
La Salle-Peru-Oglesby Jr. C., La Salle, Ill.; dist
    (jr); coed; 1924.
Lasell Jr. C., Auburndale, Mass.; pvt (jr); women;
    1851.
La Sierra C., Arlington, Cal.; pvt (SDA); coed; 1922.
La Verne C., La Verne, Cal.; pvt (Br); coed; 1891.
Lawrence C., Appleton, Wisc.; pvt; coed; 1847.
Lawrence Inst. of Tech., Detroit, Mich.; pvt; men;
    1932.
Layton Schl. of Art, Milwaukee, Wisc.; pvt; coed;
    1920.
Lebanon Valley C., Annville, Pa.; pvt (EUB); coed;
    1866.
Lee C., Cleveland, Tenn.; pvt (CG, jr); coed; 1918.

Lee C., Baytown, Tex.; dist (jr); coed; 1934.
Lees Jr. C., Jackson, Ky.; pvt (Presb, jr); coed; 1883.
Lees-McRae C., Banner Elk, N. C.; pvt (Presb, jr); coed; 1900.
Lehigh U., Bethlehem, Pa.; pvt; men; 1865.
Leland C., Baker, La.; pvt (Bapt); coed; 1870.
Le Moyne C., Syracuse, NY; pvt (RC); coed; 1946.
Le Moyne C., Memphis, Tenn.; pvt (AMA); coed; 1870.
Lenoir-Rhyne C., Hickory, N. C.; pvt (Luth); coed; 1891.
Lesley C., Cambridge, Mass.; pvt; women; 1909.
Le Tourneau Tech. Inst., Longview, Tex.; pvt; men; 1946.
Lewis and Clark C., Portland Ore.; pvt (Presb); coed; 1867.
Lewis C. of Sci. & Tech., Lockport, Ill.; pvt (RC); coed; 1930.
Limestone C., Gaffney, S. C.; pvt; women; 1845.
Lincoln Bible Inst., Lincoln, Ill.; pvt; coed; 1944.
Lincoln C., Lincoln, Ill.; pvt (jr); coed; 1865.
Lincoln Memorial U., Harrogate, Tenn.; pvt; coed; 1897.
Lincoln U., Jefferson City, Mo.; st; coed; 1866.
Lincoln U., Lincoln University, Pa.; pvt; men; 1854.
Lindenwood C. for Women, St. Charles, Mo.; pvt (Presb); women; 1827.
Lindsey Wilson C., Columbia, Ky.; pvt (Meth, jr); coed; 1923.
Linfield C., McMinnville, Ore.; pvt (Bapt); coed; 1856.
Little Rock U., Little Rock, Ark.; pvt; coed; 1927.
Livingstone C., Salisbury, N. C.; pvt (AMEZ); coed; 1879.
Long Beach City C., Long Beach, Cal.; dist (jr); coed; 1927.
Long Beach State C., Long Beach, Cal.; st; coed; 1949.
Long Island U., Brooklyn, NY; pvt; coed; 1926.
Longwood C., Farmville, Va.; st; women; 1884.
Lon Morris C., Jacksonville, Tex.; pvt (Meth, jr); coed; 1873.
Loras C., Dubuque, Ia.; pvt (RC); men; 1839.
Loretto Hts. C., Loretto, Colo.; pvt (RC); women; 1918.
Los Angeles City C., Los Angeles, Cal.; mun (jr); coed; 1929.
Los Angeles Conserv. of Music & Arts, Los Angeles, Cal.; pvt; coed; 1883.
Los Angeles Harbor Jr. C., Wilmington, Cal.; dist (jr); coed; 1949.
Los Angeles Jr. C. of Bus., Los Angeles, Cal.; mun (jr); coed; 1950.
Los Angeles Pierce Jr. C., Woodland Hills, Cal.; mun (jr); coed; 1947.
Los Angeles State C. of Applied Arts & Sci., Los Angeles, Cal.; st; coed; 1947.
Los Angeles Trade-Tech. Jr. C., Los Angeles, Cal.; mun (jr); coed; 1927.
Los Angeles Valley Jr. C., Van Nuys, Cal.; dist (jr); coed; 1949.
Louisburg C., Louisburg, N. C., pvt (Meth, jr); coed; 1787.
Louisiana C., Pineville, La., pvt (Bapt); coed; 1906.
Louisiana Polytechnic Inst., Ruston, La.; st; coed; 1894.
Louisiana State U. in New Orleans, New Orleans, La.; st; coed; 1958.
Louisiana State U. and A. & M. C., Baton Rouge, La.; st; coed; 1860.
Louisville, U. of, Louisville, Ky.; mun; coed; 1798.
Lowell Tech. Inst., Lowell, Mass.; st; coed; 1895.
Lower Columbia Jr. C., Longview, Wash.; mun (jr); coed; 1934.
Loyola C., Baltimore, Md.; pvt (RC); men; 1852.
Loyola U., Los Angeles, Cal.; pvt (RC); men; 1911.
Loyola U., Chicago, Ill.; pvt (RC); coed; 1870.
Loyola U., New Orleans, La.; pvt (RC); coed; 1912.
Luther C., Decorah, Ia.; pvt (ELuth); coed; 1861.
Luther Jr. C., Wahoo, Nebr.; pvt (Luth, jr); coed; 1883.
Luther Theol. Sem., St. Paul, Minn.; pvt (ELuth); men; 1876.
Lutheran Theol. Sem., Philadelphia, Pa.; pvt (Luth); men; 1864.
Lycoming C., Williamsport, Pa.; pvt (Meth); coed; 1812.
Lynchburg C., Lynchburg, Va.; pvt (DC); coed; 1901.
Lyons Twp. Jr. C., La Grange, Ill.; dist (jr); coed; 1929.
Macalester C., St. Paul, Minn.; pvt (Presb);coed; 1885.
MacMurray C., Jacksonville, Ill.; pvt (Meth); women; 1846.
MacPhail C. of Music, Minneapolis, Minn.; pvt; coed; 1907.
Madison C., Madison College, Tenn.; pvt; coed; 1904.
Madison C., Harrisonburg, Va.; st; women; 1908.
Madonna C., Livonia, Mich.; pvt (RC); women; 1947.
Maine, U. of, Orono, Me.; st; coed; 1865.
Maine Maritime Acad., Castine, Me.; st; men; 1941.
Manchester C., North Manchester, Ind. pvt (CBr); coed; 1895.
Manhattan C., NYC; pvt (RC); men; 1853.
Manhattan Schl. of Music, NYC; pvt; coed; 1917.
Manhattanville C. of the Sacred Heart, Purchase, NY; pvt (RC); women; 1841.
Mankato State C., Mankato, Minn.; st; coed; 1867.
Marian C., Indianapolis, Ind.; pvt (RC); coed; 1937.
Marian C., Poughkeepsie, NY; pvt (RC); men; 1946.
Marian C., Fond du Lac, Wisc.; pvt (RC); women; 1936.

Marietta C., Marietta, O.; pvt; coed; 1835.
Marin, C. of, Kentfield, Cal.; st (jr); coed; 1926.
Marion C., Marion, Ind.; pvt (Meth); coed; 1920.
Marion Inst., Marion, Ala.; pvt (jr); men; 1842.
Maritime C. (See New York, State U. of)
Marjorie Webster Jr. C., Washington, D. C., pvt (jr); women; 1920.
Marquette U., Milwaukee, Wisc.; pvt (RC); coed; 1880.
Marshall C., Huntington, W. Va.; st; coed; 1837.
Marshalltown Jr. C., Marshalltown, Ia.; dist (jr); coed; 1927.
Mars Hill C., Mars Hill, N. C.; pvt (Bapt, jr); coed; 1856.
Martin C., Pulaski, Tenn.; pvt (Meth, jr); coed; 1870.
Mary Baldwin C., Staunton, Va.; pvt (Presb); women; 1842.
Mary Hardin-Baylor C., Belton, Tex.; pvt (Bapt); women; 1845.
Mary Manse C., Toledo, O.; pvt (RC); women; 1922.
Mary Washington C., Fredericksburg, Va.; st; women; 1908.
Marycrest C., Davenport, Ia.; pvt (RC); women; 1939.
Marygrove C., Detroit, Mich.; pvt (RC); women; 1910.
Maryknoll Sem., Glen Ellyn, Ill.; pvt (RC, jr); men; 1949.
Maryknoll T. C., Maryknoll, NY; pvt; women; 1931.
Maryland, U. of, College Park, Md.; st; coed; 1807.
Maryland Inst., Schl. of Fine & Ap. Art, Baltimore, Md.; pvt; coed; 1826.
Maryland State C., Princess Anne, Md.; st;coed; 1886.
Maryland State T. C., Bowie, Md.; st; coed; 1867.
Maryland State T. C., Frostburg, Md.; st; coed; 1898.
Maryland State T. C., Salisbury, Md.; st; coed; 1925.
Maryland State T. C., Towson, Md.; st; coed; 1866.
Marylhurst C., Marylhurst, Ore.; pvt (RC); women; 1930.
Marymount C., Los Angeles, Cal.; pvt (RC); women; 1933.
Marymount C., Salina, Kans.; pvt (RC); women; 1922.
Marymount C., Tarrytown, NY; pvt (RC); women; 1907.
Marymount Jr. C., Arlington, Va.; pvt (RC, jr); women; 1955.
Maryville C., Maryville, Tenn.; pvt (Presb); coed; 1819.
Maryville C. of the Sacred Heart, St. Louis, Mo.; pvt (RC); women; 1872.
Marywood C., Scranton, Pa.; pvt (RC); women; 1915.
Mason City Jr. C., Mason City, Ia.; dist (jr); coed; 1918.
Massachusetts, U. of, Amherst, Mass.; st; coed; 1863.
Massachusetts C. of Pharmacy, Boston, Mass.; pvt; coed; 1823.
Massachusetts Inst. of Tech., Cambridge, Mass.; pvt; coed; 1861.
Massachusetts Schl. of Art, Boston, Mass.; st; coed; 1870.
Massachusetts State T. C., Boston, Mass.; st; coed; 1852.
Massachusetts State T. C., Bridgewater, Mass.; st; coed; 1840.
Massachusetts State T. C., Fitchburg, Mass.; st; coed; 1894.
Massachusetts State T. C., Framingham, Mass.; st; women; 1839.
Massachusetts State T. C., Lowell, Mass.; st; coed; 1894.
Massachusetts State T. C., North Adams, Mass.; st; coed; 1894.
Massachusetts State T. C., Salem, Mass.; st; coed; 1854.
Massachusetts State T. C., Westfield, Mass.; st; coed; 1839.
Massachusetts State T. C., Worcester, Mass.; st; coed; 1871.
McCook Jr. C., McCook, Nebr.; mun (jr); coed; 1926.
McCormick Theol. Sem., Chicago, Ill.; pvt (Presb); coed; 1829.
McKendree C., Lebanon, Ill.; pvt (Meth); coed; 1828.
McMurry C., Abilene, Tex.; pvt (Meth); coed; 1923.
McNeese State C., Lake Charles, La.; st; coed; 1939.
McPherson C., McPherson, Kans.; pvt (CBr); coed; 1887.
Meharry Medical C., Nashville, Tenn.; pvt;coed; 1876.
Memphis State C., Memphis, Tenn.; st; coed; 1912.
Menlo C., Menlo Park, Cal.; pvt; men; 1915.
Mercer U., Macon, Ga.; pvt (Bapt); coed; 1833.
Mercy C., Detroit, Mich.; pvt (RC); women; 1941.
Mercy Jr. C., Webster Groves, Mo.; pvt (RC, jr); women; 1952.
Mercyhurst C., Erie, Pa.; pvt (RC); women; 1926.
Meredith C., Raleigh, N. C.; pvt (Bapt); women; 1891.
Meridian Municipal Jr. C., Meridian, Miss.; mun (jr); coed; 1937.
Merrimack C., Andover, Mass.; pvt (RC); coed; 1947.
Mesa County Jr. C., Grand Junction, Colo.; mun (jr); coed; 1925.
Messiah C., Grantham, Pa.; pvt (Br); coed; 1909.
Miami, U. of, Coral Gables, Fla.; pvt; coed; 1925.
Miami U., Oxford, O.; st; coed; 1809.
Michigan, U. of, Ann Arbor, Mich.; st; coed; 1817.
Michigan C. of Mining & Tech., Houghton, Mich.; st; coed; 1885.

Michigan State U., E. Lansing, Mich.; st; coed; 1855.
Middle Georgia C., Cochran, Ga.; st (jr); coed; 1928.
Middle Tennessee State C., Murfreesboro, Tenn.; st; coed; 1911.
Middlebury C., Middlebury, Vt.; pvt; coed; 1800.
Midland C., Freemont, Nebr.; pvt (UL); coed; 1887.
Midwestern U., Wichita Falls, Tex.; mun; coed; 1922.
Miles C., Birmingham, Ala.; pvt (ME); coed; 1907.
Millard Fillmore C., Buffalo, NY; pvt; coed; 1923.
Milligan C., Milligan College, Tenn.; pvt; coed; 1881.
Millikin U., Decatur, Ill.; pvt (Presb); coed; 1901.
Mills C., Oakland, Cal.; pvt; women; 1852.
Mills C. of Ed., NYC; pvt; women; 1909.
Millsaps C., Jackson, Miss.; pvt (Meth); coed; 1890.
Milton C., Milton, Wisc.; pvt; coed; 1867.
Milwaukee-Downer C., Milwaukee, Wisc.; pvt; women; 1851.
Milwaukee Inst. of Tech., Milwaukee, Wisc.; mun; coed; 1951.
Milwaukee Schl. of Engineering, Milwaukee, Wisc.; pvt; men; 1903.
Minneapolis C. of Music, Minneapolis, Minn.; pvt; coed; 1928.
Minneapolis Schl. of Art, Minneapolis, Minn.; pvt; coed; 1886.
Minnesota, U. of, Minneapolis, Minn.; st; coed; 1851.
Misericordia C., Dallas, Pa.; pvt (RC); women; 1923.
Mississippi, U. of, University, Miss.; st. coed; 1848.
Mississippi C., Clinton, Miss.; pvt (Bapt); coed; 1826.
Mississippi Indust. C., Holly Springs, Miss.; pvt (Meth); coed; 1905.
Mississippi Southern C., Hattiesburg, Miss.; st; coed; 1912.
Mississippi State C., State College, Miss.; st; coed; 1878.
Mississippi State C. for Women, Columbus, Miss.; st; women; 1884.
Mississippi Vocational C., Itta Bena, Miss.; st; coed; 1950.
Missouri, U. of, Columbia, Mo.; st; coed; 1839.
Missouri Valley C., Marshall, Mo.; pvt (Presb); coed; 1888.
Mitchell C., New London, Conn.; pvt (jr); coed; 1938.
Mitchell C., Statesville, N. C.; pvt (Presb, jr); coed; 1922.
Moberly Jr. C., Moberly, Mo.; mun (jr); coed; 1927.
Modesto Jr. C., Modesto, Cal.; st (jr); coed; 1921.
Mohawk Valley Tech. Inst., New Hartford, NY; st (jr); coed; 1946.
Moline Community C., Moline, Ill.; dist (jr); coed; 1946.
Monmouth C., Monmouth, Ill.; pvt (Presb); coed; 1853.
Monmouth Jr. C., West Long Branch, N. J.; pvt (jr); coed; 1933.
Montana Schl. of Mines, Butte, Mont.; st; coed; 1893.
Montana State C., Bozeman, Mont.; st; coed; 1893.
Montana State U., Missoula, Mont.; st; coed; 1893.
Monterey Peninsula C., Monterey, Cal.; dist (jr); coed; 1947.
Montgomery Jr. C., Takoma Park, Md.; dist (jr); coed; 1946.
Monticello C., Alton, Ill.; pvt (jr); women; 1835.
Montreat-Anderson C. Inc., Montreat, N.C.; pvt (Presb, jr); coed; 1960.
Moody Bible Inst., Chicago, Ill.; pvt (jr); coed; 1886.
Moore Inst. of Art, Sci., & Indust., Philadelphia, Pa.; pvt; women; 1844.
Moorhead State C., Moorhead, Minn.; st; coed; 1887.
Moravian C., Bethlehem, Pa.; pvt (Mor); coed; 1807.
Morehead State C., Morehead, Ky.; st; coed; 1923.
Morehouse C., Atlanta, Ga.; pvt; men; 1867.
Morgan State C., Baltimore, Md.; st; coed; 1867.
Morningside C., Sioux City, Ia.; pvt (Meth); coed; 1894.
Morris Brown C., Atlanta, Ga.; pvt (AME); coed; 1881.
Morris C., Sumter, S. C.; pvt (Bapt); coed; 1908.
Morris Harvey C., Charleston, W. Va.; pvt; coed; 1888.
Morton Jr. C., Cicero, Ill.; dist (jr); coed; 1924.
Mt. Aloysius Jr. C., Cresson, Pa.; pvt (RC, jr); women; 1939.
Mt. Holyoke C., South Hadley, Mass.; pvt; women; 1837.
Mt. Marty C., Yankton, S. D.; pvt (RC); women; 1936.
Mt. Mary C., Milwaukee, Wisc.; pvt (RC); women; 1913.
Mt. Mercy C., Pittsburgh, Pa.; pvt (RC); women; 1932.
Mt. Mercy Jr. C., Cedar Rapids, Ia.; pvt (RC, jr); women; 1928.
Mt. St. Agnes C., Baltimore, Md.; pvt (RC); women; 1867.
Mt. St. Clare Jr. C., Clinton, Ia.; pvt (RC, jr); women; 1918.
Mt. St. Joseph-on-the-Ohio, C. of, Mt. St. Joseph, O.; pvt (RC); women; 1854.
Mt. St. Jos. T. C., Buffalo, NY; pvt (RC); women; 1937.
Mt. St. Mary C., Hooksett, N. H.; pvt (RC); women; 1934.
Mt. St. Mary's C., Los Angeles, Cal.; pvt (RC); women; 1925.
Mt. St. Mary's C., Emmitsburg, Md.; pvt (RC); men; 1808.

Mt. St. Scholastica C., Atchison, Kans.; pvt (RC); women; 1863.
Mt. St. Vincent, C. of, NYC; pvt (RC); women; 1910.
Mt. San Antonio C., Walnut, Cal.; st (jr); coed; 1946.
Mt. Union C., Alliance, O.; pvt (Meth); coed; 1846.
Mt. Vernon Jr. C., Washington, D. C.; pvt (jr); women; 1875.
Muhlenberg C., Allentown, Pa.; pvt (Luth); coed; 1848.
Multnomah C., Portland, Ore.; pvt (jr); coed; 1897.
Multnomah Schl. of the Bible Portland, Ore.; pvt (Inter); coed; 1936.
Mundelein C., Chicago, Ill.; pvt (RC); women; 1930.
Murray State Ag. C., Tishomingo, Okla.; st (jr); coed; 1908.
Murray State C., Murray, Ky.; st; coed; 1923.
Muscatine Jr. C., Muscatine, Ia.; mun (jr); coed; 1929.
Muskegon Community C., Muskegon, Mich.; dist (jr); coed; 1926.
Muskingum C., New Concord, O.; pvt (Presb); coed; 1837.
Muskogee Jr. C., Muskogee, Okla.; mun (jr); coed; 1920.
Napa C., Napa, Cal.; dist (jr); coed; 1942.
Nasson C., Springvale, Me.; pvt; coed; 1912.
National Ag. C., Doylestown, Pa.; pvt; men; 1896.
National C. of Ed., Evanston, Ill.; pvt; coed; 1886.
Navarro Jr. C., Corsicana, Tex.; dist (jr); coed; 1946.
Nazareth C., Louisville, Ky.; pvt (RC); women; 1920.
Nazareth C., Nazareth, Mich.; pvt (RC); women; 1897.
Nazareth C., Rochester, NY; pvt (RC); women; 1924.
Nazareth C. & Acad., Nazareth, Ky.; pvt (RC); women; 1814.
Nebraska, U. of, Lincoln, Nebr.; st; coed; 1869.
Nebraska State T. C., Chadron, Nebr.; st; coed; 1911.
Nebraska State T. C., Kearney, Nebr.; st; coed; 1905.
Nebraska State T. C., Peru, Nebr.; st; coed; 1867.
Nebraska State T. C., Wayne, Nebr.; st; coed; 1910.
Nebraska Wesleyan U., Lincoln, Nebr.; pvt (Meth); coed; 1887.
Nevada, U. of, Reno, Nev.; st; coed; 1874.
Newark C. of Engineering, Newark, N. J.; st & mun; coed; 1881.
New Bedford Inst. of Textiles & Tech., New Bedford, Mass.; st; coed; 1898.
Newberry C., Newberry, S. C.; pvt (UL); coed; 1856.
Newcomb C., New Orleans, La.; pvt; women; 1886.
New England C. of Pharmacy, Boston, Mass.; pvt; coed; 1927.
New England Conserv. of Music, Boston, Mass.; pvt; coed; 1867.
New Hampshire, U. of, Durham, N. H.; st; coed; 1866.
New Haven State T. C., New Haven, Conn.; st; coed; 1893.
New Haven YMCA Jr. C., New Haven, Conn.; pvt (YMCA, jr); coed; 1926.
New Jersey State C., Glassboro, N. J.; st; coed; 1923.
New Jersey State C., Jersey City, N. J.; st; coed; 1929.
New Jersey State C., Newark, N. J.; st; coed; 1855.
New Jersey State C., Paterson, N. J.; st; coed; 1855.
New Jersey State C., Trenton, N. J.; st; coed; 1855.
New Jersey State C., Upper Montclair, N. J.; st; coed; 1908.
New Mexico, U. of, Albuquerque, N. M.; st; coed; 1889.
New Mexico C. of A. & M. A., State College, N. M.; st; coed; 1889.
New Mexico Highlands U., Las Vegas, N. M.; st; coed; 1893.
New Mexico Inst. of Mining & Tech., Socorro, N. M.; st; coed; 1889.
New Mexico Military Inst., Roswell, N. M.; st; men; 1893.
New Mexico Western C., Silver City, N. M.; st; coed; 1893.
New Rochelle, C. of, New Rochelle, NY; pvt (RC); women; 1904.
New School for Social Research, NYC; pvt; coed; 1918.
Newton C. of the Sacred Heart, Newton, Mass.; pvt (RC); women; 1946.
Newton Jr. C., Newtonville, Mass.; mun (jr); coed; 1946.
New York, State U. of
   Agriculture, C. of, Ithaca, NY; st; coed; 1904.
   Ag. & Tech. Inst., Alfred, NY; st (jr); coed; 1908.
   Ag. & Tech. Inst., Canton, NY; st (jr); coed; 1906.
   Ag. & Tech. Inst., Cobleskill, NY; st (jr); coed; 1914.
   Ag. & Tech. Inst., Delhi, NY; st (jr); coed; 1916.
   Ag. & Tech. Inst., Farmingdale, NY; st (jr); coed; 1916.
   Ag. & Tech. Inst., Morrisville, NY; st (jr); coed; 1910.
   Ceramics C. of, Alfred, NY; st; coed; 1900.
   Downstate Medical, Brooklyn, NY; st; coed; 1857.
   Forestry, C. of, Syracuse, NY; st; coed; 1911.
   Harpur C., Endicott, NY; st; coed; 1946.
   Home Eco., C. of, Ithaca, NY; st; coed; 1925.
   Indust. & Labor Rela., Schl. of, Ithaca, NY; st; coed; 1945.
   Maritime C., Ft. Schuyler, NY; st; men; 1874.
   New York State T. C., Albany, NY; st; coed; 1844.
   New York State T. C., Brockport, NY; st; coed; 1866.
   New York State T. C., Buffalo, NY; st; coed; 1867.
   New York State T. C., Cortland, NY; st; coed; 1866.

New York State T. C., Fredonia, NY; st; coed; 1886.
New York State T. C., Geneseo, NY; st; coed; 1867.
New York State T. C., New Paltz, NY; st; coed; 1886.
New York State T. C., Oneonta, NY; st; coed; 1889.
New York State T. C., Oswego, NY; st; coed; 1861.
New York State T. C., Plattsburgh, NY; st; coed; 1889.
New York State T. C., Potsdam, NY; st; coed; 1866.
Upstate Medical Center, Syracuse, NY; st; coed; 1834.
Veterinary C., Ithaca, NY; st; coed; 1894.
New York City Community C., Brooklyn, NY; dist (jr); coed; 1946.
New York Law Schl., NYC; pvt; coed; 1891.
New York Medical C., NYC; pvt; coed; 1860.
New York Schl. of Social Work, NYC; pvt; coed; 1898.
New York U., NYC; pvt; coed; 1831.
Niagara U., Niagara University, NY; pvt (RC); coed; 1856.
Nichols Jr. C., Dudley, Mass.; pvt (jr); men; 1931.
Norfolk Jr. C., Norfolk, Nebr.; dist (jr); coed; 1942.
Norman C., Norman Park, Ga.; pvt (Bapt, jr); coed; 1900.
North Carolina, A. & T. C. of, Greensboro, N. C.; st; coed; 1891.
North Carolina, U. of, Chapel Hill, N. C.; st; coed; 1795.
North Carolina, Women's C. of the U. of, Greensboro, N. C.; st; women; 1891.
North Carolina C., Durham, N. C.; st; coed; 1910.
North Carolina State C. of Ag. & Engineering, Raleigh, N. C.; st; coed; 1889.
North Carolina State T. C., Elizabeth City, N. C.; st; coed; 1889.
North Central C., Naperville, Ill.; pvt (EUB); coed; 1861.
North Dakota, U. of, Grand Forks, N. D.; st; coed; 1883.
North Dakota Ag. C., Fargo, N. D.; st; coed; 1889.
North Dakota Schl. of Forestry, Bottineau, N. D.; st (jr); coed; 1907.
North Dakota State Normal & Indus. C., Ellendale, N. D.; st; coed; 1889.
North Dakota State Schl. of Sci., Wahpeton, N. D.; st (jr); coed; 1903.
North Dakota State T. C., Dickinson, N. D.; st; coed; 1918.
North Dakota State T. C., Mayville, N. D.; st; coed; 1889.
North Dakota State T. C., Minot, N. D.; st; coed; 1913.
North Dakota State T. C., Valley City, N. D.; st; coed; 1889.
Northeast Ag. Jr. C., Sheridan, Wyo.; st (jr); coed; 1948.
Northeast Louisiana State C., Monroe, La.; st; coed; 1931.
Northeast Mississippi Jr. C., Booneville, Miss.; dist (jr); coed; 1948.
Northeast Missouri State T. C., Kirksville, Mo.; st; coed; 1867.
Northeastern Jr. C., Sterling, Colo.; cnty (jr); coed; 1941.
Northeastern Oklahoma A. & M. C., Miami, Okla.; st (jr); coed; 1919.
Northeastern State C., Tahlequah, Okla.; st; coed; 1909.
Northeastern U., Boston, Mass.; pvt; coed; 1898.
Northern Illinois U., De Kalb, Ill.; st; coed; 1899.
Northern Michigan U., Marquette, Mich.; st; coed; 1899.
Northern Montana C., Havre, Mont.; st (jr); coed; 1929.
Northern Oklahoma Jr. C., Tonkawa, Okla.; st (jr); coed; 1901.
Northern State T. C., Aberdeen, S. D.; st; coed; 1902.
North Georgia C., Dahlonega, Ga.; st; coed; 1873.
North Greenville Jr. C., Tigerville, S. C.; pvt (Bapt, jr); coed; 1892.
North Idaho Jr. C., Coeur d'Alene, Ida.; dist (jr); coed; 1939.
Northland C., Ashland, Wisc.; pvt; coed; 1892.
North Park C. & Theol. Sem., Chicago, Ill.; pvt; coed; 1891.
North Texas State C., Denton, Tex.; st; coed; 1890.
Northwest Center, U. of Wyoming, Powell, Wyo.; st; coed; 1946.
Northwest Christian C., Eugene, Ore.; pvt (DC); coed; 1895.
Northwest Mississippi Jr. C., Senatobia, Miss.; dist (jr); coed; 1925.
Northwest Missouri State C., Maryville, Mo.; st; coed; 1905.
Northwest Nazarene C., Nampa, Ia.; pvt (Naz); coed; 1913.
Northwestern C., Minneapolis, Minn.; pvt; coed; 1902.
Northwestern C., Watertown, Wisc.; pvt (Luth); coed; 1865.
Northwestern Jr. C., Orange City, Ia.; pvt (Ref, jr); coed; 1882.
Northwestern Michigan C., Traverse City, Mich.; dist (jr); coed; 1951.
Northwestern State C., Alba, Okla.; st; coed; 1897.

Northwestern State C. of Louisiana, Natchitoches, La.; st; coed; 1884.
Northwestern U., Evanston, Ill.; pvt; coed; 1851.
Norwich U., Northfield, Vt.; pvt; men; 1819.
Notre Dame, C. of, Belmont, Cal.; pvt (RC); women; 1868.
Notre Dame, U. of, Notre Dame, Ind.; pvt (RC); men; 1842.
Notre Dame C., St. Louis, Mo.; pvt (RC, jr); women; 1925.
Notre Dame C., Staten Island, NY; pvt (RC); women; 1931.
Notre Dame C., Cleveland, O.; pvt (RC); women; 1922.
Notre Dame of Maryland, C. of, Baltimore, Md.; pvt (RC); women; 1873.
Nyack Missionary C., Nyack, NY; pvt (CMA); coed; 1882.
Oakland City C., Oakland City, Ind.; pvt (Bapt); coed; 1885.
Oakland Jr. C., Oakland, Cal.; dist (jr); coed; 1935.
Oakwood C., Huntsville, Ala.; pvt (SDA); coed; 1896.
Oberlin C., Oberlin, O.; pvt; coed; 1833.
Occidental C., Los Angeles, Cal.; pvt; coed; 1887.
Oceanside-Carlsbad C., Oceanside, Cal.; dist; coed; 1934.
Odessa C., Odessa, Tex.; dist (jr); coed; 1946.
Oglethorpe U., Atlanta, Ga.; pvt; coed; 1835.
Ohio Mechanics Inst., Cincinnati, O.; pvt (jr); coed; 1828.
Ohio Northern U., Ada, O.; pvt (Meth); coed; 1871.
Ohio State U., Columbus, O.; st; coed; 1873.
Ohio U., Athens, O.; st; coed; 1804.
Ohio Wesleyan U., Delaware, O.; pvt (Meth); coed; 1842.
Oklahoma, U. of, Norman, Okla.; st; coed; 1892.
Oklahoma Baptist U., Shawnee, Okla.; pvt (Bapt); coed; 1911.
Oklahoma City U., Oklahoma City, Okla.; pvt (Meth); coed; 1904.
Oklahoma C. for Women, Chickasha, Okla.; st; women; 1908.
Oklahoma State U. of Ag. & Applied Sci., Stillwater, Okla.; st; coed; 1891.
Olivet C., Olivet, Mich.; pvt (Cong); coed; 1844.
Olivet Nazarene C., Kankakee, Ill.; pvt (Naz); coed; 1907.
Olympic C., Bremerton, Wash.; st (jr); coed; 1946.
Omaha, U. of, Omaha, Nebr.; mun; coed; 1908.
Orange Coast C., Costa Mesa, Cal.; dist (jr); coed; 1947.
Orange County Community C., Middletown, NY; st (jr); coed; 1950.
Oregon, U. of, Eugene, Ore.; st; coed; 1872.
Oregon C. of Ed., Monmouth, Ore.; st; coed; 1856.
Oregon State C., Corvallis, Ore.; st; coed; 1868.
Oregon Tech. Inst., Oretech, Ore.; st (jr); coed; 1947.
Orlando Jr. C., Orlando, Fla.; pvt (jr); coed; 1941.
Ottawa U., Ottawa, Kans.; pvt (Bapt); coed; 1865.
Otterbein C., Westerville, O.; pvt (EUB); coed; 1847.
Ottumwa Heights C., Ottumwa, Ia.; pvt (RC, jr); women; 1925.
Ouachita Baptist C., Arkadelphia, Ark.; pvt (Bapt); coed; 1886.
Our Lady of Cincinnati C., Cincinnati, O.; pvt (RC); women; 1935.
Our Lady of the Elms, C. of, Chicopee, Mass.; pvt (RC); women; 1928.
Our Lady of the Lake C., San Antonio, Tex.; pvt (RC); women; 1912.
Owosso Bible C., Owosso, Mich.; pvt (Pilgrim Holiness); coed; 1909.
Ozarks, C. of the, Clarksville, Ark.; pvt (Presb); coed; 1834.
Pace C., NYC; pvt; coed; 1906.
Pacific, C. of the, Stockton, Cal.; pvt (Meth); coed; 1851.
Pacific Bible C., Portland, Ore.; pvt (CG); coed; 1937.
Pacific Bible C. of Azusa, Azusa, Cal.; pvt (Inter); coed; 1899.
Pacific Lutheran C., Parkland, Wash.; pvt (Luth); coed; 1894.
Pacific Union C., Angwin, Cal.; pvt (SDA); coed; 1909.
Pacific U., Forest Grove, Ore.; pvt (Cong); coed; 1849.
Paducah Jr. C., Paducah, Ky.; mun (jr); coed; 1932.
Paine C., Augusta, Ga.; pvt (Meth); coed; 1883.
Palm Beach Jr. C., Lake Worth, Fla.; cnty (jr); coed; 1933.
Palomar C., San Marcos, Cal.; dist (jr); coed; 1946.
Palo Verde Jr. C., Blythe, Cal.; dist (jr); coed; 1947.
Pan American C., Edinburg, Tex.; dist; coed; 1927.
Panhandle A. & M. C., Goodwell, Okla.; st; coed; 1909.
Panola County Jr. C., Carthage, Tex.; cnty (jr); coed; 1947.
Panzer C. of Phys. Ed., East Orange, N. J.; pvt; coed; 1917.
Paper Chemistry, Inst. of, Appleton, Wisc.; pvt; men; 1929.
Paris Jr. C., Paris, Tex.; mun (jr); coed; 1924.
Park C., Parkville, Mo.; pvt (Presb); coed; 1875.
Parks C. of Aeronautical Tech., East St. Louis, Ill.; pvt (RC); coed; 1927.
Parsons C., Fairfield, Ia.; pvt (Presb); coed; 1875.
Parsons Jr. C., Parsons, Kans.; mun (jr); coed; 1923.
Parsons Schl. of Design, NYC; pvt; coed; 1896.
Pasadena City C., Pasadena, Cal.; st (jr); coed; 1924.
Pasadena C., Pasadena, Cal.; pvt (Naz); coed; 1902.

Paul Quinn C., Waco, Tex.; pvt (AME); coed; 1872.
Paul Smith's C., Paul Smiths, NY; pvt (jr); coed; 1946.
Peabody Conserv. of Music, Baltimore, Md.; pvt; coed; 1868.
Peace C., Raleigh, N. C.; pvt (Presb, jr); women; 1857.
Pearl River Jr. C., Poplarville, Miss.; st (jr); coed; 1926.
Pembroke C., Providence, R. I.; pvt; women; 1891.
Pembroke State C., Pembroke, N. C.; st; jr; 1887.
Penn Hall Jr. C., Chambersburg, Pa.; pvt (jr); women; 1906.
Pennsylvania, U. of, Philadelphia, Pa.; pvt; coed; 1740.
Pennsylvania Military C., Chester, Pa.; pvt; men; 1821.
Pennsylvania State T. C., Bloomsburg, Pa.; st; coed; 1839.
Pennsylvania State T. C., California, Pa.; st; coed; 1852.
Pennsylvania State T. C., Cheyney, Pa.; st; coed; 1837.
Pennsylvania State T. C., Clarion, Pa.; st; coed; 1867.
Pennsylvania State T. C., East Stroudsburg, Pa.; st; coed; 1893.
Pennsylvania State T. C., Edinboro, Pa.; st; coed; 1861.
Pennsylvania State T. C., Indiana, Pa.; st; coed; 1875.
Pennsylvania State T. C., Kutztown, Pa.; st; coed; 1866.
Pennsylvania State T. C., Lock Haven, Pa.; st; coed; 1870.
Pennsylvania State T. C., Mansfield, Pa.; st; coed; 1857.
Pennsylvania State T. C., Millersville, Pa.; st; coed; 1855.
Pennsylvania State T. C., Shippensburg, Pa.; st; coed; 1871.
Pennsylvania State T. C., Slippery Rock, Pa.; st; coed; 1889.
Pennsylvania State T. C., West Chester, Pa.; st; coed; 1871.
Pennsylvania State U., University Park, Pa.; st; coed; 1855.
Pensacola Jr. C., Pensacola, Fla.; dist (jr); coed; 1948.
Pepperdine (George) C., Los Angeles, Cal.; pvt; coed; 1937.
Perkinston Jr. C., Perkinston, Miss.; mun (jr); coed; 1925.
Pestalozzi Froebel T. C., Chicago, Ill.; pvt; coed; 1896.
Pfeiffer C., Misenheimer, N. C.; pvt (Meth, jr); coed; 1885.
Philadelphia Bible Inst., Phila., Pa.; pvt; coed; 1913.
Philadelphia C. of Osteopathy, Philadelphia, Pa.; pvt; coed; 1899.
Philadelphia C. of Pharmacy & Sci., Philadelphia, Pa.; pvt; coed; 1821.
Philadelphia Museum Schl. of Art, Philadelphia, Pa.; pvt; coed; 1876.
Philadelphia Textile Inst., Philadelphia, Pa.; pvt; coed; 1884.
Philander Smith C., Little Rock, Ark.; pvt (Meth); coed; 1868.
Phillips U., Enid, Okla.; pvt (DC); coed; 1906.
Phoenix C., Phoenix, Ariz.; dist (jr); coed; 1920.
Piedmont C., Demorest, Ga.; pvt (Cong); coed; 1897.
Pikeville C., Pikeville, Ky.; pvt (Presb, jr); coed; 1889.
Pineland Jr. C. & Edwards Military Inst., Salemburg, N. C.; pvt (jr); coed; 1875.
Pine Manor Jr. C., Wellesley, Mass.; pvt (jr); women; 1911.
Pittsburgh, U. of, Pittsburgh, Pa.; pvt; coed; 1787.
Pittsburgh-Xenia Theol. Sem., Pittsburgh, Pa.; pvt (Presb); coed; 1794.
Plymouth T. C., Plymouth, N. H.; st; coed; 1871.
Polytechnic Inst. of Brooklyn, Brooklyn, NY; pvt; coed; 1854.
Pomona C., Claremont, Cal.; pvt; coed; 1887.
Porterville C., Porterville, Cal.; st & dist (jr); coed; 1927.
Port Huron Jr. C., Port Huron, Mich.; mun (jr); coed; 1923.
Portland, U. of, Portland, Ore.; pvt (RC); coed; 1901.
Portland State C., Portland, Ore.; st; coed; 1955.
Post C. (of Long Island U.), Brookville, NY; pvt; coed; 1955.
Potomac State C., Keyser, W. Va.; st (jr); coed; 1902.
Prairie View A. & M. C., Prairie View, Tex.; st; coed; 1876.
Pratt Inst., Brooklyn, NY; pvt; coed; 1887.
Pratt Jr. C., Pratt, Kans.; dist (jr); coed; 1938.
Presbyterian C., Clinton, S. C.; pvt (Presb); coed; 1880.
Presbyterian Jr. C. for Men, Maxton, N. C.; pvt (Presb, jr); men; 1929.
Presentation Jr. C., Aberdeen, S. D.; pvt (RC, jr); women; 1951.
Princeton Theol. Sem., Princeton, N. J.; pvt (Presb); coed; 1812.
Princeton U., Princeton, N. J.; pvt; men; 1746.
Principia C., Elsah, Ill.; pvt; coed; 1910.
Protestant Episcopal Theol. Sem., Alexandria, Va.; pvt (Episc); men; 1823.
Providence-Barrington Bible C., Providence, R. I.; pvt; coed; 1900.
Providence C., Providence, R. I.; pvt (RC); men; 1917.
Pueblo Jr. C., Pueblo, Colo.; st & dist (jr); coed; 1933.
Puerto Rico, Catholic U. of, Ponce, P. R.; pvt (RC); coed; 1948.

Puerto Rico, Polytech. Inst. of, San Germán, P. R.; pvt (Presb); coed; 1912.
Puerto Rico, U. of, Rio Piedras, P. R.; st; coed; 1903.
Puget Sound, C. of, Tacoma, Wash.; pvt (Meth); coed; 1888.
Purdue U., Lafayette, Ind.; st; coed; 1869.
Queens C. of the City U. of NY, Queens, NY; 1937.
Queens C., Charlotte, N. C.; pvt (Presb); women; 1857.
Queensborough Community C. of the City U. of NY, Bayside, NY; (jr); 1958.
Quincy C., Quincy, Ill.; pvt (RC); coed;¶1860.
Quinnipiac C., Hamden, Conn.; pvt; coed; 1929.
Rabbinical C. of Telshe, Cleveland, O.; pvt (Jewish); men; 1875.
Radcliffe C., Cambridge, Mass.; pvt; women; 1879.
Radford C., Radford, Va.; st; women; 1913.
Randolph-Macon C., Ashland, Va.; pvt (Meth); men; 1830.
Randolph-Macon Woman's C., Lynchburg, Va.; pvt (Meth); women; 1891.
Ranger Jr. C., Ranger, Tex.; mun (jr); coed; 1926.
RCA Institutes, NYC; pvt (jr); coed; 1909.
Redlands, U. of, Redlands, Cal.; pvt (Bapt); coed; 1907.
Reed C., Portland, Ore.; pvt; coed; 1909.
Reedley C., Reedley, Cal.; st (jr); coed; 1926.
Regis C., Denver, Colo.; pvt (RC); men; 1888.
Regis C., Weston, Mass.; pvt (RC); women; 1927.
Reinhardt C., Waleska, Ga.; pvt (Meth, jr); coed; 1883.
Rensselaer Polytechnic Inst., Troy, NY; pvt; men; 1824.
Rhode Island, U. of, Kingston, R. I.; st; coed; 1894.
Rhode Island C. of Ed., Providence, R. I.; st; coed; 1854.
Rhode Island Schl. of Design, Providence, R. I.; pvt; coed; 1877.
Rice Inst., Houston, Tex.; pvt; coed; 1891.
Richmond, U. of, Richmond, Va.; pvt (Bapt); coed; 1830.
Ricks C., Rexburg, Ida.; pvt (LDS); coed; 1888.
Rider C., Trenton, N. J.; pvt; coed; 1865.
Rio Grande C., Rio Grande, O.; pvt (Inter); coed; 1876.
Ripon C., Ripon, Wisc.; pvt; coed; 1851.
Riverside C., Riverside, Cal.; st (jr); coed; 1916.
Rivier C., Nashua, N. H.; pvt; women; 1933.
Roanoke C., Salem, Va.; pvt (Luth); coed; 1842.
Roberts Wesleyan C., North Chili, NY; pvt (Meth); coed; 1866.
Rochester, U. of, Rochester, NY; pvt; coed; 1850.
Rochester Inst. of Tech., Rochester, NY; pvt; coed; 1829.
Rochester Jr. C., Roch., Minn.; mun (jr); coed; 1915.
Rockford C., Rockford, Ill.; pvt; women; 1847.
Rockhurst C., Kansas City, Mo.; pvt (RC); men; 1910.
Rocky Mountain C., Billings, Mont.; pvt (Inter); coed; 1947.
Rollins C., Winter Park, Fla.; pvt; coed; 1885.
Roosevelt U., Chicago, Ill; pvt; coed; 1945.
Rosary C., River Forest, Ill.; pvt (RC); women; 1901.
Rosary Hill C., Buffalo, NY; pvt (RC); women; 1947.
Rose Polytechnic Inst., Terre Haute, Ind.; pvt; men; 1874.
Rosemont C., Rosemont, Pa.; pvt (RC); women; 1921.
Russell Sage C., Troy, NY; pvt; women; 1916.
Rust C., Holly Springs, Miss.; pvt (Meth); coed; 1866.
Rutgers U., New Brunswick, N. J.; st; coed; 1766.
Sacramento Jr. C., Sacramento, Cal.; mun (jr); coed; 1916.
Sacramento State C., Sacramento, Cal.; st; coed; 1947.
Sacred Heart, C. of the, Santurce, P. R.; pvt (RC); women; 1881.
Sacred Heart Dominican C., Houston, Tex.; pvt (RC); women; 1945.
Sacred Heart Jr. C. & Acad., Belmont, N. C.; pvt (RC, jr); women; 1935.
St. Ambrose C., Davenport, Ia.; pvt (RC); men; 1882.
St. Anselm's C., Manchester, N. H.; pvt (RC); men; 1889.
St. Augustine's C., Raleigh, N. C.; pvt (Episc); coed; 1867.
St. Benedict, C. of, St. Jos., Minn.; pvt; women; 1913.
St. Benedict's C., Atchison, Kans.; pvt (RC); men; 1857.
St. Bernard C., St. Bernard, Ala.; pvt (RC, jr); men; 1892.
St. Bernardine of Siena C., Loudonville, NY; pvt (RC); men; 1937.
St. Bernard's Sem. & C., Rochester, NY; pvt (RC); men; 1893.
St. Bonaventure U., St. Bonaventure, NY; pvt (RC); coed; 1856.
St. Catharine Jr. C., Springfield, Ky.; pvt (RC, jr); coed; 1931.
St. Catherine, C. of, St. Paul, Minn.; pvt (RC); women; 1905.
St. Charles Borromeo Sem., Philadelphia, Pa.; pvt (RC); men; 1832.
St. Charles C., Baltimore, Md.; pvt (RC); men; 1926.
St. Cloud State C., St. Cloud, Minn.; st; coed; 1869.
St. Edward's Sem., Kenmore, Wash.; pvt (RC); men; 1931.
St. Edward's U., Austin, Tex.; pvt (RC); men; 1885.
St. Elizabeth, C. of, Convent Station, N. J.; pvt (RC); women; 1899.
St. Francis, C. of, Joliet, Ill.; pvt (RC); women; 1920.
St. Francis C., Ft. Wayne, Ind.; pvt (RC); women; 1890.

St. Francis C., Brooklyn, NY; pvt (RC); men; 1858.
St. Francis C., Loretto, Pa.; pvt (RC); coed; 1847.
St. John C., Cleveland, O.; pvt (RC); women; 1928.
St. John Fisher C., Rochester, NY; pvt (RC); men; 1951.
St. John's C., Camarillo, Cal.; pvt (RC); men; 1939.
St. John's C., Annapolis, Md.; pvt; coed; 1696.
St. John's Lutheran C., Winfield, Kans.; pvt (Luth, jr); coed; 1893.
St. John's Sem., Brighton, Mass.; pvt (RC); men; 1884.
St. John's U., Collegeville, Minn.; pvt (RC); men; 1857.
St. John's U., Brooklyn, NY; pvt (RC); men; 1870.
St. Joseph C., West Hartford, Conn.; pvt (RC); women; 1932.
St. Joseph C., Emmitsburg, Md.; pvt (RC); women; 1809.
St. Joseph Jr. C., St. Joseph, Mo.; mun (jr); coed; 1915.
St. Joseph on the Rio Grande, C. of, Albuquerque, N. M.; pvt (RC); coed; 1940.
St. Joseph's C., Collegeville, Ind.; pvt (RC); men; 1889.
St. Joseph's C., North Windham, Me.; pvt (RC); women; 1915.
St. Joseph's C., Philadelphia, Pa.; pvt (RC); men; 1851.
St. Joseph's C. for Women, Brooklyn, NY; pvt (RC); women; 1916.
St. Joseph's Sem. & C., Yonkers, NY; pvt (RC); men; 1839.
St. Lawrence U., Canton, NY; pvt; coed; 1856.
St. Louis C. of Pharmacy & Allied Sci., St. Louis, Mo.; pvt; coed; 1864.
St. Louis Inst. of Music, St. Louis, Mo.; pvt; coed; 1924.
St. Louis Prep. Sem., St. Louis, Mo.; pvt (RC, jr); men; 1900.
St. Louis U., St. Louis, Mo.; pvt (RC); coed; 1818.
St. Martin's C., Olympia, Wash.; pvt (RC); men; 1895.
St. Mary, C. of, Omaha, Nebr.; pvt (RC); women; 1923.
St. Mary C., Xavier, Kans.; pvt (RC); women; 1923.
St. Mary of the Lake Sem., Mundelein, Ill.; pvt (RC); men; 1921.
St. Mary of the Springs, C. of, Columbus, O.; pvt (RC); women; 1911.
St. Mary-of-the-Woods C., Saint-Mary-of-the-Woods, Ind.; pvt (RC); women; 1840.
St. Mary's C., St. Mary's C., Cal.; pvt (RC); men; 1863.
St. Mary's C., Notre Dame, Ind.; pvt; (RC); women; 1843.
St. Mary's C., St. Mary's, Kans.; pvt (RC); coed; 1869.
St. Mary's C., St. Mary, Ky.; pvt; men; 1821.
St. Mary's C., Winona, Minn.; pvt (RC); men; 1912.
St. Mary's Dominican C., New Orleans, La.; pvt (RC); women; 1910.
St. Mary's Jr. C., O'Fallon, Mo.; pvt (RC, jr); women; 1921.
St. Mary's Jr. C., Raleigh, N. C., pvt (Episc, jr); women; 1842.
St. Mary's Sem. Jr. C., St. Mary's City, Md.; st (jr); women; 1839.
St. Mary's Sem. & U., Baltimore, Md.; pvt (RC); men; 1791.
St. Mary's U., San Antonio, Tex.; pvt (RC); men; 1852.
St. Meinrad Sem., St. Meinrad, Ind.; pvt (RC); men; 1861.
St. Michael's C., Santa Fe, N. M.; pvt (RC); men; 1947.
St. Michael's C., Winooski, Vt.; pvt (RC); men; 1904.
St. Olaf C., Northfield, Minn.; pvt (Luth); coed; 1874.
St. Patrick's Sem., Menlo Park, Cal.; pvt (RC); men; 1898.
St. Paul Bible Inst., St. Paul, Minn.; pvt (CMA); coed; 1916.
St. Paul Sem., St. Paul, Minn.; pvt (RC); men; 1896.
St. Paul's Polytechnic Inst., Lawrenceville, Va.; pvt (Episc); coed; 1888.
St. Peter's C., Jersey City, N. J.; pvt (RC); men; 1872.
St. Petersburg Jr. C., St. Petersburg, Fla.; dist (jr); coed; 1927.
St. Philip's C., San Antonio, Tex.; dist (jr); coed; 1902.
St. Procopius C., Lisle, Ill.; pvt (RC); men; 1887.
St. Rose, C. of, Albany, NY; pvt (RC); women; 1920.
St. Scholastica, C. of, Duluth, Minn.; pvt (RC); women; 1912.
St. Teresa, C. of, Winona, Minn.; pvt (RC); women; 1907.
St. Teresa, C. of, Kansas City, Mo.; pvt (RC); women; 1940.
St. Thomas, C. of, St. Paul, Minn.; pvt (RC); men; 1885.
St. Thomas, U. of, Houston, Tex.; pvt (RC); coed; 1947.
St. Thomas Aquinas C., Sparkill, NY; pvt (RC); women; 1952.
St. Thomas Sem., Bloomfield, Conn.; pvt (RC, jr); men; 1897.
St. Vincent C., Latrobe, Pa.; pvt (RC); men; 1846.
St. Xavier C., Chicago, Ill.; pvt (RC); women; 1846.
Salem C., Winston-Salem, N. C.; pvt (Mor); women; 1772.
Salem C., Salem, W. Va.; pvt (SDBapt); coed; 1888.

Salve Regina C., Newport, R. I.; pvt (RC); women; 1947.
Sam Houston State T. C., Huntsville, Tex.; st; coed; 1879.
San Angelo C., San Angelo, Tex.; mun (jr); coed; 1928.
San Antonio C., San Antonio, Tex.; dist (jr); coed; 1925.
San Bernardino Valley C., San Bernardino, Cal.; dist (jr); coed; 1926.
San Diego C. for Women, San Diego, Cal.; pvt (RC); women; 1952.
San Diego Jr. C., San Diego, Cal.; mun (jr); coed; 1914.
San Diego State C., San Diego, Cal.; st; coed; 1897.
San Francisco, City C. of, San Francisco, Cal.; mun; coed; 1935.
San Francisco, U. of, San Francisco, Cal.; pvt (RC); men; 1855.
San Francisco C. for Women, San Francisco, Cal.; pvt (RC); women; 1930.
San Francisco State C., San Francisco, Cal.; st; coed; 1899.
San Jose Jr. C., San Jose, Cal.; mun (jr); coed; 1921.
San Jose State C., San Jose, Cal.; st; coed; 1857.
San Luis Obispo Jr. C., San Luis Obispo, Cal.; dist (jr); coed; 1936.
San Mateo, C. of, San Mateo, Cal.; dist (jr); coed; 1922.
Santa Ana C., Santa Ana, Cal.; dist (jr); coed; 1915.
Santa Barbara C., Santa Barbara, Cal.; st; coed; 1944.
Santa Barbara Jr. C., Santa Barbara, Cal.; dist (jr); coed; 1946.
Santa Clara, U. of, Santa Clara, Cal.; pvt (RC); men; 1851.
Santa Monica City C., Santa Monica, Cal.; st (jr); coed; 1929.
Santa Rosa Jr. C., Santa Rosa, Cal.; st (jr); coed; 1918.
Sarah Lawrence C., Bronxville, NY; pvt; women; 1928.
Savannah State C., Savannah, Ga.; st; coed; 1890.
Sayre Jr. C., Sayre, Okla.; dist (jr); coed; 1938.
Scarritt C. for Christian Workers, Nashville, Tenn.; pvt (Meth); coed; 1924.
Schreiner Inst., Kerrville, Tex.; pvt (Presb, jr); men; 1923.
Scottsbluff C., Scottsbluff, Nebr.; dist (jr); coed; 1931.
Scranton, U. of, Scranton, Pa.; pvt (RC); men; 1888.
Scripps C., Claremont, Cal.; pvt; women; 1926.
Seattle Pacific C., Seattle, Wash.; pvt (FMeth); coed; 1891.
Seattle U., Seattle, Wash.; pvt (RC); coed; 1891.
Sequoias, C. of the, Visalia, Cal.; st (jr); coed; 1926.
Seton Hall U., South Orange, N. J.; pvt (RC); coed; 1856.
Seton Hill C., Greensburg, Pa.; pvt (RC); women; 1883.
Seventh-Day Adventist Theol. Sem., Washington, D. C.; pvt (SDA); coed; 1936.
Shasta C., Redding, Cal.; st (jr); coed; 1950.
Shaw U., Raleigh, N. C.; pvt (Bapt); coed; 1865.
Shelton C., Ringwood, N. J.; pvt; coed; 1885.
Shenandoah C., Dayton, Va.; pvt (EUB, jr); coed; 1875.
Shenandoah Conserv. of Music, Dayton, Va.; pvt; coed; 1875.
Shepherd State C., Shepherdstown, W. Va.; st; coed; 1871.
Sherwood Music Schl., Chicago, Ill.; pvt; coed; 1895.
Shimer C., Mt. Carroll, Ill.; pvt; coed; 1853.
Shorter C., North Little Rock, Ark.; pvt (AME); coed; 1884.
Shorter C., Rome, Ga.; pvt (Bapt); coed; 1873.
Siena C., Memphis, Tenn.; pvt; women; 1923.
Siena Heights C., Adrian, Mich.; pvt (RC); women; 1919.
Sierra C., Auburn, Cal.; st (jr); coed; 1936.
Simmons C., Boston, Mass.; pvt; women; 1899.
Simpson C., Indianola, Ia.; pvt (Meth); coed; 1860.
Sinclair C., Dayton, O.; pvt (YMCA, jr); coed; 1887.
Sioux Falls C., Sioux Falls, S. D.; pvt (Bapt); coed; 1883.
Skagit Valley Jr. C., Mt. Vernon, Wash.; dist (jr); coed; 1926.
Skidmore C., Saratoga Springs, NY; pvt; women; 1911.
Smith C., Northampton, Mass.; pvt; women; 1871.
Snead Jr. C., Boaz, Ala.; pvt (Meth, jr); coed; 1935.
Snow C., Ephraim, Utah; st (jr); coed; 1888.
South, U. of the, Sewanee, Tenn.; pvt (Episc); men; 1856.
South Carolina, Medical C. of, Charleston, S. C.; st; coed; 1823.
South Carolina, U. of, Columbia, S. C.; st; coed; 1801.
South Carolina State C., Orangeburg, S. C.; st; coed; 1896.
South Dakota, U. of, Vermillion, S. D.; st; coed; 1882.
South Dakota Schl. of Mines & Tech., Rapid City, S. D.; st; coed; 1885.
South Dakota State C. of A. & M. A., Brookings, S. D.; st; coed; 1881.
South Georgia C., Douglas, Ga.; st (jr); coed; 1906.
South Jersey, C. of, Camden, N. J.; st & pvt; coed; 1926.
South Macomb Community C., Van Dyke, Mich.; dist; coed; 1953.
South Texas C., Houston, Tex.; pvt (YMCA, jr); coed; 1923.
Southeast Center, U. of Wyoming, Torrington, Wyo.; st; coed; 1948.

Southeast Missouri State C., Cape Girardeau, Mo.; st; coed; 1873.
Southeastern Baptist Theol. Sem., Wake Forest, N.C.; pvt (Bapt); coed; 1951.
Southeastern Bible C., Birmingham, Ala.; pvt; coed; 1934.
South-Eastern Bible C., Lakeland, Fla.; pvt (AG); coed; 1935.
Southeastern Louisiana C., Hammond, La.; st; coed; 1925.
Southeastern State C., Durant, Okla.; st; coed; 1909.
Southeastern U., Washington, D. C.; pvt (YMCA); coed; 1879.
Southern Baptist C., Walnut Ridge, Ark.; pvt (Bapt, jr); coed; 1941.
Southern Baptist Theol. Sem., Louisville, Ky.; pvt (Bapt); coed; 1859.
Southern California, U. of, Los Angeles, Cal.; pvt; coed; 1880.
Southern California Bible C., Costa Mesa, Cal.; pvt (AG); coed; 1920.
Southern C. of Optometry, Memphis, Tenn.; pvt; coed; 1932.
Southern Illinois U., Carbondale, Ill.; st; coed; 1869.
Southern Methodist U., Dallas, Tex.; pvt (Meth); coed; 1911.
Southern Missionary C., Collegedale, Tenn.; pvt (SDA); coed; 1893.
Southern Oregon C. of Ed., Ashland, Ore.; st; coed; 1926.
Southern Sem. & Jr. C., Buena Vista, Va.; pvt (jr); women; 1868.
Southern State C., Magnolia, Ark.; st; coed; 1909.
Southern State T. C., Springfield, S. D.; st; coed; 1897.
Southern Union C., Wadley, Ala.; pvt (Cong, jr); coed; 1922.
Southern U., Baton Rouge, La.; st; coed; 1880.
Southern Utah, C. of, Cedar City, Utah; st; coed; 1897.
Southwest Baptist C., Bolivar, Mo.; pvt (Bapt, jr); coed; 1878.
Southwest Mississippi Jr. C., Summit, Miss.; dist (jr); coed; 1927.
Southwest Texas Jr. C., Uvalde, Tex.; dist (jr); coed; 1946.
Southwest Texas State T. C., San Marcos, Tex.; st; coed; 1903.
Southwestern Baptist Theol. Sem., Ft. Worth, Tex.; pvt (Bapt); coed; 1908.
Southwestern Bible Inst., Waxahatchie, Tex.; pvt (AG jr); coed; 1929.
Southwestern C., Winfield, Kans.; pvt (Meth); coed; 1885.
Southwestern Jr. C., Keene, Tex.; pvt (SDA, jr); coed; 1893.
Southwestern Louisiana Inst., Lafayette, La.; st; coed; 1898.
Southwestern at Memphis, Memphis, Tenn.; pvt; (Presb); coed; 1848.
Southwestern State C., Weatherford, Okla.; st; coed; 1901.
Southwestern U., Georgetown, Tex.; pvt (Meth); coed; 1840.
Spartanburg Jr. C., Spartanburg, S. C.; pvt (Meth, jr); coed; 1911.
Spelman C., Atlanta, Ga.; pvt (Bapt); women; 1881.
Spring Arbor Jr. C., Spring Arbor, Mich.; pvt (Meth, jr); coed; 1873.
Springfield C., Springfield, Mass.; pvt; coed; 1885.
Springfield Jr. C., Springfield, Ill.; pvt (RC, jr); coed; 1929.
Spring Garden Inst., Philadelphia, Pa.; pvt (jr); coed; 1851.
Spring Hill C., Spring Hill, Ala.; pvt (RC); coed; 1830.
Staley C. of the Spoken Word, Brookline, Mass.; pvt; coed; 1900.
Stanford U., Stanford, Cal.; pvt; coed; 1885.
Staten Island Community C. of the City U. of NY, Staten Island, NY; (jr); 1955.
Stephen F. Austin State C., Nacogdoches, Tex.; st; coed; 1923.
Stephens C., Columbia, Mo.; pvt (jr); women; 1833.
Sterling C., Sterling, Kans.; pvt (Presb); coed; 1887.
Stetson U., De Land, Fla.; pvt (Bapt); coed; 1883.
Steubenville, C. of, Steubenville, O.; pvt (RC); coed; 1946.
Stevens Inst. of Tech., Hoboken, N. J.; pvt; men; 1870.
Stillman C., Tuscaloosa, Ala.; pvt (Presb); coed; 1876.
Stockton C., Stockton, Cal.; mun (jr); coed; 1935.
Stonehill C., North Easton, Mass.; pvt (RC); coed; 1948.
Stratford C., Danville, Va.; pvt (jr); women; 1852.
Sue Bennett C., London, Ky.; pvt (Meth, jr); coed; 1896.
Suffolk U., Boston, Mass.; pvt; coed; 1906.
Sullins C., Bristol, Va.; pvt (jr); women; 1870.
Sul Ross State C., Alpine, Tex.; st; coed; 1920.
Sunflower Jr. C., Moorhead, Miss.; dist (jr); coed; 1926.
Suomi C. & Theol. Sem., Hancock, Mich.; pvt (Luth, jr); coed; 1896.
Susquehanna U., Selinsgrove, Pa.; pvt (Luth); coed; 1858.
Swarthmore C., Swarthmore, Pa.; pvt; coed; 1864.
Sweet Briar C., Sweet Briar, Va.; pvt; women; 1901.
Syracuse U., Syracuse, NY; pvt; coed; 1870.
Tabor C., Hillsboro, Kans.; pvt (Men); coed; 1908.

Taft C., Taft, Cal.; dist (jr); coed; 1922.
Talladega C., Talladega, Ala.; pvt; coed; 1867.
Tampa, U. of, Tampa, Fla.; pvt; coed; 1931.
Tarkio C., Tarkio, Mo.; pvt (Presb); coed; 1883.
Tarleton State C., Stephenville, Tex.; st (jr); coed; 1899.
Taylor U., Upland, Ind.; pvt; coed; 1846.
Teachers C. of Columbia U., NYC; pvt; coed; 1888.
Temple Jr. C., Temple, Tex.; mun (jr); coed; 1926.
Temple U., Philadelphia, Pa.; pvt; coed; 1884.
Tennessee, U. of, Knoxville, Tenn.; st; coed; 1794.
Tennessee Ag. & Indust. State U., Nashville, Tenn.; st; coed; 1912.
Tennessee Polytechnic Inst., Cookeville, Tenn.; st; coed; 1915.
Tennessee Wesleyan C., Athens, Tenn.; pvt (Meth); coed; 1857.
Texarkana C., Texarkana, Tex.; mun (jr); coed; 1927.
Texas, A. & M. C. of, College Station, Tex.; st; men; 1876.
Texas, U. of, Austin, Tex.; st; coed; 1881.
Texas Christian U., Fort Worth, Tex.; Disc. of Christ; coed; 1873.
Texas C., Tyler, Tex.; pvt (ME); coed; 1894.
Texas C. of Arts & Indust., Kingsville, Tex.; st; coed; 1925.
Texas Lutheran C., Seguin, Tex.; pvt (Luth); coed; 1891.
Texas Southern U., Houston, Tex.; st; coed; 1947.
Texas Southmost C., Brownsville, Tex.; mun (jr); coed; 1926.
Texas State C. for Women, Denton, Tex.; st; women; 1903.
Texas Tech. C., Lubbock, Tex.; st; coed; 1923.
Texas Wesleyan C., Ft. Worth, Tex.; pvt (Meth); coed; 1891.
Texas Western C., El Paso, Tex.; st; coed; 1913.
Thiel C., Greenville, Pa.; pvt (UL); coed; 1870.
Thornton Jr. C., Harvey, Ill.; twp (jr); coed; 1927.
Toledo, U. of, Toledo, O.; mun; coed; 1872.
Tougaloo Southern Christian C., Tougaloo, Miss.; pvt (Inter); coed; 1869.
Transylvania C., Lexington, Ky.; pvt; coed; 1780.
Trenton Jr. C., Trenton, N. J.; st & mun (jr); coed; 1947.
Trevecca Nazarene C., Nashville, Tenn.; pvt (Naz); coed; 1901.
Trinidad State Jr. C., Trinidad, Colo.; dist (jr); coed; 1925.
Trinity C., Hartford, Conn.; pvt; men; 1823.
Trinity C., Washington, D. C.; pvt (RC); women; 1897.
Trinity C., Burlington, Vt.; pvt (RC); women; 1925.
Trinity U., San Antonio, Tex.; pvt (Presb); coed; 1869.
Tri-State C., Angola, Ind.; pvt; coed; 1884.
Truett-McConnell Jr. C., Cleveland, Ga.; pvt (Bapt, jr); coed; 1946.
Tufts U., Medford, Mass.; pvt; coed; 1852.
Tulane U., New Orleans, La.; pvt; coed; 1834.
Tulsa, U. of, Tulsa, Okla.; pvt; coed; 1894.
Tusculum C., Greeneville, Tenn.; pvt (Presb); coed; 1794.
Tuskegee Inst., Tuskegee Inst., Ala.; pvt; coed; 1881.
Tyler Jr. C., Tyler, Tex.; dist (jr); coed; 1926.
Union C., Barbourville, Ky.; pvt (Meth); coed; 1879.
Union C., Lincoln, Nebr.; pvt (SDA); coed; 1891.
Union C. & U., Schenectady, NY; pvt; men; 1795.
Union Jr. C., Cranford, N. J.; pvt (jr); coed; 1933.
Union Theol. Sem., NYC; pvt; coed; 1836.
Union Theol. Sem., Richmond, Va.; pvt (Presb); men; 1812.
Union U., Jackson, Tenn., pvt (Bapt); coed; 1825.
U. S. Air Force Acad., Denver, Colo.; nat; men; 1954.
U. S. Air Force Inst. of Tech., Dayton, O.; nat; men; 1920.
U. S. Coast Guard Acad., New London, Conn.; nat; men; 1876.
U. S. Dept. of Ag. Grad. Schl., Washington, D. C.; nat; coed; 1921.
U. S. Merchant Marine Acad., Kings Point, NY; nat; men; 1943.
U. S. Military Acad., West Point, NY; nat; men; 1802.
U. S. Naval Acad., Annapolis, Md.; nat; men; 1845.
U. S. Naval Postgrad. Schl., Monterey, Cal.; nat; coed; 1909.
United Theol. Sem., Dayton, O.; pvt (EUB); coed; 1871.
Upper Iowa U., Fayette, Ia.; pvt; coed; 1857.
Upsala C., E. Orange, N.J.; pvt (Luth); coed; 1893.
Ursinus C., Collegeville, Pa.; pvt (ER); coed; 1869.
Ursuline C., Louisville, Ky.; pvt; women; 1938.
Ursuline C., Cleveland, O.; pvt (RC); women; 1871.
Utah, U. of, Salt Lake City, Utah; st; coed; 1850.
Utah State Ag. C., Logan, Utah; st; coed; 1889.
Valdosta State C., Valdosta, Ga.; st; coed; 1906.
Vallejo Jr. C., Vallejo, Cal.; dist (jr); coed; 1945.
Valley Forge Military Jr. C., Wayne, Pa.; pvt (jr); men; 1928.
Valparaiso Tech. Inst., Valparaiso, Ind.; pvt (jr); coed; 1874.
Valparaiso U., Valparaiso, Ind.; pvt (Luth); coed; 1859.
Vanderbilt U., Nashville, Tenn.; pvt; coed; 1872.
Vassar C., Poughkeepsie, NY; pvt; women; 1861.
Ventura C., Ventura, Cal.; dist (jr); coed; 1929.

Vermont, U. of, & State Ag. C., Burlington, Vt.; st; coed; 1791.

Vermont Jr. C., Montpelier, Vt.; pvt (jr); women; 1834.

Vermont State T. C., Castleton, Vt.; st; coed; 1867.

Vermont State T. C., Johnson, Vt.; st; coed; 1867.

Vermont State T. C., Lyndon Center, Vt.; st; coed; 1911.

Victoria C., Victoria, Tex.; dist (jr); coed; 1925.

Villa Madonna C., Covington, Ky.; pvt (RC); coed; 1921.

Villa Maria C., Erie, Pa.; pvt (RC); women; 1925.

Villanova U., Villanova, Pa.; pvt (RC); men; 1842.

Vincennes U., Vincennes, Ind.; pvt (jr); coed; 1806.

Virginia, Medical C. of, Richmond, Va.; st; coed; 1838.

Virginia, U. of, Charlottesville, Va.; st; men; 1819.

Virginia Intermont C., Bristol, Va.; pvt (Bapt, jr); women; 1884.

Virginia Jr. C., Virginia, Minn.; mun (jr); coed; 1921.

Virginia Military Inst., Lexington, Va.; st; men; 1839.

Virginia Polytechnic Inst., Blacksburg, Va.; st; coed; 1872.

Virginia State C., Petersburg, Va.; st; coed; 1882.

Virginia Theol. Sem. & C., Lynchburg, Va.; pvt (Bapt); coed; 1888.

Virginia Union U., Richmond, Va.; pvt (Bapt); coed; 1865.

Viterbo C., La Crosse, Wisc.; pvt; women; 1931.

Voorhees Schl. & Jr. C., Denmark, S. C.; pvt (Episc, jr); coed; 1897.

Wabash C., Crawfordsville, Ind.; pvt; men; 1832.

Wagner Lutheran C., Staten Island, NY; pvt (Luth); coed; 1883.

Wake Forest C., Winston-Salem, N. C.; pvt (Bapt); coed; 1834.

Waldorf C., Forest City, Ia.; pvt (Luth, jr); coed; 1897.

Walla Walla C., College Place, Wash.; pvt (SDA); coed; 1892.

Warren Wilson C., Swannanoa, N. C.; pvt (Presb); coed; 1893.

Wartburg C., Waverly, Ia.; pvt (AL); coed; 1852.

Washburn U., Topeka, Kans.; mun; coed; 1865.

Washington, State C. of, Pullman, Wash.; st; coed; 1890.

Washington, U. of, Seattle, Wash.; st; coed; 1861.

Washington C., Chestertown, Md.; pvt; coed; 1782.

Washington and Jefferson C., Washington, Pa.; pvt; men; 1781.

Washington Jr. C., Pensacola, Fla.; st (jr); coed; 1949.

Washington and Lee U., Lexington, Va.; pvt; men; 1749.

Washington Missionary C., Washington, D. C.; pvt (SDA); coed; 1904.

Washington U., St. Louis, Mo.; pvt; coed; 1853.

Wayland Baptist C., Plainview, Tex.; pvt (Bapt); coed; 1909.

Wayne State U., Detroit, Mich.; st; coed; 1868.

Waynesburg C., Waynesburg, Pa.; pvt (Presb); coed; 1849.

Weatherford C., Weatherford, Tex.; cnty (jr); coed; 1921.

Weber C., Ogden, Utah; st (jr); coed; 1889.

Webster C., Webster Groves, Mo.; pvt (RC); women; 1915.

Wellesley C., Wellesley, Mass.; pvt; women; 1870.

Wells C., Aurora, NY; pvt; women; 1868.

Wenatchee Jr. C., Wenatchee, Wash.; dist (jr); coed; 1939.

Wentworth Inst., Boston, Mass.; pvt (jr); men; 1904.

Wentworth Military Acad., Lexington, Mo.; pvt (jr); men; 1923.

Wesley Jr. C., Dover, Del.; pvt (Meth, jr); coed; 1873.

Wesleyan C., Macon, Ga.; pvt (Meth); women; 1836.

Wesleyan Methodist C., Central, S. C.; pvt (WesMeth, jr); coed; 1906.

Wesleyan U., Middletown, Conn.; pvt; men; 1831.

West Baden C., West Baden, Ind.; pvt (RC); men; 1934.

West Contra Costa Jr. C., Richmond, Cal.; dist (jr); coed; 1949.

West Georgia C., Carrolton, Ga.; st (jr); coed; 1933.

West Liberty State C., W. Liberty, W. Va.; st; coed; 1837.

West Texas State C., Canyon, Tex.; st; coed; 1910.

West Virginia Inst. of Tech., Montgomery, W. Va.; st; coed; 1895.

West Virginia State C., Institute, W. Va.; st; coed; 1891.

West Virginia U., Morgantown, W. Va.; st; coed; 1867.

West Virginia Wesleyan C., Buckhannon, W. Va.; pvt (Meth); coed; 1890.

Westbrook Jr. C., Portland, Me.; pvt (jr); women; 1831.

Westchester Community C., White Plains, NY; dist (jr); coed; 1946.

Western Carolina C., Cullowhee, N. C.; st; coed; 1889.

Western C. for Women, Oxford, O.; pvt; women; 1853.

Western Illinois U., Macomb, Ill.; st; coed; 1899.

Western Kentucky State C., Bowling Green, Ky.; st; coed; 1906.

Western Maryland C., Westminster, Md.; pvt; coed; 1868.

Western Michigan U. of Ed., Kalamazoo, Mich.; st; coed; 1903.

Western Montana C. of Ed., Dillon, Mont.; st; coed; 1897.

Western Reserve U., Cleveland, O.; pvt; coed; 1826.

Western State C., Gunnison, Colo.; st; coed; 1901.

Western Theol. Sem., Pittsburgh, Pa.; pvt (Presb); men; 1825.

Western Washington C. of Ed., Bellingham, Wash.; st; coed; 1899.

Westhampton C., Richmond, Va.; pvt (Bapt); women; 1914.

Westmar C., Le Mars, Ia.; pvt (EUB); coed; 1890.

Westminster Choir C., Princeton, N. J.; pvt; coed; 1926.

Westminster C., Fulton, Mo.; pvt (Presb); men; 1851.

Westminster C., New Wilmington, Pa.; pvt (Presb); coed; 1852.

Westminster C., Salt Lake City, Utah; pvt (Inter); coed; 1875.

Westminster Theol. Sem., Westminster, Md.; pvt (Meth); coed; 1882.

Westmont C., Santa Barbara, Cal.; pvt; coed; 1940.

Wharton County Jr. C., Wharton, Tex.; dist (jr); coed; 1946.

Wheaton C., Wheaton, Ill.; pvt; coed; 1860.

Wheaton C., Norton, Mass.; pvt; women; 1834.

Wheelock C., Boston, Mass.; pvt; women; 1888.

Whitman C., Walla Walla, Wash.; pvt; coed; 1859.

Whittier C., Whittier, Cal.; pvt; coed; 1901.

Whitworth C., Spokane, Wash.; pvt (Presb); coed; 1890.

Wichita, U. of, Wichita, Kans.; mun; coed; 1895.

Wilberforce U., Wilberforce, O.; pvt (AMC); coed; 1856.

Wiley C., Marshall, Tex.; pvt (Meth); coed; 1873.

Wilkes C., Wilkes-Barre, Pa.; pvt; coed; 1933.

Willamette U., Salem, Ore.; pvt (Meth); coed; 1842.

William Carey C., Hattiesburg, Miss.; pvt (Bapt); coed; 1906.

William Jennings Bryan U., Dayton, Tenn.; pvt; coed; 1930.

William Jewell C., Liberty, Mo.; pvt (Bapt); coed; 1849.

William & Mary, C. of, Williamsburg, Va.; st; coed; 1693.

William Mitchell C. of Law, St. Paul, Minn.; pvt; coed; 1900.

William Penn C., Oskaloosa, Ia.; pvt (Fr); coed; 1873.

William Smith C. (See Hobart C.)

William Woods C., Fulton, Mo.; pvt (DC, jr); women; 1890.

Williams C., Williamstown, Mass.; pvt; men; 1793.

Willimantic State T. C., Willimantic, Conn.; st; coed; 1889.

Wilmington C., Wilmington, N. C.; cnty (jr); coed; 1947.

Wilmington C., Wilmington, O.; pvt (Fr); coed; 1870.

Wilson C., Chambersburg, Pa.; pvt; women; 1869.

Wingate C., Wingate, N. C.; pvt (Bapt, jr); coed; 1896.

Winona State C., Winona, Minn.; st; coed; 1858.

Winston-Salem T. C., Winston-Salem, N. C.; st; coed; 1892.

Winthrop C., Rock Hill, S. C.; st; women; 1886.

Wisconsin, U. of, Madison, Wisc.; st; coed; 1848.

Wisconsin Inst. of Tech., Platteville, Wisc.; st; men; 1907.

Wisconsin State C., Eau Claire, Wisc.; st; coed; 1916.

Wisconsin State C., La Crosse, Wisc.; st; coed; 1909.

Wisconsin State C., Oshkosh, Wisc.; st; coed; 1871.

Wisconsin State C., Platteville, Wisc.; st; coed; 1866.

Wisconsin State C., River Falls, Wisc.; st; coed; 1874.

Wisconsin State C., Stevens Point, Wisc.; st; coed; 1894.

Wisconsin State C., Superior, Wisc.; st; coed; 1896.

Wisconsin State C., Whitewater, Wisc.; st; coed; 1868.

Wittenberg C., Springfield, O.; pvt (UL); coed; 1845.

Wofford C., Spartanburg, S. C.; pvt (Meth); men; 1854.

Woodstock C., Woodstock, Md.; pvt (RC); men; 1867.

Wooster, C. of, Wooster, O.; pvt (Presb); coed; 1866.

Worcester Jr. C., Worcester, Mass.; pvt (YMCA, jr); coed; 1938.

Worcester Polytechnic Inst., Worcester, Mass.; pvt; men; 1865.

Worthington Jr. C., Worthington, Minn.; dist (jr); coed; 1936.

Wyoming, U. of, Laramie, Wyo.; st; coed; 1887.

Wyomissing Polytechnic Inst., Wyomissing, Pa.; pvt (jr); men; 1927.

Xavier U., New Orleans, La.; pvt (RC); coed; 1925.

Xavier U., Cincinnati, O.; pvt (RC); men; 1831.

Yakima Valley Jr. C., Yakima, Wash.; dist (jr); coed; 1928.

Yale U., New Haven, Conn.; pvt; men; 1701.

Yankton C., Yankton, S. D.; pvt (Cong); coed; 1881.

Yeshiva U., NYC; pvt (Jewish); coed; 1886.

Young L. G. Harris C., Young Harris, Ga.; pvt (Meth, jr); coed; 1886.

Youngstown U., Youngstown, O.; pvt; coed; 1908.

Yuba C., Marysville, Cal.; dist (jr); coed; 1927.

Weights and Measures

LINEAR MEASURE

12 inches	= 1 foot
3 feet	= 1 yard
5½ yards	= 1 rod
40 rods	= 1 furlong
8 furlongs (5280 feet)	= 1 statute mile

MARINERS' MEASURE

6 feet	= 1 fathom
1000 fathoms (approx.)	= 1 nautical mile
3 nautical miles	= 1 league

SQUARE MEASURE

144 square inches	= 1 square foot
9 square feet	= 1 square yard
30¼ square yards	= 1 square rod
160 square rods	= 1 acre
640 acres	= 1 square mile

CUBIC MEASURE

1728 cubic inches	= 1 cubic foot
27 cubic feet	= 1 cubic yard

SURVEYORS' MEASURE

•7.92 inches	= 1 link
100 links	= 1 chain

LIQUID MEASURE

4 gills	= 1 pint
2 pints	= 1 quart
4 quarts	= 1 gallon
31½ gallons	= 1 barrel
2 barrels	= 1 hogshead

APOTHECARIES' FLUID MEASURE

60 minims	= 1 fluid dram
8 fluid drams	= 1 fluid ounce
16 fluid ounces	= 1 pint
2 pints	= 1 quart
4 quarts	= 1 gallon

DRY MEASURE

2 pints	= 1 quart
8 quarts	= 1 peck
4 pecks	= 1 bushel

WOOD MEASURE

16 cubic feet	= 1 cord foot
8 cord feet	= 1 cord

TIME MEASURE

60 seconds	= 1 minute
60 minutes	= 1 hour
24 hours	= 1 day
7 days	= 1 week
4 weeks (28 to 31 days)	= 1 month
12 months (365 or 366 days)	= 1 year
100 years	= 1 century

ANGULAR AND CIRCULAR MEASURE

60 seconds	= 1 minute
60 minutes	= 1 degree
90 degrees	= 1 right angle
180 degrees	= 1 straight angle
360 degrees	= 1 circle

TROY WEIGHT

24 grains	= 1 pennyweight
20 pennyweights	= 1 ounce
12 ounces	= 1 pound

AVOIRDUPOIS WEIGHT

27 11/32 grains	= 1 dram
16 drams	= 1 ounce
16 ounces	= 1 pound
100 pounds	= 1 short hundredweight
20 short hundredweight	= 1 short ton

APOTHECARIES' WEIGHT

20 grains	= 1 scruple
3 scruples	= 1 dram
8 drams	= 1 ounce
12 ounces	= 1 pound

THE METRIC SYSTEM*

LINEAR MEASURE

10 millimeters	= 1 centimeter
10 centimeters	= 1 decimeter
10 decimeters	= 1 meter
10 meters	= 1 decameter
10 decameters	= 1 hectometer
10 hectometers	= 1 kilometer

SQUARE MEASURE

100 sq. millimeters	= 1 sq. centimeter
100 sq. centimeters	= 1 sq. decimeter
100 sq. decimeters	= 1 sq. meter
100 sq. meters	= 1 sq. decameter
100 sq. decameters	= 1 sq. hectometer
100 sq. hectometers	= 1 sq. kilometer

CUBIC MEASURE

1000 cu. millimeters	= 1 cu. centimeter
1000 cu. centimeters	= 1 cu. decimeter
1000 cu. decimeters	= 1 cu. meter

LIQUID MEASURE

10 milliliters	= 1 centiliter
10 centiliters	= 1 deciliter
10 deciliters	= 1 liter
10 liters	= 1 decaliter
10 decaliters	= 1 hectoliter
10 hectoliters	= 1 kiloliter

WEIGHTS

10 milligrams	= 1 centigram
10 centigrams	= 1 decigram
10 decigrams	= 1 gram
10 grams	= 1 decagram
10 decagrams	= 1 hectogram
10 hectograms	= 1 kilogram
100 kilograms	= 1 quintal
10 quintals	= 1 ton

* See the entries *metric system* and *meter*[1] in the main body of this dictionary.